W9-AMU-326

5-

The National Hockey League

Official Guide & Record Book

2005

THE NATIONAL HOCKEY LEAGUE
Official Guide & Record Book/2005

TERMS & CONDITIONS FOR USING THIS BOOK

ATTENTION: PLEASE READ THIS DOCUMENT CAREFULLY BEFORE USING THIS BOOK (THE "BOOK") AND/OR THE DATA IT CONTAINS (THE "DATA"). INDIVIDUALS OR ENTITIES USING THE BOOK AND/OR THE DATA ("END USERS") AGREE TO BE BOUND BY THE TERMS OF THIS LICENSE. IF YOU DO NOT AGREE TO THE TERMS OF THIS LICENSE, DO NOT USE THE BOOK OR THE DATA AND PROMPTLY RETURN THE UNUSED BOOK AND PROOF OF PAYMENT TO THE FOLLOWING ADDRESS FOR A REFUND:

Dan Diamond & Associates, Inc.
194 Dovercourt Road, Toronto, Ontario, Canada M6J 3C8
dda.nhl@sympatico.ca.

Dan Diamond & Associates, Inc. (the "Publisher") owns, and retains ownership of, the Data. The Publisher reserves any right not expressly granted to End Users below.

1. License. End-Users are granted a limited, non-exclusive license to do only the following, subject to the restrictions set out in Section 2 below:
   (a) End-Users may use the Book and the Data for personal, non-commercial purposes.
   (b) End-Users may reproduce individual player records, tables and data panels in connection with bona fide private study and research.
   (c) End-Users who are journalists may reproduce individual player records, tables and data panels for use by the broadcast and print media.

2. Restrictions. End-Users may NOT reproduce the Book or the Data, in whole or in part, in any form or by any means, electronic or mechanical, including photocopying, recording, or by any information storage and retrieval system now known or hereafter invented, without written permission from the Publisher. End-Users may NOT sublicense, assign, or distribute (via the World Wide Web or otherwise) copies of the Book or the Data, in whole or in part, to others. END-USERS MAY NOT MODIFY, ADAPT, TRANSLATE, RENT, LEASE, LOAN, RESELL FOR PROFIT, DISTRIBUTE, OR OTHERWISE ASSIGN OR TRANSFER THE BOOK OR THE DATA, OR CREATE DERIVATIVE WORKS BASED UPON THE BOOK OR THE DATA OR ANY PART THEREOF, EXCEPT AS PROVIDED ABOVE.

3. Commercial Users. Commercial users (such as sports reference and sports gaming websites) may obtain a license to use customized Data upon payment of a reasonable fee. Please contact the Publisher at the address provided above.

4. Termination. This License is effective until terminated. This License will terminate immediately without notice from the Publisher if the End User fails to comply with any of its provisions. Upon termination End Users must destroy the Book, the Data and all copies thereof.

5. General. This License will be governed by and construed in accordance with the laws of the province of Ontario and the laws of Canada applicable therein, and shall inure to the benefit of the Publisher and End-Users and their successors, assigns and legal representatives. If any provision of this License is held by a court of competent jurisdiction to be invalid or unenforceable to any extent under applicable law, that provision will be enforced to the maximum extent permissible and the remaining provisions of this License will remain in full force and effect. Any notices or other communications to be sent to the Publisher must be mailed first class, postage prepaid, to the address provided above. This Agreement constitutes the entire agreement between the parties with respect to the subject matter hereof, and all prior proposals, agreements, representations, statements and undertakings are hereby expressly cancelled and superseded. This Agreement may not be changed or amended except by a written instrument executed by a duly authorized officer of the Publisher.

6. Acknowledgment. BY USING THE BOOK OR THE DATA, THE END-USER ACKNOWLEDGES THAT IT HAS READ THIS LICENSE, UNDERSTANDS IT, AND AGREES TO BE BOUND BY ITS TERMS AND CONDITIONS. Should you have any questions concerning this License, contact the Publisher at the address provided above.

Copyright © 2004 by the National Hockey League.

Compiled by the NHL Public Relations Department and the 30 NHL Club Public Relations Directors.

Printed in Canada. All rights reserved under the Pan-American and International Copyright Conventions.

Published in Canada by: Dan Diamond and Associates, Inc., 194 Dovercourt Road, Toronto, Ontario M6J 3C8 Canada
ISBN in Canada 0-920445-91-8

Published in the United States by: Triumph Books, 601 South LaSalle, Suite 500, Chicago, Illinois 60605   ISBN in USA 1-57243-603-4

Staff

For the NHL: Dave McCarthy, George Puro; Supervising Editor: Greg Inglis; Statistician: Benny Ercolani; Editorial Staff: John Halligan, David Keon, Dave Baker, Jackie Rinaldi, Kelley Rosset, Julie Young.

Senior Managing Editor: Ralph Dinger   **Associate Managing Editor:** Paul Bontje   **Photo Editor:** Eric Zweig
Player Register Editor: James Duplacey   **Production Editors:** John Pasternak, Alex Dubiel   **Publisher:** Dan Diamond

Data Management and Typesetting: Caledon Data Management, Orangeville, Ontario
Film Output and Scanning: Embassy Graphics, Toronto, Ontario
Printing: Fidelity National Information Solutions Canada, Scarborough, Ontario
Production Management: Dan Diamond and Associates, Inc., Toronto, Ontario
Contributors and Photo Credits: see page 639

Distribution

Trade sales and distribution in Canada by:
North 49 Books, 35 Prince Andrew Drive, Toronto, Ontario M3C 2H2   416/449-4000; Fax 416/449-9924
Dan Diamond and Associates, Inc., Toronto   416/531-6535; Fax 416/531-3939   dda.nhl@sympatico.ca   www.nhlofficialguide.com

Trade sales and distribution in the United States by:
Triumph Books, 601 South LaSalle, Suite 500, Chicago, Illinois 60605   312/939-3330; Fax 312/663-3557

International representatives:
Barkers Worldwide Publications, Unit 6/7 The Elms Centre, Glaziers Lane, Normandy, Guildford, Surrey GU3 2DF England
Tel 011/441/483/811-971; Fax 011/441/483/811-972   sales@bwpu.demon.co.uk   www.bwpu.demon.co.uk

Licensed by the National Hockey League.

NHL and the NHL Shield are registered trademarks of the National Hockey League.
All NHL logos and marks and team logos and marks depicted herein are the property of the NHL and the respective teams and may not be reproduced without the prior written consent of Enterprises, L.P. © NHL 2004. All Rights Reserved.

The National Hockey League
1251 Avenue of the Americas, 47th Floor, New York, New York 10020-1198
1800 McGill College Ave., Suite 2600, Montreal, Quebec H3A 3J6
50 Bay Street, 11th Floor, Toronto, Ontario M5J 2X8

Table of Contents

13 CLUBS   records, rosters, management

133 FINAL STATISTICS 2003-04

Table of Contents continued

Introduction

WELCOME TO THE *NHL OFFICIAL GUIDE & RECORD BOOK 2005.* This is the 73rd edition of a book that is older than the center ice red line and predates the incorrectly named "original six." While we are proud of the fact that there's a lot of the game's heritage in the *Guide's* staying power, its unofficial status as "the bible of hockey" is rooted in the editors' willingness to use the latest technologies to make a better book. Today's editorial team has worked on the project since 1984, making the *NHL Guide & Record Book* the perfect laboratory to study the impact of every advance in this era of desktop computing, from page composition to database management to photo handling and data transmission. While hot metal type was long gone by the time we came on the scene, the first editions of the book were assembled on a drafting table with a t-square, triangle and sharp knife. Rubber cement and hot wax were liberally employed in the week-long process of laying out the book. Once the Player Register was assembled, it was locked in with no easy way of adding a late signing or of deleting a sudden retirement. During assembly, if a photo was too wide, you sliced off a portion and discarded it. If you changed your mind, you were out of luck.

Today, the content of the *NHL Guide* is driven by a comprehensive database of hockey statistics that covers the NHL, minor pro leagues, junior, college and European hockey as well as international competitions such as the World Cup of Hockey and Olympics. Customized software takes this data and composes many of the sections of the book. If a player's statistics change – say he gains five pounds or we find a statistical line from when he was 16 years old – the database is changed and all the appropriate sections of the book are modified. Liberated from our drafting tables, we are free to improve the book in countless ways: to find sources of new statistics throughout every level of the game and to provide more in-depth coverage of the NHL, its member clubs and their players and prospects. Imagine the impossible jigsaw puzzle of trying to find, shoot, trim and paste-in the more than one thousand player photos that are part of the Player Register that begins on page 339 of this year's edition. Today, it's just one of those features that's an accepted and expected part of the *Official Guide & Record Book.* And, as there's no sign of a slowdown in the pace of technological change, enhancements to the *Guide* will continue with each edition.

LIKE THE *NHL OFFICIAL GUIDE & RECORD BOOK,* the 2003-04 NHL season combined history and innovation. The first regular-season NHL game played outdoors was a huge and chilly success as 57,167 fans in Commonwealth Stadium saw the Montreal Canadiens defeat the hometown Edmonton Oilers 4–3 on Saturday, November 22, 2003. The game, designated as the "Heritage Classic," took place on the anniversary date of the start of a series of meetings that culminated in the founding of the NHL in 1917.

Later in the season, goaltender Brian Boucher of the Phoenix Coyotes recorded five consecutive shutouts. At 332 minutes, this was the third longest streak all time and the longest since 1928-29 when forward passing was not permitted in the offensive zone. Miikka Kiprusoff registered a goals-against average of 1.69 and backstopped the Calgary Flames to within one game of the Stanley Cup title. Kiprusoff's mark was achieved in a season that saw him traded from San Jose to Calgary and was the lowest goals-against average since Dave Kerr's 1.54 in 1939-40. And perennial all-star netminder Martin Brodeur set a single-season record for minutes played (4,555) and recorded his ninth consecutive season with 30-or-more wins. (Goaltending Leaders, page 184; Individual Regular-Season Records for goaltenders, page 172)

New players and new teams build new hockey traditions.

The Stanley Cup playoffs culminated in a red-hot seven-game final between the Flames and the eventual champions, the Tampa Bay Lightning. For many fans, it was a chance to see some of hockey's best young players at the "big dance" for the first time. Individual awards would soon make it obvious: these guys could play. Martin St. Louis, Brad Richards, Craig Conroy, Jarome Iginla and Kiprusoff shone in the playoffs. Others, like Ilya Kovalchuk and Rick Nash, demonstrated their prowess throughout the season. (Individual Awards begin on page 199.) Records, rosters and management for each NHL club begin on page 13. Note that in each club's section, overtime losses (abbreviated OL or, elsewhere where space permits, OTL) are not included in a team's loss total. Therefore W+L+T+OTL=GP. Overtime losses are only reflected in team statistics. Goaltender and coaching statistics do not include OTLs.

Expanded coverage of the NHL's Amateur/Entry Draft since 1969 begins on page 208 with a Draft Summary table and list of first overall selections. Individual data panels on drafted forwards and defensemen are found in the *Guide's* Prospect Register (page 267). Players in the Prospect Register are active, but have yet to play in the NHL. They have been drafted, signed as free agents or invited to training camp by NHL clubs.

The NHL Player Register begins on page 339. It includes active forwards and defensemen who have appeared in an NHL regular-season or playoff game at any time. In addition to the standard GP-G-A-Pts-PIM, an NHLer's player panel includes the following statistical categories, listed from left to right as they appear in the book: power-play goals (PP), shorthand goals (SH), game-winning goals (GW), shots on goal (S), percentage of shots that score (%), plus-minus rating (+/–), total face-offs taken (TF*), face-off winning percentage (F%*), and average time-on-ice per game played (Min*). Categories marked with an asterisk (*) are NHL Real-Time statistics gathered by teams of trained spotters who, working with laptop computers and specialized software, record shots, ice-time, face-off wins, etc. "on-the-fly" at each game. These statistics were kept officially for the first time in 1998-99, so no player in this year's *NHL Guide* has more than six years of Real-Time statistics. Career totals in these Real-Time categories reflect only the past six seasons.

The order of the Registers is as follows: Prospect, NHL Player, Goaltender (page 573), Retired Player (596) and Retired Goaltender (630). Note that the Goaltender Register combines prospects and NHL goaltenders in the same section.

A key to the abbreviations and symbols used in individual player and goaltender data panels, along with useful information on how to use the Registers, is found on page 266. A list of abbreviations used for league names is found on page 337. Late additions to the Registers are found on page 338 and each NHL club's minor-pro affiliates are found on page 7. Referees and linesmen are listed on page 8.

New this year are Top 100 All-Time and Active Games Played Leaders (pages 180 and 181) and a complete list of players eligible for free agency (page 635). A season-long Trade Register begins on page 637.

As always, our thanks to readers, correspondents and members of the media who take the time to comment on the *Guide & Record Book.* Thanks as well to the people working in the communications departments of the NHL's member clubs and to their counterparts in minor pro, junior, college and European hockey.

Best wishes for a successful World Cup of Hockey and an enjoyable 2004-05 NHL season.

ACCURACY REMAINS THE *GUIDE & RECORD BOOK*'S TOP PRIORITY.

We appreciate comments and clarification from our readers. Please direct these to:

- Ralph Dinger   Senior Managing Editor, 194 Dovercourt Road, Toronto, Ontario M6J 3C8. e-mail: ralph.dda@sympatico.ca.
- Greg Inglis   47th floor, 1251 Avenue of the Americas, New York, New York 10020-1198 . . . or . . .
- David Keon   50 Bay Street, 11th Floor, Toronto, Ontario, M5J 2X8

Your involvement makes a better book.

NATIONAL HOCKEY LEAGUE

Established November 22, 1917

New York, 1251 Avenue of the Americas, 47th Floor, New York, NY 10020-1198, 212/789-2000, Fax: 212/789-2020, PR Fax: 212/789-2080
Montréal, 1800 McGill College Avenue, Suite 2600, Montréal, Québec, H3A 3J6, 514/841-9220, Fax: 514/841-1070
Toronto, 50 Bay Street, 11th Floor, Toronto, Ontario, M5J 2X8, 416/981-2777, Fax: 416/981-2779
NHL Enterprises, L.P. — 1251 Avenue of the Americas, 47th Floor, New York, NY 10020-1198, 212/789-2000, Fax: 212/789-2020
NHL Enterprises Canada, L.P. — 50 Bay Street, 11th Floor, Toronto, Ontario, M5J 2X8, 416/981-2777, Fax: 416/981-2779
NHL Productions/NHL Images — 240 Pegasus Avenue, Northvale, NJ 07647, 201/750-5800, Fax: 201/750-5850

BOARD OF GOVERNORS

Chairman of the Board – Harley N. Hotchkiss

Mighty Ducks of Anaheim

Jay Rasulo.....................................Governor
Michael D. Eisner ....Alternate Governor
Al Coates ....Alternate Governor

Atlanta Thrashers

Bruce Levenson ....Governor
Stan Kasten ....Alternate Governor
Don Waddell ....Alternate Governor
Bernie Mullin ....Alternate Governor
J. Rutherford Seydel II ....Alternate Governor

Boston Bruins

Jeremy M. Jacobs ....Governor
Jeremy M. Jacobs, Jr. ....Alternate Governor
Louis Jacobs ....Alternate Governor
Charles M. Jacobs ....Alternate Governor
Harry J. Sinden ....Alternate Governor
Mike O'Connell ....Alternate Governor

Buffalo Sabres

B. Thomas Golisano ....Governor
Lawrence Quinn ....Alternate Governor
Daniel J. DiPofi ....Alternate Governor

Calgary Flames

Harley N. Hotchkiss......................Governor
N. Murray Edwards ....Alternate Governor
Alvin Libin ....Alternate Governor
Ken King.......................................Alternate Governor

Carolina Hurricanes

Peter Karmanos, Jr. ....Governor
Jim Rutherford ....Alternate Governor
Jason Karmanos ....Alternate Governor

Chicago Blackhawks

William W. Wirtz ....Governor
Robert J. Pulford ....Alternate Governor
John A. Ziegler, Jr. ....Alternate Governor
Peter R. Wirtz...............................Alternate Governor

Colorado Avalanche

E. Stanley Kroenke.......................Governor
Pierre Lacroix ....Alternate Governor
David B. Ehrlich ....Alternate Governor

Columbus Blue Jackets

John H. McConnell ....Governor
John P. McConnell ....Alternate Governor
Doug MacLean ....Alternate Governor
Mike Priest ....Alternate Governor

Dallas Stars

Thomas O. Hicks ....Governor
James R. Lites ....Alternate Governor
Doug Armstrong ....Alternate Governor

Detroit Red Wings

Michael Ilitch ....Governor
Jim Devellano ....Alternate Governor
Christopher Ilitch ....Alternate Governor
Ken Holland ....Alternate Governor

Edmonton Oilers

Cal Nichols ....Governor
Patrick R. LaForge........................Alternate Governor
Kevin Lowe ....Alternate Governor
William K. Butler...........................Alternate Governor

Florida Panthers

Alan Cohen ....Governor
Steven Cohen ....Alternate Governor
Richard Lehman ....Alternate Governor
William A. Torrey..........................Alternate Governor
Jordan Zimmerman ....Alternate Governor

Los Angeles Kings

Timothy J. Leiweke ....Governor
Philip F. Anschutz ....Alternate Governor
David Taylor ....Alternate Governor

Minnesota Wild

Robert O. Naegele, Jr. ....Governor
Jac Sperling ....Alternate Governor
Doug Risebrough ....Alternate Governor

Montréal Canadiens

George N. Gillett, Jr. ....Governor
Pierre Boivin ....Alternate Governor
Fred Steer.....................................Alternate Governor
Bob Gainey ....Alternate Governor
Jeff Joyce ....Alternate Governor
Foster Gillett................................Alternate Governor

Nashville Predators

Craig Leipold ....Governor
Jack Diller ....Alternate Governor
David Poile ....Alternate Governor

New Jersey Devils

Lou Lamoriello..............................Governor
Michael Gilfillan ....Alternate Governor

New York Islanders

Charles B. Wang............................Governor
Sanjay Kumar ....Alternate Governor
Mike Milbury ....Alternate Governor
Michael J. Picker ....Alternate Governor
Roy E. Reichbach ....Alternate Governor

New York Rangers

James L. Dolan ....Governor
Glen Sather...................................Alternate Governor
Steve Mills ....Alternate Governor

Ottawa Senators

Eugene Melnyk..............................Governor
Roy Mlakar....................................Alternate Governor
Sheldon Plener ....Alternate Governor

Philadelphia Flyers

Edward M. Snider..........................Governor
Ronald K. Ryan ....Alternate Governor
Philip I. Weinberg..........................Alternate Governor
Bob Clarke....................................Alternate Governor

Phoenix Coyotes

Steve Ellman.................................Governor
Wayne Gretzky...............................Alternate Governor
Doug Moss ....Alternate Governor
Mike Barnett ....Alternate Governor

Pittsburgh Penguins

Kenneth Sawyer ....Governor
Craig Patrick ....Alternate Governor
Ronald Burkle...............................Alternate Governor
Anthony Liberati ....Alternate Governor

St. Louis Blues

William J. Laurie ....Governor
Richard C. Thomas ....Alternate Governor
Brent P. Karasiuk ....Alternate Governor
Mark Sauer ....Alternate Governor
Larry Pleau ....Alternate Governor

San Jose Sharks

Greg Jamison................................Governor
Kevin Compton ....Alternate Governor
Doug Wilson ....Alternate Governor

Tampa Bay Lightning

Thomas S. Wilson..........................Governor
Ronald J. Campbell ....Alternate Governor
Jay H. Feaster ....Alternate Governor

Toronto Maple Leafs

Larry Tanenbaum ....Governor
Dean Metcalf ....Alternate Governor
Dale Lastman ....Alternate Governor
Richard Peddie ....Alternate Governor
John Ferguson, Jr..........................Alternate Governor

Vancouver Canucks

John E. McCaw, Jr. ....Governor
Stanley B. McCammon..................Alternate Governor
David M. Nonis ....Alternate Governor

Washington Capitals

Richard M. Patrick ....Governor
Ted Leonsis...................................Alternate Governor
George McPhee ....Alternate Governor

NHL Clubs' Minor-League Affiliations, 2004-05

NHL CLUB	MINOR-LEAGUE AFFILIATES
Anaheim	Cincinnati Mighty Ducks (AHL) San Diego Gulls (ECHL)
Atlanta	Chicago Wolves (AHL) Gwinnett Gladiators (ECHL)
Boston	Providence Bruins (AHL)
Buffalo	Rochester Americans (AHL)
Calgary	Lowell Lock Monsters (AHL) Las Vegas Wranglers (ECHL)
Carolina	Lowell Lock Monsters (AHL) Florida Everblades (ECHL)
Chicago	Norfolk Admirals (AHL) Greenville Grrrowl (ECHL)
Colorado	Hershey Bears (AHL)
Columbus	Syracuse Crunch (AHL) Dayton Bombers (ECHL) Elmira Jackals (UHL)
Dallas	Houston Aeros (AHL) Hamilton Bulldogs (AHL)
Detroit	Grand Rapids Griffins (AHL) Toledo Storm (ECHL)
Edmonton	Edmonton Roadrunners (AHL) Greenville Grrrowl (ECHL) Odessa Jackalopes (CHL)
Florida	San Antonio Rampage (AHL)
Los Angeles	Manchester Monarchs (AHL) Reading Royals (ECHL)
Minnesota	Houston Aeros (AHL) Louisiana IceGators (ECHL)

NHL CLUB	MINOR-LEAGUE AFFILIATES
Montreal	Hamilton Bulldogs (AHL) Long Beach Ice Dogs (ECHL)
Nashville	Milwaukee Admirals (AHL)
New Jersey	Albany River Rats (AHL)
NY Islanders	Bridgeport Sound Tigers (AHL)
NY Rangers	Hartford Wolf Pack (AHL)
Ottawa	Binghamton Senators (AHL)
Philadelphia	Philadelphia Phantoms (AHL) Trenton Titans (ECHL)
Phoenix	Utah Grizzlies (AHL) Idaho Steelheads (ECHL)
Pittsburgh	Wilkes-Barre/Scranton Penguins (AHL) Wheeling Nailers (ECHL)
St. Louis	Worcester IceCats (AHL) Peoria Rivermen (ECHL)
San Jose	Cleveland Barons (AHL) Fresno Falcons (ECHL) Johnstown Chiefs (ECHL)
Tampa Bay	Springfield Falcons (AHL) Pensacola Ice Pilots (ECHL)
Toronto	St. John's Maple Leafs (AHL) Memphis RiverKings (CHL)
Vancouver	Manitoba Moose (AHL) Columbia Inferno (ECHL)
Washington	Portland Pirates (AHL) South Carolina Stingrays (ECHL)

Commissioner and League Presidents

Gary B. Bettman

Gary B. Bettman took office as the NHL's first Commissioner on February 1, 1993. Since the League was formed in 1917, there have been five League Presidents.

NHL President	Years in Office
Frank Calder	1917-1943
Mervyn "Red" Dutton	1943-1946
Clarence Campbell	1946-1977
John A. Ziegler, Jr.	1977-1992
Gil Stein	1992-1993

Hockey Hall of Fame

BCE Place
30 Yonge Street
Toronto, Ontario M5E 1X8
Phone: 416/360-7735
Executive Fax: 416/360-1501
Resource Centre Fax: 416/360-1316
www.hhof.com

Bill Hay – Chairman and Chief Executive Officer
Jeff Denomme – President, C.O.O. and Treasurer
Craig Baines – Vice President, Marketing and Facility Services
Phil Pritchard – Vice President, Hockey Operations and Curator
Ron Ellis – Director, Public Affairs and Assistant to the President
Ray Paquet – Creative Director, Exhibit Development
Sandra Walters – Controller and Office Manager
Peter Jagla – Producer, Media and E-Business
Craig Campbell – Manager, Resource Centre and Archives
Steve Ozimec – Manager, Special Events and Hospitality
Kelly Massé – Manager, Corporate and Media Relations
Craig Beckim – Manager, Merchandising and Retail Operations
Jackie Boughazale – Manager, Promotions
    and Attraction Services
Anthony Fusco – Manager, Information Systems
Pearl Rajwanth – Executive Assistant to
    the Chairman and President

National Hockey League Players' Association

777 Bay Street, Suite 2400
Toronto, Ontario M5G 2C8
Phone: 416/313-2300
Fax: 416/313-2301
www.nhlpa.com

Robert W. Goodenow – Executive Director and General Counsel
Ted Saskin – Senior Director, Business Affairs and Licensing
Mike Gartner – Director, Business Relations
Kenneth Kim – Director, Marketing
Ian Pulver, Ian Penny, Roland Lee – Associate Counsel, Labour
Mike Ouellet – Associate Counsel, Licensing
Steve Larmer – Player Relations
Greg Dick – Senior Manager, Finance and Business Administration
Kim Murdoch – Manager, Pensions and Benefits
Devin Smith – Program Manager, Goals & Dreams Fund
Dave Tredgett – Executive Producer-Television
Jonathan Weatherdon – Manager, Media Relations

NHL On-Ice Officials

Total NHL Games and 2003-04 Games columns count regular-season games only.

Referees

#	Name	Birthplace	Birthdate	First NHL Game	Total NHL Games	2003-04 Games
9	Blaine Angus	Shawville, Que.	9/25/61	10/17/92	444	54
15	Stephane Auger	Montreal, Que.	12/9/70	4/1/00	240	72
10	Paul Devorski	Guelph, Ont.	8/18/58	10/14/89	895	72
44	Harry Dumas	Mount Laurel, N.J.	7/7/73	12/27/00	28	14
39	Gord Dwyer	Halifax, N.S.	5/18/77			
2	Kerry Fraser	Sarnia, Ont.	5/30/52	4/6/75	1551	72
27	Eric Furlatt	Cap de la Madelaine, Que.	12/2/71	10/8/01	167	72
30	Mike Hasenfratz	Regina, Sask.	7/19/66	10/21/00	249	72
17	Shane Heyer	Summerland, B.C.	2/7/64	*10/1/99	[1]314	72
46	Scott Hoberg	Windsor, Ont.	1/23/71			
8	Dave Jackson	Montreal, Que.	11/28/64	12/23/90	754	72
25	Marc Joannette	Verdun, Que.	11/3/68	10/27/99	289	72
18	Greg Kimmerly	Toronto, Ont.	12/8/64	11/30/96	376	72
12	Don Koharski	Halifax, N.S.	12/2/55	10/14/77	[2]1434	72
48	Tom Kowal	Vernon, B.C.	11/2/67	10/29/99	175	26
40	Steve Kozari	Penticton, B.C.	6/20/73			
37	Bob Langdon	Woodstock, Ont.	3/11/71	11/11/01	57	29
14	Dennis LaRue	Savannah, GA	7/14/59	3/26/91	576	72
28	Chris Lee	Saint John, N.B.	7/7/70	4/2/00	147	72
3	Mike Leggo	North Bay, Ont.	10/7/64	3/3/98	368	72
6	Dan Marouelli	Edmonton, Alta.	7/16/55	11/2/84	1266	72
26	Rob Martell	Winnipeg, Man.	10/21/63	3/14/84	[3]289	72
41	Wes McCauley	Georgetown, Ont.	1/11/72	1/20/03	23	18
7	Bill McCreary	Guelph, Ont.	11/17/55	11/3/84	1305	72
19	Mick McGeough	Regina, Sask.	6/20/57	1/19/89	877	73
34	Brad Meier	Dayton, OH	4/11/67	10/23/99	291	72
36	Dean Morton	Peterborough, Ont.	2/27/68	11/11/00	31	0
13	Dan O'Halloran	Essex, Ont.	3/25/64	10/14/95	447	72
42	Dan O'Rourke	Calgary, Alta.	8/31/72	10/2/99	[4]25	23
20	Tim Peel	Toronto, Ont.	4/27/66	10/21/99	299	73
43	Brian Pochmara	Detroit, MI	11/27/76			
33	Kevin Pollock	Kincardine, Ont.	2/7/70	3/28/00	296	73
21	Chris Rooney	Boston, MA	5/26/74	11/22/00	192	72
38	Francois St. Laurent	Greenfield Park, Que.	6/26/77			
45	Justin St. Pierre	Dolbeau, Que.	2/17/72			
16	Rob Shick	Port Alberni, B.C.	12/4/57	4/6/86	1074	72
49	Jeff Smith	Hamilton, Ont.	9/2/69			
31	Craig Spada	Welland, Ont.	9/7/71	3/28/02	90	71
11	Kelly Sutherland	Victoria, B.C.	4/18/71	12/19/00	232	72
5	Don Van Massenhoven	London, Ont.	7/17/60	11/11/93	692	72
24	Stephen Walkom	North Bay, Ont.	8/8/63	10/18/92	693	72
29	Ian Walsh	Philadelphia, PA	5/9/72	10/14/00	134	70
35	Dean Warren	Toronto, Ont.	7/22/63	10/8/99	293	72
23	Brad Watson	Regina, Sask.	10/4/61	2/5/94	396	72

[1] plus 785 games as a linesman. [2] plus 163 games as a linesman. [3] plus 1 game as a linesman. [4] plus 120 games as a linesman.

Linesmen

#	Name	Birthplace	Birthdate	First NHL Game	Total NHL Games	2003-04 Games
75	Derek Amell	Port Colborne, Ont.	9/16/68	10/13/97	433	73
59	Steve Barton	Ottawa, Ont.	12/27/71	11/1/00	210	71
96	David Brisebois	Sudbury, Ont.	4/14/76	10/11/99	165	29
74	Lonnie Cameron	Victoria, B.C.	7/15/64	10/5/96	550	74
67	Pierre Champoux	Ville St-Pierre, Que.	4/18/63	10/8/88	1005	68
50	Kevin Collins	Springfield, MA	12/15/50	10/13/77	1964	71
76	Michel Cormier	Trois-Rivieres, Que.	5/28/74	10/10/03	71	71
88	Mike Cvik	Calgary, Alta.	7/6/62	10/8/87	1134	71
83	Angelo D'Amico	Etobicoke, Ont.	5/29/74	11/27/00	97	27
60	Pat Dapuzzo	Hoboken, NJ	12/29/58	12/5/84	1368	32
54	Greg Devorski	Guelph, Ont.	8/3/69	10/9/93	714	70
68	Scott Driscoll	Seaforth, Ont.	5/2/68	10/10/92	782	69
82	Ryan Galloway	Winnipeg, Man.	7/12/72	10/17/02	98	73
91	Don Henderson	Calgary, Alta.	9/23/68	3/10/95	537	74
71	Brad Kovachik	Woodstock, Ont.	3/7/71	10/10/96	521	72
86	Brad Lazarowich	Vancouver, B.C.	8/4/62	10/9/86	1228	72
78	Brian Mach	Little Falls, MN	4/15/74	10/7/00	274	71
51	Dan McCourt	Falconbridge, Ont.	8/14/54	12/27/80	1623	65
90	Andy McElman	Chicago Heights, IL	8/4/61	10/7/93	718	71
89	Steve Miller	Stratford, Ont.	6/22/72	10/7/00	264	68
97	Jean Morin	Sorel, Que.	8/10/63	10/5/91	827	60
93	Brian Murphy	Dover, NH	12/13/64	10/7/88	[5]928	70
95	Jonny Murray	Beauport, Que.	8/10/74	10/7/00	277	71
70	Derek Nansen	Ottawa, Ont.	12/6/71	10/11/02	136	71
80	Thor Nelson	Westminister, CA	1/6/68	2/16/95	439	63
77	Tim Nowak	Buffalo, NY	9/6/67	10/8/93	728	73
79	Mark Paré	Windsor, Ont.	7/26/57	10/11/79	1814	68
72	Stephane Provost	Montreal, Que.	5/5/67	1/25/95	695	72
65	Pierre Racicot	Verdun, Que.	2/15/67	10/12/93	747	71
73	Vaughan Rody	Winnipeg, Man.	12/13/68	10/8/00	267	58
52	Dan Schachte	Madison, WI	7/13/58	10/6/82	1538	71
61	Lyle Seitz	Brooks, Alta.	1/22/69	10/6/92	[6]396	73
84	Anthony Sericolo	Troy, NY	7/17/68	10/21/98	370	70
57	Jay Sharrers	Jamaica, West Indies	7/3/67	10/6/90	[7]642	69
92	Mark Shewchuk	Hamilton, Ont.	6/1/75	10/9/03	71	71
56	Mark Wheler	North Battleford, Sask.	9/20/65	10/10/92	814	74

[5] plus 88 games as a referee. [6] plus 10 games as a referee. [7] plus 136 games as a referee.

NHL History

1917 — National Hockey League organized November 22 in Montreal following suspension of operations by the National Hockey Association of Canada Limited (NHA). Montreal Canadiens, Montreal Wanderers, Ottawa Senators and Quebec Bulldogs attended founding meeting. Delegates decided to use NHA rules.

Toronto Arenas were later admitted as fifth team; Quebec decided not to operate during the first season. Quebec players allocated to remaining four teams.

Frank Calder elected president and secretary-treasurer.

First NHL games played December 19, with Toronto only arena with artificial ice. Clubs played 22-game split schedule.

1918 — Emergency meeting held January 3 due to destruction by fire of Montreal Arena which was home ice for both Canadiens and Wanderers.

Wanderers withdrew, reducing the NHL to three teams; Canadiens played remaining home games at 3,250-seat Jubilee rink.

Quebec franchise sold to P.J. Quinn of Toronto on October 18 on the condition that the team operate in Quebec City for 1918-19 season. Quinn did not attend the November League meeting and Quebec did not play in 1918-19.

1919-20 — NHL reactivated Quebec Bulldogs franchise. Former Quebec players returned to the club. New Mount Royal Arena became home of Canadiens. Toronto Arenas changed name to St. Patricks. Clubs played 24-game split schedule.

1920-21 — H.P. Thompson of Hamilton, Ontario made application for the purchase of an NHL franchise. Quebec franchise shifted to Hamilton with other NHL teams providing players to strengthen the club.

1921-22 — Split schedule abandoned. First and second place teams at the end of full schedule to play for championship.

1922-23 — Clubs agreed that players could not be sold or traded to clubs in any other league without first being offered to all other clubs in the NHL. In March, Foster Hewitt broadcasts radio's first hockey game.

1923-24 — Ottawa's new 10,000-seat arena opened. First U.S. franchise granted to Boston for following season.

Dr. Cecil Hart Trophy donated to NHL to be awarded to the player judged most useful to his team.

1924-25 — Canadian Arena Company of Montreal granted a franchise to operate Montreal Maroons. NHL now six team league with two clubs in Montreal. Inaugural game in new Montreal Forum played November 29, 1924 as Canadiens defeated Toronto 7-1. Forum was home rink for the Maroons, but no ice was available in the Canadiens arena November 29, resulting in a shift to the Forum.

Hamilton finished first in the standings, receiving a bye into the finals. But Hamilton players, demanding $200 each for additional games in the playoffs, went on strike. The NHL suspended all players, fining them $200 each. Stanley Cup finalist to be the winner of NHL semi-final between Toronto and Canadiens.

Prince of Wales and Lady Byng trophies donated to NHL.

Clubs played 30-game schedule.

1925-26 — Hamilton club dropped from NHL. Players signed by new New York Americans franchise. Pittsburgh Pirates granted franchise.

Clubs played 36-game schedule.

1926-27 — New York Rangers granted franchise May 15, 1926. Chicago Black Hawks and Detroit Cougars granted franchises September 25, 1926. NHL now ten-team league with an American and a Canadian Division.

Stanley Cup came under the control of NHL. In previous seasons, winners of the now-defunct Western or Pacific Coast leagues would play NHL champion in Cup finals.

Toronto franchise sold to a new company controlled by Hugh Aird and Conn Smythe. Name changed from St. Patricks to Maple Leafs.

Clubs played 44-game schedule.

The Montreal Canadiens donated the Vezina Trophy to be awarded to the team allowing the fewest goals-against in regular season play. The winning team would, in turn, present the trophy to the goaltender playing in the greatest number of games during the season.

1930-31 — Detroit franchise changed name from Cougars to Falcons. Pittsburgh transferred to Philadelphia for one season. Pirates changed name to Philadelphia Quakers. Trading deadline for teams set at February 15 of each year. NHL approved operation of farm teams by Rangers, Americans, Falcons and Bruins. Four-sided electric arena clock first demonstrated.

1931-32 — Philadelphia dropped out. Ottawa withdrew for one season. New Maple Leaf Gardens completed.

Clubs played 48-game schedule

1932-33 — Detroit franchise changed name from Falcons to Red Wings. Franchise application received from St. Louis but refused because of additional travel costs. Ottawa team resumed play.

1933-34 — First All-Star Game played as a benefit for injured player Ace Bailey. Leafs defeated All-Stars 7-3 in Toronto.

1934-35 — Ottawa franchise transferred to St. Louis. Team called St. Louis Eagles and consisted largely of Ottawa's players.

1935-36 — Ottawa-St. Louis franchise terminated. Montreal Canadiens finished season with very poor record. To strengthen the club, NHL gave Canadiens first call on the services of all French-Canadian players for three seasons.

1937-38 — Second benefit All-Star game staged November 2 in Montreal in aid of the family of the late Canadiens star Howie Morenz.

Montreal Maroons withdrew from the NHL on June 22, 1938, leaving seven clubs in the League.

1938-39 — Expenses for each club regulated at $5 per man per day for meals and $2.50 per man per day for accommodation.

1939-40 — Benefit All-Star Game played October 29, 1939 in Montreal for the children of the late Albert (Babe) Siebert.

1940-41 — Ross-Tyer puck adopted as the official puck of the NHL. Early in the season it was apparent that this puck was too soft. The Spalding puck was adopted in its place.

On May 16, 1941, Arthur Ross, NHL governor from Boston, donated a perpetual trophy to be awarded annually to the player voted outstanding in the league. Due to wartime restrictions, the trophy was never awarded.

1941-42 — New York Americans changed name to Brooklyn Americans.

1942-43 — Brooklyn Americans withdrew from NHL, leaving six teams: Boston, Chicago, Detroit, Montreal, New York and Toronto. Playoff format saw first-place team play third-place team and second play fourth.

Clubs played 50-game schedule.

Frank Calder, president of the NHL since its inception, died in Montreal. Meryn "Red" Dutton, former manager of the New York Americans, became president. The NHL commissioned the Calder Memorial Trophy to be awarded to the League's outstanding rookie each year.

1945-46 — Philadelphia, Los Angeles and San Francisco applied for NHL franchises.

The Philadelphia Arena Company of the American Hockey League applied for an injunction to prevent the possible operation of an NHL franchise in that city.

1946-47 — Mervyn Dutton retired as president of the NHL prior to the start of the season. He was succeeded by Clarence S. Campbell.

Individual trophy winners and all-star team members to receive $1,000 awards.

Playoff guarantees for players introduced.

Clubs played 60-game schedule.

1947-48 — The first annual All-Star Game for the benefit of the players' pension fund was played when the All-Stars defeated the Stanley Cup Champion Toronto Maple Leafs 4-3 in Toronto on October 13, 1947.

Criteria for awarding Art Ross Trophy changed. Now awarded to top scorer. Elmer Lach was its first winner.

Philadelphia and Los Angeles franchise applications refused.

National Hockey League Pension Society formed.

1949-50 — Clubs played 70-game schedule.

First intra-league draft held April 30, 1950. Clubs allowed to protect 30 players. Remaining players available for $25,000 each.

1951-52 — Referees included in the League's pension plan.

1952-53 — In May of 1952, City of Cleveland applied for NHL franchise. Application denied. In March of 1953, the Cleveland Barons of the AHL challenged the NHL champions for the Stanley Cup. The NHL governors did not accept this challenge.

1953-54 — The James Norris Memorial Trophy presented to the NHL for annual presentation to the League's best defenseman.

Intra-league draft rules amended to allow teams to protect 18 skaters and two goaltenders, claiming price reduced to $15,000.

1954-55 — Each arena to operate an "out-of-town" scoreboard. Referees and linesmen to wear shirts of black and white vertical stripes.

1956-57 — Standardized signals for referees and linesmen introduced.

1960-61 — Canadian National Exhibition, City of Toronto and NHL reach agreement for the construction of a Hockey Hall of Fame on the CNE grounds. Hall opens on August 26, 1961.

1963-64 — Player development league established with clubs operated by NHL franchises located in Minneapolis, St. Paul, Indianapolis, Omaha and, beginning in 1964-65, Tulsa. First universal amateur draft took place. All players of qualifying age (17) unaffected by sponsorship of junior teams available to be drafted.

1964-65 — Conn Smythe Trophy presented to the NHL to be awarded annually to the outstanding player in the Stanley Cup playoffs.

Minimum age of players subject to amateur draft changed to 18.

1965-66 — NHL announced expansion plans for a second six-team division to begin play in 1967-68.

1966-67 — Fourteen applications for NHL franchises received.

Lester Patrick Trophy presented to the NHL to be awarded annually for outstanding service to hockey in the United States.

NHL sponsorship of junior teams ceased, making all players of qualifying age not already on NHL-sponsored lists eligible for the amateur draft.

1967-68 — Six new teams added: California Seals, Los Angeles Kings, Minnesota North Stars, Philadelphia Flyers, Pittsburgh Penguins, St. Louis Blues. New teams to play in West Division. Remaining six teams to play in East Division.

Minimum age of players subject to amateur draft changed to 20.

Clubs played 74-game schedule.

Clarence S. Campbell Trophy awarded to team finishing the regular season in first place in West Division.

California Seals change name to Oakland Seals on December 8, 1967.

1968-69 — Clubs played 76-game schedule.

Amateur draft expanded to cover any amateur player of qualifying age throughout the world.

1970-71 — Two new teams added: Buffalo Sabres and Vancouver Canucks. These teams joined East Division: Chicago switched to West Division. Oakland Seals change name to California Golden Seals prior to season.

Clubs played 78-game schedule.

1971-72 — Playoff format amended. In each division, first to play fourth; second to play third.

1972-73 — Soviet Nationals and Canadian NHL stars play eight-game pre-season series. Canadians win 4-3-1.

Two new teams added. Atlanta Flames join West Division; New York Islanders join East Division.

1974-75 — Two new teams added: Kansas City Scouts and Washington Capitals. Teams realigned into two nine-team conferences, the Prince of Wales made up of the Norris and Adams Divisions, and the Clarence Campbell made up of the Smythe and Patrick Divisions.

Clubs played 80-game schedule.

1976-77 — California franchise transferred to Cleveland. Team named Cleveland Barons. Kansas City franchise transferred to Denver. Team named Colorado Rockies.

1977-78 — Clarence S. Campbell retires as NHL president. Succeeded by John A. Ziegler, Jr.

1978-79 — Cleveland and Minnesota franchises merge, leaving NHL with 17 teams. Merged team placed in Adams Division, playing home games in Minnesota.

Minimum age of players subject to amateur draft changed to 19.

1979-80 — Four new teams added: Edmonton Oilers, Hartford Whalers, Quebec Nordiques and Winnipeg Jets.

Minimum age of players subject to entry draft changed to 18.

1980-81 — Atlanta franchise shifted to Calgary, retaining "Flames" name.

1981-82 — Teams realigned within existing divisions. New groupings based on geographical areas. Unbalanced schedule adopted.

1982-83 — Colorado Rockies franchise shifted to East Rutherford, New Jersey. Team named New Jersey Devils. Franchise moved to Patrick Division from Smythe; Winnipeg moved to Smythe Division from Norris.

NHL History — *continued*

1991-92 — San Jose Sharks added, making the NHL a 22-team league. NHL celebrates 75th Anniversary Season. The 1991-92 regular season suspended due to a strike by members of the NHL Players' Association on April 1, 1992. Play resumed April 12, 1992.

1992-93 — Gil Stein named NHL president (October, 1992). Gary Bettman named first NHL Commissioner (February, 1993). Ottawa Senators and Tampa Bay Lightning added, making the NHL a 24-team league. NHL celebrates Stanley Cup Centennial. Clubs played 84-game schedule.

1993-94 — Mighty Ducks of Anaheim and Florida Panthers added, making the NHL a 26-team league. Minnesota franchise shifted to Dallas, team named Dallas Stars. Prince of Wales and Clarence Campbell Conferences renamed Eastern and Western. Adams, Patrick, Norris and Smythe Divisions renamed Northeast, Atlantic, Central and Pacific. Winnipeg moved to Central Division from Pacific; Tampa Bay moved to Atlantic Division from Central; Pittsburgh moved to Northeast Division from Atlantic.

1994-95 — A labor disruption forced the cancellation of 468 games from October 1, 1994 to January 19, 1995. Clubs played a 48-game schedule that began January 20, 1995 and ended May 3, 1995. No inter-conference games were played.

1995-96 — Quebec franchise transferred to Denver. Team named Colorado Avalanche and placed in Pacific Division of Western Conference. Clubs to play 82-game schedule.

1996-97 — Winnipeg franchise transferred to Phoenix. Team named Phoenix Coyotes and placed in Central Division of Western Conference.

1997-98 — Hartford franchise transferred to Raleigh. Team named Carolina Hurricanes and remains in Northeast Division of Eastern Conference.

1998-99 — The addition of the Nashville Predators made the NHL a 27-team league and brought about the creation of two new divisions and a League-wide realignment in preparation for further expansion to 30 teams by 2000-2001. Nashville was added to the Central Division of the Western Conference, while Toronto moved into the Northeast Division of the Eastern Conference. Pittsburgh was shifted from the Northeast to the Atlantic, while Carolina left the Northeast for the newly created Southeast Division of the Eastern Conference. Florida, Tampa Bay and Washington also joined the Southeast. In the Western Conference, Calgary, Colorado, Edmonton and Vancouver make up the new Northwest Division. Dallas and Phoenix moved from the Central to the Pacific Division.

The NHL retired uniform number 99 in honor of all-time scoring leader Wayne Gretzky who retired at the end of the season.

1999-2000 — Atlanta Thrashers added, making the NHL a 28-team league.

2000-01 — Columbus Blue Jackets and Minnesota Wild added, making the NHL a 30-team league.

2003-04 — First outdoor NHL game and largest crowd in League history as 57,167 attend Heritage Classic at Edmonton's Commonwealth Stadium. Montreal defeated Edmonton 4-3, November 22, 2003.

NHL Attendance

Season	Games	Regular Season Attendance	Games	Playoffs Attendance	Total Attendance
1960-61	210	2,317,142	17	242,000	2,559,142
1961-62	210	2,435,424	18	277,000	2,712,424
1962-63	210	2,590,574	16	220,906	2,811,480
1963-64	210	2,732,642	21	309,149	3,041,791
1964-65	210	2,822,635	20	303,859	3,126,494
1965-66	210	2,941,164	16	249,000	3,190,184
1966-67	210	3,084,759	16	248,336	3,333,095
1967-68[1]	444	4,938,043	40	495,089	5,433,132
1968-69	456	5,550,613	33	431,739	5,982,352
1969-70	456	5,992,065	34	461,694	6,453,759
1970-71[2]	546	7,257,677	43	707,633	7,965,310
1971-72	546	7,609,368	36	582,666	8,192,034
1972-73[3]	624	8,575,651	38	624,637	9,200,288
1973-74	624	8,640,978	38	600,442	9,241,420
1974-75[4]	720	9,521,536	51	784,181	10,305,717
1975-76	720	9,103,761	48	726,279	9,830,040
1976-77	720	8,563,890	44	646,279	9,210,169
1977-78	720	8,526,564	45	686,634	9,213,198
1978-79	680	7,758,053	45	694,521	8,452,574
1979-80[5]	840	10,533,623	63	976,699	11,510,322
1980-81	840	10,726,198	68	966,390	11,692,588
1981-82	840	10,710,894	71	1,058,948	11,769,842
1982-83	840	11,020,610	66	1,088,222	12,028,832
1983-84	840	11,359,386	70	1,107,400	12,466,786
1984-85	840	11,633,730	70	1,107,500	12,741,230
1985-86	840	11,621,000	72	1,152,503	12,773,503
1986-87	840	11,855,880	87	1,383,967	13,239,847
1987-88	840	12,117,512	83	1,336,901	13,454,413
1988-89	840	12,417,969	83	1,327,214	13,745,183
1989-90	840	12,579,651	85	1,355,593	13,935,244
1990-91	840	12,343,897	92	1,442,203	13,786,100
1991-92[6]	880	12,769,676	86	1,327,920	14,097,596
1992-93[7]	1,008	14,158,177[8]	83	1,346,034	15,504,211
1993-94[9]	1,092	16,105,604[10]	90	1,440,095	17,545,699
1994-95	624[11]	9,233,884	81	1,329,130	10,563,014
1995-96	1,066	17,041,614	86	1,540,140	18,581,754
1996-97	1,066	17,640,529	82	1,494,878	19,135,407
1997-98	1,066	17,264,678	82	1,507,416	18,772,094
1998-99[12]	1,107	18,001,741	86	1,509,411	19,511,152
1999-2000[13]	1,148	18,800,139	83	1,524,629	20,324,768
2000-01[14]	1,230	20,373,379	86	1,584,011	21,957,390
2001-02	1,230	20,614,613	90	1,691,174	22,305,787
2002-03	1,230	20,408,704	89	1,636,120	22,044,824
2003-04	1,230	20,356,199	89	1,708,691	22,064,890

[1] First expansion: Los Angeles, Pittsburgh, California (Cleveland),Philadelphia, St. Louis and Minnesota (Dallas)
[2] Second expansion: Buffalo and Vancouver
[3] Third expansion: Atlanta (Calgary) and New York Islanders
[4] Fourth expansion: Kansas City (Colorado, New Jersey) and Washington
[5] Fifth expansion: Edmonton, Hartford (Carolina), Quebec (Colorado) and Winnipeg (Phoenix)
[6] Sixth expansion: San Jose
[7] Seventh expansion: Ottawa and Tampa Bay
[8] Includes 24 neutral site games
[9] Eighth expansion: Anaheim and Florida
[10] Includes 26 neutral site games
[11] Lockout resulted in the cancellation of 468 regular-season games.
[12] Ninth expansion: Nashville
[13] Tenth expansion: Atlanta
[14] Eleventh expansion: Columbus and Minnesota

Major Rule Changes

1910-11 — Game changed from two 30-minute periods to three 20-minute periods.

1911-12 — National Hockey Association (forerunner of the NHL) originated six-man hockey, replacing seven-man game.

1917-18 — Goalies permitted to fall to the ice to make saves. Previously a goaltender was penalized for dropping to the ice.

1918-19 — Penalty rules amended. For minor fouls, substitutes not allowed until penalized player had served three minutes. For major fouls, no substitutes for five minutes. For match fouls, no substitutes allowed for the remainder of the game.

With the addition of two lines painted on the ice twenty feet from center, three playing zones were created, producing a forty-foot neutral center ice area in which forward passing was permitted. Kicking the puck was permitted in this neutral zone.

Tabulation of assists began.

1921-22 — Goaltenders allowed to pass the puck forward up to their own blue line.

Overtime limited to twenty minutes.

Minor penalties changed from three minutes to two minutes.

1923-24 — Match foul defined as actions deliberately injuring or disabling an opponent. For such actions, a player was fined not less than $50 and ruled off the ice for the balance of the game. A player assessed a match penalty may be replaced by a substitute at the end of 20 minutes. Match penalty recipients must meet with the League president who can assess additional punishment.

1925-26 — Delayed penalty rules introduced. Each team must have a minimum of four players on the ice at all times.

Two rules were amended to encourage offense: No more than two defensemen permitted to remain inside a team's own blue line when the puck has left the defensive zone. A faceoff to be called for ragging the puck unless short-handed.

Team captains only players allowed to talk to referees.

Goaltender's leg pads limited to 12-inch width.

Timekeeper's gong to mark end of periods rather than referee's whistle. Teams to dress a maximum of 12 players for each game from a roster of no more than 14 players.

1926-27 — Blue lines repositioned to sixty feet from each goal-line, thereby enlarging the neutral zone and standardizing distance from blue line to goal.

Uniform goal nets adopted throughout NHL with goal posts securely fastened to the ice.

1927-28 — To further encourage offense, forward passes allowed in defending and neutral zones and goaltender's pads reduced in width from 12 to 10 inches.

Game standardized at three twenty-minute periods of stop-time separated by ten-minute intermissions. Teams to change ends after each period.

Ten minutes of sudden-death overtime to be played if the score is tied after regulation time.

Minor penalty to be assessed to any player other than a goaltender for deliberately picking up the puck while it is in play. Minor penalty to be assessed for deliberately shooting the puck out of play.

The Art Ross goal net adopted as the official net of the NHL.

Maximum length of hockey sticks limited to 53 inches measured from heel of blade to end of handle. No minimum length stipulated.

Home teams given choice of end to defend at start of game.

1928-29 — Forward passing permitted in defensive and neutral zones and into attacking zone if pass receiver is in neutral zone when pass is made. No forward passing allowed inside attacking zone.

Minor penalty to be assessed to any player who delays the game by passing the puck back into his defensive zone.

Ten-minute overtime without sudden-death provision to be played in games tied after regulation time. Games tied after this overtime period declared a draw.

Exclusive of goaltenders, team to dress at least 8 and no more than 12 skaters.

Major Rule Changes — *continued*

1929-30 — Forward passing permitted inside all three zones but not permitted across either blue line.

Kicking the puck allowed, but a goal cannot be scored by kicking the puck in.

No more than three players including the goaltender may remain in their defensive zone when the puck has gone up ice. Minor penalties to be assessed for the first two violations of this rule in a game; major penalties thereafter.

Goaltenders forbidden to hold the puck. Pucks caught must be cleared immediately. For infringement of this rule, a faceoff to be taken ten feet in front of the goal with no player except the goaltender standing between the faceoff spot and the goal-line.

Highsticking penalties introduced.

Maximum number of players in uniform increased from 12 to 15.

December 21, 1929 — Forward passing rules instituted at the beginning of the 1929-30 season more than doubled number of goals scored. Partway through the season, these rules were further amended to read, "No attacking player allowed to precede the play when entering the opposing defensive zone." This is similar to modern offside rule.

1930-31 — A player without a complete stick ruled out of play and forbidden from taking part in further action until a new stick is obtained. A player who has broken his stick must obtain a replacement at his bench.

A further refinement of the offside rule stated that the puck must first be propelled into the attacking zone before any player of the attacking side can enter that zone; for infringement of this rule a faceoff to take place at the spot where the infraction took place.

1931-32 — Though there is no record of a team attempting to play with two goaltenders on the ice, a rule was instituted which stated that each team was allowed only one goaltender on the ice at one time.

Attacking players forbidden to impede the movement or obstruct the vision of opposing goaltenders.

Defending players with the exception of the goaltender forbidden from falling on the puck within 10 feet of the net.

1932-33 — Each team to have captain on the ice at all times.

If the goaltender is removed from the ice to serve a penalty, the manager of the club to appoint a substitute.

Match penalty with substitution after five minutes instituted for kicking another player.

1933-34 — Number of players permitted to stand in defensive zone restricted to three including goaltender.

Visible time clocks required in each rink.

Two referees replace one referee and one linesman.

1934-35 — Penalty shot awarded when a player is tripped and thus prevented from having a clear shot on goal, having no player to pass to other than the offending player. Shot taken from inside a 10-foot circle located 38 feet from the goal. The goaltender must not advance more than one foot from his goal-line when the shot is taken.

1937-38 — Rules introduced governing icing the puck.

Penalty shot awarded when a player other than a goaltender falls on the puck within 10 feet of the goal.

1938-39 — Penalty shot modified to allow puck carrier to skate in before shooting.

One referee and one linesman replace two referee system.

Blue line widened to 12 inches.

Maximum number of players in uniform increased from 14 to 15.

1939-40 — A substitute replacing a goaltender removed from ice to serve a penalty may use a goaltender's stick and gloves but no other goaltending equipment.

1940-41 — Flooding ice surface between periods made obligatory.

1941-42 — Penalty shots classified as minor and major. Minor shot to be taken from a line 28 feet from the goal. Major shot, awarded when a player is tripped with only the goaltender to beat, permits the player taking the penalty shot to skate right into the goalkeeper and shoot from point-blank range.

One referee and two linesmen employed to officiate games.

For playoffs, standby minor league goaltenders employed by NHL as emergency substitutes.

1942-43 — Because of wartime restrictions on train scheduling, regular-season overtime was discontinued on November 21, 1942.

Player limit reduced from 15 to 14. Minimum of 12 men in uniform abolished.

1943-44 — Red line at center ice introduced to speed up the game and reduce offside calls. This rule is considered to mark the beginning of the modern era in the NHL.

1945-46 — Goal indicator lights synchronized with official time clock required at all rinks.

1946-47 — System of signals by officials to indicate infractions introduced.

Linesmen from neutral cities employed for all games.

1947-48 — Goal awarded when a player with the puck has an open net to shoot at and a thrown stick prevents the shot on goal. Major penalty to any player who throws his stick in any zone other than defending zone. If a stick is thrown by a player in his defending zone but the thrown stick is not considered to have prevented a goal, a penalty shot is awarded.

All playoff games played until a winner determined, with 20-minute sudden-death overtime periods separated by 10-minute intermissions.

1949-50 — Ice surface painted white.

Clubs allowed to dress 17 players exclusive of goaltenders.

Major penalties incurred by goaltenders served by a member of the goaltender's team instead of resulting in a penalty shot.

1950-51 — Each team required to provide an emergency goaltender in attendance with full equipment at each game for use by either team in the event of illness or injury to a regular goaltender.

1951-52 — Home teams to wear basic white uniforms; visiting teams basic colored uniforms.

Goal crease enlarged from 3 × 7 feet to 4 × 8 feet.

Number of players in uniform reduced to 15 plus goaltenders.

Faceoff circles enlarged from 10-foot to 15-foot radius.

1952-53 — Teams permitted to dress 15 skaters on the road and 16 at home.

1953-54 — Number of players in uniform set at 16 plus goaltenders.

1954-55 — Number of players in uniform set at 18 plus goaltenders up to December 1 and 16 plus goaltenders thereafter. Teams agree to wear colored uniforms at home and white uniforms on the road.

1956-57 — Player serving a minor penalty allowed to return to ice when a goal is scored by opposing team.

1959-60 — Players prevented from leaving their benches to enter into an altercation. Substitutions permitted providing substitutes do not enter into altercation.

1960-61 — Number of players in uniform set at 16 plus goaltenders.

1961-62 — Penalty shots to be taken by the player against whom the foul was committed. In the event of a penalty shot called in a situation where a particular player hasn't been fouled, the penalty shot to be taken by any player on the ice when the foul was committed.

1964-65 — No body contact on faceoffs.

In playoff games, each team to have its substitute goaltender dressed in his regular uniform except for leg pads and body protector. All previous rules governing standby goaltenders terminated.

1965-66 — Teams required to dress two goaltenders for each regular-season game. Maximum stick length increased to 55 inches.

1966-67 — Substitution allowed on coincidental major penalties.

Between-periods intermissions fixed at 15 minutes.

1967-68 — If a penalty incurred by a goaltender is a co-incident major, the penalty to be served by a player of the goaltender's team on the ice at the time the penalty was called. Limit of curvature of hockey stick blade set at 1½ inches.

1969-70 — Limit of curvature of hockey stick blade set at 1 inch.

1970-71 — Home teams to wear basic white uniforms; visiting teams basic colored uniforms.

Limit of curvature of hockey stick blade set at ½ inch.

Minor penalty for deliberately shooting the puck out of the playing area.

1971-72 — Number of players in uniform set at 17 plus 2 goaltenders.

Third man to enter an altercation assessed an automatic game misconduct penalty.

1972-73 — Minimum width of stick blade reduced to 2 inches from 2½ inches.

1974-75 — Bench minor penalty imposed if a penalized player does not proceed directly and immediately to the penalty box.

1976-77 — Rule dealing with fighting amended to provide a major and game misconduct penalty for any player who is clearly the instigator of a fight.

1977-78 — Teams requesting a stick measurement to be assessed a minor penalty in the event that the measured stick does not violate the rules.

1979-80 — Wearing of helmets made mandatory for players entering the NHL.

1980-81 — Maximum stick length increased to 58 inches.

1981-82 — If both of a team's listed goaltenders are incapacitated, the team can dress and play any eligible goaltender who is available.

1982-83 — Number of players in uniform set at 18 plus 2 goaltenders.

1983-84 — Five-minute sudden-death overtime to be played in regular-season games that are tied at the end of regulation time.

1985-86 — Substitutions allowed in the event of co-incidental minor penalties. Maximum stick length increased to 60 inches.

1986-87 — Delayed off-side is no longer in effect once the players of the offending team have cleared the opponents' defensive zone.

1990-91 — The goal lines, blue lines, defensive zone face-off circles and markings all moved one foot out from the end boards, creating 11 feet of room behind the nets and shrinking the neutral zone from 60 to 58 feet.

1991-92 — Video replays employed to assist referees in goal/no goal situations. Size of goal crease increased. Crease changed to semi-circular configuration. Time clock to record tenths of a second in last minute of each period and overtime. Major and game misconduct penalty for checking from behind into boards. Penalties added for crease infringement and unnecessary contact with goaltender. Goal disallowed if puck enters net while a player of the attacking team is standing on the goal crease line, is in the goal crease or places his stick in the goal crease.

1992-93 — No substitutions allowed in the event of coincidental minor penalties called when both teams are at full strength. Wearing of helmets made optional for forwards and defensemen. Minor penalty for attempting to draw a penalty ("diving"). Major and game misconduct penalty for checking from behind into goal frame. Game misconduct penalty for instigating a fight. High sticking redefined to include any use of the stick above waist-height. Previous rule stipulated shoulder-height.

1993-94 — High sticking redefined to allow goals scored with a high stick below the height of the crossbar of the goal frame.

1996-97 — Maximum stick length increased to 63 inches.

1998-99 — The league instituted a two-referee system with each team to play 20 regular-season games with two referees and a pair of linesmen. Also, the goal lines, blue lines, defensive zone face-off circles and markings all moved two feet closer to center, creating 13 feet of room behind the nets and cutting the neutral zone from 58 to 54 feet. The goal crease was altered so that it extends only one foot beyond each goal post (eight feet across in total) and has square sides for the first 4'6". Only the top of the crease remains rounded.

1999-2000 — Each team to play 25 home and 25 road games using the two-referee system. Crease rule revised to implement a "no harm, no foul, no video review" standard. An attacking player's position, whether inside or outside the crease, does not, in itself, determine whether a goal should be allowed or disallowed. The on-ice judgement of the referee(s) — instead of video review — will determine if a goal is "good" or not. Also, regular-season games tied at the end of three periods will result in each team being awarded one point in the standings. As before, there will be a five-minute sudden death overtime when the score is tied after three periods, but each team will play "four on four," with four skaters and a goalkeeper. In the event that penalties dictate that one team has a two-man advantage, the penalized team plays with three skaters while the team with the two-man advantage adds a fifth skater. A team that scores a goal in regular-season overtime is credited with a win and earns two points in the standings. A team scored upon in regular-season overtime is credited with an overtime loss and earns one point in the standings.

2000-01 — All games to be played using the two-referee system.

2002-03 — "Hurry-up" faceoff and line-change rules implemented.

2003-04 — Home teams to wear basic colored uniforms; visiting teams basic white uniforms. Maximum length of goaltender's pads set at 38 inches.

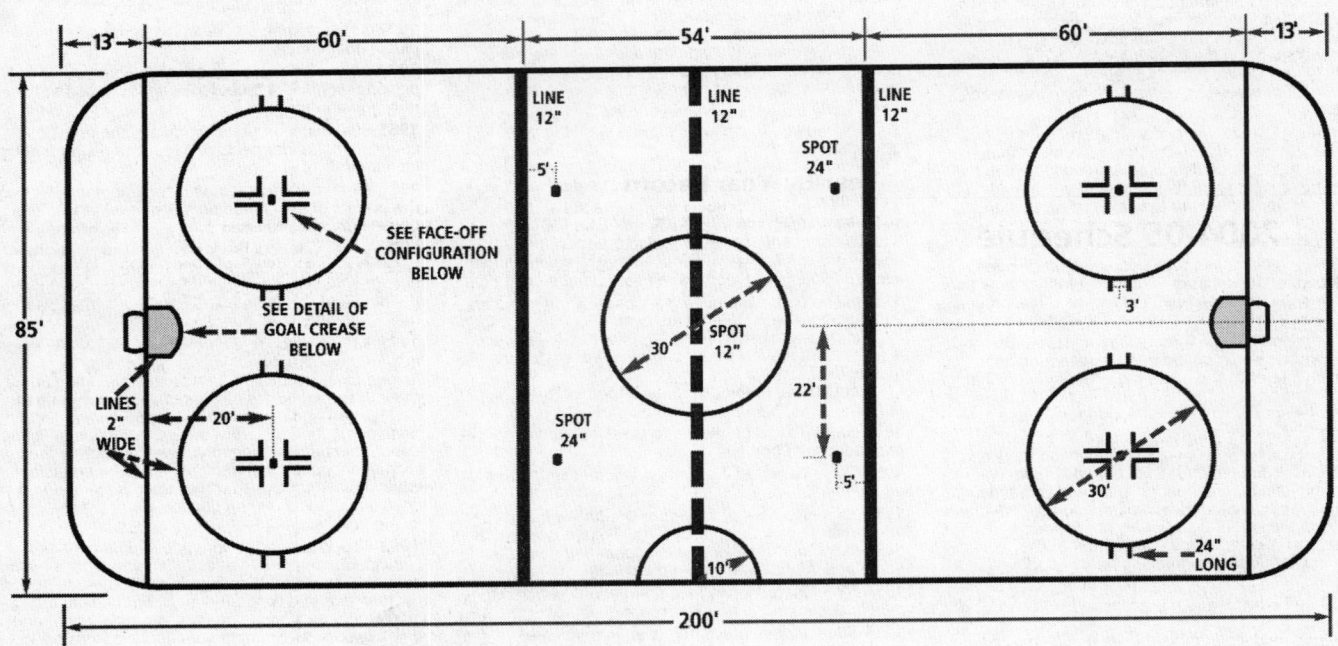

NHL RINK DIMENSIONS

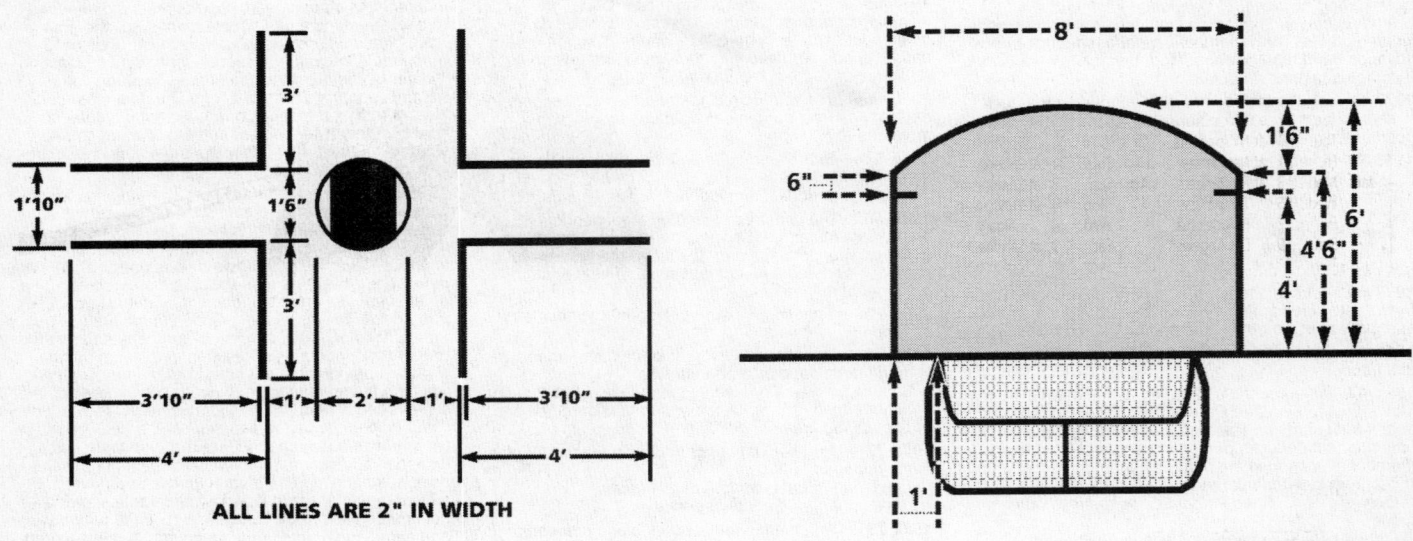

FACEOFF CONFIGURATION

CREASE DIMENSIONS

Mighty Ducks of Anaheim

2003-04 Results: 29w-35L-10T-8OTL 76PTS.
Fourth, Pacific Division

Year-by-Year Record

Season	GP	Home W	L	T	OL	Road W	L	T	OL	Overall W	L	T	OL	GF	GA	Pts.	Finished	Playoff Result
2003-04	82	19	11	7	4	10	24	3	4	29	35	10	8	184	213	76	4th, Pacific Div.	Out of Playoffs
2002-03	82	22	10	7	2	18	17	2	4	40	27	9	6	203	193	95	2nd, Pacific Div.	Lost Final
2001-02	82	15	19	5	2	14	23	3	1	29	42	8	3	175	198	69	5th, Pacific Div.	Out of Playoffs
2000-01	82	15	20	4	2	10	21	7	3	25	41	11	5	188	245	66	5th, Pacific Div.	Out of Playoffs
1999-2000	82	19	13	7	2	15	20	5	1	34	33	12	3	217	227	83	5th, Pacific Div.	Out of Playoffs
1998-99	82	21	14	6	...	14	20	7	...	35	34	13	...	215	206	83	3rd, Pacific Div.	Lost Conf. Quarter-Final
1997-98	82	12	23	6	...	14	20	7	...	26	43	13	...	205	261	65	6th, Pacific Div.	Out of Playoffs
1996-97	82	23	12	6	...	13	21	7	...	36	33	13	...	245	233	85	2nd, Pacific Div.	Lost Conf. Semi-Final
1995-96	82	22	15	4	...	13	24	4	...	35	39	8	...	234	247	78	4th, Pacific Div.	Out of Playoffs
1994-95	48	11	9	4	...	5	18	1	...	16	27	5	...	125	164	37	6th, Pacific Div.	Out of Playoffs
1993-94	84	14	26	2	...	19	20	3	...	33	46	5	...	229	251	71	4th, Pacific Div.	Out of Playoffs

2004-05 Schedule

Oct.	Wed.	13	Calgary		Wed.	12	St. Louis
	Fri.	15	San Jose		Fri.	14	Vancouver
	Sun.	17	at Los Angeles*		Mon.	17	Columbus*
	Wed.	20	Los Angeles		Wed.	19	San Jose
	Sat.	23	at Nashville		Sun.	23	at Calgary*
	Mon.	25	at Detroit		Mon.	24	at Edmonton
	Tue.	26	at Minnesota		Wed.	26	Nashville
	Thu.	28	at Chicago		Sat.	29	at Minnesota*
	Sat.	30	at Boston		Sun.	30	at Columbus*
Nov.	Wed.	3	Atlanta	**Feb.**	Tue.	1	at Detroit
	Fri.	5	Pittsburgh		Thu.	3	at Philadelphia
	Sun.	7	at Vancouver		Sat.	5	at Florida
	Tue.	9	at Calgary		Mon.	7	at Dallas
	Fri.	12	at Chicago		Thu.	10	at St. Louis
	Sat.	13	at St. Louis		Wed.	16	Phoenix
	Wed.	17	Florida		Fri.	18	Colorado
	Fri.	19	Detroit		Sun.	20	Minnesota*
	Sat.	20	at Colorado		Wed.	23	at Phoenix
	Tue.	23	at Dallas		Fri.	25	Dallas
	Wed.	24	at Phoenix		Sun.	27	St. Louis*
	Fri.	26	Chicago*	**Mar.**	Tue.	1	at San Jose
	Sun.	28	Dallas*		Wed.	2	Minnesota
Dec.	Wed.	1	Washington		Fri.	4	Buffalo
	Fri.	3	at Colorado		Sun.	6	Vancouver*
	Wed.	8	Carolina		Tue.	8	San Jose
	Sun.	12	Edmonton*		Fri.	11	NY Rangers
	Tue.	14	at Los Angeles		Sun.	13	Chicago*
	Wed.	15	Nashville		Tue.	15	at Toronto
	Fri.	17	Colorado		Thu.	17	at Ottawa
	Sun.	19	Los Angeles*		Sat.	19	at Montreal
	Wed.	22	at Dallas		Mon.	21	Detroit
	Thu.	23	at Nashville		Wed.	23	Edmonton
	Sun.	26	Phoenix*		Thu.	24	at San Jose
	Tue.	28	at Columbus		Sat.	26	Dallas
	Thu.	30	at NY Islanders		Wed.	30	Phoenix
	Fri.	31	at New Jersey		Thu.	31	at Phoenix
Jan.	Mon.	3	at NY Rangers	**Apr.**	Sun.	3	at Edmonton*
	Wed.	5	Tampa Bay		Mon.	4	at Vancouver
	Fri.	7	Philadelphia		Wed.	6	Calgary
	Sun.	9	Los Angeles*		Sat.	9	at San Jose*
	Tue.	11	at Los Angeles		Sun.	10	Columbus*

* Denotes afternoon game.

Franchise date: June 15, 1993

PACIFIC DIVISION

12th NHL Season

In his first season in Anaheim, Sergei Fedorov led the Mighty Ducks with 31 goals and 65 points. He also led with six game-winning goals and two shorthanded efforts, and tied for the team lead with nine power-play goals.

2004-05 Player Personnel

FORWARDS	HT	WT	S	Place of Birth	Date	2003-04 Club
BURNETT, Garrett	6-3	230	L	Coquitlam, B.C.	9/23/75	Anaheim
CHISTOV, Stanislav	5-10	193	R	Chelyabinsk, USSR	4/17/83	Anaheim-Cincinnati (AHL)
FEDOROV, Sergei	6-2	205	L	Pskov, USSR	12/13/69	Anaheim
GETZLAF, Ryan	6-2	205	R	Regina, Sask.	5/10/85	Calgary (WHL)
GLENCROSS, Curtis	6-1	190	L	Kindersley, Sask.	12/28/82	Alaska/Anchorage-Cincinnati (AHL)
HEDSTROM, Jonathan	6-0	200	L	Skelleftea, Sweden	12/27/77	Djurgarden
HOLMQVIST, Mikael	6-3	205	L	Stockholm, Sweden	6/8/79	Anaheim-Cincinnati (AHL)
KUNITZ, Chris	6-0	200	L	Regina, Sask.	9/26/79	Anaheim-Cincinnati (AHL)
LECLERC, Mike	6-2	208	L	Winnipeg, Man.	11/10/76	Anaheim
LUPUL, Joffrey	6-1	198	R	Edmonton, Alta.	9/23/83	Anaheim-Cincinnati (AHL)
McDONALD, Andy	5-10	186	L	Strathroy, Ont.	8/25/77	Anaheim
NIEDERMAYER, Rob	6-2	204	L	Cassiar, B.C.	12/28/74	Anaheim
PAHLSSON, Samuel	5-11	212	L	Ornskoldsvik, Sweden	12/17/77	Anaheim
PROSPAL, Vaclav	6-2	195	L	Ceske Budejovice, Czech.	2/17/75	Anaheim
RUCCHIN, Steve	6-2	211	L	Thunder Bay, Ont.	7/4/71	Anaheim
SMIRNOV, Alexei	6-3	211	L	Tver, USSR	1/28/82	Anaheim-Cincinnati (AHL)
SYKORA, Petr	6-0	190	L	Plzen, Czech.	11/19/76	Anaheim

DEFENSEMEN						
CARNEY, Keith	6-2	211	L	Providence, RI	2/3/70	Anaheim
FOSTER, Kurtis	6-5	235	R	Carp, Ont.	11/24/81	Atlanta-Chicago (AHL)
MALEC, Tomas	6-2	210	L	Skalica, Czech.	5/13/82	Carolina-Lowell
OZOLINSH, Sandis	6-3	215	L	Riga, Latvia	8/3/72	Anaheim
POPOVIC, Mark	6-1	210	L	Stoney Creek, Ont.	10/11/82	Anaheim-Cincinnati (AHL)
ROME, Aaron	6-1	225	L	Nesbitt, Man.	9/27/83	Swift Current-Moose Jaw
SALEI, Ruslan	6-1	205	L	Minsk, USSR	11/2/74	Anaheim
SKOULA, Martin	6-2	195	L	Litomerice, Czech.	10/28/79	Colorado-Anaheim
VISHNEVSKI, Vitaly	6-2	206	L	Kharkov, USSR	3/18/80	Anaheim
WARD, Lance	6-3	220	L	Lloydminster, Alta.	6/2/78	Anaheim-Cincinnati (AHL)

GOALTENDERS	HT	WT	C	Place of Birth	Date	2003-04 Club
BRYZGALOV, Ilya	6-3	198	L	Togliatti, USSR	6/22/80	Anaheim-Cincinnati (AHL)
FERHI, Eddy	6-3	181	L	Charenton, France	11/26/79	Cincinnati (AHL)
GIGUERE, Jean-Sebastien	6-1	199	L	Montreal, Que.	5/16/77	Anaheim

2003-04 Scoring

* – rookie

Regular Season

Pos	#	Player	Team	GP	G	A	Pts	+/–	PIM	PP	SH	GW	GT	S	%
C	91	Sergei Fedorov	ANA	80	31	34	65	–5	42	9	2	6	1	268	11.6
L	40	Vaclav Prospal	ANA	82	19	35	54	–9	54	7	0	4	1	185	10.3
R	39	Petr Sykora	ANA	81	23	29	52	–9	34	6	0	2	0	277	8.3
C	20	Steve Rucchin	ANA	82	20	23	43	–14	12	9	1	1	0	148	13.5
C	15	* Joffrey Lupul	ANA	75	13	21	34	–6	28	4	0	2	1	137	9.5
C	19	Andy Mcdonald	ANA	79	9	21	30	–13	24	2	1	1	1	162	5.6
C	44	Rob Niedermayer	ANA	55	12	16	28	–6	34	6	0	2	1	111	10.8
D	28	Niclas Havelid	ANA	79	6	20	26	–28	28	5	0	3	0	122	4.9
D	14	Martin Skoula	COL	58	2	14	16	2	30	0	0	0	0	54	3.7
			ANA	21	2	7	9	3	2	1	0	1	0	30	6.7
			TOTAL	79	4	21	25	5	32	1	0	1	0	84	4.8
C	26	Samuel Pahlsson	ANA	82	8	14	22	–2	52	1	0	2	0	134	6.0
L	10	Jason Krog	ANA	80	6	12	18	–4	16	1	0	1	0	111	5.4
L	23	Stanislav Chistov	ANA	56	2	16	18	–16	26	2	0	0	0	70	2.9
D	5	Vitaly Vishnevski	ANA	73	6	10	16	0	51	0	0	0	0	86	7.0
D	8	Sandis Ozolinsh	ANA	36	5	11	16	–7	24	1	0	2	1	58	8.6
D	24	Ruslan Salei	ANA	82	4	11	15	–1	110	0	1	2	0	145	2.8
L	27	Petr Schastlivy	OTT	43	2	4	6	–1	14	1	0	1	0	37	5.4
			ANA	22	2	0	2	–3	4	0	0	1	0	48	4.2
			TOTAL	65	4	4	8	–4	18	1	0	2	0	85	4.7
D	3	Keith Carney	ANA	69	2	5	7	–5	42	1	0	0	0	58	3.4
L	38	* Chris Kunitz	ANA	21	0	6	6	1	12	0	0	0	0	31	0.0
L	12	Mike Leclerc	ANA	10	1	3	4	–1	4	0	0	0	0	19	5.3
D	4	Lance Ward	ANA	46	0	4	4	–1	94	0	0	0	0	26	0.0
L	17	* Cam Severson	ANA	31	3	0	3	–3	50	1	0	0	0	24	12.5
L	55	Garrett Burnett	ANA	39	1	2	3	0	184	0	0	0	0	24	4.2
C	18	* Mikael Holmqvist	ANA	21	2	0	2	–6	25	0	0	0	0	18	11.1
C	46	* Tony Martensson	ANA	6	1	1	2	–2	0	0	0	0	0	4	25.0
D	41	Chris Armstrong	ANA	4	0	1	1	0	0	0	0	0	0	8	0.0
L	22	Alexei Smirnov	ANA	8	0	1	1	–0	0	0	0	0	0	8	0.0
D	33	* Mark Popovic	ANA	1	0	0	0	0	0	0	0	0	0	1	0.0
L	48	Casey Hankinson	ANA	4	0	0	0	0	4	0	0	0	0	0	0.0
R	21	Dan Bylsma	ANA	11	0	0	0	–3	0	0	0	0	0	6	0.0

Goaltending

No.	Goaltender	GPI	Mins	Avg	W	L	T	EN	SO	GA	SA	S%	G	A	PIM
30	* Ilja Bryzgalov	1	60	2.00	1	0	0	0	2	2	28	.929	0	0	0
29	Martin Gerber	32	1698	2.26	11	12	4	0	2	64	785	.918	0	0	4
35	J-S Giguere	55	3210	2.62	17	31	6	4	3	140	1623	.914	0	2	4
	Totals	**82**	**5000**	**2.56**	**29**	**43**	**10**	**7**	**5**	**213**	**2443**	**.913**			

Coach

BABCOCK, MIKE
Coach, Mighty Ducks of Anaheim.
Born in Manitouwadge, Ont., April 29, 1963.

The Mighty Ducks of Anaheim announced Mike Babcock as the club's head coach on May 22, 2002. In his first season behind the bench in 2002-03, he led the team to the seventh game of the Stanley Cup Finals. Babcock spent the previous two seasons as head coach of the Cincinnati Mighty Ducks, Anaheim's primary development affiliate in the American Hockey League. While with Cincinnati, he led the club to a franchise-best 41 wins and 95 points in 2000-01.

Babcock earned the honor of coaching the Canadian World Junior team in 1997, leading the club to its fifth consecutive gold medal in the tournament. In 2004, he coached Team Canada to its second straight gold medal at the World Championships.

Prior to joining the Mighty Ducks, Babcock had a successful six-year run as the head coach of the Spokane Chiefs of the Western Hockey League. While with Spokane, he had a regular-season record of 224-175-29 (.557 winning percentage, the highest in the WHL in that span). He was twice named WHL coach of the year (1996 & 2000) after taking the franchise to the league finals both seasons. Additionally, he was the head coach of the 2000 WHL West Division All-Star team.

In 1988, Babcock was named head coach at Red Deer College in Red Deer, Alberta. He spent three seasons at the school, winning the Alberta college championship and coach of the year honors in 1989. Babcock won a national championship and was again named the coach of the year while with the University of Lethbridge in 1993-94. He began his WHL career as head coach of the Moose Jaw Warriors from 1991 to 1993.

Coaching Record

Season	Team	Games	Regular Season			Games	Playoffs	
			W	L	T		W	L
1991-92	Moose Jaw (WHL)	72	33	36	3	4	0	4
1992-93	Moose Jaw (WHL)	72	27	42	3	....	....	....
1993-94	U. of Lethbridge (CIAU)	28	19	7	2	....	....	....
1994-95	Spokane (WHL)	72	32	36	4	11	6	5
1995-96	Spokane (WHL)	72	50	18	4	9	3	6
1996-97	Spokane (WHL)	65	31	30	4	9	4	5
1997-98	Spokane (WHL)	72	45	23	4	18	10	8
1998-99	Spokane (WHL)	72	19	44	9	....	....	....
1999-2000	Spokane (WHL)	72	47	21	4	20	15	5
2000-01	Cincinnati (WHL)	80	41	26	13	4	1	3
2001-02	Cincinnati (WHL)	80	33	33	14	3	1	2
2002-03	**Anaheim (NHL)**	**82**	**40**	**33**	**9**	**21**	**15**	**6**
2003-04	**Anaheim (NHL)**	**82**	**29**	**43**	**10**	**....**	**....**	**....**
	NHL Totals	**164**	**69**	**76**	**19**	**21**	**15**	**6**

Jean-Sebastien Giguere ranked 11th in the NHL with 1,623 saves in 2003-04.

Club Records

Team

(Figures in brackets for season records are games played; records for fewest points, wins, ties, losses, goals, goals against are for 70 or more games)

Most Points	95	2002-03 (82)
Most Wins	40	2002-03 (82)
Most Ties	13	1996-97 (82); 1997-98 (82); 1998-99 (82)
Most Losses	46	1993-94 (84)
Most Goals	245	1996-97 (82)
Most Goals Against	261	1997-98 (82)
Fewest Points	65	1997-98 (82)
Fewest Wins	25	2000-01 (82)
Fewest Ties	5	1993-94 (84)
Fewest Losses	27	2002-03 (82)
Fewest Goals	175	2001-02 (82)
Fewest Goals Against	193	2002-03 (82)

Longest Winning Streak

Overall	7	Feb. 20-Mar. 7/99
Home	5	Four times
Away	5	Nov. 26-Dec. 26/99

Longest Undefeated Streak

Overall	12	Feb. 22-Mar. 19/97 (7 wins, 5 ties)
Home	14	Feb. 12-Apr. 9/97 (10 wins, 4 ties)
Away	5	Five times

Longest Losing Streak

Overall	8	Oct. 12-30/96
Home	8	Jan. 10-Feb. 9/01
Away	6	Four times

Longest Winless Streak

Overall	9	Twice
Home	11	Jan. 5-Feb. 14/01 (8 losses, 3 ties)
Away	13	Nov. 1-Dec. 27/03 (11 losses, 2 ties)
Most Shutouts, Season	9	2002-03 (82)
Most PIM, Season	1,843	1997-98 (82)
Most Goals, Game	8	Three times

Individual

Most Seasons	10	Steve Rucchin
Most Games	616	Steve Rucchin
Most Goals, Career	300	Paul Kariya
Most Assists, Career	369	Paul Kariya
Most Points, Career	669	Paul Kariya (300G, 369A)
Most PIM, Career	788	Dave Karpa
Most Shutouts, Career	27	Guy Hebert

Longest Consecutive

Games Streak	237	Oleg Tverdovsky (Oct. 2/99-Mar. 24/02)
Most Goals, Season	52	Teemu Selanne (1997-98)
Most Assists, Season	62	Paul Kariya (1998-99)
Most Points, Season	109	Teemu Selanne (1996-97; 51G, 58A)
Most PIM, Season	285	Todd Ewen (1995-96)
Most Points, Defenseman, Season	56	Fredrik Olausson (1998-99; 16G, 40A)
Most Points, Center, Season	67	Steve Rucchin (1996-97; 19G, 48A)
Most Points, Right Wing, Season	109	Teemu Selanne (1996-97; 51G, 58A)
Most Points, Left Wing, Season	108	Paul Kariya (1995-96; 50G, 58A)
Most Points, Rookie, Season	39	Paul Kariya (1994-95; 18G, 21A)
Most Shutouts, Season	8	Jean-Sebastien Giguere (2002-03)
Most Goals, Game	3	Twenty-one times
Most Assists, Game	5	Dmitri Mironov (Dec. 12/97)
Most Points, Game	5	Six times

General Managers' History

Jack Ferreira, 1993-94 to 1997-98; Pierre Gauthier, 1998-99 to 2001-02; Bryan Murray, 2002-03 to 2003-04; Al Coates, 2004-05.

Coaching History

Ron Wilson, 1993-94 to 1996-97; Pierre Page, 1997-98; Craig Hartsburg, 1998-99, 1999-2000; Craig Hartsburg and Guy Charron, 2000-01; Bryan Murray, 2001-02; Mike Babcock, 2002-03 to date.

Captains' History

Troy Loney, 1993-94; Randy Ladouceur, 1994-95, 1995-96; Paul Kariya, 1996-97; Paul Kariya and Teemu Selanne, 1997-98; Paul Kariya, 1998-99 to 2002-03; Steve Rucchin, 2003-04 to date.

All-time Record vs. Other Clubs

Regular Season

	At Home								On Road								Total							
	GP	W	L	T	OL	GF	GA	PTS	GP	W	L	T	OL	GF	GA	PTS	GP	W	L	T	OL	GF	GA	PTS
Atlanta	4	2	2	0	0	12	9	4	4	3	1	0	0	16	10	6	8	5	3	0	0	28	19	10
Boston	9	2	3	2	2	18	24	8	8	4	4	0	0	24	23	8	17	6	7	2	2	42	47	16
Buffalo	9	2	7	0	0	15	30	4	9	2	4	3	0	20	25	7	18	4	11	3	0	35	55	11
Calgary	26	12	8	6	0	80	69	30	25	9	15	1	0	61	72	19	51	21	23	7	0	141	141	49
Carolina	9	5	3	1	0	29	26	11	9	3	5	1	0	19	23	7	18	8	8	2	0	48	49	18
Chicago	22	12	7	3	0	58	47	27	24	10	12	2	0	58	67	22	46	22	19	5	0	116	114	49
Colorado	21	7	10	3	1	48	53	18	21	6	10	4	1	53	65	17	42	13	20	7	2	101	118	35
Columbus	8	5	2	1	0	24	16	11	8	2	6	0	0	15	23	4	16	7	8	1	0	39	39	15
Dallas	27	11	13	3	0	61	66	25	27	5	19	2	1	52	101	13	54	16	32	5	1	113	167	38
Detroit	22	7	11	4	0	52	65	18	22	2	15	3	2	49	83	9	44	9	26	7	2	101	148	27
Edmonton	26	15	9	2	0	71	64	32	25	8	15	0	2	50	57	18	51	23	24	2	2	121	121	50
Florida	9	3	5	1	0	27	30	7	8	2	3	2	1	17	23	7	17	5	8	3	1	44	53	14
Los Angeles	30	13	6	7	4	100	80	37	30	9	17	4	0	72	89	22	60	22	23	11	4	172	169	59
Minnesota	8	5	2	0	1	19	17	11	8	3	3	2	0	14	13	8	16	8	5	2	1	33	30	19
Montreal	8	3	5	0	0	25	27	6	8	2	4	2	0	19	24	6	16	5	9	2	0	44	51	12
Nashville	12	9	1	0	2	33	20	20	12	5	5	2	0	28	24	12	24	14	6	2	2	61	44	32
New Jersey	10	4	5	1	0	26	26	9	8	1	6	0	1	14	31	3	18	5	11	1	1	40	57	12
NY Islanders	9	2	4	3	0	18	24	7	8	3	4	1	0	23	24	7	17	5	8	4	0	41	48	14
NY Rangers	8	6	1	0	1	32	25	13	9	5	2	1	0	26	23	12	17	11	3	1	2	58	48	25
Ottawa	9	4	3	2	0	21	18	10	8	3	4	1	0	19	24	7	17	7	7	3	0	40	42	17
Philadelphia	9	4	3	2	0	30	28	10	8	2	3	3	0	17	22	7	17	6	6	5	0	47	50	17
Phoenix	27	15	9	3	0	74	67	33	26	13	10	2	1	77	75	29	53	28	19	5	1	151	142	62
Pittsburgh	8	5	3	0	0	24	10	9	2	2	0	0	0	7	6	4	10	7	3	0	0	31	16	13
St. Louis	22	7	13	2	0	54	65	16	22	7	10	3	2	56	67	19	44	14	23	5	2	110	132	35
San Jose	30	11	17	2	0	78	99	24	30	14	13	2	1	80	84	31	60	25	30	4	1	158	183	55
Tampa Bay	8	4	3	1	0	24	20	9	9	5	4	0	0	23	17	10	17	9	7	1	0	47	37	19
Toronto	11	5	5	1	0	34	28	11	15	2	7	4	2	30	50	8	26	7	14	5	0	64	78	19
Vancouver	25	7	10	7	1	59	74	22	26	8	16	2	0	59	91	18	51	15	26	9	1	118	165	40
Washington	9	6	2	1	0	29	22	13	9	5	4	0	0	22	16	10	18	11	6	1	0	51	38	23
Totals	**435**	**193**	**172**	**58**	**12**	**1180**	**1163**	**456**	**435**	**145**	**228**	**49**	**13**	**1040**	**1275**	**352**	**870**	**338**	**400**	**107**	**25**	**2220**	**2438**	**808**

Playoffs

	Series	W	L	GP	W	L	T	GF	GA	Last Mtg.	Rnd.	Result
Dallas	1	1	0	6	4	2	0	14	14	2003	CSF	W 4-2
Detroit	3	1	2	12	4	8	0	24	36	2003	CQF	W 4-0
Minnesota	1	1	0	4	4	0	0	9	1	2003	CF	W 4-0
New Jersey	1	0	1	7	3	4	0	12	19	2003	F	L 3-4
Phoenix	1	1	0	7	4	3	0	17	17	1997	CQF	W 4-3
Totals	**7**	**4**	**3**	**36**	**19**	**17**	**0**	**76**	**87**			

Carolina totals include Hartford, 1993-94 to 1996-97.
Colorado totals include Quebec, 1993-94 to 1994-95.
Phoenix totals include Winnipeg, 1993-94 to 1995-96.

Playoff Results 2004-2000

Year	Round	Opponent	Result	GF	GA
2003	F	New Jersey	L 3-4	12	19
	CF	Minnesota	W 4-0	9	1
	CSF	Dallas	W 4-2	14	14
	CQF	Detroit	W 4-0	10	6

Abbreviations: Round: F - Final; CF – conference final; **CSF** – conference quarter-final; **CQF** – conference quarter-final

2003-04 Results

Oct.	8	at Dallas	1-4		9	Vancouver	2-5
	9	at Nashville	1-3		11	Columbus	2-2
	12	Phoenix	0-2		13	at Colorado	1-3
	17	Ottawa	0-3		15	at Edmonton	0-1
	19	Boston	3-4*		17	at Vancouver	2-1
	21	at San Jose	2-0		19	Calgary	1-5
	22	Philadelphia	4-3*		21	Detroit	2-2
	24	Buffalo	2-5		23	Minnesota	6-2
	26	Chicago	1-1		24	at Los Angeles	2-4
	28	at NY Rangers	3-1		28	Los Angeles	3-4*
	29	at Washington	4-2		30	Colorado	4-3*
Nov.	1	at NY Islanders	1-4	Feb.	1	at Calgary	4-6
	2	at Chicago	1-3		2	at Edmonton	1-2*
	4	at St. Louis	1-2*		4	Carolina	3-2
	8	at Phoenix	3-4*		11	Phoenix	5-3
	9	Phoenix	2-1*		13	at Calgary	1-2
	12	Toronto	5-1		14	at Vancouver	1-2
	16	St. Louis	4-3		16	Dallas	3-1
	18	at Colorado	1-2*		18	Columbus	3-1
	19	at Dallas	3-3		20	Nashville	2-3*
	21	Nashville	3-4*		22	at Dallas	0-4
	26	New Jersey	3-3		23	at Phoenix	1-1
	28	Chicago	4-3		25	Edmonton	4-2
	28	at Minnesota	1-1		28	at Los Angeles	1-2
Dec.	2	at Columbus	1-2		29	Los Angeles	6-3
	3	at Detroit	2-7	Mar.	3	Minnesota	2-0
	5	at Atlanta	2-6		5	at Chicago	5-2
	7	Dallas	4-0		6	at Pittsburgh	1-2
	10	San Jose	3-2		8	Montreal	1-2
	13	at San Jose	0-2		12	NY Islanders	1-3
	14	Edmonton	2-3		14	at Los Angeles	1-5
	19	Colorado	1-0		16	at Phoenix	3-2*
	21	San Jose	1-2		17	St. Louis	1-1
	22	at San Jose	1-2		19	San Jose	2-4
	27	at Florida	2-3		21	Detroit	8-6
	29	at Tampa Bay	2-0		23	at Nashville	2-3
	31	at Carolina	3-1		25	at St. Louis	2-3
Jan.	2	at Buffalo	2-5		26	at Columbus	1-3
	3	at Detroit	1-3		28	at Minnesota	1-2
	5	Dallas	2-2		31	Vancouver	1-3
	7	Los Angeles	4-4	Apr.	4	Calgary	2-1

* – Overtime

Entry Draft
Selections 2004-1993

2004 Pick		2001 Pick		1998 Pick		1995 Pick	
9	Ladislav Smid	5	Stanislav Chistov	5	Vitaly Vishnevski	4	Chad Kilger
39	Jordan Smith	35	Mark Popovic	32	Stephen Peat	29	Brian Wesenberg
74	Kyle Klubertanz	69	Joel Stepp	112	Viktor Wallin	55	Mike Leclerc
75	Tim Brent	102	Timo Parssinen	150	Trent Hunter	107	Igor Nikulin
172	Matt Auffrey	105	Vladimir Korsunov	178	Jesse Fibiger	133	Peter LeBoutillier
203	Gabriel Bouthillette	118	Brandon Rogers	205	David Bernier	159	Mike LaPlante
236	Matt Christie	137	Joel Perreault	233	Pelle Prestberg	185	Igor Karpenko
269	Janne Pesonen	170	Jan Tabacek	245	Andreas Andersson		

2003 Pick		2001 Pick (cont.)		1997 Pick		1994 Pick	
19	Ryan Getzlaf	224	Tony Martensson	18	Mikael Holmqvist	2	Oleg Tverdovsky
28	Corey Perry	232	Martin Gerber	45	Maxim Balmochnykh	28	Johan Davidsson
86	Shane Hynes	264	Pierre Parenteau	72	Jay Legault	67	Craig Reichert
90	Juha Alen			125	Luc Vaillancourt	80	Byron Briske
119	Nathan Saunders	**2000 Pick**		178	Tony Mohagen	106	Pavel Trnka
186	Andrew Miller	12	Alexei Smirnov	181	Mat Snesrud	132	Bates Battaglia
218	Dirk Southern	44	Ilya Bryzgalov	209	Rene Stussi	158	Rocky Welsing
250	Shane O'Brien	98	Jonas Ronnqvist	235	Tommi Degerman	184	Brad Englehart
280	Ville Mantymaa	134	Peter Podhradsky			236	Tommi Miettinen
		153	Bill Cass			262	Jeremy Stevenson

2002 Pick		1999 Pick		1996 Pick		1993 Pick	
7	Joffrey Lupul	44	Jordan Leopold	9	Ruslan Salei	4	Paul Kariya
37	Tim Brent	83	Niclas Havelid	35	Matt Cullen	30	Nikolai Tsulygin
71	Brian Lee	105	Alexandr Chagodayev	117	Brendan Buckley	56	Valeri Karpov
103	Joonas Vihko	141	Maxim Rybin	149	Blaine Russell	82	Joel Gagnon
140	George Davis	173	Jan Sandstrom	172	Timo Ahmaoja	108	Mikhail Shtalenkov
173	Luke Fritshaw	230	Petr Tenkrat	198	Kevin Kellett	134	Antti Aalto
261	Francois Caron	258	Brian Gornick	224	Tobias Johwelin	160	Matt Peterson
267	Chris Petrow					186	Tom Askey
						212	Vitali Kozel
						238	Anatoli Fedotov
						264	David Penney

Senior Vice-President/
Interim General Manager
& Alternate Governor

COATES, AL
Born in Listowel, Ont., December 3, 1945.

The Mighty Ducks announced on June 8, 2004 that Al Coates, senior vice president of business operations, had been named interim general manager, replacing Bryan Murray, who had accepted the head coaching position with the Ottawa Senators.

Coates, who has spent 34 years working in professional hockey, joined the Mighty Ducks on April 7, 2003. His responsibilities have included the overall business operations of the team, including the management of Disney ICE. He was previously an NHL general manager with the Calgary Flames from 1995 to 2000, acquiring current Flames Jarome Iginla and Robyn Regehr. While with Calgary, he also traded for current Mighty Ducks goaltender J.S. Giguere. Coates spent 20 years in the Calgary organization.

Coates joined the Ducks after spending three years with the New York Rangers and Madison Square Garden, overseeing the team and business operation of the Rangers' American Hockey League affiliate in Hartford. Coates was named vice president and general manager of the Hartford Wolfpack on July 26, 2000. Hartford realized substantial increases in attendance and revenues in year one as well as a more aggressive role within their community through reading programs and charity tournaments for the "Children's Home." Meanwhile as a member of the league executive committee, the AHL was expanding to 28 teams.

After completing a professional hockey career in Europe, Coates spent nine years in management with the Detroit Red Wings organization from 1971 to 1980; the first four years split between Detroit's American Hockey League development team in Tidewater, Va. and an experimental touring professional team based in London, England. The next five years were spent as a part of the Red Wings front office staff. Coates joined the Calgary Flames' inaugural staff in 1980-81 (after the franchise moved from Atlanta) as the team's director of public relations. Coates spent 20 years in the organization, also holding positions of assistant to the president (1982 to 1989), director of hockey administration (1989 to 1991), and assistant general manager (1991 to 1995), culminating with the position of executive vice president, general manager and alternate governor from 1995 to 2000.

While with the Flames, Coates led the team to success both on and off the ice. In addition to his role in helping the Flames to the 1989 Stanley Cup championship, he led the organization to great success in the Calgary community.

Club Directory

Arrowhead Pond of Anaheim

Mighty Ducks of Anaheim
Arrowhead Pond of Anaheim
2695 Katella Ave.
Anaheim, CA 92806
Phone **714/940-2900**
FAX 714/940-2953
Ticket Information 877/WILDWING
www.mightyducks.com
Capacity: 17,174

Executive Management
President and Governor. . . . . Jay Rasulo
Senior V.P./Interim G.M./Alternate Governor . . . . . . Al Coates
Assistant G.M./Hockey Administration. . . . . David McNab
Assistant G.M./Hockey Operations . . . . Chuck Fletcher
Executive Assistant/Team Travel Coordinator . . . . . . Maureen Nyeholt

Coaching Staff
Head Coach . . . . Mike Babcock
Assistant Coaches . . . . Lorne Henning, Paul MacLean, Greg Carvel
Goaltending Consultant . . . . François Allaire

Hockey Club Operations
Director of Player Personnel. . . . . Tim Murray
Director of Amateur Scouting . . . . Alain Chainey
Scouting Staff . . . . Ryan Barber, Jeff Crisp, Jan-Åke Danielson, Brent Flahr, Todd Hearty, Konstantin Krylov, Donald Marier, Wayne Meier , Pavel Routa, Floyd Smith, Tom Watt
Head Athletic Trainer . . . . Chris Phillips
Strength and Conditioning Coach . . . . Sean Skahan
Equipment Manager . . . . Mark O'Neill
Assistant Equipment Manager . . . . John Allaway
Training Room Assistants . . . . Vince Bennett, Guido Sendowsky
Cincinnati Mighty Ducks (AHL) Head Coach . . . . . . Brad Shaw
Team Physicians . . . . Dr. Ronald Glousman, Dr. Craig Milhouse
Oral Surgeon. . . . . Dr. Jeff Pulver
Visiting Team Equipment Attendant . . . . Chris Kincaid

Communications Department
Director, Communications and Team Services . . . . . Alex Gilchrist
Communications and Team Services Manager . . . . Merit Tully
Publications/Communications Representative . . . . . Scott Johnson
Team Photographer . . . . Debora Robinson (Lovero Group)

Finance and Administration Department
Director, Finance . . . . Mike McGee
Controller . . . . Melody Martin
Financial Analyst . . . . Rosanna Sitzman
Accounting Assistant. . . . . Rob Dumlao
Accounting Clerk . . . . Linda Dubois
Sr. EUCS Analyst . . . . Kevin Ramirez
Human Resources Business Partner . . . . Pat Navarro
Event Services Representative . . . . Jason Davis
Sr. Travel Consultant . . . . Taki Papadatos
General Manager, Disney ICE . . . . Art Trottier
Sr. Paralegal . . . . Tia Wood

Ticket Sales and Customer Service Department
Director, Ticket Sales & Customer Service . . . . Bill Chapin
Manager, Premium Sales and Service . . . . Ron Campbell
Premium Sales and Service Manager . . . . Bob Ruiz
Premium Club and Suite Marketing Representative . . . . Carolyn LaPierre
Premium Sales & Service Assistant . . . . Roxanne Gandara
Premium Ticketing Manager . . . . Dennis Keane
Ticketing Representative . . . . Gina Bulgheroni
Account Executives . . . . Bill Schaeffer, Ben Plaisted, Mike Morrow, Justin Sheppard
Group Sales Account Executives . . . . Ken Bamberg, Casey Norvall
Group Sales Secretary . . . . Jayme Johnson
Receptionist . . . . Jennifer Williams

Ticketing Department
Ticketing Operations Manager . . . . Christa Richards
Ticketing Supervisor . . . . Jonas Calicdan

Publicity and Community Development Department
Director, Publicity, Community Dev. & Synergy . . . . Charles Harris
Manager, Community Development . . . . Erin Bickmeier
Publicity/Community Relations Rep. . . . . Jesse Tyler
Website Editor . . . . Michael Corcoran
Alumni Association Director . . . . Guy Hebert

Broadcasting and Entertainment Department
Director, Broadcasting . . . . Aaron Teats
Telecast Director . . . . Mike Levy
Entertainment Manager . . . . Rod Murray
Production Manager . . . . Kent French
Television, KCAL (Ch. 9) &
   Fox Sports West 2 (Cable) . . . . John Ahlers, Brian Hayward
Radio, Flagship TBA & Mighty Ducks Radio Network . Steve Carroll

Sales and Marketing Department
Director, Sales & Marketing. . . . . Michael Williams
Marketing Manager . . . . Matt Savant
Marketing/Database Manager . . . . Veronica Tarnofsky
Marketing Representative . . . . Sara Heri
Sponsorship Services Manager . . . . Tamara Goddard
Advertising Sales Managers. . . . . James Kersten, Bryan Pringle, Matt Vicelja, Pam Kennedy
Sponsorship Services Representative . . . . Joseph Hwang

Miscellaneous
Team Colors . . . . Purple (PMS 518C), Jade (PMS 329C), Silver (PMS 429C) and White
Practice Facilities . . . . Disney ICE (300 W. Lincoln Ave.) and the Arrowhead Pond (2695 Katella Ave.)
Primary Developmental Affiliate . . . . Cincinnati Mighty Ducks (AHL)
Home Starting Times. . . . . Weeknights – 7:35 p.m.; Sundays – 5:05 p.m.
Press Box Phone 714/704-2623
Press Room . . . . 714/704-2514 or 2517

Atlanta Thrashers

2003-04 Results: 33w-37L-8T-4OTL 78PTS.
Second, Southeast Division

Year-by-Year Record

Season	GP	Home W	Home L	Home T	Home OL	Road W	Road L	Road T	Road OL	Overall W	Overall L	Overall T	Overall OL	GF	GA	Pts.	Finished	Playoff Result
2003-04	82	18	17	4	2	15	20	4	2	33	37	8	4	214	243	78	2nd, Southeast Div.	Out of Playoffs
2002-03	82	15	19	4	3	16	20	3	7	31	39	7	5	226	284	74	3rd, Southeast Div.	Out of Playoffs
2001-02	82	11	21	9	0	8	26	2	5	19	47	11	5	187	288	54	5th, Southeast Div.	Out of Playoffs
2000-01	82	10	23	6	2	13	22	6	0	23	45	12	2	211	289	60	4th, Southeast Div.	Out of Playoffs
1999-2000	82	9	26	3	3	5	31	4	1	14	57	7	4	170	313	39	5th, Southeast Div.	Out of Playoffs

2004-05 Schedule

Oct.	Thu.	14	at Carolina
	Sat.	16	Washington
	Tue.	19	at Washington
	Thu.	21	Buffalo
	Sat.	23	at NY Rangers
	Wed.	27	at Florida
	Fri.	29	Detroit
	Sat.	30	at Montreal
Nov.	Wed.	3	at Anaheim
	Thu.	4	at Los Angeles
	Sat.	6	at San Jose
	Mon.	8	New Jersey
	Wed.	10	Tampa Bay
	Fri.	12	at Carolina
	Sat.	13	at Tampa Bay
	Wed.	17	NY Rangers
	Fri.	19	NY Islanders
	Sat.	20	at Boston
	Tue.	23	Vancouver
	Fri.	26	at Philadelphia*
	Sat.	27	New Jersey
Dec.	Wed.	1	at Colorado
	Thu.	2	at Phoenix
	Sat.	4	at Nashville
	Tue.	7	Tampa Bay
	Fri.	10	Ottawa
	Sat.	11	at Washington
	Wed.	15	Carolina
	Thu.	16	at Toronto
	Sat.	18	at Carolina
	Tue.	21	NY Rangers
	Mon.	27	Carolina
	Wed.	29	Columbus
	Fri.	31	Washington*
Jan.	Sat.	1	at Ottawa
	Tue.	4	at New Jersey
	Thu.	6	Toronto
	Sat.	8	Washington*
	Tue.	11	at Buffalo
	Wed.	12	Nashville
	Fri.	14	Minnesota
	Mon.	17	at Florida*
	Wed.	19	Pittsburgh
	Fri.	21	Buffalo
	Sun.	23	Dallas
	Mon.	24	at Montreal
	Thu.	27	at NY Rangers
	Sat.	29	at Philadelphia*
	Sun.	30	at Washington
Feb.	Wed.	2	Carolina
	Fri.	4	Florida
	Sat.	5	at Tampa Bay
	Tue.	8	Boston
	Thu.	10	at Minnesota
	Tue.	15	at NY Islanders
	Wed.	16	at Chicago
	Sat.	19	at Pittsburgh
	Sun.	20	at Buffalo*
	Thu.	24	at Ottawa
	Sat.	26	at Toronto
Mar.	Tue.	1	at Pittsburgh
	Wed.	2	Philadelphia
	Fri.	4	Florida
	Sun.	6	Calgary*
	Mon.	7	at NY Islanders
	Wed.	9	Ottawa
	Fri.	11	Colorado
	Sun.	13	Edmonton*
	Tue.	15	Boston
	Thu.	17	at New Jersey
	Sat.	19	Pittsburgh
	Mon.	21	at Florida
	Wed.	23	Montreal
	Fri.	25	Toronto
	Sat.	26	at St. Louis
	Mon.	28	Florida
	Thu.	31	Philadelphia
Apr.	Sat.	2	NY Islanders
	Mon.	4	at Boston
	Wed.	6	Montreal
	Fri.	8	at Tampa Bay
	Sun.	10	Tampa Bay*

* Denotes afternoon game.

Franchise date: June 25, 1997

EASTERN NHL CONFERENCE

**SOUTHEAST
DIVISION**

**6th
NHL
Season**

Ilya Kovalchuk was busy in 2003-04, playing in 81 of 82 games and leading all NHL forwards in ice time (23:41 per game). He tied for the NHL lead with 41 goals and finished second in scoring with 87 points.

2004-05 Player Personnel

FORWARDS	HT	WT	S	Place of Birth	Date	2003-04 Club
AQUINO, Anthony	5-10	190	R	Mississauga, Ont.	8/1/82	Chicago (AHL)-Gwinnett
AUBIN, Serge	6-1	200	L	Val-d'Or, Que.	2/15/75	Atlanta
BABY, Stephen	6-5	230	R	Chicago, IL	1/31/80	Chicago (AHL)
BRENNAN, Kip	6-4	230	L	Kingston, Ont.	8/27/80	Los Angeles-Manchester-Atlanta
DOELL, Kevin	5-11	190	L	Saskatoon, Sask.	7/15/79	Gwinnett-Chicago (AHL)
HEATLEY, Dany	6-3	215	L	Freiburg, West Germany	1/21/81	Atlanta
KOVALCHUK, Ilya	6-2	220	R	Tver, USSR	4/15/83	Atlanta
KOZLOV, Vyacheslav	5-10	185	L	Voskresensk, USSR	5/3/72	Atlanta
LAROSE, Cory	6-0	190	L	Campbellton, N.B.	5/14/75	NY Rangers-Hartford
LARSEN, Brad	6-0	200	L	Nakusp, B.C.	6/28/77	Colorado-Hershey-Atlanta
LESSARD, Francis	6-2	225	R	Montreal, Que.	5/30/79	Atlanta
MacKENZIE, Derek	5-11	180	L	Sudbury, Ont.	6/11/81	Atlanta-Chicago (AHL)
MALONEY, Brian	6-1	205	L	Bassano, Alta.	9/27/78	Chicago (AHL)
McEACHERN, Shawn	5-11	200	L	Waltham, MA	2/28/69	Atlanta
MELLANBY, Scott	6-1	210	R	Montreal, Que.	6/11/66	St. Louis
PETROVICKY, Ronald	5-11	190	R	Zilina, Czechoslovakia	2/15/77	Atlanta
SANTALA, Tommi	6-2	210	R	Helsinki, Finland	6/27/79	Atlanta-Chicago (AHL)
SAVARD, Marc	5-10	195	L	Ottawa, Ont.	7/17/77	Atlanta
SCHELL, Brad	6-1	180	L	Scott, Sask.	8/5/84	Spokane
SIMON, Ben	6-0	200	L	Shaker Heights, OH	6/14/78	Milwaukee-Atlanta
STEFAN, Patrik	6-2	210	L	Pribram, Czech.	9/16/80	Atlanta
STEWART, Karl	5-10	175	L	Aurora, Ont.	6/30/83	Atlanta-Chicago (AHL)
STUART, Colin	6-1	195	L	Rochester, MN	7/8/82	Colorado College
VIGIER, J.P.	6-0	200	R	Notre Dame de Lourdes, Man.	9/11/76	Atlanta

DEFENSEMEN						
COBURN, Braydon	6-5	220	L	Calgary, Alta.	2/27/85	Portland (WHL)
DWYER, Jeff	6-1	205	L	Greenwich, CT	11/22/80	Yale-Chicago (AHL)
EXELBY, Garnet	6-1	215	L	Ste. Anne, Man.	8/16/81	Atlanta
FLACHE, Paul	6-5	220	R	Toronto, Ont.	3/4/82	Chicago (AHL)-Gwinnett
HAVELID, Niclas	6-0	200	L	Stockholm, Sweden	4/12/73	Anaheim
KLOUCEK, Tomas	6-3	225	L	Prague, Czech.	3/7/80	Nashville-Atlanta
MAJESKY, Ivan	6-5	230	R	Banska Bystrica, Czech.	9/2/76	Atlanta
MANSON, Lane	6-8	265	L	Watrous, Sask.	2/14/84	Moose Jaw
MODRY, Jaroslav	6-2	220	L	Ceske Budejovice, Czech.	2/27/71	Los Angeles
ROCHE, Travis	6-1	190	R	Grand Cache, Alta.	6/17/78	Minnesota-Houston
ROSSITER, Kyle	6-3	220	L	Edmonton, Alta.	6/9/80	Florida-San Antonio-Atlanta-Chicago (AHL)
SELLARS, Luke	6-1	210	L	Toronto, Ont.	5/21/81	Chicago (AHL)
SIPOTZ, Brian	6-7	250	R	South Bend, IN	9/16/81	Miami
SUTTON, Andy	6-6	245	L	Kingston, Ont.	3/10/75	Atlanta
TJARNQVIST, Daniel	6-2	200	L	Umea, Sweden	10/14/76	Atlanta
USTRNUL, Libor	6-5	235	L	Sternberk, Czech.	2/20/82	Chicago (AHL)

GOALTENDERS	HT	WT	C	Place of Birth	Date	2003-04 Club
BERKHOEL, Adam	5-11	190	L	St. Paul, MN	5/16/81	U. of Denver
GARNETT, Michael	6-1	200	L	Saskatoon, Sask.	11/25/82	Chicago (AHL)-Gwinnett
HURME, Jani	6-0	190	L	Turku, Finland	1/7/75	Did Not Play - Injured
LEHTONEN, Kari	6-3	205	L	Helsinki, Finland	11/16/83	Atlanta-Chicago (AHL)
NURMINEN, Pasi	5-10	215	L	Lahti, Finland	12/17/75	Atlanta

2003-04 Scoring

* - rookie

Regular Season

Pos	#	Player	Team	GP	G	A	Pts	+/–	PIM	PP	SH	GW	GT	S	%
L	17	Ilya Kovalchuk	ATL	81	41	46	87	–10	63	16	1	6	0	341	12.0
R	19	Shawn Mceachern	ATL	82	17	38	55	5	76	5	1	3	0	176	9.7
L	13	Vyacheslav Kozlov	ATL	76	20	32	52	–12	74	6	0	1	0	191	10.5
C	9	Marc Savard	ATL	45	19	33	52	–8	85	6	1	3	1	133	14.3
C	27	Patrik Stefan	ATL	82	14	26	40	–7	26	3	2	2	0	110	12.7
C	28	Randy Robitaille	ATL	69	11	26	37	–12	20	5	0	2	0	121	9.1
R	26	Ronald Petrovicky	ATL	78	16	15	31	–9	123	0	0	1	0	102	15.7
D	8	Frantisek Kaberle	ATL	67	3	26	29	2	30	2	0	1	0	94	3.2
R	15	Dany Heatley	ATL	31	13	12	25	–8	18	5	0	3	0	83	15.7
L	10	Serge Aubin	ATL	66	10	15	25	0	73	1	0	2	0	97	10.3
D	25	Andy Sutton	ATL	65	8	13	21	0	94	7	1	1	1	102	7.7
D	36	Daniel Tjarnqvist	ATL	68	5	15	20	–4	20	2	2	1	0	65	7.7
R	11	Jean-Pierre Vigier	ATL	70	10	8	18	–18	22	2	2	3	0	110	9.1
D	23	Ivan Majesky	ATL	63	3	7	10	–7	76	0	0	0	0	35	8.6
D	38	Yannick Tremblay	ATL	38	2	8	10	–13	13	1	0	1	0	47	4.3
D	2	* Garnet Exelby	ATL	71	1	9	10	–10	134	0	0	0	0	42	2.4
D	4	Chris Tamer	ATL	38	2	5	7	–9	55	0	0	1	0	40	5.0
L	29	Brad Larsen	COL	26	2	2	4	2	11	0	0	1	1	17	11.8
			ATL	6	0	0	0	–2	2	0	0	0	0	6	0.0
			TOTAL	32	2	2	4	0	13	0	0	1	1	23	8.7
D	6	Shawn Heins	ATL	17	0	4	4	–1	16	0	0	0	0	17	0.0
L	49	* Zdenek Blatny	ATL	16	3	0	3	0	6	0	0	0	0	17	17.6
C	14	Ben Simon	ATL	52	3	0	3	–10	28	0	0	0	0	30	10.0
C	24	* Tommi Santala	ATL	33	1	2	3	–7	22	0	0	1	0	23	4.3
R	20	* Francis Lessard	ATL	62	1	1	2	–5	181	0	0	0	0	19	5.3
L	39	* Kip Brennan	L.A.	18	1	0	1	–1	79	0	0	0	0	6	16.7
			ATL	5	0	0	0	0	17	0	0	0	0	2	0.0
			TOTAL	23	1	0	1	–1	96	0	0	0	0	8	12.5
C	29	Brian Swanson	ATL	2	0	1	1	0	0	0	0	0	0	0	0.0
D	47	* Kurtis Foster	ATL	3	0	1	1	0	0	0	0	0	0	1	0.0
L	42	* Karl Stewart	ATL	5	0	1	1	0	4	0	0	0	0	2	0.0
D	48	* Kyle Rossiter	FLA	4	0	0	0	–1	7	0	0	0	0	1	0.0
			ATL	2	0	1	1	0	0	0	0	0	0	0	0.0
			TOTAL	6	0	1	1	–1	7	0	0	0	0	1	0.0
C	41	Daniel Corso	ATL	7	0	1	1	–2	0	0	0	0	0	2	0.0
C	21	* Derek Mackenzie	ATL	12	0	1	1	0	10	0	0	0	0	7	0.0
D	5	Tomas Kloucek	NSH	5	0	1	1	3	10	0	0	0	0	0	0.0
			ATL	37	0	0	0	–8	25	0	0	0	0	12	0.0
			TOTAL	42	0	1	1	–5	35	0	0	0	0	12	0.0
D	43	Mike Weaver	ATL	1	0	0	0	–1	0	0	0	0	0	0	0.0
L	12	Bill Lindsay	ATL	24	0	0	0	–6	25	0	0	0	0	10	0.0

Goaltending

No.	Goaltender	GPI	Mins	Avg	W	L	T	EN	SO	GA	SA	S%	G	A	PIM
32	* Kari Lehtonen	4	240	1.25	4	0	0	0	1	5	106	.953	0	0	0
31	Pasi Nurminen	64	3738	2.78	25	30	7	12	3	173	1792	.903	0	2	35
34	Byron Dafoe	18	973	3.14	4	11	1	2	0	51	499	.898	0	0	2
	Totals	**82**	**4989**	**2.92**	**33**	**41**	**8**	**14**	**4**	**243**	**2411**	**.899**			

Vice President and General Manager

WADDELL, DON
Vice President/General Manager, Atlanta Thrashers.
Born in Detroit, MI, August 19, 1958.

As the only general manager in the history of the Atlanta Thrashers, Don Waddell has established a foundation that is anchored by two of the NHL's young superstars, Ilya Kovalchuk and Dany Heatley. Waddell has laid the groundwork for long-term success in Atlanta by infusing the club with solid veterans to support a young line-up.

Despite facing tremendous adversity following the death of Dan Snyder, Waddell's leadership saw the team narrowly miss the playoffs in 2003-04 while setting franchise records for wins (33) and points (78). The team's first step toward achieving this success came during the 2002-03 season when it made a very dramatic second-half turnaround which was keyed by Waddell's decision to hire proven Stanley Cup winner Bob Hartley as coach. Prior to hiring Hartley, Waddell made his own successful NHL coaching debut with a win at Carolina on December 27, 2002. (He served as interim head coach until January 13, 2003.)

Waddell came to the franchise on June 23, 1998 – almost a year to the day after the NHL granted Atlanta a team. He has built the core of the franchise through the NHL Entry Draft and by stockpiling impressive prospects. He selected Heatley second overall in the 2000 NHL Entry Draft, and, in 2001, he made Kovalchuk the first Russian player selected first overall in the history of the Entry Draft. In the 2002 Entry Draft, Waddell made Kari Lehtonen of Finland the highest-selected European goaltender in NHL draft history.

Waddell has a long-standing relationship with USA Hockey as a player and in management, and served as assistant general manager for the 2004 World Championship and World Cup teams. His extensive organizational experience also includes having previously built two professional hockey franchises: the San Diego Gulls and the Orlando Solar Bears of the now-defunct International Hockey League. He's also no stranger to winning through his role as assistant general manager for the Stanley Cup champion Detroit Red Wings during the 1997-98 season.

Waddell's playing experience includes more than nine seasons of professional hockey, mostly in the IHL. He was drafted by the NHL's Los Angeles Kings in 1978 and spent three years with the organization from 1980 to 1983. During a successful amateur career, Waddell helped the U.S. national team win the gold medal at the 1983 B-Pool World Championships. He played Division I hockey at Northern Michigan University from 1976 to 1980, where he majored in business management.

General Managers' History

Don Waddell, 1999-2000 to date.

Captains' History

Kelly Buchberger, 1999-2000; Steve Staios, 2000-01; Ray Ferraro, 2001-02; no captain, 2002-03; Shawn McEachern, 2003-04 to date.

Coaching History

Curt Fraser, 1999-2000 to 2001-02; Curt Fraser, Don Waddell and Bob Hartley, 2002-03; Bob Hartley, 2003-04 to date.

NHL Coaching Record

Season	Team	Regular Season				Playoffs		
		Games	W	L	T	Games	W	L
2002-03	Atlanta	10	4	5	1	....	....	....
	NHL Totals	10	4	5	1	....	....	....

Club Records

Team
(Figures in brackets for season records are games played.)

Most Points	78	2003-04 (82)
Most Wins	33	2003-04 (82)
Most Ties	12	2000-01 (82)
Most Losses	57	1999-2000 (82)
Most Goals	226	2002-03 (82)
Most Goals Against	313	1999-2000 (82)
Fewest Points	39	1999-2000 (82)
Fewest Wins	14	1999-2000 (82)
Fewest Ties	7	1999-2000 (82), 2002-03 (82)
Fewest Losses	37	2003-04 (82)
Fewest Goals	170	1999-2000 (82)
Fewest Goals Against	243	2003-04 (82)

Longest Winning Streak
Overall............4 Twice
Home............3 Three times
Away............4 Jan. 13-Feb. 7/03

Longest Undefeated Streak
Overall............5 Oct. 9-18/03 (3 wins, 2 ties)
Home............4 Oct. 9-23/03 (3 wins, 1 tie)
Away............7 Oct. 21-Nov. 13/00 (3 wins, 4 ties)

Longest Losing Streak
Overall............12 Jan. 24-Feb. 20/00
Home............*11 Jan. 24-Mar. 16/00
Away............10 Oct. 6-Nov. 18/01

Longest Winless Streak
Overall............16 Jan. 16-Feb. 20/00 (2 ties, 14 losses)
Home............*17 Jan. 19-Mar. 29/00 (2 ties, 15 losses)
Away............10 Oct. 6-Nov. 18/01 (10 losses)

Most Shutouts, Season............4 2003-04 (82)
Most PIM, Season............1,505 2003-04 (82)
Most Goals, Game............8 Twice

Individual

Most Seasons............5 Four players
Most Games, Career............350 Patrik Stefan
Most Goals, Career............108 Ilya Kovalchuk
Most Assists, Career............104 Patrik Stefan
Most Points, Career............205 Ilya Kovalchuk (108G, 97A)
Most PIM, Career............532 Jeff Odgers
Most Shutouts, Career............5 Milan Hnilicka, Pasi Nurminen

Longest Consecutive
Games Streak............136 Ilya Kovalchuk (Nov. 2/02-Feb. 25/04)
Most Goals, Season............41 Dany Heatley (2002-03), Ilya Kovalchuk (2003-04)
Most Assists, Season............49 Vyachaslev Kozlov (2002-03)
Most Points, Season............89 Dany Heatley (2002-03; 41G, 48A)
Most PIM, Season............226 Jeff Odgers (2000-01)

Most Points, Defenseman, Season............31 Yannick Tremblay (1999-2000; 10G, 21A)
Most Points, Center, Season............76 Ray Ferraro (2000-01; 29G, 47A)
Most Points, Right Wing, Season............89 Dany Heatley (2002-03; 41G, 48A)
Most Points, Left Wing, Season............87 Ilya Kovalchuk (2003-04; 41G, 46A)
Most Points, Rookie, Season............67 Dany Heatley (2001-02; 26G, 41A)
Most Shutouts, Season............3 Milan Hnilicka (2001-02), Pasi Nurminen (2003-04)
Most Goals, Game............4 Pascal Rheaume (Jan. 19/02)
Most Assists, Game............4 Andrew Brunette (Dec. 19/00), Ilya Kovalchuk (Jan. 19/02), Marc Savard (Dec. 20/03)
Most Points, Game............5 Four times

* NHL Record.

Pasi Nurminen saw the bulk of action in goal for the Thrashers last year. He set a team record with 25 wins and tied the club mark with three shutouts.

2003-04 Results

Oct.	9	Columbus	2-1		8	at Dallas	1-2
	11	at Washington	4-3		10	at San Jose	2-5
	14	NY Islanders	2-2		11	at Phoenix	1-1
	16	at NY Rangers	0-0		14	Montreal	1-2
	18	Chicago	7-2		16	Carolina	3-4
	21	at Tampa Bay	2-3*		18	at Carolina	5-2
	23	Nashville	4-2		20	Buffalo	4-1
	25	Florida	2-3		22	Colorado	1-1
	27	at Toronto	3-2*		24	NY Islanders	0-3
	30	at Minnesota	2-3		25	at New Jersey	2-3
	31	at Washington	1-2		28	St. Louis	1-1
Nov.	2	San Jose	2-2		30	Toronto	1-4
	5	at Buffalo	7-4		31	at Tampa Bay	2-5
	7	at Columbus	2-4	Feb.	3	at Boston	4-5
	8	at NY Islanders	4-3		5	Philadelphia	1-5
	11	Ottawa	3-5		10	at Calgary	2-5
	13	at Carolina	1-5		11	at Edmonton	1-5
	15	at Philadelphia	0-4		13	at Vancouver	4-1
	16	Florida	5-2		16	at Buffalo	2-7
	19	Boston	5-4*		17	at Montreal	4-1
	21	at Florida	6-3		19	at Ottawa	3-2*
	23	Phoenix	1-0		21	at Philadelphia	4-5
	25	Ottawa	3-6		25	Tampa Bay	2-4
	27	Toronto	7-4		27	at New Jersey	3-2
	29	Tampa Bay	2-1		29	NY Rangers	3-2
Dec.	1	at Pittsburgh	3-4	Mar.	2	at NY Rangers	4-3
	3	Boston	4-6		5	Carolina	2-3*
	5	Anaheim	6-2		6	at Boston	2-2
	6	at Florida	4-3*		9	NY Rangers	0-2
	10	Los Angeles	4-3*		12	at Carolina	2-4
	12	Pittsburgh	6-3		13	Washington	5-2
	13	at NY Islanders	0-4		15	Carolina	1-0*
	16	Washington	0-5		17	Buffalo	3-4*
	18	New Jersey	0-3		19	Florida	3-2
	20	at Pittsburgh	7-4		20	at Washington	2-2
	21	Philadelphia	4-1		24	Washington	3-2
	26	Tampa Bay	3-1		26	New Jersey	0-5
	28	at Ottawa	2-5		27	at Florida	3-0
	29	Montreal	1-2		29	at Toronto	1-2
	31	at Detroit	5-6*	Apr.	2	Pittsburgh	2-3
Jan.	3	at Montreal	1-5		3	at Tampa Bay	2-1

* – Overtime

All-time Record vs. Other Clubs
Regular Season

	At Home								On Road								Total							
	GP	W	L	T	OL	GF	GA	PTS	GP	W	L	T	OL	GF	GA	PTS	GP	W	L	T	OL	GF	GA	PTS
Anaheim	4	1	3	0	0	10	16	2	4	2	2	0	0	9	12	4	8	3	5	0	0	19	28	6
Boston	10	4	6	0	0	28	30	8	10	3	3	2	2	38	36	10	20	7	9	2	2	66	66	18
Buffalo	10	6	2	1	1	31	31	14	10	4	6	0	0	29	43	8	20	10	8	1	1	60	74	22
Calgary	4	3	0	1	0	8	5	7	3	0	3	0	0	6	14	0	7	3	3	1	0	14	19	7
Carolina	13	2	6	3	2	30	38	9	13	2	8	1	2	31	47	7	26	4	14	4	4	61	85	16
Chicago	4	2	2	0	0	14	10	4	2	0	2	0	0	0	6	0	6	2	4	0	0	14	16	4
Colorado	4	1	1	1	1	7	8	4	4	2	2	0	0	10	17	4	8	3	3	1	1	17	25	8
Columbus	3	2	1	0	0	5	6	4	4	2	1	0	1	11	12	5	7	4	2	0	1	16	18	9
Dallas	4	0	3	0	1	9	16	1	4	0	4	0	0	9	9	0	8	0	7	0	1	13	25	1
Detroit	3	0	3	0	0	7	19	0	4	0	2	0	2	8	17	2	7	0	5	0	2	15	36	2
Edmonton	4	2	1	0	0	3	8	4	4	1	2	1	0	11	14	3	8	3	3	1	0	14	22	5
Florida	13	5	3	4	1	40	40	15	13	8	4	1	0	44	31	17	26	13	7	5	1	84	71	32
Los Angeles	4	1	3	0	0	7	16	2	4	1	3	0	0	9	18	2	8	2	6	0	0	16	34	4
Minnesota	2	0	2	0	0	6	10	0	3	0	2	1	0	5	8	1	5	0	4	1	0	11	18	1
Montreal	10	1	7	2	0	12	31	4	10	3	7	0	0	24	34	6	20	4	14	2	0	36	65	10
Nashville	4	2	0	1	1	12	10	6	3	1	2	0	0	6	12	2	7	3	2	1	1	18	22	8
New Jersey	10	1	7	2	0	13	36	4	10	3	6	1	0	20	33	7	20	4	13	3	0	33	69	11
NY Islanders	10	2	6	2	0	27	37	6	10	5	5	0	0	25	36	10	20	7	11	2	0	52	73	16
NY Rangers	10	3	7	0	0	28	34	6	10	6	3	1	0	34	28	13	20	9	10	1	0	62	62	19
Ottawa	10	2	7	1	0	31	45	5	10	3	6	1	0	26	47	7	20	5	13	2	0	57	92	12
Philadelphia	10	2	6	1	1	24	34	6	10	1	7	2	0	28	46	4	20	3	13	3	1	52	80	10
Phoenix	4	1	3	0	0	6	12	2	5	0	4	1	0	7	16	1	9	1	7	1	0	13	28	3
Pittsburgh	10	1	8	0	1	24	39	3	10	2	7	0	1	25	39	5	20	3	15	0	2	49	78	8
St. Louis	4	1	2	1	0	14	16	3	3	0	3	0	0	1	11	0	7	1	5	1	0	15	27	3
San Jose	4	1	2	1	0	7	11	3	4	0	3	1	0	9	16	1	8	1	5	2	0	16	27	3
Tampa Bay	13	8	2	3	0	48	34	19	13	3	8	1	1	29	49	8	26	11	10	4	1	77	83	27
Toronto	9	3	5	0	1	16	31	7	9	3	6	0	0	21	33	7	18	6	10	1	1	37	64	14
Vancouver	3	1	2	0	0	11	12	2	2	1	0	1	0	5	10	3	5	2	2	1	0	16	22	5
Washington	13	2	7	1	2	28	38	14	13	1	6	3	1	29	50	6	26	3	13	5	1	57	88	20
Totals	**205**	**63**	**106**	**26**	**10**	**506**	**673**	**162**	**205**	**57**	**119**	**19**	**10**	**502**	**744**	**143**	**410**	**120**	**225**	**45**	**20**	**1008**	**1417**	**305**

Entry Draft
Selections 2004-1999

2004 Pick		2002 Pick		2000 Pick		1999 Pick	
10	Boris Valabik	2	Kari Lehtonen	2	Dany Heatley	1	Patrik Stefan
40	Grant Lewis	30	Jim Slater	31	Ilja Nikulin	30	Luke Sellars
76	Scott Lehman	116	Patrick Dwyer	42	Libor Ustrnul	68	Zdenek Blatny
106	Chad Painchaud	124	Lane Manson	107	Carl Mallette	98	David Kaczowka
142	Juraj Gracik	144	Paul Flache	108	Blake Robson	99	Rob Zepp
186	Dan Turple	167	Brad Schell	147	Matt McRae	128	Derek MacKenzie
204	Miikka Tuomainen	198	Nathan Oystrick	168	Zdenek Smid	159	Yuri Dobryshkin
237	Mitch Carefoot	230	Colton Fretter	178	Jeff Dwyer	188	Stephen Baby
270	Matthew Siddall	236	Tyler Boldt	180	Darcy Hordichuk	217	Garnet Exelby
		257	Pauli Levokari	230	Samu Isosalo	245	Tommi Santala
2003 Pick				242	Evan Nielsen	246	Raymond DiLauro
8	Braydon Coburn	2001 Pick		244	Eric Bowen		
110	James Sharrow	1	Ilya Kovalchuk	288	Mark McRae		
116	Guillaume Desbiens	80	Michael Garnett	290	Simon Gamache		
136	Michael Vannelli	100	Brian Sipotz				
145	Brett Sterling	112	Milan Gajic				
175	Mike Hamilton	135	Colin Stuart				
203	Denis Loginov	189	Pasi Nurminen				
239	Tobias Enstrom	199	Matt Suderman				
269	Rylan Kaip	201	Colin FitzRandolph				
		262	Mario Cartelli				

Coach

HARTLEY, BOB
Coach, Atlanta Thrashers. Born in Hawkesbury, Ont., September 7, 1960.

Bob Hartley, the second head coach in Thrashers history, has used his experience as a Stanley Cup champion to develop the young talent in the organization. In 2003-04, Hartley helped the team overcome the tragic loss of Dan Snyder and led the club to its best record (33-37-8-4) and a franchise-high 78 points. Hartley joined the Thrashers on January 14, 2003 and became the seventh-fastest coach in NHL history to reach 200 wins with a 4-2 Atlanta victory at New Jersey on February 7, 2003, in his 369th game.

Prior to joining the Thrashers, Hartley guided the Colorado Avalanche to the 2001 Stanley Cup championship. In the 2002 playoffs, he became the first NHL coach to lead his team to the Conference Final in each of his first four seasons with the same club. In 16 seasons as a head coach at the amateur and professional levels, Hartley's teams have qualified for the playoffs 14 times while capturing five league championships. His team's have won at least 40 games eight times and 30 or more contests on 14 occasions. His Avalanche teams won at least 42 games in four consecutive seasons from 1998 to 2002.

Hartley became the second coach of the Avalanche, and the 11th in franchise history, when he was named to the position on June 30, 1998. He served there until December 18, 2002 and is Colorado's all-time coaching victory leader (193), having guided the Avalanche to four consecutive Northwest Division titles and four straight trips to the Western Conference Final. Hartley guided the 2000-01 Avalanche to its most successful season in franchise history. Colorado established team records for points (118), wins (52) and goals against (192).

Hartley has been a proven winner at every level he has coached. Prior to joining Colorado, Hartley coached four seasons in the American Hockey League from 1994 to 1998, posting a 151-136-33 regular-season record and making four consecutive trips to the playoffs with Cornwall (1994 to 1996) and Hershey (1996 to 1998). He guided Hershey to the 1997 Calder Cup championship. After serving as an assistant coach for Cornwall in 1993-94, Hartley guided the Aces to the Southern Division title in 1994-95, and a trip to the Southern Division Final again in 1995-96. He led Laval to the Quebec Major Junior Hockey League championship and the Memorial Cup in 1993, and compiled an 81-52-7 record in two seasons with Laval from 1991 to 1993.

From 1987 to 1991, Hartley served as head coach for Hawkesbury of the Canadian Junior Hockey League. After enduring an 18-point season his rookie term behind the Hawks' bench, he guided the club to an impressive 117-45-5 mark during the next three seasons, including CJHL championships in 1990 and 1991. His teams dropped just three postseason games in 1990 and 1991, going 24-3 in that span. Overall, his teams in Hawkesbury advanced to the playoffs four consecutive seasons and finished 31-13 in the postseason during that span.

Throughout his coaching career, Hartley has shared a strong sense of dedication with his community. He was honored in his hometown of Hawkesbury, where the local ice arena was renamed Complex Bob Hartley in August 1998 in recognition of his service to the community where he grew up and coached. He has been involved in hockey camps and charitable endeavors throughout his career.

Coaching Record

Season	Team	Games	Regular Season W	L	T	Playoffs Games	W	L
1991-92	Laval (QMJHL)	70	38	27	5	10	4	6
1992-93	Laval (QMJHL)	70	43	25	2	13	12	1
1994-95	Cornwall (AHL)	80	38	33	9	15	8	7
1995-96	Cornwall (AHL)	80	34	39	7	8	3	5
1996-97	Hershey (AHL)	80	43	27	10	23	15	8
1997-98	Hershey (AHL)	80	36	37	7	7	3	4
1998-99	Colorado (NHL)	82	44	28	10	19	11	8
1999-2000	Colorado (NHL)	82	42	29	11	17	11	6
2000-01	Colorado (NHL)	82	52	20	10	23	16	7*
2001-02	Colorado (NHL)	82	45	29	8	21	11	10
2002-03	Colorado (NHL)	31	10	12	9	....	....	....
	Atlanta (NHL)	39	19	15	5	....	....	....
2003-04	Atlanta (NHL)	82	33	41	8	....	....	....
	NHL Totals	480	245	174	61	80	49	31

* Stanley Cup win.

Club Directory

Philips Arena

Atlanta Thrashers
One CNN Center
12 South, South Tower
Atlanta, GA 30303
Phone **404/827-5300**
FAX 404/827-5769
www.atlantathrashers.com
Capacity: 18,545

Executive Management – Atlanta Spirit, LLC
Board of Managers . . . . Steven Belkin, Todd Foreman, Michael Gearon, Jr., Bruce Levenson, Ed Peskowitz, Felix Riccio, Rutherford Seydel
Owner and Governor . . . . Bruce Levenson
Owner and Alternate Governor . . . . Rutherford Seydel
President and CEO/Alternate Governor . . . . Bernie Mullin
Executive Vice President and General Manager/
  Alternate Governor . . . . Don Waddell
President of Philips Arena . . . . Bob Williams
Executive Vice President and Chief Financial Officer . Bill Duffy
Executive Vice President of Business Development . . Lee Douglas
Senior Vice President of Broadcast
  and Corporate Partnerships . . . . Tracy White
Senior Vice President of Communications . . . . Tom Hughes
Senior Vice President of Ticket Sales and Service . . . Jeff Morander
Vice President and General Counsel . . . . T. Scott Wilkinson
Vice President of Community Development . . . . Tiffany Stone
Vice President of Marketing, Advertising
  and Branding . . . . Jim Pfeifer
Vice President of Strategic Planning/
  Special Assistant to President . . . . Ailey Penningroth

Hockey Operations
Assistant General Manager and Director
  of Hockey Operations . . . . Larry Simmons
Director of Player Personnel . . . . Jack Ferreira
Director of Amateur Scouting and
  Player Development . . . . Dan Marr
Senior Director of Team Services . . . . Michele Zarzaca
Video and Hockey Operations Coordinator . . . . Tony Borgford
Assistant to Don Waddell/Practice Facility
  Office Manager . . . . Leisa Strickland Ludwin

Coaching Staff
Head Coach . . . . Bob Hartley
Assistant Coaches . . . . Brad McCrimmon and Steve Weeks

Scouting Staff
Head Scout . . . . Marcel Comeau
Full-Time Scouts . . . . Mark Dobson, Bernd Freimuller, Mark Hillier, Peter Mahovlich, Bob Owen, John Perpich, Normand Poisson
Part-Time Scouts . . . . Evgeny Bogdanovich, Terry Brennan, Pat Carmichael, Pentti Katainen

Training Staff
Strength and Conditioning Coach . . . . Ray Bear
Head Athletic Trainer . . . . Scott Green
Assistant Athletic Trainer . . . . Craig Brewer
Massage Therapist . . . . Inar Treiguts

Equipment Staff
Head Equipment Manager . . . . Bobby Stewart
Assistant Equipment Managers . . . . Joe Guilmet and Jim Guilmet

Medical Staff
Team Physician . . . . Dr. Scott Gillogly
Team Internist . . . . Dr. William Whaley
Team Dentists . . . . Dr. Gary Saban, Dr. Lawrence Saltzman, Dr. Brett Silverman

Public Relations
Senior Director of Public Relations . . . . Rob Koch
Manager of Media Relations . . . . John Heid

Broadcasting – Television and Radio
Television Producer . . . . C.J. Bottitta
Television Director . . . . Jim Allen
Television Analyst/Director of Programs
  within the Community . . . . Darren Eliot
Television Play-By-Play Announcer . . . . JP Dellacamera
Director of Radio Broadcast . . . . Dan Kamal
Radio Analyst . . . . Billy Jaffe
Radio Operations Coordinator . . . . Mary Moran

Nick Boynton led Bruins defensemen at +17.

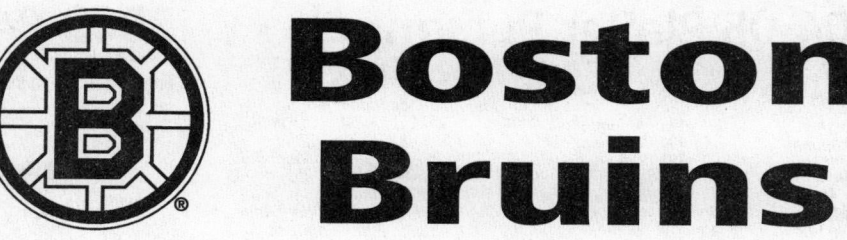

Boston Bruins

2003-04 Results: 41W-19L-15T-7OTL 104PTS.
First, Northeast Division

Year-by-Year Record

Season	GP	Home				Road				Overall				GF	GA	Pts.	Finished	Playoff Result
		W	L	T	OL	W	L	T	OL	W	L	T	OL					
2003-04	82	18	12	9	2	23	7	6	5	41	19	15	7	209	188	104	1st, Northeast Div.	Lost Conf. Quarter-Final
2002-03	82	23	11	5	2	13	20	6	2	36	31	11	4	245	237	87	3rd, Northeast Div.	Lost Conf. Quarter-Final
2001-02	82	23	11	2	5	20	13	4	4	43	24	6	9	236	201	101	1st, Northeast Div.	Lost Conf. Quarter-Final
2000-01	82	21	12	5	3	15	18	3	5	36	30	8	8	227	249	88	4th, Northeast Div.	Out of Playoffs
1999-2000	82	12	17	11	1	12	16	8	5	24	33	19	6	210	248	73	5th, Northeast Div.	Out of Playoffs
1998-99	82	22	10	9	...	17	20	4	...	39	30	13	...	214	181	91	3rd, Northeast Div.	Lost Conf. Semi-Final
1997-98	82	19	16	6	...	20	14	7	...	39	30	13	...	221	194	91	2nd, Northeast Div.	Lost Conf. Quarter-Final
1996-97	82	14	20	7	...	12	27	2	...	26	47	9	...	234	300	61	6th, Northeast Div.	Out of Playoffs
1995-96	82	22	14	5	...	18	17	6	...	40	31	11	...	282	269	91	2nd, Northeast Div.	Lost Conf. Quarter-Final
1994-95	48	15	7	2	...	12	11	1	...	27	18	3	...	150	127	57	3rd, Northeast Div.	Lost Conf. Quarter-Final
1993-94	84	20	14	8	...	22	15	5	...	42	29	13	...	289	252	97	2nd, Northeast Div.	Lost Conf. Semi-Final
1992-93	84	29	10	3	...	22	16	4	...	51	26	7	...	332	268	109	1st, Adams Div.	Lost Div. Semi-Final
1991-92	80	23	11	6	...	13	21	6	...	36	32	12	...	270	275	84	2nd, Adams Div.	Lost Conf. Championship
1990-91	80	26	9	5	...	18	15	7	...	44	24	12	...	299	264	100	1st, Adams Div.	Lost Conf. Championship
1989-90	80	23	13	4	...	23	12	5	...	46	25	9	...	289	232	101	1st, Adams Div.	Lost Final
1988-89	80	17	15	8	...	20	14	6	...	37	29	14	...	289	256	88	2nd, Adams Div.	Lost Div. Final
1987-88	80	24	13	3	...	20	17	3	...	44	30	6	...	300	251	94	2nd, Adams Div.	Lost Final
1986-87	80	25	11	4	...	14	23	3	...	39	34	7	...	301	276	85	3rd, Adams Div.	Lost Div. Semi-Final
1985-86	80	24	9	7	...	13	22	5	...	37	31	12	...	311	288	86	3rd, Adams Div.	Lost Div. Semi-Final
1984-85	80	21	15	4	...	15	19	6	...	36	34	10	...	303	287	82	4th, Adams Div.	Lost Div. Semi-Final
1983-84	80	25	12	3	...	24	13	3	...	49	25	6	...	336	261	104	1st, Adams Div.	Lost Div. Semi-Final
1982-83	80	28	6	6	...	22	14	4	...	50	20	10	...	327	228	110	1st, Adams Div.	Lost Conf. Championship
1981-82	80	24	12	4	...	19	15	6	...	43	27	10	...	323	285	96	2nd, Adams Div.	Lost Div. Final
1980-81	80	26	10	4	...	11	20	9	...	37	30	13	...	316	272	87	2nd, Adams Div.	Lost Prelim. Round
1979-80	80	27	9	4	...	19	12	9	...	46	21	13	...	310	234	105	2nd, Adams Div.	Lost Quarter-Final
1978-79	80	25	10	5	...	18	13	9	...	43	23	14	...	316	270	100	1st, Adams Div.	Lost Semi-Final
1977-78	80	29	6	5	...	22	12	6	...	51	18	11	...	333	218	113	1st, Adams Div.	Lost Final
1976-77	80	27	7	6	...	22	16	2	...	49	23	8	...	312	240	106	1st, Adams Div.	Lost Final
1975-76	80	27	5	8	...	21	10	9	...	48	15	17	...	313	237	113	1st, Adams Div.	Lost Semi-Final
1974-75	80	29	5	6	...	11	21	8	...	40	26	14	...	345	245	94	2nd, Adams Div.	Lost Prelim. Round
1973-74	78	33	4	2	...	19	13	7	...	52	17	9	...	349	221	113	1st, East Div.	Lost Final
1972-73	78	27	10	2	...	24	12	3	...	51	22	5	...	330	235	107	2nd, East Div.	Lost Quarter-Final
1971-72	78	28	4	7	...	26	9	4	...	54	13	11	...	330	204	119	**1st, East Div.**	**Won Stanley Cup**
1970-71	78	33	4	2	...	24	10	5	...	57	14	7	...	399	207	121	1st, East Div.	Lost Quarter-Final
1969-70	76	27	3	8	...	13	14	11	...	40	17	19	...	277	216	99	**2nd, East Div.**	**Won Stanley Cup**
1968-69	76	29	3	6	...	13	15	10	...	42	18	16	...	303	221	100	2nd, East Div.	Lost Semi-Final
1967-68	74	22	9	6	...	15	18	4	...	37	27	10	...	259	216	84	3rd, East Div.	Lost Quarter-Final
1966-67	70	10	21	4	...	7	22	6	...	17	43	10	...	182	253	44	6th,	Out of Playoffs
1965-66	70	15	17	3	...	6	26	3	...	21	43	6	...	174	275	48	5th,	Out of Playoffs
1964-65	70	12	17	6	...	9	26	0	...	21	43	6	...	166	253	48	6th,	Out of Playoffs
1963-64	70	13	15	7	...	5	25	5	...	18	40	12	...	170	212	48	6th,	Out of Playoffs
1962-63	70	7	18	10	...	7	21	7	...	14	39	17	...	198	281	45	6th,	Out of Playoffs
1961-62	70	9	22	4	...	6	25	4	...	15	47	8	...	177	306	38	6th,	Out of Playoffs
1960-61	70	13	17	5	...	2	25	8	...	15	42	13	...	176	254	43	6th,	Out of Playoffs
1959-60	70	21	11	3	...	7	23	5	...	28	34	8	...	220	241	64	5th,	Out of Playoffs
1958-59	70	21	11	3	...	11	18	6	...	32	29	9	...	205	215	73	2nd,	Lost Semi-Final
1957-58	70	15	14	6	...	12	14	9	...	27	28	15	...	199	194	69	4th,	Lost Final
1956-57	70	20	9	6	...	14	15	6	...	34	24	12	...	195	174	80	3rd,	Lost Final
1955-56	70	14	14	7	...	9	20	6	...	23	34	13	...	147	185	59	5th,	Out of Playoffs
1954-55	70	16	10	9	...	7	16	12	...	23	26	21	...	169	188	67	4th,	Lost Semi-Final
1953-54	70	22	8	5	...	10	20	5	...	32	28	10	...	177	181	74	4th,	Lost Semi-Final
1952-53	70	19	10	6	...	9	19	7	...	28	29	13	...	152	172	69	3rd,	Lost Final
1951-52	70	15	12	8	...	10	17	8	...	25	29	16	...	162	176	66	4th,	Lost Semi-Final
1950-51	70	13	12	10	...	9	18	8	...	22	30	18	...	178	197	62	4th,	Lost Semi-Final
1949-50	70	15	12	8	...	7	20	8	...	22	32	16	...	198	228	60	5th,	Out of Playoffs
1948-49	60	18	10	2	...	11	13	6	...	29	23	8	...	178	163	66	2nd,	Lost Semi-Final
1947-48	60	12	8	10	...	11	16	3	...	23	24	13	...	167	168	59	3rd,	Lost Semi-Final
1946-47	60	18	7	5	...	8	16	6	...	26	23	11	...	190	175	63	3rd,	Lost Semi-Final
1945-46	50	11	5	4	...	13	13	4	...	24	18	8	...	167	156	56	2nd,	Lost Final
1944-45	50	11	12	2	...	5	18	2	...	16	30	4	...	179	219	36	4th,	Lost Semi-Final
1943-44	50	15	8	2	...	4	18	3	...	19	26	5	...	223	268	43	5th,	Out of Playoffs
1942-43	50	17	3	5	...	7	14	4	...	24	17	9	...	195	176	57	2nd,	Lost Final
1941-42	48	17	4	3	...	8	13	3	...	25	17	6	...	160	118	56	3rd,	Lost Semi-Final
1940-41	48	15	4	5	...	12	4	8	...	27	8	13	...	168	102	67	**1st,**	**Won Stanley Cup**
1939-40	48	20	3	1	...	11	9	4	...	31	12	5	...	170	98	67	1st,	Lost Semi-Final
1938-39	48	20	2	2	...	16	8	0	...	36	10	2	...	156	76	74	**1st,**	**Won Stanley Cup**
1937-38	48	18	3	3	...	12	8	4	...	30	11	7	...	142	89	67	1st, Amn. Div.	Lost Semi-Final
1936-37	48	9	11	4	...	14	7	3	...	23	18	7	...	120	110	53	2nd, Amn. Div.	Lost Quarter-Final
1935-36	48	15	8	1	...	7	12	5	...	22	20	6	...	92	83	50	2nd, Amn. Div.	Lost Quarter-Final
1934-35	48	17	7	0	...	9	9	6	...	26	16	6	...	129	112	58	1st, Amn. Div.	Lost Semi-Final
1933-34	48	11	11	2	...	7	14	3	...	18	25	5	...	111	130	41	4th, Amn. Div.	Out of Playoffs
1932-33	48	19	2	3	...	6	13	5	...	25	15	8	...	124	88	58	1st, Amn. Div.	Lost Semi-Final
1931-32	48	11	10	3	...	4	11	9	...	15	21	12	...	122	117	42	4th, Amn. Div.	Out of Playoffs
1930-31	44	16	1	5	...	12	9	1	...	28	10	6	...	143	90	62	1st, Amn. Div.	Lost Semi-Final
1929-30	44	21	1	0	...	17	4	1	...	38	5	1	...	179	98	77	1st, Amn. Div.	Lost Final
1928-29	44	15	6	1	...	11	7	4	...	26	13	5	...	89	52	57	**1st, Amn. Div.**	**Won Stanley Cup**
1927-28	44	13	4	5	...	7	9	6	...	20	13	11	...	77	70	51	1st, Amn. Div.	Lost Semi-Final
1926-27	44	15	7	0	...	6	13	3	...	21	20	3	...	97	89	45	2nd, Amn. Div.	Lost Final
1925-26	36	10	7	1	...	7	8	3	...	17	15	4	...	92	85	38	4th,	Out of Playoffs
1924-25	30	3	12	0	...	3	12	0	...	6	24	0	...	49	119	12	6th,	Out of Playoffs

---

2004-05 Schedule

Oct.	Sat.	16	at Dallas	Mon.	17	Colorado*
	Sun.	17	at Colorado	Wed.	19	at Tampa Bay
	Tue.	19	at NY Islanders	Fri.	21	at Florida
	Thu.	21	Florida	Mon.	24	Florida
	Sat.	23	San Jose	Thu.	27	Washington
	Thu.	28	NY Islanders	Sat.	29	Tampa Bay*
	Sat.	30	Anaheim	Sun.	30	Buffalo*
Nov.	Mon.	1	at Ottawa	Feb. Tue.	1	at Montreal
	Wed.	3	at NY Rangers	Thu.	3	Los Angeles
	Thu.	4	Buffalo	Sat.	5	Chicago*
	Sat.	6	at Toronto	Sun.	6	at Washington*
	Thu.	11	at Philadelphia	Tue.	8	at Atlanta
	Sat.	13	Toronto	Thu.	10	Montreal
	Tue.	16	at Montreal	Tue.	15	Washington
	Thu.	18	Tampa Bay	Thu.	17	at Phoenix
	Sat.	20	Atlanta	Sat.	19	at San Jose
	Wed.	24	at Buffalo	Tue.	22	at Vancouver
	Fri.	26	Ottawa*	Fri.	25	at Edmonton
	Sat.	27	at Montreal	Sat.	26	at Calgary
Dec.	Wed.	1	at Carolina	Mon.	28	NY Islanders
	Thu.	2	Ottawa	Mar. Wed.	2	at New Jersey
	Sat.	4	Montreal	Thu.	3	at Ottawa
	Tue.	7	at Toronto	Sat.	5	Philadelphia*
	Thu.	9	at Buffalo	Mon.	7	Columbus
	Sat.	11	Buffalo*	Wed.	9	at Buffalo
	Sun.	12	at NY Rangers	Thu.	10	Pittsburgh
	Wed.	15	at Philadelphia	Sun.	13	at NY Islanders*
	Thu.	16	Philadelphia	Tue.	15	at Atlanta
	Sat.	18	at Ottawa	Thu.	17	Nashville
	Tue.	21	Toronto	Sat.	19	Carolina*
	Thu.	23	St. Louis	Mon.	21	Ottawa
	Mon.	27	at Tampa Bay	Wed.	23	at Columbus
	Wed.	29	at Florida	Thu.	24	at Carolina
	Fri.	31	at Pittsburgh*	Sat.	26	at Minnesota
Jan.	Sat.	1	Toronto	Mon.	28	Carolina
	Tue.	4	at Toronto	Thu.	31	at Washington
	Thu.	6	Montreal	Apr. Sat.	2	New Jersey*
	Sat.	8	NY Rangers*	Mon.	4	Atlanta
	Tue.	11	Detroit	Thu.	7	Pittsburgh
	Fri.	14	at New Jersey	Sat.	9	NY Rangers*
	Sat.	15	New Jersey	Sun.	10	at Pittsburgh*

* Denotes afternoon game.

Franchise date: November 1, 1924

NORTHEAST
DIVISION

81st
NHL
Season

2004-05 Player Personnel

FORWARDS	HT	WT	S	Place of Birth	Date	2003-04 Club
AXELSSON, P.J.	6-1	184	L	Kungalv, Sweden	2/26/75	Boston
BERGERON, Patrice	6-0	186	R	Ancienne-Lorette, Que.	7/24/85	Boston
BOYES, Brad	6-1	195	R	Mississauga, Ont.	4/17/82	Cleveland-S.J.-Prov (AHL)
FITZGERALD, Tom	6-0	190	R	Billerica, MA	8/28/68	Toronto
HILBERT, Andy	5-11	194	L	Lansing, MI	2/6/81	Boston-Providence (AHL)
HUML, Ivan	6-2	195	L	Kladno, Czech.	9/6/81	Boston-Providence (AHL)
LAPOINTE, Martin	5-11	215	R	Ville St-Pierre, Que.	9/12/73	Boston
LISCAK, Robert	6-0	192	L	Skalica, Czech.	4/4/78	Prov (AHL)-Aug-Trenton
ORR, Colton	6-3	210	R	Winnipeg, Man.	3/3/82	Boston-Providence (AHL)
SAMSONOV, Sergei	5-8	194	R	Moscow, USSR	10/27/78	Boston
SAMUELSSON, Martin	6-2	200	L	Upplands Vasby, Sweden	1/25/82	Boston-Providence (AHL)
STOCK, P.J.	5-10	197	L	Montreal, Que.	5/26/75	Bos-Prov (AHL)-Phi (AHL)
THORNTON, Joe	6-4	223	L	London, Ont.	7/2/79	Boston
VERNARSKY, Kris	6-3	201	L	Detroit, MI	4/5/82	Boston-Providence (AHL)
ZINOVJEV, Sergei	5-10	178	L	Novokuznetsk, USSR	3/4/80	Boston-Providence (AHL)-Kazan
DEFENSEMEN						
BOYNTON, Nick	6-2	210	R	Nobleton, Ont.	1/14/79	Boston
DALLMAN, Kevin	5-11	195	R	Niagara Falls, Ont.	2/26/81	Providence (AHL)
GILL, Hal	6-7	250	L	Concord, MA	4/6/75	Boston
GIRARD, Jonathan	5-11	201	R	Joliette, Que.	5/27/80	Boston
GONCHAR, Sergei	6-2	215	L	Chelyabinsk, USSR	4/13/74	Washington-Boston
JURCINA, Milan	6-4	198	R	Liptovsky Mikulas, Czech.	6/7/83	Providence (AHL)
KUTLAK, Zdenek	6-3	221	L	Budejovice, Czech.	2/13/80	Boston-Providence (AHL)
MORAN, Ian	6-0	200	R	Cleveland, OH	8/24/72	Boston

GOALTENDERS	HT	WT	C	Place of Birth	Date	2003-04 Club
HAMERLIK, Peter	6-1	194	L	Myjava, Czech.	1/2/82	Providence (AHL)-Augusta-Reading-Trenton
RAYCROFT, Andrew	6-0	185	L	Belleville, Ont.	5/4/80	Boston
TOIVONEN, Hannu	6-2	191	L	Kalvola, Finland	5/18/84	Providence (AHL)

Coach

SULLIVAN, MIKE
Coach, Boston Bruins. Born in Marshfield, MA, February 27, 1968.

The Boston Bruins named Mike Sullivan their head coach on June 23, 2003. He is the 25th head coach in team history and spent the 2003-04 season as the youngest coach in the NHL. In his first season behind the Bruins bench, Sullivan led the team to a first-place finish in the Northeast Division and second in the Eastern Conference with 104 points. The Bruins finished the season with the least amount of regulation losses in the league.

Sullivan began his coaching career with Providence of the AHL when he was hired on July 29, 2002. Under his watch, the Providence Bruins won the North Division with a 44-20-11-5 record and 104 points. The club established a new franchise record with a 19-game home unbeaten streak (16 wins, three ties) from December 6 to February 23. Sullivan's record behind the Providence bench was 41-17-9-4 through March 20, when he was promoted to Boston as an assistant coach under Mike O'Connell. Boston went 3-3-3-0 in the nine remaining regular season games and was eliminated by the eventual Stanley Cup champion New Jersey Devils in five games during the opening round of the playoffs. Sullivan returned to Providence following the NHL playoffs, and was behind the bench for the final three games of Providence's four-game series loss to Manitoba in their AHL playoff series.

Sullivan played four seasons of college hockey at Boston University from 1986-87 through 1989-90 with 61 goals, 77 assists and 104 penalty minutes in 141 career college games. The New York Rangers drafted the center as their fourth pick, 69th overall, in the 1987 NHL Entry Draft, but never signed with the Rangers. He turned professional in 1990, playing the 1990-91 season with San Diego of the International Hockey League before signing with the San Jose Sharks as a free agent in August, 1991 and beginning his 11-year NHL career. He played in San Jose, Calgary, Boston and Phoenix before retiring after the 2001-02 season. His career NHL playing totals were 54 goals and 82 assists for 136 points with 203 penalty minutes in 709 games.

Coaching Record

		Regular Season				Playoffs		
Season	Team	Games	W	L	T	Games	W	L
2002-03	Providence (AHL)	71	41	21	9	3	1	2
2003-04	**Boston (NHL)**	**82**	**41**	**26**	**15**	**7**	**3**	**4**
	NHL Totals	**82**	**41**	**26**	**15**	**7**	**3**	**4**

2003-04 Scoring

* - rookie

Regular Season

Pos	#	Player	Team	GP	G	A	Pts	+/–	PIM	PP	SH	GW	GT	S	%
C	19	Joe Thornton	BOS	77	23	50	73	18	98	4	0	6	0	187	12.3
R	27	Glen Murray	BOS	81	32	28	60	17	56	11	0	9	0	260	12.3
D	55	Sergei Gonchar	WSH	56	7	42	49	–20	44	4	0	0	1	127	5.5
			BOS	15	4	5	9	6	12	2	0	0	0	34	11.8
			TOTAL	71	11	47	58	–14	56	6	0	0	1	161	6.8
C	12	Brian Rolston	BOS	82	19	29	48	9	40	3	2	3	2	257	7.4
L	26	Mike Knuble	BOS	82	21	25	46	19	32	4	0	3	1	192	10.9
L	14	Sergei Samsonov	BOS	58	17	23	40	12	4	3	0	5	1	132	12.9
C	37	* Patrice Bergeron	BOS	71	16	23	39	5	22	7	0	2	0	133	12.0
D	44	Nick Boynton	BOS	81	6	24	30	17	98	1	1	1	0	178	3.4
D	6	Dan Mcgillis	BOS	80	5	23	28	–1	65	1	0	2	0	117	4.3
D	71	Jiri Slegr	VAN	16	2	5	7	6	8	1	1	1	0	15	13.3
			BOS	36	4	15	19	5	27	0	0	1	0	83	4.8
			TOTAL	52	6	20	26	11	35	1	1	2	0	98	6.1
R	20	Martin Lapointe	BOS	78	15	10	25	–5	67	9	0	2	0	136	11.0
L	11	P.J. Axelsson	BOS	68	6	14	20	2	42	0	0	1	1	107	5.6
C	39	Travis Green	BOS	64	11	5	16	–6	67	2	0	2	0	104	10.6
C	92	Michael Nylander	WSH	3	0	2	2	1	8	0	0	0	0	1	0.0
			BOS	15	1	11	12	3	14	0	0	1	0	29	3.4
			TOTAL	18	1	13	14	4	22	0	0	1	0	30	3.3
L	40	Ted Donato	BOS	63	6	5	11	2	18	0	3	1	1	35	17.1
D	21	Sean O'Donnell	BOS	82	1	10	11	10	110	0	0	0	0	72	1.4
L	17	Rob Zamuner	BOS	57	4	5	9	3	16	0	0	0	0	49	8.2
D	25	Hal Gill	BOS	82	2	7	9	16	99	0	0	0	0	104	1.9
C	33	Craig Macdonald	FLA	34	0	3	3	–5	25	0	0	0	0	42	0.0
			BOS	18	0	3	3	0	8	0	0	0	0	17	0.0
			TOTAL	52	0	6	6	–5	33	0	0	0	0	59	0.0
L	22	Michal Grosek	BOS	33	3	2	5	1	33	0	0	0	0	24	12.5
D	18	Ian Moran	BOS	35	1	4	5	3	28	0	0	0	0	54	1.9
C	52	* Carl Corazzini	BOS	12	2	0	2	2	0	0	1	0	0	16	12.5
C	16	Andy Hilbert	BOS	18	2	0	2	1	9	0	0	0	0	27	7.4
C	54	* Sergei Zinovjev	BOS	10	0	1	1	1	2	0	0	0	0	8	0.0
L	56	Doug Doull	BOS	35	0	1	1	2	132	0	0	0	0	4	0.0
C	42	P.J. Stock	BOS	1	0	0	0	0	0	0	0	0	0	1	0.0
R	75	* Colton Orr	BOS	1	0	0	0	–1	0	0	0	0	0	0	0.0
D	41	* Zdenek Kutlak	BOS	2	0	0	0	–1	0	0	0	0	0	0	0.0
C	76	* Kris Vernarsky	BOS	3	0	0	0	–1	0	0	0	0	0	0	0.0
R	55	* Patrick Leahy	BOS	6	0	0	0	1	0	0	0	0	0	2	0.0
L	43	* Martin Samuelsson	BOS	6	0	0	0	–1	0	0	0	0	0	7	0.0
L	36	Ivan Huml	BOS	7	0	0	0	–3	6	0	0	0	0	11	0.0

Goaltending

No.	Goaltender	GPI	Mins	Avg	W	L	T	EN	SO	GA	SA	S%	G	A	PIM
1	* Andrew Raycroft	57	3420	2.05	29	18	9	4	3	117	1586	.926	0	2	0
29	Felix Potvin	28	1605	2.50	12	8	6	0	4	67	690	.903	0	0	8
	Totals	**82**	**5042**	**2.24**	**41**	**26**	**15**	**4**	**7**	**188**	**2280**	**.918**			

Playoffs

Pos	#	Player	Team	GP	G	A	Pts	+/–	PIM	PP	SH	GW	GT	S	%
L	14	Sergei Samsonov	BOS	7	2	5	7	2	0	0	0	0	0	13	15.4
C	92	Michael Nylander	BOS	6	3	3	6	2	0	0	0	0	0	10	30.0
D	55	Sergei Gonchar	BOS	7	1	4	5	–4	4	1	0	1	0	19	5.3
C	37	* Patrice Bergeron	BOS	7	1	3	4	5	0	0	0	1	1	20	5.0
R	27	Glen Murray	BOS	7	2	1	3	–2	8	0	0	1	1	19	10.5
L	26	Mike Knuble	BOS	7	2	0	2	–5	0	1	0	0	0	16	12.5
D	71	Jiri Slegr	BOS	7	1	1	2	–1	0	0	0	0	0	22	4.5
D	44	Nick Boynton	BOS	7	0	2	2	1	2	0	0	0	0	18	0.0
C	16	Andy Hilbert	BOS	5	1	0	1	0	0	0	0	0	0	4	25.0
C	12	Brian Rolston	BOS	7	1	0	1	–5	8	0	0	0	0	14	7.1
C	39	Travis Green	BOS	7	0	1	1	0	8	0	0	0	0	8	0.0
D	25	Hal Gill	BOS	7	0	1	1	–2	4	0	0	0	0	11	0.0
C	33	Craig MacDonald	BOS	1	0	0	0	1	0	0	0	0	0	0	0.0
L	40	Ted Donato	BOS	2	0	0	0	0	0	0	0	0	0	1	0.0
L	17	Rob Zamuner	BOS	7	0	0	0	–1	0	0	0	0	0	3	0.0
R	20	Martin Lapointe	BOS	7	0	0	0	–2	14	0	0	0	0	7	0.0
D	21	Sean O'Donnell	BOS	7	0	0	0	1	0	0	0	0	0	2	0.0
D	6	Dan McGillis	BOS	7	0	0	0	–3	2	0	0	0	0	14	0.0
L	11	P.J. Axelsson	BOS	7	0	0	0	–2	4	0	0	0	0	10	0.0
C	19	Joe Thornton	BOS	7	0	0	0	–6	14	0	0	0	0	14	0.0

Goaltending

No.	Goaltender	GPI	Mins	Avg	W	L	EN	SO	GA	SA	S%	G	A	PIM
1	* Andrew Raycroft	7	447	2.15	3	4	3	1	16	210	.924	0	0	2
	Totals	**7**	**451**	**2.53**	**3**	**4**	**3**	**1**	**19**	**213**	**.911**			

Captains' History

No captain, 1924-25 to 1926-27; Lionel Hitchman, 1927-28 to 1930-31; George Owen, 1931-32; Dit Clapper, 1932-33 to 1937-38; Cooney Weiland, 1938-39; Dit Clapper, 1939-40 to 1945-46; Dit Clapper and John Crawford, 1946-47; John Crawford 1947-48 to 1949-50; Milt Schmidt, 1950-51 to 1953-54; Milt Schmidt, Ed Sanford, 1954-55; Fern Flaman, 1955-56 to 1960-61; Don McKenney, 1961-62, 1962-63; Leo Boivin, 1963-64 to 1965-66; John Bucyk, 1966-67; no captain, 1967-68 to 1972-73; John Bucyk, 1973-74 to 1976-77; Wayne Cashman, 1977-78 to 1982-83; Terry O'Reilly, 1983-84, 1984-85; Raymond Bourque, Rick Middleton (co-captains) 1985-86 to 1987-88; Raymond Bourque, 1988-89 to 1999-2000; Jason Allison, 2000-01; no captain, 2001-02; Joe Thornton, 2002-03 to date.

Club Records

Team

(Figures in brackets for season records are games played; records for fewest points, wins, ties, losses, goals, goals against are for 70 or more games)

Most Points **121** 1970-71 (78)
Most Wins **57** 1970-71 (78)
Most Ties **21** 1954-55 (70)
Most Losses **47** 1961-62 (70), 1996-97 (82)
Most Goals **399** 1970-71 (78)
Most Goals Against **306** 1961-62 (70)
Fewest Points **38** 1961-62 (70)
Fewest Wins **14** 1962-63 (70)
Fewest Ties **5** 1972-73 (78)
Fewest Losses **13** 1971-72 (78)
Fewest Goals **147** 1955-56 (70)
Fewest Goals Against **172** 1952-53 (70)

Longest Winning Streak
Overall .... **14** Dec. 3/29-Jan. 9/30
Home .... ***20** Dec. 3/29-Mar. 18/30
Away .... **8** Feb. 17-Mar. 8/72, Mar. 15-Apr. 14/93

Longest Undefeated Streak
Overall .... **23** Dec. 22/40-Feb. 23/41 (15 wins, 8 ties)
Home .... **27** Nov. 22/70-Mar. 20/71 (26 wins, 1 tie)
Away .... **15** Dec. 22/40-Mar. 16/41 (9 wins, 6 ties)

Longest Losing Streak
Overall .... **11** Dec. 3/24-Jan. 5/25
Home .... ***11** Dec. 8/24-Feb. 17/25
Away .... **14** Dec. 27/64-Feb. 21/65

Longest Winless Streak
Overall .... **20** Jan. 28-Mar. 11/62 (16 losses, 4 ties)
Home .... **11** Dec. 8/24-Feb. 17/25 (11 losses)
Away .... **14** Three times

Most Shutouts, Season **15** 1927-28 (44)
Most PIM, Season **2,443** 1987-88 (80)
Most Goals, Game .... **14** Jan. 21/45 (NYR 3 at Bos. 14)

Individual

Most Seasons .... **21** John Bucyk, Raymond Bourque
Most Games .... **1,518** Raymond Bourque
Most Goals, Career .... **545** John Bucyk
Most Assists, Career .... **1,111** Raymond Bourque
Most Points, Career .... **1,506** Raymond Bourque (395G, 1,111A)
Most PIM, Career .... **2,095** Terry O'Reilly
Most Shutouts, Career .... **74** Tiny Thompson
Longest Consecutive Games Streak .... **418** John Bucyk (Jan. 23/69-Mar. 2/75)
Most Goals, Season .... **76** Phil Esposito (1970-71)
Most Assists, Season .... **102** Bobby Orr (1970-71)
Most Points, Season .... **152** Phil Esposito (1970-71; 76G, 76A)
Most PIM, Season .... **302** Jay Miller (1987-88)
Most Points, Defenseman, Season .... ***139** Bobby Orr (1970-71; 37G, 102A)
Most Points, Center, Season .... **152** Phil Esposito (1970-71; 76G, 76A)
Most Points, Right Wing, Season .... **105** Ken Hodge (1970-71; 43G, 62A), (1973-74; 50G, 55A), Rick Middleton (1983-84; 47G, 58A)
Most Points, Left Wing, Season .... **116** John Bucyk (1970-71; 51G, 65A)
Most Points, Rookie, Season .... **102** Joe Juneau (1992-93; 32G, 70A)
Most Shutouts, Season .... **15** Hal Winkler (1927-28)
Most Goals, Game .... **4** Twenty times
Most Assists, Game .... **6** Ken Hodge (Feb. 9/71), Bobby Orr (Jan. 1/73)
Most Points, Game .... **7** Bobby Orr (Nov. 15/73; 3G, 4A), Phil Esposito (Dec. 19/74; 3G, 4A), Barry Pederson (Apr. 4/82; 3G, 4A), Cam Neely (Oct. 16/88; 3G, 4A)

* NHL Record.

Retired Numbers

2	Eddie Shore	1926-1940
3	Lionel Hitchman	1925-1934
4	Bobby Orr	1966-1976
5	Dit Clapper	1927-1947
7	Phil Esposito	1967-1975
8	Cam Neely	1986-1996
9	John Bucyk	1957-1978
15	Milt Schmidt	1936-1955
24	Terry O'Reilly	1971-1985
77	Raymond Bourque	1979-2000

All-time Record vs. Other Clubs

Regular Season

	At Home								On Road								Total							
	GP	W	L	T	OL	GF	GA	PTS	GP	W	L	T	OL	GF	GA	PTS	GP	W	L	T	OL	GF	GA	PTS
Anaheim	8	4	4	0	0	23	24	8	9	5	2	2	0	24	18	12	17	9	6	2	0	47	42	20
Atlanta	10	5	2	2	1	36	38	13	10	6	3	0	1	30	28	13	20	11	5	2	2	66	66	26
Buffalo	107	61	32	14	0	400	311	136	108	40	52	15	1	322	386	96	215	101	84	29	1	722	697	232
Calgary	47	28	12	6	1	165	130	63	44	22	18	4	0	154	160	48	91	50	30	10	1	319	290	111
Carolina	78	46	25	7	0	274	207	99	76	36	31	9	0	263	252	81	154	82	56	16	0	537	459	180
Chicago	284	161	89	34	0	1023	808	356	286	94	145	45	2	767	926	235	570	255	234	79	2	1790	1734	591
Colorado	62	31	21	9	1	240	192	72	66	36	24	6	0	271	234	78	128	67	45	15	1	511	426	150
Columbus	2	1	1	0	0	8	7	2	3	2	0	0	1	14	3	5	5	3	1	0	1	22	10	7
Dallas	60	41	9	10	0	258	146	92	61	30	17	13	1	220	175	74	121	71	26	23	1	478	321	166
Detroit	287	154	89	43	1	1007	761	352	285	79	153	52	1	720	952	211	572	233	242	95	2	1727	1713	563
Edmonton	30	21	6	3	0	126	80	45	29	15	11	3	0	97	98	33	59	36	17	6	0	223	178	78
Florida	22	8	10	4	0	56	57	20	21	10	8	2	1	58	57	23	43	18	18	6	1	114	114	43
Los Angeles	61	44	11	6	0	287	169	94	61	33	21	7	0	224	210	73	122	77	32	13	0	511	379	167
Minnesota	3	0	3	0	0	4	13	0	2	0	2	0	0	2	7	0	5	0	5	0	0	6	20	0
Montreal	335	155	122	56	2	990	904	368	334	98	189	47	0	790	1120	243	669	253	311	103	2	1780	2024	611
Nashville	5	2	2	1	0	14	9	5	6	4	1	0	1	16	13	9	11	6	3	1	1	30	22	14
New Jersey	56	31	15	8	2	218	171	72	53	27	13	11	2	172	139	67	109	58	28	19	4	390	310	139
NY Islanders	59	32	15	11	1	220	164	76	61	27	24	10	0	199	202	64	120	59	39	21	1	419	366	140
NY Rangers	298	160	95	42	1	1076	834	363	302	116	131	55	0	853	921	287	600	276	226	97	1	1929	1755	650
Ottawa	33	19	9	5	0	123	92	43	31	15	8	3	5	93	78	38	64	34	17	8	5	216	170	81
Philadelphia	76	46	18	11	1	283	211	104	73	31	32	10	0	211	241	72	149	77	50	21	1	494	452	176
Phoenix	30	22	4	4	0	136	92	48	30	14	13	3	0	102	101	31	60	36	17	7	0	238	193	79
Pittsburgh	78	56	16	6	0	343	218	118	80	33	31	15	1	286	273	82	158	89	47	21	1	629	491	200
St. Louis	59	35	14	9	1	247	161	80	59	23	24	9	3	198	188	58	118	58	38	18	4	445	349	138
San Jose	10	7	0	3	0	39	26	17	11	5	4	2	0	38	30	12	21	12	4	5	0	77	56	29
Tampa Bay	23	16	1	6	0	84	49	38	23	10	10	3	0	66	70	23	46	26	11	9	0	150	119	61
Toronto	298	161	89	47	1	967	786	370	299	92	156	51	0	769	1005	235	597	253	245	98	1	1736	1791	605
Vancouver	52	38	7	7	0	217	124	83	51	27	16	8	0	209	166	62	103	65	23	15	0	426	290	145
Washington	56	32	15	9	0	209	151	73	55	26	16	12	1	191	155	65	111	58	31	21	1	400	306	138
Defunct Clubs	164	112	39	13	0	525	306	237	164	79	67	18	0	496	440	176	328	191	106	31	0	1021	746	413
Totals	**2693**	**1529**	**775**	**376**	**13**	**9598**	**7241**	**3447**	**2693**	**1035**	**1222**	**415**	**21**	**7855**	**8648**	**2506**	**5386**	**2564**	**1997**	**791**	**34**	**17453**	**15889**	**5953**

Playoffs

	Series	W	L	GP	W	L	T	GF	GA	Last Mtg.	Rnd.	Result
Buffalo	7	5	2	39	21	18	0	139	130	1999	CSF	L 2-4
Carolina	3	3	0	19	12	7	0	63	48	1999	CQF	W 4-2
Chicago	6	5	1	22	16	5	1	97	63	1978	QF	W 4-0
Colorado	2	1	1	11	6	5	0	37	36	1983	DSF	W 3-1
Dallas	1	0	1	3	0	3	0	13	20	1981	PRE	L 0-3
Detroit	7	4	3	33	19	14	0	96	98	1957	SF	W 4-1
Edmonton	2	0	2	9	1	8	0	20	41	1990	F	L 1-4
Florida	1	0	1	5	1	4	0	16	22	1996	CQF	L 1-4
Los Angeles	2	2	0	13	8	5	0	56	38	1977	QF	W 4-2
Montreal	30	7	23	152	57	95	0	371	469	2004	CQF	L 3-4
New Jersey	4	1	3	23	8	15	0	60	68	2003	CQF	L 1-4
NY Islanders	2	0	2	11	3	8	0	35	49	1983	CF	L 2-4
NY Rangers	9	6	3	42	22	18	2	114	104	1973	QF	L 1-4
Philadelphia	4	2	2	20	11	9	0	60	57	1978	SF	W 4-1
Pittsburgh	4	2	2	19	9	10	0	62	67	1992	CF	L 0-4
St. Louis	2	2	0	8	8	0	0	48	15	1972	SF	W 4-0
Toronto	13	5	8	62	30	31	1	153	150	1974	QF	W 4-0
Washington	2	1	1	10	6	4	0	28	21	1998	CQF	L 2-4
Defunct Clubs	3	1	2	11	4	5	2	20	20			
Totals	**104**	**47**	**57**	**512**	**242**	**264**	**6**	**1488**	**1516**			

Calgary totals include Atlanta Flames, 1972-73 to 1979-80.
Carolina totals include Hartford, 1979-80 to 1996-97.
Colorado totals include Quebec, 1979-80 to 1994-95.
Dallas totals include Minnesota North Stars, 1967-68 to 1992-93.
New Jersey totals include Kansas City, 1974-75 to 1975-76, and Colorado Rockies, 1976-77 to 1981-82.
Phoenix totals include Winnipeg, 1979-80 to 1995-96.

Playoff Results 2004-2000

Year	Round	Opponent	Result	GF	GA
2004	CQF	Montreal	L 3-4	14	19
2003	CQF	New Jersey	L 1-4	8	13
2002	CQF	Montreal	L 2-4	18	20

Abbreviations: Round: F - Final; **CF** - conference final; **CSF** - conference semi-final; **CQF** - conference quarter-final; **DSF** - division semi-final; **SF** - semi-final; **QF** - quarter-final; **PRE** - preliminary round.

2003-04 Results

Oct.	8	New Jersey	3-3
	10	at Tampa Bay	1-5
	11	at Florida	1-1
	15	at Dallas	2-0
	18	at Los Angeles	4-3
	19	at Anaheim	4-3*
	21	at Colorado	4-1
	23	Carolina	0-2
	25	at New Jersey	5-2
	28	at Montreal	2-0
	30	Montreal	0-1*
Nov.	1	at Pittsburgh	2-3*
	6	San Jose	5-5
	8	Dallas	4-1
	11	Edmonton	4-3
	14	at Columbus	4-0
	15	Vancouver	2-1*
	19	at Atlanta	4-5*
	20	Washington	3-2
	22	at Philadelphia	2-3
	25	at St. Louis	3-4*
	28	Nashville	1-2
	30	Phoenix	3-3
Dec.	3	at Atlanta	6-4
	4	Toronto	0-6
	6	Philadelphia	1-1
	8	Ottawa	2-2
	10	at Florida	1-1
	11	at Washington	5-6
	13	at Ottawa	3-2
	16	at Montreal	1-1
	18	Calgary	0-5
	20	Carolina	1-2
	22	at NY Rangers	2-4
	23	Tampa Bay	1-1
	27	at Tampa Bay	2-4
	29	at Washington	3-1
	30	Ottawa	0-3
Jan.	1	Toronto	3-2
	3	NY Islanders	3-3
	7	at Detroit	3-0
	8	Pittsburgh	3-1
	10	Detroit	2-1*
	12	Buffalo	4-3
	15	at Buffalo	1-0
	17	at Ottawa	0-4
	19	NY Rangers	5-2
	20	at NY Rangers	4-1
	22	Buffalo	2-3
	24	Florida	1-2
	27	at NY Islanders	2-2
	29	NY Islanders	2-1*
	31	at Montreal	1-0
Feb.	1	Pittsburgh	4-1
	3	Atlanta	5-4
	5	at Buffalo	6-2
	10	at Pittsburgh	6-3
	12	at Ottawa	2-3*
	14	at Chicago	1-2*
	17	at Toronto	5-2
	19	at Philadelphia	4-3
	21	at Carolina	3-3
	23	Florida	0-2
	24	at NY Islanders	0-0
	26	Montreal	2-3*
	28	Philadelphia	3-2*
Mar.	2	at Toronto	2-3
	4	NY Rangers	3-1
	6	Atlanta	2-2
	9	at Nashville	3-2
	11	at Buffalo	3-2*
	13	Buffalo	3-2*
	16	at Toronto	2-1
	18	Minnesota	0-2
	20	Tampa Bay	5-4
	23	Ottawa	4-2
	25	Toronto	0-3
	27	Montreal	3-2*
	30	at Carolina	3-2
Apr.	1	Washington	3-3
	3	New Jersey	2-5
	4	at New Jersey	3-1

* – Overtime

Entry Draft
Selections 2004-1990

2004
Pick
63	David Krejci
64	Martins Karsums
108	Ashton Rome
134	Kris Versteeg
160	Ben Walter
224	Matt Hunwick
255	Anton Hedman

2003
Pick
21	Mark Stuart
45	Patrice Bergeron
66	Masi Marjamaki
107	Byron Bitz
118	Frank Rediker
129	Patrik Valcak
153	Mike Brown
183	Nate Thompson
247	Benoit Mondou
277	Kevin Regan

2002
Pick
29	Hannu Toivonen
56	Vladislav Evseev
130	Jan Kubista
153	Peter Hamerlik
228	Dmitri Utkin
259	Yan Stastny
290	Pavel Frolov

2001
Pick
19	Shaone Morrisonn
77	Darren McLachlan
111	Matti Kaltiainen
147	Jiri Jakes
179	Andrew Alberts
209	Jordan Sigalet
241	Milan Jurcina
282	Marcel Rodman

2000
Pick
7	Lars Jonsson
27	Martin Samuelsson
37	Andy Hilbert
59	Ivan Huml
66	Tuukka Makela
73	Sergei Zinovjev
102	Brett Nowak
174	Jarno Kultanen
204	Chris Berti
237	Zdenek Kutlak
268	Pavel Kolarik
279	Andreas Lindstrom

1999
Pick
21	Nick Boynton
56	Matt Zultek
89	Kyle Wanvig
118	Jaakko Harikkala
147	Seamus Kotyk
179	Donald Choukalos
207	Greg Barber
236	John Cronin
247	Mikko Eloranta
264	Georgy Pujacs

1998
Pick
48	Jonathan Girard
52	Bobby Allen
78	Peter Nordstrom
135	Andrew Raycroft
165	Ryan Milanovic

1997
Pick
1	Joe Thornton
8	Sergei Samsonov
27	Ben Clymer
54	Mattias Karlin
63	Lee Goren
81	Karol Bartanus
135	Denis Timofeev
162	Joel Trottier
180	Jim Baxter
191	Antti Laaksonen
218	Eric Van Acker
246	Jay Henderson

1996
Pick
8	Johnathan Aitken
45	Henry Kuster
53	Eric Naud
80	Jason Doyle
100	Trent Whitfield
132	Elias Abrahamsson
155	Chris Lane
182	Thomas Brown
208	Bob Prier
234	Anders Soderberg

1995
Pick
9	Kyle McLaren
21	Sean Brown
47	Paxton Schafer
73	Bill McCauley
99	Cameron Mann
151	Yevgeny Shaldybin
177	P.J. Axelsson
203	Sergei Zhukov
229	Jonathon Murphy

1994
Pick
21	Evgeni Ryabchikov
47	Daniel Goneau
99	Eric Nickulas
125	Darren Wright
151	Andre Roy
177	Jeremy Schaefer
229	John Grahame
255	Neil Savary
281	Andrei Yakhanov

1993
Pick
25	Kevyn Adams
51	Matt Alvey
88	Charles Paquette
103	Shawn Bates
129	Andrei Sapozhnikov
155	Milt Mastad
181	Ryan Golden
207	Hal Gill
233	Joel Prpic
259	Joakim Persson

1992
Pick
16	Dmitri Kvartalnov
55	Sergei Zholtok
112	Scott Bailey
133	Jiri Dopita
136	Grigori Panteleev
184	Kurt Seher
208	Mattias Timander
232	Chris Crombie
256	Denis Chervyakov
257	Evgeny Pavlov

1991
Pick
18	Glen Murray
40	Jozef Stumpel
62	Marcel Cousineau
84	Brad Tiley
106	Mariusz Czerkawski
150	Gary Golczewski
172	Jay Moser
194	Daniel Hodge
216	Steve Norton
238	Stephen Lombardi
260	Torsten Kienass

1990
Pick
21	Bryan Smolinski
63	Cam Stewart
84	Jerome Buckley
105	Mike Bales
126	Mark Woolf
147	Jim Mackey
168	John Gruden
189	Darren Wetherill
210	Dean Capuano
231	Andy Bezeau
252	Ted Miskolczi

Club Directory

FleetCenter

Boston Bruins
One FleetCenter Place, Suite 250
Boston, MA 02114
Phone **617/624-1900**
FAX 617/523-7184
www.bostonbruins.com
Capacity: 17,565

Executive
Owner and Governor	Jeremy M. Jacobs
Alternate Governor	Louis Jacobs, Charles Jacobs, Jeremy Jacobs Jr.
President and Alternate Governor	Harry Sinden
Senior Assistant to the President	Nate Greenberg
Chief Legal Officer	Michael Wall
Chief Financial Officer	Jessica Rahuba
Vice President, General Manager and Alternate Governor	Mike O'Connell
Assistant General Manager	Jeff Gorton
Executive Vice President	Charles Jacobs
Executive Vice President	Richard Krezwick
Director of Administration	Dale Hamilton-Powers
Assistant to the President	Joe Curnane
Assistant Director of Administration/ Travel Coordinator	Carol Gould
Administrative Assistant	Karen Ondo
Executive Secretary	Rita Brandano

Coaching Staff
Head Coach	Mike Sullivan
Assistant Coaches	Wayne Cashman, Norm Maciver
Goaltending Consultant	Bob Essensa
Video Coordinator	Brant Berglund
Team Road Services Coordinator	John Bucyk
Coach, Providence Bruins	Scott Gordon

Scouting Staff
Director of Pro Scouting & Player Development	Sean Coady
Director of Amateur Scouting	Scott Bradley
Scouting Staff	Nikolai Bobrov, Gerry Cheevers, Adam Creighton, Daniel Dore, Oto Huscak, Mike McGraw, Tom McVie, Tom Songin, Svenake Svensson

Medical & Training Staff
Strength and Conditioning Coach	John Whitesides
Athletic Trainer	Don DelNegro
Physical Therapist	Scott Waugh
Equipment Manager	Peter Henderson
Assistant Equipment Managers	Chris "Muggsy" Aldrich, Keith Robinson

Communications & Marketing Staff
Director of Media Relations	Heidi Holland
Media Relations Manager	Ryan Nadeau
Director of Marketing & Community Relations	Sue Byrne
Promotions Manager	Dave Murray
Manager of Community Development and Special Events	Kerry Collins
Marketing Services Coordinator	Chris DiPierro
Website and Editorial Coordinator	Brian Scully
Administrative Assistant, Alumni Office	Mal Viola

Ticketing & Finance Staff
Director of Ticket Operations	Matt Brennan
Assistant Director of Ticket Operations	Jim Foley
Ticket Office Receptionist	Jo-Ann Connolly-White
Controller	Rick McGlinchey
Accountant, Payroll & Benefits	Audrey Centeno
Accounts Payable	Linda Bartlett

Vice President and General Manager

O'CONNELL, MIKE
Vice President/General Manager, Boston Bruins.
Born in Chicago, IL, November 25, 1955.

Mike O'Connell was named the general manager of the Boston Bruins on November 1, 2000, becoming just the sixth man in club history to hold that position. He was involved in all aspects of the on-ice operation of the hockey team over the previous six seasons as the team's assistant general manager and was instrumental in bringing much of the young talent into the organization. In his first four seasons as the club's general manager, Boston has won two Northeast Division titles.

O'Connell's experience as both a player and assistant coach in the National Hockey League, and as a head coach in both the American and International Hockey Leagues, dates back to the 1977-78 season. Raised in Cohasset, MA, he played two years of high school hockey at Archbishop Williams High School in Braintree, MA. He then made what at the time was an unusual move for an American player, jumping to the Ontario Hockey League to play Canadian major junior hockey at the suggestion of Harry Sinden and Tom Johnson. The move proved beneficial as, after two seasons with Kingston of the OHL, he was drafted by Chicago 43rd overall in the 1975 NHL Amateur Draft.

He turned professional with the Blackhawks organization in 1975 and played five-plus seasons with Chicago and their Central Hockey League affiliate in Dallas before coming to Boston on December 18, 1980, in a trade for Al Secord. He enjoyed his best NHL seasons during his six years in a Bruins uniform, recording 50+ point campaigns for three straight years from 1982 to 1985 and representing the team in the 1984 NHL All-Star Game in New Jersey. He was traded to Detroit for Reed Larson on March 10, 1986 and concluded his playing career with the Red Wings at the end of the 1989-90 season.

O'Connell then moved into the coaching ranks, assuming the head coaching position for the IHL's San Diego Gulls in 1990-91. He then returned to the NHL, with Boston as an assistant coach. On June 12, 1992, he was named the head coach of Boston's American Hockey League affiliate in Providence. Working with many players who also wore a Boston uniform during his tenure, he compiled a 74-71-15 record over a two-year span and won a Northern Division title in 1992-93. He then returned to Boston when he was named the club's assistant general manager on July 5, 1994. He was named as a vice president of the team in 1998. During the 2002-03 season, O'Connell took over behind the bench late in the season.

NHL Coaching Record

Season	Team	Games	W	L	T	Games	W	L
			Regular Season				Playoffs	
2002-03	Boston	9	3	3	3	5	1	4
	NHL Totals	9	3	3	3	5	1	4

General Managers' History

Art Ross, 1924-25 to 1953-54; Lynn Patrick, 1954-55 to 1964-65; Hap Emms, 1965-66, 1966-67; Milt Schmidt, 1967-68 to 1971-72; Harry Sinden, 1972-73 to 1999-2000; Harry Sinden and Mike O'Connell, 2000-01; Mike O'Connell, 2001-02 to date.

Coaching History

Art Ross, 1924-25 to 1927-28; Cy Denneny, 1928-29; Art Ross, 1929-30 to 1933-34; Frank Patrick, 1934-35, 1935-36; Art Ross, 1936-37 to 1938-39; Cooney Weiland, 1939-40, 1940-41; Art Ross, 1941-42 to 1944-45; Dit Clapper, 1945-46 to 1948-49; Georges Boucher, 1949-50; Lynn Patrick, 1950-51 to 1953-54; Lynn Patrick and Milt Schmidt, 1954-55; Milt Schmidt, 1955-56 to 1960-61; Phil Watson, 1961-62; Phil Watson and Milt Schmidt, 1962-63; Milt Schmidt, 1963-64 to 1965-66; Harry Sinden, 1966-67 to 1969-70; Tom Johnson, 1970-71, 1971-72; Tom Johnson and Bep Guidolin, 1972-73; Bep Guidolin, 1973-74; Don Cherry, 1974-75 to 1978-79; Fred Creighton and Harry Sinden, 1979-80; Gerry Cheevers, 1980-81 to 1983-84; Gerry Cheevers and Harry Sinden, 1984-85; Butch Goring, 1985-86; Butch Goring and Terry O'Reilly, 1986-87; Terry O'Reilly, 1987-88, 1988-89; Mike Milbury, 1989-90, 1990-91; Rick Bowness, 1991-92; Brian Sutter, 1992-93 to 1994-95; Steve Kasper, 1995-96, 1996-97; Pat Burns, 1997-98 to 1999-2000; Pat Burns and Mike Keenan, 2000-01; Robbie Ftorek, 2001-02; Robbie Ftorek and Mike O'Connell, 2002-03; Mike Sullivan, 2003-04 to date.

Buffalo Sabres

2003-04 Results: 37W-34L-7T-4OTL 85PTS.
Fifth, Northeast Division

2004-05 Schedule

Oct.	Fri.	15	at Columbus	Thu.	13	Carolina
	Sat.	16	New Jersey	Sat.	15	at Philadelphia
	Mon.	18	Tampa Bay	Mon.	17	at Tampa Bay
	Thu.	21	at Atlanta	Wed.	19	at Florida
	Fri.	22	at Dallas	Fri.	21	at Atlanta
	Sun.	24	at Phoenix*	Sat.	22	at Ottawa
	Tue.	26	at St. Louis	Tue.	25	St. Louis
	Thu.	28	San Jose	Thu.	27	NY Islanders
	Sat.	30	Pittsburgh	Sat.	29	at NY Islanders*
Nov.	Thu.	4	at Boston	Sun.	30	at Boston*
	Fri.	5	Philadelphia	Feb. Tue.	1	Toronto
	Fri.	12	Edmonton	Thu.	3	New Jersey
	Sat.	13	at NY Rangers	Sat.	5	Pittsburgh
	Mon.	15	Toronto	Tue.	8	Ottawa
	Wed.	17	Carolina	Thu.	10	Washington
	Fri.	19	NY Rangers	Tue.	15	at Detroit
	Sat.	20	at Carolina	Fri.	18	at Toronto
	Wed.	24	Boston	Sun.	20	Atlanta*
	Fri.	26	Montreal	Tue.	22	Washington
	Sat.	27	at Toronto	Fri.	25	Tampa Bay
Dec.	Wed.	1	Minnesota	Sat.	26	at Montreal
	Fri.	3	NY Islanders	Mar. Tue.	1	at Los Angeles
	Sat.	4	at Philadelphia	Thu.	3	at San Jose
	Tue.	7	at New Jersey	Fri.	4	at Anaheim
	Thu.	9	Boston	Wed.	9	Boston
	Sat.	11	at Boston*	Fri.	11	Ottawa
	Mon.	13	Toronto	Sat.	12	at Montreal
	Wed.	15	at Florida	Tue.	15	Colorado
	Fri.	17	at Tampa Bay	Fri.	18	at NY Rangers
	Sun.	19	Florida*	Sat.	19	Nashville
	Tue.	21	at Montreal	Mon.	21	at New Jersey
	Wed.	22	Montreal	Wed.	23	Philadelphia
	Sun.	26	NY Rangers	Sat.	26	at Ottawa
	Tue.	28	at Pittsburgh	Sun.	27	Calgary*
	Wed.	29	at Chicago	Tue.	29	at Carolina
Jan.	Sat.	1	Vancouver	Thu.	31	at Pittsburgh
	Mon.	3	Chicago	Apr. Fri.	1	at Ottawa
	Wed.	5	Ottawa	Sun.	3	Florida*
	Sat.	8	at NY Islanders	Wed.	6	at Washington
	Sun.	9	at Washington	Fri.	8	Montreal
	Tue.	11	Atlanta	Sat.	9	at Toronto

Denotes afternoon game.

Franchise date: May 22, 1970

NHL
EASTERN CONFERENCE

NORTHEAST DIVISION

35th NHL Season

Center Chris Drury won 14 of 19 face-offs in his Sabres debut at Philadelphia on October 9, 2003. He finished the season 13th in face-off winning percentage with a mark of 54.9.

Year-by-Year Record

		Home				Road				Overall							
Season	GP	W	L	T	OL	W	L	T	OL	W	L	T	OL	GF	GA	Pts.	Finished	Playoff Result
2003-04	82	21	13	4	3	16	21	3	1	37	34	7	4	220	221	85	5th, Northeast Div.	Out of Playoffs
2002-03	82	18	16	5	2	9	21	5	6	27	37	10	8	190	219	72	5th, Northeast Div.	Out of Playoffs
2001-02	82	20	16	5	0	15	19	6	1	35	35	11	1	213	200	82	5th, Northeast Div.	Out of Playoffs
2000-01	82	26	12	3	0	20	18	2	1	46	30	5	1	218	184	98	2nd, Northeast Div.	Lost Conf. Semi-Final
1999-2000	82	21	14	5	1	14	18	6	3	35	32	11	4	213	204	85	3rd, Northeast Div.	Lost Conf. Quarter-Final
1998-99	82	23	12	6	...	14	16	11	...	37	28	17	...	207	175	91	4th, Northeast Div.	Lost Final
1997-98	82	20	13	8	...	16	16	9	...	36	29	17	...	211	187	89	3rd, Northeast Div.	Lost Conf. Final
1996-97	82	24	11	6	...	16	19	6	...	40	30	12	...	237	208	92	1st, Northeast Div.	Lost Conf. Semi-Final
1995-96	82	19	17	5	...	14	25	2	...	33	42	7	...	247	262	73	5th, Northeast Div.	Out of Playoffs
1994-95	48	15	8	1	...	7	11	6	...	22	19	7	...	130	119	51	4th, Northeast Div.	Lost Conf. Quarter-Final
1993-94	84	22	17	3	...	21	15	6	...	43	32	9	...	282	218	95	4th, Northeast Div.	Lost Conf. Quarter-Final
1992-93	84	25	15	2	...	13	21	8	...	38	36	10	...	335	297	86	4th, Adams Div.	Lost Div. Final
1991-92	84	22	13	5	...	9	24	7	...	31	37	12	...	289	299	74	3rd, Adams Div.	Lost Div. Semi-Final
1990-91	80	15	13	12	...	16	17	7	...	31	30	19	...	292	278	81	3rd, Adams Div.	Lost Div. Semi-Final
1989-90	80	27	11	2	...	18	16	6	...	45	27	8	...	286	248	98	2nd, Adams Div.	Lost Div. Semi-Final
1988-89	80	25	12	3	...	13	23	4	...	38	35	7	...	291	299	83	3rd, Adams Div.	Lost Div. Semi-Final
1987-88	80	19	14	7	...	18	18	4	...	37	32	11	...	283	305	85	3rd, Adams Div.	Lost Div. Semi-Final
1986-87	80	18	18	4	...	10	26	4	...	28	44	8	...	280	308	64	5th, Adams Div.	Out of Playoffs
1985-86	80	23	16	1	...	14	21	5	...	37	37	6	...	296	291	80	5th, Adams Div.	Out of Playoffs
1984-85	80	23	10	7	...	15	18	7	...	38	28	14	...	290	237	90	3rd, Adams Div.	Lost Div. Semi-Final
1983-84	80	25	9	6	...	23	16	1	...	48	25	7	...	315	257	103	2nd, Adams Div.	Lost Div. Semi-Final
1982-83	80	25	7	8	...	13	22	5	...	38	29	13	...	318	285	89	3rd, Adams Div.	Lost Div. Final
1981-82	80	23	8	9	...	16	18	6	...	39	26	15	...	307	273	93	3rd, Adams Div.	Lost Div. Semi-Final
1980-81	80	21	7	12	...	18	13	9	...	39	20	21	...	327	250	99	1st, Adams Div.	Lost Quarter-Final
1979-80	80	27	5	8	...	20	12	8	...	47	17	16	...	318	201	110	1st, Adams Div.	Lost Semi-Final
1978-79	80	19	13	8	...	17	15	8	...	36	28	16	...	280	263	88	2nd, Adams Div.	Lost Prelim. Round
1977-78	80	25	7	8	...	19	12	9	...	44	19	17	...	288	215	105	2nd, Adams Div.	Lost Quarter-Final
1976-77	80	27	8	5	...	21	16	3	...	48	24	8	...	301	220	104	2nd, Adams Div.	Lost Quarter-Final
1975-76	80	28	7	5	...	18	14	8	...	46	21	13	...	339	240	105	2nd, Adams Div.	Lost Quarter-Final
1974-75	80	28	6	6	...	21	10	9	...	49	16	15	...	354	240	113	1st, Adams Div.	Lost Final
1973-74	78	23	10	6	...	9	24	6	...	32	34	12	...	242	250	76	5th, East Div.	Out of Playoffs
1972-73	78	30	6	3	...	7	21	11	...	37	27	14	...	257	219	88	4th, East Div.	Lost Quarter-Final
1971-72	78	11	19	9	...	5	24	10	...	16	43	19	...	203	289	51	6th, East Div.	Out of Playoffs
1970-71	78	16	13	10	...	8	26	5	...	24	39	15	...	217	291	63	5th, East Div.	Out of Playoffs

2004-05 Player Personnel

FORWARDS

	HT	WT	S	Place of Birth	Date	2003-04 Club
AFINOGENOV, Maxim	6-0	190	L	Moscow, USSR	9/4/79	Buffalo
BOULTON, Eric	6-0	222	L	Halifax, N.S.	8/17/76	Buffalo
BRIERE, Daniel	5-10	178	R	Gatineau, Que.	10/6/77	Buffalo
CONNOLLY, Tim	6-1	182	R	Syracuse, NY	5/7/81	Buffalo
DRURY, Chris	5-10	180	R	Trumbull, CT	8/20/76	Buffalo
DUMONT, J.P.	6-1	205	L	Montreal, Que.	4/1/78	Buffalo
GRIER, Mike	6-1	227	R	Detroit, MI	1/5/75	Washington-Buffalo
HECHT, Jochen	6-1	200	L	Mannheim, W. Germany	6/21/77	Buffalo
KOTALIK, Ales	6-1	217	R	Jindrichuv Hradec, Czech.	12/23/78	Buffalo
MAIR, Adam	6-2	215	R	Hamilton, Ont.	2/15/79	Buffalo
PYATT, Taylor	6-4	222	L	Thunder Bay, Ont.	8/19/81	Buffalo
ROY, Derek	5-9	186	L	Ottawa, Ont.	5/4/83	Buffalo-Rochester
SATAN, Miroslav	6-3	190	L	Topolcany, Czech.	10/22/74	Slovan Bratislava-Buffalo
TAYLOR, Chris	6-2	192	L	Stratford, Ont.	3/6/72	Buffalo-Rochester

DEFENSEMEN

	HT	WT	S	Place of Birth	Date	2003-04 Club
BROWN, Brad	6-4	220	R	Baie Verte, Nfld.	12/27/75	Minnesota-Buffalo
CAMPBELL, Brian	6-0	190	L	Strathroy, Ont.	5/23/79	Buffalo
FITZPATRICK, Rory	6-2	215	R	Rochester, NY	1/11/75	Buffalo
JILLSON, Jeff	6-3	220	R	North Smithfield, RI	7/24/80	Boston-Buffalo
KALININ, Dmitri	6-3	215	L	Chelyabinsk, USSR	7/22/80	Buffalo
McKEE, Jay	6-4	212	L	Kingston, Ont.	9/8/77	Buffalo
PATRICK, James	6-2	202	R	Winnipeg, Man.	6/14/63	Buffalo
TALLINDER, Henrik	6-3	210	L	Stockholm, Sweden	1/10/79	Buffalo

GOALTENDERS

	HT	WT	C	Place of Birth	Date	2003-04 Club
BIRON, Martin	6-2	168	L	Lac-St-Charles, Que.	8/15/77	Buffalo
MILLER, Ryan	6-2	150	L	East Lansing, MI	7/17/80	Buffalo-Rochester
NORONEN, Mika	6-2	196	L	Tampere, Finland	6/17/79	Buffalo

2003-04 Scoring

* - rookie

Regular Season

Pos	#	Player	Team	GP	G	A	Pts	+/-	PIM	PP	SH	GW	GT	S	%
C	48	Daniel Briere	BUF	82	28	37	65	-7	70	11	0	3	0	194	14.4
R	81	Miroslav Satan	BUF	82	29	28	57	-15	30	11	1	5	0	206	14.1
R	17	Jean-Pierre Dumont	BUF	77	22	31	53	-9	40	10	0	1	0	156	14.1
C	23	Chris Drury	BUF	76	18	35	53	8	68	5	1	2	0	152	11.8
L	55	Jochen Hecht	BUF	64	15	37	52	17	49	2	1	0	0	174	8.6
D	45	Dmitri Kalinin	BUF	77	10	24	34	0	42	2	1	4	0	118	8.5
R	61	Maxim Afinogenov	BUF	73	17	14	31	-4	57	3	0	4	1	148	11.5
R	25	Mike Grier	WSH	68	8	12	20	-19	32	1	1	0	0	115	7.0
			BUF	14	1	8	9	10	4	0	0	0	0	18	5.6
			TOTAL	82	9	20	29	-9	36	1	1	0	0	133	6.8
D	44	Alexei Zhitnik	BUF	68	4	24	28	-13	102	2	0	0	1	134	3.0
R	12	Ales Kotalik	BUF	62	15	11	26	-1	41	2	0	3	0	142	10.6
L	24	Taylor Pyatt	BUF	63	8	12	20	-7	25	1	2	4	0	98	8.2
C	22	Adam Mair	BUF	81	6	14	20	-3	146	1	0	1	0	82	7.3
C	9	* Derek Roy	BUF	49	9	10	19	-8	12	1	0	4	0	71	12.7
D	34	Jeff Jillson	BOS	50	4	10	14	-1	35	1	0	1	0	80	5.0
			BUF	14	0	3	3	-3	19	0	0	0	0	35	0.0
			TOTAL	64	4	13	17	-4	54	1	0	1	1	115	3.5
C	16	Chris Taylor	BUF	54	6	6	12	-2	22	0	0	0	0	50	12.0
D	3	James Patrick	BUF	55	4	7	11	11	12	0	0	1	0	44	9.1
D	8	Rory Fitzpatrick	BUF	60	4	7	11	-5	44	2	0	2	0	78	5.1
D	51	Brian Campbell	BUF	53	3	8	11	-8	12	0	0	0	0	45	6.7
D	10	Henrik Tallinder	BUF	72	1	9	10	5	26	0	0	0	0	63	1.6
R	15	* Milan Bartovic	BUF	23	1	8	9	1	18	0	0	0	0	30	3.3
D	5	Andy Delmore	BUF	37	2	5	7	-5	29	2	0	0	0	40	5.0
D	74	Jay Mckee	BUF	43	2	3	5	6	41	0	0	1	0	29	6.9
L	28	Jason Botterill	BUF	19	2	1	3	0	14	1	0	0	0	20	10.0
L	26	Eric Boulton	BUF	44	1	2	3	-2	110	0	0	0	0	20	5.0
D	4	Brad Brown	MIN	30	0	1	1	-1	54	0	0	0	0	14	0.0
			BUF	13	0	2	2	3	12	0	0	0	0	6	0.0
			TOTAL	43	0	3	3	2	66	0	0	0	0	20	0.0
L	76	* Andrew Peters	BUF	42	2	0	2	-3	151	0	0	0	0	19	10.5
R	29	* Jason Pominville	BUF	1	0	0	0	0	0	0	0	0	0	3	0.0
R	19	* Norman Milley	BUF	2	0	0	0	0	2	0	0	0	0	2	0.0
C	38	Domenic Pittis	BUF	4	0	0	0	-1	4	0	0	0	0	4	0.0
D	33	* Doug Janik	BUF	4	0	0	0	0	19	0	0	0	0	3	0.0

Goaltending

No.	Goaltender	GPI	Mins	Avg	W	L	T	EN	SO	GA	SA	S%	G	A	PIM
43	Martin Biron	52	2972	2.52	26	18	5	3	2	125	1442	.913	0	2	10
35	Mika Noronen	35	1796	2.57	11	17	2	1	2	77	821	.906	1	0	0
30	* Ryan Miller	3	178	5.06	0	3	0	0	0	15	73	.795	0	0	0
	Totals	**82**	**4971**	**2.67**	**37**	**38**	**7**	**4**	**4**	**221**	**2340**	**.906**			

In his first full season in Buffalo, Daniel Briere finished second to Miroslav Satan with 28 goals and established career highs with 37 assists and 65 points.

Coaching History

Punch Imlach, 1970-71; Punch Imlach, Floyd Smith and Joe Crozier, 1971-72; Joe Crozier, 1972-73, 1973-74; Floyd Smith, 1974-75 to 1976-77; Marcel Pronovost, 1977-78; Marcel Pronovost and Billy Inglis, 1978-79; Scotty Bowman, 1979-80; Roger Neilson, 1980-81; Jim Roberts and Scotty Bowman, 1981-82; Scotty Bowman 1982-83 to 1984-85; Jim Schoenfeld and Scotty Bowman, 1985-86; Scotty Bowman, Craig Ramsay and Ted Sator, 1986-87; Ted Sator, 1987-88, 1988-89; Rick Dudley, 1989-90, 1990-91; Rick Dudley and John Muckler, 1991-92; John Muckler, 1992-93 to 1994-95; Ted Nolan, 1995-96, 1996-97; Lindy Ruff, 1997-98 to date.

Head Coach

RUFF, LINDY
Head Coach, Buffalo Sabres. Born in Warburg, Alta., February, 17, 1960.

A former captain of the Sabres, Lindy Ruff was appointed as the club's 15th head coach on July 21, 1997. In 1999, he led the Sabres to the Stanley Cup Finals for just the second time in club history. With 253 victories in seven seasons behind the bench, Ruff has surpassed Scotty Bowman (210) as the winningest coach in Sabres history. As a player, Ruff was drafted 32nd overall by the Sabres in the 1979 Entry Draft. He played both defense and left wing in an NHL career that spanned 12 seasons including 608 regular-season games with Buffalo. He became a playing assistant coach with Rochester of the AHL in 1991-92 and San Diego of the IHL in 1992-93. Ruff's San Diego club set a pro hockey record with 62 wins. In 1993-94 he became an NHL assistant coach with the Florida Panthers.

Coaching Record

			Regular Season				Playoffs		
Season	Team	Games	W	L	T		Games	W	L
1997-98	Buffalo (NHL)	82	36	29	17		15	10	5
1998-99	Buffalo (NHL)	82	37	28	17		21	14	7
1999-2000	Buffalo (NHL)	82	35	36	11		5	1	4
2000-01	Buffalo (NHL)	82	46	31	5		13	7	6
2001-02	Buffalo (NHL)	82	35	36	11		....	....	....
2002-03	Buffalo (NHL)	82	27	45	10		....	....	....
2003-04	Buffalo (NHL)	82	37	38	7		....	....	....
	NHL Totals	**574**	**253**	**243**	**78**		**54**	**32**	**22**

Captains' History

Floyd Smith, 1970-71; Gerry Meehan, 1971-72 to 1973-74; Gerry Meehan and Jim Schoenfeld, 1974-75; Jim Schoenfeld, 1975-76, 1976-77; Danny Gare, 1977-78 to 1980-81; Danny Gare and Gilbert Perreault, 1981-82; Gilbert Perreault, 1982-83 to 1985-86; Gilbert Perreault and Lindy Ruff, 1986-87; Lindy Ruff, 1987-88; Lindy Ruff and Mike Foligno, 1988-89; Mike Foligno, 1989-90; Mike Foligno and Mike Ramsey, 1990-91; Mike Ramsey, 1991-92; Mike Ramsey and Pat LaFontaine, 1992-93; Pat LaFontaine and Alexander Mogilny, 1993-94; Pat LaFontaine, 1994-95 to 1996-97; Donald Audette and Michael Peca, 1997-98; Michael Peca, 1998-99, 1999-2000; no captain, 2000-01; Stu Barnes. 2001-02, 2002-03; Miroslav Satan, Chris Drury, James Patrick, J.P. Dumont, Daniel Briere, 2003-04.

Club Records

Team

(Figures in brackets for season records are games played; records for fewest points, wins, ties, losses, goals, goals against are for 70 or more games)

Most Points	**113**	1974-75 (80)
Most Wins	**49**	1974-75 (80)
Most Ties	**21**	1980-81 (80)
Most Losses	**44**	1986-87 (80)
Most Goals	**354**	1974-75 (80)
Most Goals Against	**308**	1986-87 (80)
Fewest Points	**51**	1971-72 (78)
Fewest Wins	**16**	1971-72 (78)
Fewest Ties	**5**	2000-01 (82)
Fewest Losses	**16**	1974-75 (80)
Fewest Goals	**190**	2002-03 (82)
Fewest Goals Against	**175**	1998-99 (82)
Longest Winning Streak		
Overall	**10**	Jan. 4-23/84
Home	**12**	Nov. 12/72-Jan. 7/73, Oct. 13-Dec. 10/89
Away	***10**	Dec. 10/83-Jan. 23/84
Longest Undefeated Streak		
Overall	**14**	Mar. 6-Apr. 6/80 (8 wins, 6 ties)
Home	**21**	Oct. 8/72-Jan. 7/73 (18 wins, 3 ties)
Away	**10**	Dec. 10/83-Jan. 23/84 (10 wins)
Longest Losing Streak		
Overall	**7**	Four times
Home	**6**	Oct. 10-Nov. 10/93, Mar. 3-Apr. 3/96
Away	**7**	Oct. 14-Nov. 7/70, Feb. 6-27/71, Jan. 10-Feb. 3/96
Longest Winless Streak		
Overall	**12**	Nov. 23-Dec. 20/91 (8 losses, 4 ties)
Home	**12**	Jan. 27-Mar. 10/91 (7 losses, 5 ties)
Away	**23**	Oct. 30/71-Feb. 19/72 (15 losses, 8 ties)
Most Shutouts, Season	**13**	1997-98 (82)
Most PIM, Season	***2,713**	1991-92 (80)
Most Goals, Game	**14**	Jan. 21/75 (Wsh. 2 at Buf. 14), Mar. 19/81 (Tor. 4 at Buf. 14)

Individual

Most Seasons	**17**	Gilbert Perreault
Most Games	**1,191**	Gilbert Perreault
Most Goals, Career	**512**	Gilbert Perreault
Most Assists, Career	**814**	Gilbert Perreault
Most Points, Career	**1,326**	Gilbert Perreault (512G, 814A)
Most PIM, Career	**3,189**	Rob Ray
Most Shutouts, Career	**55**	Dominik Hasek
Longest Consecutive Games Streak	**776**	Craig Ramsay (Mar. 27/73-Feb. 10/83)
Most Goals, Season	**76**	Alexander Mogilny (1992-93)
Most Assists, Season	**95**	Pat LaFontaine (1992-93)
Most Points, Season	**148**	Pat LaFontaine (1992-93; 53G, 95A)
Most PIM, Season	**354**	Rob Ray (1991-92)
Most Points, Defenseman, Season	**81**	Phil Housley (1989-90; 21G, 60A)
Most Points, Center, Season	**148**	Pat LaFontaine (1992-93; 53G, 95A)
Most Points, Right Wing, Season	**127**	Alexander Mogilny (1992-93; 76G, 51A)
Most Points, Left Wing, Season	**95**	Rick Martin (1974-75; 52G, 43A)
Most Points, Rookie, Season	**74**	Rick Martin (1971-72; 44G, 30A)
Most Shutouts, Season	**13**	Dominik Hasek (1997-98)
Most Goals, Game	**5**	Dave Andreychuk (Feb. 6/86)
Most Assists, Game	**5**	Gilbert Perreault (Feb. 1/76, Mar. 9/80, Jan. 4/84), Dale Hawerchuk (Jan. 15/92), Pat LaFontaine (Dec. 31/92, Feb. 10/93)
Most Points, Game	**7**	Gilbert Perreault (Feb. 1/76; 2G, 5A)

* NHL Record.

Retired Numbers

2	Tim Horton	1972-1974
7	Rick Martin	1971-1981
11	Gilbert Perreault	1970-1987
14	Rene Robert	1971-1979

All-time Record vs. Other Clubs

Regular Season

	At Home								On Road								Total							
	GP	W	L	T	OL	GF	GA	PTS	GP	W	L	T	OL	GF	GA	PTS	GP	W	L	T	OL	GF	GA	PTS
Anaheim	9	4	2	3	0	25	20	11	9	7	2	0	0	30	15	14	18	11	4	3	0	55	35	25
Atlanta	10	6	4	0	0	43	29	12	10	3	5	1	1	31	31	8	20	9	9	1	1	74	60	20
Boston	108	53	39	15	1	386	322	122	107	32	60	14	1	311	400	79	215	85	99	29	2	697	722	201
Calgary	45	27	13	5	0	189	131	59	46	18	17	11	0	146	152	47	91	45	30	16	0	335	283	106
Carolina	77	46	23	7	1	309	226	100	78	35	32	11	0	230	227	81	155	81	55	18	1	539	453	181
Chicago	53	32	14	7	0	199	138	71	51	18	27	6	0	139	164	42	104	50	41	13	0	338	302	113
Colorado	63	36	18	9	0	247	204	81	64	22	31	11	0	197	227	55	127	58	49	20	0	444	431	136
Columbus	4	2	2	0	0	13	9	4	2	0	1	1	0	4	5	1	6	2	3	1	0	17	14	5
Dallas	52	28	13	11	0	188	139	67	54	21	27	6	0	156	173	48	106	49	40	17	0	344	312	115
Detroit	52	33	11	8	0	226	153	74	55	18	31	5	1	159	203	42	107	51	42	13	1	385	356	116
Edmonton	30	10	13	7	0	109	112	27	29	5	21	3	0	74	120	13	59	15	34	10	0	183	232	40
Florida	23	15	5	3	0	64	37	33	21	10	10	1	0	63	59	21	44	25	15	4	0	127	96	54
Los Angeles	53	28	16	9	0	217	157	65	54	23	22	9	0	187	185	55	107	51	38	18	0	404	342	120
Minnesota	3	1	2	0	0	7	8	2	3	2	1	0	0	7	4	4	6	3	3	0	0	14	12	6
Montreal	102	54	29	19	0	317	268	127	103	34	57	12	0	306	392	80	205	88	86	31	0	623	660	207
Nashville	4	0	3	1	0	9	16	1	5	3	2	0	0	9	10	6	9	3	5	1	0	18	26	7
New Jersey	54	31	15	8	0	213	165	70	54	26	18	9	1	177	162	62	108	57	33	17	1	390	327	132
NY Islanders	61	32	19	9	1	197	164	74	61	25	26	9	1	166	172	60	122	57	45	18	2	363	336	134
NY Rangers	68	39	19	10	0	279	212	88	66	23	27	15	1	180	214	62	134	62	46	25	1	459	426	150
Ottawa	31	21	7	3	0	99	48	45	33	16	9	7	1	86	76	40	64	37	16	10	1	185	124	85
Philadelphia	63	32	23	8	0	209	176	72	67	15	39	12	1	162	228	43	130	47	62	20	1	371	404	115
Phoenix	31	20	6	5	0	127	80	45	29	14	13	2	0	92	87	30	60	34	19	7	0	219	167	75
Pittsburgh	71	34	18	17	2	274	190	87	71	17	36	18	0	217	266	52	142	51	54	35	2	491	456	139
St. Louis	52	29	17	6	0	200	164	64	50	14	28	7	1	125	180	36	102	43	45	13	1	325	344	100
San Jose	11	11	0	0	0	52	27	22	10	1	4	4	1	33	36	7	21	12	4	4	1	85	63	29
Tampa Bay	23	13	8	2	0	63	63	28	23	14	6	3	0	70	49	31	46	27	14	5	0	133	112	59
Toronto	69	43	19	6	1	279	184	93	67	27	26	12	2	228	203	68	136	70	45	18	3	507	387	161
Vancouver	52	26	18	8	0	186	152	60	52	16	25	11	0	162	193	43	104	42	43	19	0	348	345	103
Washington	56	35	15	6	0	216	146	76	56	32	15	9	0	196	140	73	112	67	30	15	0	412	286	149
Defunct Clubs	23	13	5	5	0	94	63	31	23	12	8	3	0	97	76	27	46	25	13	8	0	191	139	58
Totals	**1353**	**754**	**396**	**197**	**6**	**5036**	**3803**	**1711**	**1353**	**503**	**626**	**212**	**12**	**4040**	**4449**	**1230**	**2706**	**1257**	**1022**	**409**	**18**	**9076**	**8252**	**2941**

Playoffs

	Series	W	L	GP	W	L	T	GF	GA	Last Mtg.	Rnd.	Result
Boston	7	2	5	39	18	21	0	130	139	1999	CSF	W 4-2
Chicago	2	2	0	9	8	1	0	36	17	1980	QF	W 4-0
Colorado	2	0	2	8	2	6	0	27	35	1985	DSF	L 2-3
Dallas	3	1	2	13	5	8	0	37	39	1999	F	L 2-4
Montreal	7	3	4	35	17	18	0	111	124	1998	CSF	W 4-0
New Jersey	1	0	1	7	3	4	0	14	14	1994	CQF	L 3-4
NY Islanders	3	0	3	16	4	12	0	45	59	1980	SF	L 2-4
NY Rangers	1	1	0	3	2	1	0	11	6	1978	PRE	W 2-1
Ottawa	2	2	0	11	8	3	0	26	19	1999	CQF	W 4-0
Philadelphia	7	2	5	37	14	23	0	96	110	2001	CQF	W 4-2
Pittsburgh	2	0	2	10	4	6	0	26	26	2001	CSF	L 3-4
St. Louis	1	1	0	3	2	1	0	7	8	1976	PRE	W 2-1
Toronto	1	1	0	5	4	1	0	21	16	1999	CF	W 4-1
Vancouver	2	2	0	7	6	1	0	28	14	1981	PRE	W 3-0
Washington	1	0	1	6	2	4	0	11	13	1998	CF	L 2-4
Totals	**42**	**17**	**25**	**209**	**99**	**110**	**0**	**626**	**639**			

Calgary totals include Atlanta Flames, 1972-73 to 1979-80. Carolina totals include Hartford, 1979-80 to 1996-97.
Colorado totals include Quebec, 1979-80 to 1994-95. Dallas totals include Minnesota North Stars, 1970-71 to 1992-93.
New Jersey totals include Kansas City, 1974-75 to 1975-76, and Colorado Rockies, 1976-77 to 1981-82.
Phoenix totals include Winnipeg, 1979-80 to 1995-96.

Playoff Results 2004-2000

Year	Round	Opponent	Result	GF	GA
2001	CSF	Pittsburgh	L 3-4	17	17
	CQF	Philadelphia	W 4-2	21	13
2000	CQF	Philadelphia	L 1-4	8	14

Abbreviations: Round: F - Final; **CF** - conference final; **CSF** - conference semi-final; **CQF** - conference quarter-final; **DSF** - division semi-final; **SF** - semi-final; **QF** - quarter-final; **PRE** - preliminary round.

2003-04 Results

Oct.	9	at Philadelphia	0-2
	11	NY Islanders	0-6
	13	Dallas	4-3
	16	at Edmonton	1-4
	18	at Calgary	2-0
	20	at Vancouver	1-6
	23	at Los Angeles	5-1
	24	at Anaheim	5-2
	26	at Colorado	3-1
	28	Minnesota	1-3
	30	Toronto	5-3
Nov.	1	at Ottawa	1-1
	5	Atlanta	4-7
	7	Montreal	2-1
	8	at Montreal	0-3
	12	New Jersey	2-2
	14	Pittsburgh	1-2*
	17	at Ottawa	2-1
	19	at New Jersey	1-4
	21	Carolina	5-0
	22	at Tampa Bay	1-2
	24	at Florida	1-2
	26	Washington	5-2
	28	Florida	4-3
	29	at Nashville	1-4
Dec.	3	at Chicago	3-2
	4	Phoenix	2-3
	6	Tampa Bay	1-3
	10	Detroit	2-7
	12	NY Rangers	1-3
	13	at Minnesota	2-3
	16	at Pittsburgh	1-2
	19	New Jersey	2-5
	23	Ottawa	2-2
	26	Carolina	3-1
	27	at Washington	3-1
	29	at Carolina	1-2
	31	Washington	7-1
Jan.	2	Anaheim	5-2
	3	at Toronto	3-3
	6	at Montreal	1-3
	7	Philadelphia	1-1
	9	Ottawa	3-2
	12	at Boston	3-4
	13	Philadelphia	6-2
	15	Boston	0-1
	17	at NY Islanders	2-4
	20	at Atlanta	1-4
	22	at Boston	3-2
	24	at Philadelphia	1-2
	25	at Carolina	4-2
	27	Montreal	4-1
	30	at NY Rangers	3-1
	31	NY Rangers	3-1
Feb.	5	Boston	2-6
	10	San Jose	2-1
	13	Los Angeles	8-3
	14	at Toronto	6-4
	16	Atlanta	7-2
	18	Florida	1-1
	20	Tampa Bay	4-3*
	21	at NY Islanders	1-4
	25	at New Jersey	2-8
	27	NY Islanders	2-4
	28	at Ottawa	1-7
Mar.	3	Ottawa	4-3
	6	at Toronto	5-1
	7	St. Louis	1-5
	10	at Washington	6-0
	11	Boston	2-3*
	13	at Boston	2-3*
	15	Toronto	5-6*
	17	at Atlanta	4-3*
	18	at Tampa Bay	1-3
	20	at Florida	2-1
	24	Montreal	2-1
	26	Pittsburgh	5-1
	27	at Pittsburgh	2-2
	29	Columbus	6-0
	31	at NY Rangers	4-3
Apr.	2	Toronto	0-2
	3	at Montreal	3-6

* – Overtime

Entry Draft
Selections 2004-1990

2004 Pick		2000 Pick		1996 Pick		1992 Pick	
13	Drew Stafford	15	Artem Kryukov	7	Erik Rasmussen	11	David Cooper
43	Michael Funk	48	Gerard Dicaire	27	Cory Sarich	35	Jozef Cierny
71	Andrej Sekera	111	Ghyslain Rousseau	33	Darren Van Oene	59	Ondrej Steiner
145	Michal Valent	149	Denis Denisov	54	Francois Methot	80	Dean Melanson
176	Patrick Kaleta	213	Vasili Bizyayev	87	Kurt Walsh	83	Matthew Barnaby
207	Mark Mancari	220	Paul Gaustad	106	Mike Martone	107	Markus Ketterer
241	Mike Card	258	Sean McMorrow	115	Alexei Tezikov	108	Yuri Khmylev
273	Dylan Hunter	277	Ryan Courtney	142	Ryan Davis	131	Paul Rushforth
				161	Darren Mortier	179	Dean Tiltgen
2003 Pick		**1999 Pick**		222	Scott Buhler	203	Todd Simon
5	Thomas Vanek	20	Barrett Heisten			227	Rick Kowalsky
65	Branislav Fabry	35	Milan Bartovic	**1995 Pick**		251	Chris Clancy
74	Clarke MacArthur	55	Doug Janik	14	Jay McKee		
106	Jan Hejda	64	Mike Zigomanis	16	Martin Biron	**1991 Pick**	
114	Denis Ezhov	73	Tim Preston	42	Mark Dutiaume	13	Philippe Boucher
150	Thomas Morrow	117	Karel Mosovsky	68	Mathieu Sunderland	35	Jason Dawe
172	Pavel Voroshnin	138	Ryan Miller	94	Matt Davidson	57	Jason Young
202	Nathan Paetsch	146	Matt Kinch	111	Marian Menhart	72	Peter Ambroziak
235	Jeff Weber	178	Seneque Hyacinthe	119	Kevin Popp	101	Steve Shields
266	Louis-Philippe Martin	206	Bret DeCecco	123	Daniel Bienvenue	123	Sean O'Donnell
		235	Brad Self	172	Brian Scott	124	Brian Holzinger
2002 Pick		263	Craig Brunel	198	Mike Zanutto	145	Chris Snell
11	Keith Ballard			224	Rob Skrlac	162	Jiri Kuntos
20	Dan Paille	**1998 Pick**				189	Tony Iob
76	Michael Tessier	18	Dmitri Kalinin	**1994 Pick**		211	Spencer Meany
82	John Adams	34	Andrew Peters	17	Wayne Primeau	233	Mikhail Volkov
108	Jakub Hulva	47	Norm Milley	43	Curtis Brown	255	Michael Smith
121	Marty Magers	50	Jaroslav Kristek	69	Rumun Ndur		
178	Maxim Schevjev	77	Mike Pandolfo	121	Sergei Klimentiev	**1990 Pick**	
208	Radoslav Hecl	137	Aaron Goldade	147	Cal Benazic	14	Brad May
241	Dennis Wideman	164	Ales Kotalik	168	Steve Plouffe	82	Brian McCarthy
271	Martin Cizek	191	Brad Moran	173	Shane Hnidy	97	Richard Smehlik
		218	David Moravec	176	Steve Webb	100	Todd Bojcun
2001 Pick		249	Edo Terglav	199	Bob Westerby	103	Brad Pascall
22	Jiri Novotny			225	Craig Millar	142	Viktor Gordiouk
32	Derek Roy	**1997 Pick**		251	Mark Polak	166	Milan Nedoma
50	Chris Thorburn	21	Mika Noronen	277	Shayne Wright	187	Jason Winch
55	Jason Pominville	48	Henrik Tallinder			208	Sylvain Naud
155	Michal Vondrka	69	Maxim Afinogenov	**1993 Pick**		229	Kenneth Martin
234	Calle Aslund	75	Jeff Martin	38	Denis Tsygurov	250	Brad Rubachuk
247	Marek Dubec	101	Luc Theoret	64	Ethan Philpott		
279	Ryan Jorde	128	Torrey DiRoberto	116	Richard Safarik		
		156	Brian Campbell	142	Kevin Pozzo		
		184	Jeremy Adduono	168	Sergei Petrenko		
		212	Kamil Piros	194	Mike Barrie		
		238	Dylan Kemp	220	Barrie Moore		
				246	Chris Davis		
				272	Scott Nichol		

General Managers' History

Punch Imlach, 1970-71 to 1977-78; John Anderson, 1978-79; Scotty Bowman, 1979-80 to 1985-86; Scotty Bowman and Gerry Meehan, 1986-87; Gerry Meehan, 1987-88 to 1992-93; John Muckler, 1993-94 to 1996-97; Darcy Regier, 1997-98 to date.

General Manager

REGIER, DARCY
General Manager, Buffalo Sabres. Born in Swift Current, Sask., Nov. 27, 1957.

Darcy Regier became the sixth general manager of the Buffalo Sabres on June 11, 1997 after a lengthy management apprenticeship in the New York Islanders organization. As a player, Regier played eight pro seasons, including part of the 1977-78 season with the Cleveland Barons and parts of the 1982-83 and 1983-84 campaigns with the New York Islanders.

He began his career as an administrator with the Islanders in 1984-85 and went on to serve in a variety of capacities including director of administration, assistant director of hockey operations, assistant coach and assistant general manager. He also served as an assistant coach with Hartford in 1991-92.

While with the Islanders, Regier benefitted from working with talented managers and coaches including Bill Torrey and Al Arbour. As a minor pro player with Indianapolis of the CHL he became associated with another important influence on his hockey career, current Detroit Red Wing executive Jim Devellano.

Club Directory

HSBC Arena

Buffalo Sabres
HSBC Arena
One Seymour H. Knox III Plaza
Buffalo, NY 14203
Phone **716/855-4100**
Fax 716/855-4110
Tickets, U.S.: 888/GO-SABRES
Capacity: 18,690

Executive
Owner . . . . B. Thomas Golisano
Managing Partner . . . . Lawrence Quinn
Chief Operating Officer . . . . Daniel DiPofi

Hockey Operations
General Manager . . . . Darcy Regier
Director of Player Development . . . . Don Luce
Director of Pro Scouting . . . . Terry Martin
Director of Amateur Scouting . . . . Jim Benning
Hockey Operations Assistant . . . . Scott Schranz
Coordinator of Hockey Administration . . . . Mike Bermingham
Travel Coordinator . . . . Neil Herman
Scouting Staff . . . . Bo Berglund, Larry Carriere, Kevin Devine, Iouri Khmylev, Paul Merritt, Darryl Plandowski, Mike Racicot, David Volek
Head Coach . . . . Lindy Ruff
Assistant Coaches . . . . Scott Arniel, Brian McCutcheon
Strength & Conditioning Coach . . . . Doug McKenney
Goaltender Coach . . . . Jim Corsi
Administrative Assistant Coach . . . . Jeff Holbrook
Head Equipment Manager . . . . Rip Simonick

Medical
Team Doctor . . . . Les Bisson, M.D.
Doctors . . . . Nicholas Aquino, M.D., William Hartrich, M.D.
Oral Surgeon . . . . Steven Jenson, DDS
Team Dentist . . . . Daniel Yustin, DDS, M.S.
Physical Therapist . . . . Joe Aquino
Team Doctor Emeritus . . . . John L. Butsch, M.D.

Legal
Director of Legal Affairs/Human Resources . . . . Richard Mugel

Administration
Director of Finance/Administration . . . . Chuck Lamatina
Director of IT . . . . Jon Lamont
IT Assistant . . . . Aaron Beauregard
Executive Assistant . . . . Eleanore MacKenzie
Receptionist . . . . Olive Anticola

Broadcast Production
Director of Technical & Broadcast Operations . . . . . Al Weissman
Staff Producer . . . . Joe Pinter
Staff Director . . . . Eric Grossman
Feature Producer/Editor . . . . Jeff Hill
Broadcast Coordinator . . . . Lisa Tzetzo
Broadcast Team . . . . Rick Jeanneret (Play-By-Play), Jim Lorentz (Color), Danny Gare (Reporter)

Finance
Senior Accountant . . . . Frank Unger
Accounting Manager . . . . Christine Ivansitz
Payroll & Human Resource Manager . . . . Birgid Haensel
Accounts Payable Clerk . . . . Kim Binkley
Accounting Clerk/Workers Comp. . . . . Ann Pastwick

Merchandise
Director of Merchandise . . . . Mike Kaminska
Assistant Store Manager . . . . Jeanne Rudyk
Merchandise Manager – Inventory Control . . . . . . Glenn Barker
Merchandise Manager – Event Sales . . . . Jeff Smith

Marketing
Director of Marketing/Game Presentation . . . . Rich Wall
Director of Creative Services . . . . Frank Cravotta

Public and Community Relations
Director of Public Relations . . . . Michael Gilbert
Manager of Media Relations . . . . Gregg Huller
Media Relations Assistant . . . . Matt Schmidt
Youth Hockey Manager . . . . Patrick Fisher
Mascot Coordinator . . . . Pat Martino
Special Events Coordinator . . . . Maria Merlino
Team Photographer . . . . Bill Wippert
Director of Alumni Relations . . . . Larry Playfair
Corporate & Community Relations Liaison . . . . Gilbert Perreault

Sales
Director of Sales . . . . John Livsey
Director of Business Development (Rochester) . . . . . Rob Kopacz
Director of Suite Sales . . . . Jody Ulrich
Director of Business Development (Canada) . . . . . . Mike Sciarra

Ticket Sales and Operations
Director of Ticket Operations & Services . . . . John Sinclair
Box Office Manager . . . . Christopher Makowski

HSBC Arena
Director of Arena Operations . . . . Stan Makowski, Jr.
Director of Event Booking . . . . Jennifer Van Rysdam
Director of Lacrosse & Amateur Athletics . . . . Kurt Silcott
Chief Engineer . . . . Barry Becker
Ice Technician . . . . Chris Harszlak

Calgary Flames

2003-04 Results: 42w-30L-7t-3OTL 94PTS.
Third, Northwest Division

2004-05 Schedule

Oct.	Wed.	13	at Anaheim		Fri.	14	Ottawa
	Fri.	15	at Los Angeles		Sun.	16	at Chicago
	Sun.	17	at Edmonton		Mon.	17	at Pittsburgh
	Tue.	19	Vancouver		Wed.	19	at Detroit
	Thu.	21	St. Louis		Fri.	21	NY Islanders
	Sat.	23	Columbus		Sun.	23	Anaheim*
	Tue.	26	at Vancouver		Tue.	25	at Dallas
	Fri.	29	at Colorado		Thu.	27	at Phoenix
	Sat.	30	at Phoenix		Sat.	29	New Jersey
Nov.	Tue.	2	Nashville	Feb.	Tue.	1	San Jose
	Thu.	4	Colorado		Thu.	3	NY Rangers
	Sat.	6	Edmonton		Sat.	5	Detroit
	Tue.	9	Anaheim		Mon.	7	at Edmonton
	Thu.	11	at Tampa Bay		Tue.	8	Phoenix
	Fri.	12	at Florida		Thu.	10	Vancouver
	Sun.	14	at Carolina*		Wed.	16	at Los Angeles
	Thu.	18	Nashville		Thu.	17	at San Jose
	Sat.	20	Chicago		Sat.	19	at Vancouver
	Tue.	23	at St. Louis		Thu.	24	Minnesota
	Wed.	24	at Detroit		Sat.	26	Boston
	Fri.	26	Colorado	Mar.	Tue.	1	at St. Louis
	Sun.	28	at Minnesota*		Wed.	2	at Dallas
	Tue.	30	Toronto		Fri.	4	at Chicago
Dec.	Thu.	2	at Vancouver		Sun.	6	at Atlanta*
	Fri.	3	Columbus		Tue.	8	at Nashville
	Sun.	5	at Colorado*		Thu.	10	Chicago
	Tue.	7	Edmonton		Sat.	12	St. Louis
	Thu.	9	Vancouver		Tue.	15	Minnesota
	Sat.	11	Detroit		Thu.	17	Phoenix
	Tue.	14	at Edmonton		Sat.	19	at Colorado
	Thu.	16	at Ottawa		Sun.	20	at Minnesota
	Sat.	18	at Toronto		Tue.	22	Washington
	Tue.	21	Edmonton		Thu.	24	Los Angeles
	Mon.	27	Minnesota		Sat.	26	at Montreal
	Wed.	29	Philadelphia		Sun.	27	at Buffalo*
	Fri.	31	Montreal		Wed.	30	at Columbus
Jan.	Mon.	3	San Jose*	Apr.	Sat.	2	Dallas
	Thu.	6	at Nashville		Mon.	4	Los Angeles
	Fri.	7	at Minnesota		Wed.	6	at Anaheim
	Sun.	9	at Columbus*		Thu.	7	at San Jose
	Tue.	11	Dallas		Sun.	10	Colorado*

* Denotes afternoon game.

Year-by-Year Record

		Home				Road				Overall						
Season	GP	W	L	T	OL	W	L	T	OL	W	L	T	OL	GF	GA	Pts.	Finished	Playoff Result
2003-04	82	21	14	5	1	21	16	2	2	42	30	7	3	200	176	94	3rd, Northwest Div.	Lost Final
2002-03	82	14	16	10	1	15	20	3	3	29	36	13	4	186	228	75	5th, Northwest Div.	Out of Playoffs
2001-02	82	20	14	5	2	12	21	7	1	32	35	12	3	201	220	79	4th, Northwest Div.	Out of Playoffs
2000-01	82	12	18	9	2	15	18	6	2	27	36	15	4	197	236	73	4th, Northwest Div.	Out of Playoffs
1999-2000	82	20	14	6	1	11	22	4	4	31	36	10	5	211	256	77	4th, Northwest Div.	Out of Playoffs
1998-99	82	15	20	6	...	15	20	6	...	30	40	12	...	211	234	72	3rd, Northwest Div.	Out of Playoffs
1997-98	82	18	17	6	...	8	24	9	...	26	41	15	...	217	252	67	5th, Pacific Div.	Out of Playoffs
1996-97	82	21	18	2	...	11	23	7	...	32	41	9	...	214	239	73	5th, Pacific Div.	Out of Playoffs
1995-96	82	18	18	5	...	16	19	6	...	34	37	11	...	241	240	79	2nd, Pacific Div.	Lost Conf. Quarter-Final
1994-95	48	15	7	2	...	9	10	5	...	24	17	7	...	163	135	55	1st, Pacific Div.	Lost Conf. Quarter-Final
1993-94	84	25	12	5	...	17	17	8	...	42	29	13	...	302	256	97	1st, Pacific Div.	Lost Conf. Quarter-Final
1992-93	84	23	14	5	...	20	16	6	...	43	30	11	...	322	282	97	2nd, Smythe Div.	Lost Div. Semi-Final
1991-92	80	19	14	7	...	12	23	5	...	31	37	12	...	296	305	74	5th, Smythe Div.	Out of Playoffs
1990-91	80	29	8	3	...	17	18	5	...	46	26	8	...	344	263	100	2nd, Smythe Div.	Lost Div. Semi-Final
1989-90	80	28	7	5	...	14	16	10	...	42	23	15	...	348	265	99	1st, Smythe Div.	Lost Div. Semi-Final
1988-89	80	32	4	4	...	22	13	5	...	54	17	9	...	354	226	117	1st, Smythe Div.	**Won Stanley Cup**
1987-88	80	26	11	3	...	22	12	6	...	48	23	9	...	397	305	105	1st, Smythe Div.	Lost Div. Final
1986-87	80	25	13	2	...	21	18	1	...	46	31	3	...	318	289	95	2nd, Smythe Div.	Lost Div. Semi-Final
1985-86	80	23	11	6	...	17	20	3	...	40	31	9	...	354	315	89	2nd, Smythe Div.	Lost Final
1984-85	80	23	11	6	...	18	16	6	...	41	27	12	...	363	302	94	3rd, Smythe Div.	Lost Div. Semi-Final
1983-84	80	22	11	7	...	12	21	7	...	34	32	14	...	311	314	82	2nd, Smythe Div.	Lost Div. Final
1982-83	80	21	12	7	...	11	22	7	...	32	34	14	...	321	317	78	2nd, Smythe Div.	Lost Div. Final
1981-82	80	20	11	9	...	9	23	8	...	29	34	17	...	334	345	75	3rd, Smythe Div.	Lost Div. Semi-Final
1980-81	80	25	5	10	...	14	22	4	...	39	27	14	...	329	298	92	3rd, Patrick Div.	Lost Semi-Final
1979-80*	80	18	15	7	...	17	17	6	...	35	32	13	...	282	269	83	4th, Patrick Div.	Lost Prelim. Round
1978-79*	80	25	11	4	...	16	20	4	...	41	31	8	...	327	280	90	4th, Patrick Div.	Lost Prelim. Round
1977-78*	80	20	13	7	...	14	14	12	...	34	27	19	...	274	252	87	3rd, Patrick Div.	Lost Prelim. Round
1976-77*	80	22	11	7	...	12	23	5	...	34	34	12	...	264	265	80	3rd, Patrick Div.	Lost Prelim. Round
1975-76*	80	19	14	7	...	16	19	5	...	35	33	12	...	262	237	82	3rd, Patrick Div.	Lost Prelim. Round
1974-75*	80	24	9	7	...	10	22	8	...	34	31	15	...	243	233	83	4th, Patrick Div.	Out of Playoffs
1973-74*	78	17	15	7	...	13	19	7	...	30	34	14	...	214	238	74	4th, West Div.	Lost Quarter-Final
1972-73	78	16	16	7	...	9	22	8	...	25	38	15	...	191	239	65	7th, West Div.	Out of Playoffs

* Atlanta Flames

Brad Ference (#21) and Mike Commodore check Tyler Bouck of the Canucks during Calgary's first-round playoff matchup with Vancouver. Commodore's huge head of red hair became a fan favorite during Calgary's surprising run to the Stanley Cup finals.

Franchise date: June 6, 1972
Transferred from Atlanta to Calgary, June 24, 1980.

NORTHWEST DIVISION

33rd NHL Season

2004-05 Player Personnel

FORWARDS	HT	WT	S	Place of Birth	Date	2003-04 Club
BELLEMARE, Thomas	6-3	236	R	Shawinigan, Que.	1/11/84	Drummondville
CLARK, Chris	6-0	200	R	South Windsor, CT	3/8/76	Calgary
DONOVAN, Shean	6-2	200	R	Timmins, Ont.	1/22/75	Calgary
GELINAS, Martin	5-11	195	L	Shawinigan, Que.	6/5/70	Calgary
GERMYN, Carsen	5-10	185	R	Campbell River, B.C.	2/22/82	Norfolk
HEINTZ, Davin	6-4	213	L	Luseland, Sask.	6/30/83	Swift Current
IGINLA, Jarome	6-1	208	R	Edmonton, Alta.	7/1/77	Calgary
JOHNER, Dustin	5-11	170	R	Estevan, Sask.	3/6/83	Seattle-South Carolina
KOBASEW, Chuck	5-11	195	L	Osoyoos, B.C.	4/17/82	Calgary
LOMBARDI, Matthew	5-11	191	L	Montreal, Que.	3/18/82	Calgary
LOYNS, Lynn	5-11	200	L	Naicam, Sask.	2/21/81	San Jose-Cleveland-Calgary-Lowell (AHL)
LYNCH, Darren	5-11	175	R	Regina, Sask.	7/7/83	Vancouver (WHL)
NIEMINEN, Ville	6-0	200	L	Tampere, Finland	4/6/77	Chicago-Calgary
NILSON, Marcus	6-2	195	R	Balsta, Sweden	3/1/78	Florida-Calgary
NILSON, Patrik	6-0	180	R	Balsta, Sweden	5/18/81	San Antonio-Laredo
NYSTROM, Eric	6-1	195	L	Syosset, NY	2/14/83	U. of Michigan
REINPRECHT, Steve	6-0	190	L	Edmonton, Alta.	5/7/76	Calgary
RITCHIE, Byron	5-10	195	L	Burnaby, B.C.	4/24/77	Florida
SAPRYKIN, Oleg	6-0	195	L	Moscow, USSR	2/12/81	Calgary
SIMON, Chris	6-4	235	L	Wawa, Ont.	1/30/72	NY Rangers-Calgary
TAYLOR, Justin	6-4	200	L	Edmonton, Alta.	1/1/83	Red Deer
WIEMER, Jason	6-1	225	L	Kimberley, B.C.	4/14/76	NY Islanders-Minnesota
YELLE, Stephane	6-1	190	L	Ottawa, Ont.	5/9/74	Calgary
DEFENSEMEN						
COMMODORE, Mike	6-4	230	R	Fort Saskatchewan, Alta.	11/7/79	Calgary-Lowell
ENGELLAND, Deryk	6-2	205	R	Edmonton, Alta.	4/5/82	Lowell-Las Vegas
EVANS, Brennan	6-3	205	L	North Battleford, Sask.	1/6/82	Calgary-Lowell
FERENCE, Andrew	5-10	196	L	Edmonton, Alta.	3/17/79	Calgary
GAUTHIER, Denis	6-2	224	L	Montreal, Que.	10/1/76	Calgary
GIORDANO, Mark	6-0	203	L	Toronto, Ont.	5/10/83	Owen Sound
LEOPOLD, Jordan	6-0	193	L	Golden Valley, MN	8/3/80	Calgary
LYDMAN, Toni	6-1	202	L	Lahti, Finland	9/25/77	Calgary
MONTADOR, Steve	6-0	210	R	Vancouver, B.C.	12/21/79	Calgary
PHANEUF, Dion	6-2	205	L	Edmonton, Alta.	4/10/85	Red Deer
REGEHR, Richie	6-0	190	R	Rosthern, Sask.	1/17/83	Portland (WHL)
REGEHR, Robyn	6-2	226	L	Recife, Brazil	4/19/80	Calgary
WARRENER, Rhett	6-2	217	R	Shaunavon, Sask.	1/27/76	Calgary
GOALTENDERS	**HT**	**WT**	**C**	**Place of Birth**	**Date**	**2003-04 Club**
KIPRUSOFF, Miikka	6-2	190	L	Turku, Finland	10/26/76	Calgary
KRAHN, Brent	6-4	200	L	Winnipeg, Man.	4/2/82	Lowell-Las Vegas-San Antonio
PARLEY, Davis	6-2	183	L	Surrey, B.C.	9/4/82	Texas
TUREK, Roman	6-3	220	R	Strakonice, Czech.	5/21/70	Calgary

Coach and General Manager

SUTTER, DARRYL
Coach/General Manager, Calgary Flames. Born in Vikings, Alta., August 19, 1958.

Darryl Sutter was named general manager of the Calgary Flames on April 11, 2003 adding the portfolio to his head coaching position. He had joined the Flames as coach on December 28, 2002. In his first full season with the Flames in 2003-04, Sutter led the team back to the playoffs after a seven-year absence and guided the club on a thrilling run to the seventh game of the Stanley Cup Finals.

Before joining the Flames, Sutter was the San Jose Sharks franchise leader in regular-season games coached (434) and wins (192). Through the 2001-02 season, Sutter became only the second coach in NHL history (Al Arbour, New York Islanders) to improve his team's point total for five consecutive years.

Prior to San Jose, Sutter coached Chicago for three years (1992 to 1995) and spent two seasons (1995 to 1997) with the Blackhawks as a consultant for special assignments. He spent the 1987-88 campaign as a Blackhawks assistant coach to Bob Murdoch and served as an associate coach for Mike Keenan during the 1990-91 and 1991-92 seasons. During his final season as associate coach, the Blackhawks advanced to the Stanley Cup Finals. Sutter spent two seasons coaching the Blackhawks top development affiliate in the IHL, which played in Saginaw (1988-89) and in Indianapolis (1989-90). Under his leadership, the Indianapolis Ice stormed through the regular season with 114 points and won the Turner Cup championship. He was named IHL coach of the year.

As a player, Sutter was selected by Chicago in the ninth round, 179th overall, in the 1978 NHL Entry Draft. During his eight-year career with the Blackhawks from 1979 to 1987, he scored 279 points (161 goals, 118 assists) with 288 penalty minutes in 406 NHL career games. Sutter served as team captain with the Blackhawks for five seasons, beginning in the 1982-83 season through 1986-87 when he was forced to retire prematurely due to a series of injuries.

Darryl is a member of the famous Sutter hockey family, who had six brothers that played in the NHL. They were all inducted into the Alberta Sports Hall of Fame in May 2000 under the Lifetime Achievement category. Along with his brothers, Darryl is very involved in the Sutter Foundation, started by he and his family in Alberta, which raises money for non-profit organizations.

NHL Coaching Record

		Regular Season				Playoffs		
Season	Team	Games	W	L	T	Games	W	L
1992-93	Chicago	84	47	25	12	4	0	4
1993-94	Chicago	84	39	36	9	6	2	4
1994-95	Chicago	48	24	19	5	16	9	7
1997-98	San Jose	82	34	38	10	6	2	4
1998-99	San Jose	82	31	33	18	6	2	4
1999-2000	San Jose	82	35	37	10	12	5	7
2000-01	San Jose	82	40	30	12	6	2	4
2001-02	San Jose	82	44	30	8	12	7	5
2002-03	San Jose	24	8	14	2	....	....	....
	Calgary	46	19	19	8	....	....	....
2003-04	Calgary	82	42	33	7	26	15	11
	NHL Totals	**778**	**363**	**314**	**101**	**94**	**44**	**50**

2003-04 Scoring

* - rookie

Regular Season

Pos	#	Player	Team	GP	G	A	Pts	+/–	PIM	PP	SH	GW	GT	S	%
R	12	Jarome Iginla	CGY	81	41	32	73	21	84	8	4	10	1	265	15.5
C	22	Craig Conroy	CGY	63	8	39	47	13	44	2	0	0	0	112	7.1
R	16	Shean Donovan	CGY	82	18	24	42	14	72	3	3	8	0	138	13.0
L	23	Martin Gelinas	CGY	76	17	18	35	10	70	5	0	3	0	139	12.2
D	4	Jordan Leopold	CGY	82	9	24	33	8	24	6	0	1	0	138	6.5
C	37	Dean Mcammond	CGY	64	17	13	30	9	18	4	1	5	0	101	16.8
C	18 *	Matthew Lombardi	CGY	79	16	13	29	4	32	3	2	4	0	130	12.3
L	19	Oleg Saprykin	CGY	69	12	17	29	1	41	4	0	0	0	151	7.9
C	27	Steven Reinprecht	CGY	44	7	22	29	1	4	3	0	1	0	68	10.3
L	15	Chris Simon	NYR	65	14	9	23	14	225	3	0	0	1	116	12.1
			CGY	13	3	2	5	1	25	1	0	0	0	31	9.7
			TOTAL	78	17	11	28	15	250	4	0	0	1	147	11.6
R	17	Chris Clark	CGY	82	10	15	25	–3	106	4	0	2	0	137	7.3
L	26	Marcus Nilson	FLA	69	6	13	19	–9	26	1	1	1	1	110	5.5
			CGY	14	5	0	5	3	14	1	0	2	0	23	21.7
			TOTAL	83	11	13	24	–6	40	2	1	3	1	133	8.3
L	24	Ville Nieminen	CHI	60	2	11	13	–15	40	1	0	0	1	56	3.6
			CGY	19	3	5	8	6	18	0	0	1	0	27	11.1
			TOTAL	79	5	16	21	–9	58	1	0	1	1	83	6.0
D	32	Toni Lydman	CGY	67	4	16	20	6	30	2	0	1	0	93	4.3
D	28	Robyn Regehr	CGY	82	4	14	18	14	74	2	0	1	0	106	3.8
R	7 *	Chuck Kobasew	CGY	70	6	11	17	–12	51	3	0	0	0	78	7.7
C	11	Stephane Yelle	CGY	53	4	13	17	1	24	1	0	0	0	76	5.3
D	44	Rhett Warrener	CGY	77	3	14	17	8	97	0	1	1	0	82	3.7
D	21	Andrew Ference	CGY	72	4	12	16	5	53	1	0	0	0	86	4.7
D	3	Denis Gauthier	CGY	80	1	15	16	4	113	0	0	0	0	90	1.1
L	33	Krzysztof Oliwa	CGY	65	3	2	5	–8	247	0	0	0	0	32	9.4
C	15	Blair Betts	CGY	20	1	2	3	–1	10	1	0	1	0	21	4.8
D	5	Steve Montador	CGY	26	1	2	3	–1	50	0	0	1	0	31	3.2
L	10	Dave Lowry	CGY	18	1	1	2	–6	11	0	0	0	0	9	11.1
L	20 *	Lynn Loyns	S.J.	2	0	0	0	–1	0	0	0	0	0	0	0.0
			CGY	12	0	2	2	–2	2	0	0	0	0	6	0.0
			TOTAL	14	0	2	2	–3	2	0	0	0	0	6	0.0
L	25	Martin Sonnenberg	CGY	5	0	0	0	–2	2	0	0	0	0	7	0.0
D	2	Mike Commodore	CGY	12	0	0	0	–4	25	0	0	0	0	10	0.0

Goaltending

No.	Goaltender	GPI	Mins	Avg	W	L	T	EN	SO	GA	SA	S%	G	A	PIM
34	Miikka Kiprusoff	38	2301	1.69	24	10	4	4	4	65	966	.933	0	1	15
33	Jamie Mclennan	26	1446	2.20	12	9	3	2	4	53	587	.910	0	1	4
1	Roman Turek	18	1031	2.33	6	11	0	2	3	40	463	.914	0	1	0
50	* Dany Sabourin	4	169	3.55	0	3	0	0	0	10	66	.848	0	1	0
	Totals	**82**	**4968**	**2.13**	**42**	**33**	**7**	**8**	**11**	**176**	**2090**	**.916**			

Playoffs

Pos	#	Player	Team	GP	G	A	Pts	+/–	PIM	PP	SH	GW	GT	S	%
R	12	Jarome Iginla	CGY	26	13	9	22	13	45	4	2	3	0	93	14.0
C	22	Craig Conroy	CGY	26	6	11	17	12	12	2	0	1	0	49	12.2
L	23	Martin Gelinas	CGY	26	8	7	15	10	35	2	0	3	2	51	15.7
L	26	Marcus Nilson	CGY	26	4	7	11	0	12	0	0	1	1	37	10.8
R	16	Shean Donovan	CGY	24	5	5	10	0	23	0	0	2	0	43	11.6
D	4	Jordan Leopold	CGY	26	0	10	10	5	6	0	0	0	0	34	0.0
D	28	Robyn Regehr	CGY	26	2	7	9	7	20	0	0	0	0	29	6.9
L	24	Ville Nieminen	CGY	24	4	4	8	0	55	1	0	0	0	41	9.8
L	15	Chris Simon	CGY	16	5	2	7	0	74	4	0	1	0	34	14.7
C	11	Stephane Yelle	CGY	23	3	3	6	–1	16	0	1	1	0	27	11.1
R	17	Chris Clark	CGY	26	3	3	6	0	30	1	0	0	0	29	10.3
L	19	Oleg Saprykin	CGY	26	3	3	6	1	14	1	0	1	1	53	5.7
C	18 *	Matthew Lombardi	CGY	13	1	5	6	1	4	0	0	1	0	15	6.7
D	5	Steve Montador	CGY	20	1	2	3	4	6	0	0	1	1	44	2.3
D	21	Andrew Ference	CGY	26	0	3	3	5	25	0	0	0	0	37	0.0
L	33	Krzysztof Oliwa	CGY	20	2	0	2	–1	6	0	0	0	0	16	12.5
D	2	Mike Commodore	CGY	20	0	2	2	1	19	0	0	0	0	13	0.0
D	3	Denis Gauthier	CGY	6	0	1	1	2	4	0	0	0	0	3	0.0
D	32	Toni Lydman	CGY	6	0	1	1	1	2	0	0	0	0	4	0.0
D	44	Rhett Warrener	CGY	24	0	1	1	1	6	0	0	0	0	27	0.0
R	7 *	Chuck Kobasew	CGY	26	0	1	1	0	24	0	0	0	0	15	0.0
D	43 *	Brennan Evans	CGY	2	0	0	0	0	0	0	0	0	0	0	0.0
L	10	Dave Lowry	CGY	10	0	0	0	–1	6	0	0	0	0	4	0.0

Goaltending

No.	Goaltender	GPI	Mins	Avg	W	L	EN	SO	GA	SA	S%	G	A	PIM
1	Roman Turek	1	19	0.00	0	0	0	0	0	3	1.000	0	0	0
34	Miikka Kiprusoff	26	1655	1.85	15	11	2	5	51	710	.928	0	1	0
	Totals	**26**	**1680**	**1.89**	**15**	**11**	**2**	**5**	**53**	**715**	**.926**			

General Managers' History

Cliff Fletcher, 1972-73 to 1990-91; Doug Risebrough, 1991-92 to 1994-95; Doug Risebrough and Al Coates, 1995-96; Al Coates, 1996-97 to 1999-2000; Craig Button, 2000-01 to 2001-02; Craig Button and Darryl Sutter, 2002-03; Darryl Sutter, 2003-04 to date.

Coaching History

Bernie Geoffrion, 1972-73, 1973-74; Bernie Geoffrion and Fred Creighton, 1974-75; Fred Creighton, 1975-76 to 1978-79; Al MacNeil, 1979-80 to 1981-82; Bob Johnson, 1982-83 to 1986-87; Terry Crisp, 1987-88 to 1989-90; Doug Risebrough, 1990-91; Doug Risebrough and Guy Charron, 1991-92; Dave King, 1992-93 to 1994-95; Pierre Page, 1995-96, 1996-97; Brian Sutter, 1997-98 to 1999-2000; Don Hay and Greg Gilbert, 2000-01; Greg Gilbert, 2001-02; Greg Gilbert, Al MacNeil and Darryl Sutter, 2002-03; Darryl Sutter, 2003-04 to date.

Club Records

Team

(Figures in brackets for season records are games played; records for fewest points, wins, ties, losses, goals, goals against are for 70 or more games)

Most Points .... 117 — 1988-89 (80)
Most Wins .... 54 — 1988-89 (80)
Most Ties .... 19 — 1977-78 (80)
Most Losses .... 41 — 1996-97 (82), 1997-98 (82), 1999-2000 (82)
Most Goals .... 397 — 1987-88 (80)
Most Goals Against .... 345 — 1981-82 (80)
Fewest Points .... 65 — 1972-73 (78)
Fewest Wins .... 25 — 1972-73 (78)
Fewest Ties .... 3 — 1986-87 (80)
Fewest Losses .... 17 — 1988-89 (80)
Fewest Goals .... 186 — 2002-03 (82)
Fewest Goals Against .... 176 — 2003-04 (82)
Longest Winning Streak
Overall .... 10 — Oct. 14-Nov. 3/78
Home .... 9 — Oct. 17-Nov. 15/78, Jan. 3-Feb. 5/89, Mar. 3-Apr. 1/90, Feb. 21-Mar. 14/91
Away .... 7 — Nov. 10-Dec. 4/88
Longest Undefeated Streak
Overall .... 13 — Nov. 10-Dec. 8/88 (12 wins, 1 tie)
Home .... 18 — Dec. 29/90-Mar. 14/91 (17 wins, 1 tie)
Away .... 9 — Feb. 20-Mar. 21/88 (6 wins, 3 ties), Nov. 11-Dec. 16/90 (6 wins, 3 ties)
Longest Losing Streak
Overall .... 11 — Dec. 14/85-Jan. 7/86
Home .... 6 — Dec. 5-31/98
Away .... 9 — Dec. 1/85-Jan. 12/86
Longest Winless Streak
Overall .... 11 — Dec. 14/85-Jan. 7/86 (11 losses), Jan. 5-26/93 (9 losses, 2 ties)
Home .... 10 — Oct. 21-Dec. 4/00 (6 losses, 4 ties)
Away .... 13 — Feb. 3-Mar. 29/73 (10 losses, 3 ties)
Most Shutouts, Season .... 11 — 2003-04 (82)
Most PIM, Season .... 2,643 — 1991-92 (80)
Most Goals, Game .... 13 — Feb. 10/93 (S.J. 1 at Cgy. 13)

Individual

Most Seasons .... 13 — Al MacInnis
Most Games .... 803 — Al MacInnis
Most Goals, Career .... 364 — Theoren Fleury
Most Assists, Career .... 609 — Al MacInnis
Most Points, Career .... 830 — Theoren Fleury (364G, 466A)
Most PIM, Career .... 2,405 — Tim Hunter
Most Shutouts, Career .... 20 — Dan Bouchard
Longest Consecutive Games Streak .... 257 — Brad Marsh (Oct. 11/78-Nov. 10/81)
Most Goals, Season .... 66 — Lanny McDonald (1982-83)
Most Assists, Season .... 82 — Kent Nilsson (1980-81)
Most Points, Season .... 131 — Kent Nilsson (1980-81; 49G, 82A)
Most PIM, Season .... 375 — Tim Hunter (1988-89)
Most Points, Defenseman, Season .... 103 — Al MacInnis (1990-91; 28G, 75A)
Most Points, Center, Season .... 131 — Kent Nilsson (1980-81; 49G, 82A)
Most Points, Right Wing, Season .... 110 — Joe Mullen (1988-89; 51G, 59A)
Most Points, Left Wing, Season .... 90 — Gary Roberts (1991-92; 53G, 37A)
Most Points, Rookie, Season .... 92 — Joe Nieuwendyk (1987-88; 51G, 41A)
Most Shutouts, Season .... 5 — Dan Bouchard (1973-74), Phil Myre (1974-75), Fred Brathwaite (1999-2000, 2000-01), Roman Turek (2001-02)
Most Goals, Game .... 5 — Joe Nieuwendyk (Jan. 11/89)
Most Assists, Game .... 6 — Guy Chouinard (Feb. 25/81), Gary Suter (Apr. 4/86)
Most Points, Game .... 7 — Sergei Makarov (Feb. 25/90; 2G, 5A)

Records include Atlanta Flames, 1972-73 through 1979-80.

Retired Numbers

9	Lanny McDonald	1981-1989

All-time Record vs. Other Clubs

Regular Season

	At Home								On Road								Total							
	GP	W	L	T	OL	GF	GA	PTS	GP	W	L	T	OL	GF	GA	PTS	GP	W	L	T	OL	GF	GA	PTS
Anaheim	25	15	9	1	0	72	61	31	26	8	10	6	2	69	80	24	51	23	19	7	2	141	141	55
Atlanta	3	3	0	0	0	14	6	6	4	0	3	1	0	5	8	1	7	3	3	1	0	19	14	7
Boston	44	18	22	4	0	160	154	40	47	13	28	6	0	130	165	32	91	31	50	10	0	290	319	72
Buffalo	46	17	18	11	0	152	146	45	45	13	26	5	1	131	189	32	91	30	44	16	1	283	335	77
Carolina	29	21	6	2	0	140	92	44	28	13	10	5	0	103	91	31	57	34	16	7	0	243	183	75
Chicago	63	29	21	13	0	201	188	71	61	22	26	13	0	179	196	57	124	51	47	26	0	380	384	128
Colorado	47	20	17	9	1	160	141	50	47	18	17	11	1	154	165	48	94	38	34	20	2	314	306	98
Columbus	8	5	3	0	0	24	18	10	8	2	6	0	0	16	26	4	16	7	9	0	0	40	44	14
Dallas	62	33	15	14	0	208	155	80	62	21	29	11	1	196	228	54	124	54	44	25	1	404	383	134
Detroit	60	34	20	6	0	228	179	74	59	18	31	10	0	174	215	46	119	52	51	16	0	402	394	120
Edmonton	81	43	29	9	0	324	275	95	81	29	41	10	1	265	306	69	162	72	70	19	1	589	581	164
Florida	8	4	3	1	0	21	20	9	9	4	3	2	0	22	21	10	17	8	6	3	0	43	41	19
Los Angeles	94	55	27	12	0	413	310	122	91	36	45	9	1	316	338	82	185	91	72	21	1	729	648	204
Minnesota	10	5	1	3	1	23	21	14	11	5	4	1	1	20	24	12	21	10	5	4	2	43	45	26
Montreal	49	16	26	7	0	146	164	39	46	12	26	8	0	112	163	32	95	28	52	15	0	258	327	71
Nashville	12	6	2	3	1	35	26	16	13	4	8	1	0	25	39	9	25	10	10	4	1	60	65	25
New Jersey	42	28	6	8	0	184	111	64	45	27	15	3	0	162	128	57	87	55	21	11	0	346	239	121
NY Islanders	49	24	14	11	0	172	145	59	51	17	25	9	0	143	191	43	100	41	39	20	0	315	336	102
NY Rangers	49	27	11	10	1	216	148	65	52	23	22	5	2	184	178	53	101	50	33	15	3	400	326	118
Ottawa	11	6	4	1	0	38	25	13	10	2	5	3	0	24	27	7	21	8	9	4	0	62	52	20
Philadelphia	52	25	18	9	0	208	172	59	51	15	33	3	0	137	199	33	103	40	51	12	0	345	371	92
Phoenix	71	39	22	9	1	295	227	88	70	25	33	11	1	238	264	62	141	64	55	20	2	533	491	150
Pittsburgh	46	27	11	8	0	204	140	62	44	10	24	10	0	133	167	30	90	37	35	18	0	337	307	92
St. Louis	62	29	26	5	2	201	180	65	64	24	31	9	0	195	229	57	126	53	57	14	2	396	409	122
San Jose	32	18	10	4	0	116	87	40	34	17	13	4	0	102	100	38	66	35	23	8	0	218	187	78
Tampa Bay	10	6	4	0	0	32	24	12	10	4	5	1	0	32	31	9	20	10	9	1	0	64	55	21
Toronto	61	34	22	5	0	239	195	73	53	18	28	7	0	189	202	43	114	52	50	12	0	428	397	116
Vancouver	98	57	26	15	0	392	283	129	99	45	35	18	1	327	335	109	197	102	61	33	1	719	618	238
Washington	38	24	7	7	0	157	93	55	41	14	21	6	0	139	153	34	79	38	28	13	0	296	246	89
Defunct Clubs	13	8	4	1	0	51	34	17	13	7	3	3	0	43	33	17	26	15	7	4	0	94	67	34
Totals	**1275**	**676**	**404**	**188**	**7**	**4826**	**3820**	**1547**	**1275**	**466**	**606**	**191**	**12**	**3965**	**4491**	**1135**	**2550**	**1142**	**1010**	**379**	**19**	**8791**	**8311**	**2682**

Playoffs

	Series	W	L	GP	W	L	T	GF	GA	Last Mtg.	Rnd.	Result
Chicago	3	2	1	12	7	5	0	37	33	1996	CQF	L 0-4
Dallas	1	0	1	6	2	4	0	18	25	1981	SF	L 2-4
Detroit	2	1	1	8	4	4	0	16	20	2004	CSF	W 4-2
Edmonton	5	1	4	30	11	19	0	96	132	1991	DSF	L 3-4
Los Angeles	6	2	4	26	13	13	0	102	105	1993	DSF	L 2-4
Montreal	2	1	1	11	5	6	0	32	31	1989	F	W 4-2
NY Rangers	1	0	1	4	1	3	0	8	14	1980	PRE	L 1-3
Philadelphia	2	1	1	11	4	7	0	28	43	1981	QF	W 4-3
St. Louis	1	1	0	7	4	3	0	28	22	1986	CF	W 4-3
San Jose	2	1	1	13	7	6	0	51	38	2004	CF	W 4-2
Tampa Bay	1	0	1	7	3	4	0	14	13	2004	F	L 3-4
Toronto	1	0	1	2	0	2	0	5	9	1979	PRE	L 0-2
Vancouver	6	4	2	32	17	15	0	101	96	2004	CQF	W 4-3
Winnipeg	3	1	2	13	6	7	0	43	45	1987	DSF	L 2-4
Totals	**36**	**15**	**21**	**182**	**84**	**98**	**0**	**579**	**626**			

Carolina totals include Hartford, 1979-80 to 1996-97.
Colorado totals include Quebec, 1979-80 to 1994-95.
Dallas totals include Minnesota North Stars, 1972-73 to 1992-93.
New Jersey totals include Kansas City, 1974-75 to 1975-76, and Colorado Rockies, 1976-77 to 1981-82.
Phoenix totals include Winnipeg, 1979-80 to 1995-96.

Playoff Results 2004-2000

Year	Round	Opponent	Result	GF	GA
2004	F	Tampa Bay	L 3-4	14	13
	CF	San Jose	W 4-2	16	12
	CSF	Detroit	W 4-2	11	12
	CQF	Vancouver	W 4-3	19	16

Abbreviations: Round: F - Final; **CF** - conference final; **CSF** - conference semi-final; **CQF** - conference quarter-final; **DSF** - division semi-final; **SF** - semi-final; **QF** - quarter-final; **PRE** - preliminary round.

2003-04 Results

Month	Day	Opponent	Score
Oct.	9	at Vancouver	1-4
	11	San Jose	3-2
	14	Edmonton	1-0
	18	Buffalo	0-2
	21	at Minnesota	3-2
	24	St. Louis	1-2
	25	at Edmonton	4-2
	28	at Colorado	2-4
	29	at Dallas	3-4*
Nov.	1	Columbus	3-0
	4	Detroit	0-3
	7	Minnesota	0-3
	9	at Columbus	3-4
	12	at Chicago	6-2
	13	at Nashville	1-4
	15	at Edmonton	1-2*
	18	Toronto	3-2*
	20	Montreal	2-1
	22	Chicago	2-1
	27	Colorado	5-6*
	29	Vancouver	4-4
Dec.	2	San Jose	3-1
	4	at Vancouver	4-1
	5	Minnesota	2-1
	7	Pittsburgh	6-1
	9	at Minnesota	1-2
	11	Carolina	1-0
	13	Colorado	1-1
	16	at Philadelphia	3-2*
	18	at Boston	5-0
	19	at Columbus	2-1
	23	Edmonton	2-1
	26	Vancouver	0-2
	28	at Edmonton	2-1
	29	Minnesota	2-2
	31	Colorado	1-2
Jan.	3	Vancouver	1-3
	5	at NY Rangers	5-0
	6	at NY Islanders	3-2
	8	at Chicago	1-3
	10	Florida	4-2
	13	at Toronto	1-4
	14	at Washington	3-3
	17	Dallas	2-3
	19	at Anaheim	5-1
	20	at Los Angeles	1-4
	22	Nashville	4-0
	24	Tampa Bay	2-6
	27	at Phoenix	2-1
	28	at San Jose	1-4
	30	Chicago	3-5
Feb.	1	Anaheim	6-4
	3	Los Angeles	4-4
	5	St. Louis	1-2
	10	Atlanta	5-2
	11	at Vancouver	3-2
	13	Anaheim	2-1
	15	at Minnesota	2-1
	19	at Montreal	1-4
	21	at Ottawa	1-2
	22	at New Jersey	1-3
	24	at Colorado	2-0
	26	Detroit	1-2
	29	Phoenix	4-2
Mar.	2	at St. Louis	4-2
	3	at Detroit	1-2
	5	at Dallas	1-5
	7	at Colorado	7-1
	9	Edmonton	1-1
	11	Ottawa	4-2
	13	at Nashville	4-4
	14	at St. Louis	3-0
	16	at Detroit	4-1
	18	Columbus	2-0
	20	Nashville	1-3
	22	Dallas	0-4
	24	at Phoenix	4-0
	25	at San Jose	2-3
	27	Los Angeles	3-2*
	31	Phoenix	1-0
Apr.	2	at Los Angeles	3-2
	4	at Anaheim	1-2

* – Overtime

Entry Draft
Selections 2004-1990

2004
Pick
24	Kris Chucko
70	Brandon Prust
98	Dustin Boyd
118	Aki Seitsonen
121	Kris Hogg
173	Adam Pardy
182	Fred Wikner
200	Matt Schneider
213	James Spratt
279	Adam Cracknell

2003
Pick
9	Dion Phaneuf
39	Tim Ramholt
97	Ryan Donally
112	Jamie Tardif
143	Greg Moore
173	Tyler Johnson
206	Thomas Bellemare
240	Cam Cunning
270	Kevin Harvey

2002
Pick
10	Eric Nystrom
39	Brian McConnell
90	Matthew Lombardi
112	Yuri Artemenkov
141	Jiri Cetkovsky
142	Emanuel Peter
146	Viktor Bobrov
159	Kristofer Persson
176	Curtis McElhinney
206	David Van Der Gulik
207	Pierre Johnsson
238	Jyri Marttinen

2001
Pick
14	Chuck Kobasew
41	Andrei Taratukhin
56	Andrei Medvedev
108	Tomi Maki
124	Yegor Shastin
145	James Hakewill
164	Yuri Trubachev
207	Garrett Bembridge
220	David Moss
233	Joe Campbell
251	Ville Hamalainen

2000
Pick
9	Brent Krahn
40	Kurtis Foster
46	Jarret Stoll
116	Levente Szuper
141	Wade Davis
155	Travis Moen
176	Jukka Hentunen
239	David Hajek
270	Micki DuPont

1999
Pick
11	Oleg Saprykin
38	Dan Cavanaugh
77	Craig Anderson
106	Roman Rozakov
135	Matt Doman
153	Jesse Cook
166	Cory Pecker
170	Matt Underhill
190	Blair Stayzer
252	Dmitri Kirilenko

1998
Pick
6	Rico Fata
33	Blair Betts
62	Paul Manning
102	Shaun Sutter
108	Dany Sabourin
120	Brent Gauvreau
192	Radek Duda
206	Jonas Frogren
234	Kevin Mitchell

1997
Pick
6	Daniel Tkaczuk
32	Evan Lindsay
42	John Tripp
51	Dimitri Kokorev
60	Derek Schutz
70	Erik Andersson
92	Chris St. Croix
100	Ryan Ready
113	Martin Moise
140	Ilja Demidov
167	Jeremy Rondeau
223	Dustin Paul

1996
Pick
13	Derek Morris
39	Travis Brigley
40	Steve Begin
73	Dmitri Vlasenkov
89	Toni Lydman
94	Christian Lefebvre
122	Josef Straka
202	Ryan Wade
228	Ronald Petrovicky

1995
Pick
20	Denis Gauthier
46	Pavel Smirnov
72	Rocky Thompson
98	Jan Labraaten
150	Clarke Wilm
176	Ryan Gillis
233	Steve Shirreffs

1994
Pick
19	Chris Dingman
45	Dmitri Ryabykin
77	Chris Clark
91	Ryan Duthie
97	Johan Finnstrom
107	Nils Ekman
123	Frank Appel
149	Patrick Haltia
175	Ladislav Kohn
201	Keith McCambridge
227	Jorgen Jonsson
253	Mike Peluso
279	Pavel Torgaev

1993
Pick
18	Jesper Mattsson
44	Jamie Allison
70	Dan Tompkins
95	Jason Smith
96	Marty Murray
121	Darryl Lafrance
122	John Emmons
148	Andreas Karlsson
200	Derek Sylvester
252	German Titov
278	Burke Murphy

1992
Pick
6	Cory Stillman
30	Chris O'Sullivan
54	Mathias Johansson
78	Robert Svehla
102	Sami Helenius
126	Ravil Yakubov
129	Joel Bouchard
150	Pavel Rajnoha
174	Ryan Mulhern
198	Brandon Carper
222	Jonas Höglund
246	Andrei Potaichuk

1991
Pick
19	Niklas Sundblad
41	Francois Groleau
52	Sandy McCarthy
63	Brian Caruso
85	Steven Magnusson
107	Jerome Butler
129	Bobby Marshall
140	Matt Hoffman
151	Kelly Harper
173	David St-Pierre
195	David Struch
217	Sergei Zolotov
239	Marko Jantunen
261	Andrei Trefilov

1990
Pick
11	Trevor Kidd
26	Nicolas Perreault
32	Vesa Viitakoski
41	Etiènne Belzile
62	Glen Mears
83	Paul Kruse
125	Chris Tschupp
146	Dimitri Frolov
167	Shawn Murray
188	Mike Murray
209	Rob Sumner
230	invalid pick
251	Leo Gudas

Club Directory

Pengrowth Saddledome

Calgary Flames
Pengrowth Saddledome
P.O. Box 1540 Station M
Calgary, Alberta T2P 3B9
Phone **403/777-4636**
FAX 403/777-2171
www.calgaryflames.com
Capacity: 17,439

Owners N. Murray Edwards, Harley N. Hotchkiss, Alvin G. Libin, Allan P. Markin, J.R. (Bud) McCaig, Clayton H. Riddell, Byron J. Seaman, Daryl K. Seaman

Executive
President & Chief Executive Officer	Ken King
General Manager & Head Coach	Darryl Sutter
Vice President, Hockey Administration	Michael Holditch
Vice-President, Building Operations	Libby Raines
Vice-President, Advertising, Sponsorship & Marketing	Jim Bagshaw
Vice-President, Sales	Rollie Cyr
Vice-President, Business Development	Jim Peplinski

Hockey Club Personnel
Head Coach & General Manager	Darryl Sutter
Vice President, Hockey Administration	Michael Holditch
Director, Hockey Administration	Mike Burke
Special Assistant to the GM	Al MacNeil
Assistant Coaches	Jim Playfair, Rich Preston, Rob Cookson
Goaltending Coach	David Marcoux
Development Coach	Jamie Hislop
Team Services Manager	Kelly Chesla
Exec. Asst. to GM and Hockey Operations	Brenda Koyich
Director of Scouting	Tod Button
Director of Amateur Scouting	Mike Sands
Western Pro Scout	Ron Sutter
Eastern Pro Scout	Tom Webster
Scouts	Tomas Jelinek, Sergei Samoilov, Al Tuer, Craig Demetrick, Fred Devereaux, Randy Hansch, Ralph Schmidt, Anders Steen
Assistant Coach, Lowell	Scott Allen

Medical/Training Staff
Athletic Therapist	Morris Boyer
Assistant Athletic Therapist	Gerry Kurylowich
Strength & Conditioning Coach	Rich Hesketh
Equipment Manager	Gus Thorson
Assistant Equipment Manager	Les Jarvis
Team Physician	Dr. Kelly Brett
Team Physician	Dr. Jim Thorne
Team Dentist	Dr. Bill Blair
Dressing Room Attendant	Jules Carriere
Visiting Dressing Room Attendant	Garland Auvigne

Communications
Director, Communications	Peter Hanlon
Manager, Media Relations	Sean O'Brien
Administrative Assistant, Communications	Bernie Hargrave
Community Relations Coordinator	Trevor Elgar
Community Relations Ambassador	Jim "Bearcat" Murray

Administration
Director of Finance	Hansine Ulberg
Controller	Karen Kingham
Assistant Controller	Trudy McInnes, Kelly Shillington
Exec. Asst. to President/CEO	Judy O'Brien
Exec. Asst. to Finance & Administration	Judith Virag

Marketing
Senior Director, Advertising	Pat Halls
Director, Executive Suites	Bob White
Business Development Manager	Kevin Gross
Sales Manager	Mike Franco
Director, Game Presentation	Dave Imbach
Director/Producer, Jumbotron	Carlo Petrini
Director, Retail/FanAttic	Kevin Lawton
Publishing	Laurie Wheeler
Exec. Asst. to VP, Advertising, Sponsorship & Marketing	Yvette Mutcheson
Mascot	Harvey the Hound

Pengrowth Saddledome
Operations Manager	George Greenwood
Food Services Manager	Art Hernandez
Concessions Manager	Sheila Parisien
Security/Parking Manager	Bob Godun

Calgary Hitmen
General Manager/Head Coach	Kelly Kisio
Asst. General Manager/Asst. Coach	Blaine Forsythe
Co-Coach	Dean Evason

Miscellaneous Data
Home ice (capacity)	Pengrowth Saddledome (17,439)
Website	www.calgaryflames.com
Practice Facility	Pengrowth Saddledome
Training Facility	Pengrowth Saddledome
Club Colours	Red, white, gold and black
Radio Affiliate	The FAN 960 (960 AM)
TV Affiliate	Rogers Sportsnet, CBC-TV, PPV, TSN
AHL Affiliate	Lowell Lock Monsters
ECHL Affiliate	Las Vegas Wranglers

Captains' History
Keith McCreary, 1972-73 to 1974-75; Pat Quinn, 1975-76, 1976-77; Tom Lysiak, 1977-78, 1978-79; Jean Pronovost, 1979-80; Brad Marsh, 1980-81; Phil Russell, 1981-82, 1982-83; Lanny McDonald, Doug Risebrough (co-captains), 1983-84; Lanny McDonald, Doug Risebrough, Jim Peplinski (tri-captains), 1984-85 to 1986-87; Lanny McDonald, Jim Peplinski (co-captains), 1987-88; Lanny McDonald, Jim Peplinski, Tim Hunter (tri-captains), 1988-89; Brad McCrimmon, 1989-90; alternating captains, 1990-91; Joe Nieuwendyk, 1991-92 to 1994-95; Theoren Fleury, 1995-96, 1996-97; Todd Simpson, 1997-98, 1998-99; Steve Smith, 1999-2000; Steve Smith and Dave Lowry, 2000-01; Dave Lowry; Bob Boughner and Craig Conroy (co-captains), 2001-02; Bob Boughner and Craig Conroy (co-captains), 2002-03; Jarome Iginla, 2003-04.

Carolina Hurricanes

2003-04 Results: 28w-34l-14t-6otl 76pts.
Third, Southeast Division

2004-05 Schedule

Oct.	Thu.	14	Atlanta	Mon.	17	Washington
	Sat.	16	at NY Islanders	Fri.	21	Tampa Bay
	Wed.	20	at Detroit	Sat.	22	at New Jersey
	Thu.	21	at Philadelphia	Mon.	24	at Toronto
	Tue.	26	at Montreal	Wed.	26	at Pittsburgh
	Wed.	27	Ottawa	Fri.	28	Ottawa
	Fri.	29	Toronto	Sat.	29	at Florida
	Sun.	31	Chicago*	Mon.	31	Phoenix
Nov.	Thu.	4	at Tampa Bay	**Feb.**	Wed. 2	at Atlanta
	Fri.	5	Montreal	Thu.	3	at St. Louis
	Sun.	7	Minnesota*	Sat.	5	at Phoenix
	Wed.	10	Dallas	Mon.	7	at Colorado
	Fri.	12	Atlanta	Wed.	9	NY Islanders
	Sun.	14	Calgary*	Thu.	10	at Ottawa
	Wed.	17	at Buffalo	Tue.	15	at Toronto
	Fri.	19	at Philadelphia	Fri.	18	Pittsburgh
	Sat.	20	Buffalo	Sat.	19	at New Jersey
	Wed.	24	NY Rangers	Mon.	21	Tampa Bay
	Sat.	27	Tampa Bay	Wed.	23	Philadelphia
	Sun.	28	Vancouver*	Sat.	26	at Washington
Dec.	Wed.	1	Boston	Sun.	27	Washington
	Fri.	3	Pittsburgh	**Mar.**	Wed. 2	at NY Rangers
	Sat.	4	at NY Islanders	Fri.	4	at Tampa Bay
	Wed.	8	at Anaheim	Sun.	6	at Dallas*
	Thu.	9	at Los Angeles	Mon.	7	Edmonton
	Sat.	11	at San Jose	Thu.	10	Colorado
	Wed.	15	at Atlanta	Sat.	12	Florida
	Fri.	17	at Florida	Tue.	15	Washington
	Sat.	18	Atlanta	Thu.	17	Montreal
	Tue.	21	New Jersey	Sat.	19	at Boston*
	Thu.	23	Toronto	Tue.	22	at NY Rangers
	Sun.	26	Florida*	Thu.	24	Boston
	Mon.	27	at Atlanta	Sat.	26	at Pittsburgh
	Thu.	30	at Ottawa	Mon.	28	at Boston
	Fri.	31	NY Islanders	Tue.	29	Buffalo
Jan.	Wed.	5	at Washington	Thu.	31	New Jersey
	Fri.	7	Columbus	**Apr.**	Sat. 2	NY Rangers
	Sat.	8	at Nashville	Mon.	4	at Washington
	Tue.	11	at Montreal	Wed.	6	at Tampa Bay
	Thu.	13	at Buffalo	Fri.	8	at Florida
	Fri.	14	Philadelphia	Sun.	10	Florida*

* Denotes afternoon game.

Franchise date: June 22, 1979
Transferred from Hartford to Carolina, June 25, 1997.

EASTERN NHL CONFERENCE
SOUTHEAST DIVISION

26th NHL Season

Year-by-Year Record

Season	GP	Home				Road				Overall				GF	GA	Pts.	Finished	Playoff Result
		W	L	T	OL	W	L	T	OL	W	L	T	OL					
2003-04	82	13	18	8	2	15	16	6	4	28	34	14	6	172	209	76	3rd, Southeast Div.	Out of Playoffs
2002-03	82	12	17	9	3	10	26	2	3	22	43	11	6	171	240	61	5th, Southeast Div.	Out of Playoffs
2001-02	82	15	13	11	2	20	13	5	3	35	26	16	5	217	217	91	1st, Southeast Div.	Lost Final
2000-01	82	23	15	3	0	15	17	6	3	38	32	9	3	212	225	88	2nd, Southeast Div.	Lost Conf. Quarter-Final
1999-2000	82	20	16	5	0	17	19	5	0	37	35	10	0	217	216	84	3rd, Southeast Div.	Out of Playoffs
1998-99	82	20	12	9	...	14	18	9	...	34	30	18	...	210	202	86	1st, Southeast Div.	Lost Conf. Quarter-Final
1997-98	82	16	18	7	...	17	23	1	...	33	41	8	...	200	219	74	6th, Northeast Div.	Out of Playoffs
1996-97*	82	23	15	3	...	9	24	8	...	32	39	11	...	226	256	75	5th, Northeast Div.	Out of Playoffs
1995-96*	82	22	15	4	...	12	24	5	...	34	39	9	...	237	259	77	4th, Northeast Div.	Out of Playoffs
1994-95*	48	12	10	2	...	7	14	3	...	19	24	5	...	127	141	43	5th, Northeast Div.	Out of Playoffs
1993-94*	84	14	22	6	...	13	26	3	...	27	48	9	...	227	288	63	6th, Northeast Div.	Out of Playoffs
1992-93*	84	12	25	5	...	14	27	1	...	26	52	6	...	284	369	58	5th, Adams Div.	Out of Playoffs
1991-92*	80	13	17	10	...	13	24	3	...	26	41	13	...	247	283	65	4th, Adams Div.	Lost Div. Semi-Final
1990-91*	80	18	16	6	...	13	22	5	...	31	38	11	...	238	276	73	4th, Adams Div.	Lost Div. Semi-Final
1989-90*	80	17	18	5	...	21	15	4	...	38	33	9	...	275	268	85	4th, Adams Div.	Lost Div. Semi-Final
1988-89*	80	21	17	2	...	16	21	3	...	37	38	5	...	299	290	79	4th, Adams Div.	Lost Div. Semi-Final
1987-88*	80	21	14	5	...	14	24	2	...	35	38	7	...	249	267	77	4th, Adams Div.	Lost Div. Semi-Final
1986-87*	80	26	9	5	...	17	21	2	...	43	30	7	...	287	270	93	1st, Adams Div.	Lost Div. Semi-Final
1985-86*	80	21	17	2	...	19	19	2	...	40	36	4	...	332	302	84	4th, Adams Div.	Lost Div. Final
1984-85*	80	17	18	5	...	13	23	4	...	30	41	9	...	268	318	69	5th, Adams Div.	Out of Playoffs
1983-84*	80	19	16	5	...	9	26	5	...	28	42	10	...	288	320	66	5th, Adams Div.	Out of Playoffs
1982-83*	80	13	22	5	...	6	32	2	...	19	54	7	...	261	403	45	5th, Adams Div.	Out of Playoffs
1981-82*	80	13	17	10	...	8	24	8	...	21	41	18	...	264	351	60	5th, Adams Div.	Out of Playoffs
1980-81*	80	14	17	9	...	7	24	9	...	21	41	18	...	292	372	60	4th, Norris Div.	Out of Playoffs
1979-80*	80	22	12	6	...	5	22	13	...	27	34	19	...	303	312	73	4th, Norris Div.	Lost Prelim. Round

* Hartford Whalers

In his fourth season in the NHL, Josef Vasicek established career highs in games played (82), goals (19), assists (26), points (65), power-play goals (6) and game-winners (5).

2004-05 Player Personnel

FORWARDS	HT	WT	S	Place of Birth	Date	2003-04 Club
ADAMS, Craig	6-0	200	R	Seria, Brunei	4/26/77	Carolina
ADAMS, Kevyn	6-1	195	R	Washington, DC	10/8/74	Carolina
BAYDA, Ryan	5-11	185	L	Saskatoon, Sask.	12/9/80	Carolina-Lowell
BOULERICE, Jesse	6-2	203	R	Plattsburgh, NY	8/10/78	Carolina-Lowell
BRENDL, Pavel	6-1	206	R	Opocno, Czech.	3/23/81	Carolina-Lowell
BRIND'AMOUR, Rod	6-1	200	L	Ottawa, Ont.	8/9/70	Carolina
COLE, Erik	6-2	200	L	Oswego, NY	11/6/78	Carolina
CULLEN, Matt	6-2	199	L	Virginia, MN	11/2/76	Florida
DEFAUW, Brad	6-2	220	L	Edina, MN	11/10/77	Lowell
DWYER, Gordie	6-3	215	L	Dalhousie, N.B.	1/25/78	Montreal-Hamilton
FORBES, Colin	6-3	205	L	New Westminster, B.C.	2/16/76	Washington-Portland (AHL)
HENKEL, Jim	6-2	180	L	Red Bank, NJ	5/25/79	Atlantic City-Grand Rapids-Wor-Lowell (AHL)-Prov (AHL)
KURKA, Tomas	5-11	190	L	Most, Czech.	12/14/81	Carolina-Lowell
MURRAY, Marty	5-9	180	L	Lylton, Man.	2/16/75	Carolina
O'NEILL, Jeff	6-1	195	R	Richmond Hill, Ont.	2/23/76	Carolina
STAAL, Eric	6-3	182	L	Thunder Bay, Ont.	10/29/84	Carolina
SURMA, Damian	5-10	200	L	Lincoln Park, MI	1/22/81	Carolina-Lowell-Florida (ECHL)
TETARENKO, Joey	6-2	215	R	Prince Albert, Sask.	3/3/78	Carolina
VASICEK, Josef	6-4	200	L	Havlickuv Brod, Czech.	9/12/80	Carolina
VRBATA, Radim	6-1	190	R	Mlada Boleslav, Czech.	6/13/81	Carolina
WILLIAMS, Justin	6-1	190	R	Cobourg, Ont.	10/4/81	Philadelphia-Carolina
ZIGOMANIS, Mike	6-1	189	R	North York, Ont.	1/17/81	Carolina-Lowell
DEFENSEMEN						
CURRY, Sean	6-4	230	R	Burnsville, MN	4/29/82	Lowell
HEDICAN, Bret	6-2	205	L	St. Paul, MN	8/10/70	Carolina
KABERLE, Frantisek	6-1	190	L	Kladno, Czech.	11/8/73	Atlanta
ROURKE, Allan	6-1	214	L	Mississauga, Ont.	3/6/80	Carolina-Lowell
ST. JACQUES, Bruno	6-2	204	L	Montreal, Que.	8/22/80	Carolina-Lowell
WALLIN, Niclas	6-3	220	L	Boden, Sweden	2/20/75	Carolina
WARD, Aaron	6-2	225	R	Windsor, Ont.	1/17/73	Carolina
WESLEY, Glen	6-1	205	L	Red Deer, Alta.	10/2/68	Carolina

GOALTENDERS	HT	WT	C	Place of Birth	Date	2003-04 Club
DesROCHERS, Patrick	6-3	209	L	Penetanguishene, Ont.	10/27/79	Lowell
GERBER, Martin	6-0	185	L	Burgdorf, Switz.	9/3/74	Anaheim
ZEPP, Rob	6-1	181	L	Scarborough, Ont.	9/7/81	Lowell-Florida (ECHL)

Coaching History

Don Blackburn, 1979-80; Don Blackburn and Larry Pleau, 1980-81; Larry Pleau, 1981-82; Larry Kish, Larry Pleau and John Cuniff, 1982- 83; Jack Evans, 1983-84 to 1986-87; Jack Evans and Larry Pleau, 1987-88; Larry Pleau, 1988-89; Rick Ley, 1989-90, 1990-91; Jim Roberts, 1991-92; Paul Holmgren, 1992-93; Paul Holmgren and Pierre Maguire, 1993-94; Paul Holmgren, 1994-95; Paul Holmgren and Paul Maurice, 1995-96; Paul Maurice, 1996-97 to 2002-03; Paul Maurice and Peter Laviolette, 2003-04; Peter Laviolette, 2004-05.

Coach

LAVIOLETTE, PETER
Coach, Carolina Hurricanes. Born in Norwood, MA, December 7, 1964

On December 15, 2003 the Carolina Hurricanes made Peter Laviolette the 11th head coach in team history. Laviolette most recently coached the New York Islanders during the 2001-02 and 2002-03 seasons, and led the Islanders to the playoffs both seasons after the team missed the postseason seven straight times between 1994 and 2001.

Prior to joining the Islanders, Laviolette served as an assistant coach with the Boston Bruins after two years of guiding Boston's AHL affiliate, Providence. In 1998-99, Laviolette led the Providence Bruins to a 56-16-8 regular-season record, and a 15-4 playoff record that culminated with Providence hoisting the Calder Cup and Laviolette being named AHL coach of the year.

Laviolette played 11 seasons of professional hockey, mostly in the AHL and IHL, but did play 12 games with the New York Rangers during the 1988-89 season. He was a member of the 1988 and 1994 U.S. Olympic hockey teams, and captained the 1994 Olympic squad.

In the spring of 2004, Laviolette helped assure the United States' spot in the 2006 Olympic Games in Torino, Italy, when he guided Team USA to a bronze medal at the 2004 World Championships in the Czech Republic. He also served as an assistant to San Jose Sharks head coach Ron Wilson behind the bench for Team USA in the 2004 World Cup of Hockey.

Coaching Record

Season	Team	Games	Regular Season			Playoffs		
			W	L	T	Games	W	L
1997-98	Wheeling (ECHL)	70	37	24	9	15	8	7
1998-99	Providence (AHL)	80	56	16	8	19	15	4
1999-00	Providence (AHL)	80	33	38	9	14	10	4
2001-02	NY Islanders (NHL)	82	42	32	8	7	3	4
2002-03	NY Islanders (NHL)	82	35	36	11	5	1	4
2003-04	Carolina (NHL)	52	20	26	6	.....	.....	.....
	NHL Totals	216	97	94	25	12	4	8

2003-04 Scoring
* - rookie

Regular Season

Pos	#	Player	Team	GP	G	A	Pts	+/-	PIM	PP	SH	GW	GT	S	%
C	63	Josef Vasicek	CAR	82	19	26	45	–3	60	6	0	5	0	161	11.8
R	11	Justin Williams	PHI	47	6	20	26	10	32	3	0	1	0	107	5.6
			CAR	32	5	13	18	2	32	1	0	0	0	96	5.2
			TOTAL	79	11	33	44	12	64	4	0	1	0	203	5.4
L	26	Erik Cole	CAR	80	18	24	42	–4	93	2	2	3	1	172	10.5
D	22	Sean Hill	CAR	80	13	26	39	–2	84	6	0	1	0	228	5.7
C	17	Rod Brind'Amour	CAR	78	12	26	38	0	28	1	0	1	0	141	8.5
R	92	Jeff O'Neill	CAR	67	14	20	34	–12	60	7	0	4	0	207	6.8
C	12	* Eric Staal	CAR	81	11	20	31	–6	40	2	1	3	0	164	6.7
R	19	Radim Vrbata	CAR	80	12	13	25	–10	24	4	0	2	0	195	6.2
D	6	Bret Hedican	CAR	81	7	17	24	–10	64	2	0	3	0	112	6.3
C	14	Kevyn Adams	CAR	73	10	12	22	6	43	0	5	1	0	141	7.1
R	27	Craig Adams	CAR	80	7	10	17	–5	69	0	1	0	0	110	6.4
C	15	Marty Murray	CAR	66	5	7	12	6	8	0	0	1	0	56	8.9
D	7	Niclas Wallin	CAR	57	3	7	10	–8	51	0	0	1	0	74	4.1
R	23	Pavel Brendl	CAR	18	5	3	8	0	8	1	0	1	1	27	18.5
D	4	Aaron Ward	CAR	49	3	5	8	1	37	2	0	0	0	51	5.9
C	36	Jesse Boulerice	CAR	76	6	1	7	–5	127	0	0	1	0	46	13.0
L	16	* Ryan Bayda	CAR	44	3	3	6	–14	22	0	0	1	0	65	4.6
D	2	Glen Wesley	CAR	74	0	6	6	18	32	0	0	0	0	82	0.0
R	62	Jaroslav Svoboda	CAR	33	3	1	4	3	6	0	0	1	0	27	11.1
D	38	* Allan Rourke	CAR	25	1	3	4	4	22	0	0	0	0	24	4.2
C	18	* Michael Zigomanis	CAR	17	0	3	3	–1	2	0	0	0	0	13	0.0
D	25	Bruno St. Jacques	CAR	35	0	2	2	–7	31	0	0	0	0	16	0.0
D	47	* Brad Fast	CAR	1	1	0	1	1	0	0	0	0	1	4	25.0
C	52	* Damian Surma	CAR	1	0	1	1	1	0	0	0	0	0	0	0.0
R	33	Joey Tetarenko	CAR	2	0	0	0	0	5	0	0	0	0	0	0.0
C	56	* Brett Lysak	CAR	2	0	0	0	–2	2	0	0	0	0	1	0.0
D	71	Tomas Malec	CAR	2	0	0	0	–1	2	0	0	0	0	1	0.0
L	37	* Tomas Kurka	CAR	3	0	0	0	0	0	0	0	0	0	3	0.0

Goaltending

No.	Goaltender	GPI	Mins	Avg	W	L	T	EN	SO	GA	SA	S%	G	A	PIM
80	Kevin Weekes	66	3765	2.33	23	30	11	5	6	146	1652	.912	0	0	6
1	Arturs Irbe	10	564	2.33	5	2	1	2	0	23	228	.899	0	0	2
1	Jamie Storr	14	660	2.91	0	8	2	1	0	32	262	.878	0	0	0
	Totals	82	5021	2.50	28	40	14	8	6	209	2150	.903			

Kevyn Adams scored five shorthanded goals to tie Kris Draper for second in the NHL behind Martin St. Louis.

Captains' History

Rick Ley, 1979-80; Rick Ley and Mike Rogers, 1980-81; Dave Keon, 1981-82; Russ Anderson, 1982-83; Mark Johnson, 1983-84; Mark Johnson and Ron Francis, 1984-85; Ron Francis, 1985-86 to 1990-91; Randy Ladouceur, 1991-92; Pat Verbeek, 1992-93 to 1994-95; Brendan Shanahan, 1995-96; Kevin Dineen, 1996-97, 1997-98; Keith Primeau, 1998-99; Keith Primeau and Ron Francis, 1999-2000; Ron Francis, 2000-01 to 2003-04.

Club Records

Team

(Figures in brackets for season records are games played; records for fewest points, wins, ties, losses, goals, goals against are for 70 or more games.)

Most Points	93	1986-87 (80)
Most Wins	43	1986-87 (80)
Most Ties	19	1979-80 (80)
Most Losses	54	1982-83 (80)
Most Goals	332	1985-86 (80)
Most Goals Against	403	1982-83 (80)
Fewest Points	45	1982-83 (80)
Fewest Wins	19	1982-83 (80)
Fewest Ties	4	1985-86 (80)
Fewest Losses	26	2001-02 (82)
Fewest Goals	171	2002-03 (82)
Fewest Goals Against	202	1998-99 (82)

Longest Winning Streak

Overall	7	Mar. 16-29/85
Home	5	Mar. 17-29/85
Away	6	Nov. 10-Dec. 7/90

Longest Undefeated Streak

Overall	10	Jan. 20-Feb. 10/82
		(6 wins, 4 ties)
Home	9	Dec. 15/00-Jan. 18/01
		(8 wins, 1 tie)
Away	8	Nov. 11-Dec. 5/96
		(4 wins, 4 ties)

Longest Losing Streak

Overall	9	Feb. 19-Mar. 8/83
Home	6	Feb. 19-Mar. 12/83,
		Feb. 10-Mar. 3/85
Away	13	Dec. 18/82-Feb. 5/83

Longest Winless Streak

Overall	14	Jan. 4-Feb. 9/92
		(8 losses, 6 ties)
Home	13	Jan. 15-Mar. 10/85
		(11 losses, 2 ties)
Away	15	Nov. 11/79-Jan. 9/80
		(11 losses, 4 ties)
Most Shutouts, Season	8	1998-99 (82)
Most PIM, Season	2,354	1992-93 (84)
Most Goals, Game	11	Feb. 12/84
		(Edm. 0 at Hfd. 11),
		Oct. 19/85
		(Mtl. 6 at Hfd. 11),
		Jan. 17/86
		(Que. 6 at Hfd. 11),
		Mar. 15/86
		(Chi. 4 at Hfd. 11)

Individual

Most Seasons	16	Ron Francis
Most Games	1,186	Ron Francis
Most Goals, Career	382	Ron Francis
Most Assists, Career	793	Ron Francis
Most Points, Career	1,175	Ron Francis
		(382G, 793A)
Most PIM, Career	1,439	Kevin Dineen
Most Shutouts, Career	20	Arturs Irbe

Longest Consecutive

Games Streak	419	Dave Tippett
		(Mar. 3/84-Oct. 7/89)
Most Goals, Season	56	Blaine Stoughton
		(1979-80)
Most Assists, Season	69	Ron Francis
		(1989-90)
Most Points, Season	105	Mike Rogers
		(1979-80; 44G, 61A),
		(1980-81; 40G, 65A)
Most PIM, Season	358	Torrie Robertson
		(1985-86)

Most Points, Defenseman, Season	69	Dave Babych
		(1985-86; 14G, 55A)
Most Points, Center, Season	105	Mike Rogers
		(1979-80; 44G, 61A),
		(1980-81; 40G, 65A)
Most Points, Right Wing, Season	100	Blaine Stoughton
		(1979-80; 56G, 44A)
Most Points, Left Wing, Season	89	Geoff Sanderson
		(1992-93; 46G, 43A)
Most Points, Rookie, Season	72	Sylvain Turgeon
		(1983-84; 40G, 32A)
Most Shutouts, Season	6	Arturs Irbe
		(1998-99, 2000-01),
		Kevin Weekes
		(2003-04)
Most Goals, Game	4	Jordy Douglas
		(Feb. 3/80),
		Ron Francis
		(Feb. 12/84)
Most Assists, Game	6	Ron Francis
		(Mar. 5/87)
Most Points, Game	6	Paul Lawless
		(Jan. 4/87; 2G, 4A),
		Ron Francis
		(Mar. 5/87; 6A)
		(Oct. 8/89; 3G, 3A)

Records include Hartford Whalers, 1979-80 through 1996-97.

All-time Record vs. Other Clubs

Regular Season

	At Home								On Road									Total						
	GP	W	L	T	OL	GF	GA	PTS	GP	W	L	T	OL	GF	GA	PTS	GP	W	L	T	OL	GF	GA	PTS
Anaheim	9	5	3	1	0	23	19	11	9	3	5	1	0	26	29	7	18	8	8	2	0	49	48	18
Atlanta	13	10	2	1	0	47	31	21	13	8	1	3	1	38	30	20	26	18	3	4	1	85	61	41
Boston	76	31	36	9	0	252	263	71	78	25	46	7	0	207	274	57	154	56	82	16	0	459	537	128
Buffalo	78	32	35	11	0	227	230	75	77	24	45	7	1	226	309	56	155	56	80	18	1	453	539	131
Calgary	28	10	13	5	0	91	103	25	29	6	21	2	0	92	140	14	57	16	34	7	0	183	243	39
Chicago	30	14	12	4	0	97	93	32	29	10	16	3	0	83	117	23	59	24	28	7	0	180	210	55
Colorado	62	24	25	12	1	203	214	61	65	17	39	9	0	191	274	43	127	41	64	21	1	394	488	104
Columbus	4	3	1	0	0	13	11	6	3	2	1	0	0	9	6	4	7	5	2	0	0	22	17	10
Dallas	32	13	15	4	0	101	110	30	29	10	16	2	1	86	115	23	61	23	31	6	1	187	225	53
Detroit	30	17	12	1	0	104	86	35	31	7	16	7	1	86	119	22	61	24	28	8	1	190	205	57
Edmonton	29	11	11	7	0	112	98	29	31	7	19	5	0	92	121	19	60	18	30	12	0	204	219	48
Florida	25	13	9	3	0	73	63	29	26	7	10	8	1	55	74	23	51	20	19	11	1	128	137	52
Los Angeles	31	15	11	5	0	114	115	35	30	10	17	3	0	113	129	23	61	25	28	8	0	227	244	58
Minnesota	2	2	0	0	0	3	0	4	4	1	1	2	0	12	9	4	6	3	1	2	0	15	9	8
Montreal	78	29	36	13	0	224	268	71	75	18	49	7	1	213	309	44	153	47	85	20	1	437	577	115
Nashville	5	2	1	1	1	14	13	6	4	1	3	0	0	7	9	2	9	3	4	1	1	21	22	8
New Jersey	44	18	18	8	0	137	132	44	45	16	24	4	1	140	158	37	89	34	42	12	1	277	290	81
NY Islanders	45	21	18	5	1	152	148	48	44	20	19	4	1	121	132	45	89	41	37	9	2	273	280	93
NY Rangers	43	24	16	3	0	145	137	51	45	14	27	4	0	115	172	32	88	38	43	7	0	260	309	83
Ottawa	27	16	7	4	0	81	65	36	29	13	12	4	0	78	81	30	56	29	19	8	0	159	146	66
Philadelphia	44	13	21	9	1	140	158	36	43	9	27	5	2	107	162	25	87	22	48	14	3	247	320	61
Phoenix	30	14	10	6	0	103	89	34	31	15	14	2	0	112	110	32	61	29	24	8	0	215	199	66
Pittsburgh	48	22	21	5	0	178	177	49	46	17	22	6	1	170	185	41	94	39	43	11	1	348	362	90
St. Louis	31	12	17	2	0	92	97	26	31	9	18	3	1	94	119	22	62	21	35	5	1	186	216	48
San Jose	11	6	5	0	0	34	23	12	11	4	7	0	0	31	50	8	22	10	12	0	0	65	73	20
Tampa Bay	27	15	4	7	1	81	65	38	26	9	14	3	0	67	73	21	53	24	18	10	1	148	138	59
Toronto	37	18	12	6	1	144	119	43	36	18	13	5	0	126	120	41	73	36	25	11	1	270	239	84
Vancouver	29	12	12	5	0	94	100	29	30	10	13	6	1	81	105	27	59	22	25	11	1	175	205	56
Washington	49	15	23	10	1	128	152	41	47	14	29	4	0	118	163	32	96	29	52	14	1	246	315	73
Totals	**997**	**437**	**406**	**147**	**7**	**3207**	**3179**	**1028**	**997**	**324**	**544**	**116**	**13**	**2896**	**3694**	**777**	**1994**	**761**	**950**	**263**	**20**	**6103**	**6873**	**1805**

Playoffs

	Series	W	L	GP	W	L	T	GF	GA	Last Mtg.
Boston	3	0	3	19	7	12	0	48	63	1999
Colorado	2	1	1	9	5	4	0	35	34	1987
Detroit	1	0	1	5	1	4	0	7	14	2002
Montreal	6	1	5	33	12	21	0	91	108	2002
New Jersey	2	1	1	12	6	6	0	17	31	2002
Toronto	1	1	0	6	4	2	0	10	6	2002
Totals	**15**	**4**	**11**	**84**	**35**	**49**	**0**	**208**	**256**	

Playoff Results 2004-2000

Year	Round	Opponent	Result	GF	GA
2002	F	Detroit	L 1-4	7	14
	CF	Toronto	W 4-2	10	6
	CSF	Montreal	W 4-2	21	12
	CQF	New Jersey	W 4-2	9	11
2001	CQF	New Jersey	L 2-4	8	20

Abbreviations: Round: F - Final; CF - conference final; CSF - conference semi-final; CQF - conference quarter-final; DSF - division semi-final.

Calgary totals include Atlanta Flames, 1979-80.
Dallas totals include Minnesota North Stars, 1979-80 to 1992-93.
Phoenix totals include Winnipeg, 1979-80 to 1995-96.

Colorado totals include Quebec, 1979-80 to 1994-95.
New Jersey totals include Colorado Rockies, 1979-80 to 1981-82.

2003-04 Results

Oct.	9	at Florida	1-3	9	at Washington	1-4
	11	New Jersey	1-2	11	Ottawa	2-2
	13	Florida	2-2	15	at Tampa Bay	4-5
	18	at NY Rangers	2-2	16	at Atlanta	4-3
	22	at Pittsburgh	1-1	18	Atlanta	2-5
	23	at Boston	2-0	20	Ottawa	1-3
	25	at Philadelphia	4-4	21	at New Jersey	2-1
	28	San Jose	1-1	23	NY Islanders	2-3
	30	at NY Rangers	1-4	25	Buffalo	2-4
Nov.	1	at Tampa Bay	3-4	27	at Toronto	2-0
	2	Toronto	1-2	29	Washington	3-5
	6	NY Rangers	6-3	31	at Detroit	4-4
	8	Los Angeles	3-2*	Feb. 3	at Colorado	1-3
	9	Tampa Bay	1-1	4	at Anaheim	2-3
	12	at Washington	1-7	12	Washington	3-3
	13	Atlanta	5-1	14	at New Jersey	1-4
	15	Washington	1-2	16	Florida	3-1
	18	Philadelphia	2-2	19	Toronto	1-2*
	20	at Ottawa	1-6	21	Boston	3-3
	21	at Buffalo	0-5	23	at Toronto	2-1
	23	Tampa Bay	0-0	25	at Washington	2-1
	26	at NY Islanders	2-0	28	at Montreal	0-1*
	28	at Philadelphia	2-4	29	at Minnesota	3-3
	29	Pittsburgh	4-3	Mar. 2	Columbus	0-3
Dec.	3	Nashville	1-2*	5	at Atlanta	3-2*
	5	Montreal	1-1	6	New Jersey	1-4
	6	at Montreal	1-3	8	at Columbus	4-1
	9	at Edmonton	3-2	10	Tampa Bay	2-4
	11	at Calgary	0-1	12	Atlanta	4-2
	14	at Vancouver	1-2*	13	at Tampa Bay	5-1
	18	Pittsburgh	2-1*	15	at Atlanta	0-1*
	20	at Boston	2-1	17	at Chicago	3-2
	22	Dallas	1-3	19	at Pittsburgh	3-4*
	26	at Buffalo	1-3	20	at Ottawa	3-2*
	27	Montreal	2-1*	23	Philadelphia	2-4
	29	Buffalo	2-1	25	Florida	3-2
	31	Anaheim	1-3	27	at NY Islanders	3-2
Jan.	2	Detroit	1-4	29	at Florida	1-3
	4	Phoenix	0-3	30	Boston	2-3
	5	St. Louis	2-0	Apr. 2	NY Islanders	4-6
	8	NY Rangers	3-2	4	at Florida	6-6

* – Overtime

Entry Draft
Selections 2004-1990

2004
Pick
4	Andrew Ladd
38	Justin Peters
69	Casey Borer
109	Brett Carson
137	Magnus Akerlund
202	Ryan Pottruff
235	Jonas Fiedler
268	Martin Vagner

2003
Pick
2	Eric Staal
31	Danny Richmond
102	Aaron Dawson
126	Kevin Nastiuk
130	Matej Trojovsky
137	Tyson Strachan
198	Shay Stephenson
230	Jamie Hoffmann
262	Ryan Rorabeck

2002
Pick
25	Cam Ward
91	Jesse Lane
160	Daniel Manzato
224	Adam Taylor

2001
Pick
15	Igor Knyazev
46	Mike Zigomanis
91	Kevin Estrada
110	Rob Zepp
181	Daniel Boisclair
211	Sean Curry
244	Carter Trevisani
274	Peter Reynolds

2000
Pick
32	Tomas Kurka
80	Ryan Bayda
97	Niclas Wallin
110	Jared Newman
181	J.D. Forrest
212	Magnus Kahnberg
235	Craig Kowalski
276	Troy Ferguson

1999
Pick
16	David Tanabe
49	Brett Lysak
84	Brad Fast
113	Ryan Murphy
174	Damian Surma
202	Jim Baxter
231	David Evans
237	Antti Jokela
259	Yevgeny Kurilin

1998
Pick
11	Jeff Heerema
70	Kevin Holdridge
71	Erik Cole
91	Josef Vasicek
93	Tommy Westlund
97	Chris Madden
184	Don Smith
208	Jaroslav Svoboda
211	Mark Kosick
239	Brent McDonald

1997
Pick
22	Nikos Tselios
28	Brad DeFauw
80	Francis Lessard
88	Shane Willis
142	Kyle Dafoe
169	Andrew Merrick
195	Niklas Nordgren
199	Randy Fitzgerald
225	Kent McDonell

1996
Pick
34	Trevor Wasyluk
61	Andrei Petrunin
88	Craig MacDonald
104	Steve Wasylko
116	Mark McMahon
143	Aaron Baker
171	Greg Kuznik
197	Kevin Marsh
223	Craig Adams
231	Ashkat Rakhmatullin

1995
Pick
13	Jean-Sebastien Giguere
35	Sergei Fedotov
85	Ian MacNeil
87	Sami Kapanen
113	Hugh Hamilton
165	Byron Ritchie
191	Milan Kostolny
217	Mike Rucinski

1994
Pick
5	Jeff O'Neill
83	Hnat Domenichelli
109	Ryan Risidore
187	Tom Buckley
213	Ashlin Halfnight
230	Matt Ball
239	Brian Regan
265	Steve Nimigon

1993
Pick
2	Chris Pronger
72	Marek Malik
84	Trevor Roenick
115	Nolan Pratt
188	Manny Legace
214	Dmitri Gorenko
240	Wes Swinson
266	Igor Chibirev

1992
Pick
9	Robert Petrovicky
47	Andrei Nikolishin
57	Jan Vopat
79	Kevin Smyth
81	Jason McBain
143	Jarrett Reid
153	Ken Belanger
177	Konstantin Korotkov
201	Greg Zwakman
225	Steven Halko
249	Joacim Esbjors

1991
Pick
9	Patrick Poulin
31	Martin Hamrlik
53	Todd Hall
59	Michael Nylander
75	Jim Storm
119	Mike Harding
141	Brian Mueller
163	Steve Yule
185	Chris Belanger
207	Jason Currie
229	Mike Santonelli
251	Rob Peters

1990
Pick
15	Mark Greig
36	Geoff Sanderson
57	Mike Lenarduzzi
78	Chris Bright
120	Cory Keenan
141	Jergus Baca
162	Martin D'Orsonnens
183	Corey Osmak
204	Espen Knutsen
225	Tommie Eriksen
246	Denis Chalifoux

Club Directory

RBC Center

Carolina Hurricanes
1400 Edwards Mill Rd.
Raleigh, NC   27607
Phone **919/861-2300**
FAX 919/462-0123
www.carolinahurricanes.com
Capacity: 18,730

Carolina Hurricanes Directory
CEO/Owner/Governor	Peter Karmanos Jr.
President/General Manager	Jim Rutherford
Vice President/Assistant General Manager	Jason Karmanos
Head Coach	Peter Laviolette
Assistant Coach	Kevin McCarthy
Assistant Coach	Jeff Daniels
Director of Media Relations	Mike Sundheim
Manager of Media Relations	Kyle Hanlin
Head Athletic Therapist/ Strength Conditioning Coach	Peter Friesen
Equipment Managers	Wally Tatomir, Bob Gorman, Skip Cunningham
RBC Center Capacity	18,730
Public Relations Phone	(919) 861-5477 or (919) 861-5429
Public Relations Fax	(919) 462-0123
Press Box Phone	(919) 861-2300 ext. 6560 or 6533
Practice Facility Phone	(919) 754-0441
Practice Facility	Rec Zone, 912 Hodges St., Raleigh
Radio	WWMY-FM (102.9), WDTF-AM (570), WMFD-AM (630)
Television	FOX Sports South FOX 50 Digital

General Managers' History

Jack Kelly, 1979-80, 1980-81; Larry Pleau, 1981-82, 1982-83; Emile Francis, 1983-84 to 1988-89; Eddie Johnston, 1989-90 to 1991-92; Brian Burke, 1992-93; Paul Holmgren, 1993-94; Jim Rutherford, 1994-95 to date.

President and General Manager

RUTHERFORD, JIM
President/General Manager, Carolina Hurricanes.
Born in Beeton, Ont., February 17, 1949.

Jim Rutherford, a former NHL goaltender, is the franchise's seventh general manager and the only general manager of the Carolina Hurricanes. Named to his position on June 28, 1994, Rutherford has always taken an aggressive approach towards improving the fortunes of the franchise through trades and the NHL draft. In 2002, the team reached the Stanley Cup Finals for the first time in history.

A veteran of 13 NHL seasons, Rutherford began his professional goaltending career in 1969 as a first-round selection of the Detroit Red Wings. While playing for Detroit, Pittsburgh, Toronto and Los Angeles, Rutherford collected 14 career shutouts. For five seasons he also served as the Red Wings' player representative. Rutherford also played for Team Canada at the World Championships in Vienna in 1977 and Moscow in 1979.

After his playing days with the Red Wings, Rutherford joined Compuware to serve as the director of hockey operations for Compuware Sports Corporation. Rutherford gained a wealth of experience in youth hockey and junior programs. As a former player, coach, and general manager, his ability to develop players and produce winning programs is widely respected throughout the hockey community.

He started his management career by guiding Compuware Sports Corporation's purchase of the Windsor Spitfires of the Ontario Hockey League in April of 1984. During the next four years, Rutherford acted as general manager of the Spitfires. After the Spitfires advanced to the 1988 Memorial Cup finals, Rutherford led Compuware's efforts to bring the first American-based OHL franchise to Detroit on December 11, 1989. Rutherford was voted the 1987 executive of the year in both the OHL and the Canadian Hockey League and won the OHL executive of the year award again in 1988.

Selected second overall behind Marc-Andre Fleury in the 2003 Entry Draft, Eric Staal came straight out of junior hockey to play 81 games in 2003-04. He ranked 10th in rookie scoring with 31 points.

Chicago Blackhawks

Kyle Calder had 21 goals in 66 games.

2003-04 Results: 20W-43L-11T-8OTL 59PTS.
Fifth, Central Division

2004-05 Schedule

Month	Day	Date	Opponent
Oct.	Wed.	13	Minnesota
	Fri.	15	at St. Louis
	Sat.	16	Columbus
	Wed.	20	Colorado
	Fri.	22	at Detroit
	Sun.	24	Dallas
	Mon.	25	at Philadelphia
	Thu.	28	Anaheim
	Sun.	31	at Carolina*
Nov.	Wed.	3	at Dallas
	Thu.	4	at Phoenix
	Sun.	7	Phoenix
	Wed.	10	Los Angeles
	Fri.	12	Anaheim
	Sun.	14	Edmonton
	Wed.	17	at Vancouver
	Thu.	18	at Edmonton
	Sat.	20	at Calgary
	Wed.	24	at San Jose
	Fri.	26	at Anaheim*
	Sat.	27	at Los Angeles
Dec.	Thu.	2	Nashville
	Fri.	3	at Detroit
	Sun.	5	Los Angeles
	Thu.	9	at Phoenix
	Fri.	10	at Colorado
	Sun.	12	New Jersey
	Tue.	14	at Detroit
	Wed.	15	San Jose
	Fri.	17	Detroit
	Sun.	19	Dallas
	Wed.	22	Tampa Bay
	Thu.	23	at Columbus
	Sun.	26	Colorado
	Tue.	28	at Nashville
	Wed.	29	Buffalo
Jan.	Sun.	2	Philadelphia
	Mon.	3	at Buffalo
	Wed.	5	Phoenix
	Fri.	7	at Pittsburgh
	Sun.	9	Detroit
	Wed.	12	at Columbus
	Fri.	14	Toronto
	Sun.	16	Calgary
	Tue.	18	at Minnesota
	Thu.	20	Nashville
	Sat.	22	at St. Louis*
	Sun.	23	Ottawa
	Wed.	26	Detroit
	Fri.	28	Columbus
	Sun.	30	St. Louis
Feb.	Tue.	1	at Tampa Bay
	Wed.	2	at Florida
	Sat.	5	at Boston*
	Tue.	8	at Nashville
	Wed.	9	at Dallas
	Wed.	16	Atlanta
	Fri.	18	Nashville
	Sun.	20	Columbus*
	Mon.	21	at NY Rangers*
	Wed.	23	Edmonton
	Fri.	25	at Columbus
	Sun.	27	San Jose*
Mar.	Tue.	1	at Washington
	Wed.	2	Montreal
	Fri.	4	Calgary
	Sun.	6	St. Louis
	Tue.	8	at Vancouver
	Thu.	10	at Calgary
	Sat.	12	at San Jose*
	Sun.	13	at Anaheim*
	Tue.	15	at Los Angeles
	Thu.	17	Vancouver
	Sun.	20	NY Islanders*
	Wed.	23	Minnesota
	Thu.	24	at Minnesota
	Sat.	26	at Nashville*
	Tue.	29	at Edmonton
	Thu.	31	at Colorado
Apr.	Fri.	1	Vancouver
	Wed.	6	St. Louis
	Sat.	9	at St. Louis*

* Denotes afternoon game.

Franchise date: September 25, 1926

WESTERN CONFERENCE

CENTRAL DIVISION

79th NHL Season

Year-by-Year Record

		Home				Road				Overall								
Season	GP	W	L	T	OL	W	L	T	OL	W	L	T	OL	GF	GA	Pts.	Finished	Playoff Result
2003-04	82	13	17	6	5	7	26	5	3	20	43	11	8	188	259	59	5th, Central Div.	Out of Playoffs
2002-03	82	17	15	7	2	13	18	6	4	30	33	13	6	207	226	79	3rd, Central Div.	Out of Playoffs
2001-02	82	28	7	5	1	13	20	8	0	41	27	13	1	216	207	96	3rd, Central Div.	Lost Conf. Quarter-Final
2000-01	82	14	21	4	2	15	19	4	3	29	40	8	5	210	246	71	4th, Central Div.	Out of Playoffs
1999-2000	82	16	19	5	1	17	18	5	1	33	37	10	2	242	245	78	3rd, Central Div.	Out of Playoffs
1998-99	82	20	17	4	...	9	24	8	...	29	41	12	...	202	248	70	3rd, Central Div.	Out of Playoffs
1997-98	82	14	19	8	...	16	20	5	...	30	39	13	...	192	199	73	5th, Central Div.	Out of Playoffs
1996-97	82	16	21	4	...	18	14	9	...	34	35	13	...	223	210	81	5th, Central Div.	Lost Conf. Quarter-Final
1995-96	82	22	13	6	...	18	15	8	...	40	28	14	...	273	220	94	2nd, Central Div.	Lost Conf. Semi-Final
1994-95	48	11	10	3	...	13	9	2	...	24	19	5	...	156	115	53	3rd, Central Div.	Lost Conf. Championship
1993-94	84	21	16	5	...	18	20	4	...	39	36	9	...	254	240	87	5th, Central Div.	Lost Conf. Quarter-Final
1992-93	84	25	11	6	...	22	14	6	...	47	25	12	...	279	230	106	1st, Norris Div.	Lost Div. Semi-Final
1991-92	80	23	9	8	...	13	20	7	...	36	29	15	...	257	236	87	2nd, Norris Div.	Lost Final
1990-91	80	28	8	4	...	21	15	4	...	49	23	8	...	284	211	106	1st, Norris Div.	Lost Div. Semi-Final
1989-90	80	25	13	2	...	16	20	4	...	41	33	6	...	316	294	88	1st, Norris Div.	Lost Conf. Championship
1988-89	80	16	14	10	...	11	27	2	...	27	41	12	...	297	335	66	4th, Norris Div.	Lost Conf. Championship
1987-88	80	21	17	2	...	9	24	7	...	30	41	9	...	284	328	69	3rd, Norris Div.	Lost Div. Semi-Final
1986-87	80	18	13	9	...	11	24	5	...	29	37	14	...	290	310	72	3rd, Norris Div.	Lost Div. Semi-Final
1985-86	80	23	12	5	...	16	21	3	...	39	33	8	...	351	349	86	1st, Norris Div.	Lost Div. Semi-Final
1984-85	80	22	16	2	...	16	19	5	...	38	35	7	...	309	299	83	2nd, Norris Div.	Lost Conf. Championship
1983-84	80	25	13	2	...	5	29	6	...	30	42	8	...	277	311	68	4th, Norris Div.	Lost Div. Semi-Final
1982-83	80	29	8	3	...	18	15	7	...	47	23	10	...	338	268	104	1st, Norris Div.	Lost Conf. Championship
1981-82	80	20	13	7	...	10	25	5	...	30	38	12	...	332	363	72	4th, Norris Div.	Lost Conf. Championship
1980-81	80	21	11	8	...	10	22	8	...	31	33	16	...	304	315	78	2nd, Smythe Div.	Lost Prelim. Round
1979-80	80	21	12	7	...	13	15	12	...	34	27	19	...	241	250	87	1st, Smythe Div.	Lost Quarter-Final
1978-79	80	18	12	10	...	11	24	5	...	29	36	15	...	244	277	73	1st, Smythe Div.	Lost Quarter-Final
1977-78	80	20	9	11	...	12	20	8	...	32	29	19	...	230	220	83	1st, Smythe Div.	Lost Quarter-Final
1976-77	80	19	16	5	...	7	27	6	...	26	43	11	...	240	298	63	3rd, Smythe Div.	Lost Prelim. Round
1975-76	80	17	15	8	...	15	15	10	...	32	30	18	...	254	261	82	1st, Smythe Div.	Lost Quarter-Final
1974-75	80	24	12	4	...	13	23	4	...	37	35	8	...	268	241	82	3rd, Smythe Div.	Lost Quarter-Final
1973-74	78	20	6	13	...	21	8	10	...	41	14	23	...	272	164	105	2nd, West Div.	Lost Semi-Final
1972-73	78	26	9	4	...	16	18	5	...	42	27	9	...	284	225	93	1st, West Div.	Lost Final
1971-72	78	28	3	8	...	18	14	7	...	46	17	15	...	256	166	107	1st, West Div.	Lost Semi-Final
1970-71	78	30	6	3	...	19	14	6	...	49	20	9	...	277	184	107	1st, West Div.	Lost Final
1969-70	76	26	7	5	...	19	15	4	...	45	22	9	...	250	170	99	1st, East Div.	Lost Semi-Final
1968-69	76	20	14	4	...	14	19	5	...	34	33	9	...	280	246	77	6th, East Div.	Out of Playoffs
1967-68	74	20	13	4	...	12	13	12	...	32	26	16	...	212	222	80	4th, East Div.	Lost Semi-Final
1966-67	70	24	5	6	...	17	12	6	...	41	17	12	...	264	170	94	1st,	Lost Semi-Final
1965-66	70	21	8	6	...	16	17	2	...	37	25	8	...	240	187	82	2nd,	Lost Semi-Final
1964-65	70	20	13	2	...	14	15	6	...	34	28	8	...	224	176	76	3rd,	Lost Final
1963-64	70	26	4	5	...	10	18	7	...	36	22	12	...	218	169	84	2nd,	Lost Semi-Final
1962-63	70	17	9	9	...	15	12	8	...	32	21	17	...	194	178	81	2nd,	Lost Semi-Final
1961-62	70	20	10	5	...	11	16	8	...	31	26	13	...	217	186	75	3rd,	Lost Final
1960-61	**70**	**20**	**6**	**9**	**...**	**9**	**18**	**8**	**...**	**29**	**24**	**17**	**...**	**198**	**180**	**75**	**3rd,**	**Won Stanley Cup**
1959-60	70	18	11	6	...	10	18	7	...	28	29	13	...	191	180	69	3rd,	Lost Semi-Final
1958-59	70	14	12	9	...	14	17	4	...	28	29	13	...	197	208	69	3rd,	Lost Semi-Final
1957-58	70	15	17	3	...	9	22	4	...	24	39	7	...	163	202	55	5th,	Out of Playoffs
1956-57	70	12	15	8	...	4	24	7	...	16	39	15	...	169	225	47	6th,	Out of Playoffs
1955-56	70	9	19	7	...	10	20	5	...	19	39	12	...	155	216	50	6th,	Out of Playoffs
1954-55	70	6	21	8	...	7	19	9	...	13	40	17	...	161	235	43	6th,	Out of Playoffs
1953-54	70	8	21	6	...	4	30	1	...	12	51	7	...	133	242	31	6th,	Out of Playoffs
1952-53	70	14	11	10	...	13	17	5	...	27	28	15	...	169	175	69	4th,	Lost Semi-Final
1951-52	70	9	19	7	...	8	25	2	...	17	44	9	...	158	241	43	6th,	Out of Playoffs
1950-51	70	8	22	5	...	5	25	5	...	13	47	10	...	171	280	36	6th,	Out of Playoffs
1949-50	70	13	18	4	...	9	20	6	...	22	38	10	...	203	244	54	6th,	Out of Playoffs
1948-49	60	13	12	5	...	8	19	3	...	21	31	8	...	173	211	50	5th,	Out of Playoffs
1947-48	60	10	17	3	...	10	17	3	...	20	34	6	...	195	225	46	6th,	Out of Playoffs
1946-47	60	10	17	3	...	9	20	1	...	19	37	4	...	193	274	42	6th,	Out of Playoffs
1945-46	50	15	5	5	...	8	15	2	...	23	20	7	...	200	178	53	3rd,	Lost Semi-Final
1944-45	50	9	14	2	...	4	16	5	...	13	30	7	...	141	194	33	5th,	Out of Playoffs
1943-44	50	15	6	4	...	7	17	1	...	22	23	5	...	178	187	49	4th,	Lost Final
1942-43	50	14	3	8	...	3	15	7	...	17	18	15	...	179	180	49	5th,	Out of Playoffs
1941-42	48	15	8	1	...	7	15	2	...	22	23	3	...	145	155	47	4th,	Lost Quarter-Final
1940-41	48	11	10	3	...	5	15	4	...	16	25	7	...	112	139	39	5th,	Lost Semi-Final
1939-40	48	15	7	2	...	8	12	4	...	23	19	6	...	112	120	52	4th,	Lost Quarter-Final
1938-39	48	5	13	6	...	7	15	2	...	12	28	8	...	91	132	32	7th,	Out of Playoffs
1937-38	**48**	**10**	**10**	**4**	**...**	**4**	**15**	**5**	**...**	**14**	**25**	**9**	**...**	**97**	**139**	**37**	**3rd, Amn. Div.**	**Won Stanley Cup**
1936-37	48	8	13	3	...	6	14	4	...	14	27	7	...	99	131	35	4th, Amn. Div.	Out of Playoffs
1935-36	48	15	7	2	...	6	12	6	...	21	19	8	...	93	92	50	3rd, Amn. Div.	Lost Quarter-Final
1934-35	48	12	9	3	...	14	8	2	...	26	17	5	...	118	88	57	2nd, Amn. Div.	Lost Quarter-Final
1933-34	**48**	**13**	**4**	**7**	**...**	**7**	**13**	**4**	**...**	**20**	**17**	**11**	**...**	**88**	**83**	**51**	**2nd, Amn. Div.**	**Won Stanley Cup**
1932-33	48	12	7	5	...	4	13	7	...	16	20	12	...	88	101	44	4th, Amn. Div.	Out of Playoffs
1931-32	48	13	5	6	...	5	14	5	...	18	19	11	...	86	101	47	2nd, Amn. Div.	Lost Quarter-Final
1930-31	44	13	8	1	...	11	9	2	...	24	17	3	...	108	78	51	2nd, Amn. Div.	Lost Final
1929-30	44	12	9	1	...	9	9	4	...	21	18	5	...	117	111	47	2nd, Amn. Div.	Lost Quarter-Final
1928-29	44	3	13	6	...	4	16	2	...	7	29	8	...	33	85	22	5th, Amn. Div.	Out of Playoffs
1927-28	44	2	18	2	...	5	16	1	...	7	34	3	...	68	134	17	5th, Amn. Div.	Out of Playoffs
1926-27	44	12	8	2	...	7	14	1	...	19	22	3	...	115	116	41	3rd, Amn. Div.	Lost Quarter-Final

2004-05 Player Personnel

FORWARDS	HT	WT	S	Place of Birth	Date	2003-04 Club
ARNASON, Tyler	5-11	192	L	Oklahoma City, OK	3/16/79	Chicago
BAINES, Ajay	5-10	179	L	Kamloops, B.C.	3/25/78	Norfolk
BARNABY, Matthew	6-0	189	L	Ottawa, Ont.	5/4/73	NY Rangers-Colorado
BELL, Mark	6-4	205	L	St. Paul's, Ont.	8/5/80	Chicago
BROWN, Curtis	6-0	196	L	Unity, Sask.	2/12/76	Buffalo-San Jose
CALDER, Kyle	5-11	176	L	Mannville, Alta.	1/5/79	Chicago
DAZE, Eric	6-6	235	L	Montreal, Que.	7/2/75	Chicago
ELLISON, Matt	6-0	192	R	Duncan, B.C.	12/8/83	Chicago-Norfolk
FRASER, Colin	6-1	182	L	Sicamous, B.C.	1/28/85	Red Deer
KEITH, Matt	6-2	200	R	Edmonton, Alta.	4/11/83	Chicago-Norfolk
LAING, Quintin	6-2	175	L	Rosetown, Sask.	6/8/79	Chicago-Norfolk
MOEN, Travis	6-2	210	L	Stewart Valley, Sask.	4/6/82	Chicago
MORGAN, Jason	6-1	200	L	St. John's, Nfld.	10/9/76	Calgary-Lowell (AHL)-Nashville-Norfolk
NICHOL, Scott	5-8	173	R	Edmonton, Alta.	12/31/74	Chicago
NICKULAS, Eric	5-11	206	R	Hyannis, MA	3/25/75	St. Louis-Chicago
RADULOV, Igor	6-1	186	L	Nizhny Tagil, USSR	8/23/82	Chicago-Norfolk
RUUTU, Tuomo	6-2	208	L	Vantaa, Finland	2/16/83	Chicago
THORNTON, Shawn	6-1	209	R	Oshawa, Ont.	7/23/77	Chicago-Norfolk
VOROBIEV, Pavel	6-0	194	L	Karaganda, USSR	5/5/82	Chicago-Norfolk
YAKUBOV, Mikhail	6-3	202	L	Barnaul, USSR	2/16/82	Chicago-Norfolk

DEFENSEMEN	HT	WT	S	Place of Birth	Date	2003-04 Club
BABCHUK, Anton	6-5	202	R	Kiev, USSR	5/6/84	Chicago-Norfolk
BARINKA, Michal	6-3	217	L	Vyskov, Czech.	6/12/84	Chicago-Norfolk
BARKER, Cam	6-3	213	L	Winnipeg, Man.	4/4/86	Medicine Hat
BERARD, Bryan	6-2	220	L	Woonsocket, RI	3/5/77	Chicago
CULLIMORE, Jassen	6-5	244	L	Simcoe, Ont.	12/4/72	Tampa Bay
KEITH, Duncan	6-0	182	L	Winnipeg, Man.	7/16/83	Norfolk
KUIPER, Nick	6-3	215	R	Beaconsfield, Que.	2/12/82	Massachusetts
KUKKONEN, Lasse	6-0	187	L	Oulu, Finland	9/18/81	Chicago-Norfolk
McCARTHY, Steve	6-1	198	L	Trail, B.C.	2/3/81	Chicago
POAPST, Steve	6-0	199	L	Cornwall, Ont.	1/3/69	Chicago
ROBIDAS, Stephane	5-11	188	R	Sherbrooke, Que.	3/3/77	Dallas-Chicago
SEABROOK, Brent	6-3	215	R	Richmond, B.C.	4/20/85	Lethbridge
VANDERMEER, Jim	6-1	218	L	Caroline, Alta.	2/21/80	Phi-Phi (AHL)-Chi
WILFORD, Marty	6-1	212	L	Cobourg, Ont.	4/17/77	Norfolk
WISNIEWSKI, James	6-0	206	R	Canton, MI	2/21/84	Plymouth

GOALTENDERS	HT	WT	C	Place of Birth	Date	2003-04 Club
ANDERSON, Craig	6-2	174	L	Park Ridge, IL	5/21/81	Chicago-Norfolk
BRODEUR, Mike	6-2	170	L	Calgary, Alta.	3/30/83	Moose Jaw
LEIGHTON, Michael	6-3	186	L	Petrolia, Ont.	5/19/81	Chicago-Norfolk
MUNRO, Adam	6-2	219	L	St. George, Ont.	11/12/82	Chicago-Norfolk-Gwinnett
THIBAULT, Jocelyn	5-11	169	L	Montreal, Que.	1/12/75	Chicago

Coach

SUTTER, BRIAN
Coach, Chicago Blackhawks. Born in Viking, Alta., October 7, 1956.

Brian Sutter became the 34th head coach in club history on May 3, 2001. He became only the 10th man in NHL history to coach in 1,000 games on February 1, 2004 at Montreal. Sutter currently ranks 12th (third among active coaches) on the NHL's all-time wins list with 451. In his inaugural season with Chicago, (2001-02) the team returned to the playoffs for the first time in five seasons. Sutter was named "The Sport News" coach of the year and was runner-up for the Jack Adams Award. He is the second member of the Sutter family to coach the Blackhawks (Darryl Sutter served as head coach from 1992 to 1995) and the fifth of the six hockey playing Sutter brothers to be associated with the Blackhawks (only Ron Sutter has not).

Sutter spent his entire 12-year NHL playing career with the St. Louis Blues. He ranks second on the all-time Blues games played list with 779, third in goals with 303, third in power-play goals with 107, third in assists with 333, and third in points with 636. He also is the Blues lifetime leader with 1,786 career penalty minutes. A great leader and an outstanding performer on the ice, Sutter's #11 was retired by the Blues on December 30, 1988.

Immediately following his playing career, Sutter became coach of the Blues in 1988-89. In four seasons, Sutter's Blues posting a mark of 153-124-43 which exceeded Scotty Bowman's record, but has since been surpassed by Joel Quenneville as the winningest coach in Blues history. Sutter won the Jack Adams Award as coach of the year in 1990-91.

Sutter became the head coach of the Boston Bruins for the 1992-93 season, a position he held for three years. After leaving the coaching ranks for two seasons, Sutter returned behind the bench in his native province of Alberta as the head coach of the Calgary Flames for the 1997-98 season.

Coaching Record

		Regular Season				Playoffs		
Season	**Team**	**Games**	**W**	**L**	**T**	**Games**	**W**	**L**
1988-89	St. Louis (NHL)	80	33	35	12	10	5	5
1989-90	St. Louis (NHL)	80	37	34	9	12	7	5
1990-91	St. Louis (NHL)	80	47	22	11	13	6	7
1991-92	St. Louis (NHL)	80	36	33	11	6	2	4
1992-93	Boston (NHL)	84	51	26	7	4	0	4
1993-94	Boston (NHL)	84	42	29	13	13	6	7
1994-95	Boston (NHL)	48	27	18	3	5	1	4
1997-98	Calgary (NHL)	82	26	41	15	....	....	....
1998-99	Calgary (NHL)	82	30	40	12	....	....	....
1999-2000	Calgary (NHL)	82	31	41	10	....	....	....
2001-02	Chicago (NHL)	82	41	28	13	5	1	4
2002-03	Chicago (NHL)	82	30	39	13	....	....	....
2003-04	Chicago (NHL)	82	20	51	11	....	....	....
	NHL Totals	**1028**	**451**	**437**	**140**	**68**	**28**	**40**

2003-04 Scoring

* - rookie

Regular Season

Pos	#	Player	Team	GP	G	A	Pts	+/–	PIM	PP	SH	GW	GT	S	%
C	39	Tyler Arnason	CHI	82	22	33	55	–13	16	6	0	2	1	222	9.9
D	4	Bryan Berard	CHI	58	13	34	47	–24	53	6	0	0	0	203	6.4
L	28	Mark Bell	CHI	82	21	24	45	–14	106	2	0	1	0	202	10.4
C	15	* Tuomo Ruutu	CHI	82	23	21	44	–31	58	10	0	3	0	174	13.2
L	19	Kyle Calder	CHI	66	21	18	39	–18	29	10	0	1	0	144	14.6
C	53	* Brett Mclean	CHI	76	11	20	31	–11	54	5	1	0	0	125	8.8
R	20	Eric Nickulas	STL	44	7	11	18	–2	44	1	0	1	0	80	8.8
			CHI	21	1	1	2	–6	8	0	0	0	0	41	2.4
			TOTAL	65	8	12	20	–8	52	1	0	1	0	121	6.6
C	12	Scott Nichol	CHI	75	7	11	18	–16	145	0	0	1	0	112	6.3
D	23	* Jim Vandermeer	PHI	23	3	2	5	–5	25	0	0	1	0	24	12.5
			CHI	23	2	10	12	–6	58	1	1	0	0	37	5.4
			TOTAL	46	5	12	17	–11	83	1	1	1	0	61	8.2
D	17	Stephane Robidas	DAL	14	1	0	1	–2	8	1	0	0	0	8	12.5
			CHI	45	2	10	12	6	33	0	1	1	0	55	3.6
			TOTAL	59	3	10	13	4	41	1	1	1	0	63	4.8
C	22	Igor Korolev	CHI	62	3	10	13	–15	22	0	0	1	0	38	7.9
L	55	Eric Daze	CHI	19	4	7	11	–7	0	1	0	0	0	76	5.3
L	50	* Igor Radulov	CHI	36	4	7	11	–2	18	0	0	0	0	47	8.5
D	2	Deron Quint	CHI	51	4	7	11	–26	18	2	0	0	0	72	5.6
C	36	* Mikhail Yakubov	CHI	30	1	7	8	–12	8	0	0	0	0	32	3.1
L	59	* Travis Moen	CHI	82	4	2	6	–17	142	0	0	2	0	51	7.8
D	44	* Burke Henry	CHI	23	2	4	6	0	24	0	0	0	0	31	6.5
R	14	Ryan Vandenbussche	CHI	65	4	1	5	–10	120	2	0	0	0	25	16.0
R	11	* Matt Keith	CHI	20	2	3	5	–5	10	1	0	0	1	21	9.5
D	8	Steve Poapst	CHI	53	2	2	4	–16	26	0	0	1	0	55	3.6
R	32	* Pavel Vorobiev	CHI	18	1	3	4	1	4	1	0	1	0	20	5.0
D	5	Steve Mccarthy	CHI	25	1	3	4	–9	8	0	0	0	0	29	3.4
D	34	Jason Strudwick	CHI	54	1	3	4	–16	73	0	0	0	0	32	3.1
D	6	* Anton Babchuk	CHI	5	0	2	2	–1	2	0	0	0	0	11	0.0
L	33	Shawn Thornton	CHI	8	1	0	1	2	23	0	0	0	0	14	7.1
L	45	* Quintin Laing	CHI	3	0	1	1	1	0	0	0	0	0	3	0.0
D	42	* Michal Barinka	CHI	9	0	1	1	–5	6	0	0	0	0	15	0.0
R	16	* Matt Ellison	CHI	10	0	1	1	–3	0	0	0	0	0	4	0.0
D	47	* Lasse Kukkonen	CHI	10	0	1	1	–2	4	0	0	0	0	9	0.0
D	56	* Johnathan Aitken	CHI	41	0	1	1	–9	70	0	0	0	0	37	0.0

Goaltending

No.	Goaltender	GPI	Mins	Avg	W	L	T	EN	SO	GA	SA	S%	G	A	PIM
31	* Craig Anderson	21	1205	2.84	6	14	0	4	1	57	602	.905	0	0	4
41	Jocelyn Thibault	14	821	2.85	5	7	2	0	1	39	450	.913	0	0	0
29	Steve Passmore	9	478	2.89	2	6	0	1	0	23	221	.896	0	0	0
49	* Michael Leighton	34	1988	2.99	6	18	8	5	2	99	987	.900	0	2	2
30	Adam Munro	7	426	3.66	1	5	1	1	0	26	217	.880	0	0	2
40	* Matt Underhill	1	61	3.93	0	1	0	0	0	4	33	.879	0	0	0
	Totals	**82**	**5008**	**3.10**	**20**	**51**	**11**	**11**	**4**	**259**	**2521**	**.897**			

General Managers' History

Major Frederic McLaughlin, 1926-27 to 1941-42; Bill Tobin, 1942-43 to 1953-54; Tommy Ivan, 1954-55 to 1976-77; Bob Pulford, 1977-78 to 1989-90; Mike Keenan, 1990-91, 1991-92; Mike Keenan and Bob Pulford, 1992-93; Bob Pulford, 1993-94 to 1996-97; Bob Murray, 1997-98, 1998-99; Bob Murray and Bob Pulford, 1999-2000; Mike Smith, 2000-01 to 2002-03; Mike Smith and Bob Pulford, 2003-04; Bob Pulford, 2004-05.

Vice President and General Manager

PULFORD, BOB
Senior Vice President/General Manager, Chicago Blackhawks.
Born in Newton Robinson, Ont., March 31, 1936.

Bob Pulford has excelled at every aspect the game of hockey offers: player, coach, and general manager. With the Toronto Maple Leafs in their glory-days of the 1960s, Pulford earned a Stanley Cup ring in 1962, 1963, 1964, and 1967. Known as an outstanding penalty killer, he registered four 20-or-more goal seasons.

Retiring from active play, Pulford accepted the position of head coach with the Los Angeles Kings in 1972. He was named coach of the year in 1974-75. Following five successful seasons in L.A., Pulford joined the Chicago Blackhawks on July 6, 1977, becoming head coach and general manager. Twice after relinquishing his coaching position to concentrate on management, Pulford reassumed the coaching role in midseason to revive a struggling Hawk team. With Pulford at the helm, Chicago won eight division titles and made the playoffs 20 consecutive seasons.

In June of 1990, Pulford became the club's senior vice president. He has reassumed the role of general manager several times over the years, most recently on October 24, 2003.

NHL Coaching Record

		Regular Season				Playoffs		
Season	**Team**	**Games**	**W**	**L**	**T**	**Games**	**W**	**L**
1972-73	Los Angeles	78	31	36	11	....	....	....
1973-74	Los Angeles	78	33	33	12	5	1	4
1974-75	Los Angeles	80	42	17	21	3	1	2
1975-76	Los Angeles	80	38	33	9	9	4	5
1976-77	Los Angeles	80	34	31	15	9	4	5
1977-78	Chicago	80	32	29	19	4	0	4
1978-79	Chicago	80	29	36	15	4	0	4
1971-82	Chicago	28	12	14	2	15	8	7
1984-85	Chicago	27	16	7	4	15	9	6
1985-86	Chicago	80	39	33	8	3	0	3
1986-87	Chicago	80	29	37	14	4	0	4
99-2000	Chicago	58	28	24	6	....	....	....
	NHL Totals	**829**	**363**	**330**	**126**	**71**	**27**	**44**

Club Records

Team

(Figures in brackets for season records are games played; records for fewest points, wins, ties, losses, goals, goals against are for 70 or more games)

Most Points	**107**	1970-71 (78), 1971-72 (78)
Most Wins	**49**	1970-71 (78), 1990-91 (80)
Most Ties	**23**	1973-74 (78)
Most Losses	**51**	1953-54 (70), 2003-04 (82)
Most Goals	**351**	1985-86 (80)
Most Goals Against	**363**	1981-82 (80)
Fewest Points	**31**	1953-54 (70)
Fewest Wins	**12**	1953-54 (70)
Fewest Ties	**6**	1989-90 (80)
Fewest Losses	**14**	1973-74 (78)
Fewest Goals	***133**	1953-54 (70)
Fewest Goals Against	**164**	1973-74 (78)
Longest Winning Streak		
Overall	**8**	Dec. 9-26/71, Jan. 4-21/81
Home	**13**	Nov. 11-Dec. 20/70
Away	**7**	Dec. 9-29/64
Longest Undefeated Streak		
Overall	**15**	Jan. 14-Feb. 16/67 (12 wins, 3 ties)
Home	**18**	Oct. 11-Dec. 20/70 (16 wins, 2 ties)
Away	**12**	Nov. 2-Dec. 16/67 (6 wins, 6 ties)
Longest Losing Streak		
Overall	**12**	Feb. 25-Mar. 25/51
Home	**9**	Feb. 8-Mar. 21/28
Away	**19**	Nov. 10-Jan. 29/04
Longest Winless Streak		
Overall	**21**	Dec. 17/50-Jan. 28/51 (18 losses, 3 ties)
Home	**15**	Dec. 16/28-Feb. 28/29 (11 losses, 4 ties)
Away	**22**	Dec. 19/50-Mar. 25/51 (20 losses, 2 ties)
Most Shutouts, Season	**15**	1969-70 (76)
Most PIM, Season	**2,663**	1991-92 (80)
Most Goals, Game	**12**	Jan. 30/69 (Chi. 12 at Phi. 0)

Individual

Most Seasons	**22**	Stan Mikita
Most Games	**1,394**	Stan Mikita
Most Goals, Career	**604**	Bobby Hull
Most Assists, Career	**926**	Stan Mikita
Most Points, Career	**1,467**	Stan Mikita (541G, 926A)
Most PIM, Career	**1,495**	Chris Chelios
Most Shutouts, Career	**74**	Tony Esposito
Longest Consecutive Games Streak	**884**	Steve Larmer (Oct. 6/82-Apr. 15/93)
Most Goals, Season	**58**	Bobby Hull (1968-69)
Most Assists, Season	**87**	Denis Savard (1981-82, 1987-88)
Most Points, Season	**131**	Denis Savard (1987-88; 44G, 87A)
Most PIM, Season	**408**	Mike Peluso (1991-92)
Most Points, Defenseman, Season	**85**	Doug Wilson (1981-82; 39G, 46A)
Most Points, Center, Season	**131**	Denis Savard (1987-88; 44G, 87A)
Most Points, Right Wing, Season	**101**	Steve Larmer (1990-91; 44G, 57A)
Most Points, Left Wing, Season	**107**	Bobby Hull (1968-69; 58G, 49A)
Most Points, Rookie, Season	**90**	Steve Larmer (1982-83; 43G, 47A)
Most Shutouts, Season	**15**	Tony Esposito (1969-70)
Most Goals, Game	**5**	Grant Mulvey (Feb. 3/82)
Most Assists, Game	**6**	Pat Stapleton (Mar. 30/69)
Most Points, Game	**7**	Max Bentley (Jan. 28/43; 4G, 3A), Grant Mulvey (Feb. 3/82; 5G, 2A)

* NHL Record.

Retired Numbers

1	Glenn Hall	1957-1967
9	Bobby Hull	1957-1972
18	Denis Savard	1980-1990, 1995-1997
21	Stan Mikita	1958-1980
35	Tony Esposito	1969-1984

All-time Record vs. Other Clubs

Regular Season

	At Home								On Road								Total							
	GP	W	L	T	OL	GF	GA	PTS	GP	W	L	T	OL	GF	GA	PTS	GP	W	L	T	OL	GF	GA	PTS
Anaheim	24	12	10	2	0	67	58	26	22	7	12	3	0	47	58	17	46	19	22	5	0	114	116	43
Atlanta	2	2	0	0	0	6	0	4	4	2	2	0	0	10	14	4	6	4	2	0	0	16	14	8
Boston	286	147	94	45	0	926	767	339	284	89	161	34	0	808	1023	212	570	236	255	79	0	1734	1790	551
Buffalo	51	27	17	6	1	164	139	61	53	14	32	7	0	138	199	35	104	41	49	13	1	302	338	96
Calgary	61	26	22	13	0	196	179	65	63	21	28	13	1	188	201	56	124	47	50	26	1	384	380	121
Carolina	29	16	9	3	1	117	83	36	30	12	14	4	0	93	97	28	59	28	23	7	1	210	180	64
Colorado	41	21	14	3	3	144	130	48	39	12	21	6	0	124	158	30	80	33	35	9	3	268	288	78
Columbus	10	7	2	1	0	30	15	15	11	4	5	1	1	34	32	10	21	11	7	2	1	64	47	25
Dallas	110	64	31	15	0	412	289	143	112	44	51	16	1	340	377	105	222	108	82	31	1	752	666	248
Detroit	338	155	130	51	2	1015	951	363	335	99	202	33	1	833	1144	232	673	254	332	84	3	1848	2095	595
Edmonton	44	21	15	7	1	167	152	50	45	18	22	5	0	147	165	41	89	39	37	12	1	314	317	91
Florida	10	5	3	2	0	34	30	12	8	5	2	1	0	30	18	11	18	10	5	3	0	64	48	23
Los Angeles	75	35	31	9	0	261	221	79	74	33	33	8	0	246	245	74	149	68	64	17	0	507	466	153
Minnesota	8	3	4	1	0	17	25	7	8	2	5	0	1	20	28	5	16	5	9	1	1	37	53	12
Montreal	273	93	125	55	0	731	761	241	276	54	173	48	1	653	1067	157	549	147	298	103	1	1384	1828	398
Nashville	17	10	5	1	1	49	39	22	16	6	6	3	1	43	48	16	33	16	11	4	2	92	87	38
New Jersey	46	24	12	10	0	176	127	58	47	16	20	11	0	142	147	43	93	40	32	21	0	318	274	101
NY Islanders	48	26	17	5	0	162	162	57	47	14	18	15	0	141	163	43	95	40	35	20	0	303	325	100
NY Rangers	286	128	115	43	0	870	792	299	285	113	117	55	0	807	841	281	571	241	232	98	0	1677	1633	580
Ottawa	8	4	2	2	0	18	18	10	10	6	4	0	0	30	31	12	18	10	6	2	0	48	49	22
Philadelphia	60	26	15	19	0	205	170	71	62	16	35	11	0	162	204	43	122	42	50	30	0	367	374	114
Phoenix	48	26	12	10	0	184	128	62	50	18	26	5	1	154	164	42	98	44	38	15	1	338	292	104
Pittsburgh	60	39	11	10	0	236	157	88	59	23	29	7	0	190	210	53	119	62	40	17	0	426	367	141
St. Louis	118	65	35	18	0	433	348	148	115	41	56	17	1	356	388	100	233	106	91	35	1	789	736	248
San Jose	25	13	9	2	1	76	77	29	26	10	12	3	1	70	72	24	51	23	21	5	2	146	149	53
Tampa Bay	14	8	4	2	0	45	35	18	11	4	4	3	0	28	26	11	25	12	8	5	0	73	61	29
Toronto	318	156	120	42	0	968	831	354	315	97	164	54	0	821	1071	248	633	253	284	96	0	1789	1902	602
Vancouver	71	47	16	7	1	267	164	102	72	22	34	15	1	210	218	60	143	69	50	22	2	477	382	162
Washington	40	22	12	6	0	151	120	50	41	15	21	5	0	127	145	35	81	37	33	11	0	278	265	85
Defunct Clubs	139	79	40	20	0	408	268	178	140	52	67	21	0	316	346	125	279	131	107	41	0	724	614	303
Totals	**2660**	**1307**	**932**	**410**	**11**	**8535**	**7236**	**3035**	**2660**	**869**	**1376**	**404**	**11**	**7308**	**8900**	**2153**	**5320**	**2176**	**2308**	**814**	**22**	**15843**	**16136**	**5188**

Playoffs

	Series	W	L	GP	W	L	T	GF	GA	Last Mtg.	Rnd.	Result
Boston	6	1	5	22	5	16	1	63	97	1978	QF	L 0-4
Buffalo	2	0	2	9	1	8	0	17	36	1980	QF	L 0-4
Calgary	3	1	2	12	5	7	0	33	37	1996	CQF	W 4-0
Colorado	2	0	2	12	4	8	0	28	49	1997	CQF	L 2-4
Dallas	6	4	2	33	19	14	0	120	118	1991	DSF	L 2-4
Detroit	14	8	6	69	38	31	0	210	190	1995	CF	L 1-4
Edmonton	4	1	3	20	8	12	0	77	102	1992	CF	W 4-0
Los Angeles	1	1	0	5	4	1	0	10	7	1974	QF	W 4-1
Montreal	17	5	12	81	29	50	2	185	261	1976	QF	L 0-4
NY Islanders	2	0	2	6	0	6	0	6	21	1979	QF	L 0-4
NY Rangers	5	4	1	24	14	10	0	66	54	1973	SF	W 4-1
Philadelphia	1	1	0	4	4	0	0	20	8	1971	QF	W 4-0
Pittsburgh	2	1	1	8	4	4	0	24	23	1992	F	L 0-4
St. Louis	10	7	3	50	28	22	0	171	142	2002	CQF	L 1-4
Toronto	9	3	6	38	15	22	1	89	111	1995	CQF	W 4-3
Vancouver	2	1	1	9	5	4	0	24	24	1995	CSF	W 4-0
Defunct Clubs	4	2	2	9	5	3	1	16	15			
Totals	**90**	**40**	**50**	**411**	**188**	**218**	**5**	**1159**	**1295**			

Calgary totals include Atlanta Flames, 1972-73 to 1979-80.
Carolina totals include Hartford, 1979-80 to 1996-97.
Colorado totals include Quebec, 1979-80 to 1994-95.
Dallas totals include Minnesota North Stars, 1967-68 to 1992-93.
New Jersey totals include Kansas City, 1974-75 to 1975-76, and Colorado Rockies, 1976-77 to 1981-82.
Phoenix totals include Winnipeg, 1979-80 to 1995-96.

Playoff Results 2004-2000

Year	Round	Opponent	Result	GF	GA
2002	CQF	St. Louis	L 1-4	5	13

Abbreviations: Round: F - Final; **CF** - conference final; **CSF** - conference semi-final; **CQF** - conference quarter-final; **DSF** - division semi-final; **SF** - semi-final; **QF** - quarter-final.

2003-04 Results

Oct.	8	Minnesota	1-0		7	at Minnesota	4-7
	10	at Colorado	0-5		8	Calgary	3-1
	12	Los Angeles	2-4		11	Colorado	4-5*
	16	at Columbus	1-2		12	at St. Louis	4-7
	18	at Atlanta	2-7		14	at Detroit	2-4
	19	Nashville	3-1		18	Los Angeles	1-2
	23	at San Jose	3-3		21	at Minnesota	2-4
	25	at Los Angeles	3-2		22	Columbus	7-0
	26	at Anaheim	1-1		24	at Columbus	3-4
	28	at Phoenix	2-2		27	at Vancouver	2-3
	30	Pittsburgh	0-1		29	at Edmonton	2-5
Nov.	1	at St. Louis	3-2		30	at Calgary	5-3
	2	Anaheim	3-1	**Feb.**	1	at Montreal	4-6
	7	at Nashville	2-1		3	at Toronto	4-1
	9	Colorado	3-4*		11	Nashville	5-2
	10	at Detroit	0-3		14	Boston	2-1*
	12	Calgary	2-6		15	Washington	0-4
	14	Detroit	3-4*		19	San Jose	3-6
	16	NY Rangers	2-2		22	St. Louis	3-2*
	18	at Edmonton	2-5		24	at Philadelphia	1-3
	20	at Vancouver	2-3*		25	at Columbus	4-3
	22	at Calgary	1-2		27	Columbus	3-4
	26	at San Jose	2-3		29	Florida	2-2
	28	at Anaheim	3-4	**Mar.**	1	at Nashville	2-2
	29	at Los Angeles	1-3		3	Tampa Bay	3-5
Dec.	3	Buffalo	2-3		5	Anaheim	2-5
	6	at NY Islanders	2-5		7	Edmonton	3-4*
	7	Phoenix	2-2		11	at New Jersey	4-6
	11	Detroit	4-3*		12	at Washington	4-3
	12	at Dallas	0-1		14	Dallas	0-4
	14	Dallas	1-1		17	Carolina	2-3
	18	at Ottawa	1-6		19	Vancouver	4-3*
	19	at Detroit	2-3		21	Phoenix	2-2
	21	New Jersey	2-2		23	at Colorado	2-2
	23	St. Louis	3-0		25	Minnesota	2-8
	26	Columbus	1-4		27	at St. Louis	3-4*
	28	Detroit	3-0		28	St. Louis	1-3
	29	at Pittsburgh	0-1		30	at Nashville	2-5
	31	Vancouver	3-4*	**Apr.**	1	Nashville	1-3
Jan.	2	San Jose	2-1		3	at Phoenix	1-2*
	4	Edmonton	3-4		4	at Dallas	2-5

* – Overtime

Entry Draft Selections 2004-1990

2004
Pick
- 3 Cam Barker
- 32 Dave Bolland
- 41 Bryan Bickell
- 45 Ryan Garlock
- 54 Jakub Sindel
- 68 Adam Berti
- 120 Mitch Maunu
- 123 Karel Hromas
- 131 Trevor Kell
- 140 Jake Dowell
- 165 Scott McCulloch
- 196 Petri Kontiola
- 214 Troy Brouwer
- 223 Jared Walker
- 229 Eric Hunter
- 256 Matthew Ford
- 260 Marko Anttila

2003
Pick
- 14 Brent Seabrook
- 52 Corey Crawford
- 59 Michal Barinka
- 151 Lasse Kukkonen
- 156 Alexei Ivanov
- 181 Johan Andersson
- 211 Mike Brodeur
- 245 Dustin Byfuglien
- 275 Michael Grenzy
- 282 Chris Porter

2002
Pick
- 21 Anton Babchuk
- 54 Duncan Keith
- 93 Alexander Kojevnikov
- 128 Matt Ellison
- 156 James Wisniewski
- 188 Kevin Kantee
- 219 Tyson Kellerman
- 251 Jason Kostadine
- 282 Adam Burish

2001
Pick
- 9 Tuomo Ruutu
- 29 Adam Munro
- 59 Matt Keith
- 73 Craig Anderson
- 104 Brent MacLellan
- 115 Vladimir Gusev
- 119 Alexei Zotkin
- 142 Tommi Jaminki
- 174 Alexander Golovin
- 186 Petr Puncochar
- 205 Teemu Jaaskelainen
- 216 Oleg Minakov
- 268 Jeff Miles

2000
Pick
- 10 Mikhail Yakubov
- 11 Pavel Vorobiev
- 49 Jonas Nordqvist
- 74 Igor Radulov
- 106 Scott Balan
- 117 Olli Malmivaara
- 151 Alexander Barkunov
- 177 Michael Ayers
- 193 Joey Martin
- 207 Cliff Loya
- 225 Vladislav Luchkin
- 240 Adam Berkhoel
- 262 Peter Flache
- 271 Reto Von Arx
- 291 Arne Ramholt

1999
Pick
- 23 Steve McCarthy
- 46 Dimitri Levinski
- 63 Stepan Mokhov
- 134 Michael Jacobsen
- 165 Michael Leighton
- 194 Mattias Wennerberg
- 195 Yorick Treille
- 223 Andrew Carver

1998
Pick
- 8 Mark Bell
- 94 Matthias Trattnig
- 156 Kent Huskins
- 158 Jari Viuhkola
- 166 Jonathan Pelletier
- 183 Tyler Arnason
- 210 Sean Griffin
- 238 Alexandre Couture
- 240 Andrei Yershov

1997
Pick
- 13 Daniel Cleary
- 16 Ty Jones
- 39 Jeremy Reich
- 67 Mike Souza
- 110 Ben Simon
- 120 Peter Gardiner
- 130 Kyle Calder
- 147 Heath Gordon
- 174 Jerad Smith
- 204 Sergei Shikhanov
- 230 Chris Feil

1996
Pick
- 31 Remi Royer
- 42 Jeff Paul
- 46 Geoff Peters
- 130 Andy Johnson
- 184 Mike Vellinga
- 210 Chris Twerdun
- 236 Andrei Kozyrev

1995
Pick
- 19 Dmitri Nabokov
- 45 Christian Laflamme
- 71 Kevin McKay
- 82 Chris Van Dyk
- 97 Pavel Kriz
- 146 Marc Magliardini
- 149 Marty Wilford
- 175 Steve Tardif
- 201 Casey Hankinson
- 227 Mike Pittman

1994
Pick
- 14 Ethan Moreau
- 40 Jean-Yves Leroux
- 85 Steve McLaren
- 118 Marc Dupuis
- 144 Jim Enson
- 170 Tyler Prosofsky
- 196 Mike Josephson
- 222 Lubomir Jandera
- 248 Lars Weibel
- 263 Rob Mara

1993
Pick
- 24 Eric Lecompte
- 50 Eric Manlow
- 54 Bogdan Savenko
- 76 Ryan Huska
- 90 Eric Daze
- 102 Patrik Pysz
- 128 Jonni Vauhkonen
- 180 Tom White
- 206 Sergei Petrov
- 232 Mike Rusk
- 258 Mike McGhan
- 284 Tom Noble

1992
Pick
- 12 Sergei Krivokrasov
- 36 Jeff Shantz
- 41 Sergei Klimovich
- 89 Andy MacIntyre
- 113 Tim Hogan
- 137 Gerry Skrypec
- 161 Mike Prokopec
- 185 Layne Roland
- 209 David Hymovitz
- 233 Richard Raymond

1991
Pick
- 22 Dean McAmmond
- 39 Michael Pomichter
- 44 Jamie Matthews
- 66 Bobby House
- 71 Igor Kravchuk
- 88 Zac Boyer
- 110 Maco Balkovec
- 112 Kevin St. Jacques
- 132 Jacques Auger
- 154 Scott Kirton
- 176 Roch Belley
- 198 Scott MacDonald
- 220 Alexander Andrievski
- 242 Mike Larkin
- 264 Scott Dean

1990
Pick
- 16 Karl Dykhuis
- 37 Ivan Droppa
- 79 Chris Tucker
- 121 Brett Stickney
- 124 Derek Edgerly
- 163 Hugo Belanger
- 184 Owen Lessard
- 205 Erik Peterson
- 226 Steve Dubinsky
- 247 Dino Grossi

Coaching History

Pete Muldoon, 1926-27; Barney Stanley and Hugh Lehman, 1927-28; Herb Gardiner and Dick Irvin, 1928-29; Tom Shaughnessy and Bill Tobin, 1929-30; Dick Irvin, 1930-31; Bill Tobin, 1931-32; Emil Iverson, Godfrey Matheson and Tommy Gorman, 1932-33; Tommy Gorman, 1933-34; Clem Loughlin, 1934-35 to 1936-37; Bill Stewart, 1937-38; Bill Stewart and Paul Thompson, 1938-39; Paul Thompson, 1939-40 to 1943-44; Paul Thompson and Johnny Gottselig, 1944-45; Johnny Gottselig, 1945-46, 1946-47; Johnny Gottselig and Charlie Conacher, 1947-48; Charlie Conacher, 1948-49, 1949-50; Ebbie Goodfellow, 1950-51, 1951-52; Sid Abel, 1952-53, 1953-54; Frank Eddolls, 1954-55; Dick Irvin, 1955-56; Tommy Ivan, 1956-57; Tommy Ivan and Rudy Pilous, 1957-58; Rudy Pilous, 1958-59 to 1962-63; Billy Reay, 1963-64 to 1975-76; Billy Reay and Bill White, 1976-77; Bob Pulford, 1977-78, 1978-79; Eddie Johnston, 1979-80; Keith Magnuson, 1980-81; Keith Magnuson and Bob Pulford, 1981-82; Orval Tessier, 1982-83, 1983-84; Orval Tessier and Bob Pulford, 1984-85; Bob Pulford, 1985-86, 1986-87; Bob Murdoch, 1987-88; Mike Keenan, 1988-89 to 1991-92; Darryl Sutter, 1992-93 to 1994-95; Craig Hartsburg, 1995-96 to 1997-98; Dirk Graham and Lorne Molleken, 1998-99; Lorne Molleken and Bob Pulford, 1999-2000; Alpo Suhonen, 2000-01; Brian Sutter, 2001-02 to date.

Captains' History

Dick Irvin, 1926-27 to 1928-29; Duke Dukowski, 1929-30; Ty Arbour, 1930-31; Cy Wentworth, 1931-32; Helge Bostrom, 1932-33; Charlie Gardiner, 1933-34; no captain, 1934-35; Johnny Gottselig, 1935-36 to 1939-40; Earl Seibert, 1940-41, 1941-42; Doug Bentley, 1942-43, 1943-44; Clint Smith 1944-45; John Mariucci, 1945-46; Red Hamill, 1946-47; John Mariucci, 1947-48; Gaye Stewart, 1948-49; Doug Bentley, 1949-50; Jack Stewart, 1950-51, 1951-52; Bill Gadsby, 1952-53, 1953-54; Gus Mortson, 1954-55 to 1956-57; no captain, 1957-58; Ed Litzenberger, 1958-59 to 1960-61; Pierre Pilote, 1961-62 to 1967-68, no captain, 1968-69; Pat Stapleton, 1969-70; no captain, 1970-71 to 1974-75; Stan Mikita and Pit Martin, 1975-76; Stan Mikita, Pit Martin and Keith Magnuson, 1976-77; Keith Magnuson, 1977-78, 1978-79; Keith Magnuson and Terry Ruskowski, 1979-80; Terry Ruskowski, 1980-81, 1981-82; Darryl Sutter, 1982-83 to 1984-85; Darryl Sutter and Bob Murray, 1985-86; Darryl Sutter, 1986-87; no captain, 1987-88; Denis Savard and Dirk Graham, 1988-89; Dirk Graham, 1989-90 to 1994-95; Chris Chelios, 1995-96 to 1998-99; Doug Gilmour, 1999-2000; Tony Amonte, 2000-01, 2001-02; Alex Zhamnov, 2002-03, 2003-04.

Club Directory

United Center

Chicago Blackhawks
United Center
1901 W. Madison Street
Chicago, IL 60612
Phone **312/455-7000**
FAX 312/455-7041
www.chicagoblackhawks.com
Capacity: 20,500

President...William W. Wirtz
Senior V.P. and General Manager..............Robert J. Pulford
Vice President......................................Jack Davison
Vice President......................................Peter R. Wirtz
Assistant General Manager.......................Dale Tallon
Head Coach..Brian Sutter
Assistant Coach....................................Denis Savard
Assistant Coach....................................Bruce Cassidy
Asst. Coach, Strength & Cond....................Phil Walker
Goaltending Consultant...........................Vladislav Tretiak
Goaltending Coach.................................Stephane Waite
Chief Amateur Scout..............................Michel Dumas
Amateur Scouts....................................Ron Anderson, Gord Donnelly, Bruce Franklin, Tim Higgins, Rob Pulford
European Scouting Coordinator..................Sakari Pietila
European Amateur Scouts.........................Matti Kautto, Karl Pavlik, Ruslan Shabanov
Executive Assistant...............................Cindy Brueck
Special Assistant to G.M..........................Stan Bowman
Manager of Team Services........................Matt Colleran
Video Coordinator.................................Ike Rhodes

Medical Staff
Team Physicians...................................Mark Bowen, Gordon Nuber, Greg Ewert, Angelo Costas
Team Dentists......................................Daniel Mackey, Dean Sana
Oral Surgeon.......................................Eric Pulver
Eye Doctor...Robert Stein
Head Trainer.......................................Michael Gapski
Assistant Trainer..................................Jeff Thomas
Massage Therapist.................................Pawel Prylinski
Equipment Manager...............................Troy Parchman
Asst. Equipment Mgr..............................Mark DePasquale

Public Relations/Marketing
Exec. Dir. of Communications....................Jim De Maria
Dir. of Comm. Relations/PR Asst................Barbara Davidson
Manager of Public Relations.....................Tony Ommen
Website Producer..................................Adam Kempenaar
Exec. Dir. of Sales & Marketing.................Jim Sofranko
Dir. of Corporate Sponsorships..................Steve Waight
Acct. Exec., Corp. Sponsorship.................David Stensby
Manager, Client Services..........................Kelly Bodnarchuk
Exec. Dir. Community Outreach & Operations.....Carol Czaplicki
Mgr. of Advertising & Promotions...............Maxine Olhava
Marketing Associate...............................Alison Finley
Administrative Assistant..........................Angela Armbruster

Finance
Controller..Tracy Hernandez
Treasurer...Robert Rinkus
Accounting Manager...............................Deb Kulir

Ticketing
Exec. Director, Ticket Operations...............James K. Bare
Director, Ticket Sales.............................Doug Ryan
Season Ticket Sales Manager....................Steve Rigney
Account Executives................................Brad Bober, Adam Collopy, Ildegardo Esparza, Evan Hall, Dustin Sublett, Andrew Wallach
Ticket Operations Manager.......................Kathie Raimondi
Customer Service Representative.................Holly Doyle

Miscellaneous Information
Team Photographer................................Bill Smith
Organist..Frank Pellico
Public Address Announcer........................Gene Honda
Website Contributor...............................Harvey Wittenberg
Radio Station.......................................WSCR (AM 670)
Television Station..................................Comcast Sports Net Chicago
Broadcasters.......................................Pat Foley, Troy Murray
Television Studio Host............................Jim Blaney
Television Studio Analyst.........................TBD
Radio Studio Host.................................Jesse Rogers

In his second full NHL season, Tyler Arnason led the Blackhawks with 55 points in 2003-04.

Colorado Avalanche

2003-04 Results: 40w-22L-13T-7OTL 100PTS.
Second, Northwest Division

2004-05 Schedule

Oct.	Wed. 13	Los Angeles
	Sat. 16	at San Jose
	Sun. 17	Boston
	Wed. 20	at Chicago
	Thu. 21	at Columbus
	Sat. 23	Tampa Bay
	Wed. 27	Phoenix
	Fri. 29	Calgary
	Sat. 30	Vancouver
Nov.	Tue. 2	at Vancouver
	Thu. 4	at Calgary
	Fri. 5	at Minnesota
	Mon. 8	Pittsburgh
	Wed. 10	Vancouver
	Thu. 11	at St. Louis
	Sat. 13	at Nashville
	Tue. 16	Edmonton
	Thu. 18	St. Louis
	Sat. 20	Anaheim
	Mon. 22	Columbus
	Fri. 26	at Calgary
	Sat. 27	at Edmonton
Dec.	Wed. 1	Atlanta
	Fri. 3	Anaheim
	Sun. 5	Calgary*
	Wed. 8	Detroit
	Fri. 10	Chicago
	Sat. 11	at Nashville
	Mon. 13	Florida
	Wed. 15	at Phoenix
	Fri. 17	at Anaheim
	Sat. 18	at Los Angeles
	Thu. 23	Ottawa
	Sun. 26	at Chicago
	Mon. 27	Toronto
	Thu. 30	at St. Louis
	Fri. 31	at Dallas
Jan.	Sun. 2	Phoenix
	Tue. 4	Edmonton
	Thu. 6	Vancouver
	Sat. 8	Detroit*

	Tue. 11	at NY Islanders
	Wed. 12	at New Jersey
	Fri. 14	at Columbus
	Mon. 17	at Boston*
	Wed. 19	Montreal
	Sat. 22	San Jose*
	Wed. 26	Dallas
	Thu. 27	at Minnesota
	Sat. 29	at Detroit*
	Mon. 31	at Vancouver
Feb.	Tue. 1	at Edmonton
	Fri. 4	Minnesota
	Mon. 7	Carolina
	Wed. 9	St. Louis
	Wed. 16	at Dallas
	Fri. 18	at Anaheim
	Sat. 19	at Los Angeles
	Tue. 22	Minnesota
	Thu. 24	at Washington
	Sat. 26	at Philadelphia*
	Sun. 27	at NY Rangers*
Mar.	Wed. 2	Nashville
	Fri. 4	Dallas
	Sun. 6	San Jose*
	Thu. 10	at Carolina
	Fri. 11	at Atlanta
	Sun. 13	at Detroit
	Tue. 15	at Buffalo
	Thu. 17	Edmonton
	Sat. 19	Calgary
	Mon. 21	at Edmonton
	Tue. 22	at Vancouver
	Fri. 25	Columbus
	Sat. 26	at Phoenix
	Mon. 28	at San Jose
	Thu. 31	Chicago
Apr.	Sat. 2	Los Angeles
	Mon. 4	at Minnesota
	Wed. 6	Minnesota
	Fri. 8	Nashville
	Sun. 10	at Calgary*

* Denotes afternoon game.

Franchise date: June 22, 1979
Transferred from Quebec to Denver, June 21, 1995

NORTHWEST DIVISION

26th NHL Season

Adam Foote played in his 738th career game on November 4, 2003, moving into third place in franchise history for games played. He led all NHL defensemen with 35.5 shifts per game in 2003-04.

Year-by-Year Record

Season	GP	Home				Road				Overall							Finished	Playoff Result
		W	L	T	OL	W	L	T	OL	W	L	T	OL	GF	GA	Pts.		
2003-04	82	19	14	6	2	21	8	7	5	40	22	13	7	236	198	100	2nd, Northwest Div.	Lost Conf. Semi-Final
2002-03	82	21	9	8	3	21	10	5	5	42	19	13	8	251	194	105	1st, Northwest Div.	Lost Conf. Quarter-Final
2001-02	82	24	12	4	1	21	16	4	0	45	28	8	1	212	169	99	1st, Northwest Div.	Lost Conf. Championship
2000-01	**82**	**28**	**6**	**5**	**2**	**24**	**10**	**5**	**2**	**52**	**16**	**10**	**4**	**270**	**192**	**118**	**1st, Northwest Div.**	**Won Stanley Cup**
1999-2000	82	25	12	4	0	17	16	7	1	42	28	11	1	233	201	96	1st, Northwest Div.	Lost Conf. Championship
1998-99	82	21	14	6	...	23	14	4	...	44	28	10	...	239	205	98	1st, Northwest Div.	Lost Conf. Championship
1997-98	82	21	10	10	...	18	16	7	...	39	26	17	...	231	205	95	1st, Pacific Div.	Lost Conf. Quarter-Final
1996-97	82	26	10	5	...	23	14	4	...	49	24	9	...	277	205	107	1st, Pacific Div.	Lost Conf. Championship
1995-96	**82**	**24**	**10**	**7**	**...**	**23**	**15**	**3**	**...**	**47**	**25**	**10**	**...**	**326**	**240**	**104**	**1st, Pacific Div.**	**Won Stanley Cup**
1994-95*	48	19	1	4	...	11	12	1	...	30	13	5	...	185	134	65	1st, Northeast Div.	Lost Conf. Quarter-Final
1993-94*	84	19	17	6	...	15	25	2	...	34	42	8	...	277	292	76	5th, Northeast Div.	Out of Playoffs
1992-93*	84	23	17	2	...	24	10	8	...	47	27	10	...	351	300	104	2nd, Adams Div.	Lost Div. Semi-Final
1991-92*	80	18	19	3	...	2	29	9	...	20	48	12	...	255	318	52	5th, Adams Div.	Out of Playoffs
1990-91*	80	9	23	8	...	7	27	6	...	16	50	14	...	236	354	46	5th, Adams Div.	Out of Playoffs
1989-90*	80	8	26	6	...	4	35	1	...	12	61	7	...	240	407	31	5th, Adams Div.	Out of Playoffs
1988-89*	80	16	20	4	...	11	26	3	...	27	46	7	...	269	342	61	5th, Adams Div.	Out of Playoffs
1987-88*	80	15	23	2	...	17	20	3	...	32	43	5	...	271	306	69	5th, Adams Div.	Out of Playoffs
1986-87*	80	20	13	7	...	11	26	3	...	31	39	10	...	267	276	72	4th, Adams Div.	Lost Div. Final
1985-86*	80	23	13	4	...	20	18	2	...	43	31	6	...	330	289	92	1st, Adams Div.	Lost Div. Semi-Final
1984-85*	80	24	12	4	...	17	18	5	...	41	30	9	...	323	275	91	2nd, Adams Div.	Lost Conf. Championship
1983-84*	80	24	11	5	...	18	17	5	...	42	28	10	...	360	278	94	3rd, Adams Div.	Lost Div. Final
1982-83*	80	23	10	7	...	11	24	5	...	34	34	12	...	343	336	80	4th, Adams Div.	Lost Div. Semi-Final
1981-82*	80	24	13	3	...	9	18	13	...	33	31	16	...	356	345	82	4th, Adams Div.	Lost Conf. Championship
1980-81*	80	18	11	11	...	12	21	7	...	30	32	18	...	314	318	78	4th, Adams Div.	Lost Prelim. Round
1979-80*	80	17	16	7	...	8	28	4	...	25	44	11	...	248	313	61	5th, Adams Div.	Out of Playoffs

* Quebec Nordiques

2004-05 Player Personnel

FORWARDS	HT	WT	S	Place of Birth	Date	2003-04 Club
BALA, Chris	6-1	196	L	Alexandria, VA	9/24/78	Houston-Hershey
BONVIE, Dennis	5-11	205	R	Antigonish, N.S.	7/23/73	Colorado-Binghamton-Hershey
DARCHE, Mathieu	6-1	210	L	St. Laurent, Que.	11/26/76	Nashville-Milwaukee
FORSBERG, Peter	6-0	205	L	Ornskoldsvik, Sweden	7/20/73	Colorado
GRATTON, Chris	6-4	225	L	Brantford, Ont.	7/5/75	Phoenix-Colorado
HAHL, Riku	6-1	205	L	Hameenlinna, Finland	11/1/80	Colorado
HEJDUK, Milan	5-11	185	R	Usti-nad-Labem, Czech.	2/14/76	Colorado
HENDRICKSON, Darby	6-1	195	L	Richfield, MN	8/28/72	Min-Houston-Col
HINOTE, Dan	6-0	190	R	Leesburg, FL	1/30/77	Colorado
KLYAZMIN, Sergei	6-4	200	L	Moscow, USSR	1/3/82	Did Not Play - Injured
KONOWALCHUK, Steve	6-2	207	L	Salt Lake City, UT	11/11/72	Washington-Colorado
LAAKSONEN, Antti	6-0	180	L	Tammela, Finland	10/3/73	Minnesota
LAPERRIERE, Ian	6-1	201	R	Montreal, Que.	1/19/74	Los Angeles
McCORMICK, Cody	6-2	200	R	London, Ont.	4/18/83	Colorado-Hershey
McLEAN, Brett	5-11	194	L	Comox, B.C.	8/14/78	Chicago-Norfolk
SAKIC, Joe	5-11	195	L	Burnaby, B.C.	7/7/69	Colorado
SAVAGE, Andre	6-0	195	R	Ottawa, Ont.	5/27/75	Phi (AHL)-Prov (AHL)
SKLADANY, Frantisek	6-0	185	L	Martin, Czech.	4/22/82	Boston University
STEEVES, Ryan	6-0	195	L	Ottawa, Ont.	12/31/82	Yale
SVAGROVSKY, David	6-3	205	R	Prague, Czech.	12/21/84	Seattle
SVATOS, Marek	5-9	170	R	Kosice, Czech.	6/17/82	Colorado
TANGUAY, Alex	6-0	190	L	Ste-Justine, Que.	11/21/79	Colorado
ULMER, Jeff	5-11	195	R	Wilcox, Sask.	4/27/77	Cardiff-Lukko
WORRELL, Peter	6-6	235	L	Pierrefonds, Que.	8/18/77	Colorado
DEFENSEMEN						
BLAKE, Rob	6-4	225	R	Simcoe, Ont.	12/10/69	Colorado
BOUGHNER, Bob	6-0	203	R	Windsor, Ont.	3/8/71	Carolina-Colorado
BOYCHUK, Johnny	6-2	215	R	Edmonton, Alta.	1/19/84	Moose Jaw
CLARK, Brett	6-1	195	L	Wapella, Sask.	12/23/76	Colorado-Hershey
FINGER, Jeff	6-2	195	L	Hancock, MI	12/18/79	Reading-Hershey
FOOTE, Adam	6-2	215	R	Toronto, Ont.	7/10/71	Colorado
LILES, John-Michael	5-10	185	L	Zionsville, IN	11/25/80	Colorado
SAUER, Kurt	6-4	225	L	St. Cloud, MN	1/16/81	Anaheim-Colorado
SAVIELS, Agris	6-1	210	L	Riga, Latvia	1/15/82	Hershey
SKRASTINS, Karlis	6-1	212	L	Riga, USSR	7/9/74	Colorado
SLOVAK, Tomas	6-1	203	R	Kosice, Czech.	4/5/83	Hershey-Reading
SMITH, D.J.	6-1	205	L	Windsor, Ont.	5/13/77	Hershey
VAANANEN, Ossi	6-4	215	L	Vantaa, Finland	8/18/80	Phoenix-Colorado
VIITANEN, Mikko	6-3	220	L	Rajamaki, Finland	2/18/82	Hershey-Reading
GOALTENDERS	**HT**	**WT**	**C**	**Place of Birth**	**Date**	**2003-04 Club**
AEBISCHER, David	6-1	190	L	Fribourg, Switz.	2/7/78	Colorado
BUDAJ, Peter	6-1	200	L	Bystrica, Czech.	9/18/82	Hershey
SAUVE, Philippe	6-0	180	L	Buffalo, NY	2/27/80	Colorado-Hershey
WEIMAN, Tyler	5-11	160	L	Saskatoon, Sask.	6/5/84	Tri-City

Coaching History

Jacques Demers, 1979-80; Maurice Filion and Michel Bergeron, 1980-81; Michel Bergeron, 1981-82 to 1986-87; Andre Savard and Ron Lapointe, 1987-88; Ron Lapointe and Jean Perron, 1988-89; Michel Bergeron, 1989-90; Dave Chambers, 1990-91; Dave Chambers and Pierre Page, 1991-92; Pierre Page, 1992-93, 1993-94; Marc Crawford, 1994-95 to 1997-98; Bob Hartley, 1998-99 to 2001-02; Bob Hartley and Tony Granato, 2002-03; Tony Granato, 2003-04; Joel Quenneville, 2004-05.

Coach

QUENNEVILLE, JOEL
Coach, Colorado Avalanche. Born in Windsor, Ont., September 15, 1958.

Joel Quenneville returned to the franchise where he began his NHL coaching career in 1994-95 when he was named the fourth head coach in Colorado Avalanche, and the 12th in franchise, history on July 7, 2004.

The former Colorado Rockies defenseman was the winningest coach in St. Louis Blues history, compiling a 307-209-77 record while spending 593 regular-season games behind the St. Louis bench, the most of any Blues coach. He reached the personal milestone of 500 career games coached on January 23, 2003 versus Chicago.

Under his guidance, the Blues reached the Western Conference Finals in 2001, the first time the team had done so since 1986, and won the Presidents' Trophy in 1999-2000 with a league-leading and franchise-high 114 points. He served as head coach of the North American All-Stars at the 2001 All-Star Game in Denver, and was named the NHL's coach of the year for 1999-00, capturing the Jack Adams Award.

The former NHL defenseman spent two-and-a-half seasons with the Colorado Avalanche/Quebec Nordiques as an assistant coach prior to being named the Blues' head coach on January 6, 1997. He was instrumental in the Avs' drive for their first Stanley Cup in 1996. He retired as an active player after the 1991-92 season, when he served as a player-coach for the St. John's Maple Leafs (AHL). Quenneville played 13 seasons in the NHL, closing out his career with 54 goals and 136 assists for 190 points adding 705 penalty minutes in 803 games played with Hartford, Washington, New Jersey, Toronto, and the Colorado Rockies. A short time later, he received his first coaching opportunity with the Springfield Indians (AHL) in 1993-94.

Coaching Record

		Regular Season				Playoffs		
Season	Team	Games	W	L	T	Games	W	L
1993-94	Springfield (AHL)	80	29	38	13	6	2	4
1996-97	**St. Louis (NHL)**	**40**	**18**	**15**	**7**	**6**	**2**	**4**
1997-98	**St. Louis (NHL)**	**82**	**45**	**29**	**8**	**10**	**6**	**4**
1998-99	**St. Louis (NHL)**	**82**	**37**	**32**	**13**	**13**	**6**	**7**
1999-2000	**St. Louis (NHL)**	**82**	**51**	**20**	**11**	**7**	**3**	**4**
2000-01	**St. Louis (NHL)**	**82**	**43**	**27**	**12**	**15**	**9**	**6**
2001-02	**St. Louis (NHL)**	**82**	**43**	**31**	**8**	**10**	**5**	**5**
2002-03	**St. Louis (NHL)**	**82**	**41**	**30**	**11**	**7**	**3**	**4**
2003-04	**St. Louis (NHL)**	**61**	**29**	**25**	**7**	....	....	....
	NHL Totals	**593**	**307**	**209**	**77**	**68**	**34**	**34**

2003-04 Scoring

* - rookie

Regular Season

Pos	#	Player	Team	GP	G	A	Pts	+/-	PIM	PP	SH	GW	GT	S	%
C	19	Joe Sakic	COL	81	33	54	87	11	42	13	1	3	1	253	13.0
L	18	Alex Tanguay	COL	69	25	54	79	30	42	7	0	5	0	117	21.4
R	23	Milan Hejduk	COL	82	35	40	75	19	20	16	0	6	0	237	14.8
C	21	Peter Forsberg	COL	39	18	37	55	16	30	3	1	5	0	85	21.2
D	4	Rob Blake	COL	74	13	33	46	6	61	8	0	3	0	242	5.4
R	38	Matthew Barnaby	NYR	69	12	20	32	15	120	0	0	1	1	80	15.0
			COL	13	4	5	9	3	37	1	0	2	0	24	16.7
			TOTAL	82	16	25	41	18	157	1	0	3	1	104	15.4
L	22	Steve Konowalchuk	WSH	6	0	1	1	–5	0	0	0	0	0	7	0.0
			COL	76	19	20	39	2	70	3	0	3	1	145	13.1
			TOTAL	82	19	21	40	–3	70	3	0	3	1	152	12.5
L	9	Paul Kariya	COL	51	11	25	36	–5	22	5	1	1	0	110	10.0
D	26 *	John-Michael Liles	COL	79	10	24	34	7	28	2	0	1	2	115	8.7
R	8	Teemu Selanne	COL	78	16	16	32	2	32	6	1	4	0	182	8.8
C	24	Chris Gratton	PHX	68	11	18	29	–19	93	3	0	1	0	122	9.0
			COL	13	2	1	3	1	18	0	0	0	0	28	7.1
			TOTAL	81	13	19	32	–18	111	3	0	1	0	150	8.7
D	52	Adam Foote	COL	73	8	22	30	13	87	5	0	1	1	105	7.6
D	3	Karlis Skrastins	COL	82	5	8	13	18	26	0	1	1	0	102	4.9
C	11	Andrei Nikolishin	COL	49	5	7	12	3	24	1	0	0	0	71	7.0
C	36 *	Steve Moore	COL	57	5	7	12	–5	37	0	0	1	0	52	9.6
R	13	Dan Hinote	COL	59	4	7	11	–6	57	0	2	0	0	53	7.5
L	60	Travis Brigley	COL	36	3	4	7	0	10	1	0	0	0	39	7.7
D	27	Ossi Vaananen	PHX	67	2	4	6	–10	87	0	0	1	0	39	5.1
			COL	12	0	0	0	–4	2	0	0	0	0	6	0.0
			TOTAL	79	2	4	6	–14	89	0	0	1	0	45	4.4
D	34	Kurt Sauer	ANA	55	1	4	5	–8	32	0	0	0	0	32	3.1
			COL	14	0	1	1	–3	19	0	0	0	0	12	0.0
			TOTAL	69	1	5	6	–11	51	0	0	0	0	44	2.3
C	7	Darby Hendrickson	MIN	14	1	0	1	–7	6	0	0	0	0	14	7.1
			COL	20	1	3	4	–8	6	0	0	0	0	21	4.8
			TOTAL	34	2	3	5	–15	12	0	0	0	0	35	5.7
C	20 *	Cody Mccormick	COL	44	2	3	5	–4	73	0	0	1	0	33	6.1
D	6	Bob Boughner	CAR	43	0	5	5	–9	80	0	0	0	0	26	0.0
			COL	11	0	0	0	–1	8	0	0	0	0	8	0.0
			TOTAL	54	0	5	5	–10	88	0	0	0	0	34	0.0
L	28	Peter Worrell	COL	49	3	1	4	2	179	0	0	0	0	32	9.4
R	17	Jim Cummins	COL	55	1	2	3	–5	147	0	0	1	0	25	4.0
R	40 *	Marek Svatos	COL	4	2	0	2	1	0	1	0	1	0	6	33.3
D	5	Brett Clark	COL	12	1	1	2	3	6	0	0	0	0	14	7.1
C	38 *	Charlie Stephens	COL	6	0	2	2	–1	4	0	0	0	0	1	0.0
C	32	Riku Hahl	COL	28	0	1	1	–7	12	0	0	0	0	40	0.0
R	37	Dennis Bonvie	COL	1	0	0	0	0	0	0	0	0	0	1	0.0
L	43 *	Mikhail Kuleshov	COL	3	0	0	0	–1	0	0	0	0	0	4	0.0
L	37 *	Jordan Krestanovich	COL	14	0	0	0	0	6	0	0	0	0	25	0.0

Goaltending

No.	Goaltender	GPI	Mins	Avg	W	L	T	EN	SO	GA	SA	S%	G	A	PIM
1	David Aebischer	62	3703	2.09	32	19	9	5	4	129	1703	.924	0	1	4
35	Tommy Salo	5	304	2.37	1	3	1	0	0	12	136	.912	0	0	0
30	* Philippe Sauve	17	986	3.04	7	7	3	2	0	50	479	.896	0	0	2
	Totals	**82**	**5018**	**2.37**	**40**	**29**	**13**	**7**	**4**	**198**	**2325**	**.915**			

Playoffs

Pos	#	Player	Team	GP	G	A	Pts	+/-	PIM	PP	SH	GW	GT	S	%
C	19	Joe Sakic	COL	11	7	5	12	0	8	1	1	2	2	35	20.0
C	21	Peter Forsberg	COL	11	4	7	11	6	12	1	0	1	0	16	25.0
R	23	Milan Hejduk	COL	11	5	2	7	6	0	2	0	0	0	30	16.7
R	40 *	Marek Svatos	COL	11	1	5	6	3	2	0	0	1	1	25	4.0
D	4	Rob Blake	COL	9	0	5	5	0	6	0	0	0	0	17	0.0
L	22	Steve Konowalchuk	COL	11	4	0	4	–4	12	4	0	1	0	25	16.0
L	18	Alex Tanguay	COL	8	2	2	4	1	2	1	0	1	0	6	33.3
D	6	Bob Boughner	COL	11	0	4	4	5	6	0	0	0	0	13	0.0
D	52	Adam Foote	COL	11	0	4	4	–2	10	0	0	0	0	6	0.0
R	8	Teemu Selanne	COL	10	0	3	3	–2	2	0	0	0	0	9	0.0
C	11	Andrei Nikolishin	COL	11	0	2	2	–3	4	0	0	0	0	7	0.0
R	38	Matthew Barnaby	COL	11	0	2	2	–3	27	0	0	0	0	10	0.0
D	3	Karlis Skrastins	COL	11	0	2	2	–2	2	0	0	0	0	14	0.0
C	7	Darby Hendrickson	COL	6	1	0	1	–1	2	0	0	0	0	5	20.0
C	32	Riku Hahl	COL	7	1	0	1	0	2	0	0	0	0	12	8.3
R	13	Dan Hinote	COL	11	1	0	1	2	0	0	1	0	0	15	6.7
L	9	Paul Kariya	COL	1	0	1	1	–1	0	0	0	0	0	2	0.0
D	27	Ossi Vaananen	COL	11	0	1	1	3	18	0	0	0	0	4	0.0
D	26 *	John-Michael Liles	COL	11	0	1	1	1	4	0	0	0	0	21	0.0
D	34	Kurt Sauer	COL	3	0	0	0	0	0	0	0	0	0	1	0.0
C	24	Chris Gratton	COL	11	0	0	0	–1	27	0	0	0	0	12	0.0

Goaltending

No.	Goaltender	GPI	Mins	Avg	W	L	EN	SO	GA	SA	S%	G	A	PIM
35	Tommy Salo	1	27	0.00	0	0	0	0	0	7	1.000	0	0	2
1	David Aebischer	11	662	2.08	6	5	1	1	23	295	.922	0	0	2
	Totals	**11**	**695**	**2.07**	**6**	**5**	**1**	**1**	**24**	**303**	**.921**			

Captains' History

Marc Tardif, 1979-80, 1980-81; Robbie Ftorek and Andre Dupont, 1981-82; Mario Marois, 1982-83 to 1984-85; Mario Marois and Peter Stastny, 1985-86; Peter Stastny, 1986-87 to 1989-90; Joe Sakic and Steven Finn, 1990-91; Mike Hough, 1991-92; Joe Sakic, 1992-93 to date.

Club Records

Team

(Figures in brackets for season records are games played; records for fewest points, wins, ties, losses, goals, goals against are for 70 or more games)

Most Points **118** 2000-01 (82)
Most Wins **52** 2000-01 (82)
Most Ties **18** 1980-81 (80)
Most Losses **61** 1989-90 (80)
Most Goals **360** 1983-84 (80)
Most Goals Against **407** 1989-90 (80)
Fewest Points **31** 1989-90 (80)
Fewest Wins **12** 1989-90 (80)
Fewest Ties **5** 1987-88 (80)
Fewest Losses **16** 2000-01 (82)
Fewest Goals **212** 2001-02 (82)
Fewest Goals Against **169** 2001-02 (82)
Longest Winning Streak
Overall .... **12** Jan. 10-Feb. 7/99
Home .... **10** Nov. 26/83-Jan. 10/84, Mar. 6-Apr. 16/95
Away .... **7** Jan. 10-Feb. 7/99
Longest Undefeated Streak
Overall .... **12** Dec. 23/96-Jan. 20/97 (9 wins, 3 ties), Jan. 10-Feb. 7/99 (12 wins)
Home .... **14** Nov. 19/83-Jan. 21/84 (11 wins, 3 ties)
Away .... **10** Jan. 10-Mar. 3/99 (8 wins, 2 ties)
Longest Losing Streak
Overall .... **14** Oct. 21-Nov. 19/90
Home .... **8** Oct. 21-Nov. 24/90
Away .... **18** Jan. 18-Apr. 1/90
Longest Winless Streak
Overall .... **17** Oct. 21-Nov. 25/90 (15 losses, 2 ties)
Home .... **11** Nov. 14-Dec. 26/89 (7 losses, 4 ties)
Away .... **33** Oct. 8/91-Feb. 27/92 (25 losses, 8 ties)
Most Shutouts, Season **11** 2001-02 (82)
Most PIM, Season **2,104** 1989-90 (80)
Most Goals, Game .... **12** Three times

Individual

Most Seasons .... **16** Joe Sakic
Most Games .... **1,155** Joe Sakic
Most Goals, Career .... **542** Joe Sakic
Most Assists, Career .... **860** Joe Sakic
Most Points, Career .... **1,402** Joe Sakic (542G, 860A)
Most PIM, Career .... **1,562** Dale Hunter
Most Shutouts, Career .... **37** Patrick Roy
Longest Consecutive Games Streak .... **312** Dale Hunter (Oct. 9/80-Mar. 13/84)
Most Goals, Season .... **57** Michel Goulet (1982-83)
Most Assists, Season .... **93** Peter Stastny (1981-82)
Most Points, Season .... **139** Peter Stastny (1981-82; 46G, 93A)
Most PIM, Season .... **301** Gord Donnelly (1987-88)
Most Points, Defenseman, Season .... **82** Steve Duchesne (1992-93; 20G, 62A)
Most Points, Center, Season .... **139** Peter Stastny (1981-82; 46G, 93A)
Most Points, Right Wing, Season .... **103** Jacques Richard (1980-81; 52G, 51A)
Most Points, Left Wing, Season .... **121** Michel Goulet (1983-84; 56G, 65A)
Most Points, Rookie, Season .... **109** Peter Stastny (1980-81; 39G, 70A)
Most Shutouts, Season .... **9** Patrick Roy (2001-02)
Most Goals, Game .... **5** Mats Sundin (Mar. 5/92), Mike Ricci (Feb. 17/94)
Most Assists, Game .... **5** Six times
Most Points, Game .... **8** Peter Stastny (Feb. 22/81; 4G, 4A), Anton Stastny (Feb. 22/81; 3G, 5A)

Records include Quebec Nordiques, 1979-80 through 1994-95.

Retired Numbers

3	J.C. Tremblay*	1972-1979
8	Marc Tardif*	1979-1983
16	Michel Goulet*	1979-1990
77	Raymond Bourque	2000-2001

* Quebec Nordiques

All-time Record vs. Other Clubs

Regular Season

	At Home								On Road								Total							
	GP	W	L	T	OL	GF	GA	PTS	GP	W	L	T	OL	GF	GA	PTS	GP	W	L	T	OL	GF	GA	PTS
Anaheim	21	11	5	4	1	65	53	27	21	11	5	3	2	53	48	27	42	22	10	7	3	118	101	54
Atlanta	4	2	1	0	1	17	10	5	4	2	1	1	0	8	7	5	8	4	2	1	1	25	17	10
Boston	66	24	36	6	0	234	271	54	62	22	31	9	0	192	240	53	128	46	67	15	0	426	511	107
Buffalo	64	31	21	11	1	227	197	74	63	18	35	9	1	204	247	46	127	49	56	20	2	431	444	120
Calgary	47	18	18	11	0	165	154	47	47	18	20	9	0	141	160	45	94	36	38	20	0	306	314	92
Carolina	65	39	17	9	0	274	191	87	62	26	24	12	0	214	203	64	127	65	41	21	0	488	394	151
Chicago	39	21	12	6	0	158	124	48	41	17	21	3	0	130	144	37	80	38	33	9	0	288	268	85
Columbus	8	8	0	0	0	38	10	16	8	6	0	1	1	31	13	14	16	14	0	1	1	69	23	30
Dallas	41	23	11	7	0	150	103	53	41	15	20	5	1	115	131	36	82	38	31	12	1	265	234	89
Detroit	42	20	17	4	1	148	142	45	40	15	23	1	1	120	142	32	82	35	40	5	2	268	284	77
Edmonton	47	24	19	4	0	179	169	52	46	17	24	4	1	137	186	39	93	41	43	8	1	316	355	91
Florida	11	4	4	3	0	30	27	11	11	10	1	0	0	48	30	20	22	14	5	3	0	78	57	31
Los Angeles	42	23	16	3	0	169	140	49	43	13	25	5	0	137	176	31	85	36	41	8	0	306	316	80
Minnesota	11	8	1	2	0	36	22	18	10	6	1	1	2	36	21	15	21	14	2	3	2	72	43	33
Montreal	63	32	26	5	0	216	222	69	64	16	38	10	0	198	261	42	127	48	64	15	0	414	483	111
Nashville	12	6	3	2	1	32	24	15	12	6	2	3	1	45	36	16	24	12	5	5	2	77	60	31
New Jersey	35	18	13	4	0	124	98	40	36	13	19	4	0	121	147	30	71	31	32	8	0	245	245	70
NY Islanders	34	20	11	3	0	123	97	43	32	13	18	1	0	109	129	27	66	33	29	4	0	232	226	70
NY Rangers	35	19	13	3	0	143	130	41	34	11	19	4	0	99	134	26	69	30	32	7	0	242	264	67
Ottawa	15	12	2	1	0	70	41	25	18	7	8	3	0	64	53	17	33	19	10	4	0	134	94	42
Philadelphia	35	12	10	12	1	124	122	37	34	10	21	2	1	91	122	23	69	22	31	14	2	215	244	60
Phoenix	41	21	15	5	0	142	133	47	40	17	15	7	1	142	144	42	81	38	30	12	1	284	277	89
Pittsburgh	32	17	13	2	0	142	122	36	37	17	15	5	0	152	145	39	69	34	28	7	0	294	267	75
St. Louis	41	20	13	7	1	138	111	48	40	14	22	4	0	124	148	32	81	34	35	11	1	262	259	80
San Jose	23	14	4	4	1	82	42	33	24	16	7	1	0	89	65	33	47	30	11	5	1	171	107	66
Tampa Bay	13	8	3	2	0	50	28	18	12	3	8	1	0	32	39	7	25	11	11	3	0	82	67	25
Toronto	29	17	7	5	0	111	87	39	35	15	16	4	0	133	118	34	64	32	23	9	0	244	205	73
Vancouver	47	22	17	8	0	157	133	52	47	23	16	7	1	181	153	54	94	45	33	15	1	338	286	106
Washington	34	15	14	5	0	105	116	35	33	11	18	4	0	105	131	26	67	26	32	9	0	210	247	61
Totals	**997**	**509**	**342**	**138**	**8**	**3649**	**3119**	**1164**	**997**	**388**	**473**	**123**	**13**	**3251**	**3573**	**912**	**1994**	**897**	**815**	**261**	**21**	**6900**	**6692**	**2076**

Playoffs

	Series	W	L	GP	W	L	T	GF	GA	Last Mtg.	Rnd.	Result
Boston	2	1	1	11	5	6	0	36	37	1983	DSF	L 1-3
Buffalo	2	2	0	8	6	2	0	35	27	1985	DSF	W 3-2
Chicago	2	2	0	12	8	4	0	49	28	1997	CQF	W 4-2
Dallas	3	1	2	19	10	9	0	48	47	2004	CQF	W 4-1
Detroit	5	3	2	30	17	13	0	79	76	2002	CF	L 3-4
Edmonton	2	1	1	12	7	5	0	35	30	1998	CQF	L 3-4
Florida	1	1	0	4	4	0	0	15	4	1996	F	W 4-0
Hartford	2	1	1	9	4	5	0	34	35	1987	DSF	W 4-2
Los Angeles	2	2	0	14	8	6	0	33	23	2002	CQF	W 4-3
Minnesota	1	0	1	7	3	4	0	17	16	2003	CQF	L 3-4
Montreal	5	2	3	31	14	17	0	85	105	1993	DSF	L 2-4
New Jersey	1	1	0	7	4	3	0	19	11	2001	F	W 4-3
NY Islanders	1	0	1	4	0	4	0	9	18	1982	CF	L 0-4
NY Rangers	1	0	1	6	2	4	0	19	25	1995	CQF	L 2-4
Philadelphia	2	0	2	11	4	7	0	29	39	1985	CF	L 2-4
Phoenix	1	1	0	5	4	1	0	17	10	2000	CQF	W 4-1
St. Louis	1	1	0	5	4	1	0	17	11	2001	CF	W 4-1
San Jose	3	2	1	19	10	9	0	51	52	2004	CSF	L 2-4
Vancouver	2	2	0	10	8	2	0	40	26	2001	CQF	W 4-0
Totals	**39**	**23**	**16**	**224**	**122**	**102**	**0**	**667**	**620**			

Calgary totals include Atlanta Flames, 1979-80.
Dallas totals include Minnesota North Stars, 1979-80 to 1992-93.
Phoenix totals include Winnipeg, 1979-80 to 1995-96.

Playoff Results 2004-2000

Year	Round	Opponent	Result	GF	GA
2004	CSF	San Jose	L 2-4	7	14
	CQF	Dallas	W 4-1	19	10
2003	CQF	Minnesota	L 3-4	17	16
2002	CF	Detroit	L 3-4	13	22
	CSF	San Jose	W 4-3	25	21
	CQF	Los Angeles	W 4-3	16	13
2001	**F**	**New Jersey**	**W 4-3**	**19**	**11**
	CF	St. Louis	W 4-1	17	11
	CSF	Los Angeles	W 4-3	17	10
	CQF	Vancouver	W 4-0	16	9
2000	CF	Dallas	L 3-4	13	14
	CSF	Detroit	W 4-1	13	8
	CQF	Phoenix	W 4-1	17	10

Abbreviations: Round: F - Final; **CF** - conference final; **CSF** - conference semi-final; **CQF** - conference quarter-final; **DSF** - division semi-final.

Carolina totals include Hartford, 1979-80 to 1996-97.
New Jersey totals include Colorado Rockies, 1979-80 to 1981-82.

2003-04 Results

Oct.	10	Chicago	5-0		11	at Chicago	5-4*
	12	St. Louis	1-2		13	Anaheim	3-1
	16	at Minnesota	5-2		15	Dallas	4-1
	18	at Edmonton	3-6		17	San Jose	1-2
	21	Boston	1-4		19	at Tampa Bay	5-4*
	23	Edmonton	6-1		21	at Florida	6-5
	25	at Nashville	5-3		22	at Atlanta	1-1
	26	Buffalo	1-3		24	at Pittsburgh	5-3
	28	Calgary	4-2		27	Edmonton	3-1
Nov.	1	at New Jersey	3-4		29	at Los Angeles	3-3
	2	at NY Rangers	3-2*		30	at Anaheim	3-4*
	4	Minnesota	4-4	**Feb.**	3	Carolina	3-1
	6	Phoenix	2-1		5	Detroit	2-3*
	9	at Chicago	4-3*		10	NY Islanders	1-1
	11	at San Jose	4-3		12	at St. Louis	4-0
	13	at Phoenix	2-3*		14	at Detroit	5-2
	15	Dallas	3-0		16	Vancouver	0-1
	18	Anaheim	2-1*		18	Edmonton	1-5
	20	NY Rangers	4-3		20	at Dallas	1-5
	22	Los Angeles	0-2		22	at Minnesota	3-1
	24	Nashville	2-3		24	Calgary	0-2
	27	at Calgary	6-5*		26	St. Louis	2-2
	28	at Edmonton	4-1		28	at Columbus	4-5*
	30	New Jersey	1-1	**Mar.**	1	Tampa Bay	0-3
Dec.	4	at San Jose	2-2		3	Vancouver	5-5
	6	Columbus	5-1		5	San Jose	5-1
	8	Washington	4-1		7	Calgary	1-7
	11	at Vancouver	1-1		8	at Vancouver	9-2
	13	at Calgary	1-1		10	at Edmonton	3-2*
	17	Minnesota	2-3		12	at Phoenix	3-2
	19	at Anaheim	0-1		14	Phoenix	4-1
	20	at Los Angeles	3-3		16	at Montreal	2-4
	26	at St. Louis	3-3		18	at Ottawa	0-2
	27	Philadelphia	3-2*		20	at Toronto	2-5
	29	Vancouver	2-3		23	Chicago	2-2
	31	at Calgary	2-1		25	Detroit	1-3
Jan.	2	at Vancouver	4-2		27	at Detroit	0-2
	4	Minnesota	3-1		29	Los Angeles	2-1
	6	Columbus	6-0		31	at Minnesota	4-5*
	8	at Nashville	3-4*	**Apr.**	2	at Columbus	4-2
	10	at Dallas	4-2		4	Nashville	1-2*

* – Overtime

Entry Draft
Selections 2004-1990

2004
Pick
- 21 Wojtek Wolski
- 55 Victor Oreskovich
- 72 Denis Parshin
- 154 Richard Demen-Willaume
- 184 Derek Peltier
- 215 Ian Keserich
- 239 Brandon Yip
- 249 J.D. Corbin
- 281 Stephen Mcclellan

2003
Pick
- 63 David Liffiton
- 131 David Svagrovsky
- 146 Mark McCutcheon
- 163 Brad Richardson
- 204 Linus Videll
- 225 Brett Hemingway
- 257 Darryl Yacboski
- 288 David Jones

2002
Pick
- 28 Jonas Johansson
- 61 Johnny Boychuk
- 94 Eric Lundberg
- 107 Mikko Kalteva
- 129 Tom Gilbert
- 164 Tyler Weiman
- 195 Taylor Christie
- 227 Ryan Steeves
- 258 Sergei Shemetov
- 289 Sean Collins

2001
Pick
- 63 Peter Budaj
- 97 Danny Bois
- 130 Colt King
- 143 Frantisek Skladany
- 144 Cody McCormick
- 149 Mikko Viitanen
- 165 Pierre-Luc Emond
- 184 Scott Horvath
- 196 Charlie Stephens
- 227 Marek Svatos

2000
Pick
- 14 Vaclav Nedorost
- 47 Jared Aulin
- 50 Sergei Soin
- 63 Agris Saviels
- 88 Kurt Sauer
- 92 Sergei Klyazmin
- 119 Brian Fahey
- 159 John-Michael Liles
- 189 Chris Bahen
- 221 Aaron Molnar
- 252 Darryl Bootland
- 266 Sean Kotary
- 285 Blake Ward

1999
Pick
- 25 Mikhail Kuleshov
- 45 Martin Grenier
- 93 Branko Radivojevic
- 112 Sanny Lindstrom
- 122 Kristian Kovac
- 142 Will Magnuson
- 152 Jordan Krestanovich
- 158 Anders Lovdahl
- 183 Riku Hahl
- 212 Radim Vrbata
- 240 Jeff Finger

1998
Pick
- 12 Alex Tanguay
- 17 Martin Skoula
- 19 Robyn Regehr
- 20 Scott Parker
- 28 Ramzi Abid
- 38 Philippe Sauve
- 53 Steve Moore
- 79 Yevgeny Lazarev
- 141 K.C. Timmons
- 167 Alexander Riazantsev

1997
Pick
- 26 Kevin Grimes
- 53 Graham Belak
- 55 Rick Berry
- 78 Ville Nieminen
- 87 Brad Larsen
- 133 Aaron Miskovich
- 161 David Aebischer
- 217 Doug Schmidt
- 243 Kyle Kidney
- 245 Stephen Lafleur

1996
Pick
- 25 Peter Ratchuk
- 51 Yuri Babenko
- 79 Mark Parrish
- 98 Ben Storey
- 107 Randy Petruk
- 134 Luke Curtin
- 146 Brian Willsie
- 160 Kai Fischer
- 167 Dan Hinote
- 176 Samuel Pahlsson
- 188 Roman Pylner
- 214 Matt Scorsune
- 240 Justin Clark

1995
Pick
- 25 Marc Denis
- 51 Nic Beaudoin
- 77 John Tripp
- 81 Tomi Kallio
- 129 Brent Johnson
- 155 John Cirjak
- 181 Dan Smith
- 207 Tomi Hirvonen
- 228 Chris George

1994
Pick
- 12 Wade Belak
- 22 Jeffrey Kealty
- 35 Josef Marha
- 61 Sebastien Bety
- 72 Chris Drury
- 87 Milan Hejduk
- 113 Tony Tuzzolino
- 139 Nicholas Windsor
- 165 Calvin Elfring
- 191 Jay Bertsch
- 217 Tim Thomas
- 243 Chris Pittman
- 285 Steven Low

1993
Pick
- 10 Jocelyn Thibault
- 14 Adam Deadmarsh
- 49 Ashley Buckberger
- 75 Bill Pierce
- 101 Ryan Tocher
- 127 Anders Myrvold
- 137 Nicholas Checco
- 153 Christian Matte
- 179 David Ling
- 205 Petr Franek
- 231 Vincent Auger
- 257 Mark Pivetz
- 283 John Hillman

1992
Pick
- 4 Todd Warriner
- 28 Paul Brousseau
- 29 Tuomas Gronman
- 52 Manny Fernandez
- 76 Ian McIntyre
- 100 Charlie Wasley
- 124 Paxton Schulte
- 148 Martin Lepage
- 172 Mike Jickling
- 196 Steve Passmore
- 220 Anson Carter
- 244 Aaron Ellis

1991
Pick
- 1 Eric Lindros
- 24 Rene Corbet
- 46 Rich Brennan
- 68 Dave Karpa
- 90 Patrick Labrecque
- 103 Bill Lindsay
- 134 Mikael Johansson
- 156 Janne Laukkanen
- 157 Aaron Asp
- 178 Adam Bartell
- 188 Brent Brekke
- 200 Paul Koch
- 222 Doug Friedman
- 244 Eric Meloche

1990
Pick
- 1 Owen Nolan
- 22 Ryan Hughes
- 43 Brad Zavisha
- 106 Jeff Parrott
- 127 Dwayne Norris
- 148 Andrei Kovalenko
- 158 Alexander Karpovtsev
- 169 Pat Mazzoli
- 190 Scott Davis
- 211 Mika Stromberg
- 232 Wade Klippenstein

General Managers' History
Maurice Filion, 1979-80 to 1987-88; Martin Madden, 1988-89; Martin Madden and Maurice Filion, 1989-90; Pierre Page, 1990-91 to 1993-94; Pierre Lacroix, 1994-95 to date.

President and General Manager

LACROIX, PIERRE
President/General Manager, Colorado Avalanche.
Born in Montreal, Que., August 3, 1948.
Pierre Lacroix was appointed to the general manager's post on May 24, 1994 after 21 years as a respected player agent. In his first season as general manager, his leadership was instrumental in moving the team from 11th to second place in the NHL. Lacroix's second season began with the club's move to Denver. The revamped Avs finished atop the Pacific Division and went on to win the Stanley Cup. He was named NHL executive of the year by *The Hockey News* and became president of the club's hockey operations in August, 1995. The Avalanche have continued to rank among the NHL's top teams, and won the Stanley Cup again in 2001. Colorado won its record-setting ninth consecutive division title in 2002-03.

Club Directory

Pepsi Center

Colorado Avalanche
Pepsi Center
1000 Chopper Circle
Denver, CO 80204
Phone **303/405-1100**
FAX 303/893-0614
Press Box 303/575-1926
www.coloradoavalanche.com
Capacity: 18,007

Owner & Governor . . . . E. Stanley Kroenke
Alternate Governor, President & General Manager . Pierre Lacroix
Head Coach . . . . Joel Quenneville
Assistant Coach . . . . Tony Granato
Assistant Coach . . . . Jacques Cloutier
Vice President of Player Personnel . . . . Michel Goulet
Assistant to the General Manager . . . . Greg Sherman
Director of Hockey Operations . . . . Eric Lacroix
Director of Player Development/
  Goaltending Consultant . . . . Craig Billington
Director of Hockey Administration . . . . Charlotte Grahame
Video Coordinator . . . . Mike McCready
Team Services Assistant . . . . Ronnie Jameson
Hockey Administration Assistant . . . . Andrea Furness
Chief Scout . . . . Jim Hammett
Pro Scouts . . . . Brad Smith, Garth Joy
Scouts . . . . Glen Cochrane, Luc Gauthier, Jason Grahame, Alan Hepple, Chris O'Sullivan, Don Paarup, Richard Pracey
European Scouts . . . . Kiril Ladygin, Joni Lehto
Computer Research Consultant . . . . John Donohue
Strength and Conditioning Coach . . . . Paul Goldberg
Head Athletic Trainer . . . . Matthew Sokolowski
Assistant Athletic Trainer . . . . Scott Woodward
Massage Therapist . . . . Gregorio Pradera
Inventory Manager . . . . Wayne Flemming
Head Equipment Manager . . . . Mark Miller
Assistant Equipment Managers . . . . Terry Geer, Cliff Halstead

Communications Department
Senior Vice President, Communications
  & Team Services . . . . Jean Martineau
Director of Special Projects/Communications . . . . . . Hayne Ellis
Assistant Director of Media Relations . . . . Damen Zier

Team Information
Press Box Location . . . . West Side – Level P
Practice Facility . . . . South Suburban Family Sports Center
Minor League Affiliate . . . . Hershey Bears (AHL)
Television Outlet . . . . Altitude Sports and Entertainment
Radio Flagship . . . . KKFN AM-950

In his first season as a number-one goaltender, David Aebischer ranked seventh in the NHL with 32 wins. His goals-against average of 2.09 ranked sixth.

Columbus Blue Jackets

2003-04 Results: 25w-45L-8T-4OTL 62PTS.
Fourth, Central Division

Year-by-Year Record

Season	GP	Home				Road				Overall							
		W	L	T	OL	W	L	T	OL	W	L	T	OL	GF	GA	Pts.	Finished	Playoff Result
2003-04	82	17	18	4	2	8	27	4	2	25	45	8	4	177	238	62	4th, Central Div.	Out of Playoffs
2002-03	82	20	14	5	2	9	28	3	1	29	42	8	3	213	263	69	5th, Central Div.	Out of Playoffs
2001-02	82	14	18	5	4	8	29	3	1	22	47	8	5	164	255	57	5th, Central Div.	Out of Playoffs
2000-01	82	19	15	4	3	9	24	5	3	28	39	9	6	190	233	71	5th, Central Div.	Out of Playoffs

2004-05 Schedule

Oct.	Fri.	15	Buffalo
	Sat.	16	at Chicago
	Tue.	19	San Jose
	Thu.	21	Colorado
	Sat.	23	at Calgary
	Sun.	24	at Vancouver
	Tue.	26	at Edmonton
	Thu.	28	at Phoenix
	Sat.	30	at Dallas
Nov.	Mon.	1	at St. Louis
	Fri.	5	Detroit
	Sun.	7	Dallas*
	Tue.	9	Edmonton
	Fri.	12	Los Angeles
	Sat.	13	at Detroit
	Thu.	18	Phoenix
	Sat.	20	at Dallas
	Mon.	22	at Colorado
	Wed.	24	Dallas
	Fri.	26	St. Louis
Dec.	Wed.	1	at Detroit
	Fri.	3	at Calgary
	Sun.	5	at Edmonton
	Mon.	6	at Vancouver
	Thu.	9	Toronto
	Sat.	11	at St. Louis
	Sun.	12	Vancouver*
	Wed.	15	Minnesota
	Fri.	17	Phoenix
	Sun.	19	Tampa Bay*
	Thu.	23	Chicago
	Sun.	26	Pittsburgh*
	Tue.	28	Anaheim
	Wed.	29	at Atlanta
	Fri.	31	St. Louis
Jan.	Sun.	2	at Minnesota*
	Thu.	6	at NY Rangers
	Fri.	7	at Carolina
	Sun.	9	Calgary*
	Wed.	12	Chicago
	Fri.	14	Colorado
	Sat.	15	at Nashville
	Mon.	17	at Anaheim*
	Thu.	20	at San Jose
	Sat.	22	at Los Angeles
	Mon.	24	Minnesota
	Wed.	26	Montreal
	Fri.	28	at Chicago
	Sun.	30	Anaheim*
Feb.	Tue.	1	at St. Louis
	Wed.	2	at Pittsburgh
	Sat.	5	at NY Islanders*
	Tue.	8	San Jose
	Thu.	10	Nashville
	Tue.	15	Edmonton
	Thu.	17	NY Rangers
	Sun.	20	at Chicago*
	Wed.	23	Nashville
	Fri.	25	Chicago
	Sat.	26	Florida
	Mon.	28	at New Jersey
Mar.	Fri.	4	Nashville
	Sat.	5	St. Louis
	Mon.	7	at Boston
	Wed.	9	Los Angeles
	Fri.	11	Detroit
	Sat.	12	at Minnesota
	Mon.	14	at Nashville
	Wed.	16	at Washington
	Fri.	18	Vancouver
	Mon.	21	at Philadelphia
	Wed.	23	Boston
	Fri.	25	at Colorado
	Sat.	26	at San Jose
	Mon.	28	at Phoenix
	Wed.	30	Calgary
Apr.	Fri.	1	at Detroit
	Sat.	2	at Ottawa
	Tue.	5	at Nashville
	Wed.	6	Detroit
	Sat.	9	at Los Angeles*
	Sun.	10	at Anaheim*

* Denotes afternoon game.

Franchise date: June 25, 1997

5th NHL Season

CENTRAL DIVISION

At 19 years, 10 months, Rick Nash became the first teenager to reach the 40-goal plateau since Jimmy Carson in 1987-88. Nash is the youngest player to lead the NHL in goals, moving past Wayne Gretzky who topped the league at age 21 in 1981-82.

2004-05 Player Personnel

FORWARDS	HT	WT	S	Place of Birth	Date	2003-04 Club
CASSELS, Andrew	6-1	185	L	Bramalea, Ont.	7/23/69	Columbus
FRITSCHE, Dan	6-1	198	R	Cleveland, OH	7/13/85	Columbus-Sarnia-Syracuse
HARTIGAN, Mark	6-0	205	L	Fort St. John, B.C.	10/15/77	Columbus-Syracuse
JACKMAN, Tim	6-4	210	R	Minot, ND	11/14/81	Columbus-Syracuse
KOMARNISKI, Zenith	6-0	200	L	Edmonton, Alta.	8/13/78	Manitoba-Columbus-Syracuse
LETOWSKI, Trevor	5-10	180	R	Thunder Bay, Ont.	4/5/77	Columbus
MALHOTRA, Manny	6-2	215	L	Mississauga, Ont.	5/18/80	Dallas-Columbus
MARCHANT, Todd	5-10	180	L	Buffalo, NY	8/12/73	Columbus
McDONELL, Kent	6-2	205	R	Williamstown, Ont.	3/1/79	Columbus-Syracuse
MOTZKO, Joe	6-0	190	R	Bemidji, MN	3/14/80	Columbus-Syracuse
NASH, Rick	6-4	206	L	Brampton, Ont.	6/16/84	Columbus
PANDOLFO, Mike	6-3	221	L	Winchester, MA	9/15/79	Columbus-Syracuse
REICH, Jeremy	6-1	204	L	Craik, Sask.	2/11/79	Columbus-Syracuse
SANDERSON, Geoff	6-0	190	L	Hay River, N.W.T.	2/1/72	Columbus-Vancouver
SHELLEY, Jody	6-4	225	L	Thompson, Man.	2/7/76	Columbus
SVITOV, Alexander	6-3	217	L	Omsk, USSR	11/3/82	Tampa Bay-Hamilton-Columbus
TRATTNIG, Matthias	6-1	208	L	Graz, Austria	4/22/79	Kassel
VYBORNY, David	5-10	189	L	Jihlava, Czech.	6/2/75	Columbus
WRIGHT, Tyler	6-0	190	R	Kamsack, Sask.	4/6/73	Columbus
ZHERDEV, Nikolai	6-0	186	R	Kiev, USSR	11/5/84	CSKA Moscow-Columbus

DEFENSEMEN						
JOHNSON, Aaron	6-0	197	L	Port Hawkesbury, N.S.	4/30/83	Columbus-Syracuse
KLESLA, Rostislav	6-3	206	L	Novy Jicin, Czech.	3/21/82	Columbus
LACHANCE, Scott	6-1	215	L	Charlottesville, VA	10/22/72	Columbus
LAKOS, Andre	6-6	230	R	Vienna, Austria	7/29/79	Vienna
RICHARDSON, Luke	6-4	215	L	Ottawa, Ont.	3/26/69	Columbus
RYAN, Prestin	6-0	192	L	Arcola, Sask.	6/29/80	U. of Maine-Syracuse
SCOVILLE, Darrel	6-3	208	L	Swift Current, Sask.	10/13/75	Columbus-Syracuse
SPACEK, Jaroslav	5-11	206	L	Rokycany, Czech.	2/11/74	Columbus
SUCHY, Radoslav	6-2	204	L	Kezmarok, Czech.	4/7/76	Phoenix
WESTCOTT, Duvie	5-11	192	R	Winnipeg, Man.	10/30/77	Columbus

GOALTENDERS	HT	WT	C	Place of Birth	Date	2003-04 Club
DENIS, Marc	6-1	190	L	Montreal, Que.	8/1/77	Columbus
IRBE, Arturs	5-8	190	L	Riga, Latvia	2/2/67	Carolina-Johnstown
LECLAIRE, Pascal	6-2	190	L	Repentigny, Que.	11/7/82	Columbus-Syracuse

General Managers' History

Doug MacLean, 2000-01 to date.

President and General Manager

MacLEAN, DOUG
President/General Manager, Columbus Blue Jackets.
Born in Summerside, P.E.I., April 12, 1954.

Doug MacLean was named the first general manager of the Blue Jackets on February 11, 1998. A month later he was named president of the organization and as its top executive, he holds the dual role of overseeing both the business and hockey operations of the franchise as well as the management of Nationwide Arena. MacLean also coached the team for parts of the 2002-03 and 2003-04 seasons.

Under MacLean's guidance, the Blue Jackets have established themselves as one of the most successful business franchises in the NHL. The Blue Jackets have made a significant impact in the Columbus community through its business operations and community service programs.

Prior to joining the Blue Jackets, MacLean served as head coach of the Florida Panthers, where he led his teams into the playoffs in both of his full seasons behind the bench (1995-96, 1996-97). In his first season as an NHL head coach, MacLean led Florida to the Stanley Cup Finals.

MacLean began his NHL coaching career in 1986 as an assistant to Jacques Martin in St. Louis. He spent two seasons with the Blues before joining the Washington Capitals in 1988, assisting Bryan Murray behind the bench. He was named coach of the Capitals' American Hockey League affiliate in Baltimore for the final 35 games of the 1989-90 season.

The following season, MacLean joined Murray on the Detroit Red Wings, serving as an assistant coach for two years. In 1992, MacLean was named assistant general manager of the Red Wings and also served as general manager of the team's AHL affiliate in Adirondack for two years. MacLean followed Murray to the Panthers in 1994, becoming the expansion club's director of player development. He was named head coach on July 24, 1995.

A collegiate hockey player at the University of Prince Edward Island, MacLean graduated with a bachelor's degree in education. He also played for the Montreal Jr. Canadiens and was invited to training camp with the St. Louis Blues in 1974. Following his playing career, MacLean enrolled at the University of Western Ontario, where he received a master's degree in educational psychology. While attending Western, MacLean began his coaching career as an assistant with London of the Ontario Hockey League.

NHL Coaching Record

			Regular Season				Playoffs		
Season	Team	Games	W	L	T		Games	W	L
1995-96	Florida	82	41	31	10		22	12	10
1996-97	Florida	82	35	28	19		5	1	4
1997-98	Florida	23	7	12	4		....	....	....
2002-03	Columbus	42	15	23	4		....	....	....
2003-04	Columbus	37	9	24	4		....	....	....
	NHL Totals	**266**	**107**	**118**	**41**		**27**	**13**	**14**

2003-04 Scoring
* - rookie

Regular Season

Pos	#	Player	Team	GP	G	A	Pts	+/-	PIM	PP	SH	GW	GT	S	%
L	61	Rick Nash	CBJ	80	41	16	57	-35	87	19	0	7	2	269	15.2
R	9	David Vyborny	CBJ	82	22	31	53	-26	40	8	4	2	0	158	13.9
R	13	* Nikolai Zherdev	CBJ	57	13	21	34	-11	54	5	0	1	0	137	9.5
C	26	Todd Marchant	CBJ	77	9	25	34	-17	34	4	0	2	0	163	5.5
R	10	Trevor Letowski	CBJ	73	15	17	32	-12	16	4	0	1	0	126	11.9
D	2	Anders Eriksson	CBJ	66	7	20	27	-6	18	2	0	1	1	84	8.3
C	25	Andrew Cassels	CBJ	58	6	20	26	-24	26	2	0	0	1	91	6.6
C	27	Manny Malhotra	DAL	9	0	0	0	-2	4	0	0	0	0	4	0.0
			CBJ	56	12	13	25	-5	24	1	0	2	0	103	11.7
			TOTAL	65	12	13	25	-7	28	1	0	2	0	107	11.2
C	19	Brian Holzinger	PIT	61	6	15	21	-27	38	1	1	1	0	82	7.3
			CBJ	13	1	0	1	-4	2	0	0	0	0	14	7.1
			TOTAL	74	7	15	22	-31	40	1	1	1	0	96	7.3
D	3	Jaroslav Spacek	CBJ	58	5	17	22	-13	45	2	1	2	0	108	4.6
R	28	Tyler Wright	CBJ	68	9	9	18	-19	63	2	0	3	0	109	8.3
D	44	Rostislav Klesla	CBJ	47	2	11	13	-16	27	0	0	1	0	74	2.7
C	16	Alexander Svitov	T.B.	11	0	3	3	0	4	0	0	0	0	16	0.0
			CBJ	29	2	6	8	-8	16	0	0	0	0	36	5.6
			TOTAL	40	2	9	11	-8	20	0	0	0	0	52	3.8
D	23	Derrick Walser	CBJ	27	1	8	9	-6	22	1	0	0	0	35	2.9
D	47	* Aaron Johnson	CBJ	29	2	6	8	-2	32	0	0	1	0	33	6.1
D	15	Duvie Westcott	CBJ	34	0	7	7	-15	39	0	0	0	0	43	0.0
L	45	Jody Shelley	CBJ	76	3	3	6	-10	228	1	0	0	0	62	4.8
D	22	Luke Richardson	CBJ	64	1	5	6	-11	48	0	0	1	0	34	2.9
C	42	* Mark Hartigan	CBJ	9	1	3	4	-2	6	1	0	0	0	15	6.7
C	21	Espen Knutsen	CBJ	14	0	4	4	-5	2	0	0	0	0	11	0.0
D	7	Scott Lachance	CBJ	77	0	4	4	-23	44	0	0	0	0	35	0.0
R	46	* Tim Jackman	CBJ	19	1	2	3	-7	16	0	0	0	0	18	5.6
R	32	Kent Mcdonell	CBJ	29	1	2	3	-7	36	0	0	0	0	23	4.3
R	17	David Ling	CBJ	50	1	2	3	-3	98	0	0	0	0	45	2.2
L	38	Andrej Nedorost	CBJ	9	2	0	2	-3	2	0	0	0	0	16	12.5
C	41	* Brad Moran	CBJ	2	1	1	2	-1	2	0	0	0	0	4	25.0
C	36	Donald Maclean	CBJ	4	1	0	1	-1	0	0	0	0	0	10	10.0
C	49	Dan Fritsche	CBJ	19	1	0	1	-5	12	0	0	0	0	19	5.3
D	37	Darrel Scoville	CBJ	8	0	1	1	-4	6	0	0	0	0	8	0.0
L	33	Jeremy Reich	CBJ	9	0	1	1	-3	20	0	0	0	0	3	0.0
D	18	Zenith Komarniski	CBJ	2	0	0	0	0	0	0	0	0	0	3	0.0
R	19	* Joe Motzko	CBJ	2	0	0	0	0	0	0	0	0	0	1	0.0
L	39	* Mike Pandolfo	CBJ	3	0	0	0	-2	0	0	0	0	0	4	0.0
C	14	* Greg Mauldin	CBJ	6	0	0	0	-2	4	0	0	0	0	6	0.0

Goaltending

No.	Goaltender	GPI	Mins	Avg	W	L	T	EN	SO	GA	SA	S%	G	A	PIM
30	Marc Denis	66	3796	2.56	21	36	7	9	5	162	1970	.918	0	2	10
40	Fred Brathwaite	21	1050	3.37	4	11	1	1	0	59	574	.897	0	0	2
31	* Pascal Leclaire	2	119	3.53	0	2	0	0	0	7	69	.899	0	0	0
	Totals	**82**	**4995**	**2.86**	**25**	**49**	**8**	**10**	**5**	**238**	**2623**	**.909**			

Coaching History

Dave King, 2000-01, 2001-02; Dave King and Doug MacLean, 2002-03; Doug MacLean and Gerard Gallant, 2003-04; Gerard Gallant, 2004-05.

Columbus selected Nikolai Zherdev fourth overall at the 2003 Entry Draft. He finished sixth in scoring among NHL rookies (13 goals, 21 assists) despite playing 14 fewer games than any other player in the top 10.

Club Records

Team

(Figures in brackets for season records are games played.)

Most Points	71	2000-01 (82)
Most Wins	29	2002-03 (82)
Most Ties	9	2000-01 (82)
Most Losses	47	2001-02 (82)
Most Goals	213	2002-03 (82)
Most Goals Against	263	2002-03 (82)
Fewest Points	57	2001-02 (82)
Fewest Wins	22	2001-02 (82)
Fewest Ties	8	2001-02 (82), 2002-03 (82), 2003-04 (82)
Fewest Losses	39	2000-01 (82)
Fewest Goals	164	2001-02 (82)
Fewest Goals Against	233	2000-01 (82)

Longest Winning Streak
Overall .... 4 Nov. 9-Nov. 16/00, Mar. 21-27/04
Home .... 4 Mar. 24-Apr. 8/01, Dec. 31/01-Jan. 16/02
Away .... 3 Jan. 8-11/03

Longest Undefeated Streak
Overall .... 4 Nov. 9-Nov. 16/00 (4 wins), Mar. 21-27/04 (4 wins)
Home .... 6 Jan. 20-Feb. 12/03 (4 wins, 2 ties)
Away .... 4 Jan. 3-11/03 (3 wins, 1 tie)

Longest Losing Streak
Overall .... 8 Nov. 17-Dec. 3/00, Mar. 3-18/04
Home .... 6 Oct. 12-Nov. 9/01
Away .... 11 Mar. 25-Oct. 29/02

Longest Winless Streak
Overall .... 9 Dec. 4-23/03 (8 losses, 1 tie)
Home .... 8 Oct. 4-Nov. 9/01 (6 losses, 2 ties), Dec. 4-31/03 (7 losses, 1 tie)
Away .... 14 Oct. 9-Dec. 23/03 (13 losses, 1 tie)

Most Shutouts, Season 5 2002-03 (82), 2003-04 (82)
Most PIM, Season 1,505 2002-03 (82)
Most Goals, Game .... 7 Three times

Individual

Most Seasons .... 4 Eight players
Most Games .... 315 David Vyborny
Most Goals, Career .... 88 Geoff Sanderson
Most Assists, Career .... 95 Ray Whitney
Most Points, Career .... 168 Geoff Sanderson (88G, 80A)
Most PIM, Career .... 693 Jody Shelley
Most Shutouts, Career .... 11 Marc Denis
Longest Consecutive Games Streak .... 161 David Vyborny (Oct. 17/02 to date)
Most Goals, Season .... 41 Rick Nash (2003-04)

Most Assists, Season .... 52 Ray Whitney (2002-03)
Most Points, Season .... 76 Ray Whitney (2002-03; 24G, 52A)
Most PIM, Season .... 249 Jody Shelley (2002-03)
Most Points, Defenseman, Season .... 45 Jaroslav Spacek (2002-03; 9G, 36A)
Most Points, Center, Season .... 68 Andrew Cassels (2002-03; 20G, 48A)
Most Points, Right Wing, Season .... 53 David Vyborny (2003-04; 22G, 31A)
Most Points, Left Wing, Season .... 76 Ray Whitney (2002-03; 24G, 52A)
Most Points, Rookie, Season .... 39 Rick Nash (2002-03; 17G, 22A)
Most Shutouts, Season .... 5 Marc Denis (2002-03, 2003-04)
Most Goals, Game .... 4 Geoff Sanderson (Jan. 11/03)
Most Assists, Game .... 5 Espen Knutsen (Mar. 24/01)
Most Points, Game .... 5 Espen Knutsen (Mar. 24/01; 5A), Geoff Sanderson (Jan. 11/03; 4G, 1A), Andrew Cassels (Jan. 11/03; 1G, 4A), David Vyborny (Feb. 28/04; 1G, 4A)

Captains' History

Lyle Odelein, 2000-01, 2001-02; Ray Whitney, 2002-03; Luke Richardson, 2003-04 to date.

All-time Record vs. Other Clubs

Regular Season

	At Home								On Road								Total							
	GP	W	L	T	OL	GF	GA	PTS	GP	W	L	T	OL	GF	GA	PTS	GP	W	L	T	OL	GF	GA	PTS
Anaheim	8	6	2	0	0	23	15	12	8	2	4	1	1	16	24	6	16	8	6	1	1	39	39	18
Atlanta	4	2	2	0	0	12	11	4	3	1	2	0	0	6	5	2	7	3	4	0	0	18	16	6
Boston	3	1	2	0	0	3	14	2	2	1	1	0	0	7	8	2	5	2	3	0	0	10	22	4
Buffalo	2	1	0	1	0	5	4	3	4	2	2	0	0	9	13	4	6	3	2	1	0	14	17	7
Calgary	8	6	1	0	1	26	16	13	8	3	5	0	0	18	24	6	16	9	6	0	1	44	40	19
Carolina	3	1	2	0	0	6	9	2	4	1	3	0	0	11	13	2	7	2	5	0	0	17	22	4
Chicago	11	6	4	1	0	32	34	13	10	2	7	1	0	15	30	5	21	8	11	2	0	47	64	18
Colorado	8	1	6	1	0	13	31	3	8	0	8	0	0	10	38	0	16	1	14	1	0	23	69	3
Dallas	8	2	6	0	0	19	26	4	8	0	7	0	1	9	26	1	16	2	13	0	1	28	52	5
Detroit	11	2	4	1	4	21	26	9	10	2	8	0	0	22	39	4	21	4	12	1	4	43	65	13
Edmonton	8	1	4	3	0	20	27	5	8	1	6	0	1	17	31	3	16	2	10	3	1	37	58	8
Florida	2	1	1	0	0	4	4	2	3	1	2	0	0	7	9	2	5	2	3	0	0	11	13	4
Los Angeles	8	5	3	0	0	21	26	10	8	3	4	1	0	16	18	7	16	8	7	1	0	37	44	17
Minnesota	7	5	1	1	0	19	7	11	8	2	5	0	1	16	25	5	15	7	6	1	1	35	32	16
Montreal	1	0	1	0	0	1	3	0	4	2	1	1	0	6	6	5	5	2	2	1	0	7	9	5
Nashville	10	5	4	0	1	23	27	11	11	3	7	1	0	24	29	7	21	8	11	1	1	47	56	18
New Jersey	4	2	2	0	0	13	13	4	2	0	1	0	1	4	5	1	6	2	3	0	1	17	18	5
NY Islanders	4	3	0	1	0	13	7	7	2	2	0	0	0	11	7	4	6	5	0	1	0	24	14	11
NY Rangers	4	3	1	0	0	16	7	6	2	0	1	1	0	5	7	1	6	3	2	1	0	21	14	7
Ottawa	2	0	1	1	0	7	9	1	3	0	2	1	0	6	12	1	5	0	3	2	0	13	21	2
Philadelphia	3	0	1	2	0	6	7	2	2	0	2	0	0	3	7	0	5	0	3	2	0	9	14	2
Phoenix	8	4	3	1	0	19	14	9	8	0	5	3	0	15	24	3	16	4	8	4	0	34	38	12
Pittsburgh	3	1	0	0	2	10	9	4	3	1	2	0	0	9	12	2	6	2	2	0	2	19	21	6
St. Louis	10	4	3	2	1	22	26	11	11	1	8	1	1	23	45	4	21	5	11	3	2	45	71	15
San Jose	8	3	4	0	1	21	20	7	8	1	6	1	0	12	32	3	16	4	10	0	2	33	52	10
Tampa Bay	3	1	1	1	0	5	4	3	3	1	2	0	0	3	5	2	6	2	3	1	0	8	9	5
Toronto	1	1	0	0	0	3	1	2	4	0	4	0	0	4	10	0	5	1	4	0	0	8	13	3
Vancouver	8	2	4	2	0	17	29	6	8	2	5	1	0	23	34	5	16	4	9	3	0	40	63	11
Washington	4	1	2	0	1	11	15	3	2	0	2	0	0	5	8	1	6	1	4	0	1	16	23	4
Totals	**164**	**70**	**65**	**18**	**11**	**412**	**443**	**169**	**164**	**34**	**108**	**15**	**7**	**332**	**546**	**90**	**328**	**104**	**173**	**33**	**18**	**744**	**989**	**259**

2003-04 Results

Oct.	9	at Atlanta	1-2		10	at Los Angeles	2-2
	11	NY Rangers	5-0		11	at Anaheim	2-2
	13	Vancouver	3-2		15	at St. Louis	3-5
	16	Chicago	2-1		16	Los Angeles	3-2*
	18	at Nashville	2-3		18	Edmonton	4-4
	22	at Detroit	1-4		21	St. Louis	3-1
	23	Tampa Bay	0-1		22	at Chicago	0-7
	25	Dallas	2-3		24	Chicago	4-3
	28	at Vancouver	3-6		27	New Jersey	3-4
	30	at Edmonton	3-4*		29	Nashville	4-6
Nov.	1	at Calgary	0-3		31	Minnesota	2-1*
	7	Atlanta	4-2	Feb.	2	at Phoenix	3-3
	9	Calgary	4-3		4	at Dallas	0-1
	11	at Montreal	1-1		11	Los Angeles	3-2*
	13	at Ottawa	2-5		12	at Toronto	1-4
	14	Boston	0-4		14	San Jose	1-2*
	16	Phoenix	2-2		16	Nashville	4-2
	19	at Detroit	1-5		18	at Anaheim	1-3
	20	Detroit	3-0		20	at Phoenix	2-3
	22	NY Islanders	2-1		21	at Los Angeles	3-4
	25	Edmonton	3-3		23	at San Jose	2-4
	26	at Nashville	2-4		25	Chicago	3-4
	29	Washington	3-5		27	at Chicago	4-3
Dec.	2	Anaheim	2-1		28	Colorado	5-4*
	4	Nashville	2-4	Mar.	2	at Carolina	3-0
	6	at Colorado	1-5		3	at Dallas	2-4
	10	Philadelphia	1-1		6	Vancouver	0-4
	12	St. Louis	2-3*		8	Carolina	1-4
	13	at Pittsburgh	3-5		11	Detroit	2-4
	16	at St. Louis	1-2*		13	at St. Louis	3-5
	19	Calgary	1-2		14	at Minnesota	2-3
	20	at Minnesota	2-5		16	at Edmonton	2-3
	23	Phoenix	1-2		18	at Calgary	0-2
	26	at Chicago	4-1		21	at Vancouver	5-4
	27	Dallas	3-4		24	Minnesota	2-0
	29	St. Louis	2-3		26	Anaheim	3-1
	31	San Jose	0-1		27	at Nashville	3-2*
Jan.	2	at Tampa Bay	2-0		29	at Buffalo	0-6
	3	at Florida	0-1		31	Detroit	2-3
	6	at Colorado	0-6	Apr.	2	Colorado	2-3
	8	at San Jose	3-2*		3	at Detroit	4-1

* – Overtime

Entry Draft
Selections 2004-2000

2004
Pick
8	Alexandre Picard
46	Adam Pineault
59	Kyle Wharton
93	Dan Lacosta
96	Andrei Plehanov
133	Petr Pohl
167	Rob Page
190	Lennart Petrell
198	Justin Vienneau
231	Brian Mcguirk
233	Matt Greer
271	Grant Clitsome

2003
Pick
4	Nikolai Zherdev
46	Dan Fritsche
71	Dmitri Kosmachev
103	Kevin Jarman
104	Philippe Dupuis
138	Arsi Piispanen
168	Marc Methot
200	Alexander Guskov
233	Mathieu Gravel
283	Trevor Hendrikx

2002
Pick
1	Rick Nash
41	Joakim Lindstrom
65	Ole-Kristian Tollefsen
96	Jeff Genovy
98	Ivan Tkachenko
119	Jekabs Redlihs
133	Lasse Pirjeta
168	Tim Konsorada
184	Jaroslav Balastik
199	Greg Mauldin
225	Steve Goertzen
231	Jaroslav Kracik
263	Sergei Mozyakin

2001
Pick
8	Pascal Leclaire
38	Tim Jackman
53	Kiel McLeod
85	Aaron Johnson
87	Per Mars
141	Cole Jarrett
173	Justin Aikins
187	Artem Vostrikov
204	Raffaele Sannitz
236	Ryan Bowness
242	Andrew Murray

2000
Pick
4	Rostislav Klesla
69	Ben Knopp
133	Petteri Nummelin
138	Scott Heffernan
150	Tyler Kolarik
169	Shane Bendera
200	Janne Jokila
231	Peter Zingoni
278	Martin Paroulek
286	Andrej Nedorost
292	Louis Mandeville

Coach

GALLANT, GERARD
Coach, Columbus Blue Jackets.
Born in Summerside, P.E.I., September 2, 1963.

Former NHL All-Star Gerard Gallant joined the Blue Jackets organization July 18, 2000 and served as an assistant coach for three and a half seasons. He took over as the club's interim head coach on January 1, 2004 and was officially named to the position of head coach on June 25.

Originally the Red Wings' sixth pick, 107th overall, in the 1981 Entry Draft, Gallant spent two seasons with Adirondack, Detroit's AHL affiliate. His NHL career began with the Red Wings in 1984 when he notched six goals and 12 assists for 18 points in 32 games as a rookie. Over the next eight years, he averaged 56 points and 72 games played with Detroit, including four consecutive seasons with 70 or more points from 1986 to 1990. Gallant helped Detroit capture three division titles and in 1988-89 he was named a Second Team NHL All-Star after posting a career-high 39 goals, 54 assists and 93 points in 76 games.

Gallant wrapped up his Red Wings career following the 1992-93 season having registered 207 goals, 260 assists, 467 points and 1,600 penalty minutes in 563 games. He signed with the Tampa Bay Lightning as a free agent and played in 51 games during the 1993-94 season. He concluded his NHL career with 211 goals, 269 assists, 480 points and 1,674 penalty minutes in 615 games.

Gallant spent the next five years coaching at the junior hockey and minor pro levels before joining the Blue Jackets organization. He began his coaching career with the Summerside (PEI) Western Capitals, a Canadian Junior A team, midway through the 1995-96 season. In 1996-97, his first full season with the club, he led the squad to the Royal Bank Cup championship, Canada's Junior A national championship tournament, and a 33-11-11 regular season mark. He remained with the club through 1997-98.

Gallant then served as an assistant coach with the Fort Wayne Komets of the International Hockey League in 1998-99 and the following season joined the Louisville Panthers of the American Hockey League as the club's top assistant coach.

Coaching Record

			Regular Season			Playoffs		
Season	Team	Games	W	L	T	Games	W	L
2003-04	Columbus (NHL)	45	16	25	4	....	....	....
	NHL Totals	45	16	25	4	....	....	....

Club Directory

Nationwide Arena

Columbus Blue Jackets
Nationwide Arena
200 W. Nationwide Blvd.
Columbus, Ohio 43215
Phone 614/246-4625
FAX 614/246-4007
www.BlueJackets.com
Capacity: 18,136

Ownership
Majority Owner/Governor	John H. McConnell
Alternate Governor	John P. McConnell

Executive Staff
President/General Manager/Alternate Governor	Doug MacLean
Executive Vice-President/Assistant General Manager	Jim Clark
Vice-President of Marketing	David Paitson
Vice-President of Corporate Development	Paul D'Aiuto
Vice-President of Ticket Sales	Dan Froelich
Chief Financial Officer	T.J. LaMendola
General Counsel	Greg Kirstein

Hockey Operations
Head Coach	Gerard Gallant
Associate Coach	Dean Blais
Assistant Coach	Gord Murphy
Goaltending Coach, Pro Scout	Rick Wamsley
Director of Amateur Scouting	Don Boyd
Director of Pro Scouting	Bob Strumm
Director of Player Development	Paul Castron
Player Development/Special Assignment	Kevin Dineen
Manager of Hockey Operations	Chris MacFarland
Manager of Team Services	Jim Rankin
Video Coordinator	Dan Singleton
Administrative Assistant, Hockey Operations	Julie Uhler
Amateur Scouts	Sam McMaster, Wayne Smith, John Williams
Pro Scout	Peter Dineen
European Scout	Kjell Larsson
Regional Scouts	Brian Bates, Scott Fitzgerald, Jukka Holtari, Denis LeBlanc, John McNamara, Artem Telepin Nicholaevich, Bryan Raymond, Andrew Shaw, Milan Tichy
Head Athletic Trainer	Chris Mizer
Equipment Manager	Tim LeRoy
Assistant Equipment Manager	Jamie Healy
Equipment Assistant	Andre Szucko

Business Operations
Executive Director of Marketing	Marc Gregory
Director of Communications	Todd Sharrock
Director of Client Services	Brent Baker
Director of Event Presentation/Production	Kimberly Kershaw
Director of Fan Development	J.D. Kershaw
Director of Community Development	Wendy Bradshaw
Director of Human Resources	Kelley Walton
Director of Retail Operations	Chris Weller
Director of Corporate Sales	Scott Klein
Director of Corporate Sales – Columbus Destroyers	Jeff Abbot
Assistant Director of Communications	Jason Rothwell
Manager of Multimedia	Jay Levin
Graphic Designer/Manager of Print Production	Will Bennett
Client Services Manager	Heather Popa, Cheri Masdea
Manager of Advertising and Promotions	Chris Sprague
Manager of Video Production	David Bakalik
Manager of Event Presentation	Matt Bettinger
Manager of Fan Development	Joel Siegman
Manager of Community Development	Heather Hall
Mascot Coordinator	Jason Zumpano
Business Development Representative	Brice Clark
Video Broadcast Engineer	John Bonitatibus
Retail Operations Warehouse Manager	Ron Smith
Human Resources Coordinator	Jennifer Pritz
Blueline Store Manager	Terry Lowe
Blueline Sales Associate	Katie Weber
Executive Assistant to Doug MacLean	Kari Rucker
Administrative Assistant to Business Development	Gretchen Kyle
Administrative Assistant to Greg Kirstein	Nikki Ward
Administrative Assistant to David Paitson	Heather do Forno

Finance
Controller	Rich Gross
Financial Analyst	Dana Fletcher
Staff Accountants	Nora Ludwig, Pete Nyikes
Accounts Payable	Malika Dickerson, Rose Phillips
Payroll Administrator	Christine Parthemore
Accounts Receivable	Shelly Phillips
MIS Manager	Jim Connolly
Office Manager	Rachel Durham
Receptionist	Beth Trexler

Ticket Operations
Director of Ticket Operations/Customer Service	Mark Morris
Managers of Ticket Operations/Customer Service	Karen Bierley, Mark Metz
Account Executives – PSL	Ted Hritz, David Melfi
Account Executives – Group Sales	Heather Bardocz, Adam Russell, Scott Schiff
Sales Associates	Clint Fettty, D.J. Nowalski, Eben Bierle, Eric Hill
Premium and Suite Services	Melissa DeGraw
Database Coordinator	Krista Romano
Season Ticket Service Coordinator	Liz Burri

Broadcasting
Director of Broadcasting	Russ Mollohan
Fox Sports Net Play-By-Play Announcer	Jeff Rimer
Fox Sports Net Color Analyst	TBA
Radio Play-By-Play Announcer	George Matthews
Radio Color Analyst	Bill Davidge

Dallas Stars

2003-04 Results: 41W-26L-13T-2OTL 97PTS.
Second, Pacific Division

2004-05 Schedule

Oct.	Wed.	13	at Phoenix		Tue.	11	at Calgary
	Thu.	14	Phoenix		Thu.	13	at Edmonton
	Sat.	16	Boston		Sat.	15	at Montreal
	Wed.	20	Nashville		Mon.	17	at Detroit
	Fri.	22	Buffalo		Wed.	19	Nashville
	Sun.	24	at Chicago		Fri.	21	Detroit
	Wed.	27	at Detroit		Sun.	23	at Atlanta
	Fri.	29	Edmonton		Tue.	25	Calgary
	Sat.	30	Columbus		Wed.	26	at Colorado
Nov.	Mon.	1	Minnesota		Fri.	28	at San Jose
	Wed.	3	Chicago		Mon.	31	Los Angeles
	Sun.	7	at Columbus*	Feb.	Wed.	2	Minnesota
	Wed.	10	at Carolina		Sat.	5	at St. Louis*
	Fri.	12	at New Jersey		Mon.	7	Anaheim
	Sat.	13	at NY Islanders		Wed.	9	Chicago
	Tue.	16	at Toronto		Wed.	16	Colorado
	Thu.	18	at Ottawa		Sat.	19	at St. Louis*
	Sat.	20	Columbus		Sun.	20	Washington
	Tue.	23	Anaheim		Wed.	23	at Los Angeles
	Wed.	24	at Columbus		Fri.	25	at Anaheim
	Fri.	26	San Jose		Sun.	27	Vancouver
	Sun.	28	at Anaheim*	Mar.	Wed.	2	Calgary
	Tue.	30	at Los Angeles		Fri.	4	at Colorado
Dec.	Thu.	2	at San Jose		Sun.	6	Carolina*
	Sat.	4	at Phoenix		Wed.	9	NY Rangers
	Wed.	8	Philadelphia		Fri.	11	Los Angeles
	Sat.	11	at Minnesota		Sat.	12	at Nashville
	Mon.	13	San Jose		Mon.	14	Tampa Bay
	Wed.	15	St. Louis		Wed.	16	Pittsburgh
	Fri.	17	at Washington		Fri.	18	Edmonton
	Sun.	19	at Chicago		Sun.	20	Vancouver*
	Mon.	20	at Minnesota		Wed.	23	Florida
	Wed.	22	Anaheim		Sat.	26	at Anaheim
	Sun.	26	at Nashville		Mon.	28	at Los Angeles
	Mon.	27	Detroit		Wed.	30	at Vancouver
	Wed.	29	Los Angeles	Apr.	Fri.	1	at Edmonton
	Fri.	31	Colorado		Sat.	2	at Calgary
Jan.	Sun.	2	at Tampa Bay		Mon.	4	San Jose
	Tue.	4	Phoenix		Wed.	6	Phoenix
	Thu.	6	at San Jose		Fri.	8	at Phoenix
	Sat.	8	at Vancouver		Sun.	10	St. Louis*

*Denotes afternoon game.

Franchise date: June 5, 1967
Transferred from Minnesota to Dallas, June 9, 1993.

PACIFIC DIVISION

38th NHL Season

Brenden Morrow established new career highs in goals (25), points (49) and power-play goals (9) in 2003-04. His 25 goals were second on the Stars behind Bill Guerin.

Year-by-Year Record

Season	GP	Home W	L	T	OL	Road W	L	T	OL	Overall W	L	T	OL	GF	GA	Pts.	Finished	Playoff Result
2003-04	82	26	7	8	0	15	19	5	2	41	26	13	2	194	175	97	2nd, Pacific Div.	Lost Conf. Quarter-Final
2002-03	82	28	5	6	2	18	12	9	2	46	17	15	4	245	169	111	1st, Pacific Div.	Lost Conf. Semi-Final
2001-02	82	18	13	6	4	18	15	7	1	36	28	13	5	215	213	90	4th, Pacific Div.	Out of Playoffs
2000-01	82	26	10	5	0	22	14	3	2	48	24	8	2	241	187	106	1st, Pacific Div.	Lost Conf. Semi-Final
1999-2000	82	21	11	5	4	22	12	5	2	43	23	10	6	211	184	102	1st, Pacific Div.	Lost Final
1998-99	**82**	**29**	**8**	**4**	**...**	**22**	**11**	**8**	**...**	**51**	**19**	**12**	**...**	**236**	**168**	**114**	**1st, Pacific Div.**	**Won Stanley Cup**
1997-98	82	26	8	7	...	23	14	4	...	49	22	11	...	242	167	109	1st, Central Div.	Lost Conf. Final
1996-97	82	25	13	3	...	23	13	5	...	48	26	8	...	252	198	104	1st, Central Div.	Lost Conf. Quarter-Final
1995-96	82	14	18	9	...	12	24	5	...	26	42	14	...	227	280	66	6th, Central Div.	Out of Playoffs
1994-95	48	9	10	5	...	8	13	3	...	17	23	8	...	136	135	42	5th, Central Div.	Lost Conf. Quarter-Final
1993-94	84	23	12	7	...	19	17	6	...	42	29	13	...	286	265	97	3rd, Central Div.	Lost Conf. Semi-Final
1992-93*	84	18	17	7	...	18	21	3	...	36	38	10	...	272	293	82	5th, Norris Div.	Out of Playoffs
1991-92*	80	20	16	4	...	12	26	2	...	32	42	6	...	246	278	70	4th, Norris Div.	Lost Div. Semi-Final
1990-91*	80	19	15	6	...	8	24	8	...	27	39	14	...	256	266	68	4th, Norris Div.	Lost Final
1989-90*	80	26	12	2	...	10	28	2	...	36	40	4	...	284	291	76	4th, Norris Div.	Lost Div. Semi-Final
1988-89*	80	17	15	8	...	10	22	8	...	27	37	16	...	258	278	70	3rd, Norris Div.	Lost Div. Semi-Final
1987-88*	80	10	24	6	...	9	24	7	...	19	48	13	...	242	349	51	5th, Norris Div.	Out of Playoffs
1986-87*	80	17	20	3	...	13	20	7	...	30	40	10	...	296	314	70	5th, Norris Div.	Out of Playoffs
1985-86*	80	21	15	4	...	17	18	5	...	38	33	9	...	327	305	85	2nd, Norris Div.	Lost Div. Semi-Final
1984-85*	80	14	19	7	...	11	24	5	...	25	43	12	...	268	321	62	4th, Norris Div.	Lost Div. Final
1983-84*	80	22	14	4	...	17	17	6	...	39	31	10	...	345	344	88	1st, Norris Div.	Lost Conf. Championship
1982-83*	80	23	6	11	...	17	18	5	...	40	24	16	...	321	290	96	2nd, Norris Div.	Lost Div. Final
1981-82*	80	21	7	12	...	16	16	8	...	37	23	20	...	346	288	94	1st, Norris Div.	Lost Div. Semi-Final
1980-81*	80	23	10	7	...	12	18	10	...	35	28	17	...	291	263	87	3rd, Adams Div.	Lost Final
1979-80*	80	25	8	7	...	11	20	9	...	36	28	16	...	311	253	88	3rd, Adams Div.	Lost Semi-Final
1978-79*	80	19	15	6	...	9	25	6	...	28	40	12	...	257	289	68	4th, Adams Div.	Out of Playoffs
1977-78*	80	12	24	4	...	6	29	5	...	18	53	9	...	218	325	45	5th, Smythe Div.	Out of Playoffs
1976-77*	80	17	14	9	...	6	25	9	...	23	39	18	...	240	310	64	2nd, Smythe Div.	Lost Prelim. Round
1975-76*	80	15	22	3	...	5	31	4	...	20	53	7	...	195	303	47	4th, Smythe Div.	Out of Playoffs
1974-75*	80	17	20	3	...	6	30	4	...	23	50	7	...	221	341	53	4th, Smythe Div.	Out of Playoffs
1973-74*	78	18	15	6	...	5	23	11	...	23	38	17	...	235	275	63	7th, West Div.	Out of Playoffs
1972-73*	78	26	8	5	...	11	22	6	...	37	30	11	...	254	230	85	3rd, West Div.	Lost Quarter-Final
1971-72*	78	22	11	6	...	15	18	6	...	37	29	12	...	212	191	86	2nd, West Div.	Lost Quarter-Final
1970-71*	78	16	15	8	...	12	19	8	...	28	34	16	...	191	223	72	4th, West Div.	Lost Semi-Final
1969-70*	76	11	16	11	...	8	19	11	...	19	35	22	...	224	257	60	3rd, West Div.	Lost Quarter-Final
1968-69*	76	11	21	6	...	7	22	9	...	18	43	15	...	189	270	51	6th, West Div.	Out of Playoffs
1967-68*	74	17	12	8	...	10	20	7	...	27	32	15	...	191	226	69	4th, West Div.	Lost Semi-Final

*Minnesota North Stars

2004-05 Player Personnel

FORWARDS	HT	WT	S	Place of Birth	Date	2003-04 Club
ARNOTT, Jason	6-4	220	R	Collingwood, Ont.	10/11/74	Dallas
BARARUK, David	6-0	175	L	Moose Jaw, Sask.	5/26/83	Utah-Idaho
BARNES, Stu	5-11	180	R	Spruce Grove, Alta.	12/25/70	Dallas
DiMAIO, Rob	5-10	190	R	Calgary, Alta.	2/19/68	Dallas
DOWNEY, Aaron	6-1	216	R	Shelburne, Ont.	8/27/74	Dallas
GUERIN, Bill	6-2	210	R	Worcester, MA	11/9/70	Dallas
HOLTET, Marius	6-0	183	R	Hamar, Norway	8/31/84	Bofors
KAPANEN, Niko	5-9	180	L	Hattula, Finland	4/29/78	Dallas
LEHTINEN, Jere	6-0	200	R	Espoo, Finland	6/24/73	Dallas
LESSARD, Junior	6-0	195	R	St-Joseph-de-Beauce, Que.	5/26/80	Minnesota-Duluth
MIETTINEN, Antti	5-11	180	R	Hameenlinna, Finland	7/3/80	Dallas-Utah
MODANO, Mike	6-3	205	L	Livonia, MI	6/7/70	Dallas
MORROW, Brenden	5-11	210	L	Carlyle, Sask.	1/16/79	Dallas
OTT, Steve	6-0	185	L	Summerside, P.E.I.	8/19/82	Dallas
SIKLENKA, Mike	6-5	224	R	Meadow Lake, Sask.	12/18/79	NY Rangers-Trenton-Phi (AHL)-Utah
SVOBODA, Jaroslav	6-2	190	L	Cervenka, Czech.	6/1/80	Carolina-Lowell
TJARNQVIST, Mathias	6-1	183	L	Umea, Sweden	4/15/79	Dallas-Utah
TURGEON, Pierre	6-1	199	L	Rouyn, Que.	8/28/69	Dallas
DEFENSEMEN						
BOUCHER, Philippe	6-3	221	R	Ste-Apollinaire, Que.	3/24/73	Dallas
DALEY, Trevor	5-9	197	L	Toronto, Ont.	10/9/83	Dallas-Utah
ERSKINE, John	6-4	215	L	Kingston, Ont.	6/26/80	Dallas-Utah
JANCEVSKI, Dan	6-3	212	L	Windsor, Ont.	6/15/81	Utah
KLEMM, Jon	6-2	200	R	Cranbrook, B.C.	1/8/70	Chicago-Dallas
NICKERSON, Matt	6-4	230	R	New Haven, CT	1/11/85	Clarkson
SWEENEY, Don	5-10	185	L	St. Stephen, N.B.	8/17/66	Dallas
ZUBOV, Sergei	6-1	200	R	Moscow, USSR	7/22/70	Dallas

GOALTENDERS	HT	WT	C	Place of Birth	Date	2003-04 Club
ELLIS, Dan	6-0	185	L	Saskatoon, Sask.	6/19/80	Dallas-Utah-Idaho
SMITH, Mike	6-3	189	L	Kingston, Ont.	3/22/82	Utah
TURCO, Marty	5-11	183	L	Sault Ste. Marie, Ont.	8/13/75	Dallas

2003-04 Scoring

* - rookie

Regular Season

Pos	#	Player	Team	GP	G	A	Pts	+/–	PIM	PP	SH	GW	GT	S	%
R	13	Bill Guerin	DAL	82	34	35	69	14	109	9	0	10	1	263	12.9
C	44	Jason Arnott	DAL	73	21	36	57	23	66	5	0	5	0	143	14.7
R	17	Valeri Bure	FLA	55	20	25	45	0	20	8	0	4	1	175	11.4
			DAL	13	2	5	7	3	6	0	0	0	0	34	5.9
			TOTAL	68	22	30	52	3	26	8	0	4	1	209	10.5
L	10	Brenden Morrow	DAL	81	25	24	49	10	121	9	0	3	1	132	18.9
C	9	Mike Modano	DAL	76	14	30	44	–21	46	6	0	0	0	152	9.2
D	56	Sergei Zubov	DAL	77	7	35	42	0	20	4	1	1	1	154	4.5
C	77	Pierre Turgeon	DAL	76	15	25	40	17	20	6	0	1	1	104	14.4
C	14	Stu Barnes	DAL	77	11	18	29	7	18	0	1	4	0	135	8.1
R	26	Jere Lehtinen	DAL	58	13	13	26	0	20	4	1	4	0	138	9.4
R	18	Rob Dimaio	DAL	69	9	15	24	2	52	0	1	1	1	76	11.8
D	43	Philippe Boucher	DAL	70	8	16	24	15	64	2	0	2	0	134	6.0
D	24	Richard Matvichuk	DAL	75	1	20	21	0	36	0	0	1	0	85	1.2
D	27	Teppo Numminen	DAL	62	3	14	17	–5	18	0	0	0	1	83	3.6
R	48	Scott Young	DAL	53	8	8	16	–15	14	2	0	2	0	134	6.0
R	28	David Oliver	DAL	36	7	5	12	6	12	3	0	1	0	30	23.3
C	29	Steve Ott	DAL	73	2	10	12	–2	152	0	0	1	0	74	2.7
D	32	Don Sweeney	DAL	63	0	11	11	22	18	0	0	0	0	39	0.0
L	72	Shayne Corson	DAL	17	5	5	10	12	29	0	1	1	0	21	23.8
D	6	Chris Therien	PHI	56	1	9	10	2	50	0	0	0	0	59	1.7
			DAL	11	0	0	0	4	2	0	0	0	0	9	0.0
			TOTAL	67	1	9	10	6	52	0	0	0	0	68	1.5
D	42	Jon Klemm	CHI	19	0	1	1	6	20	0	0	0	0	19	0.0
			DAL	58	2	4	6	10	24	0	0	1	0	52	3.8
			TOTAL	77	2	5	7	16	44	0	0	1	0	71	2.8
D	5 *	Trevor Daley	DAL	27	1	5	6	–6	14	1	0	0	0	34	2.9
C	39	Niko Kapanen	DAL	67	1	5	6	–15	16	0	0	0	0	57	1.8
D	37	Lubomir Sekeras	DAL	4	1	1	2	0	2	0	0	0	0	2	50.0
L	23 *	Mathias Tjarnqvist	DAL	18	1	1	2	–6	2	0	0	1	0	11	9.1
R	47	Aaron Downey	DAL	37	1	1	2	2	77	0	0	1	0	11	9.1
L	20 *	Antti Miettinen	DAL	16	1	0	1	–9	0	0	0	1	0	17	5.9
D	55	John Erskine	DAL	32	0	1	1	–9	84	0	0	0	0	23	0.0
D	37 *	Jeff Macmillan	DAL	4	0	0	0	–2	0	0	0	0	0	3	0.0
C	40	Gavin Morgan	DAL	6	0	0	0	0	21	0	0	0	0	7	0.0
R	11	Rob Valicevic	DAL	7	0	0	0	–1	2	0	0	0	0	4	0.0
L	36 *	Steve Gainey	DAL	7	0	0	0	1	7	0	0	0	0	0	0.0
R	16	Blake Sloan	DAL	28	0	0	0	–1	7	0	0	0	0	23	0.0

Goaltending

No.	Goaltender	GPI	Mins	Avg	W	L	T	EN	SO	GA	SA	S%	G	A	PIM
35	Marty Turco	73	4359	1.98	37	21	13	6	9	144	1648	.913	0	1	32
31	Ron Tugnutt	11	548	2.41	3	7	0	0	1	22	220	.900	0	0	0
1	* Dan Ellis	1	60	3.00	1	0	0	0	0	3	28	.893	0	0	0
	Totals	**82**	**4993**	**2.10**	**41**	**28**	**13**	**6**	**10**	**175**	**1902**	**.908**			

Playoffs

Pos	#	Player	Team	GP	G	A	Pts	+/–	PIM	PP	SH	GW	GT	S	%
C	77	Pierre Turgeon	DAL	5	1	3	4	–2	2	0	0	0	0	9	11.1
C	9	Mike Modano	DAL	5	1	2	3	–4	8	1	0	0	0	12	8.3
R	17	Valeri Bure	DAL	5	0	3	3	–1	0	0	0	0	0	9	0.0
D	6	Chris Therien	DAL	5	2	0	2	1	0	0	0	0	0	6	33.3
D	56	Sergei Zubov	DAL	5	1	1	2	–5	0	1	0	0	0	14	7.1
C	44	Jason Arnott	DAL	5	1	1	2	–1	2	1	0	0	0	11	9.1
C	39	Niko Kapanen	DAL	1	1	0	1	0	0	0	0	0	0	2	50.0
R	48	Scott Young	DAL	4	1	0	1	1	2	1	0	0	0	9	11.1
C	29	Steve Ott	DAL	4	1	0	1	0	0	0	0	1	1	3	33.3
D	43	Philippe Boucher	DAL	5	1	0	1	–1	6	0	0	0	0	15	6.7
D	27	Teppo Numminen	DAL	4	0	1	1	–1	0	0	0	0	0	3	0.0
L	72	Shayne Corson	DAL	5	0	1	1	–5	12	0	0	0	0	2	0.0
R	18	Rob DiMaio	DAL	5	0	1	1	–2	2	0	0	0	0	2	0.0
R	13	Bill Guerin	DAL	5	0	1	1	–1	4	0	0	0	0	23	0.0
D	24	Richard Matvichuk	DAL	5	0	1	1	–4	8	0	0	0	0	5	0.0
L	10	Brenden Morrow	DAL	5	0	1	1	0	4	0	0	0	0	10	0.0
R	28	David Oliver	DAL	1	0	0	0	0	0	0	0	0	0	0	0.0
D	5 *	Trevor Daley	DAL	1	0	0	0	0	0	0	0	0	0	0	0.0
D	32	Don Sweeney	DAL	5	0	0	0	–2	2	0	0	0	0	2	0.0
C	14	Stu Barnes	DAL	5	0	0	0	–6	0	0	0	0	0	8	0.0
R	26	Jere Lehtinen	DAL	5	0	0	0	–4	0	0	0	0	0	11	0.0

Goaltending

No.	Goaltender	GPI	Mins	Avg	W	L	EN	SO	GA	SA	S%	G	A	PIM
35	Marty Turco	5	325	3.32	1	4	1	0	18	119	.849	0	0	0
	Totals	**5**	**327**	**3.49**	**1**	**4**	**1**	**0**	**19**	**120**	**.842**			

Coach

TIPPETT, DAVE
Coach, Dallas Stars. Born in Moosomin, Sask., August 25, 1961.

Dallas Stars general manager Doug Armstrong announced the hiring of Dave Tippett as the club's head coach on May 16, 2002. In his first season behind the bench in 2002-03, he led the Stars to the best record in the Western Conference and the second best in the NHL. Tippett had spent the previous three seasons as an assistant coach with the Los Angeles Kings. He served a five-game stint as interim head coach in 2002 while head coach Andy Murray recovered from an auto accident. In all three seasons Tippett was in Los Angeles the Kings qualified for the playoffs. They had reached the postseason just once out of the previous six seasons.

Under Tippett's direction, the Kings power-play led the NHL in 2001-02 with a 20.7 percent success rate. The year before Tippett came aboard the Kings, in 1998-99, the Kings power-play unit ranked 24th in the league. As a highly regarded minor league coach with tremendous work ethic, Tippett posted two 50-win seasons at Houston (International Hockey League) and led the Aeros to the 1999 Turner Cup championship while serving as general manager/head coach. He was also named IHL coach of the year.

Prior to becoming a coach, Tippett played 11 years as a forward in the National Hockey League with the Hartford Whalers, Washington Capitals, Pittsburgh Penguins and Philadelphia Flyers. He ended his playing career in 1995 as a player-assistant coach with the Houston Aeros (IHL). Internationally, he captained the 1984 Canadian Olympic team in Sarajevo, Yugoslavia, and he earned a silver medal as a member of the Canadian Olympic team in Albertville, France, in 1992. He was a member of the 1982 NCAA Division I championship squad at the University of North Dakota with former Stars defenseman Craig Ludwig.

Coaching Record

		Regular Season				Playoffs		
Season	Team	Games	W	L	T	Games	W	L
1995-96	Houston (IHL)	42	17	18	7	....	....	....
1996-97	Houston (IHL)	82	44	30	8	13	8	5
1997-98	Houston (IHL)	82	50	22	10	4	1	3
1998-99	Houston (IHL)	82	54	15	13	19	11	8
2002-03	**Dallas (NHL)**	**82**	**46**	**21**	**15**	**12**	**6**	**6**
2003-04	**Dallas (NHL)**	**82**	**41**	**28**	**13**	**5**	**1**	**4**
	NHL Totals	**164**	**87**	**49**	**28**	**17**	**7**	**10**

Coaching History

Wren Blair, 1967-68; Wren Blair and John Muckler, 1968-69; Wren Blair and Charlie Burns, 1969-70; Jack Gordon, 1970-71 to 1972-73; Jack Gordon and Parker MacDonald, 1973-74; Jack Gordon and Charlie Burns, 1974-75; Ted Harris, 1975-76, 1976-77; Ted Harris, André Beaulieu and Lou Nanne, 1977-78; Harry Howell and Glen Sonmor, 1978-79; Glen Sonmor, 1979-80 to 1981-82; Glen Sonmor and Murray Oliver, 1982-83; Bill Mahoney, 1983-84, 1984-85; Lorne Henning, 1985-86; Lorne Henning and Glen Sonmor, 1986-87; Herb Brooks, 1987-88; Pierre Page, 1988-89, 1989-90; Bob Gainey, 1990-91 to 1994-95; Bob Gainey and Ken Hitchcock, 1995-96; Ken Hitchcock, 1996-97 to 2000-01; Ken Hitchcock and Rick Wilson, 2001-02; Dave Tippett, 2002-03 to date.

Club Records

Team

(Figures in brackets for season records are games played; records for fewest points, wins, ties, losses, goals, goals against are for 70 or more games)

Most Points	**114**	1998-99 (82)
Most Wins	**51**	1998-99 (82)
Most Ties	**22**	1969-70 (76)
Most Losses	**53**	1975-76, 1977-78 (80)
Most Goals	**346**	1981-82 (80)
Most Goals Against	**349**	1987-88 (80)
Fewest Points	**45**	1977-78 (80)
Fewest Wins	**18**	1968-69 (76), 1977-78 (80)
Fewest Ties	**4**	1989-90 (80)
Fewest Losses	**17**	2002-03 (82)
Fewest Goals	**189**	1968-69 (76)
Fewest Goals Against	**167**	1997-98 (82)
Longest Winning Streak		
Overall	**7**	Mar. 16-28/80, Mar. 16-Apr. 2/97, Nov. 22-Dec. 5/97
Home	**11**	Nov. 4-Dec. 27/72
Away	**7**	Three times
Longest Undefeated Streak		
Overall	**17**	Jan. 23-Mar. 20/04 (13 wins, 4 ties)
Home	**13**	Oct. 28-Dec. 27/72 (12 wins, 1 tie), Nov. 21/79-Jan. 9/80 (10 wins, 3 ties), Jan. 17-Mar. 17/91 (11 wins, 2 ties)
Away	**10**	Jan. 12-Mar. 4/99 (8 wins, 2 ties)
Longest Losing Streak		
Overall	**10**	Feb. 1-20/76
Home	**6**	Jan. 17-Feb. 4/70
Away	**8**	Oct. 19-Nov. 13/75, Jan. 28-Mar. 3/88
Longest Winless Streak		
Overall	**20**	Jan. 15-Feb. 28/70 (15 losses, 5 ties)
Home	**12**	Jan. 17-Feb. 25/70 (8 losses, 4 ties)
Away	**23**	Oct. 25/74-Jan. 28/75 (19 losses, 4 ties)
Most Shutouts, Season	**11**	2000-01 (82), 2002-03 (82)
Most PIM, Season	**2,313**	1987-88 (80)
Most Goals, Game	**15**	Nov. 11/81 (Wpg. 2 at Min. 15)

Individual

Most Seasons	**16**	Neal Broten, Mike Modano
Most Games	**1,101**	Mike Modano
Most Goals, Career	**458**	Mike Modano
Most Assists, Career	**648**	Mike Modano
Most Points, Career	**1,106**	Mike Modano (458G, 648A)
Most PIM, Career	**1,883**	Shane Churla
Most Shutouts, Career	**27**	Ed Belfour
Longest Consecutive Games Streak	**442**	Danny Grant (Dec. 4/68-Apr. 7/74)
Most Goals, Season	**55**	Dino Ciccarelli (1981-82), Brian Bellows (1989-90)
Most Assists, Season	**76**	Neal Broten (1985-86)
Most Points, Season	**114**	Bobby Smith (1981-82; 43G, 71A)
Most PIM, Season	**382**	Basil McRae (1987-88)
Most Points, Defenseman, Season	**77**	Craig Hartsburg (1981-82; 17G, 60A)
Most Points, Center, Season	**114**	Bobby Smith (1981-82; 43G, 71A)
Most Points, Right Wing, Season	**106**	Dino Ciccarelli (1981-82; 55G, 51A)
Most Points, Left Wing, Season	**99**	Brian Bellows (1989-90; 55G, 44A)
Most Points, Rookie, Season	**98**	Neal Broten (1981-82; 38G, 60A)
Most Shutouts, Season	**9**	Ed Belfour (1997-98)
Most Goals, Game	**5**	Tim Young (Jan. 15/79)
Most Assists, Game	**5**	Murray Oliver (Oct. 24/71), Larry Murphy (Oct. 17/89)
Most Points, Game	**7**	Bobby Smith (Nov. 11/81; 4G, 3A)

Records include Minnesota North Stars, 1967-68 through 1992-93.

Retired Numbers

7	Neal Broten	1980-1995, 1996-1997
8	Bill Goldsworthy*	1967-1976
19	Bill Masterton*	1967-1968

* Minnesota North Stars

All-time Record vs. Other Clubs

Regular Season

	At Home								On Road								Total							
	GP	W	L	T	OL	GF	GA	PTS	GP	W	L	T	OL	GF	GA	PTS	GP	W	L	T	OL	GF	GA	PTS
Anaheim	27	20	5	2	0	101	52	42	27	13	11	3	0	66	61	29	54	33	16	5	0	167	113	71
Atlanta	4	4	0	0	0	9	4	8	4	4	0	0	0	16	9	8	8	8	0	0	0	25	13	16
Boston	61	18	30	13	0	175	220	49	60	9	41	10	0	146	258	28	121	27	71	23	0	321	478	77
Buffalo	54	27	21	6	0	173	156	60	52	13	28	11	0	139	188	37	106	40	49	17	0	312	344	97
Calgary	62	30	20	11	1	228	196	72	62	15	31	14	2	155	208	46	124	45	51	25	3	383	404	118
Carolina	29	17	10	2	0	115	86	36	32	15	13	4	0	110	101	34	61	32	23	6	0	225	187	70
Chicago	112	52	43	16	1	377	340	121	110	31	64	15	0	289	412	77	222	83	107	31	1	666	752	198
Colorado	41	21	13	5	2	131	115	49	41	11	22	7	1	103	150	30	82	32	35	12	3	234	265	79
Columbus	8	8	0	0	0	26	9	16	8	6	2	0	0	26	19	12	16	14	2	0	0	52	28	28
Detroit	106	51	36	18	1	370	319	121	106	37	53	16	0	336	406	90	212	88	89	34	1	706	725	211
Edmonton	45	24	14	7	0	163	126	55	44	15	20	8	1	145	176	39	89	39	34	15	1	308	302	94
Florida	8	3	2	2	1	25	22	9	10	5	4	1	0	28	22	11	18	8	6	3	1	53	44	20
Los Angeles	84	52	19	13	0	323	218	117	82	28	35	19	0	234	277	75	166	80	54	32	0	557	495	192
Minnesota	8	4	2	1	1	27	18	10	8	4	4	0	0	19	23	8	16	8	6	1	1	46	41	18
Montreal	59	17	30	12	0	153	203	46	58	12	37	9	0	144	250	33	117	29	67	21	0	297	453	79
Nashville	12	10	2	0	0	36	14	20	12	5	6	1	0	23	28	11	24	15	8	1	0	59	42	31
New Jersey	45	26	13	6	0	164	117	58	43	19	21	3	0	132	146	41	88	45	34	9	0	296	263	99
NY Islanders	47	18	20	8	1	139	170	45	48	14	25	8	1	134	176	37	95	32	45	16	2	273	346	82
NY Rangers	61	20	30	11	0	187	221	51	62	15	36	11	0	165	213	41	123	35	66	22	0	352	434	92
Ottawa	11	7	4	0	0	44	28	14	9	5	3	0	1	24	22	11	20	12	7	0	1	68	50	25
Philadelphia	66	27	23	16	0	216	212	70	67	9	42	16	0	150	255	34	133	36	65	32	0	366	467	104
Phoenix	55	27	19	9	0	199	166	63	54	27	23	4	0	182	170	58	109	54	42	13	0	381	336	121
Pittsburgh	64	37	21	6	0	246	213	80	63	19	38	6	0	178	236	44	127	56	59	12	0	424	449	124
St. Louis	115	53	39	22	1	383	334	129	117	32	63	21	1	330	424	86	232	85	102	43	2	713	758	215
San Jose	29	15	10	4	0	81	64	34	30	18	10	1	1	85	68	38	59	33	20	5	1	166	132	72
Tampa Bay	11	7	3	1	0	39	27	15	13	10	1	2	0	37	20	22	24	17	4	3	0	76	47	37
Toronto	97	50	36	11	0	365	306	111	101	35	49	17	0	319	356	87	198	85	85	28	0	684	662	198
Vancouver	71	37	22	12	0	259	211	86	71	30	30	10	1	218	252	71	142	67	52	22	1	477	463	157
Washington	41	21	11	8	1	152	110	51	40	17	15	8	0	129	120	42	81	38	26	16	1	281	230	93
Defunct Clubs	33	19	8	6	0	123	86	44	32	10	16	6	0	84	105	26	65	29	24	12	0	207	191	70
Totals	**1466**	**722**	**506**	**228**	**10**	**5029**	**4363**	**1682**	**1466**	**483**	**743**	**231**	**9**	**4146**	**5151**	**1206**	**2932**	**1205**	**1249**	**459**	**19**	**9175**	**9514**	**2888**

Playoffs

	Series	W	L	GP	W	L	T	GF	GA	Last Mtg.	Rnd.	Result
Anaheim	1	0	1	6	2	4	0	14	14	2003	CSF	L 2-4
Boston	1	1	0	3	3	0	0	20	13	1981	PRE	W 3-0
Buffalo	3	2	1	13	8	5	0	39	37	1999	F	W 4-2
Calgary	1	1	0	6	4	2	0	25	18	1981	SF	W 4-2
Chicago	6	2	4	33	14	19	0	118	120	1991	DSF	W 4-2
Colorado	3	2	1	19	9	10	0	47	48	2004	CQF	L 1-4
Detroit	3	0	3	18	6	12	0	40	55	1998	CF	L 2-4
Edmonton	8	6	2	42	27	15	0	118	104	2003	CQF	W 4-2
Los Angeles	1	1	0	7	4	3	0	26	21	1968	QF	W 4-3
Montreal	2	1	1	13	6	7	0	37	48	1980	QF	W 4-3
New Jersey	1	0	1	6	2	4	0	9	15	2000	F	L 2-4
NY Islanders	1	0	1	5	1	4	0	16	26	1981	F	L 1-4
Philadelphia	2	0	2	11	3	8	0	26	41	1980	SF	L 1-4
Pittsburgh	1	0	1	6	2	4	0	16	28	1991	F	L 2-4
St. Louis	12	6	6	66	34	32	0	197	187	2001	CSF	L 0-4
San Jose	2	2	0	11	8	3	0	31	19	2000	CSF	W 4-1
Toronto	2	2	0	7	6	1	0	35	26	1983	DSF	W 3-1
Vancouver	1	0	1	5	1	4	0	11	18	1994	CSF	L 1-4
Totals	**51**	**26**	**25**	**277**	**140**	**137**	**0**	**825**	**838**			

Calgary totals include Atlanta Flames, 1972-73 to 1979-80. Carolina totals include Hartford, 1979-80 to 1996-97.
Colorado totals include Quebec, 1979-80 to 1994-95.
New Jersey totals include Kansas City, 1974-75 to 1975-76, and Colorado Rockies, 1976-77 to 1981-82.
Phoenix totals include Winnipeg, 1979-80 to 1995-96.

Playoff Results 2004-2000

Year	Round	Opponent	Result	GF	GA
2004	CQF	Colorado	L 1-4	10	19
2003	CSF	Anaheim	L 2-4	14	14
	CQF	Edmonton	W 4-2	20	11
2001	CSF	St. Louis	L 0-4	6	13
	CQF	Edmonton	W 4-2	16	13
2000	F	New Jersey	L 2-4	9	15
	CF	Colorado	W 4-3	14	13
	CSF	San Jose	W 4-1	15	7
	CQF	Edmonton	W 4-1	14	11

Abbreviations: Round: F - Final; **CF** - conference final; **CSF** - conference semi-final; **CQF** - conference quarter-final; **DSF** - division semi-final; **SF** - semi-final; **QF** - quarter-final; **PRE** - preliminary round.

2003-04 Results

Oct.	8	Anaheim	4-1		5	at Anaheim	2-2
	11	at Nashville	3-1		8	Atlanta	2-1
	13	at Buffalo	3-4		10	Colorado	2-4
	15	Boston	0-2		13	at San Jose	3-0
	17	Washington	4-2		15	at Colorado	1-4
	19	Minnesota	3-1		17	at Calgary	3-2
	22	Toronto	1-3		19	at Vancouver	3-2
	24	at Detroit	0-4		20	at Edmonton	0-3
	25	at Columbus	3-2		23	St. Louis	2-0
	29	Calgary	4-3*		24	at St. Louis	3-2
Nov.	1	at Nashville	1-1		26	Detroit	2-2
	2	Nashville	7-3		28	Ottawa	5-3
	4	at NY Rangers	0-3		30	San Jose	3-1
	6	at NY Islanders	1-4		31	at Phoenix	5-4
	8	at Boston	1-4	**Feb.**	4	Columbus	1-0
	12	Detroit	2-6		11	NY Islanders	4-4
	14	Phoenix	3-3		14	at Phoenix	2-3
	15	at Colorado	0-3		16	at Anaheim	1-3
	19	Anaheim	3-3		18	at Los Angeles	4-3
	21	Los Angeles	3-1		20	Colorado	5-1
	22	at St. Louis	1-2		22	Anaheim	4-0
	24	Phoenix	5-2		25	Los Angeles	1-1
	26	at Minnesota	3-1		27	Minnesota	3-1
	28	New Jersey	2-0		29	Edmonton	5-4*
	30	Los Angeles	1-2	**Mar.**	3	Columbus	4-2
Dec.	4	at Los Angeles	0-3		5	Calgary	5-1
	6	at San Jose	1-2		7	San Jose	4-0
	7	at Anaheim	0-4		9	at Pittsburgh	0-4
	10	at Phoenix	1-2		11	at Philadelphia	2-2
	12	Chicago	1-0		13	at Detroit	0-3
	14	at Chicago	1-1		14	at Chicago	4-0
	17	Vancouver	3-1		16	San Jose	3-3
	19	at Florida	0-1		18	Vancouver	3-0
	20	at Tampa Bay	2-1		20	St. Louis	3-1
	22	at Carolina	3-1		22	at Calgary	4-0
	26	Nashville	2-1		24	at Edmonton	4-3*
	27	at Columbus	4-3		27	at Vancouver	2-3*
	29	Philadelphia	2-2		28	at San Jose	1-2*
	31	Montreal	1-1		31	Edmonton	1-3
Jan.	2	Phoenix	0-6	**Apr.**	2	at Minnesota	2-4
	3	at Los Angeles	2-2		4	Chicago	5-2

* – Overtime

Entry Draft
Selections 2004-1990

2004	2001	1997	1993
Pick	**Pick**	**Pick**	**Pick**
28 Mark Fistric	26 Jason Bacashihua	25 Brenden Morrow	9 Todd Harvey
34 Johan Fransson	70 Yared Hagos	52 Roman Lyashenko	35 Jamie Langenbrunner
52 Raymond Sawada	92 Anthony Aquino	77 Steve Gainey	87 Chad Lang
56 Nicklas Grossman	126 Daniel Volrab	105 Marcus Kristoffersson	136 Rick Mrozik
86 John Lammers	161 Mike Smith	132 Teemu Elomo	139 Per Svartvadet
104 Fredrik Naslund	167 Michal Blazek	160 Alexei Timkin	165 Jeremy Stasiuk
183 Trevor Ludwig	192 Jussi Jokinen	189 Jeff McKercher	191 Rob Lurtsema
218 Sergei Kukushin	255 Marco Rosa	216 Alexei Komarov	243 Jordan Willis
248 Lukas Vomela	265 Dale Sullivan	242 Brett McLean	249 Bill Lang
280 Matt Mcknight	285 Marek Tomica		269 Cory Peterson

2003	2000	1996	1992
Pick	**Pick**	**Pick**	**Pick**
33 Loui Eriksson	25 Steve Ott	5 Ric Jackman	34 Jarkko Varvio
36 Vojtech Polak	60 Dan Ellis	70 Jon Sim	58 Jeff Bes
54 Brandon Crombeen	68 Joel Lundqvist	90 Mike Hurley	88 Jere Lehtinen
99 Matt Nickerson	91 Alexei Tereschenko	112 Ryan Christie	130 Michael Johnson
134 Alexander Naurov	123 Vadim Khomitsky	113 Yevgeny Tsybuk	154 Kyle Peterson
144 Eero Kilpelainen	139 Ruslan Bernikov	166 Eoin McInerney	178 Juha Lind
165 Gino Guyer	162 Artem Chernov	194 Joel Kwiatkowski	202 Lars Edstrom
185 Francis Wathier	192 Ladislav Vlcek	220 Nick Bootland	226 Jeff Romfo
195 Drew Bagnall	219 Marco Tuokko		250 Jeffrey Moen
196 Elias Granath	224 Antti Miettinen	**1995**	
259 Niko Vainio		**Pick**	**1991**
	1999	11 Jarome Iginla	**Pick**
2002	**Pick**	37 Patrick Cote	8 Richard Matvichuk
Pick	32 Michael Ryan	63 Petr Buzek	74 Mike Torchia
26 Martin Vagner	66 Dan Jancevski	69 Sergey Gusev	97 Mike Kennedy
32 Janos Vas	96 Mathias Tjarnqvist	115 Wade Strand	118 Mark Lawrence
34 Tobias Stephan	126 Jeff Bateman	141 Dominic Marleau	137 Geoff Finch
42 Marius Holtet	156 Gregor Baumgartner	173 Jeff Dewar	174 Michael Burkett
43 Trevor Daley	184 Justin Cox	193 Anatoli Koveshnikov	184 Derek Herlofsky
78 Geoff Waugh	186 Brett Draney	202 Sergei Luchinkin	206 Tom Nemeth
110 Jarkko A. Immonen	215 Jeff MacMillan	219 Stephen Lowe	228 Shayne Green
147 David Bararuk	243 Brian Sullivan		250 Jukka Suomalainen
180 Kirill Sidorenko	265 Jamie Chamberlain	**1994**	
210 Bryan Hamm	272 Mikhail Donika	**Pick**	**1990**
243 Tuomas Mikkonen		20 Jason Botterill	**Pick**
273 Ned Havern	**1998**	46 Lee Jinman	8 Derian Hatcher
	Pick	98 Jamie Wright	50 Laurie Billeck
	39 John Erskine	124 Marty Turco	70 Cal McGowan
	57 Tyler Bouck	150 Evgeny Petrochinin	71 Frank Kovacs
	86 Gabriel Karlsson	228 Marty Flichel	92 Enrico Ciccone
	153 Pavel Patera	254 Jimmy Roy	113 Roman Turek
	173 Niko Kapanen	280 Chris Szysky	134 Jeff Levy
	200 Scott Perry		155 Doug Barrault
			176 Joe Biondi
			197 Troy Binnie
			218 Ole-Eskild Dahlstrom
			239 John McKersie

Captains' History
Bob Woytowich, 1967-68; Moose Vasko, 1968-69; Claude Larose, 1969-70; Ted Harris, 1970-71 to 1973-74; Bill Goldsworthy, 1974-75, 1975-76; Bill Hogaboam, 1976-77; Nick Beverley, 1977-78; J.P. Parise, 1978-79; Paul Shmyr, 1979-80, 1980-81; Tim Young, 1981-82; Craig Hartsburg, 1982-83; Craig Hartsburg and Brian Bellows, 1983-84; Craig Hartsburg, 1984-85 to 1987-88; Curt Fraser, Bob Rouse and Curt Giles, 1988-89; Curt Giles, 1989-90, 1990-91; Mark Tinordi, 1991-92 to 1993-94; Neal Broten and Derian Hatcher, 1994-95; Derian Hatcher, 1995-96 to 2002-03; Mike Modano, 2003-04 to date.

General Managers' History
Wren Blair, 1967-68 to 1973-74; Jack Gordon, 1974-75 to 1976-77; Lou Nanne, 1977-78 to 1987-88; Jack Ferreira, 1988-89, 1989-90; Bob Clarke 1990-91, 1991-92; Bob Gainey, 1992-93 to 2000-01; Bob Gainey and Doug Armstrong, 2001-02; Doug Armstrong, 2002-03 to date.

General Manager

ARMSTRONG, DOUG
General Manager, Dallas Stars. Born in Sarnia, Ont., September 24, 1964.

Doug Armstrong was in his ninth season as an assistant to Bob Gainey when he was elevated to the position of general manager on January 25, 2002. In his first full season on the job in 2002-03, the Stars had the best record in the Western Conference and the second best in the NHL. Armstrong originally joined the club in 1991. As Gainey's assistant, he worked on contract information and season scheduling and handled the day-to-day operations of the hockey department. In five seasons from 1996 to 2001, he helped Gainey build a team that won five straight division championships, as well as the Presidents' Trophy for the best regular-season record in the NHL twice, and the 1999 Stanley Cup. At the international level, Armstrong served as Team Canada's assistant general manger at the 2002 World Championships in Sweden.

A native of Sarnia, Ontario, Armstrong attended Western Michigan University for two years before transferring to Florida State University in Tallahassee, where he earned his B.S. in Business Administration with a major in marketing.

Club Directory

American Airlines Center

Dallas Stars
2601 Ave. of the Stars
Frisco, TX 75034
Office Address:
Dr Pepper StarCenter
211 Cowboys Parkway
Irving, TX 75063
Phone **214/387-5600**
FAX 214/387-5610
Ticket Information 214/GO STARS
www.dallasstars.com
Capacity: 18,532

Chairman of the Board and Owner . . . . Thomas O. Hicks
President. . . . . James R. Lites
Executive Vice President, Sales & Marketing . . . . . . Geoff Moore
Executive Vice President, Finance & CFO . . . . Robert Hutson
Executive Vice President, Corporate Sales . . . . Tom Fireoved
Executive Vice President, Business Operations . . . . . Randy Locey
Assistant to the President . . . . Cheryl Hocker

Hockey Operations
General Manager . . . . Doug Armstrong
Assistant General Manager . . . . Francois Giguere
Assistant General Manager . . . . Les Jackson
Assistant General Manager . . . . Guy Carbonneau
Head Coach . . . . Dave Tippett
Associate Coach . . . . Rick Wilson
Assistant Coach . . . . Mark Lamb
Assistant/Goaltending Coach . . . . Andy Moog
Coaching Assistant/Video Coordinator . . . . Derek MacKinnon
Director, Hockey Administration and Team Services . Lesa Moake
Administrative Assistant, Hockey Operations . . . . . Pam Wenzel
Director, Amateur Scouting . . . . Tim Bernhardt
Director, Professional Scouting . . . . Doug Overton
Scout . . . . Bob Gernander
Professional Scout . . . . Paul McIntosh
Regional Scouts. . . . . Hands Edlund, Jack Foley, Jiri Hrdina, Dennis Holland, Jimmy Johnston, Jim Pederson, Brad Robson, Karri Takko
Head Athletic Trainer . . . . Dave Surprenant
Head Equipment Manager . . . . Steve Sumner
Strength and Conditioning Coach. . . . . J.J. McQueen
Assistant Equipment Manager . . . . Tony Addeo
Assistant Athletic Trainer. . . . . Tommy Alva

Communications
Senior Director of Hockey Communications . . . . . . Rob Scichili
Director of Media Relations . . . . Mark Janko
Director, Community Relations . . . . Julie Berkhouse
Manager, Publications and Media Relations . . . . . . Jason Rademan
Desktop/LAN Support . . . . Bill Jennings
Office Manager. . . . . Christine Hill

Broadcasting
Announcers, TV/Radio. . . . . Ralph Strangis, Daryl Reaugh
Arena Announcer . . . . Bill Oellermann

Business Operations
Department Analyst . . . . Christy Norton

Corporate Sales
Director, Corporate Sales . . . . Jeff Tummonds
Broadcast and Sales Services Manager. . . . . Brooke Fendrick
Sponsorship Manager . . . . Ben Young

Marketing
Vice President, Marketing . . . . Christy Martinez
Manager, In-Arena Production . . . . Scott Robertson
Manager, Marketing . . . . Ashley House
Manager, New Media . . . . Lane Pate

Merchandising
District Manager, Merchandise . . . . Jason Atkinson
Merchandising Analyst and Buyer . . . . Jill Moore
Inventory Controller . . . . Gary Peterson

Ticket Operations
Director, Ticket Operations . . . . Stacey Marthaler
Assistant Director, Ticket Operations . . . . Matt McKee
Box Office Assistants . . . . Jessica Everdale, Kenna Talley, Sharon Talley

Ticket Sales
Vice President, Ticket Sales . . . . Jamie Norman
Director, Stars Season Tickets Sales . . . . Colin Faulkner
Account Executives . . . . Brad Brawner, Ben Cahalane, Rodney Ferrell, Shelly Ford, Andrea Myers, Nick Ralston, Blake Teegarden
Customer Service Representatives . . . . Jeremy Gray

Kris Draper set career highs with 24 goals and 40 points.

Detroit Red Wings

2003-04 Results: 48W-21L-11T-2OTL 109PTS.
First, Central Division

Year-by-Year Record

		Home				Road				Overall								
Season	GP	W	L	T	OL	W	L	T	OL	W	L	T	OL	GF	GA	Pts.	Finished	Playoff Result
2003-04	82	30	7	4	0	18	14	7	2	48	21	11	2	255	189	109	1st, Central Div.	Lost Conf. Semi-Final
2002-03	82	28	6	5	2	20	14	5	2	48	20	10	4	269	203	110	1st, Central Div.	Lost Conf. Quarter-Final
2001-02	**82**	**28**	**7**	**5**	**1**	**23**	**10**	**5**	**3**	**51**	**17**	**10**	**4**	**251**	**187**	**116**	**1st, Central Div.**	**Won Stanley Cup**
2000-01	82	27	9	3	2	22	11	6	2	49	20	9	4	253	202	111	1st, Central Div.	Lost Conf. Quarter-Final
1999-2000	82	28	9	3	1	20	13	7	1	48	22	10	2	278	210	108	2nd, Central Div.	Lost Conf. Semi-Final
1998-99	82	27	12	2	...	16	20	5	...	43	32	7	...	245	202	93	1st, Central Div.	Lost Conf. Semi-Final
1997-98	**82**	**25**	**8**	**8**	**...**	**19**	**15**	**7**	**...**	**44**	**23**	**15**	**...**	**250**	**196**	**103**	**2nd, Central Div.**	**Won Stanley Cup**
1996-97	**82**	**20**	**12**	**9**	**...**	**18**	**14**	**9**	**...**	**38**	**26**	**18**	**...**	**253**	**197**	**94**	**2nd, Central Div.**	**Won Stanley Cup**
1995-96	82	36	3	2	...	26	10	5	...	62	13	7	...	325	181	131	1st, Central Div.	Lost Conf. Championship
1994-95	48	17	4	3	...	16	7	1	...	33	11	4	...	180	117	70	1st, Central Div.	Lost Final
1993-94	84	23	13	6	...	23	17	2	...	46	30	8	...	356	275	100	1st, Central Div.	Lost Conf. Quarter-Final
1992-93	84	25	14	3	...	22	14	6	...	47	28	9	...	369	280	103	2nd, Norris Div.	Lost Div. Semi-Final
1991-92	80	24	12	4	...	19	13	8	...	43	25	12	...	320	256	98	1st, Norris Div.	Lost Div. Final
1990-91	80	26	14	0	...	8	24	8	...	34	38	8	...	273	298	76	3rd, Norris Div.	Lost Div. Semi-Final
1989-90	80	20	14	6	...	8	24	8	...	28	38	14	...	288	323	70	5th, Norris Div.	Out of Playoffs
1988-89	80	20	14	6	...	14	20	6	...	34	34	12	...	313	316	80	1st, Norris Div.	Lost Div. Semi-Final
1987-88	80	24	10	6	...	17	18	5	...	41	28	11	...	322	269	93	1st, Norris Div.	Lost Conf. Championship
1986-87	80	20	14	6	...	14	22	4	...	34	36	10	...	260	274	78	2nd, Norris Div.	Lost Conf. Championship
1985-86	80	10	26	4	...	7	31	2	...	17	57	6	...	266	415	40	5th, Norris Div.	Out of Playoffs
1984-85	80	19	14	7	...	8	27	5	...	27	41	12	...	313	357	66	3rd, Norris Div.	Lost Div. Semi-Final
1983-84	80	18	20	2	...	13	22	5	...	31	42	7	...	298	323	69	3rd, Norris Div.	Lost Div. Semi-Final
1982-83	80	14	19	7	...	7	25	8	...	21	44	15	...	263	344	57	5th, Norris Div.	Out of Playoffs
1981-82	80	15	19	6	...	6	28	6	...	21	47	12	...	270	351	54	6th, Norris Div.	Out of Playoffs
1980-81	80	16	15	9	...	3	28	9	...	19	43	18	...	252	339	56	5th, Norris Div.	Out of Playoffs
1979-80	80	14	21	5	...	12	22	6	...	26	43	11	...	268	306	63	5th, Norris Div.	Out of Playoffs
1978-79	80	15	17	8	...	8	24	8	...	23	41	16	...	252	295	62	5th, Norris Div.	Out of Playoffs
1977-78	80	22	11	7	...	10	23	7	...	32	34	14	...	252	266	78	2nd, Norris Div.	Lost Quarter-Final
1976-77	80	12	22	6	...	4	33	3	...	16	55	9	...	183	309	41	5th, Norris Div.	Out of Playoffs
1975-76	80	17	15	8	...	9	29	2	...	26	44	10	...	226	300	62	4th, Norris Div.	Out of Playoffs
1974-75	80	17	17	6	...	6	28	6	...	23	45	12	...	259	335	58	4th, Norris Div.	Out of Playoffs
1973-74	78	21	12	6	...	8	27	4	...	29	39	10	...	255	319	68	6th, East Div.	Out of Playoffs
1972-73	78	22	12	5	...	15	17	7	...	37	29	12	...	265	243	86	5th, East Div.	Out of Playoffs
1971-72	78	25	11	3	...	8	24	7	...	33	35	10	...	261	262	76	5th, East Div.	Out of Playoffs
1970-71	78	17	15	7	...	5	30	4	...	22	45	11	...	209	308	55	7th, East Div.	Out of Playoffs
1969-70	76	20	11	7	...	20	10	8	...	40	21	15	...	246	199	95	3rd, East Div.	Lost Quarter-Final
1968-69	76	23	8	7	...	10	23	5	...	33	31	12	...	239	221	78	5th, East Div.	Out of Playoffs
1967-68	74	18	15	4	...	9	20	8	...	27	35	12	...	245	257	66	6th, East Div.	Out of Playoffs
1966-67	70	21	11	3	...	6	28	1	...	27	39	4	...	212	241	58	5th,	Out of Playoffs
1965-66	70	20	8	7	...	11	19	5	...	31	27	12	...	221	194	74	4th,	Lost Final
1964-65	70	25	7	3	...	15	16	4	...	40	23	7	...	224	175	87	1st,	Lost Semi-Final
1963-64	70	23	9	3	...	7	20	8	...	30	29	11	...	191	204	71	4th,	Lost Final
1962-63	70	19	10	6	...	13	15	7	...	32	25	13	...	200	194	77	4th,	Lost Final
1961-62	70	17	11	7	...	6	22	7	...	23	33	14	...	184	219	60	5th,	Out of Playoffs
1960-61	70	15	13	7	...	10	16	9	...	25	29	16	...	195	215	66	4th,	Lost Final
1959-60	70	18	14	3	...	8	15	12	...	26	29	15	...	186	197	67	4th,	Lost Semi-Final
1958-59	70	13	17	5	...	12	20	3	...	25	37	8	...	167	218	58	6th,	Out of Playoffs
1957-58	70	16	11	8	...	13	18	4	...	29	29	12	...	176	207	70	3rd,	Lost Semi-Final
1956-57	70	23	7	5	...	15	13	7	...	38	20	12	...	198	157	88	1st,	Lost Semi-Final
1955-56	70	21	6	8	...	9	18	8	...	30	24	16	...	183	148	76	2nd,	Lost Final
1954-55	**70**	**25**	**5**	**5**	**...**	**17**	**12**	**6**	**...**	**42**	**17**	**11**	**...**	**204**	**134**	**95**	**1st,**	**Won Stanley Cup**
1953-54	**70**	**24**	**4**	**7**	**...**	**13**	**15**	**7**	**...**	**37**	**19**	**14**	**...**	**191**	**132**	**88**	**1st,**	**Won Stanley Cup**
1952-53	70	20	5	10	...	16	11	8	...	36	16	18	...	222	133	90	1st,	Lost Semi-Final
1951-52	**70**	**24**	**7**	**4**	**...**	**20**	**7**	**8**	**...**	**44**	**14**	**12**	**...**	**215**	**133**	**100**	**1st,**	**Won Stanley Cup**
1950-51	70	25	3	7	...	19	10	6	...	44	13	13	...	236	139	101	1st,	Lost Semi-Final
1949-50	**70**	**19**	**9**	**7**	**...**	**18**	**10**	**7**	**...**	**37**	**19**	**14**	**...**	**229**	**164**	**88**	**1st,**	**Won Stanley Cup**
1948-49	60	21	6	3	...	13	13	4	...	34	19	7	...	195	145	75	1st,	Lost Final
1947-48	60	16	9	5	...	14	9	7	...	30	18	12	...	187	148	72	2nd,	Lost Final
1946-47	60	14	10	6	...	8	17	5	...	22	27	11	...	190	193	55	4th,	Lost Semi-Final
1945-46	50	16	5	4	...	4	15	6	...	20	20	10	...	146	159	50	4th,	Lost Semi-Final
1944-45	50	19	5	1	...	12	9	4	...	31	14	5	...	218	161	67	2nd,	Lost Final
1943-44	50	18	5	2	...	8	13	4	...	26	18	6	...	214	177	58	2nd,	Lost Semi-Final
1942-43	**50**	**16**	**4**	**5**	**...**	**9**	**10**	**6**	**...**	**25**	**14**	**11**	**...**	**169**	**124**	**61**	**1st,**	**Won Stanley Cup**
1941-42	48	14	7	3	...	5	18	1	...	19	25	4	...	140	147	42	5th,	Lost Final
1940-41	48	14	5	5	...	7	11	6	...	21	16	11	...	112	102	53	3rd,	Lost Final
1939-40	48	11	10	3	...	5	16	3	...	16	26	6	...	91	126	38	5th,	Lost Semi-Final
1938-39	48	14	8	2	...	4	16	4	...	18	24	6	...	107	128	42	5th,	Lost Semi-Final
1937-38	48	8	10	6	...	4	15	5	...	12	25	11	...	99	133	35	4th, Amn. Div.	Out of Playoffs
1936-37	**48**	**14**	**5**	**5**	**...**	**11**	**9**	**4**	**...**	**25**	**14**	**9**	**...**	**128**	**102**	**59**	**1st, Amn. Div.**	**Won Stanley Cup**
1935-36	**48**	**14**	**5**	**5**	**...**	**10**	**11**	**3**	**...**	**24**	**16**	**8**	**...**	**124**	**103**	**56**	**1st, Amn. Div.**	**Won Stanley Cup**
1934-35	48	11	8	5	...	8	14	2	...	19	22	7	...	127	114	45	4th, Amn. Div.	Out of Playoffs
1933-34	48	15	5	4	...	9	9	6	...	24	14	10	...	113	98	58	1st, Amn. Div.	Lost Final
1932-33*	48	17	3	4	...	8	12	4	...	25	15	8	...	111	93	58	2nd, Amn. Div.	Lost Semi-Final
1931-32	48	15	3	6	...	3	17	4	...	18	20	10	...	95	108	46	3rd, Amn. Div.	Lost Quarter-Final
1930-31**	44	10	7	5	...	6	14	2	...	16	21	7	...	102	105	39	4th, Amn. Div.	Out of Playoffs
1929-30	44	9	10	3	...	5	14	3	...	14	24	6	...	117	133	34	4th, Amn. Div.	Out of Playoffs
1928-29	44	11	6	5	...	8	10	4	...	19	16	9	...	72	63	47	3rd, Amn. Div.	Lost Quarter-Final
1927-28	44	9	10	3	...	10	9	3	...	19	19	6	...	88	79	44	4th, Amn. Div.	Out of Playoffs
1926-27***	44	5	16	0	...	7	12	4	...	12	28	4	...	76	105	28	5th, Amn. Div.	Out of Playoffs

* Team name changed to Red Wings. ** Team name changed to Falcons. *** Team named Cougars.

2004-05 Schedule

Oct.	Thu.	14	at Edmonton		Sun.	9	at Chicago
	Sat.	16	at Vancouver		Tue.	11	at Boston
	Wed.	20	Carolina		Thu.	13	Nashville
	Fri.	22	Chicago		Sat.	15	Toronto
	Sat.	23	at New Jersey		Mon.	17	Dallas
	Mon.	25	Anaheim		Wed.	19	Calgary
	Wed.	27	Dallas		Fri.	21	at Dallas
	Fri.	29	at Atlanta		Sat.	22	at Phoenix
	Sat.	30	at Nashville		Wed.	26	at Chicago
Nov.	Tue.	2	Edmonton		Sat.	29	Colorado*
	Fri.	5	at Columbus	**Feb.**	Tue.	1	Anaheim
	Sat.	6	Phoenix		Thu.	3	at Edmonton
	Tue.	9	Los Angeles		Sat.	5	at Calgary
	Thu.	11	at Washington		Wed.	9	Los Angeles
	Sat.	13	Columbus		Tue.	15	Buffalo
	Wed.	17	at San Jose		Thu.	17	St. Louis
	Fri.	19	at Anaheim		Sat.	19	at Tampa Bay*
	Sat.	20	at Los Angeles		Sun.	20	at Florida*
	Wed.	24	Calgary		Wed.	23	New Jersey
	Fri.	26	Minnesota		Sat.	26	San Jose*
	Sat.	27	at St. Louis		Sun.	27	at Nashville*
	Mon.	29	San Jose	**Mar.**	Tue.	1	Edmonton
Dec.	Wed.	1	Columbus		Thu.	3	Montreal
	Fri.	3	Chicago		Sat.	5	Pittsburgh
	Sat.	4	at Pittsburgh		Tue.	8	Phoenix
	Mon.	6	St. Louis		Thu.	10	at Minnesota
	Wed.	8	at Colorado		Fri.	11	at Columbus
	Fri.	10	at Vancouver		Sun.	13	Colorado
	Sat.	11	at Calgary		Wed.	16	Nashville
	Tue.	14	Chicago		Sat.	19	at San Jose*
	Thu.	16	Vancouver		Mon.	21	at Anaheim
	Fri.	17	at Chicago		Tue.	22	at Los Angeles
	Sun.	19	Ottawa		Thu.	24	St. Louis
	Tue.	21	NY Islanders		Sat.	26	NY Rangers
	Sun.	26	at St. Louis		Mon.	28	at St. Louis
	Mon.	27	at Dallas		Thu.	31	at Nashville
	Wed.	29	at Phoenix	**Apr.**	Fri.	1	Columbus
	Fri.	31	Vancouver		Sun.	3	at Philadelphia*
Jan.	Sun.	2	at NY Islanders*		Wed.	6	at Columbus
	Wed.	5	Nashville		Fri.	8	Minnesota
	Sat.	8	at Colorado*		Sun.	10	at Minnesota*

* Denotes afternoon game.

Franchise date: September 25, 1926

WESTERN NHL CONFERENCE

CENTRAL DIVISION

79th NHL Season

2004-05 Player Personnel

FORWARDS	HT	WT	S	Place of Birth	Date	2003-04 Club
BARNES, Ryan	6-1	201	L	Dunnville, Ont.	1/30/80	Detroit-Grand Rapids
BOOTLAND, Darryl	6-1	194	R	Toronto, Ont.	11/2/81	Detroit-Grand Rapids
DANDENAULT, Mathieu	6-0	200	R	Sherbrooke, Que.	2/3/76	Detroit
DATSYUK, Pavel	5-11	180	L	Sverdlovsk, USSR	7/20/78	Detroit
DRAPER, Kris	5-11	190	L	Toronto, Ont.	5/24/71	Detroit
HIMELFARB, Eric	5-9	161	R	Thornhill, Ont.	1/1/83	Grand Rapids-Kingston
HOLMSTROM, Tomas	6-0	200	L	Pitea, Sweden	1/23/73	Detroit
HUDLER, Jiri	5-9	178	L	Olomouc, Czech.	1/4/84	Detroit-Grand Rapids
JACKSON, Todd	5-11	170	R	Syracuse, NY	4/10/81	U. of Maine
KOPECKY, Tomas	6-3	187	L	Ilava, Czech.	2/5/82	Grand Rapids
LANG, Robert	6-2	216	R	Teplice, Czech.	12/19/70	Washington-Detroit
MALTBY, Kirk	6-0	180	R	Guelph, Ont.	12/22/72	Detroit
MANLOW, Eric	6-0	180	L	Belleville, Ont.	4/7/75	NY Islanders-Bridgeport
McCARTY, Darren	6-1	210	R	Burnaby, B.C.	4/1/72	Detroit
MOWERS, Mark	5-11	187	R	Whitesboro, NY	2/16/74	Detroit-Grand Rapids
ROBINSON, Nathan	5-9	180	L	Kingston, Ont.	12/31/81	Detroit-Grand Rapids
SHANAHAN, Brendan	6-3	218	R	Mimico, Ont.	1/23/69	Detroit
VANDERMEER, Peter	6-0	210	L	Carolina, Alta.	10/14/75	Philadelphia (AHL)
WHITNEY, Ray	5-10	175	R	Fort Saskatchewan, Alta.	5/8/72	Detroit
WILLIAMS, Jason	5-11	185	R	London, Ont.	8/11/80	Detroit
YZERMAN, Steve	5-11	185	R	Cranbrook, B.C.	5/9/65	Detroit
ZETTERBERG, Henrik	5-11	176	L	Njurunda, Sweden	10/9/80	Detroit
DEFENSEMEN						
BALLANTYNE, Paul	6-3	200	R	Waterloo, Ont.	7/16/82	Grand Rapids-Toledo-Louisiana
CHELIOS, Chris	6-1	190	R	Chicago, IL	1/25/62	Detroit
FISCHER, Jiri	6-5	225	L	Horovice, Czech.	7/31/80	Detroit
GROULX, Danny	6-0	205	L	LaSalle, Que.	6/23/81	Grand Rapids
HATCHER, Derian	6-5	235	L	Sterling Hts., MI	6/4/72	Detroit
HELMER, Bryan	6-1	200	R	Sault Ste. Marie, Ont.	7/15/72	Phoenix-Springfield
KRONWALL, Niklas	5-11	165	L	Stockholm, Sweden	1/12/81	Detroit-Grand Rapids
LEBDA, Brett	5-11	194	L	Buffalo Grove, IL	1/15/82	U. of Notre Dame-Grand Rapids
LIDSTROM, Nicklas	6-2	185	L	Vasteras, Sweden	4/28/70	Detroit
MEECH, Derek	5-11	182	L	Winnipeg, Man.	4/21/84	Red Deer
RIVERS, Jamie	6-0	195	L	Ottawa, Ont.	3/16/75	Detroit-Grand Rapids
SCHNEIDER, Mathieu	5-10	192	L	New York, NY	6/12/69	Detroit
WOOLLEY, Jason	6-0	203	L	Toronto, Ont.	7/27/69	Detroit

GOALTENDERS	HT	WT	C	Place of Birth	Date	2003-04 Club
JOSEPH, Curtis	5-11	190	L	Keswick, Ont.	4/29/67	Detroit-Grand Rapids
LEGACE, Manny	5-9	162	L	Toronto, Ont.	2/4/73	Detroit
MacINTYRE, Drew	6-0	173	L	Charlottetown, P.E.I.	6/24/83	Toledo

Coach

LEWIS, DAVE
Coach, Detroit Red Wings. Born in Kindersley, Sask,. July 3, 1953.

A member of the Red Wings coaching staff since retiring as a player on November 6, 1987, Dave Lewis was officially named to replace Scotty Bowman as Detroit's head coach on July 17, 2002. In his first two seasons as the club's head coach, Lewis guided the Red Wings to back-to-back Central Division titles, giving the team four straight division crowns and five in the last six years. Detroit won the Presidents' Trophy in 2003-04. In his 14 seasons as an assistant coach, Lewis worked under Jacques Demers, Bryan Murray and Bowman. He served as an associate coach alongside Barry Smith during Bowman's nine-year tenure as head coach. Lewis excelled as both a motivator and a tactician. Besides the ability to shape the young talent on the Red Wings roster, Lewis also earned the respect of the Wings veterans like Steve Yzerman, Chris Chelios, Nicklas Lidstrom and Brett Hull. His primary focus was the team's defensive corps. His other duties included extensive video work used in scouting opponents.

Lewis joined the Red Wings organization as a player when he was signed as a free agent on July 27, 1986. He played his 1,000th NHL game with Detroit on April 1, 1987. Lewis was originally selected 33rd overall by the New York Islanders in the 1973 Amateur Draft and entered the NHL for the 1973-74 season directly out of junior hockey with the Saskatoon Blades. He never played a game in the minor leagues. In all, Lewis played 1,008 games with the Islanders, Los Angeles, New Jersey and Detroit. He recorded 36 goals, 187 assists and 953 penalty minutes. He was never a Stanley Cup winner during 15 years as a player, but he helped the Red Wings win the championship three times (1997, 1998 and 2002) as an assistant coach.

Off the ice, Lewis has been actively involved with the Make-A-Wish Foundation. He has organized the Dave Lewis Detroit Red Wings Fantasy Camp and celebrity auctions to raise funds for the charitable organization.

Coaching Record

		Regular Season				Playoffs		
Season	Team	Games	W	L	T	Games	W	L
1998-99	Detroit (NHL)	5	4	1	0	....	....	....
2002-03	Detroit (NHL)	82	48	24	10	4	0	4
2003-04	Detroit (NHL)	82	48	23	11	12	6	6
	NHL Totals	169	100	48	21	16	6	10

Shared a 4-1-0 record with associate coach Barry Smith while serving as co-head coaches until Scotty Bowman received medical clearance and returned to coaching on October 23, 1998.

2003-04 Scoring

* - rookie

Regular Season

Pos	#	Player	Team	GP	G	A	Pts	+/-	PIM	PP	SH	GW	GT	S	%
C	20	Robert Lang	WSH	63	29	45	74	2	24	10	0	2	1	149	19.5
			DET	6	1	4	5	2	0	0	0	1	0	14	7.1
			TOTAL	69	30	49	79	4	24	10	0	3	1	163	18.4
C	13	Pavel Datsyuk	DET	75	30	38	68	–2	35	8	1	4	0	136	22.1
R	17	Brett Hull	DET	81	25	43	68	–4	12	10	0	6	1	200	12.5
L	14	Brendan Shanahan	DET	82	25	28	53	15	117	8	0	7	0	280	8.9
C	19	Steve Yzerman	DET	75	18	33	51	10	46	7	0	3	1	141	12.8
D	23	Mathieu Schneider	DET	78	14	32	46	22	56	4	1	4	0	165	8.5
L	40	Henrik Zetterberg	DET	61	15	28	43	15	14	7	1	2	1	137	10.9
L	41	Ray Whitney	DET	67	14	29	43	7	22	3	1	4	0	119	11.8
C	33	Kris Draper	DET	67	24	16	40	22	31	2	5	1	1	149	16.1
D	5	Nicklas Lidstrom	DET	81	10	28	38	19	18	3	1	3	1	194	5.2
L	18	Kirk Maltby	DET	79	14	19	33	24	80	1	4	4	0	123	11.4
L	96	Tomas Holmstrom	DET	67	15	15	30	8	38	6	0	0	1	74	20.3
R	32	Steve Thomas	DET	44	10	12	22	8	25	0	0	3	0	80	12.5
D	24	Chris Chelios	DET	69	2	19	21	12	61	0	0	0	0	113	1.8
D	15	Jason Woolley	DET	55	4	15	19	19	28	0	0	1	0	60	6.7
D	8	Jiri Fischer	DET	81	4	15	19	0	75	1	0	0	0	115	3.5
C	21	Boyd Devereaux	DET	61	6	9	15	–1	20	0	0	2	0	62	9.7
C	29	Jason Williams	DET	49	6	7	13	1	15	0	0	0	0	44	13.6
D	11	Mathieu Dandenault	DET	65	3	9	12	9	40	0	1	0	0	68	4.4
R	25	Darren Mccarty	DET	43	6	5	11	2	50	1	0	0	0	61	9.8
R	44	Mark Mowers	DET	52	3	8	11	3	4	1	0	1	0	48	6.3
D	4	Jamie Rivers	DET	50	3	4	7	9	41	0	0	0	0	31	9.7
D	55 *	Niklas Kronwall	DET	20	1	4	5	5	16	0	0	1	0	18	5.6
D	2	Derian Hatcher	DET	15	0	4	4	4	8	0	0	0	0	18	0.0
C	26 *	Jiri Hudler	DET	12	1	2	3	–1	10	1	0	0	0	8	12.5
R	27 *	Darryl Bootland	DET	22	1	1	2	–3	74	0	0	1	0	13	7.7
C	28	Kevin Miller	DET	4	0	2	2	2	0	0	0	0	0	2	0.0
D	22	Anders Myrvold	DET	8	0	1	1	–1	2	0	0	0	0	6	0.0
L	52 *	Ryan Barnes	DET	2	0	0	0	0	0	0	0	0	0	0	0.0
L	38 *	Nathan Robinson	DET	5	0	0	0	–1	2	0	0	0	0	5	0.0

Goaltending

No.	Goaltender	GPI	Mins	Avg	W	L	T	EN	SO	GA	SA	S%	G	A	PIM
35	Marc Lamothe	2	125	1.44	1	0	1	0	0	3	58	.948	0	0	0
34	Manny Legace	41	2325	2.12	23	10	5	3	3	82	1019	.920	0	0	0
39	Dominik Hasek	14	817	2.20	8	3	2	1	2	30	324	.907	0	2	2
31	Curtis Joseph	31	1708	2.39	16	10	3	2	2	68	744	.909	0	0	2
	Totals	**82**	**4991**	**2.27**	**48**	**23**	**11**	**6**	**7**	**189**	**2151**	**.912**			

Playoffs

Pos	#	Player	Team	GP	G	A	Pts	+/-	PIM	PP	SH	GW	GT	S	%
C	20	Robert Lang	DET	12	4	5	9	–1	6	0	0	0	0	20	20.0
D	5	Nicklas Lidstrom	DET	12	2	5	7	4	4	2	0	0	0	27	7.4
L	14	Brendan Shanahan	DET	12	1	5	6	4	20	0	1	0	0	41	2.4
C	13	Pavel Datsyuk	DET	12	0	6	6	1	2	0	0	0	0	19	0.0
C	19	Steve Yzerman	DET	11	3	2	5	–1	0	0	0	1	0	18	16.7
R	17	Brett Hull	DET	12	3	2	5	0	4	1	0	1	0	39	7.7
L	96	Tomas Holmstrom	DET	12	2	2	4	0	10	1	0	1	0	20	10.0
L	40	Henrik Zetterberg	DET	12	2	2	4	0	4	0	0	0	0	23	8.7
C	33	Kris Draper	DET	12	1	3	4	1	6	0	0	0	0	23	4.3
L	41	Ray Whitney	DET	12	1	3	4	–4	4	0	0	1	0	21	4.8
L	18	Kirk Maltby	DET	12	1	3	4	2	11	0	0	0	0	18	5.6
D	23	Mathieu Schneider	DET	12	1	2	3	2	8	1	0	1	0	32	3.1
D	11	Mathieu Dandenault	DET	12	1	1	2	–1	6	0	0	1	0	17	5.9
C	21	Boyd Devereaux	DET	3	1	0	1	0	0	0	0	0	0	3	33.3
D	8	Jiri Fischer	DET	11	1	0	1	–2	16	0	0	0	0	8	12.5
R	32	Steve Thomas	DET	6	0	1	1	1	2	0	0	0	0	10	0.0
D	24	Chris Chelios	DET	8	0	1	1	1	4	0	0	0	0	14	0.0
D	2	Derian Hatcher	DET	12	0	1	1	0	15	0	0	0	0	12	0.0
R	25	Darren McCarty	DET	12	0	1	1	0	7	0	0	0	0	15	0.0
D	4	Jamie Rivers	DET	2	0	0	0	0	2	0	0	0	0	0	0.0
C	29	Jason Williams	DET	3	0	0	0	0	2	0	0	0	0	2	0.0
D	15	Jason Woolley	DET	4	0	0	0	–1	0	0	0	0	0	3	0.0

Goaltending

No.	Goaltender	GPI	Mins	Avg	W	L	EN	SO	GA	SA	S%	G	A	PIM
31	Curtis Joseph	9	518	1.39	4	4	0	1	12	197	.939	0	0	2
34	Manny Legace	4	220	2.18	2	2	0	0	8	84	.905	0	1	0
	Totals	**12**	**742**	**1.62**	**6**	**6**	**0**	**1**	**20**	**281**	**.929**			

Coaching History

Art Duncan, 1926-27; Jack Adams, 1927-28 to 1946-47; Tommy Ivan, 1947-48 to 1953-54; Jimmy Skinner, 1954-55 to 1956-57; Jimmy Skinner and Sid Abel, 1957-58; Sid Abel, 1958-59 to 1967-68; Bill Gadsby, 1968-69; Bill Gadsby and Sid Abel, 1969-70; Ned Harkness and Doug Barkley, 1970-71; Doug Barkley and Johnny Wilson, 1971-72; Johnny Wilson, 1972-73; Ted Garvin and Alex Delvecchio, 1973-74; Alex Delvecchio, 1974-75; Doug Barkley and Alex Delvecchio, 1975-76; Alex Delvecchio and Larry Wilson, 1976-77; Bobby Kromm, 1977-78, 1978-79; Bobby Kromm and Ted Lindsay, 1979-80; Ted Lindsay and Wayne Maxner, 1980-81; Wayne Maxner and Billy Dea, 1981-82; Nick Polano, 1982-83 to 1984-85; Harry Neale and Brad Park, 1985-86; Jacques Demers, 1986-87 to 1989-90; Bryan Murray, 1990-91 to 1992-93; Scotty Bowman, 1993-94 to 1997-98; Dave Lewis, Barry Smith (co-coaches) and Scotty Bowman, 1998-99; Scotty Bowman, 1999-2000 to 2001-02; Dave Lewis, 2002-03 to date.

Club Records

Team

(Figures in brackets for season records are games played; records for fewest points, wins, ties, losses, goals, goals against are for 70 or more games)

Most Points	**131**	1995-96 (82)
Most Wins	***62**	1995-96 (82)
Most Ties	**18**	1952-53 (70), 1980-81 (80), 1996-97 (82)
Most Losses	**57**	1985-86 (80)
Most Goals	**369**	1992-93 (84)
Most Goals Against	**415**	1985-86 (80)
Fewest Points	**40**	1985-86 (80)
Fewest Wins	**16**	1976-77 (80)
Fewest Ties	**4**	1966-67 (70)
Fewest Losses	**13**	1950-51 (70), 1995-96 (82)
Fewest Goals	**167**	1958-59 (70)
Fewest Goals Against	**132**	1953-54 (70)
Longest Winning Streak		
Overall	**9**	Mar. 3-21/51, Feb. 27-Mar. 20/55, Dec. 12-31/95, Mar. 3-22/96
Home	**14**	Jan. 21-Mar. 25/65
Away	**7**	Mar. 25-Apr. 14/95, Feb. 18-Mar. 20/96
Longest Undefeated Streak		
Overall	**15**	Nov. 27-Dec. 28/52 (8 wins, 7 ties)
Home	**19**	Dec. 31/00-Apr.7/01 (17 wins, 2 ties)
Away	**15**	Oct. 18-Dec. 20/51 (10 wins, 5 ties)
Longest Losing Streak		
Overall	**14**	Feb. 24-Mar. 25/82
Home	**7**	Feb. 20-Mar. 25/82
Away	**14**	Oct. 19-Dec. 21/66
Longest Winless Streak		
Overall	**19**	Feb. 26-Apr. 3/77 (18 losses, 1 tie)
Home	**10**	Dec. 11/85-Jan. 18/86 (9 losses, 1 tie)
Away	**26**	Dec. 15/76-Apr. 3/77 (23 losses, 3 ties)
Most Shutouts, Season	**13**	1953-54 (70)
Most. PIM, Season	**2,393**	1985-86 (80)
Most Goals, Game	**15**	Jan. 23/44 (NYR 0 at Det. 15)

Individual

Most Seasons	**25**	Gordie Howe
Most Games	**1,687**	Gordie Howe
Most Goals, Career	**786**	Gordie Howe
Most Assists, Career	**1,023**	Gordie Howe
Most Points, Career	**1,809**	Gordie Howe (786G, 1,023A)
Most PIM, Career	**2,090**	Bob Probert
Most Shutouts, Career	**85**	Terry Sawchuk
Longest Consecutive Games Streak	**548**	Alex Delvecchio (Dec. 13/56-Nov. 11/64)
Most Goals, Season	**65**	Steve Yzerman (1988-89)
Most Assists, Season	**90**	Steve Yzerman (1988-89)
Most Points, Season	**155**	Steve Yzerman (1988-89; 65G, 90A)
Most PIM, Season	**398**	Bob Probert (1987-88)
Most Points, Defenseman, Season	**77**	Paul Coffey (1993-94; 14G, 63A)
Most Points, Center, Season	**155**	Steve Yzerman (1988-89; 65G, 90A)
Most Points, Right Wing, Season	**103**	Gordie Howe (1968-69; 44G, 59A)
Most Points, Left Wing, Season	**105**	John Ogrodnick (1984-85; 55G, 50A)
Most Points, Rookie, Season	**87**	Steve Yzerman (1983-84; 39G, 48A)
Most Shutouts, Season	**12**	Terry Sawchuk (1951-52, 1953-54, 1954-55), Glenn Hall (1955-56)
Most Goals, Game	**6**	Syd Howe (Feb. 3/44)
Most Assists, Game	***7**	Billy Taylor (Mar. 16/47)
Most Points, Game	**7**	Carl Liscombe (Nov. 5/42; 3G, 4A), Don Grosso (Feb. 3/44; 1G, 6A), Billy Taylor (Mar. 16/47; 7A)

* NHL Record.

Retired Numbers

1	Terry Sawchuk	1949-55, 57-64, 68-69
7	Ted Lindsay	1944-57, 64-65
9	Gordie Howe	1946-1971
10	Alex Delvecchio	1951-1973
12	Sid Abel	1938-43, 45-52

All-time Record vs. Other Clubs

Regular Season

	At Home								On Road								Total							
	GP	W	L	T	OL	GF	GA	PTS	GP	W	L	T	OL	GF	GA	PTS	GP	W	L	T	OL	GF	GA	PTS
Anaheim	22	17	2	3	0	83	49	37	22	11	7	4	0	65	52	26	44	28	9	7	0	148	101	63
Atlanta	4	4	0	0	0	17	8	8	3	3	0	0	0	19	7	6	7	7	0	0	0	36	15	14
Boston	285	154	79	52	0	952	720	360	287	90	153	43	1	761	1007	224	572	244	232	95	1	1713	1727	584
Buffalo	55	32	18	5	0	203	159	69	52	11	33	8	0	153	226	30	107	43	51	13	0	356	385	99
Calgary	59	31	18	10	0	215	174	72	60	20	34	6	0	179	228	46	119	51	52	16	0	394	402	118
Carolina	31	17	7	7	0	119	86	41	30	12	17	1	0	86	104	25	61	29	24	8	0	205	190	66
Chicago	335	203	98	33	1	1144	833	440	338	132	152	51	3	951	1015	318	673	335	250	84	4	2095	1848	758
Colorado	40	24	15	1	0	142	120	49	42	18	20	4	0	142	148	40	82	42	35	5	0	284	268	89
Columbus	10	8	2	0	0	39	22	16	11	8	2	1	0	26	21	17	21	16	4	1	0	65	43	33
Dallas	106	53	37	16	0	406	336	122	106	37	51	18	0	319	370	92	212	90	88	34	0	725	706	214
Edmonton	44	25	15	3	1	172	146	54	44	14	19	10	1	155	168	39	88	39	34	13	2	327	314	93
Florida	8	4	1	3	0	30	21	11	9	6	1	2	0	27	17	14	17	10	2	5	0	57	38	25
Los Angeles	79	36	30	13	0	300	271	85	80	24	41	14	1	246	321	63	159	60	71	27	1	546	592	148
Minnesota	8	5	2	1	0	32	20	11	8	4	1	2	1	21	18	11	16	9	3	3	1	53	38	22
Montreal	280	130	97	53	0	805	717	313	282	67	172	43	0	636	994	177	562	197	269	96	0	1441	1711	490
Nashville	17	13	1	2	1	69	38	29	16	7	6	2	1	45	40	17	33	20	7	4	2	114	78	46
New Jersey	40	25	13	2	0	164	129	52	40	10	21	9	0	103	138	29	80	35	34	11	0	267	267	81
NY Islanders	45	26	17	2	0	165	135	54	46	19	23	4	0	137	164	42	91	45	40	6	0	302	299	96
NY Rangers	285	164	76	45	0	1004	699	373	284	92	134	58	0	738	868	242	569	256	210	103	0	1742	1567	615
Ottawa	9	6	3	0	0	33	19	12	10	6	3	1	0	29	28	13	19	12	6	1	0	62	47	25
Philadelphia	59	31	18	10	0	210	182	72	58	13	34	11	0	168	230	37	117	44	52	21	0	378	412	109
Phoenix	51	25	18	8	0	200	170	58	49	18	17	14	0	153	149	50	100	43	35	22	0	353	319	108
Pittsburgh	65	40	13	12	0	253	178	92	65	17	44	4	0	195	281	38	130	57	57	16	0	448	459	130
St. Louis	110	52	41	17	0	404	336	121	110	34	54	20	2	308	375	90	220	86	95	37	2	712	711	211
San Jose	25	22	2	1	0	104	45	45	26	14	9	3	0	100	83	31	51	36	11	4	0	204	128	76
Tampa Bay	12	10	1	1	0	47	21	21	14	9	4	1	0	61	43	19	26	19	5	2	0	108	64	40
Toronto	322	168	106	46	2	968	792	384	316	105	164	47	0	846	1045	257	638	273	270	93	2	1814	1837	641
Vancouver	66	41	16	8	1	275	188	91	65	26	29	10	0	210	235	62	131	67	45	18	1	485	423	153
Washington	47	21	15	11	0	161	135	53	46	20	21	5	0	147	168	45	93	41	36	16	0	308	303	98
Defunct Clubs	141	76	40	25	0	430	307	177	141	49	63	29	0	364	375	127	282	125	103	54	0	794	682	304
Totals	**2660**	**1463**	**801**	**390**	**6**	**9146**	**7056**	**3322**	**2660**	**896**	**1329**	**425**	**10**	**7390**	**8918**	**2227**	**5320**	**2359**	**2130**	**815**	**16**	**16536**	**15974**	**5549**

Playoffs

	Series	W	L	GP	W	L	T	GF	GA	Last Mtg.	Rnd.	Result
Anaheim	3	2	1	12	8	4	0	36	24	2003	CQF	L 0-4
Boston	7	3	4	33	14	19	0	98	96	1957	SF	L 1-4
Calgary	2	1	1	8	4	4	0	20	16	2004	CSF	L 2-4
Carolina	1	1	0	5	4	1	0	14	7	2002	F	W 4-1
Chicago	14	6	8	69	31	38	0	190	210	1995	CF	W 4-1
Colorado	5	2	3	30	13	17	0	76	79	2002	CF	W 4-3
Dallas	3	3	0	18	12	6	0	55	40	1998	CF	W 4-2
Edmonton	2	0	2	10	2	8	0	26	39	1988	CF	L 1-4
Los Angeles	2	1	1	10	6	4	0	32	21	2001	CQF	L 2-4
Montreal	12	7	5	62	29	33	0	149	161	1978	QF	L 1-4
Nashville	1	1	0	6	4	2	0	12	9	2004	CQF	W 4-2
New Jersey	1	0	1	4	0	4	0	7	16	1995	F	L 0-4
NY Rangers	5	4	1	23	13	10	0	57	49	1950	F	W 4-3
Philadelphia	1	1	0	4	4	0	0	16	6	1997	F	W 4-0
Phoenix	2	2	0	12	8	4	0	44	28	1998	CQF	W 4-2
St. Louis	7	5	2	40	24	16	0	125	103	2002	CSF	W 4-1
San Jose	2	1	1	11	7	4	0	51	27	1995	CSF	W 4-0
Toronto	23	11	12	117	59	58	0	321	311	1993	DSF	L 3-4
Vancouver	1	1	0	6	4	2	0	22	16	2002	CQF	W 4-2
Washington	1	1	0	4	4	0	0	13	7	1998	F	W 4-0
Defunct Clubs	4	3	1	10	7	2	1	21	13			
Totals	**99**	**56**	**43**	**494**	**257**	**236**	**1**	**1385**	**1278**			

Calgary totals include Atlanta Flames, 1972-73 to 1979-80.
Colorado totals include Quebec, 1979-80 to 1994-95.
New Jersey totals include Kansas City, 1974-75 to 1975-76, and Colorado Rockies, 1976-77 to 1981-82.
Phoenix totals include Winnipeg, 1979-80 to 1995-96.
Carolina totals include Hartford, 1979-80 to 1996-97.
Dallas totals include Minnesota North Stars, 1967-68 to 1992-93.

Playoff Results 2004-2000

Year	Round	Opponent	Result	GF	GA
2004	CSF	Calgary	L 2-4	12	11
	CQF	Nashville	W 4-2	12	9
2003	CQF	Anaheim	L 0-4	6	10
2002	**F**	**Carolina**	**W 4-1**	**14**	**7**
	CF	Colorado	W 4-3	22	13
	CSF	St. Louis	W 4-1	14	11
	CQF	Vancouver	W 4-2	22	16
2001	CQF	Los Angeles	L 2-4	17	15
2000	CSF	Colorado	L 1-4	8	13
	CQF	Los Angeles	W 4-0	15	6

Abbreviations: Round: F - Final; **CF** - conference final; **CSF** - conference semi-final; **CQF** - conference quarter-final; **DSF** - division semi-final; **SF** - semi-final; **QF** - quarter-final.

2003-04 Results

Oct.	9	Los Angeles	3-2		3	Anaheim	3-1
	11	at Ottawa	3-2*		5	Nashville	6-0
	16	Vancouver	3-2		7	Boston	0-3
	18	at Pittsburgh	3-4		10	at Boston	1-2*
	20	at Montreal	1-2		14	Chicago	4-2
	22	Columbus	4-1		16	Phoenix	3-3
	24	Dallas	4-0		19	at San Jose	1-2
	25	at NY Rangers	1-3		21	at Anaheim	2-2
	29	St. Louis	5-6		22	at Los Angeles	5-4
	30	at Nashville	3-5		24	at Phoenix	2-5
Nov.	1	at Edmonton	4-4		26	at Dallas	2-2
	3	at Vancouver	1-5		29	New Jersey	5-2
	4	at Calgary	3-0		31	Carolina	4-4
	8	Nashville	3-4	**Feb.**	3	at Nashville	4-1
	10	Chicago	3-0		5	at Colorado	3-2*
	12	at Dallas	6-2		11	San Jose	4-2
	14	at Chicago	4-3*		14	Colorado	2-5
	15	at Minnesota	1-1		16	Edmonton	2-1
	19	Columbus	5-1		18	Phoenix	5-2
	20	at Columbus	0-3		20	St. Louis	5-1
	22	at Minnesota	5-2		23	at Edmonton	1-1
	24	Washington	1-4		24	at Vancouver	2-4
	26	Edmonton	7-1		26	at Calgary	2-1
	28	NY Islanders	6-0		29	Philadelphia	4-2
	29	at St. Louis	2-1	**Mar.**	3	Calgary	2-1
Dec.	3	Anaheim	7-2		5	Vancouver	3-1
	4	at St. Louis	4-4		8	Tampa Bay	1-1
	6	at Toronto	2-5		11	at Columbus	4-2
	8	Los Angeles	3-2*		13	Dallas	3-0
	10	at Buffalo	7-2		14	Nashville	3-2*
	11	at Chicago	3-4*		16	Calgary	1-4
	13	at Washington	5-1		18	at Phoenix	1-1
	15	Florida	4-1		20	at Los Angeles	4-2
	17	San Jose	3-2*		21	at Anaheim	6-8
	19	Chicago	3-2		23	at San Jose	2-5
	20	at Nashville	0-1		25	at Colorado	3-1
	22	St. Louis	2-1		27	Colorado	2-0
	26	Minnesota	2-2		29	Minnesota	5-3
	28	at Chicago	0-3		31	at Columbus	3-2
	31	Atlanta	6-5*	**Apr.**	1	at St. Louis	3-2
Jan.	2	at Carolina	4-1		3	Columbus	1-4

* – Overtime

Entry Draft
Selections 2004-1990

2004
Pick
97   Johan Franzen
128 Evan McGrath
151 Siarhei Kolasau
162 Tyler Haskins
192 Anton Axelsson
226 Steven Covington
257 Gennady Stolyarov
290 Nils Backstrom

2003
Pick
64   James Howard
132 Kyle Quincey
164 Ryan Oulahen
170 Andreas Sundin
194 Stefan Blom
226 Tomas Kollar
258 Vladimir Kutny
289 Mikael Johansson

2002
Pick
58   Jiri Hudler
63   Tomas Fleischmann
95   Valtteri Filppula
131 Johan Berggren
166 Logan Koopmans
197 Jimmy Cuddihy
229 Derek Meech
260 Pierre-Olivier Beaulieu
262 Christian Soderstrom
291 Jonathan Ericsson

2001
Pick
62   Igor Grigorenko
121 Drew MacIntyre
129 Miroslav Blatak
157 Andreas Jamtin
195 Nick Pannoni
258 Dmitri Bykov
288 Francois Senez

2000
Pick
29   Niklas Kronwall
38   Tomas Kopecky
102 Stefan Liv
127 Dmitri Semenov
128 Alexander Seluyanov
130 Aaron Van Leusen
187 Per Backer
196 Paul Ballantyne
228 Jimmie Svensson
251 Todd Jackson
260 Yevgeny Bumagin

1999
Pick
120 Jari Tolsa
149 Andrei Maximenko
181 Kent McDonell
210 Henrik Zetterberg
238 Anton Borodkin
266 Ken Davis

1998
Pick
25   Jiri Fischer
55   Ryan Barnes
56   Tomek Valtonen
84   Jake McCracken
111 Brent Hobday
142 Calle Steen
151 Adam DeLeeuw
171 Pavel Datsyuk
198 Jeremy Goetzinger
226 David Petrasek
256 Petja Pietilainen

1997
Pick
49   Yuri Butsayev
76   Petr Sykora
102 Quintin Laing
129 John Wikstrom
157 B.J. Young
186 Mike Laceby
213 Steve Willejto
239 Greg Willers

1996
Pick
26   Jesse Wallin
52   Aren Miller
108 Johan Forsander
135 Michal Podolka
144 Magnus Nilsson
162 Alexandre Jacques
189 Colin Beardsmore
215 Craig Stahl
241 Eugeny Afanasiev

1995
Pick
26   Maxim Kuznetsov
52   Philippe Audet
58   Darryl Laplante
104 Anatoli Ustyugov
125 Chad Wilchynski
126 David Arsenault
156 Tyler Perry
182 Per Eklund
208 Andrei Samokhvalov
234 David Engblom

1994
Pick
23   Yan Golubovsky
49   Mathieu Dandenault
75   Sean Gillam
114 Frederic Deschenes
127 Doug Battaglia
153 Pavel Agarkov
205 Jason Elliot
231 Jeff Mikesch
257 Tomas Holmstrom
283 Toivo Suursoo

1993
Pick
22   Anders Eriksson
48   Jon Coleman
74   Kevin Hilton
97   John Jakopin
100 Benoit Larose
126 Norm Maracle
152 Tim Spitzig
178 Yuri Yeresko
204 Vitezslav Skuta
230 Ryan Shanahan
256 James Kosecki
282 Gordon Hunt

1992
Pick
22   Curtis Bowen
46   Darren McCarty
70   Sylvain Cloutier
118 Mike Sullivan
142 Jason MacDonald
166 Greg Scott
183 Justin Krall
189 C. J. Denomme
214 Jeff Walker
238 Dan McGillis
262 Ryan Bach

1991
Pick
10   Martin Lapointe
32   Jamie Pushor
54   Chris Osgood
76   Mike Knuble
98   Dimitri Motkov
142 Igor Malykhin
186 Jim Bermingham
208 Jason Firth
230 Bart Turner
252 Andrew Miller

1990
Pick
3   Keith Primeau
45   Vyacheslav Kozlov
66   Stewart Malgunas
87   Tony Burns
108 Claude Barthe
129 Jason York
150 Wes McCauley
171 Anthony Gruba
192 Travis Tucker
213 Brett Larson
234 John Hendry

Club Directory

Joe Louis Arena

Detroit Red Wings
Joe Louis Arena
600 Civic Center Drive
Detroit, MI 48226
Phone 313/396-7544
FAX PR: 313/567-0296
Media Hotline: 313/396-7599
www.detroitredwings.com
Capacity: 20,058

Owner/Governor	Mike Ilitch
Owner/Secretary-Treasurer	Marian Ilitch
Senior Vice-President/Alternate Governor	Jim Devellano
President & CEO, Ilitch Holdings/ Vice-President and Alt. Governor, Red Wings	Christopher Ilitch
General Counsel	Rob Carr
General Manager/Alternate Governor	Ken Holland
Assistant General Manager	Jim Nill
Head Coach	Dave Lewis
Associate Coach	Barry Smith
Assistant Coach	Joe Kocur
Consultant	Scotty Bowman
Goaltending Coach	Jim Bedard
NHL Scout	Dan Belisle
NHL Scout	Mark Howe
NHL Scout	Bob McCammon
Amateur Scout	Glenn Merkosky
Amateur Scout	Joe McDonnell
Amateur Scout	Bruce Haralson
Amateur Scout	Mark Leach
Part-Time Scout	Marty Stein
Director of European Scouting	Hakan Andersson
European Scout	Vladimir Havluj
Part-Time European Scout	Evgeni Erfilov
Vice-President of Finance	Paul MacDonald
Executive Assistant	Nancy Beard
Administrative and Scouting Coordinator	David Kolb
Accounting Assistant	Bridget Merritt
Athletic Therapist	Piet Van Zant
Assistant Athletic Therapist	Russ Baumann
Equipment Manager	Paul Boyer
Assistant Equipment Manager	Tim Abbott
Team Masseur	Sergei Tchekmarev
Senior Director of Communications	John Hahn
Media Relations Manager	Michael Kuta
Community Relations Manager	Anne Marie Krappmann
Team Photographer	Dave Reginek
Medical Director	David Collon, M.D.
Team Physician	Anthony Colucci, D.O., F.A.C.E.P.
Team Dentist	C.J. Regula, D.M.D.
Radio Broadcasters, AM 1270 - WXYT	Ken Kal, Paul Woods
Television Broadcasters, FOX Sports Net Detroit	Ken Daniels, Mickey Redmond

General Manager

HOLLAND, KEN
General Manager, Detroit Red Wings. Born in Vernon, B.C., Nov. 10, 1955.
Ken Holland is entering his eighth season as a general manager and his 22nd year with the Red Wings organization. In his seven seasons as Detroit's general manager, Holland has established himself as one of the most innovative and aggressive GMs in the National Hockey League. Detroit's Stanley Cup victory in 2002 marked the team's second championship under his leadership. Holland began his tenure as the club's general manager after serving as assistant general manager for the previous three seasons. He was elevated to his present position July 18, 1997.

Holland oversees all aspects of hockey operations including all matters relating to player personnel, development, contract negotiations and player movements. He also continues to be Detroit's point person at the NHL Entry Draft, as he has been for the past 13 years.

Holland has deftly handled several different front-office duties for the club over the past 20 years. At the conclusion of his playing days as a goaltender, spending most of his pro career at the American Hockey League level, Holland began his off-ice career in 1985 as a western Canada scout followed by five years as an amateur scouting director before promotions led to his current position as general manager.

A native of Vernon, BC, Holland played in the junior ranks for Medicine Hat (WHL) in 1974-75. He was Toronto's 13th pick (188th overall) in the 1975 draft but never saw action with the Maple Leafs. Holland twice signed with NHL teams as a free agent — in 1980 with Hartford and 1983 with Detroit. He spent most of his pro career with AHL clubs in Binghamton and Springfield, along with Adirondack, but did appear in four NHL games, making his debut with Hartford in 1980-81 and playing three contests for Detroit in 1983-84.

General Managers' History
Art Duncan and Duke Keats, 1926-27; Jack Adams, 1927-28 to 1961-62; Sid Abel, 1962-63 to 1969-70; Sid Abel and Ned Harkness, 1970-71; Ned Harkness, 1971-72 to 1973-74; Alex Delvecchio, 1974-75, 1975-76; Alex Delvecchio and Ted Lindsay, 1976-77; Ted Lindsay, 1977-78 to 1979-80; Jimmy Skinner, 1980-81, 1981-82; Jim Devellano, 1982-83 to 1989-90; Bryan Murray, 1990-91 to 1993-94; Jim Devellano (Senior Vice-President), 1994-95 to 1996-97; Ken Holland, 1997-98 to date.

Captains' History
Art Duncan, 1926-27; Reg Noble, 1927-28 to 1929-30; George Hay, 1930-31; Carson Cooper, 1931-32; Larry Aurie, 1932-33; Herbie Lewis, 1933-34; Ebbie Goodfellow, 1934-35; Doug Young, 1935-36 to 1937-38; Ebbie Goodfellow, 1938-39 to 1940-41; Ebbie Goodfellow and Syd Howe, 1941-42; Sid Abel, 1942-43; Mud Bruneteau, Flash Hollett (co-captains), 1943-44; Flash Hollett, 1944-45; Flash Hollett and Sid Abel, 1945-46; Sid Abel, 1946-47 to 1951-52; Ted Lindsay, 1952-53 to 1955-56; Red Kelly, 1956-57, 1957-58; Gordie Howe, 1958-59 to 1961-62; Alex Delvecchio, 1962-63 to 1972-73; Alex Delvecchio, Nick Libett, Red Berenson, Gary Bergman, Ted Harris, Mickey Redmond and Larry Johnston, 1973-74; Marcel Dionne, 1974-75; Danny Grant and Terry Harper, 1975-76; Danny Grant and Dennis Polonich, 1976-77; Dan Maloney and Dennis Hextall, 1977-78; Dennis Hextall, Nick Libett and Paul Woods, 1978-79; Dale McCourt, 1979-80; Errol Thompson and Reed Larson, 1980-81; Reed Larson, 1981-82; Danny Gare, 1982-83 to 1985-86; Steve Yzerman, 1986-87 to date.

Edmonton Oilers

2003-04 Results: 36w-29l-12t-5otl 89pts.
Fourth, Northwest Division

Year-by-Year Record

Season	GP	Home W	L	T	OL	Road W	L	T	OL	Overall W	L	T	OL	GF	GA	Pts.	Finished	Playoff Result
2003-04	82	22	12	4	3	14	17	8	2	36	29	12	5	221	208	89	4th, Northwest Div.	Out of Playoffs
2002-03	82	20	12	5	4	16	14	6	5	36	26	11	9	231	230	92	4th, Northwest Div.	Lost Conf. Quarter-Final
2001-02	82	23	14	4	0	15	14	8	4	38	28	12	4	205	182	92	3rd, Northwest Div.	Out of Playoffs
2000-01	82	23	9	7	2	16	19	5	1	39	28	12	3	243	222	93	2nd, Northwest Div.	Lost Conf. Quarter-Final
1999-2000	82	18	11	9	3	14	15	7	5	32	26	16	8	226	212	88	2nd, Northwest Div.	Lost Conf. Quarter-Final
1998-99	82	17	19	5	...	16	18	7	...	33	37	12	...	230	226	78	2nd, Northwest Div.	Lost Conf. Quarter-Final
1997-98	82	20	16	5	...	15	21	5	...	35	37	10	...	215	224	80	3rd, Pacific Div.	Lost Conf. Semi-Final
1996-97	82	21	16	4	...	15	21	5	...	36	37	9	...	252	247	81	3rd, Pacific Div.	Lost Conf. Semi-Final
1995-96	82	15	21	5	...	15	23	3	...	30	44	8	...	240	304	68	5th, Pacific Div.	Out of Playoffs
1994-95	48	11	12	1	...	6	15	3	...	17	27	4	...	136	183	38	5th, Pacific Div.	Out of Playoffs
1993-94	84	17	22	3	...	8	23	11	...	25	45	14	...	261	305	64	6th, Pacific Div.	Out of Playoffs
1992-93	84	16	21	5	...	10	29	3	...	26	50	8	...	242	337	60	5th, Smythe Div.	Out of Playoffs
1991-92	80	22	13	5	...	14	21	5	...	36	34	10	...	295	297	82	3rd, Smythe Div.	Lost Conf. Championship
1990-91	80	22	15	3	...	15	22	3	...	37	37	6	...	272	272	80	3rd, Smythe Div.	Lost Conf. Championship
1989-90	**80**	**23**	**11**	**6**	...	**15**	**17**	**8**	...	**38**	**28**	**14**	...	**315**	**283**	**90**	**2nd, Smythe Div.**	**Won Stanley Cup**
1988-89	80	21	16	3	...	17	18	5	...	38	34	8	...	325	306	84	3rd, Smythe Div.	Lost Div. Semi-Final
1987-88	**80**	**28**	**8**	**4**	...	**16**	**17**	**7**	...	**44**	**25**	**11**	...	**363**	**288**	**99**	**2nd, Smythe Div.**	**Won Stanley Cup**
1986-87	**80**	**29**	**6**	**5**	...	**21**	**18**	**1**	...	**50**	**24**	**6**	...	**372**	**284**	**106**	**1st, Smythe Div.**	**Won Stanley Cup**
1985-86	80	32	6	2	...	24	11	5	...	56	17	7	...	426	310	119	1st, Smythe Div.	Lost Div. Final
1984-85	**80**	**26**	**7**	**7**	...	**23**	**13**	**4**	...	**49**	**20**	**11**	...	**401**	**298**	**109**	**1st, Smythe Div.**	**Won Stanley Cup**
1983-84	**80**	**31**	**5**	**4**	...	**26**	**13**	**1**	...	**57**	**18**	**5**	...	**446**	**314**	**119**	**1st, Smythe Div.**	**Won Stanley Cup**
1982-83	80	25	9	6	...	22	12	6	...	47	21	12	...	424	315	106	1st, Smythe Div.	Lost Final
1981-82	80	31	5	4	...	17	12	11	...	48	17	15	...	417	295	111	1st, Smythe Div.	Lost Div. Semi-Final
1980-81	80	17	13	10	...	12	22	6	...	29	35	16	...	328	327	74	4th, Smythe Div.	Lost Quarter-Final
1979-80	80	17	14	9	...	11	25	4	...	28	39	13	...	301	322	69	4th, Smythe Div.	Lost Prelim. Round

---

2004-05 Schedule

Oct.	Thu.	14	Detroit
	Sun.	17	Calgary
	Tue.	19	at Minnesota
	Thu.	21	Minnesota
	Sat.	23	St. Louis
	Tue.	26	Columbus
	Fri.	29	at Dallas
	Sat.	30	at Minnesota
Nov.	Tue.	2	at Detroit
	Thu.	4	Nashville
	Sat.	6	at Calgary
	Tue.	9	at Columbus
	Thu.	11	at Pittsburgh
	Fri.	12	at Buffalo
	Sun.	14	at Chicago
	Tue.	16	at Colorado
	Thu.	18	Chicago
	Sat.	20	Minnesota
	Mon.	22	Nashville
	Wed.	24	at Minnesota
	Thu.	25	at Nashville
	Sat.	27	Colorado
Dec.	Thu.	2	Toronto
	Sun.	5	Columbus
	Tue.	7	at Calgary
	Thu.	9	at San Jose
	Sat.	11	at Los Angeles*
	Sun.	12	at Anaheim*
	Tue.	14	Calgary
	Sat.	18	at Vancouver
	Tue.	21	at Calgary
	Thu.	23	Los Angeles
	Sun.	26	Vancouver
	Tue.	28	Minnesota
	Thu.	30	Philadelphia
Jan.	Sat.	1	Montreal
	Sun.	2	San Jose
	Tue.	4	at Colorado
	Thu.	6	at St. Louis
	Sat.	8	at Phoenix
	Tue.	11	San Jose

	Thu.	13	Dallas
	Sat.	15	Ottawa
	Mon.	17	at San Jose*
	Tue.	18	at Los Angeles
	Thu.	20	NY Islanders
	Sat.	22	Vancouver
	Mon.	24	Anaheim
	Thu.	27	at Vancouver
	Fri.	28	New Jersey
Feb.	Tue.	1	Colorado
	Thu.	3	Detroit
	Sat.	5	NY Rangers
	Mon.	7	Calgary
	Wed.	9	Phoenix
	Tue.	15	at Columbus
	Thu.	17	at Montreal
	Sat.	19	at Toronto
	Mon.	21	at Ottawa
	Wed.	23	at Chicago
	Fri.	25	Boston
	Sun.	27	Phoenix*
Mar.	Tue.	1	at Detroit
	Thu.	3	at St. Louis
	Sun.	6	at Nashville*
	Mon.	7	at Carolina
	Wed.	9	at Florida
	Fri.	11	at Tampa Bay
	Sun.	13	at Atlanta*
	Tue.	15	St. Louis
	Thu.	17	at Colorado
	Fri.	18	at Dallas
	Mon.	21	Colorado
	Wed.	23	at Anaheim
	Thu.	24	at Phoenix
	Sat.	26	Washington
	Tue.	29	Chicago
Apr.	Fri.	1	Dallas
	Sun.	3	Anaheim*
	Tue.	5	Los Angeles
	Thu.	7	at Vancouver
	Sat.	9	Vancouver

Denotes afternoon game.

Franchise date: June 22, 1979

WESTERN CONFERENCE

NORTHWEST DIVISION

26th NHL Season

Ty Conklin spent his first full year in the NHL in 2003-04. He recorded his first win in his first career start on October 20 and would finish the season as Edmonton's number-one goaltender.

2004-05 Player Personnel

FORWARDS

	HT	WT	S	Place of Birth	Date	2003-04 Club
BAUM, Dan	6-1	189	L	Biggar, Sask.	6/4/83	Tor (AHL)-Columbus (ECHL)
BISHAI, Mike	5-11	185	L	Edmonton, Alta.	5/30/79	Edmonton-Toronto (AHL)
BRODZIAK, Kyle	6-2	198	R	St. Paul, Alta.	5/25/84	Moose Jaw
CARON, Ed	6-2	228	L	Nashua, NH	4/30/82	New Hampshire
CULLEN, Joe	6-1	210	L	Virginia, MN	2/14/81	Toronto (AHL)
DiCASMIRRO, Nate	5-11	205	L	Burnsville, MN	9/27/78	Toronto (AHL)
DVORAK, Radek	6-2	200	R	Tabor, Czech.	3/9/77	Edmonton
HEMSKY, Ales	6-0	192	R	Pardubice, Czech.	8/13/83	Edmonton
HORCOFF, Shawn	6-1	204	L	Trail, B.C.	9/17/78	Edmonton
HUNTER, J.J.	6-1	185	L	Shaunavon, Sask.	7/6/80	Tor (AHL)-Columbus (ECHL)
ISBISTER, Brad	6-4	231	R	Edmonton, Alta.	5/7/77	Edmonton
LARAQUE, Georges	6-3	243	L	Montreal, Que.	12/7/76	Edmonton
McASLAN, Sean	6-1	190	R	Okotoks, Alta.	1/12/80	Toronto (AHL)
MOREAU, Ethan	6-2	220	L	Huntsville, Ont.	9/22/75	Edmonton
NEDVED, Petr	6-3	195	L	Liberec, Czech.	12/9/71	NY Rangers-Edmonton
NIINIMAKI, Jesse	6-2	183	L	Tampere, Finland	8/19/83	Ilves
PETERSEN, Toby	5-10	197	L	Minneapolis, MN	10/27/78	Wilkes-Barre
PISANI, Fernando	6-1	205	L	Edmonton, Alta.	12/27/76	Edmonton
POULIOT, Marc-Antoine	6-1	195	R	Quebec City, Que.	5/22/85	Rimouski
RADUNSKE, Brock	6-4	196	L	Kitchener, Ont.	4/5/83	Michigan State
REASONER, Marty	6-1	200	L	Honeoye Falls, NY	2/26/77	Edmonton
RITA, Jani	6-1	206	L	Helsinki, Finland	7/25/81	Edmonton-Toronto (AHL)
SALMELAINEN, Tony	5-9	185	L	Espoo, Finland	8/8/81	Edmonton-Toronto (AHL)
SCHREMP, Rob	5-11	197	L	Syracuse, NY	7/1/86	Mississauga-U.S. Nat. U-18-London
SMYTH, Ryan	6-1	190	L	Banff, Alta.	2/21/76	Edmonton
STOLL, Jarret	6-1	200	R	Melville, Sask.	6/25/82	Edmonton
TORRES, Raffi	6-0	216	L	Toronto, Ont.	10/8/81	Edmonton
WINCHESTER, Brad	6-5	215	L	Madison, WI	3/1/81	Toronto (AHL)
WRIGHT, Jamie	6-0	195	L	Kitchener, Ont.	5/13/76	Toronto (AHL)
YORK, Mike	5-10	185	R	Waterford, MI	1/3/78	Edmonton

DEFENSEMEN

	HT	WT	S	Place of Birth	Date	2003-04 Club
BERGERON, Marc-Andre	5-10	197	L	St-Louis-de-France, Que.	10/13/80	Edmonton-Toronto (AHL)
BREWER, Eric	6-4	225	L	Vernon, B.C.	4/17/79	Edmonton
CROSS, Cory	6-5	225	L	Lloydminster, Alta.	1/3/71	Edmonton
LYNCH, Doug	6-3	214	L	North Vancouver, B.C.	4/4/83	Edmonton-Toronto (AHL)
PLATT, Jason	6-1	210	L	San Francisco, CA	4/29/81	Providence College-Toronto (AHL)
ROY, Mathieu	6-2	214	R	St-Georges, Que.	8/10/83	Tor (AHL)-Columbus (ECHL)
SEMENOV, Alexei	6-6	235	L	Murmansk, USSR	4/10/81	Edmonton
SMITH, Dan	6-2	200	L	Fernie, B.C.	10/19/76	Toronto (AHL)
SMITH, Jason	6-3	215	R	Calgary, Alta.	11/2/73	Edmonton
SMITH, Kenny	6-2	209	R	Stoneham, MA	12/31/81	Harvard
STAIOS, Steve	6-1	200	L	Hamilton, Ont.	7/28/73	Edmonton
THOMPSON, Rocky	6-2	205	R	Calgary, Alta.	8/8/77	Toronto (AHL)
ULANOV, Igor	6-3	220	L	Krasnokamsk, USSR	10/1/69	Edmonton-Toronto (AHL)
WOYWITKA, Jeff	6-2	209	L	Vermilion, Alta.	9/1/83	Phi (AHL)-Tor (AHL)

GOALTENDERS

	HT	WT	C	Place of Birth	Date	2003-04 Club
CONKLIN, Ty	6-0	184	L	Anchorage, AK	3/30/76	Edmonton
DESLAURIERS, Jeff	6-3	175	R	St-Jean-Richelieu, Que.	5/15/84	Chicoutimi
DUBNYK, Devan	6-5	194	L	Regina, Sask.	5/4/86	Kamloops
MARKKANEN, Jussi	6-0	182	L	Imatra, Finland	5/8/75	NY Rangers-Edmonton
MORRISON, Mike	6-3	194	R	Medford, MA	7/11/79	Toronto (AHL)

2003-04 Scoring

* - rookie

Regular Season

Pos	#	Player	Team	GP	G	A	Pts	+/-	PIM	PP	SH	GW	GT	S	%
L	94	Ryan Smyth	EDM	82	23	36	59	11	70	8	2	6	0	245	9.4
R	20	Radek Dvorak	EDM	78	15	35	50	18	26	6	0	0	2	188	8.0
C	93	Petr Nedved	NYR	65	14	17	31	-9	42	5	0	3	0	153	9.2
			EDM	16	5	10	15	1	4	2	0	0	0	37	13.5
			TOTAL	81	19	27	46	-8	46	7	0	3	0	190	10.0
L	16	Mike York	EDM	61	16	26	42	18	15	1	2	0	1	144	11.1
C	10	Shawn Horcoff	EDM	80	15	25	40	0	73	0	2	3	1	110	13.6
L	14	Raffi Torres	EDM	80	20	14	34	12	65	5	0	3	1	136	14.7
R	83	Ales Hemsky	EDM	71	12	22	34	-7	14	4	0	3	1	87	13.8
L	18	Ethan Moreau	EDM	81	20	12	32	7	96	0	3	5	2	180	11.1
R	34	Fernando Pisani	EDM	76	16	14	30	14	46	4	1	1	0	99	16.2
C	24	Steve Staios	EDM	82	6	22	28	17	86	1	0	1	0	153	3.9
D	47	* Marc-Andre Bergeron	EDM	54	9	17	26	13	26	3	0	0	0	105	8.6
D	2	Eric Brewer	EDM	77	7	18	25	-6	67	3	0	1	1	135	5.2
C	36	* Jarret Stoll	EDM	68	10	11	21	8	42	1	1	2	0	107	9.3
D	23	Cory Cross	EDM	68	7	14	21	9	56	1	0	0	0	83	8.4
D	21	Jason Smith	EDM	68	7	12	19	13	98	0	1	1	0	84	8.3
L	15	Brad Isbister	EDM	51	10	8	18	-2	54	1	0	2	1	80	12.5
D	55	Igor Ulanov	EDM	42	5	13	18	19	28	1	0	3	0	49	10.2
R	77	Adam Oates	EDM	60	2	16	18	0	8	1	0	1	0	32	6.3
R	27	Georges Laraque	EDM	66	6	11	17	7	99	1	0	1	0	54	11.1
L	28	Jason Chimera	EDM	60	4	8	12	-1	57	0	0	1	0	79	5.1
C	19	Marty Reasoner	EDM	17	2	6	8	5	10	0	1	0	0	28	7.1
D	32	Scott Ferguson	EDM	52	1	5	6	-5	80	0	0	1	0	38	2.6
D	5	Alexei Semenov	EDM	46	2	3	5	8	32	1	0	0	0	36	5.6
C	12	* Mike Bishai	EDM	14	0	2	2	0	19	0	0	0	0	14	0.0
C	33	* Peter Sarno	EDM	6	1	0	1	2	2	0	0	0	0	5	20.0
D	26	Mikko Luoma	EDM	3	0	1	1	0	0	0	0	0	0	4	0.0
L	42	* Tony Salmelainen	EDM	13	0	1	1	-1	4	0	0	0	0	17	0.0
L	22	* Jani Rita	EDM	2	0	0	0	0	0	0	0	0	0	1	0.0
D	44	* Doug Lynch	EDM	2	0	0	0	0	0	0	0	0	0	2	0.0

Goaltending

No.	Goaltender	GPI	Mins	Avg	W	L	T	EN	SO	GA	SA	S%	G	A	PIM
30	Jussi Markkanen	7	394	1.83	2	2	2	0	0	12	182	.934	0	0	2
1	Ty Conklin	38	2086	2.42	17	14	4	2	1	84	959	.912	0	0	17
35	Tommy Salo	44	2487	2.58	17	18	6	1	3	107	1024	.896	0	1	2
45	Stephen Valiquette	1	14	8.57	0	0	0	0	0	2	7	.714	0	0	0
	Totals	**82**	**5007**	**2.49**	**36**	**34**	**12**	**3**	**4**	**208**	**2175**	**.904**			

Ryan Smyth led the Oilers in goals, assists, points, power-play goals and game-winning goals. He was 16th in the NHL with 245 shots on goal.

Coaching History

Glen Sather, 1979-80; Bryan Watson and Glen Sather, 1980-81; Glen Sather, 1981-82 to 1988-89; John Muckler, 1989-90, 1990-91; Ted Green, 1991-92, 1992-93; Ted Green and Glen Sather, 1993-94; George Burnett and Ron Low, 1994-95; Ron Low, 1995-96 to 1998-99; Kevin Lowe, 1999-2000; Craig MacTavish, 2000-01 to date.

Coach

MacTAVISH, CRAIG
Coach, Edmonton Oilers. Born in London, Ont., August 15, 1958.

The Edmonton Oilers named Craig MacTavish as their head coach on June 22, 2000. He became the eighth person in the club's NHL history to hold the position. MacTavish joined Kevin Lowe and Glen Sather as head coaches who were former captains of the Oilers.

MacTavish played for 18 seasons in the NHL, including eight-and-three-quarter campaigns with the Oilers. He was instrumental in helping his teams win four Stanley Cup titles; three with Edmonton and one with the New York Rangers. Although he was the last player in the NHL to play without a helmet, MacTavish was known for his aggressive style, combined with above average skills.

MacTavish retired as a player in 1997 and was immediately named an assistant coach with the New York Rangers. He was with the Rangers for two seasons prior to joining the Oilers' coaching staff as an assistant under Kevin Lowe in 1999-2000.

Coaching Record

Season	Team	Games	Regular Season W	L	T	Playoffs Games	W	L
2000-01	Edmonton (NHL)	82	39	31	12	6	2	4
2001-02	Edmonton (NHL)	82	38	32	12	....	....	....
2002-03	Edmonton (NHL)	82	36	35	11	6	2	4
2003-04	Edmonton (NHL)	82	36	34	12	....	....	....
	NHL Totals	328	149	132	47	12	4	8

Club Records

Team

(Figures in brackets for season records are games played; records for fewest points, wins, ties, losses, goals, goals against are for 70 or more games)

Most Points	**119**	1983-84 (80), 1985-86 (80)
Most Wins	**57**	1983-84 (80)
Most Ties	**16**	1980-81 (80), 1999-2000 (82)
Most Losses	**50**	1992-93 (84)
Most Goals	***446**	1983-84 (80)
Most Goals Against	**337**	1992-93 (84)
Fewest Points	**60**	1992-93 (84)
Fewest Wins	**25**	1993-94 (84)
Fewest Ties	**5**	1983-84 (80)
Fewest Losses	**17**	1981-82 (80), 1985-86 (80)
Fewest Goals	**205**	2001-02 (82)
Fewest Goals Against	**182**	2001-02 (82)
Longest Winning Streak		
Overall	**9**	Feb. 20-Mar. 13/01
Home	**8**	Jan. 19-Feb. 22/85, Feb. 24-Apr. 2/86
Away	**8**	Dec. 9/86-Jan. 17/87
Longest Undefeated Streak		
Overall	**15**	Oct. 11-Nov. 9/84 (12 wins, 3 ties)
Home	**14**	Nov. 15/89-Jan. 6/90 (11 wins, 3 ties)
Away	**9**	Jan. 17-Mar. 2/82 (6 wins, 3 ties), Nov. 23/82-Jan. 18/83 (7 wins, 2 ties)
Longest Losing Streak		
Overall	**11**	Oct. 16-Nov. 7/93
Home	**9**	Oct. 16-Nov. 24/93
Away	**9**	Nov. 25-Dec. 30/80
Longest Winless Streak		
Overall	**14**	Oct. 11-Nov. 7/93 (13 losses, 1 tie)
Home	**9**	Oct. 16-Nov. 24/93 (9 losses)
Away	**11**	Dec. 18/01-Feb. 8/02 (7 losses, 4 ties)
Most Shutouts, Season	**8**	1997-98 (82); 2000-01 (82); 2001-02 (82)
Most PIM, Season	**2,173**	1987-88 (80)
Most Goals, Game	**13**	Nov. 19/83 (N.J. 4 at Edm. 13), Nov. 8/85 (Van. 0 at Edm. 13)

Individual

Most Seasons	**15**	Kevin Lowe
Most Games	**1,037**	Kevin Lowe
Most Goals, Career	**583**	Wayne Gretzky
Most Assists, Career	**1,086**	Wayne Gretzky
Most Points, Career	**1,669**	Wayne Gretzky (583G, 1,086A)
Most PIM, Career	**1,747**	Kelly Buchberger
Most Shutouts, Career	**23**	Tommy Salo
Longest Consecutive Games Streak	**519**	Craig MacTavish (Oct. 11/86-Jan. 2/93)
Most Goals, Season	***92**	Wayne Gretzky (1981-82)
Most Assists, Season	***163**	Wayne Gretzky (1985-86)
Most Points, Season	***215**	Wayne Gretzky (1985-86; 52G, 163A)
Most PIM, Season	**286**	Steve Smith (1987-88)
Most Points, Defenseman, Season	**138**	Paul Coffey (1985-86; 48G, 90A)
Most Points, Center, Season	***215**	Wayne Gretzky (1985-86; 52G, 163A)
Most Points, Right Wing, Season	**135**	Jari Kurri (1984-85; 71G, 64A)
Most Points, Left Wing, Season	**106**	Mark Messier (1982-83; 48G, 58A)
Most Points, Rookie, Season	**75**	Jari Kurri (1980-81; 32G, 43A)
Most Shutouts, Season	**8**	Curtis Joseph (1997-98), Tommy Salo (2000-01)
Most Goals, Game	**5**	Wayne Gretzky (Feb. 18/81, Dec. 30/81, Dec. 15/84, Dec. 6/87), Jari Kurri (Nov. 19/83), Pat Hughes (Feb. 3/84)
Most Assists, Game	***7**	Wayne Gretzky (Feb. 15/80, Dec. 11/85, Feb. 14/86)
Most Points, Game	**8**	Wayne Gretzky (Nov. 19/83; 3G, 5A), (Jan. 4/84; 4G, 4A), Paul Coffey (Mar. 14/86; 2G, 6A)

* NHL Record.

Retired Numbers

3	Al Hamilton	1972-1980
17	Jari Kurri	1980-1990
31	Grant Fuhr	1981-1991
99	Wayne Gretzky	1979-1988

Captains' History

Ron Chipperfield, 1979-80; Blair MacDonald and Lee Fogolin, Jr., 1980-81; Lee Fogolin, Jr., 1981-82, 1982-83; Wayne Gretzky, 1983-84 to 1987-88; Mark Messier, 1988-89 to 1990-91; Kevin Lowe, 1991-92; Craig MacTavish, 1992-93, 1993-94; Shayne Corson, 1994-95; Kelly Buchberger, 1995-96 to 1998-99; Doug Weight, 1999-2000, 2000-01; Jason Smith, 2001-02 to date.

All-time Record vs. Other Clubs

Regular Season

	At Home								On Road								Total							
	GP	W	L	T	OL	GF	GA	PTS	GP	W	L	T	OL	GF	GA	PTS	GP	W	L	T	OL	GF	GA	PTS
Anaheim	25	17	8	0	0	57	50	34	26	9	15	2	0	64	71	20	51	26	23	2	0	121	121	54
Atlanta	4	2	1	1	0	14	11	5	3	2	1	0	0	8	3	4	7	4	2	1	0	22	14	9
Boston	29	11	15	3	0	98	97	25	30	6	20	3	1	80	126	16	59	17	35	6	1	178	223	41
Buffalo	29	21	5	3	0	120	74	45	30	13	10	7	0	112	109	33	59	34	15	10	0	232	183	78
Calgary	81	42	28	10	1	306	265	95	81	29	43	9	0	275	324	67	162	71	71	19	1	581	589	162
Carolina	31	19	7	5	0	121	92	43	29	11	11	7	0	98	112	29	60	30	18	12	0	219	204	72
Chicago	45	22	18	5	0	165	147	49	44	16	21	7	0	152	167	39	89	38	39	12	0	317	314	88
Colorado	46	25	16	4	1	186	137	55	47	19	24	4	0	169	179	42	93	44	40	8	1	355	316	97
Columbus	8	7	1	0	0	31	17	14	8	4	1	3	0	27	20	11	16	11	2	3	0	58	37	25
Dallas	44	21	13	8	2	176	145	52	45	14	23	7	1	126	163	36	89	35	36	15	3	302	308	88
Detroit	44	20	14	10	0	168	155	50	44	16	23	3	2	146	172	37	88	36	37	13	2	314	327	87
Florida	7	4	2	1	0	24	16	9	9	2	5	2	0	24	24	6	16	6	7	3	0	48	40	15
Los Angeles	77	39	23	15	0	347	275	93	77	34	27	15	1	318	298	84	154	73	50	30	1	665	573	177
Minnesota	11	6	1	3	1	24	14	16	10	7	1	1	1	29	22	16	21	13	2	4	2	53	36	32
Montreal	35	18	17	0	0	117	113	36	30	10	16	4	0	95	105	24	65	28	33	4	0	212	218	60
Nashville	12	6	4	0	2	36	34	14	13	6	4	3	0	37	32	15	25	12	8	3	2	73	66	29
New Jersey	31	14	10	6	1	136	114	35	33	16	13	3	1	112	111	36	64	30	23	9	2	248	225	71
NY Islanders	29	16	8	5	0	107	87	37	31	7	15	9	0	110	128	23	60	23	23	14	0	217	215	60
NY Rangers	28	12	13	3	0	101	94	27	30	14	9	6	1	113	112	35	58	26	22	9	1	214	206	62
Ottawa	11	7	2	2	0	39	25	16	10	5	3	2	0	26	19	12	21	12	5	4	0	65	44	28
Philadelphia	28	14	8	6	0	98	83	34	31	9	20	2	0	85	128	20	59	23	28	8	0	183	211	54
Phoenix	72	46	20	6	0	313	234	98	71	37	26	5	3	314	284	82	143	83	46	11	3	627	518	180
Pittsburgh	30	22	7	1	0	148	98	45	30	12	14	3	1	127	117	28	60	34	21	4	1	275	215	73
St. Louis	44	23	17	4	0	161	144	50	44	16	20	7	1	153	157	40	88	39	37	11	1	314	301	90
San Jose	33	19	7	7	0	112	71	45	32	11	14	5	2	100	112	29	65	30	21	12	2	212	183	74
Tampa Bay	10	7	3	0	0	26	21	14	11	6	3	2	0	35	31	14	21	13	6	2	0	61	52	28
Toronto	43	23	13	6	1	178	138	53	37	15	20	2	0	154	154	32	80	38	33	8	1	332	292	85
Vancouver	81	49	22	7	3	356	256	108	82	38	30	12	2	320	295	90	163	87	52	19	5	676	551	198
Washington	29	15	10	4	0	120	91	34	29	9	18	2	0	93	118	20	58	24	28	6	0	213	209	54
Totals	**997**	**547**	**313**	**125**	**12**	**3885**	**3098**	**1231**	**997**	**393**	**450**	**137**	**17**	**3502**	**3693**	**940**	**1994**	**940**	**763**	**262**	**29**	**7387**	**6791**	**2171**

Playoffs

	Series	W	L	GP	W	L	T	GF	GA	Last Mtg.	Rnd.	Result
Boston	2	2	0	9	8	1	0	41	20	1990	F	W 4-1
Calgary	5	4	1	30	19	11	0	132	96	1991	DSF	W 4-3
Chicago	4	3	1	20	12	8	0	102	77	1992	CF	L 0-4
Colorado	2	1	1	12	5	7	0	30	35	1998	CQF	W 4-3
Dallas	8	2	6	42	15	27	0	104	118	2003	CQF	L 2-4
Detroit	2	2	0	10	8	2	0	39	26	1988	CF	W 4-1
Los Angeles	7	5	2	36	24	12	0	154	127	1992	DSF	W 4-2
Montreal	1	1	0	3	3	0	0	15	6	1981	PRE	W 3-0
NY Islanders	3	1	2	15	6	9	0	47	58	1984	F	W 4-1
Philadelphia	3	2	1	15	8	7	0	49	44	1987	F	W 4-3
Vancouver	2	2	0	9	7	2	0	35	20	1992	DF	W 4-2
Winnipeg	6	6	0	26	22	4	0	120	75	1990	DSF	W 4-3
Totals	**45**	**31**	**14**	**227**	**137**	**90**	**0**	**868**	**702**			

Playoff Results 2004-2000

Year	Round	Opponent	Result	GF	GA
2003	CQF	Dallas	L 2-4	11	20
2001	CQF	Dallas	L 2-4	13	16
2000	CQF	Dallas	L 1-4	11	14

Abbreviations: Round: F - Final; **CF** - conference final; **CQF** - conference quarter-final; **DF** - division final;**DSF** - division semi-final; **PRE** - preliminary round.

Calgary totals include Atlanta Flames, 1979-80.
Colorado totals include Quebec, 1979-80 to 1994-95.
New Jersey totals include Colorado Rockies, 1979-80 to 1981-82.
Carolina totals include Hartford, 1979-80 to 1996-97.
Dallas totals include Minnesota North Stars, 1979-80 to 1992-93.
Phoenix totals include Winnipeg, 1979-80 to 1995-96.

2003-04 Results

Oct.	9	San Jose	5-2
	11	at Vancouver	0-3
	14	at Calgary	0-1
	16	Buffalo	4-1
	18	Colorado	6-3
	21	St. Louis	4-6
	23	at Colorado	1-6
	25	Calgary	2-4
	30	Columbus	4-3*
Nov.	1	Detroit	4-4
	4	at Montreal	4-2
	6	at Ottawa	3-3
	8	at Toronto	1-4
	10	at NY Rangers	5-4
	11	at Boston	3-4
	13	at Minnesota	2-0
	15	Calgary	2-1*
	18	Chicago	5-2
	20	Toronto	3-2
	22	Montreal	3-4
	25	at Columbus	3-3
	26	at Detroit	1-7
	28	Colorado	1-4
	30	San Jose	1-2
Dec.	3	Minnesota	0-1
	6	Pittsburgh	4-3
	9	Carolina	2-3
	11	at San Jose	2-2
	12	at Phoenix	3-3
	14	at Anaheim	3-2
	16	at Los Angeles	2-4
	18	Minnesota	1-1
	20	Vancouver	0-3
	23	at Calgary	1-2
	27	at Vancouver	6-2
	28	Calgary	1-2
	30	Minnesota	2-2
Jan.	2	at Minnesota	2-1
	4	at Chicago	4-3
	5	at New Jersey	2-3*
	8	at NY Islanders	2-3
	10	at Philadelphia	3-0
	11	at Washington	0-1
	13	Florida	4-2
	15	Anaheim	1-0
	17	at Nashville	1-2
	18	at Columbus	4-4
	20	Dallas	3-0
	22	Tampa Bay	2-3
	24	Nashville	3-4
	27	at Colorado	1-3
	29	Chicago	5-2
	31	Los Angeles	3-4
Feb.	2	Anaheim	2-1*
	4	St. Louis	5-3
	11	Atlanta	5-1
	13	at Minnesota	0-3
	15	at Nashville	2-2
	16	at Detroit	1-2
	18	at Colorado	5-1
	21	Vancouver	4-3*
	23	Detroit	1-1
	25	at Anaheim	2-4
	27	at Phoenix	7-2
	29	at Dallas	4-5*
Mar.	2	Phoenix	5-4*
	4	at St. Louis	1-1
	7	at Chicago	4-3*
	9	at Calgary	1-1
	10	Colorado	2-3*
	12	Vancouver	3-4*
	14	Ottawa	3-1
	16	Columbus	3-2
	19	Nashville	5-4
	21	at San Jose	5-2
	22	at Los Angeles	2-1
	24	Dallas	3-4*
	26	Los Angeles	3-1
	28	Phoenix	4-2
	30	at St. Louis	0-1
	31	at Dallas	3-1
Apr.	3	at Vancouver	2-5

* – Overtime

Entry Draft
Selections 2004-1990

2004 Pick		2001 Pick		1997 Pick		1993 Pick	
14	Devan Dubnyk	13	Ales Hemsky	14	Michel Riesen	7	Jason Arnott
25	Rob Schremp	43	Doug Lynch	41	Patrick Dovigi	16	Nick Stajduhar
44	Roman Teslyuk	52	Ed Caron	68	Sergei Yerkovich	33	David Vyborny
57	Geoff Paukovich	84	Kenny Smith	94	Jonas Elofsson	59	Kevin Paden
112	Liam Reddox	133	Jussi Markkanen	121	Jason Chimera	60	Alexander Kerch
146	Bryan Young	154	Jake Brenk	141	Peter Sarno	111	Miroslav Satan
177	Max Gordichuk	185	Mikael Svensk	176	Kevin Bolibruck	163	Alexander Zhurik
208	Stephane Goulet	215	Dan Baum	187	Chad Hinz	189	Martin Bakula
242	Tyler Spurgeon	248	Kari Haakana	205	Chris Kerr	215	Brad Norton
274	Bjorn Bjurling	272	Ales Pisa	231	Alexander Fomitchev	241	Oleg Maltsev
		278	Shay Stephenson			267	Ilja Byakin

2003 Pick		2000 Pick		1996 Pick		1992 Pick	
22	Marc-Antoine Pouliot			6	Boyd Devereaux	13	Joe Hulbig
51	Colin McDonald	17	Alexei Mikhnov	19	Matthieu Descoteaux	37	Martin Reichel
68	Jean-Francois Jacques	35	Brad Winchester	32	Chris Hajt	61	Simon Roy
72	Mishail Joukov	83	Alexander Liubimov	59	Tom Poti	65	Kirk Maltby
94	Zachery Stortini	113	Lou Dickenson	114	Brian Urick	96	Ralph Intranuovo
147	Kalle Olsson	152	Paul Flache	141	Bryan Randall	109	Joaquin Gage
154	David Rohlfs	184	Shaun Norrie	168	David Bernier	157	Steve Gibson
184	Dragan Umicevic	211	Joe Cullen	170	Brandon Lafrance	181	Kyuin Shim
214	Kyle Brodziak	215	Matthew Lombardi	195	Fernando Pisani	190	Colin Schmidt
215	Mathieu Roy	247	Jason Platt	221	John Hultberg	205	Marko Tuomainen
248	Josef Hrabal	274	Yevgeny Muratov			253	Bryan Rasmussen
278	Troy Bodie						

2002 Pick		1999 Pick		1995 Pick		1991 Pick	
15	Jesse Niinimaki	13	Jani Rita	6	Steve Kelly	12	Tyler Wright
31	Jeff Deslauriers	36	Alexei Semenov	31	Georges Laraque	20	Martin Rucinsky
36	Jarret Stoll	41	Tony Salmelainen	57	Lukas Zib	34	Andrew Verner
44	Matt Greene	81	Adam Hauser	83	Mike Minard	56	George Breen
79	Brock Radunske	91	Mike Comrie	109	Jan Snopek	78	Mario Nobili
106	Ivan Koltsov	139	Jonathan Fauteux	161	Martin Cerven	93	Ryan Haggerty
111	Jonas Almtorp	171	Chris Legg	187	Stephen Douglas	144	David Oliver
123	invalid pick	199	Christian Chartier	213	Jiri Antonin	166	Gary Kitching
148	Glenn Fisher	256	Tamas Groschl			210	Vegar Barlie
181	Mikko Luoma			1994 Pick		232	Yevgeny Belosheiken
205	J.F. Dufort	1998 Pick		4	Jason Bonsignore	254	Juha Riihijarvi
211	Patrick Murphy	13	Michael Henrich	6	Ryan Smyth		
244	Dwight Helminen	67	Alex Henry	32	Mike Watt	1990 Pick	
245	Tomas Micka	99	Shawn Horcoff	53	Corey Neilson	17	Scott Allison
274	Fredrik Johansson	113	Kristian Antila	60	Brad Symes	38	Alexandre Legault
		128	Paul Elliott	79	Adam Copeland	59	Joe Crowley
		144	Oleg Smirnov	95	Jussi Tarvainen	67	Joel Blain
		159	Trevor Ettinger	110	Jon Gaskins	101	Greg Louder
		186	Mike Morrison	136	Terry Marchant	122	Keijo Sailynoja
		213	Christian Lefebvre	160	Curtis Sheptak	143	Mike Power
		241	Maxim Spiridonov	162	Dmitri Shulga	164	Roman Mejzlik
				179	Chris Wickenheiser	185	Richard Zemlicka
				185	Rob Guinn	206	Petr Korinek
				188	Jason Reid	227	invalid pick
				214	Jeremy Jablonski	248	Sami Nuutinen
				266	Ladislav Benysek		

General Managers' History

Larry Gordon, 1979-80; Glen Sather, 1980-81 to 1999-2000; Kevin Lowe, 2000-01 to date.

Vice President and General Manager

LOWE, KEVIN
Executive Vice President/General Manager, Edmonton Oilers.
Born in Lachute, Que., April 15, 1959.

The Edmonton Oilers named Kevin Lowe as their general manager on June 9, 2000, filling the position left vacant when Glen Sather resigned on May 19th. Lowe moved into the front office after spending the 1999-2000 season as coach of the Oilers. In his role as Oilers' g.m., Lowe has worked with Wayne Gretzky as assistant executive director of Canada's gold medal-winning team at the 2002 Winter Olympics and at the 2004 World Cup of Hockey.

After a brilliant 19-year playing career with the Edmonton Oilers and New York Rangers, Lowe announced his retirement on July 30, 1998 and joined the Edmonton Oilers coaching staff. He replaced Ron Low as head coach on June 18, 1999.

Lowe was the Oilers' first-ever draft pick when he was selected 1st overall in the 1979 NHL Entry Draft. He went on to play in 1,254 regular-season games and 214 playoff games, winning six Stanley Cup championships; the first five with Edmonton (1984, 1985, 1987, 1988, 1990) followed by a sixth title with the Rangers in 1994.

Besides being the first draft choice in Oilers history, Lowe also scored the first goal in team history on October 10, 1979. He holds the Oilers' record for most games played in both the regular season (1,037) and playoffs (172), and became the sixth captain in team history in 1990-91. He was no less a leader off the ice, becoming the only player to win the King Clancy Memorial Trophy and the Budweiser/NHL Man of the Year Award in the same season (1989-90). Both awards are presented for leadership qualities and humanitarian contributions. His work with the Edmonton Christmas Bureau has set the standard for the Oilers' commitment to community involvement.

NHL Coaching Record

Season	Team	Games	Regular Season W	L	T	Playoffs Games	W	L
1999-2000	Edmonton	82	32	34	16	5	1	4
	NHL Totals	**82**	**32**	**34**	**16**	**5**	**1**	**4**

Club Directory

Rexall Place

Edmonton Oilers
11230 – 110 Street
Edmonton, Alberta T5G 3H7
Phone **780/414-4000**
Press Box 780/414-4235
Ticketing 780/414-4400
Media Lounge 780/414-4173
FAX 780/414-4659
www.edmontonoilers.com
Capacity: 16,389

Owner	Edmonton Investors Group Ltd.
Governor	Cal Nichols
Alternate Governors	Patrick R. LaForge, Kevin Lowe, William Butler
President & Chief Executive Officer	Patrick R. LaForge
Executive Vice-President & General Manager	Kevin Lowe
Vice-President, Hockey Operations	Kevin Prendergast
Assistant General Manager	Scott Howson
Head Coach	Craig MacTavish
Assistant Coaches	Charlie Huddy, Bill Moores, Craig Simpson
Goaltending Coach	Pete Peeters
Video Coach	Brian Ross
European Scout/Development Coach	Frank Musil
Vice President, Public Relations	Bill Tuele
Information Coordinator	Steve Knowles
Public Relations Coordinator, Hockey	J.J. Hebert
Director of Research, Analysis and Software Development	Sean Draper
Scouting Staff	Bob Brown, Bill Dandy, Brad Davis, Lorne Davis, Morey Gare, Stu MacGregor, Chris McCarthy, Kent Nilsson, Dave Semenko, John Stevenson
Executive Assistant to the President	Donna Perman
Executive Assistant to the General Manager	Valerie Rendell
Security Advisor	Gary Goulet

Medical and Training Staff

Head Medical Trainer	Ken Lowe
Assistant Medical Trainer	Ryan McInnes
Head Equipment Manager	Barrie Stafford
Equipment Manager	Lyle Kulchisky
Assistant Equipment Manager	Jeff Lang
Massage Therapist	Stewart Poirier
Team Medical Chief of Staff/Director of Glen Sather Sports Medicine Clinic	Dr. David C. Reid
Team Physicians	Dr. John Clarke
Team Dermatologist	Dr. Don Groot
Team Dentists	Dr. Ben Eastwood, Dr. Tony Sneazwell
Fitness Consultants	Dr. Art Quinney, Dr. Gordon Bell
Physical Therapy Consultant	Dr. Dave Magee
Team Optometrist	Dr. Brent Saik
Strength & Conditioning Consultant	Daryl Duke

Finance & Administration

Vice-President of Finance and Chief Financial Officer	Darryl Boessenkool
Controller	Jason Quilley
Facilities Manager	Craig Tkachuk
Assistant Controller	Colleen Rolston
Legal	Antoinette Mongillo
IT Manager	Terry Rhoades
Systems Administrator	Rod Pruden
Human Resource Manager	Tandy Kustiak
Payroll Manager	Shawna Quigley
Accounts Receivable Coordinator	Corinne McGregor
Accounts Payable Coordinator	Linda Balicki
Executive Assistant	Sherry Smith

Marketing & Communications

Vice-President, Marketing & Communications	Allan Watt
Director, Corporate Communications & Marketing	Natalie Minckler
Marketing & Communications Coordinator	Darren Krill
Marketing & Promotions Coordinator	Stacey Brockhoff
Director of Broadcast	Don Metz
Game Night Operations	Glenn Wiun, Marilyn Riddell
Director, Licensing & Merchandising	Nick Wilson
New Media Production Manager	Andreas Schwabe
Publications Coordinator	Steve Sandor
Receptionist	Lisa Saskiw

Community Relations

Director Community Relations & Executive Director, Edmonton Oilers Community Foundation	Gillian Andries
Community Relations Coordinators	Heidi Lippert, Christopher Field
ICE School Coordinator	Sandy VanRiper

Sales

Director of Sales	Eric Upton

Sponsorships Sales

Manager, Corporate Sponsorships	Brad MacGregor
National Accounts Managers	Sean Price, Michael Lake, Daryl Zelinski
Sponsorship Services Managers	Connie Lloyd, Amanda Nichols, Jocelyn Hickey

Suite Sales

Manager, Executive Suite Operations	Bob Haromy
Suite Coordinator	Chella Barott

Ticket Sales

Director of Ticket Sales	Ken Brown
Ticket Sales Department Coordinator/ Office Administrator	Cheryl Thomas
Corporate Account Executives	Dan Brodeur, Randy Keller, Sheldon Smart, Tyler Waye
Group Account Executive	Janice Wimberly
Inside Sales Representatives	Brad Bistritz, Tabitha Kobeluck
Credit Supervisor	Deborah Barnes
Credit Clerk	Candace Lega

Ticket Operations

Box Office Manager	Christine Dmytryshyn
Customer Service Coordinator	Shari Hands
Ticketing Services Representatives	Sandy Langley, Sheila McCaskill, Jamie Schenknecht

Team Information

Television Outlets	Sportsnet , CBXT TV & TSN
Radio Flagship Station	630 CHED (AM); Rod Phillips (Play-by-play) & Morley Scott (colour)

Florida Panthers

2003-04 Results: 28w-35L-15T-4OTL 75PTS.
Fourth, Southeast Division

2004-05 Schedule

Oct.	Thu.	14	Philadelphia
	Sat.	16	at Tampa Bay
	Tue.	19	at Toronto
	Thu.	21	at Boston
	Sat.	23	Pittsburgh
	Wed.	27	Atlanta
	Fri.	29	Nashville
	Sun.	31	Washington*
Nov.	Wed.	3	Montreal
	Fri.	5	at NY Rangers
	Sat.	6	at NY Islanders
	Tue.	9	at Ottawa
	Fri.	12	Calgary
	Sun.	14	Los Angeles*
	Wed.	17	at Anaheim
	Thu.	18	at Los Angeles
	Sat.	20	at San Jose
	Wed.	24	New Jersey
	Fri.	26	Vancouver
	Sun.	28	at Washington*
	Mon.	29	at Pittsburgh
Dec.	Wed.	1	St. Louis
	Sat.	4	at Tampa Bay
	Wed.	8	Montreal
	Sat.	11	at Phoenix
	Mon.	13	at Colorado
	Wed.	15	Buffalo
	Fri.	17	Carolina
	Sun.	19	at Buffalo*
	Tue.	21	at Philadelphia
	Thu.	23	at NY Rangers
	Sun.	26	at Carolina*
	Mon.	27	New Jersey
	Wed.	29	Boston
	Fri.	31	NY Rangers*
Jan.	Tue.	4	at NY Islanders
	Thu.	6	at Ottawa
	Sat.	8	at Montreal
	Wed.	12	Washington
	Sat.	15	Tampa Bay
	Mon.	17	Atlanta*

	Wed.	19	Buffalo
	Fri.	21	Boston
	Sat.	22	at Washington
	Mon.	24	at Boston
	Wed.	26	Toronto
	Fri.	28	Pittsburgh
	Sat.	29	Carolina
Feb.	Wed.	2	Chicago
	Fri.	4	at Atlanta
	Sat.	5	Anaheim
	Tue.	8	at New Jersey
	Wed.	9	at Pittsburgh
	Wed.	16	Ottawa
	Sat.	19	NY Islanders
	Sun.	20	Detroit*
	Tue.	22	at Toronto
	Thu.	24	at Montreal
	Sat.	26	at Columbus
	Sun.	27	at Minnesota*
Mar.	Wed.	2	Toronto
	Fri.	4	at Atlanta
	Sat.	5	Tampa Bay
	Mon.	7	Ottawa
	Wed.	9	Edmonton
	Fri.	11	Washington
	Sat.	12	at Carolina
	Tue.	15	Philadelphia
	Fri.	18	at Washington
	Sat.	19	Tampa Bay
	Mon.	21	Atlanta
	Wed.	23	at Dallas
	Thu.	24	at Nashville
	Sat.	26	at Tampa Bay
	Mon.	28	at Atlanta
	Wed.	30	NY Rangers
Apr.	Fri.	1	NY Islanders
	Sun.	3	at Buffalo*
	Tue.	5	at Philadelphia
	Wed.	6	at New Jersey
	Fri.	8	Carolina
	Sun.	10	at Carolina*

* Denotes afternoon game.

Year-by-Year Record

| | | Home | | | | Road | | | | Overall | | | | | | |
Season	GP	W	L	T	OL	W	L	T	OL	W	L	T	OL	GF	GA	Pts.	Finished	Playoff Result
2003-04	82	16	15	7	3	12	20	8	1	28	35	15	4	188	221	75	4th, Southeast Div.	Out of Playoffs
2002-03	82	8	21	7	5	16	15	6	4	24	36	13	9	176	237	70	4th, Southeast Div.	Out of Playoffs
2001-02	82	11	23	3	4	11	21	7	6	22	44	10	6	180	250	60	4th, Southeast Div.	Out of Playoffs
2000-01	82	12	18	7	4	10	20	6	5	22	38	13	9	200	246	66	3rd, Southeast Div.	Out of Playoffs
1999-2000	82	26	9	4	2	17	18	2	4	43	27	6	6	244	209	98	2nd, Southeast Div.	Lost Conf. Quarter-Final
1998-99	82	17	17	7	...	13	17	11	...	30	34	18	...	210	228	78	2nd, Southeast Div.	Out of Playoffs
1997-98	82	11	24	6	...	13	19	9	...	24	43	15	...	203	256	63	6th, Atlantic Div.	Out of Playoffs
1996-97	82	21	12	8	...	14	16	11	...	35	28	19	...	221	201	89	3rd, Atlantic Div.	Lost Conf. Quarter-Final
1995-96	82	25	12	4	...	16	19	6	...	41	31	10	...	254	234	92	3rd, Atlantic Div.	Lost Final
1994-95	48	9	12	3	...	11	10	3	...	20	22	6	...	115	127	46	5th, Atlantic Div.	Out of Playoffs
1993-94	84	15	18	9	...	18	16	8	...	33	34	17	...	233	233	83	5th, Atlantic Div.	Out of Playoffs

Franchise date: June 14, 1993

SOUTHEAST
DIVISION

12th
NHL
Season

Roberto Luongo set new Panthers records for games (72), minutes (4,252), saves (2,303), shots faced (2,475) and shutouts (7). He was fifth in the NHL in shutouts, third in save percentage (.931) and finished third in voting for the Vezina Trophy.

2004-05 Player Personnel

FORWARDS	HT	WT	S	Place of Birth	Date	2003-04 Club
BEAUDOIN, Eric	6-5	210	L	Ottawa, Ont.	5/3/80	Florida-San Antonio
BERGLUND, Christian	5-11	190	L	Orebro, Sweden	3/12/80	New Jersey-Florida
CAMPBELL, Gregory	6-0	191	L	London, Ont.	12/17/83	Florida-San Antonio
HAGMAN, Niklas	6-0	200	L	Espoo, Finland	12/5/79	Florida
HORDICHUK, Darcy	6-1	215	L	Kamsack, Sask.	8/10/80	Florida
HORTON, Nathan	6-2	201	R	Welland, Ont.	5/29/85	Florida
HUSELIUS, Kristian	6-1	190	L	Osterhaninge, Sweden	11/10/78	Florida
JARDINE, Ryan	6-0	210	L	Ottawa, Ont.	3/15/80	San Antonio
JOKINEN, Olli	6-3	205	L	Kuopio, Finland	12/5/78	Florida
JONES, Ty	6-3	218	R	Richland, WA	2/22/79	Norfolk-Florida-San Antonio
KOLNIK, Juraj	5-10	190	R	Nitra, Czech.	11/13/80	Florida-San Antonio
NEDOROST, Vaclav	6-1	190	L	Budejovice, Czech.	3/16/82	Florida-San Antonio
OLESZ, Rostislav	6-1	207	L	Bilovec, Czechoslovakia	10/10/85	Vitkovice-Vitkovice Jr.
OLSON, Josh	6-5	225	L	Grand Forks, ND	7/13/81	Florida-San Antonio
PAYER, Serge	6-0	192	L	Rockland, Ont.	5/7/79	Ottawa-Binghamton
PIROS, Kamil	6-0	200	L	Most, Czech.	11/20/78	Atl-Chi (AHL)-Fla-San Antonio
STEWART, Anthony	6-1	225	R	Lasalle, Que.	1/5/85	Kingston
TATICEK, Petr	6-3	195	L	Rakovnik, Czech.	9/22/83	San Antonio
WEISS, Stephen	5-11	185	L	Toronto, Ont.	4/3/83	Florida-San Antonio

DEFENSEMEN						
BIRON, Mathieu	6-6	220	R	Lac-St-Charles, Que.	4/29/80	Florida
BOUWMEESTER, Jay	6-4	210	L	Edmonton, Alta.	9/27/83	Florida-San Antonio
CAIRNS, Eric	6-6	230	L	Oakville, Ont.	6/27/74	NY Islanders
HILL, Sean	6-0	205	R	Duluth, MN	2/14/70	Carolina
KADLEC, Petr	5-11	180	L	Prague, Czech.	1/5/77	Slavia Praha
KARPOVTSEV, Alexander	6-3	221	R	Moscow, USSR	4/7/70	Chicago-NY Islanders
KRAJICEK, Lukas	6-2	185	L	Prostejov, Czech.	3/11/83	Florida-San Antonio
KWIATKOWSKI, Joel	6-2	210	L	Kindersley, Sask.	3/22/77	Washington
McNEILL, Grant	6-2	210	L	Vermillion, Alta.	6/8/83	Florida-San Antonio
MEZEI, Branislav	6-5	236	L	Nitra, Czech.	10/8/80	Florida
NOVAK, Filip	6-1	185	L	Ceske Budejovice, Czech.	5/7/82	Did Not Play - Injured
UCHEVATOV, Victor	6-4	225	L	Angarsk, USSR	2/10/83	Albany-San Antonio
VAN RYN, Mike	6-1	202	R	London, Ont.	5/14/79	Florida

GOALTENDERS	HT	WT	C	Place of Birth	Date	2003-04 Club
LUONGO, Roberto	6-3	205	L	Montreal, Que.	4/4/79	Florida
McLENNAN, Jamie	6-0	190	L	Edmonton, Alta.	6/30/71	Calgary-NY Rangers
SCOTT, Travis	6-2	185	L	Kanata, Ont.	9/14/75	San Antonio

2003-04 Scoring
* - rookie

Regular Season

Pos	#	Player	Team	GP	G	A	Pts	+/-	PIM	PP	SH	GW	GT	S	%
C	12	Olli Jokinen	FLA	82	26	32	58	-16	81	8	2	8	1	280	9.3
D	26	Mike Van Ryn	FLA	79	13	24	37	-16	52	6	1	0	1	136	9.6
L	22	Kristian Huselius	FLA	76	10	21	31	-6	24	2	0	2	1	168	6.0
C	9	Stephen Weiss	FLA	50	12	17	29	-10	10	3	0	2	1	82	14.6
R	13	Juraj Kolnik	FLA	53	14	11	25	-7	14	2	0	1	0	100	14.0
L	14	Niklas Hagman	FLA	75	10	13	23	-5	22	0	1	2	0	122	8.2
L	16	* Nathan Horton	FLA	55	14	8	22	-5	57	6	1	0	0	81	17.3
R	28	Donald Audette	MTL	23	3	5	8	-4	16	0	0	0	0	41	7.3
			FLA	28	6	7	13	-9	22	5	0	0	0	66	9.1
			TOTAL	51	9	12	21	-13	38	5	0	0	0	107	8.4
D	4	Jay Bouwmeester	FLA	61	2	18	20	-15	30	0	0	0	0	85	2.4
C	17	Matt Cullen	FLA	56	6	13	19	-2	24	1	0	2	0	75	8.0
D	2	Lyle Odelein	FLA	82	4	12	16	-7	88	2	0	0	0	67	6.0
D	7	Pavel Trnka	FLA	67	3	13	16	2	51	1	0	0	0	66	4.5
D	34	Mathieu Biron	FLA	57	3	10	13	-13	51	0	0	1	0	75	4.0
C	19	Byron Ritchie	FLA	50	5	6	11	-10	84	0	0	2	0	65	7.7
L	27	Christian Berglund	N.J.	23	2	3	5	-4	4	0	0	0	0	33	6.1
			FLA	10	3	1	4	-2	10	0	0	0	0	17	17.6
			TOTAL	33	5	4	9	-6	14	0	0	0	0	50	10.0
R	11	Mikael Samuelsson	FLA	37	3	6	9	0	35	0	0	1	0	50	6.0
C	40	Vaclav Nedorost	FLA	32	4	3	7	-6	12	2	0	0	0	38	10.5
D	6	Andreas Lilja	FLA	79	3	4	7	-8	90	0	0	0	0	79	3.8
D	23	* Lukas Krajicek	FLA	18	1	6	7	-2	12	1	0	0	0	16	6.3
D	5	Branislav Mezei	FLA	45	0	7	7	-4	80	0	0	0	0	26	0.0
L	38	Eric Beaudoin	FLA	30	2	4	6	-6	12	0	0	0	0	30	6.7
L	24	Darcy Hordichuk	FLA	57	3	1	4	-10	158	0	0	1	0	27	11.1
L	15	Eric Messier	FLA	21	0	3	3	-2	16	0	0	0	0	13	0.0
R	27	Jaroslav Bednar	FLA	13	1	1	2	2	4	0	0	0	0	19	5.3
R	20	* Kamil Piros	ATL	14	0	1	1	-3	4	0	0	0	0	10	0.0
			FLA	3	1	0	1	-1	0	1	0	0	0	1	100.0
			TOTAL	17	1	1	2	-4	4	1	0	0	0	11	9.1
L	20	* Josh Olson	FLA	5	1	0	1	1	0	0	0	0	0	6	16.7
R	23	Lee Goren	FLA	2	0	1	1	-4	0	0	0	0	0	5	0.0
R	21	Denis Shvidki	FLA	2	0	0	0	0	0	0	0	0	0	4	0.0
D	33	* Kristian Kudroc	FLA	2	0	0	0	-1	5	0	0	0	0	0	0.0
C	44	* Gregory Campbell	FLA	2	0	0	0	-1	0	0	0	0	0	0	0.0
D	32	* Grant Mcneill	FLA	3	0	0	0	0	0	0	0	0	0	0	0.0
R	15	* Ty Jones	FLA	6	0	0	0	0	0	0	0	0	0	1	0.0

Goaltending

No.	Goaltender	GPI	Mins	Avg	W	L	T	EN	SO	GA	SA	S%	G	A	PIM
1	Roberto Luongo	72	4252	2.43	25	33	14	7	7	172	2475	.931	0	3	2
31	Steve Shields	16	732	3.44	3	6	1	0	0	42	346	.879	0	0	6
	Totals	82	5017	2.64	28	39	15	7	7	221	2828	.922			

Olli Jokinen led the Panthers in goals, assists, points, power-play goals, shorthanded goals, game-winning goals and shots on goal. His 280 shots tied for fourth in the NHL.

General Managers' History

Bob Clarke, 1993-94; Bryan Murray, 1994-95 to 1999-2000; Bryan Murray and Bill Torrey, 2000-01; Bill Torrey and Chuck Fletcher, 2001-02; Rick Dudley, 2002-03, 2003-04; Mike Keenan, 2004-05.

Coach

MARTIN, JACQUES
Coach, Florida Panthers. Born in St. Pascal, Ont., October 1, 1952.

Jacques Martin was hired as coach of the Florida Panthers on May 26, 2004, joining the team after eight-and-a-half seasons with the Ottawa Senators. Martin guided Ottawa to a 43-23-10-6 mark with 102 points in 2003-04. For his career with the Senators, he posted a 341-255-96 regular-season record and stands as the franchise's all-time leader in games coached (692), regular-season wins (341), playoff wins (31) and playoff games coached (69). He becomes the ninth coach in Panthers history.

Under Martin's guidance, the Senators earned their first Presidents' Trophy and Eastern Conference title, posting a 52-21-8-1 mark in 2002-03. He led Ottawa to its first trip to the Eastern Conference Finals, losing to the eventual Stanley Cup champion New Jersey Devils. Martin has been nominated for the Jack Adams Award as coach of the year four times. He won the award in 1998-99 and was nominated in 1996-97, 2000-01 and 2002-03. Martin was named as an associate coach for Team Canada's men's hockey team that won gold at the 2002 Olympic Winter Games in Salt Lake City and served in the same capacity with Team Canada at this year's World Cup of Hockey.

Martin joined Ottawa after spending the first half of the 1995-96 season with the Stanley Cup champion Colorado Avalanche, where he served as an assistant coach to Marc Crawford and was widely recognized as one of the architects of that championship team. Martin entered the NHL as head coach of the St. Louis Blues in 1986-87 and 1987-88, leading the Blues to the Norris Division championship in his rookie season. He joined the Blues after guiding the Ontario Hockey League's Guelph Platers to the 1986 Memorial Cup championship and winning OHL coach of the year honors for his efforts. Before joining Guelph, Martin spent two years with the Peterborough Petes (OHL) and 10 years honing his coaching skills at Ottawa's Algonquin College and in the Central Junior Hockey League.

Coaching Record

		Regular Season				Playoffs		
Season	Team	Games	W	L	T	Games	W	L
1983-84	Peterborough (OHL)	70	43	23	4	....	....	....
1984-85	Peterborough (OHL)	66	42	20	4	....	....	....
1985-86	Guelph (OHL)	66	41	23	2	....	....	....
1986-87	St. Louis (NHL)	80	32	33	15	6	2	4
1987-88	St. Louis (NHL)	80	34	38	8	10	5	5
1993-94	Cornwall (AHL)	80	33	36	11	13	8	5
1995-96	Ottawa (NHL)	38	10	24	4	....	....	....
1996-97	Ottawa (NHL)	82	31	36	15	7	3	4
1997-98	Ottawa (NHL)	82	34	33	15	11	5	6
1998-99	Ottawa (NHL)	82	44	23	15	4	0	4
1999-2000	Ottawa (NHL)	82	41	30	11	6	2	4
2000-01	Ottawa (NHL)	82	48	25	9	4	0	4
2001-02	Ottawa (NHL)	80	38	33	9	12	7	5
2002-03	Ottawa (NHL)	82	52	22	8	18	11	7
2003-04	Ottawa (NHL)	82	43	29	10	7	3	4
	NHL Totals	852	407	326	119	85	38	47

Martin stepped aside (with NHL permission) during the final two games of the 2001-02 season in order to allow assistant coach Roger Neilson to reach the 1,000-game plateau, April 11 and 13, 2002.

Club Records

Team

(Figures in brackets for season records are games played; records for fewest points, wins, ties, losses, goals, goals against are for 70 or more games)

Most Points **98** 1999-2000 (82)
Most Wins **43** 1999-2000 (82)
Most Ties **19** 1996-97 (82)
Most Losses **44** 2001-02 (82)
Most Goals **254** 1995-96 (82)
Most Goals Against **256** 1997-98 (82)
Fewest Points **60** 2001-02 (82)
Fewest Wins **22** 2000-01 (82), 2001-02 (82)
Fewest Ties **6** 1999-2000 (82)
Fewest Losses **27** 1999-2000 (82)
Fewest Goals **176** 2002-03 (82)
Fewest Goals Against **201** 1996-97 (82)

Longest Winning Streak
Overall .... **7** Nov. 2-14/95
Home .... **5** Nov. 5-14/95
Away .... **4** Four times

Longest Undefeated Streak
Overall .... **12** Oct. 5-30/96 (8 wins, 4 ties)
Home .... **8** Nov. 5-26/95 (7 wins, 1 tie)
Away .... **7** Twice

Longest Losing Streak
Overall .... **13** Feb. 7-Mar. 23/98
Home .... **6** Feb. 25-Mar. 23/98
Away .... **9** Feb. 9-Mar. 25/02

Longest Winless Streak
Overall .... **15** Feb. 1-Mar. 23/98 (14 losses, 1 tie)
Home .... **13** Feb. 5-Mar. 24/03 (11 losses, 2 ties)
Away .... **16** Jan. 2-Mar. 21/98 (12 losses, 4 ties)

Most Shutouts, Season **7** 2002-03 (82)
Most PIM, Season **1,994** 2001-02 (82)
Most Goals, Game .... **10** Nov. 26/97 (Bos. 5 at Fla. 10)

Individual

Most Seasons .... **9** Paul Laus
Most Games .... **573** Robert Svehla
Most Goals, Career .... **157** Scott Mellanby
Most Assists, Career ...... **229** Robert Svehla
Most Points, Career ...... **354** Scott Mellanby (157G, 197A)
Most PIM, Career .... **1,702** Paul Laus
Most Shutouts, Career ...... **22** Roberto Luongo

Longest Consecutive
Games Streak .... **300** Robert Svehla (Dec. 23/98-Apr. 14/02)
Most Goals, Season .... **59** Pavel Bure (2000-01)
Most Assists, Season .... **53** Viktor Kozlov (1999-2000)
Most Points, Season .... **94** Pavel Bure (1999-2000; 58G, 36A)
Most PIM, Season .... **354** Peter Worrell (2001-02)

Most Points, Defenseman,
Season .... **57** Robert Svehla (1995-96; 8G, 49A)
Most Points, Center,
Season .... **70** Viktor Kozlov (1999-2000; 17G, 53A)
Most Points, Right Wing,
Season .... **94** Pavel Bure (1999-2000; 58G, 36A)
Most Points, Left Wing,
Season .... **71** Ray Whitney (1999-2000; 29G, 42A)
Most Points, Rookie,
Season .... **50** Jesse Belanger (1993-94; 17G, 33A)
Most Shutouts, Season .... **7** Roberto Luongo (2003-04)
Most Goals, Game .... **4** Mark Parrish (Oct. 30/98); Pavel Bure (Jan. 1/00, Feb. 10/01)
Most Assists, Game .... **4** Scott Mellanby (Nov. 26/97); Ray Whitney (Oct. 30/00)
Most Points, Game .... **5** Pavel Bure (Feb. 10/01; 4G, 1A)

Coaching History

Roger Neilson, 1993-94, 1994-95; Doug MacLean, 1995-96, 1996-97; Doug MacLean and Bryan Murray, 1997-98; Terry Murray, 1998-99, 1999-2000; Terry Murray and Duane Sutter, 2000-01; Duane Sutter and Mike Keenan, 2001-02; Mike Keenan, 2002-03; Mike Keenan, Rick Dudley and John Torchetti, 2003-04; Jacques Martin, 2004-05.

Captains' History

Brian Skrudland, 1993-94 to 1996-97; Scott Mellanby, 1997-98 to 2000-01; Pavel Bure, 2001-02; no captain, 2002-03; Olli Jokinen, 2003-04.

All-time Record vs. Other Clubs

Regular Season

		At Home						On Road						Total					
	GP	W	L	T	OL	GF	GA	PTS	GP	W	L	T	OL	GF	GA	PTS	GP	W	L	T	OL	GF	GA	PTS
Anaheim	8	4	2	0	0	23	17	10	9	5	2	1	1	30	27	12	17	9	4	1	1	53	44	22
Atlanta	13	4	7	1	1	31	44	10	13	4	3	4	2	40	40	14	26	8	10	5	3	71	84	24
Boston	21	9	9	2	1	57	58	21	22	10	8	4	0	57	56	24	43	19	17	6	1	114	114	45
Buffalo	21	10	10	1	0	59	63	21	23	5	14	3	1	37	64	14	44	15	24	4	1	96	127	35
Calgary	9	3	3	2	1	21	22	9	8	3	4	1	0	20	21	7	17	6	7	3	1	41	43	16
Carolina	26	11	5	8	2	74	55	32	25	9	12	3	1	63	73	22	51	20	17	11	3	137	128	54
Chicago	8	2	5	1	0	18	30	5	10	3	5	2	0	30	34	8	18	5	10	3	0	48	64	13
Colorado	11	1	10	0	0	30	48	2	11	4	4	3	0	27	30	11	22	5	14	3	0	57	78	13
Columbus	3	2	0	0	1	9	7	5	2	1	1	0	0	4	4	2	5	3	1	0	1	13	11	7
Dallas	10	4	5	1	0	22	28	9	8	3	3	2	0	22	25	8	18	7	8	3	0	44	53	17
Detroit	9	1	4	2	2	17	27	6	8	1	4	1	2	21	30	5	17	2	8	3	4	38	57	11
Edmonton	9	5	2	2	0	24	24	12	7	2	4	1	0	16	24	5	16	7	6	3	0	40	48	17
Los Angeles	8	4	1	3	0	23	14	11	9	4	5	0	0	29	27	8	17	8	6	3	0	52	41	19
Minnesota	3	1	1	0	1	11	8	3	2	1	0	1	0	10	1	6	4	1	1	1	0	7	18	3
Montreal	22	11	8	0	3	68	61	25	21	10	7	3	1	49	54	24	43	21	15	6	1	117	115	49
Nashville	4	2	0	1	1	11	8	6	5	2	1	2	0	10	8	6	9	4	1	3	1	21	16	12
New Jersey	25	7	13	4	1	53	66	19	24	7	12	3	2	49	72	19	49	14	25	7	3	102	138	38
NY Islanders	25	11	8	6	0	76	74	28	25	11	11	1	1	65	64	25	50	22	19	8	1	141	138	53
NY Rangers	25	10	12	1	1	64	69	23	24	8	12	4	0	59	74	20	49	18	24	6	1	123	143	43
Ottawa	22	9	11	1	1	64	67	20	22	10	8	2	2	60	61	24	44	19	19	3	3	124	128	44
Philadelphia	24	5	17	1	1	57	88	12	25	9	10	6	0	60	65	24	49	14	27	7	1	117	153	36
Phoenix	8	3	5	0	0	23	21	6	10	4	3	2	1	31	25	11	18	7	8	2	1	54	46	18
Pittsburgh	22	13	8	0	1	64	50	27	23	8	10	3	2	68	72	21	45	21	18	3	3	132	122	48
St. Louis	9	2	4	2	1	17	20	7	9	1	7	1	0	12	25	3	18	3	11	3	1	29	45	10
San Jose	9	2	2	5	0	25	27	9	9	2	5	2	0	17	26	6	18	4	7	7	0	42	53	15
Tampa Bay	28	16	6	4	2	81	62	38	28	12	10	6	0	77	60	30	56	28	16	10	2	158	122	68
Toronto	17	5	7	5	0	48	51	15	15	4	9	2	0	34	53	10	32	9	16	7	0	82	104	25
Vancouver	8	3	3	1	1	21	27	8	9	2	5	2	0	19	25	7	17	4	6	3	1	40	52	15
Washington	28	11	12	4	1	70	71	27	28	8	13	5	2	61	86	23	56	19	25	9	3	131	157	50
Totals	**435**	**171**	**181**	**65**	**18**	**1156**	**1207**	**425**	**435**	**151**	**191**	**77**	**34**	**1068**	**1235**	**395**	**870**	**322**	**372**	**142**	**34**	**2224**	**2442**	**820**

Playoffs

	Series	W	L	GP	W	L	T	GF	GA	Last Mtg.	Rnd.	Result
Boston	1	1	0	5	4	1	0	22	16	1996	CQF	W 4-1
Colorado	1	0	1	4	0	4	0	4	15	1996	F	L 0-4
New Jersey	1	0	1	4	0	4	0	6	12	2000	CQF	L 0-4
NY Rangers	1	0	1	5	1	4	0	10	13	1997	CQF	L 1-4
Philadelphia	1	1	0	6	4	2	0	15	11	1996	CSF	W 4-2
Pittsburgh	1	1	0	7	4	3	0	20	15	1996	CF	W 4-3
Totals	**6**	**3**	**3**	**31**	**13**	**18**	**0**	**77**	**82**			

Colorado totals include Quebec, 1993-94 to 1994-95.
Phoenix totals include Winnipeg, 1993-94 to 1995-96.

Carolina totals include Hartford, 1993-94 to 1996-97.

Playoff Results 2004-2000

Year	Round	Opponent	Result	GF	GA
2000	CQF	New Jersey	L 0-4	6	12

Abbreviations: Round: F - Final;
CF - conference final; **CSF** - conference semi-final;
CQF - conference quarter-final.

2003-04 Results

Oct.	9	Carolina	3-1	8	at Philadelphia	4-3*
	11	Boston	1-1	10	at Calgary	2-4
	13	at Carolina	2-2	11	at Vancouver	2-2
	15	Phoenix	1-2	13	at Edmonton	2-4
	18	at NY Islanders	1-2	17	Tampa Bay	2-1
	20	at NY Rangers	1-3	19	St. Louis	1-2*
	22	at New Jersey	2-1	21	Colorado	5-6
	24	Minnesota	3-4	23	Washington	4-1
	25	at Atlanta	3-2	24	at Boston	2-1
	29	at Philadelphia	1-5	26	at NY Rangers	2-5
	30	at Ottawa	3-2	28	Philadelphia	3-3
Nov.	1	San Jose	2-6	31	at NY Islanders	2-4
	5	Los Angeles	2-3	Feb. 3	at San Jose	0-3
	7	Pittsburgh	6-3	4	at Phoenix	5-4*
	8	at St. Louis	0-2	10	Montreal	2-1
	11	Tampa Bay	4-0	12	Pittsburgh	5-1
	13	at New Jersey	3-2	14	at Tampa Bay	2-4
	15	at Pittsburgh	3-2	16	at Carolina	1-3
	16	at Atlanta	2-5	18	at Buffalo	1-1
	19	NY Islanders	3-4	20	at Pittsburgh	2-0
	21	Atlanta	3-6	21	at Washington	2-2
	22	at Washington	3-2*	23	at Boston	2-0
	24	Buffalo	3-2*	25	Toronto	4-0
	26	NY Rangers	3-3	27	Washington	1-4
	28	at Buffalo	3-4	29	at Chicago	2-2
	29	at Montreal	1-1	Mar. 2	at Washington	1-0
Dec.	3	Ottawa	0-4	3	New Jersey	2-5
	6	Atlanta	3-4*	6	Tampa Bay	3-5
	10	Boston	1-1	9	at Toronto	0-5
	12	Montreal	4-2	11	at Montreal	3-2*
	13	at Nashville	2-2	13	NY Rangers	3-2*
	15	at Detroit	1-4	17	NY Islanders	6-4
	17	Washington	2-2	19	at Atlanta	2-3
	19	Dallas	1-0	20	Buffalo	1-2
	22	at Ottawa	2-3*	23	New Jersey	3-4*
	23	at Toronto	2-5	25	at Carolina	2-3
	27	Anaheim	3-2	27	Atlanta	0-3
	29	Toronto	4-4	29	Carolina	3-1
	31	at Tampa Bay	2-2	31	Ottawa	2-2
Jan.	2	Philadelphia	1-2	Apr. 1	at Tampa Bay	3-4
	3	Columbus	1-0	4	at Carolina	6-6

* – Overtime

Entry Draft
Selections 2004-1993

2004 Pick		2001 Pick		1998 Pick		1995 Pick	
7	Rostislav Olesz	4	Stephen Weiss	30	Kyle Rossiter	10	Radek Dvorak
37	David Shantz	24	Lukas Krajicek	61	Joe DiPenta	36	Aaron MacDonald
53	David Booth	34	Greg Watson	63	Lance Ward	62	Mike O'Grady
105	Evan Schafer	64	Tomas Malec	89	Ryan Jardine	80	Dave Duerden
152	Bret Nasby	68	Grant McNeill	117	Jaroslav Spacek	88	Daniel Tjarnqvist
267	Spencer Dillon	117	Mike Woodford	148	Chris Ovington	114	Francois Cloutier
283	Luke Beaverson	136	Billy Thompson	176	B.J. Ketcheson	166	Peter Worrell
		169	Dustin Johner	203	Ian Jacobs	192	Filip Kuba
2003 Pick		200	Toni Koivisto	231	Adrian Wichser	218	David Lemanowicz
3	Nathan Horton	231	Kyle Bruce				
25	Anthony Stewart	263	Jan Blanar	**1997 Pick**		**1994 Pick**	
38	Kamil Kreps	267	Ivan Majesky	20	Mike Brown	1	Ed Jovanovski
55	Stefan Meyer			47	Kristian Huselius	27	Rhett Warrener
105	Martin Lojek	**2000 Pick**		56	Vratislav Cech	31	Jason Podollan
124	James Pemberton	58	Vladimir Sapozhnikov	74	Nick Smith	36	Ryan Johnson
141	Dan Travis	77	Robert Fried	95	Ivan Novoseltsev	84	David Nemirovsky
162	Martin Tuma	82	Sean O'Connor	127	Pat Parthenais	105	Dave Geris
171	Denis Stasyuk	115	Chris Eade	155	Keith Delaney	157	Matt O'Dette
223	Dany Roussin	120	Davis Parley	183	Tyler Palmer	183	Jason Boudrias
234	Petr Kadlec	190	Josh Olson	211	Doug Schueller	235	Tero Lehtera
264	John Hecimovic	234	Janis Sprukts	237	Benoit Cote	261	Per Gustafsson
265	Tanner Glass	253	Mathew Sommerfeld				
				1996 Pick		**1993 Pick**	
2002 Pick		**1999 Pick**		20	Marcus Nilson	5	Rob Niedermayer
3	Jay Bouwmeester	12	Denis Shvidki	60	Chris Allen	41	Kevin Weekes
9	Petr Taticek	40	Alexander Auld	65	Oleg Kvasha	57	Chris Armstrong
40	Rob Globke	70	Niklas Hagman	82	Joey Tetarenko	67	Mikael Tjallden
67	Gregory Campbell	80	Jean-Francois Laniel	129	Andrew Long	78	Steve Washburn
134	Topi Jaakola	103	Morgan McCormick	156	Gaetan Poirier	83	Bill McCauley
158	Vince Bellissimo	109	Rod Sarich	183	Alexandre Couture	109	Todd MacDonald
169	Jeremy Swanson	169	Brad Woods	209	Denis Khloptonov	135	Alain Nasreddine
196	Mikael Vuorio	198	Travis Eagles	235	Russell Smith	161	Trevor Doyle
200	Denis Yachmenev	227	Jonathon Charron			187	Briane Thompson
232	Peter Hafner					213	Chad Cabana
						239	John Demarco
						265	Eric Montreuil

General Manager

KEENAN, MIKE
General Manager, Florida Panthers.
Born in Bowmanville, Ont., October 21, 1949.

Mike Keenan became the sixth general manager of the Florida Panthers on May 26, 2004. Previously, he served as interim general manager with Vancouver (1997-98) and as general manager in St. Louis (1994 to 1996) and Chicago (1988 to 1992). During his tenure with these clubs, he traded for players such as Wayne Gretzky (St. Louis), Craig Conroy (St. Louis), Chris Pronger (St. Louis), Todd Bertuzzi (Vancouver), Chris Chelios (Chicago), Michel Goulet (Chicago) and Brent Sutter (Chicago). Serving as both coach and g.m. in Chicago, Keenan posted a mark of 153-126-41 and led the Blackhawks to the Stanley Cup Finals in 1992. His Chicago teams made the playoffs all four years, finishing 33-27 (.550) in the postseason and winning seven of 11 playoff series.

A coaching veteran of 18 seasons, Keenan has spent time behind the bench for seven different NHL clubs including Florida, Boston, Vancouver, St. Louis , NY Rangers, Chicago and Philadelphia. His resume includes three Presidents' Trophies (1985, 1991 and 1994), six division titles (1985, 1986, 1987, 1990, 1991 and 1994), three 50+ win seasons (1984-85, 1985-86 and 1993-94), and five 100+ point seasons (1984-85, 1985-86, 1986-87, 1990-91 and 1993-94). Keenan ranks fifth on the all-time coaching list in both games coached (1,222) and victories (584). Most significantly, he led the Rangers to the 1994 Stanley Cup championship. The Rangers went 52-24-8 under Keenan, going from a non-playoff team to the Presidents' Trophy winner and Stanley Cup champion in a single year. Additionally, Keenan was the general manager/head coach of the championship Team Canada squads that participated in the Canada Cup in 1991 and 1987.

Keenan and Jacques Martin last worked together in Chicago (1988 to 1990), when Keenan served as the team's head coach/general manager and Martin was an assistant coach. Prior to that, the pair worked together when they led the Peterborough Petes to the Memorial Cup Finals in 1980. The duo also played hockey together at St. Lawrence University.

NHL Coaching Record

Season	Team	Regular Season				Playoffs		
		Games	W	L	T	Games	W	L
1984-85	Philadelphia	80	53	20	7	19	12	7
1985-86	Philadelphia	80	53	23	4	5	2	3
1986-87	Philadelphia	80	46	26	8	26	15	11
1987-88	Philadelphia	80	38	33	9	7	3	4
1988-89	Chicago	80	27	41	12	16	9	7
1989-90	Chicago	80	41	33	6	20	10	10
1990-91	Chicago	80	49	23	8	6	2	4
1991-92	Chicago	80	36	29	15	18	12	6
1993-94	NY Rangers	84	52	24	8	23	16	7*
1994-95	St. Louis	48	28	15	5	7	3	4
1995-96	St. Louis	82	32	34	16	13	7	6
1996-97	St. Louis	33	15	17	1	....	....	....
1997-98	Vancouver	63	21	30	12	....	....	....
1998-99	Vancouver	45	15	24	6	....	....	....
2000-01	Boston	74	33	34	7	....	....	....
2001-02	Florida	56	16	32	8	....	....	....
2002-03	Florida	82	24	45	13	....	....	....
2003-04	Florida	15	5	8	2	....	....	....
	NHL Totals	1222	584	491	147	160	91	69

* Stanley Cup win.

Club Directory

Office Depot Center

Florida Panthers
Office Depot Center
One Panthers Parkway
Sunrise, FL 33323
Phone **954/835-7000**
FAX 954/835-7700
www.floridapanthers.com
Capacity: 19,250

Executive
General Partner and Chairman of the Board/
  Chief Executive Officer/Governor . . . . Alan Cohen
Partner/President, Panthers Hockey LLLP &
  Alternate Governor . . . . Jordan Zimmerman
Partners . . . . Steve Cohen, David Epstein, Dr. Elliott Hahn, H. Wayne Huizenga, Bernie Kosar, Richard Lehman M.D., Al Maroone, Michael Maroone, Cliff Viner
Alternate Governor . . . . William A. Torrey
Chief Operating Officer . . . . Michael R. Yormark
Exec. VP, Business Ops. & Chief Marketing Officer . Chris Overholt
Sr. VP & GM, Office Depot Center . . . . Steve Dangerfield
Executive Assistants . . . . Korrynn Lancaster, Cathy Stevenson
Assistant to Chief Operating Officer . . . . Matt Rickoff

Hockey Operations
General Manager . . . . Mike Keenan
Head Coach . . . . Jacques Martin
Assistant Coach . . . . Guy Charron
Goaltending Coach . . . . Clint Malarchuk
Director, Hockey Operations . . . . Jack Birch
Director, Player Development . . . . Duane Sutter
Director, Scouting . . . . Scott Luce
Pro Scout . . . . Grant Sonier
Head Amateur Scout . . . . Darwin Bennett
Amateur Scouts . . . . Erin Ginnell, Ron Harris
Part-time Scouts . . . . . . Dale Degray, Luke Williams, Vadim Podrezov
European Scouts . . . . Niklas Blomgren, Jari Kekalainen
Executive Assistant to General Manager . . . . Janine Shea
Head Medical Trainer . . . . TBA
Head Equipment Manager . . . . Mark Brennan
Associate Equipment Manager . . . . Scott Tinkler
Coordinator, Team Services . . . . TBA
Head Coach – San Antonio . . . . Steve Ludzik
Director, Hockey Operations – San Antonio . . . . . . Matt Loughran
Orthopedic Surgeon . . . . Al A. DeSimone M.D.
Internist . . . . Howard Bush M.D.
Team Dentist . . . . Martin Robins D.D.S.
Orthodontist . . . . Larry Kawa D.D.S
Neuropsychologist . . . . Nicholas Suite M.D.
Laser Vision Specialist . . . . Cory Lessner M.D.
Chiropractic Medicine . . . . Nicholas J. Ruggiero .C.
Podiatrist . . . . Sean Liffiton D.P.M.
Plastic Surgeon . . . . Gregory Albert M.D.

Community Development and Youth Hockey
Director, Broadcasting,
  Community Development & Youth Hockey . . . . . Randy Moller
Manager, Community Development . . . . Jean Marshall
Coordinator, Youth & Amateur Hockey . . . . Andee Boiman

Corporate Partnerships
Vice President, Corporate Partnerships . . . . Chris Hibbs
Senior Director, Sponsorship Sales . . . . Jarrett Nasca
Senior Director, Marketing Partnerships . . . . Brette Sadler
Director, New Business Development . . . . Bob Ohrablo
Manager, Marketing Partnerships . . . . Heather Germano, Jeff Dow
Manager, Corporate Marketing . . . . Susan Ferro
Account Executive, Corporate Partnerships . . . . . . Kevin Rooney

Finance and Business Support
Vice President, Finance/Chief Financial Officer . . . . . Evelyn Lopez
Vice President, Human Resources/Payroll . . . . Carol Duncanson
Director, Accounting . . . . Michele Gilbert
Director, Information Technology . . . . Kelly Moyer
Office Manager . . . . Laura Barrera
Manager, Human Resources . . . . Cheryl Udrich

Game and Event Presentation
Director, Game Presentation & Events . . . . Matthew Coppola
Coordinator, Game/Event Presentation . . . . Kristen Hewitt
Coordinators, Special Events . . . . Phil Crowhurst, Eric Wasser

Marketing
Director, Marketing . . . . Gabrielle Valdez

Media Relations and Publications
Director, Media Relations . . . . Randy Sieminski
Coordinator, Media Relations . . . . Justin Copertino
Coordinator, Internet Services . . . . Erika Hodges
Associate, Media Relations . . . . Mike Wasserman

New Business Development and Service
Vice President, Sales & Service . . . . Chad Johnson
Director, Client & Premium Services . . . . Carrie Rubin
Manager, Inside Sales . . . . Ryan Bringger
Manager, Sales . . . . Mike Ragan
Coordinator, Sales & Service . . . . Lauren Preziosi

Suite Sales and Service
Senior Director, Sales & Premium Seating . . . . RJ Martino
Manager, Premium Seating Sales . . . . Jason McDonough

Ticket Office
Director, Ticket Operations . . . . Jennifer Womack
Managers, Box Office . . . . . . Kevin Doherty, Orvandis Almonte, Megan Hanney

General Information
Television . . . . Fox Sports Net
Television Announcers . . . . Play-by-Play (TBA), Denis Potvin, Craig Minervini
Radio Flagship . . . . WQAM (560 AM)
Radio Announcers . . . . Steve Goldstein, Randy Moller
Practice Facility . . . . incredible ICE

Los Angeles Kings

2003-04 Results: 28W-29L-16T-9OTL 81PTS.
Third, Pacific Division

2004-05 Schedule

Oct.	Wed.	13	at Colorado		Tue.	11	Anaheim
	Fri.	15	Calgary		Thu.	13	at San Jose
	Sun.	17	Anaheim*		Sat.	15	Vancouver
	Wed.	20	at Anaheim		Tue.	18	Edmonton
	Sat.	23	Phoenix		Thu.	20	at Phoenix
	Tue.	26	at Toronto		Sat.	22	Columbus
	Thu.	28	at Ottawa		Thu.	27	San Jose
	Sat.	30	at NY Islanders		Sat.	29	Nashville*
Nov.	Mon.	1	at NY Rangers		Mon.	31	at Dallas
	Thu.	4	Atlanta	Feb.	Wed.	2	at New Jersey
	Sat.	6	Pittsburgh		Thu.	3	at Boston
	Tue.	9	at Detroit		Sat.	5	at Montreal*
	Wed.	10	at Chicago		Tue.	8	at Philadelphia
	Fri.	12	at Columbus		Wed.	9	at Detroit
	Sun.	14	at Florida*		Wed.	16	Calgary
	Tue.	16	at Nashville		Fri.	18	Minnesota
	Thu.	18	Florida		Sat.	19	Colorado
	Sat.	20	Detroit		Mon.	21	Phoenix
	Fri.	26	at Phoenix		Wed.	23	Dallas
	Sat.	27	Chicago		Fri.	25	at Phoenix
	Tue.	30	Dallas		Sat.	26	St. Louis
Dec.	Thu.	2	Washington	Mar.	Tue.	1	Buffalo
	Sat.	4	at St. Louis		Thu.	3	Minnesota
	Sun.	5	at Chicago		Sat.	5	Vancouver
	Tue.	7	at Minnesota		Tue.	8	at Minnesota
	Thu.	9	Carolina		Wed.	9	at Columbus
	Sat.	11	Edmonton*		Fri.	11	at Dallas
	Tue.	14	Anaheim		Sun.	13	Phoenix
	Thu.	16	Nashville		Tue.	15	Chicago
	Sat.	18	Colorado		Thu.	17	NY Islanders
	Sun.	19	at Anaheim*		Sat.	19	St. Louis*
	Tue.	21	at Vancouver		Tue.	22	Detroit
	Thu.	23	at Edmonton		Thu.	24	at Calgary
	Sun.	26	at San Jose*		Sat.	26	at Vancouver
	Mon.	27	San Jose		Mon.	28	Dallas
	Wed.	29	at Dallas		Wed.	30	San Jose
Jan.	Sat.	1	at Nashville*		Thu.	31	at San Jose
	Sun.	2	at St. Louis	Apr.	Sat.	2	at Colorado
	Thu.	6	Tampa Bay		Mon.	4	at Calgary
	Sat.	8	Philadelphia		Tue.	5	at Edmonton
	Sun.	9	at Anaheim*		Sat.	9	Columbus*

Denotes afternoon game.

Franchise date: June 5, 1967

PACIFIC DIVISION

38th NHL Season

After leading all Kings rookies in scoring in 2002-03, Alexander Frolov topped the club with 24 goals last season and finished second to Luc Robitaille with 48 points.

Year-by-Year Record

		Home				Road				Overall							
Season	GP	W	L	T	OL	W	L	T	OL	W	L	T	OL	GF	GA	Pts.	Finished	Playoff Result
2003-04	82	15	16	9	1	13	13	7	8	28	29	16	9	205	217	81	3rd, Pacific Div.	Out of Playoffs
2002-03	82	19	19	2	1	14	18	4	5	33	37	6	6	203	221	78	3rd, Pacific Div.	Out of Playoffs
2001-02	82	22	12	6	1	18	15	5	3	40	27	11	4	214	190	95	3rd, Pacific Div.	Lost Conf. Quarter-Final
2000-01	82	20	12	8	1	18	16	5	2	38	28	13	3	252	228	92	3rd, Pacific Div.	Lost Conf. Semi-Final
1999-2000	82	21	13	5	2	18	14	7	2	39	27	12	4	245	228	94	2nd, Pacific Div.	Lost Conf. Quater-Final
1998-99	82	18	20	3	...	14	25	2	...	32	45	5	...	189	222	69	5th, Pacific Div.	Out of Playoffs
1997-98	82	22	16	3	...	16	17	8	...	38	33	11	...	227	225	87	2nd, Pacific Div.	Lost Conf. Quater-Final
1996-97	82	18	16	7	...	10	27	4	...	28	43	11	...	214	268	67	6th, Pacific Div.	Out of Playoffs
1995-96	82	16	16	9	...	8	24	9	...	24	40	18	...	256	302	66	6th, Pacific Div.	Out of Playoffs
1994-95	48	7	11	6	...	9	12	3	...	16	23	9	...	142	174	41	4th, Pacific Div.	Out of Playoffs
1993-94	84	18	19	5	...	9	26	7	...	27	45	12	...	294	322	66	5th, Pacific Div.	Out of Playoffs
1992-93	84	22	15	5	...	17	20	5	...	39	35	10	...	338	340	88	3rd, Smythe Div.	Lost Final
1991-92	80	20	11	9	...	15	20	5	...	35	31	14	...	287	296	84	2nd, Smythe Div.	Lost Div. Semi-Final
1990-91	80	26	9	5	...	20	15	5	...	46	24	10	...	340	254	102	1st, Smythe Div.	Lost Div. Final
1989-90	80	21	16	3	...	13	23	4	...	34	39	7	...	338	337	75	4th, Smythe Div.	Lost Div. Final
1988-89	80	25	12	3	...	17	19	4	...	42	31	7	...	376	335	91	2nd, Smythe Div.	Lost Div. Final
1987-88	80	19	18	3	...	11	24	5	...	30	42	8	...	318	359	68	4th, Smythe Div.	Lost Div. Semi-Final
1986-87	80	20	17	3	...	11	24	5	...	31	41	8	...	318	341	70	4th, Smythe Div.	Lost Div. Semi-Final
1985-86	80	9	27	4	...	14	22	4	...	23	49	8	...	284	389	54	5th, Smythe Div.	Out of Playoffs
1984-85	80	20	14	6	...	14	18	8	...	34	32	14	...	339	326	82	4th, Smythe Div.	Lost Div. Semi-Final
1983-84	80	13	19	8	...	10	25	5	...	23	44	13	...	309	376	59	5th, Smythe Div.	Out of Playoffs
1982-83	80	20	13	7	...	7	28	5	...	27	41	12	...	308	365	66	5th, Smythe Div.	Out of Playoffs
1981-82	80	19	15	6	...	5	26	9	...	24	41	15	...	314	369	63	4th, Smythe Div.	Lost Div. Final
1980-81	80	22	11	7	...	21	13	6	...	43	24	13	...	337	290	99	2nd, Norris Div.	Lost Prelim. Round
1979-80	80	18	13	9	...	12	23	5	...	30	36	14	...	290	313	74	2nd, Norris Div.	Lost Prelim. Round
1978-79	80	20	13	7	...	14	21	5	...	34	34	12	...	292	286	80	3rd, Norris Div.	Lost Prelim. Round
1977-78	80	18	16	6	...	13	18	9	...	31	34	15	...	243	245	77	3rd, Norris Div.	Lost Prelim. Round
1976-77	80	20	13	7	...	14	18	8	...	34	31	15	...	271	241	83	2nd, Norris Div.	Lost Quarter-Final
1975-76	80	22	13	5	...	16	20	4	...	38	33	9	...	263	265	85	2nd, Norris Div.	Lost Quarter-Final
1974-75	80	22	7	11	...	20	10	10	...	42	17	21	...	269	185	105	2nd, Norris Div.	Lost Prelim. Round
1973-74	78	22	13	4	...	11	20	8	...	33	33	12	...	233	231	78	3rd, West Div.	Lost Quarter-Final
1972-73	78	21	11	7	...	10	25	4	...	31	36	11	...	232	245	73	6th, West Div.	Out of Playoffs
1971-72	78	14	23	2	...	6	26	7	...	20	49	9	...	206	305	49	7th, West Div.	Out of Playoffs
1970-71	78	17	14	8	...	8	26	5	...	25	40	13	...	239	303	63	5th, West Div.	Out of Playoffs
1969-70	76	12	22	4	...	2	30	6	...	14	52	10	...	168	290	38	6th, West Div.	Out of Playoffs
1968-69	76	19	14	5	...	5	28	5	...	24	42	10	...	185	260	58	4th, West Div.	Lost Semi-Final
1967-68	74	20	13	4	...	11	20	6	...	31	33	10	...	200	224	72	2nd, West Div.	Lost Quarter-Final

2004-05 Player Personnel

FORWARDS	HT	WT	S	Place of Birth	Date	2003-04 Club
ARMSTRONG, Derek	6-0	195	R	Ottawa, Ont.	4/23/73	Los Angeles
AVERY, Sean	5-10	185	L	Pickering, Ont.	4/10/80	Los Angeles
BARNEY, Scott	6-4	208	R	Oshawa, Ont.	3/27/79	Manchester-Los Angeles
BELANGER, Eric	6-0	185	L	Sherbrooke, Que.	12/16/77	Los Angeles
BROWN, Dustin	6-0	195	R	Ithaca, NY	11/4/84	Los Angeles
CAMMALLERI, Michael	5-9	180	L	Richmond Hill, Ont.	6/8/82	Los Angeles-Manchester
CLARKE, Noah	5-9	185	L	LaVerne, CA	6/11/79	Los Angeles-Manchester
CONROY, Craig	6-2	197	R	Potsdam, NY	9/4/71	Calgary
COWAN, Jeff	6-2	210	L	Scarborough, Ont.	9/27/76	Atlanta-Los Angeles
FLINN, Ryan	6-5	248	L	Halifax, N.S.	4/20/80	Manchester
FROLOV, Alexander	6-3	210	R	Moscow, USSR	6/19/82	Nizhny Novgorod-Los Angeles
HOGEBOOM, Greg	6-0	190	R	Toronto, Ont.	9/26/82	Miami-Manchester
KANKO, Petr	5-9	195	L	Pribram, Czech.	2/7/84	Kitchener-Manchester
KLATT, Trent	6-1	210	R	Robbinsdale, MN	1/30/71	Los Angeles
LEHOUX, Yanick	6-1	200	R	Montreal, Que.	4/8/82	Manchester
PARROS, George	6-4	210	R	Washington, PA	12/29/79	Manchester
PIRNES, Esa	6-0	189	L	Oulu, Finland	4/1/77	Los Angeles-Manchester
ROBITAILLE, Luc	6-1	215	L	Montreal, Que.	2/17/66	Los Angeles
SCHMIDT, Chris	6-3	212	L	Beaver Lodge, Alta.	3/1/76	Manchester
SMYTH, Brad	6-0	195	R	Ottawa, Ont.	3/13/73	Karpat
STRAKA, Martin	5-9	178	L	Plzen, Czech.	9/3/72	Pittsburgh-Los Angeles

DEFENSEMEN						
CORVO, Joe	6-1	205	R	Oak Park, IL	6/20/77	Los Angeles
DEMPSEY, Nathan	6-0	190	R	Spruce Grove, Alta.	7/14/74	Chicago-Los Angeles
GLEASON, Tim	6-1	202	L	Southfield, MI	1/29/83	Los Angeles-Manchester
GREBESHKOV, Denis	6-1	200	L	Yaroslavl, USSR	10/11/83	Los Angeles-Manchester
HOLLAND, Jason	6-3	219	R	Morinville, Alta.	4/30/76	Los Angeles
MILLER, Aaron	6-4	200	R	Buffalo, NY	8/11/71	Los Angeles
NORSTROM, Mattias	6-2	210	L	Stockholm, Sweden	1/2/72	Los Angeles
QUINTAL, Stephane	6-3	231	R	Boucherville, Que.	10/22/68	Montreal
VISNOVSKY, Lubomir	5-10	188	L	Topolcany, Czech.	8/11/76	Los Angeles
WEAVER, Mike	5-9	180	R	Bramalea, Ont.	5/2/78	Atlanta-Chicago (AHL)
ZIZKA, Tomas	6-1	198	L	Sternberk, Czech.	10/10/79	Los Angeles-Manchester

GOALTENDERS	HT	WT	C	Place of Birth	Date	2003-04 Club
BRUST, Barry	6-2	210	L	Swan River, Man.	8/8/83	Spokane-Calgary (WHL)
CECHMANEK, Roman	6-3	187	L	Gottwaldov, Czech.	3/2/71	Los Angeles
GARON, Mathieu	6-2	192	R	Chandler, Que.	1/9/78	Montreal
HAUSER, Adam	6-2	195	L	Bovey, MN	5/27/80	Manchester-Reading

2003-04 Scoring

* - rookie

Regular Season

Pos	#	Player	Team	GP	G	A	Pts	+/-	PIM	PP	SH	GW	GT	S	%
L	20	Luc Robitaille	L.A.	80	22	29	51	4	56	12	0	4	2	221	10.0
L	24	Alexander Frolov	L.A.	77	24	24	48	8	24	5	2	3	1	168	14.3
R	26	Trent Klatt	L.A.	82	17	26	43	2	46	6	0	2	1	160	10.6
R	33	Ziggy Palffy	L.A.	35	16	25	41	18	12	3	3	2	0	109	14.7
C	15	Jozef Stumpel	L.A.	64	8	29	37	5	16	4	0	0	0	78	10.3
C	7	Derek Armstrong	L.A.	57	14	21	35	4	33	5	0	1	1	101	13.9
C	25	Eric Belanger	L.A.	81	13	20	33	-16	44	0	1	2	0	132	9.8
D	10	Nathan Dempsey	CHI	58	8	17	25	-5	30	2	0	1	0	155	5.2
			L.A.	17	4	3	7	-7	2	1	0	0	0	28	14.3
			TOTAL	75	12	20	32	-12	32	3	0	1	0	183	6.6
D	44	Jaroslav Modry	L.A.	79	5	27	32	11	44	1	0	1	0	196	2.6
D	17	Lubomir Visnovsky	L.A.	58	8	21	29	8	26	5	0	0	0	114	7.0
R	11	Anson Carter	NYR	43	10	7	17	-12	14	4	1	2	0	63	15.9
			WSH	19	5	5	10	2	6	2	0	2	0	33	15.2
			L.A.	15	0	1	1	-5	0	0	0	0	0	18	0.0
			TOTAL	77	15	13	28	-15	20	6	1	4	0	114	13.2
C	19	Sean Avery	L.A.	76	9	19	28	2	261	0	0	2	1	125	7.2
L	8	Jeff Cowan	ATL	58	9	15	24	2	68	1	0	1	1	74	12.2
			L.A.	13	2	1	3	-1	24	1	0	0	0	15	13.3
			TOTAL	71	11	16	27	1	92	2	0	1	1	89	12.4
C	82	Martin Straka	PIT	22	4	8	12	-16	16	1	0	0	0	34	11.8
			L.A.	32	6	8	14	-9	4	1	1	0	1	34	17.6
			TOTAL	54	10	16	26	-25	20	2	1	0	1	68	14.7
D	27	Joseph Corvo	L.A.	72	8	17	25	7	36	0	0	3	0	150	5.3
R	22	Ian Laperriere	L.A.	62	10	12	22	-4	58	1	0	3	0	59	16.9
C	13	Michael Cammalleri	L.A.	31	9	6	15	1	20	2	0	2	0	53	17.0
D	14	Mattias Norstrom	L.A.	74	1	13	14	-3	44	0	0	0	0	65	1.5
R	62	* Scott Barney	L.A.	19	5	6	11	3	4	2	0	0	0	31	16.1
C	12	Esa Pirnes	L.A.	57	3	8	11	-9	12	0	1	0	0	57	5.3
R	29	Brad Chartrand	L.A.	53	3	4	7	-3	30	0	1	0	0	63	4.8
D	42	* Tim Gleason	L.A.	47	0	7	7	1	21	0	0	0	0	45	0.0
D	53	Jason Holland	L.A.	52	3	3	6	5	24	0	0	1	0	64	4.7
R	21	John Tripp	L.A.	34	1	5	6	-4	33	0	0	0	0	45	2.2
D	5	* Tomas Zizka	L.A.	15	2	3	5	-4	12	1	0	0	0	24	8.3
R	23	* Dustin Brown	L.A.	31	1	4	5	0	18	0	0	0	0	40	2.5
D	3	Aaron Miller	L.A.	35	1	2	3	-3	32	0	0	0	0	26	3.8
R	55	Pavel Rosa	L.A.	2	1	1	2	1	0	0	0	0	0	4	25.0
D	2	Bryan Muir	L.A.	2	0	1	1	1	2	0	0	0	0	2	0.0
L	39	* Noah Clarke	L.A.	2	0	1	1	0	0	0	0	0	0	3	0.0
D	38	* Denis Grebeshkov	L.A.	4	0	1	1	-4	0	0	0	0	0	5	0.0
C	52	* Jerred Smithson	L.A.	8	0	1	1	0	4	0	0	0	0	2	0.0
D	6	Maxim Kuznetsov	L.A.	16	0	1	1	-5	20	0	0	0	0	11	0.0
C	11	Steve Kelly	L.A.	3	0	0	0	0	0	0	0	0	0	5	0.0

Goaltending

No.	Goaltender	GPI	Mins	Avg	W	L	T	EN	SO	GA	SA	S%	G	A	PIM
46	* Mathieu Chouinard	1	3	0.00	0	0	0	0	0	0	2	1.000	0	0	0
35	Cristobal Huet	41	2199	2.43	10	16	10	7	3	89	961	.907	0	0	4
32	Roman Cechmanek	49	2701	2.51	18	21	6	3	5	113	1198	.906	0	0	2
1	Milan Hnilicka	2	80	3.75	0	1	0	0	0	5	42	.881	0	0	0
	Totals	82	5029	2.59	28	38	16	10	8	217	2213	.902			

Vice President and General Manager

TAYLOR, DAVE
Senior Vice President/General Manager, Los Angeles Kings.
Born in Levack, Ont., December 4, 1955.

No player in the history of the Kings ever wore the uniform with more distinction and class than Dave Taylor. For 17 seasons, Taylor gave his all, both on and off the ice, receiving All-Star status for his outstanding play.

Fittingly, after finishing his illustrious career during the 1993-94 season, Taylor remains a key part of the Kings organization, now serving as vice president and general manager for the NHL club. Taylor assumed his current responsibilities on April 22, 1997, becoming the seventh g.m. in team history. He joined the Kings front office four years earlier as an assistant to his predecessor, Sam McMaster.

An All-American hockey player while at Clarkson College, Taylor was relatively unknown when the Kings picked him in the 15th round of the 1975 draft. His grit and work ethic kept him around long enough to hook up with a center named Marcel Dionne, who virtually ignited Taylor's career. As a member of the renowned Triple Crown line with Dionne and left winger Charlie Simmer, Taylor became a prolific scorer and a fearsome checker. Taylor's NHL career stats include a Kings-record 1,111 games, 431 goals, 638 assists and 1,069 points.

A four-time NHL All-Star Game selection, Taylor served as the Kings captain for four seasons (1985-89). After posting career highs in goals (47) and points (112) during the 1980-81 season, Taylor earned a spot on the NHL Second All-Star Team. On April 3, 1995, Taylor's jersey No. 18 was retired, joining Rogie Vachon (No. 30) and Marcel Dionne (No. 16). For all his individual accomplishments in hockey, his crowning glory was reaching the Stanley Cup Finals with the 1992-93 Kings.

Away from the ice, Taylor has worked tirelessly for numerous charities throughout the years. Each year he hosts the Dave Taylor Golf Classic benefiting the Cystic Fibrosis Foundation, which annually raises more than $125,000. In 1991, the NHL honored Taylor's contributions to hockey and the community by awarding him both the Bill Masterton and King Clancy trophies.

General Managers' History

Larry Regan, 1967-68 to 1972-73; Larry Regan and Jake Milford, 1973-74; Jake Milford, 1974-75 to 1976-77; George Maguire, 1977-78 to 1982-83; George Maguire and Rogie Vachon, 1983-84; Rogie Vachon, 1984-85 to 1991-92; Nick Beverley, 1992-93, 1993-94; Sam McMaster, 1994-95 to 1996-97; Dave Taylor, 1997-98 to date.

Captains' History

Bob Wall, 1967-68, 1968-69; Larry Cahan, 1969-70, 1970-71; Bob Pulford, 1971-72, 1972-73; Terry Harper, 1973-74, 1974-75; Mike Murphy, 1975-76 to 1980-81; Dave Lewis, 1981-82, 1982-83; Terry Ruskowski, 1983-84, 1984-85; Dave Taylor, 1985-86 to 1988-89; Wayne Gretzky, 1989-90 to 1991-92; Wayne Gretzky and Luc Robitaille, 1992-93; Wayne Gretzky, 1993-94, 1994-95; Wayne Gretzky and Rob Blake, 1995-96; Rob Blake, 1996-97 to 2000-01; Mattias Norstrom, 2001-02 to date.

Club Records

Team

(Figures in brackets for season records are games played; records for fewest points, wins, ties, losses, goals, goals against are for 70 or more games)

Most Points	**105**	1974-75 (80)
Most Wins	**46**	1990-91 (80)
Most Ties	**21**	1974-75 (80)
Most Losses	**52**	1969-70 (76)
Most Goals	**376**	1988-89 (80)
Most Goals Against	**389**	1985-86 (80)
Fewest Points	**38**	1969-70 (76)
Fewest Wins	**14**	1969-70 (76)
Fewest Ties	**5**	1998-99 (82)
Fewest Losses	**17**	1974-75 (80)
Fewest Goals	**168**	1969-70 (76)
Fewest Goals Against	**185**	1974-75 (80)
Longest Winning Streak		
Overall	**8**	Oct. 21-Nov. 7/72, Feb. 23-Mar. 9/92
Home	**12**	Oct. 10-Dec. 5/92
Away	**8**	Dec. 18/74-Jan. 16/75
Longest Undefeated Streak		
Overall	**11**	Feb. 28-Mar. 24/74 (9 wins, 2 ties)
Home	**13**	Oct. 10-Dec. 8/92 (12 wins, 1 tie)
Away	**11**	Oct. 10-Dec. 11/74 (6 wins, 5 ties)
Longest Losing Streak		
Overall	**11**	Mar. 16-Apr. 4/04
Home	**9**	Feb. 8-Mar. 12/86
Away	**12**	Jan. 11-Feb. 15/70
Longest Winless Streak		
Overall	**17**	Jan. 29-Mar. 5/70 (13 losses, 4 ties)
Home	**9**	Jan. 29-Mar. 5/70 (8 losses, 1 tie), Feb. 8-Mar. 12/86 (9 losses)
Away	**21**	Jan. 11-Apr. 3/70 (17 losses, 4 ties)
Most Shutouts, Season	**10**	2000-01 (82)
Most PIM, Season	**2,247**	1992-93 (84)
Most Goals, Game	**12**	Nov. 29/84 (Van. 1 at L.A. 12)

Individual

Most Seasons	**17**	Dave Taylor
Most Games	**1,111**	Dave Taylor
Most Goals, Career	**550**	Marcel Dionne
Most Assists, Career	**757**	Marcel Dionne
Most Points Career	**1,307**	Marcel Dionne (550G, 757A)
Most PIM, Career	**1,846**	Marty McSorley
Most Shutouts, Career	**32**	Rogie Vachon
Longest Consecutive Games Streak	**324**	Marcel Dionne (Jan. 7/78-Jan. 9/82)
Most Goals, Season	**70**	Bernie Nicholls (1988-89)
Most Assists, Season	**122**	Wayne Gretzky (1990-91)
Most Points, Season	**168**	Wayne Gretzky (1988-89; 54G, 114A)
Most PIM, Season	**399**	Marty McSorley (1992-93)
Most Points, Defenseman, Season	**76**	Larry Murphy (1980-81; 16G, 60A)
Most Points, Center, Season	**168**	Wayne Gretzky (1988-89; 54G, 114A)
Most Points, Right Wing, Season	**112**	Dave Taylor (1980-81; 47G, 65A)
Most Points, Left Wing, Season	***125**	Luc Robitaille (1992-93; 63G, 62A)
Most Points, Rookie, Season	**84**	Luc Robitaille (1986-87; 45G, 39A)
Most Shutouts, Season	**8**	Rogie Vachon (1976-77)
Most Goals, Game	**4**	Sixteen times
Most Assists, Game	**6**	Bernie Nicholls (Dec. 1/88), Tomas Sandstrom (Oct. 9/93)
Most Points, Game	**8**	Bernie Nicholls (Dec. 1/88; 2G, 6A)

* NHL Record.

Coaching History

Red Kelly, 1967-68, 1968-69; Hal Laycoe and Johnny Wilson, 1969-70; Larry Regan, 1970-71; Larry Regan and Fred Glover, 1971-72; Bob Pulford, 1972-73 to 1976-77; Ron Stewart, 1977-78; Bob Berry, 1978-79 to 1980-81; Parker MacDonald and Don Perry, 1981-82; Don Perry, 1982-83; Don Perry, Rogie Vachon and Roger Neilson, 1983-84; Pat Quinn, 1984-85, 1985-86; Pat Quinn and Mike Murphy 1986-87; Mike Murphy, Rogie Vachon and Robbie Ftorek, 1987-88; Robbie Ftorek, 1988-89; Tom Webster, 1989-90 to 1991-92; Barry Melrose, 1992-93, 1993-94; Barry Melrose and Rogie Vachon, 1994-95; Larry Robinson, 1995-96 to 1998-99; Andy Murray, 1999-2000 to date.

Retired Numbers

16	Marcel Dionne	1975-1987
18	Dave Taylor	1977-1994
30	Rogie Vachon	1971-1978
99	Wayne Gretzky	1988-1996

All-time Record vs. Other Clubs

Regular Season

	At Home								On Road								Total							
	GP	W	L	T	OL	GF	GA	PTS	GP	W	L	T	OL	GF	GA	PTS	GP	W	L	T	OL	GF	GA	PTS
Anaheim	30	17	9	4	0	89	72	38	30	10	13	7	0	80	100	27	60	27	22	11	0	169	172	65
Atlanta	4	3	0	0	1	18	9	7	4	3	0	0	1	16	7	7	8	6	0	0	2	34	16	14
Boston	61	21	32	7	1	210	224	50	61	11	44	6	0	169	287	28	122	32	76	13	1	379	511	78
Buffalo	54	22	23	9	0	185	187	53	53	16	28	9	0	157	217	41	107	38	51	18	0	342	404	94
Calgary	91	46	36	9	0	338	316	101	94	27	52	12	3	310	413	69	185	73	88	21	3	648	729	170
Carolina	30	17	10	3	0	129	113	37	31	11	13	5	2	115	114	29	61	28	23	8	2	244	227	66
Chicago	74	33	33	8	0	245	246	74	75	31	34	9	1	221	261	72	149	64	67	17	1	466	507	146
Colorado	43	25	13	5	0	176	137	55	42	16	23	3	0	140	169	35	85	41	36	8	0	316	306	90
Columbus	8	4	3	1	0	18	16	9	8	3	3	0	2	26	21	8	16	7	6	1	2	44	37	17
Dallas	82	35	28	19	0	277	234	89	84	19	50	13	2	218	323	53	166	54	78	32	2	495	557	142
Detroit	80	42	24	14	0	321	246	98	79	30	35	13	1	271	300	74	159	72	59	27	1	592	546	172
Edmonton	77	28	34	15	0	298	318	71	77	23	39	15	0	275	347	61	154	51	73	30	0	573	665	132
Florida	9	5	4	0	0	27	29	10	8	1	4	3	0	14	23	5	17	6	8	3	0	41	52	15
Minnesota	8	2	4	2	0	17	21	6	8	4	1	3	0	21	13	11	16	6	5	5	0	38	34	17
Montreal	65	19	37	9	0	199	256	47	64	8	45	11	0	160	289	27	129	27	82	20	0	359	545	74
Nashville	12	7	4	0	1	36	28	15	12	8	1	3	0	31	16	19	24	15	5	3	1	67	44	34
New Jersey	42	28	8	6	0	201	130	62	43	19	18	5	1	148	142	44	85	47	26	11	1	349	272	106
NY Islanders	45	21	17	7	0	163	143	49	44	15	24	5	0	123	156	35	89	36	41	12	0	286	299	84
NY Rangers	60	23	26	10	1	199	216	57	58	17	35	6	0	172	233	40	118	40	61	16	1	371	449	97
Ottawa	10	8	1	1	0	46	21	17	9	4	4	1	0	28	30	9	19	12	5	2	0	74	51	26
Philadelphia	66	21	37	8	0	193	223	50	63	16	40	7	0	156	244	39	129	37	77	15	0	349	467	89
Phoenix	74	28	31	14	1	294	288	71	76	27	37	11	1	250	301	66	150	55	68	25	2	544	589	137
Pittsburgh	69	44	17	8	0	265	183	96	73	25	38	10	0	233	265	60	142	69	55	18	0	498	448	156
St. Louis	78	35	31	12	0	261	226	82	78	18	49	10	1	195	293	47	156	53	80	22	1	456	519	129
San Jose	37	23	10	4	0	116	88	50	37	12	19	3	3	102	128	30	74	35	29	7	3	218	216	80
Tampa Bay	11	1	8	2	0	24	36	4	10	5	5	0	0	22	23	10	21	6	13	2	0	46	59	14
Toronto	65	34	21	10	0	234	191	78	68	22	34	11	1	223	266	56	133	56	55	21	1	457	457	134
Vancouver	99	51	32	16	0	393	310	118	97	31	49	16	1	300	365	79	196	82	81	32	1	693	675	197
Washington	47	27	13	6	1	187	144	61	46	21	18	7	0	171	185	49	93	48	31	13	1	358	329	110
Defunct Clubs	35	27	6	2	0	141	76	56	34	11	14	9	0	91	109	31	69	38	20	11	0	232	185	87
Totals	**1466**	**697**	**552**	**211**	**6**	**5300**	**4727**	**1611**	**1466**	**464**	**769**	**213**	**20**	**4438**	**5640**	**1161**	**2932**	**1161**	**1321**	**424**	**26**	**9738**	**10367**	**2772**

Playoffs

	Series	W	L	GP	W	L	T	GF	GA	Last Mtg.	Rnd.	Result
Boston	2	0	2	13	5	8	0	38	56	1977	QF	L 2-4
Calgary	6	4	2	26	13	13	0	105	102	1993	DSF	W 4-2
Chicago	1	0	1	5	1	4	0	7	10	1974	QF	L 1-4
Colorado	2	0	2	14	6	8	0	23	33	2002	CQF	L 3-4
Dallas	1	0	1	7	3	4	0	21	26	1968	QF	L 3-4
Detroit	2	1	1	10	4	6	0	21	32	2001	CQF	W 4-2
Edmonton	7	2	5	36	12	24	0	127	154	1992	DSF	L 2-4
Montreal	1	0	1	5	1	4	0	12	15	1993	F	L 1-4
NY Islanders	1	0	1	4	1	3	0	10	21	1980	PRE	L 1-3
NY Rangers	2	0	2	6	1	5	0	14	32	1981	PRE	L 1-3
St. Louis	2	0	2	8	0	8	0	13	32	1998	CQF	L 0-4
Toronto	3	1	2	12	5	7	0	31	41	1993	CF	W 4-3
Vancouver	3	2	1	17	9	8	0	66	60	1993	DF	W 4-2
Defunct Clubs	1	1	0	7	4	3	0	23	25			
Totals	**34**	**11**	**23**	**170**	**65**	**105**	**0**	**511**	**639**			

Calgary totals include Atlanta Flames, 1972-73 to 1979-80.
Colorado totals include Quebec, 1979-80 to 1994-95.
New Jersey totals include Kansas City, 1974-75 to 1975-76, and Colorado Rockies, 1976-77 to 1981-82.
Phoenix totals include Winnipeg, 1979-80 to 1995-96.
Carolina totals include Hartford, 1979-80 to 1996-97.
Dallas totals include Minnesota North Stars, 1967-68 to 1992-93.

Playoff Results 2004-2000

Year	Round	Opponent	Result	GF	GA
2002	CQF	Colorado	L 3-4	13	16
2001	CSF	Colorado	L 3-4	10	17
	CQF	Detroit	W 4-2	15	17
2000	CQF	Detroit	L 0-4	6	15

Abbreviations: Round: F - Final; **CF** - conference final; **CSF** - conference semi-final; **CQF** - conference quarter-final; **DF** - division final; **DSF** - division semi-final; **QF** - quarter-final; **PRE** - preliminary round.

2003-04 Results

Oct.	9	at Detroit	2-3		10	Columbus	2-2
	10	at Pittsburgh	3-0		13	at Nashville	0-0
	12	at Chicago	4-2		14	at Minnesota	2-2
	15	Ottawa	4-3		16	at Columbus	2-3*
	18	Boston	3-4		18	at Chicago	2-1
	21	Philadelphia	4-0		20	Calgary	4-1
	23	Buffalo	1-5		22	Detroit	4-5
	25	Chicago	2-3		24	Anaheim	4-2
	30	Vancouver	1-3		26	Minnesota	2-2
Nov.	1	Phoenix	7-3		28	at Anaheim	4-3*
	5	at Florida	3-2		29	Colorado	3-3
	6	at Tampa Bay	1-0*		31	at Edmonton	4-3
	8	at Carolina	2-3*	**Feb.**	3	at Calgary	4-4
	10	at Washington	3-2		10	at Minnesota	3-1
	13	Toronto	4-4		11	at Columbus	2-3*
	15	St. Louis	0-1		13	at Buffalo	3-8
	19	Nashville	3-0		15	at New Jersey	2-3*
	21	at Dallas	1-3		16	at NY Islanders	1-1
	22	at Colorado	2-0		18	Dallas	3-4
	25	New Jersey	0-4		21	Columbus	4-3
	27	at Phoenix	4-6		23	Nashville	3-0
	29	Chicago	3-1		25	at Dallas	1-1
	30	at Dallas	2-1		28	Anaheim	2-1
Dec.	2	at St. Louis	1-4		29	at Anaheim	3-6
	4	Dallas	3-0	**Mar.**	4	Minnesota	1-1
	6	Washington	7-3		6	Montreal	2-4
	8	at Detroit	2-3*		9	Phoenix	3-2
	10	at Atlanta	3-4*		10	at Phoenix	3-1
	11	at Nashville	4-1		13	at San Jose	1-3
	13	at St. Louis	1-2		14	Anaheim	5-1
	16	Edmonton	4-2		16	St. Louis	3-5
	18	Phoenix	4-4		18	San Jose	3-5
	20	Colorado	3-3		20	Detroit	2-4
	22	at Vancouver	4-4		22	Edmonton	1-2
	26	at San Jose	0-5		24	at Vancouver	0-1
	27	San Jose	4-4		26	at Edmonton	1-3
	30	NY Rangers	2-3*		27	at Calgary	2-3*
	31	at Phoenix	0-4		29	at Colorado	1-2
Jan.	3	Dallas	2-2		31	San Jose	0-3
	7	at Anaheim	4-4	**Apr.**	2	Calgary	2-3
	8	Vancouver	1-3		4	at San Jose	3-4*

* – Overtime

Entry Draft
Selections 2004-1990

2004
Pick
11	Lauri Tukonen
95	Paul Baier
110	Ned Lukacevic
143	Eric Neilson
174	Scott Parse
205	John Curry
220	Maxim Semenov
221	Daniel Taylor
238	Yutaka Fukufuji
264	Valtteri Tenkanen

2003
Pick
13	Dustin Brown
26	Brian Boyle
27	Jeff Tambellini
44	Konstantin Pushkarev
82	Ryan Munce
152	Brady Murray
174	Esa Pirnes
231	Matt Zaba
244	Mike Sullivan
274	Marty Guerin

2002
Pick
18	Denis Grebeshkov
50	Sergei Anshakov
66	Petr Kanko
104	Aaron Rome
115	Mark Rooneem
152	Greg Hogeboom
157	Joel Andresen
185	Ryan Murphy
215	Mikhail Lyubushin
248	Tuukka Pulliainen
279	Connor James

2001
Pick
18	Jens Karlsson
30	Dave Steckel
49	Michael Cammalleri
51	Jaroslav Bednar
83	Henrik Juntunen
116	Richard Petiot
152	Terry Denike
153	Tuukka Mantyla
214	Cristobal Huet
237	Mike Gabinet
277	Sebastien Laplante

2000
Pick
20	Alexander Frolov
54	Andreas Lilja
86	Yanick Lehoux
118	Lubomir Visnovsky
165	Nathan Marsters
201	Yevgeny Fedorov
206	Tim Eriksson
218	Craig Olynick
245	Dan Welch
250	Flavien Conne
282	Carl Grahn

1999
Pick
43	Andrei Shefer
74	Jason Crain
76	Frantisek Kaberle
92	Cory Campbell
104	Brian McGrattan
125	Daniel Johansson
133	Jean-Francois Nogues
193	Kevin Baker
222	George Parros
250	Noah Clarke

1998
Pick
21	Mathieu Biron
46	Justin Papineau
76	Alexei Volkov
103	Kip Brennan
133	Joe Rullier
163	Tomas Zizka
190	Tommi Hannus
217	Jim Henkel
248	Matthew Yeats

1997
Pick
3	Olli Jokinen
15	Matt Zultek
29	Scott Barney
83	Joe Corvo
99	Sean Blanchard
137	Richard Seeley
150	Jeff Katcher
193	Jay Kopischke
220	Konrad Brand

1996
Pick
30	Josh Green
37	Marian Cisar
57	Greg Phillips
84	Mikael Simons
96	Eric Belanger
120	Jesse Black
123	Peter Hogan
190	Stephen Valiquette
193	Kai Nurminen
219	Sebastien Simard

1995
Pick
3	Aki Berg
33	Don MacLean
50	Pavel Rosa
59	Vladimir Tsyplakov
118	Jason Morgan
137	Igor Melyakov
157	Benoit Larose
163	Juha Vuorivirta
215	Brian Stewart

1994
Pick
7	Jamie Storr
33	Matt Johnson
59	Vitali Yachmenev
111	Chris Schmidt
163	Luc Gagne
189	Andrew Dale
215	Jan Nemecek
241	Sergei Shalomai

1993
Pick
42	Shayne Toporowski
68	Jeff Mitchell
94	Bob Wren
105	Frederick Beaubien
117	Jason Saal
120	Tomas Vlasak
146	Jere Karalahti
172	Justin Martin
198	John-Tra Dillabough
224	Martin Strbak
250	Kimmo Timonen
276	Patrick Howald

1992
Pick
39	Justin Hocking
63	Sandy Allan
87	Kevin Brown
111	Jeff Shevalier
135	Rem Murray
207	Magnus Wernblom
231	Ryan Pisiak
255	Jukka Tiilikainen

1991
Pick
42	Guy Leveque
79	Keith Redmond
81	Alexei Zhitnik
108	Pauli Jaks
130	Brett Seguin
152	Kelly Fairchild
196	Craig Brown
218	Mattias Olsson
240	Andre Bouliane
262	Mike Gaul

1990
Pick
7	Darryl Sydor
28	Brandy Semchuk
49	Bill Berg
91	David Goverde
112	Erik Andersson
133	Robert Lang
154	Dean Hulett
175	Denis Leblanc
196	Patrik Ross
217	K.J.(Kevin) White
238	Troy Mohns

Club Directory

STAPLES Center

Los Angeles Kings
STAPLES Center
1111 South Figueroa Street
Los Angeles, CA 90015
Phone **213/742-7100**
GM FAX 310/535-4507
www.lakings.com
Capacity: 18,118

Executive
Owner	Philip F. Anschutz
Owner	Edward P. Roski
President	Timothy J. Lieweke

Hockey Operations
Senior Vice President/General Manager	Dave Taylor
Vice President, Hockey Operations/ Assistant General Manager	Kevin Gilmore
Director of Player Personnel	Bill O'Flaherty
Assistant to the General Manager	John Wolf
Executive Assistant to the General Manager	Marcia Galloway
Head Coach	Andy Murray
Assistant Coach	Mark Hardy, Ray Bennett, John Van Boxmeer
Video Coordinator	Bill Gurney
Pro Scout - Director of European Evaluation	Rob Laird
Scouts	Vaclav Nedomansky, Brian Putnam, John Stanton, Jan Vopat, Ari Vuori, Michel Boucher, Jim Cassidy, Mike Donnelly, Viacheslav Golovin, Gary Harker, Jerry Sodomlak, Victor Tjumenev

Medical
Athletic Trainer	Peter Demers
Assistant Athletic Trainer	Rick Burrill
Rehabilitation Trainer	Robert Zolg
Massage Therapist	Marco Yrjovouri
Head Strength and Conditioning Coach	Mike Kadar

Equipment Staff
Equipment Manager	Peter Millar
Assistant Equipment Manager	Rick Garcia

Media Relations/Team Services
Vice President, Communications & Broadcasting	Mike Altieri
Director, Communications	Jeff Moeller
Manager, Communications	Lee Callans

Broadcasters
TV Play-by-Play Announcer	Bob Miller
Radio Play-by-Play Announcer	Nick Nickson
TV Color Commentator	Jim Fox
Radio Color Commentator	Daryl Evans
Training Center	HealthSouth Training Center
Team Colors	Purple, Silver, Black, White
Television	Fox Sports Net
Radio Flagship	ESPN Radio - KSPN 710
Minor League Affiliates	Manchester Monarchs (AHL), Reading Royals (ECHL)

Coach

MURRAY, ANDY
Coach, Los Angeles Kings. Born in Gladstone, Man., March 3, 1951.

Andy Murray became the 19th head coach in Kings history on June 14, 1999. His coaching experience dates back to 1974 and includes seven seasons as an NHL assistant or associate coach with the Winnipeg Jets (1993 to 1995), Minnesota North Stars (1990 to 1992) and Philadelphia Flyers (1988 to 1990). As an assistant coach in Minnesota, Murray reached the Stanley Cup Finals in 1991.

In addition to his NHL service, Murry brings to the Kings a tremendous amount of internatial coaching experience. As head coach of the Canadian national team, he guided his team to a 77-29-14 record. He also won the gold medal at the 1997 and 2003 World Championships.

From 1976 to 1978, Murray served his first head coaching position with the Brandon Travelers of the Manitoba Junior Hockey League. He moved on to become head coach for Brandon University from 1978 to 1981, leading the Bobcats to the #1 ranking in Canadian university hockey during his final year. In 1981-82, Murray moved to Switzerland, where for the next seven years he coached several Swiss-A Division teams.

Murray returned to North America as an assistant coach for the Hershey Bears of the American Hockey League in 1987 and helped guide the Bears to the 1988 Calder Cup championship. In 1992, Murray returned to Europe to coach Lugano in Switzerland and then Eisbaren Berlin in Germany a year later. Most recently, Murray served as the head coach for Shattuck-St. Mary's in Faribault, Minnesota, where he led the prep school to a 70-9-2 record and the Midget Triple A USA Hockey national championship in 1998-99.

Coaching Record

Season	Team	Regular Season				Playoffs		
		Games	W	L	T	Games	W	L
1999-2000	Los Angeles (NHL)	82	39	31	12	4	0	4
2000-01	Los Angeles (NHL)	82	38	31	13	13	7	6
2001-02	Los Angeles (NHL)	82	40	31	11	7	3	4
2002-03	Los Angeles (NHL)	82	33	43	6	....	....	....
2003-04	Los Angeles (NHL)	82	28	38	16	....	....	....
	NHL Totals	**410**	**178**	**174**	**58**	**80**	**49**	**31**

Assistant coach Dave Tippett posted a 2-2-1 record as replacement coach when Murray was sidelined following a car accident, February 26 to March 6, 2002. All games are credited to Murray's coaching record.

Trent Klatt scored 17 goals in his first season with Los Angeles in 2003-04, the second highest total of his career. He scored 24 goals with Philadelphia in 1996-97.

Minnesota Wild

2003-04 Results: 30w-29L-20T-3OTL 83PTS.
Fifth, Northwest Division

Year-by-Year Record

Season	GP	Home W	Home L	Home T	Home OL	Road W	Road L	Road T	Road OL	Overall W	Overall L	T	OL	GF	GA	Pts.	Finished	Playoff Result
2003-04	82	19	13	7	2	11	16	13	1	30	29	20	3	188	183	83	5th, Northwest Div.	Out of Playoffs
2002-03	82	25	13	3	0	17	16	7	1	42	29	10	1	198	178	95	3rd, Northwest Div.	Lost Conf. Championship
2001-02	82	14	14	8	5	12	21	4	4	26	35	12	9	195	238	73	5th, Northwest Div.	Out of Playoffs
2000-01	82	14	13	10	4	11	26	3	1	25	39	13	5	168	210	68	5th, Northwest Div.	Out of Playoffs

2004-05 Schedule

Oct.	Wed.	13	at Chicago	Wed.	12	at Tampa Bay
	Thu.	14	at Nashville	Fri.	14	at Atlanta
	Sat.	16	Phoenix	Sun.	16	at Washington*
	Tue.	19	Edmonton	Tue.	18	Chicago
	Thu.	21	at Edmonton	Thu.	20	Vancouver
	Fri.	22	at Vancouver	Sat.	22	Nashville
	Tue.	26	Anaheim	Mon.	24	at Columbus
	Thu.	28	Vancouver	Tue.	25	San Jose
	Sat.	30	Edmonton	Thu.	27	Colorado
Nov.	Mon.	1	at Dallas	Sat.	29	Anaheim*
	Wed.	3	NY Islanders	**Feb.** Wed.	2	at Dallas
	Fri.	5	Colorado	Fri.	4	at Colorado
	Sun.	7	at Carolina*	Sat.	5	at Nashville
	Tue.	9	Phoenix	Mon.	7	St. Louis
	Thu.	11	at San Jose	Thu.	10	Atlanta
	Sat.	13	at Phoenix	Wed.	16	NY Rangers
	Wed.	17	St. Louis	Fri.	18	at Los Angeles
	Sat.	20	at Edmonton	Sun.	20	at Anaheim*
	Sun.	21	at Vancouver	Tue.	22	at Colorado
	Wed.	24	Edmonton	Thu.	24	at Calgary
	Fri.	26	at Detroit	Sun.	27	Florida*
	Sun.	28	Calgary*	**Mar.** Wed.	2	at Anaheim
	Tue.	30	at Montreal	Thu.	3	at Los Angeles
Dec.	Wed.	1	at Buffalo	Sat.	5	at Phoenix
	Sat.	4	at Ottawa	Tue.	8	Los Angeles
	Tue.	7	Los Angeles	Thu.	10	Detroit
	Thu.	9	New Jersey	Sat.	12	Columbus
	Sat.	11	Dallas	Mon.	14	at Vancouver
	Wed.	15	at Columbus	Tue.	15	at Calgary
	Thu.	16	San Jose	Thu.	17	at Toronto
	Sat.	18	Pittsburgh	Sun.	20	Calgary
	Mon.	20	Dallas	Wed.	23	at Chicago
	Thu.	23	Tampa Bay	Thu.	24	Chicago
	Mon.	27	at Calgary	Sat.	26	Boston
	Tue.	28	at Edmonton	Tue.	29	Nashville
	Thu.	30	at San Jose	Thu.	31	at St. Louis
Jan.	Sun.	2	Columbus*	**Apr.** Sat.	2	Vancouver
	Wed.	5	Philadelphia	Mon.	4	Colorado
	Fri.	7	Calgary	Wed.	6	at Colorado
	Sat.	8	at St. Louis	Fri.	8	at Detroit
	Mon.	10	at New Jersey	Sun.	10	Detroit*

* Denotes afternoon game.

Franchise date: June 25, 1997

NORTHWEST DIVISION

5th NHL Season

The Wild made things difficult for opposing shooters in 2003-04, allowing only 183 goals against. Dwayne Roloson edged out Calgary's Miikka Kiprusoff for the league lead with a .933 save percentage and was second to Kiprusoff with a 1.88 goals-against average.

2004-05 Player Personnel

FORWARDS	HT	WT	S	Place of Birth	Date	2003-04 Club
BOUCHARD, Pierre-Marc	5-10	165	L	Sherbrooke, Que.	4/27/84	Minnesota
BRANDNER, Christoph	6-4	224	L	Bruck an der Mur, Austria	7/5/75	Minnesota-Houston
BRUNETTE, Andrew	6-1	210	L	Sudbury, Ont.	8/24/73	Minnesota
CAVANAUGH, Dan	6-1	190	R	Springfield, MA	3/3/80	Houston
CAVOSIE, Marc	6-0	173	L	Albany, NY	8/6/81	Houston
CHOUINARD, Marc	6-5	218	R	Charlesbourg, Que.	5/6/77	Minnesota
CULLEN, Mark	5-11	175	L	Moorhead, MN	10/28/78	Houston
DAIGLE, Alexandre	6-0	195	L	Montreal, Que.	2/7/75	Minnesota
DUPUIS, Pascal	6-0	196	L	Laval, Que.	4/7/79	Minnesota
FOY, Matt	6-2	219	R	Oakville, Ont.	5/18/83	Houston
GABORIK, Marian	6-1	190	L	Trencin, Czech.	2/14/82	Minnesota-Dukla Trencin
HANNULA, Mika	5-11	180	L	Huddinge, Sweden	4/2/79	Houston
JOHNSON, Matt	6-5	235	L	Welland, Ont.	11/23/75	Minnesota
KRESTANOVICH, Jordan	6-1	180	L	Langley, B.C.	6/14/81	Colorado-Hershey-Houston
LAW, Kirby	6-1	185	R	McCreary, Man.	3/11/77	Phi-Phi (AHL)
PARK, Richard	5-11	190	R	Seoul, South Korea	5/27/76	Minnesota
ROLSTON, Brian	6-2	210	L	Flint, MI	2/21/73	Boston
VEILLEUX, Stephane	6-1	187	L	Beauceville, Que.	11/16/81	Minnesota-Houston
WALLIN, Rickard	6-2	185	L	Stockholm, Sweden	4/19/80	Minnesota-Houston
WALZ, Wes	5-10	180	R	Calgary, Alta.	5/15/70	Minnesota
WANVIG, Kyle	6-2	219	R	Calgary, Alta.	1/29/81	Minnesota-Houston

DEFENSEMEN	HT	WT	S	Place of Birth	Date	2003-04 Club
BECKETT, Jason	6-3	218	R	Lethbridge, Alta.	7/23/80	Houston
BURNS, Brent	6-4	200	R	Ajax, Ont.	3/9/85	Minnesota-Houston
GIROUX, Raymond	6-1	190	L	North Bay, Ont.	7/20/76	New Jersey-Albany
HEID, Chris	6-2	205	L	Langley, B.C.	3/14/83	Houston
HENRY, Alex	6-5	220	L	Elliot Lake, Ont.	10/18/79	Minnesota
KUBA, Filip	6-3	205	L	Ostrava, Czech.	12/29/76	Minnesota
MICHALEK, Zbynek	6-1	199	R	Jindrichuv Hradec, Czech.	12/23/82	Minnesota-Houston
MITCHELL, Willie	6-3	205	L	Port McNeill, B.C.	4/23/77	Minnesota
REITZ, Erik	6-1	210	R	Detroit, MI	7/29/82	Houston
SCHULTZ, Nick	6-1	207	L	Strasbourg, Sask.	8/25/82	Minnesota
ZYUZIN, Andrei	6-1	215	L	Ufa, USSR	1/21/78	Minnesota

GOALTENDERS	HT	WT	C	Place of Birth	Date	2003-04 Club
FERNANDEZ, Manny	6-0	180	L	Etobicoke, Ont.	8/27/74	Minnesota
HARDING, Josh	6-1	180	R	Regina, Sask.	6/18/84	Regina-Brandon
KETTLES, Kyle	6-3	180	L	Lac du Bonnet, Man.	2/19/81	Houston
ROLOSON, Dwayne	6-1	178	L	Simcoe, Ont.	10/12/69	Minnesota

2003-04 Scoring

* - rookie

Regular Season

Pos	#	Player	Team	GP	G	A	Pts	+/-	PIM	PP	SH	GW	GT	S	%
C	9	Alexandre Daigle	MIN	78	20	31	51	-4	14	6	0	3	0	145	13.8
L	15	Andrew Brunette	MIN	82	15	34	49	3	12	7	0	3	1	90	16.7
R	10	Marian Gaborik	MIN	65	18	22	40	10	20	3	0	4	0	220	8.2
L	24	Antti Laaksonen	MIN	77	12	14	26	0	20	0	1	1	0	100	12.0
L	11	Pascal Dupuis	MIN	59	11	15	26	5	20	2	0	1	0	127	8.7
R	18	Richard Park	MIN	73	13	12	25	0	28	4	0	1	1	142	9.2
C	37	Wes Walz	MIN	57	12	13	25	5	32	0	3	2	0	70	17.1
D	17	Filip Kuba	MIN	77	5	19	24	-7	28	2	1	2	0	114	4.4
C	28	Jason Wiemer	NYI	13	1	3	4	-1	24	0	0	0	0	14	7.1
			MIN	62	7	11	18	-6	106	1	0	2	0	89	7.9
			TOTAL	75	8	14	22	-7	130	1	0	2	0	103	7.8
L	96	Pierre-Marc Bouchard	MIN	61	4	18	22	-7	22	2	0	0	0	60	6.7
C	32	Marc Chouinard	MIN	45	11	10	21	4	17	3	1	2	0	70	15.7
D	20	Andrei Zyuzin	MIN	65	8	13	21	4	48	4	0	1	1	104	7.7
D	55	Nick Schultz	MIN	79	6	10	16	12	16	1	0	1	0	72	8.3
D	2	Willie Mitchell	MIN	70	1	13	14	12	83	0	0	0	0	58	1.7
R	21	Eric Chouinard	PHI	17	3	0	3	-3	0	0	0	0	1	15	20.0
			MIN	31	3	4	7	-7	6	0	0	1	0	45	6.7
			TOTAL	48	6	4	10	-10	6	0	0	1	1	60	10.0
L	19	Stephane Veilleux	MIN	19	2	8	10	0	20	1	1	1	0	37	5.4
C	25 *	Rickard Wallin	MIN	15	5	4	9	5	14	3	0	1	0	16	31.3
L	26	Christoph Brandner	MIN	35	4	5	9	-2	8	1	0	0	0	50	8.0
C	12	Matt Johnson	MIN	57	7	1	8	4	177	0	0	1	0	21	33.3
D	36	Alex Henry	MIN	71	2	4	6	4	106	0	0	0	0	37	5.4
R	8 *	Brent Burns	MIN	36	1	5	6	-10	12	0	0	0	0	34	2.9
D	6 *	Zbynek Michalek	MIN	22	1	1	2	-7	4	0	0	0	0	17	5.9
D	71 *	Travis Roche	MIN	5	0	1	1	-3	0	0	0	0	0	5	0.0
R	27 *	Kyle Wanvig	MIN	6	0	1	1	-2	10	0	0	0	0	16	0.0

Goaltending

No.	Goaltender	GPI	Mins	Avg	W	L	T	EN	SO	GA	SA	S%	G	A	PIM
30	Dwayne Roloson	48	2847	1.88	19	18	11	2	5	89	1323	.933	0	1	8
35	Emmanuel Fernandez	37	2166	2.49	11	14	9	2	2	90	1056	.915	0	0	2
	Totals	**82**	**5033**	**2.18**	**30**	**32**	**20**	**4**	**7**	**183**	**2383**	**.923**			

Coach

LEMAIRE, JACQUES
Coach, Minnesota Wild. Born in LaSalle, Que., September 7, 1945.

The Minnesota Wild announced the signing of Jacques Lemaire as the club's first head coach on June 19, 2000. In 2002-03, he led Minnesota into the playoffs after just three seasons and all the way to the Western Conference Final. He also won the Jack Adams Award as coach of the year. Prior to joining the Wild, Lemaire had spent parts of the previous two seasons as a senior consultant to the general manager for the Montreal Canadiens, the franchise with which he captured eight Stanley Cup championships as a player.

Lemaire spent five seasons behind the New Jersey Devils bench and compiled a 199-122-57 mark. In 1994-95, he coached the Devils to their first Stanley Cup championship. In his first season with the team (1993-94), he was awarded the Jack Adams Award for the first time.

Lemaire began his NHL coaching career with the Montreal Canadiens in 1983-84. He stepped aside as head coach following the 1984-85 campaign and moved to the front office where he held the position of assistant to the managing director. In that role, Lemaire played a part in Montreal's Stanley Cup championships of 1986 and 1993.

Lemaire spent his entire NHL playing career with Montreal from 1967 to 1979 winning the Stanley Cup eight times. He then began his coaching career in Switzerland where he served as player/coach of the Sierre club. He returned to North America in 1981 and was named the first head coach of the Quebec Major Junior Hockey League's expansion Longueuil Chevaliers. In his only season at the helm (1982-83), Lemaire guided the team to the QMJHL finals.

Coaching Record

Season	Team	Games	Regular Season W	L	T	Playoffs Games	W	L
1979-80	Sierre (Switzerland)				UNAVAILABLE			
1980-81	Sierre (Switzerland)				UNAVAILABLE			
1982-83	Longueuil (QMJHL)	70	37	29	4	15	9	6
1983-84	**Montreal (NHL)**	17	7	10	0	15	9	6
1984-85	**Montreal (NHL)**	80	41	27	12	12	6	6
1993-94	**New Jersey (NHL)**	84	47	25	12	20	11	9
1994-95	**New Jersey (NHL)**	48	22	18	8	20	16	4*
1995-96	**New Jersey (NHL)**	82	37	33	12	....	....	....
1996-97	**New Jersey (NHL)**	82	45	23	14	10	5	5
1997-98	**New Jersey (NHL)**	82	48	23	11	6	2	4
2000-01	**Minnesota (NHL)**	82	25	44	13	....	....	....
2001-02	**Minnesota (NHL)**	82	26	44	12	....	....	....
2002-03	**Minnesota (NHL)**	82	42	30	10	18	8	10
2003-04	**Minnesota (NHL)**	82	30	32	20			
	NHL Totals	**803**	**370**	**309**	**124**	**101**	**57**	**44**

* Stanley Cup win.

Alexandre Daigle led the Wild in scoring in his first season in Minnesota, putting up numbers that matched his early days in Ottawa.

Club Records

Team

(Figures in brackets for season records are games played.)

Most Points	95	2002-03 (82)
Most Wins	42	2002-03 (82)
Most Ties	20	2003-04 (82)
Most Losses	39	2000-01 (82)
Most Goals	198	2002-03 (82)
Most Goals Against	238	2001-02 (82)
Fewest Points	68	2000-01 (82)
Fewest Wins	25	2000-01 (82)
Fewest Ties	10	2002-03 (82)
Fewest Losses	29	2002-03 (82), 2003-04 (82)
Fewest Goals	168	2000-01 (82)
Fewest Goals Against	178	2002-03 (82)

Longest Winning Streak
Overall ..... 3 — Twelve times
Home ..... 5 — Feb. 23-Mar. 23/03
Away ..... 2 — Eleven times

Longest Undefeated Streak
Overall ..... 9 — Dec. 13-30/03 (4 wins, 5 ties)
Home ..... 9 — Dec. 13/00-Jan. 10/01 (5 wins, 4 ties)
Away ..... 7 — Dec. 6-30/03 (2 wins, 5 ties)

Longest Losing Streak
Overall ..... 5 — Mar. 11-19/01, Jan. 28-Feb. 8/02, Mar. 29-Apr. 5/02
Home ..... 4 — Oct. 29-Nov. 15/00
Away ..... 5 — Three times

Longest Winless Streak
Overall ..... 12 — Mar. 11-Apr. 4/01 (9 losses, 3 ties)
Home ..... 8 — Feb. 26-Mar. 28/01 (5 losses, 3 ties)
Away ..... 12 — Dec. 18/03-Jan. 31/04 (5 losses, 7 ties)

Most Shutouts, Season ..... 7 — 2003-04 (82)
Most PIM, Season ..... 1,209 — 2001-02 (82)
Most Goals, Game ..... 8 — Mar. 25/04 (Min. 8 at Chi. 2)

Individual

Most Seasons ..... 4 — Many players
Most Games ..... 323 — Antti Laaksonen
Most Goals, Career ..... 96 — Marian Gaborik
Most Assists, Career ..... 112 — Marian Gaborik
Most Points, Career ..... 208 — Marian Gaborik (96G, 112A)
Most PIM, Career ..... 698 — Matt Johnson
Most Shutouts, Career ..... 14 — Dwayne Roloson
Longest Consecutive Games Streak ..... 288 — Antti Laaksonen (Oct. 6/00-Dec. 29/03)
Most Goals, Season ..... 30 — Marian Gaborik (2001-02, 2002-03)
Most Assists, Season ..... 48 — Andrew Brunette (2001-02)
Most Points, Season ..... 69 — Andrew Brunette (2001-02; 21G, 48A)
Most PIM, Season ..... 201 — Matt Johnson (2002-03)

Most Points, Defenseman, Season ..... 34 — Lubomir Sekeras (2000-01; 11G, 23A)
Most Points, Center, Season ..... 48 — Cliff Ronning (2002-03; 17G, 31A)
Most Points, Right Wing, Season ..... 67 — Marian Gaborik (2001-02; 30G, 37A)
Most Points, Left Wing, Season ..... 69 — Andrew Brunette (2001-02; 21G, 48A)
Most Points, Rookie, Season ..... 36 — Marian Gaborik (2000-01; 18G, 18A)
Most Shutouts, Season ..... 5 — Dwayne Roloson (2001-02, 2003-04)
Most Goals, Game ..... 3 — Antti Laaksonen (Nov. 26/00), Marian Gaborik (Seven times)
Most Assists, Game ..... 4 — Andrew Brunette (Mar. 10/02), Marian Gaborik (Oct. 26/02), Pascal Dupuis (Mar. 25/04)
Most Points, Game ..... 6 — Marian Gaborik (Oct. 26/02; 2G, 4A)

General Managers' History

Doug Risebrough, 2000-01 to date.

Coaching History

Jacques Lemaire, 2000-01 to date.

Captains' History

Sean O'Donnell, Scott Pellerin, Wes Walz, Brad Bombardir, Darby Hendrickson, 2000-01; Jim Dowd, Filip Kuba, Brad Brown, Andrew Brunette, 2001-02; Brad Bombardir, Matt Johnson, Sergei Zholtok, 2002-03; Brad Brown, Andrew Brunette, Richard Park, Brad Bombardir, Jim Dowd, 2003-04.

All-time Record vs. Other Clubs

Regular Season

	At Home								On Road								Total							
	GP	W	L	T	OL	GF	GA	PTS	GP	W	L	T	OL	GF	GA	PTS	GP	W	L	T	OL	GF	GA	PTS
Anaheim	8	3	2	2	1	13	14	9	8	3	4	0	1	17	19	7	16	6	6	2	2	30	33	16
Atlanta	3	2	0	1	0	8	5	5	2	2	0	0	0	10	6	4	5	4	0	1	0	18	11	9
Boston	2	2	0	0	0	7	2	4	3	3	0	0	0	13	4	6	5	5	0	0	0	20	6	10
Buffalo	3	1	2	0	0	4	7	2	3	2	1	0	0	8	7	4	6	3	3	0	0	12	14	6
Calgary	11	5	4	1	1	24	20	12	10	2	5	3	0	21	23	7	21	7	9	4	1	45	43	19
Carolina	4	1	1	2	0	9	12	4	2	0	2	0	0	0	3	0	6	1	3	2	0	9	15	4
Chicago	8	6	2	0	0	28	20	12	8	4	3	1	0	25	17	9	16	10	5	1	0	53	37	21
Colorado	10	3	5	1	1	21	36	8	11	1	8	2	0	22	36	4	21	4	13	3	1	43	72	12
Columbus	8	6	2	0	0	25	16	12	7	1	4	1	1	7	19	4	15	7	6	1	1	32	35	16
Dallas	8	4	4	0	0	23	19	8	8	3	4	1	0	18	27	7	16	7	8	1	0	41	46	15
Detroit	8	2	3	2	1	18	21	7	8	2	5	1	0	20	32	5	16	4	8	3	1	38	53	12
Edmonton	10	2	6	1	1	22	29	6	11	2	4	3	2	14	24	9	21	4	10	4	3	36	53	15
Florida	3	2	0	1	0	10	1	5	3	2	1	0	0	8	6	4	6	4	1	1	0	18	7	9
Los Angeles	8	1	4	0	3	13	21	5	8	4	2	2	0	21	17	10	16	5	6	2	3	34	38	15
Montreal	2	1	0	0	1	6	5	3	2	1	1	0	0	8	9	2	4	2	1	0	1	14	14	6
Nashville	8	3	2	3	0	20	18	9	8	1	5	2	0	11	21	4	16	4	7	5	0	31	39	13
New Jersey	3	1	1	1	0	7	8	3	3	0	2	1	0	8	13	1	6	1	3	2	0	15	21	4
NY Islanders	3	2	1	0	0	9	9	4	3	1	2	0	0	6	6	2	6	3	3	0	0	15	15	6
NY Rangers	4	1	2	0	1	11	13	3	3	1	2	0	0	7	10	2	7	2	4	0	1	18	23	5
Ottawa	3	1	0	1	1	10	8	4	2	1	1	0	0	4	6	2	5	2	1	1	1	14	14	6
Philadelphia	2	1	0	1	0	5	3	3	4	0	3	1	0	3	11	2	6	1	3	2	0	8	14	5
Phoenix	8	2	3	2	1	15	17	7	8	4	2	1	0	16	23	6	16	6	5	3	1	31	40	13
Pittsburgh	3	2	0	1	0	9	5	5	3	1	2	0	0	12	6	4	6	3	2	1	0	21	11	9
St. Louis	8	3	1	2	2	19	13	10	8	2	3	1	2	11	15	7	16	5	4	3	2	30	28	17
San Jose	8	4	3	1	0	19	17	9	8	4	1	0	4	14	21	7	16	7	4	1	2	33	38	16
Tampa Bay	3	3	0	0	0	13	8	6	3	1	1	1	0	9	8	3	6	4	1	1	0	22	16	9
Toronto	1	0	1	0	0	0	1	0	3	0	3	0	0	3	11	0	4	0	4	0	0	3	12	0
Vancouver	11	5	4	0	0	27	27	12	10	3	2	3	2	26	28	11	21	8	6	5	2	53	55	23
Washington	3	3	0	0	0	6	1	6	2	0	2	0	0	6	6	1	5	3	2	0	0	12	7	6
Totals	**164**	**72**	**53**	**28**	**11**	**401**	**376**	**183**	**164**	**51**	**79**	**27**	**7**	**348**	**433**	**136**	**328**	**123**	**132**	**55**	**18**	**749**	**809**	**319**

Playoffs

	Series	W	L	GP	W	L	T	GF	GA	Last Mtg.	Rnd.	Result
Anaheim	1	0	1	4	0	4	0	1	9	2003	CF	L 0-4
Colorado	1	1	0	7	4	3	0	16	17	2003	CQF	W 4-3
Vancouver	1	1	0	7	4	3	0	26	17	2003	CSF	W 4-3
Totals	**3**	**2**	**1**	**18**	**8**	**10**	**0**	**43**	**43**			

Playoff Results 2004-2000

Year	Round	Opponent	Result	GF	GA
2003	CF	Anaheim	L 0-4	1	9
	CSF	Vancouver	W 4-3	26	17
	CQF	Colorado	W 4-3	16	17

Abbreviations: Round: CF – conference final; CSF – conference semi-final; CQF – conference quarter-final.

2003-04 Results

Oct.	8	at Chicago	0-1		7	Chicago	7-4
	10	NY Rangers	5-3		9	Phoenix	0-2
	12	San Jose	2-3		12	Nashville	3-3
	16	Colorado	2-5		14	Los Angeles	2-2
	18	Vancouver	2-2		16	Pittsburgh	4-2
	19	at Dallas	1-3		17	at St. Louis	2-2
	21	Calgary	2-3		19	at Nashville	0-2
	24	at Florida	4-3		21	Chicago	4-2
	25	at Tampa Bay	2-3		23	at Anaheim	2-6
	28	at Buffalo	3-1		24	at San Jose	0-4
	30	Atlanta	3-2		26	at Los Angeles	2-2
Nov.	1	Washington	2-1		29	Montreal	2-3*
	4	at Colorado	4-4		31	at Columbus	1-2*
	7	at Calgary	3-0	Feb.	2	St. Louis	4-0
	8	at Vancouver	3-4		4	at NY Rangers	4-3
	11	Vancouver	1-0		10	Los Angeles	1-3
	13	Edmonton	0-2		13	Edmonton	3-0
	15	Detroit	1-1		15	Calgary	1-2
	19	at Pittsburgh	6-2		17	at New Jersey	4-4
	20	at Philadelphia	1-3		19	Vancouver	6-2
	22	Detroit	2-5		22	Colorado	1-3
	26	Dallas	1-3		26	at Nashville	0-4
	28	San Jose	1-2		27	at Dallas	1-3
	30	Anaheim	1-1		29	Carolina	3-3
Dec.	3	at Edmonton	1-0	Mar.	3	at Anaheim	0-2
	5	at Calgary	1-2		4	at Los Angeles	1-1
	6	at Vancouver	1-1		7	at Phoenix	1-1
	9	Calgary	2-1		9	at San Jose	4-3
	11	Toronto	0-1		10	at Vancouver	1-1
	13	Buffalo	3-2		14	Columbus	3-2
	15	at Phoenix	5-2		16	Ottawa	5-2
	17	at Colorado	3-2		18	at Boston	2-0
	18	at Edmonton	1-1		19	at NY Islanders	1-3
	20	Columbus	5-2		22	Phoenix	2-3*
	23	Nashville	3-3		24	at Columbus	0-2
	26	at Detroit	2-2		25	at Chicago	8-2
	29	Calgary	2-2		28	Anaheim	2-1
	30	at Edmonton	2-2		29	at Detroit	3-5
Jan.	2	Edmonton	1-2		31	Colorado	5-4*
	4	at Colorado	1-3	Apr.	2	Dallas	2-2
	5	at St. Louis	1-1		4	St. Louis	3-0

* – Overtime

Entry Draft
Selections 2004-2000

2004 Pick		2003 Pick		2002 Pick		2001 Pick	
12	A.J. Thelen	20	Brent Burns	8	Pierre-Marc Bouchard	6	Mikko Koivu
42	Roman Voloshenko	56	Patrick O'Sullivan	38	Josh Harding	36	Kyle Wanvig
78	Peter Olvecky	78	Danny Irmen	72	Mike Erickson	74	Chris Heid
79	Clayton Stoner	157	Marcin Kolusz	73	Barry Brust	93	Stephane Veilleux
111	Ryan Jones	187	Miroslav Kopriva	155	Armands Berzins	103	Tony Virta
114	Patrick Bordeleau	207	Grigory Misharin	175	Matt Foy	202	Derek Boogaard
117	Julien Sprunger	219	Adam Courchaine	204	Niklas Eckerblom	239	Jake Riddle
161	Jean-Claude Sawyer	251	Mathieu Melanson	237	Christoph Brandner		
175	Aaron Boogaard	281	Jean-Michel Bolduc	268	Mikhail Tyulyapkin	**2000** Pick	
195	Jean-Michel Rizk			269	Mika Hannula	3	Marian Gaborik
206	Anton Khudobin					33	Nick Schultz
272	Kyle Wilson					99	Marc Cavosie
						132	Maxim Sushinsky
						170	Erik Reitz
						199	Brian Passmore
						214	Peter Bartos
						232	Lubomir Sekeras
						255	Eric Johansson

President and General Manager

RISEBROUGH, DOUG
President/General Manager, Minnesota Wild.
Born in Guelph, Ont., January 29, 1954.

Doug Risebrough was hired as the first executive vice president and general manager of the Minnesota Wild on September 2, 1999. He is responsible for the club's overall hockey operations. His efforts to build a winner through the draft has been exemplified by the success of Martin Gaborik, the club's first-round choice in 2000. The Wild qualified for the playoffs after just three seasons, going all the way to the 2003 Western Conference Final.

After ending his 13-year NHL playing career with the Flames in 1987, Risebrough was named as assistant coach with Calgary and joined Terry Crisp behind the bench. Risebrough was appointed head coach of the Flames on May 18, 1990 and on May 16, 1991, he also assumed the role of general manager. Late in the 1991-92 campaign he directed his energies full-time to general manager, handing the coaching responsibilities over to Guy Charron for the balance of the season. Risebrough served as g.m. in Calgary through the start of the 1995-96 season. He was vice president of hockey operations for the Edmonton Oilers from 1996 to 1999.

Risebrough was Montreal's first selection, seventh overall, in the 1974 Amateur Draft. During his nine years with the Canadiens, he helped his club to four consecutive Stanley Cup championships between 1976 and 1979. He joined the Flames prior to the start of the club's 1982 training camp. During his NHL career, his clubs have won five Stanley Cup titles (1976-1979 as a player and 1989 as an assistant coach with Calgary) and two Presidents' Trophies (1987-88 and 1988-89 as an assistant coach).

NHL Coaching Record

Season	Team	Games	Regular Season				Playoffs		
			W	L	T	Games	W	L
1990-91	Calgary	80	46	26	8	7	3	4
1991-92	Calgary	64	25	30	9	....	....	....
	NHL Totals	**144**	**71**	**56**	**17**	**7**	**3**	**4**

Club Directory

Xcel Energy Center

Minnesota Wild
317 Washington Street
St. Paul, MN 55102
Phone **651/602-6000**
FAX 651/222-1055
Tickets 651/222-9453
www.wild.com
Capacity: 18,064

Executive Management
Chairman . . . . Bob Naegele, Jr.
Chief Executive Officer . . . . Jac Sperling
President/General Manager. . . . . Doug Risebrough
Executive Vice President, Chief Financial Officer. . . . Pamela Wheelock
Executive Vice President, Business Operations . . . Matt Majka
Vice President, Sales and Service . . . . Steve Griggs
Vice President/General Manager, RiverCentre . . . . . Jim Ibister
Vice President, Information Technology. . . . . Brian Jore
Vice President/General Manager,
  Xcel Energy Center . . . . Jack Larson
Vice President, Finance and Corporate Controller . . Mike Nealy
Vice President, Administration. . . . . Mike Reeves
Vice President, Communications and Broadcasting . . Bill Robertson
Executive Assistant . . . . Stephanie Huseby
Executive Assistant, Hockey Operations. . . . . Laura Kinzel

Hockey Operations
Assistant General Manager/Hockey Operations . . . . Tom Lynn
Assistant General Manager/Player Personnel . . . . . Tom Thompson
Head Coach . . . . Jacques Lemaire
Assistant Coaches . . . . Mike Ramsey, Mario Tremblay
Goaltending Consultant . . . . Bob Mason
Strength and Conditioning . . . . George Kinnear
Strength and Conditioning Coach. . . . . Kirk Olson
Coordinator of Amateur Scouting . . . . Guy Lapointe
Coordinator of Player Development . . . . Barry MacKenzie
Amateur Scouts . . . . Paul Charles, Marc Chamard, Glen Sonmor,
Ernie Vargas, Doug Mosher, Tim Sweeney,
Herb Hammond, Darryl Porter
Pro Scouts. . . . . Rich Sutter, Frank Effinger, Bruce Southern
European Scouts. . . . . Matti Vaisanen, Thomas Steen, Branislav
Gaborik, Ken Hoodikoff, Jiri Koluch
Head Athletic Therapist. . . . . Don Fuller
Head Equipment Manager . . . . Tony DaCosta
Assistant Athletic Trainer. . . . . Mike Vogt
Assistant Equipment Managers . . . . Brent Proulx, Matt Benz
Video Coach . . . . Todd Woodcroft
Hockey Operations Administrator . . . . Cindy Sweiger
Hockey Operations Coordinator . . . . Denny Scanlon
Medical Director . . . . Dr. Sheldon Burns
Orthopedic Surgeon . . . . Dr. Joel Boyd

Customer Sales And Service
Administrative Assistant . . . . Tawnya Vidnovic
Director, Customer Sales and Service. . . . . Jamie Spencer
Director, Group and Event Suite Sales . . . . Kelly McGrath
Director, Premium Service and Operations. . . . . . . Rachael Johnson
Director, Ticket Operations . . . . Chris Turns
Coordinator, Group Sales . . . . Karen Reisinger
Account Executive, Event Suite Sales . . . . Cory Effertz
New Business Development. . . . . Mike Kimbell, Nick Guzzo, Michael Brinkman
Manager, Customer Service . . . . Maria Troje
Managers, Premium Service and Operations . . . . . Heather Erickson, Katie Bellows
Manager, Suite Sales. Matt Cords
Customer Service Representatives . . . . Jora Deziel, Rob Armstrong, Pat Varecka
Senior Manager, Retail Operations . . . . Nikki Stewart

Communications And Broadcasting
Administrative Assistant . . . . Kristie Hewitt
Manager, Media Relations and Team Services . . . . . Brad Smith
Manager, Media Relations for Xcel Energy Center . . Chris Kelleher
Manager, Communications . . . . Aaron Sickman
Director, Community Relations . . . . Marlene Wall
Broadcast Coordinator . . . . Maggie Kukar
Associate Radio Producer . . . . Kevin Falness
Radio Play-by-Play . . . . Bob Kurtz
Radio Analyst . . . . Tom Reid
Television Play-by-Play . . . . Matt McConnell
Television Analyst . . . . Mike Greenlay

Corporate Partnerships
Senior Director, Corporate Services . . . . Carin Anderson
Account Executives . . . . Chris Poitras, Mike Snee, Erin Collins,
Kelly Flinn, John Swing

Marketing
Senior Director, Creative Services . . . . John Maher
Director, Graphic Services and Publications . . . . . . Brian Israel
Director, Advertising and Promotions . . . . Wayne Petersen
Manager, Production Services . . . . Hank Dolan
Coordinator, Graphic and Advertising Design . . . . . Ron Ramirez
Coordinator, Creative Services. . . . . Glen Andresen
Coordinator, Advertising and Promotions . . . . Annie Gleason
Team Curator . . . . Roger Godin

Information Technology
Director, Technology Services . . . . Chris Monicatti
Manager, Internet Services . . . . Jason Ball
Manager, Technology Support . . . . Matt Spraguer
Computer Support Specialist. . . . . Derek Farsund

Miscellaneous
Training Site . . . . Parade Ice Garden
Radio Network Flagship. . . . . WCCO (830 AM)
Television Networks . . . . FOX 9 – KMSP (over-the-air),
Fox Sports Net (Cable)
Team Photographer . . . . Bruce Kluckhohn
Public Address Announcer. . . . . Adam Abrams

Center Mike Ribeiro led the Canadiens with 45 assists and 65 points in 2003-04.

Montreal Canadiens

2003-04 Results: 41W-30L-7T-4OTL 93PTS.
Fourth, Northeast Division

2004-05 Schedule

Month	Day	Date	Opponent
Oct.	Wed.	13	at Ottawa
	Sat.	16	Philadelphia
	Tue.	19	Pittsburgh
	Thu.	21	at Washington
	Sat.	23	Toronto
	Tue.	26	Carolina
	Thu.	28	at Philadelphia
	Sat.	30	Atlanta
Nov.	Wed.	3	at Florida
	Fri.	5	at Carolina
	Sat.	6	at St. Louis
	Tue.	9	Washington
	Fri.	12	at Ottawa
	Sat.	13	Ottawa
	Tue.	16	Boston
	Wed.	17	at Pittsburgh
	Sat.	20	NY Rangers
	Wed.	24	at NY Islanders
	Fri.	26	at Buffalo
	Sat.	27	Boston
	Tue.	30	Minnesota
Dec.	Fri.	3	at New Jersey
	Sat.	4	at Boston
	Wed.	8	at Florida
	Thu.	9	at Tampa Bay
	Sat.	11	at Toronto
	Tue.	14	Tampa Bay
	Fri.	17	at New Jersey
	Sat.	18	New Jersey
	Tue.	21	Buffalo
	Wed.	22	at Buffalo
	Wed.	29	at Vancouver
	Fri.	31	at Calgary
Jan.	Sat.	1	at Edmonton
	Tue.	4	Pittsburgh
	Thu.	6	at Boston
	Sat.	8	Florida
	Mon.	10	at NY Rangers
	Tue.	11	Carolina
	Sat.	15	Dallas
	Mon.	17	at Nashville*
	Wed.	19	at Colorado
	Sat.	22	Toronto
	Mon.	24	Atlanta
	Wed.	26	at Columbus
	Fri.	28	at Washington
	Sat.	29	NY Rangers
Feb.	Tue.	1	Boston
	Thu.	3	San Jose
	Sat.	5	Los Angeles*
	Sun.	6	NY Islanders*
	Tue.	8	Vancouver
	Thu.	10	at Boston
	Tue.	15	Philadelphia
	Thu.	17	Edmonton
	Sat.	19	Ottawa*
	Sun.	20	at Philadelphia
	Tue.	22	NY Islanders
	Thu.	24	Florida
	Sat.	26	Buffalo
	Sun.	27	at Pittsburgh*
Mar.	Wed.	2	at Chicago
	Thu.	3	at Detroit
	Sat.	5	at Toronto
	Tue.	8	Washington
	Fri.	11	at NY Islanders
	Sat.	12	Buffalo
	Tue.	15	at Ottawa
	Thu.	17	at Carolina
	Sat.	19	Anaheim
	Mon.	21	Phoenix
	Wed.	23	at Atlanta
	Thu.	24	at Tampa Bay
	Sat.	26	Calgary
	Mon.	28	at NY Rangers
	Tue.	29	Tampa Bay
	Thu.	31	Toronto
Apr.	Sat.	2	at Toronto
	Mon.	4	New Jersey
	Wed.	6	at Atlanta
	Fri.	8	at Buffalo
	Sat.	9	Ottawa

* Denotes afternoon game.

Franchise date: November 22, 1917

EASTERN CONFERENCE NORTHEAST DIVISION

88th NHL Season

Year-by-Year Record

		Home				Road				Overall								
Season	**GP**	**W**	**L**	**T**	**OL**	**W**	**L**	**T**	**OL**	**W**	**L**	**T**	**OL**	**GF**	**GA**	**Pts.**	**Finished**	**Playoff Result**
2003-04	82	23	13	4	1	18	17	3	3	41	30	7	4	208	192	93	4th, Northeast Div.	Lost Conf. Semi-Final
2002-03	82	16	16	5	4	14	19	3	5	30	35	8	9	206	234	77	4th, Northeast Div.	Out of Playoffs
2001-02	82	21	13	6	1	15	18	6	2	36	31	12	3	207	209	87	4th, Northeast Div.	Lost Conf. Semi-Final
2000-01	82	15	20	4	2	13	20	4	4	28	40	8	6	206	232	70	5th, Northeast Div.	Out of Playoffs
1999-2000	82	18	17	5	1	17	17	4	3	35	34	9	4	196	194	83	4th, Northeast Div.	Out of Playoffs
1998-99	82	21	15	5	...	11	24	6	...	32	39	11	...	184	209	75	5th, Northeast Div.	Out of Playoffs
1997-98	82	15	17	9	...	22	15	4	...	37	32	13	...	235	208	87	4th, Northeast Div.	Lost Conf. Semi-Final
1996-97	82	17	17	7	...	14	19	8	...	31	36	15	...	249	276	77	4th, Northeast Div.	Lost Conf. Quarter-Final
1995-96	82	23	12	6	...	17	20	4	...	40	32	10	...	265	248	90	3rd, Northeast Div.	Lost Conf. Quarter-Final
1994-95	48	15	5	4	...	3	18	3	...	18	23	7	...	125	148	43	6th, Northeast Div.	Out of Playoffs
1993-94	84	26	12	4	...	15	17	10	...	41	29	14	...	283	248	96	3rd, Northeast Div.	Lost Conf. Quarter-Final
1992-93	**84**	**27**	**13**	**2**	**...**	**21**	**17**	**4**	**...**	**48**	**30**	**6**	**...**	**326**	**280**	**102**	**3rd, Adams Div.**	**Won Stanley Cup**
1991-92	80	27	8	5	...	14	20	6	...	41	28	11	...	267	207	93	1st, Adams Div.	Lost Div. Final
1990-91	80	23	12	5	...	16	18	6	...	39	30	11	...	273	249	89	2nd, Adams Div.	Lost Div. Final
1989-90	80	26	8	6	...	15	20	5	...	41	28	11	...	288	234	93	3rd, Adams Div.	Lost Div. Final
1988-89	80	30	6	4	...	23	12	5	...	53	18	9	...	315	218	115	1st, Adams Div.	Lost Final
1987-88	80	26	8	6	...	19	14	7	...	45	22	13	...	298	238	103	1st, Adams Div.	Lost Div. Final
1986-87	80	27	9	4	...	14	20	6	...	41	29	10	...	277	241	92	2nd, Adams Div.	Lost Conf. Championship
1985-86	**80**	**25**	**11**	**4**	**...**	**15**	**22**	**3**	**...**	**40**	**33**	**7**	**...**	**330**	**280**	**87**	**2nd, Adams Div.**	**Won Stanley Cup**
1984-85	80	24	10	6	...	17	17	6	...	41	27	12	...	309	262	94	1st, Adams Div.	Lost Div. Final
1983-84	80	19	19	2	...	16	21	3	...	35	40	5	...	286	295	75	4th, Adams Div.	Lost Conf. Championship
1982-83	80	25	6	9	...	17	18	5	...	42	24	14	...	350	286	98	2nd, Adams Div.	Lost Div. Semi-Final
1981-82	80	25	6	9	...	21	11	8	...	46	17	17	...	360	223	109	1st, Adams Div.	Lost Div. Semi-Final
1980-81	80	31	7	2	...	14	15	11	...	45	22	13	...	332	232	103	1st, Norris Div.	Lost Prelim. Round
1979-80	80	30	7	3	...	17	13	10	...	47	20	13	...	328	240	107	1st, Norris Div.	Lost Quarter-Final
1978-79	**80**	**29**	**6**	**5**	**...**	**23**	**11**	**6**	**...**	**52**	**17**	**11**	**...**	**337**	**204**	**115**	**1st, Norris Div.**	**Won Stanley Cup**
1977-78	**80**	**32**	**4**	**4**	**...**	**27**	**6**	**7**	**...**	**59**	**10**	**11**	**...**	**359**	**183**	**129**	**1st, Norris Div.**	**Won Stanley Cup**
1976-77	**80**	**33**	**1**	**6**	**...**	**27**	**7**	**6**	**...**	**60**	**8**	**12**	**...**	**387**	**171**	**132**	**1st, Norris Div.**	**Won Stanley Cup**
1975-76	**80**	**32**	**3**	**5**	**...**	**26**	**8**	**6**	**...**	**58**	**11**	**11**	**...**	**337**	**174**	**127**	**1st, Norris Div.**	**Won Stanley Cup**
1974-75	80	27	8	5	...	20	6	14	...	47	14	19	...	374	225	113	1st, Norris Div.	Lost Semi-Final
1973-74	78	24	12	3	...	21	12	6	...	45	24	9	...	293	240	99	2nd, East Div.	Lost Quarter-inal
1972-73	**78**	**29**	**4**	**6**	**...**	**23**	**6**	**10**	**...**	**52**	**10**	**16**	**...**	**329**	**184**	**120**	**1st, East Div.**	**Won Stanley Cup**
1971-72	78	29	3	7	...	17	13	9	...	46	16	16	...	307	205	108	3rd, East Div.	Lost Quarter-Final
1970-71	**78**	**29**	**7**	**3**	**...**	**13**	**16**	**10**	**...**	**42**	**23**	**13**	**...**	**291**	**216**	**97**	**3rd, East Div.**	**Won Stanley Cup**
1969-70	76	21	9	8	...	17	13	8	...	38	22	16	...	244	201	92	5th, East Div.	Out of Playoffs
1968-69	**76**	**26**	**7**	**5**	**...**	**20**	**12**	**6**	**...**	**46**	**19**	**11**	**...**	**271**	**202**	**103**	**1st, East Div.**	**Won Stanley Cup**
1967-68	**74**	**26**	**5**	**6**	**...**	**16**	**17**	**4**	**...**	**42**	**22**	**10**	**...**	**236**	**167**	**94**	**1st, East Div.**	**Won Stanley Cup**
1966-67	70	19	9	7	...	13	16	6	...	32	25	13	...	202	188	77	2nd,	Lost Final
1965-66	**70**	**23**	**11**	**1**	**...**	**18**	**10**	**7**	**...**	**41**	**21**	**8**	**...**	**239**	**173**	**90**	**1st,**	**Won Stanley Cup**
1964-65	**70**	**20**	**8**	**7**	**...**	**16**	**15**	**4**	**...**	**36**	**23**	**11**	**...**	**211**	**185**	**83**	**2nd,**	**Won Stanley Cup**
1963-64	70	22	7	6	...	14	14	7	...	36	21	13	...	209	167	85	1st,	Lost Semi-Final
1962-63	70	15	10	10	...	13	9	13	...	28	19	23	...	225	183	79	3rd,	Lost Semi-Final
1961-62	70	26	2	7	...	16	12	7	...	42	14	14	...	259	166	98	1st,	Lost Semi-Final
1960-61	70	24	6	5	...	17	13	5	...	41	19	10	...	254	188	92	1st,	Lost Semi-Final
1959-60	**70**	**23**	**4**	**8**	**...**	**17**	**14**	**4**	**...**	**40**	**18**	**12**	**...**	**255**	**178**	**92**	**1st,**	**Won Stanley Cup**
1958-59	**70**	**21**	**8**	**6**	**...**	**18**	**10**	**7**	**...**	**39**	**18**	**13**	**...**	**258**	**158**	**91**	**1st,**	**Won Stanley Cup**
1957-58	**70**	**23**	**8**	**4**	**...**	**20**	**9**	**6**	**...**	**43**	**17**	**10**	**...**	**250**	**158**	**96**	**1st,**	**Won Stanley Cup**
1956-57	**70**	**23**	**6**	**6**	**...**	**12**	**17**	**6**	**...**	**35**	**23**	**12**	**...**	**210**	**155**	**82**	**2nd,**	**Won Stanley Cup**
1955-56	**70**	**29**	**5**	**1**	**...**	**16**	**10**	**9**	**...**	**45**	**15**	**10**	**...**	**222**	**131**	**100**	**1st,**	**Won Stanley Cup**
1954-55	70	26	5	4	...	15	13	7	...	41	18	11	...	228	157	93	2nd,	Lost Final
1953-54	70	27	5	3	...	8	19	8	...	35	24	11	...	195	141	81	2nd,	Lost Final
1952-53	**70**	**18**	**12**	**5**	**...**	**10**	**11**	**14**	**...**	**28**	**23**	**19**	**...**	**155**	**148**	**75**	**2nd,**	**Won Stanley Cup**
1951-52	70	22	8	5	...	12	18	5	...	34	26	10	...	195	164	78	2nd,	Lost Final
1950-51	70	17	10	8	...	8	20	7	...	25	30	15	...	173	184	65	3rd,	Lost Final
1949-50	70	17	8	10	...	12	14	9	...	29	22	19	...	172	150	77	2nd,	Lost Semi-Final
1948-49	60	19	8	3	...	9	15	6	...	28	23	9	...	152	126	65	3rd,	Lost Semi-Final
1947-48	60	13	13	4	...	7	16	7	...	20	29	11	...	147	169	51	5th,	Out of Playoffs
1946-47	60	19	6	5	...	15	10	5	...	34	16	10	...	189	138	78	1st,	Lost Final
1945-46	**50**	**16**	**6**	**3**	**...**	**12**	**11**	**2**	**...**	**28**	**17**	**5**	**...**	**172**	**134**	**61**	**1st,**	**Won Stanley Cup**
1944-45	50	21	2	2	...	17	6	2	...	38	8	4	...	228	121	80	1st,	Lost Semi-Final
1943-44	**50**	**22**	**0**	**3**	**...**	**16**	**5**	**4**	**...**	**38**	**5**	**7**	**...**	**234**	**109**	**83**	**1st,**	**Won Stanley Cup**
1942-43	50	14	4	7	...	5	15	5	...	19	19	12	...	181	191	50	4th,	Lost Semi-Final
1941-42	48	12	10	2	...	6	17	1	...	18	27	3	...	134	173	39	6th,	Lost Quarter-Final
1940-41	48	11	9	4	...	5	17	2	...	16	26	6	...	121	147	38	6th,	Lost Quarter-Final
1939-40	48	5	14	5	...	5	19	0	...	10	33	5	...	90	167	25	7th,	Out of Playoffs
1938-39	48	8	11	5	...	7	13	4	...	15	24	9	...	115	146	39	6th,	Lost Quarter-Final
1937-38	48	13	4	7	...	5	13	6	...	18	17	13	...	123	128	49	3rd, Cdn. Div.	Lost Quarter-Final
1936-37	48	16	8	0	...	8	10	6	...	24	18	6	...	115	111	54	1st, Cdn. Div.	Lost Semi-Final
1935-36	48	5	11	8	...	6	15	3	...	11	26	11	...	82	123	33	4th, Cdn. Div.	Out of Playoffs
1934-35	48	11	11	2	...	8	12	4	...	19	23	6	...	110	145	44	3rd, Cdn. Div.	Lost Quarter-Final
1933-34	48	16	6	2	...	6	14	4	...	22	20	6	...	99	101	50	2nd, Cdn. Div.	Lost Quarter-Final
1932-33	48	15	5	4	...	3	20	1	...	18	25	5	...	92	115	41	3rd, Cdn. Div.	Lost Quarter-Final
1931-32	48	18	3	3	...	7	13	4	...	25	16	7	...	128	111	57	1st, Cdn. Div.	Lost Semi-Final
1930-31	**44**	**15**	**3**	**4**	**...**	**11**	**7**	**4**	**...**	**26**	**10**	**8**	**...**	**129**	**89**	**60**	**1st, Cdn. Div.**	**Won Stanley Cup**
1929-30	**44**	**13**	**5**	**4**	**...**	**8**	**9**	**5**	**...**	**21**	**14**	**9**	**...**	**142**	**114**	**51**	**2nd, Cdn. Div.**	**Won Stanley Cup**
1928-29	44	12	4	6	...	10	3	9	...	22	7	15	...	71	43	59	1st, Cdn. Div.	Lost Semi-Final
1927-28	44	12	7	3	...	14	4	4	...	26	11	7	...	116	48	59	1st, Cdn. Div.	Lost Semi-Final
1926-27	44	15	5	2	...	13	9	0	...	28	14	2	...	99	67	58	2nd, Cdn. Div.	Lost Semi-Final
1925-26	36	5	12	1	...	6	12	0	...	11	24	1	...	79	108	23	7th,	Out of Playoffs
1924-25	30	10	5	0	...	7	6	2	...	17	11	2	...	93	56	36	3rd,	Lost Final
1923-24	**24**	**10**	**2**	**0**	**...**	**3**	**9**	**0**	**...**	**13**	**11**	**0**	**...**	**59**	**48**	**26**	**2nd,**	**Won Stanley Cup**
1922-23	24	10	2	0	...	3	7	2	...	13	9	2	...	73	61	28	2nd,	Lost NHL Final
1921-22	24	8	3	1	...	4	8	0	...	12	11	1	...	88	94	25	3rd,	Out of Playoffs
1920-21	24	9	3	0	...	4	8	0	...	13	11	0	...	112	99	26	3rd and 2nd*	Out of Playoffs
1919-20	24	8	4	0	...	5	7	0	...	13	11	0	...	129	113	26	2nd and 3rd*	Out of Playoffs
1918-19	18	7	2	0	...	3	6	0	...	10	8	0	...	88	78	20	1st and 2nd*	Cup Final but no Decision
1917-18	22	8	3	0	...	5	6	0	...	13	9	0	...	115	84	26	1st and 3rd*	Lost NHL Final

* Season played in two halves with no combined standing at end.
From 1917-18 through 1925-26, NHL champions played against PCHA/WCHL champions for Stanley Cup.

2004-05 Player Personnel

FORWARDS	HT	WT	S	Place of Birth	Date	2003-04 Club
BEGIN, Steve	5-11	195	L	Trois-Rivieres, Que.	6/14/78	Montreal
BONK, Radek	6-3	220	L	Krnov, Czech.	1/9/76	Ottawa
BULIS, Jan	6-1	208	L	Pardubice, Czech.	3/18/78	Montreal
DAGENAIS, Pierre	6-4	217	L	Blainville, Que.	3/4/78	Montreal-Hamilton
HOSSA, Marcel	6-2	215	L	Ilava, Czech.	10/12/81	Montreal-Hamilton
IVANANS, Raitis	6-3	220	L	Riga, Latvia	1/1/79	Milwaukee-Rockford
KOIVU, Saku	5-10	181	L	Turku, Finland	11/23/74	Montreal
RIBEIRO, Mike	6-0	177	L	Montreal, Que.	2/10/80	Montreal
RYDER, Michael	6-1	196	R	St. John's, Nfld.	3/31/80	Montreal
SUNDSTROM, Niklas	6-0	191	L	Ornskoldsvik, Sweden	6/6/75	Montreal
WARD, Jason	6-3	203	R	Chapleau, Ont.	1/16/79	Montreal-Hamilton
ZEDNIK, Richard	6-1	196	L	Bystrica, Czech.	1/6/76	Montreal
DEFENSEMEN						
BOUILLON, Francis	5-8	196	L	New York, NY	10/17/75	Montreal
BRISEBOIS, Patrice	6-2	203	R	Montreal, Que.	1/27/71	Montreal
DYKHUIS, Karl	6-3	209	L	Sept-Iles, Que.	7/8/72	Montreal-Hamilton
HAINSEY, Ron	6-3	211	L	Bolton, CT	3/24/81	Montreal-Hamilton
KOMISAREK, Mike	6-4	237	R	Islip Terrace, NY	1/19/82	Montreal-Hamilton
MARKOV, Andrei	6-0	208	L	Voskresensk, USSR	12/20/78	Montreal
RIVET, Craig	6-2	207	R	North Bay, Ont.	9/13/74	Montreal
SOURAY, Sheldon	6-4	227	L	Elk Point, Alta.	7/13/76	Montreal

GOALTENDERS	HT	WT	C	Place of Birth	Date	2003-04 Club
HUET, Cristobal	6-0	194	L	St. Martin D'Heres, France	9/3/75	Los Angeles
MICHAUD, Olivier	5-11	179	L	Beloeil, Que.	9/14/83	Columbus (ECHL)-Hamilton
THEODORE, Jose	5-11	182	R	Laval, Que.	9/13/76	Montreal

Coaching History

Jack Laviolette, 1909-10; Adolphe Lecours, 1910-11; Napoleon Dorval, 1911-12, 1912-13; Jimmy Gardner, 1913-14, 1914-15; Newsy Lalonde, 1915-16 to 1920-21; Newsy Lalonde and Léo Dandurand, 1921-22; Léo Dandurand, 1922-23 to 1925-26; Cecil Hart, 1926-27 to 1931-32; Newsy Lalonde, 1932-33, 1933-34; Newsy Lalonde and Léo Dandurand, 1934-35; Sylvio Mantha, 1935-36; Cecil Hart, 1936-37, 1937-38; Cecil Hart and Jules Dugal, 1938-39; Babe Siebert, 1939*; Pit Lepine, 1939-40; Dick Irvin 1940-41 to 1954-55; Toe Blake, 1955-56 to 1967-68; Claude Ruel, 1968-69, 1969-70; Claude Ruel and Al MacNeil, 1970-71; Scotty Bowman, 1971-72 to 1978-79; Bernie Geoffrion and Claude Ruel, 1979-80; Claude Ruel, 1980-81; Bob Berry, 1981-82, 1982-83; Bob Berry and Jacques Lemaire, 1983-84; Jacques Lemaire, 1984-85; Jean Perron, 1985-86 to 1987-88; Pat Burns, 1988-89 to 1991-92; Jacques Demers, 1992-93 to 1994-95; Jacques Demers and Mario Tremblay, 1995-96; Mario Tremblay, 1996-97; Alain Vigneault, 1997-98 to 1999-2000; Alain Vigneault and Michel Therrien, 2000-01; Michel Therrien, 2001-02; Michel Therrien and Claude Julien, 2002-03; Claude Julien, 2003-04 to date.

* Named coach in summer but died before 1939-40 season began.

Vice President and General Manager

GAINEY, BOB
Executive Vice President/General Manager, Montreal Canadiens.
Born in Peterborough, Ont., December 13, 1953.

On June 2, 2003, the Montreal Canadiens announced the appointment of Bob Gainey as executive vice president and general manager, effective July 1, 2003. As a player in Montreal, Gainey brought many elements to the Canadiens over his 16-year career.

Described as the world's best all-around player by legendary Soviet national team coach Viktor Tikhonov, Gainey was a tenacious competitor, relentless checker and a respected team leader. His presence helped the Canadiens win the Stanley Cup five times in the decade between 1976 and 1986. He won the Conn Smythe Trophy as playoff MVP in 1979 and was a four-time winner of the Selke Trophy as the NHL's best defensive forward. Gainey was captain of the Canadiens from 1981 until his retirement in 1989. He was elected to the Hockey Hall of Fame in 1992.

Gainey spent a year as a player-coach of the Epinal franchise in France before becoming head coach of the Minnesota North Stars in 1990-91. He was given the g.m.'s job in 1992 and was in the dual role when the Stars relocated to Dallas in 1993. Gainey stepped down as coach on January 8, 1996 to focus solely on the duties of general manager and built a powerhouse club that won five straight division titles from 1996-97 to 2000-01, the Presidents' Trophy in 1998 and 1999, and the Stanley Cup in 1999.

NHL Coaching Record

		Regular Season				Playoffs		
Season	Team	Games	W	L	T	Games	W	L
1990-91	Minnesota	80	27	39	14	23	14	9
1991-92	Minnesota	80	32	42	6	7	3	4
1992-93	Minnesota	84	36	38	10	....	....	....
1993-94	Dallas	84	42	29	13	9	5	4
1994-95	Dallas	48	17	23	8	5	1	4
1995-96	Dallas	39	11	19	9	....	....	....
	NHL Totals	**415**	**165**	**190**	**60**	**44**	**23**	**21**

2003-04 Scoring

* - rookie

Regular Season

Pos	#	Player	Team	GP	G	A	Pts	+/–	PIM	PP	SH	GW	GT	S	%
C	71	Mike Ribeiro	MTL	81	20	45	65	15	34	7	0	5	1	103	19.4
R	73	* Michael Ryder	MTL	81	25	38	63	10	26	10	0	4	0	215	11.6
C	11	Saku Koivu	MTL	68	14	41	55	–5	52	5	0	3	0	112	12.5
R	20	Richard Zednik	MTL	81	26	24	50	5	63	7	0	9	0	218	11.9
R	27	Alex Kovalev	NYR	66	13	29	42	–5	54	3	0	0	1	178	7.3
			MTL	12	1	2	3	–4	12	0	0	1	0	29	3.4
			TOTAL	78	14	31	45	–9	66	3	0	1	1	207	6.8
D	44	Sheldon Souray	MTL	63	15	20	35	4	104	6	1	3	0	186	8.1
C	94	Yanic Perreault	MTL	69	16	15	31	–10	40	5	0	3	0	114	14.0
D	43	Patrice Brisebois	MTL	71	4	27	31	17	22	2	0	0	0	96	4.2
C	38	Jan Bulis	MTL	72	13	17	30	–8	30	1	1	4	0	147	8.8
C	34	Jim Dowd	MIN	55	4	20	24	6	38	2	0	2	0	41	9.8
			MTL	14	3	2	5	6	6	0	1	0	0	13	23.1
			TOTAL	69	7	22	29	12	44	2	1	2	0	54	13.0
D	79	Andrei Markov	MTL	69	6	22	28	–2	20	2	0	0	0	105	5.7
R	26	Pierre Dagenais	MTL	50	17	10	27	15	24	4	0	3	0	149	11.4
R	37	Niklas Sundstrom	MTL	66	8	12	20	3	18	0	0	2	1	67	11.9
D	51	Francis Bouillon	MTL	73	2	16	18	1	70	0	0	0	0	86	2.3
C	22	Steve Begin	MTL	52	10	5	15	6	41	0	1	1	0	91	11.0
C	90	Joe Juneau	MTL	70	5	10	15	–4	20	2	1	1	0	76	6.6
R	17	Jason Ward	MTL	53	5	7	12	3	21	2	0	1	0	56	8.9
R	24	Andreas Dackell	MTL	60	4	8	12	8	10	0	0	0	0	50	8.0
D	52	Craig Rivet	MTL	80	4	8	12	–1	98	2	0	1	0	96	4.2
D	5	Stephane Quintal	MTL	73	3	5	8	10	82	0	0	0	0	86	3.5
D	8	* Michael Komisarek	MTL	46	0	4	4	4	34	0	0	0	0	40	0.0
L	15	Darren Langdon	MTL	64	0	3	3	–2	135	0	0	0	0	22	0.0
D	65	* Ron Hainsey	MTL	11	1	1	2	3	4	0	0	0	0	11	9.1
L	81	Marcel Hossa	MTL	15	1	1	2	–3	8	0	0	0	0	19	5.3
C	46	Benoit Gratton	MTL	4	0	1	1	0	4	0	0	0	0	3	0.0
L	32	Gordie Dwyer	MTL	2	0	0	0	0	7	0	0	0	0	0	0.0
L	35	* Tomas Plekanec	MTL	2	0	0	0	0	0	0	0	0	0	0	0.0
C	88	* Christopher Higgins	MTL	2	0	0	0	0	0	0	0	0	0	0	0.0
D	28	Karl Dykhuis	MTL	9	0	0	0	–2	2	0	0	0	0	6	0.0

Goaltending

No.	Goaltender	GPI	Mins	Avg	W	L	T	EN	SO	GA	SA	S%	G	A	PIM
30	Mathieu Garon	19	1003	2.27	8	6	2	1	0	38	480	.921	0	0	2
60	Jose Theodore	67	3961	2.27	33	28	5	3	6	150	1860	.919	0	3	4
	Totals	**82**	**4979**	**2.31**	**41**	**34**	**7**	**4**	**6**	**192**	**2344**	**.918**			

Playoffs

Pos	#	Player	Team	GP	G	A	Pts	+/–	PIM	PP	SH	GW	GT	S	%
C	11	Saku Koivu	MTL	11	3	8	11	1	10	2	0	0	0	27	11.1
R	27	Alex Kovalev	MTL	11	6	4	10	2	8	1	0	1	0	29	20.7
R	20	Richard Zednik	MTL	11	3	3	6	7	2	0	0	1	0	32	9.4
D	52	Craig Rivet	MTL	11	1	4	5	2	2	1	0	0	0	16	6.3
D	79	Andrei Markov	MTL	11	1	4	5	3	8	0	0	1	0	18	5.6
C	94	Yanic Perreault	MTL	9	2	2	4	–3	0	0	0	1	0	15	13.3
D	43	Patrice Brisebois	MTL	11	2	1	3	–5	4	1	0	0	0	10	20.0
C	71	Mike Ribeiro	MTL	11	2	1	3	0	18	0	0	0	0	14	14.3
R	73	* Michael Ryder	MTL	11	1	2	3	–5	4	0	0	0	0	36	2.8
C	38	Jan Bulis	MTL	11	1	1	2	–6	4	0	0	0	0	15	6.7
R	17	Jason Ward	MTL	5	0	2	2	–2	2	0	0	0	0	4	0.0
C	34	Jim Dowd	MTL	11	0	2	2	–3	2	0	0	0	0	10	0.0
D	44	Sheldon Souray	MTL	11	0	2	2	–2	39	0	0	0	0	31	0.0
R	37	Niklas Sundstrom	MTL	4	1	0	1	–1	2	0	0	0	0	5	20.0
L	15	Darren Langdon	MTL	9	1	0	1	0	6	0	0	0	0	2	50.0
L	26	Pierre Dagenais	MTL	8	0	1	1	–1	6	0	0	0	0	17	0.0
C	22	Steve Begin	MTL	9	0	1	1	0	10	0	0	0	0	9	0.0
C	90	Joe Juneau	MTL	11	0	1	1	–2	4	0	0	0	0	10	0.0
D	5	Stephane Quintal	MTL	4	0	0	0	–1	2	0	0	0	0	1	0.0
D	8	* Mike Komisarek	MTL	7	0	0	0	1	8	0	0	0	0	6	0.0
D	51	Francis Bouillon	MTL	11	0	0	0	–6	7	0	0	0	0	13	0.0

Goaltending

No.	Goaltender	GPI	Mins	Avg	W	L	EN	SO	GA	SA	S%	G	A	PIM
30	Mathieu Garon	1	12	0.00	0	0	0	0	0	6	1.000	0	0	0
60	Jose Theodore	11	678	2.39	4	7	1	1	27	333	.919	0	2	0
	Totals	**11**	**692**	**2.43**	**4**	**7**	**1**	**1**	**28**	**340**	**.918**			

General Managers' History

Jack Laviolette and Joseph Cattarinich, 1909-1910; George Kennedy, 1910-11 to 1920-21; Leo Dandurand, 1921-22 to 1934-35; Ernest Savard, 1935-36; Cecil Hart, 1936-37 to 1938-39; Jules Dugal, 1939-40; Tom P. Gorman, 1940-41 to 1945-46; Frank J. Selke, 1946-47 to 1963-64; Sam Pollock, 1964-65 to 1977-78; Irving Grundman, 1978-79 to 1982-83; Serge Savard, 1983-84 to 1994-95; Serge Savard and Réjean Houle, 1995-96; Réjean Houle, 1996-97 to 1999-2000; Réjean Houle and Andre Savard, 2000-01; Andre Savard, 2001-02, 2002-03; Bob Gainey, 2003-04 to date.

Captains' History

Jack Laviolette, 1909-10; Newsy Lalonde, 1910-11; Jack Laviolette, 1911-12; Newsy Lalonde, 1912-13; Jimmy Gardner, 1913-14, 1914-15; Howard McNamara, 1915-16; Newsy Lalonde, 1916-17 to 1921-22; Sprague Cleghorn, 1922-23 to 1924-25; Bill Coutu, 1925-26; Sylvio Mantha, 1926-27 to 1931-32; George Hainsworth, 1932-33; Sylvio Mantha, 1933-34 to 1935-36; Babe Siebert, 1936-37 to 1938-39; Walt Buswell, 1939-40; Toe Blake, 1940-41 to 1946-47; Toe Blake and Bill Durnan, 1947-48; Butch Bouchard, 1948-49 to 1955-56; Maurice Richard, 1956-57 to 1959-60; Doug Harvey, 1960-61; Jean Béliveau, 1961-62 to 1970-71; Henri Richard, 1971-72 to 1974-75; Yvan Cournoyer, 1975-76 to 1978-79; Serge Savard, 1979-80, 1980-81; Bob Gainey, 1981-82 to 1988-89; Guy Carbonneau and Chris Chelios (co-captains), 1989-90; Guy Carbonneau, 1990-91 to 1993-94; Kirk Muller and Mike Keane, 1994-95; Mike Keane and Pierre Turgeon, 1995-96; Pierre Turgeon and Vincent Damphousse, 1996-97; Vincent Damphousse, 1997-98, 1998-99; Saku Koivu, 1999-2000 to date.

Club Records

Team

(Figures in brackets for season records are games played; records for fewest points, wins, ties, losses, goals, goals against are for 70 or more games)

Record		
Most Points	***132**	1976-77 (80)
Most Wins	**60**	1976-77 (80)
Most Ties	**23**	1962-63 (70)
Most Losses	**40**	1983-84 (80), 2000-01 (82)
Most Goals	**387**	1976-77 (80)
Most Goals Against	**295**	1983-84 (80)
Fewest Points	**65**	1950-51 (70)
Fewest Wins	**25**	1950-51 (70)
Fewest Ties	**5**	1983-84 (80)
Fewest Losses	***8**	1976-77 (80)
Fewest Goals	**155**	1952-53 (70)
Fewest Goals Against	***131**	1955-56 (70)
Longest Winning Streak		
Overall	**12**	Jan. 6-Feb. 3/68
Home	**13**	Nov. 2/43-Jan. 8/44, Jan. 30-Mar. 26/77
Away	**8**	Dec. 18/77-Jan. 18/78, Jan. 21-Feb. 21/82
Longest Undefeated Streak		
Overall	**28**	Dec. 18/77-Feb. 23/78 (23 wins, 5 ties)
Home	***34**	Nov. 1/76-Apr. 2/77 (28 wins, 6 ties)
Away	***23**	Nov. 27/74-Mar. 12/75 (14 wins, 9 ties)
Longest Losing Streak		
Overall	**12**	Feb. 13-Mar. 13/26
Home	**7**	Dec. 16/39-Jan. 18/40, Oct. 28-Nov. 25/00
Away	**10**	Jan. 16-Mar. 13/26
Longest Winless Streak		
Overall	**12**	Feb. 13-Mar. 13/26 (12 losses), Nov. 28-Dec. 29/35 (8 losses, 4 ties)
Home	**15**	Dec. 16/39-Mar. 7/40 (12 losses, 3 ties)
Away	**12**	Nov. 26/33-Jan. 28/34 (8 losses, 4 ties), Oct. 20/50-Dec. 13/51 (8 losses, 4 ties)
Most Shutouts, Season	***22**	1928-29 (44)
Most PIM, Season	**1,847**	1995-96 (82)
Most Goals, Game	***16**	Mar. 3/20 (Mtl. 16 at Que. 3)

Individual

Record		
Most Seasons	**20**	Henri Richard, Jean Béliveau
Most Games	**1,256**	Henri Richard
Most Goals, Career	**544**	Maurice Richard
Most Assists, Career	**728**	Guy Lafleur
Most Points, Career	**1,246**	Guy Lafleur (518G, 728A)
Most PIM, Career	**2,248**	Chris Nilan
Most Shutouts, Career	**75**	George Hainsworth
Longest Consecutive Games Streak	**560**	Doug Jarvis (Oct. 8/75-Apr. 4/82)
Most Goals, Season	**60**	Steve Shutt (1976-77), Guy Lafleur (1977-78)
Most Assists, Season	**82**	Pete Mahovlich (1974-75)
Most Points, Season	**136**	Guy Lafleur (1976-77; 56G, 80A)
Most PIM, Season	**358**	Chris Nilan (1984-85)
Most Points, Defenseman, Season	**85**	Larry Robinson (1976-77; 19G, 66A)
Most Points, Center, Season	**117**	Pete Mahovlich (1974-75; 35G, 82A)
Most Points, Right Wing, Season	**136**	Guy Lafleur (1976-77; 56G, 80A)
Most Points, Left Wing, Season	**110**	Mats Naslund (1985-86; 43G, 67A)
Most Points, Rookie, Season	**71**	Mats Naslund (1982-83; 26G, 45A), Kjell Dahlin (1985-86; 32G, 39A)
Most Shutouts, Season	***22**	George Hainsworth (1928-29)
Most Goals, Game	**6**	Newsy Lalonde (Jan. 10/20)
Most Assists, Game	**6**	Elmer Lach (Feb. 6/43)
Most Points, Game	**8**	Maurice Richard (Dec. 28/44; 5G, 3A), Bert Olmstead (Jan. 9/54; 4G, 4A)

* NHL Record.

Retired Numbers

1	Jacques Plante	1952-1963
2	Doug Harvey	1947-1961
4	Jean Béliveau	1950-1971
7	Howie Morenz	1923-1937
9	Maurice Richard	1942-1960
10	Guy Lafleur	1971-1984
16	Henri Richard	1955-1975

All-time Record vs. Other Clubs

Regular Season

	At Home								On Road								Total							
	GP	W	L	T	OL	GF	GA	PTS	GP	W	L	T	OL	GF	GA	PTS	GP	W	L	T	OL	GF	GA	PTS
Anaheim	8	4	2	2	0	24	19	10	8	5	3	0	0	27	25	10	16	9	5	2	0	51	44	20
Atlanta	10	7	3	0	0	34	24	14	10	7	1	2	0	31	12	16	20	14	4	2	0	65	36	30
Boston	334	189	97	47	1	1120	790	426	335	124	152	56	3	904	990	307	669	313	249	103	4	2024	1780	733
Buffalo	103	57	34	12	0	392	306	126	102	29	53	19	1	268	317	78	205	86	87	31	1	660	623	204
Calgary	46	26	12	8	0	163	112	60	49	26	15	7	1	164	146	60	95	52	27	15	1	327	258	120
Carolina	75	50	17	7	1	309	213	108	78	36	27	13	2	268	224	87	153	86	44	20	3	577	437	195
Chicago	276	174	54	48	0	1067	653	396	273	125	93	55	0	761	731	305	549	299	147	103	0	1828	1384	701
Colorado	64	38	15	10	1	261	198	87	63	26	31	5	1	222	216	58	127	64	46	15	2	483	414	145
Columbus	4	1	1	1	1	6	6	4	1	1	0	0	0	3	1	2	5	2	1	1	1	9	7	6
Dallas	58	37	12	9	0	250	144	83	59	30	17	12	0	203	153	72	117	67	29	21	0	453	297	155
Detroit	282	172	67	43	0	994	636	387	280	97	129	53	1	717	805	248	562	269	196	96	1	1711	1441	635
Edmonton	30	16	9	4	1	105	95	37	35	17	16	0	2	113	117	36	65	33	25	4	3	218	212	73
Florida	21	8	9	3	1	54	49	20	22	8	11	3	0	61	68	19	43	16	20	6	1	115	117	39
Los Angeles	64	45	8	11	0	289	160	101	65	37	19	9	0	256	199	83	129	82	27	20	0	545	359	184
Minnesota	3	1	1	1	0	9	8	3	2	1	1	0	0	5	6	2	5	2	2	1	0	14	14	5
Nashville	4	4	0	0	0	15	9	8	4	1	2	1	0	7	14	3	8	5	2	1	0	22	23	11
New Jersey	54	33	15	6	0	182	134	72	54	25	25	4	0	190	160	54	108	58	40	10	0	372	294	126
NY Islanders	60	36	15	9	0	217	168	81	60	24	28	6	2	167	187	56	120	60	43	15	2	384	355	137
NY Rangers	290	190	60	40	0	1125	669	420	290	118	117	54	1	844	835	291	580	308	177	94	1	1969	1504	711
Ottawa	33	17	12	4	0	97	95	38	31	15	14	1	1	87	90	32	64	32	26	5	1	184	185	70
Philadelphia	74	34	25	14	1	254	229	83	73	28	29	16	0	215	223	72	147	62	54	30	1	469	452	155
Phoenix	29	24	3	2	0	142	66	50	29	13	9	7	0	112	94	33	58	37	12	9	0	254	160	83
Pittsburgh	82	62	10	10	0	383	203	134	82	41	28	13	0	290	238	95	164	103	38	23	0	673	441	229
St. Louis	59	41	11	7	0	255	161	89	57	28	14	15	0	195	147	71	116	69	25	22	0	450	308	160
San Jose	11	7	2	2	0	36	20	16	11	4	4	2	1	28	33	11	22	11	6	4	1	64	53	27
Tampa Bay	22	11	10	1	0	59	53	23	23	9	9	5	0	61	55	23	45	20	19	6	0	120	108	46
Toronto	333	198	91	43	1	1162	827	440	333	116	172	45	0	865	1007	277	666	314	263	88	1	2027	1834	717
Vancouver	53	38	10	5	0	244	135	81	55	33	13	8	1	202	146	75	108	71	23	13	1	446	281	156
Washington	60	35	16	8	1	229	127	79	59	24	26	9	0	177	163	57	119	59	42	17	1	406	290	136
Defunct Clubs	231	148	58	25	0	779	469	321	230	98	97	35	0	586	606	231	461	246	155	60	0	1365	1075	552
Totals	**2773**	**1703**	**679**	**382**	**9**	**10256**	**6778**	**3797**	**2773**	**1146**	**1155**	**455**	**17**	**8029**	**8008**	**2764**	**5546**	**2849**	**1834**	**837**	**26**	**18285**	**14786**	**6561**

Playoffs

	Series	W	L	GP	W	L	T	GF	GA	Last Mtg.	Rnd.	Result
Boston	30	23	7	152	95	57	0	469	371	2004	CQF	W 4-3
Buffalo	7	4	3	35	18	17	0	124	111	1998	CSF	L 0-4
Calgary	2	1	1	11	6	5	0	31	32	1989	F	L 2-4
Carolina	6	5	1	33	21	12	0	108	91	2002	CSF	L 2-4
Chicago	17	12	5	81	50	29	2	261	185	1976	QF	W 4-0
Colorado	5	3	2	31	17	14	0	105	85	1993	DSF	W 4-2
Dallas	2	1	1	13	7	6	0	48	37	1980	QF	L 3-4
Detroit	12	5	7	62	33	29	0	161	149	1978	QF	W 4-1
Edmonton	1	0	1	3	0	3	0	6	15	1981	PRE	L 0-3
Los Angeles	1	1	0	5	4	1	0	15	12	1993	F	W 4-1
New Jersey	1	0	1	5	1	4	0	11	22	1997	CQF	L 1-4
NY Islanders	4	3	1	22	14	8	0	64	55	1993	CF	W 4-1
NY Rangers	14	7	7	61	34	25	2	188	158	1996	CQF	L 2-4
Philadelphia	4	3	1	21	14	7	0	72	52	1989	CF	W 4-2
Pittsburgh	1	1	0	6	4	2	0	18	15	1998	CQF	W 4-2
St. Louis	3	3	0	12	12	0	0	42	14	1977	QF	W 4-0
Tampa Bay	1	0	1	4	0	4	0	5	14	2004	CSF	L 0-4
Toronto	15	8	7	71	42	29	0	215	160	1979	QF	W 4-0
Vancouver	1	1	0	5	4	1	0	20	9	1975	QF	W 4-1
Defunct Clubs	11*	6	4	28	15	9	4	70	71			
Totals	**138***	**87**	**50**	**661**	**391**	**262**	**8**	**2033**	**1658**			

* 1919 Final incomplete due to influenza epidemic.

Playoff Results 2004-2000

Year	Round	Opponent	Result	GF	GA
2004	CSF	Tampa Bay	L 0-4	5	14
	CQF	Boston	W 4-3	19	14
2002	CSF	Carolina	L 2-4	12	21
	CQF	Boston	W 4-2	20	18

Abbreviations: Round: F - Final; **CF** - conference final; **CSF** - conference semi-final; **CQF** - conference quarter-final; **DSF** - division semi-final; **QF** - quarter-final; **PRE** - preliminary round.

Calgary totals include Atlanta Flames, 1972-73 to 1979-80.
Colorado totals include Quebec, 1979-80 to 1994-95.
New Jersey totals include Kansas City, 1974-75 to 1975-76, and Colorado Rockies, 1976-77 to 1981-82.
Phoenix totals include Winnipeg, 1979-80 to 1995-96.
Carolina totals include Hartford, 1979-80 to 1996-97.
Dallas totals include Minnesota North Stars, 1967-68 to 1992-93.

2003-04 Results

Oct.	9	at Ottawa	2-5
	11	at Toronto	4-0
	14	Washington	5-1
	16	Pittsburgh	4-1
	18	Toronto	0-1
	20	Detroit	2-1
	23	NY Islanders	3-0
	25	Ottawa	2-6
	27	at Philadelphia	0-5
	28	Boston	0-2
	30	at Boston	1-0*
Nov.	1	NY Rangers	1-5
	4	Edmonton	2-4
	7	at Buffalo	1-2
	8	Buffalo	3-0
	11	Columbus	1-1
	13	at NY Islanders	1-3
	15	at Ottawa	3-2
	18	at Vancouver	4-5*
	20	at Calgary	1-2
	22	at Edmonton	4-3
	25	Vancouver	2-5
	28	at Washington	5-3
	29	Florida	1-1
Dec.	2	Tampa Bay	3-2
	5	at Carolina	1-1
	6	Carolina	3-1
	8	Philadelphia	2-3
	10	at NY Rangers	2-1
	12	at Florida	2-4
	13	at Tampa Bay	5-2
	16	Boston	1-1
	18	Nashville	5-4*
	20	at Toronto	2-4
	22	Pittsburgh	4-1
	23	at Washington	2-3
	27	at Carolina	1-2*
	29	at Atlanta	2-1
	31	at Dallas	1-1
Jan.	3	Atlanta	5-1
	4	Washington	4-1
	6	Buffalo	3-1
	8	Tampa Bay	1-4
	10	at Pittsburgh	8-0
	13	St. Louis	5-2
	14	at Atlanta	2-1
	17	NY Rangers	2-2
	20	at Philadelphia	4-1
	23	at New Jersey	0-2
	24	Toronto	1-4
	27	at Buffalo	1-4
	29	at Minnesota	3-2*
	31	Boston	0-1
Feb.	1	Chicago	6-4
	3	at Pittsburgh	4-3
	5	NY Islanders	2-1
	10	at Florida	1-2
	12	at Tampa Bay	3-5
	14	at Ottawa	2-5
	17	Atlanta	1-4
	19	Calgary	4-1
	21	at Toronto	4-5
	23	at NY Rangers	4-1
	24	Ottawa	4-2
	26	at Boston	3-2*
	28	Carolina	1-0*
Mar.	1	New Jersey	2-1
	3	at San Jose	3-4
	5	at Phoenix	4-3
	6	at Los Angeles	4-2
	8	at Anaheim	5-2
	11	Florida	2-3*
	13	Toronto	4-3
	16	Colorado	4-2
	19	at New Jersey	1-1
	20	New Jersey	3-2
	24	at Buffalo	1-2
	25	Ottawa	0-4
	27	at Boston	2-3*
	31	at NY Islanders	1-5
Apr.	1	Philadelphia	0-2
	3	Buffalo	6-3

* – Overtime

Entry Draft Selections 2004-1990

2004
Pick
18 Kyle Chipchura
84 Alexei Yemelin
100 James Wyman
150 Mikhail Grabovsky
181 Loic Lacasse
212 Jon Gleed
246 Gregory Stewart
262 Mark Streit
278 Alex Dulac-Lemelin

2003
Pick
10 Andrei Kostitsyn
40 Cory Urquhart
61 Maxim Lapierre
79 Ryan O'Byrne
113 Corey Locke
123 Danny Stewart
177 Christopher Heino-Lindberg
188 Mark Flood
217 Oskari Korpikari
241 Jimmy Bonneau
271 Jaroslav Halak

2002
Pick
14 Christopher Higgins
45 Tomas Linhart
99 Michael Lambert
182 Andre Deveaux
212 Jonathan Ferland
275 Konstantin Korneev

2001
Pick
7 Mike Komisarek
25 Alexander Perezhogin
37 Duncan Milroy
71 Tomas Plekanec
109 Martti Jarventie
171 Eric Himelfarb
203 Andrew Archer
266 Viktor Ujcik

2000
Pick
13 Ron Hainsey
16 Marcel Hossa
78 Jozef Balej
79 Tyler Hanchuck
109 Johan Eneqvist
114 Christian Larrivee
145 Ryan Glenn
172 Scott Selig
182 Petr Chvojka
243 Joni Puurula
275 Jonathan Gauthier

1999
Pick
39 Alexander Buturlin
58 Matt Carkner
97 Chris Dyment
107 Evan Lindsay
136 Dusty Jamieson
145 Marc-Andre Thinel
150 Matt Shasby
167 Sean Dixon
196 Vadim Tarasov
225 Mikko Hyytia
253 Jerome Marois

1998
Pick
16 Eric Chouinard
45 Mike Ribeiro
75 Francois Beauchemin
132 Andrei Bashkirov
152 Gordie Dwyer
162 Andrei Markov
189 Andrei Kruchinin
201 Craig Murray
216 Michael Ryder
247 Darcy Harris

1997
Pick
11 Jason Ward
37 Gregor Baumgartner
65 Ilkka Mikkola
91 Daniel Tetrault
118 Konstantin Sidulov
122 Gennady Razin
145 Jonathan Desroches
172 Ben Guite
197 Petr Kubos
202 Andrei Sidyakin
228 Jarl Espen Ygranes

1996
Pick
18 Matt Higgins
44 Mathieu Garon
71 Arron Asham
92 Kim Staal
99 Etienne Drapeau
127 Daniel Archambault
154 Brett Clark
181 Timo Vertala
207 Mattia Baldi
233 Michel Tremblay

1995
Pick
8 Terry Ryan
60 Miloslav Guren
74 Martin Hohenberger
86 Jonathan Delisle
112 Niklas Anger
138 Boyd Olson
164 Stephane Robidas
190 Greg Hart
216 Eric Houde

1994
Pick
18 Brad Brown
44 Jose Theodore
54 Chris Murray
70 Marko Kiprusoff
74 Martin Belanger
96 Arto Kuki
122 Jimmy Drolet
148 Joel Irving
174 Jessie Rezansoff
200 Peter Strom
226 Tomas Vokoun
252 Chris Aldous
278 Ross Parsons

1993
Pick
21 Saku Koivu
47 Rory Fitzpatrick
73 Sebastien Bordeleau
85 Adam Wiesel
99 Jean-Francois Houle
113 Jeff Lank
125 Dion Darling
151 Darcy Tucker
177 David Ruhly
203 Alan Letang
229 Alexandre Duchesne
255 Brian Larochelle
281 Russell Guzior

1992
Pick
20 David Wilkie
33 Valeri Bure
44 Keli Corpse
68 Craig Rivet
82 Louis Bernard
92 Marc Lamothe
116 Don Chase
140 Martin Sychra
164 Christian Proulx
188 Michael Burman
212 Earl Cronan
236 Trent Cavicchi
260 Hiroyuki Miura

1991
Pick
17 Brent Bilodeau
28 Jim Campbell
43 Craig Darby
61 Yves Sarault
73 Vladimir Vujtek
83 Sylvain Lapointe
100 Brad Layzell
105 Tony Prpic
127 Oleg Petrov
149 Brady Kramer
171 Brian Savage
193 Scott Fraser
215 Greg MacEachern
237 Paul Lepler
259 Dale Hooper

1990
Pick
12 Turner Stevenson
39 Ryan Kuwabara
58 Charles Poulin
60 Robert Guillet
81 Gilbert Dionne
102 Paul DiPietro
123 Craig Conroy
144 Stephen Rohr
165 Brent Fleetwood
186 Derek Maguire
207 Mark Kettelhut
228 John Uniac
249 Sergei Martynyuk

Coach

JULIEN, CLAUDE
Coach, Montreal Canadiens. Born in Blind River, Ont., April 23, 1960.

Claude Julien became head coach of the Montreal Canadiens on January 17, 2003. At the time, he was in his third season as head coach of the Hamilton Bulldogs, the Canadiens' affiliate team in the American Hockey League. In his first full season behind the bench in 2003-04, the Canadiens posted their best record in 10 years and reached the second round of the playoffs.

Julien started his coaching career at the helm of the Ottawa Senators of the Central Junior Hockey League in 1993-94. He later became an assistant coach with the Hull Olympiques of the QMJHL and was promoted to head coach in 1996-97, leading Hull to the Memorial Cup championship that year. Internationally, Julien earned a silver medal as assistant coach and a bronze medal as head coach at the World Junior Championships in 1999 and 2000.

Julien suited up for a total of 14 games as a player in the NHL with the Quebec Nordiques in 1984-85 and 1985-86. He had 40 goals and 206 assists in 409 games as a defenseman in the American Hockey League.

Coaching Record

		Regular Season				Playoffs		
Season	**Team**	**Games**	**W**	**L**	**T**	**Games**	**W**	**L**
1996-97	Hull (QMJHL)	70	48	19	3	14	12	2
1997-98	Hull (QMJHL)	70	32	37	1	11	6	5
1998-99	Hull (QMJHL)	70	23	38	9	23	15	8
1999-00	Hull (QMJHL)	72	42	24	6	15	9	6
2000-01	Hamilton (AHL)	80	28	46	6	....	....	....
2001-02	Hamilton (AHL)	80	37	33	10	15	10	5
2002-03	Hamilton (AHL)	45	33	9	3	....	....	....
2002-03	**Montreal (NHL)**	**36**	**12**	**21**	**3**	**....**	**....**	**....**
2003-04	**Montreal (NHL)**	**82**	**41**	**34**	**7**	**11**	**4**	**7**
	NHL Totals	**118**	**53**	**55**	**10**	**11**	**4**	**7**

Club Directory

Bell Centre

Bell Centre
1260 de La Gauchetière Street W.
Montréal, QC H3B 5E8
Phone: **514/932-2582**
Media Hotline: 514/989-2835
Fax Lines (all area code 514):
Communications 932-8285
Hockey 989-2717
Press Lounge 932-5258
Marketing 925-2145
Community Relations 925-2144
www.canadiens.com
Capacity: 21,273

Executive Management
Chairman and Governor . . . . . George N. Gillett, Jr.
Vice-Chairman . . . . . Jeff Joyce
President of Club de Hockey Canadien/ Bell Centre & Alternate Governor . . . . . Pierre Boivin
Assistant to the President & Alternate Governor . . . Foster Gillett
Administrative Assistant to the President . . . . . Lise Beaudry
Exec. VP Hockey, GM & Alternate Governor . . . . . Bob Gainey
Chief Financial Officer & Alternate Governor . . . . . Fred Steer
Vice-President, Marketing and Sales . . . . . Ray Lalonde
Vice-President, Communications and Community Relations . . . . . Donald Beauchamp
Vice-President, Operations, Bell Centre . . . . . Alain Gauthier
President, Gillett Entertainment Group . . . . . Aldo Giampaolo

Hockey
Assistant General Manager . . . . . André Savard
Director of Hockey Operations & Legal Affairs . . . . . Julien BriseBois
Director of Player Personnel . . . . . Trevor Timmins
Director of Professional Scouting . . . . . Pierre Gauthier
Head Coach . . . . . Claude Julien
Assistant Coaches . . . . . Roland Melanson, Rick Green
Professional Scouts . . . . . Gordie Roberts, Richard Green
Amateur Scouting Coordinator . . . . . Pierre Dorion
Scouting Staff . . . . . Patrick Allvin, Elmer Benning, William A. Berglund, Hannu Laine, Dave Mayville, Trent McCleary, Antonin Routa, Craig Sarner, Nikolai Vakourov
Team Services & Hockey Administration Manager . . Claudine Crépin
Administrative Assistant to the General Manager . . Suzanne Charlebois

Medical and Training Staff
Club Physician and Chief Surgeon . . . . . Dr. David Mulder
Consultant Orthopedic Surgeon . . . . . Dr. Eric Lenczner
Dentist . . . . . Dr. Pierre Desautels
Consultant Ophthalmologist . . . . . Dr. John Little
Consultant Sports Medicine . . . . . Dr. Vincent Lacroix
Head Athletic Therapist . . . . . Graham Rynbend
Assistant to the Athletic Therapist . . . . . Jodi van Rees
Strength & Conditioning Coordinator . . . . . Scott Livingston
Video Supervisor . . . . . Mario Leblanc
Equipment Manager . . . . . Pierre Gervais
Assistants to the Equipment Manager . . . . . Robert Boulanger, Pierre Ouellette
Visiting Team Coordinator . . . . . Richard Généreux

Communications
Director of Media Relations . . . . . Dominick Saillant
Administrative Assistant to VP Communications . . . Sylvie Lambert
Communications Coordinator . . . . . Frédéric Daigle

Community Relations
President, Canadiens Alumni . . . . . Réjean Houle
CEO, Canadiens Children's Foundation . . . . . Robert Sirois
Manager of Community Relations . . . . . Frédérique Cardinal
Community Relations Coordinator . . . . . Geneviève Paquette
Coordinators, Canadiens Children's Foundation . . . Normande Herget, Francoise Archambault

Marketing and Sales
Executive Director, Premium Sales & Services . . . . . Richard Primeau
Group Manager, Marketing . . . . . Paul-André Côté
Group Manager, Game Day Sales & Promotions . . . Vincent Lucier
Administrative Asst, to VP, Marketing & Sales . . . . . Danielle Laporte
Manager, Game Presentation . . . . . Chantal Bunnett
Manager, Internet Services . . . . . Jon Trzcienski
Manager, Editorial . . . . . Carl Lavigne
Manager, Group Sales . . . . . Pierre Constant
Manager, Sponsor Promotions . . . . . Marc Fisher
Manager, Fan Development . . . . . Matt Zalkowitz
Team Photographer . . . . . Bob Fisher
Photography Coordinator . . . . . Marie-Christine Boucher

Advertising and Sponsorship Sales
EFFIX Inc. . . . . . François-Xavier Seigneur

Ticket Sales and Building Operations
Director of Ticket Office . . . . . Cathy D'Ascoli
Assistant Director of Ticket Office . . . . . Lucie Masse
Director of Building Operations . . . . . Xavier Luydlin
Administrative Assistant to the VP Operations . . . . . Maryse Cartwright

Finance
Executive Director, Finance . . . . . Jacques Aubé
Controller, Budgeting & Analysis . . . . . Dennis McKinley
Director of Information Technology . . . . . Pierre-Éric Belzile
Administrative Assistant, Chief Financial Officer . . . Christine Ouellette

AHL Affiliation
Hamilton Bulldogs . . . . . www.hamiltonbulldogs.com
Arena . . . . . Copps Coliseum, 85 York Blvd. Hamilton, ONT, L8R 3L4 905/529-8500
Chairman of Board & Governor . . . . . Michael Andlauer
General Manager & Alternate Governor . . . . . André Savard
Head Coach . . . . . Doug Jarvis
Assistant Coach . . . . . Ron Wilson
Equipment Manager . . . . . Patrick Langlois
Assistant to the Equipment Manager . . . . . Stéphane Gauthier
Head Athletic Therapist . . . . . Luc Leblanc
Director of Communications . . . . . Craig Downey
Broadcast Rightsholders
Radio/TV Flagship Stations . . . . . RDS (Cable 33), CKAC (730 AM), CJAD (800 AM)
Play-by-play – Radio/TV . . . . . Pierre Houde (RDS), Martin McGuire (CKAC), Rick Moffat (CJAD)
Colormen – Radio/TV . . . . . Yvon Pedneault (RDS), Dany Dubé (CKAC), Murray Wilson (CJAD)

Nashville Predators

2003-04 Results: 38w-29L-11T-4OTL 91PTS.
Third, Central Division

2004-05 Schedule

Oct.	Thu.	14	Minnesota
	Sat.	16	St. Louis
	Wed.	20	at Dallas
	Thu.	21	San Jose
	Sat.	23	Anaheim
	Wed.	27	at Tampa Bay
	Fri.	29	at Florida
	Sat.	30	Detroit
Nov.	Tue.	2	at Calgary
	Thu.	4	at Edmonton
	Fri.	5	at Vancouver
	Mon.	8	at NY Rangers
	Wed.	10	at New Jersey
	Thu.	11	at NY Islanders
	Sat.	13	Colorado
	Tue.	16	Los Angeles
	Thu.	18	at Calgary
	Fri.	19	at Vancouver
	Mon.	22	at Edmonton
	Thu.	25	Edmonton
	Sat.	27	San Jose
	Tue.	30	Vancouver
Dec.	Thu.	2	at Chicago
	Sat.	4	Atlanta
	Tue.	7	Philadelphia
	Wed.	8	at St. Louis
	Sat.	11	Colorado
	Wed.	15	at Anaheim
	Thu.	16	at Los Angeles
	Sat.	18	at San Jose
	Tue.	21	Ottawa
	Thu.	23	Anaheim
	Sun.	26	Dallas
	Tue.	28	Chicago
	Thu.	30	Toronto
Jan.	Sat.	1	Los Angeles*
	Mon.	3	at Washington
	Wed.	5	at Detroit
	Thu.	6	Calgary
	Sat.	8	Carolina
	Mon.	10	St. Louis

	Wed.	12	at Atlanta
	Thu.	13	at Detroit
	Sat.	15	Columbus
	Mon.	17	Montreal*
	Wed.	19	at Dallas
	Thu.	20	at Chicago
	Sat.	22	at Minnesota
	Tue.	25	at Phoenix
	Wed.	26	at Anaheim
	Sat.	29	at Los Angeles*
	Sun.	30	at San Jose*
Feb.	Thu.	3	Phoenix
	Sat.	5	Minnesota
	Tue.	8	Chicago
	Thu.	10	at Columbus
	Tue.	15	at St. Louis
	Fri.	18	at Chicago
	Sun.	20	New Jersey*
	Wed.	23	at Columbus
	Fri.	25	Vancouver
	Sun.	27	Detroit*
Mar.	Wed.	2	at Colorado
	Fri.	4	at Columbus
	Sun.	6	Edmonton*
	Tue.	8	Calgary
	Thu.	10	Phoenix
	Sat.	12	Dallas
	Mon.	14	Columbus
	Wed.	16	at Detroit
	Thu.	17	at Boston
	Sat.	19	at Buffalo
	Tue.	22	Pittsburgh
	Thu.	24	Florida
	Sat.	26	Chicago*
	Tue.	29	at Minnesota
	Thu.	31	Detroit
Apr.	Sat.	2	St. Louis*
	Sun.	3	at St. Louis*
	Tue.	5	Columbus
	Fri.	8	at Colorado
	Sun.	10	at Phoenix*

* Denotes afternoon game.

Year-by-Year Record

Season	GP	Home				Road				Overall				GF	GA	Pts.	Finished	Playoff Result
		W	L	T	OL	W	L	T	OL	W	L	T	OL					
2003-04	82	22	10	7	2	16	19	4	2	38	29	11	4	216	217	91	3rd, Central Div.	Lost Conf. Quarter-Final
2002-03	82	18	17	5	1	9	18	8	6	27	35	13	7	183	206	74	4th, Central Div.	Out of Playoffs
2001-02	82	17	16	8	0	11	25	5	0	28	41	13	0	196	230	69	4th, Central Div.	Out of Playoffs
2000-01	82	16	18	7	0	18	18	2	3	34	36	9	3	186	200	80	3rd, Central Div.	Out of Playoffs
1999-2000	82	15	21	3	2	13	19	4	5	28	40	7	7	199	240	70	4th, Central Div.	Out of Playoffs
1998-99	82	15	22	4	...	13	25	3	...	28	47	7	...	190	261	63	4th, Central Div.	Out of Playoffs

Steve Sullivan had 30 points (nine goals, 21 assists) in just 24 games after being dealt to Nashville as he helped the Predators reach the playoffs for the first time in franchise history.

Franchise date: June 25, 1997

CENTRAL DIVISION

7th NHL Season

2004-05 Player Personnel

FORWARDS	HT	WT	S	Place of Birth	Date	2003-04 Club
ARKHIPOV, Denis	6-3	214	L	Kazan, USSR	5/19/79	Nashville
ERAT, Martin	6-0	195	L	Trebic, Czech.	8/29/81	Nashville
FIDDLER, Vernon	5-11	197	L	Edmonton, Alta.	5/9/80	Nashville-Milwaukee
HALL, Adam	6-3	205	R	Kalamazoo, MI	8/14/80	Nashville
HARTNELL, Scott	6-2	205	L	Regina, Sask.	4/18/82	Nashville
HAYDAR, Darren	5-9	170	L	Toronto, Ont.	10/22/79	Milwaukee
HRKAC, Tony	5-10	190	L	Thunder Bay, Ont.	7/7/66	Milwaukee
JOHNSON, Greg	5-11	200	L	Thunder Bay, Ont.	3/16/71	Nashville
LEGWAND, David	6-2	190	L	Detroit, MI	8/17/80	Nashville
McKENZIE, Jim	6-4	230	L	Gull Lake, Sask.	11/3/69	Nashville
ORSZAGH, Vladimir	5-11	195	L	Banska Bystrica, Czech.	5/24/77	Nashville
PIVKO, Libor	6-2	205	L	Novy Vicin, Czech.	3/29/80	Nashville-Milwaukee
SEGAL, Brandon	6-3	214	R	Richmond, B.C.	7/12/83	Milwaukee
SEVERSON, Cam	6-1	215	L	Canora, Sask.	1/15/78	Anaheim-Cincinnati (AHL)
SHISHKANOV, Timofei	6-1	213	R	Moscow, USSR	6/10/83	Nashville-Milwaukee
SMITH, Wyatt	5-11	200	L	Thief River Falls, MN	2/13/77	Nashville-Milwaukee
SMITHSON, Jerred	6-2	197	R	Vernon, B.C.	2/4/79	Los Angeles-Manchester
STEVENSON, Jeremy	6-1	215	L	San Bernardino, CA	7/28/74	Minnesota-Nashville
SULLIVAN, Steve	5-9	155	R	Timmins, Ont.	7/6/74	Chicago-Nashville
TOOTOO, Jordin	5-9	195	R	Churchill, Man.	2/2/83	Nashville
UPSHALL, Scottie	6-0	187	L	Fort McMurray, Alta.	10/7/83	Nashville-Milwaukee
WALKER, Scott	5-10	196	R	Cambridge, Ont.	7/19/73	Nashville
YABLONSKI, Jeremy	6-0	232	R	Meadow Lake, Sask.	3/21/80	StL-Peoria-Wor-Milwaukee
DEFENSEMEN						
ALLISON, Jamie	6-1	200	L	Lindsay, Ont.	5/13/75	Nashville
EATON, Mark	6-2	208	L	Wilmington, DE	5/6/77	Nashville
HAMHUIS, Dan	6-0	205	L	Smithers, B.C.	12/13/82	Nashville
HNIDY, Shane	6-2	204	R	Neepawa, Man.	11/8/75	Ottawa-Nashville
HUTCHINSON, Andrew	6-2	204	R	Evanston, IL	3/24/80	Nashville-Milwaukee
LILJA, Andreas	6-3	228	L	Landskrona, Sweden	7/13/75	Florida
MUKHACHEV, Andrei	6-3	196	L	Sverdlovsk, USSR	7/21/80	CSKA Moscow
TIMONEN, Kimmo	5-10	196	L	Kuopio, Finland	3/18/75	Nashville
ZANON, Greg	5-11	190	L	Burnaby, B.C.	6/5/80	Milwaukee
ZIDLICKY, Marek	5-11	187	R	Most, Czech.	2/3/77	Nashville

GOALTENDERS	HT	WT	C	Place of Birth	Date	2003-04 Club
FINLEY, Brian	6-3	205	R	Sault Ste. Marie, Ont.	7/13/81	Milwaukee
MASON, Chris	6-0	195	L	Red Deer, Alta.	4/20/76	Nashville-Milwaukee
VOKOUN, Tomas	6-0	195	R	Karlovy Vary, Czech.	7/2/76	Nashville

Vice President and General Manager

POILE, DAVID
Executive Vice President/General Manager, Nashville Predators.
Born in Toronto, Ont., February 14, 1949.

Since joining the Predators as general manager on July 9, 1997, David Poile has made a commitment to building for the future, surrounding himself with one of the youngest and most talented staffs in the National Hockey League. In 2003-04, Nashville reached the playoffs for the first time in franchise history. Poile has an impressive reputation as an NHL leader and in 2001 he received the Lester Patrick Trophy for his contributions to hockey in the United States. His father, Norman "Bud" Poile, had won the honor in 1989.

Prior to joining Nashville, Poile spent 15 seasons as vice president/general manager of the Washington Capitals. During his tenure in Washington, the Capitals made 14 postseason appearances, winning their only Patrick Division title in 1989 and advancing to the Conference Finals in 1990. During Poile's 15 years in Washington, the Capitals compiled a record of 594-454-132, finished second in the Patrick Division seven times and recorded 90-or-more points seven different seasons.

Poile started his professional hockey career as an administrative assistant for the Atlanta Flames in 1972, shortly after graduating from Northeastern University in Boston. At Northeastern, he was hockey team captain, leading scorer and most valuable player for two years.

In 1977, he was named assistant general manager of the Atlanta Flames (who moved to Calgary in 1980), serving as the manager and coordinator of the Flames farm club.

Poile is a member of the NHL's general managers committee and was instrumental in the NHL's adoption of the instant replay rule in 1991. He was awarded *Inside Hockey*'s man of the year for his leadership on the issue. He was also twice honored as *The Sporting News* NHL executive of the year following the 1982-83 and 1983-84 seasons. Poile served as general manager of the 1998 and 1999 U.S. national team for the World Championships.

Poile was introduced to hockey by watching his father play seven seasons in the NHL. Bud Poile later became general manager for the Vancouver Canucks and the Philadelphia Flyers, both NHL expansion franchises at the time. He was inducted into the Hockey Hall of Fame in 1990.

2003-04 Scoring

* - rookie

Regular Season

Pos	#	Player	Team	GP	G	A	Pts	+/–	PIM	PP	SH	GW	GT	S	%
R	26	Steve Sullivan	CHI	56	15	28	43	–7	36	4	2	4	0	140	10.7
			NSH	24	9	21	30	8	12	7	0	0	0	78	11.5
			TOTAL	80	24	49	73	1	48	11	2	4	0	218	11.0
R	24	Scott Walker	NSH	75	25	42	67	4	94	9	3	3	0	157	15.9
D	3	Marek Zidlicky	NSH	82	14	39	53	–16	82	9	0	4	0	143	9.8
L	10	Martin Erat	NSH	76	16	33	49	10	38	4	0	2	1	137	11.7
C	11	David Legwand	NSH	82	18	29	47	9	46	5	1	5	0	165	10.9
D	44	Kimmo Timonen	NSH	77	12	32	44	–7	52	8	0	1	0	180	6.7
R	33	Vladimir Orszagh	NSH	82	16	21	37	–4	74	2	2	3	0	124	12.9
L	17	Scott Hartnell	NSH	59	18	15	33	–5	87	5	0	3	0	154	11.7
C	22	Greg Johnson	NSH	82	14	18	32	–21	33	1	4	4	0	100	14.0
C	9	Sergei Zholtok	MIN	59	13	16	29	4	19	3	0	3	1	115	11.3
			NSH	11	1	1	2	–2	0	0	0	0	0	17	5.9
			TOTAL	70	14	17	31	2	19	3	0	3	1	132	10.6
R	18	Adam Hall	NSH	79	13	14	27	–8	37	6	0	1	1	151	8.6
L	21	Andreas Johansson	NSH	47	12	15	27	–2	26	3	1	1	0	108	11.1
D	2 *	Dan Hamhuis	NSH	80	7	19	26	–12	57	2	0	4	0	115	6.1
C	25	Denis Arkhipov	NSH	72	9	12	21	–2	22	3	0	3	0	91	9.9
C	15	Rem Murray	NSH	39	8	9	17	–1	12	0	2	1	0	58	13.8
D	27	Jason York	NSH	67	2	13	15	–4	64	0	0	1	0	80	2.5
D	4	Mark Eaton	NSH	75	4	9	13	16	26	0	0	1	0	82	4.9
L	28	Jeremy Stevenson	MIN	3	0	0	0	–1	2	0	0	0	0	5	0.0
			NSH	53	5	4	9	–2	103	3	0	0	0	62	8.1
			TOTAL	56	5	4	9	–3	105	3	0	0	0	67	7.5
D	42 *	Andrew Hutchinson	NSH	18	4	4	8	1	4	2	0	1	0	24	16.7
R	55 *	Jordin Tootoo	NSH	70	4	4	8	–6	137	2	0	0	0	92	4.3
D	34	Shane Hnidy	OTT	37	0	5	5	2	72	0	0	0	0	16	0.0
			NSH	9	0	2	2	3	10	0	0	0	0	12	0.0
			TOTAL	46	0	7	7	5	82	0	0	0	0	28	0.0
C	46	Wyatt Smith	NSH	18	3	1	4	2	2	0	1	0	0	21	14.3
L	19	Jim Mckenzie	NSH	61	1	3	4	–13	88	0	0	0	0	10	10.0
C	45	Jason Morgan	CGY	13	0	2	2	1	2	0	0	0	0	14	0.0
			NSH	6	0	2	2	0	2	0	0	0	0	6	0.0
			TOTAL	19	0	4	4	1	4	0	0	0	0	20	0.0
D	5	Brad Bombardir	MIN	56	1	2	3	–10	21	0	0	1	0	38	2.6
			NSH	13	0	0	0	1	4	0	0	0	0	9	0.0
			TOTAL	69	1	2	3	–9	25	0	0	1	0	47	2.1
D	36 *	Robert Schnabel	NSH	20	0	3	3	6	34	0	0	0	0	10	0.0
D	23	Jamie Allison	NSH	47	0	3	3	–7	76	0	0	0	0	19	0.0
L	20 *	Simon Gamache	ATL	2	0	1	1	0	0	0	0	0	0	1	0.0
			NSH	7	1	0	1	–3	0	1	0	0	0	4	25.0
			TOTAL	9	1	1	2	–3	0	1	0	0	0	5	20.0
D	6	Stan Neckar	NSH	1	0	1	1	2	0	0	0	0	0	0	0.0
R	7 *	Scottie Upshall	NSH	7	0	1	1	–2	0	0	0	0	0	6	0.0
D	40 *	Michael Farrell	NSH	1	0	0	0	0	0	0	0	0	0	0	0.0
L	47 *	Libor Pivko	NSH	1	0	0	0	0	0	0	0	0	0	2	0.0
L	32	Mathieu Darche	NSH	2	0	0	0	–1	0	0	0	0	0	1	0.0
R	16 *	Timofei Shishkanov	NSH	2	0	0	0	–1	0	0	0	0	0	0	0.0
C	38 *	Vernon Fiddler	NSH	17	0	0	0	–6	23	0	0	0	0	8	0.0

Goaltending

No.	Goaltender	GPI	Mins	Avg	W	L	T	EN	SO	GA	SA	S%	G	A	PIM
30	Chris Mason	17	744	2.18	4	4	1	3	1	27	365	.926	0	0	4
29	Tomas Vokoun	73	4221	2.53	34	29	10	9	3	178	1958	.909	0	2	35
	Totals	**82**	**4999**	**2.60**	**38**	**33**	**11**	**12**	**4**	**217**	**2335**	**.907**			

Playoffs

Pos	#	Player	Team	GP	G	A	Pts	+/–	PIM	PP	SH	GW	GT	S	%
R	18	Adam Hall	NSH	6	2	1	3	3	2	0	0	1	0	13	15.4
C	22	Greg Johnson	NSH	6	1	2	3	4	0	0	0	0	0	7	14.3
L	17	Scott Hartnell	NSH	6	1	2	3	3	2	0	0	0	0	11	9.1
D	27	Jason York	NSH	6	0	3	3	2	4	0	0	0	0	9	0.0
R	33	Vladimir Orszagh	NSH	6	2	0	2	–2	4	0	0	0	0	5	40.0
R	26	Steve Sullivan	NSH	6	1	1	2	–4	6	0	0	1	0	13	7.7
D	2 *	Dan Hamhuis	NSH	6	0	2	2	–2	6	0	0	0	0	4	0.0
C	9	Sergei Zholtok	NSH	6	1	0	1	–3	0	1	0	0	0	6	16.7
C	11	David Legwand	NSH	6	1	0	1	1	8	0	1	0	0	8	12.5
D	5	Brad Bombardir	NSH	6	0	1	1	1	2	0	0	0	0	3	0.0
R	24	Scott Walker	NSH	6	0	1	1	–3	6	0	0	0	0	14	0.0
L	10	Martin Erat	NSH	6	0	1	1	–2	6	0	0	0	0	6	0.0
L	19	Jim McKenzie	NSH	1	0	0	0	0	0	0	0	0	0	0	0.0
D	3	Marek Zidlicky	NSH	1	0	0	0	0	0	0	0	0	0	0	0.0
D	34	Shane Hnidy	NSH	5	0	0	0	0	6	0	0	0	0	4	0.0
R	55 *	Jordin Tootoo	NSH	5	0	0	0	0	4	0	0	0	0	2	0.0
L	21	Andreas Johansson	NSH	6	0	0	0	–3	0	0	0	0	0	5	0.0
L	28	Jeremy Stevenson	NSH	6	0	0	0	–1	8	0	0	0	0	3	0.0
D	44	Kimmo Timonen	NSH	6	0	0	0	–3	10	0	0	0	0	9	0.0
D	4	Mark Eaton	NSH	6	0	0	0	–2	2	0	0	0	0	6	0.0

Goaltending

No.	Goaltender	GPI	Mins	Avg	W	L	EN	SO	GA	SA	S%	G	A	PIM
29	Tomas Vokoun	6	356	2.02	2	4	0	1	12	197	.939	0	0	0
	Totals	**6**	**360**	**2.00**	**2**	**4**	**0**	**1**	**12**	**197**	**.939**			

Club Records

Team

(Figures in brackets for season records are games played; records for fewest points, wins, ties, losses, goals, goals against are for 70 or more games)

Most Points	91	2003-04 (82)
Most Wins	38	2003-04 (82)
Most Ties	13	2001-02 (82), 2002-03 (82)
Most Losses	47	1998-99 (82)
Most Goals	216	2003-04 (82)
Most Goals Against	261	1998-99 (82)
Fewest Points	63	1998-99 (82)
Fewest Wins	27	2002-03 (82)
Fewest Ties	7	1998-99 (82) 1999-2000 (82)
Fewest Losses	29	2003-04 (82)
Fewest Goals	183	2002-03 (82)
Fewest Goals Against	200	2000-01 (82)

Longest Winning Streak
Overall.................6 — Nov. 11-Dec. 4/03
Home....................7 — Feb. 13-Mar. 1/03
Away....................4 — Nov. 11-Dec. 4/03, Mar. 20-Apr. 4/04

Longest Undefeated Streak
Overall.................8 — Dec. 18/99-Jan. 1/00 (5 wins, 3 ties)
Home...................11 — Twice
Away....................4 — Twice

Longest Losing Streak
Overall.................7 — Nov. 20-Dec. 2/99
Home....................6 — Jan. 21-Feb. 15/99, Feb. 26-Mar. 21/02 Five times
Away....................5

Longest Winless Streak
Overall................15 — Mar. 10-Apr. 6/03 (12 losses (2 in OT), 3 ties)
Home....................9 — Jan. 21-Mar. 2/99 (8 losses, 1 tie)
Away....................9 — Three times
Most Shutouts, Season...6 — 2000-01 (82)
Most PIM, Season...1,420 — 1998-99 (82)
Most Goals, Game........9 — Mar. 4/04 (Nsh. 9 at Pit. 4)

Individual

Most Seasons	6	Many players
Most Games	434	Greg Johnson
Most Goals, Career	91	Scott Walker
Most Assists, Career	145	Cliff Ronning
Most Points, Career	231	Scott Walker (91G, 140A)
Most PIM, Career	429	Scott Walker
Most Shutouts, Career	12	Tomas Vokoun

Longest Consecutive Games Streak..........269 — Karlis Skrastins (Feb. 21/00-Apr. 6/03)
Most Goals, Season......26 — Cliff Ronning (1999-2000)
Most Assists, Season....43 — Cliff Ronning (2000-01)
Most Points, Season.....67 — Scott Walker (2003-04; 25G, 42A)

Most PIM, Season	242	Patrick Cote (1999-2000)
Most Points, Defenseman, Season	53	Marek Zidlicky (2003-04; 14G, 39A)
Most Points, Center, Season	62	Cliff Ronning (1999-2000; 26G, 36A) (2000-01; 19G, 43A)
Most Points, Right Wing, Season	67	Scott Walker (2003-04; 25G, 42A)
Most Points, Left Wing, Season	49	Martin Erat (2003-04; 16G, 33A)
Most Points, Rookie, Season	53	Marek Zidlicky (2003-04; 14G, 39A)
Most Shutouts, Season	4	Mike Dunham (2000-01)
Most Goals, Game	3	Seven times
Most Assists, Game	5	Mark Zidlicky (Feb. 18/04)
Most Points, Game	5	Mark Zidlicky (Feb. 18/04; 5A), Dan Hamhuis (Mar. 4/04; 1G-4A)

General Managers' History

David Poile, 1998-99 to date.

Coaching History

Barry Trotz, 1998-99 to date.

Captains' History

Tom Fitzgerald, 1998-99 to 2001-02;
Greg Johnson, 2002-03 to date.

All-time Record vs. Other Clubs

Regular Season

	At Home								On Road								Total							
	GP	W	L	T	OL	GF	GA	PTS	GP	W	L	T	OL	GF	GA	PTS	GP	W	L	T	OL	GF	GA	PTS
Anaheim	12	5	4	2	1	24	28	13	12	3	8	0	1	20	33	7	24	8	12	2	2	44	61	20
Atlanta	3	1	0	0	0	12	6	4	4	1	2	1	0	10	12	3	7	3	1	3	0	22	18	7
Boston	6	2	4	0	0	13	16	4	5	2	2	1	0	9	14	5	11	4	6	1	0	22	30	9
Buffalo	5	2	2	0	1	10	9	5	4	3	0	1	0	16	9	7	9	5	2	1	1	26	18	12
Calgary	13	8	4	1	0	39	25	17	12	3	4	3	2	26	35	11	25	11	8	4	2	65	60	28
Carolina	4	3	1	0	0	9	7	6	5	2	2	1	0	13	14	5	9	5	3	1	0	22	21	11
Chicago	16	7	6	3	0	48	43	17	17	6	10	1	0	39	49	13	33	13	16	4	0	87	92	30
Colorado	12	3	6	3	0	36	45	9	12	4	5	2	1	24	32	11	24	7	11	5	1	60	77	20
Columbus	11	7	2	1	1	29	24	16	10	5	5	0	0	27	23	10	21	12	7	1	1	56	47	26
Dallas	12	6	5	1	0	28	23	13	12	2	9	0	1	14	36	5	24	8	14	1	1	42	59	18
Detroit	16	7	7	2	0	40	45	16	17	2	11	2	2	38	69	8	33	9	18	4	2	78	114	24
Edmonton	13	4	6	3	0	32	37	11	12	6	5	0	1	34	36	13	25	10	11	3	1	66	73	24
Florida	5	1	2	2	0	8	10	4	4	1	2	1	0	8	11	3	9	2	4	3	0	16	21	7
Los Angeles	12	1	8	3	0	16	31	5	12	5	5	0	2	28	36	12	24	6	13	3	2	44	67	17
Minnesota	8	5	1	2	0	21	11	12	8	2	3	3	0	18	20	7	16	7	4	5	0	39	31	19
Montreal	4	2	1	1	0	14	7	5	4	0	3	0	1	9	15	1	8	2	4	1	1	23	22	6
New Jersey	5	1	4	0	0	9	14	2	5	3	1	0	1	14	15	7	10	4	5	0	1	23	29	9
NY Islanders	5	3	2	0	0	14	16	6	4	2	1	0	1	12	11	5	9	5	3	0	1	26	27	11
NY Rangers	4	2	2	0	0	13	14	4	6	3	2	1	0	15	18	7	10	5	4	1	0	28	32	11
Ottawa	4	2	2	0	0	8	11	4	3	1	4	0	0	7	15	2	7	3	6	0	0	15	26	6
Philadelphia	4	0	2	2	0	4	7	2	5	2	2	1	0	9	17	5	9	2	4	3	0	13	24	7
Phoenix	12	5	5	2	0	32	34	12	12	5	6	0	1	35	33	11	24	10	11	2	1	67	67	23
Pittsburgh	6	4	2	0	0	21	10	8	5	2	1	0	2	17	14	6	11	6	3	0	2	38	24	14
St. Louis	17	5	9	3	0	35	46	13	16	3	10	1	2	23	53	9	33	8	19	4	2	58	99	22
San Jose	12	5	6	1	0	29	34	11	12	4	5	1	2	31	30	11	24	9	11	2	2	60	64	22
Tampa Bay	6	2	4	0	0	12	16	4	4	1	1	2	0	10	13	4	10	3	5	2	0	22	27	8
Toronto	1	1	0	0	0	3	2	2	4	0	3	0	1	18	13	7	4	2	3	0	1	21	15	9
Vancouver	13	5	5	1	2	35	40	13	12	2	9	1	0	28	48	5	25	7	14	2	2	63	88	18
Washington	5	3	1	1	0	16	11	7	4	1	3	0	0	8	10	2	9	4	4	1	0	24	21	9
Totals	**246**	**103**	**104**	**34**	**5**	**610**	**622**	**245**	**246**	**80**	**124**	**26**	**16**	**560**	**732**	**202**	**492**	**183**	**228**	**60**	**21**	**1170**	**1354**	**447**

Playoffs

	Series	W	L	GP	W	L	T	GF	GA	Last Mtg.	Rnd.	Result
Detroit	1	0	1	6	2	4	0	9	12	2004	CQF	L 2-4
Totals	**1**	**0**	**1**	**6**	**2**	**4**	**0**	**9**	**12**			

Playoff Results 2004-2000

Year	Round	Opponent	Result	GF	GA
2004	CQF	Detroit	L 2-4	9	12

Abbreviations: Round: CQF - conference quarter-final.

2003-04 Results

Oct.	9	Anaheim	3-1		10	St. Louis	3-1
	11	Dallas	1-3		12	at Minnesota	3-3
	16	St. Louis	4-1		13	Los Angeles	0-0
	18	Columbus	3-2		15	Phoenix	4-3
	19	at Chicago	1-3		17	Edmonton	2-1
	23	at Atlanta	2-4		19	Minnesota	2-0
	25	Colorado	3-5		22	at Calgary	0-4
	28	at St. Louis	0-1		24	at Edmonton	4-3
	30	Detroit	5-3		25	at Vancouver	1-4
Nov.	1	Dallas	1-1		29	at Columbus	6-4
	2	at Dallas	3-7		31	San Jose	3-2*
	5	Vancouver	3-4	**Feb.**	3	Detroit	1-4
	7	Chicago	1-2		5	Tampa Bay	2-5
	8	at Detroit	4-3		11	at Chicago	2-5
	13	Calgary	4-1		13	Washington	5-2
	15	NY Islanders	4-3		15	Edmonton	2-2
	19	at Los Angeles	0-3		16	at Columbus	2-4
	21	at Anaheim	4-3*		18	San Jose	7-3
	22	at San Jose	1-3		20	at Anaheim	3-2*
	24	at Colorado	3-2		21	at Phoenix	8-2
	26	Columbus	2-5		23	at Los Angeles	0-3
	28	at Boston	2-1		26	Minnesota	4-0
	29	Buffalo	4-1		28	NY Rangers	2-1*
Dec.	3	at Carolina	2-1*	**Mar.**	1	Chicago	2-2
	4	at Columbus	2-4		2	at Philadelphia	2-5
	6	at St. Louis	1-4		4	at Pittsburgh	9-4
	11	Los Angeles	1-4		6	at Ottawa	2-4
	13	Florida	2-2		9	Boston	2-3
	16	Vancouver	1-2*		11	at St. Louis	1-1
	18	at Montreal	4-5*		13	Calgary	4-4
	20	Detroit	1-0		14	at Detroit	2-3*
	22	Phoenix	3-3		16	at Vancouver	2-2
	23	at Minnesota	3-3		19	at Edmonton	4-5
	26	at Dallas	1-2		20	at Calgary	3-1
	27	at Phoenix	3-1		23	Anaheim	1-4
	29	at San Jose	2-5		25	at NY Rangers	2-1*
Jan.	1	Pittsburgh	3-2		27	Columbus	2-3*
	3	New Jersey	3-2		30	Chicago	5-2
	5	at Detroit	0-6	**Apr.**	1	at Chicago	3-1
	6	at Toronto	1-2		3	St. Louis	1-4
	8	Colorado	4-3*		4	at Colorado	2-1*

* – Overtime

Entry Draft
Selections 2004-1998

2004
Pick
15	Alexander Radulov
81	Vaclav Meidl
107	Nick Fugere
139	Kyle Moir
147	Janne Niskala
178	Michael Santorelli
193	Kevin Schaeffer
209	Stanislav Balan
243	Denis Kulyash
258	Pekka Rinne
275	Craig Switzer

2003
Pick
7	Ryan Suter
35	Konstantin Glazachev
37	Kevin Klein
49	Shea Weber
76	Richard Stehlik
89	Paul Brown
92	Alexander Sulzer
98	Grigory Shafigulin
117	Teemu Lassila
133	Rustam Sidikov
210	Andrei Mukhachev
213	Miroslav Hanuljak
268	Lauris Darzins

2002
Pick
6	Scottie Upshall
102	Brandon Segal
138	Patrick Jarrett
172	Mike McKenna
203	Josh Morrow
235	Kaleb Betts
264	Matt Davis
266	Steve Spencer

2001
Pick
12	Dan Hamhuis
33	Timofei Shishkanov
42	Tomas Slovak
75	Denis Platonov
76	Oliver Setzinger
98	Jordin Tootoo
178	Anton Lavrentiev
240	Gustav Grasberg
271	Mikko Lehtonen

2000
Pick
6	Scott Hartnell
36	Daniel Widing
72	Mattias Nilsson
89	Libor Pivko
131	Matt Hendricks
137	Mike Stuart
154	Matt Koalska
173	Tomas Harant
197	Zbynek Irgl
203	Jure Penko
236	Mats Christeen
284	Martin Hohener

1999
Pick
6	Brian Finley
33	Jonas Andersson
52	Adam Hall
54	Andrew Hutchinson
61	Ed Hill
65	Jan Lasak
72	Brett Angel
121	Yevgeny Pavlov
124	Alexandre Krevsun
131	Konstantin Panov
162	Timo Helbling
191	Martin Erat
205	Kyle Kettles
220	Miroslav Durak
248	Darren Haydar

1998
Pick
2	David Legwand
60	Denis Arkhipov
85	Geoff Koch
88	Kent Sauer
138	Martin Beauchesne
147	Craig Brunel
202	Martin Bartek
230	Karlis Skrastins

Coach

TROTZ, BARRY
Coach, Nashville Predators. Born in Winnipeg, Man., July 15, 1962.

Barry Trotz realized his dream of becoming an NHL head coach on August 6, 1997, after serving four seasons as head coach and director of hockey operations for the American Hockey League's Portland Pirates. He and assistant Paul Gardner spent the 1997-98 season scouting in preparation for the inaugural season of the Predators. In his sixth season behind the bench in 2003-04, Trotz led Nashville into the playoffs for the first time.

Trotz began his coaching career in 1984 as assistant coach with the University of Manitoba for one season, before serving two seasons as the head coach and general manager of the Dauphin Kings Junior Hockey Club from 1985 to 1987. He became head coach of the University of Manitoba during the 1987 season and also served as a scout for the Spokane Chiefs of the Western Hockey League that season. Trotz joined the Washington Capitals organization as their chief western scout during the 1988 season. The Winnipeg, Manitoba native was appointed an assistant coach of the Capitals' American Hockey League affiliate in Baltimore prior to the 1991 season before being named head coach prior to the 1992 season. When the franchise relocated to Portland, he guided the Pirates to two AHL Calder Cup Final appearances in the club's first four seasons. He led the Pirates to a league-best 43-27-10 record, captured the Calder Cup championship and was named the American Hockey League coach of the year following the 1994-95 season.

In 1995, Trotz guided Portland to a new North American professional hockey league record 17-game unbeaten streak (14-0-3) to start the season. He was named head coach for the U.S. team at the American Hockey League All-Star Game in 1996.

Prior to his coaching career, Trotz played junior hockey for the Western Hockey League's Regina Pats from 1979-83. During that time, he recorded 39 goals, 121 assists for 160 points, along with 490 penalty minutes in 204 games.

Coaching Record

			Regular Season				Playoffs		
Season	Team	Games	W	L	T	Games	W	L
1992-93	Baltimore (AHL)	80	28	40	12	7	3	4
1993-94	Portland (AHL)	80	43	27	10	8	6	2
1994-95	Portland (AHL)	80	46	22	12	7	3	4
1995-96	Portland (AHL)	80	32	38	10	24	14	10
1996-97	Portland (AHL)	80	37	33	10	5	2	3
1998-99	**Nashville (NHL)**	82	28	47	7	....	....	....
1999-2000	**Nashville (NHL)**	82	28	47	7	....	....	....
2000-01	**Nashville (NHL)**	82	34	39	9	....	....	....
2001-02	**Nashville (NHL)**	82	28	41	13	....	....	....
2002-03	**Nashville (NHL)**	82	27	42	13	....	....	....
2003-04	**Nashville (NHL)**	82	38	33	11	6	2	4
	NHL Totals	**492**	**183**	**249**	**60**	**6**	**2**	**4**

Club Directory

Gaylord Entertainment Center

Nashville Predators
Gaylord Entertainment Center
501 Broadway
Nashville, TN 37203
Phone **615/770-2300**
FAX 615/770-2309
Ticket Information 615/770-PUCK
www.nashvillepredators.com
Capacity: 17,113

Owner, Chairman and Governor	Craig Leipold
General Partner	Nashville Predators, LLC
Limited Partner	Gaylord Entertainment Company
President, COO and Alternate Governor	Jack Diller
Executive Vice President/General Manager and Alternate Governor	David Poile
Executive Vice President of Finance & Administration/CFO	Ed Lang
Senior Vice President/Communications & Development	Gerry Helper

Hockey Operations
Assistant General Manager	Ray Shero
Head Coach	Barry Trotz
Associate Coach	Brent Peterson
Assistant Coach	Peter Horachek
Goaltending Coach	Mitch Korn
Video Coach	Robert Bouchard
Strength and Conditioning Coach	Dave Good
Director of Player Personnel/Chief Scout	Paul Fenton
Assistant Director of Amateur Scouting	Greg Royce
Amateur and Professional Scout	Rick Knickle
Professional Scout	Dan MacKinnon
US Amateur & Quebec Scout	Jeff Kealty
Western Canada Scout	Mike Rooney
Western Canada Scout	Glen Sanders
Quebec Scout	Trent Mann
Minnesota/USHL Scout	David Westby
Head European Scout	Alexei Dementiev
European Scout	Lucas Bergman
European Scout	Janne Kekalainen
European Scout	Martin Divis
Head Athletic Trainer	Dan Redmond
Assistant Athletic Trainer	Eric Claas
Equipment Manager	Pete Rogers
Assistant Equipment Manager	Chris Scoppetto
Equipment Assistant	Chris Moody
Locker Room Attendant	Craig "Partner" Baugh
Director of Team Services	Gregory Harvey
Hockey Operations Coordinator	Brandon Walker
Executive Assistant	Jessica Halperin

Team Doctors
Team Physician	Dr. Michael J. Pagnani, MD
Assistant Team Physician	Dr. Blake Garside, MD
Team Dentist	
Team Ophthalmologist	Dr. Daniel Weikert, MD
Team Plastic Surgeon	Dr. Bryan D. Oslin, MD, Dr. Donald Griffin, MD
Team Neuropsychologist	Dr. Gary S. Solomon, Ph. D.
Team Neurosurgeon	Dr. Carl Hampf, MD
Team Internist	Dr. Richard W. Garman, MD

Communications/Development
Director of Communications	Ken Anderson
Communications Coordinator	Tim Darling
Community Relations and Amateur Hockey Mgr.	Marc Spigel
Team Photographer	John Russell

Business/Marketing/Corporate sales
Vice President of Corporate Partnerships	David Nivison
Account Executives – Corporate Partnerships	David Morse, Tom Moulton
Senior Sponsor Services Account Manager	Kristin Fricke
Sponsor Services Account Manager	Tiffany Williams
Vice President of Marketing	Randy Campbell
Marketing and Special Events Manager	Christel Foley
Advertising Manager	Carrie Poss
Entertainment Coordinator	Adam DeVault
Graphic Artist, Marketing & Communications	Jennifer Sheets

Finance/Human Resources/Administration
Vice President of Business Administration	Susie Masotti
Senior Director of Finance	Beth Snider
Senior Director of Human Resources	Stephanie Ditenhafer
Payroll Manager	Susan Charnley
Premium Seating Manager	Britt Kincheloe
Senior Accountant, Predators	Sjar Toney
Finance and Human Resources Coordinator	Jonathan Norris
Information Systems Manager	Jeff Beck
Executive Assistant	Elaine Lewis

Broadcast/Game Presentation Department
Director of Broadcasting	Erik Barnhart
Director of Game Operations	Bryan Shaffer
Director of Technical Operations	Blake Grant
Play-by-Play Announcer	Pete Weber
Color Analyst	Terry Crisp

Ticket Operations
Vice President of Ticket Sales	Scott Wampold
Ticket Operations Coordinator	Brad MacLachlan
Season Ticket Sales Manager	Nat Harden
Suite and Group Sales Manager	Chris Junghans
Account Executives	Ed Chamberlain, Sean Mahoney, Bob Milhizer, Jason Mott, Tom Patterson, Tim Wilson
Fan Relations Supervisor	Brad Gillispie

Miscellaneous
Minor League Affiliate	Milwaukee Admirals (AHL)
Radio Flagship	TBA
TV Flagship	Fox Sports Net
FOR TICKET INFORMATION	(615) 770-PUCK

New Jersey Devils

2003-04 Results: 43W-25L-12T-2OTL 100PTS.
Second, Atlantic Division

Year-by-Year Record

Season	GP	Home W	L	T	OL	Road W	L	T	OL	Overall W	L	T	OL	GF	GA	Pts.	Finished	Playoff Result
2003-04	82	22	13	5	1	21	12	7	1	43	25	12	2	213	164	100	2nd, Atlantic Div.	Lost Conf. Quarter-Final
2002-03	**82**	**25**	**11**	**3**	**2**	**21**	**9**	**7**	**4**	**46**	**20**	**10**	**6**	**216**	**166**	**108**	**1st, Atlantic Div.**	**Won Stanley Cup**
2001-02	82	22	13	4	2	19	15	5	2	41	28	9	4	205	187	95	3rd, Atlantic Div.	Lost Conf. Quarter-Final
2000-01	82	24	11	6	0	24	8	6	3	48	19	12	3	295	195	111	1st, Atlantic Div.	Lost Final
1999-2000	**82**	**28**	**9**	**3**	**1**	**17**	**15**	**5**	**4**	**45**	**24**	**8**	**5**	**251**	**203**	**103**	**2nd, Atlantic Div.**	**Won Stanley Cup**
1998-99	82	19	14	8	...	28	10	3	...	47	24	11	...	248	196	105	1st, Atlantic Div.	Lost Conf. Quarter-Final
1997-98	82	29	10	2	...	19	13	9	...	48	23	11	...	225	166	107	1st, Atlantic Div.	Lost Conf. Quarter-Final
1996-97	82	23	9	9	...	22	14	5	...	45	23	14	...	231	182	104	1st, Atlantic Div.	Lost Conf. Semi-Final
1995-96	82	22	17	2	...	15	16	10	...	37	33	12	...	215	202	86	6th, Atlantic Div.	Out of Playoffs
1994-95	**48**	**14**	**4**	**6**	**...**	**8**	**14**	**2**	**...**	**22**	**18**	**8**	**...**	**136**	**121**	**52**	**2nd, Atlantic Div.**	**Won Stanley Cup**
1993-94	84	29	11	2	...	18	14	10	...	47	25	12	...	306	220	106	2nd, Atlantic Div.	Lost Conf. Championship
1992-93	84	24	14	4	...	16	23	3	...	40	37	7	...	308	299	87	4th, Patrick Div.	Lost Div. Semi-Final
1991-92	80	24	12	4	...	14	19	3	...	38	31	11	...	289	259	87	4th, Patrick Div.	Lost Div. Semi-Final
1990-91	80	23	10	7	...	9	23	8	...	32	33	15	...	272	264	79	4th, Patrick Div.	Lost Div. Semi-Final
1989-90	80	22	15	3	...	15	19	6	...	37	34	9	...	295	288	83	2nd, Patrick Div.	Lost Div. Semi-Final
1988-89	80	17	18	5	...	10	23	7	...	27	41	12	...	281	325	66	5th, Patrick Div.	Out of Playoffs
1987-88	80	23	16	1	...	15	20	5	...	38	36	6	...	295	296	82	4th, Patrick Div.	Lost Conf. Championship
1986-87	80	20	17	3	...	9	28	3	...	29	45	6	...	293	368	64	6th, Patrick Div.	Out of Playoffs
1985-86	80	17	21	2	...	11	28	1	...	28	49	3	...	300	374	59	6th, Patrick Div.	Out of Playoffs
1984-85	80	13	21	6	...	9	27	4	...	22	48	10	...	264	346	54	5th, Patrick Div.	Out of Playoffs
1983-84	80	10	28	2	...	7	28	5	...	17	56	7	...	231	350	41	5th, Patrick Div.	Out of Playoffs
1982-83	80	11	20	9	...	6	29	5	...	17	49	14	...	230	338	48	5th, Patrick Div.	Out of Playoffs
1981-82**	80	14	21	5	...	4	28	8	...	18	49	13	...	241	362	49	5th, Smythe Div.	Out of Playoffs
1980-81**	80	15	16	9	...	7	29	4	...	22	45	13	...	258	344	57	5th, Smythe Div.	Out of Playoffs
1979-80**	80	12	20	8	...	7	28	5	...	19	48	13	...	234	308	51	6th, Smythe Div.	Out of Playoffs
1978-79**	80	8	24	8	...	7	29	4	...	15	53	12	...	210	331	42	4th, Smythe Div.	Out of Playoffs
1977-78**	80	17	14	9	...	2	26	12	...	19	40	21	...	257	305	59	2nd, Smythe Div.	Lost Prelim. Round
1976-77**	80	12	20	8	...	8	26	6	...	20	46	14	...	226	307	54	5th, Smythe Div.	Out of Playoffs
1975-76*	80	8	24	8	...	4	32	4	...	12	56	12	...	190	351	36	5th, Smythe Div.	Out of Playoffs
1974-75*	80	12	20	8	...	3	34	3	...	15	54	11	...	184	328	41	5th, Smythe Div.	Out of Playoffs

* Kansas City Scouts. ** Colorado Rockies.

2004-05 Schedule

Oct.	Fri.	15	Toronto
	Sat.	16	at Buffalo
	Wed.	20	NY Islanders
	Sat.	23	Detroit
	Tue.	26	at NY Islanders
	Fri.	29	St. Louis
	Sat.	30	at Ottawa
Nov.	Tue.	2	at Philadelphia
	Wed.	3	at Washington
	Sat.	6	Tampa Bay*
	Mon.	8	at Atlanta
	Wed.	10	Nashville
	Fri.	12	Dallas
	Sat.	13	at Washington
	Tue.	16	Ottawa
	Thu.	18	Toronto
	Sat.	20	Pittsburgh*
	Mon.	22	at Pittsburgh
	Wed.	24	at Florida
	Fri.	26	at Tampa Bay
	Sat.	27	at Atlanta
Dec.	Wed.	1	NY Rangers
	Fri.	3	Montreal
	Sat.	4	at NY Rangers
	Tue.	7	Buffalo
	Thu.	9	at Minnesota
	Sat.	11	NY Rangers*
	Sun.	12	at Chicago
	Wed.	15	Tampa Bay
	Fri.	17	Montreal
	Sat.	18	at Montreal
	Tue.	21	at Carolina
	Thu.	23	NY Islanders
	Mon.	27	at Florida
	Wed.	29	at Tampa Bay
	Fri.	31	Anaheim
Jan.	Tue.	4	Atlanta
	Thu.	6	at NY Islanders
	Sat.	8	at Toronto
	Mon.	10	Minnesota
	Wed.	12	Colorado

	Fri.	14	Boston
	Sat.	15	at Boston
	Tue.	18	Philadelphia
	Thu.	20	at NY Rangers
	Sat.	22	Carolina
	Tue.	25	at Vancouver
	Fri.	28	at Edmonton
	Sat.	29	at Calgary
Feb.	Wed.	2	Los Angeles
	Thu.	3	at Buffalo
	Sat.	5	at Philadelphia*
	Tue.	8	Florida
	Thu.	10	NY Rangers
	Tue.	15	Pittsburgh
	Thu.	17	at Philadelphia
	Sat.	19	Carolina
	Sun.	20	at Nashville*
	Wed.	23	at Detroit
	Thu.	24	at Toronto
	Sat.	26	NY Islanders*
	Mon.	28	Columbus
Mar.	Wed.	2	Boston
	Fri.	4	Washington
	Sat.	5	at Ottawa
	Mon.	7	Philadelphia
	Thu.	10	at San Jose
	Sat.	12	at Phoenix
	Wed.	16	at NY Rangers
	Thu.	17	Atlanta
	Sat.	19	Philadelphia*
	Mon.	21	Buffalo
	Thu.	24	at Pittsburgh
	Sat.	26	at NY Islanders
	Sun.	27	Pittsburgh*
	Tue.	29	Ottawa
	Thu.	31	at Carolina
Apr.	Sat.	2	at Boston*
	Mon.	4	at Montreal
	Wed.	6	Florida
	Fri.	8	at Pittsburgh
	Sat.	9	Washington

* Denotes afternoon game.

Franchise date: June 11, 1974

Transferred from Denver to New Jersey, June 30, 1982.
Previously transferred from Kansas City to Denver.

EASTERN NHL CONFERENCE

ATLANTIC DIVISION

31st NHL Season

Scott Niedermayer served as Devils' captain after January 9 in the absence of Scott Stevens. He was nominated for the Norris Trophy for the first time, and won the award over Zdeno Chara and Chris Pronger.

2004-05 Player Personnel

FORWARDS	HT	WT	S	Place of Birth	Date	2003-04 Club
BICEK, Jiri	5-10	190	L	Kosice, Czech.	12/3/78	New Jersey-Albany
BRYLIN, Sergei	5-10	190	L	Moscow, USSR	1/13/74	New Jersey
CLOUTHIER, Brett	6-5	225	L	Ottawa, Ont.	6/9/81	Albany-Cincinnati (ECHL)
ELIAS, Patrik	6-1	195	L	Trebic, Czech.	4/13/76	New Jersey
FOSTER, Adrian	6-0	205	L	Lethbridge, Alta.	1/15/82	Albany
FRIESEN, Jeff	6-1	205	L	Meadow Lake, Sask.	8/5/76	New Jersey
GIONTA, Brian	5-7	175	R	Rochester, NY	1/18/79	New Jersey
GOMEZ, Scott	5-11	200	L	Anchorage, AK	12/23/79	New Jersey
HRDINA, Jan	6-0	205	R	Hradec Kralove, Czech.	2/5/76	Phoenix-New Jersey
JANSSEN, Cam	5-11	205	R	St. Louis, MO	4/15/84	Windsor-Guelph
JOHANSSON, Eric	6-0	195	L	Edmonton, Alta.	1/7/82	Albany
KHOMUTOV, Ivan	6-3	205	L	Saratov, USSR	3/11/85	London
KOZLOV, Viktor	6-5	235	R	Togliatti, USSR	2/14/75	Florida-New Jersey
LANGDON, Darren	6-1	205	L	Deer Lake, Nfld.	1/8/71	Montreal
LANGENBRUNNER, Jamie	6-1	200	R	Cloquet, MN	7/24/75	New Jersey
LEBLOND-LETOURNEAU, P-L	6-2	210	L	Levis, Que.	6/4/85	Baie-Comeau
MADDEN, John	5-11	190	L	Barrie, Ont.	5/4/73	New Jersey
MARSHALL, Grant	6-1	200	R	Mississauga, Ont.	6/9/73	New Jersey
MURPHY, Ryan	6-1	210	L	Van Nuys, CA	3/21/79	Albany
NITTEL, Ahren	6-3	225	L	Waterloo, Ont.	12/6/83	Albany-Adirondack
OLIWA, Krzysztof	6-5	245	L	Tychy, Poland	4/12/73	Calgary
PANDOLFO, Jay	6-1	190	L	Winchester, MA	12/27/74	New Jersey
PARISE, Zach	5-11	185	L	Minneapolis, MN	7/28/84	North Dakota
PIHLMAN, Tuomas	6-3	210	L	Espoo, Finland	11/13/82	New Jersey-Albany
PIKKARAINEN, Ilkka	6-2	200	R	Sonkajarvi, Finland	4/19/81	Albany
RASMUSSEN, Erik	6-1	210	L	Minneapolis, MN	3/28/77	New Jersey
RHEAUME, Pascal	6-1	220	L	Quebec City, Que.	6/21/73	NY Rangers-Hartford-St. Louis
SKRLAC, Rob	6-5	245	L	Port McNeill, B.C.	6/10/76	New Jersey-Albany
SUGLOBOV, Aleksander	6-0	200	L	Elektrostal, USSR	1/15/82	New Jersey-Albany
VOROS, Aaron	6-4	190	L	Vancouver, B.C.	7/2/81	Alaska-Fairbanks-Albany
VRANA, Petr	5-10	175	L	Sternberk, Czech.	3/29/85	Halifax
DEFENSEMEN						
ALLEN, Bobby	6-1	205	L	Braintree, MA	11/14/78	Toronto (AHL)
BROOKS, Alex	6-1	205	R	Madison, WI	8/21/76	Albany
BROWN, Sean	6-3	215	L	Oshawa, Ont.	11/5/76	New Jersey-Albany
COLE, Phil	6-4	205	L	Winnipeg, Man.	9/6/82	Albany-Cincinnati (ECHL)
DeMARCHI, Matt	6-3	190	L	Bemidji, MN	5/4/81	Albany
HALE, David	6-1	215	L	Colorado Springs, CO	6/18/81	New Jersey
KADEYKIN, Anton	6-3	205	L	Elektrostal, USSR	5/17/84	Sarnia
KESA, Teemu	6-1	190	R	Helsinki, Finland	6/7/81	Lukko
MARTIN, Paul	6-1	190	L	Minneapolis, MN	3/5/81	New Jersey
MATVICHUK, Richard	6-2	215	L	Edmonton, Alta.	2/5/73	Dallas
NIEDERMAYER, Scott	6-1	200	L	Edmonton, Alta.	8/31/73	New Jersey
RAFALSKI, Brian	5-10	190	R	Dearborn, MI	9/28/73	New Jersey
REDLIHS, Krisjanis	6-3	190	L	Riga, Latvia	1/15/81	Albany
SCHULTZ, Ray	6-2	215	L	Red Deer, Alta.	11/14/76	Milwaukee
SPENCER, Steven	6-3	220	L	Regina, Sask.	6/16/82	South Carolina
STEVENS, Scott	6-2	215	L	Kitchener, Ont.	4/1/64	New Jersey
WHITE, Colin	6-4	215	L	New Glasgow, N.S.	12/12/77	New Jersey

GOALTENDERS	HT	WT	C	Place of Birth	Date	2003-04 Club
AHONEN, Ari	6-2	195	L	Jyvaskyla, Finland	2/6/81	Albany
BRODEUR, Martin	6-2	210	L	Montreal, Que.	5/6/72	New Jersey
CLEMMENSEN, Scott	6-3	205	L	Des Moines, IA	7/23/77	New Jersey-Albany
DISHER, Josh	6-1	165	L	Chatham, Ont.	6/24/85	Erie (OHL)
KOSTUR, Matus	6-1	195	L	Banska Bystrica, Czech.	3/28/80	Columbus (ECHL)-Albany

Coaching History

Bep Guidolin, 1974-75; Bep Guidolin, Sid Abel and Eddie Bush, 1975-76; Johnny Wilson, 1976-77; Pat Kelly, 1977-78; Pat Kelly and Aldo Guidolin, 1978-79; Don Cherry, 1979-80; Bill MacMillan, 1980-81; Bert Marshall and Marshall Johnston, 1981-82; Bill MacMillan, 1982-83; Bill MacMillan and Tom McVie, 1983-84; Doug Carpenter, 1984-85 to 1986-87; Doug Carpenter and Jim Schoenfeld, 1987-88; Jim Schoenfeld, 1988-89; Jim Schoenfeld and John Cunniff, 1989-90; John Cunniff and Tom McVie, 1990-91; Tom McVie, 1991-92; Herb Brooks, 1992-93; Jacques Lemaire, 1993-94 to 1997-98; Robbie Ftorek, 1998-99; Robbie Ftorek and Larry Robinson, 1999-2000; Larry Robinson, 2000-01; Larry Robinson and Kevin Constantine, 2001-02; Pat Burns, 2002-03 to date.

Coach

BURNS, PAT
Coach, New Jersey Devils. Born in St-Henri, Que., April 4, 1952.

Pat Burns was hired as head coach of the New Jersey Devils on June 13, 2002. In his first season with the club, he guided the Devils to the 2003 Stanley Cup title. He was diagnosed with colon cancer during the first round of the 2004 playoffs.

Before joining New Jersey, Burns had been out of coaching for more than a year after being fired by Boston early in 2000-01. He had joined the Bruins in 1997-98 and won the Jack Adams Award as coach of the year in 1998 after his Bruins showed a 30-point improvement over the previous season. He became the first man in NHL history to win the award three times, having won it previously with Toronto (1993) and Montreal (1989).

Burns began his coaching career with the Hull Olympiques of the QMJHL in 1983. He spent four seasons with the club, guiding them to a berth in the Memorial Cup finals in 1986. He moved into the professional ranks in 1987 with Montreal's AHL affiliate and took over the Canadiens the following year. Burns was the winningest coach in the NHL during his four-year tenure with the Canadiens, posting a record of 174-104-42. He was hired by the Toronto Maple Leafs on May 29, 1992, and promptly led the team to a club-record 32-point improvement on their 1991-92 record with a mark of 44-29-11 and 99 points.

2003-04 Scoring

* - rookie

Regular Season

Pos	#	Player	Team	GP	G	A	Pts	+/–	PIM	PP	SH	GW	GT	S	%
C	26	Patrik Elias	N.J.	82	38	43	81	26	44	9	3	9	0	300	12.7
C	23	Scott Gomez	N.J.	80	14	56	70	18	70	3	0	1	0	189	7.4
D	27	Scott Niedermayer	N.J.	81	14	40	54	20	44	9	0	3	0	165	8.5
L	12	Jeff Friesen	N.J.	81	17	20	37	8	26	5	0	4	0	177	9.6
D	28	Brian Rafalski	N.J.	69	6	30	36	6	24	2	0	1	0	130	4.6
C	11	John Madden	N.J.	80	12	23	35	7	22	1	1	1	0	210	5.7
C	18	Sergei Brylin	N.J.	82	14	19	33	10	20	7	0	1	1	98	14.3
R	22	Viktor Kozlov	FLA	48	11	16	27	–4	16	3	1	1	1	117	9.4
			N.J.	11	2	4	6	0	2	0	0	0	0	26	7.7
			TOTAL	59	13	20	33	–4	18	3	1	1	1	143	9.1
C	16	Jan Hrdina	PHX	55	11	15	26	–10	30	5	0	1	1	62	17.7
			N.J.	13	1	6	7	4	10	0	0	0	0	11	9.1
			TOTAL	68	12	21	33	–6	40	5	0	1	1	73	16.4
R	14	Brian Gionta	N.J.	75	21	8	29	19	36	0	0	8	1	174	12.1
R	24	Turner Stevenson	N.J.	61	14	13	27	0	76	4	0	2	0	76	18.4
L	20	Jay Pandolfo	N.J.	82	13	13	26	5	14	1	2	4	1	140	9.3
R	15	Jamie Langenbrunner	N.J.	53	10	16	26	9	43	1	2	2	0	130	7.7
D	7	* Paul Martin	N.J.	70	6	18	24	12	4	2	0	2	0	82	7.3
R	29	Grant Marshall	N.J.	65	8	7	15	–9	67	5	0	2	0	76	10.5
C	10	Erik Rasmussen	N.J.	69	7	6	13	5	41	0	0	0	1	68	10.3
D	5	Colin White	N.J.	75	2	11	13	10	96	0	0	0	0	61	3.3
D	4	Scott Stevens	N.J.	38	3	9	12	3	22	1	0	1	0	68	4.4
C	8	Igor Larionov	N.J.	49	1	10	11	3	20	0	0	0	0	25	4.0
D	6	Tommy Albelin	N.J.	45	1	3	4	7	4	0	0	0	0	27	3.7
D	25	* David Hale	N.J.	65	0	4	4	12	72	0	0	0	0	45	0.0
D	19	Raymond Giroux	N.J.	11	0	3	3	–3	4	0	0	0	0	17	0.0
D	2	Sean Brown	N.J.	39	0	3	3	5	44	0	0	0	0	25	0.0
R	32	Rob Skrlac	N.J.	8	1	0	1	1	22	0	0	1	0	3	33.3
R	9	Jiri Bicek	N.J.	12	0	1	1	0	0	0	0	0	0	10	0.0
R	21	* Aleksander Suglobov	N.J.	1	0	0	0	0	0	0	0	0	0	2	0.0
C	22	Craig Darby	N.J.	2	0	0	0	–1	0	0	0	0	0	0	0.0
L	19	* Thomas Pihlman	N.J.	2	0	0	0	0	2	0	0	0	0	1	0.0

Goaltending

No.	Goaltender	GPI	Mins	Avg	W	L	T	EN	SO	GA	SA	S%	G	A	PIM
35	Corey Schwab	3	187	0.64	2	0	1	0	1	2	68	.971	0	1	2
40	Scott Clemmensen	4	238	1.01	3	1	0	0	2	4	84	.952	0	0	0
30	Martin Brodeur	75	4555	2.03	38	26	11	4	11	154	1845	.917	0	0	4
	Totals	**82**	**5002**	**1.97**	**43**	**27**	**12**	**4**	**14**	**164**	**2001**	**.918**			

Playoffs

Pos	#	Player	Team	GP	G	A	Pts	+/–	PIM	PP	SH	GW	GT	S	%
C	23	Scott Gomez	N.J.	5	0	6	6	–2	0	0	0	0	0	17	0.0
C	26	Patrik Elias	N.J.	5	3	2	5	–3	2	1	0	1	0	18	16.7
R	14	Brian Gionta	N.J.	5	2	3	5	–2	0	1	0	0	0	9	22.2
C	16	Jan Hrdina	N.J.	5	2	0	2	0	2	0	0	0	0	7	28.6
D	7	* Paul Martin	N.J.	5	1	1	2	–4	4	1	0	0	0	9	11.1
R	15	Jamie Langenbrunner	N.J.	5	0	2	2	0	2	0	0	0	0	11	0.0
C	10	Erik Rasmussen	N.J.	5	0	2	2	1	2	0	0	0	0	4	0.0
D	27	Scott Niedermayer	N.J.	5	1	0	1	–5	6	0	0	0	0	12	8.3
D	6	Tommy Albelin	N.J.	4	0	1	1	1	0	0	0	0	0	2	0.0
D	28	Brian Rafalski	N.J.	5	0	1	1	0	0	0	0	0	0	9	0.0
C	8	Igor Larionov	N.J.	1	0	0	0	–1	0	0	0	0	0	0	0.0
D	2	Sean Brown	N.J.	1	0	0	0	–1	2	0	0	0	0	0	0.0
D	25	* David Hale	N.J.	1	0	0	0	1	0	0	0	0	0	0	0.0
R	22	Viktor Kozlov	N.J.	2	0	0	0	–1	0	0	0	0	0	2	0.0
R	9	Jiri Bicek	N.J.	2	0	0	0	–1	0	0	0	0	0	4	0.0
D	19	Raymond Giroux	N.J.	4	0	0	0	1	0	0	0	0	0	3	0.0
R	24	Turner Stevenson	N.J.	5	0	0	0	–2	0	0	0	0	0	9	0.0
C	18	Sergei Brylin	N.J.	5	0	0	0	0	0	0	0	0	0	9	0.0
L	20	Jay Pandolfo	N.J.	5	0	0	0	0	0	0	0	0	0	4	0.0
L	12	Jeff Friesen	N.J.	5	0	0	0	–2	4	0	0	0	0	11	0.0
D	5	Colin White	N.J.	5	0	0	0	–1	4	0	0	0	0	2	0.0
C	11	John Madden	N.J.	5	0	0	0	0	0	0	0	0	0	13	0.0

Goaltending

No.	Goaltender	GPI	Mins	Avg	W	L	EN	SO	GA	SA	S%	G	A	PIM
30	Martin Brodeur	5	298	2.62	1	4	1	0	13	133	.902	0	0	0
	Totals	**5**	**300**	**2.80**	**1**	**4**	**1**	**0**	**14**	**134**	**.896**			

Coaching Record

			Regular Season				Playoffs	
Season	Team	Games	W	L	T	Games	W	L
1983-84	Hull (QMJHL)	70	25	45	0	....	....	....
1984-85	Hull (QMJHL)	68	33	34	1	5	1	4
1985-86	Hull (QMJHL)	72	54	18	0	15	15	0
1986-87	Hull (QMJHL)	70	26	39	5	8	4	4
1987-88	Sherbrooke (AHL)	80	42	34	4	6	2	4
1988-89	**Montreal (NHL)**	**80**	**53**	**18**	**9**	**21**	**14**	**7**
1989-90	**Montreal (NHL)**	**80**	**41**	**28**	**11**	**11**	**5**	**6**
1990-91	**Montreal (NHL)**	**80**	**39**	**30**	**11**	**13**	**7**	**6**
1991-92	**Montreal (NHL)**	**80**	**41**	**28**	**11**	**11**	**4**	**7**
1992-93	**Toronto (NHL)**	**84**	**44**	**29**	**11**	**21**	**11**	**10**
1993-94	**Toronto (NHL)**	**84**	**43**	**29**	**12**	**18**	**9**	**9**
1994-95	**Toronto (NHL)**	**48**	**21**	**19**	**8**	**7**	**3**	**4**
1995-96	**Toronto (NHL)**	**65**	**25**	**30**	**10**	....	....	....
1997-98	**Boston (NHL)**	**82**	**39**	**30**	**13**	**6**	**2**	**4**
1998-99	**Boston (NHL)**	**82**	**39**	**30**	**13**	**12**	**6**	**6**
1999-2000	**Boston (NHL)**	**82**	**24**	**39**	**19**	....	....	....
2000-01	**Boston (NHL)**	**8**	**3**	**4**	**1**	....	....	....
2002-03	**New Jersey (NHL)**	**82**	**46**	**26**	**10**	**24**	**16**	**8***
2003-04	**New Jersey (NHL)**	**82**	**43**	**27**	**12**	**5**	**1**	**4**
	NHL Totals	**1019**	**501**	**367**	**151**	**149**	**78**	**71**

* Stanley Cup win.

Club Records

Team

(Figures in brackets for season records are games played; records for fewest points, wins, ties, losses, goals, goals against are for 70 or more games)

Most Points	**111**	2000-01 (82)
Most Wins	**48**	1997-98 (82), 2000-01 (82)
Most Ties	**21**	1977-78 (80)
Most Losses	**56**	1975-76 (80), 1983-84 (80)
Most Goals	**308**	1992-93 (84)
Most Goals Against	**374**	1985-86 (80)
Fewest Points	***36**	1975-76 (80)
	41	1983-84 (80)
Fewest Wins	***12**	1975-76 (80)
	17	1982-83 (80), 1983-84 (80)
Fewest Ties	**3**	1985-86 (80)
Fewest Losses	**19**	2000-01 (82)
Fewest Goals	***184**	1974-75 (80)
	205	2001-02 (82)
Fewest Goals Against	**164**	2003-04 (82)
Longest Winning Streak		
Overall	**13**	Feb. 26-Mar. 23/01
Home	**8**	Oct. 9-Nov. 7/87, Jan. 3-Feb. 4/03
Away	****10**	Feb. 27-Apr. 7/01
Longest Undefeated Streak		
Overall	**13**	Four times
Home	**15**	Jan. 8-Mar. 15/97 (9 wins, 6 ties)
Away	**10**	Feb. 27-Apr. 7/01 (10 wins)
Longest Losing Streak		
Overall	***14**	Dec. 30/75-Jan. 29/76
	10	Oct. 14-Nov. 4/83
Home	**9**	Dec. 22/85-Feb. 6/86
Away	**12**	Oct. 19-Dec. 1/83
Longest Winless Streak		
Overall	***27**	Feb. 12-Apr. 4/76 (21 losses, 6 ties)
	18	Oct. 20-Nov. 26/82 (14 losses 4 ties)
Home	***14**	Feb. 12-Mar. 30/76 (10 losses, 4 ties), Feb. 4-Mar. 31/79 (12 losses, 2 ties)
	9	Dec. 22/85-Feb. 6/86 (9 losses)
Away	***32**	Nov. 12/77-Mar. 15/78 (22 losses, 10 ties)
	14	Dec. 26/82-Mar. 5/83 (13 losses, 1 tie)
Most Shutouts, Season	**14**	2003-04 (82)
Most PIM, Season	**2,494**	1988-89 (80)
Most Goals, Game	**9**	Nine times

Individual

Most Seasons	**20**	Ken Daneyko
Most Games	**1,283**	Ken Daneyko
Most Goals, Career	**347**	John MacLean
Most Assists, Career	**364**	Scott Niedermayer
Most Points, Career	**701**	John MacLean (347G, 354A)
Most PIM, Career	**2,519**	Ken Daneyko
Most Shutouts, Career	**75**	Martin Brodeur
Longest Consecutive Games Streak	**388**	Ken Daneyko (Nov. 4/89-Mar. 29/94)
Most Goals, Season	**46**	Pat Verbeek (1987-88)
Most Assists, Season	**60**	Scott Stevens (1993-94)
Most Points, Season	**96**	Patrik Elias (2000-01; 40G, 56A)
Most PIM, Season	**295**	Krzysztof Oliwa (1997-98)
Most Points, Defenseman, Season	**78**	Scott Stevens (1993-94; 18G, 60A)
Most Points, Center, Season	**94**	Kirk Muller (1987-88; 37G, 57A)
Most Points, Right Wing, Season	***87**	Wilf Paiement (1977-78; 31G, 56A)
	87	John MacLean (1988-89; 42G, 45A)
Most Points, Left Wing, Season	**96**	Patrik Elias (2000-01; 40G, 56A)
Most Points, Rookie, Season	**70**	Scott Gomez (1999-2000; 19G, 51A)
Most Shutouts, Season	**11**	Martin Brodeur (2003-04)
Most Goals, Game	**4**	Five times
Most Assists, Game	**5**	Greg Adams (Oct. 10/85), Kirk Muller (Mar. 25/87), Tom Kurvers (Feb. 13/89), Scott Gomez (Mar. 30/03)
Most Points, Game	**6**	Kirk Muller (Nov. 29/86; 3G, 3A)

* Records include Kansas City Scouts and Colorado Rockies, 1974-75 through 1981-82.

** NHL Record.

Captains' History

Simon Nolet, 1974-75 to 1976-77; Wilf Paiement, 1977-78; Gary Croteau, 1978-79; Mike Christie, Rene Robert and Lanny McDonald, 1979-80; Lanny McDonald, 1980-81; Lanny McDonald and Rob Ramage, 1981-82; Don Lever, 1982-83; Don Lever and Mel Bridgman, 1983-84; Mel Bridgman, 1984-85 to 1986-87; Kirk Muller, 1987-88 to 1990-91; Bruce Driver, 1991-92; Scott Stevens, 1992-93 to date.

All-time Record vs. Other Clubs

Regular Season

	At Home								On Road								Total							
	GP	W	L	T	OL	GF	GA	PTS	GP	W	L	T	OL	GF	GA	PTS	GP	W	L	T	OL	GF	GA	PTS
Anaheim	8	7	1	0	0	31	14	14	10	5	4	1	0	26	26	11	18	12	5	1	0	57	40	25
Atlanta	10	6	3	1	0	33	20	13	10	7	1	2	0	36	13	16	20	13	4	3	0	69	33	29
Boston	53	15	27	11	0	139	172	41	56	17	29	8	2	171	218	44	109	32	56	19	2	310	390	85
Buffalo	54	19	26	9	0	162	177	47	54	15	31	8	0	165	213	38	108	34	57	17	0	327	390	85
Calgary	45	15	27	3	0	128	162	33	42	6	27	8	1	111	184	21	87	21	54	11	1	239	346	54
Carolina	45	25	16	4	0	158	140	54	44	18	17	8	1	132	137	45	89	43	33	12	1	290	277	99
Chicago	47	20	16	11	0	147	142	51	46	12	24	10	0	127	176	34	93	32	40	21	0	274	318	85
Colorado	36	19	13	4	0	147	121	42	35	13	18	4	0	98	124	30	71	32	31	8	0	245	245	72
Columbus	2	1	0	1	0	5	4	3	4	2	2	0	0	13	13	4	6	3	2	1	0	18	17	7
Dallas	43	21	19	3	0	146	132	45	45	13	25	6	1	117	164	33	88	34	44	9	1	263	296	78
Detroit	40	21	10	9	0	138	103	51	40	13	24	2	1	129	164	29	80	34	34	11	1	267	267	80
Edmonton	33	14	16	3	0	111	112	31	31	11	14	6	0	114	136	28	64	25	30	9	0	225	248	59
Florida	24	14	7	3	0	72	49	31	25	14	7	4	0	66	53	32	49	28	14	7	0	138	102	63
Los Angeles	43	19	19	5	0	142	148	43	42	8	27	6	1	130	201	23	85	27	46	11	1	272	349	66
Minnesota	3	2	0	1	0	13	8	5	3	1	1	1	0	8	7	3	6	3	1	2	0	21	15	8
Montreal	54	25	25	4	0	160	190	54	54	15	32	6	1	134	182	37	108	40	57	10	1	294	372	91
Nashville	5	2	3	0	0	15	14	4	5	4	1	0	0	14	9	8	10	6	4	0	0	29	23	12
NY Islanders	84	36	36	11	1	281	289	84	85	19	55	11	0	247	355	49	169	55	91	22	1	528	644	133
NY Rangers	86	45	34	7	0	301	280	97	84	24	39	20	1	255	323	69	170	69	73	27	1	556	603	166
Ottawa	23	13	8	2	0	66	54	28	24	15	5	3	1	60	47	34	47	28	13	5	1	126	101	62
Philadelphia	83	42	33	8	0	283	285	92	85	24	51	10	0	214	322	58	168	66	84	18	0	497	607	150
Phoenix	29	12	11	6	0	95	87	30	31	7	21	3	0	81	114	17	60	19	32	9	0	176	201	47
Pittsburgh	81	39	29	13	0	295	269	91	79	35	39	4	1	269	289	75	160	74	68	17	1	564	558	166
St. Louis	46	22	17	7	0	146	128	51	46	12	26	7	1	143	192	32	92	34	43	14	1	289	320	83
San Jose	12	7	4	1	0	44	24	15	10	6	2	1	1	32	24	14	22	13	6	2	1	76	48	29
Tampa Bay	26	18	5	2	1	93	44	39	25	12	7	5	1	75	59	30	51	30	12	7	2	168	103	69
Toronto	46	17	13	15	1	155	136	50	48	12	31	5	0	138	182	29	94	29	44	20	1	293	318	79
Vancouver	49	20	21	6	2	151	159	48	47	9	27	11	0	130	175	29	96	29	48	17	2	281	334	77
Washington	79	39	32	7	1	240	226	86	79	24	49	6	0	223	308	54	158	63	81	13	1	463	534	140
Defunct Clubs	8	4	2	2	0	25	19	10	8	2	3	3	0	19	27	7	16	6	5	5	0	44	46	17
Totals	**1197**	**559**	**473**	**159**	**6**	**3922**	**3708**	**1283**	**1197**	**375**	**639**	**169**	**14**	**3477**	**4437**	**933**	**2394**	**934**	**1112**	**328**	**20**	**7399**	**8145**	**2216**

Playoffs

	Series	W	L	GP	W	L	T	GF	GA	Last Mtg.	Rnd.	Result
Anaheim	1	1	0	7	4	3	0	19	12	2003	F	W 4-3
Boston	4	3	1	23	15	8	0	68	60	2003	CQF	W 4-1
Buffalo	1	1	0	7	4	3	0	14	14	1994	CQF	W 4-3
Carolina	2	1	1	12	6	6	0	31	17	2002	CQF	L 2-4
Colorado	1	0	1	7	3	4	0	11	19	2001	F	L 3-4
Dallas	1	1	0	6	4	2	0	15	9	2000	F	W 4-2
Detroit	1	1	0	4	4	0	0	16	7	1995	F	W 4-0
Florida	1	1	0	4	4	0	0	12	6	2000	CQF	W 4-0
Montreal	1	1	0	5	4	1	0	22	11	1997	CQF	W 4-1
NY Islanders	1	1	0	6	4	2	0	23	18	1988	DSF	W 4-2
NY Rangers	3	0	3	19	7	12	0	46	56	1997	CSF	L 1-4
Ottawa	2	1	1	13	6	7	0	29	26	2003	CF	W 4-3
Philadelphia	4	2	2	20	9	11	0	50	49	2004	CQF	L 1-4
Pittsburgh	5	2	3	29	15	14	0	86	80	2001	CF	W 4-1
Tampa Bay	1	1	0	5	4	1	0	14	8	2003	CSF	W 4-1
Toronto	2	2	0	13	8	5	0	37	27	2001	CSF	W 4-3
Washington	2	1	1	13	6	7	0	43	44	1990	DSF	L 2-4
Totals	**33**	**20**	**13**	**193**	**107**	**86**	**0**	**536**	**463**			

Playoff Results 2004-2000

Year	Round	Opponent	Result	GF	GA
2004	CQF	Philadelphia	L 1-4	9	14
2003	**F**	**Anaheim**	**W 4-3**	**19**	**12**
	CF	Ottawa	W 4-3	17	13
	CSF	Tampa Bay	W 4-1	14	8
	CQF	Boston	W 4-1	13	8
2002	CQF	Carolina	L 2-4	11	9
2001	F	Colorado	L 3-4	11	19
	CF	Pittsburgh	W 4-1	17	7
	CSF	Toronto	W 4-3	21	18
	CQF	Carolina	W 4-2	20	8
2000	**F**	**Dallas**	**W 4-2**	**15**	**9**
	CF	Philadelphia	W 4-3	18	15
	CSF	Toronto	W 4-2	16	9
	CQF	Florida	W 4-0	12	6

Abbreviations: Round: F – Final; **CF** – conference final; **CSF** – conference semi-final; **CQF** – conference quarter-final; **DSF** – division semi-final.

Calgary totals include Atlanta Flames, 1974-75 to 1979-80.
Colorado totals include Quebec, 1979-80 to 1994-95.
Phoenix totals include Winnipeg, 1979-80 to 1995-96.
Carolina totals include Hartford, 1979-80 to 1996-97.
Dallas totals include Minnesota North Stars, 1974-75 to 1992-93.

2003-04 Results

Oct.	8	at Boston	3-3
	11	at Carolina	2-1
	16	Toronto	2-2
	18	Tampa Bay	2-3
	22	Florida	1-2
	24	at Pittsburgh	2-1
	25	Boston	2-5
	28	at NY Islanders	4-0
	30	Philadelphia	3-2
Nov.	1	Colorado	4-3
	5	San Jose	3-2*
	7	Toronto	1-1
	8	at Ottawa	1-0
	12	at Buffalo	2-2
	13	Florida	3-1
	15	NY Rangers	5-0
	19	Buffalo	4-1
	21	Pittsburgh	2-1*
	25	at Los Angeles	4-0
	26	at Anaheim	3-3
	28	at Dallas	0-2
	30	at Colorado	1-1
Dec.	2	Phoenix	1-3
	4	Washington	3-0
	6	at Ottawa	2-1
	10	NY Islanders	1-0*
	12	Philadelphia	3-3
	13	at Philadelphia	2-0
	16	at NY Islanders	4-5
	18	at Atlanta	3-0
	19	at Buffalo	5-2
	21	at Chicago	2-2
	26	NY Islanders	3-4*
	27	at Pittsburgh	2-0
	29	at NY Islanders	1-3
Jan.	1	at Washington	2-2
	3	at Nashville	2-3
	5	Edmonton	3-2*
	7	Pittsburgh	2-4
	9	Tampa Bay	1-4
	10	at Toronto	1-0
	13	Ottawa	0-4
	15	at NY Rangers	3-3
	17	Washington	2-1*
	20	at Pittsburgh	3-0
	21	Carolina	1-2
	23	Montreal	2-0
	25	Atlanta	3-2
	27	at Columbus	4-3
	29	at Detroit	2-5
	31	at St. Louis	4-1
Feb.	3	Ottawa	2-1
	5	Vancouver	0-4
	10	at Philadelphia	1-4
	11	NY Rangers	1-3
	14	Carolina	4-1
	15	Los Angeles	3-2*
	17	Minnesota	4-4
	19	at Washington	1-3
	21	at NY Rangers	7-3
	22	Calgary	3-1
	25	Buffalo	8-2
	27	Atlanta	2-3
	28	at Toronto	0-3
Mar.	1	at Montreal	1-2
	3	at Florida	5-2
	5	at Tampa Bay	2-3*
	6	at Carolina	4-1
	9	Philadelphia	1-3
	11	Chicago	6-4
	13	at Philadelphia	1-2
	15	at NY Rangers	3-1
	17	Pittsburgh	6-1
	19	Montreal	1-1
	20	at Montreal	2-3
	23	at Florida	4-3*
	25	at Tampa Bay	1-2
	26	at Atlanta	5-0
	28	NY Islanders	3-2
	30	NY Rangers	5-0
Apr.	3	at Boston	5-2
	4	Boston	1-3

* – Overtime

Entry Draft
Selections 2004-1990

2004
Pick
20	Travis Zajac
155	Alexander Mikhailishin
185	Josh Disher
216	Pierre-Luc Leblond-Letourneau
217	Tyler Eckford
250	Nathan Perkovich
282	Valeri Klimov

2003
Pick
17	Zach Parise
42	Petr Vrana
93	Ivan Khomutov
167	Zach Tarkir
197	Jason Smith
261	Joey Tenute
292	Arseny Bondarev

2002
Pick
51	Anton Kadeykin
53	Barry Tallackson
64	Jason Ryznar
84	Marek Chvatal
85	Ahren Nittel
117	Cam Janssen
154	Krisjanis Redlihs
187	Eric Johansson
218	Ilkka Pikkarainen
250	Dan Glover
281	Bill Kinkel

2001
Pick
28	Adrian Foster
44	Igor Pohanka
48	Thomas Pihlman
60	Victor Uchevatov
67	Robin Leblanc
72	Brandon Nolan
128	Andrei Posnov
163	Andreas Salomonsson
194	James Massen
229	Aaron Voros
257	Yevgeny Gamalei

2000
Pick
22	David Hale
39	Teemu Laine
56	Aleksander Suglobov
57	Matt DeMarchi
62	Paul Martin
67	Max Birbraer
76	Mike Rupp
125	Phil Cole
135	Mike Danton
164	Matus Kostur
194	Deryk Engelland
198	Ken Magowan
257	Warren McCutcheon

1999
Pick
27	Ari Ahonen
42	Mike Commodore
50	Brett Clouthier
95	Andre Lakos
100	Teemu Kesa
185	Scott Cameron
214	Chris Hartsburg
242	Justin Dziama

1998
Pick
26	Mike Van Ryn
27	Scott Gomez
37	Christian Berglund
82	Brian Gionta
96	Mikko Jokela
105	Pierre Dagenais
119	Anton But
143	Ryan Flinn
172	Jacques Lariviere
199	Erik Jensen
227	Marko Ahosilta
257	Ryan Held

1997
Pick
24	Jean-Francois Damphousse
38	Stanislav Gron
104	Lucas Nehrling
131	Jiri Bicek
159	Sascha Goc
188	Mathieu Benoit
215	Scott Clemmensen
241	Jan Srdinko

1996
Pick
10	Lance Ward
38	Wes Mason
41	Josh DeWolf
47	Pierre Dagenais
49	Colin White
63	Scott Parker
91	Josef Boumedienne
101	Josh MacNevin
118	Glenn Crawford
145	Sean Ritchlin
173	Daryl Andrews
199	Willie Mitchell
205	Jay Bertsch
225	Pasi Petrilainen

1995
Pick
18	Petr Sykora
44	Nathan Perrott
70	Sergei Vyshedkevich
78	David Gosselin
79	Alyn McCauley
96	Henrik Rehnberg
122	Chris Mason
148	Adam Young
174	Richard Rochefort
200	Frederic Henry
226	Colin O'Hara

1994
Pick
25	Vadim Sharifijanov
51	Patrik Elias
71	Sheldon Souray
103	Zdenek Skorepa
129	Christian Gosselin
134	Ryan Smart
155	Luciano Caravaggio
181	Jeff Williams
207	Eric Bertrand
233	Steve Sullivan
259	Scott Swanjord
269	Mike Hanson

1993
Pick
13	Denis Pederson
32	Jay Pandolfo
39	Brendan Morrison
65	Krzysztof Oliwa
110	John Guirestante
143	Steve Brule
169	Nikolai Zavarukhin
195	Thomas Cullen
221	Judd Lambert
247	Jimmy Provencher
273	Mike Legg

1992
Pick
18	Jason Smith
42	Sergei Brylin
66	Cale Hulse
90	Vitali Tomilin
94	Scott McCabe
114	Ryan Black
138	Dan Trebil
162	Geordie Kinnear
186	Stephane Yelle
210	Jeff Toms
234	Heath Weenk
258	Vladislav Yakovenko

1991
Pick
3	Scott Niedermayer
11	Brian Rolston
33	Donevan Hextall
55	Fredrik Lindquist
77	Bradley Willner
121	Curt Regnier
143	David Craievich
165	Paul Wolanski
187	Daniel Reimann
231	Kevin Riehl
253	Jason Hehr

1990
Pick
20	Martin Brodeur
24	David Harlock
29	Chris Gotziaman
53	Mike Dunham
56	Brad Bombardir
64	Mike Bodnarchuk
95	Dean Malkoc
104	Petr Kuchyna
116	Lubomir Kolnik
137	Chris McAlpine
179	Jaroslav Modry
200	Corey Schwab
221	Valeri Zelepukin
242	Todd Reirden

General Managers' History
Sid Abel, 1974-75, 1975-76; Ray Miron, 1976-77 to 1980-81; Bill MacMillan, 1981-82, 1982-83; Bill MacMillan and Max McNab, 1983-84; Max McNab 1984-85 to 1986-87; Lou Lamoriello, 1987-88 to date.

President and General Manager

LAMORIELLO, LOU
CEO/President/General Manager, New Jersey Devils.
Born in Providence, RI, October 21, 1942.

Lou Lamoriello's life-long dedication to the game of hockey was rewarded in 1992 when he was named a recipient of the Lester Patrick Trophy for outstanding service to hockey in the United States. Lamoriello is entering his 18th season as president and general manager of the Devils following more than 20 years with Providence College as a player, coach and administrator. His trades, signings and draft choices helped lead the Devils to their first Stanley Cup championship in 1995 and were followed by victories again in 2000 and 2003. A member of the varsity hockey Friars during his undergraduate days, he became an assistant coach with the college club after graduating in 1963. Lamoriello was later named head coach and in the ensuing 15 years, led his teams to a 248-179-13 record and appearances in 10 post-season tournaments, including the 1983 NCAA Final Four. Lamoriello also served a five-year term as athletic director at Providence and was a co-founder of Hockey East, one of the strongest collegiate hockey conferences in the U.S. He remained as athletic director until he was hired as president of the Devils on April 30, 1987. He assumed the responsibility of general manager on September 10, 1987. He was g.m. of Team USA for the first World Cup of Hockey in 1996 as the U.S. captured the championship. He was also the g.m. for the 1998 U.S. Olympic team.

Club Directory

Continental Airlines Arena

New Jersey Devils
Continental Airlines Arena
50 Route 120 North
P.O. Box 504
East Rutherford, NJ 07073
Phone **201/935-6050**
FAX 201/935-2127
www.newjerseydevils.com
Capacity: 19,040

Chairman	Jeffrey Vanderbeek
CEO/President/General Manager	Louis A. Lamoriello
Executive Vice President	Peter S. McMullen
Executive Vice President	Chris Modrzynski
Vice President, General Counsel	Joseph C. Benedetti
Vice President, Ticket Operations	Terry Farmer
Vice President, Corporate Partnerships	Kenneth F. Ferriter
Vice President, Information/Publications	Mike Levine
Vice President, Marketing/Community Development	Jason Siegel
Vice President, Finance	Scott Struble

Hockey Club Personnel
Head Coach	Pat Burns
Assistant Coaches	Jacques Laperriere, Bob Carpenter, John MacLean
Goaltending Coach	Jacques Caron
Special Assignment Coach	Larry Robinson
Director, Scouting	David Conte
Assistant Director, Scouting	Claude Carrier
Scouting Staff	Glen Dirk, Milt Fisher, Ferny Flaman, Dan Labraaten, Chris Lamoriello, Vladimir Lokotko, Larry Perris, Marcel Pronovost, Lou Reycroft, Vaclav Slansky, Jr., Geoff Stevens, Ed Thomlinson, Les Widdifield
Pro Scouting Staff	Andre Boudrias, Bob Hoffmeyer, Jan Ludvig
Special Assignment Scouts	Geordie Kinnear, Kurt Kleinendorst, Gates Orlando
Hockey Operations Video Coordinator	Taran Singleton
Scouting Staff Assistant	Callie A. Smith
Medical Trainer	Bill Murray
Strength/Conditioning Coordinator	Michael Vasalani
Equipment Manager	Rich Matthews
Assistant Equipment Managers	Alex Abasto, Josh Penn
Assistant Trainer	Curtis Bell
Team Cardiologist	Dr. Joseph Niznik
Team Dentist	Dr. H. Hugh Gardy
Team Optometrist	Dr. Paul Berman
Team Orthopedists	Dr. Barry Fisher, Dr. Len Jaffe
Fitness Consultant	Vladimir Bure
Exercise Physiologist	Dr. Garret Caffrey
Physical Therapist	David Feniger
Video Consultant	Mitch Kaufman
Head Coach, Albany	Robbie Ftorek
Goaltending Coach, Albany	Chris Terreri
Athletic Trainer, Albany	Chris Palmer
Equipment Manager, Albany	Jason McGrath
Asst. Equip. Mgr., Albany	Stephen Bratspis

President's Office
Hockey Ops. Exec. Asst. to CEO/Pres./G.M.	Marie Carnevale
Corporate Exec. Asst. to CEO/Pres./G.M.	Mary K. Morrison
Legal Assistant	Lisa Romero

Operations
Receptionist	Jelsa Belotta
Staff Assistants	Pat Maione, Alfredo Vastola

Ticket Operations
Director, Ticket Operations	Tom Bates
Ticket Service Managers	Andrea Marchesani, Frank Calandrillo
Director, Group Sales	Neil Desormeaux
Managers, Group Accounts	Don Gleeson, Vincent Occhipinti

Corporate Partnerships
Director, Corporate Accounts	Michael DeMartino
Coordinator, Corporate Partner Services	Matt Dugan

Sales
Director, Ticket Sales/Customer Service	David Beck
Assistant Director, Ticket Sales	Todd Hyland
Account Managers	John Baier, Kirk Beckman, Joe Davis, Michael Desmond, George Duffy, Sarah Johnston, Michael McManus, Jeremy Steiner
Receptionist, Sales	Caryn Blood

Marketing/Community Development
Director, Merchandising	David Perricone
Merchandising Assistant	Adam Manger
Director, Grass Roots Programs	Michael Merolla
Director, Game Entertainment	Anthony Gioia
Manager, Game Entertainment	Bruce Cohn
Game Presentation Assistant	Michael Dilworth
Coordinator, Website Operations	Anthony Bovasso
Staff Assistant	Jennifer Schubert

Communications
Director, Public Relations	Jeff Altstadter
Staff Assistants	Erica Luthman, Pete Albietz

Finance
Assistant Controller	Craig S. Wolman
Staff Accountants	Frederick Bunker, Steven Seid
Administrative Assistant	Eileen Philips

Computer Operations
Director, Programming/Computer Operations	Jack Skelley
Programmer/Analyst	Joseph Wyks
Systems Administrator	Mike Tukes

Nets & Devils Foundation
Program/Grants Manager	Daniel McNeal

Television/Radio
Television Outlet	FOX Sports Net New York
Broadcasters	Mike Emrick, Play-by-Play; Glenn Resch, Color
Radio Outlet	Sports Radio 66 WFAN
Broadcasters	John Hennessy, Play-by-Play; Randy Velischek, Color

New York Islanders

2003-04 Results: 38w-29L-11T-4OTL 91PTS.
Third, Atlantic Division

2004-05 Schedule

Oct.	Sat.	16	Carolina
	Tue.	19	Boston
	Wed.	20	at New Jersey
	Sat.	23	at Washington
	Tue.	26	New Jersey
	Thu.	28	at Boston
	Sat.	30	Los Angeles
Nov.	Mon.	1	Tampa Bay
	Wed.	3	at Minnesota
	Thu.	4	at St. Louis
	Sat.	6	Florida
	Tue.	9	Toronto
	Thu.	11	Nashville
	Sat.	13	Dallas
	Mon.	15	NY Rangers
	Wed.	17	at Philadelphia
	Fri.	19	at Atlanta
	Sat.	20	at Washington
	Mon.	22	at NY Rangers
	Wed.	24	Montreal
	Fri.	26	Pittsburgh*
	Sat.	27	Philadelphia
	Tue.	30	Ottawa
Dec.	Fri.	3	at Buffalo
	Sat.	4	Carolina
	Mon.	6	Washington
	Fri.	10	at Philadelphia
	Sat.	11	at Pittsburgh
	Tue.	14	at Toronto
	Fri.	17	at NY Rangers
	Sat.	18	Washington
	Tue.	21	at Detroit
	Thu.	23	at New Jersey
	Sun.	26	at Ottawa
	Thu.	30	Anaheim
	Fri.	31	at Carolina
Jan.	Sun.	2	Detroit*
	Tue.	4	Florida
	Thu.	6	New Jersey
	Sat.	8	Buffalo
	Tue.	11	Colorado

	Fri.	14	at Pittsburgh
	Sat.	15	Phoenix
	Tue.	18	at Toronto
	Thu.	20	at Edmonton
	Fri.	21	at Calgary
	Sun.	23	at Vancouver
	Tue.	25	NY Rangers
	Thu.	27	at Buffalo
	Sat.	29	Buffalo*
Feb.	Tue.	1	Philadelphia
	Thu.	3	Ottawa
	Sat.	5	Columbus*
	Sun.	6	at Montreal*
	Wed.	9	at Carolina
	Thu.	10	at Tampa Bay
	Tue.	15	Atlanta
	Thu.	17	at Tampa Bay
	Sat.	19	at Florida
	Mon.	21	Pittsburgh*
	Tue.	22	at Montreal
	Thu.	24	San Jose
	Sat.	26	at New Jersey*
	Mon.	28	at Boston
Mar.	Fri.	4	at Pittsburgh
	Sat.	5	NY Rangers
	Mon.	7	Atlanta
	Fri.	11	Montreal
	Sun.	13	Boston*
	Tue.	15	at Phoenix
	Thu.	17	at Los Angeles
	Sun.	20	at Chicago*
	Tue.	22	Tampa Bay
	Fri.	25	at NY Rangers
	Sat.	26	New Jersey
	Mon.	28	at Philadelphia
	Tue.	29	Pittsburgh
Apr.	Fri.	1	at Florida
	Sat.	2	at Atlanta
	Tue.	5	Toronto
	Fri.	8	at Ottawa
	Sat.	9	Philadelphia

Denotes afternoon game.

Jason Blake followed up a 25-goal season in 2002-03 with 22 goals last year. His career-high four shorthanded goals ranked him among the NHL leaders behind Martin St. Louis, Kris Draper and Kevyn Adams.

Franchise date: June 6, 1972

**ATLANTIC
DIVISION**

**33rd
NHL
Season**

Year-by-Year Record

		Home				Road				Overall							
Season	GP	W	L	T	OL	W	L	T	OL	W	L	T	OL	GF	GA	Pts.	Finished	Playoff Result
2003-04	82	25	11	4	1	13	18	7	3	38	29	11	4	237	210	91	3rd, Atlantic Div.	Lost Conf. Quarter-Final
2002-03	82	18	18	5	0	17	16	6	2	35	34	11	2	224	231	83	3rd, Atlantic Div.	Lost Conf. Quarter-Final
2001-02	82	21	13	5	2	21	15	3	2	42	28	8	4	239	220	96	2nd, Atlantic Div.	Lost Conf. Quarter-Final
2000-01	82	12	27	1	1	9	24	6	2	21	51	7	3	185	268	52	5th, Atlantic Div.	Out of Playoffs
1999-2000	82	10	25	5	1	14	23	4	0	24	48	9	1	194	275	58	5th, Atlantic Div.	Out of Playoffs
1998-99	82	11	23	7	...	13	25	3	...	24	48	10		194	244	58	5th, Atlantic Div.	Out of Playoffs
1997-98	82	17	20	4	...	13	21	7	...	30	41	11		212	225	71	4th, Atlantic Div.	Out of Playoffs
1996-97	82	19	18	4	...	10	23	8	...	29	41	12		240	250	70	7th, Atlantic Div.	Out of Playoffs
1995-96	82	14	21	6	...	8	29	4	...	22	50	10		229	315	54	7th, Atlantic Div.	Out of Playoffs
1994-95	48	10	11	3	...	5	17	2	...	15	28	5		126	158	35	7th, Atlantic Div.	Out of Playoffs
1993-94	84	23	15	4	...	13	21	8	...	36	36	12		282	264	84	4th, Atlantic Div.	Lost Conf. Quarter-Final
1992-93	84	20	19	3	...	20	18	4	...	40	37	7		335	297	87	3rd, Patrick Div.	Lost Conf. Championship
1991-92	80	20	15	5	...	14	20	6	...	34	35	11		291	299	79	5th, Patrick Div.	Out of Playoffs
1990-91	80	15	19	6	...	10	26	4	...	25	45	10		223	290	60	6th, Patrick Div.	Out of Playoffs
1989-90	80	15	17	8	...	16	21	3	...	31	38	11		281	288	73	4th, Patrick Div.	Lost Div. Semi-Final
1988-89	80	19	18	3	...	9	29	2	...	28	47	5		265	325	61	6th, Patrick Div.	Out of Playoffs
1987-88	80	24	10	6	...	15	21	4	...	39	31	10		308	267	88	1st, Patrick Div.	Lost Div. Semi-Final
1986-87	80	20	15	5	...	15	18	7	...	35	33	12		279	281	82	3rd, Patrick Div.	Lost Div. Final
1985-86	80	22	11	7	...	17	18	5	...	39	29	12		327	284	90	3rd, Patrick Div.	Lost Div. Semi-Final
1984-85	80	26	11	3	...	14	23	3	...	40	34	6		345	312	86	3rd, Patrick Div.	Lost Div. Final
1983-84	80	28	11	1	...	22	15	3	...	50	26	4		357	269	104	1st, Patrick Div.	Lost Final
1982-83	**80**	**26**	**11**	**3**	...	**16**	**15**	**9**	...	**42**	**26**	**12**		**302**	**226**	**96**	**2nd, Patrick Div.**	**Won Stanley Cup**
1981-82	**80**	**33**	**3**	**4**	...	**21**	**13**	**6**	...	**54**	**16**	**10**		**385**	**250**	**118**	**1st, Patrick Div.**	**Won Stanley Cup**
1980-81	**80**	**23**	**6**	**11**	...	**25**	**12**	**3**	...	**48**	**18**	**14**		**355**	**260**	**110**	**1st, Patrick Div.**	**Won Stanley Cup**
1979-80	**80**	**26**	**9**	**5**	...	**13**	**19**	**8**	...	**39**	**28**	**13**		**281**	**247**	**91**	**2nd, Patrick Div.**	**Won Stanley Cup**
1978-79	80	31	3	6	...	20	12	8	...	51	15	14		358	214	116	1st, Patrick Div.	Lost Semi-Final
1977-78	80	29	3	8	...	19	14	7	...	48	17	15		334	210	111	1st, Patrick Div.	Lost Quarter-Final
1976-77	80	24	11	5	...	23	10	7	...	47	21	12		288	193	106	2nd, Patrick Div.	Lost Semi-Final
1975-76	80	24	8	8	...	18	13	9	...	42	21	17		297	190	101	2nd, Patrick Div.	Lost Semi-Final
1974-75	80	22	6	12	...	11	19	10	...	33	25	22		264	221	88	3rd, Patrick Div.	Lost Semi-Final
1973-74	78	13	17	9	...	6	24	9	...	19	41	18		182	247	56	8th, East Div.	Out of Playoffs
1972-73	78	10	25	4	...	2	35	2	...	12	60	6		170	347	30	8th, East Div.	Out of Playoffs

2004-05 Player Personnel

FORWARDS	HT	WT	S	Place of Birth	Date	2003-04 Club
ASHAM, Arron	5-11	209	R	Portage La Prairie, Man.	4/13/78	NY Islanders
BATES, Shawn	6-0	205	R	Melrose, MA	4/3/75	NY Islanders
BELAK, Graham	6-5	230	L	Saskatoon, Sask.	8/1/79	Bridgeport
BLAKE, Jason	5-10	180	L	Moorhead, MN	9/2/73	NY Islanders
COLLEY, Kevin	5-10	175	R	New Haven, CT	1/4/79	Bridgeport
COLLINS, Rob	5-10	174	R	Kitchener, Ont.	3/15/74	Bridgeport
DOWN, Blaine	5-11	170	L	Whitby, Ont.	7/16/82	Bridgeport
GODARD, Eric	6-4	227	R	Vernon, B.C.	3/7/80	NY Islanders-Bridgeport
HAMILTON, Jeff	5-10	180	R	Englewood, OH	9/4/77	NY Islanders-Bridgeport
HUNTER, Trent	6-3	191	R	Red Deer, Alta.	7/5/80	NY Islanders
KRAFT, Ryan	5-9	181	L	Bottineau, ND	11/7/75	Bridgeport
KVASHA, Oleg	6-5	230	R	Moscow, USSR	7/26/78	NY Islanders
MAPLETOFT, Justin	6-1	180	L	Lloydminster, Sask.	1/11/81	NY Islanders-Bridgeport
PAPINEAU, Justin	5-10	178	L	Ottawa, Ont.	1/15/80	NY Islanders
PARRISH, Mark	5-11	200	R	Bloomington, MN	2/2/77	NY Islanders
PECA, Michael	5-11	190	R	Toronto, Ont.	3/26/74	NY Islanders
SCATCHARD, Dave	6-2	224	R	Hinton, Alta.	2/20/76	NY Islanders
WEINHANDL, Mattias	6-0	183	R	Ljungby, Sweden	6/1/80	NY Islanders-Bridgeport
YASHIN, Alexei	6-3	225	R	Sverdlovsk, USSR	11/5/73	NY Islanders
DEFENSEMEN						
AUCOIN, Adrian	6-2	214	R	Ottawa, Ont.	7/3/73	NY Islanders
BUTENSCHON, Sven	6-4	215	L	Itzehoe, West Germany	3/22/76	NY Islanders-Bridgeport
CALDWELL, Ryan	6-2	174	L	Deloraine, Man.	6/15/81	U. of Denver
GERVAIS, Bruno	6-0	188	R	Longueuil, Que.	10/3/84	Acadie-Bathurst
HAMRLIK, Roman	6-2	200	L	Zlin, Czech.	4/12/74	NY Islanders
JARRETT, Cole	6-0	195	L	Sault Ste. Marie, Ont.	1/4/83	Bridgeport
JONSSON, Kenny	6-3	217	L	Angelholm, Sweden	10/6/74	NY Islanders
LETANG, Alan	6-1	201	L	Renfrew, Ont.	9/4/75	Bridgeport
MARTINEK, Radek	6-1	200	R	Havlickuv Brod, Czech.	8/31/76	NY Islanders
NIINIMAA, Janne	6-1	220	L	Raahe, Finland	5/22/75	NY Islanders
PETTINEN, Tomi	6-3	220	L	Ylojarvi, Finland	6/17/77	NY Islanders-Bridgeport
ROBINSON, Jody	6-2	205	L	New Haven, CT	9/23/78	Bridgeport
SMITH, Brandon	6-1	209	L	Hazelton, B.C.	2/25/73	Bridgeport

GOALTENDERS	HT	WT	C	Place of Birth	Date	2003-04 Club
DiPIETRO, Rick	5-11	185	R	Winthrop, MA	9/19/81	NY Islanders-Bridgeport
DUBIELEWICZ, Wade	5-10	178	L	Invermere, B.C.	1/30/78	NY Islanders-Bridgeport
KOCHAN, Dieter	6-1	180	L	Saskatoon, Sask.	5/11/74	Bridgeport

Coach

STIRLING, STEVE
Coach, New York Islanders. Born in Clarkson, Ont., November 19, 1949.

In his first season in 2003-04, Steve Stirling led the Islanders to their third consecutive playoff berth, amassing 91 points. Stirling was named head coach on June 3, 2003, after two successful seasons as skipper of the team's top AHL affiliate in Bridgeport. As the Sound Tigers' first head coach, Stirling led the team to the Calder Cup Finals in the 2001-02 inaugural season, and was named *The Hockey News* Minor Pro Coach of the Year.

Stirling joined the Islanders' organization as a scout in 1997. He served as an assistant coach for the Lowell Lock Monsters, the Islanders' AHL affiliate, from 1998 through 2000 and for the Islanders themselves during the 2000-01 season. He was named the first head coach of the Sound Tigers on July 26, 2001 and led Bridgeport to the AHL's 2001-02 Kilpatrick Trophy regular season championship and Eastern Conference playoff championship before losing to the Chicago Wolves in the 2002 Calder Cup Final.

Stirling first moved into the coaching ranks with the NCAA's Babson College Beavers from 1978 through 1983 and 1985 through 1993. He was the NCAA Division II / III coach of the year in 1980 and again in 1982 and also served as Babson's athletic director from 1986 through 1997. Stirling coached Division I Providence College from 1983 though 1985, leading the Friars to an appearance in the 1985 NCAA National Championship Game.

As a player, Stirling led the Boston University Terriers to appearances in the Beanpot Tournament during each of his three seasons at the school, 1968 to 1971, winning the tournament in 1970 and 1971. As a senior and BU's team captain in 1970-71, he was named Beanpot Most Valuable Player and led the Terriers to the NCAA National Championship. Stirling was inducted into the Beanpot Hall of Fame in February 2003.

Stirling played six seasons, (1971 to 1977), of professional hockey in the AHL and North American Hockey League, as well as in Austria. He spent the bulk of his professional-playing career in the AHL with the Boston Braves (1971 to 1974) and Rochester Americans (1974 to 1977).

Coaching Record

		Regular Season				Playoffs		
Season	Team	Games	W	L	T	Games	W	L
2001-02	Bridgeport (AHL)	80	43	29	8	20	12	8
2002-03	Bridgeport (AHL)	80	40	29	11	9	5	4
2003-04	**NY Islanders (NHL)**	**82**	**38**	**33**	**11**	**5**	**1**	**4**
	NHL Totals	**82**	**38**	**33**	**11**	**5**	**1**	**4**

2003-04 Scoring

* - rookie

Regular Season

Pos	#	Player	Team	GP	G	A	Pts	+/-	PIM	PP	SH	GW	GT	S	%
R	7	* Trent Hunter	NYI	77	25	26	51	23	16	4	0	7	0	187	13.4
L	12	Oleg Kvasha	NYI	81	15	36	51	4	48	5	3	3	0	147	10.2
R	21	Mariusz Czerkawski	NYI	81	25	24	49	8	16	9	0	2	2	157	15.9
C	55	Jason Blake	NYI	75	22	25	47	11	56	1	4	3	0	243	9.1
D	3	Adrian Aucoin	NYI	81	13	31	44	29	54	4	0	2	1	213	6.1
C	27	Michael Peca	NYI	76	11	29	40	17	71	0	1	0	0	117	9.4
R	37	Mark Parrish	NYI	59	24	11	35	8	18	6	0	6	0	105	22.9
C	79	Alexei Yashin	NYI	47	15	19	34	–1	10	3	0	1	0	148	10.1
C	17	Shawn Bates	NYI	69	9	23	32	–8	46	0	1	1	0	115	7.8
D	4	Roman Hamrlik	NYI	81	7	22	29	2	68	2	0	2	0	182	3.8
D	29	Kenny Jonsson	NYI	79	5	24	29	25	22	3	0	2	0	106	4.7
D	44	Janne Niinimaa	NYI	82	9	19	28	12	64	4	0	2	0	97	9.3
C	38	Dave Scatchard	NYI	61	9	16	25	12	78	1	1	1	0	111	8.1
R	45	Arron Asham	NYI	79	12	12	24	–12	92	1	0	0	1	108	11.1
C	77	Cliff Ronning	NYI	40	9	15	24	3	2	2	0	0	0	55	16.4
R	11	Mattias Weinhandl	NYI	55	8	12	20	9	26	4	0	2	0	49	16.3
C	26	* Justin Papineau	NYI	64	8	5	13	4	8	5	0	2	0	44	18.2
D	33	Eric Cairns	NYI	72	2	6	8	–5	189	0	0	0	0	24	8.3
D	25	Alexander Karpovtsev	CHI	24	0	7	7	–17	14	0	0	0	0	31	0.0
			NYI	3	0	1	1	1	4	0	0	0	0	3	0.0
			TOTAL	27	0	8	8	–16	18	0	0	0	0	34	0.0
D	24	Radek Martinek	NYI	47	4	3	7	–9	43	0	0	1	0	48	8.3
D	52	Sven Butenschon	NYI	41	1	6	7	–3	30	0	0	0	0	17	5.9
C	16	* Justin Mapletoft	NYI	27	1	4	5	–1	6	0	0	0	0	15	6.7
L	10	* Sean Bergenheim	NYI	18	1	1	2	–4	4	0	1	0	0	12	8.3
C	20	Eric Manlow	NYI	18	0	2	2	–2	2	0	0	0	0	10	0.0
R	49	* Eric Godard	NYI	31	0	1	1	–2	97	0	0	0	0	5	0.0
C	18	Jeffrey Hamilton	NYI	1	0	0	0	0	0	0	0	0	0	1	0.0
L	41	Derek Bekar	NYI	4	0	0	0	0	2	0	0	0	0	3	0.0
D	8	Tomi Pettinen	NYI	4	0	0	0	–2	2	0	0	0	0	2	0.0
R	20	Steve Webb	PIT	5	0	0	0	–3	2	0	0	0	0	3	0.0
			NYI	5	0	0	0	–1	2	0	0	0	0	0	0.0
			TOTAL	10	0	0	0	–4	4	0	0	0	0	3	0.0

Goaltending

No.	Goaltender	GPI	Mins	Avg	W	L	T	EN	SO	GA	SA	S%	G	A	PIM
34	* Wade Dubielewicz	2	105	1.71	1	0	1	0	0	3	50	.940	0	0	0
39	Rick Dipietro	50	2844	2.36	23	18	5	1	5	112	1261	.911	0	2	22
30	Garth Snow	39	2015	2.80	14	15	5	0	1	94	932	.899	0	1	28
	Totals	**82**	**4985**	**2.53**	**38**	**33**	**11**	**1**	**6**	**210**	**2244**	**.906**			

Playoffs

Pos	#	Player	Team	GP	G	A	Pts	+/-	PIM	PP	SH	GW	GT	S	%
D	44	Janne Niinimaa	NYI	5	1	2	3	–2	2	1	0	1	0	4	25.0
R	37	Mark Parrish	NYI	5	1	2	3	–4	0	0	0	0	0	12	8.3
C	55	Jason Blake	NYI	4	2	0	2	–2	2	0	0	0	0	9	22.2
L	12	Oleg Kvasha	NYI	5	1	0	1	–1	0	1	0	0	0	8	12.5
R	21	Mariusz Czerkawski	NYI	5	0	1	1	–1	0	0	0	0	0	7	0.0
D	4	Roman Hamrlik	NYI	5	0	1	1	0	2	0	0	0	0	10	0.0
C	79	Alexei Yashin	NYI	5	0	1	1	–2	0	0	0	0	0	15	0.0
C	38	Dave Scatchard	NYI	5	0	1	1	–3	6	0	0	0	0	12	0.0
R	45	Arron Asham	NYI	5	0	1	1	0	4	0	0	0	0	8	0.0
D	24	Radek Martinek	NYI	5	0	1	1	2	0	0	0	0	0	4	0.0
D	33	Eric Cairns	NYI	1	0	0	0	–2	0	0	0	0	0	0	0.0
R	20	Steve Webb	NYI	2	0	0	0	–1	6	0	0	0	0	1	0.0
C	77	Cliff Ronning	NYI	4	0	0	0	–2	0	0	0	0	0	3	0.0
D	52	Sven Butenschon	NYI	4	0	0	0	–1	0	0	0	0	0	1	0.0
C	27	Michael Peca	NYI	5	0	0	0	–1	6	0	0	0	0	12	0.0
D	3	Adrian Aucoin	NYI	5	0	0	0	–6	6	0	0	0	0	12	0.0
D	29	Kenny Jonsson	NYI	5	0	0	0	–4	2	0	0	0	0	2	0.0
C	17	Shawn Bates	NYI	5	0	0	0	–2	4	0	0	0	0	6	0.0
R	7	* Trent Hunter	NYI	5	0	0	0	–2	4	0	0	0	0	6	0.0
R	11	Mattias Weinhandl	NYI	5	0	0	0	–2	2	0	0	0	0	10	0.0

Goaltending

No.	Goaltender	GPI	Mins	Avg	W	L	EN	SO	GA	SA	S%	G	A	PIM
39	Rick DiPietro	5	303	2.18	1	4	1	1	11	120	.908	0	0	0
	Totals	**5**	**304**	**2.37**	**1**	**4**	**1**	**1**	**12**	**121**	**.901**			

Coaching History

Phil Goyette and Earl Ingarfield, 1972-73; Al Arbour, 1973-74 to 1985-86; Terry Simpson, 1986-87, 1987-88; Terry Simpson and Al Arbour, 1988-89; Al Arbour, 1989-90 to 1993-94; Lorne Henning, 1994-95; Mike Milbury, 1995-96; Mike Milbury and Rick Bowness, 1996-97; Rick Bowness and Mike Milbury, 1997-98; Mike Milbury and Bill Stewart, 1998-99; Butch Goring, 1999-2000; Butch Goring and Lorne Henning, 2000-01; Peter Laviolette, 2001-02, 2002-03; Steve Stirling, 2003-04 to date.

Club Records

Team

(Figures in brackets for season records are games played; records for fewest points, wins, ties, losses, goals, goals against are for 70 or more games)

Most Points 118 1981-82 (80)
Most Wins 54 1981-82 (80)
Most Ties 22 1974-75 (80)
Most Losses 60 1972-73 (78)
Most Goals 385 1981-82 (80)
Most Goals Against 347 1972-73 (78)
Fewest Points 30 1972-73 (78)
Fewest Wins 12 1972-73 (78)
Fewest Ties 4 1983-84 (80)
Fewest Losses 15 1978-79 (80)
Fewest Goals 170 1972-73 (78)
Fewest Goals Against 190 1975-76 (80)

Longest Winning Streak
- **Overall** .... 15 Jan. 21-Feb. 20/82
- **Home** .... 14 Jan. 2-Feb. 25/82
- **Away** .... 8 Feb. 27-Mar. 29/81

Longest Undefeated Streak
- **Overall** .... 15 Three times
- **Home** .... 23 Oct. 17/78-Jan. 27/79 (19 wins, 4 ties), Jan. 2-Apr. 3/82 (21 wins, 2 ties)
- **Away** .... 8 Three times

Longest Losing Streak
- **Overall** .... 12 Dec. 27/72-Jan. 16/73, Nov. 22-Dec. 15/88
- **Home** .... 7 Nov. 13-Dec. 14/99
- **Away** .... 15 Jan. 20-Mar. 31/73

Longest Winless Streak
- **Overall** .... 15 Nov. 22-Dec. 21/72 (12 losses, 3 ties)
- **Home** .... 9 Mar. 2-Apr. 6/99 (7 losses, 2 ties)
- **Away** .... 20 Nov. 3/72-Jan. 13/73 (19 losses, 1 tie)

Most Shutouts, Season 10 1975-76 (80)
Most PIM, Season 1,857 1986-87 (80)
Most Goals, Game .... 11 Dec. 20/83 (Pit. 3 at NYI 11), Mar. 3/84 (NYI 11 at Tor. 6)

Individual

Most Seasons .... 17 Billy Smith
Most Games .... 1,123 Bryan Trottier
Most Goals, Career .... 573 Mike Bossy
Most Assists, Career .... 853 Bryan Trottier
Most Points, Career .... 1,353 Bryan Trottier (500G, 853A)
Most PIM, Career .... 1,879 Mick Vukota
Most Shutouts, Career .... 25 Glenn Resch
Longest Consecutive Games Streak .... 576 Billy Harris (Oct. 7/72-Nov. 30/79)
Most Goals, Season .... 69 Mike Bossy (1978-79)
Most Assists, Season .... 87 Bryan Trottier (1978-79)
Most Points, Season .... 147 Mike Bossy (1981-82; 64G, 83A)
Most PIM, Season .... 356 Brian Curran (1986-87)
Most Points, Defenseman, Season .... 101 Denis Potvin (1978-79; 31G, 70A)
Most Points, Center, Season .... 134 Bryan Trottier (1978-79; 47G, 87A)
Most Points, Right Wing, Season .... 147 Mike Bossy (1981-82; 64G, 83A)
Most Points, Left Wing, Season .... 100 John Tonelli (1984-85; 42G, 58A)
Most Points, Rookie, Season .... 95 Bryan Trottier (1975-76; 32G, 63A)
Most Shutouts, Season .... 7 Glenn Resch (1975-76)
Most Goals, Game .... 5 Bryan Trottier (Dec. 23/78, Feb. 13/82), John Tonelli (Jan. 6/81)
Most Assists, Game .... 6 Mike Bossy (Jan. 6/81)
Most Points, Game .... 8 Bryan Trottier (Dec. 23/78; 5G, 3A)

Captains' History

Ed Westfall, 1972-73 to 1975-76; Ed Westfall and Clark Gillies, 1976-77; Clark Gillies, 1977-78, 1978-79; Denis Potvin, 1979-80 to 1986-87; Brent Sutter, 1987-88 to 1990-91; Brent Sutter and Pat Flatley, 1991-92; Pat Flatley, 1992-93 to 1995-96; no captain, 1996-97; Bryan McCabe and Trevor Linden, 1997-98; Trevor Linden, 1998-99; Kenny Jonsson, 1999-2000, 2000-01; Michael Peca, 2001-02 to date.

Retired Numbers

5	Denis Potvin	1973-1988
9	Clark Gillies	1974-1986
19	Bryan Trottier	1975-1990
22	Mike Bossy	1977-1987
23	Bob Nystrom	1972-1986
31	Billy Smith	1972-1989

All-time Record vs. Other Clubs

Regular Season

	At Home								On Road								Total							
	GP	W	L	T	OL	GF	GA	PTS	GP	W	L	T	OL	GF	GA	PTS	GP	W	L	T	OL	GF	GA	PTS
Anaheim	8	4	3	1	0	24	23	9	9	4	2	3	0	24	18	11	17	8	5	4	0	48	41	20
Atlanta	10	5	5	0	0	36	25	10	10	6	2	2	0	37	27	14	20	11	7	2	0	73	52	24
Boston	61	24	27	10	0	202	199	58	59	16	31	11	1	164	220	44	120	40	58	21	1	366	419	102
Buffalo	61	27	25	9	0	172	166	63	61	20	31	9	1	164	197	50	122	47	56	18	1	336	363	113
Calgary	51	25	17	9	0	191	143	59	49	14	24	11	0	145	172	39	100	39	41	20	0	336	315	98
Carolina	44	20	20	4	0	132	121	44	45	19	21	5	0	148	152	43	89	39	41	9	0	280	273	87
Chicago	47	18	14	15	0	163	141	51	48	17	26	5	0	162	162	39	95	35	40	20	0	325	303	90
Colorado	32	18	13	1	0	129	109	37	34	11	20	3	0	97	123	25	66	29	33	4	0	226	232	62
Columbus	2	0	2	0	0	7	11	0	4	0	3	1	0	7	13	1	6	0	5	1	0	14	24	1
Dallas	48	26	14	8	0	176	134	60	47	21	18	8	0	170	139	50	95	47	32	16	0	346	273	110
Detroit	46	23	18	4	1	164	137	51	45	17	26	2	0	135	165	36	91	40	44	6	1	299	302	87
Edmonton	31	15	7	9	0	128	110	39	29	8	16	5	0	87	107	21	60	23	23	14	0	215	217	60
Florida	25	12	11	2	0	64	65	26	25	8	11	6	0	74	76	22	50	20	22	8	0	138	141	48
Los Angeles	44	24	15	5	0	156	123	53	45	17	21	7	0	143	163	41	89	41	36	12	0	299	286	94
Minnesota	3	2	1	0	0	6	6	4	3	1	2	0	0	9	9	2	6	3	3	0	0	15	15	6
Montreal	60	30	24	6	0	187	167	66	60	15	36	9	0	168	217	39	120	45	60	15	0	355	384	105
Nashville	4	2	2	0	0	11	12	4	5	2	3	0	0	16	14	4	9	4	5	0	0	27	26	8
New Jersey	85	55	19	11	0	355	247	121	84	37	34	11	2	289	281	87	169	92	53	22	2	644	528	208
NY Rangers	96	54	33	8	1	371	306	117	96	30	55	11	0	284	358	71	192	84	88	19	1	655	664	188
Ottawa	24	5	12	6	1	78	89	17	23	5	13	5	0	62	78	15	47	10	25	11	1	140	167	32
Philadelphia	98	50	33	15	0	356	289	115	95	29	55	11	0	268	340	69	193	79	88	26	0	624	629	184
Phoenix	30	13	9	8	0	113	91	34	30	15	11	4	0	105	96	34	60	28	20	12	0	218	187	68
Pittsburgh	86	46	30	8	2	348	285	102	88	34	39	14	1	310	329	83	174	80	69	22	3	658	614	185
St. Louis	49	25	13	11	0	183	131	61	47	20	17	9	1	153	166	50	96	45	30	20	1	336	297	111
San Jose	11	5	4	2	0	40	35	12	12	6	5	1	0	40	30	13	23	11	9	3	0	80	65	25
Tampa Bay	25	13	11	1	0	78	69	27	26	12	11	2	1	80	67	27	51	25	22	3	1	158	136	54
Toronto	53	30	20	3	0	208	155	63	55	23	27	4	1	184	189	51	108	53	47	7	1	392	344	114
Vancouver	47	26	11	10	0	174	129	62	47	21	23	3	0	153	155	45	94	47	34	13	0	327	284	107
Washington	81	42	37	2	0	298	255	86	81	30	39	11	1	251	267	72	162	72	76	13	1	549	522	158
Defunct Clubs	13	11	0	2	0	75	33	24	13	4	5	4	0	35	41	12	26	15	5	6	0	110	74	36
Totals	**1275**	**650**	**450**	**170**	**5**	**4625**	**3806**	**1475**	**1275**	**462**	**627**	**177**	**9**	**3964**	**4371**	**1110**	**2550**	**1112**	**1077**	**347**	**14**	**8589**	**8177**	**2585**

Playoffs

	Series	W	L	GP	W	L	T	GF	GA	Last Mtg.	Rnd.	Result
Boston	2	2	0	11	8	3	0	49	35	1983	CF	W 4-2
Buffalo	3	3	0	16	12	4	0	59	45	1980	SF	W 4-2
Chicago	2	2	0	6	6	0	0	21	6	1979	QF	W 4-0
Colorado	1	1	0	4	4	0	0	18	9	1982	CF	W 4-0
Dallas	1	1	0	5	4	1	0	26	16	1981	F	W 4-1
Edmonton	3	2	1	15	9	6	0	58	47	1984	F	L 1-4
Los Angeles	1	1	0	4	3	1	0	21	10	1980	PRE	W 3-1
Montreal	4	1	3	22	8	14	0	55	64	1993	CF	L 1-4
New Jersey	1	0	1	6	2	4	0	18	23	1988	DSF	L 2-4
NY Rangers	8	5	3	39	20	19	0	129	132	1994	CQF	L 0-4
Ottawa	1	0	1	5	1	4	0	7	13	2003	CQF	L 1-4
Philadelphia	4	1	3	25	11	14	0	69	83	1987	DF	L 3-4
Pittsburgh	3	3	0	19	11	8	0	67	58	1993	DF	W 4-3
Tampa Bay	1	0	1	5	1	4	0	5	12	2004	CQF	L 1-4
Toronto	3	1	2	17	9	8	0	54	42	2002	CQF	L 3-4
Vancouver	2	2	0	6	6	0	0	26	14	1982	F	W 4-0
Washington	6	5	1	30	18	12	0	99	88	1993	DSF	W 4-2
Totals	**46**	**30**	**16**	**235**	**133**	**102**	**0**	**781**	**697**			

Calgary totals include Atlanta Flames, 1972-73 to 1979-80.
Colorado totals include Quebec, 1979-80 to 1994-95.
New Jersey totals include Kansas City, 1974-75 to 1975-76, and Colorado Rockies, 1976-77 to 1981-82.
Phoenix totals include Winnipeg, 1979-80 to 1995-96.
Carolina totals include Hartford, 1979-80 to 1996-97.
Dallas totals include Minnesota North Stars, 1972-73 to 1992-93.

Playoff Results 2004-2000

Year	Round	Opponent	Result	GF	GA
2004	CQF	Tampa Bay	L 1-4	5	12
2003	CQF	Ottawa	L 1-4	7	13
2002	CQF	Toronto	L 3-4	21	22

Abbreviations: Round: F – Final; **CF** – conference final; **CQF** – conference quarter-final; **DF** – division final; **DSF** – division semi-final; **SF** – semi-final; **QF** – quarter-final; **PRE** – preliminary round.

2003-04 Results

Oct.	9	at Washington	1-6		10	NY Rangers	2-3
	11	at Buffalo	6-0		13	at NY Rangers	1-4
	14	at Atlanta	2-2		15	at Ottawa	4-4
	18	Florida	2-1		17	Buffalo	4-2
	20	Toronto	5-2		19	Ottawa	5-2
	23	at Montreal	0-3		20	at Toronto	0-2
	25	Pittsburgh	7-2		23	at Carolina	3-2
	28	New Jersey	0-4		24	at Atlanta	3-0
	29	at Pittsburgh	4-4		27	Boston	2-2
Nov.	1	Anaheim	4-1		29	at Boston	1-2*
	3	Ottawa	6-3		31	Florida	4-2
	6	Dallas	4-1	**Feb.**	3	Vancouver	5-4*
	8	Atlanta	3-4		5	at Montreal	1-2
	11	at Philadelphia	1-2		10	at Colorado	1-1
	13	Montreal	3-1		11	at Dallas	4-4
	15	at Nashville	3-4		13	at Phoenix	5-2
	19	at Florida	4-1		16	Los Angeles	1-1
	20	at Tampa Bay	2-3		18	Pittsburgh	4-3
	22	at Columbus	1-2		19	at NY Rangers	2-6
	26	Carolina	0-2		21	Buffalo	4-1
	28	at Detroit	0-6		24	Boston	0-0
	29	Philadelphia	1-5		26	NY Rangers	3-6
Dec.	2	Washington	1-4		27	at Buffalo	4-2
	4	NY Rangers	2-4		29	Pittsburgh	2-3*
	6	Chicago	5-2	**Mar.**	2	at Pittsburgh	3-3
	9	Tampa Bay	5-2		4	at Toronto	2-6
	10	at New Jersey	0-1*		6	St. Louis	2-4
	13	Atlanta	4-0		9	at St. Louis	2-3*
	16	New Jersey	5-4		11	at San Jose	4-5
	18	at NY Rangers	3-4		12	at Anaheim	3-1
	20	at Philadelphia	1-3		16	at Tampa Bay	3-1
	21	at Washington	5-4		17	at Florida	4-6
	23	Philadelphia	4-2		19	Minnesota	3-1
	26	at New Jersey	4-3*		21	Tampa Bay	3-0
	27	Toronto	3-1		23	Washington	3-0
	29	New Jersey	3-1		25	at Philadelphia	4-2
	31	at Pittsburgh	6-1		27	Carolina	2-3
Jan.	1	at Ottawa	0-1		28	at New Jersey	2-3
	3	at Boston	3-3		31	Montreal	5-1
	6	Calgary	2-3	**Apr.**	2	at Carolina	6-4
	8	Edmonton	3-2		4	Philadelphia	3-3

* – Overtime

Entry Draft
Selections 2004-1990

2004
Pick
16	Petteri Nokelainen
47	Blake Comeau
82	Sergei Ogorodnikov
115	Wes O'Neill
148	Steve Regier
179	Jaroslav Mrazek
210	Emil Axelsson
227	Chris Campoli
244	Jason Pitton
276	Sylvain Michaud

2003
Pick
15	Robert Nilsson
48	Dmitri Chernykh
53	Yevgeny Tunik
58	Jeremy Colliton
120	Stefan Blaho
182	Bruno Gervais
212	Denis Rehak
238	Cody Blanshan
246	Igor Volkov

2002
Pick
22	Sean Bergenheim
87	Frans Nielsen
149	Marcus Paulsson
189	Alexei Stonkus
220	Brad Topping
252	Martin Chabada
283	Per Braxenholm

2001
Pick
101	Cory Stillman
132	Dusan Salficky
166	Andy Chiodo
197	Jan Holub
228	Mike Bray
260	Bryan Perez
280	Roman Kuhtinov
287	Juha-Pekka Ketola

2000
Pick
1	Rick DiPietro
5	Raffi Torres
101	Arto Tukio
105	Vladimir Gorbunov
136	Dmitri Upper
148	Kristofer Ottosson
202	Ryan Caldwell
264	Dmitri Altarev
267	Tomi Pettinen

1999
Pick
5	Tim Connolly
8	Taylor Pyatt
10	Branislav Mezei
28	Kristian Kudroc
78	Mattias Weinhandl
87	Brian Collins
101	Juraj Kolnik
102	Johan Halvardsson
130	Justin Mapletoft
140	Adam Johnson
163	Bjorn Melin
228	Radek Martinek
255	Brett Henning
268	Tyler Scott

1998
Pick
9	Mike Rupp
36	Chris Nielsen
95	Andy Burnham
123	Jiri Dopita
155	Kevin Clauson
182	Evgeny Korolev
209	Frederik Brindamour
237	Ben Blais
242	Jason Doyle
250	Radek Matejovsky

1997
Pick
4	Roberto Luongo
5	Eric Brewer
31	Jeff Zehr
59	Jarrett Smith
79	Robert Schnabel
85	Petr Mika
115	Adam Edinger
139	Bobby Leavins
166	Kris Knoblauch
196	Jeremy Symington
222	Ryan Clark

1996
Pick
3	J.P. Dumont
29	Dan LaCouture
56	Zdeno Chara
83	Tyrone Garner
109	Bubba Berenzweig
128	Petr Sachl
138	Todd Miller
165	J.R. Prestifilippo
192	Evgeny Korolev
218	Mike Muzechka

1995
Pick
2	Wade Redden
28	Jan Hlavac
41	D.J. Smith
106	Vladimir Orszagh
158	Andrew Taylor
210	David MacDonald
211	Mike Broda

1994
Pick
9	Brett Lindros
38	Jason Holland
63	Jason Strudwick
90	Brad Lukowich
112	Mark McArthur
116	Albert O'Connell
142	Jason Stewart
194	Mike Loach
203	Peter Hogardh
220	Gord Walsh
246	Kirk Dewaele
272	Dick Tarnstrom

1993
Pick
23	Todd Bertuzzi
40	Bryan McCabe
66	Vladimir Chebaturkin
92	Warren Luhning
118	Tommy Salo
144	Peter LeBoutillier
170	Darren Van Impe
196	Rod Hinks
222	Daniel Johansson
248	Stephane Larocque
274	Carl Charland

1992
Pick
5	Darius Kasparaitis
56	Jarrett Deuling
104	Thomas Klimt
105	Ryan Duthie
128	Derek Armstrong
152	Vladimir Grachev
159	Steve O'Rourke
176	Jason Widmer
200	Daniel Paradis
224	David Wainwright
248	Andrei Vasilyev

1991
Pick
4	Scott Lachance
26	Ziggy Palffy
48	Jamie McLennan
70	Milan Hnilicka
92	Steve Junker
114	Rob Valicevic
136	Andreas Johansson
158	Todd Sparks
180	John Johnson
202	Robert Canavan
224	Marcus Thuresson
246	Marty Schriner

1990
Pick
6	Scott Scissons
27	Chris Taylor
48	Dan Plante
90	Chris Marinucci
111	Joni Lehto
132	Michael Guilbert
153	Sylvain Fleury
174	John Joyce
195	Richard Enga
216	Martin Lacroix
237	Andy Shier

General Managers' History
Bill Torrey, 1972-73 to 1991-92; Don Maloney, 1992-93 to 1994-95; Don Maloney and Mike Milbury, 1995-96; Mike Milbury, 1996-97 to date.

General Manager

MILBURY, MIKE
General Manager, New York Islanders. Born in Walpole, MA, June 17, 1952.

Mike Milbury came to the Islanders with 20 years of professional hockey experience with the Boston Bruins — as a player, assistant coach, assistant general manager, general manager and coach on both the NHL and AHL levels. Milbury took over as general manager from Don Maloney on December 12, 1995.

Milbury's recent trades have brought the Islanders established stars like Alexei Yashin, Michael Peca and Adrian Aucoin, while his eye for young talent has yielded new NHL stars such as 2003-04 Calder Trophy nominee Trent Hunter, Mattias Weinhandl and starting goaltender Rick DiPietro. Under Milbury's direction, the Islanders have earned a playoff spot in each of the last three seasons.

Milbury joined the Boston organization after graduating from Colgate University with a degree in urban sociology and enjoyed a 10-year playing career with the team. He retired May 6, 1985 and took over as assistant coach. He returned to the ice late in the 1985-86 season when injuries decimated the Bruins defense.

Milbury's playing career concluded after the 1986-87 season and on July 16, 1987 he took over as coach of the Maine Mariners, Boston's top AHL affiliate. In his first year with the team he guided the Mariners to the AHL's Northern Division title and was named both AHL coach of the year and *The Hockey News* minor league coach of the year.

NHL Coaching Record

Season	Team	Games	Regular Season			Games	Playoffs		
			W	L	T		W	L	
1989-90	Boston	80	46	25	9	21	13	8	
1990-91	Boston	80	44	24	12	19	10	9	
1995-96	NY Islanders	82	22	50	10	....	....	....	
1996-97	NY Islanders	45	13	23	9	....	....	....	
1997-98	NY Islanders	19	8	9	2	....	....	....	
	NHL Totals	**306**	**133**	**131**	**42**	**40**	**23**	**17**	

Club Directory

Nassau Veterans' Memorial Coliseum

New York Islanders
Executive Office
1535 Old Country Rd.
Plainview, NY 11803
Phone **516/501-6700**
FAX 516/501-6762
www.newyorkislanders.com
Arena
Nassau Veterans'
Memorial Coliseum
Uniondale, NY 11553
Capacity: 16,234

Owner/Governor	Charles B. Wang
Operations	
Sr. VP of Operations/Alternate Governor	Michael J. Picker
General Counsel/Alternate Governor	Roy Reichbach
Sr. VP/CFO	Art McCarthy
Manager of Human Resources & Adminstration	Theresa Dewar
Controller	Ralph Sellitti
Assistant Controller	Ginna Cotton
Payroll Manager	Christine Bowler
Accounts Payable	Janet Nelson
Staff Accountant	Laura Ferretti
Accounting Assistant	Teressa Farino
Ticket Manager	Maria Corvino
Assistant Ticket Manager	Adam Ortiz
Sales	
Sr. VP of Sales	Paul Lancey
Sales Assistant	Jessica Rotoli
VP/Regional Managers	Bill Kain, Larry Fitzpatrick
Regional Managers	Mary Dolan Grippo, Chris Lombardo
Account Managers	Emily Derkasch, Steven Beisel, Mike Bellinzoni, Kate Larson, Brian Reynolds, Cliff Gault
Account Manager	Ted Van Zelst, Anthony Mercogliano, Erik Scheibe
Client Service Representatives	Kerry Cornils, Jeff Guida, Marc Steffa, Mike Surrey, Erin Leavy
Marketing	
VP of Marketing	Dori White
VP, Communications	Chris Botta
VP, Game Operations	Tim Beach
Manager, Marketing/Iceworks	Jessica Sousa
Merchandise	Danny DiPierri
Avid Editor	Nima Foroush
Manager, Creative Services	Thomas Takoczy
Director, Community Relations/Foundation	Heather Umen
Marketing Coordinator	Jennifer Meilan
Hockey Operations	
General Manager	Michael Milbury
Manager, Hockey Administration	Joanne Holewa
Assistant Manager, Hockey Administration	Kerry Gwydir
Head Coach	Steve Stirling
Assistant Coach	Jeff Jackson
Goaltending Coach	Sudarshan Maharaj
Strength and Conditioning Coach	Garrett Timms
Video Coordinator	Bob Smith
Head Amateur Scout	Tony Feltrin
Director of Pro Scouting	Kenn Morrow
Assistant Director of Pro Scouting	Kevin Maxwell
Chief US Scout	Jay Heinbuck
Chief Canada Scout	Doug Gibson
Ontario Scout	Harkie Singh
Chief European Amateur Scout	Ryan Jankowski
European Scout	Anders Kallur
Czech and Slovak Scout	Karel Pavlik
Russian Scout	Yuri Karmanov
Head Athletic Trainer	Rich Campbell
Assistant Athletic Trainer	Andy Wetstein
Head Equipment Manager	Scott Moon
Equipment Assistant	Tom Kitz
Director of Medical Services	Dr. Elliot Pellman
Internist	Dr. Clifford Cooper
Team Orthopedists	Drs. Elliott Hershman, Kenneth Montgomery, David Gazzaniga
Team Dentists	Drs. Bruce Michnick, Jan Sherman

Bobby Holik had 25 goals in 82 games.

New York Rangers

2003-04 Results: 27W-40L-7T-8OTL 69PTS.
Fourth, Atlantic Division

Year-by-Year Record

Season	GP	Home W	L	T	OL	Road W	L	T	OL	Overall W	L	T	OL	GF	GA	Pts.	Finished	Playoff Result
2003-04	82	13	21	3	4	14	19	4	4	27	40	7	8	206	250	69	4th, Atlantic Div.	Out of Playoffs
2002-03	82	17	18	4	2	15	18	6	2	32	36	10	4	210	231	78	4th, Atlantic Div.	Out of Playoffs
2001-02	82	19	19	2	1	17	19	2	3	36	38	4	4	227	258	80	4th, Atlantic Div.	Out of Playoffs
2000-01	82	17	20	3	1	16	23	2	0	33	43	5	1	250	290	72	4th, Atlantic Div.	Out of Playoffs
1999-2000	82	15	20	5	1	14	18	7	2	29	38	12	3	218	246	73	4th, Atlantic Div.	Out of Playoffs
1998-99	82	17	19	5	...	16	19	6	...	33	38	11	...	217	227	77	4th, Atlantic Div.	Out of Playoffs
1997-98	82	14	18	9	...	11	21	9	...	25	39	18	...	197	231	68	5th, Atlantic Div.	Out of Playoffs
1996-97	82	21	14	6	...	17	20	4	...	38	34	10	...	258	231	86	4th, Atlantic Div.	Lost Conf. Final
1995-96	82	22	10	9	...	19	17	5	...	41	27	14	...	272	237	96	2nd, Atlantic Div.	Lost Conf. Semi-Final
1994-95	48	11	10	3	...	11	13	0	...	22	23	3	...	139	134	47	4th, Atlantic Div.	Lost Conf. Semi-Final
1993-94	84	28	8	6	...	24	16	2	...	52	24	8	...	299	231	112	1st, Atlantic Div.	Won Stanley Cup
1992-93	84	20	17	5	...	14	22	6	...	34	39	11	...	304	308	79	6th, Patrick Div.	Out of Playoffs
1991-92	80	28	8	4	...	22	17	1	...	50	25	5	...	321	246	105	1st, Patrick Div.	Lost Div. Final
1990-91	80	22	11	7	...	14	20	6	...	36	31	13	...	297	265	85	2nd, Patrick Div.	Lost Div. Semi-Final
1989-90	80	20	11	9	...	16	20	4	...	36	31	13	...	279	267	85	1st, Patrick Div.	Lost Div. Final
1988-89	80	21	17	2	...	16	18	6	...	37	35	8	...	310	307	82	3rd, Patrick Div.	Lost Div. Semi-Final
1987-88	80	22	13	5	...	14	21	5	...	36	34	10	...	300	283	82	5th, Patrick Div.	Out of Playoffs
1986-87	80	18	18	4	...	16	20	4	...	34	38	8	...	307	323	76	4th, Patrick Div.	Lost Div. Semi-Final
1985-86	80	20	18	2	...	16	20	4	...	36	38	6	...	280	276	78	4th, Patrick Div.	Lost Conf. Championship
1984-85	80	16	18	6	...	10	26	4	...	26	44	10	...	295	345	62	4th, Patrick Div.	Lost Div. Semi-Final
1983-84	80	27	12	1	...	15	17	8	...	42	29	9	...	314	304	93	4th, Patrick Div.	Lost Div. Semi-Final
1982-83	80	24	13	3	...	11	22	7	...	35	35	10	...	306	287	80	4th, Patrick Div.	Lost Div. Final
1981-82	80	19	15	6	...	20	12	8	...	39	27	14	...	316	306	92	2nd, Patrick Div.	Lost Div. Final
1980-81	80	17	13	10	...	13	23	4	...	30	36	14	...	312	317	74	4th, Patrick Div.	Lost Semi-Final
1979-80	80	22	10	8	...	16	22	2	...	38	32	10	...	308	284	86	3rd, Patrick Div.	Lost Quarter-Final
1978-79	80	19	13	8	...	21	16	3	...	40	29	11	...	316	292	91	3rd, Patrick Div.	Lost Final
1977-78	80	18	15	7	...	12	22	6	...	30	37	13	...	279	280	73	4th, Patrick Div.	Lost Prelim. Round
1976-77	80	17	18	5	...	12	19	9	...	29	37	14	...	272	310	72	4th, Patrick Div.	Out of Playoffs
1975-76	80	16	16	8	...	13	26	1	...	29	42	9	...	262	333	67	4th, Patrick Div.	Out of Playoffs
1974-75	80	21	11	8	...	16	18	6	...	37	29	14	...	319	276	88	2nd, Patrick Div.	Lost Prelim. Round
1973-74	78	26	7	6	...	14	17	8	...	40	24	14	...	300	251	94	3rd, East Div.	Lost Semi-Final
1972-73	78	26	8	5	...	21	15	3	...	47	23	8	...	297	208	102	3rd, East Div.	Lost Semi-Final
1971-72	78	26	6	7	...	22	11	6	...	48	17	13	...	317	192	109	2nd, East Div.	Lost Final
1970-71	78	30	2	7	...	19	16	4	...	49	18	11	...	259	177	109	2nd, East Div.	Lost Semi-Final
1969-70	76	22	8	8	...	16	14	8	...	38	22	16	...	246	189	92	4th, East Div.	Lost Quarter-Final
1968-69	76	27	7	4	...	14	19	5	...	41	26	9	...	231	196	91	3rd, East Div.	Lost Quarter-Final
1967-68	74	22	8	7	...	17	15	5	...	39	23	12	...	226	183	90	2nd, East Div.	Lost Quarter-Final
1966-67	70	18	12	5	...	12	16	7	...	30	28	12	...	188	189	72	4th,	Lost Semi-Final
1965-66	70	12	16	7	...	6	25	4	...	18	41	11	...	195	261	47	6th,	Out of Playoffs
1964-65	70	8	19	8	...	12	19	4	...	20	38	12	...	179	246	52	5th,	Out of Playoffs
1963-64	70	14	13	8	...	8	25	2	...	22	38	10	...	186	242	54	5th,	Out of Playoffs
1962-63	70	12	17	6	...	10	19	6	...	22	36	12	...	211	233	56	5th,	Out of Playoffs
1961-62	70	16	11	8	...	10	21	4	...	26	32	12	...	195	207	64	4th,	Lost Semi-Final
1960-61	70	15	15	5	...	7	23	5	...	22	38	10	...	204	248	54	5th,	Out of Playoffs
1959-60	70	10	15	10	...	7	23	5	...	17	38	15	...	187	247	49	6th,	Out of Playoffs
1958-59	70	14	16	5	...	12	16	7	...	26	32	12	...	201	217	64	5th,	Out of Playoffs
1957-58	70	14	15	6	...	18	10	7	...	32	25	13	...	195	188	77	2nd,	Lost Semi-Final
1956-57	70	15	12	8	...	11	18	6	...	26	30	14	...	184	227	66	4th,	Lost Semi-Final
1955-56	70	20	7	8	...	12	21	2	...	32	28	10	...	204	203	74	3rd,	Lost Semi-Final
1954-55	70	10	12	13	...	7	23	5	...	17	35	18	...	150	210	52	5th,	Out of Playoffs
1953-54	70	18	12	5	...	11	19	5	...	29	31	10	...	161	182	68	5th,	Out of Playoffs
1952-53	70	11	14	10	...	6	23	6	...	17	37	16	...	152	211	50	6th,	Out of Playoffs
1951-52	70	16	13	6	...	7	21	7	...	23	34	13	...	192	219	59	5th,	Out of Playoffs
1950-51	70	14	11	10	...	6	18	11	...	20	29	21	...	169	201	61	5th,	Out of Playoffs
1949-50	70	19	12	4	...	9	19	7	...	28	31	11	...	170	189	67	4th,	Lost Final
1948-49	60	13	12	5	...	5	19	6	...	18	31	11	...	133	172	47	6th,	Out of Playoffs
1947-48	60	11	12	7	...	10	14	6	...	21	26	13	...	176	201	55	4th,	Lost Semi-Final
1946-47	60	11	14	5	...	11	18	1	...	22	32	6	...	167	186	50	5th,	Out of Playoffs
1945-46	50	8	12	5	...	5	16	4	...	13	28	9	...	144	191	35	6th,	Out of Playoffs
1944-45	50	5	7	13	...	4	18	3	...	11	29	10	...	154	247	32	6th,	Out of Playoffs
1943-44	50	4	17	4	...	2	22	1	...	6	39	5	...	162	310	17	6th,	Out of Playoffs
1942-43	50	7	13	5	...	4	18	3	...	11	31	8	...	161	253	30	6th,	Out of Playoffs
1941-42	48	15	8	1	...	14	9	1	...	29	17	2	...	177	143	60	1st,	Lost Semi-Final
1940-41	48	8	12	4	...	8	12	4	...	21	19	8	...	143	125	50	4th,	Lost Quarter-Final
1939-40	48	17	4	3	...	10	7	7	...	27	11	10	...	136	77	64	2nd,	Won Stanley Cup
1938-39	48	13	8	3	...	13	8	3	...	26	16	6	...	149	105	58	2nd,	Lost Semi-Final
1937-38	48	15	5	4	...	12	10	2	...	27	15	6	...	149	96	60	2nd, Amn. Div.	Lost Quarter-Final
1936-37	48	9	7	8	...	10	13	1	...	19	20	9	...	117	106	47	3rd, Amn. Div.	Lost Final
1935-36	48	11	6	7	...	8	11	5	...	19	17	12	...	91	96	50	3rd, Amn. Div.	Out of Playoffs
1934-35	48	11	8	5	...	11	12	1	...	22	20	6	...	137	139	50	3rd, Amn. Div.	Lost Semi-Final
1933-34	48	11	7	6	...	10	12	2	...	21	19	8	...	120	113	50	3rd, Amn. Div.	Lost Quarter-Final
1932-33	48	12	7	5	...	11	10	3	...	23	17	8	...	135	107	54	3rd, Amn. Div.	Won Stanley Cup
1931-32	48	13	4	7	...	10	10	4	...	23	17	8	...	134	112	54	1st, Amn. Div.	Lost Final
1930-31	44	10	9	3	...	9	7	6	...	19	16	9	...	106	87	47	3rd, Amn. Div.	Lost Semi-Final
1929-30	44	11	6	5	...	6	12	4	...	17	17	10	...	136	143	44	3rd, Amn. Div.	Lost Semi-Final
1928-29	44	12	6	4	...	9	7	6	...	21	13	10	...	72	65	52	2nd, Amn. Div.	Lost Final
1927-28	44	10	8	4	...	9	8	5	...	19	16	9	...	94	79	47	2nd, Amn. Div.	Won Stanley Cup
1926-27	44	13	5	4	...	12	8	2	...	25	13	6	...	95	72	56	1st, Amn. Div.	Lost Quarter-Final

2004-05 Schedule

Oct.	Fri.	15	Pittsburgh
	Sat.	16	at Pittsburgh
	Wed.	20	Philadelphia
	Sat.	23	Atlanta
	Mon.	25	San Jose
	Fri.	29	at Pittsburgh
	Sat.	30	at Toronto
Nov.	Mon.	1	Los Angeles
	Wed.	3	Boston
	Fri.	5	Florida
	Sat.	6	at Ottawa
	Mon.	8	Nashville
	Thu.	11	Toronto
	Sat.	13	Buffalo
	Mon.	15	at NY Islanders
	Wed.	17	at Atlanta
	Fri.	19	at Buffalo
	Sat.	20	at Montreal
	Mon.	22	NY Islanders
	Wed.	24	at Carolina
	Fri.	26	at Washington*
	Sun.	28	Pittsburgh
Dec.	Wed.	1	at New Jersey
	Thu.	2	at Philadelphia
	Sat.	4	New Jersey
	Mon.	6	Ottawa
	Thu.	9	Washington
	Sat.	11	at New Jersey*
	Sun.	12	Boston
	Tue.	14	at Washington
	Fri.	17	NY Islanders
	Sat.	18	at Philadelphia
	Tue.	21	at Atlanta
	Thu.	23	Florida
	Sun.	26	at Buffalo
	Fri.	31	at Florida*
Jan.	Sat.	1	at Tampa Bay*
	Mon.	3	Anaheim
	Thu.	6	Columbus
	Sat.	8	at Boston*
	Mon.	10	Montreal
	Thu.	13	Phoenix
	Sat.	15	Pittsburgh
	Tue.	18	at Ottawa
	Thu.	20	New Jersey
	Sat.	22	Philadelphia*
	Mon.	24	St. Louis
	Tue.	25	at NY Islanders
	Thu.	27	Atlanta
	Sat.	29	at Montreal
Feb.	Wed.	2	at Vancouver
	Thu.	3	at Calgary
	Sat.	5	at Edmonton
	Tue.	8	Toronto
	Thu.	10	at New Jersey
	Wed.	16	at Minnesota
	Thu.	17	at Columbus
	Sat.	19	Philadelphia*
	Mon.	21	Chicago*
	Wed.	23	Tampa Bay
	Sat.	26	at Pittsburgh
	Sun.	27	Colorado*
Mar.	Wed.	2	Carolina
	Sat.	5	at NY Islanders
	Mon.	7	Washington
	Wed.	9	at Dallas
	Fri.	11	at Anaheim
	Sun.	13	at San Jose
	Wed.	16	New Jersey
	Fri.	18	Buffalo
	Sat.	19	at Toronto
	Tue.	22	Carolina
	Fri.	25	NY Islanders
	Sat.	26	at Detroit
	Mon.	28	Montreal
	Wed.	30	at Florida
	Thu.	31	at Tampa Bay
Apr.	Sat.	2	at Carolina
	Mon.	4	Tampa Bay
	Wed.	6	Ottawa
	Thu.	7	at Philadelphia
	Sat.	9	at Boston*

Denotes afternoon game.

Franchise date: May 15, 1926

EASTERN CONFERENCE NHL
ATLANTIC DIVISION

79th NHL Season

2004-05 Player Personnel

FORWARDS	HT	WT	S	Place of Birth	Date	2003-04 Club
BALEJ, Jozef	6-1	187	R	Myjava, Czech.	2/22/82	Mtl-Hamilton-NYR-Hart
BETTS, Blair	6-1	200	L	Edmonton, Alta.	2/16/80	Calgary
GERNANDER, Ken	5-10	175	L	Coleraine, MN	6/30/69	NY Rangers-Hartford
GILLIES, Trevor	6-3	210	L	Cambridge, Ont.	1/30/79	Springfield
GIROUX, Alexandre	6-3	190	L	Quebec City, Que.	6/16/81	Binghamton-Hartford
HELMINEN, Dwight	6-0	200	L	Hancock, MI	6/22/83	U. of Michigan
HOLIK, Bobby	6-4	230	R	Jihlava, Czech.	1/1/71	NY Rangers
HOLLWEG, Ryan	5-9	201	L	Downey, CA	4/23/83	Medicine Hat
JAGR, Jaromir	6-2	234	L	Kladno, Czech.	2/15/72	Washington-NY Rangers
LAWSON, Lucas	6-1	195	L	Braeside, Ont.	8/10/79	Hartford-Charlotte
LUNDMARK, Jamie	6-0	174	R	Edmonton, Alta.	1/16/81	NY Rangers
MOORE, Dominic	6-0	180	L	Thornhill, Ont.	8/3/80	NY Rangers-Hartford
MURRAY, Garth	6-1	205	L	Regina, Sask.	9/17/82	NY Rangers-Hartford
NYLANDER, Michael	6-1	195	L	Stockholm, Sweden	10/3/72	Washington-Boston
ORTMEYER, Jed	6-1	186	R	Omaha, NE	9/3/78	NY Rangers-Hartford
SCOTT, Richard	6-2	195	L	Orillia, Ont.	8/1/78	NY Rangers-Hartford
STRUDWICK, Jason	6-3	210	L	Edmonton, Alta.	7/17/75	Chicago
ULMER, Layne	6-1	205	L	North Battleford, Sask.	9/14/80	NY Rangers-Hartford
WISEMAN, Chad	6-0	190	L	Burlington, Ont.	3/25/81	NY Rangers-Hartford
DEFENSEMEN						
GRENIER, Martin	6-5	245	L	Laval, Que.	11/2/80	Vancouver-Manitoba-Hartford
KASPARAITIS, Darius	5-11	212	L	Elektrenai, USSR	10/16/72	NY Rangers
KONDRATIEV, Maxim	6-1	176	L	Togliatti, USSR	1/20/83	Tor-St.J's-Lada Togliatti
LAMPMAN, Bryce	6-1	193	L	Rochester, MN	8/31/82	NY Rangers-Hartford
LIFFITON, David	6-2	201	L	Windsor, Ont.	10/18/84	Plymouth
MacMILLAN, Jeff	6-3	206	L	Durham, Ont.	3/30/79	Dallas-Utah
NYCHOLAT, Lawrence	6-0	192	L	Calgary, Alta.	5/7/79	NY Rangers-Hartford
POCK, Thomas	6-1	208	L	Klagenfurt, Austria	12/2/81	Massachusetts-NY Rangers
POTI, Tom	6-3	215	L	Worcester, MA	3/22/77	NY Rangers
PURINTON, Dale	6-3	214	L	Fort Wayne, IN	10/11/76	NY Rangers
RACHUNEK, Karel	6-2	211	R	Zlin, Czech.	8/27/79	Ottawa-NY Rangers
RAWLYK, Rory	6-3	175	R	Edmonton, Alta.	9/9/83	Hartford-Charlotte
TAYLOR, Jake	6-4	220	R	Rochester, MN	8/1/83	U. of Minnesota
TJUTIN, Fedor	6-2	196	L	Izhevsk, USSR	7/19/83	NY Rangers-Hartford
WELLER, Craig	6-3	195	R	Calgary, Alta.	1/17/81	Hartford

GOALTENDERS	HT	WT	C	Place of Birth	Date	2003-04 Club
BLACKBURN, Dan	6-0	180	L	Montreal, Que.	5/20/83	Did Not Play - Injured
DUNHAM, Mike	6-3	200	L	Johnson City, NY	6/1/72	NY Rangers
LABARBERA, Jason	6-2	205	L	Prince George, B.C.	1/18/80	NY Rangers-Hartford
VALIQUETTE, Stephen	6-5	205	L	Etobicoke, Ont.	8/20/77	Edm-Tor (AHL)-NYR-Hart

Coach

RENNEY, TOM

Coach, New York Rangers. Born in Cranbrook, B.C., March 1, 1955.

Tom Renney took over as interim coach of the New York Rangers on February 25, 2004. He was officially named the 33rd head coach in franchise history on July 6. Renney joined the Rangers on July 31, 2000 as director of player personnel and was promoted to vice president, player development on June 21, 2002. In that position, he oversaw all facets of the team's amateur scouting operations, while also assisting with the professional scouting process and player development within the organization. Renney joined the Rangers coaching staff as an assistant coach on July 21, 2003.

From June of 1996 through November, 1997, Renney served as head coach of the Vancouver Canucks. Prior to his return to the National Hockey League in New York, Renney held the position of vice president and head coach of the Canadian national team. Renney rejoined the Canadian Hockey Association in May, 1998. He began his affiliation with the Canadian national team in 1992 and coached Canada's Olympic hockey team to a silver medal at the 1994 Winter Games in Lillehammer, Norway. Later that year, he served as an assistant coach on Team Canada's gold medal-winning team at the World Championships. Previously, he won the Memorial Cup with the Kamloops Blazers in 1992.

Coaching Record

		Regular Season				Playoffs, Olympics or World Championships			
Year	Team	Games	W	L	T	Games	W	L	T
1990-91	Kamloops (WHL)	72	50	20	2	12	5	7	0
1991-92	Kamloops (WHL)	72	51	17	4	16	11	5	0
1993-94	Canadian National	63	33	26	4	8	5	2	1*
1994-95	Canadian National	57	37	17	3	8	4	2	2**
1995-96	Canadian National	53	33	12	8	8	4	2	2***
1996-97	**Vancouver (NHL)**	**82**	**35**	**40**	**7**	....	....	....	....
1997-98	**Vancouver (NHL)**	**19**	**4**	**13**	**2**	....	....	....	....
1999-00	Canadian National	56	27	23	6	....	....	....	....
2003-04	**NY Rangers (NHL)**	**20**	**5**	**15**	**0**	....	....	....	....
	NHL Totals	**121**	**44**	**68**	**9**	....	....	....	....

* Olympics (silver medal)
** World Championships (bronze)
*** World Championships (silver)

2003-04 Scoring

* - rookie

Regular Season

Pos	#	Player	Team	GP	G	A	Pts	+/-	PIM	PP	SH	GW	GT	S	%
R	68	Jaromir Jagr	WSH	46	16	29	45	–4	26	6	0	1	1	159	10.1
			NYR	31	15	14	29	–1	12	4	0	2	0	98	15.3
			TOTAL	77	31	43	74	–5	38	10	0	3	1	257	12.1
C	16	Bobby Holik	NYR	82	25	31	56	4	96	8	0	4	0	225	11.1
C	11	Mark Messier	NYR	76	18	25	43	3	42	1	2	3	1	104	17.3
C	88	Eric Lindros	NYR	39	10	22	32	7	60	3	0	0	0	83	12.0
L	37	Jan Hlavac	NYR	72	5	21	26	–8	16	2	0	0	0	125	4.0
D	3	Tom Poti	NYR	67	10	14	24	–1	47	4	0	5	0	124	8.1
D	23	Karel Rachunek	OTT	60	1	16	17	17	29	0	0	0	0	99	1.0
			NYR	12	1	3	4	–9	4	1	0	0	0	21	4.8
			TOTAL	72	2	19	21	8	33	1	0	0	0	120	1.7
D	29	Boris Mironov	NYR	75	3	13	16	1	86	1	0	1	1	129	2.3
L	44	Josh Green	CGY	36	2	4	6	–3	24	0	0	0	0	47	4.3
			NYR	14	3	2	5	0	8	0	0	1	0	29	10.3
			TOTAL	50	5	6	11	–3	32	0	0	1	0	76	6.6
C	21	Jamie Lundmark	NYR	56	2	8	10	–8	33	0	0	1	0	68	2.9
D	6	Darius Kasparaitis	NYR	44	1	9	10	11	48	0	0	0	0	29	3.4
D	74	Joel Bouchard	NYR	28	1	7	8	2	10	0	0	0	0	34	2.9
L	39	Dan Lacouture	NYR	59	5	2	7	–13	82	1	0	1	0	39	12.8
D	51 *	Fedor Tyutin	NYR	25	2	5	7	–4	14	0	1	0	0	33	6.1
R	41 *	Jed Ortmeyer	NYR	58	2	4	6	–10	16	0	0	0	0	48	4.2
R	10	Sandy Mccarthy	BOS	37	3	1	4	0	28	0	0	1	0	27	11.1
			NYR	13	1	0	1	–8	2	1	0	0	0	11	9.1
			TOTAL	50	4	1	5	–8	30	1	0	1	0	38	10.5
R	10	Sandy Mccarthy	NYR	50	4	1	5	–8	30	1	0	1	0	38	10.5
R	20 *	Jozef Balej	MTL	4	0	0	0	–1	0	0	0	0	0	4	0.0
			NYR	13	1	4	5	0	4	0	0	0	0	25	4.0
			TOTAL	17	1	4	5	–1	4	0	0	0	0	29	3.4
D	22 *	Thomas Pock	NYR	6	2	2	4	–4	0	0	0	0	0	8	25.0
C	47 *	Mike Green	FLA	11	0	1	1	0	2	0	0	0	0	7	0.0
			NYR	13	1	2	3	0	2	0	0	0	0	13	7.7
			TOTAL	24	1	3	4	0	4	0	0	0	0	20	5.0
C	28 *	Dominic Moore	NYR	5	0	3	3	0	0	0	0	0	0	3	0.0
D	5	Dale Purinton	NYR	40	1	1	2	–9	117	0	0	0	0	31	3.2
L	15 *	Chad Wiseman	NYR	4	1	0	1	–1	0	0	0	0	0	3	33.3
C	25 *	Garth Murray	NYR	20	1	0	1	–5	24	0	0	0	0	18	5.6
R	18	Cory Larose	NYR	7	0	1	1	–2	4	0	0	0	0	10	0.0
D	24	Chris Mcallister	COL	34	0	0	0	–2	62	0	0	0	0	11	0.0
			NYR	12	0	1	1	–4	12	0	0	0	0	8	0.0
			TOTAL	46	0	1	1	–6	74	0	0	0	0	19	0.0
R	18 *	Mike Siklenka	NYR	1	0	0	0	0	0	0	0	0	0	0	0.0
C	53 *	Layne Ulmer	NYR	1	0	0	0	–1	0	0	0	0	0	1	0.0
C	12	Ken Gernander	NYR	2	0	0	0	–1	2	0	0	0	0	0	0.0
C	22 *	Benoit Dusablon	NYR	3	0	0	0	–1	2	0	0	0	0	3	0.0
R	43	Jason Macdonald	NYR	4	0	0	0	–1	19	0	0	0	0	3	0.0
R	25	Paul Healey	NYR	4	0	0	0	0	0	0	0	0	0	0	0.0
R	13 *	Richard Scott	NYR	5	0	0	0	0	23	0	0	0	0	1	0.0
D	38 *	Bryce Lampman	NYR	8	0	0	0	–4	0	0	0	0	0	7	0.0
D	28 *	Lawrence Nycholat	NYR	9	0	0	0	–2	6	0	0	0	0	6	0.0
D	24	Jamie Pushor	CBJ	7	0	0	0	–2	2	0	0	0	0	6	0.0
			NYR	7	0	0	0	–3	0	0	0	0	0	4	0.0
			TOTAL	14	0	0	0	–5	2	0	0	0	0	10	0.0

Goaltending

No.	Goaltender	GPI	Mins	Avg	W	L	T	EN	SO	GA	SA	S%	G	A	PIM
30	Jussi Markkanen	26	1244	2.56	8	12	1	2	2	53	611	.913	0	0	0
33	Jamie Mclennan	4	244	2.95	1	3	0	1	0	12	97	.876	0	0	0
45	Stephen Valiquette	2	120	3.00	1	1	0	0	0	6	71	.915	0	0	0
30	Mike Dunham	57	3148	3.03	16	30	6	1	2	159	1522	.896	0	0	0
34	* Jason Labarbera	4	198	4.85	1	2	0	0	0	16	91	.824	0	1	2
	Totals	**82**	**4979**	**3.01**	**27**	**48**	**7**	**4**	**4**	**250**	**2396**	**.896**			

Captains' History

Bill Cook, 1926-27 to 1936-37; Art Coulter, 1937-38 to 1941-42; Ott Heller, 1942-43 to 1944-45; Neil Colville 1945-46 to 1948-49; Buddy O'Connor, 1949-50; Frank Eddolls, 1950-51; Frank Eddolls and Allan Stanley, 1951-52; Allan Stanley, 1952-53; Allan Stanley and Don Raleigh, 1953-54; Don Raleigh, 1954-55; Harry Howell, 1955-56, 1956-57; Red Sullivan, 1957-58 to 1960-61; Andy Bathgate, 1961-62, 1962-63; Andy Bathgate and Camille Henry, 1963-64; Camille Henry and Bob Nevin, 1964-65; Bob Nevin 1965-66 to 1970-71; Vic Hadfield, 1971-72 to 1973-74; Brad Park, 1974-75; Brad Park and Phil Esposito, 1975-76; Phil Esposito, 1976-77, 1977-78; Dave Maloney, 1978-79, 1979-80; Dave Maloney, Walt Tkaczuk and Barry Beck, 1980-81; Barry Beck, 1981-82 to 1985-86; Ron Greschner, 1986-87; Ron Greschner and Kelly Kisio, 1987-88; Kelly Kisio, 1988-89 to 1990-91; Mark Messier, 1991-92 to 1996-97; Brian Leetch, 1997-98 to 1999-2000; Mark Messier, 2000-01 to 2003-04.

Coaching History

Lester Patrick, 1926-27 to 1938-39; Frank Boucher, 1939-40 to 1947-48; Frank Boucher and Lynn Patrick, 1948-49; Lynn Patrick, 1949-50; Neil Colville, 1950-51; Neil Colville and Bill Cook, 1951-52; Bill Cook, 1952-53; Frank Boucher and Muzz Patrick, 1953-54; Muzz Patrick, 1954-55; Phil Watson, 1955-56 to 1958-59; Phil Watson and Alf Pike, 1959-60; Alf Pike, 1960-61; Doug Harvey, 1961-62; Muzz Patrick and Red Sullivan, 1962-63; Red Sullivan, 1963-64, 1964-65; Red Sullivan and Emile Francis, 1965-66; Emile Francis, 1966-67, 1967-68; Bernie Geoffrion and Emile Francis, 1968-69; Emile Francis, 1969-70 to 1972-73; Larry Popein and Emile Francis, 1973-74; Emile Francis, 1974-75; Ron Stewart and John Ferguson, 1975-76; John Ferguson, 1976-77; Jean-Guy Talbot, 1977-78; Fred Shero, 1978-79, 1979-80; Fred Shero and Craig Patrick, 1980-81; Herb Brooks, 1981-82 to 1983-84; Herb Brooks and Craig Patrick, 1984-85; Ted Sator, 1985-86; Ted Sator, Tom Webster and Phil Esposito, 1986-87; Michel Bergeron, 1987-88; Michel Bergeron and Phil Esposito, 1988-89; Roger Neilson, 1989-90 to 1991-92; Roger Neilson and Ron Smith, 1992-93; Mike Keenan, 1993-94; Colin Campbell, 1994-95 to 1996-97; Colin Campbell and John Muckler, 1997-98; John Muckler, 1998-99; John Muckler and John Tortorella, 1999-2000; Ron Low, 2000-01, 2001-02; Bryan Trottier and Glen Sather, 2002-03; Glen Sather and Tom Renney, 2003-04; Tom Renney, 2004-05.

Club Records

Team

(Figures in brackets for season records are games played; records for fewest points, wins, ties, losses, goals, goals against are for 70 or more games)

Most Points **112** 1993-94 (84)
Most Wins **52** 1993-94 (84)
Most Ties **21** 1950-51 (70)
Most Losses **44** 1984-85 (80)
Most Goals **321** 1991-92 (80)
Most Goals Against **345** 1984-85 (80)
Fewest Points **47** 1965-66 (70)
Fewest Wins **17** 1952-53 (70), 1954-55 (70), 1959-60 (70)
Fewest Ties **4** 2001-02 (82)
Fewest Losses **17** 1971-72 (78)
Fewest Goals **150** 1954-55 (70)
Fewest Goals Against **177** 1970-71 (78)
Longest Winning Streak
Overall .... **10** Dec. 19/39-Jan. 13/40, Jan. 19-Feb. 10/73
Home .... **14** Dec. 19/39-Feb. 25/40
Away .... **7** Jan. 12-Feb. 12/35, Oct. 28-Nov. 29/78
Longest Undefeated Streak
Overall .... **19** Nov. 23/39-Jan. 13/40 (14 wins, 5 ties)
Home .... **26** Mar. 29/70-Jan. 31/71 (19 wins, 7 ties)
Away .... **11** Nov. 5/39-Jan. 13/40 (6 wins, 5 ties)
Longest Losing Streak
Overall .... **11** Oct. 30-Nov. 27/43
Home .... **7** Oct. 20-Nov. 14/76, Mar. 24-Apr. 14/93
Away .... **10** Oct. 30-Dec. 23/43, Feb. 2-Mar. 15/61
Longest Winless Streak
Overall .... **21** Jan. 23-Mar. 19/44 (17 losses, 4 ties)
Home .... **10** Jan. 30-Mar. 19/44 (7 losses, 3 ties)
Away .... **16** Oct. 9-Dec. 20/52 (12 losses, 4 ties)
Most Shutouts, Season **13** 1928-29 (44)
Most PIM, Season **2,018** 1989-90 (80)
Most Goals, Game .... **12** Nov. 21/71 (Cal. 1 at NYR 12)

Individual

Most Seasons .... **18** Rod Gilbert
Most Games .... **1,160** Harry Howell
Most Goals, Career .... **406** Rod Gilbert
Most Assists, Career .... **741** Brian Leetch
Most Points, Career .... **1,021** Rod Gilbert (406G, 615A)
Most PIM, Career .... **1,226** Ron Greschner
Most Shutouts, Career .... **49** Ed Giacomin
Longest Consecutive Games Streak .... **560** Andy Hebenton (Oct. 7/55-Mar. 24/63)
Most Goals, Season .... **52** Adam Graves (1993-94)
Most Assists, Season .... **80** Brian Leetch (1991-92)
Most Points, Season .... **109** Jean Ratelle (1971-72; 46G, 63A)
Most PIM, Season .... **305** Troy Mallette (1989-90)
Most Points, Defenseman, Season .... **102** Brian Leetch (1991-92; 22G, 80A)
Most Points, Center, Season .... **109** Jean Ratelle (1971-72; 46G, 63A)
Most Points, Right Wing, Season .... **97** Rod Gilbert (1971-72; 43G, 54A), (1974-75; 36G, 61A)
Most Points, Left Wing, Season .... **106** Vic Hadfield (1971-72; 50G, 56A)
Most Points, Rookie, Season .... **76** Mark Pavelich (1981-82; 33G, 43A)
Most Shutouts, Season .... **13** John Ross Roach (1928-29)
Most Goals, Game .... **5** Don Murdoch (Oct. 12/76), Mark Pavelich (Feb. 23/83)
Most Assists, Game .... **5** Walt Tkaczuk (Feb. 12/72), Rod Gilbert (Mar. 2/75, Mar. 30/75, Oct. 8/76), Don Maloney (Jan. 3/87), Brian Leetch (Apr. 18/95), Wayne Gretzky (Feb. 15/99)
Most Points, Game .... **7** Steve Vickers (Feb. 18/76; 3G, 4A)

Retired Numbers

1	Ed Giacomin	1965-1976
7	Rod Gilbert	1960-1978
35	Mike Richter	1989-2003

All-time Record vs. Other Clubs

Regular Season

	At Home								On Road								Total							
	GP	W	L	T	OL	GF	GA	PTS	GP	W	L	T	OL	GF	GA	PTS	GP	W	L	T	OL	GF	GA	PTS
Anaheim	9	3	5	1	0	23	26	7	8	2	6	0	0	25	32	4	17	5	11	1	0	48	58	11
Atlanta	10	3	5	1	1	28	34	8	10	7	3	0	0	34	28	14	20	10	8	1	1	62	62	22
Boston	302	131	116	55	0	921	853	317	298	96	160	42	0	834	1076	234	600	227	276	97	0	1755	1929	551
Buffalo	66	28	23	15	0	214	180	71	68	19	39	10	0	212	279	48	134	47	62	25	0	426	459	119
Calgary	52	24	23	5	0	178	184	53	49	12	27	10	0	148	216	34	101	36	50	15	0	326	400	87
Carolina	45	27	13	4	1	172	115	59	43	16	24	3	0	137	145	35	88	43	37	7	1	309	260	94
Chicago	285	117	113	55	0	841	807	289	286	115	128	43	0	792	870	273	571	232	241	98	0	1633	1677	562
Colorado	34	19	9	4	2	134	99	44	35	13	18	3	1	130	143	30	69	32	27	7	3	264	242	74
Columbus	2	1	0	1	0	7	5	3	4	1	3	0	0	7	16	2	6	2	3	1	0	14	21	5
Dallas	62	36	15	11	0	213	165	83	61	30	19	11	1	221	187	72	123	66	34	22	1	434	352	155
Detroit	284	134	92	58	0	868	738	326	285	76	164	45	0	699	1004	197	569	210	256	103	0	1567	1742	523
Edmonton	30	10	14	6	0	112	113	26	28	13	12	3	0	94	101	29	58	23	26	9	0	206	214	55
Florida	24	12	8	4	0	74	59	28	25	13	9	2	1	69	64	29	49	25	17	6	1	143	123	57
Los Angeles	58	35	17	6	0	233	172	76	60	27	23	10	0	216	199	64	118	62	40	16	0	449	371	140
Minnesota	3	2	1	0	0	10	7	4	4	3	1	0	0	13	11	6	7	5	2	0	0	23	18	10
Montreal	290	118	118	54	0	835	844	290	290	60	190	40	0	669	1125	160	580	178	308	94	0	1504	1969	450
Nashville	6	2	2	1	1	18	15	6	4	2	1	0	1	14	13	5	10	4	3	1	2	32	28	11
New Jersey	84	40	24	20	0	323	255	100	86	34	45	7	0	280	301	75	170	74	69	27	0	603	556	175
NY Islanders	96	55	30	11	0	358	284	121	96	34	54	8	0	306	371	76	192	89	84	19	0	664	655	197
Ottawa	23	11	12	0	0	74	70	22	23	11	8	3	1	65	69	26	46	22	20	3	1	139	139	48
Philadelphia	110	47	39	23	1	353	321	118	109	39	55	14	1	297	355	93	219	86	94	37	2	650	676	211
Phoenix	29	18	9	2	0	128	102	38	31	14	13	4	0	101	107	32	60	32	22	6	0	229	209	70
Pittsburgh	101	51	41	9	0	393	346	111	100	43	40	14	3	365	359	103	201	94	81	23	3	758	705	214
St. Louis	60	44	10	6	0	245	143	94	63	28	25	10	0	202	188	66	123	72	35	16	0	447	331	160
San Jose	10	7	2	1	0	40	29	15	13	9	2	2	0	49	31	20	23	16	4	3	0	89	60	35
Tampa Bay	27	13	11	2	1	87	85	29	25	11	11	3	0	83	86	25	52	24	22	5	1	170	171	54
Toronto	283	120	106	56	1	873	836	297	282	84	158	39	1	741	974	208	565	204	264	95	2	1614	1810	505
Vancouver	54	38	11	5	0	237	139	81	51	33	15	3	0	204	163	69	105	71	26	8	0	441	302	150
Washington	82	38	34	9	1	304	281	86	84	33	41	9	1	273	315	76	166	71	75	18	2	577	596	162
Defunct Clubs	139	87	30	22	0	460	290	196	139	82	34	23	0	441	291	187	278	169	64	45	0	901	581	383
Totals	**2660**	**1271**	**933**	**447**	**9**	**8756**	**7597**	**2998**	**2660**	**960**	**1328**	**361**	**11**	**7721**	**9119**	**2292**	**5320**	**2231**	**2261**	**808**	**20**	**16477**	**16716**	**5290**

Playoffs

	Series	W	L	GP	W	L	T	GF	GA	Last Mtg.	Rnd.	Result
Boston	9	3	6	42	18	22	2	104	114	1973	QF	W 4-1
Buffalo	1	0	1	3	1	2	0	6	11	1978	PRE	L 1-2
Calgary	1	1	0	4	3	1	0	14	8	1980	PRE	W 3-1
Chicago	5	1	4	24	10	14	0	54	66	1973	SF	L 1-4
Colorado	1	1	0	6	4	2	0	25	19	1995	CQF	W 4-2
Detroit	5	1	4	23	10	13	0	49	57	1950	F	L 3-4
Florida	1	1	0	5	4	1	0	13	10	1997	CQF	W 4-1
Los Angeles	2	2	0	6	5	1	0	32	14	1981	PRE	W 3-1
Montreal	14	7	7	61	25	34	2	158	188	1996	CQF	W 4-2
New Jersey	3	3	0	19	12	7	0	56	46	1997	CSF	W 4-1
NY Islanders	8	3	5	39	19	20	0	132	129	1994	CQF	W 4-0
Philadelphia	10	4	6	47	20	27	0	153	157	1997	CF	L 1-4
Pittsburgh	3	0	3	15	3	12	0	45	64	1996	CSF	L 1-4
St. Louis	1	1	0	6	4	2	0	29	22	1981	QF	W 4-2
Toronto	8	5	3	35	19	16	0	86	86	1971	QF	W 4-2
Vancouver	1	1	0	7	4	3	0	21	19	1994	F	W 4-3
Washington	4	2	2	22	11	11	0	71	75	1994	CSF	W 4-1
Defunct Clubs	9	6	3	22	11	7	4	43	29			
Totals	**86**	**42**	**44**	**386**	**183**	**195**	**8**	**1091**	**1114**			

Calgary totals include Atlanta Flames, 1972-73 to 1979-80.
Colorado totals include Quebec, 1979-80 to 1994-95.
Carolina totals include Hartford, 1979-80 to 1996-97.
Dallas totals include Minnesota North Stars, 1967-68 to 1992-93.
New Jersey totals include Kansas City, 1974-75 to 1975-76, and Colorado Rockies, 1976-77 to 1981-82.
Phoenix totals include Winnipeg, 1979-80 to 1995-96.

Playoff Results 2004-2000

(Last playoff appearance: 1997)

Abbreviations: Round: F – Final;
CF – conference final; **CSF** – conference semi-final;
CQF – conference quarter-final; **SF** – semi-final;
QF – quarter-final; **PRE** – preliminary round.

2003-04 Results

Oct.	10	at Minnesota	3-5		11	Tampa Bay	1-2*
	11	at Columbus	0-5		13	NY Islanders	4-1
	16	Atlanta	0-0		15	New Jersey	3-3
	18	Carolina	2-2		17	at Montreal	2-2
	20	Florida	3-1		19	at Boston	2-5
	25	Detroit	3-1		20	Boston	1-4
	28	Anaheim	1-3		22	Philadelphia	2-4
	30	Carolina	4-1		24	at Ottawa	1-9
Nov.	1	at Montreal	5-1		26	Florida	5-2
	2	Colorado	2-3*		28	Washington	1-2
	4	Dallas	3-0		30	Buffalo	1-3
	6	at Carolina	3-6		31	at Buffalo	1-3
	8	Philadelphia	1-2*	**Feb.**	2	Vancouver	4-3
	10	Edmonton	4-5		4	Minnesota	3-4
	12	Pittsburgh	6-2		11	at New Jersey	3-1
	15	at New Jersey	0-5		12	Philadelphia	1-2
	16	at Chicago	2-2		14	at Philadelphia	2-6
	18	at San Jose	2-2		16	Ottawa	1-4
	20	at Colorado	3-4		19	NY Islanders	6-2
	23	Ottawa	6-2		21	New Jersey	3-7
	25	at Tampa Bay	2-0		23	Montreal	1-4
	26	at Florida	3-3		26	at NY Islanders	6-3
	28	at Pittsburgh	4-1		28	at Nashville	1-2*
	30	Toronto	2-4		29	at Atlanta	2-3
Dec.	2	at Toronto	4-5	**Mar.**	2	Atlanta	3-4
	4	at NY Islanders	4-2		4	at Boston	1-3
	7	Tampa Bay	2-3		5	Washington	3-2
	10	Montreal	1-2		7	Pittsburgh	4-7
	12	at Buffalo	3-1		9	at Atlanta	2-0
	13	at Toronto	1-3		12	at Tampa Bay	2-5
	18	NY Islanders	4-3		13	at Florida	2-3*
	20	at Ottawa	1-3		15	New Jersey	1-3
	22	Boston	4-2		18	at Washington	3-4*
	26	Toronto	5-6*		20	at Philadelphia	0-3
	29	at Phoenix	3-2*		21	at Pittsburgh	3-4*
	30	at Los Angeles	3-2*		23	Pittsburgh	2-5
Jan.	1	at St. Louis	4-5		25	Nashville	2-4
	3	at Pittsburgh	4-1		27	at Philadelphia	3-1
	5	Calgary	0-5		30	at New Jersey	0-5
	8	at Carolina	2-3		31	Buffalo	3-4
	10	at NY Islanders	3-2	**Apr.**	3	at Washington	3-2*

* – Overtime

Entry Draft
Selections 2004-1990

2004
Pick
6	Al Montoya
19	Lauri Korpikoski
36	Darin Olver
48	Dane Byers
51	Bruce Graham
60	Brandon Dubinsky
73	Zdenek Bahensky
80	Billy Ryan
127	Ryan Callahan
135	Roman Psurny
169	Jordan Foote
247	Jonathan Paiement
266	Jakub Petruzalek

2003
Pick
12	Hugh Jessiman
50	Ivan Baranka
75	Ken Roche
122	Corey Potter
149	Nigel Dawes
176	Ivan Dornic
179	Philippe Furrer
180	Chris Holt
209	Dylan Reese
243	Jan Marek

2002
Pick
33	Lee Falardeau
81	Marcus Jonasen
127	Nate Guenin
143	Mike Walsh
177	Jake Taylor
194	Kim Hirschovits
226	Joey Crabb
240	Petr Prucha
270	Rob Flynn

2001
Pick
10	Dan Blackburn
40	Fedor Tjutin
79	Garth Murray
113	Bryce Lampman
139	Shawn Collymore
176	Marek Zidlicky
206	Petr Preucil
226	Pontus Petterstrom
226	Pontus Petterstrom
230	Leonid Zhvachkin
238	Ryan Hollweg
269	Juris Stals

2000
Pick
64	Filip Novak
95	Dominic Moore
112	Premysl Duben
140	Nathan Martz
143	Brandon Snee
175	Sven Helfenstein
205	Henrik Lundqvist
238	Danny Eberly
269	Martin Richter

1999
Pick
4	Pavel Brendl
9	Jamie Lundmark
59	David Inman
79	Johan Asplund
90	Patrick Aufiero
137	Garrett Bembridge
177	Jay Dardis
197	Arto Laatikainen
226	Yevgeny Gusakov
251	Petter Henning
254	Alexei Bulatov

1998
Pick
7	Manny Malhotra
40	Randy Copley
66	Jason Labarbera
114	Boyd Kane
122	Patrick Leahy
131	Tomas Kloucek
180	Stefan Lundqvist
207	Johan Witehall
235	Jan Mertzig

1997
Pick
19	Stefan Cherneski
46	Wes Jarvis
73	Burke Henry
93	Tomi Kallarsson
126	Jason McLean
134	Johan Lindbom
136	Mike York
154	Shawn Degagne
175	Johan Holmqvist
182	Mike Mottau
210	Andrew Proskurnicki
236	Richard Miller

1996
Pick
22	Jeff Brown
48	Daniel Goneau
76	Dmitri Subbotin
131	Colin Pepperall
158	Ola Sandberg
185	Jeff Dessner
211	Ryan McKie
237	Ronnie Sundin

1995
Pick
39	Christian Dube
65	Mike Martin
91	Marc Savard
110	Alexei Vasiliev
117	Dale Purinton
143	Peter Slamiar
169	Jeff Heil
195	Ilja Gorokhov
221	Bob Maudie

1994
Pick
26	Dan Cloutier
52	Rudolf Vercik
78	Adam Smith
100	Alexander Korobolin
104	Sylvain Blouin
130	Martin Ethier
135	Yuri Litvinov
156	David Brosseau
182	Alexei Lazarenko
208	Craig Anderson
209	Vitali Yeremeyev
234	Eric Boulton
260	Radoslav Kropac
267	Jamie Butt
286	Kim Johnsson

1993
Pick
8	Niklas Sundstrom
34	Lee Sorochan
61	Maxim Galanov
86	Sergei Olimpiyev
112	Gary Roach
138	Dave Trofimenkoff
162	Sergei Kondrashkin
164	Todd Marchant
190	Ed Campbell
216	Ken Shepard
242	Andrei Kudinov
261	Pavel Komarov
268	Maxim Smelnitsky

1992
Pick
24	Peter Ferraro
48	Mattias Norstrom
72	Eric Cairns
85	Chris Ferraro
120	Dmitri Starostenko
144	David Dal Grande
168	Matt Oates
192	Mickey Elick
216	Daniel Brierley
240	Vladimir Vorobiev

1991
Pick
15	Alex Kovalev
37	Darcy Werenka
96	Corey Machanic
125	Fredrik Jax
128	Barry Young
147	John Rushin
169	Corey Hirsch
191	Vyachesl Uvayev
213	Jamie Ram
235	Vitali Chinakhov
257	Brian Wiseman

1990
Pick
13	Michael Stewart
34	Doug Weight
55	John Vary
69	Jeff Nielsen
76	Rick Willis
85	Sergei Zubov
99	Lubos Rob
118	Jason Weinrich
139	Brian Lonsinger
160	Todd Hedlund
181	Andrew Silverman
202	Jon Hillebrandt
223	Brett Lievers
244	Sergei Nemchinov

Club Directory

New York Rangers
14th Floor
2 Pennsylvania Plaza
New York, New York 10121
Phone **212/465-6000**
PR FAX 212/465-6494
www.newyorkrangers.com
Capacity: 18,200

Madison Square Garden

Office of the Chairman, Madison Square Garden
President and CEO, Cablevision Systems Corporation; Chairman, Madison Square Garden	James L. Dolan
Vice Chairman, Cablevision Systems Corporation; Vice Chairman, Madison Square Garden	Hank J. Ratner
President and COO, MSG Sports	Steve Mills
President, G.M., NY Rangers	Glen Sather
President, Basketball Operations, NY Knicks	Isiah Thomas

Team Executive Management
President, G.M. and Alternate Governor	Glen Sather
Senior Vice President, Finance and Controller	John Cudmore
Senior Vice President, Business Operations	Mark Piazza
Senior Vice President, Legal Affairs, MSG	Marc Schoenfeld
Vice President, Marketing	Jeanie Baumgartner
Vice President, Public Relations	John Rosasco
Vice President, Publicity – MSG Sports Teams	Dan Schoenberg

Madison Square Garden Management
President, MSG Networks	Mike McCarthy
Executive Vice President, Finance	Robert Pollichino
Executive Vice President, Ad Sales	Neil Davis
Executive Vice President, Facilities	Tim Hassett
Senior V.P., Sports and Facility Event Sales	Joel Fisher
Senior V.P., Communications	Barry Watkins
Senior V.P., Team Sales, Tickets/Suites	Brian Lafemina

Hockey Club Personnel
V.P., Player Personnel and Asst. G.M.	Don Maloney
Head Coach and V.P., Player Development	Tom Renney
V.P., Hockey Admin., Research and Development	Cameron Hope
Assistant Coaches	Benoit Allaire, Perry Pearn
Amateur Scouting Staff	Rich Brown, Ray Clearwater, Andre Beaulieu, Jan Gajdosik, Ernie Gare, Vladimir Lutchenko, Christer Rockstom, Bob Crocker, Shanon Sather
Head Professional Scout	Dave Brown
Professional Scouting Staff	Gordie Clark, Gilles Leger, Peter Stephan
Medical Trainer	Jim Ramsay
Equipment Manager	Acacio Marques
Assistant Equipment Manager	James Johnson
Massage Therapist	Bruce Lifrieri
Strength and Conditioning Coordinator	Reg Grant
Video Analyst	Jerry Dineen
Manager, MSG Training Center	Pat Boller

Operations
Director, Business Operations	Barbara Dand
Director, Legal and Business Affairs	Rana Dershowitz
Director, Team Operations	Darren Blake
Director, Finance	Nicole Florit
Exec. Assistant to the Pres. and G.M.	Sara Adamson
Operations Coordinator	Victor Saljanin
Senior Accountant	Jeanine McGrory
Senior Administrative Asst., Finance	Carrie Delorme

Public Relations
Director, Public Relations	Jason Vogel
Manager, Public Relations	Keith Soutar
Coordinator, Public Relations	TBA

Marketing
Director, Marketing Partnerships	Rob Scolaro
Director, Marketing	Janet Duch
Manager, Game Presentation	Ryan Halkett
Manager, Marketing Partnerships	Kelly Jutras
Manager, Website	Jeff Schwartzenberg
Marketing Coordinator	Adam Evert

Community Development
Director, Community Development	Rob Capilli
Director, Special Projects and Community Relations Representative	Rod Gilbert

Medical/Training Staff
Team Physician and Orthopedic Surgeon	Dr. Andrew Feldman
Assistant Team Physician	Dr. Anthony Maddalo
Medical Consultant	Dr. Ronald Weissman
Team Dentists	Drs. Joe Esposito, Don Salomon, Jeff Shapiro
Sports Psychologist – MSG Sports Teams	Dr. Kimberly Amirault

Additional Information
Television Network	MSG Network
Radio Network	MSG Radio
Practice Facility	Madison Square Garden Training Center

President and General Manager

SATHER, GLEN
President/General Manager, New York Rangers.
Born in High River, Alta., September 2, 1943.

Glen Sather, who spent parts of four seasons with the New York Rangers as a player from 1970 to 1974, became the franchise's 12th president and tenth general manager on June 2, 2000. He also served as coach of the team from January 30, 2003, to February 25, 2004.

Sather joined the Rangers following a 24-year career with the Edmonton Oilers, where he was the architect of five Stanley Cup championships between 1984 and 1990. One of the most respected executives in the National Hockey League, Sather was honored for his tremendous achievements in 1997 by becoming the first member of the Oilers organization to be selected to the Hockey Hall of Fame.

Named coach and vice president of hockey operations for the Oilers when the franchise joined the NHL in June of 1979, Sather became general manager and club president in May of 1980. He coached through the 1988-89 season and also returned for 60 games behind the bench in 1993-94. Sather-coached teams won the Stanley Cup four times in the 1980s. As general manager, Sather was instrumental in the Oilers' fifth Cup triumph in 1990.

He played for six different teams during a 10-year NHL career. He scored 80 goals in 658 games.

NHL Coaching Record

		Regular Season				Playoffs		
Season	Team	Games	W	L	T	Games	W	L
1979-80	Edmonton	80	28	39	13	3	0	3
1980-81	Edmonton	62	25	26	11	9	5	4
1981-82	Edmonton	80	48	17	15	5	2	3
1982-83	Edmonton	80	47	21	12	16	11	5
1983-84	Edmonton	80	57	18	5	19	15	4*
1984-85	Edmonton	80	49	20	11	18	15	3*
1985-86	Edmonton	80	56	17	7	10	6	4
1986-87	Edmonton	80	50	24	6	21	16	5*
1987-88	Edmonton	80	44	25	11	18	16	2*
1988-89	Edmonton	80	38	34	8	7	3	4
1993-94	Edmonton	60	22	27	11	....	....	....
2002-03	NY Rangers	28	11	13	4	....	....	....
2003-04	NY Rangers	62	22	33	7	....	....	....
	NHL Totals	**932**	**497**	**314**	**121**	**126**	**89**	**37**

* Stanley Cup win.

General Managers' History

Lester Patrick, 1926-27 to 1945-46; Frank Boucher, 1946-47 to 1954-55; Muzz Patrick, 1955-56 to 1963-64; Emile Francis, 1964-65 to 1974-75; Emile Francis and John Ferguson, 1975-76; John Ferguson, 1976-77, 1977-78; John Ferguson and Fred Shero, 1978-79; Fred Shero, 1979-80; Fred Shero and Craig Patrick, 1980-81; Craig Patrick, 1981-82 to 1985-86; Phil Esposito, 1986-87 to 1988-89; Neil Smith, 1989-90 to 1999-2000; Glen Sather, 2000-01 to date.

Ottawa Senators

2003-04 Results: 43W-23L-10T-6OTL 102PTS.
Third, Northeast Division

Year-by-Year Record

Season	GP	Home W	L	T	OL	Road W	L	T	OL	Overall W	L	T	OL	GF	GA	Pts.	Finished	Playoff Result
2003-04	82	23	8	5	5	20	15	5	1	43	23	10	6	262	189	102	3rd, Northeast Div.	Lost Conf. Quarter-Final
2002-03	82	28	9	3	1	24	12	5	0	52	21	8	1	263	182	113	1st, Northeast Div.	Lost Conf. Championship
2001-02	82	21	13	3	4	18	14	6	3	39	27	9	7	243	208	94	3rd, Northeast Div.	Lost Conf. Semi-Final
2000-01	82	26	7	5	3	22	14	4	1	48	21	9	4	274	205	109	1st, Northeast Div.	Lost Conf. Quarter-Final
1999-2000	82	24	10	5	2	17	18	6	0	41	28	11	2	244	210	95	2nd, Northeast Div.	Lost Conf. Quarter-Final
1998-99	82	22	11	8	...	22	12	7	...	44	23	15	...	239	179	103	1st, Northeast Div.	Lost Conf. Quarter-Final
1997-98	82	18	16	7	...	16	17	8	...	34	33	15	...	193	200	83	5th, Northeast Div.	Lost Conf. Semi-Final
1996-97	82	16	17	8	...	15	19	7	...	31	36	15	...	226	234	77	3rd, Northeast Div.	Lost Conf. Quarter-Final
1995-96	82	8	28	5	...	10	31	0	...	18	59	5	...	191	291	41	6th, Northeast Div.	Out of Playoffs
1994-95	48	5	16	3	...	4	18	2	...	9	34	5	...	117	174	23	7th, Northeast Div.	Out of Playoffs
1993-94	84	8	30	4	...	6	31	5	...	14	61	9	...	201	397	37	7th, Northeast Div.	Out of Playoffs
1992-93	84	9	29	4	...	1	41	0	...	10	70	4	...	202	395	24	6th, Adams Div.	Out of Playoffs

2004-05 Schedule

Oct.	Wed.	13	Montreal
	Sat.	16	at Toronto
	Thu.	21	Toronto
	Sat.	23	Philadelphia
	Wed.	27	at Carolina
	Thu.	28	Los Angeles
	Sat.	30	New Jersey
Nov.	Mon.	1	Boston
	Fri.	5	at Washington
	Sat.	6	NY Rangers
	Tue.	9	Florida
	Fri.	12	Montreal
	Sat.	13	at Montreal
	Tue.	16	at New Jersey
	Thu.	18	Dallas
	Sat.	20	Tampa Bay
	Wed.	24	at Pittsburgh
	Fri.	26	at Boston*
	Tue.	30	at NY Islanders
Dec.	Thu.	2	at Boston
	Sat.	4	Minnesota
	Mon.	6	at NY Rangers
	Tue.	7	at Pittsburgh
	Fri.	10	at Atlanta
	Sat.	11	at Tampa Bay
	Mon.	13	Philadelphia
	Thu.	16	Calgary
	Sat.	18	Boston
	Sun.	19	at Detroit
	Tue.	21	at Nashville
	Thu.	23	at Colorado
	Sun.	26	NY Islanders
	Tue.	28	at Washington
	Thu.	30	Carolina
Jan.	Sat.	1	Atlanta
	Wed.	5	at Buffalo
	Thu.	6	Florida
	Sat.	8	Pittsburgh
	Mon.	10	Toronto
	Wed.	12	at Vancouver
	Fri.	14	at Calgary
	Sat.	15	at Edmonton
	Tue.	18	NY Rangers
	Thu.	20	Toronto
	Sat.	22	Buffalo
	Sun.	23	at Chicago
	Tue.	25	Pittsburgh
	Fri.	28	at Carolina
	Sat.	29	at Toronto
Feb.	Tue.	1	Washington
	Thu.	3	at NY Islanders
	Sat.	5	San Jose
	Mon.	7	Vancouver
	Tue.	8	at Buffalo
	Thu.	10	Carolina
	Tue.	15	at Tampa Bay
	Wed.	16	at Florida
	Sat.	19	at Montreal*
	Mon.	21	Edmonton
	Thu.	24	Atlanta
	Sat.	26	Tampa Bay
	Mon.	28	at Philadelphia
Mar.	Thu.	3	Boston
	Sat.	5	New Jersey
	Mon.	7	at Florida
	Wed.	9	at Atlanta
	Fri.	11	at Buffalo
	Sat.	12	at Toronto
	Tue.	15	Montreal
	Thu.	17	Anaheim
	Sat.	19	Phoenix
	Mon.	21	at Boston
	Tue.	22	at St. Louis
	Thu.	24	at Philadelphia
	Sat.	26	Buffalo
	Mon.	28	Washington
	Tue.	29	at New Jersey
Apr.	Fri.	1	Buffalo
	Sat.	2	at Columbus
	Wed.	6	at NY Rangers
	Fri.	8	NY Islanders
	Sat.	9	at Montreal

* Denotes afternoon game.

Franchise date: December 16, 1991

EASTERN CONFERENCE

NORTHEAST DIVISION

13th NHL Season

Zdeno Chara established new career highs in goals (16), points (41), power-play goals (7), game-winning goals (3) and plus/minus (+33) last season. He was runner-up to Scott Niedermayer in voting for the Norris Trophy.

2004-05 Player Personnel

FORWARDS	HT	WT	S	Place of Birth	Date	2003-04 Club
ALFREDSSON, Daniel	5-11	199	R	Goteborg, Sweden	12/11/72	Ottawa
FISHER, Mike	6-1	200	R	Peterborough, Ont.	6/5/80	Ottawa
HAMEL, Denis	6-1	201	L	Lachute, Que.	5/10/77	Ottawa-Binghamton
HAVLAT, Martin	6-1	190	L	Mlada Boleslav, Czech.	4/19/81	Sparta Praha-Ottawa
HOSSA, Marian	6-1	208	L	Stara Lubovna, Czech.	1/12/79	Ottawa
KAVANAGH, Pat	6-3	192	R	Ottawa, Ont.	3/14/79	Vancouver-Manitoba
KELLY, Chris	6-0	190	L	Toronto, Ont.	11/11/80	Ottawa-Binghamton
LANGFELD, Josh	6-3	216	R	Fridley, MN	7/17/77	Ottawa-Binghamton
McGRATTAN, Brian	6-4	225	L	Hamilton, Ont.	9/2/81	Binghamton
NEIL, Chris	6-0	213	R	Markdale, Ont.	6/18/79	Ottawa
POTULNY, Grant	6-3	205	L	Grand Forks, ND	3/4/80	U. of Minnesota-Binghamton
SCHAEFER, Peter	5-11	195	L	Yellow Grass, Sask.	7/12/77	Ottawa
SMOLINSKI, Bryan	6-1	208	R	Toledo, OH	12/27/71	Ottawa
SPEZZA, Jason	6-2	206	R	Mississauga, Ont.	6/13/83	Ottawa
STEPHENS, Charlie	6-3	220	R	London, Ont.	4/5/81	Col-Her-Quad City-Binghamton
VARADA, Vaclav	6-0	208	L	Vsetin, Czech.	4/26/76	Ottawa
VERMETTE, Antoine	6-1	184	L	St-Agapit, Que.	7/20/82	Ottawa-Binghamton
WATSON, Greg	6-0	205	L	Eastend, Sask.	3/2/83	Binghamton
WHITE, Todd	5-10	194	L	Kanata, Ont.	5/21/75	Ottawa

DEFENSEMEN						
CHARA, Zdeno	6-9	260	L	Trencin, Czech.	3/18/77	Ottawa
de VRIES, Greg	6-3	215	L	Sundridge, Ont.	1/4/73	NY Rangers-Ottawa
FIBIGER, Jesse	6-3	210	L	Victoria, B.C.	4/4/78	Cleveland
HEDLUND, Andy	6-3	215	L	Osseo, MN	5/16/78	Binghamton
KOMADOSKI, Neil	6-2	215	L	Chesterfield, MO	2/10/82	U. of Notre Dame-Binghamton
PHILLIPS, Chris	6-3	215	L	Calgary, Alta.	3/9/78	Ottawa
PLATIL, Jan	6-2	195	L	Kladno, Czech.	2/9/83	Binghamton
POTHIER, Brian	6-0	195	R	New Bedford, MA	4/15/77	Ottawa
REDDEN, Wade	6-2	205	L	Lloydminster, Sask.	6/12/77	Ottawa
SCHUBERT, Christoph	6-2	210	L	Munich, West Germany	2/5/82	Binghamton
VOLCHENKOV, Anton	6-1	227	L	Moscow, USSR	2/25/82	Ottawa

GOALTENDERS	HT	WT	C	Place of Birth	Date	2003-04 Club
EMERY, Ray	6-3	198	L	Cayuga, Ont.	9/28/82	Ottawa-Binghamton
GUARD, Kelly	6-1	203	L	Prince Albert, Sask.	6/10/83	Kelowna
HASEK, Dominik	5-11	180	L	Pardubice, Czech.	1/29/65	Detroit
PRUSEK, Martin	6-1	176	L	Ostrava, Czech.	12/11/75	Ottawa
THOMPSON, Billy	6-2	200	L	Saskatoon, Sask.	9/24/82	Binghamton

2003-04 Scoring

* - rookie

Regular Season

Pos	#	Player	Team	GP	G	A	Pts	+/-	PIM	PP	SH	GW	GT	S	%
R	18	Marian Hossa	OTT	81	36	46	82	4	46	14	1	5	1	233	15.5
R	11	Daniel Alfredsson	OTT	77	32	48	80	12	24	9	0	5	1	230	13.9
R	9	Martin Havlat	OTT	68	31	37	68	12	46	13	0	7	0	175	17.7
C	39	Jason Spezza	OTT	78	22	33	55	22	71	5	0	3	0	142	15.5
L	10	Peter Bondra	WSH	54	21	14	35	-17	22	12	0	4	0	136	15.4
			OTT	23	5	9	14	1	16	2	0	1	0	52	9.6
			TOTAL	77	26	23	49	-16	38	14	0	5	0	188	13.8
C	21	Bryan Smolinski	OTT	80	19	27	46	22	49	4	0	3	0	182	10.4
C	14	Radek Bonk	OTT	66	12	32	44	2	66	6	0	1	0	98	12.2
D	6	Wade Redden	OTT	81	17	26	43	21	65	12	0	3	1	175	9.7
D	3	Zdeno Chara	OTT	79	16	25	41	33	147	7	0	3	2	185	8.6
L	15	Peter Schaefer	OTT	81	15	24	39	22	26	2	2	3	0	112	13.4
C	28	Todd White	OTT	53	9	20	29	12	22	1	1	2	0	98	9.2
D	4	Chris Phillips	OTT	82	7	16	23	15	46	0	0	1	0	93	7.5
R	33	Josh Langfeld	OTT	38	7	10	17	6	16	2	0	2	0	59	11.9
R	25	Chris Neil	OTT	82	8	8	16	13	194	0	0	1	0	76	10.5
D	5	Greg De Vries	NYR	53	3	12	15	12	37	0	0	0	0	58	5.2
			OTT	13	0	0	0	0	12	0	0	0	0	12	0.0
			TOTAL	66	3	13	16	12	43	0	0	0	0	70	4.3
L	20	* Antoine Vermette	OTT	57	7	7	14	5	16	0	1	0	1	63	11.1
C	22	Shaun Van Allen	OTT	73	2	10	12	6	80	0	1	0	1	41	4.9
L	26	Vaclav Varada	OTT	30	5	5	10	2	26	0	0	1	0	47	10.6
C	12	Mike Fisher	OTT	24	4	6	10	-3	39	1	0	0	0	47	8.5
D	27	Todd Simpson	ANA	46	4	3	7	-6	105	0	0	0	0	42	9.5
			OTT	16	0	1	1	-1	47	0	0	0	0	10	0.0
			TOTAL	62	4	4	8	-7	152	0	0	0	0	52	7.7
D	2	Brian Pothier	OTT	55	2	6	8	6	24	1	0	1	0	78	2.6
D	7	Curtis Leschyshyn	OTT	56	1	4	5	13	16	0	0	0	0	30	3.3
D	24	Anton Volchenkov	OTT	19	1	2	3	1	8	0	0	0	0	15	6.7
R	32	Rob Ray	OTT	6	1	0	1	0	14	0	0	0	0	3	33.3
C	43	Serge Payer	OTT	5	0	1	1	1	2	0	0	0	0	2	0.0
L	16	Jody Hull	OTT	1	0	0	0	0	0	0	0	0	0	1	0.0
D	42	* Julien Vauclair	OTT	1	0	0	0	1	2	0	0	0	0	0	0.0
C	49	Chris Kelly	OTT	1	0	0	0	-2	0	0	0	0	0	0	0.0
R	45	Denis Hamel	OTT	5	0	0	0	-3	0	0	0	0	0	6	0.0

Goaltending

No.	Goaltender	GPI	Mins	Avg	W	L	T	EN	SO	GA	SA	S%	G	A	PIM
31	Martin Prusek	29	1528	2.12	16	6	3	0	3	54	651	.917	0	1	0
40	Patrick Lalime	57	3324	2.29	25	23	7	3	5	127	1334	.905	0	2	17
1	* Ray Emery	3	126	2.38	2	0	0	0	0	5	52	.904	0	0	2
	Totals	82	4996	2.27	43	29	10	3	8	189	2040	.907			

Playoffs

Pos	#	Player	Team	GP	G	A	Pts	+/-	PIM	PP	SH	GW	GT	S	%
R	18	Marian Hossa	OTT	7	3	1	4	0	0	1	0	2	0	32	9.4
R	11	Daniel Alfredsson	OTT	7	1	2	3	0	2	0	0	0	0	29	3.4
R	9	Martin Havlat	OTT	7	0	3	3	-1	2	0	0	0	0	14	0.0
C	21	Bryan Smolinski	OTT	7	1	1	2	-2	4	0	0	0	0	10	10.0
L	26	Vaclav Varada	OTT	7	1	1	2	0	4	0	0	0	0	10	10.0
D	3	Zdeno Chara	OTT	7	1	1	2	2	6	0	0	0	0	12	8.3
C	14	Radek Bonk	OTT	7	0	2	2	2	0	0	0	0	0	15	0.0
L	15	Peter Schaefer	OTT	7	0	2	2	1	0	0	0	0	0	15	0.0
D	6	Wade Redden	OTT	7	1	0	1	-5	2	1	0	0	0	18	5.6
D	4	Chris Phillips	OTT	7	1	0	1	2	12	1	0	0	0	15	6.7
C	28	Todd White	OTT	7	1	0	1	0	4	0	0	0	0	13	7.7
C	12	Mike Fisher	OTT	7	1	0	1	0	4	0	0	1	1	13	7.7
L	20	* Antoine Vermette	OTT	4	0	1	1	-1	4	0	0	0	0	5	0.0
D	5	Greg de Vries	OTT	7	0	1	1	0	6	0	0	0	0	10	0.0
R	25	Chris Neil	OTT	7	0	1	1	0	19	0	0	0	0	6	0.0
D	7	Curtis Leschyshyn	OTT	2	0	0	0	-1	0	0	0	0	0	4	0.0
C	39	Jason Spezza	OTT	3	0	0	0	1	2	0	0	0	0	4	0.0
D	24	Anton Volchenkov	OTT	5	0	0	0	0	4	0	0	0	0	5	0.0
L	10	Peter Bondra	OTT	7	0	0	0	-4	6	0	0	0	0	16	0.0
D	2	Brian Pothier	OTT	7	0	0	0	-2	6	0	0	0	0	8	0.0

Goaltending

No.	Goaltender	GPI	Mins	Avg	W	L	EN	SO	GA	SA	S%	G	A	PIM
31	Martin Prusek	1	40	1.50	0	0	0	1	15	.933	0	0	0	
40	Patrick Lalime	7	398	1.96	3	4	0	0	13	139	.906	0	0	2
	Totals	7	442	1.90	3	4	0	0	14	154	.909			

General Manager

MUCKLER, JOHN
General Manager, Ottawa Senators. Born in Midland, Ont., April 3, 1934.

John Muckler was named the sixth general manager in Senators history on June 12, 2002. Prior to his arrival in Ottawa, Muckler served as coach of the New York Rangers from 1997-98 to 1999-2000. Previously, he was general manager of the Buffalo Sabres from 1993 to 1997, and was named NHL executive of the year by *The Sporting News* for the 1996-97 season. Muckler is the first g.m. hired by the Senators to have previous NHL experience as a general manager.

Working for Glen Sather, Muckler enjoyed Edmonton's great 1980s run. He was an assistant coach with the Stanley Cup winners in 1984 and 1985, and designated co-coach during the 1987 and 1988 championship seasons. When Sather gave up the Oilers' coaching reins in 1989, Muckler stepped in and led the team to its fifth Stanley Cup in seven years. In 1991, he left the Oilers for the Buffalo Sabres.

Muckler has been involved in professional hockey since the 1949-50 season. He was a defenseman in the minor leagues for 13 seasons, playing the bulk of his career in the old Eastern Hockey League. His professional coaching career began while he was still a player in 1959 when he took over the New York Rovers of the EHL. He had great success with the team in the 1960s when they were known as the Long Island Ducks. Muckler joined the Minnesota North Stars after NHL expansion in 1967 and spent six seasons in the organization, mostly as a coach and g.m. in the minor leagues. His first NHL coaching job came with the North Stars midway through the 1968-69 season. He later worked in the Rangers and Canucks organizations before joining the Oilers as coach of their Wichita farm club in 1981.

NHL Coaching Record

			Regular Season				Playoffs		
Season	Team	Games	W	L	T	Games	W	L
1968-69	Minnesota	35	6	23	6	....	....	....
1989-90	Edmonton	80	38	28	14	22	16	6*
1990-91	Edmonton	80	37	37	6	18	9	9
1991-92	Buffalo	52	22	22	8	7	3	4
1992-93	Buffalo	84	38	36	10	8	4	4
1993-94	Buffalo	84	43	32	9	7	3	4
1994-95	Buffalo	48	22	19	7	5	1	4
1997-98	NY Rangers	25	8	15	2	....	....	....
1998-99	NY Rangers	82	33	38	11	....	....	....
1999-2000	NY Rangers	78	29	38	11	....	....	....
	NHL Totals	**648**	**276**	**288**	**84**	**67**	**36**	**31**

* Stanley Cup win.

General Managers' History

Mel Bridgman, 1992-93; Randy Sexton, 1993-94, 1994-95; Randy Sexton and Pierre Gauthier, 1995-96; Pierre Gauthier, 1996-97, 1997-98; Rick Dudley, 1998-99; Marshall Johnston, 1999-2000 to 2001-02; John Muckler, 2002-03 to date.

Club Records

Team

(Figures in brackets for season records are games played; records for fewest points, wins, ties, losses, goals, goals against are for 70 or more games)

Most Points	113	2002-03 (82)
Most Wins	52	2002-03 (82)
Most Ties	15	1996-97 (82), 1997-98 (82), 1998-99 (82)
Most Losses	70	1992-93 (84)
Most Goals	274	2000-01 (82)
Most Goals Against	397	1993-94 (84)
Fewest Points	24	1992-93 (84)
Fewest Wins	10	1992-93 (84)
Fewest Ties	4	1992-93 (84)
Fewest Losses	21	2000-01 (82), 2002-03 (82)
Fewest Goals	191	1995-96 (82)
Fewest Goals Against	179	1998-99 (82)

Longest Winning Streak

Overall	7	Oct. 25-Nov. 13/01
Home	8	Nov. 14-Dec. 14/02
Away	6	Mar. 18-Apr. 5/03

Longest Undefeated Streak

Overall	11	Three times
Home	12	Dec. 18/03-Jan. 24/04 (10 wins, 2 ties)
Away	7	Three times

** NHL records do not include neutral site games

Longest Losing Streak

Overall	14	Mar. 2-Apr. 7/93
Home	*11	Oct. 27-Dec. 8/93
Away	*38	Oct. 10/92-Apr. 3/93**

Longest Winless Streak

Overall	21	Oct. 10-Nov. 23/92 (20 losses, 1 tie)
Home	*17	Oct. 28/95-Jan. 27/96 (15 losses, 2 ties)
Away	*38	Oct. 10/92-Apr. 3/93 (38 losses)

Most Shutouts, Season	10	2001-02 (82)
Most PIM, Season	1,716	1992-93 (84)
Most Goals, Game	11	Nov. 13/01 (Ott. 11 at Wsh. 5)

Individual

Most Seasons	10	Radek Bonk
Most Games, Career	689	Radek Bonk
Most Goals, Career	219	Daniel Alfredsson
Most Assists, Career	349	Daniel Alfredsson
Most Points, Career	568	Daniel Alfredsson (219G, 349A)
Most PIM, Career	625	Dennis Vial
Most Shutouts, Career	30	Patrick Lalime

Longest Consecutive

Games Streak	292	Alexei Yashin (Dec. 31/95-Apr. 17/99)

Most Goals, Season	45	Marian Hossa (2002-03)
Most Assists, Season	51	Daniel Alfredsson (2002-03)
Most Points, Season	94	Alexei Yashin (1998-99; 44G, 50A)
Most PIM, Season	318	Mike Peluso (1992-93)
Most Points, Defenseman, Season	63	Norm Maciver (1992-93; 17G, 46A)
Most Points, Center, Season	94	Alexei Yashin (1998-99; 44G, 50A)
Most Points, Right Wing, Season	82	Marian Hossa (2003-04; 36G, 46A)
Most Points, Left Wing, Season	72	Shawn McEachern (2000-01; 32G, 40A)
Most Points, Rookie, Season	79	Alexei Yashin (1993-94; 30G, 49A)
Most Shutouts, Season	8	Patrick Lalime (2002-03)
Most Goals, Game	4	Marian Hossa (Jan. 2/03)
Most Assists, Game	5	Marian Hossa (Jan. 4/01)
Most Points, Game	6	Dan Quinn (Oct. 15/95; 3G, 3A), Radek Bonk (Jan. 4/01; 3G, 3A)

* NHL Record.

Coaching History

Rick Bowness, 1992-93 to 1994-95; Rick Bowness, Dave Allison and Jacques Martin, 1995-96; Jacques Martin, 1996-97 to 2000-01; Jacques Martin and Roger Neilson, 2001-02; Jacques Martin, 2002-03, 2003-04; Bryan Murray, 2004-05.

Captains' History

Laurie Boschman, 1992-93; Brad Shaw, Mark Lamb and Gord Dineen, 1993-94; Randy Cunneyworth, 1994-95 to 1997-98; Alexei Yashin, 1998-99; Daniel Alfredsson, 1999-2000 to date.

Retired Numbers

8	Frank Finnigan	1924-1934

All-time Record vs. Other Clubs

Regular Season

	At Home								On Road								Total							
	GP	W	L	T	OL	GF	GA	PTS	GP	W	L	T	OL	GF	GA	PTS	GP	W	L	T	OL	GF	GA	PTS
Anaheim	8	4	3	1	0	24	19	9	9	3	4	2	0	18	21	8	17	7	7	3	0	42	40	17
Atlanta	10	6	1	1	2	47	26	15	10	7	1	1	1	45	31	16	20	13	2	2	3	92	57	31
Boston	31	13	15	3	0	78	93	29	33	9	19	5	0	92	123	23	64	22	34	8	0	170	216	52
Buffalo	33	10	13	7	3	76	86	30	31	7	20	3	1	48	99	18	64	17	33	10	4	124	185	48
Calgary	10	5	1	3	1	27	24	14	11	4	6	1	0	25	38	9	21	9	7	4	1	52	62	23
Carolina	29	12	11	4	2	81	78	30	27	7	16	4	0	65	81	18	56	19	27	8	2	146	159	48
Chicago	10	4	5	0	1	31	30	9	8	2	4	2	0	18	18	6	18	6	9	2	1	49	48	15
Colorado	18	8	7	3	0	53	64	19	15	2	12	1	0	41	70	5	33	10	19	4	0	94	134	24
Columbus	3	2	0	1	0	12	6	5	2	1	0	1	0	9	7	3	5	3	0	2	0	21	13	8
Dallas	9	4	5	0	0	22	24	8	11	4	7	0	0	28	44	8	20	8	12	0	0	50	68	16
Detroit	10	3	5	1	1	28	29	8	9	3	5	0	1	19	33	7	19	6	10	1	2	47	62	15
Edmonton	10	3	5	2	0	19	26	8	11	2	7	1	0	25	39	6	21	5	12	4	0	44	65	14
Florida	22	10	10	2	0	61	60	22	22	12	9	1	0	67	64	25	44	22	19	3	0	128	124	47
Los Angeles	9	4	3	1	1	30	28	10	10	1	8	1	0	21	46	3	19	5	11	2	1	51	74	13
Minnesota	2	1	1	0	0	4	4	2	1	1	0	0	0	8	10	3	5	2	1	0	0	12	14	5
Montreal	31	15	15	1	0	90	87	31	33	12	17	4	0	95	97	28	64	27	32	5	0	185	184	59
Nashville	5	4	1	0	0	15	7	8	4	2	2	0	0	11	8	4	9	6	3	0	0	26	15	12
New Jersey	24	6	14	3	1	47	60	16	23	8	12	2	1	54	66	19	47	14	26	5	2	101	126	35
NY Islanders	23	13	5	5	0	78	62	31	24	13	5	6	0	89	78	32	47	26	10	11	0	167	140	63
NY Rangers	23	9	11	3	0	69	65	21	23	12	11	0	0	70	74	24	46	21	22	3	0	139	139	45
Philadelphia	24	8	10	6	0	65	72	22	23	8	13	2	0	63	73	18	47	16	23	8	0	128	145	40
Phoenix	11	4	6	1	0	29	34	9	10	5	4	1	0	38	34	11	21	9	10	2	0	67	68	20
Pittsburgh	27	8	14	5	0	70	87	21	27	6	16	4	1	64	97	17	54	14	30	9	1	134	184	38
St. Louis	10	4	6	0	0	23	36	8	9	3	4	2	0	25	27	8	19	7	10	2	0	48	63	16
San Jose	9	4	1	4	0	36	26	12	9	4	5	0	0	16	18	8	18	8	6	4	0	52	44	20
Tampa Bay	23	15	8	0	0	88	50	30	23	13	8	2	0	80	70	28	46	28	16	2	0	168	120	58
Toronto	20	12	6	1	1	56	53	26	22	10	10	2	0	60	59	22	42	22	16	3	1	116	112	48
Vancouver	10	5	3	1	1	24	24	12	11	5	5	1	0	26	33	11	21	10	8	2	1	50	57	23
Washington	23	12	9	1	1	84	70	26	24	9	11	4	0	68	76	22	47	21	20	5	1	152	146	48
Totals	**477**	**208**	**194**	**60**	**15**	**1367**	**1330**	**491**	**477**	**175**	**242**	**55**	**5**	**1288**	**1534**	**410**	**954**	**383**	**436**	**115**	**20**	**2655**	**2864**	**901**

Playoffs

	Series	W	L	GP	W	L	T	GF	GA	Last Mtg.	Rnd.	Result
Buffalo	2	0	2	11	3	8	0	19	26	1999	CQF	L 0-4
New Jersey	2	1	1	13	7	6	0	26	29	2003	CF	L 3-4
NY Islanders	1	1	0	5	4	1	0	13	7	2003	CQF	W 4-1
Philadelphia	2	2	0	11	8	3	0	28	12	2003	CSF	W 4-2
Toronto	4	0	4	24	8	16	0	42	57	2004	CQF	L 3-4
Washington	1	0	1	5	1	4	0	7	18	1998	CSF	L 1-4
Totals	**12**	**4**	**8**	**69**	**31**	**38**	**0**	**135**	**149**			

Playoff Results 2004-2000

Year	Round	Opponent	Result	GF	GA
2004	CQF	Toronto	L 3-4	11	14
2003	CF	New Jersey	L 3-4	13	17
	CSF	Philadelphia	W 4-2	17	10
	CQF	NY Islanders	W 4-1	13	7
2002	CSF	Toronto	L 3-4	18	16
	CQF	Philadelphia	W 4-1	11	2
2001	CQF	Toronto	L 0-4	3	10
2000	CQF	Toronto	L 2-4	10	17

Abbreviations: Round: CF – conference final; **CSF** – conference semi-final; **CQF** – conference quarter-final.

Colorado totals include Quebec, 1992-93 to 1994-95.
Dallas totals include Minnesota North Stars, 1992-93.
Carolina totals include Hartford, 1992-93 to 1996-97.
Phoenix totals include Winnipeg, 1992-93 to 1995-96.

2003-04 Results

Oct.	9	Montreal	5-2	11	at Carolina	2-2
	11	Detroit	2-3*	13	at New Jersey	4-0
	15	at Los Angeles	3-4	15	NY Islanders	4-4
	17	at Anaheim	3-0	17	Boston	4-0
	18	San Jose	4-1	19	at NY Islanders	2-5
	23	Washington	5-1	20	at Carolina	3-1
	25	at Montreal	6-2	22	Pittsburgh	6-5
Nov.	1	Buffalo	1-1	24	NY Rangers	3-5
	3	at NY Islanders	3-6	28	at Dallas	3-5
	6	Edmonton	3-3	29	at Phoenix	4-1
	8	New Jersey	0-1	31	at Toronto	1-5
	11	at Atlanta	5-3	**Feb.** 3	at New Jersey	1-2
	13	Columbus	5-2	5	Toronto	4-5*
	15	Montreal	2-3	10	St. Louis	3-1
	17	Buffalo	1-2	12	Boston	3-2*
	20	Carolina	6-1	14	Montreal	5-2
	22	at Pittsburgh	1-2*	16	at NY Rangers	4-1
	23	at NY Rangers	2-6	17	at Washington	1-1
	25	at Atlanta	6-3	19	Atlanta	2-3*
	27	Vancouver	2-3*	21	Calgary	1-1
	29	Toronto	1-2	22	at Pittsburgh	6-3
Dec.	1	Philadelphia	4-1	24	at Montreal	2-4
	3	at Florida	4-0	26	Philadelphia	1-1
	4	at Tampa Bay	4-1	28	Buffalo	7-1
	6	New Jersey	1-2	**Mar.** 3	at Buffalo	3-4
	8	at Boston	2-2	5	at Philadelphia	3-5
	11	Tampa Bay	3-2	6	Nashville	2-3
	13	Boston	2-3	8	at Washington	4-1
	18	Chicago	6-1	11	at Calgary	2-4
	20	NY Rangers	1-2	13	at Vancouver	2-1
	22	Florida	3-2*	14	at Edmonton	1-3
	23	at Buffalo	2-2	16	at Minnesota	2-5
	26	Pittsburgh	3-3	18	Colorado	2-0
	28	Atlanta	3-3	20	Carolina	2-3*
	30	at Boston	3-0	23	at Boston	2-4
Jan.	1	NY Islanders	1-0	25	at Montreal	4-0
	3	Washington	5-2	27	at Toronto	2-2
	6	Tampa Bay	5-2	29	at Tampa Bay	5-4*
	8	at Toronto	7-1	31	at Florida	5-4
	9	at Buffalo	2-3	**Apr.** 2	at Philadelphia	3-1
				3	Toronto	0-6

* – Overtime

Entry Draft
Selections 2004-1992

2004
Pick
23 Andrej Meszaros
58 Kirill Lyamin
77 Shawn Weller
87 Peter Regin Jensen
89 Jeff Glass
122 Alexander Nikulin
141 Jim McKenzie
156 Roman Wick
219 Joe Cooper
251 Matthew McIlvane
284 John Wikner

2003
Pick
29 Patrick Eaves
67 Igor Mirnov
100 Philippe Seydoux
135 Mattias Karlsson
142 Tim Cook
166 Sergei Gimaev
228 Will Colbert
260 Ossi Louhivaara
291 Brian Elliott

2002
Pick
16 Jakub Klepis
47 Alexei Kaigorodov
75 Arttu Luttinen
113 Scott Dobben
125 Johan Bjork
150 Brock Hooton
246 Josef Vavra
276 Vitali Atyushov

2001
Pick
2 Jason Spezza
23 Tim Gleason
81 Neil Komadoski
99 Ray Emery
127 Christoph Schubert
162 Stefan Schauer
193 Brooks Laich
218 Jan Platil
223 Brandon Bochenski
235 Neil Petruic
256 Gregg Johnson
286 Toni Dahlman

2000
Pick
21 Anton Volchenkov
45 Mathieu Chouinard
55 Antoine Vermette
87 Jan Bohac
122 Derrick Byfuglien
156 Greg Zanon
157 Grant Potulny
158 Sean Connolly
188 Jason Maleyko
283 James Demone

1999
Pick
26 Martin Havlat
48 Simon Lajeunesse
62 Teemu Sainomaa
94 Chris Kelly
154 Andrew Ianiero
164 Martin Prusek
201 Mikko Ruutu
209 Layne Ulmer
213 Alexandre Giroux
269 Konstantin Gorovikov

1998
Pick
15 Mathieu Chouinard
44 Mike Fisher
58 Chris Bala
74 Julien Vauclair
101 Petr Schastlivy
130 Gavin McLeod
161 Chris Neil
188 Michel Periard
223 Sergei Verenikin
246 Rastislav Pavlikovsky

1997
Pick
12 Marian Hossa
58 Jani Hurme
66 Josh Langfeld
119 Magnus Arvedson
146 Jeff Sullivan
173 Robin Bacul
203 Nick Gillis
229 Karel Rachunek

1996
Pick
1 Chris Phillips
81 Antti-Jussi Niemi
136 Andreas Dackell
163 Francois Hardy
212 Erich Goldmann
216 Ivan Ciernik
239 Sami Salo

1995
Pick
1 Bryan Berard
27 Marc Moro
53 Brad Larsen
89 Kevin Bolibruck
103 Kevin Boyd
131 David Hruska
183 Kaj Linna
184 Ray Schultz
231 Erik Kaminski

1994
Pick
3 Radek Bonk
29 Stan Neckar
81 Bryan Masotta
131 Mike Gaffney
133 Daniel Alfredsson
159 Doug Sproule
210 Frederic Cassivi
211 Danny Dupont
237 Stephen MacKinnon
274 Antti Tormanen

1993
Pick
1 Alexandre Daigle
27 Radim Bicanek
53 Patrick Charbonneau
91 Cosmo Dupaul
131 Rick Bodkin
157 Sergei Poleschuk
183 Jason Disher
209 Toby Kvalevog
227 Pavol Demitra
235 Rick Schuwerk

1992
Pick
2 Alexei Yashin
25 Chad Penney
50 Patrick Traverse
73 Radek Hamr
98 Daniel Guerard
121 Al Sinclair
146 Jaroslav Miklenda
169 Jay Kenney
194 Claude Savoie
217 Jake Grimes
242 Tomas Jelinek
264 Petter Ronnqvist

Club Directory

Corel Centre

Ottawa Senators
Corel Centre
1000 Palladium Drive
Ottawa, Ontario
K2V 1A5
Phone **613/599-0250**
FAX 613/599-0358
www.ottawasenators.com
Capacity: 18,500

Executive
Owner, governor and chairman . . . . Eugene Melnyk
President and CEO . . . . Roy Mlakar
Chief operating officer . . . . Cyril Leeder
Vice-president and executive officer, Corel Centre . . . Tom Conroy
General Manager . . . . John Muckler

Hockey Operations
Assistant general manager . . . . Peter Chiarelli
Director of player personnel . . . . Anders Hedberg
Assistant to the general manager . . . . Allison Vaughan
Head coach . . . . Bryan Murray
Assistant coach . . . . John Paddock
Strength and conditioning coach . . . . Randy Lee
Goaltending coach and pro scout . . . . Ron Low
Video coordinator . . . . Pierre Groulx
Chief amateur scout . . . . Frank Jay
Scouts . . . . Nick Polano, Mike Abbamont, Lewis
Mongelluzzo, Gord Pell, George Fargher,
Bob Janecyk, Patrick Savard, Vaclav Burda,
Boris Shagas
Head athletic therapist . . . . Gerry Townend
Massage therapist . . . . Brad Joyal
Assistant equipment manager . . . . Chris Cook
Team doctor . . . . Don Chow, M.D.
Scouting and travel coordinator . . . . Alex Lepore

Communications
Vice-president, communications . . . . Phil Legault
Director, communications . . . . Steve Keogh
Manager, communications . . . . Tim Pattyson

Broadcasting
Vice-president, broadcast . . . . Jim Steel

Miscellaneous
Minor league affiliate . . . . Binghamton Senators (AHL)
Team colours . . . . Red, white and black
Radio . . . . Sports Radio 1200 The Team (English)
Radio 1150 CJRC (French)
Television . . . . Rogers Sportsnet, The New RO, RDS
Team photographer . . . . Freestyle photography (Andre Ringuette)
Anthem singer . . . . Lyndon Slewidge
Mascot . . . . Spartacat

Coach

MURRAY, BRYAN
Coach, Ottawa Senators. Born in Shawville, Que., December 5, 1942.

Bryan Murray was announced on June 8, 2004, as the fifth head coach in the franchise's new era since returning to the NHL for the 1992-93 season. Murray, who had just completed his 23rd consecutive season in the NHL, resigned as senior vice president and general anager of the Mighty Ducks of Anaheim. He'd been promoted to that post in May 2002, moulding the Ducks into Western Conference champions in 2002-03 before losing in the Stanley Cup to the New Jersey Devils. Murray, named the Ducks' fifth head coach for the 2001-02 season, selected Mike Babcock as his replacement.

Murray joined the NHL coaching fraternity with the Washington Capitals on Nov. 11, 1981, replacing interim head coach Roger Crozier. He remained at the helm of the Capitals for the following eight and half seasons. Beginning with his first full campaign behind the Washington bench (1982-83), the club had winning records and averaged 95 points per season over the next seven years (all playoff teams). Murray won the Jack Adams Award in 1983-84 as the NHL's coach of the year. He enters the 2004-05 season ranked sixth in the NHL in all-time games coached (1,057) and seventh in wins (513). He coached his 1,000th NHL game with Anaheim on November 28, 2001 and earned his 500th victory on January 25, 2002.

A former student of Macdonald College at McGill University, Murray spent four years as the athletic director and coach at the school. He left that post to become head coach of the Regina Pats of the Western Hockey League in 1979-80 where he led the Pats to the WHL championship. Murray took over as coach of the American Hockey League's (AHL) Hershey Bears the next season and was named minor league coach of the year by The Hockey News, after leading Hershey to its best record in 40 years.

Coaching Record

Season	Team	Games	Regular Season W	L	T	Playoffs Games	W	L
1981-82	Washington (NHL)	66	25	28	13	....	....	....
1982-83	Washington (NHL)	80	39	25	16	4	1	3
1983-84	Washington (NHL)	80	48	27	5	8	4	4
1984-85	Washington (NHL)	80	46	25	9	5	2	3
1985-86	Washington (NHL)	80	50	23	7	9	5	4
1986-87	Washington (NHL)	80	38	32	10	7	3	4
1987-88	Washington (NHL)	80	38	33	9	14	7	7
1988-89	Washington (NHL)	80	41	29	10	6	2	4
1989-90	Washington (NHL)	46	18	24	4	....	....*	....
1990-91	Detroit (NHL)	80	34	38	8	7	3	4
1991-92	Detroit (NHL)	80	43	25	12	11	4	7
1992-93	Detroit (NHL)	84	47	28	9	7	3	4
1997-98	Florida (NHL)	59	17	31	11	....	....	....
2001-02	Anaheim (NHL)	82	29	45	8	....	....	....
	NHL Totals	**1057**	**513**	**413**	**131**	**78**	**34**	**44**

Philadelphia Flyers

2003-04 Results: 40w-21L-15T-6OTL 101PTS.
First, Atlantic Division

2004-05 Schedule

Oct.	Wed.	13	at Tampa Bay		
	Thu.	14	at Florida		
	Sat.	16	at Montreal		
	Wed.	20	at NY Rangers		
	Thu.	21	Carolina		
	Sat.	23	at Ottawa		
	Mon.	25	Chicago		
	Thu.	28	Montreal		
Nov.	Tue.	2	New Jersey		
	Fri.	5	at Buffalo		
	Sat.	6	Washington		
	Mon.	8	St. Louis		
	Thu.	11	Boston		
	Sat.	13	at Pittsburgh		
	Wed.	17	NY Islanders		
	Fri.	19	Carolina		
	Sat.	20	at Toronto		
	Wed.	24	at Washington		
	Fri.	26	Atlanta*		
	Sat.	27	at NY Islanders		
	Tue.	30	Tampa Bay		
Dec.	Thu.	2	NY Rangers		
	Sat.	4	Buffalo		
	Tue.	7	at Nashville		
	Wed.	8	at Dallas		
	Fri.	10	NY Islanders		
	Mon.	13	at Ottawa		
	Wed.	15	Boston		
	Thu.	16	at Boston		
	Sat.	18	NY Rangers		
	Tue.	21	Florida		
	Thu.	23	at Pittsburgh		
	Mon.	27	at Vancouver		
	Wed.	29	at Calgary		
	Thu.	30	at Edmonton		
Jan.	Sun.	2	at Chicago		
	Wed.	5	at Minnesota		
	Fri.	7	at Anaheim		
	Sat.	8	at Los Angeles		
	Wed.	12	Phoenix		
	Fri.	14	at Carolina		
	Sat.	15	Buffalo		
	Tue.	18	at New Jersey		
	Thu.	20	Pittsburgh		
	Sat.	22	at NY Rangers*		
	Mon.	24	at Washington		
	Tue.	25	Tampa Bay		
	Sat.	29	Atlanta*		
Feb.	Tue.	1	at NY Islanders		
	Thu.	3	Anaheim		
	Sat.	5	New Jersey*		
	Tue.	8	Los Angeles		
	Thu.	10	San Jose		
	Tue.	15	at Montreal		
	Thu.	17	New Jersey		
	Sat.	19	at NY Rangers*		
	Sun.	20	Montreal		
	Wed.	23	at Carolina		
	Thu.	24	Pittsburgh		
	Sat.	26	Colorado*		
	Mon.	28	Ottawa		
Mar.	Wed.	2	at Atlanta		
	Thu.	3	Washington		
	Sat.	5	at Boston*		
	Mon.	7	at New Jersey		
	Tue.	8	at Toronto		
	Thu.	10	Toronto		
	Sat.	12	at Pittsburgh*		
	Tue.	15	at Florida		
	Wed.	16	at Tampa Bay		
	Sat.	19	at New Jersey*		
	Mon.	21	Columbus		
	Wed.	23	at Buffalo		
	Thu.	24	Ottawa		
	Sat.	26	Toronto		
	Mon.	28	NY Islanders		
	Thu.	31	at Atlanta		
Apr.	Sat.	2	at Pittsburgh*		
	Sun.	3	Detroit*		
	Tue.	5	Florida		
	Thu.	7	NY Rangers		
	Sat.	9	at NY Islanders		

* Denotes afternoon game.

Year-by-Year Record

Season	GP	Home W	L	T	OL	Road W	L	T	OL	Overall W	L	T	OL	GF	GA	Pts	Finished	Playoff Result
2003-04	82	24	11	3	3	16	10	12	3	40	21	15	6	229	186	101	1st, Atlantic Div.	Lost Conf. Final
2002-03	82	21	10	8	2	24	10	5	2	45	20	13	4	211	166	107	2nd, Atlantic Div.	Lost Conf. Semi-Final
2001-02	82	20	13	5	3	22	14	5	4	42	27	10	3	234	192	97	1st, Atlantic Div.	Lost Conf. Quarter-Final
2000-01	82	26	11	4	0	17	14	7	3	43	25	11	3	240	207	100	2nd, Atlantic Div.	Lost Conf. Quarter-Final
1999-2000	82	25	6	7	3	20	16	5	0	45	22	12	3	237	179	105	1st, Atlantic Div.	Lost Conf. Championship
1998-99	82	21	9	11	...	16	17	8	...	37	26	19	...	231	196	93	2nd, Atlantic Div.	Lost Conf. Quarter-Final
1997-98	82	24	11	6	...	18	18	5	...	42	29	11	...	242	193	95	2nd, Atlantic Div.	Lost Conf. Quarter-Final
1996-97	82	23	12	6	...	22	12	7	...	45	24	13	...	274	217	103	2nd, Atlantic Div.	Lost Final
1995-96	82	27	9	5	...	18	15	8	...	45	24	13	...	282	208	103	1st, Atlantic Div.	Lost Conf. Semi-Final
1994-95	48	16	7	1	...	12	9	3	...	28	16	4	...	150	132	60	1st, Atlantic Div.	Lost Conf. Championship
1993-94	84	19	20	3	...	16	19	7	...	35	39	10	...	294	314	80	6th, Atlantic Div.	Out of Playoffs
1992-93	84	23	14	5	...	13	23	6	...	36	37	11	...	319	319	83	5th, Patrick Div.	Out of Playoffs
1991-92	80	22	11	7	...	10	26	4	...	32	37	11	...	252	273	75	6th, Patrick Div.	Out of Playoffs
1990-91	80	18	16	6	...	15	21	4	...	33	37	10	...	252	267	76	5th, Patrick Div.	Out of Playoffs
1989-90	80	17	19	4	...	13	20	7	...	30	39	11	...	290	297	71	6th, Patrick Div.	Out of Playoffs
1988-89	80	22	15	3	...	14	21	5	...	36	36	8	...	307	285	80	4th, Patrick Div.	Lost Conf. Championship
1987-88	80	20	14	6	...	18	19	3	...	38	33	9	...	292	292	85	3rd, Patrick Div.	Lost Div. Semi-Final
1986-87	80	29	9	2	...	17	17	6	...	46	26	8	...	310	245	100	1st, Patrick Div.	Lost Final
1985-86	80	33	6	1	...	20	17	3	...	53	23	4	...	335	241	110	1st, Patrick Div.	Lost Div. Semi-Final
1984-85	80	32	4	4	...	21	16	3	...	53	20	7	...	348	241	113	1st, Patrick Div.	Lost Final
1983-84	80	25	10	5	...	19	16	5	...	44	26	10	...	350	290	98	3rd, Patrick Div.	Lost Div. Semi-Final
1982-83	80	29	8	3	...	20	15	5	...	49	23	8	...	326	240	106	1st, Patrick Div.	Lost Div. Semi-Final
1981-82	80	25	10	5	...	13	21	6	...	38	31	11	...	325	313	87	3rd, Patrick Div.	Lost Div. Semi-Final
1980-81	80	23	9	8	...	18	15	7	...	41	24	15	...	313	249	97	2nd, Patrick Div.	Lost Quarter-Final
1979-80	80	27	5	8	...	21	7	12	...	48	12	20	...	327	254	116	1st, Patrick Div.	Lost Final
1978-79	80	26	10	4	...	14	15	11	...	40	25	15	...	281	248	95	2nd, Patrick Div.	Lost Quarter-Final
1977-78	80	29	6	5	...	16	14	10	...	45	20	15	...	296	200	105	2nd, Patrick Div.	Lost Semi-Final
1976-77	80	33	6	1	...	15	10	15	...	48	16	16	...	323	213	112	1st, Patrick Div.	Lost Semi-Final
1975-76	80	36	2	2	...	15	11	14	...	51	13	16	...	348	209	118	1st, Patrick Div.	Lost Final
1974-75	80	32	6	2	...	19	12	9	...	51	18	11	...	293	181	113	1st, Patrick Div.	**Won Stanley Cup**
1973-74	78	28	6	5	...	22	10	7	...	50	16	12	...	273	164	112	1st, West Div.	**Won Stanley Cup**
1972-73	78	27	8	4	...	10	22	7	...	37	30	11	...	296	256	85	2nd, West Div.	Lost Semi-Final
1971-72	78	19	13	7	...	7	25	7	...	26	38	14	...	200	236	66	5th, West Div.	Out of Playoffs
1970-71	78	20	10	9	...	8	23	8	...	28	33	17	...	207	225	73	3rd, West Div.	Lost Quarter-Final
1969-70	76	11	14	13	...	6	21	11	...	17	35	24	...	197	225	58	5th, West Div.	Out of Playoffs
1968-69	76	14	16	8	...	6	19	13	...	20	35	21	...	174	225	61	3rd, West Div.	Lost Quarter-Final
1967-68	74	17	13	7	...	14	19	4	...	31	32	11	...	173	179	73	1st, West Div.	Lost Quarter-Final

Robert Esche won the Pelle Lindbergh Trophy awarded to the most improved Flyer as voted by his teammates. He ranked fifth in the NHL with a 2.04 goals-against average.

Franchise date: June 5, 1967

ATLANTIC DIVISION

38th NHL Season

2004-05 Player Personnel

FORWARDS	HT	WT	S	Place of Birth	Date	2003-04 Club
AMONTE, Tony	6-0	200	L	Hingham, MA	8/2/70	Philadelphia
BRASHEAR, Donald	6-2	235	L	Bedford, IN	1/7/72	Philadelphia
CARTER, Jeff	6-3	182	R	London, Ont.	1/1/85	Sault Ste. Marie-Phi (AHL)
FEDORUK, Todd	6-2	235	L	Redwater, Alta.	2/13/79	Phi-Phi (AHL)
GAGNE, Simon	6-0	190	L	Ste-Foy, Que.	2/29/80	Philadelphia
HANDZUS, Michal	6-5	217	L	Banska Bystrica, Czech.	3/11/77	Philadelphia
KANE, Boyd	6-2	218	L	Swift Current, Sask.	4/18/78	Phi-Phi (AHL)
KAPANEN, Sami	5-10	185	L	Vantaa, Finland	6/14/73	Philadelphia
KNUBLE, Mike	6-3	228	R	Toronto, Ont.	7/4/72	Boston
LAPOINTE, Claude	5-9	188	L	Lachine, Que.	10/11/68	Phi-Phi (AHL)
LeCLAIR, John	6-3	226	L	St. Albans, VT	7/5/69	Philadelphia
MELOCHE, Eric	5-10	197	R	Montreal, Que.	5/1/76	Pittsburgh-Wilkes-Barre
PRIMEAU, Keith	6-5	220	L	Toronto, Ont.	11/24/71	Philadelphia
RADIVOJEVIC, Branko	6-1	209	R	Piestany, Czech.	11/24/80	Phoenix-Philadelphia
RICHARDS, Mike	5-11	185	L	Kenora, Ont.	2/11/85	Kitchener
ROENICK, Jeremy	6-1	196	R	Boston, MA	1/17/70	Philadelphia
SHARP, Patrick	6-0	197	R	Thunder Bay, Ont.	12/27/81	Phi-Phi (AHL)
SOMIK, Radovan	6-2	194	R	Martin, Czech.	5/5/77	Phi-Phi (AHL)
STEVENSON, Turner	6-3	220	R	Prince George, B.C.	5/18/72	New Jersey
UMBERGER, R.J.	6-2	200	L	Pittsburgh, PA	5/3/82	Did Not Play - Injured
WHITE, Peter	5-11	200	L	Montreal, Que.	3/15/69	Phi-Phi (AHL)
DEFENSEMEN						
DESJARDINS, Eric	6-1	205	R	Rouyn, Que.	6/14/69	Philadelphia
JOHNSSON, Kim	6-1	205	L	Malmo, Sweden	3/16/76	Philadelphia
JONES, Randy	6-2	200	L	Quispamsis, N.B.	7/23/81	Phi-Phi (AHL)
MARKOV, Danny	6-1	190	L	Moscow, USSR	7/30/76	Carolina-Philadelphia
MEYER, Freddy	5-10	192	L	Sanbornville, NH	1/4/81	Phi-Phi (AHL)
PITKANEN, Joni	6-3	200	L	Oulu, Finland	9/19/83	Philadelphia
RAGNARSSON, Marcus	6-1	215	L	Ostervala, Sweden	8/13/71	Philadelphia
SEIDENBERG, Dennis	6-0	200	L	Schwenningen, W. Ger.	7/18/81	Phi-Phi (AHL)
SLANEY, John	6-0	189	L	St. John's, Nfld.	2/7/72	Phi-Phi (AHL)

GOALTENDERS	HT	WT	C	Place of Birth	Date	2003-04 Club
BURKE, Sean	6-4	211	L	Windsor, Ont.	1/29/67	Phoenix-Philadelphia
ESCHE, Robert	6-1	210	L	Whitesboro, NY	1/22/78	Philadelphia
LITTLE, Neil	6-1	193	L	Medicine Hat, Alta.	12/18/71	Phi-Phi (AHL)
NIITTYMAKI, Antero	6-0	195	L	Turku, Finland	6/18/80	Phi-Phi (AHL)

Captains' History

Lou Angotti, 1967-68; Ed Van Impe, 1968-69 to 1971-72; Ed Van Impe and Bobby Clarke, 1972-73; Bobby Clarke, 1973-74 to 1978-79; Mel Bridgman, 1979-80, 1980-81; Bill Barber, 1981-82; Bill Barber and Bobby Clarke, 1982-83; Bobby Clarke, 1983-84; Dave Poulin, 1984-85 to 1988-89; Dave Poulin and Ron Sutter, 1989-90; Ron Sutter, 1990-91; Rick Tocchet, 1991-92; no captain, 1992-93; Kevin Dineen, 1993-94; Eric Lindros, 1994-95 to 1998-99; Eric Lindros and Eric Desjardins, 1999-2000; Eric Desjardins, 2000-01; Eric Desjardins and Keith Primeau, 2001-02; Keith Primeau, 2002-03 to date.

Coach

HITCHCOCK, KEN
Coach, Philadelphia Flyers. Born in Edmonton, Alta., December 17, 1951.

The Philadelphia Flyers named Ken Hitchcock as their head coach on May 14, 2002. Hitchcock is the 15th head coach in Flyers history. Prior to joining the Flyers, he won a gold medal as an associate coach with Team Canada at the 2002 Winter Olympic Games. (He served the same role with Canada's team at the 2004 World Cup.) Hitchcock served as head coach of the Dallas Stars for parts of seven seasons (1995-96 to 2001-02), compiling a 277-166-60 record in 503 regular season games. Hitchcock served as head coach of Dallas' International Hockey League affiliate, the Kalamazoo Wings/Michigan K-Wings for three seasons, from the 1993-94 season until being named Stars' head coach on January 8, 1996. Prior to joining the Stars' organization, Hitchcock served three seasons as an assistant coach with the Flyers (1990-91 through 1992-93).

Hitchcock joined the Flyers after six seasons as head coach of the Kamloops Blazers of the Western Hockey League from 1984-85 through 1989-90. His .693 winning percentage as head coach at Kamloops is the second highest in the history of the WHL (291-125-15). His international experience also includes serving as an assistant coach for the Team Canada team that captured the gold medal at the 1987 World Junior Championships.

Coaching Record

		Regular Season				Playoffs		
Season	Team	Games	W	L	T	Games	W	L
1984-85	Kamloops (WHL)	71	52	17	2	15	10	5
1985-86	Kamloops (WHL)	72	49	19	4	16	14	2
1986-87	Kamloops (WHL)	72	55	14	3	13	8	5
1987-88	Kamloops (WHL)	72	45	26	1	18	12	6
1988-89	Kamloops (WHL)	72	34	33	5	16	8	8
1989-90	Kamloops (WHL)	72	56	16	0	17	14	3
1993-94	Kalamazoo (IHL)	81	48	26	7	5	1	4
1994-95	Kalamazoo (IHL)	81	43	24	14	16	10	6
1995-96	Michigan (IHL)	40	19	10	11	....	....	....
	Dallas (NHL)	**43**	**15**	**23**	**5**	....	....	....
1996-97	**Dallas (NHL)**	**82**	**48**	**26**	**8**	**7**	**3**	**4**
1997-98	**Dallas (NHL)**	**82**	**49**	**22**	**11**	**17**	**10**	**7**
1998-99	**Dallas (NHL)**	**82**	**51**	**19**	**12**	**23**	**16**	**7***
1999-2000	**Dallas (NHL)**	**82**	**43**	**29**	**10**	**23**	**14**	**9**
2000-01	**Dallas (NHL)**	**82**	**48**	**26**	**8**	**10**	**4**	**6**
2001-02	**Dallas (NHL)**	**50**	**23**	**21**	**6**	....	....	....
2002-03	**Philadelphia (NHL)**	**82**	**45**	**24**	**13**	**13**	**6**	**7**
2003-04	**Philadelphia (NHL)**	**82**	**40**	**27**	**15**	**18**	**11**	**7**
	NHL Totals	**667**	**362**	**217**	**88**	**111**	**64**	**47**

* Stanley Cup win.

2003-04 Scoring

* - rookie

Regular Season

Pos	#	Player	Team	GP	G	A	Pts	+/–	PIM	PP	SH	GW	GT	S	%
R	8	Mark Recchi	PHI	82	26	49	75	18	47	14	1	5	2	167	15.6
C	26	Michal Handzus	PHI	82	20	38	58	18	82	7	1	2	0	135	14.8
L	10	John Leclair	PHI	75	23	32	55	20	51	8	0	4	0	182	12.6
R	11	Tony Amonte	PHI	80	20	33	53	13	38	4	0	3	0	173	11.6
C	97	Jeremy Roenick	PHI	62	19	28	47	1	62	10	1	1	0	128	14.8
L	12	Simon Gagne	PHI	80	24	21	45	12	29	6	0	6	2	211	11.4
D	5	Kim Johnsson	PHI	80	13	29	42	16	26	4	0	3	1	189	6.9
C	23	Alex Zhamnov	CHI	23	6	12	18	–8	14	1	0	1	0	63	9.5
			PHI	20	5	13	18	7	14	0	0	0	0	33	15.2
			TOTAL	43	11	25	36	–1	28	1	0	1	0	96	11.5
R	19	Branko Radivojevic	PHX	53	9	14	23	–5	36	2	1	2	1	83	10.8
			PHI	24	1	8	9	0	36	0	0	0	0	24	4.2
			TOTAL	77	10	22	32	–5	72	2	1	2	1	107	9.3
L	24	Sami Kapanen	PHI	74	12	18	30	9	14	0	1	2	1	149	8.1
D	44 *	Joni Pitkanen	PHI	71	8	19	27	15	44	5	0	2	0	133	6.0
C	25	Keith Primeau	PHI	54	7	15	22	11	80	0	1	2	1	86	8.1
D	55	Danny Markov	CAR	44	4	10	14	–6	37	2	0	1	0	73	5.5
			PHI	34	2	3	5	0	58	1	0	1	0	27	7.4
			TOTAL	78	6	13	19	–6	95	3	0	2	0	100	6.0
D	2	Vladimir Malakhov	NYR	56	3	15	18	–5	53	1	0	0	0	83	3.6
			PHI	6	0	1	1	–1	2	0	0	0	0	12	0.0
			TOTAL	62	3	16	19	–6	55	1	0	0	0	95	3.2
D	28	Marcus Ragnarsson	PHI	70	7	9	16	12	58	2	0	2	0	82	8.5
L	20	Radovan Somik	PHI	53	4	10	14	–2	17	0	0	0	0	41	9.8
L	87	Donald Brashear	PHI	64	6	7	13	–1	212	0	0	0	0	72	8.3
D	37	Eric Desjardins	PHI	48	1	11	12	11	28	0	0	0	0	92	1.1
C	13	Claude Lapointe	PHI	42	5	3	8	2	32	0	1	1	0	26	19.2
C	9 *	Patrick Sharp	PHI	41	5	2	7	–3	55	0	0	1	0	44	11.4
D	3	Mattias Timander	NYI	5	1	1	2	2	2	0	0	1	0	3	33.3
			PHI	34	1	4	5	13	19	0	1	0	0	43	2.3
			TOTAL	39	2	5	7	15	21	0	1	1	0	46	4.3
L	29	Todd Fedoruk	PHI	49	1	4	5	–4	136	0	0	1	0	33	3.0
D	45	John Slaney	PHI	4	0	2	2	0	0	0	0	0	0	0	0.0
R	47	Kirby Law	PHI	6	0	1	1	0	2	0	0	0	0	1	0.0
R	22	Mike Peluso	PHI	1	0	0	0	0	0	0	0	0	0	2	0.0
D	48 *	Frederick Meyer	PHI	1	0	0	0	0	0	0	0	0	0	1	0.0
C	15	Peter White	PHI	3	0	0	0	–1	2	0	0	0	0	2	0.0
D	36	Dennis Seidenberg	PHI	5	0	0	0	–4	2	0	0	0	0	14	0.0
D	51 *	Randy Jones	PHI	5	0	0	0	1	0	0	0	0	0	5	0.0
L	21 *	Boyd Kane	PHI	7	0	0	0	–4	7	0	0	0	0	6	0.0

Goaltending

No.	Goaltender	GPI	Mins	Avg	W	L	T	EN	SO	GA	SA	S%	G	A	PIM
30	* Antero Niittymaki	3	180	1.00	3	0	0	0	0	3	77	.961	0	0	0
42	Robert Esche	40	2322	2.04	21	11	7	1	3	79	932	.915	0	0	31
33	Jeff Hackett	27	1630	2.39	10	10	6	1	3	65	684	.905	0	0	0
41	Sean Burke	15	825	2.55	6	5	2	0	1	35	389	.910	0	0	0
35	Neil Little	1	33	3.64	0	1	0	0	0	2	8	.750	0	0	0
	Totals	**82**	**5011**	**2.23**	**40**	**27**	**15**	**2**	**7**	**186**	**2092**	**.911**			

Playoffs

Pos	#	Player	Team	GP	G	A	Pts	+/–	PIM	PP	SH	GW	GT	S	%
C	25	Keith Primeau	PHI	18	9	7	16	11	22	0	2	3	0	44	20.5
C	23	Alex Zhamnov	PHI	18	4	10	14	–1	8	1	0	1	0	31	12.9
C	97	Jeremy Roenick	PHI	18	4	9	13	4	8	2	0	1	1	49	8.2
C	26	Michal Handzus	PHI	18	5	5	10	7	10	0	0	0	0	23	21.7
L	24	Sami Kapanen	PHI	18	3	7	10	5	6	0	1	1	0	24	12.5
L	12	Simon Gagne	PHI	18	5	4	9	10	12	0	0	1	1	44	11.4
R	11	Tony Amonte	PHI	18	3	5	8	7	6	2	0	0	0	26	11.5
D	5	Kim Johnsson	PHI	15	2	6	8	–3	8	0	0	1	0	22	9.1
R	8	Mark Recchi	PHI	18	4	2	6	–3	4	2	0	0	0	33	12.1
D	3	Mattias Timander	PHI	18	2	4	6	2	6	0	0	1	0	17	11.8
D	2	Vladimir Malakhov	PHI	17	1	5	6	9	12	0	0	0	0	38	2.6
D	28	Marcus Ragnarsson	PHI	14	1	4	5	3	14	0	0	1	0	12	8.3
L	10	John LeClair	PHI	18	2	2	4	2	8	0	0	0	0	27	7.4
L	87	Donald Brashear	PHI	18	1	3	4	0	61	1	0	0	0	18	5.6
D	55	Danny Markov	PHI	18	1	2	3	17	25	0	0	1	0	19	5.3
D	44 *	Joni Pitkanen	PHI	15	0	3	3	–6	6	0	0	0	0	15	0.0
L	20	Radovan Somik	PHI	10	1	1	2	1	4	0	0	0	0	5	20.0
R	19	Branko Radivojevic	PHI	18	1	1	2	–1	32	0	0	0	0	19	5.3
C	9 *	Patrick Sharp	PHI	12	1	0	1	–2	2	0	0	0	0	11	9.1
C	13	Claude Lapointe	PHI	1	0	0	0	0	0	0	0	0	0	2	0.0
L	29	Todd Fedoruk	PHI	1	0	0	0	–2	2	0	0	0	0	1	0.0
D	36	Dennis Seidenberg	PHI	3	0	0	0	1	0	0	0	0	0	2	0.0

Goaltending

No.	Goaltender	GPI	Mins	Avg	W	L	EN	SO	GA	SA	S%	G	A	PIM
41	Sean Burke	1	40	1.50	0	0	0	0	1	9	.889	0	0	0
42	Robert Esche	18	1061	2.32	11	7	1	1	41	498	.918	0	0	8
	Totals	**18**	**1106**	**2.33**	**11**	**7**	**1**	**1**	**43**	**508**	**.915**			

Coaching History

Keith Allen, 1967-68, 1968-69; Vic Stasiuk, 1969-70, 1970-71; Fred Shero, 1971-72 to 1977-78; Bob McCammon and Pat Quinn, 1978-79; Pat Quinn, 1979-80, 1980-81; Pat Quinn and Bob McCammon, 1981-82; Bob McCammon, 1982-83, 1983-84; Mike Keenan, 1984-85 to 1987-88; Paul Holmgren, 1988-89 to 1990-91; Paul Holmgren and Bill Dineen, 1991-92; Bill Dineen, 1992-93; Terry Simpson, 1993-94; Terry Murray, 1994-95 to 1996-97; Wayne Cashman and Roger Neilson, 1997-98; Roger Neilson, 1998-99, 1999-2000; Craig Ramsay and Bill Barber, 2000-01; Bill Barber, 2001-02; Ken Hitchcock, 2002-03 to date.

Club Records

Team

(Figures in brackets for season records are games played; records for fewest points, wins, ties, losses, goals, goals against are for 70 or more games)

Most Points	**118**	1975-76 (80)
Most Wins	**53**	1984-85 (80), 1985-86 (80)
Most Ties	***24**	1969-70 (76)
Most Losses	**39**	1989-90 (80), 1993-94 (84)
Most Goals	**350**	1983-84 (80)
Most Goals Against	**319**	1992-93 (84)
Fewest Points	**58**	1969-70 (76)
Fewest Wins	**17**	1969-70 (76)
Fewest Ties	**4**	1985-86 (80)
Fewest Losses	**12**	1979-80 (80)
Fewest Goals	**173**	1967-68 (74)
Fewest Goals Against	**164**	1973-74 (78)
Longest Winning Streak		
Overall	**13**	Oct. 19-Nov. 17/85
Home	***20**	Jan. 4-Apr. 3/76
Away	**8**	Dec. 22/82-Jan. 16/83
Longest Undefeated Streak		
Overall	***35**	Oct. 14/79-Jan. 6/80 (25 wins, 10 ties)
Home	**26**	Oct. 11/79-Feb. 3/80 (19 wins, 7 ties)
Away	**16**	Oct. 20/79-Jan. 6/80 (11 wins, 5 ties)
Longest Losing Streak		
Overall	**6**	Mar. 25-Apr. 4/70, Dec. 5-17/92, Jan. 25-Feb. 5/94
Home	**5**	Jan. 30-Feb. 15/69, Dec. 19/89-Jan. 23/90
Away	**8**	Oct. 25-Nov. 26/72, Mar. 3-29/88
Longest Winless Streak		
Overall	**12**	Feb. 24-Mar. 16/99 (8 losses, 4 ties)
Home	**8**	Dec. 19/68-Jan. 18/69 (4 losses, 4 ties), Nov. 17-Dec. 14/91 (4 losses, 4 ties)
Away	**19**	Oct. 23/71-Jan. 27/72 (15 losses, 4 ties)
Most Shutouts, Season	**13**	1974-75 (80)
Most PIM, Season	**2,621**	1980-81 (80)
Most Goals, Game	**13**	Mar. 22/84 (Pit. 4 at Phi. 13), Oct. 18/84 (Van. 2 at Phi. 13)

Individual

Most Seasons	**15**	Bobby Clarke
Most Games	**1,144**	Bobby Clarke
Most Goals, Career	**420**	Bill Barber
Most Assists, Career	**852**	Bobby Clarke
Most Points, Career	**1,210**	Bobby Clarke (358G, 852A)
Most PIM, Career	**1,817**	Rick Tocchet
Most Shutouts, Career	**50**	Bernie Parent
Longest Consecutive Game Streak	**484**	Rod Brind'Amour (Feb. 24/93-Apr. 18/99)
Most Goals, Season	**61**	Reggie Leach (1975-76)
Most Assists, Season	**89**	Bobby Clarke (1974-75, 1975-76)
Most Points, Season	**123**	Mark Recchi (1992-93; 53G, 70A)
Most PIM, Season	***472**	Dave Schultz (1974-75)
Most Points, Defenseman, Season	**82**	Mark Howe (1985-86; 24G, 58A)
Most Points, Center, Season	**119**	Bobby Clarke (1975-76; 30G, 89A)
Most Points, Right Wing, Season	**123**	Mark Recchi (1992-93; 53G, 70A)
Most Points, Left Wing, Season	**112**	Bill Barber (1975-76; 50G, 62A)
Most Points, Rookie, Season	**82**	Mikael Renberg (1993-94; 38G, 44A)
Most Shutouts, Season	**12**	Bernie Parent (1973-74, 1974-75)
Most Goals, Game	**4**	Sixteen times
Most Assists, Game	**6**	Eric Lindros (Feb. 26/97)
Most Points, Game	**8**	Tom Bladon (Dec. 11/77; 4G, 4A)

* NHL Record.

Retired Numbers

1	Bernie Parent	1967-1971, 1973-1979
4	Barry Ashbee	1970-1974
7	Bill Barber	1972-1985
16	Bobby Clarke	1969-1984

All-time Record vs. Other Clubs

Regular Season

	At Home								On Road								Total							
	GP	W	L	T	OL	GF	GA	PTS	GP	W	L	T	OL	GF	GA	PTS	GP	W	L	T	OL	GF	GA	PTS
Anaheim	8	3	2	3	0	22	17	9	9	3	3	2	1	28	30	9	17	6	5	5	1	50	47	18
Atlanta	10	7	1	2	0	46	28	16	10	7	2	1	0	34	24	15	20	14	3	3	0	80	52	31
Boston	73	32	30	10	1	241	211	75	76	19	44	11	2	211	283	51	149	51	74	21	3	452	494	126
Buffalo	67	40	15	12	0	228	162	92	63	23	32	8	0	176	209	54	130	63	47	20	0	404	371	146
Calgary	51	33	14	3	1	199	137	70	52	18	25	9	0	172	208	45	103	51	39	12	1	371	345	115
Carolina	43	29	9	5	0	162	107	63	44	22	13	9	0	158	140	53	87	51	22	14	0	320	247	116
Chicago	62	35	16	11	0	204	162	81	60	15	26	19	0	170	205	49	122	50	42	30	0	374	367	130
Colorado	34	22	9	2	1	122	91	47	35	11	11	12	1	122	124	35	69	33	20	14	2	244	215	82
Columbus	2	1	0	1	0	7	3	3	3	1	0	2	0	7	6	4	5	2	0	3	0	14	9	7
Dallas	67	42	9	16	0	255	150	100	66	23	27	16	0	212	216	62	133	65	36	32	0	467	366	162
Detroit	58	34	13	11	0	230	168	79	59	18	31	10	0	182	210	46	117	52	44	21	0	412	378	125
Edmonton	31	20	9	2	0	128	85	42	28	8	14	6	0	83	98	22	59	28	23	8	0	211	183	64
Florida	25	10	8	6	1	65	60	27	24	18	5	1	0	88	57	37	49	28	13	7	1	153	117	64
Los Angeles	63	40	15	7	1	244	156	88	66	37	21	8	0	223	193	82	129	77	36	15	1	467	349	170
Minnesota	4	3	1	0	0	11	3	6	2	0	1	1	0	3	5	1	6	3	2	1	0	14	8	7
Montreal	73	29	27	16	1	223	215	75	74	26	33	14	1	229	254	67	147	55	60	30	2	452	469	142
Nashville	5	2	1	1	1	17	9	6	4	2	0	2	0	7	4	6	9	4	1	3	1	24	13	12
New Jersey	85	51	23	10	1	322	214	113	83	33	42	8	0	285	283	74	168	84	65	18	1	607	497	187
NY Islanders	95	55	27	11	2	340	268	123	98	33	49	15	1	289	356	82	193	88	76	26	3	629	624	205
NY Rangers	109	56	39	14	0	355	297	126	110	40	46	23	1	321	353	104	219	96	85	37	1	676	650	230
Ottawa	23	13	8	2	0	73	63	28	24	10	8	6	0	72	65	26	47	23	16	8	0	145	128	54
Phoenix	31	23	8	0	0	134	83	46	31	16	13	2	0	106	99	34	62	39	21	2	0	240	182	80
Pittsburgh	106	81	17	8	0	446	257	170	106	38	46	22	0	346	373	98	212	119	63	30	0	792	630	268
St. Louis	67	45	12	10	0	264	153	100	68	35	26	7	0	219	194	77	135	80	38	17	0	483	347	177
San Jose	11	6	3	2	0	36	27	14	12	7	3	2	0	31	22	16	23	13	6	4	0	67	49	30
Tampa Bay	25	14	3	7	1	79	46	36	26	16	9	1	0	78	71	33	51	30	12	8	1	157	117	69
Toronto	67	43	16	8	0	254	154	94	67	30	23	14	0	225	210	74	134	73	39	22	0	479	364	168
Vancouver	54	37	16	1	0	234	159	75	51	29	10	12	0	203	144	70	105	66	26	13	0	437	303	145
Washington	83	53	24	6	0	312	219	112	80	34	32	13	1	259	261	82	163	87	56	19	1	571	480	194
Defunct Clubs	34	24	4	6	0	137	67	54	35	13	14	8	0	102	89	34	69	37	18	14	0	239	156	88
Totals	**1466**	**883**	**379**	**193**	**11**	**5390**	**3771**	**1970**	**1466**	**585**	**609**	**264**	**8**	**4641**	**4786**	**1442**	**2932**	**1468**	**988**	**457**	**19**	**10031**	**8557**	**3412**

Playoffs

	Series	W	L	GP	W	L	T	GF	GA	Last Mtg.	Rnd.	Result
Boston	4	2	2	20	9	11	0	57	60	1978	SF	L 1-4
Buffalo	7	5	2	37	23	14	0	110	96	2001	CQF	L 2-4
Calgary	2	1	1	11	7	4	0	43	28	1981	QF	L 3-4
Chicago	1	0	1	4	0	4	0	8	20	1971	QF	L 0-4
Colorado	2	2	0	11	7	4	0	39	29	1985	CF	W 4-2
Dallas	2	2	0	11	8	3	0	41	26	1980	SF	W 4-1
Detroit	1	0	1	4	0	4	0	6	16	1997	F	L 0-4
Edmonton	3	1	2	15	7	8	0	44	49	1987	F	L 3-4
Florida	1	0	1	6	2	4	0	11	15	1996	CSF	L 2-4
Montreal	4	1	3	21	7	14	0	52	72	1989	CF	L 2-4
New Jersey	4	2	2	20	11	9	0	49	50	2004	CQF	W 4-1
NY Islanders	4	3	1	25	14	11	0	83	69	1987	DF	W 4-3
NY Rangers	10	6	4	47	27	20	0	157	153	1997	CF	W 4-1
Ottawa	2	0	2	11	3	8	0	12	28	2003	CSF	L 2-4
Pittsburgh	3	3	0	18	12	6	0	66	51	2000	CSF	W 4-2
St. Louis	2	0	2	11	3	8	0	20	34	1969	QF	L 0-4
Tampa Bay	2	1	1	13	7	6	0	45	34	2004	CF	L 3-4
Toronto	6	5	1	36	22	14	0	119	85	2004	CSF	W 4-2
Vancouver	1	1	0	3	2	1	0	15	9	1979	PRE	W 2-1
Washington	3	1	2	16	7	9	0	55	65	1989	DSF	W 4-2
Totals	**64**	**36**	**28**	**340**	**178**	**162**	**0**	**1032**	**989**			

Playoff Results 2004-2000

Year	Round	Opponent	Result	GF	GA
2004	CF	Tampa Bay	L 3-4	19	21
	CSF	Toronto	W 4-2	17	13
	CQF	New Jersey	W 4-1	14	9
2003	CSF	Ottawa	L 2-4	10	17
	CQF	Toronto	W 4-3	24	16
2002	CQF	Ottawa	L 1-4	2	11
2001	CQF	Buffalo	L 2-4	13	21
2000	CF	New Jersey	L 3-4	15	18
	CSF	Pittsburgh	W 4-2	15	14
	CQF	Buffalo	W 4-1	14	8

Abbreviations: Round: F – Final;
CF – conference final; **CSF** – conference semi-final;
CQF – conference quarter-final; **DF** – division final;
DSF – division semi-final; **SF** – semi-final;
QF – quarter-final; **PRE** – preliminary round.

Calgary totals include Atlanta Flames, 1972-73 to 1979-80.
Carolina totals include Hartford, 1979-80 to 1996-97.
Colorado totals include Quebec, 1979-80 to 1994-95.
Dallas totals include Minnesota North Stars, 1967-68 to 1992-93.
New Jersey totals include Kansas City, 1974-75 to 1975-76, and Colorado Rockies, 1976-77 to 1981-82.
Phoenix totals include Winnipeg, 1979-80 to 1995-96.

2003-04 Results

Oct.	9	Buffalo	2-0
	11	Pittsburgh	3-3
	16	at San Jose	0-0
	18	at Phoenix	5-4
	21	at Los Angeles	0-4
	22	at Anaheim	3-4*
	25	Carolina	4-4
	27	Montreal	5-0
	29	Florida	5-1
	30	at New Jersey	2-3
Nov.	1	at Toronto	7-1
	6	Washington	4-2
	8	at NY Rangers	2-1*
	11	NY Islanders	2-1
	13	Vancouver	4-3*
	15	Atlanta	4-0
	18	at Carolina	2-2
	20	Minnesota	3-1
	22	Boston	3-2
	26	at Pittsburgh	1-1
	28	Carolina	4-2
	29	at NY Islanders	5-1
Dec.	1	at Ottawa	1-4
	3	Pittsburgh	5-2
	5	Phoenix	3-2
	6	at Boston	1-1
	8	at Montreal	3-2
	10	at Columbus	1-1
	12	at New Jersey	3-3
	13	New Jersey	0-2
	16	Calgary	2-3*
	18	Tampa Bay	4-5*
	20	NY Islanders	3-1
	21	at Atlanta	1-4
	23	at NY Islanders	2-4
	27	at Colorado	2-3*
	29	at Dallas	2-2
	30	at St. Louis	7-2
Jan.	2	at Florida	2-1
	3	at Tampa Bay	1-6
	7	at Buffalo	1-1
	8	Florida	3-4*
	10	Edmonton	0-3
	12	Pittsburgh	1-2
	13	at Buffalo	2-6
	16	Toronto	4-1
	17	at Toronto	4-0
	20	Montreal	1-4
	22	at NY Rangers	4-2
	24	Buffalo	2-1
	25	at Washington	4-1
	28	at Florida	3-3
	31	at Pittsburgh	5-3
Feb.	2	Tampa Bay	1-2
	4	Washington	5-1
	5	at Atlanta	5-1
	10	New Jersey	4-1
	12	at NY Rangers	2-1
	14	NY Rangers	6-2
	16	San Jose	2-5
	17	at Tampa Bay	2-5
	19	Boston	3-4
	21	Atlanta	5-4
	24	Chicago	3-1
	26	at Ottawa	1-1
	28	at Boston	2-3*
	29	at Detroit	2-4
Mar.	3	Nashville	5-2
	5	Ottawa	5-3
	6	at Washington	1-2
	9	at New Jersey	3-1
	11	Dallas	2-2
	13	New Jersey	2-1
	14	at Pittsburgh	3-3
	18	Toronto	2-3
	20	NY Rangers	3-0
	23	at Carolina	4-2
	25	NY Islanders	2-4
	27	NY Rangers	1-3
Apr.	1	at Montreal	2-0
	2	Ottawa	1-3
	4	at NY Islanders	3-3

* – Overtime

Entry Draft
Selections 2004-1990

2004 Pick		2000 Pick		1996 Pick		1992 Pick	
92	Rob Bellamy	28	Justin Williams	15	Dainius Zubrus	7	Ryan Sittler
101	R.J. Anderson	94	Alexander Drozdetsky	64	Chester Gallant	15	Jason Bowen
124	David Laliberte	171	Roman Cechmanek	124	Per-Ragna Bergqvist	31	Denis Metlyuk
144	Chris Zarb	195	Colin Shields	133	Jesse Boulerice	103	Vladislav Buljin
149	Gino Pisellini	210	John Eichelberger	187	Roman Malov	127	Roman Zolotov
170	Ladislav Scurko	227	Guillaume Lefebvre	213	Jeff Milleker	151	Kirk Daubenspeck
171	Frederik Cabana	259	Regan Kelly			175	Claude Jr. Jutras
232	Martin Houle	287	Milan Kopecky	**1995 Pick**		199	Jonas Hakansson
253	Travis Gawryletz			22	Brian Boucher	223	Chris Herperger
286	Triston Grant	**1999 Pick**		48	Shane Kenny	247	Patrice Paquin
291	John Carter	22	Maxime Ouellet	100	Radovan Somik		
		119	Jeff Feniak	132	Dmitri Tertyshny	**1991 Pick**	
2003 Pick		160	Konstantin Rudenko	135	Jamie Sokolsky	6	Peter Forsberg
11	Jeff Carter	200	Pavel Kasparik	152	Martin Spanhel	50	Yanick Dupre
24	Mike Richards	208	Vaclav Pletka	178	Martin Streit	86	Aris Brimanis
69	Colin Fraser	224	David Nystrom	204	Ruslan Shafikov	94	Yanick Degrace
81	Stefan Ruzicka			230	Jeff Lank	116	Clayton Norris
85	Alexandre Picard	**1998 Pick**				122	Dmitry Yushkevich
87	Ryan Potulny	22	Simon Gagne	**1994 Pick**		138	Andrei Lomakin
95	Rick Kozak	42	Jason Beckett	62	Artem Anisimov	182	James Bode
108	Kevin Romy	51	Ian Forbes	88	Adam Magarrell	204	Josh Bartell
140	David Tremblay	109	Jean-Philippe Morin	101	Sebastien Vallee	226	Neil Little
191	Rejean Beauchemin	124	Francis Belanger	140	Alex Selivanov	248	John Porco
193	Ville Hostikka	139	Garrett Prosofsky	166	Colin Forbes		
		168	Antero Niittymaki	192	Derek Diener	**1990 Pick**	
2002 Pick		175	Cam Ondrik	202	Raymond Giroux	4	Mike Ricci
4	Joni Pitkanen	195	Tomas Divisek	218	Johan Hedberg	25	Chris Simon
105	Rosario Ruggeri	222	Lubomir Pistek	244	Andre Payette	40	Mikael Renberg
126	Konstantin Baranov	243	Petr Hubacek	270	Jan Lipiansky	42	Terran Sandwith
161	Dov Grumet-Morris	253	Bruno St. Jacques			44	Kimbi Daniels
192	Nikita Korovkin	258	Sergei Skrobot	**1993 Pick**		46	Bill Armstrong
193	Joey Mormina			36	Janne Niinimaa	47	Chris Therien
201	Mathieu Brunelle	**1997 Pick**		71	Vaclav Prospal	52	Al Kinisky
		30	Jean-Marc Pelletier	77	Milos Holan	88	Dan Kordic
2001 Pick		50	Pat Kavanagh	114	Vladimir Krechin	109	Viacheslav Butsayev
27	Jeff Woywitka	62	Kris Mallette	140	Mike Crowley	151	Patrik Englund
95	Patrick Sharp	103	Mikhail Chernov	166	Aaron Israel	172	Toni Porkka
146	Jussi Timonen	158	Jordon Flodell	192	Paul Healey	193	Greg Hanson
150	Bernd Bruckler	164	Todd Fedoruk	218	Tripp Tracy	214	Tommy Soderstrom
158	Roman Malek	214	Marko Kauppinen	226	E.J. Bradley	235	William Lund
172	Dennis Seidenberg	240	Par Styf	244	Jeff Staples		
177	Andrei Razin			270	Ken Hemenway		
208	Thierry Douville						
225	David Printz						

General Managers' History

Bud Poile, 1967-68, 1968-69; Bud Poile and Keith Allen, 1969-70; Keith Allen, 1970-71 to 1982-83; Bob McCammon, 1983-84; Bob Clarke, 1984-85 to 1989-90; Russ Farwell, 1990-91 to 1993-94; Bob Clarke, 1994-95 to date.

General Manager

CLARKE, BOB
General Manager, Philadelphia Flyers.
Born in Flin Flon, Man., August 13, 1949.

Bob Clarke was named general manager of the Philadelphia Flyers on June 15, 1994. Clarke's appointment marked the second time he has served as the Flyers' general manager. The Flin Flon native was the Flyers' vice president and general manager from 1984 to 1990. During his 16 years as the team's general manager, the Flyers have won seven divisional titles, three conference championships, reached the Stanley Cup semifinals seven times and the finals three times.

Prior to re-joining the Flyers' family in 1994, Clarke served as vice president and general manager of the Florida Panthers. In 1993-94, their first season in the NHL, the Panthers established NHL records for wins (33) and points (83) by an expansion franchise. Clarke also served as the vice president and general manager of the Minnesota North Stars from 1990 to 1992, guiding the team to the Stanley Cup Finals in 1991.

As a player, the former Philadelphia captain led his club to Stanley Cup championships in 1974 and 1975 and captured numerous individual awards, including the Hart Trophy as the league's most valuable player in 1973, 1975 and 1976. The four-time All-Star also received the Bill Masterton Memorial Trophy (perseverance and dedication) in 1972 and the Frank J. Selke Trophy (top defensive forward) in 1983. He appeared in eight All-Star Games and was elected to the Hockey Hall of Fame in 1987. He was awarded the Lester Patrick Trophy in 1979-80 in recognition of his contribution to hockey in the United States. Clarke appeared in 1,144 regular season games, recording 358 goals and 852 assists for 1,210 points. He also added 119 points in 136 playoff games.

Club Directory

Wachovia Center

Philadelphia Flyers
Wachovia Center
3601 South Broad Street
Philadelphia, PA 19148-5290
Phone **215/465-4500**
PR FAX 215/389-9403
www.philadelphiaflyers.com
Capacity: 19,523

Executive Management
Chairman	Ed Snider
Limited Partners	Pat Croce, Jay Snider, Sylvan and Fran Tobin
President	Ron Ryan
General Manager	Bob Clarke
Executive Vice President	Keith Allen
Governor	Ed Snider
Alternate Governors	Bob Clarke, Ron Ryan, Phil Weinberg
Executive Assistants	Lisa D'Aprile, Gina Pelle
President of Comcast-Spectacor Marketing	Dave Coskey
Office Manager	Patty Butler
Senior Vice President, Sales	Joe Croce
Administrative Assistant	Kate Dreyer
Vice President, Marketing and Communications	Shawn Tilger

Hockey Club Personnel
Assistant General Manager	Paul Holmgren
Head Coach	Ken Hitchcock
Assistant Coach	Wayne Fleming
Assistant Coach	Craig Hartsburg
Assistant Coach	Terry Murray
Goaltending Coach	Reggie Lemelin
Director of Pro Hockey Personnel	Ron Hextall
Chief Scout	Dennis Patterson
Scouting Staff	Serge Boudreault, John Chapman, Inge Hammarstrom, Simon Nolet, Chris Pryor, Ilkka Sinisalo, Vaclav Slansky, Evgeny Zimin
Pro Scouts	Al Hill, Dean Lombardi
Assistant to the General Manager	Barry Hanrahan
Video Coordinator	Adam Patterson
Scouting Information Coordinator	Bryan Hardenbergh
Executive Assistant	Dianna Taylor
Receptionist	Sharon Allison

Training Staff
Athletic Trainer/Strength and Conditioning Coach	Jim McCrossin
Massage Therapist	Brad Smith
Head Equipment Manager	Jim Evers
Equipment Managers	Anthony Oratorio, Harry Bricker, Luke Clarke
Training Center Maintenance	Mike Craytor

Communications Department
Senior Director of Communications	Zack Hill
Assistant Director of Communications	Jill Lipson
Director of Media Services and Publications	Joe Klueg
Manager of Interactive Media	Kevin Kurz
Communications Assistant	Katie Hammer
Archivist and Special Projects Manager	Kerrianne Brady

Community Relations Department
Community Relations Manager	Maureen McGuckin
Executive Director of Fan Development	Eric Turner
Fan Development Coordinators	Rob Baer, Jason Brinn, Bill Scheier
Ambassador of Hockey	Bob Kelly

Customer Service Department
Customer Service Manager	Cindy Stutman
Customer Service Account Manager	Missy Keeler
Director of Fan Relations	Joe Kadlec

Marketing Department
Director of Marketing	Linda Mantai
Manager of Game Presentation	Michael Wurman
Assistants to the VP, Marketing	Scott Bohrer, Debbie Brown
Receptionist	Ashley Key

Ticket Sales Department
Vice President of Ticket Sales	Jim Van Stone
Director of Ticket Sales	Tara Ritting
Manager, Sales Administration	Jacqueline Halligan
Inside Sales Manager	Andrew Palsky
Corporate Sales Consultants	Leigh Castergine, Flavil Hampsten

Ticketing Department
Vice President, Ticket Operations	Cecilia Baker
Ticket Office Administration	Joan Kadlec

Finance Department
Director of Finance	Dave Jablonski
Controller	Lisa Cataldo
Payroll Accountant	Susann Schaffer
Accounts Payable	Marilyn Trout

Advertising Sales Department
Vice President of Advertising Sales	Brian Monihan
National Sales Manager	Lee Stein
Director of Sales	Adrian Staiti
Sales Manager	Drew Camerota
Senior Account Executives	Mike Garrity, Bo Koelle, Ray Lyons, Joe Watson
Account Executives	Stephanie Bennett, Bryan Collins, Joe Heyer, Andrew Humphreys, Traci Kloss, Jon Roche, Rich Rodowicz
Sponsorship Manager	Maura Thomson
Manager of Television Services	Shannan Archer
Director of Client Services	Thea Crum-Vogel

Premium Seating Department
V.P. of Premium Seating – Sales & Services	Rick Campbell
Corporate Sales Manager	Dennis Shea
Manager of Finance and Inventory	Amanda Keen
Sales Executives	Jimmy Dunk, Chris Genther, Anthony Monaco, Pete Seelaus

Comcast-Spectacor Foundation/Flyers Wives Fight for Lives
Executive Director	Fran Tobin
Director	Rita Johanson

Phoenix Coyotes

2003-04 Results: 22w-36L-18T-6OTL 68PTS.
Fifth, Pacific Division

Year-by-Year Record

Season	GP	Home				Road				Overall				GF	GA	Pts.	Finished	Playoff Result
		W	L	T	OL	W	L	T	OL	W	L	T	OL					
2003-04	82	11	19	7	4	11	17	11	2	22	36	18	6	188	245	68	5th, Pacific Div.	Out of Playoffs
2002-03	82	17	16	6	2	14	19	5	3	31	35	11	5	204	230	78	4th, Pacific Div.	Out of Playoffs
2001-02	82	27	8	3	3	13	19	6	3	40	27	9	6	228	210	95	2nd, Pacific Div.	Lost Conf. Quarter-Final
2000-01	82	21	11	7	2	14	16	10	1	35	27	17	3	214	212	90	4th, Pacific Div.	Out of Playoffs
1999-2000	82	22	16	2	1	17	15	6	...	39	31	8	4	232	228	90	3rd, Pacific Div.	Lost Conf. Quarter-Final
1998-99	82	23	13	5	...	16	18	7	...	39	31	12	...	205	197	90	2nd, Pacific Div.	Lost Conf. Quarter-Final
1997-98	82	19	16	6	...	16	19	6	...	35	35	12	...	224	227	82	4th, Central Div.	Lost Conf. Quarter-Final
1996-97	82	15	19	7	...	23	18	0	...	38	37	7	...	240	243	83	3rd, Central Div.	Lost Conf. Quarter-Final
1995-96*	82	22	16	3	...	14	24	3	...	36	40	6	...	275	291	78	5th, Central Div.	Lost Conf. Quarter-Final
1994-95*	48	10	10	4	...	6	15	3	...	16	25	7	...	157	177	39	6th, Central Div.	Out of Playoffs
1993-94*	84	15	23	4	...	9	28	5	...	24	51	9	...	245	344	57	6th, Central Div.	Out of Playoffs
1992-93*	84	23	16	3	...	17	21	4	...	40	37	7	...	322	320	87	4th, Smythe Div.	Lost Div. Semi-Final
1991-92*	80	20	14	6	...	13	18	9	...	33	32	15	...	251	244	81	4th, Smythe Div.	Lost Div. Semi-Final
1990-91*	80	17	18	5	...	9	25	6	...	26	43	11	...	260	288	63	5th, Smythe Div.	Out of Playoffs
1989-90*	80	22	13	5	...	15	19	6	...	37	32	11	...	298	290	85	3rd, Smythe Div.	Lost Div. Semi-Final
1988-89*	80	17	18	5	...	9	24	7	...	26	42	12	...	300	355	64	5th, Smythe Div.	Out of Playoffs
1987-88*	80	20	14	6	...	13	22	5	...	33	36	11	...	292	310	77	3rd, Smythe Div.	Lost Div. Semi-Final
1986-87*	80	25	12	3	...	15	20	5	...	40	32	8	...	279	271	88	3rd, Smythe Div.	Lost Div. Final
1985-86*	80	18	18	4	...	8	28	4	...	26	47	7	...	295	372	59	3rd, Smythe Div.	Lost Div. Semi-Final
1984-85*	80	21	13	6	...	22	14	4	...	43	27	10	...	358	332	96	2nd, Smythe Div.	Lost Div. Final
1983-84*	80	17	15	8	...	14	23	3	...	31	38	11	...	340	374	73	4th, Smythe Div.	Lost Div. Semi-Final
1982-83*	80	22	16	2	...	11	23	6	...	33	39	8	...	311	333	74	4th, Smythe Div.	Lost Div. Semi-Final
1981-82*	80	18	13	9	...	15	20	5	...	33	33	14	...	319	332	80	2nd, Norris Div.	Lost Div. Semi-Final
1980-81*	80	7	25	8	...	2	32	6	...	9	57	14	...	246	400	32	6th, Smythe Div.	Out of Playoffs
1979-80*	80	13	19	8	...	7	30	3	...	20	49	11	...	214	314	51	5th, Smythe Div.	Out of Playoffs

* Winnipeg Jets

2004-05 Schedule

Oct.	Wed.	13	Dallas	Thu.	13	at NY Rangers
	Thu.	14	at Dallas	Sat.	15	at NY Islanders
	Sat.	16	at Minnesota	Mon.	17	St. Louis*
	Thu.	21	Tampa Bay	Thu.	20	Los Angeles
	Sat.	23	at Los Angeles	Sat.	22	Detroit
	Sun.	24	Buffalo*	Tue.	25	Nashville
	Wed.	27	at Colorado	Thu.	27	Calgary
	Thu.	28	Columbus	Sat.	29	at St. Louis
	Sat.	30	Calgary	Mon.	31	at Carolina
Nov.	Wed.	3	at San Jose	**Feb.** Thu.	3	at Nashville
	Thu.	4	Chicago	Sat.	5	Carolina
	Sat.	6	at Detroit	Tue.	8	at Calgary
	Sun.	7	at Chicago	Wed.	9	at Edmonton
	Tue.	9	at Minnesota	Wed.	16	at Anaheim
	Thu.	11	Vancouver	Thu.	17	Boston
	Sat.	13	Minnesota	Sat.	19	Washington
	Mon.	15	at Pittsburgh	Mon.	21	at Los Angeles
	Tue.	16	at Washington	Wed.	23	Anaheim
	Thu.	18	at Columbus	Fri.	25	Los Angeles
	Sat.	20	St. Louis	Sun.	27	at Edmonton*
	Mon.	22	San Jose	**Mar.** Tue.	1	at Vancouver
	Wed.	24	Anaheim	Thu.	3	Vancouver
	Fri.	26	Los Angeles	Sat.	5	Minnesota
Dec.	Thu.	2	Atlanta	Tue.	8	at Detroit
	Sat.	4	Dallas	Thu.	10	at Nashville
	Tue.	7	at San Jose	Sat.	12	New Jersey
	Thu.	9	Chicago	Sun.	13	at Los Angeles
	Sat.	11	Florida	Tue.	15	NY Islanders
	Wed.	15	Colorado	Thu.	17	at Calgary
	Fri.	17	at Columbus	Sat.	19	at Ottawa
	Sat.	18	at St. Louis	Mon.	21	at Montreal
	Wed.	22	at San Jose	Tue.	22	at Toronto
	Thu.	23	at Vancouver	Thu.	24	Edmonton
	Sun.	26	at Anaheim*	Sat.	26	Colorado
	Wed.	29	Detroit	Mon.	28	Columbus
	Fri.	31	San Jose*	Wed.	30	at Anaheim
Jan.	Sun.	2	at Colorado	Thu.	31	Anaheim
	Tue.	4	at Dallas	**Apr.** Sat.	2	San Jose
	Wed.	5	at Chicago	Wed.	6	at Dallas
	Sat.	8	Edmonton	Fri.	8	Dallas
	Wed.	12	at Philadelphia	Sun.	10	Nashville*

* Denotes afternoon game.

Franchise date: June 22, 1979
Transferred from Winnipeg to Phoenix, July 1, 1996

PACIFIC DIVISION

26th NHL Season

Acquired from Colorado at the trade deadline, Derek Morris wound up playing 83 games last year to tie for the league lead with Marcus Nilson (Florida and Calgary). Morris averaged over 25 minutes of ice time in his 14 games with the Coyotes.

2004-05 Player Personnel

FORWARDS	HT	WT	S	Place of Birth	Date	2003-04 Club
CHIMERA, Jason	6-2	206	L	Edmonton, Alta.	5/2/79	Edmonton
CLEARY, Daniel	6-0	211	L	Carbonear, Nfld.	12/18/78	Phoenix
COMRIE, Mike	5-9	185	L	Edmonton, Alta.	9/11/80	Philadelphia-Phoenix
DEVEREAUX, Boyd	6-2	195	L	Seaforth, Ont.	4/16/78	Detroit
DOAN, Shane	6-2	216	R	Halkirk, Alta.	10/10/76	Phoenix
GELECH, Randall	6-3	212	R	Wynard, Sask.	2/2/84	Kelowna
HULL, Brett	5-11	203	R	Belleville, Ont.	8/9/64	Detroit
JASPERS, Jason	5-11	207	L	Thunder Bay, Ont.	4/8/81	Phoenix-Springfield
JOHNSON, Mike	6-2	201	R	Scarborough, Ont.	10/3/74	Phoenix
KEEFE, Sheldon	5-11	185	R	Brampton, Ont.	9/17/80	Hershey
KOLANOS, Krystofer	6-3	206	R	Calgary, Alta.	7/27/81	Phoenix-Springfield
KOREIS, Jakub	6-3	213	L	Plzen, Czech	6/26/84	Guelph
KOUBA, Ladislav	6-2	213	L	Vimperk, Czech.	9/10/83	R.Deer-Sprfld-Adirondack
LANGKOW, Daymond	5-11	192	L	Edmonton, Alta.	9/27/76	Phoenix
LUKES, Frantisek	5-9	173	R	Kadan, Czech.	9/25/82	Springfield
McLACHLAN, Darren	6-1	223	L	Penticton, B.C.	2/16/83	Springfield-Adirondack
McLEOD, Kiel	6-6	240	R	Ft. Saskatchewan, Alta.	12/30/82	Springfield
MONYCH, Lance	6-3	194	R	Red Deer, Alta.	7/25/84	Brandon
NAGY, Ladislav	5-11	192	L	Saca, Czech.	6/1/79	Phoenix
NASH, Tyson	5-11	191	L	Edmonton, Alta.	3/11/75	Phoenix
NAZAROV, Andrei	6-5	242	R	Chelyabinsk, USSR	5/22/74	Phoenix
PODLESAK, Martin	6-6	219	L	Melnik, Czech.	9/26/82	Springfield
RICCI, Mike	6-0	200	L	Scarborough, Ont.	10/27/71	San Jose
RUPP, Mike	6-5	230	L	Cleveland, OH	1/13/80	New Jersey-Phoenix
SAVAGE, Brian	6-1	200	L	Sudbury, Ont.	2/24/71	Phoenix-St. Louis
SJOSTROM, Fredrik	6-1	217	L	Fargelanda, Sweden	5/6/83	Phoenix-Springfield
STUTZEL, Mike	6-2	216	L	Victoria, B.C.	2/28/79	Phoenix-Springfield
TAFFE, Jeff	6-3	201	L	Hastings, MN	2/19/81	Phoenix-Springfield
WESTRUM, Erik	6-0	204	L	Minneapolis, MN	7/26/79	Phoenix-Springfield
DEFENSEMEN						
BALLARD, Keith	5-11	202	L	Baudette, MN	11/26/82	U. of Minnesota
CALLAHAN, Joe	6-3	219	R	Brockton, MA	12/20/82	Yale-Springfield
FERENCE, Brad	6-3	218	R	Calgary, Alta.	4/2/79	Phoenix
HULSE, Cale	6-3	220	R	Edmonton, Alta.	11/10/73	Phoenix
KNYAZEV, Igor	6-0	208	L	Elektrostal, USSR	1/27/83	Springfield
MARA, Paul	6-4	219	L	Ridgewood, NJ	9/7/79	Phoenix
MORRIS, Derek	6-0	220	R	Edmonton, Alta.	8/24/78	Colorado-Phoenix
O'DONNELL, Sean	6-3	227	L	Ottawa, Ont.	10/13/71	Boston
SPILLER, Matthew	6-5	233	L	Daysland, Alta.	2/7/83	Phoenix-Springfield
TANABE, David	6-1	212	R	White Bear Lake, MN	7/19/80	Phoenix
TSELIOS, Nikos	6-5	226	L	Oak Park, IL	1/20/79	Springfield
WOOD, Dustin	6-0	185	L	Scarborough, Ont.	5/21/81	Springfield-Adirondack

GOALTENDERS	HT	WT	C	Place of Birth	Date	2003-04 Club
BOUCHER, Brian	6-2	198	L	Woonsocket, RI	1/2/77	Phoenix
JOHNSON, Brent	6-3	196	L	Farmington, MI	3/12/77	St. Louis-Worcester-Phoenix
LENEVEU, David	6-1	187	L	Fernie, B.C.	5/23/83	Springfield
PELLETIER, Jean-Marc	6-3	209	L	Atlanta, GA	3/4/78	Phoenix-Springfield

Shane Doan led the team (and set new career highs) in goals, assists, points and power-play goals last season. He ranked 25th in the NHL in scoring.

Coaching History

Tom McVie and Bill Sutherland, 1979-80; Tom McVie, Bill Sutherland and Mike Smith, 1980-81; Tom Watt, 1981-82, 1982-83; Tom Watt and Barry Long, 1983-84; Barry Long, 1984-85; Barry Long and John Ferguson, 1985-86; Dan Maloney, 1986-87, 1987-88; Dan Maloney and Rick Bowness, 1988-89; Bob Murdoch, 1989-90, 1990-91; John Paddock, 1991-92 to 1993-94; John Paddock and Terry Simpson, 1994-95; Terry Simpson, 1995-96; Don Hay, 1996-97; Jim Schoenfeld, 1997-98, 1998-99; Bob Francis, 1999-2000 to 2002-03; Bob Francis and Rick Bowness, 2003-04; Rick Bowness, 2004-05.

2003-04 Scoring

* - rookie

Regular Season

Pos	#	Player	Team	GP	G	A	Pts	+/-	PIM	PP	SH	GW	GT	S	%
R	19	Shane Doan	PHX	79	27	41	68	–11	47	9	2	1	3	254	10.6
L	17	Ladislav Nagy	PHX	55	24	28	52	11	46	11	0	6	1	160	15.0
C	11	Daymond Langkow	PHX	81	21	31	52	4	40	4	1	2	2	174	12.1
D	23	Paul Mara	PHX	81	6	36	42	–11	48	1	0	0	0	140	4.3
D	2	Derek Morris	COL	69	6	22	28	4	47	2	0	1	0	139	4.3
			PHX	14	0	4	4	–5	2	0	0	0	0	28	0.0
			TOTAL	83	6	26	32	–1	49	2	0	1	0	167	3.6
C	89	Mike Comrie	PHI	21	4	5	9	2	12	0	0	1	0	36	11.1
			PHX	28	8	7	15	–8	16	1	1	1	1	65	12.3
			TOTAL	49	12	12	24	–6	28	1	1	2	1	101	11.9
D	15	Radoslav Suchy	PHX	82	7	14	21	1	8	2	0	2	0	82	8.5
D	32	Cale Hulse	PHX	82	3	17	20	–4	123	1	0	0	0	115	2.6
C	14 *	Jeff Taffe	PHX	59	8	10	18	–8	20	5	0	0	0	67	11.9
R	8	Daniel Cleary	PHX	68	6	11	17	–8	42	0	3	0	0	83	7.2
R	20 *	Fredrik Sjostrom	PHX	57	7	6	13	–7	22	0	0	1	0	73	9.6
R	13	Michael Rupp	N.J.	51	6	5	11	–1	41	1	0	1	0	64	9.4
			PHX	6	0	1	1	–3	6	0	0	0	0	12	0.0
			TOTAL	57	6	6	12	–4	47	1	0	1	0	76	7.9
D	5	David Tanabe	PHX	45	5	7	12	4	22	2	0	2	0	88	5.7
C	36	Krystofer Kolanos	PHX	41	4	6	10	–9	24	1	0	1	1	61	6.6
R	12	Mike Johnson	PHX	11	1	9	10	–1	10	1	0	0	0	17	5.9
L	18	Tyson Nash	PHX	69	3	5	8	–6	110	0	0	0	0	83	3.6
R	7	Ivan Novoseltsev	FLA	17	1	4	5	–6	8	0	0	0	0	25	4.0
			PHX	17	2	0	2	–7	6	0	0	0	0	23	8.7
			TOTAL	34	3	4	7	–13	14	0	0	0	0	48	6.3
D	45	Brad Ference	PHX	63	0	5	5	–19	103	0	0	0	0	39	0.0
L	44	Andrei Nazarov	PHX	33	1	2	3	–7	125	0	0	0	0	17	5.9
C	39 *	Erik Westrum	PHX	15	1	1	2	–3	20	0	0	0	1	29	3.4
D	2	Todd Reirden	PHX	7	0	2	2	–4	4	0	0	0	0	9	0.0
D	3	Bryan Helmer	PHX	17	0	1	1	–5	10	0	0	0	0	10	0.0
C	21 *	Jason Jaspers	PHX	3	0	0	0	–1	2	0	0	0	0	3	0.0
D	57 *	Goran Bezina	PHX	3	0	0	0	–1	2	0	0	0	0	0	0.0
L	43 *	Mike Stutzel	PHX	9	0	0	0	–4	0	0	0	0	0	3	0.0
D	6 *	Matthew Spiller	PHX	51	0	0	0	–11	54	0	0	0	0	22	0.0
C	21 *	Jason Jaspers	PHX	2	0	0	0	–1	0	0	0	0	0	0	0.0
C	36	Krystofer Kolanos	PHX	2	0	0	0	0	0	0	0	0	0	8	0.0
D	52 *	Martin Grenier	PHX	3	0	0	0	–1	0	0	0	0	0	0	0.0
R	34	Frank Banham	PHX	5	0	0	0	–1	2	0	0	0	0	5	0.0

Goaltending

No.	Goaltender	GPI	Mins	Avg	W	L	T	EN	SO	GA	SA	S%	G	A	PIM
1	Brent Johnson	8	486	2.59	1	6	1	0	0	21	243	.914	0	0	0
33	Brian Boucher	40	2364	2.74	10	19	10	5	5	108	1150	.906	0	0	2
41	Sean Burke	32	1795	2.81	10	15	5	3	1	84	913	.908	0	2	8
35	Zac Bierk	4	190	3.79	0	1	2	0	0	12	108	.889	0	0	2
30	* Jean-Marc Pelletier	4	175	4.11	1	1	0	0	0	12	84	.857	0	0	0
	Totals	**82**	**5038**	**2.92**	**22**	**42**	**18**	**8**	**6**	**245**	**2506**	**.902**			

Coach

BOWNESS, RICK
Coach, Phoenix Coyotes. Born in Moncton, N.B., January 25, 1955.

Rick Bowness was promoted from assistant coach to head coach on February 24, 2004. He was in his fifth season with the Coyotes and his 21st season of coaching in professional hockey. He had previously served as head coach with four NHL clubs, Winnipeg, Boston, Ottawa and the New York Islanders. Prior to his coaching career, Bowness played seven seasons (1975 to 1982) in the NHL as a right winger with Atlanta, Detroit, St. Louis and Winnipeg. He played in 173 games, recording 18 goals and 37 assists for 55 points with 191 penalty minutes.

Bowness began his career in coaching with the American Hockey League's Sherbrooke Jets as a player/coach during the 1982-83 season. He served the next four seasons (1983-84 to 1986-87) as an assistant coach for the Winnipeg Jets before returning to his hometown in 1987 as coach and general manager of the Moncton Hawks, the Jets' AHL developmental team. In February 1989, Bowness had his first NHL head coaching stint when he took over as interim head coach of the Jets for the final 28 games of the 1988-89 season.

The following season, Bowness joined the Boston Bruins organization, coaching the AHL's Maine Mariners for two seasons before assuming the head coaching duties for the Bruins in 1991-92. He was then named the first head coach of the Ottawa Senators on June 15, 1992. Despite the tough times, Bowness was highly regarded for his positive style and was credited for the development of many of the Senators' young stars. Bowness remained behind the Senators bench until November 20, 1995. He was then hired by the Islanders on December 30, 1995 and worked two seasons as an associate coach. Bowness took over the head coaching duties of the Islanders from January 23, 1997 to March 11, 1998. He was instrumental in the development of many of the Islanders young players.

Coaching Record

		Regular Season				Playoffs		
Season	Team	Games	W	L	T	Games	W	L
1987-88	Moncton (AHL)	80	27	45	8	....	....	....
1988-89	Moncton (AHL)	53	28	20	5	....	....	....
	Winnipeg (NHL)	**28**	**8**	**17**	**3**	....	....	....
1989-90	Maine (AHL)	80	31	38	11	....	....	....
1990-91	Maine (AHL)	80	34	34	12	2	0	2
1991-92	**Boston (NHL)**	**80**	**36**	**32**	**12**	**15**	**8**	**7**
1992-93	**Ottawa (NHL)**	**84**	**10**	**70**	**4**	....	....	....
1993-94	**Ottawa (NHL)**	**84**	**14**	**61**	**9**	....	....	....
1994-95	**Ottawa (NHL)**	**48**	**9**	**34**	**5**	....	....	....
1995-96	**Ottawa (NHL)**	**19**	**6**	**13**	**0**	....	....	....
1996-97	**NY Islanders (NHL)**	**37**	**16**	**18**	**3**	....	....	....
1997-98	**NY Islanders (NHL)**	**63**	**22**	**32**	**9**	....	....	....
2003-04	**Phoenix (NHL)**	**20**	**2**	**15**	**3**	....	....	....
	NHL Total	**463**	**123**	**292**	**48**	**15**	**8**	**7**

Club Records

Team

(Figures in brackets for season records are games played; records for fewest points, wins, ties, losses, goals, goals against are for 70 or more games)

Most Points **96** 1984-85 (80)
Most Wins **43** 1984-85 (80)
Most Ties **18** 2003-04 (82)
Most Losses **57** 1980-81 (80)
Most Goals **358** 1984-85 (80)
Most Goals Against **400** 1980-81 (80)
Fewest Points **32** 1980-81 (80)
Fewest Wins **9** 1980-81 (80)
Fewest Ties **6** 1995-96 (82)
Fewest Losses **27** 1984-85 (80), 2000-01 (82), 2001-02 (82)
Fewest Goals **188** 2003-04 (82)
Fewest Goals Against **197** 1998-99 (82)
Longest Winning Streak
  Overall .... **9** Mar. 8-27/85
  Home .... **9** Dec. 27/92-Jan. 23/93
  Away .... **8** Feb. 25-Apr. 6/85
Longest Undefeated Streak
  Overall .... **14** Oct. 25-Nov. 28/98 (12 wins, 2 ties)
  Home .... **11** Dec. 23/83-Feb. 5/84 (6 wins, 5 ties), Oct. 15-Dec. 20/98 (10 wins, 1 tie)
  Away .... **9** Feb. 25-Apr. 7/85 (8 wins, 1 tie), Dec. 7/03-Jan. 9/04 (5 wins, 4 ties)
Longest Losing Streak
  Overall .... **10** Nov. 30-Dec. 20/80, Feb. 6-25/94
  Home .... **5** Oct. 29-Nov. 13/93 Mar. 13-23/00
  Away .... **13** Jan. 26-Apr. 14/94
Longest Winless Streak
  Overall .... ***30** Oct. 19-Dec. 20/80 (23 losses, 7 ties)
  Home .... **14** Oct. 19-Dec. 14/80 (9 losses, 5 ties)
  Away .... **18** Oct. 10-Dec. 20/80 (16 losses, 2 ties)
Most Shutouts, Season **9** 1998-99 (82)
Most PIM, Season **2,278** 1987-88 (80)
Most Goals, Game .... **12** Feb. 25/85 (Wpg. 12 at NYR 5)

Individual

Most Seasons .... **15** Teppo Numminen
Most Games .... **1,098** Teppo Numminen
Most Goals, Career .... **379** Dale Hawerchuk
Most Assists, Career .... **553** Thomas Steen
Most Points, Career .... **929** Dale Hawerchuk (379G, 550A)
Most PIM, Career .... **1,508** Keith Tkachuk
Most Shutouts, Career .... **21** Nikolai Khabibulin
Longest Consecutive Games Streak .... **475** Dale Hawerchuk (Dec. 19/82-Dec. 10/88)
Most Goals, Season .... **76** Teemu Selanne (1992-93)
Most Assists, Season .... **79** Phil Housley (1992-93)
Most Points, Season .... **132** Teemu Selanne (1992-93; 76G, 56A)
Most PIM, Season .... **347** Tie Domi (1993-94)
Most Points, Defenseman, Season .... **97** Phil Housley (1992-93; 18G, 79A)
Most Points, Center, Season .... **130** Dale Hawerchuk (1984-85; 53G, 77A)
Most Points, Right Wing, Season .... **132** Teemu Selanne (1992-93; 76G, 56A)
Most Points, Left Wing, Season .... **98** Keith Tkachuk (1995-96; 50G, 48A)
Most Points, Rookie, Season .... ***132** Teemu Selanne (1992-93; 76G, 56A)
Most Shutouts, Season .... **8** Nikolai Khabibulin (1998-99)
Most Goals, Game .... **5** Willy Lindstrom (Mar. 2/82), Alexei Zhamnov (Apr. 1/95)
Most Assists, Game .... **5** Dale Hawerchuk (Mar. 6/84, Mar. 18/89, Mar. 4/90), Phil Housley (Jan. 18/93), Keith Tkachuk (Feb. 23/01)
Most Points, Game .... **6** Willy Lindstrom (Mar. 2/82; 5G, 1A), Dale Hawerchuk (Dec. 14/83; 3G, 3A, Mar. 5/88; 2G, 4A, Mar. 18/89; 1G, 5A), Thomas Steen (Oct. 24/84; 2G, 4A), Ed Olczyk (Dec. 21/91; 2G, 4A)

* NHL Record.
Records include Winnipeg Jets, 1979-80 through 1995-96.

Winnipeg Jets Retired Numbers

*9	Bobby Hull	1972-1980
25	Thomas Steen	1981-1995

* Brett Hull will wear this number for Phoenix.

Captains' History

Lars-Erik Sjoberg, 1979-80; Morris Lukowich, 1980-81; Dave Christian, 1981-82; Dave Christian and Lucien DeBlois, 1982-83; Lucien DeBlois, 1983-84; Dale Hawerchuk, 1984-85 to 1988-89; Randy Carlyle, Dale Hawerchuk and Thomas Steen (tri-captains), 1989-90; Randy Carlyle and Thomas Steen (co-captains), 1990-91; Troy Murray, 1991-92; Troy Murray and Dean Kennedy, 1992-93; Dean Kennedy and Keith Tkachuk, 1993-94; Keith Tkachuk, 1994-95; Kris King, 1995-96; Keith Tkachuk, 1996-97 to 2000-01; Teppo Numminen, 2001-02, 2002-03; Shane Doan, 2003-04 to date.

All-time Record vs. Other Clubs

Regular Season

	At Home								On Road								Total							
	GP	W	L	T	OL	GF	GA	PTS	GP	W	L	T	OL	GF	GA	PTS	GP	W	L	T	OL	GF	GA	PTS
Anaheim	26	11	10	2	3	75	77	27	27	9	13	3	2	67	74	23	53	20	23	5	5	142	151	50
Atlanta	5	4	0	1	0	16	7	9	4	3	1	0	0	12	6	6	9	7	1	1	0	28	13	15
Boston	30	13	14	3	0	101	102	29	30	4	22	4	0	92	136	12	60	17	36	7	0	193	238	41
Buffalo	29	13	14	2	0	87	92	28	31	6	20	5	0	80	127	17	60	19	34	7	0	167	219	45
Calgary	70	34	25	11	0	264	238	79	71	23	39	9	0	227	295	55	141	57	64	20	0	491	533	134
Carolina	31	14	14	2	1	110	112	31	30	10	13	6	1	89	103	27	61	24	27	8	2	199	215	58
Chicago	50	27	18	5	0	164	154	59	48	12	26	10	0	128	184	34	98	39	44	15	0	292	338	93
Colorado	40	16	17	7	0	144	142	39	41	15	19	5	2	133	142	37	81	31	36	12	2	277	284	76
Columbus	8	5	0	3	0	24	15	13	8	3	4	1	0	14	19	7	16	8	4	4	0	38	34	20
Dallas	54	23	27	4	0	170	182	50	55	19	27	9	0	166	199	47	109	42	54	13	0	336	381	97
Detroit	49	17	18	14	0	149	153	48	51	18	25	8	0	170	200	44	100	35	43	22	0	319	353	92
Edmonton	71	29	36	5	1	284	314	64	72	20	44	6	2	234	313	48	143	49	80	11	3	518	627	112
Florida	10	3	3	3	1	25	31	10	8	5	3	0	0	21	23	10	18	8	6	3	1	46	54	20
Los Angeles	76	38	26	11	1	301	250	88	74	32	27	14	1	288	294	79	150	70	53	25	2	589	544	167
Minnesota	8	5	2	1	0	23	16	11	8	4	2	2	0	17	15	10	16	9	4	3	0	40	31	21
Montreal	29	9	13	7	0	94	112	25	29	3	24	2	0	66	142	8	58	12	37	9	0	160	254	33
Nashville	12	7	4	0	1	33	35	15	12	5	3	2	2	34	32	14	24	12	7	2	3	67	67	29
New Jersey	31	21	7	3	0	114	81	45	29	11	12	6	0	87	95	28	60	32	19	9	0	201	176	73
NY Islanders	30	11	15	4	0	96	105	26	30	9	13	8	0	91	113	26	60	20	28	12	0	187	218	52
NY Rangers	31	13	13	4	1	107	101	31	29	9	17	2	1	102	128	21	60	22	30	6	2	209	229	52
Ottawa	10	4	5	1	0	34	38	9	11	6	4	1	0	34	29	13	21	10	9	2	0	68	67	22
Philadelphia	31	13	16	2	0	99	106	28	31	8	23	0	0	83	134	16	62	21	39	2	0	182	240	44
Pittsburgh	31	14	13	3	1	116	107	32	30	10	20	0	0	86	120	20	61	24	33	3	1	202	227	52
St. Louis	51	26	18	7	0	166	156	59	50	13	26	11	0	136	182	37	101	39	44	18	0	302	338	96
San Jose	35	18	12	3	2	108	99	41	32	13	15	4	0	99	110	30	67	31	27	7	2	207	209	71
Tampa Bay	11	6	5	0	0	28	26	12	10	5	5	0	0	33	33	10	21	11	10	0	0	61	59	22
Toronto	39	20	13	6	0	161	142	46	43	21	20	2	0	161	157	44	82	41	33	8	0	322	299	90
Vancouver	69	33	26	10	0	256	245	76	72	19	43	10	0	201	272	48	141	52	69	20	0	457	517	124
Washington	30	15	8	7	0	112	105	37	31	8	17	5	1	85	119	22	61	23	25	12	1	197	224	59
Totals	**997**	**462**	**392**	**131**	**12**	**3461**	**3343**	**1067**	**997**	**323**	**527**	**135**	**12**	**3036**	**3796**	**793**	**1994**	**785**	**919**	**266**	**24**	**6497**	**7139**	**1860**

Playoffs

	Series	W	L	GP	W	L	T	GF	GA	Last Mtg.	Rnd.	Result
Anaheim	1	0	1	7	3	4	0	17	17	1997	CQF	L 3-4
Calgary	3	2	1	13	7	6	0	45	43	1987	DSF	W 4-2
Colorado	1	0	1	5	1	4	0	10	17	2000	CQF	L 1-4
Detroit	2	0	2	12	4	8	0	28	44	1998	CQF	L 2-4
Edmonton	6	0	6	26	4	22	0	75	120	1990	DSF	L 3-4
St. Louis	2	0	2	11	4	7	0	29	39	1999	CQF	L 3-4
San Jose	1	0	1	5	1	4	0	7	13	2002	CQF	L 1-4
Vancouver	2	0	2	13	5	8	0	34	50	1993	DSF	L 2-4
Totals	**18**	**2**	**16**	**92**	**29**	**63**	**0**	**245**	**343**			

Calgary totals include Atlanta Flames, 1979-80.
Colorado totals include Quebec, 1979-80 to 1994-95.
New Jersey totals include Colorado Rockies, 1979-80 to 1981-82.
Carolina totals include Hartford, 1979-80 to 1996-97.
Dallas totals include Minnesota North Stars, 1979-80 to 1992-93.

Playoff Results 2004-2000

Year	Round	Opponent	Result	GF	GA
2002	CQF	San Jose	L 1-4	7	13
2000	CQF	Colorado	L 1-4	10	17

Abbreviations: Round: CQF – conference quarter-final; **DSF** – division semi-final.

2003-04 Results

Oct.	10	St. Louis	2-1*		11	Atlanta	1-1
	12	at Anaheim	2-0		13	Vancouver	1-4
	15	at Florida	2-1		15	at Nashville	3-4
	16	at Tampa Bay	1-5		16	at Detroit	3-3
	18	Philadelphia	4-5		21	San Jose	2-4
	23	Toronto	4-5		22	at San Jose	2-1
	25	at San Jose	4-4		24	Detroit	5-2
	26	at Vancouver	3-3		27	Calgary	1-2
	28	Chicago	2-2		29	Ottawa	1-4
	31	Vancouver	1-4		31	Dallas	4-5
Nov.	1	at Los Angeles	3-7	**Feb.**	2	Columbus	3-3
	6	at Colorado	1-2		4	Florida	4-5*
	8	Anaheim	4-3*		5	at San Jose	0-5
	9	at Anaheim	1-2*		11	at Anaheim	3-5
	13	Colorado	3-2*		13	NY Islanders	2-5
	14	at Dallas	3-3		14	Dallas	3-2
	16	at Columbus	2-2		16	at St. Louis	2-4
	19	St. Louis	5-4		18	at Detroit	2-5
	21	San Jose	0-5		20	Columbus	3-2
	23	at Atlanta	0-1		21	Nashville	2-8
	24	at Dallas	2-5		23	Anaheim	1-1
	27	Los Angeles	6-4		25	Pittsburgh	3-4*
	30	at Boston	3-3		27	Edmonton	2-7
Dec.	2	at New Jersey	3-1		29	at Calgary	2-4
	4	at Buffalo	3-2	**Mar.**	2	at Edmonton	4-5*
	5	at Philadelphia	2-3		5	Montreal	3-4
	7	at Chicago	2-2		7	Minnesota	1-1
	10	Dallas	2-1		9	at Los Angeles	2-3
	12	Edmonton	3-3		10	Los Angeles	1-3
	15	Minnesota	2-5		12	Colorado	2-3
	18	at Los Angeles	4-4		14	at Colorado	1-4
	20	at St. Louis	1-1		16	Anaheim	2-3*
	22	at Nashville	3-3		18	Detroit	1-1
	23	at Columbus	2-1		21	at Chicago	2-2
	27	Nashville	1-3		22	at Minnesota	3-2*
	29	NY Rangers	2-3*		24	Calgary	0-4
	31	Los Angeles	4-0		26	San Jose	0-3
Jan.	2	at Dallas	6-0		28	at Edmonton	2-4
	4	at Carolina	3-0		29	at Vancouver	1-6
	7	at Washington	3-0		31	at Calgary	0-1
	9	at Minnesota	2-0	**Apr.**	3	Chicago	2-1*

* – Overtime

Entry Draft
Selections 2004-1990

2004 Pick		2000 Pick		1995 Pick		1992 Pick	
5	Blake Wheeler	19	Krystofer Kolanos	7	Shane Doan	17	Sergei Bautin
35	Logan Stephenson	53	Alexander Tatarinov	32	Marc Chouinard	27	Boris Mironov
50	Enver Lisin	85	Ramzi Abid	34	Jason Doig	60	Jeremy Stevenson
103	Roman Tomanek	160	Nate Kiser	67	Brad Isbister	84	Mark Visheau
119	Kevin Porter	186	Brent Gauvreau	84	Justin Kurtz	132	Alexander Alexeyev
168	Kevin Cormier	217	Igor Samoilov	121	Brian Elder	155	Artur Oktyabrev
199	Chad Kolarik	249	Sami Venalainen	136	Sylvain Daigle	156	Andrei Raisky
240	Aaron Gagnon	281	Peter Fabus	162	Paul Traynor	204	Nikolai Khabibulin
261	William Engasser			188	Jaroslav Obsut	228	Yevgeny Garanin
265	Daniel Winnik	**1999 Pick**		189	Fredrik Loven	229	Teemu Numminen
		15	Scott Kelman	214	Rob Deciantis	252	Andrei Karpovstev
2003 Pick		19	Kirill Safronov			254	Ivan Vologzhaninov
77	Tyler Redenbach	53	Brad Ralph	**1994 Pick**			
80	Dmitri Pestunov	71	Jason Jaspers	30	Deron Quint	**1991 Pick**	
115	Liam Lindstrom	116	Ryan Lauzon	56	Dorian Anneck	5	Aaron Ward
178	Ryan Gibbons	123	Preston Mizzi	58	Tavis Hansen	49	Dmitri Filimonov
208	Randall Gelech	168	Erik Lewerstrom	82	Steve Cheredaryk	91	Juha Ylonen
242	Eduard Lewandowski	234	Goran Bezina	108	Craig Mills	99	Yan Kaminsky
272	Sean Sullivan	262	Alexei Litvinenko	143	Steve Vezina	115	Jeff Sebastian
290	Loic Burkhalter			146	Chris Kibermanis	159	Jeff Ricciardi
		1998 Pick		186	Ramil Saifullin	181	Sean Gauthier
2002 Pick		14	Patrick DesRochers	212	Henrik Smangs	203	Igor Ulanov
19	Jakub Koreis	43	Ossi Vaananen	238	Mike Mader	225	Jason Jennings
23	Ben Eager	73	Pat O'Leary	264	Jason Issel	247	Sergei Sorokin
46	David Leneveu	100	Ryan Vanbuskirk				
70	Joe Callahan	115	Jay Leach	**1993 Pick**		**1990 Pick**	
80	Matt Jones	116	Josh Blackburn	15	Mats Lindgren	19	Keith Tkachuk
97	Lance Monych	129	Robert Schnabel	31	Scott Langkow	35	Mike Muller
132	John Zeiler	160	Rickard Wallin	43	Alexei Budayev	74	Roman Meluzin
186	Jeff Pietrasiak	187	Erik Westrum	79	Ruslan Batyrshin	75	Scott Levins
216	Ladislav Kouba	214	Justin Hansen	93	Ravil Gusmanov	77	Alex Zhamnov
249	Marcus Smith			119	Larry Courville	98	Craig Martin
280	Russell Spence	**1997 Pick**		145	Michal Grosek	119	Daniel Jardemyr
		43	Juha Gustafsson	171	Martin Woods	140	John Lilley
2001 Pick		96	Scott McCallum	197	Adrian Murray	161	Henrik Andersson
11	Fredrik Sjostrom	123	Curtis Suter	217	Vladimir Potapov	182	Rauli Raitanen
31	Matthew Spiller	151	Robert Francz	223	Ilja Stashenkov	203	Mika Alatalo
45	Martin Podlesak	207	Alexander Andreyev	228	Harijs Vitolinsh	224	Sergei Selyanin
78	Beat Forster	233	Wyatt Smith	285	Russ Hewson	245	Keith Morris
148	David Klema						
180	Scott Polaski	**1996 Pick**					
210	Steve Belanger	11	Dan Focht				
243	Frantisek Lukes	24	Daniel Briere				
273	Severin Blindenbacher	62	Per-Anton Lundstrom				
		119	Richard Lintner				
		139	Robert Esche				
		174	Trevor Letowski				
		200	Nicholas Lent				
		226	Marc-Etienne Hubert				

General Managers' History

John Ferguson, 1979-80 to 1987-88; John Ferguson and Mike Smith, 1988-89; Mike Smith, 1989-90 to 1992-93; Mike Smith and John Paddock, 1993-94; John Paddock, 1994-95, 1995-96; John Paddock and Bobby Smith, 1996-97; Bobby Smith, 1997-98 to 1999-2000; Bobby Smith and Cliff Fletcher, 2000-01; Cliff Fletcher and Michael Barnett, 2001-02; Michael Barnett, 2002-03 to date.

Vice President and General Manager

BARNETT, MICHAEL
Executive Vice President/General Manager, Phoenix Coyotes.
Born in Olds, Alta., October 9, 1948.

Michael Barnett joined the Coyotes as vice president and general manager on August 28, 2001 after serving as president of International Management Group's (IMG) hockey division since 1990. Barnett is the sixth general manager in franchise history and follows in the footsteps of Brian Burke (Vancouver Canucks), Pierre Lacroix (Colorado Avalanche) and Dean Lombardi (San Jose Sharks) as former player agents who have become NHL general managers.

With over 20 years of experience in the game prior to joining the Coyotes, Barnett left IMG as one of hockey's most distinguished and well-respected player agents. Over the years, Barnett earned acclaim for his integrity, vision and success as a negotiator. He developed a reputation within the NHL as one of the most creative and well-informed agents in the industry. He is reunited in Phoenix with his longtime friend Wayne Gretzky, the Coyotes' managing partner. Barnett served as Gretzky's agent for 20 years. He also represented some of the NHL's most high-profile players including Jaromir Jagr, Brett Hull, Paul Coffey, Alexander Mogilny, Owen Nolan, Mats Sundin and Joe Thornton.

Barnett actually began his career in hockey as a player. He played hockey at St. Lawrence University in Canton, New York and later attended the University of Calgary, where he played both intercollegiate hockey and football for three years. In 1973-74, he turned professional with the Chicago Cougars (WHA) playing left wing for their minor league affiliate, the Long Island Cougars (NAHL). The following season (1974-75), while playing for the Roanoke-Valley Rebels (SHL) — the Houston Aeros' (WHA) minor league affiliate — Barnett suffered a career ending eye injury.

In 1980, Barnett opened a Western Canadian sports management agency and began his long-lasting relationship with Gretzky by signing him on as his top client. In 1990, Barnett merged his company with Mark McCormack's IMG and became president of IMG hockey operations.

Club Directory

Glendale Arena

Phoenix Coyotes
5800 W. Glenn Drive, Suite 350
Glendale, AZ 85301
Phone **623/463-8800**
FAX 623/463-8810
Tickets 480/563-PUCK

Glendale Arena
9400 W. Maryland Avenue
Glendale, AZ 85303
Phone 623/772-3200
FAX 623/772-3201
Capacity: 17,799
www.PhoenixCoyotes.com

Chairman and Governor	Steve Ellman
Co-Owner	Jerry Moyes
Managing Partner & Alternate Governor	Wayne Gretzky
President, COO & Alternate Governor	Douglas Moss
Senior Exec. V.P. of Hockey Operations	Cliff Fletcher
General Manager & Alternate Governor	Michael Barnett
Vice President & Asst. General Manager	Laurence Gilman
General Counsel	Bob Kaufman
Senior V.P. & Chief Marketing Officer	Mike Bucek
Senior V.P., Corporate Sales	Dave Groff
Senior V.P., Finance & Administration	Vaibhav Gupta
Executive Assistant to the Chairman	Dawn Lovstad
Executive Assistant to the President	Cheryl Taylor
Executive Assistant to the General Manager	Maryjane DeBiasio

Hockey Operations

Head Coach	Rick Bowness
Assistant Coach	TBD
Goaltending Coach	Grant Fuhr
Special Teams Consultant	Paul Coffey
V.P., Scouting & Dir. of Player Personnel	Dave Draper
Director of Amateur Scouting	Vaughn Karpan
Professional Scouts	Tom Kurvers, Warren Rychel
Director of Player Development	Eddie Mio
Amateur Scouts	Shane Churla, Keith Gretzky, Steve Lyons, Blair Reid, Evzen Slansky, Boris Yemeljanov
Scouting Consultant	Charles Henry
Athletic Therapist	Gord Hart
Massage Therapist	Jukka Nieminen
Head Equipment Manager	Stan Wilson
Equipment Manager	Tony Silva
Assistant Equipment Manager	Jason Rudee
Strength & Conditioning Coordinator	Stieg Theander
Video Coordinator	Steve Peters
Manager of Team Services	Lesa Guth
Team Internist	Robert Luberto, D.O.
Team Dentists	Dr. Lawrence Emmott, Dr. Ron Foeldi
Utah Grizzlies (AHL) Head Coach	Pat Conacher
Utah Grizzlies (AHL) Asst. Coach	Gord Dineen

Communications

Vice President of Communications	Richard Nairn
Director of Media Relations	Rick Braunstein

Broadcasting

TV/Radio Play-by-Play Announcer	Curt Keilback
TV/Radio Color Analyst	Charlie Simmer
TV/Radio Host	Todd Walsh
Radio Studio Host	Bob Heethuis
Manager of Broadcasting	Graham Taylor

Community Relations

Community Relations Manager	Melissa Doyle
Community Relations Coordinator	Elizabeth Apodaca

Corporate Sales and Service

Vice President of Corporate Sales	Cullen Maxey
Senior Manager of Corporate Sales	John Allen
Senior Manager of Corporate Sales Services	Ashley Ritt
Manager of Advertising Sales	Angie Ness
Corporate Sales Account Executive	Kathleen Borschke, Stacie Nelson

Finance and Administration

Vice President and Controller	Joe Leibfried
Payroll Administrator	Cheri Sedor

Marketing

Vice President, Marketing	Becky Thielen
Director of Game Operations	Greg Hanover
Advertising and Promotions Manager	Jen Byron
Web Editorial Director	Damon Markiewicz

Ticket Sales and Service

Vice President, Ticket Sales & Service	Augie Manfredo
Director of Ticket Sales & Service	Nicole Allison
Director of Premium Seating	E.A. McDonough
Director of Ticket Operations	David Drake
Manager of Ticket Operations	Kevin Prebil

Security

Director of Security	Jim O'Neal

Suite Sales

Director of Luxury Suite Sales	Mike Briody
Luxury Suite Coordinator	Kristin Anderson

Phoenix Coyotes and Arena Management Group

Director of Human Resources	Julie Atherton
Legal Counsel	Steve Weinrich
Director of IT	Frank Peters

Team Information

Broadcast Television Stations	KTVK- NewsChannel 3, KASW TV-WB6
Cable Television Station	Fox Sports Net
Radio Stations	KDKB 93.3 FM, KDUS 1060 AM

Pittsburgh Penguins

2003-04 Results: 23W-47L-8T-4OTL 58PTS.
Fifth, Atlantic Division

Selected first overall in the 2003 NHL Entry Draft, Marc-Andre Fleury spent 21 games with the Penguins last year. He also posted a 1.98 goals-against average at Cape Breton in the QMJHL and won his second silver medal at the World Junior Championships.

2004-05 Schedule

Oct.	Fri.	15	at NY Rangers	Mon.	17	Calgary	
	Sat.	16	NY Rangers	Wed.	19	at Atlanta	
	Tue.	19	at Montreal	Thu.	20	at Philadelphia	
	Sat.	23	at Florida	Sat.	22	Tampa Bay	
	Tue.	26	San Jose	Tue.	25	at Ottawa	
	Fri.	29	NY Rangers	Wed.	26	Carolina	
	Sat.	30	at Buffalo	Fri.	28	at Florida	
Nov.	Fri.	5	at Anaheim	Sun.	30	at Tampa Bay*	
	Sat.	6	at Los Angeles	Feb. Wed.	2	Columbus	
	Mon.	8	at Colorado	Fri.	4	Washington	
	Thu.	11	Edmonton	Sat.	5	at Buffalo	
	Sat.	13	Philadelphia	Wed.	9	Florida	
	Mon.	15	Phoenix	Thu.	10	at Toronto	
	Wed.	17	Montreal	Tue.	15	at New Jersey	
	Thu.	18	at Washington	Fri.	18	at Carolina	
	Sat.	20	at New Jersey*	Sat.	19	Atlanta	
	Mon.	22	New Jersey	Mon.	21	at NY Islanders*	
	Wed.	24	Ottawa	Thu.	24	at Philadelphia	
	Fri.	26	at NY Islanders*	Sat.	26	NY Rangers	
	Sun.	28	at NY Rangers	Sun.	27	Montreal*	
	Mon.	29	Florida	Mar. Tue.	1	Atlanta	
Dec.	Fri.	3	at Carolina	Fri.	4	NY Islanders	
	Sat.	4	Detroit	Sat.	5	at Detroit	
	Tue.	7	Ottawa	Tue.	8	Tampa Bay	
	Thu.	9	St. Louis	Thu.	10	at Boston	
	Sat.	11	NY Islanders	Sat.	12	at Philadelphia*	
	Tue.	14	Vancouver	Sun.	13	Toronto*	
	Thu.	16	at St. Louis	Wed.	16	at Dallas	
	Sat.	18	at Minnesota	Fri.	18	at Tampa Bay	
	Tue.	21	Washington	Sat.	19	at Atlanta	
	Thu.	23	Philadelphia	Tue.	22	at Nashville	
	Sun.	26	at Columbus*	Thu.	24	New Jersey	
	Tue.	28	Buffalo	Sat.	26	Carolina	
	Fri.	31	Boston*	Sun.	27	at New Jersey*	
Jan.	Sat.	1	at Washington	Tue.	29	at NY Islanders	
	Tue.	4	at Montreal	Thu.	31	Buffalo	
	Fri.	7	Chicago	Apr. Sat.	2	Philadelphia*	
	Sat.	8	at Ottawa	Sun.	3	Toronto*	
	Tue.	11	at Toronto	Thu.	7	at Boston	
	Fri.	14	NY Islanders	Fri.	8	New Jersey*	
	Sat.	15	at NY Rangers	Sun.	10	Boston*	

* Denotes afternoon game.

Franchise date: June 5, 1967

EASTERN CONFERENCE

ATLANTIC DIVISION

38th NHL Season

Year-by-Year Record

Season	GP	Home				Road				Overall				GF	GA	Pts.	Finished	Playoff Result
		W	L	T	OL	W	L	T	OL	W	L	T	OL					
2003-04	82	13	22	6	0	10	25	2	4	23	47	8	4	190	303	58	5th, Atlantic Div.	Out of Playoffs
2002-03	82	15	22	2	2	12	22	4	3	27	44	6	5	189	255	65	5th, Atlantic Div.	Out of Playoffs
2001-02	82	16	20	4	1	12	21	4	4	28	41	8	5	198	249	69	5th, Atlantic Div.	Out of Playoffs
2000-01	82	24	15	2	0	18	13	7	3	42	28	9	3	281	256	96	3rd, Atlantic Div.	Lost Conf. Championship
1999-2000	82	23	11	7	0	14	20	1	6	37	31	8	6	241	236	88	3rd, Atlantic Div.	Lost Conf. Semi-Final
1998-99	82	21	10	10	...	17	20	4	...	38	30	14	...	242	225	90	3rd, Atlantic Div.	Lost Conf. Semi-Final
1997-98	82	21	10	10	...	19	14	8	...	40	24	18	...	228	188	98	1st, Northeast Div.	Lost Conf. Quarter-Final
1996-97	82	25	11	5	...	13	25	3	...	38	36	8	...	285	280	84	2nd, Northeast Div.	Lost Conf. Quarter-Final
1995-96	82	32	9	0	...	17	20	4	...	49	29	4	...	362	284	102	1st, Northeast Div.	Lost Conf. Championship
1994-95	48	18	5	1	...	11	11	2	...	29	16	3	...	181	158	61	2nd, Northeast Div.	Lost Conf. Semi-Final
1993-94	84	25	9	8	...	19	18	5	...	44	27	13	...	299	285	101	1st, Northeast Div.	Lost Conf. Quarter-Final
1992-93	84	32	6	4	...	24	15	3	...	56	21	7	...	367	268	119	1st, Patrick Div.	Lost Div. Final
1991-92	**80**	**21**	**13**	**6**	**...**	**18**	**19**	**3**	**...**	**39**	**32**	**9**	**...**	**343**	**308**	**87**	**3rd, Patrick Div.**	**Won Stanley Cup**
1990-91	**80**	**25**	**12**	**3**	**...**	**16**	**21**	**3**	**...**	**41**	**33**	**6**	**...**	**342**	**305**	**88**	**1st, Patrick Div.**	**Won Stanley Cup**
1989-90	80	22	15	3	...	10	25	5	...	32	40	8	...	318	359	72	5th, Patrick Div.	Out of Playoffs
1988-89	80	24	13	3	...	16	20	4	...	40	33	7	...	347	349	87	2nd, Patrick Div.	Lost Div. Final
1987-88	80	22	12	6	...	14	23	3	...	36	35	9	...	319	316	81	6th, Patrick Div.	Out of Playoffs
1986-87	80	19	15	6	...	11	23	6	...	30	38	12	...	297	290	72	5th, Patrick Div.	Out of Playoffs
1985-86	80	20	15	5	...	14	23	3	...	34	38	8	...	313	305	76	5th, Patrick Div.	Out of Playoffs
1984-85	80	17	20	3	...	7	31	2	...	24	51	5	...	276	385	53	6th, Patrick Div.	Out of Playoffs
1983-84	80	7	29	4	...	9	29	2	...	16	58	6	...	254	390	38	6th, Patrick Div.	Out of Playoffs
1982-83	80	14	22	4	...	4	31	5	...	18	53	9	...	257	394	45	6th, Patrick Div.	Out of Playoffs
1981-82	80	21	11	8	...	10	25	5	...	31	36	13	...	310	337	75	4th, Patrick Div.	Lost Div. Semi-Final
1980-81	80	21	16	3	...	9	21	10	...	30	37	13	...	302	345	73	3rd, Norris Div.	Lost Prelim. Round
1979-80	80	20	13	7	...	10	24	6	...	30	37	13	...	251	303	73	3rd, Norris Div.	Lost Prelim. Round
1978-79	80	23	12	5	...	13	19	8	...	36	31	13	...	281	279	85	2nd, Norris Div.	Lost Quarter-Final
1977-78	80	16	15	9	...	9	22	9	...	25	37	18	...	254	321	68	4th, Norris Div.	Out of Playoffs
1976-77	80	22	12	6	...	12	21	7	...	34	33	13	...	240	252	81	3rd, Norris Div.	Lost Prelim. Round
1975-76	80	23	11	6	...	12	22	6	...	35	33	12	...	339	303	82	3rd, Norris Div.	Lost Prelim. Round
1974-75	80	25	5	10	...	12	23	5	...	37	28	15	...	326	289	89	3rd, Norris Div.	Lost Quarter-Final
1973-74	78	15	18	6	...	13	23	3	...	28	41	9	...	242	273	65	5th, West Div.	Out of Playoffs
1972-73	78	24	11	4	...	8	26	5	...	32	37	9	...	257	265	73	5th, West Div.	Out of Playoffs
1971-72	78	18	15	6	...	8	23	8	...	26	38	14	...	220	258	66	4th, West Div.	Lost Quarter-Final
1970-71	78	18	12	9	...	3	25	11	...	21	37	20	...	221	240	62	6th, West Div.	Out of Playoffs
1969-70	76	17	13	8	...	9	25	4	...	26	38	12	...	182	238	64	2nd, West Div.	Lost Semi-Final
1968-69	76	12	20	6	...	8	25	5	...	20	45	11	...	189	252	51	5th, West Div.	Out of Playoffs
1967-68	74	15	12	10	...	12	22	3	...	27	34	13	...	195	216	67	5th, West Div.	Out of Playoffs

2004-05 Player Personnel

FORWARDS	HT	WT	S	Place of Birth	Date	2003-04 Club
ABID, Ramzi	6-2	210	L	Montreal, Que.	3/24/80	Pittsburgh
ARMSTRONG, Colby	6-2	195	R	Lloydminster, Sask.	11/23/82	Wilkes-Barre
BEECH, Kris	6-2	208	L	Salmon Arm, B.C.	2/5/81	Pittsburgh-Wilkes-Barre
BRADLEY, Matt	6-3	199	R	Stittsville, Ont.	6/13/78	Pittsburgh
CHRISTENSEN, Erik	6-1	191	L	Edmonton, Alta.	12/17/83	Kamloops-Brandon
CRAMPTON, Steve	6-3	205	R	Winnipeg, Man.	4/12/82	Wheeling
EASTWOOD, Mike	6-3	216	R	Ottawa, Ont.	7/1/67	Pittsburgh
EAVES, Ben	5-8	180	R	Minneapolis, MN	3/27/82	Boston College
ENDICOTT, Shane	6-3	214	L	Saskatoon, Sask.	12/21/81	Wilkes-Barre
FATA, Rico	6-0	205	L	Sault Ste. Marie, Ont.	2/12/80	Pittsburgh
HUSSEY, Matt	6-2	215	L	New Haven, CT	5/28/79	Pittsburgh-Wilkes-Barre
KOLTSOV, Konstantin	6-0	206	L	Minsk, USSR	4/17/81	Pittsburgh-Wilkes-Barre
KRAFT, Milan	6-4	212	R	Plzen, Czech.	1/17/80	Pittsburgh
LEFEBVRE, Guillaume	6-1	202	L	Amos, Que.	5/7/81	Wilkes-Barre
LEMIEUX, Mario	6-4	230	R	Montreal, Que.	10/5/65	Pittsburgh
MALONE, Ryan	6-4	216	L	Pittsburgh, PA	12/1/79	Pittsburgh
MOROZOV, Aleksey	6-1	204	L	Moscow, USSR	2/16/77	Pittsburgh
MURLEY, Matt	6-1	206	L	Troy, NY	12/17/79	Pittsburgh-Wilkes-Barre
OUELLET, Michel	6-0	201	R	Rimouski, Que.	3/5/82	Wilkes-Barre
PADDOCK, Cam	6-1	191	R	Vancouver, B.C.	3/22/83	Kelowna-Wilkes-Barre
PIRJETA, Lasse	6-4	225	L	Oulu, Finland	4/4/74	Columbus-Syracuse-Pittsburgh
RECCHI, Mark	5-10	190	L	Kamloops, B.C.	2/1/68	Philadelphia
SUROVY, Tomas	6-1	205	L	Banska Bystrica, Czech.	9/24/81	Pittsburgh-Wilkes-Barre
VANDENBUSSCHE, Ryan	6-0	200	R	Simcoe, Ont.	2/28/73	Chicago

DEFENSEMEN						
FATA, Drew	6-1	220	L	Sault Ste. Marie, Ont.	7/28/83	Wilkes-Barre-Wheeling
JACKMAN, Ric	6-2	197	R	Toronto, Ont.	6/28/78	Toronto-Pittsburgh
KOCI, David	6-6	230	L	Prague, Czech.	5/12/81	Wilkes-Barre
LUPASCHUK, Ross	6-1	210	R	Edmonton, Alta.	1/19/81	Wilkes-Barre
MELICHAR, Josef	6-2	220	L	Ceske Budejovice, Czech.	1/20/79	Pittsburgh
ORPIK, Brooks	6-2	228	L	San Francisco, CA	9/26/80	Pittsburgh-Wilkes-Barre
ROBINSON, Darcy	6-3	235	R	Kamloops, B.C.	5/3/81	Wilkes-Barre
ROULEAU, Alexandre	6-1	192	L	Mont-Laurier, Que.	7/29/83	Wheeling-Wilkes-Barre
ROZSIVAL, Michal	6-1	212	R	Vlasim, Czech.	9/3/78	Wilkes-Barre
SCUDERI, Rob	6-0	214	L	Syosset, NY	12/30/78	Pittsburgh-Wilkes-Barre
STRBAK, Martin	6-3	210	L	Presov, Czech.	1/15/75	L.A.-Manchester-Pit
TARNSTROM, Dick	6-1	205	L	Sundbyberg, Sweden	1/20/75	Pittsburgh
WHITNEY, Ryan	6-4	202	L	Boston, MA	2/19/83	Boston University-Wilkes-Barre

GOALTENDERS	HT	WT	C	Place of Birth	Date	2003-04 Club
CARON, Sebastian	6-1	170	L	Amqui, Que.	6/25/80	Pittsburgh
CHIODO, Andy	5-11	192	L	Toronto, Ont.	4/25/83	Pittsburgh-Wheeling-Wilkes-Barre
FLEURY, Marc-Andre	6-1	175	L	Sorel, Que.	11/28/84	Pittsburgh-Cape Breton-Wilkes-Barre

2003-04 Scoring

* - rookie

Regular Season

Pos	#	Player	Team	GP	G	A	Pts	+/-	PIM	PP	SH	GW	GT	S	%
D	32	Dick Tarnstrom	PIT	80	16	36	52	-37	38	12	0	0	0	158	10.1
R	95	Aleksey Morozov	PIT	75	16	34	50	-24	24	8	0	5	1	132	12.1
L	12	* Ryan Malone	PIT	81	22	21	43	-23	64	5	3	4	0	139	15.8
C	14	Milan Kraft	PIT	66	19	21	40	-22	18	6	0	1	0	134	14.2
C	9	Rico Fata	PIT	73	16	18	34	-46	54	6	2	1	0	163	9.8
D	55	Ric Jackman	TOR	29	2	4	6	-11	13	1	0	1	0	35	5.7
			PIT	25	7	17	24	-5	14	6	0	1	0	56	12.5
			TOTAL	54	9	21	30	-16	27	7	0	2	0	91	9.9
R	71	* Konstantin Koltsov	PIT	82	9	20	29	-30	30	2	0	3	1	123	7.3
R	43	Tomas Surovy	PIT	47	11	12	23	-8	16	3	0	1	0	112	9.8
R	36	Tom Kostopoulos	PIT	60	9	13	22	-14	67	2	1	1	0	101	8.9
C	11	Lasse Pirjeta	CBJ	57	2	8	10	-6	20	0	0	0	0	78	2.6
			PIT	13	6	6	12	3	0	1	0	1	0	33	18.2
			TOTAL	70	8	14	22	-3	20	1	0	1	0	111	7.2
C	20	Mike Eastwood	PIT	82	4	15	19	-18	40	0	0	1	0	55	7.3
L	34	* Ramzi Abid	PHX	30	10	8	18	1	30	4	0	3	0	52	19.2
			PIT	3	0	0	0	-5	2	0	0	0	0	7	0.0
			TOTAL	33	10	8	18	-4	32	4	0	3	0	59	16.9
L	39	Jonathan Sim	L.A.	48	6	7	13	0	27	0	0	1	0	73	8.2
			PIT	15	2	3	5	-4	6	0	0	1	0	27	7.4
			TOTAL	63	8	10	18	-4	33	0	0	2	0	100	8.0
R	8	Matt Bradley	PIT	82	7	9	16	-27	65	0	0	1	0	85	8.2
D	6	Martin Strbak	L.A.	5	2	0	2	1	8	0	0	0	0	7	28.6
			PIT	44	3	11	14	-11	38	0	0	0	0	47	6.4
			TOTAL	49	5	11	16	-10	46	0	0	0	0	54	9.3
R	26	Landon Wilson	PHX	35	3	1	4	-3	16	0	0	0	0	41	2.4
			PIT	19	5	1	6	0	31	2	0	0	0	35	14.3
			TOTAL	54	6	4	10	-3	47	2	0	0	0	76	7.9
R	72	Eric Meloche	PIT	25	3	7	10	-6	20	0	0	0	0	28	10.7
D	44	* Brooks Orpik	PIT	79	1	9	10	-36	127	0	0	0	0	56	1.8
C	66	Mario Lemieux	PIT	10	1	8	9	-2	6	0	0	0	0	21	4.8
D	2	Josef Melichar	PIT	82	3	5	8	-17	62	0	0	0	0	78	3.8
D	5	Patrick Boileau	PIT	16	3	4	7	-16	8	3	0	0	0	41	7.3
L	19	Ramzi Abid	PIT	16	3	2	5	-5	27	2	0	1	0	35	8.6
D	4	Dan Focht	PIT	52	2	3	5	-23	105	0	0	0	0	56	3.6
L	7	Kelly Buchberger	PIT	71	1	3	4	-19	109	0	0	0	0	34	2.9
C	49	* Matt Hussey	PIT	3	2	1	3	-1	0	2	0	0	0	8	25.0
D	45	* Robert Scuderi	PIT	13	1	2	3	-2	8	0	0	0	0	4	25.0
L	23	Steve Mckenna	PIT	49	1	2	3	-10	85	0	0	0	0	30	3.3
L	22	* Matt Murley	PIT	18	1	1	2	-6	14	0	0	0	0	20	5.0
C	16	Kris Beech	PIT	4	0	1	1	0	6	0	0	0	0	6	0.0
L	33	Reid Simpson	PIT	2	0	0	0	0	17	0	0	0	0	2	0.0

Goaltending

No.	Goaltender	GPI	Mins	Avg	W	L	T	EN	SO	GA	SA	S%	G	A	PIM
50	Martin Brochu	1	33	1.82	0	0	0	0	1	19	.947	0	0	0
30	J-Sebastien Aubin	22	1067	2.98	7	9	4	1	53	574	.908	0	0	2
40	* Andy Chiodo	8	486	3.46	3	4	1	0	28	260	.892	0	0	0
29	* Marc-Andre Fleury	21	1154	3.64	4	14	2	3	1	70	675	.896	0	0	6
31	* Sebastien Caron	40	2213	3.74	9	24	5	6	1	138	1179	.883	0	0	6
	Totals	82	4984	3.65	23	51	8	13	3	303	2720	.889			

General Managers' History

Jack Riley, 1967-68 to 1969-70; Red Kelly, 1970-71; Red Kelly and Jack Riley, 1971-72; Jack Riley, 1972-73; Jack Riley and Jack Button, 1973-74; Jack Button, 1974-75; Wren Blair, 1975-76; Wren Blair and Baz Bastien, 1976-77; Baz Bastien, 1977-78 to 1982-83; Eddie Johnston, 1983-84 to 1987-88; Tony Esposito, 1988-89; Tony Esposito and Craig Patrick, 1989-90; Craig Patrick, 1990-91 to date.

Coach

OLCZYK, EDDIE
Coach, Pittsburgh Penguins. Born in Chicago, IL, August 16, 1966.

Craig Patrick named former Penguins forward Eddie Olczyk as the successor to Rick Kehoe behind the Pittsburgh bench on June 11, 2003. Olczyk is the 21st head coach in club history and the 18th different person to hold the position. He is also the fifth former Penguins player to guide the team, joining Ken Schinkel, Lou Angotti, Gene Ubriaco and Kehoe. At the time of his hiring, he had no previous coaching experience.

The Chicago native moved to the bench from the broadcast booth, having spent the three previous seasons as a color commentator for Penguins broadcasts on Fox Sports Net. He also covered the Stanley Cup playoffs for ESPN and NHL Radio. Olczyk moved behind the microphone in 2000 after completing a successful 16-year NHL career. Selected by his hometown Blackhawks third overall in the 1984 draft, "Edzo" went on to record 342 goals and 794 points in 1,031 games with Chicago, Toronto, Winnipeg, the New York Rangers, Los Angeles and Pittsburgh. He topped the 30-goal mark five consecutive seasons (1987 to 1992), netted a single-season high 42 goals with the Maple Leafs in 1987-88 and captured the Stanley Cup as a member of the Rangers in 1994.

Olczyk joined the Penguins at the 1997 trade deadline, coming to Pittsburgh from Los Angeles for Glen Murray. He recorded 33 points (15 goals, 18 assists) in 68 regular season games with the Pens and added three goals in 11 postseason contests.

Coaching Record

			Regular Season				Playoffs		
Season	Team	Games	W	L	T	Games	W	L
2003-04	Pittsburgh (NHL)	82	23	51	8	....	....	....
	NHL Totals	82	23	51	8	....	....	....

Coaching History

Red Sullivan, 1967-68, 1968-69; Red Kelly, 1969-70 to 1971-72; Red Kelly and Ken Schinkel, 1972-73; Ken Schinkel and Marc Boileau, 1973-74; Marc Boileau, 1974-75; Marc Boileau and Ken Schinkel, 1975-76; Ken Schinkel, 1976-77; Johnny Wilson, 1977-78 to 1979-80; Eddie Johnston, 1980-81 to 1982-83; Lou Angotti, 1983-84; Bob Berry, 1984-85 to 1986-87; Pierre Creamer, 1987-88; Gene Ubriaco, 1988-89; Gene Ubriaco and Craig Patrick, 1989-90; Bob Johnson, 1990-91, 1991-92; Scotty Bowman, 1991-92, 1992-93; Eddie Johnston, 1993-94 to 1995-96; Eddie Johnston and Craig Patrick, 1996-97; Kevin Constantine, 1997-98, 1998-99; Kevin Constantine and Herb Brooks, 1999-2000; Ivan Hlinka, 2000-01; Ivan Hlinka and Rick Kehoe, 2001-02; Rick Kehoe, 2002-03; Eddie Olczyk, 2003-04 to date.

Club Records

Team

(Figures in brackets for season records are games played; records for fewest points, wins, ties, losses, goals, goals against are for 70 or more games)

Most Points **119** 1992-93 (84)
Most Wins **56** 1992-93 (84)
Most Ties **20** 1970-71 (78)
Most Losses **58** 1983-84 (80)
Most Goals **367** 1992-93 (84)
Most Goals Against **394** 1982-83 (80)
Fewest Points **38** 1983-84 (80)
Fewest Wins **16** 1983-84 (80)
Fewest Ties **4** 1995-96 (82)
Fewest Losses **21** 1992-93 (84)
Fewest Goals **182** 1969-70 (76)
Fewest Goals Against **188** 1997-98 (82)
Longest Winning Streak
Overall .... ***17** Mar. 9-Apr. 10/93
Home .... **11** Jan. 5-Mar. 7/91
Away .... **7** Mar. 14-Apr. 9/93
Longest Undefeated Streak
Overall .... **18** Mar. 9-Apr. 14/93 (17 wins, 1 tie)
Home .... **20** Nov. 30/74-Feb. 22/75 (12 wins, 8 ties)
Away .... **8** Mar. 14-Apr. 14/93 (7 wins, 1 tie)
Longest Losing Streak
Overall .... **18** Jan. 13-Feb. 22/04
Home .... **14** Dec. 31/03-Feb. 22/04
Away .... **18** Dec. 23/82-Mar. 4/83
Longest Winless Streak
Overall .... **18** Jan. 2-Feb. 10/83 (17 losses, 1 tie), Jan. 13-Feb. 22/04 (18 losses)
Home .... **16** Dec. 31/03-Mar. 4/04 (15 losses, 1 tie)
Away .... **18** Oct. 25/70-Jan. 14/71 (11 losses, 7 ties), Dec. 23/82-Mar. 4/83 (18 losses)
Most Shutouts, Season **9** 1998-99 (82)
Most PIM, Season **2,670** 1988-89 (80)
Most Goals, Game .... **12** Mar. 15/75 (Wsh. 1 at Pit. 12), Dec. 26/91 (Tor. 1 at Pit. 12)

Individual

Most Seasons .... **16** Mario Lemieux
Most Games .... **889** Mario Lemieux
Most Goals, Career .... **683** Mario Lemieux
Most Assists, Career .... **1,018** Mario Lemieux
Most Points, Career .... **1,701** Mario Lemieux (683G, 1,018A)
Most PIM, Career .... **1,023** Kevin Stevens
Most Shutouts, Career .... **22** Tom Barrasso
Longest Consecutive Games Streak .... **320** Ron Schock (Oct. 24/73-Apr. 3/77)
Most Goals, Season .... **85** Mario Lemieux (1988-89)
Most Assists, Season .... **114** Mario Lemieux (1988-89)
Most Points, Season .... **199** Mario Lemieux (1988-89; 85G, 114A)
Most PIM, Season .... **409** Paul Baxter (1981-82)
Most Points, Defenseman, Season .... **113** Paul Coffey (1988-89; 30G, 83A)
Most Points, Center, Season .... **199** Mario Lemieux (1988-89; 85G, 114A)
Most Points, Right Wing, Season .... ***149** Jaromir Jagr (1995-96; 62G, 87A)
Most Points, Left Wing, Season .... **123** Kevin Stevens (1991-92; 54G, 69A)
Most Points, Rookie, Season .... **100** Mario Lemieux (1984-85; 43G, 57A)
Most Shutouts, Season .... **7** Tom Barrasso (1997-98)
Most Goals, Game .... **5** Mario Lemieux (Three times)
Most Assists, Game .... **6** Ron Stackhouse (Mar. 8/75), Greg Malone (Nov. 28/79), Mario Lemieux (Three times)
Most Points, Game .... **8** Mario Lemieux (Oct. 15/88; 2G, 6A, Dec. 31/88; 5G, 3A)

* NHL Record.

Captains' History

Ab McDonald, 1967-68; no captain, 1968-69 to 1972-73; Ron Schock, 1973-74 to 1976-77; Jean Pronovost, 1977-78; Orest Kindrachuk, 1978-79 to 1980-81; Randy Carlyle, 1981-82 to 1983-84; Mike Bullard, 1984-85, 1985-86; Mike Bullard and Terry Ruskowski, 1986-87; Dan Frawley and Mario Lemieux, 1987-88; Mario Lemieux, 1988-89 to 1993-94; Ron Francis, 1994-95; Mario Lemieux, 1995-96, 1996-97; Ron Francis, 1997-98; Jaromir Jagr, 1998-99 to 2000-01; Mario Lemieux, 2001-02 to date.

Retired Numbers

21 Michel Brière 1969-1970

All-time Record vs. Other Clubs

Regular Season

	At Home								On Road								Total							
	GP	W	L	T	OL	GF	GA	PTS	GP	W	L	T	OL	GF	GA	PTS	GP	W	L	T	OL	GF	GA	PTS
Anaheim	9	5	2	2	0	29	27	12	8	3	4	0	1	24	29	7	17	8	6	2	1	53	56	19
Atlanta	10	8	1	0	1	39	25	17	10	9	1	0	0	39	24	18	20	17	2	0	1	78	49	35
Boston	80	32	33	15	0	273	286	79	78	16	56	6	0	218	343	38	158	48	89	21	0	491	629	117
Buffalo	71	36	17	18	0	266	217	90	71	20	34	17	0	190	274	57	142	56	51	35	0	456	491	147
Calgary	44	24	10	10	0	167	133	58	46	11	27	8	0	140	204	30	90	35	37	18	0	307	337	88
Carolina	46	23	17	6	0	185	170	52	48	21	21	5	1	177	178	48	94	44	38	11	1	362	348	100
Chicago	59	29	23	7	0	210	190	65	60	11	39	10	0	157	236	32	119	40	62	17	0	367	426	97
Colorado	37	15	17	5	0	145	152	35	32	13	16	2	1	122	142	29	69	28	33	7	1	267	294	64
Columbus	3	2	1	0	0	12	9	4	3	2	1	0	0	9	10	4	6	4	2	0	0	21	19	8
Dallas	63	38	19	6	0	236	178	82	64	21	36	6	1	213	246	49	127	59	55	12	1	449	424	131
Detroit	65	44	17	4	0	281	195	92	65	13	39	12	1	178	253	39	130	57	56	16	1	459	448	131
Edmonton	30	15	12	3	0	117	127	33	30	7	22	1	0	98	148	15	60	22	34	4	0	215	275	48
Florida	23	12	8	3	0	72	68	27	22	8	11	1	2	50	64	19	45	20	19	4	2	122	132	46
Los Angeles	73	38	25	10	0	265	233	86	69	17	43	8	1	183	265	43	142	55	68	18	1	448	498	129
Minnesota	3	1	2	0	0	6	12	2	3	0	2	1	0	5	9	1	6	1	4	1	0	11	21	3
Montreal	82	28	40	13	1	238	290	70	82	10	60	10	2	203	383	32	164	38	100	23	3	441	673	102
Nashville	5	1	2	2	0	14	17	4	6	2	4	0	0	10	21	4	11	3	6	2	0	24	38	8
New Jersey	79	40	34	4	1	289	269	85	81	29	38	13	1	269	295	72	160	69	72	17	2	558	564	157
NY Islanders	88	40	34	14	0	329	310	94	86	32	46	8	0	285	348	72	174	72	80	22	0	614	658	166
NY Rangers	100	43	43	14	0	359	365	100	101	41	51	9	0	346	393	91	201	84	94	23	0	705	758	191
Ottawa	27	17	6	4	0	97	64	38	27	14	8	5	0	87	70	33	54	31	14	9	0	184	134	71
Philadelphia	106	46	38	22	0	373	346	114	106	17	78	8	3	257	446	45	212	63	116	30	3	630	792	159
Phoenix	30	20	10	0	0	120	86	40	31	14	14	3	0	107	116	31	61	34	24	3	0	227	202	71
St. Louis	64	32	20	12	0	238	190	76	64	15	41	6	2	171	247	38	128	47	61	18	2	409	437	114
San Jose	9	4	4	1	0	41	32	9	13	6	5	2	0	54	34	14	22	10	9	3	0	95	66	23
Tampa Bay	23	15	5	3	0	90	59	33	23	9	11	2	1	60	75	21	46	24	16	5	1	150	134	54
Toronto	69	36	27	6	0	278	228	78	67	24	31	11	1	213	264	60	136	60	58	17	1	491	492	138
Vancouver	50	33	10	7	0	227	171	73	50	23	22	4	1	187	180	51	100	56	32	11	1	414	351	124
Washington	83	47	29	7	0	322	261	101	86	32	44	9	1	312	358	74	169	79	73	16	1	634	619	175
Defunct Clubs	35	22	6	7	0	148	93	51	34	13	10	11	0	108	101	37	69	35	16	18	0	256	194	88
Totals	**1466**	**746**	**512**	**205**	**3**	**5466**	**4803**	**1700**	**1466**	**453**	**815**	**178**	**20**	**4472**	**5756**	**1104**	**2932**	**1199**	**1327**	**383**	**23**	**9938**	**10559**	**2804**

Playoffs

	Series	W	L	GP	W	L	T	GF	GA	Last Mtg.	Rnd.	Result
Boston	4	2	2	19	10	9	0	67	62	1992	CF	W 4-0
Buffalo	2	2	0	10	6	4	0	26	26	2001	CSF	W 4-3
Chicago	2	1	1	8	4	4	0	23	24	1992	F	W 4-0
Dallas	1	1	0	6	4	2	0	28	16	1991	F	W 4-2
Florida	1	0	1	7	3	4	0	15	20	1996	CF	L 3-4
Montreal	1	0	1	6	2	4	0	15	18	1998	CQF	L 2-4
New Jersey	5	3	2	29	14	15	0	80	86	2001	CF	L 1-4
NY Islanders	3	0	3	19	8	11	0	58	67	1993	DF	L 3-4
NY Rangers	3	3	0	15	12	3	0	64	45	1996	CSF	W 4-1
Philadelphia	3	0	3	18	6	12	0	51	66	2000	CSF	L 2-4
St. Louis	3	1	2	13	6	7	0	40	45	1981	PRE	L 2-3
Toronto	3	0	3	12	4	8	0	27	39	1999	CSF	L 2-4
Washington	7	6	1	42	26	16	0	137	121	2001	CQF	W 4-2
Defunct Clubs	1	1	0	4	4	0	0	13	6			
Totals	**39**	**20**	**19**	**208**	**109**	**99**	**0**	**644**	**641**			

Calgary totals include Atlanta Flames, 1972-73 to 1979-80. Carolina totals include Hartford, 1979-80 to 1996-97.
Colorado totals include Quebec, 1979-80 to 1994-95. Dallas totals include Minnesota North Stars, 1967-68 to 1992-93.
New Jersey totals include Kansas City, 1974-75 to 1975-76, and Colorado Rockies, 1976-77 to 1981-82.
Phoenix totals include Winnipeg, 1979-80 to 1995-96.

Playoff Results 2004-2000

Year	Round	Opponent	Result	GF	GA
2001	CF	New Jersey	L 1-4	7	17
	CSF	Buffalo	W 4-3	17	17
	CQF	Washington	W 4-2	14	10
2000	CSF	Philadelphia	L 2-4	14	15
	CQF	Washington	W 4-1	17	8

Abbreviations: Round: F – Final;
CF – conference final; **CSF** – conference semi-final;
CQF – conference quarter-final; **DF** – division final;
PRE – preliminary round.

2003-04 Results

Oct.	10	Los Angeles	0-3		8	at Boston	1-3
	11	at Philadelphia	3-3		10	Montreal	0-8
	16	at Montreal	1-4		12	at Philadelphia	2-1
	18	Detroit	4-3		13	Tampa Bay	1-3
	22	Carolina	1-1		16	at Minnesota	2-4
	24	New Jersey	1-2		18	at Washington	3-4
	25	at NY Islanders	2-7		20	New Jersey	0-3
	29	NY Islanders	4-4		22	at Ottawa	5-6
	30	at Chicago	1-0		24	Colorado	3-5
Nov.	1	Boston	3-2*		27	Tampa Bay	2-6
	4	at Toronto	2-4		29	at Tampa Bay	1-5
	7	at Florida	3-6		31	Philadelphia	3-5
	8	at Tampa Bay	0-9	**Feb.**	1	at Boston	1-4
	12	at NY Rangers	2-6		3	Montreal	3-4
	14	at Buffalo	2-1*		10	Boston	3-6
	15	Florida	2-3		12	at Florida	1-5
	19	Minnesota	2-6		14	at St. Louis	2-3*
	21	at New Jersey	1-2*		16	Toronto	4-8
	22	Ottawa	2-1*		18	at NY Islanders	3-4
	26	Philadelphia	1-1		20	Florida	0-2
	28	NY Rangers	1-4		22	Ottawa	3-6
	29	at Carolina	3-4		25	at Phoenix	4-3*
Dec.	1	Atlanta	4-3		27	at San Jose	2-4
	3	at Philadelphia	2-5		29	at NY Islanders	3-2*
	6	at Edmonton	3-4	**Mar.**	2	NY Islanders	3-3
	7	at Calgary	1-6		4	Nashville	4-9
	9	at Vancouver	3-4*		6	Anaheim	2-1
	12	at Atlanta	3-6		7	at NY Rangers	7-4
	13	Columbus	5-3		9	Dallas	4-0
	16	Buffalo	2-1		11	at Toronto	3-2
	18	at Carolina	1-2*		14	Philadelphia	3-3
	20	Atlanta	4-7		16	Washington	4-1
	22	at Montreal	1-4		17	at New Jersey	1-6
	26	at Ottawa	3-3		19	Carolina	4-3*
	27	New Jersey	0-2		21	NY Rangers	4-3*
	29	Chicago	1-0		23	at NY Rangers	5-2
	31	NY Islanders	1-6		26	at Buffalo	1-5
Jan.	1	at Nashville	2-3		27	Buffalo	2-2
	3	NY Rangers	1-4		30	at Washington	2-4
	5	Toronto	0-5	**Apr.**	2	at Atlanta	3-2
	7	at New Jersey	4-2		4	Washington	4-3

* – Overtime

Entry Draft
Selections 2004-1990

2004
Pick
- 2 Evgeni Malkin
- 31 Johannes Salmonsson
- 61 Alex Goligoski
- 67 Nick Johnson
- 85 Brian Gifford
- 99 Tyler Kennedy
- 130 Michal Sersen
- 164 Moises Gutierrez
- 194 Chris Peluso
- 222 Jordan Morrison
- 228 David Brown
- 259 Dan Ihnacak

2003
Pick
- 1 Marc-Andre Fleury
- 32 Ryan Stone
- 70 Jonathan Filewich
- 73 Daniel Carcillo
- 121 Paul Bissonnette
- 161 Yevgeny Isakov
- 169 Lukas Bolf
- 199 Andy Chiodo
- 229 Stephen Dixon
- 232 Joe Jensen
- 263 Matt Moulson

2002
Pick
- 5 Ryan Whitney
- 35 Ondrej Nemec
- 69 Erik Christensen
- 101 Daniel Fernholm
- 136 Andrew Sertich
- 137 Cam Paddock
- 171 Robert Goepfert
- 202 Patrik Bartschi
- 234 Maxime Talbot
- 239 Ryan Lannon
- 265 Dwight Labrosse

2001
Pick
- 21 Colby Armstrong
- 54 Noah Welch
- 86 Drew Fata
- 96 Alexandre Rouleau
- 120 Tomas Surovy
- 131 Ben Eaves
- 156 Andrew Schneider
- 217 Tomas Duba
- 250 Brandon Crawford-West

2000
Pick
- 18 Brooks Orpik
- 52 Shane Endicott
- 84 Peter Hamerlik
- 124 Michel Ouellet
- 146 David Koci
- 185 Patrick Foley
- 216 Jim Abbott
- 248 Steve Crampton
- 273 Roman Simicek
- 280 Nick Boucher

1999
Pick
- 18 Konstantin Koltsov
- 51 Matt Murley
- 57 Jeremy Van Hoof
- 86 Sebastian Caron
- 115 Ryan Malone
- 144 Tomas Skvaridlo
- 157 Vladimir Malenkykh
- 176 Doug Meyer
- 204 Tom Kostopoulos
- 233 Darcy Robinson
- 261 Andrew McPherson

1998
Pick
- 23 Milan Kraft
- 54 Alexander Zevakhin
- 80 David Cameron
- 110 Scott Myers
- 134 Rob Scuderi
- 169 Jan Fadrny
- 196 Joel Scherban
- 224 Mika Lehto
- 244 Toby Petersen
- 254 Matt Hussey

1997
Pick
- 17 Robert Dome
- 44 Brian Gaffaney
- 71 Josef Melichar
- 97 Alexandre Mathieu
- 124 Harlan Pratt
- 152 Petr Havelka
- 179 Mark Moore
- 208 Andrew Ference
- 234 Eric Lind

1996
Pick
- 23 Craig Hillier
- 28 Pavel Skrbek
- 72 Boyd Kane
- 77 Boris Protsenko
- 105 Michal Rozsival
- 150 Peter Bergman
- 186 Eric Meloche
- 238 Timo Seikkula

1995
Pick
- 24 Aleksey Morozov
- 76 Jean-Sebastien Aubin
- 102 Oleg Belov
- 128 Jan Hrdina
- 154 Alexei Kolkunov
- 180 Derrick Pyke
- 206 Sergei Voronov
- 232 Frank Ivankovic

1994
Pick
- 24 Chris Wells
- 50 Richard Park
- 57 Sven Butenschon
- 73 Greg Crozier
- 76 Alexei Krivchenkov
- 102 Tom O'Connor
- 128 Clint Johnson
- 154 Valentin Morozov
- 161 Serge Aubin
- 180 Drew Palmer
- 206 Boris Zelenko
- 232 Jason Godbout
- 258 Mikhail Kazakevich
- 284 Brian Leitza

1993
Pick
- 26 Stefan Bergkvist
- 52 Domenic Pittis
- 62 Dave Roche
- 104 Jonas Andersson-Junkka
- 130 Chris Kelleher
- 156 Patrick Lalime
- 182 Sean Selmser
- 208 Larry McMorran
- 234 Timothy Harberts
- 260 Leonid Toropchenko
- 286 Hans Jonsson

1992
Pick
- 19 Martin Straka
- 43 Marc Hussey
- 67 Travis Thiessen
- 91 Todd Klassen
- 115 Philippe DeRouville
- 139 Artem Kopot
- 163 Jan Alinc
- 187 Fran Bussey
- 211 Brian Bonin
- 235 Brian Callahan

1991
Pick
- 16 Markus Naslund
- 38 Rusty Fitzgerald
- 60 Shane Peacock
- 82 Joe Tamminen
- 104 Robert Melanson
- 126 Brian Clifford
- 148 Ed Patterson
- 170 Peter McLaughlin
- 192 Jeff Lembke
- 214 Chris Tok
- 236 Paul Dyck
- 258 Pasi Huura

1990
Pick
- 5 Jaromir Jagr
- 61 Joe Dziedzic
- 68 Chris Tamer
- 89 Brian Farrell
- 107 Ian Moran
- 110 Denis Casey
- 130 Mika Valila
- 131 Ken Plaquin
- 145 Pat Neaton
- 152 Petteri Koskimaki
- 173 Ladislav Karabin
- 194 Timothy Fingerhut
- 215 Michael Thompson
- 236 Brian Bruininks

Club Directory

Mellon Arena

Pittsburgh Penguins
Mellon Arena
66 Mario Lemieux Place
Pittsburgh, PA 15219
Phone **412/642-1300**
FAX 412/642-1859
Media Relations FAX 412/642-1322
Capacity: 16,958

Ownership .... Mario Lemieux and the Lemieux Group LP

Administration
Chairman/CEO .... Mario Lemieux
President and Governor .... Ken Sawyer
Executive VP/General Manager .... Craig Patrick
Vice President & General Counsel .... Ted Black
Vice President & Controller .... Kevin Hart
Vice President, Communications/Marketing . Tom McMillan
Vice President, Sales .... David Soltesz
Executive Assistant .... Fay McNamara
Receptionist .... Kelly Hart
Mailroom Supervisor .... Brett Hart

Hockey Operations
General Manager .... Craig Patrick
Assistant General Manager .... Ed Johnston
Head Coach .... Eddie Olczyk
Assistant Coaches .... Randy Hillier, Joe Mullen
Head Scout .... Greg Malone
Goaltending Coach/Scout .... Gilles Meloche
Scouts .... Wayne Daniels, Chuck Grillo, Charlie Hodge, Mark Kelley, Richard Rose, Neil Shea
Pro Scouts .... Rick Kehoe, Glenn Patrick
Head Coach, Wilkes-Barre/Scranton (AHL) . Michel Therrien
Assistant Coach, Wilkes-Barre/Scranton (AHL) .... Mike Yeo
Strength & Conditioning Coach .... John Welday
Equipment Manager .... Steve Latin
Assistant Equipment Manager .... Paul Flati
Equipment Staff .... Paul DeFazio
Team Physician .... Dr. Charles Burke
Head Athletic Trainer .... Mark Mortland
Assistant Athletic Trainer .... Scott Johnson
Massage Therapist .... Tom Plasko
Executive Assistant .... Tracey Botsford
Team Staff .... Michael Lang
Video Coordinator .... Paul Fink

Communications/Marketing
Vice President, Communications/Marketing ...... Tom McMillan
Director of Media Relations .... Keith Wehner
Manager, Media Relations .... Todd Lepovsky
Director of Publications .... Brian Coe
Multi Media Manager .... Chris Devivo
New Media Manager .... Brett Robinson
Director of Marketing .... Brian Magness
Creative Director .... Barb Pilarski
Director of Public/Alumni Relations ... Cindy Himes
Manager, Video Production .... Joe Hale
Manager, Art and Graphics .... Dori Minnis
Director of Amateur Hockey .... Mark Shuttleworth
Director of Alumni Relations .... Jack Riley
Exec. Producer, Penguins Radio Network .. Ray Walker

Finance
Vice President & Controller .... Kevin Hart
Assistant Controller .... Michael McCullough
Accounting Staff .... Tawni Love, Troy Ussack, Andrea Winschel

Ticketing
Vice President, Sales .... David Soltesz
Senior Director of Ticketing .... James Santilli
Director, Premium Seating .... Terri Smith
Director, Ticketing .... Chad Slencak
Manager, Group Sales .... Mike Guiffre
Premium Seating Account Representative . Bonnie Golinski, George Murphy
Ticket Sales Representatives .... George Birman, Jason Florian, Mike McLaughlin, Ross Miller, Chuck Pukansky
Box Office Manager .... Carol Coulson
Box Office Staff .... Kelly Gabany, Jason Onufer
Customer Service Representatives ...... Kathy Davis, Jill Weisbrod
Data Base Manager .... Jill Shaw

Corporates Sales
Vice President, Sales .... David Soltesz
Senior Director, Corporate Sales ...... Kimberly Bogesdorfer
Directors, Corporate Sales .... Carl D'Alicandro, Mark DeAndrea
Sales Service .... Kelly Maza
Corporate Sales Liason .... Pierre Larouche

General Information
Home Ice .... Mellon Arena
Dimensions of Rink .... 200 feet by 85 feet
Seating Capacity 16,940
Team Colors .... Black, Gold and White
TV Station .... Fox Sports Net Pittsburgh
TV Announcers .... Mike Lange, Bob Errey
Radio Announcers .... Paul Steigerwald, Phil Bourque
Flagship Radio Station .... 3WS (94.5FM), Fox Sports Radio 970AM

Vice President and General Manager

PATRICK, CRAIG
Executive Vice President/General Manager, Pittsburgh Penguins.
Born in Detroit, MI, May 20, 1946.

Known for his calm and patient management style, Craig Patrick has led the Penguins to two Stanley Cup championships, one Presidents' Trophy title and five division championships since taking over as general manager on December 5, 1989. In 2000, he and Mario Lemieux were recipients of the Lester Patrick Trophy for their contributions to hockey in the United States. He was elected to the Hockey Hall of Fame in 2001.

A member of one of hockey's most famous families — including grandfather Lester, father Lynn and uncle Muzz — Patrick played collegiate hockey at the University of Denver and captained the Pioneers to the NCAA championship in 1969. He played eight NHL seasons with four different teams, registering 72 goals and 163 points in 401 games before retiring in 1979. He made the transition to management and coaching when he landed the dual role of assistant coach and assistant g.m. of the 1980 U.S. Olympic team that won the gold medal at Lake Placid.

Patrick joined the New York Rangers organization as director of operations in 1980 and became the youngest general manager in club history one year later. He served in that capacity through the 1985-86 season, leading his team to the playoffs every year.

Prior to joining the Penguins, Patrick spent two years as director of athletics and recreation at the University of Denver.

NHL Coaching Record

| Season | Team | Games | Regular Season | | | Games | Playoffs | |
			W	L	T		W	L
1980-81	NY Rangers	60	26	23	11	14	7	7
1984-85	NY Rangers	35	11	22	2	3	0	3
1989-90	Pittsburgh	54	22	26	6	....	....	....
1996-97	Pittsburgh	20	7	10	3	5	1	4
	NHL Totals	**169**	**66**	**81**	**22**	**22**	**8**	**14**

St. Louis Blues

2003-04 Results: 39w-30L-11T-2OTL 91PTS.
Second, Central Division

2004-05 Schedule

Oct.	Fri.	15	Chicago
	Sat.	16	at Nashville
	Wed.	20	at Vancouver
	Thu.	21	at Calgary
	Sat.	23	at Edmonton
	Tue.	26	Buffalo
	Fri.	29	at New Jersey
	Sat.	30	San Jose
Nov.	Mon.	1	Columbus
	Thu.	4	NY Islanders
	Sat.	6	Montreal
	Mon.	8	at Philadelphia
	Thu.	11	Colorado
	Sat.	13	Anaheim
	Wed.	17	at Minnesota
	Thu.	18	at Colorado
	Sat.	20	at Phoenix
	Tue.	23	Calgary
	Fri.	26	at Columbus
	Sat.	27	Detroit
Dec.	Wed.	1	at Florida
	Thu.	2	at Tampa Bay
	Sat.	4	Los Angeles
	Mon.	6	at Detroit
	Wed.	8	Nashville
	Thu.	9	at Pittsburgh
	Sat.	11	Columbus
	Wed.	15	at Dallas
	Thu.	16	Pittsburgh
	Sat.	18	Phoenix
	Wed.	22	at Washington
	Thu.	23	at Boston
	Sun.	26	Detroit
	Tue.	28	Toronto
	Thu.	30	Colorado
	Fri.	31	at Columbus
Jan.	Sun.	2	Los Angeles
	Tue.	4	Vancouver
	Thu.	6	Edmonton
	Sat.	8	Minnesota
	Mon.	10	at Nashville

	Wed.	12	at Anaheim
	Sat.	15	at San Jose
	Mon.	17	at Phoenix*
	Thu.	20	Washington
	Sat.	22	Chicago*
	Mon.	24	at NY Rangers
	Tue.	25	at Buffalo
	Sat.	29	Phoenix
	Sun.	30	at Chicago
Feb.	Tue.	1	Columbus
	Thu.	3	Carolina
	Sat.	5	Dallas*
	Mon.	7	at Minnesota
	Wed.	9	at Colorado
	Thu.	10	Anaheim
	Tue.	15	Nashville
	Thu.	17	at Detroit
	Sat.	19	Dallas*
	Mon.	21	San Jose*
	Thu.	24	Vancouver
	Sat.	26	at Los Angeles
	Sun.	27	at Anaheim*
Mar.	Tue.	1	Calgary
	Thu.	3	Edmonton
	Sat.	5	at Columbus
	Sun.	6	at Chicago
	Thu.	10	at Vancouver
	Sat.	12	at Calgary
	Tue.	15	at Edmonton
	Thu.	17	at San Jose
	Sat.	19	at Los Angeles*
	Tue.	22	Ottawa
	Thu.	24	at Detroit
	Sat.	26	Atlanta
	Mon.	28	Detroit
	Thu.	31	Minnesota
Apr.	Sat.	2	at Nashville*
	Sun.	3	Nashville*
	Wed.	6	at Chicago
	Sat.	9	Chicago*
	Sun.	10	at Dallas*

* Denotes afternoon game.

Franchise date: June 5, 1967

CENTRAL DIVISION

38th NHL Season

Keith Tkachuk led the Blues with 33 goals last season, marking the ninth time in his career that he has reached the 30-goal plateau. He scored his 400th career goal on October 12, 2003.

Year-by-Year Record

Season	GP	Home				Road				Overall				GF	GA	Pts.	Finished	Playoff Result
		W	L	T	OL	W	L	T	OL	W	L	T	OL					
2003-04	82	23	11	7	0	16	19	4	2	39	30	11	2	191	198	91	2nd, Central Div.	Lost Conf. Quarter-Final
2002-03	82	23	11	4	3	18	13	7	3	41	24	11	6	253	222	99	2nd, Central Div.	Lost Conf. Quarter-Final
2001-02	82	27	12	1	1	16	15	7	3	43	27	8	4	227	188	98	2nd, Central Div.	Lost Conf. Semi-Final
2000-01	82	28	5	5	3	15	17	7	2	43	22	12	5	249	195	103	2nd, Central Div.	Lost Conf. Championship
1999-2000	82	24	9	7	1	27	10	4	0	51	19	11	1	248	165	114	1st, Central Div.	Lost Conf. Quarter-Final
1998-99	82	18	17	6	...	19	15	7	...	37	32	13	...	237	209	87	3rd, Central Div.	Lost Conf. Semi-Final
1997-98	82	26	10	5	...	19	19	3	...	45	29	8	...	256	204	98	3rd, Central Div.	Lost Conf. Semi-Final
1996-97	82	17	20	4	...	19	15	7	...	36	35	11	...	236	239	83	4th, Central Div.	Lost Conf. Quarter-Final
1995-96	82	15	17	9	...	17	17	7	...	32	34	16	...	219	248	80	4th, Central Div.	Lost Conf. Semi-Final
1994-95	48	16	6	2	...	12	9	3	...	28	15	5	...	178	135	61	4th, Central Div.	Lost Conf. Quarter-Final
1993-94	84	23	11	8	...	17	22	3	...	40	33	11	...	270	283	91	4th, Central Div.	Lost Conf. Quarter-Final
1992-93	84	22	13	7	...	15	23	4	...	37	36	11	...	282	278	85	4th, Norris Div.	Lost Div. Final
1991-92	80	25	12	3	...	11	21	8	...	36	33	11	...	279	266	83	3rd, Norris Div.	Lost Div. Semi-Final
1990-91	80	24	9	7	...	23	13	4	...	47	22	11	...	310	250	105	2nd, Norris Div.	Lost Div. Final
1989-90	80	20	15	5	...	17	19	4	...	37	34	9	...	295	279	83	2nd, Norris Div.	Lost Div. Final
1988-89	80	22	11	7	...	11	24	5	...	33	35	12	...	275	285	78	2nd, Norris Div.	Lost Div. Final
1987-88	80	18	17	5	...	16	21	3	...	34	38	8	...	278	294	76	2nd, Norris Div.	Lost Div. Final
1986-87	80	21	12	7	...	11	21	8	...	32	33	15	...	281	293	79	1st, Norris Div.	Lost Div. Semi-Final
1985-86	80	23	11	6	...	14	23	3	...	37	34	9	...	302	291	83	3rd, Norris Div.	Lost Conf. Championship
1984-85	80	21	12	7	...	16	19	5	...	37	31	12	...	299	288	86	1st, Norris Div.	Lost Div. Semi-Final
1983-84	80	23	14	3	...	9	27	4	...	32	41	7	...	293	316	71	2nd, Norris Div.	Lost Div. Final
1982-83	80	16	16	8	...	9	24	7	...	25	40	15	...	285	316	65	4th, Norris Div.	Lost Div. Semi-Final
1981-82	80	22	14	4	...	10	26	4	...	32	40	8	...	315	349	72	3rd, Norris Div.	Lost Div. Final
1980-81	80	29	7	4	...	16	11	13	...	45	18	17	...	352	281	107	1st, Smythe Div.	Lost Quarter-Final
1979-80	80	20	13	7	...	14	21	5	...	34	34	12	...	266	278	80	2nd, Smythe Div.	Lost Prelim. Round
1978-79	80	14	20	6	...	4	30	6	...	18	50	12	...	249	348	48	3rd, Smythe Div.	Out of Playoffs
1977-78	80	12	20	8	...	8	27	5	...	20	47	13	...	195	304	53	4th, Smythe Div.	Out of Playoffs
1976-77	80	22	13	5	...	10	26	4	...	32	39	9	...	239	276	73	1st, Smythe Div.	Lost Quarter-Final
1975-76	80	20	12	8	...	9	25	6	...	29	37	14	...	249	290	72	3rd, Smythe Div.	Lost Prelim. Round
1974-75	80	23	13	4	...	12	18	10	...	35	31	14	...	269	267	84	2nd, Smythe Div.	Lost Prelim. Round
1973-74	78	16	16	7	...	10	24	5	...	26	40	12	...	206	248	64	6th, West Div.	Out of Playoffs
1972-73	78	21	11	7	...	11	23	5	...	32	34	12	...	233	251	76	4th, West Div.	Lost Quarter-Final
1971-72	78	17	17	5	...	11	22	6	...	28	39	11	...	208	247	67	3rd, West Div.	Lost Semi-Final
1970-71	78	23	7	9	...	11	18	10	...	34	25	19	...	223	208	87	2nd, West Div.	Lost Quarter-Final
1969-70	76	24	9	5	...	13	18	7	...	37	27	12	...	224	179	86	1st, West Div.	Lost Final
1968-69	76	21	8	9	...	16	17	5	...	37	25	14	...	204	157	88	1st, West Div.	Lost Final
1967-68	74	18	12	7	...	9	19	9	...	27	31	16	...	177	191	70	3rd, West Div.	Lost Final

2004-05 Player Personnel

FORWARDS	HT	WT	S	Place of Birth	Date	2003-04 Club
BOGUNIECKI, Eric	5-8	192	R	New Haven, CT	5/6/75	St. Louis-Worcester
CAJANEK, Petr	5-11	176	L	Gottwaldov, Czech.	8/18/75	St. Louis
DISALVATORE, Jon	6-1	200	R	Bangor, ME	3/30/81	Cleveland
DRAKE, Dallas	6-1	190	L	Trail, B.C.	2/4/69	St. Louis
EVANS, Blake	6-1	210	R	Smiley, Sask.	7/2/80	Worcester
GLUMAC, Mike	6-2	205	R	Niagara Falls, Ont.	4/5/80	Worcester
JOHNSON, Ryan	6-1	200	L	Thunder Bay, Ont.	6/14/76	St. Louis
LOW, Reed	6-3	222	R	Moose Jaw, Sask.	6/21/76	St. Louis
MAYERS, Jamal	6-1	217	R	Toronto, Ont.	10/24/74	St. Louis
McCLEMENT, Jay	6-1	193	L	Kingston, Ont.	3/2/83	Worcester
POHL, John	6-0	186	R	Rochester, MN	6/29/79	St. Louis-Worcester
RYCROFT, Mark	5-11	192	R	Penticton, B.C.	7/12/78	St. Louis
SEJNA, Peter	5-11	198	L	Liptovski Mikulas, Czech.	10/5/79	St. Louis-Worcester
SILLINGER, Mike	5-11	196	R	Regina, Sask.	6/29/71	Phoenix-St. Louis
TKACHUK, Keith	6-2	225	L	Melrose, MA	3/28/72	St. Louis
WEIGHT, Doug	5-11	200	L	Warren, MI	1/21/71	St. Louis
DEFENSEMEN						
BACKMAN, Christian	6-4	198	L	Alingsas, Sweden	4/28/80	St. Louis-Worcester
BRIMANIS, Aris	6-3	215	R	Cleveland, OH	3/14/72	St. Louis-Worcester
JACKMAN, Barret	6-1	197	L	Trail, B.C.	3/5/81	St. Louis
KHAVANOV, Alexander	6-2	205	L	Moscow, USSR	1/30/72	St. Louis
MacINNIS, Al	6-2	204	R	Inverness, N.S.	7/11/63	St. Louis
MacKENZIE, Aaron	6-0	193	L	Terrace Bay, Ont.	3/7/81	Worcester
POLLOCK, Jame	6-1	210	R	Quebec City, Que.	6/16/79	St. Louis-Worcester
PRONGER, Chris	6-6	220	L	Dryden, Ont.	10/10/74	St. Louis
ROACH, Andy	5-11	181	R	Mattawan, MI	8/22/73	Mannheim
SALVADOR, Bryce	6-2	215	L	Brandon, Man.	2/11/76	St. Louis-Worcester
STUART, Mike	6-0	200	R	Rochester, MN	8/31/80	St. Louis-Worcester
WALKER, Matt	6-2	236	R	Beaverlodge, Alta.	4/7/80	St. Louis-Worcester
WEINRICH, Eric	6-1	207	L	Roanoke, VA	12/19/66	Philadelphia-St. Louis

GOALTENDERS	HT	WT	C	Place of Birth	Date	2003-04 Club
BACASHIHUA, Jason	5-11	175	L	Garden City, MI	9/20/82	Utah
DIVIS, Reinhard	5-11	200	L	Vienna, Austria	7/4/75	St. Louis-Worcester
LALIME, Patrick	6-3	185	L	St-Bonaventure, Que.	7/7/74	Ottawa
SANFORD, Curtis	5-10	187	R	Owen Sound, Ont.	10/5/79	Worcester

Coaching History

Lynn Patrick and Scotty Bowman, 1967-68; Scotty Bowman, 1968-69, 1969-70; Al Arbour and Scotty Bowman, 1970-71; Sid Abel, Bill McCreary and Al Arbour, 1971-72; Al Arbour and Jean-Guy Talbot, 1972-73; Jean-Guy Talbot and Lou Angotti, 1973-74; Lou Angotti, Lynn Patrick and Garry Young, 1974-75; Garry Young, Lynn Patrick and Leo Boivin, 1975-76; Emile Francis, 1976-77; Leo Boivin and Barclay Plager, 1977-78; Barclay Plager, 1978-79; Barclay Plager and Red Berenson, 1979-80; Red Berenson, 1980-81; Red Berenson and Emile Francis, 1981-82; Emile Francis and Barclay Plager, 1982-83; Jacques Demers, 1983-84 to 1985-86; Jacques Martin, 1986-87, 1987-88; Brian Sutter, 1988-89 to 1991-92; Bob Plager and Bob Berry, 1992-93; Bob Berry, 1993-94; Mike Keenan, 1994-95, 1995-96; Mike Keenan, Jim Roberts and Joel Quenneville, 1996-97; Joel Quenneville, 1997-98 to 2002-03; Joel Quenneville and Mike Kitchen, 2003-04; Mike Kitchen, 2004-05.

Coach

KITCHEN, MIKE
Coach, St. Louis Blues. Born in Newmarket, Ont., February 1, 1956.

Mike Kitchen was named head coach of the St. Louis Blues on February 24, 2004. His first game as head coach was on February 26, 2004 at Colorado. Kitchen spent six and a half seasons as the Blues' assistant coach, joining the staff on September 1, 1998. Prior to joining the Blues, he spent nine seasons as an assistant coach for the Toronto Maple Leafs. He joined the Leafs on August 8, 1989 after spending one season as an assistant coach for Newmarket in the American Hockey League.

Kitchen spent eight seasons in the National Hockey League as a defenseman with the Colorado Rockies and the New Jersey Devils. He appeared in 474 games, while recording 12 goals, 62 assists and 370 penalty minutes. Kansas City originally drafted him as the 38th overall choice in the 1976 Entry Draft.

Prior to playing in the NHL, Kitchen spent three seasons with the Toronto Marlboros of the OHA, accumulating 79 points (14 goals, 65 assists) and 429 penalty minutes in 202 games played. He also spent one season with the Rhode Island Reds of the AHL, registering 10 assists and 14 penalty minutes in 14 games played.

Coaching Record

		Regular Season				Playoffs		
Season	Team	Games	W	L	T	Games	W	L
2003-04	St. Louis (NHL)	21	10	7	4	5	1	4
	NHL Totals	21	10	7	4	5	1	4

2003-04 Scoring

* - rookie

Regular Season

Pos	#	Player	Team	GP	G	A	Pts	+/–	PIM	PP	SH	GW	GT	S	%
L	7	Keith Tkachuk	STL	75	33	38	71	8	83	18	0	8	2	233	14.2
C	39	Doug Weight	STL	75	14	51	65	–3	37	6	0	5	1	198	7.1
C	38	Pavol Demitra	STL	68	23	35	58	1	18	8	0	5	1	179	12.8
D	44	Chris Pronger	STL	80	14	40	54	–1	88	7	0	3	0	203	6.9
R	10	Dallas Drake	STL	79	13	22	35	10	65	3	2	1	0	121	10.7
L	49	Brian Savage	PHX	61	12	13	25	–5	36	3	0	1	0	101	11.9
			STL	13	4	3	7	–3	2	1	0	1	0	23	17.4
			TOTAL	74	16	16	32	–8	38	4	0	2	0	124	12.9
R	19	Scott Mellanby	STL	68	14	17	31	–7	76	6	0	3	0	103	13.6
C	26	Petr Cajanek	STL	70	12	14	26	12	16	3	0	4	0	126	9.5
C	18	Mike Sillinger	PHX	60	8	6	14	–14	54	0	1	0	0	66	12.1
			STL	16	5	5	10	4	14	0	1	0	0	40	12.5
			TOTAL	76	13	11	24	–10	68	0	2	0	0	106	12.3
R	42	* Mark Rycroft	STL	71	9	12	21	2	32	0	0	0	0	110	8.2
D	6	Eric Weinrich	PHI	54	2	7	9	11	32	1	0	1	0	56	3.6
			STL	26	2	8	10	1	14	1	0	0	1	27	7.4
			TOTAL	80	4	15	19	12	46	2	0	1	1	83	4.8
D	55	* Christian Backman	STL	66	5	13	18	3	16	1	0	0	0	92	5.4
C	22	* Mike Danton	STL	68	7	5	12	–8	141	0	1	0	0	72	9.7
R	21	Jamal Mayers	STL	80	6	5	11	–19	91	0	1	3	0	130	4.6
C	17	Ryan Johnson	STL	69	4	7	11	–2	8	0	1	1	0	36	11.1
R	33	Eric Boguniecki	STL	27	6	4	10	–1	20	2	0	2	0	40	15.0
D	29	Alexander Khavanov	STL	48	3	7	10	2	18	2	0	0	0	62	4.8
D	27	Bryce Salvador	STL	69	3	5	8	–4	47	0	0	1	0	60	5.0
D	23	Murray Baron	STL	80	1	5	6	–6	61	0	0	0	0	57	1.8
L	15	* Peter Sejna	STL	20	2	2	4	–9	4	2	0	0	0	36	5.6
C	25	Pascal Rheaume	NYR	17	0	0	0	–3	5	0	0	0	0	15	0.0
			STL	25	1	3	4	–3	4	0	0	0	0	23	4.3
			TOTAL	42	1	3	4	–6	9	0	0	0	0	38	2.6
D	5	Barret Jackman	STL	15	1	2	3	–1	41	0	0	0	0	11	9.1
R	9	* Jeff Heerema	STL	22	1	2	3	–5	4	0	0	1	0	28	3.6
D	2	Al Macinnis	STL	3	0	2	2	–1	6	0	0	0	0	9	0.0
R	34	Reed Low	STL	57	0	2	2	–6	141	0	0	0	0	28	0.0
C	12	Steve Martins	STL	25	1	0	1	–7	22	0	1	0	0	27	3.7
D	28	* Matt Walker	STL	14	0	1	1	0	25	0	0	0	0	8	0.0
D	46	Christian Laflamme	STL	16	0	1	1	–3	20	0	0	0	0	9	0.0
D	37	Jeff Finley	STL	53	0	1	1	–9	34	0	0	0	0	25	0.0
C	25	* John Pohl	STL	1	0	0	0	–2	0	0	0	0	0	1	0.0
R	70	* Jeremy Yablonski	STL	1	0	0	0	–1	5	0	0	0	0	1	0.0
L	18	Scott Pellerin	STL	2	0	0	0	–3	2	0	0	0	0	1	0.0
D	43	* Mike Stuart	STL	2	0	0	0	0	0	0	0	0	0	0	0.0
L	80	Steve Mclaren	STL	6	0	0	0	0	25	0	0	0	0	2	0.0
D	9	* Jame Pollock	STL	9	0	0	0	–1	6	0	0	0	0	19	0.0
D	32	Aris Brimanis	STL	13	0	0	0	0	4	0	0	0	0	3	0.0

Goaltending

No.	Goaltender	GPI	Mins	Avg	W	L	T	EN	SO	GA	SA	S%	G	A	PIM
30	Chris Osgood	67	3861	2.24	31	25	8	3	3	144	1604	.910	0	0	10
1	Brent Johnson	10	493	2.43	4	3	1	0	1	20	203	.901	0	0	0
50	Reinhard Divis	13	629	2.77	4	4	2	2	0	29	291	.900	0	0	2
	Totals	**82**	**5014**	**2.37**	**39**	**32**	**11**	**5**	**4**	**198**	**2103**	**.906**			

Playoffs

Pos	#	Player	Team	GP	G	A	Pts	+/–	PIM	PP	SH	GW	GT	S	%
C	18	Mike Sillinger	STL	5	3	1	4	5	6	0	1	0	0	12	25.0
C	39	Doug Weight	STL	5	2	1	3	–4	6	1	1	0	0	14	14.3
R	10	Dallas Drake	STL	5	1	1	2	–1	2	0	0	1	0	7	14.3
L	49	Brian Savage	STL	5	1	1	2	–3	0	0	0	0	0	10	10.0
L	7	Keith Tkachuk	STL	5	0	2	2	–1	10	0	0	0	0	12	0.0
D	55	* Christian Backman	STL	5	0	2	2	2	4	0	0	0	0	6	0.0
C	26	Petr Cajanek	STL	5	0	2	2	3	2	0	0	0	0	8	0.0
C	38	Pavol Demitra	STL	5	1	0	1	1	4	0	0	0	0	13	7.7
C	22	* Mike Danton	STL	5	1	0	1	1	2	0	0	0	0	1	100.0
R	19	Scott Mellanby	STL	4	0	1	1	–4	2	0	0	0	0	3	0.0
D	6	Eric Weinrich	STL	5	0	1	1	–1	0	0	0	0	0	6	0.0
D	44	Chris Pronger	STL	5	0	1	1	1	16	0	0	0	0	8	0.0
D	37	Jeff Finley	STL	1	0	0	0	0	2	0	0	0	0	0	0.0
R	33	Eric Boguniecki	STL	1	0	0	0	0	0	0	0	0	0	2	0.0
C	12	Steve Martins	STL	1	0	0	0	–1	0	0	0	0	0	0	0.0
C	25	Pascal Rheaume	STL	3	0	0	0	–1	2	0	0	0	0	2	0.0
C	17	Ryan Johnson	STL	3	0	0	0	0	0	0	0	0	0	2	0.0
R	42	* Mark Rycroft	STL	3	0	0	0	–1	2	0	0	0	0	1	0.0
D	28	* Matt Walker	STL	4	0	0	0	–2	0	0	0	0	0	3	0.0
D	23	Murray Baron	STL	5	0	0	0	0	6	0	0	0	0	6	0.0
R	21	Jamal Mayers	STL	5	0	0	0	1	0	0	0	0	0	6	0.0
D	27	Bryce Salvador	STL	5	0	0	0	–2	2	0	0	0	0	6	0.0

Goaltending

No.	Goaltender	GPI	Mins	Avg	W	L	EN	SO	GA	SA	S%	G	A	PIM
50	Reinhard Divis	1	18	0.00	0	0	0	0	0	8	1.000	0	0	0
30	Chris Osgood	5	287	2.51	1	4	0	0	12	109	.890	0	1	0
	Totals	**5**	**309**	**2.33**	**1**	**4**	**0**	**0**	**12**	**117**	**.897**			

Captains' History

Al Arbour, 1967-68 to 1969-70; Red Berenson and Barclay Plager, 1970-71; Barclay Plager, 1971-72 to 1975-76; no captain, 1976-77; Red Berenson, 1977-78; Barry Gibbs, 1978-79; Brian Sutter, 1979-80 to 1987-88; Bernie Federko, 1988-89; Rick Meagher, 1989-90; Scott Stevens, 1990-91; Garth Butcher, 1991-92; Brett Hull, 1992-93 to 1994-95; Brett Hull, Shayne Corson and Wayne Gretzky, 1995-96; no captain, 1996-97; Chris Pronger, 1997-98 to 2001-02; Al MacInnis, 2002-03 to date.

Club Records

Team

(Figures in brackets for season records are games played; records for fewest points, wins, ties, losses, goals, goals against are for 70 or more games)

Most Points	**114**	1999-2000 (82)
Most Wins	**51**	1999-2000 (82)
Most Ties	**19**	1970-71 (78)
Most Losses	**50**	1978-79 (80)
Most Goals	**352**	1980-81 (80)
Most Goals Against	**349**	1981-82 (80)
Fewest Points	**48**	1978-79 (80)
Fewest Wins	**18**	1978-79 (80)
Fewest Ties	**7**	1983-84 (80)
Fewest Losses	**18**	1980-81 (80)
Fewest Goals	**177**	1967-68 (74)
Fewest Goals Against	**157**	1968-69 (76)
Longest Winning Streak		
Overall	**10**	Jan. 3-23/02
Home	**9**	Jan. 26-Feb. 26/91
Away	***10**	Jan. 21-Mar. 2/00
Longest Undefeated Streak		
Overall	**12**	Nov. 10-Dec. 8/68 (5 wins, 7 ties), Nov. 24-Dec. 26/00 (11 wins, 1 tie)
Home	**11**	Four times
Away	**11**	Jan. 21-Mar. 4/00 (10 wins, 1 tie)
Longest Losing Streak		
Overall	**7**	Nov. 12-26/67, Feb. 12-25/89
Home	**6**	Nov. 23-Dec. 19/96
Away	**10**	Jan. 20-Mar. 8/82
Longest Winless Streak		
Overall	**12**	Jan. 17-Feb. 15/78 (10 losses, 2 ties)
Home	**7**	Dec. 28/82-Jan. 25/83 (5 losses, 2 ties)
Away	**17**	Jan. 23-Oct. 9/74 (13 losses, 4 ties)
Most Shutouts, Season	**13**	1968-69 (76)
Most PIM, Season	**2,041**	1990-91 (80)
Most Goals, Game	**11**	Feb. 26/94 (St.L. 11 at Ott. 1)

Individual

Most Seasons	**13**	Bernie Federko
Most Games	**927**	Bernie Federko
Most Goals, Career	**527**	Brett Hull
Most Assists, Career	**721**	Bernie Federko
Most Points, Career	**1,073**	Bernie Federko (352G, 721A)
Most PIM, Career	**1,786**	Brian Sutter
Most Shutouts, Career	**16**	Glenn Hall
Longest Consecutive Games Streak	**662**	Garry Unger (Feb. 7/71-Apr. 8/79)
Most Goals, Season	**86**	Brett Hull (1990-91)
Most Assists, Season	**90**	Adam Oates (1990-91)
Most Points, Season	**131**	Brett Hull (1990-91) (86G, 45A)
Most PIM, Season	**306**	Bob Gassoff (1975-76)
Most Points, Defenseman, Season	**78**	Jeff Brown (1992-93; 25G, 53A)
Most Points, Center, Season	**115**	Adam Oates (1990-91; 25G, 90A)
Most Points, Right Wing, Season	**131**	Brett Hull (1990-91; 86G, 45A)
Most Points, Left Wing, Season	**102**	Brendan Shanahan (1993-94; 52G, 50A)
Most Points, Rookie, Season	**73**	Jorgen Pettersson (1980-81; 37G, 36A)
Most Shutouts, Season	**8**	Glenn Hall (1968-69)
Most Goals, Game	**6**	Red Berenson (Nov. 7/68)
Most Assists, Game	**5**	Brian Sutter (Nov. 22/83), Bernie Federko (Feb. 27/88), Adam Oates (Jan. 26/91), Dallas Drake (Oct. 29/03)
Most Points, Game	**7**	Red Berenson (Nov. 7/68; 6G, 1A), Garry Unger (Mar. 13/71; 3G, 4A)

* NHL Record.

Retired Numbers

3	Bob Gassoff	1973-1977
8	Barclay Plager	1967-1977
11	Brian Sutter	1976-1988
24	Bernie Federko	1976-1989

All-time Record vs. Other Clubs

Regular Season

	At Home								On Road								Total							
	GP	W	L	T	OL	GF	GA	PTS	GP	W	L	T	OL	GF	GA	PTS	GP	W	L	T	OL	GF	GA	PTS
Anaheim	22	12	7	3	0	67	56	27	22	13	7	2	0	65	54	28	44	25	14	5	0	132	110	55
Atlanta	3	3	0	0	0	11	1	6	4	2	1	1	0	16	14	5	7	5	1	1	0	27	15	11
Boston	59	27	23	9	0	188	198	63	59	15	35	9	0	161	247	39	118	42	58	18	0	349	445	102
Buffalo	50	29	14	7	0	180	125	65	52	17	29	6	0	164	200	40	102	46	43	13	0	344	325	105
Calgary	64	31	24	9	0	229	195	71	62	28	28	5	1	180	201	62	126	59	52	14	1	409	396	133
Carolina	31	19	9	3	0	119	94	41	31	17	12	2	0	97	92	36	62	36	21	5	0	216	186	77
Chicago	115	57	40	17	1	388	356	132	118	35	63	18	2	348	433	90	233	92	103	35	3	736	789	222
Colorado	40	22	14	4	0	148	124	48	41	14	20	7	0	111	138	35	81	36	34	11	0	259	262	83
Columbus	11	9	1	1	0	45	23	19	10	4	3	2	1	26	22	11	21	13	4	3	1	71	45	30
Dallas	117	64	32	21	0	424	330	149	115	40	53	22	0	334	383	102	232	104	85	43	0	758	713	251
Detroit	110	56	34	20	0	375	308	132	110	41	51	17	1	336	404	100	220	97	85	37	1	711	712	232
Edmonton	44	21	16	7	0	157	153	49	44	17	23	4	0	144	161	38	88	38	39	11	0	301	314	87
Florida	9	7	1	1	0	25	12	15	9	5	2	2	0	20	17	12	18	12	3	3	0	45	29	27
Los Angeles	78	50	18	10	0	293	195	110	78	31	35	12	0	226	261	74	156	81	53	22	0	519	456	184
Minnesota	8	3	2	3	0	15	11	9	8	3	3	2	0	13	19	8	16	6	5	5	0	28	30	17
Montreal	57	14	28	15	0	147	195	43	59	11	41	7	0	161	255	29	116	25	69	22	0	308	450	72
Nashville	16	12	3	1	0	53	23	25	17	9	4	3	1	46	35	22	33	21	7	4	1	99	58	47
New Jersey	46	27	11	7	1	192	143	62	46	17	22	7	0	128	146	41	92	44	33	14	1	320	289	103
NY Islanders	47	18	18	9	2	166	153	47	49	13	25	11	0	131	183	37	96	31	43	20	2	297	336	84
NY Rangers	63	25	28	10	0	188	202	60	60	10	44	6	0	143	245	26	123	35	72	16	0	331	447	86
Ottawa	9	4	3	2	0	27	25	10	10	6	4	0	0	36	23	12	19	10	7	2	0	63	48	22
Philadelphia	68	26	33	7	2	194	219	61	67	12	45	10	0	153	264	34	135	38	78	17	2	347	483	95
Phoenix	50	26	13	11	0	182	136	63	51	18	25	7	1	156	166	44	101	44	38	18	1	338	302	107
Pittsburgh	64	43	15	6	0	247	171	92	64	20	31	12	1	190	238	53	128	63	46	18	1	437	409	145
San Jose	28	18	8	1	1	93	65	38	24	19	4	1	0	85	51	39	52	37	12	2	1	178	116	77
Tampa Bay	11	10	1	0	0	44	24	20	13	5	4	3	1	42	38	14	24	15	5	3	1	86	62	34
Toronto	102	58	29	14	1	348	283	131	99	30	58	11	0	292	369	71	201	88	87	25	1	640	652	202
Vancouver	71	41	21	9	0	265	205	91	72	33	29	9	1	230	214	76	143	74	50	18	1	495	419	167
Washington	41	20	13	8	0	165	127	48	39	15	20	4	0	117	136	34	80	35	33	12	0	282	263	82
Defunct Clubs	32	25	4	3	0	131	55	53	33	11	10	12	0	95	100	34	65	36	14	15	0	226	155	87
Totals	**1466**	**777**	**463**	**218**	**8**	**5106**	**4207**	**1780**	**1466**	**511**	**731**	**214**	**10**	**4246**	**5109**	**1246**	**2932**	**1288**	**1194**	**432**	**18**	**9352**	**9316**	**3026**

Playoffs

	Series	W	L	GP	W	L	T	GF	GA	Last Mtg.	Rnd.	Result
Boston	2	0	2	8	0	8	0	15	48	1972	SF	L 0-4
Buffalo	1	0	1	3	1	2	0	8	7	1976	PRE	L 1-2
Calgary	1	0	1	7	3	4	0	22	28	1986	CF	L 3-4
Chicago	10	3	7	50	22	28	0	142	171	2002	CQF	W 4-1
Colorado	1	0	1	5	1	4	0	11	17	2001	CF	L 1-4
Dallas	12	6	6	66	32	34	0	187	197	2001	CSF	W 4-0
Detroit	7	2	5	40	16	24	0	103	125	2002	CSF	L 1-4
Los Angeles	2	2	0	8	8	0	0	32	13	1998	CQF	W 4-0
Montreal	3	0	3	12	0	12	0	14	42	1977	QF	L 0-4
NY Rangers	1	0	1	6	2	4	0	22	29	1981	QF	L 2-4
Philadelphia	2	2	0	11	8	3	0	34	20	1969	QF	W 4-0
Phoenix	2	2	0	11	7	4	0	39	29	1999	CQF	W 4-3
Pittsburgh	3	2	1	13	7	6	0	45	40	1981	PRE	W 3-2
San Jose	3	1	2	18	8	10	0	47	43	2004	CQF	L 1-4
Toronto	5	3	2	31	17	14	0	88	90	1996	CQF	W 4-2
Vancouver	2	0	2	14	6	8	0	48	44	2003	CQF	L 3-4
Totals	**57**	**23**	**34**	**303**	**138**	**165**	**0**	**857**	**943**			

Calgary totals include Atlanta Flames, 1972-73 to 1979-80.
Carolina totals include Hartford, 1979-80 to 1996-97.
Colorado totals include Quebec, 1979-80 to 1994-95.
Dallas totals include Minnesota North Stars, 1967-68 to 1992-93.
New Jersey totals include Kansas City, 1974-75 to 1975-76, and Colorado Rockies, 1976-77 to 1981-82.
Phoenix totals include Winnipeg, 1979-80 to 1995-96.

Playoff Results 2004-2000

Year	Round	Opponent	Result	GF	GA
2004	CQF	San Jose	L 1-4	9	12
2003	CQF	Vancouver	L 3-4	21	17
2002	CSF	Detroit	L 1-4	11	14
	CQF	Chicago	W 4-1	13	5
2001	CF	Colorado	L 1-4	11	17
	CSF	Dallas	W 4-0	13	6
	CQF	San Jose	W 4-2	16	11
2000	CQF	San Jose	L 3-4	22	20

Abbreviations: Round: CF – conference final; **CSF** – conference semi-final; **CQF** – conference quarter-final; **SF** – semi-final; **QF** – quarter-final; **PRE** – preliminary round.

2003-04 Results

Oct.	10	at Phoenix	1-2*
	12	at Colorado	2-1
	16	at Nashville	1-4
	18	Washington	4-1
	21	at Edmonton	6-4
	22	at Vancouver	2-3
	24	at Calgary	2-1
	28	Nashville	1-0
	29	at Detroit	6-5
Nov.	1	Chicago	2-3
	4	Anaheim	2-1*
	6	Vancouver	3-2
	8	Florida	2-0
	13	at San Jose	4-3*
	15	at Los Angeles	1-0
	16	at Anaheim	3-4
	19	at Phoenix	4-5
	22	Dallas	2-1
	25	Boston	4-3*
	28	at Tampa Bay	2-2
	29	Detroit	1-2
Dec.	2	Los Angeles	4-1
	4	Detroit	4-4
	6	Nashville	4-1
	9	at Toronto	3-2*
	12	at Columbus	3-2*
	13	Los Angeles	2-1
	16	Columbus	2-1*
	18	San Jose	4-2
	20	Phoenix	1-1
	22	at Detroit	1-2
	23	at Chicago	0-3
	26	Colorado	3-3
	29	at Columbus	3-2
	30	Philadelphia	2-7
Jan.	1	NY Rangers	5-4
	3	San Jose	1-3
	5	Minnesota	1-1
	6	at Carolina	0-2
	10	at Nashville	1-3
	12	Chicago	7-4
	13	at Montreal	2-5
	15	Columbus	5-3
	17	Minnesota	2-2
	19	at Florida	2-1*
	21	at Columbus	1-3
	23	at Dallas	0-2
	24	Dallas	2-3
	28	at Atlanta	1-1
	29	Vancouver	2-4
	31	New Jersey	1-4
Feb.	2	at Minnesota	0-4
	4	at Edmonton	3-5
	5	at Calgary	2-1
	10	at Ottawa	1-3
	12	Colorado	0-4
	14	Pittsburgh	3-2*
	16	Phoenix	4-2
	19	Tampa Bay	4-3*
	20	at Detroit	1-5
	22	at Chicago	2-3*
	26	at Colorado	2-2
	28	at Vancouver	0-2
	29	at San Jose	0-1
Mar.	2	Calgary	2-4
	4	Edmonton	1-1
	6	at NY Islanders	4-2
	7	at Buffalo	5-1
	9	NY Islanders	3-2*
	11	Nashville	1-1
	13	Columbus	5-3
	14	Calgary	0-3
	16	at Los Angeles	5-3
	17	at Anaheim	1-1
	20	at Dallas	1-3
	25	Anaheim	3-2
	27	Chicago	4-3*
	28	at Chicago	3-1
	30	Edmonton	1-0
Apr.	1	Detroit	2-3
	3	at Nashville	4-1
	4	at Minnesota	0-3

* – Overtime

Entry Draft
Selections 2004-1990

2004
Pick
17	Marek Schwarz
49	Carl Soderberg
83	Viktor Alexandrov
116	Michal Birner
136	Nikita Nikitin
180	Roman Polak
211	David Fredriksson
277	Jonathan Michel
	Boutin

2003
Pick
30	Shawn Belle
62	David Backes
84	Konstantin Barulin
88	Zack Fitzgerald
101	Konstantin Zakharov
127	Alexandre Bolduc
148	Lee Stempniak
159	Chris Beckford-Tseu
189	Jonathan Lehun
221	Yevgeny Skachkov
253	Andrei Pervyshin
284	Juhamatti Aaltonen

2002
Pick
48	Alexei Shkotov
62	Andrei Mikhnov
89	Tomas Troliga
120	Robin Jonsson
165	Justin Maiser
191	D.J. King
221	Jonas Johnson
253	Tom Koivisto
284	Ryan MacMurchy

2001
Pick
57	Jay McClement
89	Tuomas Nissinen
122	Igor Valeev
159	Dmitri Semin
190	Brett Scheffelmaier
253	Petr Cajanek
270	Grant Jacobsen
283	Simon Skoog

2000
Pick
30	Jeff Taffe
65	Dave Morisset
75	Justin Papineau
96	Antoine Bergeron
129	Troy Riddle
167	Craig Weller
229	Brett Lutes
261	Reinhard Divis
293	Lauri Kinos

1999
Pick
17	Barret Jackman
85	Peter Smrek
114	Chad Starling
143	Trevor Byrne
180	Tore Vikingstad
203	Phil Osaer
221	Colin Hemingway
232	Alexander Khavanov
260	Brian McMeekin
270	James Desmarais

1998
Pick
24	Christian Backman
41	Maxim Linnik
83	Matt Walker
157	Brad Voth
170	Andrei Troschinsky
197	Brad Twordik
225	Yevgeny Pastukh
255	John Pohl

1997
Pick
40	Tyler Rennette
86	Didier Tremblay
98	Jan Horacek
106	Jame Pollock
149	Nicholas Bilotto
177	Ladislav Nagy
206	Bobby Haglund
232	Dmitri Plekhanov
244	Marek Ivan

1996
Pick
14	Marty Reasoner
67	Gordie Dwyer
95	Jonathan Zukiwsky
97	Andrei Petrakov
159	Stephen Wagner
169	Daniel Corso
177	Reed Low
196	Andrej Podkonicky
203	Tony Hutchins
229	Konstantin Shafranov

1995
Pick
49	Jochen Hecht
75	Scott Roche
101	Michal Handzus
127	Jeff Ambrosio
153	Denis Hamel
179	Jean-Luc Grand-Pierre
205	Derek Bekar
209	Libor Zabransky

1994
Pick
68	Stephane Roy
94	Tyler Harlton
120	Edvin Frylen
172	Roman Vopat
198	Steve Noble
224	Marc Stephan
250	Kevin Harper
276	Scott Fankhouser

1993
Pick
37	Maxim Bets
63	Jamie Rivers
89	Jamal Mayers
141	Todd Kelman
167	Mike Buzak
193	Eric Boguniecki
219	Mike Grier
245	Libor Prochazka
271	Alexander Vasilevski
275	Christer Olsson

1992
Pick
38	Igor Korolev
62	Vitali Karamnov
64	Vitali Prokhorov
86	Lee Leslie
134	Bob Lachance
158	Ian Laperriere
160	Lance Burns
180	Igor Boldin
182	Nick Naumenko
206	Todd Harris
230	Yuri Gunko
259	Wade Salzman

1991
Pick
27	Steve Staios
64	Kyle Reeves
65	Nathan LaFayette
87	Grayden Reid
109	Jeff Callinan
131	Bruce Gardiner
153	Terry Hollinger
175	Chris Kenady
197	Jed Fiebelkorn
219	Chris MacKenzie
241	Kevin Rappana
263	Mike Veisor

1990
Pick
33	Craig Johnson
54	Patrice Tardif
96	Jason Ruff
117	Kurtis Miller
138	Wayne Conlan
180	Parris Duffus
201	Steve Widmeyer
222	Joe Hawley
243	Joe Fleming

General Managers' History

Lynn Patrick, 1967-68; Scotty Bowman, 1968-69 to 1970-71; Lynn Patrick, 1971-72; Sid Abel, 1972-73; Charles Catto, 1973-74; Gerry Ehman, 1974-75; Dennis Ball, 1975-76; Emile Francis, 1976-77 to 1982-83; Ron Caron, 1983-84 to 1993-94; Mike Keenan, 1994-95, 1995-96; Mike Keenan and Ron Caron, 1996-97; Larry Pleau, 1997-98 to date.

Vice President and General Manager

PLEAU, LARRY
Senior Vice President/General Manager, St. Louis Blues.
Born in Lynn, MA, June 29, 1947.

Larry Pleau was named general manager on June 9, 1997, becoming the tenth person to hold that position in team history. He has built the Blues into one of the NHL's top teams, winning the President's Trophy in 1999-2000 and reaching the Western Conference Finals in 2000-01. In international hockey, he served as associate general manager of the silver medal-winning 2002 U.S. Olympic team and as general manager of Team USA at the World Championships in 2003 and 2004 (bronze medal) and at the 2004 World Cup.

Pleau joined the Blues after spending eight seasons with the New York Rangers organization, reaching the position of vice president of player personnel. He joined the Rangers in 1989 as assistant general manager of player development. During Pleau's tenure in New York, the Rangers drafted NHL stars Sergei Zubov, Doug Weight, Alex Kovalev and Niklas Sundstrom. Prior to joining the Rangers, Pleau spent 17 seasons with the Hartford Whalers organization as a player, assistant coach, head coach, general manager and minor league general manager and head coach. He was also instrumental in drafting Ray Ferraro, Ron Francis, Kevin Dineen and Ulf Samuelsson while a member of the Whalers organization.

Pleau played three seasons with the Montreal Canadiens (1969-1972) in the National Hockey League before being the first player signed by the Hartford Whalers of the World Hockey Association. He was a center/left wing for the Whalers from 1972 until his retirement in 1979. He played in 468 regular season games for Hartford, accumulating 157 goals and 215 assists for 372 points. He also played for the 1968 United States Olympic team, the 1969 U.S. national team and went to training camp with Team USA for the 1976 Canada Cup tournament.

NHL Coaching Record

Season	Team	Games	Regular Season W	L	T	Playoffs Games	W	L
1980-81	Hartford	20	6	12	2	....	....	....
1981-82	Hartford	80	21	41	18	....	....	....
1982-83	Hartford	18	4	13	1	....	....	....
1987-88	Hartford	26	13	13	0	6	2	4
1988-89	Hartford	80	37	38	5	4	0	4
	NHL Totals	**224**	**81**	**117**	**26**	**10**	**2**	**8**

Club Directory

Savvis Center

St. Louis Blues
Savvis Center
1401 Clark Avenue
St. Louis, MO 63103
Phone **314/622-2500**
FAX 314/622-2582
www.stlouisblues.com
Capacity: 19,022

Executive Management
Owner and Chairman	Bill Laurie
President, Paige Sports Entertainment	Richard Thomas
COO & General Counsel, Paige Sports Entertainment	Brent Karasiuk
President and CEO	Mark Sauer
Sr. Vice President and General Manager	Larry Pleau
Sr. Vice President of Finance and Hockey Administration	Jerry Jasiek
Sr. Vice President of Marketing and Communications	Jim Woodcock
Sr. Vice President and General Manager, Savvis Center	Dennis Petrullo
Vice President of Sales	Bruce Affleck
Vice President of Marketing	Jo Ann Miles
Vice President of Human Resources	Dave Coverstone
Vice President of Building Operations	Fred Corsi
Executive Assistant to the President	Lisa Cwiklowski
Executive Assistant to the General Manager	Donna Lembke
Executive Assistant to the General Manager, Savvis Center	Cherri Haynes

Hockey Operations
Head Coach	Mike Kitchen
Assistant Coach	Don Lever
Goaltending Coach	Keith Allain
Video/Assistant Strength and Conditioning Coach	Jamie Kompon
Director of Player Evaluation	Ted Hampson
Athletic Trainer	Ray Barile
Equipment Manager	Bert Godin
Assistant Equipment Manager	Steve Wissman
Massage Therapist	Jeff Wright
Exercise Physiologist	Dr. Howie Wenger
Director of Team Services	Mike Caruso
Director of Professional Scouting	Kevin McDonald
Director of Amateur Scouting	Jarmo Kekalainen
Professional Scouts	Bob Berry, Wayne Mundey
Amateur Scouts	Mike Antonovich, Craig Channell, Paul Gallagher, Dan Ginnell, Vladimir Havluj, Jr., Veli-Pekka Kautonen, Stephen Leach, Rick Meagher, Barclay Parneta, Ville Siren, Georgi Zhuravlev

Team Doctors
Dr. Jerome Gilden, Dr. Rick Wright, Dr. Matt Matava, Dr. Aaron Birenbaum, Dr. William Birenbaum, Dr. Ralph Dacey, Dr. Michael Brunt, Dr. Tom Francel, Dr. Glenn Edwards, Dr. Gill Grand, Dr. Rex Ghormley

Communications
Director of Communications	Chuck Menke
Communications Assistants	Scott Bonanni, Rich Jankowski
Assistant Director of Multimedia	Renee Orr
Marketing/Public Relations Assistant	Donna Ferguson
Team Photographer	Mark Buckner

Marketing and Sales
Director of Corporate Sponsorships	Chris Arger
Director of Marketing Programs	Lou Siville
Event Presentation Director	Chris Frome
Manager of Community Relations and Youth Marketing	Kim Mulherin
Sr. Manager of Corporate Sales and Promotions	Rob Rixford, Mary Greener
Manager of Corporate Sales and Promotions	Jeff Floerke
Manager of Fan Services	Bob Laurie
Senior Director of Sales	Kyle Draper
Director of Group Sales	Jennifer Nevins
Manager of Customer Service	Jill Hahn
Assistant Manager of Customer Service	Paula Munder
Customer Service Representatives	Kim Derringer, Josh Hardin
Ticket Sales Representatives	Katie Proctor, Mike McGrath, Jill Serve, Kari Palmer, JoAnna Dettmann
Database Administrator	Sean Puchta
Sales Coordinator	Belinda Kirchgessner

Finance
Director of MIS/Accounting	Phil Siddle
Manager of Accounting	Craig Bryant
Accounting Supervisor	Ron Catlett
Payroll Supervisor	Pam Pflasterer
Accounting	Deann Cromer, Traci Hinterser, Mindy Wallace, Chantay Kane

Team Broadcasters
Radio Station	KTRS 550 AM
Radio Broadcasters	Chris Kerber, Kelly Chase
Television Station	KPLR-TV WB 11
Television Broadcasters	John Kelly, Bernie Federko, Dan McLaughlin
Regional Sports Network	Fox Sports Net (Midwest)

San Jose Sharks

2003-04 Results: 43W-21L-12T-6OTL 104PTS.
First, Pacific Division

2004-05 Schedule

Oct.	Wed.	13	Vancouver		Thu.	13	Los Angeles
	Fri.	15	at Anaheim		Sat.	15	St. Louis
	Sat.	16	Colorado		Mon.	17	Edmonton*
	Tue.	19	at Columbus		Wed.	19	at Anaheim
	Thu.	21	at Nashville		Thu.	20	Columbus
	Sat.	23	at Boston		Sat.	22	at Colorado*
	Mon.	25	at NY Rangers		Tue.	25	at Minnesota
	Tue.	26	at Pittsburgh		Thu.	27	at Los Angeles
	Thu.	28	at Buffalo		Fri.	28	Dallas
	Sat.	30	at St. Louis		Sun.	30	Nashville*
Nov.	Wed.	3	Phoenix	Feb.	Tue.	1	at Calgary
	Sat.	6	Atlanta		Thu.	3	at Montreal
	Thu.	11	Minnesota		Sat.	5	at Ottawa
	Sat.	13	Vancouver		Mon.	7	at Toronto
	Wed.	17	Detroit		Tue.	8	at Columbus
	Sat.	20	Florida		Thu.	10	at Philadelphia
	Mon.	22	at Phoenix		Tue.	15	at Vancouver
	Wed.	24	Chicago		Thu.	17	Calgary
	Fri.	26	at Dallas		Sat.	19	Boston
	Sat.	27	at Nashville		Mon.	21	at St. Louis*
	Mon.	29	at Detroit		Thu.	24	at NY Islanders
Dec.	Thu.	2	Dallas		Sat.	26	at Detroit*
	Sat.	4	Washington		Sun.	27	at Chicago*
	Tue.	7	Phoenix	Mar.	Tue.	1	Anaheim
	Thu.	9	Edmonton		Thu.	3	Buffalo
	Sat.	11	Carolina		Sun.	6	at Colorado*
	Mon.	13	at Dallas		Tue.	8	at Anaheim
	Wed.	15	at Chicago		Thu.	10	New Jersey
	Thu.	16	at Minnesota		Sat.	12	Chicago*
	Sat.	18	Nashville		Sun.	13	NY Rangers*
	Wed.	22	Phoenix		Thu.	17	St. Louis
	Sun.	26	Los Angeles*		Sat.	19	Detroit*
	Mon.	27	at Los Angeles		Thu.	24	Anaheim
	Thu.	30	Minnesota		Sat.	26	Columbus
	Fri.	31	at Phoenix*		Mon.	28	Colorado
Jan.	Sun.	2	at Edmonton		Wed.	30	at Los Angeles
	Mon.	3	at Calgary*		Thu.	31	Los Angeles
	Thu.	6	Dallas	Apr.	Sat.	2	at Phoenix
	Sat.	8	Tampa Bay		Mon.	4	at Dallas
	Mon.	10	at Vancouver		Thu.	7	Calgary
	Tue.	11	at Edmonton		Sat.	9	Anaheim*

Denotes afternoon game.

Year-by-Year Record

Season	GP	Home W	L	T	OL	Road W	L	T	OL	Overall W	L	T	OL	GF	GA	Pts.	Finished	Playoff Result
2003-04	82	24	8	7	2	19	13	5	4	43	21	12	6	219	183	104	1st, Pacific Div.	Lost Conf. Final
2002-03	82	17	16	5	3	11	21	4	5	28	37	9	8	214	239	73	5th, Pacific Div.	Out of Playoffs
2001-02	82	25	11	3	2	19	16	5	1	44	27	8	3	248	199	99	1st, Pacific Div.	Lost Conf. Semi-Final
2000-01	82	22	14	4	1	18	13	8	2	40	27	12	3	217	192	95	2nd, Pacific Div.	Lost Conf. Quarter-Final
1999-2000	82	21	14	3	3	14	16	7	4	35	30	10	7	225	214	87	4th, Pacific Div.	Lost Conf. Semi-Final
1998-99	82	17	15	9	…	14	18	9	…	31	33	18	…	196	191	80	4th, Pacific Div.	Lost Conf. Quarter-Final
1997-98	82	17	19	5	…	17	19	5	…	34	38	10	…	210	216	78	4th, Pacific Div.	Lost Conf. Quarter-Final
1996-97	82	14	23	4	…	13	24	4	…	27	47	8	…	211	278	62	7th, Pacific Div.	Out of Playoffs
1995-96	82	12	26	3	…	8	29	4	…	20	55	7	…	252	357	47	7th, Pacific Div.	Out of Playoffs
1994-95	48	10	13	1	…	9	12	3	…	19	25	4	…	129	161	42	3rd, Pacific Div.	Lost Conf. Semi-Final
1993-94	84	19	13	10	…	14	22	6	…	33	35	16	…	252	265	82	3rd, Pacific Div.	Lost Conf. Semi-Final
1992-93	84	8	33	1	…	3	38	1	…	11	71	2	…	218	414	24	6th, Smythe Div.	Out of Playoffs
1991-92	80	14	23	3	…	3	35	2	…	17	58	5	…	219	359	39	6th, Smythe Div.	Out of Playoffs

Franchise date: May 9, 1990

WESTERN NHL CONFERENCE

PACIFIC DIVISION

14th NHL Season

Defensive excellence was a key reason why San Jose set a franchise record with 104 points last season. Scott Hannan played in all 82 games and ranked 14th among NHL defensemen in total ice time.

2004-05 Player Personnel

FORWARDS	HT	WT	S	Place of Birth	Date	2003-04 Club
BERNIER, Steve	6-2	230	R	Quebec City, Que.	3/31/85	Moncton
CHEECHOO, Jonathan	6-1	190	R	Moose Factory, Ont.	7/15/80	San Jose
CLOWE, Ryan	6-2	215	R	St. John's, Nfld.	9/30/82	Cleveland
DAMPHOUSSE, Vincent	6-1	200	L	Montreal, Que.	12/17/67	San Jose
DIMITRAKOS, Niko	5-10	205	R	Sommerville, MA	5/21/79	San Jose-Cleveland
EKMAN, Nils	6-0	185	L	Stockholm, Sweden	3/11/76	San Jose
GILL, Aaron	6-0	180	R	Rochester, MN	3/5/80	Notre Dame-Cleveland
GOC, Marcel	6-0	195	L	Calw, West Germany	8/24/83	Cleveland-San Jose
HARVEY, Todd	6-0	210	R	Hamilton, Ont.	2/17/75	San Jose-Cleveland
JOSEPH, Shane	5-9	170	R	Brooks, Alta.	7/23/81	Minnesota State-Cleveland
KOROLYUK, Alexander	5-9	190	L	Moscow, USSR	1/15/76	San Jose
MARLEAU, Patrick	6-2	220	L	Aneroid, Sask.	9/15/79	San Jose
McCAULEY, Alyn	5-11	200	L	Brockville, Ont.	5/29/77	San Jose
MICHALEK, Milan	6-2	220	L	Jindrichuv Hradec, Czech.	12/7/84	San Jose-Cleveland
OLSON, Glenn	6-4	230	L	Fort McNeil, B.C.	5/1/84	Kootenay
PARKER, Scott	6-5	230	R	Hanford, CA	1/29/78	San Jose
PLIHAL, Tomas	6-1	195	L	Frydlant v Cechach, Czech.	3/28/83	Cleveland
PRIMEAU, Wayne	6-4	230	L	Scarborough, Ont.	6/4/76	San Jose
RISSMILLER, Pat	6-4	210	L	Belmont, MA	10/26/78	San Jose-Cleveland
SMITH, Mark	5-10	215	L	Edmonton, Alta.	10/24/77	San Jose
STEVENSON, Grant	5-11	170	R	Spruce Grove, Alta.	10/15/81	Cleveland
STURM, Marco	6-0	195	L	Dingolfing, West Germany	9/8/78	San Jose
THORNTON, Scott	6-3	225	L	London, Ont.	1/9/71	San Jose
VALETTE, Craig	6-0	190	L	Shellbrook, Sask.	10/7/82	Cleveland
ZALESAK, Miroslav	6-0	200	L	Skalica, Czech.	1/2/80	San Jose-Cleveland
DEFENSEMEN						
CARKNER, Matt	6-4	235	R	Winchester, Ont.	11/3/80	Cleveland
CLOUTIER, David	6-1	200	R	Quebec City, Que.	12/17/81	Cleveland
DAVISON, Rob	6-2	225	L	St. Catharines, Ont.	5/1/80	San Jose
EHRHOFF, Christian	6-2	195	L	Moers, West Germany	7/6/82	San Jose-Cleveland
FAHEY, Jim	6-0	205	R	Boston, MA	5/11/79	San Jose-Cleveland
FORD, Scott	6-3	225	R	Charlie Lake, B.C.	12/24/79	Brown
GORGES, Josh	6-1	190	L	Kelowna, B.C.	8/14/84	Kelowna
HANNAN, Scott	6-1	220	L	Richmond, B.C.	1/23/79	San Jose
MARSHALL, Jason	6-2	200	R	Cranbrook, B.C.	2/22/71	Minnesota-Houston-San Jose
McLAREN, Kyle	6-4	225	L	Humboldt, Sask.	6/18/77	San Jose
MURRAY, Doug	6-3	245	L	Bromma, Sweden	3/12/80	Cleveland
PREISSING, Tom	6-0	205	R	Rosemount, MN	12/3/78	San Jose
RATHJE, Mike	6-5	235	L	Mannville, Alta.	5/11/74	San Jose
STAFFORD, Garrett	6-0	190	R	Los Angeles, CA	1/28/80	Cleveland
STUART, Brad	6-2	220	L	Rocky Mountain House, Alta.	11/6/79	San Jose

GOALTENDERS	HT	WT	C	Place of Birth	Date	2003-04 Club
NABOKOV, Evgeni	6-0	200	L	Ust-Kamenogorsk, USSR	7/25/75	San Jose
PATZOLD, Dimitri	6-0	200	L	Ust-Kamenogorsk, USSR	2/3/83	Cleveland-Johnstown
SCHAEFER, Nolan	6-2	200	R	Yellow Grass, Sask.	1/15/80	Cleveland-Fresno
TOSKALA, Vesa	5-10	190	L	Tampere, Finland	5/20/77	San Jose

Coach

WILSON, RON
Coach, San Jose Sharks. Born in Windsor, Ont., May 28, 1955.

Named head coach of the Sharks on December 4, 2002, Ron Wilson's first full season behind the San Jose bench saw the team rebound from a disappointing 2002-03 campaign in which they finished last in the Pacific Division and 14th in the Western Conference to capture its second Pacific Division title with a franchise-best 104 points. The Sharks finished second overall in the Western Conference and reached the Western Conference Final for the first time.

Prior to spending five seasons with the Washington Capitals, Wilson had served as the first head coach of the expansion Mighty Ducks of Anaheim in 1993 and led the team to its first trip to the Stanley Cup playoffs in 1996-97. In four seasons behind the Anaheim bench, he posted a record of 120-145-31.

Throughout his professional and amateur career, Wilson has enjoyed a long-standing relationship with USA Hockey. In 1996, he led Team USA to the gold medal at the inaugural World Cup of Hockey. He coached the team again at the 2004 tournament. Wilson also coached the U.S. national team at the 1994 and 1996 World Championships, where his teams finished fourth and third respectively. Wilson also served as head coach for Team USA at the 1998 Nagano Winter Olympics.

Born in Windsor, Ontario, but raised in Riverside Rhode Island, Wilson was selected by the Toronto Maple Leafs in the seventh round (132nd overall) of the 1975 NHL Entry Draft. He began his professional career with the Dallas Blackhawks (Central Hockey League) in the spring of 1977 and joined the Maple Leafs for the 1977-78 season. In 177 career games with Toronto and the Minnesota North Stars, Wilson posted 93 points (26 goals, 67 assists). He also played for the U.S. national team in 1975, 1981, 1983 and 1987.

2003-04 Scoring

* - rookie

Regular Season

Pos	#	Player	Team	GP	G	A	Pts	+/–	PIM	PP	SH	GW	GT	S	%
C	12	Patrick Marleau	S.J.	80	28	29	57	–5	24	9	0	5	0	220	12.7
L	28	Nils Ekman	S.J.	82	22	33	55	30	34	1	4	5	1	147	15.0
R	14	Jonathan Cheechoo	S.J.	81	28	19	47	5	33	8	0	9	1	175	16.0
C	10	Alyn Mccauley	S.J.	82	20	27	47	23	28	5	0	4	0	146	13.7
L	19	Marco Sturm	S.J.	64	21	20	41	0	36	10	2	6	2	158	13.3
C	25	Vincent Damphousse	S.J.	82	12	29	41	–5	66	7	0	4	0	156	7.7
D	7	Brad Stuart	S.J.	77	9	30	39	9	34	5	0	0	0	129	7.0
L	94	Alexander Korolyuk	S.J.	63	19	18	37	20	18	4	0	2	0	108	17.6
C	15	Wayne Primeau	S.J.	72	9	20	29	4	90	0	1	1	0	142	6.3
L	17	Scott Thornton	S.J.	80	13	14	27	–6	84	1	0	1	1	127	10.2
C	18	Mike Ricci	S.J.	71	7	19	26	8	40	2	0	0	0	48	14.6
C	37	Curtis Brown	BUF	68	9	12	21	2	30	2	1	2	0	117	7.7
			S.J.	12	2	2	4	1	6	0	0	0	0	21	9.5
			TOTAL	80	11	14	25	3	36	2	1	2	0	138	8.0
R	23 *	Nicholas Dimitrakos	S.J.	68	9	15	24	6	49	2	0	4	0	116	7.8
D	4	Kyle Mclaren	S.J.	64	2	22	24	10	60	0	1	0	0	67	3.0
D	22	Scott Hannan	S.J.	82	6	15	21	10	48	0	0	0	0	114	5.3
D	42 *	Tom Preissing	S.J.	69	2	17	19	8	12	2	0	1	1	89	2.2
D	2	Mike Rathje	S.J.	80	2	17	19	18	46	0	1	0	0	105	1.9
D	44 *	Christian Ehrhoff	S.J.	41	1	11	12	4	14	0	0	1	0	58	1.7
R	13	Todd Harvey	S.J.	47	4	5	9	3	38	0	0	0	0	51	7.8
D	6	Jason Marshall	MIN	12	1	4	5	–1	18	1	0	0	0	16	6.3
			S.J.	12	0	2	2	–2	8	0	0	0	0	14	0.0
			TOTAL	24	1	6	7	–3	26	1	0	0	0	30	3.3
C	16	Mark Smith	S.J.	36	1	3	4	–5	72	0	0	0	0	31	3.2
R	27	Scott Parker	S.J.	50	1	3	4	0	101	0	0	0	0	20	5.0
D	5 *	Rob Davison	S.J.	55	0	3	3	–3	92	0	0	0	0	33	0.0
D	21	Jim Fahey	S.J.	15	0	2	2	–2	18	0	0	0	0	19	0.0
R	9 *	Milan Michalek	S.J.	2	1	0	1	1	4	0	0	0	0	1	100.0
C	24 *	Brad Boyes	S.J.	1	0	0	0	–2	2	0	0	0	0	0	0.0
R	32 *	Miroslav Zalesak	S.J.	2	0	0	0	–1	0	0	0	0	0	3	0.0
C	34 *	Pat Rissmiller	S.J.	4	0	0	0	0	0	0	0	0	0	2	0.0

Goaltending

No.	Goaltender	GPI	Mins	Avg	W	L	T	EN	SO	GA	SA	S%	G	A	PIM
35	Vesa Toskala	28	1541	2.06	12	8	4	3	1	53	760	.930	0	1	2
20	Evgeni Nabokov	59	3456	2.20	31	19	8	0	9	127	1610	.921	0	0	14
	Totals	**82**	**5016**	**2.19**	**43**	**27**	**12**	**3**	**11**	**183**	**2373**	**.923**			

Evgeni Nabokov and Vesa Toskala shared a shutout vs. Phoenix on Nov. 21, 2003.

Playoffs

Pos	#	Player	Team	GP	G	A	Pts	+/–	PIM	PP	SH	GW	GT	S	%
C	25	Vincent Damphousse	S.J.	17	7	7	14	0	20	3	0	3	0	37	18.9
C	12	Patrick Marleau	S.J.	17	8	4	12	0	6	4	1	2	0	45	17.8
R	14	Jonathan Cheechoo	S.J.	17	4	6	10	4	10	1	0	0	0	34	11.8
R	23 *	Niko Dimitrakos	S.J.	15	1	8	9	2	8	0	0	1	1	22	4.5
L	94	Alexander Korolyuk	S.J.	17	5	2	7	0	10	2	0	1	0	42	11.9
D	2	Mike Rathje	S.J.	17	1	5	6	1	13	0	0	0	0	14	7.1
D	22	Scott Hannan	S.J.	17	1	5	6	7	22	1	0	1	0	25	4.0
D	7	Brad Stuart	S.J.	17	1	5	6	–4	13	0	0	0	0	28	3.6
C	18	Mike Ricci	S.J.	17	2	3	5	5	4	0	0	0	0	13	15.4
L	17	Scott Thornton	S.J.	12	2	2	4	1	22	0	0	0	0	15	13.3
C	10	Alyn McCauley	S.J.	11	2	1	3	0	2	0	0	0	0	11	18.2
R	13	Todd Harvey	S.J.	16	1	2	3	–3	2	0	0	0	0	11	9.1
C	15	Wayne Primeau	S.J.	17	1	2	3	–7	4	0	0	0	0	28	3.6
L	28	Nils Ekman	S.J.	16	0	3	3	–2	8	0	0	0	0	29	0.0
D	4	Kyle McLaren	S.J.	16	0	3	3	–1	10	0	0	0	0	12	0.0
C	57 *	Marcel Goc	S.J.	5	1	1	2	1	0	0	0	1	0	1	100.0
D	5 *	Rob Davison	S.J.	5	0	2	2	0	4	0	0	0	0	2	0.0
C	37	Curtis Brown	S.J.	17	0	2	2	–5	18	0	0	0	0	23	0.0
C	16	Mark Smith	S.J.	10	1	0	1	2	11	0	0	1	0	3	33.3
D	42 *	Tom Preissing	S.J.	11	0	1	1	0	0	0	0	0	0	7	0.0
D	6	Jason Marshall	S.J.	17	0	1	1	1	25	0	0	0	0	13	0.0
D	21	Jim Fahey	S.J.	2	0	0	0	0	0	0	0	0	0	0	0.0

Goaltending

No.	Goaltender	GPI	Mins	Avg	W	L	EN	SO	GA	SA	S%	G	A	PIM
20	Evgeni Nabokov	17	1052	1.71	10	7	2	3	30	461	.935	0	0	4
	Totals	**17**	**1055**	**1.82**	**10**	**7**	**2**	**3**	**32**	**463**	**.931**			

Coaching History

George Kingston, 1991-92, 1992-93; Kevin Constantine, 1993-94, 1994-95; Kevin Constantine and Jim Wiley, 1995-96; Al Sims, 1996-97; Darryl Sutter, 1997-98 to 2001-02; Darryl Sutter and Ron Wilson, 2002-03; Ron Wilson, 2003-04 to date.

Coaching Record

		Regular Season				Playoffs		
Season	**Team**	**Games**	**W**	**L**	**T**	**Games**	**W**	**L**
1993-94	Anaheim (NHL)	84	33	46	5	....	....	....
1994-95	Anaheim (NHL)	48	16	27	5	....	....	....
1995-96	Anaheim (NHL)	82	35	39	8	....	....	....
1996-97	Anaheim (NHL)	82	36	33	13	11	4	7
1997-98	Washington (NHL)	82	40	30	12	21	12	9
1998-99	Washington (NHL)	82	31	45	6	....	....	....
1999-2000	Washington (NHL)	82	44	26	12	5	1	4
2000-01	Washington (NHL)	82	41	31	10	6	2	4
2001-02	Washington (NHL)	82	36	35	11	....	....	....
2002-03	San Jose (NHL)	57	19	31	7	....	....	....
2003-04	San Jose (NHL)	82	43	27	12	17	10	7
	NHL Totals	**845**	**374**	**370**	**101**	**60**	**29**	**31**

Club Records

Team

(Figures in brackets for season records are games played; records for fewest points, wins, ties, losses, goals, goals against are for 70 or more games)

Most Points	104	2003-04 (82)
Most Wins	44	2001-02 (82)
Most Ties	18	1998-99 (82)
Most Losses	*71	1992-93 (84)
Most Goals	252	1993-94 (84), 1995-96 (82)
Most Goals Against	414	1992-93 (84)
Fewest Points	24	1992-93 (84)
Fewest Wins	11	1992-93 (84)
Fewest Ties	*2	1992-93 (84)
Fewest Losses	33	1998-99 (82)
Fewest Goals	196	1998-99 (82)
Fewest Goals Against	183	2003-04 (82)

Longest Winning Streak
Overall	7	Mar. 24-Apr. 5/94, Jan. 30-Feb. 28/02
Home	5	Jan. 21-Feb. 15/95, Oct. 11-Nov. 3/01
Away	6	Nov. 30-Dec. 19/01

Longest Undefeated Streak
Overall	10	Nov. 27-Dec. 19/01 (9 wins, 1 tie)
Home	7	Oct. 12-Nov. 22/00 (6 wins, 1 tie)
Away	10	Dec. 26/00-Feb. 16/01 (6 wins, 4 ties)

Longest Losing Streak
Overall	*17	Jan. 4-Feb. 12/93
Home	9	Nov. 19-Dec. 19/92
Away	19	Nov. 27/92-Feb. 12/93

Longest Winless Streak
Overall	20	Dec. 29/92-Feb. 12/93 (19 losses, 1 tie)
Home	9	Nov. 19-Dec. 19/92 (9 losses)
Away	19	Nov. 27/92-Feb. 12/93 (19 losses)

Most Shutouts, Season	9	2000-01 (82), 2001-02 (82)
Most PIM, Season	2,134	1992-93 (84)
Most Goals, Game	10	Jan. 13/96 (S.J. 10 at Pit. 8), Mar. 30/02 (CBJ 2 at S.J. 10)

Individual

Most Seasons	11	Mike Rathje
Most Games, Career	671	Mike Rathje
Most Goals, Career	206	Owen Nolan
Most Assists, Career	225	Owen Nolan
Most Points, Career	431	Owen Nolan (206G, 225A)
Most PIM, Career	1,001	Jeff Odgers
Most Shutouts, Career	26	Evgeni Nabokov

Longest Consecutive
Games Streak	228	Mike Ricci (Nov. 22/97-Oct. 20/00)
Most Goals, Season	44	Owen Nolan (1999-2000)
Most Assists, Season	52	Kelly Kisio (1992-93)
Most Points, Season	84	Owen Nolan (1999-2000; 44G, 40A)

Most PIM, Season	326	Link Gaetz (1991-92)
Most Points, Defenseman, Season	64	Sandis Ozolinsh (1993-94; 26G, 38A)
Most Points, Center, Season	78	Kelly Kisio (1992-93; 26G, 52A)
Most Points, Right Wing, Season	84	Owen Nolan (1999-2000; 44G, 40A)
Most Points, Left Wing, Season	66	Johan Garpenlov (1992-93; 22G, 44A)
Most Points, Rookie, Season	59	Pat Falloon (1991-92; 25G, 34A)
Most Shutouts, Season	9	Evgeni Nabokov (2003-04)
Most Goals, Game	4	Owen Nolan (Dec. 19/95)
Most Assists, Game	4	Seven times
Most Points, Game	6	Owen Nolan (Oct. 4/99; 3G, 3A)

* NHL Record.

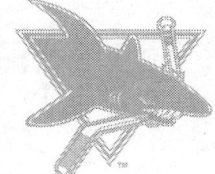

Captains' History

Doug Wilson, 1991-92, 1992-93; Bob Errey, 1993-94; Bob Errey and Jeff Odgers, 1994-95; Jeff Odgers, 1995-96; Todd Gill, 1996-97, 1997-98; Owen Nolan, 1998-99 to 2002-03; Mike Ricci, Vincent Damphousse, Alyn McCauley, Patrick Marleau, 2003-04.

All-time Record vs. Other Clubs

Regular Season

			At Home								On Road								Total				
	GP	W	L	T	OL	GF	GA	PTS	GP	W	L	T	OL	GF	GA	PTS	GP	W	L	T	OL	GF	GA	PTS
Anaheim	30	14	13	2	1	84	80	31	30	17	10	2	1	99	78	37	60	31	23	4	2	183	158	68
Atlanta	4	3	0	1	0	16	7	7	4	2	0	1	1	11	7	6	8	5	0	2	1	27	14	13
Boston	11	4	5	2	0	38	10	10	10	0	7	3	0	26	39	3	21	4	12	5	0	56	77	13
Buffalo	10	5	1	4	0	36	33	14	11	0	11	0	0	27	52	0	21	5	12	4	0	63	85	14
Calgary	34	13	17	4	0	100	102	30	32	10	17	4	1	87	116	25	66	23	34	8	1	187	218	55
Carolina	11	7	4	0	0	50	31	14	11	5	5	0	0	23	34	10	22	12	10	0	0	73	65	24
Chicago	26	13	9	3	1	72	70	30	25	10	11	2	2	77	76	24	51	23	20	5	3	149	146	54
Colorado	24	7	16	1	0	65	89	15	23	5	14	4	0	42	82	14	47	12	30	5	0	107	171	29
Columbus	8	7	0	0	1	32	12	15	8	5	3	0	0	20	21	10	16	12	3	0	1	52	33	25
Dallas	30	11	16	1	2	68	85	25	29	10	15	4	0	64	81	24	59	21	31	5	2	132	166	49
Detroit	26	9	13	4	0	83	100	22	25	2	21	1	1	45	104	6	51	11	34	5	1	128	204	28
Edmonton	32	16	11	5	0	112	100	37	33	7	19	7	0	71	112	21	65	23	30	12	0	183	212	58
Florida	9	5	2	2	0	26	17	12	9	2	2	5	0	27	25	9	18	7	4	7	0	53	42	21
Los Angeles	37	22	12	3	0	128	102	47	37	10	21	4	2	88	116	26	74	32	33	7	2	216	218	73
Minnesota	8	4	3	1	0	21	14	9	8	3	3	1	1	17	19	8	16	7	6	2	1	38	33	17
Montreal	11	5	3	2	1	33	28	13	11	2	7	2	0	20	36	6	22	7	10	4	1	53*	64	19
Nashville	12	6	5	1	0	30	31	13	12	6	4	1	1	34	29	14	24	12	9	2	1	64	60	27
New Jersey	10	3	5	1	1	24	32	8	12	4	6	1	1	24	44	10	22	7	11	2	2	48	76	18
NY Islanders	12	5	5	1	1	30	40	12	11	4	5	2	0	35	40	10	23	9	10	3	1	65	80	22
NY Rangers	13	5	2	4	2	31	49	6	10	2	6	1	1	29	40	6	23	4	15	3	1	60	89	12
Ottawa	9	5	4	0	0	18	16	10	9	1	4	4	0	26	36	6	18	6	8	4	0	44	52	16
Philadelphia	12	3	7	2	0	22	31	8	11	3	6	2	0	27	36	8	23	6	13	4	0	49	67	16
Phoenix	32	15	12	4	1	110	99	35	35	14	17	3	1	99	108	32	67	29	29	7	2	209	207	67
Pittsburgh	13	5	6	2	0	34	54	12	9	4	4	1	0	32	41	9	22	9	10	3	0	66	95	21
St. Louis	24	4	18	1	1	51	85	10	28	9	17	1	1	65	93	20	52	13	35	2	2	116	178	30
Tampa Bay	10	3	6	1	0	32	36	7	12	4	6	1	1	31	32	10	22	7	12	2	1	63	68	17
Toronto	15	5	7	3	0	32	40	13	18	4	12	2	0	47	69	10	33	9	19	5	0	79	109	23
Vancouver	34	13	16	5	0	98	106	31	32	10	17	4	1	84	115	25	66	23	33	9	1	182	221	56
Washington	10	6	3	1	0	29	26	13	12	7	5	0	0	36	34	14	22	13	8	1	0	65	60	27
Totals	**517**	**220**	**228**	**58**	**11**	**1497**	**1553**	**509**	**517**	**162**	**276**	**63**	**16**	**1313**	**1715**	**403**	**1034**	**382**	**504**	**121**	**27**	**2810**	**3268**	**912**

Playoffs

	Series	W	L	GP	W	L	T	GF	GA	Last Mtg.	Rnd.	Result
Calgary	2	1	1	13	6	7	0	38	51	2004	CF	L 2-4
Colorado	3	1	2	19	9	10	0	52	51	2004	CSF	W 4-2
Dallas	2	0	2	11	3	8	0	19	31	2000	CSF	L 1-4
Detroit	2	1	1	11	4	7	0	27	51	1995	CSF	L 0-4
Phoenix	1	1	0	5	4	1	0	13	7	2002	CQF	W 4-1
St. Louis	3	2	1	18	10	8	0	43	47	2004	CQF	W 4-1
Toronto	1	0	1	7	3	4	0	21	26	1994	CSF	L 3-4
Totals	**14**	**6**	**8**	**84**	**39**	**45**	**0**	**213**	**264**			

Playoff Results 2004-2000

Year	Round	Opponent	Result	GF	GA
2004	CF	Calgary	L 2-4	12	16
	CSF	Colorado	W 4-2	14	7
	CQF	St. Louis	W 4-1	12	9
2002	CSF	Colorado	L 3-4	21	25
	CQF	Phoenix	W 4-1	13	7
2001	CQF	St. Louis	L 2-4	11	16
2000	CSF	Dallas	L 1-4	19	15
	CQF	St. Louis	W 4-3	20	22

Abbreviations: Round: CF – conference final; **CSF** – conference semi-final; **CQF** – conference quarter-final.

Carolina totals include Hartford, 1991-92 to 1996-97.
Dallas totals include Minnesota North Stars, 1991-92 to 1992-93.

Colorado totals include Quebec, 1991-92 to 1994-95.
Phoenix totals include Winnipeg, 1991-92 to 1995-96.

2003-04 Results

Oct.	9	at Edmonton	2-5		8	Columbus	2-3*
	11	at Calgary	2-3		10	Atlanta	5-2
	12	at Minnesota	3-2		13	Dallas	0-3
	16	Philadelphia	0-0		15	Vancouver	3-1
	18	Ottawa	1-4		17	at Colorado	2-1
	21	Anaheim	0-2		19	Detroit	2-1
	23	Chicago	3-3		21	at Phoenix	4-2
	25	Phoenix	4-4		22	Phoenix	1-2
	28	at Carolina	0-3		24	Minnesota	4-0
	30	at Tampa Bay	2-2		28	Calgary	4-1
Nov.	1	at Florida	6-2		30	at Dallas	1-3
	2	at Atlanta	2-2		31	at Nashville	2-3*
	5	at New Jersey	2-3*	Feb.	3	Florida	3-0
	6	at Boston	5-5		5	Phoenix	5-0
	8	at Washington	3-2		10	at Buffalo	1-2
	11	Colorado	3-4		11	at Detroit	2-4
	13	St. Louis	3-4*		14	at Columbus	2-1*
	15	Toronto	2-2		16	at Philadelphia	5-2
	18	NY Rangers	2-2		18	at Nashville	3-7
	21	at Phoenix	5-0		19	at Chicago	6-3
	22	Nashville	3-1		23	Columbus	4-2
	26	Chicago	3-2		26	at Vancouver	2-3*
	28	at Minnesota	2-1		27	Pittsburgh	4-2
	30	at Edmonton	2-1		29	St. Louis	1-0
Dec.	2	at Calgary	1-3	Mar.	3	Montreal	4-3
	4	Colorado	2-2		5	at Colorado	1-5
	6	Dallas	2-1		7	at Dallas	0-4
	10	at Anaheim	2-3		9	Minnesota	3-4
	11	Edmonton	2-2		11	NY Islanders	5-4
	13	Anaheim	2-0		13	Los Angeles	3-1
	17	at Detroit	2-3*		16	at Dallas	3-3
	18	at St. Louis	2-4		18	at Los Angeles	5-3
	21	at Anaheim	2-1		19	at Anaheim	4-2
	22	Anaheim	2-1		21	Edmonton	2-5
	26	Los Angeles	5-0		23	Detroit	5-2
	27	at Los Angeles	4-4		25	Calgary	3-2
	29	Nashville	3-1		26	at Phoenix	3-0
	31	at Columbus	1-0		28	Dallas	2-1*
Jan.	2	at Chicago	1-2		31	at Los Angeles	3-0
	3	at St. Louis	3-1	Apr.	2	Vancouver	1-4
	5	at Vancouver	2-1		4	Los Angeles	4-3*

* – Overtime

Entry Draft
Selections 2004-1991

2004
Pick
22	Lukas Kaspar
94	Thomas Greiss
126	Torrey Mitchell
129	Jason Churchill
153	Steven Zalewski
201	Michael Vernace
225	David MacDonald
234	Derek MacIntyre
288	Brian Mahoney-Wilson
289	Christian Jensen

2003
Pick
6	Milan Michalek
16	Steve Bernier
43	Joshua Hennessy
47	Matthew Carle
139	Patrick Ehelechner
201	Jonathan Tremblay
205	Joe Pavelski
216	Kai Hospelt
236	Alexander Hult
267	Brian O'Hanley
276	Carter Lee

2002
Pick
27	Mike Morris
52	Dan Spang
86	Jonas Fiedler
139	Kris Newbury
163	Tom Walsh
217	Tim Conboy
288	Michael Hutchins

2001
Pick
20	Marcel Goc
106	Christian Ehrhoff
107	Dimitri Patzold
140	Tomas Plihal
175	Ryan Clowe
182	Tom Cavanagh

2000
Pick
41	Tero Maatta
104	Jon Disalvatore
142	Michal Pinc
166	Nolan Schaefer
183	Michal Macho
246	Chad Wiseman
256	Pasi Saarinen

1999
Pick
14	Jeff Jillson
82	Mark Concannon
111	Willie Levesque
155	Niko Dimitrakos
229	Eric Betournay
241	Doug Murray
257	Hannes Hyvonen

1998
Pick
3	Brad Stuart
29	Jonathan Cheechoo
65	Eric Laplante
98	Rob Davison
104	Miroslav Zalesak
127	Brandon Coalter
145	Mikael Samuelsson
185	Robert Mulick
212	Jim Fahey

1997
Pick
2	Patrick Marleau
23	Scott Hannan
82	Adam Colagiacomo
107	Adam Nittel
163	Joe Dusbabek
192	Cam Severson
219	Mark Smith

1996
Pick
2	Andrei Zyuzin
21	Marco Sturm
55	Terry Friesen
102	Matt Bradley
137	Michel Larocque
164	Jake Deadmarsh
191	Cory Cyrenne
217	David Thibeault

1995
Pick
12	Teemu Riihijarvi
38	Peter Roed
64	Marko Makinen
90	Vesa Toskala
116	Miikka Kiprusoff
130	Michal Bros
140	Timo Hakanen
142	Jaroslav Kudrna
167	Brad Mehalko
168	Robert Jindrich
194	Ryan Kraft
220	Mikko Markkanen

1994
Pick
11	Jeff Friesen
37	Angel Nikolov
66	Alexei Yegorov
89	Vaclav Varada
115	Brian Swanson
141	Alexander Korolyuk
167	Sergei Gorbachev
193	Eric Landry
219	Evgeni Nabokov
240	Tomas Pisa
245	Aniket Dhadphale
271	David Beauregard

1993
Pick
6	Viktor Kozlov
28	Shean Donovan
45	Vlastimil Kroupa
58	Ville Peltonen
80	Alexander Osadchy
106	Andrei Buschan
132	Petri Varis
154	Fredrik Oduya
158	Anatoli Filatov
184	Todd Holt
210	Jonas Forsberg
236	Jeff Salajko
262	Jamie Matthews

1992
Pick
3	Mike Rathje
10	Andrei Nazarov
51	Alexander Cherbayev
75	Jan Caloun
99	Marcus Ragnarsson
123	Michal Sykora
147	Eric Bellerose
171	Ryan Smith
195	Chris Burns
219	Alexander Kholomeyev
243	Victor Ignatjev

1991
Pick
2	Pat Falloon
23	Ray Whitney
30	Sandis Ozolinsh
45	Dody Wood
67	Kerry Toporowski
89	Dan Ryder
111	Frank Nilsson
133	Jaroslav Otevrel
155	Dean Grillo
177	Corwin Saurdiff
199	Dale Craigwell
221	Aaron Kriss
243	Mikhail Kravets

General Managers' History

Jack Ferreira, 1991-92; Chuck Grillo (V.P. Director of Player Personnel), 1992-93 to 1995-96; Dean Lombardi, 1996-97 to 2002-03; Doug Wilson, 2003-04 to date.

Vice President and General Manager

WILSON, DOUG
Executive Vice President/General Manager, San Jose Sharks.
Born in Ottawa, Ont., July 5, 1957.

Doug Wilson is the architect of the current San Jose Sharks team that soared to unprecedented heights in 2003-04. After missing the playoffs in 2002-03, the Sharks rebounded to capture the Pacific Division title, setting a franchise record with 104 points, earning the second seed in the Western Conference playoffs and reaching the Western Conference Finals for the first time. The Sharks' record of 43-21-12-8 in 2003-04 was the third-best mark in the NHL and the team's 31-point improvement over the previous season was the largest turnaround in the NHL. The team also finished tied for fourth in the NHL with a franchise-best 183 goals against and was tied for sixth with a 85.3 percent penalty kill.

Doug Wilson officially took over as the Sharks' executive vice president and general manager on May 13, 2003. In his current role, he has overall authority regarding all hockey-related operations. He oversees all player personnel decisions, negotiates player contracts, coordinates the efforts of the team's scouting department, leads the team in its draft-day preparations and administers the club's player evaluation process at all professional, minor and junior levels.

In his previous role as the team's director of pro development (1997 to 2003), the 16-year NHL veteran's primary responsibilities included evaluating talent at all professional and minor league levels and continuous assessment of the Sharks roster and reserve list. In addition, he provided valuable input assisting the club's player development programs and consulting with the hockey department on all major personnel issues, special assignments and contract negotiations.

A first-round choice (sixth overall) of the Blackhawks in 1977 after a stellar junior career with the Ottawa 67s, Wilson played 14 seasons in Chicago and still ranks as the club's highest scoring defenseman in goals (225), assists (554) and points (779). In addition, he led all Blackhawks defensemen in scoring from 10 consecutive seasons (1980-81 through 1990-91) and captured the 1982 Norris Trophy, symbolic of the NHL's top defenseman, when he tallied 39 goals and 85 points – still Blackhawks single-season records for goals and points by a defenseman.

Club Directory

HP Pavilion at San Jose

San Jose Sharks
HP Pavilion at San Jose
525 West Santa Clara Street
San Jose, CA 95113
Phone **408/287-7070**
FAX 408/999-5797
www.sjsharks.com
Capacity: 17,496

San Jose Sports & Entertainment Enterprises Board Members
Kevin Compton, Greg Reyes, Greg Jamison, Tom McEnery, Brent Jones

Investors in SJSEE include
Blue Line Associates (Kevin Compton, Greg Reyes, Hasso Plattner, Stratton Sclavos, Gary Valenzuela, Harvey Armstrong), William DelBiaggio, George Gund III, Greg Jamison, Floyd Kvamme, Tom McEnery, Gordon Russell, Rudy Staedler

Executive Staff
President & Chief Executive Officer	Greg Jamison
Executive V.P. of Business Operations	Malcolm Bordelon
Executive V.P. & G.M. (HP Pavilion at San Jose)	Jim Goddard
Executive V.P. & General Counsel	Don Gralnek
Executive V.P. & G.M. (Sharks)	Doug Wilson
Executive V.P. & Chief Financial Officer	Charlie Faas
Vice President of Finance	Ken Caveney
Vice President of Sales & Marketing	Kent Russell
Vice President of Building Operations	Rich Sotelo
Vice President and Assistant G.M. (Sharks)	Wayne Thomas
Executive Assistants	Tricia Sullivan, Michelle Simmons, Janelle Garcia

Hockey Operations
Head Coach	Ron Wilson
Assistant Coach	Tim Hunter
Assistant Coach	Rob Zettler
Goaltender Coach	Warren Strelow
Special Consultant to the General Manager	John Ferguson
Professional Scouts	Barry Long, Cap Raeder
Director of Amateur Scouting	Tim Burke
Chief Scout	Ray Payne
Assistant to the General Manager	Joe Will
Scouts	Gilles Cote, Pat Funk, Rob Grillo, Brian Gross, Karel Masopust
Director of Hockey Administration	Rosemary Maher
Video Scouting Coordinator	Bob Friedlander
Team Services Coordinator	Marshall Dickerson
Head Athletic Trainer	Ray Tufts, A.T.,C
Athletic Trainer	Tom Woodcock, A.T.,C,L
Strength & Conditioning Coordinator	Mac Read
Massage Therapist	Wes Howard
Equipment Manager	Mike Aldrich
Assistant Equipment Manager	Kurt Harvey
Equipment Assistant & Equipment Transportation	Roy Sneesby
Head Coach, Cleveland Barons (AHL)	Roy Sommer
Assistant Coach, Cleveland Barons (AHL)	David Cunniff
Head Trainer, Cleveland Barons (AHL)	Dave Zenobi
Equipment Manager, Cleveland Barons (AHL)	Rob Kennedy
Assistant Equipment Mngr., Cleveland Barons (AHL)	Phil Simon
Team Physician	Arthur J. Ting, M.D.
Team Dentist	Robert Bonahoom, D.D.S.
Team Internist	John Chiu, M.D.
Team Vision Specialist	Vincent S. Zuccaro, O.D., F.A.A.O.
Medical Staff	Warren King, M.D., Mark Sontag, M.D.

SVS&E/Business Operations
Senior Director of Communications	Ken Arnold
Senior Sponsorship Sales Manager	Bryan Deierling
Senior Ticket Operations Manager	Scott Fitzsimmons
Director of Broadcasting	Frank Albin
Director of Ticket Sales	John Castro
Director of Media Relations	Scott Emmert
Director of Fan Development/The Sharks Foundation	Rob Jaynes
Director of Event Presentation	Steve Maroni
Director of Suite Hospitality	Jay O'Sullivan
Director of Sponsorship Sales	Chris Parker
Director of Internet Services	Roger Ross
Sponsorship Sales Managers	Jennifer Birmingham, Jonathan Chin, Eric Kwait, Bob Rowatt
Public Relations Manager	Jim Sparaco

Finance
Director of Information Technology	James Struckle
Human Resources Manager	Cathy Chandler
Payroll Administrator	Sue Feachen
Controller	Stephanie Reitz

Building Operations
Director of Ticket Operations	Daniel DeBoer
Director of Booking & Events	Steve Kirsner
Director of Guest Services	Ken Sweezey
Facilities Technical Director	Greg Carrolan
Director of Building Services	Monte Chavez
Chief Engineer	Mark Mullins

Miscellaneous
Television Station	FOX Sports Net
Radio Network Flagship	98.5 K-FOX (KUFX FM)
Television Play-By-Play Broadcaster	Randy Hahn
Television Color Analyst	Drew Remenda
Radio Play-By-Play Broadcaster	Dan Rusanowsky
In Game TV Host	Glen Kuiper
Team Photographers	Don Smith, Rocky Widner
P.A. Announcer	Joe Ike
In Game Host	Danny Miller
Mascot	S.J. Sharkie

Tampa Bay Lightning

2003-04 Results: 46w-22L-8T-6OTL 106PTS.
First, Southeast Division

EASTERN
NHL
CONFERENCE

SOUTHEAST
DIVISION

13th
NHL
Season

Franchise date: December 16, 1991

2004-05 Schedule

Oct.	Wed.	13	Philadelphia		Sat.	15	at Florida
	Sat.	16	Florida		Mon.	17	Buffalo
	Mon.	18	at Buffalo		Wed.	19	Boston
	Thu.	21	at Phoenix		Fri.	21	at Carolina
	Sat.	23	at Colorado		Sat.	22	at Pittsburgh
	Wed.	27	Nashville		Tue.	25	at Philadelphia
	Fri.	29	Washington		Thu.	27	Toronto
Nov.	Mon.	1	at NY Islanders		Sat.	29	at Boston*
	Tue.	2	at Toronto		Sun.	30	Pittsburgh*
	Thu.	4	Carolina	Feb.	Tue.	1	Chicago
	Sat.	6	at New Jersey*		Sat.	5	Atlanta
	Wed.	10	at Atlanta		Tue.	8	at Washington
	Thu.	11	Calgary		Thu.	10	NY Islanders
	Sat.	13	Atlanta		Tue.	15	Ottawa
	Thu.	18	at Boston		Thu.	17	NY Islanders
	Sat.	20	at Ottawa		Sat.	19	Detroit*
	Wed.	24	Vancouver		Mon.	21	at Carolina
	Fri.	26	New Jersey		Wed.	23	at NY Rangers
	Sat.	27	at Carolina		Fri.	25	at Buffalo
	Tue.	30	at Philadelphia		Sat.	26	at Ottawa
Dec.	Thu.	2	St. Louis	Mar.	Tue.	1	Toronto
	Sat.	4	Florida		Fri.	4	Carolina
	Tue.	7	at Atlanta		Sat.	5	at Florida
	Thu.	9	Montreal		Tue.	8	at Pittsburgh
	Sat.	11	Ottawa		Fri.	11	Edmonton
	Tue.	14	at Montreal		Sat.	12	Washington
	Wed.	15	at New Jersey		Mon.	14	at Dallas
	Fri.	17	Buffalo		Wed.	16	Philadelphia
	Sun.	19	at Columbus*		Fri.	18	Pittsburgh
	Wed.	22	at Chicago		Sat.	19	at Florida
	Thu.	23	at Minnesota		Tue.	22	at NY Islanders
	Sun.	26	at Washington*		Thu.	24	Montreal
	Mon.	27	Boston		Sat.	26	Florida
	Wed.	29	New Jersey		Mon.	28	at Toronto
Jan.	Sat.	1	NY Rangers*		Tue.	29	at Montreal
	Sun.	2	Dallas		Thu.	31	NY Rangers
	Wed.	5	at Anaheim	Apr.	Sat.	2	at Washington
	Thu.	6	at Los Angeles		Mon.	4	at NY Rangers
	Sat.	8	at San Jose		Wed.	6	Carolina
	Wed.	12	Minnesota		Fri.	8	Atlanta
	Fri.	14	Washington		Sun.	10	at Atlanta*

* Denotes afternoon game.

Year-by-Year Record

Season	GP	Home				Road				Overall				GF	GA	Pts.	Finished	Playoff Result
		W	L	T	OL	W	L	T	OL	W	L	T	OL					
2003-04	**82**	**24**	**10**	**4**	**3**	**22**	**12**	**4**	**3**	**46**	**22**	**8**	**6**	**245**	**192**	**106**	**1st, Southeast Div.**	**Won Stanley Cup**
2002-03	82	22	9	7	3	14	16	9	2	36	25	16	5	219	210	93	1st, Southeast Div.	Lost Conf. Semi-Final
2001-02	82	16	17	5	3	11	23	6	1	27	40	11	4	178	219	69	3rd, Southeast Div.	Out of Playoffs
2000-01	82	17	19	3	2	7	28	3	3	24	47	6	5	201	280	59	5th, Southeast Div.	Out of Playoffs
1999-2000	82	13	20	4	4	6	27	5	3	19	47	9	7	204	310	54	4th, Southeast Div.	Out of Playoffs
1998-99	82	12	25	4	...	7	29	5	...	19	54	9	...	179	292	47	4th, Southeast Div.	Out of Playoffs
1997-98	82	11	23	7	...	6	32	3	...	17	55	10	...	151	269	44	7th, Atlantic Div.	Out of Playoffs
1996-97	82	15	18	8	...	17	22	2	...	32	40	10	...	217	247	74	6th, Atlantic Div.	Out of Playoffs
1995-96	82	22	14	5	...	16	18	7	...	38	32	12	...	238	248	88	5th, Atlantic Div.	Lost Conf. Quarter-Final
1994-95	48	10	14	0	...	7	14	3	...	17	28	3	...	120	144	37	6th, Atlantic Div.	Out of Playoffs
1993-94	84	14	22	6	...	16	21	5	...	30	43	11	...	224	251	71	7th, Atlantic Div.	Out of Playoffs
1992-93	84	12	27	3	...	11	27	4	...	23	54	7	...	245	332	53	6th, Norris Div.	Out of Playoffs

Vincent Lecavalier's 32 goals last season were second on the team behind Martin St. Louis. His plus/minus rating of +23 ranked among the league leaders and marked the first in his career that he had a positive rating.

2004-05 Player Personnel

FORWARDS

	HT	WT	S	Place of Birth	Date	2003-04 Club
AFANASENKOV, Dmitry	6-2	200	R	Arkhangelsk, USSR	5/12/80	Tampa Bay
ALEXEEV, Nikita	6-5	225	L	Murmansk, USSR	12/27/81	Hershey
ANDREYCHUK, Dave	6-4	220	R	Hamilton, Ont.	9/29/63	Tampa Bay
ARTUKHIN, Evgeni	6-4	215	L	Moscow, USSR	4/4/83	Hershey-Pensacola
CIBAK, Martin	6-1	195	L	Liptovsky Mikulas, Czech.	5/17/80	Tampa Bay-Hershey
DARBY, Craig	6-4	205	R	Oneida, NY	9/26/72	New Jersey-Albany
DINGMAN, Chris	6-4	235	L	Edmonton, Alta.	7/6/76	Tampa Bay
FEDOTENKO, Ruslan	6-2	195	L	Kiev, Ukraine	1/18/79	Tampa Bay
LECAVALIER, Vincent	6-4	205	L	Ile Bizard, Que.	4/21/80	Tampa Bay
MODIN, Fredrik	6-4	225	L	Sundsvall, Sweden	10/8/74	Tampa Bay
PERRIN, Eric	5-9	176	L	Laval, Que.	11/1/75	Tampa Bay-Hershey
RICHARDS, Brad	6-1	198	L	Murray Harbour, P.E.I.	5/2/80	Tampa Bay
ROY, Andre	6-4	221	L	Port Chester, NY	2/8/75	Tampa Bay
ST. LOUIS, Martin	5-9	185	L	Laval, Que.	6/18/75	Tampa Bay
SKALDE, Jarrod	6-0	185	L	Niagara Falls, Ont.	2/26/71	Utah
SOMERVUORI, Eero	5-10	185	R	Jarvenpaa, Finland	2/7/79	Hamilton
STILLMAN, Cory	6-0	194	L	Peterborough, Ont.	12/20/73	Tampa Bay
TAYLOR, Tim	6-1	189	L	Stratford, Ont.	2/6/69	Tampa Bay
WILLIS, Shane	6-1	190	R	Edmonton, Alta.	6/13/77	Tampa Bay-Hershey

DEFENSEMEN

	HT	WT	S	Place of Birth	Date	2003-04 Club
BOYLE, Dan	5-11	190	R	Ottawa, Ont.	7/12/76	Tampa Bay
DICAIRE, Gerard	6-2	190	L	Faro, Yukon	9/14/82	Utah
KUBINA, Pavel	6-4	230	R	Celadna, Czech.	4/15/77	Tampa Bay
LUKOWICH, Brad	6-1	200	L	Cranbrook, B.C.	8/12/76	Tampa Bay
McLAREN, Steve	6-0	210	L	Owen Sound, Ont.	2/3/75	St. Louis-Worcester
PRATT, Nolan	6-3	200	L	Fort McMurray, Alta.	8/14/75	Tampa Bay
SARICH, Cory	6-5	204	R	Saskatoon, Sask.	8/16/78	Tampa Bay
SYDOR, Darryl	6-1	205	L	Edmonton, Alta.	5/13/72	Columbus-Tampa Bay

GOALTENDERS

	HT	WT	C	Place of Birth	Date	2003-04 Club
EKLUND, Brian	6-5	205	L	Braintree, MA	5/24/80	Pensacola
GRAHAME, John	6-2	220	L	Denver, CO	8/31/75	Tampa Bay
KHABIBULIN, Nikolai	6-1	203	L	Sverdlovsk, USSR	1/13/73	Tampa Bay

General Managers' History

Phil Esposito, 1992-93 to 1997-98; Jacques Demers, 1998-99; Rick Dudley, 1999-2000, 2000-01; Rick Dudley and Jay Feaster, 2001-02; Jay Feaster, 2002-03 to date.

Coaching History

Terry Crisp, 1992-93 to 1996-97; Terry Crisp, Rick Paterson and Jacques Demers, 1997-98; Jacques Demers, 1998-99; Steve Ludzik, 1999-2000; Steve Ludzik and John Tortorella, 2000-01; John Tortorella, 2001-02 to date.

Coach

TORTORELLA, JOHN
Coach, Tampa Bay Lightning. Born in Boston, MA, June 24, 1958.

John Tortorella is entering his fourth full season as head coach of the Lightning after leading the team to its first Eastern Conference and Stanley Cup championships, as well as its second consecutive Southeast Division championship in 2003-04. He was the winner of the Jack Adams Award as the National Hockey League's top coach after leading the Lightning to franchise records with 46 wins and 106 points before embarking on the successful playoff campaign. His 2003-04 team tallied a franchise-record 245 goals and many of his Lightning players established personal bests in goals, assists and points. He now has 121 wins with the Lightning, ranking him second on the team's all-time wins list.

A 14-year NHL coaching veteran, Tortorella became the fourth head coach in team history when he was named to that position on January 6, 2001. Recognized as one of the top teaching coaches in the game, the Boston native joined the Lightning organization when he was hired on as an associate coach prior to the 2000-01 season.

Tortorella began his playing career at Salem State College before transferring to the University of Maine. He spent three seasons with the Black Bears and was twice named an ECAC All-Star. After playing in Sweden, Tortorella played in the Atlantic Coast Hockey League with Virginia, Hampton Roads, and Erie. He spent two seasons as general manager and head coach of the Virginia Lancers (ACHL) from 1986 to 1988, where he garnered coach of the year honors both years while leading his 1986-87 team to the league championship. He was hired as an assistant coach with the New Haven Nighthawks of the American Hockey League in 1988-89 and became an assistant coach with the Buffalo Sabres the following season. Tortorella remained with the Sabres organization through the 1996-97 season, including two years as coach of their AHL affiliate in Rochester.

Tortorella returned to the NHL in 1997 as an assistant with the Phoenix Coyotes, where he spent two seasons before joining the Rangers for 1999-2000. He served as the Rangers' interim head coach for the final four games of the '99-00 season before joining the Lightning staff.

2003-04 Scoring

- rookie

Regular Season

Pos	#	Player	Team	GP	G	A	Pts	+/-	PIM	PP	SH	GW	GT	S	%
R	26	Martin St. Louis	T.B.	82	38	56	94	35	24	8	8	7	0	212	17.9
L	61	Cory Stillman	T.B.	81	25	55	80	18	36	11	1	6	0	178	14.0
C	19	Brad Richards	T.B.	82	26	53	79	14	12	5	1	6	0	244	10.7
C	4	Vincent Lecavalier	T.B.	81	32	34	66	23	52	5	2	6	0	242	13.2
L	33	Fredrik Modin	T.B.	82	29	28	57	31	32	5	1	2	1	206	14.1
L	25	Dave Andreychuk	T.B.	82	21	18	39	-9	42	10	0	5	1	165	12.7
R	17	Ruslan Fedotenko	T.B.	77	17	22	39	14	30	0	0	3	0	116	14.7
D	22	Dan Boyle	T.B.	78	9	30	39	23	60	3	0	2	0	137	6.6
D	13	Pavel Kubina	T.B.	81	17	18	35	9	85	8	1	4	0	153	11.1
C	27	Tim Taylor	T.B.	82	7	15	22	-5	25	0	0	1	0	95	7.4
D	55	Darryl Sydor	CBJ	49	2	13	15	-19	26	1	0	0	0	80	2.5
			T.B.	31	1	6	7	3	6	0	0	0	0	42	2.4
			TOTAL	80	3	19	22	-16	32	1	0	0	0	122	2.5
D	37	Brad Lukowich	T.B.	79	5	14	19	29	24	0	0	1	0	86	5.8
D	21	Cory Sarich	T.B.	82	3	16	19	5	89	0	1	1	0	93	3.2
C	29	* Dimitry Afanasenkov	T.B.	71	6	10	16	-4	12	0	0	1	0	98	6.1
R	7	Ben Clymer	T.B.	66	2	8	10	5	50	0	0	0	0	96	2.1
C	8	Martin Cibak	T.B.	63	2	7	9	-1	30	0	0	0	0	44	4.5
D	5	Jassen Cullimore	T.B.	79	2	5	7	8	58	0	0	1	0	78	2.6
L	11	Chris Dingman	T.B.	74	1	5	6	-9	140	0	0	0	0	65	1.5
R	24	Shane Willis	T.B.	12	0	6	6	1	2	0	0	0	0	27	0.0
D	44	Nolan Pratt	T.B.	58	1	3	4	11	42	0	0	0	0	35	2.9
L	36	Andre Roy	T.B.	33	1	1	2	-5	78	0	0	0	0	24	4.2
C	9	Eric Perrin	T.B.	4	0	0	0	-1	0	0	0	0	0	3	0.0
D	38	Darren Rumble	T.B.	5	0	0	0	-2	2	0	0	0	0	5	0.0

Goaltending

No.	Goaltender	GPI	Mins	Avg	W	L	T	EN	SO	GA	SA	S%	G	A	PIM
47	John Grahame	29	1688	2.06	18	9	1	2	1	58	664	.913	0	0	4
35	Nikolai Khabibulin	55	3274	2.33	28	19	7	5	3	127	1414	.910	0	2	12
	Totals	**82**	**4988**	**2.31**	**46**	**28**	**8**	**7**	**4**	**192**	**2085**	**.908**			

Playoffs

Pos	#	Player	Team	GP	G	A	Pts	+/-	PIM	PP	SH	GW	GT	S	%
C	19	Brad Richards	T.B.	23	12	14	26	5	4	7	0	7	1	88	13.6
R	26	Martin St. Louis	T.B.	23	9	15	24	6	14	3	1	3	2	58	15.5
L	33	Fredrik Modin	T.B.	23	8	11	19	7	10	3	0	2	0	50	16.0
C	4	Vincent Lecavalier	T.B.	23	9	7	16	-2	25	2	0	0	0	76	11.8
R	17	Ruslan Fedotenko	T.B.	22	12	2	14	0	14	5	0	3	0	43	27.9
L	25	Dave Andreychuk	T.B.	23	1	13	14	-2	14	0	0	0	0	30	3.3
D	22	Dan Boyle	T.B.	23	2	8	10	7	16	1	0	0	0	25	8.0
L	61	Cory Stillman	T.B.	21	2	5	7	2	15	0	1	0	0	35	5.7
D	55	Darryl Sydor	T.B.	23	0	6	6	4	9	0	0	0	0	25	0.0
C	27	Tim Taylor	T.B.	22	2	3	5	-2	31	0	0	0	0	21	9.5
D	13	Pavel Kubina	T.B.	22	0	4	4	0	50	0	0	0	0	29	0.0
L	36	Andre Roy	T.B.	21	1	2	3	3	61	0	0	1	0	11	9.1
L	29	* Dimitry Afanasenkov	T.B.	23	1	2	3	-3	6	0	0	0	0	27	3.7
L	11	Chris Dingman	T.B.	23	1	1	2	1	63	0	0	0	0	13	7.7
D	5	Jassen Cullimore	T.B.	11	0	2	2	7	6	0	0	0	0	7	0.0
D	37	Brad Lukowich	T.B.	18	0	2	2	4	6	0	0	0	0	10	0.0
D	21	Cory Sarich	T.B.	23	0	2	2	1	25	0	0	0	0	32	0.0
C	8	Martin Cibak	T.B.	6	0	1	1	1	6	0	0	0	0	5	0.0
C	9	Eric Perrin	T.B.	12	0	1	1	0	6	0	0	0	0	9	0.0
D	2	Stan Neckar	T.B.	2	0	0	0	1	0	0	0	0	0	1	0.0
R	7	Ben Clymer	T.B.	5	0	0	0	0	0	0	0	0	0	2	0.0
D	44	Nolan Pratt	T.B.	20	0	0	0	0	8	0	0	0	0	10	0.0

Goaltending

No.	Goaltender	GPI	Mins	Avg	W	L	EN	SO	GA	SA	S%	G	A	PIM
35	Nikolai Khabibulin	23	1401	1.71	16	7	1	5	40	598	.933	0	0	0
47	John Grahame	1	34	3.53	0	0	0	0	2	17	.882	0	0	0
	Totals	**23**	**1439**	**1.79**	**16**	**7**	**1**	**5**	**43**	**616**	**.930**			

Coaching Record

			Regular Season				Playoffs		
Season	Team	Games	W	L	T		Games	W	L
1995-96	Rochester (AHL)	80	37	38	5		19	15	4
1996-97	Rochester (AHL)	80	40	30	9		10	6	4
1999-2000	NY Rangers (NHL)	4	0	3	1		....	....	....
2000-01	Tampa Bay (NHL)	43	12	30	1		....	....	....
2001-02	Tampa Bay (NHL)	82	27	44	11		....	....	....
2002-03	Tampa Bay (NHL)	82	36	30	16		11	5	6
2003-04	Tampa Bay (NHL)	82	46	28	8		23	16	7
	NHL Totals	**293**	**121**	**135**	**37**		**34**	**21**	**13**

Club Records

Team

(Figures in brackets for season records are games played; records for fewest points, wins, ties, losses, goals, goals against are for 70 or more games)

Most Points	106	2003-04 (82)
Most Wins	46	2003-04 (82)
Most Ties	16	2002-03 (82)
Most Losses	55	1997-98 (82)
Most Goals	245	1992-93 (84), 2003-04 (82)
Most Goals Against	332	1992-93 (84)
Fewest Points	44	1997-98 (82)
Fewest Wins	17	1997-98 (82)
Fewest Ties	6	2000-01 (82)
Fewest Losses	22	2003-04 (82)
Fewest Goals	151	1997-98 (82)
Fewest Goals Against	192	2003-04 (82)

Longest Winning Streak
Overall..................5 Twice
Home...................6 Feb. 15-Mar. 10/96, Nov. 17-Dec. 21/01
Away...................4 Jan. 6-13/97

Longest Undefeated Streak
Overall..................13 Mar. 7-Apr. 2/03 (7 wins, 6 ties)
Home...................9 Feb. 25-Apr. 2/03 (5 wins, 4 ties)
Away...................6 Twice

Longest Losing Streak
Overall..................13 Jan. 3-Feb. 2/98
Home...................10 Jan. 3-Feb. 26/98
Away...................11 Oct. 24-Dec. 10/97

Longest Winless Streak
Overall..................16 Twice
Home...................11 Jan. 2-Feb. 26/98 (10 losses, 1 tie)
Away...................17 Dec. 2/99-Feb. 19/00 (14 losses, 3 ties)

Most Shutouts, Season........9 2001-02 (82)
Most PIM, Season..........1,823 1997-98 (82)
Most Goals, Game............9 Nov. 8/03 (Pit. 0 at T.B. 9)

Individual

Most Seasons...............7 Five players
Most Games, Career........475 Rob Zamuner
Most Goals, Career........146 Vincent Lecavalier
Most Assists, Career........193 Brad Richards
Most Points, Career........327 Vincent Lecavalier (146G, 171A)
Most PIM, Career...........782 Chris Gratton
Most Shutouts, Career........14 Nikolai Khabibulin

Longest Consecutive
Games Streak............226 Rob Zamuner (Nov. 1/95-Mar. 30/98)
Most Goals, Season.........42 Brian Bradley (1992-93)
Most Assists, Season.........57 Vaclav Prospal, Brad Richards (2002-03)

Most Points, Season.........94 Martin St. Louis (2003-04; 38G, 56A)
Most PIM, Season..........258 Enrico Ciccone (1995-96)
Most Points, Defenseman, Season...................65 Roman Hamrlik (1995-96; 16G, 49A)
Most Points, Center, Season...................86 Brian Bradley (1992-93; 42G, 44A)
Most Points, Right Wing, Season...................94 Martin St. Louis (2003-04; 38G, 56A)
Most Points, Left Wing, Season...................80 Cory Stillman (2003-04; 25G, 55A)
Most Points, Rookie, Season...................62 Brad Richards (2000-01; 21G, 41A)
Most Shutouts, Season........7 Nikolai Khabibulin (2001-02)
Most Goals, Game............4 Chris Kontos (Oct. 7/92)
Most Assists, Game...........4 Four times
Most Points, Game............6 Doug Crossman (Nov. 7/92; 3G, 3A)

Captains' History

No captain, 1992-93 to 1994-95; Paul Ysebaert, 1995-96, 1996-97; Paul Ysebaert and Mikael Renberg, 1997-98; Rob Zamuner, 1998-99; Bill Houlder, Chris Gratton and Vincent Lecavalier, 1999-2000; Vincent Lecavalier, 2000-01; no captain, 2001-02; Dave Andreychuk, 2002-03 to date.

All-time Record vs. Other Clubs

Regular Season

	At Home								On Road								Total							
	GP	W	L	T	OL	GF	GA	PTS	GP	W	L	T	OL	GF	GA	PTS	GP	W	L	T	OL	GF	GA	PTS
Anaheim	9	4	5	0	0	17	23	8	8	3	4	1	0	20	24	7	17	7	9	1	0	37	47	15
Atlanta	13	9	2	1	1	49	29	20	13	2	8	3	0	34	48	7	26	11	10	4	1	83	77	27
Boston	23	10	8	3	2	70	66	25	23	1	15	6	1	49	84	9	46	11	23	9	3	119	150	34
Buffalo	23	6	13	3	1	49	70	16	23	8	12	2	1	63	63	19	46	14	25	5	2	112	133	35
Calgary	10	5	4	1	0	31	32	11	10	4	5	0	1	24	32	9	20	9	9	1	1	55	64	20
Carolina	26	14	9	3	0	73	67	31	27	5	14	7	1	65	81	18	53	19	23	10	1	138	148	49
Chicago	11	4	3	3	1	26	28	12	14	4	8	2	0	35	45	10	25	8	11	5	1	61	73	22
Colorado	12	8	2	1	1	39	32	18	13	3	8	2	0	28	50	8	25	11	10	3	1	67	82	26
Columbus	3	2	1	0	0	5	3	4	3	1	1	1	0	4	5	3	6	3	2	1	0	9	8	7
Dallas	13	1	10	2	0	20	37	4	11	3	7	1	0	27	39	7	24	4	17	3	0	47	76	11
Detroit	14	4	8	1	1	43	61	10	12	1	10	1	0	21	47	3	26	5	18	2	1	64	108	13
Edmonton	11	3	5	2	1	31	35	9	10	3	7	1	0	21	26	6	21	6	12	2	1	52	61	15
Florida	28	10	12	6	0	60	77	26	28	8	14	4	2	62	81	22	56	18	26	10	2	122	158	48
Los Angeles	10	5	4	0	1	23	22	11	11	8	1	2	0	36	24	18	21	13	5	2	1	59	46	29
Minnesota	3	1	1	1	0	8	9	3	3	0	3	0	0	8	13	0	6	1	4	1	0	16	22	3
Montreal	23	9	8	5	1	55	61	24	22	10	11	1	0	53	59	21	45	19	19	6	1	108	120	45
Nashville	4	1	1	2	0	11	10	4	4	4	2	0	0	16	12	8	8	5	3	2	0	27	22	12
New Jersey	25	8	12	5	0	59	75	21	26	6	18	2	0	44	93	14	51	14	30	7	0	103	168	35
NY Islanders	26	12	12	2	0	67	80	26	25	11	12	1	1	69	78	24	51	23	24	3	1	136	158	50
NY Rangers	25	11	10	3	1	86	83	26	27	12	12	2	1	50	87	27	52	23	22	5	2	171	170	53
Ottawa	23	8	12	2	1	70	80	19	23	8	15	0	0	50	88	16	46	16	27	2	1	120	168	35
Philadelphia	26	9	15	1	1	71	78	20	25	4	14	7	0	46	79	15	51	13	29	8	1	117	157	35
Phoenix	10	5	5	0	0	33	33	10	11	5	6	0	0	26	28	10	21	10	11	0	0	59	61	20
Pittsburgh	23	12	9	2	0	75	60	26	23	5	14	3	1	59	90	14	46	17	23	5	1	134	150	40
St. Louis	13	5	5	3	0	38	42	13	11	1	9	1	0	24	44	3	24	6	14	3	1	62	86	16
San Jose	12	7	4	1	0	32	31	15	10	6	3	1	0	36	32	13	22	13	7	2	0	68	63	28
Toronto	20	3	15	1	1	42	71	8	21	7	12	1	1	55	76	16	41	10	27	2	2	97	147	24
Vancouver	9	3	5	0	1	31	37	7	9	0	8	1	0	17	40	3	18	3	13	1	1	48	77	10
Washington	29	9	18	2	0	65	93	20	29	7	18	4	0	51	101	18	58	16	36	6	0	130	194	38
Totals	**477**	**188**	**218**	**56**	**15**	**1279**	**1425**	**447**	**477**	**140**	**269**	**56**	**12**	**1142**	**1569**	**348**	**954**	**328**	**487**	**112**	**27**	**2421**	**2994**	**795**

Playoffs

	Series	W	L	GP	W	L	T	GF	GA	Last Mtg.	Rnd.	Result
Calgary	1	1	0	7	4	3	0	13	14	2004	F	W 4-3
Montreal	1	1	0	4	4	0	0	14	5	2004	CSF	W 4-0
New Jersey	1	0	1	5	1	4	0	8	14	2003	CSF	L 1-4
NY Islanders	1	1	0	5	4	1	0	12	5	2004	CQF	W 4-1
Philadelphia	2	1	1	13	6	7	0	34	45	2004	CF	W 4-3
Washington	1	1	0	6	4	2	0	14	15	2003	CQF	W 4-2
Totals	**7**	**5**	**2**	**40**	**23**	**17**	**0**	**95**	**98**			

Playoff Results 2004-2000

Year	Round	Opponent	Result	GF	GA
2004	F	Calgary	W 4-3	13	14
	CF	Philadelphia	W 4-3	21	19
	CSF	Montreal	W 4-0	14	5
	CQF	NY Islanders	W 4-1	12	5
2003	CSF	New Jersey	L 1-4	8	14
	CQF	Washington	W 4-2	14	15

Abbreviations: Round: F – Final; **CF** – conference final; **CSF** – conference semi-final; **CQF** – conference quarter-final.

Carolina totals include Hartford, 1992-93 to 1996-97.
Dallas totals include Minnesota North Stars, 1992-93.
Colorado totals include Quebec, 1992-93 to 1994-95.
Phoenix totals include Winnipeg, 1992-93 to 1995-96.

2003-04 Results

Oct.	10	Boston	5-1		13	at Pittsburgh	3-1	
	16	Phoenix	5-1		15	Carolina	5-4	
	18	at New Jersey	3-2		17	at Florida	1-2	
	21	Atlanta	3-2*		19	Colorado	4-5*	
	23	at Columbus	1-0		21	at Vancouver	4-5*	
	25	Minnesota	3-2		22	at Edmonton	3-2	
	30	San Jose	2-2		24	at Calgary	6-2	
Nov.	1	Carolina	4-3		27	at Pittsburgh	6-2	
	4	Washington	1-5		29	Pittsburgh	5-1	
	6	Los Angeles	0-1*		31	Atlanta	4-1	
	8	Pittsburgh	9-0	Feb.	2	at Philadelphia	2-1	
	9	at Carolina	1-1		3	at Washington	1-2	
	11	at Florida	0-4		5	at Nashville	5-2	
	14	at Washington	5-2		10	Toronto	4-4	
	20	NY Islanders	3-2		12	Montreal	5-3	
	22	Buffalo	2-1		14	Florida	3-2	
	23	at Carolina	0-0		17	Philadelphia	5-2	
	25	NY Rangers	2-2		19	at St. Louis	3-4*	
	28	St. Louis	2-2		20	at Buffalo	3-4*	
	29	at Atlanta	1-2		23	at Washington	6-3	
Dec.	2	at Montreal	2-3		25	at Atlanta	4-2	
	4	at Ottawa	1-4		26	Toronto	4-3	
	6	at Buffalo	3-1		28	Washington	4-2	
	7	at NY Rangers	3-2	Mar.	1	at Colorado	3-0	
	9	at Chicago	2-5		3	at Chicago	5-3	
	11	at Ottawa	3-2		5	New Jersey	3-2*	
	13	Montreal	2-5		6	at Florida	5-3	
	16	at Toronto	0-3		8	at Detroit	1-1	
	18	at Philadelphia	5-4*		10	at Carolina	4-1	
	20	Dallas	1-2		12	NY Rangers	5-2	
	23	at Boston	1-1		13	Carolina	1-5	
	26	at Atlanta	1-3		16	NY Islanders	1-3	
	27	Boston	4-2		18	Buffalo	3-1	
	29	Anaheim	0-2		20	at Boston	4-5	
	31	Florida	2-2		21	at NY Islanders	0-3	
Jan.	2	Columbus	0-2		23	at Toronto	7-2	
	3	Philadelphia	6-1		25	New Jersey	2-1	
	6	at Ottawa	2-5		27	Washington	4-1	
	8	at Montreal	4-1		29	Ottawa	4-5*	
	9	at New Jersey	4-1	Apr.	1	Florida	4-3	
	11	at NY Rangers	2-1*		3	Atlanta	1-2	

* – Overtime

Entry Draft Selections 2004-1992

2004 Pick		2001 Pick		1998 Pick		1994 Pick	
30	Andy Rogers	3	Alexander Svitov	1	Vincent Lecavalier	8	Jason Wiemer
65	Mark Tobin	47	Alexander Polushin	64	Brad Richards	34	Colin Cloutier
102	Mike Lundin	61	Andreas Holmqvist	72	Dmitry Afanasenkov	55	Vadim Epanchintsev
158	Brandon Elliott	94	Evgeni Artukhin	92	Eric Beaudoin	86	Dmitri Klevakin
163	Dustin Collins	123	Aaron Lobb	121	Curtis Rich	137	Daniel Juden
188	Jan Zapletal	138	Paul Lynch	146	Sergei Kuznetsov	138	Bryce Salvador
191	Karri Ramo	188	Arthur Femenella	174	Brett Allan	164	Chris Maillet
245	Justin Keller	219	Dennis Packard	194	Oak Hewer	190	Alexei Baranov
		222	Jeremy Van Hoof	221	Daniel Hulak	216	Yuri Smirnov
2003 Pick		252	J.F. Soucy	229	Chris Lyness	242	Shawn Gervais
34	Mike Egener	259	Dmitri Bezrukov	252	Martin Cibak	268	Brian White
41	Matt Smaby	261	Vitali Smolyaninov				
96	Jonathan Boutin	281	Ilja Solarev	**1997 Pick**		**1993 Pick**	
192	Doug O'Brien	289	Henrik Bergfors	7	Paul Mara	3	Chris Gratton
224	Gerald Coleman			33	Kyle Kos	29	Tyler Moss
227	Jay Rosehill	**2000 Pick**		61	Matt Elich	55	Allan Egeland
255	Raimonds Danilics	8	Nikita Alexeev	108	Mark Thompson	81	Marian Kacir
256	Brady Greco	34	Ruslan Zainullin	109	Jan Sulc	107	Ryan Brown
273	Albert Vishnyakov	81	Alexander Kharitonov	112	Karel Betik	133	Kiley Hill
286	Zbynek Hrdel	126	Johan Hagglund	153	Andrei Skopintsev	159	Matthieu Raby
287	Nick Tarnasky	161	Pavel Sedov	168	Justin Jack	185	Ryan Nauss
		191	Aaron Gionet	170	Eero Somervuori	211	Alexandre Laporte
2002 Pick		222	Marek Priechodsky	185	Samuel St-Pierre	237	Brett Duncan
60	Adam Henrich	226	Brian Eklund	198	Shawn Skolney	263	Mark Szoke
100	Dmitri Kazionov	233	Alexander Polukeyev	224	Paul Comrie		
135	Joseph Pearce	263	Thomas Ziegler			**1992 Pick**	
162	Gerard Dicaire			**1996 Pick**		1	Roman Hamrlik
170	P.J. Atherton	**1999 Pick**		16	Mario Larocque	26	Drew Bannister
174	Karri Akkanen	47	Sheldon Keefe	69	Curtis Tipler	49	Brent Gretzky
183	Paul Ranger	67	Evgeny Konstantinov	125	Jason Robinson	74	Aaron Gavey
213	Fredrik Norrena	75	Brett Scheffelmaier	152	Nikolai Ignatov	97	Brantt Myhres
233	Vasily Koshechkin	88	Jimmie Olvestad	157	Xavier Delisle	122	Martin Tanguay
255	Ryan Craig	127	Kaspars Astashenko	179	Pavel Kubina	145	Derek Wilkinson
256	Darren Reid	148	Michal Lanicek			170	Dennis Maxwell
286	Alexei Glukhov	182	Fedor Fedorov	**1995 Pick**		193	Andrew Kemper
287	John Toffey	187	Ivan Rachunek	5	Daymond Langkow	218	Marc Tardif
		216	Erkki Rajamaki	30	Mike McBain	241	Tom MacDonald
		244	Mikko Kuparinen	56	Shane Willis		
				108	Konstantin Golokhvastov		
				134	Eduard Pershin		
				160	Cory Murphy		
				186	Joe Cardarelli		
				212	Zac Bierk		

Vice President and General Manager

FEASTER, JAY
Executive Vice President/General Manager, Tampa Bay Lightning.
Born in Williamstown, PA, July 30, 1962.

Jay Feaster enters his fourth season (third full season) as the executive vice president and general manager of the Tampa Bay Lightning after leading the team to its first Stanley Cup championship and being named NHL executive of the year by *The Sporting News*. The Lightning enjoyed a storybook season under Feaster's direction in 2003-04, winning a second consecutive Southeast Division title, capturing the top seed in the Eastern Conference and skating off with Lord Stanley's Cup after a hard-fought seven game series against the Calgary Flames. He has been widely praised for bringing continuity and stability to the Lightning franchise.

Feaster, named the fourth general manager in franchise history on February 10, 2002, joined the Lightning on October 20, 1998, from the Hershey Bears of the American Hockey League. He spent three-plus seasons as Tampa Bay's assistant general manager, overseeing all contractual, collective bargaining and NHL legal issues, as well as the organization's scouting department and its minor league affiliates. As general manager, Feaster has developed the Lightning into one of the most competitive and entertaining teams in the NHL. He also served as co-general manager of Team USA for the 2003 World Championships along with Larry Pleau of St. Louis.

To join the Lightning, Feaster resigned his post as president of the Hershey Bears and vice president of Hershey Sports and Entertainment. In that capacity, Feaster oversaw the operations of the Bears, the Hershey Wildcats professional soccer team and HersheyPark Arena/Stadium. In his nine years with the Bears, he led the team to a division title (1993-94) and a Calder Cup Championship (1997), while establishing three consecutive single-season attendance records (1991-92 to 1993-94) and entering into a five-year affiliation agreement with the NHL's Colorado Avalanche.

While in Hershey, Feaster spent time on the advisory boards of the Big 33 Scholarship Foundation, the Four Diamonds Fund at the Pennsylvania State University Milton S. Hershey Medical Center, and the Central PA Chapter of the National Multiple Sclerosis Society. He also taught business law and hotel law as a visiting faculty member at the Lebanon Valley College in Annville, Pennsylvania. Prior to joining the Hershey Company, Feaster practiced law with the firm of McNees, Wallace & Nurick in Harrisburg, Pennsylvania. He is a Summa Cum Laude graduate of Susquehanna University and a Cum Laude graduate of The Georgetown Law Center in Washington, D.C.

Club Directory

St. Pete Times Forum

Tampa Bay Lightning
St. Pete Times Forum
401 Channelside Drive
Tampa, FL 33602
Phone **813/301-6500**
FAX 813/301-1480
Ticket Info. 813/301-6600
www.tampabaylightning.com
Capacity: 19,758

Executive Staff
Owner	Palace Sports & Entertainment, Bill Davidson
Pres. of Palace Sports & Entertainment/Governor	Tom Wilson
Pres. of Tampa Bay Lightning/Alt. Governor	Ron Campbell
Executive Vice President/Chief Operating Officer	Sean Henry
Sr Vice President of Corporate Development	Greg Myford
Sr Vice President of Sponsorship Sales	Todd Wiseman
Sr Vice President of Marketing & Branding	Ken Lehner
Executive Assistant	Julie Stein
Executive Vice President, G.M. & Alt. Governor	Jay H. Feaster
Sr Vice President Communications	Bill Wickett
Vice President, Legal Affairs/Legal Counsel	Paul Davis
Vice President, Chief Financial Officer	Joe Fada

Hockey Operations
Executive Vice President, General Manager & Alternate Governor	Jay H. Feaster
Director of Player Personnel	Bill Barber
Hockey Operations Assiatant	Kathy Paterson
Assistant to the General Manager	Ryan Belec
Head Coach	John Tortorella
Associate Coach	Craig Ramsay
Assistant Coach	Jeff Reese
Strength & Conditioning Coach	Eric Lawson
Video Coach	Nigel Kirwan
Chief Scout	Jake Goertzen
Chief Professional Scout	Rick Paterson
Scouting Staff	Mikael Andersson, Stephen Baker, Larry Bernard, Dave Heitz, Kari Kettunen, Gerry O'Flaherty, Miroslav Prihoda, Yuri Yanchenkov, Darrell Young, Glen Zacharias
Director of Team Services	Phil Thibodeau
Head Medical Trainer	Thomas Mulligan
Assistant Medical Trainer	Adam Rambo
Massage Therapist	Mike Griebel
Equipment Manager	Ray Thill
Assistant Equipment Managers	Dana Heinze, Jim Pickard
Team Physician	Dr. Ira Guttentag
Director of Alumni	John Tucker

Premium Services
Director of Premium Services	Karrie Yager
Premium Services Ticket Manager	Missy Davis
Premium Services Suite Manager	Lakisha Sharpe
Premium Services Manager	Amanda Graul

Finance
Senior Accountants	Doug Riefler, Dave Weber
Accounts Payable	Donna Clark
Staff Accountants	Jane Sheill, Richard Ghizzone

Internal Support Staff
Vice President, Information Services	David Everett
Assistant Information Services Manager	Roberto Camejo, Rosie Chhuor
Database Marketing Manager	Josh Brady

Box Office
Director of Ticket Operations	Jim Mannino
Assistant Box Office Manager	Alex Bohne

Ticket Sales
Vice President of Ticket Sales	Dave Bullock
Sr Director of Sales	Todd Lambert
Director of Sales	Brad Lott
Asst Dir of Storm Sales/Sr Corp Acct Mgr	Alex English
Outside Sales Manager	Patrick Duffy
Sr Suites Sales Managers	Chris Diiorio, Joe Ondrejko
Premium Seating Manager	Paul Wallace
Sr Corporate Account Managers	Ryan McCoy, Derek Beeman
Corporate Account Managers	Dan Collins, Mike Clough, Tim Post, Alec Nguyen, Ryan West, Mike Warren, Robert Mulhearn, Sam Margolis, Justin Wilson

Sponsorship Sales & Marketing
Director of Promotions	Mark Gullett
Director of Outside Entertainment	Jason Franke
Director of Marketing Partnerships	Alaina Miller
Director of Event Marketing	Holly Brown
Director of Broadcast Production & Game Ops	Jim Ciotoli
Director of Fan Development	David Cole
Director of Web Services	Martin Quessenberry
Web Audio Manager	Tom Gilbert
Sr Marketing Partnerships Manager	Kelly McCoy
Marketing Partnerships Managers	Kasey Rodgers, Lauren DeLaney, Craig Smith
Corporate Marketing Managers	Amy Baldridge, Brienne Calcotte
Sr Corporate Marketing Managers	Scott Shepherd, Scott Morrison,
Director of National Sales	Ted Major
Marketing Manager	Karen Cohn

Communications
Director of Public Relations	Jay Preble
Media Relations Manager	Brian Breseman
Executive Director of Lightning Foundation	Nancy Crane
Public Relations Coordinator	Mary China
Community Relations Assistant	Liz Stowell

Broadcast Information
Director of Broadcasting & Programming	Jason Dixon
Television	Sunshine Network
Television Broadcasters	Rick Peckham, Bobby Taylor, Paul Kennedy
Radio	WDAE 620 AM, WHOO 1080 AM (Orlando), WIXC 1060 AM (Melbourne), WDGF 1350 AM (Dade City)
Radio Broadcasters	David Mishkin, Phil Esposito

Toronto Maple Leafs

Bryan McCabe was a Second-Team All-Star in 2003-04.

2003-04 Results: 45w-24L-10T-3OTL 103PTS.
Second, Northeast Division

Year-by-Year Record

Season	GP	Home				Road				Overall				GF	GA	Pts	Finished	Playoff Result
		W	L	T	OL	W	L	T	OL	W	L	T	OL					
2003-04	82	22	14	3	2	23	10	7	1	45	24	10	3	242	204	103	2nd, Northeast Div.	Lost Conf. Semi-Final
2002-03	82	24	13	4	0	20	15	3	3	44	28	7	3	236	208	98	2nd, Northeast Div.	Lost Conf. Quarter-Final
2001-02	82	24	11	6	0	19	14	4	4	43	25	10	4	249	207	100	2nd, Northeast Div.	Lost Conf. Championship
2000-01	82	19	11	7	4	18	18	4	1	37	29	11	5	232	207	90	3rd, Northeast Div.	Lost Conf. Semi-Final
1999-2000	82	24	12	5	0	21	15	2	3	45	27	7	3	246	222	100	1st, Northeast Div.	Lost Conf. Semi-Final
1998-99	82	23	13	5	...	22	17	2	...	45	30	7	...	268	231	97	2nd, Northeast Div.	Lost Conf. Championship
1997-98	82	16	20	5	...	14	23	4	...	30	43	9	...	194	237	69	6th, Central Div.	Out of Playoffs
1996-97	82	18	20	3	...	12	24	5	...	30	44	8	...	230	273	68	6th, Central Div.	Out of Playoffs
1995-96	82	19	15	7	...	15	21	5	...	34	36	12	...	247	252	80	3rd, Central Div.	Lost Conf. Quarter-Final
1994-95	48	15	7	2	...	6	12	6	...	21	19	8	...	135	146	50	4th, Central Div.	Lost Conf. Quarter-Final
1993-94	84	23	15	4	...	20	14	8	...	43	29	12	...	280	243	98	2nd, Central Div.	Lost Conf. Championship
1992-93	84	25	11	6	...	19	18	5	...	44	29	11	...	288	241	99	3rd, Norris Div.	Lost Conf. Championship
1991-92	80	21	16	3	...	9	27	4	...	30	43	7	...	234	294	67	5th, Norris Div.	Out of Playoffs
1990-91	80	15	21	4	...	8	25	7	...	23	46	11	...	241	318	57	5th, Norris Div.	Out of Playoffs
1989-90	80	24	14	2	...	14	24	2	...	38	38	4	...	337	358	80	3rd, Norris Div.	Lost Div. Semi-Final
1988-89	80	15	20	5	...	13	26	1	...	28	46	6	...	259	342	62	5th, Norris Div.	Out of Playoffs
1987-88	80	14	20	6	...	7	29	4	...	21	49	10	...	273	345	52	4th, Norris Div.	Lost Div. Semi-Final
1986-87	80	22	14	4	...	10	28	2	...	32	42	6	...	286	319	70	4th, Norris Div.	Lost Div. Final
1985-86	80	16	21	3	...	9	27	4	...	25	48	7	...	311	386	57	4th, Norris Div.	Lost Div. Final
1984-85	80	10	28	2	...	10	24	6	...	20	52	8	...	253	358	48	5th, Norris Div.	Out of Playoffs
1983-84	80	17	16	7	...	9	29	2	...	26	45	9	...	303	387	• 61	5th, Norris Div.	Out of Playoffs
1982-83	80	20	15	5	...	8	25	7	...	28	40	12	...	293	330	68	3rd, Norris Div.	Lost Div. Semi-Final
1981-82	80	12	20	8	...	8	24	8	...	20	44	16	...	298	380	56	5th, Norris Div.	Out of Playoffs
1980-81	80	14	21	5	...	14	16	10	...	28	37	15	...	322	367	71	5th, Adams Div.	Lost Prelim. Round
1979-80	80	17	19	4	...	18	21	1	...	35	40	5	...	304	327	75	4th, Adams Div.	Lost Prelim. Round
1978-79	80	20	12	8	...	14	21	5	...	34	33	13	...	267	252	81	3rd, Adams Div.	Lost Quarter-Final
1977-78	80	21	13	6	...	20	16	4	...	41	29	10	...	271	237	92	3rd, Adams Div.	Lost Semi-Final
1976-77	80	18	13	9	...	15	19	6	...	33	32	15	...	301	285	81	3rd, Adams Div.	Lost Quarter-Final
1975-76	80	23	12	5	...	11	19	10	...	34	31	15	...	294	276	83	3rd, Adams Div.	Lost Quarter-Final
1974-75	80	19	12	9	...	12	21	7	...	31	33	16	...	280	309	78	3rd, Adams Div.	Lost Quarter-Final
1973-74	78	21	11	7	...	14	16	9	...	35	27	16	...	274	230	86	4th, East Div.	Lost Quarter-Final
1972-73	78	20	12	7	...	7	29	3	...	27	41	10	...	247	279	64	6th, East Div.	Out of Playoffs
1971-72	78	21	11	7	...	12	20	7	...	33	31	14	...	209	208	80	4th, East Div.	Lost Quarter-Final
1970-71	78	24	9	6	...	13	24	2	...	37	33	8	...	248	211	82	4th, East Div.	Lost Quarter-Final
1969-70	76	18	13	7	...	11	21	6	...	29	34	13	...	222	242	71	6th, East Div.	Out of Playoffs
1968-69	76	20	8	10	...	15	18	5	...	35	26	15	...	234	217	85	4th, East Div.	Lost Quarter-Final
1967-68	74	24	9	4	...	9	22	6	...	33	31	10	...	209	176	76	5th, East Div.	Out of Playoffs
1966-67	70	21	8	6	...	11	19	5	...	32	27	11	...	204	211	75	**3rd,**	**Won Stanley Cup**
1965-66	70	22	9	4	...	12	16	7	...	34	25	11	...	208	187	79	3rd,	Lost Semi-Final
1964-65	70	17	15	3	...	13	11	11	...	30	26	14	...	204	173	74	4th,	Lost Semi-Final
1963-64	70	22	7	6	...	11	18	6	...	33	25	12	...	192	172	78	**3rd,**	**Won Stanley Cup**
1962-63	70	21	8	6	...	14	15	6	...	35	23	12	...	221	180	82	**1st,**	**Won Stanley Cup**
1961-62	70	25	5	5	...	12	17	6	...	37	22	11	...	232	180	85	**2nd,**	**Won Stanley Cup**
1960-61	70	21	6	8	...	18	13	4	...	39	19	12	...	234	176	90	2nd,	Lost Semi-Final
1959-60	70	20	9	6	...	15	17	3	...	35	26	9	...	199	195	79	2nd,	Lost Final
1958-59	70	17	13	5	...	10	19	6	...	27	32	11	...	189	201	65	4th,	Lost Final
1957-58	70	12	16	7	...	9	22	4	...	21	38	11	...	192	226	53	6th,	Out of Playoffs
1956-57	70	12	16	7	...	9	18	8	...	21	34	15	...	174	192	57	5th,	Out of Playoffs
1955-56	70	19	10	6	...	5	23	7	...	24	33	13	...	153	181	61	4th,	Lost Semi-Final
1954-55	70	14	10	11	...	10	14	11	...	24	24	22	...	147	135	70	3rd,	Lost Semi-Final
1953-54	70	22	6	7	...	10	18	7	...	32	24	14	...	152	131	78	3rd,	Lost Semi-Final
1952-53	70	17	12	6	...	10	18	7	...	27	30	13	...	156	167	67	5th,	Out of Playoffs
1951-52	70	17	10	8	...	12	15	8	...	29	25	16	...	168	157	74	3rd,	Lost Semi-Final
1950-51	70	22	8	5	...	19	8	8	...	41	16	13	...	212	138	95	**2nd,**	**Won Stanley Cup**
1949-50	70	18	9	8	...	13	18	4	...	31	27	12	...	176	173	74	3rd,	Lost Semi-Final
1948-49	60	12	8	10	...	10	17	3	...	22	25	13	...	147	161	57	**4th,**	**Won Stanley Cup**
1947-48	60	22	3	5	...	10	12	8	...	32	15	13	...	182	143	77	**1st,**	**Won Stanley Cup**
1946-47	60	20	8	2	...	11	11	8	...	31	19	10	...	209	172	72	**2nd,**	**Won Stanley Cup**
1945-46	50	10	13	2	...	9	11	5	...	19	24	7	...	174	185	45	5th,	Out of Playoffs
1944-45	50	13	9	3	...	11	13	1	...	24	22	4	...	183	161	52	**3rd,**	**Won Stanley Cup**
1943-44	50	13	11	1	...	10	12	3	...	23	23	4	...	214	174	50	3rd,	Lost Semi-Final
1942-43	50	13	9	3	...	9	13	3	...	22	19	9	...	198	159	53	3rd,	Lost Semi-Final
1941-42	48	18	6	0	...	9	12	3	...	27	18	3	...	158	136	57	**2nd,**	**Won Stanley Cup**
1940-41	48	16	5	3	...	12	9	3	...	28	14	6	...	145	99	62	3rd,	Lost Semi-Final
1939-40	48	15	6	3	...	10	14	0	...	25	17	6	...	134	110	56	3rd,	Lost Final
1938-39	48	13	8	3	...	6	12	6	...	19	20	9	...	114	107	47	3rd,	Lost Final
1937-38	48	13	6	5	...	11	9	4	...	24	15	9	...	151	127	57	1st, Cdn. Div.	Lost Final
1936-37	48	14	9	1	...	8	12	4	...	22	21	5	...	119	115	49	3rd, Cdn. Div.	Lost Quarter-Final
1935-36	48	15	4	5	...	8	15	1	...	23	19	6	...	126	106	52	2nd, Cdn. Div.	Lost Final
1934-35	48	16	6	2	...	14	8	2	...	30	14	4	...	157	111	64	1st, Cdn. Div.	Lost Final
1933-34	48	19	5	0	...	7	11	6	...	26	13	9	...	174	119	61	1st, Cdn. Div.	Lost Semi-Final
1932-33	48	16	4	4	...	8	14	2	...	24	18	6	...	119	111	54	1st, Cdn. Div.	Lost Final
1931-32	48	17	4	3	...	6	14	4	...	23	18	7	...	155	127	53	**2nd, Cdn. Div.**	**Won Stanley Cup**
1930-31	44	15	5	2	...	7	13	2	...	22	13	9	...	118	99	53	2nd, Cdn. Div.	Lost Quarter-Final
1929-30	44	10	8	4	...	7	13	2	...	17	21	6	...	116	124	40	4th, Cdn. Div.	Out of Playoffs
1928-29	44	15	5	2	...	6	13	3	...	21	18	5	...	85	69	47	3rd, Cdn. Div.	Lost Semi-Final
1927-28	44	9	8	5	...	9	10	3	...	18	18	8	...	89	88	44	4th, Cdn. Div.	Out of Playoffs
1926-27*	44	10	10	2	...	5	14	3	...	15	24	5	...	79	94	35	5th, Cdn. Div.	Out of Playoffs
1925-26	36	11	5	2	...	1	16	1	...	12	21	3	...	92	114	27	6th,	Out of Playoffs
1924-25	30	10	5	0	...	9	6	0	...	19	11	0	...	90	84	38	2nd,	Lost NHL S-Final
1923-24	24	7	5	0	...	3	9	0	...	10	14	0	...	59	85	20	3rd,	Out of Playoffs
1922-23	24	9	3	0	...	4	9	0	...	13	10	1	...	82	88	27	3rd,	Out of Playoffs
1921-22	24	8	4	0	...	5	6	1	...	13	10	1	...	98	97	27	**2nd,**	**Won Stanley Cup**
1920-21	24	9	3	0	...	6	6	0	...	15	9	0	...	105	100	30	2nd and 1st***	Lost NHL Final
1919-20**	24	8	4	0	...	4	8	0	...	12	12	0	...	119	106	24	3rd and 2nd***	Out of Playoffs
1918-19	18	5	4	0	...	0	9	0	...	5	13	0	...	64	92	10	3rd and 3rd***	Out of Playoffs
1917-18	22	10	1	0	...	3	8	0	...	13	9	0	...	108	109	26	**2nd and 1st***	**Won Stanley Cup**

* Name changed from St. Patricks to Maple Leafs (February, 1927). ** Name changed from Arenas to St. Patricks.
*** Season played in two halves with no combined standing at end.
From 1917-18 through 1925-26, NHL champions played against PCHA/WCHL champions for Stanley Cup.

2004-05 Schedule

Oct.	Fri.	15	at New Jersey		Sat.	15	at Detroit	
	Sat.	16	Ottawa		Tue.	18	NY Islanders	
	Tue.	19	Florida		Thu.	20	at Ottawa	
	Thu.	21	at Ottawa		Sat.	22	at Montreal	
	Sat.	23	at Montreal		Mon.	24	Carolina	
	Tue.	26	Los Angeles		Wed.	26	at Florida	
	Fri.	29	at Carolina		Thu.	27	at Tampa Bay	
	Sat.	30	NY Rangers		Sat.	29	Ottawa	
Nov.	Tue.	2	Tampa Bay	Feb.	Tue.	1	at Buffalo	
	Sat.	6	Boston		Thu.	3	Washington	
	Tue.	9	at NY Islanders		Sat.	5	Vancouver	
	Thu.	11	at NY Rangers		Mon.	7	San Jose	
	Sat.	13	at Boston		Tue.	8	at NY Rangers	
	Mon.	15	at Buffalo		Thu.	10	Pittsburgh	
	Tue.	16	Dallas		Tue.	15	Carolina	
	Thu.	18	at New Jersey		Fri.	18	Buffalo	
	Sat.	20	Philadelphia		Sat.	19	Edmonton	
	Tue.	23	Washington		Tue.	22	Florida	
	Sat.	27	Buffalo		Thu.	24	New Jersey	
	Tue.	30	at Calgary		Sat.	26	Atlanta	
Dec.	Thu.	2	at Edmonton	Mar.	Tue.	1	at Tampa Bay	
	Sat.	4	Vancouver		Wed.	2	at Florida	
	Tue.	7	Boston		Sat.	5	Montreal	
	Thu.	9	at Columbus		Tue.	8	Philadelphia	
	Sat.	11	Montreal		Thu.	10	at Philadelphia	
	Mon.	13	at Buffalo		Sat.	12	Ottawa	
	Tue.	14	NY Islanders		Sun.	13	at Pittsburgh*	
	Thu.	16	Atlanta		Tue.	15	Anaheim	
	Sat.	18	Calgary		Thu.	17	Minnesota	
	Tue.	21	at Boston		Sat.	19	NY Rangers	
	Thu.	23	at Carolina		Sun.	20	at Washington	
	Mon.	27	at Colorado		Tue.	22	Phoenix	
	Tue.	28	at St. Louis		Fri.	25	at Atlanta	
	Thu.	30	at Nashville		Sat.	26	at Philadelphia	
Jan.	Sat.	1	at Boston		Mon.	28	Tampa Bay	
	Tue.	4	Boston		Thu.	31	at Montreal	
	Thu.	6	at Atlanta	Apr.	Sat.	2	Montreal	
	Sat.	8	New Jersey		Sun.	3	at Pittsburgh*	
	Mon.	10	at Ottawa		Tue.	5	at NY Islanders	
	Tue.	11	Pittsburgh		Fri.	8	at Washington	
	Fri.	14	at Chicago		Sat.	9	Buffalo	

* Denotes afternoon game.

Franchise date: November 22, 1917

EASTERN NHL CONFERENCE

NORTHEAST DIVISION

88th NHL Season

2004-05 Player Personnel

FORWARDS	HT	WT	S	Place of Birth	Date	2003-04 Club
ANTROPOV, Nik	6-6	220	L	Vost, USSR	2/18/80	Toronto
BARRETT, Nathan	6-0	189	L	Vancouver, B.C.	8/3/81	St. John's
DOMI, Tie	5-10	213	R	Windsor, Ont.	11/1/69	Toronto
DRUKEN, Harold	6-0	200	L	St. John's, Nfld.	1/26/79	Toronto-St. John's
KILGER, Chad	6-4	224	L	Cornwall, Ont.	11/27/76	Montreal-Hamilton-Toronto
LEEB, Brad	5-11	187	R	Red Deer, Alta.	8/27/79	Toronto-St. John's
MOGILNY, Alexander	6-0	209	L	Khabarovsk, USSR	2/18/69	Toronto
NIEUWENDYK, Joe	6-2	205	L	Oshawa, Ont.	9/10/66	Toronto
NOLAN, Owen	6-1	215	R	Belfast, Ireland	2/12/72	Toronto
ONDRUS, Ben	6-0	185	R	Sherwood Park, Alta.	6/25/82	St. John's
PERROTT, Nathan	6-0	225	R	Owen Sound, Ont.	12/8/76	Toronto
PONIKAROVSKY, Alexei	6-4	220	L	Kiev, USSR	4/9/80	Toronto
ROBERTS, Gary	6-2	215	L	North York, Ont.	5/23/66	Toronto
ST. JACQUES, Chris	5-8	181	R	Edmonton, Alta.	1/22/83	Medicine Hat
STAJAN, Matt	6-1	180	L	Mississauga, Ont.	12/19/83	Toronto
SUNDIN, Mats	6-5	231	R	Bromma, Sweden	2/13/71	Toronto
TUCKER, Darcy	5-10	178	L	Castor, Alta.	3/15/75	Toronto
WELLWOOD, Kyle	5-10	190	R	Windsor, Ont.	5/16/83	Toronto-St. John's
WILLIAMS, Jeremy	5-11	184	R	Regina, Sask.	1/26/84	Swift Current-St. John's
WILM, Clarke	6-0	202	L	Central Butte, Sask.	10/24/76	Toronto-St. John's
DEFENSEMEN						
BELAK, Wade	6-5	221	R	Saskatoon, Sask.	7/3/76	Toronto
BELL, Brendan	6-1	205	L	Ottawa, Ont.	3/31/83	St. John's
BERG, Aki	6-3	213	L	Turku, Finland	7/28/77	Toronto
CHARTIER, Christian	6-0	216	L	Russell, Man.	12/29/80	St. John's
COLAIACOVO, Carlo	6-1	188	L	Toronto, Ont.	1/27/83	Toronto-St. John's
D'AMOUR, Dominic	6-3	202	L	La Salle, Que.	1/28/84	Gatineau
HARRISON, Jay	6-4	211	L	Oshawa, Ont.	11/3/82	St. John's
HEDIN, Pierre	6-1	198	L	Ornskoldsvik, Sweden	2/19/78	Toronto-St. John's
KABERLE, Tomas	6-1	198	L	Rakovnik, Czech.	3/2/78	Toronto
KELLY, Regan	6-2	200	L	Watrous, Sask.	3/9/81	St. John's
KLEE, Ken	6-0	210	R	Indianapolis, IN	4/24/71	Toronto
LEETCH, Brian	6-1	190	L	Corpus Christi, TX	3/3/68	NY Rangers-Toronto
MARSH, Tyson	6-1	190	L	Quesnel, B.C	6/20/84	Vancouver (WHL)
McCABE, Bryan	6-2	220	L	St. Catharines, Ont.	6/8/75	Toronto
MORO, Marc	6-1	218	L	Toronto, Ont.	7/17/77	St. John's
PILAR, Karel	6-3	207	R	Prague, Czech.	12/23/77	Toronto-St. John's
TURON, David	6-3	202	R	Havirov, Czech.	10/4/83	St. John's-Memphis
WHITE, Ian	5-10	185	R	Winnipeg, Man.	6/4/84	Swift Current-St. John's
WOZNIEWSKI, Andy	6-4	220	L	Buffalo Grove, IL	5/25/80	U. of Wisconsin-St. John's

GOALTENDERS	HT	WT	C	Place of Birth	Date	2003-04 Club
BELFOUR, Ed	5-11	202	L	Carman, Man.	4/21/65	Toronto
FORD, Todd	6-4	176	L	Calgary, Alta.	5/1/84	Prince George-Vancouver (WHL)
RACINE, Jean-Francois	6-3	194	L	St-Hyacinthe, Que.	4/27/82	Memphis-St. John's
TELLQVIST, Mikael	5-11	194	L	Sundbyberg, Sweden	9/19/79	Toronto-St. John's

Coaching History

Dick Carroll, 1917-18, 1918-19; Frank Heffernan and Harry Sproule, 1919-20; Frank Carroll, 1920-21; George O'Donohue, 1921-22; George O'Donohue and Charles Querrie, 1922-23; Charles Querrie, 1923-24; Eddie Powers, 1924-25, 1925-26; Charles Querrie, Mike Rodden and Alex Romeril, 1926-27; Conn Smythe, 1927-28 to 1929-30; Conn Smythe and Art Duncan, 1930-31; Art Duncan and Dick Irvin, 1931-32; Dick Irvin, 1932-33 to 1939-40; Hap Day, 1940-41 to 1949-50; Joe Primeau, 1950-51 to 1952-53; King Clancy, 1953-54 to 1955-56; Howie Meeker, 1956-57; Billy Reay, 1957-58; Billy Reay and Punch Imlach, 1958-59; Punch Imlach, 1959-60 to 1968-69; John McLellan, 1969-70 to 1972-73; Red Kelly, 1973-74 to 1976-77; Roger Neilson, 1977-78, 1978-79; Floyd Smith, Dick Duff and Punch Imlach, 1979-80; Punch Imlach, Joe Crozier and Mike Nykoluk, 1980-81; Mike Nykoluk, 1981-82 to 1983-84; Dan Maloney, 1984-85, 1985-86; John Brophy, 1986-87, 1987-88; John Brophy and George Armstrong, 1988-89; Doug Carpenter, 1989-90; Doug Carpenter and Tom Watt, 1990-91; Tom Watt, 1991-92; Pat Burns, 1992-93 to 1994-95; Pat Burns and Nick Beverley, 1995-96; Mike Murphy, 1996-97, 1997-98; Pat Quinn, 1998-99 to date.

General Managers' History

Charles Querrie, 1917-18 to 1926-27; Conn Smythe, 1927-28 to 1956-57; Hap Day, 1957-58; Punch Imlach, 1958-59 to 1968-69; Jim Gregory, 1969-70 to 1978-79; Punch Imlach, 1979-80, 1980-81; Punch Imlach and Gerry McNamara, 1981-82; Gerry McNamara, 1982-83 to 1987-88; Gord Stellick, 1988-89; Floyd Smith, 1989-90, 1990-91; Cliff Fletcher, 1991-92 to 1996-97; Ken Dryden, 1997-98, 1998-99; Pat Quinn, 1999-2000 to 2002-03; John Ferguson, 2003-04 to date.

General Manager

FERGUSON, JOHN
General Manager, Toronto Maple Leafs. Born in Montreal, Que., July 7, 1969.

John Ferguson became the 12th person to hold the role of general manager of the Toronto Maple Leafs on August 29, 2003. He is the youngest current general manager in the NHL. In his first year on the job in 2003-04, the Maple Leafs set a club record with 103 points.

Prior to his arrival in Toronto, Ferguson had served as vice-president and director of hockey operations for the St. Louis Blues since February 26, 2001. Prior to that he spent five seasons as assistant general manager with the club. Ferguson was also the president and general manager of the Worcester IceCats, the Blues' top minor league affiliate. He is a former chairman of the American Hockey League's Competition Committee and also served on the league's Legal Affairs Committee.

The son of former Montreal Canadiens great John Ferguson, John Jr. played hockey at Providence College and spent four professional seasons at the American Hockey League level with the Montreal Canadiens and Ottawa Senators organizations from 1989 to 1993. From 1993 to 1996 he was a member of the Ottawa Senators scouting staff as an amateur and professional scout. Before joining the Blues, he served as a player agent.

2003-04 Scoring

* - rookie

Regular Season

Pos	#	Player	Team	GP	G	A	Pts	+/-	PIM	PP	SH	GW	GT	S	%
C	13	Mats Sundin	TOR	81	31	44	75	11	52	11	1	10	0	226	13.7
D	24	Bryan Mccabe	TOR	75	16	37	53	22	86	8	0	2	1	168	9.5
D	2	Brian Leetch	NYR	57	13	23	36	–5	24	4	1	1	0	165	7.9
			TOR	15	2	13	15	11	10	1	0	1	0	41	4.9
			TOTAL	72	15	36	51	6	34	5	1	2	0	206	7.3
C	25	Joe Nieuwendyk	TOR	64	22	28	50	7	26	10	1	5	0	131	16.8
L	7	Gary Roberts	TOR	72	28	20	48	9	84	11	1	7	2	124	22.6
R	11	Owen Nolan	TOR	65	19	29	48	4	110	7	2	3	2	154	12.3
C	10	Ron Francis	CAR	68	10	20	30	–12	14	5	0	1	2	79	12.7
			TOR	12	3	7	10	3	0	2	0	1	0	12	25.0
			TOTAL	80	13	27	40	–9	14	7	0	2	2	91	14.3
R	16	Darcy Tucker	TOR	64	21	11	32	4	68	8	1	2	0	146	14.4
C	80	Nik Antropov	TOR	62	13	18	31	7	62	1	1	2	0	89	14.6
D	15	Tomas Kaberle	TOR	71	3	28	31	16	18	0	0	1	0	88	3.4
C	21	Robert Reichel	TOR	69	11	19	30	2	30	2	0	2	0	100	11.0
R	89	Alexander Mogilny	TOR	37	8	22	30	9	12	4	1	1	0	92	8.7
D	22	Ken Klee	TOR	66	4	25	29	–1	36	3	0	1	0	85	4.7
L	23	Alexei Ponikarovsky	TOR	73	9	19	28	14	44	1	0	2	0	110	8.2
C	14 *	Matt Stajan	TOR	69	14	13	27	7	22	0	0	0	1	63	22.2
R	19	Mikael Renberg	TOR	59	12	13	25	–1	50	2	0	1	0	88	13.6
D	55	Drake Berehowsky	PIT	47	5	16	21	–16	50	3	0	0	0	62	8.1
			TOR	9	1	2	3	5	17	0	0	0	0	8	12.5
			TOTAL	56	6	18	24	–11	67	3	0	0	0	70	8.6
R	28	Tie Domi	TOR	80	7	13	20	–2	208	1	0	0	0	84	8.3
D	29	Karel Pilar	TOR	50	2	17	19	2	22	1	0	1	0	74	2.7
R	12	Tom Fitzgerald	TOR	69	7	10	17	–2	52	1	0	1	0	81	8.6
D	8	Aki Berg	TOR	79	2	7	9	–1	40	0	0	0	0	69	2.9
L	18	Chad Kilger	MTL	36	2	2	4	2	14	0	0	0	0	29	6.9
			TOR	5	1	1	2	2	2	0	0	1	0	6	16.7
			TOTAL	41	3	3	6	4	16	0	0	1	0	35	8.6
D	9	Calle Johansson	TOR	8	0	6	6	5	0	0	0	0	0	8	0.0
D	27	Bryan Marchment	TOR	75	1	3	4	4	106	0	0	0	0	56	1.8
C	18	Harold Druken	TOR	9	0	4	4	4	2	0	0	0	0	19	0.0
R	26	Nathan Perrott	TOR	40	1	2	3	–1	116	0	0	0	0	47	2.1
R	3	Wade Belak	TOR	34	1	1	2	0	109	0	0	0	0	15	6.7
D	45 *	Carlo Colaiacovo	TOR	2	0	1	1	1	2	0	0	0	0	0	0.0
D	3 *	Pierre Hedin	TOR	3	0	1	1	–1	0	0	0	0	0	4	0.0
C	9	Josh Holden	TOR	1	0	0	0	0	0	0	0	0	0	0	0.0
R	38 *	Brad Leeb	TOR	1	0	0	0	–1	0	0	0	0	0	1	0.0
C	42 *	Kyle Wellwood	TOR	1	0	0	0	–1	0	0	0	0	0	1	0.0
D	34 *	Maxim Kondratiev	TOR	7	0	0	0	0	2	0	0	0	0	6	0.0
C	39	Clarke Wilm	TOR	10	0	0	0	0	7	0	0	0	0	10	0.0

Goaltending

No.	Goaltender	GPI	Mins	Avg	W	L	T	EN	SO	GA	SA	S%	G	A	PIM
20	Ed Belfour	59	3444	2.13	34	19	6	2	10	122	1483	.918	0	2	16
32	* Mikael Tellqvist	11	647	2.87	5	3	2	0	0	31	293	.894	0	0	0
37	Trevor Kidd	15	883	3.26	6	5	2	1	1	48	388	.876	0	2	2
	Totals	**82**	**4991**	**2.45**	**45**	**27**	**10**	**3**	**11**	**204**	**2167**	**.906**			

Playoffs

Pos	#	Player	Team	GP	G	A	Pts	+/-	PIM	PP	SH	GW	GT	S	%
C	13	Mats Sundin	TOR	9	4	5	9	–2	8	0	0	1	0	19	21.1
L	7	Gary Roberts	TOR	13	4	4	8	–3	10	2	0	1	0	19	21.1
D	24	Bryan McCabe	TOR	13	3	5	8	0	14	2	0	0	0	26	11.5
D	2	Brian Leetch	TOR	13	0	8	8	1	6	0	0	0	0	23	0.0
C	25	Joe Nieuwendyk	TOR	9	6	0	6	0	4	1	0	2	0	23	26.1
R	89	Alexander Mogilny	TOR	13	2	4	6	–1	8	0	0	0	0	16	12.5
R	28	Tie Domi	TOR	13	2	2	4	4	41	0	0	1	0	27	7.4
L	23	Alexei Ponikarovsky	TOR	13	1	3	4	–1	8	0	0	1	0	23	4.3
C	10	Ron Francis	TOR	12	0	4	4	0	2	0	0	0	0	14	0.0
L	18	Chad Kilger	TOR	13	2	1	3	0	0	0	0	0	0	16	12.5
D	15	Tomas Kaberle	TOR	13	0	3	3	1	6	0	0	0	0	14	0.0
R	16	Darcy Tucker	TOR	12	2	0	2	–3	14	1	0	0	0	16	12.5
C	21	Robert Reichel	TOR	12	0	2	2	4	8	0	0	0	0	18	0.0
C	80	Nik Antropov	TOR	13	0	2	2	1	18	0	0	0	0	18	0.0
D	29	Karel Pilar	TOR	1	1	0	1	1	0	0	0	0	0	2	50.0
C	39	Clarke Wilm	TOR	5	0	1	1	–1	2	0	0	0	0	5	0.0
G	37	Trevor Kidd	TOR	1	0	0	0	0	0	0	0	0	0	0	0.0
R	19	Mikael Renberg	TOR	2	0	0	0	0	4	0	0	0	0	2	0.0
C	14 *	Matt Stajan	TOR	3	0	0	0	0	2	0	0	0	0	3	0.0
D	9	Calle Johansson	TOR	4	0	0	0	–1	2	0	0	0	0	3	0.0
R	3	Wade Belak	TOR	4	0	0	0	0	14	0	0	0	0	0	0.0
R	12	Tom Fitzgerald	TOR	10	0	0	0	0	6	0	0	0	0	9	0.0
D	8	Aki Berg	TOR	10	0	0	0	–3	2	0	0	0	0	7	0.0
D	22	Ken Klee	TOR	11	0	0	0	–1	6	0	0	0	0	6	0.0
D	27	Bryan Marchment	TOR	13	0	0	0	0	8	0	0	0	0	2	0.0

Goaltending

No.	Goaltender	GPI	Mins	Avg	W	L	EN	SO	GA	SA	S%	G	A	PIM
37	Trevor Kidd	1	33	1.82	0	0	0	0	1	11	.909	0	0	0
20	Ed Belfour	13	774	2.09	6	7	0	3	27	379	.929	0	0	8
	Totals	**13**	**809**	**2.08**	**6**	**7**	**0**	**3**	**28**	**390**	**.928**			

Captains' History

Hap Day, 1927-28 to 1936-37; Charlie Conacher, 1937-38; Red Horner, 1938-39, 1939-40; Syl Apps, 1940-41 to 1942-43; Bob Davidson, 1943-44, 1944-45; Syl Apps, 1945-46 to 1947-48; Ted Kennedy, 1948-49 to 1954-55; Sid Smith, 1955-56; Jimmy Thomson, Ted Kennedy, 1956-57; George Armstrong, 1957-58 to 1968-69; Dave Keon, 1969-70 to 1974-75; Darryl Sittler, 1975-76 to 1980-81; Rick Vaive, 1981-82 to 1985-86; no captain, 1986-87 to 1988-89; Rob Ramage, 1989-90, 1990-91; Wendel Clark, 1991-92 to 1993-94; Doug Gilmour, 1994-95 to 1996-97; Mats Sundin, 1997-98 to date.

Club Records

Team

(Figures in brackets for season records are games played; records for fewest points, wins, ties, losses, goals, goals against are for 70 or more games)

Most Points	**100**	1999-2000 (82), 2001-02 (82)
Most Wins	**45**	1998-99 (82), 1999-2000 (82)
Most Ties	**22**	1954-55 (70)
Most Losses	**52**	1984-85 (80)
Most Goals	**337**	1989-90 (80)
Most Goals Against	**387**	1983-84 (80)
Fewest Points	**48**	1984-85 (80)
Fewest Wins	**20**	1981-82 (80), 1984-85 (80)
Fewest Ties	**4**	1989-90 (80)
Fewest Losses	**16**	1950-51 (70)
Fewest Goals	**147**	1954-55 (70)
Fewest Goals Against	***131**	1953-54 (70)
Longest Winning Streak		
Overall	**10**	Oct. 7-28/93
Home	**9**	Nov. 11-Dec. 26/53
Away	**7**	Nov. 14-Dec. 15/40, Dec. 4/60-Jan. 5/61
Longest Undefeated Streak		
Overall	**11**	Oct. 15-Nov. 8/50 (8 wins, 3 ties), Jan. 6-Feb. 1/94 (7 wins, 4 ties)
Home	**18**	Nov. 28/33-Mar. 10/34 (15 wins, 3 ties), Oct. 31/53-Jan. 23/54 (16 wins, 2 ties)
Away	**9**	Nov. 30/47-Jan. 11/48 (4 wins, 5 ties)
Longest Losing Streak		
Overall	**10**	Jan. 15-Feb. 8/67
Home	**7**	Nov. 11-Dec. 5/84
Away	**11**	Feb. 20-Apr. 1/88
Longest Winless Streak		
Overall	**15**	Dec. 26/87-Jan. 25/88 (11 losses, 4 ties)
Home	**11**	Dec. 19/87-Jan. 25/88 (7 losses, 4 ties)
Away	**18**	Oct. 6/82-Jan. 5/83 (13 losses, 5 ties)
Most Shutouts, Season	**13**	1953-54 (70)
Most PIM, Season	**2,419**	1989-90 (80)
Most Goals, Game	**14**	Mar. 16/57 (NYR 1 at Tor. 14)

Individual

Most Seasons	**21**	George Armstrong
Most Games	**1,187**	George Armstrong
Most Goals, Career	**389**	Darryl Sittler
Most Assists, Career	**620**	Borje Salming
Most Points, Career	**916**	Darryl Sittler (389G, 527A)
Most PIM, Career	**1,777**	Tie Domi
Most Shutouts, Career	**62**	Turk Broda
Longest Consecutive Games Streak	**486**	Tim Horton (Feb. 11/61-Feb. 4/68)
Most Goals, Season	**54**	Rick Vaive (1981-82)
Most Assists, Season	**95**	Doug Gilmour (1992-93)
Most Points, Season	**127**	Doug Gilmour (1992-93; 32G, 95A)
Most PIM, Season	**365**	Tie Domi (1997-98)
Most Points, Defenseman, Season	**79**	Ian Turnbull (1976-77; 22G, 57A)
Most Points, Center, Season	**127**	Doug Gilmour (1992-93; 32G, 95A)
Most Points, Right Wing, Season	**97**	Wilf Paiement (1980-81; 40G, 57A)
Most Points, Left Wing, Season	**99**	Dave Andreychuk (1993-94; 53G, 46A)
Most Points, Rookie, Season	**66**	Peter Ihnacak (1982-83; 28G, 38A)
Most Shutouts, Season	**13**	Harry Lumley (1953-54)
Most Goals, Game	**6**	Corb Denneny (Jan. 26/21), Darryl Sittler (Feb. 7/76)
Most Assists, Game	**6**	Babe Pratt (Jan. 8/44), Doug Gilmour (Feb. 13/93)
Most Points, Game	***10**	Darryl Sittler (Feb. 7/76; 6G, 4A)

* NHL Record.

Retired Numbers

5	Bill Barilko	1946-1951
6	Ace Bailey	1926-1934

Honored Numbers

1	Turk Broda	1936-43, 45-52
	Johnny Bower	1958-1970
7	King Clancy	1930-1937
	Tim Horton	1949-50, 51-70
9	Charlie Conacher	1929-1938
	Ted Kennedy	1942-55, 56-57
10	Syl Apps	1936-43, 45-48
	George Armstrong	1949-50, 51-71
27	Frank Mahovlich	1956-1968
	Darryl Sittler	1970-1982

All-time Record vs. Other Clubs

Regular Season

	At Home								On Road								Total							
	GP	W	L	T	OL	GF	GA	PTS	GP	W	L	T	OL	GF	GA	PTS	GP	W	L	T	OL	GF	GA	PTS
Anaheim	15	9	2	4	0	50	30	22	11	5	5	1	0	28	34	11	26	14	7	5	0	78	64	33
Atlanta	9	5	2	1	1	33	21	12	9	6	3	0	0	31	16	12	18	11	5	1	1	64	37	24
Boston	299	156	92	51	0	1005	769	363	298	90	159	47	2	786	967	229	597	246	251	98	2	1791	1736	592
Buffalo	67	28	27	12	0	203	228	68	69	20	43	6	0	184	279	46	136	48	70	18	0	387	507	114
Calgary	53	28	17	7	1	202	189	64	61	22	32	5	2	195	239	51	114	50	49	12	3	397	428	115
Carolina	36	13	18	5	0	120	126	31	37	13	18	6	0	119	144	32	73	26	36	11	0	239	270	63
Chicago	315	164	97	54	0	1071	821	382	318	120	156	42	0	831	968	282	633	284	253	96	0	1902	1789	664
Colorado	35	16	15	4	0	118	133	36	29	7	17	5	0	87	111	19	64	23	32	9	0	205	244	55
Columbus	3	2	0	1	0	10	4	5	1	0	0	0	1	3	4	1	4	2	0	1	1	13	8	6
Dallas	101	49	35	17	0	356	319	115	97	36	50	11	0	306	365	83	198	85	85	28	0	662	684	198
Detroit	316	164	105	47	0	1045	846	375	322	108	168	46	0	792	968	262	638	272	273	93	0	1837	1814	637
Edmonton	37	20	15	2	0	154	154	42	43	14	22	6	1	138	178	35	80	34	37	8	1	292	332	77
Florida	15	9	4	2	0	53	34	20	17	7	5	5	0	51	48	19	32	16	9	7	0	104	82	39
Los Angeles	68	35	22	11	0	266	223	81	65	21	34	10	0	191	234	52	133	56	56	21	0	457	457	133
Minnesota	3	3	0	0	0	11	3	6	1	1	0	0	0	1	0	2	4	4	0	0	0	12	3	8
Montreal	333	172	116	45	0	1007	865	389	333	92	198	43	0	827	1162	227	666	264	314	88	0	1834	2027	616
Nashville	6	2	3	1	0	13	18	5	1	0	0	0	1	2	3	1	7	2	3	1	1	15	21	6
New Jersey	48	31	12	5	0	182	138	67	46	14	16	15	1	136	155	44	94	45	28	20	1	318	293	111
NY Islanders	55	28	23	4	0	189	184	60	53	20	30	3	0	155	208	43	108	48	53	7	0	344	392	103
NY Rangers	282	159	84	39	0	974	741	357	283	107	118	56	2	836	873	272	565	266	202	95	2	1810	1614	629
Ottawa	22	10	9	2	1	59	60	23	20	7	11	1	1	53	56	16	42	17	20	3	2	112	116	39
Philadelphia	67	23	29	14	1	210	225	61	67	16	42	8	1	154	254	41	134	39	71	22	2	364	479	102
Phoenix	43	20	21	2	0	157	161	42	39	13	20	6	0	142	161	32	82	33	41	8	0	299	322	74
Pittsburgh	67	32	24	11	0	264	213	75	69	27	36	6	0	228	278	60	136	59	60	17	0	492	491	135
St. Louis	99	58	28	11	2	369	292	129	102	30	58	14	0	283	348	74	201	88	86	25	2	652	640	203
San Jose	18	12	4	2	0	69	47	26	15	7	5	3	0	40	32	17	33	19	9	5	0	109	79	43
Tampa Bay	21	13	7	1	0	76	55	27	20	16	3	1	0	71	42	33	41	29	10	2	0	147	97	60
Vancouver	60	28	21	11	0	219	195	67	64	24	29	11	0	216	225	59	124	52	50	22	0	435	420	126
Washington	48	26	16	6	0	211	163	58	50	18	28	4	0	144	182	40	98	44	44	10	0	355	345	98
Defunct Clubs	232	158	53	21	0	860	515	337	233	84	120	29	0	607	745	197	465	242	173	50	0	1467	1260	534
Totals	**2773**	**1473**	**901**	**393**	**6**	**9556**	**7772**	**3345**	**2773**	**945**	**1426**	**390**	**12**	**7637**	**9279**	**2292**	**5546**	**2418**	**2327**	**783**	**18**	**17193**	**17051**	**5637**

Playoffs

	Series	W	L	GP	W	L	T	GF	GA	Last Mtg.	Rnd.	Result
Boston	13	8	5	62	31	30	1	150	153	1974	QF	L 0-4
Buffalo	1	0	1	5	1	4	0	16	21	1999	CF	L 1-4
Calgary	1	1	0	2	2	0	0	9	5	1979	PRE	W 2-0
Carolina	1	0	1	6	2	4	0	6	10	2002	CF	L 2-4
Chicago	9	6	3	38	22	15	1	111	89	1995	CQF	L 3-4
Dallas	2	0	2	7	1	6	0	26	35	1983	DSF	L 1-3
Detroit	23	12	11	117	58	59	0	311	321	1993	DSF	W 4-3
Los Angeles	3	2	1	12	7	5	0	41	31	1993	CF	L 3-4
Montreal	15	7	8	71	29	42	0	160	215	1979	QF	L 0-4
New Jersey	2	0	2	13	5	8	0	27	37	2001	CSF	L 3-4
NY Islanders	3	2	1	17	8	9	0	42	54	2002	CQF	W 4-3
NY Rangers	8	3	5	35	16	19	0	86	86	1971	QF	L 2-4
Ottawa	4	4	0	24	16	8	0	57	42	2004	CQF	W 4-3
Philadelphia	6	1	5	36	14	22	0	85	119	2004	CSF	L 2-4
Pittsburgh	3	3	0	12	8	4	0	39	27	1999	CSF	W 4-2
St. Louis	5	2	3	31	14	17	0	90	88	1996	CQF	L 2-4
San Jose	1	1	0	7	4	3	0	26	21	1994	CSF	W 4-3
Vancouver	1	0	1	5	1	4	0	9	16	1994	CF	L 1-4
Defunct Clubs	8	6	2	24	12	10	2	59	57			
Totals	**109**	**58**	**51**	**524**	**251**	**269**	**4**	**1350**	**1427**			

Calgary totals include Atlanta Flames, 1972-73 to 1979-80.
Colorado totals include Quebec, 1979-80 to 1994-95.
New Jersey totals include Kansas City, 1974-75 to 1975-76, and Colorado Rockies, 1976-77 to 1981-82.
Phoenix totals include Winnipeg, 1979-80 to 1995-96.
Carolina totals include Hartford, 1979-80 to 1996-97.
Dallas totals include Minnesota North Stars, 1967-68 to 1992-93.

Playoff Results 2004-2000

Year	Round	Opponent	Result	GF	GA
2004	CSF	Philadelphia	L 2-4	13	17
	CQF	Ottawa	W 4-3	14	11
2003	CQF	Philadelphia	L 3-4	16	24
2002	CF	Carolina	L 2-4	6	10
	CSF	Ottawa	W 4-3	16	18
	CQF	NY Islanders	W 4-3	22	21
2001	CSF	New Jersey	L 3-4	18	21
	CQF	Ottawa	W 4-0	10	3
2000	CSF	New Jersey	L 2-4	9	16
	CQF	Ottawa	W 4-2	17	10

Abbreviations: Round: CF – conference final; **CSF** – conference semi-final; **CQF** – conference quarter-final; **DSF** – division semi-final; **QF** – quarter-final; **PRE** – preliminary round.

2003-04 Results

Oct.	11	Montreal	0-4
	13	Washington	2-2
	16	at New Jersey	2-2
	18	at Montreal	1-0
	20	at NY Islanders	2-5
	22	at Dallas	3-1
	23	at Phoenix	5-4
	25	Washington	4-1
	27	Atlanta	2-3*
	30	at Buffalo	3-5
Nov.	1	Philadelphia	1-7
	2	at Carolina	2-1
	4	Pittsburgh	4-2
	7	at New Jersey	1-1
	8	Edmonton	4-1
	12	at Anaheim	1-5
	13	at Los Angeles	4-4
	15	at San Jose	2-2
	18	at Calgary	2-3*
	20	at Edmonton	2-3
	22	at Vancouver	5-3
	24	Vancouver	2-1
	27	at Atlanta	3-1
	29	at Ottawa	2-1
	30	at NY Rangers	4-2
Dec.	2	NY Rangers	5-4
	4	at Boston	6-0
	6	Detroit	5-2
	9	St. Louis	2-3*
	11	at Minnesota	1-0
	13	NY Rangers	3-1
	16	Tampa Bay	3-0
	19	at Washington	2-2
	20	Montreal	4-2
	23	Florida	5-2
	26	at NY Rangers	6-5*
	27	at NY Islanders	1-3
	29	at Florida	4-4
Jan.	1	at Boston	2-3
	3	Buffalo	3-3
	5	at Pittsburgh	5-0
	6	Nashville	2-1
	8	Ottawa	1-7
	10	New Jersey	0-1
	13	Calgary	4-1
	16	at Philadelphia	1-4
	17	Philadelphia	0-4
	20	NY Islanders	2-0
	21	at Washington	3-2
	24	at Montreal	4-1
	27	Carolina	0-2
	30	at Atlanta	4-1
	31	Ottawa	5-1
Feb.	3	Chicago	1-4
	5	at Ottawa	5-4*
	10	at Tampa Bay	4-4
	12	Columbus	4-1
	14	Buffalo	4-6
	16	at Pittsburgh	8-4
	17	Boston	2-5
	19	at Carolina	2-1*
	21	Montreal	5-4
	23	Carolina	1-2
	25	at Florida	0-4
	26	at Tampa Bay	3-4
	28	New Jersey	3-0
Mar.	2	Boston	3-2
	4	NY Islanders	6-2
	6	Buffalo	1-5
	9	Florida	5-0
	11	Pittsburgh	2-3
	13	at Montreal	3-4
	15	at Buffalo	6-5*
	16	Boston	1-2
	18	at Philadelphia	3-2
	20	Colorado	5-2
	23	Tampa Bay	2-7
	25	at Boston	3-0
	27	Ottawa	2-2
	29	Atlanta	4-2
Apr.	2	at Buffalo	2-0
	3	at Ottawa	6-0

* – Overtime

Entry Draft
Selections 2004-1990

2004		2000		1996		1992	
Pick		**Pick**		**Pick**		**Pick**	
90	Justin Pogge	24	Brad Boyes	36	Marek Posmyk	8	Brandon Convery
113	Roman Kukumberg	51	Kris Vernarsky	50	Francis Larivee	23	Grant Marshall
157	Dmitri Vorobiev	70	Mikael Tellqvist	66	Mike Lankshear	77	Nikolai Borschevsky
187	Robert Earl	90	Jean-Francois Racine	68	Konstantin Kalmikov	95	Mark Raiter
252	Jan Steber	100	Miguel Delisle	86	Jason Sessa	101	Janne Gronvall
285	Pierce Norton	179	Vadim Sozinov	103	Vladimir Antipov	106	Chris Deruiter
		209	Markus Seikola	110	Peter Cava	125	Mikael Hakansson
2003		223	Lubos Velebny	111	Brandon Sugden	149	Patrik Augusta
Pick		254	Alexander Shinkar	140	Dmitri Yakushin	173	Ryan Vandenbussche
57	John Doherty	265	Jean-Philippe Cote	148	Chris Bogas	197	Wayne Clarke
91	Martin Sagat			151	Lucio DeMartinis	221	Sergei Simonov
125	Konstantin Volkov	**1999**		178	Reggie Berg	245	Nathan Dempsey
158	John Mitchell	**Pick**		204	Tomas Kaberle		
220	Jeremy Williams	24	Luca Cereda	230	Jared Hope	**1991**	
237	Shaun Landolt	60	Peter Reynolds			**Pick**	
		108	Mirko Murovic	**1995**		47	Yanic Perreault
2002		110	Jon Zion	**Pick**		69	Terry Chitaroni
Pick		151	Vaclav Zavoral	15	Jeff Ware	102	Alexei Kudashov
24	Alexander Steen	161	Jan Sochor	54	Ryan Pepperall	113	Jeff Perry
57	Matt Stajan	211	Vladimir Kulikov	139	Doug Bonner	120	Alexander Kuzminsky
74	Todd Ford	239	Pierre Hedin	145	Yannick Tremblay	135	Martin Prochazka
88	Dominic D'Amour	267	Peter Metcalf	171	Marek Melenovsky	160	Dmitri Mironov
122	David Turon			197	Mark Murphy	164	Robb McIntyre
191	Ian White	**1998**		223	Danny Markov	167	Tomas Kucharcik
222	Scott May	**Pick**				179	Guy Lehoux
254	Jarkko Immonen	10	Nik Antropov	**1994**		201	Gary Miller
285	Staffan Kronvall	35	Petr Svoboda	**Pick**		223	Johnathon Kelley
		69	Jamie Hodson	16	Eric Fichaud	245	Chris O'Rourke
2001		87	Alexei Ponikarovsky	48	Sean Haggerty		
Pick		126	Morgan Warren	64	Fredrik Modin	**1990**	
17	Carlo Colaiacovo	154	Allan Rourke	126	Mark Deyell	**Pick**	
39	Karel Pilar	181	Jonathan Gagnon	152	Kam White	10	Drake Berehowsky
65	Brendan Bell	215	Dwight Wolfe	178	Tommi Rajamaki	31	Felix Potvin
82	Jay Harrison	228	Michal Travnicek	204	Rob Butler	73	Darby Hendrickson
88	Nicolas Corbeil	236	Sergei Rostov	256	Sergei Berezin	80	Greg Walters
134	Kyle Wellwood			282	Doug Nolan	115	Alexander Godynyuk
168	Maxim Kondratiev	**1997**				136	Eric Lacroix
183	Jaroslav Sklenar	**Pick**		**1993**		157	Dan Stiver
198	Ivan Kolozvary	57	Jeff Farkas	**Pick**		178	Robert Horyna
213	Jan Chovan	84	Adam Mair	12	Kenny Jonsson	199	Rob Chebator
246	Tomas Mojzis	111	Frantisek Mrazek	19	Landon Wilson	220	Scott Malone
276	Mike Knoepfli	138	Eric Gooldy	123	Zdenek Nedved	241	Nick Vachon
		165	Hugo Marchand	149	Paul Vincent		
		190	Shawn Thornton	175	Jeff Andrews		
		194	Russ Bartlett	201	David Brumby		
		221	Jonathan Hedstrom	253	Kyle Ferguson		
				279	Mikhail Lapin		

Coach

QUINN, PAT
Coach, Toronto Maple Leafs. Born in Hamilton, Ont., January 29, 1943.

Pat Quinn became the 25th head coach of the Toronto Maple Leafs on June 26, 1998. He added the responsibilities of general manager to his coaching duties on July 14, 1999 and held both jobs until the appointment of John Ferguson on August 29, 2003.

The Maple Leafs have reached the playoffs in each of Quinn's six seasons behind the bench and set a club record with 103 points in 2003-04. He is fourth all-time in regular-season NHL games coached (1,236) and wins (616) and is only the fourth coach in franchise history to reach the 200-win mark with the club, joining Punch Imlach, Hap Day and Dick Irvin. Previous to his arrival in Toronto he served as coach and/or general manager with Philadelphia, Los Angeles and Vancouver.

In February 2002, Quinn served as head coach of the Canadian Olympic team and guided Canada to its first hockey gold medal in 50 years of Olympic competition. He also coached Team Canada at the 2004 World Cup.

Quinn received the Jake Milford Award for dedicated service and contribution to hockey in British Columbia in 1994. In 2002, he was inducted into the British Columbia Hockey Hall of Fame and he has also been inducted into the Hamilton Gallery of Distinction. He is active in the community, holding his annual Pat Quinn and Friends golf tournament with the proceeds going to Kids Help Phone, RCMP Drugs and Sport and Hockey Canada.

NHL Coaching Record

Season	Team		Regular Season				Playoffs		
		Games	W	L	T	Games	W	L	
1978-79	Philadelphia	30	18	8	4	8	3	5	
1979-80	Philadelphia	80	48	12	20	19	13	6	
1980-81	Philadelphia	80	41	24	15	12	6	6	
1981-82	Philadelphia	72	34	29	9	....	....	....	
1984-85	Los Angeles	80	34	32	14	3	0	3	
1985-86	Los Angeles	80	23	49	8	....	....	....	
1986-87	Los Angeles	42	18	20	4	....	....	....	
1990-91	Vancouver	26	9	13	4	6	2	4	
1991-92	Vancouver	80	42	26	12	13	6	7	
1992-93	Vancouver	84	46	29	9	12	6	6	
1993-94	Vancouver	84	41	40	3	24	15	9	
1995-96	Vancouver	6	3	3	0	6	2	4	
1998-99	Toronto	82	45	30	7	17	9	8	
1999-2000	Toronto	82	45	30	7	12	6	6	
2000-01	Toronto	82	37	34	11	11	7	4	
2001-02	Toronto	82	43	29	10	20	10	10	
2002-03	Toronto	82	44	31	7	7	3	4	
2003-04	Toronto	82	45	27	10	13	6	7	
	NHL Totals	**1236**	**616**	**466**	**154**	**183**	**94**	**89**	

Assistant coach Rick Ley posted a 1-1 record as replacement coach when Quinn was sidelined with heart arrythmia, May 21 and 25, 2002. Both games are credited to Quinn's coaching record.

Club Directory

Air Canada Centre

Toronto Maple Leafs
Air Canada Centre
40 Bay St., Suite 400
Toronto, Ontario M5J 2X2
Phone **416/815-5700**
FAX 416/359-9331
www.mapleleafs.com
Capacity: 18,819

Board of Directors
Larry M. Tanenbaum, Robert G. Bertram, James W. Leech, Dean Metcalf, Ivan Fecan, John MacIntyre, Dale H. Lastman, Richard Peddie

Maple Leaf Sports & Entertainment Ltd.
Chairman, NHL Governor	Larry M. Tanenbaum
President, CEO and Alternate NHL Governor	Richard Peddie
Alternate NHL Governor	John Ferguson
Alternate NHL Governor	Dale H. Lastman
Alternate NHL Governor	Dean Metcalf
Executive V.P., Chief Operating Officer	Tom Anselmi
Executive V.P., CFO And Business Development	Ian Clarke
Executive V.P., G.M., Air Canada Centre	Bob Hunter
Sr. V.P., General Counsel & Corporate Secretary	Robin Brudner
V.P., Communications & Community Development	John Lashway
V.P., People	Mardi Walker
V.P., Programming, Exec. Producer, Leafs TV	John Shannon
V.P., Corporate Sales & Service	Dave Hopkinson
V.P., Finance	Kevin Nonomura
V.P., Marketing	Beth Robertson
V.P., Operations	Diego Roccasalva

Maple Leafs Management
General Manager	John Ferguson
Head Coach	Pat Quinn
Assistant General Manager & Director of Player Personnel	Mike Penny
Assistant Coaches	Keith Acton, Rick Ley
Player Development Coach & Scouting Coordinator	Paul Dennis
Video Analyst	Reid Mitchell
Strength & Conditioning Coach	Matt Nichol
Community Representatives	Wendel Clark, Darryl Sittler
Director, Amateur Scouting	Barry Trapp
Scouts	George Armstrong, Garth Malarchuk, Dave Morrison, Murray Oliver, Mike Palmateer, Mark Yannetti
European Scouts	Thommie Bergman, Jan Kovac, Nikolai Ladygin, Peter Ahola
Director, Team Services	Casey Vanden Heuvel
Travel Coordinator	Mary Speck
Executive Assistant	Ann Clark
Executive Assistant to the General Manager	Maria Tomasevic

Maple Leafs Communications and Community Development
Vice-President, Communications & Community Development	John Lashway
Director, Media Relations	Pat Park
Coordinator, Media Relations	Dave Griffiths
Manager, Corporate Communications	Rajani Kamath
Director, Community Relations	Beverley Deeth
Manager, Community Relations	Dave De Freitas
Coordinators, Community Relations	Paula Dal Maso, Ryan Janzen
Coordinator, Youth & Amateur Hockey Development	Greg Schell
Assistant Coordinator, Youth & Amateur Hockey Development	Geoff George
Executive Assistant, Communications & Community Development	Rose Politi
Acting Director, Go Kids Go! The Leafs Fund	Mary Rowe
Coordinators, Go Kids Go! The Leafs Fund	Ted Warner, Brad Young
Manager, Game Presentation	Mike Ferriman
Manager, Game Operations	Nancy Gilks
Assistant, Game Operations	Stephenie Summerhill
Head Audio Engineer	Courtney Ross
Alumni Relations	Susanna Tyson
Team Photographer	Graig Abel

Maple Leafs Medical and Training Staff
Head Athletic Therapist	Chris Broadhurst
Athletic Therapist	Brent Smith
Massage Therapist	Tony Scott
Equipment Manager	Brian Papineau
Assistant Equipment Managers	Bobby Hastings, Scott McKay
Team Doctors	Dr. Michael Clarfield, Dr. Darrell Ogilvie-Harris, Dr. Leith Douglas, Dr. Rob Devenyi, Dr. Simon McGrail
Team Dentist	Dr. Allan Hawryluk

Broadcast Information
Radio Play-By-Play	Joe Bowen, Dennis Beyak
Radio Analyst	Jim Ralph
Television Play-By-Play	Bob Cole, Joe Bowen
Television Analyst	Harry Neale

Air Canada Centre
Director, Finance	Suzanne Scott
Director, Consumer Products	Marc Petitpas
Director, Event Operations and Production	Jim Roe
Director, Executive Suite Services	Kristy Fletcher
Director, Food & Beverage	Michael Doyle
Director, Retail Finance	Alldrick Britto
Director, Guest Services	Chris Gibbs
Director, Information Technology	Sasha Puric
Director, People Relations	Craig Richardson
Director, Programming and Event Marketing	Patti-Anne Tarlton
Director, Restaurant Operations, Executive Chef	Brad Long
Director, Sales	Jim Edmands
Director, Service and Ticketing	Paul Beirne
Director, Ticket Operations	Donna Henderson
Legal Counsel	Peter Miller
Operations Manager, Leafs TV	Duncan Blair
Coordinating Producer, Leafs TV	Frank Hayward
Manager, Video and Scoreboard Production	Curtis Emerson

Vancouver Canucks

2003-04 Results: 43w-24L-10T-5OTL 101PTS.
First, Northwest Division

2004-05 Schedule

Oct.	Wed.	13	at San Jose		Sat.	8	Dallas
	Sat.	16	Detroit		Mon.	10	San Jose
	Tue.	19	at Calgary		Wed.	12	Ottawa
	Wed.	20	St. Louis		Fri.	14	at Anaheim
	Fri.	22	Minnesota		Sat.	15	at Los Angeles
	Sun.	24	Columbus		Thu.	20	at Minnesota
	Tue.	26	Calgary		Sat.	22	at Edmonton
	Thu.	28	at Minnesota		Sun.	23	NY Islanders
	Sat.	30	at Colorado		Tue.	25	New Jersey
Nov.	Tue.	2	Colorado		Thu.	27	Edmonton
	Fri.	5	Nashville		Mon.	31	Colorado
	Sun.	7	Anaheim	Feb.	Wed.	2	NY Rangers
	Wed.	10	at Colorado		Sat.	5	at Toronto
	Thu.	11	at Phoenix		Mon.	7	at Ottawa
	Sat.	13	at San Jose		Tue.	8	at Montreal
	Wed.	17	Chicago		Thu.	10	at Calgary
	Fri.	19	Nashville		Tue.	15	San Jose
	Sun.	21	Minnesota		Sat.	19	Calgary
	Tue.	23	at Atlanta		Tue.	22	Boston
	Wed.	24	at Tampa Bay		Thu.	24	at St. Louis
	Fri.	26	at Florida		Fri.	25	at Nashville
	Sun.	28	at Carolina*		Sun.	27	at Dallas
	Tue.	30	at Nashville	Mar.	Tue.	1	Phoenix
Dec.	Thu.	2	Calgary		Thu.	3	at Phoenix
	Sat.	4	Toronto		Sat.	5	at Los Angeles
	Mon.	6	Columbus		Sun.	6	at Anaheim*
	Thu.	9	at Calgary		Tue.	8	Chicago
	Fri.	10	Detroit		Thu.	10	St. Louis
	Sun.	12	at Columbus*		Mon.	14	Minnesota
	Tue.	14	at Pittsburgh		Thu.	17	at Chicago
	Thu.	16	at Detroit		Fri.	18	at Columbus
	Sat.	18	Edmonton		Sun.	20	at Dallas*
	Tue.	21	Los Angeles		Tue.	22	Colorado
	Thu.	23	Phoenix		Thu.	24	Washington
	Sun.	26	at Edmonton		Sat.	26	Los Angeles
	Mon.	27	Philadelphia		Wed.	30	Dallas
	Wed.	29	Montreal	Apr.	Fri.	1	at Chicago
	Fri.	31	at Detroit		Sat.	2	at Minnesota
Jan.	Sat.	1	at Buffalo		Mon.	4	Anaheim
	Tue.	4	at St. Louis		Thu.	7	Edmonton
	Thu.	6	at Colorado		Sat.	9	at Edmonton

* Denotes afternoon game.

Year-by-Year Record

Season	GP	Home				Road				Overall						Pts.	Finished	Playoff Result
		W	L	T	OL	W	L	T	OL	W	L	T	OL	GF	GA			
2003-04	82	21	13	7	0	22	11	3	5	43	24	10	5	235	194	101	1st, Northwest Div.	Lost Conf. Quarter-Final
2002-03	82	22	13	6	0	23	10	7	1	45	23	13	1	264	208	104	2nd, Northwest Div.	Lost Conf. Semi-Final
2001-02	82	23	11	5	2	19	19	2	1	42	30	7	3	254	211	94	2nd, Northwest Div.	Lost Conf. Quarter-Final
2000-01	82	21	12	5	3	15	16	6	4	36	28	11	7	239	238	90	3rd, Northwest Div.	Lost Conf. Quarter-Final
1999-2000	82	16	14	5	6	14	15	10	2	30	29	15	8	227	237	83	3rd, Northwest Div.	Out of Playoffs
1998-99	82	14	21	6	...	9	26	6	...	23	47	12	...	192	258	58	4th, Northwest Div.	Out of Playoffs
1997-98	82	15	22	4	...	10	21	10	...	25	43	14	...	224	273	64	7th, Pacific Div.	Out of Playoffs
1996-97	82	20	17	4	...	15	23	3	...	35	40	7	...	257	273	77	4th, Pacific Div.	Out of Playoffs
1995-96	82	15	19	7	...	17	16	8	...	32	35	15	...	278	278	79	3rd, Pacific Div.	Lost Conf. Quarter-Final
1994-95	48	10	8	6	...	8	10	6	...	18	18	12	...	153	148	48	2nd, Pacific Div.	Lost Conf. Semi-Final
1993-94	84	20	19	3	...	21	21	0	...	41	40	3	...	279	276	85	2nd, Pacific Div.	Lost Final
1992-93	84	27	11	4	...	19	18	5	...	46	29	9	...	346	278	101	1st, Smythe Div.	Lost Div. Final
1991-92	80	23	10	7	...	19	16	5	...	42	26	12	...	285	250	96	1st, Smythe Div.	Lost Div. Final
1990-91	80	18	17	5	...	10	26	4	...	28	43	9	...	243	315	65	4th, Smythe Div.	Lost Div. Semi-Final
1989-90	80	13	16	11	...	12	25	3	...	25	41	14	...	245	306	64	5th, Smythe Div.	Out of Playoffs
1988-89	80	19	15	6	...	14	24	2	...	33	39	8	...	251	253	74	4th, Smythe Div.	Lost Div. Semi-Final
1987-88	80	15	20	5	...	10	26	4	...	25	46	9	...	272	320	59	5th, Smythe Div.	Out of Playoffs
1986-87	80	17	19	4	...	12	24	4	...	29	43	8	...	282	314	66	5th, Smythe Div.	Out of Playoffs
1985-86	80	17	18	5	...	6	26	8	...	23	44	13	...	282	333	59	4th, Smythe Div.	Lost Div. Semi-Final
1984-85	80	15	21	4	...	10	25	5	...	25	46	9	...	284	401	59	5th, Smythe Div.	Out of Playoffs
1983-84	80	20	16	4	...	12	23	5	...	32	39	9	...	306	328	73	3rd, Smythe Div.	Lost Div. Semi-Final
1982-83	80	20	12	8	...	10	23	7	...	30	35	15	...	303	309	75	3rd, Smythe Div.	Lost Div. Semi-Final
1981-82	80	20	8	12	...	10	25	5	...	30	33	17	...	290	286	77	2nd, Smythe Div.	Lost Final
1980-81	80	17	12	11	...	11	20	9	...	28	32	20	...	289	301	76	3rd, Smythe Div.	Lost Prelim. Round
1979-80	80	14	17	9	...	13	20	7	...	27	37	16	...	256	281	70	3rd, Smythe Div.	Lost Prelim. Round
1978-79	80	15	18	7	...	10	24	6	...	25	42	13	...	217	291	63	2nd, Smythe Div.	Lost Prelim. Round
1977-78	80	13	15	12	...	7	28	5	...	20	43	17	...	239	320	57	3rd, Smythe Div.	Out of Playoffs
1976-77	80	13	21	6	...	12	21	7	...	25	42	13	...	235	294	63	4th, Smythe Div.	Out of Playoffs
1975-76	80	22	11	7	...	11	21	8	...	33	32	15	...	271	272	81	2nd, Smythe Div.	Lost Prelim. Round
1974-75	80	23	12	5	...	15	20	5	...	38	32	10	...	271	254	86	1st, Smythe Div.	Lost Quarter-Final
1973-74	78	14	18	7	...	10	25	4	...	24	43	11	...	224	296	59	7th, East Div.	Out of Playoffs
1972-73	78	17	18	4	...	5	29	5	...	22	47	9	...	233	339	53	7th, East Div.	Out of Playoffs
1971-72	78	14	20	5	...	6	30	3	...	20	50	8	...	203	297	48	7th, East Div.	Out of Playoffs
1970-71	78	17	18	4	...	7	28	4	...	24	46	8	...	229	296	56	6th, East Div.	Out of Playoffs

Franchise date: May 22, 1970

NORTHWEST DIVISION

35th NHL Season

After posting a +23 rating in 69 games for Vancouver in 2002-03, Marek Malik tied Martin St. Louis for the league-lead at +35 in 2003-04 despite the fact that St. Louis outscored him by 35 goals and 75 points.

2004-05 Player Personnel

FORWARDS	HT	WT	S	Place of Birth	Date	2003-04 Club
BERTUZZI, Todd	6-3	245	L	Sudbury, Ont.	2/2/75	Vancouver
BOUCK, Tyler	6-0	196	L	Camrose, Alta.	1/13/80	Vancouver-Manitoba
CHUBAROV, Artem	6-1	189	L	Gorky, USSR	12/12/79	Vancouver
COOKE, Matt	5-11	205	L	Belleville, Ont.	9/7/78	Vancouver
FEDOROV, Fedor	6-3	230	L	Appatity, USSR	6/11/81	Vancouver-Manitoba
GOREN, Lee	6-3	205	R	Winnipeg, Man.	12/26/77	Florida-San Antonio
KESLER, Ryan	6-1	195	R	Detroit, MI	8/31/84	Vancouver-Manitoba
KING, Jason	6-1	195	L	Corner Brook, Nfld.	9/14/81	Vancouver-Manitoba
LINDEN, Trevor	6-4	215	R	Medicine Hat, Alta.	4/11/70	Vancouver
MAY, Brad	6-1	217	L	Toronto, Ont.	11/29/71	Vancouver
MORRISON, Brendan	5-11	190	L	Pitt Meadows, B.C.	8/15/75	Vancouver
MORRISON, Justin	6-3	205	R	Los Angeles, CA	9/10/79	Manitoba
NASLUND, Markus	5-11	195	L	Ornskoldsvik, Sweden	7/30/73	Vancouver
NOLAN, Brandon	6-0	180	L	Sault Ste. Marie, Ont.	7/18/83	Manitoba-Columbia
RUUTU, Jarkko	6-2	194	L	Vantaa, Finland	8/23/75	Vancouver
SARNO, Peter	5-11	185	L	Toronto, Ont.	7/26/79	Edmonton-Tor (AHL)-Manitoba
SEDIN, Daniel	6-1	200	L	Ornskoldsvik, Sweden	9/26/80	Vancouver
SEDIN, Henrik	6-2	200	L	Ornskoldsvik, Sweden	9/26/80	Vancouver
SMITH, Nathan	6-2	192	L	Edmonton, Alta.	2/9/82	Vancouver-Manitoba
SMITH, Tim	5-9	160	L	Whitecourt, Alta.	7/21/81	Columbia-Manitoba
DEFENSEMEN						
AITKEN, Johnathan	6-4	230	L	Edmonton, Alta.	5/24/78	Chicago-Norfolk
ALLEN, Bryan	6-4	220	L	Kingston, Ont.	8/21/80	Vancouver
BIEKSA, Kevin	6-1	190	R	Grimsby, Ont.	6/16/81	Bowling Green-Manitoba
BROOKBANK, Wade	6-4	225	L	Lanigan, Sask.	9/29/77	Nsh-Milwaukee-Binghamton-Van-Manitoba
JOVANOVSKI, Ed	6-2	210	L	Windsor, Ont.	6/26/76	Vancouver
KOLTSOV, Kirill	5-11	183	L	Chelyabinsk, USSR	2/1/83	Manitoba
MALIK, Marek	6-5	215	L	Ostrava, Czech.	6/24/75	Vancouver
MOJZIS, Tomas	6-1	186	L	Kolin, Czech.	5/2/82	Manitoba
OHLUND, Mattias	6-2	220	L	Pitea, Sweden	9/9/76	Vancouver
SALO, Sami	6-3	215	R	Turku, Finland	9/2/74	Vancouver
SOPEL, Brent	6-1	205	R	Calgary, Alta.	1/7/77	Vancouver

GOALTENDERS	HT	WT	C	Place of Birth	Date	2003-04 Club
AULD, Alexander	6-4	197	L	Cold Lake, Alta.	1/7/81	Vancouver-Manitoba
CLOUTIER, Dan	6-1	182	L	Mont-Laurier, Que.	4/22/76	Vancouver
FLAHERTY, Wade	6-0	185	L	Terrace, B.C.	1/11/68	Milwaukee
McVICAR, Rob	6-4	195	L	Hay River, NWT	1/15/82	Manitoba-Columbia

Vice President and General Manager

NONIS, DAVID
Senior Vice President/General Manager, Vancouver Canucks.
Born in Burnaby, B.C., May 25, 1966.

David Nonis was given his first assignment as general manager of an NHL hockey club when he was named to the position by the Vancouver Canucks on May 6, 2004. Nonis had spent the previous six seasons as senior vice president, director of hockey operations and was the Canucks' chief negotiator of player contracts. In his first act as general manager, Nonis appointed Steve Tambellini assistant general manager.

A native of Vancouver, Nonis broke into the NHL with the Canucks in 1990. In his first years he was primarily responsible for corporate contracts, computer scouting and team services. Prior to being named senior vice president in 1998, Nonis served as the National Hockey League's manager of hockey operations for four seasons. In his role with the NHL, Nonis gained a vast knowledge of the collective bargaining agreement and helped finalize sections of the document when the previous edition was drafted during the 1994-95 season. He also worked with the league's arbitration team, which included helping teams prepare for arbitration, researching salaries and interpreting contract language.

Nonis played for the Burnaby Blackhawks of the British Columbia Junior Hockey League from 1982 to 1984. He then played for the University of Maine where he served as captain for two seasons and graduated with a B.A. in 1988. Nonis played one season professionally in Denmark, then returned to Maine in 1989 to serve as graduate assistant under head coach Shawn Walsh. Nonis earned an MBA from the University of Maine in 1990.

2003-04 Scoring

* - rookie

Regular Season

Pos	#	Player	Team	GP	G	A	Pts	+/–	PIM	PP	SH	GW	GT	S	%
L	19	Markus Naslund	VAN	78	35	49	84	24	58	5	0	6	0	296	11.8
C	7	Brendan Morrison	VAN	82	22	38	60	16	50	5	1	4	1	161	13.7
R	44	Todd Bertuzzi	VAN	69	17	43	60	21	122	8	0	2	0	156	10.9
L	22	Daniel Sedin	VAN	82	18	36	54	18	18	1	0	3	0	153	11.8
L	26	Martin Rucinsky	NYR	69	13	29	42	13	62	0	1	2	0	161	8.1
			VAN	13	1	2	3	2	10	0	0	0	0	45	2.2
			TOTAL	82	14	31	45	15	72	0	1	2	0	206	6.8
C	33	Henrik Sedin	VAN	76	11	31	42	23	32	2	0	2	2	99	11.1
D	3	Brent Sopel	VAN	80	10	32	42	11	36	6	0	2	0	173	5.8
L	14	Geoff Sanderson	CBJ	67	13	16	29	–9	34	5	0	1	0	191	6.8
			VAN	13	3	4	7	–1	4	1	0	1	1	36	8.3
			TOTAL	80	16	20	36	–10	38	6	0	2	1	227	7.0
C	16	Trevor Linden	VAN	82	14	22	36	–6	26	4	0	1	1	97	14.4
D	2	Mattias Ohlund	VAN	82	14	20	34	14	73	5	0	3	1	129	10.9
D	6	Sami Salo	VAN	74	7	19	26	8	22	5	0	2	0	143	4.9
C	24	Matt Cooke	VAN	53	11	12	23	5	73	1	1	4	0	79	13.9
D	55	Ed Jovanovski	VAN	56	7	16	23	2	64	2	0	1	1	143	4.9
C	17	* Jason King	VAN	47	12	9	21	0	8	6	0	1	0	107	11.2
C	13	Artem Chubarov	VAN	65	12	7	19	1	14	1	1	3	0	93	12.9
D	8	Marek Malik	VAN	78	3	16	19	35	45	0	0	0	0	61	4.9
L	9	Mike Keane	VAN	64	8	9	17	7	20	0	0	2	0	41	19.5
L	21	Magnus Arvedson	VAN	41	8	7	15	7	12	2	0	4	0	54	14.8
L	37	Jarkko Ruutu	VAN	71	6	8	14	–13	133	1	0	0	1	70	8.6
L	10	Brad May	VAN	70	5	6	11	–2	137	0	0	0	0	75	6.7
D	23	Marc Bergevin	PIT	52	1	8	9	–8	27	0	0	0	1	23	4.3
			VAN	9	0	2	2	2	2	0	0	0	0	7	0.0
			TOTAL	61	1	10	11	–6	29	0	0	0	1	30	3.3
D	5	Bryan Allen	VAN	74	2	5	7	–10	94	0	0	0	0	70	2.9
C	20	* Ryan Kesler	VAN	28	2	3	5	–2	16	0	0	0	0	23	8.7
R	32	Tyler Bouck	VAN	18	1	2	3	–4	23	0	1	0	0	12	8.3
D	4	Nolan Baumgartner	PIT	5	0	0	0	–7	2	0	0	0	0	6	0.0
			VAN	9	0	3	3	3	2	0	0	0	0	9	0.0
			TOTAL	14	0	3	3	–4	4	0	0	0	0	15	0.0
D	28	* Wade Brookbank	NSH	9	0	0	0	–4	38	0	0	0	0	1	0.0
			VAN	20	2	0	2	3	95	0	0	1	0	6	33.3
			TOTAL	29	2	0	2	–1	133	0	0	1	0	7	28.6
R	15	* Pat Kavanagh	VAN	3	1	0	1	0	0	0	0	0	0	1	100.0
D	23	* Martin Grenier	VAN	7	1	0	1	3	9	0	0	0	0	6	16.7
C	15	Sean Pronger	VAN	3	0	1	1	–1	4	0	0	0	0	6	0.0
C	14	* Brandon Reid	VAN	3	0	1	1	1	0	0	0	0	0	2	0.0
C	18	* Fedor Fedorov	VAN	8	0	1	1	0	4	0	0	0	0	10	0.0
C	29	* Nathan Smith	VAN	2	0	0	0	–1	0	0	0	0	0	1	0.0

Goaltending

No.	Goaltender	GPI	Mins	Avg	W	L	T	EN	SO	GA	SA	S%	G	A	PIM
35	* Alexander Auld	6	349	2.06	2	2	2	0	0	12	168	.929	0	0	0
39	Dan Cloutier	60	3539	2.27	33	21	6	2	5	134	1554	.914	0	1	22
1	Johan Hedberg	21	1098	2.51	8	6	2	0	3	46	459	.900	0	0	10
	Totals	**82**	**5015**	**2.32**	**43**	**29**	**10**	**2**	**8**	**194**	**2183**	**.911**			

Playoffs

Pos	#	Player	Team	GP	G	A	Pts	+/–	PIM	PP	SH	GW	GT	S	%
L	19	Markus Naslund	VAN	7	2	7	9	1	2	2	0	0	0	32	6.3
C	7	Brendan Morrison	VAN	7	2	3	5	2	8	1	0	1	1	13	15.4
D	2	Mattias Ohlund	VAN	7	1	4	5	–6	13	0	0	1	0	15	6.7
C	24	Matt Cooke	VAN	7	3	1	4	3	12	0	0	1	0	15	20.0
C	33	Henrik Sedin	VAN	7	2	2	4	0	2	2	0	0	0	11	18.2
D	55	Ed Jovanovski	VAN	7	0	4	4	2	6	0	0	0	0	17	0.0
D	6	Sami Salo	VAN	7	1	2	3	–3	2	1	0	0	0	19	5.3
L	22	Daniel Sedin	VAN	7	1	2	3	0	0	1	0	0	0	13	7.7
L	14	Geoff Sanderson	VAN	7	1	1	2	–1	4	0	0	0	0	10	10.0
L	26	Martin Rucinsky	VAN	7	1	1	2	–3	6	1	0	0	0	15	6.7
L	10	Brad May	VAN	6	1	0	1	–3	6	0	0	0	0	6	16.7
L	37	Jarkko Ruutu	VAN	6	1	0	1	–3	10	0	0	0	0	2	50.0
D	3	Brent Sopel	VAN	7	0	1	1	–4	0	0	0	0	0	16	0.0
C	13	Artem Chubarov	VAN	7	0	1	1	–3	0	0	0	0	0	5	0.0
R	32	Tyler Bouck	VAN	1	0	0	0	–1	0	0	0	0	0	0	0.0
C	17	* Jason King	VAN	1	0	0	0	0	0	0	0	0	0	0	0.0
D	23	Marc Bergevin	VAN	3	0	0	0	0	2	0	0	0	0	2	0.0
D	5	Bryan Allen	VAN	4	0	0	0	0	2	0	0	0	0	1	0.0
L	9	Mike Keane	VAN	7	0	0	0	–3	4	0	0	0	0	4	0.0
C	16	Trevor Linden	VAN	7	0	0	0	–3	6	0	0	0	0	4	0.0
D	8	Marek Malik	VAN	7	0	0	0	1	10	0	0	0	0	6	0.0

Goaltending

No.	Goaltender	GPI	Mins	Avg	W	L	EN	SO	GA	SA	S%	G	A	PIM
39	Dan Cloutier	3	138	2.17	1	1	0	0	5	64	.922	0	0	2
35	* Alexander Auld	3	222	2.43	1	2	0	0	9	88	.898	0	0	0
1	Johan Hedberg	2	98	2.45	1	1	1	0	4	51	.922	0	0	0
	Totals	**7**	**464**	**2.46**	**3**	**4**	**1**	**0**	**19**	**204**	**.907**			

Coaching History

Hal Laycoe, 1970-71, 1971-72; Vic Stasiuk, 1972-73; Bill McCreary and Phil Maloney, 1973-74; Phil Maloney, 1974-75, 1975-76; Phil Maloney and Orland Kurtenbach, 1976-77; Orland Kurtenbach, 1977-78; Harry Neale, 1978-79 to 1980-81; Harry Neale and Roger Neilson, 1981-82; Roger Neilson, 1982-83; Roger Neilson and Harry Neale, 1983-84; Bill Laforge and Harry Neale, 1984-85; Tom Watt, 1985-86, 1986-87; Bob McCammon, 1987-88 to 1989-90; Bob McCammon and Pat Quinn, 1990-91; Pat Quinn, 1991-92 to 1993-94; Rick Ley, 1994-95; Rick Ley and Pat Quinn, 1995-96; Tom Renney, 1996-97; Tom Renney and Mike Keenan, 1997-98; Mike Keenan and Marc Crawford, 1998-99; Marc Crawford, 1999-2000 to date.

Club Records

Team

(Figures in brackets for season records are games played; records for fewest points, wins, ties, losses, goals, goals against are for 70 or more games)

Most Points **104** 2002-03 (82)
Most Wins **46** 1992-93 (84)
Most Ties **20** 1980-81 (80)
Most Losses **50** 1971-72 (78)
Most Goals **346** 1992-93 (84)
Most Goals Against **401** 1984-85 (80)
Fewest Points **48** 1971-72 (78)
Fewest Wins **20** 1971-72 (78), 1977-78 (80)
Fewest Ties **3** 1993-94 (84)
Fewest Losses **24** 2002-03 (82)
Fewest Goals **192** 1998-99 (82)
Fewest Goals Against **194** 2003-04 (82)
Longest Winning Streak
Overall .... **10** Nov. 9-30/02
Home .... **9** Nov. 6-Dec. 9/92
Away .... **8** Dec. 20/03-Jan. 13/04
Longest Undefeated Streak
Overall .... **14** Jan.26-Feb. 25/03 (10 wins, 4 ties)
Home .... **18** Nov. 4/92-Jan. 16/93 (16 wins, 2 ties)
Away .... **9** Feb. 4-Mar. 3/03 (6 wins, 3 ties)
Longest Losing Streak
Overall .... **10** Oct. 23-Nov. 11/97
Home .... **6** Dec. 18/70-Jan. 20/71
Away .... **12** Nov. 28/81-Feb. 6/82
Longest Winless Streak
Overall .... **13** Nov. 9-Dec. 7/73 (10 losses, 3 ties)
Home .... **11** Dec. 18/70-Feb. 6/71 (10 losses, 1 tie)
Away .... **20** Jan. 2-Apr. 2/86 (14 losses, 6 ties)
Most Shutouts, Season **8** 1974-75 (80), 2001-02 (82)
Most PIM, Season **2,326** 1992-93 (84)
Most Goals, Game .... **11** Mar. 28/71 (Cal. 5 at Van. 11), Nov. 25/86 (L.A. 5 at Van. 11), Mar. 1/92 (Cgy. 0 at Van. 11)

Individual

Most Seasons .... **13** Stan Smyl
Most Games .... **919** Trevor Linden
Most Goals, Career .... **292** Trevor Linden
Most Assists, Career .... **411** Stan Smyl
Most Points, Career .... **680** Trevor Linden (292G, 388A)
Most PIM, Career .... **2,127** Gino Odjick
Most Shutouts, Career .... **20** Kirk McLean
Longest Consecutive Games Streak .... **482** Trevor Linden (Oct. 4/90-Dec. 7/96)
Most Goals, Season .... **60** Pavel Bure (1992-93, 1993-94)
Most Assists, Season .... **62** André Boudrias (1974-75)
Most Points, Season .... **110** Pavel Bure (1992-93; 60G, 50A)
Most PIM, Season .... **372** Donald Brashear (1997-98)
Most Points, Defenseman, Season .... **63** Doug Lidster (1986-87; 12G, 51A)
Most Points, Center, Season .... **91** Patrik Sundstrom (1983-84; 38G, 53A)
Most Points, Right Wing, Season .... **110** Pavel Bure (1992-93; 60G, 50A)
Most Points, Left Wing, Season .... **104** Markus Naslund (2002-03; 48G, 56A)
Most Points, Rookie, Season .... **60** Ivan Hlinka (1981-82; 23G, 37A), Pavel Bure (1991-92; 34G, 26A)
Most Shutouts, Season .... **7** Dan Cloutier (2001-02)
Most Goals, Game .... **4** Eleven times
Most Assists, Game .... **6** Patrik Sundstrom (Feb. 29/84)
Most Points, Game .... **7** Patrik Sundstrom (Feb. 29/84; 1G, 6A)

Retired Numbers

12	Stan Smyl	1978-1991

General Managers' History

Bud Poile, 1970-71 to 1972-73; Hal Laycoe, 1973-74; Phil Maloney, 1974-75 to 1976-77; Jake Milford, 1977-78 to 1981-82; Harry Neale, 1982-83 to 1984-85; Jack Gordon, 1985-86, 1986-87; Pat Quinn, 1987-88 to 1997-98; Brian Burke, 1998-99 to 2003-04; David Nonis, 2004-05.

Captains' History

Orland Kurtenbach, 1970-71 to 1973-74; no captain, 1974-75; Andre Boudrias, 1975-76; Chris Oddleifson, 1976-77; Don Lever, 1977-78; Don Lever and Kevin McCarthy, 1978-79; Kevin McCarthy, 1979-80 to 1981-82; Stan Smyl, 1982-83 to 1989-90; Dan Quinn, Doug Lidster and Trevor Linden, 1990-91; Trevor Linden, 1991-92 to 1996-97; Mark Messier, 1997-98 to 1999-2000; Markus Naslund, 2000-01 to date.

All-time Record vs. Other Clubs

Regular Season

	At Home								On Road								Total							
	GP	W	L	T	OL	GF	GA	PTS	GP	W	L	T	OL	GF	GA	PTS	GP	W	L	T	OL	GF	GA	PTS
Anaheim	26	16	8	2	0	91	59	34	25	11	7	7	0	74	59	29	51	27	15	9	0	165	118	63
Atlanta	3	1	1	1	0	10	5	3	3	2	1	0	0	12	11	4	6	3	2	1	0	22	16	7
Boston	51	16	26	8	1	166	209	41	52	7	37	7	1	124	217	22	103	23	63	15	2	290	426	63
Buffalo	52	25	16	11	0	193	162	61	52	18	26	8	0	152	186	44	104	43	42	19	0	345	348	105
Calgary	99	36	44	18	1	335	327	91	98	26	57	15	0	283	392	67	197	62	101	33	1	618	719	158
Carolina	30	14	10	6	0	105	81	34	29	12	12	5	0	100	94	29	59	26	22	11	0	205	175	63
Chicago	72	35	22	15	0	218	210	85	71	17	45	7	2	164	267	43	143	52	67	22	2	382	477	128
Colorado	47	17	22	7	1	153	181	42	47	17	21	8	1	133	157	43	94	34	43	15	2	286	338	85
Columbus	8	6	2	0	0	34	23	12	8	4	1	2	1	29	17	11	16	10	3	2	1	63	40	23
Dallas	71	31	29	10	1	252	218	73	71	22	37	12	0	211	259	56	142	53	66	22	1	463	477	129
Detroit	65	29	26	10	0	235	210	68	66	17	40	8	1	188	275	43	131	46	66	18	1	423	485	111
Edmonton	82	32	37	12	1	295	320	77	81	25	47	7	2	256	356	59	163	57	84	19	3	551	676	136
Florida	9	3	1	5	0	25	19	11	8	4	3	1	0	27	21	9	17	7	4	6	0	52	40	20
Los Angeles	97	50	31	16	0	365	300	116	99	32	50	16	1	310	393	81	196	82	81	32	1	675	693	197
Minnesota	10	4	2	3	1	28	26	12	11	4	5	2	0	27	27	10	21	8	7	5	1	55	53	22
Montreal	55	14	33	8	0	146	202	36	53	10	38	5	0	135	244	25	108	24	71	13	0	281	446	61
Nashville	12	9	2	1	0	48	28	19	13	7	5	1	0	40	35	15	25	16	7	2	0	88	63	34
New Jersey	47	27	9	11	0	175	130	65	49	23	20	6	0	159	151	52	96	50	29	17	0	334	281	117
NY Islanders	47	23	21	3	0	155	153	49	47	11	25	10	1	129	174	33	94	34	46	13	1	284	327	82
NY Rangers	51	15	33	3	0	163	204	33	54	11	38	5	0	139	237	27	105	26	71	8	0	302	441	60
Ottawa	11	5	5	1	0	33	26	11	10	4	5	1	0	24	24	9	21	9	10	2	0	57	50	20
Philadelphia	51	10	28	12	1	144	203	33	54	16	36	1	1	159	234	34	105	26	64	13	2	303	437	67
Phoenix	72	43	18	10	1	272	201	97	69	26	32	10	1	245	256	63	141	69	50	20	2	517	457	160
Pittsburgh	50	23	23	4	0	180	187	50	50	10	33	7	0	171	227	27	100	33	56	11	0	351	414	77
St. Louis	72	30	33	9	0	214	230	69	71	21	41	9	0	205	265	51	143	51	74	18	0	419	495	120
San Jose	32	18	10	4	0	115	84	40	34	16	13	5	0	106	98	37	66	34	23	9	0	221	182	77
Tampa Bay	9	7	0	2	0	40	17	16	9	6	3	0	0	37	31	12	18	13	3	2	0	77	48	28
Toronto	64	29	22	11	2	225	216	71	60	21	28	11	0	195	219	53	124	50	50	22	2	420	435	124
Washington	39	18	15	5	1	136	123	42	40	14	21	4	1	120	132	33	79	32	36	9	2	256	255	75
Defunct Clubs	19	14	3	2	0	82	48	30	19	10	8	1	0	71	68	21	38	24	11	3	0	153	116	51
Totals	**1353**	**600**	**532**	**210**	**11**	**4633**	**4402**	**1421**	**1353**	**424**	**735**	**181**	**13**	**4025**	**5126**	**1042**	**2706**	**1024**	**1267**	**391**	**24**	**8658**	**9528**	**2463**

Playoffs

	Series	W	L	GP	W	L	T	GF	GA	Last Mtg.	Rnd.	Result
Buffalo	2	0	2	7	1	6	0	14	28	1981	PRE	L 0-3
Calgary	6	2	4	32	15	17	0	96	101	2004	CQF	L 3-4
Chicago	2	1	1	9	4	5	0	24	24	1995	CSF	L 0-4
Colorado	2	0	2	10	2	8	0	26	40	2001	CQF	L 0-4
Dallas	1	1	0	5	4	1	0	18	11	1994	CSF	W 4-1
Detroit	1	0	1	6	2	4	0	16	22	2002	CQF	L 2-4
Edmonton	2	0	2	9	2	7	0	20	35	1992	DF	L 2-4
Los Angeles	3	1	2	17	8	9	0	60	66	1993	DF	L 2-4
Minnesota	1	0	1	7	3	4	0	17	26	2003	CSF	L 3-4
Montreal	1	0	1	5	1	4	0	9	20	1975	QF	L 1-4
NY Islanders	2	0	2	6	0	6	0	14	26	1982	F	L 0-4
NY Rangers	1	0	1	7	3	4	0	19	21	1994	F	L 3-4
Philadelphia	1	0	1	3	1	2	0	9	15	1979	PRE	L 1-2
St. Louis	2	2	0	14	8	6	0	44	48	2003	CQF	W 4-3
Toronto	1	1	0	5	4	1	0	16	9	1994	CF	W 4-1
Winnipeg	2	2	0	13	8	5	0	50	34	1993	DSF	W 4-2
Totals	**30**	**10**	**20**	**155**	**66**	**89**	**0**	**452**	**526**			

Playoff Results 2004-2000

Year	Round	Opponent	Result	GF	GA
2004	CQF	Calgary	L 3-4	16	19
2003	CSF	Minnesota	L 3-4	17	26
	CQF	St. Louis	W 4-3	17	21
2002	CQF	Detroit	L 2-4	16	22
2001	CQF	Colorado	L 0-4	9	16

Abbreviations: Round: F – Final; **CF** – conference final; **CSF** – conference semi-final; **CQF** – conference quarter-final; **DF** – division final; **DSF** – division semi-final; **QF** – quarter-final; **PRE** – preliminary round.

Calgary totals include Atlanta Flames, 1972-73 to 1979-80. Carolina totals include Hartford, 1979-80 to 1996-97.
Colorado totals include Quebec, 1979-80 to 1994-95. Dallas totals include Minnesota North Stars, 1970-71 to 1992-93.
New Jersey totals include Kansas City, 1974-75 to 1975-76, and Colorado Rockies, 1976-77 to 1981-82.
Phoenix totals include Winnipeg, 1979-80 to 1995-96.

2003-04 Results

Oct.	9	Calgary	4-1		8	at Los Angeles	3-1
	11	Edmonton	3-0		9	at Anaheim	5-2
	13	at Columbus	2-3		11	Florida	2-2
	16	at Detroit	2-3		13	at Phoenix	4-1
	18	at Minnesota	2-2		15	at San Jose	1-3
	20	Buffalo	6-1		17	Anaheim	1-2
	22	St. Louis	3-2		19	Dallas	2-3
	26	Phoenix	3-3		21	Tampa Bay	5-4*
	28	Columbus	6-3		25	Nashville	4-1
	30	at Los Angeles	3-1		27	Chicago	3-2
	31	at Phoenix	4-1		29	at St. Louis	4-2
Nov.	3	Detroit	5-1		31	at Washington	6-1
	5	at Nashville	4-3	**Feb.**	2	at NY Rangers	3-4
	6	at St. Louis	2-3		3	at NY Islanders	4-5*
	8	Minnesota	4-3		5	at New Jersey	4-0
	11	at Minnesota	0-1		11	Calgary	2-3
	13	at Philadelphia	3-4*		13	Atlanta	1-4
	15	at Boston	1-2*		14	Anaheim	1-2
	18	Montreal	5-4*		16	at Colorado	1-0
	20	Chicago	3-2*		19	at Minnesota	2-6
	22	Toronto	3-5		21	at Edmonton	3-4*
	24	at Toronto	1-2		24	Detroit	4-2
	25	at Montreal	5-2		26	San Jose	3-2*
	27	at Ottawa	3-2*		28	St. Louis	2-0
	29	at Calgary	4-4	**Mar.**	3	at Colorado	5-5
Dec.	4	Calgary	1-4		5	at Detroit	1-3
	6	Minnesota	1-1		6	at Columbus	4-0
	9	Pittsburgh	4-3*		8	Colorado	2-9
	11	Colorado	1-1		10	Minnesota	1-1
	14	Carolina	2-1*		12	at Edmonton	4-3*
	16	at Nashville	2-1*		13	Ottawa	1-2
	17	at Dallas	1-3		16	Nashville	2-2
	20	at Edmonton	3-0		18	at Dallas	0-3
	22	Los Angeles	4-4		19	at Chicago	3-4*
	26	at Calgary	2-0		21	Columbus	4-5
	27	Edmonton	2-6		24	Los Angeles	1-0
	29	at Colorado	3-2		27	Dallas	3-2*
	31	at Chicago	4-3*		29	Phoenix	6-1
Jan.	2	Colorado	2-4		31	at Anaheim	2-1
	3	at Calgary	3-1	**Apr.**	2	at San Jose	4-1
	5	San Jose	1-2		3	Edmonton	5-2

* – Overtime

Entry Draft
Selections 2004-1990

2004 Pick		2000 Pick		1996 Pick		1992	
26	Cory Schneider	23	Nathan Smith	12	Josh Holden	21	Libor Polasek
91	Alexander Edler	71	Thatcher Bell	75	Zenith Komarniski	40	Michael Peca
125	Andrew Sarauer	93	Tim Branham	93	Jonas Soling	45	Mike Fountain
159	Mike Brown	144	Pavel Duma	121	Tyler Prosofsky	69	Jeff Connolly
189	Julien Ellis-Plante	208	Brandon Reid	147	Nolan McDonald	93	Brent Tully
254	David Schulz	241	Nathan Barrett	175	Clint Cabana	110	Brian Loney
287	Jannik Hansen	272	Tim Smith	201	Jeff Scissons	117	Adrian Aucoin
				227	Lubomir Vaic	141	Jason Clark
2003 Pick		**1999 Pick**				165	Scott Hollis
23	Ryan Kesler	2	Daniel Sedin	**1995 Pick**		213	Sonny Mignacca
60	Marc-Andre Bernier	3	Henrik Sedin	40	Chris McAllister	237	Mark Wotton
111	Brandon Nolan	69	Rene Vydareny	61	Larry Courville	261	Aaron Boh
128	Ty Morris	129	Ryan Thorpe	66	Peter Schaefer		
160	Nicklas Danielsson	172	Josh Reed	92	Lloyd Shaw	**1991 Pick**	
190	Chad Brownlee	189	Kevin Swanson	120	Todd Norman	7	Alek Stojanov
222	Francois-Pierre Guenette	218	Markus Kankaanpera	144	Brent Sopel	29	Jassen Cullimore
252	Sergei Topol	271	Darrell Hay	170	Stewart Bodtker	51	Sean Pronger
254	Nathan Mciver			196	Tyler Willis	95	Dan Kesa
285	Matthew Hansen	**1998 Pick**		222	Jason Cugnet	117	John Namestnikov
		4	Bryan Allen			139	Brent Thurston
2002 Pick		31	Artem Chubarov	**1994 Pick**		161	Eric Johnson
49	Kirill Koltsov	68	Jarkko Ruutu	13	Mattias Ohlund	183	David Neilson
55	Denis Grot	81	Justin Morrison	39	Robb Gordon	205	Brad Barton
68	Brett Skinner	90	Regan Darby	42	Dave Scatchard	227	Jason Fitzsimmons
83	Lukas Mensator	136	David Ytfeldt	65	Chad Allan	249	Xavier Majic
114	John Laliberte	140	Rick Bertran	92	Mike Dubinsky		
151	Rob McVicar	149	Paul Cabana	117	Yanick Dube	**1990 Pick**	
214	Marc-Andre Roy	177	Vincent Malts	169	Yuri Kuznetsov	2	Petr Nedved
223	Ilja Krikunov	204	Greg Mischler	195	Rob Trumbley	18	Shawn Antoski
247	Matt Violin	219	Curtis Valentine	221	Bill Muckalt	23	Jiri Slegr
277	Thomas Nussli	232	Jason Metcalfe	247	Tyson Nash	65	Darin Bader
278	Matt Gens	**1997 Pick**		273	Robert Longpre	86	Gino Odjick
		10	Brad Ference			128	Daryl Filipek
2001 Pick		34	Ryan Bonni	**1993 Pick**		149	Paul O'Hagan
16	R.J. Umberger	36	Harold Druken	20	Mike Wilson	170	Mark Cipriano
66	Fedor Fedorov	64	Kyle Freadrich	46	Rick Girard	191	Troy Neumier
114	Evgeny Gladskikh	90	Chris Stanley	98	Dieter Kochan	212	Tyler Ertel
151	Kevin Bieksa	114	David Darguzas	124	Scott Walker	233	Karri Kivi
212	Jason King	117	Matt Cockell	150	Troy Creurer		
245	Konstantin Mikhailov	144	Matt Cooke	176	Yevgeni Babariko		
		148	Larry Shapley	202	Sean Tallaire		
		171	Rod Leroux	254	Bert Robertsson		
		201	Denis Martynyuk	280	Sergei Tkachenko		
		227	Peter Brady				

Coach

CRAWFORD, MARC
Coach, Vancouver Canucks. Born in Belleville, Ont., February 13, 1961.

Marc Crawford became the Canucks' 15th head coach on January 24, 1999.

Crawford began his NHL coaching career with the Quebec Nordiques in 1994 and won a Stanley Cup in 1996 when the team moved to Denver to become the Colorado Avalanche. As coach of the Canucks, he led the team to 83 points in his first full season behind the bench in 1999-2000, then guided the Canucks back into the playoffs in 2000-01. Under Crawford, the Canucks recorded a franchise high 104 points in 2002-03 and won the Northwest Division title in 2003-04.

Crawford was the head coach for Team Canada at the 1998 Olympics and was an assistant at the 1996 World Cup of Hockey. He began his coaching career as a playing assistant with Fredericton (AHL) for the 1987-88 season. At the end of the year he moved to Milwaukee where he served as an assistant coach for the Canucks' IHL affiliate in 1988-89. He then moved to Cornwall where he served as the Royals' general manager and head coach in 1989-90.

After two seasons with Cornwall, Crawford went on to coach the St. John's Maple Leafs of the AHL before joining the Nordiques in 1994. He received the 1995 Jack Adams Award as the NHL coach of the year, becoming the first rookie coach to win the award since it was inaugurated in 1974.

Crawford played every game of his six-year NHL career with the Vancouver Canucks, recording 19 goals and 31 assists in 176 games.

Coaching Record

Season	Team	Games	Regular Season W	L	T	Playoffs Games	W	L
1989-90	Cornwall (OHL)	66	24	38	4	6	2	4
1990-91	Cornwall (OHL)	66	23	42	1	....	....	....
1991-92	St. John's (AHL)	80	39	29	12	16	11	5
1992-93	St. John's (AHL)	80	41	26	13	9	4	5
1993-94	St. John's (AHL)	80	45	23	12	11	6	5
1994-95	Quebec (NHL)	48	30	13	5	6	2	4
1995-96	Colorado (NHL)	82	47	25	10	22	16	6*
1996-97	Colorado (NHL)	82	49	24	9	17	10	7
1997-98	Colorado (NHL)	82	39	26	17	7	3	4
1998-99	Vancouver (NHL)	37	8	23	6	....	....	....
1999-2000	Vancouver (NHL)	82	30	37	15	....	....	....
2000-01	Vancouver (NHL)	82	36	35	11	4	0	4
2001-02	Vancouver (NHL)	82	42	33	7	6	2	4
2002-03	Vancouver (NHL)	82	45	24	13	14	7	7
2003-04	Vancouver (NHL)	82	43	29	10	7	3	4
	NHL Totals	**741**	**369**	**269**	**103**	**83**	**43**	**40**

* Stanley Cup win.

Club Directory

Vancouver Canucks
General Motors Place
800 Griffiths Way
Vancouver, B.C. V6B 6G1
Phone **604/899-4600**
FAX 604/899-4640
www.canucks.com
Capacity: 18,630

General Motors Place

Executive
Chairman, OBSE; Governor, NHL	John E. McCaw Jr.
President, Chief Executive Officer	Stanley B. McCammon
Senior Vice President, General Manager & Alternate Governor	David M. Nonis
Chief Operating Officer	TBD
Corporate Counsel	James Conrad
Vice President, Finance	Victor de Bonis
Vice President, People Development	Susanne Haine
Vice President, Broadcast & New Media	Chris Hebb
Vice President & G.M., Arena Operations	Harvey Jones
Vice President, Customer Sales & Service	John Rocha
Vice President, Business Development	Ric Thomsen
Executive Assistant	Wendy Bennett

Hockey Operations
Senior Vice President, General Manager & Alternate Governor	David M. Nonis
Executive Assistant	Chris Stephens
Vice President & Assistant General Manager	Steve Tambellini
Head Coach	Marc Crawford
Associate Coaches	Jack McIlhargey, Mike Johnston
Director, Player Development	Stan Smyl
Director, Player Personnel	Bob Murray
General Manager, Manitoba Moose	Craig Heisinger
Head Coach, Manitoba Moose	Randy Carlyle
Assistant Coach, Manitoba Moose	Eric Crawford
Assistant Coach, Video	Barry Smith
Strength & Conditioning Coach	Roger Takahashi
Goaltending Coach	Ian Clark
Senior Editor, Alumni Liaison	Norm Jewison
Director, Media Relations	Chris Brumwell
Manager, Media Relations	T.C. Carling
Coordinator, Media & Team Services	TBD
Director, Community Relations	TBD
Manager, Community Relations	Allanah Mooney
Accountant, Canucks for Kids Fund	Maria Haycock

Scouting
Chief Scout	Ron Delorme
Professional Scout	Lucien DeBlois
European Scout	Thomas Gradin
Russian Scout	Sergei Chibisov
Amateur Scouts	Jack McCartan, Barry Dean, Mario Marois, John McMorrow, Gary Lupul, Ken Slater, Tim Lenardon, Branislav Pulis
Coordinator, Scouting & Player Information	Jonathan Wall

Medical and Training Staff
Medical Trainer	Mike Burnstein
Assistant Medical Trainers	Jon Sanderson, Marty Dudgeon
Equipment Manager	Pat O'Neill
Assistant Equipment Manager	Darren Granger
Assistant Equipment Trainer	Jamie Hendricks
Game Dressing Room Attendants	John Jukitch, Ron Shute, Brian Hamilton
Team Doctors	Dr. Rui Avelar, Dr. Bill Regan
Team Dentist	Dr. David Lawson
Team Chiropractor	Dr. Sid Sheard
Team Optometrist	Dr. Alan R. Boyco

Corporate Communications
Manager, Creative Services	Jackie Boucher
Photo Editor/Librarian	Kathy McAdam
Graphic Designers	Ken Jones, Kim Sissons

Broadcast
Director, Facilities and In-house Productions	Paul Brettell
Director, Production Services	Mike Hall
Director, Technical Services	Vic Araujo
Radio Affiliation	CKNW 98 (AM 980)
Television Affiliation	Sportsnet (Channel 22)

Business Development
Directors, Business Development	David Altman, Sharon Butler, Dave Cannon, Tom Mauthe
Sr. Manager, Suite and Sponsorship Services	Darren Moscovitch
Manager, Suite and Sponsorship Services	Deborah Boren
Manager, Business Development	Lui Garcea

Customer Sales and Service
Director, Customer Sales & Service	Caley Denton
Director, Customer Sales	Jordan Thorsteinson
Managers, Customer Sales	Greg Kettner, Andrew Merai
Account Managers	Josh Bender, Martha Vassos

Marketing and Game Entertainment
Director, Marketing	Paul Dal Monte

Central Services, Travel, People Development
Director of Finance	Chris Samis
Assistant Controllers	Patricia Bigonzi, Miranda Meyer
Travel Manager	Cathie Moroney
Manager, People Development	Tracey Arnish (Brenda Cholowski)

Authentix, Fan Apparel and Collectibles
Director, Merchandise	Dennis Kim
Merchandise Manager	TBD
Arena, Store Manager	Alan Cook

Washington Capitals

2003-04 Results: 23w-46L-10T-3OTL 59PTS.
Fifth, Southeast Division

2004-05 Schedule

Oct.
Sat. 16 at Atlanta
Tue. 19 Atlanta
Thu. 21 Montreal
Sat. 23 NY Islanders
Fri. 29 at Tampa Bay
Sun. 31 at Florida*

Nov. Wed. 3 New Jersey
Fri. 5 Ottawa
Sat. 6 at Philadelphia
Tue. 9 at Montreal
Thu. 11 Detroit
Sat. 13 New Jersey
Tue. 16 Phoenix
Thu. 18 Pittsburgh
Sat. 20 NY Islanders
Tue. 23 at Toronto
Wed. 24 Philadelphia
Fri. 26 NY Rangers*
Sun. 28 Florida*

Dec. Wed. 1 at Anaheim
Thu. 2 at Los Angeles
Sat. 4 at San Jose
Mon. 6 at NY Islanders
Thu. 9 at NY Rangers
Sat. 11 Atlanta
Tue. 14 NY Rangers
Fri. 17 Dallas
Sat. 18 at NY Islanders
Tue. 21 at Pittsburgh
Wed. 22 St. Louis
Sun. 26 Tampa Bay*
Tue. 28 Ottawa
Fri. 31 at Atlanta*

Jan. Sat. 1 Pittsburgh
Mon. 3 Nashville
Wed. 5 Carolina
Sat. 8 at Atlanta*
Sun. 9 Buffalo
Wed. 12 at Florida
Fri. 14 at Tampa Bay
Sun. 16 Minnesota*

Mon. 17 at Carolina
Thu. 20 at St. Louis
Sat. 22 Florida
Mon. 24 Philadelphia
Thu. 27 at Boston
Fri. 28 Montreal
Sun. 30 Atlanta

Feb. Tue. 1 at Ottawa
Thu. 3 at Toronto
Fri. 4 at Pittsburgh
Sun. 6 Boston*
Tue. 8 Tampa Bay
Thu. 10 at Buffalo
Tue. 15 at Boston
Sat. 19 at Phoenix
Sun. 20 at Dallas
Tue. 22 at Buffalo
Thu. 24 Colorado
Sat. 26 Carolina
Sun. 27 at Carolina

Mar. Tue. 1 Chicago
Thu. 3 at Philadelphia
Fri. 4 at New Jersey
Mon. 7 at NY Rangers
Tue. 8 at Montreal
Fri. 11 at Florida
Sat. 12 at Tampa Bay
Tue. 15 at Carolina
Wed. 16 Columbus
Fri. 18 Florida
Sun. 20 Toronto
Tue. 22 at Calgary
Thu. 24 at Vancouver
Sat. 26 at Edmonton
Mon. 28 at Ottawa
Thu. 31 Boston

Apr. Sat. 2 Tampa Bay
Mon. 4 Carolina
Wed. 6 Buffalo
Fri. 8 Toronto
Sat. 9 at New Jersey

* Denotes afternoon game.

Year-by-Year Record

Season	GP	Home W	L	T	OL	Road W	L	T	OL	Overall W	L	T	OL	GF	GA	Pts.	Finished	Playoff Result
2003-04	82	13	20	6	2	10	26	4	1	23	46	10	3	186	253	59	5th, Southeast Div.	Out of Playoffs
2002-03	82	24	13	2	...	15	16	6	4	39	29	8	6	224	220	92	2nd, Southeast Div.	Lost Conf. Quarter-Final
2001-02	82	21	12	6	2	15	21	5	0	36	33	11	2	228	240	85	2nd, Southeast Div.	Out of Playoffs
2000-01	82	24	9	6	2	17	18	4	2	41	27	10	4	233	211	96	1st, Southeast Div.	Lost Conf. Quarter-Final
1999-2000	82	26	5	8	2	18	19	4	0	44	24	12	2	227	194	102	1st, Southeast Div.	Lost Conf. Quarter-Final
1998-99	82	16	23	2	...	15	22	4	...	31	45	6	...	200	218	68	3rd, Southeast Div.	Out of Playoffs
1997-98	82	23	12	6	...	17	18	6	...	40	30	12	...	219	202	92	3rd, Atlantic Div.	Lost Final
1996-97	82	19	17	5	...	14	23	4	...	33	40	9	...	214	231	75	5th, Atlantic Div.	Out of Playoffs
1995-96	82	21	15	5	...	18	17	6	...	39	32	11	...	234	204	89	4th, Atlantic Div.	Lost Conf. Quarter-Final
1994-95	48	15	6	3	...	7	12	5	...	22	18	8	...	136	120	52	3rd, Atlantic Div.	Lost Conf. Quarter-Final
1993-94	84	17	16	9	...	22	19	1	...	39	35	10	...	277	263	88	3rd, Atlantic Div.	Lost Conf. Semi-Final
1992-93	84	21	15	6	...	22	19	1	...	43	34	7	...	325	286	93	2nd, Patrick Div.	Lost Div. Semi-Final
1991-92	80	25	12	3	...	20	15	5	...	45	27	8	...	330	275	98	2nd, Patrick Div.	Lost Div. Semi-Final
1990-91	80	21	14	5	...	16	22	2	...	37	36	7	...	258	258	81	3rd, Patrick Div.	Lost Div. Final
1989-90	80	19	18	3	...	17	20	3	...	36	38	6	...	284	275	78	3rd, Patrick Div.	Lost Conf. Championship
1988-89	80	25	12	3	...	16	17	7	...	41	29	10	...	305	259	92	1st, Patrick Div.	Lost Div. Semi-Final
1987-88	80	22	14	4	...	16	19	5	...	38	33	9	...	281	249	85	2nd, Patrick Div.	Lost Div. Final
1986-87	80	22	15	3	...	16	17	7	...	38	32	10	...	285	278	86	2nd, Patrick Div.	Lost Div. Semi-Final
1985-86	80	30	8	2	...	20	15	5	...	50	23	7	...	315	272	107	2nd, Patrick Div.	Lost Div. Final
1984-85	80	27	11	2	...	19	14	7	...	46	25	9	...	322	240	101	2nd, Patrick Div.	Lost Div. Semi-Final
1983-84	80	26	11	3	...	22	16	2	...	48	27	5	...	308	226	101	2nd, Patrick Div.	Lost Div. Final
1982-83	80	22	12	6	...	17	13	10	...	39	25	16	...	306	283	94	3rd, Patrick Div.	Lost Div. Semi-Final
1981-82	80	16	16	8	...	10	25	5	...	26	41	13	...	319	338	65	5th, Patrick Div.	Out of Playoffs
1980-81	80	16	17	7	...	10	19	11	...	26	36	18	...	286	317	70	5th, Patrick Div.	Out of Playoffs
1979-80	80	20	14	6	...	7	26	7	...	27	40	13	...	261	293	67	5th, Patrick Div.	Out of Playoffs
1978-79	80	15	19	6	...	9	22	9	...	24	41	15	...	273	338	63	4th, Norris Div.	Out of Playoffs
1977-78	80	10	23	7	...	7	26	7	...	17	49	14	...	195	321	48	5th, Norris Div.	Out of Playoffs
1976-77	80	17	15	8	...	7	27	6	...	24	42	14	...	221	307	62	4th, Norris Div.	Out of Playoffs
1975-76	80	6	26	8	...	5	33	2	...	11	59	10	...	224	394	32	5th, Norris Div.	Out of Playoffs
1974-75	80	7	28	5	...	1	39	0	...	8	67	5	...	181	446	21	5th, Norris Div.	Out of Playoffs

Brendan Witt is a hard-hitting defensive defenseman who focuses his energy on protecting his own net.

Franchise date: June 11, 1974

SOUTHEAST DIVISION

31st NHL Season

2004-05 Player Personnel

FORWARDS	HT	WT	S	Place of Birth	Date	2003-04 Club
AULIN, Jared	6-0	192	R	Calgary, Alta.	3/15/82	Portland (AHL)
FLEISCHMANN, Tomas	6-0	165	L	Koprivnice, Czech.	5/16/84	Moose Jaw
FUSSEY, Owen	6-0	195	L	Winnipeg, Man.	4/2/83	Washington-Portland (AHL)
GORDON, Boyd	6-0	198	R	Unity, Sask.	10/19/83	Washington-Portland (AHL)
HALPERN, Jeff	6-0	198	R	Potomac, MD	5/3/76	Washington
JOHANSSON, Jonas	6-1	180	R	Jonkoping, Sweden	3/18/84	Kamloops
KLEPIS, Jakub	6-0	200	R	Prague, Czech.	6/5/84	Slavia Praha
LAICH, Brooks	6-2	199	L	Wawota, Alta.	6/23/83	Ottawa-Binghamton-Washington-Portland (AHL)
MINK, Graham	6-3	217	R	Stowe, VT	5/21/79	Washington-Portland (AHL)
OVECHKIN, Alexander	6-2	212	R	Moscow, USSR	9/17/85	Dynamo Moscow
PEAT, Stephen	6-3	230	R	Princeton, B.C.	3/10/80	Washington
PETTINGER, Matt	6-1	205	L	Edmonton, Alta.	10/22/80	Washington
SEMIN, Alexander	6-0	181	L	Krasnoyarsk, USSR	3/3/84	Washington-Portland (AHL)
STROSHEIN, Garret	6-7	245	R	Edmonton, Alta.	4/4/80	Washington-Portland (AHL)
SUTHERBY, Brian	6-3	205	L	Edmonton, Alta.	3/1/82	Washington
VEROT, Darcy	6-0	199	L	Radville, Sask.	7/13/76	Washington-Portland (AHL)
WHITFIELD, Trent	5-11	204	L	Estevan, Sask.	6/17/77	Washington-Portland (AHL)
WILLSIE, Brian	6-1	195	R	London, Ont.	3/16/78	Washington
ZUBRUS, Dainius	6-4	226	L	Elektrenai, USSR	6/16/78	Washington
DEFENSEMEN						
BOUMEDIENNE, Josef	6-2	205	L	Stockholm, Sweden	1/12/78	Washington-Portland (AHL)
CUTTA, Jakub	6-3	210	L	Jablonec nad Nisou, Czech.	12/29/81	Washington-Portland (AHL)
DOIG, Jason	6-3	230	R	Montreal, Que.	1/29/77	Washington
EMINGER, Steve	6-2	203	R	Woodbridge, Ont.	10/31/83	Washington-Portland (AHL)
MORRISONN, Shaone	6-3	205	L	Vancouver, B.C.	12/23/82	Boston-Providence (AHL)-Washington-Portland (AHL)
PAUL, Jeff	6-4	225	R	London, Ont.	3/1/78	San Antonio-Hartford
WITT, Brendan	6-2	219	L	Humboldt, Sask.	2/20/75	Washington
YONKMAN, Nolan	6-6	245	R	Punnichy, Sask.	4/1/81	Washington-Portland (AHL)
ZINGER, Dwayne	6-4	216	L	Coronation, Alta.	7/5/76	Washington-Portland (AHL)
GOALTENDERS	HT	WT	C	Place of Birth	Date	2003-04 Club
DAIGNEAULT, Maxime	6-3	202	L	St-Jacques-le-Mineur, Que.	1/23/84	Val-d'Or
KOLZIG, Olie	6-3	225	L	Johannesburg, South Africa	4/6/70	Washington
OUELLET, Maxime	6-2	195	L	Beauport, Que.	6/17/81	Washington-Portland (AHL)
STANA, Rastislav	6-2	184	L	Kosice, Czech.	1/10/80	Washington-Portland (AHL)

2003-04 Scoring

* - rookie

Regular Season

Pos	#	Player	Team	GP	G	A	Pts	+/-	PIM	PP	SH	GW	GT	S	%
C	11	Jeff Halpern	WSH	79	19	27	46	-21	56	7	0	2	1	114	16.7
L	14	Kip Miller	WSH	66	9	22	31	-10	8	6	0	2	0	74	12.2
R	9	Dainius Zubrus	WSH	54	12	15	27	-16	38	6	1	2	1	115	10.4
L	28	* Alexander Semin	WSH	52	10	12	22	-2	36	4	0	2	0	92	10.9
R	24	Brian Willsie	WSH	49	10	5	15	-7	18	1	1	1	0	85	11.8
D	2	* Josef Boumedienne	WSH	37	2	12	14	-10	30	2	0	0	0	44	4.5
L	18	Matt Pettinger	WSH	71	7	5	12	-9	37	1	0	1	0	92	7.6
D	29	Joel Kwiatkowski	WSH	80	6	6	12	-28	89	2	0	0	1	90	6.7
D	19	Brendan Witt	WSH	72	2	10	12	-22	123	0	0	0	0	91	2.2
C	23	Trent Whitfield	WSH	44	6	5	11	-2	14	0	1	2	0	38	15.8
L	13	Bates Battaglia	COL	4	0	1	1	-1	4	0	0	0	0	1	0.0
			WSH	66	4	6	10	-23	38	0	1	0	0	69	5.8
			TOTAL	70	4	7	11	-24	42	0	1	0	0	70	5.7
L	27	Craig Johnson	ANA	39	1	2	3	-4	14	0	0	0	0	45	2.2
			TOR	10	1	1	2	0	6	0	0	0	0	12	8.3
			WSH	15	0	6	6	-6	8	0	0	0	0	20	0.0
			TOTAL	64	2	9	11	-10	28	0	0	0	0	77	2.6
D	3	Jason Doig	WSH	65	2	9	11	-12	105	0	0	0	0	59	3.4
D	26	* Shaone Morrisonn	BOS	30	1	7	8	10	10	0	0	0	0	13	7.7
			WSH	3	0	0	0	0	0	0	0	0	0	1	0.0
			TOTAL	33	1	7	8	10	10	0	0	0	0	14	7.1
R	15	* Boyd Gordon	WSH	41	1	5	6	-9	8	0	0	0	0	42	2.4
D	4	Rick Berry	WSH	65	0	6	6	-5	108	0	0	0	0	43	0.0
R	51	Stephen Peat	WSH	64	5	0	5	-10	90	0	0	0	0	21	23.8
R	34	J-Luc Grand-Pierre	CBJ	16	0	0	0	-3	12	0	0	0	0	15	0.0
			ATL	27	2	2	4	-7	26	0	1	0	0	19	10.5
			WSH	13	1	0	1	-2	14	0	0	0	0	19	5.3
			TOTAL	56	3	2	5	-12	52	0	1	0	0	53	5.7
D	38	Todd Rohloff	CBJ	24	0	2	2	-12	8	0	0	0	0	16	0.0
			WSH	35	0	3	3	-5	18	0	0	0	0	19	0.0
			TOTAL	59	0	5	5	-17	26	0	0	0	0	35	0.0
D	8	* Steve Eminger	WSH	41	0	4	4	-11	45	0	0	0	0	12	0.0
C	16	Brian Sutherby	WSH	30	2	0	2	-5	28	0	0	1	0	24	8.3
L	27	Ivan Ciernik	WSH	7	1	1	2	1	0	0	0	0	0	8	12.5
D	41	Brad Norton	L.A.	20	0	1	1	-1	77	0	0	0	0	10	0.0
			WSH	16	0	1	1	-4	17	0	0	0	0	6	0.0
			TOTAL	36	0	2	2	-5	94	0	0	0	0	16	0.0
C	76	Darcy Verot	WSH	37	0	2	2	-6	135	0	0	0	0	11	0.0
D	17	John Gruden	WSH	11	1	0	1	-1	6	0	0	1	0	7	14.3
R	63	* Owen Fussey	WSH	4	0	1	1	-1	0	0	0	0	0	1	0.0
C	21	* Brooks Laich	OTT	1	0	0	0	0	2	0	0	0	0	1	0.0
			WSH	4	0	1	1	-1	0	0	0	0	0	2	0.0
			TOTAL	5	0	1	1	-1	2	0	0	0	0	3	0.0
D	49	Dwayne Zinger	WSH	7	0	1	1	2	9	0	0	0	0	3	0.0
R	64	* Roman Tvrdon	WSH	9	0	1	1	-3	2	0	0	0	0	7	0.0
D	40	* Nolan Yonkman	WSH	1	0	0	0	0	0	0	0	0	0	0	0.0
L	69	Mel Angelstad	WSH	2	0	0	0	0	7	0	0	0	0	1	0.0
C	36	Colin Forbes	WSH	2	0	0	0	0	0	0	0	0	0	2	0.0
C	65	* Andrej Podkonicky	WSH	2	0	0	0	0	0	0	0	0	0	1	0.0
D	58	Jean-Francois Fortin	WSH	2	0	0	0	-1	0	0	0	0	0	0	0.0
L	39	Graham Mink	WSH	3	0	0	0	-1	2	0	0	0	0	4	0.0
D	36	* Jakub Cutta	WSH	3	0	0	0	0	0	0	0	0	0	1	0.0
R	56	* Garret Stroshein	WSH	3	0	0	0	-1	14	0	0	0	0	0	0.0
D	75	* Chris Hajt	WSH	5	0	0	0	0	0	0	0	0	0	1	0.0

Goaltending

No.	Goaltender	GPI	Mins	Avg	W	L	T	EN	SO	GA	SA	S%	G	A	PIM
37	Olaf Kolzig	63	3738	2.89	19	35	9	7	2	180	1958	.908	0	1	6
31	* Matthew Yeats	5	258	3.02	1	3	0	0	0	13	141	.908	0	0	2
33	* Maxime Ouellet	6	365	3.12	2	3	1	0	1	19	210	.910	0	1	0
1	* Rastislav Stana	6	211	3.13	1	2	0	0	0	11	100	.890	0	0	0
35	Sebastien Charpentier	7	369	3.41	0	6	0	2	0	21	168	.875	0	0	0
	Totals	82	4976	3.05	23	49	10	9	3	253	2586	.902			

Coach

HANLON, GLEN
Coach, Washington Capitals. Born in Brandon, Man., February 20, 1957.

Glen Hanlon was in his second season as an assistant coach when he was promoted to the position of head coach on December 10, 2003. Previously, Hanlon had served as head coach for Washington's minor-league affiliate, the Portland Pirates, for three seasons.

During his first season at the helm of the Pirates in 1999-2000, Hanlon was named the American Hockey League's coach of the year after guiding Portland to a 46-23-10-1 record and a league-best 48-point turnaround. The Pirates finished with 103 points overall, second best in the AHL's New England Division.

In three seasons leading the Pirates, Hanlon guided the club to two Calder Cup playoff appearances. He finished his tenure posting the second-highest win total (110) in Pirates history.

Before arriving in Portland, Hanlon served eight seasons with the Vancouver Canucks as an assistant coach (1994 to 1999) and goaltending coach (1991 to 1994). He helped lead the Canucks to their first 40-win season in franchise history in 1991-92, and the team advanced to the Stanley Cup Finals in 1994. He also served as an assistant coach with the Canadian national team at the 1998 World Championships in Zurich, Switzerland.

Hanlon appeared in 477 NHL games in 14 seasons as a goaltender between 1977 and 1991, playing with the Vancouver Canucks, St. Louis Blues, New York Rangers and Detroit Red Wings. He posted a career record of 167-202-61, a 3.60 goals-against average and 13 shutouts. He also played 35 career NHL playoff games, compiling an 11-15-0 record, a 3.14 goals-against average and four shutouts.

Coaching Record

			Regular Season				Playoffs		
Season	Team	Games	W	L	T	Games	W	L	
1999-00	Portland (AHL)	80	46	24	10	4	1	3	
2000-01	Portland (AHL)	80	34	42	4	3	0	3	
2001-02	Portland (AHL)	80	30	35	15	....	....	....	
2003-04	**Washington (NHL)**	**54**	**15**	**30**	**9**	....	....	....	
	NHL Totals	54	15	30	9	....	....	....	

Coaching History

Jim Anderson, Red Sullivan and Milt Schmidt, 1974-75; Milt Schmidt and Tom McVie, 1975-76; Tom McVie, 1976-77, 1977-78; Danny Belisle, 1978-79; Danny Belisle and Gary Green, 1979-80; Gary Green, 1980-81; Gary Green, Roger Crozier and Bryan Murray, 1981-82; Bryan Murray, 1982-83 to 1988-89; Bryan Murray and Terry Murray, 1989-90; Terry Murray, 1990-91 to 1992-93; Terry Murray and Jim Schoenfeld, 1993-94; Jim Schoenfeld, 1994-95 to 1996-97; Ron Wilson, 1997-98 to 2001-02; Bruce Cassidy, 2002-03; Bruce Cassidy and Glen Hanlon, 2003-04; Glen Hanlon, 2004-05.

Club Records

Team

(Figures in brackets for season records are games played; records for fewest points, wins, ties, losses, goals, goals against are for 70 or more games)

Most Points	107	1985-86 (80)	
Most Wins	50	1985-86 (80)	
Most Ties	18	1980-81 (80)	
Most Losses	67	1974-75 (80)	
Most Goals	330	1991-92 (80)	
Most Goals Against	*446	1974-75 (80)	
Fewest Points	*21	1974-75 (80)	
Fewest Wins	*8	1974-75 (80)	
Fewest Ties	5	1974-75 (80), 1983-84 (80)	
Fewest Losses	23	1985-86 (80)	
Fewest Goals	181	1974-75 (80)	
Fewest Goals Against	202	1997-98 (82)	

Longest Winning Streak
- Overall ... 10 Jan. 27-Feb. 18/84
- Home ... 10 Jan. 4-Feb. 23/00
- Away ... 6 Feb. 26-Apr. 1/84

Longest Undefeated Streak
- Overall ... 14 Nov. 24-Dec. 23/82 (9 wins, 5 ties), Jan. 17-Feb. 18/84 (13 wins, 1 tie)
- Home ... 13 Nov. 25/92-Jan. 31/93 (9 wins, 4 ties), Dec. 27/99-Feb. 23/00 (11 wins, 2 ties)
- Away ... 10 Nov. 24/82-Jan. 8/83 (6 wins, 4 ties)

Longest Losing Streak
- Overall ... *17 Feb. 18-Mar. 26/75
- Home ... *11 Feb. 18-Mar. 30/75
- Away ... 37 Oct. 9/74-Mar. 26/75

Longest Winless Streak
- Overall ... 25 Nov. 29/75-Jan. 21/76 (22 losses, 3 ties)
- Home ... 14 Dec. 3/75-Jan. 21/76 (11 losses, 3 ties)
- Away ... 37 Oct. 9/74-Mar. 26/75 (37 losses)

Most Shutouts, Season ... 9 1995-96 (82)
Most PIM, Season ... 2,204 1989-90 (80)
Most Goals, Game ... 12 Feb. 6/90 (Que. 2 at Wsh. 12), Jan. 11/03 (Fla. 2 at Wsh. 12)

Individual

Most Seasons	15	Calle Johansson
Most Games	983	Calle Johansson
Most Goals, Career	472	Peter Bondra
Most Assists, Career	418	Michal Pivonka
Most Points, Career	825	Peter Bondra (472G, 353A)
Most PIM, Career	2,003	Dale Hunter
Most Shutouts, Career	35	Olaf Kolzig

Longest Consecutive
Games Streak ... 422 Bob Carpenter (Oct. 7/81-Nov. 22/86)

Most Goals, Season ... 60 Dennis Maruk (1981-82)
Most Assists, Season ... 76 Dennis Maruk (1981-82)
Most Points, Season ... 136 Dennis Maruk (1981-82; 60G, 76A)
Most PIM, Season ... 339 Alan May (1989-90)

Most Points, Defenseman, Season ... 81 Larry Murphy (1986-87; 23G, 58A)

Most Points, Center, Season ... 136 Dennis Maruk (1981-82; 60G, 76A)

Most Points, Right Wing, Season ... 102 Mike Gartner (1984-85; 50G, 52A)

Most Points, Left Wing, Season ... 87 Ryan Walter (1981-82; 38G, 49A)

Most Points, Rookie, Season ... 67 Bob Carpenter (1981-82; 32G, 35A), Chris Valentine (1981-82; 30G, 37A)

Most Shutouts, Season ... 9 Jim Carey (1995-96)

Most Goals, Game ... 5 Bengt Gustafsson (Jan. 8/84), Peter Bondra (Feb. 5/94)

Most Assists, Game ... 6 Mike Ridley (Jan. 7/89)

Most Points, Game ... 7 Dino Ciccarelli (Mar. 18/89; 4G, 3A)

* NHL Record.

Retired Numbers

5	Rod Langway	1982-1993
7	Yvon Labre	1974-1981
32	Dale Hunter	1987-1999

Captains' History

Doug Mohns, 1974-75; Bill Clement and Yvon Labre, 1975-76; Yvon Labre, 1976-77, 1977-78; Guy Charron, 1978-79; Ryan Walter, 1979-80 to 1981-82; Rod Langway, 1982-83 to 1991-92; Rod Langway and Kevin Hatcher, 1992-93; Kevin Hatcher, 1993-94; Dale Hunter, 1994-95 to 1998-99; Adam Oates, 1999-2000, 2000-01; Brendan Witt and Steve Konowalchuk, 2001-02; Steve Konowalchuk, 2002-03, 2003-04.

All-time Record vs. Other Clubs

Regular Season

		At Home							On Road							Total					
	GP	W	L	T	OL	GF	GA	PTS	GP	W	L	T	OL	GF	GA	PTS	GP	W	L	T	OL	GF	GA	PTS
Anaheim	9	4	5	0	0	16	22	8	9	2	6	1	0	22	29	5	18	6	11	1	0	38	51	13
Atlanta	13	9	1	3	0	50	29	21	13	5	6	2	0	38	28	12	26	14	7	5	0	88	57	33
Boston	55	17	26	12	0	155	191	46	56	15	31	9	1	151	209	40	111	32	57	21	1	306	400	86
Buffalo	56	15	31	9	1	140	196	40	56	15	35	6	0	146	216	36	112	30	66	15	1	286	412	76
Calgary	41	21	14	6	0	153	139	48	38	7	24	7	0	93	157	21	79	28	38	13	0	246	296	69
Carolina	47	29	14	4	0	163	118	62	49	24	14	10	1	152	128	59	96	53	28	14	1	315	246	121
Chicago	41	21	15	5	0	145	127	47	40	12	22	6	0	120	151	30	81	33	37	11	0	265	278	77
Colorado	33	18	10	4	1	131	105	41	34	14	15	5	0	116	105	33	67	32	25	9	1	247	210	74
Columbus	2	1	0	1	0	8	5	3	4	3	1	0	0	15	11	6	6	4	1	1	0	23	16	9
Dallas	40	15	17	8	0	120	129	38	41	12	21	8	0	110	152	32	81	27	38	16	0	230	281	70
Detroit	46	21	20	5	0	168	147	47	47	15	20	11	1	135	161	42	93	36	40	16	1	303	308	89
Edmonton	29	18	9	2	0	118	93	38	29	10	15	4	0	91	120	24	58	28	24	6	0	209	213	62
Florida	28	15	7	5	1	86	61	36	28	13	11	4	0	71	70	30	56	28	18	9	1	157	131	66
Los Angeles	46	18	21	7	0	185	171	43	47	14	27	6	0	144	187	34	93	32	48	13	0	329	358	77
Minnesota	3	2	1	0	0	7	6	4	3	0	3	0	0	1	6	0	6	2	4	0	0	8	12	4
Montreal	59	26	24	9	0	163	177	61	60	17	35	8	0	127	229	42	119	43	59	17	0	290	406	103
Nashville	4	3	1	0	0	10	8	6	5	1	3	1	0	11	16	3	9	4	4	1	0	21	24	9
New Jersey	79	49	23	6	1	308	223	105	79	33	36	7	3	226	240	76	158	82	59	13	4	534	463	181
NY Islanders	81	40	30	11	0	267	251	91	81	37	42	2	0	255	298	76	162	77	72	13	0	522	549	167
NY Rangers	84	42	30	9	3	315	273	96	82	35	38	9	0	281	304	79	166	77	68	18	3	596	577	175
Ottawa	24	11	9	4	0	76	68	26	23	10	12	1	0	70	84	21	47	21	21	5	0	146	152	47
Philadelphia	80	33	34	13	0	261	259	79	83	24	53	6	0	219	312	54	163	57	87	19	0	480	571	133
Phoenix	31	18	7	5	1	119	85	42	30	8	15	7	0	105	112	23	61	26	22	12	1	224	197	65
Pittsburgh	86	45	31	9	1	358	312	100	83	29	47	7	0	261	322	65	169	74	78	16	1	619	634	165
St. Louis	39	20	15	4	0	136	117	44	41	13	20	8	0	127	165	34	80	33	35	12	0	263	282	78
San Jose	12	5	7	0	0	34	36	10	10	3	6	1	0	26	29	7	22	8	13	1	0	60	65	17
Tampa Bay	29	18	7	4	0	101	65	40	29	18	9	2	0	93	65	38	58	36	16	6	0	194	130	78
Toronto	50	28	17	4	1	182	144	61	48	16	25	6	1	163	211	39	98	44	42	10	2	345	355	100
Vancouver	40	22	14	4	0	132	120	48	39	16	18	5	0	123	136	37	79	38	32	9	0	255	256	85
Defunct Clubs	10	2	8	0	0	28	42	4	10	4	5	1	0	30	39	9	20	6	13	1	0	58	81	13
Totals	1197	586	448	153	10	4135	3719	1335	1197	425	615	150	7	3522	4292	1007	2394	1011	1063	303	17	7657	8011	2342

Playoffs

	Series	W	L	GP	W	L	T	GF	GA	Last Mtg.	Rnd.	Result
Boston	2	1	1	10	4	6	0	21	28	1998	CQF	W 4-2
Buffalo	1	1	0	6	4	2	0	13	11	1998	CF	W 4-2
Detroit	1	0	1	4	0	4	0	7	13	1998	F	L 0-4
New Jersey	2	1	1	13	7	6	0	43	1990	DSF	W 4-2
NY Islanders	6	1	5	30	12	18	0	88	99	1993	DSF	L 2-4
NY Rangers	4	2	2	22	11	11	0	75	71	1994	CSF	L 1-4
Ottawa	1	1	0	5	4	1	0	18	7	1998	CSF	W 4-1
Philadelphia	3	2	1	16	9	7	0	65	55	1989	DSF	L 2-4
Pittsburgh	7	1	6	42	16	26	0	121	137	2001	CQF	L 2-4
Tampa Bay	1	0	1	6	2	4	0	15	14	2003	CQF	L 2-4
Totals	28	10	18	154	69	85	0	467	478			

Calgary totals include Atlanta Flames, 1974-75 to 1979-80.
Colorado totals include Quebec, 1979-80 to 1994-95.
New Jersey totals include Kansas City, 1974-75 to 1975-76, and Colorado Rockies, 1976-77 to 1981-82.
Phoenix totals include Winnipeg, 1979-80, 1995-96.

Carolina totals include Hartford, 1979-80 to 1996-97.
Dallas totals include Minnesota North Stars, 1974-75 to 1992-93.

Playoff Results 2004-2000

Year	Round	Opponent	Result	GF	GA
2003	CQF	Tampa Bay	L 2-4	15	14
2001	CQF	Pittsburgh	L 2-4	10	14
2000	CQF	Pittsburgh	L 1-4	8	17

Abbreviations: Round: F – Final; **CF** – conference final; **CSF** – conference semi-final; **CQF** – conference quarter-final; **DSF** – division semi-final.

2003-04 Results

Oct.	9	NY Islanders	6-1		7	Phoenix	0-3
	11	Atlanta	3-4		9	Carolina	4-1
	13	at Toronto	2-2		11	Edmonton	1-0
	14	at Montreal	1-5		14	Calgary	3-3
	17	at Dallas	2-4		17	at New Jersey	1-2*
	18	at St. Louis	1-4		18	Pittsburgh	4-3
	23	at Ottawa	1-5		21	Toronto	2-3
	25	at Toronto	1-4		23	at Florida	1-4
	29	Anaheim	2-4		25	Philadelphia	1-4
	31	Atlanta	2-1		28	at NY Rangers	2-1
Nov.	1	at Minnesota	1-2		29	at Carolina	5-3
	4	at Tampa Bay	5-1		31	Vancouver	1-6
	6	at Philadelphia	2-4	Feb.	1	Tampa Bay	2-1
	8	San Jose	2-3		4	at Philadelphia	1-5
	10	Los Angeles	2-3		12	at Carolina	3-3
	12	Carolina	7-1		13	at Nashville	2-5
	14	Tampa Bay	2-5		15	at Chicago	4-0
	15	at Carolina	2-1		17	Ottawa	1-1
	20	at Boston	2-3		19	New Jersey	3-1
	22	Florida	2-3*		21	Florida	2-2
	24	at Detroit	4-1		23	Tampa Bay	3-6
	26	at Buffalo	2-5		25	Carolina	1-2
	28	Montreal	3-5		27	at Florida	4-1
	29	at Columbus	5-3		28	at Tampa Bay	2-4
Dec.	2	at NY Islanders	4-1	Mar.	2	Florida	0-1
	4	at New Jersey	0-3		5	at NY Rangers	2-3
	6	at Los Angeles	3-7		6	Philadelphia	2-1
	8	at Colorado	1-4		8	Ottawa	1-4
	11	Boston	6-5		10	Buffalo	0-6
	13	Detroit	1-5		12	Chicago	3-4
	16	at Atlanta	5-0		13	at Atlanta	2-5
	17	at Florida	2-2		16	at Pittsburgh	1-4
	19	Toronto	2-2		18	NY Rangers	4-3*
	21	NY Islanders	4-5		20	Atlanta	2-2
	23	Montreal	3-2		23	at NY Rangers	0-3
	27	Buffalo	1-3		24	at Atlanta	2-3
	29	Boston	1-3		27	at Tampa Bay	1-4
	31	at Buffalo	1-7		30	Pittsburgh	4-2
Jan.	1	New Jersey	2-2	Apr.	1	at Boston	3-3
	3	at Ottawa	2-5		3	NY Rangers	2-3*
	4	at Montreal	1-4		4	at Pittsburgh	3-4

* – Overtime

Entry Draft
Selections 2004-1990

2004 Pick		2000 Pick		1996 Pick		1992 Pick	
1	Alexander Ovechkin	26	Brian Sutherby	4	Alexandre Volchkov	14	Sergei Gonchar
27	Jeff Schultz	43	Matt Pettinger	17	Jaroslav Svejkovsky	32	Jim Carey
29	Mike Green	61	Jakub Cutta	43	Jan Bulis	53	Stefan Ustorf
33	Christopher Bourque	121	Ryan Vanbuskirk	58	Sergei Zimakov	71	Martin Gendron
62	Mikhail Yunkov	163	Ivan Nepryayev	74	Dave Weninger	119	John Varga
66	Sami Lepisto	289	Bjorn Nord	78	Shawn McNeil	167	Mark Matier
88	Clayton Barthel			85	Justin Davis	191	Mike Mathers
132	Oscar Hedman	**1999**		126	Matthew Lahey	215	Brian Stagg
138	Pasi Salonen	**Pick**		153	Andrew Van Bruggen	239	Gregory Callahan
166	Peter Guggisberg	7	Kris Beech	180	Michael Anderson	263	Billy Jo MacPherson
197	Andrew Gordon	29	Michal Sivek	206	Oleg Orekhovsky		
230	Justin Mrazek	31	Charlie Stephens	232	Chad Cavanagh	**1991**	
263	Travis Morin	34	Ross Lupaschuk			**Pick**	
		37	Nolan Yonkman	**1995**		14	Pat Peake
2003		132	Roman Tvrdon	**Pick**		21	Trevor Halverson
Pick		175	Kyle Clark	17	Brad Church	25	Eric Lavigne
18	Eric Fehr	192	David Bornhammar	23	Miika Elomo	36	Jeff Nelson
83	Steve Werner	219	Maxim Orlov	43	Dwayne Hay	58	Steve Konowalchuk
109	Andreas Valdix	249	Igor Shadilov	93	Sebastien Charpentier	80	Justin Morrison
155	Josh Robertson			95	Joel Theriault	146	Dave Morissette
249	Andrew Joudrey	**1998**		105	Benoit Gratton	168	Rick Corriveau
279	Mark Olafson	**Pick**		124	Joel Cort	190	Trevor Duhaime
		49	Jomar Cruz	147	Frederick Jobin	209	Rob Leask
2002		59	Todd Hornung	199	Vasili Turkovsky	212	Carl Leblanc
Pick		106	Krys Barch	225	Scott Swanson	234	Rob Puchniak
12	Steve Eminger	107	Chris Corrinet			256	Bill Kovacs
13	Alexander Semin	118	Mike Siklenka	**1994**			
17	Boyd Gordon	125	Erik Wendell	**Pick**		**1990**	
59	Maxime Daigneault	179	Nate Forster	10	Nolan Baumgartner	**Pick**	
77	Patrick Wellar	193	Rastislav Stana	15	Alexander Kharlamov	9	John Slaney
92	Derek Krestanovich	220	Mike Farrell	41	Scott Cherrey	30	Rod Pasma
109	Jevon Desautels	251	Blake Evans	93	Matt Herr	51	Chris Longo
118	Petr Dvorak			119	Yanick Jean	72	Randy Pearce
145	Rob Gherson	**1997**		145	Dmitri Mekeshkin	93	Brian Sakic
179	Marian Havel	**Pick**		171	Daniel Reja	94	Mark Ouimet
209	Joni Lindlof	9	Nick Boynton	197	Chris Patrick	114	Andrei Kovalev
242	Igor Ignatushkin	35	Jean-Francois Fortin	223	John Tuohy	135	Roman Kontsek
272	Patric Blomdahl	89	Curtis Cruickshank	249	Richard Zednik	156	Peter Bondra
		116	Kevin Caulfield	275	Sergei Tertyshny	159	Steve Martell
2001		143	Henrik Petre			177	Ken Klee
Pick		200	Pierre-Luc Therrien	**1993**		198	Michael Boback
58	Nathan Paetsch	226	Matt Oikawa	**Pick**		219	Alan Brown
90	Owen Fussey			11	Brendan Witt	240	Todd Hlushko
125	Jeff Lucky			17	Jason Allison		
160	Artem Ternavsky			69	Patrick Boileau		
191	Zbynek Novak			147	Frank Banham		
221	John Oduya			173	Daniel Hendrickson		
249	Matt Maglione			174	Andrew Brunette		
254	Peter Polcik			199	Joel Poirier		
275	Robert Muller			225	Jason Gladney		
284	Viktor Hubl			251	Mark Seliger		
				277	Dany Bousquet		

General Managers' History

Milt Schmidt, 1974-75; Milt Schmidt and Max McNab, 1975-76; Max McNab, 1976-77 to 1980-81; Max McNab and Roger Crozier, 1981-82; David Poile, 1982-83 to 1996-97; George McPhee, 1997-98 to date.

Vice President and General Manager

McPHEE, GEORGE
Vice President/General Manager, Washington Capitals.
Born in Guelph, Ont., July 2, 1958.

On June 9, 1997, George McPhee became the fifth general manager of the Washington Capitals. In his first year on the job, McPhee led the Caps to the Stanley Cup Finals for the first time in franchise history. He has begun rebuilding the Capitals with younger players and used the first overall choice at the 2004 NHL Entry Draft to select Alexander Ovechkin.

Prior to joining the Capitals, McPhee spent five years in the front office of the Vancouver Canucks where he served as vice president of hockey operations and alternate governor. He has earned degrees in both law and business and, while attending law school at Rutgers University, interned at the United States Court of International Trade in 1991.

A back injury forced McPhee to retire as an active player at the conclusion of the 1988-89 season, after a seven year playing career with the New York Rangers and New Jersey Devils. McPhee originally signed as a free agent with the Rangers in July, 1982, after graduating from Bowling Green State University with a business degree. McPhee did not waste any time in college, tallying 40 goals and 48 assists in his freshman season and easily winning CCHA rookie of the year honors. His outstanding collegiate hockey career was capped off when he was named the recipient of the Hobey Baker Award as the top U.S. collegiate player in his senior season. McPhee also earned All-America honors as a senior and finished his career at Bowling Green as the CCHA's all-time leading scorer with 114-153-267. He was the first player in CCHA history to make the Conference's all-academic team three straight seasons.

Club Directory

MCI Center

Washington Capitals
401 Ninth Street, NW, Suite 750
Washington, DC 20004
Phone **202/226-2200**
PR FAX 202/266-2360
www.WashingtonCaps.com
Capacity: 18,277

Ownership (Lincoln Holdings LLC)
Chairman & Majority Owner . . . . Ted Leonsis
President & Owner . . . . Dick Patrick
Owners . . . . Jack Davies, Richard Fairbank, Raul Fernandez, Joshua M. Freeman, Richard Kay, Jeong Kim, Mark D. Lerner, George Stamas
Executive Assistant . . . . Michelle Trostle

Hockey Operations
Vice President & General Manager . . . . George McPhee
Assistant General Manager . . . . Frank Provenzano
Director of Player Personnel . . . . Brian MacLellan
Head Coach . . . . Glen Hanlon
Assistant Coach . . . . Jay Leach
Goaltending Coach . . . . Dave Prior
Strength & Conditioning Coach . . . . Dana White
Scouting Coordinator . . . . Kris Wagner
Piney Orchard Staff . . . . Alex Walker
Security Representative . . . . James Wiseman
Executive Assistant . . . . Katy Headman

Scouting Staff
Director of Amateur Scouting . . . . Ross Mahoney
Pro Scout . . . . Mike Backman
Ontario Scout . . . . Steve Bowman
Quebec Scout . . . . Martin Pouliot
Western U.S. Scout . . . . Steve Richmond
Eastern U.S. Scout . . . . Ed McColgan
European Scout . . . . Gleb Chistyakov
European Scout . . . . Vojtech Kucera

Medical Staff
Head Athletic Trainer . . . . Greg Smith
Assistant Athletic Trainer . . . . Tim Clark
Massage Therapist . . . . Curt Millar
Team Physician . . . . Ben Shaffer, MD
Team Internist . . . . Richard Feldman, MD
Team Ophthalmologist . . . . Michael Herr, MD
Team Dentist . . . . Howard Salob, DDS

Training Staff
Head Equipment Manager . . . . Doug Shearer
Assistant Equipment Manager . . . . Craig Leydig
Equipment Assistant . . . . Brian Metzger

Business Operations
Director of Operations . . . . George Parr
Director of Sponsorship Partnerships . . . . Chris Hudgins
Information Technology Manager . . . . Kevin McDermott
Mailroom Coordinator . . . . Jennifer Whittington

Communications
Senior Director of Communications . . . . Kurt Kehl
Manager of Media Relations . . . . Brian Potter
Manager of Community Relations . . . . Elizabeth Wodatch
Communications Coordinator . . . . Stephanie Offen
New Media Manager . . . . Sean Parker
Senior Sports Media Producer . . . . Mike Vogel
Website & Publications Coordinator . . . . Ben Solomon

Finance
Controller . . . . Keith Burrows
Senior Accountant . . . . Michael Mercer
Accounts Payable Manager . . . . Jennifer Simpson
Staff Accountant . . . . Jill Ruehle

Marketing
Vice President of Marketing . . . . John Vidalin
Director of Game Operations . . . . Mark Tamar
Manager, Fan Development/Alumni Relations . . . . . . Chris Lewis
Fan Development Coordinator . . . . Ryan Ahern
Promotions Coordinator . . . . Erin Young

Sales
Vice President of Sales . . . . Kevin Morgan
Director, Group Sales . . . . Darren Montgomery
Senior Regional Sales Manager . . . . Tim Bronaugh
Regional Sales Managers . . . . Deanne Andringa, Anthony Aspaas, Dave Boettinger, Letitia Petrillo, Doug Pristach, Audrius Zubrus
Executive Assistant . . . . Carolyn Weaver

Ticket Operations & Guest Services
Director, Ticket Operations . . . . Gary Brosius
Coordinator, Ticket Operations Plans . . . . Lori Murphy
Coordinator, Ticket Operations, Internet . . . . Jeff Keeney
Director, Guest Services . . . . Greg Monares
Assistant Manager, Guest Services . . . . Megan Donohoo
Coordinator, Guest Services . . . . Eric Garvey

Miscellaneous
Home Arena . . . . MCI Center (18,277)
Television Rights Holder . . . . Comcast SportsNet
Radio Flagship . . . . SportsTalk 980
Team Photographer . . . . Mitchell Layton
Television Play-by-Play . . . . Joe Beninati
Television Analyst . . . . Craig Laughlin
Radio Play-by-Play . . . . Steve Kolbe
Radio Analyst . . . . Ken Sabourin

2003-2004 Final Statistics

Standings

Abbreviations: GP – games played; **W** – wins; **L** – losses; **T** – ties; **OTL** – overtime losses; **GF** – goals for; **GA** – goals against; **PTS** – points.

EASTERN CONFERENCE

Northeast Division

	GP	W	L	T	OTL	GF	GA	PTS
Boston	82	41	19	15	7	209	188	104
Toronto	82	45	24	10	3	242	204	103
Ottawa	82	43	23	10	6	262	189	102
Montreal	82	41	30	7	4	208	192	93
Buffalo	82	37	34	7	4	220	221	85

Atlantic Division

	GP	W	L	T	OTL	GF	GA	PTS
Philadelphia	82	40	21	15	6	229	186	101
New Jersey	82	43	25	12	2	213	164	100
NY Islanders	82	38	29	11	4	237	210	91
NY Rangers	82	27	40	7	8	206	250	69
Pittsburgh	82	23	47	8	4	190	303	58

Southeast Division

	GP	W	L	T	OTL	GF	GA	PTS
Tampa Bay	82	46	22	8	6	245	192	106
Atlanta	82	33	37	8	4	214	243	78
Carolina	82	28	34	14	6	172	209	76
Florida	82	28	35	15	4	188	221	75
Washington	82	23	46	10	3	186	253	59

WESTERN CONFERENCE

Central Division

	GP	W	L	T	OTL	GF	GA	PTS
Detroit	82	48	21	11	2	255	189	109
St. Louis	82	39	30	11	2	191	198	91
Nashville	82	38	29	11	4	216	217	91
Columbus	82	25	45	8	4	177	238	62
Chicago	82	20	43	11	8	188	259	59

Pacific Division

	GP	W	L	T	OTL	GF	GA	PTS
San Jose	82	43	21	12	6	219	183	104
Dallas	82	41	26	13	2	194	175	97
Los Angeles	82	28	29	16	9	205	217	81
Anaheim	82	29	35	10	8	184	213	76
Phoenix	82	22	36	18	6	188	245	68

Northwest Division

	GP	W	L	T	OTL	GF	GA	PTS
Vancouver	82	43	24	10	5	235	194	101
Colorado	82	40	22	13	7	236	198	100
Calgary	82	42	30	7	3	200	176	94
Edmonton	82	36	29	12	5	221	208	89
Minnesota	82	30	29	20	3	188	183	83

INDIVIDUAL LEADERS

Goal Scoring

Player	Team	GP	G
Rick Nash	Columbus	80	41
Jarome Iginla	Calgary	81	41
Ilya Kovalchuk	Atlanta	81	41
Patrik Elias	New Jersey	82	38
Martin St. Louis	Tampa Bay	82	38
Marian Hossa	Ottawa	81	36
Markus Naslund	Vancouver	78	35
Milan Hejduk	Colorado	82	35
Bill Guerin	Dallas	82	34
Keith Tkachuk	St. Louis	75	33
Joe Sakic	Colorado	81	33

Assists

Player	Team	GP	A
Scott Gomez	New Jersey	80	56
Martin St. Louis	Tampa Bay	82	56
Cory Stillman	Tampa Bay	81	55
Alex Tanguay	Colorado	69	54
Joe Sakic	Colorado	81	54
Brad Richards	Tampa Bay	82	53
Doug Weight	St. Louis	75	51
Joe Thornton	Boston	77	50

Power-play Goals

Player	Team	GP	PP
Rick Nash	Columbus	80	19
Keith Tkachuk	St. Louis	75	18
Ilya Kovalchuk	Atlanta	81	16
Milan Hejduk	Colorado	82	16
Peter Bondra	Wsh.-Ott.	77	14
Marian Hossa	Ottawa	81	14
Mark Recchi	Philadelphia	82	14

Short-handed Goals

Player	Team	GP	SH
Martin St. Louis	Tampa Bay	82	8
Kris Draper	Detroit	67	5
Kevyn Adams	Carolina	73	5
Jason Blake	NY Islanders	75	4
Kirk Maltby	Detroit	79	4
Jarome Iginla	Calgary	81	4
Greg Johnson	Nashville	82	4
David Vyborny	Columbus	82	4
Nils Ekman	San Jose	82	4

Game-winning Goals

Player	Team	GP	GW
Mats Sundin	Toronto	81	10
Jarome Iginla	Calgary	81	10
Bill Guerin	Dallas	82	10

Game-tying Goals

Player	Team	GP	GT
Shane Doan	Phoenix	79	3
18 Players with			2

Shots

Player	Team	GP	S
Ilya Kovalchuk	Atlanta	81	341
Patrik Elias	New Jersey	82	300
Markus Naslund	Vancouver	78	296
Brendan Shanahan	Detroit	82	280
Olli Jokinen	Florida	82	280

Shooting Percentage

(minimum 82 shots)

Player	Team	GP	G	S	%
Mark Parrish	NY Islanders	59	24	105	22.9
Gary Roberts	Toronto	72	28	124	22.6
Pavel Datsyuk	Detroit	75	30	136	22.1
Alex Tanguay	Colorado	69	25	117	21.4
Peter Forsberg	Colorado	39	18	85	21.2

Penalty Minutes

Player	Team	GP	PIM
Sean Avery	Los Angeles	76	261
Chris Simon	NYR-Cgy.	78	250
Krzysztof Oliwa	Calgary	65	247
Jody Shelley	Columbus	76	228
Donald Brashear	Philadelphia	64	212

Plus/Minus

Player	Team	GP	+/–
Marek Malik	Vancouver	78	35
Martin St. Louis	Tampa Bay	82	35
Zdeno Chara	Ottawa	79	33
Fredrik Modin	Tampa Bay	82	31
Alex Tanguay	Colorado	69	30
Nils Ekman	San Jose	82	30

In addition to tying Ilya Kovalchuk and Jarome Iginla for the league lead with 41 goals, Rick Nash of Columbus topped all scorers with 19 power-play goals.

Individual Leaders

Abbreviations: GP – games played; **G** – goals; **A** – assists; **Pts** – points; **+/–** – difference between Goals For (**GF**) scored when a player is on the ice with his team at even strength or short-handed and Goals Against (**GA**) scored when the same player is on the ice with his team at even strength or on a power play; **PIM** – penalties in minutes; **PP** – power play goals; **SH** – short-handed goals; **GW** – game-winning goals; **GT** – game-tying goals; **S** – shots on goal; **%** – percentage of shots on goal resulting in goals.

Individual Scoring Leaders for Art Ross Trophy

Player	Team	GP	G	A	Pts	+/–	PIM	PP	SH	GW	GT	S	%
Martin St. Louis	Tampa Bay	82	38	56	94	35	24	8	8	7	0	212	17.9
Ilya Kovalchuk	Atlanta	81	41	46	87	–10	63	16	1	6	0	341	12.0
Joe Sakic	Colorado	81	33	54	87	11	.42	13	1	3	1	253	13.0
Markus Naslund	Vancouver	78	35	49	84	24	58	5	0	6	0	296	11.8
Marian Hossa	Ottawa	81	36	46	82	4	46	14	1	5	1	233	15.5
Patrik Elias	New Jersey	82	38	43	81	26	44	9	3	9	0	300	12.7
Daniel Alfredsson	Ottawa	77	32	48	80	12	24	9	0	5	1	230	13.9
Cory Stillman	Tampa Bay	81	25	55	80	18	36	11	1	6	0	178	14.0
Robert Lang	Wsh.-Det.	69	30	49	79	4	24	10	0	3	1	163	18.4
Brad Richards	Tampa Bay	82	26	53	79	14	12	5	1	6	0	244	10.7
Alex Tanguay	Colorado	69	25	54	79	30	42	7	0	5	0	117	21.4
Milan Hejduk	Colorado	82	35	40	75	19	20	16	0	6	0	237	14.8
Mats Sundin	Toronto	81	31	44	75	11	52	11	1	10	0	226	13.7
Mark Recchi	Philadelphia	82	26	49	75	18	47	14	1	5	2	167	15.6
Jaromir Jagr	Wsh.-NYR	77	31	43	74	–5	38	10	0	3	1	257	12.1
Jarome Iginla	Calgary	81	41	32	73	21	84	8	4	10	1	265	15.5
Steve Sullivan	Chi.-Nsh.	80	24	49	73	1	48	11	2	4	0	218	11.0
Joe Thornton	Boston	77	23	50	73	18	98	4	0	6	0	187	12.3
Keith Tkachuk	St. Louis	75	33	38	71	8	83	18	0	8	2	233	14.2
Scott Gomez	New Jersey	80	14	56	70	18	70	3	0	1	0	189	7.4
Bill Guerin	Dallas	82	34	35	69	14	109	9	0	10	1	263	12.9
Martin Havlat	Ottawa	68	31	37	68	12	46	13	0	7	0	175	17.7
Pavel Datsyuk	Detroit	75	30	38	68	–2	35	8	1	4	0	136	22.1
Shane Doan	Phoenix	79	27	41	68	–11	47	9	2	1	3	254	10.6
Brett Hull	Detroit	81	25	43	68	–4	12	10	0	6	1	200	12.5
Scott Walker	Nashville	75	25	42	67	4	94	9	3	3	0	157	15.9

Defencemen Scoring Leaders

Player	Team	GP	G	A	Pts	+/–	PIM	PP	SH	GW	GT	S	%
Sergei Gonchar	Wsh.-Bos.	71	11	47	58	–14	56	6	0	0	1	161	6.8
Chris Pronger	St. Louis	80	14	40	54	–1	88	7	0	3	0	203	6.9
Scott Niedermayer	New Jersey	81	14	40	54	20	44	9	0	3	0	165	8.5
Bryan McCabe	Toronto	75	16	37	53	22	86	8	0	2	1	168	9.5
Marek Zidlicky	Nashville	82	14	39	53	–16	82	9	0	4	0	143	9.8
Dick Tarnstrom	Pittsburgh	80	16	36	52	–37	38	12	0	0	0	158	10.1
Brian Leetch	NYR-Tor.	72	15	36	51	6	34	5	1	2	0	206	7.3
Bryan Berard	Chicago	58	13	34	47	–24	53	6	0	0	0	203	6.4
Mathieu Schneider	Detroit	78	14	32	46	22	56	4	1	4	0	165	8.5
Rob Blake	Colorado	74	13	33	46	6	61	8	0	3	0	242	5.4

Martin St. Louis captured the Art Ross Trophy as the NHL's scoring leader with a career-high 94 points (38 goals, 56 assists). He also led the league in shorthanded goals (eight) and points (11) and tied for the lead in assists and plus-minus (+35).

CONSECUTIVE SCORING STREAKS

Goals

Games	Player	Team	G
7	Brett Hull	Detroit	7
6	Glen Murray	Boston	9
6	Shean Donovan	Calgary	9
6	Pavel Datsyuk	Detroit	8
5	Patrik Elias	New Jersey	8
5	Jarome Iginla	Calgary	6
5	Rick Nash	Columbus	6
5	Vyacheslav Kozlov	Atlanta	5
5	Pavel Datsyuk	Detroit	5

Assists

Games	Player	Team	A
8	Martin St. Louis	Tampa Bay	9
8	Mario Lemieux	Pittsburgh	8
7	Mark Recchi	Philadelphia	12
7	Peter Forsberg	Colorado	11
7	Brad Richards	Tampa Bay	9
7	Alexei Zhamnov	Chicago	7
7	Mike Ribeiro	Montreal	7
6	Scott Gomez	New Jersey	13
6	Markus Naslund	Vancouver	9
6	Martin St. Louis	Tampa Bay	9
6	John LeClair	Philadelphia	8
6	Mathieu Schneider	Detroit	8
6	Alex Kovalev	NY Rangers	8
6	Jason Arnott	Dallas	8
6	Daymond Langkow	Phoenix	8
6	Brett Hull	Detroit	7
6	Cory Stillman	Tampa Bay	7
6	Saku Koivu	Montreal	7
6	Marc Savard	Atlanta	7
6	Mike Modano	Dallas	6
6	Bryan McCabe	Toronto	6
6	Richard Zednik	Montreal	6
6	Bryan Berard	Chicago	6
6	Marek Zidlicky	Nashville	6

Points

Games	Player	Team	G	A	PTS
16	Robert Lang	Washington	11	14	25
14	Robert Lang	Wsh.-Det.	6	13	19
13	Martin St. Louis	Tampa Bay	8	15	23
12	Jaromir Jagr	Washington	6	14	20
12	Brad Richards	Tampa Bay	6	14	20
12	Brett Hull	Detroit	7	10	17
10	Martin St. Louis	Tampa Bay	9	9	18
9	Mark Recchi	Philadelphia	5	12	17
9	Alex Tanguay	Colorado	5	11	16
9	Tony Amonte	Philadelphia	6	7	13
9	Pavol Demitra	St. Louis	5	8	13
9	Radek Bonk	Ottawa	4	8	12
9	Brendan Morrison	Vancouver	5	6	11
9	Patrick Marleau	San Jose	4	6	10

Dick Tarnstrom led the Penguins in scoring with 52 points. His 16 goals tied Toronto's Bryan McCabe for the second most among NHL defensemen, behind Wade Redden and Pavel Kubina (17).

The second Ruutu brother to reach the NHL, Tuomo Ruutu of the Blackhawks ranked third among NHL rookies with 23 goals and 44 points.

Individual Rookie Scoring Leaders

Rookie	Team	GP	G	A	Pts	+/−	PIM	PP	SH	GW	GT	S	%
Michael Ryder	Montreal	81	25	38	63	10	26	10	0	4	0	215	11.6
Trent Hunter	NY Islanders	77	25	26	51	23	16	4	0	7	0	187	13.4
Tuomo Ruutu	Chicago	82	23	21	44	−31	58	10	0	3	0	174	13.2
Ryan Malone	Pittsburgh	81	22	21	43	−23	64	5	3	4	0	139	15.8
Patrice Bergeron	Boston	71	16	23	39	5	22	7	0	2	0	133	12.0
Nikolai Zherdev	Columbus	57	13	21	34	−11	54	5	0	1	0	137	9.5
Joffrey Lupul	Anaheim	75	13	21	34	−6	28	4	0	2	1	137	9.5
John-Michael Liles	Colorado	79	10	24	34	7	28	2	0	1	2	115	8.7
Brett McLean	Chicago	76	11	20	31	−11	54	5	1	0	0	125	8.8
Eric Staal	Carolina	81	11	20	31	−6	40	2	1	3	0	164	6.7

Goal Scoring

Name	Team	GP	G
Trent Hunter	NY Islanders	77	25
Michael Ryder	Montreal	81	25
Tuomo Ruutu	Chicago	82	23
Ryan Malone	Pittsburgh	81	22
Patrice Bergeron	Boston	71	16
Matthew Lombardi	Calgary	79	16
Nathan Horton	Florida	55	14
Matt Stajan	Toronto	69	14
Nikolai Zherdev	Columbus	57	13
Joffrey Lupul	Anaheim	75	13
Jason King	Vancouver	47	12

Assists

Name	Team	GP	A
Michael Ryder	Montreal	81	38
Trent Hunter	NY Islanders	77	26
John-Michael Liles	Colorado	79	24
Patrice Bergeron	Boston	71	23
Nikolai Zherdev	Columbus	57	21
Joffrey Lupul	Anaheim	75	21
Ryan Malone	Pittsburgh	81	21
Tuomo Ruutu	Chicago	82	21
Brett McLean	Chicago	76	20
Eric Staal	Carolina	81	20
Konstantin Koltsov	Pittsburgh	82	20

Power-play Goals

Name	Team	GP	PP
Michael Ryder	Montreal	81	10
Tuomo Ruutu	Chicago	82	10
Patrice Bergeron	Boston	71	7
Jason King	Vancouver	47	6
Nathan Horton	Florida	55	6

Short-handed Goals

Name	Team	GP	SH
Ryan Malone	Pittsburgh	81	3
Matthew Lombardi	Calgary	79	2
10 Players with			1

Game-winning Goals

Name	Team	GP	GW
Trent Hunter	NY Islanders	77	7
Derek Roy	Buffalo	49	4
Niko Dimitrakos	San Jose	68	4
Matthew Lombardi	Calgary	79	4
Dan Hamhuis	Nashville	80	4
Michael Ryder	Montreal	81	4
Ryan Malone	Pittsburgh	81	4
Eric Staal	Carolina	81	3
Konstantin Koltsov	Pittsburgh	82	3
Tuomo Ruutu	Chicago	82	3

Game-tying Goals

Name	Team	GP	GT
John-Michael Liles	Colorado	79	2
Brad Fast	Carolina	1	1
Erik Westrum	Phoenix	15	1
Matt Keith	Chicago	20	1
Antoine Vermette	Ottawa	57	1
Matt Stajan	Toronto	69	1
Tom Preissing	San Jose	69	1
Joffrey Lupul	Anaheim	75	1
Konstantin Koltsov	Pittsburgh	82	1

Shots

Name	Team	GP	S
Michael Ryder	Montreal	81	215
Trent Hunter	NY Islanders	77	187
Tuomo Ruutu	Chicago	82	174
Eric Staal	Carolina	81	164
Ryan Malone	Pittsburgh	81	139

Shooting Percentage

(minimum 82 shots)

Name	Team	GP	G	S	%
Ryan Malone	Pittsburgh	81	22	139	15.8
Trent Hunter	NY Islanders	77	25	187	13.4
Tuomo Ruutu	Chicago	82	23	174	13.2
Matthew Lombardi	Calgary	79	16	130	12.3
Patrice Bergeron	Boston	71	16	133	12.0

Penalty Minutes

Name	Team	GP	PIM
Francis Lessard	Atlanta	62	181
Andrew Peters	Buffalo	42	151
Travis Moen	Chicago	82	142
Mike Danton	St. Louis	68	141
Jordin Tootoo	Nashville	70	137

Plus/Minus

Name	Team	GP	+/−
Trent Hunter	NY Islanders	77	23
Joni Pitkanen	Philadelphia	71	15
Marc-Andre Bergeron	Edmonton	54	13
David Hale	New Jersey	65	12
Paul Martin	New Jersey	70	12

Three-or-More-Goal Games

Player	Team	Date	Final Score			G
Maxim Afinogenov	Buffalo	Dec. 31	Wsh. 1	Buf. 7		3
Tyler Arnason	Chicago	Mar. 19	Van. 3	Chi. 4		3
Jason Arnott	Dallas	Feb. 20	Col. 1	Dal. 5		3
Jason Blake	NY Islanders	Mar. 19	Min. 1	NYI 3		3
Peter Bondra	Washington	Nov. 29	Wsh. 5	CBJ 3		3
Shean Donovan	Calgary	Dec. 07	Pit. 1	Cgy. 6		3
Peter Forsberg	Colorado	Oct. 23	Edm. 1	Col. 6		3
Marian Gaborik	Minnesota	Feb. 17	Min. 4	N.J. 4		3
Marian Gaborik	Minnesota	Mar. 16	Ott. 2	Min. 5		3
Bill Guerin	Dallas	Oct. 29	Cgy. 3	Dal. 4		3
Bill Guerin	Dallas	Nov. 02	Nsh. 3	Dal. 7		3
Bill Guerin	Dallas	Mar. 03	CBJ 3	Dal. 4		3
Martin Havlat	Ottawa	Feb. 22	Ott. 6	Pit. 3		3
Milan Hejduk	Colorado	Mar. 08	Col. 9	Van. 2		3
Jarome Iginla	Calgary	Feb. 03	L.A. 4	Cgy. 4		3
Ilya Kovalchuk	Atlanta	Oct. 18	Chi. 2	Atl. 7		3
Ilya Kovalchuk	Atlanta	Oct. 23	Nsh. 2	Atl. 4		3
Robert Lang	Washington	Nov. 12	Car. 1	Wsh. 7		3
Vincent Lecavalier	Tampa Bay	Nov. 08	Pit. 0	T.B. 9		3
*Matthew Lombardi	Calgary	Nov. 12	Cgy. 6	Chi. 2		3
Alyn McCauley	San Jose	Nov. 01	S.J. 6	Fla. 2		3
Fredrik Modin	Tampa Bay	Jan. 03	Phi. 1	T.B. 6		3
Brendan Morrison	Vancouver	Nov. 29	Van. 4	Cgy. 4		3
Brenden Morrow	Dallas	Jan. 31	Dal. 5	Phx. 4		3
Glen Murray	Boston	Feb. 01	Pit. 1	Bos 4		3
Ladislav Nagy	Phoenix	Nov. 27	L.A. 4	Phx. 6		3
Markus Naslund	Vancouver	Dec. 09	Pit. 3	Van. 4		4
Jeff O'Neill	Carolina	Jan. 16	Car. 4	Atl. 3		3
Vladimir Orszagh	Nashville	Nov. 29	Buf. 1	Nsh. 4		3
Vaclav Prospal	Anaheim	Jan. 23	Min. 2	Ana. 6		3
Joe Sakic	Colorado	Dec. 20	Col. 3	L.A. 3		3
Joe Sakic	Colorado	Mar. 03	Van. 5	Col. 5		3
Miroslav Satan	Buffalo	Dec. 31	Wsh. 1	Buf. 7		3
Miroslav Satan	Buffalo	Feb. 16	Atl. 2	Buf. 7		4
Daniel Sedin	Vancouver	Feb. 24	Det. 2	Van. 4		4
Brendan Shanahan	Detroit	Mar. 14	Nsh. 2	Det. 3		3
Sheldon Souray	Montreal	Dec. 18	Nsh. 4	Mtl. 5		3
Martin St. Louis	Tampa Bay	Jan. 15	Car. 4	T.B. 5		3
Martin St. Louis	Tampa Bay	Jan. 24	T.B. 6	Cgy. 2		3
Steve Sullivan	Nashville	Feb. 18	S.J. 3	Nsh. 7		3
Alex Tanguay	Colorado	Jan. 21	Col. 6	Fla. 5		3
Josef Vasicek	Carolina	Oct. 28	S.J. 0	Car. 3		3
Radim Vrbata	Carolina	Nov. 29	Pit. 3	Car. 4		3
David Vyborny	Columbus	Nov. 07	Atl. 2	CBJ 4		3
Scott Walker	Nashville	Dec. 22	Phx. 2	Nsh. 3		3
Doug Weight	St. Louis	Oct. 29	St.L. 6	Det. 5		3

* indicates rookie

2003-04 Penalty Shots

Scored

Marian Hossa (Ottawa) scored against Evgeni Nabokov (San Jose), October 18. Final score: Ottawa 4 at San Jose 1.

Patrik Stefan (Atlanta) scored against Martin Biron (Buffalo), November 5. Final score: Atlanta 7 at Buffalo 4.

Jan Hlavac (NY Rangers) scored against Kevin Weekes (Carolina), November 6. Final score: NY Rangers 3 at Carolina 6.

Marian Gaborik (Minnesota) scored against Sebastien Caron (Pittsburgh), November 19. Final score: Minnesota 6 at Pittsburgh 2.

Shean Donovan (Calgary) scored against Vesa Toskala (San Jose), December 2. Final score: San Jose 1 at Calgary 3.

Nils Ekman (San Jose) scored against Ron Tugnutt (Dallas), December 6. Final score: Dallas 1 at San Jose 2.

Dainius Zubrus (Washington) scored against Andrew Raycroft (Boston), December 11. Final score: Boston 5 at Washington 6.

Richard Park (Minnesota) scored against Miikka Kiprusoff (Calgary), December 29. Final score: Minnesota 2 at Calgary 2.

Nathan Horton (Florida) scored against Jeff Hackett (Philadelphia), January 8. Final score: Florida 4 at Philadelphia 3.

Milan Hejduk (Colorado) scored against Michael Leighton (Chicago), January 11. Final score: Colorado 5 at Chicago 4.

Milan Hejduk (Colorado) scored against Nikolai Khabibulin (Tampa Bay), January 19. Final score: Colorado 5 at Tampa Bay 4.

Shean Donovan (Calgary) scored against Sean Burke (Phoenix), January 27. Final score: Calgary 2 at Phoenix 1.

Wes Walz (Minnesota) scored against Reinhard Divis (St. Louis), February 2. Final score: St. Louis 0 at Minnesota 4.

David Vyborny (Columbus) scored against Brian Boucher (Phoenix), February 2. Final score: Columbus 3 at Phoenix 3.

Antti Laaksonen (Minnesota) scored against Dan Cloutier (Vancouver), February 19. Final score: Vancouver 2 at Minnesota 6.

Simon Gagne (Philadelphia) scored against Pasi Nurminen (Atlanta), February 21. Final score: Atlanta 4 at Philadelphia 5.

Jonathan Cheechoo (San Jose) scored against Pascal Leclaire (Columbus), February 23. Final score: Columbus 2 at San Jose 4.

Jason Ward (Montreal) scored against Andrew Raycroft (Boston), March 27. Final score: Montreal 2 at Boston 3.

Stopped

Marc-Andre Fleury (Pittsburgh) stopped Esa Pirnes (Los Angeles), October 10. Final score: Los Angeles 3 at Pittsburgh 0.

Jocelyn Thibault (Chicago) stopped Esa Pirnes (Los Angeles), October 12. Final score: Los Angeles 4 at Chicago 2.

Johan Hedberg (Vancouver) stopped Antti Laaksonen (Minnesota), October 18. Final score: Vancouver 2 at Minnesota 2.

Tommy Salo (Edmonton) stopped Brendan Shanahan (Detroit), November 1. Final score: Detroit 4 at Edmonton 4.

Dan Cloutier (Vancouver) stopped Eric Nickulas (St. Louis), November 6. Final score: Vancouver 2 at St. Louis 3.

Dwayne Roloson (Minnesota) stopped Pavel Datsyuk (Detroit), November 15. Final score: Detroit 1 at Minnesota 2.

Mikael Tellqvist (Toronto) stopped Marco Sturm (San Jose), November 15. Final score: Toronto 2 at San Jose 2.

Roberto Luongo (Florida) stopped Michael Peca (NY Islanders), November 19. Final score: NY Islanders 4 at Florida 1.

Marty Turco (Dallas) stopped Keith Tkachuk (St. Louis), November 22. Final score: Dallas 1 at St. Louis 2.

Sebastien Caron (Pittsburgh) stopped Erik Cole (Carolina), November 29. Final score: Pittsburgh 3 at Carolina 4.

Garth Snow (NY Islanders) stopped Patrik Elias (New Jersey), December 10. Final score: NY Islanders 0 at New Jersey 1.

Olaf Kolzig (Washington) stopped Brett Hull (Detroit), December 13. Final score: Detroit 5 at Washington 1.

Tomas Vokoun (Nashville) stopped Vaclav Nedorost (Florida), December 13. Final score: Florida 2 at Nashville 2.

Marc Denis (Columbus) stopped Pavol Demitra (St. Louis), December 16. Final score: Columbus 1 at St. Louis 2.

Dan Cloutier (Vancouver) stopped Oleg Saprykin (Calgary), December 26. Final score: Vancouver 2 at Calgary 0.

Jussi Markkanen (NY Rangers) stopped Eric Meloche (Pittsburgh), January 3. Final score: NY Rangers 4 at Pittsburgh 1.

Alexander Auld (Vancouver) stopped Jarome Iginla (Calgary), January 3. Final score: Vancouver 3 at Calgary 1.

Jean-Sebastien Giguere (Anaheim) stopped Daniel Sedin (Vancouver), January 17. Final score: Anaheim 2 at Vancouver 1.

Robert Esche (Philadelphia) stopped Richard Zednik (Montreal), January 20. Final score: Montreal 4 at Philadelphia 1.

Jose Theodore (Montreal) stopped Grant Marshall (New Jersey), January 23. Final score: Montreal 0 at New Jersey 2.

Chris Osgood (St. Louis) stopped Mike Modano (Dallas), January 23. Final score: St. Louis 0 at Dallas 2.

Roberto Luongo (Florida) stopped P.J. Axelsson (Boston), January 24. Final score: Florida 2 at Boston 1.

Pasi Nurminen (Atlanta) stopped Jason Blake (NY Islanders), January 24. Final score: NY Islanders 3 at Atlanta 0.

Marc-Andre Fleury (Pittsburgh) stopped Dan Boyle (Tampa Bay), January 27. Final score: Tampa Bay 6 at Pittsburgh 2.

John Grahame (Tampa Bay) stopped Brian Holzinger (Pittsburgh), January 27. Final score: Tampa Bay 6 at Pittsburgh 2.

Roberto Luongo (Florida) stopped Alexander Korolyuk (San Jose), February 3. Final score: Florida 0 at San Jose 3.

Pasi Nurminen (Atlanta) stopped Jarkko Ruutu (Vancouver), February 13. Final score: Atlanta 4 at Vancouver 1.

Patrick Lalime (Ottawa) stopped Matthew Barnaby (NY Rangers), February 16. Final score: Ottawa 4 at NY Rangers 1.

Michael Leighton (Chicago) stopped Alex Zhamnov (Philadelphia), February 24. Final score: Chicago 1 at Philadelphia 3.

Marc Denis (Columbus) stopped Paul Kariya (Colorado), February 28. Final score: Colorado 4 at Columbus 5.

Johan Hedberg (Vancouver) stopped Pavol Demitra (St. Louis), February 28. Final score: St. Louis 0 at Vancouver 2.

Chris Osgood (St. Louis) stopped Ryan Smyth (Edmonton), March 4. Final score: Edmonton 1 at St. Louis 1.

Marty Turco (Dallas) stopped Shean Donovan (Calgary), March 5. Final score: Calgary 1 at Dallas 5.

Tommy Salo (Colorado) stopped Mike Comrie (Phoenix), March 14. Final score: Phoenix 1 at Colorado 4.

Jose Theodore (Montreal) stopped Peter Bondra (Ottawa), March 25. Final score: Ottawa 4 at Montreal 0.

Rick DiPietro (NY Islanders) stopped Erik Cole (Carolina), April 2. Final score: NY Islanders 6 at Carolina 4.

Adam Munro (Chicago) stopped Ivan Novoseltsev (Phoenix), April 3. Final score: Chicago 1 at Phoenix 2.

Kari Lehtonen (Atlanta) stopped Vincent Lecavalier (Tampa Bay), April 3. Final score: Atlanta 2 at Tampa Bay 1.

Reinhard Divis (St. Louis) stopped Marian Gaborik (Minnesota), April 4. Final score: St. Louis 0 at Minnesota 3.

Summary

57 penalty shots resulted in 18 goals.

Goaltending Leaders

Minimum 25 games

Goals Against Average

Goaltender	Team	GPI	MINS	GA	Avg
Miikka Kiprusoff	S.J.-Cgy.	38	2301	65	1.69
Dwayne Roloson	Minnesota	48	2847	89	1.88
Marty Turco	Dallas	73	4359	144	1.98
Martin Brodeur	New Jersey	75	4555	154	2.03
Robert Esche	Philadelphia	40	2322	79	2.04

Save Percentage

Goaltender	Team	GPI	MINS	GA	SA	S%	W	L	T
Dwayne Roloson	Minnesota	48	2847	89	1323	.933	19	18	11
Miikka Kiprusoff	S.J.-Cgy.	38	2301	65	966	.933	24	10	4
Roberto Luongo	Florida	72	4252	172	2475	.931	25	33	14
Vesa Toskala	San Jose	28	1541	53	760	.930	12	8	4
*Andrew Raycroft	Boston	57	3420	117	1586	.926	29	18	9

Wins

Goaltender	Team	GPI	MINS	W	L	T
Martin Brodeur	New Jersey	75	4555	38	26	11
Marty Turco	Dallas	73	4359	37	21	13
Ed Belfour	Toronto	59	3444	34	19	6
Tomas Vokoun	Nashville	73	4221	34	29	10
Dan Cloutier	Vancouver	60	3539	33	21	6
Jose Theodore	Montreal	67	3961	33	28	5

Shutouts

Goaltender	Team	GPI	MINS	SO	W	L	T
Martin Brodeur	New Jersey	75	4555	11	38	26	11
Ed Belfour	Toronto	59	3444	10	34	19	6
Evgeni Nabokov	San Jose	59	3456	9	31	19	8
Marty Turco	Dallas	73	4359	9	37	21	13
Roberto Luongo	Florida	72	4252	7	25	33	14

Team-by-Team Point Totals

1999-2000 to 2003-04
(Ranked by five-year point %)

Team	03-04	02-03	01-02	00-01	99-00	Pts%
Detroit	109	110	116	111	108	.676
Colorado	100	105	99	118	96	.632
New Jersey	100	108	95	111	103	.630
Ottawa	102	113	94	109	95	.626
Philadelphia	101	107	97	100	105	.622
Dallas	97	111	90	106	102	.617
St. Louis	91	99	98	103	114	.616
Toronto	103	98	100	90	100	.599
Vancouver	101	104	94	90	83	.576
San Jose	104	73	99	95	87	.559
Edmonton	89	92	92	93	88	.554
Boston	104	87	101	88	73	.552
Los Angeles	81	78	95	92	94	.537
Washington	60	92	85	96	102	.530
Buffalo	85	72	82	98	85	.515
Phoenix	68	78	95	90	90	.513
Montreal	93	77	87	70	83	.500
Carolina	76	61	91	88	84	.488
Minnesota	83	95	73	68	—	.486
Calgary	94	75	79	73	77	.485
Anaheim	76	95	69	66	83	.474
Nashville	91	74	69	80	70	.468
Chicago	59	79	96	71	78	.467
Tampa Bay	106	93	69	59	54	.465
NY Islanders	91	83	96	52	58	.463
Pittsburgh	58	65	69	96	88	.459
NY Rangers	69	78	80	72	73	.454
Florida	75	70	60	66	98	.450
Columbus	62	69	57	71	—	.395
Atlanta	78	74	54	60	39	.372

Team Record When Scoring First Goal of a Game

Team	FG	W	L	T
Anaheim	38	20	14	4
Atlanta	31	21	8	2
Boston	34	20	7	7
Buffalo	46	28	13	5
Calgary	41	29	8	4
Carolina	30	17	6	7
Chicago	33	11	15	7
Colorado	47	28	12	7
Columbus	37	15	18	4
Dallas	41	30	6	5
Detroit	47	**37**	6	4
Edmonton	35	23	8	4
Florida	36	19	12	5
Los Angeles	44	24	13	7
Minnesota	46	22	11	13
Montreal	**51**	34	12	5
Nashville	41	25	9	7
New Jersey	48	37	4	7
NY Islanders	39	27	7	5
NY Rangers	40	20	17	3
Ottawa	45	30	11	4
Philadelphia	44	28	8	8
Phoenix	36	16	11	9
Pittsburgh	31	18	10	3
San Jose	45	30	8	7
St. Louis	42	26	11	5
Tampa Bay	50	34	12	4
Toronto	43	32	7	4
Vancouver	48	31	13	4
Washington	36	17	14	5

Team Plus/Minus Differential

Team	GF	PPGF	Net GF	GA	PPGA	Net GA	Goal Differential
Ottawa	262	80	182	189	57	132	+50
Detroit	255	63	192	189	42	147	+45
Tampa Bay	245	55	190	192	42	150	+40
New Jersey	213	51	162	164	39	125	+37
Philadelphia	229	65	164	186	58	128	+36
Vancouver	235	56	179	194	50	144	+35
Edmonton	221	44	177	208	66	142	+35
Boston	209	48	161	188	55	133	+28
Toronto	242	75	167	204	64	140	+27
San Jose	219	56	163	183	47	136	+27
NY Islanders	237	54	183	210	52	158	+25
Calgary	200	54	146	176	53	123	+23
Colorado	236	74	162	198	58	140	+22
Montreal	208	55	153	192	55	137	+16
Dallas	194	52	142	175	44	131	+11
Los Angeles	205	50	155	217	65	152	+3
Minnesota	188	46	142	183	44	139	+3
Buffalo	220	58	162	221	53	168	-6
Nashville	216	72	144	217	64	153	-9
NY Rangers	206	46	160	250	80	170	-10
St. Louis	191	61	130	198	57	141	-11
Carolina	172	41	131	209	66	143	-12
Atlanta	214	60	154	243	58	185	-31
Anaheim	184	56	128	213	54	159	-31
Florida	188	52	136	221	51	170	-34
Phoenix	188	51	137	245	71	174	-37
Washington	186	64	122	253	75	178	-56
Chicago	188	55	133	259	63	196	-63
Columbus	177	58	119	238	50	188	-69
Pittsburgh	190	65	125	303	84	219	-94

Team Record When Leading, Trailing, Tied

Team	Leading after 1 period W	L	T	Leading after 2 periods W	L	T	Trailing after 1 period W	L	T	Trailing after 2 periods W	L	T	Tied after 1 period W	L	T	Tied after 2 periods W	L	T
Anaheim	10	6	2	19	4	1	5	23	2	3	29	4	14	14	6	7	10	5
Atlanta	12	4	2	21	1	1	6	24	3	7	31	3	15	13	3	5	9	4
Boston	16	1	2	24	3	4	12	16	4	9	21	3	13	9	9	8	2	8
Buffalo	18	4	3	24	5	2	2	16	1	4	28	0	17	18	3	9	5	5
Calgary	20	1	0	27	4	2	10	15	2	4	23	0	12	17	5	11	6	5
Carolina	12	3	4	23	1	4	7	23	2	3	27	0	9	14	8	2	12	10
Chicago	9	6	5	14	6	5	4	21	2	2	39	3	7	24	4	2	6	3
Colorado	21	7	3	28	3	4	9	11	3	5	17	5	10	11	7	7	9	4
Columbus	9	2	2	19	4	2	7	21	2	3	32	1	9	26	4	3	13	5
Dallas	24	2	2	27	1	5	4	11	4	5	22	1	13	15	7	9	5	7
Detroit	24	7	1	37	3	4	4	12	5	2	16	5	20	4	5	9	4	2
Edmonton	15	9	3	24	2	1	9	17	3	3	27	6	12	12	6	9	6	6
Florida	12	8	4	17	7	4	6	19	4	1	25	3	10	12	7	10	7	8
Los Angeles	13	10	4	24	3	6	4	22	4	1	27	3	11	6	8	3	8	7
Minnesota	16	9	6	20	4	8	4	14	6	3	23	3	10	9	8	7	5	9
Montreal	20	5	2	30	4	0	2	14	1	3	25	2	19	15	4	8	5	5
Nashville	20	3	6	28	5	3	6	19	2	5	23	2	12	11	3	5	9	6
New Jersey	23	2	3	32	2	4	6	15	3	1	18	2	14	10	6	10	7	6
NY Islanders	21	5	1	26	0	5	5	18	1	3	25	3	12	11	5	9	8	3
NY Rangers	17	6	1	22	5	1	2	21	3	2	36	1	8	21	3	4	9	4
Ottawa	25	5	2	33	7	1	2	14	2	0	14	3	16	9	6	9	6	6
Philadelphia	23	3	3	33	1	2	6	12	5	2	23	4	11	12	7	5	3	9
Phoenix	9	6	5	14	2	3	2	28	6	4	30	7	11	8	7	4	10	8
Pittsburgh	10	8	2	14	5	3	4	37	5	3	42	2	9	6	1	6	7	2
San Jose	25	4	7	34	2	3	1	13	1	0	18	4	17	10	4	9	5	3
St. Louis	23	5	2	27	3	3	3	13	5	3	25	0	13	14	4	9	5	5
Tampa Bay	27	5	2	32	5	1	4	11	0	4	16	3	15	12	6	9	4	4
Toronto	23	3	3	33	3	4	4	13	3	3	21	5	18	11	4	7	3	6
Vancouver	19	9	4	26	3	1	6	8	4	7	17	7	18	12	2	10	9	2
Washington	14	4	1	20	0	3	2	29	3	2	40	3	7	16	6	1	9	4

Boston's Andrew Raycroft earned the Calder Trophy as rookie of the year. His .926 save percentage ranked fifth in the NHL, while his 2.05 goals-against average was sixth.

Team Statistics

TEAMS' HOME AND ROAD RECORD

Eastern Conference

	Home								Road							
Team	GP	W	L	T	OTL	GF	GA	PTS	GP	W	L	T	OTL	GF	GA	PTS
T.B.	41	24	10	4	3	127	97	55	41	22	12	4	3	118	95	51
BOS	41	18	12	9	2	94	99	47	41	23	7	6	5	115	89	57
TOR	41	22	14	3	2	114	104	49	41	23	10	7	1	128	100	54
OTT	41	23	8	5	5	134	85	56	41	20	15	5	1	128	104	46
PHI	41	24	11	3	3	123	90	54	41	16	10	12	3	106	96	47
N.J.	41	22	13	5	1	107	87	50	41	21	12	7	1	106	77	50
MTL	41	23	13	4	1	104	88	51	41	18	17	3	3	104	104	42
NYI	41	25	11	4	1	129	92	55	41	13	18	7	3	108	118	36
BUF	41	21	13	4	3	126	108	49	41	16	21	3	1	94	113	36
ATL	41	18	17	4	2	103	109	42	41	15	20	4	2	111	134	36
CAR	41	13	18	8	2	85	100	36	41	15	16	6	4	87	109	40
FLA	41	16	15	7	3	109	111	42	41	12	20	8	1	79	110	33
NYR	41	13	21	3	4	108	123	33	41	14	19	4	4	98	127	36
WSH	41	13	20	6	2	97	119	34	41	10	26	4	1	89	134	25
PIT	41	13	22	6	0	95	145	32	41	10	25	2	4	95	158	26
Total	**615**	**288**	**218**	**75**	**34**	**1655**	**1557**	**685**	**615**	**248**	**248**	**82**	**37**	**1566**	**1668**	**615**

Western Conference

DET	41	30	7	4	0	142	82	64	41	18	14	7	2	113	107	45
S.J.	41	24	8	7	2	114	82	57	41	19	13	5	4	105	101	47
VAN	41	21	13	7	0	118	102	49	41	22	11	3	5	117	92	52
COL	41	19	14	6	2	102	83	46	41	21	8	7	5	134	115	54
DAL	41	26	7	8	0	118	77	60	41	15	19	5	2	76	98	37
CGY	41	21	14	5	1	93	85	48	41	21	16	2	2	107	91	46
ST.L.	41	23	11	7	0	106	95	53	41	16	19	4	2	85	103	38
NSH	41	22	10	7	2	112	93	53	41	16	19	4	2	104	124	38
EDM	41	22	12	4	3	123	102	51	41	14	17	8	2	98	106	38
MIN	41	19	13	7	2	104	89	47	41	11	16	13	1	84	94	36
L.A.	41	15	16	9	1	115	108	40	41	13	13	7	8	90	109	41
ANA	41	19	11	7	4	113	106	49	41	10	24	3	4	71	107	27
PHX	41	11	19	7	4	95	132	33	41	11	17	11	2	93	113	35
CBJ	41	17	18	4	2	98	103	40	41	8	27	4	2	79	135	22
CHI	41	13	17	6	5	98	116	37	41	7	26	5	3	90	143	22
Total	**615**	**302**	**190**	**95**	**28**	**1651**	**1455**	**727**	**615**	**222**	**259**	**88**	**46**	**1446**	**1638**	**578**
	1230	**590**	**408**	**170**	**62**	**3306**	**3012**	**1412**	**1230**	**470**	**507**	**170**	**83**	**3012**	**3306**	**1193**

TEAMS' DIVISIONAL RECORD

Northeast Division

	Against Own Division								Against Other Divisions							
	GP	W	L	T	OTL	GF	GA	PTS	GP	W	L	T	OTL	GF	GA	PTS
BOS	24	13	6	2	3	51	52	31	58	28	13	13	4	158	136	73
TOR	24	13	9	2	0	74	66	28	58	32	15	8	3	168	138	75
OTT	24	9	10	4	1	71	58	23	58	34	13	6	5	191	131	79
MTL	24	9	13	1	1	50	62	20	58	32	17	6	3	158	130	73
BUF	24	10	8	3	3	61	69	26	58	27	26	4	1	159	152	59
Total	**120**	**54**	**46**	**12**	**8**	**307**	**307**	**128**	**290**	**153**	**84**	**37**	**16**	**834**	**687**	**359**

Atlantic Division

PHI	24	13	6	5	0	67	48	31	58	27	15	10	6	162	138	70
N.J.	24	14	7	2	1	68	45	31	58	29	18	10	1	145	119	69
NYI	24	8	11	3	2	67	76	21	58	30	18	8	2	170	134	70
NYR	24	11	10	1	2	69	75	25	58	16	30	6	6	137	175	44
PIT	24	6	12	5	1	57	84	18	58	17	35	3	3	133	219	40
Total	**120**	**52**	**46**	**16**	**6**	**328**	**328**	**126**	**290**	**119**	**116**	**37**	**18**	**747**	**785**	**293**

Southeast Division

T.B.	24	13	8	3	0	66	59	29	58	33	14	5	6	179	133	77
ATL	24	13	8	1	2	65	62	29	58	20	29	7	2	149	181	49
CAR	24	8	10	5	1	60	68	22	58	20	24	9	5	112	141	54
FLA	24	8	10	5	1	59	65	22	58	20	25	10	3	129	156	53
WSH	24	9	10	4	1	64	60	23	58	14	36	6	2	122	193	36
Total	**120**	**51**	**46**	**18**	**5**	**314**	**314**	**125**	**290**	**107**	**128**	**37**	**18**	**691**	**804**	**269**

Central Division

DET	24	15	7	1	1	74	55	32	58	33	14	10	1	181	134	77
ST.L.	24	12	9	2	1	64	62	27	58	27	21	9	1	127	136	64
NSH	24	11	9	2	2	58	63	26	58	27	20	9	2	158	154	65
CBJ	24	9	13	0	2	61	76	20	58	16	32	8	2	116	162	42
CHI	24	10	11	1	2	65	66	23	58	10	32	10	6	123	193	36
Total	**120**	**57**	**49**	**6**	**8**	**322**	**322**	**128**	**290**	**113**	**119**	**46**	**12**	**705**	**779**	**284**

Pacific Division

S.J.	24	15	6	3	0	66	43	33	58	28	15	9	6	153	140	71
DAL	24	9	8	6	1	56	53	25	58	32	18	7	1	138	122	72
L.A.	24	9	9	5	1	66	72	24	58	19	20	11	8	139	145	57
ANA	24	8	10	4	2	53	61	22	58	21	25	6	6	131	152	54
PHX	24	8	10	4	2	61	73	22	58	14	26	14	4	127	172	46
Total	**120**	**49**	**43**	**22**	**6**	**302**	**302**	**126**	**290**	**114**	**104**	**47**	**25**	**688**	**731**	**300**

Northwest Division

VAN	24	10	7	6	1	60	63	27	58	33	17	4	4	175	131	74
COL	24	12	7	4	1	76	64	29	58	28	15	9	6	160	134	71
CGY	24	11	7	4	2	52	48	28	58	31	23	3	1	148	128	66
EDM	24	7	12	3	2	45	59	19	58	29	17	9	3	176	149	70
MIN	24	8	9	7	0	49	48	23	58	22	20	13	3	139	135	60
Total	**120**	**48**	**42**	**24**	**6**	**282**	**282**	**126**	**290**	**143**	**92**	**38**	**17**	**798**	**677**	**341**

TEAM STREAKS

Consecutive Wins

Games	Team	From	To
8	Toronto	Nov. 22	Dec. 6
8	Tampa Bay	Feb. 23	Mar. 6
6	Tampa Bay	Oct. 10	Oct. 25
6	Philadelphia	Nov. 1	Nov. 15
6	Nashville	Nov. 24	Dec. 4
6	St. Louis	Dec. 6	Dec. 18
6	NY Islanders	Dec. 21	Dec. 31
6	Ottawa	Dec. 28	Jan. 8
6	Tampa Bay	Jan. 22	Feb. 2
6	Boston	Jan. 29	Feb. 10
6	Vancouver	Mar. 24	Apr. 3

Consecutive Home Wins

Games	Team	From	To
11	Philadelphia	Oct. 27	Dec. 5
8	Detroit	Nov. 26	Dec. 22
8	San Jose	Jan. 24	Mar. 3
7	NY Islanders	Dec. 6	Dec. 29
7	Tampa Bay	Feb. 12	Mar. 12
6	Detroit	Feb. 16	Mar. 5
5	Vancouver	Oct. 28	Nov. 20
5	St. Louis	Nov. 4	Nov. 25
5	Toronto	Nov. 4	Dec. 6
5	Montreal	Dec. 18	Jan. 6
5	Anaheim	Jan. 30	Feb. 18
5	Dallas	Feb. 27	Mar. 7

Consecutive Road Wins

Games	Team	From	To
8	Vancouver	Dec. 20	Jan. 13
6	Boston	Oct. 15	Oct. 28
6	Toronto	Nov. 22	Dec. 11
6	Calgary	Dec. 16	Jan. 6
5	Phoenix	Dec. 23	Jan. 9
5	Tampa Bay	Feb. 23	Mar. 6
5	Boston	Mar. 9	Apr. 4
5	Toronto	Mar. 15	Apr. 3

Consecutive Undefeated

Games	Team	W	T	From	To
13	New Jersey	10	3	Oct. 28	Nov. 26
12	Philadelphia	10	2	Nov. 1	Nov. 29
11	Ottawa	9	2	Dec. 18	Jan. 8
11	Tampa Bay	10	1	Feb. 23	Mar. 12
9	Vancouver	7	2	Oct. 18	Nov. 5
9	St. Louis	7	2	Dec. 2	Dec. 20
9	Minnesota	4	5	Dec. 13	Dec. 30
9	Dallas	8	1	Feb. 18	Mar. 7
8	Tampa Bay	7	1	Oct. 10	Nov. 1
8	Toronto	8	0	Nov. 22	Dec. 6
8	Colorado	4	4	Nov. 27	Dec. 13
8	Dallas	6	2	Jan. 23	Feb. 11
8	Detroit	7	1	Feb. 26	Mar. 14

Consecutive Home Undefeated

Games	Team	W	T	From	To
17	Dallas	13	4	Jan. 23	Mar. 20
14	Philadelphia	12	2	Oct. 9	Dec. 5
12	Detroit	11	1	Nov. 26	Jan. 5
12	Ottawa	10	2	Dec. 18	Jan. 24
11	San Jose	7	4	Nov. 15	Dec. 29
11	Nashville	9	2	Dec. 20	Jan. 31
10	Vancouver	9	1	Oct. 9	Nov. 20
10	Tampa Bay	9	1	Jan. 29	Mar. 12
9	NY Islanders	6	3	Jan. 17	Feb. 24
9	Detroit	8	1	Feb. 16	Mar. 14
8	New Jersey	7	1	Oct. 30	Nov. 21
8	St. Louis	5	3	Dec. 2	Dec. 26
8	San Jose	8	0	Jan. 24	Mar. 3
8	Pittsburgh	6	2	Mar. 6	Apr. 4

Consecutive Road Undefeated

Games	Team	W	T	From	To
9	Phoenix	5	4	Dec. 7	Jan. 9
8	New Jersey	5	3	Oct. 8	Nov. 26
8	Toronto	7	1	Nov. 22	Dec. 26
8	Vancouver	8	0	Dec. 20	Jan. 13
7	Boston	6	1	Oct. 11	Oct. 28
7	Ottawa	5	2	Nov. 25	Jan. 8
7	Minnesota	2	5	Dec. 6	Dec. 30
7	Colorado	5	2	Jan. 10	Jan. 29
7	Philadelphia	6	1	Jan. 17	Feb. 12
7	Toronto	6	1	Jan. 21	Feb. 19
7	Tampa Bay	6	1	Feb. 23	Mar. 10
6	Chicago	3	3	Oct. 23	Nov. 7
6	Calgary	6	0	Dec. 16	Jan. 6
6	Dallas	4	2	Dec. 20	Jan. 13
6	Florida	3	3	Feb. 18	Mar. 2

TEAM PENALTIES

Abbreviations: GP – games played; **PEN** – total penalty minutes including bench minutes; **BMI** – total bench minor minutes; **AVG** – average penalty minutes/game calculated by dividing total penalty minutes by games played

Team	GP	PEN	BMI	AVG
N.J.	82	894	14	10.9
DET	82	966	22	11.8
T.B.	82	985	34	12.0
MIN	82	1035	44	12.6
MTL	82	1039	16	12.7
S.J.	82	1091	18	13.3
CAR	82	1102	16	13.4
ANA	82	1131	14	13.8
DAL	82	1143	20	13.9
L.A.	82	1163	6	14.2
NYI	82	1168	16	14.2
FLA	82	1192	22	14.5
BOS	82	1208	22	14.7
CBJ	82	1209	22	14.7
EDM	82	1220	22	14.9
OTT	82	1270	20	15.5
PIT	82	1270	32	15.5
ST.L.	82	1274	28	15.5
VAN	82	1274	28	15.5
WSH	82	1282	12	15.6
BUF	82	1289	28	15.7
COL	82	1293	28	15.8
PHX	82	1300	24	15.9
CHI	82	1318	18	16.1
PHI	82	1357	22	16.5
NSH	82	1360	28	16.6
CGY	82	1428	42	17.4
TOR	82	1452	20	17.7
NYR	82	1459	30	17.8
ATL	82	1505	32	18.4
Total	**1230**	**36677**	**700**	
Two-Team Avg. PIM/GP				**29.8**

Milan Hejduk scored 16 of his 35 goals last season while Colorado was on the power-play. Both totals ranked him among the NHL leaders.

TEAMS' POWER-PLAY RECORD

Abbreviations: ADV – total advantages; **PPGF** – power-play goals for; **%** – calculated by dividing number of power-play goals by total advantages.

	Home					Road					Overall				
	Team	GP	ADV	PPGF	%	Team	GP	ADV	PPGF	%	Team	GP	ADV	PPGF	%
1	OTT	41	199	47	23.6	COL	41	182	44	24.2	OTT	82	371	80	21.6
2	DET	41	165	39	23.6	TOR	41	182	36	19.8	PHI	82	314	65	20.7
3	PHI	41	160	37	23.1	OTT	41	172	33	19.2	COL	82	363	74	20.4
4	DAL	41	176	39	22.2	PIT	41	180	34	18.9	DET	82	314	63	20.1
5	ST.L.	41	171	37	21.6	PHI	41	154	28	18.2	TOR	82	373	75	20.1
6	FLA	41	157	33	21.0	MTL	41	139	25	18.0	WSH	82	334	64	19.2
7	WSH	41	176	36	20.5	ATL	41	207	37	17.9	ANA	82	310	56	18.1
8	TOR	41	191	39	20.4	WSH	41	158	28	17.7	PIT	82	360	65	18.1
9	ANA	41	164	32	19.5	N.J.	41	165	28	17.0	ST.L.	82	341	61	17.9
10	BUF	41	195	36	18.5	T.B.	41	157	26	16.6	MTL	82	319	55	17.2
11	CHI	41	184	33	17.9	ANA	41	146	24	16.4	NSH	82	426	72	16.9
12	NSH	41	234	41	17.5	S.J.	41	165	27	16.4	FLA	82	310	52	16.8
13	EDM	41	177	31	17.5	DET	41	149	24	16.1	NYI	82	323	54	16.7
14	NYI	41	171	30	17.5	NSH	41	192	31	16.1	S.J.	82	337	56	16.6
15	PIT	41	180	31	17.2	NYI	41	152	24	15.8	N.J.	82	312	51	16.3
16	S.J.	41	172	29	16.9	PHX	41	158	25	15.8	T.B.	82	339	55	16.2
17	CBJ	41	227	38	16.7	BOS	41	147	23	15.6	BOS	82	300	48	16.0
18	MTL	41	180	30	16.7	VAN	41	174	27	15.5	DAL	82	328	52	15.9
19	COL	41	181	30	16.6	NYR	41	167	24	14.4	CHI	82	349	55	15.8
20	CGY	41	182	30	16.5	MIN	41	175	25	14.3	BUF	82	367	58	15.8
21	L.A.	41	200	33	16.5	ST.L.	41	170	24	14.1	CGY	82	357	54	15.1
22	BOS	41	153	25	16.3	CGY	41	175	24	13.7	VAN	82	374	56	15.0
23	T.B.	41	182	29	15.9	CHI	41	165	22	13.3	ATL	82	409	60	14.7
24	N.J.	41	147	23	15.6	BUF	41	172	22	12.8	CBJ	82	401	58	14.5
25	VAN	41	200	29	14.5	FLA	41	153	19	12.4	NYR	82	322	46	14.3
26	NYR	41	155	22	14.2	CAR	41	188	22	11.7	PHX	82	358	51	14.2
27	PHX	41	200	26	13.0	CBJ	41	174	20	11.5	L.A.	82	356	50	14.0
28	MIN	41	163	21	12.9	L.A.	41	156	17	10.9	MIN	82	338	46	13.6
29	ATL	41	202	23	11.4	DAL	41	152	13	8.6	EDM	82	338	44	13.0
30	CAR	41	196	19	9.7	EDM	41	161	13	8.1	CAR	82	384	41	10.7
TOTAL		**1230**	**5440**	**948**	**17.4**		**1230**	**4987**	**769**	**15.4**		**1230**	**10427**	**1717**	**16.5**

TEAMS' PENALTY KILLING RECORD

Abbreviations: TSH – total times short-handed; **PPGA** – power-play goals against; **%** – calculated by dividing times short minus power-play goals against by times short.

	Home					Road					Overall				
	Team	GP	TSH	PPGA	%	Team	GP	TSH	PPGA	%	Team	GP	TSH	PPGA	%
1	S.J.	41	145	13	91.0	N.J.	41	136	18	86.8.	DET	82	317	42	86.8
2	ATL	41	201	22	89.1	DET	41	176	24	86.4	FLA	82	374	51	86.4
3	NYI	41	163	19	88.3	CHI	41	201	29	85.6	VAN	82	357	50	86.0
4	CBJ	41	152	18	88.2	VAN	41	171	25	85.4	DAL	82	311	44	85.9
5	FLA	41	177	21	88.1	MIN	41	141	21	85.1	NYI	82	359	52	85.5
6	OTT	41	180	22	87.8	DAL	41	147	22	85.0	N.J.	82	266	39	85.3
7	DET	41	141	18	87.2	FLA	41	197	30	84.8	S.J.	82	319	47	85.3
8	CGY	41	158	21	86.7	T.B.	41	132	20	84.8	ATL	82	391	58	85.2
9	DAL	41	164	22	86.6	PHX	41	195	30	84.6	CBJ	82	337	50	85.2
10	VAN	41	186	25	86.6	ST.L.	41	200	31	84.5	T.B.	82	278	42	84.9
11	NSH	41	176	24	86.4	ANA	41	186	29	84.4	BUF	82	348	53	84.8
12	COL	41	162	22	86.4	BUF	41	183	29	84.2	ANA	82	353	54	84.7
13	MTL	41	160	22	86.3	BOS	41	177	28	84.2	CGY	82	346	53	84.7
14	BUF	41	165	24	85.5	PHI	41	186	31	83.3	ST.L.	82	369	57	84.6
15	EDM	41	163	24	85.3	NYI	41	196	33	83.2	MIN	82	283	44	84.5
16	ANA	41	167	25	85.0	CGY	41	188	32	83.0	COL	82	357	58	83.8
17	T.B.	41	146	22	84.9	CBJ	41	185	32	82.7	BOS	82	335	55	83.6
18	ST.L.	41	169	26	84.6	TOR	41	196	34	82.7	OTT	82	347	57	83.6
19	TOR	41	190	30	84.2	CAR	41	198	35	82.3	CHI	82	381	63	83.5
20	MIN	41	142	23	83.8	WSH	41	222	40	82.0	TOR	82	386	64	83.4
21	N.J.	41	130	21	83.8	L.A.	41	168	31	81.5	PHI	82	348	58	83.3
22	PHI	41	162	27	83.3	COL	41	195	36	81.5	MTL	82	314	55	82.5
23	BOS	41	158	27	82.9	ATL	41	190	36	81.1	PHX	82	398	71	82.2
24	CHI	41	180	34	81.1	S.J.	41	174	34	80.5	NSH	82	351	64	81.8
25	CAR	41	161	31	80.7	PIT	41	208	43	79.3	CAR	82	359	66	81.6
26	WSH	41	179	35	80.4	OTT	41	167	35	79.0	WSH	82	401	75	81.3
27	NYR	41	178	35	80.3	MTL	41	154	33	78.6	EDM	82	349	66	81.1
28	PHX	41	203	41	79.8	NYR	41	210	45	78.6	L.A.	82	336	65	80.7
29	L.A.	41	168	34	79.8	EDM	41	186	42	77.4	NYR	82	388	80	79.4
30	PIT	41	161	41	74.5	NSH	41	175	40	77.1	PIT	82	369	84	77.2
TOTAL		**1230**	**4987**	**769**	**84.6**		**1230**	**5440**	**948**	**82.6**		**1230**	**10427**	**1717**	**83.5**

SHORT-HANDED GOALS FOR

	Home			Road			Overall		
	Team	GP	SHGF	Team	GP	SHGF	Team	GP	SHGF
1	DET	41	10	ATL	41	8	DET	82	15
2	NSH	41	10	EDM	41	7	T.B	82	15
3	T.B.	41	10	NYI	41	6	NSH	82	14
4	EDM	41	6	BOS	41	6	EDM	82	13
5	CGY	41	6	COL	41	6	NYI	82	11
6	L.A.	41	6	CGY	41	5	ATL	82	11
7	FLA	41	5	CHI	41	5	CGY	82	11
8	MIN	41	5	DET	41	5	CAR	82	9
9	CAR	41	5	PHX	41	5	L.A	82	9
10	N.J.	41	5	T.B	41	5	S.J	82	9
11	S.J.	41	5	MTL	41	4	PHX	82	9
12	NYI	41	5	BUF	41	4	N.J	82	8
13	ST.L.	41	5	CAR	41	4	TOR	82	8
14	PHX	41	4	S.J	41	4	BOS	82	7
15	TOR	41	4	NYR	41	4	MIN	82	7
16	PHI	41	3	PIT	41	4	PHI	82	7
17	ATL	41	3	VAN	41	4	BUF	82	7
18	PIT	41	3	OTT	41	4	FLA	82	7
19	BUF	41	3	TOR	41	4	PIT	82	7
20	DAL	41	2	PHI	41	4	COL	82	7
21	OTT	41	2	NSH	41	4	ST.L.	82	7
22	CBJ	41	2	N.J	41	3	OTT	82	6
23	ANA	41	2	ANA	41	3	NYR	82	6
24	NYR	41	2	CBJ	41	3	DAL	82	5
25	BOS	41	1	L.A	41	3	ANA	82	5
26	WSH	41	1	DAL	41	3	CHI	82	5
27	VAN	41	1	WSH	41	3	MTL	82	5
28	COL	41	1	MIN	41	2	CBJ	82	5
29	MTL	41	1	ST.L.	41	2	VAN	82	5
30	CHI	41	0	FLA	41	2	WSH	82	4
TOTAL		**1230**	**118**		**1230**	**126**		**1230**	**244**

SHORT-HANDED GOALS AGAINST

	Home			Road			Overall		
	Team	GP	SHGA	Team	GP	SHGA	Team	GP	SHGA
1	DET	41	0	L.A	41	0	CGY	82	2
2	PHI	41	2	CGY	41	0	PHI	82	3
3	EDM	41	2	T.B	41	0	ANA	82	4
4	MIN	41	2	OTT	41	1	L.A	82	4
5	CGY	41	2	PHI	41	1	T.B	82	4
6	ANA	41	2	N.J	41	2	N.J	82	5
7	NYI	41	2	ANA	41	2	WSH	82	5
8	WSH	41	3	WSH	41	2	NYI	82	5
9	ATL	41	3	TOR	41	2	DET	82	5
10	NSH	41	3	MTL	41	3	MTL	82	6
11	MTL	41	3	NYI	41	3	MIN	82	7
12	N.J.	41	3	NYR	41	3	ATL	82	7
13	ST.L.	41	3	VAN	41	3	OTT	82	8
14	T.B.	41	4	CAR	41	4	NSH	82	8
15	PHX	41	4	S.J	41	4	EDM	82	8
16	BUF	41	4	ATL	41	4	VAN	82	8
17	L.A.	41	4	PHX	41	4	NYR	82	8
18	DAL	41	5	MIN	41	5	PHX	82	8
19	VAN	41	5	BUF	41	5	TOR	82	8
20	CAR	41	5	DET	41	5	BUF	82	9
21	NYR	41	5	NSH	41	5	CAR	82	9
22	S.J.	41	5	CHI	41	6	S.J	82	9
23	BOS	41	6	PIT	41	6	DAL	82	11
24	FLA	41	6	DAL	41	6	ST.L.	82	11
25	COL	41	6	EDM	41	6	FLA	82	12
26	TOR	41	6	FLA	41	6	BOS	82	13
27	OTT	41	7	CBJ	41	7	CHI	82	14
28	CBJ	41	7	BOS	41	7	CBJ	82	14
29	CHI	41	8	ST.L.	41	8	COL	82	14
30	PIT	41	9	COL	41	8	PIT	82	15
TOTAL		**1230**	**126**		**1230**	**118**		**1230**	**244**

Regular-Season Overtime Results

1984-85 to 2003-04

Team	2003-04 GP	W	L	T	2002-03 GP	W	L	T	2001-02 GP	W	L	T	2000-01 GP	W	L	T	1999-2000 GP	W	L	T	1998-99 GP	W	L	T	1997-98 GP	W	L	T	1996-97 GP	W	L	T	1995-96 GP	W	L	T	1994-95 GP	W	L	T
ANA	22	4	8	10	21	6	6	9	14	3	3	8	20	4	5	11	18	3	3	12	17	1	3	13	20	3	4	13	16	3	0	13	16	6	2	8	7	2	0	5
ATL	18	6	4	8	19	7	5	7	19	3	5	11	16	2	2	12	11	0	4	7																				
BOS	30	8	7	15	21	6	4	11	24	9	9	6	20	4	8	8	26	1	6	19	17	2	2	13	17	3	1	13	15	3	3	9	15	2	6	7	8	2	3	3
BUF	13	2	4	7	21	3	8	10	16	4	1	11	10	4	1	5	20	5	4	11	23	3	3	17	21	3	1	17	16	3	4	9	16	2	3	11	9	1	1	7
CGY	13	3	3	7	19	2	6	11	17	2	3	12	22	3	4	15	26	11	5	10	16	3	1	12	22	4	3	15	16	3	4	9	16	3	2	11	9	1	1	7
CAR/HFD	25	5	6	14	15	4	3	8	27	6	5	16	18	6	3	9	14	4	0	10	24	1	5	18	12	2	2	8	18	1	4	13	19	1	5	13	9	1	1	7
CHI	23	4	8	11	23	6	4	13	17	3	1	13	15	2	5	8	17	5	2	10	15	1	2	12	18	1	4	13	15	1	5	13	15	2	3	10	7	2	0	5
COL/QUE	28	8	7	13	23	4	6	13	13	4	1	8	20	6	4	10	17	5	1	11	12	2	0	10	22	2	3	17	15	2	3	10	6	1	0	5	8	0	0	8
CBJ	18	6	4	8	28	7	8	13	15	2	5	8	18	3	6	9																								
DAL/MIN	18	3	2	13	24	5	4	15	21	3	5	13	16	2	8	6	19	3	6	10	16	3	1	12	17	5	1	11	15	4	3	8	15	1	0	14	9	0	1	8
DET	20	7	2	11	21	7	4	10	24	10	4	10	23	10	4	9	16	4	2	10	10	2	1	7	15	0	0	15	27	7	2	18	11	3	1	7	4	0	0	4
EDM	23	6	5	12	27	7	9	11	19	3	4	12	20	5	3	12	27	3	8	16	20	3	5	12	15	3	2	10	16	1	6	9	14	4	2	8	7	1	2	4
FLA	24	5	4	15	26	4	9	13	16	0	6	10	24	2	9	13	15	3	6	6	21	1	2	18	20	3	2	15	26	3	4	19	13	0	3	10	9	0	3	6
L.A.	27	2	9	16	19	6	7	6	18	3	4	11	19	3	3	13	21	5	4	12	12	5	2	5	16	3	2	11	14	0	3	11	23	3	2	18	9	0	0	9
MIN	24	1	3	20	19	8	1	10	21	0	9	12	22	4	5	13																								
MTL	16	5	4	7	19	2	9	8	17	2	3	12	16	2	6	8	18	4	7	7	15	0	4	11	20	3	4	13	21	2	4	15					10	1	2	7
NSH	22	7	4	11	24	8	6	10	18	5	0	13	17	5	3	9																								
N.J.	21	7	2	12	25	5	7	13	19	6	4	9	20	5	3	12	16	3	5	8	15	3	1	11	16	2	3	11	17	1	2	14	17	2	5	10	11	1	2	8
NYI	17	2	4	11	18	6	4	8	13	5	4	4	12	2	3	7	21	5	1	9	17	1	6	10	13	0	2	11	17	3	2	12	17	2	1	14	7	1	1	5
NYR	18	3	8	7	20	6	4	10	13	5	4	4	11	5	1	5	15	2	2	11	19	5	3	11	24	2	4	18	13	3	0	10	17	0	2	15	3	0	0	3
OTT	19	3	6	10	16	7	1	8	19	3	7	9	16	3	4	9	15	2	2	11	15	1	2	12	15	3	1	11	17	2	0	15	18	0	3	15	7	1	1	5
PHI	23	2	6	15	20	4	5	11	16	3	3	10	19	5	3	11	16	4	4	8	15	2	1	12	14	0	2	12	14	0	2	12	8	2	0	6	9	0	2	7
PHX/WPG	29	5	6	18	20	4	5	11	19	4	6	9	22	7	1	14	16	4	4	8	22	7	1	14	14	0	2	12	16	5	4	7	9	3	2	4	9	0	2	7
PIT	19	7	4	8	14	3	5	6	20	7	5	8	15	3	3	9	17	3	6	8	15	1	1	13	12	2	2	8	13	1	1	11	18	1	1	16	5	1	1	3
ST.L.	24	11	2	11	19	2	8	9	18	6	4	8	23	6	5	12	21	4	7	10	21	1	2	18	12	2	2	10	12	2	2	8	9	1	1	7	5	1	0	4
S.J.	21	3	6	12	23	6	6	11	17	3	8	3	22	7	3	12	21	4	7	10	10	0	7	9	21	1	2	18	12	3	1	8	18	3	3	12	7	2	2	3
T.B.	18	4	6	8	23	2	5	16	19	4	4	11	13	2	5	6	17	7	3	7	16	0	7	9	13	0	1	9	10	1	0	9	18	3	3	12	8	0	0	8
TOR	17	4	3	10	17	7	3	7	17	3	4	10	19	3	5	11	17	7	3	7	14	6	1	7	10	1	0	9	10	1	1	8	17	4	6	7	13	0	1	12
VAN	26	11	5	10	19	5	1	13	14	4	3	7	23	5	7	11	27	4	8	15	13	0	1	12	17	0	3	14	14	5	2	7	16	1	4	11	9	0	1	8
WSH	14	1	3	10	20	6	6	8	19	6	2	11	16	2	4	10	19	5	2	12	11	2	3	6	17	4	1	12	17	4	1	12	16	4	1	11				
Totals	**315**	**145**	**170**		**313**	**156**	**157**		**270**	**121**	**149**		**274**	**122**	**152**		**260**	**114**	**146**		**222**	**60**	**162**		**219**	**54**	**165**		**214**	**70**	**144**		**201**	**64**	**137**		**101**	**26**	**75**	

2003-04

Home Team Wins: 83
Visiting Team Wins: 62

Team	1993-94 GP	W	L	T	1992-93 GP	W	L	T	1991-92 GP	W	L	T	1990-91 GP	W	L	T	1989-90 GP	W	L	T	1988-89 GP	W	L	T	1987-88 GP	W	L	T	1986-87 GP	W	L	T	1985-86 GP	W	L	T	1984-85 GP	W	L	T
ANA	12	2	5	5																																				
ATL																																								
BOS	17	2	2	13	15	5	3	7	20	6	2	12	17	5	0	12	14	3	2	14	19	3	2	14	14	4	4	6	12	2	3	7	17	2	3	12	18	4	4	10
BUF	13	0	4	9	18	4	4	10	16	2	2	12	24	3	2	19	15	4	3	8	13	2	4	7	12	0	1	11	13	1	4	8	9	1	2	6	17	0	3	14
CGY	18	3	2	13	19	4	4	11	19	2	5	12	19	2	5	12	21	3	3	15	17	5	3	9	15	2	4	9	9	2	0	7	12	1	1	10	14	1	1	12
CAR/HFD	14	4	1	9	18	3	9	6	18	2	3	13	9	1	1	7	10	2	2	6	10	1	4	5	17	2	3	12	12	3	2	7	7	1	2	4	17	4	4	9
CHI	16	2	5	9	16	1	3	12	19	2	2	15	12	3	1	8	10	2	2	6	15	4	2	9	15	4	2	9	5	1	0	4	11	4	1	6	12	2	3	7
COL/QUE	15	3	3	9	15	4	1	10	17	0	5	12	18	1	3	14	8	0	1	7	8	0	1	7	10	2	1	7	9	2	2	5	14	0	4	10	14	3	2	9
CBJ																																								
DAL/MIN	22	6	3	13	10	0	0	10	8	0	2	6	17	0	3	14	11	3	4	4	17	3	4	10	16	1	2	13	14	2	2	10	15	4	2	9	15	1	2	12
DET	15	5	2	8	15	2	0	9	16	3	1	12	14	2	4	8	17	2	1	14	16	3	1	12	16	2	3	11	14	5	3	6	13	4	5	6	12	0	1	11
EDM	21	1	6	14	17	5	4	8	12	0	2	10	15	4	5	6	20	5	1	14	15	4	3	8	16	3	2	11	14	5	3	6	14	5	2	7	12	0	1	11
FLA	24	2	5	17																																				
L.A.	18	3	3	12	13	2	1	10	16	1	1	14	16	4	2	10	12	3	2	7	14	6	1	7	12	1	3	8	12	2	2	8	14	3	3	8	19	3	2	14
MIN																																								
MTL	19	3	2	14	14	5	3	6	20	6	3	11	17	3	3	11	17	4	2	11	11	2	0	9	16	1	2	13	16	2	4	10	14	1	6	7	18	3	3	12
NSH																																								
N.J.	14	1	1	12	11	4	0	7	17	2	4	11	17	1	1	15	16	3	4	9	17	1	4	12	12	4	2	6	13	3	4	6	10	4	3	3	12	0	2	10
NYI	19	5	2	12	13	3	3	7	16	3	2	11	15	2	3	10	16	3	2	11	13	2	2	9	11	2	1	8	19	4	3	12	15	1	8	6	17	2	5	10
NYR	12	3	1	8	17	2	4	11	11	5	1	5	16	1	2	13	17	2	2	13	10	1	1	8	11	0	1	10	19	5	6	8	13	0	7	6	17	2	5	10
OTT	17	4	4	9	10	0	6	4																																
PHI	18	3	5	10	17	4	2	11	17	2	4	11	14	1	0	10	18	2	5	11	14	1	5	8	13	1	3	9	10	1	1	8	8	0	1	7	9	1	1	7
PHX/WPG	15	1	5	9	11	2	2	7	20	1	4	15	14	1	2	11	19	4	4	11	20	6	2	12	21	8	2	11	11	2	1	8	11	2	1	8	14	3	1	10
PIT	19	4	2	13	10	3	0	7	12	2	1	9	12	4	2	6	12	4	3	5	10	2	1	7	16	5	2	9	16	5	4	7	17	3	3	8	8	3	0	5
ST.L.	17	2	4	11	10	3	5	2	15	2	2	11	18	3	4	11	15	2	1	12	16	3	1	12	14	2	4	8	21	4	2	15	17	5	3	9	15	2	1	12
S.J.	19	2	1	16	10	3	5	2	9	1	3	5																												
T.B.	18	3	4	11	14	3	4	7																																
TOR	17	4	1	12	13	1	1	11	11	4	0	7	17	4	2	11	11	1	4	6	11	1	4	6	13	1	2	10	13	3	4	6	17	4	6	7	15	5	2	8
VAN	12	5	4	3	10	1	0	9	17	4	1	12	15	3	3	9	14	4	3	7	16	2	4	10	11	0	2	9	10	2	0	8	16	1	2	13	17	7	1	9
WSH	14	2	2	10	11	2	2	7	12	2	2	8	14	4	3	7	9	2	1	6	16	2	4	10	15	2	4	9	11	5	2	10	11	4	0	7	12	3	0	9
Totals	**214**	**74**	**140**		**165**	**65**	**100**		**169**	**52**	**117**		**166**	**54**	**112**		**155**	**55**	**100**		**149**	**52**	**97**		**146**	**49**	**97**		**147**	**54**	**93**		**135**	**56**	**79**		**152**	**48**	**104**	

NHL Record Book

Year-By-Year Final Standings & Leading Scorers

*Stanley Cup winner

1917-18

First Half

Team	GP	W	L	T	GF	GA	PTS
Montreal	14	10	4	0	81	47	20
Toronto	14	8	6	0	71	75	16
Ottawa	14	5	9	0	67	79	10
**Mtl. Wanderers	6	1	5	0	17	35	2

**Montreal Arena burned down and Wanderers forced to withdraw from League. Montreal Canadiens and Toronto each counted a win for defaulted games with Wanderers.

Second Half

Team	GP	W	L	T	GF	GA	PTS
*Toronto	8	5	3	0	37	34	10
Ottawa	8	4	4	0	35	35	8
Montreal	8	3	5	0	34	37	6

Leading Scorers

Player	Club	GP	G	A	PTS	PIM
Malone, Joe	Montreal	20	44	4	48	30
Denneny, Cy	Ottawa	20	36	10	46	80
Noble, Reg	Toronto	20	30	10	40	35
Lalonde, Newsy	Montreal	14	23	7	30	51
Denneny, Corb	Toronto	21	20	9	29	14
Cameron, Harry	Toronto	21	17	10	27	28
Pitre, Didier	Montreal	20	17	6	23	29
Gerard, Eddie	Ottawa	20	13	7	20	26
Darragh, Jack	Ottawa	18	14	5	19	26
Nighbor, Frank	Ottawa	10	11	8	19	6
Meeking, Harry	Toronto	21	10	9	19	28

1918-19

First Half

Team	GP	W	L	T	GF	GA	PTS
• Montreal	10	7	3	0	57	50	14
Ottawa	10	5	5	0	39	39	10
Toronto	10	3	7	0	42	49	6

Second Half

Team	GP	W	L	T	GF	GA	PTS
Ottawa	8	7	1	0	32	14	14
Montreal	8	3	5	0	31	28	6
Toronto	8	2	6	0	22	43	4

• NHL Champion. Stanley Cup not awarded due to influenza epidemic.

Leading Scorers

Player	Club	GP	G	A	PTS	PIM
Lalonde, Newsy	Montreal	17	22	10	32	40
Cleghorn, Odie	Montreal	17	22	6	28	22
Nighbor, Frank	Ottawa	18	19	9	28	27
Denneny, Cy	Ottawa	18	18	4	22	58
Pitre, Didier	Montreal	17	14	5	19	12
Skinner, Alf	Toronto	17	12	4	16	26
Cameron, Harry	Tor., Ott.	14	11	3	14	35
Darragh, Jack	Ottawa	14	11	3	14	33
Randall, Ken	Toronto	15	8	6	14	27
Cleghorn, Sprague	Ottawa	18	7	6	13	27

1919-20

First Half

Team	GP	W	L	T	GF	GA	PTS
Ottawa	12	9	3	0	59	23	18
Montreal	12	8	4	0	62	51	16
Toronto	12	5	7	0	52	62	10
Quebec	12	2	10	0	44	81	4

Second Half

Team	GP	W	L	T	GF	GA	PTS
*Ottawa	12	10	2	0	62	41	20
Toronto	12	7	5	0	67	44	14
Montreal	12	5	7	0	67	62	10
Quebec	12	2	10	0	47	96	4

Leading Scorers

Player	Club	GP	G	A	PTS	PIM
Malone, Joe	Quebec	24	39	10	49	12
Lalonde, Newsy	Montreal	23	37	9	46	34
Nighbor, Frank	Ottawa	23	26	15	41	18
Denneny, Corb	Toronto	24	24	12	36	20
Darragh, Jack	Ottawa	23	22	14	36	22
Noble, Reg	Toronto	24	24	9	33	52
Arbour, Amos	Montreal	22	21	5	26	13
Wilson, Cully	Toronto	23	20	6	26	86
Pitre, Didier	Montreal	22	14	12	26	6
Broadbent, Punch	Ottawa	21	19	6	25	40

1920-21

First Half

Team	GP	W	L	T	GF	GA	PTS
*Ottawa	10	8	2	0	49	23	16
Toronto	10	5	5	0	39	47	10
Montreal	10	4	6	0	37	51	8
Hamilton	10	3	7	0	34	38	6

Second Half

Team	GP	W	L	T	GF	GA	PTS
Toronto	14	10	4	0	66	53	20
Montreal	14	9	5	0	75	48	18
Ottawa	14	6	8	0	48	52	12
Hamilton	14	3	11	0	58	94	6

Leading Scorers

Player	Club	GP	G	A	PTS	PIM
Lalonde, Newsy	Montreal	24	33	10	43	36
Dye, Babe	Ham., Tor.	24	35	5	40	32
Denneny, Cy	Ottawa	24	34	5	39	10
Malone, Joe	Hamilton	20	28	9	37	6
Nighbor, Frank	Ottawa	24	19	10	29	10
Noble, Reg	Toronto	24	19	8	27	54
Cameron, Harry	Toronto	24	18	9	27	35
Prodgers, Goldie	Hamilton	24	18	9	27	8
Denneny, Corb	Toronto	20	19	7	26	29
Darragh, Jack	Ottawa	24	11	15	26	20

All-Time Standings of NHL Teams

(ranked by percentage)

Active Clubs

Team	Games	Wins	Losses	Ties	OT Losses	Goals For	Goals Against	Points	Pts %	First Season
Montreal	5546	2849	1834	837	26	18285	14786	6561	.590	1917-18
Philadelphia	2932	1468	988	457	19	10031	8557	3412	.578	1967-68
Boston	5386	2564	1997	791	34	17453	15889	5953	.550	1924-25
Buffalo	2706	1257	1022	409	18	9076	8252	2941	.540	1970-71
Edmonton	1994	940	763	262	29	7387	6791	2171	.538	1979-80
Calgary	2550	1142	1010	379	19	8791	8311	2682	.521	1972-73
Detroit	5320	2359	2130	815	16	16536	15974	5549	.519	1926-27
Colorado	1994	897	815	261	21	6900	6692	2076	.514	1979-80
St. Louis	2932	1288	1194	432	18	9352	9316	3026	.511	1967-68
Toronto	5546	2418	2327	783	18	17193	17051	5637	.506	1917-18
NY Islanders	2550	1112	1077	347	14	8589	8177	2585	.503	1972-73
NY Rangers	5320	2231	2261	808	20	16477	16716	5290	.495	1926-27
Dallas	2932	1205	1249	459	19	9175	9514	2888	.489	1967-68
Chicago	5320	2176	2308	814	22	15843	16136	5188	.486	1926-27
Washington	2394	1011	1063	303	17	7657	8011	2342	.485	1974-75
Pittsburgh	2932	1199	1327	383	23	9938	10559	2804	.474	1967-68
Los Angeles	2932	1161	1321	424	26	9738	10367	2772	.469	1967-68
Minnesota	328	123	132	55	18	749	809	319	.464	2000-01
Ottawa	954	383	436	115	20	2655	2864	901	.462	1992-93
Phoenix	1994	785	919	266	24	6497	7139	1860	.461	1979-80
Florida	870	322	372	142	34	2224	2442	820	.459	1993-94
New Jersey	2394	934	1112	328	20	7399	8145	2216	.457	1974-75
Anaheim	870	338	400	107	25	2220	2438	808	.452	1993-94
Vancouver	2706	1024	1267	391	24	8658	9528	2463	.450	1970-71
Carolina	1994	761	950	263	20	6103	6873	1805	.447	1979-80
San Jose	1034	382	504	121	27	2810	3268	912	.431	1991-92
Nashville	492	183	228	60	21	1170	1354	447	.430	1998-99
Tampa Bay	954	328	487	112	27	2421	2994	795	.408	1992-93
Columbus	328	104	173	33	18	744	989	259	.371	2000-01
Atlanta	410	120	225	45	20	1008	1417	305	.349	1999-2000

Defunct Clubs

Team	Games	Wins	Losses	Ties	Goals For	Goals Against	Points	Pts %	First Season	Last Season
Ottawa Senators	542	258	221	63	1458	1333	579	.534	1917-18	1933-34
Montreal Maroons	622	271	260	91	1474	1405	633	.509	1924-25	1937-38
NY/Brooklyn Americans	784	255	402	127	1643	2182	637	.406	1925-26	1941-42
Hamilton Tigers	126	47	78	1	414	475	95	.377	1920-21	1924-25
Cleveland Barons	160	47	87	26	470	617	120	.375	1976-77	1977-78
Pittsburgh Pirates	212	67	122	23	376	519	157	.370	1925-26	1929-30
Calif./Oakland Seals	698	182	401	115	1826	2580	479	.343	1967-68	1975-76
St. Louis Eagles	48	11	31	6	86	144	28	.292	1934-35	1934-35
Quebec Bulldogs	24	4	20	0	91	177	8	.167	1919-20	1919-20
Montreal Wanderers	6	1	5	0	17	35	2	.167	1917-18	1917-18
Philadelphia Quakers	44	4	36	4	76	184	12	.136	1930-31	1930-31

Calgary totals include Atlanta Flames, 1972-73 to 1979-80.
Carolina totals include Hartford, 1979-80 to 1996-97.
Colorado totals include Quebec, 1979-80 to 1994-95.
Dallas totals include Minnesota North Stars, 1967-68 to 1992-93.
Detroit totals include Cougars, 1926-27 to 1929-30, and Falcons, 1930-31 to 1931-32.
New Jersey totals include Kansas City, 1974-75 to 1975-76, and Colorado Rockies, 1976-77 to 1981-82.
Phoenix totals include Winnipeg, 1979-80 to 1995-96.
Toronto totals include Arenas, 1917-18 to 1918-19, and St. Patricks, 1919-20 to 1925-26.

1921-22

Team	GP	W	L	T	GF	GA	PTS
Ottawa	24	14	8	2	106	84	30
*Toronto	24	13	10	1	98	97	27
Montreal	24	12	11	1	88	94	25
Hamilton	24	7	17	0	88	105	14

Leading Scorers

Player	Club	GP	G	A	PTS	PIM
Broadbent, Punch	Ottawa	24	32	14	46	28
Denneny, Cy	Ottawa	22	27	12	39	20
Dye, Babe	Toronto	24	31	7	38	39
Cameron, Harry	Toronto	24	18	17	35	22
Malone, Joe	Hamilton	24	24	7	31	4
Denneny, Corb	Toronto	24	19	9	28	28
Noble, Reg	Toronto	24	17	11	28	19
Cleghorn, Sprague	Montreal	24	17	9	26	80
Boucher, Georges	Ottawa	23	13	12	25	12
Cleghorn, Odie	Montreal	23	21	3	24	26

1922-23

Team	GP	W	L	T	GF	GA	PTS
*Ottawa	24	14	9	1	77	54	29
Montreal	24	13	9	2	73	61	28
Toronto	24	13	10	1	82	88	27
Hamilton	24	6	18	0	81	110	12

Leading Scorers

Player	Club	GP	G	A	PTS	PIM
Dye, Babe	Toronto	22	26	11	37	19
Denneny, Cy	Ottawa	24	23	11	34	28
Boucher, Billy	Montreal	24	24	7	31	55
Adams, Jack	Toronto	23	19	9	28	42
Roach, Mickey	Hamilton	24	17	10	27	8
Cleghorn, Odie	Montreal	24	19	6	25	18
Boucher, Georges	Ottawa	24	14	9	23	58
Noble, Reg	Toronto	24	12	11	23	47
Wilson, Cully	Hamilton	23	16	5	21	46
Joliat, Aurel	Montreal	24	12	9	21	37

1923-24

Team	GP	W	L	T	GF	GA	PTS
Ottawa	24	16	8	0	74	54	32
*Montreal	24	13	11	0	59	48	26
Toronto	24	10	14	0	59	85	20
Hamilton	24	9	15	0	63	68	18

Leading Scorers

Player	Club	GP	G	A	PTS	PIM
Denneny, Cy	Ottawa	22	22	2	24	10
Boucher, Georges	Ottawa	21	13	10	23	38
Boucher, Billy	Montreal	23	16	6	22	48
Burch, Billy	Hamilton	24	16	6	22	6
Joliat, Aurel	Montreal	24	15	5	20	27
Dye, Babe	Toronto	19	16	3	19	23
Adams, Jack	Toronto	22	14	4	18	51
Noble, Reg	Toronto	23	12	5	17	79
Morenz, Howie	Montreal	24	13	3	16	20
Clancy, King	Ottawa	24	8	8	16	79

1924-25

Team	GP	W	L	T	GF	GA	PTS
Hamilton	30	19	10	1	90	60	39
Toronto	30	19	11	0	90	84	38
• Montreal	30	17	11	2	93	56	36
Ottawa	30	17	12	1	83	66	35
Mtl. Maroons	30	9	19	2	45	65	20
Boston	30	6	24	0	49	119	12

• NHL Champion (Stanley Cup won by Victoria Cougars, WCHL)

Leading Scorers

Player	Club	GP	G	A	PTS	PIM
Dye, Babe	Toronto	29	38	6	46	41
Denneny, Cy	Ottawa	29	27	15	42	16
Joliat, Aurel	Montreal	25	30	11	41	85
Morenz, Howie	Montreal	30	28	11	39	46
Green, Red	Hamilton	30	19	15	34	81
Adams, Jack	Toronto	27	21	10	31	67
Boucher, Billy	Montreal	30	17	13	30	92
Burch, Billy	Hamilton	27	20	7	27	10
Herberts, Jimmy	Boston	30	17	7	24	55
Smith, Hooley	Ottawa	30	10	13	23	81

1925-26

Team	GP	W	L	T	GF	GA	PTS
Ottawa	36	24	8	4	77	42	52
*Mtl. Maroons	36	20	11	5	91	73	45
Pittsburgh	36	19	16	1	82	70	39
Boston	36	17	15	4	92	85	38
NY Americans	36	12	20	4	68	89	28
Toronto	36	12	21	3	92	114	27
Montreal	36	11	24	1	79	108	23

Leading Scorers

Player	Club	GP	G	A	PTS	PIM
Stewart, Nels	Mtl. Maroons	36	34	8	42	119
Denneny, Cy	Ottawa	36	24	12	36	18
Cooper, Carson	Boston	36	28	3	31	10
Herberts, Jimmy	Boston	36	26	5	31	47
Morenz, Howie	Montreal	31	23	3	26	39
Adams, Jack	Toronto	36	21	5	26	52
Joliat, Aurel	Montreal	35	17	9	26	52
Burch, Billy	NY Americans	36	22	3	25	33
Smith, Hooley	Ottawa	28	16	9	25	53
Nighbor, Frank	Ottawa	35	12	13	25	40

1926-27

Canadian Division

Team	GP	W	L	T	GF	GA	PTS
*Ottawa	44	30	10	4	86	69	64
Montreal	44	28	14	2	99	67	58
Mtl. Maroons	44	20	20	4	71	68	44
NY Americans	44	17	25	2	82	91	36
Toronto	44	15	24	5	79	94	35

American Division

Team	GP	W	L	T	GF	GA	PTS
NY Rangers	44	25	13	6	95	72	56
Boston	44	21	20	3	97	89	45
Chicago	44	19	22	3	115	116	41
Pittsburgh	44	15	26	3	79	108	33
Detroit	44	12	28	4	76	105	28

Leading Scorers

Player	Club	GP	G	A	PTS	PIM
Cook, Bill	NY Rangers	44	33	4	37	58
Irvin, Dick	Chicago	43	18	18	36	34
Morenz, Howie	Montreal	44	25	7	32	49
Fredrickson, Frank	Det., Bos.	41	18	13	31	46
Dye, Babe	Chicago	41	25	5	30	14
Bailey, Ace	Toronto	42	15	13	28	82
Boucher, Frank	NY Rangers	44	13	15	28	17
Burch, Billy	NY Americans	43	19	8	27	40
Oliver, Harry	Boston	42	18	6	24	17
Keats, Duke	Bos., Det.	42	16	8	24	52

1927-28

Canadian Division

Team	GP	W	L	T	GF	GA	PTS
Montreal	44	26	11	7	116	48	59
Mtl. Maroons	44	24	14	6	96	77	54
Ottawa	44	20	14	10	78	57	50
Toronto	44	18	18	8	89	88	44
NY Americans	44	11	27	6	63	128	28

American Division

Team	GP	W	L	T	GF	GA	PTS
Boston	44	20	13	11	77	70	51
*NY Rangers	44	19	16	9	94	79	47
Pittsburgh	44	19	17	8	67	76	46
Detroit	44	19	19	6	88	79	44
Chicago	44	7	34	3	68	134	17

Leading Scorers

Player	Club	GP	G	A	PTS	PIM
Morenz, Howie	Montreal	43	33	18	51	66
Joliat, Aurel	Montreal	44	28	11	39	105
Boucher, Frank	NY Rangers	44	23	12	35	15
Hay, George	Detroit	42	22	13	35	20
Stewart, Nels	Mtl. Maroons	41	27	7	34	104
Gagne, Art	Montreal	44	20	10	30	75
Cook, Bun	NY Rangers	44	14	14	28	45
Carson, Bill	Toronto	32	20	6	26	36
Finnigan, Frank	Ottawa	38	20	5	25	34
Cook, Bill	NY Rangers	43	18	6	24	42
Keats, Duke	Det., Chi.	38	14	10	24	60

1928-29

Canadian Division

Team	GP	W	L	T	GF	GA	PTS
Montreal	44	22	7	15	71	43	59
NY Americans	44	19	13	12	53	53	50
Toronto	44	21	18	5	85	69	47
Ottawa	44	14	17	13	54	67	41
Mtl. Maroons	44	15	20	9	67	65	39

American Division

Team	GP	W	L	T	GF	GA	PTS
*Boston	44	26	13	5	89	52	57
NY Rangers	44	21	13	10	72	65	52
Detroit	44	19	16	9	72	63	47
Pittsburgh	44	9	27	8	46	80	26
Chicago	44	7	29	8	33	85	22

Leading Scorers

Player	Club	GP	G	A	PTS	PIM
Bailey, Ace	Toronto	44	22	10	32	78
Stewart, Nels	Mtl. Maroons	44	21	8	29	74
Cooper, Carson	Detroit	43	18	9	27	14
Morenz, Howie	Montreal	42	17	10	27	47
Blair, Andy	Toronto	44	12	15	27	41
Boucher, Frank	NY Rangers	44	10	16	26	8
Oliver, Harry	Boston	43	17	6	23	24
Cook, Bill	NY Rangers	43	15	8	23	41
Ward, Jimmy	Mtl. Maroons	43	14	8	22	46

Seven players tied with 19 points

1929-30

Canadian Division

Team	GP	W	L	T	GF	GA	PTS
Mtl. Maroons	44	23	16	5	141	114	51
*Montreal	44	21	14	9	142	114	51
Ottawa	44	21	15	8	138	118	50
Toronto	44	17	21	6	116	124	40
NY Americans	44	14	25	5	113	161	33

American Division

Team	GP	W	L	T	GF	GA	PTS
Boston	44	38	5	1	179	98	77
Chicago	44	21	18	5	117	111	47
NY Rangers	44	17	17	10	136	143	44
Detroit	44	14	24	6	117	133	34
Pittsburgh	44	5	36	3	102	185	13

Leading Scorers

Player	Club	GP	G	A	PTS	PIM
Weiland, Cooney	Boston	44	43	30	73	27
Boucher, Frank	NY Rangers	42	26	36	62	16
Clapper, Dit	Boston	44	41	20	61	48
Cook, Bill	NY Rangers	44	29	30	59	56
Kilrea, Hec	Ottawa	44	36	22	58	72
Stewart, Nels	Mtl. Maroons	44	39	16	55	81
Morenz, Howie	Montreal	44	40	10	50	72
Himes, Normie	NY Americans	44	28	22	50	15
Lamb, Joe	Ottawa	44	29	20	49	119
Gainor, Dutch	Boston	42	18	31	49	39

1930-31

Canadian Division

Team	GP	W	L	T	GF	GA	PTS
*Montreal	44	26	10	8	129	89	60
Toronto	44	22	13	9	118	99	53
Mtl. Maroons	44	20	18	6	105	106	46
NY Americans	44	18	16	10	76	74	46
Ottawa	44	10	30	4	91	142	24

American Division

Team	GP	W	L	T	GF	GA	PTS
Boston	44	28	10	6	143	90	62
Chicago	44	24	17	3	108	78	51
NY Rangers	44	19	16	9	106	87	47
Detroit	44	16	21	7	102	105	39
Philadelphia	44	4	36	4	76	184	12

Leading Scorers

Player	Club	GP	G	A	PTS	PIM
Morenz, Howie	Montreal	39	28	23	51	49
Goodfellow, Ebbie	Detroit	44	25	23	48	32
Conacher, Charlie	Toronto	37	31	12	43	78
Cook, Bill	NY Rangers	43	30	12	42	39
Bailey, Ace	Toronto	40	23	19	42	46
Primeau, Joe	Toronto	38	9	32	41	18
Stewart, Nels	Mtl. Maroons	42	25	14	39	75
Boucher, Frank	NY Rangers	44	12	27	39	20
Weiland, Cooney	Boston	44	25	13	38	14
Cook, Bun	NY Rangers	44	18	17	35	72
Joliat, Aurel	Montreal	43	13	22	35	73

1931-32

Canadian Division

Team	GP	W	L	T	GF	GA	PTS
Montreal	48	25	16	7	128	111	57
*Toronto	48	23	18	7	155	127	53
Mtl. Maroons	48	19	22	7	142	139	45
NY Americans	48	16	24	8	95	142	40

American Division

Team	GP	W	L	T	GF	GA	PTS
NY Rangers	48	23	17	8	134	112	54
Chicago	48	18	19	11	86	101	47
Detroit	48	18	20	10	95	108	46
Boston	48	15	21	12	122	117	42

Leading Scorers

Player	Club	GP	G	A	PTS	PIM
Jackson, Busher	Toronto	48	28	25	53	63
Primeau, Joe	Toronto	46	13	37	50	25
Morenz, Howie	Montreal	48	24	25	49	46
Conacher, Charlie	Toronto	44	34	14	48	66
Cook, Bill	NY Rangers	48	34	14	48	33
Trottier, Dave	Mtl. Maroons	48	26	18	44	94
Smith, Hooley	Mtl. Maroons	43	11	33	44	49
Siebert, Babe	Mtl. Maroons	48	21	18	39	64
Clapper, Dit	Boston	48	17	22	39	21
Joliat, Aurel	Montreal	48	15	24	39	46

1932-33

Canadian Division

Team	GP	W	L	T	GF	GA	PTS
Toronto	48	24	18	6	119	111	54
Mtl. Maroons	48	22	20	6	135	119	50
Montreal	48	18	25	5	92	115	41
NY Americans	48	15	22	11	91	118	41
Ottawa	48	11	27	10	88	131	32

American Division

Team	GP	W	L	T	GF	GA	PTS
Boston	48	25	15	8	124	88	58
Detroit	48	25	15	8	111	93	58
*NY Rangers	48	23	17	8	135	107	54
Chicago	48	16	20	12	88	101	44

Leading Scorers

Player	Club	GP	G	A	PTS	PIM
Cook, Bill	NY Rangers	48	28	22	50	51
Jackson, Busher	Toronto	48	27	17	44	43
Northcott, Baldy	Mtl. Maroons	48	22	21	43	30
Smith, Hooley	Mtl. Maroons	48	20	21	41	66
Haynes, Paul	Mtl. Maroons	48	16	25	41	18
Joliat, Aurel	Montreal	48	18	21	39	53
Barry, Marty	Boston	48	24	13	37	40
Cook, Bun	NY Rangers	48	22	15	37	35
Stewart, Nels	Boston	47	18	18	36	62
Morenz, Howie	Montreal	46	14	21	35	32
Gagnon, Johnny	Montreal	48	12	23	35	64
Shore, Eddie	Boston	48	8	27	35	102
Boucher, Frank	NY Rangers	46	7	28	35	4

1933-34

Canadian Division

Team	GP	W	L	T	GF	GA	PTS
Toronto	48	26	13	9	174	119	61
Montreal	48	22	20	6	99	101	50
Mtl. Maroons	48	19	18	11	117	122	49
NY Americans	48	15	23	10	104	132	40
Ottawa	48	13	29	6	115	143	32

American Division

Team	GP	W	L	T	GF	GA	PTS
Detroit	48	24	14	10	113	98	58
*Chicago	48	20	17	11	88	83	51
NY Rangers	48	21	19	8	120	113	50
Boston	48	18	25	5	111	130	41

Leading Scorers

Player	Club	GP	G	A	PTS	PIM
Conacher, Charlie	Toronto	42	32	20	52	38
Primeau, Joe	Toronto	45	14	32	46	8
Boucher, Frank	NY Rangers	48	14	30	44	4
Barry, Marty	Boston	48	27	12	39	12
Dillon, Cecil	NY Rangers	48	13	26	39	10
Stewart, Nels	Boston	48	21	17	38	68
Jackson, Busher	Toronto	38	20	18	38	38
Joliat, Aurel	Montreal	48	22	15	37	27
Smith, Reg	Mtl. Maroons	47	18	19	37	58
Thompson, Paul	Chicago	48	20	16	36	17

1934-35

Canadian Division

Team	GP	W	L	T	GF	GA	PTS
Toronto	48	30	14	4	157	111	64
*Mtl. Maroons	48	24	19	5	123	92	53
Montreal	48	19	23	6	110	145	44
NY Americans	48	12	27	9	100	142	33
St. Louis	48	11	31	6	86	144	28

American Division

Team	GP	W	L	T	GF	GA	PTS
Boston	48	26	16	6	129	112	58
Chicago	48	26	17	5	118	88	57
NY Rangers	48	22	20	6	137	139	50
Detroit	48	19	22	7	127	114	45

Leading Scorers

Player	Club	GP	G	A	PTS	PIM
Conacher, Charlie	Toronto	47	36	21	57	24
Howe, Syd	St.L., Det.	50	22	25	47	34
Aurie, Larry	Detroit	48	17	29	46	24
Boucher, Frank	NY Rangers	48	13	32	45	2
Jackson, Busher	Toronto	42	22	22	44	27
Lewis, Herbie	Detroit	47	16	27	43	26
Chapman, Art	NY Americans	47	9	34	43	4
Barry, Marty	Boston	48	20	20	40	33
Schriner, Sweeney	NY Americans	48	18	22	40	6
Stewart, Nels	Boston	47	21	18	39	45
Thompson, Paul	Chicago	48	16	23	39	20

1935-36

Canadian Division

Team	GP	W	L	T	GF	GA	PTS
Mtl. Maroons	48	22	16	10	114	106	54
Toronto	48	23	19	6	126	106	52
*NY Americans	48	16	25	7	109	122	39
Montreal	48	11	26	11	82	123	33

American Division

Team	GP	W	L	T	GF	GA	PTS
*Detroit	48	24	16	8	124	103	56
Boston	48	22	20	6	92	83	50
Chicago	48	21	19	8	93	92	50
NY Rangers	48	19	17	12	91	96	50

Leading Scorers

Player	Club	GP	G	A	PTS	PIM
Schriner, Sweeney	NY Americans	48	19	26	45	8
Barry, Marty	Detroit	48	21	19	40	16
Thompson, Paul	Chicago	45	17	23	40	19
Thoms, Bill	Toronto	48	23	15	38	29
Conacher, Charlie	Toronto	44	23	15	38	74
Smith, Hooley	Mtl. Maroons	47	19	19	38	75
Romnes, Doc	Chicago	48	13	25	38	6
Chapman, Art	NY Americans	47	10	28	38	14
Lewis, Herbie	Detroit	45	14	23	37	25
Northcott, Baldy	Mtl. Maroons	48	15	21	36	41

1936-37

Canadian Division

Team	GP	W	L	T	GF	GA	PTS
Montreal	48	24	18	6	115	111	54
Mtl. Maroons	48	22	17	9	126	110	53
Toronto	48	22	21	5	119	115	49
NY Americans	48	15	29	4	122	161	34

American Division

Team	GP	W	L	T	GF	GA	PTS
*Detroit	48	25	14	9	128	102	59
Boston	48	23	18	7	120	110	53
NY Rangers	48	19	20	9	117	106	47
Chicago	48	14	27	7	99	131	35

Leading Scorers

Player	Club	GP	G	A	PTS	PIM
Schriner, Sweeney	NY Americans	48	21	25	46	17
Apps, Syl	Toronto	48	16	29	45	10
Barry, Marty	Detroit	48	17	27	44	6
Aurie, Larry	Detroit	45	23	20	43	20
Jackson, Busher	Toronto	46	21	19	40	12
Gagnon, Johnny	Montreal	48	20	16	36	38
Gracie, Bob	Mtl. Maroons	47	11	25	36	18
Stewart, Nels	Bos., NYA	43	23	12	35	37
Thompson, Paul	Chicago	47	17	18	35	28
Cowley, Bill	Boston	46	13	22	35	4

1937-38

Canadian Division

Team	GP	W	L	T	GF	GA	PTS
Toronto	48	24	15	9	151	127	57
NY Americans	48	19	18	11	110	111	49
Montreal	48	18	17	13	123	128	49
Mtl. Maroons	48	12	30	6	101	149	30

American Division

Team	GP	W	L	T	GF	GA	PTS
Boston	48	30	11	7	142	89	67
NY Rangers	48	27	15	6	149	96	60
*Chicago	48	14	25	9	97	139	37
Detroit	48	12	25	11	99	133	35

Leading Scorers

Player	Club	GP	G	A	PTS	PIM
Drillon, Gordie	Toronto	48	26	26	52	4
Apps, Syl	Toronto	47	21	29	50	9
Thompson, Paul	Chicago	48	22	22	44	14
Mantha, Georges	Montreal	47	23	19	42	12
Dillon, Cecil	NY Rangers	48	21	18	39	6
Cowley, Bill	Boston	48	17	22	39	8
Schriner, Sweeney	NY Americans	49	21	17	38	22
Thoms, Bill	Toronto	48	14	24	38	14
Smith, Clint	NY Rangers	48	14	23	37	0
Stewart, Nels	NY Americans	48	19	17	36	6
Colville, Neil	NY Rangers	45	17	19	36	11

1938-39

Team	GP	W	L	T	GF	GA	PTS
*Boston	48	36	10	2	156	76	74
NY Rangers	48	26	16	6	149	105	58
Toronto	48	19	20	9	114	107	47
NY Americans	48	17	21	10	119	157	44
Detroit	48	18	24	6	107	128	42
Montreal	48	15	24	9	115	146	39
Chicago	48	12	28	8	91	132	32

Leading Scorers

Player	Club	GP	G	A	PTS	PIM
Blake, Toe	Montreal	48	24	23	47	10
Schriner, Sweeney	NY Americans	48	13	31	44	20
Cowley, Bill	Boston	34	8	34	42	2
Smith, Clint	NY Rangers	48	21	20	41	2
Barry, Marty	Detroit	48	13	28	41	4
Apps, Syl	Toronto	44	15	25	40	4
Anderson, Tom	NY Americans	48	13	27	40	14
Gottselig, Johnny	Chicago	48	16	23	39	15
Haynes, Paul	Montreal	47	5	33	38	27
Conacher, Roy	Boston	47	26	11	37	12
Carr, Lorne	NY Americans	46	19	18	37	16
Colville, Neil	NY Rangers	48	18	19	37	12
Watson, Phil	NY Rangers	48	15	22	37	42

1939-40

Team	GP	W	L	T	GF	GA	PTS
Boston	48	31	12	5	170	98	67
*NY Rangers	48	27	11	10	136	77	64
Toronto	48	25	17	6	134	110	56
Chicago	48	23	19	6	112	120	52
Detroit	48	16	26	6	91	126	38
NY Americans	48	15	29	4	106	140	34
Montreal	48	10	33	5	90	168	25

Leading Scorers

Player	Club	GP	G	A	PTS	PIM
Schmidt, Milt	Boston	48	22	30	52	37
Dumart, Woody	Boston	48	22	21	43	16
Bauer, Bobby	Boston	48	17	26	43	2
Drillon, Gordie	Toronto	43	21	19	40	13
Cowley, Bill	Boston	48	13	27	40	24
Hextall, Bryan	NY Rangers	48	24	15	39	52
Colville, Neil	NY Rangers	48	19	19	38	22
Howe, Syd	Detroit	46	14	23	37	17
Blake, Toe	Montreal	48	17	19	36	48
Armstrong, Murray	NY Americans	48	16	20	36	12

1940-41

Team	GP	W	L	T	GF	GA	PTS
*Boston	48	27	8	13	168	102	67
Toronto	48	28	14	6	145	99	62
Detroit	48	21	16	11	112	102	53
NY Rangers	48	21	19	8	143	125	50
Chicago	48	16	25	7	112	139	39
Montreal	48	16	26	6	121	147	38
NY Americans	48	8	29	11	99	186	27

Leading Scorers

Player	Club	GP	G	A	PTS	PIM
Cowley, Bill	Boston	46	17	45	62	16
Hextall, Bryan	NY Rangers	48	26	18	44	16
Drillon, Gordie	Toronto	42	23	21	44	2
Apps, Syl	Toronto	41	20	24	44	6
Patrick, Lynn	NY Rangers	48	20	24	44	12
Howe, Syd	Detroit	48	20	24	44	8
Colville, Neil	NY Rangers	48	14	28	42	28
Wiseman, Eddie	Boston	48	16	24	40	10
Bauer, Bobby	Boston	48	17	22	39	2
Schriner, Sweeney	Toronto	48	24	14	38	6
Conacher, Roy	Boston	40	24	14	38	7
Schmidt, Milt	Boston	44	13	25	38	23

1941-42

Team	GP	W	L	T	GF	GA	PTS
NY Rangers	48	29	17	2	177	143	60
*Toronto	48	27	18	3	158	136	57
Boston	48	25	17	6	160	118	56
Chicago	48	22	23	3	145	155	47
Detroit	48	19	25	4	140	147	42
Montreal	48	18	27	3	134	173	39
Brooklyn	48	16	29	3	133	175	35

Leading Scorers

Player	Club	GP	G	A	PTS	PIM
Hextall, Bryan	NY Rangers	48	24	32	56	30
Patrick, Lynn	NY Rangers	47	32	22	54	18
Grosso, Don	Detroit	48	23	30	53	13
Watson, Phil	NY Rangers	48	15	37	52	48
Abel, Sid	Detroit	48	18	31	49	45
Blake, Toe	Montreal	47	17	28	45	19
Thoms, Bill	Chicago	47	15	30	45	8
Drillon, Gordie	Toronto	48	23	18	41	6
Apps, Syl	Toronto	38	18	23	41	0
Anderson, Tom	Brooklyn	48	12	29	41	54

1942-43

Team	GP	W	L	T	GF	GA	PTS
*Detroit	50	25	14	11	169	124	61
Boston	50	24	17	9	195	176	57
Toronto	50	22	19	9	198	159	53
Montreal	50	19	19	12	181	191	50
Chicago	50	17	18	15	179	180	49
NY Rangers	50	11	31	8	161	253	30

Leading Scorers

Player	Club	GP	G	A	PTS	PIM
Bentley, Doug	Chicago	50	33	40	73	18
Cowley, Bill	Boston	48	27	45	72	10
Bentley, Max	Chicago	47	26	44	70	2
Patrick, Lynn	NY Rangers	50	22	39	61	28
Carr, Lorne	Toronto	50	27	33	60	15
Taylor, Billy	Toronto	50	18	42	60	2
Hextall, Bryan	NY Rangers	50	27	32	59	28
Blake, Toe	Montreal	48	23	36	59	28
Lach, Elmer	Montreal	45	18	40	58	14
O'Connor, Buddy	Montreal	50	15	43	58	2

1943-44

Team	GP	W	L	T	GF	GA	PTS
*Montreal	50	38	5	7	234	109	83
Detroit	50	26	18	6	214	177	58
Toronto	50	23	23	4	214	174	50
Chicago	50	22	23	5	178	187	49
Boston	50	19	26	5	223	268	43
NY Rangers	50	6	39	5	162	310	17

Leading Scorers

Player	Club	GP	G	A	PTS	PIM
Cain, Herb	Boston	48	36	46	82	4
Bentley, Doug	Chicago	50	38	39	77	22
Carr, Lorne	Toronto	50	36	38	74	9
Liscombe, Carl	Detroit	50	36	37	73	17
Lach, Elmer	Montreal	48	24	48	72	23
Smith, Clint	Chicago	50	23	49	72	4
Cowley, Bill	Boston	36	30	41	71	12
Mosienko, Bill	Chicago	50	32	38	70	10
Jackson, Art	Boston	49	28	41	69	8
Bodnar, Gus	Toronto	50	22	40	62	18

1944-45

Team	GP	W	L	T	GF	GA	PTS
Montreal	50	38	8	4	228	121	80
Detroit	50	31	14	5	218	161	67
*Toronto	50	24	22	4	183	161	52
Boston	50	16	30	4	179	219	36
Chicago	50	13	30	7	141	194	33
NY Rangers	50	11	29	10	154	247	32

Leading Scorers

Player	Club	GP	G	A	PTS	PIM
Lach, Elmer	Montreal	50	26	54	80	37
Richard, Maurice	Montreal	50	50	23	73	36
Blake, Toe	Montreal	49	29	38	67	15
Cowley, Bill	Boston	49	25	40	65	2
Kennedy, Ted	Toronto	49	29	25	54	14
Mosienko, Bill	Chicago	50	28	26	54	0
Carveth, Joe	Detroit	50	26	28	54	6
DeMarco, Ab	NY Rangers	50	24	30	54	10
Smith, Clint	Chicago	50	23	31	54	0
Howe, Syd	Detroit	46	17	36	53	6

1945-46

Team	GP	W	L	T	GF	GA	PTS
*Montreal	50	28	17	5	172	134	61
Boston	50	24	18	8	167	156	56
Chicago	50	23	20	7	200	178	53
Detroit	50	20	20	10	146	159	50
Toronto	50	19	24	7	174	185	45
NY Rangers	50	13	28	9	144	191	35

Leading Scorers

Player	Club	GP	G	A	PTS	PIM
Bentley, Max	Chicago	47	31	30	61	6
Stewart, Gaye	Toronto	50	37	15	52	8
Blake, Toe	Montreal	50	29	21	50	2
Smith, Clint	Chicago	50	26	24	50	2
Richard, Maurice	Montreal	50	27	21	48	50
Mosienko, Bill	Chicago	40	18	30	48	12
DeMarco, Ab	NY Rangers	50	20	27	47	20
Lach, Elmer	Montreal	50	13	34	47	34
Kaleta, Alex	Chicago	49	19	27	46	17
Taylor, Billy	Toronto	48	23	18	41	14
Horeck, Pete	Chicago	50	20	21	41	34

1946-47

Team	GP	W	L	T	GF	GA	PTS
Montreal	60	34	16	10	189	138	78
*Toronto	60	31	19	10	209	172	72
Boston	60	26	23	11	190	175	63
Detroit	60	22	27	11	190	193	55
NY Rangers	60	22	32	6	167	186	50
Chicago	60	19	37	4	193	274	42

Leading Scorers

Player	Club	GP	G	A	PTS	PIM
Bentley, Max	Chicago	60	29	43	72	12
Richard, Maurice	Montreal	60	45	26	71	69
Taylor, Billy	Detroit	60	17	46	63	35
Schmidt, Milt	Boston	59	27	35	62	40
Kennedy, Ted	Toronto	60	28	32	60	27
Bentley, Doug	Chicago	52	21	34	55	18
Bauer, Bobby	Boston	58	30	24	54	4
Conacher, Roy	Detroit	60	30	24	54	6
Mosienko, Bill	Chicago	59	25	27	52	2
Dumart, Woody	Boston	60	24	28	52	12

1947-48

Team	GP	W	L	T	GF	GA	PTS
*Toronto	60	32	15	13	182	143	77
Detroit	60	30	18	12	187	148	72
Boston	60	23	24	13	167	168	59
NY Rangers	60	21	26	13	176	201	55
Montreal	60	20	29	11	147	169	51
Chicago	60	20	34	6	195	225	46

Leading Scorers

Player	Club	GP	G	A	PTS	PIM
Lach, Elmer	Montreal	60	30	31	61	72
O'Connor, Buddy	NY Rangers	60	24	36	60	8
Bentley, Doug	Chicago	60	20	37	57	16
Stewart, Gaye	Tor., Chi.	61	27	29	56	83
Bentley, Max	Chi., Tor.	59	26	28	54	14
Poile, Bud	Tor., Chi.	58	25	29	54	17
Richard, Maurice	Montreal	53	28	25	53	89
Apps, Syl	Toronto	55	26	27	53	12
Lindsay, Ted	Detroit	60	33	19	52	95
Conacher, Roy	Chicago	52	22	27	49	4

1948-49

Team	GP	W	L	T	GF	GA	PTS
Detroit	60	34	19	7	195	145	75
Boston	60	29	23	8	178	163	66
Montreal	60	28	23	9	152	126	65
*Toronto	60	22	25	13	147	161	57
Chicago	60	21	31	8	173	211	50
NY Rangers	60	18	31	11	133	172	47

Leading Scorers

Player	Club	GP	G	A	PTS	PIM
Conacher, Roy	Chicago	60	26	42	68	8
Bentley, Doug	Chicago	58	23	43	66	38
Abel, Sid	Detroit	60	28	26	54	49
Lindsay, Ted	Detroit	50	26	28	54	97
Conacher, Jim	Det., Chi.	59	26	23	49	43
Ronty, Paul	Boston	60	20	29	49	11
Watson, Harry	Toronto	60	26	19	45	0
Reay, Billy	Montreal	60	22	23	45	33
Bodnar, Gus	Chicago	59	19	26	45	14
Peirson, Johnny	Boston	59	22	21	43	45

1949-50

Team	GP	W	L	T	GF	GA	PTS
*Detroit	70	37	19	14	229	164	88
Montreal	70	29	22	19	172	150	77
Toronto	70	31	27	12	176	173	74
NY Rangers	70	28	31	11	170	189	67
Boston	70	22	32	16	198	228	60
Chicago	70	22	38	10	203	244	54

Leading Scorers

Player	Club	GP	G	A	PTS	PIM
Lindsay, Ted	Detroit	69	23	55	78	141
Abel, Sid	Detroit	69	34	35	69	46
Howe, Gordie	Detroit	70	35	33	68	69
Richard, Maurice	Montreal	70	43	22	65	114
Ronty, Paul	Boston	70	23	36	59	8
Conacher, Roy	Chicago	70	25	31	56	16
Bentley, Doug	Chicago	64	20	33	53	28
Peirson, Johnny	Boston	57	27	25	52	49
Prystai, Metro	Chicago	65	29	22	51	31
Guidolin, Bep	Chicago	70	17	34	51	42

1950-51

Team	GP	W	L	T	GF	GA	PTS
Detroit	70	44	13	13	236	139	101
*Toronto	70	41	16	13	212	138	95
Montreal	70	25	30	15	173	184	65
Boston	70	22	30	18	178	197	62
NY Rangers	70	20	29	21	169	201	61
Chicago	70	13	47	10	171	280	36

Leading Scorers

Player	Club	GP	G	A	PTS	PIM
Howe, Gordie	Detroit	70	43	43	86	74
Richard, Maurice	Montreal	65	42	24	66	97
Bentley, Max	Toronto	67	21	41	62	34
Abel, Sid	Detroit	69	23	38	61	30
Schmidt, Milt	Boston	62	22	39	61	33
Kennedy, Ted	Toronto	63	18	43	61	32
Lindsay, Ted	Detroit	67	24	35	59	110
Sloan, Tod	Toronto	70	31	25	56	105
Kelly, Red	Detroit	70	17	37	54	24
Smith, Sid	Toronto	70	30	21	51	10
Gardner, Cal	Toronto	66	23	28	51	42

1951-52

Team	GP	W	L	T	GF	GA	PTS
*Detroit	70	44	14	12	215	133	100
Montreal	70	34	26	10	195	164	78
Toronto	70	29	25	16	168	157	74
Boston	70	25	29	16	162	176	66
NY Rangers	70	23	34	13	192	219	59
Chicago	70	17	44	9	158	241	43

Leading Scorers

Player	Club	GP	G	A	PTS	PIM
Howe, Gordie	Detroit	70	47	39	86	78
Lindsay, Ted	Detroit	70	30	39	69	123
Lach, Elmer	Montreal	70	15	50	65	36
Raleigh, Don	NY Rangers	70	19	42	61	14
Smith, Sid	Toronto	70	27	30	57	6
Geoffrion, Bernie	Montreal	67	30	24	54	66
Mosienko, Bill	Chicago	70	31	22	53	10
Abel, Sid	Detroit	62	17	36	53	32
Kennedy, Ted	Toronto	70	19	33	52	33
Schmidt, Milt	Boston	69	21	29	50	57
Peirson, Johnny	Boston	68	20	30	50	30

1952-53

Team	GP	W	L	T	GF	GA	PTS
Detroit	70	36	16	18	222	133	90
*Montreal	70	28	23	19	155	148	75
Boston	70	28	29	13	152	172	69
Chicago	70	27	28	15	169	175	69
Toronto	70	27	30	13	156	167	67
NY Rangers	70	17	37	16	152	211	50

Leading Scorers

Player	Club	GP	G	A	PTS	PIM
Howe, Gordie	Detroit	70	49	46	95	57
Lindsay, Ted	Detroit	70	32	39	71	111
Richard, Maurice	Montreal	70	28	33	61	112
Hergesheimer, Wally	NY Rangers	70	30	29	59	10
Delvecchio, Alex	Detroit	70	16	43	59	28
Ronty, Paul	NY Rangers	70	16	38	54	20
Prystai, Metro	Detroit	70	16	34	50	12
Kelly, Red	Detroit	70	19	27	46	8
Olmstead, Bert	Montreal	69	17	28	45	83
Mackell, Fleming	Boston	65	27	17	44	63
McFadden, Jim	Chicago	70	23	21	44	29

1953-54

Team	GP	W	L	T	GF	GA	PTS
*Detroit	70	37	19	14	191	132	88
Montreal	70	35	24	11	195	141	81
Toronto	70	32	24	14	152	131	78
Boston	70	32	28	10	177	181	74
NY Rangers	70	29	31	10	161	182	68
Chicago	70	12	51	7	133	242	31

Leading Scorers

Player	Club	GP	G	A	PTS	PIM
Howe, Gordie	Detroit	70	33	48	81	109
Richard, Maurice	Montreal	70	37	30	67	112
Lindsay, Ted	Detroit	70	26	36	62	110
Geoffrion, Bernie	Montreal	54	29	25	54	87
Olmstead, Bert	Montreal	70	15	37	52	85
Kelly, Red	Detroit	62	16	33	49	18
Reibel, Dutch	Detroit	69	15	33	48	18
Sandford, Ed	Boston	70	16	31	47	42
Mackell, Fleming	Boston	67	15	32	47	60
Mosdell, Ken	Montreal	67	22	24	46	64
Ronty, Paul	NY Rangers	70	13	33	46	18

1954-55

Team	GP	W	L	T	GF	GA	PTS
*Detroit	70	42	17	11	204	134	95
Montreal	70	41	18	11	228	157	93
Toronto	70	24	24	22	147	135	70
Boston	70	23	26	21	169	188	67
NY Rangers	70	17	35	18	150	210	52
Chicago	70	13	40	17	161	235	43

Leading Scorers

Player	Club	GP	G	A	PTS	PIM
Geoffrion, Bernie	Montreal	70	38	37	75	57
Richard, Maurice	Montreal	67	38	36	74	125
Béliveau, Jean	Montreal	70	37	36	73	58
Reibel, Dutch	Detroit	70	25	41	66	15
Howe, Gordie	Detroit	64	29	33	62	68
Sullivan, Red	Chicago	69	19	42	61	51
Olmstead, Bert	Montreal	70	10	48	58	103
Smith, Sid	Toronto	70	33	21	54	14
Mosdell, Ken	Montreal	70	22	32	54	82
Lewicki, Danny	NY Rangers	70	29	24	53	8

1955-56

Team	GP	W	L	T	GF	GA	PTS
*Montreal	70	45	15	10	222	131	100
Detroit	70	30	24	16	183	148	76
NY Rangers	70	32	28	10	204	203	74
Toronto	70	24	33	13	153	181	61
Boston	70	23	34	13	147	185	59
Chicago	70	19	39	12	155	216	50

Leading Scorers

Player	Club	GP	G	A	PTS	PIM
Béliveau, Jean	Montreal	70	47	41	88	143
Howe, Gordie	Detroit	70	38	41	79	100
Richard, Maurice	Montreal	70	38	33	71	89
Olmstead, Bert	Montreal	70	14	56	70	94
Sloan, Tod	Toronto	70	37	29	66	100
Bathgate, Andy	NY Rangers	70	19	47	66	59
Geoffrion, Bernie	Montreal	59	29	33	62	66
Reibel, Dutch	Detroit	68	17	39	56	10
Delvecchio, Alex	Detroit	70	25	26	51	24
Creighton, Dave	NY Rangers	70	20	31	51	43
Gadsby, Bill	NY Rangers	70	9	42	51	84

1956-57

Team	GP	W	L	T	GF	GA	PTS
Detroit	70	38	20	12	198	157	88
*Montreal	70	35	23	12	210	155	82
Boston	70	34	24	12	195	174	80
NY Rangers	70	26	30	14	184	227	66
Toronto	70	21	34	15	174	192	57
Chicago	70	16	39	15	169	225	47

Leading Scorers

Player	Club	GP	G	A	PTS	PIM
Howe, Gordie	Detroit	70	44	45	89	72
Lindsay, Ted	Detroit	70	30	55	85	103
Béliveau, Jean	Montreal	69	33	51	84	105
Bathgate, Andy	NY Rangers	70	27	50	77	60
Litzenberger, Ed	Chicago	70	32	32	64	48
Richard, Maurice	Montreal	63	33	29	62	74
McKenney, Don	Boston	69	21	39	60	31
Moore, Dickie	Montreal	70	29	29	58	56
Richard, Henri	Montreal	63	18	36	54	71
Ullman, Norm	Detroit	64	16	36	52	47

1957-58

Team	GP	W	L	T	GF	GA	PTS
*Montreal	70	43	17	10	250	158	96
NY Rangers	70	32	25	13	195	188	77
Detroit	70	29	29	12	176	207	70
Boston	70	27	28	15	199	194	69
Chicago	70	24	39	7	163	202	55
Toronto	70	21	38	11	192	226	53

Leading Scorers

Player	Club	GP	G	A	PTS	PIM
Moore, Dickie	Montreal	70	36	48	84	65
Richard, Henri	Montreal	67	28	52	80	56
Bathgate, Andy	NY Rangers	65	30	48	78	42
Howe, Gordie	Detroit	64	33	44	77	40
Horvath, Bronco	Boston	67	30	36	66	71
Litzenberger, Ed	Chicago	70	32	30	62	63
Mackell, Fleming	Boston	70	20	40	60	72
Béliveau, Jean	Montreal	55	27	32	59	93
Delvecchio, Alex	Detroit	70	21	38	59	22
McKenney, Don	Boston	70	28	30	58	22

1958-59

Team	GP	W	L	T	GF	GA	PTS
*Montreal	70	39	18	13	258	158	91
Boston	70	32	29	9	205	215	73
Chicago	70	28	29	13	197	208	69
Toronto	70	27	32	11	189	201	65
NY Rangers	70	26	32	12	201	217	64
Detroit	70	25	37	8	167	218	58

Leading Scorers

Player	Club	GP	G	A	PTS	PIM
Moore, Dickie	Montreal	70	41	55	96	61
Béliveau, Jean	Montreal	64	45	46	91	67
Bathgate, Andy	NY Rangers	70	40	48	88	48
Howe, Gordie	Detroit	70	32	46	78	57
Litzenberger, Ed	Chicago	70	33	44	77	37
Geoffrion, Bernie	Montreal	59	22	44	66	30
Sullivan, Red	NY Rangers	70	21	42	63	56
Hebenton, Andy	NY Rangers	70	33	29	62	8
McKenney, Don	Boston	70	32	30	62	20
Sloan, Tod	Chicago	59	27	35	62	79

1959-60

Team	GP	W	L	T	GF	GA	PTS
*Montreal	70	40	18	12	255	178	92
Toronto	70	35	26	9	199	195	79
Chicago	70	28	29	13	191	180	69
Detroit	70	26	29	15	186	197	67
Boston	70	28	34	8	220	241	64
NY Rangers	70	17	38	15	187	247	49

Leading Scorers

Player	Club	GP	G	A	PTS	PIM
Hull, Bobby	Chicago	70	39	42	81	68
Horvath, Bronco	Boston	68	39	41	80	60
Béliveau, Jean	Montreal	60	34	40	74	57
Bathgate, Andy	NY Rangers	70	26	48	74	28
Richard, Henri	Montreal	70	30	43	73	66
Howe, Gordie	Detroit	70	28	45	73	46
Geoffrion, Bernie	Montreal	59	30	41	71	36
McKenney, Don	Boston	70	20	49	69	28
Stasiuk, Vic	Boston	69	29	39	68	121
Prentice, Dean	NY Rangers	70	32	34	66	43

1960-61

Team	GP	W	L	T	GF	GA	PTS
Montreal	70	41	19	10	254	188	92
Toronto	70	39	19	12	234	176	90
*Chicago	70	29	24	17	198	180	75
Detroit	70	25	29	16	195	215	66
NY Rangers	70	22	38	10	204	248	54
Boston	70	15	42	13	176	254	43

Leading Scorers

Player	Club	GP	G	A	PTS	PIM
Geoffrion, Bernie	Montreal	64	50	45	95	29
Béliveau, Jean	Montreal	69	32	58	90	57
Mahovlich, Frank	Toronto	70	48	36	84	131
Bathgate, Andy	NY Rangers	70	29	48	77	22
Howe, Gordie	Detroit	64	23	49	72	30
Ullman, Norm	Detroit	70	28	42	70	34
Kelly, Red	Toronto	64	20	50	70	12
Moore, Dickie	Montreal	57	35	34	69	62
Richard, Henri	Montreal	70	24	44	68	91
Delvecchio, Alex	Detroit	70	27	35	62	26

1961-62

Team	GP	W	L	T	GF	GA	PTS
Montreal	70	42	14	14	259	166	98
*Toronto	70	37	22	11	232	180	85
Chicago	70	31	26	13	217	186	75
NY Rangers	70	26	32	12	195	207	64
Detroit	70	23	33	14	184	219	60
Boston	70	15	47	8	177	306	38

Leading Scorers

Player	Club	GP	G	A	PTS	PIM
Hull, Bobby	Chicago	70	50	34	84	35
Bathgate, Andy	NY Rangers	70	28	56	84	44
Howe, Gordie	Detroit	70	33	44	77	54
Mikita, Stan	Chicago	70	25	52	77	97
Mahovlich, Frank	Toronto	70	33	38	71	87
Delvecchio, Alex	Detroit	70	26	43	69	18
Backstrom, Ralph	Montreal	66	27	38	65	29
Ullman, Norm	Detroit	70	26	38	64	54
Hay, Bill	Chicago	60	11	52	63	34
Provost, Claude	Montreal	70	33	29	62	22

1962-63

Team	GP	W	L	T	GF	GA	PTS
*Toronto	70	35	23	12	221	180	82
Chicago	70	32	21	17	194	178	81
Montreal	70	28	19	23	225	183	79
Detroit	70	32	25	13	200	194	77
NY Rangers	70	22	36	12	211	233	56
Boston	70	14	39	17	198	281	45

Leading Scorers

Player	Club	GP	G	A	PTS	PIM
Howe, Gordie	Detroit	70	38	48	86	100
Bathgate, Andy	NY Rangers	70	35	46	81	54
Mikita, Stan	Chicago	65	31	45	76	69
Mahovlich, Frank	Toronto	67	36	37	73	56
Richard, Henri	Montreal	67	23	50	73	57
Béliveau, Jean	Montreal	69	18	49	67	68
Bucyk, John	Boston	69	27	39	66	36
Delvecchio, Alex	Detroit	70	20	44	64	8
Hull, Bobby	Chicago	65	31	31	62	27
Oliver, Murray	Boston	65	22	40	62	38

1963-64

Team	GP	W	L	T	GF	GA	PTS
Montreal	70	36	21	13	209	167	85
Chicago	70	36	22	12	218	169	84
*Toronto	70	33	25	12	192	172	78
Detroit	70	30	29	11	191	204	71
NY Rangers	70	22	38	10	186	242	54
Boston	70	18	40	12	170	212	48

Leading Scorers

Player	Club	GP	G	A	PTS	PIM
Mikita, Stan	Chicago	70	39	50	89	146
Hull, Bobby	Chicago	70	43	44	87	50
Béliveau, Jean	Montreal	68	28	50	78	42
Bathgate, Andy	NYR, Tor.	71	19	58	77	34
Howe, Gordie	Detroit	69	26	47	73	70
Wharram, Kenny	Chicago	70	39	32	71	18
Oliver, Murray	Boston	70	24	44	68	41
Goyette, Phil	NY Rangers	67	24	41	65	15
Gilbert, Rod	NY Rangers	70	24	40	64	62
Keon, Dave	Toronto	70	23	37	60	6

1964-65

Team	GP	W	L	T	GF	GA	PTS
Detroit	70	40	23	7	224	175	87
*Montreal	70	36	23	11	211	185	83
Chicago	70	34	28	8	224	176	76
Toronto	70	30	26	14	204	173	74
NY Rangers	70	20	38	12	179	246	52
Boston	70	21	43	6	166	253	48

Leading Scorers

Player	Club	GP	G	A	PTS	PIM
Mikita, Stan	Chicago	70	28	59	87	154
Ullman, Norm	Detroit	70	42	41	83	70
Howe, Gordie	Detroit	70	29	47	76	104
Hull, Bobby	Chicago	61	39	32	71	32
Delvecchio, Alex	Detroit	68	25	42	67	16
Provost, Claude	Montreal	70	27	37	64	28
Gilbert, Rod	NY Rangers	70	25	36	61	52
Pilote, Pierre	Chicago	68	14	45	59	162
Bucyk, John	Boston	68	26	29	55	24
Backstrom, Ralph	Montreal	70	25	30	55	41
Esposito, Phil	Chicago	70	23	32	55	44

1965-66

Team	GP	W	L	T	GF	GA	PTS
*Montreal	70	41	21	8	239	173	90
Chicago	70	37	25	8	240	187	82
Toronto	70	34	25	11	208	187	79
Detroit	70	31	27	12	221	194	74
Boston	70	21	43	6	174	275	48
NY Rangers	70	18	41	11	195	261	47

Leading Scorers

Player	Club	GP	G	A	PTS	PIM
Hull, Bobby	Chicago	65	54	43	97	70
Mikita, Stan	Chicago	68	30	48	78	58
Rousseau, Bobby	Montreal	70	30	48	78	20
Béliveau, Jean	Montreal	67	29	48	77	50
Howe, Gordie	Detroit	70	29	46	75	83
Ullman, Norm	Detroit	70	31	41	72	35
Delvecchio, Alex	Detroit	70	31	38	69	16
Nevin, Bob	NY Rangers	69	29	33	62	10
Richard, Henri	Montreal	62	22	39	61	47
Oliver, Murray	Boston	70	18	42	60	30

1966-67

Team	GP	W	L	T	GF	GA	PTS
Chicago	70	41	17	12	264	170	94
Montreal	70	32	25	13	202	188	77
*Toronto	70	32	27	11	204	211	75
NY Rangers	70	30	28	12	188	189	72
Detroit	70	27	39	4	212	241	58
Boston	70	17	43	10	182	253	44

Leading Scorers

Player	Club	GP	G	A	PTS	PIM
Mikita, Stan	Chicago	70	35	62	97	12
Hull, Bobby	Chicago	66	52	28	80	52
Ullman, Norm	Detroit	68	26	44	70	26
Wharram, Kenny	Chicago	70	31	34	65	21
Howe, Gordie	Detroit	69	25	40	65	53
Rousseau, Bobby	Montreal	68	19	44	63	58
Esposito, Phil	Chicago	69	21	40	61	40
Goyette, Phil	NY Rangers	70	12	49	61	6
Mohns, Doug	Chicago	61	25	35	60	58
Richard, Henri	Montreal	65	21	34	55	28
Delvecchio, Alex	Detroit	70	17	38	55	10

1967-68

East Division

Team	GP	W	L	T	GF	GA	PTS
*Montreal	74	42	22	10	236	167	94
NY Rangers	74	39	23	12	226	183	90
Boston	74	37	27	10	259	216	84
Chicago	74	32	26	16	212	222	80
Toronto	74	33	31	10	209	176	76
Detroit	74	27	35	12	245	257	66

West Division

Team	GP	W	L	T	GF	GA	PTS
Philadelphia	74	31	32	11	173	179	73
Los Angeles	74	31	33	10	200	224	72
St. Louis	74	27	31	16	177	191	70
Minnesota	74	27	32	15	191	226	69
Pittsburgh	74	27	34	13	195	216	67
Oakland	74	15	42	17	153	219	47

Leading Scorers

Player	Club	GP	G	A	PTS	PIM
Mikita, Stan	Chicago	72	40	47	87	14
Esposito, Phil	Boston	74	35	49	84	21
Howe, Gordie	Detroit	74	39	43	82	53
Ratelle, Jean	NY Rangers	74	32	46	78	18
Gilbert, Rod	NY Rangers	73	29	48	77	12
Hull, Bobby	Chicago	71	44	31	75	39
Ullman, Norm	Det., Tor.	71	35	37	72	28
Delvecchio, Alex	Detroit	74	22	48	70	14
Bucyk, John	Boston	72	30	39	69	8
Wharram, Kenny	Chicago	74	27	42	69	18

1968-69

East Division

Team	GP	W	L	T	GF	GA	PTS
*Montreal	76	46	19	11	271	202	103
Boston	76	42	18	16	303	221	100
NY Rangers	76	41	26	9	231	196	91
Toronto	76	35	26	15	234	217	85
Detroit	76	33	31	12	239	221	78
Chicago	76	34	33	9	280	246	77

West Division

Team	GP	W	L	T	GF	GA	PTS
St. Louis	76	37	25	14	204	157	88
Oakland	76	29	36	11	219	251	69
Philadelphia	76	20	35	21	174	225	61
Los Angeles	76	24	42	10	185	260	58
Pittsburgh	76	20	45	11	189	252	51
Minnesota	76	18	43	15	189	270	51

Leading Scorers

Player	Club	GP	G	A	PTS	PIM
Esposito, Phil	Boston	74	49	77	126	79
Hull, Bobby	Chicago	74	58	49	107	48
Howe, Gordie	Detroit	76	44	59	103	58
Mikita, Stan	Chicago	74	30	67	97	52
Hodge, Ken	Boston	75	45	45	90	75
Cournoyer, Yvan	Montreal	76	43	44	87	31
Delvecchio, Alex	Detroit	72	25	58	83	8
Berenson, Red	St. Louis	76	35	47	82	43
Béliveau, Jean	Montreal	69	33	49	82	55
Mahovlich, Frank	Detroit	76	49	29	78	38
Ratelle, Jean	NY Rangers	75	32	46	78	26

1969-70

East Division

Team	GP	W	L	T	GF	GA	PTS
Chicago	76	45	22	9	250	170	99
*Boston	76	40	17	19	277	216	99
Detroit	76	40	21	15	246	199	95
NY Rangers	76	38	22	16	246	189	92
Montreal	76	38	22	16	244	201	92
Toronto	76	29	34	13	222	242	71

West Division

Team	GP	W	L	T	GF	GA	PTS
St. Louis	76	37	27	12	224	179	86
Pittsburgh	76	26	38	12	182	238	64
Minnesota	76	19	35	22	224	257	60
Oakland	76	22	40	14	169	243	58
Philadelphia	76	17	35	24	197	225	58
Los Angeles	76	14	52	10	168	290	38

Leading Scorers

Player	Club	GP	G	A	PTS	PIM
Orr, Bobby	Boston	76	33	87	120	125
Esposito, Phil	Boston	76	43	56	99	50
Mikita, Stan	Chicago	76	39	47	86	50
Goyette, Phil	St. Louis	72	29	49	78	16
Tkaczuk, Walt	NY Rangers	76	27	50	77	38
Ratelle, Jean	NY Rangers	75	32	42	74	28
Berenson, Red	St. Louis	67	33	39	72	38
Parise, Jean-Paul	Minnesota	74	24	48	72	72
Howe, Gordie	Detroit	76	31	40	71	58
Mahovlich, Frank	Detroit	74	38	32	70	59
Balon, Dave	NY Rangers	76	33	37	70	100
McKenzie, John	Boston	72	29	41	70	114

1970-71

East Division

Team	GP	W	L	T	GF	GA	PTS
Boston	78	57	14	7	399	207	121
NY Rangers	78	49	18	11	259	177	109
*Montreal	78	42	23	13	291	216	97
Toronto	78	37	33	8	248	211	82
Buffalo	78	24	39	15	217	291	63
Vancouver	78	24	46	8	229	296	56
Detroit	78	22	45	11	209	308	55

West Division

Team	GP	W	L	T	GF	GA	PTS
Chicago	78	49	20	9	277	184	107
St. Louis	78	34	25	19	223	208	87
Philadelphia	78	28	33	17	207	225	73
Minnesota	78	28	34	16	191	223	72
Los Angeles	78	25	40	13	239	303	63
Pittsburgh	78	21	37	20	221	240	62
California	78	20	53	5	199	320	45

Leading Scorers

Player	Club	GP	G	A	PTS	PIM
Esposito, Phil	Boston	78	76	76	152	71
Orr, Bobby	Boston	78	37	102	139	91
Bucyk, John	Boston	78	51	65	116	8
Hodge, Ken	Boston	78	43	62	105	113
Hull, Bobby	Chicago	78	44	52	96	32
Ullman, Norm	Toronto	73	34	51	85	24
Cashman, Wayne	Boston	77	21	58	79	100
McKenzie, John	Boston	65	31	46	77	120
Keon, Dave	Toronto	76	38	38	76	4
Béliveau, Jean	Montreal	70	25	51	76	40
Stanfield, Fred	Boston	75	24	52	76	12

1971-72

East Division

Team	GP	W	L	T	GF	GA	PTS
*Boston	78	54	13	11	330	204	119
NY Rangers	78	48	17	13	317	192	109
Montreal	78	46	16	16	307	205	108
Toronto	78	33	31	14	209	208	80
Detroit	78	33	35	10	261	262	76
Buffalo	78	16	43	19	203	289	51
Vancouver	78	20	50	8	203	297	48

West Division

Team	GP	W	L	T	GF	GA	PTS
Chicago	78	46	17	15	256	166	107
Minnesota	78	37	29	12	212	191	86
St. Louis	78	28	39	11	208	247	67
Pittsburgh	78	26	38	14	220	258	66
Philadelphia	78	26	38	14	200	236	66
California	78	21	39	18	216	288	60
Los Angeles	78	20	49	9	206	305	49

Leading Scorers

Player	Club	GP	G	A	PTS	PIM
Esposito, Phil	Boston	76	66	67	133	76
Orr, Bobby	Boston	76	37	80	117	106
Ratelle, Jean	NY Rangers	63	46	63	109	4
Hadfield, Vic	NY Rangers	78	50	56	106	142
Gilbert, Rod	NY Rangers	73	43	54	97	64
Mahovlich, Frank	Montreal	76	43	53	96	36
Hull, Bobby	Chicago	78	50	43	93	24
Cournoyer, Yvan	Montreal	73	47	36	83	15
Bucyk, John	Boston	78	32	51	83	4
Clarke, Bobby	Philadelphia	78	35	46	81	87
Lemaire, Jacques	Montreal	77	32	49	81	26

1972-73

East Division

Team	GP	W	L	T	GF	GA	PTS
*Montreal	78	52	10	16	329	184	120
Boston	78	51	22	5	330	235	107
NY Rangers	78	47	23	8	297	208	102
Buffalo	78	37	27	14	257	219	88
Detroit	78	37	29	12	265	243	86
Toronto	78	27	41	10	247	279	64
Vancouver	78	22	47	9	233	339	53
NY Islanders	78	12	60	6	170	347	30

West Division

Team	GP	W	L	T	GF	GA	PTS
Chicago	78	42	27	9	284	225	93
Philadelphia	78	37	30	11	296	256	85
Minnesota	78	37	30	11	254	230	85
St. Louis	78	32	34	12	233	251	76
Pittsburgh	78	32	37	9	257	265	73
Los Angeles	78	31	36	11	232	245	73
Atlanta	78	25	38	15	191	239	65
California	78	16	46	16	213	323	48

Leading Scorers

Player	Club	GP	G	A	PTS	PIM
Esposito, Phil	Boston	78	55	75	130	87
Clarke, Bobby	Philadelphia	78	37	67	104	80
Orr, Bobby	Boston	63	29	72	101	99
MacLeish, Rick	Philadelphia	78	50	50	100	69
Lemaire, Jacques	Montreal	77	44	51	95	16
Ratelle, Jean	NY Rangers	78	41	53	94	12
Redmond, Mickey	Detroit	76	52	41	93	24
Bucyk, John	Boston	78	40	53	93	12
Mahovlich, Frank	Montreal	78	38	55	93	51
Pappin, Jim	Chicago	76	41	51	92	82

Norm Ullman ranked among the NHL's top-10 scorers seven times in his career, including the 1964-65 season when he led the league with 42 goals.

1973-74

East Division

Team	GP	W	L	T	GF	GA	PTS
Boston	78	52	17	9	349	221	113
Montreal	78	45	24	9	293	240	99
NY Rangers	78	40	24	14	300	251	94
Toronto	78	35	27	16	274	230	86
Buffalo	78	32	34	12	242	250	76
Detroit	78	29	39	10	255	319	68
Vancouver	78	24	43	11	224	296	59
NY Islanders	78	19	41	18	182	247	56

West Division

Team	GP	W	L	T	GF	GA	PTS
*Philadelphia	78	50	16	12	273	164	112
Chicago	78	41	14	23	272	164	105
Los Angeles	78	33	33	12	233	231	78
Atlanta	78	30	34	14	214	238	74
Pittsburgh	78	28	41	9	242	273	65
St. Louis	78	26	40	12	206	248	64
Minnesota	78	23	38	17	235	275	63
California	78	13	55	10	195	342	36

Leading Scorers

Player	Club	GP	G	A	PTS	PIM
Esposito, Phil	Boston	78	68	77	145	58
Orr, Bobby	Boston	74	32	90	122	82
Hodge, Ken	Boston	76	50	55	105	43
Cashman, Wayne	Boston	78	30	59	89	111
Clarke, Bobby	Philadelphia	77	35	52	87	113
Martin, Rick	Buffalo	78	52	34	86	38
Apps Jr., Syl	Pittsburgh	75	24	61	85	37
Sittler, Darryl	Toronto	78	38	46	84	55
MacDonald, Lowell	Pittsburgh	78	43	39	82	14
Park, Brad	NY Rangers	78	25	57	82	148
Hextall, Dennis	Minnesota	78	20	62	82	138

1974-75

PRINCE OF WALES CONFERENCE

Norris Division

Team	GP	W	L	T	GF	GA	PTS
Montreal	80	47	14	19	374	225	113
Los Angeles	80	42	17	21	269	185	105
Pittsburgh	80	37	28	15	326	289	89
Detroit	80	23	45	12	259	335	58
Washington	80	8	67	5	181	446	21

Adams Division

Team	GP	W	L	T	GF	GA	PTS
Buffalo	80	49	16	15	354	240	113
Boston	80	40	26	14	345	245	94
Toronto	80	31	33	16	280	309	78
California	80	19	48	13	212	316	51

CLARENCE CAMPBELL CONFERENCE

Patrick Division

Team	GP	W	L	T	GF	GA	PTS
*Philadelphia	80	51	18	11	293	181	113
NY Rangers	80	37	29	14	319	276	88
NY Islanders	80	33	25	22	264	221	88
Atlanta	80	34	31	15	243	233	83

Smythe Division

Team	GP	W	L	T	GF	GA	PTS
Vancouver	80	38	32	10	271	254	86
St. Louis	80	35	31	14	269	267	84
Chicago	80	37	35	8	268	241	82
Minnesota	80	23	50	7	221	341	53
Kansas City	80	15	54	11	184	328	41

Leading Scorers

Player	Club	GP	G	A	PTS	PIM
Orr, Bobby	Boston	80	46	89	135	101
Esposito, Phil	Boston	79	61	66	127	62
Dionne, Marcel	Detroit	80	47	74	121	14
Lafleur, Guy	Montreal	70	53	66	119	37
Mahovlich, Pete	Montreal	80	35	82	117	64
Clarke, Bobby	Philadelphia	80	27	89	116	125
Robert, Rene	Buffalo	74	40	60	100	75
Gilbert, Rod	NY Rangers	76	36	61	97	22
Perreault, Gilbert	Buffalo	68	39	57	96	36
Martin, Rick	Buffalo	68	52	43	95	72

1975-76

PRINCE OF WALES CONFERENCE

Norris Division

Team	GP	W	L	T	GF	GA	PTS
*Montreal	80	58	11	11	337	174	127
Los Angeles	80	38	33	9	263	265	85
Pittsburgh	80	35	33	12	339	303	82
Detroit	80	26	44	10	226	300	62
Washington	80	11	59	10	224	394	32

Adams Division

Team	GP	W	L	T	GF	GA	PTS
Boston	80	48	15	17	313	237	113
Buffalo	80	46	21	13	339	240	105
Toronto	80	34	31	15	294	276	83
California	80	27	42	11	250	278	65

CLARENCE CAMPBELL CONFERENCE

Patrick Division

Team	GP	W	L	T	GF	GA	PTS
Philadelphia	80	51	13	16	348	209	118
NY Islanders	80	42	21	17	297	190	101
Atlanta	80	35	33	12	262	237	82
NY Rangers	80	29	42	9	262	333	67

Smythe Division

Team	GP	W	L	T	GF	GA	PTS
Chicago	80	32	30	18	254	261	82
Vancouver	80	33	32	15	271	272	81
St. Louis	80	29	37	14	249	290	72
Minnesota	80	20	53	7	195	303	47
Kansas City	80	12	56	12	190	351	36

Leading Scorers

Player	Club	GP	G	A	PTS	PIM
Lafleur, Guy	Montreal	80	56	69	125	36
Clarke, Bobby	Philadelphia	76	30	89	119	136
Perreault, Gilbert	Buffalo	80	44	69	113	36
Barber, Bill	Philadelphia	80	50	62	112	104
Larouche, Pierre	Pittsburgh	76	53	58	111	33
Ratelle, Jean	Bos., NYR	80	36	69	105	18
Mahovlich, Pete	Montreal	80	34	71	105	76
Pronovost, Jean	Pittsburgh	80	52	52	104	24
Sittler, Darryl	Toronto	79	41	59	100	90
Apps Jr., Syl	Pittsburgh	80	32	67	99	24

1976-77

PRINCE OF WALES CONFERENCE

Norris Division

Team	GP	W	L	T	GF	GA	PTS
*Montreal	80	60	8	12	387	171	132
Los Angeles	80	34	31	15	271	241	83
Pittsburgh	80	34	33	13	240	252	81
Washington	80	24	42	14	221	307	62
Detroit	80	16	55	9	183	309	41

Adams Division

Team	GP	W	L	T	GF	GA	PTS
Boston	80	49	23	8	312	240	106
Buffalo	80	48	24	8	301	220	104
Toronto	80	33	32	15	301	285	81
Cleveland	80	25	42	13	240	292	63

CLARENCE CAMPBELL CONFERENCE

Patrick Division

Team	GP	W	L	T	GF	GA	PTS
Philadelphia	80	48	16	16	323	213	112
NY Islanders	80	47	21	12	288	193	106
Atlanta	80	34	34	12	264	265	80
NY Rangers	80	29	37	14	272	310	72

Smythe Division

Team	GP	W	L	T	GF	GA	PTS
St. Louis	80	32	39	9	239	276	73
Minnesota	80	23	39	18	240	310	64
Chicago	80	26	43	11	240	298	63
Vancouver	80	25	42	13	235	294	63
Colorado	80	20	46	14	226	307	54

Leading Scorers

Player	Club	GP	G	A	PTS	PIM
Lafleur, Guy	Montreal	80	56	80	136	20
Dionne, Marcel	Los Angeles	80	53	69	122	12
Shutt, Steve	Montreal	80	60	45	105	28
MacLeish, Rick	Philadelphia	79	49	48	97	42
Perreault, Gilbert	Buffalo	80	39	56	95	30
Young, Tim	Minnesota	80	29	66	95	58
Ratelle, Jean	Boston	78	33	61	94	22
McDonald, Lanny	Toronto	80	46	44	90	77
Sittler, Darryl	Toronto	73	38	52	90	89
Clarke, Bobby	Philadelphia	80	27	63	90	71

1977-78

PRINCE OF WALES CONFERENCE

Norris Division

Team	GP	W	L	T	GF	GA	PTS
*Montreal	80	59	10	11	359	183	129
Detroit	80	32	34	14	252	266	78
Los Angeles	80	31	34	15	243	245	77
Pittsburgh	80	25	37	18	254	321	68
Washington	80	17	49	14	195	321	48

Adams Division

Team	GP	W	L	T	GF	GA	PTS
Boston	80	51	18	11	333	218	113
Buffalo	80	44	19	17	288	215	105
Toronto	80	41	29	10	271	237	92
Cleveland	80	22	45	13	230	325	57

CLARENCE CAMPBELL CONFERENCE

Patrick Division

Team	GP	W	L	T	GF	GA	PTS
NY Islanders	80	48	17	15	334	210	111
Philadelphia	80	45	20	15	296	200	105
Atlanta	80	34	27	19	274	252	87
NY Rangers	80	30	37	13	279	280	73

Smythe Division

Team	GP	W	L	T	GF	GA	PTS
Chicago	80	32	29	19	230	220	83
Colorado	80	19	40	21	257	305	59
Vancouver	80	20	43	17	239	320	57
St. Louis	80	20	47	13	195	304	53
Minnesota	80	18	53	9	218	325	45

Leading Scorers

Player	Club	GP	G	A	PTS	PIM
Lafleur, Guy	Montreal	78	60	72	132	26
Trottier, Bryan	NY Islanders	77	46	77	123	46
Sittler, Darryl	Toronto	80	45	72	117	100
Lemaire, Jacques	Montreal	76	36	61	97	14
Potvin, Denis	NY Islanders	80	30	64	94	81
Bossy, Mike	NY Islanders	73	53	38	91	6
O'Reilly, Terry	Boston	77	29	61	90	211
Perreault, Gilbert	Buffalo	79	41	48	89	20
Clarke, Bobby	Philadelphia	71	21	68	89	83
McDonald, Lanny	Toronto	74	47	40	87	54
Paiement, Wilf	Colorado	80	31	56	87	114

1978-79

PRINCE OF WALES CONFERENCE

Norris Division

Team	GP	W	L	T	GF	GA	PTS
*Montreal	80	52	17	11	337	204	115
Pittsburgh	80	36	31	13	281	279	85
Los Angeles	80	34	34	12	292	286	80
Washington	80	24	41	15	273	338	63
Detroit	80	23	41	16	252	295	62

Adams Division

Team	GP	W	L	T	GF	GA	PTS
Boston	80	43	23	14	316	270	100
Buffalo	80	36	28	16	280	263	88
Toronto	80	34	33	13	267	252	81
Minnesota	80	28	40	12	257	289	68

CLARENCE CAMPBELL CONFERENCE

Patrick Division

Team	GP	W	L	T	GF	GA	PTS
NY Islanders	80	51	15	14	358	214	116
Philadelphia	80	40	25	15	281	248	95
NY Rangers	80	40	29	11	316	292	91
Atlanta	80	41	31	8	327	280	90

Smythe Division

Team	GP	W	L	T	GF	GA	PTS
Chicago	80	29	36	15	244	277	73
Vancouver	80	25	42	13	217	291	63
St. Louis	80	18	50	12	249	348	48
Colorado	80	15	53	12	210	331	42

Leading Scorers

Player	Club	GP	G	A	PTS	PIM
Trottier, Bryan	NY Islanders	76	47	87	134	50
Dionne, Marcel	Los Angeles	80	59	71	130	30
Lafleur, Guy	Montreal	80	52	77	129	28
Bossy, Mike	NY Islanders	80	69	57	126	25
MacMillan, Bob	Atlanta	79	37	71	108	14
Chouinard, Guy	Atlanta	80	50	57	107	14
Potvin, Denis	NY Islanders	73	31	70	101	58
Federko, Bernie	St. Louis	74	31	64	95	14
Taylor, Dave	Los Angeles	78	43	48	91	124
Gillies, Clark	NY Islanders	75	35	56	91	68

1979-80
PRINCE OF WALES CONFERENCE
Norris Division

Team	GP	W	L	T	GF	GA	PTS
Montreal	80	47	20	13	328	240	107
Los Angeles	80	30	36	14	290	313	74
Pittsburgh	80	30	37	13	251	303	73
Hartford	80	27	34	19	303	312	73
Detroit	80	26	43	11	268	306	63

Adams Division

Buffalo	80	47	17	16	318	201	110
Boston	80	46	21	13	310	234	105
Minnesota	80	36	28	16	311	253	88
Toronto	80	35	40	5	304	327	75
Quebec	80	25	44	11	248	313	61

CLARENCE CAMPBELL CONFERENCE
Patrick Division

Philadelphia	80	48	12	20	327	254	116
*NY Islanders	80	39	28	13	281	247	91
NY Rangers	80	38	32	10	308	284	86
Atlanta	80	35	32	13	282	269	83
Washington	80	27	40	13	261	293	67

Smythe Division

Chicago	80	34	27	19	241	250	87
St. Louis	80	34	34	12	266	278	80
Vancouver	80	27	37	16	256	281	70
Edmonton	80	28	39	13	301	322	69
Winnipeg	80	20	49	11	214	314	51
Colorado	80	19	48	13	234	308	51

Leading Scorers

Player	Club	GP	G	A	PTS	PIM
Dionne, Marcel	Los Angeles	80	53	84	137	32
Gretzky, Wayne	Edmonton	79	51	86	137	21
Lafleur, Guy	Montreal	74	50	75	125	12
Perreault, Gilbert	Buffalo	80	40	66	106	57
Rogers, Mike	Hartford	80	44	61	105	10
Trottier, Bryan	NY Islanders	78	42	62	104	68
Simmer, Charlie	Los Angeles	64	56	45	101	65
Stoughton, Blaine	Hartford	80	56	44	100	16
Sittler, Darryl	Toronto	73	40	57	97	62
MacDonald, Blair	Edmonton	80	46	48	94	6
Federko, Bernie	St. Louis	79	38	56	94	24

1980-81
PRINCE OF WALES CONFERENCE
Norris Division

Team	GP	W	L	T	GF	GA	PTS
Montreal	80	45	22	13	332	232	103
Los Angeles	80	43	24	13	337	290	99
Pittsburgh	80	30	37	13	302	345	73
Hartford	80	21	41	18	292	372	60
Detroit	80	19	43	18	252	339	56

Adams Division

Buffalo	80	39	20	21	327	250	99
Boston	80	37	30	13	316	272	87
Minnesota	80	35	28	17	291	263	87
Quebec	80	30	32	18	314	318	78
Toronto	80	28	37	15	322	367	71

CLARENCE CAMPBELL CONFERENCE
Patrick Division

*NY Islanders	80	48	18	14	355	260	110
Philadelphia	80	41	24	15	313	249	97
Calgary	80	39	27	14	329	298	92
NY Rangers	80	30	36	14	312	317	74
Washington	80	26	36	18	286	317	70

Smythe Division

St. Louis	80	45	18	17	352	281	107
Chicago	80	31	33	16	304	315	78
Vancouver	80	28	32	20	289	301	76
Edmonton	80	29	35	16	328	327	74
Colorado	80	22	45	13	258	344	57
Winnipeg	80	9	57	14	246	400	32

Leading Scorers

Player	Club	GP	G	A	PTS	PIM
Gretzky, Wayne	Edmonton	80	55	109	164	28
Dionne, Marcel	Los Angeles	80	58	77	135	70
Nilsson, Kent	Calgary	80	49	82	131	26
Bossy, Mike	NY Islanders	79	68	51	119	32
Taylor, Dave	Los Angeles	72	47	65	112	130
Stastny, Peter	Quebec	77	39	70	109	37
Simmer, Charlie	Los Angeles	65	56	49	105	62
Rogers, Mike	Hartford	80	40	65	105	32
Federko, Bernie	St. Louis	78	31	73	104	47
Richard, Jacques	Quebec	78	52	51	103	39
Middleton, Rick	Boston	80	44	59	103	16
Trottier, Bryan	NY Islanders	73	31	72	103	74

1981-82
CLARENCE CAMPBELL CONFERENCE
Norris Division

Team	GP	W	L	T	GF	GA	PTS
Minnesota	80	37	23	20	346	288	94
Winnipeg	80	33	33	14	319	332	80
St. Louis	80	32	40	8	315	349	72
Chicago	80	30	38	12	332	363	72
Toronto	80	20	44	16	298	380	56
Detroit	80	21	47	12	270	351	54

Smythe Division

Edmonton	80	48	17	15	417	295	111
Vancouver	80	30	33	17	290	286	77
Calgary	80	29	34	17	334	345	75
Los Angeles	80	24	41	15	314	369	63
Colorado	80	18	49	13	241	362	49

PRINCE OF WALES CONFERENCE
Adams Division

Montreal	80	46	17	17	360	223	109
Boston	80	43	27	10	323	285	96
Buffalo	80	39	26	15	307	273	93
Quebec	80	33	31	16	356	345	82
Hartford	80	21	41	18	264	351	60

Patrick Division

*NY Islanders	80	54	16	10	385	250	118
NY Rangers	80	39	27	14	316	306	92
Philadelphia	80	38	31	11	325	313	87
Pittsburgh	80	31	36	13	310	337	75
Washington	80	26	41	13	319	338	65

Leading Scorers

Player	Club	GP	G	A	PTS	PIM
Gretzky, Wayne	Edmonton	80	92	120	212	26
Bossy, Mike	NY Islanders	80	64	83	147	22
Stastny, Peter	Quebec	80	46	93	139	91
Maruk, Dennis	Washington	80	60	76	136	128
Trottier, Bryan	NY Islanders	80	50	79	129	88
Savard, Denis	Chicago	80	32	87	119	82
Dionne, Marcel	Los Angeles	78	50	67	117	50
Smith, Bobby	Minnesota	80	43	71	114	82
Ciccarelli, Dino	Minnesota	76	55	51	106	138
Taylor, Dave	Los Angeles	78	39	67	106	130

1982-83
CLARENCE CAMPBELL CONFERENCE
Norris Division

Team	GP	W	L	T	GF	GA	PTS
Chicago	80	47	23	10	338	268	104
Minnesota	80	40	24	16	321	290	96
Toronto	80	28	40	12	293	330	68
St. Louis	80	25	40	15	285	316	65
Detroit	80	21	44	15	263	344	57

Smythe Division

Edmonton	80	47	21	12	424	315	106
Calgary	80	32	34	14	321	317	78
Vancouver	80	30	35	15	303	309	75
Winnipeg	80	33	39	8	311	333	74
Los Angeles	80	27	41	12	308	365	66

PRINCE OF WALES CONFERENCE
Adams Division

Boston	80	50	20	10	327	228	110
Montreal	80	42	24	14	350	286	98
Buffalo	80	38	29	13	318	285	89
Quebec	80	34	34	12	343	336	80
Hartford	80	19	54	7	261	403	45

Patrick Division

Philadelphia	80	49	23	8	326	240	106
*NY Islanders	80	42	26	12	302	226	96
Washington	80	39	25	16	306	283	94
NY Rangers	80	35	35	10	306	287	80
New Jersey	80	17	49	14	230	338	48
Pittsburgh	80	18	53	9	257	394	45

Leading Scorers

Player	Club	GP	G	A	PTS	PIM
Gretzky, Wayne	Edmonton	80	71	125	196	59
Stastny, Peter	Quebec	75	47	77	124	78
Savard, Denis	Chicago	78	35	86	121	99
Bossy, Mike	NY Islanders	79	60	58	118	20
Dionne, Marcel	Los Angeles	80	56	51	107	22
Pederson, Barry	Boston	77	46	61	107	47
Messier, Mark	Edmonton	77	48	58	106	72
Goulet, Michel	Quebec	80	57	48	105	51
Anderson, Glenn	Edmonton	72	48	56	104	70
Nilsson, Kent	Calgary	80	46	58	104	10
Kurri, Jari	Edmonton	80	45	59	104	22

1983-84
CLARENCE CAMPBELL CONFERENCE
Norris Division

Team	GP	W	L	T	GF	GA	PTS
Minnesota	80	39	31	10	345	344	88
St. Louis	80	32	41	7	293	316	71
Detroit	80	31	42	7	298	323	69
Chicago	80	30	42	8	277	311	68
Toronto	80	26	45	9	303	387	61

Smythe Division

*Edmonton	80	57	18	5	446	314	119
Calgary	80	34	32	14	311	314	82
Vancouver	80	32	39	9	306	328	73
Winnipeg	80	31	38	11	340	374	73
Los Angeles	80	23	44	13	309	376	59

PRINCE OF WALES CONFERENCE
Adams Division

Boston	80	49	25	6	336	261	104
Buffalo	80	48	25	7	315	257	103
Quebec	80	42	28	10	360	278	94
Montreal	80	35	40	5	286	295	75
Hartford	80	28	42	10	288	320	66

Patrick Division

NY Islanders	80	50	26	4	357	269	104
Washington	80	48	27	5	308	226	101
Philadelphia	80	44	26	10	350	290	98
NY Rangers	80	42	29	9	314	304	93
New Jersey	80	17	56	7	231	350	41
Pittsburgh	80	16	58	6	254	390	38

Leading Scorers

Player	Club	GP	G	A	PTS	PIM
Gretzky, Wayne	Edmonton	74	87	118	205	39
Coffey, Paul	Edmonton	80	40	86	126	104
Goulet, Michel	Quebec	75	56	65	121	76
Stastny, Peter	Quebec	80	46	73	119	73
Bossy, Mike	NY Islanders	67	51	67	118	8
Pederson, Barry	Boston	80	39	77	116	64
Kurri, Jari	Edmonton	64	52	61	113	14
Trottier, Bryan	NY Islanders	68	40	71	111	59
Federko, Bernie	St. Louis	79	41	66	107	43
Middleton, Rick	Boston	80	47	58	105	14

1984-85
CLARENCE CAMPBELL CONFERENCE
Norris Division

Team	GP	W	L	T	GF	GA	PTS
St. Louis	80	37	31	12	299	288	86
Chicago	80	38	35	7	309	299	83
Detroit	80	27	41	12	313	357	66
Minnesota	80	25	43	12	268	321	62
Toronto	80	20	52	8	253	358	48

Smythe Division

*Edmonton	80	49	20	11	401	298	109
Winnipeg	80	43	27	10	358	332	96
Calgary	80	41	27	12	363	302	94
Los Angeles	80	34	32	14	339	326	82
Vancouver	80	25	46	9	284	401	59

PRINCE OF WALES CONFERENCE
Adams Division

Montreal	80	41	27	12	309	262	94
Quebec	80	41	30	9	323	275	91
Buffalo	80	38	28	14	290	237	90
Boston	80	36	34	10	303	287	82
Hartford	80	30	41	9	268	318	69

Patrick Division

Philadelphia	80	53	20	7	348	241	113
Washington	80	46	25	9	322	240	101
NY Islanders	80	40	34	6	345	312	86
NY Rangers	80	26	44	10	295	345	62
New Jersey	80	22	48	10	264	346	54
Pittsburgh	80	24	51	5	276	385	53

Leading Scorers

Player	Club	GP	G	A	PTS	PIM
Gretzky, Wayne	Edmonton	80	73	135	208	52
Kurri, Jari	Edmonton	73	71	64	135	30
Hawerchuk, Dale	Winnipeg	80	53	77	130	74
Dionne, Marcel	Los Angeles	80	46	80	126	46
Coffey, Paul	Edmonton	80	37	84	121	97
Bossy, Mike	NY Islanders	76	58	59	117	38
Ogrodnick, John	Detroit	79	55	50	105	30
Savard, Denis	Chicago	79	38	67	105	56
Federko, Bernie	St. Louis	76	30	73	103	27
Gartner, Mike	Washington	80	50	52	102	71

1985-86

CLARENCE CAMPBELL CONFERENCE

Norris Division

Team	GP	W	L	T	GF	GA	PTS
Chicago	80	39	33	8	351	349	86
Minnesota	80	38	33	9	327	305	85
St. Louis	80	37	34	9	302	291	83
Toronto	80	25	48	7	311	386	57
Detroit	80	17	57	6	266	415	40

Smythe Division

Team	GP	W	L	T	GF	GA	PTS
Edmonton	80	56	17	7	426	310	119
Calgary	80	40	31	9	354	315	89
Winnipeg	80	26	47	7	295	372	59
Vancouver	80	23	44	13	282	333	59
Los Angeles	80	23	49	8	284	389	54

PRINCE OF WALES CONFERENCE

Adams Division

Team	GP	W	L	T	GF	GA	PTS
Quebec	80	43	31	6	330	289	92
*Montreal	80	40	33	7	330	280	87
Boston	80	37	31	12	311	288	86
Hartford	80	40	36	4	332	302	84
Buffalo	80	37	37	6	296	291	80

Patrick Division

Team	GP	W	L	T	GF	GA	PTS
Philadelphia	80	53	23	4	335	241	110
Washington	80	50	23	7	315	272	107
NY Islanders	80	39	29	12	327	284	90
NY Rangers	80	36	38	6	280	276	78
Pittsburgh	80	34	38	8	313	305	76
New Jersey	80	28	49	3	300	374	59

Leading Scorers

Player	Club	GP	G	A	PTS	PIM
Gretzky, Wayne	Edmonton	80	52	163	215	52
Lemieux, Mario	Pittsburgh	79	48	93	141	43
Coffey, Paul	Edmonton	79	48	90	138	120
Kurri, Jari	Edmonton	78	68	63	131	22
Bossy, Mike	NY Islanders	80	61	62	123	14
Stastny, Peter	Quebec	76	41	81	122	60
Savard, Denis	Chicago	80	47	69	116	111
Naslund, Mats	Montreal	80	43	67	110	16
Hawerchuk, Dale	Winnipeg	80	46	59	105	44
Broten, Neal	Minnesota	80	29	76	105	47

1986-87

CLARENCE CAMPBELL CONFERENCE

Norris Division

Team	GP	W	L	T	GF	GA	PTS
St. Louis	80	32	33	15	281	293	79
Detroit	80	34	36	10	260	274	78
Chicago	80	29	37	14	290	310	72
Toronto	80	32	42	6	286	319	70
Minnesota	80	30	40	10	296	314	70

Smythe Division

Team	GP	W	L	T	GF	GA	PTS
*Edmonton	80	50	24	6	372	284	106
Calgary	80	46	31	3	318	289	95
Winnipeg	80	40	32	8	279	271	88
Los Angeles	80	31	41	8	318	341	70
Vancouver	80	29	43	8	282	314	66

PRINCE OF WALES CONFERENCE

Adams Division

Team	GP	W	L	T	GF	GA	PTS
Hartford	80	43	30	7	287	270	93
Montreal	80	41	29	10	277	241	92
Boston	80	39	34	7	301	276	85
Quebec	80	31	39	10	267	276	72
Buffalo	80	28	44	8	280	308	64

Patrick Division

Team	GP	W	L	T	GF	GA	PTS
Philadelphia	80	46	26	8	310	245	100
Washington	80	38	32	10	285	278	86
NY Islanders	80	35	33	12	279	281	82
NY Rangers	80	34	38	8	307	323	76
Pittsburgh	80	30	38	12	297	290	72
New Jersey	80	29	45	6	293	368	64

Leading Scorers

Player	Club	GP	G	A	PTS	PIM
Gretzky, Wayne	Edmonton	79	62	121	183	28
Kurri, Jari	Edmonton	79	54	54	108	41
Lemieux, Mario	Pittsburgh	63	54	53	107	57
Messier, Mark	Edmonton	77	37	70	107	73
Gilmour, Doug	St. Louis	80	42	63	105	58
Ciccarelli, Dino	Minnesota	80	52	51	103	92
Hawerchuk, Dale	Winnipeg	80	47	53	100	54
Goulet, Michel	Quebec	75	49	47	96	61
Kerr, Tim	Philadelphia	75	58	37	95	57
Bourque, Raymond	Boston	78	23	72	95	36

1987-88

CLARENCE CAMPBELL CONFERENCE

Norris Division

Team	GP	W	L	T	GF	GA	PTS
Detroit	80	41	28	11	322	269	93
St. Louis	80	34	38	8	278	294	76
Chicago	80	30	41	9	284	328	69
Toronto	80	21	49	10	273	345	52
Minnesota	80	19	48	13	242	349	51

Smythe Division

Team	GP	W	L	T	GF	GA	PTS
Calgary	80	48	23	9	397	305	105
*Edmonton	80	44	25	11	363	288	99
Winnipeg	80	33	36	11	292	310	77
Los Angeles	80	30	42	8	318	359	68
Vancouver	80	25	46	9	272	320	59

PRINCE OF WALES CONFERENCE

Adams Division

Team	GP	W	L	T	GF	GA	PTS
Montreal	80	45	22	13	298	238	103
Boston	80	44	30	6	300	251	94
Buffalo	80	37	32	11	283	305	85
Hartford	80	35	38	7	249	267	77
Quebec	80	32	43	5	271	306	69

Patrick Division

Team	GP	W	L	T	GF	GA	PTS
NY Islanders	80	39	31	10	308	267	88
Washington	80	38	33	9	281	249	85
Philadelphia	80	38	33	9	292	292	85
New Jersey	80	38	36	6	295	296	82
NY Rangers	80	36	34	10	300	283	82
Pittsburgh	80	36	35	9	319	316	81

Leading Scorers

Player	Club	GP	G	A	PTS	PIM
Lemieux, Mario	Pittsburgh	77	70	98	168	92
Gretzky, Wayne	Edmonton	64	40	109	149	24
Savard, Denis	Chicago	80	44	87	131	95
Hawerchuk, Dale	Winnipeg	80	44	77	121	59
Robitaille, Luc	Los Angeles	80	53	58	111	82
Stastny, Peter	Quebec	76	46	65	111	69
Messier, Mark	Edmonton	77	37	74	111	103
Carson, Jimmy	Los Angeles	80	55	52	107	45
Loob, Hakan	Calgary	80	50	56	106	47
Goulet, Michel	Quebec	80	48	58	106	56

1988-89

CLARENCE CAMPBELL CONFERENCE

Norris Division

Team	GP	W	L	T	GF	GA	PTS
Detroit	80	34	34	12	313	316	80
St. Louis	80	33	35	12	275	285	78
Minnesota	80	27	37	16	258	278	70
Chicago	80	27	41	12	297	335	66
Toronto	80	28	46	6	259	342	62

Smythe Division

Team	GP	W	L	T	GF	GA	PTS
*Calgary	80	54	17	9	354	226	117
Los Angeles	80	42	31	7	376	335	91
Edmonton	80	38	34	8	325	306	84
Vancouver	80	33	39	8	251	253	74
Winnipeg	80	26	42	12	300	355	64

PRINCE OF WALES CONFERENCE

Adams Division

Team	GP	W	L	T	GF	GA	PTS
Montreal	80	53	18	9	315	218	115
Boston	80	37	29	14	289	256	88
Buffalo	80	38	35	7	291	299	83
Hartford	80	37	38	5	299	290	79
Quebec	80	27	46	7	269	342	61

Patrick Division

Team	GP	W	L	T	GF	GA	PTS
Washington	80	41	29	10	305	259	92
Pittsburgh	80	40	33	7	347	349	87
NY Rangers	80	37	35	8	310	307	82
Philadelphia	80	36	36	8	307	285	80
New Jersey	80	27	41	12	281	325	66
NY Islanders	80	28	47	5	265	325	61

Leading Scorers

Player	Club	GP	G	A	PTS	PIM
Lemieux, Mario	Pittsburgh	76	85	114	199	100
Gretzky, Wayne	Los Angeles	78	54	114	168	26
Yzerman, Steve	Detroit	80	65	90	155	61
Nicholls, Bernie	Los Angeles	79	70	80	150	96
Brown, Rob	Pittsburgh	68	49	66	115	118
Coffey, Paul	Pittsburgh	75	30	83	113	193
Mullen, Joe	Calgary	79	51	59	110	16
Kurri, Jari	Edmonton	76	44	58	102	69
Carson, Jimmy	Edmonton	80	49	51	100	36
Robitaille, Luc	Los Angeles	78	46	52	98	65

1989-90

CLARENCE CAMPBELL CONFERENCE

Norris Division

Team	GP	W	L	T	GF	GA	PTS
Chicago	80	41	33	6	316	294	88
St. Louis	80	37	34	9	295	279	83
Toronto	80	38	38	4	337	358	80
Minnesota	80	36	40	4	284	291	76
Detroit	80	28	38	14	288	323	70

Smythe Division

Team	GP	W	L	T	GF	GA	PTS
Calgary	80	42	23	15	348	265	99
*Edmonton	80	38	28	14	315	283	90
Winnipeg	80	37	32	11	298	290	85
Los Angeles	80	34	39	7	338	337	75
Vancouver	80	25	41	14	245	306	64

PRINCE OF WALES CONFERENCE

Adams Division

Team	GP	W	L	T	GF	GA	PTS
Boston	80	46	25	9	289	232	101
Buffalo	80	45	27	8	286	248	98
Montreal	80	41	28	11	288	234	93
Hartford	80	38	33	9	275	268	85
Quebec	80	12	61	7	240	407	31

Patrick Division

Team	GP	W	L	T	GF	GA	PTS
NY Rangers	80	36	31	13	279	267	85
New Jersey	80	37	34	9	295	288	83
Washington	80	36	38	6	284	275	78
NY Islanders	80	31	38	11	281	288	73
Pittsburgh	80	32	40	8	318	359	72
Philadelphia	80	30	39	11	290	297	71

Leading Scorers

Player	Club	GP	G	A	PTS	PIM
Gretzky, Wayne	Los Angeles	73	40	102	142	42
Messier, Mark	Edmonton	79	45	84	129	79
Yzerman, Steve	Detroit	79	62	65	127	79
Lemieux, Mario	Pittsburgh	59	45	78	123	78
Hull, Brett	St. Louis	80	72	41	113	24
Nicholls, Bernie	L.A., NYR	79	39	73	112	86
Turgeon, Pierre	Buffalo	80	40	66	106	29
LaFontaine, Pat	NY Islanders	74	54	51	105	38
Coffey, Paul	Pittsburgh	80	29	74	103	95
Sakic, Joe	Quebec	80	39	63	102	27
Oates, Adam	St. Louis	80	23	79	102	30

1990-91

CLARENCE CAMPBELL CONFERENCE

Norris Division

Team	GP	W	L	T	GF	GA	PTS
Chicago	80	49	23	8	284	211	106
St. Louis	80	47	22	11	310	250	105
Detroit	80	34	38	8	273	298	76
Minnesota	80	27	39	14	256	266	68
Toronto	80	23	46	11	241	318	57

Smythe Division

Team	GP	W	L	T	GF	GA	PTS
Los Angeles	80	46	24	10	340	254	102
Calgary	80	46	26	8	344	263	100
Edmonton	80	37	37	6	272	272	80
Vancouver	80	28	43	9	243	315	65
Winnipeg	80	26	43	11	260	288	63

PRINCE OF WALES CONFERENCE

Adams Division

Team	GP	W	L	T	GF	GA	PTS
Boston	80	44	24	12	299	264	100
Montreal	80	39	30	11	273	249	89
Buffalo	80	31	30	19	292	278	81
Hartford	80	31	38	11	238	276	73
Quebec	80	16	50	14	236	354	46

Patrick Division

Team	GP	W	L	T	GF	GA	PTS
*Pittsburgh	80	41	33	6	342	305	88
NY Rangers	80	36	31	13	297	265	85
Washington	80	37	36	7	258	258	81
New Jersey	80	32	33	15	272	264	79
Philadelphia	80	33	37	10	252	267	76
NY Islanders	80	25	45	10	223	290	60

Leading Scorers

Player	Club	GP	G	A	PTS	PIM
Gretzky, Wayne	Los Angeles	78	41	122	163	16
Hull, Brett	St. Louis	78	86	45	131	22
Oates, Adam	St. Louis	61	25	90	115	29
Recchi, Mark	Pittsburgh	78	40	73	113	48
Cullen, John	Pit., Hfd.	78	39	71	110	101
Sakic, Joe	Quebec	80	48	61	109	24
Yzerman, Steve	Detroit	80	51	57	108	34
Fleury, Theoren	Calgary	79	51	53	104	136
MacInnis, Al	Calgary	78	28	75	103	90
Larmer, Steve	Chicago	80	44	57	101	79

1991-92
CLARENCE CAMPBELL CONFERENCE
Norris Division

Team	GP	W	L	T	GF	GA	PTS
Detroit	80	43	25	12	320	256	98
Chicago	80	36	29	15	257	236	87
St. Louis	80	36	33	11	279	266	83
Minnesota	80	32	42	6	246	278	70
Toronto	80	30	43	7	234	294	67

Smythe Division

	GP	W	L	T	GF	GA	PTS
Vancouver	80	42	26	12	285	250	96
Los Angeles	80	35	31	14	287	296	84
Edmonton	80	36	34	10	295	297	82
Winnipeg	80	33	32	15	251	244	81
Calgary	80	31	37	12	296	305	74
San Jose	80	17	58	5	219	359	39

PRINCE OF WALES CONFERENCE
Adams Division

	GP	W	L	T	GF	GA	PTS
Montreal	80	41	28	11	267	207	93
Boston	80	36	32	12	270	275	84
Buffalo	80	31	37	12	289	299	74
Hartford	80	26	41	13	247	283	65
Quebec	80	20	48	12	255	318	52

Patrick Division

	GP	W	L	T	GF	GA	PTS
NY Rangers	80	50	25	5	321	246	105
Washington	80	45	27	8	330	275	98
*Pittsburgh	80	39	32	9	343	308	87
New Jersey	80	38	31	11	289	259	87
NY Islanders	80	34	35	11	291	299	79
Philadelphia	80	32	37	11	252	273	75

Leading Scorers

Player	Club	GP	G	A	PTS	PIM
Lemieux, Mario	Pittsburgh	64	44	87	131	94
Stevens, Kevin	Pittsburgh	80	54	69	123	254
Gretzky, Wayne	Los Angeles	74	31	90	121	34
Hull, Brett	St. Louis	73	70	39	109	48
Robitaille, Luc	Los Angeles	80	44	63	107	95
Messier, Mark	NY Rangers	79	35	72	107	76
Roenick, Jeremy	Chicago	80	53	50	103	23
Yzerman, Steve	Detroit	79	45	58	103	64
Leetch, Brian	NY Rangers	80	22	80	102	26
Oates, Adam	St.L., Bos.	80	20	79	99	22

1992-93
CLARENCE CAMPBELL CONFERENCE
Norris Division

Team	GP	W	L	T	GF	GA	PTS
Chicago	84	47	25	12	279	230	106
Detroit	84	47	28	9	369	280	103
Toronto	84	44	29	11	288	241	99
St. Louis	84	37	36	11	282	278	85
Minnesota	84	36	38	10	272	293	82
Tampa Bay	84	23	54	7	245	332	53

Smythe Division

	GP	W	L	T	GF	GA	PTS
Vancouver	84	46	29	9	346	278	101
Calgary	84	43	30	11	322	282	97
Los Angeles	84	39	35	10	338	340	88
Winnipeg	84	40	37	7	322	320	87
Edmonton	84	26	50	8	242	337	60
San Jose	84	11	71	2	218	414	24

PRINCE OF WALES CONFERENCE
Adams Division

	GP	W	L	T	GF	GA	PTS
Boston	84	51	26	7	332	268	109
Quebec	84	47	27	10	351	300	104
*Montreal	84	48	30	6	326	280	102
Buffalo	84	38	36	10	335	297	86
Hartford	84	26	52	6	284	369	58
Ottawa	84	10	70	4	202	395	24

Patrick Division

	GP	W	L	T	GF	GA	PTS
Pittsburgh	84	56	21	7	367	268	119
Washington	84	43	34	7	325	286	93
NY Islanders	84	40	37	7	335	297	87
New Jersey	84	40	37	7	308	299	87
Philadelphia	84	36	37	11	319	319	83
NY Rangers	84	34	39	11	304	308	79

Leading Scorers

Player	Club	GP	G	A	PTS	PIM
Lemieux, Mario	Pittsburgh	60	69	91	160	38
LaFontaine, Pat	Buffalo	84	53	95	148	63
Oates, Adam	Boston	84	45	97	142	32
Yzerman, Steve	Detroit	84	58	79	137	44
Selanne, Teemu	Winnipeg	84	76	56	132	45
Turgeon, Pierre	NY Islanders	83	58	74	132	26
Mogilny, Alexander	Buffalo	77	76	51	127	40
Gilmour, Doug	Toronto	83	32	95	127	100
Robitaille, Luc	Los Angeles	84	63	62	125	100
Recchi, Mark	Philadelphia	84	53	70	123	95

1993-94
EASTERN CONFERENCE
Northeast Division

Team	GP	W	L	T	GF	GA	PTS
Pittsburgh	84	44	27	13	299	285	101
Boston	84	42	29	13	289	252	97
Montreal	84	41	29	14	283	248	96
Buffalo	84	43	32	9	282	218	95
Quebec	84	34	42	8	277	292	76
Hartford	84	27	48	9	227	288	63
Ottawa	84	14	61	9	201	397	37

Atlantic Division

	GP	W	L	T	GF	GA	PTS
*NY Rangers	84	52	24	8	299	231	112
New Jersey	84	47	25	12	306	220	106
Washington	84	39	35	10	277	263	88
NY Islanders	84	36	36	12	282	264	84
Florida	84	33	34	17	233	233	83
Philadelphia	84	35	39	10	294	314	80
Tampa Bay	84	30	43	11	224	251	71

WESTERN CONFERENCE
Central Division

	GP	W	L	T	GF	GA	PTS
Detroit	84	46	30	8	356	275	100
Toronto	84	43	29	12	280	243	98
Dallas	84	42	29	13	286	265	97
St. Louis	84	40	33	11	270	283	91
Chicago	84	39	36	9	254	240	87
Winnipeg	84	24	51	9	245	344	57

Pacific Division

	GP	W	L	T	GF	GA	PTS
Calgary	84	42	29	13	302	256	97
Vancouver	84	41	40	3	279	276	85
San Jose	84	33	35	16	252	265	82
Anaheim	84	33	46	5	229	251	71
Los Angeles	84	27	45	12	294	322	66
Edmonton	84	25	45	14	261	305	64

Leading Scorers

Player	Club	GP	G	A	PTS	PIM
Gretzky, Wayne	Los Angeles	81	38	92	130	20
Fedorov, Sergei	Detroit	82	56	64	120	34
Oates, Adam	Boston	77	32	80	112	45
Gilmour, Doug	Toronto	83	27	84	111	105
Bure, Pavel	Vancouver	76	60	47	107	86
Roenick, Jeremy	Chicago	84	46	61	107	125
Recchi, Mark	Philadelphia	84	40	67	107	46
Shanahan, Brendan	St. Louis	81	52	50	102	211
Andreychuk, Dave	Toronto	83	53	46	99	98
Jagr, Jaromir	Pittsburgh	80	32	67	99	61

1994-95
EASTERN CONFERENCE
Northeast Division

Team	GP	W	L	T	GF	GA	PTS
Quebec	48	30	13	5	185	134	65
Pittsburgh	48	29	16	3	181	158	61
Boston	48	27	18	3	150	127	57
Buffalo	48	22	19	7	130	119	51
Hartford	48	19	24	5	127	141	43
Montreal	48	18	23	7	125	148	43
Ottawa	48	9	34	5	117	174	23

Atlantic Division

	GP	W	L	T	GF	GA	PTS
Philadelphia	48	28	16	4	150	132	60
*New Jersey	48	22	18	8	136	121	52
Washington	48	22	18	8	136	120	52
NY Rangers	48	22	23	3	139	134	47
Florida	48	20	22	6	115	127	46
Tampa Bay	48	17	28	3	120	144	37
NY Islanders	48	15	28	5	126	158	35

WESTERN CONFERENCE
Central Division

	GP	W	L	T	GF	GA	PTS
Detroit	48	33	11	4	180	117	70
St. Louis	48	28	15	5	178	135	61
Chicago	48	24	19	5	156	115	53
Toronto	48	21	19	8	135	146	50
Dallas	48	17	23	8	136	135	42
Winnipeg	48	16	25	7	157	177	39

Pacific Division

	GP	W	L	T	GF	GA	PTS
Calgary	48	24	17	7	163	135	55
Vancouver	48	18	18	12	153	148	48
San Jose	48	19	25	4	129	161	42
Los Angeles	48	16	23	9	142	174	41
Edmonton	48	17	27	4	136	183	38
Anaheim	48	16	27	5	125	164	37

Leading Scorers

Player	Club	GP	G	A	PTS	PIM
Jagr, Jaromir	Pittsburgh	48	32	38	70	37
Lindros, Eric	Philadelphia	46	29	41	70	60
Zhamnov, Alex	Winnipeg	48	30	35	65	20
Sakic, Joe	Quebec	47	19	43	62	30
Francis, Ron	Pittsburgh	44	11	48	59	18
Fleury, Theoren	Calgary	47	29	29	58	112
Coffey, Paul	Detroit	45	14	44	58	72
Renberg, Mikael	Philadelphia	47	26	31	57	20
LeClair, John	Mtl., Phi.	46	26	28	54	30
Messier, Mark	NY Rangers	46	14	39	53	40
Oates, Adam	Boston	48	12	41	53	8

Twice a top-10 scorer, Pierre Turgeon had his best season in 1992-93 when he established career highs with 58 goals, 74 assists and 132 points. He was sixth in the NHL in scoring that year.

1995-96

EASTERN CONFERENCE
Northeast Division

Team	GP	W	L	T	GF	GA	PTS
Pittsburgh	82	49	29	4	362	284	102
Boston	82	40	31	11	282	269	91
Montreal	82	40	32	10	265	248	90
Hartford	82	34	39	9	237	259	77
Buffalo	82	33	42	7	247	262	73
Ottawa	82	18	59	5	191	291	41

Atlantic Division

Team	GP	W	L	T	GF	GA	PTS
Philadelphia	82	45	24	13	282	208	103
NY Rangers	82	41	27	14	272	237	96
Florida	82	41	31	10	254	234	92
Washington	82	39	32	11	234	204	89
Tampa Bay	82	38	32	12	238	248	88
New Jersey	82	37	33	12	215	202	86
NY Islanders	82	22	50	10	229	315	54

WESTERN CONFERENCE
Central Division

Team	GP	W	L	T	GF	GA	PTS
Detroit	82	62	13	7	325	181	131
Chicago	82	40	28	14	273	220	94
Toronto	82	34	36	12	247	252	80
St. Louis	82	32	34	16	219	248	80
Winnipeg	82	36	40	6	275	291	78
Dallas	82	26	42	14	227	280	66

Pacific Division

Team	GP	W	L	T	GF	GA	PTS
*Colorado	82	47	25	10	326	240	104
Calgary	82	34	37	11	241	240	79
Vancouver	82	32	35	15	278	278	79
Anaheim	82	35	39	8	234	247	78
Edmonton	82	30	44	8	240	304	68
Los Angeles	82	24	40	18	256	302	66
San Jose	82	20	55	7	252	357	47

Leading Scorers

Player	Club	GP	G	A	PTS	PIM
Lemieux, Mario	Pittsburgh	70	69	92	161	54
Jagr, Jaromir	Pittsburgh	82	62	87	149	96
Sakic, Joe	Colorado	82	51	69	120	44
Francis, Ron	Pittsburgh	77	27	92	119	56
Forsberg, Peter	Colorado	82	30	86	116	47
Lindros, Eric	Philadelphia	73	47	68	115	163
Kariya, Paul	Anaheim	82	50	58	108	20
Selanne, Teemu	Wpg., Ana.	79	40	68	108	22
Mogilny, Alexander	Vancouver	79	55	52	107	16
Fedorov, Sergei	Detroit	78	39	68	107	48

1996-97

EASTERN CONFERENCE
Northeast Division

Team	GP	W	L	T	GF	GA	PTS
Buffalo	82	40	30	12	237	208	92
Pittsburgh	82	38	36	8	285	280	84
Ottawa	82	31	36	15	226	234	77
Montreal	82	31	36	15	249	276	77
Hartford	82	32	39	11	226	256	75
Boston	82	26	47	9	234	300	61

Atlantic Division

Team	GP	W	L	T	GF	GA	PTS
New Jersey	82	45	23	14	231	182	104
Philadelphia	82	45	24	13	274	217	103
Florida	82	35	28	19	221	201	89
NY Rangers	82	38	34	10	258	231	86
Washington	82	33	40	9	214	231	75
Tampa Bay	82	32	40	10	217	247	74
NY Islanders	82	29	41	12	240	250	70

WESTERN CONFERENCE
Central Division

Team	GP	W	L	T	GF	GA	PTS
Dallas	82	48	26	8	252	198	104
*Detroit	82	38	26	18	253	197	94
Phoenix	82	38	37	7	240	243	83
St. Louis	82	36	35	11	236	239	83
Chicago	82	34	35	13	223	210	81
Toronto	82	30	44	8	230	273	68

Pacific Division

Team	GP	W	L	T	GF	GA	PTS
Colorado	82	49	24	9	277	205	107
Anaheim	82	36	33	13	245	233	85
Edmonton	82	36	37	9	252	247	81
Vancouver	82	35	40	7	257	273	77
Calgary	82	32	41	9	214	239	73
Los Angeles	82	28	43	11	214	268	67
San Jose	82	27	47	8	211	278	62

Leading Scorers

Player	Club	GP	G	A	PTS	PIM
Lemieux, Mario	Pittsburgh	76	50	72	122	65
Selanne, Teemu	Anaheim	78	51	58	109	34
Kariya, Paul	Anaheim	69	44	55	99	6
LeClair, John	Philadelphia	82	50	47	97	58
Gretzky, Wayne	NY Rangers	82	25	72	97	28
Jagr, Jaromir	Pittsburgh	63	47	48	95	40
Sundin, Mats	Toronto	82	41	53	94	59
Palffy, Ziggy	NY Islanders	80	48	42	90	43
Francis, Ron	Pittsburgh	81	27	63	90	20
Shanahan, Brendan	Hfd., Det.	81	47	41	88	131

1997-98

EASTERN CONFERENCE
Northeast Division

Team	GP	W	L	T	GF	GA	PTS
Pittsburgh	82	40	24	18	228	188	98
Boston	82	39	30	13	221	194	91
Buffalo	82	36	29	17	211	187	89
Montreal	82	37	32	13	235	208	87
Ottawa	82	34	33	15	193	200	83
Carolina	82	33	41	8	200	219	74

Atlantic Division

Team	GP	W	L	T	GF	GA	PTS
New Jersey	82	48	23	11	225	166	107
Philadelphia	82	42	29	11	242	193	95
Washington	82	40	30	12	219	202	92
NY Islanders	82	30	41	11	212	225	71
NY Rangers	82	25	39	18	197	231	68
Florida	82	24	43	15	203	256	63
Tampa Bay	82	17	55	10	151	269	44

WESTERN CONFERENCE
Central Division

Team	GP	W	L	T	GF	GA	PTS
Dallas	82	49	22	11	242	167	109
*Detroit	82	44	23	15	250	196	103
St. Louis	82	45	29	8	256	204	98
Phoenix	82	35	35	12	224	227	82
Chicago	82	30	39	13	192	199	73
Toronto	82	30	43	9	194	237	69

Pacific Division

Team	GP	W	L	T	GF	GA	PTS
Colorado	82	39	26	17	231	205	95
Los Angeles	82	38	33	11	227	225	87
Edmonton	82	35	37	10	215	224	80
San Jose	82	34	38	10	210	216	78
Calgary	82	26	41	15	217	252	67
Anaheim	82	26	43	13	205	261	65
Vancouver	82	25	43	14	224	273	64

Leading Scorers

Player	Club	GP	G	A	PTS	PIM
Jagr, Jaromir	Pittsburgh	77	35	67	102	64
Forsberg, Peter	Colorado	72	25	66	91	94
Bure, Pavel	Vancouver	82	51	39	90	48
Gretzky, Wayne	NY Rangers	82	23	67	90	28
LeClair, John	Philadelphia	82	51	36	87	32
Palffy, Ziggy	NY Islanders	82	45	42	87	34
Francis, Ron	Pittsburgh	81	25	62	87	20
Selanne, Teemu	Anaheim	73	52	34	86	30
Allison, Jason	Boston	81	33	50	83	60
Stumpel, Jozef	Los Angeles	77	21	58	79	53

Ron Francis made his first appearance among the NHL's top-10 scorers in 1994-95.

Alex Zhamnov scored a career-high 30 goals in 1994-95 and finished third in scoring.

The 1994-95 season marked Theo Fleury's second (and final) appearance among the top-10 scorers.

1998-99
EASTERN CONFERENCE
Northeast Division

Team	GP	W	L	T	GF	GA	PTS
Ottawa	82	44	23	15	239	179	103
Toronto	82	45	30	7	268	231	97
Boston	82	39	30	13	214	181	91
Buffalo	82	37	28	17	207	175	91
Montreal	82	32	39	11	184	209	75

Atlantic Division

Team	GP	W	L	T	GF	GA	PTS
New Jersey	82	47	24	11	248	196	105
Philadelphia	82	37	26	19	231	196	93
Pittsburgh	82	38	30	14	242	225	90
NY Rangers	82	33	38	11	217	227	77
NY Islanders	82	24	48	10	194	244	58

Southeast Division

Team	GP	W	L	T	GF	GA	PTS
Carolina	82	34	30	18	210	202	86
Florida	82	30	34	18	210	228	78
Washington	82	31	45	6	200	218	68
Tampa Bay	82	19	54	9	179	292	47

WESTERN CONFERENCE
Central Division

Team	GP	W	L	T	GF	GA	PTS
Detroit	82	43	32	7	245	202	93
St Louis	82	37	32	13	237	209	87
Chicago	82	29	41	12	202	248	70
Nashville	82	28	47	7	190	261	63

Pacific Division

Team	GP	W	L	T	GF	GA	PTS
*Dallas	82	51	19	12	236	168	114
Phoenix	82	39	31	12	205	197	90
Anaheim	82	35	34	13	215	206	83
San Jose	82	31	33	18	196	191	80
Los Angeles	82	32	45	5	189	222	69

Northwest Division

Team	GP	W	L	T	GF	GA	PTS
Colorado	82	44	28	10	239	205	98
Edmonton	82	33	37	12	230	226	78
Calgary	82	30	40	12	211	234	72
Vancouver	82	23	47	12	192	258	58

Leading Scorers

Player	Club	GP	G	A	PTS	PIM
Jagr, Jaromir	Pittsburgh	81	44	83	127	66
Selanne, Teemu	Anaheim	75	47	60	107	30
Kariya, Paul	Anaheim	82	39	62	101	40
Forsberg, Peter	Colorado	78	30	67	97	108
Sakic, Joe	Colorado	73	41	55	96	29
Yashin, Alexei	Ottawa	82	44	50	94	54
Lindros, Eric	Philadelphia	71	40	53	93	120
Fleury, Theoren	Cgy., Col.	75	40	53	93	86
LeClair, John	Philadelphia	76	43	47	90	30
Demitra, Pavol	St Louis	82	37	52	89	16

1999-2000
EASTERN CONFERENCE
Northeast Division

Team	GP	W	L	T	OTL	GF	GA	PTS
Toronto	82	45	27	7	3	246	222	100
Ottawa	82	41	28	11	2	244	210	95
Buffalo	82	35	32	11	4	213	204	85
Montreal	82	35	34	9	4	196	194	83
Boston	82	24	33	19	6	210	248	73

Atlantic Division

Team	GP	W	L	T	OTL	GF	GA	PTS
Philadelphia	82	45	22	12	3	237	179	105
*New Jersey	82	45	24	8	5	251	203	103
Pittsburgh	82	37	31	8	6	241	236	88
NY Rangers	82	29	38	12	3	218	246	73
NY Islanders	82	24	48	9	1	194	275	58

Southeast Division

Team	GP	W	L	T	OTL	GF	GA	PTS
Washington	82	44	24	12	2	227	194	102
Florida	82	43	27	6	6	244	209	98
Carolina	82	37	35	10	0	217	216	84
Tampa Bay	82	19	47	9	7	204	310	54
Atlanta	82	14	57	7	4	170	313	39

WESTERN CONFERENCE
Central Division

Team	GP	W	L	T	OTL	GF	GA	PTS
St. Louis	82	51	19	11	1	248	165	114
Detroit	82	48	22	10	2	278	210	108
Chicago	82	33	37	10	2	242	245	78
Nashville	82	28	40	7	7	199	240	70

Pacific Division

Team	GP	W	L	T	OTL	GF	GA	PTS
Dallas	82	43	23	10	6	211	184	102
Los Angeles	82	39	27	12	4	245	228	94
Phoenix	82	39	31	8	4	232	228	90
San Jose	82	35	30	10	7	225	214	87
Anaheim	82	34	33	12	3	217	227	83

Northwest Division

Team	GP	W	L	T	OTL	GF	GA	PTS
Colorado	82	42	28	11	1	233	201	96
Edmonton	82	32	26	16	8	226	212	88
Vancouver	82	30	29	15	8	227	237	83
Calgary	82	31	36	10	5	211	256	77

Leading Scorers

Player	Club	GP	G	A	PTS	PIM
Jagr, Jaromir	Pittsburgh	63	42	54	96	50
Bure, Pavel	Florida	74	58	36	94	16
Recchi, Mark	Philadelphia	82	28	63	91	50
Kariya, Paul	Anaheim	74	42	44	86	24
Selanne, Teemu	Anaheim	79	33	52	85	12
Nolan, Owen	San Jose	78	44	40	84	110
Amonte, Tony	Chicago	82	43	41	84	48
Modano, Mike	Dallas	77	38	43	81	48
Sakic, Joe	Colorado	60	28	53	81	28
Yzerman, Steve	Detroit	78	35	44	79	34

2000-2001
EASTERN CONFERENCE
Northeast Division

Team	GP	W	L	T	OTL	GF	GA	PTS
Ottawa	82	48	21	9	4	274	205	109
Buffalo	82	46	30	5	1	218	184	98
Toronto	82	37	29	11	5	232	207	90
Boston	82	36	30	8	8	227	249	88
Montreal	82	28	40	8	6	206	232	70

Atlantic Division

Team	GP	W	L	T	OTL	GF	GA	PTS
New Jersey	82	48	19	12	3	295	195	111
Philadelphia	82	43	25	11	3	240	207	100
Pittsburgh	82	42	28	9	3	281	256	96
NY Rangers	82	33	43	5	1	250	290	72
NY Islanders	82	21	51	7	3	185	268	52

Southeast Division

Team	GP	W	L	T	OTL	GF	GA	PTS
Washington	82	41	27	10	4	233	211	96
Carolina	82	38	32	9	3	212	225	88
Florida	82	22	38	13	9	200	246	66
Atlanta	82	23	45	12	2	211	289	60
Tampa Bay	82	24	47	6	5	201	280	59

WESTERN CONFERENCE
Central Division

Team	GP	W	L	T	OTL	GF	GA	PTS
Detroit	82	49	20	9	4	253	202	111
St. Louis	82	43	22	12	5	249	195	103
Nashville	82	34	36	9	3	186	200	80
Chicago	82	29	40	8	5	210	246	71
Columbus	82	28	39	9	6	190	233	71

Pacific Division

Team	GP	W	L	T	OTL	GF	GA	PTS
Dallas	82	48	24	8	2	241	187	106
San Jose	82	40	27	12	3	217	192	95
Los Angeles	82	38	28	13	3	252	228	92
Phoenix	82	35	27	17	3	214	212	90
Anaheim	82	25	41	11	5	188	245	66

Northwest Division

Team	GP	W	L	T	OTL	GF	GA	PTS
*Colorado	82	52	16	10	4	270	192	118
Edmonton	82	39	28	12	3	243	222	93
Vancouver	82	36	28	11	7	239	238	90
Calgary	82	27	36	15	4	197	236	73
Minnesota	82	25	39	13	5	168	210	68

Leading Scorers

Player	Club	GP	G	A	PTS	PIM
Jagr, Jaromir	Pittsburgh	81	52	69	121	42
Sakic, Joe	Colorado	82	54	64	118	30
Elias, Patrik	New Jersey	82	40	56	96	51
Kovalev, Alex	Pittsburgh	79	44	51	95	96
Allison, Jason	Boston	82	36	59	95	85
Straka, Martin	Pittsburgh	82	27	68	95	38
Bure, Pavel	Florida	82	59	33	92	58
Weight, Doug	Edmonton	82	25	65	90	91
Palffy, Ziggy	Los Angeles	73	38	51	89	20
Forsberg, Peter	Colorado	73	27	62	89	54

Joe Sakic made his ninth appearance among the NHL's top 10 scorers in 2003-04. He ranked among the league leaders in goals (33), assists (54) and points (87).

2001-2002

EASTERN CONFERENCE
Northeast Division

Team	GP	W	L	T	OTL	GF	GA	PTS
Boston	82	43	24	6	9	236	201	101
Toronto	82	43	25	10	4	249	207	100
Ottawa	82	39	27	9	7	243	208	94
Montreal	82	36	31	12	3	207	209	87
Buffalo	82	35	35	1·1	1	213	200	82

Atlantic Division

Team	GP	W	L	T	OTL	GF	GA	PTS
Philadelphia	82	42	27	10	3	234	192	97
NY Islanders	82	42	28	8	4	239	220	96
New Jersey	82	41	28	9	4	205	187	95
NY Rangers	82	36	38	4	4	227	258	80
Pittsburgh	82	28	41	8	5	198	249	69

Southeast Division

Team	GP	W	L	T	OTL	GF	GA	PTS
Carolina	82	35	26	16	6	217	217	91
Washington	82	36	33	11	2	228	240	85
Tampa Bay	82	27	40	11	4	178	219	69
Florida	82	22	44	10	6	180	250	60
Atlanta	82	19	47	11	5	187	288	54

WESTERN CONFERENCE
Central Division

Team	GP	W	L	T	OTL	GF	GA	PTS
*Detroit	82	51	17	10	4	251	187	116
St. Louis	82	43	27	8	4	227	188	98
Chicago	82	41	27	13	1	216	207	96
Nashville	82	28	41	13	0	196	230	69
Columbus	82	22	47	8	5	164	255	57

Pacific Division

Team	GP	W	L	T	OTL	GF	GA	PTS
San Jose	82	44	27	8	3	248	199	99
Phoenix	82	40	27	9	6	228	210	95
Los Angeles	82	40	27	11	4	214	190	95
Dallas	82	36	28	13	5	215	213	90
Anaheim	82	29	42	8	3	175	198	69

Northwest Division

Team	GP	W	L	T	OTL	GF	GA	PTS
Colorado	82	45	28	8	1	212	169	99
Vancouver	82	42	30	7	3	254	211	94
Edmonton	82	38	28	12	4	205	182	92
Calgary	82	32	35	12	3	201	220	79
Minnesota	82	26	35	12	9	195	238	73

Leading Scorers

Player	Club	GP	G	A	PTS	PIM
Iginla, Jarome	Calgary	82	52	44	96	77
Naslund, Markus	Vancouver	81	40	50	90	50
Bertuzzi, Todd	Vancouver	72	36	49	85	110
Sundin, Mats	Toronto	82	41	39	80	94
Jagr, Jaromir	Washington	69	31	48	79	30
Sakic, Joe	Colorado	82	26	53	79	18
Demitra, Pavol	St. Louis	82	35	43	78	46
Oates, Adam	Wsh., Phi.	80	14	64	78	28
Modano, Mike	Dallas	78	34	43	77	38
Francis, Ron	Carolina	80	27	50	77	18

2002-2003

EASTERN CONFERENCE
Northeast Division

Team	GP	W	L	T	OTL	GF	GA	PTS
Ottawa	82	52	21	8	1	263	182	113
Toronto	82	44	28	7	3	236	208	98
Boston	82	36	31	11	4	245	237	87
Montreal	82	30	35	8	9	206	234	77
Buffalo	82	27	37	10	8	190	219	72

Atlantic Division

Team	GP	W	L	T	OTL	GF	GA	PTS
*New Jersey	82	46	20	10	6	216	166	108
Philadelphia	82	45	20	13	4	211	166	107
NY Islanders	82	35	34	11	2	224	231	83
NY Rangers	82	32	36	10	4	210	231	78
Pittsburgh	82	27	44	6	5	189	255	65

Southeast Division

Team	GP	W	L	T	OTL	GF	GA	PTS
Tampa Bay	82	36	25	16	5	219	210	93
Washington	82	39	29	8	6	224	220	92
Atlanta	82	31	39	7	5	226	284	74
Florida	82	24	36	13	9	176	237	70
Carolina	82	22	43	11	6	171	240	61

WESTERN CONFERENCE
Central Division

Team	GP	W	L	T	OTL	GF	GA	PTS
Detroit	82	48	20	10	4	269	203	110
St. Louis	82	41	24	11	6	253	222	99
Chicago	82	30	33	13	6	207	226	79
Nashville	82	27	35	13	7	183	206	74
Columbus	82	29	42	8	3	213	263	69

Pacific Division

Team	GP	W	L	T	OTL	GF	GA	PTS
Dallas	82	46	17	15	4	245	169	111
Anaheim	82	40	27	9	6	203	193	95
Los Angeles	82	33	37	6	6	203	221	78
Phoenix	82	31	35	11	5	204	230	78
San Jose	82	28	37	9	8	214	239	73

Northwest Division

Team	GP	W	L	T	OTL	GF	GA	PTS
Colorado	82	42	19	13	8	251	194	105
Vancouver	82	45	23	13	1	264	208	104
Minnesota	82	42	29	10	1	198	178	95
Edmonton	82	36	26	11	9	231	230	92
Calgary	82	29	36	13	4	186	228	75

Leading Scorers

Player	Club	GP	G	A	PTS	PIM
Forsberg, Peter	Colorado	75	29	77	106	70
Naslund, Markus	Vancouver	82	48	56	104	52
Thornton, Joe	Boston	77	36	65	101	109
Hejduk, Milan	Colorado	82	50	48	98	52
Bertuzzi, Todd	Vancouver	82	46	51	97	144
Demitra, Pavol	St. Louis	78	36	57	93	32
Murray, Glen	Boston	82	44	48	92	64
Lemieux, Mario	Pittsburgh	67	28	63	91	43
Heatley, Danny	Atlanta	77	41	48	89	58
Palffy, Ziggy	Los Angeles	76	37	48	85	47
Modano, Mike	Dallas	79	28	57	85	30

2003-2004

EASTERN CONFERENCE
Northeast Division

Team	GP	W	L	T	OTL	GF	GA	PTS
Boston	82	41	19	15	7	209	188	104
Toronto	82	45	24	10	3	242	204	103
Ottawa	82	43	23	10	6	262	189	102
Montreal	82	41	30	7	4	208	192	93
Buffalo	82	37	34	7	4	220	221	85

Atlantic Division

Team	GP	W	L	T	OTL	GF	GA	PTS
Philadelphia	82	40	21	15	6	229	186	101
New Jersey	82	43	25	12	2	213	164	100
NY Islanders	82	38	29	11	4	237	210	91
NY Rangers	82	27	40	7	8	206	250	69
Pittsburgh	82	23	47	8	4	190	303	58

Southeast Division

Team	GP	W	L	T	OTL	GF	GA	PTS
*Tampa Bay	82	46	22	8	6	245	192	106
Atlanta	82	33	37	8	4	214	243	78
Carolina	82	28	34	14	6	172	209	76
Florida	82	28	35	15	4	188	221	75
Washington	82	23	46	10	3	186	253	59

WESTERN CONFERENCE
Central Division

Team	GP	W	L	T	OTL	GF	GA	PTS
Detroit	82	48	21	11	2	255	189	109
St. Louis	82	39	30	11	2	191	198	91
Nashville	82	38	29	11	4	216	217	91
Columbus	82	25	45	8	4	177	238	62
Chicago	82	20	43	11	8	188	259	59

Pacific Division

Team	GP	W	L	T	OTL	GF	GA	PTS
San Jose	82	43	21	12	6	219	183	104
Dallas	82	41	26	13	2	·194	175	97
Los Angeles	82	28	29	16	9	205	217	81
Anaheim	82	29	35	10	8	184	213	76
Phoenix	82	22	36	18	6	188	245	68

Northwest Division

Team	GP	W	L	T	OTL	GF	GA	PTS
Vancouver	82	43	24	10	5	235	194	101
Colorado	82	40	22	13	7	236	198	100
Calgary	82	42	30	7	3	200	176	94
Edmonton	82	36	29	12	5	221	208	89
Minnesota	82	30	29	20	3	188	183	83

Leading Scorers

Player	Club	GP	G	A	PTS	PIM
St. Louis, Martin	Tampa Bay	82	38	56	94	24
Kovalchuk, Ilya	Atlanta	81	41	46	87	63
Sakic, Joe	Colorado	81	33	54	87	42
Naslund, Markus	Vancouver	78	35	49	84	58
Hossa, Marian	Ottawa	81	36	46	82	46
Elias, Patrik	New Jersey	82	38	43	81	44
Alfredsson, Daniel	Ottawa	77	32	48	80	24
Stillman, Cory	Tampa Bay	81	25	55	80	36
Lang, Robert	Wsh., Det.	69	30	49	79	24
Richards, Brad	Tampa Bay	82	26	53	79	12
Tanguay, Alex	Colorado	69	25	54	79	42

Note: Detailed statistics for 2003-2004 are listed in the Final Statistics, 2003-2004 section of the *NHL Guide & Record Book*. **See page 133.**

Atlanta's Ilya Kovalchuk (far left) tied for the NHL lead with 41 goals, while Tampa Bay's Brad Richards (left) ranked sixth in the league with 53 assists.

Team Records

Regular Season

FINAL STANDINGS

MOST POINTS, ONE SEASON:
  132 – Montreal Canadiens, 1976-77. 60w-8l-12t. 80gp
  131 – Detroit Red Wings, 1995-96. 62w-13l-7t. 82gp
  129 – Montreal Canadiens, 1977-78. 59w-10l-11t. 80gp

BEST POINTS PERCENTAGE, ONE SEASON:
  .875 – Boston Bruins, 1929-30. 38w-5l-1t. 77pts in 44gp
  .830 – Montreal Canadiens, 1943-44. 38w-5l-7t. 83pts in 50gp
  .825 – Montreal Canadiens, 1976-77. 60w-8l-12t. 132pts in 80gp
  .806 – Montreal Canadiens, 1977-78. 59w-10l-11t. 129pts in 80gp
  .800 – Montreal Canadiens, 1944-45. 38w-8l-4t. 80pts in 50gp

FEWEST POINTS, ONE SEASON:
  8 – Quebec Bulldogs, 1919-20. 4w-20l-0t. 24gp
  10 – Toronto Arenas, 1918-19. 5w-13l-0t. 18gp
  12 – Hamilton Tigers, 1920-21. 6w-18l-0t. 24gp
   – Hamilton Tigers, 1922-23. 6w-18l-0t. 24gp
   – Boston Bruins, 1924-25. 6w-24l-0t. 30gp
   – Philadelphia Quakers, 1930-31. 4w-36l-4t. 44gp

FEWEST POINTS, ONE SEASON (MINIMUM 70-GAME SCHEDULE):
  21 – Washington Capitals, 1974-75. 8w-67l-5t. 80gp
  24 – Ottawa Senators, 1992-93. 10w-70l-4t. 84gp
   – San Jose Sharks, 1992-93. 11w-71l-2t. 84gp
  30 – New York Islanders, 1972-73. 12w-60l-6t. 78gp

WORST POINTS PERCENTAGE, ONE SEASON:
  .131 – Washington Capitals, 1974-75. 8w-67l-5t. 21pts in 80gp
  .136 – Philadelphia Quakers, 1930-31. 4w-36l-4t. 12pts in 44gp
  .143 – Ottawa Senators, 1992-93. 10w-70l-4t. 24pts in 84gp
   – San Jose Sharks, 1992-93. 11w-71l-2t. 24pts in 84gp
  .148 – Pittsburgh Pirates, 1929-30. 5w-36l-3t. 13pts in 44gp

TEAM WINS

Most Wins

MOST WINS, ONE SEASON:
  62 – Detroit Red Wings, 1995-96. 82gp
  60 – Montreal Canadiens, 1976-77. 80gp
  59 – Montreal Canadiens, 1977-78. 80gp

MOST HOME WINS, ONE SEASON:
  36 – Philadelphia Flyers, 1975-76. 40gp
   – Detroit Red Wings, 1995-96. 41gp
  33 – Boston Bruins, 1970-71. 39gp
   – Boston Bruins, 1973-74. 39gp
   – Montreal Canadiens, 1976-77. 40gp
   – Philadelphia Flyers, 1976-77. 40gp
   – New York Islanders, 1981-82. 40gp
   – Philadelphia Flyers, 1985-86. 40gp

MOST ROAD WINS, ONE SEASON:
  28 – New Jersey Devils, 1998-99. 41gp
  27 – Montreal Canadiens, 1976-77. 40gp
   – Montreal Canadiens, 1977-78. 40gp
   – St. Louis Blues, 1999-2000. 41gp
  26 – Boston Bruins, 1971-72. 39gp
   – Montreal Canadiens, 1975-76. 40gp
   – Edmonton Oilers, 1983-84. 40gp
   – Detroit Red Wings, 1995-96. 41gp

Fewest Wins

FEWEST WINS, ONE SEASON:
  4 – Quebec Bulldogs, 1919-20. 24gp
   – Philadelphia Quakers, 1930-31. 44gp
  5 – Toronto Arenas, 1918-19. 18gp
   Pittsburgh Pirates, 1929-30. 44gp

FEWEST WINS, ONE SEASON (MINIMUM 70-GAME SCHEDULE):
  8 – Washington Capitals, 1974-75. 80gp
  9 – Winnipeg Jets, 1980-81. 80gp
  10 – Ottawa Senators, 1992-93. 84gp

FEWEST HOME WINS, ONE SEASON:
  2 – Chicago Blackhawks, 1927-28. 22gp
  3 – Boston Bruins, 1924-25. 15gp
   – Chicago Blackhawks, 1928-29. 22gp
   – Philadelphia Quakers, 1930-31. 22gp

FEWEST HOME WINS, ONE SEASON (MINIMUM 70-GAME SCHEDULE):
  6 – Chicago Blackhawks, 1954-55. 35gp
   – Washington Capitals, 1975-76. 40gp
  7 – Boston Bruins, 1962-63. 35gp
   – Washington Capitals, 1974-75. 40gp
   – Winnipeg Jets, 1980-81. 40gp
   – Pittsburgh Penguins, 1983-84. 40gp

FEWEST ROAD WINS, ONE SEASON:
  0 – Toronto Arenas, 1918-19. 9gp
   – Quebec Bulldogs, 1919-20. 12gp
   – Pittsburgh Pirates, 1929-30. 22gp
  1 – Hamilton Tigers, 1921-22. 12gp
   – Toronto St. Patricks, 1925-26. 18gp
   – Philadelphia Quakers, 1930-31. 22gp
   – New York Americans, 1940-41. 24gp
   – Washington Capitals, 1974-75. 40gp
  * – Ottawa Senators, 1992-93. 41gp

FEWEST ROAD WINS, ONE SEASON (MINIMUM 70-GAME SCHEDULE):
  1 – Washington Capitals, 1974-75. 40gp
  * **– Ottawa Senators**, 1992-93. 41gp
  2 – Boston Bruins, 1960-61. 35gp
   – Los Angeles Kings, 1969-70. 38gp
   – New York Islanders, 1972-73. 39gp
   – California Golden Seals, 1973-74. 39gp
   – Colorado Rockies, 1977-78. 40gp
   – Winnipeg Jets, 1980-81. 40gp
   – Quebec Nordiques, 1991-92. 40gp

TEAM LOSSES

Fewest Losses

FEWEST LOSSES, ONE SEASON:
  5 – Ottawa Senators, 1919-20. 24gp
   – Boston Bruins, 1929-30. 44gp
   – Montreal Canadiens, 1943-44. 50gp

FEWEST HOME LOSSES, ONE SEASON:
  0 – Ottawa Senators, 1922-23. 12gp
   – Montreal Canadiens, 1943-44. 25gp
  1 – Toronto Arenas, 1917-18. 11gp
   – Ottawa Senators, 1918-19. 9gp
   – Ottawa Senators, 1919-20. 12gp
   – Toronto St. Patricks, 1922-23. 12gp
   – Boston Bruins, 1929-30. 22gp
   – Boston Bruins, 1930-31. 22gp
   – Montreal Canadiens, 1976-77. 40gp
   – Quebec Nordiques, 1994-95. 24gp

FEWEST ROAD LOSSES, ONE SEASON:
  3 – Montreal Canadiens, 1928-29. 22gp
  4 – Ottawa Senators, 1919-20. 12gp
   – Montreal Canadiens, 1927-28. 22gp
   – Boston Bruins, 1929-30. 20gp
   – Boston Bruins, 1940-41. 24gp

FEWEST LOSSES, ONE SEASON (MINIMUM 70-GAME SCHEDULE):
  8 – Montreal Canadiens, 1976-77. 80gp
  10 – Montreal Canadiens, 1972-73. 78gp
   – Montreal Canadiens, 1977-78. 80gp
  11 – Montreal Canadiens, 1975-76. 80gp

FEWEST HOME LOSSES, ONE SEASON (MINIMUM 70-GAME SCHEDULE):
  1 – Montreal Canadiens, 1976-77. 40gp
  2 – Montreal Canadiens, 1961-62. 35gp
   – New York Rangers, 1970-71. 39gp
   – Philadelphia Flyers, 1975-76. 40gp

FEWEST ROAD LOSSES, ONE SEASON (MINIMUM 70-GAME SCHEDULE):
  6 – Montreal Canadiens, 1972-73. 39gp
   – Montreal Canadiens, 1974-75. 40gp
   – Montreal Canadiens, 1977-78. 40gp
  7 – Detroit Red Wings, 1951-52. 35gp
   – Montreal Canadiens, 1976-77. 40gp
   – Philadelphia Flyers, 1979-80. 40gp
   – Boston Bruins, 2003-04. 41gp

Most Losses

MOST LOSSES, ONE SEASON:
  71 – San Jose Sharks, 1992-93. 84gp
  70 – Ottawa Senators, 1992-93. 84gp
  67 – Washington Capitals, 1974-75. 80gp
  61 – Quebec Nordiques, 1989-90. 80gp
   – Ottawa Senators, 1993-94. 84gp

MOST HOME LOSSES, ONE SEASON:
  ***32 – San Jose Sharks**, 1992-93. 41gp
  29 – Pittsburgh Penguins, 1983-84. 40gp
  * – Ottawa Senators, 1993-94. 41gp

MOST ROAD LOSSES, ONE SEASON:
  ***40 – Ottawa Senators**, 1992-93. 41gp
  39 – Washington Capitals, 1974-75. 40gp
  37 – California Golden Seals, 1973-74. 39gp
  * – San Jose Sharks, 1992-93. 41gp

* – Does not include neutral site games

TEAM TIES

Most Ties

MOST TIES, ONE SEASON:
24 – Philadelphia Flyers, 1969-70. 76GP
23 – Montreal Canadiens, 1962-63. 70GP
– Chicago Blackhawks, 1973-74. 78GP

MOST HOME TIES, ONE SEASON:
13 – New York Rangers, 1954-55. 35GP
– **Philadelphia Flyers**, 1969-70. 38GP
– **California Golden Seals**, 1971-72. 39GP
– **California Golden Seals**, 1972-73. 39GP
– **Chicago Blackhawks**, 1973-74. 39GP

MOST ROAD TIES, ONE SEASON:
15 – Philadelphia Flyers, 1976-77. 40GP
14 – Montreal Canadiens, 1952-53. 35GP
– Montreal Canadiens, 1974-75. 40GP
– Philadelphia Flyers, 1975-76. 40GP

Fewest Ties

FEWEST TIES, ONE SEASON (Since 1926-27):
1 – Boston Bruins, 1929-30. 44GP
2 – Montreal Canadiens, 1926-27. 44GP
– New York Americans, 1926-27. 44GP
– Boston Bruins, 1938-39. 48GP
– New York Rangers, 1941-42. 48GP
– San Jose Sharks, 1992-93. 84GP

FEWEST TIES, ONE SEASON (MINIMUM 70-GAME SCHEDULE):
2 – San Jose Sharks, 1992-93. 84GP
3 – New Jersey Devils, 1985-86. 80GP
– Calgary Flames, 1986-87. 80GP
– Vancouver Canucks, 1993-94. 84GP

WINNING STREAKS

LONGEST WINNING STREAK, ONE SEASON:
17 Games – Pittsburgh Penguins, Mar. 9 – Apr. 10, 1993.
15 Games – New York Islanders, Jan. 21 – Feb. 20, 1982.
14 Games – Boston Bruins, Dec. 3, 1929 – Jan. 9, 1930.

LONGEST HOME WINNING STREAK, ONE SEASON:
20 Games – Boston Bruins, Dec. 3, 1924 – Mar. 18, 1930.
– **Philadelphia Flyers**, Jan. 4 – Apr. 3, 1976.

LONGEST ROAD WINNING STREAK, ONE SEASON:
10 Games – Buffalo Sabres, Dec. 10, 1983 – Jan. 23, 1984.
– **St. Louis Blues**, Jan. 21 – Mar. 2, 2000.
– **New Jersey Devils**, Feb. 27 – Apr. 7, 2001.
8 Games – Boston Bruins, Feb. 17 – Mar. 8, 1972.
– Los Angeles Kings, Dec. 18, 1974 – Jan. 16, 1975.
– Montreal Canadiens, Dec. 18, 1977 – Jan. 18, 1978.
– New York Islanders, Feb. 27 – Mar. 29, 1981.
– Montreal Canadiens, Jan. 21 – Feb. 21, 1982.
– Philadelphia Flyers, Dec. 22, 1982 – Jan. 16, 1983.
– Winnipeg Jets, Feb. 25 – Apr. 6, 1985.
– Edmonton Oilers, Dec. 9, 1986 – Jan. 17, 1987.
– Boston Bruins, Mar. 15 – Apr. 14, 1993.
– Detroit Red Wings, Feb. 4 – Mar. 9, 2002.
– Vancouver Canucks, Dec. 20, 2003 – Jan. 13, 2004.

LONGEST WINNING STREAK FROM START OF SEASON:
10 Games – Toronto Maple Leafs, 1993-94.
8 Games – Toronto Maple Leafs, 1934-35.
– Buffalo Sabres, 1975-76.
7 Games – Edmonton Oilers, 1983-84.
– Quebec Nordiques, 1985-86.
– Pittsburgh Penguins, 1986-87.
– Pittsburgh Penguins, 1994-95.

LONGEST HOME WINNING STREAK FROM START OF SEASON:
11 Games – Chicago Blackhawks, 1963-64.
10 Games – Ottawa Senators, 1925-26.
9 Games – Montreal Canadiens, 1953-54.
– Chicago Blackhawks, 1971-72.

LONGEST ROAD WINNING STREAK FROM START OF SEASON:
7 Games – Toronto Maple Leafs, Nov. 14 – Dec. 15, 1940.
– **Philadelphia Flyers**, Oct. 12 – Nov. 16, 1985.

LONGEST WINNING STREAK, INCLUDING PLAYOFFS:
15 Games – Detroit Red Wings, Feb. 27 – Apr. 5, 1955.
(9 regular-season games, 6 playoff games)

LONGEST HOME WINNING STREAK, INCLUDING PLAYOFFS:
24 Games – Philadelphia Flyers, Jan. 4 – Apr. 25, 1976.
(20 regular-season games, 4 playoff games)

LONGEST ROAD WINNING STREAK, INCLUDING PLAYOFFS:
11 Games – New Jersey Devils, Feb. 27 – Apr. 17, 2001.
(10 regular-season games, 1 playoff game)

UNDEFEATED STREAKS

LONGEST UNDEFEATED STREAK, ONE SEASON:
35 Games – Philadelphia Flyers, Oct. 14, 1979 – Jan. 6, 1980. 25W-10T
28 Games – Montreal Canadiens, Dec. 18, 1977 – Feb. 23, 1978. 23W-5T

LONGEST HOME UNDEFEATED STREAK, ONE SEASON:
34 Games – Montreal Canadiens, Nov. 1, 1976 – Apr. 2, 1977. 28W-6T
27 Games – Boston Bruins, Nov. 22, 1970 – Mar. 20, 1971. 26W-1T

LONGEST ROAD UNDEFEATED STREAK, ONE SEASON:
23 Games – Montreal Canadiens, Nov. 27, 1974 – Mar. 12, 1975. 14W-9T
17 Games – Montreal Canadiens, Dec. 18, 1977 – Mar. 1, 1978. 14W-3T

LONGEST UNDEFEATED STREAK FROM START OF SEASON:
15 Games – Edmonton Oilers, 1984-85. 12W-3T
14 Games – Montreal Canadiens, 1943-44. 11W-3T

LONGEST HOME UNDEFEATED STREAK FROM START OF SEASON:
26 Games – Philadelphia Flyers, Oct. 11, 1979 – Feb. 3, 1980. 19W-7T

LONGEST ROAD UNDEFEATED STREAK FROM START OF SEASON:
15 Games – Detroit Red Wings, Oct. 18 – Dec. 20, 1951. 10W-5T

LONGEST UNDEFEATED STREAK, INCLUDING PLAYOFFS:
21 Games – Pittsburgh Penguins, Mar. 9 – Apr. 22, 1993.
17W-1T in regular season and 3W in playoffs.

LONGEST HOME UNDEFEATED STREAK, INCLUDING PLAYOFFS:
38 Games – Montreal Canadiens, Nov. 1, 1976 – Apr. 26, 1977.
28W-6T in regular season and 4W in playoffs.

LONGEST ROAD UNDEFEATED STREAK, INCLUDING PLAYOFFS:
13 Games – Philadelphia Flyers, Feb. 26 – Apr. 21, 1977. 6W-4T in
regular season and 3W in playoffs.
– **Montreal Canadiens**, Feb. 26 – Apr. 20, 1980. 6W-4T in
regular season and 3W in playoffs.
– **New York Islanders**, Mar. 16 – May 1, 1980. 3W-3T in regular
season and 7W in playoffs.

LOSING STREAKS

LONGEST LOSING STREAK, ONE SEASON:
17 Games – Washington Capitals, Feb. 18 – Mar. 26, 1975.
– **San Jose Sharks**, Jan. 4 – Feb. 12, 1993.
15 Games – Philadelphia Quakers, Nov. 29, 1930 – Jan. 8, 1931.

LONGEST HOME LOSING STREAK, ONE SEASON:
14 Games – Pittsburgh Penguins, Dec. 31, 2003 – Feb. 22, 2004.
11 Games – Boston Bruins, Dec. 8, 1924 – Feb. 17, 1925.
– Washington Capitals, Feb. 18 – Mar. 30, 1975.
– Ottawa Senators, Oct. 27 – Dec. 8, 1993.
– Atlanta Thrashers, Jan. 24 – Mar. 16, 2000.

LONGEST ROAD LOSING STREAK, ONE SEASON:
*38 Games – Ottawa Senators, Oct. 10, 1992 – Apr. 3, 1993.
37 Games – Washington Capitals, Oct. 9, 1974 – Mar. 26, 1975.

LONGEST LOSING STREAK FROM START OF SEASON:
11 Games – New York Rangers, 1943-44.
7 Games – Montreal Canadiens, 1938-39.
– Chicago Blackhawks, 1947-48.
– Washington Capitals, 1983-84.
– Chicago Blackhawks, 1997-98.

LONGEST HOME LOSING STREAK FROM START OF SEASON:
8 Games – Los Angeles Kings, Oct. 13 – Nov. 6, 1971.

LONGEST ROAD LOSING STREAK FROM START OF SEASON:
*38 Games – Ottawa Senators, Oct. 10, 1992 – Apr. 3, 1993.

WINLESS STREAKS

LONGEST WINLESS STREAK, ONE SEASON:
30 Games – Winnipeg Jets, Oct. 19 – Dec. 20, 1980. 23L-7T
27 Games – Kansas City Scouts, Feb. 12 – Apr. 4, 1976. 21L-6T
25 Games – Washington Capitals, Nov. 29, 1975 – Jan. 21, 1976. 22L-3T

LONGEST HOME WINLESS STREAK, ONE SEASON:
17 Games – Ottawa Senators, Oct. 28, 1995 – Jan. 27, 1996. 15L-2T
– **Atlanta Thrashers**, Jan. 19 – Mar. 29, 2000. 15L-2T
16 Games – Pittsburgh Penguins, Dec. 31, 2003 – Mar. 4, 2004. 15L-1T

LONGEST ROAD WINLESS STREAK, ONE SEASON:
*38 Games – Ottawa Senators, Oct. 10, 1992 – Apr. 3, 1993. 38L
37 Games – Washington Capitals, Oct. 9, 1974 – Mar. 26, 1975. 37L

LONGEST WINLESS STREAK FROM START OF SEASON:
15 Games – New York Rangers, 1943-44. 14L-1T
11 Games – Pittsburgh Pirates, 1927-28. 8L-3T
– Minnesota North Stars, 1973-74. 5L-6T
– San Jose Sharks, 1995-96. 7L-4T

LONGEST HOME WINLESS STREAK FROM START OF SEASON:
11 Games – Pittsburgh Penguins, Oct. 8 – Nov. 19, 1983. 9L-2T

LONGEST ROAD WINLESS STREAK FROM START OF SEASON:
*38 Games – Ottawa Senators, Oct. 10, 1992 – Apr. 3, 1993. 38L

NON-SHUTOUT STREAKS

LONGEST NON-SHUTOUT STREAK:
264 Games – Calgary Flames, Nov. 12, 1981 – Jan. 9, 1985.
  261 Games – Los Angeles Kings, Mar. 15, 1986 – Oct. 22, 1989.
  244 Games – Washington Capitals, Oct. 31, 1989 – Nov. 11, 1993.
  236 Games – New York Rangers, Dec. 20, 1989 – Dec. 13, 1992.
  230 Games – Quebec Nordiques, Feb. 10, 1980 – Jan. 12, 1983.

LONGEST NON-SHUTOUT STREAK, INCLUDING PLAYOFFS:
264 Games – Los Angeles Kings, Mar. 15, 1986 – Apr. 6, 1989.
  (5 playoff games in 1987; 5 in 1988; 2 in 1989).
  262 Games – Chicago Blackhawks, Mar. 14, 1970 – Feb. 21, 1973.
  (8 playoff games in 1970; 18 in 1971; 8 in 1972).
  251 Games – Quebec Nordiques, Feb. 10, 1980 – Jan. 12, 1983.
  (5 playoff games in 1981; 16 in 1982).
  246 Games – Pittsburgh Penguins, Jan. 7, 1989 – Oct. 26, 1991.
  (11 playoff games in 1989; 24 in 1991).

TEAM GOALS

Most Goals

MOST GOALS, ONE SEASON:
446 – Edmonton Oilers, 1983-84. 80GP
  426 – Edmonton Oilers, 1985-86. 80GP
  424 – Edmonton Oilers, 1982-83. 80GP
  417 – Edmonton Oilers, 1981-82. 80GP
  401 – Edmonton Oilers, 1984-85. 80GP

MOST GOALS, ONE TEAM, ONE GAME:
16 – Montreal Canadiens, Mar. 3, 1920, at Quebec. Montreal won 16-3.

MOST GOALS, BOTH TEAMS, ONE GAME:
21 – Montreal Canadiens (14), Toronto St. Patricks (7), Jan. 10, 1920,
  at Montreal.
  – Edmonton Oilers (12), Chicago Blackhawks (9), Dec. 11, 1985,
  at Chicago.
  20 – Edmonton Oilers (12), Minnesota North Stars (8), Jan. 4, 1984,
  at Edmonton.
  – Toronto Maple Leafs (11), Edmonton Oilers (9), Jan. 8, 1986,
  at Toronto.
  19 – Montreal Wanderers (10), Toronto Arenas (9), Dec. 19, 1917,
  at Montreal.
  – Montreal Canadiens (16), Quebec Bulldogs (3), Mar. 3, 1920,
  at Quebec.
  – Montreal Canadiens (13), Hamilton Tigers (6), Feb. 26, 1921,
  at Montreal.
  – Boston Bruins (10), New York Rangers (9), Mar. 4, 1944, at Boston.
  – Detroit Red Wings (10), Boston Bruins (9), Mar. 16, 1944, at Detroit.
  – Vancouver Canucks (10), Minnesota North Stars (9), Oct. 7, 1983,
  at Vancouver.

MOST GOALS, ONE TEAM, ONE PERIOD:
9 – Buffalo Sabres, Mar. 19, 1981, at Buffalo, second period during
  14-4 win over Toronto.
  8 – Detroit Red Wings, Jan. 23, 1944, at Detroit, third period during
  15-0 win over NY Rangers.
  – Boston Bruins, Mar. 16, 1969, at Boston, second period during
  11-3 win over Toronto.
  – New York Rangers, Nov. 21, 1971, at NY Rangers, third period during
  12-1 win over California.
  – Philadelphia Flyers, Mar. 31, 1973, at Philadelphia, second period
  during 10-2 win over NY Islanders.
  – Buffalo Sabres, Dec. 21, 1975, at Buffalo, third period during
  14-2 win over Washington.
  – Minnesota North Stars, Nov. 11, 1981, at Minnesota, second
  period during 15-2 win over Winnipeg.
  – Pittsburgh Penguins, Dec. 17, 1991, at Pittsburgh, second period
  during 10-2 win over San Jose.
  – Washington Capitals, Feb. 3, 1999, at Washington, second period
  during 10-1 win over Tampa Bay.

MOST GOALS, BOTH TEAMS, ONE PERIOD:
12 – Buffalo Sabres (9), Toronto Maple Leafs (3), Mar. 19, 1981,
  at Buffalo, second period. Buffalo won 14-4.
  – Edmonton Oilers (6), Chicago Blackhawks (6), Dec. 11, 1985,
  at Chicago, second period. Edmonton won 12-9.
  10 – New York Rangers (7), New York Americans (3), Mar. 16, 1939, at
  NY Americans, third period. NY Rangers won 11-5.
  – Toronto Maple Leafs (6), Detroit Red Wings (4), Mar. 17, 1946,
  at Detroit, third period. Toronto won 11-7.
  – Buffalo Sabres (6), Vancouver Canucks (4), Jan. 8, 1976,
  at Buffalo, third period. Buffalo won 8-5.
  – Buffalo Sabres (5), Montreal Canadiens (5), Oct. 26, 1982,
  at Montreal, first period. Teams tied 7-7.
  – Quebec Nordiques (6), Boston Bruins (4), Dec. 7, 1982,
  at Quebec, second period. Quebec won 10-5.
  – Vancouver Canucks (6), Calgary Flames (4), Jan. 16, 1987,
  at Vancouver, first period. Vancouver won 9-5.
  – Detroit Red Wings (7), Winnipeg Jets (3), Nov. 25, 1987,
  at Detroit, third period. Detroit won 10-8.
  – Chicago Blackhawks (5), St. Louis Blues (5), Mar. 15, 1988,
  at St. Louis, third period. Teams tied 7-7.

MOST CONSECUTIVE GOALS, ONE TEAM, ONE GAME:
15 – Detroit Red Wings, Jan. 23, 1944, at Detroit during 15-0 win over
  NY Rangers.

Fewest Goals

FEWEST GOALS, ONE SEASON:
33 – Chicago Blackhawks, 1928-29. 44GP
  45 – Montreal Maroons, 1924-25. 30GP
  46 – Pittsburgh Pirates, 1928-29. 44GP

FEWEST GOALS, ONE SEASON (MINIMUM 70-GAME SCHEDULE):
133 – Chicago Blackhawks, 1953-54. 70GP
  147 – Toronto Maple Leafs, 1954-55. 70GP
  – Boston Bruins, 1955-56. 70GP
  150 – New York Rangers, 1954-55. 70GP

TEAM POWER-PLAY GOALS

MOST POWER-PLAY GOALS, ONE SEASON:
119 – Pittsburgh Penguins, 1988-89. 80GP
  113 – Detroit Red Wings, 1992-93. 84GP
  111 – New York Rangers, 1987-88. 80GP
  110 – Pittsburgh Penguins, 1987-88. 80GP
  – Winnipeg Jets, 1987-88, 80GP

TEAM SHORTHAND GOALS

MOST SHORTHAND GOALS, ONE SEASON:
36 – Edmonton Oilers, 1983-84. 80GP
  28 – Edmonton Oilers, 1986-87. 80GP
  27 – Edmonton Oilers, 1985-86. 80GP
  – Edmonton Oilers, 1988-89. 80GP

TEAM GOALS-PER-GAME

HIGHEST GOALS-PER-GAME AVERAGE, ONE SEASON:
5.58 – Edmonton Oilers, 1983-84. 446G in 80GP.
  5.38 – Montreal Canadiens, 1919-20. 129G in 24GP.
  5.33 – Edmonton Oilers, 1985-86. 426G in 80GP.
  5.30 – Edmonton Oilers, 1982-83. 424G in 80GP.
  5.23 – Montreal Canadiens, 1917-18. 115G in 22GP.

LOWEST GOALS-PER-GAME AVERAGE, ONE SEASON:
0.75 – Chicago Blackhawks, 1928-29. 33G in 44GP.
  1.05 – Pittsburgh Pirates, 1928-29. 46G in 44GP.
  1.20 – New York Americans, 1928-29. 53G in 44GP.

TEAM ASSISTS

MOST ASSISTS, ONE SEASON:
737 – Edmonton Oilers, 1985-86. 80GP
  736 – Edmonton Oilers, 1983-84. 80GP
  706 – Edmonton Oilers, 1981-82. 80GP

FEWEST ASSISTS, ONE SEASON (Since 1926-27):
45 – New York Rangers, 1926-27. 44GP

FEWEST ASSISTS, ONE SEASON (MINIMUM 70-GAME SCHEDULE):
206 – Chicago Blackhawks, 1953-54. 70GP

TEAM TOTAL POINTS

MOST SCORING POINTS, ONE SEASON:
1,182 – Edmonton Oilers, 1983-84. 80GP
  1,163 – Edmonton Oilers, 1985-86. 80GP
  1,123 – Edmonton Oilers, 1981-82. 80GP

MOST SCORING POINTS, ONE TEAM, ONE GAME:
40 – Buffalo Sabres, Dec. 21, 1975, at Buffalo.
  Buffalo defeated Washington 14-2, and had 26A.
  39 – Minnesota North Stars, Nov. 11, 1981, at Minnesota.
  Minnesota defeated Winnipeg 15-2, and had 24A.
  37 – Detroit Red Wings, Jan. 23, 1944, at Detroit.
  Detroit defeated NY Rangers 15-0, and had 22A.
  – Toronto Maple Leafs, Mar. 16, 1957, at Toronto.
  Toronto defeated NY Rangers 14-1, and had 23A.
  – Buffalo Sabres, Feb. 25, 1978, at Cleveland.
  Buffalo defeated Cleveland 13-3, and had 24A.
  – Calgary Flames, Feb. 10, 1993, at Calgary.
  Calgary defeated San Jose 13-1, and had 24A.

MOST SCORING POINTS, BOTH TEAMS, ONE GAME:
62 – Edmonton Oilers, Chicago Blackhawks, Dec. 11, 1985, at Chicago.
  Edmonton won 12-9. Edmonton had 24A, Chicago, 17A.
  53 – Quebec Nordiques, Washington Capitals, Feb. 22, 1981, at Washington.
  Quebec won 11-7. Quebec had 22A, Washington, 13A.
  – Edmonton Oilers, Minnesota North Stars, Jan. 4, 1984, at Edmonton.
  Edmonton won 12-8. Edmonton had 20A, Minnesota, 13A.
  – Minnesota North Stars, St. Louis Blues, Jan. 27, 1984, at St. Louis.
  Minnesota won 10-8. Minnesota had 19A, St. Louis, 16A.
  – Toronto Maple Leafs, Edmonton Oilers, Jan. 8, 1986, at Toronto.
  Toronto won 11-9. Toronto had 17A, Edmonton, 16A.
  52 – Montreal Maroons, New York Americans, Feb. 18, 1936, at
  NY Americans. Teams tied 8-8. NY Americans had 20A, Montreal, 16A.
  (3A allowed for each goal.)
  – Vancouver Canucks, Minnesota North Stars, Oct. 7, 1983, at Vancouver.
  Vancouver won 10-9. Vancouver had 16A, Minnesota, 17A.

MOST SCORING POINTS, ONE TEAM, ONE PERIOD:

23 – New York Rangers, Nov. 21, 1971, at NY Rangers, third period during 12-1 win over California. NY Rangers had 8G, 15A.
- **Buffalo Sabres**, Dec. 21, 1975, at Buffalo, third period during 14-2 win over Washington. Buffalo had 8G, 15A.
- **Buffalo Sabres**, Mar. 19, 1981, at Buffalo, second period during 14-4 win over Toronto. Buffalo had 9G, 14A.
22 – Detroit Red Wings, Jan. 23, 1944, at Detroit, third period during 15-0 win over NY Rangers. Detroit had 8G, 14A.
- Boston Bruins, Mar. 16, 1969, at Boston, second period during 11-3 win over Toronto. Boston had 8G, 14A.
- Minnesota North Stars, Nov. 11, 1981, at Minnesota, second period during 15-2 win over Winnipeg. Minnesota had 8G, 14A.
- Pittsburgh Penguins, Dec. 17, 1991, at Pittsburgh, second period during 10-2 win over San Jose. Pittsburgh had 8G, 14A.
- Washington Capitals, Feb. 3, 1999, at Washington, second period during 10-1 win over Tampa Bay. Washington had 8G, 14A.

MOST SCORING POINTS, BOTH TEAMS, ONE PERIOD:

35 – Edmonton, Oilers, Chicago Blackhawks, Dec. 11, 1985, at Chicago, second period. Edmonton won 12-9. Edmonton had 6G, 12A; Chicago, 6G, 11A.
31 – Buffalo Sabres, Toronto Maple Leafs, Mar. 19, 1981, at Buffalo, second period. Buffalo won 14-4. Buffalo had 9G, 14A; Toronto, 3G, 5A.
29 – Winnipeg Jets, Detroit Red Wings, Nov. 25, 1987, at Detroit, third period. Detroit won 10-8. Detroit had 7G, 13A; Winnipeg, 3G, 6A.
- Chicago Blackhawks, St. Louis Blues, Mar. 15, 1988, at St. Louis, third period. Teams tied 7-7. St. Louis had 5G, 10A; Chicago, 5G, 9A.

FASTEST GOALS

FASTEST SIX GOALS, BOTH TEAMS:

3:00 – Quebec Nordiques, Washington Capitals, Feb. 22, 1981, at Washington. Scorers: Peter Stastny, Quebec, 18:51; Pierre Lacroix, Quebec, 19:57 (first period); Anton Stastny, Quebec, 0:34; Jacques Richard, Quebec, 1:07 and 1:37; Rick Green, Washington, 1:51 (second period). Quebec won 11-7.
3:15 – Montreal Canadiens, Toronto Maple Leafs, Jan. 4, 1944, at Montreal, first period. Scorers: Maurice Richard, Montreal, 14:10; Don Webster, Toronto, 15:13; Fern Majeau, Montreal, 15:41; Phil Watson, Montreal, 15:52; Lorne Carr, Toronto, 16:55; Butch Bouchard, Montreal, 17:25. Montreal won 6-3.

FASTEST FIVE GOALS, BOTH TEAMS:

1:24 – Chicago Blackhawks, Toronto Maple Leafs, Oct. 15, 1983, at Toronto, second period. Scorers: Gaston Gingras, Toronto, 16:49; Denis Savard, Chicago, 17:12; Steve Larmer, Chicago, 17:27; Denis Savard, Chicago, 17:42; John Anderson, Toronto, 18:13. Toronto won 10-8.
1:39 – Detroit Red Wings, Toronto Maple Leafs, Nov. 15, 1944, at Toronto, third period. Scorers: Ted Kennedy, Toronto, 10:36 and 10:55; Harold Jackson, Detroit, 11:48; Steve Wojciechowski, Detroit, 12:02; Don Grosso, Detroit, 12:15. Detroit won 8-4.

FASTEST FIVE GOALS, ONE TEAM:

2:07 – Pittsburgh Penguins, Nov. 22, 1972, at Pittsburgh, third period. Scorers: Bryan Hextall, Jr., 12:00; Jean Pronovost, 12:18; Al McDonough, 13:40; Ken Schinkel, 13:49; Ron Schock, 14:07. Pittsburgh defeated St. Louis 10-4.
2:37 – New York Islanders, Jan. 26, 1982, at NY Islanders, first period. Scorers: Duane Sutter, 1:31; John Tonelli, 2:30; Bryan Trottier, 2:46 and 3:31; Duane Sutter, 4:08. NY Islanders defeated Pittsburgh 9-2.
2:55 – Boston Bruins, Dec. 19, 1974, at Boston. Scorers: Bobby Schmautz, 19:13 (first period); Ken Hodge, 0:18; Phil Esposito, 0:43; Don Marcotte, 0:58; John Bucyk, 2:08 (second period). Boston defeated NY Rangers 11-3.

FASTEST FOUR GOALS, BOTH TEAMS:

0:53 – Chicago Blackhawks, Toronto Maple Leafs, Oct. 15, 1983, at Toronto, second period. Scorers: Gaston Gingras, Toronto, 16:49; Denis Savard, Chicago, 17:12; Steve Larmer, Chicago, 17:27; Denis Savard, Chicago, 17:42. Toronto won 10-8.
0:57 – Quebec Nordiques, Detroit Red Wings, Jan. 27, 1990, at Quebec, first period. Scorers: Paul Gillis, Quebec, 18:01; Claude Loiselle, Quebec, 18:12; Joe Sakic, Quebec, 18:27; Jimmy Carson, Detroit, 18:58. Detroit won 8-6.
1:01 – Colorado Rockies, New York Rangers, Jan. 15, 1980, at NY Rangers, first period. Scorers: Doug Sulliman, NY Rangers, 7:52; Eddie Johnstone, NY Rangers, 7:57; Warren Miller, NY Rangers, 8:20; Rob Ramage, Colorado, 8:53. Teams tied 6-6.
- Chicago Blackhawks, Toronto Maple Leafs, Oct. 15, 1983, at Toronto, second period. Scorers: Denis Savard, Chicago, 17:12; Steve Larmer, Chicago, 17:27; Denis Savard, Chicago, 17:42; John Anderson, Toronto, 18:13. Toronto won 10-8.

FASTEST FOUR GOALS, ONE TEAM:

1:20 – Boston Bruins, Jan. 21, 1945, at Boston, second period. Scorers: Bill Thoms, 6:34; Frank Mario, 7:08 and 7:27; Ken Smith, 7:54. Boston defeated NY Rangers 14-3.

FASTEST THREE GOALS, BOTH TEAMS:

0:15 – Minnesota North Stars, New York Rangers, Feb. 10, 1983, at Minnesota, second period. Scorers: Mark Pavelich, NY Rangers, 19:18; Ron Greschner, NY Rangers, 19:27; Willi Plett, Minnesota, 19:33. Minnesota won 7-5.
0:18 – Montreal Canadiens, New York Rangers, Dec. 12, 1963, at Montreal, first period. Scorers: Dave Balon, Montreal, 0:58; Gilles Tremblay, Montreal, 1:04; Camille Henry, NY Rangers, 1:16. Montreal won 6-4.
- California Golden Seals, Buffalo Sabres, Feb. 1, 1976, at California, third period. Scorers: Jim Moxey, California, 19:38; Wayne Merrick, California, 19:45; Danny Gare, Buffalo, 19:56. Buffalo won 9-5.

FASTEST THREE GOALS, ONE TEAM:

0:20 – Boston Bruins, Feb. 25, 1971, at Boston, third period. Scorers: John Bucyk, 4:50; Ed Westfall, 5:02; Ted Green, 5:10. Boston defeated Vancouver 8-3.
0:21 – Chicago Blackhawks, Mar. 23, 1952, at NY Rangers, third period. Bill Mosienko scored all three goals, at 6:09, 6:20 and 6:30. Chicago defeated NY Rangers 7-6.
- Washington Capitals, Nov. 23, 1990, at Washington, first period. Scorers: Michal Pivonka, 16:18; Stephen Leach, 16:29 and 16:39. Washington defeated Pittsburgh 7-3.

FASTEST THREE GOALS FROM START OF PERIOD, BOTH TEAMS:

1:05 – Hartford Whalers, Montreal Canadiens, Mar. 11, 1989, at Montreal, second period. Scorers: Kevin Dineen, Hartford, 0:11; Guy Carbonneau, Montreal, 0:36; Petr Svoboda, Montreal, 1:05. Montreal won 5-3.

FASTEST THREE GOALS FROM START OF PERIOD, ONE TEAM:

0:53 – Calgary Flames, Feb. 10, 1993, at Calgary, third period. Scorers: Gary Suter, 0:17; Chris Lindberg, 0:40; Ron Stern, 0:53. Calgary defeated San Jose 13-1.

FASTEST TWO GOALS, BOTH TEAMS:

0:02 – St. Louis Blues, Boston Bruins, Dec. 19, 1987, at Boston, third period. Scorers: Ken Linseman, Boston, 19:50; Doug Gilmour, St. Louis, 19:52. St. Louis won 7-5.
0:03 – Chicago Blackhawks, Minnesota North Stars, Nov. 5, 1988, at Minnesota, third period. Scorers: Steve Thomas, Chicago, 6:03; Dave Gagner, Minnesota, 6:06. Teams tied 5-5.

FASTEST TWO GOALS, ONE TEAM:

0:03 – Minnesota Wild, Jan. 21, 2004, at Minnesota, third period. Scorers: Jim Dowd, 19:44; Richard Park, 19:47. Minnesota defeated Chicago 4-2.
0:04 – Montreal Maroons, Jan. 3, 1931, at Montreal, third period. Nels Stewart scored both goals, at 8:24 and 8:28. Mtl. Maroons defeated Boston 5-3.
- Buffalo Sabres, Oct. 17, 1974, at Buffalo, third period. Scorers: Lee Fogolin, Jr., 14:55; Don Luce, 14:59. Buffalo defeated California 6-1.
- Toronto Maple Leafs, Dec. 29, 1988, at Quebec, third period. Scorers: Ed Olczyk, 5:24; Gary Leeman, 5:28. Toronto defeated Quebec 6-5.
- Calgary Flames, Oct. 17, 1989, at Quebec, third period. Scorers: Doug Gilmour, 19:45; Paul Ranheim, 19:49. Teams tied 8-8.
- Winnipeg Jets, Dec. 15, 1995, at Winnipeg, second period. Deron Quint scored both goals, at 7:51 and 7:55. Winnipeg defeated Edmonton 9-4.

FASTEST TWO GOALS FROM START OF GAME, ONE TEAM:

0:24 – Edmonton Oilers, Mar. 28, 1982, at Los Angeles. Scorers: Mark Messier, 0:14; Dave Lumley, 0:24. Edmonton defeated Los Angeles 6-2.
0:27 – Boston Bruins, Feb. 14, 2003, at Florida. Mike Knuble scored both goals, at 0:10 and 0:27. Calgary defeated Hartford 6-1.
0:29 – Pittsburgh Penguins, Dec. 6, 1980, at Pittsburgh. Scorers: George Ferguson, 0:17; Greg Malone, 0:29. Pittsburgh defeated Chicago 6-4.

FASTEST TWO GOALS FROM START OF PERIOD, BOTH TEAMS:

0:14 – New York Rangers, Quebec Nordiques, Nov. 5, 1983, at Quebec, third period. Scorers: Andre Savard, Quebec, 0:08; Pierre Larouche, NY Rangers, 0:14. Teams tied 4-4.
0:26 – Buffalo Sabres, St. Louis Blues, Jan. 3, 1993, at Buffalo, third period. Scorers: Alexander Mogilny, Buffalo, 0:08; Philippe Bozon, St. Louis, 0:26. Buffalo won 6-5.
0:28 – Boston Bruins, Montreal Canadiens, Oct. 11, 1989, at Montreal, third period. Scorers: Jim Wiemer, Boston, 0:10; Tom Chorske, Montreal, 0:28. Montreal won 4-2.

FASTEST TWO GOALS FROM START OF PERIOD, ONE TEAM:

0:21 – Chicago Blackhawks, Nov. 5, 1983, at Minnesota, second period. Scorers: Ken Yaremchuk, 0:12; Darryl Sutter, 0:21. Minnesota defeated Chicago 10-5.
0:24 – Edmonton Oilers, Mar. 28, 1982, at Los Angeles, first period. Scorers: Mark Messier, 0:14; Dave Lumley, 0:24. Edmonton defeated Los Angeles 6-2.
0:29 – Pittsburgh Penguins, Dec. 6, 1980, at Pittsburgh, first period. Scorers: George Ferguson, 0:17; Greg Malone, 0:29. Pittsburgh defeated Chicago 6-4.

Gilbert Perreault scored the first, fourth and seventh goals when the Buffalo Sabres scored a record nine times in the second period versus Toronto on March 19, 1981.

50, 40, 30, 20-GOAL SCORERS

MOST 50-OR-MORE GOAL SCORERS, ONE SEASON:

3 – **Edmonton Oilers**, 1983-84. 80GP. Wayne Gretzky, 87; Glenn Anderson, 54; Jari Kurri, 52.
– **Edmonton Oilers**, 1985-86. 80GP. Jari Kurri, 68; Glenn Anderson, 54; Wayne Gretzky, 52.

2 – Boston Bruins, 1970-71. 78GP. Phil Esposito, 76; John Bucyk, 51.
– Boston Bruins, 1973-74. 78GP. Phil Esposito, 68; Ken Hodge, 50.
– Philadelphia Flyers, 1975-76. 80GP. Reggie Leach, 61; Bill Barber, 50.
– Pittsburgh Penguins, 1975-76. 80GP. Pierre Larouche, 53; Jean Pronovost, 52.
– Montreal Canadiens, 1976-77. 80GP. Steve Shutt, 60; Guy Lafleur, 56.
– Los Angeles Kings, 1979-80. 80GP. Charlie Simmer, 56; Marcel Dionne, 53.
– Montreal Canadiens, 1979-80. 80GP. Pierre Larouche, 50; Guy Lafleur, 50.
– Los Angeles Kings, 1980-81. 80GP. Marcel Dionne, 58; Charlie Simmer, 56.
– Edmonton Oilers, 1981-82. 80GP. Wayne Gretzky, 92; Mark Messier, 50.
– New York Islanders, 1981-82. 80GP. Mike Bossy, 64; Bryan Trottier, 50.
– Edmonton Oilers, 1984-85. 80GP. Wayne Gretzky, 73; Jari Kurri, 71.
– Washington Capitals, 1984-85. 80GP. Bob Carpenter, 53; Mike Gartner, 50.
– Edmonton Oilers, 1986-87. 80GP. Wayne Gretzky, 62; Jari Kurri, 54.
– Calgary Flames, 1987-88. 80GP. Joe Nieuwendyk, 51; Hakan Loob, 50.
– Los Angeles Kings, 1987-88. 80GP. Jimmy Carson, 55; Luc Robitaille, 53.
– Los Angeles Kings, 1988-89. 80GP. Bernie Nicholls, 70; Wayne Gretzky, 54.
– Calgary Flames, 1988-89. 80GP. Joe Nieuwendyk, 51; Joe Mullen, 51.
– Buffalo Sabres, 1992-93. 84GP. Alexander Mogilny, 76; Pat LaFontaine, 53.
– Pittsburgh Penguins, 1992-93. 84GP. Mario Lemieux, 69; Kevin Stevens, 55.
– St. Louis Blues, 1992-93. 84GP. Brett Hull, 54; Brendan Shanahan, 51.
– St. Louis Blues, 1993-94. 84GP. Brett Hull, 57; Brendan Shanahan, 52.
– Detroit Red Wings, 1993-94. 84GP. Sergei Fedorov, 56; Ray Sheppard, 52.
– Pittsburgh Penguins, 1995-96. 82GP. Mario Lemieux, 69; Jaromir Jagr, 62.

MOST 40-OR-MORE GOAL SCORERS, ONE SEASON:

4 – **Edmonton Oilers**, 1982-83. 80GP. Wayne Gretzky, 71; Glenn Anderson, 48; Mark Messier, 48; Jari Kurri, 45.
– **Edmonton Oilers**, 1983-84. 80GP. Wayne Gretzky, 87; Glenn Anderson, 54; Jari Kurri, 52; Paul Coffey, 40.
– **Edmonton Oilers**, 1984-85. 80GP. Wayne Gretzky, 73; Jari Kurri, 71; Mike Krushelnyski, 43; Glenn Anderson, 42.
– **Edmonton Oilers**, 1985-86. 80GP. Jari Kurri, 68; Glenn Anderson, 54; Wayne Gretzky, 52; Paul Coffey, 48.
– **Calgary Flames**, 1987-88. 80GP. Joe Nieuwendyk, 51; Hakan Loob, 50; Mike Bullard, 48; Joe Mullen, 40.

3 – Boston Bruins, 1970-71. 78GP. Phil Esposito, 76; John Bucyk, 51; Ken Hodge, 43.
– New York Rangers, 1971-72. 78GP. Vic Hadfield, 50; Jean Ratelle, 46; Rod Gilbert, 43.
– Buffalo Sabres, 1975-76. 80GP. Danny Gare, 50; Rick Martin, 49; Gilbert Perreault, 44.
– Montreal Canadiens, 1979-80. 80GP. Guy Lafleur, 50; Pierre Larouche, 50; Steve Shutt, 47.
– Buffalo Sabres, 1979-80. 80GP. Danny Gare, 56; Rick Martin, 45; Gilbert Perreault, 40.
– Los Angeles Kings, 1980-81. 80GP. Marcel Dionne, 58; Charlie Simmer, 56; Dave Taylor, 47.
– Los Angeles Kings, 1984-85. 80GP. Marcel Dionne, 46; Bernie Nicholls, 46; Dave Taylor, 41.
– New York Islanders, 1984-85. 80GP. Mike Bossy, 58; Brent Sutter, 42; John Tonelli, 42.
– Chicago Blackhawks, 1985-86. 80GP. Denis Savard, 47; Troy Murray, 45; Al Secord, 40.
– Chicago Blackhawks, 1987-88. 80GP. Denis Savard, 44; Rick Vaive, 43; Steve Larmer, 41.
– Edmonton Oilers, 1987-88. 80GP. Craig Simpson, 43; Jari Kurri, 43; Wayne Gretzky, 40.
– Los Angeles Kings, 1988-89. 80GP. Bernie Nicholls, 70; Wayne Gretzky, 54; Luc Robitaille, 46.
– Los Angeles Kings, 1990-91. 80GP. Luc Robitaille, 45; Tomas Sandstrom, 45; Wayne Gretzky, 41.
– Pittsburgh Penguins, 1991-92. 80GP. Kevin Stevens, 54; Mario Lemieux, 44; Joe Mullen, 42.
– Pittsburgh Penguins, 1992-93. 84GP. Mario Lemieux, 69; Kevin Stevens, 55; Rick Tocchet, 48.
– Calgary Flames, 1993-94. 84GP. Gary Roberts, 41; Robert Reichel, 40; Theoren Fleury, 40.
– Pittsburgh Penguins, 1995-96. 82GP. Mario Lemieux, 69; Jaromir Jagr, 62; Petr Nedved, 45.

MOST 30-OR-MORE GOAL SCORERS, ONE SEASON:

6 – **Buffalo Sabres**, 1974-75. 80GP. Rick Martin, 52; Rene Robert, 40; Gilbert Perreault, 39; Don Luce, 33; Rick Dudley, 31; Danny Gare, 31.
– **New York Islanders**, 1977-78. 80GP. Mike Bossy, 53; Bryan Trottier, 46; Clark Gillies, 35; Denis Potvin, 30; Bob Nystrom, 30; Bob Bourne, 30.
– **Winnipeg Jets**, 1984-85. 80GP. Dale Hawerchuk, 53; Paul MacLean, 41; Laurie Boschman, 32; Brian Mullen, 32; Doug Smail, 31; Thomas Steen, 30.

5 – Chicago Blackhawks, 1968-69. 76GP
– Boston Bruins, 1970-71. 78GP
– Montreal Canadiens, 1971-72. 78GP
– Philadelphia Flyers, 1972-73. 78GP
– Boston Bruins, 1973-74. 78GP
– Montreal Canadiens, 1974-75. 80GP
– Montreal Canadiens, 1975-76. 80GP
– Pittsburgh Penguins, 1975-76. 80GP
– New York Islanders, 1978-79. 80GP
– Detroit Red Wings, 1979-80. 80GP
– Philadelphia Flyers, 1979-80. 80GP
– New York Islanders, 1980-81. 80GP
– St. Louis Blues, 1980-81. 80GP
– Chicago Blackhawks, 1981-82. 80GP
– Edmonton Oilers, 1981-82. 80GP
– Montreal Canadiens, 1981-82. 80GP
– Quebec Nordiques, 1981-82. 80GP
– Washington Capitals, 1981-82. 80GP
– Edmonton Oilers, 1982-83. 80GP
– Edmonton Oilers, 1983-84. 80GP
– Edmonton Oilers, 1984-85. 80GP
– Los Angeles Kings, 1984-85. 80GP
– Edmonton Oilers, 1985-86. 80GP
– Edmonton Oilers, 1986-87. 80GP
– Edmonton Oilers, 1987-88. 80GP
– Edmonton Oilers, 1988-89. 80GP
– Detroit Red Wings, 1991-92. 80GP
– New York Rangers, 1991-92. 80GP
– Pittsburgh Penguins, 1991-92. 80GP
– Detroit Red Wings, 1992-93. 84GP
– Pittsburgh Penguins, 1992-93. 84GP

MOST 20-OR-MORE GOAL SCORERS, ONE SEASON:

11 – **Boston Bruins**, 1977-78. 80GP. Peter McNab, 41; Terry O'Reilly, 29; Bobby Schmautz, 27; Stan Jonathan, 27; Jean Ratelle, 25; Rick Middleton, 25; Wayne Cashman, 24; Gregg Sheppard, 23; Brad Park, 22; Don Marcotte, 20; Bob Miller, 20.
10 – Boston Bruins, 1970-71. 78GP
– Montreal Canadiens, 1974-75. 80GP
– St. Louis Blues, 1980-81. 80GP

George Hainsworth of the Montreal Canadiens allowed just 43 goals in 44 games during the 1928-29 season. His 22 shutouts is one of the oldest entries in the NHL record book.

100-POINT SCORERS

MOST 100 OR-MORE-POINT SCORERS, ONE SEASON:
4 – **Boston Bruins**, 1970-71. 78GP. Phil Esposito, 76G–76A–152PTS;
Bobby Orr, 37G–102A–139PTS; John Bucyk, 51G–65A–116PTS;
Ken Hodge, 43G–62A–105PTS.
– **Edmonton Oilers**, 1982-83. 80GP. Wayne Gretzky, 71G–125A–196PTS;
Mark Messier, 48G–58A–106PTS; Glenn Anderson, 48G–56A–104PTS;
Jari Kurri, 45G–59A–104PTS.
– **Edmonton Oilers**, 1983-84. 80GP. Wayne Gretzky, 87G–118A–205PTS;
Paul Coffey, 40G–86A–126PTS; Jari Kurri, 52G–61A–113PTS;
Mark Messier, 37G–64A–101PTS.
– **Edmonton Oilers**, 1985-86. 80GP. Wayne Gretzky, 52G–163A–215PTS;
Paul Coffey, 48G–90A–138PTS; Jari Kurri, 68G–63A–131PTS;
Glenn Anderson, 54G–48A–102PTS.
– **Pittsburgh Penguins**, 1992-93. 84GP. Mario Lemieux, 69G–91A–160PTS;
Kevin Stevens, 55G–56A–111PTS; Rick Tocchet, 48G–61A–109PTS;
Ron Francis, 24G–76A–100PTS.
3 – Boston Bruins, 1973-74. 78GP. Phil Esposito, 68G–77A–145PTS;
Bobby Orr, 32G–90A–122PTS; Ken Hodge, 50G–55A–105PTS.
– New York Islanders, 1978-79. 80GP. Bryan Trottier, 47G–87A–134PTS;
Mike Bossy, 69G–57A–126PTS; Denis Potvin, 31G–70A–101PTS.
– Los Angeles Kings, 1980-81. 80GP. Marcel Dionne, 58G–77A–135PTS;
Dave Taylor, 47G–65A–112PTS; Charlie Simmer, 56G–49A–105PTS.
– Edmonton Oilers, 1984-85. 80GP. Wayne Gretzky, 73G–135A–208PTS;
Jari Kurri, 71G–64A–135PTS; Paul Coffey, 37G–84A–121PTS.
– New York Islanders, 1984-85. 80GP. Mike Bossy, 58G–59A–117PTS;
Brent Sutter, 42G–60A–102PTS; John Tonelli, 42G–58A–100PTS.
– Edmonton Oilers, 1986-87. 80GP. Wayne Gretzky, 62G–121A–183PTS;
Jari Kurri, 54G–54A–108PTS; Mark Messier, 37G–70A–107PTS.
– Pittsburgh Penguins, 1988-89. 80GP. Mario Lemieux, 85G–114A–199PTS;
Rob Brown, 49G–66A–115PTS; Paul Coffey, 30G–83A–113PTS.
– Pittsburgh Penguins, 1995-96. 82GP. Mario Lemieux, 69G–92A–161PTS;
Jaromir Jagr, 62G–87A–149PTS; Ron Francis, 27G–92A–119PTS.

SHOTS ON GOAL

MOST SHOTS, BOTH TEAMS, ONE GAME:
141 – **New York Americans, Pittsburgh Pirates**, Dec. 26, 1925, at
NY Americans. NY Americans won 3-1 with 73 shots; Pittsburgh had 68
shots.

MOST SHOTS, ONE TEAM, ONE GAME:
83 – **Boston Bruins**, Mar. 4, 1941, at Boston. Boston defeated Chicago 3-2.
73 – New York Americans, Dec. 26, 1925, at NY Americans. NY Americans
defeated Pittsburgh 3-1.
– Boston Bruins, Mar. 21, 1991, at Boston. Boston tied Quebec 3-3.
72 – Boston Bruins, Dec. 10, 1970, at Boston. Boston defeated Buffalo 8-2.

MOST SHOTS, ONE TEAM, ONE PERIOD:
33 – **Boston Bruins**, Mar. 4, 1941, at Boston, second period.
Boston defeated Chicago 3-2.

TEAM GOALS AGAINST

Fewest Goals Against

FEWEST GOALS AGAINST, ONE SEASON:
42 – **Ottawa Senators**, 1925-26. 36GP
43 – Montreal Canadiens, 1928-29. 44GP
48 – Montreal Canadiens, 1923-24. 24GP
– Montreal Canadiens, 1927-28. 44GP

**FEWEST GOALS AGAINST, ONE SEASON
(MINIMUM 70-GAME SCHEDULE):**
131 – **Toronto Maple Leafs**, 1953-54. 70GP
– **Montreal Canadiens**, 1955-56. 70GP
132 – Detroit Red Wings, 1953-54. 70GP
133 – Detroit Red Wings, 1951-52. 70GP
– Detroit Red Wings, 1952-53. 70GP

LOWEST GOALS-AGAINST-PER-GAME AVERAGE, ONE SEASON:
0.98 – **Montreal Canadiens**, 1928-29. 43GA in 44GP.
1.09 – Montreal Canadiens, 1927-28. 48GA in 44GP.
1.17 – Ottawa Senators, 1925-26. 42GA in 36GP.

Most Goals Against

MOST GOALS AGAINST, ONE SEASON:
446 – **Washington Capitals**, 1974-75. 80GP
415 – Detroit Red Wings, 1985-86. 80GP
414 – San Jose Sharks, 1992-93. 84GP
407 – Quebec Nordiques, 1989-90. 80GP
403 – Hartford Whalers, 1982-83. 80GP

HIGHEST GOALS-AGAINST-PER-GAME AVERAGE, ONE SEASON:
7.38 – **Quebec Bulldogs**, 1919-20. 177GA in 24GP.
6.20 – New York Rangers, 1943-44. 310GA in 50GP.
5.58 – Washington Capitals, 1974-75. 446GA in 80GP.

MOST POWER-PLAY GOALS AGAINST, ONE SEASON:
122 – **Chicago Blackhawks**, 1988-89. 80GP
120 – Pittsburgh Penguins, 1987-88. 80GP
115 – New Jersey Devils, 1988-89. 80GP
– Ottawa Senators, 1992-93. 84GP
114 – Los Angeles Kings, 1992-93. 84GP

MOST SHORTHAND GOALS AGAINST, ONE SEASON:
22 – **Pittsburgh Penguins**, 1984-85. 80GP
– **Minnesota North Stars**, 1991-92. 80GP
– **Colorado Avalanche**, 1995-96. 82GP
21 – Calgary Flames, 1984-85. 80GP
– Pittsburgh Penguins, 1989-90. 80GP

SHUTOUTS

MOST SHUTOUTS, ONE SEASON:
22 – **Montreal Canadiens**, 1928-29. All by George Hainsworth. 44GP
16 – New York Americans, 1928-29. Roy Worters 13; Flat Walsh 3. 44GP
15 – Ottawa Senators, 1925-26. All by Alex Connell. 36GP
– Ottawa Senators, 1927-28. All by Alex Connell. 44GP
– Boston Bruins, 1927-28. All by Hal Winkler. 44GP
– Chicago Blackhawks, 1969-70. All by Tony Esposito. 76GP

MOST CONSECUTIVE SHUTOUTS, ONE SEASON:
6 – **Ottawa Senators**, Jan. 31 – Feb. 18, 1928. All by Alex Connell.

MOST CONSECUTIVE SHUTOUTS TO START SEASON:
5 – **Toronto Maple Leafs**, Nov. 13 – 22, 1930. Lorne Chabot 3,
Benny Grant 2.

MOST GAMES SHUTOUT, ONE SEASON:
20 – **Chicago Blackhawks**, 1928-29. 44GP

MOST CONSECUTIVE GAMES SHUTOUT:
8 – **Chicago Blackhawks**, Feb. 7 – 28, 1929.

MOST CONSECUTIVE GAMES SHUTOUT TO START SEASON:
3 – **Montreal Maroons**, Nov. 11 – 18, 1930.

TEAM PENALTIES

MOST PENALTY MINUTES, ONE SEASON:
2,713 – **Buffalo Sabres**, 1991-92. 80GP
2,670 – Pittsburgh Penguins, 1988-89. 80GP
2,663 – Chicago Blackhawks, 1991-92. 80GP
2,643 – Calgary Flames, 1991-92. 80GP
2,621 – Philadelphia Flyers, 1980-81. 80GP

MOST PENALTIES, BOTH TEAMS, ONE GAME:
85 – **Edmonton Oilers (44), Los Angeles Kings (41)**, Feb. 28, 1990, at
Los Angeles. Edmonton received 26 minors, 7 majors, 6 10-minute
misconducts, 4 game misconducts and 1 match penalty; Los Angeles
received 26 minors, 9 majors, 3 10-minute misconducts and 3 game
misconducts.

MOST PENALTY MINUTES, BOTH TEAMS, ONE GAME:
419 – **Ottawa Senators (206), Philadelphia Flyers (213)**, Mar. 5, 2004, at
Philadelphia. Ottawa received 8 minors, 10 majors, 4 10-minute
misconducts and 10 game misconducts. Philadelphia received 9 minors,
11 majors, 4 10-minute misconducts and 10 game misconducts.

MOST PENALTIES, ONE TEAM, ONE GAME:
44 – **Edmonton Oilers**, Feb. 28, 1990, at Los Angeles. Edmonton received
26 minors, 7 majors, 6 10-minute misconducts, 4 game misconducts
and 1 match penalty.
42 – Minnesota North Stars, Feb. 26, 1981, at Boston. Minnesota received
18 minors, 13 majors, 4 10-minute misconducts and 7 game misconducts.
– Boston Bruins, Feb. 26, 1981, at Boston vs. Minnesota. Boston received
20 minors, 13 majors, 3 10-minute misconducts and 6 game misconducts.

MOST PENALTY MINUTES, ONE TEAM, ONE GAME:
213 – **Philadelphia Flyers**, Mar. 5, 2004, at Philadelphia. Philadelphia received
9 minors, 11 majors, 4 10-minute misconducts and 10 game misconducts.

MOST PENALTIES, BOTH TEAMS, ONE PERIOD:
67 – **Minnesota North Stars (34), Boston Bruins (33)**, Feb. 26, 1981, at
Boston, first period. Minnesota received 15 minors, 8 majors, 4 10-minute
misconducts and 7 game misconducts. Boston had 16 minors, 8 majors,
3 10-minute misconducts and 6 game misconducts.

MOST PENALTY MINUTES, BOTH TEAMS, ONE PERIOD:
409 – **Ottawa Senators (200), Philadelphia Flyers (209)**, Mar. 5, 2004, at
Philadelphia, third period. Ottawa received 5 minors, 10 majors, 4 10-
minute misconducts and 10 game misconducts. Philadelphia received 7
minors, 11 majors, 4 10-minute misconducts and 10 game misconducts.

MOST PENALTIES, ONE TEAM, ONE PERIOD:
34 – **Minnesota North Stars**, Feb. 26, 1981, at Boston, first period.
Minnesota received 15 minors, 8 majors, 4 10-minute misconducts and
7 game misconducts.

MOST PENALTY MINUTES, ONE TEAM, ONE PERIOD:
209 – **Philadelphia Flyers**, Mar. 5, 2004, at Philadelphia vs. Ottawa, third
period. Philadelphia received 7 minors, 11 majors, 4 10-minute
misconducts and 10 game misconducts.
200 – Ottawa Senators, Mar. 5, 2004, at Philadelphia, third period.
Ottawa received 5 minors, 10 majors, 4 10-minute misconducts and
10 game misconducts.

NHL Individual Scoring Records - History

Six individual scoring records stand as benchmarks in the history of the game: most goals, single-season and career; most assists, single-season and career; and most points, single-season and career. The evolution of these six records is traced here, beginning with 1917-18, the NHL's first season. New research has resulted in changes to scoring records in the NHL's first nine seasons.

MOST GOALS, ONE SEASON

44 —Joe Malone, Montreal, 1917-18.
Scored goal #44 against Toronto's Harry Holmes on March 2, 1918 and finished season with 44 goals.

50 —Maurice Richard, Montreal, 1944-45.
Scored goal #45 against Toronto's Frank McCool on February 25, 1945 and finished the season with 50 goals.

50 —Bernie Geoffrion, Montreal, 1960-61.
Scored goal #50 against Toronto's Cesare Maniago on March 16, 1961 and finished the season with 50 goals.

50 —Bobby Hull, Chicago, 1961-62.
Scored goal #50 against NY Rangers' Gump Worsley on March 25, 1962 and finished the season with 50 goals.

54 —Bobby Hull, Chicago, 1965-66.
Scored goal #51 against NY Rangers' Cesare Maniago on March 12, 1966 and finished the season with 54 goals.

58 —Bobby Hull, Chicago, 1968-69.
Scored goal #55 against Boston's Gerry Cheevers on March 20, 1969 and finished the season with 58 goals.

76 —Phil Esposito, Boston, 1970-71.
Scored goal #59 against Los Angeles' Denis DeJordy on March 11, 1971 and finished the season with 76 goals.

92 —Wayne Gretzky, Edmonton, 1981-82.
Scored goal #77 against Buffalo's Don Edwards on February 24, 1982 and finished the season with 92 goals.

MOST ASSISTS, ONE SEASON

10 —Cy Denneny, Ottawa, 1917-18.
   —Reg Noble, Toronto, 1917-18.
   —Harry Cameron, Toronto, 1917-18.
   —Newsy Lalonde, Montreal, 1918-19.
15 —Frank Nighbor, Ottawa, 1919-20.
   —Jack Darragh, Ottawa, 1920-21.
17 —Harry Cameron, Toronto, 1921-22.
18 —Dick Irvin, Chicago, 1926-27.
   —Howie Morenz, Montreal, 1927-28.
36 —Frank Boucher, NY Rangers, 1929-30.
37 —Joe Primeau, Toronto, 1931-32.
45 —Bill Cowley, Boston, 1940-41.
   —Bill Cowley, Boston, 1942-43.
49 —Clint Smith, Chicago, 1943-44.
54 —Elmer Lach, Montreal, 1944-45.
55 —Ted Lindsay, Detroit, 1949-50.
56 —Bert Olmstead, Montreal, 1955-56.
58 —Jean Beliveau, Montreal, 1960-61.
   —Andy Bathgate, NY Rangers/Toronto, 1963-64.
59 —Stan Mikita, Chicago, 1964-65.
62 —Stan Mikita, Chicago, 1966-67.
77 —Phil Esposito, Boston, 1968-69.
87 —Bobby Orr, Boston, 1969-70.
102 —Bobby Orr, Boston, 1970-71.
109 —Wayne Gretzky, Edmonton, 1980-81.
120 —Wayne Gretzky, Edmonton, 1981-82.
125 —Wayne Gretzky, Edmonton, 1982-83.
135 —Wayne Gretzky, Edmonton, 1984-85.
163 —Wayne Gretzky, Edmonton, 1985-86.

MOST POINTS, ONE SEASON

48 —Joe Malone, Montreal, 1917-18.
49 —Joe Malone, Montreal, 1919-20.
51 —Howie Morenz, Montreal, 1927-28.
73 —Cooney Weiland, Boston, 1929-30.
   —Doug Bentley, Chicago, 1942-43.
82 —Herb Cain, Boston, 1943-44.
86 —Gordie Howe, Detroit, 1950-51.
95 —Gordie Howe, Detroit, 1952-53.
96 —Dickie Moore, Montreal, 1958-59.
97 —Bobby Hull, Chicago, 1965-66.
   —Stan Mikita, Chicago, 1966-67.
126 —Phil Esposito, Boston, 1968-69.
152 —Phil Esposito, Boston, 1970-71.
164 —Wayne Gretzky, Edmonton, 1980-81.
212 —Wayne Gretzky, Edmonton, 1981-82.
215 —Wayne Gretzky, Edmonton, 1985-86.

MOST REGULAR-SEASON GOALS, CAREER

44 —Joe Malone, 1917-18, Montreal.
Malone led the NHL in goals in the league's first season and finished with 44 goals in 22 games in 1917-18.

54 —Cy Denneny, 1918-19, Ottawa.
Denneny passed Malone during the 1918-19 season, finishing the year with a two-year total of 54 goals. He held the career goal-scoring mark until 1919-20.

143 —Joe Malone, Montreal, Quebec Bulldogs, Hamilton.
Malone passed Denneny in 1919-20 and remained the NHL's career goal-scoring leader until 1922-23.

248 —Cy Denneny, Ottawa, Boston.
Denneny passed Malone with goal #144 in 1922-23 and remained the NHL's career goal-scoring leader until his retirement. He finished with a career total of 248 goals.

271 —Howie Morenz, Montreal, Chicago, NY Rangers.
Morenz passed Denneny with goal #249 in 1933-34 and finished his career with 271 goals.

324 —Nels Stewart, Montreal Maroons, Boston, NY Americans.
Stewart passed Morenz with goal #272 in 1936-37 and remained the NHL's career goal-scoring leader until his retirement. He finished his career with 324 goals.

544 —Maurice Richard, Montreal.
Richard passed Nels Stewart with goal #325 on Nov. 8, 1952 and remained the NHL's career goal-scoring leader until his retirement. He finished his career with 544 goals.

801 —Gordie Howe, Detroit, Hartford.
Howe passed Richard with goal #545 on Nov. 10, 1963 and remained the NHL's career goal-scoring leader until his retirement. He finished his career with 801 goals.

894 —Wayne Gretzky, Edmonton, Los Angeles, St. Louis, NY Rangers.
Gretzky passed Gordie Howe with goal #802 on March 23, 1994. He retired as the NHL's current goal-scoring leader with 894.

MOST REGULAR-SEASON ASSISTS, CAREER

(minimum 100 assists)

100 —Frank Boucher, Ottawa, NY Rangers.
In 1930-31, Boucher became the first NHL player to reach the 100-assist milestone.

263 —Frank Boucher, Ottawa, NY Rangers.
Boucher retired as the NHL's career assist leader in 1938 with 253. He returned to the NHL in 1943-44 and remained the NHL's career assist leader until he was overtaken by Bill Cowley in 1943-44. He finished his career with 263 assists.

353 —Bill Cowley, St. Louis Eagles, Boston.
Cowley passed Boucher with assist #264 in 1943-44. He retired as the NHL's career assist leader in 1947 with 353.

408 —Elmer Lach, Montreal.
Lach passed Cowley with assist #354 in 1951-52. He retired as the NHL's career assist leader in 1954 with 408.

1,049 —Gordie Howe, Detroit, Hartford.
Howe passed Lach with assist #409 in 1957-58. He retired as the NHL's career assist leader in 1980 with 1,049.

1,963 —Wayne Gretzky, Edmonton, Los Angeles, St. Louis, NY Rangers.
Gretzky passed Howe with assist #1,050 in 1988-89. He retired as the NHL's current career assist leader with 1,963.

MOST REGULAR-SEASON POINTS, CAREER

(minimum 100 points)

100 —Joe Malone, Montreal, Quebec Bulldogs, Hamilton.
In 1919-20, Malone became the first player in NHL history to record 100 points.

200 —Cy Denneny, Ottawa.
In 1923-24, Denneny became the first player in NHL history to record 200 points.

300 —Cy Denneny, Ottawa.
In 1926-27, Denneny became the first player in NHL history to record 300 points.

333 —Cy Denneny, Ottawa, Boston.
Denneny retired as the NHL's career point-scoring leader in 1929 with 333 points.

472 —Howie Morenz, Montreal, Chicago, NY Rangers.
Morenz passed Cy Denneny with point #334 in 1931-32. At the time his career ended in 1937, he was the NHL's career point-scoring leader with 472 points.

515 —Nels Stewart, Montreal Maroons, Boston, NY Americans.
Stewart passed Morenz with point #473 in 1938-39. He retired as the NHL's career point-scoring leader in 1940 with 515 points.

528 —Syd Howe, Ottawa, Philadelphia Quakers, Toronto, St. Louis Eagles, Detroit.
Howe passed Nels Stewart with point #516 on March 8, 1945. He retired as the NHL's career point-scoring leader in 1946 with 528 points.

548 —Bill Cowley, St. Louis Eagles, Boston.
Cowley passed Syd Howe with point #529 on Feb. 12, 1947. He retired as the NHL's career point-scoring leader in 1947 with 548 points.

610 —Elmer Lach, Montreal.
Lach passed Bill Cowley with point #549 on Feb. 23, 1952. He remained the NHL's career point-scoring leader until he was overtaken by Maurice Richard in 1953-54. He finished his career with 623 points.

946 —Maurice Richard, Montreal.
Richard passed teammate Elmer Lach with point #611 on Dec. 12, 1953. He remained the NHL's career point-scoring leader until he was overtaken by Gordie Howe in 1959-60. He finished his career with 965 points.

1,850 —Gordie Howe, Detroit, Hartford.
Howe passed Richard with point #947 on Jan. 16, 1960. He retired as the NHL's career point-scoring leader in 1980 with 1,850 points.

2,857 —Wayne Gretzky, Edmonton, Los Angeles, St. Louis, NY Rangers.
Gretzky passed Howe with point #1,851 on Oct. 15, 1989. He retired as the NHL's current career points leader with 2,857.

With his fourth goal of the 1933-34 season, Howie Morenz (left) passed Cy Denneny as the leading scorer in NHL history. Morenz had scored 271 goals at the time of the injury that ended his career (and cut short his life) on January 28, 1937. Remembered primarily for his skating speed and scoring exploits, Morenz could also set up his teammates. His 18 assists in 1927-28 were an NHL record before the introduction of more modern passing rules just two years later. Frank Boucher (facing page, centering brothers Bun and Bill Cook) doubled Morenz's assist record in 1929-30. Boucher was considered the best playmaker in hockey and the game's most sportsmanlike player during his days with the New York Rangers. The combination of Frank Boucher and the Cook brothers is considered to be the NHL's first great forward line.

Individual Records

Regular Season

SEASONS

MOST SEASONS:
26 – Gordie Howe, Detroit, 1946-47 – 1970-71; Hartford, 1979-80.
25 – Mark Messier, Edmonton, NY Rangers, Vancouver,
1979-80 – 2003-04.
24 – Alex Delvecchio, Detroit, 1950-51 – 1973-74.
– Tim Horton, Toronto, NY Rangers, Pittsburgh, Buffalo,
1949-50, 1951-52 – 1973-74.
23 – John Bucyk, Detroit, Boston, 1955-56 – 1977-78.
– Ron Francis, Hartford, Pittsburgh, Carolina, Toronto, 1981-82 – 2003-04.
– Al MacInnis, Calgary, St. Louis, 1981-82 – 2003-04.

GAMES

MOST GAMES:
1,767 – Gordie Howe, Detroit, 1946-47 – 1970-71; Hartford, 1979-80.
1,756 – Mark Messier, Edmonton, NY Rangers, Vancouver, 1979-80 – 2003-04.
1,731 – Ron Francis, Hartford, Pittsburgh, Carolina, Toronto, 1981-82 – 2003-04.
1,635 – Scott Stevens, Washington, St. Louis, New Jersey, 1982-83 – 2003-04.
1,615 – Larry Murphy, Los Angeles, Washington, Minnesota, Pittsburgh, Toronto, Detroit, 1980-81 – 2000-01.

MOST GAMES, INCLUDING PLAYOFFS:
1,992 – Mark Messier, Edmonton, NY Rangers, Vancouver,
1,756 regular-season games, 236 playoff games.
1,924 – Gordie Howe, Detroit, Hartford, 1,767 regular-season games,
157 playoff games.
1,902 – Ron Francis, Hartford, Pittsburgh, Carolina, Toronto, 1,731 regular-season games, 171 playoff games.
1,868 – Scott Stevens, Washington, St. Louis, New Jersey, 1,635 regular-season games, 233 playoff games.
1,830 – Larry Murphy, Los Angeles, Washington, Minnesota, Pittsburgh, Toronto, Detroit, 1,615 regular-season games, 215 playoff games.

MOST CONSECUTIVE GAMES:
964 – Doug Jarvis, Montreal, Washington, Hartford,
Oct. 8, 1975 – Oct. 10, 1987.
914 – Garry Unger, Toronto, Detroit, St. Louis, Atlanta,
Feb. 24, 1968 – Dec. 21, 1979.
884 – Steve Larmer, Chicago, Oct. 6, 1982 – Apr. 15, 1993.
776 – Craig Ramsay, Buffalo, Mar. 27, 1973 – Feb. 10, 1983.
630 – Andy Hebenton, NY Rangers, Boston, Oct. 7, 1955 – Mar. 22, 1964.

GOALS

MOST GOALS:
894 – Wayne Gretzky, Edmonton, Los Angeles, St. Louis, NY Rangers,
in 20 seasons. 1,487GP
801 – Gordie Howe, Detroit, Hartford, in 26 seasons. 1,767GP
741 – Brett Hull, Calgary, St. Louis, Dallas, Detroit, in 18 seasons. 1,264GP
731 – Marcel Dionne, Detroit, Los Angeles, NY Rangers, in 18 seasons. 1,348GP
717 – Phil Esposito, Chicago, Boston, NY Rangers, in 18 seasons. 1,282GP

MOST GOALS, INCLUDING PLAYOFFS:
1,016 – Wayne Gretzky, Edmonton, Los Angeles, St. Louis, NY Rangers,
894G in 1,487 regular-season games, 122G in 208 playoff games.
869 – Gordie Howe, Detroit, Hartford, 801G in 1,767 regular-season games,
68G in 157 playoff games.
844 – Brett Hull, Calgary, St. Louis, Dallas, Detroit, 741G in 1,264 regular-season games, 103G in 202 playoff games.
803 – Mark Messier, Edmonton, NY Rangers, Vancouver, 694G in 1,756 regular-season games, 109G in 236 playoff games.
778 – Phil Esposito, Chicago, Boston, NY Rangers, 717G in 1,282 regular-season games, 61G in 130 playoff games.

MOST GOALS, ONE SEASON:
92 – Wayne Gretzky, Edmonton, 1981-82. 80GP – 80 game schedule.
87 – Wayne Gretzky, Edmonton, 1983-84. 74GP – 80 game schedule.
86 – Brett Hull, St. Louis, 1990-91. 78GP – 80 game schedule.
85 – Mario Lemieux, Pittsburgh, 1988-89. 76GP – 80 game schedule.
76 – Phil Esposito, Boston, 1970-71. 78GP – 78 game schedule.
– Alexander Mogilny, Buffalo, 1992-93. 77GP – 84 game schedule.
– Teemu Selanne, Winnipeg, 1992-93. 84GP – 84 game schedule.
73 – Wayne Gretzky, Edmonton, 1984-85. 80GP – 80 game schedule.
72 – Brett Hull, St. Louis, 1989-90. 80GP – 80 game schedule.
71 – Wayne Gretzky, Edmonton, 1982-83. 80GP – 80 game schedule.
– Jari Kurri, Edmonton, 1984-85. 73GP – 80 game schedule.
70 – Mario Lemieux, Pittsburgh, 1987-88. 77GP – 80 game schedule.
– Bernie Nicholls, Los Angeles, 1988-89. 79GP – 80 game schedule.
– Brett Hull, St. Louis, 1991-92. 73GP – 80 game schedule.

MOST GOALS, ONE SEASON, INCLUDING PLAYOFFS:
100 – Wayne Gretzky, Edmonton, 1983-84,
87G in 74 regular-season games, 13G in 19 playoff games.
97 – Wayne Gretzky, Edmonton, 1981-82,
92G in 80 regular-season games, 5G in 5 playoff games.
– Mario Lemieux, Pittsburgh, 1988-89,
85G in 76 regular-season games, 12G in 11 playoff games.
– Brett Hull, St. Louis, 1990-91,
86G in 78 regular-season games, 11G in 13 playoff games.
90 – Wayne Gretzky, Edmonton, 1984-85,
73G in 80 regular-season games, 17G in 18 playoff games.
– Jari Kurri, Edmonton, 1984-85,
71G in 80 regular-season games, 19G in 18 playoff games.
85 – Mike Bossy, NY Islanders, 1980-81,
68G in 79 regular-season games, 17G in 18 playoff games.
– Brett Hull, St. Louis, 1989-90,
72G in 80 regular-season games, 13G in 12 playoff games.
83 – Wayne Gretzky, Edmonton, 1982-83,
71G in 73 regular-season games, 12G in 16 playoff games.
– Alexander Mogilny, Buffalo, 1992-93,
76G in 77 regular-season games, 7G in 7 playoff games.

MOST GOALS, 50 GAMES FROM START OF SEASON:
61 – Wayne Gretzky, Edmonton, 1981-82.
Oct. 7, 1981 – Jan. 22, 1982. (80-game schedule)
– Wayne Gretzky, Edmonton, 1983-84.
Oct. 5, 1983 – Jan. 25, 1984. (80-game schedule)
54 – Mario Lemieux, Pittsburgh, 1988-89.
Oct. 7, 1988 – Jan. 31, 1989. (80-game schedule)
53 – Wayne Gretzky, Edmonton, 1984-85.
Oct. 11, 1984 – Jan. 28, 1985. (80-game schedule)
52 – Brett Hull, St. Louis, 1990-91.
Oct. 4, 1990 – Jan. 26, 1991. (80-game schedule)
50 – Maurice Richard, Montreal, 1944-45.
Oct. 28, 1944 – Mar. 18, 1945. (50-game schedule)
– Mike Bossy, NY Islanders, 1980-81.
Oct. 11, 1980 – Jan. 24, 1981. (80-game schedule)
– Brett Hull, St. Louis, 1991-92.
Oct. 5, 1991 – Jan. 28, 1992. (80-game schedule)

MOST GOALS, ONE GAME:
7 – Joe Malone, Quebec, Jan. 31, 1920, at Quebec.
Quebec 10, Toronto 6.
6 – Newsy Lalonde, Montreal, Jan. 10, 1920, at Montreal.
Montreal 14, Toronto 7.
– Joe Malone, Quebec, Mar. 10, 1920, at Quebec.
Quebec 10, Ottawa 4.
– Corb Denneny, Toronto, Jan. 26, 1921, at Toronto.
Toronto 10, Hamilton 3.
– Cy Denneny, Ottawa, Mar. 7, 1921, at Ottawa.
Ottawa 12, Hamilton 5.
– Syd Howe, Detroit, Feb. 3, 1944, at Detroit.
Detroit 12, NY Rangers 2.
– Red Berenson, St. Louis, Nov. 7, 1968, at Philadelphia.
St. Louis 8, Philadelphia 0.
– Darryl Sittler, Toronto, Feb. 7, 1976, at Toronto.
Toronto 11, Boston 4.

Like his 801 goals, Gordie Howe's total of 1,767 games played was long considered unbreakable. Mark Messier pulled to within 11 games of Howe in 2003-04 and has surpassed his record for most games played including playoffs.

Edouard "Newsy" Lalonde of the Montreal Canadiens (top left) became the first player in NHL history to score six goals in a game on January 10, 1920. His record lasted three weeks before Joe Malone scored seven times in one game.

MOST GOALS, ONE ROAD GAME:
6 – Red Berenson, St. Louis, Nov. 7, 1968, at Philadelphia. St. Louis 8, Philadelphia 0.
5 – Joe Malone, Montreal, Dec. 19, 1917, at Ottawa. Montreal 7, Ottawa 4.
– Red Green, Hamilton, Dec. 5, 1924, at Toronto. Hamilton 10, Toronto 3.
– Babe Dye, Toronto, Dec. 22, 1924, at Boston. Toronto 10, Boston 1.
– Punch Broadbent, Mtl. Maroons, Jan. 7, 1925, at Hamilton. Mtl. Maroons 6, Hamilton 2.
– Don Murdoch, NY Rangers, Oct. 12, 1976, at Minnesota. NY Rangers 10, Minnesota 4.
– Tim Young, Minnesota, Jan. 15, 1979, at NY Rangers. Minnesota 8, NY Rangers 1.
– Willy Lindstrom, Winnipeg, Mar. 2, 1982, at Philadelphia. Winnipeg 7, Philadelphia 6.
– Bengt Gustafsson, Washington, Jan. 8, 1984, at Philadelphia. Washington 7, Philadelphia 1.
– Wayne Gretzky, Edmonton, Dec. 15, 1984, at St. Louis. Edmonton 8, St. Louis 2.
– Dave Andreychuk, Buffalo, Feb. 6, 1986, at Boston. Buffalo 8, Boston 6.
– Mats Sundin, Quebec, Mar. 5, 1992, at Hartford. Quebec 10, Hartford 4.
– Mario Lemieux, Pittsburgh, Apr. 9, 1993, at NY Rangers. Pittsburgh 10, NY Rangers 4.
– Mike Ricci, Quebec, Feb. 17, 1994, at San Jose. Quebec 8, San Jose 2.
– Alex Zhamnov, Winnipeg, Apr. 1, 1995, at Los Angeles. Winnipeg 7, Los Angeles 7.

MOST GOALS, ONE PERIOD:
4 – Busher Jackson, Toronto, Nov. 20, 1934, at St. Louis, third period. Toronto 5, St. Louis 2.
– Max Bentley, Chicago, Jan. 28, 1943, at Chicago, third period. Chicago 10, NY Rangers 1.
– Clint Smith, Chicago, Mar. 4, 1945, at Chicago, third period. Chicago 6, Montreal 4.
– Red Berenson, St. Louis, Nov. 7, 1968, at Philadelphia, second period. St. Louis 8, Philadelphia 0.
– Wayne Gretzky, Edmonton, Feb. 18, 1981, at Edmonton, third period. Edmonton 9, St. Louis 2.
– Grant Mulvey, Chicago, Feb. 3, 1982, at Chicago, first period. Chicago 9, St. Louis 5.
– Bryan Trottier, NY Islanders, Feb. 13, 1982, at NY Islanders, second period. NY Islanders 8, Philadelphia 2.
– Al Secord, Chicago, Jan. 7, 1987, at Chicago, second period. Chicago 6, Toronto 4.
– Joe Nieuwendyk, Calgary, Jan. 11, 1989, at Calgary, second period. Calgary 8, Winnipeg 3.
– Peter Bondra, Washington, Feb. 5, 1994, at Washington, first period. Washington 6, Tampa Bay 3.
– Mario Lemieux, Pittsburgh, Jan. 26, 1997, at Montreal, third period. Pittsburgh 5, Montreal 2.

ASSISTS

MOST ASSISTS:
1,963 – Wayne Gretzky, Edmonton, Los Angeles, St. Louis, NY Rangers, in 20 seasons. 1,487GP
1,249 – Ron Francis, Hartford, Pittsburgh, Carolina, Toronto, in 23 seasons. 1,731GP
1,193 – Mark Messier, Edmonton, NY Rangers, Vancouver, in 25 seasons. 1,756GP
1,169 – Raymond Bourque, Boston, Colorado, in 22 seasons. 1,612GP
1,135 – Paul Coffey, Edmonton, Pittsburgh, Los Angeles, Detroit, Hartford, Philadelphia, Chicago, Carolina, Boston, in 21 seasons. 1,409GP

MOST ASSISTS, INCLUDING PLAYOFFS:
2,223 – Wayne Gretzky, Edmonton, Los Angeles, St. Louis, NY Rangers, 1,963A in 1,487 regular-season games, 260A in 208 playoff games.
1,379 – Mark Messier, Edmonton, NY Rangers, Vancouver, 1,193A in 1,756 regular-season games, 186A in 236 playoff games.
1,346 – Ron Francis, Hartford, Pittsburgh, Carolina, Toronto, 1,249A in 1,731 regular-season games, 97A in 171 playoff games.
1,308 – Raymond Bourque, Boston, Colorado, 1,169A in 1,612 regular-season games, 139A in 214 playoff games.
1,272 – Paul Coffey, Edmonton, Pittsburgh, Los Angeles, Detroit, Hartford, Philadelphia, Chicago, Carolina, Boston, 1,135A in 1,409 regular-season games, 137A in 194 playoff games.

MOST ASSISTS, ONE SEASON:
163 – Wayne Gretzky, Edmonton, 1985-86. 80GP – 80 game schedule.
135 – Wayne Gretzky, Edmonton, 1984-85. 80GP – 80 game schedule.
125 – Wayne Gretzky, Edmonton, 1982-83. 80GP – 80 game schedule.
122 – Wayne Gretzky, Los Angeles, 1990-91. 78GP – 80 game schedule.
121 – Wayne Gretzky, Edmonton, 1986-87. 79GP – 80 game schedule.
120 – Wayne Gretzky, Edmonton, 1981-82. 80GP – 80 game schedule.
118 – Wayne Gretzky, Edmonton, 1983-84. 74GP – 80 game schedule.
114 – Wayne Gretzky, Los Angeles, 1988-89. 78GP – 80 game schedule.
– Mario Lemieux, Pittsburgh, 1988-89. 76GP – 80 game schedule.
109 – Wayne Gretzky, Edmonton, 1980-81. 80GP – 80 game schedule.
– Wayne Gretzky, Edmonton, 1987-88. 64GP – 80 game schedule.
102 – Bobby Orr, Boston, 1970-71. 78GP – 78 game schedule.
– Wayne Gretzky, Los Angeles, 1989-90. 73GP – 80 game schedule.

MOST ASSISTS, ONE SEASON, INCLUDING PLAYOFFS:
174 – Wayne Gretzky, Edmonton, 1985-86,
163A in 80 regular-season games, 11A in 10 playoff games.
165 – Wayne Gretzky, Edmonton, 1984-85,
135A in 80 regular-season games, 30A in 18 playoff games.
151 – Wayne Gretzky, Edmonton, 1982-83,
125A in 80 regular-season games, 26A in 16 playoff games.
150 – Wayne Gretzky, Edmonton, 1986-87,
121A in 79 regular-season games, 29A in 21 playoff games.
140 – Wayne Gretzky, Edmonton, 1983-84,
118A in 74 regular-season games, 22A in 19 playoff games.
    – Wayne Gretzky, Edmonton, 1987-88,
109A in 64 regular-season games, 31A in 19 playoff games.
133 – Wayne Gretzky, Los Angeles, 1990-91,
122A in 78 regular-season games, 11A in 12 playoff games.
131 – Wayne Gretzky, Los Angeles, 1988-89,
114A in 78 regular-season games, 17A in 11 playoff games.
127 – Wayne Gretzky, Edmonton, 1981-82,
120A in 80 regular-season games, 7A in 5 playoff games.
123 – Wayne Gretzky, Edmonton, 1980-81,
109A in 80 regular-season games, 14A in 9 playoff games.
121 – Mario Lemieux, Pittsburgh, 1988-89,
114A in 76 regular-season games, 7A in 11 playoff games.

MOST ASSISTS, ONE GAME:
7 – Billy Taylor, Detroit, Mar. 16, 1947, at Chicago. Detroit 10, Chicago 6.
  – Wayne Gretzky, Edmonton, Feb. 15, 1980, at Edmonton.
Edmonton 8, Washington 2.
  – Wayne Gretzky, Edmonton, Dec. 11, 1985, at Chicago.
Edmonton 12, Chicago 9.
  – Wayne Gretzky, Edmonton, Feb. 14, 1986, at Edmonton.
Edmonton 8, Quebec 2.
6 – Six assists have been recorded in one game on 24 occasions since
Elmer Lach of Montreal first accomplished the feat vs. Boston on
Feb. 6, 1943. The most recent player is Eric Lindros of Philadelphia
on Feb. 26, 1997 at Ottawa.

MOST ASSISTS, ONE ROAD GAME:
7 – Billy Taylor, Detroit, Mar. 16, 1947, at Chicago. Detroit 10, Chicago 6.
  – Wayne Gretzky, Edmonton, Dec. 11, 1985, at Chicago.
Edmonton 12, Chicago 9.
6 – Bobby Orr, Boston, Jan. 1, 1973, at Vancouver. Boston 8, Vancouver 2.
  – Patrik Sundstrom, Vancouver, Feb. 29, 1984, at Pittsburgh.
Vancouver 9, Pittsburgh 5.
  – Mario Lemieux, Pittsburgh, Dec. 5, 1992, at San Jose.
Pittsburgh 9, San Jose 4.
  – Eric Lindros, Philadelphia, Feb. 26, 1997, at Ottawa.
Philadelphia 8, Ottawa 5.

MOST ASSISTS, ONE PERIOD:
5 – Dale Hawerchuk, Winnipeg, Mar. 6, 1984, at Los Angeles,
second period. Winnipeg 7, Los Angeles 3.
4 – Four assists have been recorded in one period on 63 occasions since
Mickey Roach of Hamilton first accomplished the feat vs. Toronto
on Feb. 23, 1921. The most recent player is Paul Kariya of Anaheim
on Dec. 16, 1998 vs. Nashville.

POINTS

MOST POINTS:
2,857 – Wayne Gretzky, Edmonton, Los Angeles, St. Louis, NY Rangers,
in 20 seasons. 1,487GP (894G–1,963A)
1,887 – Mark Messier, Edmonton, NY Rangers, Vancouver,
in 25 seasons. 1,756GP (694G–1,193A)
1,850 – Gordie Howe, Detroit, Hartford, in 26 seasons. 1,767GP (801G–1,049A)
1,798 – Ron Francis, Hartford, Pittsburgh, Carolina, Toronto,
in 23 seasons. 1,731GP (549G–1,249A)
1,771 – Marcel Dionne, Detroit, Los Angeles, NY Rangers,
in 18 seasons. 1,348GP (731G–1,040A)

MOST POINTS, INCLUDING PLAYOFFS:
3,239 – Wayne Gretzky, Edmonton, Los Angeles, St. Louis, NY Rangers,
2,857PTS in 1,487 regular-season games, 382PTS in 208 playoff games.
2,182 – Mark Messier, Edmonton, NY Rangers, Vancouver,
1,887PTS in 1,756 regular-season games, 295PTS in 236 playoff games.
2,010 – Gordie Howe, Detroit, Hartford,
1,850PTS in 1,767 regular-season games, 160PTS in 157 playoff games.
1,941 – Ron Francis, Hartford, Pittsburgh, Carolina, Toronto,
1,798PTS in 1,731 regular-season games, 143PTS in 171 playoff games
1,902 – Steve Yzerman, Detroit,
1,721PTS in 1,453 regular-season games, 181PTS in 192 playoff games.

MOST POINTS, ONE SEASON:
215 – Wayne Gretzky, Edmonton, 1985-86. 80GP – 80 game schedule.
212 – Wayne Gretzky, Edmonton, 1981-82. 80GP – 80 game schedule.
208 – Wayne Gretzky, Edmonton, 1984-85. 80GP – 80 game schedule.
205 – Wayne Gretzky, Edmonton, 1983-84. 74GP – 80 game schedule.
199 – Mario Lemieux, Pittsburgh, 1988-89. 76GP – 80 game schedule.
196 – Wayne Gretzky, Edmonton, 1982-83. 80GP – 80 game schedule.
183 – Wayne Gretzky, Edmonton, 1986-87. 79GP – 80 game schedule.
168 – Mario Lemieux, Pittsburgh, 1987-88. 77GP – 80 game schedule.
    – Wayne Gretzky, Los Angeles, 1988-89. 78GP – 80 game schedule.
164 – Wayne Gretzky, Edmonton, 1980-81. 80GP – 80 game schedule.
163 – Wayne Gretzky, Los Angeles, 1990-91. 78GP – 80 game schedule.
161 – Mario Lemieux, Pittsburgh, 1995-96. 70GP – 82 game schedule.
160 – Mario Lemieux, Pittsburgh, 1992-93. 60GP – 84 game schedule.

MOST POINTS, ONE SEASON, INCLUDING PLAYOFFS:
255 – Wayne Gretzky, Edmonton, 1984-85,
208PTS in 80 regular-season games, 47PTS in 18 playoff games.
240 – Wayne Gretzky, Edmonton, 1983-84,
205PTS in 74 regular-season games, 35PTS in 19 playoff games.
234 – Wayne Gretzky, Edmonton, 1982-83,
196PTS in 80 regular-season games, 38PTS in 16 playoff games.
    – Wayne Gretzky, Edmonton, 1985-86,
215PTS in 80 regular-season games, 19PTS in 10 playoff games.
224 – Wayne Gretzky, Edmonton, 1981-82,
212PTS in 80 regular-season games, 12PTS in 5 playoff games.
218 – Mario Lemieux, Pittsburgh, 1988-89,
199PTS in 76 regular-season games, 19PTS in 11 playoff games.
217 – Wayne Gretzky, Edmonton, 1986-87,
183PTS in 79 regular-season games, 34PTS in 21 playoff games.
192 – Wayne Gretzky, Edmonton, 1987-88,
149PTS in 64 regular-season games, 43PTS in 19 playoff games.
190 – Wayne Gretzky, Los Angeles, 1988-89,
168PTS in 78 regular-season games, 22PTS in 11 playoff games.
188 – Mario Lemieux, Pittsburgh, 1995-96,
161PTS in 70 regular-season games, 27PTS in 18 playoff games.
185 – Wayne Gretzky, Edmonton, 1980-81,
164PTS in 80 regular-season games, 21PTS in 9 playoff games.

Wayne Gretzky celebrates one of the early goals among the 894 regular-season tallies during his brilliant career. Gretzky holds or shares almost every significant record for goals, assists and points during a game, season and career.

MOST POINTS, ONE GAME:

10 – Darryl Sittler, Toronto, Feb. 7, 1976, at Toronto, 6G-4A.
Toronto 11, Boston 4.
8 – Maurice Richard, Montreal, Dec. 28, 1944, at Montreal, 5G-3A.
Montreal 9, Detroit 1.
– Bert Olmstead, Montreal, Jan. 9, 1954, at Montreal, 4G-4A.
Montreal 12, Chicago 1.
– Tom Bladon, Philadelphia, Dec. 11, 1977, at Philadelphia, 4G-4A.
Philadelphia 11, Cleveland 1.
– Bryan Trottier, NY Islanders, Dec. 23, 1978, at NY Islanders, 5G-3A.
NY Islanders 9, NY Rangers 4.
– Peter Stastny, Quebec, Feb. 22, 1981, at Washington, 4G-4A.
Quebec 11, Washington 7.
– Anton Stastny, Quebec, Feb. 22, 1981, at Washington, 3G-5A.
Quebec 11, Washington 7.
– Wayne Gretzky, Edmonton, Nov. 19, 1983, at Edmonton, 3G-5A.
Edmonton 13, New Jersey 4.
– Wayne Gretzky, Edmonton, Jan. 4, 1984, at Edmonton, 4G-4A.
Edmonton 12, Minnesota 8.
– Paul Coffey, Edmonton, Mar. 14, 1986, at Edmonton, 2G-6A.
Edmonton 12, Detroit 3.
– Mario Lemieux, Pittsburgh, Oct. 15, 1988, at Pittsburgh, 2G-6A.
Pittsburgh 9, St. Louis 2.
– Bernie Nicholls, Los Angeles, Dec. 1, 1988, at Los Angeles, 2G-6A.
Los Angeles 9, Toronto 3.
– Mario Lemieux, Pittsburgh, Dec. 31, 1988, at Pittsburgh, 5G-3A.
Pittsburgh 8, New Jersey 6.

MOST POINTS, ONE ROAD GAME:

8 – Peter Stastny, Quebec, Feb. 22, 1981, at Washington. 4G-4A.
Quebec 11, Washington 7.
– **Anton Stastny**, Quebec, Feb. 22, 1981, at Washington. 3G-5A.
Quebec 11, Washington 7.
7 – Red Green, Hamilton, Dec. 5, 1924, at Toronto. 5G-2A.
Hamilton 10, Toronto 3.
– Billy Taylor, Detroit, Mar. 16, 1947, at Chicago. 7A. Detroit 10, Chicago 6.
– Red Berenson, St. Louis, Nov. 7, 1968, at Philadelphia, 6G-1A.
St. Louis 8, Philadelphia 0.
– Gilbert Perreault, Buffalo, Feb. 1, 1976, at California. 2G-5A.
Buffalo 9, California 5.
– Peter Stastny, Quebec, Apr. 1, 1982, at Boston. 3G-4A. Quebec 8, Boston 5.
– Wayne Gretzky, Edmonton, Nov. 6, 1983, at Winnipeg. 4G-3A.
Edmonton 8, Winnipeg 5.
– Patrik Sundstrom, Vancouver, Feb. 29, 1984, at Pittsburgh. 1G-6A.
Vancouver 9, Pittsburgh 5.
– Wayne Gretzky, Edmonton, Dec. 11, 1985, at Chicago. 7A.
Edmonton 12, Chicago 9.
– Cam Neely, Boston, Oct. 16, 1988, at Chicago. 3G-4A.
Boston 10, Chicago 3.
– Mario Lemieux, Pittsburgh, Jan. 21, 1989, at Edmonton. 2G-5A.
Pittsburgh 7, Edmonton 4.
– Dino Ciccarelli, Washington, Mar. 18, 1989, at Hartford. 4G-3A.
Washington 8, Hartford 2.
– Mats Sundin, Quebec, Mar. 5, 1992, at Hartford. 5G-2A.
Quebec 10, Hartford 4.
– Mario Lemieux, Pittsburgh, Dec. 5, 1992, at San Jose. 1G-6A.
Pittsburgh 9, San Jose 4.
– Eric Lindros, Philadelphia, Feb. 26, 1997, at Ottawa. 1G-6A.
Philadelphia 8, Ottawa 5.

MOST POINTS, ONE PERIOD:

6 – Bryan Trottier, NY Islanders, Dec. 23, 1978, at NY Islanders,
second period. 3G-3A. NY Islanders 9, NY Rangers 4.
5 – Bill Cook, NY Rangers, Mar. 12, 1933, at NY Americans
third period. 3G-2A. NY Rangers 8, NY Americans 2.
– Les Cunningham, Chicago, Jan. 28, 1940, at Chicago,
third period. 2G-3A. Chicago 8, Montreal 1.
– Max Bentley, Chicago, Jan. 28, 1943, at Chicago,
third period. 4G-1A. Chicago 10, NY Rangers 1.
– Leo Labine, Boston, Nov. 28, 1954, at Boston,
second period. 3G-2A. Boston 6, Detroit 2.
– Darryl Sittler, Toronto, Feb. 7, 1976, at Toronto,
second period. 5G. Toronto 11, Boston 4.
– Grant Mulvey, Chicago, Feb. 3, 1982, at Chicago,
first period. 4G-1A. Chicago 9, St. Louis 5.
– Dale Hawerchuk, Winnipeg, Mar. 6, 1984, at Los Angeles,
second period. 5A. Winnipeg 7, Los Angeles 3.
– Jari Kurri, Edmonton, Oct. 26, 1984, at Edmonton,
second period. 2G-3A. Edmonton 8, Los Angeles 2.
– Pat Elynuik, Winnipeg, Jan. 20, 1989, at Winnipeg,
second period. 2G-3A. Winnipeg 7, Pittsburgh 3.
– Ray Ferraro, Hartford, Dec. 9, 1989, at Hartford,
first period. 3G-2A. Hartford 7, New Jersey 3.
– Stephane Richer, Montreal, Feb. 14, 1990, at Montreal,
first period. 2G-3A. Montreal 10, Vancouver 1.
– Cliff Ronning, Vancouver, Apr. 15, 1993, at Los Angeles,
third period. 3G-2A. Vancouver 8, Los Angeles 6.
– Peter Forsberg, Colorado, Mar. 3, 1999, at Florida,
third period. 2G-3A. Colorado 7, Florida 5.

POWER-PLAY AND SHORTHAND GOALS

MOST POWER-PLAY GOALS, CAREER:

270 – Dave Andreychuk, Buffalo, Toronto, New Jersey, Boston, Colorado,
Tampa Bay, in 22 seasons. 1,597GP.
265 – Brett Hull, Calgary, St. Louis, Dallas, Detroit, in 18 seasons. 1,264GP.
249 – Phil Esposito, Chicago, Boston, NY Rangers, in 18 seasons. 1,282GP.

MOST POWER-PLAY GOALS, ONE SEASON:

34 – Tim Kerr, Philadelphia, 1985-86. 76GP – 80 game schedule.
32 – Dave Andreychuk, Buffalo, Toronto, 1992-93. 83GP – 84 game schedule.
31 – Joe Nieuwendyk, Calgary, 1987-88. 75GP – 80 game schedule.
– Mario Lemieux, Pittsburgh, 1988-89. 76GP – 80 game schedule.
– Mario Lemieux, Pittsburgh, 1995-96. 70GP – 82 game schedule.
29 – Michel Goulet, Quebec, 1987-88. 80GP – 80 game schedule.
– Brett Hull, St. Louis, 1990-91. 78GP – 80 game schedule.
– Brett Hull, St. Louis, 1992-93. 80GP – 84 game schedule.

MOST SHORTHAND GOALS, ONE SEASON:

13 – Mario Lemieux, Pittsburgh, 1988-89. 76GP – 80 game schedule.
12 – Wayne Gretzky, Edmonton, 1983-84. 74GP – 80 game schedule.
11 – Wayne Gretzky, Edmonton, 1984-85. 80GP – 80 game schedule.
10 – Marcel Dionne, Detroit, 1974-75. 80GP – 80 game schedule.
– Mario Lemieux, Pittsburgh, 1987-88. 77GP – 80 game schedule.
– Dirk Graham, Chicago, 1988-89. 80GP – 80 game schedule.

MOST SHORTHAND GOALS, ONE GAME:

3 – Theoren Fleury, Calgary, Mar. 9, 1991, at St. Louis. Calgary 8,
St. Louis 4.

OVERTIME SCORING

MOST OVERTIME GOALS, CAREER:

13 – Steve Thomas, Toronto, Chicago, NY Islanders, New Jersey, Anaheim.
– **Sergei Fedorov**, Detroit, Anaheim.
– **Mats Sundin**, Quebec, Toronto.
12 – Jaromir Jagr, Pittsburgh, Washington.
– Brett Hull, St. Louis, Dallas, Detroit.
11 – Mario Lemieux, Pittsburgh.
– Theoren Fleury, Calgary, Colorado, NY Rangers, Chicago.
– Pierre Turgeon, Buffalo, NY Islanders, Montreal, St. Louis, Dallas.

MOST OVERTIME ASSISTS, CAREER:

18 – Mark Messier, Edmonton, NY Rangers, Vancouver.
17 – Adam Oates, Detroit, St. Louis, Boston, Washington, Philadelphia,
Anaheim.
16 – Nicklas Lidstrom, Detroit.
15 – Wayne Gretzky, Edmonton, Los Angeles, St. Louis, NY Rangers.
– Doug Gilmour, St. Louis, Calgary, Toronto, New Jersey, Chicago,
Buffalo, Montreal.

MOST OVERTIME POINTS, CAREER:

26 – Mark Messier, Edmonton, NY Rangers, Vancouver. 8G-18A
24 – Sergei Fedorov, Detroit, Anaheim. 13G-11A
23 – Steve Thomas, Toronto, Chicago, NY Islanders, New Jersey, Chicago,
Anaheim. 13G-10A
22 – Mario Lemieux, Pittsburgh. 11G-11A
– Adam Oates, Detroit, St. Louis, Boston, Washington, Philadelphia,
Anaheim. 5G-17A
– Pierre Turgeon, Buffalo, NY Islanders, Montreal, St. Louis, Dallas.
11G-11A

*Toronto's Mats Sundin tied Bill Guerin and Jarome Iginla for the NHL lead
with 10 game-winning goals in 2003-04. His overtime winner against the
Rangers on December 26, 2003 gave him a share of the record for most
career regular-season overtime goals.*

SCORING BY A CENTER

MOST GOALS BY A CENTER, CAREER

894 – Wayne Gretzky, Edmonton, Los Angeles, St. Louis, NY Rangers, in 20 seasons. 1,487GP

731 – Marcel Dionne, Detroit, Los Angeles, NY Rangers, in 18 seasons. 1,348GP

717 – Phil Esposito, Chicago, Boston, NY Rangers, in 18 seasons. 1,282GP

694 – Mark Messier, Edmonton, NY Rangers, Vancouver, in 25 seasons. 1,756GP

683 – Mario Lemieux, Pittsburgh, in 16 seasons. 889GP

MOST GOALS BY A CENTER, ONE SEASON

92 – Wayne Gretzky, Edmonton, 1981-82. 80GP – 80 game schedule.

87 – Wayne Gretzky, Edmonton, 1983-84. 74GP – 80 game schedule.

85 – Mario Lemieux, Pittsburgh, 1988-89. 76GP – 80 game schedule.

76 – Phil Esposito, Boston, 1970-71. 78GP – 78 game schedule.

73 – Wayne Gretzky, Edmonton, 1984-85. 80GP – 80 game schedule.

MOST ASSISTS BY A CENTER, CAREER:

1,963 – Wayne Gretzky, Edmonton, Los Angeles, St. Louis, NY Rangers, in 20 seasons. 1,487GP

1,249 – Ron Francis, Hartford, Pittsburgh, Carolina, Toronto, in 23 seasons. 1,731GP

1,193 – Mark Messier, Edmonton, NY Rangers, Vancouver, in 25 seasons. 1,756GP

1,079 – Adam Oates, Detroit, St. Louis, Boston, Washington, Philadelphia, Anaheim, Edmonton, in 19 seasons. 1,337GP

1,043 – Steve Yzerman, Detroit, in 21 seasons. 1,453GP

MOST ASSISTS BY A CENTER, ONE SEASON:

163 – Wayne Gretzky, Edmonton, 1985-86. 80GP – 80 game schedule.

135 – Wayne Gretzky, Edmonton, 1984-85. 80GP – 80 game schedule.

125 – Wayne Gretzky, Edmonton, 1982-83. 80GP – 80 game schedule.

122 – Wayne Gretzky, Los Angeles, 1990-91. 78GP – 80 game schedule.

121 – Wayne Gretzky, Edmonton, 1986-87. 79GP – 80 game schedule.

MOST POINTS BY A CENTER, CAREER:

2,857 – Wayne Gretzky, Edmonton, Los Angeles, St. Louis, NY Rangers, in 20 seasons. 1,487GP (894G–1,963A)

1,887 – Mark Messier, Edmonton, NY Rangers, Vancouver, in 25 seasons. 1,756GP (694G–1,193A)

1,798 – Ron Francis, Hartford, Pittsburgh, Carolina, Toronto, in 23 seasons. 1,731GP (549G–1,249A)

1,771 – Marcel Dionne, Detroit, Los Angeles, NY Rangers, in 18 seasons. 1,348GP (731G–1,040A)

1,721 – Steve Yzerman, Detroit, in 21 seasons. 1,453GP (678G–1,043A)

MOST POINTS BY A CENTER, ONE SEASON:

215 – Wayne Gretzky, Edmonton, 1985-86. 80GP – 80 game schedule.

212 – Wayne Gretzky, Edmonton, 1981-82. 80GP – 80 game schedule.

208 – Wayne Gretzky, Edmonton, 1984-85. 80GP – 80 game schedule.

205 – Wayne Gretzky, Edmonton, 1983-84. 74GP – 80 game schedule.

199 – Mario Lemieux, Pittsburgh, 1988-89. 76GP – 80 game schedule.

SCORING BY A LEFT WING

MOST GOALS BY A LEFT WING, CAREER:

653 – Luc Robitaille, Los Angeles, Pittsburgh, NY Rangers, Detroit, in 18 seasons. 1,366GP

634 – Dave Andreychuk, Buffalo, Toronto, New Jersey, Boston, Colorado, Tampa Bay, in 22 seasons. 1,597GP

610 – Bobby Hull, Chicago, Winnipeg, Hartford, in 16 seasons. 1,063GP

558 – Brendan Shanahan, New Jersey, St. Louis, Hartford, Detroit, in 17 seasons. 1,268GP

556 – John Bucyk, Detroit, Boston, in 23 seasons. 1,540GP

Though his record for points by a left winger was surpassed by Luc Robitaille in 2003-04, John Bucyk still has a healthy lead on the competition when it comes to career assists.

MOST GOALS BY A LEFT WING, ONE SEASON:

63 – Luc Robitaille, Los Angeles, 1992-93. 84GP – 84 game schedule.

60 – Steve Shutt, Montreal, 1976-77. 80GP – 80 game schedule.

58 – Bobby Hull, Chicago, 1968-69. 74GP – 76 game schedule.

57 – Michel Goulet, Quebec, 1982-83. 80GP – 80 game schedule.

56 – Charlie Simmer, Los Angeles, 1979-80. 64GP – 80 game schedule.
– Charlie Simmer, Los Angeles, 1980-81. 65GP – 80 game schedule.
– Michel Goulet, Quebec, 1983-84. 75GP – 80 game schedule.

MOST ASSISTS BY A LEFT WING, CAREER:

813 – John Bucyk, Detroit, Boston, in 23 seasons. 1,540GP

717 – Luc Robitaille, Los Angeles, Pittsburgh, NY Rangers, Detroit, in 18 seasons. 1,366GP

706 – Dave Andreychuk, Buffalo, Toronto, New Jersey, Boston, Colorado, Tampa Bay, in 22 seasons. 1,597GP

604 – Michel Goulet, Quebec, Chicago, in 15 seasons. 1,089GP

598 – Brendan Shanahan, New Jersey, St. Louis, Hartford, Detroit, in 17 seasons. 1,268GP

MOST ASSISTS BY A LEFT WING, ONE SEASON:

70 – Joe Juneau, Boston, 1992-93. 84GP – 84 game schedule.

69 – Kevin Stevens, Pittsburgh, 1991-92. 80GP – 80 game schedule.

67 – Mats Naslund, Montreal, 1985-86. 80GP – 80 game schedule.

65 – John Bucyk, Boston, 1970-71. 78GP – 78 game schedule.
– Michel Goulet, Quebec, 1983-84. 75GP – 80 game schedule.

64 – Mark Messier, Edmonton, 1983-84. 73GP – 80 game schedule.

MOST POINTS BY A LEFT WING, CAREER:

1,370 – Luc Robitaille, Los Angeles, Pittsburgh, NY Rangers, Detroit, in 18 seasons. 1,366GP (653G–717A)

1,369 – John Bucyk, Detroit, Boston, in 23 seasons. 1,540GP (556G–813A)

1,320 – Dave Andreychuk, Buffalo, Toronto, New Jersey, Boston, Colorado, Tampa Bay, in 22 seasons. 1,597GP (634G–686A)

1,170 – Bobby Hull, Chicago, Winnipeg, Hartford, in 16 seasons. 1,063GP (610G–560A)

1,152 – Michel Goulet, Quebec, Chicago, in 15 seasons. 1,089GP (548G–604A)

MOST POINTS BY A LEFT WING, ONE SEASON:

125 – Luc Robitaille, Los Angeles, 1992-93. 84GP – 84 game schedule.

123 – Kevin Stevens, Pittsburgh, 1991-92. 80GP – 80 game schedule.

121 – Michel Goulet, Quebec, 1983-84. 75GP – 80 game schedule.

116 – John Bucyk, Boston, 1970-71. 78GP – 78 game schedule.

112 – Bill Barber, Philadelphia, 1975-76. 80GP – 80 game schedule.

SCORING BY A RIGHT WING

MOST GOALS BY A RIGHT WING, CAREER:

801 – Gordie Howe, Detroit, Hartford, in 26 seasons. 1,767GP

741 – Brett Hull, Calgary, St. Louis, Dallas, Detroit, in 18 seasons. 1,264GP

708 – Mike Gartner, Washington, Minnesota, NY Rangers, Toronto, Phoenix, in 19 seasons. 1,432GP

608 – Dino Ciccarelli, Minnesota, Washington, Detroit, Tampa Bay, Florida, in 19 seasons. 1,232GP

601 – Jari Kurri, Edmonton, Los Angeles, NY Rangers, Anaheim, Colorado, in 17 seasons. 1,251GP

MOST GOALS BY A RIGHT WING, ONE SEASON:

86 – Brett Hull, St. Louis, 1990-91. 78GP – 80 game schedule.

76 – Alexander Mogilny, Buffalo, 1992-93. 77GP – 84 game schedule.
– Teemu Selanne, Winnipeg, 1992-93. 84GP – 84 game schedule.

72 – Brett Hull, St. Louis, 1989-90. 80GP – 80 game schedule.

71 – Jari Kurri, Edmonton, 1984-85. 73GP – 80 game schedule.

70 – Brett Hull, St. Louis, 1991-92. 73GP – 80 game schedule.

MOST ASSISTS BY A RIGHT WING, CAREER:

1,049 – Gordie Howe, Detroit, Hartford, in 26 seasons. 1,767GP

797 – Jari Kurri, Edmonton, Los Angeles, NY Rangers, Anaheim, Colorado, in 17 seasons. 1,251GP

793 – Guy Lafleur, Montreal, NY Rangers, Quebec, in 17 seasons. 1,126GP

772 – Jaromir Jagr, Pittsburgh, Washington, NY Rangers, in 14 seasons. 1,027GP

745 – Mark Recchi, Pittsburgh, Philadelphia, Montreal, in 16 seasons. 1,173GP

MOST ASSISTS BY A RIGHT WING, ONE SEASON:

87 – Jaromir Jagr, Pittsburgh, 1995-96. 82GP – 82 game schedule.

83 – Mike Bossy, NY Islanders, 1981-82. 80GP – 80 game schedule.
– Jaromir Jagr, Pittsburgh, 1998-99. 81GP – 82 game schedule.

80 – Guy Lafleur, Montreal, 1976-77. 80GP – 80 game schedule.

77 – Guy Lafleur, Montreal, 1978-79. 80GP – 80 game schedule.

MOST POINTS BY A RIGHT WING, CAREER:
  1,850 – Gordie Howe, Detroit, Hartford, in 26 seasons. 1,767GP (801G-1,049A)
  1,398 – Jari Kurri, Edmonton, Los Angeles, NY Rangers, Anaheim, Colorado, in 17 seasons. 1,251GP (601G-797A)
  1,390 – Brett Hull, Calgary, St. Louis, Dallas, Detroit, in 18 seasons. 1,264GP (741G-649A)
  1,353 – Guy Lafleur, Montreal, NY Rangers, Quebec, in 17 seasons. 1,126GP (560G-793A)
  1,335 – Mike Gartner, Washington, Minnesota, NY Rangers, Toronto, Phoenix, in 19 seasons. 1,432GP (708G-627A)

MOST POINTS BY A RIGHT WING, ONE SEASON:
  149 – Jaromir Jagr, Pittsburgh, 1995-96. 82GP – 82 game schedule.
  147 – Mike Bossy, NY Islanders, 1981-82. 80GP – 80 game schedule.
  136 – Guy Lafleur, Montreal, 1976-77. 80GP – 80 game schedule.
  135 – Jari Kurri, Edmonton, 1984-85. 73GP – 80 game schedule.
  132 – Guy Lafleur, Montreal, 1977-78. 78GP – 80 game schedule.
     – Teemu Selanne, Winnipeg, 1992-93. 84GP – 84 game schedule.

SCORING BY A DEFENSEMAN

MOST GOALS BY A DEFENSEMAN, CAREER:
  410 – Raymond Bourque, Boston, Colorado, in 22 seasons. 1,612GP
  396 – Paul Coffey, Edmonton, Pittsburgh, Los Angeles, Detroit, Hartford, Philadelphia, Chicago, Carolina, Boston, in 21 seasons. 1,409GP
  340 – Al MacInnis, Calgary, St. Louis, in 23 seasons. 1,416GP
  338 – Phil Housley, Buffalo, Winnipeg, St. Louis, Calgary, New Jersey, Washington, Chicago, Toronto, in 21 seasons. 1,495GP
  310 – Denis Potvin, NY Islanders, in 15 seasons. 1,060GP

MOST GOALS BY A DEFENSEMAN, ONE SEASON:
  48 – Paul Coffey, Edmonton, 1985-86. 79GP – 80 game schedule.
  46 – Bobby Orr, Boston, 1974-75. 80GP – 80 game schedule.
  40 – Paul Coffey, Edmonton, 1983-84. 80GP – 80 game schedule.
  39 – Doug Wilson, Chicago, 1981-82. 76GP – 80 game schedule.
  37 – Bobby Orr, Boston, 1970-71. 78GP – 78 game schedule.
     – Bobby Orr, Boston, 1971-72. 76GP – 78 game schedule.
     – Paul Coffey, Edmonton, 1984-85. 80GP – 80 game schedule.

MOST GOALS BY A DEFENSEMAN, ONE GAME:
  5 – Ian Turnbull, Toronto, Feb. 2, 1977, at Toronto. Toronto 9, Detroit 1.
  4 – Harry Cameron, Toronto, Dec. 26, 1917, at Toronto. Toronto 7, Montreal 5.
    – Harry Cameron, Montreal, Mar. 3, 1920, at Quebec. Montreal 16, Quebec 3.
    – Sprague Cleghorn, Montreal, Jan. 14, 1922, at Montreal. Montreal 10, Hamilton 6.
    – John McKinnon, Pittsburgh, Nov. 19, 1929, at Pittsburgh. Pittsburgh 10, Toronto 5.
    – Hap Day, Toronto, Nov. 19, 1929, at Pittsburgh. Pittsburgh 10, Toronto 5.
    – Tom Bladon, Philadelphia, Dec. 11, 1977, at Philadelphia. Philadelphia 11, Cleveland 1.
    – Ian Turnbull, Los Angeles, Dec. 12, 1981, at Los Angeles. Los Angeles 7, Vancouver 5.
    – Paul Coffey, Edmonton, Oct. 26, 1984, at Calgary. Edmonton 6, Calgary 5.

MOST ASSISTS BY A DEFENSEMAN, CAREER:
  1,169 – Raymond Bourque, Boston, Colorado, in 22 seasons. 1,612GP
  1,135 – Paul Coffey, Edmonton, Pittsburgh, Los Angeles, Detroit, Hartford, Philadelphia, Chicago, Carolina, Boston, in 21 seasons. 1,409GP
  934 – Al MacInnis, Calgary, St. Louis, in 23 seasons. 1,416GP
  929 – Larry Murphy, Los Angeles, Washington, Minnesota, Pittsburgh, Toronto, Detroit, in 21 seasons. 1,615GP
  894 – Phil Housley, Buffalo, Winnipeg, St. Louis, Calgary, New Jersey, Washington, Chicago, Toronto, in 21 seasons. 1,495GP

MOST ASSISTS BY A DEFENSEMAN, ONE SEASON:
  102 – Bobby Orr, Boston, 1970-71. 78GP – 78 game schedule.
  90 – Bobby Orr, Boston, 1973-74. 74GP – 78 game schedule.
    – Paul Coffey, Edmonton, 1985-86. 79GP – 80 game schedule.
  89 – Bobby Orr, Boston, 1974-75. 80GP – 80 game schedule.
  87 – Bobby Orr, Boston, 1969-70. 76GP – 78 game schedule.

MOST ASSISTS BY A DEFENSEMAN, ONE GAME:
  6 – Babe Pratt, Toronto, Jan. 8, 1944, at Toronto. Toronto 12, Boston 3.
    – Pat Stapleton, Chicago, Mar. 30, 1969, at Chicago. Chicago 9, Detroit 5.
    – Bobby Orr, Boston, Jan. 1, 1973, at Vancouver. Boston 8, Vancouver 2.
    – Ron Stackhouse, Pittsburgh, Mar. 8, 1975, at Pittsburgh. Pittsburgh 8, Philadelphia 2.
    – Paul Coffey, Edmonton, Mar. 14, 1986, at Edmonton. Edmonton 12, Detroit 3.
    – Gary Suter, Calgary, Apr. 4, 1986, at Calgary. Calgary 9, Edmonton 3.

MOST POINTS BY A DEFENSEMAN, CAREER:
  1,579 – Raymond Bourque, Boston, Colorado, in 22 seasons. 1,612GP (410G-1,169A)
  1,531 – Paul Coffey, Edmonton, Pittsburgh, Los Angeles, Detroit, Hartford, Philadelphia, Chicago, Carolina, Boston, in 21 seasons. 1,409GP (396G-1,135A)
  1,274 – Al MacInnis, Calgary, St. Louis, in 23 seasons. 1,416GP (340G-934A)
  1,232 – Phil Housley, Buffalo, Winnipeg, New Jersey, St. Louis, Calgary, Washington, Chicago, Toronto, in 21 seasons. 1,495GP (338G-894A)
  1,216 – Larry Murphy, Los Angeles, Washington, Minnesota, Pittsburgh, Toronto, Detroit, in 21 seasons. 1,615GP (287G-929A)

MOST POINTS BY A DEFENSEMAN, ONE SEASON:
  139 – Bobby Orr, Boston, 1970-71. 78GP – 78 game schedule.
  138 – Paul Coffey, Edmonton, 1985-86. 79GP – 80 game schedule.
  135 – Bobby Orr, Boston, 1974-75. 80GP – 80 game schedule.
  126 – Paul Coffey, Edmonton, 1983-84. 80GP – 80 game schedule.
  122 – Bobby Orr, Boston, 1973-74. 74GP – 78 game schedule.

MOST POINTS BY A DEFENSEMAN, ONE GAME:
  8 – Tom Bladon, Philadelphia, Dec. 11, 1977, at Philadelphia. Philadelphia 11, Cleveland 1. 4G-4A.
    – Paul Coffey, Edmonton, Mar. 14, 1986, at Edmonton. Edmonton 12, Detroit 3. 2G-6A.
  7 – Bobby Orr, Boston, Nov. 15, 1973, at Boston. Boston 10, NY Rangers 2. 3G-4A.

SCORING BY A GOALTENDER

MOST POINTS BY A GOALTENDER, CAREER:
  48 – Tom Barrasso, Buffalo, Pittsburgh, Ottawa, Carolina, Toronto, St. Louis, in 19 seasons. 777GP
  46 – Grant Fuhr, Edmonton, Toronto, Buffalo, Los Angeles, St. Louis, Calgary, in 19 seasons. 868GP

MOST POINTS BY A GOALTENDER, ONE SEASON:
  14 – Grant Fuhr, Edmonton, 1983-84. 45GP – 80 game schedule.
  9 – Curtis Joseph, St. Louis, 1991-92. 60GP – 80 game schedule.
  8 – Mike Palmateer, Washington, 1980-81. 49GP – 80 game schedule.
    – Grant Fuhr, Edmonton, 1987-88. 75GP – 80 game schedule.
    – Ron Hextall, Philadelphia, 1988-89. 64GP – 80 game schedule.
    – Tom Barrasso, Pittsburgh, 1992-93. 63GP – 84 game schedule.

MOST POINTS BY A GOALTENDER, ONE GAME:
  3 – Jeff Reese, Calgary, Feb. 10, 1993, at Calgary. Calgary 13, San Jose 1.

Defenseman Ian Turnbull had been shutout for 30 straight games before exploding for a record five goals on five shots against Detroit on February 2, 1977. Turnbull's 22 goals that season share the record for most scored by a Leafs defenseman.

SCORING BY A ROOKIE

MOST GOALS BY A ROOKIE, ONE SEASON:
76 – **Teemu Selanne**, Winnipeg, 1992-93. 84GP – 84 game schedule.
53 – Mike Bossy, NY Islanders, 1977-78. 73GP – 80 game schedule.
51 – Joe Nieuwendyk, Calgary, 1987-88. 75GP – 80 game schedule.
45 – Dale Hawerchuk, Winnipeg, 1981-82. 80GP – 80 game schedule.
    – Luc Robitaille, Los Angeles, 1986-87. 79GP – 80 game schedule.

MOST GOALS BY A PLAYER IN HIS FIRST NHL SEASON, ONE GAME:
5 – **Howie Meeker**, Toronto, Jan. 8, 1947, at Toronto. Toronto 10, Chicago 4.
    – **Don Murdoch**, NY Rangers, Oct. 12, 1976, at Minnesota.
    NY Rangers 10, Minnesota 4.

MOST GOALS BY A PLAYER IN HIS FIRST NHL GAME:
3 – **Alex Smart**, Montreal, Jan. 14, 1943, at Montreal. Montreal 5, Chicago 1.
    – **Real Cloutier**, Quebec, Oct. 10, 1979, at Quebec. Atlanta 5, Quebec 3.

MOST ASSISTS BY A ROOKIE, ONE SEASON:
70 – **Peter Stastny**, Quebec, 1980-81. 77GP – 80 game schedule.
    – **Joe Juneau**, Boston, 1992-93. 84GP – 84 game schedule.
63 – Bryan Trottier, NY Islanders, 1975-76. 80GP – 80 game schedule.
62 – Sergei Makarov, Calgary, 1989-90. 80GP – 80 game schedule.
60 – Larry Murphy, Los Angeles, 1980-81. 80GP – 80 game schedule.

MOST ASSISTS BY A PLAYER IN HIS FIRST NHL SEASON, ONE GAME:
7 – **Wayne Gretzky**, Edmonton, Feb. 15, 1980, at Edmonton.
    Edmonton 8, Washington 2.
6 – Gary Suter, Calgary, Apr. 4, 1986, at Calgary. Calgary 9, Edmonton 3.

MOST ASSISTS BY A PLAYER IN HIS FIRST NHL GAME:
4 – **Dutch Reibel**, Detroit, Oct. 8, 1953, at Detroit. Detroit 4, NY Rangers 1.
    – **Roland Eriksson**, Minnesota, Oct. 6, 1976, at NY Rangers.
    NY Rangers 6, Minnesota 5.
3 – Al Hill, Philadelphia, Feb. 14, 1977, at Philadelphia. Philadelphia 6,
    St. Louis 4.
    – Jarno Kultanen, Boston, Oct. 5, 2000, at Boston. Boston 4, Ottawa 4.
    – Stanislav Chistov, Anaheim, Oct. 10, 2002, at St. Louis. Anaheim 4,
    St. Louis 3.
    – Dominic Moore, NY Rangers, Nov. 1, 2003, at Montreal. NY Rangers 5,
    Montreal 1.

MOST POINTS BY A ROOKIE, ONE SEASON:
132 – **Teemu Selanne**, Winnipeg, 1992-93. 84GP – 84 game schedule.
109 – Peter Stastny, Quebec, 1980-81. 77GP – 80 game schedule.
103 – Dale Hawerchuk, Winnipeg, 1981-82. 80GP – 80 game schedule.
102 – Joe Juneau, Boston, 1992-93. 84GP – 84 game schedule.
100 – Mario Lemieux, Pittsburgh, 1984-85. 73GP – 80 game schedule.

MOST POINTS BY A PLAYER IN HIS FIRST NHL SEASON, ONE GAME:
8 – **Peter Stastny**, Quebec, Feb. 22, 1981, at Washington. 4G-4A.
    Quebec 11, Washington 7.
    – **Anton Stastny**, Quebec, Feb. 22, 1981, at Washington. 3G-5A.
    Quebec 11, Washington 7.
7 – Wayne Gretzky, Edmonton, Feb. 15, 1980, at Edmonton. 7A.
    Edmonton 8, Washington 2.
    – Sergei Makarov, Calgary, Feb. 25, 1990, at Calgary. 2G-5A.
    Calgary 10, Edmonton 4.
6 – Wayne Gretzky, Edmonton, Mar. 29, 1980, at Toronto. 2G-4A.
    Edmonton 8, Toronto 5.
    – Gary Suter, Calgary, Apr. 4, 1986, at Calgary. 6A.
    Calgary 9, Edmonton 3.

MOST POINTS BY A PLAYER IN HIS FIRST NHL GAME:
5 – **Al Hill**, Philadelphia, Feb. 14, 1977, at Philadelphia. 2G-3A.
    Philadelphia 6, St. Louis 4.
4 – Alex Smart, Montreal, Jan. 14, 1943, at Montreal. 3G-1A.
    Montreal 5, Chicago 1.
    – Dutch Reibel, Detroit, Oct. 8, 1953, at Detroit. 4A.
    Detroit 4, NY Rangers 1.
    – Roland Eriksson, Minnesota, Oct. 6, 1976, at NY Rangers. 4A.
    NY Rangers 6, Minnesota 5.
    – Stanislav Chistov, Anaheim, Oct. 10, 2002, at St. Louis. 1G-3A.
    Anaheim 4, St. Louis 3.

SCORING BY A ROOKIE DEFENSEMAN

MOST GOALS BY A ROOKIE DEFENSEMAN, ONE SEASON:
23 – **Brian Leetch**, NY Rangers, 1988-89. 68GP – 80 game schedule.
22 – Barry Beck, Colorado, 1977-78. 75GP – 80 game schedule.
19 – Reed Larson, Detroit, 1977-78. 75GP – 80 game schedule.
    – Phil Housley, Buffalo, 1982-83. 77GP – 80 game schedule.

MOST ASSISTS BY A ROOKIE DEFENSEMAN, ONE SEASON:
60 – **Larry Murphy**, Los Angeles, 1980-81. 80GP – 80 game schedule.
55 – Chris Chelios, Montreal, 1984-85. 74GP – 80 game schedule.
50 – Stefan Persson, NY Islanders, 1977-78. 66GP – 80 game schedule.
    – Gary Suter, Calgary, 1985-86. 80GP – 80 game schedule.
49 – Nicklas Lidstrom, Detroit, 1991-92. 80GP – 80 game schedule.

MOST POINTS BY A ROOKIE DEFENSEMAN, ONE SEASON:
76 – **Larry Murphy**, Los Angeles, 1980-81. 80GP – 80 game schedule.
71 – Brian Leetch, NY Rangers, 1988-89. 68GP – 80 game schedule.
68 – Gary Suter, Calgary, 1985-86. 80GP – 80 game schedule.
66 – Phil Housley, Buffalo, 1982-83. 77GP – 80 game schedule.
65 – Raymond Bourque, Boston, 1979-80. 80GP – 80 game schedule.

Before Barry Beck scored 22 goals as a rookie in 1977-78, the only defensemen to have scored that many times in a single season were Bobby Orr, Denis Potvin, Guy Lapointe, Brad Park, Ian Turnbull and Dick Redmond.

PER-GAME SCORING AVERAGES

HIGHEST GOALS-PER-GAME AVERAGE, CAREER
(AMONG PLAYERS WITH 200-OR-MORE GOALS):
.768 – Mario Lemieux, Pittsburgh, 1984-85 – 1996-97,
2000-01 – 2003-04, with 683G in 889GP.
.762 – Mike Bossy, NY Islanders, 1977-78 – 1986-87, with 573G in 752GP.
.756 – Cy Denneny, Ottawa, Boston, 1917-18 – 1928-29, with 248G in 328GP.
.742 – Babe Dye, Toronto, Hamilton, Chicago, NY Americans,
1919-20 – 1930-31, with 201G in 271GP.
.623 – Pavel Bure, Vancouver, Florida, NY Rangers, 1991-92 – 2002-03,
with 437G in 702GP.

HIGHEST GOALS-PER-GAME AVERAGE, ONE SEASON
(AMONG PLAYERS WITH 20-OR-MORE GOALS):
2.20 – Joe Malone, Montreal, 1917-18, with 44G in 20GP.
1.80 – Cy Denneny, Ottawa, 1917-18, with 36G in 20GP.
1.64 – Newsy Lalonde, Montreal, 1917-18, with 23G in 14GP.
1.63 – Joe Malone, Quebec, 1919-20, with 39G in 24GP.
1.61 – Newsy Lalonde, Montreal, 1919-20, with 37G in 23GP.

HIGHEST GOALS-PER-GAME AVERAGE, ONE SEASON
(AMONG PLAYERS WITH 50-OR-MORE GOALS):
1.18 – Wayne Gretzky, Edmonton, 1983-84, with 87G in 74GP.
1.15 – Wayne Gretzky, Edmonton, 1981-82, with 92G in 80GP.
– Mario Lemieux, Pittsburgh, 1992-93, with 69G in 60GP.
1.12 – Mario Lemieux, Pittsburgh, 1988-89, with 85G in 76GP.
1.10 – Brett Hull, St. Louis, 1990-91, with 86G in 78GP.
1.02 – Cam Neely, Boston, 1993-94, with 50G in 49GP.
1.00 – Maurice Richard, Montreal, 1944-45, with 50G in 50GP.

HIGHEST ASSISTS-PER-GAME AVERAGE, CAREER
(AMONG PLAYERS WITH 300-OR-MORE ASSISTS):
1.320 – Wayne Gretzky, Edmonton, Los Angeles, St. Louis, NY Rangers,
1979-80 – 1998-99, with 1,963A in 1,487GP.
1.145 – Mario Lemieux, Pittsburgh, 1984-85 – 1996-97,
2000-01 – 2003-04, with 1,018A in 889GP.
.982 – Bobby Orr, Boston, Chicago, 1966-67 – 1978-79, with 645A in 657GP.
.905 – Peter Forsberg, Quebec, Colorado, 1994-95 – 2000-01, 2002-03 –
2003-04 with 525A in 580GP.
.808 – Peter Stastny, Quebec, New Jersey, St. Louis, 1980-81 – 1994-95, with
789A in 977GP.

HIGHEST ASSISTS-PER-GAME AVERAGE, ONE SEASON
(AMONG PLAYERS WITH 35-OR-MORE ASSISTS):
2.04 – Wayne Gretzky, Edmonton, 1985-86, with 163A in 80GP.
1.70 – Wayne Gretzky, Edmonton, 1987-88, with 109A in 64GP.
1.69 – Wayne Gretzky, Edmonton, 1984-85, with 135A in 80GP.
1.59 – Wayne Gretzky, Edmonton, 1983-84, with 118A in 74GP.
1.56 – Wayne Gretzky, Edmonton, 1982-83, with 125A in 80GP.
– Wayne Gretzky, Los Angeles, 1990-91, with 122A in 78GP.
1.53 – Wayne Gretzky, Edmonton, 1986-87, with 121A in 79GP.
1.52 – Mario Lemieux, Pittsburgh, 1992-93, with 91A in 60GP.
1.50 – Wayne Gretzky, Edmonton, 1981-82, with 120A in 80GP.
– Mario Lemieux, Pittsburgh, 1988-89, with 114A in 76GP.

HIGHEST POINTS-PER-GAME AVERAGE, CAREER:
(AMONG PLAYERS WITH 500-OR-MORE POINTS):
1.921 – Wayne Gretzky, Edmonton, Los Angeles, St. Louis, NY Rangers,
1979-80 – 1998-99, with 2,857PTS (894G-1,963A) in 1,487GP.
1.913 – Mario Lemieux, Pittsburgh, 1984-85 – 1996-97,
2000-01 – 2003-04, with 1,701PTS (683G-1,018A) in 889GP.
1.497 – Mike Bossy, NY Islanders, 1977-78 – 1986-87, with 1,126PTS (573G-553A)
in 752GP.
1.393 – Bobby Orr, Boston, Chicago, 1966-67 – 1978-79, with 915PTS
(270G-645A) in 657GP.
1.314 – Marcel Dionne, Detroit, Los Angeles, NY Rangers, 1971-72 – 1988-89, with
1,771PTS (731G-1,040A) in 1,348GP.

HIGHEST POINTS-PER-GAME AVERAGE, ONE SEASON
(AMONG PLAYERS WITH 50-OR-MORE POINTS):
2.77 – Wayne Gretzky, Edmonton, 1983-84, with 205PTS in 74GP.
2.69 – Wayne Gretzky, Edmonton, 1985-86, with 215PTS in 80GP.
2.67 – Mario Lemieux, Pittsburgh, 1992-93, with 160PTS in 60GP.
2.65 – Wayne Gretzky, Edmonton, 1981-82, with 212PTS in 80GP.
2.62 – Mario Lemieux, Pittsburgh, 1988-89, with 199PTS in 76GP.
2.60 – Wayne Gretzky, Edmonton, 1984-85, with 208PTS in 80GP.
2.45 – Wayne Gretzky, Edmonton, 1982-83, with 196PTS in 80GP.
2.33 – Wayne Gretzky, Edmonton, 1987-88, with 149PTS in 64GP.
2.32 – Wayne Gretzky, Edmonton, 1986-87, with 183PTS in 79GP.
2.30 – Mario Lemieux, Pittsburgh, 1995-96, with 161PTS in 70GP.
2.18 – Mario Lemieux, Pittsburgh, 1987-88, with 168PTS in 77GP.
2.15 – Wayne Gretzky, Los Angeles, 1988-89, with 168PTS in 78GP.
2.09 – Wayne Gretzky, Los Angeles, 1990-91, with 163PTS in 78GP.
2.08 – Mario Lemieux, Pittsburgh, 1989-90, with 123PTS in 59GP.

SCORING PLATEAUS

MOST 20-OR-MORE GOAL SEASONS:
22 – Gordie Howe, Detroit, Hartford, in 26 seasons.
20 – Ron Francis, Hartford, Pittsburgh, Carolina, Toronto, in 23 seasons.
19 – Dave Andreychuk, Buffalo, Toronto, New Jersey, Boston, Colorado,
Tampa Bay, in 22 seasons.
17 – Marcel Dionne, Detroit, Los Angeles, NY Rangers, in 18 seasons.
– Mike Gartner, Washington, Minnesota, NY Rangers, Toronto,
Phoenix, in 19 seasons.
– Wayne Gretzky, Edmonton, Los Angeles, St. Louis, NY Rangers,
in 20 seasons.
– Mark Messier, Edmonton, NY Rangers, Vancouver, in 25 seasons.
– Brett Hull, Calgary, St. Louis, Dallas, Detroit, in 18 seasons.

MOST CONSECUTIVE 20-OR-MORE GOAL SEASONS:
22 – Gordie Howe, Detroit, 1949-50 – 1970-71.
17 – Marcel Dionne, Detroit, Los Angeles, NY Rangers, 1971-72 – 1987-88.
– Brett Hull, Calgary, St. Louis, Dallas, Detroit, 1987-88 – 2003-04.
16 – Phil Esposito, Chicago, Boston, NY Rangers, 1964-65 – 1979-80.
– Brendan Shanahan, New Jersey, St. Louis, Hartford, Detroit,
1988-89 – 2003-04.
15 – Mike Gartner, Washington, Minnesota, NY Rangers, Toronto,
1979-80 – 1993-94.

*With 25 goals for Detroit last season, Brett Hull has now
scored at least 20 goals for 17 consecutive seasons.
His 741 career goals place him third among
the all-time leaders behind Wayne Gretzky
and Gordie Howe.*

MOST 30-OR-MORE GOAL SEASONS:

17 – Mike Gartner, Washington, Minnesota, NY Rangers, Toronto, Phoenix, in 19 seasons.
14 – Gordie Howe, Detroit, Hartford, in 26 seasons.
 – Marcel Dionne, Detroit, Los Angeles, NY Rangers, in 18 seasons.
 – Wayne Gretzky, Edmonton, Los Angeles, St. Louis, NY Rangers, in 20 seasons.
13 – Bobby Hull, Chicago, Winnipeg, Hartford, in 16 seasons.
 – Phil Esposito, Chicago, Boston, NY Rangers, in 18 seasons.
 – Jaromir Jagr, Pittsburgh, Washington, NY Rangers, in 14 seasons.
 – Brett Hull, Calgary, St. Louis, Dallas, Detroit, in 18 seasons.

MOST CONSECUTIVE 30-OR-MORE GOAL SEASONS:

15 – Mike Gartner, Washington, Minnesota, NY Rangers, Toronto, 1979-80 – 1993-94.
13 – Bobby Hull, Chicago, 1959-60 – 1971-72.
 – Phil Esposito, Boston, NY Rangers, 1967-68 – 1979-80.
 – Wayne Gretzky, Edmonton, Los Angeles, 1979-80 – 1991-92.
 – Jaromir Jagr, Pittsburgh, Washington, NY Rangers, 1991-92 – 2003-04.

MOST 40-OR-MORE GOAL SEASONS:

12 – Wayne Gretzky, Edmonton, Los Angeles, St. Louis, NY Rangers, in 20 seasons.
10 – Marcel Dionne, Detroit, Los Angeles, NY Rangers, in 18 seasons.
 – Mario Lemieux, Pittsburgh, in 15 seasons.
 9 – Mike Bossy, NY Islanders, in 10 seasons.
 – Mike Gartner, Washington, Minnesota, NY Rangers, Toronto, Phoenix, in 19 seasons.

MOST CONSECUTIVE 40-OR-MORE GOAL SEASONS:

12 – Wayne Gretzky, Edmonton, Los Angeles, 1979-80 – 1990-91.
 9 – Mike Bossy, NY Islanders, 1977-78 – 1985-86.
 8 – Luc Robitaille, Los Angeles, 1986-87 – 1993-94.
 7 – Phil Esposito, Boston, 1968-69 – 1974-75.
 – Michel Goulet, Quebec, 1981-82 – 1987-88.
 – Jari Kurri, Edmonton, 1982-83 – 1988-89.

MOST 50-OR-MORE GOAL SEASONS:

9 – Mike Bossy, NY Islanders, in 10 seasons.
 – **Wayne Gretzky**, Edmonton, Los Angeles, St. Louis, NY Rangers, in 20 seasons.
 6 – Guy Lafleur, Montreal, NY Rangers, Quebec, in 17 seasons.
 – Marcel Dionne, Detroit, Los Angeles, NY Rangers, in 18 seasons.
 – Mario Lemieux, Pittsburgh, in 15 seasons.
 5 – Bobby Hull, Chicago, Winnipeg, Hartford, in 16 seasons.
 – Phil Esposito, Chicago, Boston, NY Rangers, in 18 seasons.
 – Brett Hull, Calgary, St. Louis, Dallas, Detroit, in 17 seasons.
 – Steve Yzerman, Detroit, in 20 seasons.
 – Pavel Bure, Vancouver, Florida, NY Rangers, in 12 seasons.

MOST CONSECUTIVE 50-OR-MORE GOAL SEASONS:

9 – Mike Bossy, NY Islanders, 1977-78 – 1985-86.
 8 – Wayne Gretzky, Edmonton, 1979-80 – 1986-87.
 6 – Guy Lafleur, Montreal, 1974-75 – 1979-80.
 5 – Phil Esposito, Boston, 1970-71 – 1974-75.
 – Marcel Dionne, Los Angeles, 1978-79 – 1982-83.
 – Brett Hull, St. Louis, 1989-90 – 1993-94.

MOST 60-OR-MORE GOAL SEASONS:

5 – Mike Bossy, NY Islanders, in 10 seasons.
 – **Wayne Gretzky**, Edmonton, Los Angeles, St. Louis, NY Rangers, in 20 seasons.
 4 – Phil Esposito, Chicago, Boston, NY Rangers, in 18 seasons.
 – Mario Lemieux, Pittsburgh, in 15 seasons.

MOST CONSECUTIVE 60-OR-MORE GOAL SEASONS:

4 – Wayne Gretzky, Edmonton, 1981-82 – 1984-85.
 3 – Mike Bossy, NY Islanders, 1980-81 – 1982-83.
 – Brett Hull, St. Louis, 1989-90 – 1991-92.
 2 – Phil Esposito, Boston, 1970-71 – 1971-72, 1973-74 – 1974-75.
 – Jari Kurri, Edmonton, 1984-85 – 1985-86.
 – Mario Lemieux, Pittsburgh, 1987-88 – 1988-89.
 – Steve Yzerman, Detroit, 1988-89 – 1989-90.
 – Pavel Bure, Vancouver, 1992-93 – 1993-94.

MOST 100-OR-MORE POINT SEASONS:

15 – Wayne Gretzky, Edmonton, Los Angeles, St. Louis, NY Rangers, in 20 seasons.
10 – Mario Lemieux, Pittsburgh, in 15 seasons.
 8 – Marcel Dionne, Detroit, Los Angeles, NY Rangers, in 18 seasons.
 7 – Mike Bossy, NY Islanders, in 10 seasons.
 – Peter Stastny, Quebec, New Jersey, St. Louis, in 15 seasons.

MOST CONSECUTIVE 100-OR-MORE POINT SEASONS:

13 – Wayne Gretzky, Edmonton, Los Angeles, 1979-80 – 1991-92.
 6 – Bobby Orr, Boston, 1969-70 – 1974-75.
 – Guy Lafleur, Montreal, 1974-75 – 1979-80.
 – Mike Bossy, NY Islanders, 1980-81 – 1985-86.
 – Peter Stastny, Quebec, 1980-81 – 1985-86.
 – Mario Lemieux, Pittsburgh, 1984-85 – 1989-90.
 – Steve Yzerman, Detroit, 1987-88 – 1992-93.

Jaromir Jagr scored his 30th goal of the 2003-04 season with the Rangers on March 18, 2004. Jagr has now scored 30 or more goals in 13 consecutive NHL seasons.

THREE-OR-MORE-GOAL GAMES

MOST THREE-OR-MORE GOAL GAMES, CAREER:

50 – Wayne Gretzky, Edmonton, Los Angeles, St. Louis, NY Rangers, in 20 seasons, 37 three-goal games, 9 four-goal games, 4 five-goal games.
40 – Mario Lemieux, Pittsburgh, in 16 seasons, 27 three-goal games, 10 four-goal games, 3 five-goal games.
39 – Mike Bossy, NY Islanders, in 10 seasons, 30 three-goal games, 9 four-goal games.
33 – Brett Hull, Calgary, St. Louis, Dallas, Detroit, in 18 seasons, 30 three-goal games, 3 four-goal games.
32 – Phil Esposito, Chicago, Boston, NY Rangers, in 18 seasons, 27 three-goal games, 5 four-goal games.

MOST THREE-OR-MORE GOAL GAMES, ONE SEASON:

10 – Wayne Gretzky, Edmonton, 1981-82. 6 three-goal games, 3 four-goal games, 1 five-goal game.
 – **Wayne Gretzky**, Edmonton, 1983-84. 6 three-goal games, 4 four-goal games.
 9 – Mike Bossy, NY Islanders, 1980-81. 6 three-goal games, 3 four-goal games.
 – Mario Lemieux, Pittsburgh, 1988-89. 7 three-goal games, 1 four-goal game, 1 five-goal game.
 8 – Brett Hull, St. Louis, 1991-92. 8 three-goal games.
 7 – Joe Malone, Montreal, 1917-18. 2 three-goal games, 2 four-goal games, 3 five-goal games.
 – Phil Esposito, Boston, 1970-71. 7 three-goal games.
 – Rick Martin, Buffalo, 1975-76. 6 three-goal games, 1 four-goal game.
 – Alexander Mogilny, Buffalo, 1992-93. 5 three-goal games, 2 four-goal games.

SCORING STREAKS

LONGEST CONSECUTIVE GOAL-SCORING STREAK:
16 Games – Punch Broadbent, Ottawa, 1921-22. 27G
14 Games – Joe Malone, Montreal, 1917-18. 35G
13 Games – Newsy Lalonde, Montreal, 1920-21. 24G
– Charlie Simmer, Los Angeles, 1979-80. 17G
12 Games – Cy Denneny, Ottawa, 1917-18. 23G
– Dave Lumley, Edmonton, 1981-82. 15G
– Mario Lemieux, Pittsburgh, 1992-93. 18G

LONGEST CONSECUTIVE ASSIST-SCORING STREAK:
23 Games – Wayne Gretzky, Los Angeles, 1990-91. 48A
18 Games – Adam Oates, Boston, 1992-93. 28A
17 Games – Wayne Gretzky, Edmonton, 1983-84. 38A
– Paul Coffey, Edmonton, 1985-86. 27A
– Wayne Gretzky, Los Angeles, 1989-90. 35A
16 Games – Jaromir Jagr, Pittsburgh, 2000-01. 24A

LONGEST CONSECUTIVE POINT-SCORING STREAK:
51 Games – Wayne Gretzky, Edmonton, 1983-84. 61G-92A-153PTS
46 Games – Mario Lemieux, Pittsburgh, 1989-90. 39G-64A-103PTS
39 Games – Wayne Gretzky, Edmonton, 1985-86. 33G-75A-108PTS
30 Games – Wayne Gretzky, Edmonton, 1982-83. 24G-52A-76PTS
– Mats Sundin, Quebec, 1992-93. 21G-25A-46PTS

LONGEST CONSECUTIVE POINT-SCORING STREAK
FROM START OF SEASON:
51 Games – Wayne Gretzky, Edmonton, 1983-84. 61G-92A-153PTS. Streak ended by Los Angeles and goaltender Markus Mattsson on Jan. 28, 1984.

LONGEST CONSECUTIVE POINT-SCORING STREAK BY A DEFENSEMAN:
28 Games – Paul Coffey, Edmonton, 1985-86. 16G-39A-55PTS
19 Games – Raymond Bourque, Boston, 1987-88. 6G-21A-27PTS
17 Games – Raymond Bourque, Boston, 1984-85. 4G-24A-28PTS
– Brian Leetch, NY Rangers, 1991-92. 5G-24A-29PTS
16 Games – Gary Suter, Calgary, 1987-88. 8G-17A-25PTS
15 Games – Bobby Orr, Boston, 1970-71. 10G-23A-33PTS
– Bobby Orr, Boston, 1973-74. 8G-15A-23PTS
– Steve Duchesne, Quebec, 1992-93. 4G-17A-21PTS
– Chris Chelios, Chicago, 1995-96. 4G-16A-20PTS

FASTEST GOALS AND ASSISTS

FASTEST GOAL FROM START OF A GAME:
0:05 – Doug Smail, Winnipeg, Dec. 20, 1981, at Winnipeg. Winnipeg 5, St. Louis 4.
– **Bryan Trottier**, NY Islanders, Mar. 22, 1984, at Boston. NY Islanders 3, Boston 3.
– **Alexander Mogilny**, Buffalo, Dec. 21, 1991, at Toronto. Buffalo 4, Toronto 1.
0:06 – Henry Boucha, Detroit, Jan. 28, 1973, at Montreal. Detroit 4, Montreal 2.
– Jean Pronovost, Pittsburgh, Mar. 25, 1976, at St. Louis. St. Louis 5, Pittsburgh 2.
0:07 – Charlie Conacher, Toronto, Feb. 6, 1932, at Toronto. Toronto 6, Boston 0.
– Danny Gare, Buffalo, Dec. 17, 1978, at Buffalo. Buffalo 6, Vancouver 3.
– Tiger Williams, Los Angeles, Feb. 14, 1987, at Los Angeles. Los Angeles 5, Harford 2.
0:08 – Ron Martin, NY Americans, Dec. 4, 1932, at NY Americans. NY Americans 4, Montreal 2.
– Chuck Arnason, Colorado, Jan. 28, 1977, at Atlanta. Colorado 3, Atlanta 3.
– Wayne Gretzky, Edmonton, Dec. 14, 1983, at NY Rangers. Edmonton 9, NY Rangers 4.
– Gaetan Duchesne, Washington, Mar. 14, 1987, at St. Louis. Washington 3, St. Louis 3.
– Tim Kerr, Philadelphia, Mar. 7, 1989, at Philadelphia. Philadelphia 4, Edmonton 4.
– Grant Ledyard, Buffalo, Dec. 4, 1991, at Winnipeg. Buffalo 4, Winnipeg 4.
– Brent Sutter, Chicago, Feb. 5, 1995, at Vancouver. Chicago 9, Vancouver 4.
– Paul Kariya, Anaheim, Mar. 9, 1997, at Colorado. Anaheim 2, Colorado 2.
– Tony Hrkac, Dallas, Nov. 7, 1998, at Los Angeles. Dallas 4, Los Angeles 3.
– Sergei Fedorov, Detroit, Nov. 21, 1998, at Vancouver. Detroit 4, Vancouver 2.
– Ronald Petrovicky, Atlanta, Dec. 20, 2003, at Pittsburgh. Atlanta 7, Pittsburgh 4.
– Mike Modano, Dallas, Dec. 27, 2003, at Columbus. Dallas 4, Columbus 3.

FASTEST GOAL FROM START OF A PERIOD:
0:04 – Claude Provost, Montreal, Nov. 9, 1957, at Montreal, second period. Montreal 3, Boston 2.
– **Denis Savard**, Chicago, Jan. 12, 1986, at Chicago, third period. Chicago 4, Hartford 2.

FASTEST GOAL BY A PLAYER IN HIS FIRST NHL GAME:
0:15 – Gus Bodnar, Toronto, Oct. 30, 1943, at Toronto. Toronto 5, NY Rangers 2.
0:18 – Danny Gare, Buffalo, Oct. 10, 1974, at Buffalo. Buffalo 9, Boston 5.
0:20 – Alexander Mogilny, Buffalo, Oct. 5, 1989, at Buffalo. Buffalo 4, Quebec 3.

FASTEST TWO GOALS FROM START OF A GAME:
0:27 – Mike Knuble, Boston, Feb. 14, 2003, at Florida at 0:10 and 0:27. Boston 6, Florida 5.

FASTEST TWO GOALS:
0:04 – Nels Stewart, Mtl. Maroons, Jan. 3, 1931, at Mtl. Maroons at 8:24 and 8:28, third period. Mtl. Maroons 5, Boston 3.
– **Deron Quint**, Winnipeg, Dec. 15, 1995, at Winnipeg at 7:51 and 7:55, second period. Winnipeg 9, Edmonton 4.
0:05 – Pete Mahovlich, Montreal, Feb. 20, 1971, at Montreal at 12:16 and 12:21, third period. Montreal 7, Chicago 1.
0:06 – Jim Pappin, Chicago, Feb. 16, 1972, at Chicago at 2:57 and 3:03, third period. Chicago 3, Philadelphia 3.
– Ralph Backstrom, Los Angeles, Nov. 2, 1972, at Los Angeles at 8:30 and 8:36, third period. Los Angeles 5, Boston 2.
– Lanny McDonald, Calgary, Mar. 22, 1984, at Calgary at 16:23 and 16:29, first period. Detroit 6, Calgary 4.
– Sylvain Turgeon, Hartford, Mar. 28, 1987, at Hartford at 13:59 and 14:05, second period. Hartford 5, Pittsburgh 4.

FASTEST THREE GOALS:
0:21 – Bill Mosienko, Chicago, Mar. 23, 1952, at NY Rangers, against goaltender Lorne Anderson. Mosienko scored at 6:09, 6:20 and 6:30 of third period, all with both teams at full strength. Chicago 7, NY Rangers 6.
0:44 – Jean Béliveau, Montreal, Nov. 5, 1955, against goaltender Terry Sawchuk. Béliveau scored at 0:42, 1:08 and 1:26 of second period, all with Montreal holding a 6-4 man advantage. Montreal 4, Boston 2.

FASTEST THREE ASSISTS:
0:21 – Gus Bodnar, Chicago, Mar. 23, 1952, at NY Rangers, Bodnar assisted on Bill Mosienko's three goals at 6:09, 6:20 and 6:30 of third period. Chicago 7, NY Rangers 6.
0:44 – Bert Olmstead, Montreal, Nov. 5, 1955, at Montreal, Olmstead assisted on Jean Béliveau's three goals at 0:42, 1:08 and 1:26 of second period. Montreal 4, Boston 2.

SHOTS ON GOAL

MOST SHOTS ON GOAL, ONE SEASON:
550 – Phil Esposito, Boston, 1970-71. 78GP – 78 game schedule.
429 – Paul Kariya, Anaheim, 1998-99. 82GP – 82 game schedule.
426 – Phil Esposito, Boston, 1971-72. 76GP – 78 game schedule.
414 – Bobby Hull, Chicago, 1968-69. 74GP – 76 game schedule.

PENALTIES

MOST PENALTY MINUTES, CAREER:
3,966 – Tiger Williams, Toronto, Vancouver, Detroit, Los Angeles, Hartford, in 14 seasons. 962GP
3,565 – Dale Hunter, Quebec, Washington, Colorado, in 19 seasons. 1,407GP
3,406 – Tie Domi, Toronto, NY Rangers, Winnipeg, in 15 seasons. 943GP
3,381 – Marty McSorley, Pittsburgh, Edmonton, Los Angeles, NY Rangers, San Jose, Boston, in 17 seasons. 961GP
3,300 – Bob Probert, Detroit, Chicago, in 17 seasons. 935GP

MOST PENALTY MINUTES, CAREER, INCLUDING PLAYOFFS:
4,421 – Tiger Williams, Toronto, Vancouver, Detroit, Los Angeles, Hartford, 3,966 in 962 regular-season games; 455 in 83 playoff games.
4,294 – Dale Hunter, Quebec, Washington, Colorado, 3,565 in 1,407 regular-season games; 729 in 186 playoff games.
3,755 – Marty McSorley, Pittsburgh, Edmonton, Los Angeles, NY Rangers, San Jose, Boston, 3,381 in 961 regular-season games; 374 in 115 playoff games.
3,644 – Tie Domi, Toronto, NY Rangers, Winnipeg, 3,406 in 943 regular-season games; 238 in 98 playoff games.
3,584 – Chris Nilan, Montreal, NY Rangers, Boston, 3,043 in 688 regular-season games; 541 in 111 playoff games.

MOST PENALTY MINUTES, ONE SEASON:
472 – Dave Schultz, Philadelphia, 1974-75.
409 – Paul Baxter, Pittsburgh, 1981-82.
408 – Mike Peluso, Chicago, 1991-92.
405 – Dave Schultz, Los Angeles, Pittsburgh, 1977-78.

MOST PENALTIES, ONE GAME:
10 – Chris Nilan, Boston, Mar. 31, 1991, at Boston vs. Hartford. 6 minors, 2 majors, 1 10-minute misconduct, 1 game misconduct.
9 – Jim Dorey, Toronto, Oct. 16, 1968, at Toronto vs. Pittsburgh. 4 minors, 2 majors, 2 10-minute misconducts, 1 game misconduct.
– Dave Schultz, Pittsburgh, Apr. 6, 1978, at Detroit. 5 minors, 2 majors, 2 10-minute misconducts.
– Randy Holt, Los Angeles, Mar. 11, 1979, at Philadelphia. 1 minor, 3 majors, 2 10-minute misconducts, 3 game misconducts.
– Russ Anderson, Pittsburgh, Jan. 19, 1980, at Pittsburgh vs. Edmonton. 3 minors, 3 majors, 3 game misconducts.
– Kim Clackson, Quebec, Mar. 8, 1981, at Quebec vs. Chicago. 4 minors, 3 majors, 2 game misconducts.
– Terry O'Reilly, Boston, Dec. 19, 1984, at Hartford. 5 minors, 3 majors, 1 game misconduct.
– Larry Playfair, Los Angeles, Dec. 9, 1986, at NY Islanders. 6 minors, 2 majors, 1 10-minute misconduct.
– Marty McSorley, Los Angeles, Apr. 14, 1992, at Vancouver. 5 minors, 2 majors, 1 10-minute misconduct, 1 game misconduct.
– Reed Low, St. Louis, Dec. 31, 2002, at Detroit. 4 minors, 1 major, 1 10-minute misconduct, 3 game misconducts.

MOST PENALTY MINUTES, ONE GAME:
67 – Randy Holt, Los Angeles, Mar. 11, 1979, at Philadelphia. 1 minor, 3 majors, 2 10-minute misconducts, 3 game misconducts.
57 – Brad Smith, Toronto, Nov. 15, 1986, at Toronto vs. Detroit. 1 minor, 3 majors, 2 10-minute misconducts, 2 game misconducts.
– Reed Low, St. Louis, Feb. 28, 2002, at St. Louis vs. Calgary. 1 minor, 3 majors, 1 10-minute misconduct, 3 game misconducts.

MOST PENALTIES, ONE PERIOD:
  9 – **Randy Holt**, Los Angeles, Mar. 11, 1979, at Philadelphia, first period.
  1 minor, 3 majors, 2 10-minute misconducts, 3 game misconducts.

MOST PENALTY MINUTES, ONE PERIOD:
  67 – **Randy Holt**, Los Angeles, Mar. 11, 1979, at Philadelphia, first period.
  1 minor, 3 majors, 2 10-minute misconducts, 3 game misconducts.

GOALTENDING

MOST GAMES APPEARED IN BY A GOALTENDER, CAREER:
  1,029 – Patrick Roy, Montreal, Colorado,1984-85 – 2002-03.
  971 – Terry Sawchuk, Detroit, Boston, Toronto, Los Angeles, NY Rangers, 1949-50 – 1969-70.
  906 – Glenn Hall, Detroit, Chicago, St. Louis, 1952-53 – 1970-71.
  886 – Tony Esposito, Montreal, Chicago, 1968-69 – 1983-84.
  882 – John Vanbiesbrouck, NY Rangers, Florida, Philadelphia, NY Islanders, New Jersey, 1981-82 – 2001-02.

MOST CONSECUTIVE COMPLETE GAMES BY A GOALTENDER:
  502 – Glenn Hall, Detroit, Chicago. Played 502 games from beginning of 1955-56 season through first 12 games of 1962-63 season. In his 503rd straight game, Nov. 7, 1962, at Chicago, Hall was removed from the game against Boston with a back injury in the first period.

MOST GAMES APPEARED IN BY A GOALTENDER, ONE SEASON:
  79 – Grant Fuhr, St. Louis, 1995-96.
  77 – Martin Brodeur, New Jersey, 1995-96.
  – Bill Ranford, Edmonton, Boston, 1995-96.
  – Arturs Irbe, Carolina, 2000-01.
  – Marc Denis, Columbus, 2002-03.

MOST MINUTES PLAYED BY A GOALTENDER, CAREER:
  60,235 – Patrick Roy, Montreal, Colorado, 1984-85 – 2002-03.
  57,194 – Terry Sawchuk, Detroit, Boston, Toronto, Los Angeles, NY Rangers, 1949-50 – 1969-70.

MOST MINUTES PLAYED BY A GOALTENDER, ONE SEASON:
  4,555 – Martin Brodeur, New Jersey, 2003-04.
  4,511 – Marc Denis, Columbus, 2002-03.

MOST SHUTOUTS, CAREER:
  103 – Terry Sawchuk, Detroit, Boston, Toronto, Los Angeles, NY Rangers, in 21 seasons.
  94 – George Hainsworth, Montreal, Toronto, in 11 seasons.
  84 – Glenn Hall, Detroit, Chicago, St. Louis, in 18 seasons.

MOST SHUTOUTS, ONE SEASON:
  22 – George Hainsworth, Montreal, 1928-29. 44GP
  15 – Alec Connell, Ottawa, 1925-26. 36GP
  – Alec Connell, Ottawa, 1927-28. 44GP
  – Hal Winkler, Boston, 1927-28. 44GP
  – Tony Esposito, Chicago, 1969-70. 63GP
  14 – George Hainsworth, Montreal, 1926-27. 44GP

LONGEST SHUTOUT SEQUENCE BY A GOALTENDER:
  461:29 – Alec Connell, Ottawa, 1927-28, six consecutive shutouts.
  (Forward passing not permitted in attacking zones in 1927-28.)
  343:05 – George Hainsworth, Montreal, 1928-29, four consecutive shutouts.
  (Forward passing not permitted in attacking zones in 1928-29.)
  332:01 – Brian Boucher, Phoenix, 2003-04, five consecutive shutouts.
  324:40 – Roy Worters, NY Americans, 1930-31, four consecutive shutouts.
  309:21 – Bill Durnan, Montreal, 1948-49, four consecutive shutouts.

MOST WINS BY A GOALTENDER, CAREER:
  551 – Patrick Roy, Montreal, Colorado, in 19 seasons. 1,029GP
  447 – Terry Sawchuk, Detroit, Boston, Toronto, Los Angeles, NY Rangers, in 21 seasons. 971GP
  435 – Jacques Plante, Montreal, NY Rangers, St. Louis, Toronto, Boston, in 18 seasons. 837GP
  – Ed Belfour, Chicago, San Jose, Dallas, Toronto, in 15 seasons. 856GP
  423 – Tony Esposito, Montreal, Chicago, in 16 seasons. 886GP

MOST WINS BY A GOALTENDER, ONE SEASON:
  47 – Bernie Parent, Philadelphia, 1973-74. 73GP
  44 – Bernie Parent, Philadelphia, 1974-75. 68GP
  – Terry Sawchuk, Detroit, 1950-51. 70GP
  – Terry Sawchuk, Detroit, 1951-52. 70GP

LONGEST WINNING STREAK BY A GOALTENDER, ONE SEASON:
  17 – Gilles Gilbert, Boston, 1975-76.
  14 – Tiny Thompson, Boston, 1929-30.
  – Ross Brooks, Boston, 1973-74.
  – Don Beaupre, Minnesota, 1985-86.
  – Tom Barrasso, Pittsburgh, 1992-93.

LONGEST UNDEFEATED STREAK BY A GOALTENDER, ONE SEASON:
  32 Games – Gerry Cheevers, Boston, 1971-72. 24w-8T
  31 Games – Pete Peeters, Boston, 1982-83. 26w-5T
  27 Games – Pete Peeters, Philadelphia, 1979-80. 22w-5T

LONGEST UNDEFEATED STREAK BY A GOALTENDER IN HIS FIRST NHL SEASON:
  23 Games – Grant Fuhr, Edmonton, 1981-82. 15w-8T

LONGEST UNDEFEATED STREAK BY A GOALTENDER FROM START OF CAREER:
  16 Games – Patrick Lalime, Pittsburgh, 1996-97. 14w-2T

MOST 40-OR-MORE WIN SEASONS BY A GOALTENDER:
  4 – Martin Brodeur, New Jersey, in 12 seasons.
  3 – Terry Sawchuk, Detroit, Boston, Toronto, Los Angeles, NY Rangers, in 21 seasons.
  – Jacques Plante, Montreal, NY Rangers, St. Louis, Toronto, Boston, in 18 seasons.
  2 – Bernie Parent, Boston, Philadelphia, in 13 seasons.
  – Ken Dryden, Montreal, in 8 seasons.
  – Ed Belfour, Chicago, San Jose, Dallas, Toronto, in 15 seasons.

MOST CONSECUTIVE 40-OR-MORE WIN SEASONS BY A GOALTENDER:
  2 – Terry Sawchuk, Detroit, 1950-51 – 1951-52.
  – **Bernie Parent**, Philadelphia, 1973-74 – 1974-75.
  – **Ken Dryden**, Montreal, 1975-76 – 1976-77.
  – **Martin Brodeur**, New Jersey, 1999-2000 – 2000-01.

MOST 30-OR-MORE WIN SEASONS BY A GOALTENDER:
  13 – Patrick Roy, Montreal, Colorado, in 19 seasons.
  9 – Martin Brodeur, New Jersey, in 12 seasons.
  – Ed Belfour, Chicago, San Jose, Dallas, Toronto, in 15 seasons.
  8 – Tony Esposito, Montreal, Chicago, in 16 seasons.
  7 – Jacques Plante, Montreal, NY Rangers, St. Louis, Toronto, Boston, in 18 seasons.
  – Ken Dryden, Montreal, in 8 seasons.

MOST CONSECUTIVE 30-OR-MORE WIN SEASONS BY A GOALTENDER:
  9 – Martin Brodeur, New Jersey, 1995-96 – 2003-04.
  8 – Patrick Roy, Montreal, Colorado, 1995-96 – 2002-03.
  7 – Tony Esposito, Chicago, 1969-70 – 1975-76.
  6 – Jacques Plante, Montreal, 1954-55 – 1959-60.
  5 – Terry Sawchuk, Detroit, 1950-51 – 1954-55.
  – Ken Dryden, Montreal, 1974-75 – 1978-79.

MOST LOSSES BY A GOALTENDER, CAREER:
  352 – Gump Worsley, NY Rangers, Montreal, Minnesota, in 21 seasons. 861GP
  351 – Gilles Meloche, Chicago, California, Cleveland, Minnesota, Pittsburgh, in 18 seasons. 788GP
  346 – John Vanbiesbrouck, NY Rangers, Florida, Philadelphia, NY Islanders, New Jersey, in 20 seasons. 882GP
  332 – Terry Sawchuk, Detroit, Boston, Toronto, Los Angeles, NY Rangers, in 21 seasons. 971GP

MOST LOSSES BY A GOALTENDER, ONE SEASON:
  48 – Gary Smith, California, 1970-71. 71GP
  47 – Al Rollins, Chicago, 1953-54. 66GP
  46 – Peter Sidorkiewicz, Ottawa, 1992-93. 64GP
  44 – Harry Lumley, Chicago, 1951-52. 70GP

New Jersey's Martin Brodeur has led NHL goaltenders in wins six times in the last seven seasons. His 38 victories in 2003-04 gave him a record ninth consecutive 30-win season. His 4,555 minutes played also set a new NHL record.

Active NHL Players' Three-or-More-Goal Games

Regular Season

Teams named are the ones the players were with at the time of their multiple-scoring games. Players listed alphabetically.

Miroslav Satan had two hat tricks last season, including the first four-goal game of his career in Buffalo's 7-2 win over Atlanta on February 16, 2004.

Player	Team	3-Goals	4-Goals	5-Goals
Alfredsson, Daniel	Ottawa	4	—	—
Allison, Jason	Boston	4	—	—
Amonte, Tony	NYR, Chi.	7	—	—
Andreychuk, Dave	Buf., Tor., Bos.	7	3	1
Antropov, Nik	Toronto	1	—	—
Arnason, Tyler	Chicago	1	—	—
Arnott, Jason	Edm., N.J., Dal.	4	—	—
Arvedson, Magnus	Ottawa	1	—	—
Audette, Donald	Buf., Atl.	4	—	—
Barnes, Stu	Wpg., Pit.	3	—	—
Battaglia, Bates	Carolina	1	—	—
Belanger, Eric	Los Angeles	1	—	—
Bertuzzi, Todd	Vancouver	3	—	—
Blake, Jason	NY Islanders	1	—	—
Blake, Rob	Los Angeles	1	—	—
Bondra, Peter	Washington	12	5	1
Bonk, Radek	Ottawa	1	—	—
Brind'Amour, Rod	Phi., Car.	2	—	—
Brown, Curtis	Buffalo	1	—	—
Buchberger, Kelly	Edmonton	1	—	—
Bure, Valeri	Calgary	1	—	—
Carter, Anson	Boston	1	—	—
Cassels, Andrew	Vancouver	1	—	—
Cole, Erik	Carolina	2	—	—
Conroy, Craig	St. Louis	1	—	—
Corson, Shayne	Mtl., Edm.	3	—	—
Czerkawski, Mariusz	Edm., NYI	4	—	—
Dackell, Andreas	Ottawa	1	—	—
Daigle, Alexandre	Ott., Phi.	2	—	—
Damphousse, Vincent	Tor., Edm., Mtl., S.J.	11	1	—
Daze, Eric	Chicago	5	1	—
Deadmarsh, Adam	Col., L.A.	2	—	—
Demitra, Pavol	St. Louis	3	—	—
Devereaux, Boyd	Edmonton	1	—	—
Donovan, Shean	Atlanta	1	—	—
Druken, Harold	Vancouver	1	—	—
Dumont, Jean-Pierre	Chi., Buf.	3	—	—
Dvorak, Radek	NY Rangers	1	1	—
Eastwood, Mike	St. Louis	1	—	—
Elias, Patrik	New Jersey	5	1	—
Fedorov, Sergei	Detroit	4	1	1
Forsberg, Peter	Colorado	6	—	—
Francis, Ron	Hfd., Pit.	10	1	—
Friesen, Jeff	San Jose	2	—	—
Gaborik, Marian	Minnesota	5	—	—
Gagne, Simon	Philadelphia	1	—	—
Gelinas, Martin	Edm., Van.	2	1	—
Gomez, Scott	New Jersey	1	—	—
Gonchar, Sergei	Washington	1	—	—
Gratton, Chris	Tampa Bay	1	—	—
Green, Travis	NY Islanders	1	—	—
Grier, Mike	Edmonton	1	—	—
Grosek, Michal	Buffalo	1	—	—
Guerin, Bill	N.J., Bos.	3	—	—
Handzus, Michal	St. Louis	1	—	—
Harvey, Todd	Dal., S.J.	2	—	—
Havlat, Martin	Ottawa	3	—	—
Heatley, Dany	Atlanta	2	—	—
Hejduk, Milan	Colorado	1	—	—
Hlavac, Jan	NYR, Car.	3	—	—
Holik, Bobby	New Jersey	3	—	—
Holmstrom, Tomas	Detroit	1	—	—
Hossa, Marian	Ottawa	3	1	—
Hull, Brett	Cgy., St.L., Dal., Det.	30	3	—
Iginla, Jarome	Calgary	3	1	—
Jagr, Jaromir	Pittsburgh	10	1	—
Johansson, Andreas	Nashville	1	—	—
Kapanen, Sami	Carolina	3	—	—
Kariya, Paul	Anaheim	8	—	—
Klatt, Trent	Philadelphia	1	—	—
Koivu, Saku	Montreal	1	—	—
Konowalchuk, Steve	Washington	3	—	—
Korolev, Igor	Winnipeg	1	—	—
Kovalchuk, Ilya	Atlanta	3	—	—
Kovalev, Alex	NYR, Pit.	10	—	—
Kozlov, Viktor	Florida	1	—	—
Kozlov, Vyacheslav	Detroit	2	1	—
Laaksonen, Antti	Minnesota	1	—	—
Lang, Robert	Washington	1	—	—
Langkow, Daymond	Phoenix	2	—	—
Laperriere, Ian	Los Angeles	1	—	—
Lapointe, Martin	Det., Bos.	2	—	—
Laraque, Georges	Edmonton	1	—	—
Lecavalier, Vincent	Tampa Bay	3	—	—
LeClair, John	Philadelphia	8	3	—
Lehtinen, Jere	Dallas	2	—	—
Lemieux, Mario	Pittsburgh	27	10	3
Linden, Trevor	Van., Mtl.	5	—	—
Lindros, Eric	Phi., NYR	12	1	—
Lombardi, Matthew	Calgary	1	—	—
MacInnis, Al	Cgy., St.L.	3	—	—
Madden, John	New Jersey	1	1	—
Malakhov, Vladimir	Montreal	1	—	—
Maltby, Kirk	Detroit	1	—	—
Marleau, Patrick	San Jose	1	—	—
McCauley, Alyn	San Jose	1	—	—
McEachern, Shawn	Ott., Atl.	2	—	—
McKenzie, Jim	Phoenix	1	—	—
Mellanby, Scott	St. Louis	—	1	—
Messier, Mark	Edm., NYR	15	4	—
Miller, Kevin	Det., St.L., S.J.	4	—	—
Modano, Mike	Min., Dal.	6	1	—
Modin, Fredrik	Tampa Bay	2	—	—
Mogilny, Alexander	Buf., Van., N.J., Tor.	15	2	—
Morozov, Aleksey	Pittsburgh	2	—	—
Morrison, Brendan	Vancouver	1	—	—
Morrow, Brendan	Dallas	1	—	—
Murray, Glen	L.A., Bos.	5	—	—
Murray, Rem	Edmonton	1	—	—
Nagy, Ladislav	Phoenix	1	—	—
Naslund, Markus	Pit., Van.	8	2	—
Nedved, Petr	Pit., NYR	6	1	—
Nieuwendyk, Joe	Cgy., Dal.	9	3	1
Nolan, Owen	Que., S.J.	9	1	—
Nylander, Michael	Hfd., Chi.	1	1	—
Odelein, Lyle	Montreal	1	—	—
Oliver, David	Edmonton	1	—	—
O'Neill, Jeff	Hfd., Car.	2	—	—
Orszagh, Vladimir	Nashville	1	—	—
Ozolinsh, Sandis	Col., Car.	2	—	—
Palffy, Ziggy	NYI, L.A.	8	—	—
Parrish, Mark	Fla., NYI	3	1	—
Peca, Michael	Buffalo	1	—	—
Perreault, Yanic	L.A., Tor., Mtl.	3	1	—
Petersen, Toby	Pittsburgh	1	—	—
Piros, Kamil	Atlanta	1	—	—
Pisani, Fernando	Edmonton	1	—	—
Primeau, Keith	Philadelphia	1	—	—
Prospal, Vaclav	Anaheim	1	—	—
Pyatt, Taylor	Buffalo	1	—	—
Quint, Deron	Columbus	1	—	—
Recchi, Mark	Pit., Mtl., Phi.	5	—	—
Reichel, Robert	Cgy., Tor.	5	—	—
Reinprecht, Steve	Colorado	2	—	—
Rheaume, Pascal	Atlanta	—	1	—
Ricci, Mike	Que., S.J.	1	—	1
Roberts, Gary	Cgy., Car., Tor.	12	1	—
Robitaille, Luc	L.A., Pit.	11	3	—
Roenick, Jeremy	Chi., Phx.	7	2	—
Rolston, Brian	New Jersey	1	—	—
Ronning, Cliff	St.L., Van.	3	—	—
Rucinsky, Martin	Montreal	2	—	—
Sakic, Joe	Que., Col.	13	1	—
Salo, Sami	Ottawa	1	—	—
Samsonov, Sergei	Boston	1	—	—
Sanderson, Geoff	Har., Buf., CBJ	7	1	—
Satan, Miroslav	Buffalo	5	1	—
Savage, Brian	Montreal	6	1	—
Savard, Marc	Calgary	1	1	—
Scatchard, Dave	NY Islanders	2	—	—
Sedin, Daniel	Vancouver	—	1	—
Selanne, Teemu	Wpg., Ana., S.J.	16	2	—
Shanahan, Brendan	N.J., St.L., Hfd., Det.	15	1	—
Smolinski, Bryan	Bos., L.A.	3	—	—
Smyth, Ryan	Edmonton	4	—	—
Souray, Sheldon	Montreal	1	—	—
St. Louis, Martin	Tampa Bay	3	—	—
Stillman, Cory	Cgy., St.L.	3	—	—
Straka, Martin	Pittsburgh	4	—	—
Stumpel, Jozef	Bos., L.A.	2	—	—
Sturm, Marco	San Jose	1	—	—
Sullivan, Steve	Tor., Chi., Nsh.	3	1	—
Sundin, Mats	Que., Tor.	5	—	1
Sydor, Darryl	Dallas	1	—	—
Tanguay, Alex	Colorado	2	—	—
Tenkrat, Petr	Nashville	1	—	—
Thomas, Steve	Chi., NYI	4	2	—
Thornton, Joe	Boston	2	—	—
Thornton, Scott	San Jose	1	—	—
Tkachuk, Keith	Phoenix	7	2	—
Toms, Jeff	NY Rangers	1	—	—
Turgeon, Pierre	Buf., NYI, Mtl., St.L.	15	—	—
Valicevic, Robert	Nashville	1	—	—
Vasicek, Josef	Carolina	1	—	—
Vrbata, Radim	Col., Car.	1	—	—
Vyborny, David	Columbus	1	—	—
Walker, Scott	Nashville	2	—	—
Weight, Doug	Edm., St.L.	1	—	—
Wesley, Glen	Boston	1	—	—
Whitney, Ray	Columbus	1	—	—
Wiemer, Jason	Tampa Bay	1	—	—
Willis, Shane	Carolina	1	—	—
Wright, Tyler	Columbus	1	—	—
Yachmenev, Vitali	Los Angeles	1	—	—
Yashin, Alexei	Ott., NYI	8	—	—
Young, Scott	Que., Col.	4	—	—
Yzerman, Steve	Detroit	17	1	—
Zamuner, Rob	Tampa Bay	1	—	—
Zednik, Richard	Washington	1	—	—
Zhamnov, Alex	Wpg., Chi.	5	—	1
Zubrus, Dainus	Montreal	1	—	—

Top 100 All-Time Goal-Scoring Leaders

* active player

Player	Seasons	Games	Goals	Goals per game
1. Wayne Gretzky, Edm., L.A., St.L., NYR .	20	1487	894	.601
2. Gordie Howe, Det., Hfd.	26	1767	801	.453
* 3. Brett Hull, Cgy., St.L., Dal., Det.	19	1264	741	.586
4. Marcel Dionne, Det., L.A., NYR	18	1348	731	.542
5. Phil Esposito, Chi., Bos., NYR	18	1282	717	.559
6. Mike Gartner, Wsh., Min., NYR, Tor., Phx.	19	1432	708	.494
* 7. Mark Messier, Edm., NYR, Van.	25	1756	694	.395
* 8. Mario Lemieux, Pit.	17	889	683	.768
* 9. Steve Yzerman, Det.	21	1453	678	.467
* 10. Luc Robitaille, L.A., Pit., NYR, Det.	18	1366	653	.478
* 11. Dave Andreychuk, Buf., Tor., N.J., Bos., Col., T.B.	22	1597	634	.397
12. Bobby Hull, Chi., Wpg., Hfd.	16	1063	610	.574
13. Dino Ciccarelli, Min., Wsh., Det., T.B., Fla.	19	1232	608	.494
14. Jari Kurri, Edm., L.A., NYR, Ana., Col. . .	17	1251	601	.480
15. Mike Bossy, NYI	10	752	573	.762
16. Guy Lafleur, Mtl., NYR, Que.	17	1126	560	.497
* 17. Brendan Shanahan, N.J., St.L., Hfd., Det.	17	1268	558	.440
18. John Bucyk, Det., Bos.	23	1540	556	.361
* 19. Ron Francis, Hfd., Pit., Car., Tor.	23	1731	549	.317
20. Michel Goulet, Que., Chi.	15	1089	548	.503
21. Maurice Richard, Mtl.	18	978	544	.556
* 22. Joe Sakic, Que., Col.	16	1155	542	.469
23. Stan Mikita, Chi.	22	1394	541	.388
* 24. Jaromir Jagr, Pit., Wsh., NYI	14	1027	537	.523
* 25. Joe Nieuwendyk, Cgy., Dal., N.J., Tor. . .	18	1177	533	.453
26. Frank Mahovlich, Tor., Det., Mtl.	18	1181	533	.451
27. Bryan Trottier, NYI, Pit.	18	1279	524	.410
28. Pat Verbeek, N.J., Hfd., NYR, Dal., Det. . .	20	1424	522	.367
29. Dale Hawerchuk, Wpg., Buf., St.L., Phi. .	16	1188	518	.436
30. Gilbert Perreault, Buf.	17	1191	512	.430
31. Jean Beliveau, Mtl.	20	1125	507	.451
32. Joe Mullen, St.L., Cgy., Pit., Bos. . . .	17	1062	502	.473
33. Lanny McDonald, Tor., Col., Cgy.	16	1111	500	.450
34. Glenn Anderson, Edm., Tor., NYR, St.L.	16	1129	498	.441
* 35. Pierre Turgeon, Buf., NYI, Mtl., St.L., Dal.	17	1215	495	.407
36. Jean Ratelle, NYR, Bos.	21	1281	491	.383
37. Norm Ullman, Det., Tor.	20	1410	490	.348
38. Brian Bellows, Min., Mtl., T.B., Ana., Wsh.	17	1188	485	.408
39. Darryl Sittler, Tor., Phi., Det.	15	1096	484	.442
* 40. Peter Bondra, Wsh., Ott.	14	984	477	.485
* 41. Jeremy Roenick, Chi., Phx., Phi.	16	1124	475	.423
42. Bernie Nicholls, L.A., NYR, Edm., N.J., Chi., S.J.	18	1127	475	.421
43. Denis Savard, Chi., Mtl., T.B.	17	1196	473	.395
44. Pat LaFontaine, NYI, Buf., NYR.	15	865	468	.541
* 45. Mats Sundin, Que., Tor.	14	1086	465	.428
* 46. Alexander Mogilny, Buf., Van., N.J., Tor.	15	956	461	.482
* 47. Mike Modano, Min., Dal.	16	1101	458	.416
* 48. Mark Recchi, Pit., Phi., Mtl.	16	1173	456	.389
49. Alex Delvecchio, Det.	24	1549	456	.294
50. Theoren Fleury, Cgy., Col., NYR, Chi. .	15	1084	455	.420
* 51. Teemu Selanne, Wpg., Ana., S.J., Col. .	12	879	452	.514
52. Doug Gilmour, St.L., Cgy., Tor., N.J., Chi., Buf., Mtl.	20	1474	450	.305
53. Peter Stastny, Que., N.J., St.L.	15	977	450	.461
54. Rick Middleton, NYR, Bos.	14	1005	448	.446
55. Rick Vaive, Van., Tor., Chi., Buf.	13	876	441	.503
56. Steve Larmer, Chi., NYR.	15	1006	441	.438
57. Rick Tocchet, Phi., Pit., L.A., Bos., Wsh., Phx.	18	1144	440	.385
58. Pavel Bure, Van., Fla., NYR	12	702	437	.623
59. Vincent Damphousse, Tor., Edm., Mtl., S.J.	18	1378	432	.313
* 60. Keith Tkachuk, Wpg., Phx., St.L. . . .	13	856	431	.504
61. Dave Taylor, L.A.	17	1111	431	.388
* 62. Sergei Fedorov, Det., Ana.	14	988	431	.436
63. Yvan Cournoyer, Mtl.	16	968	428	.442
64. Brian Propp, Phi., Bos., Min., Hfd. . . .	15	1016	425	.418
65. Steve Shutt, Mtl., L.A.	13	930	424	.456
* 66. Steve Thomas, Tor., Chi., NYI, N.J., Ana., Det.	20	1235	421	.341
67. Stephane Richer, Mtl., N.J., T.B., St.L., Pit.	17	1054	421	.399
68. Bill Barber, Phi.	14	903	420	.465
69. John MacLean, N.J., S.J., NYR, Dal. . . .	18	1194	413	.346
70. Garry Unger, Tor., Det., St.L., Atl., L.A., Edm.	16	1105	413	.374
71. Raymond Bourque, Bos., Col.	22	1612	410	.254
72. Ray Ferraro, Hfd., NYI, NYR, L.A., Atl., St.L.	18	1258	408	.324
73. Rod Gilbert, NYR	18	1065	406	.381
74. John Ogrodnick, Det., Que., NYR	14	928	402	.433

Pat Verbeek is the only player in NHL history to score more than 500 goals and accumulate more than 2,000 penalty minutes. His career-high 46 goals for New Jersey in 1987-88 is still the Devils' franchise record.

Player	Seasons	Games	Goals	Goals per game
* 75. Gary Roberts, Cgy., Car., Tor.	18	1029	397	.386
76. Paul Coffey, Edm., Pit., L.A., Det., Hfd., Phi., Chi., Car., Bos.	21	1409	396	.281
77. Dave Keon, Tor., Hfd.	18	1296	396	.306
78. Cam Neely, Van., Bos.	13	726	395	.544
79. Pierre Larouche, Pit., Mtl., Hfd., NYR . .	14	812	395	.486
80. Tomas Sandstrom, NYR, L.A., Pit., Det., Ana.	15	983	394	.401
81. Bernie Geoffrion, Mtl., NYR	16	883	393	.445
* 82. Tony Amonte, NYR, Chi., Phx., Phi. . . .	14	1013	392	.387
83. Jean Pronovost, Pit., Atl., Wsh.	14	998	391	.392
84. Dean Prentice, NYR, Bos., Det., Pit., Min.	22	1378	391	.284
85. Rick Martin, Buf., L.A.	11	685	384	.561
* 86. John LeClair, Mtl., Phi.	14	873	382	.438
87. Reggie Leach, Bos., Cal., Phi., Det. . . .	13	934	381	.408
88. Ted Lindsay, Det., Chi.	17	1068	379	.355
89. Claude Lemieux, Mtl., N.J., Col., Phx., Dal.	20	1197	379	.317
90. Butch Goring, L.A., NYI, Bos.	16	1107	375	.339
91. Rick Kehoe, Tor., Pit.	14	906	371	.409
92. Tim Kerr, Phi., NYR, Hfd.	13	655	370	.565
93. Bernie Federko, St.L., Det.	14	1000	369	.369
94. Geoff Courtnall, Bos., Edm., Wsh., St.L., Van.	17	1048	367	.350
95. Jacques Lemaire, Mtl.	12	853	366	.429
96. Peter McNab, Buf., Bos., Van., N.J. . . .	14	954	363	.381
97. Brent Sutter, NYI, Chi.	18	1111	363	.327
98. Ivan Boldirev, Bos., Cal., Chi., Atl., Van., Det.	15	1052	361	.343
99. Henri Richard, Mtl.	20	1256	358	.285
100. Bobby Clarke, Phi.	15	1144	358	.313

Top 100 Active Goal-Scoring Leaders

	Player	Seasons	Games	Goals	Goals per game
1.	**Brett Hull**, Cgy., St.L., Dal., Det.	19	1264	**741**	.586
2.	**Mark Messier**, Edm., NYR, Van.	25	1756	**694**	.395
3.	**Mario Lemieux**, Pit.	17	889	**683**	.768
4.	**Steve Yzerman**, Det.	21	1453	**678**	.467
5.	**Luc Robitaille**, L.A., Pit., NYR, Det.	18	1366	**653**	.478
6.	**Dave Andreychuk**, Buf., Tor., N.J., Bos., Col., T.B.	22	1597	**634**	.397
7.	**Brendan Shanahan**, N.J., St.L., Hfd., Det.	17	1268	**558**	.440
8.	**Ron Francis**, Hfd., Pit., Car., Tor.	23	1731	**549**	.317
9.	**Joe Sakic**, Que., Col.	16	1155	**542**	.469
10.	**Jaromir Jagr**, Pit., Wsh., NYI	14	1027	**537**	.523
11.	**Joe Nieuwendyk**, Cgy., Dal., N.J., Tor.	18	1177	**533**	.453
12.	**Pierre Turgeon**, Buf., NYI, Mtl., St.L., Dal.	17	1215	**495**	.407
13.	**Peter Bondra**, Wsh., Ott.	14	984	**477**	.485
14.	**Jeremy Roenick**, Chi., Phx., Phi.	16	1124	**475**	.423
15.	**Mats Sundin**, Que., Tor.	14	1086	**465**	.428
16.	**Alexander Mogilny**, Buf., Van., N.J., Tor.	15	956	**461**	.482
17.	**Mike Modano**, Min., Dal.	16	1101	**458**	.416
18.	**Mark Recchi**, Pit., Phi., Mtl.	16	1173	**456**	.389
19.	**Teemu Selanne**, Wpg., Ana., S.J., Col.	12	879	**452**	.514
20.	**Vincent Damphousse**, Tor., Edm., Mtl., S.J.	18	1378	**432**	.313
21.	**Keith Tkachuk**, Wpg., Phx., St.L.	13	856	**431**	.504
22.	**Sergei Fedorov**, Det., Ana.	14	988	**431**	.436
23.	**Steve Thomas**, Tor., Chi., NYI, N.J., Ana., Det.	20	1235	**421**	.341
24.	**Gary Roberts**, Cgy., Car., Tor.	18	1029	**397**	.386
25.	**Tony Amonte**, NYR, Chi., Phx., Phi.	14	1013	**392**	.387
26.	**John LeClair**, Mtl., Phi.	14	873	**382**	.438
27.	**Eric Lindros**, Phi., NYR, NYI	11	678	**356**	.525
28.	**Rod Brind'Amour**, St.L., Phi., Car.	16	1109	**351**	.317
29.	**Owen Nolan**, Que., Col., S.J., Tor.	14	915	**349**	.381
30.	**Trevor Linden**, Van., NYI, Mtl., Wsh.	16	1161	**349**	.301
31.	**Scott Mellanby**, Phi., Edm., Fla., St.L.	19	1291	**340**	.263
32.	**Al MacInnis**, Cgy., St.L.	23	1416	**340**	.240
33.	**Scott Young**, Hfd., Pit., Que., Col., Ana., St.L., Dal.	16	1102	**324**	.294
34.	**Ziggy Palffy**, NYI, L.A.	11	642	**318**	.495
35.	**Geoff Sanderson**, Hfd., Car., Van., Buf., CBJ	14	928	**316**	.341
36.	**Bill Guerin**, N.J., Edm., Bos., Dal.	13	879	**315**	.358
37.	**Paul Kariya**, Ana., Col.	10	657	**311**	.473
38.	**Cliff Ronning**, St.L., Van., Phx., Nsh., L.A., Min., NYI	18	1137	**306**	.269
39.	**Petr Nedved**, Van., St.L., NYR, Pit., Edm.	13	889	**301**	.339
40.	**Alex Kovalev**, NYR, Pit., Mtl.	12	849	**292**	.344
41.	**Alexei Yashin**, Ott., NYI	10	710	**291**	.410
42.	**Markus Naslund**, Pit., Van.	11	790	**290**	.367
43.	**Bobby Holik**, Hfd., N.J., NYR	14	1024	**281**	.274
44.	**Martin Gelinas**, Edm., Que., Van., Car., Cgy.	16	1052	**269**	.256
45.	**Glen Murray**, Bos., Pit., L.A.	13	823	**268**	.326
46.	**Keith Primeau**, Det., Hfd., Car., Phi.	14	900	**265**	.294
47.	**Donald Audette**, Buf., L.A., Atl., Dal., Mtl., Fla.	15	735	**260**	.354
48.	**Miroslav Satan**, Edm., Buf.	9	704	**259**	.368
49.	**Shawn McEachern**, Pit., L.A., Bos., Ott., Atl.	13	883	**254**	.288
50.	**Vyacheslav Kozlov**, Det., Buf., Atl.	13	800	**252**	.315
51.	**Robert Reichel**, Cgy., NYI, Phx., Tor.	11	830	**252**	.304
52.	**Jarome Iginla**, Cgy.	9	626	**250**	.399
53.	**Alex Zhamnov**, Wpg., Chi., Phi.	12	783	**248**	.317
54.	**Jason Arnott**, Edm., N.J., Dal.	11	743	**244**	.328
55.	**Brian Leetch**, NYR, NYI, Tor.	17	1144	**242**	.212
56.	**Mike Ricci**, Phi., Que., Col., S.J.	14	1014	**233**	.230
57.	**Bryan Smolinski**, Bos., Pit., NYI, L.A., Ott.	12	829	**231**	.279
58.	**Eric Daze**, Chi.	10	600	**226**	.377
59.	**Doug Weight**, NYR, Edm., St.L.	14	912	**224**	.246
60.	**Stu Barnes**, Wpg., Fla., Pit., Buf., Dal.	13	897	**221**	.246
61.	**Daniel Alfredsson**, Ott.	9	629	**219**	.348
62.	**Peter Forsberg**, Que., Col.	10	580	**216**	.372
63.	**Pavol Demitra**, Ott., St.L.	11	553	**216**	.391
64.	**Jeff Friesen**, S.J., Ana., N.J.	10	770	**208**	.270
65.	**Martin Rucinsky**, Edm., Que., Col., Mtl., Dal., NYR, St.L., Van.	13	817	**208**	.255
66.	**Mariusz Czerkawski**, Bos., Edm., NYI, Mtl.	11	710	**207**	.292
67.	**Patrik Elias**, N.J.	9	558	**207**	.371
68.	**Ray Whitney**, S.J., Edm., Fla., CBJ, Det.	13	700	**205**	.293
69.	**Petr Sykora**, N.J., Ana.	9	608	**202**	.332
70.	**Andrew Cassels**, Mtl., Hfd., Cgy., Van., CBJ	15	984	**200**	.203
71.	**Todd Bertuzzi**, NYI, Van.	9	628	**198**	.315

Bill Guerin's 34 goals in 2003-04 ranked him among the NHL leaders. His first of two goals in a 3-0 Dallas win over San Jose on January 13, 2004 marked the 300th of his career.

	Player	Seasons	Games	Goals	Goals per game
72.	**Jeff O'Neill**, Hfd., Car.	9	673	**198**	.294
73.	**Ryan Smyth**, Edm.	10	642	**198**	.308
74.	**Milan Hejduk**, Col.	6	470	**197**	.419
75.	**Scott Stevens**, Wsh., St.L., N.J.	22	1635	**196**	.120
76.	**Yanic Perreault**, Tor., L.A., Mtl.	11	671	**195**	.291
77.	**Martin Straka**, Pit., Ott., NYI, Fla., L.A.	12	730	**192**	.263
78.	**Brian Rolston**, N.J., Col., Bos.	10	736	**190**	.258
79.	**Marian Hossa**, Ott.	7	467	**188**	.403
80.	**Rob Blake**, L.A., Col.	15	903	**186**	.206
81.	**Adam Deadmarsh**, Que., Col., L.A.	9	567	**184**	.325
82.	**Cory Stillman**, Cgy., St.L., T.B.	10	645	**184**	.285
83.	**Brian Savage**, Mtl., Phx., St.L.	11	608	**183**	.301
84.	**Travis Green**, NYI, Ana., Phx., Tor., Bos.	12	857	**182**	.212
85.	**Chris Chelios**, Mtl., Chi., Det.	21	1395	**178**	.128
86.	**Steve Sullivan**, N.J., Tor., Chi., Nsh.	9	597	**175**	.293
87.	**Robert Lang**, L.A., Bos., Pit., Wsh., Det.	11	646	**174**	.269
88.	**Chris Gratton**, T.B., Phi., Buf., Phx., Col.	11	851	**174**	.204
89.	**Valeri Bure**, Mtl., Cgy., Fla., St.L., Dal.	10	621	**174**	.280
90.	**Nicklas Lidstrom**, Det.	13	1016	**173**	.170
91.	**Mathieu Schneider**, Mtl., NYI, Tor., NYR, L.A., Det.	16	992	**168**	.169
92.	**Mike Keane**, Mtl., Col., NYR, Dal., St.L., Van.	16	1161	**168**	.145
93.	**Dallas Drake**, Det., Wpg., Phx., St.L.	12	822	**166**	.202
94.	**Mike Sillinger**, Det., Ana., Van., Phi., T.B., Fla., Ott., CBJ, Phx., St.L.	14	829	**166**	.200
95.	**Steve Konowalchuk**, Wsh., Col.	13	769	**165**	.215
96.	**Dave Lowry**, Van., St.L., Fla., S.J., Cgy.	19	1084	**164**	.151
97.	**Sami Kapanen**, Hfd., Car., Phi.	9	622	**161**	.259
98.	**Joe Thornton**, Bos.	7	509	**160**	.314
99.	**Anson Carter**, Wsh., Bos., Edm., NYR, NYI, L.A.	8	529	**158**	.299
100.	**Sandis Ozolinsh**, S.J., Col., Car., Fla., Ana.	12	779	**158**	.203

Top 100 All-Time Assist Leaders

* active player

Player	Seasons	Games	Assists	Assists per game
1. **Wayne Gretzky**, Edm., L.A., St.L., NYR .	20	1487	**1963**	1.320
* 2. **Ron Francis**, Hfd., Pit., Car., Tor.	23	1731	**1249**	.722
* 3. **Mark Messier**, Edm., NYR, Van.	25	1756	**1193**	.679
4. **Raymond Bourque**, Bos., Col.	22	1612	**1169**	.725
5. **Paul Coffey**, Edm., Pit., L.A., Det., Hfd., Phi., Chi., Car., Bos.	21	1409	**1135**	.806
6. **Adam Oates**, Det., St.L., Bos., Wsh., Phi., Ana., Edm.	19	1337	**1079**	.807
7. **Gordie Howe**, Det., Hfd.	26	1767	**1049**	.594
* 8. **Steve Yzerman**, Det.	21	1453	**1043**	.718
9. **Marcel Dionne**, Det., L.A., NYR	18	1348	**1040**	.772
* 10. **Mario Lemieux**, Pit.	17	889	**1018**	1.145
11. **Doug Gilmour**, St.L., Cgy., Tor., N.J., Chi., Buf., Mtl.	20	1474	**964**	.654
* 12. **Al MacInnis**, Cgy., St.L.	23	1416	**934**	.660
13. **Larry Murphy**, L.A., Wsh., Min., Pit., Tor., Det.	21	1615	**929**	.575
14. **Stan Mikita**, Chi.	22	1394	**926**	.664
15. **Bryan Trottier**, NYI, Pit.	18	1279	**901**	.704
16. **Phil Housley**, Buf., Wpg., St.L., Cgy., N.J., Wsh., Chi., Tor.	21	1495	**894**	.598
17. **Dale Hawerchuk**, Wpg., Buf., St.L., Phi.	16	1188	**891**	.750
18. **Phil Esposito**, Chi., Bos., NYR	18	1282	**873**	.681
19. **Denis Savard**, Chi., Mtl., T.B.	17	1196	**865**	.723
* 20. **Joe Sakic**, Que., Col.	16	1155	**860**	.745
21. **Bobby Clarke**, Phi.	15	1144	**852**	.745
22. **Alex Delvecchio**, Det.	24	1549	**825**	.533
23. **Gilbert Perreault**, Buf.	17	1191	**814**	.683
24. **John Bucyk**, Det., Bos.	23	1540	**813**	.528
25. **Jari Kurri**, Edm., L.A., NYR, Ana., Col. . .	17	1251	**797**	.637
26. **Guy Lafleur**, Mtl., NYR, Que.	17	1126	**793**	.704
27. **Peter Stastny**, Que., N.J., St.L.	15	977	**789**	.808
* 28. **Pierre Turgeon**, Buf., NYI, Mtl., St.L., Dal.	17	1215	**779**	.641
29. **Jean Ratelle**, NYR, Bos.	21	1281	**776**	.606
* 30. **Vincent Damphousse**, Tor., Edm., Mtl., S.J.	18	1378	**773**	.561
* 31. **Jaromir Jagr**, Pit., Wsh., NYI	14	1027	**772**	.752
32. **Bernie Federko**, St.L., Det.	14	1000	**761**	.761
* 33. **Brian Leetch**, NYR, NYI, Tor.	17	1144	**754**	.659
34. **Larry Robinson**, Mtl., L.A.	20	1384	**750**	.542
* 35. **Mark Recchi**, Pit., Phi., Mtl.	16	1173	**745**	.635
36. **Denis Potvin**, NYI	15	1060	**742**	.700
37. **Norm Ullman**, Det., Tor.	20	1410	**739**	.524
* 38. **Chris Chelios**, Mtl., Chi., Det.	21	1395	**736**	.528
39. **Bernie Nicholls**, L.A., NYR, Edm., N.J., Chi., S.J.	18	1127	**734**	.651
* 40. **Luc Robitaille**, L.A., Pit., NYR, Det. . .	18	1366	**717**	.525
41. **Jean Beliveau**, Mtl.	20	1125	**712**	.633
* 42. **Scott Stevens**, Wsh., St.L., N.J.	22	1635	**712**	.435
43. **Dale Hunter**, Que., Wsh., Col.	19	1407	**697**	.495
44. **Henri Richard**, Mtl.	20	1256	**688**	.548
* 45. **Dave Andreychuk**, Buf., Tor., N.J., Bos., Col., T.B.	22	1597	**686**	.430
46. **Brad Park**, NYR, Bos., Det.	17	1113	**683**	.614
47. **Bobby Smith**, Min., Mtl.	15	1077	**679**	.630
* 48. **Brett Hull**, Cgy., St.L., Dal., Det.	19	1264	**649**	.513
* 49. **Mike Modano**, Min., Dal.	16	1101	**648**	.589
* 50. **Jeremy Roenick**, Chi., Phx., Phi.	16	1124	**645**	.574
51. **Bobby Orr**, Bos., Chi.	12	657	**645**	.982
52. **Gary Suter**, Cgy., Chi., S.J.	17	1145	**641**	.560
53. **Dave Taylor**, L.A.	17	1111	**638**	.574
54. **Darryl Sittler**, Tor., Phi., Det.	15	1096	**637**	.581
55. **Borje Salming**, Tor., Det.	17	1148	**637**	.555
56. **Neal Broten**, Min., Dal., N.J., L.A. . . .	17	1099	**634**	.577
57. **Theoren Fleury**, Cgy., Col., NYR, Chi. . .	15	1084	**633**	.584
58. **Mike Gartner**, Wsh., Min., NYR, Tor., Phx.	19	1432	**627**	.438
59. **Andy Bathgate**, NYR, Tor., Det., Pit. . . .	17	1069	**624**	.584
* 60. **Mats Sundin**, Que., Tor.	14	1086	**624**	.575
61. **Rod Gilbert**, NYR	18	1065	**615**	.577
62. **Michel Goulet**, Que., Chi.	15	1089	**604**	.555
* 63. **Doug Weight**, NYR, Edm., St.L.	14	912	**604**	.662
64. **Kirk Muller**, N.J., Mtl., NYI, Tor., Fla., Dal.	19	1349	**602**	.446
65. **Glenn Anderson**, Edm., Tor., NYR, St.L.	16	1129	**601**	.532
* 66. **Brendan Shanahan**, N.J., St.L., Hfd., Det.	17	1268	**593**	.468
67. **Dino Ciccarelli**, Min., Wsh., Det., T.B., Fla.	19	1232	**592**	.481
68. **Dave Keon**, Tor., Hfd.	18	1296	**590**	.455
69. **Doug Wilson**, Chi., S.J.	16	1024	**590**	.576
* 70. **Sergei Fedorov**, Det., Ana.	14	988	**588**	.595
71. **Dave Babych**, Wpg., Hfd., Van., Phi., L.A.	19	1195	**581**	.486
72. **Brian Propp**, Phi., Bos., Min., Hfd.	15	1016	**579**	.570

A top sniper during his years with Los Angeles, Bernie Nicholls was also an effective playmaker. He had 80 assists along with his 70 goals in 1988-89 and a total of 734 helpers in his career.

Player	Seasons	Games	Assists	Assist per game
73. **Steve Larmer**, Chi., NYR	15	1006	**571**	.568
74. **Frank Mahovlich**, Tor., Det., Mtl.	18	1181	**570**	.483
75. **Craig Janney**, Bos., St.L., S.J., Wpg., Phx., T.B., NYI	12	760	**563**	.741
* 76. **Cliff Ronning**, St.L., Van., Phx., Nsh., L.A., Min., NYI	18	1137	**563**	.495
77. **Joe Mullen**, St.L., Cgy., Pit., Bos.	17	1062	**561**	.528
78. **Bobby Hull**, Chi., Wpg., Hfd.	16	1063	**560**	.527
* 79. **Rod Brind'Amour**, St.L., Phi., Car.	16	1109	**560**	.505
* 80. **Nicklas Lidstrom**, Det.	13	1016	**553**	.544
81. **Thomas Steen**, Wpg.	14	950	**553**	.582
82. **Mike Bossy**, NYI	10	752	**553**	.735
83. **Tom Lysiak**, Atl., Chi.	13	919	**551**	.600
84. **Ken Linseman**, Phi., Edm., Bos., Tor. . . .	14	860	**551**	.641
* 85. **Alexander Mogilny**, Buf., Van., N.J., Tor.	15	956	**546**	.571
86. **Mark Howe**, Hfd., Phi., Det.	16	929	**545**	.587
87. **Pat LaFontaine**, NYI, Buf., NYR	15	865	**545**	.630
88. **Red Kelly**, Det., Tor.	20	1316	**542**	.412
89. **Pat Verbeek**, N.J., Hfd., NYR, Dal., Det.	20	1424	**541**	.380
90. **Rick Middleton**, NYR, Bos.	14	1005	**540**	.537
91. **Brian Bellows**, Min., Mtl., T.B., Ana., Wsh.	17	1188	**537**	.452
* 92. **Joe Nieuwendyk**, Cgy., Dal., N.J., Tor.	18	1177	**529**	.449
* 93. **Peter Forsberg**, Que., Col.	10	580	**525**	.905
94. **Steve Duchesne**, L.A., Phi., Que., St.L., Ott., Det.	14	1113	**525**	.472
95. **Dennis Maruk**, Cal., Cle., Min., Wsh. . .	14	888	**522**	.588
* 96. **Andrew Cassels**, Mtl., Hfd., Cgy., Van., CBJ	15	984	**520**	.528
97. **Wayne Cashman**, Bos.	17	1027	**516**	.502
98. **Butch Goring**, L.A., NYI, Bos.	16	1107	**513**	.463
* 99. **Steve Thomas**, Tor., Chi., NYI, N.J., Ana., Det.	20	1235	**512**	.415
100. **Rick Tocchet**, Phi., Pit., L.A., Bos., Wsh., Phx.	18	1144	**512**	.448

Top 100 Active Assist Leaders

	Player	Seasons	Games	Assists	Assists per game
1.	**Ron Francis**, Hfd., Pit., Car., Tor.	23	1731	**1249**	.722
2.	**Mark Messier**, Edm., NYR, Van.	25	1756	**1193**	.679
3.	**Steve Yzerman**, Det.	21	1453	**1043**	.718
4.	**Mario Lemieux**, Pit.	17	889	**1018**	1.145
5.	**Al MacInnis**, Cgy., St.L.	23	1416	**934**	.660
6.	**Joe Sakic**, Que., Col.	16	1155	**860**	.745
7.	**Pierre Turgeon**, Buf., NYI, Mtl., St.L., Dal.	17	1215	**779**	.641
8.	**Vincent Damphousse**, Tor., Edm., Mtl., S.J.	18	1378	**773**	.561
9.	**Jaromir Jagr**, Pit., Wsh., NYI	14	1027	**772**	.752
10.	**Brian Leetch**, NYR, NYI, Tor.	17	1144	**754**	.659
11.	**Mark Recchi**, Pit., Phi., Mtl.	16	1173	**745**	.635
12.	**Chris Chelios**, Mtl., Chi., Det.	21	1395	**736**	.528
13.	**Luc Robitaille**, L.A., Pit., NYR, Det.	18	1366	**717**	.525
14.	**Scott Stevens**, Wsh., St.L., N.J.	22	1635	**712**	.435
15.	**Dave Andreychuk**, Buf., Tor., N.J., Bos., Col., T.B.	22	1597	**686**	.430
16.	**Brett Hull**, Cgy., St.L., Dal., Det.	19	1264	**649**	.513
17.	**Mike Modano**, Min., Dal.	16	1101	**648**	.589
18.	**Jeremy Roenick**, Chi., Phx., Phi.	16	1124	**645**	.574
19.	**Mats Sundin**, Que., Tor.	14	1086	**624**	.575
20.	**Doug Weight**, NYR, Edm., St.L.	14	912	**604**	.662
21.	**Brendan Shanahan**, N.J., St.L., Hfd., Det.	17	1268	**593**	.468
22.	**Sergei Fedorov**, Det., Ana.	14	988	**588**	.595
23.	**Cliff Ronning**, St.L., Van., Phx., Nsh., L.A., Min., NYI	18	1137	**563**	.495
24.	**Rod Brind'Amour**, St.L., Phi., Car.	16	1109	**560**	.505
25.	**Nicklas Lidstrom**, Det.	13	1016	**553**	.544
26.	**Alexander Mogilny**, Buf., Van., N.J., Tor.	15	956	**546**	.571
27.	**Joe Nieuwendyk**, Cgy., Dal., N.J., Tor.	18	1177	**529**	.449
28.	**Peter Forsberg**, Que., Col.	10	580	**525**	.905
29.	**Andrew Cassels**, Mtl., Hfd., Cgy., Van., CBJ	15	984	**520**	.528
30.	**Steve Thomas**, Tor., Chi., NYI, N.J., Ana., Det.	20	1235	**512**	.415
31.	**Teemu Selanne**, Wpg., Ana., S.J., Col.	12	879	**499**	.568
32.	**James Patrick**, NYR, Hfd., Cgy., Buf.	21	1280	**490**	.383
33.	**Sergei Zubov**, NYR, Pit., Dal.	12	856	**484**	.565
34.	**Trevor Linden**, Van., NYI, Mtl., Wsh.	16	1161	**465**	.401
35.	**Eric Lindros**, Phi., NYR, NYI.	11	678	**461**	.680
36.	**Alex Zhamnov**, Wpg., Chi., Phi.	12	783	**461**	.589
37.	**Teppo Numminen**, Wpg., Phx., Dal.	16	1160	**440**	.379
38.	**Tony Amonte**, NYR, Chi., Phx., Phi.	14	1013	**436**	.430
39.	**Scott Mellanby**, Phi., Edm., Fla., St.L.	19	1291	**430**	.333
40.	**Eric Desjardins**, Mtl., Phi.	16	1098	**419**	.382
41.	**Gary Roberts**, Cgy., Car., Tor.	18	1029	**409**	.397
42.	**Keith Tkachuk**, Wpg., Phx., St.L.	13	856	**401**	.468
43.	**Rob Blake**, L.A., Col.	15	903	**400**	.443
44.	**Jozef Stumpel**, Bos., L.A.	13	758	**397**	.524
45.	**Paul Kariya**, Ana., Col.	10	657	**394**	.600
46.	**Alex Kovalev**, NYR, Pit., Mtl.	12	849	**388**	.457
47.	**Owen Nolan**, Que., Col., S.J., Tor.	14	915	**386**	.422
48.	**Scott Young**, Hfd., Pit., Que., Col., Ana., St.L., Dal.	16	1102	**384**	.348
49.	**Mathieu Schneider**, Mtl., NYI, Tor., NYR, L.A., Det.	16	992	**384**	.387
50.	**Glen Wesley**, Bos., Hfd., Car., Tor.	17	1247	**382**	.306
51.	**Petr Nedved**, Van., St.L., NYR, Pit., Edm.	13	889	**379**	.426
52.	**John LeClair**, Mtl., Phi.	14	873	**379**	.434
53.	**Robert Reichel**, Cgy., NYI, Phx., Tor.	11	830	**378**	.455
54.	**Alexei Yashin**, Ott., NYI	10	710	**374**	.527
55.	**Sandis Ozolinsh**, S.J., Col., Car., Fla., Ana.	12	779	**367**	.471
56.	**Scott Niedermayer**, N.J.	13	892	**364**	.408
57.	**Peter Bondra**, Wsh., Ott.	14	984	**362**	.368
58.	**Bobby Holik**, Hfd., N.J., NYR	14	1024	**361**	.353
59.	**Mike Ricci**, Phi., Que., Col., S.J.	14	1014	**355**	.350
60.	**Ziggy Palffy**, NYI, L.A.	11	642	**353**	.550
61.	**Daniel Alfredsson**, Ott.	9	629	**349**	.555
62.	**Keith Primeau**, Det., Hfd., Car., Phi.	14	900	**347**	.386
63.	**Darryl Sydor**, L.A., Dal., CBJ, T.B.	13	943	**342**	.363
64.	**Markus Naslund**, Pit., Van.	11	790	**339**	.429
65.	**Martin Straka**, Pit., Ott., NYI, Fla., L.A.	12	730	**338**	.463
66.	**Ray Whitney**, S.J., Edm., Fla., CBJ, Det.	13	700	**330**	.471
67.	**Roman Hamrlik**, T.B., Edm., NYI	12	873	**324**	.371
68.	**Jason Arnott**, Edm., N.J., Dal.	11	743	**324**	.436
69.	**Shawn McEachern**, Pit., L.A., Bos., Ott., Atl.	13	883	**317**	.359
70.	**Alexei Zhitnik**, L.A., Buf.	12	882	**315**	.357
71.	**Bill Guerin**, N.J., Edm., Bos., Dal.	13	879	**308**	.350
72.	**Vyacheslav Kozlov**, Det., Buf., Atl.	13	800	**307**	.384

St. Louis set-up man Doug Weight was seventh in the NHL with 51 assists in 2003-04. He received an NHL milestone award for collecting his 600th career assist on March 27, 2004.

	Player	Games	Assists	Assists per game
73.	**Michael Nylander**, Hfd., Cgy., T.B., Chi., Wsh., Bos.	11	648	**307**	.474
74.	**Chris Pronger**, Hfd., St.L.	11	722	**306**	.424
75.	**Pavol Demitra**, Ott., St.L.	11	553	**303**	.548
76.	**Bryan Smolinski**, Bos., Pit., NYI, L.A., Ott.	12	829	**303**	.366
77.	**Eric Weinrich**, N.J., Hfd., Chi., Mtl., Bos., Phi., St.L.	16	1082	**302**	.279
78.	**Mike Keane**, Mtl., Col., NYR, Dal., St.L., Van.	16	1161	**302**	.260
79.	**Martin Rucinsky**, Edm., Que., Col., Mtl., Dal., NYR, St.L., Van.	13	817	**300**	.367
80.	**Chris Gratton**, T.B., Phi., Buf., Phx., Col.	11	851	**296**	.348
81.	**Geoff Sanderson**, Hfd., Car., Van., Buf., CBJ	14	928	**296**	.319
82.	**Robert Lang**, L.A., Bos., Pit., Wsh., Det.	11	646	**293**	.454
83.	**Stu Barnes**, Wpg., Fla., Pit., Buf., Dal.	13	897	**292**	.326
84.	**Jason Allison**, Wsh., Bos., L.A.	10	486	**288**	.593
85.	**Martin Gelinas**, Edm., Que., Van., Car., Cgy.	16	1052	**286**	.272
86.	**Jeff Friesen**, S.J., Ana., N.J.	10	770	**285**	.370
87.	**Steve Rucchin**, Ana.	10	616	**279**	.453
88.	**Saku Koivu**, Mtl.	9	497	**278**	.559
89.	**Sergei Gonchar**, Wsh., Bos.	10	669	**277**	.414
90.	**Steve Sullivan**, N.J., Tor., Chi., Nsh.	9	597	**274**	.459
91.	**Dallas Drake**, Det., Wpg., Phx., St.L.	12	822	**267**	.325
92.	**Patrice Brisebois**, Mtl.	14	791	**263**	.332
93.	**Joe Thornton**, Bos.	7	509	**261**	.513
94.	**Miroslav Satan**, Edm., Buf.	9	704	**260**	.369
95.	**Todd Bertuzzi**, NYI, Van.	9	628	**260**	.414
96.	**Petr Sykora**, N.J., Ana.	9	608	**259**	.426
97.	**Vladimir Malakhov**, NYI, Mtl., N.J., NYR, Phi.	12	683	**255**	.373
98.	**Glen Murray**, Bos., Pit., L.A.	13	823	**255**	.310
99.	**Jarome Iginla**, Cgy.	9	626	**253**	.404
100.	**Patrik Elias**, N.J.	9	558	**252**	.452

Top 100 All-Time Point Leaders

* active player

With two goals in a game on November 4, 2003, Mark Messier moved past Gordie Howe into second place on the NHL's all-time scoring list. Messier had 682 goals and 1,169 assists for 1,851 points.

	Player	Seasons	Games	Goals	Assists	Points	Points per game
1.	Wayne Gretzky, Edm., L.A., St.L., NYR	20	1487	894	1963	**2857**	1.921
* 2.	Mark Messier, Edm., NYR, Van.	25	1756	694	1193	**1887**	1.075
3.	Gordie Howe, Det., Hfd.	26	1767	801	1049	**1850**	1.047
* 4.	Ron Francis, Hfd., Pit., Car., Tor.	23	1731	549	1249	**1798**	1.039
5.	Marcel Dionne, Det., L.A., NYR	18	1348	731	1040	**1771**	1.314
* 6.	Steve Yzerman, Det.	21	1453	678	1043	**1721**	1.184
* 7.	Mario Lemieux, Pit.	17	889	683	1018	**1701**	1.913
8.	Phil Esposito, Chi., Bos., NYR	18	1282	717	873	**1590**	1.240
9.	Raymond Bourque, Bos., Col.	22	1612	410	1169	**1579**	.980
10.	Paul Coffey, Edm., Pit., L.A., Det., Hfd., Phi., Chi., Car., Bos.	21	1409	396	1135	**1531**	1.087
11.	Stan Mikita, Chi.	22	1394	541	926	**1467**	1.052
12.	Bryan Trottier, NYI, Pit.	18	1279	524	901	**1425**	1.114
13.	Adam Oates, Det., St.L., Bos., Wsh., Phi., Ana., Edm.	19	1337	341	1079	**1420**	1.062
14.	Doug Gilmour, St.L., Cgy., Tor., N.J., Chi., Buf., Mtl.	20	1474	450	964	**1414**	.959
15.	Dale Hawerchuk, Wpg., Buf., St.L., Phi.	16	1188	518	891	**1409**	1.186
* 16.	Joe Sakic, Que., Col.	16	1155	542	860	**1402**	1.214
17.	Jari Kurri, Edm., L.A., NYR, Ana., Col.	17	1251	601	797	**1398**	1.118
* 18.	Brett Hull, Cgy., St.L., Dal., Det.	19	1264	741	649	**1390**	1.100
* 19.	Luc Robitaille, L.A., Pit., NYR, Det.	18	1366	653	717	**1370**	1.003
20.	John Bucyk, Det., Bos.	23	1540	556	813	**1369**	.889
21.	Guy Lafleur, Mtl., NYR, Que.	17	1126	560	793	**1353**	1.202
22.	Denis Savard, Chi., Mtl., T.B.	17	1196	473	865	**1338**	1.119
23.	Mike Gartner, Wsh., Min., NYR, Tor., Phx.	19	1432	708	627	**1335**	.932
24.	Gilbert Perreault, Buf.	17	1191	512	814	**1326**	1.113
* 25.	Dave Andreychuk, Buf., Tor., N.J., Bos., Col., T.B.	22	1597	634	686	**1320**	.827
* 26.	Jaromir Jagr, Pit., Wsh., NYI	14	1027	537	772	**1309**	1.275
27.	Alex Delvecchio, Det.	24	1549	456	825	**1281**	.827
* 28.	Pierre Turgeon, Buf., NYI, Mtl., St.L., Dal.	17	1215	495	779	**1274**	1.049
* 29.	Al MacInnis, Cgy., St.L.	23	1416	340	934	**1274**	.900
30.	Jean Ratelle, NYR, Bos.	21	1281	491	776	**1267**	.989
31.	Peter Stastny, Que., N.J., St.L.	15	977	450	789	**1239**	1.268
32.	Phil Housley, Buf., Wpg., St.L., Cgy., N.J., Wsh., Chi., Tor.	21	1495	338	894	**1232**	.824
33.	Norm Ullman, Det., Tor.	20	1410	490	739	**1229**	.872
34.	Jean Beliveau, Mtl.	20	1125	507	712	**1219**	1.084
35.	Larry Murphy, L.A., Wsh., Min., Pit., Tor., Det.	21	1615	287	929	**1216**	.753
36.	Bobby Clarke, Phi.	15	1144	358	852	**1210**	1.058
37.	Bernie Nicholls, L.A., NYR, Edm., N.J., Chi., S.J.	18	1127	475	734	**1209**	1.073
* 38.	Vincent Damphousse, Tor., Edm., Mtl., S.J.	18	1378	432	773	**1205**	.874
* 39.	Mark Recchi, Pit., Phi., Mtl.	16	1173	456	745	**1201**	1.024
40.	Dino Ciccarelli, Min., Wsh., Det., T.B., Fla.	19	1232	608	592	**1200**	.974
41.	Bobby Hull, Chi., Wpg., Hfd.	16	1063	610	560	**1170**	1.101
42.	Michel Goulet, Que., Chi.	15	1089	548	604	**1152**	1.058
* 43.	Brendan Shanahan, N.J., St.L., Hfd., Det.	17	1268	558	593	**1151**	.908
44.	Bernie Federko, St.L., Det.	14	1000	369	761	**1130**	1.130
45.	Mike Bossy, NYI	10	752	573	553	**1126**	1.497
46.	Darryl Sittler, Tor., Phi., Det.	15	1096	484	637	**1121**	1.023
* 47.	Jeremy Roenick, Chi., Phx., Phi.	16	1124	475	645	**1120**	.996
* 48.	Mike Modano, Min., Dal.	16	1101	458	648	**1106**	1.005
49.	Frank Mahovlich, Tor., Det., NYR, St.L., Mtl.	18	1181	533	570	**1103**	.934
50.	Glenn Anderson, Edm., Tor., NYR, St.L.	16	1129	498	601	**1099**	.973
* 51.	Mats Sundin, Que., Tor.	14	1086	465	624	**1089**	1.003
52.	Theoren Fleury, Cgy., Col., NYR, Chi.	15	1084	455	633	**1088**	1.004
53.	Dave Taylor, L.A.	17	1111	431	638	**1069**	.962
54.	Pat Verbeek, N.J., Hfd., NYR, Dal., Det.	20	1424	522	541	**1063**	.746
55.	Joe Mullen, St.L., Cgy., Pit., Bos.	17	1062	502	561	**1063**	1.001
* 56.	Joe Nieuwendyk, Cgy., Dal., N.J., Tor.	18	1177	533	529	**1062**	.902
57.	Denis Potvin, NYI	15	1060	310	742	**1052**	.992
58.	Henri Richard, Mtl.	20	1256	358	688	**1046**	.833
59.	Bobby Smith, Min., Mtl.	15	1077	357	679	**1036**	.962
60.	Brian Bellows, Min., Mtl., T.B., Ana., Wsh.	17	1188	485	537	**1022**	.860
61.	Rod Gilbert, NYR.	18	1065	406	615	**1021**	.959
62.	Dale Hunter, Que., Wsh., Col.	19	1407	323	697	**1020**	.725
* 63.	Sergei Fedorov, Det., Ana.	14	988	431	588	**1019**	1.031
64.	Pat LaFontaine, NYI, Buf., NYR	15	865	468	545	**1013**	1.171
65.	Steve Larmer, Chi., NYR	15	1006	441	571	**1012**	1.006
* 66.	Alexander Mogilny, Buf., Van., N.J., Tor.	15	956	461	546	**1007**	1.053
67.	Lanny McDonald, Tor., Col., Cgy.	16	1111	500	506	**1006**	.905
68.	Brian Propp, Phi., Bos., Min., Hfd.	15	1016	425	579	**1004**	.988
* 69.	Brian Leetch, NYR, NYI, Tor.	17	1144	242	754	**996**	.871
70.	Rick Middleton, NYR, Bos.	14	1005	448	540	**988**	.983
71.	Dave Keon, Tor., Hfd.	18	1296	396	590	**986**	.761
72.	Andy Bathgate, NYR, Tor., Det., Pit.	17	1069	349	624	**973**	.910
73.	Maurice Richard, Mtl.	18	978	544	421	**965**	.987
74.	Kirk Muller, N.J., Mtl., NYI, Tor., Fla., Dal.	19	1349	357	602	**959**	.711
75.	Larry Robinson, Mtl., L.A.	20	1384	208	750	**958**	.692
76.	Rick Tocchet, Phi., Pit., L.A., Bos., Wsh., Phx.	18	1144	440	512	**952**	.832
* 77.	Teemu Selanne, Wpg., Ana., S.J., Col.	12	879	452	499	**951**	1.082
* 78.	Steve Thomas, Tor., Chi., NYI, N.J., Ana., Det.	20	1235	421	512	**933**	.755
79.	Neal Broten, Min., Dal., N.J., L.A.	17	1099	289	634	**923**	.840
80.	Bobby Orr, Bos., Chi.	12	657	270	645	**915**	1.393
* 81.	Chris Chelios, Mtl., Chi., Det.	21	1395	178	736	**914**	.655
* 82.	Rod Brind'Amour, St.L., Phi., Car.	16	1109	351	560	**911**	.821
* 83.	Scott Stevens, Wsh., St.L., N.J.	22	1635	196	712	**908**	.555
84.	Ray Ferraro, Hfd., NYI, NYR, L.A., Atl., St.L.	18	1258	408	490	**898**	.714
85.	Brad Park, NYR, Bos., Det.	17	1113	213	683	**896**	.805
86.	Butch Goring, L.A., NYI, Bos.	16	1107	375	513	**888**	.802
87.	Bill Barber, Phi.	14	903	420	463	**883**	.978
88.	Dennis Maruk, Cal., Cle., Min., Wsh.	14	888	356	522	**878**	.989
* 89.	Cliff Ronning, St.L., Van., Phx., Nsh., L.A., Min., NYI	18	1137	306	563	**869**	.764
90.	Ivan Boldirev, Bos., Cal., Chi., Atl., Van., Det.	15	1052	361	505	**866**	.823
91.	Yvan Cournoyer, Mtl.	16	968	428	435	**863**	.892
92.	Dean Prentice, NYR, Bos., Det., Pit., Min.	22	1378	391	469	**860**	.624
93.	Tomas Sandstrom, NYR, L.A., Pit., Det., Ana.	15	983	394	462	**856**	.871
94.	Ted Lindsay, Det., Chi.	17	1068	379	472	**851**	.797
95.	Gary Suter, Cgy., Chi., S.J.	17	1145	203	641	**844**	.737
96.	Tom Lysiak, Atl., Chi.	13	919	292	551	**843**	.917
97.	John MacLean, N.J., S.J., NYR, Dal.	18	1194	413	429	**842**	.705
* 98.	Peter Bondra, Wsh., Ott.	14	984	477	362	**839**	.853
99.	John Tonelli, NYI, Cgy., L.A., Chi., Que.	14	1028	325	511	**836**	.813
100.	Jacques Lemaire, Mtl.	12	853	366	469	**835**	.979

Top 100 Active Points Leaders

Ottawa's Daniel Alfredsson finished seventh in the NHL with 80 points in 2003-04. He has scored a total of 568 points in nine seasons with the Senators.

	Player	Seasons	Games	Goals	Assists	Points	Points per game
1.	Mark Messier, Edm., NYR, Van.	25	1756	694	1193	**1887**	1.075
2.	Ron Francis, Hfd., Pit., Car., Tor.	23	1731	549	1249	**1798**	1.039
3.	Steve Yzerman, Det.	21	1453	678	1043	**1721**	1.184
4.	Mario Lemieux, Pit.	17	889	683	1018	**1701**	1.913
5.	Joe Sakic, Que., Col.	16	1155	542	860	**1402**	1.214
6.	Brett Hull, Cgy., St.L., Dal., Det.	19	1264	741	649	**1390**	1.100
7.	Luc Robitaille, L.A., Pit., NYR, Det.	18	1366	653	717	**1370**	1.003
8.	Dave Andreychuk, Buf., Tor., N.J., Bos., Col., T.B.	22	1597	634	686	**1320**	.827
9.	Jaromir Jagr, Pit., Wsh., NYI	14	1027	537	772	**1309**	1.275
10.	Al MacInnis, Cgy., St.L.	23	1416	340	934	**1274**	.900
11.	Pierre Turgeon, Buf., NYI, Mtl., St.L., Dal.	17	1215	495	779	**1274**	1.049
12.	Vincent Damphousse, Tor., Edm., Mtl., S.J.	18	1378	432	773	**1205**	.874
13.	Mark Recchi, Pit., Phi., Mtl.	16	1173	456	745	**1201**	1.024
14.	Brendan Shanahan, N.J., St.L., Hfd., Det.	17	1268	558	593	**1151**	.908
15.	Jeremy Roenick, Chi., Phx., Phi.	16	1124	475	645	**1120**	.996
16.	Mike Modano, Min., Dal.	16	1101	458	648	**1106**	1.005
17.	Mats Sundin, Que., Tor.	14	1086	465	624	**1089**	1.003
18.	Joe Nieuwendyk, Cgy., Dal., N.J., Tor.	18	1177	533	529	**1062**	.902
19.	Sergei Fedorov, Det., Ana.	14	988	431	588	**1019**	1.031
20.	Alexander Mogilny, Buf., Van., N.J., Tor.	15	956	461	546	**1007**	1.053
21.	Brian Leetch, NYR, NYI, Tor.	17	1144	242	754	**996**	.871
22.	Teemu Selanne, Wpg., Ana., S.J., Col.	12	879	452	499	**951**	1.082
23.	Steve Thomas, Tor., Chi., NYI, N.J., Ana., Det.	20	1235	421	512	**933**	.755
24.	Chris Chelios, Mtl., Chi., Det.	21	1395	178	736	**914**	.655
25.	Rod Brind'Amour, St.L., Phi., Car.	16	1109	351	560	**911**	.821
26.	Scott Stevens, Wsh., St.L., N.J.	22	1635	196	712	**908**	.555
27.	Cliff Ronning, St.L., Van., Phx., Nsh., L.A., Min., NYI	18	1137	306	563	**869**	.764
28.	Peter Bondra, Wsh., Ott.	14	984	477	362	**839**	.853
29.	Keith Tkachuk, Wpg., Phx., St.L.	13	856	431	401	**832**	.972
30.	Tony Amonte, NYR, Chi., Phx., St.L.	14	1013	392	436	**828**	.817
31.	Doug Weight, NYR, Edm., St.L.	14	912	224	604	**828**	.908
32.	Eric Lindros, Phi., NYR, NYI	11	678	356	461	**817**	1.205
33.	Trevor Linden, Van., NYI, Mtl., Wsh.	16	1161	349	465	**814**	.701
34.	Gary Roberts, Cgy., Car., Tor.	18	1029	397	409	**806**	.783
35.	Scott Mellanby, Phi., Edm., Fla., Atl.	19	1291	340	430	**770**	.596
36.	John LeClair, Mtl., Phi.	14	873	382	379	**761**	.872
37.	Peter Forsberg, Que., Col.	10	580	216	525	**741**	1.278
38.	Owen Nolan, Que., Col., S.J., Tor.	14	915	349	386	**735**	.803
39.	Nicklas Lidstrom, Det.	13	1016	173	553	**726**	.715
40.	Andrew Cassels, Mtl., Hfd., Cgy., Van., CBJ.	15	984	200	520	**720**	.732
41.	Alex Zhamnov, Wpg., Chi., Phi.	12	783	248	461	**709**	.905
42.	Scott Young, Hfd., Pit., Que., Col., Ana., St.L., Dal.	16	1102	324	384	**708**	.642
43.	Paul Kariya, Ana., Col.	10	657	311	394	**705**	1.073
44.	Petr Nedved, Van., St.L., NYR, Pit., Edm.	13	889	301	379	**680**	.765
45.	Alex Kovalev, NYR, Pit., Mtl.	12	849	292	388	**680**	.801
46.	Ziggy Palffy, NYI, L.A.	11	642	318	353	**671**	1.045
47.	Alexei Yashin, Ott., NYI	10	710	291	374	**665**	.937
48.	Bobby Holik, Hfd., N.J., NYR	14	1024	281	361	**642**	.627
49.	James Patrick, NYR, Hfd., Cgy., Buf.	21	1280	149	490	**639**	.499
50.	Robert Reichel, Cgy., NYI, Phx., Tor.	11	830	252	378	**630**	.759
51.	Markus Naslund, Pit., Van.	11	790	290	339	**629**	.796
52.	Bill Guerin, N.J., Edm., Bos., Dal.	13	879	315	308	**623**	.709
53.	Geoff Sanderson, Hfd., Car., Van., Buf., CBJ	14	928	316	296	**612**	.659
54.	Keith Primeau, Det., Hfd., Car., Phi.	14	900	265	347	**612**	.680
55.	Sergei Zubov, NYR, Pit., Dal.	12	856	123	484	**607**	.709
56.	Mike Ricci, Phi., Que., Col., S.J.	14	1014	233	355	**588**	.580

	Player	Seasons	Games	Goals	Assists	Points	Points per game
57.	Rob Blake, L.A., Col.	15	903	186	400	**586**	.649
58.	Joe Juneau, Bos., Wsh., Buf., Ott., Phx., Mtl.	13	828	156	416	**572**	.691
59.	Shawn McEachern, Pit., L.A., Bos., Ott., Atl.	13	883	254	317	**571**	.647
60.	Daniel Alfredsson, Ott.	9	629	219	349	**568**	.903
61.	Jason Arnott, Edm., N.J., Dal.	11	743	244	324	**568**	.764
62.	Vyacheslav Kozlov, Det., Buf., Atl.	13	800	252	307	**559**	.699
63.	Martin Gelinas, Edm., Que., Van., Car., Cgy.	16	1052	269	286	**555**	.528
64.	Mathieu Schneider, Mtl., NYI, Tor., NYR, L.A., Det.	16	992	168	384	**552**	.556
65.	Eric Desjardins, Mtl., Phi.	16	1098	132	419	**551**	.502
66.	Teppo Numminen, Wpg., Phx., Dal.	16	1160	111	440	**551**	.475
67.	Jozef Stumpel, Bos., L.A.	13	758	151	397	**548**	.723
68.	Ray Whitney, S.J., Edm., Fla., CBJ, Det.	13	700	205	330	**535**	.764
69.	Bryan Smolinski, Bos., Pit., NYI, L.A., Ott.	12	829	231	303	**534**	.644
70.	Martin Straka, Pit., Ott., NYI, Fla., L.A.	12	730	192	338	**530**	.726
71.	Sandis Ozolinsh, S.J., Col., Car., Fla., Ana.	12	779	158	367	**525**	.674
72.	Glen Murray, Bos., Pit., L.A.	13	823	268	255	**523**	.635
73.	Miroslav Satan, Edm., Buf.	9	704	259	260	**519**	.737
74.	Pavol Demitra, Ott., St.L.	11	553	216	303	**519**	.939
75.	Stu Barnes, Wpg., Fla., Pit., Buf., Dal.	13	897	221	292	**513**	.572
76.	Donald Audette, Buf., L.A., Atl., Dal., Mtl., Fla.	15	735	260	249	**509**	.693
77.	Martin Rucinsky, Edm., Que., Col., Mtl., Dal., NYR, St.L., Van.	13	817	208	300	**508**	.622
78.	Glen Wesley, Bos., Hfd., Car., Tor.	17	1247	124	382	**506**	.406.
79.	Jarome Iginla, Cgy.	9	626	250	253	**503**	.804
80.	Jeff Friesen, S.J., Ana., N.J.	10	770	208	285	**493**	.640
81.	Scott Niedermayer, N.J.	13	892	112	364	**476**	.534
82.	Mike Keane, Mtl., Col., NYR, Dal., St.L., Van.	16	1161	168	302	**470**	.405
83.	Chris Gratton, T.B., Phi., Buf., Phx., Col.	11	851	174	296	**470**	.552
84.	Robert Lang, L.A., Bos., Pit., Wsh., Det.	11	646	174	293	**467**	.723
85.	Petr Sykora, N.J., Ana.	9	608	202	259	**461**	.758
86.	Patrik Elias, N.J.	9	558	207	252	**459**	.823
87.	Todd Bertuzzi, NYI, Van.	9	628	198	260	**458**	.729
88.	Steve Sullivan, N.J., Tor., Chi., Nsh.	9	597	175	274	**449**	.752
89.	Michael Nylander, Hfd., Cgy., T.B., Chi., Wsh., Bos.	11	648	140	307	**447**	.690
90.	Roman Hamrlik, T.B., Edm., NYI	12	873	117	324	**441**	.505
91.	Cory Stillman, Cgy., St.L., T.B.	10	645	184	250	**434**	.673
92.	Dallas Drake, Det., Wpg., Phx., St.L.	12	822	166	267	**433**	.527
93.	Steve Rucchin, Ana.	10	616	153	279	**432**	.701
94.	Brian Rolston, N.J., Col., Bos.	10	736	190	242	**432**	.587
95.	Travis Green, NYI, Ana., Phx., Tor., Bos.	12	857	182	249	**431**	.503
96.	Ryan Smyth, Edm.	10	642	198	232	**430**	.670
97.	Darryl Sydor, L.A., Dal., CBJ, T.B.	13	943	85	342	**427**	.453
98.	Jason Allison, Wsh., Bos., L.A.	10	486	137	288	**425**	.874
99.	Sergei Gonchar, Wsh., Bos.	10	669	148	277	**425**	.635
100.	Mariusz Czerkawski, Bos., Edm., NYI, Mtl.	11	710	207	218	**425**	.599

Top 100 All-Time Games Played Leaders

* active player

Player	Seasons	Games Played
1. **Gordie Howe**, Det., Hfd.	26	**1767**
* 2. **Mark Messier**, Edm., NYR, Van.	25	**1756**
* 3. **Ron Francis**, Hfd., Pit., Car., Tor.	23	**1731**
* 4. **Scott Stevens**, Wsh., St.L., N.J.	22	**1635**
5. **Larry Murphy**, L.A., Wsh., Min., Pit., Tor., Det.	21	**1615**
6. **Raymond Bourque**, Bos., Col.	22	**1612**
* 7. **Dave Andreychuk**, Buf., Tor., N.J., Bos., Col., T.B.	22	**1597**
8. **Alex Delvecchio**, Det.	24	**1549**
9. **John Bucyk**, Det., Bos.	23	**1540**
10. **Phil Housley**, Buf., Wpg., St.L., Cgy., N.J., Wsh., Chi., Tor.	21	**1495**
11. **Wayne Gretzky**, Edm., L.A., St.L., NYR	20	**1487**
12. **Doug Gilmour**, St.L., Cgy., Tor., N.J., Chi., Buf., Mtl.	20	**1474**
* 13. **Steve Yzerman**, Det.	21	**1453**
14. **Tim Horton**, Tor., NYR, Pit., Buf.	24	**1446**
15. **Mike Gartner**, Wsh., Min., NYR, Tor., Phx.	19	**1432**
16. **Pat Verbeek**, N.J., Hfd., NYR, Dal., Det.	20	**1424**
* 17. **Al MacInnis**, Cgy., St.L.	23	**1416**
18. **Harry Howell**, NYR, Oak., Cal., L.A.	21	**1411**
19. **Norm Ullman**, Det., Tor.	20	**1410**
20. **Paul Coffey**, Edm., Pit., L.A., Det., Hfd., Phi., Chi., Car., Bos.	21	**1409**
21. **Dale Hunter**, Que., Wsh., Col.	19	**1407**
* 22. **Chris Chelios**, Mtl., Chi., Det.	21	**1395**
23. **Stan Mikita**, Chi.	22	**1394**
24. **Doug Mohns**, Bos., Chi., Min., Atl., Wsh.	22	**1390**
25. **Larry Robinson**, Mtl., L.A.	20	**1384**
* 26. **Vincent Damphousse**, Tor., Edm., Mtl., S.J.	18	**1378**
27. **Dean Prentice**, NYR, Bos., Det., Pit., Min.	22	**1378**
* 28. **Luc Robitaille**, L.A., Pit., NYR, Det.	18	**1366**
29. **Ron Stewart**, Tor., Bos., St.L., NYR, Van., NYI	21	**1353**
30. **Kirk Muller**, N.J., Mtl., NYI, Tor., Fla., Dal.	19	**1349**
31. **Marcel Dionne**, Det., L.A., NYR	18	**1348**
32. **Adam Oates**, Det., St.L., Bos., Wsh., Phi., Ana., Edm.	19	**1337**
33. **Guy Carbonneau**, Mtl., St.L., Dal.	19	**1318**
34. **Red Kelly**, Det., Tor.	20	**1316**
35. **Dave Keon**, Tor., Hfd.	18	**1296**
* 36. **Scott Mellanby**, Phi., Edm., Fla., St.L.	19	**1291**
37. **Ken Daneyko**, N.J.	20	**1283**
38. **Phil Esposito**, Chi., Bos., NYR	18	**1282**
39. **Jean Ratelle**, NYR, Bos.	21	**1281**
* 40. **James Patrick**, NYR, Hfd., Cgy., Buf.	21	**1280**
41. **Bryan Trottier**, NYI, Pit.	18	**1279**
* 42. **Brendan Shanahan**, N.J., St.L., Hfd., Det.	17	**1268**
* 43. **Brett Hull**, Cgy., St.L., Dal., Det.	19	**1264**
44. **Ray Ferraro**, Hfd., NYI, NYR, L.A., Atl., St.L.	18	**1258**
45. **Craig Ludwig**, Mtl., NYI, Min., Dal.	17	**1256**
46. **Henri Richard**, Mtl.	20	**1256**
47. **Kevin Lowe**, Edm., NYR.	19	**1254**
48. **Jari Kurri**, Edm., L.A., NYR, Ana., Col.	17	**1251**
49. **Bill Gadsby**, Chi., NYR, Det.	20	**1248**
* 50. **Luke Richardson**, Tor., Edm., Phi., CBJ	17	**1247**
* 51. **Glen Wesley**, Bos., Hfd., Car., Tor.	17	**1247**
52. **Allan Stanley**, NYR, Chi., Bos., Tor., Phi.	21	**1244**
* 53. **Steve Thomas**, Tor., Chi., NYI, N.J., Ana., Det.	20	**1235**
54. **Dino Ciccarelli**, Min., Wsh., Det., T.B., Fla.	19	**1232**
55. **Brad McCrimmon**, Bos., Phi., Cgy., Det., Hfd., Phx.	18	**1222**
56. **Ed Westfall**, Bos., NYI	18	**1220**
57. **Eric Nesterenko**, Tor., Chi.	21	**1219**
* 58. **Pierre Turgeon**, Buf., NYI, Mtl., St.L., Dal.	17	**1215**
59. **Marcel Pronovost**, Det., Tor.	21	**1206**
60. **Claude Lemieux**, Mtl., N.J., Col., Phx., Dal.	20	**1197**
61. **Denis Savard**, Chi., Mtl., T.B.	17	**1196**
62. **Dave Babych**, Wpg., Hfd., Van., Phi., L.A.	19	**1195**
63. **John MacLean**, N.J., S.J., NYR, Dal.	18	**1194**
64. **Gilbert Perreault**, Buf.	17	**1191**
* 65. **Marc Bergevin**, Chi., NYI, Hfd., T.B., Det., St.L., Pit., Van.	20	**1191**
66. **Dale Hawerchuk**, Wpg., Buf., St.L., Phi.	16	**1188**
67. **Brian Bellows**, Min., Mtl., T.B., Ana., Wsh.	17	**1188**
68. **Kevin Dineen**, Hfd., Phi., Car., Ott., CBJ	19	**1188**
69. **George Armstrong**, Tor.	21	**1187**
* 70. **Kelly Buchberger**, Edm., Atl., L.A., Phx., Pit.	18	**1182**
71. **Frank Mahovlich**, Tor., Det., Mtl.	18	**1181**
72. **Bob Carpenter**, Wsh., NYR, L.A., Bos., N.J.	19	**1178**
* 73. **Joe Nieuwendyk**, Cgy., Dal., N.J., Tor.	18	**1177**
74. **Don Marshall**, Mtl., NYR, Buf., Tor.	19	**1176**
* 75. **Mark Recchi**, Pit., Phi., Mtl.	16	**1173**
76. **Sylvain Cote**, Hfd., Wsh., Tor., Chi., Dal.	19	**1171**
* 77. **Mike Keane**, Mtl., Col., NYR, Dal., St.L., Van.	16	**1161**

Larry Murphy was the first to surpass Tim Horton's NHL record of 1,446 games played on defense. Murphy played 1,615 games with six teams over a 21-year career. He will be inducted into the Hockey Hall of Fame this year alongside Raymond Bourque and Paul Coffey.

Player	Seasons	Games Played
* 78. **Trevor Linden**, Van., NYI, Mtl., Wsh.	16	**1161**
79. **Bob Gainey**, Mtl.	16	**1160**
* 80. **Teppo Numminen**, Wpg., Phx., Dal.	16	**1160**
81. **Kevin Hatcher**, Wsh., Dal., Pit., NYR, Car.	17	**1157**
82. **Shayne Corson**, Mtl., Edm., St.L., Tor., Dal.	19	**1156**
* 83. **Joe Sakic**, Que., Col.	16	**1155**
84. **Adam Graves**, Det., Edm., NYR, S.J.	16	**1152**
85. **Leo Boivin**, Tor., Bos., Det., Pit., Min.	19	**1150**
86. **Garry Galley**, L.A., Wsh., Bos., Phi., Buf., NYI	17	**1149**
87. **Borje Salming**, Tor., Det.	17	**1148**
88. **Gary Suter**, Cgy., Chi., S.J.	17	**1145**
89. **Bobby Clarke**, Phi.	15	**1144**
* 90. **Brian Leetch**, NYR, Tor.	17	**1144**
91. **Rick Tocchet**, Phi., Pit., L.A., Bos., Wsh., Phx.	18	**1144**
* 92. **Cliff Ronning**, St.L., Van., Phx., Nsh., L.A., Min., NYI	18	**1137**
93. **Glenn Anderson**, Edm., Tor., NYR, St.L.	16	**1129**
94. **Dave Ellett**, Wpg., Tor., N.J., Bos., St.L.	16	**1129**
95. **Jamie Macoun**, Cgy., Tor., Det.	16	**1128**
96. **Bob Nevin**, Tor., NYR, Min., L.A.	18	**1128**
97. **Murray Oliver**, Det., Bos., Tor., Min.	17	**1127**
98. **Bernie Nicholls**, L.A., NYR, Edm., N.J., Chi., S.J.	18	**1127**
99. **Guy Lafleur**, Mtl., NYR, Que.	17	**1126**
100. **Jean Beliveau**, Mtl.	20	**1125**

Top 100 Active Games Played Leaders

Player	Seasons	Games Played
1. **Mark Messier**, Edm., NYR, Van.	25	**1756**
2. **Ron Francis**, Hfd., Pit., Car., Tor.	23	**1731**
3. **Scott Stevens**, Wsh., St.L., N.J.	22	**1635**
4. **Dave Andreychuk**, Buf., Tor., N.J., Bos., Col., T.B.	22	**1597**
5. **Steve Yzerman**, Det.	21	**1453**
6. **Al MacInnis**, Cgy., St.L.	23	**1416**
7. **Chris Chelios**, Mtl., Chi., Det.	21	**1395**
8. **Vincent Damphousse**, Tor., Edm., Mtl., S.J.	18	**1378**
9. **Luc Robitaille**, L.A., Pit., NYR, Det.	18	**1366**
10. **Scott Mellanby**, Phi., Edm., Fla., St.L.	19	**1291**
11. **James Patrick**, NYR, Hfd., Cgy., Buf.	21	**1280**
12. **Brendan Shanahan**, N.J., St.L., Hfd., Det.	17	**1268**
13. **Brett Hull**, Cgy., St.L., Dal., Det.	19	**1264**
14. **Luke Richardson**, Tor., Edm., Phi., CBJ	17	**1247**
15. **Glen Wesley**, Bos., Hfd., Car., Tor.	17	**1247**
16. **Steve Thomas**, Tor., Chi., NYI, N.J., Ana., Det.	20	**1235**
17. **Pierre Turgeon**, Buf., NYI, Mtl., St.L., Dal.	17	**1215**
18. **Marc Bergevin**, Chi., NYI, Hfd., T.B., Det., St.L., Pit., Van.	20	**1191**
19. **Kelly Buchberger**, Edm., Atl., L.A., Phx., Pit.	18	**1182**
20. **Joe Nieuwendyk**, Cgy., Dal., N.J., Tor.	18	**1177**
21. **Mark Recchi**, Pit., Phi., Mtl.	16	**1173**
22. **Mike Keane**, Mtl., Col., NYR, Dal., St.L., Van.	16	**1161**
23. **Trevor Linden**, Van., NYI, Mtl., Wsh.	16	**1161**
24. **Teppo Numminen**, Wpg., Phx., Dal.	16	**1160**
25. **Joe Sakic**, Que., Col.	16	**1155**
26. **Brian Leetch**, NYR, Tor.	17	**1144**
27. **Cliff Ronning**, St.L., Van., Phx., Nsh., L.A., Min., NYI	18	**1137**
28. **Jeremy Roenick**, Chi., Phx., Phi.	16	**1124**
29. **Don Sweeney**, Bos., Dal.	16	**1115**
30. **Rod Brind'Amour**, St.L., Phi., Car.	16	**1109**
31. **Scott Young**, Hfd., Pit., Que., Col., Ana., St.L., Dal.	16	**1102**
32. **Mike Modano**, Min., Dal.	16	**1101**
33. **Eric Desjardins**, Mtl., Phi.	16	**1098**
34. **Mats Sundin**, Que., Tor.	14	**1086**
35. **Dave Lowry**, Van., St.L., Fla., S.J., Cgy.	19	**1084**
36. **Eric Weinrich**, N.J., Hfd., Mtl., Bos., Phi., St.L.	16	**1082**
37. **Martin Gelinas**, Edm., Que., Van., Car., Cgy.	16	**1052**
38. **Stephane Quintal**, Bos., St.L., Wpg., Mtl., NYR, Chi.	16	**1037**
39. **Curtis Leschyshyn**, Que., Col., Wsh., Hfd., Car., Min., Ott.	16	**1033**
40. **Lyle Odelein**, Mtl., N.J., Phx., CBJ, Chi., Dal., Fla.	15	**1029**
41. **Gary Roberts**, Cgy., Car., Tor.	18	**1029**
42. **Jaromir Jagr**, Pit., Wsh., NYR.	14	**1027**
43. **Tom Fitzgerald**, NYI, Fla., Col., Nsh., Chi., Tor.	16	**1026**
44. **Bobby Holik**, Hfd., N.J., NYR	14	**1024**
45. **Nicklas Lidstrom**, Det.	13	**1016**
46. **Mike Ricci**, Phi., Que., Col., S.J.	14	**1014**
47. **Tony Amonte**, NYR, Chi., Phx., Phi.	14	**1013**
48. **Mathieu Schneider**, Mtl., NYI, Tor., NYR, L.A., Det.	16	**992**
49. **Sergei Fedorov**, Det., Ana.	14	**988**
50. **Murray Baron**, Phi., St.L., Mtl., Phx., Van.	15	**988**
51. **Peter Bondra**, Wsh., Ott.	14	**984**
52. **Andrew Cassels**, Mtl., Hfd., Cgy., Van., CBJ	15	**984**
53. **Alexander Mogilny**, Buf., Van., N.J., Tor.	15	**956**
54. **Darryl Sydor**, L.A., Dal., CBJ, T.B.	13	**943**
55. **Tie Domi**, Tor., NYR, Wpg.	15	**943**
56. **Geoff Sanderson**, Hfd., Car., Van., Buf., CBJ	14	**928**
57. **Tommy Albelin**, Que., N.J., Cgy.	17	**916**
58. **Owen Nolan**, Que., Col., S.J., Tor.	14	**915**
59. **Doug Weight**, NYR, Edm., St.L.	14	**912**
60. **Rob Blake**, L.A., Col.	15	**903**
61. **Keith Primeau**, Det., Hfd., Car., Phi.	14	**900**
62. **Rob Ray**, Buf., Ott.	15	**900**
63. **Stu Barnes**, Wpg., Fla., Pit., Buf., Dal.	13	**897**
64. **Scott Niedermayer**, N.J.	13	**892**
65. **Petr Nedved**, Van., St.L., NYR, Pit., Edm.	13	**889**
66. **Bryan Marchment**, Wpg., Chi., Hfd., Edm., T.B., S.J., Col., Tor.	16	**889**
67. **Mario Lemieux**, Pit.	17	**889**
68. **Shawn McEachern**, Pit., L.A., Bos., Ott., Atl.	13	**883**
69. **Alexei Zhitnik**, L.A., Buf.	12	**882**
70. **Jim McKenzie**, Hfd., Dal., Pit., Wpg., Phx., Ana., Wsh., N.J., Nsh.	15	**880**
71. **Teemu Selanne**, Wpg., Ana., S.J., Col.	12	**879**
72. **Bill Guerin**, N.J., Edm., Bos., Dal.	13	**879**
73. **Claude Lapointe**, Que., Col., Cgy., NYI, Phi.	14	**879**
74. **Roman Hamrlik**, T.B., Edm., NYI	12	**873**
75. **John LeClair**, Mtl., Phi.	14	**873**
76. **Travis Green**, NYI, Ana., Phx., Tor., Bos.	12	**857**
77. **Sergei Zubov**, NYR, Pit., Dal.	12	**856**
78. **Keith Tkachuk**, Wpg., Phx., St.L.	13	**856**

One of the most rugged performers in NHL history, New Jersey's Scott Stevens passed Larry Murphy as the NHL's all-time leader in games played by a defenseman when he played in his 1,616th game on November 28, 2003.

Player	Seasons	Games Played
79. **Chris Gratton**, T.B., Phi., Buf., Phx., Col.	11	**851**
80. **Alex Kovalev**, NYR, Pit., Mtl.	12	**849**
81. **Derian Hatcher**, Min., Dal., Det.	13	**842**
82. **Rob DiMaio**, NYI, T.B., Phi., Bos., NYR, Car., Dal.	16	**833**
83. **Jody Hull**, Hfd., NYR, Ott., Fla., T.B., Phi.	16	**831**
84. **Robert Reichel**, Cgy., NYI, Phx., Tor.	11	**830**
85. **Bryan Smolinski**, Bos., Pit., NYI, L.A., Ott.	12	**829**
86. **Mike Sillinger**, Det., Ana., Van., Phi., T.B., Fla., Ott., CBJ, Phx., St.L.	14	**829**
87. **Glen Murray**, Bos., Pit., L.A.	13	**823**
88. **Dallas Drake**, Det., Wpg., Phx., St.L.	12	**822**
89. **Scott Lachance**, NYI, Mtl., Van., CBJ	13	**819**
90. **Martin Rucinsky**, Edm., Que., Col., Mtl., Dal., NYR, St.L., Van.	13	**817**
91. **Brad May**, Buf., Van., Phx.	13	**804**
92. **Vyacheslav Kozlov**, Det., Buf., Atl.	13	**800**
93. **Adam Foote**, Que., Col.	13	**799**
94. **Keith Carney**, Buf., Chi., Phx., Ana.	13	**798**
95. **Bret Hedican**, St.L., Van., Fla., Car.	13	**798**
96. **Rob Zamuner**, NYR, T.B., Ott., Bos.	13	**798**
97. **Igor Korolev**, St.L., Wpg., Phx., Tor., Chi.	12	**795**
98. **Shaun Van Allen**, Edm., Ana., Ott., Dal., Mtl.	13	**794**
99. **Patrice Brisebois**, Mtl.	14	**791**
100. **Markus Naslund**, Pit., Van.	11	**790**

Goaltending Records

All-Time Shutout Leaders (Minimum 41 Shutouts)

Goaltender	Team	Seasons	Games	Shutouts
Terry Sawchuk	Detroit	14	734	85
(1949-1970)	Boston	2	102	11
	Toronto	3	91	4
	Los Angeles	1	36	2
	NY Rangers	1	8	1
	Total	21	971	**103**
George Hainsworth	Montreal	7½	318	75
(1926-1937)	Toronto	3½	147	19
	Total	11	465	**94**
Glenn Hall	Detroit	4	148	17
(1952-1971)	Chicago	10	618	51
	St. Louis	4	140	16
	Total	18	906	**84**
Jacques Plante	Montreal	11	556	58
(1952-1973)	NY Rangers	2	98	5
	St. Louis	2	69	10
	Toronto	2¾	106	7
	Boston	¼	8	2
	Total	18	837	**82**
Tiny Thompson	Boston	10¼	468	74
(1928-1940)	Detroit	1¾	85	7
	Total	12	553	**81**
Alex Connell	Ottawa	8	293	64
(1924-1937)	Detroit	1	48	6
	NY Americans	1	1	0
	Mtl. Maroons	2	75	11
	Total	12	417	**81**
Tony Esposito	Montreal	1	13	2
(1968-1984)	Chicago	15	873	74
	Total	16	886	**76**
Martin Brodeur	New Jersey	12	740	**75**
(1991-2004)				
Ed Belfour	Chicago	7⅔	415	30
(1988-2004)	San Jose	⅓	13	1
	Dallas	5	307	27
	Toronto	2	121	17
	Total	15	856	**75**
Lorne Chabot	NY Rangers	2	80	21
(1926-1937)	Toronto	5	214	33
	Montreal	1	47	8
	Chicago	1	48	8
	Mtl. Maroons	1	16	2
	NY Americans	1	6	1
	Total	11	411	**73**
Harry Lumley	Detroit	6½	324	26
(1943-1960)	NY Rangers	½	1	0
	Chicago	2	134	5
	Toronto	4	267	34
	Boston	3	78	6
	Total	16	804	**71**
Roy Worters	Pittsburgh Pirates	3	123	22
(1925-1937)	NY Americans	9	360	45
	* Montreal		1	0
	Total	12	484	**67**

Goaltender	Team	Seasons	Games	Shutouts
Patrick Roy	Montreal	11½	551	29
(1984-2003)	Colorado	6½	478	37
	Total	19	1,029	**66**
Turk Broda	Toronto	14	629	**62**
(1936-1952)				
Dominik Hasek	Chicago	2	25	1
(1990-2004)	Buffalo	9	491	55
	Detroit	1	65	5
	Total	12	581	**61**
Clint Benedict	Ottawa	7	158	19
(1917-1930)	Mtl. Maroons	6	204	39
	Total	13	362	**58**
John Ross Roach	Toronto	7	222	13
(1921-1935)	NY Rangers	4	89	30
	Detroit	3	180	15
	Total	14	491	**58**
Bernie Parent	Boston	2	57	1
(1965-1979)	Philadelphia	9½	486	50
	Toronto	1½	65	3
	Total	13	608	**54**
Ed Giacomin	NY Rangers	10¼	539	49
(1965-1978)	Detroit	2¾	71	5
	Total	13	610	**54**
Dave Kerr	Mtl. Maroons	3	101	11
(1930-1941)	NY Americans	1	1	0
	NY Rangers	7	324	40
	Total	11	426	**51**
Rogie Vachon	Montreal	5¼	206	13
(1966-1982)	Los Angeles	6¾	389	32
	Detroit	2	109	4
	Boston	2	91	2
	Total	16	795	**51**
Ken Dryden	Montreal	8	397	**46**
(1970-1979)				
Curtis Joseph	St. Louis	6	280	5
(1989-2004)	Edmonton	3	177	14
	Toronto	4	249	17
	Detroit	2	92	7
	Total	15	498	**43**
Gump Worsley	NY Rangers	10	582	24
(1952-1974)	Montreal	6½	172	16
	Minnesota	4½	107	3
	Total	21	861	**43**
Charlie Gardiner	Chicago	7	316	**42**
(1927-1934)				
Chris Osgood	Detroit	8	389	30
(1993-2004)	NY Islanders	1¾	103	6
	St. Louis	1¼	76	5
	Total	11	568	**41**

*Played 1 game for Montreal in 1929-30.

Ten or More Shutouts, One Season

Number of Shutouts	Goaltender	Team	Season	Length of Schedule
22	George Hainsworth	Montreal	1928-29	44
15	Alex Connell	Ottawa	1925-26	36
	Alex Connell	Ottawa	1927-28	44
	Hal Winkler	Boston	1927-28	44
	Tony Esposito	Chicago	1969-70	76
14	George Hainsworth	Montreal	1926-27	44
13	Clint Benedict	Mtl. Maroons	1926-27	44
	Alex Connell	Ottawa	1926-27	44
	George Hainsworth	Montreal	1927-28	44
	John Ross Roach	NY Rangers	1928-29	44
	Roy Worters	NY Americans	1928-29	44
	Harry Lumley	Toronto	1953-54	70
	Dominik Hasek	Buffalo	1997-98	82
12	Lorne Chabot	Toronto	1928-29	44
	Tiny Thompson	Boston	1928-29	44
	Charlie Gardiner	Chicago	1930-31	44
	Terry Sawchuk	Detroit	1951-52	70
	Terry Sawchuk	Detroit	1953-54	70
	Terry Sawchuk	Detroit	1954-55	70
	Glenn Hall	Detroit	1955-56	70
	Bernie Parent	Philadelphia	1973-74	78
	Bernie Parent	Philadelphia	1974-75	80
11	Lorne Chabot	NY Rangers	1927-28	44
	Hap Holmes	Detroit	1927-28	44
	Roy Worters	Pittsburgh Pirates	1927-28	44
	Clint Benedict	Mtl. Maroons	1928-29	44
	Joe Miller	Pittsburgh Pirates	1928-29	44
	Tiny Thompson	Boston	1932-33	48
	Terry Sawchuk	Detroit	1950-51	70
	Dominik Hasek	Buffalo	2000-01	82
	Martin Brodeur	New Jersey	**2003-04**	82
10	Lorne Chabot	NY Rangers	1926-27	44
	Dolly Dolson	Detroit	1928-29	44
	John Ross Roach	Detroit	1932-33	48
	Charlie Gardiner	Chicago	1933-34	48
	Tiny Thompson	Boston	1935-36	48
	Frank Brimsek	Boston	1938-39	48
	Bill Durnan	Montreal	1948-49	60
	Harry Lumley	Toronto	1952-53	70
	Gerry McNeil	Montreal	1952-53	70
	Tony Esposito	Chicago	1973-74	78
	Ken Dryden	Montreal	1976-77	80
	Martin Brodeur	New Jersey	1996-97	82
	Martin Brodeur	New Jersey	1997-98	82
	Byron Dafoe	Boston	1998-99	82
	Roman Cechmanek	Philadelphia	2000-01	82
	Ed Belfour	Toronto	**2003-04**	82

All-Time Win Leaders

(Minimum 230 Wins)

Wins	Goaltender	GP	Dec.	Losses	Ties
551	Patrick Roy	1029	997	315	131
447	Terry Sawchuk	971	949	330	172
437	Jacques Plante	837	827	247	145
435	* Ed Belfour	856	827	281	111
423	Tony Esposito	886	880	306	151
407	Glenn Hall	906	896	326	163
403	* Martin Brodeur	740	665	217	105
403	Grant Fuhr	868	812	295	114
396	* Curtis Joseph	798	767	289	90
385	Mike Vernon	781	750	273	92
374	John Vanbiesbrouck	882	839	346	119
372	Andy Moog	713	669	209	88
369	Tom Barrasso	777	732	277	86
355	Rogie Vachon	795	773	291	127
335	Gump Worsley	861	837	352	150
330	Harry Lumley	803	801	329	142
305	* Chris Osgood	568	548	177	66
305	Billy Smith	680	643	233	105
304	* Sean Burke	762	726	321	101
302	Turk Broda	629	627	224	101
301	Mike Richter	666	632	258	73
296	* Dominik Hasek	595	570	192	82
296	Ron Hextall	608	579	214	69
294	Mike Liut	663	639	271	74
289	Ed Giacomin	610	594	208	97
286	Dan Bouchard	655	631	232	113
284	Tiny Thompson	553	553	194	75
271	Bernie Parent	608	590	198	121
271	Kelly Hrudey	677	624	265	88
270	Gilles Meloche	788	752	351	131
268	Don Beaupre	667	620	277	75
266	* Felix Potvin	635	611	260	85
258	Ken Dryden	397	389	57	74
252	Frank Brimsek	514	514	182	80
250	Johnny Bower	552	535	195	90
246	George Hainsworth	465	465	145	74
246	Pete Peeters	489	452	155	51
245	Kirk McLean	612	579	262	72
240	Bill Ranford	647	595	279	76
236	Reggie Lemelin	507	461	162	63
234	* Olie Kolzig	544	517	220	63
234	Eddie Johnston	592	571	257	80
231	Glenn Resch	571	537	224	82
230	Gerry Cheevers	418	406	102	74

* active player

Active Shutout Leaders

(Minimum 25 Shutouts)

Goaltender	Teams	Seasons	Games	Shutouts
Martin Brodeur	New Jersey	12	740	75
Ed Belfour	Chi., S.J., Dal., Tor.	15	856	75
Dominik Hasek	Chi., Buf., Det.	13	595	63
Curtis Joseph	St.L., Edm., Tor., Det.	15	798	43
Chris Osgood	Det., NYI, St.L.	11	568	41
Tommy Salo	NY Islanders, Edmonton	10	521	37
Jocelyn Thibault	Que., Col., Mtl., Chi.	11	536	36
Nikolai Khabibulin	Wpg., Phx., T.B.	9	476	35
Sean Burke	N.J., Hfd., Car., Van., Phi., Fla., Phx.	16	762	35
Patrick Lalime	Pittsburgh, Ottawa	6	322	33
Olaf Kolzig	Washington	13	544	33
Arturs Irbe	S.J., Dal., Van., Car.	13	568	33
Felix Potvin	Tor., NYI, Van., L.A., Bos.	13	635	32
Roman Turek	Dal., St.L., Cal.	8	328	27
Evgeni Nabokov	San Jose	5	258	26
Byron Dafoe	Wsh., L.A., Bos., Atl.	12	415	26
Ron Tugnutt	Que., Edm., Ana., Mtl., Ott., Pit., CBJ, Dal.	16	537	26
Roman Cechmanek	Philadelphia, Los Angeles	4	212	25

All-Time Penalty-Minute Leaders

* active player

(Regular season.)

	Player	Seasons	Games	Penalty Minutes	Mins. per game
1.	**Tiger Williams**, Tor., Van., Det., L.A., Hfd.	14	962	**3966**	4.12
2.	**Dale Hunter**, Que., Wsh., Col.	19	1407	**3565**	2.53
* 3.	**Tie Domi**, Tor., NYR, Wpg.	15	943	**3406**	3.61
4.	**Marty McSorley**, Pit., Edm., L.A., NYR, S.J., Bos.	17	961	**3381**	3.52
5.	**Bob Probert**, Det., Chi.	16	935	**3300**	3.53
* 6.	**Rob Ray**, Buf., Ott.	15	900	**3207**	3.56
7.	**Craig Berube**, Phi., Tor., Cgy., Wsh., NYI	17	1054	**3149**	2.99
8.	**Tim Hunter**, Cgy., Que., Van., S.J.	16	815	**3146**	3.86
9.	**Chris Nilan**, Mtl., NYR, Bos.	13	688	**3043**	4.42
10.	**Rick Tocchet**, Phi., Pit., L.A., Bos., Wsh., Phx.	18	1144	**2972**	2.60

Goals Against Average Leaders (Minimum 25 games played)

(Exceptions: Minimum 13 games played, 1994-95; minimum 26 games played, 1992-93 to 1993-94; minimum 15 games played, 1917-18 to 1925-26)

Season	Goaltender and Club	GP	Mins.	GA	SO	AVG.
2003-04	Miikka Kiprusoff, San Jose, Calgary	38	2,301	65	4	1.69
2002-03	Marty Turco, Dallas	55	3,203	92	7	1.72
2001-02	Patrick Roy, Colorado	63	3,773	122	9	1.94
2000-01	Marty Turco, Dallas	26	1,266	40	3	1.90
99-2000	Brian Boucher, Philadelphia	35	2,038	65	4	1.91
1998-99	Ron Tugnutt, Ottawa	43	2,508	75	3	1.79
1997-98	Ed Belfour, Dallas	61	3,581	112	9	1.88
1996-97	Martin Brodeur, New Jersey	67	3,838	120	10	1.88
1995-96	Ron Hextall, Philadelphia	53	3,102	112	4	2.17
1994-95	Dominik Hasek, Buffalo	41	2,416	85	5	2.11
1993-94	Dominik Hasek, Buffalo	58	3,358	109	7	1.95
1992-93	Felix Potvin, Toronto	48	2,781	116	2	2.50
1991-92	Patrick Roy, Montreal	67	3,935	155	5	2.36
1990-91	Ed Belfour, Chicago	74	4,127	170	4	2.47
1989-90	Mike Liut, Hartford, Washington	37	2,161	91	4	2.53
1988-89	Patrick Roy, Montreal	48	2,744	113	4	2.47
1987-88	Pete Peeters, Washington	35	1,896	88	2	2.78
1986-87	Brian Hayward, Montreal	37	2,178	102	1	2.81
1985-86	Bob Froese, Philadelphia	51	2,728	116	5	2.55
1984-85	Tom Barrasso, Buffalo	54	3,248	144	5	2.66
1983-84	Pat Riggin, Washington	41	2,299	102	4	2.66
1982-83	Pete Peeters, Boston	62	3,611	142	8	2.36
1981-82	Denis Herron, Montreal	27	1,547	68	3	2.64
1980-81	Richard Sevigny, Montreal	33	1,777	71	2	2.40
1979-80	Bob Sauve, Buffalo	32	1,880	74	4	2.36
1978-79	Ken Dryden, Montreal	47	2,814	108	5	2.30
1977-78	Ken Dryden, Montreal	52	3,071	105	5	2.05
1976-77	Michel Larocque, Montreal	26	1,525	53	4	2.09
1975-76	Ken Dryden, Montreal	62	3,580	121	8	2.03
1974-75	Bernie Parent, Philadelphia	68	4,041	137	12	2.03
1973-74	Bernie Parent, Philadelphia	73	4,314	136	12	1.89
1972-73	Ken Dryden, Montreal	54	3,165	119	6	2.26
1971-72	Tony Esposito, Chicago	48	2,780	82	9	1.77
1970-71	Jacques Plante, Toronto	40	2,329	73	4	1.88
1969-70	Ernie Wakely, St. Louis	30	1,651	58	4	2.11
1968-69	Jacques Plante, St. Louis	37	2,139	70	5	1.96
1967-68	Gump Worsley, Montreal	40	2,213	73	6	1.98
1966-67	Glenn Hall, Chicago	32	1,664	66	2	2.38
1965-66	Johnny Bower, Toronto	35	1,998	75	3	2.25
1964-65	Johnny Bower, Toronto	34	2,040	81	3	2.38
1963-64	Johnny Bower, Toronto	51	3,009	106	5	2.11
1962-63	Don Simmons, Toronto	28	1,680	69	1	2.46
1961-62	Jacques Plante, Montreal	70	4,200	166	4	2.37
1960-61	Charlie Hodge, Montreal	30	1,800	74	4	2.47
1959-60	Jacques Plante, Montreal	69	4,140	175	3	2.54
1958-59	Jacques Plante, Montreal	67	4,000	144	9	2.16
1957-58	Jacques Plante, Montreal	57	3,386	119	9	2.11
1956-57	Jacques Plante, Montreal	61	3,660	122	9	2.00
1955-56	Jacques Plante, Montreal	64	3,840	119	7	1.86
1954-55	Harry Lumley, Toronto	69	4,140	134	8	1.94
1953-54	Harry Lumley, Toronto	69	4,140	128	13	1.86
1952-53	Terry Sawchuk, Detroit	63	3,780	120	9	1.90
1951-52	Terry Sawchuk, Detroit	70	4,200	133	12	1.90
1950-51	Al Rollins, Toronto	40	2,367	70	5	1.77
1949-50	Bill Durnan, Montreal	64	3,840	141	8	2.20
1948-49	Bill Durnan, Montreal	60	3,600	126	10	2.10
1947-48	Turk Broda, Toronto	60	3,600	143	5	2.38
1946-47	Bill Durnan, Montreal	60	3,600	138	4	2.30
1945-46	Bill Durnan, Montreal	40	2,400	104	4	2.60
1944-45	Bill Durnan, Montreal	50	3,000	121	1	2.42
1943-44	Bill Durnan, Montreal	50	3,000	109	2	2.18
1942-43	Johnny Mowers, Detroit	50	3,010	124	6	2.47
1941-42	Frank Brimsek, Boston	47	2,930	115	3	2.35
1940-41	Turk Broda, Toronto	48	2,970	99	5	2.00
1939-40	Dave Kerr, NY Rangers	48	3,000	77	8	1.54
1938-39	Frank Brimsek, Boston	43	2,610	68	10	1.56
1937-38	Tiny Thompson, Boston	48	2,970	89	7	1.80
1936-37	Normie Smith, Detroit	48	2,980	102	6	2.05
1935-36	Tiny Thompson, Boston	48	2,930	82	10	1.68
1934-35	Lorne Chabot, Chicago	48	2,940	88	8	1.80
1933-34	Wilf Cude, Detroit, Montreal	30	1,920	47	5	1.47
1932-33	Tiny Thompson, Boston	48	3,000	88	11	1.76
1931-32	Charlie Gardiner, Chicago	48	2,989	92	4	1.85
1930-31	Roy Worters, NY Americans	44	2,760	74	8	1.61
1929-30	Tiny Thompson, Boston	44	2,680	98	3	2.19
1928-29	George Hainsworth, Montreal	44	2,800	43	22	0.92
1927-28	George Hainsworth, Montreal	44	2,730	48	13	1.05
1926-27	Clint Benedict, Mtl. Maroons	44	2,748	65	13	1.42
1925-26	Alex Connell, Ottawa	36	2,251	42	15	1.12
1924-25	Georges Vezina, Montreal	30	1,860	56	5	1.81
1923-24	Georges Vezina, Montreal	24	1,459	48	3	1.97
1922-23	Clint Benedict, Ottawa	24	1,478	54	4	2.18
1921-22	Clint Benedict, Ottawa	24	1,508	84	2	3.34
1920-21	Clint Benedict, Ottawa	24	1,457	75	2	3.09
1919-20	Clint Benedict, Ottawa	24	1,444	64	5	2.66
1918-19	Clint Benedict, Ottawa	18	1,113	53	2	2.86
1917-18	Georges Vezina, Montreal	21	1,282	84	1	3.93

All-Time Regular Season NHL Coaching Register

Regular Season, 1917-2004

Coach	Team	Games Coached	Wins	Losses	Ties	Years	Cup Wins	Career
Abel, Sid	Chicago	140	39	79	22	2		
	Detroit	811	340	339	132	12		
	St. Louis	10	3	6	1	1		
	Kansas City	3	0	3	0	1		
	Total	964	382	427	155	16		1952-76
Adams, Jack	Detroit	964	413	390	161	20	3	1927-47
Allen, Keith	Philadelphia	150	51	67	32	2		1967-69
Allison, Dave	Ottawa	25	2	22	1	1		1995-96
Anderson, Jim	Washington	54	4	45	5	1		1974-75
Angotti, Lou	St. Louis	32	6	20	6	2		
	Pittsburgh	80	16	58	6	1		
	Total	112	22	78	12	3		1973-84
Arbour, Al	St. Louis	107	42	40	25	3		
	NY Islanders	1499	739	537	223	19	4	1970-94
	Total	1606	781	577	248	22	4	1988-89
Armstrong, George	Toronto	47	17	26	4	1		1988-89
Babcock, Mike	Anaheim	164	69	76	19	2		2002-04
Barber, Bill	Philadelphia	136	73	46	17	2		2000-02
Barkley, Doug	Detroit	77	20	46	11	3		1970-76
Beaulieu, Andre	Minnesota	32	6	23	3	1		1977-78
Belisle, Danny	Washington	96	28	51	17	2		1978-80
Berenson, Red	St. Louis	204	100	72	32	3		1979-82
Bergeron, Michel	Quebec	634	265	283	86	8		
	NY Rangers	158	73	67	18	2		
	Total	792	338	350	104	10		1980-90
Berry, Bob	Los Angeles	240	107	94	39	3		
	Montreal	223	116	71	36	3		
	Pittsburgh	240	88	127	25	3		
	St. Louis	157	73	63	21	2		
	Total	860	384	355	121	11		1978-94
Beverley, Nick	Toronto	17	9	6	2	1		1995-96
Blackburn, Don	Hartford	140	42	63	35	2		1979-81
Blair, Wren	Minnesota	147	48	65	34	3		1967-70
Blake, Toe	Montreal	914	500	255	159	13	8	1955-68
Boileau, Marc	Pittsburgh	151	66	61	24	3		1973-76
Boivin, Leo	St. Louis	97	28	53	16	2		1975-78
Boucher, Frank	NY Rangers	527	181	263	83	11	1	1939-54
Boucher, Georges	Mtl. Maroons	12	6	5	1	1		
	Ottawa	48	13	29	6	1		
	St. Louis	35	9	20	6	1		
	Boston	70	22	32	16	1		
	Total	165	50	86	29	4		1930-50
Bowman, Scotty	St. Louis	238	110	83	45	4		
	Montreal	634	419	110	105	8	5	
	Buffalo	404	210	134	60	7		
	Pittsburgh	164	95	53	16	2	1	
	Detroit	701	410	204	87	9	3	
	Total	2141	1244	584	313	30	9	1967-02
Bowness, Rick	Winnipeg	28	8	17	3	1		
	Boston	80	36	32	12	1		
	Ottawa	235	39	178	18	4		
	NY Islanders	100	38	50	12	2		
	Phoenix	20	2	15	3	1		
	Total	463	123	292	48	9		1988-04
Brooks, Herb	NY Rangers	285	131	113	41	4		
	Minnesota	80	19	48	13	1		
	New Jersey	84	40	37	7	1		
	Pittsburgh	58	29	24	5	1		
	Total	507	219	222	66	7		1981-00
Brophy, John	Toronto	193	64	111	18	3		1986-89
Burnett, George	Edmonton	35	12	20	3	1		1994-95
Burns, Charlie	Minnesota	86	22	50	14	2		1969-75
Burns, Pat	Montreal	320	174	104	42	4		
	Toronto	281	133	107	41	4		
	Boston	254	105	103	46	4		
	New Jersey	164	89	53	22	2	1	
	Total	1019	501	367	151	14	1	1988-04
Bush, Eddie	Kansas City	32	1	23	8	1		1975-76
Campbell, Colin	NY Rangers	269	118	108	43	4		1994-98
Carpenter, Doug	New Jersey	290	100	166	24	4		
	Toronto	91	39	47	5	2		
	Total	381	139	213	29	6		1984-91
Carroll, Dick	Toronto	40	18	22	0	2	1	1917-19
Carroll, Frank	Toronto	24	15	9	0	1		1920-21
Cashman, Wayne	Philadelphia	61	32	20	9	1		1997-98
Cassidy, Bruce	Washington	110	47	54	9	2		2002-04
Chambers, Dave	Quebec	98	19	64	15	2		1990-92
Charron, Guy	Calgary	16	6	7	3	1		
	Anaheim	49	14	28	7	1		
	Total	65	20	35	10	2		1991-01
Cheevers, Gerry	Boston	376	204	126	46	5		1980-85
Cherry, Don	Boston	400	231	105	64	5		
	Colorado	80	19	48	13	1		
	Total	480	250	153	77	6		1974-80

Coach	Team	Games Coached	Wins	Losses	Ties	Years	Cup Wins	Career
Clancy, King	Mtl. Maroons	18	6	11	1	1		
	Toronto	210	80	81	49	3		
	Total	228	86	92	50	4		1937-56
Clapper, Dit	Boston	230	102	88	40	4		1945-49
Cleghorn, Odie	Pittsburgh	168	62	86	20	4		1925-29
Cleghorn, Sprague	Mtl. Maroons	48	19	22	7	1		1931-32
Colville, Neil	NY Rangers	93	26	41	26	2		1950-52
Conacher, Charlie	Chicago	162	56	84	22	3		1947-50
Conacher, Lionel	NY Americans	44	14	25	5	1		1929-30
Constantine, Kevin	San Jose	157	55	78	24	3		
	Pittsburgh	188	86	67	35	3		
	New Jersey	31	20	9	2	1		
	Total	376	161	154	61	7		1993-02
Cook, Bill	NY Rangers	117	34	59	24	2		1951-53
Crawford, Marc	Quebec	48	30	13	5	1		
	Colorado	246	135	75	36	3	1	
	Vancouver	447	204	181	62	6		
	Total	741	369	269	103	10	1	1994-04
Creamer, Pierre	Pittsburgh	80	36	35	9	1		1987-88
Creighton, Fred	Atlanta	348	156	136	56	5		
	Boston	73	40	20	13	1		
	Total	421	196	156	69	6		1974-80
Crisp, Terry	Calgary	240	144	63	33	3	1	
	Tampa Bay	391	142	204	45	6		
	Total	631	286	267	78	9	1	1987-98
Crozier, Joe	Buffalo	192	77	80	35	3		
	Toronto	40	13	22	5	1		
	Total	232	90	102	40	4		1971-81
Crozier, Roger	Washington	1	0	1	0	1		1981-82
Cunniff, John	Hartford	13	3	9	1	1		
	New Jersey	133	59	56	18	2		
	Total	146	62	65	19	3		1982-91
Curry, Alex	Ottawa	36	24	8	4	1		1925-26
Dandurand, Leo	Montreal	163	78	76	9	6	1	1921-35
Day, Hap	Toronto	546	259	206	81	10	5	1940-50
Dea, Billy	Detroit	11	3	8	0	1		1981-82
Delvecchio, Alex	Detroit	245	82	131	32	4		1973-77
Demers, Jacques	Quebec	80	25	44	11	1		
	St. Louis	240	106	106	28	3		
	Detroit	320	137	136	47	4		
	Montreal	221	107	87	27	4	1	
	Tampa Bay	145	34	94	17	2		
	Total	1006	409	467	130	14	1	1979-99
Denneny, Cy	Boston	44	26	13	5	1	1	
	Ottawa	48	11	27	10	1		
	Total	92	37	40	15	2	1	1928-33
Dineen, Bill	Philadelphia	140	60	60	20	2		1991-93
Dudley, Rick	Buffalo	188	85	72	31	3		
	Florida	40	13	18	9	1		
	Total	228	98	90	40	4		1989-04
Duff, Dick	Toronto	2	0	2	0	1		1979-80
Dugal, Jules	Montreal	18	9	6	3	1		1938-39
Duncan, Art	Detroit	33	10	21	2	1		
	Toronto	47	21	16	10	2	1	
	Total	80	31	37	12	3	1	1926-32
Dutton, Red	NY Americans	288	90	151	47	6		
	Brooklyn	48	16	29	3	1		
	Total	336	106	180	50	7		1935-42
Eddolls, Frank	Chicago	70	13	40	17	1		1954-55
Esposito, Phil	NY Rangers	45	24	21	0	2		1986-89
Evans, Jack	California	80	27	42	11	2		
	Cleveland	160	47	87	26	2		
	Hartford	374	163	174	37	5		
	Total	614	237	303	74	8		1975-88
Fashoway, Gordie	Oakland	10	4	5	1	1		1967-68
Ferguson, John	NY Rangers	121	43	59	19	2		
	Winnipeg	14	7	6	1	1		
	Total	135	50	65	20	3		1975-86
Filion, Maurice	Quebec	6	1	3	2	1		1980-81
Francis, Bob	Phoenix	390	165	165	60	5		1999-04
Francis, Emile	NY Rangers	654	342	209	103	10		
	St. Louis	124	46	64	14	3		
	Total	778	388	273	117	13		1965-83
Fraser, Curt	Atlanta	279	64	184	31	4		1999-03
Fredrickson, Frank	Pittsburgh	44	5	36	3	1		1929-30
Ftorek, Robbie	Los Angeles	132	65	56	11	2		
	New Jersey	156	88	49	19	2		
	Boston	155	76	65	14	2		
	Total	443	229	170	44	6		1987-03
Gadsby, Bill	Detroit	78	35	31	12	2		1968-70
Gainey, Bob	Minnesota	244	95	119	30	3		
	Dallas	171	70	71	30	3		
	Total	415	165	190	60	6		1990-96
Gallant, Gerard	Columbus	45	16	25	4	1		2003-04
Gardiner, Herb	Chicago	32	5	23	4	1		1929-30
Gardner, Jimmy	Hamilton	30	19	10	1	1		1924-25
Garvin, Ted	Detroit	11	2	8	1	1		1973-74
Geoffrion, Bernie	NY Rangers	43	22	18	3	1		
	Atlanta	208	77	92	39	3		
	Montreal	30	15	9	6	1		
	Total	281	114	119	48	5		1968-80
Gerard, Eddie	Ottawa	22	9	13	0	1		
	Mtl. Maroons	294	129	122	43	7	1	
	NY Americans	92	34	40	18	2		
	St. Louis	13	2	11	0	1		
	Total	421	174	186	61	11	1	1917-35

Coach	Team	Games Coached	Wins	Losses	Ties	Years	Cup Wins	Career
Gilbert, Greg	Calgary	121	42	62	17	3		2000-03
Gill, David	Ottawa	132	64	41	27	3	1	1926-29
Glover, Fred	Oakland	152	51	76	25	2		
	California	204	45	131	28	4		
	Los Angeles	68	18	42	8	1		
	Total	424	114	249	61	7		1968-74
Goodfellow, Ebbie	Chicago	140	30	91	19	2		1950-52
Gordon, Jackie	Minnesota	289	116	123	50	5		1970-75
Goring, Butch	Boston	93	42	38	13	2		
	NY Islanders	147	41	92	14	2		
	Total	240	83	130	27	4		1985-01
Gorman, Tommy	NY Americans	80	31	33	16	2		
	Chicago	73	28	28	17	2	1	
	Mtl. Maroons	174	74	71	29	4	1	
	Total	327	133	132	62	8	2	1925-38
Gottselig, Johnny	Chicago	187	62	105	20	4		1944-48
Goyette, Phil	NY Islanders	48	6	38	4	1		1972-73
Graham, Dirk	Chicago	59	16	35	8	1		1998-99
Granato, Tony	Colorado	133	72	44	17	2		2002-04
Green, Gary	Washington	157	50	78	29	3		1979-82
Green, Pete	Ottawa	150	94	52	4	6	3	1919-25
Green, Shorty	NY Americans	44	11	27	6	1		1927-28
Green, Ted	Edmonton	188	65	102	21	3		1991-94
Guidolin, Aldo	Colorado	59	12	39	8	1		1978-79
Guidolin, Bep	Boston	104	72	23	9	2		
	Kansas City	125	26	84	15	2		
	Total	229	98	107	24	4		1972-76
Hanlon, Glen	Washington	54	15	30	9	1		2003-04
Harkness, Ned	Detroit	38	12	22	4	1		1970-71
Harris, Ted	Minnesota	179	48	104	27	3		1975-78
Hart, Cecil	Montreal	394	196	125	73	9	2	1926-39
Hartley, Bob	Colorado	359	193	118	48	5	1	
	Atlanta	121	52	56	13	2		
	Total	480	245	174	61	6	1	1998-04
Hartsburg, Craig	Chicago	246	104	102	40	3		
	Anaheim	197	80	88	29	3		
	Total	443	184	190	69	6		1995-01
Harvey, Doug	NY Rangers	70	26	32	12	1		1961-62
Hay, Don	Phoenix	82	38	37	7	1		
	Calgary	68	23	32	13	1		
	Total	150	61	69	20	2		1996-01
Heffernan, Frank	Toronto	12	5	7	0	1		1919-20
Henning, Lorne	Minnesota	158	68	72	18	2		
	NY Islanders	65	19	39	7	2		
	Total	223	87	111	25	4		1985-01
Hitchcock, Ken	Dallas	503	277	166	60	7		
	Philadelphia	164	85	51	28	2		
	Total	667	362	217	88	9	1	1995-04
Hlinka, Ivan	Pittsburgh	86	42	35	9	2		2000-02
Holmgren, Paul	Philadelphia	264	107	126	31	4		
	Hartford	161	54	93	14	4		
	Total	425	161	219	45	8		1988-96
Howell, Harry	Minnesota	11	3	6	2	1		1978-79
Imlach, Punch	Toronto	770	370	275	125	12	4	
	Buffalo	119	32	62	25	2		
	Total	889	402	337	150	14	4	1958-80
Ingarfield, Earl	NY Islanders	30	6	22	2	1		1972-73
Inglis, Bill	Buffalo	56	28	18	10	1		1978-79
Irvin, Dick	Chicago	126	45	62	19	3		
	Toronto	427	216	152	59	9	1	
	Montreal	896	431	313	152	15	3	
	Total	1449	692	527	230	27	4	1928-56
Ivan, Tommy	Detroit	470	262	118	90	7	3	
	Chicago	103	26	56	21	2		
	Total	573	288	174	111	9	3	1947-58
Iverson, Emil	Chicago	21	8	7	6	1		1932-33
Johnson, Bob	Calgary	400	193	155	52	5		
	Pittsburgh	80	41	33	6	1	1	
	Total	480	234	188	58	6	1	1982-91
Johnson, Tom	Boston	208	142	43	23	3	1	1970-73
Johnston, Eddie	Chicago	80	34	27	19	1		
	Pittsburgh	516	232	224	60	7		
	Total	596	266	251	79	8		1979-97
Johnston, Marshall	California	69	13	45	11	2		
	Colorado	56	15	32	9	1		
	Total	125	28	77	20	3		1973-82
Julien, Claude	Montreal	118	53	55	10	2		2002-04
Kasper, Steve	Boston	164	66	78	20	2		1995-97
Keats, Duke	Detroit	11	2	7	2	1		1926-27
Keenan, Mike	Philadelphia	320	190	102	28	4		
	Chicago	320	153	126	41	4		
	NY Rangers	84	52	24	8	1	1	
	St. Louis	163	75	66	22	3		
	Vancouver	108	36	54	18	2		
	Boston	74	33	34	7	1		
	Florida	153	45	85	23	3		
	Total	1222	584	491	147	18	1	1984-04
Kehoe, Rick	Pittsburgh	160	55	91	14	2		2001-03
Kelly, Pat	Colorado	101	22	54	25	2		1977-79
Kelly, Red	Los Angeles	150	55	75	20	2		
	Pittsburgh	274	90	132	52	4		
	Toronto	318	133	123	62	4		
	Total	742	278	330	134	10		1967-77
King, Dave	Calgary	216	109	76	31	3		
	Columbus	204	64	119	21	3		
	Total	420	173	195	52	6		1992-03
Kingston, George	San Jose	164	28	129	7	2		1991-93
Kish, Larry	Hartford	49	12	32	5	1		1982-83
Kitchen, Mike	St. Louis	21	10	7	4	1		2003-04
Kromm, Bobby	Detroit	231	79	111	41	3		1977-80
Kurtenbach, Orland	Vancouver	125	36	62	27	2		1976-78
LaForge, Bill	Vancouver	20	4	14	2	1		1984-85
Lalonde, Newsy	Montreal	207	96	97	14	8		
	NY Americans	44	17	25	2	1		
	Ottawa	88	31	45	12	2		
	Total	339	144	167	28	11		1917-35
Lapointe, Ron	Quebec	89	33	50	6	2		1987-89
Laviolette, Peter	NY Islanders	164	77	68	19	2		
	Carolina	52	20	26	6	1		
	Total	216	97	94	25	3		2001-04
Laycoe, Hal	Los Angeles	24	5	18	1	1		
	Vancouver	156	44	96	16	2		
	Total	180	49	114	17	3		1969-72
Lehman, Hugh	Chicago	21	3	17	1	1		1927-28
Lemaire, Jacques	Montreal	97	48	37	12	2		
	New Jersey	378	199	122	57	5	1	
	Minnesota	328	123	150	55	4		
	Total	803	370	309	124	11	1	1983-04
Lepine, Pit	Montreal	48	10	33	5	1		1939-40
LeSueur, Percy	Hamilton	10	3	7	0	1		1923-24
Lewis, Dave*	Detroit	169	100	48	21	3		1998-04

*Shared a record of 4-1-0 with co-coach Barry Smith in 1998-99

Coach	Team	Games Coached	Wins	Losses	Ties	Years	Cup Wins	Career
Ley, Rick	Hartford	160	69	71	20	2		
	Vancouver	124	47	50	27	2		
	Total	284	116	121	47	4		1989-96
Lindsay, Ted	Detroit	29	5	21	3	2		1979-81
Long, Barry	Winnipeg	205	87	93	25	3		1983-86
Loughlin, Clem	Chicago	144	61	63	20	3		1934-37
Lowe, Ron	Edmonton	341	139	162	40	5		
	NY Rangers	164	69	86	9	2		
	Total	505	208	248	49	7		1994-02
Lowe, Kevin	Edmonton	82	32	34	16	1		1999-00
Ludzik, Steve	Tampa Bay	121	31	76	14	2		1999-01
MacDonald, Parker	Minnesota	61	20	30	11	1		
	Los Angeles	42	13	24	5	1		
	Total	103	33	54	16	2		1973-82
MacLean, Doug	Florida	187	83	71	33	3		
	Columbus	79	24	47	8	2		
	Total	266	107	118	41	5		1995-04
MacMillan, Bill	Colorado	80	22	45	13	1		
	New Jersey	100	19	67	14	2		
	Total	180	41	112	27	3		1980-84
MacNeil, Al	Montreal	55	31	15	9	1	1	
	Atlanta	80	35	32	13	1		
	Calgary	171	72	66	33	3		
	Total	306	138	113	55	5		1970-03
MacTavish, Craig	Edmonton	328	149	132	47	4		2000-04
Magnuson, Keith	Chicago	132	49	57	26	2		1980-82
Mahoney, Bill	Minnesota	93	42	39	12	2		1983-85
Maloney, Dan	Toronto	160	45	100	15	2		
	Winnipeg	212	91	93	28	3		
	Total	372	136	193	43	5		1984-89
Maloney, Phil	Vancouver	232	95	105	32	4		1973-77
Mantha, Sylvio	Montreal	48	11	26	11	1		1935-36
Marshall, Bert	Colorado	24	3	17	4	1		1981-82
Martin, Jacques	St. Louis	160	66	71	23	2		
	Ottawa	692	341	255	96	9		
	Total	852	407	326	119	11		1986-04
Matheson, Godfrey	Chicago	2	0	2	0	1		1932-33
Maurice, Paul	Hartford	152	61	72	19	2		
	Carolina	522	207	235	80	7		
	Total	674	268	307	99	9		1995-04
Maxner, Wayne	Detroit	129	34	68	27	2		1980-82
McCammon, Bob	Philadelphia	218	119	68	31	4		
	Vancouver	294	102	156	36	4		
	Total	512	221	224	67	8		1978-91
McCreary, Bill	St. Louis	24	6	14	4	1		
	Vancouver	41	9	25	7	1		
	California	32	8	20	4	1		
	Total	97	23	59	15	3		1971-75
McGuire, Pierre	Hartford	67	23	37	7	1		1993-94
McLellan, John	Toronto	310	126	139	45	4		1969-73
McVie, Tom	Washington	204	49	122	33	3		
	Winnipeg	105	20	67	18	2		
	New Jersey	153	57	74	22	3		
	Total	462	126	263	73	8		1975-92
Meeker, Howie	Toronto	70	21	34	15	1		1956-57
Melrose, Barry	Los Angeles	209	79	101	29	3		1992-95
Milbury, Mike	Boston	160	90	49	21	2		
	NY Islanders	191	56	111	24	4		
	Total	351	146	160	45	6		1989-99
Molleken, Lorne	Chicago	47	18	21	8	2		1998-00
Muckler, John	Minnesota	35	6	23	6	1		
	Edmonton	160	75	65	20	2	1	
	Buffalo	268	125	109	34	4		
	NY Rangers	185	70	91	24	3		
	Total	648	276	288	84	10	1	1968-00
Muldoon, Pete	Chicago	44	19	22	3	1		1926-27

Coach	Team	Games Coached	Wins	Losses	Ties	Years	Cup Wins	Career
Munro, Dunc	Mtl. Maroons	76	37	29	10	2		1929-31
Murdoch, Bob	Chicago	80	30	41	9	1		
	Winnipeg	160	63	75	22	2		
	Total	240	93	116	31	3		1987-91
Murphy, Mike	Los Angeles	65	20	37	8	2		
	Toronto	164	60	87	17	2		
	Total	229	80	124	25	4		1986-98
Murray, Andy	Los Angeles	410	178	174	58	5		1999-04
Murray, Bryan	Washington	672	343	246	83	9		
	Detroit	244	124	91	29	3		
	Florida	59	17	31	11	1		
	Anaheim	82	29	45	8	1		
	Total	1057	513	413	131	14		1981-02
Murray, Terry	Washington	325	163	134	28	5		
	Philadelphia	212	118	64	30	3		
	Florida	200	79	90	31	3		
	Total	737	360	288	89	11		1989-01
Nanne, Lou	Minnesota	29	7	18	4	1		1977-78
Neale, Harry	Vancouver	407	142	189	76	6		
	Detroit	35	8	23	4	1		
	Total	442	150	212	80	7		1978-86
Neilson, Roger	Toronto	160	75	62	23	2		
	Buffalo	80	39	20	21	1		
	Vancouver	133	51	61	21	3		
	Los Angeles	28	8	17	3	1		
	NY Rangers	280	141	104	35	4		
	Florida	132	53	56	23	2		
	Philadelphia	185	92	60	33	3		
	Ottawa	2	1	1	0	1		
	Total	1000	460	381	159	17		1977-02
Nolan, Ted	Buffalo	164	73	72	19	2		1995-97
Nykoluk, Mike	Toronto	280	89	144	47	4		1980-84
O'Connell, Mike	Boston	9	3	3	3	1		2002-03
O'Donoghue, George	Toronto	29	15	13	1	2	1	1921-23
O'Reilly, Terry	Boston	227	115	86	26	3		1986-89
Olcyck, Ed	Pittsburgh	82	23	51	8	1		2003-04
Oliver, Murray	Minnesota	41	21	12	8	2		1981-83
Olmstead, Bert	Oakland	64	11	37	16	1		1967-68
Paddock, John	Winnipeg	281	106	138	37	4		1991-95
Page, Pierre	Minnesota	160	63	77	20	2		
	Quebec	230	98	103	29	3		
	Calgary	164	66	78	20	2		
	Anaheim	82	26	43	13	1		
	Total	636	253	301	82	8		1988-98
Park, Brad	Detroit	45	9	34	2	1		1985-86
Paterson, Rick	Tampa Bay	8	0	8	0	1		1997-98
Patrick, Craig	NY Rangers	95	37	45	13	2		
	Pittsburgh	74	29	36	9	2		
	Total	169	66	81	22	4		1980-97
Patrick, Frank	Boston	96	48	36	12	2		1934-36
Patrick, Lester	NY Rangers	604	281	216	107	13	2	1926-39
Patrick, Lynn	NY Rangers	107	40	51	16	2		
	Boston	310	117	130	63	5		
	St. Louis	26	8	15	3	1		
	Total	443	165	196	82	10		1948-76
Patrick, Muzz	NY Rangers	136	43	66	27	4		1953-63
Perron, Jean	Montreal	240	126	84	30	3	1	
	Quebec	47	16	26	5	1		
	Total	287	142	110	35	4	1	1985-89
Perry, Don	Los Angeles	168	52	85	31	3		1981-84
Pike, Alf	NY Rangers	123	36	66	21	2		1959-61
Pilous, Rudy	Chicago	387	162	151	74	6	1	1957-63
Plager, Barclay	St. Louis	178	49	96	33	4		1977-83
Plager, Bob	St. Louis	11	4	6	1	1		1992-93
Pleau, Larry	Hartford	224	81	117	26	5		1980-89
Polano, Nick	Detroit	240	79	127	34	3		1982-85
Popein, Larry	NY Rangers	41	18	14	9	1		1973-74
Powers, Eddie	Toronto	66	31	32	3	2		1924-26
Primeau, Joe	Toronto	210	97	71	42	3	1	1950-53
Pronovost, Marcel	Buffalo	104	52	29	23	2		1977-79
Pulford, Bob	Los Angeles	396	178	150	68	5		
	Chicago	433	185	180	68	7		
	Total	829	363	330	136	12		1972-00
Quenneville, Joel	St. Louis	593	307	209	77	8		1996-04
Querrie, Charles	Toronto	72	29	38	5	3		1922-27
Quinn, Mike	Quebec	24	4	20	0	1		1919-20
Quinn, Pat	Philadelphia	262	141	73	48	4		
	Los Angeles	202	75	101	26	3		
	Vancouver	280	141	111	28	5		
	Toronto	492	259	181	52	6		
	Total	1236	616	466	154	17		1978-04
Raeder, Cap	San Jose	1	1	0	0	1		2002-03
Ramsay, Craig	Buffalo	21	4	15	2	1		
	Philadelphia	28	12	12	4	1		
	Total	49	16	27	6	2		1986-01
Randall, Ken	Hamilton	14	6	8	0	1		1923-24
Reay, Billy	Toronto	90	26	50	14	2		
	Chicago	1012	516	335	161	14		
	Total	1102	542	385	175	16		1957-77
Regan, Larry	Los Angeles	88	27	47	14	2		1970-72
Renney, Tom	Vancouver	101	39	53	9	2		
	NY Rangers	20	5	15	0	1		
	Total	121	44	68	9	3		1996-04

Coach	Team	Games Coached	Wins	Losses	Ties	Years	Cup Wins	Career
Risebrough, Doug	Calgary	144	71	56	17	2		1990-92
Roberts, Jim	Buffalo	45	21	16	8	1		
	Hartford	80	26	41	13	1		
	St. Louis	9	3	3	3	1		
	Total	134	50	60	24	3		1981-97
Robinson, Larry	Los Angeles	328	122	161	45	4		
	New Jersey	141	73	49	19	3	1	
	Total	469	195	210	64	7	1	1995-02
Rodden, Mike	Toronto	2	0	2	0	1		1926-27
Romeril, Alex	Toronto	13	7	5	1	1		1926-27
Ross, Art	Mtl. Wanderers	6	1	5	0	1		
	Hamilton	24	6	18	0	1		
	Boston	728	361	277	90	16	1	
	Total	758	368	300	90	18	1	1917-45
Ruel, Claude	Montreal	305	172	82	51	5	2	1968-81
Ruff, Lindy	Buffalo	574	253	243	78	7		1997-04
Sather, Glen	Edmonton	842	464	268	110	11	4	
	NY Rangers	90	33	46	11	2		
	Total	932	497	314	121	13		1979-04
Sator, Ted	NY Rangers	99	41	48	10	2		
	Buffalo	207	96	89	22	3		
	Total	306	137	137	32	5		1985-89
Savard, Andre	Quebec	24	10	13	1	1		1987-88
Schinkel, Ken	Pittsburgh	203	83	92	28	4		1972-77
Schmidt, Milt	Boston	726	245	360	121	11		
	Washington	44	5	34	5	2		
	Total	770	250	394	126	13		1954-76
Schoenfeld, Jim	Buffalo	43	19	19	5	1		
	New Jersey	124	50	59	15	3		
	Washington	249	113	102	34	4		
	Phoenix	164	74	66	24	2		
	Total	580	256	248	78	10		1985-99
Shaughnessy, Tom	Chicago	21	10	8	3	1		1929-30
Shero, Fred	Philadelphia	554	308	151	95	7	2	
	NY Rangers	180	82	74	24	3		
	Total	734	390	225	119	10	2	1971-81
Simpson, Joe	NY Americans	144	42	72	30	3		1932-35
Simpson, Terry	NY Islanders	187	81	82	24	3		
	Philadelphia	84	35	39	10	1		
	Winnipeg	97	43	47	7	2		
	Total	368	159	168	41	6		1986-96
Sims, Al	San Jose	82	27	47	8	1		1996-97
Sinden, Harry	Boston	327	153	116	58	6	1	1966-85
Skinner, Jimmy	Detroit	247	123	78	46	4	1	1954-58
Smeaton, Cooper	Philadelphia	44	4	36	4	1		1930-31
Smith, Alf	Ottawa	18	12	6	0	1		1918-19
Smith, Barry*	Detroit	5	4	1	0	1		1998-99
*Results shared with co-coach Dave Lewis								
Smith, Floyd	Buffalo	241	143	62	36	4		
	Toronto	68	30	33	5	1		
	Total	309	173	95	41	5		1971-80
Smith, Mike	Winnipeg	23	2	17	4	1		1980-81
Smith, Ron	NY Rangers	44	15	22	7	1		1992-93
Smythe, Conn	Toronto	134	57	57	20	4		1927-31
Sonmor, Glen	Minnesota	417	174	161	82	7		1978-87
Sproule, Harry	Toronto	12	7	5	0	1		1919-20
Stanley, Barney	Chicago	23	4	17	2	1		1927-28
Stasiuk, Vic	Philadelphia	154	45	68	41	2		
	California	75	21	38	16	1		
	Vancouver	78	22	47	9	1		
	Total	307	88	153	66	4		1969-73
Stewart, Bill	Chicago	69	22	35	12	2	1	1937-39
Stewart, Bill	NY Islanders	37	11	19	7	1		1998-99
Stewart, Ron	NY Rangers	39	15	20	4	1		
	Los Angeles	80	31	34	15	1		
	Total	119	46	54	19	2		1975-78
Stirling, Steve	NY Islanders	82	38	33	11	1		2003-04
Suhonen, Alpo	Chicago	82	29	45	8	1		2000-01
Sullivan, Red	NY Rangers	196	58	103	35	4		
	Pittsburgh	150	47	79	24	2		
	Washington	18	2	16	0	1		
	Total	364	107	198	59	7		1962-75
Sullivan, Mike	Boston	82	41	26	15	1		2003-04
Sutherland, Bill	Winnipeg	32	7	22	3	2		1979-81
Sutter, Brian	St. Louis	320	153	124	43	4		
	Boston	216	120	73	23	3		
	Calgary	246	87	122	37	3		
	Chicago	246	91	118	37	3		
	Total	1028	451	437	140	13		1988-04
Sutter, Darryl	Chicago	216	110	80	26	3		
	San Jose	434	192	182	60	6		
	Calgary	128	61	52	15	2		
	Total	778	363	314	101	10		1992-04
Sutter, Duane	Florida	72	22	42	8	2		2000-02
Talbot, Jean-Guy	St. Louis	120	52	53	15	2		
	NY Rangers	80	30	37	13	1		
	Total	200	82	90	28	3		1972-78
Tessier, Orval	Chicago	213	99	93	21	3		1982-85
Therrien, Michel	Montreal	190	77	90	23	3		2000-03
Thompson, Paul	Chicago	272	104	127	41	7		1938-45
Thompson, Percy	Hamilton	48	13	35	0	2		1920-22
Tippett, Dave	Dallas	164	87	49	28	2		2002-04
Tobin, Bill	Chicago	71	29	29	13	2		1929-32

Coach	Team	Games Coached	Wins	Losses	Ties	Years	Cup Wins	Career
Torchetti, John	**Florida**	27	10	13	4	1		2003-04
Tortorella, John	NY Rangers	4	0	3	1	1		
	Tampa Bay	289	121	132	36	4	1	
	Total	293	121	135	37	5	1	1999-04
Tremblay, Mario	**Montreal**	159	71	63	25	2		1995-97
Trottier, Bryan	**NY Rangers**	54	21	27	6	1		2002-03
Trotz, Barry	**Nashville**	492	183	249	60	6		1998-04
Ubriaco, Gene	**Pittsburgh**	106	50	47	9	2		1988-90
Vachon, Rogie	**Los Angeles**	10	4	3	3	3		1983-95
Vigneault, Alain	**Montreal**	266	109	122	35	4		1997-01
Waddell, Don	**Atlanta**	10	4	5	1	1		2002-03
Watson, Bryan	**Edmonton**	18	4	9	5	1		1980-81
Watson, Phil	NY Rangers	295	119	124	52	5		
	Boston	84	16	55	13	2		
	Total	379	135	179	65	7		1955-63
Watt, Tom	Winnipeg	181	72	85	24	3		
	Vancouver	160	52	87	21	2		
	Toronto	149	52	80	17	2		
	Total	490	176	252	62	7		1981-92
Webster, Tom	NY Rangers	18	5	9	4	1		
	Los Angeles	240	115	94	31	3		
	Total	258	120	103	35	4		1986-92
Weiland, Cooney	**Boston**	96	58	20	18	2	1	1939-41
White, Bill	**Chicago**	46	16	24	6	1		1976-77
Wiley, Jim	**San Jose**	57	17	37	3	1		1995-96
Wilson, Johnny	Los Angeles	52	9	34	9	1		
	Detroit	145	67	56	22	2		
	Colorado	80	20	46	14	1		
	Pittsburgh	240	91	105	44	3		
	Total	517	187	241	89	7		1969-80
Wilson, Larry	**Detroit**	36	3	29	4	1		1976-77
Wilson, Rick	**Dallas**	32	13	12	7	1		2001-02
Wilson, Ron	Anaheim	296	120	145	31	4		
	Washington	410	192	167	51	5		
	San Jose	139	62	58	19	2		
	Total	845	374	370	101	11		1993-04
	Total	706	312	312	82	9		1993-02
Young, Garry	California	12	2	7	3	1		
	St. Louis	98	41	41	16	2		
	Total	110	43	48	19	3		1972-76

The three newest members of the NHL coaching fraternity: Mike Kitchen (top right) broke into the NHL with the Colorado Rockies in 1976-77 and played eight seasons in the league. He made his head coaching debut with St. Louis at Colorado on February 26, 2004. Glen Hanlon (below left) appeared in 477 NHL games in 14 seasons as a goaltender between 1977 and 1991, playing with the Vancouver Canucks, St. Louis Blues, New York Rangers and Detroit Red Wings. He took over as head coach of the Washington Capitals on December 10, 2003. Gerard Gallant (below right) played nine years with Detroit and two seasons with Tampa Bay, earning a Second-Team All-Star selection in 1988-89 when he had 39 goals and 54 assists. He took over as the interim coach of the Columbus Blue Jackets on January 1, 2004 and was officially named to the position of head coach on June 25.

Year-by-Year Individual Regular-Season Leaders

Season	Goals	G	Assists	A	Points	Pts.	Penalty Minutes	PIM
1917-18	Joe Malone	44	Cy Denneny, Reg Noble, Harry Cameron	10	Joe Malone	48	Joe Hall	100
1918-19	Newsy Lalonde	22	Newsy Lalonde, Eddie Gerard	10	Newsy Lalonde	32	Joe Hall	135
1919-20	Joe Malone	39	Frank Nighbor	15	Joe Malone	49	Cully Wilson	86
1920-21	Babe Dye	35	Jack Darragh	15	Newsy Lalonde	43	Bert Corbeau	86
1921-22	Punch Broadbent	32	Harry Cameron	17	Punch Broadbent	46	Sprague Cleghorn	63
1922-23	Babe Dye	26	Edmond Bouchard	12	Babe Dye	37	Georges Boucher	58
1923-24	Cy Denneny	22	Georges Boucher	10	Cy Denneny	24	Bert Corbeau	55
1924-25	Babe Dye	38	Cy Denneny, Red Green	15	Babe Dye	46	Georges Boucher	95
1925-26	Nels Stewart	34	Frank Nighbor	13	Nels Stewart	42	Bert Corbeau	121
1926-27	Bill Cook	33	Dick Irvin	18	Bill Cook	37	Nels Stewart	133
1927-28	Howie Morenz	33	Howie Morenz	18	Howie Morenz	51	Eddie Shore	165
1928-29	Ace Bailey	22	Frank Boucher	16	Ace Bailey	32	Red Dutton	139
1929-30	Cooney Weiland	43	Frank Boucher	36	Cooney Weiland	73	Joe Lamb	119
1930-31	Charlie Conacher	31	Joe Primeau	32	Howie Morenz	51	Harvey Rockburn	118
1931-32	Charlie Conacher, Bill Cook	34	Joe Primeau	37	Busher Jackson	53	Red Dutton	107
1932-33	Bill Cook	28	Frank Boucher	28	Bill Cook	50	Red Horner	144
1933-34	Charlie Conacher	32	Joe Primeau	32	Charlie Conacher	52	Red Horner	126 *
1934-35	Charlie Conacher	36	Art Chapman	34	Charlie Conacher	57	Red Horner	125
1935-36	Charlie Conacher, Bill Thoms	23	Art Chapman	28	Sweeney Schriner	45	Red Horner	167
1936-37	Larry Aurie, Nels Stewart	23	Syl Apps	29	Sweeney Schriner	46	Red Horner	124
1937-38	Gordie Drillon	26	Syl Apps	29	Gordie Drillon	52	Red Horner	82 *
1938-39	Roy Conacher	26	Bill Cowley	34	Toe Blake	47	Red Horner	85
1939-40	Bryan Hextall	24	Milt Schmidt	30	Milt Schmidt	52	Red Horner	87
1940-41	Bryan Hextall	26	Bill Cowley	45	Bill Cowley	62	Jimmy Orlando	99
1941-42	Lynn Patrick	32	Phil Watson	37	Bryan Hextall	56	Pat Egan	124
1942-43	Doug Bentley	33	Bill Cowley	45	Doug Bentley	73	Jimmy Orlando	89 *
1943-44	Doug Bentley	38	Clint Smith	49	Herb Cain	82	Mike McMahon	98
1944-45	Maurice Richard	50	Elmer Lach	54	Elmer Lach	80	Pat Egan	86
1945-46	Gaye Stewart	37	Elmer Lach	34	Max Bentley	61	Jack Stewart	73
1946-47	Maurice Richard	45	Billy Taylor	46	Max Bentley	72	Gus Mortson	133
1947-48	Ted Lindsay	33	Doug Bentley	37	Elmer Lach	61	Bill Barilko	147
1948-49	Sid Abel	28	Doug Bentley	43	Roy Conacher	68	Bill Ezinicki	145
1949-50	Maurice Richard	43	Ted Lindsay	55	Ted Lindsay	78	Bill Ezinicki	144
1950-51	Gordie Howe	43	Gordie Howe, Ted Kennedy	43	Gordie Howe	86	Gus Mortson	142
1951-52	Gordie Howe	47	Elmer Lach	50	Gordie Howe	86	Gus Kyle	127
1952-53	Gordie Howe	49	Gordie Howe	46	Gordie Howe	95	Maurice Richard	112
1953-54	Maurice Richard	37	Gordie Howe	48	Gordie Howe	81	Gus Mortson	132
1954-55	Maurice Richard, Bernie Geoffrion	38	Bert Olmstead	48	Bernie Geoffrion	75	Fern Flaman	150
1955-56	Jean Beliveau	47	Bert Olmstead	56	Jean Beliveau	88	Lou Fontinato	202
1956-57	Gordie Howe	44	Ted Lindsay	55	Gordie Howe	89	Gus Mortson	147
1957-58	Dickie Moore	36	Henri Richard	52	Dickie Moore	84	Lou Fontinato	152
1958-59	Jean Beliveau	45	Dickie Moore	55	Dickie Moore	96	Ted Lindsay	184
1959-60	Bobby Hull, Bronco Horvath	39	Don McKenney	49	Bobby Hull	81	Carl Brewer	150
1960-61	Bernie Geoffrion	50	Jean Beliveau	58	Bernie Geoffrion	95	Pierre Pilote	165
1961-62	Bobby Hull	50	Andy Bathgate	56	Bobby Hull, Andy Bathgate	84	Lou Fontinato	167
1962-63	Gordie Howe	38	Henri Richard	50	Gordie Howe	86	Howie Young	273
1963-64	Bobby Hull	43	Andy Bathgate	58	Stan Mikita	89	Vic Hadfield	151
1964-65	Norm Ullman	42	Stan Mikita	59	Stan Mikita	87	Carl Brewer	177
1965-66	Bobby Hull	54	Stan Mikita, Bobby Rousseau, Jean Beliveau	48	Bobby Hull	97	Reggie Fleming	166
1966-67	Bobby Hull	52	Stan Mikita	62	Stan Mikita	97	John Ferguson	177
1967-68	Bobby Hull	44	Phil Esposito	49	Stan Mikita	87	Barclay Plager	153
1968-69	Bobby Hull	58	Phil Esposito	77	Phil Esposito	126	Forbes Kennedy	219
1969-70	Phil Esposito	43	Bobby Orr	87	Bobby Orr	120	Keith Magnuson	213
1970-71	Phil Esposito	76	Bobby Orr	102	Phil Esposito	152	Keith Magnuson	291
1971-72	Phil Esposito	66	Bobby Orr	80	Phil Esposito	133	Bryan Watson	212
1972-73	Phil Esposito	55	Phil Esposito	75	Phil Esposito	130	Dave Schultz	259
1973-74	Phil Esposito	68	Bobby Orr	90	Phil Esposito	145	Dave Schultz	348
1974-75	Phil Esposito	61	Bobby Orr, Bobby Clarke	89	Bobby Orr	135	Dave Schultz	472
1975-76	Reggie Leach	61	Bobby Clarke	89	Guy Lafleur	125	Steve Durbano	370
1976-77	Steve Shutt	60	Guy Lafleur	80	Guy Lafleur	136	Tiger Williams	338
1977-78	Guy Lafleur	60	Bryan Trottier	77	Guy Lafleur	132	Dave Schultz	405
1978-79	Mike Bossy	69	Bryan Trottier	87	Bryan Trottier	134	Tiger Williams	298
1979-80	Charlie Simmer, Danny Gare, Blaine Stoughton	56	Wayne Gretzky	86	Marcel Dionne, Wayne Gretzky	137	Jimmy Mann	287
1980-81	Mike Bossy	68	Wayne Gretzky	109	Wayne Gretzky	164	Tiger Williams	343
1981-82	Wayne Gretzky	92	Wayne Gretzky	120	Wayne Gretzky	212	Paul Baxter	409
1982-83	Wayne Gretzky	71	Wayne Gretzky	125	Wayne Gretzky	196	Randy Holt	275
1983-84	Wayne Gretzky	87	Wayne Gretzky	118	Wayne Gretzky	205	Chris Nilan	338
1984-85	Wayne Gretzky	73	Wayne Gretzky	135	Wayne Gretzky	208	Chris Nilan	358
1985-86	Jari Kurri	68	Wayne Gretzky	163	Wayne Gretzky	215	Joe Kocur	377
1986-87	Wayne Gretzky	62	Wayne Gretzky	121	Wayne Gretzky	183	Tim Hunter	361
1987-88	Mario Lemieux	70	Wayne Gretzky	109	Mario Lemieux	168	Bob Probert	398
1988-89	Mario Lemieux	85	Mario Lemieux, Wayne Gretzky	114	Mario Lemieux	199	Tim Hunter	375
1989-90	Brett Hull	72	Wayne Gretzky	102	Wayne Gretzky	142	Basil McRae	351
1990-91	Brett Hull	86	Wayne Gretzky	122	Wayne Gretzky	163	Rob Ray	350
1991-92	Brett Hull	70	Wayne Gretzky	90	Mario Lemieux	131	Mike Peluso	408
1992-93	Teemu Selanne, Alexander Mogilny	76	Adam Oates	97	Mario Lemieux	160	Marty McSorley	399
1993-94	Pavel Bure	60	Wayne Gretzky	92	Wayne Gretzky	130	Tie Domi	347
1994-95	Peter Bondra	34	Ron Francis	48	Jaromir Jagr, Eric Lindros	70	Enrico Ciccone	225
1995-96	Mario Lemieux	69	Mario Lemieux, Wayne Gretzky	92	Mario Lemieux	161	Matthew Barnaby	335
1996-97	Keith Tkachuk	52	Mario Lemieux, Wayne Gretzky	72	Mario Lemieux	122	Gino Odjick	371
1997-98	Teemu Selanne, Peter Bondra	52	Jaromir Jagr	67	Jaromir Jagr	102	Donald Brashear	372
1998-99	Teemu Selanne	47	Jaromir Jagr	83	Jaromir Jagr	127	Rob Ray	261
99-2000	Pavel Bure	58	Mark Recchi	63	Jaromir Jagr	96	Denny Lambert	219
2000-01	Pavel Bure	59	Jaromir Jagr, Adam Oates	69	Jaromir Jagr	121	Matthew Barnaby	265
2001-02	Jarome Iginla	52	Adam Oates	64	Jarome Iginla	96	Peter Worell	354
2002-03	Milan Hejduk	50	Peter Forsberg	77	Peter Forsberg	106	Jody Shelley	249
2003-04	Rick Nash, Jarome Iginla, Ilya Kovalchuk	41	Scott Gomez, Martin St. Louis	56	Martin St. Louis	94	Sean Avery	261

* Match Misconduct penalty not included in total penalty minutes.
1946-47 was the first season that a Match penalty was automatically written into the player's total penalty minutes as 20 minutes.
Beginning in 1947-48 all penalties, Match, Game Misconduct, and Misconduct, are written as 10 minutes.

One Season Scoring Records

Goals-Per-Game Leaders, One Season

(Among players with 20 goals or more in one season)

Player	Team	Season	Games	Goals	Average
Joe Malone	Montreal	1917-18	20	44	2.20
Cy Denneny	Ottawa	1917-18	20	36	1.80
Newsy Lalonde	Montreal	1917-18	14	23	1.64
Joe Malone	Quebec	1919-20	24	39	1.63
Newsy Lalonde	Montreal	1919-20	23	37	1.61
Reg Noble	Toronto	1917-18	20	30	1.50
Babe Dye	Ham., Tor.	1920-21	24	35	1.46
Cy Denneny	Ottawa	1920-21	24	34	1.42
Joe Malone	Hamilton	1920-21	20	28	1.40
Newsy Lalonde	Montreal	1920-21	24	33	1.38
Punch Broadbent	Ottawa	1921-22	24	32	1.33
Babe Dye	Toronto	1924-25	29	38	1.31
Babe Dye	Toronto	1921-22	24	31	1.29
Newsy Lalonde	Montreal	1918-19	17	22	1.29
Odie Cleghorn	Montreal	1918-19	17	22	1.29
Cy Denneny	Ottawa	1921-22	22	27	1.23
Aurel Joliat	Montreal	1924-25	25	30	1.20
Wayne Gretzky	Edmonton	1983-84	74	87	1.18
Babe Dye	Toronto	1922-23	22	26	1.18
Wayne Gretzky	Edmonton	1981-82	80	92	1.15
Mario Lemieux	Pittsburgh	1992-93	60	69	1.15
Frank Nighbor	Ottawa	1919-20	23	26	1.13
Mario Lemieux	Pittsburgh	1988-89	76	85	1.12
Brett Hull	St. Louis	1990-91	78	86	1.10
Cam Neely	Boston	1993-94	49	50	1.02
Maurice Richard	Montreal	1944-45	50	50	1.00
Reg Noble	Toronto	1919-20	24	24	1.00
Corb Denneny	Toronto	1919-20	24	24	1.00
Joe Malone	Hamilton	1921-22	24	24	1.00
Billy Boucher	Montreal	1922-23	24	24	1.00
Cy Denneny	Ottawa	1923-24	22	22	1.00
Alexander Mogilny	Buffalo	1992-93	77	76	0.99
Mario Lemieux	Pittsburgh	1995-96	70	69	0.99
Cooney Weiland	Boston	1929-30	44	43	0.98
Phil Esposito	Boston	1970-71	78	76	0.97
Jari Kurri	Edmonton	1984-85	73	71	0.97

Cam Neely and Maurice Richard are the only players in NHL history to average at least a goal a game while scoring exactly 50 goals. Neely had 50 goals in just 49 games as injuries forced him to miss more than 30 games in 1993-94.

Assists-Per-Game Leaders, One Season

(Among players with 35 assists or more in one season)

Player	Team	Season	Games	Assists	Average
Wayne Gretzky	Edmonton	1985-86	80	163	2.04
Wayne Gretzky	Edmonton	1987-88	64	109	1.70
Wayne Gretzky	Edmonton	1984-85	80	135	1.69
Wayne Gretzky	Edmonton	1983-84	74	118	1.59
Wayne Gretzky	Edmonton	1982-83	80	125	1.56
Wayne Gretzky	Los Angeles	1990-91	78	122	1.56
Wayne Gretzky	Edmonton	1986-87	79	121	1.53
Mario Lemieux	Pittsburgh	1992-93	60	91	1.52
Wayne Gretzky	Edmonton	1981-82	80	120	1.50
Mario Lemieux	Pittsburgh	1988-89	76	114	1.50
Adam Oates	St. Louis	1990-91	61	90	1.48
Wayne Gretzky	Los Angeles	1988-89	78	114	1.46
Wayne Gretzky	Los Angeles	1989-90	73	102	1.40
Wayne Gretzky	Edmonton	1980-81	80	109	1.36
Mario Lemieux	Pittsburgh	1991-92	64	87	1.36
Mario Lemieux	Pittsburgh	1989-90	59	78	1.32
Bobby Orr	Boston	1970-71	78	102	1.31
Mario Lemieux	Pittsburgh	1995-96	70	92	1.31
Mario Lemieux	Pittsburgh	1987-88	77	98	1.27
Bobby Orr	Boston	1973-74	74	90	1.22
Wayne Gretzky	Los Angeles	1991-92	74	90	1.22
Ron Francis	Pittsburgh	1995-96	77	92	1.19
Mario Lemieux	Pittsburgh	1985-86	79	93	1.18
Bobby Clarke	Philadelphia	1975-76	76	89	1.17
Peter Stastny	Quebec	1981-82	80	93	1.16
Adam Oates	Boston	1992-93	84	97	1.15
Doug Gilmour	Toronto	1992-93	83	95	1.14
Wayne Gretzky	Los Angeles	1993-94	81	92	1.14
Paul Coffey	Edmonton	1985-86	79	90	1.14
Bobby Orr	Boston	1969-70	76	87	1.14
Bryan Trottier	NY Islanders	1978-79	76	87	1.14
Bobby Orr	Boston	1972-73	63	72	1.14
Bill Cowley	Boston	1943-44	36	41	1.14
Pat LaFontaine	Buffalo	1992-93	84	95	1.13
Steve Yzerman	Detroit	1988-89	80	90	1.13
Paul Coffey	Pittsburgh	1987-88	46	52	1.13
Bobby Orr	Boston	1974-75	80	89	1.11
Bobby Clarke	Philadelphia	1974-75	80	89	1.11
Paul Coffey	Pittsburgh	1988-89	75	83	1.11
Wayne Gretzky	Los Angeles	1992-93	45	49	1.11
Denis Savard	Chicago	1982-83	78	86	1.10
Denis Savard	Chicago	1981-82	80	87	1.09
Denis Savard	Chicago	1987-88	80	87	1.09
Wayne Gretzky	Edmonton	1979-80	79	86	1.09
Ron Francis	Pittsburgh	1994-95	44	48	1.09
Paul Coffey	Edmonton	1983-84	80	86	1.08
Elmer Lach	Montreal	1944-45	50	54	1.08
Peter Stastny	Quebec	1985-86	76	81	1.07
Jaromir Jagr	Pittsburgh	1995-96	82	87	1.06
Mark Messier	Edmonton	1989-90	79	84	1.06
Peter Forsberg	Colorado	1995-96	82	86	1.05
Paul Coffey	Edmonton	1984-85	80	84	1.05
Marcel Dionne	Los Angeles	1979-80	80	84	1.05
Bobby Orr	Boston	1971-72	76	80	1.05
Mike Bossy	NY Islanders	1981-82	80	83	1.04
Adam Oates	Boston	1993-94	77	80	1.04
Phil Esposito	Boston	1968-69	74	77	1.04
Bryan Trottier	NY Islanders	1983-84	68	71	1.04
Pete Mahovlich	Montreal	1974-75	80	82	1.03
Kent Nilsson	Calgary	1980-81	80	82	1.03
Peter Stastny	Quebec	1982-83	75	77	1.03
Denis Savard	Chicago	1988-89	58	59	1.02
Jaromir Jagr	Pittsburgh	1998-99	81	83	1.02
Doug Gilmour	Toronto	1993-94	83	84	1.01
Bernie Nicholls	Los Angeles	1988-89	79	80	1.01
Guy Lafleur	Montreal	1979-80	74	75	1.01
Guy Lafleur	Montreal	1976-77	80	80	1.00
Marcel Dionne	Los Angeles	1984-85	80	80	1.00
Brian Leetch	NY Rangers	1991-92	80	80	1.00
Bryan Trottier	NY Islanders	1977-78	77	77	1.00
Mike Bossy	NY Islanders	1983-84	67	67	1.00
Jean Ratelle	NY Rangers	1971-72	63	63	1.00
Steve Yzerman	Detroit	1993-94	58	58	1.00
Ron Francis	Hartford	1985-86	53	53	1.00
Guy Chouinard	Calgary	1980-81	52	52	1.00
Elmer Lach	Montreal	1943-44	48	48	1.00

Points-Per-Game Leaders, One Season

(Among players with 50 points or more in one season)

Player	Team	Season	Games	Points	Average	Player	Team	Season	Games	Points	Average
Wayne Gretzky	Edmonton	1983-84	74	205	2.77	Peter Stastny	Quebec	1982-83	75	124	1.65
Wayne Gretzky	Edmonton	1985-86	80	215	2.69	Bobby Orr	Boston	1973-74	74	122	1.65
Mario Lemieux	Pittsburgh	1992-93	60	160	2.67	Kent Nilsson	Calgary	1980-81	80	131	1.64
Wayne Gretzky	Edmonton	1981-82	80	212	2.65	Denis Savard	Chicago	1987-88	80	131	1.64
Mario Lemieux	Pittsburgh	1988-89	76	199	2.62	Wayne Gretzky	Los Angeles	1991-92	74	121	1.64
Wayne Gretzky	Edmonton	1984-85	80	208	2.60	Steve Yzerman	Detroit	1992-93	84	137	1.63
Wayne Gretzky	Edmonton	1982-83	80	196	2.45	Marcel Dionne	Los Angeles	1978-79	80	130	1.63
Wayne Gretzky	Edmonton	1987-88	64	149	2.33	Dale Hawerchuk	Winnipeg	1984-85	80	130	1.63
Wayne Gretzky	Edmonton	1986-87	79	183	2.32	Mark Messier	Edmonton	1989-90	79	129	1.63
Mario Lemieux	Pittsburgh	1995-96	70	161	2.30	Bryan Trottier	NY Islanders	1983-84	68	111	1.63
Mario Lemieux	Pittsburgh	1987-88	77	168	2.18	Pat LaFontaine	Buffalo	1991-92	57	93	1.63
Wayne Gretzky	Los Angeles	1988-89	78	168	2.15	Charlie Simmer	Los Angeles	1980-81	65	105	1.62
Wayne Gretzky	Los Angeles	1990-91	78	163	2.09	Guy Lafleur	Montreal	1978-79	80	129	1.61
Mario Lemieux	Pittsburgh	1989-90	59	123	2.08	Bryan Trottier	NY Islanders	1981-82	80	129	1.61
Wayne Gretzky	Edmonton	1980-81	80	164	2.05	Phil Esposito	Boston	1974-75	79	127	1.61
Mario Lemieux	Pittsburgh	1991-92	64	131	2.05	Steve Yzerman	Detroit	1989-90	79	127	1.61
Bill Cowley	Boston	1943-44	36	71	1.97	Peter Stastny	Quebec	1985-86	76	122	1.61
Phil Esposito	Boston	1970-71	78	152	1.95	Mario Lemieux	Pittsburgh	1996-97	76	122	1.61
Wayne Gretzky	Los Angeles	1989-90	73	142	1.95	Michel Goulet	Quebec	1983-84	75	121	1.61
Steve Yzerman	Detroit	1988-89	80	155	1.94	Wayne Gretzky	Los Angeles	1993-94	81	130	1.60
Bernie Nicholls	Los Angeles	1988-89	79	150	1.90	Bryan Trottier	NY Islanders	1977-78	77	123	1.60
Adam Oates	St. Louis	1990-91	61	115	1.89	Bobby Orr	Boston	1972-73	63	101	1.60
Phil Esposito	Boston	1973-74	78	145	1.86	Guy Chouinard	Calgary	1980-81	52	83	1.60
Jari Kurri	Edmonton	1984-85	73	135	1.85	Elmer Lach	Montreal	1944-45	50	80	1.60
Mike Bossy	NY Islanders	1981-82	80	147	1.84	Pierre Turgeon	NY Islanders	1992-93	83	132	1.59
Jaromir Jagr	Pittsburgh	1995-96	82	149	1.82	Steve Yzerman	Detroit	1987-88	64	102	1.59
Mario Lemieux	Pittsburgh	1985-86	79	141	1.78	Mike Bossy	NY Islanders	1978-79	80	126	1.58
Bobby Orr	Boston	1970-71	78	139	1.78	Paul Coffey	Edmonton	1983-84	80	126	1.58
Jari Kurri	Edmonton	1983-84	64	113	1.77	Marcel Dionne	Los Angeles	1984-85	80	126	1.58
Mario Lemieux	Pittsburgh	2000-01	43	76	1.77	Bobby Orr	Boston	1969-70	76	120	1.58
Pat LaFontaine	Buffalo	1992-93	84	148	1.76	Eric Lindros	Philadelphia	1995-96	73	115	1.58
Bryan Trottier	NY Islanders	1978-79	76	134	1.76	Charlie Simmer	Los Angeles	1979-80	64	101	1.58
Mike Bossy	NY Islanders	1983-84	67	118	1.76	Teemu Selanne	Winnipeg	1992-93	84	132	1.57
Paul Coffey	Edmonton	1985-86	79	138	1.75	Jaromir Jagr	Pittsburgh	1998-99	81	127	1.57
Phil Esposito	Boston	1971-72	76	133	1.75	Bobby Clarke	Philadelphia	1975-76	76	119	1.57
Peter Stastny	Quebec	1981-82	80	139	1.74	Guy Lafleur	Montreal	1975-76	80	125	1.56
Wayne Gretzky	Edmonton	1979-80	79	137	1.73	Dave Taylor	Los Angeles	1980-81	72	112	1.56
Jean Ratelle	NY Rangers	1971-72	63	109	1.73	Denis Savard	Chicago	1982-83	78	121	1.55
Marcel Dionne	Los Angeles	1979-80	80	137	1.71	Ron Francis	Pittsburgh	1995-96	77	119	1.55
Herb Cain	Boston	1943-44	48	82	1.71	Mike Bossy	NY Islanders	1985-86	80	123	1.54
Guy Lafleur	Montreal	1976-77	80	136	1.70	Kevin Stevens	Pittsburgh	1991-92	80	123	1.54
Dennis Maruk	Washington	1981-82	80	136	1.70	Bobby Orr	Boston	1971-72	76	117	1.54
Phil Esposito	Boston	1968-69	74	126	1.70	Mike Bossy	NY Islanders	1984-85	76	117	1.54
Guy Lafleur	Montreal	1974-75	70	119	1.70	Kevin Stevens	Pittsburgh	1992-93	72	111	1.54
Mario Lemieux	Pittsburgh	1986-87	63	107	1.70	Doug Bentley	Chicago	1943-44	50	77	1.54
Adam Oates	Boston	1992-93	84	142	1.69	Doug Gilmour	Toronto	1992-93	83	127	1.53
Bobby Orr	Boston	1974-75	80	135	1.69	Marcel Dionne	Los Angeles	1976-77	80	122	1.53
Marcel Dionne	Los Angeles	1980-81	80	135	1.69	Jaromir Jagr	Pittsburgh	99-2000	63	96	1.52
Guy Lafleur	Montreal	1977-78	78	132	1.69	Eric Lindros	Philadelphia	1996-97	52	79	1.52
Guy Lafleur	Montreal	1979-80	74	125	1.69	Eric Lindros	Philadelphia	1994-95	46	70	1.52
Rob Brown	Pittsburgh	1988-89	68	115	1.69	Marcel Dionne	Detroit	1974-75	80	121	1.51
Jari Kurri	Edmonton	1985-86	78	131	1.68	Mike Bossy	NY Islanders	1980-81	79	119	1.51
Brett Hull	St. Louis	1990-91	78	131	1.68	Paul Coffey	Edmonton	1984-85	80	121	1.51
Phil Esposito	Boston	1972-73	78	130	1.67	Dale Hawerchuk	Winnipeg	1987-88	80	121	1.51
Cooney Weiland	Boston	1929-30	44	73	1.66	Paul Coffey	Pittsburgh	1988-89	75	113	1.51
Alexander Mogilny	Buffalo	1992-93	77	127	1.65	Jaromir Jagr	Pittsburgh	1996-97	63	95	1.51

Paul Coffey and Bobby Orr are the only defensemen to average more than 1.5 points per game in an NHL season. Coffey's 48 goals in 1985-86 are a record for defensemen, while his 138 points that year are one short of Orr's record set in 1970-71.

Montreal's Michael Ryder (left) led all NHL rookies with 63 points in 2003-04. His 25 goals tied Islanders freshman Trent Hunter. Teemu Selanne (right) set rookie records with 76 goals and 132 points for the Winnipeg Jets in 1992-93.

Rookie Scoring Records

All-Time Top 50 Goal-Scoring Rookies

	Rookie	Team	Position	Season	GP	G	A	PTS
1.	* Teemu Selanne	Winnipeg	Right wing	1992-93	84	**76**	56	132
2.	* Mike Bossy	NY Islanders	Right wing	1977-78	73	**53**	38	91
3.	* Joe Nieuwendyk	Calgary	Center	1987-88	75	**51**	41	92
4.	* Dale Hawerchuk	Winnipeg	Center	1981-82	80	**45**	58	103
	* Luc Robitaille	Los Angeles	Left wing	1986-87	79	**45**	39	84
6.	Rick Martin	Buffalo	Left wing	1971-72	73	**44**	30	74
	Barry Pederson	Boston	Center	1981-82	80	**44**	48	92
8.	Steve Larmer	Chicago	Right wing	1982-83	80	**43**	47	90
	* Mario Lemieux	Pittsburgh	Center	1984-85	73	**43**	57	100
10.	Eric Lindros	Philadelphia	Center	1992-93	61	**41**	34	75
11.	Darryl Sutter	Chicago	Left wing	1980-81	76	**40**	22	62
	Sylvain Turgeon	Hartford	Left wing	1983-84	76	**40**	32	72
	Warren Young	Pittsburgh	Left wing	1984-85	80	**40**	32	72
14.	* Eric Vail	Atlanta	Left wing	1974-75	72	**39**	21	60
	Anton Stastny	Quebec	Left wing	1980-81	80	**39**	46	85
	* Peter Stastny	Quebec	Center	1980-81	77	**39**	70	109
	Steve Yzerman	Detroit	Center	1983-84	80	**39**	48	87
18.	* Gilbert Perreault	Buffalo	Center	1970-71	78	**38**	34	72
	Neal Broten	Minnesota	Center	1981-82	73	**38**	60	98
	Ray Sheppard	Buffalo	Right wing	1987-88	74	**38**	27	65
	Mikael Renberg	Philadelphia	Left wing	1993-94	83	**38**	44	82
22.	Jorgen Pettersson	St. Louis	Left wing	1980-81	62	**37**	36	73
	Jimmy Carson	Los Angeles	Center	1986-87	80	**37**	42	79
24.	Mike Foligno	Detroit	Right wing	1979-80	80	**36**	35	71
	Mike Bullard	Pittsburgh	Center	1981-82	75	**36**	27	63
	Paul MacLean	Winnipeg	Right wing	1981-82	74	**36**	25	61
	Tony Granato	NY Rangers	Right wing	1988-89	78	**36**	27	63
28.	Marian Stastny	Quebec	Right wing	1981-82	74	**35**	54	89
	Brian Bellows	Minnesota	Center	1982-83	78	**35**	30	65
	Tony Amonte	NY Rangers	Right wing	1991-92	79	**35**	34	69
31.	Nels Stewart	Mtl. Maroons	Center	1925-26	36	**34**	8	42
	* Danny Grant	Minnesota	Left wing	1968-69	75	**34**	31	65
	Norm Ferguson	Oakland	Right wing	1968-69	76	**34**	20	54
	Brian Propp	Philadelphia	Left wing	1979-80	80	**34**	41	75
	Wendel Clark	Toronto	Left wing	1985-86	66	**34**	11	45
	* Pavel Bure	Vancouver	Right wing	1991-92	65	**34**	26	60
37.	* Willi Plett	Atlanta	Right wing	1976-77	64	**33**	23	56
	Dale McCourt	Detroit	Center	1977-78	76	**33**	39	72
	Mark Pavelich	NY Rangers	Center	1981-82	79	**33**	43	76
	Ron Flockhart	Philadelphia	Center	1981-82	72	**33**	39	72
	Steve Bozek	Los Angeles	Center	1981-82	71	**33**	23	56
	Jason Arnott	Edmonton	Center	1993-94	78	**33**	35	68
43.	Bill Mosienko	Chicago	Right wing	1943-44	50	**32**	38	70
	Michel Bergeron	Detroit	Right wing	1975-76	72	**32**	27	59
	* Bryan Trottier	NY Islanders	Center	1975-76	80	**32**	63	95
	Don Murdoch	NY Rangers	Right wing	1976-77	59	**32**	24	56
	Jari Kurri	Edmonton	Left wing	1980-81	75	**32**	43	75
	Bobby Carpenter	Washington	Center	1981-82	80	**32**	35	67
	Kjell Dahlin	Montreal	Right wing	1985-86	77	**32**	39	71
	Petr Klima	Detroit	Left wing	1985-86	74	**32**	24	56
	Darren Turcotte	NY Rangers	Center	1989-90	76	**32**	34	66
	Joe Juneau	Boston	Center	1992-93	84	**32**	70	102

All-Time Top 50 Point-Scoring Rookies

	Rookie	Team	Position	Season	GP	G	A	PTS
1.	* Teemu Selanne	Winnipeg	Right wing	1992-93	84	76	56	**132**
2.	* Peter Stastny	Quebec	Center	1980-81	77	39	70	**109**
3.	* Dale Hawerchuk	Winnipeg	Center	1981-82	80	45	58	**103**
4.	Joe Juneau	Boston	Center	1992-93	84	32	70	**102**
5.	* Mario Lemieux	Pittsburgh	Center	1984-85	73	43	57	**100**
6.	Neal Broten	Minnesota	Center	1981-82	73	38	60	**98**
7.	* Bryan Trottier	NY Islanders	Center	1975-76	80	32	63	**95**
8.	Barry Pederson	Boston	Center	1981-82	80	44	48	**92**
	* Joe Nieuwendyk	Calgary	Center	1987-88	75	51	41	**92**
10.	* Mike Bossy	NY Islanders	Right wing	1977-78	73	53	38	**91**
11.	* Steve Larmer	Chicago	Right wing	1982-83	80	43	47	**90**
12.	Marian Stastny	Quebec	Right wing	1981-82	74	35	54	**89**
13.	Steve Yzerman	Detroit	Center	1983-84	80	39	48	**87**
14.	* Sergei Makarov	Calgary	Right wing	1989-90	80	24	62	**86**
15.	Anton Stastny	Quebec	Left wing	1980-81	80	39	46	**85**
16.	* Luc Robitaille	Los Angeles	Left wing	1986-87	79	45	39	**84**
17.	Mikael Renberg	Philadelphia	Left wing	1993-94	83	38	44	**82**
18.	Jimmy Carson	Los Angeles	Center	1986-87	80	37	42	**79**
	Sergei Fedorov	Detroit	Center	1990-91	77	31	48	**79**
	Alexei Yashin	Ottawa	Center	1993-94	83	30	49	**79**
21.	Marcel Dionne	Detroit	Center	1971-72	78	28	49	**77**
22.	Larry Murphy	Los Angeles	Defense	1980-81	80	16	60	**76**
	Mark Pavelich	NY Rangers	Center	1981-82	79	33	43	**76**
	Dave Poulin	Philadelphia	Center	1983-84	73	31	45	**76**
25.	Brian Propp	Philadelphia	Left wing	1979-80	80	34	41	**75**
	Jari Kurri	Edmonton	Left wing	1980-81	75	32	43	**75**
	Denis Savard	Chicago	Center	1980-81	76	28	47	**75**
	Mike Modano	Minnesota	Center	1989-90	80	29	46	**75**
	Eric Lindros	Philadelphia	Center	1992-93	61	41	34	**75**
30.	Rick Martin	Buffalo	Left wing	1971-72	73	44	30	**74**
	* Bobby Smith	Minnesota	Center	1978-79	80	30	44	**74**
32.	Jorgen Pettersson	St. Louis	Left wing	1980-81	62	37	36	**73**
33.	* Gilbert Perreault	Buffalo	Center	1970-71	78	38	34	**72**
	Dale McCourt	Detroit	Center	1977-78	76	33	39	**72**
	Ron Flockhart	Philadelphia	Center	1981-82	72	33	39	**72**
	Sylvain Turgeon	Hartford	Left wing	1983-84	76	40	32	**72**
	Warren Young	Pittsburgh	Left wing	1984-85	80	40	32	**72**
	Carey Wilson	Calgary	Center	1984-85	74	24	48	**72**
	Alex Zhamnov	Winnipeg	Center	1992-93	68	25	47	**72**
40.	Mike Foligno	Detroit	Right wing	1979-80	80	36	35	**71**
	Dave Christian	Winnipeg	Center	1980-81	80	28	43	**71**
	Mats Naslund	Montreal	Left wing	1982-83	74	26	45	**71**
	Kjell Dahlin	Montreal	Right wing	1985-86	77	32	39	**71**
	* Brian Leetch	NY Rangers	Defense	1988-89	68	23	48	**71**
45.	Bill Mosienko	Chicago	Right wing	1943-44	50	32	38	**70**
	* Scott Gomez	New Jersey	Center	99-2000	82	19	51	**70**
47.	Roland Eriksson	Minnesota	Center	1976-77	80	25	44	**69**
	Tony Amonte	NY Rangers	Right wing	1991-92	79	35	34	**69**
49.	Jude Drouin	Minnesota	Center	1970-71	75	16	52	**68**
	Pierre Larouche	Pittsburgh	Center	1974-75	79	31	37	**68**
	Ron Francis	Hartford	Center	1981-82	59	25	43	**68**
	* Gary Suter	Calgary	Defense	1985-86	80	18	50	**68**
	Jason Arnott	Edmonton	Center	1993-94	84	33	35	**68**

* Calder Trophy Winner

Peter Bondra

Pavel Bure

Joe Sakic

50-Goal Seasons

Player	Team	Date of 50th Goal	Score	Goaltender	Player's Game No.	Team Game No.	Total Goals	Total Games	Age When First 50th Scored (Yrs. & Mos.)
Maurice Richard	Mtl.	18-3-45	Mtl. 4 at Bos. 2	Harvey Bennett	50	50	50	50	23.7
Bernie Geoffrion	Mtl.	16-3-61	Tor. 2 at Mtl. 5	Cesare Maniago	62	68	50	64	30.1
Bobby Hull	Chi.	25-3-62	Chi. 1 at NYR 4	Gump Worsley	70	70	50	70	23.2
Bobby Hull	Chi.	2-3-66	Det. 4 at Chi. 5	Hank Bassen	52	57	54	65	
Bobby Hull	Chi.	18-3-67	Chi. 5 at Tor. 9	Bruce Gamble	63	66	52	66	
Bobby Hull	Chi.	5-3-69	NYR 4 at Chi. 4	Ed Giacomin	64	66	58	74	
Phil Esposito	Bos.	20-2-71	Bos. 4 at L.A. 5	Denis DeJordy	58	58	76	78	29.0
John Bucyk	Bos.	16-3-71	Bos. 11 at Det. 4	Roy Edwards	69	69	51	78	35.10
Phil Esposito	Bos.	20-2-72	Bos. 3 at Chi. 1	Tony Esposito	60	60	66	76	
Bobby Hull	Chi.	2-4-72	Det. 1 at Chi. 6	Andy Brown	78	78	50	78	
Vic Hadfield	NYR	2-4-72	Mtl. 6 at NYR 5	Denis DeJordy	78	78	50	78	31.6
Phil Esposito	Bos.	25-3-73	Buf. 1 at Bos. 6	Roger Crozier	75	75	55	78	
Mickey Redmond	Det.	27-3-73	Det. 8 at Tor. 1	Ron Low	73	75	52	76	25.3
Rick MacLeish	Phi.	1-4-73	Phi. 4 at Pit. 5	Cam Newton	78	78	50	78	23.2
Phil Esposito	Bos.	20-2-74	Bos. 5 at Min. 5	Cesare Maniago	56	56	68	78	
Mickey Redmond	Det.	23-3-74	NYR 3 at Det. 5	Ed Giacomin	69	71	51	76	
Ken Hodge	Bos.	6-4-74	Bos. 2 at Mtl. 6	Michel Larocque	75	77	50	78	29.10
Rick Martin	Buf.	7-4-74	St.L. 2 at Buf. 5	Wayne Stephenson	78	78	52	78	22.9
Phil Esposito	Bos.	8-2-75	Bos. 8 at Det. 5	Jim Rutherford	54	54	61	79	
Guy Lafleur	Mtl.	29-3-75	K.C. 1 at Mtl. 4	Denis Herron	66	76	53	70	23.6
Danny Grant	Det.	2-4-75	Wsh. 3 at Det. 8	John Adams	78	78	50	80	29.2
Rick Martin	Buf.	3-4-75	Bos. 2 at Buf. 4	Ken Broderick	67	79	52	68	
Reggie Leach	Phi.	14-3-76	Atl. 1 at Phi. 6	Dan Bouchard	69	69	61	80	25.11
Jean Pronovost	Pit.	24-3-76	Bos. 5 at Pit. 5	Gilles Gilbert	74	74	52	80	30.3
Guy Lafleur	Mtl.	27-3-76	K.C. 2 at Mtl. 8	Denis Herron	76	76	56	80	
Bill Barber	Phi.	3-4-76	Buf. 2 at Phi. 5	Al Smith	79	79	50	80	23.9
Pierre Larouche	Pit.	3-4-76	Wsh. 5 at Pit. 4	Ron Low	75	79	53	76	20.5
Danny Gare	Buf.	4-4-76	Tor. 2 at Buf. 5	Gord McRae	79	80	50	79	21.11
Steve Shutt	Mtl.	1-3-77	Mtl. 5 at NYI 4	Glenn Resch	65	65	60	80	24.8
Guy Lafleur	Mtl.	6-3-77	Mtl. 1 at Buf. 4	Don Edwards	68	68	56	80	
Marcel Dionne	L.A.	2-4-77	Min. 2 at L.A. 7	Pete LoPresti	79	79	53	80	25.8
Guy Lafleur	Mtl.	8-3-78	Wsh. 3 at Mtl. 4	Jim Bedard	63	65	60	78	
Mike Bossy	NYI	1-4-78	Wsh. 2 at NYI 3	Bernie Wolfe	69	76	53	73	21.2
Mike Bossy	NYI	24-2-79	Det. 1 at NYI 3	Rogie Vachon	58	58	69	80	
Marcel Dionne	L.A.	11-3-79	L.A. 3 at Phi. 6	Wayne Stephenson	68	68	59	80	
Guy Lafleur	Mtl.	31-3-79	Pit. 3 at Mtl. 5	Denis Herron	76	76	52	80	
Guy Chouinard	Atl.	6-4-79	NYR 2 at Atl. 9	John Davidson	79	79	50	80	22.5
Marcel Dionne	L.A.	12-3-80	L.A. 2 at Pit. 4	Nick Ricci	70	70	53	80	
Mike Bossy	NYI	16-3-80	NYI 6 at Chi. 1	Tony Esposito	68	71	51	75	
Charlie Simmer	L.A.	19-3-80	Det. 3 at L.A. 4	Jim Rutherford	57	73	56	64	26.0
Pierre Larouche	Mtl.	25-3-80	Chi. 4 at Mtl. 8	Tony Esposito	72	75	50	73	
Danny Gare	Buf.	27-3-80	Det. 1 at Buf. 10	Jim Rutherford	71	75	56	76	
Blaine Stoughton	Hfd.	28-3-80	Hfd. 4 at Van. 4	Glen Hanlon	75	75	56	80	27.0
Guy Lafleur	Mtl.	2-4-80	Mtl. 7 at Det. 2	Rogie Vachon	72	78	50	74	
Wayne Gretzky	Edm.	2-4-80	Min. 1 at Edm. 1	Gary Edwards	78	79	51	79	19.2
Reggie Leach	Phi.	3-4-80	Wsh. 2 at Phi. 4	empty net	75	79	50	76	
Mike Bossy	NYI	24-1-81	Que. 3 at NYI 7	Ron Grahame	50	50	68	79	
Charlie Simmer	L.A.	26-1-81	L.A. 7 at Que. 5	Michel Dion	51	51	56	65	
Marcel Dionne	L.A.	8-3-81	L.A. 4 at Wpg. 1	Markus Mattsson	68	68	58	80	
Wayne Babych	St.L.	12-3-81	St.L. 3 at Mtl. 4	Richard Sevigny	70	68	54	78	22.9
Wayne Gretzky	Edm.	15-3-81	Edm. 3 at Cgy. 3	Pat Riggin	69	69	55	80	
Rick Kehoe	Pit.	16-3-81	Pit. 7 at Edm. 6	Eddie Mio	70	70	55	80	29.7
Jacques Richard	Que.	29-3-81	Mtl. 0 at Que. 4	Richard Sevigny	76	75	52	78	28.6
Dennis Maruk	Wsh.	5-4-81	Det. 2 at Wsh. 7	Larry Lozinski	80	80	50	80	25.3
Wayne Gretzky	Edm.	30-12-81	Phi. 5 at Edm. 7	empty net	39	39	92	80	
Dennis Maruk	Wsh.	21-2-82	Wpg. 3 at Wsh. 6	Doug Soetaert	61	61	60	80	
Mike Bossy	NYI	4-3-82	Tor. 1 at NYI 10	Michel Larocque	66	66	64	80	
Dino Ciccarelli	Min.	8-3-82	St.L. 1 at Min. 8	Mike Liut	67	68	55	76	22.1
Rick Vaive	Tor.	24-3-82	St.L. 3 at Tor. 4	Mike Liut	72	75	54	77	22.10
Blaine Stoughton	Hfd.	28-3-82	Min. 5 at Hfd. 2	Gilles Meloche	76	76	52	80	
Rick Middleton	Bos.	28-3-82	Bos. 5 at Buf. 9	Paul Harrison	72	77	51	75	28.11
Marcel Dionne	L.A.	30-3-82	Cgy. 7 at L.A. 5	Pat Riggin	75	77	50	78	
Mark Messier	Edm.	31-3-82	L.A. 3 at Edm. 7	Mario Lessard	78	79	50	78	21.3
Bryan Trottier	NYI	3-4-82	Phi. 3 at NYI 6	Pete Peeters	79	79	50	80	25.9
Lanny McDonald	Cgy.	18-2-83	Cgy. 1 at Buf. 5	Bob Sauve	60	60	66	80	30.0
Wayne Gretzky	Edm.	19-2-83	Edm. 10 at Pit. 7	Nick Ricci	60	60	71	80	
Michel Goulet	Que.	5-3-83	Hfd. 3 at Que. 10	Mike Veisor	67	67	57	80	22.11
Mike Bossy	NYI	12-3-83	Wsh. 2 at NYI 6	Al Jensen	70	71	60	79	
Marcel Dionne	L.A.	17-3-83	Que. 3 at L.A. 4	Dan Bouchard	71	71	56	80	
Al Secord	Chi.	20-3-83	Tor. 3 at Chi. 7	Mike Palmateer	73	73	54	80	25.0
Rick Vaive	Tor.	30-3-83	Tor. 4 at Det. 2	Gilles Gilbert	76	78	51	78	
Wayne Gretzky	Edm.	7-1-84	Hfd. 3 at Edm. 5	Greg Millen	42	42	87	74	
Michel Goulet	Que.	8-3-84	Que. 8 at Pit. 6	Denis Herron	63	69	56	75	
Rick Vaive	Tor.	14-3-84	Min. 3 at Tor. 3	Gilles Meloche	69	72	52	76	
Mike Bullard	Pit.	14-3-84	Pit. 6 at L.A. 7	Markus Mattsson	71	72	51	76	23.0
Jari Kurri	Edm.	15-3-84	Edm. 2 at Mtl. 3	Rick Wamsley	57	73	52	64	23.10
Glenn Anderson	Edm.	21-3-84	Hfd. 3 at Edm. 5	Greg Millen	76	76	54	80	23.6
Tim Kerr	Phi.	22-3-84	Pit. 4 at Phi. 13	Denis Herron	74	75	54	79	24.3
Mike Bossy	NYI	31-3-84	NYI 3 at Wsh. 1	Pat Riggin	67	79	51	67	
Wayne Gretzky	Edm.	26-1-85	Pit. 3 at Edm. 6	Denis Herron	49	49	73	80	
Jari Kurri	Edm.	3-2-85	Hfd. 3 at Edm. 6	Greg Millen	50	53	71	73	
Mike Bossy	NYI	5-3-85	Phi. 5 at NYI 4	Bob Froese	61	65	58	76	
Michel Goulet	Que.	6-3-85	Buf. 3 at Que. 4	Tom Barrasso	62	73	55	69	
Tim Kerr	Phi.	7-3-85	Wsh. 6 at Phi. 9	Pat Riggin	63	65	54	74	
John Ogrodnick	Det.	13-3-85	Det. 6 at Edm. 7	Grant Fuhr	69	69	55	79	25.9
Bob Carpenter	Wsh.	21-3-85	Wsh. 2 at Mtl. 3	Steve Penney	72	72	53	80	21.9

Player	Team	Date of 50th Goal	Score			Goaltender	Player's Game No.	Team Game No.	Total Goals	Total Games	Age When First 50th Scored (Yrs. & Mos.)
Dale Hawerchuk	Wpg.	29-3-85	Chi. 5	at	Wpg. 5	W. Skorodenski	77	77	53	80	21.11
Mike Gartner	Wsh.	7-4-85	Pit. 3	at	Wsh. 7	Brian Ford	80	80	50	80	25.5
Jari Kurri	Edm.	4-3-86	Edm. 6	at	Van. 2	Richard Brodeur	63	65	68	78	
Mike Bossy	NYI	11-3-86	Cgy. 4	at	NYI 8	Reggie Lemelin	67	67	61	80	
Glenn Anderson	Edm.	14-3-86	Det. 3	at	Edm. 12	Greg Stefan	63	71	54	72	
Michel Goulet	Que.	17-3-86	Que. 8	at	Mtl. 6	Patrick Roy	67	72	53	75	
Wayne Gretzky	Edm.	18-3-86	Wpg. 2	at	Edm. 6	Brian Hayward	72	72	52	80	
Tim Kerr	Phi.	20-3-86	Pit. 1	at	Phi. 5	Roberto Romano	68	72	58	76	
Wayne Gretzky	Edm.	4-2-87	Edm. 6	at	Min. 5	Don Beaupre	55	55	62	79	
Dino Ciccarelli	Min.	7-3-87	Pit. 7	at	Min. 3	Gilles Meloche	66	66	52	80	
Mario Lemieux	Pit.	12-3-87	Que. 3	at	Pit. 6	Mario Gosselin	53	70	54	63	21.5
Tim Kerr	Phi.	17-3-87	NYR 1	at	Phi. 4	J. Vanbiesbrouck	67	71	58	75	
Jari Kurri	Edm.	17-3-87	N.J. 4	at	Edm. 7	Craig Billington	69	70	54	79	
Mario Lemieux	Pit.	2-2-88	Wsh. 2	at	Pit. 3	Pete Peeters	51	54	70	77	
Steve Yzerman	Det.	1-3-88	Buf. 0	at	Det. 4	Tom Barrasso	64	64	50	64	22.10
Joe Nieuwendyk	Cgy.	12-3-88	Buf. 4	at	Cgy. 10	Tom Barrasso	66	70	51	75	21.5
Craig Simpson	Edm.	15-3-88	Buf. 4	at	Edm. 6	Jacques Cloutier	71	71	56	80	21.1
Jimmy Carson	L.A.	26-3-88	Chi. 5	at	L.A. 9	Darren Pang	77	77	55	88	19.8
Luc Robitaille	L.A.	1-4-88	L.A. 6	at	Cgy. 3	Mike Vernon	79	79	53	80	21.10
Hakan Loob	Cgy.	3-4-88	Min. 1	at	Cgy. 4	Don Beaupre	80	80	50	80	27.9
Stephane Richer	Mtl.	3-4-88	Mtl. 4	at	Buf. 4	Tom Barrasso	72	80	50	72	21.10
Mario Lemieux	Pit.	20-1-89	Pit. 3	at	Wpg. 7	Pokey Reddick	44	46	85	76	
Bernie Nicholls	L.A.	28-1-89	Edm.7	at	L.A. 6	Grant Fuhr	51	51	70	79	27.7
Steve Yzerman	Det.	5-2-89	Det. 6	at	Wpg. 2	Pokey Reddick	55	55	65	80	
Wayne Gretzky	L.A.	4-3-89	Phi. 2	at	L.A. 6	Ron Hextall	66	67	54	78	
Joe Nieuwendyk	Cgy.	21-3-89	NYI 1	at	Cgy. 4	Mark Fitzpatrick	72	74	51	77	
Joe Mullen	Cgy.	31-3-89	Wpg. 1	at	Cgy. 4	Bob Essensa	78	79	51	79	32.1
Brett Hull	St.L.	6-2-90	Tor. 4	at	St.L. 5	Jeff Reese	54	54	72	80	25.6
Steve Yzerman	Det.	24-2-90	Det. 3	at	NYI 3	Glenn Healy	63	63	62	79	
Cam Neely	Bos.	10-3-90	Bos. 3	at	NYI 3	Mark Fitzpatrick	69	71	55	76	24.9
Luc Robitaille	L.A.	31-3-90	L.A. 3	at	Van. 6	Kirk McLean	79	79	52	80	
Brian Bellows	Min.	22-3-90	Min. 5	at	Det. 1	Tim Cheveldae	75	75	55	80	25.6
Pat LaFontaine	NYI	24-3-90	NYI 5	at	Edm. 5	Bill Ranford	71	77	54	74	25.1
Stephane Richer	Mtl.	24-3-90	Mtl. 4	at	Hfd. 7	Peter Sidorkiewicz	75	77	51	75	
Gary Leeman	Tor.	28-3-90	NYI 6	at	Tor. 3	Mark Fitzpatrick	78	78	51	80	26.1
Brett Hull	St.L.	25-1-91	St.L. 9•	at	Det. 4	David Gagnon	49	49	86	78	
Cam Neely	Bos.	26-3-91	Bos. 7	at	Que. 4	empty net	67	78	51	69	
Theoren Fleury	Cgy.	26-3-91	Van. 2	at	Cgy. 7	Bob Mason	77	77	51	79	22.9
Steve Yzerman	Det.	30-3-91	NYR 5	at	Det. 6	Mike Richter	79	79	51	80	
Brett Hull	St.L.	28-1-92	St.L. 3	at	L.A. 3	Kelly Hrudey	50	50	70	73	
Jeremy Roenick	Chi.	7-3-92	Chi. 2	at	Bos. 1	Daniel Berthiaume	67	67	53	80	22.2
Kevin Stevens	Pit.	24-3-92	Pit. 3	at	Det. 4	Tim Cheveldae	74	74	54	80	26.11
Gary Roberts	Cgy.	31-3-92	Edm. 2	at	Cgy. 5	Bill Ranford	73	77	53	76	25.10
Alexander Mogilny	Buf.	3-2-93	Hfd. 2	at	Buf. 3	Sean Burke	46	53	76	77	23.11
Teemu Selanne	Wpg.	28-2-93	Min. 6	at	Wpg. 7	Darcy Wakaluk	63	63	76	84	22.6
Pavel Bure	Van.	1-3-93	Van. 5	at	Buf. 2*	Grant Fuhr	63	63	60	83	21.11
Steve Yzerman	Det.	10-3-93	Det. 6	at	Edm. 3	Bill Ranford	70	70	58	84	
Luc Robitaille	L.A.	15-3-93	L.A. 4	at	Buf. 2	Grant Fuhr	69	69	63	84	
Brett Hull	St.L.	20-3-93	St.L. 2	at	L.A. 3	Robb Stauber	73	73	54	80	
Mario Lemieux	Pit.	21-3-93	Pit. 6	at	Edm. 4**	Ron Tugnutt	48	72	69	60	
Kevin Stevens	Pit.	21-3-93	Pit. 6	at	Edm. 4**	Ron Tugnutt	62	72	55	72	
Dave Andreychuk	Tor.	23-3-93	Tor. 5	at	Wpg. 4	Bob Essensa	72	73	54	83	29.6
Pat LaFontaine	Buf.	28-3-93	Ott. 1	at	Buf. 3	Peter Sidorkiewicz	75	75	53	84	
Pierre Turgeon	NYI	2-4-93	NYI 3	at	NYR 2	Mike Richter	75	76	58	83	23.8
Mark Recchi	Phi.	3-4-93	T.B. 2	at	Phi. 6	J-C Bergeron	77	77	53	84	25.2
Jeremy Roenick	Chi.	15-4-93	Tor. 2	at	Chi. 3	Felix Potvin	84	84	50	84	
Brendan Shanahan	St.L.	15-4-93	T.B. 5	at	St.L. 6	Pat Jablonski	71	84	51	71	24.3
Cam Neely	Bos.	7-3-94	Wsh. 3	at	Bos. 6	Don Beaupre	44	66	50	49	
Sergei Fedorov	Det.	15-3-94	Van. 2	at	Det. 5	Kirk McLean	67	69	56	82	24.3
Pavel Bure	Van.	23-3-94	Van. 6	at	L.A. 3	empty net	65	73	60	76	
Adam Graves	NYR	23-3-94	NYR 5	at	Edm. 3	Bill Ranford	74	74	51	84	25.11
Dave Andreychuk	Tor.	24-3-94	S.J. 2	at	Tor. 1	Arturs Irbe	73	74	53	83	
Brett Hull	St.L.	25-3-94	Dal. 3	at	St.L. 5	Andy Moog	71	74	52	81	
Ray Sheppard	Det.	29-3-94	Hfd. 2	at	Det. 6	Sean Burke	74	76	52	82	27.10
Brendan Shanahan	St.L.	12-4-94	St.L. 5	at	Dal. 9	Andy Moog	80	83	52	81	
Mike Modano	Dal.	12-4-94	St.L. 5	at	Dal. 9	Curtis Joseph	75	83	50	76	23.11
Mario Lemieux	Pit.	23-2-96	Hfd. 4	at	Pit. 5	Sean Burke	50	59	69	70	
Jaromir Jagr	Pit.	23-2-96	Hfd. 4	at	Pit. 5	Sean Burke	59	59	62	82	24.0
Alexander Mogilny	Van.	29-2-96	St.L. 2	at	Van. 2	Grant Fuhr	60	63	55	79	
Peter Bondra	Wsh.	3-4-96	Wsh. 5	at	Buf. 1	Andrei Trefilov	62	77	52	67	28.1
Joe Sakic	Col.	7-4-96	Col. 4	at	Dal. 1	empty net	79	79	51	82	26.7
John LeClair	Phi.	10-4-96	Phi. 5	at	N.J. 1	Corey Schwab	80	80	51	82	26.7
Keith Tkachuk	Wpg.	12-4-96	L.A. 3	at	Wpg. 5	empty net	75	81	50	76	24.0
Paul Kariya	Ana.	14-4-96	Wpg. 2	at	Ana. 5	N. Khabibulin	82	82	50	82	21.5
Keith Tkachuk	Phx.	6-4-97	Phx. 1	at	Col. 2	Patrick Roy	78	79	52	81	
Teemu Selanne	Ana.	9-4-97	L.A. 1	at	Ana. 4	empty net	77	81	51	78	
Mario Lemieux	Pit.	11-4-97	Pit. 2	at	Fla. 4	J. Vanbiesbrouck	75	81	50	76	
John LeClair	Phi.	13-4-97	N.J. 4	at	Phi. 5	Mike Dunham	82	82	50	82	
Teemu Selanne	Ana.	25-3-98	Ana. 3	at	Chi. 2	Jeff Hackett	66	71	52	73	
John LeClair	Phi.	13-4-98	Phi. 1	at	Buf. 2	Dominik Hasek	79	79	51	82	
Pavel Bure	Van.	17-4-98	Cgy. 4	at	Van. 2	Dwayne Roloson	81	81	51	82	
Peter Bondra	Wsh.	18-4-98	Wsh. 4	at	Car. 3	Mike Fountain	75	80	52	76	
Pavel Bure	Fla.	18-3-00	Fla. 4	at	NYI 2	empty net	63	71	58	74	
Pavel Bure	Fla.	16-3-01	Pit. 6	at	Fla. 3	Johan Hedberg	72	72	59	82	
Joe Sakic	Col.	4-4-01	Ana. 1	at	Col. 1	J-S Giguere	80	80	54	82	
Jaromir Jagr	Pit.	4-4-01	T.B. 2	at	Pit. 4	Kevin Weekes	80	80	52	81	
Jarome Iginla	Cgy.	7-4-02	Cgy. 2	at	Chi. 3	Jocelyn Thibault	79	79	52	82	24.9
Milan Hejduk	Col.	6-4-03	St.L. 2	at	Col. 5	Brent Johnson	82	82	50	82	27.1

* neutral site game played at Hamilton; ** neutral site game played at Cleveland

Jaromir Jagr

Jarome Iginla

Milan Hejduk

Bobby Orr

Bryan Trottier

Dale Hawerchuk

100-Point Seasons

Player	Team	Date of 100th Point	G or A	Score		Player's Game No.	Team Game No.	G - A PTS	Total Games	Age when first 100th point scored (Yrs. & Mos.)
Phil Esposito	Bos.	2-3-69	(G)	Pit. 0	at Bos. 4	60	62	49-77 — 126	74	27.1
Bobby Hull	Chi.	20-3-69	(G)	Chi. 5	at Bos. 5	71	71	58-49 — 107	76	30.2
Gordie Howe	Det.	30-3-69	(G)	Det. 5	at Chi. 9	76	76	44-59 — 103	76	41.0
Bobby Orr	Bos.	15-3-70	(G)	Det. 5	at Bos. 5	67	67	33-87 — 120	76	22.11
Phil Esposito	Bos.	6-2-71	(A)	Buf. 3	at Bos. 4	51	51	76-76 — 152	78	
Bobby Orr	Bos.	20-2-71	(A)	Bos. 4	at L.A. 5	58	58	37-102 — 139	78	
John Bucyk	Bos.	13-3-71	(A)	Bos. 6	at Van. 3	68	68	51-65 — 116	78	35.10
Ken Hodge	Bos.	21-3-71	(A)	Buf. 7	at Bos. 5	72	72	43-62 — 105	78	26.9
Jean Ratelle	NYR	18-2-72	(A)	NYR 2	at Cal. 2	58	58	46-63 — 109	63	31.4
Phil Esposito	Bos.	19-2-72	(A)	Bos. 6	at Min. 4	59	59	66-67 — 133	76	
Bobby Orr	Bos.	2-3-72	(A)	Van. 3	at Bos. 3	64	64	37-80 — 117	76	
Vic Hadfield	NYR	25-3-72	(A)	NYR 3	at Mtl. 3	74	74	50-56 — 106	78	31.5
Phil Esposito	Bos.	3-3-73	(A)	Bos. 1	at Mtl. 5	64	64	55-75 — 130	78	
Bobby Clarke	Phi.	29-3-73	(G)	Atl. 2	at Phi. 4	76	76	37-67 — 104	78	23.7
Bobby Orr	Bos.	31-3-73	(G)	Bos. 3	at Tor. 7	62	77	29-72 — 101	63	
Rick MacLeish	Phi.	1-4-73	(G)	Phi. 4	at Pit. 5	78	78	50-50 — 100	78	23.3
Phil Esposito	Bos.	13-2-74	(A)	Bos. 9	at Cal. 6	53	53	68-77 — 145	78	
Bobby Orr	Bos.	12-3-74	(A)	Buf. 0	at Bos. 4	62	66	32-90 — 122	74	
Ken Hodge	Bos.	24-3-74	(A)	Mtl. 3	at Bos. 6	72	72	50-55 — 105	76	
Phil Esposito	Bos.	8-2-75	(A)	Bos. 8	at Det. 5	54	54	61-66 — 127	79	
Bobby Orr	Bos.	13-2-75	(A)	Bos. 1	at Buf. 3	57	57	46-89 — 135	80	
Guy Lafleur	Mtl.	7-3-75	(G)	Wsh. 4	at Mtl. 8	56	66	53-66 — 119	70	24.6
Pete Mahovlich	Mtl.	9-3-75	(A)	Mtl. 5	at NYR 3	67	67	35-82 — 117	80	29.5
Marcel Dionne	Det.	9-3-75	(A)	Det. 5	at Phi. 8	67	67	47-74 — 121	80	23.7
Bobby Clarke	Phi.	22-3-75	(A)	Min. 0	at Phi. 4	72	72	27-89 — 116	80	
Rene Robert	Buf.	5-4-75	(A)	Buf. 4	at Tor. 2	74	80	40-60 — 100	74	26.4
Guy Lafleur	Mtl.	10-3-76	(G)	Mtl. 5	at Chi. 1	69	69	56-69 — 125	80	
Bobby Clarke	Phi.	11-3-76	(A)	Buf. 1	at Phi. 6	64	68	30-89 — 119	76	
Bill Barber	Phi.	18-3-76	(A)	Van. 2	at Phi. 3	71	71	50-62 — 112	80	23.8
Gilbert Perreault	Buf.	21-3-76	(A)	K.C. 1	at Buf. 3	73	73	44-69 — 113	80	25.4
Pierre Larouche	Pit.	24-3-76	(A)	Bos. 5	at Pit. 5	70	74	53-58 — 111	76	20.4
Pete Mahovlich	Mtl.	28-3-76	(A)	Mtl. 2	at Bos. 2	77	77	34-71 — 105	80	
Jean Ratelle	Bos.	30-3-76	(A)	Buf. 4	at Bos. 4	77	77	36-69 — 105	80	
Jean Pronovost	Pit.	3-4-76	(A)	Wsh. 5	at Pit. 4	79	79	52-52 — 104	80	30.4
Darryl Sittler	Tor.	3-4-76	(A)	Bos. 4	at Tor. 2	78	79	41-59 — 100	79	25.7
Guy Lafleur	Mtl.	26-2-77	(A)	Cle. 3	at Mtl. 5	63	63	56-80 — 136	80	
Marcel Dionne	L.A.	5-3-77	(G)	Pit. 3	at L.A. 3	67	67	53-69 — 122	80	
Steve Shutt	Mtl.	27-3-77	(A)	Mtl. 6	at Det. 0	77	77	60-45 — 105	80	24.9
Bryan Trottier	NYI	25-2-78	(A)	Chi. 1	at NYI 7	59	60	46-77 — 123	77	21.7
Guy Lafleur	Mtl.	28-2-78	(G)	Det. 3	at Mtl. 9	69	61	60-72 — 132	78	
Darryl Sittler	Tor.	12-3-78	(A)	Tor. 7	at Pit. 1	67	67	45-72 — 117	80	
Guy Lafleur	Mtl.	27-2-79	(A)	Mtl. 3	at NYI 7	61	61	52-77 — 129	80	
Bryan Trottier	NYI	6-3-79	(A)	Buf. 3	at NYI 2	59	63	47-87 — 134	76	
Marcel Dionne	L.A.	8-3-79	(A)	L.A. 4	at Buf. 6	66	66	59-71 — 130	80	
Mike Bossy	NYI	11-3-79	(G)	NYI 4	at Bos. 4	66	66	69-57 — 126	80	22.2
Bob MacMillan	Atl.	15-3-79	(A)	Atl. 4	at Phi. 5	68	69	37-71 — 108	79	26.6
Guy Chouinard	Atl.	30-3-79	(A)	L.A. 3	at Atl. 5	75	75	50-57 — 107	80	22.5
Denis Potvin	NYI	8-4-79	(A)	NYI 5	at NYR 2	73	80	31-70 — 101	73	25.5
Marcel Dionne	L.A.	6-2-80	(A)	L.A. 3	at Hfd. 7	53	53	53-84 — 137	80	
Guy Lafleur	Mtl.	10-2-80	(A)	Mtl. 3	at Bos. 2	55	55	50-75 — 125	74	
Wayne Gretzky	Edm.	24-2-80	(A)	Bos. 4	at Edm. 2	61	62	51-86 — 137	79	19.2
Bryan Trottier	NYI	30-3-80	(A)	NYI 9	at Que. 6	75	77	42-62 — 104	80	
Gilbert Perreault	Buf.	1-4-80	(A)	Buf. 5	at Atl. 2	77	77	40-66 — 106	80	
Mike Rogers	Hfd.	4-4-80	(A)	Que. 2	at Hfd. 9	79	79	44-61 — 105	80	25.5
Charlie Simmer	L.A.	5-4-80	(G)	Van. 5	at L.A. 3	64	80	56-45 — 101	64	26.0
Blaine Stoughton	Hfd.	6-4-80	(A)	Det. 3	at Hfd. 5	80	80	56-44 — 100	80	27.0
Wayne Gretzky	Edm.	6-2-81	(G)	Wpg. 4	at Edm. 10	53	53	55-109 — 164	80	
Marcel Dionne	L.A.	12-2-81	(A)	L.A. 5	at Chi. 5	58	58	58-77 — 135	80	
Charlie Simmer	L.A.	14-2-81	(A)	Bos. 5	at L.A. 4	59	59	56-49 — 105	65	
Kent Nilsson	Cgy.	27-2-81	(G)	Hfd. 1	at Cgy. 5	64	64	49-82 — 131	80	24.6
Mike Bossy	NYI	3-3-81	(G)	Edm. 8	at NYI 8	65	66	68-51 — 119	79	
Dave Taylor	L.A.	14-3-81	(G)	Min. 4	at L.A. 10	63	70	47-65 — 112	72	25.3
Mike Rogers	Hfd.	22-3-81	(G)	Tor. 3	at Hfd. 3	74	74	40-65 — 105	80	
Bernie Federko	St.L.	28-3-81	(A)	Buf. 4	at St.L. 7	74	76	31-73 — 104	78	24.10
Rick Middleton	Bos.	28-3-81	(A)	Chi. 2	at Bos. 5	76	76	44-59 — 103	80	27.4
Jacques Richard	Que.	29-3-81	(G)	Mtl. 0	at Que. 4	75	76	52-51 — 103	78	28.6
Bryan Trottier	NYI	29-3-81	(A)	NYI 5	at Wsh. 4	69	76	31-72 — 103	73	
Peter Stastny	Que.	29-3-81	(A)	Mtl. 0	at Que. 4	73	76	39-70 — 109	77	24.6
Wayne Gretzky	Edm.	27-12-81	(G)	L.A. 3	at Edm. 10	38	38	92-120 — 212	80	
Mike Bossy	NYI	13-2-82	(A)	Phi. 2	at NYI 8	55	55	64-83 — 147	80	
Peter Stastny	Que.	16-2-82	(A)	Wpg. 3	at Que. 7	60	60	46-93 — 139	80	
Dennis Maruk	Wsh.	20-2-82	(G)	Wsh. 3	at Min. 7	60	60	60-76 — 136	80	26.3
Bryan Trottier	NYI	23-2-82	(G)	Chi. 1	at NYI 5	61	61	50-79 — 129	80	
Denis Savard	Chi.	27-2-82	(A)	Chi. 5	at L.A. 3	64	64	32-87 — 119	80	21.1
Bobby Smith	Min.	3-3-82	(A)	Det. 4	at Min. 6	66	66	43-71 — 114	80	24.1
Marcel Dionne	L.A.	6-3-82	(G)	L.A. 6	at Hfd. 7	64	66	50-67 — 117	78	
Dave Taylor	L.A.	20-3-82	(A)	Pit. 5	at L.A. 7	71	72	39-67 — 106	78	
Dale Hawerchuk	Wpg.	24-3-82	(A)	L.A. 3	at Wpg. 5	74	74	45-58 — 103	80	18.11
Dino Ciccarelli	Min.	27-3-82	(A)	Min. 6	at Bos. 5	72	76	55-52 — 107	76	21.8
Glenn Anderson	Edm.	28-3-82	(G)	Edm. 6	at L.A. 2	78	78	38-67 — 105	80	21.7
Mike Rogers	NYR	2-4-82	(G)	Pit. 7	at NYR 5	79	79	38-65 — 103	80	

Player	Team	Date of 100th Point	G or A	Score	Player's Game No.	Team Game No.	G - A — PTS	Total Games	Age when first 100th point scored (Yrs. & Mos.)
Wayne Gretzky	Edm.	5-1-83	(A)	Edm. 8 at Wpg. 3	42	42	71-125 — 196	80	
Mike Bossy	NYI	3-3-83	(A)	Tor. 1 at NYI 5	66	67	60-58 — 118	79	
Peter Stastny	Que.	5-3-83	(A)	Hfd. 3 at Que. 10	62	67	47-77 — 124	75	
Denis Savard	Chi.	6-3-83	(G)	Mtl. 4 at Chi. 5	65	67	35-86 — 121	78	
Mark Messier	Edm.	23-3-83	(G)	Edm. 4 at Wpg. 7	73	76	48-58 — 106	77	22.2
Barry Pederson	Bos.	26-3-83	(A)	Hfd. 4 at Bos. 7	73	76	46-61 — 107	77	22.0
Marcel Dionne	L.A.	26-3-83	(A)	Edm. 9 at L.A. 3	75	75	56-51 — 107	80	
Michel Goulet	Que.	27-3-83	(A)	Que. 6 at Buf. 6	77	77	57-48 — 105	80	22.11
Glenn Anderson	Edm.	29-3-83	(A)	Edm. 7 at Van. 4	70	78	48-56 — 104	72	
Jari Kurri	Edm.	29-3-83	(A)	Edm. 7 at Van. 4	78	78	45-59 — 104	80	22.10
Kent Nilsson	Cgy.	29-3-83	(G)	L.A. 3 at Cgy. 5	78	78	46-58 — 104	80	
Wayne Gretzky	Edm.	18-12-83	(G)	Edm. 7 at Wpg. 5	34	34	87-118 — 205	74	
Paul Coffey	Edm.	4-3-84	(A)	Mtl. 1 at Edm. 6	68	68	40-86 — 126	80	22.9
Michel Goulet	Que.	4-3-84	(A)	Que. 1 at Buf. 1	62	67	56-65 — 121	75	
Jari Kurri	Edm.	7-3-84	(G)	Chi. 4 at Edm. 7	53	69	52-61 — 113	64	
Peter Stastny	Que.	8-3-84	(A)	Que. 8 at Pit. 6	69	69	46-73 — 119	80	
Mike Bossy	NYI	8-3-84	(A)	Tor. 5 at NYI 9	56	68	51-67 — 118	67	
Barry Pederson	Bos.	14-3-84	(A)	Bos. 4 at Det. 2	71	71	39-77 — 116	80	
Bryan Trottier	NYI	18-3-84	(G)	NYI 4 at Hfd. 5	62	73	40-71 — 111	68	
Bernie Federko	St.L.	20-3-84	(A)	Wpg. 3 at St.L. 9	75	76	41-66 — 107	79	
Rick Middleton	Bos.	27-3-84	(G)	Bos. 6 at Que. 4	77	77	47-58 — 105	80	
Dale Hawerchuk	Wpg.	27-3-84	(G)	Wpg. 3 at L.A. 3	77	77	37-65 — 102	80	
Mark Messier	Edm.	27-3-84	(G)	Edm. 9 at Cgy. 2	72	79	37-64 — 101	73	
Wayne Gretzky	Edm.	29-12-84	(A)	Det. 3 at Edm. 6	35	35	73-135 — 208	80	
Jari Kurri	Edm.	29-1-85	(A)	Edm. 4 at Cgy. 2	48	51	71-64 — 135	73	
Mike Bossy	NYI	23-2-85	(G)	Bos. 1 at NYI 7	56	60	58-59 — 117	76	
Dale Hawerchuk	Wpg.	25-2-85	(A)	Wpg. 12 at NYR 5	64	64	53-77 — 130	80	
Marcel Dionne	L.A.	5-3-85	(A)	Pit. 0 at L.A. 6	66	66	46-80 — 126	80	
Brent Sutter	NYI	12-3-85	(A)	NYI 6 at St.L. 5	68	68	42-60 — 102	72	22.10
John Ogrodnick	Det.	22-3-85	(A)	NYR 3 at Det. 5	73	73	55-50 — 105	79	25.9
Paul Coffey	Edm.	26-3-85	(G)	Edm. 7 at NYI 5	74	74	37-84 — 121	80	
Denis Savard	Chi.	29-3-85	(A)	Chi. 5 at Wpg. 5	75	76	38-67 — 105	79	
Peter Stastny	Que.	2-4-85	(A)	Bos. 4 at Que. 6	74	77	32-68 — 100	75	
Bernie Federko	St.L.	4-4-85	(A)	NYR 5 at St.L. 4	74	78	30-73 — 103	76	
John Tonelli	NYI	6-4-85	(G)	N.J. 5 at NYI 5	80	80	42-58 — 100	80	28.1
Paul MacLean	Wpg.	6-4-85	(A)	Wpg. 6 at Edm. 5	78	79	41-60 — 101	79	27.1
Bernie Nicholls	L.A.	6-4-85	(A)	Van. 4 at L.A. 4	80	80	46-54 — 100	80	22.9
Mike Gartner	Wsh.	7-4-85	(A)	Pit. 3 at Wsh. 7	80	80	50-52 — 102	80	25.6
Mario Lemieux	Pit.	7-4-85	(G)	Pit. 3 at Wsh. 7	73	80	43-57 — 100	73	19.6
Wayne Gretzky	Edm.	4-1-86	(A)	Hfd. 3 at Edm. 4	39	39	52-163 — 215	80	
Mario Lemieux	Pit.	15-2-86	(G)	Van. 4 at Pit. 9	55	56	48-93 — 141	79	
Paul Coffey	Edm.	19-2-86	(A)	Tor. 5 at Edm. 9	59	60	48-90 — 138	79	
Peter Stastny	Que.	1-3-86	(A)	Buf. 8 at Que. 4	66	68	41-81 — 122	76	
Jari Kurri	Edm.	2-3-86	(G)	Phi. 1 at Edm. 2	62	64	68-63 — 131	78	
Mike Bossy	NYI	8-3-86	(G)	Wsh. 6 at NYI 2	65	65	61-62 — 123	80	
Denis Savard	Chi.	12-3-86	(A)	Buf. 7 at Chi. 6	69	69	47-69 — 116	80	
Mats Naslund	Mtl.	13-3-86	(A)	Mtl. 2 at Bos. 3	70	70	43-67 — 110	80	26.4
Michel Goulet	Que.	24-3-86	(A)	Que. 1 at Min. 0	70	75	53-50 — 103	75	
Glenn Anderson	Edm.	25-3-86	(G)	Edm. 7 at Det. 2	66	74	54-48 — 102	72	
Neal Broten	Min.	26-3-86	(A)	Min. 6 at Tor. 1	76	76	29-76 — 105	80	26.4
Dale Hawerchuk	Wpg.	31-3-86	(G)	Wpg. 5 at L.A. 2	78	78	46-59 — 105	80	
Bernie Federko	St.L.	5-4-86	(G)	Chi. 5 at St.L. 7	79	79	34-68 — 102	80	
Wayne Gretzky	Edm.	11-1-87	(A)	Cgy. 3 at Edm. 5	42	42	62-121 — 183	79	
Jari Kurri	Edm.	14-3-87	(A)	Buf. 3 at Edm. 5	67	68	54-54 — 108	79	
Mario Lemieux	Pit.	18-3-87	(A)	St.L. 4 at Pit. 5	55	72	54-53 — 107	63	
Mark Messier	Edm.	19-3-87	(A)	Edm. 4 at Cgy. 5	71	71	37-70 — 107	77	
Dino Ciccarelli	Min.	30-3-87	(A)	NYR 6 at Min. 5	78	78	52-51 — 103	80	
Doug Gilmour	St.L.	2-4-87	(A)	Buf. 3 at St.L. 5	78	78	42-63 — 105	80	23.10
Dale Hawerchuk	Wpg.	5-4-87	(A)	Wpg. 3 at Cgy. 1	80	80	47-53 — 100	80	
Mario Lemieux	Pit.	20-1-88	(G)	Pit. 8 at Chi. 3	45	48	70-98 — 168	77	
Wayne Gretzky	Edm.	11-2-88	(A)	Edm. 7 at Van. 2	43	56	40-109 — 149	64	
Denis Savard	Chi.	12-2-88	(A)	St.L. 3 at Chi. 4	57	57	44-87 — 131	80	
Dale Hawerchuk	Wpg.	23-2-88	(G)	Wpg. 4 at Pit. 3	61	61	44-77 — 121	80	
Steve Yzerman	Det.	27-2-88	(A)	Det. 4 at Que. 5	63	63	50-52 — 102	64	22.10
Peter Stastny	Que.	8-3-88	(A)	Hfd. 4 at Que. 6	63	67	46-65 — 111	76	
Mark Messier	Edm.	15-3-88	(A)	Buf. 4 at Edm. 6	68	71	37-74 — 111	77	
Jimmy Carson	L.A.	26-3-88	(A)	Chi. 5 at L.A. 9	77	77	55-52 — 107	80	19.8
Hakan Loob	Cgy.	26-3-88	(A)	Van. 1 at Cgy. 6	76	76	50-56 — 106	80	27.9
Mike Bullard	Cgy.	26-3-88	(A)	Van. 1 at Cgy. 6	76	76	48-55 — 103	79	27.1
Michel Goulet	Que.	27-3-88	(A)	Pit. 6 at Que. 3	76	76	48-58 — 106	80	
Luc Robitaille	L.A.	30-3-88	(G)	Cgy. 7 at L.A. 9	78	78	53-58 — 111	80	22.1
Mario Lemieux	Pit.	31-12-88	(A)	N.J. 6 at Pit. 8	36	38	85-114 — 199	76	
Wayne Gretzky	L.A.	21-1-89	(A)	L.A. 4 at Hfd. 5	47	48	54-114 — 168	78	
Bernie Nicholls	L.A.	21-1-89	(A)	L.A. 4 at Hfd. 5	48	48	70-80 — 150	79	
Steve Yzerman	Det.	27-1-89	(G)	Tor. 1 at Det. 8	50	50	65-90 — 155	80	
Rob Brown	Pit.	16-3-89	(A)	Pit. 2 at N.J. 1	60	72	49-66 — 115	68	20.11
Paul Coffey	Pit.	20-3-89	(A)	Pit. 2 at Min. 7	69	74	30-83 — 113	75	
Joe Mullen	Cgy.	23-3-89	(A)	L.A. 2 at Cgy. 4	74	75	51-59 — 110	79	32.1
Jari Kurri	Edm.	29-3-89	(A)	Edm. 5 at Van. 2	75	79	44-58 — 102	76	
Jimmy Carson	Edm.	2-4-89	(A)	Edm. 2 at Cgy. 4	80	80	49-51 — 100	80	
Mario Lemieux	Pit.	28-1-90	(G)	Pit. 2 at Buf. 7	50	50	45-78 — 123	59	
Wayne Gretzky	L.A.	30-1-90	(A)	N.J. 2 at L.A. 5	51	51	40-102 — 142	73	
Steve Yzerman	Det.	19-2-90	(A)	Mtl. 3 at Det. 5	61	61	62-65 — 127	79	
Mark Messier	Edm.	20-2-90	(A)	Edm. 4 at Van. 2	62	62	45-84 — 129	79	
Brett Hull	St.L.	3-3-90	(A)	NYI 4 at St.L. 5	67	67	72-41 — 113	80	25.7
Bernie Nicholls	NYR	12-3-90	(A)	L.A. 6 at NYR 2	70	71	39-73 — 112	79	
Pierre Turgeon	Buf.	25-3-90	(A)	N.J. 4 at Buf. 3	76	76	40-66 — 106	80	20.7
Paul Coffey	Pit.	25-3-90	(A)	Pit. 2 at Hfd. 4	77	77	29-74 — 103	80	25.1
Pat LaFontaine	NYI	27-3-90	(G)	Cgy. 4 at NYI 2	72	78	54-51 — 105	74	
Adam Oates	St.L.	29-3-90	(G)	Pit 4 at St.L. 5	79	79	23-79 — 102	80	27.7

Michel Goulet

Doug Gilmour and Denis Savard

Joe Mullen

Mark Recchi

Jeremy Roenick

Paul Kariya

Player	Team	Date of 100th Point	G or A	Score		Player's Game No.	Team Game No.	G - A PTS	Total Games	Age when first 100th point scored (Yrs. & Mos.)
Joe Sakic	Que.	31-3-90	(G)	Hfd. 3	at Que. 2	79	79	39-63 — 102	80	20.8
Ron Francis	Hfd.	31-3-90	(G)	Hfd. 3	at Que. 2	79	79	32-69 — 101	80	27.0
Luc Robitaille	L.A.	1-4-90	(A)	L.A. 4	at Cgy. 8	80	80	52-49 — 101	80	
Wayne Gretzky	L.A.	30-1-91	(A)	N.J. 4	at L.A. 2	50	51	41-122 — 163	78	
Brett Hull	St.L.	23-2-91	(G)	Bos. 2	at St.L. 9	60	62	86-45 — 131	78	
Mark Recchi	Pit.	5-3-91	(A)	Van. 1	at Pit. 4	66	67	40-73 — 113	78	23.1
Steve Yzerman	Det.	10-3-91	(G)	Det. 4	at St.L. 1	72	72	51-57 — 108	80	
John Cullen	Hfd.	16-3-91	(G)	N.J. 2	at Hfd. 6	71	71	39-71 — 110	78	26.7
Adam Oates	St.L.	17-3-91	(A)	St.L. 4	at Chi. 6	54	73	25-90 — 115	61	
Joe Sakic	Que.	19-3-91	(G)	Edm. 7	at Que. 6	74	74	48-61 — 109	80	
Steve Larmer	Chi.	24-3-91	(A)	Min. 4	at Chi. 5	76	76	44-57 — 101	80	29.9
Theoren Fleury	Cgy.	26-3-91	(G)	Van. 2	at Cgy. 7	77	77	51-53 — 104	79	22.9
Al MacInnis	Cgy.	28-3-91	(A)	Edm. 4	at Cgy. 4	78	78	28-75 — 103	78	27.8
Brett Hull	St.L.	2-3-92	(G)	St.L. 5	at Van. 3	66	66	70-39 — 109	73	
Wayne Gretzky	L.A.	3-3-92	(A)	Phi. 1	at L.A. 4	60	66	31-90 — 121	74	
Kevin Stevens	Pit.	7-3-92	(A)	Pit. 3	at L.A. 5	66	66	54-69 — 123	80	26.11
Mario Lemieux	Pit.	10-3-92	(A)	Cgy. 2	at Pit. 5	53	67	44-87 — 131	64	
Luc Robitaille	L.A.	17-3-92	(A)	Wpg. 4	at L.A. 5	73	73	44-63 — 107	80	
Mark Messier	NYR	22-3-92	(G)	N.J. 3	at NYR 6	74	75	35-72 — 107	79	
Jeremy Roenick	Chi.	29-3-92	(A)	Tor. 1	at Chi. 5	77	77	53-50 — 103	80	22.2
Steve Yzerman	Det.	14-4-92	(G)	Det. 7	at Min. 4	79	80	45-58 — 103	80	
Brian Leetch	NYR	16-4-92	(G)	Pit. 1	at NYR 7	80	80	22-80 — 102	80	24.1
Mario Lemieux	Pit.	31-12-92	(G)	Tor. 3	at Pit. 3	38	39	69-91 — 160	60	
Pat LaFontaine	Buf.	10-2-93	(A)	Buf. 6	at Wpg. 2	55	55	53-95 — 148	84	
Adam Oates	Bos.	14-2-93	(A)	Bos. 3	at T.B. 3	58	58	45-97 — 142	84	
Steve Yzerman	Det.	24-2-93	(A)	Det. 7	at Buf. 10	64	64	58-79 — 137	84	
Pierre Turgeon	NYI	28-2-93	(G)	NYI 7	at Hfd. 6	62	63	58-74 — 132	83	
Doug Gilmour	Tor.	3-3-93	(A)	Min. 1	at Tor. 3	64	64	32-95 — 127	83	
Alexander Mogilny	Buf.	5-3-93	(A)	Hfd. 4	at Buf. 2	58	65	76-51 — 127	77	24.1
Mark Recchi	Phi.	7-3-93	(G)	Phi. 3	at N.J. 7	66	66	53-70 — 123	84	
Teemu Selanne	Wpg.	9-3-93	(G)	Wpg. 4	at T.B. 3	68	68	76-56 — 132	84	22.7
Luc Robitaille	L.A.	15-3-93	(A)	L.A. 4	at Buf. 2	69	69	63-62 — 125	84	
Kevin Stevens	Pit.	23-3-93	(A)	S.J. 2	at Pit. 7	63	73	55-56 — 111	72	
Mats Sundin	Que.	27-3-93	(G)	Phi. 3	at Que. 8	71	75	47-67 — 114	80	22.1
Pavel Bure	Van.	1-4-93	(G)	Van. 5	at T.B. 3	77	77	60-50 — 110	83	22.0
Jeremy Roenick	Chi.	4-4-93	(G)	St.L. 4	at Chi. 5	79	79	50-57 — 107	84	
Craig Janney	St.L.	4-4-93	(G)	St.L. 4	at Chi. 5	79	79	24-82 — 106	84	25.7
Rick Tocchet	Pit.	7-4-93	(G)	Mtl. 3	at Pit. 4	77	81	48-61 — 109	80	28.11
Joe Sakic	Que.	8-4-93	(A)	Que. 2	at Bos. 6	75	81	48-57 — 105	78	
Ron Francis	Pit.	9-4-93	(A)	Pit. 10	at NYR 4	82	82	24-76 — 100	84	
Brett Hull	St.L.	11-4-93	(G)	Min. 1	at St.L. 5	78	82	54-47 — 101	80	
Theoren Fleury	Cgy.	11-4-93	(A)	Cgy. 3	at Van. 6	82	82	34-66 — 100	83	
Joe Juneau	Bos.	14-4-93	(A)	Bos. 4	at Ott. 2	84	84	32-70 — 102	84	25.3
Wayne Gretzky	L.A.	14-2-94	(A)	Bos. 3	at L.A. 2	56	56	38-92 — 130	81	
Sergei Fedorov	Det.	1-3-94	(A)	Cgy. 2	at Det. 5	63	63	56-64 — 120	82	24.2
Doug Gilmour	Tor.	23-3-94	(A)	Tor. 1	at Fla. 1	74	74	27-84 — 111	83	
Adam Oates	Bos.	26-3-94	(A)	Mtl. 3	at Bos. 6	68	75	32-80 — 112	77	
Mark Recchi	Phi.	27-3-94	(A)	Ana. 3	at Phi. 2	76	76	40-67 — 107	84	
Pavel Bure	Van.	28-3-94	(G)	Tor. 2	at Van. 3	68	76	60-47 — 107	76	
Jeremy Roenick	Chi.	31-3-94	(G)	Chi. 3	at Wsh. 6	78	78	46-61 — 107	84	
Brendan Shanahan	St.L.	12-4-94	(G)	St.L. 5	at Dal. 9	80	83	52-50 — 102	81	25.2
Mario Lemieux	Pit.	16-1-96	(G)	Col. 5	at Pit. 2	38	44	69-92 — 161	70	
Jaromir Jagr	Pit.	6-2-96	(G)	Bos. 5	at Pit. 6	52	52	62-87 — 149	82	23.11
Ron Francis	Pit.	9-3-96	(A)	N.J. 4	at Pit. 3	61	66	27-92 — 119	77	
Peter Forsberg	Col.	9-3-96	(A)	Col. 7	at Van. 5	68	68	30-86 — 116	82	22.7
Joe Sakic	Col.	17-3-96	(A)	Edm. 1	at Col. 8	70	70	51-69 — 120	82	
Teemu Selanne	Ana.	25-3-96	(A)	Ana. 1	at Det. 5	70	73	40-68 — 108	79	
Alexander Mogilny	Van.	25-3-96	(A)	L.A. 1	at Van. 4	72	75	55-52 — 107	79	
Eric Lindros	Phi.	25-3-96	(A)	Hfd. 0	at Phi. 3	65	73	47-68 — 115	73	23.0
Wayne Gretzky	St.L.	28-3-96	(G)	N.J. 4	at St.L. 4	76	75	23-79 — 102	80	
Doug Weight	Edm.	30-3-96	(G)	Tor. 4	at Edm. 3	76	76	25-79 — 104	82	25.3
Sergei Fedorov	Det.	2-4-96	(A)	Det. 3	at S.J. 6	72	76	39-68 — 107	78	
Paul Kariya	Ana.	7-4-96	(G)	Ana. 5	at S.J. 3	78	78	50-58 — 108	82	21.5
Mario Lemieux	Pit.	8-3-97	(A)	Phi. 2	at Pit. 3	61	65	50-72 — 122	76	
Teemu Selanne	Ana.	1-4-97	(A)	Chi. 3	at Ana. 3	74	78	51-58 — 109	78	
Jaromir Jagr	Pit.	15-4-98	(G)	T.B. 1	at Pit. 5	76	80	35-67 — 102	77	
Jaromir Jagr	Pit.	13-3-99	(G)	Phi. 0	at Pit. 4	65	65	44-83 — 127	81	
Teemu Selanne	Ana.	5-4-99	(A)	Ana. 2	at Det. 3	69	76	47-60 — 107	75	
Paul Kariya	Ana.	17-4-99	(G)	Ana. 3	at S.J. 3	82	82	39-62 — 101	82	
Jaromir Jagr	Pit.	10-3-01	(G)	Cgy. 3	at Pit. 6	68	68	52-69 — 121	81	
Joe Sakic	Col.	18-3-01	(G)	Min. 3	at Col. 4	72	72	54-64 — 118	82	
Markus Naslund	Van.	27-3-03	(A)	Phx. 1	at Van. 5	78	78	48-56 — 104	82	
Peter Forsberg	Col.	31-3-03	(A)	S.J. 1	at Col. 3	72	79	29-77 — 106	79	
Joe Thornton	Bos.	4-4-03	(A)	Buf. 5	at Bos. 8	77	82	36-65 — 101	77	

Five-or-more-Goal Games

Player	Team	Date	Score	Opposing Goaltender
SEVEN GOALS				
Joe Malone	Quebec Bulldogs	Jan. 31/20	Tor. 6 at Que. 10	Ivan Mitchell
SIX GOALS				
Newsy Lalonde	Montreal	Jan. 10/20	Tor. 7 at Mtl. 14	Ivan Mitchell
Joe Malone	Quebec Bulldogs	Mar. 10/20	Ott. 4 at Que. 10	Clint Benedict
Corb Denneny	Toronto St. Pats	Jan. 26/21	Ham. 3 at Tor. 10	Howard Lockhart
Cy Denneny	Ottawa Senators	Mar. 7/21	Ham. 5 at Ott. 12	Howard Lockhart
Syd Howe	Detroit	Feb. 3/44	NYR 2 at Det. 12	Ken McAuley
Red Berenson	St. Louis	Nov. 7/68	St.L. 8 at Phi. 0	Doug Favell
Darryl Sittler	Toronto	Feb. 7/76	Bos. 4 at Tor. 11	Dave Reece
FIVE GOALS				
Joe Malone	Montreal	Dec. 19/17	Mtl. 7 at Ott. 4	Clint Benedict
Harry Hyland	Mtl. Wanderers	Dec. 19/17	Tor. 9 at Mtl. W. 10	Art Brooks, Sammy Hebert
Joe Malone	Montreal	Jan. 12/18	Ott. 4 at Mtl. 9	Clint Benedict
Joe Malone	Montreal	Feb. 2/18	Tor. 2 at Mtl. 11	Hap Holmes
Mickey Roach	Toronto St. Pats	Mar. 6/20	Que. 2 at Tor. 11	Howard Lockhart
Newsy Lalonde	Montreal	Feb. 16/21	Ham. 5 at Mtl. 10	Howard Lockhart
Babe Dye	Toronto St. Pats	Dec. 16/22	Mtl. 2 at Tor. 7	Georges Vezina
Red Green	Hamilton Tigers	Dec. 5/24	Ham. 10 at Tor. 3	John Ross Roach
Babe Dye	Toronto St. Pats	Dec. 22/24	Tor. 10 at Bos. 1	Hec Fowler
Punch Broadbent	Mtl. Maroons	Jan. 7/25	Mtl. 6 at Ham. 2	Jake Forbes
Pit Lepine	Montreal	Dec. 14/29	Ott. 4 at Mtl. 6	Alex Connell
Howie Morenz	Montreal	Mar. 18/30	NYA 3 at Mtl. 8	Roy Worters
Charlie Conacher	Toronto	Jan. 19/32	NYA 3 at Tor. 11	Roy Worters, Al Shields
Ray Getliffe	Montreal	Feb. 6/43	Bos. 3 at Mtl. 8	Frank Brimsek
Maurice Richard	Montreal	Dec. 28/44	Det. 1 at Mtl. 9	Harry Lumley
Howie Meeker	Toronto	Jan. 8/47	Chi. 4 at Tor. 10	Paul Bibeault
Bernie Geoffrion	Montreal	Feb. 19/55	NYR 2 at Mtl. 10	Gump Worsley
Bobby Rousseau	Montreal	Feb. 1/64	Det. 3 at Mtl. 8	Roger Crozier
Yvan Cournoyer	Montreal	Feb. 15/75	Chi. 3 at Mtl. 12	Mike Veisor
Don Murdoch	NY Rangers	Oct. 12/76	NYR 10 at Min. 4	Gary Smith
Ian Turnbull	Toronto	Feb. 2/77	Det. 1 at Tor. 9	Ed Giacomin (2), Jim Rutherford (3)
Bryan Trottier	NY Islanders	Dec. 23/78	NYR 4 at NYI 9	Wayne Thomas (4), John Davidson (1)
Tim Young	Minnesota	Jan. 15/79	Min. 8 at NYR 1	Doug Soetaert (3), Wayne Thomas (2)
John Tonelli	NY Islanders	Jan. 6/81	Tor. 3 at NYI 6	Jiri Crha (4), empty net (1)
Wayne Gretzky	Edmonton	Feb. 18/81	St.L. 2 at Edm. 9	Mike Liut (3), Ed Staniowski (2)
Wayne Gretzky	Edmonton	Dec. 30/81	Phi. 5 at Edm. 7	Pete Peeters (4), empty net (1)
Grant Mulvey	Chicago	Feb. 3/82	St.L. 5 at Chi. 9	Mike Liut (4), Gary Edwards (1)
Bryan Trottier	NY Islanders	Feb. 13/82	Phi. 2 at NYI 8	Pete Peeters
Willy Lindstrom	Winnipeg	Mar. 2/82	Wpg. 7 at Phi. 6	Pete Peeters
Mark Pavelich	NY Rangers	Feb. 23/83	Hfd. 3 at NYR 11	Greg Millen
Jari Kurri	Edmonton	Nov. 19/83	N.J. 4 at Edm. 13	Glenn Resch (3), Ron Low (2)
Bengt Gustafsson	Washington	Jan. 8/84	Wsh. 7 at Phi. 1	Pelle Lindbergh
Pat Hughes	Edmonton	Feb. 3/84	Cgy. 5 at Edm. 10	Don Edwards (3), Reggie Lemelin (2)
Wayne Gretzky	Edmonton	Dec. 15/84	Edm. 8 at St.L. 2	Rick Wamsley (4), Mike Liut(1)
Dave Andreychuk	Buffalo	Feb. 6/86	Buf. 8 at Bos. 6	Pat Riggin (1), Doug Keans (4)
Wayne Gretzky	Edmonton	Dec. 6/87	Min. 4 at Edm. 10	Don Beaupre (4), Kari Takko (1)
Mario Lemieux	Pittsburgh	Dec. 31/88	N.J. 6 at Pit. 8	Bob Sauve (3), Chris Terreri (2)
Joe Nieuwendyk	Calgary	Jan. 11/89	Wpg. 3 at Cgy. 8	Daniel Berthiaume, Peter Sidorkiewicz (3)
Mats Sundin	Quebec	Mar. 5/92	Que. 10 at Hfd. 4	Kay Whitmore (2)
Mario Lemieux	Pittsburgh	Apr. 9/93	Pit. 10 at NYR 4	Corey Hirsch (3), Mike Richter (2)
Peter Bondra	Washington	Feb. 5/94	T.B. 3 at Wsh. 6	Daren Puppa (4), Pat Jablonski (1)
Mike Ricci	Quebec	Feb. 17/94	Que. 8 at S.J. 2	Arturs Irbe (3), Jimmy Waite (2)
Alex Zhamnov	Winnipeg	Apr. 1/95	Wpg. 7 at L.A. 7	Kelly Hrudey (3), Grant Fuhr (2)
Mario Lemieux	Pittsburgh	Mar. 26/96	St.L. 4 at Pit. 8	Grant Fuhr (1), Jon Casey (4)
Sergei Fedorov	Detroit	Dec. 26/96	Wsh. 4 at Det. 5	Jim Carey

Players' 500th Goals

Regular Season

Lanny McDonald is the only player in NHL history to score exactly 500 goals in his career. He also reached 1,000 points in his final season of 1988-89 and scored the insurance goal that gave Calgary the 1989 Stanley Cup championship.

Player	Team	Date	Game No.	Score	Opposing Goaltender	Total Goals	Total Games
Maurice Richard	Montreal	Oct. 19/57	863	Chi. 1 at Mtl. 3	Glenn Hall	544	978
Gordie Howe	Detroit	Mar. 14/62	1,045	Det. 2 at NYR 3	Gump Worsley	801	1,767
Bobby Hull	Chicago	Feb. 21/70	861	NYR. 2 at Chi. 4	Ed Giacomin	610	1,063
Jean Béliveau	Montreal	Feb. 11/71	1,101	Min. 2 at Mtl. 6	Gilles Gilbert	507	1,125
Frank Mahovlich	Montreal	Mar. 21/73	1,105	Van. 2 at Mtl. 3	Dunc Wilson	533	1,181
Phil Esposito	Boston	Dec. 22/74	803	Det. 4 at Bos. 5	Jim Rutherford	717	1,282
John Bucyk	Boston	Oct. 30/75	1,370	St.L. 2 at Bos. 3	Yves Bélanger	556	1,540
Stan Mikita	Chicago	Feb. 27/77	1,221	Van. 4 at Chi. 3	Cesare Maniago	541	1,394
Marcel Dionne	Los Angeles	Dec. 14/82	887	L.A. 2 at Wsh. 7	Al Jensen	731	1,348
Guy Lafleur	Montreal	Dec. 20/83	918	Mtl. 6 at N.J. 0	Glenn Resch	560	1,126
Mike Bossy	NY Islanders	Jan. 2/86	647	Bos. 5 at NYI 7	empty net	573	752
Gilbert Perreault	Buffalo	Mar. 9/86	1,159	N.J. 3 at Buf. 4	Alain Chevrier	512	1,191
Wayne Gretzky	Edmonton	Nov. 22/86	575	Van. 2 at Edm. 5	empty net	894	1,487
Lanny McDonald	Calgary	Mar. 21/89	1,107	NYI 1 at Cgy. 4	Mark Fitzpatrick	500	1,111
Bryan Trottier	NY Islanders	Feb. 13/90	1,104	Cgy. 4 at NYI 2	Rick Wamsley	524	1,279
Mike Gartner	NY Rangers	Oct. 14/91	936	Wsh. 5 at NYR 3	Mike Liut	708	1,432
Michel Goulet	Chicago	Feb. 16/92	951	Cgy. 5 at Chi. 5	Jeff Reese	548	1,089
Jari Kurri	Los Angeles	Oct. 17/92	833	Bos. 6 at L.A. 8	empty net	601	1,251
Dino Ciccarelli	Detroit	Jan. 8/94	946	Det. 4 at L.A. 3	Kelly Hrudey	608	1,232
*Mario Lemieux	Pittsburgh	Oct. 26/95	605	Pit. 7 at NYI 5	Tommy Soderstrom	683	889
*Mark Messier	NY Rangers	Nov. 6/95	1,141	Cgy. 2 at NYR 4	Rick Tabaracci	694	1,756
*Steve Yzerman	Detroit	Jan. 17/96	906	Col. 2 at Det. 3	Patrick Roy	678	1,453
Dale Hawerchuk	St. Louis	Jan. 31/96	1,103	St.L. 4 at Tor. 0	Felix Potvin	518	1,188
*Brett Hull	St. Louis	Dec. 22/96	693	L.A. 4 at St.L. 7	Stephane Fiset	741	1,264
Joe Mullen	Pittsburgh	Mar. 14/97	1,052	Pit. 3 at Col. 6	Patrick Roy	502	1,062
*Dave Andreychuk	New Jersey	Mar. 15/97	1,070	Wsh. 2 at N.J. 3	Bill Ranford	634	1,597
*Luc Robitaille	Los Angeles	Jan. 7/99	928	Buf. 2 at L.A. 4	Dwayne Roloson	653	1,366
Pat Verbeek	Detroit	Mar. 22/00	1,285	Cgy. 2 at Det. 2	Fred Brathwaite	522	1,424
*Ron Francis	Carolina	Jan. 2/02	1,533	Bos. 6 at Car. 3	Byron Dafoe	549	1,731
*Brendan Shanahan	Detroit	Mar. 23/02	1,100	Det. 2 at Col. 0	Patrick Roy	558	1,268
*Joe Sakic	Colorado	Dec. 11/02	1,044	Col. 1 at Van. 3	Dan Cloutier	542	1,155
*Joe Nieuwendyk	New Jersey	Jan. 17/03	1,094	N.J. 2 at Car. 1	Kevin Weekes	533	1,177
*Jaromir Jagr	Washington	Feb. 4/03	928	Wsh. 5 at T.B. 1	John Grahame	537	1,027

*Active

Players' 1,000th Points

Regular Season

Player	Team	Date	Game No.	G or A	Score				Total Points G A PTS			Total Games
Gordie Howe	Detroit	Nov. 27/60	938	(A)	Tor. 0	at	Det. 2		801–1,049	–1,850		1,767
Jean Béliveau	Montreal	Mar. 3/68	911	(G)	Mtl. 2	at	Det. 5		507–712	–1,219		1,125
Alex Delvecchio	Detroit	Feb. 16/69	1,143	(A)	L.A. 3	at	Det. 6		456–825	–1,281		1,549
Bobby Hull	Chicago	Dec. 13/70	909	(A)	Min. 2	at	Chi. 5		610–560	–1,170		1,063
Norm Ullman	Toronto	Oct. 16/71	1,113	(A)	NYR 5	at	Tor. 3		490–739	–1,229		1,410
Stan Mikita	Chicago	Oct. 15/72	924	(A)	St.L. 3	at	Chi. 1		541–926	–1,467		1,394
John Bucyk	Boston	Nov. 9/72	1,144	(G)	Det. 3	at	Bos. 8		556–813	–1,369		1,540
Frank Mahovlich	Montreal	Feb. 17/73	1,090	(A)	Phi. 7	at	Mtl. 6		533–570	–1,103		1,181
Henri Richard	Montreal	Dec. 20/73	1,194	(A)	Mtl. 2	at	Buf. 2		358–688	–1,046		1,256
Phil Esposito	Boston	Feb. 15/74	745	(A)	Bos. 4	at	Van. 2		717–873	–1,590		1,282
Rod Gilbert	NY Rangers	Feb. 19/77	1,027	(G)	NYR 2	at	NYI 5		406–615	–1,021		1,065
Jean Ratelle	Boston	Apr. 3/77	1,007	(A)	Tor. 4	at	Bos. 7		491–776	–1,267		1,281
Marcel Dionne	Los Angeles	Jan. 7/81	740	(G)	L.A. 5	at	Hfd. 3		731–1,040	–1,771		1,348
Guy Lafleur	Montreal	Mar. 4/81	720	(G)	Mtl. 9	at	Wpg. 3		560–793	–1,353		1,126
Bobby Clarke	Philadelphia	Mar. 19/81	922	(G)	Bos. 3	at	Phi. 5		358–852	–1,210		1,144
Gilbert Perreault	Buffalo	Apr. 3/82	871	(A)	Buf. 5	at	Mtl. 4		512–814	–1,326		1,191
Darryl Sittler	Philadelphia	Jan. 20/83	927	(G)	Cgy. 2	at	Phi. 5		484–637	–1,121		1,096
Wayne Gretzky	Edmonton	Dec. 19/84	424	(A)	L.A. 3	at	Edm. 7		894–1,963	–2,875		1,487
Bryan Trottier	NY Islanders	Jan. 29/85	726	(A)	Min. 4	at	NYI 4		524–901	–1,425		1,279
Mike Bossy	NY Islanders	Jan. 24/86	656	(G)	NYI 7	at	Wsh. 5		573–553	–1,126		752
Denis Potvin	NY Islanders	Apr. 4/87	987	(G)	Buf. 6	at	NYI 6		310–742	–1,052		1,060
Bernie Federko	St. Louis	Mar. 19/88	855	(A)	Hfd. 5	at	St.L. 3		369–761	–1,130		1,000
Lanny McDonald	Calgary	Mar. 7/89	1,101	(G)	Wpg. 5	at	Cgy. 9		500–506	–1,006		1,111
Peter Stastny	Quebec	Oct. 19/89	682	(G)	Que. 5	at	Chi. 3		450–789	–1,239		977
Jari Kurri	Edmonton	Jan. 2/90	716	(A)	Edm. 6	at	St.L. 4		601–797	–1,398		1,251
Denis Savard	Chicago	Mar. 11/90	727	(A)	St.L. 6	at	Chi. 4		473–865	–1,338		1,196
Paul Coffey	Pittsburgh	Dec. 22/90	770	(A)	Pit. 4	at	NYI 3		396–1,135	–1,531		1,409
*Mark Messier	Edmonton	Jan. 13/91	822	(A)	Edm. 5	at	Phi. 3		694–1,193	–1,887		1,756
Dave Taylor	Los Angeles	Feb. 5/91	930	(A)	L.A. 3	at	Phi. 2		431–638	–1,069		1,111
Michel Goulet	Chicago	Feb. 23/91	878	(G)	Chi. 3	at	Min. 3		548–604	–1,152		1,089
Dale Hawerchuk	Buffalo	Mar. 8/91	781	(G)	Chi. 5	at	Buf. 3		518–891	–1,409		1,188
Bobby Smith	Minnesota	Nov. 30/91	986	(A)	Min. 4	at	Tor. 3		357–679	–1,036		1,077
Mike Gartner	NY Rangers	Jan. 4/92	971	(A)	NYR 4	at	N.J. 6		708–627	–1,335		1,432
Raymond Bourque	Boston	Feb. 29/92	933	(A)	Wsh. 5	at	Bos. 5		410–1,169	–1,579		1,612
*Mario Lemieux	Pittsburgh	Mar. 24/92	513	(A)	Pit. 3	at	Det. 4		683–1,018	–1,701		889
Glenn Anderson	Toronto	Feb. 22/93	954	(G)	Tor. 8	at	Van. 1		498–601	–1,099		1,129
*Steve Yzerman	Detroit	Feb. 24/93	737	(A)	Det. 7	at	Buf. 10		678–1,043	–1,721		1,453
*Ron Francis	Pittsburgh	Oct. 28/93	893	(G)	Que. 7	at	Pit. 3		549–1,249	–1,798		1,731
Bernie Nicholls	New Jersey	Feb. 13/94	858	(G)	N.J. 3	at	T.B. 3		475–734	–1,209		1,127
Dino Ciccarelli	Detroit	Mar. 9/94	957	(G)	Det. 5	at	Cgy. 1		608–592	–1,200		1,232
Brian Propp	Hartford	Mar. 19/94	1,008	(A)	Hfd. 3	at	Phi. 3		425–579	–1,004		1,016
Joe Mullen	Pittsburgh	Feb. 7/95	935	(A)	Fla. 3	at	Pit. 7		502–561	–1,063		1,062
Steve Larmer	NY Rangers	Mar. 8/95	983	(A)	N.J. 4	at	NYR 6		441–571	–1,012		1,006
Doug Gilmour	Toronto	Dec. 23/95	935	(A)	Edm. 1	at	Tor. 6		450–964	–1,414		1,474
Larry Murphy	Toronto	Mar. 27/96	1,228	(G)	Tor. 6	at	Van. 2		287–929	–1,216		1,615
*Dave Andreychuk	New Jersey	Apr. 7/96	998	(G)	NYR 2	at	N.J. 4		634–686	–1,320		1,597
Adam Oates	Washington	Oct. 8/97	830	(G)	Wsh. 6	at	NYI 3		341–1,079	–1,420		1,337
Phil Housley	Washington	Nov. 8/97	1,081	(A)	Edm. 1	at	Wsh. 2		338–894	–1,232		1,495
Dale Hunter	Washington	Jan. 9/98	1,308	(A)	Phi. 1	at	Wsh. 4		323–697	–1,020		1,407
Pat LaFontaine	NY Rangers	Jan. 22/98	847	(A)	Phi. 4	at	NYR 3		468–545	–1,013		865
*Luc Robitaille	Los Angeles	Jan. 29/98	882	(A)	Cgy. 3	at	L.A. 5		653–717	–1,370		1,366
*Al MacInnis	St. Louis	Apr. 7/98	1,056	(A)	St.L. 3	at	Det. 5		340–934	–1,274		1,416
*Brett Hull	Dallas	Nov. 14/98	815	(A)	Dal. 3	at	Bos. 1		741–649	–1,390		1,264
Brian Bellows	Washington	Jan. 2/99	1,147	(A)	Tor. 2	at	Wsh. 5		485–537	–1,022		1,188
*Pierre Turgeon	St. Louis	Oct. 9/99	881	(G)	St.L. 4	at	Edm. 3		495–779	–1,274		1,215
*Joe Sakic	Colorado	Dec. 27/99	810	(A)	St.L. 1	at	Col. 5		542–860	–1,402		1,155
Pat Verbeek	Detroit	Feb. 27/00	1,275	(A)	T.B. 1	at	Det. 3		522–541	–1,063		1,424
*V. Damphousse	San Jose	Oct. 14/00	1,090	(A)	Bos. 2	at	S.J. 5		432–773	–1,205		1,378
*Jaromir Jagr	Pittsburgh	Dec. 30/00	763	(G)	Ott. 3	at	Pit. 5		537–772	–1,309		1,027
*Mark Recchi	Philadelphia	Mar. 13/01	920	(G)	St.L. 2	at	Phi. 5		456–745	–1,201		1,173
Theoren Fleury	NY Rangers	Oct. 29/01	960	(A)	Dal. 2	at	NYR 4		455–633	–1,088		1,084
*B. Shanahan	Detroit	Jan. 12/02	1,073	(G)	Dal. 2	at	Det. 5		558–593	–1,151		1,268
*Jeremy Roenick	Philadelphia	Jan. 30/02	961	(G)	Phi. 1	at	Ott. 3		475–645	–1,120		1,124
*Mike Modano	Dallas	Nov. 15/02	965	(A)	Col. 2	at	Dal. 4		458–648	–1,106		1,101
*Joe Nieuwendyk	New Jersey	Feb. 23/03	1,094	(G)	N.J. 4	at	Pit. 3		533–529	–1,062		1,177
*Mats Sundin	Toronto	Mar. 10/03	994	(G)	Tor. 3	at	Edm. 2		465–624	–1,089		1,086
*Sergei Fedorov	Anaheim	Feb. 14/04	965	(A)	Ana. 2	at	Van. 1		431–588	–1,019		988
*Alexander Mogilny	Toronto	Mar. 15/04	946	(A)	Tor. 6	at	Buf. 5		461–546	–1,007		956

*Active

Sergei Fedorov (top) became the first Russian to reach the 1,000-point plateau on February 14, 2004. One month later, Alexander Mogilny became the second.

Individual Awards

Hart Memorial Trophy

Art Ross Trophy

Calder Memorial Trophy

James Norris Memorial Trophy

HART MEMORIAL TROPHY

An annual award "to the player adjudged to be the most valuable to his team." Winner selected in a poll by the Professional Hockey Writers' Association in the 30 NHL cities at the end of the regular schedule. The winner receives $10,000 and the runners-up $6,000 and $4,000.

History: The Hart Memorial Trophy was presented by the National Hockey League in 1960 after the original Hart Trophy was retired to the Hockey Hall of Fame. The original Hart Trophy was donated to the NHL in 1923 by Dr. David A. Hart, father of Cecil Hart, former manager-coach of the Montreal Canadiens.

2003-04 Winner: **Martin St. Louis, Tampa Bay Lightning**
Runners-up: Jarome Iginla, Calgary Flames
Martin Brodeur, New Jersey Devils

Right winger Martin St. Louis of the Tampa Bay Lightning captured the Hart Memorial Trophy by a comfortable margin over Jarome Iginla of the Calgary Flames and New Jersey Devils goaltender Martin Brodeur. St. Louis was named on all 105 ballots and received 97 first-place votes for 1,016 points. Iginla received votes on 49 ballots and earned two first-place votes for 253 points. Brodeur also had two first-place votes and a total of 213 points.

St. Louis captured the Art Ross Trophy as the NHL's scoring leader with a career-high 94 points (38 goals, 56 assists), led the league in assists, shorthanded goals (eight) and points (11) and tied for the lead in plus-minus (+35). During a two-month stretch from January 3 through March 3, St. Louis tallied points in 27 of 30 games, collecting 21-28-49 in that span. The Lightning went on to post a franchise-best 46-22-8-6 record for 106 points and first place overall in the Eastern Conference. St. Louis was voted to the Eastern Conference All-Star starting lineup and played in the All-Star game for the second straight year. He was named to the NHL's First All-Star Team at season's end.

CALDER MEMORIAL TROPHY

An annual award "to the player selected as the most proficient in his first year of competition in the National Hockey League." Winner selected in a poll by the Professional Hockey Writers' Association at the end of the regular schedule. The winner receives $10,000 and the runners-up $6,000 and $4,000.

History: From 1936-37 until his death in 1943, Frank Calder, NHL President, bought a trophy each year to be given permanently to the outstanding rookie. After Calder's death, the NHL presented the Calder Memorial Trophy in his memory and the trophy is to be kept in perpetuity. To be eligible for the award, a player cannot have played more than 25 games in any single preceding season nor in six or more games in each of any two preceding seasons in any major professional league. Beginning in 1990-91, to be eligible for this award a player must not have attained his twenty-sixth birthday by September 15th of the season in which he is eligible.

2003-04 Winner: **Andrew Raycroft, Boston Bruins**
Runners-up: Michael Ryder, Montreal Canadiens
Trent Hunter, New York Islanders

Goaltender Andrew Raycroft of the Boston Bruins was elected the winner of the Calder Memorial Trophy. Raycroft received 93 of 105 first-place votes and was the second choice on eight other ballots for 1,002 points. Montreal Canadiens forward Michael Ryder, named on 104 of 105 ballots, including 11 first-place votes, was second with 723 points. Trent Hunter of the New York Islanders received one first-place vote and garnered 470 points.

Raycroft appeared in 57 games and posted a 29-18-9 record with three shutouts, a 2.05 goals-against average (sixth in the NHL) and a .926 save percentage (fifth). He finished the season with a flourish, going 14-6-3 in his last 23 games and 20-8-3 in his last 31. Boston's fifth-round pick in the 1998 Entry Draft, Raycroft played in the 2004 NHL YoungStars Game and was named Rookie of the Month for March. He is the first Bruins goaltender to win the Calder Memorial Trophy since Jack Gelineau in 1950.

ART ROSS TROPHY

An annual award "to the player who leads the league in scoring points at the end of the regular season." The winner receives $10,000 and the runners-up $6,000 and $4,000.

History: Arthur Howie Ross, former manager-coach of the Boston Bruins, presented the trophy to the National Hockey League in 1947. If two players finish the schedule with the same number of points, the trophy is awarded in the following manner: 1. Player with most goals. 2. Player with fewer games played. 3. Player scoring first goal of the season.

2003-04 Winner: **Martin St. Louis, Tampa Bay Lightning**
Runners-up: Ilya Kovalchuk, Atlanta Thrashers
Joe Sakic, Colorado Avalanche

Right winger Martin St. Louis of the Tampa Bay Lightning won the Art Ross Trophy for the first time. St. Louis posted a career-high 94 points (38 goals, 56 assists). He also led the league in assists (56) shorthanded goals (eight) and points (11) and tied for the lead in plus-minus (+35). He had at least one point in 13 straight games from February 5 to March 3 and scored two hat tricks (January 15 vs. Carolina and January 24 vs. Calgary). He was named the NHL Offensive Player of the Month for February and March, 2004. St. Louis finished seven points in front of both Ilya Kovalchuk of Atlanta and Colorado's Joe Sakic. Kovalchuk had 87 points on 41 goals and 46 assists while Sakic had 87 points on 33 goals and 54 assists.

JAMES NORRIS MEMORIAL TROPHY

An annual award "to the defense player who demonstrates throughout the season the greatest all-round ability in the position." Winner selected in a poll by the Professional Hockey Writers' Association at the end of the regular schedule. The winner receives $10,000 and the runners-up $6,000 and $4,000.

History: The James Norris Memorial Trophy was presented in 1953 by the four children of the late James Norris in memory of the former owner-president of the Detroit Red Wings.

2003-04 Winner: **Scott Niedermayer, New Jersey Devils**
Runners-up: Zdeno Chara, Ottawa Senators
Chris Pronger, St. Louis Blues

Scott Niedermayer of the New Jersey Devils won the James Norris Memorial Trophy for the first time. Niedermayer, who was a Norris finalist for the first time, was named on 100 of 104 ballots and received 72 first-place votes for 872 points, ahead of fellow first-time nominee Zdeno Chara of the Ottawa Senators (19 first-place votes and 563 points) and 2000 Norris Trophy winner Chris Pronger of St. Louis (seven first-place votes, 345 points).

Niedermayer tied for second among NHL defensemen in scoring with 54 points (14 goals, 40 assists), the second-highest point total of his NHL career. Serving as Devils captain from January 9 in the absence of Scott Stevens, Niedermayer appeared in 81 games, led the club in average ice time per game (25:53) and ranked second in plus-minus (+20).

Vezina Trophy

Lady Byng Memorial Trophy

Frank J. Selke Trophy

Conn Smythe Trophy

VEZINA TROPHY

An annual award "to the goalkeeper adjudged to be the best at his position" as voted by the general managers of each of the 30 clubs. The winner receives $10,000 and the runners-up $6,000 and $4,000.

History: Leo Dandurand, Louis Letourneau and Joe Cattarinich, former owners of the Montreal Canadiens, presented the trophy to the National Hockey League in 1926-27 in memory of Georges Vezina, outstanding goalkeeper of the Canadiens who collapsed during an NHL game on November 28, 1925, and died of tuberculosis a few months later. Until the 1981-82 season, the goalkeeper(s) of the team allowing the fewest number of goals during the regular season were awarded the Vezina Trophy.

2003-04 Winner: **Martin Brodeur, New Jersey Devils**
Runners-up: **Miikka Kiprusoff, Calgary Flames**
          Roberto Luongo, Florida Panthers

Martin Brodeur of the New Jersey Devils captured the Vezina Trophy for the second consecutive season. Brodeur was nominated for the fifth time, having finished second in voting in 1997 and 1998, and third in 2001. Brodeur received votes on 21 of 30 ballots this year, including 15 first-place votes, for 89 points. The Calgary Flames' Miikka Kiprusoff, in his first year as a finalist, was named on 17 of 30 ballots, including five first-place votes, for 55 points to finish second. Florida's Roberto Luongo had six first-place votes and 45 points.

Brodeur posted a 38-26-11 record (his 9th consecutive season with 30 or more wins), had a 2.03 goals-against average in 75 games, led all goaltenders in victories and shutouts (11), set a record for most minutes played (4,555) by a goaltender in one season and won the Jennings Trophy for fewest regular-season goals against for the fourth time.

CONN SMYTHE TROPHY

An annual award "to the most valuable player for his team in the playoffs." Winner selected by the Professional Hockey Writers' Association at the conclusion of the final game in the Stanley Cup Finals. The winner receives $10,000.

History: Presented by Maple Leaf Gardens Limited in 1964 to honor Conn Smythe, the former coach, manager, president and owner-governor of the Toronto Maple Leafs.

2003-04 Winner: **Brad Richards, Tampa Bay Lightning.**

Center Brad Richards of the Tampa Bay Lightning is the first native of Prince Edward Island to win the Conn Smythe Trophy after leading all playoff performers with 26 points (12 goals, 14 assists) in 23 games. Richards established a new NHL playoff record with seven game-winning goals as the Lightning posted a perfect 9-0 record in games in which he had at least one goal. Richards assisted on Martin St. Louis' double overtime goal in game six of the Stanley Cup finals, and set up Ruslan Fedetenko for the key first goal in game seven. He is the first forward to win the Conn Smythe Trophy since Joe Nieuwendyk in 1999.

LADY BYNG MEMORIAL TROPHY

An annual award "to the player adjudged to have exhibited the best type of sportsmanship and gentlemanly conduct combined with a high standard of playing ability." Winner selected in a poll by the Professional Hockey Writers' Association at the end of the regular schedule. The winner receives $10,000 and the runners-up $6,000 and $4,000.

History: Lady Byng, wife of Canada's Governor-General at the time, presented the Lady Byng Trophy in the 1924-25 season. After Frank Boucher of the New York Rangers won the award seven times in eight seasons, he was given the trophy to keep and Lady Byng donated another trophy in 1936. After Lady Byng's death in 1949, the National Hockey League presented a new trophy, changing the name to Lady Byng Memorial Trophy.

2003-04 Winner: **Brad Richards, Tampa Bay Lightning**
Runners-up: **Daniel Alfredsson, Ottawa Senators**
          Martin St. Louis, Tampa Bay Lightning

Tampa Bay Lightning center Brad Richards won the Lady Byng Memorial Trophy in his first time as a finalist. Richards was named on 66 of 105 ballots and received 25 first-place votes for 425 points, ahead of Ottawa Senators right winger Daniel Alfredsson (14 first-place votes, 316 points) and teammate Martin St. Louis (19 and 314). Richards surpassed the 50-assist and 70-point marks for the second consecutive season, tallying 26 goals and 53 assists. He finished sixth in the NHL in assists and 10th overall in points. Despite playing an average of 20:25 per game and appearing in each of the Lightning's 82 games, Richards was assessed just 12 minutes in penalties.

FRANK J. SELKE TROPHY

An annual award "to the forward who best excels in the defensive aspects of the game." Winner selected in a poll by the Professional Hockey Writers' Association at the end of the regular schedule. The winner receives $10,000 and the runners-up $6,000 and $4,000.

History: Presented to the National Hockey League in 1977 by the Board of Governors of the NHL in honor of Frank J. Selke, one of the great architects of Montreal and Toronto championship teams.

2003-04 Winner: **Kris Draper, Detroit Red Wings**
Runners-up: **John Madden, New Jersey Devils**
          Alyn McCauley, San Jose Sharks

Detroit Red Wings center Kris Draper captured the Frank J. Selke Trophy in his first time as a nominee. Draper outdistanced the field by receiving 66 first-place votes and was named on 95 of 105 ballots for 839 points. New Jersey Devils center John Madden, the 2001 Selke winner, was second for the second consecutive season with 368 points, including six first-place votes. San Jose's Alyn McCauley, another first-time nominee, finished third with nine first-place votes and 271 points.

Draper anchored the NHL's top penalty-killing unit in 2003-04 as the Red Wings allowed just 42 goals in 317 times shorthanded for a 86.8% success rate. He tied for second in the league with five shorthanded goals, was eighth in face-off-winning percentage (56.9%) and posted a +22 rating. Draper also excelled in the offensive zone, recording a career-high 40 points (24 goals, 16 assists) in 67 games.

WILLIAM M. JENNINGS TROPHY

An annual award "to the goalkeeper(s) having played a minimum of 25 games for the team with the fewest goals scored against it." Winners selected on regular-season play. The winner receives $10,000, and the runners-up $6,000 and $4,000.

History: The Jennings Trophy was presented in 1981-82 by the National Hockey League's Board of Governors to honor the late William M. Jennings, longtime governor and president of the New York Rangers and one of the great builders of hockey in the United States.

2003-04 Winner: **Martin Brodeur, New Jersey Devils**
Runners-up: **Marty Turco, Dallas Stars**
          Miikka Kiprusoff, Calgary Flames

The New Jersey Devils' Martin Brodeur was presented with the William M. Jennings Trophy for the fourth time. It was his second win in as many seasons. Brodeur appeared in 75 games, led all goaltenders in victories (38) and ranked fourth in goals-against average (2.03). The Devils allowed a league-low 164 goals en route to a 43-25-12-2 record for 100 points and second place in the Atlantic Division. Marty Turco appeared in 73 games for Dallas, who let in 175 goals as a team. His goals-against average of 1.98 was third in the NHL. Miikka Kiprusoff appeared in 38 games for Calgary. His goals-against average of 1.69 was the NHL's lowest since 1939-40. The Flames allowed 176 goals.

William M. Jennings Trophy

Jack Adams Award

Bill Masterton Trophy

Lester Patrick Trophy

Lester B. Pearson Award

JACK ADAMS AWARD

An annual award presented by the National Hockey League Broadcasters' Association to "the NHL coach adjudged to have contributed the most to his team's success." Winner selected by a poll among members of the NHL Broadcasters' Association at the end of the regular season. The winner receives $1,000 from the NHLBA.

History: The award was presented by the NHL Broadcasters' Association in 1974 to commemorate the late Jack Adams, coach and general manager of the Detroit Red Wings, whose lifetime dedication to hockey serves as an inspiration to all who aspire to further the game.

2003-04 Winner: John Tortorella, Tampa Bay Lightning
Runners-up Ron Wilson, San Jose Sharks
Darryl Sutter, Calgary Flames

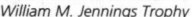

Tampa Bay [...] coach John Tortorella captured the Jack Adams Award after [...]ing in his first time as a finalist in 2002-03. Tortorella [...] 231 points. San Jose's Ron Wilson, who finished third [...]med first on 16 ballots and had 167 points. Darryl Sutter [...]ine first-place votes and 87 points.

[...] to the Southeast Division title and, for the first time, [...]ce with a franchise-best 46-22-8-6 record for 106 [...] Lightning made headlines by earning a point in 26 [...] capped off the season by winning the Stanley [...] e Lightning's point total has increased in each of

[BILL MASTERTON] MEMORIAL TROPHY

An [...] under the trusteeship of the Professional Hockey Writers' Ass[...] the National Hockey League player who best exemplifies the qualities of p[...]nce, sportsmanship and dedication to hockey." Winner selected by a poll among the 30 chapters of the PHWA at the end of the regular season. A $2,500 grant from the PHWA is awarded annually to the Bill Masterton Scholarship Fund, based in Bloomington, MN, in the name of the Masterton Trophy winner.

History: The trophy was presented by the NHL Writers' Association in 1968 to commemorate the late Bill Masterton, a player with the Minnesota North Stars, who exhibited to a high degree the qualities of perseverance, sportsmanship and dedication to hockey, and who died January 15, 1968.

2003-04 Winner: Bryan Berard, Chicago Blackhawks
Runners-up: Dave Andreychuk, Tampa Bay Lightning
Sheldon Souray, Montreal Canadiens

Chicago Blackhawks defenseman Bryan Berard missed the entire 2000-01 season recovering from an eye injury that many thought would be the end of his career. Instead, Berard worked his way back to the NHL in 2001-02 with the New York Rangers.

Despite damaged vision in one eye, Berard has continued to play at an elite level. He appeared in 58 games with the Blackhawks in 2003-04, recording 13 goals and 34 assists for 47 points – just one fewer than his career high with the New York Islanders in his Calder Trophy season of 1996-97 – and averaged nearly 22 minutes of ice time per game. Berard ranked second on the Blackhawks and eighth among NHL defensemen in scoring, despite appearing in far fewer games than the other leaders. Berard celebrated another milestone in his inspirational comeback when he appeared in his 500th career regular-season game March 17 against the Carolina Hurricanes.

LESTER PATRICK TROPHY

An annual award "for outstanding service to hockey in the United States." Eligible recipients are players, officials, coaches, executives and referees. Winners are selected by an award committee consisting of the commissioner of the NHL, an NHL governor, a representative of the New York Rangers, a member of the Hockey Hall of Fame builder's section, a member of the Hockey Hall of Fame player's section, a member of the U.S. Hockey Hall of Fame, a member of the NHL Broadcasters' Association and a member of the Professional Hockey Writers' Association. Each except the League Commissioner is rotated annually. The winner receives a miniature of the trophy.

History: Presented by the New York Rangers in 1966 to honor the late Lester Patrick, longtime general manager and coach of the New York Rangers, whose teams finished out of the playoffs only once in his first 16 years with the club.

2003-04 Winners: Mike Emrick
John Davidson
Ray Miron

Mike Emrick has been familiar to NHL fans across America for nearly 20 years and has spent the last five seasons as a play-by-play voice on ABC's National Hockey League coverage. Emrick's national credits include the past 17 Stanley Cup playoffs, seven Stanley Cup finals, five NHL All-Star Games, and three Olympic Winter Games (1992, 1994, 1998). "Doc" has spent most of his NHL broadcasting career in the New York area, including 14 seasons (11 consecutively) as the lead television play-by-play man for the New Jersey Devils.

John Davidson has appeared on all four major American television networks' hockey coverage, and currently is ABC's lead studio analyst. He also has served as the color commentator on New York Rangers telecasts for the Madison Square Garden Network for the past 18 seasons. An 11-year NHL goaltender, "J.D." was drafted in 1973 by St. Louis, where he played for two years, before moving to the Rangers. Forced into retirement by injury in 1983, Davidson quickly and smoothly made the shift into broadcasting. He is widely hailed as one of the most knowledgeable men associated with the sport.

Ray Miron managed and coached teams across North America for more than 50 years and also held many executive positions, serving as founder and president of a "new" Central Hockey League from 1992 to 1997 and commissioner of the Atlantic Coast Hockey League from 1983 to 1987. Miron also was general manager of the NHL's Colorado Rockies from 1976 to 1981. A native of Cornwall, Ontario, Miron began managing and coaching teams in hockey, lacrosse and baseball at age 16. Miron found a home in the Toronto Maple Leafs organization from 1964-65 through 1975-76, serving as coach and general manager for CHL affiliates Tulsa and Oklahoma City. In 1967-68, his Tulsa Oilers won the Adams Cup, the CHL championship.

LESTER B. PEARSON AWARD

An annual award presented to the NHL's outstanding player as selected by the members of the National Hockey League Players' Association. The winner receives $20,000, and the two runners-up receive $10,000 each to donate to the grassroots hockey program of their choice, through the NHLPA's Goals & Dreams Fund.

History: The award was first presented in 1970-71 by the NHLPA in honor of the late Lester B. Pearson, former Prime Minister of Canada.

2003-04 Winner: Martin St. Louis, Tampa Bay Lightning
Runners-up: Roberto Luongo, Florida Panthers
Joe Sakic, Colorado Avalanche

Martin St. Louis, having won his first Stanley Cup as a member of the Tampa Bay Lightning, polished off his career-year by winning the Lester B. Pearson Award. St. Louis, in his 6th NHL season, led the league in total points (94), assists (56), plus/minus (+35), and shorthanded goals (8), on his way to being voted by his peers as most outstanding player. As the winner, St. Louis allocated the $20,000 that accompanies the award to be divided equally amongst the Delta Association of Minor Hockey in Laval, Quebec and the Burlington Youth Hockey Association in Vermont. As finalists, Roberto Luongo designated his $10,000 to be shared between Bourassa Minor Hockey in Quebec and Air Canada's Dreams Take Flight program, while Joe Sakic distributed $10,000 evenly between the Minor Hockey Associations in Littleton, Colorado and White Rock, British Columbia.

King Clancy Memorial Trophy

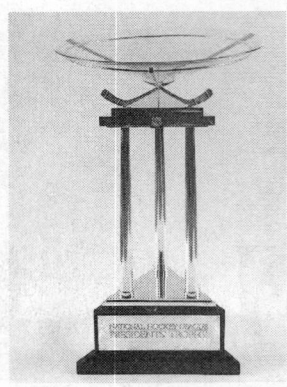

Presidents' Trophy

Maurice "Rocket" Richard Trophy

Bud Light Plus-Minus Award

KING CLANCY MEMORIAL TROPHY

An annual award "to the player who best exemplifies leadership qualities on and off the ice and has made a noteworthy humanitarian contribution in his community."

History: The King Clancy Memorial Trophy was presented to the National Hockey League by the Board of Governors in 1988 to honor the late Frank "King" Clancy.

2003-04 Winner: Jarome Iginla, Calgary Flames

Jarome Iginla's giving nature and warm approach to the people of Calgary makes him an excellent choice for the 2003-04 King Clancy Memorial Trophy. Since joining the Flames in 1996, he has made a priority of giving back to the community and has done so in a variety of ways.

Iginla takes an active role in all Flames' community programs, most notably as spokesperson for the club's "Reading ... Give It a Shot" program over the past six seasons. Through his participation in photo shoots, public service announcements and school visits, Iginla sends an effective message to kids on the importance of reading. The Flames captain also leads his teammates at their annual celebrity golf classic, celebrity waiter dinner, SuperSkills competition, holiday hospital visits and wheelchair hockey game against the Townsend Tigers.

Since 2000-01, Iginla has donated $1,000 for each goal he scores – including a league-leading 41 this season – to KidSport Calgary, which assists children in low-income families so they can participate in sports. In addition to making monetary donations to KidSport Calgary, Iginla fullfills his role as local spokesman by helping KidSport create awareness through filming PSA's, being involved in poster shoots and attending special events.

For the past two summers, Iginla has hosted his own non-profit summer hockey school in Calgary, providing 100 young players the opportunity to receive personal on and off-ice instruction and raising $7,000 for Easter Seal's Camp Horizon.

Two years ago Iginla was named an Honorary Special Events Chair for the Juvenile Diabetes Research Foundation of Calgary. He is an annual participant in their annual golf tournament and supports other JDRF special events, including their Awareness Month launch and Walk For A Cure.

Jarome Iginla also takes a special interest in the Canadian Spinal Research Organization, and in particular Shoot For a Cure, a program that raises money for spinal cord research, promotes safe hockey and increases awareness of neck injuries. He has lent his support through filming of public service announcements and donations to their programs.

PRESIDENTS' TROPHY

An annual award to the club finishing the regular-season with the best overall record. The winner receives $350,000, to be split between the team and its players.

History: Presented to the National Hockey League in 1985-86 by the NHL Board of Governors to recognize the team compiling the top regular-season record.

2003-04 Winner: Detroit Red Wings
Runners-up: Tampa Bay Lightning
San Jose Sharks

The Detroit Red Wings won the Presidents' Trophy for the second time in three years and the fourth time since 1995. The Red Wings led the NHL with a record of 48-21-11-2, which was good for 109 points. They also had the league's best home record at 30-7-4-0 and were second in the NHL with 255 goals scored. Detroit has won the Central Division three years in a row, four times in the last five seasons and seven times in the last ten. Tampa Bay won the Southeast Division title for the second straight season, and earned the top seed in the Eastern Conference with a franchise-best 46-22-8-6 record for 106 points. San Jose rebounded from a disappointing year to win the Pacific Division title for the second time in three seasons, posting a record of 43-21-12-6 for a franchise-record 104 points.

MAURICE "ROCKET" RICHARD TROPHY

An annual award "presented to the player finishing the regular season as the League's goal-scoring leader." The winner receives $10,000.

History: A gift to the NHL from the Montreal Canadiens in 1999, the Maurice "Rocket" Richard Trophy honors one of the game's greatest stars. During his 18-year career with the Canadiens from 1942-43 through 1959-60, Richard was the first player in NHL history to score 50 goals in a season and 500 in his career. He played on eight Stanley Cup champions and led the League in goal scoring five times.

2003-04 Winners: Rick Nash, Columbus Blue Jackets
Jarome Iginla, Calgary Flames
Ilya Kovalchuk, Atlanta Thrashers

Left wingers Rick Nash of the Columbus Blue Jackets and Ilya Kovalchuk of the Atlanta Thrashers, plus right winger Jarome Iginla of the Calgary Flames are co-winners of the 2003-04 Maurice "Rocket" Richard Trophy. Each tallied 41 goals.

At 19 years, 10 months, Nash became the youngest player to lead the NHL in goals – 14 months younger than 21-year-old Wayne Gretzky in 1981-82 – and was the first teenager to reach the 40-goal mark since the Los Angeles Kings' Jimmy Carson in 1987-88. Nash accounted for 23.2 percent of the Blue Jackets' goals this season (41 of 177), the highest percentage in the NHL. He notched a league-leading 19 power-play goals and tallied seven game-winners.

Kovalchuk began the season with 11 goals in his first 10 games and went on to record a career-high 41. Kovalchuk tallied 16 power-play goals, tied for third in the NHL, had six game-winning goals, led the League in shots on goal (341) and led all forwards in average ice time per game (23:41).

A shorthanded goal at Anaheim on the final day of the regular season earned Iginla a share of the trophy. Iginla, who captured the award for the second time in three years, had started the season slowly, with just four tallies in his first 21 games, but was the league's hottest scorer down the stretch, notching 20 goals in his last 30 contests.

BUD LIGHT PLUS-MINUS AWARD

An annual award "to the player, having played a minimum of 60 games, who leads the League in plus/minus statistics" at the end of the regular season.
Bud Light will contribute $5,000 on behalf of the winner to the charity of his choice.

History: This award was first presented to the NHL in 1997-98 by Anheuser-Busch Inc. to recognize the League leader in plus-minus statistics. Plus-minus statistics are calculated by giving a player a "plus" when on-ice for an even-strength or short-handed goal scored by his team. He receives a "minus" when on-ice for an even-strength or short-handed goal scored by the opposing team. A plus-minus award has been presented since the 1982-83 season.

2003-04 Winners: Marek Malik, Vancouver Canucks
Martin St. Louis, Tampa Bay Lightning
Runners-up: Zdeno Chara, Ottawa Senators
Fredrik Modin, Tampa Bay Lightning

Right winger Martin St. Louis of the Tampa Bay Lightning and defenseman Marek Malik of the Vancouver Canucks were co-winners of the Bud Light Plus-Minus Award. Both players had a plus-minus rating of +35. St. Louis, with 94 points, led the NHL in scoring and helped Tampa Bay to the best record in the Eastern Conference (46-22-8-6, 106 points). Malik helped lead Vancouver to a first-place finish in the Northwest Division and third overall in the Western Conference (43-24-10-5, 101 points) St. Louis and Marek were followed by Zdeno Chara of Ottawa (+33), and St. Louis' Tampa Bay teammate Fredrik Modin (+31). Colorado teammates Alex Tanguay and Nils Ekman were both +30.

*MBNA/Mastercard Roger Crozier
Saving Grace Award*

*Bud Light NHL All-Star Game
MVP Award*

MBNA/MASTERCARD
ROGER CROZIER SAVING GRACE AWARD

An award "presented to the goaltender having played a minimum of 25 games with the NHL's best save percentage during the regular season." The winner receives $25,000 to be donated to the youth hockey or educational program of his choice.

History: This award was first presented to the league in 1999-2000 by MBNA Corporation. It is named for Roger Crozier, one of the NHL's top goaltenders during his career. Crozier joined MBNA America Bank in 1983. He passed away on Jan. 11, 1996. Save percentage is calculated by dividing total saves by total shots faced.

2003-04 Winner: **Dwayne Roloson, Minnesota Wild**
Runners-up: **Miikka Kiprusoff, Calgary Flames**
Roberto Luongo, Flordia Panthers

Dwayne Roloson of the Minnesota Wild won the MBNA/MasterCard Roger Crozier Saving Grace Award by compiling a .932728 save percentage (1,323 shots, 1,234 saves) in 48 games. Roloson narrowly edged Miikka Kiprusoff of the Calgary Flames, who finished with a .932712 save percentage (966 shots, 901 saves) in 38 appearances, by just .000016. The Wild netminder made 24 saves in shutting out the St. Louis Blues on the final day of the season to surpass Kiprusoff. Rounding out the top five were Roberto Luongo of the Florida Panthers (.931), Vesa Toskala of the San Jose Sharks (.930) and Andrew Raycroft of the Boston Bruins (.926). Roloson received a trophy and a check for $25,000 (U.S.), which he donated to the The Norfolk Pros Foundation, a Simcoe, Ontario-based organization dedicated to helping youth by working toward the relief of poverty and the advancement of education.

BUD LIGHT NHL ALL-STAR GAME MVP AWARD

1962	Eddie Shack, Tor.	1984	Don Maloney, NYR
1963	Frank Mahovlich, Tor.	1985	Mario Lemieux, Pit.
1964	Jean Beliveau, Mtl.	1986	Grant Fuhr, Edm.
1965	Gordie Howe, Det.	1988	Mario Lemieux, Pit.
1967	Henri Richard, Mtl.	1989	Wayne Gretzky, L.A.
1968	Bruce Gamble, Tor.	1990	Mario Lemieux, Pit.
1969	Frank Mahovlich, Det.	1991	Vincent Damphousse, Tor.
1970	Bobby Hull, Chi.	1992	Brett Hull, St.L.
1971	Bobby Hull, Chi.	1993	Mike Gartner, NYR
1972	Bobby Orr, Bos.	1994	Mike Richter, NYR
1973	Greg Polis, Pit.	1996	Raymond Bourque, Bos.
1974	Garry Unger, St.L.	1997	Mark Recchi, Mtl.
1975	Syl Apps Jr., Pit.	1998	Teemu Selanne, Ana.
1976	Pete Mahovlich, Mtl.	1999	Wayne Gretzky, NYR
1977	Rick Martin, Buf.	2000	Pavel Bure, Fla.
1978	Billy Smith, NYI	2001	Bill Guerin, Bos.
1980	Reggie Leach, Phi.	2002	Eric Daze, Chi.
1981	Mike Liut, St.L.	2003	Dany Heatley, Atl.
1982	Mike Bossy, NYI	2004	Joe Sakic, Col.
1983	Wayne Gretzky, Edm.		

NHL/SHERATON ROAD PERFORMER AWARD

An award "to the players who accumulate the most road points." The player with the most road points at the end of each month is recognized as the monthly winner. At season's end, the player who accrues the most road points during the regular season wins year-end honors. Sheraton will donate one million Starpoints ® to the charity of the player's choice. Points can be used for travel expenses including hotel stays, airline tickets and more.

History: This award was introduced for the 2003-04 season by the NHL and Sheraton Hotels & Resorts Worldwide, Inc

2003-04 Winner: **Joe Sakic, Colorado Avalanche**
Runners-up: **Ilya Kovalchuk, Atlanta**
Alex Tanguay, Colorado
Martin St. Louis, Tampa Bay

Joe Sakic of the Colorado Avalanche, with 49 points (22 goals, 27 assists) in 41 road games, captured the inaugural NHL/Sheraton Road Performer Award. Ilya Kovalchuk of the Atlanta Thrashers was runner-up with 48 road points. Alex Tanguay and Martin St. Louis tied for third with 47 road points. Sakic and Tanguay helped the Avalanche compile the best road record in the Western Conference with a mark of 21-8-7-5 and 54 points. As the winner, Sakic receives a Sheraton Sweet Sleeper BedSM. Sheraton will donate a million Starpoints ® on behalf of Sakic to the A-T Children's Project. The A-T Children's Project raises funds to support and coordinate biomedical research projects, scientific conferences and a clinical center aimed at finding a cure for ataxia-telangiectasia, a rare genetic disease that causes progressive loss of motor control, cancer and immune system problems.

Islanders goalie Rick DiPietro began the season with a shutout streak of 115 minutes and 59 seconds, including his first career shutout on October 11. He was 2-0-1 with a 0.83 average to open the season as the NHL's Defensive Player of the Week.

Washington Capitals center Jeff Halpern led all NHL players in scoring with eight points (four goals, four assists) and a +8 rating in four games to win NHL Offensive Player of the Week honors for the final week of the 2003-04 season.

NHL AWARD MONEY BREAKDOWN — 2003-04

(Players on each club determine how team award money is divided.)

TEAM AWARDS

Stanley Cup Playoffs	Number of Clubs	Share Per Club	Total
Conference Quarter-Final Losers	8	$ 276,575	$2,212,600
Conference Semi-Final Losers	4	481,525	1,926,100
Conference Championship Losers	2	1,053,525	2,107,050
Stanley Cup Loser	1	1,713,150	1,713,150
Stanley Cup Winner	1	2,501,100	2,501,000
TOTAL PLAYOFF AWARD MONEY			$10,460,000

Final Standings, Regular Season	Number of Clubs	Share Per Club	Total
Presidents' Trophy*			
Club's Share	1	$ 100,000	$ 100,000
Players' Share	1	250,000	250,000
Conference First Place*	2	500,000	1,000,000
Conference Second Place*	2	375,000	750,000
Conference Third Place*	2	250,000	500,000
Conference Fourth Place*	2	125,000	250,000
*based on points.			
TOTAL REGULAR-SEASON AWARD MONEY			$2,850,000

INDIVIDUAL AWARDS	Winner	First Runner-up	Second Runner-up
Hart, Calder, Norris, Ross, Vezina, Byng, Selke, Jennings, Masterton Trophies	$10,000	$6,000	$4,000
King Clancy Trophy	$ 3,000	$1,000	
Conn Smythe and Maurice Richard Trophies	$10,000		
TOTAL INDIVIDUAL AWARD MONEY			$204,000

ALL-STARS	Number of winners	Per Player	Total
First Team All-Stars	6	$10,000	$ 60,000
Second Team All-Stars	6	5,000	$ 30,000
TOTAL ALL-STAR AWARD MONEY			$ 90,000
TOTAL AWARD MONEY			**$13,604,000**

2003-04 NHL Player of the Week/Month Award Winners

Player of the Week/Month

Period Ending	Offensive Player	Defensive Player
Oct. 19	**Ilya Kovalchuk**, Atlanta	**Rick DiPietro**, NY Islanders
Oct. 26	**Ilya Kovalchuk**, Atlanta	**Martin Biron**, Buffalo
October	**Ilya Kovalchuk**, Atlanta	**Nikolai Khabibulin**, Tampa Bay
Nov. 2	**Bill Guerin**, Dallas	**Robert Esche**, Philadelphia
Nov. 9	**Markus Naslund**, Vancouver	**Adrian Aucoin**, NY Islanders
Nov. 16	**Robert Lang**, Washington	**Ty Conklin**, Edmonton
Nov. 23	**Martin Rucinsky**, NY Rangers	**Jassen Cullimore**, Tampa Bay
		Corey Sarich, Tampa Bay
Nov. 30	**Markus Naslund**, Vancouver	**Tomas Vokoun**, Nashville
November	**Robert Lang**, Washington	**Martin Brodeur**, New Jersey
Dec. 7	**Shean Donovan**, Calgary	**Miikka Kiprusoff**, Calgary
Dec. 14	**Pavel Datsyuk**, Detroit	**Martin Brodeur**, New Jersey
Dec. 21	**Robert Lang**, Washington	**Dwayne Roloson**, Minnesota
Dec. 28	**Scott Walker**, Nashville	**Michael Leighton**, Chicago
December	**Pavel Datsyuk**, Detroit	**Miikka Kiprusoff**, Calgary
Jan. 4	**Mark Messier**, NY Rangers	**Brian Boucher**, Phoenix
Jan. 11	**Jarome Iginla**, Calgary	**Brian Boucher**, Phoenix
Jan. 18	**Martin Havlat**, Ottawa	**Chris Pronger**, St. Louis
Jan. 25	**Milan Hejduk**, Colorado	**Ed Belfour**, Toronto
January	**Martin St. Louis**, Tampa Bay	**Wade Redden**, Ottawa
Feb. 1	**Glen Murray**, Boston	**Andrew Raycroft**, Boston
Feb. 15	**Vincent Lecavalier**, Tampa Bay	**Miikka Kiprusoff**, Calgary
Feb. 22	**Steve Sullivan**, Nashville	**Olaf Kolzig**, Washington
Feb. 29	**David Vyborny**, Columbus	**Jose Theodore**, Montreal
February	**Martin St. Louis**, Tampa Bay	**Evgeni Nabokov**, San Jose
Mar. 7	**Richard Zednik**, Montreal	**Nikolai Khabibulin**, Tampa Bay
Mar. 14	**Joe Sakic**, Colorado	**Robert Esche**, Philadelphia
Mar. 21	**Brian Leetch**, Toronto	**Adrian Aucoin**, NY Islanders
Mar. 28	**Patrick Elias**, New Jersey	**Evgeni Nabokov**, San Jose
March	**Scott Gomez**, New Jersey	**Chris Osgood**, St. Louis
Apr. 4	**Jeff Halpern**, Washington	**Ed Belfour**, Toronto

Rookie of the Month

Month	Player
October	**Marc-Andre Fleury**, Pittsburgh
November	**Jason King**, Vancouver
December	**Trent Hunter**, NY Islanders
January	**Andrew Raycroft**, Boston
February	**Michael Ryder**, Montreal
March	**Tuomo Ruutu**, Chicago

NATIONAL HOCKEY LEAGUE INDIVIDUAL AWARD WINNERS

ART ROSS TROPHY

	Winner	Runner-up
2004	Martin St. Louis, T.B.	Ilya Kovalchuk, Atl.
2003	Peter Forsberg, Col.	Markus Naslund, Van.
2002	Jarome Iginla, Cgy.	Markus Naslund, Van.
2001	Jaromir Jagr, Pit.	Joe Sakic, Col.
2000	Jaromir Jagr, Pit.	Pavel Bure, Fla.
1999	Jaromir Jagr, Pit.	Teemu Selanne, Ana.
1998	Jaromir Jagr, Pit.	Peter Forsberg, Col.
1997	Mario Lemieux, Pit.	Teemu Selanne, Ana.
1996	Mario Lemieux, Pit.	Jaromir Jagr, Pit.
1995	Jaromir Jagr, Pit.	Eric Lindros, Phi.
1994	Wayne Gretzky, L.A.	Sergei Fedorov, Det.
1993	Mario Lemieux, Pit.	Pat LaFontaine, Buf.
1992	Mario Lemieux, Pit.	Kevin Stevens, Pit.
1991	Wayne Gretzky, L.A.	Brett Hull, St.L.
1990	Wayne Gretzky, L.A.	Mark Messier, Edm.
1989	Mario Lemieux, Pit.	Wayne Gretzky, L.A.
1988	Mario Lemieux, Pit.	Wayne Gretzky, Edm.
1987	Wayne Gretzky, Edm.	Jari Kurri, Edm.
1986	Wayne Gretzky, Edm.	Mario Lemieux, Pit.
1985	Wayne Gretzky, Edm.	Jari Kurri, Edm.
1984	Wayne Gretzky, Edm.	Paul Coffey, Edm.
1983	Wayne Gretzky, Edm.	Peter Stastny, Que.
1982	Wayne Gretzky, Edm.	Mike Bossy, NYI
1981	Wayne Gretzky, Edm.	Marcel Dionne, L.A.
1980	Marcel Dionne, L.A.	Wayne Gretzky, Edm.
1979	Bryan Trottier, NYI	Marcel Dionne, L.A.
1978	Guy Lafleur, Mtl.	Bryan Trottier, NYI
1977	Guy Lafleur, Mtl.	Marcel Dionne, L.A.
1976	Guy Lafleur, Mtl.	Bobby Clarke, Phi.
1975	Bobby Orr, Bos.	Phil Esposito, Bos.
1974	Phil Esposito, Bos.	Bobby Orr, Bos.
1973	Phil Esposito, Bos.	Bobby Clarke, Phi.
1972	Phil Esposito, Bos.	Bobby Orr, Bos.
1971	Phil Esposito, Bos.	Bobby Orr, Bos.
1970	Bobby Orr, Bos.	Phil Esposito, Bos.
1969	Phil Esposito, Bos.	Bobby Hull, Chi.
1968	Stan Mikita, Chi.	Phil Esposito, Bos.
1967	Stan Mikita, Chi.	Bobby Hull, Chi.
1966	Bobby Hull, Chi.	Stan Mikita, Chi.
1965	Stan Mikita, Chi.	Norm Ullman, Det.
1964	Stan Mikita, Chi.	Bobby Hull, Chi.
1963	Gordie Howe, Det.	Andy Bathgate, NYR
1962	Bobby Hull, Chi.	Andy Bathgate, NYR
1961	Bernie Geoffrion, Mtl.	Jean Beliveau, Mtl.
1960	Bobby Hull, Chi.	Bronco Horvath, Bos.
1959	Dickie Moore, Mtl.	Jean Beliveau, Mtl.
1958	Dickie Moore, Mtl.	Henri Richard, Mtl.
1957	Gordie Howe, Det.	Ted Lindsay, Det.
1956	Jean Beliveau, Mtl.	Gordie Howe, Det.
1955	Bernie Geoffrion, Mtl.	Maurice Richard, Mtl.
1954	Gordie Howe, Det.	Maurice Richard, Mtl.
1953	Gordie Howe, Det.	Ted Lindsay, Det.
1952	Gordie Howe, Det.	Ted Lindsay, Det.
1951	Gordie Howe, Det.	Maurice Richard, Mtl.
1950	Ted Lindsay, Det.	Sid Abel, Det.
1949	Roy Conacher, Chi.	Doug Bentley, Chi.
1948*	Elmer Lach, Mtl.	Buddy O'Connor, NYR
1947	Max Bentley, Chi.	Maurice Richard, Mtl.
1946	Max Bentley, Chi.	Gaye Stewart, Tor.
1945	Elmer Lach, Mtl.	Maurice Richard, Mtl.
1944	Herb Cain, Bos.	Doug Bentley, Chi.
1943	Doug Bentley, Chi.	Bill Cowley, Bos.
1942	Bryan Hextall, NYR	Lynn Patrick, NYR
1941	Bill Cowley, Bos.	Bryan Hextall, NYR
1940	Milt Schmidt, Bos.	Woody Dumart, Bos.
1939	Toe Blake, Mtl.	Sweeney Schriner, NYA
1938	Gordie Drillon, Tor.	Syl Apps, Tor.
1937	Sweeney Schriner, NYA	Syl Apps, Tor.
1936	Sweeney Schriner, NYA	Marty Barry, Det.
1935	Charlie Conacher, Tor.	Syd Howe, St.L., Det.
1934	Charlie Conacher, Tor.	Joe Primeau, Tor
1933	Bill Cook, NYR	Busher Jackson, Tor.
1932	Busher Jackson, Tor.	Joe Primeau, Tor.
1931	Howie Morenz, Mtl.	Ebbie Goodfellow, Det.
1930	Cooney Weiland, Bos.	Frank Boucher, NYR
1929	Ace Bailey, Tor.	Nels Stewart, Mtl.M
1928	Howie Morenz, Mtl.	Aurel Joliat, Mtl.
1927	Bill Cook, NYR	Dick Irvin, Chi.
1926	Nels Stewart, Mtl.M.	Cy Denneny, Ott.
1925	Babe Dye, Tor.	Cy Denneny, Ott.
1924	Cy Denneny, Ott.	Billy Boucher, Mtl.
1923	Babe Dye, Tor.	Cy Denneny, Ott.
1922	Punch Broadbent, Ott.	Cy Denneny, Ott.
1921	Newsy Lalonde, Mtl.	Babe Dye, Ham., Tor.
1920	Joe Malone, Que.	Newsy Lalonde, Mtl.
1919	Newsy Lalonde, Mtl.	Odie Cleghorn, Mtl.
1918	Joe Malone, Mtl.	Cy Denneny, Ott.

* Trophy first awarded in 1948.
Scoring leaders listed from 1918 to 1947.

HART MEMORIAL TROPHY

	Winner	Runner-up
2004	Martin St. Louis, T.B.	Jarome Iginla, Cgy.
2003	Peter Forsberg, Col.	Markus Naslund, Van.
2002	Jose Theodore, Mtl.	Jarome Iginla, Cgy.
2001	Joe Sakic, Col.	Mario Lemieux, Pit.
2000	Chris Pronger, St.L.	Jaromir Jagr, Pit.
1999	Jaromir Jagr, Pit.	Alexei Yashin, Ott.
1998	Dominik Hasek, Buf.	Jaromir Jagr, Pit.
1997	Dominik Hasek, Buf.	Paul Kariya, Ana.
1996	Mario Lemieux, Pit.	Mark Messier, NYR
1995	Eric Lindros, Phi.	Jaromir Jagr, Pit.
1994	Sergei Fedorov, Det.	Dominik Hasek, Buf.
1993	Mario Lemieux, Pit.	Doug Gilmour, Tor.
1992	Mark Messier, NYR	Patrick Roy, Mtl.
1991	Brett Hull, St.L.	Wayne Gretzky, L.A.
1990	Mark Messier, Edm.	Raymond Bourque, Bos.
1989	Wayne Gretzky, L.A.	Mario Lemieux, Pit.
1988	Mario Lemieux, Pit.	Grant Fuhr, Edm.
1987	Wayne Gretzky, Edm.	Raymond Bourque, Bos.
1986	Wayne Gretzky, Edm.	Mario Lemieux, Pit.
1985	Wayne Gretzky, Edm.	Dale Hawerchuk, Wpg.
1984	Wayne Gretzky, Edm.	Rod Langway, Wsh.
1983	Wayne Gretzky, Edm.	Pete Peeters, Bos.
1982	Wayne Gretzky, Edm.	Bryan Trottier, NYI
1981	Wayne Gretzky, Edm.	Mike Liut, St.L.
1980	Wayne Gretzky, Edm.	Marcel Dionne, L.A.
1979	Bryan Trottier, NYI	Guy Lafleur, Mtl
1978	Guy Lafleur, Mtl.	Bryan Trottier, NYI
1977	Guy Lafleur, Mtl.	Bobby Clarke, Phi.
1976	Bobby Clarke, Phi.	Denis Potvin, NYI
1975	Bobby Clarke, Phi.	Rogie Vachon, L.A.
1974	Phil Esposito, Bos.	Bernie Parent, Phi.
1973	Bobby Clarke, Phi.	Phil Esposito, Bos.
1972	Bobby Orr, Bos.	Ken Dryden, Mtl.
1971	Bobby Orr, Bos.	Phil Esposito, Bos.
1970	Bobby Orr, Bos.	Tony Esposito, Chi.
1969	Phil Esposito, Bos.	Jean Beliveau, Mtl.
1968	Stan Mikita, Chi.	Jean Beliveau, Mtl.
1967	Stan Mikita, Chi.	Ed Giacomin, NYR
1966	Bobby Hull, Chi.	Jean Beliveau, Mtl.
1965	Bobby Hull, Chi.	Norm Ullman, Det.
1964	Jean Beliveau, Mtl.	Bobby Hull, Chi.
1963	Gordie Howe, Det.	Stan Mikita, Chi.
1962	Jacques Plante, Mtl.	Doug Harvey, NYR
1961	Bernie Geoffrion, Mtl.	Johnny Bower, Tor.
1960	Gordie Howe, Det.	Bobby Hull, Chi.
1959	Andy Bathgate, NYR	Gordie Howe, Det.
1958	Gordie Howe, Det.	Andy Bathgate, NYR
1957	Gordie Howe, Det.	Jean Beliveau, Mtl.
1956	Jean Beliveau, Mtl.	Tod Sloan, Tor.
1955	Ted Kennedy, Tor.	Harry Lumley, Tor.
1954	Al Rollins, Chi.	Red Kelly, Det.
1953	Gordie Howe, Det.	Al Rollins, Chi.
1952	Gordie Howe, Det.	Elmer Lach, Mtl.
1951	Milt Schmidt, Bos.	Maurice Richard, Mtl.
1950	Chuck Rayner, NYR	Ted Kennedy, Tor.
1949	Sid Abel, Det.	Bill Durnan, Mtl.
1948	Buddy O'Connor, NYR	Frank Brimsek, Bos.
1947	Maurice Richard, Mtl.	Milt Schmidt, Bos.
1946	Max Bentley, Chi.	Gaye Stewart, Tor.
1945	Elmer Lach, Mtl.	Maurice Richard, Mtl.
1944	Babe Pratt, Tor.	Bill Cowley, Bos.
1943	Bill Cowley, Bos.	Doug Bentley, Chi.
1942	Tom Anderson, Bro.	Syl Apps, Tor.
1941	Bill Cowley, Bos.	Dit Clapper, Bos.
1940	Ebbie Goodfellow, Det.	Syl Apps, Tor.
1939	Toe Blake, Mtl.	Syl Apps, Tor.
1938	Eddie Shore, Bos.	Paul Thompson, Chi.
1937	Babe Siebert, Mtl.	Lionel Conacher, Mtl.M
1936	Eddie Shore, Bos.	Hooley Smith, Mtl.M
1935	Eddie Shore, Bos.	Charlie Conacher, Tor.
1934	Aurel Joliat, Mtl.	Lionel Conacher, Chi.
1933	Eddie Shore, Bos.	Bill Cook, NYR
1932	Howie Morenz, Mtl.	Ching Johnson, NYR
1931	Howie Morenz, Mtl.	Eddie Shore, Bos.
1930	Nels Stewart, Mtl.M.	Lionel Hitchman, Bos.
1929	Roy Worters, NYA	Ace Bailey, Tor.
1928	Howie Morenz, Mtl.	Roy Worters, Pit.
1927	Herb Gardiner, Mtl.	Bill Cook, NYR
1926	Nels Stewart, Mtl.M.	Sprague Cleghorn, Bos.
1925	Billy Burch, Ham.	Howie Morenz, Mtl.
1924	Frank Nighbor, Ott.	Sprague Cleghorn, Mtl.

WILLIAM M. JENNINGS TROPHY

	Winner	Runner-up
2004	Martin Brodeur, N.J.	Marty Turco, Dal.
2003	Martin Brodeur, N.J.	Marty Turco, Dal.
	Roman Cechmanek, Phi.	Ron Tugnutt, Dal.
	Robert Esche, Phi.	
2002	Patrick Roy, Col.	Tommy Salo, Edm.
2001	Dominik Hasek, Buf.	Ed Belfour, Dal.
		Marty Turco, Dal.
2000	Roman Turek, St.L.	John Vanbiesbrouck, Phi.
		Brian Boucher, Phi.
1999	Ed Belfour, Dal.	Dominik Hasek, Buf.
	Roman Turek, Dal.	
1998	Martin Brodeur, N.J.	Ed Belfour, Dal.
1997	Martin Brodeur, N.J.	Chris Osgood, Det.
	Mike Dunham, N.J.	Mike Vernon, Det.
1996	Chris Osgood, Det.	Martin Brodeur, N.J.
	Mike Vernon, Det.	
1995	Ed Belfour, Chi.	Mike Vernon, Det.
		Chris Osgood, Det.
1994	Dominik Hasek, Buf.	Martin Brodeur, N.J.
	Grant Fuhr, Buf.	Chris Terreri, N.J.
1993	Ed Belfour, Chi.	Felix Potvin, Tor.
		Grant Fuhr, Tor.
1992	Patrick Roy, Mtl.	Ed Belfour, Chi.
1991	Ed Belfour, Chi.	Patrick Roy, Mtl.
1990	Andy Moog, Bos.	Patrick Roy, Mtl.
	Reggie Lemelin, Bos.	Brian Hayward, Mtl.
1989	Patrick Roy, Mtl.	Mike Vernon, Cgy.
	Brian Hayward, Mtl.	Rick Wamsley, Cgy.
1988	Patrick Roy, Mtl.	Clint Malarchuk, Wsh.
	Brian Hayward, Mtl.	Pete Peeters, Wsh.
1987	Patrick Roy, Mtl.	Ron Hextall, Phi.
	Brian Hayward, Mtl.	
1986	Bob Froese, Phi.	Al Jensen, Wsh.
	Darren Jensen, Phi.	Pete Peeters, Wsh.
1985	Tom Barrasso, Buf.	Pat Riggin, Wsh.
	Bob Sauve, Buf.	
1984	Al Jensen, Wsh.	Tom Barrasso, Buf.
	Pat Riggin, Wsh.	Bob Sauve, Buf.
1983	Roland Melanson, NYI	Pete Peeters, Bos.
	Billy Smith, NYI	
1982	Rick Wamsley, Mtl.	Billy Smith, NYI
	Denis Herron, Mtl.	Roland Melanson, NYI

BILL MASTERTON MEMORIAL TROPHY

2004	Bryan Berard	Chicago
2003	Steve Yzerman	Detroit
2002	Saku Koivu	Montreal
2001	Adam Graves	NY Rangers
2000	Ken Daneyko	New Jersey
1999	John Cullen	Tampa Bay
1998	Jamie McLennan	St. Louis
1997	Tony Granato	San Jose
1996	Gary Roberts	Calgary
1995	Pat LaFontaine	Buffalo
1994	Cam Neely	Boston
1993	Mario Lemieux	Pittsburgh
1992	Mark Fitzpatrick	NY Islanders
1991	Dave Taylor	Los Angeles
1990	Gord Kluzak	Boston
1989	Tim Kerr	Philadelphia
1988	Bob Bourne	Los Angeles
1987	Doug Jarvis	Hartford
1986	Charlie Simmer	Boston
1985	Anders Hedberg	NY Rangers
1984	Brad Park	Detroit
1983	Lanny McDonald	Calgary
1982	Glenn Resch	Colorado
1981	Blake Dunlop	St. Louis
1980	Al MacAdam	Minnesota
1979	Serge Savard	Montreal
1978	Butch Goring	Los Angeles
1977	Ed Westfall	NY Islanders
1976	Rod Gilbert	NY Rangers
1975	Don Luce	Buffalo
1974	Henri Richard	Montreal
1973	Lowell MacDonald	Pittsburgh
1972	Bobby Clarke	Philadelphia
1971	Jean Ratelle	NY Rangers
1970	Pit Martin	Chicago
1969	Ted Hampson	Oakland
1968	Claude Provost	Montreal

BUD LIGHT PLUS-MINUS AWARD

2004	Marek Malik	Vancouver
	Martin St. Louis	Tampa Bay
2003	Peter Forsberg	Colorado
	Milan Hejduk	Colorado
2002	Chris Chelios	Detroit
2001	Patrik Elias	New Jersey
	Joe Sakic	Colorado

NHL/SHERATON ROAD PERFORMER AWARD

2004	Joe Sakic	Colorado

LADY BYNG MEMORIAL TROPHY

	Winner	Runner-up
2004	Brad Richards, T.B.	Daniel Alfredsson, Ott.
2003	Alexander Mogilny, Tor.	Nicklas Lidstrom, Det.
2002	Ron Francis, Car.	Joe Sakic, Col.
2001	Joe Sakic, Col.	Nicklas Lidstrom, Det.
2000	Pavol Demitra, St.L.	Nicklas Lidstrom, Det.
1999	Wayne Gretzky, NYR.	Nicklas Lidstrom, Det.
1998	Ron Francis, Pit.	Teemu Selanne, Ana.
1997	Paul Kariya, Ana.	Teemu Selanne, Ana.
1996	Paul Kariya, Ana.	Adam Oates, Bos.
1995	Ron Francis, Pit.	Adam Oates, Bos.
1994	Wayne Gretzky, L.A.	Adam Oates, Bos.
1993	Pierre Turgeon, NYI	Adam Oates, Bos.
1992	Wayne Gretzky, L.A.	Joe Sakic, Que.
1991	Wayne Gretzky, L.A.	Brett Hull, St.L.
1990	Brett Hull, St.L.	Wayne Gretzky, L.A.
1989	Joe Mullen, Cgy.	Wayne Gretzky, L.A.
1988	Mats Naslund, Mtl.	Wayne Gretzky, Edm.
1987	Joe Mullen, Cgy.	Wayne Gretzky, Edm.
1986	Mike Bossy, NYI	Jari Kurri, Edm.
1985	Jari Kurri, Edm.	Joe Mullen, St.L.
1984	Mike Bossy, NYI	Rick Middleton, Bos.
1983	Mike Bossy, NYI	Rick Middleton, Bos.
1982	Rick Middleton, Bos.	Mike Bossy, NYI
1981	Rick Kehoe, Pit.	Wayne Gretzky, Edm.
1980	Wayne Gretzky, Edm.	Marcel Dionne, L.A.
1979	Bob MacMillan, Atl.	Marcel Dionne, L.A.
1978	Butch Goring, L.A.	Peter McNab, Bos.
1977	Marcel Dionne, L.A.	Jean Ratelle, Bos.
1976	Jean Ratelle, NYR-Bos.	Jean Pronovost, Pit.
1975	Marcel Dionne, Det.	John Bucyk, Bos.
1974	John Bucyk, Bos.	Lowell MacDonald, Pit.
1973	Gilbert Perreault, Buf.	Jean Ratelle, NYR
1972	Jean Ratelle, NYR	John Bucyk, Bos.
1971	John Bucyk, Bos.	Dave Keon, Tor.
1970	Phil Goyette, St.L.	John Bucyk, Bos.
1969	Alex Delvecchio, Det.	Ted Hampson, Oak.
1968	Stan Mikita, Chi.	John Bucyk, Bos.
1967	Stan Mikita, Chi.	Dave Keon, Tor.
1966	Alex Delvecchio, Det.	Bobby Rousseau, Mtl.
1965	Bobby Hull, Chi.	Alex Delvecchio, Det.
1964	Kenny Wharram, Chi.	Dave Keon, Tor.
1963	Dave Keon, Tor.	Camille Henry, NYR
1962	Dave Keon, Tor.	Claude Provost, Mtl.
1961	Red Kelly, Tor.	Norm Ullman, Det.
1960	Don McKenney, Bos.	Andy Hebenton, NYR
1959	Alex Delvecchio, Det.	Andy Hebenton, NYR
1958	Camille Henry, NYR	Don Marshall, Mtl.
1957	Andy Hebenton, NYR	Dutch Reibel, Det.
1956	Dutch Reibel, Det.	Floyd Curry, Mtl.
1955	Sid Smith, Tor.	Danny Lewicki, NYR
1954	Red Kelly, Det.	Don Raleigh, NYR
1953	Red Kelly, Det.	Wally Hergesheimer, NYR
1952	Sid Smith, Tor.	Red Kelly, Det.
1951	Red Kelly, Det.	Woody Dumart, Bos.
1950	Edgar Laprade, NYR	Red Kelly, Det.
1949	Bill Quackenbush, Det.	Harry Watson, Tor.
1948	Buddy O'Connor, NYR	Syl Apps, Tor.
1947	Bobby Bauer, Bos.	Syl Apps, Tor.
1946	Toe Blake, Mtl.	Clint Smith, Chi.
1945	Bill Mosienko, Chi.	Syd Howe, Det.
1944	Clint Smith, Chi.	Herb Cain, Bos.
1943	Max Bentley, Chi.	Buddy O'Connor, Mtl.
1942	Syl Apps, Tor.	Gordie Drillon, Tor.
1941	Bobby Bauer, Bos.	Gordie Drillon, Tor.
1940	Bobby Bauer, Bos.	Clint Smith, NYR
1939	Clint Smith, NYR	Marty Barry, Det.
1938	Gordie Drillon, Tor.	Clint Smith, NYR
1937	Marty Barry, Det.	Gordie Drillon, Tor.
1936	Doc Romnes, Chi.	Sweeney Schriner, NYA
1935	Frank Boucher, NYR	Russ Blinco, Mtl.M
1934	Frank Boucher, NYR	Joe Primeau, Tor.
1933	Frank Boucher, NYR	Joe Primeau, Tor.
1932	Joe Primeau, Tor.	Frank Boucher, NYR
1931	Frank Boucher, NYR	Normie Himes, NYA
1930	Frank Boucher, NYR	Normie Himes, NYA
1929	Frank Boucher, NYR	Harold Darragh, Pit.
1928	Frank Boucher, NYR	George Hay, Det.
1927	Billy Burch, NYA	Dick Irvin, Chi.
1926	Frank Nighbor, Ott.	Billy Burch, NYA
1925	Frank Nighbor, Ott.	none

KING CLANCY MEMORIAL TROPHY

2004	Jarome Iginla	Calgary
2003	Brendan Shanahan	Detroit
2002	Ron Francis	Carolina
2001	Shjon Podein	Colorado
2000	Curtis Joseph	Toronto
1999	Rob Ray	Buffalo
1998	Kelly Chase	St. Louis
1997	Trevor Linden	Vancouver
1996	Kris King	Winnipeg
1995	Joe Nieuwendyk	Calgary
1994	Adam Graves	NY Rangers
1993	Dave Poulin	Boston
1992	Raymond Bourque	Boston
1991	Dave Taylor	Los Angeles
1990	Kevin Lowe	Edmonton
1989	Bryan Trottier	NY Islanders
1988	Lanny McDonald	Calgary

VEZINA TROPHY

	Winner	Runner-up
2004	Martin Brodeur, N.J.	Miikka Kiprusoff, Cgy.
2003	Martin Brodeur, N.J.	Marty Turco, Dal.
2002	Jose Theodore, Mtl.	Patrick Roy, Col.
2001	Dominik Hasek, Buf.	Roman Cechmanek, Phi.
2000	Olaf Kolzig, Wsh.	Roman Turek, St.L.
1999	Dominik Hasek, Buf.	Curtis Joseph, Tor.
1998	Dominik Hasek, Buf.	Martin Brodeur, N.J.
1997	Dominik Hasek, Buf.	Martin Brodeur, N.J.
1996	Jim Carey, Wsh.	Chris Osgood, Det.
1995	Dominik Hasek, Buf.	Ed Belfour, Chi.
1994	Dominik Hasek, Buf.	John Vanbiesbrouck, Fla.
1993	Ed Belfour, Chi.	Tom Barrasso, Pit.
1992	Patrick Roy, Mtl.	Kirk McLean, Van.
1991	Ed Belfour, Chi.	Patrick Roy, Mtl.
1990	Patrick Roy, Mtl.	Daren Puppa, Buf.
1989	Patrick Roy, Mtl.	Mike Vernon, Cgy.
1988	Grant Fuhr, Edm.	Tom Barrasso, Buf.
1987	Ron Hextall, Phi.	Mike Liut, Hfd.
1986	John Vanbiesbrouck, NYR	Bob Froese, Phi.
1985	Pelle Lindbergh, Phi.	Tom Barrasso, Buf.
1984	Tom Barrasso, Buf.	Reggie Lemelin, Cgy.
1983	Pete Peeters, Bos.	Roland Melanson, NYI
1982	Billy Smith, NYI	Grant Fuhr, Edm.
1981	Richard Sevigny, Mtl.	Pete Peeters, Phi.
	Denis Herron, Mtl.	Rick St. Croix, Phi.
	Michel Larocque, Mtl.	
1980	Bob Sauve, Buf.	Gerry Cheevers, Bos.
	Don Edwards, Buf.	Gilles Gilbert, Bos.
1979	Ken Dryden, Mtl.	Glenn Resch, NYI
	Michel Larocque, Mtl.	Billy Smith, NYI
1978	Ken Dryden, Mtl.	Bernie Parent, Phi.
	Michel Larocque, Mtl.	Wayne Stephenson, Phi.
1977	Ken Dryden, Mtl.	Glenn Resch, NYI
	Michel Larocque, Mtl.	Billy Smith, NYI
1976	Ken Dryden, Mtl.	Glenn Resch, NYI
		Billy Smith, NYI
1975	Bernie Parent, Phi.	Rogie Vachon, L.A.
		Gary Edwards, L.A.
1974	Bernie Parent, Phi. (tie)	Gilles Gilbert, Bos.
	Tony Esposito, Chi. (tie)	
1973	Ken Dryden, Mtl.	Ed Giacomin, NYR
		Gilles Villemure, NYR
1972	Tony Esposito, Chi.	Cesare Maniago, Min.
	Gary Smith, Chi.	Gump Worsley, Min.
1971	Ed Giacomin, NYR	Tony Esposito, Chi.
	Gilles Villemure, NYR	
1970	Tony Esposito, Chi.	Jacques Plante, St.L.
		Ernie Wakely, St.L.
1969	Jacques Plante, St.L.	Ed Giacomin, NYR
	Glenn Hall, St.L.	
1968	Gump Worsley, Mtl.	Johnny Bower, Tor.
	Rogie Vachon, Mtl.	Bruce Gamble, Tor.
1967	Glenn Hall, Chi.	Charlie Hodge, Mtl.
	Denis Dejordy, Chi.	
1966	Gump Worsley, Mtl.	Glenn Hall, Chi.
	Charlie Hodge, Mtl.	
1965	Terry Sawchuk, Tor.	Roger Crozier, Det.
	Johnny Bower, Tor.	
1964	Charlie Hodge, Mtl.	Glenn Hall, Chi.
1963	Glenn Hall, Chi.	Johnny Bower, Tor.
		Don Simmons, Tor.
1962	Jacques Plante, Mtl.	Johnny Bower, Tor.
1961	Johnny Bower, Tor.	Glenn Hall, Chi.
1960	Jacques Plante, Mtl.	Glenn Hall, Chi.
1959	Jacques Plante, Mtl.	Johnny Bower, Tor.
		Ed Chadwick, Tor.
1958	Jacques Plante, Mtl.	Gump Worsley, NYR
		Marcel Paille, NYR
1957	Jacques Plante, Mtl.	Glenn Hall, Det.
1956	Jacques Plante, Mtl.	Glenn Hall, Det.
1955	Terry Sawchuk, Det.	Harry Lumley, Tor.
1954	Harry Lumley, Tor.	Terry Sawchuk, Det.
1953	Terry Sawchuk, Det.	Gerry McNeil, Mtl.
1952	Terry Sawchuk, Det.	Al Rollins, Tor.
1951	Al Rollins, Tor.	Terry Sawchuk, Det.
1950	Bill Durnan, Mtl.	Harry Lumley, Det.
1949	Bill Durnan, Mtl.	Harry Lumley, Det.
1948	Turk Broda, Tor.	Harry Lumley, Det.
1947	Bill Durnan, Mtl.	Turk Broda, Tor.
1946	Bill Durnan, Mtl.	Frank Brimsek, Bos.
1945	Bill Durnan, Mtl.	Frank McCool, Tor. (tie)
		Harry Lumley, Det. (tie)
1944	Bill Durnan, Mtl.	Paul Bibeault, Tor.
1943	Johnny Mowers, Det.	Turk Broda, Tor.
1942	Frank Brimsek, Bos.	Turk Broda, Tor.
1941	Turk Broda, Tor.	Frank Brimsek, Bos. (tie)
		Johnny Mowers, Det. (tie)
1940	Dave Kerr, NYR	Frank Brimsek, Bos.
1939	Frank Brimsek, Bos.	Dave Kerr, NYR
1938	Tiny Thompson, Bos.	Dave Kerr, NYR
1937	Normie Smith, Det.	Dave Kerr, NYR
1936	Tiny Thompson, Bos.	Mike Karakas, Chi.
1935	Lorne Chabot, Chi.	Alex Connell, Mtl.M
1934	Charlie Gardiner, Chi.	Wilf Cude, Det.
1933	Tiny Thompson, Bos.	John Ross Roach, Det.
1932	Charlie Gardiner, Chi.	Alex Connell, Det.
1931	Roy Worters, NYA	Charlie Gardiner, Chi.
1930	Tiny Thompson, Bos.	Charlie Gardiner, Chi.
1929	George Hainsworth, Mtl.	Tiny Thompson, Bos.
1928	George Hainsworth, Mtl.	Alex Connell, Ott.
1927	George Hainsworth, Mtl.	Clint Benedict, Mtl.M

CALDER MEMORIAL TROPHY

	Winner	Runner-up
2004	Andrew Raycroft, Bos.	Michael Ryder, Mtl.
2003	Barret Jackman, St.L.	Henrik Zetterberg, Det.
2002	Dany Heatley, Atl.	Ilya Kovalchuk, Atl.
2001	Evgeni Nabokov, S.J.	Brad Richards, T.B.
2000	Scott Gomez, N.J.	Brad Stuart, S.J.
1999	Chris Drury, Col.	Marian Hossa, Ott.
1998	Sergei Samsonov, Bos.	Mattias Ohlund, Van.
1997	Bryan Berard, NYI	Jarome Iginla, Cgy.
1996	Daniel Alfredsson, Ott.	Eric Daze, Chi.
1995	Peter Forsberg, Que.	Jim Carey, Wsh.
1994	Martin Brodeur, N.J.	Jason Arnott, Edm.
1993	Teemu Selanne, Wpg.	Joe Juneau, Bos.
1992	Pavel Bure, Van.	Nicklas Lidstrom, Det
1991	Ed Belfour, Chi.	Sergei Fedorov, Det.
1990	Sergei Makarov, Cgy.	Mike Modano, Min.
1989	Brian Leetch, NYR	Trevor Linden, Van.
1988	Joe Nieuwendyk, Cgy.	Ray Sheppard, Buf.
1987	Luc Robitaille, L.A.	Ron Hextall, Phi.
1986	Gary Suter, Cgy.	Wendel Clark, Tor.
1985	Mario Lemieux, Pit.	Chris Chelios, Mtl.
1984	Tom Barrasso, Buf.	Steve Yzerman, Det.
1983	Steve Larmer, Chi.	Phil Housley, Buf.
1982	Dale Hawerchuk, Wpg.	Barry Pederson, Bos.
1981	Peter Stastny, Que.	Larry Murphy, L.A.
1980	Raymond Bourque, Bos.	Mike Foligno, Det.
1979	Bobby Smith, Min	Ryan Walter, Wsh.
1978	Mike Bossy, NYI	Barry Beck, Col.
1977	Willi Plett, Atl.	Don Murdoch, NYR
1976	Bryan Trottier, NYI	Glenn Resch, NYI
1975	Eric Vail, Atl.	Pierre Larouche, Pit.
1974	Denis Potvin, NYI	Tom Lysiak, Atl.
1973	Steve Vickers, NYR	Bill Barber, Phi.
1972	Ken Dryden, Mtl.	Rick Martin, Buf.
1971	Gilbert Perreault, Buf.	Jude Drouin, Min.
1970	Tony Esposito, Chi.	Bill Fairbairn, NYR
1969	Danny Grant, Min.	Norm Ferguson, Oak.
1968	Derek Sanderson, Bos.	Jacques Lemaire, Mtl.
1967	Bobby Orr, Bos.	Ed Van Impe, Chi.
1966	Brit Selby, Tor.	Bert Marshall, Det.
1965	Roger Crozier, Det.	Ron Ellis, Tor.
1964	Jacques Laperriere, Mtl.	John Ferguson, Mtl.
1963	Kent Douglas, Tor.	Doug Barkley, Det.
1962	Bobby Rousseau, Mtl.	Cliff Pennington, Bos.
1961	Dave Keon, Tor.	Bob Nevin, Tor.
1960	Bill Hay, Chi.	Murray Oliver, Det.
1959	Ralph Backstrom, Mtl.	Carl Brewer, Tor.
1958	Frank Mahovlich, Tor.	Bobby Hull, Chi.
1957	Larry Regan, Bos.	Ed Chadwick, Tor.
1956	Glenn Hall, Det.	Andy Hebenton, NYR
1955	Ed Litzenberger, Chi.	Don McKenney, Bos.
1954	Camille Henry, NYR	Dutch Reibel, Det.
1953	Gump Worsley, NYR	Gord Hannigan, Tor.
1952	Bernie Geoffrion, Mtl.	Hy Buller, NYR
1951	Terry Sawchuk, Det.	Al Rollins, Tor.
1950	Jack Gelineau, Bos.	Phil Maloney, Bos.
1949	Pentti Lund, NYR	Allan Stanley, NYR
1948	Jim McFadden, Det.	Pete Babando, Bos.
1947	Howie Meeker, Tor.	Jim Conacher, Det.
1946	Edgar Laprade, NYR	George Gee, Chi.
1945	Frank McCool, Tor.	Ken Smith, Bos.
1944	Gus Bodnar, Tor.	Bill Durnan, Mtl.
1943	Gaye Stewart, Tor.	Glen Harmon, Mtl.
1942	Grant Warwick, NYR	Buddy O'Connor, Mtl.
1941	John Quilty, Mtl.	Johnny Mowers, Det.
1940	Kilby MacDonald, NYR	Wally Stanowski, Tor.
1939	Frank Brimsek, Bos.	Roy Conacher, Bos.
1938	Cully Dahlstrom, Chi.	Murph Chamberlain, Tor.
1937	Syl Apps, Tor.	Gordie Drillon, Tor.
1936	Mike Karakas, Chi.	Bucko McDonald, Det.
1935	Sweeney Schriner, NYA	Bert Connelly, NYR
1934	Russ Blinco, Mtl.M.	none
1933	Carl Voss, Det.	none

FRANK J. SELKE TROPHY

	Winner	Runner-up
2004	Kris Draper, Det.	John Madden, N.J.
2003	Jere Lehtinen, Dal.	John Madden, N.J.
2002	Michael Peca, NYI	Craig Conroy, Cgy.
2001	John Madden, N.J.	Joe Sakic, Col.
2000	Steve Yzerman, Det.	Michal Handzus, St.L.
1999	Jere Lehtinen, Dal.	Magnus Arvedson, Ott.
1998	Jere Lehtinen, Dal.	Michael Peca, Buf.
1997	Michael Peca, Buf.	Peter Forsberg, Col.
1996	Sergei Fedorov, Det.	Ron Francis, Pit.
1995	Ron Francis, Pit.	Esa Tikkanen, St.L.
1994	Sergei Fedorov, Det.	Doug Gilmour, Tor.
1993	Doug Gilmour, Tor.	Dave Poulin, Bos.
1992	Guy Carbonneau, Mtl.	Sergei Fedorov, Det.
1991	Dirk Graham, Chi.	Esa Tikkanen, Edm.
1990	Rick Meagher, St.L.	Guy Carbonneau, Mtl.
1989	Guy Carbonneau, Mtl.	Esa Tikkanen, Edm.
1988	Guy Carbonneau, Mtl.	Steve Kasper, Bos.
1987	Dave Poulin, Phi.	Guy Carbonneau, Mtl.
1986	Troy Murray, Chi.	Ron Sutter, Phi.
1985	Craig Ramsay, Buf.	Doug Jarvis, Wsh.
1984	Doug Jarvis, Wsh.	Bryan Trottier, NYI
1983	Bobby Clarke, Phi.	Jari Kurri, Edm.
1982	Steve Kasper, Bos.	Bob Gainey, Mtl.
1981	Bob Gainey, Mtl.	Craig Ramsay, Buf.
1980	Bob Gainey, Mtl.	Craig Ramsay, Buf.
1979	Bob Gainey, Mtl.	Don Marcotte, Bos.
1978	Bob Gainey, Mtl.	Craig Ramsay, Buf.

CONN SMYTHE TROPHY

2004	Brad Richards	Tampa Bay
2003	Jean-Sebastien Giguere	Anaheim
2002	Nicklas Lidstrom	Detroit
2001	Patrick Roy	Colorado
2000	Scott Stevens	New Jersey
1999	Joe Nieuwendyk	Dallas
1998	Steve Yzerman	Detroit
1997	Mike Vernon	Detroit
1996	Joe Sakic	Colorado
1995	Claude Lemieux	New Jersey
1994	Brian Leetch	NY Rangers
1993	Patrick Roy	Montreal
1992	Mario Lemieux	Pittsburgh
1991	Mario Lemieux	Pittsburgh
1990	Bill Ranford	Edmonton
1989	Al MacInnis	Calgary
1988	Wayne Gretzky	Edmonton
1987	Ron Hextall	Philadelphia
1986	Patrick Roy	Montreal
1985	Wayne Gretzky	Edmonton
1984	Mark Messier	Edmonton
1983	Billy Smith	NY Islanders
1982	Mike Bossy	NY Islanders
1981	Butch Goring	NY Islanders
1980	Bryan Trottier	NY Islanders
1979	Bob Gainey	Montreal
1978	Larry Robinson	Montreal
1977	Guy Lafleur	Montreal
1976	Reggie Leach	Philadelphia
1975	Bernie Parent	Philadelphia
1974	Bernie Parent	Philadelphia
1973	Yvan Cournoyer	Montreal
1972	Bobby Orr	Boston
1971	Ken Dryden	Montreal
1970	Bobby Orr	Boston
1969	Serge Savard	Montreal
1968	Glenn Hall	St. Louis
1967	Dave Keon	Toronto
1966	Roger Crozier	Detroit
1965	Jean Beliveau	Montreal

JAMES NORRIS MEMORIAL TROPHY

	Winner	Runner-up
2004	Scott Niedermayer, N.J.	Zdeno Chara, Ott.
2003	Nicklas Lidstrom, Det.	Al MacInnis, St.L.
2002	Nicklas Lidstrom, Det.	Chris Chelios, Det.
2001	Nicklas Lidstrom, Det.	Raymond Bourque, Col.
2000	Chris Pronger, St.L.	Nicklas Lidstrom, Det.
1999	Al MacInnis, St.L.	Nicklas Lidstrom, Det.
1998	Rob Blake, L.A.	Nicklas Lidstrom, Det.
1997	Brian Leetch, NYR	V. Konstantinov, Det.
1996	Chris Chelios, Chi.	Raymond Bourque, Bos.
1995	Paul Coffey, Det.	Chris Chelios, Chi.
1994	Raymond Bourque, Bos.	Scott Stevens, N.J.
1993	Chris Chelios, Chi.	Raymond Bourque, Bos.
1992	Brian Leetch, NYR	Raymond Bourque, Bos.
1991	Raymond Bourque, Bos.	Al MacInnis, Cgy.
1990	Raymond Bourque, Bos.	Al MacInnis, Cgy.
1989	Chris Chelios, Mtl	Paul Coffey, Pit.
1988	Raymond Bourque, Bos.	Scott Stevens, Wsh.
1987	Raymond Bourque, Bos.	Mark Howe, Phi.
1986	Paul Coffey, Edm.	Mark Howe, Phi.
1985	Paul Coffey, Edm.	Raymond Bourque, Bos.
1984	Rod Langway, Wsh.	Paul Coffey, Edm.
1983	Rod Langway, Wsh.	Mark Howe, Phi.
1982	Doug Wilson, Chi.	Raymond Bourque, Bos.
1981	Randy Carlyle, Pit.	Denis Potvin, NYI
1980	Larry Robinson, Mtl.	Borje Salming, Tor.
1979	Denis Potvin, NYI	Larry Robinson, Mtl.
1978	Denis Potvin, NYI	Brad Park, Bos.
1977	Larry Robinson, Mtl.	Borje Salming, Tor.
1976	Denis Potvin, NYI	Brad Park, NYR-Bos.
1975	Bobby Orr, Bos.	Denis Potvin, NYI
1974	Bobby Orr, Bos.	Brad Park, NYR
1973	Bobby Orr, Bos.	Guy Lapointe, Mtl.
1972	Bobby Orr, Bos.	Brad Park, NYR
1971	Bobby Orr, Bos.	Brad Park, NYR
1970	Bobby Orr, Bos.	Brad Park, NYR
1969	Bobby Orr, Bos.	Tim Horton, Tor.
1968	Bobby Orr, Bos.	J.C. Tremblay, Mtl
1967	Harry Howell, NYR	Pierre Pilote, Chi.
1966	Jacques Laperriere, Mtl.	Pierre Pilote, Chi.
1965	Pierre Pilote, Chi.	Jacques Laperriere, Mtl.
1964	Pierre Pilote, Chi.	Tim Horton, Tor.
1963	Pierre Pilote, Chi.	Carl Brewer, Tor.
1962	Doug Harvey, NYR	Pierre Pilote, Chi.
1961	Doug Harvey, Mtl.	Marcel Pronovost, Det.
1960	Doug Harvey, Mtl.	Allan Stanley, Tor.
1959	Tom Johnson, Mtl.	Bill Gadsby, NYR
1958	Doug Harvey, Mtl.	Bill Gadsby, NYR
1957	Doug Harvey, Mtl.	Red Kelly, Det.
1956	Doug Harvey, Mtl.	Bill Gadsby, NYR
1955	Doug Harvey, Mtl.	Red Kelly, Det.
1954	Red Kelly, Det.	Doug Harvey, Mtl.

MAURICE "ROCKET" RICHARD TROPHY

2004	Rick Nash	Columbus
	Jarome Iginla	Calgary
	Ilya Kovalchuk	Atlanta
2003	Milan Hejduk	Colorado
2002	Jarome Iginla	Calgary
2001	Pavel Bure	Florida
2000	Pavel Bure	Florida
1999	Teemu Selanne	Anaheim

LESTER PATRICK TROPHY

2004	Mike Emrick
	John Davidson
	Ray Miron
2003	Raymond Bourque
	Ron DeGregorio
	Willie O'Ree
2002	1960 U.S. Olympic Hockey Team
	Herb Brooks
	Larry Pleau
2001	Scotty Bowman
	David Poile
	Gary Bettman
2000	Mario Lemieux
	Craig Patrick
	Lou Vairo
1999	Harry Sinden
	1998 U.S. Olympic Women's Hockey Team
1998	Peter Karmanos
	Neal Broten
	John Mayasich
	Max McNab
1997	Seymour H. Knox III
	Bill Cleary
	Pat LaFontaine
1996	George Gund
	Ken Morrow
	Milt Schmidt
1995	Joe Mullen
	Brian Mullen
	Bob Fleming
1994	Wayne Gretzky
	Robert Ridder
1993	*Frank Boucher
	*Mervyn "Red" Dutton
	Bruce McNall
	Gil Stein
1992	Al Arbour
	Art Berglund
	Lou Lamoriello
1991	Rod Gilbert
	Mike Ilitch
1990	Len Ceglarski
1989	Dan Kelly
	Lou Nanne
	*Lynn Patrick
	Bud Poile
1988	Keith Allen
	Fred Cusick
	Bob Johnson
1987	*Hobey Baker
	Frank Mathers
1986	John MacInnes
	Jack Riley
1985	Jack Butterfield
	Arthur M. Wirtz
1984	John A. Ziegler, Jr.
	*Arthur Howie Ross
1983	Bill Torrey
1982	Emile P. Francis
1981	Charles M. Schulz
1980	Bobby Clarke
	Edward M. Snider
	Frederick A. Shero
	1980 U.S. Olympic Hockey Team
1979	Bobby Orr
1978	Phil Esposito
	Tom Fitzgerald
	William T. Tutt
	William W. Wirtz
1977	John P. Bucyk
	Murray A. Armstrong
	John Mariucci
1976	Stanley Mikita
	George A. Leader
	Bruce A. Norris
1975	Donald M. Clark
	William L. Chadwick
	Thomas N. Ivan
1974	Alex Delvecchio
	Murray Murdoch
	*Weston W. Adams, Sr.
	*Charles L. Crovat
1973	Walter L. Bush, Jr.
1972	Clarence S. Campbell
	John A. "Snooks" Kelly
	Ralph "Cooney" Weiland
	*James D. Norris
1971	William M. Jennings
	*John B. Sollenberger
	*Terrance G. Sawchuk
1970	Edward W. Shore
	*James C. V. Hendy
1969	Robert M. Hull
	*Edward J. Jeremiah
1968	Thomas F. Lockhart
	*Walter A. Brown
	*Gen. John R. Kilpatrick
1967	Gordon Howe
	*Charles F. Adams
	*James Norris, Sr.
1966	J.J. "Jack" Adams
	* awarded posthumously

PRESIDENTS' TROPHY

	Winner	Runner-up
2004	Detroit Red Wings	Tampa Bay Lightning
2003	Ottawa Senators	Dallas Stars
2002	Detroit Red Wings	Boston Bruins
2001	Colorado Avalanche	Detroit Red Wings
2000	St. Louis Blues	Detroit Red Wings
1999	Dallas Stars	New Jersey Devils
1998	Dallas Stars	New Jersey Devils
1997	Colorado Avalanche	Dallas Stars
1996	Detroit Red Wings	Colorado Avalanche
1995	Detroit Red Wings	Quebec Nordiques
1994	New York Rangers	New Jersey Devils
1993	Pittsburgh Penguins	Boston Bruins
1992	New York Rangers	Washington Capitals
1991	Chicago Blackhawks	St. Louis Blues
1990	Boston Bruins	Calgary Flames
1989	Calgary Flames	Montreal Canadiens
1988	Calgary Flames	Montreal Canadiens
1987	Edmonton Oilers	Philadelphia Flyers
1986	Edmonton Oilers	Philadelphia Flyers

LESTER B. PEARSON AWARD

2004	Martin St. Louis	Tampa Bay
2003	Markus Naslund	Vancouver
2002	Jarome Iginla	Calgary
2001	Joe Sakic	Colorado
2000	Jaromir Jagr	Pittsburgh
1999	Jaromir Jagr	Pittsburgh
1998	Dominik Hasek	Buffalo
1997	Dominik Hasek	Buffalo
1996	Mario Lemieux	Pittsburgh
1995	Eric Lindros	Philadelphia
1994	Sergei Fedorov	Detroit
1993	Mario Lemieux	Pittsburgh
1992	Mark Messier	NY Rangers
1991	Brett Hull	St. Louis
1990	Mark Messier	Edmonton
1989	Steve Yzerman	Detroit
1988	Mario Lemieux	Pittsburgh
1987	Wayne Gretzky	Edmonton
1986	Mario Lemieux	Pittsburgh
1985	Wayne Gretzky	Edmonton
1984	Wayne Gretzky	Edmonton
1983	Wayne Gretzky	Edmonton
1982	Wayne Gretzky	Edmonton
1981	Mike Liut	St. Louis
1980	Marcel Dionne	Los Angeles
1979	Marcel Dionne	Los Angeles
1978	Guy Lafleur	Montreal
1977	Guy Lafleur	Montreal
1976	Guy Lafleur	Montreal
1975	Bobby Orr	Boston
1974	Phil Esposito	Boston
1973	Bobby Clarke	Philadelphia
1972	Jean Ratelle	NY Rangers
1971	Phil Esposito	Boston

JACK ADAMS AWARD

	Winner	Runner-up
2004	John Tortorella, T.B.	Ron Wilson, S.J.
2003	Jacques Lemaire, Min.	John Tortorella, T.B.
2002	Bob Francis, Phx.	Brian Sutter, Chi.
2001	Bill Barber, Phi.	Scotty Bowman, Det.
2000	Joel Quenneville, St.L.	Alain Vigneault, Mtl.
1999	Jacques Martin, Ott.	Pat Quinn, Tor.
1998	Pat Burns, Bos.	Larry Robinson, L.A.
1997	Ted Nolan, Buf.	Ken Hitchcock, Dal.
1996	Scotty Bowman, Det.	Doug MacLean, Fla.
1995	Marc Crawford, Que.	Scotty Bowman, Det.
1994	Jacques Lemaire, N.J.	Kevin Constantine, S.J.
1993	Pat Burns, Tor.	Brian Sutter, Bos.
1992	Pat Quinn, Van.	Roger Neilson, NYR
1991	Brian Sutter, St.L.	Tom Webster, L.A.
1990	Bob Murdoch, Wpg.	Mike Milbury, Bos.
1989	Pat Burns, Mtl.	Bob McCammon, Van.
1988	Jacques Demers, Det.	Terry Crisp, Cgy.
1987	Jacques Demers, Det.	Jack Evans, Hfd.
1986	Glen Sather, Edm.	Jacques Demers, St.L.
1985	Mike Keenan, Phi.	Barry Long, Wpg.
1984	Bryan Murray, Wsh.	Scotty Bowman, Buf.
1983	Orval Tessier, Chi.	
1982	Tom Watt, Wpg.	
1981	Red Berenson, St.L.	Bob Berry, L.A.
1980	Pat Quinn, Phi.	
1979	Al Arbour, NYI	Fred Shero, NYR
1978	Bobby Kromm, Det.	Don Cherry, Bos.
1977	Scotty Bowman, Mtl.	Tom McVie, Wsh.
1976	Don Cherry, Bos.	
1975	Bob Pulford, L.A.	
1974	Fred Shero, Phi.	

MBNA/MASTERCARD
ROGER CROZIER SAVING GRACE AWARD

	Winner	Runner-up
2004	Dwayne Roloson, Min.	Miikka Kiprusoff, Cgy.
2003	Marty Turco, Dal.	Dwayne Roloson, Min.
2002	Jose Theodore, Mtl.	Patrick Roy, Col.
2001	Marty Turco, Dal.	Mike Dunham, N.J.
2000	Ed Belfour, Dal.	Jose Theodore, Mtl.

NHL Entry Draft

History

Year	Location	Date	Players Drafted
1963	Queen Elizabeth Hotel, Montreal	June 5	21
1964	Queen Elizabeth Hotel, Montreal	June 11	24
1965	Queen Elizabeth Hotel, Montreal	April 27	11
1966	Mount Royal Hotel, Montreal	April 25	24
1967	Queen Elizabeth Hotel, Montreal	June 7	18
1968	Queen Elizabeth Hotel, Montreal	June 13	24
1969	Queen Elizabeth Hotel, Montreal	June 12	84
1970	Queen Elizabeth Hotel, Montreal	June 11	115
1971	Queen Elizabeth Hotel, Montreal	June 10	117
1972	Queen Elizabeth Hotel, Montreal	June 8	152
1973	Mount Royal Hotel, Montreal	May 15	168
1974	NHL Montreal Office	May 28	247
1975	NHL Montreal Office	June 3	217
1976	NHL Montreal Office	June 1	135
1977	NHL Montreal Office	June 14	185
1978	Queen Elizabeth Hotel, Montreal	June 15	234
1979	Queen Elizabeth Hotel, Montreal	August 9	126
1980	Montreal Forum	June 11	210
1981	Montreal Forum	June 10	211
1982	Montreal Forum	June 9	252
1983	Montreal Forum	June 8	242
1984	Montreal Forum	June 9	250
1985	Toronto Convention Centre	June 15	252
1986	Montreal Forum	June 21	252
1987	Joe Louis Arena, Detroit	June 13	252
1988	Montreal Forum	June 11	252
1989	Met Sports Center, Bloomington	June 17	252
1990	B.C. Place, Vancouver	June 16	250
1991	Memorial Auditorium, Buffalo	June 22	264
1992	Montreal Forum	June 20	264
1993	Le Colisee, Quebec	June 26	286
1994	Hartford Civic Center	June 28-29	286
1995	Edmonton Coliseum	July 8	234
1996	Kiel Center, St. Louis	June 22	241
1997	Civic Arena, Pittsburgh	June 21	246
1998	Marine Midland Arena, Buffalo	June 27	258
1999	FleetCenter, Boston	June 26	272
2000	Saddledome, Calgary	June 24-25	293
2001	National Car Rental Center, Florida	June 23-24	289
2002	Air Canada Centre, Toronto	June 22-23	290
2003	Gaylord Entertainment Center, Nashville	June 21-22	292
2004	RBC Center, Raleigh, NC	June 26-27	291

First Selections

Year	Player	Pos	Team	Drafted From	Age
1963	Garry Monahan	LW	Montreal	St. Michael's Juveniles	16.7
1964	Claude Gauthier		Detroit	Comite des jeunes (Rosemont)	
1965	Andre Veilleux	RW	NY Rangers	Montreal Ranger Jr. B	
1966	Barry Gibbs	D	Boston	Estevan Bruins	17.7
1967	Rick Pagnutti	D	Los Angeles	Garson Native Sons	20.6
1968	Michel Plasse	G	Montreal	Drummondville Rangers	20.0
1969	Rejean Houle	LW	Montreal	Montreal Jr. Canadiens	19.8
1970	Gilbert Perreault	C	Buffalo	Montreal Jr. Canadiens	19.7
1971	Guy Lafleur	RW	Montreal	Quebec Remparts	19.9
1972	Billy Harris	RW	NY Islanders	Toronto Marlboros	20.4
1973	Denis Potvin	D	NY Islanders	Ottawa 67s	19.7
1974	Greg Joly	D	Washington	Regina Pats	20.0
1975	Mel Bridgman	C	Philadelphia	Victoria Cougars	20.1
1976	Rick Green	D	Washington	London Knights	20.3
1977	Dale McCourt	C	Detroit	St. Catharines Fincups	20.4
1978	Bobby Smith	C	Minnesota	Ottawa 67's	20.4
1979	Rob Ramage	D	Colorado	London Knights	20.5
1980	Doug Wickenheiser	C	Montreal	Regina Pats	19.2
1981	Dale Hawerchuk	C	Winnipeg	Cornwall Royals	18.2
1982	Gord Kluzak	D	Boston	Nanaimo Islanders	18.3
1983	Brian Lawton	C	Minnesota	Mount St. Charles HS	18.11
1984	Mario Lemieux	C	Pittsburgh	Laval Voisins	18.8
1985	Wendel Clark	LW/D	Toronto	Saskatoon Blades	18.7
1986	Joe Murphy	C	Detroit	Michigan State	18.8
1987	Pierre Turgeon	C	Buffalo	Granby Bisons	17.10
1988	Mike Modano	C	Minnesota	Prince Albert Raiders	18.0
1989	Mats Sundin	RW	Quebec	Nacka (Sweden)	18.4
1990	Owen Nolan	RW	Quebec	Cornwall Royals	18.4
1991	Eric Lindros	C	Quebec	Oshawa Generals	18.3
1992	Roman Hamrlik	D	Tampa Bay	ZPS Zlin (Czech.)	18.2
1993	Alexandre Daigle	C	Ottawa	Victoriaville Tigres	18.5
1994	Ed Jovanovski	D	Florida	Windsor Spitfires	18.0
1995	Bryan Berard	D	Ottawa	Detroit Jr. Red Wings	18.4
1996	Chris Phillips	D	Ottawa	Prince Albert Raiders	18.3
1997	Joe Thornton	C	Boston	Sault Ste. Marie	17.11
1998	Vincent Lecavalier	C	Tampa Bay	Rimouski Oceanic	18.2
1999	Patrik Stefan	C	Atlanta	Long Beach Ice Dogs (IHL)	18.9
2000	Rick DiPietro	G	NY Islanders	Boston University	18.9
2001	Ilya Kovalchuk	RW	Atlanta	Spartak (Russia)	18.2
2002	Rick Nash	LW	Columbus	London Knights	18.0
2003	Marc-Andre Fleury	G	Pittsburgh	Cape Breton Screaming Eagles	18.0
2004	Alexander Ovechkin	LW	Washington	Dynamo Moscow (Russia)	18.9

Draft Summary

Following is a summary of the players drafted from the Ontario Hockey League (OHL), Quebec Major Junior Hockey League (QMJHL), Western Hockey League (WHL), United States colleges, United States high schools, European leagues and other North American leagues since 1969. "Other" may include Canadian and U.S. Jr. A and Jr. B, minor professional leagues (AHL, IHL), midget and other teams playing in leagues not listed above.

Year	Total Picks	OHL Picks	%	QMJHL Picks	%	WHL Picks	%	College Picks	%	Hi School Picks	%	Int'l Picks	%	Other Picks	%
1969	84	36	42.9	11	13.1	20	23.8	7	8.3	-	-	1	1.2	9	10.7
1970	115	51	44.3	13	11.3	22	19.1	16	13.9	-	-	-	-	13	11.3
1971	117	41	35.0	13	11.1	28	23.9	22	18.8	-	-	-	-	13	11.1
1972	152	46	30.3	30	19.7	44	28.9	21	13.8	-	-	-	-	11	7.2
1973	168	56	33.3	24	14.3	49	29.2	25	14.9	-	-	-	-	14	8.3
1974	247	69	27.9	40	16.2	66	26.7	41	16.6	-	-	6	2.4	25	10.1
1975	217	55	25.3	28	12.9	57	26.3	59	27.2	-	-	6	2.8	12	5.5
1976	135	47	34.8	18	13.3	33	24.4	26	19.3	-	-	8	5.9	3	2.2
1977	185	42	22.7	40	21.6	44	23.8	49	26.5	-	-	5	2.7	5	2.7
1978	234	59	25.2	22	9.4	48	20.5	73	31.2	-	-	16	6.8	16	6.8
1979	126	48	38.1	19	15.1	37	29.4	15	11.9	-	-	6	4.8	1	0.8
1980	210	73	34.8	24	11.4	41	19.5	42	20.0	7	3.3	13	6.2	10	4.8
1981	211	59	28.0	28	13.3	37	17.5	21	10.0	17	8.1	32	15.2	17	8.1
1982	252	60	23.8	17	6.7	55	21.8	20	7.9	47	18.7	35	13.9	18	7.1
1983	242	57	23.6	24	9.9	41	16.9	14	5.8	35	14.5	34	14.0	37	15.3
1984	250	55	22.0	16	6.4	37	14.8	22	8.8	44	17.6	40	16.0	36	14.4
1985	252	59	23.4	15	6.0	48	19.0	20	7.9	48	19.0	31	12.3	31	12.3
1986	252	66	26.2	22	8.7	32	12.7	22	8.7	40	15.9	28	11.1	42	16.7
1987	252	32	12.7	17	6.7	36	14.3	40	15.9	69	27.4	38	15.1	20	7.9
1988	252	32	12.7	22	8.7	30	11.9	48	19.0	56	22.2	39	15.5	25	9.9
1989	252	39	15.5	16	6.3	44	17.5	48	19.0	47	18.7	38	15.1	20	7.9
1990	250	39	15.6	14	5.6	33	13.2	38	15.2	57	22.8	53	21.2	16	6.4
1991	264	43	16.3	25	9.5	40	15.2	43	16.3	37	14.0	55	20.8	21	8.0
1992	264	57	21.6	22	8.3	45	17.0	9	3.4	25	9.5	84	31.8	22	8.3
1993	286	60	21.0	23	8.0	44	15.4	17	5.9	33	11.5	78	27.3	31	10.8
1994	286	45	15.7	28	9.8	66	23.1	6	2.1	28	9.8	80	28.0	33	11.5
1995	234	54	23.1	35	15.0	55	23.5	5	2.1	2	0.9	69	29.5	14	6.0
1996	241	51	21.2	31	12.9	54	22.4	25	10.4	6	2.5	58	24.1	16	6.6
1997	246	52	21.1	19	7.7	63	25.6	26	10.6	4	1.6	63	25.6	19	7.7
1998	258	50	19.4	41	15.9	44	17.1	27	10.5	7	2.7	75	29.1	14	5.4
1999	272	52	19.1	20	7.4	40	14.7	36	13.2	9	3.3	94	34.6	21	7.7
2000	293	39	13.3	21	7.2	41	14.0	35	11.9	7	2.4	123	42.0	27	9.2
2001	289	41	14.2	26	9.0	45	15.6	24	8.3	8	2.8	119	41.2	26	9.0
2002	290	35	12.1	23	7.9	43	14.8	41	14.1	6	2.1	110	37.9	32	11.0
2003	292	44	15.1	38	13.0	41	14.0	23	7.9	10	3.4	93	31.8	43	14.7
2004	291	42	14.4	44	15.1	27	9.3	28	9.6	18	6.2	88	30.2	44	15.1
Total		**1786**	**21.6**	**1547**	**18.7**	**852**	**10.3**	**1034**	**12.5**	**667**	**8.1**	**1618**	**19.6**	**757**	**9.2**

Total Players Drafted (1969-2004): 8,261

Alexander Ovechkin (Dynamo Moscow, LW, 1st by Washington), Al Montoya (U. of Michigan, G, 6th by NY Rangers), Andrew Ladd (Calgary Hitmen, LW, 4th by Carolina), Lauri Tukonen (Espoo Blues, RW, 11th by Los Angeles), Ladislav Smid (Liberec, D, 9th by Anaheim), Cam Barker (Medicine Hat, D, 3rd by Chicago), Marek Schwarz (Sparta Praha, G, 17th by St. Louis), Rostislav Olesz (Vitkovice, C, 7th by Florida), Kyle Chipchura (Prince Albert, C, 18th by Montreal), Alexandre Picard (Lewiston, LW, 8th by Columbus), Boris Valabik (Kitchener, D, 10th by Atlanta), Evgeni Malkin (Magnitogorsk, C, 2nd by Pittsburgh), Devan Dubnyk (Kamloops, G, 14th by Edmonton), Wojtek Wolski (Brampton, LW, 21st by Colorado).

Ontario Hockey League

Club	'69	'70	'71	'72	'73	'74	'75	'76	'77	'78	'79	'80	'81	'82	'83	'84	'85	'86	'87	'88	'89	'90	'91	'92	'93	'94	'95	'96	'97	'98	'99	'00	'01	'02	'03	'04	Total
Peterborough	5	5	4	5	9	4	8	1	4	6	9	10	3	5	7	3	9	2	5	2	2	4	3	4	4	2	5	4	5	1	4	1	2	1	5	5	158
Oshawa	5	4	3	5	5	7	6	6	1	3	3	2	9	5	5	6	6	6	3	2	4	2	4	4	4	1	10	1	3	4	3	2	1	3	3	3	144
London	4	9	1	5	6	6	3	5	4	3	6	2	5	5	3	7	1	3	2	6	3	3	1	3	4	1	1	4	1	8	4	1	2	2	4	6	134
Kitchener	1	6	2	8	4	13	3	1	3	4	4	4	5	5	8	4	6	3	2	1	7	5	3	1	4	2	4	2	3	5	–	1	1	4	1	2	132
Ottawa	2	4	3	4	6	5	6	5	5	5	3	8	4	9	2	2	3	3	2	1	–	5	5	6	4	1	1	2	5	2	6	2	3	–	2	3	129
S.S. Marie	–	–	–	–	4	5	2	5	1	5	3	3	8	1	6	4	5	7	1	2	3	1	2	7	3	4	3	4	1	4	1	1	1	2	1	3	103
Sudbury	–	–	–	–	6	6	4	5	4	4	3	7	2	4	–	2	5	3	1	–	1	2	8	2	10	2	2	1	3	5	5	–	2	1	1	0	101
Kingston	–	–	–	–	–	4	4	6	4	9	2	8	5	2	1	3	3	4	1	1	–	2	2	3	5	2	3	4	4	1	4	–	2	1	1	–	91
Windsor	–	–	–	–	–	–	–	2	1	4	2	3	5	3	2	2	3	7	–	5	2	1	–	3	–	3	4	1	5	1	2	2	2	2	2	2	71
Guelph	–	–	–	–	–	–	–	–	–	–	–	–	–	–	1	5	3	8	2	–	4	–	–	2	2	7	5	6	1	5	3	1	4	2	1	2	64
Saginaw/North Bay	–	–	–	–	–	–	–	–	–	–	–	–	–	–	4	4	3	3	3	3	1	4	2	5	2	7	2	1	1	2	2	2	3	2	2	1	59
Belleville	–	–	–	–	–	–	–	–	–	–	–	–	–	–	3	4	4	5	2	–	4	2	1	4	–	3	3	–	5	2	5	1	3	2	–	–	53
Plymouth	–	–	–	–	–	–	–	–	–	–	–	–	–	–	–	–	–	–	–	–	–	–	2	2	7	2	6	3	4	2	2	6	3	3	3	3	48
Sarnia	–	–	–	–	–	–	–	–	–	–	–	–	–	–	–	–	–	–	–	–	–	–	–	–	–	–	1	7	2	3	1	3	1	2	5	–	25
Owen Sound	–	–	–	–	–	–	–	–	–	–	–	–	–	–	–	–	–	–	–	–	–	1	1	2	4	3	2	3	2	1	–	1	–	1	1	1	23
Barrie	–	–	–	–	–	–	–	–	–	–	–	–	–	–	–	–	–	–	–	–	–	–	–	–	–	–	–	2	4	3	6	3	1	1	1	–	21
Brampton	–	–	–	–	–	–	–	–	–	–	–	–	–	–	–	–	–	–	–	–	–	–	–	–	–	–	–	–	–	–	2	6	3	3	4	2	20
St. Michael's	–	–	–	–	–	–	–	–	–	–	–	–	–	–	–	–	–	–	–	–	–	–	–	–	–	–	–	–	–	–	–	1	5	1	5	4	16
Erie	–	–	–	–	–	–	–	–	–	–	–	–	–	–	–	–	–	–	–	–	–	–	–	–	–	–	–	–	3	1	2	3	2	2	–	2	15
Mississauga	–	–	–	–	–	–	–	–	–	–	–	–	–	–	–	–	–	–	–	–	–	–	–	–	–	–	–	–	–	–	–	2	–	–	2	3	7

Teams no longer operating

Club	'69	'70	'71	'72	'73	'74	'75	'76	'77	'78	'79	'80	'81	'82	'83	'84	'85	'86	'87	'88	'89	'90	'91	'92	'93	'94	'95	'96	'97	'98	'99	'00	'01	'02	'03	'04	Total
Toronto	3	7	6	5	6	8	4	4	7	5	4	10	2	6	4	4	3	4	1	2	2	–	–	–	–	–	–	–	–	–	–	–	–	–	–	–	97
Niagara Falls	4	2	1	4	–	–	–	–	2	3	5	8	6	6	–	–	–	–	–	–	4	4	4	4	4	3	2	6	–	–	–	–	–	–	–	–	72
Hamilton	2	3	5	4	6	4	7	3	–	8	1	–	–	–	–	–	3	6	4	4	–	–	2	–	–	–	–	–	–	–	–	–	–	–	–	–	62
St. Catharines	5	5	8	5	4	7	8	4	6	–	–	–	–	–	–	–	–	–	–	–	–	–	–	–	–	–	–	–	–	–	–	–	–	–	–	–	52
Cornwall	–	–	–	–	–	–	–	–	–	–	–	–	–	7	4	3	2	2	3	3	2	3	3	5	–	–	–	–	–	–	–	–	–	–	–	–	37
Brantford	–	–	–	–	–	–	–	–	–	–	3	8	5	2	7	2	–	–	–	–	–	–	–	–	–	–	–	–	–	–	–	–	–	–	–	–	27
Montreal	5	6	8	1	–	–	–	–	–	–	–	–	–	–	–	–	–	–	–	–	–	–	–	–	–	–	–	–	–	–	–	–	–	–	–	–	20
Newmarket	–	–	–	–	–	–	–	–	–	–	–	–	–	–	–	–	–	–	–	–	–	–	–	–	3	2	–	–	–	–	–	–	–	–	–	–	5

Quebec Major Junior Hockey League

Club	'69	'70	'71	'72	'73	'74	'75	'76	'77	'78	'79	'80	'81	'82	'83	'84	'85	'86	'87	'88	'89	'90	'91	'92	'93	'94	'95	'96	'97	'98	'99	'00	'01	'02	'03	'04	Total
Shawinigan	3	2	1	6	1	5	3	–	3	–	–	2	2	5	5	2	–	2	1	–	2	–	2	3	1	1	2	4	1	3	1	1	1	2	2	3	72
Gatineau/Hull	–	–	–	–	–	–	3	2	2	3	–	3	1	–	3	1	–	4	3	2	2	3	3	3	3	1	3	3	–	3	4	–	2	5	4	4	70
Lewiston/Sherbrooke		–	2	2	4	3	7	5	6	3	4	1	5	2	–	–	–	–	–	–	–	–	–	–	3	2	4	–	1	5	–	–	3	–	1	2	65
Drummondville	2	4	1	4	2	1	–	–	–	–	–	–	–	–	–	1	2	2	2	4	1	–	4	2	2	1	4	3	2	2	–	1	1	–	1	1	50
Chicoutimi	–	–	–	–	–	1	–	–	5	1	1	3	6	1	3	–	3	1	2	2	1	1	–	1	1	3	2	–	2	1	–	1	1	3	1	–	47
Halifax	–	–	–	–	–	–	–	–	–	–	–	–	–	–	–	–	–	–	–	–	–	–	–	–	–	–	3	1	3	3	–	2	3	–	6	3	24
Rimouski	–	–	–	–	–	–	–	–	–	–	–	–	–	–	–	–	–	–	–	–	–	–	–	–	–	–	–	–	–	5	2	2	4	–	4	3	20
Val-d'Or	–	–	–	–	–	–	–	–	–	–	–	–	–	–	–	–	–	–	–	–	–	–	–	–	–	1	2	4	2	–	3	2	2	1	1	1	19
Quebec	–	–	–	–	–	–	–	–	–	–	–	–	–	–	–	–	–	–	–	–	–	–	–	–	–	–	–	–	–	4	3	–	3	1	3	1	15
Baie-Comeau	–	–	–	–	–	–	–	–	–	–	–	–	–	–	–	–	–	–	–	–	–	–	–	–	–	–	–	–	–	3	–	2	3	1	2	3	14
Moncton	–	–	–	–	–	–	–	–	–	–	–	–	–	–	–	–	–	–	–	–	–	–	–	–	–	–	–	1	1	2	2	–	–	2	3	2	13
Cape Breton	–	–	–	–	–	–	–	–	–	–	–	–	–	–	–	–	–	–	–	–	–	–	–	–	–	–	–	–	–	3	–	1	1	2	2	3	12
Rouyn-Noranda	–	–	–	–	–	–	–	–	–	–	–	–	–	–	–	–	–	–	–	–	–	–	–	–	–	–	–	–	–	3	1	4	–	–	2	–	10
PEI/Montreal Rocket	–	–	–	–	–	–	–	–	–	–	–	–	–	–	–	–	–	–	–	–	–	–	–	–	–	–	–	–	–	–	–	2	1	1	3	1	8
Acadie-Bathurst	–	–	–	–	–	–	–	–	–	–	–	–	–	–	–	–	–	–	–	–	–	–	–	–	–	–	–	–	–	–	2	–	–	2	3	–	7

Teams no longer operating

Club	'69	'70	'71	'72	'73	'74	'75	'76	'77	'78	'79	'80	'81	'82	'83	'84	'85	'86	'87	'88	'89	'90	'91	'92	'93	'94	'95	'96	'97	'98	'99	'00	'01	'02	'03	'04	Total
Laval	–	–	–	1	–	2	1	1	4	2	1	–	–	2	1	2	–	5	3	1	3	3	4	1	2	5	4	2	1	3	–	–	–	–	–	–	54
Quebec	1	1	2	4	6	6	1	3	7	1	3	2	2	1	2	2	3	–	–	–	–	–	–	–	–	–	–	–	–	–	–	–	–	–	–	–	47
Trois Rivieres	–	1	2	2	2	2	3	2	6	3	2	2	2	1	3	–	3	–	1	3	3	1	2	1	–	–	–	–	–	–	–	–	–	–	–	–	47
Cornwall	2	1	2	6	4	8	1	3	1	6	1	5	5	–	–	–	–	–	–	–	–	–	–	–	–	–	–	–	–	–	–	–	–	–	–	–	45
Montreal	–	–	–	–	4	4	8	1	3	2	4	3	–	3	–	–	–	–	–	–	–	–	–	–	–	–	–	–	–	–	–	–	–	–	–	–	32
Granby	–	–	–	–	–	–	–	–	–	–	–	–	–	2	1	3	2	2	4	–	2	–	2	–	1	5	2	3	1	–	–	–	–	–	–	–	30
Victoriaville	–	–	–	–	–	–	–	–	–	–	–	–	–	–	–	–	–	–	–	4	–	1	–	2	6	1	1	3	2	1	2	3	1	3	–	–	30
Sorel	2	3	1	3	1	8	1	1	3	–	–	–	5	–	–	–	–	–	–	–	–	–	–	–	–	–	–	–	–	–	–	–	–	–	–	–	28
Verdun	–	1	1	2	–	–	–	–	–	1	3	3	–	–	3	3	–	3	0	3	1	–	–	3	–	–	–	–	–	–	–	–	–	–	–	–	27
Beauport	–	–	–	–	–	–	–	–	–	–	–	–	–	–	–	–	–	–	–	–	–	–	1	3	1	3	7	3	3	–	–	–	–	–	–	–	21
St. Jean	–	–	–	–	–	–	–	–	–	–	–	–	–	–	2	–	1	1	0	3	1	–	3	1	2	1	1	–	–	–	–	–	–	–	–	–	16
St. Hyacinthe	–	–	–	–	–	–	–	–	–	–	–	–	–	–	–	–	–	–	–	–	–	3	1	2	1	4	–	4	–	–	–	–	–	–	–	–	15
Longueuil	–	–	–	–	–	–	–	–	–	–	–	–	–	–	1	2	1	2	1	–	–	2	3	–	–	–	–	–	–	–	–	–	–	–	–	–	12
St. Jerome	1	–	1	–	–	–	–	–	–	–	–	–	–	–	–	–	–	–	–	–	–	–	–	–	–	–	–	–	–	–	–	–	–	–	–	–	2

Western Hockey League

Club	'69	'70	'71	'72	'73	'74	'75	'76	'77	'78	'79	'80	'81	'82	'83	'84	'85	'86	'87	'88	'89	'90	'91	'92	'93	'94	'95	'96	'97	'98	'99	'00	'01	'02	'03	'04	Total
Regina	–	–	5	5	1	8	5	3	1	4	1	3	5	6	8	4	4	3	2	–	5	1	–	4	–	3	2	4	3	2	4	2	2	1	2	0	103
Kamloops	–	–	–	–	–	4	4	4	4	–	–	–	–	2	4	4	4	4	3	1	5	4	6	3	2	9	5	4	3	1	4	4	2	5	2	5	102
Portland	–	–	–	–	–	–	–	–	4	8	7	8	6	7	7	5	2	4	3	1	4	1	1	4	4	3	2	1	3	3	1	6	–	2	1	2	100
Saskatoon	1	–	1	3	8	4	5	3	4	1	2	2	3	5	5	3	1	5	4	4	3	2	2	3	2	4	2	2	2	2	4	1	4	–	–	1	98
Medicine Hat	–	–	–	4	6	4	5	3	5	4	–	4	2	1	2	1	6	2	5	1	4	1	3	3	1	6	2	7	2	3	1	–	2	3	3	2	97
Brandon	–	3	1	5	2	7	4	–	3	1	10	5	2	2	1	3	2	1	3	3	–	1	1	1	2	5	6	2	5	4	–	–	2	4	3	0	94
Seattle	–	–	–	–	–	–	–	–	–	4	2	3	–	6	–	1	3	1	2	4	2	6	3	2	4	5	5	1	8	2	6	4	5	1	5	2	87
Lethbridge	–	–	–	–	–	–	3	2	3	5	4	1	4	7	2	1	5	1	–	3	3	4	7	3	4	3	3	1	5	1	–	3	1	2	2	2	85
Prince Albert	–	–	–	–	–	–	–	–	–	–	–	–	–	4	2	2	6	6	1	3	3	4	6	2	5	3	4	3	5	3	3	2	4	1	2	4	78
Swift Current	1	–	1	–	3	6	–	–	–	–	–	–	–	–	–	–	–	–	5	2	2	2	1	1	5	4	4	1	2	2	1	3	1	4	2	2	55
Moose Jaw	–	–	–	–	–	–	–	–	–	–	–	–	–	–	–	–	4	1	3	–	3	1	2	3	2	3	4	4	4	2	1	5	3	3	3	3	54
Spokane	–	–	–	–	–	–	–	–	–	–	–	–	1	–	–	–	–	–	1	3	2	1	5	7	4	4	4	5	4	1	1	2	3	3	–	1	52
Tri-City	–	–	–	–	–	–	–	–	–	–	–	–	–	–	–	–	–	–	–	–	4	3	3	5	2	2	6	6	1	4	1	2	2	3	1	4	49
Red Deer	–	–	–	–	–	–	–	–	–	–	–	–	–	–	–	–	–	–	–	–	–	–	–	–	3	5	2	4	3	5	1	1	6	4	4	1	39
Calgary	–	–	–	–	–	–	–	–	–	–	–	–	–	–	–	–	–	–	–	–	–	–	–	–	–	–	–	3	–	3	6	4	1	2	3	5	27
Kelowna	–	–	–	–	–	–	–	–	–	–	–	–	–	–	–	–	–	–	–	–	–	–	–	–	–	–	–	4	7	2	2	1	1	1	4	4	26
Prince George	–	–	–	–	–	–	–	–	–	–	–	–	–	–	–	–	–	–	–	–	–	–	–	–	–	–	2	2	2	4	2	–	4	–	2	2	20
Kootenay	–	–	–	–	–	–	–	–	–	–	–	–	–	–	–	–	–	–	–	–	–	–	–	–	–	–	–	–	–	–	2	1	2	3	1	2	11
Vancouver	–	–	–	–	–	–	–	–	–	–	–	–	–	–	–	–	–	–	–	–	–	–	–	–	–	–	–	–	–	–	–	–	–	1	1	2	4

Teams no longer operating

Club	'69	'70	'71	'72	'73	'74	'75	'76	'77	'78	'79	'80	'81	'82	'83	'84	'85	'86	'87	'88	'89	'90	'91	'92	'93	'94	'95	'96	'97	'98	'99	'00	'01	'02	'03	'04	Total
Victoria	–	–	–	2	2	5	7	4	3	3	1	8	6	2	3	4	2	1	2	4	4	2	–	1	2	2	–	–	–	–	–	–	–	–	–	–	70
Calgary	3	5	2	7	4	8	4	4	4	3	–	2	5	4	3	3	3	2	–	–	–	–	–	–	–	–	–	–	–	–	–	–	–	–	–	–	66
New Westm'r	–	–	–	6	8	7	9	5	8	6	5	1	–	–	–	2	1	1	2	1	–	–	–	–	–	–	–	–	–	–	–	–	–	–	–	–	62
Flin Flon	4	4	5	2	4	7	4	3	1	5	–	–	–	–	–	–	–	–	–	–	–	–	–	–	–	–	–	–	–	–	–	–	–	–	–	–	39
Edmonton	4	4	5	6	6	2	3	2	–	–	2	–	–	–	–	–	–	–	–	–	–	–	–	–	–	–	–	–	4	–	–	–	–	–	–	–	38
Winnipeg	3	2	4	2	5	4	4	–	4	–	–	–	1	4	1	–	–	–	–	–	–	–	–	–	–	–	–	–	–	–	–	–	–	–	–	–	34
Billings	–	–	–	–	–	–	–	–	–	4	3	4	2	–	–	–	–	–	–	–	–	–	–	–	–	–	–	–	–	–	–	–	–	–	–	–	13
Estevan	4	4	4	–	–	–	–	–	–	–	–	–	–	–	–	–	–	–	–	–	–	–	–	–	–	–	–	–	–	–	–	–	–	–	–	–	12
Tacoma	–	–	–	–	–	–	–	–	–	–	–	–	–	–	–	–	–	–	–	–	–	–	–	3	2	5	2	–	–	–	–	–	–	–	–	–	12

San Jose selected Patrick Marleau (top) second overall from Seattle of the WHL in the 1997 NHL Entry Draft. Atlanta took Dany Heatley from the University of Wisconsin with the second pick in 2000.

Western Hockey League *continued*

Kelowna	–	–	–	–	–	–	–	–	–	–	–	–	–	–	2	4	5	–	–	–	–	–	–	–	–	–	–	–	–	–	–	–	–	–	–	–	11
Nanaimo	–	–	–	–	–	–	–	–	–	–	–	–	–	5	1	–	–	–	–	–	–	–	–	–	–	–	–	–	–	–	–	–	–	–	–	–	6
Vancouver	–	–	–	2	–	–	–	–	–	–	–	–	–	–	–	–	–	–	–	–	–	–	–	–	–	–	–	–	–	–	–	–	–	–	–	–	2

U.S. College Hockey

School	'69	'70	'71	'72	'73	'74	'75	'76	'77	'78	'79	'80	'81	'82	'83	'84	'85	'86	'87	'88	'89	'90	'91	'92	'93	'94	'95	'96	'97	'98	'99	'00	'01	'02	'03	'04	Total
Minnesota	1	3	2	–	–	9	4	4	5	5	2	3	1	1	1	–	–	2	1	1	1	–	–	–	–	–	2	3	2	1	3	3	–	3	2	0	65
Michigan	1	–	–	–	2	2	3	3	1	6	–	4	–	–	–	1	1	–	1	2	3	5	4	2	1	1	–	3	1	3	2	1	2	3	2	3	63
Boston U.	–	4	–	–	1	1	1	1	4	5	1	–	1	–	–	1	1	2	2	3	1	2	2	1	1	–	1	1	1	2	3	1	2	3	–	1	50
Michigan State	–	–	1	–	1	1	1	1	–	–	–	2	–	2	–	2	–	1	1	4	4	5	4	1	1	1	–	1	1	1	2	2	–	4	1	2	47
Michigan Tech	–	–	3	1	2	5	4	4	1	2	1	4	–	1	–	2	2	2	1	1	2	1	2	–	1	2	–	1	–	–	–	–	1	–	–	–	46
Yale	–	–	–	1	–	–	1	–	–	2	–	1	–	–	–	–	–	1	2	–	1	–	–	–	1	–	–	–	–	–	–	–	–	3	–	2	43
Denver	1	3	2	4	2	3	1	2	2	2	2	1	–	1	–	–	1	2	4	1	1	–	–	–	–	–	–	–	3	–	1	–	–	1	–	1	41
Wisconsin	–	1	2	4	5	4	4	2	3	–	1	–	3	2	–	1	1	–	1	–	1	–	1	–	–	–	–	–	–	–	2	3	–	–	–	–	41
North Dakota	2	3	3	1	4	2	1	–	1	2	3	3	1	–	–	1	–	–	–	–	2	1	1	–	–	–	–	–	2	–	1	1	–	1	1	1	38
Boston College	–	1	–	–	–	–	1	1	–	5	–	2	1	1	–	–	–	1	2	–	2	–	–	–	–	–	–	2	3	3	–	3	2	3	1	1	35
Providence	–	–	–	–	–	–	3	2	3	4	–	5	4	1	2	–	1	1	–	–	–	1	–	–	–	–	–	–	1	2	–	2	–	1	1	0	34
Cornell	–	–	–	2	1	1	–	1	1	1	–	1	1	1	–	1	2	–	1	2	5	2	–	–	–	–	–	–	1	–	2	2	–	1	2	2	33
Harvard	–	–	2	–	–	–	2	–	2	2	–	–	–	1	1	–	2	–	1	1	2	–	–	–	2	1	–	3	1	2	1	2	2	3	–	–	33
Clarkson	–	–	2	2	1	–	2	–	2	2	1	1	1	1	1	1	–	–	1	1	1	3	2	1	1	–	–	–	–	3	1	1	–	–	–	–	32
Colorado	2	1	–	–	–	1	3	1	2	2	–	1	–	–	–	3	–	1	–	1	–	2	–	–	–	–	1	–	–	3	1	2	1	1	2	0	31
New Hampshire	–	–	–	1	1	3	6	–	4	1	1	2	1	1	1	2	–	–	–	1	–	–	–	–	–	–	–	–	1	–	1	2	–	1	–	1	31
Notre Dame	–	–	2	3	–	–	7	2	–	3	1	1	–	–	–	–	–	–	–	–	–	–	–	–	–	–	–	1	2	–	2	1	1	2	–	2	30
Bowling Green	–	–	–	–	–	1	3	2	1	1	1	1	–	–	1	–	–	–	–	3	2	1	3	1	–	–	–	–	1	1	1	–	1	1	–	–	26
RPI	–	–	–	–	1	–	–	–	1	3	–	1	2	1	1	–	1	–	2	2	–	–	3	1	–	–	–	–	1	–	2	2	1	–	–	–	25
Lake Superior	–	–	–	–	1	1	1	–	–	3	–	–	–	–	–	1	–	3	–	3	2	3	1	–	1	–	–	1	1	–	1	–	–	1	–	–	24
St. Lawrence	–	–	–	–	–	–	1	–	1	4	–	–	–	3	–	1	1	1	1	1	1	1	2	–	1	–	–	1	1	–	1	–	–	1	–	–	23
W. Michigan	–	–	–	–	–	–	–	–	2	–	–	2	–	–	2	2	–	2	1	1	1	1	4	–	2	–	–	–	1	1	–	–	–	1	–	–	23
Northern Mich.	–	–	–	–	–	–	–	–	–	4	–	1	2	1	–	–	–	–	4	1	2	–	1	–	–	–	–	1	–	–	–	1	–	–	2	2	22
Maine	–	–	–	–	–	–	–	–	–	–	–	–	–	1	1	–	–	1	–	3	2	1	–	–	1	–	–	1	1	1	4	1	–	–	2	1	21
Ohio State	–	–	–	–	–	–	–	–	2	1	–	–	–	–	–	1	–	–	2	2	–	1	1	1	1	–	–	1	1	–	1	–	2	2	1	0	20
Vermont	–	–	–	–	1	–	4	–	1	1	–	1	1	–	1	1	2	–	–	1	–	–	1	–	–	1	–	1	–	–	–	–	2	–	–	–	19
Miami of Ohio	–	–	–	–	–	–	–	–	–	–	–	–	–	–	–	–	1	–	2	4	2	–	2	1	1	–	–	–	–	1	–	–	1	1	–	2	18
Brown	–	–	–	–	1	2	1	–	3	2	–	–	–	1	–	–	–	–	–	–	–	–	1	–	–	–	–	–	–	–	–	1	–	–	–	1	13
Minn.-Duluth	–	–	2	1	–	–	–	–	1	1	–	–	1	–	–	–	–	–	–	2	1	2	1	–	–	–	–	–	–	1	–	–	–	–	–	–	13
Colgate	–	–	–	–	–	1	–	–	–	2	1	–	–	–	–	–	–	–	–	1	1	2	2	–	–	–	–	–	–	–	–	–	–	1	–	1	12
Northeastern	–	–	–	–	–	1	–	–	–	1	–	1	–	–	1	–	1	1	–	–	1	1	–	–	–	–	–	–	–	1	1	–	–	–	–	–	10
Princeton	–	–	–	–	–	–	1	–	–	1	–	1	1	–	1	–	–	–	1	–	1	–	–	–	1	–	–	–	–	1	–	–	1	–	–	–	10

Colleges with fewer than 10 players drafted: 9 - Dartmouth; 8 - Ferris State, Merrimack; 7 - Mass.-Lowell, St.Cloud State; 6 - Illinois-Chicago, St. Louis; 5 - Pennsylvania, Union College; 4 - Alaska-Anchorage, Nebraska-Omaha; 3 - Babson College, Mass.-Amherst; 2 - Alaska-Fairbanks, Minnesota State (Mankato); 1 - Air Force, American International College, Army, Bemidji State, Greenway, Hamilton, St. Anselem College, St. Thomas, Salem State, San Diego U., Wisconsin-River Falls.

U.S. High Schools and Prep Schools (10 or more players drafted)

School	'80	'81	'82	'83	'84	'85	'86	'87	'88	'89	'90	'91	'92	'93	'94	'95	'96	'97	'98	'99	'00	'01	'02	'03	'04	Total
Northwood Prep (NY)	–	–	2	1	–	2	2	4	1	1	3	1	–	1	1	–	–	–	–	–	1	–	–	–	1	21
Cushing Acad. (MA)	–	–	–	–	1	–	–	–	3	2	3	1	–	2	2	–	1	1	–	–	–	1	–	–	2	19
Edina (MN)	–	1	4	2	2	–	–	1	2	2	1	–	1	–	–	–	–	–	–	–	–	–	–	–	–	16
Belmont Hill (MA)	–	–	–	1	–	2	1	2	1	3	2	1	2	–	1	–	–	–	–	–	–	–	–	–	–	16
Hill-Murray (MN)	–	–	–	–	3	–	3	3	–	2	3	–	–	–	1	–	–	–	–	–	–	–	–	–	–	15
Catholic Memorial (MA)	–	–	–	–	–	2	–	1	1	2	–	–	2	1	2	–	–	–	1	–	–	–	–	–	2	14
Deerfield (IL)	–	–	–	–	1	1	–	1	1	2	–	1	–	–	–	–	–	–	–	1	2	–	1	1	1	13
Mount St. Charles (RI)	–	1	–	3	1	–	2	1	2	1	1	–	–	–	–	–	–	–	–	–	–	–	–	–	–	12
Culver Mil. Acad. (IN)	–	–	–	–	–	–	–	2	1	2	2	1	2	2	–	–	–	–	–	–	–	–	–	–	–	12
St. Sebastien's (MA)	–	–	–	–	–	–	–	–	–	–	–	–	2	2	1	–	–	–	1	–	–	1	1	4	–	12
Hotchkiss (CT)	–	–	–	–	–	1	–	–	1	–	1	–	–	–	3	1	2	–	–	–	–	1	–	–	1	11
Canterbury (CT)	–	–	–	–	–	–	2	–	3	–	2	–	2	1	–	–	–	–	–	–	–	–	–	1	–	11
Matignon (MA)	1	1	1	–	3	–	–	3	–	–	–	1	–	–	–	–	–	–	–	–	–	–	–	–	–	10
Roseau (MN)	1	–	1	1	1	–	1	–	–	1	3	1	–	–	–	–	–	–	–	–	–	–	–	–	–	10
Choate (CT)	–	–	–	–	–	1	–	2	3	–	1	1	1	–	–	–	–	–	–	–	1	–	–	–	–	10

U.S. College and High School Firsts

1967 – First U.S. College Player Drafted
Michigan Tech center Al Karlander was selected 17th overall by the Detroit Red Wings.

1979 – First U.S. College First-Round Selection
Minnesota-born defenseman Mike Ramsey (currently an assistant coach with the Minnesota Wild) was selected 11th overall by the Buffalo Sabres.

1980 – First U.S. High School Player Drafted
Center Jay North of Bloomington-Jefferson H.S. was taken 62nd overall by the Buffalo Sabres in 1980.

1981 – First U.S. High School First- Round Selection
Center Bob Carpenter of St. John's prep school was selected third overall by Washington in 1981.

1983 – First U.S. High School Player Drafted First Overall
Minnesota North Stars selected left winger Brian Lawton from Mount St. Charles H.S. first overall in 1983.

1986 – First U.S. College Player Drafted First Overall
Detroit selected right winger Joe Murphy from Michigan State first overall in 1986.

2003 – Most U.S. College Players Selected in the First Round
The 2003 draft saw seven U.S. college players selected in the first round, the most in Entry Draft history. Six were selected in the first round in 2000, five in 2002, four in 2001 and three in each of the 1986 and 1999 Entry Drafts.

Draft Evolution and Eligibility

The 41st edition of NHL Entry Draft was held on June 26-27, 2004 at the home of the Carolina Hurricanes, the RBC Center in Raleigh, North Carolina. Since 1963, the event has grown from a small gathering of hockey executives to a spectacle seen by hundreds of thousands of hockey fans throughout the world.

Inception of the Amateur Draft

In an effort to eliminate the sponsorship of amateur teams and players by its member clubs, the National Hockey League began developing a drafting system that would provide each team with an equal opportunity to acquire amateur players.

"I'm trying to work out a system whereby all amateur players who will attain their 17th birthdays before August of each year will be available for drafting by NHL teams in the reverse order of the standing," said NHL President Clarence Campbell during the 1962-63 season. "We're ultimately hopeful it will produce a uniform opportunity for each team to acquire a star player."

The end result was the establishment of the NHL's Amateur Draft.

The first NHL Amateur Draft was held at the Queen Elizabeth Hotel in Montreal on June 5, 1963. All amateur players, 17 years of age and older who were not already sponsored by an NHL club, were eligible to be drafted. Garry Monahan, a 17-year-old center from the St. Michael's Juveniles of Toronto, was selected first overall by the Montreal Canadiens.

The 1969 Draft marked the first year that the effects of NHL amateur sponsorship would not be seen, as every junior of qualifying age (20 years) was available for selection. Eighty-four players were selected that year, more than four times the average number of players chosen in the first six years of the Draft.

Entry Draft Replaces the Amateur Draft

In 1979, the name of the Draft was changed from "Amateur" to "Entry" to reflect the inclusion of young players eligible for selection who had played professionally in the now-defunct World Hockey Association.

Draft Eligibility

Beginning with the 1980 Entry Draft and continuing today, all 18, 19 and 20-year old North American and non-North American-born players have been eligible to be drafted. In addition, non-North American players aged 21-years or older are eligible for claim. From 1987 to 1991, the selection of 18 and 19-year-old players was restricted to the first three rounds of the draft, unless the player met qualifying criteria that dealt with hockey experience in major junior, U.S. college and high school or European hockey. Starting with the 1992 Draft, those players were available in all rounds.

International

Country	'69	'70	'71	'72	'73	'74	'75	'76	'77	'78	'79	'80	'81	'82	'83	'84	'85	'86	'87	'88	'89	'90	'91	'92	'93	'94	'95	'96	'97	'98	'99	'00	'01	'02	'03	'04	Total
USSR/CIS/Russia	–	–	–	–	–	1	–	–	2	–	–	3	5	1	2	1	2	11	18	14	25	45	31	35	27	17	16	22	29	44	36	33	32	24	–	–	476
Sweden	–	–	–	–	–	5	2	5	2	8	5	9	14	14	14	16	9	15	14	9	7	11	11	18	17	8	16	14	19	24	24	14	24	19	18	–	395
Czech Republic and Slovakia	–	–	–	–	–	–	–	2	1	–	4	13	9	13	8	6	11	5	8	21	9	17	15	18	21	14	17	20	20	28	28	21	20	24	–	–	373
Finland	1	–	–	–	–	1	3	2	3	2	–	4	12	5	9	10	4	10	6	7	3	9	6	8	9	8	12	7	11	12	17	19	29	26	12	14	281
Switzerland	–	–	–	–	–	–	–	1	–	–	–	–	–	–	–	–	–	–	–	–	–	1	–	2	1	–	1	3	2	3	7	5	4	5	4	–	39
Germany	–	–	–	–	–	–	–	2	–	–	2	–	1	2	1	–	1	2	–	–	1	1	3	1	1	1	3	1	–	–	1	7	1	4	1	–	36
Norway	–	–	–	–	–	–	–	–	–	–	–	–	–	–	–	2	–	2	1	–	–	–	1	–	–	–	1	–	1	7	1	4	1	–	–	–	7
Denmark	–	–	–	–	–	–	–	–	–	–	–	–	–	–	1	1	–	–	–	–	–	–	–	–	–	–	–	–	–	–	–	–	–	–	–	–	2
Poland	–	–	–	–	–	–	–	–	–	–	–	–	–	–	–	–	1	–	–	–	–	–	1	–	–	–	–	–	–	–	–	–	–	–	–	–	2
Scotland	–	–	–	–	–	–	–	–	–	–	–	–	–	1	–	–	–	–	–	–	–	–	–	–	–	–	–	–	–	–	1	–	–	–	–	–	1
Japan	–	–	–	–	–	–	–	–	–	–	–	–	–	–	–	–	–	–	1	–	–	–	–	–	–	–	–	–	–	–	–	–	–	1	–	–	1
Hungary	–	–	–	–	–	–	–	–	–	–	–	–	–	–	–	–	–	–	–	–	–	–	–	–	–	1	–	–	–	–	–	–	–	–	–	–	1

Czech Republic and Slovakia

Club	'69	'70	'71	'72	'73	'74	'75	'76	'77	'78	'79	'80	'81	'82	'83	'84	'85	'86	'87	'88	'89	'90	'91	'92	'93	'94	'95	'96	'97	'98	'99	'00	'01	'02	'03	'04	Total
Chemopetrol Litvinov[1]	–	–	–	–	–	–	–	–	–	–	3	1	2	–	–	2	2	1	3	2	4	2	2	2	1	1	–	1	–	2	3						33
Dukla Jihlava	–	–	–	–	–	–	–	–	–	2	4	3	1	–	3	1	1	3	2	1	1	2	2	–	1	–	–	1								29
HC Ceske Budejovice[2]	–	–	–	–	–	–	–	2	1	1	–	–	1	2	–	–	1	2	3	1	2	1	1	3	2												26
Slavia Praha	–	–	–	–	–	–	–	1	–	–	1	–	–	–	–	1	–	4	5	2	3	5	2	2	1												26
Dukla Trencin	–	–	–	–	–	–	–	–	2	–	–	1	1	2	–	2	–	1	2	1	2	1	–	2	3	2	–	3	4								27
Slovan Bratislava	–	–	–	–	–	1	1	1	–	2	–	1	1	1	–	1	–	3	–	1	1	1	1	2	1	3											22
Sparta Praha	–	–	–	–	–	–	1	–	2	1	1	2	1	2	–	1	1	1	–	1	1	–	1	2	1	1	4										25
HC Kladno[3]	–	–	–	–	–	2	1	–	1	1	–	–	1	2	–	1	2	2	1	1	1	1	–	2													19
ZPS Zlin[4]	–	–	–	–	–	–	1	–	1	1	1	–	2	2	1	–	2	–	1	2	2	–	2														20
HC Vitkovice[5]	–	–	–	–	1	1	–	1	–	1	–	1	1	3	1	1	1	1	1	1	–	2	–	2													17
HC Kosice[6]	–	–	–	–	–	–	–	1	2	–	2	–	1	–	1	1	1	1	1	–	1																13
HC Pardubice[7]	–	–	–	–	–	–	–	2	–	2	–	1	–	–	2	1	–	1	–	1	3																13
Interconex Plzen[8]	–	–	–	–	–	–	–	–	–	1	1	–	3	–	1	1	–	1	1	2	–																13
HC Vsetin	–	–	–	–	–	–	–	–	–	–	–	–	–	–	–	–	2	1	2	2	3	1	1														12
Zetor Brno	–	–	–	–	–	–	1	–	3	–	1	–	2	–	1																						8
HC Olomouc[9]	–	–	–	–	–	–	–	–	–	–	2	–	2	–	–	1	1	2	–																		7
AC Nitra	–	–	–	–	–	–	–	–	–	–	–	–	2	–	1	–	1	1	–	1	1																7
ZTK Zvolen	–	–	–	–	–	–	–	–	–	–	–	1	1	–	1	–	1	2	2																		7
ZTS Martin	–	–	–	–	–	–	–	–	–	1	–	1	–	–	2	–	1	1	6																		6
Zelezarny Trinec	–	–	–	–	–	–	–	–	–	–	–	–	–	–	2	1	1	1	1																		6
HC Karlovy Vary	–	–	–	–	–	–	–	–	–	–	–	–	–	–	–	1	1	1	1																		4
Havirov	–	–	–	–	–	–	–	–	–	–	–	–	–	–	–	1	2	–	3																		3
HC Liberec	–	–	–	–	–	–	–	–	–	–	–	–	–	–	–	2	–	1	3																		3

Former club names: [1]–CHZ Litvinov, [2]–Motor Ceske Budejovice, [3]–Poldi Kladno, [4]–TJ Gottwaldov, TJ Zlin, [5]–TJ Vitkovice, [6]–VSZ Kosice, [7]–Tesla Pardubice, [8]–Skoda Plzen, [9]–DS Olomouc.

Teams with two players selected: Ingstav Brno, IS Banska Bystrica, Michalovce, Partizan Liptovsky Mikulas, VTJ Pisek, ZPA Presov, Spisska Nova Ves.

Teams with one player selected: Banik Sokolov, KLH Chomutov, Dubnica, Havlickuv Brod, Ostrava, KC SKP Poprad, Povazska Bystrica, KC Skalica, Topolcany, HK Trnava, KHM Zvolen.

Finland

Country	'69	'70	'71	'72	'73	'74	'75	'76	'77	'78	'79	'80	'81	'82	'83	'84	'85	'86	'87	'88	'89	'90	'91	'92	'93	'94	'95	'96	'97	'98	'99	'00	'01	'02	'03	'04	Total
HIFK Helsinki	1	–	–	–	–	1	–	1	–	–	1	1	2	2	1	–	–	2	1	–	–	2	–	1	–	1	2	4	2	2	5	–	2				34
Jokerit	–	–	–	–	–	–	–	2	1	–	–	1	1	–	2	–	3	–	1	–	1	1	1	3	3	4	6	2	1								34
TPS Turku	–	–	–	–	–	–	1	6	–	–	1	1	–	–	–	–	3	2	3	1	3	3	1	1	3	1	1	1									34
Ilves	–	–	–	1	2	–	2	–	2	2	–	1	–	1	1	1	–	2	–	2	1	3	4	2	1												27
Karpat	–	–	–	–	–	–	1	1	–	1	1	2	2	–	–	1	1	–	1	–	3	3	3	2													22
Tappara	–	–	1	–	–	–	2	–	–	4	–	1	–	1	–	1	1	2	1	2	2	1	1	1													20
Lukko	–	2	1	–	–	–	2	–	1	–	1	1	2	1	3	1	1	1																			18
Blues Espoo	–	–	–	–	–	–	–	1	1	–	1	1	1	–	2	–	1	–	2	1	1	1															15
Assat	–	–	–	–	–	1	2	–	1	–	1	1	1	1	2	1	–	1																			14
JyP Jyvaskyla	–	–	–	–	–	–	–	–	–	–	2	1	–	3	–	1	2	–	1																		11
HPK Hameenlinna	–	–	–	–	–	–	–	1	1	2	–	1	1	1	3	1	1	–																			11
KalPa Kuopio	–	–	–	–	–	–	–	–	–	–	–	1	–	1	1	1	2	–	1	–																	9
Reipas Lahti	–	–	–	–	–	1	1	1	–	–	–	2	–	1	–	1	–	1																			8
SaiPa Lappeenranta	–	–	–	–	–	–	–	–	–	–	2	–	1	–	1	–	1	1	–	1	1																6
Kiekoo-67 Turku	–	–	–	–	–	–	–	–	–	–	–	–	–	3	–	–	–	–																			3

Teams with two players selected: KooKoo Kouvola, Sapko Savonlinna, Sport Vaasa, TuTo.

Teams with one player selected: Ahmat Hyvinkaa, GrIFK Kauniainen, S-Kiekko Seinajoki, Junkkarit Kalajoki, Hermes Kokkola, LeKi.

New Jersey Patrik Elias (top) spent one more season in the Czech Republic after being drafted in 1994. Ladislav Nagy of Phoenix was drafted by St. Louis in 1997. He left Slovakia for a year of junior hockey in Quebec in 1998-99.

Opting-In and Re-Entering the Draft

Opting-in to the Entry Draft

Beginning with the 1995 Entry Draft, all players 18 years of age are required to opt-in to be eligible for selection. For 2004, any player born between Sept. 16, 1985 and Sept. 15, 1986 is considered to be 18 years of age and, therefore, must opt-in to the Entry Draft.

Any player born prior to Sept. 16, 1985 is automatically eligible for selection and is *not* required to opt-in.

A player has until the later of May 1, 2004 or up until seven days of his team's last game to opt-in to be considered eligible for selection.

Re-Entering the Draft

In 1978, the NHL saw the first players re-enter the Entry Draft after being selected in 1977.

Any player 20 years of age or younger who has not signed a contract within two years of being drafted or has not received a bona fide offer from the NHL club that drafted him within one year of being drafted is subject to re-enter the Entry Draft.

European players who have not signed a contract or whose rights have been released by the NHL club that drafted them, without playing in North America as an 18, 19 or 20-year-old, are subject to re-entry.

If a player is drafted twice and remains without a contract, he is not subject to re-entry.

Draft Becomes an Event for Fans

Prior to 1980, the Entry Draft was closed to the public. The 1980 Draft was held in the Montreal Forum in front of 2,500 fans.

The Canadian Broadcasting Corporation (CBC) and Radio-Canada provided the first live network television coverage in both English and French in 1984. Coverage in the U.S. was first provided by SportsChannel America in 1989.

In recent years the NHL has staged a Top Prospects Preview, introducing the top-rated players of the current year to fans and members of the media.

USSR/CIS/Russia

Club	'69	'70	'71	'72	'73	'74	'75	'76	'77	'78	'79	'80	'81	'82	'83	'84	'85	'86	'87	'88	'89	'90	'91	'92	'93	'94	'95	'96	'97	'98	'99	'00	'01	'02	'03	'04	Total
CSKA Moscow	–	–	–	–	–	–	1	–	–	–	–	1	4	–	1	1	1	5	8	3	4	7	3	5	2	3	–	1	3	–	–	–	3	3	59
Dynamo Moscow														2	3	4	7	10	2	1	7	1	1	1	2	2	–	1	1	45
Krylja Sovetov Moscow	–	–	–	–	–	–	–	–	–	1	1	2	4	3	1	5	3	2	1	1	2	1	1	–	2	31
Lokomotiv-2 Yaroslavl[1]	–																						1	2	2	4	–	9	1	1	3	–	23
Spartak Moscow	–	–	–	–	1	–	1	–	1	–	–	1	4	–	6	1	–	1	–	6	–	22
Lokomotiv Yaroslavl[1]	–											1	2	–	1	–	1	5	1	1	3	1	1	–	2	4	–	22
Traktor Chelyabinsk	–													2	–	–	2	7	1	1	1	–	1	9	2	–	16
Elemash Elektrostal	–																3	–	–	1	–	1	–	1	9	2	1	16
Dynamo-2 Moscow	–													2	1	2	–	–	3	3	–	4	–	1	–	16
Lada Togliatti	–													1	2	–	1	3	1	2	–	1	2	2	–	2	–	16
Khimik Voskresensk	–	–	–	–	–	–	1	–	–	1	3	1	2	–	1	1	–	2	1	1	–	14
Severstal Cherepovets[2]	–														1	1	–	1	1	–	5	1	–	2	–	12
SKA St. Peterburg[3]	–	–	–	–	1	–	1	–	1	–	–	–	2	1	1	–	1	1	–	2	–	11
Sokol Kiev	–													–	1	–	1	2	3	1	2	1	–	11
HC CSKA Moscow	–																					2	5	–	4	11
Pardaugava Riga[4]	–	–	–	–	–	1	–	1	–	–	–	1	–	2	–	1	4	1	–	10
Torpedo Ust-Kamenogorsk	–														1	1	2	1	–	1	–	1	–	9
Salavat Yulayev Ufa	–															2	2	1	1	1	–	1	–	9
Avangard Omsk	–														3	–	1	–	3	1	–	9
CSKA-2 Moscow	–														1	–	2	2	–	–	2	1	8
Metallurg Novokuznetsk	–																	–	2	2	1	–	1	1	7
Neftekhimik Nizhnekamsk	–																	1	–	2	2	–	–	1	6
THC Tver	–																					2	1	–	3	3	6
Molot-Prikamje Perm	–															1	1	–	–	1	1	1	–	5
AK Bars Kazan	–														1	–	1	1	–	1	1	–	5
Lada-2 Togliatti	–																1	1	2	2	–	5
Metallurg Magnitogorsk	–																			3	1	1	–	5
Avangard-2 Omsk	–																			3	–	1	1	5
Tivali Minsk[5]	–									1	–	1	–	2	1	–	4
Torpedo Nizhny Novgorod[6]	–																	–	1	1	1	–	4
Krylja Sovetov Moscow 2	–																			3	–	1	4
CSK VVS Samara	–															1	–	1	–	1	1	–	4
Dynamo-Energiya Yekaterinburg[7]	–														1	–	1	–	1	–	3
Kristall Saratov	–																		1	1	–	1	–	3
Severstal-2 Cherepovets	–																	1	1	–	1	–	3
Ak-Bars-2 Kazan	–																				1	1	–	1	3

Former club names: [1]–Torpedo Yaroslavl, [2]–Metallurg Cherepovets, [3]–SKA Leningrad, [4]–Dynamo Riga, HC Riga, [5]–Dynamo Minsk, [6]–Torpedo Gorky, [7]–Avtomobilist Yekaterinburg

Teams with two players selected: Dizelist Penza, Metallurg-2 Novokuznetsk, Spartak-2 Moscow, Torpedo Nizhny Novgorod 2, Yunost Minsk.

Teams with one player selected: Amur Khabarovsk, Argus Moscow, HC CSKA Moscow 2, Dynamo Khazov, Dynamo-81 Riga, Gazovik Tyumen, Izohets St. Petersburg, Kapitan Stupino, Khimik Novopolotsk, Khimik Voskresensk 2, Mechel Chelyabinsk, Metallurg Magnitogorsk 2, Metalurgs Liepaja, Mostovik Kurgan, Neftekhimik Nizhnekamsk, Neftekhimik Nizhnekamsk 2, Salavat Novoil Ufa, SKA-2 St. Petersburg, Sibir-2 Novosibirsk-1, Stalkers-Juniors, Torpedo Nizhny Novgorod 2, THC Tver, Vityaz Podolsk, Vityaz-2 Podolsk.

Sweden

Club	'69	'70	'71	'72	'73	'74	'75	'76	'77	'78	'79	'80	'81	'82	'83	'84	'85	'86	'87	'88	'89	'90	'91	'92	'93	'94	'95	'96	'97	'98	'99	'00	'01	'02	'03	'04	Total
Djurgarden Stockholm	–	–	–	–	1	1	1	–	1	–	1	–	2	1	–	1	2	–	1	2	–	1	1	2	1	–	3	2	2	–	1	4	1	2	–	2	36
MoDo Ornskoldsvik	–	–	–	–	–	–	–	–	1	–	1	–	1	–	2	–	1	–	2	2	5	–	3	3	–	7	3	–	3	–	1	34
Farjestad Karlstad	–	–	–	–	2	2	–	1	2	1	1	1	–	1	1	1	–	1	2	–	1	2	3	6	1	–	1	2	–	2	32
Leksand	–	–	1	–	–	1	–	–	1	1	–	2	2	1	2	1	2	–	2	–	2	2	1	1	–	2	5	–	2	–	28
Vastra Frolunda Goteborg	–	–	–	–	–	–	–	–	–	2	1	1	1	1	–	1	1	–	1	–	3	1	1	–	1	2	4	3	3	2	4	27
AIK Solna	–	–	–	–	1	–	–	1	–	1	1	–	2	3	1	–	4	–	1	–	1	1	–	1	–	1	1	1	–	2	–	24
Brynas Gavle	–	–	–	1	–	1	1	1	1	–	1	2	–	4	–	1	–	1	1	–	1	1	–	2	1	1	2	–	2	23
HV 71 Jonkoping	–	–	–	–	–	–	–	–	–	–	–	–	1	1	–	1	–	2	–	2	1	4	3	1	1	–	1	1	2	21
Sodertalje	–	–	–	–	–	1	–	1	2	2	2	–	1	–	–	–	1	–	–	1	–	1	–	4	1	1	14
Malmo	–	–	–	–	–	–	–	–	–	–	–	1	1	2	1	–	1	–	–	1	–	1	1	10
Skelleftea	–	–	–	–	–	1	1	–	1	–	–	–	1	1	–	1	–	1	–	1	1	11
Lulea	–	–	–	–	–	–	–	–	–	–	–	–	–	–	2	2	1	1	–	–	–	1	–	1	–	1	1	11
Vasteras	–	–	–	–	–	–	–	–	–	–	–	–	–	1	2	–	1	–	2	2	1	–	9
Rogle Angelholm	–	–	–	–	–	–	–	–	–	–	–	–	1	1	1	1	–	1	3	–	9
Hammarby Stockholm	–	–	–	–	–	–	–	–	1	1	–	–	–	–	–	1	1	1	–	–	3	–	8
Timra	–	–	–	–	–	–	–	1	–	1	2	–	1	–	–	1	6
Huddinge	–	–	–	–	–	–	–	–	1	–	–	–	1	1	1	–	1	6
Mora	–	–	–	–	–	–	–	–	–	–	–	1	1	–	1	1	–	1	6
Bjorkloven Umea	–	–	–	–	–	–	–	2	1	–	1	–	1	6
Orebro	–	–	–	–	1	–	1	–	–	–	–	2	–	4
Nacka	–	–	–	–	–	–	–	–	1	–	2	3
Troja/Ljungby	–	–	–	–	–	–	–	1	–	1	1	3
Falun	–	–	–	–	–	–	1	–	1	–	1	3
Team Kiruna	–	–	1	–	1	–	1	3
Boden	–	–	–	–	–	–	1	–	1	1	3
Pitea	–	–	–	–	–	–	1	1	1	3
Grums	–	–	–	–	–	–	1	1	1	3
Morrum	–	–	–	–	–	–	–	1	2	–	3
Stocksund	–	–	–	–	1	–	–	–	2	3

Teams with two players selected: Hasten, Linkoping, Ostersund.

Teams with one player selected: Almtuna, Arboga, Arvika, Danderyd Hockey, Fagersta, Jamtland, Karskoga, Linkoping, Stocksund, S/G Hockey 83 Gavle, Talje, Tingsryd, Tunabro, Uppsala, Vallentuna, Bofors, Sunne.

2004 Entry Draft Analysis

Country of Origin

Country	Players Drafted
Canada	125
USA	64
Czech Republic	21
Sweden	19
Russia	18
Finland	14
Slovakia	10
Switzerland	4
Belarus	3
Germany	3
Kazakhstan	3
Denmark	2
Great Britain	1
Japan	1
Latvia	1
Poland	1
Serbia	1

Birth Year

Year	Players Drafted
1986	151
1985	98
1984	33
1983	1
1982	3
1981	1
1980	1
1979	2
1978	0
1977	1

Position

Position	Players Drafted
Defense	86
Center	66
Right Wing	56
Left Wing	50
Goaltender	33

Note: Players drafted in the international category played outside North America in their draft year. European-born players drafted from the OHL, QMJHL, WHL, U.S. colleges or other North American leagues are not counted as International players. See Country of Origin above

---

European Draft Firsts

1969 – First European (and Finn) Selected The first European-trained player selected was left winger Tommi Salmelainen taken 66th overall by the St. Louis Blues in 1969.

1974 – First Swede Selected Center Per Alexandersson was selected by the Toronto Maple Leafs 49th overall in 1974. Four other Swedish-born players were selected that year, including defenseman Stefan Persson (214th overall, NY Islanders) who became the first European to play on a Stanley Cup winner. (four times, 1980-83).

1975 – First Russian Selected The Philadelphia Flyers selected center Viktor Khatulev 160th overall in 1975.

1976 – First European Taken in the First Round The California Seals selected Swedish defenseman Bjorn Johansson with their first pick, fifth overall, in the 1976 Amateur Draft.

1976 – First Swiss Player Selected The St. Louis Blues selected center Jacques Soguel 121st overall in 1976.

1978 – First Czechoslovak Selected The Detroit Red Wings selected left winger Ladislav Svozil 194th overall in 1978

1978 – First German Selected The first German players were also drafted in 1978. The Atlanta Flames selected goaltender Bernard Englbrecht 196th overall and St. Louis selected forward Gerd Truntschka 200th overall.

1989 – First European Taken First Overall The Quebec Nordiques selected Swedish center Mats Sundin first overall in 1989.

Notes on 2004 First-Round Selections

1. WASHINGTON • **ALEXANDER OVECHKIN** • LW • An offensive star who also takes care of his defensive responsibilities, Alexander Ovechkin is the complete package. He is a superb skater and stickhandler who moves well through traffic and can hit and take a hit when needed. His shot is precise and deceptive, and he has a quick release on his wrist shot and snap shot. Ovechkin sees the ice extremely well and has superb hockey sense. His mother won two Olympic gold medals in basketball and his father played pro soccer.

2. PITTSBURGH • **EVGENI MALKIN** • C • A strong skater with fine balance and agility, Evgeni Malkin is a great mix of size (6'3", 186 lbs.), skill and hockey sense. An excellent stickhandler with smooth hands, he is an excellent playmaker and has a quick, accurate slap and wrist shot. He can score in many ways. Malkin competes hard for the puck and can play a finesse or a physical game. He captained Russia to a gold medal at the 2004 World Junior Under-18 Championships.

3. CHICAGO • **CAM BARKER** • D • An offensive-minded defenseman, Cam Barker is a strong skater with very good balance and agility. He moves the puck well both on his forehand and the backhand and makes good use of his partner in the defensive zone. Barker is effective at joining the rush and makes good decisions. He has a hard wrist and slap shot and passes the puck well. He captained the Canadian team at the Junior Under-18 World Cup in the summer of 2003.

4. CAROLINA • **ANDREW LADD** • LW • With a good shot and a quick release from either wing, Andrew Ladd is difficult to contain in one-on-one situations. He is a fluid skater with outstanding speed and is solid on his skates. His speed and tenacious forechecking cause turnovers and scoring chances and he is adept at making short, soft passes in tight quarters. Ladd is an unselfish player who stands up for teammates. He led the WHL in plus-minus (+39) as a rookie in 2003-04.

5. PHOENIX • **BLAKE WHEELER** • RW • Selected straight out of high school, Blake Wheeler is a big (6'3", 185 lbs.) rangy forward with a wide stance and very good balance. He is a good skater with great agility and balance. Wheeler drives hard to the net and is very good at deking a goaltender. He also has a good wrist and slap shot. He is a competitive and aggressive forechecker who takes the body in the corners and along the boards. Wheeler starred in hockey and football.

6. NY RANGERS • **AL MONTOYA** • G • A very focused competitor who thrives on big games, Al Montoya has a well-balanced butterfly stance and a good glove hand. He has good instincts for anticipating the play and handles the puck well. A product of the U.S. National Team Development Program, Montoya was named the tournament's top goaltender when the U.S. won gold at the 2004 World Junior Championships.

7. FLORIDA • **ROSTISLAV OLESZ** • C • An unselfish team player who is loaded with skill, Rostislav Olesz is very mature both physically and mentally for his age. A good, solid skater with fine speed and balance, he is a skillful forward with a good selection of shots who is also reliable defensively. Olesz has good hockey sense and vision. He is a finesse player who also likes to play an aggressive style and is a hard hitter.

8. COLUMBUS • **ALEXANDRE PICARD** • LW • A player who is not afraid to pay the price for his goals, Alexandre Picard has very good hockey sense and a great work ethic. He is a bent-over skater with a good stride, balance and deceptive speed. He accelerates quickly in the offensive zone and can beat opposing defensemen to the outside. Picard reads the play well. He goes to the net hard and is a smart passer.

9. ANAHEIM • **LADISLAV SMID** • D • A big defenseman with good puck skills, Ladislav Smid skates well for his size (6'3", 202 lbs.) and plays with confidence and intelligence. He is a good, smooth passer with superb vision and fine playmaking skills. He makes the right decisions at all times and is good offensively, though he doesn't shoot much. His father had a good career in the Czechoslovakian league.

10. ATLANTA • **BORIS VALABIK** • D • Standing 6'7" and using his long reach to his advantage, Boris Valabik is effective at clearing shooting lanes in front of his goaltender or pinning opposition forwards to the boards. He is big and rangy with a long stride and can move the puck effectively. He has a good wrist and slap shot and can use both effectively on the power-play. Valabik is also a solid bodychecker.

11. LOS ANGELES • **LAURI TUKONEN** • RW • A strong skater with good balance, Lauri Tukonen is a nice mix of skill and physical play. He is a fine stickhandler with a good, quick wrist shot and is difficult to knock off the puck. He is a solid, hard-working team player who can drive though an opponent's defense. He was the youngest player in the Finnish league and was one of four players tied for the scoring lead (5-6-11) at the 2004 World Junior Under-18 Championships.

12. MINNESOTA • **A.J. THELEN** • D • The top-scoring defenseman in U.S. college hockey as a freshman in 2003-04, A.J. Thelen has an excellent shot which is hard and accurate from the point. He is a very good skater with balance and agility who can read the play well and is seldom caught out of position. At 6'3" and 205 lbs., he is big and strong and uses his body in the corners and along the boards. Thelen is a product of the U.S. National Team Development Program.

13. BUFFALO • **DREW STAFFORD** • RW • A good checker who takes his man out with authority, Drew Stafford is a dependable, hard-working winger. A smart player, he has excellent hands with a quick release and can beat an opponent one-on-one. Stafford sees the ice very well and goes to the net to create scoring opportunities for himself and his teammates. He was a late addition to the U.S. team that won gold at the 2004 World Junior Championships.

14. EDMONTON • **DEVAN DUBNYK** • G • At 6'5" and 194 pounds, Devan Dubnyk is a very big goalie who uses his size to his advantage. A strong skater with good reflexes and quickness, he is quick to get his pads down and his size from the butterfly position allows him to protect the upper portion of the net. Dubnyk possesses a good glove and blocker and follows the puck well on screen shots and in tight situations. He holds his ground well in traffic and competes hard.

15. NASHVILLE • **ALEXANDER RADULOV** • LW • A good skater with balance and agility, Alexander Radulov is strong on his skates and likes to play at top speed. A good puck-handler with soft hands and good vision, Radulov creates scoring changes for himself and teammates with his quick moves in the offensive zone. An emotional player with a good work ethic, he was a member of Russia's gold medal-winning team at the 2004 World Junior Under-18 Championships.

16. NY ISLANDERS • **PETTERI NOKELAINEN** • C • An effective two-way player, Petteri Nokelainen works hard in all three zones. He is effective in shorthand situations and can pass and create scoring chances while under pressure. He is an agile skater with speed, intensity and balance who can make things happen around the net. Solid defensively, he was one of four players tied for the scoring lead (5-6-11) at the 2004 World Junior Under-18 Championships.

17. ST. LOUIS • **MAREK SCHWARZ** • G • An ultra competitive goaltender who gives his teammates confidence, Marek Schwarz has exceptional quickness and very good reflexes. He plays a butterfly style, has an excellent glove hand and controls rebounds very well. Schwarz likes to challenge shooters and plays well under pressure.. He played at both the 2004 World Junior and World Under-18 Championships.

18. MONTREAL • **KYLE CHIPCHURA** • C • An excellent two-way player who is strong on face-offs, Kyle Chipchura has excellent vision and very good hockey sense. He has a good shot with a quick release and is a good playmaker in traffic. Chipchura is a character player who is very competitive and finishes his checks with authority. He does not hesitate to go into traffic and will take a hit to make a play.

19. NY RANGERS • **LAURI KORPIKOSKI** • LW • A fast skater with great acceleration and good top speed, Lauri Korpikoski can score in many ways but is also a great playmaker. He likes to go straight to the net to create chances. Along with linemates Lauri Tukonen and Petteri Nokelainen, he was one of four players tied for the scoring lead (5-6-11) at the 2004 World Junior Under-18 Championships.

20. NEW JERSEY • **TRAVIS ZAJAC** • C • Though he did not play at the top junior level, Travis Zajac is a go-to guy in clutch situations. He is a good skater with a fluid stride and excellent balance who can control the pace of a game. He carries the puck with poise and confidence and is very patient when drawing opponents to him. He has a strong work ethic and is willing to battle opponents one-on-one for puck possession.

21. COLORADO • **WOJTEK WOLSKI** • LW • Born in Poland but raised in southern Ontario, Wojtek Wolski is a very good competitor who does not shy away from traffic. He skates very well, with good acceleration and balance. He has remarkable on-ice vision and handles the puck well in traffic. He uses his size (6'3", 200 lbs) effectively to protect the puck and has a good shot with a quick release. His cousin, Sebastien Mila, plays for Poland's national soccer team.

22. SAN JOSE • **LUKAS KASPAR** • RW • An offensive-minded winger with a good overall skill level, Lukas Kaspar is good with the puck and effective around the net with a wide selection of shots. He is a solid skater with a decent burst of speed and a smart player who is productive in the offensive zone. A solid competitor, he is not afraid of the rough stuff and can use his size and strength (6'2", 202 lbs.) when fighting along the boards or in front of the net.

23. OTTAWA • **ANDREJ MESZAROS** • D • A rushing, mobile defenseman who reads the game extremely well, Andrej Meszaros is a smart player who is a fine competitor and who leads on and off the ice. He captained Slovakia to a silver medal at the 2003 World Junior Under-18 Championships. In 2004, he represented Slovakia at both the World Junior Championships and the World Championships, where he was the youngest player at the tournament.

24. CALGARY • **KRIS CHUCKO** • LW • A good skater who is strong on his skates, Kris Chucko drives hard to the net with good puck protection tactics. He has a hard, accurate shot with a good one timer. Chucko can control the puck along the boards and advance it to the dangerous scoring areas. He is a power winger who is willing to play the game physically to get the job done. He is aggressive in one-on-one situations.

25. EDMONTON • **ROB SCHREMP** • C • A real opportunist with an uncanny ability to anticipate scoring chances, Rob Schremp's playmaking abilities and his finish around the net make him and his linemates a threat to score on any given shift. He has excellent hands, possessing a quick release and is very good at shooting the puck directly off the pass. He was named player of the game at the 2004 Top Prospects game.

26. VANCOUVER • **CORY SCHNEIDER** • G • Captain of his high school hockey team, Cory Schneider is a butterfly goaltender who gets his pads down and out quickly. He is a good skater with quickness, agility and balance, has a good catching hand and controls rebounds well. He follows the puck well on screen shots and is tough to beat on breakaways. He starred on the U.S. team at the 2003 Junior World Cup and at the 2004 World Junior Under-18 Championships.

27. WASHINGTON • **JEFF SCHULTZ** • D • Though he stands 6'6" and weighs 212 pounds, Jeff Schultz is not a punishing checker but will eliminate opponents from the play. He is a good skater who is strong and agile on his skates. He gives a quick first pass and likes to throw the long pass up the middle for breakaways. He has good hockey sense and can jump into the play to create odd-man rushes. He does not panic under pressure and is effective at tying up the man.

28. DALLAS • **MARK FISTRIC** • D • A defensive defenseman who is aware of his responsibilities, Mark Fistric plays his best when he is physical. He is a good skater whose willingness and determination make up for his lack of top speed. He is hard to knock off the puck and pivots smartly to keep onrushing forwards to the outside. He likes to use his strength when taking out opponents and makes forwards pay the price for standing in front of his net.

29. WASHINGTON • **MIKE GREEN** • D • A very good skater with excellent mobility and agility, Mike Green pivots well in both directions and has good balance and lateral movement. He is a smart player who anticipates the play in front of him and can quarterback the power-play. He is a good end-to-end rusher and has a hard shot from the point. He made his debut in the WHL at age 14 and captained his team last year.

30. TAMPA BAY • **ANDY ROGERS** • D • A very tall player at 6'5", Andy Rogers covers a lot of ice with his long stride and has good straightaway speed once in motion. His long reach makes him effective at poke-checking opponents and his good balance makes it hard to knock him off the puck. He has a good shot, but is more of a stay-at-home defenseman. He does not back down from a physical game.

Players selected first through tenth in the 2004 NHL Entry Draft (All rows left to right): Top row: 1. Alexander Ovechkin, LW, Washington; 2. Evgeni Malkin, C, Pittsburgh. Second row: 3. Cam Barker, D, Chicago; 4. Andrew Ladd, LW, Carolina. Third row: 5. Blake Wheeler, RW, Phxoenix; 6. Al Montoya, G, NY Rangers. Fourth row: 7. Rostislav Olesz, C, Florida; 8. Alexandre Picard, LW, Columbus. Bottom row: 9. Ladislav Smid, D, Anaheim; 10. Boris Valabik, D, Atlanta.

2004 NHL ENTRY DRAFT

Pick	Claimed by	Amateur Club	Position

FIRST ROUND

Pick	Claimed by	Amateur Club	Position
1	Wsh.	Alexander Ovechkin	Dynamo	LW
2	Pit.	Evgeni Malkin	Magnitogorsk	C
3	Chi.	Cam Barker	Medicine Hat	D
4	Car.	Andrew Ladd	Calgary	LW
5	Phx.	Blake Wheeler	Breck	RW
6	NYR	Al Montoya	U. of Michigan	G
7	Fla.	Rostislav Olesz	Vitkovice	LW
8	CBJ	Alexandre Picard	Lewiston	LW
9	Ana.	Ladislav Smid	Liberec	D
10	Atl.	Boris Valabik	Kitchener	D
11	L.A.	Lauri Tukonen	Blues Espoo	RW
12	Min.	A.J. Thelen	Michigan State	D
13	Buf.	Drew Stafford	U. of North Dakota	RW
14	Edm.	Devan Dubnyk	Kamloops	G
15	Nsh.	Alexander Radulov	Tver	LW
16	NYI	Petteri Nokelainen	SaiPa	C
17	St.L.	Marek Schwarz	Sparta Praha	G
18	Mtl.	Kyle Chipchura	Prince Albert	C
19	NYR	Lauri Korpikoski	TPS Turku Jr.	LW
20	N.J.	Travis Zajac	Salmon Arm	C
21	Col.	Wojtek Wolski	Brampton	LW
22	S.J.	Lukas Kaspar	Litvinov	RW
23	Ott.	Andrej Meszaros	Trencin	D
24	Cgy.	Kris Chucko	Salmon Arm	LW
25	Edm.	Rob Schremp	London	C
26	Van.	Cory Schneider	Phillips-Andover	G
27	Wsh.	Jeff Schultz	Calgary	D
28	Dal.	Mark Fistric	Vancouver	D
29	Wsh.	Mike Green	Saskatoon	D
30	T.B.	Andy Rogers	Calgary	D

SECOND ROUND

Pick	Claimed by	Amateur Club	Position
31	Pit.	Johannes Salmonsson	Djurgarden	LW
32	Chi.	Dave Bolland	London	C/RW
33	Wsh.	Christopher Bourque	Cushing Academy	C
34	Dal.	Johan Fransson	Lulea	D
35	Phx.	Logan Stephenson	Tri-City	D
36	NYR	Darin Olver	Northern Michigan	C
37	Fla.	David Shantz	Mississauga	G
38	Car.	Justin Peters	St. Michael's	G
39	Ana.	Jordan Smith	Sault Ste. Marie	D
40	Atl.	Grant Lewis	Dartmouth	D
41	Chi.	Bryan Bickell	Ottawa	LW
42	Min.	Roman Voloshenko	Krylja Sovetov	LW
43	Buf.	Michael Funk	Portland	D
44	Edm.	Roman Teslyuk	Kamloops	D
45	Chi.	Ryan Garlock	Windsor	C
46	CBJ	Adam Pineault	Boston College	RW
47	NYI	Blake Comeau	Kelowna	RW
48	NYR	Dane Byers	Prince Albert	LW
49	St.L.	Carl Soderberg	Malmo	C
50	Phx.	Enver Lisin	Saratov	RW
51	NYR	Bruce Graham	Moncton	C
52	Dal.	Raymond Sawada	Nanaimo	RW
53	Fla.	David Booth	Michigan State	LW
54	Chi.	Jakub Sindel	Sparta Praha	C
55	Col.	Victor Oreskovich	Green Bay	RW
56	Dal.	Niklas Grossman	Sodertalje Jr.	D
57	Edm.	Geoff Paukovich	U.S. Nat'l U-18	LW
58	Ott.	Kirill Lyamin	CSKA Moscow	D
59	CBJ	Kyle Wharton	Ottawa	D
60	NYR	Brandon Dubinsky	Portland	C
61	Pit.	Alex Goligoski	Sioux Falls	D
62	Wsh.	Michail Yunkov	Krylja	C
63	Bos.	David Krejci	Kladno Jr.	C
64	Bos.	Martins Karsums	Moncton	RW
65	T.B.	Mark Tobin	Rimouski	LW

THIRD ROUND

Pick	Claimed by	Amateur Club	Position
66	Wsh.	Sami Lepisto	Jokerit	D
67	Pit.	Nick Johnson	St. Albert	RW
68	Chi.	Adam Berti	Oshawa	LW
69	Car.	Casey Borer	St. Cloud State	D
70	Cgy.	Brandon Prust	London	C/LW
71	Buf.	Andrej Sekera	Trencin Jr.	D
72	Col.	Denis Parshin	CSKA Moscow 2	RW
73	NYR	Zdenek Bahensky	Litvinov	RW
74	Ana.	Kyle Klubertanz	Green Bay	D
75	Ana.	Tim Brent	St. Michael's	C
76	Atl.	Scott Lehman	St. Michael's	D
77	Ott.	Shawn Weller	Capital District	LW
78	Min.	Peter Olvecky	Trencin Jr.	C
79	Min.	Clayton Stoner	Tri-City	D
80	NYR	Billy Ryan	Cushing Academy	C
81	Nsh.	Vaclav Meidl	Plymouth	C
82	NYI	Sergei Ogorodnikov	Tver	C
83	St.L.	Victor Alexandrov	Novokuznetsk	LW
84	Mtl.	Alexei Yemelin	Samara	D
85	Pit.	Brian Gifford	Moorhead	C
86	Dal.	John Lammers	Lethbridge	LW
87	Ott.	Peter Regin Jensen	Herning	C
88	Wsh.	Clayton Barthel	Seattle	D
89	Ott.	Jeff Glass	Kootenay	G

Pick	Claimed by	Amateur Club	Position
90	Tor.	Justin Pogge	Prince George	G
91	Van.	Alexander Edler	Jamtland	D
92	Phi.	Rob Bellamy	New England	RW
93	CBJ	Daniel Lacosta	Owen Sound	G
94	S.J.	Thomas Greiss	Koln	G
95	L.A.	Paul Baier	Deerfield Academy	D
96	CBJ	Andrei Plehanov	Nizhnekamsk 2	D
97	Det.	Johan Franzen	Linkoping	C
98	Cgy.	Dustin Boyd	Moose Jaw	C

FOURTH ROUND

Pick	Claimed by	Amateur Club	Position
99	Pit.	Tyler Kennedy	Sault Ste. Marie	C
100	Mtl.	James Wyman	Blake	RW
101	Phi.	R.J. Anderson	Centennial	D
102	T.B.	Mike Lundin	U. of Maine	D
103	Phx.	Roman Tomanek	Povazka Bystrica	RW
104	Dal.	Fredrik Naslund	Vasteras	LW
105	Fla.	Evan Schafer	Prince Albert	D
106	Atl.	Chad Painchaud	Mississauga	LW
107	Nsh.	Nick Fugere	Gatineau	LW
108	Bos.	Ashton Rome	Moose Jaw	RW
109	Car.	Brett Carson	Calgary	D
110	L.A.	Ned Lukacevic	Spokane	LW
111	Min.	Ryan Jones	Chatham	RW
112	Edm.	Liam Reddox	Peterborough	LW
113	Tor.	Roman Kukumberg	Trencin	C
114	Min.	Patrick Bordeleau	Val D'Or	LW
115	NYI	Wes O'Neill	U. of Notre Dame	D
116	St.L.	Michal Birner	Slavia Praha Jr.	LW
117	Min.	Julien Sprunger	Fribourg	RW
118	Cgy.	Aki Seitsonen	Prince Albert	C
119	Phx.	Kevin Porter	U.S. Nat'l U-18	C/LW
120	Chi.	Mitch Maunu	Windsor	D
121	Cgy.	Kristopher Hogg	Kamloops	LW
122	Ott.	Alexander Nikulin	CSKA Moscow 2	C
123	Chi.	Karel Hromas	Sparta Praha Jr.	LW
124	Phi.	David Laliberte	Prince Edward Island	RW
125	Van.	Andrew Sarauer	Langley	LW
126	S.J.	Torrey Mitchell	Hotchkiss	C
127	NYR	Ryan Callahan	Guelph	RW
128	Det.	Evan McGrath	Kitchener	C
129	S.J.	Jason Churchill	Halifax	G

FIFTH ROUND

Pick	Claimed by	Amateur Club	Position
130	Pit.	Michal Sersen	Rimouski	D
131	Chi.	Trevor Kell	London	RW
132	Wsh.	Oscar Hedman	MoDo	D
133	CBJ	Petr Pohl	Gatineau	RW
134	Bos.	Kris Versteeg	Lethbridge	RW
135	NYR	Roman Psurny	Zlin Jr.	LW
136	St.L.	Nikita Nikitin	Omsk 2	D
137	Car.	Magnus Akerlund	HV 71 Jr.	G
138	Wsh.	Pasi Salonen	HIFK Helsinki Jr.	LW
139	Nsh.	Kyle Moir	Swift Current	G
140	Chi.	Jacob Dowell	U. of Wisconsin	C
141	Ott.	Jim McKenzie	Sioux Falls	RW
142	Atl.	Juraj Gracik	Topolcany	RW
143	L.A.	Eric Neilson	Rimouski	RW
144	Phi.	Chris Zarb	Tri-City	D
145	Buf.	Michal Valent	Martin Jr.	G
146	Edm.	Bryan Young	Peterborough	D
147	Nsh.	Janne Niskala	Lukko	D
148	NYI	Steve Regier	Medicine Hat	LW
149	Phi.	Gino Pisellini	Plymouth	RW
150	Mtl.	Mikhail Grabovski	Nizhnekamsk	C
151	Det.	Sergei Kolesov	Minsk	D
152	Fla.	Bret Nasby	Oshawa	D
153	S.J.	Steven Zalewski	Northwood Prep	C
154	Col.	Richard Demen-Willaume	Frolunda Jr.	D
155	N.J.	Alexander Mikhailishin	Spartak 2	D
156	Ott.	Roman Wick	Kloten	RW
157	Tor.	Dimitri Vorobiev	Togliatti	D
158	T.B.	Brandon Elliott	Mississauga	D
159	Van.	Mike Brown	U. of Michigan	RW
160	Bos.	Ben Walter	Mass-Lowell	C
161	Min.	Jean-Claude Sawyer	Cape Breton	D
162	Det.	Tyler Haskins	St. Michael's	C
163	T.B.	Dustin Collins	Northern Michigan	C/LW

SIXTH ROUND

Pick	Claimed by	Amateur Club	Position
164	Pit.	Moises Gutierrez	Kamloops	RW
165	Chi.	Scott McCulloch	Grande Prairie	LW
166	Wsh.	Peter Guggisberg	Davos	RW
167	CBJ	Rob Page	Blake	D
168	Phx.	Kevin Cormier	Moncton Jr A	LW
169	NYR	Jordan Foote	Nanaimo	LW
170	Phi.	Ladislav Scurko	Spisska Nova Ves Jr.	C
171	Phi.	Frederik Cabana	Halifax	C/LW
172	Ana.	Matt Auffrey	U.S. Nat'l U-18	RW
173	Cgy.	Adam Pardy	Cape Breton	D
174	L.A.	Scott Parse	U. of Nebraska-Omaha	C
175	Min.	Aaron Boogaard	Tri-City	RW
176	Buf.	Patrick Kaleta	Peterborough	RW
177	Edm.	Max Gordichuk	Kamloops	D
178	Nsh.	Michael Santorelli	Vernon	C
179	NYI	Jaroslav Mrazek	Sparta Praha Jr.	D
180	St.L.	Roman Polak	Vitkovice Jr.	D

Pick	Claimed by		Amateur Club	Position
181	Mtl.	Loic Lacasse	Baie Comeau	G
182	Cgy.	Fred Wikner	Frolunda Jr.	C
183	Dal.	Trevor Ludwig	Texas	D
184	Col.	Derek Peltier	Cedar Rapids	D
185	N.J.	Josh Disher	Erie	G
186	Atl.	Dan Turple	Oshawa	G
187	Tor.	Robert Earl	U. of Wisconsin	LW
188	T.B.	Jan Zapletal	Vsetin Jr.	D
189	Van.	Julien Ellis-Plante	Shawinigan	G
190	CBJ	Lennart Petrell	HIFK Helsinki Jr.	C
191	T.B.	Karri Ramo	Pelicans Jr.	G
192	Det.	Anton Axelsson	Frolunda Jr.	LW
193	Nsh.	Kevin Schaeffer	Boston U.	D

SEVENTH ROUND

Pick	Claimed by		Amateur Club	Position
194	Pit.	Chris Peluso	Brainerd	D
195	Min.	Jean-Michel Rizk	Saginaw	RW
196	Chi.	Petri Kontiola	Tappara	C
197	Wsh.	Andrew Gordon	Notre Dame	RW
198	CBJ	Justin Vienneau	Shawinigan	D
199	Phx.	Chad Kolarik	U.S. Nat'l U-18	C
200	Cgy.	Matt Schneider	Tri-City	C
201	S.J.	Michael Vernace	Brampton	D
202	Car.	Ryan Pottruff	London	D
203	Ana.	Gabriel Bouthillette	Gatineau	G
204	Atl.	Miikka Tuomainen	TuTo	LW
205	L.A.	John Curry	Sioux City	RW
206	Min.	Anton Khudobin	Magnitogorsk 2	G
207	Buf.	Mark Mancari	Ottawa	RW
208	Edm.	Stephane Goulet	Quebec	RW
209	Nsh.	Stanislav Balan	Zlin Jr.	C
210	NYI	Emil Axelsson	Orebro	D
211	St.L.	David Fredriksson	HV 71 Jr.	RW
212	Mtl.	Jon Gleed	Cornell	D
213	Cgy.	James Spratt	Sioux City	G
214	Chi.	Troy Brouwer	Moose Jaw	RW
215	Col.	Ian Keserich	Cleveland	G
216	N.J.	P.L. Leblond-Letourneau	Baie Comeau	LW
217	N.J.	Tyler Eckford	South Surrey	D
218	Dal.	Sergei Kukushkin	Junost Minsk	C
219	Ott.	Joe Cooper	Miami University	RW
220	Tor.	Maxim Semenov	Togliatti	D
221	L.A.	Daniel Taylor	Guelph	G
222	Pit.	Jordan Morrison	Peterborough	C
223	Chi.	Jared Walker	Red Deer	C
224	Bos.	Matt Hunwick	U. of Michigan	D
225	S.J.	David MacDonald	New England	D
226	Det.	Steven Covington	Calgary	RW
227	NYI	Chris Campoli	Erie	D

EIGHTH ROUND

Pick	Claimed by		Amateur Club	Position
228	Pit.	David Brown	U. of Notre Dame	G
229	Chi.	Eric Hunter	Prince George	C
230	Wsh.	Justin Mrazek	Estevan	G
231	CBJ	Brian McGuirk	Governor Dummer	LW
232	Phi.	Martin Houle	Cape Breton	G
233	CBJ	Matt Greer	White Bear Lake H.S.	RW
234	S.J.	Derek MacIntyre	Soo	G
235	Car.	Jonas Fiedler	Plymouth	RW
236	Ana.	Matt Christie	Miami University	C
237	Atl.	Mitch Carefoot	Cornell	C
238	L.A.	Yutaka Fukufuji	Japanese National Team	G
239	Col.	Brandon Yip	Coquitlam	RW
240	Phx.	Aaron Gagnon	Seattle	C
241	Buf.	Mike Card	Kelowna	D
242	Edm.	Tyler Spurgeon	Kelowna	C
243	Nsh.	Denis Kulyash	CSKA Moscow	D
244	NYI	Jason Pitton	Sault Ste. Marie	LW
245	T.B.	Justin Keller	Kelowna	LW
246	Mtl.	Gregory Stewart	Peterborough	LW
247	NYR	Jonathan Paiement	Lewiston	D
248	Dal.	Lukas Vomela	Budejovice	D
249	Col.	J.D. Corbin	U. of Denver	LW
250	N.J.	Nathan Perkovich	Cedar Rapids	RW
251	Ott.	Matthew McIlvane	Chicago	C
252	Tor.	Jan Steber	Halifax	D
253	Phi.	Travis Gawryletz	Trail	D
254	Van.	David Schulz	Swift Current	D
255	Bos.	Anton Hedman	Stocksund	LW
256	Chi.	Matthew Ford	Sioux Falls	RW
257	Det.	Gennady Stolyarov	Tver	LW
258	Nsh.	Pekka Rinne	Karpat	G

NINTH ROUND

Pick	Claimed by		Amateur Club	Position
259	Pit.	Brian Ihnacak	Brown University	C
260	Chi.	Marko Anttila	Lempaala	RW
261	Phx.	William Engasser	Blake	LW
262	Mtl.	Mark Streit	Zurich	D
263	Wsh.	Travis Morin	Minnesota State	C
264	L.A.	Valtteri Tenkanen	Jyvaskyla	C
265	Phx.	Daniel Winnik	U. of New Hampshire	C/LW
266	NYR	Jakub Petruzalek	Litvinov	RW
267	Fla.	Spencer Dillon	Salmon Arm	D
268	Car.	Martin Vagner	Gatineau	D
269	Ana.	Janne Pesonen	Karpat	LW
270	Atl.	Matthew Siddall	Powell River	RW
271	CBJ	Grant Clitsome	Nepean	D
272	Min.	Kyle Wilson	Colgate	C

Pick	Claimed by		Amateur Club	Position
273	Buf.	Dylan Hunter	London	LW
274	Edm.	Bjorn Bjurling	Djurgarden	G
275	Nsh.	Craig Switzer	Salmon Arm	D
276	NYI	Sylvain Michaud	Drummondville	G
277	St.L.	Jonathan Michel Boutin	Shawinigan	RW
278	Mtl.	Alex Dulac-Lemelin	Baie Comeau	D
279	Cgy.	Adam Cracknell	Kootenay	RW
280	Dal.	Matt McKnight	Camrose	C
281	Col.	Stephen McClellan	Catholic Memorial	D
282	N.J.	Valeri Klimov	Spartak 2	D
283	Fla.	Luke Beaverson	Green Bay	D
284	Ott.	John Wikner	Frolunda Jr.	LW
285	Tor.	Pierce Norton	Thayer Academy	RW
286	Phi.	Triston Grant	Vancouver	LW
287	Van.	Jannik Hansen	Malmo Jr.	RW
288	S.J.	Brian Mahoney-Wilson	Catholic Memorial	G
289	S.J.	Christian Jensen	New Jersey Jr. Titans	D
290	Det.	Nils Backstrom	Stocksund	D
291	Phi.	John Carter	Brewster Bulldogs	C

First Two Rounds
2003–2001

2003

FIRST ROUND

Pick	Claimed by		Amateur Club	Position
1	Pit.	Marc-Andre Fleury	Cape Breton	G
2	Car.	Eric Staal	Peterborough	C
3	Fla.	Nathan Horton	Oshawa	C
4	CBJ	Nikolai Zherdev	CSKA Moscow	W
5	Buf.	Thomas Vanek	U. of Minnesota	LW
6	S.J.	Milan Michalek	Budejovice	RW
7	Nsh.	Ryan Suter	U.S. National U-18	D
8	Atl.	Braydon Coburn	Portland	D
9	Cgy.	Dion Phaneuf	Red Deer	D
10	Mtl.	Andrei Kostitsyn	CSKA Moscow 2	RW
11	Phi.	Jeff Carter	Sault Ste. Marie	C
12	NYR	Hugh Jessiman	Dartmouth	RW
13	L.A.	Dustin Brown	Guelph	RW
14	Chi.	Brent Seabrook	Lethbridge	D
15	NYI	Robert Nilsson	Leksand	RW
16	S.J.	Steve Bernier	Moncton	RW
17	N.J.	Zach Parise	North Dakota	C
18	Wsh.	Eric Fehr	Brandon	RW
19	Ana.	Ryan Getzlaf	Calgary	C
20	Min.	Brent Burns	Brampton	RW
21	Bos.	Mark Stuart	Colorado College	D
22	Edm.	Marc-Antoine Pouliot	Rimouski	C
23	Van.	Ryan Kesler	Ohio State	C
24	Phi.	Mike Richards	Kitchener	C
25	Fla.	Anthony Stewart	Kingston	C
26	L.A.	Brian Boyle	St. Sebastian's H.S.	C
27	L.A.	Jeff Tambellini	U. of Michigan	C
28	Ana.	Corey Perry	London	RW
29	Ott.	Patrick Eaves	Boston College	RW
30	St.L.	Shawn Belle	Tri-City	D

SECOND ROUND

Pick	Claimed by		Amateur Club	Position
31	Car.	Danny Richmond	U. of Michigan	D
32	Pit.	Ryan Stone	Brandon	C
33	Dal.	Loui Eriksson	Vastra Frolunda Jr.	LW
34	T.B.	Mike Egener	Calgary	D
35	Nsh.	Konstantin Glazachev	Yaroslavl	LW
36	Dal.	Vojtech Polak	Karlovy Vary	LW
37	Nsh.	Kevin Klein	St. Michael's	D
38	Fla.	Kamil Kreps	Brampton	C

Selected 45th overall in 2003, 18-year-old Patrice Bergeron was the NHL's youngest player last season. He ranked fifth among rookies with 16 goals and 39 points.

Pick	Claimed by		Amateur Club	Position
39	Cgy.	Tim Ramholt	Zurich	D
40	Mtl.	Cory Urquhart	Montreal	C
41	T.B.	Matt Smaby	Shattuck St. Mary's H.S.	D
42	N.J.	Petr Vrana	Halifax	LW
43	S.J.	Joshua Hennessy	Quebec	C
44	L.A.	Konstantin Pushkarev	Ust-Kamenogorsk	RW
45	Bos.	Patrice Bergeron-Cleary	Acadie-Bathurst	C
46	CBJ	Dan Fritsche	Sarnia	C
47	S.J.	Matthew Carle	River City	D
48	NYI	Dmitri Chernykh	Khimik Voskresensk	RW
49	Nsh.	Shea Weber	Kelowna	D
50	NYR	Ivan Baranka	Dubnica Jr.	D
51	Edm.	Colin McDonald	New England	RW
52	Chi.	Corey Crawford	Moncton	G
53	NYI	Yevgeni Tunik	Elektrostal	C
54	Dal.	Brandon Crombeen	Barrie	RW
55	Fla.	Stefan Meyer	Medicine Hat	LW
56	Min.	Patrick O'Sullivan	Mississauga	C
57	Tor.	John Doherty	Phillips-Andover	D
58	NYI	Jeremy Colliton	Prince Albert	C
59	Chi.	Michal Barinka	Budejovice	D
60	Van.	Marc-Andre Bernier	Halifax	RW
61	Mtl.	Maxim Lapierre	Montreal	C
62	St.L.	David Backes	Lincoln	C
63	Col.	David Liffiton	Plymouth	D
64	Det.	James Howard	U. of Maine	G
65	Buf.	Branislav Fabry	Bratislava Jr.	LW
66	Bos.	Masi Marjamaki	Red Deer	LW
67	Ott.	Igor Mirnov	Dynamo	LW
68	Edm.	Jean-Francois Jacques	Baie-Comeau	LW

2002

FIRST ROUND

Pick	Claimed by		Amateur Club	Position
1	CBJ	Rick Nash	London	LW
2	Atl.	Kari Lehtonen	Jokerit	G
3	Fla.	Jay Bouwmeester	Medicine Hat	D
4	Phi.	Joni Pitkanen	Karpat	D
5	Pit.	Ryan Whitney	Boston U.	D
6	Nsh.	Scottie Upshall	Kamloops	RW
7	Ana.	Joffrey Lupul	Medicine Hat	C
8	Min.	Pierre-Marc Bouchard	Chicoutimi	C
9	Fla.	Petr Taticek	Sault Ste. Marie	C
10	Cgy.	Eric Nystrom	U. of Michigan	LW
11	Buf.	Keith Ballard	U. of Minnesota	D
12	Wsh.	Steve Eminger	Kitchener	D
13	Wsh.	Alexander Semin	Chelyabinsk	LW
14	Mtl.	Christopher Higgins	Yale	C
15	Edm.	Jesse Niinimaki	Ilves Tampere	C
16	Ott.	Jakub Klepis	Portland	C
17	Wsh.	Boyd Gordon	Red Deer	RW
18	L.A.	Denis Grebeshkov	Yaroslavl	D
19	Phx.	Jakub Koreis	Plzen	C
20	Buf.	Dan Paille	Guelph	LW
21	Chi.	Anton Babchuk	Elektrostal	D
22	NYI	Sean Bergenheim	Jokerit	C
23	Phx.	Ben Eager	Oshawa	LW
24	Tor.	Alexander Steen	Vastra Frolunda	C
25	Car.	Cam Ward	Red Deer	G
26	Dal.	Martin Vagner	Hull	D
27	S.J.	Mike Morris	St. Sebastian's H.S.	RW
28	Col.	Jonas Johansson	HV 71 Jonkoping Jr.	RW
29	Bos.	Hannu Toivonen	HPK Jr.	G
30	Atl.	Jim Slater	Michigan State	C

SECOND ROUND

Pick	Claimed by		Amateur Club	Position
31	Edm.	Jeff Deslauriers	Chicoutimi	G
32	Dal.	Janos Vas	Malmo Jr.	LW
33	NYR	Lee Falardeau	Michigan State	C
34	Dal.	Tobias Stephan	Chur	G
35	Pit.	Ondrej Nemec	Vsetin	D
36	Edm.	Jarret Stoll	Kootenay	C
37	Min.	Tim Brent	St. Michael's	C
38	Min.	Josh Harding	Regina	G
39	Cgy.	Brian McConnell	Boston U.	C
40	Fla.	Rob Globke	Notre Dame	C
41	CBJ	Joakim Lindstrom	MoDo Ornskoldsvik	C
42	Dal.	Marius Holtet	Farjestad Jr.	C
43	Dal.	Trevor Daley	Sault Ste. Marie	D
44	Edm.	Matt Greene	Green Bay	D
45	Mtl.	Tomas Linhart	Pardubice Jr.	D
46	Phx.	David Leneveu	Cornell	G
47	Ott.	Alexei Kaigorodov	Magnitogorsk	C
48	St.L.	Alexei Shkotov	Elektrostal Jr.	RW
49	Van.	Kirill Koltsov	Omsk	D
50	L.A.	Sergei Anshakov	CSKA Moscow	LW
51	N.J.	Anton Kadeikin	Elektrostal	D
52	S.J.	Dan Spang	Winchester H.S.	D
53	N.J.	Barry Tallackson	U. of Minnesota	RW
54	Chi.	Duncan Keith	Michigan State	D
55	Van.	Denis Grot	Elektrostal	D
56	Bos.	Vladislav Yevseyev	CSKA Moscow	LW
57	Tor.	Matt Stajan	Belleville	C
58	Det.	Jiri Hudler	Vsetin	C
59	Wsh.	Maxime Daigneault	Val-d'Or	G
60	T.B.	Adam Henrich	Brampton	LW
61	Col.	Johnny Boychuk	Calgary	D
62	St.L.	Andrei Mikhnov	Sudbury	C
63	Det.	Tomas Fleischmann	Vitkovice Jr.	LW

Pick	Claimed by	Amateur Club	Position

2001
FIRST ROUND

1	Atl.	Ilya Kovalchuk	Krylja Sovetov	LW
2	Ott.	Jason Spezza	Windsor	C
3	T.B.	Alexander Svitov	Avangard Omsk	C
4	Fla.	Stephen Weiss	Plymouth	C
5	Ana.	Stanislav Chistov	Avangard Omsk	LW
6	Min.	Mikko Koivu	TPS Turku	C
7	Mtl.	Mike Komisarek	U. of Michigan	D
8	CBJ	Pascal Leclaire	Halifax	G
9	Chi.	Tuomo Ruutu	Jokerit	C/LW
10	NYR	Dan Blackburn	Kootenay	G
11	Phx.	Fredrik Sjostrom	Vastra Frolunda	RW
12	Nsh.	Dan Hamhuis	Prince George	D
13	Edm.	Ales Hemsky	Hull	RW
14	Cgy.	Chuck Kobasew	Boston College	C
15	Car.	Igor Knyazev	Spartak	D
16	Van.	R.J. Umberger	Ohio State	C
17	Tor.	Carlo Colaiacovo	Erie	D
18	L.A.	Jens Karlsson	Vastra Frolunda	RW
19	Bos.	Shaone Morrisonn	Kamloops	D
20	S.J.	Marcel Goc	Schwenningen	C
21	Pit.	Colby Armstrong	Red Deer	RW
22	Buf.	Jiri Novotny	Budejovice	C
23	Ott.	Tim Gleason	Windsor	D
24	Fla.	Lukas Krajicek	Peterborough	D
25	Mtl.	Alexander Perezhogin	Avangard Omsk	C
26	Dal.	Jason Bacashihua	Chicago (NAHL)	G
27	Phi.	Jeff Woywitka	Red Deer	D
28	N.J.	Adrian Foster	Saskatoon	C
29	Chi.	Adam Munro	Erie	G
30	L.A.	Dave Steckel	Ohio State	C

SECOND ROUND

31	Phx.	Matthew Spiller	Seattle	D
32	Buf.	Derek Roy	Kitchener	C
33	Nsh.	Timofei Shishkanov	Spartak	LW
34	Fla.	Greg Watson	Prince Albert	C
35	Ana.	Mark Popovic	St. Michael's	D
36	Min.	Kyle Wanvig	Red Deer	RW
37	Mtl.	Duncan Milroy	Swift Current	RW
38	CBJ	Tim Jackman	Minnesota State	RW
39	Tor.	Karel Pilar	Litvinov	D
40	NYR	Fedor Tutin	St. Petersburg	D
41	Cgy.	Andrei Taratukhin	Omsk	C
42	Nsh.	Tomas Slovak	Kosice	D
43	Edm.	Doug Lynch	Red Deer	D
44	N.J.	Igor Pohanka	Prince Albert	C
45	Phx.	Martin Podlesak	Lethbridge	C
46	Car.	Mike Zigomanis	Kingston	C
47	T.B.	Alexander Polushin	Tver	C
48	N.J.	Thomas Pihlman	JYP Jyvaskyla	LW
49	L.A.	Mike Cammalleri	U. of Michigan	C
50	Buf.	Chris Thorburn	North Bay	C
51	L.A.	Jaroslav Bednar	HIFK Helsinki	RW
52	Edm.	Ed Caron	Phillips-Exeter	C
53	CBJ	Kiel McLeod	Kelowna	C
54	Pit.	Noah Welch	St. Sebastian's H.S.	D
55	Buf.	Jason Pominville	Shawinigan	RW
56	Cgy.	Andrei Medvedev	Spartak	G
57	St.L.	Jay McClement	Brampton	C
58	Wsh.	Nathan Paetsch	Moose Jaw	D
59	Chi.	Matt Keith	Spokane	RW
60	N.J.	Victor Uchevatov	Yaroslavl	D
61	T.B.	Andreas Holmqvist	Hammarby	D
62	Det.	Igor Grigorenko	Lada Togliatti	RW
63	Col.	Peter Budaj	St. Michael's	G

First Round and Other Notable Selections 2000–1969

2000
FIRST ROUND

1	NYI	Rick DiPietro	Boston U.	G
2	Atl.	Dany Heatley	U. of Wisconsin	RW
3	Min.	Marian Gaborik	Dukla Trencin	RW
4	CBJ	Rostislav Klesla	Brampton	D
5	NYI	Raffi Torres	Brampton	LW
6	Nsh.	Scott Hartnell	Prince Albert	LW
7	Bos.	Lars Jonsson	Leksand	D
8	T.B.	Nikita Alexeev	Erie	RW
9	Cgy.	Brent Krahn	Calgary	G
10	Chi.	Mikhail Yakubov	Lada Togliatti	C
11	Chi.	Pavel Vorobiev	Yaroslavl	RW
12	Ana.	Alexei Smirnov	Tver	LW
13	Mtl.	Ron Hainsey	U. of Mass-Lowell	D
14	Col.	Vaclav Nedorost	Budejovice	C
15	Buf.	Artem Kryukov	Yaroslavl	C
16	Mtl.	Marcel Hossa	Portland	LW
17	Edm.	Alexei Mikhnov	Yaroslavl	LW

(center-top column)

18	Pit.	Brooks Orpik	Boston College	D
19	Phx.	Krys Kolanos	Boston College	C
20	L.A.	Alexander Frolov	Yaroslavl 2	LW
21	Ott.	Anton Volchenkov	HC Moscow	D
22	N.J.	David Hale	Sioux City	D
23	Van.	Nathan Smith	Swift Current	C
24	Tor.	Brad Boyes	Erie	C
25	Dal.	Steve Ott	Windsor	C
26	Wsh.	Brian Sutherby	Moose Jaw	C
27	Bos.	Martin Samuelsson	MoDo Ornskoldsvik	RW
28	Phi.	Justin Williams	Plymouth	RW
29	Det.	Niklas Kronwall	Djurgarden	D
30	St.L.	Jeff Taffe	U. of Minnesota	C

OTHER NOTABLE SELECTIONS

33	Min.	Nick Schultz	Prince Albert	D
43	Wsh.	Matt Pettinger	Calgary	LW
46	Cgy.	Jarrett Stoll	Kootenay	C
54	L.A.	Andreas Lilja	Malmo	D
76	N.J.	Michael Rupp	Erie	LW
97	Car.	Niclas Wallin	Brynas	D
118	L.A.	Lubomir Visnovsky	Bratislava	D
135	N.J.	Mike Danton	Barrie	D
155	Cgy.	Travis Moen	Kelowna	LW
159	Col.	John-Michael Liles	Michigan State	D
171	Phi.	Roman Cechmanek	Vsetin	G
232	Min.	Lubomir Sekeras	Trinec	D

1999
FIRST ROUND

1	Atl.	Patrik Stefan	Long Beach	C
2	Van.	Daniel Sedin	MoDo Ornskoldsvik	LW
3	Van.	Henrik Sedin	MoDo Ornskoldsvik	C
4	NYR	Pavel Brendl	Calgary	RW
5	NYI	Tim Connolly	Erie	C
6	Nsh.	Brian Finley	Barrie	G
7	Wsh.	Kris Beech	Calgary	C
8	NYI	Taylor Pyatt	Sudbury	LW
9	NYR	Jamie Lundmark	Moose Jaw	C
10	NYI	Branislav Mezei	Belleville	D
11	Cgy.	Oleg Saprykin	Seattle	LW
12	Fla.	Denis Shvidki	Barrie	RW
13	Edm.	Jani Rita	Jokerit	LW
14	S.J.	Jeff Jillson	U. of Michigan	D
15	Phx.	Scott Kelman	Seattle	C
16	Car.	David Tanabe	U. of Wisconsin	D
17	St.L.	Barret Jackman	Regina	D
18	Pit.	Konstantin Koltsov	Cherepovets	RW
19	Phx.	Kirill Safronov	St. Petersburg	D
20	Buf.	Barrett Heisten	U. of Maine	LW
21	Bos.	Nick Boynton	Ottawa	D
22	Phi.	Maxime Ouellet	Quebec	G
23	Chi.	Steve McCarthy	Kootenay	D
24	Tor.	Luca Cereda	Ambri	C
25	Col.	Mikhail Kuleshov	Cherepovets	LW
26	Ott.	Martin Havlat	Trinec	RW
27	N.J.	Ari Ahonen	JyP HT Jr.	G
28	NYI	Kristian Kudroc	Michalovce	D

OTHER NOTABLE SELECTIONS

42	N.J.	Mike Commodore	North Dakota	D
70	Fla.	Niklas Hagman	HIFK Helsinki	LW
76	L.A.	Frantisek Kaberle	MoDo Ornskoldsvik	D
83	Ana.	Niclas Havelid	Malmo	D
91	Edm.	Mike Comrie	U. of Michigan	C
115	Pit.	Ryan Malone	Omaha	LW
191	Nsh.	Martin Erat	ZPS Zlin Jr.	LW
210	Det.	Henrik Zetterberg	Timra	C
212	Col.	Radim Vrbata	Hull	RW
230	Ana.	Petr Tenkrat	Kladno	RW
232	St.L.	Alexander Khavanov	Dynamo	D
247	Bos.	Mikko Eloranta	TPS Turku	LW

1998
FIRST ROUND

1	T.B.	Vincent Lecavalier	Rimouski	C
2	Nsh.	David Legwand	Plymouth	C
3	S.J.	Brad Stuart	Regina	D
4	Van.	Bryan Allen	Oshawa	D
5	Ana.	Vitaly Vishnevski	Yaroslavl 2	D
6	Cgy.	Rico Fata	London	RW
7	NYR	Manny Malhotra	Guelph	C
8	Chi.	Mark Bell	Ottawa	C
9	NYI	Mike Rupp	Erie	RW
10	Tor.	Nik Antropov	Ust-Kamenogorsk	C
11	Car.	Jeff Heerema	Sarnia	RW
12	Col.	Alex Tanguay	Halifax	LW
13	Edm.	Michael Henrich	Barrie	RW
14	Phx.	Patrick DesRochers	Sarnia	G
15	Ott.	Mathieu Chouinard	Shawinigan	G
16	Mtl.	Eric Chouinard	Quebec	LW
17	Col.	Martin Skoula	Barrie	D
18	Buf.	Dmitri Kalinin	Chelyabinsk	D
19	Col.	Robyn Regehr	Kamloops	D
20	Col.	Scott Parker	Kelowna	RW
21	L.A.	Mathieu Biron	Shawinigan	D
22	Phi.	Simon Gagne	Quebec	LW

(right-top column)

23	Pit.	Milan Kraft	Keramika Plzen Jr.	C
24	St.L.	Christian Backman	Vastra Frolunda Jr.	D
25	Det.	Jiri Fischer	Hull	D
26	N.J.	Mike Van Ryn	U. of Michigan	D
27	N.J.	Scott Gomez	Tri-City	C

San Jose's second pick, 29th overall, in 1998, Jonathan Cheechoo in 2003-04.

OTHER NOTABLE SELECTIONS

29	S.J.	Jonathan Cheechoo	Belleville	RW
43	Phx.	Ossi Vaananen	Jokerit Jr.	D
44	Ott.	Mike Fisher	Sudbury	C
48	Bos.	Jonathan Girard	Laval	D
60	Nsh.	Denis Arkhipov	Ak Bars Kazan	C
64	T.B.	Brad Richards	Rimouski	C
91	Car.	Josef Vasicek	Slavia Praha Jr.	C
99	Edm.	Shawn Horcoff	Michigan State	C
117	Fla.	Jaroslav Spacek	Farjestad Karlstad	D
135	Bos.	Andrew Raycroft	Sudbury	G
150	Ana.	Trent Hunter	Prince George	RW
171	Det.	Pavel Datsyuk	Yekateringburg	C
216	Mtl.	Michael Rider	Hull	RW
230	Nsh.	Karlis Skrastins	TPS Turku	D

1997
FIRST ROUND

1	Bos.	Joe Thornton	Sault Ste. Marie	C
2	S.J.	Patrick Marleau	Seattle	C
3	L.A.	Olli Jokinen	HIFK Helsinki	C
4	NYI	Roberto Luongo	Val-d'Or	G
5	NYI	Eric Brewer	Prince George	D
6	Cgy.	Daniel Tkaczuk	Barrie	C
7	T.B.	Paul Mara	Sudbury	D
8	Bos.	Sergei Samsonov	Detroit	LW
9	Wsh.	Nick Boynton	Ottawa	D
10	Van.	Brad Ference	Spokane	D
11	Mtl.	Jason Ward	Erie	RW
12	Ott.	Marian Hossa	Dukla Trencin	RW
13	Chi.	Daniel Cleary	Belleville	RW
14	Edm.	Michel Riesen	Biel-Bienne	RW
15	L.A.	Matt Zultek	Ottawa	LW
16	Chi.	Ty Jones	Spokane	C
17	Pit.	Robert Dome	Las Vegas (IHL)	RW
18	Ana.	Mikael Holmqvist	Djurgarden	C
19	NYR	Stefan Cherneski	Brandon	RW
20	Fla.	Mike Brown	Red Deer	LW
21	Buf.	Mika Noronen	Tappara Tampere	G
22	Car.	Nikos Tselios	Belleville	D
23	S.J.	Scott Hannan	Kelowna	D
24	N.J.	J-F Damphousse	Moncton	G
25	Dal.	Brenden Morrow	Portland	LW
26	Col.	Kevin Grimes	Kingston	D

OTHER NOTABLE SELECTIONS

27	Bos.	Ben Clymer	Minnesota-Duluth	LW
70	Cgy.	Erik Andersson	U. of Denver	C
95	Fla.	Ivan Novoseltsev	Krylja Sovetov	RW
119	Ott.	Magnus Arvedson	Farjestad Karlstad	LW
130	Chi.	Kyle Calder	Regina	LW
136	NYR	Mike York	Michigan State	LW
144	Van.	Matt Cooke	Windsor	C
177	St.L.	Ladislav Nagy	Dragon Presov	LW
191	Bos.	Antti Laaksonen	U. of Denver	LW
242	Chi.	Brett McLean	Kelowna	C

Pick	Claimed by	Amateur Club	Position

1996
FIRST ROUND

Pick	Claimed by	Amateur Club	Position
1	Ott.	Chris Phillips	Prince Albert	D
2	S.J.	Andrei Zyuzin	Salavat Yulayev Ufa	D
3	NYI	J.P. Dumont	Val-d'Or	RW
4	Wsh.	Alexandre Volchkov	Barrie	C
5	Dal.	Ric Jackman	Sault Ste. Marie	D
6	Edm.	Boyd Devereaux	Kitchener	C
7	Buf.	Erik Rasmussen	Minnesota-Duluth	LW/C
8	Bos.	Johnathan Aitken	Medicine Hat	D
9	Ana.	Ruslan Salei	Las Vegas (IHL)	D
10	N.J.	Lance Ward	Red Deer	D
11	Phx.	Dan Focht	Tri-City	D
12	Van.	Josh Holden	Regina	C
13	Cgy.	Derek Morris	Regina	D
14	St.L.	Marty Reasoner	Boston College	C
15	Phi.	Dainius Zubrus	Pembroke Jr. A	RW
16	T.B.	Mario Larocque	Hull	D
17	Wsh.	Jaroslav Svejkovsky	Tri-City	RW
18	Mtl.	Matt Higgins	Moose Jaw	C
19	Edm.	Matthieu Descoteaux	Shawinigan	D
20	Fla.	Marcus Nilson	Djurgarden	LW
21	S.J.	Marco Sturm	Landshut	LW
22	NYR	Jeff Brown	Sarnia	D
23	Pit.	Craig Hillier	Ottawa	G
24	Phx.	Daniel Briere	Drummondville	C
25	Col.	Peter Ratchuk	Shattuck St. Mary's H.S.	D
26	Det.	Jesse Wallin	Red Deer	D

OTHER NOTABLE SELECTIONS

Pick	Claimed by	Amateur Club	Position
35	Ana.	Matt Cullen	St. Cloud State	C
49	N.J.	Colin White	Hull	D
56	NYI	Zdeno Chara	Dukla Trencin	D
59	Edm.	Tom Poti	Cushing Academy	D
65	Fla.	Oleg Kvasha	CSKA Moscow	LW/C
79	Col.	Mark Parrish	St. Cloud State	RW
136	Ott.	Andreas Dackell	Brynas Gavle	RW
139	Phx.	Robert Esche	Detroit	G
174	Phx.	Trevor Letowski	Sarnia	RW
179	T.B.	Pavel Kubina	Vitkovice	D
204	Tor.	Tomas Kaberle	Kladno	D

1995
FIRST ROUND

Pick	Claimed by	Amateur Club	Position
1	Ott.	Bryan Berard	Detroit	D
2	NYI	Wade Redden	Brandon	D
3	L.A.	Aki Berg	Kiekko-67 Turku	D
4	Ana.	Chad Kilger	Kingston	C
5	T.B.	Daymond Langkow	Tri-City	C
6	Edm.	Steve Kelly	Prince Albert	C
7	Wpg.	Shane Doan	Kamloops	RW
8	Mtl.	Terry Ryan	Tri-City	LW
9	Bos.	Kyle McLaren	Tacoma	D
10	Fla.	Radek Dvorak	HC Ceske Budejovice	RW
11	Dal.	Jarome Iginla	Kamloops	RW
12	S.J.	Teemu Riihijarvi	Kiekko-Espoo	LW
13	Hfd.	Jean-Sebastien Giguere	Halifax	G
14	Buf.	Jay McKee	Niagara Falls	D
15	Tor.	Jeff Ware	Oshawa	D
16	Buf.	Martin Biron	Beauport	G
17	Wsh.	Brad Church	Prince Albert	LW
18	N.J.	Petr Sykora	Detroit	RW
19	Chi.	Dmitri Nabokov	Krylja Sovetov	C/LW
20	Cgy.	Denis Gauthier	Drummondville	D
21	Bos.	Sean Brown	Belleville	D
22	Phi.	Brian Boucher	Tri-City	G
23	Wsh.	Miika Elomo	Kiekko-67 Turku	LW
24	Pit.	Aleksey Morozov	Krylja Sovetov	RW
25	Col.	Marc Denis	Chicoutimi	G
26	Det.	Maxim Kuznetsov	Dynamo	D

OTHER NOTABLE SELECTIONS

Pick	Claimed by	Amateur Club	Position
31	Edm.	Georges Laraque	St-Jean	RW
45	Chi.	Christian Laflamme	Beauport	D
59	L.A.	Vladimir Tsyplakov	Fort Wayne IHL	LW
67	Wpg.	Brad Isbister	Portland	LW
79	N.J.	Alyn McCauley	Ottawa	C
87	Hfd.	Sami Kapanen	HIFK Helsinki	RW
91	NYR	Marc Savard	Oshawa	C
101	St.L.	Michal Handzus	IS Banska Bystrica	C
116	S.J.	Miikka Kiprusoff	TPS Turku Jr.	G
128	Pit.	Jan Hrdina	Seattle	C
145	Tor.	Yannick Tremblay	Beauport	D
166	Fla.	Peter Worrell	Hull	LW
177	Bos.	P.J. Axelsson	Vastra Frolunda	LW
223	Tor.	Danny Markov	Spartak	D

1994
FIRST ROUND

Pick	Claimed by	Amateur Club	Position
1	Fla.	Ed Jovanovski	Windsor	D
2	Ana.	Oleg Tverdovsky	Krylja Sovetov	D
3	Ott.	Radek Bonk	Las Vegas (IHL)	C
4	Edm.	Jason Bonsignore	Niagara Falls	C
5	Hfd.	Jeff O'Neill	Guelph	RW
6	Edm.	Ryan Smyth	Moose Jaw	LW

Pick	Claimed by	Amateur Club	Position
7	L.A.	Jamie Storr	Owen Sound	G
8	T.B.	Jason Wiemer	Portland	C
9	NYI	Brett Lindros	Kingston	RW
10	Wsh.	Nolan Baumgartner	Kamloops	D
11	S.J.	Jeff Friesen	Regina	LW
12	Que.	Wade Belak	Saskatoon	D/RW
13	Van.	Mattias Ohlund	Pitea	D
14	Chi.	Ethan Moreau	Niagara Falls	LW
15	Wsh.	Alexander Kharlamov	CSKA Moscow	C
16	Tor.	Eric Fichaud	Chictoutimi	G
17	Buf.	Wayne Primeau	Owen Sound	C
18	Mtl.	Brad Brown	North Bay	D
19	Cgy.	Chris Dingman	Brandon	LW
20	Dal.	Jason Botterill	U. of Michigan	LW
21	Bos.	Evgeni Ryabchikov	Molot Perm	G
22	Que.	Jeffrey Kealty	Catholic Memorial H.S.	D
23	Det.	Yan Golubovsky	Dynamo 2	D
24	Pit.	Chris Wells	Seattle	C
25	N.J.	Vadim Sharifijanov	Salavat Yulayev Ufa	LW
26	NYR	Dan Cloutier	Sault Ste. Marie	G

OTHER NOTABLE SELECTIONS

Pick	Claimed by	Amateur Club	Position
27	Fla.	Rhett Warrener	Saskatoon	D
43	Buf.	Curtis Brown	Moose Jaw	C/LW
49	Det.	Mathieu Dandenault	Sherbrooke	RW/D
51	N.J.	Patrik Elias	Kladno	LW
64	Tor.	Fredrik Modin	Timra	LW
87	Que.	Milan Hejduk	Pardubice	RW
124	Dal.	Marty Turco	Cambridge Jr. A	G
132	Ana.	Bates Battaglia	Caledon Jr. A	LW
133	Ott.	Daniel Alfredsson	Vastra Frolunda	RW
210	N.J.	Steve Sullivan	Sault Ste. Marie	RW
219	S.J.	Evegeni Nabokov	Ust-Kamengorsk	G
272	NYR	Dick Tarnstrom	AIK Solna	D

1993
FIRST ROUND

Pick	Claimed by	Amateur Club	Position
1	Ott.	Alexandre Daigle	Victoriaville	C
2	Hfd.	Chris Pronger	Peterborough	D
3	T.B.	Chris Gratton	Kingston	C
4	Ana.	Paul Kariya	U. of Maine	LW
5	Fla.	Rob Niedermayer	Medicine Hat	C
6	Det.	Benoit Larose	Laval	D
7	S.J.	Viktor Kozlov	Dynamo	C
8	Edm.	Jason Arnott	Oshawa	C
9	NYR	Niklas Sundstrom	MoDo Ornskoldsvik	RW
10	Dal.	Todd Harvey	Detroit	RW/C
11	Que.	Jocelyn Thibault	Sherbrooke	G
12	Wsh.	Brendan Witt	Seattle	D
13	Tor.	Kenny Jonsson	Rogle Angelholm	D
14	N.J.	Denis Pederson	Prince Albert	C/RW
15	Que.	Adam Deadmarsh	Portland	RW
16	Wpg.	Mats Lindgren	Skelleftea	C/LW
17	Edm.	Nick Stajduhar	London	D
18	Wsh.	Jason Allison	London	C
19	Cgy.	Jesper Mattsson	Malmo	C
20	Tor.	Landon Wilson	Dubuque Jr. A	RW
21	Van.	Mike Wilson	Sudbury	D
22	Mtl.	Saku Koivu	TPS Turku	C
23	Det.	Anders Eriksson	MoDo Ornskoldsvik	D
24	NYI	Todd Bertuzzi	Guelph	RW
25	Chi.	Eric Lecompte	Hull	LW
26	Bos.	Kevyn Adams	Miami of Ohio	C
26	Pit.	Stefan Bergkvist	Leksand	D

Picked 124th overall by Vancouver in 1993, Scott Walker helped Nashville reach the playoffs for the first time with a team-leading 25 goals in 2003-04.

Pick	Claimed by	Amateur Club	Position

OTHER NOTABLE SELECTIONS

Pick	Claimed by	Amateur Club	Position
28	S.J.	Shean Donovan	Ottawa	RW
71	Phi.	Vaclav Prospal	Motor Ceske Budejovice	C
72	Hfd.	Marek Malik	Vitkovice	D
90	Chi.	Eric Daze	Beauport	RW
111	Edm.	Miroslav Satan	Dukla Trencin	LW
118	NYI	Tommy Salo	Vasteras	G
124	Van.	Scott Walker	Owen Sound	RW
151	Buf.	Darcy Tucker	Kamloops	RW
164	NYR	Todd Marchant	Clarkson	C
207	Bos.	Hal Gill	Nashoba H.S.	D
219	St.L.	Mike Grier	St. Sebastian's H.S.	RW
227	Ott.	Pavol Demitra	Dukla Trencin	LW
252	Cgy.	German Titov	TPS Turku	LW

New Jersey's first choice, 18th overall, in 1992, Jason Smith played for the Devils and Maple Leafs before finding a home in Edmonton. He's been captain of the Oilers since 2001-02.

1992
FIRST ROUND

Pick	Claimed by	Amateur Club	Position
1	T.B.	Roman Hamrlik	ZPS Zlin	D
2	Ott.	Alexei Yashin	Dynamo	C
3	S.J.	Mike Rathje	Medicine Hat	D
4	Que.	Todd Warriner	Windsor	LW
5	NYI	Darius Kasparaitis	Dynamo	D
6	Cgy.	Cory Stillman	Windsor	LW
7	Phi.	Ryan Sittler	Nichols H.S.	LW
8	Tor.	Brandon Convery	Sudbury	C
9	Hfd.	Robert Petrovicky	Dukla Trencin	C
10	S.J.	Andrei Nazarov	Dynamo	LW
11	Buf.	David Cooper	Medicine Hat	D
12	Chi.	Sergei Krivokrasov	CSKA Moscow	RW
13	Edm.	Joe Hulbig	St. Sebastian's H.S.	LW
14	Wsh.	Sergei Gonchar	Chelyabinsk	D
15	Phi.	Jason Bowen	Tri-City	D
16	Bos.	Dmitri Kvartalnov	San Diego (IHL)	LW
17	Wpg.	Sergei Bautin	Dynamo	D
18	N.J.	Jason Smith	Regina	D
19	Pit.	Martin Straka	HC Skoda Plzen	C
20	Mtl.	David Wilkie	Kamloops	D
21	Van.	Libor Polasek	Vitkovice	C
22	Det.	Curtis Bowen	Ottawa	LW
23	Tor.	Grant Marshall	Ottawa	RW
24	NYR	Peter Ferraro	Waterloo Jr. A	LW

OTHER NOTABLE SELECTIONS

Pick	Claimed by	Amateur Club	Position
27	Wpg.	Boris Mironov	CSKA Moscow	D
33	Mtl.	Valeri Bure	Spokane	RW
36	Chi.	Jeff Shantz	Regina	C
38	St.L.	Igor Korolev	Dynamo	C
40	Van.	Michael Peca	Ottawa	C
42	N.J.	Sergei Brylin	CSKA Moscow	C
46	Det.	Darren McCarty	Belleville	RW
48	NYR	Mattias Norstrom	AIK Solna	D
65	Edm.	Kirk Maltby	Owen Sound	RW
78	Cgy.	Robert Svehla	Dukla Trencin	D
83	Buf.	Matthew Barnaby	Beauport	RW
158	St.L.	Ian Laperriere	Drummondville	C/RW
186	N.J.	Stephane Yelle	Oshawa	C
204	Wpg.	Nikolai Khabibulin	CSKA Moscow	G

1991
FIRST ROUND

Pick	Claimed by	Amateur Club	Position
1	Que.	Eric Lindros	Oshawa	C
2	S.J.	Pat Falloon	Spokane	RW
3	N.J.	Scott Niedermayer	Kamloops	D
4	NYI	Scott Lachance	Boston U.	D
5	Wpg.	Aaron Ward	U. of Michigan	D
6	Phi.	Peter Forsberg	MoDo Ornskoldsvik	C

Pick	Claimed by		Amateur Club	Position
7	Van.	Alek Stojanov	Hamilton	RW
8	Min.	Richard Matvichuk	Saskatoon	D
9	Hfd.	Patrick Poulin	St-Hyacinthe	C
10	Det.	Martin Lapointe	Laval	RW
11	N.J.	Brian Rolston	Detroit Compuware Jr. A	C/RW
12	Edm.	Tyler Wright	Swift Current	C
13	Buf.	Philippe Boucher	Granby	D
14	Wsh.	Pat Peake	Detroit	C
15	NYR	Alex Kovalev	Dynamo	RW
16	Pit.	Markus Naslund	MoDo Ornskoldsvik	LW
17	Mtl.	Brent Bilodeau	Seattle	D
18	Bos.	Glen Murray	Sudbury	RW
19	Cgy.	Niklas Sundblad	AIK Solna	RW
20	Edm.	Martin Rucinsky	CHZ Litvinov	LW
21	Wsh.	Trevor Halverson	North Bay	LW
22	Chi.	Dean McAmmond	Prince Albert	LW

OTHER NOTABLE SELECTIONS

Pick	Claimed by		Amateur Club	Position
23	S.J.	Ray Whitney	Spokane	LW
26	NYI	Ziggy Palffy	AC Nitra	RW
30	S.J.	Sandis Ozolinsh	Dynamo Riga	D
40	Bos.	Jozef Stumpel	AC Nitra	C
52	Cgy.	Sandy McCarthy	Laval	RW
58	Wsh.	Steve Konowalchuk	Portland	LW
59	Hfd.	Michael Nylander	Huddinge	C
71	Chi.	Igor Kravchuk	CSKA Moscow	D
81	L.A.	Alexei Zhitnik	Sokol Kiev	D
103	Que.	Bill Lindsay	Tri-City	RW
106	Bos.	Mariusz Czerkawski	GKS Tychy	RW
122	Phi.	Dmitry Yushkevich	Yaroslavl	D
203	Wpg.	Igor Ulanov	Khimik Voskresensk	D

1990

FIRST ROUND

Pick	Claimed by		Amateur Club	Position
1	Que.	Owen Nolan	Cornwall	RW
2	Van.	Petr Nedved	Seattle	C
3	Det.	Keith Primeau	Niagara Falls	C
4	Phi.	Mike Ricci	Peterborough	C
5	Pit.	Jaromir Jagr	Kladno	RW
6	NYI	Scott Scissons	Saskatoon	C
7	L.A.	Darryl Sydor	Kamloops	D
8	Min.	Derian Hatcher	North Bay	D
9	Wsh.	John Slaney	Cornwall	D
10	Tor.	Drake Berehowsky	Kingston	D
11	Cgy.	Trevor Kidd	Brandon	G
12	Mtl.	Turner Stevenson	Seattle	RW
13	NYR	Michael Stewart	Michigan State	D
14	Buf.	Brad May	Niagara Falls	LW
15	Hfd.	Mark Greig	Lethbridge	RW
16	Chi.	Karl Dykhuis	Hull	D
17	Edm.	Scott Allison	Prince Albert	C
18	Van.	Shawn Antoski	North Bay	LW
19	Wpg.	Keith Tkachuk	Malden Catholic H.S.	LW
20	N.J.	Martin Brodeur	St-Hyacinthe	G
21	Bos.	Bryan Smolinski	Michigan State	C

OTHER NOTABLE SELECTIONS

Pick	Claimed by		Amateur Club	Position
23	Van.	Jiri Slegr	CHZ Litvinov	D
31	Tor.	Felix Potvin	Chicoutimi	G
34	NYR	Doug Weight	Lake Superior State	C
36	Hfd.	Geoff Sanderson	Swift Current	LW
45	Det.	Vyacheslav Kozlov	Khimik Voskresensk	RW
85	NYR	Sergei Zubov	CSKA Moscow	D
86	Van.	Gino Odjick	Laval	RW
97	Buf.	Richard Smehlik	Vitkovice	D
133	L.A.	Robert Lang	CHZ Litvinov	C
156	Wsh.	Peter Bondra	Kosice	RW
177	Wsh.	Ken Klee	Bowling Green	D
244	NYR	Sergei Nemchinov	Krylja Sovetov	LW

1989

FIRST ROUND

Pick	Claimed by		Amateur Club	Position
1	Que.	Mats Sundin	Nacka	C
2	NYI	Dave Chyzowski	Kamloops	LW
3	Tor.	Scott Thornton	Belleville	LW
4	Wpg.	Stu Barnes	Tri-City	C
5	N.J.	Bill Guerin	Springfield Jr. B	RW
6	Chi.	Adam Bennett	Sudbury	D
7	Min.	Doug Zmolek	John Marshall H.S.	D
8	Van.	Jason Herter	North Dakota	D
9	St.L.	Jason Marshall	Vernon Jr. A	D
10	Hfd.	Bobby Holik	Dukla Jihlava	C
11	Det.	Mike Sillinger	Regina	C
12	Tor.	Rob Pearson	Belleville	RW
13	Mtl.	Lindsay Vallis	Seattle	D
14	Buf.	Kevin Haller	Regina	D
15	Edm.	Jason Soules	Niagara Falls	D
16	Pit.	Jamie Heward	Regina	D
17	Bos.	Shayne Stevenson	Kitchener	RW
18	N.J.	Jason Miller	Medicine Hat	LW
19	Wsh.	Olie Kolzig	Tri-City	G
20	NYR	Steven Rice	Kitchener	RW
21	Tor.	Steve Bancroft	Belleville	D

OTHER NOTABLE SELECTIONS

Pick	Claimed by		Amateur Club	Position
22	Que.	Adam Foote	Sault Ste. Marie	D
23	NYI	Travis Green	Spokane	C
53	Det.	Nicklas Lidstrom	Vasteras	D
62	Wpg.	Kris Draper	Canadian National	C
73	Hfd.	Jim McKenzie	Victoria	LW
74	Det.	Sergei Fedorov	CSKA Moscow	C
82	Wsh.	Trent Klatt	Osseo H.S.	RW
113	Van.	Pavel Bure	CSKA Moscow	RW
116	Det.	Dallas Drake	Northern Michigan	RW
183	Buf.	Donald Audette	Laval	RW
196	Min.	Arturs Irbe	Dynamo Riga	G
221	Det.	Vladimir Konstantinov	CSKA Moscow	D

1988

FIRST ROUND

Pick	Claimed by		Amateur Club	Position
1	Min.	Mike Modano	Prince Albert	C
2	Van.	Trevor Linden	Medicine Hat	RW
3	Que.	Curtis Leschyshyn	Saskatoon	D
4	Pit.	Darrin Shannon	Windsor	LW
5	Que.	Daniel Dore	Drummondville	RW
6	Tor.	Scott Pearson	Kingston	LW
7	L.A.	Martin Gelinas	Hull	LW
8	Chi.	Jeremy Roenick	Thayer Academy	C
9	St.L.	Rod Brind'Amour	Notre Dame Jr. A	C
10	Wpg.	Teemu Selanne	Jokerit	RW
11	Hfd.	Chris Govedaris	Toronto	LW
12	N.J.	Corey Foster	Peterborough	D
13	Buf.	Joel Savage	Victoria	RW
14	Phi.	Claude Boivin	Drummondville	LW
15	Wsh.	Reggie Savage	Victoriaville	C
16	NYI	Kevin Cheveldayoff	Brandon	D
17	Det.	Kory Kocur	Saskatoon	RW
18	Bos.	Rob Cimetta	Toronto	W
19	Edm.	Francois Leroux	St-Jean	D
20	Mtl.	Eric Charron	Trois-Rivieres	D
21	Cgy.	Jason Muzzatti	Michigan State	G

OTHER NOTABLE SELECTIONS

Pick	Claimed by		Amateur Club	Position
27	Tor.	Tie Domi	Peterborough	RW
60	Bos.	Steve Heinze	Lawrence Academy	RW
67	Pit.	Mark Recchi	Kamloops	RW
68	NYR	Tony Amonte	Thayer Academy	RW
89	Buf.	Alexander Mogilny	CSKA Moscow	RW
97	Buf.	Rob Ray	Cornwall	RW
120	Wsh.	Dmitri Khristich	Sokol Kiev	LW/C
163	NYI	Marty McInnis	Milton Academy	RW
198	St.L.	Bret Hedican	North St. Paul H.S.	D
234	Que.	Claude Lapointe	Laval	LW/C

1987

FIRST ROUND

Pick	Claimed by		Amateur Club	Position
1	Buf.	Pierre Turgeon	Granby	C
2	N.J.	Brendan Shanahan	London	LW
3	Bos.	Glen Wesley	Portland	D
4	L.A.	Wayne McBean	Medicine Hat	D
5	Pit.	Chris Joseph	Seattle	D
6	Min.	Dave Archibald	Portland	C/LW
7	Tor.	Luke Richardson	Peterborough	D
8	Chi.	Jimmy Waite	Chicoutimi	G
9	Que.	Bryan Fogarty	Kingston	D
10	NYR	Jay More	New Westminster	D
11	Det.	Yves Racine	Longueuil	D
12	St.L.	Keith Osborne	North Bay	RW
13	NYI	Dean Chynoweth	Medicine Hat	D
14	Bos.	Stephane Quintal	Granby	D
15	Que.	Joe Sakic	Swift Current	C
16	Wpg.	Bryan Marchment	Belleville	D
17	Mtl.	Andrew Cassels	Ottawa	C
18	Hfd.	Jody Hull	Peterborough	RW
19	Cgy.	Bryan Deasley	U. of Michigan	LW
20	Phi.	Darren Rumble	Kitchener	D
21	Edm.	Peter Soberlak	Swift Current	LW

OTHER NOTABLE SELECTIONS

Pick	Claimed by		Amateur Club	Position
25	Cgy.	Stephane Matteau	Hull	LW
33	Mtl.	John LeClair	Bellows Academy	LW
38	Mtl.	Eric Desjardins	Granby	D
44	Mtl.	Mathieu Schneider	Cornwall	D
71	Tor.	Joe Sacco	Medford H.S.	RW
108	Van.	Garry Valk	Sherwood Park Jr. A	RW
110	Pit.	Shawn McEachern	Matignon H.S.	RW
159	St.L.	Guy Hebert	Hamilton College	G
166	Cgy.	Theoren Fleury	Moose Jaw	RW

1986

FIRST ROUND

Pick	Claimed by		Amateur Club	Position
1	Det.	Joe Murphy	Michigan State	RW
2	L.A.	Jimmy Carson	Verdun	C
3	N.J.	Neil Brady	Medicine Hat	C
4	Pit.	Zarley Zalapski	Canadian National	D
5	Buf.	Shawn Anderson	Canadian National	D
6	Tor.	Vincent Damphousse	Laval	C
7	Van.	Dan Woodley	Portland	RW
8	Wpg.	Pat Elynuik	Prince Albert	RW
9	NYR	Brian Leetch	Avon Old Farms H.S.	D
10	St.L.	Jocelyn Lemieux	Laval	RW
11	Hfd.	Scott Young	Boston U.	RW
12	Min.	Warren Babe	Lethbridge	LW
13	Bos.	Craig Janney	Boston College	C
14	Chi.	Everett Sanipass	Verdun	LW
15	Mtl.	Mark Pederson	Medicine Hat	LW
16	Cgy.	George Pelawa	Bemidji H.S.	RW
17	NYI	Tom Fitzgerald	Austin Prep	RW
18	Que.	Ken McRae	Sudbury	C
19	Wsh.	Jeff Greenlaw	Canadian National	LW
20	Phi.	Kerry Huffman	Guelph	D
21	Edm.	Kim Issel	Prince Albert	RW

OTHER NOTABLE SELECTIONS

Pick	Claimed by		Amateur Club	Position
22	Det.	Adam Graves	Windsor	LW
27	Mtl.	Benoit Brunet	Hull	LW
29	Wpg.	Teppo Numminen	Tappara Tampere	D
47	Buf.	Bob Corkum	U. of Maine	C
57	Mtl.	Jyrki Lumme	Ilves Tampere	D
67	Pit.	Rob Brown	Kamloops	RW
72	NYR	Mark Janssens	Regina	C
85	Det.	Johan Garpenlov	Nacka	LW
114	NYR	Darren Turcotte	North Bay	C
141	Mtl.	Lyle Odelein	Moose Jaw	D
143	NYI	Rich Pilon	Prince Albert AAA	D
167	Phi.	Murray Baron	Vernon Jr. A	D

1985

FIRST ROUND

Pick	Claimed by		Amateur Club	Position
1	Tor.	Wendel Clark	Saskatoon	LW/D
2	Pit.	Craig Simpson	Michigan State	LW
3	N.J.	Craig Wolanin	Kitchener	D
4	Van.	Jim Sandlak	London	RW
5	Hfd.	Dana Murzyn	Calgary	D
6	NYI	Brad Dalgarno	Hamilton	RW
7	NYR	Ulf Dahlen	Ostersund	LW
8	Det.	Brent Fedyk	Regina	LW
9	L.A.	Craig Duncanson	Sudbury	LW
10	L.A.	Dan Gratton	Oshawa	C
11	Chi.	Dave Manson	Prince Albert	D
12	Mtl.	Jose Charbonneau	Drummondville	RW
13	NYI	Derek King	Sault Ste. Marie	LW
14	Buf.	Calle Johansson	Vastra Frolunda	D
15	Que.	David Latta	Kitchener	LW
16	Mtl.	Tom Chorske	Minneapolis SW H.S.	LW
17	Cgy.	Chris Biotti	Belmont Hill H.S.	D
18	Wpg.	Ryan Stewart	Kamloops	C
19	Wsh.	Yvon Corriveau	Toronto	LW
20	Edm.	Scott Metcalfe	Kingston	LW
21	Phi.	Glen Seabrooke	Peterborough	C

OTHER NOTABLE SELECTIONS

Pick	Claimed by		Amateur Club	Position
24	N.J.	Sean Burke	Toronto	G
27	Cgy.	Joe Nieuwendyk	Cornell	C
28	NYR	Mike Richter	Northwood Prep	G
32	N.J.	Eric Weinrich	North Yarmouth Academy	D
35	Buf.	Benoit Hogue	St-Jean	C
44	St.L.	Nelson Emerson	Stratford Jr.A	RW
52	Bos.	Bill Ranford	New Westminster	G
81	Wpg.	Fredrik Olausson	Farjestad Karlstad	D
113	Det.	Randy McKay	Michigan Tech	RW
119	Buf.	Joe Reekie	Cornwall	D
188	Edm.	Kelly Buchberger	Moose Jaw	RW
214	Van.	Igor Larionov	CSKA Moscow	C

1984

FIRST ROUND

Pick	Claimed by		Amateur Club	Position
1	Pit.	Mario Lemieux	Laval	C
2	N.J.	Kirk Muller	Guelph	LW
3	Chi.	Eddie Olczyk	Team USA	C
4	Tor.	Al Iafrate	Belleville	D
5	Mtl.	Petr Svoboda	CHZ Litvinov	D
6	L.A.	Craig Redmond	U. of Denver	D
7	Det.	Shawn Burr	Kitchener	LW/C
8	Mtl.	Shayne Corson	Brantford	LW
9	Pit.	Doug Bodger	Kamloops	D
10	Van.	J.J. Daigneault	Longueuil	D
11	Hfd.	Sylvain Cote	Quebec	D
12	Cgy.	Gary Roberts	Ottawa	LW
13	Min.	David Quinn	Kent H.S.	D
14	NYR	Terry Carkner	Peterborough	D
15	Que.	Trevor Stienburg	Guelph	RW
16	Pit.	Roger Belanger	Kingston	C
17	Wsh.	Kevin Hatcher	North Bay	D
18	Buf.	Mikael Andersson	Vastra Frolunda	LW
19	Bos.	Dave Pasin	Prince Albert	RW
20	NYI	Duncan MacPherson	Saskatoon	D
21	Edm.	Selmar Odelein	Regina	D

OTHER NOTABLE SELECTIONS

Pick	Claimed by		Amateur Club	Position
25	Tor.	Todd Gill	Windsor	D
27	Phi.	Scott Mellanby	Henry Carr Jr. B	RW
29	Mtl.	Stephane Richer	Granby	RW
38	Cgy.	Paul Ranheim	Edina H.S.	LW
51	Mtl.	Patrick Roy	Granby	G
59	Wsh.	Michal Pivonka	Kladno	C
60	Buf.	Ray Sheppard	Cornwall	RW
117	Cgy.	Brett Hull	Penticton Jr. A	RW

Pick	Claimed by	Amateur Club	Position
119 NYR	Kjell Samuelsson	Leksand	D
134 St.L.	Cliff Ronning	New Westminster	C
166 Bos.	Don Sweeney	St. Paul's H.S.	D
171 L.A.	Luc Robitaille	Hull	LW
180 Cgy.	Gary Suter	U. of Wisconsin	D

1983
FIRST ROUND

Pick	Claimed by	Amateur Club	Position
1 Min.	Brian Lawton	Mount St. Charles H.S.	LW
2 Hfd.	Sylvain Turgeon	Hull	LW
3 NYI	Pat LaFontaine	Verdun	C
4 Det.	Steve Yzerman	Peterborough	C
5 Buf.	Tom Barrasso	Acton-Boxborough	G
6 N.J.	John MacLean	Oshawa	RW
7 Tor.	Russ Courtnall	Victoria	RW
8 Wpg.	Andrew McBain	North Bay	C
9 Van.	Cam Neely	Portland	RW
10 Buf.	Normand Lacombe	New Hampshire	RW
11 Buf.	Adam Creighton	Ottawa	C
12 NYR	Dave Gagner	Brantford	C
13 Cgy.	Dan Quinn	Belleville	C
14 Wpg.	Bobby Dollas	Laval	D
15 Pit.	Bob Errey	Peterborough	LW
16 NYI	Gerald Diduck	Lethbridge	D
17 Mtl.	Alfie Turcotte	Portland	C
18 Chi.	Bruce Cassidy	Ottawa	D
19 Edm.	Jeff Beukeboom	Sault Ste. Marie	D
20 Hfd.	David Jensen	Lawrence Academy	C
21 Bos.	Nevin Markwart	Regina	LW

OTHER NOTABLE SELECTIONS

Pick	Claimed by	Amateur Club	Position
26 Mtl.	Claude Lemieux	Trois-Rivieres	RW
46 Det.	Bob Probert	Brantford	LW
60 Chi.	Marc Bergevin	Chicoutimi	D
82 Edm.	Esa Tikkanen	HIFK Helsinki	LW
88 Det.	Petr Klima	Dukla Jihlava	W
91 Det.	Joe Kocur	Saskatoon	RW
103 L.A.	Garry Galley	Bowling Green	D
114 Van.	Dave Lowry	London	LW
125 Phi.	Rick Tocchet	Sault Ste. Marie	RW
150 N.J.	Viacheslav Fetisov	CSKA Moscow	D
207 Chi.	Dominik Hasek	Pardubice	G
223 Buf.	Uwe Krupp	Koln	D
241 Cgy.	Sergei Makarov	CSKA Moscow	RW

1982
FIRST ROUND

Pick	Claimed by	Amateur Club	Position
1 Bos.	Gord Kluzak	Billings	D
2 Min.	Brian Bellows	Kitchener	LW
3 Tor.	Gary Nylund	Portland	D
4 Phi.	Ron Sutter	Lethbridge	C
5 Wsh.	Scott Stevens	Kitchener	D
6 Buf.	Phil Housley	South St. Paul H.S.	D
7 Chi.	Ken Yaremchuk	Portland	C
8 N.J.	Rocky Trottier	Nanaimo	RW
9 Buf.	Paul Cyr	Victoria	LW
10 Pit.	Rich Sutter	Lethbridge	RW
11 Van.	Michel Petit	Sherbrooke	D
12 Wpg.	Jim Kyte	Cornwall	D
13 Que.	David Shaw	Kitchener	D
14 Hfd.	Paul Lawless	Windsor	LW
15 NYR	Chris Kontos	Toronto	LW/C
16 Buf.	Dave Andreychuk	Oshawa	LW
17 Det.	Murray Craven	Medicine Hat	LW
18 N.J.	Ken Daneyko	Seattle	D
19 Mtl.	Alain Heroux	Chicoutimi	LW
20 Edm.	Jim Playfair	Portland	D
21 NYI	Pat Flatley	U. of Wisconsin	RW

OTHER NOTABLE SELECTIONS

Pick	Claimed by	Amateur Club	Position
36 NYR	Tomas Sandstrom	Farjestad Karlstad	RW
43 N.J.	Pat Verbeek	Sudbury	RW
45 Tor.	Ken Wregget	Lethbridge	G
56 Hfd.	Kevin Dineen	U. of Denver	RW
60 Bos.	Dave Reid	Peterborough	LW
67 Hfd.	Ulf Samuelsson	Leksand	D
75 Wpg.	Dave Ellett	Ottawa Jr. A	D
80 Min.	Bob Rouse	Nanaimo	D
88 Hfd.	Ray Ferraro	Penticton Jr. A	C
119 Phi.	Ron Hextall	Brandon	G
120 NYR	Tony Granato	Northwood Prep	RW
134 St.L.	Doug Gilmour	Cornwall	C
140 Phi.	Dave Brown	Saskatoon	RW
181 Que.	Mike Hough	Kitchener	LW
183 NYR	Kelly Miller	Michigan State	LW

1981
FIRST ROUND

Pick	Claimed by	Amateur Club	Position
1 Wpg.	Dale Hawerchuk	Cornwall	C
2 L.A.	Doug Smith	Ottawa	C
3 Wsh.	Bob Carpenter	St. John's Prep	C
4 Hfd.	Ron Francis	Sault Ste. Marie	C
5 Col.	Joe Cirella	Oshawa	D
6 Tor.	Jim Benning	Portland	D
7 Mtl.	Mark Hunter	Brantford	RW
8 Edm.	Grant Fuhr	Victoria	G
9 NYR	James Patrick	Prince Albert	D
10 Van.	Garth Butcher	Regina	D
11 Que.	Randy Moller	Lethbridge	D
12 Chi.	Tony Tanti	Oshawa	RW
13 Min.	Ron Meighan	Niagara Falls	D
14 Bos.	Normand Leveille	Chicoutimi	LW
15 Cgy.	Al MacInnis	Kitchener	D
16 Phi.	Steve Smith	Sault Ste. Marie	D
17 Buf.	Jiri Dudacek	Kladno	RW
18 Mtl.	Gilbert Delorme	Chicoutimi	D
19 Mtl.	Jan Ingman	Farjestad Karlstad	LW
20 St.L.	Marty Ruff	Lethbridge	D
21 NYI	Paul Boutilier	Sherbrooke	D

OTHER NOTABLE SELECTIONS

Pick	Claimed by	Amateur Club	Position
40 Mtl.	Chris Chelios	Moose Jaw	D
56 Cgy.	Mike Vernon	Calgary	G
72 NYR	John Vanbiesbrouck	Sault Ste. Marie	G
108 Col.	Bruce Driver	U. of Wisconsin	D
111 Edm.	Steve Smith	London	D
116 Que.	Mike Eagles	Kitchener	C/LW
145 Mtl.	Tom Kurvers	Minnesota-Duluth	D
152 Wsh.	Gaetan Duchesne	Quebec	LW

1980
FIRST ROUND

Pick	Claimed by	Amateur Club	Position
1 Mtl.	Doug Wickenheiser	Regina	C
2 Wpg.	Dave Babych	Portland	D
3 Chi.	Denis Savard	Montreal	C
4 L.A.	Larry Murphy	Peterborough	D
5 Wsh.	Darren Veitch	Regina	D
6 Edm.	Paul Coffey	Kitchener	D
7 Van.	Rick Lanz	Oshawa	D
8 Hfd.	Fred Arthur	Cornwall	D
9 Pit.	Mike Bullard	Brantford	C
10 L.A.	Jim Fox	Ottawa	RW
11 Det.	Mike Blaisdell	Regina	RW
12 St.L.	Rik Wilson	Kingston	D
13 Cgy.	Denis Cyr	Montreal	RW
14 NYR	Jim Malone	Toronto	C
15 Chi.	Jerome Dupont	Toronto	D
16 Min.	Brad Palmer	Victoria	LW
17 NYI	Brent Sutter	Red Deer Jr. A.	C
18 Bos.	Barry Pederson	Victoria	C
19 Col.	Paul Gagne	Windsor	LW
20 Buf.	Steve Patrick	Brandon	RW
21 Phi.	Mike Stothers	Kingston	D

OTHER NOTABLE SELECTIONS

Pick	Claimed by	Amateur Club	Position
37 Min.	Don Beaupre	Sudbury	G
38 NYI	Kelly Hrudey	Medicine Hat	G
39 Cgy.	Steve Konroyd	Oshawa	D
46 Det.	Mark Osborne	Niagara Falls	LW
61 Mtl.	Craig Ludwig	North Dakota	D
69 Edm.	Jari Kurri	Jokerit	RW
73 L.A.	Bernie Nicholls	Kingston	C
80 NYI	Greg Gilbert	Toronto	LW
81 Bos.	Steve Kasper	Verdun	C
106 Col.	Aaron Broten	Minnesota-Duluth	LW/C
120 Chi.	Steve Larmer	Niagara Falls	RW
124 Mtl.	Mike McPhee	RPI	LW
128 Wpg.	Brian Mullen	U.S. Jr. National	RW
132 Edm.	Andy Moog	Billings	G
133 Van.	Doug Lidster	Colorado College	D
167 Buf.	Randy Cunneyworth	Ottawa	LW

Drafted by Boston in 1980, Steve Kasper is best remembered for shadowing Wayne Gretzky but he also scored at least 16 goals in eight of his 12 NHL seasons. He had a high of 26 in 1987-88.

1979
FIRST ROUND

Pick	Claimed by	Amateur Club	Position
1 Col.	Rob Ramage	London	D
2 St.L.	Perry Turnbull	Portland	C
3 Det.	Mike Foligno	Sudbury	RW
4 Wsh.	Mike Gartner	Niagara Falls	RW
5 Van.	Rick Vaive	Sherbrooke	RW
6 Min.	Craig Hartsburg	Sault Ste. Marie	D
7 Chi.	Keith Brown	Portland	D
8 Bos.	Raymond Bourque	Verdun	D
9 Tor.	Laurie Boschman	Brandon	C
10 Min.	Tom McCarthy	Oshawa	LW
11 Buf.	Mike Ramsey	U. of Minnesota	D
12 Atl.	Paul Reinhart	Kitchener	D
13 NYR	Doug Sulliman	Kitchener	RW
14 Phi.	Brian Propp	Brandon	LW
15 Bos.	Brad McCrimmon	Brandon	D
16 L.A.	Jay Wells	Kingston	D
17 NYI	Duane Sutter	Lethbridge	RW
18 Hfd.	Ray Allison	Brandon	RW
19 Wpg.	Jimmy Mann	Sherbrooke	RW
20 Que.	Michel Goulet	Quebec	LW
21 Edm.	Kevin Lowe	Quebec	D

OTHER NOTABLE SELECTIONS

Pick	Claimed by	Amateur Club	Position
26 Van.	Brent Ashton	Saskatoon	LW
30 L.A.	Mark Hardy	Montreal	D
32 Buf.	Lindy Ruff	Lethbridge	D/LW
37 Mtl.	Mats Naslund	Brynas Gavle	LW
40 Wpg.	Dave Christian	North Dakota	RW
41 Que.	Dale Hunter	Sudbury	C
42 Min.	Neal Broten	Minnesota-Duluth	C
44 Mtl.	Guy Carbonneau	Chicoutimi	C
48 Mtl.	Mark Messier	St. Albert Jr. A.	C
54 Atl.	Tim Hunter	Seattle	RW
66 Det.	John Ogrodnick	New Westminster	LW
69 Edm.	Glenn Anderson	U. of Denver	RW
75 Atl.	Jim Peplinski	Toronto	C
83 Que.	Anton Stastny	Slovan Bratislava	LW
89 Van.	Dirk Graham	Regina	RW/LW
103 Wpg.	Thomas Steen	Leksand	C
120 Bos.	Mike Krushelnyski	Montreal	LW/C

1978
FIRST ROUND

Pick	Claimed by	Amateur Club	Position
1 Min.	Bobby Smith	Ottawa	C
2 Wsh.	Ryan Walter	Seattle	C/LW
3 St.L.	Wayne Babych	Portland	RW
4 Van.	Bill Derlago	Brandon	C
5 Col.	Mike Gillis	Kingston	LW
6 Phi.	Behn Wilson	Kingston	D
7 Phi.	Ken Linseman	Kingston	C
8 Mtl.	Danny Geoffrion	Cornwall	RW
9 Det.	Willie Huber	Hamilton	D
10 Chi.	Tim Higgins	Ottawa	RW
11 Atl.	Brad Marsh	London	D
12 Det.	Brent Peterson	Portland	C
13 Buf.	Larry Playfair	Portland	D
14 Phi.	Danny Lucas	Sault Ste. Marie	RW
15 NYI	Steve Tambellini	Lethbridge	C
16 Bos.	Al Secord	Hamilton	LW
17 Mtl.	Dave Hunter	Sudbury	LW
18 Wsh.	Tim Coulis	Hamilton	LW

OTHER NOTABLE SELECTIONS

Pick	Claimed by	Amateur Club	Position
19 Min.	Steve Payne	Ottawa	LW
21 Tor.	Joel Quenneville	Windsor	D
26 NYR	Don Maloney	Kitchener	LW
32 Buf.	Tony McKegney	Kingston	LW
40 Van.	Stan Smyl	New Westminster	RW
54 Min.	Curt Giles	Minnesota-Duluth	D
55 Wsh.	Bengt-Ake Gustafsson	Farjestad Karlstad	RW
93 NYR	Tom Laidlaw	Northern Michigan	D
103 Mtl.	Keith Acton	Peterborough	C
109 St.L.	Paul MacLean	Hull	RW
153 Bos.	Craig MacTavish	University of Lowell	C
173 Que.	Risto Siltanen	Ilves Tampere	D
179 Chi.	Darryl Sutter	Lethbridge	LW
231 Mtl.	Chris Nilan	Northeastern	RW

1977
FIRST ROUND

Pick	Claimed by	Amateur Club	Position
1 Det.	Dale McCourt	St. Catharines	C
2 Col.	Barry Beck	New Westminster	D
3 Wsh.	Robert Picard	Montreal	D
4 Van.	Jere Gillis	Sherbrooke	LW
5 Cle.	Mike Crombeen	Kingston	RW
6 Chi.	Doug Wilson	Ottawa	D
7 Min.	Brad Maxwell	New Westminster	D
8 NYR	Lucien DeBlois	Sorel	C
9 St.L.	Scott Campbell	London	D
10 Mtl.	Mark Napier	Toronto	RW
11 Tor.	John Anderson	Toronto	RW
12 Tor.	Trevor Johansen	Toronto	D
13 NYR	Ron Duguay	Sudbury	C/RW

14	Buf.	Ric Seiling	St. Catharines	RW/C
15	NYI	Mike Bossy	Laval	RW
16	Bos.	Dwight Foster	Kitchener	RW
17	Phi.	Kevin McCarthy	Winnipeg	D
18	Mtl.	Norm Dupont	Montreal	LW

OTHER NOTABLE SELECTIONS

25	Min.	Dave Semenko	Brandon	LW
33	NYI	John Tonelli	Toronto	LW
36	Mtl.	Rod Langway	New Hampshire	D
43	Mtl.	Alain Cote	Chicoutimi	D
54	Mtl.	Gordie Roberts	Victoria	D
62	NYR	Mario Marois	Quebec	D
66	Pit.	Mark Johnson	U. of Wisconsin	C
102	Pit.	Greg Millen	Peterborough	G
118	Atl.	Bobby Gould	New Hampshire	C
135	Phi.	Pete Peeters	Medicine Hat	G
162	Mtl.	Craig Laughlin	Clarkson	RW

1976
FIRST ROUND

1	Wsh.	Rick Green	London	D
2	Pit.	Blair Chapman	Saskatoon	RW
3	Min.	Glen Sharpley	Hull	C
4	Det.	Fred Williams	Saskatoon	C
5	Cal.	Bjorn Johansson	Orebro	D
6	NYR	Don Murdoch	Medicine Hat	RW
7	St.L.	Bernie Federko	Saskatoon	C
8	Atl.	Dave Shand	Peterborough	D
9	Chi.	Real Cloutier	Quebec	RW
10	Atl.	Harold Phillipoff	New Westminster	LW
11	K.C.	Paul Gardner	Oshawa	C
12	Mtl.	Peter Lee	Ottawa	RW
13	Mtl.	Rod Schutt	Sudbury	LW
14	NYI	Alex McKendry	Sudbury	W
15	Wsh.	Greg Carroll	Medicine Hat	C
16	Bos.	Clayton Pachal	New Westminster	C/LW
17	Phi.	Mark Suzor	Kingston	D
18	Mtl.	Bruce Baker	Ottawa	RW

OTHER NOTABLE SELECTIONS

20	St.L.	Brian Sutter	Lethbridge	LW
22	Det.	Reed Larson	Minnesota-Duluth	D
30	Tor.	Randy Carlyle	Sudbury	D
42	NYR	Mike McEwen	Toronto	D
45	Chi.	Thomas Gradin	MoDo Ornskoldsvik	C
47	Pit.	Morris Lukowich	Medicine Hat	LW
56	St.L.	Mike Liut	Bowling Green	G
64	Atl.	Kent Nilsson	Djurgarden	C
68	NYI	Ken Morrow	Bowling Green	D
133	Mtl.	Ron Wilson	St. Catharines	C

1975
FIRST ROUND

1	Phi.	Mel Bridgman	Victoria	C
2	K.C.	Barry Dean	Medicine Hat	LW
3	Cal.	Ralph Klassen	Saskatoon	C
4	Min.	Bryan Maxwell	Medicine Hat	D
5	Det.	Rick Lapointe	Victoria	D
6	Tor.	Don Ashby	Calgary	C
7	Chi.	Greg Vaydik	Medicine Hat	C
8	Atl.	Richard Mulhern	Sherbrooke	D
9	Mtl.	Robin Sadler	Edmonton	D
10	Van.	Rick Blight	Brandon	RW
11	NYI	Pat Price	Saskatoon	D
12	NYR	Wayne Dillon	Toronto	C
13	Pit.	Gord Laxton	New Westminster	G
14	Bos.	Doug Halward	Peterborough	D
15	Mtl.	Pierre Mondou	Montreal	C
16	L.A.	Tim Young	Ottawa	C

OTHER NOTABLE SELECTIONS

17	Buf.	Bob Sauve	Laval	G
21	Cal.	Dennis Maruk	London	C
24	Tor.	Doug Jarvis	Peterborough	C
43	Chi.	Mike O'Connell	Kingston	D
57	Cal.	Greg Smith	Colorado College	D
80	Atl.	Willi Plett	St. Catharines	RW
108	Phi.	Paul Holmgren	U. of Minnesota	RW
210	L.A.	Dave Taylor	Clarkson	RW

1974
FIRST ROUND

1	Wsh.	Greg Joly	Regina	D
2	K.C.	Wilf Paiement	St. Catharines	RW
3	Cal.	Rick Hampton	St. Catharines	LW/D
4	NYI	Clark Gillies	Regina	LW
5	Mtl.	Cam Connor	Flin Flon	RW
6	Min.	Doug Hicks	Flin Flon	D
7	Mtl.	Doug Risebrough	Kitchener	C
8	Pit.	Pierre Larouche	Sorel	C
9	Det.	Bill Lochead	Oshawa	LW
10	Mtl.	Rick Chartraw	Kitchener	D/RW
11	Buf.	Lee Fogolin Jr.	Oshawa	D
12	Mtl.	Mario Tremblay	Montreal	RW
13	Tor.	Jack Valiquette	Sault Ste. Marie	C
14	NYR	Dave Maloney	Kitchener	D

15	Mtl.	Gord McTavish	Sudbury	C
16	Chi.	Grant Mulvey	Calgary	RW
17	Cal.	Ron Chipperfield	Brandon	C
18	Bos.	Don Larway	Swift Current	RW

OTHER NOTABLE SELECTIONS

22	NYI	Bryan Trottier	Swift Current	C
25	Bos.	Mark Howe	Toronto	D
29	Buf.	Danny Gare	Calgary	RW
31	Tor.	Tiger Williams	Swift Current	LW
32	NYR	Ron Greschner	New Westminster	D
38	K.C.	Bob Bourne	Saskatoon	C
39	Cal.	Charlie Simmer	Sault Ste. Marie	LW
52	Chi.	Bob Murray	Cornwall	D
59	Van.	Harold Snepsts	Edmonton	D
70	Chi.	Terry Ruskowski	Swift Current	C
125	Phi.	Reggie Lemelin	Sherbrooke	G
199	Mtl.	Dave Lumley	New Hampshire	RW
214	NYI	Stefan Persson	Brynas Gavle	D

1973
FIRST ROUND

1	NYI	Denis Potvin	Ottawa	D
2	Atl.	Tom Lysiak	Medicine Hat	C
3	Van.	Dennis Ververgaert	London	RW
4	Tor.	Lanny McDonald	Medicine Hat	RW
5	St.L.	John Davidson	Calgary	G
6	Bos.	Andre Savard	Quebec	C
7	Pit.	Blaine Stoughton	Flin Flon	RW
8	Mtl.	Bob Gainey	Peterborough	LW
9	Van.	Bob Dailey	Toronto	D
10	Tor.	Bob Neely	Peterborough	D
11	Det.	Terry Richardson	New Westminster	G
12	Buf.	Morris Titanic	Sudbury	LW
13	Chi.	Darcy Rota	Edmonton	LW
14	NYR	Rick Middleton	Oshawa	RW
15	Tor.	Ian Turnbull	Ottawa	D
16	Atl.	Vic Mercredi	New Westminster	C

OTHER NOTABLE SELECTIONS

21	Atl.	Eric Vail	Sudbury	LW
27	Pit.	Colin Campbell	Peterborough	D
30	NYR	Pat Hickey	Hamilton	LW
33	NYI	Dave Lewis	Saskatoon	D
49	NYI	Andre St. Laurent	Montreal	C
85	Cal.	Ken Houston	Chatham Jr. B	RW
130	Cal.	Larry Patey	Braintree H.S.	C
134	Pit.	Gord Lane	New Westminster	D
162	Mtl.	Greg Fox	U. of Michigan	D

1972
FIRST ROUND

1	NYI	Billy Harris	Toronto	RW
2	Atl.	Jacques Richard	Quebec	LW
3	Van.	Don Lever	Niagara Falls	LW
4	Mtl.	Steve Shutt	Toronto	LW
5	Buf.	Jim Schoenfeld	Niagara Falls	D
6	Mtl.	Michel Larocque	Ottawa	G
7	Phi.	Bill Barber	Kitchener	LW
8	Mtl.	Dave Gardner	Toronto	C
9	St.L.	Wayne Merrick	Ottawa	C
10	NYR	Al Blanchard	Kitchener	LW
11	Tor.	George Ferguson	Toronto	C
12	Min.	Jerry Byers	Kitchener	LW
13	Chi.	Phil Russell	Edmonton	D
14	Mtl.	John Van Boxmeer	Guelph	D
15	NYR	Bob MacMillan	St. Catharines	RW
16	Bos.	Mike Bloom	St. Catharines	LW

OTHER NOTABLE SELECTIONS

17	NYI	Lorne Henning	New Westminster	C
23	Phi.	Tom Bladon	Edmonton	D
33	NYI	Bob Nystrom	Calgary	RW
39	Phi.	Jimmy Watson	Calgary	D
55	Phi.	Al MacAdam	University of PEI	RW
85	Buf.	Peter McNab	U. of Denver	C
97	NYR	Richard Brodeur	Cornwall	G
139	Tor.	Pat Boutette	Minnesota-Duluth	C/RW
144	NYI	Garry Howatt	Flin Flon	LW

1971
FIRST ROUND

1	Mtl.	Guy Lafleur	Quebec	RW
2	Det.	Marcel Dionne	St. Catharines	C
3	Van.	Jocelyn Guevremont	Montreal	D
4	St.L.	Gene Carr	Flin Flon	C
5	Buf.	Rick Martin	Montreal	LW
6	Bos.	Ron Jones	Edmonton	D
7	Mtl.	Chuck Arnason	Flin Flon	RW
8	Phi.	Larry Wright	Regina	C
9	Phi.	Pierre Plante	Drummondville	RW
10	NYR	Steve Vickers	Toronto	LW
11	Mtl.	Murray Wilson	Ottawa	LW
12	Chi.	Dan Spring	Edmonton	C
13	NYR	Steve Durbano	Toronto	D
14	Bos.	Terry O'Reilly	Oshawa	RW

OTHER NOTABLE SELECTIONS

17	Van.	Bobby Lalonde	Montreal	C
19	Buf.	Craig Ramsay	Peterborough	LW
20	Mtl.	Larry Robinson	Kitchener	D
22	Tor.	Rick Kehoe	Hamilton	RW
33	Buf.	Bill Hajt	Saskatoon	D
48	L.A.	Neil Komadoski	Winnipeg	D
55	NYR	Jerry Butler	Hamilton	RW

1970
FIRST ROUND

1	Buf.	Gilbert Perreault	Montreal	C
2	Van.	Dale Tallon	Toronto	D
3	Bos.	Reggie Leach	Flin Flon	RW
4	Bos.	Rick MacLeish	Peterborough	C
5	Mtl.	Ray Martyniuk	Flin Flon	G
6	Mtl.	Chuck Lefley	Canadian National	LW
7	Pit.	Greg Polis	Estevan	LW
8	Tor.	Darryl Sittler	London	C
9	Bos.	Ron Plumb	Peterborough	D
10	Cal.	Chris Oddleifson	Winnipeg	C
11	NYR	Norm Gratton	Montreal	LW
12	Det.	Serge Lajeunesse	Montreal	D/RW
13	Bos.	Bob Stewart	Oshawa	D
14	Chi.	Dan Maloney	London	LW

OTHER NOTABLE SELECTIONS

18	Phi.	Bill Clement	Ottawa	C
22	Tor.	Errol Thompson	Charlottetown Sr.	LW
25	NYR	Mike Murphy	Toronto	RW
27	Bos.	Dan Bouchard	London	G
32	Phi.	Bob Kelly	Oshawa	LW
40	Det.	Yvon Lambert	Drummondville	LW
59	L.A.	Billy Smith	Cornwall	G
70	Chi.	Gilles Meloche	Verdun	G
88	Oak.	Terry Murray	Ottawa	D
103	Tor.	Ron Low	Dauphin Jr. A	G

1969
FIRST ROUND

1	Mtl.	Rejean Houle	Montreal	W
2	Mtl.	Marc Tardif	Montreal	LW
3	Bos.	Don Tannahill	Niagara Falls	LW
4	Bos.	Frank Spring	Edmonton	RW
5	Min.	Dick Redmond	St. Catharines	D
6	Phi.	Bob Currier	Cornwall	C
7	Oak.	Tony Featherstone	Peterborough	RW
8	NYR	Andre Dupont	Montreal	D
9	Tor.	Ernie Moser	Estevan	RW
10	Det.	Jim Rutherford	Hamilton	G
11	Bos.	Ivan Boldirev	Oshawa	C
12	NYR	Pierre Jarry	Ottawa	LW

OTHER NOTABLE SELECTIONS

17	Phi.	Bobby Clarke	Flin Flon	C
18	Oak.	Ron Stackhouse	Peterborough	D
25	Min.	Gilles Gilbert	London	G
26	Pit.	Michel Briere	Shawinigan	C
51	L.A.	Butch Goring	Dauphin Jr. A	C
52	Phi.	Dave Schultz	Sorel	LW
55	Tor.	Brian Spencer	Swift Current	LW
64	Phi.	Don Saleski	Regina	RW

Drafted in 1969, Butch Goring played in Los Angeles until 1980, earning a reputation as a hustler who played within the rules. Traded to the New York Islanders on March 10, 1980, he is credited with putting a talented team over the top.

NHL All-Stars

Active Players' All-Star Selection Records

	First Team Selections		Second Team Selections	Total
GOALTENDERS				
Dominik Hasek	(6)	1993-94; 1994-95; 1996-97; 1997-98; 1998-99; 2000-01.	(0)	6
Martin Brodeur	(2)	2002-03; 2003-04.	(2) 1996-97; 1997-98.	4
Ed Belfour	(2)	1990-91; 1992-93.	(1) 1994-95	3
Olie Kolzig	(1)	99-2000.	(0)	1
Chris Osgood	(0)		(1) 1995-96.	1
Byron Dafoe	(0)		(1) 1998-99.	1
Roman Turek	(0)		(1) 99-2000.	1
Roman Cechmanek	(0)		(1) 2000-01.	1
Jose Theodore	(0)		(1) 2001-02.	1
Marty Turco	(0)		(1) 2002-03.	1
Roberto Luongo	(0)		(1) 2003-04.	1
DEFENSEMEN				
Chris Chelios	(5)	1988-89; 1992-93; 1994-95; 1995-96; 2001-02.	(2) 1990-91; 1996-97.	7
Al MacInnis	(4)	1989-90; 1990-91; 1998-99; 2002-03.	(3) 1986-87; 1988-89; 1993-94.	7
Nicklas Lidstrom	(6)	1997-98; 1998-99; 99-2000; 2000-01; 2001-02; 2002-03.	(0)	6
Brian Leetch	(2)	1991-92; 1996-97.	(3) 1990-91; 1993-94; 1995-96.	5
Scott Stevens	(2)	1987-88; 1993-94.	(3) 1991-92; 1996-97; 2000-01.	5
Rob Blake	(1)	1997-98.	(3) 99-2000; 2000-01; 2001-02.	4
Chris Pronger	(1)	99-2000.	(2) 1997-98; 2003-04.	3
Scott Niedermayer	(1)	2003-04.	(1) 2002-03.	2
Eric Desjardins	(0)		(2) 1998-99; 99-2000.	2
Sergei Gonchar	(0)		(2) 2001-02; 2002-03.	2
Sandis Ozolinsh	(1)	1996-97.	(0)	1
Zdeno Chara	(1)	2003-04.	(0)	1
Derian Hatcher	(0)		(1) 2002-03.	1
Bryan McCabe	(0)		(1) 2003-04.	1
CENTERS				
Mario Lemieux	(5)	1987-88; 1988-89; 1992-93; 1995-96; 1996-97.	(4) 1985-86; 1986-87; 1991-92; 2000-01.	9
Peter Forsberg	(3)	1997-98; 1998-99; 2002-03.	(0)	3
Joe Sakic	(3)	2000-01; 2001-02; 2003-04.	(0)	3
Mark Messier	(2)	1989-90; 1991-92.	(0)	2
Eric Lindros	(1)	1994-95.	(1) 1995-96.	2
Mats Sundin	(0)		(2) 2001-02; 2003-04.	2
Sergei Fedorov	(1)	1993-94.	(0)	1
Steve Yzerman	(1)	99-2000.	(0)	1
Alex Zhamnov	(0)		(1) 1994-95.	1
Alexei Yashin	(0)		(1) 1998-99.	1
Mike Modano	(0)		(1) 99-2000.	1
Joe Thornton	(0)		(1) 2002-03.	1
RIGHT WINGERS				
Jaromir Jagr	(6)	1994-95; 1995-96; 1997-98; 1998-99; 99-2000; 2000-01.	(1) 1996-97.	7
Teemu Selanne	(2)	1992-93; 1996-97.	(2) 1997-98; 1998-99.	4
Brett Hull	(3)	1989-90; 1990-91; 1991-92.	(0)	3
Jarome Iginla	(1)	2001-02.	(1) 2003-04.	2
Alexander Mogilny	(0)		(2) 1992-93; 1995-96.	2
Todd Bertuzzi	(1)	2002-03.	(0)	1
Martin St. Louis	(1)	2003-04.	(0)	1
Mark Recchi	(0)		(1) 1991-92.	1
Bill Guerin	(0)		(1) 2001-02.	1
Milan Hejduk	(0)		(1) 2002-03.	1
LEFT WINGERS				
Luc Robitaille	(5)	1987-88; 1988-89; 1989-90; 1990-91; 1992-93.	(3) 1986-87; 1991-92; 2000-01.	8
Paul Kariya	(3)	1995-96; 1996-97; 1998-99.	(2) 99-2000; 2002-03.	5
John LeClair	(2)	1994-95; 1997-98.	(3) 1995-96; 1996-97; 1998-99.	5
Mark Messier	(2)	1981-82; 1982-83.	(1) 1983-84.	3
Markus Naslund	(3)	2001-02; 2002-03; 2003-04.	(0)	3
Brendan Shanahan	(2)	1993-94; 99-2000.	(1) 2001-02.	3
Keith Tkachuk	(0)		(2) 1994-95; 1997-98.	2
Patrik Elias	(1)	2000-01.	(0)	1
Ilya Kovalchuk	(0)		(1) 2003-04.	1

Leading NHL All-Stars 1930-31 to 2003-04

Player	Pos	Team	NHL Seasons	First Team Selections	Second Team Selections	Total Selections
Howe, Gordie	RW	Detroit	26	12	9	21
Bourque, Raymond	D	Bos., Col.	22	13	6	19
Gretzky, Wayne	C	Edm., L.A., NYR	20	8	7	15
Richard, Maurice	RW	Montreal	18	8	6	14
Hull, Bobby	LW	Chicago	16	10	2	12
Harvey, Doug	D	Mtl., NYR	19	10	1	11
Hall, Glenn	G	Det., Chi., St.L.	18	7	4	11
Beliveau, Jean	C	Montreal	20	6	4	10
Seibert, Earl	D	NYR, Chi.	15	4	6	10
Orr, Bobby	D	Boston	12	8	1	9
Lindsay, Ted	LW	Detroit	17	8	1	9
* Lemieux, Mario	C	Pittsburgh	16	5	4	9
Mahovlich, Frank	LW	Tor., Det., Mtl.	18	3	6	9
Shore, Eddie	D	Boston	14	7	1	8
Esposito, Phil	C	Boston	18	6	2	8
Kelly, Red	D	Detroit	20	6	2	8
Mikita, Stan	C	Chicago	22	6	2	8
Bossy, Mike	RW	NY Islanders	10	5	3	8
Pilote, Pierre	D	Chicago	14	5	3	8
* Robitaille, Luc	LW	Los Angeles	18	5	3	8
Coffey, Paul	D	Edm., Pit., Det.	21	4	4	8
Brimsek, Frank	G	Boston	10	2	6	8
* Jagr, Jaromir	RW	Pittsburgh	14	6	1	7
Potvin, Denis	D	NY Islanders	15	5	2	7
Park, Brad	D	NYR, Bos.	17	5	2	7
* Chelios, Chris	D	Mtl., Chi.	21	5	2	7
* MacInnis, Al	D	Cgy., St.L.	23	4	3	7
Plante, Jacques	G	Mtl., Tor.	18	3	4	7
Gadsby, Bill	D	Chi., NYR, Det.	20	3	4	7
Sawchuk, Terry	G	Detroit	21	3	4	7
Durnan, Bill	G	Montreal	7	6	0	6
* Hasek, Dominik	G	Buffalo	12	6	0	6
* Lidstrom, Niklas	D	Detroit	13	6	0	6
Lafleur, Guy	RW	Montreal	17	6	0	6
Dryden, Ken	G	Montreal	8	5	1	6
Roy, Patrick	G	Montreal	19	4	2	6
Clapper, Dit	RW/D	Boston	20	3	3	6
Robinson, Larry	D	Montreal	20	3	3	6
Horton, Tim	D	Toronto	24	3	3	6
Salming, Borje	D	Toronto	17	1	5	6
Cowley, Bill	C	Boston	13	4	1	5
Jackson, Busher	LW	Toronto	15	4	1	5
* Messier, Mark	LW/C	Edm., NYR	25	4	1	5
* Kariya, Paul	LW	Anaheim	10	3	2	5
Conacher, Charlie	RW	Toronto	12	3	2	5
Stewart, Jack	D	Detroit	12	3	2	5
Blake, Toe	LW	Montreal	14	3	2	5
Lach, Elmer	C	Montreal	14	3	2	5
Quackenbush, Bill	D	Det., Bos.	14	3	2	5
Goulet, Michel	LW	Quebec	15	3	2	5
Esposito, Tony	G	Chicago	16	3	2	5
Reardon, Ken	D	Montreal	7	2	3	5
Apps, Syl	C	Toronto	10	2	3	5
* LeClair, John	LW	Mtl., Phi.	14	2	3	5
Giacomin, Ed	G	NY Rangers	13	2	3	5
* Leetch, Brian	D	NY Rangers	16	2	3	5
Kurri, Jari	RW	Edmonton	17	2	3	5
* Stevens, Scott	D	Wsh., N.J.	21	2	3	5

Position Leaders in All-Star Selections

Position	Player	First Team	Second Team	Total	Position	Player	First Team	Second Team	Total
GOAL	Glenn Hall	7	4	11	LEFT WING	Bobby Hull	10	2	12
	Frank Brimsek	2	6	8		Ted Lindsay	8	1	9
	Jacques Plante	3	4	7		Frank Mahovlich	3	6	9
	Terry Sawchuk	3	4	7		* Luc Robitaille	5	3	8
	Bill Durnan	6	0	6					
	* Dominik Hasek	6	0	6	RIGHT WING	Gordie Howe	12	9	21
	Ken Dryden	5	1	6		Maurice Richard	8	6	14
	Patrick Roy	4	2	6		Mike Bossy	5	3	8
						* Jaromir Jagr	6	1	7
DEFENSE	Raymond Bourque	13	6	19		Guy Lafleur	6	0	6
	Doug Harvey	10	1	11					
	Earl Seibert	4	6	10	CENTER	Wayne Gretzky	8	7	15
	Bobby Orr	8	1	9		Jean Beliveau	6	4	10
	Eddie Shore	7	1	8		* Mario Lemieux	5	4	9
	Red Kelly	6	2	8		Phil Esposito	6	2	8
	Pierre Pilote	5	3	8		Stan Mikita	6	2	8
	Paul Coffey	4	4	8					
						* active player			

All-Star Teams

1930-2004

Voting for the NHL All-Star Team is conducted among the representatives of the Professional Hockey Writers' Association at the end of the season.

Following is a list of the First and Second All-Star Teams since their inception in 1930-31.

2003-04

First Team		Second Team
Martin Brodeur, N.J.	G	Roberto Luongo, Fla.
Scott Niedermayer, N.J.	D	Chris Pronger, St.L.
Zdeno Chara, Ott.	D	Bryan McCabe, Tor.
Joe Sakic, Col.	C	Mats Sundin, Tor.
Martin St. Louis, T.B.	RW	Jarome Iginla, Cgy.
Markus Naslund, Van.	LW	Ilya Kovalchuk, Atl.

2002-03

First Team		Second Team
Martin Brodeur, N.J.	G	Marty Turco, Dal.
Al MacInnis, St.L.	D	Sergei Gonchar, Wsh.
Nicklas Lidstrom, Det.	D	Derian Hatcher, Dal.
Peter Forsberg, Col.	C	Joe Thornton, Bos.
Todd Bertuzzi, Van.	RW	Milan Hejduk, Col.
Markus Naslund, Van.	LW	Paul Kariya, Ana.

2001-02

First Team		Second Team
Patrick Roy, Col.	G	Jose Theodore, Mtl.
Nicklas Lidstrom, Det.	D	Rob Blake, L.A. Col.
Chris Chelios, Det.	D	Sergei Gonchar, Wsh.
Joe Sakic, Col.	C	Mats Sundin, Tor.
Jarome Iginla, Cgy.	RW	Bill Guerin, Bos.
Markus Naslund, Van.	LW	Brendan Shanahan, Det.

2000-01

First Team		Second Team
Dominik Hasek, Buf.	G	Roman Cechmanek, Phi.
Nicklas Lidstrom, Det.	D	Rob Blake, L.A. Col.
Raymond Bourque, Col.	D	Scott Stevens, N.J.
Joe Sakic, Col.	C	Mario Lemieux, Pit.
Jaromir Jagr, Pit.	RW	Pavel Bure, Fla.
Patrik Elias, N.J.	LW	Luc Robitaille, L.A.

1999-2000

First Team		Second Team
Olaf Kolzig, Wsh.	G	Roman Turek, St.L.
Chris Pronger, St.L.	D	Rob Blake, L.A.
Nicklas Lidstrom, Det.	D	Eric Desjardins, Phi.
Steve Yzerman, Det.	C	Mike Modano, Dal.
Jaromir Jagr, Pit.	RW	Pavel Bure, Fla.
Brendan Shanahan, Det.	LW	Paul Kariya, Ana.

1998-99

First Team		Second Team
Dominik Hasek, Buf.	G	Byron Dafoe, Bos.
Al MacInnis, St.L.	D	Raymond Bourque, Bos.
Nicklas Lidstrom, Det.	D	Eric Desjardins, Phi.
Peter Forsberg, Col.	C	Alexei Yashin, Ott.
Jaromir Jagr, Pit.	RW	Teemu Selanne, Ana.
Paul Kariya, Ana.	LW	John LeClair, Phi.

1997-98

First Team		Second Team
Dominik Hasek, Buf.	G	Martin Brodeur, N.J.
Nicklas Lidstrom, Det.	D	Chris Pronger, St.L.
Rob Blake, L.A.	D	Scott Niedermayer, N.J.
Peter Forsberg, Col.	C	Wayne Gretzky, NYR
Jaromir Jagr, Pit.	RW	Teemu Selanne, Ana.
John LeClair, Phi.	LW	Keith Tkachuk, Phx.

1996-97

First Team		Second Team
Dominik Hasek, Buf.	G	Martin Brodeur, N.J.
Brian Leetch, NYR	D	Chris Chelios, Chi.
Sandis Ozolinsh, Col.	D	Scott Stevens, N.J.
Mario Lemieux, Pit.	C	Wayne Gretzky, NYR
Teemu Selanne, Ana.	RW	Jaromir Jagr, Pit.
Paul Kariya, Ana.	LW	John LeClair, Phi.

1995-96

First Team		Second Team
Jim Carey, Wsh.	G	Chris Osgood, Det.
Chris Chelios, Chi.	D	V. Konstantinov, Det.
Raymond Bourque, Bos.	D	Brian Leetch, NYR
Mario Lemieux, Pit.	C	Eric Lindros, Phi.
Jaromir Jagr, Pit.	RW	Alexander Mogilny, Van.
Paul Kariya, Ana.	LW	John LeClair, Phi.

1994-95

First Team		Second Team
Dominik Hasek, Buf.	G	Ed Belfour, Chi.
Paul Coffey, Det.	D	Raymond Bourque, Bos.
Chris Chelios, Chi.	D	Larry Murphy, Pit.
Eric Lindros, Phi.	C	Alexei Zhamnov, Wpg.
Jaromir Jagr, Pit.	RW	Theoren Fleury, Cgy.
John LeClair, Mtl., Phi.	LW	Keith Tkachuk, Wpg.

1993-94

First Team		Second Team
Dominik Hasek, Buf.	G	John Vanbiesbrouck, Fla.
Raymond Bourque, Bos.	D	Al MacInnis, Cgy.
Scott Stevens, N.J.	D	Brian Leetch, NYR
Sergei Fedorov, Det.	C	Wayne Gretzky, L.A.
Pavel Bure, Van.	RW	Cam Neely, Bos.
Brendan Shanahan, St.L.	LW	Adam Graves, NYR

1992-93

First Team		Second Team
Ed Belfour, Chi.	G	Tom Barrasso, Pit.
Chris Chelios, Chi.	D	Larry Murphy, Pit.
Raymond Bourque, Bos.	D	Al Iafrate, Wsh.
Mario Lemieux, Pit.	C	Pat LaFontaine, Buf.
Teemu Selanne, Wpg.	RW	Alexander Mogilny, Buf.
Luc Robitaille, L.A.	LW	Kevin Stevens, Pit.

1991-92

First Team		Second Team
Patrick Roy, Mtl.	G	Kirk McLean, Van.
Brian Leetch, NYR	D	Phil Housley, Wpg.
Raymond Bourque, Bos.	D	Scott Stevens, N.J.
Mark Messier, NYR	C	Mario Lemieux, Pit.
Brett Hull, St.L.	RW	Mark Recchi, Pit., Phi.
Kevin Stevens, Pit.	LW	Luc Robitaille, L.A.

1990-91

First Team		Second Team
Ed Belfour, Chi.	G	Patrick Roy, Mtl.
Raymond Bourque, Bos.	D	Chris Chelios, Chi.
Al MacInnis, Cgy.	D	Brian Leetch, NYR
Wayne Gretzky, L.A.	C	Adam Oates, St.L.
Brett Hull, St.L.	RW	Cam Neely, Bos.
Luc Robitaille, L.A.	LW	Kevin Stevens, Pit.

1989-90

First Team		Second Team
Patrick Roy, Mtl.	G	Daren Puppa, Buf.
Raymond Bourque, Bos.	D	Paul Coffey, Pit.
Al MacInnis, Cgy.	D	Doug Wilson, Chi.
Mark Messier, Edm.	C	Wayne Gretzky, L.A.
Brett Hull, St.L.	RW	Cam Neely, Bos.
Luc Robitaille, L.A.	LW	Brian Bellows, Min.

1988-89

First Team		Second Team
Patrick Roy, Mtl.	G	Mike Vernon, Cgy.
Chris Chelios, Mtl.	D	Al MacInnis, Cgy.
Paul Coffey, Pit.	D	Raymond Bourque, Bos.
Mario Lemieux, Pit.	C	Wayne Gretzky, L.A.
Joe Mullen, Cgy.	RW	Jari Kurri, Edm.
Luc Robitaille, L.A.	LW	Gerard Gallant, Det.

1987-88

First Team		Second Team
Grant Fuhr, Edm.	G	Patrick Roy, Mtl.
Raymond Bourque, Bos.	D	Gary Suter, Cgy.
Scott Stevens, Wsh.	D	Brad McCrimmon, Cgy.
Mario Lemieux, Pit.	C	Wayne Gretzky, Edm.
Hakan Loob, Cgy.	RW	Cam Neely, Bos.
Luc Robitaille, L.A.	LW	Michel Goulet, Que.

1986-87

First Team		Second Team
Ron Hextall, Phi.	G	Mike Liut, Hfd.
Raymond Bourque, Bos.	D	Larry Murphy, Wsh.
Mark Howe, Phi.	D	Al MacInnis, Cgy.
Wayne Gretzky, Edm.	C	Mario Lemieux, Pit.
Jari Kurri, Edm.	RW	Tim Kerr, Phi.
Michel Goulet, Que.	LW	Luc Robitaille, L.A.

1985-86

First Team		Second Team
John Vanbiesbrouck, NYR	G	Bob Froese, Phi.
Paul Coffey, Edm.	D	Larry Robinson, Mtl.
Mark Howe, Phi.	D	Raymond Bourque, Bos.
Wayne Gretzky, Edm.	C	Mario Lemieux, Pit.
Mike Bossy, NYI	RW	Jari Kurri, Edm.
Michel Goulet, Que.	LW	Mats Naslund, Mtl.

1984-85

First Team		Second Team
Pelle Lindbergh, Phi.	G	Tom Barrasso, Buf.
Paul Coffey, Edm.	D	Rod Langway, Wsh.
Raymond Bourque, Bos.	D	Doug Wilson, Chi.
Wayne Gretzky, Edm.	C	Dale Hawerchuk, Wpg.
Jari Kurri, Edm.	RW	Mike Bossy, NYI
John Ogrodnick, Det.	LW	John Tonelli, NYI

1983-84

First Team		Second Team
Tom Barrasso, Buf.	G	Pat Riggin, Wsh.
Rod Langway, Wsh.	D	Paul Coffey, Edm.
Raymond Bourque, Bos.	D	Denis Potvin, NYI
Wayne Gretzky, Edm.	C	Bryan Trottier, NYI
Mike Bossy, NYI	RW	Jari Kurri, Edm.
Michel Goulet, Que.	LW	Mark Messier, Edm.

1982-83

First Team		Second Team
Pete Peeters, Bos.	G	Roland Melanson, NYI
Mark Howe, Phi.	D	Raymond Bourque, Bos.
Rod Langway, Wsh.	D	Paul Coffey, Edm.
Wayne Gretzky, Edm.	C	Denis Savard, Chi.
Mike Bossy, NYI	RW	Lanny McDonald, Cgy.
Mark Messier, Edm.	LW	Michel Goulet, Que.

1981-82

First Team		Second Team
Billy Smith, NYI	G	Grant Fuhr, Edm.
Doug Wilson, Chi.	D	Paul Coffey, Edm.
Raymond Bourque, Bos.	D	Brian Engblom, Mtl.
Wayne Gretzky, Edm.	C	Bryan Trottier, NYI
Mike Bossy, NYI	RW	Rick Middleton, Bos.
Mark Messier, Edm.	LW	John Tonelli, NYI

1980-81

First Team		Second Team
Mike Liut, St.L.	G	Mario Lessard, L.A.
Denis Potvin, NYI	D	Larry Robinson, Mtl.
Randy Carlyle, Pit.	D	Raymond Bourque, Bos.
Wayne Gretzky, Edm.	C	Marcel Dionne, L.A.
Mike Bossy, NYI	RW	Dave Taylor, L.A.
Charlie Simmer, L.A.	LW	Bill Barber, Phi.

First Team		Second Team

1979-80

Tony Esposito, Chi.	G	Don Edwards, Buf.
Larry Robinson, Mtl.	D	Borje Salming, Tor.
Raymond Bourque, Bos.	D	Jim Schoenfeld, Buf.
Marcel Dionne, L.A.	C	Wayne Gretzky, Edm.
Guy Lafleur, Mtl.	RW	Danny Gare, Buf.
Charlie Simmer, L.A.	LW	Steve Shutt, Mtl.

1978-79

Ken Dryden, Mtl.	G	Glenn Resch, NYI
Denis Potvin, NYI	D	Borje Salming, Tor.
Larry Robinson, Mtl.	D	Serge Savard, Mtl.
Bryan Trottier, NYI	C	Marcel Dionne, L.A.
Guy Lafleur, Mtl.	RW	Mike Bossy, NYI
Clark Gillies, NYI	LW	Bill Barber, Phi.

1977-78

Ken Dryden, Mtl.	G	Don Edwards, Buf.
Denis Potvin, NYI	D	Larry Robinson, Mtl.
Brad Park, Bos.	D	Borje Salming, Tor.
Bryan Trottier, NYI	C	Darryl Sittler, Tor.
Guy Lafleur, Mtl.	RW	Mike Bossy, NYI
Clark Gillies, NYI	LW	Steve Shutt, Mtl.

1976-77

Ken Dryden, Mtl.	G	Rogie Vachon, L.A.
Larry Robinson, Mtl.	D	Denis Potvin, NYI
Borje Salming, Tor.	D	Guy Lapointe, Mtl.
Marcel Dionne, L.A.	C	Gilbert Perreault, Buf.
Guy Lafleur, Mtl.	RW	Lanny McDonald, Tor.
Steve Shutt, Mtl.	LW	Rick Martin, Buf.

1975-76

Ken Dryden, Mtl.	G	Glenn Resch, NYI
Denis Potvin, NYI	D	Borje Salming, Tor.
Brad Park, Bos.	D	Guy Lapointe, Mtl.
Bobby Clarke, Phi.	C	Gilbert Perreault, Buf.
Guy Lafleur, Mtl.	RW	Reggie Leach, Phi.
Bill Barber, Phi.	LW	Rick Martin, Buf.

1974-75

Bernie Parent, Phi.	G	Rogie Vachon, L.A.
Bobby Orr, Bos.	D	Guy Lapointe, Mtl.
Denis Potvin, NYI	D	Borje Salming, Tor.
Bobby Clarke, Phi.	C	Phil Esposito, Bos.
Guy Lafleur, Mtl.	RW	René Robert, Buf.
Rick Martin, Buf.	LW	Steve Vickers, NYR

1973-74

Bernie Parent, Phi.	G	Tony Esposito, Chi.
Bobby Orr, Bos.	D	Bill White, Chi.
Brad Park, NYR	D	Barry Ashbee, Phi.
Phil Esposito, Bos.	C	Bobby Clarke, Phi.
Ken Hodge, Bos.	RW	Mickey Redmond, Det.
Rick Martin, Buf.	LW	Wayne Cashman, Bos.

1972-73

Ken Dryden, Mtl.	G	Tony Esposito, Chi.
Bobby Orr, Bos.	D	Brad Park, NYR
Guy Lapointe, Mtl.	D	Bill White, Chi.
Phil Esposito, Bos.	C	Bobby Clarke, Phi.
Mickey Redmond, Det.	RW	Yvan Cournoyer, Mtl.
Frank Mahovlich, Mtl.	LW	Dennis Hull, Chi.

1971-72

Tony Esposito, Chi.	G	Ken Dryden, Mtl.
Bobby Orr, Bos.	D	Bill White, Chi.
Brad Park, NYR	D	Pat Stapleton, Chi.
Phil Esposito, Bos.	C	Jean Ratelle, NYR
Rod Gilbert, NYR	RW	Yvan Cournoyer, Mtl.
Bobby Hull, Chi.	LW	Vic Hadfield, NYR

1970-71

Ed Giacomin, NYR	G	Jacques Plante, Tor.
Bobby Orr, Bos.	D	Brad Park, NYR
J.C. Tremblay, Mtl.	D	Pat Stapleton, Chi.
Phil Esposito, Bos.	C	Dave Keon, Tor.
Ken Hodge, Bos.	RW	Yvan Cournoyer, Mtl.
John Bucyk, Bos.	LW	Bobby Hull, Chi.

1969-70

Tony Esposito, Chi.	G	Ed Giacomin, NYR
Bobby Orr, Bos.	D	Carl Brewer, Det.
Brad Park, NYR	D	Jacques Laperriere, Mtl.
Phil Esposito, Bos.	C	Stan Mikita, Chi.
Gordie Howe, Det.	RW	John McKenzie, Bos.
Bobby Hull, Chi.	LW	Frank Mahovlich, Det.

1968-69

Glenn Hall, St.L.	G	Ed Giacomin, NYR
Bobby Orr, Bos.	D	Ted Green, Bos.
Tim Horton, Tor.	D	Ted Harris, Mtl.
Phil Esposito, Bos.	C	Jean Béliveau, Mtl.
Gordie Howe, Det.	RW	Yvan Cournoyer, Mtl.
Bobby Hull, Chi.	LW	Frank Mahovlich, Det.

1967-68

Gump Worsley, Mtl.	G	Ed Giacomin, NYR
Bobby Orr, Bos.	D	J.C. Tremblay, Mtl.
Tim Horton, Tor.	D	Jim Neilson, NYR
Stan Mikita, Chi.	C	Phil Esposito, Bos.
Gordie Howe, Det.	RW	Rod Gilbert, NYR
Bobby Hull, Chi.	LW	John Bucyk, Bos.

1966-67

Ed Giacomin, NYR	G	Glenn Hall, Chi.
Pierre Pilote, Chi.	D	Tim Horton, Tor.
Harry Howell, NYR	D	Bobby Orr, Bos.
Stan Mikita, Chi.	C	Norm Ullman, Det.
Kenny Wharram, Chi.	RW	Gordie Howe, Det.
Bobby Hull, Chi.	LW	Don Marshall, NYR

1965-66

Glenn Hall, Chi.	G	Gump Worsley, Mtl.
Jacques Laperriere, Mtl.	D	Allan Stanley, Tor.
Pierre Pilote, Chi.	D	Pat Stapleton, Chi.
Stan Mikita, Chi.	C	Jean Béliveau, Mtl.
Gordie Howe, Det.	RW	Bobby Rousseau, Mtl.
Bobby Hull, Chi.	LW	Frank Mahovlich, Tor.

1964-65

Roger Crozier, Det.	G	Charlie Hodge, Mtl.
Pierre Pilote, Chi.	D	Bill Gadsby, Det.
Jacques Laperriere, Mtl.	D	Carl Brewer, Tor.
Norm Ullman, Det.	C	Stan Mikita, Chi.
Claude Provost, Mtl.	RW	Gordie Howe, Det.
Bobby Hull, Chi.	LW	Frank Mahovlich, Tor.

1963-64

Glenn Hall, Chi.	G	Charlie Hodge, Mtl.
Pierre Pilote, Chi.	D	Moose Vasko, Chi.
Tim Horton, Tor.	D	Jacques Laperriere, Mtl.
Stan Mikita, Chi.	C	Jean Béliveau, Mtl.
Kenny Wharram, Chi.	RW	Gordie Howe, Det.
Bobby Hull, Chi.	LW	Frank Mahovlich, Tor.

1962-63

Glenn Hall, Chi.	G	Terry Sawchuk, Det.
Pierre Pilote, Chi.	D	Tim Horton, Tor.
Carl Brewer, Tor.	D	Moose Vasko, Chi.
Stan Mikita, Chi.	C	Henri Richard, Mtl.
Gordie Howe, Det.	RW	Andy Bathgate, NYR
Frank Mahovlich, Tor.	LW	Bobby Hull, Chi.

1961-62

Jacques Plante, Mtl.	G	Glenn Hall, Chi.
Doug Harvey, NYR	D	Carl Brewer, Tor.
Jean-Guy Talbot, Mtl.	D	Pierre Pilote, Chi.
Stan Mikita, Chi.	C	Dave Keon, Tor.
Andy Bathgate, NYR	RW	Gordie Howe, Det.
Bobby Hull, Chi.	LW	Frank Mahovlich, Tor.

1960-61

Johnny Bower, Tor.	G	Glenn Hall, Chi.
Doug Harvey, Mtl.	D	Allan Stanley, Tor.
Marcel Pronovost, Det.	D	Pierre Pilote, Chi.
Jean Béliveau, Mtl.	C	Henri Richard, Mtl.
Bernie Geoffrion, Mtl.	RW	Gordie Howe, Det.
Frank Mahovlich, Tor.	LW	Dickie Moore, Mtl.

1959-60

Glenn Hall, Chi.	G	Jacques Plante, Mtl.
Doug Harvey, Mtl.	D	Allan Stanley, Tor.
Marcel Pronovost, Det.	D	Pierre Pilote, Chi.
Jean Béliveau, Mtl.	C	Bronco Horvath, Bos.
Gordie Howe, Det.	RW	Bernie Geoffrion, Mtl.
Bobby Hull, Chi.	LW	Dean Prentice, NYR

1958-59

Jacques Plante, Mtl.	G	Terry Sawchuk, Det.
Tom Johnson, Mtl.	D	Marcel Pronovost, Det.
Bill Gadsby, NYR	D	Doug Harvey, Mtl.
Jean Béliveau, Mtl.	C	Henri Richard, Mtl.
Andy Bathgate, NYR	RW	Gordie Howe, Det.
Dickie Moore, Mtl.	LW	Alex Delvecchio, Det.

1957-58

Glenn Hall, Chi.	G	Jacques Plante, Mtl.
Doug Harvey, Mtl.	D	Fern Flaman, Bos.
Bill Gadsby, NYR	D	Marcel Pronovost, Det.
Henri Richard, Mtl.	C	Jean Béliveau, Mtl.
Gordie Howe, Det.	RW	Andy Bathgate, NYR
Dickie Moore, Mtl.	LW	Camille Henry, NYR

1956-57

Glenn Hall, Det.	G	Jacques Plante, Mtl.
Doug Harvey, Mtl.	D	Fern Flaman, Bos.
Red Kelly, Det.	D	Bill Gadsby, NYR
Jean Béliveau, Mtl.	C	Ed Litzenberger, Chi.
Gordie Howe, Det.	RW	Maurice Richard, Mtl.
Ted Lindsay, Det.	LW	Real Chevrefils, Bos.

1955-56

Jacques Plante, Mtl.	G	Glenn Hall, Det.
Doug Harvey, Mtl.	D	Red Kelly, Det.
Bill Gadsby, NYR	D	Tom Johnson, Mtl.
Jean Béliveau, Mtl.	C	Tod Sloan, Tor.
Maurice Richard, Mtl.	RW	Gordie Howe, Det.
Ted Lindsay, Det.	LW	Bert Olmstead, Mtl.

1954-55

Harry Lumley, Tor.	G	Terry Sawchuk, Det.
Doug Harvey, Mtl.	D	Bob Goldham, Det.
Red Kelly, Det.	D	Fern Flaman, Bos.
Jean Béliveau, Mtl.	C	Ken Mosdell, Mtl.
Maurice Richard, Mtl.	RW	Bernie Geoffrion, Mtl.
Sid Smith, Tor.	LW	Danny Lewicki, NYR

1953-54

Harry Lumley, Tor.	G	Terry Sawchuk, Det.
Red Kelly, Det.	D	Bill Gadsby, Chi.
Doug Harvey, Mtl.	D	Tim Horton, Tor.
Ken Mosdell, Mtl.	C	Ted Kennedy, Tor.
Gordie Howe, Det.	RW	Maurice Richard, Mtl.
Ted Lindsay, Det.	LW	Ed Sandford, Bos.

1952-53

First Team	Pos	Second Team
Terry Sawchuk, Det.	G	Gerry McNeil, Mtl.
Red Kelly, Det.	D	Bill Quackenbush, Bos.
Doug Harvey, Mtl.	D	Bill Gadsby, Chi.
Fleming MacKell, Bos.	C	Alex Delvecchio, Det.
Gordie Howe, Det.	RW	Maurice Richard, Mtl.
Ted Lindsay, Det.	LW	Bert Olmstead, Mtl.

1951-52

First Team	Pos	Second Team
Terry Sawchuk, Det.	G	Jim Henry, Bos.
Red Kelly, Det.	D	Hy Buller, NYR
Doug Harvey, Mtl.	D	Jimmy Thomson, Tor.
Elmer Lach, Mtl.	C	Milt Schmidt, Bos.
Gordie Howe, Det.	RW	Maurice Richard, Mtl.
Ted Lindsay, Det.	LW	Sid Smith, Tor.

1950-51

First Team	Pos	Second Team
Terry Sawchuk, Det.	G	Chuck Rayner, NYR
Red Kelly, Det.	D	Jimmy Thomson, Tor.
Bill Quackenbush, Bos.	D	Leo Reise Jr., Det.
Milt Schmidt, Bos.	C	Sid Abel, Det.
		Ted Kennedy (tied), Tor.
Gordie Howe, Det.	RW	Maurice Richard, Mtl.
Ted Lindsay, Det.	LW	Sid Smith, Tor.

1949-50

First Team	Pos	Second Team
Bill Durnan, Mtl.	G	Chuck Rayner, NYR
Gus Mortson, Tor.	D	Leo Reise Jr., Det.
Ken Reardon, Mtl.	D	Red Kelly, Det.
Sid Abel, Det.	C	Ted Kennedy, Tor.
Maurice Richard, Mtl.	RW	Gordie Howe, Det.
Ted Lindsay, Det.	LW	Tony Leswick, NYR

1948-49

First Team	Pos	Second Team
Bill Durnan, Mtl.	G	Chuck Rayner, NYR
Bill Quackenbush, Det.	D	Glen Harmon, Mtl.
Jack Stewart, Det.	D	Ken Reardon, Mtl.
Sid Abel, Det.	C	Doug Bentley, Chi.
Maurice Richard, Mtl.	RW	Gordie Howe, Det.
Roy Conacher, Chi.	LW	Ted Lindsay, Det.

1947-48

First Team	Pos	Second Team
Turk Broda, Tor.	G	Frank Brimsek, Bos.
Bill Quackenbush, Det.	D	Ken Reardon, Mtl.
Jack Stewart, Det.	D	Neil Colville, NYR
Elmer Lach, Mtl.	C	Buddy O'Connor, NYR
Maurice Richard, Mtl.	RW	Bud Poile, Chi.
Ted Lindsay, Det.	LW	Gaye Stewart, Chi.

1946-47

First Team	Pos	Second Team
Bill Durnan, Mtl.	G	Frank Brimsek, Bos.
Ken Reardon, Mtl.	D	Jack Stewart, Det.
Butch Bouchard, Mtl.	D	Bill Quackenbush, Det.
Milt Schmidt, Bos.	C	Max Bentley, Chi.
Maurice Richard, Mtl.	RW	Bobby Bauer, Bos.
Doug Bentley, Chi.	LW	Woody Dumart, Bos.

1945-46

First Team	Pos	Second Team
Bill Durnan, Mtl.	G	Frank Brimsek, Bos.
Jack Crawford, Bos.	D	Ken Reardon, Mtl.
Butch Bouchard, Mtl.	D	Jack Stewart, Det.
Max Bentley, Chi.	C	Elmer Lach, Mtl.
Maurice Richard, Mtl.	RW	Bill Mosienko, Chi.
Gaye Stewart, Tor.	LW	Toe Blake, Mtl.
Dick Irvin, Mtl.	Coach	Johnny Gottselig, Chi.

1944-45

First Team	Pos	Second Team
Bill Durnan, Mtl.	G	Mike Karakas, Chi.
Butch Bouchard, Mtl.	D	Glen Harmon, Mtl.
Flash Hollett, Det.	D	Babe Pratt, Tor.
Elmer Lach, Mtl.	C	Bill Cowley, Bos.
Maurice Richard, Mtl.	RW	Bill Mosienko, Chi.
Toe Blake, Mtl.	LW	Syd Howe, Det.
Dick Irvin, Mtl.	Coach	Jack Adams, Det.

1943-44

First Team	Pos	Second Team
Bill Durnan, Mtl.	G	Paul Bibeault, Tor.
Earl Seibert, Chi.	D	Butch Bouchard, Mtl.
Babe Pratt, Tor.	D	Dit Clapper, Bos.
Bill Cowley, Bos.	C	Elmer Lach, Mtl.
Lorne Carr, Tor.	RW	Maurice Richard, Mtl.
Doug Bentley, Chi.	LW	Herb Cain, Bos.
Dick Irvin, Mtl.	Coach	Hap Day, Tor.

1942-43

First Team	Pos	Second Team
Johnny Mowers, Det.	G	Frank Brimsek, Bos.
Earl Seibert, Chi.	D	Jack Crawford, Bos.
Jack Stewart, Det.	D	Flash Hollett, Bos.
Bill Cowley, Bos.	C	Syl Apps, Tor.
Lorne Carr, Tor.	RW	Bryan Hextall, NYR
Doug Bentley, Chi.	LW	Lynn Patrick, NYR
Jack Adams, Det.	Coach	Art Ross, Bos.

1941-42

First Team	Pos	Second Team
Frank Brimsek, Bos.	G	Turk Broda, Tor.
Earl Seibert, Chi.	D	Pat Egan, Bro.
Tom Anderson, Bro.	D	Bucko McDonald, Tor.
Syl Apps, Tor.	C	Phil Watson, NYR
Bryan Hextall, NYR	RW	Gordie Drillon, Tor.
Lynn Patrick, NYR	LW	Sid Abel, Det.
Frank Boucher, NYR	Coach	Paul Thompson, Chi.

1940-41

First Team	Pos	Second Team
Turk Broda, Tor.	G	Frank Brimsek, Bos.
Dit Clapper, Bos.	D	Earl Seibert, Chi.
Wally Stanowski, Tor.	D	Ott Heller, NYR
Bill Cowley, Bos.	C	Syl Apps, Tor.
Bryan Hextall, NYR	RW	Bobby Bauer, Bos.
Sweeney Schriner, Tor.	LW	Woody Dumart, Bos.
Cooney Weiland, Bos.	Coach	Dick Irvin, Mtl.

1939-40

First Team	Pos	Second Team
Dave Kerr, NYR	G	Frank Brimsek, Bos.
Dit Clapper, Bos.	D	Art Coulter, NYR
Ebbie Goodfellow, Det.	D	Earl Seibert, Chi.
Milt Schmidt, Bos.	C	Neil Colville, NYR
Bryan Hextall, NYR	RW	Bobby Bauer, Bos.
Toe Blake, Mtl.	LW	Woody Dumart, Bos.
Paul Thompson, Chi.	Coach	Frank Boucher, NYR

1938-39

First Team	Pos	Second Team
Frank Brimsek, Bos.	G	Earl Robertson, NYA
Eddie Shore, Bos.	D	Earl Seibert, Chi.
Dit Clapper, Bos.	D	Art Coulter, NYR
Syl Apps, Tor.	C	Neil Colville, NYR
Gordie Drillon, Tor.	RW	Bobby Bauer, Bos.
Toe Blake, Mtl.	LW	Johnny Gottselig, Chi.
Art Ross, Bos.	Coach	Red Dutton, NYA

1937-38

First Team	Pos	Second Team
Tiny Thompson, Bos.	G	Dave Kerr, NYR
Eddie Shore, Bos.	D	Art Coulter, NYR
Babe Siebert, Mtl.	D	Earl Seibert, Chi.
Bill Cowley, Bos.	C	Syl Apps, Tor.
Cecil Dillon, NYR	RW	
Gordie Drillon, Tor.	(tied)	
Paul Thompson, Chi.	LW	Toe Blake, Mtl.
Lester Patrick, NYR	Coach	Art Ross, Bos.

1936-37

First Team	Pos	Second Team
Normie Smith, Det.	G	Wilf Cude, Mtl.
Babe Siebert, Mtl.	D	Earl Seibert, Chi.
Ebbie Goodfellow, Det.	D	Lionel Conacher, Mtl. M.
Marty Barry, Det.	C	Art Chapman, NYA
Larry Aurie, Det.	RW	Cecil Dillon, NYR
Busher Jackson, Tor.	LW	Sweeney Schriner, NYA
Jack Adams, Det.	Coach	Cecil Hart, Mtl.

1935-36

First Team	Pos	Second Team
Tiny Thompson, Bos.	G	Wilf Cude, Mtl.
Eddie Shore, Bos.	D	Earl Seibert, Chi.
Babe Siebert, Bos.	D	Ebbie Goodfellow, Det.
Hooley Smith, Mtl. M.	C	Bill Thoms, Tor.
Charlie Conacher, Tor.	RW	Cecil Dillon, NYR
Sweeney Schriner, NYA	LW	Paul Thompson, Chi.
Lester Patrick, NYR	Coach	Tommy Gorman, Mtl. M.

1934-35

First Team	Pos	Second Team
Lorne Chabot, Chi.	G	Tiny Thompson, Bos.
Eddie Shore, Bos.	D	Cy Wentworth, Mtl. M.
Earl Seibert, NYR	D	Art Coulter, Chi.
Frank Boucher, NYR	C	Cooney Weiland, Det.
Charlie Conacher, Tor.	RW	Dit Clapper, Bos.
Busher Jackson, Tor.	LW	Aurel Joliat, Mtl.
Lester Patrick, NYR	Coach	Dick Irvin, Tor.

1933-34

First Team	Pos	Second Team
Charlie Gardiner, Chi.	G	Roy Worters, NYA
King Clancy, Tor.	D	Eddie Shore, Bos.
Lionel Conacher, Chi.	D	Ching Johnson, NYR
Frank Boucher, NYR	C	Joe Primeau, Tor.
Charlie Conacher, Tor.	RW	Bill Cook, NYR
Busher Jackson, Tor.	LW	Aurel Joliat, Mtl.
Lester Patrick, NYR	Coach	Dick Irvin, Tor.

1932-33

First Team	Pos	Second Team
John Ross Roach, Det.	G	Charlie Gardiner, Chi.
Eddie Shore, Bos.	D	King Clancy, Tor.
Ching Johnson, NYR	D	Lionel Conacher, Mtl. M.
Frank Boucher, NYR	C	Howie Morenz, Mtl.
Bill Cook, NYR	RW	Charlie Conacher, Tor.
Baldy Northcott, Mtl M.	LW	Busher Jackson, Tor.
Lester Patrick, NYR	Coach	Dick Irvin, Tor.

1931-32

First Team	Pos	Second Team
Charlie Gardiner, Chi.	G	Roy Worters, NYA
Eddie Shore, Bos.	D	Sylvio Mantha, Mtl.
Ching Johnson, NYR	D	King Clancy, Tor.
Howie Morenz, Mtl.	C	Hooley Smith, Mtl. M.
Bill Cook, NYR	RW	Charlie Conacher, Tor.
Busher Jackson, Tor.	LW	Aurel Joliat, Mtl.
Lester Patrick, NYR	Coach	Dick Irvin, Tor.

1930-31

First Team	Pos	Second Team
Charlie Gardiner, Chi.	G	Tiny Thompson, Bos.
Eddie Shore, Bos.	D	Sylvio Mantha, Mtl.
King Clancy, Tor.	D	Ching Johnson, NYR
Howie Morenz, Mtl.	C	Frank Boucher, NYR
Bill Cook, NYR	RW	Dit Clapper, Bos.
Aurel Joliat, Mtl.	LW	Bun Cook, NYR
Lester Patrick, NYR	Coach	Dick Irvin, Chi.

Dave Kerr was a Second-Team All-Star in 1937-38. In 1939-40, he led the Rangers to the Stanley Cup, won the Vezina Trophy and was named to the First All-Star Team. No one since then has posted an average below his mark of 1.54.

All-Star Game Results

Year	Venue	Score	Coaches	Attendance
2004	Minnesota	East 6, West 4	Pat Quinn, Dave Lewis	19,434
2003	Florida	West 6, East 5	Marc Crawford, Jacques Martin	19,250
2002	Los Angeles	World 8, North America 5	Scotty Bowman, Pat Quinn	18,118
2001	Colorado	North America 14, World 12	Joel Quenneville, Jacques Martin	18,646
2000	Toronto	World 9, North America 4	Scotty Bowman, Pat Quinn	19,300
1999	Tampa Bay	North America 8, World 6	Lindy Ruff, Ken Hitchcock	19,758
1998	Vancouver	North America 8, World 7	Jacques Lemaire, Ken Hitchcock	18,422
1997	San Jose	East 11, West 7	Doug MacLean, Ken Hitchcock	17,422
1996	Boston	East 5, West 4	Doug MacLean, Scotty Bowman	17,565
1994	NY Rangers	East 9, West 8	Jacques Demers, Barry Melrose	18,200
1993	Montreal	Wales 16, Campbell 6	Scotty Bowman, Mike Keenan	17,137
1992	Philadelphia	Campbell 10, Wales 6	Bob Gainey, Scotty Bowman	17,380
1991	Chicago	Campbell 11, Wales 5	John Muckler, Mike Milbury	18,472
1990	Pittsburgh	Wales 12, Campbell 7	Pat Burns, Terry Crisp	16,236
1989	Edmonton	Campbell 9, Wales 5	Glen Sather, Terry O'Reilly	17,503
1988	St. Louis	Wales 6, Campbell 5 OT	Mike Keenan, Glen Sather	17,878
1986	Hartford	Wales 4, Campbell 3 OT	Mike Keenan, Glen Sather	15,100
1985	Calgary	Wales 6, Campbell 4	Al Arbour, Glen Sather	16,825
1984	New Jersey	Wales 7, Campbell 6	Al Arbour, Glen Sather	18,939
1983	NY Islanders	Campbell 9, Wales 3	Roger Neilson, Al Arbour	15,230
1982	Washington	Wales 4, Campbell 2	Al Arbour, Glen Sonmor	18,130
1981	Los Angeles	Campbell 4, Wales 1	Pat Quinn, Scotty Bowman	15,761
1980	Detroit	Wales 6, Campbell 3	Scotty Bowman, Al Arbour	21,002
1978	Buffalo	Wales 3, Campbell 2 OT	Scotty Bowman, Fred Shero	16,433
1977	Vancouver	Wales 4, Campbell 3	Scotty Bowman, Fred Shero	15,607
1976	Philadelphia	Wales 7, Campbell 5	Floyd Smith, Fred Shero	16,436
1975	Montreal	Wales 7, Campbell 1	Bep Guidolin, Fred Shero	16,080
1974	Chicago	West 6, East 4	Billy Reay, Scotty Bowman	16,426
1973	NY Rangers	East 5, West 4	Tom Johnson, Billy Reay	16,986
1972	Minnesota	East 3, West 2	Al MacNeil, Billy Reay	15,423
1971	Boston	West 2, East 1	Scotty Bowman, Harry Sinden	14,790
1970	St. Louis	East 4, West 1	Claude Ruel, Scotty Bowman	16,587
1969	Montreal	East 3, West 3	Toe Blake, Scotty Bowman	16,260
1968	Toronto	Toronto 4, All-Stars 3	Punch Imlach, Toe Blake	15,753
1967	Montreal	Montreal 3, All-Stars 0	Toe Blake, Sid Abel	14,284
1965	Montreal	All-Stars 5, Montreal 2	Billy Reay, Toe Blake	13,529
1964	Toronto	All-Stars 3, Toronto 2	Sid Abel, Punch Imlach	14,232
1963	Toronto	All-Stars 3, Toronto 3	Sid Abel, Punch Imlach	14,034
1962	Toronto	Toronto 4, All-Stars 1	Punch Imlach, Rudy Pilous	14,236
1961	Chicago	All-Stars 3, Chicago 1	Sid Abel, Rudy Pilous	14,534
1960	Montreal	All-Stars 2, Montreal 1	Punch Imlach, Toe Blake	13,949
1959	Montreal	Montreal 6, All-Stars 1	Toe Blake, Punch Imlach	13,818
1958	Montreal	Montreal 6, All-Stars 3	Toe Blake, Milt Schmidt	13,989
1957	Montreal	All-Stars 5, Montreal 3	Milt Schmidt, Toe Blake	13,003
1956	Montreal	All-Stars 1, Montreal 1	Jim Skinner, Toe Blake	13,095
1955	Detroit	Detroit 3, All-Stars 1	Jim Skinner, Dick Irvin	10,111
1954	Detroit	All-Stars 2, Detroit 2	King Clancy, Jim Skinner	10,689
1953	Montreal	All-Stars 3, Montreal 1	Lynn Patrick, Dick Irvin	14,153
1952	Detroit	1st Team 1, 2nd Team 1	Tommy Ivan, Dick Irvin	10,680
1951	Toronto	1st Team 2, 2nd Team 2	Joe Primeau, Dick Irvin	11,469
1950	Detroit	Detroit 7, All-Stars 1	Tommy Ivan, Lynn Patrick	9,166
1949	Toronto	All-Stars 3, Toronto 1	Tommy Ivan, Hap Day	13,541
1948	Chicago	All-Stars 3, Toronto 1	Tommy Ivan, Hap Day	12,794
1947	Toronto	All-Stars 4, Toronto 3	Dick Irvin, Hap Day	14,169

There was no All-Star contest during the calendar year of 1966 because the game was moved from the start of season to mid-season. In 1979, the Challenge Cup series between the Soviet Union and Team NHL replaced the All-Star Game. In 1987, Rendez-Vous '87, two games between the Soviet Union and Team NHL replaced the All-Star Game. Rendez-Vous '87 scores: game one, NHL All-Stars

2003-04 All-Star Game Summary

February 8, 2004 at St. Paul, MN   East 6, West 4

PLAYERS ON ICE: **East** — Brodeur, Luongo, Theodore, S. Niedermayer, Souray, Aucoin, Boynton, Rafalski, Kubina, St. Louis, Thornton, Kovalchuk, Lang, Sundin, Jagr, M. Messier, Alfredsson, Roenick, K. Primeau, Roberts, G. Murray

West — Turco, Roloson, Vokoun, R. Blake, Lidstrom, Timonen, C. Pronger, Norstrom, Kuba, Bertuzzi, Modano, Guerin, Doan, Datsyuk, Naslund, Iginla, Marleau, R. Nash, Tkachuk, Sakic, Tanguay

SUMMARY
First Period

1. East	Aucoin	(Jagr, Messier)	5:44
2. West	Sakic	(Naslund, Bertuzzi)	13:37

PENALTIES: None

Second Period

3. East	Alfredsson	(unassisted)	0:51
4. West	Sakic	(Naslund, Bertuzzi)	5:44
5. West	Doan	(Lidstrom, Tkachuk)	13:02
6. East	Messier	(Niedermayer, Lang)	13:48
7. East	Roberts	(Alfredsson, Sundin)	14:41
8. East	Alfredsson	(Sundin, Roberts)	18:04

PENALTIES: None

Third Period

9. East	Kovalchuk	(Souray)	4:03
10. West	Sakic	(Naslund)	7:22

PENALTIES: None

SHOTS ON GOAL BY:

East	10	12	7	**29**
West	11	12	9	**32**

	Goaltenders:	Time	SA	GA	ENG	Dec
East	Brodeur	20:00	11	1	0	
East	Theodore	20:00	12	2	0	W
East	Luongo	20:00	9	1	0	
West	Turco	20:00	10	1	0	
West	Vokoun	20:00	12	4	0	L
West	Roloson	18:51	7	1	0	

PP Conversions: East 0/0; West 0/0.

Referees: Blaine Angus, Stephen Walkom
Linesmen: Scott Driscoll, Thor Nelson
Attendance: 19,434

NHL ALL-ROOKIE TEAM

Voting for the NHL All-Rookie Team is conducted among the representatives of the Professional Hockey Writers' Association at the end of the season. The rookie all-star team was first selected for the 1982-83 season.

	2003-04		**1998-99**	**1993-94**	**1988-89**	**1983-84**
Goal	Andrew Raycroft, Boston		Jamie Storr, Los Angeles	Martin Brodeur, New Jersey	Peter Sidorkiewicz, Hartford	Tom Barrasso, Buffalo
Defense	John-Michael Liles, Colorado		Tom Poti, Edmonton	Chris Pronger, Hartford	Brian Leetch, NY Rangers	Thomas Eriksson, Philadelphia
Defense	Joni Pitkanen, Philadelphia		Sami Salo, Ottawa	Boris Mironov, Wpg./Edm.	Zarley Zalapski, Pittsburgh	Jamie Macoun, Calgary
Forward	Trent Hunter, NY Islanders		Chris Drury, Colorado	Jason Arnott, Edmonton	Trevor Linden, Vancouver	Steve Yzerman, Detroit
Forward	Ryan Malone, Pittsburgh		Milan Hejduk, Colorado	Mikael Renberg, Philadelphia	Tony Granato, NY Rangers	Hakan Loob, Calgary
Forward	Michael Ryder,•Montreal		Marian Hossa, Ottawa	Oleg Petrov, Montreal	David Volek, NY Islanders	Sylvain Turgeon, Hartford
	2002-03		**1997-98**	**1992-93**	**1987-88**	**1982-83**
Goal	Sebastian Caron, Pittsburgh		Jamie Storr, Los Angeles	Felix Potvin, Toronto	Darren Pang, Chicago	Pelle Lindbergh, Philadelphia
Defense	Jay Bouwmeester, Florida		Mattias Ohlund, Vancouver	Vladimir Malakhov, NY Islanders	Glen Wesley, Boston	Scott Stevens, Washington
Defense	Barret Jackman, St. Louis		Derek Morris, Calgary	Scott Niedermayer, New Jersey	Calle Johansson, Buffalo	Phil Housley, Buffalo
Forward	Tyler Arnason, Chicago		Sergei Samsonov, Boston	Eric Lindros, Philadelphia	Joe Nieuwendyk, Calgary	Dan Daoust, Mtl./Tor.
Forward	Rick Nash, Columbus		Patrick Elias, New Jersey	Teemu Selanne, Winnipeg	Ray Sheppard, Buffalo	Steve Larmer, Chicago
Forward	Henrik Zetterberg, Detroit		Mike Johnson, Toronto	Joe Juneau, Boston	Iain Duncan, Winnipeg	Mats Naslund, Montreal
	2001-02		**1996-97**	**1991-92**	**1986-87**	
Goal	Dan Blackburn, NY Rangers		Patrick Lalime, Pittsburgh	Dominik Hasek, Chicago	Ron Hextall, Philadelphia	
Defense	Nick Boynton, Boston		Bryan Berard, NY Islanders	Nicklas Lidstrom, Detroit	Steve Duchesne, Los Angeles	
Defense	Rostislav Klesla, Columbus		Janne Niinimaa, Philadelphia	Vladimir Konstantinov, Detroit	Brian Benning, St. Louis	
Forward	Dany Heatley, Atlanta		Jarome Iginla, Calgary	Kevin Todd, New Jersey	Jimmy Carson, Los Angeles	
Forward	Ilya Kovalchuk, Atlanta		Jim Campbell, St. Louis	Tony Amonte, NY Rangers	Jim Sandlak, Vancouver	
Forward	Kristian Huselius, Florida		Sergei Berezin, Toronto	Gilbert Dionne, Montreal	Luc Robitaille, Los Angeles	
	2000-01		**1995-96**	**1990-91**	**1985-86**	
Goal	Evgeni Nabokov, San Jose		Corey Hirsch, Vancouver	Ed Belfour, Chicago	Patrick Roy, Montreal	
Defense	Lubomir Visnovsky, Los Angeles		Ed Jovanovski, Florida	Eric Weinrich, New Jersey	Gary Suter, Calgary	
Defense	Colin White, New Jersey		Kyle McLaren, Boston	Rob Blake, Los Angeles	Dana Murzyn, Hartford	
Forward	Martin Havlat, Ottawa		Daniel Alfredsson, Ottawa	Sergei Fedorov, Detroit	Mike Ridley, NY Rangers	
Forward	Brad Richards, Tampa Bay		Eric Daze, Chicago	Ken Hodge, Boston	Kjell Dahlin, Montreal	
Forward	Shane Willis, Carolina		Petr Sykora, New Jersey	Jaromir Jagr, Pittsburgh	Wendel Clark, Toronto	
	1999-2000		**1994-95**	**1989-90**	**1984-85**	
Goal	Brian Boucher, Philadelphia		Jim Carey, Washington	Bob Essensa, Winnipeg	Steve Penney, Montreal	
Defense	Brian Rafalski, New Jersey		Chris Therien, Philadelphia	Brad Shaw, Hartford	Chris Chelios, Montreal	
Defense	Brad Stuart, San Jose		Kenny Jonsson, Toronto	Geoff Smith, Edmonton	Bruce Bell, Quebec	
Forward	Simon Gagne, Philadelphia		Peter Forsberg, Quebec	Mike Modano, Minnesota	Mario Lemieux, Pittsburgh	
Forward	Scott Gomez, New Jersey		Jeff Friesen, San Jose	Sergei Makarov, Calgary	Tomas Sandstrom, NY Rangers	
Forward	Michael York, NY Rangers		Paul Kariya, Anaheim	Rod Brind'Amour, St. Louis	Warren Young, Pittsburgh	

All-Star Game Records 1947 through 2004

TEAM RECORDS

MOST GOALS, BOTH TEAMS, ONE GAME:
26 — North America 14, World 12, 2001 at Colorado
22 — Wales 16, Campbell 6, 1993 at Montreal
19 — Wales 12, Campbell 7, 1990 at Pittsburgh
18 — East 11, West 7, 1997 at San Jose
17 — East 9, West 8, 1994 at NY Rangers
16 — Campbell 11, Wales 5, 1991 at Chicago
  — Campbell 10, Wales 6, 1992 at Philadelphia
15 — North America 8, World 7, 1998 at Vancouver

FEWEST GOALS, BOTH TEAMS, ONE GAME:
2 — First Team All-Stars 1, Second Team All-Stars 1, 1952 at Detroit
  — NHL All-Stars 1, Montreal Canadiens 1, 1956 at Montreal
3 — NHL All-Stars 2, Montreal Canadiens 1, 1960 at Montreal
  — Montreal Canadiens 3, NHL All-Stars 0, 1967 at Montreal
  — West 2, East 1, 1971 at Boston

MOST GOALS, ONE TEAM, ONE GAME:
16 — Wales 16, Campbell 6, 1993 at Montreal
14 — North America 14, World 12, 2001 at Colorado
12 — Wales 12, Campbell 7, 1990 at Pittsburgh
  — World 12, North America 14, 2001 at Colorado
11 — Campbell 11, Wales 5, 1991 at Chicago
  — East 11, West 7, 1997 at San Jose

FEWEST GOALS, ONE TEAM, ONE GAME:
0 — NHL All-Stars 0, Montreal Canadiens 3, 1967 at Montreal
1 — 17 times (1981, 1975, 1971, 1970, 1962, 1961, 1960, 1959, both teams 1956, 1955, 1953, both teams 1952, 1950, 1949, 1948)

MOST SHOTS, BOTH TEAMS, ONE GAME (SINCE 1955):
102 — 1994 at NY Rangers — East 9 (56 shots), West 8 (46 shots)
98 — 2001 at Colorado — North America 14 (53 shots), World 12 (45 shots)
90 — 1993 at Montreal — Wales 16 (49 shots), Campbell 6 (41 shots)
89 — 2002 at Los Angeles — World 8 (39 shots), North America 5 (50 shots)

FEWEST SHOTS, BOTH TEAMS, ONE GAME (SINCE 1955):
52 — 1978 at Buffalo — Campbell 2 (12 shots), Wales 3 (40 shots)
53 — 1960 at Montreal — NHL All-Stars 2 (27 shots), Montreal Canadiens 1 (26 shots)
55 — 1956 at Montreal — NHL All-Stars 1 (28 shots), Montreal Canadiens 1 (27 shots)
  — 1971 at Boston — West 2 (28 shots), East 1 (27 shots)

MOST SHOTS, ONE TEAM, ONE GAME (SINCE 1955):
56 — 1994 at NY Rangers — East (9-8 vs. West)
53 — 2001 at Colorado — North America (14-12 vs. World)
50 — 2002 at Los Angeles — North America (5-8 vs. World)
49 — 1993 at Montreal — Wales (16-6 vs. Campbell)
  — 1999 at Tampa Bay — North America (8-6 vs. World)

FEWEST SHOTS, ONE TEAM, ONE GAME (SINCE 1955):
12 — 1978 at Buffalo — Campbell (2-3 vs. Wales)
17 — 1970 at St. Louis — West (1-4 vs. East)
23 — 1961 at Chicago — Chicago Black Hawks (1-3 vs. NHL All-Stars)
24 — 1976 at Philadelphia — Campbell (5-7 vs. Wales)

MOST POWER-PLAY GOALS, BOTH TEAMS, ONE GAME (SINCE 1950):
3 — 1953 at Montreal — NHL All-Stars 3 (2 power-play goals), Montreal Canadiens 1 (1 power-play goal)
  — 1954 at Detroit — NHL All-Stars 2 (1 power-play goal), Detroit Red Wings 2 (2 power-play goals)
  — 1958 at Montreal — NHL All-Stars 3 (1 power-play goal), Montreal Canadiens 6 (2 power-play goals)

FEWEST POWER-PLAY GOALS, BOTH TEAMS, ONE GAME (SINCE 1950):
0 — 22 times (1952, 1959, 1960, 1967, 1968, 1969, 1972, 1973, 1976, 1980, 1981, 1984, 1985, 1992, 1994, 1996, 1999, 2000, 2001, 2002, 2003, 2004)

FASTEST TWO GOALS, BOTH TEAMS, FROM START OF GAME:
0:37 — 1970 at St. Louis — Jacques Laperriere of East scored at 0:20 and Dean Prentice of West scored at 0:37. Final score: East 4, West 1.
2:15 — 1998 at Vancouver — Teemu Selanee scored at 0:53 and Jaromir Jagr scored at 2:15 for World. Final score: North America 8, World 7.
3:37 — 1993 at Montreal — Mike Gartner scored at 3:15 and at 3:37 for Wales. Final score: Wales 16, Campbell 6.

FASTEST TWO GOALS, BOTH TEAMS:
0:08 — 1997 at San Jose — Owen Nolan scored at 18:54 and 19:02 of second period for West. Final Score: East 11, West 7.
0:10 — 1976 at Philadelphia — Dennis Ververgaert scored at 4:33 and at 4:43 of third period for Campbell. Final score: Wales 7, Campbell 5.
0:13 — 1998 at Vancouver — Teemu Selanne scored at 4:00 of first period for World and John LeClair scored at 4:13 for North America. Final score: North America 8, World 7.

FASTEST THREE GOALS, BOTH TEAMS:
1:08 — 1993 at Montreal — all by Wales — Mike Gartner scored at 3:15 and at 3:37 of first period; Peter Bondra scored at 4:23. Final score: Wales 16, Campbell 6.
1:14 — 1994 at NY Rangers — Bob Kudelski scored at 9:46 of first period for East; Sergei Fedorov scored at 10:20 for West; Eric Lindros scored at 11:00 for East. Final score: East 9, West 8.
1:23 — 1999 at Tampa Bay — Mats Sundin scored at 2:57 of third period for World; Darryl Sydor scored at 4:02 for North America; Sergei Zubov scored at 4:20 for World. Final score: North America 8, World 6.

FASTEST FOUR GOALS, BOTH TEAMS:
2:24 — 1997 at San Jose — Brendan Shanahan scored at 16:38 of second period for West; Dale Hawerchuk scored at 17:28 for East; Owen Nolan scored at 18:54 and 19:02 for West. Final score: East 11, West 7.
2:57 — 2002 at Los Angeles — Sergei Fedorov scored at 16:59 of third period for World; Markus Naslund scored at 18:17 for World; Alex Zhamnov scored at 19:12 for World; Sami Kapanen scored at 19:56 for World. Final score: World 8, North America 5.
3:04 — 1997 at San Jose — Mark Recchi scored at 15:32 of first period for East; Dale Hawerchuk scored at 16:19 for East; Pavel Bure scored at 17:36 for West; Paul Kariya scored at 18:36 for West. Final score: East 11, West 7.

FASTEST TWO GOALS, ONE TEAM, FROM START OF GAME:
2:15 — 1998 at Vancouver — World — Teemu Selanee scored at 0:53 and Jaromir Jagr scored at 2:15. Final score: North America 8, World 7.
3:37 — 1993 at Montreal — Wales — Mike Gartner scored at 3:15 and at 3:37. Final score: Wales 16, Campbell 6.
4:19 — 1980 at Detroit — Wales — Larry Robinson scored at 3:58 and Steve Payne scored at 4:19. Final score: Wales 6, Campbell 3.

FASTEST TWO GOALS, ONE TEAM:
0:08 — 1997 at San Jose — West — Owen Nolan scored at 18:54 and at 19:02 of second period. Final score: East 11, West 7.
0:10 — 1976 at Philadelphia — Campbell — Dennis Ververgaert scored at 4:33 and at 4:43 of third period. Final score: Wales 7, Campbell 5.
0:14 — 1989 at Edmonton — Campbell — Steve Yzerman and Gary Leeman scored at 17:21 and 17:35 of second period. Final score: Campbell 9, Wales 5.

FASTEST THREE GOALS, ONE TEAM:
1:08 — 1993 at Montreal — Wales — Mike Gartner scored at 3:15 and 3:37 of first period; Peter Bondra scored at 4:23. Final score: Wales 16, Campbell 6.
1:32 — 1980 at Detroit — Wales — Ron Stackhouse scored at 11:40 of third period; Craig Hartsburg scored at 12:40; Reed Larson scored at 13:12. Final score: Wales 6, Campbell 3.
1:39 — 2002 at Los Angeles — Markus Naslund scored at 18:17 of third period; Alex Zhamnov scored at 19:12; Sami Kapanen scored at 19:56. Final score: World 8, North America 5.

FASTEST FOUR GOALS, ONE TEAM:
2:57 — 2002 at Los Angeles — World — Sergei Fedorov scored at 16:59 of third period; Markus Naslund scored at 18:17; Alex Zhamnov scored at 19:12; Sami Kapanen scored at 19:56. Final score: World 8, North America 5.
4:19 — 1992 at Philadelphia — Campbell — Brian Bellows scored at 7:40 of second period; Jeremy Roenick scored at 8:13; Theoren Fleury scored at 11:06; Brett Hull scored at 11:59. Final score: Campbell 10, Wales 6.
4:26 — 1980 at Detroit — Wales — Ron Stackhouse scored at 11:40 of third period; Craig Hartsburg scored at 12:40; Reed Larson scored at 13:12; Real Cloutier scored at 16:06. Final score: Wales 6, Campbell 3.

MOST GOALS, BOTH TEAMS, ONE PERIOD:
10 — 1997 at San Jose — Second period — East (6), West (4). Final score: East 11, West 7.
  — 2001 at Colorado — Second period — North America (6), World (4). Final score: North America 14, World 12.
  — 2001 at Colorado — Third period — North America (5), World (5). Final score: North America 14, World 12.
9 — 1990 at Pittsburgh — First period — Wales (7), Campbell (2). Final score: Wales 12, Campbell 7.

MOST GOALS, ONE TEAM, ONE PERIOD:
7 — 1990 at Pittsburgh — First period — Wales. Final score: Wales 12, Campbell 7.
6 — 1983 at NY Islanders — Third period — Campbell.
Final score: Campbell 9, Wales 3.
— 1992 at Philadelphia — Second period — Campbell.
Final score: Campbell 10, Wales 6.
— 1993 at Montreal — First period — Wales.
Final score: Wales 16, Campbell 6.
— 1993 at Montreal — Second period — Wales.
Final score: Wales 16, Campbell 6.
— 1997 at San Jose — Second period — East.
Final score: East 11, West 7.
— 2001 at Colorado — Second period — North America.
Final score: North America 14, World 12.

MOST SHOTS, BOTH TEAMS, ONE PERIOD:
39 — 1994 at NY Rangers — Second period — West (21), East (18).
Final score: East 9, West 8.
— 2001 at Colorado — Third period — World (23), North America (16).
Final score: North America 14, World 12.
36 — 1990 at Pittsburgh — Third period — Campbell (22), Wales (14).
Final score: Wales 12, Campbell 7.
— 1994 at NY Rangers — First period — East (19), West (17).
Final score: East 9, West 8.
— 2002 at Los Angeles — Third period — North America (20), World (16).
Final score: World 8, North America 5.

MOST SHOTS, ONE TEAM, ONE PERIOD:
23 — 2001 at Colorado — Third period — World.
Final score: North America 14, World 12.
22 — 1990 at Pittsburgh — Third period — Campbell.
Final score: Wales 12, Campbell 7.
— 1991 at Chicago — Third period — Wales.
Final score: Campbell 11, Wales 5.
— 1993 at Montreal — First period — Wales.
Final score: Wales 16, Campbell 6.

FEWEST SHOTS, BOTH TEAMS, ONE PERIOD:
9 — 1971 at Boston — Third period — East (2), West (7).
Final score: West 2, East 1.
— 1980 at Detroit — Second period — Campbell (4), Wales (5).
Final score: Wales 6, Campbell 3.
13 — 1982 at Washington — Third period — Campbell (6), Wales (7).
Final score: Wales 4, Campbell 2.
14 — 1978 at Buffalo — First period — Campbell (7), Wales (7).
Final score: Wales 3, Campbell 2.
— 1986 at Hartford — First period — Campbell (6), Wales (8).
Final score: Wales 4, Campbell 3.

FEWEST SHOTS, ONE TEAM, ONE PERIOD:
2 — 1971 at Boston — Third period — East.
Final score: West 2, East 1.
— 1978 at Buffalo — Second period — Campbell.
Final score: Wales 3, Campbell 2.
3 — 1978 at Buffalo — Third period — Campbell.
Final score: Wales 3, Campbell 2.
4 — 1955 at Detroit — First period — NHL All-Stars.
Final score: Detroit Red Wings 3, NHL All-Stars 1.
— 1980 at Detroit — Second period — Campbell.
Final score: Wales 6, Campbell 3.

INDIVIDUAL RECORDS

Games

MOST GAMES PLAYED:
23 — **Gordie Howe** from 1948 through 1980
19 — Raymond Bourque from 1981 through 2001
18 — Wayne Gretzky from 1980 through 1999
15 — Frank Mahovlich from 1959 through 1974
— Mark Messier from 1982 through 2004

Goals

MOST GOALS (CAREER):
13 — **Wayne Gretzky** in 18GP
— **Mario Lemieux** in 10GP
10 — Gordie Howe in 23GP
8 — Frank Mahovlich in 15GP
— Luc Robitaille in 8GP
— Teemu Selanne in 9GP

MOST GOALS, ONE GAME:
4 — **Wayne Gretzky,** Campbell, 1983
— **Mario Lemieux,** Wales, 1990
— **Vince Damphousse,** Campbell, 1991
— **Mike Gartner,** Wales, 1993
— **Dany Heatley,** East, 2003
3 — Ted Lindsay, Detroit, 1950
— Mario Lemieux, Wales, 1988
— Pierre Turgeon, Wales, 1993
— Mark Recchi, East, 1997
— Owen Nolan, West, 1997
— Teemu Selanne, World, 1998
— Pavel Bure, World, 2000
— Bill Guerin, North America, 2001
— Joe Sakic, West, 2004

MOST GOALS, ONE PERIOD:
4 — **Wayne Gretzky,** Campbell, Third period, 1983
3 — Mario Lemieux, Wales, First period, 1990
— Vince Damphousse, Campbell, Third period, 1991
— Mike Gartner, Wales, First period, 1993

Assists

MOST ASSISTS (CAREER):
14 — **Mark Messier** in 15GP
13 — Raymond Bourque in 19GP
12 — Adam Oates in 5GP
— Mats Sundin in 8GP
— Joe Sakic in 11GP
— Wayne Gretzky in 18GP

MOST ASSISTS, ONE GAME:
5 — **Mats Naslund,** Wales, 1988
4 — Raymond Bourque, Wales, 1985
— Adam Oates, Campbell, 1991
— Adam Oates, Wales, 1993
— Mark Recchi, Wales, 1993
— Pierre Turgeon, East, 1994
— Fredrik Modin, World, 2001

MOST ASSISTS, ONE PERIOD:
4 — **Adam Oates,** Wales, First period, 1993
3 — Mark Messier, Campbell, Third period, 1983

The Islanders' Adrian Aucoin (covered by Vancouver's Markus Naslund) scored the first goal as the Eastern Conference beat the Western Conference 6-4. Aucoin also blasted a slapshot of 102.2 miles per hour to win the hardest shot competition.

Points

MOST POINTS, CAREER:
25 — Wayne Gretzky (13G-12A in 18GP)
23 — Mario Lemieux (13G-10A in 10GP)
20 — Mark Messier (6G-14A in 15GP)
19 — Gordie Howe (10G-9A in 23GP)
18 — Joe Sakic (6G-12A in 11GP)

MOST POINTS, ONE GAME:
6 — Mario Lemieux, Wales, 1988 (3G-3A)
5 — Mats Naslund, Wales, 1988 (5A)
 — Adam Oates, Campbell, 1991 (1G-4A)
 — Mike Gartner, Wales, 1993 (4G-1A)
 — Mark Recchi, Wales, 1993 (1G-4A)
 — Pierre Turgeon, Wales, 1993 (3G-2A)
 — Bill Guerin, North America, 2001 (3G-2A)
 — Dany Heatley, East, 2003 (4G-1A)

MOST POINTS, ONE PERIOD:
4 — Wayne Gretzky, Campbell, Third period, 1983 (4G)
 — Mike Gartner, Wales, First period, 1993 (3G-1A)
 — Adam Oates, Wales, First period, 1993 (4A)
3 — Gordie Howe, NHL All-Stars, Second period, 1965 (1G-2A)
 — Pete Mahovlich, Wales, First period, 1976 (1G-2A)
 — Mark Messier, Campbell, Third period, 1983 (3A)
 — Mario Lemieux, Wales, Second period, 1988 (1G-2A)
 — Mario Lemieux, Wales, First period, 1990 (3G)
 — Vince Damphousse, Campbell, Third period, 1991 (3G)
 — Mark Recchi, Wales, Second period, 1993 (1G-2A)
 — Tony Amonte, North America, Second period, 2001 (2G-1A)
 — Daniel Alfredsson, East, Second period, 2004 (2G-1A)

Power-Play Goals

MOST POWER-PLAY GOALS, CAREER:
6 — Gordie Howe in 23GP
3 — Bobby Hull in 12GP
 — Maurice Richard in 13GP

Fastest Goals

FASTEST GOAL FROM START OF GAME:
0:19 — Ted Lindsay, Detroit, 1950
0:20 — Jacques Laperriere, East, 1970
0:21 — Mario Lemieux, Wales, 1990
0:35 — Vincent Damphousse, North America, 2002
0:36 — Chico Maki, West, 1971

FASTEST GOAL FROM START OF A PERIOD:
0:17 — Raymond Bourque, North America, 1999 (second period)
0:19 — Ted Lindsay, Detroit, 1950 (first period)
 — Rick Tocchet, Wales, 1993 (second period)
0:20 — Jacques Laperriere, East, 1970 (first period)
0:21 — Mario Lemieux, Wales, 1990 (first period)
0:26 — Wayne Gretzky, Campbell, 1982 (second period)

FASTEST TWO GOALS (ONE PLAYER) FROM START OF GAME:
3:37 — Mike Gartner, Wales, 1993, at 3:15 and 3:37.
4:00 — Teemu Selanne, World, 1998, at 0:53 and 4:00
5:25 — Wally Hergesheimer, NHL All-Stars, 1953, at 4:06 and 5:25.

FASTEST TWO GOALS (ONE PLAYER) FROM START OF A PERIOD:
3:37 — Mike Gartner, Wales, 1993, at 3:15 and 3:37 of first period.
4:00 — Teemu Selanne, World, 1998, at 0:53 and 4:00 of first period.
4:43 — Dennis Ververgaert, Campbell, 1976, at 4:33 and 4:43 of third period.

FASTEST TWO GOALS (ONE PLAYER):
0:08 — Owen Nolan, West, 1997. Scored at 18:54 and 19:02 of second period.
0:10 — Dennis Ververgaert, Campbell, 1976. Scored at 4:33 and 4:43 of third period.
0:22 — Mike Gartner, Wales, 1993. Scored at 3:15 and 3:37 of first period.

Penalties

MOST PENALTY MINUTES:
25 — Gordie Howe in 23GP
21 — Gus Mortson in 9GP
16 — Harry Howell in 7GP

Goaltenders

MOST GAMES PLAYED:
13 — Glenn Hall from 1955 through 1969
11 — Terry Sawchuk from 1950 through 1968
 — Patrick Roy from 1988 through 2003
 8 — Jacques Plante from 1956 through 1970
 — Martin Brodeur from 1996 through 2004

MOST MINUTES PLAYED:
540 — Glenn Hall in 13GP
467 — Terry Sawchuk in 11GP
370 — Jacques Plante in 8GP
230 — Patrick Roy in 11GP
209 — Turk Broda in 4GP

MOST GOALS AGAINST:
29 — Patrick Roy in 11GP
22 — Glenn Hall in 13GP
21 — Mike Vernon in 5GP
19 — Terry Sawchuk in 11GP
18 — Jacques Plante in 8GP
 — Andy Moog in 4GP

BEST GOALS-AGAINST-AVERAGE AMONG THOSE WITH AT LEAST TWO GAMES PLAYED:
0.68 — Gilles Villemure in 3GP
1.49 — Gerry McNeil in 3GP
1.50 — Johnny Bower in 4GP
1.51 — Frank Brimsek in 3GP
1.64 — Gump Worsley in 4GP

Rangers goalie Gilles Villemure, peering out from behind Boston's Ken Hodge, has the lowest goals-against average in All-Star Game history, surrendering just one goal in 88 minutes of action in three games from 1971 to 1973.

Hockey Hall of Fame

(Year of induction is listed after each Honoured Members name)

Location: BCE Place, at the corner of Front and Yonge Streets in the heart of downtown Toronto. Easy access from all major highways running into Toronto. Close to TTC and Union Station.

Telephone: administration (416) 360-7735; information (416) 360-7765.

Public Hours of Operation: Open every day except Christmas Day, New Year's Day and Induction Day (November 8, 2004). Please call our information number (above) or visit our website (below) for times.

The Hockey Hall of Fame can be booked for private functions after hours.

Website address: www.hhof.com

History: The Hockey Hall of Fame was established in 1943. Members were first honoured in 1945. On August 26, 1961, the Hockey Hall of Fame opened its doors to the public in a building located on the grounds of the Canadian National Exhibition in Toronto. The Hockey Hall of Fame relocated to its new site at BCE Place and welcomed the hockey world on June 18, 1993.

Honour Roll: There are 336 Honoured Members in the Hockey Hall of Fame. 230 have been inducted as players, 92 as builders and 14 as Referees/Linesmen. In addition, there are 72 media honourees.

Founding/Premiere Sponsors: IBM Canada, Imperial Oil, International Ice Hockey Federation, Kodak Canada, Molson Canada, National Hockey League, National Hockey League Players' Association, Panasonic Canada, Pepsi-Cola Canada, Sun Media (Toronto)/The Toronto Sun, The Sports Network (TSN/RDS), MCI Canada.

Raymond Bourque enters the Hockey Hall of Fame this year with fellow blueliners Paul Coffey and Larry Murphy, as well as builder Cliff Fletcher. Bourque, Coffey and Murphy rank first, second and fifth in all-time scoring by defensemen.

PLAYERS

* Abel, Sidney Gerald 1969
* Adams, John James "Jack" 1959
* Apps, Charles Joseph Sylvanus "Syl" 1961
  Armstrong, George Edward 1975
* Bailey, Irvine Wallace "Ace" 1975
* Bain, Donald H. "Dan" 1945
* Baker, Hobart "Hobey" 1945
  Barber, William Charles "Bill" 1990
* Barry, Martin J. "Marty" 1965
  Bathgate, Andrew James "Andy" 1978
* Bauer, Robert Theodore "Bobby" 1996
  Béliveau, Jean Arthur 1972
* Benedict, Clinton S. 1965
* Bentley, Douglas Wagner 1964
* Bentley, Maxwell H. L. 1966
* Blake, Hector "Toe" 1966
  Boivin, Leo Joseph 1986
* Boon, Richard R. "Dickie" 1952
  Bossy, Michael 1991
  Bouchard, Emile Joseph "Butch" 1966
* Boucher, Frank 1958
* Boucher, Georges "Buck" 1960
  Bourque, Raymond 2004
  Bower, John William 1976
* Bowie, Russell 1945
* Brimsek, Francis Charles 1966
* Broadbent, Harry L. "Punch" 1962
* Broda, Walter Edward "Turk" 1967
  Bucyk, John Paul 1981
* Burch, Billy 1974
* Cameron, Harold Hugh "Harry" 1962
  Cheevers, Gerald Michael "Gerry" 1985
* Clancy, Francis Michael "King" 1958
* Clapper, Aubrey "Dit" 1947
  Clarke, Robert "Bobby" 1987
* Cleghorn, Sprague 1958
  Coffey, Paul 2004
* Colville, Neil MacNeil 1967
* Conacher, Charles W. 1961
* Conacher, Lionel Pretoria 1994
* Conacher, Roy Gordon 1998
* Connell, Alex 1958
* Cook, Fred "Bun" 1995
* Cook, William Osser 1952
* Coulter, Arthur Edmund 1974
  Cournoyer, Yvan Serge 1982
* Cowley, William Mailes 1968
* Crawford, Samuel Russell "Rusty" 1962
* Darragh, John Proctor "Jack" 1962
* Davidson, Allan M. "Scotty" 1950
* Day, Clarence Henry "Hap" 1961
  Delvecchio, Alex 1977
* Denneny, Cyril "Cy" 1959
  Dionne, Marcel 1992
* Drillon, Gordon Arthur 1975

* Drinkwater, Charles Graham 1950
  Dryden, Kenneth Wayne 1983
* Dumart, Woodrow "Woody" 1992
* Dunderdale, Thomas 1974
* Durnan, William Ronald 1964
* Dutton, Mervyn A. "Red" 1958
* Dye, Cecil Henry "Babe" 1970
  Esposito, Anthony James "Tony" 1988
  Esposito, Philip Anthony 1984
* Farrell, Arthur F. 1965
  Federko, Bernie 2002
  Fetisov, Viacheslav 2001
* Flaman, Ferdinand Charles "Fern" 1990
* Foyston, Frank 1958
* Fredrickson, Frank 1958
  Fuhr, Grant S. 2003
  Gadsby, William Alexander 1970
  Gainey, Bob 1992
* Gardiner, Charles Robert "Chuck" 1945
* Gardiner, Herbert Martin "Herb" 1958
* Gardner, James Henry "Jimmy" 1962
  Gartner, Michael Alfred 2001
  Geoffrion, Jos. A. Bernard "Boom Boom" 1972
* Gerard, Eddie 1945
  Giacomin, Edward "Eddie" 1987
  Gilbert, Rodrigue Gabriel "Rod" 1982
  Gillies, Clark 2002
* Gilmour, Hamilton Livingstone "Billy" 1962
  Goheen, Frank Xavier "Moose" 1952
* Goodfellow, Ebenezer R. "Ebbie" 1963
  Goulet, Michel 1998
* Grant, Michael "Mike" 1950
* Green, Wilfred "Shorty" 1962
  Gretzky, Wayne Douglas 1999
* Griffis, Silas Seth "Si" 1950
* Hainsworth, George 1961
  Hall, Glenn Henry 1975
* Hall, Joseph Henry 1961
* Harvey, Douglas Norman 1973
  Hawerchuk, Dale Martin 2001
* Hay, George 1958
* Hern, William Milton "Riley" 1962
* Hextall, Bryan Aldwyn 1969
* Holmes, Harry "Hap" 1972
* Hooper, Charles Thomas "Tom" 1962
  Horner, George Reginald "Red" 1965
* Horton, Miles Gilbert "Tim" 1977
  Howe, Gordon 1972
* Howe, Sydney Harris 1965
  Howell, Henry Vernon "Harry" 1979
  Hull, Robert Marvin 1983
* Hutton, John Bower "Bouse" 1962
* Hyland, Harry M. 1962
* Irvin, James Dickenson "Dick" 1958
* Jackson, Harvey "Busher" 1971

* Johnson, Ernest "Moose" 1952
* Johnson, Ivan "Ching" 1958
  Johnson, Thomas Christian 1970
* Joliat, Aurel 1947
* Keats, Gordon "Duke" 1958
  Kelly, Leonard Patrick "Red" 1969
  Kennedy, Theodore Samuel "Teeder" 1966
  Keon, David Michael 1986
  Kurri, Jari 2001
  Lach, Elmer James 1966
  Lafleur, Guy Damien 1988
  LaFontaine, Pat 2003
* Lalonde, Edouard Charles "Newsy" 1950
  Langway, Rod Corry 2002
  Laperriere, Jacques 1987
  Lapointe, Guy 1993
  Laprade, Edgar 1993
* Laviolette, Jean Baptiste "Jack" 1962
* Lehman, Hugh 1958
  Lemaire, Jacques Gerard 1984
  Lemieux, Mario 1997
* LeSueur, Percy 1961
* Lewis, Herbert A. 1989
  Lindsay, Robert Blake Theodore "Ted" 1966
* Lumley, Harry 1980
* MacKay, Duncan "Mickey" 1952
  Mahovlich, Frank William 1981
* Malone, Joseph "Joe" 1950
* Mantha, Sylvio 1960
* Marshall, John "Jack" 1965
* Maxwell, Fred G. "Steamer" 1962
  McDonald, Lanny 1992
* McGee, Frank 1945
* McGimsie, William George "Billy" 1962
* McNamara, George 1958
  Mikita, Stanley 1983
  Moore, Richard Winston "Dickie" 1974
* Moran, Patrick Joseph "Paddy" 1958
* Morenz, Howie 1945
* Mosienko, William "Billy" 1965
  Mullen, Joseph P. 2000
  Murphy, Larry 2004
* Nighbor, Frank 1947
* Noble, Edward Reginald "Reg" 1962
* O'Connor, Herbert William "Buddy" 1988
* Oliver, Harry 1967
  Olmstead, Murray Bert "Bert" 1985
  Orr, Robert Gordon 1979
  Parent, Bernard Marcel 1984
  Park, Douglas Bradford "Brad" 1988
* Patrick, Joseph Lynn 1980
* Patrick, Lester 1947
  Perreault, Gilbert 1990
* Phillips, Tommy 1945
  Pilote, Joseph Albert Pierre Paul 1975

* Pitre, Didier "Pit" 1962
* Plante, Joseph Jacques Omer 1978
  Potvin, Denis 1991
* Pratt, Walter "Babe" 1966
* Primeau, A. Joseph 1963
  Pronovost, Joseph René Marcel 1978
  Pulford, Bob 1991
* Pulford, Harvey 1945
* Quackenbush, Hubert George "Bill" 1976
* Rankin, Frank 1961
  Ratelle, Joseph Gilbert Yvan Jean "Jean" 1985
* Rayner, Claude Earl "Chuck" 1973
  Reardon, Kenneth Joseph 1966
  Richard, Joseph Henri 1979
* Richard, Joseph Henri Maurice "Rocket" 1961
  Richardson, George Taylor 1950
* Roberts, Gordon 1971
  Robinson, Larry 1995
* Ross, Arthur Howie 1945
* Russel, Blair 1965
* Russell, Ernest 1965
* Ruttan, J.D. "Jack" 1962
  Salming, Börje Anders 1996
  Savard, Denis Joseph 2000
  Savard, Serge A. 1986
* Sawchuk, Terrance Gordon "Terry" 1971
* Scanlan, Fred 1965
  Schmidt, Milton Conrad "Milt" 1961
* Schriner, David "Sweeney" 1962
* Seibert, Earl Walter 1963
* Seibert, Oliver Levi 1961
* Shore, Edward W. "Eddie" 1947
  Shutt, Stephen 1993
* Siebert, Albert C. "Babe" 1964
* Simpson, Harold Edward "Bullet Joe" 1962
  Sittler, Darryl Glen 1989
* Smith, Alfred E. 1962
  Smith, Clint 1991
* Smith, Reginald "Hooley" 1972
* Smith, Thomas James 1973
  Smith, William John "Billy" 1993
  Stanley, Allan Herbert 1981
* Stanley, Russell "Barney" 1962
  Stastny, Peter 1998
* Stewart, John Sherratt "Black Jack" 1964
* Stewart, Nelson "Nels" 1962
* Stuart, Bruce 1961
* Stuart, Hod 1945
* Taylor, Frederick "Cyclone" (O.B.E.) 1947
* Thompson, Cecil R. "Tiny" 1959
  Tretiak, Vladislav 1989
* Trihey, Col. Harry J. 1950
  Trottier, Bryan 1997
  Ullman, Norman V. Alexander "Norm" 1982
* Vezina, Georges 1945
* Walker, John Phillip "Jack" 1960
* Walsh, Martin "Marty" 1962
* Watson, Harry E. 1962
  Watson, Harry 1994
* Weiland, Ralph "Cooney" 1971
* Westwick, Harry 1962
* Whitcroft, Fred 1962
* Wilson, Gordon Allan "Phat" 1962
  Worsley, Lorne John "Gump" 1980
* Worters, Roy 1969

BUILDERS

* Adams, Charles 1960
* Adams, Weston W. 1972
* Ahearn, Thomas Franklin "Frank" 1962
* Ahearne, John Francis "Bunny" 1977
* Allan, Sir Montagu (C.V.O.) 1945
  Allen, Keith 1992
  Arbour, Alger Joseph "Al" 1996
* Ballard, Harold Edwin 1977
* Bauer, Father David 1989
* Bickell, John Paris 1978
  Bowman, Scotty 1991
* Brown, George V. 1961
* Brown, Walter A. 1962
* Buckland, Frank 1975
  Bush, Walter Sr. 2000
  Butterfield, Jack Arlington 1980
* Calder, Frank 1947
* Campbell, Angus D. 1964
* Campbell, Clarence Sutherland 1966
* Cattarinich, Joseph 1977
* Dandurand, Joseph Viateur "Leo" 1963
* Dilio, Francis Paul 1964

* Dudley, George S. 1958
* Dunn, James A. 1968
  Fletcher, Cliff 2004
  Francis, Emile 1982
* Gibson, Dr. John L. "Jack" 1976
* Gorman, Thomas Patrick "Tommy" 1963
* Griffiths, Frank A. 1993
* Hanley, William 1986
* Hay, Charles 1974
* Hendy, James C. 1968
* Hewitt, Foster 1965
* Hewitt, William Abraham 1947
* Hume, Fred J. 1962
  Illitch, Mike 2003
* Imlach, George "Punch" 1984
* Ivan, Thomas N. 1974
* Jennings, William M. 1975
* Johnson, Bob 1992
* Juckes, Gordon W. 1979
* Kilpatrick, Gen. John Reed 1960
  Kilrea, Brian Blair 2003
* Knox, Seymour H. III 1993
* Leader, George Alfred 1969
* LeBel, Robert 1970
* Lockhart, Thomas F. 1965
* Loicq, Paul 1961
* Mariucci, John 1985
  Mathers, Frank 1992
* McLaughlin, Major Frederic 1963
* Milford, John "Jake" 1984
* Molson, Hon. Hartland de Montarville 1973
  Morrison, Ian "Scotty" 1999
* Murray, Monsignor Athol 1998
* Neilson, Roger 2002
* Nelson, Francis 1947
* Norris, Bruce A. 1969
* Norris, Sr., James 1958
* Norris, James Dougan 1962
* Northey, William M. 1947
* O'Brien, John Ambrose 1962
  O'Neill, Brian 1994
* Page, Fred 1993
  Patrick, Craig 2001
* Patrick, Frank 1958
* Pickard, Allan W. 1958
* Pilous, Rudy 1985
  Poile, Norman "Bud" 1990
  Pollock, Samuel Patterson Smyth 1978
* Raymond, Sen. Donat 1958
* Robertson, John Ross 1947
* Robinson, Claude C. 1947
* Ross, Philip D. 1976
* Sabetzki, Dr. Gunther 1995
  Sather, Glen 1997
* Selke, Frank J. 1960
  Sinden, Harry James 1983
* Smith, Frank D. 1962
* Smythe, Conn 1958
  Snider, Edward M. 1988
* Stanley of Preston, Lord (G.C.B.) 1945
* Sutherland, Cap. James T. 1947
* Tarasov, Anatoli V. 1974
  Torrey, Bill 1995
* Turner, Lloyd 1958
* Tutt, William Thayer 1978
* Voss, Carl Potter 1974
* Waghorne, Fred 1961
* Wirtz, Arthur Michael 1971
  Wirtz, William W. "Bill" 1976
  Ziegler, John A. Jr. 1987

REFEREES/LINESMEN

  Armstrong, Neil 1991
  Ashley, John George 1981
  Chadwick, William L. 1964
  D'Amico, John 1993
* Elliott, Chaucer 1961
* Hayes, George William 1988
* Hewitson, Robert W. 1963
* Ion, Fred J. "Mickey" 1961
  Pavelich, Matt 1987
* Rodden, Michael J. "Mike" 1962
  Storey, Roy Alvin "Red" 1967
  Udvari, Frank Joseph 1973
  Van Hellemond, Andy 1999

6th Annual Hockey Hall of Fame Game
Saturday, November 6, 2004
Boston Bruins vs. Toronto Maple Leafs
at Air Canada Centre in Toronto.

Elmer Ferguson Memorial Award Winners

In recognition of distinguished members of the newspaper profession whose words have brought honor to journalism and to hockey. Selected by the Professional Hockey Writers' Association.

* Barton, Charlie, Buffalo-Courier Express 1985
* Beauchamp, Jacques, Montreal Matin/Journal de Montréal 1984
* Brennan, Bill, Detroit News 1987
* Burchard, Jim, New York World Telegram 1984
* Burnett, Red, Toronto Star 1984
* Carroll, Dink, Montreal Gazette 1984
* Coleman, Jim, Southam Newspapers 1984
  Conway, Russ, Eagle-Tribune 1999
* Damata, Ted, Chicago Tribune 1984
  Delano, Hugh, New York Post 1991
  Desjardins, Marcel, Montréal La Presse 1984
  Duhatschek, Eric, Calgary Herald/Globe and Mail 2001
* Dulmage, Jack, Windsor Star 1984
  Dunnell, Milt, Toronto Star 1984
  Dupont, Kevin Paul, Boston Globe 2002
  Farber, Michael, Montreal Gazette/Sports Illustrated 2003
* Ferguson, Elmer, Montreal Herald/Star 1984
* Fitzgerald, Tom, Boston Globe 1984
  Frayne, Trent, Toronto Telegram/Globe and Mail/Sun 1984
  Gatecliff, Jack, St. Catherines Standard 1995
  Gross, George, Toronto Telegram/Sun 1985
  Johnston, Dick, Buffalo News 1986
  Kelley, Jim, Buffalo News 2004
* Laney, Al, New York Herald-Tribune 1984
* Larochelle, Claude, Le Soleil 1989
  L'Esperance, Zotique, Journal de Montréal/le Petit Journal 1985
* MacLeod, Rex, Toronto Globe and Mail/Star 1987
  Matheson, Jim, Edmonton Journal 2000
* Mayer, Charles, Journal de Montréal/la Patrie 1985
* McKenzie, Ken, The Hockey News 1997
  Monahan, Leo, Boston Daily Record/Record-American/Herald American 1986
  Moriarty, Tim, UPI/Newsday 1986
* Nichols, Joe, New York Times 1984
* O'Brien, Andy, Weekend Magazine 1985
  Orr, Frank, Toronto Star 1989
  Olan, Ben, New York Associated Press 1987
* O'Meara, Basil, Montreal Star 1984
  Pedneault, Yvon, La Presse/Journal de Montréal 1998
* Proudfoot, Jim, Toronto Star 1988
  Raymond, Bertrand, Journal de Montréal 1990
  Rosa, Fran, Boston Globe 1987
  Strachan, Al, Globe and Mail/Toronto Sun 1993
* Vipond, Jim, Toronto Globe and Mail 1984
  Walter, Lewis, Detroit Times 1984
  Young, Scott, Toronto Globe and Mail/Telegram 1988

Foster Hewitt Memorial Award Winners

In recognition of members of the radio and television industry who made outstanding contributions to their profession and the game during their career in hockey broadcasting. Selected by the NHL Broadcasters' Association.

  Cole, Bob, Hockey Night in Canada 1996
  Cusick, Fred, Boston 1984
* Darling, Ted, Buffalo 1994
* Gallivan, Danny, Montreal 1984
  Garneau, Richard, Montreal 1999
* Hart, Gene, Philadelphia 1997
* Hewitt, Foster, Toronto 1984
  Irvin, Dick, Montreal 1988
  Kaiton, Chuck, Hartford/Carolina 2004
* Kelly, Dan, St. Louis 1989
  Lange, Mike, Pittsburgh 2001
* Lecavelier, René, Montreal 1984
  Lynch, Budd, Detroit 1985
  Martyn, Bruce, Detroit 1991
  McDonald, Jiggs, Los Angeles, Atlanta, NY Islanders 1990
  McFarlane, Brian, Hockey Night in Canada 1995
* McKnight, Wes, Toronto 1986
  Meeker, Howie, Hockey Night in Canada 1998
  Miller, Bob, Los Angeles 2000
  Pettit, Lloyd, Chicago 1986
  Phillips, Rod, Edmonton 2003
  Robson, Jim, Vancouver 1992
  Shaver, Al, Minnesota 1993
* Smith, Doug, Montreal 1985
  Tremblay, Gilles, La Soirée du Hockey 2002
  Wilson, Bob, Boston 1987

* Deceased

United States
Hockey Hall of Fame

The United States Hockey Hall of Fame was opened on June 21, 1973 as the national shrine of American Hockey. It is dedicated to honoring the sport of ice hockey in the United States by preserving those precious memories and legends of the game. It is located in Eveleth, Minnesota, 60 miles north of Duluth on Highway 53. The facility is open Monday to Saturday, 9 a.m. to 5 p.m. and Sundays from 10 a.m. to 3 p.m. Admission is $8.00 for adults, $7.00 for seniors and youths (13-17) and $6.00 for children (6-12). Children under 6 are free. Call for any further information: 1-800-443-7825 or 218-744-5167.
Web site address: www.ushockeyhall.com

There are now 123 enshrined members consisting of 75 players, 24 coaches, 20 administrators, one player/administrator, one referee and two teams. New members are inducted annually in the fall and must have made a significant contribution towards hockey in the United States during the course of their career. A special Wayne Gretzky Award pays tribute to international individuals who have made major contributions to hockey in the USA. Support for the Hall of Fame comes from sponsorships, admissions, gift store sales, special events and grants from the hockey community and government agencies.

EVELETH, MN

PLAYERS
* Abel, Clarence "Taffy" 1973
* Baker, Hobart "Hobey" 1973
* Bartholome, Earl 1977
* Bessone, Peter 1978
Blake, Robert 1985
Boucha, Henry 1995
* Brimsek, Frank 1973
Broten, Neal 2000
Cavanagh, Joe 1994
* Chaisson, Ray 1974
* Chase, John P. 1973
Christian, Dave 2001
Christian, Roger 1989
Christian, William "Bill" 1984
Cleary, Robert 1981
Cleary, William 1976
* Conroy, Anthony 1975
Coppo, Paul, 2004
Curran, Mike 1998
* Dahlstrom, Carl "Cully" 1973
* Desjardins, Victor 1974
* Desmond, Richard 1988
* Dill, Robert 1979
Dougherty, Richard "Dick"
* Everett, Doug 1974
Fusco, Mark 2002
Fusco, Scott 2002
Ftorek, Robbie 1991
* Garrison, John B. 1973
Garrity, Jack 1986
* Goheen, Frank "Moose" 1973
Grant, Wally 1994
* Harding, Austin "Austie" 1975
Housley, Phil 2004
Howe, Mark 2003
* Iglehart, Stewart 1975
Johnson, Mark 2004
Johnson, Paul 2001
* Johnson, Virgil 1974
* Karakas, Mike 1973
Kirrane, Jack 1987
Lafontaine, Pat 2003
* Lane, Myles J. 1973
Langevin, David R. 1993
Langway, Rod 1999
Larson, Reed 1996
* Linder, Joseph 1975
* LoPresti, Sam L. 1973
* Mariucci, John 1973
Matchefts, John 1991
* Mather, Bruce 1998
Mayasich, John 1976
McCartan, Jack 1983
* Moe, William 1974
Morrow, Ken 1995
* Moseley, Fred 1975
Mullen, Joe 1998
* Murray, Sr., Hugh "Muzz" 1987
* Nelson, Hubert "Hub" 1978
* Nyrop, William D. 1997
* Olson , Eddie 1977
* Owen, Jr., George 1973
* Palmer, Winthrop 1973
Paradise, Robert 1989
* Purpur, Clifford "Fido" 1974
Ramsey, Mike 2001
*Riley, Joe 2002
Riley, William 1977
Roberts, Gordie 1999
* Romnes, Elwin "Doc" 1973
* Rondeau, Richard 1985
Sheehy, Timothy K. 1997
* Williams, Thomas 1981
* Winters, Frank "Coddy" 1973
* Yackel, Ken 1986

COACHES
* Almquist, Oscar 1983
Bessone, Amo 1992
Brooks, Herbert 1990
Ceglarski, Len 1992
* Cuniff, John
* Fullerton, James 1992
Gambucci, Sergio 1996
* Gordon, Malcolm K. 1973
Harkness, Nevin D. "Ned" 1994
Heyliger, Victor 1974
* Holt, Jr. Charles E. 1997
Ikola, Willard 1990
* Jeremiah, Edward J. 1973
* Johnson, Bob 1991
* Kelley, John "Snooks" 1974
Kelley, John H. "Jack" 1993
Patrick, Craig 1996
* Pleban, Jon "Connie" 1990
Riley, Jack 1979
* Ross, Larry 1988
* Thompson, Clifford, R. 1973
* Stewart, William 1982
* Winsor, Alfred "Ralph" 1973
Woog, Doug 2002

ADMINISTRATORS
* Brown, George V. 1973
* Brown, Walter A. 1973
Bush, Walter 1980
* Clark, Donald 1978
Claypool, James 1995
* Gibson, J.C. "Doc" 1973
Ilitch, Mike 2004
* Jennings, William M. 1981
* Kahler, Nick 1980
* Lockhart, Thomas F. 1973
* Marvin, Cal 1982
Palazzari, Doug 2000
Pleau, Larry 2000
* Ridder, Robert 1976
* Schulz, Charles M. 1993
Trumble, Harold 1985
* Tutt, William Thayer 1973
* Watson, Sid 1999
Wirtz, William W. "Bill" 1984
* Wright, Lyle Z.1973

PLAYER/ADMINISTRATOR
Nanne, Lou 1998

REFEREE
Chadwick, William 1974

TEAM
1960 Olympic Team, 2000
1980 Olympic Team, 2003

WAYNE GRETZKY INTERNATIONAL AWARD
Wayne Gretzky 1999
The Howe family 2000
Scotty Morrison 2001
Scotty Bowman 2002
Bobby Hull 2003
* Herb Brooks 2004

*Deceased

Jumping to the NHL with the Buffalo Sabres directly from high school in 1982-83, Phil Housley went on to play 21 seasons, appearing in more games (1,495) and collecting more points (1,232) than any other U.S.-born and developed player.

Notes

Results

2004 Stanley Cup Playoffs

CONFERENCE QUARTER-FINALS
(Best-of-seven series)

Eastern Conference

Series 'A'
Thu. Apr. 8	NY Islanders 0	at	Tampa Bay 3
Sat. Apr. 10	NY Islanders 3	at	Tampa Bay 0
Mon. Apr. 12	Tampa Bay 3	at	NY Islanders 0
Wed. Apr. 14	Tampa Bay 3	at	NY Islanders 0
Fri. Apr. 16	NY Islanders 2	at	Tampa Bay 3*

*Martin St. Louis scored at 4:07 of overtime

(Tampa Bay won series 4-1)

Series 'B'
Wed. Apr. 7	Montreal 0	at	Boston 3
Fri. Apr. 9	Montreal 1	at	Boston 2*
Sun. Apr. 11	Boston 2	at	Montreal 3
Tue. Apr. 13	Boston 4	at	Montreal 3**
Thu. Apr. 15	Montreal 5	at	Boston 1
Sat. Apr. 17	Boston 2	at	Montreal 5
Mon. Apr. 19	Montreal 2	at	Boston 0

*Patrice Bergeron scored at 1:26 of overtime
**Glen Murray scored at 29:27 of overtime

(Montreal won series 4-3)

Series 'C'
Thu. Apr. 8	New Jersey 2	at	Philadelphia 3
Sat. Apr. 10	New Jersey 2	at	Philadelphia 3
Mon. Apr. 12	Philadelphia 2	at	New Jersey 4
Wed. Apr. 14	Philadelphia 3	at	New Jersey 0
Sat. Apr. 17	New Jersey 1	at	Philadelphia 3

(Philadelphia won series 4-1)

Series 'D'
Thu. Apr. 8	Ottawa 4	at	Toronto 2
Sat. Apr. 10	Ottawa 0	at	Toronto 2
Mon. Apr. 12	Toronto 2	at	Ottawa 0
Wed. Apr. 14	Toronto 1	at	Ottawa 4
Fri. Apr. 16	Ottawa 0	at	Toronto 2
Sun. Apr. 18	Toronto 1	at	Ottawa 2*
Tue. Apr. 20	Ottawa 1	at	Toronto 4

*Mike Fisher scored at 21:47 of overtime

(Toronto won series 4-3)

Western Conference

Series 'E'
Wed. Apr. 7	Nashville 1	at	Detroit 3
Sat. Apr. 10	Nashville 1	at	Detroit 2
Sun. Apr. 11	Detroit 1	at	Nashville 3
Tue. Apr. 13	Detroit 0	at	Nashville 3
Thu. Apr. 15	Nashville 1	at	Detroit 4
Sat. Apr. 17	Detroit 2	at	Nashville 0

(Detroit won series 4-2)

Series 'F'
Thu. Apr. 8	St. Louis 0	at	San Jose 1*
Sat. Apr. 10	St. Louis 1	at	San Jose 3
Mon. Apr. 12	San Jose 1	at	St. Louis 4
Tue. Apr. 13	San Jose 4	at	St. Louis 3
Thu. Apr. 15	St. Louis 1	at	San Jose 3

*Niko Dimitrakos scored at 9:16 of overtime

(San Jose won series 4-1)

Series 'G'
Wed. Apr. 7	Calgary 3	at	Vancouver 5
Fri. Apr. 9	Calgary 2	at	Vancouver 1
Sun. Apr. 11	Vancouver 2	at	Calgary 1
Tue. Apr. 13	Vancouver 0	at	Calgary 4
Thu. Apr. 15	Calgary 2	at	Vancouver 1
Sat. Apr. 17	Vancouver 5	at	Calgary 4*
Mon. Apr. 19	Calgary 3	at	Vancouver 2**

*Brendan Morrison scored at 42:28 of overtime
**Martin Gelinas scored at 1:25 of overtime

(Calgary won series 4-3)

Series 'H'
Wed. Apr. 7	Dallas 1	at	Colorado 3
Fri. Apr. 9	Dallas 2	at	Colorado 5
Mon. Apr. 12	Colorado 3	at	Dallas 4*
Wed. Apr. 14	Colorado 3	at	Dallas 2**
Sat. Apr. 17	Dallas 1	at	Colorado 5

*Steve Ott scored at 2:11 of overtime
**Marek Svatos scored at 25:18 of overtime

(Colorado won series 4-1)

CONFERENCE SEMI-FINALS
(Best-of-seven series)

Eastern Conference

Series 'I'
Fri. Apr. 23	Montreal 0	at	Tampa Bay 4
Sun. Apr. 25	Montreal 1	at	Tampa Bay 3
Tue. Apr. 27	Tampa Bay 4	at	Montreal 3*
Thu. Apr. 29	Tampa Bay 3	at	Montreal 1

*Brad Richards scored at 1:05 of overtime

(Tampa Bay won series 4-0)

Series 'J'
Thu. Apr. 22	Toronto 1	at	Philadelphia 3
Sun. Apr. 25	Toronto 1	at	Philadelphia 2
Wed. Apr. 28	Philadelphia 1	at	Toronto 4
Fri. Apr. 30	Philadelphia 1	at	Toronto 3
Sun. May 2	Toronto 2	at	Philadelphia 7
Tue. May 4	Philadelphia 3	at	Toronto 2*

*Jeremy Roenick scored at 7:39 of overtime

(Philadelphia won series 4-2)

Western Conference

Series 'K'
Thu. Apr. 22	Calgary 2	at	Detroit 1*
Sat. Apr. 24	Calgary 2	at	Detroit 5
Tue. Apr. 27	Detroit 2	at	Calgary 3
Thu. Apr. 29	Detroit 4	at	Calgary 2
Sat. May 1	Calgary 1	at	Detroit 0
Mon. May 3	Detroit 0	at	Calgary 1**

*Marcus Nilson scored at 2:39 of overtime
**Martin Gelinas scored at 19:13 of overtime

(Calgary won series 4-2)

Series 'L'
Thu. Apr. 22	Colorado 2	at	San Jose 5
Sat. Apr. 24	Colorado 1	at	San Jose 4
Mon. Apr. 26	San Jose 1	at	Colorado 0
Wed. Apr. 28	San Jose 0	at	Colorado 1*
Sat. May 1	Colorado 2	at	San Jose 1**
Tue. May 4	San Jose 3	at	Colorado 1

*Joe Sakic scored at 5:15 of overtime
**Joe Sakic scored at 1:54 of overtime

(San Jose won series 4-2)

CONFERENCE FINALS
(Best-of-seven series)

Eastern Conference

Series 'M'
Sat. May 8	Philadelphia 1	at	Tampa Bay 3
Mon. May 10	Philadelphia 6	at	Tampa Bay 2
Thu. May 13	Tampa Bay 4	at	Philadelphia 1
Sat. May 15	Tampa Bay 2	at	Philadelphia 3
Tue. May 18	Philadelphia 2	at	Tampa Bay 4
Thu. May 20	Tampa Bay 4	at	Philadelphia 5*
Sat. May 22	Philadelphia 1	at	Tampa Bay 2

*Simon Gagne scored at 18:18 of overtime

(Tampa Bay won series 4-3)

Western Conference

Series 'N'
Sun. May 9	Calgary 4	at	San Jose 3*
Tue. May 11	Calgary 4	at	San Jose 1
Thu. May 13	San Jose 3	at	Calgary 0
Sun. May 16	San Jose 4	at	Calgary 2
Mon. May 17	Calgary 3	at	San Jose 0
Wed. May 19	San Jose 1	at	Calgary 3

*Steve Montador scored at 18:43 of overtime

(Calgary won series 4-2)

STANLEY CUP CHAMPIONSHIP
(Best-of-seven series)

Series 'O'
Tue. May 25	Calgary 4	at	Tampa Bay 1
Thu. May 27	Calgary 1	at	Tampa Bay 4
Sat. May 29	Tampa Bay 0	at	Calgary 3
Mon. May 31	Tampa Bay 1	at	Calgary 0
Thu. June 3	Calgary 3	at	Tampa Bay 2*
Sat. June 5	Tampa Bay 3	at	Calgary 2**
Mon. June 7	Calgary 1	at	Tampa Bay 2

*Oleg Saprykin scored at 14:40 of overtime
**Martin St. Louis scored at 20:33 of overtime

(Tampa Bay won series 4-3)

Team Playoff Records

	GP	W	L	GF	GA	%
Tampa Bay	23	16	7	60	43	.696
Calgary	26	15	11	60	53	.577
Philadelphia	18	11	7	50	43	.611
San Jose	17	10	7	38	32	.588
Colorado	11	6	5	26	24	.545
Detroit	12	6	6	24	20	.500
Toronto	13	6	7	27	28	.462
Montreal	11	4	7	24	28	.364
Vancouver	7	3	4	16	19	.429
Ottawa	7	3	4	11	14	.429
Boston	7	3	4	14	19	.429
Nashville	6	2	4	9	12	.333
St. Louis	5	1	4	9	12	.200
New Jersey	5	1	4	9	14	.200
NY Islanders	5	1	4	5	12	.200
Dallas	5	1	4	10	19	.200

Individual Leaders

Abbreviations: GP – games played; **G** – goals; **A** – assists; **Pts** – points; **+/−** – difference between Goals For (**GF**) scored when a player is on the ice with his team at even strength or short-handed and Goals Against (**GA**) scored when the same player is on the ice with his team at even strength or on a power play; **PIM** – penalties in minutes; **PP** – power play goals; **SH** – short-handed goals; **GW** – game-winning goals; **OT** – overtime goals; **S** – shots on goal; **%** – percentage of shots resulting in goals.

Playoff Scoring Leaders

Player	Team	GP	G	A	PTS	+/−	PIM	PP	SH	GW	OT	S	%
Brad Richards	Tampa Bay	23	12	14	26	5	4	7	0	7	1	88	13.6
Martin St. Louis	Tampa Bay	23	9	15	24	6	14	3	1	3	2	58	15.5
Jarome Iginla	Calgary	26	13	9	22	13	45	4	2	3	0	93	14.0
Fredrik Modin	Tampa Bay	23	8	11	19	7	10	3	0	2	0	50	16.0
Craig Conroy	Calgary	26	6	11	17	12	12	2	0	1	0	49	12.2
Keith Primeau	Philadelphia	18	9	7	16	11	22	0	2	3	0	44	20.5
Vincent Lecavalier	Tampa Bay	23	9	7	16	−2	25	2	0	0	0	76	11.8
Martin Gelinas	Calgary	26	8	7	15	10	35	2	0	3	2	51	15.7
Ruslan Fedotenko	Tampa Bay	22	12	2	14	0	14	5	0	3	0	43	27.9
Vincent Damphousse	San Jose	17	7	7	14	0	20	3	0	3	0	37	18.9
Alex Zhamnov	Philadelphia	18	4	10	14	−1	8	1	0	1	0	31	12.9
Dave Andreychuk	Tampa Bay	23	1	13	14	−2	14	0	0	0	0	30	3.3
Jeremy Roenick	Philadelphia	18	4	9	13	4	8	2	0	1	1	49	8.2
Patrick Marleau	San Jose	17	8	4	12	0	6	4	1	0	0	45	17.8
Joe Sakic	Colorado	11	5	7	12	0	8	1	1	2	2	35	20.0
Peter Forsberg	Colorado	11	4	7	11	6	12	1	0	1	0	16	25.0
Marcus Nilson	Calgary	26	4	7	11	0	12	0	0	1	0	37	10.8
Saku Koivu	Montreal	11	3	8	11	1	10	2	0	0	0	27	11.1
Alex Kovalev	Montreal	11	6	4	10	2	8	1	0	1	0	29	20.7
Michal Handzus	Philadelphia	18	5	5	10	7	10	0	0	0	0	23	21.7
Shean Donovan	Calgary	24	5	5	10	0	23	0	0	2	0	43	11.6
Jonathan Cheechoo	San Jose	17	4	6	10	4	10	1	0	0	0	34	11.8
Sami Kapanen	Philadelphia	18	3	7	10	5	6	0	1	1	0	24	12.5
Dan Boyle	Tampa Bay	23	2	8	10	7	16	1	0	0	0	25	8.0
Jordan Leopold	Calgary	26	0	10	10	5	6	0	0	0	0	34	0.0

Playoff Defencemen Scoring Leaders

Player	Team	GP	G	A	PTS	+/−	PIM	PP	SH	GW	OT	S	%
Dan Boyle	Tampa Bay	23	2	8	10	7	16	1	0	0	0	25	8.0
Jordan Leopold	Calgary	26	0	10	10	5	6	0	0	0	0	34	0.0
Robyn Regehr	Calgary	26	2	7	9	7	20	0	0	0	0	29	6.9
Bryan McCabe	Toronto	13	3	5	8	0	14	2	0	0	0	26	11.5
Kim Johnsson	Philadelphia	15	2	6	8	−3	8	0	0	1	0	22	9.1
Brian Leetch	Toronto	13	0	8	8	1	6	0	0	0	0	23	0.0
Nicklas Lidstrom	Detroit	12	2	5	7	4	4	2	0	0	0	27	7.4
Mattias Timander	Philadelphia	18	2	4	6	2	6	0	0	1	0	17	11.8
Vladimir Malakhov	Philadelphia	17	1	5	6	9	12	0	0	0	0	38	2.6
Mike Rathje	San Jose	17	1	5	6	1	13	0	0	0	0	14	7.1
Scott Hannan	San Jose	17	1	5	6	7	22	1	0	1	0	25	4.0
Brad Stuart	San Jose	17	1	5	6	−4	13	0	0	0	0	28	3.6
Darryl Sydor	Tampa Bay	23	0	6	6	−4	9	0	0	0	0	25	0.0

GOALTENDING LEADERS

Goals Against Average

Goaltender	Team	GP	Mins	GA	Avg.
Curtis Joseph	Detroit	9	518	12	1.39
Nikolai Khabibulin	Tampa Bay	23	1401	40	1.71
Evgeni Nabokov	San Jose	17	1052	30	1.71
Miikka Kiprusoff	Calgary	26	1655	51	1.85
Patrick Lalime	Ottawa	7	398	13	1.96

Wins

Goaltender	Team	GP	Mins	W	L
Nikolai Khabibulin	Tampa Bay	23	1401	16	7
Miikka Kiprusoff	Calgary	26	1655	15	11
Robert Esche	Philadelphia	18	1061	11	7
Evgeni Nabokov	San Jose	17	1052	10	7
David Aebischer	Colorado	11	662	6	5
Ed Belfour	Toronto	13	774	6	7

Save Percentage

Goaltender	Team	GP	Mins	GA	SA	S%	W	L
Curtis Joseph	Detroit	9	518	12	197	.939	4	4
Tomas Vokoun	Nashville	6	356	12	197	.939	2	4
Evgeni Nabokov	San Jose	17	1052	30	461	.935	10	7
Nikolai Khabibulin	Tampa Bay	23	1401	40	598	.933	16	7
Ed Belfour	Toronto	13	774	27	379	.929	6	7

Shutouts

Goaltender	Team	GP	Mins	SO
Nikolai Khabibulin	Tampa Bay	23	1401	5
Miikka Kiprusoff	Calgary	26	1655	5
Ed Belfour	Toronto	13	774	3
Evgeni Nabokov	San Jose	17	1052	3

Goal Scoring

Name	Team	GP	G
Jarome Iginla	Calgary	26	13
Ruslan Fedotenko	Tampa Bay	22	12
Brad Richards	Tampa Bay	23	12
Keith Primeau	Philadelphia	18	9
Martin St. Louis	Tampa Bay	23	9
Vincent Lecavalier	Tampa Bay	23	9
Patrick Marleau	San Jose	17	8
Fredrik Modin	Tampa Bay	23	8
Martin Gelinas	Calgary	26	8
Joe Sakic	Colorado	11	7
Vincent Damphousse	San Jose	17	7

Assists

Name	Team	GP	A
Martin St. Louis	Tampa Bay	23	15
Brad Richards	Tampa Bay	23	14
Dave Andreychuk	Tampa Bay	23	13
Fredrik Modin	Tampa Bay	23	11
Craig Conroy	Calgary	26	11
Alex Zhamnov	Philadelphia	18	10
Jordan Leopold	Calgary	26	10
Jeremy Roenick	Philadelphia	18	9
Jarome Iginla	Calgary	26	9
Saku Koivu	Montreal	11	8
Brian Leetch	Toronto	13	8
*Niko Dimitrakos	San Jose	15	8

Power-play Goals

Name	Team	GP	PP
Brad Richards	Tampa Bay	23	7
Ruslan Fedotenko	Tampa Bay	22	5
Steve Konowalchuk	Colorado	11	4
Chris Simon	Calgary	16	4
Patrick Marleau	San Jose	17	4
Jarome Iginla	Calgary	26	4
Vincent Damphousse	San Jose	17	3
Fredrik Modin	Tampa Bay	23	3
Martin St. Louis	Tampa Bay	23	3

Game-winning Goals

Name	Team	GP	GW
Brad Richards	Tampa Bay	23	7
Vincent Damphousse	San Jose	17	3
Keith Primeau	Philadelphia	18	3
Ruslan Fedotenko	Tampa Bay	22	3
Martin St. Louis	Tampa Bay	23	3
Martin Gelinas	Calgary	26	3
Jarome Iginla	Calgary	26	3

Short-handed Goals

Name	Team	GP	SH
Keith Primeau	Philadelphia	18	2
Jarome Iginla	Calgary	26	2
10 players with one			

Overtime Goals

Name	Team	GP	OT
Joe Sakic	Colorado	11	2
Martin St. Louis	Tampa Bay	23	2
Martin Gelinas	Calgary	26	2

Shots

Name	Team	GP	S
Jarome Iginla	Calgary	26	93
Brad Richards	Tampa Bay	23	88
Vincent Lecavalier	Tampa Bay	23	76
Martin St. Louis	Tampa Bay	23	58
Oleg Saprykin	Calgary	26	53

Plus/Minus

Name	Team	GP	+/−
Danny Markov	Philadelphia	18	17
Jarome Iginla	Calgary	26	13
Craig Conroy	Calgary	26	12
Keith Primeau	Philadelphia	18	11
Simon Gagne	Philadelphia	18	10

TEAMS' PLAYOFF HOME/ROAD RECORD

90 games played.

			HOME							ROAD			
	GP	W	L	GF	GA	%	GP	W	L	GF	GA	%
T.B.	13	9	4	33	25	.692	10	7	3	27	18	.700
CGY	12	5	7	25	25	.417	14	10	4	35	28	.714
PHI	9	8	1	30	19	.889	9	3	6	20	24	.333
S.J.	9	5	4	21	18	.556	8	5	3	17	14	.625
COL	6	4	2	15	8	.667	5	2	3	11	16	.400
DET	6	4	2	15	8	.667	6	2	4	9	12	.333
TOR	7	5	2	19	10	.714	6	1	5	8	18	.167
MTL	5	2	3	15	15	.400	6	2	4	9	13	.333
VAN	4	1	3	9	10	.250	3	2	1	7	9	.667
OTT	3	2	1	6	4	.667	4	1	3	5	10	.250
BOS	4	2	2	6	8	.500	3	1	2	8	11	.333
NSH	3	2	1	6	3	.667	3	0	3	3	9	.000
ST.L.	2	1	1	7	5	.500	3	0	3	2	7	.000
N.J.	2	1	1	4	5	.500	3	0	3	5	9	.000
NYI	2	0	2	0	6	.000	3	1	2	5	6	.333
DAL	2	1	1	6	6	.500	3	0	3	4	13	.000
Total	**89**	**52**	**37**	**217**	**175**	**.584**	**89**	**37**	**52**	**175**	**217**	**.416**

TEAMS' POWER-PLAY RECORD

Abbreviations: ADV-total advantages; **PPGF**-power play goals for; **%** arrived by dividing number of power-play goals by total advantages. 89 games played.

			HOME						ROAD						OVERALL		
	Team	GP	ADV	PPGF	%	Team	GP	ADV	PPGF	%	Team	GP	ADV	PPGF	%			
1	DAL	2	7	3	42.9	T.B.	10	38	10	26.3	T.B.	23	100	21	21.0			
2	N.J.	2	9	3	33.3	COL	5	18	4	22.2	VAN	7	39	8	20.5			
3	VAN	4	22	6	27.3	NYI	3	10	2	20.0	COL	11	48	9	18.8			
4	T.B.	13	62	11	17.7	MTL	6	25	4	16.0	DAL	5	22	4	18.2			
5	COL	6	30	5	16.7	CGY	14	57	9	15.8	N.J.	5	18	3	16.7			
6	DET	6	33	5	15.2	S.J.	8	30	4	13.3	CGY	26	108	15	13.9			
7	ST.L.	2	7	1	14.3	PHI	9	30	4	13.3	S.J.	17	81	11	13.6			
8	S.J.	9	51	7	13.7	VAN	3	17	2	11.8	PHI	18	61	8	13.1			
9	PHI	9	31	4	12.9	TOR	6	27	3	11.1	NYI	5	16	2	12.5			
10	BOS	4	17	2	11.8	OTT	4	21	2	9.5	MTL	11	40	5	12.5			
11	CGY	12	51	6	11.8	NSH	3	14	1	7.1	TOR	13	59	6	10.2			
12	TOR	7	32	3	9.4	DAL	3	15	1	6.7	DET	12	52	5	9.6			
13	OTT	3	14	1	7.1	BOS	3	8	0	0.0	OTT	7	35	3	8.6			
14	MTL	5	15	1	6.7	N.J.	3	9	0	0.0	BOS	7	25	2	8.0			
15	NYI	2	6	0	0.0	ST.L.	3	15	0	0.0	ST.L.	5	22	1	4.5			
16	NSH	3	15	0	0.0	DET	6	19	0	0.0	NSH	6	29	1	3.4			
	Total		**402**	**58**	**14.4**			**353**	**46**	**13.0**			**755**	**104**	**13.8**			

TEAMS' PENALTY KILLING RECORD

Abbreviations: TSH – Total times short-handed; **PPGA** – power-play goals against; **%** arrived by dividing times short-handed minus power-play goals against by times short. 89 games played.

			HOME					ROAD						OVERALL		
	Team	GP	TSH	PPGA	%	Team	GP	TSH	PPGA	%	Team	GP	TSH	PPGA	%	
1	NSH	3	13	0	100.0	BOS	3	10	0	100.0	DET	12	50	2	96.0	
2	DET	6	25	1	96.0	DET	6	25	1	96.0	NSH	6	29	2	93.1	
3	COL	6	21	1	95.2	NYI	3	19	1	94.7	S.J.	17	73	6	91.7	
4	S.J.	9	36	2	94.4	VAN	3	17	1	94.1	NYI	5	23	2	91.3	
5	ST.L.	2	10	1	90.0	ST.L.	3	21	2	90.5	ST.L.	5	31	3	90.3	
6	TOR	7	29	3	89.7	T.B.	10	30	3	90.0	BOS	7	30	3	90.0	
7	MTL	5	17	2	88.2	TOR	6	29	3	89.7	TOR	13	58	6	89.7	
8	OTT	3	14	2	85.7	OTT	4	18	2	88.9	MTL	11	42	5	88.1	
9	PHI	9	34	5	85.3	S.J.	8	36	4	88.9	OTT	7	32	4	87.5	
10	BOS	4	20	3	85.0	MTL	6	25	3	88.0	T.B.	23	76	11	85.5	
11	CGY	12	50	8	84.0	NSH	3	16	2	87.5	VAN	7	40	6	85.0	
12	T.B.	13	46	8	82.6	CGY	14	71	13	81.7	CGY	26	121	21	82.6	
13	VAN	4	23	5	78.3	PHI	9	37	9	75.7	COL	11	47	9	80.9	
14	NYI	2	4	1	75.0	DAL	3	16	4	75.0	PHI	18	71	14	80.3	
15	N.J.	2	6	2	66.7	COL	5	26	8	69.2	DAL	5	21	6	71.4	
16	DAL	2	5	2	60.0	N.J.	3	6	2	66.7	N.J.	5	12	4	66.7	
	Total		**353**	**46**	**87.0**			**402**	**58**	**85.6**			**755**	**104**	**86.2**	

SHORT HAND GOALS

89 games played.

GOALS FOR			GOALS AGAINST		
Team	GP	GF	Team	GP	GA
PHI	18	3	CGY	26	0
CGY	26	3	PHI	18	0
ST.L.	5	2	COL	11	0
COL	11	2	BOS	7	0
T.B.	23	2	OTT	7	0
NSH	6	1	N.J.	5	0
DET	12	1	TOR	13	1
S.J.	17	1	DET	12	1
NYI	5	0	MTL	11	1
N.J.	5	0	VAN	7	1
DAL	5	0	NSH	6	1
BOS	7	0	NYI	5	1
OTT	7	0	ST.L.	5	1
VAN	7	0	DAL	5	2
MTL	11	0	T.B.	23	3
TOR	13	0	S.J.	17	3
Total		**15**	**Total**		**15**

TEAM PENALTIES

Abbreviations: GP – games played; **PEN** – total penalty minutes, including bench penalties; **BMI** – total bench minor minutes; **AVG** – average penalty minutes per game. 89 games played.

Team	GP	PEN	BMI	AVG
N.J.	5	28	0	5.6
NYI	5	50	4	10.0
BOS	7	72	2	10.3
DAL	5	56	4	11.2
DET	12	135	0	11.3
NSH	6	76	0	12.7
S.J.	17	216	0	12.7
MTL	11	148	0	13.5
ST.L.	5	68	0	13.6
COL	11	154	4	14.0
OTT	7	99	0	14.1
VAN	7	99	2	14.1
PHI	18	272	8	15.1
TOR	13	201	0	15.5
T.B.	23	387	4	16.8
CGY	26	444	0	17.1
Total		**2505**	**28**	
Two-Team average. PIM/GP				**28.1**

After tying for the regular-season lead with 41 goals, Calgary's Jarome Iginla led all playoff performers with 13 goals in 26 games as the Flames made a thrilling run to the seventh game of the Stanley Cup finals.

Stanley Cup Record Book

History: The Stanley Cup, the oldest trophy competed for by professional athletes in North America, was donated by Frederick Arthur, Lord Stanley of Preston and son of the Earl of Derby, in 1893. Lord Stanley purchased the trophy for 10 guineas ($50 at that time) for presentation to the amateur hockey champions of Canada. Since 1910, when the National Hockey Association took possession of the Stanley Cup, the trophy has been the symbol of professional hockey supremacy. It has been competed for only by NHL teams since 1926-27 and has been under the exclusive control of the NHL since 1947.

Stanley Cup Standings

1918-2004
(ranked by Cup wins)

Teams	Cup Wins	Yrs.	Series	Wins	Losses	Games Wins	Losses	Ties	Goals For	Goals Against	Winning %
Montreal	23 [1]	74	137 [2]	86	50	661	391	262	8	2033	1658	.598
Toronto	13	64	109	58	51	524	251	269	4	1350	1427	.483
Detroit	10	53	99	56	43	494	257	236	1	1385	1278	.521
Boston	5	62	104	47	45	512	242	264	6	1488	1516	.479
Edmonton	5	19	45	31	14	227	137	90	0	868	702	.604
NY Rangers	4	48	86	42	44	386	183	195	8	1091	1114	.484
NY Islanders	4	20	46	30	16	235	133	102	0	781	697	.566
Chicago	3	53	90	40	50	411	188	218	5	1176	1311	.464
New Jersey[3]	3	16	33	20	13	193	107	86	0	536	463	.554
Philadelphia	2	30	64	36	28	340	178	162	0	1032	989	.524
Pittsburgh	2	21	39	20	19	208	109	99	0	644	641	.524
Colorado[4]	2	18	39	23	16	224	122	102	0	667	620	.545
Dallas[5]	1	26	51	26	25	277	140	137	0	825	838	.505
Calgary[6]	1	22	36	15	21	182	84	98	0	579	626	.462
Tampa Bay	1	3	7	5	2	40	23	17	0	95	98	.575
St. Louis	0	34	57	23	34	303	138	165	0	857	943	.455
Buffalo	0	25	42	17	25	209	99	110	0	626	639	.474
Los Angeles	0	23	34	11	23	170	65	105	0	511	649	.382
Vancouver	0	20	30	10	20	155	66	89	0	452	526	.426
Washington	0	18	28	10	18	154	69	85	0	467	478	.448
Phoenix[7]	0	16	18	2	16	92	29	63	0	245	343	.315
Carolina[8]	0	11	15	4	11	84	35	49	0	208	256	.417
San Jose	0	8	14	6	8	84	39	45	0	213	264	.464
Ottawa[9]	0	8	12	4	8	69	31	38	0	135	149	.449
Florida	0	3	6	3	3	31	13	18	0	77	82	.419
Anaheim	0	3	7	4	3	36	19	17	0	76	87	.528
Minnesota	0	1	3	2	1	18	8	10	0	43	43	.444

[1] Montreal also won the Stanley Cup in 1916.
[2] 1919 final incomplete due to influenza epidemic.
[3] Includes totals of Colorado Rockies 1976-82.
[4] Includes totals of Quebec 1979-95.
[5] Includes totals of Minnesota North Stars 1967-93.
[6] Includes totals of Atlanta Flames 1972-80.
[7] Includes totals of Winnipeg 1979-96.
[8] Includes totals of Hartford 1979-97.
[9] Modern Ottawa franchise only 1992 to date.

Stanley Cup Winners Prior to Formation of NHL in 1917

Season	Champions	Manager	Coach
1916-17	Seattle Metropolitans	Pete Muldoon	Pete Muldoon
1915-16	Montreal Canadiens	George Kennedy	George Kennedy
1914-15	Vancouver Millionaires	Frank Patrick	Frank Patrick
1913-14	Toronto Blueshirts	Jack Marshall	Scotty Davidson*
1912-13**	Quebec Bulldogs	M.J. Quinn	Joe Malone*
1911-12	Quebec Bulldogs	M.J. Quinn	C. Nolan*
1910-11	Ottawa Senators		Bruce Stuart*
1909-10	Montreal Wanderers (Mar. 1910)	Dickie Boon	Pud Glass*
1909-10	Ottawa Senators (Jan. 1910)		Bruce Stuart*
1908-09	Ottawa Senators		Bruce Stuart*
1907-08	Montreal Wanderers	Dickie Boon	Cecil Blachford
1906-07	Montreal Wanderers (Mar. 1907)	Dickie Boon	Cecil Blachford
1906-07	Kenora Thistles (Jan./Mar. 1907)	F.A. Hudson	Tom Phillips*
1905-06	Montreal Wanderers (Mar. 1906)	Cecil Blachford*	
1905-06	Ottawa Silver Seven (Feb. 1906)		Alf Smith
1904-05	Ottawa Silver Seven		Alf Smith
1903-04	Ottawa Silver Seven		Alf Smith
1902-03	Ottawa Silver Seven (Mar. 1903)		Alf Smith
1902-03	Montreal A.A.A. (Feb. 1903)		C. McKerrow
1901-02	Montreal A.A.A. (Mar. 1902)		C. McKerrow
1901-02	Winnipeg Victorias (Jan. 1902)		
1900-01	Winnipeg Victorias		Dan Bain*
1899-1900	Montreal Shamrocks		Harry Trihey*
1898-99	Montreal Shamrocks (Mar. 1899)		Harry Trihey*
1898-99	Montreal Victorias (Feb. 1899)		Mike Grant*
1897-98	Montreal Victorias		Frank Richardson
1896-97	Montreal Victorias		Mike Grant*
1895-96	Montreal Victorias (Dec. 1896)		Mike Grant*
1895-96	Winnipeg Victorias (Feb. 1896)		Jack Armitage
1894-95	Montreal Victorias		Mike Grant*
1893-94	Montreal A.A.A.		
1892-93	Montreal A.A.A.		

* In the early years the teams were frequently run by the Captain. *Indicates Captain

Stanley Cup Winners

Year	W-L-T in Finals	Winner	Coach	Finalist	Coach
2004	4-3	Tampa Bay	John Tortorella	Calgary	Darryl Sutter
2003	4-3	New Jersey	Pat Burns	Anaheim	Mike Babcock
2002	4-1	Detroit	Scotty Bowman	Carolina	Paul Maurice
2001	4-3	Colorado	Bob Hartley	New Jersey	Larry Robinson
2000	4-2	New Jersey	Larry Robinson	Dallas	Ken Hitchcock
1999	4-2	Dallas	Ken Hitchcock	Buffalo	Lindy Ruff
1998	4-0	Detroit	Scotty Bowman	Washington	Ron Wilson
1997	4-0	Detroit	Scotty Bowman	Philadelphia	Terry Murray
1996	4-0	Colorado	Marc Crawford	Florida	Doug MacLean
1995	4-0	New Jersey	Jacques Lemaire	Detroit	Scotty Bowman
1994	4-3	NY Rangers	Mike Keenan	Vancouver	Pat Quinn
1993	4-1	Montreal	Jacques Demers	Los Angeles	Barry Melrose
1992	4-0	Pittsburgh	Scotty Bowman	Chicago	Mike Keenan
1991	4-2	Pittsburgh	Bob Johnson	Minnesota	Bob Gainey
1990	4-1	Edmonton	John Muckler	Boston	Mike Milbury
1989	4-2	Calgary	Terry Crisp	Montreal	Pat Burns
1988	4-0	Edmonton	Glen Sather	Boston	Terry O'Reilly
1987	4-3	Edmonton	Glen Sather	Philadelphia	Mike Keenan
1986	4-1	Montreal	Jean Perron	Calgary	Bob Johnson
1985	4-1	Edmonton	Glen Sather	Philadelphia	Mike Keenan
1984	4-1	Edmonton	Glen Sather	NY Islanders	Al Arbour
1983	4-0	NY Islanders	Al Arbour	Edmonton	Glen Sather
1982	4-0	NY Islanders	Al Arbour	Vancouver	Roger Neilson
1981	4-1	NY Islanders	Al Arbour	Minnesota	Glen Sonmor
1980	4-2	NY Islanders	Al Arbour	Philadelphia	Pat Quinn
1979	4-1	Montreal	Scotty Bowman	NY Rangers	Fred Shero
1978	4-2	Montreal	Scotty Bowman	Boston	Don Cherry
1977	4-0	Montreal	Scotty Bowman	Boston	Don Cherry
1976	4-0	Montreal	Scotty Bowman	Philadelphia	Fred Shero
1975	4-2	Philadelphia	Fred Shero	Buffalo	Floyd Smith
1974	4-2	Philadelphia	Fred Shero	Boston	Bep Guidolin
1973	4-2	Montreal	Scotty Bowman	Chicago	Billy Reay
1972	4-2	Boston	Tom Johnson	NY Rangers	Emile Francis
1971	4-3	Montreal	Al MacNeil	Chicago	Billy Reay
1970	4-0	Boston	Harry Sinden	St. Louis	Scotty Bowman
1969	4-0	Montreal	Claude Ruel	St. Louis	Scotty Bowman
1968	4-0	Montreal	Toe Blake	St. Louis	Scotty Bowman
1967	4-2	Toronto	Punch Imlach	Montreal	Toe Blake
1966	4-2	Montreal	Toe Blake	Detroit	Sid Abel
1965	4-3	Montreal	Toe Blake	Chicago	Billy Reay
1964	4-3	Toronto	Punch Imlach	Detroit	Sid Abel
1963	4-1	Toronto	Punch Imlach	Detroit	Sid Abel
1962	4-2	Toronto	Punch Imlach	Chicago	Rudy Pilous
1961	4-2	Chicago	Rudy Pilous	Detroit	Sid Abel
1960	4-0	Montreal	Toe Blake	Toronto	Punch Imlach
1959	4-1	Montreal	Toe Blake	Toronto	Punch Imlach
1958	4-2	Montreal	Toe Blake	Boston	Milt Schmidt
1957	4-1	Montreal	Toe Blake	Boston	Milt Schmidt
1956	4-1	Montreal	Toe Blake	Detroit	Jimmy Skinner
1955	4-3	Detroit	Jimmy Skinner	Montreal	Dick Irvin
1954	4-3	Detroit	Tommy Ivan	Montreal	Dick Irvin
1953	4-1	Montreal	Dick Irvin	Boston	Lynn Patrick
1952	4-0	Detroit	Tommy Ivan	Montreal	Dick Irvin
1951	4-1	Toronto	Joe Primeau	Montreal	Dick Irvin
1950	4-3	Detroit	Tommy Ivan	NY Rangers	Lynn Patrick
1949	4-0	Toronto	Hap Day	Detroit	Tommy Ivan
1948	4-0	Toronto	Hap Day	Detroit	Tommy Ivan
1947	4-2	Toronto	Hap Day	Montreal	Dick Irvin
1946	4-1	Montreal	Dick Irvin	Boston	Dit Clapper
1945	4-3	Toronto	Hap Day	Detroit	Jack Adams
1944	4-0	Montreal	Dick Irvin	Chicago	Paul Thompson
1943	4-0	Detroit	Jack Adams	Boston	Art Ross
1942	4-3	Toronto	Hap Day	Detroit	Jack Adams
1941	4-0	Boston	Cooney Weiland	Detroit	Ebbie Goodfellow
1940	4-2	NY Rangers	Frank Boucher	Toronto	Dick Irvin
1939	4-1	Boston	Art Ross	Toronto	Dick Irvin
1938	3-1	Chicago	Bill Stewart	Toronto	Dick Irvin
1937	3-2	Detroit	Jack Adams	NY Rangers	Lester Patrick
1936	3-1	Detroit	Jack Adams	Toronto	Dick Irvin
1935	3-0	Mtl. Maroons	Tommy Gorman	Toronto	Dick Irvin
1934	3-1	Chicago	Tommy Gorman	Detroit	Herbie Lewis
1933	3-1	NY Rangers	Lester Patrick	Toronto	Dick Irvin
1932	3-0	Toronto	Dick Irvin	NY Rangers	Lester Patrick
1931	3-2	Montreal	Cecil Hart	Chicago	Dick Irvin
1930	2-0	Montreal	Cecil Hart	Boston	Art Ross
1929	2-0	Boston	Cy Denneny	NY Rangers	Lester Patrick
1928	3-2	NY Rangers	Lester Patrick	Mtl. Maroons	Eddie Gerard
1927	2-0-2	Ottawa	Dave Gill	Boston	Art Ross

The National Hockey League assumed control of Stanley Cup competition after 1926

Year	W-L-T in Finals	Winner	Coach	Finalist	Coach
1926	3-1	Mtl. Maroons	Eddie Gerard	Victoria	Lester Patrick
1925	3-1	Victoria	Lester Patrick	Montreal	Leo Dandurand
1924	2-0	Montreal	Leo Dandurand	Cgy. Tigers	Eddie Oatman
	2-0			Van. Maroons	Art Duncan/Frank Patrick
1923	2-0	Ottawa	Pete Green	Edm. Eskimos	Ken McKenzie
	3-1			Van. Maroons	Lloyd Cook/Frank Patrick
1922	3-2	Tor. St. Pats	George O'Donoghue	Van. Millionaires	Lloyd Cook/Frank Patrick
1921	3-2	Ottawa	Pete Green	Van. Millionaires	Lloyd Cook/Frank Patrick
1920	3-2	Ottawa	Pete Green	Seattle	Pete Muldoon
1919	2-2-1	No decision - series between Montreal and Seattle cancelled due to influenza epidemic			
1918	3-2	Tor. Arenas	Dick Carroll	Van. Millionaires	Frank Patrick

Championship Trophies

PRINCE OF WALES TROPHY

Beginning with the 1993-94 season, the club which advances to the Stanley Cup Finals as the winner of the Eastern Conference Championship is presented with the Prince of Wales Trophy.

History: His Royal Highness, the Prince of Wales, donated the trophy to the National Hockey League in 1924. From 1927-28 through 1937-38, the award was presented to the team finishing first in the American Division of the NHL. (The team finishing first in the Canadian Division received the O'Brien Trophy during these years.) From 1938-39, when the NHL reverted to one section, to 1966-67, it was presented to the team winning the NHL regular-season championship. With expansion in 1967-68, it again became a divisional trophy, awarded to the regular-season champions of the East Division through to the end of the 1973-74 season. Beginning in 1974-75, it was awarded to the regular-season winner of the conference bearing the name of the trophy. From 1981-82 to 1992-93 the trophy was presented to the playoff champion in the Wales Conference. Since 1993-94, the trophy has been presented to the playoff champion in the Eastern Conference.

2003-04 Winner: Tampa Bay Lightning

The Tampa Bay Lightning won their first Prince of Wales Trophy on May 22, 2004 after defeating the Philadelphia Flyers 2-1 in game seven of the Eastern Conference Championship series. Before defeating the Flyers, the Lightning had series wins over the New York Islanders and Montreal Canadiens.

PRINCE OF WALES TROPHY WINNERS

2003-04	Tampa Bay Lightning	1962-63	Toronto Maple Leafs
2002-03	New Jersey Devils	1961-62	Montreal Canadiens
2001-02	Carolina Hurricanes	1960-61	Montreal Canadiens
2000-01	New Jersey Devils	1959-60	Montreal Canadiens
99-2000	New Jersey Devils	1958-59	Montreal Canadiens
1998-99	Buffalo Sabres	1957-58	Montreal Canadiens
1997-98	Washington Capitals	1956-57	Detroit Red Wings
1996-97	Philadelphia Flyers	1955-56	Montreal Canadiens
1995-96	Florida Panthers	1954-55	Detroit Red Wings
1994-95	New Jersey Devils	1953-54	Detroit Red Wings
1993-94	New York Rangers	1952-53	Detroit Red Wings
1992-93	Montreal Canadiens	1951-52	Detroit Red Wings
1991-92	Pittsburgh Penguins	1950-51	Detroit Red Wings
1990-91	Pittsburgh Penguins	1949-50	Detroit Red Wings
1989-90	Boston Bruins	1948-49	Detroit Red Wings
1988-89	Montreal Canadiens	1947-48	Toronto Maple Leafs
1987-88	Boston Bruins	1946-47	Montreal Canadiens
1986-87	Philadelphia Flyers	1945-46	Montreal Canadiens
1985-86	Montreal Canadiens	1944-45	Montreal Canadiens
1984-85	Philadelphia Flyers	1943-44	Montreal Canadiens
1983-84	New York Islanders	1942-43	Detroit Red Wings
1982-83	New York Islanders	1941-42	New York Rangers
1981-82	New York Islanders	1940-41	Boston Bruins
1980-81	Montreal Canadiens	1939-40	Boston Bruins
1979-80	Buffalo Sabres	1938-39	Boston Bruins
1978-79	Montreal Canadiens	1937-38	Boston Bruins
1977-78	Montreal Canadiens	1936-37	Detroit Red Wings
1976-77	Montreal Canadiens	1935-36	Detroit Red Wings
1975-76	Montreal Canadiens	1934-35	Detroit Red Wings
1974-75	Buffalo Sabres	1933-34	Detroit Red Wings
1973-74	Boston Bruins	1932-33	Boston Bruins
1972-73	Montreal Canadiens	1931-32	New York Rangers
1971-72	Boston Bruins	1930-31	Boston Bruins
1970-71	Boston Bruins	1929-30	Boston Bruins
1969-70	Chicago Blackhawks	1928-29	Boston Bruins
1968-69	Montreal Canadiens	1927-28	Boston Bruins
1967-68	Chicago Blackhawks	1926-27	Ottawa Senators
1966-67	Chicago Blackhawks	1925-26	Montreal Maroons
1965-66	Montreal Canadiens	1924-25	Montreal Canadiens
1964-65	Detroit Red Wings	1923-24	Montreal Canadiens
1963-64	Montreal Canadiens		

CLARENCE S. CAMPBELL BOWL

Beginning with the 1993-94 season, the club which advances to the Stanley Cup Finals as the winner of the Western Conference Championship is presented with the Clarence S. Campbell Bowl.

History: Presented by the member clubs in 1968 for perpetual competition by the National Hockey League in recognition of the services of Clarence S. Campbell, President of the NHL from 1946 to 1977. From 1967-68 through 1973-74, the trophy was awarded to the regular-season champions of the West Division. Beginning in 1974-75, it was awarded to the regular-season winner of the conference bearing the name of the trophy. From 1981-82 to 1992-93 the trophy was presented to the playoff champion in the Campbell Conference. Since 1993-94, the trophy has been presented to the playoff champion in the Western Conference. The trophy itself is a hallmark piece made of sterling silver and was crafted by a British silversmith in 1878.

2003-04 Winner: Calgary Flames

The Calgary Flames won their first Clarence Campbell Bowl since 1989 on May 19, 2004 after defeating the San Jose Sharks 3-1 in game six of the Western Conference Championship series. Before defeating the Sharks, the Flames had series wins over the Vancouver Canucks and Detroit Red Wings.

CLARENCE S. CAMPBELL BOWL WINNERS

2003-04	Calgary Flames	1984-85	Edmonton Oilers
2002-03	Anaheim Mighty Ducks	1983-84	Edmonton Oilers
2001-02	Detroit Red Wings	1982-83	Edmonton Oilers
2000-01	Colorado Avalanche	1981-82	Vancouver Canucks
99-2000	Dallas Stars	1980-81	New York Islanders
1998-99	Dallas Stars	1979-80	Philadelphia Flyers
1997-98	Detroit Red Wings	1978-79	New York Islanders
1996-97	Detroit Red Wings	1977-78	New York Islanders
1995-96	Colorado Avalanche	1976-77	Philadelphia Flyers
1994-95	Detroit Red Wings	1975-76	Philadelphia Flyers
1993-94	Vancouver Canucks	1974-75	Philadelphia Flyers
1992-93	Los Angeles Kings	1973-74	Philadelphia Flyers
1991-92	Chicago Blackhawks	1972-73	Chicago Blackhawks
1990-91	Minnesota North Stars	1971-72	Chicago Blackhawks
1989-90	Edmonton Oilers	1970-71	Chicago Blackhawks
1988-89	Calgary Flames	1969-70	St. Louis Blues
1987-88	Edmonton Oilers	1968-69	St. Louis Blues
1986-87	Edmonton Oilers	1967-68	Philadelphia Flyers
1985-86	Calgary Flames		

Prince of Wales Trophy

Clarence S. Campbell Bowl

Stanley Cup

Stanley Cup Winners

Rosters and Final Series Scores

2003-04 — Tampa Bay Lightning — Dave Andreychuk (Captain), Dimitry Afanasenkov, Dan Boyle, Martin Cibak, Ben Clymer, Jassen Cullimore, Chris Dingman, Ruslan Fedotenko, John Grahame, Nikolai Khabibulin, Pavel Kubina, Vincent Lecavalier, Brad Lukowich, Fredrik Modin, Stan Neckar, Eric Perrin, Nolan Pratt, Brad Richards, Andre Roy, Darren Rumble, Martin St. Louis, Cory Sarich, Cory Stillman, Darryl Sydor, Tim Taylor, Bill Davidson (Owner), Tom Wilson (Governor), Ron Campbell (President), Jay Feaster (General Manager), Bill Barber (Director of Player Personnel), John Tortorella (Head Coach), Craig Ramsay (Associate Coach), Jeff Reese (Assistant Coach), Eric Lawson (Strength and Conditioning Coach), Nigel Kirwan (Video Coach), Jake Goertzen (Head Scout), Rick Paterson (Chief Professional Scout), Dirk Graham (Pro Scout), Ryan Belec (Assistant to the GM), Kathy Paterson (Hockey Operations Executive Assistant), Phil Thibodeau (Director of Team Services), Thomas Mulligan (Trainer), Adam Rambo (Assistant Trainer), Mike Griebel (Massage Therapist), Ray Thill (Equipment Manager), Dana Heinze, Jim Pickard (Assistant Equipment Managers).

*List of names for 2004 not finalized at press time.

Scores: May 25, at Tampa Bay - Calgary 4, Tampa Bay 1; May 27, at Tampa Bay - Tampa Bay 4, Calgary 1; May 29, at Calgary - Calgary 3, Tampa Bay 0; May 31, at Calgary - Tampa Bay 1, Calgary 0; June 3, at Tampa Bay - Calgary 3, Tampa Bay 2; June 5, at Calgary - Tampa Bay 3, Calgary 2; June 7, at Tampa Bay - Tampa Bay 2, Calgary 1.

2002-03 — New Jersey Devils — Scott Stevens (Captain), Tommy Albelin, Jiri Bicek, Martin Brodeur, Sergei Brylin, Ken Daneyko, Patrik Elias, Jeff Friesen, Brian Gionta, Scott Gomez, Jamie Langenbrunner, John Madden, Grant Marshall, Jim McKenzie, Scott Niedermayer, Joe Nieuwendyk, Jay Pandolfo, Brian Rafalski, Pascal Rheaume, Michael Rupp, Corey Schwab, Richard Smehlik, Oleg Tverdovsky, Colin White, Raymond G. Chambers (Owner), Lewis Katz (Owner), Peter Simon (Chairman), Lou Lamoriello (CEO/President/General Manager), Pat Burns (Head Coach), Bob Carpenter (Assistant Coach), John MacLean (Assistant Coach), Jacques Caron (Goaltending Coach), Larry Robinson (Special Assignment Coach), David Conte (Director, Scouting), Claude Carrier (Assistant Director, Scouting), Chris Lamoriello (Scout/Albany GM), Milt Fisher (Scout), Dan Labraaten (Scout), Marcel Pronovost (Scout), Bob Hoffmeyer (Pro Scout), Jan Ludvig (Pro Scout), Dr. Barry Fisher (Orthopedist), Chris Modrzynski (Exec. VP), Terry Farmer (VP), Vladimir Bure (Fitness Consultant), Taran Singleton (Hockey Operations), Bill Murray (Medical Trainer), Michael Vasalani (Strength/Conditioning Coordinator), Rich Matthews (Equipment Manager), Juergen Merz (Massage Therapist), Alex Abasto (Assistant Equipment Manager).

Scores: May 27, at New Jersey - New Jersey 3, Anaheim 0; May 29, at New Jersey - New Jersey 3, Anaheim 0; May 31, at Anaheim - Anaheim 3, New Jersey 2; June 2, at Anaheim - Anaheim 1, New Jersey 0; June 5, at New Jersey - New Jersey 6, Anaheim 3; June 7, at Anaheim - Anaheim 5, New Jersey 2; June 9, at New Jersey - New Jersey 3, Anaheim 0.

2001-02 — Detroit Red Wings — Steve Yzerman (Captain), Chris Chelios, Mathieu Dandenault, Pavel Datsyuk, Boyd Devereaux, Kris Draper, Steve Duchesne, Sergei Fedorov, Jiri Fischer, Dominik Hasek, Tomas Holmstrom, Brett Hull, Igor Larionov, Manny Legace, Nicklas Lidstrom, Kirk Maltby, Darren McCarty, Fredrik Olausson, Luc Robitaille, Brendan Shanahan, Jiri Slegr, Jason Williams, Michael Ilitch (Owner/Governor) Marian Ilitch (Owner/Secretary Treasurer), Ronald Ilitch, Michael Ilitch Jr., Lisa Ilitch Murray, Atanas Ilitch, Carole Ilitch, Jim Devallano (Senior Vice President), Christopher Ilitch (Vice President), Denise Ilitch (Alternate Governor), Ken Holland (General Manager), Jim Nill (Assistant General Manager), Scotty Bowman (Head Coach), Dave Lewis (Associate Coach), Barry Smith (Associate Coach), Jim Bedard (Goaltending Consultant), Joe Kocur (Video Coordinator), John Wharton (Athletic Trainer), Paul Boyer (Equipment Manager), Piet Van Zant (Assistant Athletic Trainer), Paul MacDonald (Senior Director of Finance), Nancy Beard (Executive Assistant), Dan Belisle (Pro Scout), Mark Howe (Pro Scout), Bob McCammon (Pro Scout), Hakan Andersson (Director of European Scouting), Mark Leach (Scout), Bruce Haralson (Scout), Joe McDonnell (Scout), Glenn Merkosky (Scout).

Scores: June 4, at Detroit - Carolina 3, Detroit 2; June 6, at Detroit - Detroit 3, Carolina 1; June 8, at Carolina - Detroit 3, Carolina 2; June 10, at Carolina - Detroit 3, Carolina 0; June 13, at Detroit - Detroit 3, Carolina 1.

2000-01 — Colorado Avalanche — Joe Sakic (Captain), David Aebischer, Rob Blake, Raymond Bourque, Greg de Vries, Chris Dingman, Chris Drury, Adam Foote, Peter Forsberg, Milan Hejduk, Dan Hinote, Jon Klemm, Eric Messier, Bryan Muir, Ville Nieminen, Scott Parker, Shjon Podein, Nolan Pratt, Dave Reid, Steve Reinprecht, Patrick Roy, Martin Skoula, Alex Tanguay, Stephane Yelle, E. Stanley Kroenke (Owner/Governor), Pierre Lacroix (President and General Manager), Bob Hartley (Head Coach), Jacques Cloutier (Assistant Coach), Bryan Trottier (Assistant Coach), Paul Fixter (Video Coach), Francois Giguere (Vice President of Hockey Operations), Brian MacDonald (Assistant General Manager), Michel Goulet (Vice President of Player Personnel), Jean Martineau (Vice President of Communications/Team Services), Pat Karns (Head Athletic Trainer), Matthew Sokolowski (Assistant Athletic Trainer), Wayne Flemming (Equipment Manager), Mark Miller (Equipment Manager), Dave Randolph (Assistant Equipment Manager), Paul Goldberg (Strength and Conditioning Coach), Gregorio Pradera (Massage Therapist), Brad Smith (Pro Scout), Jim Hammett (Chief Scout), Garth Joy, Steve Lyons, Joni Lehto, Orval Tessier (Scouts), Charlotte Grahame (Director of Hockey Operations).

Scores: May 26, at Colorado - Colorado 5, New Jersey 0; May 29, at Colorado - New Jersey 2, Colorado 1; May 31, at New Jersey - Colorado 3, New Jersey 1; June 2, at New Jersey - New Jersey 3, Colorado 2; June 4, at Colorado - New Jersey 4, Colorado 1; June 7, at New Jersey - Colorado 4, New Jersey 0; June 9, at Colorado - Colorado 3, New Jersey 1.

1999-2000 — New Jersey Devils — Scott Stevens (Captain), Jason Arnott, Brad Bombardir, Martin Brodeur, Steve Brule, Sergei Brylin, Ken Daneyko, Patrik Elias, Scott Gomez, Bobby Holik, Steve Kelly, Claude Lemieux, John Madden, Vladimir Malakhov, Randy McKay, Alexander Mogilny, Sergei Nemchinov, Scott Niedermayer, Krzysztof Oliwa, Jay Pandolfo, Brian Rafalski, Ken Sutton, Petr Sykora, Chris Terreri, Colin White, Dr. John J. McMullen (Owner/Chairman), Peter S. McMullen (Owner), Lou Lamoriello (President/General Manager), Larry Robinson (Head Coach), Viacheslav Fetisov (Assistant Coach), Bob Carpenter (Assistant Coach), Jacques Caron (Goaltending Coach), John Cunniff (AHL Coach), David Conte (Director of Scouting), Milt Fisher (Scout), Claude Carrier (Assistant Director of Scouting), Dan Labraaten (Scout), Marcel Pronovost (Scout), Bob Hoffmeyer (Pro Scout), Dr. Barry Fisher (Orthopedist), Dennis Gendron (AHL Assistant Coach), Robbie Ftorek (Coach), Vladimir Bure (Consultant), Taran Singleton (Hockey Operations), Marie Carnevale (Hockey Operations), Callie Smith (Hockey Operations), Bill Murray (Medical Trainer), Michael Vasalani (Strength/Conditioning Coordinator), Dana McGuane (Equipment Manager), Juergen Merz (Massage Therapist), Harry Bricker (Assistant Equipment Manager), Lou Centanni (Assistant Equipment Manager).

Scores: May 30, at New Jersey - New Jersey 7, Dallas 3; June 1, at New Jersey - Dallas 2, New Jersey 1; June 3, at Dallas - New Jersey 2, Dallas 1; June 5, at Dallas - New Jersey 3, Dallas 1; June 8, at New Jersey - Dallas 1 - New Jersey 0; at Dallas, New Jersey 2 - Dallas 1.

1998-99 — Dallas Stars — Derian Hatcher (Captain), Ed Belfour, Guy Carbonneau, Shawn Chambers, Benoit Hogue, Tony Hrkac, Brett Hull, Mike Keane, Jamie Langenbrunner, Jere Lehtinen, Craig Ludwig, Grant Marshall, Richard Matvichuk, Mike Modano, Joe Nieuwendyk, Derek Plante, Dave Reid, Jon Sim, Brian Skrudland, Blake Sloan, Darryl Sydor, Roman Turek, Pat Verbeek, Sergei Zubov, Thomas Hicks (Chairman of the Board and Owner), Jim Lites (President), Bob Gainey (Vice President, Hockey Operations and General Manager), Doug Armstrong (Assistant General Manager), Craig Button (Director of Player Personnel), Ken Hitchcock (Head Coach), Doug Jarvis (Assistant Coach), Rick Wilson (Assistant Coach), Rick McLaughlin (Vice President and Chief Financial Officer), Jeff Cogen (Vice President, Marketing and Promotion), Bill Strong (Vice President, Marketing and Broadcasting), Tim Bernhardt (Director of Amateur Scouting), Doug Overton (Director of Pro Scouting), Bob Gernander (Chief Scout), Stu MacGregor (Western Scout), Dave Suprenant (Medical Trainer), Dave Smith (Equipment Manager), Rich Matthews (Equipment Manager), J.J. McQueen (Strength and Conditioning Coach), Rick St. Croix (Goaltending Consultant), Dan Stuchal (Director of Team Services), Larry Kelly (Director of Public Relations).

Scores: June 8, at Dallas - Buffalo 3, Dallas 2; June 10, at Dallas - Dallas 4, Buffalo 2; June 12, at Buffalo - Dallas 2, Buffalo 1; June 15, at Buffalo - Buffalo 2, Dallas 1; June 17, at Dallas - Dallas 2, Buffalo 0; June 19, at Buffalo - Dallas 2, Buffalo 1.

1997-98 — Detroit Red Wings — Steve Yzerman (Captain), Doug Brown, Mathieu Dandenault, Kris Draper, Anders Eriksson, Sergei Fedorov, Viacheslav Fetisov, Brent Gilchrist, Kevin Hodson, Tomas Holmstrom, Mike Knuble, Joe Kocur, Vladimir Konstantinov, Vyacheslav Kozlov, Martin Lapointe, Igor Larionov, Nicklas Lidstrom, Jamie Macoun, Kirk Maltby, Darren McCarty, Dmitri Mironov, Larry Murphy, Chris Osgood, Bob Rouse, Brendan Shanahan, Aaron Ward, Mike Ilitch, (Owner/Chairman), Marian Ilitch (Owner), Atanas Ilitch (Vice President), Christopher Ilitch (Vice President), Denise Ilitch, Ronald Ilitch, Michael Ilitch Jr., Lisa Ilitch Murray, Carole Ilitch Trepeck, Jim Devellano (Senior Vice President), Scotty Bowman (Head Coach), Ken Holland (General Manager), Don Waddell (Assistant General Manager), Barry Smith (Associate Coach), Dave Lewis (Associate Coach), Jim Bedard (Goaltending Consultant), Jim Nill (Director of Player Development), Dan Belisle (Pro Scout), Mark Howe (Pro Scout), Hakan Andersson (Director of European Scouting), Mark Leach (USA Scout), Moe McDonnell (Eastern Scout), Bruce Haralson (Western Scout), John Wharton (Athletic Trainer), Paul Boyer (Equipment Manager) Tim Abbott (Assistant Equipment Manager), Bob Huddleston (Masseur), Sergei Mnatsakanov (Masseur), Wally Crossman (Dressing Room Assistant).

Scores: June 9, at Detroit — Detroit 2, Washington 1; June 11, at Detroit — Detroit 5, Washington 4; June 13, at Washington — Detroit 2, Washington 1; June 16, at Washington — Detroit 4, Washington 1.

1996-97 — Detroit Red Wings — Steve Yzerman (Captain), Doug Brown, Mathieu Dandenault, Kris Draper, Sergei Fedorov, Viacheslav Fetisov, Kevin Hodson, Tomas Holmstrom, Joe Kocur, Vladimir Konstantinov, Vyacheslav Kozlov, Martin Lapointe, Igor Larionov, Nicklas Lidstrom, Kirk Maltby, Darren McCarty, Larry Murphy, Chris Osgood, Jamie Pushor, Bob Rouse, Tomas Sandstrom, Brendan Shanahan, Tim Taylor, Mike Vernon, Aaron Ward, Mike Ilitch (Owner/Chairman), Marian Ilitch (Owner), Atanas Ilitch (Vice President), Christopher Ilitch (Vice President), Denise Ilitch Lites, Ronald Ilitch, Michael Ilitch, Jr., Lisa Ilitch Murray, Carole Ilitch Trepeck, Jim Devellano (Senior Vice President), Scotty Bowman (Head Coach/Director of Player Personnel), Ken Holland (Assistant General Manager), Barry Smith (Associate Coach), Dave Lewis (Associate Coach), Mike Krushelnyski (Assistant Coach). Jim Nill (Director of Player Development), Dan Belisle (Pro Scout), Mark Howe (Pro Scout), Hakan Andersson (Director of European Scouting), John Wharton (Athletic Trainer), Paul Boyer (Equipment Manager) Tim Abbott (Assistant Equipment Manager), Sergei Mnatsakanov (Masseur).

Scores: May 31, at Philadelphia — Detroit 4, Philadelphia 2; June 3, at Philadelphia — Detroit 4, Philadelphia 2; June 5, at Detroit — Detroit 6, Philadelphia 1; June 7, at Detroit — Detroit 2, Philadelphia 1.

1995-96 — Colorado Avalanche — Joe Sakic (Captain), Rene Corbet, Adam Deadmarsh, Stephane Fiset, Adam Foote, Peter Forsberg, Alexei Gusarov, Dave Hannan, Valeri Kamensky, Mike Keane, Jon Klemm, Uwe Krupp, Sylvain Lefebvre, Claude Lemieux, Curtis Leschyshyn, Troy Murray, Sandis Ozolinsh, Mike Ricci, Patrick Roy, Warren Rychel, Chris Simon, Craig Wolanin, Stephane Yelle, Scott Young, Charlie Lyons (Chairman, CEO), Pierre Lacroix (Exec. V.P., G.M.), Marc Crawford (Head Coach), Joel Quenneville (Assistant Coach), Jacques Cloutier (Assistant Coach), Francois Giguere (Assistant General Manager), Michel Goulet (Director of Player Personnel), Dave Draper (Chief Scout), Jean Martineau (Director of Public Relations), Pat Karns (Trainer), Matthew Sokolowski (Assistant Trainer), Rob McLean (Equipment Manager), Mike Kramer (Assistant Equipment Manager), Brock Gibbins (Assistant Equipment Manager), Skip Allen (Strength and Conditioning Coach), Paul Fixter (Video Coordinator), Leo Vyssokov (Massage Therapist).

Scores: June 4, at Colorado — Colorado 3, Florida 1; June 6, at Colorado — Colorado 8, Florida 1; June 8, at Florida — Colorado 3, Florida 2; June 10, at Florida — Colorado 1, Florida 0.

1994-95 — New Jersey Devils — Scott Stevens (Captain), Tommy Albelin, Martin Brodeur, Neal Broten, Sergei Brylin, Bob Carpenter, Shawn Chambers, Tom Chorske, Danton Cole, Ken Daneyko, Kevin Dean, Jim Dowd, Bruce Driver (Alternate Captain), Bill Guerin, Bobby Holik, Claude Lemieux, John MacLean (Alternate Captain), Chris McAlpine, Randy McKay, Scott Niedermayer, Mike Peluso, Stephane Richer, Brian Rolston, Chris Terreri, Valeri Zelepukin, Dr. John J. McMullen (Owner/Chairman), Peter S. McMullen (Owner), Lou Lamoriello (President/General Manager), Jacques Lemaire (Head Coach), Jacques Caron (Goaltender Coach), Dennis Gendron (Assistant Coach), Larry Robinson (Assistant Coach), Robbie Ftorek (AHL Coach), Alex Abasto (Assistant Equipment Manager), Bob Huddleston (Massage Therapist), David Nichols (Equipment Manager), Ted Schuch (Medical Trainer), Mike Vasalani (Strength Coach), David Conte (Director of Scouting) Claude Carrier (Scout), Milt Fisher (Scout), Dan Labraaten (Scout), Marcel Pronovost (Scout).

Scores: June 17, at Detroit — New Jersey 2, Detroit 1; June 20, at Detroit — New Jersey 4, Detroit 2; June 22, at New Jersey — New Jersey 5, Detroit 2; June 24, at New Jersey — New Jersey 5, Detroit 2.

1993-94 — New York Rangers — Mark Messier (Captain), Brian Leetch, Kevin Lowe, Adam Graves, Steve Larmer, Glenn Anderson, Jeff Beukeboom, Greg Gilbert, Mike Hartman, Glenn Healy, Mike Hudson, Alexander Karpovtsev, Joe Kocur, Alexei Kovalev, Nick Kypreos, Doug Lidster, Stephane Matteau, Craig MacTavish, Sergei Nemchinov, Brian Noonan, Ed Olczyk, Mike Richter, Esa Tikkanen, Jay Wells, Sergei Zubov, Neil Smith (President, General Manager and Governor), Robert Gutkowski, Stanley Jaffe, Kenneth Munoz (Governors), Larry Pleau (Assistant General Manager), Mike Keenan (Head Coach), Colin Campbell (Associate Coach), Dick Todd (Assistant Coach), Matthew Loughren (Manager, Team Operations), Barry Watkins (Director, Communications), Christer Rockstrom, Tony Feltrin, Martin Madden, Herb Hammond, Darwin Bennett (Scouts), Dave Smith, Joe Murphy, Mike Folga, Bruce Lifrieri (Trainers).

Scores: May 31, at New York — Vancouver 3, NY Rangers 2; June 2, at New York — NY Rangers 3, Vancouver 1; June 4, at Vancouver — NY Rangers 5, Vancouver 1; June 7, at Vancouver — NY Rangers 4, Vancouver 2; June 9, at New York — Vancouver 6, at NY Rangers 3; June 11, at Vancouver — Vancouver 4, NY Rangers 1; June 14, at New York — NY Rangers 3, Vancouver 2.

1992-93 — Montreal Canadiens — Guy Carbonneau (Captain), Patrick Roy, Mike Keane, Eric Desjardins, Stephan Lebeau, Mathieu Schneider, J-J Daigneault, Denis Savard, Lyle Odelein, Todd Ewen, Kirk Muller, John LeClair, Gilbert Dionne, Benoit Brunet, Patrice Brisebois, Paul Di Pietro, Andre Racicot, Donald Dufresne, Mario Roberge, Sean Hill, Ed Ronan, Kevin Haller, Vincent Damphousse, Brian Bellows, Gary Leeman, Rob Ramage, Ronald Corey (President), Serge Savard (Managing Director & Vice-President Hockey), Jacques Demers (Head Coach), Jacques Laperriere (Assistant Coach), Charles Thiffault (Assistant Coach), Francois Allaire (Goaltending Instructor), Jean Béliveau (Senior Vice-President, Corporate Affairs), Fred Steer (Vice-President, Finance & Adminstration), Aldo Giampaolo (Vice-President, Operations), Bernard Brisset (Vice-President, Marketing & Communications), André Boudrias (Assistant to the Managing Director & Director of Scouting), Jacques Lemaire (Assistant to the Managing Director), Gaeten Lefebvre (Athletic Trainer), John Shipman (Assistant to the Athletic Trainer), Eddy Palchak (Equipment Manager), Pierre Gervais (Assistant to the Equipment Manager), Robert Boulanger (Assistant to the Equipment Manager), Pierre Ouellete (Assistant to the Equipment Manager).

Scores: June 1, at Montreal — Los Angeles 4, Montreal 1; June 2, at Montreal — Montreal 3, Los Angeles 2; June 5, at Los Angeles — Montreal 4, Los Angeles 3; June 7, at Los Angeles — Montreal 3, Los Angeles 2; June 9, at Montreal — Montreal 4, Los Angeles 1.

1991-92 — Pittsburgh Penguins — Mario Lemieux (Captain), Ron Francis, Bryan Trottier, Kevin Stevens, Bob Errey, Phil Bourque, Troy Loney, Rick Tocchet, Joe Mullen, Jaromir Jagr, Jiri Hrdina, Shawn McEachern, Ulf Samuelsson, Kjell Samuelsson, Larry Murphy, Gordie Roberts, Jim Paek, Paul Stanton, Tom Barrasso, Ken Wregget, Jay Caufield, Jamie Leach, Wendell Young, Grant Jennings, Peter Taglianetti, Jock Callander, Dave Michayluk, Mike Needham, Jeff Chychrun, Ken Priestlay, Jeff Daniels, Howard Baldwin (Owner and President), Morris Belzberg (Owner), Thomas Ruta (Owner), Donn Patton (Executive Vice President and Chief Financial Officer), Paul Martha (Executive Vice President and General Counsel), Craig Patrick (Executive Vice President and General Manager), Bob Johnson (Coach), Scotty Bowman (Director of Player Development and Coach), Barry Smith, Rick Kehoe, Pierre McGuire, Gilles Meloche, Rick Paterson (Assistant Coaches), Steve Latin (Equipment Manager), Skip Thayer (Trainer), John Welday (Strength and Conditioning Coach), Greg Malone, Les Binkley, Charlie Hodge, John Gill, Ralph Cox (Scouts).
Scores: May 26, at Pittsburgh — Pittsburgh 5, Chicago 4; May 28, at Pittsburgh — Pittsburgh 3, Chicago 1; May 30, at Chicago — Pittsburgh 1, Chicago 0; June 1, at Chicago — Pittsburgh 6, Chicago 5.

1990-91 — Pittsburgh Penguins — Mario Lemieux (Captain), Paul Coffey, Randy Hillier, Bob Errey, Tom Barrasso, Phil Bourque, Jay Caufield, Ron Francis, Randy Gilhen, Jiri Hrdina, Jaromir Jagr, Grant Jennings, Troy Loney, Joe Mullen, Larry Murphy, Jim Paek, Frank Pietrangelo, Barry Pederson, Mark Recchi, Gordie Roberts, Ulf Samuelsson, Paul Stanton, Kevin Stevens, Peter Taglianetti, Bryan Trottier, Scott Young, Wendell Young, Edward J. DeBartolo, Sr. (Owner), Marie D. DeBartolo York (President), Paul Martha (Vice-President & General Counsel), Craig Patrick (General Manager), Scotty Bowman (Director of Player Development & Recruitment), Bob Johnson (Coach), Rick Kehoe (Assistant Coach), Gilles Meloche (Goaltending Coach & Scout), Rick Paterson (Assistant Coach), Barry Smith (Assistant Coach), Steve Latin (Equipment Manager), Skip Thayer (Trainer), John Welday (Strength & Conditioning Coach), Greg Malone (Scout).
Scores: May 15, at Pittsburgh — Minnesota 5, Pittsburgh 4; May 17, at Pittsburgh — Pittsburgh 4, Minnesota 1; May 19, at Minnesota — Minnesota 3, Pittsburgh 1; May 21, at Minnesota — Pittsburgh 5, Minnesota 3; May 23, at Pittsburgh — Pittsburgh 6, Minnesota 4; May 25, at Minnesota — Pittsburgh 8, Minnesota 0.

1989-90 — Edmonton Oilers — Kevin Lowe, Steve Smith, Jeff Beukeboom, Mark Lamb, Joe Murphy, Glenn Anderson, Mark Messier (Captain), Adam Graves, Craig MacTavish, Kelly Buchberger, Jari Kurri, Craig Simpson, Martin Gelinas, Randy Gregg, Charlie Huddy, Geoff Smith, Reijo Ruotsalainen, Craig Muni, Bill Ranford, Dave Brown, Pokey Reddick, Petr Klima, Esa Tikkanen, Grant Fuhr, Peter Pocklington (Owner), Glen Sather (President/General Manager), John Muckler (Coach), Ted Green (Co-Coach), Ron Low (Ass't Coach), Bruce MacGregor (Ass't General Manager), Barry Fraser (Director of Player Personnel), John Blackwell (Director of Operations, AHL), Ace Bailey, Ed Chadwick, Lorne Davis, Harry Howell, Matti Vaisanen and Albert Reeves (Scouts), Bill Tuele (Director of Public Relations), Werner Baum (Controller), Dr. Gordon Cameron (Medical Chief of Staff), Dr. David Reid (Team Physician), Barrie Stafford (Athletic Trainer), Ken Lowe (Athletic Therapist), Stuart Poirier (Massage Therapist), Lyle Kulchisky (Ass't Trainer).
Scores: May 15, at Boston — Edmonton 3, Boston 2; May 18, at Boston — Edmonton 7, Boston 2; May 20, at Edmonton — Boston 2, Edmonton 1; May 22, at Edmonton — Edmonton 5, Boston 1; May 24, at Boston — Edmonton 4, Boston 1.

1988-89 — Calgary Flames — Mike Vernon, Rick Wamsley, Al MacInnis, Brad McCrimmon, Dana Murzyn, Ric Nattress, Joe Mullen, Lanny McDonald (Co-captain), Gary Roberts, Colin Patterson, Hakan Loob, Theoren Fleury, Jiri Hrdina, Tim Hunter (Ass't. captain), Gary Suter, Mark Hunter, Jim Peplinski (Co-captain), Joe Nieuwendyk, Brian MacLellan, Joel Otto, Jamie Macoun, Doug Gilmour, Rob Ramage. Norman Green, Harley Hotchkiss, Norman Kwong, Sonia Scurfield, B.J. Seaman, D.K. Seaman (Owners), Cliff Fletcher (President and General Manager), Al MacNeil (Ass't General Manager), Al Coates (Ass't to the President), Terry Crisp (Head Coach), Doug Risebrough, Tom Watt (Ass't Coaches), Glenn Hall (Goaltending Consultant), Jim Murray (Trainer), Bob Stewart (Equipment Manager), Al Murray (Ass't Trainer).
Scores: May 14, at Calgary — Calgary 3, Montreal 2; May 17, at Calgary— Montreal 4, Calgary 2; May 19, at Montreal — Montreal 4, Calgary 3; May 21, at Montreal — Calgary 4, Montreal 2; May 23, at Calgary — Calgary 3, Montreal 2; May 25, at Montreal — Calgary 4, Montreal 2.

1987-88 — Edmonton Oilers — Keith Acton, Glenn Anderson, Jeff Beukeboom, Geoff Courtnall, Grant Fuhr, Randy Gregg, Wayne Gretzky (Captain), Dave Hannan, Charlie Huddy, Mike Krushelnyski, Jari Kurri, Normand Lacombe, Kevin Lowe, Craig MacTavish, Kevin McClelland, Marty McSorley, Mark Messier, Craig Muni, Bill Ranford, Craig Simpson, Steve Smith, Esa Tikkanen, Peter Pocklington (Owner), Glen Sather (General Manager/Coach), John Muckler (Co-Coach), Ted Green (Ass't Coach), Bruce MacGregor (Ass't General Manager), Barry Fraser (Director of Player Personnel), Bill Tuele (Director of Public Relations), Dr. Gordon Cameron (Team Physician), Peter Millar (Athletic Therapist), Barrie Stafford (Trainer), Juergen Mers (Massage Therapist), Lyle Kulchisky (Ass't Trainer).
Scores: May 18, at Edmonton — Edmonton 2, Boston 1; May 20, at Edmonton — Edmonton 4, Boston 2; May 22, at Boston — Edmonton 6, Boston 3; May 24, at Boston — Boston 3, Edmonton 3 (suspended due to power failure); May 26, at Edmonton — Edmonton 6, Boston 3.

1986-87 — Edmonton Oilers — Glenn Anderson, Jeff Beukeboom, Kelly Buchberger, Paul Coffey, Grant Fuhr, Randy Gregg, Wayne Gretzky (Captain), Charlie Huddy, Dave Hunter, Mike Krushelnyski, Jari Kurri, Moe Lemay, Kevin Lowe, Craig MacTavish, Kevin McClelland, Marty McSorley, Mark Messier, Andy Moog, Craig Muni, Kent Nilsson, Jaroslav Pouzar, Reijo Ruotsalainen, Steve Smith, Esa Tikkanen, Peter Pocklington (Owner), Glen Sather (General Manager/Coach), John Muckler (Co-Coach), Ted Green (Ass't. Coach), Ron Low (Ass't. Coach), Bruce MacGregor (Ass't. General Manager), Barry Fraser (Director of Player Personnel), Peter Millar (Athletic Therapist), Barrie Stafford (Trainer), Lyle Kulchisky (Ass't Trainer).
Scores: May 17, at Edmonton — Edmonton 4, Philadelphia 2; May 20, at Edmonton — Edmonton 3, Philadelphia 2; May 22, at Philadelphia — Philadelphia 5, Edmonton 3; May 24, at Philadelphia — Edmonton 4, Philadelphia 1; May 26, at Edmonton — Philadelphia 4, Edmonton 3; May 28, at Philadelphia — Philadelphia 3, Edmonton 2; May 31, at Edmonton — Edmonton 3, Philadelphia 1.

1985-86 — Montreal Canadiens — Bob Gainey (Captain), Doug Soetaert, Patrick Roy, Rick Green, David Maley, Ryan Walter, Serge Boisvert, Mario Tremblay, Bobby Smith, Craig Ludwig, Tom Kurvers, Kjell Dahlin, Larry Robinson, Guy Carbonneau, Chris Chelios, Petr Svoboda, Mats Naslund, Lucien DeBlois, Steve Rooney, Gaston Gingras, Mike Lalor, Chris Nilan, John Kordic, Claude Lemieux, Mike McPhee, Brian Skrudland, Stephane Richer, Ronald Corey (President), Serge Savard (General Manager), Jean Perron (Coach), Jacques Laperrière (Ass't. Coach), Jean Béliveau (Vice President), Francois-Xavier Seigneur (Vice President), Fred Steer (Vice President), Jacques Lemaire (Ass't. General Manager), André Boudrias (Ass't. General Manager), Claude Ruel (Scouting), Yves Belanger (Athletic Therapist), Gaetan Lefebvre (Ass't. Athletic Therapist), Eddy Palchak (Trainer), Sylvain Toupin (Ass't. Trainer).
Scores: May 16, at Calgary — Calgary 5, Montreal 2; May 18, at Calgary — Montreal 3, Calgary 2; May 20, at Montreal — Montreal 5, Calgary 3; May 22, at Montreal — Montreal 1, Calgary 0; May 24, at Calgary — Montreal 4, Calgary 3.

1984-85 — Edmonton Oilers — Glenn Anderson, Billy Carroll, Paul Coffey, Lee Fogolin, Grant Fuhr, Randy Gregg, Wayne Gretzky (Captain), Charlie Huddy, Pat Hughes, Dave Hunter, Don Jackson, Mike Krushelnyski, Jari Kurri, Willy Lindstrom, Kevin Lowe, Dave Lumley, Kevin McClelland, Larry Melnyk, Mark Messier, Andy Moog, Mark Napier, Jaroslav Pouzar, Dave Semenko, Esa Tikkanen, Peter Pocklington (Owner), Glen Sather (General Manager/Coach), John Muckler (Ass't. Coach), Ted Green (Ass't. Coach), Bruce MacGregor (Ass't. General Manager), Barry Fraser (Director of Player Personnel/Chief Scout), Peter Millar (Athletic Therapist), Barrie Stafford, Lyle Kulchisky (Trainers)
Scores: May 21, at Philadelphia — Philadelphia 4, Edmonton 1; May 23, at Philadelphia — Edmonton 3, Philadelphia 1; May 25, at Edmonton — Edmonton 4, Philadelphia 3; May 28, at Edmonton — Edmonton 5, Philadelphia 3; May 30, at Edmonton — Edmonton 8, Philadelphia 3.

1983-84 — Edmonton Oilers — Glenn Anderson, Paul Coffey, Pat Conacher, Lee Fogolin, Grant Fuhr, Randy Gregg, Wayne Gretzky (Captain), Charlie Huddy, Pat Hughes, Dave Hunter, Don Jackson, Jari Kurri, Willy Lindstrom, Ken Linseman, Kevin Lowe, Dave Lumley, Kevin McClelland, Mark Messier, Andy Moog, Jaroslav Pouzar, Dave Semenko, Peter Pocklington (Owner), Glen Sather (General Manager/Coach), John Muckler (Ass't. Coach), Ted Green (Ass't. Coach), Bruce MacGregor (Ass't. General Manager), Barry Fraser (Director of Player Personnel/Chief Scout), Peter Millar (Athletic Therapist), Barrie Stafford (Trainer)
Scores: May 10, at New York — Edmonton 1, NY Islanders 0; May 12, at New York — NY Islanders 6, Edmonton 1; May 15, at Edmonton — Edmonton 7, NY Islanders 2; May 17, at Edmonton — Edmonton 7, NY Islanders 2; May 19, at Edmonton — Edmonton 5, NY Islanders 2.

1982-83 — New York Islanders — Mike Bossy, Bob Bourne, Paul Boutilier, Billy Carroll, Greg Gilbert, Clark Gillies, Butch Goring, Mats Hallin, Tomas Jonsson, Anders Kallur, Gord Lane, Dave Langevin, Mike McEwen, Rollie Melanson, Wayne Merrick, Ken Morrow, Bob Nystrom, Stefan Persson, Denis Potvin (Captain), Billy Smith, Brent Sutter, Duane Sutter, John Tonelli, Bryan Trottier, Al Arbour (Coach), Lorne Henning (Ass't. Coach), Bill Torrey (General Manager), Ron Waske, Jim Pickard (Trainers)
Scores: May 10, at Edmonton — NY Islanders 2, Edmonton 0; May 12, at Edmonton — NY Islanders 6, Edmonton 3; May 14, at New York — NY Islanders 5, Edmonton 1; May 17, at New York — NY Islanders 4, Edmonton 2

1981-82 — New York Islanders — Mike Bossy, Bob Bourne, Billy Carroll, Butch Goring, Greg Gilbert, Clark Gillies, Tomas Jonsson, Anders Kallur, Gord Lane, Dave Langevin, Hector Marini, Mike McEwen, Rollie Melanson, Wayne Merrick, Ken Morrow, Bob Nystrom, Stefan Persson, Denis Potvin (Captain), Billy Smith, Brent Sutter, Duane Sutter, John Tonelli, Bryan Trottier, Al Arbour (Coach), Lorne Henning (Ass't. Coach), Bill Torrey (General Manager), Jim Devellano (ass't. general manager/dir. of scouting), Ron Waske, Jim Pickard (Trainers)
Scores: May 8, at New York — NY Islanders 6, Vancouver 5; May 11, at New York — NY Islanders 6, Vancouver 4; May 13, at Vancouver — NY Islanders 3, Vancouver 0; May 16, at Vancouver — NY Islanders 3, Vancouver 1

1980-81 — New York Islanders — Denis Potvin (Captain), Mike McEwen, Ken Morrow, Gord Lane, Bob Lorimer, Stefan Persson, Dave Langevin, Mike Bossy, Bryan Trottier, Butch Goring, Wayne Merrick, Clark Gillies, John Tonelli, Bob Nystrom, Billy Carroll, Bob Bourne, Hector Marini, Anders Kallur, Duane Sutter, Garry Howatt, Lorne Henning, Billy Smith, Rollie Melanson, Al Arbour (Coach), Bill Torrey (General Manager), Jim Devellano (Chief Scout), Ron Waske, Jim Pickard (Trainers).
Scores: May 12, at New York — NY Islanders 6, Minnesota 3; May 14, at New York — NY Islanders 6, Minnesota 3; May 17, at Minnesota — NY Islanders 7, Minnesota 5; May 19, at Minnesota— Minnesota 4, NY Islanders 2; May 21, at New York — NY Islanders 5, Minnesota 1.

1979-80 — New York Islanders — Gord Lane, Jean Potvin, Bob Lorimer, Denis Potvin (Captain), Stefan Persson, Ken Morrow, Dave Langevin, Duane Sutter, Garry Howatt, Clark Gillies, Lorne Henning, Wayne Merrick, Bob Bourne, Steve Tambellini, Bryan Trottier, Mike Bossy, Bob Nystrom, John Tonelli, Anders Kallur, Butch Goring, Alex McKendry, Glenn Resch, Billy Smith, Al Arbour (Coach), Bill Torrey (General Manager), Jim Devellano (Chief Scout), Ron Waske, Jim Pickard (Trainers).
Scores: May 13, at Philadelphia — NY Islanders 4, Philadelphia 3; May 15, at Philadelphia — Philadelphia 8, NY Islanders 3; May 17, at New York — NY Islanders 6, Philadelphia 2; May 19, at New York — NY Islanders 5, Philadelphia 2; May 22 at Philadelphia — Philadelphia 6, NY Islanders 3; May 24, at New York — NY Islanders 5, Philadelphia 4.

1978-79 — Montreal Canadiens — Ken Dryden, Larry Robinson, Serge Savard, Guy Lapointe, Brian Engblom, Gilles Lupien, Rick Chartraw, Guy Lafleur, Steve Shutt, Jacques Lemaire, Yvan Cournoyer (Captain), Réjean Houle, Pierre Mondou, Bob Gainey, Doug Jarvis, Yvon Lambert, Doug Risebrough, Pierre Larouche, Mario Tremblay, Cam Connor, Pat Hughes, Rod Langway, Mark Napier, Michel Larocque, Richard Sévigny, Scotty Bowman (Coach), Irving Grundman (Managing Director), Eddy Palchak, Pierre Meilleur (Trainers).
Scores: May 13, at Montreal — NY Rangers 4, Montreal 1; May 15, at Montreal — Montreal 6, NY Rangers 2; May 17, at New York — Montreal 4, NY Rangers 1; May 19, at New York — Montreal 4, NY Rangers 3; May 21, at Montreal — Montreal 4, NY Rangers 1.

1977-78 — Montreal Canadiens — Ken Dryden, Larry Robinson, Serge Savard, Guy Lapointe, Bill Nyrop, Pierre Bouchard, Brian Engblom, Gilles Lupien, Rick Chartraw, Guy Lafleur, Steve Shutt, Jacques Lemaire, Yvan Cournoyer (Captain), Réjean Houle, Pierre Mondou, Bob Gainey, Doug Jarvis, Yvon Lambert, Doug Risebrough, Pierre Larouche, Mario Tremblay, Michel Larocque, Murray Wilson, Scotty Bowman (Coach), Sam Pollock (General Manager), Eddy Palchak, Pierre Meilleur (Trainers).
Scores: May 13, at Montreal — Montreal 4, Boston 1; May 16, at Montreal — Montreal 3, Boston 2; May 18, at Boston — Boston 4, Montreal 0; May 21, at Boston — Boston 4, Montreal 3; May 23, at Montreal — Montreal 4, Boston 1; May 25, at Boston — Montreal 4, Boston 1.

1976-77 — Montreal Canadiens — Ken Dryden, Guy Lapointe, Larry Robinson, Serge Savard, Jimmy Roberts, Rick Chartraw, Bill Nyrop, Pierre Bouchard, Brian Engblom, Yvan Cournoyer (Captain), Guy Lafleur, Jacques Lemaire, Steve Shutt, Pete Mahovlich, Murray Wilson, Doug Jarvis, Yvon Lambert, Bob Gainey, Doug Risebrough, Mario Tremblay, Réjean Houle, Pierre Mondou, Mike Polich, Michel Larocque, Scotty Bowman (Coach), Sam Pollock (General Manager), Eddy Palchak, Pierre Meilleur (Trainers).
Scores: May 7, at Montreal — Montreal 7, Boston 3; May 10, at Montreal — Montreal 3, Boston 0; May 12, at Boston — Montreal 4, Boston 2; May 14, at Boston — Montreal 2, Boston 1.

1975-76 — Montreal Canadiens — Ken Dryden, Serge Savard, Guy Lapointe, Larry Robinson, Bill Nyrop, Pierre Bouchard, Jimmy Roberts, Guy Lafleur, Steve Shutt, Pete Mahovlich, Yvan Cournoyer (Captain), Jacques Lemaire, Yvon Lambert, Doug Jarvis, Doug Risebrough, Murray Wilson, Mario Tremblay, Rick Chartraw, Michel Larocque, Scotty Bowman (Coach), Sam Pollock (General Manager), Eddy Palchak, Pierre Meilleur (Trainers).
Scores: May 9, at Montreal — Montreal 4, Philadelphia 3; May 11, at Montreal — Montreal 2, Philadelphia 1; May 13, at Philadelphia — Montreal 3, Philadelphia 2; May 16, at Philadelphia — Montreal 5, Philadelphia 3.

1974-75 — Philadelphia Flyers — Bernie Parent, Wayne Stephenson, Ed Van Impe, Tom Bladon, André Dupont, Joe Watson, Jimmy Watson, Ted Harris, Larry Goodenough, Rick MacLeish, Bobby Clarke (Captain), Bill Barber, Reggie Leach, Gary Dornhoefer, Ross Lonsberry, Bob Kelly, Terry Crisp, Don Saleski, Dave Schultz, Orest Kindrachuk, Bill Clement, Fred Shero (Coach), Keith Allen (general manager), Frank Lewis, Jim McKenzie (Trainers).
Scores: May 15, at Philadelphia — Philadelphia 4, Buffalo 1; May 18, at Philadelphia — Philadelphia 2, Buffalo 1; May 20, at Buffalo — Buffalo 5, Philadelphia 4; May 22, at Buffalo — Buffalo 4, Philadelphia 2; May 25, at Philadelphia — Philadelphia 5, Buffalo 1; May 27, at Buffalo — Philadelphia 2, Buffalo 0.

1973-74 — Philadelphia Flyers — Bernie Parent, Ed Van Impe, Tom Bladon, André Dupont, Joe Watson, Jimmy Watson, Barry Ashbee, Bill Barber, Dave Schultz, Don Saleski, Gary Dornhoefer, Terry Crisp, Bobby Clarke (Captain), Simon Nolet, Ross Lonsberry, Rick MacLeish, Bill Flett, Orest Kindrachuk, Bill Clement, Bob Kelly, Bruce Cowick, Al MacAdam, Bobby Taylor, Fred Shero (Coach), Keith Allen (General Manager), Frank Lewis, Jim McKenzie (Trainers).
Scores: May 7, at Boston — Boston 3, Philadelphia 2; May 9, at Boston — Philadelphia 3, Boston 2; May 12, at Philadelphia — Philadelphia 4, Boston 1; May 14, at Philadelphia — Philadelphia 4, Boston 2; May 16, at Boston — Boston 5, Philadelphia 1; May 19, at Philadelphia — Philadelphia 1, Boston 0.

1972-73 — Montreal Canadiens — Ken Dryden, Guy Lapointe, Serge Savard, Larry Robinson, Jacques Laperrière, Bob Murdoch, Pierre Bouchard, Jimmy Roberts, Yvan Cournoyer, Frank Mahovlich, Jacques Lemaire, Pete Mahovlich, Marc Tardif, Henri Richard (Captain), Réjean Houle, Guy Lafleur, Chuck Lefley, Claude Larose, Murray Wilson, Steve Shutt, Michel Plasse, Scotty Bowman (Coach), Sam Pollock (General Manager), Eddy Palchak, Bob Williams (Trainers).
Scores: April 29, at Montreal — Montreal 8, Chicago 3; May 1, at Montreal — Montreal 4, Chicago 1; May 3, at Chicago — Chicago 7, Montreal 4; May 6, at Chicago — Montreal 4, Chicago 0; May 8, at Montreal — Chicago 8, Montreal 7; May 10, at Chicago — Montreal 6, Chicago 4.

1971-72 — Boston Bruins — Gerry Cheevers, Eddie Johnston, Bobby Orr, Ted Green, Carol Vadnais, Dallas Smith, Don Awrey, Phil Esposito, Ken Hodge, John Bucyk, Mike Walton, Wayne Cashman, Garnet Bailey, Derek Sanderson, Fred Stanfield, Ed Westfall, John McKenzie, Don Marcotte, Garry Peters, Chris Hayes, Tom Johnson (Coach), Milt Schmidt (General Manager), Dan Canney, John Forristall (Trainers).
Scores: April 30, at Boston — Boston 6, NY Rangers 5; May 2, at Boston — Boston 2, NY Rangers 1; May 4, at New York — NY Rangers 5, Boston 2; May 7, at New York — Boston 3, NY Rangers 2; May 9, at Boston — NY Rangers 3, Boston 2; May 11, at New York — Boston 3, NY Rangers 0.

1970-71 — Montreal Canadiens — Ken Dryden, Rogie Vachon, Jacques Laperrière, J.C. Tremblay, Guy Lapointe, Terry Harper, Pierre Bouchard, Jean Béliveau (Captain), Marc Tardif, Yvan Cournoyer, Réjean Houle, Claude Larose, Henri Richard, Phil Roberto, Pete Mahovlich, Leon Rochefort, John Ferguson, Bobby Sheehan, Jacques Lemaire, Frank Mahovlich, Bob Murdoch, Chuck Lefley, Al MacNeil (Coach), Sam Pollock (General Manager), Yvon Belanger, Eddy Palchak (Trainers).
Scores: May 4, at Chicago — Chicago 2, Montreal 1; May 6, at Chicago — Chicago 5, Montreal 3; May 9, at Montreal — Montreal 4, Chicago 2; May 11, at Montreal — Montreal 5, Chicago 2; May 13, at Chicago — Chicago 2, Montreal 0; May 16, at Montreal — Montreal 4, Chicago 3; May 18, at Chicago — Montreal 3, Chicago 2.

1969-70 — Boston Bruins — Gerry Cheevers, Eddie Johnston, Bobby Orr, Rick Smith, Dallas Smith, Bill Speer, Gary Doak, Don Awrey, Phil Esposito, Ken Hodge, John Bucyk, Wayne Carleton, Wayne Cashman, Derek Sanderson, Fred Stanfield, Ed Westfall, John McKenzie, Jim Lorentz, Don Marcotte, Bill Lesuk, Danny Schock, Harry Sinden (Coach), Milt Schmidt (General Manager), Dan Canney, John Forristall (Trainers).
Scores: May 3, at St. Louis — Boston 6, St. Louis 1; May 5, at St. Louis — Boston 6, St. Louis 2; May 7, at Boston — Boston 4, St. Louis 1; May 10, at Boston — Boston 4, St. Louis 3.

1968-69 — Montreal Canadiens — Gump Worsley, Rogie Vachon, Jacques Laperrière, J.C. Tremblay, Ted Harris, Serge Savard, Terry Harper, Larry Hillman, Jean Béliveau (Captain), Ralph Backstrom, Dick Duff, Yvan Cournoyer, Claude Provost, Bobby Rousseau, Henri Richard, Jacques Lemaire, Lucien Grenier, Tony Esposito, Claude Ruel (Coach), Sam Pollock (General Manager), Larry Aubut, Eddy Palchak (Trainers).
Scores: April 27, at Montreal — Montreal 3, St. Louis 1; April 29, at Montreal — Montreal 3, St. Louis 1; May 1 at St. Louis — Montreal 4, St. Louis 0; May 4, at St. Louis — Montreal 2, St. Louis 1.

1967-68 — Montreal Canadiens — Gump Worsley, Rogie Vachon, Jacques Laperrière, J.C. Tremblay, Ted Harris, Serge Savard, Terry Harper, Carol Vadnais, Jean Béliveau (Captain), Gilles Tremblay, Ralph Backstrom, Dick Duff, Claude Larose, Yvan Cournoyer, Claude Provost, Bobby Rousseau, Henri Richard, John Ferguson, Danny Grant, Jacques Lemaire, Mickey Redmond, Toe Blake (Coach), Sam Pollock (General Manager), Larry Aubut, Eddy Palchak (Trainers).
Scores: May 5, at St. Louis — Montreal 3, St. Louis 2; May 7, at St. Louis — Montreal 1, St. Louis 0; May 9, at Montreal — Montreal 4, St. Louis 3; May 11, at Montreal — Montreal 3, St. Louis 2.

1966-67 — Toronto Maple Leafs — Johnny Bower, Terry Sawchuk, Larry Hillman, Marcel Pronovost, Tim Horton, Bob Baun, Aut Erickson, Allan Stanley, Red Kelly, Ron Ellis, George Armstrong (Captain), Pete Stemkowski, Dave Keon, Mike Walton, Jim Pappin, Bob Pulford, Brian Conacher, Eddie Shack, Frank Mahovlich, Milan Marcetta, Larry Jeffrey, Bruce Gamble, Punch Imlach (Manager-Coach), Bob Haggart (Trainer).
Scores: April 20, at Montreal — Toronto 2, Montreal 6; April 22, at Montreal — Toronto 3, Montreal 0; April 25, at Toronto — Toronto 3, Montreal 2; April 27, at Toronto — Toronto 6, Montreal 6; April 29, at Montreal — Toronto 4, Montreal 1; May 2, at Toronto — Toronto 3, Montreal 1.

1965-66 — Montreal Canadiens — Gump Worsley, Charlie Hodge, J.C. Tremblay, Ted Harris, Jean-Guy Talbot, Terry Harper, Jacques Laperrière, Noel Price, Jean Béliveau (Captain), Ralph Backstrom, Dick Duff, Gilles Tremblay, Claude Larose, Yvan Cournoyer, Claude Provost, Bobby Rousseau, Henri Richard, Dave Balon, John Ferguson, Leon Rochefort, Jimmy Roberts, Toe Blake (Coach), Sam Pollock (general manager), Larry Aubut, Andy Galley (Trainers).
Scores: April 24, at Montreal — Montreal 3, Detroit 1; April 26, at Montreal — Detroit 5, Montreal 2; April 28, at Detroit — Montreal 4, Detroit 2; May 1, at Detroit — Montreal 2, Detroit 1; May 3, at Montreal — Montreal 5, Detroit 1; May 5, at Detroit — Montreal 3, Detroit 2.

1964-65 — Montreal Canadiens — Gump Worsley, Charlie Hodge, J.C. Tremblay, Ted Harris, Jean-Guy Talbot, Terry Harper, Jacques Laperrière, Jean Gauthier, Noel Picard, Jean Béliveau (Captain), Ralph Backstrom, Dick Duff, Claude Larose, Yvan Cournoyer, Claude Provost, Bobby Rousseau, Henri Richard, Dave Balon, John Ferguson, Red Berenson, Jimmy Roberts, Toe Blake (Coach), Sam Pollock (general manager), Larry Aubut, Andy Galley (Trainers).
Scores: April 17, at Montreal — Montreal 3, Chicago 2; April 20, at Montreal — Montreal 2, Chicago 0; April 22, at Chicago — Montreal 1, Chicago 3; April 25, at Chicago — Montreal 1, Chicago 5; April 7, at Montreal — Montreal 6, Chicago 0; April 29, at Chicago — Montreal 1, Chicago 2; May 1, at Montreal — Montreal 4, Chicago 0.

1963-64 — Toronto Maple Leafs — Johnny Bower, Don Simmons, Carl Brewer, Tim Horton, Bob Baun, Allan Stanley, Larry Hillman, Al Arbour, Red Kelly, Gerry Ehman, Andy Bathgate, George Armstrong (Captain), Ron Stewart, Dave Keon, Billy Harris, Don McKenney, Jim Pappin, Bob Pulford, Eddie Shack, Frank Mahovlich, Ed Litzenberger, Punch Imlach (Manager-Coach), Bob Haggart (Trainer).
Scores April 11, at Toronto — Toronto 3, Detroit 2; April 14, at Toronto — Toronto 4; April 16, at Detroit — Toronto 3, Detroit 4; April 18, at Detroit — Toronto 4, Detroit 2; April 21, at Toronto — Toronto 1, Detroit 2; April 23, at Detroit — Toronto 4, Detroit 3; April 25, at Toronto — Toronto 4, Detroit 0.

1962-63 — Toronto Maple Leafs — Johnny Bower, Don Simmons, Carl Brewer, Tim Horton, Kent Douglas, Allan Stanley, Bob Baun, Larry Hillman, Red Kelly, Dick Duff, George Armstrong (Captain), Bob Nevin, Ron Stewart, Dave Keon, Billy Harris, Bob Pulford, Eddie Shack, Ed Litzenberger, Frank Mahovlich, John MacMillan, Punch Imlach (Manager-Coach), Bob Haggert (Trainer).
Scores: April 9, at Toronto — Toronto 4, Detroit 2; April 11, at Toronto — Toronto 4, Detroit 2; April 14, at Detroit — Toronto 2, Detroit 3; April 16, at Detroit — Toronto 4, Detroit 2; April 18, at Toronto — Toronto 3, Detroit 1.

1961-62 — Toronto Maple Leafs — Johnny Bower, Don Simmons, Carl Brewer, Tim Horton, Bob Baun, Allan Stanley, Al Arbour, Larry Hillman, Red Kelly, Dick Duff, George Armstrong (Captain), Frank Mahovlich, Bob Nevin, Ron Stewart, Billy Harris, Bert Olmstead, Bob Pulford, Eddie Shack, Dave Keon, Ed Litzenberger, John MacMillan, Punch Imlach (Manager-Coach), Bob Haggert (Trainer).
Scores: April 10, at Toronto — Toronto 4, Chicago 1; April 12, at Toronto — Toronto 3, Chicago 2; April 15, at Chicago — Toronto 0, Chicago 3; April 17, at Chicago — Toronto 1, Chicago 4; April 19, at Toronto —Toronto 8, Chicago 4; April 22, at Chicago — Toronto 2, Chicago 1.

1960-61 — Chicago Black Hawks — Glenn Hall, Al Arbour, Pierre Pilote, Moose Vasko, Jack Evans, Dollard St. Laurent, Reggie Fleming, Tod Sloan, Ron Murphy, Ed Litzenberger (Captain), Bill Hay, Wayne Hillman, Bobby Hull, Ab McDonald, Eric Nesterenko, Kenny Wharram, Earl Balfour, Stan Mikita, Murray Balfour, Chico Maki, Wayne Hicks, Tommy Ivan (Manager), Rudy Pilous (Coach), Nick Garen (Trainer).
Scores: April 6, at Chicago — Chicago 3, Detroit 2; April 8, at Detroit — Detroit 3, Chicago 1; April 10, at Chicago — Chicago 3, Detroit 1; April 12, at Detroit — Detroit 2, Chicago 1; April 14, at Chicago — Chicago 6, Detroit 3; April 16, at Detroit — Chicago 5, Detroit 1.

1959-60 — Montreal Canadiens — Jacques Plante, Charlie Hodge, Doug Harvey, Tom Johnson, Bob Turner, Jean-Guy Talbot, Albert Langlois, Ralph Backstrom, Jean Béliveau, Marcel Bonin, Bernie Geoffrion, Phil Goyette, Bill Hicke, Don Marshall, Ab McDonald, Dickie Moore, André Pronovost, Claude Provost, Henri Richard, Maurice Richard (Captain), Frank Selke (Manager), Toe Blake (Coach), Hector Dubois, Larry Aubut (Trainers).
Scores: April 7, at Montreal — Montreal 4, Toronto 2; April 9, at Montreal — Montreal 2, Toronto 1; April 12, at Toronto — Montreal 5, Toronto 2; April 14, at Toronto — Montreal 4, Toronto 0.

1958-59 — Montreal Canadiens — Jacques Plante, Charlie Hodge, Doug Harvey, Tom Johnson, Bob Turner, Jean-Guy Talbot, Albert Langlois, Bernie Geoffrion, Ralph Backstrom, Bill Hicke, Maurice Richard (Captain), Marcel Bonin, Phil Goyette, Don Marshall, André Pronovost, Jean Béliveau, Ab McDonald, Henri Richard, Frank Selke (Manager), Toe Blake (Coach), Hector Dubois, Larry Aubut (Trainers).
Scores: April 9, at Montreal — Montreal 5, Toronto 3; April 11, at Montreal — Montreal 3, Toronto 1; April 14, at Toronto — Montreal 2, Toronto 3; April 16, at Toronto — Montreal 3, Toronto 2; April 18, at Montreal — Montreal 5, Toronto 3.

1957-58 — Montreal Canadiens — Jacques Plante, Gerry McNeil, Doug Harvey, Tom Johnson, Bob Turner, Dollard St-Laurent, Jean-Guy Talbot, Albert Langlois, Jean Béliveau, Bernie Geoffrion, Maurice Richard (Captain), Dickie Moore, Claude Provost, Floyd Curry, Bert Olmstead, Henri Richard, Marcel Bonin, Phil Goyette, Don Marshall, André Pronovost, Connie Broden, Ab McDonald, Frank Selke (Manager), Toe Blake (Coach), Hector Dubois, Larry Aubut (Trainers).
Scores: April 8, at Montreal —Montreal 2, Boston 1; April 10, at Montreal — Boston 5, Montreal 2; April 13, at Boston — Montreal 3, Boston 0; April 15, at Boston — Boston 3, Montreal 1; April 17, at Montreal — Montreal 3, Boston 2; April 20, at Boston — Montreal 5, Boston 3.

1956-57 — Montreal Canadiens — Jacques Plante, Gerry McNeil, Doug Harvey, Tom Johnson, Bob Turner, Dollard St-Laurent, Jean-Guy Talbot, Jean Béliveau, Bernie Geoffrion, Floyd Curry, Dickie Moore, Maurice Richard (Captain), Claude Provost, Bert Olmstead, Henri Richard, Phil Goyette, Don Marshall, André Pronovost, Connie Broden, Frank Selke (Manager), Toe Blake (Coach), Hector Dubois, Larry Aubut (Trainers).
Scores: April 6, at Montreal — Montreal 5, Boston 1; April 9, at Montreal — Montreal 1, Boston 0; April 11, at Boston — Montreal 4, Boston 2; April 14, at Boston — Boston 2, Montreal 0; April 16, at Montreal — Montreal 5, Boston 1.

1955-56 — Montreal Canadiens — Jacques Plante, Doug Harvey, Butch Bouchard (Captain), Bob Turner, Tom Johnson, Jean-Guy Talbot, Dollard St-Laurent, Jean Béliveau, Bernie Geoffrion, Bert Olmstead, Floyd Curry, Jackie Leclair, Maurice Richard, Dickie Moore, Henri Richard, Ken Mosdell, Don Marshall, Claude Provost, Frank Selke (Manager), Toe Blake (Coach), Hector Dubois (Trainer).
Scores: March 31, at Montreal — Montreal 6, Detroit 4; April 3, at Montreal — Montreal 5, Detroit 1; April 5, at Detroit — Detroit 3, Montreal 1; April 8, at Detroit — Montreal 3, Detroit 0; April 10, at Montreal — Montreal 3, Detroit 1.

1954-55 — Detroit Red Wings — Terry Sawchuk, Red Kelly, Bob Goldham, Marcel Pronovost, Benny Woit, Jim Hay, Larry Hillman, Ted Lindsay (Captain), Tony Leswick, Gordie Howe, Alex Delvecchio, Marty Pavelich, Glen Skov, Earl Reibel, Johnny Wilson, Bill Dineen, Vic Stasiuk, Marcel Bonin, Jack Adams (Manager), Jimmy Skinner (Coach), Carl Mattson (Trainer).
Scores: April 3, at Detroit — Detroit 4, Montreal 2; April 5, at Detroit — Detroit 7, Montreal 1, April 7, at Montreal — Montreal 4, Detroit 2; April 9, at Montreal — Montreal 5, Detroit 3; April 10, at Detroit — Detroit 5, Montreal 1; April 12, at Montreal — Montreal 6, Detroit 3; April 14, at Detroit — Detroit 3, Montreal 1.

1953-54 — Detroit Red Wings — Terry Sawchuk, Red Kelly, Bob Goldham, Benny Woit, Marcel Pronovost, Al Arbour, Keith Allen, Ted Lindsay (Captain), Tony Leswick, Gordie Howe, Marty Pavelich, Alex Delvecchio, Gilles Dube, Glen Skov, Johnny Wilson, Bill Dineen, Jimmy Peters, Earl Reibel, Vic Stasiuk, Jack Adams (Manager), Tommy Ivan (Coach), Carl Mattson (Trainer).
Scores: April 4, at Detroit — Detroit 3, Montreal 1; April 6, at Detroit — Montreal 3, Detroit 1; April 8, at Montreal — Montreal 5, Detroit 2; April 10, at Montreal — Detroit 2, Montreal 0; April 11, at Detroit — Montreal 1, Detroit 0; April 13, at Montreal — Montreal 4, Detroit 1; April 16, at Detroit — Detroit 2, Montreal 1.

1952-53 — Montreal Canadiens — Gerry McNeil, Jacques Plante, Doug Harvey, Butch Bouchard (Captain), Tom Johnson, Dollard St. Laurent, Bud MacPherson, Maurice Richard, Elmer Lach, Paul Meger, Bert Olmstead, Floyd Curry, Paul Masnick, Billy Reay, Dickie Moore, Ken Mosdell, Dick Gamble, John McCormack, Lorne Davis, Calum MacKay, Eddie Mazur, Frank Selke (Manager), Dick Irvin (Coach), Hector Dubois (Trainer).
Scores: April 9, at Montreal — Montreal 4, Boston 2; April 11, at Montreal — Boston 4, Montreal 1; April 12, at Boston — Montreal 3, Boston 0; April 14, at Boston — Montreal 7, Boston 3; April 16, at Montreal — Montreal 1, Boston 0.

1951-52 — Detroit Red Wings — Terry Sawchuk, Bob Goldham, Benny Woit, Red Kelly, Leo Reise Jr., Marcel Pronovost, Ted Lindsay, Tony Leswick, Gordie Howe, Metro Prystai, Marty Pavelich, Sid Abel (Captain), Glen Skov, Alex Delvecchio, John Wilson, Vic Stasiuk, Larry Zeidel, Jack Adams (Manager) Tommy Ivan (Coach), Carl Mattson (Trainer).
Scores: April 10, at Montreal — Detroit 3, Montreal 1; April 12, at Montreal — Detroit 2, Montreal 1; April 13, at Detroit — Detroit 3, Montreal 0; April 15, at Detroit — Detroit 3, Montreal 0.

1950-51 — Toronto Maple Leafs — Turk Broda, Al Rollins, Jimmy Thomson, Gus Mortson, Bill Barilko, Bill Juzda, Fern Flaman, Hugh Bolton, Ted Kennedy (Captain), Sid Smith, Tod Sloan, Cal Gardner, Howie Meeker, Harry Watson, Max Bentley, Joe Klukay, Danny Lewicki, Ray Timgren, Fleming Mackell, John McCormack, Bob Hassard, Conn Smythe (Manager), Joe Primeau (Coach), Tim Daly (Trainer).
Scores: April 11, at Toronto — Toronto 3, Montreal 2; April 14, at Toronto — Montreal 3, Toronto 2; April 17, at Montreal — Toronto 2, Montreal 1; April 19, at Montreal — Toronto 3, Montreal 2; April 21, at Toronto — Toronto 3, Montreal 2.

1949-50 — Detroit Red Wings — Harry Lumley, Jack Stewart, Leo Reise Jr., Clare Martin, Doug McKay, Al Dewsbury, Lee Fogolin, Marcel Pronovost, Red Kelly, Gord Haidy, Ted Lindsay, Sid Abel (Captain), Gordie Howe, George Gee, Jimmy Peters, Marty Pavelich, Jim McFadden, Pete Babando, Max McNab, Gerry Couture, Joe Carveth, Steve Black, Johnny Wilson, Larry Wilson, Jack Adams (Manager), Tommy Ivan (Coach), Carl Mattson (Trainer).
Scores: April 11, at Detroit — Detroit 4, NY Rangers 1; April 13, at Toronto* — NY Rangers 3, Detroit 1; April 15, at Toronto — Detroit 4, NY Rangers 0; April 18, at Detroit — NY Rangers 4, Detroit 3; April 20, at Detroit — NY Rangers 2, Detroit 1; April 22, at Detroit — Detroit 5, NY Rangers 4; April 23, at Detroit — Detroit 4, NY Rangers 3.

* Ice was unavailable in Madison Square Garden and Rangers elected to play second and third games on Toronto ice.

The Canadiens celebrate their 1966 Stanley Cup championship in the visiting dressing room at the Detroit Olympia after beating the Red Wings in overtime in the sixth game of the Finals.

1948-49 — Toronto Maple Leafs — Turk Broda, Jimmy Thomson, Gus Mortson, Bill Barilko, Garth Boesch, Bill Juzda, Ted Kennedy (Captain), Howie Meeker, Vic Lynn, Harry Watson, Bill Ezinicki, Cal Gardner, Max Bentley, Joe Klukay, Sid Smith, Don Metz, Ray Timgren, Fleming Mackell, Harry Taylor, Bob Dawes, Tod Sloan, Conn Smythe (Manager), Hap Day (Coach), Tim Daly (Trainer).
Scores: April 8, at Detroit — Toronto 3, Detroit 2; April 10, at Detroit — Toronto 3, Detroit 1; April 13, at Toronto — Toronto 3, Detroit 1; April 16, at Toronto — Toronto 3, Detroit 1.

1947-48 — Toronto Maple Leafs — Turk Broda, Jimmy Thomson, Wally Stanowski, Garth Boesch, Bill Barilko, Gus Mortson, Phil Samis, Syl Apps (Captain), Bill Ezinicki, Harry Watson, Ted Kennedy, Howie Meeker, Vic Lynn, Nick Metz, Max Bentley, Joe Klukay, Les Costello, Don Metz, Sid Smith, Conn Smythe (Manager), Hap Day (Coach), Tim Daly (Trainer).
Scores: April 7, at Toronto — Toronto 5, Detroit 3; April 10, at Toronto — Toronto 4, Detroit 2; April 11, at Detroit — Toronto 2, Detroit 0; April 14, at Detroit — Toronto 7, Detroit 2.

1946-47 — Toronto Maple Leafs — Turk Broda, Garth Boesch, Gus Mortson, Jimmy Thomson, Wally Stanowski, Bill Barilko, Harry Watson, Bud Poile, Ted Kennedy, Syl Apps (Captain), Don Metz, Nick Metz, Bill Ezinicki, Vic Lynn, Howie Meeker, Gaye Stewart, Joe Klukay, Gus Bodnar, Bob Goldham, Conn Smythe (Manager), Hap Day (Coach), Tim Daly (Trainer).
Scores: April 8, at Montreal — Montreal 6, Toronto 0; April 10, at Montreal — Toronto 4, Montreal 0; April 12, at Toronto — Toronto 4, Montreal 2; April 15, at Toronto — Toronto 2, Montreal 1; April 17, at Montreal — Montreal 3, Toronto 1; April 19, at Toronto — Toronto 2, Montreal 1.

1945-46 — Montreal Canadiens — Elmer Lach, Toe Blake (Captain), Maurice Richard, Bob Fillion, Dutch Hiller, Murph Chamberlain, Ken Mosdell, Buddy O'Connor, Glen Harmon, Jimmy Peters, Butch Bouchard, Billy Reay, Ken Reardon, Leo Lamoureux, Frank Eddolls, Gerry Plamondon, Bill Durnan, Tommy Gorman (Manager), Dick Irvin (Coach), Ernie Cook (Trainer).
Scores: March 30, at Montreal — Montreal 4, Boston 3; April 2, at Montreal — Montreal 3, Boston 2; April 4, at Boston — Montreal 4, Boston 2; April 7, at Boston — Boston 3, Montreal 2; April 9, at Montreal — Montreal 6, Boston 3.

1944-45 — Toronto Maple Leafs — Don Metz, Frank McCool, Wally Stanowski, Reg Hamilton, Moe Morris, John McCreedy, Tom O'Neill, Ted Kennedy, Babe Pratt, Gus Bodnar, Art Jackson, Jack McLean, Mel Hill, Nick Metz, Bob Davidson (Captain), Sweeney Schriner, Lorne Carr, Conn Smythe (Manager), Frank Selke (Business Manager), Hap Day (Coach), Tim Daly (Trainer).
Scores: April 6, at Detroit — Toronto 1, Detroit 0; April 8, at Detroit — Toronto 2, Detroit 0; April 12, at Toronto — Toronto 1, Detroit 0; April 14, at Toronto — Detroit 5, Toronto 3; April 19, at Detroit — Detroit 2, Toronto 0; April 21, at Toronto — Detroit 1, Toronto 0; April 22, at Detroit — Toronto 2, Detroit 1.

1943-44 — Montreal Canadiens — Toe Blake (Captain), Maurice Richard, Elmer Lach, Ray Getliffe, Murph Chamberlain, Phil Watson, Butch Bouchard, Glen Harmon, Buddy O'Connor, Gerry Heffernan, Mike McMahon, Leo Lamoureux, Fern Majeau, Bob Fillion, Bill Durnan, Tommy Gorman (Manager), Dick Irvin (Coach), Ernie Cook (Trainer).
Scores: April 4, at Montreal — Montreal 5, Chicago 1; April 6, at Chicago — Montreal 3, Chicago 1; April 9, at Chicago — Montreal 3, Chicago 2; April 13, at Montreal — Montreal 5, Chicago 4.

1942-43 — Detroit Red Wings — Jack Stewart, Jimmy Orlando, Sid Abel (Captain), Alex Motter, Harry Watson, Joe Carveth, Mud Bruneteau, Eddie Wares, Johnny Mowers, Cully Simon, Don Grosso, Carl Liscombe, Connie Brown, Syd Howe, Les Douglas, Harold Jackson, Joe Fisher, Jack Adams (Manager), Ebbie Goodfellow (Playing Coach), Honey Walker (Trainer).
Scores: April 1, at Detroit — Detroit 6, Boston 2; April 4, at Detroit — Detroit 4, Boston 3; April 7, at Boston — Detroit 4, Boston 0; April 8, at Boston — Detroit 2, Boston 0.

1941-42 — Toronto Maple Leafs — Wally Stanowski, Syl Apps (Captain), Bob Goldham, Gordie Drillon, Hank Goldup, Ernie Dickens, Sweeney Schriner, Bucko McDonald, Bob Davidson, Nick Metz, Bingo Kampman, Don Metz, Gaye Stewart, Turk Broda, John McCreedy, Lorne Carr, Pete Langelle, Billy Taylor, Conn Smythe (Manager), Hap Day (Coach), Frank Selke (Business Manager), Tim Daly (Trainer).
Scores: April 4, at Toronto — Detroit 3, Toronto 2; April 7, at Toronto — Detroit 4, Toronto 2; April 9, at Detroit — Detroit 5, Toronto 2; April 12, at Detroit — Toronto 4, Detroit 3; April 14, at Toronto — Toronto 9, Detroit 3; April 16, at Detroit — Toronto 3, Detroit 0; April 18, at Toronto — Toronto 3, Detroit 1.

1940-41 — Boston Bruins — Bill Cowley, Des Smith, Dit Clapper (Captain), Frank Brimsek, Flash Hollett, Jack Crawford, Bobby Bauer, Pat McReavy, Herb Cain, Mel Hill, Milt Schmidt, Woody Dumart, Roy Conacher, Terry Reardon, Art Jackson, Eddie Wiseman, Art Ross (Manager), Cooney Weiland (Coach), Win Green (Trainer).
Scores: April 6, at Boston — Detroit 2, Boston 3; April 8, at Boston — Detroit 1, Boston 2; April 10, at Detroit — Boston 4, Detroit 2; April 12, at Detroit — Boston 3, Detroit 1.

1939-40 — New York Rangers — Dave Kerr, Art Coulter (Captain), Ott Heller, Alex Shibicky, Mac Colville, Neil Colville, Phil Watson, Lynn Patrick, Clint Smith, Muzz Patrick, Babe Pratt, Bryan Hextall, Kilby MacDonald, Dutch Hiller, Alf Pike, Stan Smith, Lester Patrick (Manager), Frank Boucher (Coach), Harry Westerby (Trainer).
Scores: April 2, at New York — NY Rangers 2, Toronto 1; April 3, at New York — NY Rangers 6, Toronto 2; April 6, at Toronto — NY Rangers 1, Toronto 2; April 9, at Toronto — NY Rangers 0, Toronto 3; April 11, at Toronto — NY Rangers 2, Toronto 1; April 13, at Toronto — NY Rangers 3, Toronto 2.

1938-39 — Boston Bruins — Bobby Bauer, Mel Hill, Flash Hollett, Roy Conacher, Gord Pettinger, Charlie Sands, Milt Schmidt, Woody Dumart, Jack Crawford, Ray Getliffe, Frank Brimsek, Eddie Shore, Dit Clapper, Bill Cowley, Jack Portland, Red Hamill, Cooney Weiland (Captain), Art Ross (Manager-Coach), Win Green (Trainer).
Scores: April 6, at Boston — Toronto 1, Boston 2; April 9, at Boston — Toronto 3, Boston 2; April 11, at Toronto — Toronto 1, Boston 3; April 13, at Toronto — Toronto 0, Boston 2; April 16, at Boston — Toronto 1, Boston 3.

1937-38 — Chicago Black Hawks — Art Wiebe, Carl Voss, Harold Jackson, Mike Karakas, Mush March, Jack Shill, Earl Seibert, Cully Dahlstrom, Alex Levinsky, Johnny Gottselig (Captain), Lou Trudel, Pete Palangio, Bill MacKenzie, Doc Romnes, Paul Thompson, Roger Jenkins, Alfie Moore, Bert Connelly, Virgil Johnson, Paul Goodman, Bill Stewart (Manager-Coach), Eddie Froelich (Trainer).
Scores: April 5, at Toronto — Chicago 3, Toronto 1; April 7, at Toronto — Chicago 1, Toronto 5; April 10, at Chicago — Chicago 2, Toronto 1; April 12, at Chicago — Chicago 4, Toronto 1.

1936-37 — Detroit Red Wings — Normie Smith, Pete Kelly, Larry Aurie, Herbie Lewis, Hec Kilrea, Mud Bruneteau, Syd Howe, Wally Kilrea, Jimmy Franks, Bucko McDonald, Gord Pettinger, Ebbie Goodfellow, John Gallagher, Ralph Bowman, John Sorrell, Marty Barry, Earl Robertson, John Sherf, Howie Mackie, Rolly Roulston, Doug Young (Captain), Jack Adams (Manager-Coach), Honey Walker (Trainer).
Scores: April 6, at New York — Detroit 1, NY Rangers 5; April 8, at Detroit — Detroit 4, NY Rangers 2; April 11, at Detroit — Detroit 0, NY Rangers 1; April 13, at Detroit — Detroit 1, NY Rangers 0; April 15, at Detroit — Detroit 3, NY Rangers 0.

1935-36 — Detroit Red Wings — John Sorrell, Syd Howe, Marty Barry, Herbie Lewis, Mud Bruneteau, Wally Kilrea, Hec Kilrea, Gord Pettinger, Bucko McDonald, Ralph Bowman, Pete Kelly, Doug Young (Captain), Ebbie Goodfellow, Normie Smith, Larry Aurie, Jack Adams (Manager-Coach), Honey Walker (Trainer).
Scores: April 5, at Detroit — Detroit 3, Toronto 1; April 7, at Detroit — Detroit 9, Toronto 4; April 9, at Toronto — Detroit 3, Toronto 4; April 11, at Toronto — Detroit 3, Toronto 2.

1934-35 — Montreal Maroons — Lionel Conacher, Cy Wentworth, Alex Connell, Toe Blake, Stewart Evans, Earl Robinson, Bill Miller, Dave Trottier, Jimmy Ward, Baldy Northcott, Hooley Smith, Russ Blinco, Al Shields, Sammy McManus, Gus Marker, Bob Gracie, Herb Cain, Tommy Gorman (Manager-Coach), Bill O'Brien (Trainer).
Scores: April 4, at Toronto — Mtl. Maroons 3, Toronto 2; April 6, at Toronto — Mtl. Maroons 3, Toronto 1; April 9, at Montreal — Mtl. Maroons 4, Toronto 1.

1933-34 — Chicago Black Hawks — Clarence Abel, Rosie Couture, Lou Trudel, Lionel Conacher, Paul Thompson, Leroy Goldsworthy, Art Coulter, Roger Jenkins, Don McFadyen, Tom Cook, Doc Romnes, Johnny Gottselig, Mush March, Johnny Sheppard, Charlie Gardiner (Captain), Bill Kendall, Tommy Gorman (Manager-Coach), Eddie Froelich (Trainer).
Scores: April 3, at Detroit — Chicago 2, Detroit 1; April 5, at Detroit — Chicago 4, Detroit 1; April 8, at Chicago — Detroit 5, Chicago 2; April 10, at Chicago — Chicago 1, Detroit 0.

1932-33 — New York Rangers — Ching Johnson, Butch Keeling, Frank Boucher, Art Somers, Babe Siebert, Bun Cook, Andy Aitkenhead, Ott Heller, Oscar Asmundson, Gord Pettinger, Doug Brennan, Cecil Dillon, Bill Cook (Captain), Murray Murdoch, Earl Seibert, Lester Patrick (Manager-Coach), Harry Westerby (Trainer).
Scores: April 4, at New York — NY Rangers 5, Toronto 1; April 8, at Toronto — NY Rangers 3, Toronto 1; April 11, at Toronto — Toronto 3, NY Rangers 2; April 13, at Toronto — NY Rangers 1, Toronto 0.

1931-32 — Toronto Maple Leafs — Charlie Conacher, Busher Jackson, King Clancy, Andy Blair, Red Horner, Lorne Chabot, Alex Levinsky, Joe Primeau, Harold Darragh, Baldy Cotton, Frank Finnigan, Hap Day (Captain), Ace Bailey, Bob Gracie, Fred Robertson, Earl Miller, Conn Smythe (Manager), Dick Irvin (Coach), Tim Daly (Trainer).
Scores: April 5, at New York — Toronto 6, NY Rangers 4; April 7, at Boston* — Toronto 6, NY Rangers 2; April 9, at Toronto — Toronto 6, NY Rangers 4.

* Ice was unavailable in Madison Square Garden and Rangers elected to play the second game on neutral ice.

1930-31 — Montreal Canadiens — George Hainsworth, Wildor Larochelle, Marty Burke, Sylvio Mantha (Captain), Howie Morenz, Johnny Gagnon, Aurel Joliat, Armand Mondou, Pit Lepine, Albert Leduc, Georges Mantha, Art Lesieur, Nick Wasnie, Bert McCaffrey, Gus Rivers, Jean Pusie, Léo Dandurand (Manager), Cecil Hart (Coach), Ed Dufour (Trainer).
Scores: April 3, at Chicago — Montreal 2, Chicago 1; April 5, at Chicago — Chicago 2, Montreal 1; April 9, at Montreal — Chicago 3, Montreal 2; April 11, at Montreal — Montreal 4, Chicago 2; April 14, at Montreal — Montreal 2, Chicago 0.

1929-30 — Montreal Canadiens — George Hainsworth, Marty Burke, Sylvio Mantha (Captain), Howie Morenz, Bert McCaffrey, Aurel Joliat, Albert Leduc, Pit Lepine, Wildor Larochelle, Nick Wasnie, Gerry Carson, Armand Mondou, Georges Mantha, Gus Rivers, Léo Dandurand (Manager), Cecil Hart (Coach), Ed Dufour (Trainer).
Scores: April 1, at Boston — Montreal 3, Boston 0; April 3, at Montreal — Montreal 4, Boston 3.

1928-29 — Boston Bruins — Tiny Thompson, Eddie Shore, Lionel Hitchman (Captain), Percy Galbraith, Mickey Mackay, Red Green, Dutch Gainor, Harry Oliver, Eddie Rodden, Dit Clapper, Cooney Weiland, Lloyd Klein, Cy Denneny (Playing Coach), Bill Carson, George Owen, Myles Lane, Art Ross (Manager), Win Green (Trainer).
Scores: March 28, at Boston — Boston 2, NY Rangers 0; March 29, at New York — Boston 2, NY Rangers 1.

1927-28 — New York Rangers — Lorne Chabot, Clarence Abel, Leo Bourgeault, Ching Johnson, Bill Cook (Captain), Bun Cook, Frank Boucher, Bill Boyd, Murray Murdoch, Paul Thompson, Alex Gray, Joe Miller, Patsy Callighen, Lester Patrick (Manager-Coach), Harry Westerby (Trainer).
Scores: April 5, at Montreal — Mtl. Maroons 2, NY Rangers 0; April 7, at Montreal — NY Rangers 2, Mtl. Maroons 1; April 10, at Montreal — Mtl. Maroons 2, NY Rangers 0; April 12, at Montreal — NY Rangers 1, Mtl. Maroons 0; April 14, at Montreal — NY Rangers 2, Mtl. Maroons 1.

1926-27 — Ottawa Senators — Alex Connell, King Clancy, Georges Boucher, Ed Gorman, Frank Finnigan, Alex Smith, Hec Kilrea, Hooley Smith, Cy Denneny, Frank Nighbor, Jack Adams, Milt Halliday, Dave Gill (Manager-Coach).
Scores: April 7, at Boston — Ottawa 0, Boston 0; April 9, at Boston — Ottawa 3, Boston 1; April 11, at Ottawa — Boston 1, Ottawa 1; April 13, at Ottawa — Ottawa 3, Boston 1.

1925-26 — Montreal Maroons — Clint Benedict, Reg Noble, Frank Carson, Dunc Munro, Nels Stewart, Punch Broadbent, Babe Siebert, Chuck Dinsmore, Merlyn Phillips, Hobie Kitchen, Sam Rothschild, Albert Holway, George Horne, Bernie Brophy, Eddie Gerard (Manager-Coach), Bill O'Brien (Trainer).
Scores: March 30, at Montreal — Mtl. Maroons 3, Victoria 0; April 1, at Montreal — Mtl. Maroons 3, Victoria 0; April 3, at Montreal — Victoria 3, Mtl. Maroons 2; April 6, at Montreal — Mtl. Maroons 2, Victoria 0.

The series in the spring of 1926 ended the annual playoffs between the champions of the East and the champions of the West. Since 1926-27 the annual playoffs in the National Hockey League have decided the Stanley Cup champions.

1924-25 — Victoria Cougars — Hap Holmes, Clem Loughlin, Gord Fraser, Frank Fredrickson, Jack Walker, Gizzy Hart, Harold Halderson, Frank Foyston, Wally Elmer, Harry Meeking, Jocko Anderson, Lester Patrick (Manager-Coach).
Scores: March 21, at Victoria — Victoria 5, Montreal 2; March 23, at Vancouver — Victoria 3, Montreal 1; March 27, at Victoria — Montreal 4, Victoria 2; March 30, at Victoria — Victoria 6, Montreal 1.

WESTERN CHAMPIONS 1924-25

WORLD CHAMPIONS 1924-25

HARRY MEEKING · HAROLD HART · "HAPPY" HOLMES · CLEM LOUGHLIN CAPT. · FRANK TREDRICKSON · "SLIM" HALDERSON · "JOCKO" ANDERSON

GORDON FRASER · FRANK FOYSTON · MANAGER LESTER PATRICK · JACK WALKER · WALLY ELMER

VICTORIA COUGARS

W.C.H.L. CUP

STANLEY CUP

The 1925 Victoria Cougars of the Western Canada Hockey League are the last non-NHL team to win the Stanley Cup. Victoria lost the Cup to the Montreal Maroons in 1926. Stanley Cup competition has been exclusive to the NHL since 1927.

1923-24 — Montreal Canadiens — Georges Vezina, Sprague Cleghorn (Captain), Billy Coutu, Howie Morenz, Aurel Joliat, Billy Boucher, Odie Cleghorn, Sylvio Mantha, Bobby Boucher, Billy Bell, Billy Cameron, Joe Malone, Charles Fortier, Leo Dandurand (Manager-Coach).
Scores: March 18, at Montreal — Montreal 3, Van. Maroons 2; March 20, at Montreal — Montreal 2, Van. Maroons 1. March 22, at Montreal — Montreal 6, Cgy. Tigers 1; March 25, at Ottawa* — Montreal 3, Cgy. Tigers 0.
* Game transferred to Ottawa to benefit from artificial ice surface.

1922-23 — Ottawa Senators — Georges Boucher, Lionel Hitchman, Frank Nighbor, King Clancy, Harry Helman, Clint Benedict, Jack Darragh, Eddie Gerard, Cy Denneny, Punch Broadbent, Tommy Gorman (Manager), Pete Green (Coach), F. Dolan (Trainer).
Scores: March 16, at Vancouver — Ottawa 1, Van. Maroons 0; March 19, at Vancouver — Van. Maroons 4, Ottawa 1; March 23, at Vancouver — Ottawa 3, Van. Maroons 2; March 26, at Vancouver — Ottawa 5, Van. Maroons 1; March 29, at Vancouver — Ottawa 2, Edm. Eskimos 1; March 31, at Vancouver — Ottawa 1, Edm. Eskimos 0.

1921-22 — Toronto St. Pats — Ted Stackhouse, Corb Denneny, Rod Smylie, Lloyd Andrews, John Ross Roach, Harry Cameron, Billy Stuart, Babe Dye, Ken Randall, Reg Noble, Eddie Gerard (borrowed for one game from Ottawa), Stan Jackson, Ivan Mitchell, Charlie Querrie (Manager), George O'Donoghue (Coach).
Scores: March 17, at Toronto — Van. Millionaires 4, Toronto 3; March 20, at Toronto — Toronto 2, Van. Millionaires 1; March 23, at Toronto — Van. Millionaires 3, Toronto 0; March 25, at Toronto — Toronto 6, Van. Millionaires 0; March 28, at Toronto — Toronto 5, Van. Millionaires 1.

1920-21 — Ottawa Senators — Jack MacKell, Jack Darragh, Morley Bruce, Georges Boucher, Eddie Gerard, Clint Benedict, Sprague Cleghorn, Frank Nighbor, Punch Broadbent, Cy Denneny, Leth Graham, Tommy Gorman (Manager), Pete Green (Coach), F. Dolan (Trainer).
Scores: March 21, at Vancouver — Van. Millionaires 2, Ottawa 1; March 24, at Vancouver — Ottawa 4, Van. Millionaires 3; March 28, at Vancouver — Ottawa 3, Van. Millionaires 2; March 31, at Vancouver — Van. Millionaires 3, Ottawa 2; April 4, at Vancouver — Ottawa 2, Van. Millionaires 1

1919-20 — Ottawa Senators — Jack MacKell, Jack Darragh, Morley Bruce, Horrace Merrill, Georges Boucher, Eddie Gerard, Clint Benedict, Sprague Cleghorn, Frank Nighbor, Punch Broadbent, Cy Denneny, Tommy Gorman (Manager), Pete Green (Coach).
Scores: March 22, at Ottawa — Ottawa 3, Seattle 2; March 24, at Ottawa — Ottawa 3, Seattle 0; March 27, at Ottawa — Seattle 3, Ottawa 1; March 30, at Toronto* — Seattle 5, Ottawa 2; April 1, at Toronto* — Ottawa 6, Seattle 1.
* Games transferred to Toronto to benefit from artificial ice surface.

1918-19 — No decision, Series halted by Spanish influenza epidemic, illness of several players and death of Joe Hall of Montreal Canadiens from flu. Five games had been played when the series was halted, each team having won two and tied one. The results are shown:
Scores: March 19, at Seattle — Seattle 7, Montreal 0; March 22, at Seattle — Montreal 4, Seattle 2; March 24, at Seattle — Seattle 7, Montreal 2; March 26, at Seattle — Montreal 0, Seattle 0; March 30, at Seattle — Montreal 4, Seattle 3.

1917-18 — Toronto Arenas — Rusty Crawford, Harry Meeking, Ken Randall, Corb Denneny, Harry Cameron, Jack Adams, Alf Skinner, Harry Mummery, Hap Holmes, Reg Noble, Sammy Hebert, Jack Marks, Jack Coughlin, Charlie Querrie (Manager), Dick Carroll (Coach), Frank Carroll (Trainer).
Scores: March 20, at Toronto — Toronto 5, Van. Millionaires 3; March 23, at Toronto — Van. Millionaires 6, Toronto 4; March 26, at Toronto — Toronto 6, Van. Millionaires 3; March 28, at Toronto — Van. Millionaires 8, Toronto 1; March 30, at Toronto — Toronto 2, Van. Millionaires 1.

1916-17 — Seattle Metropolitans — Hap Holmes, Ed Carpenter, Cully Wilson, Jack Walker, Bernie Morris, Frank Foyston, Roy Rickey, Jim Riley, Bobby Rowe (Captain), Peter Muldoon (Manager).
Scores: March 17, at Seattle — Montreal 8, Seattle 4; March 20, at Seattle — Seattle 6, Montreal 1; March 23, at Seattle — Seattle 4, Montreal 1; March 25, at Seattle — Seattle 9, Montreal 1.

1915-16 — Montreal Canadiens — Georges Vezina, Bert Corbeau, Jack Laviolette, Newsy Lalonde, Louis Berlinquette, Goldie Prodgers, Howard McNamara (Captain), Didier Pitre, Skene Ronan, Amos Arbour, Skinner Poulin, Jack Fournier, George Kennedy (Manager).
Scores: March 20, at Montreal — Portland 2, Montreal 0; March 22, at Montreal — Montreal 2, Portland 1; March 25, at Montreal — Montreal 6, Portland 3; March 28, at Montreal — Portland 6, Montreal 5; March 30, at Montreal — Montreal 2, Portland 1.

1914-15 — Vancouver Millionaires — Ken Mallen, Frank Nighbor, Cyclone Taylor, Hugh Lehman, Lloyd Cook, Mickey Mackay, Barney Stanley, Jim Seaborn, Si Griffis (Captain), Johnny Matz, Frank Patrick (Playing Manager).
Scores: March 22, at Vancouver — Van. Millionaires 6, Ottawa 2; March 24, at Vancouver — Van. Millionaires 8, Ottawa 3; March 26, at Vancouver — Van. Millionaires 12, Ottawa 3.

1913-14 — Toronto Blueshirts — Con Corbeau, Roy McGiffen, Jack Walker, George McNamara, Cully Wilson, Frank Foyston, Harry Cameron, Hap Holmes, Scotty Davidson (Captain), Harriston, Jack Marshall (Playing Manager), Frank and Dick Carroll (Trainers).
Scores: March 14, at Toronto — Toronto 5, Victoria 2; March 17, at Toronto — Toronto 6, Victoria 5; March 19, at Toronto — Toronto 2, Victoria 1.

1912-13 — Quebec Bulldogs — Joe Malone, Joe Hall, Paddy Moran, Harry Mummery, Tommy Smith, Jack Marks, Rusty Crawford, Billy Creighton, Jeff Malone, Rocket Power, M.J. Quinn (Manager), D. Beland (Trainer).
Scores: March 8, at Quebec — Que. Bulldogs 14, Sydney 3; March 10, at Quebec — Que. Bulldogs 6, Sydney 2.

Victoria challenged Quebec but the Bulldogs refused to put the Stanley Cup in competition so the two teams played an exhibition series with Victoria winning two games to one by scores of 7-5, 3-6, 6-1. It was the first meeting between the Eastern champions and the Western champions. The following year, and until the Western Hockey League disbanded after the 1926 playoffs, the Cup went to the winner of the series between East and West.

1911-12 — Quebec Bulldogs — Goldie Prodgers, Joe Hall, Walter Rooney, Paddy Moran, Jack Marks, Jack McDonald, Eddie Oatman, George Leonard, Joe Malone (Captain), C. Nolan (Coach), M.J. Quinn (Manager), D. Beland (Trainer).
Scores: March 11, at Quebec — Que. Bulldogs 9, Moncton 3; March 13, at Quebec — Que. Bulldogs 8, Moncton 0.

Prior to 1912, teams could challenge the Stanley Cup champions for the title, thus there was more than one Championship Series played in most of the seasons between 1894 and 1911.

1910-11 — Ottawa Senators — Hamby Shore, Percy LeSueur, Jack Darragh, Bruce Stuart, Marty Walsh, Bruce Ridpath, Fred Lake, Dubbie Kerr, Alex Currie, Horace Gaul.
Scores: March 13, at Ottawa — Ottawa 7, Galt 4; March 16, at Ottawa — Ottawa 13, Port Arthur 4.

1909-10 (March) **— Montreal Wanderers —** Cecil Blachford, Moose Johnson, Ernie Russell, Riley Hern, Harry Hyland, Jack Marshall, Pud Glass (Captain), Jimmy Gardner, Dickie Boon (Manager).
Scores: March 12, at Montreal — Mtl. Wanderers 7, Berlin (Kitchener) 3.

1909-10 (January) **— Ottawa Senators —** Dubbie Kerr, Fred Lake, Percy LeSueur, Ken Mallen, Bruce Ridpath, Gord Roberts, Hamby Shore, Bruce Stuart, Marty Walsh.
Scores: January 5, at Ottawa — Ottawa 12, Galt 3; January 7, at Ottawa — Ottawa 3, Galt 1; January 18, at Ottawa — Ottawa 8, Edmonton 4; January 20, at Ottawa — Ottawa 13, Edmonton 7.

1908-09 — Ottawa Senators — Fred Lake, Percy LeSueur, Cyclone Taylor, Billy Gilmour, Dubbie Kerr, Edgar Dey, Marty Walsh, Bruce Stuart (Captain).
Scores: Ottawa, as champions of the Eastern Canada Hockey Association took over the Stanley Cup in 1909 and, although a challenge was accepted by the Cup trustees from Winnipeg Shamrocks, games could not be arranged because of the lateness of the season. No other challenges were made in 1909. The following season — 1909-10 — however, the Senators accepted two challenges as defending Cup Champions. The first was against Galt in a two-game, total-goals series, and the second against Edmonton, also a two-game, total-goals series. Results: January 5, at Ottawa —Ottawa 12, Galt 3; January 7, at Ottawa — Ottawa 3, Galt 1. January 18, at Ottawa — Ottawa 8, Edm. Eskimos 4; January 20, at Ottawa — Ottawa 13, Edm. Eskimos 7.

1907-08 — Montreal Wanderers — Riley Hern, Art Ross, Walter Smaill, Pud Glass, Bruce Stuart, Ernie Russell, Moose Johnson, Cecil Blachford (Captain), Tom Hooper, Larry Gilmour, Ernie Liffiton, Dickie Boon (Manager).
Scores: Wanderers accepted four challenges for the Cup: January 9, at Montreal — Mtl. Wanderers 9, Ott. Victorias 3; January 13, at Montreal — Mtl. Wanderers 13, Ott. Victorias 1; March 10, at Montreal — Mtl. Wanderers 11, Wpg. Maple Leafs 5; March 12, at Montreal — Mtl. Wanderers 9, Wpg. Maple Leafs 3; March 14, at Montreal — Mtl. Wanderers 6, Toronto (OPHL) 4. At start of following season, 1908-09, Wanderers were challenged by Edmonton. Results: December 28, at Montreal — Mtl. Wanderers 7, Edm. Eskimos 3; December 30, at Montreal — Edm. Eskimos 7, Mtl. Wanderers 6. Total goals: Mtl. Wanderers 13, Edm. Eskimos 10.

1906-07 — (March 25) **— Montreal Wanderers —** Billy Strachan, Riley Hern, Lester Patrick, Hod Stuart, Pud Glass, Ernie Russell, Cecil Blachford (Captain), Moose Johnson, Rod Kennedy, Jack Marshall, Dickie Boon (Manager).

1906-07 — (March 18) **— Kenora Thistles —** Eddie Giroux, Si Griffis, Tom Hooper, Fred Whitcroft, Alf Smith, Harry Westwick, Roxy Beaudro, Tom Phillips (Captain), Russell Phillips.
Scores: March 16, at Winnipeg — Kenora 8, Brandon 6; March 18, at Winnipeg — Kenora 4, Brandon 1; March 23, at Winnipeg — Mtl. Wanderers 7, Kenora 2; March 25, at Winnipeg — Kenora 6, Mtl. Wanderers 5. Total goals: Mtl. Wanderers 12, Kenora 8.

1906-07 — (January) **— Kenora Thistles —** Eddie Giroux, Art Ross, Si Griffis, Tom Hooper, Billy McGimsie, Roxy Beaudro, Tommy Phillips (Captain), Joe Hall, Russell Phillips.
Scores: January 17, at Montreal — Kenora 4, Mtl. Wanderers 2; Jan. 21, at Montreal — Kenora 8, Mtl. Wanderers 6.

1905-06 — (March) **— Montreal Wanderers —** Henri Menard, Billy Strachan, Rod Kennedy, Lester Patrick, Pud Glass, Ernie Russell, Moose Johnson, Cecil Blachford (Captain), Josh Arnold, Dickie Boon (Manager).
Scores: March 14, at Montreal — Mtl. Wanderers 9, Ottawa 1; March 17, at Ottawa — Ottawa 9, Mtl. Wanderers 3. Total goals: Mtl. Wanderers 12, Ottawa 10. Wanderers accepted a challenge from New Glasgow, N.S., prior to the start of the 1906-07 season. Results: December 27, at Montreal — Mtl. Wanderers 10, New Glasgow 3; December 29, at Montreal — Mtl. Wanderers 7, New Glasgow 2.

1905-06 — (February) **— Ottawa Silver Seven —** Harvey Pulford (Captain), Arthur Moore, Harry Westwick, Frank McGee, Alf Smith (Playing Coach), Billy Gilmour, Billy Hague, Percy LeSueur, Harry Smith, Tommy Smith, Dion, Ebbs.
Scores: February 27, at Ottawa — Ottawa 16, Queen's University 7; February 28, at Ottawa — Ottawa 12, Queen's University 7; March 6, at Ottawa — Ottawa 6, Smiths Falls 5; March 8, at Ottawa — Ottawa 8, Smiths Falls 2.

1904-05 — Ottawa Silver Seven — Dave Finnie, Harvey Pulford (Captain), Arthur Moore, Harry Westwick, Frank McGee, Alf Smith (Playing Coach), Billy Gilmour, Frank White, Horace Gaul, Hamby Shore, Bones Allen.
Scores: January 13, at Ottawa — Ottawa 9, Dawson City 2; January 16, at Ottawa — Ottawa 23, Dawson City 2; March 7, at Ottawa — Rat Portage 9, Ottawa 3; March 9, at Ottawa — Ottawa 4, Rat Portage 2; March 11, at Ottawa — Ottawa 5, Rat Portage 4.

1903-04 — Ottawa Silver Seven — Suddy Gilmour, Arthur Moore, Frank McGee, Bouse Hutton, Billy Gilmour, Jim McGee, Harry Westwick, Harvey Pulford (Captain), Scott, Alf Smith (Playing Coach).
Scores: December 30, at Ottawa — Ottawa 9, Wpg. Rowing Club 1; January 1, at Ottawa — Wpg. Rowing Club 6, Ottawa 2; January 4, at Ottawa — Ottawa 2, Wpg. Rowing Club 0. February 23, at Ottawa — Ottawa 6, Tor. Marlboros 3; February 25, at Ottawa — Ottawa 11, Tor. Marlboros 2; March 2, at Montreal — Ottawa 5, Mtl. Wanderers 5. Following the tie game, a new two-game series was ordered to be played in Ottawa but the Wanderers refused unless the tie game was replayed in Montreal. When no settlement could be reached, the series was abandoned and Ottawa retained the Cup and accepted a two-game challenge from Brandon. Results: (both games at Ottawa), March 9, Ottawa 6, Brandon 3; March 11, Ottawa 9, Brandon 3.

1902-03 — (March) **— Ottawa Silver Seven —** Suddy Gilmour, Percy Sims, Bouse Hutton, Dave Gilmour, Billy Gilmour, Harry Westwick, Frank McGee, F.H. Wood, A.A. Fraser, Charles Spittal, Harvey Pulford (Captain), Arthur Moore, Alf Smith (coach.)
Scores: March 7, at Montreal — Ottawa 1, Mtl. Victorias 1; March 10, at Ottawa — Ottawa 8, Mtl. Victorias 0. Total goals: Ottawa 9, Mtl. Victorias 1; March 12, at Ottawa — Ottawa 6, Rat Portage 2; March 14, at Ottawa — Ottawa 4, Rat Portage 2.

1902-03 — (February) **— Montreal AAA —** Tom Hodge, Dickie Boon, Billy Nicholson, Tommy Phillips, Art Hooper, Billy Bellingham, Charles Liffiton, Jack Marshall, Jimmy Gardner, Cecil Blachford, George Smith.
Scores: January 29, at Montreal — Mtl. AAA 8, Wpg. Victorias 1; January 31, at Montreal — Wpg. Victorias 2, Mtl. AAA 2; February 2, at Montreal — Wpg. Victorias 4, Mtl. AAA 2; February 4, at Montreal — Mtl. AAA 5, Wpg. Victorias 1.

1901-02 — (March) **— Montreal AAA —** Tom Hodge, Dickie Boon, Billy Nicholson, Archie Hooper, Billy Bellingham, Charles Liffiton, Jack Marshall, Roland Elliott, Jimmy Gardner.
Scores: March 13, at Winnipeg — Wpg. Victorias 1, Mtl. AAA 0; March 15, at Winnipeg — Mtl. AAA 5, Wpg. Victorias 0; March 17, at Winnipeg — Mtl. AAA 2, Wpg. Victorias 1.

1901-02 — (January) **— Winnipeg Victorias —** Burke Wood, Tony Gingras, Charles Johnstone, Rod Flett, Magnus Flett, Dan Bain (Captain), Fred Scanlon, F. Cadham, G. Brown.
Scores: January 21, at Winnipeg — Wpg. Victorias 5, Tor Wellingtons 3; January 23, at Winnipeg — Wpg. Victorias 5, Tor. Wellingtons 3.

1900-01 — Winnipeg Victorias — Burke Wood, Jack Marshall, Tony Gingras, Charles Johnstone, Rod Flett, Magnus Flett, Dan Bain (Captain), Art Brown.
Scores: January 29, at Montreal — Wpg. Victorias 4, Mtl. Shamrocks 3; January 31, at Montreal — Wpg. Victorias 2, Mtl. Shamrocks 1.

1899-1900 — Montreal Shamrocks — Joe McKenna, Frank Tansey, Frank Wall, Art Farrell, Fred Scanlon, Harry Trihey (Captain), Jack Brannen.
Scores: February 12, at Montreal — Mtl. Shamrocks 4, Wpg. Victorias 3; February 14, at Montreal — Wpg. Victorias 3, Mtl. Shamrocks 2; February 16, at Montreal — Mtl. Shamrocks 5, Wpg. Victorias 4; March 5, at Montreal — Mtl. Shamrocks 10, Halifax 2; March 7, at Montreal — Mtl. Shamrocks 11, Halifax 0.

1898-99 — (March) **— Montreal Shamrocks —** Joe McKenna, Frank Tansey, Frank Wall, Harry Trihey (Captain), Art Farrell, Fred Scanlon, Jack Brannen, John Dobby, Charles Hoerner.
Scores: March 14, at Montreal — Mtl. Shamrocks 6, Queen's University 2.

1898-99 — (February) **— Montreal Victorias —** Gordon Lewis, Mike Grant, Graham Drinkwater, Cam Davidson, Bob McDougall, Ernie McLea, Frank Richardson, Jack Ewing, Russell Bowie, Douglas Acer, Fred McRobie.
Scores: February 15, at Montreal — Mtl. Victorias 2, Wpg. Victorias 1; February 18, at Montreal — Mtl. Victorias 3, Wpg. Victorias 2.

1897-98 — Montreal Victorias — Gordon Lewis, Hartland McDougall, Mike Grant, Graham Drinkwater, Cam Davidson, Bob McDougall, Ernie McLea, Frank Richardson (Captain), Jack Ewing. The Victorias as champions of the Amateur Hockey Association, retained the Cup and were not called upon to defend it.

1896-97 — Montreal Victorias — Gordon Lewis, Harold Henderson, Mike Grant (Captain), Cam Davidson, Graham Drinkwater, Bob McDougall, Ernie McLea, Shirley Davidson, Hartland McDougall, Jack Ewing, Percy Molson, David Gillilan, McLellan.
Scores: December 27, at Montreal — Mtl. Victorias 15, Ott. Capitals 2.

1895-96 — (December) **— Montreal Victorias —** Harold Henderson, Mike Grant (Captain), Bob McDougall, Graham Drinkwater, Shirley Davidson, Ernie McLea, W. Wallace, Robert Jones, Cam Davidson, David Gillilan, Stanley Willett.
Scores: December 30, at Winnipeg — Mtl. Victorias 6, Wpg. Victorias 5.

1895-96 — (February) **— Winnipeg Victorias —** Whitey Merritt, Rod Flett, Fred Higginbotham, Jack Armitage (Captain), Tote Campbell, Dan Bain, Bobby Benson, Attie Howard.
Scores: February 14, at Montreal — Wpg. Victorias 2, Mtl. Victorias 0.

1894-95 — Montreal Victorias — Robert Jones, Harold Henderson, Mike Grant (Captain), Shirley Davidson, Bob McDougall, Norman Rankin, Graham Drinkwater, Roland Elliot, William Pullan, Hartland McDougall, Art Fenwick, A. McDougall. Montreal Victorias, as champions of the Amateur Hockey Association, were prepared to defend the Stanley Cup. However, the Stanley Cup trustees had already accepted a challenge match between the 1894 champion Montreal AAA and Queen's University. It was declared that if Montreal AAA defeated Queen's University, Montreal Victorias would be declared Stanley Cup champions. If Queen's University won, the Cup would go to the university club. In a game played March 9, 1895, Montreal AAA defeated Queen's University 5-1. As a result, Montreal Victorias were awarded the Stanley Cup.

1893-94 — Montreal AAA — Herb Collins, Allan Cameron, George James, Billy Barlow, Clare Mussen, Archie Hodgson, Haviland Routh, Alex Irving, James Stewart, E. O'Brien, A.C. (Toad) Wand, A.B. Kingan.
Scores: March 17, at Mtl. Victorias — Mtl. AAA 3, Mtl. Victorias 2; March 22, at Montreal — Mtl. AAA 3, Ott. Capitals 1.

1892-93 — Montreal AAA — Tom Paton, James Stewart, Allan Cameron, Haviland Routh, Archie Hodgson, Billy Barlow, A.B. Kingan, G.S. Lowe.
In accordance with the terms governing the presentation of the Stanley Cup, it was awarded for the first time to the Montreal AAA as champions of the Amateur Hockey Association in 1893. Once Montreal AAA had been declared holders of the Stanley Cup, any Canadian hockey team could challenge for the trophy.

All-Time NHL Playoff Formats

1917-18 — The regular-season was split into two halves. The winners of both halves faced each other in a two-game, total-goals series for the NHL championship and the right to meet the PCHA champion in the best-of-five Stanley Cup Finals.

1918-19 — Same as 1917-18, except that the Stanley Cup Finals was extended to a best-of-seven series.

1919-20 — Same as 1917-1918, except that Ottawa won both halves of the split regular-season schedule to earn an automatic berth into the best-of-five Stanley Cup Finals against the PCHA champions.

1921-22 — The top two teams at the conclusion of the regular-season faced each other in a two-game, total-goals series for the NHL championship. The NHL champion then moved on to play the winner of the PCHA-WCHL playoff series in the best-of-five Stanley Cup Finals.

1922-23 — The top two teams at the conclusion of the regular-season faced each other in a two-game, total-goals series for the NHL championship. The NHL champion then moved on to play the PCHA champion in the best-of-three Stanley Cup Semi-Finals, and the winner of the Semi-Finals played the WCHL champion, which had been given a bye, in the best-of-three Stanley Cup Finals.

1923-24 — The top two teams at the conclusion of the regular-season faced each other in a two-game, total-goals series for the NHL championship. The NHL champion then moved on to play the loser of the PCHA-WCHL playoff (the winner of the PCHA-WCHL playoff earned a bye into the Stanley Cup Finals) in the best-of-three Stanley Cup Semi-Finals. The winner of this series met the PCHA-WCHL playoff winner in the best-of-three Stanley Cup Finals.

1924-25 — The first place team (Hamilton) at the conclusion of the regular-season was supposed to play the winner of a two-game, total-goals series between the second (Toronto) and third (Montreal) place clubs. However, Hamilton refused to abide by this new format, demanding greater compensation than offered by the League. Thus, Toronto and Montreal played their two-game, total-goals series, and the winner (Montreal) earned the NHL title and then played the WCHL champion (Victoria) in the best-of-five Stanley Cup Finals.

1925-26 — The format which was intended for 1924-25 went into effect. The winner of the two-game, total-goals series between the second and third place teams squared off against the first place team in the two-game, total-goals NHL championship series. The NHL champion then moved on to play the WHL champion in the best-of-five Stanley Cup Finals.

After the 1925-26 season, the NHL was the only major professional hockey league still in existence and consequently took over sole control of the Stanley Cup competition.

1926-27 — The 10-team league was divided into two divisions — Canadian and American — of five teams apiece. In each division, the winner of the two-game, total-goals series between the second and third place teams faced the first place team in a two-game, total-goals series for the division title. The two division title winners then met in the best-of-five Stanley Cup Finals.

1928-29 — Both first place teams in the two divisions played each other in a best-of-five series. Both second place teams in the two divisions played each other in a two-game, total-goals series as did the two third place teams. The winners of these latter two series then played each other in a best-of-three series for the right to meet the winner of the series between the two first place clubs. This Stanley Cup Final was a best-of-three.

Series A: First in Canadian Division vs. first in American (best-of-five)
Series B: Second in Canadian Division vs. second in American (two-game, total-goals)
Series C: Third in Canadian Division vs. third in American (two-game, total-goals)
Series D: Winner of Series B vs. winner of Series C (best-of-three)
Series E: Winner of Series A vs. winner of Series D (best-of-three) for Stanley Cup

1931-32 — Same as 1928-29, except that Series D was changed to a two-game, total-goals format and Series E was changed to best-of-five.

1936-37 — Same as 1931-32, except that Series B, C, and D were each best-of-three.

1938-39 — With the NHL reduced to seven teams, the two-division system was replaced by one seven-team league. Based on final regular-season standings, the following playoff format was adopted:

Series A: First vs. Second (best-of-seven)
Series B: Third vs. Fourth (best-of-three)
Series C: Fifth vs. Sixth (best-of-three)
Series D: Winner of Series B vs. winner of Series C (best-of-three)
Series E: Winner of Series A vs. winner of Series D (best-of-seven)

1942-43 — With the NHL reduced to six teams (the "original six"), only the top four finishers qualified for playoff action. The best-of-seven Semi-Finals pitted Team #1 vs. Team #3 and Team #2 vs. Team #4. The winners of each Semi-Final series met in the best-of-seven Stanley Cup Finals.

1967-68 — When it doubled in size from 6 to 12 teams, the NHL once again was divided into two divisions — East and West — of six teams apiece. The top four clubs in each division qualified for the playoffs (all series were best-of-seven):

Series A: Team #1 (East) vs. Team #3 (East)
Series B: Team #2 (East) vs. Team #4 (East)
Series C: Team #1 (West) vs. Team #3 (West)
Series D: Team #2 (West) vs. Team #4 (West)
Series E: Winner of Series A vs. winner of Series B
Series F: Winner of Series C vs. winner of Series D
Series G: Winner of Series E vs. Winner of Series F

1970-71 — Same as 1967-68 except that Series E matched the winners of Series A and D, and Series F matched the winners of Series B and C.

1971-72 — Same as 1970-71, except that Series A and C matched Team #1 vs. Team #4, and Series B and D matched Team #2 vs. Team #3.

1974-75 — With the League now expanded to 18 teams in four divisions, a completely new playoff format was introduced. First, the #2 and #3 teams in each of the four divisions were pooled together in the Preliminary round. These eight (#2 and #3) clubs were ranked #1 to #8 based on regular-season record:

Series A: Team #1 vs. Team #8 (best-of-three)
Series B: Team #2 vs. Team #7 (best-of-three)
Series C: Team #3 vs. Team #6 (best-of-three)
Series D: Team #4 vs. Team #5 (best-of-three)
The winners of this Preliminary round then pooled together with the four division winners, which had received byes into this Quarter-Final round. These eight teams were again ranked #1 to #8 based on regular-season record:
Series E: Team #1 vs. Team #8 (best-of-seven)
Series F: Team #2 vs. Team #7 (best-of-seven)
Series G: Team #3 vs. Team #6 (best-of-seven)
Series H: Team #4 vs. Team #5 (best-of-seven)
The four Quarter-Finals winners, which moved on to the Semi-Finals, were then ranked #1 to #4 based on regular season record:
Series I: Team #1 vs. Team #4 (best-of-seven)
Series J: Team #2 vs. Team #3 (best-of-seven)
Series K: Winner of Series I vs. winner of Series J (best-of-seven)

1977-78 — Same as 1974-75, except that the Preliminary round consisted of the #2 teams in the four divisions and the next four teams based on regular-season record (not their standings within their divisions).

1979-80 — With the addition of four WHA franchises, the League expanded its playoff structure to include 16 of its 21 teams. The four first place teams in the four divisions automatically earned playoff berths. Among the 17 other clubs, the top 12, according to regular-season record, also earned berths. All 16 teams were then pooled together and ranked #1 to #16 based on regular-season record:

Series A: Team #1 vs. Team #16 (best-of-five)
Series B: Team #2 vs. Team #15 (best-of-five)
Series C: Team #3 vs. Team #14 (best-of-five)
Series D: Team #4 vs. Team #13 (best-of-five)
Series E: Team #5 vs. Team #12 (best-of-five)
Series F: Team #6 vs. Team #11 (best-of-five)
Series G: Team #7 vs. Team #10 (best-of-five)
Series H: Team #8 vs. Team # 9 (best-of-five)

The eight Preliminary round winners, ranked #1 to #8 based on regular-season record, moved on to the Quarter-Finals:
Series I: Team #1 vs. Team #8 (best-of-seven)
Series J: Team #2 vs. Team #7 (best-of-seven)
Series K: Team #3 vs. Team #6 (best-of-seven)
Series L: Team #4 vs. Team #5 (best-of-seven)
The four Quarter-Finals winners, ranked #1 to #4 based on regular-season record, moved on to the semi-finals:
Series M: Team #1 vs. Team #4 (best-of-seven)
Series N: Team #2 vs. Team #3 (best-of-seven)
Series O: Winner of Series M vs. winner of Series N (best-of-seven)

1981-82 — The first four teams in each division earned playoff berths. In each division, the first-place team opposed the fourth-place team and the second-place team opposed the third-place team in a best-of-five Division Semi-Final series (DSF). In each division, the two winners of the DSF met in a best-of-seven Division Final series (DF). The two DF winners in each conference met in a best-of-seven Conference Final series (CF). In the Prince of Wales Conference, the Adams Division winner opposed the Patrick Division winner; in the Clarence Campbell Conference, the Smythe Division winner opposed the Norris Division winner. The two CF winners met in a best-of-seven Stanley Cup Final (F) series.

1986-87 — Division Semi-Final series changed from best-of-five to best-of-seven.

1993-94 — The NHL's playoff draw is conference-based rather than division-based. At the conclusion of the regular season, the top eight teams in each of the Eastern and Western Conferences qualify for the playoffs. The teams that finish in first place in each of the League's divisions are seeded first and second in each conference's playoff draw and are assured of home ice advantage in the first two playoff rounds. The remaining teams are seeded based on their regular-season point totals. In each conference, the team seeded #1 plays #8; #2 vs. #7; #3 vs. #6; and #4 vs. #5. All series are best-of-seven with home ice rotating on a 2-2-1-1-1 basis, with the exception of matchups between Central and Pacific Division teams. These matchups will be played on a 2-3-2 basis to reduce travel. In a 2-3-2 series, the team with the most points will have its choice to start the series at home or on the road. The Eastern Conference champion will face the Western Conference champion in the Stanley Cup Final.

1994-95 — Same as 1993-94, except that in first, second or third-round playoff series involving Central and Pacific Division teams, the team with the better record has the choice of using either a 2-3-2 or a 2-2-1-1-1 format. When a 2-3-2 format is selected, the higher-ranked team also has the choice of playing games 1, 2, 6 and 7 at home or playing games 3, 4 and 5 at home. The format for the Stanley Cup Final remains 2-2-1-1-1.

1998-99 — The NHL's clubs are re-aligned into two conferences each consisting of three divisions. The number of teams qualifying for the Stanley Cup Playoffs remains unchanged at 16.

First-round playoff berths will be awarded to the first-place team in each division as well as to the next five best teams based on regular-season point totals in each conference. The three division winners in each conference will be seeded first through third, in order of points, for the playoffs and the next five best teams, in order of points, will be seeded fourth through eighth. In each conference, the team seeded #1 will play #8; #2 vs. #7; #3 vs. #6; and #4 vs. #5 in the quarterfinal round. Home-ice in the Conference Quarter-Finals is granted to those teams seeded first through fourth in each conference.

In the Conference Semi-Finals and Conference Finals, teams will be re-seeded according to the same criteria as the Conference Quarter-Finals. Higher seeded teams will have home-ice advantage.

Home-ice advantage for the Stanley Cup Finals will be determined by points.

All series remain best-of-seven.

Members of the 1935-36 Detroit Red Wings dispense good cheer from the Stanley Cup following the team's first of 10 championships. Only Montreal and Toronto have celebrated more Stanley Cup championships in NHL history.

Team Records

1918-2004

GAMES PLAYED

MOST GAMES PLAYED BY ALL TEAMS, ONE PLAYOFF YEAR:
92 — 1991. There were 51 DSF, 24 DF, 11 CF and 6 F games.
90 — 1994. There were 48 CQF, 23 CSF, 12 CF and 7 F games.
— 2002. There were 47 CQF, 25 CSF, 13 CF and 5 F games.

MOST GAMES PLAYED, ONE TEAM, ONE PLAYOFF YEAR:
26 — Philadelphia Flyers, 1987. Won DSF 4-2 vs. NY Rangers, DF 4-3 vs. NY Islanders, CF 4-2 vs. Montreal, and lost F 4-3 vs. Edmonton.
— **Calgary Flames,** 2004. Won DSF 4-3 vs. Vancouver, DF 4-2 vs. Detroit, CF 4-2 vs. San Jose, and lost F 4-3 vs. Tampa Bay.
25 — New Jersey Devils, 2001. Won CQF 4-2 vs. Carolina, CSF 4-3 vs. Toronto, CF 4-1 vs. Pittsburgh, and lost F 4-3 vs. Colorado.

PLAYOFF APPEARANCES

MOST STANLEY CUP CHAMPIONSHIPS:
23 — Montreal Canadiens (1924-30-31-44-46-53-56-57-58-59-60-65-66-68-69-71-73-76-77-78-79-86-93)
13 — Toronto Maple Leafs (1918-22-32-42-45-47-48-49-51-62-63-64-67)
10 — Detroit Red Wings (1936-37-43-50-52-54-55-97-98-02)

MOST CONSECUTIVE STANLEY CUP CHAMPIONSHIPS:
5 — Montreal Canadiens (1956-57-58-59-60)
4 — Montreal Canadiens (1976-77-78-79)
— NY Islanders (1980-81-82-83)

MOST FINAL SERIES APPEARANCES:
32 — Montreal Canadiens in 86-year history.
22 — Detroit Red Wings in 77-year history.
21 — Toronto Maple Leafs in 86-year history.

MOST CONSECUTIVE FINAL SERIES APPEARANCES:
10 — Montreal Canadiens, (1951-60, inclusive)
5 — Montreal Canadiens, (1965-69, inclusive)
— NY Islanders, (1980-84, inclusive)

MOST YEARS IN PLAYOFFS:
74 — Montreal Canadiens in 87-year history.
64 — Toronto Maple Leafs in 87-year history.
62 — Boston Bruins in 80-year history.

MOST CONSECUTIVE PLAYOFF APPEARANCES:
29 — Boston Bruins (1968-96, inclusive)
28 — Chicago Blackhawks (1970-97, inclusive)
25 — St. Louis Blues (1980-2004, inclusive)
24 — Montreal Canadiens (1971-94, inclusive)
21 — Montreal Canadiens (1949-69, inclusive)

TEAM WINS

MOST HOME WINS, ONE TEAM, ONE PLAYOFF YEAR:
12 — New Jersey Devils, 2003 in 13 home games.
11 — Edmonton Oilers, 1988 in 11 home games.
10 — Edmonton Oilers, 1985 in 10 home games.
— Montreal Canadiens, 1986 in 11 home games.
— Montreal Canadiens, 1993 in 11 home games.

MOST ROAD WINS, ONE TEAM, ONE PLAYOFF YEAR:
10 — New Jersey Devils, 1995. Won three at Boston in CQF; two at Pittsburgh in CSF; three at Philadelphia in CF; and two at Detroit in F.
— **New Jersey Devils,** 2000. Won two at Florida in CQF; two at Toronto in CSF; three at Philadelphia in CF; and three at Dallas in F.
— **Calgary Flames,** 2004. Won three at Vancouver in DSF; two at Detroit in DF; three at San Jose in CF; and two at Tampa Bay in F.
8 — NY Islanders, 1980. Won two at Los Angeles in PR; three at Boston in QF; two at Buffalo in SF; and one at Philadelphia in F.
— Philadelphia Flyers, 1987. Won two at NY Rangers in DSF; two at NY Islanders in DF; three at Montreal in CF; and one at Edmonton in F.
— Edmonton Oilers, 1990. Won one at Winnipeg in DSF; two at Los Angeles in DF; two at Chicago in CF and three at Boston in F.
— Pittsburgh Penguins, 1992. Won two at Washington in DSF; two at NY Rangers in DF; two at Boston in CF; and two at Chicago in F.
— Vancouver Canucks, 1994. Won three at Calgary in DSF; two at Dallas in CSF; one at Toronto in CF; and two at NY Rangers in F.
— Colorado Avalanche, 1996. Won two at Vancouver in CQF; two at Chicago in CSF; two at Detroit in CF; and two at Florida in F.
— Detroit Red Wings, 1998. Won two at Phoenix in CQF; three at St. Louis in CSF; one at Dallas in CF; and two at Washington in F.
— Colorado Avalanche, 1999. Won three at San Jose in CQF; three at Detroit in CSF; and two at Dallas in CF.
— New Jersey Devils, 2001. Won two at Carolina in CQF; two at Toronto in CSF; two at Pittsburgh in CF; and two at Colorado in F.
— Detroit Red Wings, 2002. Won three at Vancouver in CQF; one at St. Louis in CSF; two at Colorado in CF; and two at Carolina in F.

MOST ROAD WINS, ALL TEAMS, ONE PLAYOFF YEAR:
46 — 1987. Of 87 games played, road teams won 46 (22 DSF, 14 DF, 8 CF and 2 in F).

MOST OVERTIME WINS, ONE TEAM, ONE PLAYOFF YEAR:
10 — Montreal Canadiens, 1993. Won two vs. Quebec in DSF; three vs. Buffalo in DF; two vs. NY Islanders in CF; and three vs. Los Angeles in F.
7 — Carolina Hurricanes, 2002. Won two vs. New Jersey in CQF; one vs. Montreal in CSF; three vs. Toronto in CF; and one vs. Detroit in F.
— Anaheim Mighty Ducks, 2003. Won two vs. Detroit in CQF; two vs. Dallas in CSF; one vs. Minnestoa in CF; and two vs. New Jersey in F.

MOST OVERTIME WINS AT HOME, ONE TEAM, ONE PLAYOFF YEAR:
4 — St. Louis Blues, 1968. Won one vs. Philadelphia in QF; three vs. Minnesota in SF.
— **Montreal Canadiens, 1993.** Won one vs. Quebec in DSF; one vs. Buffalo in DF, one vs. NY Islanders in CF; one vs. Los Angeles in F.

MOST OVERTIME WINS ON THE ROAD, ONE TEAM, ONE PLAYOFF YEAR:
6 — Montreal Canadiens, 1993. Won one vs. Quebec in DSF; two vs. Buffalo in DF; one vs. NY Islanders in CF; two vs. Los Angeles in F.

TEAM LOSSES

MOST LOSSES, ONE TEAM, ONE PLAYOFF YEAR:
11 — **Philadelphia Flyers, 1987.** Lost two vs. NY Rangers in DSF; three vs. NY Islanders in DF; two vs. Montreal in CF; four vs. Edmonton in F.
— **Calgary Flames, 2004.** Lost three vs. Vancouver in CQF; two vs. Detroit in CSF; two vs. San Jose in CF; four vs. Tampa Bay in F

MOST HOME LOSSES, ONE TEAM, ONE PLAYOFF YEAR:
7 — **Calgary Flames, 2004.** Lost two vs. Vancouver in DSF; one vs. Detroit in DF; two vs. San Jose in CF; two vs. Tampa Bay in F.
6 — Philadelphia Flyers, 1987. Lost one vs. NY Rangers in DSF; two vs. NY Islanders in DF; two vs. Montreal in CF; one vs. Edmonton in F.
— Washington Capitals, 1998. Lost two vs. Boston in CQF; two vs. Buffalo in CF; two vs. Detroit in F.
— Colorado Avalanche, 1999. Lost two vs. San Jose in CQF; two vs. Detroit in CSF; two vs. Dallas in CF.
— New Jersey Devils, 2001. Lost one vs. Carolina in CQF; two vs. Toronto in CSF; one vs. Pittsburgh in CF; two vs Colorado in F.
— Minnesota Wild, 2003. Lost two vs. Colorado in CQF; two vs. Vancouver in CSF; two vs. Anaheim in CF.

MOST ROAD LOSSES, ONE TEAM, ONE PLAYOFF YEAR:
7 — **New Jersey Devils, 2003.** Lost one at Boston in CQF; one at Tampa Bay in CSF; two at Ottawa in CF; three at Anaheim in F.

MOST OVERTIME LOSSES, ONE TEAM, ONE PLAYOFF YEAR:
4 — **Montreal Canadiens, 1951.** Lost four vs. Toronto in F.
— **St. Louis Blues, 1968.** Lost one vs. Philadelphia in QF; one vs. Minnesota in SF; two vs. Montreal in F.
— **New York Rangers, 1979.** Lost one vs. Philadelphia in QF; two vs. NY Islanders in SF; one vs. Montreal in F.
— **Los Angeles Kings, 1991.** Lost one vs. Vancouver in DSF; three vs. Edmonton in DF.
— **Los Angeles Kings, 1993.** Lost one vs. Toronto in CF; three vs. Montreal in F.
— **New Jersey Devils, 1994.** Lost one vs. Buffalo in CQF; one vs. Boston in CSF; two vs. NY Rangers in CF.
— **Chicago Blackhawks, 1995.** Lost one vs. Toronto in CQF; three vs. Detroit in CF.
— **Philadelphia Flyers, 1996.** Lost two vs. Tampa Bay in CQF; two vs. Florida in CSF.
— **Dallas Stars, 1999.** Lost two vs. St. Louis in CSF; one vs. Colorado in CF; one vs. Buffalo in F.
— **Detroit Red Wings, 2002.** Lost one vs. Vancouver in CQF; two vs. Colorado in CF; one vs. Carolina in F.
— **New Jersey Devils, 2003.** Lost two vs. Ottawa in CF; two vs. Anaheim in F.

MOST OVERTIME LOSSES AT HOME, ONE TEAM, ONE PLAYOFF YEAR:
4 — **Detroit Red Wings, 2002.** Lost one vs. Vancouver in CQF; two vs. Colorado in CF; one vs. Carolina in F.

MOST OVERTIME LOSSES ON THE ROAD, ONE TEAM, ONE PLAYOFF YEAR:
3 — **Los Angeles Kings, 1991.** Lost one at Vancouver in DSF; two at Edmonton in DF.
— **Chicago Blackhawks, 1995.** Lost one at Toronto in CQF; two at Detroit in CF.
— **St. Louis Blues, 1996.** Lost two at Toronto in CQF; one at Detroit in CSF.
— **Dallas Stars, 1999.** Lost two at St. Louis in CSF; one at Colorado in CF.
— **New Jersey Devils, 2003.** Lost one at Ottawa in CF; two at Anaheim in F.

PLAYOFF WINNING STREAKS

LONGEST PLAYOFF WINNING STREAK:
14 — **Pittsburgh Penguins.** Streak started on May 9, 1992 as Pittsburgh won the first of three straight games in DF vs. NY Rangers. Continued with four wins vs. Boston in 1992 CF and four wins vs. Boston in 1992 F. Pittsburgh then won the first three games of 1993 DSF vs. New Jersey. New Jersey ended the streak April 25, 1993, at New Jersey with a 4-1 win vs. Pittsburgh in the fourth game of 1993 DSF.
12 — Edmonton Oilers. Streak started on May 15, 1984 as Edmonton won the first of three straight games in F vs. NY Islanders. Continued with three wins vs. Los Angeles in 1985 DSF and four wins vs. Winnipeg in 1985 DF. Edmonton then won the first two games of 1985 CF vs. Chicago. Chicago ended the streak May 9, 1985, at Chicago with a 5-2 win vs. Edmonton in the third game of 1985 CF.

MOST CONSECUTIVE WINS, ONE TEAM, ONE PLAYOFF YEAR:
11 — **Chicago Blackhawks** in 1992. Chicago won last three games of DSF vs. St. Louis to win series 4-2, defeated Detroit 4-0 in DF and Edmonton 4-0 in CF.
— **Pittsburgh Penguins** in 1992. Pittsburgh won last three games of DF vs. NY Rangers to win series 4-2, defeated Boston 4-0 in CF and Chicago 4-0 in F.
— **Montreal Canadiens** in 1993. Montreal won last four games of DSF vs. Quebec to win series 4-2, defeated Buffalo 4-0 in DF and won first three games of CF vs. NY Islanders.

PLAYOFF LOSING STREAKS

LONGEST PLAYOFF LOSING STREAK:
16 — **Chicago Black Hawks.** Streak started April 20, 1975 at Chicago with a 6-2 loss in fourth game of QF vs. Buffalo won by Buffalo 4-1. Continued with four consecutive losses vs. Montreal in 1976 QF and two straight losses vs. NY Islanders in 1977 best-of-three PRE. Chicago then lost four games vs. Boston in 1978 QF and four games vs. NY Islanders in 1979 QF. Chicago ended the streak April 8, 1980, at Chicago with a 3-2 win vs. St. Louis in the opening game of 1980 PRE.
— Los Angeles Kings. Streak started June 3, 1993 at Montreal with a 3-2 loss in second game of F vs. Montreal, won by Montreal 4-1. Los Angeles failed to qualify for the playoffs for the next four years. Then Los Angeles lost four games vs. St. Louis in 1998 CQF; missed the 1999 playoffs and lost four games vs. Detroit in 2000 CQF. Los Angeles then lost the first two games of 2001 CQF vs. Detroit. Los Angeles ended the streak April 15, 2001, at Los Angeles with a 2-1 win.

Patrick Roy led the 1992-93 Montreal Canadiens to the Stanley Cup championship. The Canadiens won 11 playoff games in a row at one stretch, and recorded 10 of their 16 postseason victories in overtime.

MOST GOALS IN A SERIES, ONE TEAM

MOST GOALS, ONE TEAM, ONE PLAYOFF SERIES:
44 — **Edmonton Oilers** in 1985 CF. Edmonton won best-of-seven series 4-2, outscoring Chicago 44-25.
35 — **Edmonton Oilers** in 1983 DF. Edmonton won best-of-seven series 4-1, outscoring Calgary 35-13.
— **Calgary Flames** in 1995 CQF. Calgary lost best-of-seven series 4-3, outscoring San Jose 35-26.

MOST GOALS, ONE TEAM, TWO-GAME SERIES:
11 — **Buffalo Sabres** in 1977 PRE. Buffalo won best-of-three series 2-0, outscoring Minnesota 11-3.
— **Toronto Maple Leafs** in 1978 PRE. Toronto won best-of-three series 2-0, outscoring Los Angeles 11-3.

MOST GOALS, ONE TEAM, THREE-GAME SERIES:
23 — **Chicago Blackhawks** in 1985 DSF. Chicago won best-of-five series 3-0, outscoring Detroit 23-8.
20 — **Minnesota North Stars** in 1981 PRE. Minnesota won best-of-five series 3-0, outscoring Boston 20-13.
— **NY Islanders** in 1981 PRE. NY Islanders won best-of-five series 3-0, outscoring Toronto 20-4.

MOST GOALS, ONE TEAM, FOUR-GAME SERIES:
28 — **Boston Bruins** in 1972 SF. Boston won best-of-seven series 4-0, outscoring St. Louis 28-8.

MOST GOALS, ONE TEAM, FIVE-GAME SERIES:
35 — **Edmonton Oilers** in 1983 DF. Edmonton won best-of-seven series 4-1, outscoring Calgary 35-13.
32 — **Edmonton Oilers** in 1987 DSF. Edmonton won best-of-seven series 4-1, outscoring Los Angeles 32-20.
30 — **Calgary Flames** in 1988 DSF. Calgary won best-of-seven series 4-1, outscoring Los Angeles 30-18.

MOST GOALS, ONE TEAM, SIX-GAME SERIES:
44 — **Edmonton Oilers** in 1985 CF. Edmonton won best-of-seven series 4-2, outscoring Chicago 44-25.
33 — **Montreal Canadiens** in 1973 F. Montreal won best-of-seven series 4-2, outscoring Chicago 33-23.
— **Chicago Blackhawks** in 1985 DF. Chicago won best-of-seven series 4-2, outscoring Minnesota 33-29.
— **Los Angeles Kings** in 1993 DSF. Los Angeles won best-of-seven series 4-2, outscoring Calgary 33-28.

MOST GOALS, ONE TEAM, SEVEN-GAME SERIES:
35 — **Calgary Flames** in 1995 CQF. Calgary lost best-of-seven series 4-3, outscoring San Jose 35-26.
33 — **Philadelphia Flyers** in 1976 QF. Philadelphia won best-of-seven series 4-3, outscoring Toronto 33-23.
— **Boston Bruins** in 1983 DF. Boston won best-of-seven series 4-3, outscoring Buffalo 33-23.
— **Edmonton Oilers** in 1984 DF. Edmonton won best-of-seven series 4-3, outscoring Calgary 33-27.

FEWEST GOALS IN A SERIES, ONE TEAM

FEWEST GOALS, ONE TEAM, TWO-GAME SERIES:
0 — **New York Americans** in 1929 SF. NY Americans lost two-game, total-goals series 1-0 vs. NY Rangers.
— **Chicago Black Hawks** in 1935 SF. Chicago lost two-game, total-goals series 1-0 vs. Mtl. Maroons.
— **Montreal Maroons** in 1937 SF. Mtl. Maroons lost best-of-three series 2-0, outscored by NY Rangers 5-0.
— **New York Americans** in 1939 QF. NY Americans lost best-of-three series 2-0, outscored by Toronto 5-0.

FEWEST GOALS, ONE TEAM, THREE-GAME SERIES:
1 — **Montreal Maroons** in 1936 SF. Mtl. Maroons lost best-of-five series 3-0, outscored by Detroit 6-1.

FEWEST GOALS, ONE TEAM, FOUR-GAME SERIES:
1 — **Minnesota Wild** in 2003 CF. Minnesota lost best-of-seven series 4-0, outscored by Anaheim 9-1.

FEWEST GOALS, ONE TEAM, FIVE-GAME SERIES:
2 — **Philadelphia Flyers** in 2002 CQF. Ottawa won best-of-seven series 4-1, while outscoring Philadelphia 11-2.

FEWEST GOALS, ONE TEAM, SIX-GAME SERIES:
5 — **Boston Bruins** in 1951 SF. Toronto won best-of-seven series 4-1 with 1 tie, outscoring Boston 17-5.

FEWEST GOALS, ONE TEAM, SEVEN-GAME SERIES:
9 — **Toronto Maple Leafs,** in 1945 F. Toronto won best-of- seven series 4-3; teams tied in scoring 9-9.
— **Detroit Red Wings,** in 1945 F. Toronto won best-of-seven series 4-3; teams tied in scoring 9-9.

Boston scored a record 28 goals in a four-game sweep of St. Louis in the 1972 semifinals. Phil Esposito tied Bruins teammates John Bucyk and Ken Hodge with a playoff-leading nine goals that year. He and Bobby Orr both had 24 points.

MOST GOALS IN A SERIES, BOTH TEAMS

MOST GOALS, BOTH TEAMS, ONE PLAYOFF SERIES:
69 — **Edmonton Oilers (44), Chicago Black Hawks (25)** in 1985 CF. Edmonton won best-of-seven series 4-2.
62 — Chicago Black Hawks (33), Minnesota North Stars (29) in 1985 DF. Chicago won best-of-seven series 4-2.
61 — Los Angeles Kings (33), Calgary Flames (28) in 1993 DSF. Los Angeles won best-of-seven series 4-2.
— Calgary Flames (35), San Jose Sharks (26) in 1995 CQF. San Jose won best-of-seven series 4-3.

MOST GOALS, BOTH TEAMS, TWO-GAME SERIES:
17 — **Toronto St. Patricks (10), Montreal Canadiens (7)** in 1918 NHL F. Toronto won two-game total-goals series.
15 — Boston Bruins (10), Chicago Black Hawks (5) in 1927 QF. Boston won two-game total-goals series.
— Pittsburgh Penguins (9), St. Louis Blues (6) in 1975 PRE. Pittsburgh won best-of-three series 2-0.

MOST GOALS, BOTH TEAMS, THREE-GAME SERIES:
33 — **Minnesota North Stars (20), Boston Bruins (13)** in 1981 PRE. Minnesota won best-of-five series 3-0.
31 — Chicago Black Hawks (23), Detroit Red Wings (8) in 1985 DSF. Chicago won best-of-five series 3-0.
28 — Toronto Maple Leafs (18), New York Rangers (10) in 1932 F. Toronto won best-of-five series 3-0.

MOST GOALS, BOTH TEAMS, FOUR-GAME SERIES:
36 — **Boston Bruins (28), St. Louis Blues (8)** in 1972 SF. Boston won best-of-seven series 4-0.
— **Minnesota North Stars (18), Toronto Maple Leafs (18)** in 1983 DSF. Minnesota won best-of-five series 3-1.
— **Edmonton Oilers (25), Chicago Black Hawks (11)** in 1983 CF. Edmonton won best-of-seven series 4-0.
35 — New York Rangers (23), Los Angeles Kings (12) in 1981 PRE. NY Rangers won best-of-five series 3-1.

MOST GOALS, BOTH TEAMS, FIVE-GAME SERIES:
52 — Edmonton Oilers (32), Los Angeles Kings (20) in 1987 DSF. Edmonton won best-of-seven series 4-1.
50 — Los Angeles Kings (27), Edmonton Oilers (23) in 1982 DSF. Los Angeles won best-of-five series 3-2.
48 — Edmonton Oilers (35), Calgary Flames (13) in 1983 DF. Edmonton won best-of-seven series 4-1.
 — Calgary Flames (30), Los Angeles Kings (18) in 1988 DSF. Calgary won best-of-seven series 4-1.

MOST GOALS, BOTH TEAMS, SIX-GAME SERIES:
69 — Edmonton Oilers (44), Chicago Black Hawks (25) in 1985 CF. Edmonton won best-of-seven series 4-2.
62 — Chicago Black Hawks (33), Minnesota North Stars (29) in 1985 DF. Chicago won best-of-seven series 4-2.
61 — Los Angeles Kings (33), Calgary Flames (28) in 1993 DSF. Los Angeles won best-of-seven series 4-2.

MOST GOALS, BOTH TEAMS, SEVEN-GAME SERIES:
61 — Calgary Flames (35), San Jose Sharks (26) in 1995 CQF. San Jose won best-of-seven series 4-3.
60 — Edmonton Oilers (33), Calgary Flames (27) in 1984 DF. Edmonton won best-of-seven series 4-3.

FEWEST GOALS IN A SERIES, BOTH TEAMS

FEWEST GOALS, BOTH TEAMS, TWO-GAME SERIES:
1 — New York Rangers (1), New York Americans (0) in 1929 SF. NY Rangers won two-game total-goals series.
 — **Montreal Maroons (1), Chicago Black Hawks (0)** in 1935 SF. Mtl. Maroons won two-game total-goals series.

FEWEST GOALS, BOTH TEAMS, THREE-GAME SERIES:
7 — Boston Bruins (5), Montreal Canadiens (2) in 1929 SF. Boston won best-of-five series 3-0.
 — **Detroit Red Wings (6), Montreal Maroons (1)** in 1936 SF. Detroit won best-of-five series 3-0.

FEWEST GOALS, BOTH TEAMS, FOUR-GAME SERIES:
9 — Toronto Maple Leafs (7), Boston Bruins (2) in 1935 SF. Toronto won best-of-five series 3-1.

FEWEST GOALS, BOTH TEAMS, FIVE-GAME SERIES:
11 — Montreal Maroons (6), New York Rangers (5) in 1928 F. NY Rangers won best-of-five series 3-2.

FEWEST GOALS, BOTH TEAMS, SIX-GAME SERIES:
16 — Carolina Hurricanes (10), Toronto Maple Leafs (6) in 2002 CF. Carolina won best-of-seven series 4-2.

FEWEST GOALS, BOTH TEAMS, SEVEN-GAME SERIES:
18 — Toronto Maple Leafs (9), Detroit Red Wings (9) in 1945 F. Toronto won best-of-seven series 4-3.

MOST GOALS IN A GAME OR PERIOD

MOST GOALS, ONE TEAM, ONE GAME:
13 — Edmonton Oilers April 9, 1987, vs. Los Angeles at Edmonton. Edmonton won 13-3.
12 — Los Angeles Kings, April 10, 1990, vs. Calgary at Los Angeles. Los Angeles won 12-4.
11 — Montreal Canadiens, March 30, 1944, vs. Toronto at Montreal. Montreal won 11-0.
 — Edmonton Oilers, May 4, 1985, vs. Chicago at Edmonton. Edmonton won 11-2.

MOST GOALS, ONE TEAM, ONE PERIOD:
7 — Montreal Canadiens (6), March 30, 1944, vs. Toronto at Montreal, third period. Montreal won 11-0.

MOST GOALS, BOTH TEAMS, ONE GAME:
18 — Los Angeles Kings (10), Edmonton Oilers (8), April 7, 1982, at Edmonton. Los Angeles won best-of-five DSF 3-2.
17 — Pittsburgh Penguins (10), Philadelphia Flyers (7), April 25, 1989, at Pittsburgh. Pittsburgh won best-of-seven DF 4-3.
16 — Edmonton Oilers (13), Los Angeles Kings (3), April 9, 1987, at Edmonton. Edmonton won best-of-seven DSF 4-1.
 — Los Angeles Kings (12), Calgary Flames (4), April 10, 1990, at Los Angeles. Los Angeles won best-of-seven DF 4-2.

MOST GOALS, BOTH TEAMS, ONE PERIOD:
9 — New York Rangers (6), Philadelphia Flyers (3), April 24, 1979, third period, at Philadelphia. NY Rangers won 8-3.
 — **Los Angeles Kings (5), Calgary Flames (4),** April 10, 1990, second period, at Los Angeles. Los Angeles won 12-4.
8 — Chicago Black Hawks (5), Montreal Canadiens (3), May 8, 1973, second period, at Montreal. Chicago won 8-7.
 — Chicago Black Hawks (5), Edmonton Oilers (3), May 12, 1985, first period, at Chicago. Chicago won 8-6.
 — Edmonton Oilers (6), Winnipeg Jets (2), April 6, 1988, third period, at Edmonton. Edmonton won 7-4.
 — Hartford Whalers (5), Montreal Canadiens (3), April 10, 1988, third period, at Montreal. Hartford won 7-5.
 — Vancouver Canucks (5), New York Rangers (3), June 9, 1994, third period, at NY Rangers. Vancouver won 6-3.

TEAM POWER-PLAY GOALS

MOST POWER-PLAY GOALS BY ALL TEAMS, ONE PLAYOFF YEAR:
199 — 1988 in 83 games.

MOST POWER-PLAY GOALS, ONE TEAM, ONE PLAYOFF YEAR:
35 — Minnesota North Stars, 1991 in 23 games.
32 — Edmonton Oilers, 1988 in 18 games.
31 — New York Islanders, 1981 in 18 games.

MOST POWER-PLAY GOALS, ONE TEAM, ONE SERIES:
15 — New York Islanders in 1980 F vs. Philadelphia. NY Islanders won series 4-2.
 — **Minnesota North Stars** in 1991 DSF vs. Chicago. Minnesota won series 4-2.
13 — New York Islanders in 1981 QF vs. Edmonton. NY Islanders won series 4-2.
 — Calgary Flames in 1986 CF vs. St. Louis. Calgary won series 4-3.
12 — Toronto Maple Leafs in 1976 QF vs. Philadelphia. Philadelphia won series 4-3.

MOST POWER-PLAY GOALS, BOTH TEAMS, ONE SERIES:
21 — New York Islanders (15), Philadelphia Flyers (6) in 1980 best-of-seven F won by NY Islanders 4-2.
 — **New York Islanders (13), Edmonton Oilers (8)** in 1981 best-of-seven QF won by NY Islanders 4-2.
 — **Philadelphia Flyers (11), Pittsburgh Penguins (10)** in 1989 best-of-seven DF won by Philadelphia 4-3.
 — **Minnesota North Stars (15), Chicago Black Hawks (6)** in 1991 best-of-seven DSF won by Minnesota 4-2.
20 — Toronto Maple Leafs (12), Philadelphia Flyers (8) in 1976 best-of-seven QF won by Philadelphia 4-3.

MOST POWER-PLAY GOALS, ONE TEAM, ONE GAME:
6 — Boston Bruins, April 2, 1969, at Boston vs. Toronto. Boston won 10-0.

MOST POWER-PLAY GOALS, BOTH TEAMS, ONE GAME:
8 — Minnesota North Stars (4), St. Louis Blues (4), April 24, 1991, at Minnesota. Minnesota won 8-4.
7 — Minnesota North Stars (4), Edmonton Oilers (3), April 28, 1984, at Minnesota. Edmonton won 8-5.
 — Philadelphia Flyers (4), NY Rangers (3), April 13, 1985, at NY Rangers. Philadelphia won 6-5.
 — Chicago Black Hawks (5), Edmonton Oilers (2), April 28, 1984, at Minnesota. Edmonton won 8-5.
 — Edmonton Oilers (5), Los Angeles Kings (2), April 9, 1987, at Edmonton. Edmonton won 13-3.
 — Vancouver Canucks (4), Calgary Flames (3), April 9, 1989, at Vancouver. Vancouver won 5-3.

MOST POWER-PLAY GOALS, ONE TEAM, ONE PERIOD:
4 — Toronto Maple Leafs, March 26, 1936, second period vs. Boston at Toronto. Toronto won 8-3.
 — **Minnesota North Stars,** April 28, 1984, second period vs. Edmonton at Minnesota. Edmonton won 8-5.
 — **Boston Bruins,** April 11, 1991, third period vs. Hartford at Boston. Boston won 6-1.
 — **Minnesota North Stars,** April 24, 1991, second period vs. St. Louis at Minnesota. Minnesota won 8-4.
 — **St. Louis Blues,** April 27, 1998, third period at Los Angeles. St. Louis won 4-3.

MOST POWER-PLAY GOALS, BOTH TEAMS, ONE PERIOD:
5 — Minnesota North Stars (4), Edmonton Oilers (1), April 28, 1984, at Minnesota.
 — **Vancouver Canucks (3), Calgary Flames (2),** April 9, 1989, at Vancouver. Vancouver won 5-3.
 — **Minnesota North Stars (4), St. Louis Blues (1),** April 24, 1991, at Minnesota. Minnesota won 8-4.

TEAM SHORTHAND GOALS

MOST SHORTHAND GOALS BY ALL TEAMS, ONE PLAYOFF YEAR:
33 — 1988, in 83 games.

MOST SHORTHAND GOALS, ONE TEAM, ONE PLAYOFF YEAR:
10 — Edmonton Oilers, 1983, in 16 games.
9 — New York Islanders, 1981, in 19 games.
8 — Philadelphia Flyers, 1989, in 19 games.

MOST SHORTHAND GOALS, ONE TEAM, ONE SERIES:
6 — Calgary Flames in 1995 vs. San Jose in best-of-seven CQF won by San Jose 4-3.
— **Vancouver Canucks** in 1995 vs. St. Louis in best-of-seven CQF won by Vancouver 4-3.
5 — NY Rangers in 1979 vs. Philadelphia in best-of-seven QF won by NY Rangers 4-1.
— Edmonton Oilers in 1983 vs. Calgary in best-of-seven DF won by Edmonton 4-1.

MOST SHORTHAND GOALS, BOTH TEAMS, ONE SERIES:
7 — Boston Bruins (4), NY Rangers (3), in 1958 SF won by Boston 4-2.
— **Edmonton Oilers (5), Calgary Flames (2),** in 1983 DF won by Edmonton 4-1.
— **Vancouver Canucks (6), St. Louis Blues (1),** in 1995 CQF won by Vancouver 4-3.

MOST SHORTHAND GOALS, ONE TEAM, ONE GAME:
3 — Boston Bruins, April 11, 1981, at Minnesota North Stars. Minnesota won 6-3.
— **New York Islanders,** April 17, 1983, at NY Rangers. NY Rangers won 7-6.
— **Toronto Maple Leafs,** May 8, 1994, at San Jose Sharks. Toronto won 8-3.

MOST SHORTHAND GOALS, BOTH TEAMS, ONE GAME:
4 — Boston Bruins (3), Minnesota North Stars (1), April 11, 1981, at Minnesota. Minnesota won 6-3.
— **New York Islanders (3), New York Rangers (1),** April 17, 1983, at NY Rangers. NY Rangers won 7-6.
— **Toronto Maple Leafs (3), San Jose Sharks (1),** May 8, 1994, at San Jose. Toronto won 8-3.
3 — Toronto Maple Leafs (2), Detroit Red Wings (1), April 5, 1947, at Toronto. Toronto won 6-1.
— New York Rangers (2), Boston Bruins (1), April 1, 1958, at Boston. NY Rangers won 5-2.
— Minnesota North Stars (2), Philadelphia Flyers (1), May 4, 1980, at Minnesota. Philadelphia won 5-3.
— Winnipeg Jets (2), Edmonton Oilers (1), April 9, 1988, at Winnipeg. Winnipeg won 6-4.
— New York Islanders (2), New Jersey Devils (1), April 14, 1988, at New Jersey. New Jersey won 6-5.
— Montreal Canadiens (2), New Jersey Devils (1), April 17, 1997, at New Jersey. New Jersey won 5-2.
— Dallas Stars (2), San Jose Sharks (1), May 5, 2000, at San Jose. Dallas won 5-4.

MOST SHORTHAND GOALS, ONE TEAM, ONE PERIOD:
2 — Toronto Maple Leafs, April 5, 1947, first period vs. Detroit at Toronto. Toronto won 6-1.
— **Toronto Maple Leafs,** April 13, 1965, first period vs. Montreal at Toronto. Montreal won 4-3.
— **Boston Bruins,** April 20, 1969, first period vs. Montreal at Boston. Boston won 3-2.
— **Boston Bruins,** April 8, 1970, second period vs. NY Rangers at Boston. Boston won 8-2.
— **Boston Bruins,** April 30, 1972, first period vs. NY Rangers at Boston. Boston won 6-5.
— **Chicago Black Hawks,** May 3, 1973, first period vs. Montreal at Chicago. Chicago won 7-4.
— **Montreal Canadiens,** April 23, 1978, first period at Detroit. Montreal won 8-0.
— **New York Islanders,** April 8, 1980, second period vs. Los Angeles at NY Islanders. NY Islanders won 8-1.
— **Los Angeles Kings,** April 9, 1980, first period at NY Islanders. Los Angeles won 6-3.
— **Boston Bruins,** April 13, 1980, second period at Pittsburgh. Boston won 8-3.
— **Minnesota North Stars,** May 4, 1980, second period vs. Philadelphia at Minnesota. Philadelphia won 5-3.
— **Boston Bruins,** April 11, 1981, third period at Minnesota North Stars. Minnesota won 6-3.
— **New York Islanders,** May 12, 1981, first period vs. Minnesota North Stars at NY Islanders. NY Islanders won 6-3.
— **Montreal Canadiens,** April 7, 1982, third period vs. Quebec at Montreal. Montreal won 5-1.
— **Edmonton Oilers,** April 24, 1983, third period vs. Chicago at Edmonton. Edmonton won 8-4.
— **Winnipeg Jets,** April 14, 1985, second period at Calgary. Winnipeg won 5-3.
— **Boston Bruins,** April 6, 1988, first period vs. Buffalo at Boston. Boston won 7-3.
— **New York Islanders,** April 14, 1988, third period at New Jersey. New Jersey won 6-5.
— **Detroit Red Wings,** April 29, 1993, second period at Toronto. Detroit won 7-3.
— **Toronto Maple Leafs,** May 8, 1994, third period at San Jose. Toronto won 8-3.
— **Calgary Flames,** May 11, 1995, first period at San Jose. Calgary won 9-2.
— **Vancouver Canucks,** May 15, 1995, second period at St. Louis. Vancouver won 6-5.
— **Montreal Canadiens,** April 17, 1997, second period at New Jersey. New Jersey won 5-2.
— **Philadelphia Flyers,** April 26, 1997, first period vs. Pittsburgh at Philadelphia. Philadelphia won 6-3.
— **Phoenix Coyotes,** April 24, 1998, second period at Detroit. Phoenix won 7-4.
— **Buffalo Sabres,** April 27, 1998, second period vs. Philadelphia at Buffalo. Buffalo won 6-1.
— **San Jose Sharks,** April 30, 1999, third period at Colorado. San Jose won 7-3.
— **Detroit Red Wings,** April 27, 2002, second period at Vancouver. Detroit won 6-4.

MOST SHORTHAND GOALS, BOTH TEAMS, ONE PERIOD:
3 — Toronto Maple Leafs (2), Detroit Red Wings (1), April 5, 1947, first period at Toronto. Toronto won 6-1.
— **Toronto Maple Leafs (2), San Jose Sharks (1),** May 8, 1994, third period at San Jose. Toronto won 8-3.

FASTEST GOALS

FASTEST FIVE GOALS, BOTH TEAMS:
3:06 — Minnesota North Stars, Chicago Black Hawks, April 21, 1985, at Chicago. Keith Brown scored for Chicago at 1:12 of the second period; Ken Yaremchuk, Chicago, 1:27; Dino Ciccarelli, Minnesota, 2:48; Tony McKegney, Minnesota, 4:07; and Curt Fraser, Chicago, 4:18. Chicago won 6-2 and won best-of-seven DF 4-2.
3:20 — Minnesota North Stars, Philadelphia Flyers, April 29, 1980, at Philadelphia. Paul Shmyr scored for Minnesota at 13:20 of the first period; Steve Christoff, Minnesota, 13:59; Ken Linseman, Philadelphia, 14:54; Tom Gorence, Philadelphia, 15:36; and Ken Linseman, Philadelphia, 16:40. Minnesota won 6-5. Philadelphia won best-of-seven SF 4-1.
4:00 — Los Angeles Kings, Detroit Red Wings, April 15, 2000, at Detroit. Brendan Shanahan scored for Detroit at 0:55 of the first period; Martin Lapointe, Detroit, 1:33; Luc Robitaille, Los Angeles, 2:04; Kris Draper, Detroit, 3:32; and Ziggy Palffy, Los Angeles, 4:55. Detroit won 8-5 and best-of-seven CQF 4-0.

FASTEST FIVE GOALS, ONE TEAM:
3:36 — Montreal Canadiens, March 30, 1944, at Montreal vs. Toronto. Toe Blake scored at 7:58 and 8:37 of the third period; Maurice Richard, 9:17; Ray Getliffe, 10:33; and Buddy O'Connor, 11:34. Canadiens won 11-0 and best-of-seven SF 4-1.

FASTEST FOUR GOALS, BOTH TEAMS:
1:33 — Toronto Maple Leafs, Philadelphia Flyers, April 20, 1976, at Philadelphia. Don Saleski scored for Philadelphia at 10:04 of the second period; Bob Neely, Toronto, 10:42; Gary Dornhoefer, Philadelphia, 11:24; and Don Saleski, Philadelphia, 11:37. Philadelphia won 7-1 and best-of-seven SF 4-3.
1:34 — Calgary Flames, Montreal Canadiens, May 20, 1986, at Montreal. Joel Otto scored for Calgary at 17:59 of the first period; Bobby Smith, Montreal, 18:25; Mats Naslund, Montreal, 19:17; and Bob Gainey, Montreal, 19:33. Montreal won 5-3 and best-of-seven F 4-1.
1:38 — Boston Bruins, Philadelphia Flyers, April 26, 1977, at Philadelphia. Gregg Sheppard scored for Boston at 14:01 of the second period; Mike Milbury, Boston, 15:01; Gary Dornhoefer, Philadelphia, 15:16; and Jean Ratelle, Boston, 15:39. Boston won 5-4 and best-of-seven SF 4-0.

FASTEST FOUR GOALS, ONE TEAM:
2:35 — Montreal Canadiens, March 30, 1944, at Montreal. Toe Blake scored at 7:58 and 8:37 of the third period; Maurice Richard, 9:17; and Ray Getliffe, 10:33. Montreal won 11-0 and best-of-seven SF 4-1.

FASTEST THREE GOALS, BOTH TEAMS:
0:21 — Chicago Black Hawks, Edmonton Oilers, May 7, 1985, at Edmonton. Behn Wilson scored for Chicago at 19:22 of the third period; Jari Kurri, Edmonton, 19:36; and Glenn Anderson, Edmonton, 19:43. Edmonton won 7-3 and best-of-seven CF 4-2.
0:27 — Phoenix Coyotes, Detroit Red Wings, April 24, 1998, at Detroit. Jeremy Roenick scored for Phoenix at 13:24 of the second period; Mathieu Dandenault, Detroit, 13:32; and Keith Tkachuk, Phoenix, 13:51. Phoenix won 7-4. Detroit won best-of-seven CQF 4-2.
0:30 — Pittsburgh Penguins, Chicago Black Hawks, June 1, 1992, at Chicago. Dirk Graham scored for Chicago at 6:21 of the first period; Kevin Stevens, Pittsburgh, 6:33; and Dirk Graham, Chicago, 6:51. Pittsburgh won 6-5 and best-of-seven F 4-0.

FASTEST THREE GOALS, ONE TEAM:
0:23 — Toronto Maple Leafs, April 12, 1979, at Toronto vs. Atlanta Flames. Darryl Sittler scored at 4:04 and 4:16 of the first period; and Ron Ellis, 4:27. Toronto won 7-4 and best-of-three 2-0.
0:38 — New York Rangers, April 12, 1986, at NY Rangers vs. Philadelphia. Jim Weimer scored at 12:29 of the third period; Bob Brooke, 12:43; and Ron Greschner, 13:07. NY Rangers won 5-2 and best-of-five DSF 3-2.
— Colorado Avalanche, April 18, 2001, at Vancouver. Peter Forsberg scored at 9:11 of the third period; Joe Sakic, 9:28; and Eric Messier, 9:49. Colorado won 5-1 and best-of-seven CQF 4-0.

FASTEST TWO GOALS, BOTH TEAMS:
0:05 — Pittsburgh Penguins, Buffalo Sabres, April 14, 1979, at Buffalo. Gilbert Perreault scored for Buffalo at 12:59 of the first period; and Jim Hamilton, Pittsburgh, 13:04. Pittsburgh won 4-3 and best-of-three PRE 2-1.
0:08 — St. Louis Blues, Minnesota North Stars, April 9, 1989, at Minnesota. Bernie Federko scored for St. Louis at 2:28 of the third period; and Perry Berezan, Minnesota, 2:36. Minnesota won 5-4. St. Louis won best-of-seven DSF 4-1.
— Phoenix Coyotes, Detroit Red Wings, April 24, 1998, at Detroit. Jeremy Roenick scored for Phoenix at 13:24 of the second period; and Mathieu Dandenault, Detroit, 13:32. Phoenix won 7-4. Detroit won best-of-seven CQF 4-2.

FASTEST TWO GOALS, ONE TEAM:
0:05 — Detroit Red Wings, April 11, 1965, at Detroit vs. Chicago. Norm Ullman scored at 17:35 and 17:40 of the second period. Detroit won 4-2. Chicago won best-of-seven SF 4-3.

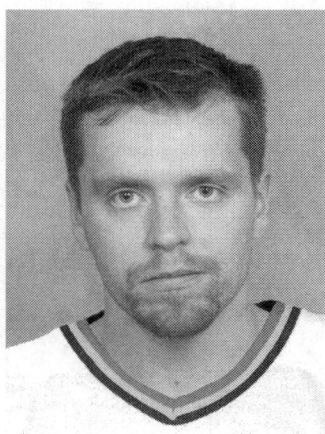

Tampa Bay's Nikolai Khabibulin (top) and Calgary's Miikka Kiprusoff (bottom) both had five shutouts during the 2004 playoffs. All teams combined for 23 postseason shutouts, with 11 of 16 teams having at least one.

OVERTIME

SHORTEST OVERTIME:
0:09 — Montreal Canadiens, Calgary Flames, May 18, 1986, at Calgary. Montreal won 3-2 on Brian Skrudland's goal at 0:09 of the first overtime period. Montreal won best-of-seven F 4-1.
0:11 — New York Islanders, New York Rangers, April 11, 1975, at NY Rangers. NY Islanders won 4-3 on J.P. Parise's goal at 0:11 of the first overtime period. NY Islanders won best-of-three PRE 2-1.

LONGEST OVERTIME:
116:30 — Detroit Red Wings, Montreal Maroons, March 24, 1936, at Montreal. Mtl. Maroons won 1-0 on Mud Bruneteau's goal at 16:30 of the sixth overtime period. Detroit won best-of-five SF 3-0.

MOST OVERTIME GAMES, ONE PLAYOFF YEAR:
28 — 1993. Of 85 games played, 28 went into overtime.
26 — 2001. Of 86 games played, 26 went into overtime.
22 — 2003. Of 89 games played, 22 went into overtime.
21 — 1999. Of 86 games played, 21 went into overtime.

FEWEST OVERTIME GAMES, ONE PLAYOFF YEAR:
0 — 1963. None of the 16 games went into overtime, the only year since 1926 that no overtime was required in any playoff series.

MOST OVERTIME GAMES, ONE SERIES:
5 — Toronto Maple Leafs, Montreal Canadiens in 1951. Toronto won best-of-seven F 4-1.
4 — Toronto Maple Leafs, Boston Bruins in 1933. Toronto won best-of-five SF 3-2.
— Boston Bruins, NY Rangers in 1939. Boston won best-of-seven SF 4-3.
— St. Louis Blues, Minnesota North Stars in 1968. St. Louis won best-of-seven SF 4-3.
— Dallas Stars, St. Louis Blues in 1999. Dallas won best-of-seven CSF 4-2.
— Dallas Stars, Edmonton Oilers in 2001. Dallas won best-of-seven CQF 4-2.

THREE-OR-MORE GOAL GAMES

MOST THREE-OR-MORE GOAL GAMES BY ALL TEAMS, ONE PLAYOFF YEAR:
12 — 1983 in 66 games.
— **1988** in 83 games.
11 — 1985 in 70 games.
— 1992 in 86 games.

MOST THREE-OR-MORE GOAL GAMES, ONE TEAM, ONE PLAYOFF YEAR:
6 — Edmonton Oilers in 16 games, 1983.
— **Edmonton Oilers** in 18 games, 1985.

SHUTOUTS

MOST SHUTOUTS, ONE PLAYOFF YEAR, ALL TEAMS:
25 — 2002. Of 90 games played, Detroit had 6; Ottawa had 4; Carolina, Colorado, St. Louis and Toronto had 3 each; while Los Angeles, New Jersey and Philadelphia had 1 each.
23 — 2004. Of 89 games played, Tampa Bay, Calgary had 5 each; Toronto, San Jose had 3 each; while Boston, Colorado, Detroit, Montreal, Nashville, NY Islanders and Philadelphia had 1 each.
19 — 2001. Of 86 games played, Colorado, New Jersey had 4 each, Toronto had 3, Pittsburgh and Los Angeles had 2 each, while Buffalo, Washington, Detroit and San Jose had 1 each.

FEWEST SHUTOUTS, ONE PLAYOFF YEAR, ALL TEAMS:
0 — 1959. 18 games played.

MOST SHUTOUTS, BOTH TEAMS, ONE SERIES:
5 — Toronto Maple Leafs (3), Detroit Red Wings (2), in 1945. Toronto won best-of-seven series F 4-3.
— **Toronto Maple Leafs (3), Detroit Red Wings (2),** in 1950. Toronto won best-of-seven SF 4-3.

TEAM PENALTIES

FEWEST PENALTIES, BOTH TEAMS, BEST-OF-SEVEN SERIES:
19 — Detroit Red Wings, Toronto Maple Leafs in 1945 F. Detroit received 10 minors, Toronto received 9 minors. Detroit won best-of-seven series 4-3.

FEWEST PENALTIES, ONE TEAM, BEST-OF-SEVEN SERIES:
9 — Toronto Maple Leafs in 1945 F vs. Detroit. Toronto received 9 minors. Detroit won best-of-seven series 4-3.

MOST PENALTIES, BOTH TEAMS, ONE SERIES:
218 — New Jersey Devils, Washington Capitals in 1988 DF. New Jersey received 97 minors, 11 majors, 9 misconducts and 1 match penalty. Washington received 80 minors, 11 majors, 8 misconducts and 1 match penalty. New Jersey won best-of-seven series 4-3.

MOST PENALTY MINUTES, BOTH TEAMS, ONE SERIES:
654 — New Jersey Devils (349), Washington Capitals (305) in 1988 DF. New Jersey won best-of-seven series 4-3.

MOST PENALTIES, ONE TEAM, ONE SERIES:
118 — New Jersey Devils in 1988 DF vs. Washington. New Jersey received 97 minors, 11 majors, 9 misconducts and 1 match penalty. New Jersey won best-of-seven series 4-3.

MOST PENALTY MINUTES, ONE TEAM, ONE SERIES:
349 — New Jersey Devils in 1988 DF vs. Washington. New Jersey won best-of-seven series 4-3.

MOST PENALTIES, BOTH TEAMS, ONE GAME:
66 — Detroit Red Wings (33), St. Louis Blues (33), April 12, 1991, at St. Louis. St. Louis won 6-1.
63 — Minnesota North Stars (34), Chicago Black Hawks (29), April 6, 1990, at Chicago. Chicago won 5-3.
62 — New Jersey Devils (32), Washington Capitals (30), April 22, 1988, at New Jersey. New Jersey won 10-4.

MOST PENALTY MINUTES, BOTH TEAMS, ONE GAME:
298 — Detroit Red Wings (152), St. Louis Blues (146), April 12, 1991, at St. Louis. Detroit received 33 penalties; St. Louis received 33 penalties. St. Louis won 6-1.
267 — New York Rangers (142), Los Angeles Kings (125), April 9, 1981, at Los Angeles. NY Rangers received 31 penalties; Los Angeles received 28 penalties. Los Angeles won 5-4.

MOST PENALTIES, ONE TEAM, ONE GAME:
34 — Minnesota North Stars, April 6, 1990, at Chicago. Chicago won 5-3.
33 — Detroit Red Wings, April 12, 1991, at St. Louis. St. Louis won 6-1.
— St. Louis Blues, April 12, 1991, at St. Louis vs. Detroit. St. Louis won 6-1.

MOST PENALTY MINUTES, ONE TEAM, ONE GAME:
152 — Detroit Red Wings, April 12, 1991, at St. Louis. St. Louis won 6-1.
146 — St. Louis Blues, April 12, 1991, at St. Louis vs. Detroit. St. Louis won 6-1.
142 — New York Rangers, April 9, 1981, at Los Angeles. Los Angeles won 5-4.

MOST PENALTIES, BOTH TEAMS, ONE PERIOD:
43 — New York Rangers (24), Los Angeles Kings (19), April 9, 1981, first period at Los Angeles. Los Angeles won 5-4.

MOST PENALTY MINUTES, BOTH TEAMS, ONE PERIOD:
248 — New York Islanders (124), Boston Bruins (124), April 17, 1980, first period at Boston. NY Islanders won 5-4.

MOST PENALTIES, ONE TEAM, ONE PERIOD:
24 — New York Rangers, April 9, 1981, first period at Los Angeles. Los Angeles won 5-4.

MOST PENALTY MINUTES, ONE TEAM, ONE PERIOD:
125 — New York Rangers, April 9, 1981, first period at Los Angeles. Los Angeles won 5-4.

Individual Records

GAMES PLAYED

MOST YEARS IN PLAYOFFS:
21 — Raymond Bourque, Boston, Colorado (1980-96 inclusive; 98-2001 inclusive)
20 — Gordie Howe, Detroit, Hartford
— Larry Robinson, Montreal, Los Angeles
— Larry Murphy, Los Angeles, Washington, Minnesota, Pittsburgh, Toronto, Detroit
— Scott Stevens, Washington, St. Louis, New Jersey
— Chris Chelios, Montreal, Chicago, Detroit

MOST CONSECUTIVE YEARS IN PLAYOFFS:
20 — Larry Robinson, Montreal, Los Angeles (1973-92, inclusive).
19 — Brett Hull, Calgary, St. Louis, Dallas, Detroit (1986-2004, inclusive).
18 — Larry Murphy, Los Angeles, Washington, Minnesota, Pittsburgh, Toronto, Detroit (1984-2001, inclusive).
17 — Brad Park, NY Rangers, Boston, Detroit (1969-85, inclusive).
— Raymond Bourque, Boston (1980-96, inclusive).

MOST PLAYOFF GAMES:
240 — Patrick Roy, Montreal, Colorado
236 — Mark Messier, Edmonton, NY Rangers
233 — Claude Lemieux, Montreal, New Jersey, Colorado, Phoenix
231 — Guy Carbonneau, Montreal, St. Louis, Dallas
227 — Larry Robinson, Montreal, Los Angeles

GOALS

MOST GOALS IN PLAYOFFS (CAREER):
122 — Wayne Gretzky, Edmonton, Los Angeles, St. Louis, NY Rangers
109 — Mark Messier, Edmonton, NY Rangers
106 — Jari Kurri, Edmonton, Los Angeles, NY Rangers, Anaheim
100 — Brett Hull, Calgary, St. Louis, Dallas, Detroit
93 — Glenn Anderson, Edmonton, Toronto, NY Rangers, St. Louis

MOST GOALS, ONE PLAYOFF YEAR:
19 — Reggie Leach, Philadelphia, 1976. 16 games.
— Jari Kurri, Edmonton, 1985. 18 games.
18 — Joe Sakic, Colorado, 1996. 22 games.
17 — Newsy Lalonde, Montreal, 1919. 10 games.
— Mike Bossy, NY Islanders, 1981. 18 games.
— Steve Payne, Minnesota, 1981. 19 games.
— Mike Bossy, NY Islanders, 1982. 19 games.
— Mike Bossy, NY Islanders, 1983. 19 games
— Wayne Gretzky, Edmonton, 1985. 18 games.
— Kevin Stevens, Pittsburgh, 1991. 24 games.

MOST GOALS IN ONE SERIES (OTHER THAN FINAL):
12 — Jari Kurri, Edmonton, in 1985 CF, 6 games vs. Chicago.
11 — Newsy Lalonde, Montreal, in 1919 NHL F, 5 games vs. Ottawa.
10 — Tim Kerr, Philadelphia, in 1989 DF, 7 games vs. Pittsburgh.
9 — Reggie Leach, Philadelphia, in 1976 SF, 5 games vs. Boston.
— Bill Barber, Philadelphia, in 1980 SF, 5 games vs. Minnesota.
— Mike Bossy, NY Islanders, in 1983 DF, 6 games vs. Boston.
— Mario Lemieux, Pittsburgh, in 1989 DF, 7 games vs. Philadelphia.

MOST GOALS IN FINAL SERIES (NHL PLAYERS ONLY):
9 — Babe Dye, Toronto, in 1922, 5 games vs. Van. Millionaires.
8 — Alf Skinner, Toronto, in 1918, 5 games vs. Van. Millionaires.
7 — Jean Beliveau, Montreal, in 1956, 5 games vs. Detroit.
— Mike Bossy, NY Islanders, in 1982, 4 games vs. Vancouver.
— Wayne Gretzky, Edmonton, in 1985, 5 games vs. Philadelphia.

MOST GOALS, ONE GAME:
5 — Newsy Lalonde, Montreal, March 1, 1919, at Montreal. Final score: Montreal 6, Ottawa 3.
— Maurice Richard, Montreal, March 23, 1944, at Montreal. Final score: Montreal 5, Toronto 1.
— Darryl Sittler, Toronto, April 22, 1976, at Toronto. Final score: Toronto 8, Philadelphia 5.
— Reggie Leach, Philadelphia, May 6, 1976, at Philadelphia. Final score: Philadelphia 6, Boston 3.
— Mario Lemieux, Pittsburgh, April 25, 1989, at Pittsburgh. Final score: Pittsburgh 10, Philadelphia 7.

MOST GOALS, ONE PERIOD:
4 — Tim Kerr, Philadelphia, April 13, 1985, at NY Rangers, second period. Final score: Philadelphia 6, NY Rangers 5.
— Mario Lemieux, Pittsburgh, April 25, 1989, at Pittsburgh vs. Philadelphia, first period. Final score: Pittsburgh 10, Philadelphia 7.

ASSISTS

MOST ASSISTS IN PLAYOFFS (CAREER):
260 — Wayne Gretzky, Edmonton, Los Angeles, St. Louis, NY Rangers
186 — Mark Messier, Edmonton, NY Rangers
139 — Raymond Bourque, Boston, Colorado
137 — Paul Coffey, Edmonton, Pittsburgh, Los Angeles, Detroit, Philadelphia, Carolina
128 — Doug Gilmour, St. Louis, Calgary, Toronto, New Jersey, Buffalo, Montreal

MOST ASSISTS, ONE PLAYOFF YEAR:
31 — Wayne Gretzky, Edmonton, 1988. 19 games.
30 — Wayne Gretzky, Edmonton, 1985. 18 games.
29 — Wayne Gretzky, Edmonton, 1987. 21 games.
28 — Mario Lemieux, Pittsburgh, 1991. 23 games.
26 — Wayne Gretzky, Edmonton, 1983. 16 games.

MOST ASSISTS IN ONE SERIES (OTHER THAN FINAL):
14 — Rick Middleton, Boston, in 1983 DF, 7 games vs. Buffalo.
— Wayne Gretzky, Edmonton, in 1985 CF, 6 games vs. Chicago.
13 — Wayne Gretzky, Edmonton, in 1987 DSF, 5 games vs. Los Angeles.
— Doug Gilmour, Toronto, in 1994 CSF, 7 games vs. San Jose.
11 — Al MacInnis, Calgary, in 1984 DF, 7 games vs. Edmonton.
— Mark Messier, Edmonton, in 1989 DSF, 7 games vs. Los Angeles.
— Mike Ridley, Washington, in 1992 DSF, 7 games vs. Pittsburgh.
— Ron Francis, Pittsburgh, in 1995 CQF, 7 games vs. Washington.
10 — Fleming Mackell, Boston, in 1958 SF, 6 games vs. NY Rangers.
— Stan Mikita, Chicago, in 1962 SF, 6 games vs. Montreal.
— Bob Bourne, NY Islanders, in 1983 DF, 6 games vs. NY Rangers.
— Wayne Gretzky, Edmonton, in 1988 DSF, 5 games vs. Winnipeg.
— Mario Lemieux, Pittsburgh, in 1992 DSF, 6 games vs. Washington.

MOST ASSISTS IN FINAL SERIES:
10 — Wayne Gretzky, Edmonton, in 1988, 4 games plus suspended game vs. Boston.
9 — Jacques Lemaire, Montreal, in 1973, 6 games vs. Chicago.
— Wayne Gretzky, Edmonton, in 1987, 7 games vs. Philadelphia.
— Larry Murphy, Pittsburgh, in 1991, 6 games vs. Minnesota.

MOST ASSISTS, ONE GAME:
6 — Mikko Leinonen, NY Rangers, April 8, 1982, at NY Rangers. Final score: NY Rangers 7, Philadelphia 3.
— Wayne Gretzky, Edmonton, April 9, 1987, at Edmonton. Final score: Edmonton 13, Los Angeles 3.
5 — Toe Blake, Montreal, March 23, 1944, at Montreal. Final score: Montreal 5, Toronto 1.
— Maurice Richard, Montreal, March 27, 1956, at Montreal. Final score: Montreal 7, NY Rangers 0.
— Bert Olmstead, Montreal, March 30, 1957, at Montreal. Final score: Montreal 8, NY Rangers 3.
— Don McKenney, Boston, April 5, 1958, at Boston. Final score: Boston 8, NY Rangers 2.
— Stan Mikita, Chicago, April 4, 1973, at Chicago. Final score: Chicago 7, St. Louis 1.
— Wayne Gretzky, Edmonton, April 8, 1981, at Montreal. Final score: Edmonton 6, Montreal 3.
— Paul Coffey, Edmonton, May 14, 1985, at Edmonton. Final score: Edmonton 10, Chicago 5.
— Doug Gilmour, St. Louis, April 15, 1986, at Minnesota. Final score: St. Louis 6, Minnesota 3.
— Risto Siltanen, Quebec, April 14, 1987, at Hartford. Final score: Quebec 7, Hartford 5.
— Patrik Sundstrom, New Jersey, April 22, 1988, at New Jersey. Final score: New Jersey 10, Washington 4.
— Geoff Courtnall, St. Louis, April 23, 1998, at St. Louis. Final score: St. Louis 8, Los Angeles 3.

MOST ASSISTS, ONE PERIOD:
3 — Three assists by one player in one period of a playoff game has been recorded on 74 occasions. Chris Chelios of the Detroit Red Wings is the most recent to equal this mark with 3 assists in the second period at Vancouver, April 27, 2002. Final score: Detroit 6, Vancouver 4.
— Wayne Gretzky has had 3 assists in one period 5 times; Raymond Bourque, 3 times; Toe Blake, Jean Beliveau, Doug Harvey and Bobby Orr, twice each. Joe Primeau of Toronto was the first player to be credited with 3 assists in one period of a playoff game; third period at Boston vs. NY Rangers, April 7, 1932. Final score: Toronto 6, NY Rangers 2.

POINTS

MOST POINTS IN PLAYOFFS (CAREER):
382 — Wayne Gretzky, Edmonton, Los Angeles, St. Louis, NY Rangers, 122G, 260A
295 — Mark Messier, Edmonton, NY Rangers, 109G, 186A
233 — Jari Kurri, Edmonton, Los Angeles, NY Rangers, Anaheim, 106G, 127A
214 — Glenn Anderson, Edmonton, Toronto, NY Rangers, St. Louis, 93G, 121A
196 — Paul Coffey, Edmonton, Pittsburgh, Los Angeles, Detroit, Philadelphia, Carolina, 59G, 137A

MOST POINTS, ONE PLAYOFF YEAR:
47 — Wayne Gretzky, Edmonton, in 1985. 17 goals, 30 assists in 18 games.
44 — Mario Lemieux, Pittsburgh, in 1991. 16 goals, 28 assists in 23 games.
43 — Wayne Gretzky, Edmonton, in 1988. 12 goals, 31 assists in 19 games.
40 — Wayne Gretzky, Los Angeles, in 1993. 15 goals, 25 assists in 24 games.
38 — Wayne Gretzky, Edmonton, in 1983. 12 goals, 26 assists in 16 games.

MOST POINTS IN ONE SERIES (OTHER THAN FINAL):

19 — Rick Middleton, Boston, in 1983 DF, 7 games vs. Buffalo. 5 goals, 14 assists.

18 — Wayne Gretzky, Edmonton, in 1985 CF, 6 games vs. Chicago. 4 goals, 14 assists.

17 — Mario Lemieux, Pittsburgh, in 1992 DSF, 6 games vs. Washington. 7 goals, 10 assists.

16 — Barry Pederson, Boston, in 1983 DF, 7 games vs. Buffalo. 7 goals, 9 assists.
— Doug Gilmour, Toronto, in 1994 CSF, 7 games vs. San Jose. 3 goals, 13 assists.

15 — Jari Kurri, Edmonton, in 1985 CF, 6 games vs. Chicago. 12 goals, 3 assists.
— Wayne Gretzky, Edmonton, in 1987 DSF, 5 games vs. Los Angeles. 2 goals, 13 assists.
— Tim Kerr, Philadelphia, in 1989 DF, 7 games vs. Pittsburgh. 10 goals, 5 assists.
— Mario Lemieux, Pittsburgh, in 1991 CF, 6 games vs. Boston. 6 goals, 9 assists.

MOST POINTS IN FINAL SERIES:

13 — Wayne Gretzky, Edmonton, in 1988, 4 games plus suspended game vs. Boston. 3 goals, 10 assists.

12 — Gordie Howe, Detroit, in 1955, 7 games vs. Montreal. 5 goals, 7 assists.
— Yvan Cournoyer, Montreal, in 1973, 6 games vs. Chicago. 6 goals, 6 assists.
— Jacques Lemaire, Montreal, in 1973, 6 games vs. Chicago. 3 goals, 9 assists.
— Mario Lemieux, Pittsburgh, in 1991, 5 games vs. Minnesota. 5 goals, 7 assists.

MOST POINTS, ONE GAME:

8 — Patrik Sundstrom, New Jersey, April 22, 1988, at New Jersey in 10-4 win over Washington. Sundstrom had 3 goals, 5 assists.
— **Mario Lemieux, Pittsburgh,** April 25, 1989, at Pittsburgh in 10-7 win over Philadelphia. Lemieux had 5 goals, 3 assists.

7 — Wayne Gretzky, Edmonton, April 17, 1983, at Calgary in 10-2 win. Gretzky had 4 goals, 3 assists.
— Wayne Gretzky, Edmonton, April 25,1985, at Winnipeg in 8-3 win. Gretzky had 3 goals, 4 assists.
— Wayne Gretzky, Edmonton, April 9, 1987, at Edmonton in 13-3 win over Los Angeles. Gretzky had 1 goal, 6 assists.

6 — Dickie Moore, Montreal, March 25, 1954, at Montreal in 8-1 win over Boston. Moore had 2 goals, 4 assists.
— Phil Esposito, Boston, April 2, 1969, at Boston in 10-0 win over Toronto. Esposito had 4 goals, 2 assists.
— Darryl Sittler, Toronto, April 22, 1976, at Toronto in 8-5 win over Philadelphia. Sittler had 5 goals, 1 assist.
— Guy Lafleur, Montreal, April 11, 1977, at Montreal in 7-2 win over St. Louis. Lafleur had 3 goals, 3 assists.
— Mikko Leinonen, NY Rangers, April 8, 1982, at NY Rangers in 7-3 win over Philadelphia. Leinonen had 6 assists.
— Paul Coffey, Edmonton, May 14, 1985, at Edmonton in 10-5 win over Chicago. Coffey had 1 goal, 5 assists.
— John Anderson, Hartford, April 12, 1986, at Hartford in 9-4 win over Quebec. Anderson had 2 goals, 4 assists.
— Mario Lemieux, Pittsburgh, April 23, 1992, at Pittsburgh in 6-4 win over Washington. Lemieux had 3 goals, 3 assists.
— Geoff Courtnall, St. Louis, April 23, 1998, at St. Louis in 8-3 win over Los Angeles. Courtnall had 1 goal, 5 assists.

MOST POINTS, ONE PERIOD:

4 — Maurice Richard, Montreal, March 29, 1945, at Montreal, third period, in 10-3 win vs. Toronto. 3 goals, 1 assist.
— **Dickie Moore,** Montreal, March 25, 1954, at Montreal, first period, in 8-1 win vs. Boston. 2 goals, 2 assists.
— **Barry Pederson,** Boston, April 8, 1982, at Boston, second period, in 7-3 win vs. Buffalo. 3 goals, 1 assist.
— **Peter McNab,** Boston, April 11, 1982, at Buffalo, second period, in 5-2 win vs. Buffalo. 1 goal, 3 assists.
— **Tim Kerr,** Philadelphia, April 13, 1985, at NY Rangers, second period, in 6-5 win vs. NY Rangers. 4 goals.
— **Ken Linseman,** Boston, April 14, 1985, at Boston, second period, in 7-6 win vs. Montreal. 2 goals, 2 assists.
— **Wayne Gretzky,** Edmonton, April 12, 1987, at Los Angeles, third period, in 6-3 win vs. Los Angeles. 1 goal, 3 assists.
— **Glenn Anderson,** Edmonton, April 6, 1988, at Edmonton, third period, in 7-4 win vs. Winnipeg. 3 goals, 1 assist.
— **Mario Lemieux,** Pittsburgh, April 25, 1989, at Pittsburgh, first period, in 10-7 win vs. Philadelphia. 4 goals.
— **Dave Gagner,** Minnesota North Stars, April 8, 1991, at Minnesota, first period, in 6-5 loss vs. Chicago. 2 goals, 2 assists.
— **Mario Lemieux,** Pittsburgh, April 23, 1992, at Pittsburgh, second period, in 6-4 win vs. Washington. 2 goals, 2 assists.
— **Alexander Mogilny,** New Jersey, April 28, 2001, at New Jersey, second period, in 6-5 win vs. Toronto. 1 goal, 3 assists.

POWER-PLAY GOALS

MOST POWER-PLAY GOALS IN PLAYOFFS (CAREER):

38 — Brett Hull, St. Louis, Dallas, Detroit
35 — Mike Bossy, NY Islanders
34 — Dino Ciccarelli, Minnesota, Washington, Detroit
— Wayne Gretzky, Edmonton, Los Angeles, St. Louis, NY Rangers
29 — Mario Lemieux, Pittsburgh

MOST POWER-PLAY GOALS, ONE PLAYOFF YEAR:

9 — Mike Bossy, NY Islanders, 1981. 18 games vs. Toronto, Edmonton, NY Rangers and Minnesota.
— **Cam Neely, Boston,** 1991. 19 games vs. Hartford, Montreal and Pittsburgh.
8 — Tim Kerr, Philadelphia, 1989. 19 games.
— John Druce, Washington, 1990. 15 games.
— Brian Propp, Minnesota, 1991. 23 games.
— Mario Lemieux, Pittsburgh, 1992. 15 games.

MOST POWER-PLAY GOALS, ONE PLAYOFF SERIES:

6 — Chris Kontos, Los Angeles, 1989 DSF vs. Edmonton, won by Los Angeles 4-3.

5 — Andy Bathgate, Detroit, 1966 SF vs. Chicago, won by Detroit 4-2.
— Denis Potvin, NY Islanders, 1981 QF vs. Edmonton, won by NY Islanders 4-2.
— Ken Houston, Calgary, 1981 QF vs. Philadelphia, won by Calgary 4-3.
— Rick Vaive, Chicago, 1988 DSF vs. St. Louis, won by St. Louis 4-1.
— Tim Kerr, Philadelphia, 1989 DF vs. Pittsburgh, won by Philadelphia 4-3.
— Mario Lemieux, Pittsburgh, 1989 DF vs. Philadelphia, won by Philadelphia 4-3.
— John Druce, Washington, 1990 DF vs. NY Rangers, won by Washington 4-1.
— Pat LaFontaine, Buffalo, 1992 DSF vs. Boston, won by Boston 4-3.
— Adam Graves, NY Rangers, 1996 CQF vs Montreal, won by NY Rangers 4-2.

MOST POWER-PLAY GOALS, ONE GAME:

3 — Syd Howe, Detroit, March 23, 1939, at Detroit vs. Montreal. Detroit won 7-3.
— **Sid Smith, Toronto,** April 10, 1949, at Detroit. Toronto won 3-1.
— **Phil Esposito, Boston,** April 2, 1969, at Boston vs. Toronto. Boston won 10-0.
— **John Bucyk, Boston,** April 21, 1974, at Boston vs. Chicago. Boston won 8-6.
— **Denis Potvin, NY Islanders,** April 17, 1981, at NY Islanders vs. Edmonton. NY Islanders won 6-3.
— **Tim Kerr, Philadelphia,** April 13, 1985, at NY Rangers. Philadelphia won 6-5.
— **Jari Kurri, Edmonton,** April 9, 1987, at Edmonton vs. Los Angeles. Edmonton won 13-3.
— **Mark Johnson, New Jersey,** April 22, 1988, at New Jersey vs. Washington. New Jersey won 10-4.
— **Dino Ciccarelli, Detroit,** April 29, 1993, at Toronto. Detroit won 7-3.
— **Dino Ciccarelli, Detroit,** May 11, 1995, at Dallas. Detroit won 5-1.
— **Valeri Kamensky, Colorado,** April 24, 1997, at Colorado vs. Chicago. Colorado won 7-0.

MOST POWER-PLAY GOALS, ONE PERIOD:

3 — Tim Kerr, Philadelphia, April 13, 1985, at NY Rangers, second period in 6-5 win.

2 — Two power-play goals have been scored by one player in one period on 55 occasions. Charlie Conacher of Toronto was the first to score two power-play goals in one period, setting the mark with two power-play goals in the second period at Toronto vs. Boston, March 26, 1936. Final score: Toronto 8, Boston 3. Brad Richards of the Tampa Bay Lightning is the most recent to equal this mark with two power-play goals in the second period at Calgary, June 5, 2004. Final score: Tampa Bay 3, Calgary 2.

SHORTHAND GOALS

MOST SHORTHAND GOALS IN PLAYOFFS (CAREER):

14 — Mark Messier, Edmonton, NY Rangers
11 — Wayne Gretzky, Edmonton, Los Angeles, St. Louis
10 — Jari Kurri, Edmonton, Los Angeles, NY Rangers
8 — Ed Westfall, Boston, NY Islanders
— Hakan Loob, Calgary

MOST SHORTHAND GOALS, ONE PLAYOFF YEAR:

3 — Derek Sanderson, Boston, 1969. 1 vs. Toronto in QF, won by Boston 4-0; 2 vs. Montreal in SF, won by Montreal, 4-2.
— **Bill Barber, Philadelphia,** 1980. All vs. Minnesota in SF, won by Philadelphia 4-1.
— **Lorne Henning, NY Islanders,** 1980. 1 vs. Boston in QF, won by NY Islanders 4-1; 1 vs. Buffalo in SF, won by NY Islanders 4-2, 1 vs. Philadelphia in F, won by NY Islanders 4-2.
— **Wayne Gretzky, Edmonton,** 1983. 2 vs. Winnipeg in DSF, won by Edmonton 3-0; 1 vs. Calgary in DF, won by Edmonton 4-1.
— **Wayne Presley, Chicago,** 1989. All vs. Detroit in DSF, won by Chicago 4-2.
— **Todd Marchant, Edmonton,** 1997. 1 vs. Dallas in CQF, won by Edmonton 4-3; 2 vs. Colorado in CSF, won by Colorado 4-1.

Keith Primeau's nine goals for the Flyers in the 2004 playoffs matched his previous career total for playoff goals. Two of those nine goals came while Philadelphia was shorthanded.

MOST SHORTHAND GOALS, ONE PLAYOFF SERIES:
3 — **Bill Barber, Philadelphia,** 1980 SF vs. Minnesota, won by Philadelphia 4-1.
— **Wayne Presley, Chicago,** 1989 DSF vs. Detroit, won by Chicago 4-2.
2 — Mac Colville, NY Rangers, 1940 SF vs. Boston, won by NY Rangers 4-2.
— Jerry Toppazzini, Boston, 1958 SF vs. NY Rangers, won by Boston 4-2.
— Dave Keon, Toronto, 1963 F vs. Detroit, won by Toronto 4-1.
— Bob Pulford, Toronto, 1964 F vs. Detroit, won by Toronto 4-3.
— Serge Savard, Montreal, 1968 F vs. St. Louis, won by Montreal 4-0.
— Derek Sanderson, Boston, 1969 SF vs. Montreal, won by Montreal 4-2.
— Bryan Trottier, NY Islanders, 1980 PR vs. Los Angeles, won by NY Islanders 3-1.
— Bobby Lalonde, Boston, 1981 PR vs. Minnesota, won by Minnesota 3-0.
— Butch Goring, NY Islanders, 1981 SF vs. NY Rangers, won by NY Islanders 4-0.
— Wayne Gretzky, Edmonton, 1983 DSF vs. Winnipeg, won by Edmonton 3-0.
— Mark Messier, Edmonton, 1983 DF vs. Calgary, won by Edmonton 4-1.
— Jari Kurri, Edmonton, 1983 CF vs. Chicago, won by Edmonton 4-0.
— Wayne Gretzky, Edmonton, 1985 DF vs. Winnipeg, won by Edmonton 4-0.
— Kevin Lowe, Edmonton, 1987 F vs. Philadelphia, won by Edmonton 4-3.
— Bob Gould, Washington, 1988 DSF vs. Philadelphia, won by Washington 4-3.
— Dave Poulin, Philadelphia, 1989 DF vs. Pittsburgh, won by Philadelphia 4-3.
— Russ Courtnall, Montreal, 1991 DF vs. Boston, won by Boston 4-3.
— Sergei Fedorov, Detroit, 1992 DSF vs. Minnesota, won by Detroit 4-3.
— Mark Messier, NY Rangers, 1992 DSF vs. New Jersey, won by NY Rangers 4-3.
— Tom Fitzgerald, NY Islanders, 1993 DF vs. Pittsburgh, won by NY Islanders 4-3.
— Mark Osborne, Toronto, 1994 CSF vs. San Jose, won by Toronto 4-3.
— Tony Amonte, Chicago, 1997 CQF vs. Colorado, won by Colorado 4-2.
— Brian Rolston, New Jersey, 1997 CQF vs. Montreal, won by New Jersey 4-1.
— Rod Brind'Amour, Philadelphia, 1997 CQF vs. Pittsburgh, won by Philadelphia 4-1.
— Todd Marchant, Edmonton, 1997 CSF vs. Colorado, won by Colorado 4-1.
— Jeremy Roenick, Phoenix, 1998 CQF vs. Detroit, won by Detroit 4-2.
— Vincent Damphousse, San Jose, 1999 CQF vs. Colorado, won by Colorado 4-2.
— Dixon Ward, Buffalo, 1999 CF vs. Toronto, won by Buffalo 4-1.
— Curtis Brown, Buffalo, 2001 CSF vs. Pittsburgh, won by Pittsburgh 4-3.

MOST SHORTHAND GOALS, ONE GAME:
2 — **Dave Keon, Toronto,** April 18, 1963, at Toronto, in 3-1 win vs. Detroit.
— **Bryan Trottier, NY Islanders,** April 8, 1980, at NY Islanders, in 8-1 win vs. Los Angeles.
— **Bobby Lalonde, Boston,** April 11, 1981, at Minnesota, in 6-3 loss vs. Minnesota.
— **Wayne Gretzky, Edmonton,** April 6, 1983, at Edmonton, in 6-3 win vs. Winnipeg.
— **Jari Kurri, Edmonton,** April 24, 1983, at Edmonton, in 8-3 win vs. Chicago.
— **Mark Messier, NY Rangers,** April 21, 1992, at NY Rangers, in 7-3 loss vs. New Jersey.
— **Tom Fitzgerald, NY Islanders,** May 8, 1993, at NY Islanders, in 6-5 win vs. Pittsburgh.
— **Rod Brind'Amour, Philadelphia,** April 26, 1997, at Philadelphia, in 6-3 win vs. Pittsburgh.
— **Jeremy Roenick, Phoenix,** April 24, 1998, at Detroit, in 7-4 win vs. Detroit.
— **Vincent Damphousse, San Jose,** April 30, 1999, at Colorado, in 7-3 win by San Jose.

MOST SHORTHAND GOALS, ONE PERIOD:
2 — **Bryan Trottier, NY Islanders,** April 8, 1980, second period, at NY Islanders, in 8-1 win vs. Los Angeles.
— **Bobby Lalonde, Boston,** April 11, 1981, third period, at Minnesota, in 6-3 loss vs. Minnesota.
— **Jari Kurri, Edmonton,** April 24, 1983, third period, at Edmonton, in 8-4 win vs. Chicago.
— **Rod Brind'Amour, Philadelphia,** April 26, 1997, first period, at Philadelphia, in 6-3 win vs. Pittsburgh.
— **Jeremy Roenick, Phoenix,** April 24, 1998, second period, at Detroit, in 7-4 win by Phoenix.
— **Vincent Damphousse, San Jose,** April 30, 1999, third period, at Colorado, in 7-3 win vs. Colorado.

GAME-WINNING GOALS

MOST GAME-WINNING GOALS IN PLAYOFFS, CAREER:
24 — **Wayne Gretzky, Edmonton, Los Angeles, St. Louis, NY Rangers**
— **Brett Hull, St. Louis, Dallas, Detroit**
19 — Claude Lemieux, Montreal, New Jersey, Colorado
18 — Maurice Richard, Montreal
17 — Mike Bossy, NY Islanders
— Glenn Anderson, Edmonton, Toronto, NY Rangers, St. Louis
— Joe Sakic, Colorado

MOST GAME-WINNING GOALS, ONE PLAYOFF YEAR:
7 — **Brad Richards, Tampa Bay,** 2004. 23 games.
6 — Joe Sakic, Colorado, 1996. 22 games.
— Joe Nieuwendyk, Dallas, 1999. 23 games.
5 — Mike Bossy, NY Islanders, 1983. 19 games.
— Jari Kurri, Edmonton, 1987. 21 games.
— Bobby Smith, Minnesota, 1991. 23 games.
— Mario Lemieux, Pittsburgh, 1992. 15 games.

MOST GAME-WINNING GOALS, ONE PLAYOFF SERIES:
4 — **Mike Bossy, NY Islanders,** 1983 CF vs. Boston, won by NY Islanders 4-2.

OVERTIME GOALS

MOST OVERTIME GOALS IN PLAYOFFS, CAREER:
6 — **Maurice Richard, Montreal** (1 in 1946; 3 in 1951; 1 in 1957; 1 in 1958)
— **Joe Sakic, Colorado** (2 in 1996; 1 in 1998; 1 in 2001; 2 in 2004)
5 — Glenn Anderson, Edmonton, Toronto, St. Louis
4 — Bob Nystrom, NY Islanders
— Dale Hunter, Quebec, Washington
— Wayne Gretzky, Edmonton, Los Angeles
— Stephane Richer, Montreal, New Jersey
— Joe Murphy, Edmonton, Chicago
— Esa Tikkanen, Edmonton, NY Rangers
— Jaromir Jagr, Pittsburgh
— Kirk Muller, Montreal, Dallas
— Jeremy Roenick, Chicago, Philadelphia

MOST OVERTIME GOALS, ONE PLAYOFF YEAR:
3 — **Mel Hill, Boston,** 1939. All vs. NY Rangers in best-of-seven SF, won by Boston 4-3.
— **Maurice Richard, Montreal,** 1951. 2 vs. Detroit in best-of-seven SF, won by Montreal 4-2; 1 vs. Toronto best-of-seven F, won by Toronto 4-1.

MOST OVERTIME GOALS, ONE PLAYOFF SERIES:
3 — **Mel Hill, Boston,** 1939, SF vs. NY Rangers, won by Boston 4-3. Hill scored at 59:25 of overtime March 21 for a 2-1 win; at 8:24 of overtime, March 23 for a 3-2 win; and at 48:00 of overtime, April 2 for a 2-1 win.

By scoring a pair of overtime goals in Colorado's Western Semifinal series with San Jose, Joe Sakic tied the legendary Maurice Richard with six career playoff overtime goals.

SCORING BY A DEFENSEMAN

MOST GOALS BY A DEFENSEMAN, ONE PLAYOFF YEAR:
12 — Paul Coffey, Edmonton, 1985. 18 games.
11 — Brian Leetch, NY Rangers, 1994. 23 games.
9 — Bobby Orr, Boston, 1970. 14 games.
 — Brad Park, Boston, 1978. 15 games.
8 — Denis Potvin, NY Islanders, 1981. 18 games.
 — Raymond Bourque, Boston, 1983. 17 games.
 — Denis Potvin, NY Islanders, 1983. 20 games.
 — Paul Coffey, Edmonton, 1984. 19 games.

MOST GOALS BY A DEFENSEMAN, ONE GAME:
3 — **Bobby Orr, Boston,** April 11, 1971, at Montreal. Final score:
Boston 5, Montreal 2.
 — **Dick Redmond, Chicago,** April 4, 1973, at Chicago. Final score:
Chicago 7, St. Louis 1.
 — **Denis Potvin, NY Islanders,** April 17, 1981, at NY Islanders. Final score:
NY Islanders 6, Edmonton 3.
 — **Paul Reinhart, Calgary,** April 14, 1983, at Edmonton. Final score:
Edmonton 6, Calgary 3.
 — **Doug Halward, Vancouver,** April 7, 1984, at Vancouver. Final score:
Vancouver 7, Calgary 0.
 — **Paul Reinhart, Calgary,** April 8, 1984, at Vancouver. Final score:
Calgary 5, Vancouver 1.
 — **Al Iafrate, Washington,** April 26, 1993, at Washington. Final score:
Washington 6, NY Islanders 4.
 — **Eric Desjardins, Montreal,** June 3, 1993, at Montreal. Final score:
Montreal 3, Los Angeles 2.
 — **Gary Suter, Chicago,** April 24, 1994, at Chicago. Final score:
Chicago 4, Toronto 3.
 — **Brian Leetch, NY Rangers,** May 22, 1995, at Philadelphia. Final score:
Philadelphia 4, NY Rangers 3.
 — **Andy Delmore, Philadelphia,** May 7, 2000, at Philadelphia. Final score:
Philadelphia 6, Pittsburgh 3.

MOST ASSISTS BY A DEFENSEMAN, ONE PLAYOFF YEAR:
25 — Paul Coffey, Edmonton, 1985. 18 games.
24 — Al MacInnis, Calgary, 1989. 22 games.
23 — Brian Leetch, NY Rangers, 1994. 23 games.
19 — Bobby Orr, Boston, 1972. 15 games.
18 — Raymond Bourque, Boston, 1988. 23 games.
 — Raymond Bourque, Boston, 1991. 19 games.
 — Larry Murphy, Pittsburgh, 1991. 23 games.

MOST ASSISTS BY A DEFENSEMAN, ONE GAME:
5 — **Paul Coffey, Edmonton,** May 14, 1985 at Edmonton vs. Chicago.
Edmonton won 10-5.
 — **Risto Siltanen, Quebec,** April 14, 1987 at Hartford. Quebec won 7-5.

MOST POINTS BY A DEFENSEMAN, ONE PLAYOFF YEAR:
37 — Paul Coffey, Edmonton, 1985. 12 goals, 25 assists in 18 games.
34 — Brian Leetch, NY Rangers, 1994. 11 goals, 23 assists in 23 games.
31 — Al MacInnis, Calgary, 1989. 7 goals, 24 assists in 22 games.
25 — Denis Potvin, NY Islanders, 1981. 8 goals, 17 assists in 18 games.
 — Raymond Bourque, Boston, 1991. 7 goals, 18 assists in 19 games.

MOST POINTS BY A DEFENSEMAN, ONE GAME:
6 — **Paul Coffey, Edmonton,** May 14, 1985 at Edmonton vs. Chicago. 1 goal,
5 assists. Edmonton won 10-5.
5 — Eddie Bush, Detroit, April 9, 1942, at Detroit vs. Toronto. 1 goal, 4 assists.
Detroit won 5-2.
 — Bob Dailey, Philadelphia, May 1, 1980, at Philadelphia vs. Minnesota. 1 goal,
4 assists. Philadelphia won 7-0.
 — Denis Potvin, NY Islanders, April 17, 1981, at NY Islanders vs. Edmonton.
3 goals, 2 assists. NY Islanders won 6-3.
 — Risto Siltanen, Quebec, April 14, 1987, at Hartford. 5 assists. Quebec
won 7-5.

SCORING BY A ROOKIE

MOST GOALS BY A ROOKIE, ONE PLAYOFF YEAR:
14 — Dino Ciccarelli, Minnesota, 1981. 19 games.
11 — Jeremy Roenick, Chicago, 1990. 20 games.
10 — Claude Lemieux, Montreal, 1986. 20 games.
9 — Pat Flatley, NY Islanders, 1984. 21 games
8 — Steve Christoff, Minnesota, 1980. 14 games.
 — Brad Palmer, Minnesota, 1981. 14 games.
 — Mike Krushelnyski, Boston, 1983. 17 games.
 — Bob Joyce, Boston, 1988. 23 games.

MOST POINTS BY A ROOKIE, ONE PLAYOFF YEAR:
21 — Dino Ciccarelli, Minnesota, 1981. 14 goals, 7 assists in 19 games.
20 — Don Maloney, NY Rangers, 1979. 7 goals, 13 assists in 18 games.

THREE-OR-MORE-GOAL GAMES

MOST THREE-OR-MORE-GOAL GAMES IN PLAYOFFS, CAREER:
10 — Wayne Gretzky, Edmonton, Los Angeles, NY Rangers. Eight three-goal
games; two four-goal games.
7 — Maurice Richard, Montreal. Four three-goal games; two four-goal games; one
five-goal game.
 — Jari Kurri, Edmonton. Six three-goal games; one four-goal game.
6 — Dino Ciccarelli, Minnesota, Washington, Detroit. Five three-goal games; one
four-goal game.
5 — Mike Bossy, NY Islanders. Four three-goal games; one four-goal game.

MOST THREE-OR-MORE-GOAL GAMES, ONE PLAYOFF YEAR:
4 — **Jari Kurri, Edmonton,** 1985. 1 four-goal game, 3 three-goal games.
3 — Mark Messier, Edmonton, 1983. 3 three-goal games.
 — Mike Bossy, NY Islanders, 1983. 1 four-goal game, 2 three-goal games
2 — Newsy Lalonde, Montreal, 1919. 1 five-goal game, 1 four-goal game.
 — Maurice Richard, Montreal, 1944. 1 five-goal game; 1 three-goal game.
 — Doug Bentley, Chicago, 1944. 2 three-goal games.
 — Norm Ullman, Detroit, 1964. 2 three-goal games.
 — Phil Esposito, Boston, 1970. 2 three-goal games.
 — Pit Martin, Chicago, 1973. 2 three-goal games.
 — Rick MacLeish, Philadelphia, 1975. 2 three-goal games.
 — Lanny McDonald, Toronto, 1977. 1 four-goal game; 1 three-goal game.
 — Wayne Gretzky, Edmonton, 1981. 2 three-goal games.
 — Wayne Gretzky, Edmonton, 1983. 2 four-goal games.
 — Wayne Gretzky, Edmonton, 1985. 2 three-goal games.
 — Petr Klima, Detroit, 1988. 2 three-goal games.
 — Cam Neely, Boston, 1991. 2 three-goal games.
 — Wayne Gretzky, NY Rangers, 1997. 2 three-goal games.
 — Daniel Alfredsson, Ottawa, 1998. 2 three-goal games.
 — Patrick Marleau, San Jose, 2004. 2 three-goal games.

MOST THREE-OR-MORE-GOAL GAMES, ONE PLAYOFF SERIES:
3 — **Jari Kurri, Edmonton,** 1985 CF vs. Chicago, won by Edmonton 4-2. Kurri
scored 3 goals May 7 at Edmonton in 7-3 win, 3 goals May 14 at Edmonton
in 10-5 win and 4 goals May 16 at Chicago in 8-2 win.
2 — Doug Bentley, Chicago, 1944 SF vs. Detroit, won by Chicago 4-1. Bentley
scored 3 goals Mar. 28 at Chicago in 7-1 win and 3 goals Mar. 30 at Detroit
in 5-2 win.
 — Norm Ullman, Detroit, 1964 SF vs. Chicago, won by Detroit 4-3. Ullman
scored 3 goals Mar. 29 at Chicago in 5-4 win and 3 goals April 7 at Detroit in
7-2 win.
 — Mark Messier, Edmonton, 1983 DF vs. Calgary, won by Edmonton 4-1.
Messier scored 4 goals April 14 at Edmonton in 6-3 win and 3 goals April 17
at Calgary in 10-2 win.
 — Mike Bossy, NY Islanders, 1983 CF vs. Boston, won by NY Islanders 4-2. Bossy
scored 3 goals May 3 at NY Islanders in 8-3 win and 4 goals May 7 at New
York in 8-4 win.

SCORING STREAKS

LONGEST CONSECUTIVE GOAL-SCORING STREAK, ONE PLAYOFF YEAR:
10 Games — Reggie Leach, Philadelphia, 1976. Streak started April 17 at Toronto
and ended May 9 at Montreal. He scored one goal in each of eight
games; two in one game; and five in another; a total of 15 goals.

LONGEST CONSECUTIVE POINT-SCORING STREAK, ONE PLAYOFF YEAR:
18 games — Bryan Trottier, NY Islanders, 1981. 11 goals, 18 assists, 29 points.
17 games — Wayne Gretzky, Edmonton, 1988. 12 goals, 29 assists, 41 points.
 — Al MacInnis, Calgary, 1989. 7 goals, 19 assists, 26 points.

LONGEST CONSECUTIVE POINT-SCORING STREAK, MORE THAN ONE PLAYOFF YEAR:
27 games — Bryan Trottier, NY Islanders, 1980, 1981 and 1982. 7 games in
1980 (3 goals, 5 assists, 8 points), 18 games in 1981 (11 goals, 18
assists, 29 points), and two games in 1982 (2 goals, 3 assists, 5
points). Total points, 42.
19 games — Wayne Gretzky, Edmonton, Los Angeles, 1988 and 1989. 17 games in
1988 (12 goals, 29 assists, 41 points with Edmonton), 2 games in
1989 (1 goal, 2 assists, 3 points with Los Angeles). Total points, 44.
 —Al MacInnis, Calgary, 1989 and 1990. 17 games in 1989 (7 goals, 19
assists, 26 points), and two games in 1990 (2 goals, 1 assist, 3 points).
Total points, 29.

FASTEST GOALS

FASTEST GOAL FROM START OF GAME:
0:06 — Don Kozak, Los Angeles, April 17, 1977, at Los Angeles vs. Boston and
goaltender Gerry Cheevers. Los Angeles won 7-4.
0:07 — Bob Gainey, Montreal, May 5, 1977, at NY Islanders vs. goaltender Chico
Resch. Montreal won 2-1.
 — Terry Murray, Philadelphia, April 12, 1981, at Quebec vs. goaltender Dan
Bouchard. Quebec won 4-3 in overtime.

FASTEST GOAL FROM START OF PERIOD (OTHER THAN FIRST):
0:06 — Pelle Eklund, Philadelphia, April 25, 1989, at Pittsburgh vs. goaltender
Tom Barrasso, second period. Pittsburgh won 10-7.
0:09 — Bill Collins, Minnesota, April 9, 1968, at Minnesota vs. Los Angeles and
goaltender Wayne Rutledge, third period. Minnesota won 7-5.
 — Dave Balon, Minnesota, April 25, 1968, at St. Louis vs. goaltender Glenn
Hall, third period. Minnesota won 5-1.
 — Murray Oliver, Minnesota, April 8, 1971, at St. Louis vs. goaltender Ernie
Wakely, third period. St. Louis won 4-2.
 — Clark Gillies, NY Islanders, April 15, 1977, at Buffalo vs. goaltender Don
Edwards, third period. NY Islanders won 4-3.
 — Eric Vail, Atlanta, April 11, 1978, at Atlanta vs. Detroit and goaltender
Ron Low, third period. Detroit won 5-3.
 — Stan Smyl, Vancouver, April 10, 1979, at Philadelphia vs. goaltender
Wayne Stephenson, third period. Vancouver won 3-2.
 — Wayne Gretzky, Edmonton, April 6, 1983, at Edmonton vs. Winnipeg and
goaltender Brian Hayward, second period. Edmonton won 6-3.
 — Mark Messier, Edmonton, April 16, 1984, at Calgary vs. goaltender Don
Edwards, third period. Edmonton won 5-3.
 — Brian Skrudland, Montreal, May 18, 1986, at Calgary vs. goaltender Mike
Vernon, first overtime period. Montreal won 3-2.

FASTEST TWO GOALS:
0:05 — Norm Ullman, Detroit, April 11, 1965, at Detroit vs. Chicago and
goaltender Glenn Hall. Ullman scored at 17:35 and 17:40 of second
period. Detroit won 4-2.

FASTEST TWO GOALS FROM START OF A GAME:
1:08 — **Dick Duff, Toronto,** April 9, 1963, at Toronto vs. Detroit and goaltender Terry Sawchuk. Duff scored at 0:49 and 1:08. Toronto won 4-2.

FASTEST TWO GOALS FROM START OF A PERIOD:
0:35 — **Pat LaFontaine, NY Islanders,** May 19, 1984, at Edmonton vs. goaltender Andy Moog. LaFontaine scored at 0:13 and 0:35 of third period. Edmonton won 5-2.

PENALTIES

MOST PENALTY MINUTES IN PLAYOFFS, CAREER:
729 — **Dale Hunter, Quebec, Washington, Colorado**
541 — Chris Nilan, Montreal, NY Rangers, Boston
529 — Claude Lemieux, Montreal, New Jersey, Colorado, Phoenix
471 — Rick Tocchet, Philadelphia, Pittsburgh, Boston, Phoenix
466 — Willi Plett, Atlanta, Calgary, Minnesota, Boston

MOST PENALTIES, ONE GAME:
8 — **Forbes Kennedy, Toronto,** April 2, 1969, at Boston. Kennedy was assessed 4 minors, 2 majors, 1 10-minute misconduct, 1 game misconduct. Boston won 10-0.
— **Kim Clackson, Pittsburgh,** April 14, 1980, at Boston. Clackson was assessed 5 minors, 2 majors, 1 10-minute misconduct. Boston won 6-2.

MOST PENALTY MINUTES, ONE GAME:
42 — **Dave Schultz, Philadelphia,** April 22, 1976, at Toronto. Schultz was assessed 1 minor, 2 majors, 1 10-minute misconduct and 2 game-misconducts. Toronto won 8-5.

MOST PENALTIES, ONE PERIOD AND MOST PENALTY MINUTES, ONE PERIOD:
6 Penalties; 39 Minutes — **Ed Hospodar, NY Rangers,** April 9, 1981, at Los Angeles, first period. Hospodar was assessed 2 minors, 1 major, 1 10-minute misconduct, 2 game misconducts. Los Angeles won 5-4.

GOALTENDING

MOST PLAYOFF GAMES APPEARED IN BY A GOALTENDER, CAREER:
247 — **Patrick Roy, Montreal, Colorado**
161 — Ed Belfour, Chicago, Dallas, Toronto
150 — Grant Fuhr, Edmonton, Buffalo, St. Louis
144 — Martin Brodeur, New Jersey
138 — Mike Vernon, Calgary, Detroit, San Jose, Florida

MOST MINUTES PLAYED BY A GOALTENDER, CAREER:
15,209 — **Patrick Roy, Montreal, Colorado**
9,945 — Ed Belfour, Chicago, Dallas, Toronto
9,000 — Martin Brodeur, New Jersey
8,834 — Grant Fuhr, Edmonton, Buffalo, St. Louis
8,214 — Mike Vernon, Calgary, Detroit, San Jose, Florida

MOST MINUTES PLAYED BY A GOALTENDER, ONE PLAYOFF YEAR:
1,655 — **Miikka Kiprusoff, Calgary,** 2004. 26 games.
1,544 — Kirk McLean, Vancouver, 1994. 24 games.
— Ed Belfour, Dallas, 1999. 23 games.
1,540 — Ron Hextall, Philadelphia, 1987. 26 games.
1,505 — Martin Brodeur, New Jersey, 2001. 25 games.

MOST SHUTOUTS IN PLAYOFFS (CAREER):
23 — **Patrick Roy, Montreal, Colorado**
20 — Martin Brodeur, New Jersey
16 — Curtis Joseph, St. Louis, Edmonton, Toronto
14 — Clint Benedict, Ottawa, Mtl. Maroons
— Jacques Plante, Montreal, St. Louis
— Ed Belfour, Chicago, Dallas, Toronto

MOST SHUTOUTS, ONE PLAYOFF YEAR:
7 — **Martin Brodeur, New Jersey,** 2003. 24 games.
6 — Dominik Hasek, Detroit, 2002. 23 games.
5 — Jean-Sebastien Giguere, Anaheim, 2003. 21 games.
— Nikolai Khabibulin, Tampa Bay, 2004. 23 games.
— Miikka Kiprusoff, Calgary, 2004. 26 games.

MOST SHUTOUTS, ONE PLAYOFF SERIES:
3 — **Clint Benedict, Mtl. Maroons,** 1926 F vs. Victoria. 4 games.
— **Dave Kerr, NY Rangers,** 1940 SF vs. Boston. 6 games.
— **Frank McCool, Toronto,** 1945 F vs. Detroit. 7 games.
— **Turk Broda, Toronto,** 1950 SF vs. Detroit. 7 games.
— **Felix Potvin, Toronto,** 1994 CQF vs. Chicago. 6 games.
— **Martin Brodeur, New Jersey,** 1995 CQF vs. Boston. 7 games.
— **Brent Johnson, St. Louis,** 2002 CQF vs. Chicago. 5 games.
— **Patrick Lalime, Ottawa,** 2002 CQF vs. Philadelphia. 5 games.
— **Jean-Sebastien Giguere, Anaheim,** 2003 CF vs. Minnesota. 4 games.
— **Martin Brodeur, New Jersey,** 2003 F vs. Anaheim. 7 games.
— **Ed Belfour, Toronto,** 2004 CQF vs. Ottawa. 7 games.
— **Nikolai Khabibulin, Tampa Bay,** 2004 CQF vs. NY Islanders. 5 games.

MOST WINS BY A GOALTENDER, (CAREER):
151 — **Patrick Roy, Montreal, Colorado**
92 — Grant Fuhr, Edmonton, Buffalo, St. Louis
88 — Billy Smith, NY Islanders
— Ed Belfour, Chicago, Dallas, Toronto
84 — Martin Brodeur, New Jersey

MOST WINS BY A GOALTENDER, ONE PLAYOFF YEAR:
16 — Sixteen wins by a goaltender in one playoff year has been recorded on 16 occasions. Nikolai Khabibulin of the Tampa Bay Lightning is the most recent to equal this mark, posting a record of 16 wins and 7 losses in 23 games in 2004. It was first accomplished by Grant Fuhr in 1988.

MOST CONSECUTIVE WINS BY A GOALTENDER, MORE THAN ONE PLAYOFF YEAR:
14 — **Tom Barrasso, Pittsburgh,** 1992, 1993; 3 wins vs. NY Rangers in 1992 DF, won by Pittsburgh 4-2; 4 wins vs. Boston in 1992 CF, won by Pittsburgh 4-0; 4 wins vs. Chicago in 1992 F, won by Pittsburgh 4-0; 3 wins vs. New Jersey in 1993 DSF, won by Pittsburgh 4-1.

MOST CONSECUTIVE WINS BY A GOALTENDER, ONE PLAYOFF YEAR:
11 — **Ed Belfour, Chicago,** 1992. 3 wins vs. St. Louis in DSF, won by Chicago 4-2; 4 wins vs. Detroit in DF, won by Chicago 4-0; and 4 wins vs. Edmonton in CF, won by Chicago 4-0.
— **Tom Barrasso, Pittsburgh,** 1992. 3 wins vs. NY Rangers in DF, won by Pittsburgh 4-2; 4 wins vs. Boston in CF, won by Pittsburgh 4-0; and 4 wins vs. Chicago in F, won by Pittsburgh 4-0.
— **Patrick Roy, Montreal,** 1993. 4 wins vs. Quebec in DSF, won by Montreal 4-2; 4 wins vs. Buffalo in DF, won by Montreal 4-0; and 3 wins vs. NY Islanders in CF, won by Montreal 4-1.

LONGEST SHUTOUT SEQUENCE:
270:08 — **George Hainsworth,** Montreal, 1930. Hainsworth's shutout streak began after Murray Murdoch scored a goal for the NY Rangers at 15:34 of the first period in the first game of a SF series on March 28, 1930. Hainsworth did not allow another goal in the final 113:18 of that game, won by Montreal 2-1 at 8:52 of the 4th overtime period. Hainsworth then shutout the NY Rangers in the next and final game of the series on March 30, 1930, won by Montreal 2-0. The streak continued with a 3-0 win over Boston in the opening game of the F series on April 1, 1930. His streak ended on April 3, 1930 when Boston's Eddie Shore scored at 16:50 of the second period in the second game of the F series.

MOST CONSECUTIVE SHUTOUTS:
3 — **Clint Benedict, Mtl. Maroons,** 1926. Benedict shut out Ottawa 1-0, Mar. 27; he then shut out Victoria twice, 3-0, Mar. 30; 3-0, Apr. 1. Mtl. Maroons won NHL F vs. Ottawa 2 goals to 1 and won the best-of-five F vs. Victoria 3-1.
— **John Ross Roach, NY Rangers,** 1929. Roach shut out NY Americans twice, 0-0, Mar. 19; 1-0, Mar. 21; he then shut out Toronto 1-0, Mar. 24. NY Rangers won QF vs. NY Americans 1 goal to 0 and won the best-of-three SF vs. Toronto 2-0.
— **Frank McCool, Toronto,** 1945. McCool shut out Detroit 1-0, April 6; 2-0, April 8; 1-0, April 12. Toronto won the best-of-seven F 4-3.
— **Brent Johnson, St. Louis,** 2002. Johnson shut out Chicago three times; 2-0, April 20; 4-0, April 21; 1-0, April 23. St. Louis won the best-of-seven CQF 4-1.
— **Patrick Lalime, Ottawa,** 2002. Lalime shut out Philadelphia three times; 3-0, April 20; 3-0, April 22; 3-0, April 24. Ottawa won the best-of-seven CQF 4-1.
— **Jean-Sebastien Giguere, Anaheim,** 2003. Giguere shut out Minnesota 1-0, May 10; 2-0, May 12; 4-0, May 14. Anaheim won the best-of-seven CF 4-0.

Early Playoff Records

1893-1918
Team Records

MOST GOALS, BOTH TEAMS, ONE GAME:
25 — **Ottawa Silver Seven, Dawson City** at Ottawa, Jan. 16, 1905. Ottawa 23, Dawson City 2. Ottawa won best-of-three series 2-0.

MOST GOALS, ONE TEAM, ONE GAME:
23 — **Ottawa Silver Seven** at Ottawa, Jan. 16, 1905. Ottawa defeated Dawson City 23-2.

MOST GOALS, BOTH TEAMS, BEST-OF-THREE SERIES:
42 — **Ottawa Silver Seven, Queen's University** at Ottawa, 1906. Ottawa defeated Queen's 16-7, Feb. 27, and 12-7, Feb. 28.

MOST GOALS, ONE TEAM, BEST-OF-THREE SERIES:
32 — **Ottawa Silver Seven** in 1905 at Ottawa. Defeated Dawson City 9-2, Jan. 13, and 23-2, Jan. 16.

MOST GOALS, BOTH TEAMS, BEST-OF-FIVE SERIES:
39 — **Toronto Arenas, Vancouver Millionaires** at Toronto, 1918. Toronto won 5-3, Mar. 20; 6-3, Mar. 26; 2-1, Mar. 30. Vancouver won 6-4, Mar. 23, and 8-1, Mar. 28. Toronto scored 18 goals; Vancouver 21.

MOST GOALS, ONE TEAM, BEST-OF-FIVE SERIES:
26 — **Vancouver Millionaires** in 1915 at Vancouver. Defeated Ottawa Senators 6-2, Mar. 22; 8-3, Mar. 24; and 12-3, Mar. 26.

Individual Records

MOST GOALS IN PLAYOFFS:
63 — **Frank McGee, Ottawa Silver Seven,** in 22 playoff games. Seven goals in four games, 1903; 21 goals in eight games, 1904; 18 goals in four games, 1905; 17 goals in six games, 1906.

MOST GOALS, ONE PLAYOFF SERIES:
15 — **Frank McGee, Ottawa Silver Seven,** in two games in 1905 at Ottawa. Scored one goal, Jan. 13, in 9-2 victory over Dawson City and 14 goals, Jan. 16, in 23-2 victory.

MOST GOALS, ONE PLAYOFF GAME:
14 — **Frank McGee, Ottawa Silver Seven,** at Ottawa, Jan. 16, 1905, in 23-2 victory over Dawson City.

FASTEST THREE GOALS:
40 Seconds — **Marty Walsh, Ottawa Senators,** at Ottawa, March 16, 1911, at 3:00, 3:10, and 3:40 of third period. Ottawa defeated Port Arthur 13-4.

All-Time Playoff Goal Leaders since 1918

(40 or more goals)

Player	Teams	Yrs.	GP	G
Wayne Gretzky	Edm., L.A., St.L., NYR	16	208	122
*Mark Messier	Edm., NYR, Van.	17	236	109
Jari Kurri	Edm., L.A., NYR, Ana., Col.	15	200	106
*Brett Hull	Cgy., St.L., Dal., Det.	19	202	103
Glenn Anderson	Edm., Tor., NYR, St.L.	15	225	93
Mike Bossy	NYI	10	129	85
Maurice Richard	Mtl.	15	133	82
Claude Lemieux	Mtl., N.J., Col., Phx., Dal.	17	233	80
Jean Beliveau	Mtl.	17	162	79
*Joe Sakic	Que., Col.	11	153	78
*Mario Lemieux	Pit.	8	107	76
Dino Ciccarelli	Min., Wsh., Det., T.B., Fla.	14	141	73
Esa Tikkanen	Edm., NYR, St.L., N.J., Van., Fla., Wsh.	13	186	72
Bryan Trottier	NYI, Pit.	17	221	71
*Steve Yzerman	Det.	19	192	70
Gordie Howe	Det., Hfd.	20	157	68
*Jaromir Jagr	Pit., Wsh., NYI	12	146	67
*Joe Nieuwendyk	Cgy., Dal., N.J., Tor.	16	158	66
Denis Savard	Chi., Mtl., T.B.	16	169	66
Yvan Cournoyer	Mtl.	12	147	64
Brian Propp	Phi., Bos., Min., Hfd.	13	160	64
Bobby Smith	Min., Mtl.	13	184	64
Bobby Hull	Chi., Wpg., Hfd.	14	119	62
Phil Esposito	Chi., Bos., NYR	15	130	61
Jacques Lemaire	Mtl.	11	145	61
Joe Mullen	St.L., Cgy., Pit., Bos.	15	143	60
Doug Gilmour	St.L., Cgy., Tor., N.J., Chi., Buf., Mtl.	17	182	60
Stan Mikita	Chi.	18	155	59
Paul Coffey	Edm., Pit., L.A., Det., Hfd., Phi., Chi., Car., Bos.	16	194	59
Guy Lafleur	Mtl., NYR, Que.	14	128	58
Bernie Geoffrion	Mtl., NYR	16	132	58
*Luc Robitaille	L.A., Pit., NYR, Det.	15	159	58
Cam Neely	Van., Bos.	9	93	57
*Peter Forsberg	Que., Col.	10	133	57
Steve Larmer	Chi., NYR	13	140	56
Denis Potvin	NYI	14	185	56
Rick MacLeish	Phi., Hfd., Pit., Det.	11	114	54
*Steve Thomas	Tor., Chi., NYI, N.J., Ana., Det.	16	174	54
Bill Barber	Phi.	11	129	53
Stephane Richer	Mtl., N.J., T.B., St.L., Pit.	13	134	53
Rick Tocchet	Phi., Pit., L.A., Bos., Wsh., Phx.	13	145	52
*Brendan Shanahan	N.J., St.L., Hfd., Det.	15	151	52
*Jeremy Roenick	Chi., Phx., Phi.	15	136	51
Frank Mahovlich	Tor., Det., Mtl.	14	137	51
Brian Bellows	Min., Mtl., T.B., Ana., Wsh.	13	143	51
*Mike Modano	Min., Dal.	12	144	51
Steve Shutt	Mtl., L.A.	12	99	50
*Sergei Fedorov	Det., Ana.	13	162	50
Henri Richard	Mtl.	18	180	49
Reggie Leach	Bos., Cal., Phi., Det.	8	94	47
Ted Lindsay	Det., Chi.	16	133	47
Clark Gillies	NYI, Buf.	13	164	47
Kevin Stevens	Pit., Bos., L.A., NYR, Phi.	7	103	46
Dickie Moore	Mtl., Tor., St.L.	14	135	46
*Ron Francis	Hfd., Pit., Car., Tor.	17	171	46
Rick Middleton	NYR, Bos.	12	114	45
Lanny McDonald	Tor., Col., Cgy.	13	117	44
*Scott Young	Hfd., Pit., Que., Col., Ana., St.L., Dal.	14	141	44
Ken Linseman	Phi., Edm., Bos., Tor.	11	113	43
Mike Gartner	Wsh., Min., NYR, Tor., Phx.	15	122	43
*Dave Andreychuk	Buf., Tor., N.J., Bos., Col., T.B.	18	162	43
*Vyacheslav Kozlov	Det., Buf., Atl.	9	114	42
Bernie Nicholls	L.A., NYR, Edm., N.J., Chi., S.J.	13	118	42
Bobby Clarke	Phi.	13	136	42
*John LeClair	Mtl., Phi.	14	154	42
Adam Oates	Det., St.L., Bos., Wsh., Phi., Ana., Edm.	15	163	42
Dale Hunter	Que., Wsh., Col.	18	186	42
John Bucyk	Det., Bos.	14	124	41
*Vincent Damphousse	Tor., Edm., Mtl., S.J.	14	140	41
Raymond Bourque	Bos., Col.	21	214	41
Tim Kerr	Phi., NYR, Hfd.	10	81	40
Peter McNab	Buf., Bos., Van., N.J.	10	107	40
*Mark Recchi	Pit., Phi., Mtl.	10	110	40
Bob Bourne	NYI, L.A.	13	139	40
John Tonelli	NYI, Cgy., L.A., Chi., Que.	13	172	40

* Active

All-Time Playoff Assist Leaders since 1918

(60 or more assists)

Player	Teams	Yrs.	GP	A
Wayne Gretzky	Edm., L.A., St.L., NYR	16	208	260
*Mark Messier	Edm., NYR, Van.	17	236	186
Raymond Bourque	Bos., Col.	21	214	139
Paul Coffey	Edm., Pit., L.A., Det., Hfd., Phi., Chi., Car., Bos.	16	194	137
Doug Gilmour	St.L., Cgy., Tor., N.J., Chi., Buf., Mtl.	17	182	128
Jari Kurri	Edm., L.A., NYR, Ana., Col.	15	200	127
*Al MacInnis	Cgy., St.L.	19	177	121
Glenn Anderson	Edm., Tor., NYR, St.L.	15	225	121
Larry Robinson	Mtl., L.A.	20	227	116
Larry Murphy	L.A., Wsh., Min., Pit., Tor., Det.	20	215	115
Adam Oates	Det., St.L., Bos., Wsh., Phi., Ana., Edm.	15	163	114
*Sergei Fedorov	Det., Ana.	13	162	113
Bryan Trottier	NYI, Pit.	17	221	113
*Steve Yzerman	Det.	19	192	111
Denis Savard	Chi., Mtl., T.B.	16	169	109
Denis Potvin	NYI	14	185	108
*Chris Chelios	Mtl., Chi., Det.	20	222	107
*Peter Forsberg	Que., Col.	10	133	97
Jean Beliveau	Mtl.	17	162	97
*Ron Francis	Hfd., Pit., Car., Tor.	17	171	97
*Mario Lemieux	Pit.	8	107	96
Bobby Smith	Min., Mtl.	13	184	96
Gordie Howe	Det., Hfd.	20	157	92
*Scott Stevens	Wsh., St.L., N.J.	20	233	92
*Joe Sakic	Que., Col.	11	153	91
Stan Mikita	Chi.	18	155	91
Brad Park	NYR, Bos., Det.	17	161	90
*Jaromir Jagr	Pit., Wsh., NYI	12	146	87
*Brett Hull	Cgy., St.L., Dal., Det.	19	202	87
Craig Janney	Bos., St.L., S.J., Wpg., Phx., T.B., NYI	11	120	86
Brian Propp	Phi., Bos., Min., Hfd.	13	160	84
*Nicklas Lidstrom	Det.	13	168	82
Henri Richard	Mtl.	18	180	80
*Sergei Zubov	NYR, Pit., Dal.	10	142	79
Jacques Lemaire	Mtl.	11	145	78
Claude Lemieux	Mtl., N.J., Col., Phx., Dal.	17	233	78
Ken Linseman	Phi., Edm., Bos., Tor.	11	113	77
Bobby Clarke	Phi.	13	136	77
Guy Lafleur	Mtl., NYR, Que.	14	128	76
Phil Esposito	Chi., Bos., NYR	15	130	76
*Mike Modano	Min., Dal.	12	144	76
Dale Hunter	Que., Wsh., Col.	18	186	76
Mike Bossy	NYI	10	129	75
Steve Larmer	Chi., NYR	13	140	75
John Tonelli	NYI, Cgy., L.A., Chi., Que.	13	172	75
Peter Stastny	Que., N.J., St.L.	12	93	72
Bernie Nicholls	L.A., NYR, Edm., N.J., Chi., S.J.	13	118	72
Brian Bellows	Min., Mtl., T.B., Ana., Wsh.	13	143	71
Gilbert Perreault	Buf.	11	90	70
Geoff Courtnall	Bos., Edm., Wsh., St.L., Van.	15	156	70
*Brian Leetch	NYR, NYI, Tor.	8	95	69
Dale Hawerchuk	Wpg., Buf., St.L., Phi.	15	97	69
Alex Delvecchio	Det.	14	121	69
*Luc Robitaille	L.A., Pit., NYR, Det.	15	159	69
Bobby Hull	Chi., Wpg., Hfd.	14	119	67
*Sandis Ozolinsh	S.J., Col., Car., Fla., Ana.	9	134	67
Frank Mahovlich	Tor., Det., Mtl.	14	137	67
Igor Larionov	Van., S.J., Det., Fla., N.J.	13	150	67
Bobby Orr	Bos., Chi.	8	74	66
Bernie Federko	St.L., Det.	11	91	66
Jean Ratelle	NYR, Bos.	15	123	66
Charlie Huddy	Edm., L.A., Buf., St.L.	14	183	66
*Jeremy Roenick	Chi., Phx., Phi.	15	136	65
*Brendan Shanahan	N.J., St.L., Hfd., Det.	15	151	65
Dickie Moore	Mtl., Tor., St.L.	14	135	64
Doug Harvey	Mtl., NYR, Det., St.L.	15	137	64
Neal Broten	Min., Dal., N.J., L.A.	13	135	63
*Vincent Damphousse	Tor., Edm., Mtl., S.J.	14	140	63
Yvan Cournoyer	Mtl.	12	147	63
John Bucyk	Det., Bos.	14	124	62
Doug Wilson	Chi., S.J.	12	95	61
Steve Duchesne	L.A., Phi., Que., St.L., Ott., Det.	14	121	61
Kevin Stevens	Pit., Bos., L.A., NYR, Phi.	7	103	60
*Pierre Turgeon	Buf., NYI, Mtl., St.L., Dal.	14	104	60
*Trevor Linden	Van., NYI, Mtl., Wsh.	11	112	60
Bernie Geoffrion	Mtl., NYR	16	132	60
Rick Tocchet	Phi., Pit., L.A., Bos., Wsh., Phx.	13	145	60
Esa Tikkanen	Edm., NYR, St.L., N.J., Van., Fla., Wsh.	13	186	60

All-Time Playoff Point Leaders since 1918

(105 or more points)

Player	Teams	Yrs.	GP	G	A	Pts.
Wayne Gretzky	Edm., L.A., St.L., NYR	16	208	122	260	382
*Mark Messier	Edm., NYR, Van.	17	236	109	186	295
Jari Kurri	Edm., L.A., NYR, Ana., Col.	15	200	106	127	233
Glenn Anderson	Edm., Tor., NYR, St.L.	15	225	93	121	214
Paul Coffey	Edm., Pit., L.A., Det., Hfd., Phi., Chi., Car., Bos.	16	194	59	137	196
*Brett Hull	Cgy., St.L., Dal., Det.	19	202	103	87	190
Doug Gilmour	St.L., Cgy., Tor., N.J., Chi., Buf., Mtl.	17	182	60	128	188
Bryan Trottier	NYI, Pit.	17	221	71	113	184
*Steve Yzerman	Det.	19	192	70	111	181
Raymond Bourque	Bos., Col.	21	214	41	139	180
Jean Beliveau	Mtl.	17	162	79	97	176
Denis Savard	Chi., Mtl., T.B.	16	169	66	109	175
*Mario Lemieux	Pit.	8	107	76	96	172
*Joe Sakic	Que., Col.	11	153	78	91	169
Denis Potvin	NYI	14	185	56	108	164
*Sergei Fedorov	Det., Ana.	13	162	50	113	163
Mike Bossy	NYI	10	129	85	75	160
Gordie Howe	Det., Hfd.	20	157	68	92	160
*Al MacInnis	Cgy., St.L.	19	177	39	121	160
Bobby Smith	Min., Mtl.	13	184	64	96	160
Claude Lemieux	Mtl., N.J., Col., Phx., Dal.	17	233	80	78	158
Adam Oates	Det., St.L., Bos., Wsh., Phi., Ana., Edm.	15	163	42	114	156
*Peter Forsberg	Que., Col.	10	133	57	97	154
*Jaromir Jagr	Pit., Wsh., NYI	12	146	67	87	154
Larry Murphy	L.A., Wsh., Min., Pit., Tor., Det.	20	215	37	115	152
Stan Mikita	Chi.	18	155	59	91	150
Brian Propp	Phi., Bos., Min., Hfd.	13	160	64	84	148
Larry Robinson	Mtl., L.A.	20	227	28	116	144
*Ron Francis	Hfd., Pit., Car., Tor.	17	171	46	97	143
Jacques Lemaire	Mtl.	11	145	61	78	139
Phil Esposito	Chi., Bos., NYR	15	130	61	76	137
*Chris Chelios	Mtl., Chi., Det.	20	222	30	107	137
Guy Lafleur	Mtl., NYR, Que.	14	128	58	76	134
Esa Tikkanen	Edm., NYR, St.L., N.J., Van., Fla., Wsh.	13	186	72	60	132
Steve Larmer	Chi., NYR	13	140	56	75	131
Bobby Hull	Chi., Wpg., Hfd.	14	119	62	67	129
Henri Richard	Mtl.	18	180	49	80	129
*Mike Modano	Min., Dal.	12	144	51	76	127
Yvan Cournoyer	Mtl.	12	147	64	63	127
*Luc Robitaille	L.A., Pit., NYR, Det.	15	159	58	69	127
Maurice Richard	Mtl.	15	133	82	44	126
Brad Park	NYR, Bos., Det.	17	161	35	90	125
Brian Bellows	Min., Mtl., T.B., Ana., Wsh.	13	143	51	71	122
Ken Linseman	Phi., Edm., Bos., Tor.	11	113	43	77	120
Bobby Clarke	Phi.	13	136	42	77	119
Bernie Geoffrion	Mtl., NYR	16	132	58	60	118
Frank Mahovlich	Tor., Det., Mtl.	14	137	51	67	118
Dino Ciccarelli	Min., Wsh., Det., T.B., Fla.	14	141	73	45	118
Dale Hunter	Que., Wsh., Col.	18	186	42	76	118
*Scott Stevens	Wsh., St.L., N.J.	20	233	26	92	118
*Brendan Shanahan	N.J., St.L., Hfd., Det.	15	151	52	65	117
*Jeremy Roenick	Chi., Phx., Phi.	15	136	51	65	116
*Joe Nieuwendyk	Cgy., Dal., N.J., Tor.	16	158	66	50	116
*Nicklas Lidstrom	Det.	13	168	34	82	116
John Tonelli	NYI, Cgy., L.A., Chi., Que.	13	172	40	75	115
Bernie Nicholls	L.A., NYR, Edm., N.J., Chi., S.J.	13	118	42	72	114
Rick Tocchet	Phi., Pit., L.A., Bos., Wsh., Phx.	13	145	52	60	112
Craig Janney	Bos., St.L., S.J., Wpg., Phx., T.B., NYI	11	120	24	86	110
Dickie Moore	Mtl., Tor., St.L.	14	135	46	64	110
Geoff Courtnall	Bos., Edm., Wsh., St.L., Van.	15	156	39	70	109
Bill Barber	Phi.	11	129	53	55	108
Rick MacLeish	Phi., Hfd., Pit., Det.	11	114	54	53	107
*Steve Thomas	Tor., Chi., NYI, N.J., Ana., Det.	16	174	54	53	107
Kevin Stevens	Pit., Bos., L.A., NYR, Phi.	7	103	46	60	106
Joe Mullen	St.L., Cgy., Pit., Bos.	15	143	60	46	106
Peter Stastny	Que., N.J., St.L.	12	93	33	72	105

Three-or-more-Goal Games, Playoffs 1918 –2004

Player	Team	Date	City	Total Goals	Opposing Goaltender	Score	
Wayne Gretzky (10)	Edm.	Apr. 11/81	Edm.	3	Richard Sevigny	Edm. 6	Mtl. 2
		Apr. 19/81	Edm.	3	Billy Smith	Edm. 5	NYI 2
		Apr. 6/83	Edm.	4	Brian Hayward	Edm. 6	Wpg. 3
		Apr. 17/83	Cgy.	4	Reggie Lemelin	Edm. 10	Cgy. 2
		Apr. 25/85	Wpg.	3	Brian Hayward (2)		
					Marc Behrend (1)	Edm. 8	Wpg. 3
		May 25/85	Edm.	3	Pelle Lindbergh	Edm. 4	Phi. 3
		Apr. 24/86	Cgy.	3	Mike Vernon	Edm. 7	Cgy. 4
	L.A.	May 29/93	Tor.	3	Felix Potvin	L.A. 5	Tor. 4
	NYR	Apr. 23/97	NYR	3	John Vanbiesbrouck	NYR 3	Fla. 2
		May 18/97	Phi.	3	Garth Snow	NYR 5	Phi. 4
Maurice Richard (7)	Mtl.	Mar. 23/44	Mtl.	5	Paul Bibeault	Mtl. 5	Tor. 1
		Apr. 6/44	Chi.	3	Mike Karakas	Mtl. 3	Chi. 1
		Mar. 29/45	Mtl.	4	Frank McCool	Mtl. 10	Tor. 3
		Apr. 14/53	Bos.	3	Gord Henry	Mtl. 7	Bos. 3
		Mar. 20/56	Mtl.	3	Gump Worsley	Mtl. 7	NYR 1
		Apr. 6/57	Mtl.	4	Don Simmons	Mtl. 5	Bos. 1
		Apr. 1/58	Det.	3	Terry Sawchuk	Mtl. 4	Det. 3
Jari Kurri (7)	Edm.	Apr. 4/84	Edm.	3	Doug Soetaert (1)		
					Mike Veisor (2)	Edm. 9	Wpg. 2
		Apr. 25/85	Wpg.	3	Brian Hayward (2)		
					Marc Behrend (1)	Edm. 8	Wpg. 3
		May 7/85	Edm.	3	Murray Bannerman	Edm. 7	Chi. 3
		May 14/85	Edm.	3	Murray Bannerman	Edm. 10	Chi. 5
		May 16/85	Chi.	4	Murray Bannerman	Edm. 8	Chi. 2
		Apr. 9/87	Edm.	4	Rollie Melanson (2)		
					Darren Eliot (2)	Edm. 13	L.A. 3
		May 18/90	Bos.	3	Andy Moog (2)		
					Reggie Lemelin (1)	Edm. 7	Bos. 2
Dino Ciccarelli (6)	Min.	May 5/81	Min.	3	Pat Riggin	Min. 7	Cgy. 4
		Apr. 10/82	Min.	3	Murray Bannerman	Min. 7	Chi. 1
	Wsh.	Apr. 5/90	N.J.	3	Sean Burke	Wsh. 5	N.J. 4
		Apr. 25/92	Pit.	4	Tom Barrasso (1)		
					Ken Wregget (3)	Wsh. 7	Pit. 2
	Det.	Apr. 29/93	Tor.	3	Felix Potvin (2)		
					Daren Puppa (1)	Det. 7	Tor. 3
		May 11/95	Dal.	3	Andy Moog (2)		
					Darcy Wakaluk (1)	Det. 5	Dal. 1
Mike Bossy (5)	NYI	Apr. 16/79	NYI	3	Tony Esposito	NYI 6	Chi. 2
		May 8/82	NYI	3	Richard Brodeur	NYI 6	Van. 5
		Apr. 10/83	Wsh.	3	Al Jensen	NYI 6	Wsh. 3
		May 3/83	NYI	3	Pete Peeters	NYI 8	Bos. 3
		May 7/83	NYI	4	Pete Peeters	NYI 8	Bos. 4
Phil Esposito (4)	Bos.	Apr. 2/69	Bos.	4	Bruce Gamble	Bos. 10	Tor. 0
		Apr. 8/70	Bos.	3	Ed Giacomin	Bos. 8	NYR 2
		Apr. 19/70	Chi.	3	Tony Esposito	Bos. 6	Chi. 3
		Apr. 8/75	Bos.	3	Tony Esposito (2)		
					Michel Dumas (1)	Bos. 8	Chi. 2
Mark Messier (4)	Edm.	Apr. 14/83	Edm.	4	Reggie Lemelin	Edm. 6	Cgy. 3
		Apr. 17/83	Cgy.	3	Reggie Lemelin (1)	Edm. 10	Cgy. 2
					Don Edwards (2)		
		Apr. 26/83	Edm.	3	Murray Bannerman	Edm. 8	Chi. 2
	NYR	May 25/94	N.J.	3	Martin Brodeur (2)	NYR 4	N.J. 2
					ENG (1)		
Steve Yzerman (4)	Det.	Apr. 6/89	Det.	3	Alain Chevrier	Chi. 5	Det. 4
		Apr. 4/91	St.L.	3	Vincent Riendeau (2)	Det. 6	St.L. 3
					Pat Jablonski (1)		
		May 8/96	St.L.	3	Jon Casey	St.L. 5	Det. 4
		Apr. 21/99	Det.	3	Guy Hebert (2)	Det. 5	Ana. 3
					Pat Jablonski (1)		
Bernie Geoffrion (3)	Mtl.	Mar. 27/52	Mtl.	3	Jim Henry	Mtl. 4	Bos. 0
		Apr. 7/55	Mtl.	3	Terry Sawchuk	Mtl. 4	Det. 2
		Mar. 30/57	Mtl.	3	Gump Worsley	Mtl. 8	NYR 3
Norm Ullman (3)	Det.	Mar. 29/64	Chi.	3	Glenn Hall	Det. 5	Chi. 4
		Apr. 7/64	Det.	3	Glenn Hall (2)		
					Denis DeJordy (1)	Det. 7	Chi. 2
		Apr. 11/65	Det.	3	Glenn Hall	Det. 4	Chi. 2
John Bucyk (3)	Bos.	May 3/70	St.L.	3	Jacques Plante (1)		
					Ernie Wakely (2)	Bos. 6	St.L. 1
		Apr. 20/72	Bos.	3	Jacques Caron (1)		
					Ernie Wakely (2)	Bos. 10	St.L. 2
		Apr. 21/74	Bos.	3	Tony Esposito	Bos. 8	Chi. 6
Rick MacLeish (3)	Phi.	Apr. 11/74	Phi.	3	Phil Myre	Phi. 5	Atl. 1
		Apr. 13/75	Phi.	3	Gord McRae	Phi. 6	Tor. 3
		May 13/75	Phi.	3	Glenn Resch	Phi. 4	NYI 1
Denis Savard (3)	Chi.	Apr. 19/82	Chi.	3	Mike Liut	Chi. 7	StL. 4
		Apr. 10/86	Chi.	4	Ken Wregget	Tor. 6	Chi. 4
		Apr. 9/88	St.L.	3	Greg Millen	Chi. 6	St.L. 3
Tim Kerr (3)	Phi.	Apr. 13/85	NYR	4	Glen Hanlon	Phi. 6	NYR 5
		Apr. 20/87	Phi.	3	Kelly Hrudey	Phi. 4	NYI 2
		Apr. 19/89	Pit.	3	Tom Barrasso	Phi. 4	Pit. 2
Cam Neely (3)	Bos.	Apr. 9/87	Mtl.	3	Patrick Roy	Mtl. 4	Bos. 3
		Apr. 5/91	Bos.	3	Peter Sidorkiewicz	Bos. 4	Hfd. 3
		Apr. 25/91	Bos.	3	Patrick Roy	Bos. 4	Mtl. 1
Petr Klima (3)	Det.	Apr. 7/88	Tor.	3	Alan Bester (2)		
					Ken Wregett (1)	Det. 6	Tor. 2
		Apr. 21/88	St.L.	3	Greg Millen	Det. 6	St.L. 0
	Edm.	May 4/91	Edm.	3	Jon Casey	Edm. 7	Min. 2
Esa Tikkanen (3)	Edm.	May 22/88	Edm.	3	Reggie Lemelin	Edm. 6	Bos. 3
		Apr. 16/91	Cgy.	3	Mike Vernon	Edm. 5	Cgy. 4
		Apr. 26/92	L.A.	3	Kelly Hrudey (2)	Edm. 5	L.A. 2
					Tom Askey (1)		
Mike Gartner (3)	NYR	Apr. 13/90	NYR	3	Mark Fitzpatrick (2)		
					Glenn Healy (1)	NYR 6	NYI 5
		Apr. 27/92	NYR	3	Chris Terreri	NYR 8	N.J. 5
	Tor.	Apr. 25/96	Tor.	3	Jon Casey	Tor. 5	St.L. 4
Mario Lemieux (3)	Pit.	Apr. 25/89	Pit.	5	Ron Hextall	Pit. 10	Phi. 7
		Apr. 23/92	Pit.	3	Don Beaupre	Pit. 6	Wsh. 4
		May 11/96	Pit.	3	Mike Richter	Pit. 7	NYR 3
Newsy Lalonde (2)	Mtl.	Mar. 1/19	Mtl.	5	Clint Benedict	Mtl. 6	Ott. 3
		Mar. 22/19	Sea.	4	Hap Holmes	Mtl. 4	Sea. 2

Player	Team	Date	City	Total Goals	Opposing Goaltender	Score	
Howie Morenz (2)	Mtl.	Mar. 22/24	Mtl.	3	Charles Reid	Mtl. 6	Cgy.T. 1
		Mar. 27/25	Mtl.	3	Hap Holmes	Mtl. 4	Vic. 2
Doug Bentley (2)	Chi.	Mar. 28/44	Chi.	3	Connie Dion	Chi. 7	Det. 1
		Mar. 30/44	Det.	3	Connie Dion	Chi. 5	Det. 2
Toe Blake (2)	Mtl.	Mar. 22/38	Mtl.	3	Mike Karakas	Mtl. 6	Chi. 4
		Mar. 26/46	Chi.	3	Mike Karakas	Mtl. 7	Chi. 2
Ted Kennedy (2)	Tor.	Apr. 14/45	Tor.	3	Harry Lumley	Det. 5	Tor. 3
		Mar. 27/48	Tor.	4	Frank Brimsek	Tor. 5	Bos. 3
F. St. Marseille (2)	St.L.	Apr. 28/70	St.L.	3	Al Smith	St.L. 5	Pit. 0
		Apr. 6/72	Min.	3	Cesare Maniago	Min. 6	St.L. 5
Bobby Hull (2)	Chi.	Apr. 7/63	Det.	3	Terry Sawchuk	Det. 7	Chi. 4
		Apr. 9/72	Pit.	3	Jim Rutherford	Chi. 6	Pit. 5
Pit Martin (2)	Chi.	Apr. 4/73	Chi.	3	Wayne Stephenson	Chi. 7	St.L. 1
		May 10/73	Chi.	3	Ken Dryden	Mtl. 6	Chi. 4
Yvan Cournoyer (2)	Mtl.	Apr. 5/73	Mtl.	3	Dave Dryden	Mtl. 7	Buf. 3
		Apr. 11/74	Mtl.	3	Ed Giacomin	Mtl. 4	NYR 1
Guy Lafleur (2)	Mtl.	May 1/75	Mtl.	3	Roger Crozier (1)		
					Gerry Desjardins (2)	Mtl. 7	Buf. 0
		Apr. 11/77	Mtl.	3	Ed Staniowski	Mtl. 7	St.L. 2
Lanny McDonald (2)	Tor.	Apr. 9/77	Pit.	3	Denis Herron	Tor. 5	Pit. 2
		Apr. 17/77	Tor.	4	Wayne Stephenson	Phi. 6	Tor. 5
Bill Barber (2)	Phi.	May 4/80	Min.	4	Gilles Meloche	Phi. 5	Min. 3
		Apr. 9/81	Phi.	3	Dan Bouchard	Phi. 8	Que. 5
Bryan Trottier (2)	NYI	Apr. 8/80	NYI	3	Doug Keans	NYI 8	L.A. 1
		Apr. 9/81	NYI	3	Michel Larocque	NYI 5	Tor. 1
Butch Goring (2)	L.A.	Apr. 9/77	L.A.	3	Phil Myre	L.A. 4	Atl. 2
	NYI	May 17/81	Min.	3	Gilles Meloche	NYI 7	Min. 5
Paul Reinhart (2)	Cgy.	Apr. 14/83	Edm.	3	Andy Moog	Edm. 6	Cgy. 3
		Apr. 8/84	Van	3	Richard Brodeur	Cgy. 5	Van. 1
Brian Propp (2)	Phi.	Apr. 22/81	Phi.	3	Pat Riggin	Phi. 9	Cgy. 4
		Apr. 21/85	Phi.	3	Billy Smith	Phi. 5	NYI 2
Peter Stastny (2)	Que.	Apr. 5/83	Bos.	3	Pete Peeters	Bos. 4	Que. 3
		Apr. 11/87	Que.	3	Mike Liut (2)		
					Steve Weeks (1)	Que. 5	Hfd. 1
Michel Goulet (2)	Que.	Apr. 23/85	Que.	3	Steve Penney	Que. 7	Mtl. 6
		Apr. 12/87	Que.	3	Mike Liut	Que. 4	Hfd. 1
Glenn Anderson (2)	Edm.	Apr. 26/83	Edm.	4	Murray Bannerman	Edm. 8	Chi. 2
		Apr. 6/88	Wpg.	3	Daniel Berthiaume	Edm. 7	Wpg. 4
Peter Zezel (2)	Phi.	Apr. 13/86	NYR	3	John Vanbiesbrouck	Phi. 7	NYR 1
	St.L.	Apr. 11/89	St.L.	3	Jon Casey (2)		
					Kari Takko (1)	St.L. 6	Min. 1
Geoff Courtnall (2)	Van.	Apr. 4/91	L.A.	3	Kelly Hrudey	Van. 6	L.A. 5
		Apr. 30/92	Van.	3	Rick Tabaracci	Van. 5	Win. 0
Joe Sakic (2)	Que.	May 6/95	Que.	3	Mike Richter	Que. 5	NYR 4
	Col.	Apr. 25/96	Col.	3	Corey Hirsch	Col. 5	Van. 4
Daniel Alfredsson (2)	Ott.	Apr. 28/98	Ott.	3	Martin Brodeur	Ott. 4	N.J. 3
		May 11/98	Ott.	3	Olaf Kolzig	Ott. 4	Wsh. 3
Patrick Marleau (2)	S.J.	Apr. 10/04	S.J.	3	Chris Osgood	S.J. 3	St.L. 1
		Apr. 22/04	S.J.	3	David Aebischer	S.J. 5	Col. 2
Harry Meeking	Tor.	Mar. 11/18	Tor.	3	Georges Vezina	Tor. 7	Mtl. 3
Alf Skinner	Tor.	Mar. 23/18	Tor.	3	Hugh Lehman	Van.M. 6	Tor. 4
Joe Malone	Mtl.	Feb. 23/19	Mtl.	3	Clint Benedict	Mtl. 8	Ott. 4
Odie Cleghorn	Mtl.	Feb. 27/19	Ott.	3	Clint Benedict	Mtl. 5	Ott. 3
Jack Darragh	Ott.	Apr. 1/20	Tor.	3	Hap Holmes	Ott. 6	Sea. 1
George Boucher	Ott.	Mar. 10/21	Ott.	3	Jake Forbes	Ott. 5	Tor. 0
Babe Dye	Tor.	Mar. 28/22	Tor.	4	Hugh Lehman	Tor. 5	Van.M. 1
Percy Galbraith	Bos.	Mar. 31/27	Bos.	3	Hugh Lehman	Bos. 4	Chi. 4
Busher Jackson	Tor.	Apr. 5/32	NYR	3	John Ross Roach	Tor. 6	NYR 4
Frank Boucher	NYR	Apr. 9/32	Tor.	3	Lorne Chabot	Tor. 6	NYR 4
Charlie Conacher	Tor.	Mar. 26/36	Tor.	3	Tiny Thompson	Tor. 8	Bos. 3
Syd Howe	Det.	Mar. 23/39	Det.	3	Claude Bourque	Det. 7	Mtl. 3
Bryan Hextall	NYR	Apr. 3/40	NYR	3	Turk Broda	NYR 6	Tor. 2
Joe Benoit	Mtl.	Mar. 22/41	Mtl.	3	Sam LoPresti	Mtl. 4	Chi. 3
Syl Apps	Tor.	Mar. 25/41	Tor.	3	Frank Brimsek	Tor. 7	Bos. 2
Jack McGill	Bos.	Mar. 29/42	Bos.	3	Johnny Mowers	Det. 6	Bos. 4
Don Metz	Tor.	Apr. 14/42	Tor.	3	Johnny Mowers	Tor. 9	Det. 3
Mud Bruneteau	Det.	Apr. 1/43	Det.	3	Frank Brimsek	Det. 6	Bos. 2
Don Grosso	Det.	Apr. 7/43	Bos.	3	Frank Brimsek	Det. 4	Bos. 0
Carl Liscombe	Det.	Apr. 3/45	Bos.	4	Paul Bibeault	Det. 5	Bos. 3
Billy Reay	Mtl.	Apr. 1/47	Bos.	4	Frank Brimsek	Mtl. 5	Bos. 1
Gerry Plamondon	Mtl.	Mar. 24/49	Det.	3	Harry Lumley	Mtl. 4	Det. 3
Sid Smith	Tor.	Apr. 10/49	Det.	3	Harry Lumley	Tor. 3	Det. 1
Pentti Lund	NYR	Apr. 2/50	NYR	3	Bill Durnan	NYR 4	Mtl. 1
Ted Lindsay	Det.	Apr. 5/55	Det.	4	Charlie Hodge (1)		
					Jacques Plante (3)	Det. 7	Mtl. 1
Gordie Howe	Det.	Apr. 10/55	Det.	3	Jacques Plante	Det. 5	Mtl. 1
Phil Goyette	Mtl.	Mar. 25/58	Mtl.	3	Terry Sawchuk	Mtl. 8	Det. 1
Jerry Toppazzini	Bos.	Apr. 5/58	Bos.	3	Gump Worsley	Bos. 8	NYR 2
Bob Pulford	Tor.	Apr. 19/62	Tor.	3	Glenn Hall	Tor. 8	Chi. 4
Dave Keon	Tor.	Apr. 9/64	Mtl.	3	Charlie Hodge (2)	Tor. 3	Mtl. 1
					ENG (1)		
Henri Richard	Mtl.	Apr. 20/67	Mtl.	3	Terry Sawchuk (2)		
					Johnny Bower (1)	Mtl. 6	Tor. 2
Rosaire Paiement	Phi.	Apr. 13/68	Phi.	3	Glenn Hall (1)		
					Seth Martin (2)	Phi. 6	St.L. 1
Jean Beliveau	Mtl.	Apr. 20/68	Mtl.	3	Denis DeJordy	Mtl. 4	Chi. 1
Red Berenson	St.L.	Apr. 15/69	St.L.	3	Gerry Desjardins	St.L. 4	L.A. 0
Ken Schinkel	Pit.	Apr. 11/70	Oak.	3	Gary Smith	Pit. 5	Oak. 2
Jim Pappin	Chi.	Apr. 11/71	Phi.	3	Bruce Gamble	Chi. 6	Phi. 2
Bobby Orr	Bos.	Apr. 11/71	Mtl.	3	Ken Dryden	Bos. 5	Mtl. 2
Jacques Lemaire	Mtl.	Apr. 20/71	Mtl.	3	Gump Worsley	Mtl. 7	Min. 2
Vic Hadfield	NYR	Apr. 22/71	NYR	3	Tony Esposito	NYR 4	Chi. 1
Fred Stanfield	Bos.	Apr. 18/72	Bos.	3	Jacques Caron	Bos. 6	St.L. 1
Ken Hodge	Bos.	Apr. 30/72	Bos.	3	Ed Giacomin	Bos. 6	NYR 5
Dick Redmond	Chi.	Apr. 4/73	Chi.	3	Wayne Stephenson	Chi. 7	St.L. 1
Steve Vickers	NYR	Apr. 10/73	Bos.	3	Ross Brooks (2)		
					Eddie Johnston (1)	NYR 6	Bos. 3
Tom Williams	L.A.	Apr. 14/74	L.A.	3	Mike Veisor	L.A. 5	Chi. 1
Marcel Dionne	L.A.	Apr. 15/76	L.A.	3	Gilles Gilbert	L.A. 6	Bos. 4
Don Saleski	Phi.	Apr. 20/76	Phi.	3	Wayne Thomas	Phi. 7	Tor. 1
Darryl Sittler	Tor.	Apr. 22/76	Tor.	5	Bernie Parent	Tor. 8	Phi. 5

Player	Team	Date	City	Total Goals	Opposing Goaltender	Score
Reggie Leach	Phi.	May 6/76	Phi.	5	Gilles Gilbert	Phi. 6 Bos. 3
Jim Lorentz	Buf.	Apr. 7/77	Min.	3	Pete LoPresti (2) Gary Smith (1)	Buf. 7 Min. 1
Bobby Schmautz	Bos.	Apr. 11/77	Bos.	3	Rogie Vachon	Bos. 8 L.A. 3
Billy Harris	NYI	Apr. 23/77	Mtl.	3	Ken Dryden	Mtl. 4 NYI 3
George Ferguson	Tor.	Apr. 11/78	Tor.	3	Rogie Vachon	Tor. 7 L.A. 3
Jean Ratelle	Bos.	May 3/79	Bos.	3	Ken Dryden	Bos. 4 Mtl. 3
Stan Jonathan	Bos.	May 8/79	Bos.	3	Ken Dryden	Bos. 5 Mtl. 2
Ron Duguay	NYR	Apr. 20/80	NYR	3	Pete Peeters	NYR 4 Phi. 2
Steve Shutt	Mtl.	Apr. 22/80	Mtl.	3	Gilles Meloche	Mtl. 6 Min. 2
Gilbert Perreault	Buf.	May 6/80	NYI	3	Billy Smith (2) ENG (1)	Buf. 7 NYI 4
Paul Holmgren	Phi.	May 15/80	Phi.	3	Billy Smith	Phi. 8 NYI 3
Steve Payne	Min.	Apr. 8/81	Bos.	3	Rogie Vachon	Min. 5 Bos. 4
Denis Potvin	NYI	Apr. 17/81	NYI	3	Andy Moog	NYI 6 Edm. 3
Barry Pederson	Bos.	Apr. 8/82	Bos.	3	Don Edwards	Bos. 7 Buf. 3
Duane Sutter	NYI	Apr. 15/83	NYI	3	Glen Hanlon	NYI 5 NYR 0
Doug Halward	Van.	Apr. 7/84	Van.	3	Reggie Lemelin (2) Don Edwards (1)	Van. 7 Cgy. 0
Jorgen Pettersson	St.L.	Apr. 8/84	Det.	3	Eddie Mio	St.L. 3 Det. 2
Clark Gillies	NYI	May 12/84	NYI	3	Grant Fuhr	NYI 6 Edm. 1
Ken Linseman	Bos.	Apr. 14/85	Bos.	3	Steve Penney	Bos. 7 Mtl. 6
Dave Andreychuk	Buf.	Apr. 14/85	Buf.	3	Dan Bouchard	Buf. 7 Que. 4
Greg Paslawski	St.L.	Apr. 15/86	Min.	3	Don Beaupre	St.L. 6 Min. 3
Doug Risebrough	Cgy.	May 4/86	Cgy.	3	Rick Wamsley	Cgy. 8 St.L. 2
Mike McPhee	Mtl.	Apr. 11/87	Bos.	3	Doug Keans	Mtl. 5 Bos. 4
John Ogrodnick	Que.	Apr. 14/87	Hfd.	3	Mike Liut	Que. 7 Hfd. 5
Pelle Eklund	Phi.	May 10/87	Mtl.	3	Patrick Roy (1) Brian Hayward (2)	Phi. 6 Mtl. 3
John Tucker	Buf.	Apr. 9/88	Bos.	4	Andy Moog	Buf. 6 Bos. 2
Tony Hrkac	St.L.	Apr. 10/88	St.L.	4	Darren Pang	St.L. 6 Chi. 5
Hakan Loob	Cgy.	Apr. 10/88	Cgy.	3	Glenn Healy	Cgy. 7 L.A. 3
Ed Olczyk	Tor.	Apr. 12/88	Tor.	3	Greg Stefan (2) Glen Hanlon (1)	Tor. 6 Det. 5
Aaron Broten	N.J.	Apr. 20/88	N.J.	3	Pete Peeters	N.J. 5 Wsh. 2
Mark Johnson	N.J.	Apr. 22/88	Wsh.	4	Pete Peeters	N.J. 10 Wsh. 4
Patrik Sundstrom	N.J.	Apr. 22/88	Wsh.	3	Pete Peeters (2) Clint Malarchuk (1)	N.J. 10 Wsh. 4
Bob Brooke	Min.	Apr. 5/89	St.L.	3	Greg Millen	St.L. 4 Min. 3
Chris Kontos	L.A.	Apr. 6/89	L.A.	3	Grant Fuhr	L.A. 5 Edm. 2
Wayne Presley	Chi.	Apr. 13/89	Chi.	3	Greg Stefan (1) Glen Hanlon (2)	Chi. 7 Det. 1
Tony Granato	L.A.	Apr. 10/90	L.A.	3	Mike Vernon (1) Rick Wamsley (2)	L.A. 12 Cgy. 4
Tomas Sandstrom	L.A.	Apr. 10/90	L.A.	3	Mike Vernon (1) Rick Wamsley (2)	L.A. 12 Cgy. 4
Dave Taylor	L.A.	Apr. 10/90	L.A.	3	Mike Vernon (1) Rick Wamsley (2)	L.A. 12 Cgy. 4
Bernie Nicholls	NYR	Apr. 19/90	NYR	3	Mike Liut	NYR 7 Wsh. 3
John Druce	Wsh.	Apr. 21/90	NYR	3	John Vanbiesbrouck	Wsh. 6 NYR 3
Adam Oates	St.L.	Apr. 12/91	St.L.	3	Tim Chevaldae	St.L. 6 Det. 1
Luc Robitaille	L.A.	Apr. 26/91	L.A.	3	Grant Fuhr	L.A. 5 Edm. 2
Ray Sheppard	Det.	Apr. 24/92	Min.	3	Jon Casey	Min. 5 Det. 2
Pavel Bure	Van.	Apr. 28/92	Wpg.	3	Rick Tabaracci	Van. 8 Wpg. 3
Joe Murphy	Edm.	May 6/92	Edm.	3	Kirk McLean	Edm. 5 Van. 2
Ron Francis	Pit.	May 9/92	Pit.	3	Mike Richter (2) John V'brouck (1)	Pit. 5 NYR. 4
Kevin Stevens	Pit.	May 21/92	Bos.	4	Andy Moog	Pit. 5 Bos. 2
Dirk Graham	Chi.	Jun. 1/92	Chi.	3	Tom Barrasso	Pit. 6 Chi. 5
Brian Noonan	Chi.	Apr. 18/93	Chi.	3	Curtis Joseph	St.L. 4 Chi. 3
Dale Hunter	Wsh.	Apr. 20/93	Wsh.	3	Glenn Healy	NYI 5 Wsh. 4
Teemu Selanne	Wpg.	Apr. 23/93	Wpg.	3	Kirk McLean	Wpg. 5 Van. 4
Ray Ferraro	NYI	Apr. 26/93	Wsh.	4	Don Beaupre	Wsh. 6 NYI 4
Al Iafrate	Wsh.	Apr. 26/93	Wsh.	3	Glenn Healy (2) Mark Fitzpatrick (1)	Wsh. 6 NYI 4
Paul Di Pietro	Mtl.	Apr. 28/93	Mtl.	3	Ron Hextall	Mtl. 6 Que. 2
Wendel Clark	Tor.	May 27/93	L.A.	3	Kelly Hrudey	L.A. 5 Tor. 4
Eric Desjardins	Mtl.	Jun. 3/93	Mtl.	3	Kelly Hrudey	Mtl. 3 L.A. 2
Tony Amonte	Chi.	Apr. 23/94	Chi.	4	Felix Potvin	Chi. 5 Tor. 4
Gary Suter	Chi.	Apr. 24/94	Chi.	3	Felix Potvin	Chi. 4 Tor. 3
Ulf Dahlen	S.J.	May 6/94	S.J.	3	Felix Potvin	S.J. 5 Tor. 2
Mike Sullivan	Cgy.	May 11/95	S.J.	3	Arturs Irbe (2) Wade Flaherty (1)	Cgy. 9 S.J. 2
Theoren Fleury	Cgy.	May 13/95	S.J.	4	Arturs Irbe (3) ENG (1)	Cgy. 6 S.J. 4
Brendan Shanahan	St.L.	May 13/95	Van.	3	Kirk McLean	St.L. 5 Van. 2
John LeClair	Phi.	May 21/95	Phi.	3	Mike Richter	Phi. 5 NYR 4
Brian Leetch	NYR	May 22/95	Phi.	3	Ron Hextall	Phi. 4 NYR 3
Trevor Linden	Van.	Apr. 25/96	Col.	3	Patrick Roy	Col. 5 Van. 4
Jaromir Jagr	Pit.	May 11/96	Pit.	3	Mike Richter	Pit. 7 NYR 3
Peter Forsberg	Col.	Jun. 6/96	Col.	3	John Vanbiesbrouck	Col. 8 Fla. 1
Valeri Zelepukin	N.J.	Apr. 22/97	Mtl.	3	Jocelyn Thibault	N.J. 6 Mtl. 4
Valeri Kamensky	Col.	Apr. 24/97	Col.	3	Jeff Hackett (2) Chris Terreri (1)	Col. 7 Chi. 0
Eric Lindros	Phi.	May 20/97	NYR	3	Mike Richter	Phi. 6 NYR 3
Matthew Barnaby	Buf.	May 10/98	Buf.	3	Andy Moog (2) ENG (1)	Buf. 6 Mtl. 3
Martin Straka	Pit.	Apr. 25/99	Pit.	3	Martin Brodeur	Pit. 4 N.J. 2
Martin Lapointe	Det.	Apr. 15/00	Det.	3	Stephane Fiset (2) Jamie Storr (1)	Det. 8 L.A. 5
Doug Weight	Edm.	Apr. 16/00	Edm.	3	Ed Belfour	Edm. 5 Dal. 2
Bill Guerin	Edm.	Apr. 18/00	Edm.	3	Ed Belfour	Dal. 4 Edm. 3
Scott Young	St.L.	Apr. 23/00	S.J.	3	Steve Shields	St.L. 6 S.J. 2
Andy Delmore	Phi.	May 7/00	Phi.	3	Ron Tugnutt (2) Peter Skudra (1)	Phi. 6 Pit. 3
Brett Hull	Det.	Apr. 27/02	Van.	3	Peter Skudra	Det. 6 Van. 4
Keith Tkachuk	St.L.	May 7/02	St.L.	3	Dominik Hasek	St.L. 6 Det. 1
Darren McCarty	Det.	May 18/02	Det.	3	Patrick Roy	Det. 5 Col. 3
Alexander Mogilny	Tor.	Apr. 9/03	Phi.	3	Roman Cechmanek (2) ENG (1)	Tor. 5 Phi. 3
Mike Sillinger	St.L.	Apr. 12/04	St.L.	3	Evgeni Nabokov (2) ENG (1)	St.L. 4 S.J. 1
Keith Primeau	Phi.	May 2/04	Phi.	3	Ed Belfour (2) Trevor Kidd (1)	Phi. 7 Tor. 2

Leading Playoff Scorers, 1918–2004

Season	Player and Club	Games Played	Goals	Assists	Points
2003-04	Brad Richards, Tampa Bay	23	12	14	26
2002-03	Jamie Langenbrunner, New Jersey	24	11	7	18
	Scott Niedermayer, New Jersey	24	2	16	18
2001-02	Peter Forsberg, Colorado	20	9	18	27
2000-01	Joe Sakic, Colorado	21	13	13	26
99-2000	Brett Hull, Dallas	23	11	13	24
1998-99	Peter Forsberg, Colorado	19	8	16	24
1997-98	Steve Yzerman, Detroit	22	6	18	24
1996-97	Eric Lindros, Philadelphia	19	12	14	26
1995-96	Joe Sakic, Colorado	22	18	16	34
1994-95	Sergei Fedorov, Detroit	17	7	17	24
1993-94	Brian Leetch, NY Rangers	23	11	23	34
1992-93	Wayne Gretzky, Los Angeles	24	15	25	40
1991-92	Mario Lemieux, Pittsburgh	15	16	18	34
1990-91	Mario Lemieux, Pittsburgh	23	16	28	44
1989-90	Craig Simpson, Edmonton	22	16	15	31
	Mark Messier, Edmonton	22	9	22	31
1988-89	Al MacInnis, Calgary	22	7	24	31
1987-88	Wayne Gretzky, Edmonton	19	12	31	43
1986-87	Wayne Gretzky, Edmonton	21	5	29	34
1985-86	Doug Gilmour, St. Louis	19	9	12	21
	Bernie Federko, St. Louis	19	7	14	21
1984-85	Wayne Gretzky, Edmonton	18	17	30	47
1983-84	Wayne Gretzky, Edmonton	19	13	22	35
1982-83	Wayne Gretzky, Edmonton	16	12	26	38
1981-82	Bryan Trottier, NY Islanders	19	6	23	29
1980-81	Mike Bossy, NY Islanders	18	17	18	35
1979-80	Bryan Trottier, NY Islanders	21	12	17	29
1978-79	Jacques Lemaire, Montreal	16	11	12	23
	Guy Lafleur, Montreal	16	10	13	23
1977-78	Guy Lafleur, Montreal	15	10	11	21
	Larry Robinson, Montreal	15	4	17	21
1976-77	Guy Lafleur, Montreal	14	9	17	26
1975-76	Reggie Leach, Philadelphia	16	19	5	24
1974-75	Rick MacLeish, Philadelphia	17	11	9	20
1973-74	Rick MacLeish, Philadelphia	17	13	9	22
1972-73	Yvan Cournoyer, Montreal	17	15	10	25
1971-72	Phil Esposito, Boston	15	9	15	24
	Bobby Orr, Boston	15	5	19	24
1970-71	Frank Mahovlich, Montreal	20	14	13	27
1969-70	Phil Esposito, Boston	14	13	14	27
1968-69	Phil Esposito, Boston	10	8	10	18
1967-68	Bill Goldsworthy, Minnesota	14	8	7	15
1966-67	Jim Pappin, Toronto	12	7	8	15
1965-66	Norm Ullman, Detroit	12	6	9	15
1964-65	Bobby Hull, Chicago	14	10	7	17
1963-64	Gordie Howe, Detroit	14	9	10	19
1962-63	Gordie Howe, Detroit	11	7	9	16
	Norm Ullman, Detroit	11	4	12	16
1961-62	Stan Mikita, Chicago	12	6	15	21
1960-61	Gordie Howe, Detroit	11	4	11	15
	Pierre Pilote, Chicago	12	3	12	15
1959-60	Henri Richard, Montreal	8	3	9	12
	Bernie Geoffrion, Montreal	8	2	10	12
1958-59	Dickie Moore, Montreal	11	5	12	17
1957-58	Fleming Mackell, Boston	12	5	14	19
1956-57	Bernie Geoffrion, Montreal	11	11	7	18
1955-56	Jean Béliveau, Montreal	10	12	7	19
1954-55	Gordie Howe, Detroit	11	9	11	20
1953-54	Dickie Moore, Montreal	11	5	8	13
1952-53	Ed Sandford, Boston	11	8	3	11
1951-52	Ted Lindsay, Detroit	8	5	2	7
	Floyd Curry, Montreal	11	4	3	7
	Metro Prystai, Detroit	8	2	5	7
	Gordie Howe, Detroit	8	2	5	7
1950-51	Maurice Richard, Montreal	11	9	4	13
	Max Bentley, Toronto	11	2	11	13
1949-50	Pentti Lund, NY Rangers	12	6	5	11
1948-49	Gordie Howe, Detroit	11	8	3	11
1947-48	Ted Kennedy, Toronto	9	8	6	14
1946-47	Maurice Richard, Montreal	10	6	5	11
1945-46	Elmer Lach, Montreal	9	5	12	17
1944-45	Joe Carveth, Detroit	14	5	6	11
1943-44	Toe Blake, Montreal	9	7	11	18
1942-43	Carl Liscombe, Detroit	10	6	8	14
1941-42	Don Grosso, Detroit	12	8	6	14
	Syl Apps, Toronto	13	5	9	14
1940-41	Milt Schmidt, Boston	11	5	6	11
1939-40	Phil Watson, NY Rangers	12	3	6	9
	Neil Colville, NY Rangers	12	2	7	9
1938-39	Bill Cowley, Boston	12	3	11	14
1937-38	Johnny Gottselig, Chicago	10	5	3	8
	Gordie Drillon, Toronto	7	7	1	8
1936-37	Marty Barry, Detroit	10	4	7	11
1935-36	Frank Boll, Toronto	9	7	3	10
1934-35	Baldy Northcott, Mtl. Maroons	7	4	1	5
	Busher Jackson, Toronto	7	3	2	5
	Cy Wentworth, Mtl. Maroons	7	3	2	5
	Charlie Conacher, Toronto	7	1	4	5
1933-34	Larry Aurie, Detroit	9	3	7	10
1932-33	Cecil Dillon, NY Rangers	8	8	2	10
1931-32	Frank Boucher, NY Rangers	7	3	6	9
1930-31	Cooney Weiland, Boston	5	6	3	9
1929-30	Marty Barry, Boston	6	3	3	6
	Cooney Weiland, Boston	6	1	5	6
1928-29	Andy Blair, Toronto	4	3	0	3
	Butch Keeling, NY Rangers	6	3	0	3
	Ace Bailey, Toronto	4	1	2	3
1927-28	Frank Boucher, NY Rangers	9	7	3	10
1926-27	Harry Oliver, Boston	8	4	2	6
	Percy Galbraith, Boston	8	3	3	6
1925-26	Nels Stewart, Mtl. Maroons	8	6	3	9
1924-25	Howie Morenz, Montreal	6	7	1	8
1923-24	Howie Morenz, Montreal	6	7	3	10
1922-23	Punch Broadbent, Ottawa	8	6	1	7
1921-22	Babe Dye, Toronto	7	11	1	12
1920-21	Cy Denneny, Ottawa	7	4	2	6
1919-20	Frank Nighbor, Ottawa	5	6	1	7
	Jack Darragh, Ottawa	5	5	2	7
1918-19	Newsy Lalonde, Montreal	10	17	2	19
1917-18	Alf Skinner, Toronto	7	8	3	11

Overtime Games since 1918

Abbreviations: Teams/Cities: — **Ana.** - Anaheim; **Atl.** - Atlanta; **Bos.** - Boston; **Buf.** - Buffalo; **Cgy.** - Calgary; **Cgy. T.** - Calgary Tigers (Western Canada Hockey League); **Chi.** - Chicago; **Col.** - Colorado; **Dal.** - Dallas; **Det.** - Detroit; **Edm.** - Edmonton; **Edm. E.** - Edmonton Eskimos (WCHL); **Fla.** - Florida; **Hfd.** - Hartford; **L.A.** - Los Angeles; **Min.** - Minnesota; **Mtl.** - Montreal; **Mtl. M.** - Montreal Maroons; **N.J.** - New Jersey; **NYA** - NY Americans; **NYI** - New York Islanders; **NYR** - New York Rangers; **Oak.** - Oakland; **Ott.** - Ottawa; **Phi.** - Philadelphia; **Phx.** - Phoenix; **Pit.** - Pittsburgh; **Que.** - Quebec; **St.L.** - St. Louis; **Sea.** - Seattle Metropolitans (Pacific Coast Hockey Association); **S.J.** - San Jose; **T.B.** - Tampa Bay; **Tor.** - Toronto; **Van.** - Vancouver; **Van. M.** - Vancouver Millionaires (PCHA); **Vic.** - Victoria Cougars (WCHL); **Wpg.** - Winnipeg; **Wsh.** - Washington.

SERIES — **CF** - conference final; **CQF** - conference quarter-final; **CSF** - conference semi-final; **DF** - division final; **DSF** - division semi-final; **F** - final; **PRE** - preliminary round; **QF** - quarter-final; **SF** - semi-final.

Date	City	Series	Score		Scorer	Overtime	Series Winner
Mar. 26/19	Sea.	F	Mtl. 0	Sea. 0	no scorer	20:00	....
Mar. 30/19	Sea.	F	Mtl. 4	Sea. 3	Odie Cleghorn	15:57	....
Mar. 20/22	Tor.	F	Tor. 2	Van. M. 1	Babe Dye	4:50	Tor.
Mar. 29/23	Van.	F	Ott. 2	Edm. E. 1	Cy Denneny	2:08	Ott.
Mar. 31/27	Mtl.	QF	Mtl. 1	Mtl. M. 0	Howie Morenz	12:05	Mtl.
Apr. 7/27	Bos.	F	Ott. 0	Bos. 0	no scorer	20:00	Ott.
Apr. 11/27	Ott.	F	Bos. 1	Ott. 1	no scorer	20:00	Ott.
Apr. 3/28	Mtl.	QF	Mtl. M. 1	Mtl. 0	Russell Oatman	8:20	Mtl. M.
Apr. 7/28	Mtl.	F	NYR 2	Mtl. M. 1	Frank Boucher	7:05	NYR
Mar. 21/29	NYR	QF	NYR 1	NYA 0	Butch Keeling	29:50	NYR
Mar. 26/29	Tor.	SF	NYR 2	Tor. 1	Frank Boucher	2:03	NYR
Mar. 20/30	Mtl.	SF	Bos. 2	Mtl. M. 1	Harry Oliver	45:35	Bos.
Mar. 25/30	Bos.	SF	Mtl. M. 1	Bos. 0	Archie Wilcox	26:27	Bos.
Mar. 26/30	Mtl.	QF	Chi. 2	Mtl. 2	Howie Morenz (Mtl.)	51:43	Mtl.
Mar. 28/30	Mtl.	SF	Mtl. 2	NYR 1	Gus Rivers	68:52	Mtl.
Mar. 24/31	Bos.	SF	Bos. 5	Mtl. 4	Cooney Weiland	18:56	Mtl.
Mar. 26/31	Chi.	QF	Chi. 2	Tor. 1	Stew Adams	19:20	Chi.
Mar. 28/31	Mtl.	SF	Mtl. 4	Bos. 3	Georges Mantha	5:10	Mtl.
Apr. 1/31	Mtl.	SF	Mtl. 3	Bos. 2	Wildor Larochelle	19:00	Mtl.
Apr. 5/31	Chi.	F	Chi. 2	Mtl. 1	Johnny Gottselig	24:50	Mtl.
Apr. 9/31	Mtl.	F	Chi. 3	Mtl. 2	Cy Wentworth	53:50	Mtl.
Mar. 26/32	Mtl.	SF	NYR 4	Mtl. 3	Fred Cook	59:32	NYR
Apr. 2/32	Tor.	SF	Tor. 3	Mtl. M. 2	Bob Gracie	17:59	Tor.
Mar. 25/33	Bos.	SF	Bos. 2	Tor. 1	Marty Barry	14:14	Tor.
Mar. 28/33	Bos.	SF	Tor. 1	Bos. 0	Busher Jackson	15:03	Tor.
Mar. 30/33	Tor.	SF	Bos. 2	Tor. 1	Eddie Shore	4:23	Tor.
Apr. 3/33	Tor.	SF	Tor. 1	Bos. 0	Ken Doraty	104:46	Tor.
Apr. 13/33	Tor.	F	NYR 1	Tor. 0	Bill Cook	7:33	NYR
Mar. 22/34	Tor.	SF	Det. 2	Tor. 1	Herbie Lewis	1:33	Det.
Mar. 25/34	Chi.	QF	Chi. 1	Mtl. 1	Mush March (Chi)	11:05	Chi.
Apr. 3/34	Det.	F	Chi. 2	Det. 1	Paul Thompson	21:10	Chi.
Apr. 10/34	Chi.	F	Chi. 1	Det. 0	Mush March	30:05	Chi.
Mar. 23/35	Bos.	SF	Bos. 1	Tor. 0	Dit Clapper	33:26	Tor.
Mar. 26/35	Chi.	QF	Mtl. M. 1	Chi. 0	Baldy Northcott	4:02	Mtl. M.
Mar. 30/35	Tor.	SF	Tor. 2	Bos. 1	Pep Kelly	1:36	Tor.
Apr. 4/35	Tor.	F	Mtl. M. 3	Tor. 2	Dave Trottier	5:28	Mtl. M.
Mar. 24/36	Mtl.	SF	Det. 1	Mtl. M. 0	Mud Bruneteau	116:30	Det.
Apr. 9/36	Tor.	F	Tor. 4	Det. 3	Buzz Boll	0:31	Det.
Mar. 25/37	NYR	QF	NYR 2	Tor. 1	Babe Pratt	13:05	NYR
Apr. 1/37	Mtl.	SF	Det. 2	Mtl. 1	Hec Kilrea	51:49	Det.
Mar. 22/38	NYR	QF	NYA 2	NYR 1	John Sorrell	21:25	NYA
Mar. 24/38	Tor.	SF	Tor. 1	Bos. 0	George Parsons	21:31	Tor.
Mar. 26/38	Mtl.	QF	Chi. 3	Mtl. 2	Paul Thompson	11:49	Chi.
Mar. 27/38	NYR	QF	NYA 3	NYR 2	Lorne Carr	60:40	NYA
Mar. 29/38	Bos.	SF	Tor. 3	Bos. 2	Gordie Drillon	10:04	Tor.
Mar. 31/38	Chi.	SF	Chi. 1	NYA 0	Cully Dahlstrom	33:01	Chi.
Mar. 21/39	NYR	SF	Bos. 2	NYR 1	Mel Hill	59:25	Bos.
Mar. 23/39	Bos.	SF	Bos. 3	NYR 2	Mel Hill	8:24	Bos.
Mar. 26/39	Det.	QF	Det. 1	Mtl. 0	Marty Barry	7:47	Det.
Mar. 30/39	Bos.	SF	NYR 2	Bos. 1	Clint Smith	17:19	Bos.
Apr. 1/39	Tor.	SF	Tor. 5	Det. 4	Gordie Drillon	5:42	Tor.
Apr. 2/39	Bos.	SF	Bos. 2	NYR 1	Mel Hill	48:00	Bos.
Apr. 9/39	Bos.	F	Tor. 3	Bos. 2	Doc Romnes	10:38	Bos.
Mar. 19/40	Det.	QF	Det. 2	NYA 1	Syd Howe	0:25	Det.
Mar. 19/40	Tor.	QF	Tor. 3	Chi. 2	Syl Apps	6:35	Tor.
Apr. 2/40	NYR	F	NYR 2	Tor. 1	Alf Pike	15:30	NYR
Apr. 11/40	Tor.	F	NYR 2	Tor. 1	Muzz Patrick	31:43	NYR
Apr. 13/40	Tor.	F	NYR 3	Tor. 2	Bryan Hextall	2:07	NYR
Mar. 20/41	Det.	QF	Det. 2	NYR 1	Gus Giesebrecht	12:01	Det.
Mar. 22/41	Mtl.	QF	Mtl. 4	Chi. 3	Charlie Sands	34:04	Chi.
Mar. 29/41	Bos.	SF	Tor. 2	Bos. 1	Pete Langelle	17:31	Bos.
Mar. 30/41	Chi.	SF	Det. 2	Chi. 1	Gus Giesebrecht	9:15	Det.
Mar. 22/42	Chi.	QF	Bos. 2	Chi. 1	Des Smith	6:51	Bos.
Mar. 21/43	Bos.	SF	Bos. 5	Mtl. 4	Don Gallinger	12:30	Bos.
Mar. 23/43	Det.	SF	Tor. 3	Det. 2	Jack McLean	70:18	Det.
Mar. 25/43	Mtl.	SF	Bos. 3	Mtl. 2	Busher Jackson	3:20	Bos.
Mar. 30/43	Tor.	SF	Det. 3	Tor. 2	Adam Brown	9:21	Det.
Mar. 30/43	Bos.	SF	Bos. 5	Mtl. 4	Ab DeMarco	3:41	Bos.
Apr. 13/44	Mtl.	F	Mtl. 5	Chi. 4	Toe Blake	9:12	Mtl.
Mar. 27/45	Tor.	SF	Tor. 4	Mtl. 3	Gus Bodnar	12:36	Tor.
Mar. 29/45	Det.	SF	Det. 3	Bos. 2	Mud Bruneteau	17:12	Det.
Apr. 21/45	Tor.	F	Det. 1	Tor. 0	Ed Bruneteau	14:16	Tor.
Mar. 28/46	Bos.	SF	Bos. 4	Det. 3	Don Gallinger	9:51	Bos.
Mar. 30/46	Mtl.	F	Mtl. 4	Bos. 3	Maurice Richard	9:08	Mtl.
Apr. 2/46	Mtl.	F	Mtl. 3	Bos. 2	Jimmy Peters	16:55	Mtl.
Apr. 7/46	Bos.	F	Bos. 3	Mtl. 2	Terry Reardon	15:13	Mtl.
Mar. 26/47	Tor.	SF	Tor. 3	Det. 2	Howie Meeker	3:05	Tor.
Mar. 27/47	Mtl.	SF	Mtl. 2	Bos. 1	Ken Mosdell	5:38	Mtl.
Apr. 3/47	Mtl.	SF	Mtl. 4	Bos. 3	John Quilty	36:40	Mtl.
Apr. 15/47	Tor.	F	Tor. 2	Mtl. 1	Syl Apps	16:36	Tor.
Mar. 24/48	Tor.	SF	Tor. 5	Bos. 4	Nick Metz	17:03	Tor.
Mar. 22/49	Det.	SF	Det. 2	Mtl. 1	Max McNab	44:52	Det.
Mar. 24/49	Det.	SF	Mtl. 4	Det. 3	Gerry Plamondon	2:59	Det.
Mar. 26/49	Tor.	SF	Bos. 5	Tor. 4	Woody Dumart	16:14	Tor.
Apr. 8/49	Det.	F	Tor. 3	Det. 2	Joe Klukay	17:31	Tor.
Apr. 4/50	Tor.	SF	Det. 2	Tor. 1	Leo Reise Jr.	20:38	Det.
Apr. 4/50	Mtl.	SF	Mtl. 3	NYR 2	Elmer Lach	15:19	NYR
Apr. 9/50	Det.	SF	Det. 1	Tor. 0	Leo Reise Jr.	8:39	Det.
Apr. 18/50	Det.	F	NYR 4	Det. 3	Don Raleigh	8:34	Det.
Apr. 20/50	Det.	F	NYR 2	Det. 1	Don Raleigh	1:38	Det.
Apr. 23/50	Det.	F	Det. 4	NYR 3	Pete Babando	28:31	Det.
Mar. 27/51	Det.	SF	Mtl. 3	Det. 2	Maurice Richard	61:09	Mtl.
Mar. 29/51	Det.	SF	Mtl. 1	Det. 0	Maurice Richard	42:20	Mtl.
Mar. 31/51	Tor.	SF	Bos. 1	Tor. 1	no scorer	20:00	Tor.
Apr. 11/51	Tor.	F	Tor. 3	Mtl. 2	Sid Smith	5:51	Tor.
Apr. 14/51	Tor.	F	Mtl. 3	Tor. 2	Maurice Richard	2:55	Tor.
Apr. 17/51	Mtl.	F	Tor. 2	Mtl. 1	Ted Kennedy	4:47	Tor.
Apr. 19/51	Mtl.	F	Tor. 3	Mtl. 2	Harry Watson	5:15	Tor.
Apr. 21/51	Tor.	F	Tor. 3	Mtl. 2	Bill Barilko	2:53	Tor.
Apr. 6/52	Bos.	SF	Mtl. 3	Bos. 2	Paul Masnick	27:49	Mtl.
Mar. 29/53	Bos.	SF	Bos. 2	Det. 1	Jack McIntyre	12:29	Bos.
Mar. 29/53	Chi.	SF	Chi. 2	Mtl. 1	Al Dewsbury	5:18	Mtl.
Apr. 16/53	Mtl.	F	Mtl. 1	Bos. 0	Elmer Lach	1:22	Mtl.
Apr. 1/54	Det.	SF	Det. 4	Tor. 3	Ted Lindsay	21:01	Det.
Apr. 11/54	Det.	F	Mtl. 1	Det. 0	Ken Mosdell	5:45	Det.
Apr. 16/54	Det.	F	Det. 2	Mtl. 1	Tony Leswick	4:29	Det.
Mar. 29/55	Bos.	SF	Mtl. 4	Bos. 3	Don Marshall	3:05	Mtl.
Mar. 24/56	Tor.	SF	Det. 5	Tor. 4	Ted Lindsay	4:22	Det.
Mar. 28/57	NYR	SF	NYR 4	Mtl. 3	Andy Hebenton	13:38	Mtl.
Apr. 4/57	Mtl.	SF	Mtl. 4	NYR 3	Maurice Richard	1:11	Mtl.
Mar. 27/58	NYR	SF	Bos. 4	NYR 3	Jerry Toppazzini	4:46	Bos.
Mar. 30/58	Det.	SF	Mtl. 2	Det. 1	André Pronovost	11:52	Mtl.
Apr. 17/58	Mtl.	F	Mtl. 3	Bos. 2	Maurice Richard	5:45	Mtl.
Mar. 28/59	Tor.	SF	Tor. 3	Bos. 2	Gerry Ehman	5:02	Tor.
Mar. 31/59	Tor.	SF	Tor. 3	Bos. 2	Frank Mahovlich	11:21	Tor.
Apr. 14/59	Tor.	F	Tor. 3	Mtl. 2	Dick Duff	10:06	Mtl.
Mar. 26/60	Mtl.	SF	Mtl. 4	Chi. 3	Doug Harvey	8:38	Mtl.
Mar. 27/60	Det.	SF	Tor. 5	Det. 4	Frank Mahovlich	43:00	Tor.
Mar. 29/60	Det.	SF	Det. 2	Tor. 1	Gerry Melnyk	1:54	Tor.
Mar. 22/61	Tor.	SF	Tor. 3	Det. 2	George Armstrong	24:51	Det.
Mar. 26/61	Chi.	SF	Chi. 2	Mtl. 1	Murray Balfour	52:12	Chi.
Apr. 5/62	Tor.	SF	Tor. 3	NYR 2	Red Kelly	24:23	Tor.
Apr. 2/64	Det.	SF	Chi. 3	Det. 2	Murray Balfour	8:21	Det.
Apr. 14/64	Tor.	F	Det. 4	Tor. 3	Larry Jeffrey	7:52	Tor.
Apr. 23/64	Det.	F	Tor. 4	Det. 3	Bob Baun	1:43	Tor.
Apr. 6/65	Tor.	SF	Tor. 3	Mtl. 2	Dave Keon	4:17	Mtl.
Apr. 13/65	Tor.	SF	Mtl. 4	Tor. 3	Claude Provost	16:33	Mtl.
May 5/66	Det.	F	Mtl. 3	Det. 2	Henri Richard	2:20	Mtl.
Apr. 13/67	NYR	SF	Mtl. 2	NYR 1	John Ferguson	6:28	Mtl.
Apr. 25/67	Tor.	F	Tor. 3	Mtl. 2	Bob Pulford	28:26	Tor.
Apr. 10/68	St.L.	QF	St.L. 3	Phi. 2	Larry Keenan	24:10	St.L.
Apr. 16/68	St.L.	QF	Phi. 2	St.L. 1	Don Blackburn	31:18	St.L.
Apr. 16/68	Min.	QF	Min. 4	L.A. 3	Milan Marcetta	9:11	Min.
Apr. 22/68	Min.	SF	Min. 3	St.L. 2	Parker MacDonald	3:41	St.L.
Apr. 27/68	St.L.	SF	St.L. 4	Min. 3	Gary Sabourin	1:32	St.L.
Apr. 28/68	Mtl.	SF	Mtl. 4	Chi. 3	Jacques Lemaire	2:14	Mtl.
Apr. 29/68	St.L.	SF	St.L. 3	Min. 2	Bill McCreary	17:27	St.L.
May 3/68	St.L.	SF	St.L. 2	Min. 1	Ron Schock	22:50	St.L.
May 5/68	St.L.	F	Mtl. 3	St.L. 2	Jacques Lemaire	1:41	Mtl.
May 9/68	Mtl.	F	Mtl. 4	St.L. 3	Bobby Rousseau	1:13	Mtl.
Apr. 2/69	Oak.	QF	L.A. 5	Oak. 4	Ted Irvine	0:19	L.A.
Apr. 10/69	Mtl.	SF	Mtl. 3	Bos. 2	Ralph Backstrom	0:42	Mtl.
Apr. 13/69	Mtl.	SF	Mtl. 4	Bos. 3	Mickey Redmond	4:55	Mtl.
Apr. 24/69	Bos.	SF	Mtl. 2	Bos. 1	Jean Béliveau	31:28	Mtl.
Apr. 12/70	Oak.	QF	Pit. 3	Oak. 2	Michel Briere	8:28	Pit.
May 10/70	Bos.	F	Bos. 4	St.L. 3	Bobby Orr	0:40	Bos.
Apr. 15/71	Tor.	QF	NYR 2	Tor. 1	Bob Nevin	9:07	NYR
Apr. 18/71	Chi.	SF	NYR 2	Chi. 1	Pete Stemkowski	1:37	Chi.
Apr. 27/71	Chi.	SF	Chi. 3	NYR 2	Bobby Hull	6:35	Chi.
Apr. 29/71	NYR	SF	NYR 3	Chi. 2	Pete Stemkowski	41:29	Chi.
May 4/71	Chi.	F	Chi. 2	Mtl. 1	Jim Pappin	21:11	Mtl.
Apr. 6/72	Bos.	QF	Tor. 4	Bos. 3	Jim Harrison	2:58	Bos.
Apr. 6/72	Min.	QF	Min. 6	St.L. 5	Bill Goldsworthy	1:36	St.L.
Apr. 9/72	Pit.	QF	Chi. 6	Pit. 5	Pit Martin	0:12	Chi.
Apr. 16/72	Min.	QF	St.L. 2	Min. 1	Kevin O'Shea	10:07	St.L.
Apr. 1/73	Mtl.	QF	Buf. 3	Mtl. 2	René Robert	9:18	Mtl.
Apr. 10/73	Phi.	QF	Phi. 3	Min. 2	Gary Dornhoefer	8:35	Phi.
Apr. 14/73	Mtl.	SF	Phi. 5	Mtl. 4	Rick MacLeish	2:56	Mtl.
Apr. 17/73	Mtl.	SF	Mtl. 4	Phi. 3	Larry Robinson	6:45	Mtl.
Apr. 14/74	Tor.	QF	Bos. 4	Tor. 3	Ken Hodge	1:27	Bos.
Apr. 14/74	Atl.	QF	Phi. 4	Atl. 3	Dave Schultz	5:40	Phi.
Apr. 16/74	Mtl.	QF	NYR 3	Mtl. 2	Ron Harris	4:07	NYR
Apr. 23/74	Chi.	SF	Chi. 4	Bos. 3	Jim Pappin	3:48	Bos.
Apr. 28/74	NYR	SF	NYR 2	Phi. 1	Rod Gilbert	4:20	Phi.
May 9/74	Bos.	F	Phi. 3	Bos. 2	Bobby Clarke	12:01	Phi.
Apr. 8/75	L.A.	PRE	L.A. 3	Tor. 2	Mike Murphy	8:53	Tor.
Apr. 10/75	Tor.	PRE	Tor. 3	L.A. 2	Blaine Stoughton	10:19	Tor.
Apr. 10/75	Chi.	PRE	Chi. 4	Bos. 3	Ivan Boldirev	7:33	Chi.
Apr. 11/75	NYR	PRE	NYI 4	NYR 3	Jean-Paul Parise	0:11	NYI
Apr. 17/75	Chi.	QF	Chi. 5	Buf. 4	Stan Mikita	2:31	Buf.
Apr. 19/75	Tor.	QF	Phi. 4	Tor. 3	André Dupont	1:45	Phi.
Apr. 22/75	Mtl.	QF	Mtl. 5	Van. 4	Guy Lafleur	17:06	Mtl.
Apr. 27/75	Buf.	SF	Buf. 6	Mtl. 5	Danny Gare	4:42	Buf.
May 1/75	Phi.	SF	Phi. 5	NYI 4	Bobby Clarke	2:56	Phi.
May 6/75	Buf.	SF	Buf. 5	Mtl. 4	René Robert	5:56	Buf.
May 7/75	NYI	SF	NYI 4	Phi. 3	Jude Drouin	1:53	Phi.
May 20/75	Buf.	F	Buf. 5	Phi. 4	René Robert	18:29	Phi.
Apr. 8/76	Buf.	PRE	Buf. 3	St.L. 2	Danny Gare	11:43	Buf.
Apr. 9/76	Buf.	PRE	Buf. 2	St.L. 1	Don Luce	14:27	Buf.
Apr. 13/76	Bos.	QF	L.A. 3	Bos. 2	Butch Goring	0:27	Bos.
Apr. 13/76	Buf.	QF	Buf. 3	NYI 2	Danny Gare	14:04	NYI
Apr. 22/76	L.A.	QF	L.A. 4	Bos. 3	Butch Goring	18:28	Bos.
Apr. 29/76	Phi.	SF	Phi. 2	Bos. 1	Reggie Leach	13:38	Phi.
Apr. 15/77	Tor.	QF	Phi. 4	Tor. 3	Rick MacLeish	2:55	Phi.
Apr. 17/77	Tor.	QF	Phi. 6	Tor. 5	Reggie Leach	19:10	Phi.
Apr. 24/77	Phi.	SF	Bos. 4	Phi. 3	Rick Middleton	2:57	Bos.
Apr. 26/77	Phi.	SF	Bos. 5	Phi. 4	Terry O'Reilly	30:07	Bos.
May 3/77	Mtl.	SF	NYI 4	Mtl. 3	Billy Harris	3:58	Mtl.

Date	City	Series	Score		Scorer	Overtime	Series Winner
May 14/77	Bos.	F	Mtl. 2	Bos. 1	Jacques Lemaire	4:32	Mtl.
Apr. 11/78	Phi.	PRE	Phi. 3	Col. 2	Mel Bridgman	0:23	Phi.
Apr. 13/78	NYR	PRE	NYR 4	Buf. 3	Don Murdoch	1:37	Buf.
Apr. 19/78	Bos.	QF	Bos. 4	Chi. 3	Terry O'Reilly	1:50	Bos.
Apr. 19/78	NYI	QF	NYI 3	Tor. 2	Mike Bossy	2:50	Tor.
Apr. 21/78	Chi.	QF	Bos. 4	Chi. 3	Peter McNab	10:17	Bos.
Apr. 25/78	NYI	QF	NYI 2	Tor. 1	Bob Nystrom	8:02	Tor.
Apr. 29/78	NYI	QF	Tor. 2	NYI 1	Lanny McDonald	4:13	Tor.
May 2/78	Bos.	SF	Bos. 3	Phi. 2	Rick Middleton	1:43	Bos.
May 16/78	Mtl.	F	Mtl. 3	Bos. 2	Guy Lafleur	13:09	Mtl.
May 21/78	Bos.	F	Bos. 4	Mtl. 3	Bobby Schmautz	6:22	Mtl.
Apr. 12/79	L.A.	PRE	NYR 2	L.A. 1	Phil Esposito	6:11	NYR
Apr. 14/79	Buf.	PRE	Pit. 4	Buf. 3	George Ferguson	0:47	Pit.
Apr. 16/79	Phi.	QF	Phi. 3	NYR 2	Ken Linseman	0:44	NYR
Apr. 18/79	NYI	QF	NYI 1	Chi. 0	Mike Bossy	2:31	NYI
Apr. 21/79	Tor.	QF	Mtl. 4	Tor. 3	Cam Connor	25:25	Mtl.
Apr. 22/79	Tor.	QF	Mtl. 5	Tor. 4	Larry Robinson	4:14	Mtl.
Apr. 28/79	NYI	SF	NYI 4	NYR 3	Denis Potvin	8:02	NYR
May 3/79	NYR	SF	NYI 3	NYR 2	Bob Nystrom	3:40	NYR
May 3/79	Bos.	SF	Bos. 4	Mtl. 3	Jean Ratelle	3:46	Mtl.
May 10/79	Mtl.	SF	Mtl. 5	Bos. 4	Yvon Lambert	9:33	Mtl.
May 19/79	NYR	F	Mtl. 4	NYR 3	Serge Savard	7:25	Mtl.
Apr. 8/80	NYR	PRE	NYR 2	Atl. 1	Steve Vickers	0:33	NYR
Apr. 8/80	Phi.	PRE	Phi. 4	Edm. 3	Bobby Clarke	8:06	Phi.
Apr. 8/80	Chi.	PRE	Chi. 3	St.L. 2	Doug Lecuyer	12:34	Chi.
Apr. 11/80	Hfd.	PRE	Mtl. 4	Hfd. 3	Yvon Lambert	0:29	Mtl.
Apr. 11/80	Tor.	PRE	Min. 4	Tor. 3	Al MacAdam	0:32	Min.
Apr. 11/80	L.A.	PRE	NYI 4	L.A. 3	Ken Morrow	6:55	NYI
Apr. 11/80	Edm.	PRE	Phi. 3	Edm. 2	Ken Linseman	23:56	Phi.
Apr. 16/80	Bos.	QF	NYI 2	Bos. 1	Clark Gillies	1:02	NYI
Apr. 17/80	Bos.	QF	NYI 5	Bos. 4	Bob Bourne	1:24	NYI
Apr. 21/80	NYI	QF	Bos. 4	NYI 3	Terry O'Reilly	17:13	NYI
May 1/80	Buf.	SF	NYI 2	Buf. 1	Bob Nystrom	21:20	NYI
May 13/80	Phi.	F	NYI 4	Phi. 3	Denis Potvin	4:07	NYI
May 24/80	NYI	F	NYI 5	Phi. 4	Bob Nystrom	7:11	NYI
Apr. 8/81	Buf.	PRE	Buf. 3	Van. 2	Alan Haworth	5:00	Buf.
Apr. 8/81	Bos.	PRE	Min. 5	Bos. 4	Steve Payne	3:34	Min.
Apr. 11/81	Chi.	PRE	Cgy. 5	Chi. 4	Willi Plett	35:17	Cgy.
Apr. 12/81	Que.	PRE	Que. 4	Phi. 3	Dale Hunter	0:37	Phi.
Apr. 14/81	St.L.	PRE	St.L. 4	Pit. 3	Mike Crombeen	25:16	St.L.
Apr. 16/81	Buf.	QF	Min. 4	Buf. 3	Steve Payne	0:22	Min.
Apr. 20/81	Min.	QF	Buf. 5	Min. 4	Craig Ramsay	16:32	Min.
Apr. 20/81	Edm.	QF	NYI 5	Edm. 4	Ken Morrow	5:41	NYI
Apr. 7/82	Min.	DSF	Chi. 3	Min. 2	Greg Fox	3:34	Chi.
Apr. 8/82	Edm.	DSF	Edm. 3	L.A. 2	Wayne Gretzky	6:20	L.A.
Apr. 8/82	Van.	DSF	Van. 2	Cgy. 1	Dave Williams	14:20	Van.
Apr. 10/82	Pit.	DSF	Pit. 2	NYI 1	Rick Kehoe	4:14	NYI
Apr. 10/82	L.A.	DSF	L.A. 6	Edm. 5	Daryl Evans	2:35	L.A.
Apr. 13/82	Mtl.	DSF	Que. 3	Mtl. 2	Dale Hunter	0:22	Que.
Apr. 13/82	NYI	DSF	NYI 4	Pit. 3	John Tonelli	6:19	NYI
Apr. 16/82	Van.	DF	L.A. 3	Van. 2	Steve Bozek	4:33	Van.
Apr. 18/82	Que.	DF	Que. 3	Bos. 2	Wilf Paiement	11:44	Que.
Apr. 18/82	NYR	DF	NYI 4	NYR 3	Bryan Trottier	3:00	NYI
Apr. 18/82	L.A.	DF	Van. 4	L.A. 3	Colin Campbell	1:23	Van.
Apr. 21/82	St.L.	DF	St.L. 3	Chi. 2	Bernie Federko	3:28	Chi.
Apr. 23/82	Que.	DF	Bos. 6	Que. 5	Peter McNab	10:54	Que.
Apr. 27/82	Chi.	CF	Van. 2	Chi. 1	Jim Nill	28:58	Van.
May 1/82	Que.	CF	NYI 5	Que. 4	Wayne Merrick	16:52	NYI
May 8/82	NYI	F	NYI 6	Van. 5	Mike Bossy	19:58	NYI
Apr. 5/83	Bos.	DSF	Bos. 4	Que. 3	Barry Pederson	1:46	Bos.
Apr. 6/83	Cgy.	DSF	Cgy. 4	Van. 3	Eddy Beers	12:27	Cgy.
Apr. 7/83	Min.	DSF	Min. 5	Tor. 4	Bobby Smith	5:03	Min.
Apr. 10/83	Tor.	DSF	Min. 5	Tor. 4	Dino Ciccarelli	8:05	Min.
Apr. 10/83	Van.	DSF	Cgy. 4	Van. 3	Greg Meredith	1:06	Cgy.
Apr. 18/83	Min.	DF	Chi. 4	Min. 3	Rich Preston	10:34	Chi.
Apr. 24/83	Bos.	DF	Bos. 3	Buf. 2	Brad Park	1:52	Bos.
Apr. 5/84	Edm.	DSF	Edm. 5	Wpg. 4	Randy Gregg	0:21	Edm.
Apr. 7/84	Det.	DSF	St.L. 4	Det. 3	Mark Reeds	37:07	St.L.
Apr. 8/84	Det.	DSF	St.L. 3	Det. 2	Jorgen Pettersson	2:42	St.L.
Apr. 10/84	NYI	DSF	NYI 3	NYR 2	Ken Morrow	8:56	NYI
Apr. 13/84	Min.	DF	St.L. 4	Min. 3	Doug Gilmour	16:16	Min.
Apr. 13/84	Edm.	DF	Cgy. 6	Edm. 5	Carey Wilson	3:42	Edm.
Apr. 13/84	NYI	DF	NYI 5	Wsh. 4	Anders Kallur	7:35	NYI
Apr. 16/84	Mtl.	DF	Que. 4	Mtl. 3	Bo Berglund	3:00	Mtl.
Apr. 20/84	Cgy.	DF	Cgy. 5	Edm. 4	Lanny McDonald	1:04	Edm.
Apr. 22/84	Min.	DF	Min. 4	St.L. 3	Steve Payne	6:00	Min.
Apr. 10/85	Phi.	DSF	Phi. 5	NYR 4	Mark Howe	8:01	Phi.
Apr. 10/85	Wsh.	DSF	Wsh. 4	NYI 3	Alan Haworth	2:28	NYI
Apr. 10/85	Edm.	DSF	Edm. 3	L.A. 2	Lee Fogolin	3:01	Edm.
Apr. 10/85	Wpg.	DSF	Wpg. 5	Cgy. 4	Brian Mullen	7:56	Wpg.
Apr. 11/85	Wsh.	DSF	Wsh. 2	NYI 1	Mike Gartner	21:23	NYI
Apr. 13/85	L.A.	DSF	Edm. 4	L.A. 3	Glenn Anderson	0:46	Edm.
Apr. 18/85	Mtl.	DF	Que. 2	Mtl. 1	Mark Kumpel	12:23	Que.
Apr. 23/85	Que.	DF	Que. 7	Mtl. 6	Dale Hunter	18:36	Que.
Apr. 25/85	Min.	DF	Chi. 7	Min. 6	Darryl Sutter	21:57	Chi.
Apr. 28/85	Chi.	DF	Min. 5	Chi. 4	Dennis Maruk	1:14	Chi.
Apr. 30/85	Min.	DF	Chi. 6	Min. 5	Darryl Sutter	15:41	Chi.
May 2/85	Mtl.	DF	Que. 3	Mtl. 2	Peter Stastny	2:22	Que.
May 5/85	Que.	CF	Que. 2	Phi. 1	Peter Stastny	6:20	Phi.
Apr. 9/86	Que.	DSF	Hfd. 3	Que. 2	Sylvain Turgeon	2:36	Hfd.
Apr. 12/86	Wpg.	DSF	Cgy. 4	Wpg. 3	Lanny McDonald	8:25	Cgy.
Apr. 17/86	Wsh.	DF	NYR 4	Wsh. 3	Brian MacLellan	1:16	NYR
Apr. 20/86	Edm.	DF	Edm. 6	Cgy. 5	Glenn Anderson	1:04	Cgy.
Apr. 23/86	Hfd.	DF	Hfd. 2	Mtl. 1	Kevin Dineen	1:07	Mtl.
Apr. 23/86	NYR	DF	NYR 6	Wsh. 5	Bob Brooke	2:40	NYR
Apr. 26/86	St L.	DF	St L. 4	Tor. 3	Mark Reeds	7:11	St L.
Apr. 29/86	Mtl.	DF	Mtl. 2	Hfd. 1	Claude Lemieux	5:55	Mtl.
May 5/86	NYR	CF	Mtl. 4	NYR 3	Claude Lemieux	9:41	Mtl.
May 12/86	St L.	CF	St L. 6	Cgy. 5	Doug Wickenheiser	7:30	Cgy.
May 18/86	Cgy.	F	Mtl. 3	Cgy. 2	Brian Skrudland	0:09	Mtl.
Apr. 8/87	Hfd.	DSF	Hfd. 3	Que. 2	Paul MacDermid	2:20	Que.
Apr. 9/87	Mtl.	DSF	Mtl. 4	Bos. 3	Mats Naslund	2:38	Mtl.
Apr. 9/87	St.L.	DSF	Tor. 3	St.L. 2	Rick Lanz	10:17	Tor.

Date	City	Series	Score		Scorer	Overtime	Series Winner
Apr. 11/87	Wpg.	DSF	Cgy. 3	Wpg. 2	Mike Bullard	3:53	Wpg.
Apr. 11/87	Chi.	DSF	Det. 4	Chi. 3	Shawn Burr	4:51	Det.
Apr. 16/87	Que.	DSF	Que. 5	Hfd. 4	Peter Stastny	6:05	Que.
Apr. 18/87	Wsh.	DSF	NYI 3	Wsh. 2	Pat LaFontaine	68:47	NYI
Apr. 21/87	Edm.	DF	Edm. 3	Wpg. 2	Glenn Anderson	0:36	Edm.
Apr. 26/87	Que.	DF	Mtl. 3	Que. 2	Mats Naslund	5:30	Mtl.
Apr. 27/87	Tor.	DF	Tor. 3	Det. 2	Mike Allison	9:31	Det.
May 4/87	Phi.	CF	Phi. 4	Mtl. 3	Ilkka Sinislao	9:11	Phi.
May 20/87	Edm.	F	Edm. 3	Phi. 2	Jari Kurri	6:50	Edm.
Apr. 6/88	NYI	DSF	NYI 4	N.J. 3	Pat LaFontaine	6:11	N.J.
Apr. 10/88	Phi.	DSF	Phi. 5	Wsh. 4	Murray Craven	1:18	Wsh.
Apr. 10/88	N.J.	DSF	NYI 5	N.J. 4	Brent Sutter	15:07	N.J.
Apr. 10/88	Buf.	DSF	Buf. 6	Bos. 5	John Tucker	5:32	Bos.
Apr. 12/88	Det.	DSF	Tor. 6	Det. 5	Ed Olczyk	0:34	Det.
Apr. 16/88	Wsh.	DSF	Wsh. 5	Phi. 4	Dale Hunter	5:57	Wsh.
Apr. 21/88	Cgy.	DF	Edm. 5	Cgy. 4	Wayne Gretzky	7:54	Edm.
May 4/88	Bos.	CF	N.J. 3	Bos. 2	Doug Brown	17:46	Bos.
May 9/88	Det.	CF	Edm. 4	Det. 3	Jari Kurri	11:02	Edm.
Apr. 5/89	St.L.	DSF	St.L. 4	Min. 3	Brett Hull	11:55	St.L.
Apr. 5/89	Cgy.	DSF	Van. 4	Cgy. 3	Paul Reinhart	2:47	Cgy.
Apr. 6/89	St.L.	DSF	St.L. 4	Min. 3	Rick Meagher	5:30	St.L.
Apr. 6/89	Det.	DSF	Chi. 5	Det. 4	Duane Sutter	14:36	Chi.
Apr. 8/89	Hfd.	DSF	Mtl. 5	Hfd. 4	Stephane Richer	5:01	Mtl.
Apr. 8/89	Phi.	DSF	Wsh. 4	Phi. 3	Kelly Miller	0:51	Phi.
Apr. 9/89	Hfd.	DSF	Mtl. 4	Hfd. 3	Russ Courtnall	15:12	Mtl.
Apr. 15/89	Cgy.	DSF	Cgy. 4	Van. 3	Joel Otto	19:21	Cgy.
Apr. 18/89	Cgy.	DF	Cgy. 4	L.A. 3	Doug Gilmour	7:47	Cgy.
Apr. 19/89	Mtl.	DF	Mtl. 3	Bos. 2	Bobby Smith	12:24	Mtl.
Apr. 20/89	St.L.	DF	St.L. 5	Chi. 4	Tony Hrkac	33:49	Chi.
Apr. 21/89	Phi.	DF	Pit. 4	Phi. 3	Phil Bourque	12:08	Phi.
May 8/89	Chi.	CF	Cgy. 2	Chi. 1	Al MacInnis	15:05	Cgy.
May 9/89	Mtl.	CF	Phi. 2	Mtl. 1	Dave Poulin	5:02	Mtl.
May 19/89	Mtl.	F	Mtl. 4	Cgy. 3	Ryan Walter	38:08	Cgy.
Apr. 5/90	N.J.	DSF	Wsh. 5	N.J. 4	Dino Ciccarelli	5:34	Wsh.
Apr. 6/90	Edm.	DSF	Edm. 3	Wpg. 2	Mark Lamb	4:21	Edm.
Apr. 8/90	Tor.	DSF	St.L. 6	Tor. 5	Sergio Momesso	6:04	St.L.
Apr. 8/90	L.A.	DSF	L.A. 2	Cgy. 1	Tony Granato	8:37	L.A.
Apr. 9/90	Mtl.	DSF	Mtl. 2	Buf. 1	Brian Skrudland	12:35	Mtl.
Apr. 9/90	NYI	DSF	NYI 4	NYR 3	Brent Sutter	20:59	NYR
Apr. 10/90	Wpg.	DSF	Wpg. 4	Edm. 3	Dave Ellett	21:08	Edm.
Apr. 14/90	L.A.	DSF	L.A. 4	Cgy. 3	Mike Krushelnyski	23:14	L.A.
Apr. 15/90	Hfd.	DSF	Hfd. 3	Bos. 2	Kevin Dineen	12:30	Bos.
Apr. 21/90	Bos.	DF	Bos. 5	Mtl. 4	Garry Galley	3:42	Bos.
Apr. 24/90	L.A.	DF	Edm. 6	L.A. 5	Joe Murphy	4:42	Edm.
Apr. 25/90	Wsh.	DF	Wsh. 4	NYR 3	Rod Langway	0:34	Wsh.
Apr. 27/90	NYR	DF	Wsh. 2	NYR 1	John Druce	6:48	Wsh.
May 15/90	Bos.	F	Edm. 3	Bos. 2	Petr Klima	55:13	Edm.
Apr. 4/91	Chi.	DSF	Min. 4	Chi. 3	Brian Propp	4:14	Min.
Apr. 5/91	Pit.	DSF	Pit. 5	N.J. 4	Jaromir Jagr	8:52	Pit.
Apr. 6/91	L.A.	DSF	L.A. 3	Van. 2	Wayne Gretzky	11:08	L.A.
Apr. 8/91	Van.	DSF	Van. 2	L.A. 1	Cliff Ronning	3:12	L.A.
Apr. 11/91	NYR	DSF	Wsh. 5	NYR 4	Dino Ciccarelli	6:44	Wsh.
Apr. 11/91	Mtl.	DSF	Mtl. 4	Buf. 3	Russ Courtnall	5:56	Mtl.
Apr. 14/91	Edm.	DSF	Cgy. 2	Edm. 1	Theoren Fleury	4:40	Edm.
Apr. 16/91	Cgy.	DSF	Edm. 5	Cgy. 4	Esa Tikkanen	6:58	Edm.
Apr. 18/91	L.A.	DF	L.A. 4	Edm. 3	Luc Robitaille	2:13	Edm.
Apr. 19/91	Bos.	DF	Mtl. 4	Bos. 3	Stephane Richer	0:27	Bos.
Apr. 19/91	Pit.	DF	Pit. 7	Wsh. 6	Kevin Stevens	8:10	Pit.
Apr. 20/91	L.A.	DF	Edm. 4	L.A. 3	Petr Klima	24:48	Edm.
Apr. 22/91	Edm.	DF	Edm. 4	L.A. 3	Esa Tikkanen	20:48	Edm.
Apr. 27/91	Mtl.	DF	Mtl. 3	Bos. 2	Shayne Corson	17:47	Bos.
Apr. 28/91	Edm.	DF	Edm. 4	L.A. 3	Craig MacTavish	16:57	Edm.
May 3/91	Bos.	CF	Bos. 5	Pit. 4	Vladimir Ruzicka	8:14	Pit.
Apr. 21/92	Bos.	DSF	Bos. 3	Buf. 2	Adam Oates	11:14	Bos.
Apr. 22/92	Min.	DSF	Det. 5	Min. 4	Yves Racine	1:15	Det.
Apr. 22/92	St.L.	DSF	St.L. 5	Chi. 4	Brett Hull	23:33	Chi.
Apr. 25/92	Buf.	DSF	Bos. 5	Buf. 4	Ted Donato	2:08	Bos.
Apr. 28/92	Min.	DSF	Det. 1	Min. 0	Sergei Fedorov	16:13	Det.
Apr. 29/92	Hfd.	DSF	Hfd. 2	Mtl. 1	Yvon Corriveau	0:24	Mtl.
May 1/92	Mtl.	DSF	Mtl. 3	Hfd. 2	Russ Courtnall	25:26	Mtl.
May 3/92	Van.	DF	Edm. 4	Van. 3	Joe Murphy	8:36	Edm.
May 5/92	Mtl.	DF	Bos. 3	Mtl. 2	Peter Douris	3:12	Bos.
May 7/92	Pit.	DF	NYR 6	Pit. 5	Kris King	1:29	Pit.
May 9/92	Pit.	DF	Pit. 5	NYR 4	Ron Francis	2:47	Pit.
May 17/92	Pit.	CF	Pit. 4	Bos. 3	Jaromir Jagr	9:44	Pit.
May 20/92	Edm.	CF	Chi. 4	Edm. 3	Jeremy Roenick	2:45	Chi.
Apr. 18/93	Bos.	DSF	Buf. 5	Bos. 4	Bob Sweeney	11:03	Buf.
Apr. 18/93	Que.	DSF	Que. 3	Mtl. 2	Scott Young	16:49	Mtl.
Apr. 20/93	Wsh.	DSF	NYI 5	Wsh. 4	Brian Mullen	34:50	NYI
Apr. 22/93	Mtl.	DSF	Mtl. 2	Que. 1	Vincent Damphousse	10:30	Mtl.
Apr. 22/93	Buf.	DSF	Buf. 4	Bos. 3	Yuri Khmylev	1:05	Buf.
Apr. 22/93	NYI	DSF	NYI 4	Wsh. 3	Ray Ferraro	4:46	NYI
Apr. 24/93	Buf.	DSF	Buf. 6	Bos. 5	Brad May	4:48	Buf.
Apr. 24/93	NYI	DSF	NYI 4	Wsh. 3	Ray Ferraro	25:40	NYI
Apr. 25/93	St.L.	DSF	St.L. 4	Chi. 3	Craig Janney	10:43	St.L.
Apr. 26/93	Que.	DSF	Mtl. 5	Que. 4	Kirk Muller	8:17	Mtl.
Apr. 27/93	Det.	DSF	Tor. 5	Det. 4	Mike Foligno	2:05	Tor.
Apr. 27/93	Van.	DSF	Wpg. 4	Van. 3	Teemu Selanne	6:18	Van.
Apr. 29/93	Wpg.	DSF	Van. 4	Wpg. 3	Greg Adams	4:30	Van.
May 1/93	Det.	DSF	Tor. 4	Det. 3	Nikolai Borschevsky	2:35	Tor.
May 3/93	Tor.	DF	Tor. 2	St.L. 1	Doug Gilmour	23:16	Tor.
May 4/93	Mtl.	DF	Mtl. 4	Buf. 3	Guy Carbonneau	2:50	Mtl.
May 5/93	Tor.	DF	St.L. 2	Tor. 1	Jeff Brown	23:03	Tor.
May 6/93	Buf.	DF	Mtl. 4	Buf. 3	Gilbert Dionne	8:28	Mtl.
May 8/93	Buf.	DF	Mtl. 4	Buf. 3	Kirk Muller	11:37	Mtl.
May 11/93	Van.	DF	L.A. 4	Van. 3	Gary Shuchuk	26:31	L.A.
May 14/93	Pit.	DF	NYI 4	Pit. 3	Dave Volek	5:16	NYI
May 18/93	Mtl.	CF	Mtl. 4	NYI 3	Stephan Lebeau	26:21	Mtl.
May 20/93	NYI	CF	Mtl. 2	NYI 1	Guy Carbonneau	12:34	Mtl.
May 25/93	Tor.	CF	Tor. 3	L.A. 2	Glenn Anderson	19:20	L.A.
May 27/93	L.A.	CF	L.A. 5	Tor. 4	Wayne Gretzky	1:41	L.A.
Jun. 3/93	Mtl.	F	Mtl. 3	L.A. 2	Eric Desjardins	0:51	Mtl.
Jun. 5/93	L.A.	F	Mtl. 4	L.A. 3	John LeClair	0:34	Mtl.

Date	City	Series	Score		Scorer	Overtime	Series Winner
Jun. 7/93	L.A.	F	Mtl. 3	L.A. 2	John LeClair	14:37	Mtl.
Apr. 20/94	Tor.	CQF	Tor. 1	Chi. 0	Todd Gill	2:15	Tor.
Apr. 22/94	St.L.	CQF	Dal. 5	St.L. 4	Paul Cavallini	8:34	Dal.
Apr. 24/94	Chi.	CQF	Chi. 4	Tor. 3	Jeremy Roenick	1:23	Tor.
Apr. 25/94	Bos.	CQF	Mtl. 2	Bos. 1	Kirk Muller	17:18	Bos.
Apr. 26/94	Cgy.	CQF	Van. 2	Cgy. 1	Geoff Courtnall	7:15	Van.
Apr. 27/94	Buf.	CQF	Buf. 1	N.J. 0	Dave Hannan	65:43	N.J.
Apr. 28/94	Van.	CQF	Van. 3	Cgy. 2	Trevor Linden	16:43	Van.
Apr. 30/94	Cgy.	CQF	Van. 4	Cgy. 3	Pavel Bure	22:20	Van.
May 3/94	N.J.	CSF	Bos. 6	N.J. 5	Don Sweeney	9:08	N.J.
May 7/94	Bos.	CSF	N.J. 5	Bos. 4	Stephane Richer	14:19	N.J.
May 8/94	Van.	CSF	Van. 2	Dal. 1	Sergio Momesso	11:01	Van.
May 12/94	Tor.	CSF	Tor. 3	S.J. 2	Mike Gartner	8:53	Tor.
May 15/94	NYR	CF	N.J. 4	NYR 3	Stephane Richer	35:23	NYR
May 16/94	Tor.	CF	Tor. 3	Van. 2	Peter Zezel	16:55	Van.
May 19/94	N.J.	CF	NYR 3	N.J. 2	Stephane Matteau	26:13	NYR
May 24/94	Van.	CF	Van. 4	Tor. 3	Greg Adams	20:14	Van.
May 27/94	NYR	CF	NYR 2	N.J. 1	Stephane Matteau	24:24	NYR
May 31/94	NYR	F	Van. 3	NYR 2	Greg Adams	19:26	NYR
May 7/95	Phi.	CQF	Phi. 4	Buf. 3	Karl Dykhuis	10:06	Phi.
May 9/95	Cgy.	CQF	S.J. 5	Cgy. 4	Ulf Dahlen	12:21	S.J.
May 12/95	NYR	CQF	NYR 3	Que. 2	Steve Larmer	8:09	NYR
May 12/95	N.J.	CQF	N.J. 1	Bos. 0	Randy McKay	8:51	N.J.
May 14/95	Pit.	CQF	Pit. 6	Wsh. 5	Luc Robitaille	4:30	Pit.
May 15/95	St.L.	CQF	Van. 6	St.L. 5	Cliff Ronning	1:48	Van.
May 17/95	Tor.	CQF	Tor. 5	Chi. 4	Randy Wood	10:00	Chi.
May 19/95	Cgy.	CQF	S.J. 5	Cgy. 4	Ray Whitney	21:54	S.J.
May 21/95	Phi.	CSF	Phi. 5	NYR 4	Eric Desjardins	7:03	Phi.
May 21/95	Chi.	CSF	Chi. 2	Van. 1	Joe Murphy	9:04	Chi.
May 22/95	Phi.	CSF	Phi. 4	NYR 3	Kevin Haller	0:25	Phi.
May 25/95	Van.	CSF	Chi. 3	Van. 2	Chris Chelios	6:22	Chi.
May 26/95	N.J.	CSF	N.J. 2	Pit. 1	Neal Broten	18:36	N.J.
May 27/95	Van.	CSF	Chi. 4	Van. 3	Chris Chelios	5:35	Chi.
Jun. 1/95	Det.	CF	Det. 2	Chi. 1	Nicklas Lidstrom	1:01	Det.
Jun. 6/95	Chi.	CF	Det. 4	Chi. 3	Vladimir Konstantinov	29:25	Det.
Jun. 7/95	N.J.	CF	Phi. 3	N.J. 2	Eric Lindros	4:19	N.J.
Jun. 11/95	Det.	CF	Det. 2	Chi. 1	Vyacheslav Kozlov	22:25	Det.
Apr. 16/96	NYR	CQF	Mtl. 3	NYR 2	Vincent Damphousse	5:04	NYR
Apr. 18/96	Tor.	CQF	Tor. 5	St.L. 4	Mats Sundin	4:02	St.L.
Apr. 18/96	Phi.	CQF	T.B. 2	Phi. 1	Brian Bellows	9:05	Phi.
Apr. 21/96	St.L.	CQF	St.L. 3	Tor. 2	Glenn Anderson	1:24	St.L.
Apr. 21/96	T.B.	CQF	T.B. 5	Phi. 4	Alexander Selivanov	2:04	Phi.
Apr. 23/96	Cgy.	CQF	Chi. 2	Cgy. 1	Joe Murphy	50:02	Chi.
Apr. 24/96	Wsh.	CQF	Pit. 3	Wsh. 2	Petr Nedved	79:15	Pit.
Apr. 25/96	Col.	CQF	Col. 5	Van. 4	Joe Sakic	0:51	Col.
Apr. 25/96	Tor.	CQF	Tor. 5	St.L. 4	Mike Gartner	7:31	St.L.
May 2/96	Col.	CSF	Chi. 3	Col. 2	Jeremy Roenick	6:29	Col.
May 6/96	Chi.	CSF	Chi. 4	Col. 3	Sergei Krivokrasov	0:46	Col.
May 8/96	St.L.	CSF	St.L. 5	Det. 4	Igor Kravchuk	3:23	Det.
May 8/96	Chi.	CSF	Col. 3	Chi. 2	Joe Sakic	44:33	Col.
May 9/96	Fla.	CSF	Fla. 4	Phi. 3	Dave Lowry	4:06	Fla.
May 12/96	Phi.	CSF	Fla. 2	Phi. 1	Mike Hough	28:05	Fla.
May 13/96	Chi.	CSF	Col. 4	Chi. 3	Sandis Ozolinsh	25:18	Col.
May 16/96	Det.	CSF	Det. 1	St.L. 0	Steve Yzerman	21:15	Det.
May 19/96	Det.	CF	Col. 3	Det. 2	Mike Keane	17:31	Col.
Jun. 10/96	Fla.	F	Col. 1	Fla. 0	Uwe Krupp	44:31	Col.
Apr. 20/97	Chi.	CQF	Chi. 4	Col. 3	Sergei Krivokrasov	31:03	Col.
Apr. 20/97	Edm.	CQF	Edm. 4	Dal. 3	Kelly Buchberger	9:15	Edm.
Apr. 22/97	NYR	CQF	NYR 4	Fla. 3	Esa Tikkanen	16:29	NYR
Apr. 23/97	Ott.	CQF	Ott. 1	Buf. 0	Daniel Alfredsson	2:34	Buf.
Apr. 24/97	Mtl.	CQF	Mtl. 4	N.J. 3	Patrice Brisebois	47:37	N.J.
Apr. 25/97	Fla.	CQF	NYR 3	Fla. 2	Esa Tikkanen	12:02	NYR
Apr. 25/97	Dal.	CQF	Edm. 1	Dal. 0	Ryan Smyth	20:22	Edm.
Apr. 27/97	Phx.	CQF	Ana. 3	Phx. 2	Paul Kariya	7:29	Ana.
Apr. 29/97	Buf.	CQF	Buf. 3	Ott. 2	Derek Plante	5:24	Buf.
Apr. 29/97	Dal.	CQF	Edm. 4	Dal. 3	Todd Marchant	12:26	Edm.
May 2/97	Det.	CSF	Det. 2	Ana. 1	Martin Lapointe	0:59	Det.
May 4/97	Det.	CSF	Det. 3	Ana. 2	Vyacheslav Kozlov	41:31	Det.
May 8/97	Ana.	CSF	Det. 3	Ana. 2	Brendan Shanahan	37:03	Det.
May 9/97	Phi.	CSF	Buf. 5	Phi. 4	Ed Ronan	6:24	Phi.
May 9/97	Edm.	CSF	Col. 3	Edm. 2	Claude Lemieux	8:35	Col.
May 11/97	N.J.	CSF	NYR 2	N.J. 1	Adam Graves	14:08	NYR
Apr. 22/98	N.J.	CQF	Ott. 2	N.J. 1	Bruce Gardiner	5:58	Ott.
Apr. 23/98	Pit.	CQF	Mtl. 3	Pit. 2	Benoit Brunet	18:43	Mtl.
Apr. 24/98	Wsh.	CQF	Bos. 4	Wsh. 3	Darren Van Impe	20:54	Wsh.
Apr. 26/98	Ott.	CQF	Ott. 2	N.J. 1	Alexei Yashin	2:47	Ott.
Apr. 26/98	Bos.	CQF	Wsh. 3	Bos. 2	Joe Juneau	26:31	Wsh.
Apr. 26/98	Edm.	CQF	Col. 5	Edm. 4	Joe Sakic	15:25	Edm.
Apr. 28/98	S.J.	CQF	S.J. 1	Dal. 0	Andrei Zyuzin	6:31	Dal.
May 1/98	Phi.	CQF	Buf. 3	Phi. 2	Michal Grosek	5:40	Buf.
May 2/98	S.J.	CQF	Dal. 3	S.J. 2	Mike Keane	3:43	Dal.
May 3/98	Bos.	CQF	Wsh. 3	Bos. 2	Brian Bellows	15:24	Wsh.
May 3/98	Buf.	CSF	Buf. 3	Mtl. 2	Geoff Sanderson	2:37	Buf.
May 11/98	Edm.	CSF	Dal. 1	Edm. 0	Benoit Hogue	13:07	Dal.
May 12/98	Mtl.	CSF	Buf. 5	Mtl. 4	Michael Peca	21:24	Buf.
May 12/98	St.L.	CSF	Det. 3	St.L. 2	Brendan Shanahan	31:12	Det.
May 25/98	Wsh.	CF	Wsh. 3	Buf. 2	Todd Krygier	3:01	Wsh.
May 28/98	Buf.	CF	Wsh. 4	Buf. 3	Peter Bondra	9:37	Wsh.
Jun. 3/98	Dal.	CF	Dal. 3	Det. 2	Jamie Langenbrunner	0:46	Det.
Jun. 4/98	Buf.	CF	Wsh. 3	Buf. 2	Joe Juneau	6:24	Wsh.
Jun. 11/98	Det.	F	Det. 5	Wsh. 4	Kris Draper	15:24	Det.
Apr. 23/99	Ott.	CQF	Buf. 3	Ott. 2	Miroslav Satan	30:35	Buf.
Apr. 24/99	Car.	CQF	Car. 3	Bos. 2	Ray Sheppard	17:05	Bos.
Apr. 24/99	Phx.	CQF	Phx. 4	St.L. 3	Shane Doan	8:58	St.L.
Apr. 26/99	S.J.	CQF	Col. 2	S.J. 1	Milan Hejduk	7:53	Col.
Apr. 27/99	Edm.	CQF	Dal. 3	Edm. 2	Joe Nieuwendyk	57:34	Dal.
Apr. 30/99	Tor.	CQF	Tor. 2	Phi. 1	Yanic Perreault	11:51	Tor.
Apr. 30/99	Car.	CQF	Bos. 4	Car. 3	Anson Carter	34:45	Bos.
Apr. 30/99	Phx..	CQF	St.L. 2	Phx. 1	Scott Young	5:43	St.L.
May 2/99	Pit.	CQF	Pit. 3	N.J. 2	Jaromir Jagr	8:59	Pit.
May 3/99	S.J.	CQF	Col. 3	S.J. 2	Milan Hejduk	13:12	Col.
May 4/99	Phx.	CQF	St.L. 1	Phx. 0	Pierre Turgeon	17:59	St.L.
May 7/99	Col.	CSF	Det. 3	Col. 2	Kirk Maltby	4:18	Col.
May 8/99	Dal.	CSF	Dal. 5	St.L. 4	Joe Nieuwendyk	8:22	Dal.
May 10/99	St.L.	CSF	St.L. 3	Dal. 2	Pavol Demitra	2:43	Dal.
May 12/99	St.L.	CSF	St.L. 3	Dal. 2	Pierre Turgeon	5:52	Dal.
May 13/99	Pit.	CSF	Tor. 3	Pit. 2	Sergei Berezin	2:18	Tor.
May 17/99	Pit.	CSF	Tor. 4	Pit. 3	Garry Valk	1:57	Tor.
May 17/99	St.L.	CSF	Dal. 2	St.L. 1	Mike Modano	2:21	Dal.
May 28/99	Col.	CF	Col. 3	Dal. 2	Chris Drury	19:29	Dal.
Jun. 8/99	Dal.	F	Buf. 3	Dal. 2	Jason Woolley	15:30	Dal.
Jun. 19/99	Buf.	F	Dal. 2	Buf. 1	Brett Hull	54:51	Dal.
Apr. 15/00	Pit.	CQF	Pit. 2	Wsh. 1	Jaromir Jagr	5:49	Pit.
Apr. 18/00	Buf.	CQF	Buf. 3	Phi. 2	Stu Barnes	4:42	Phi.
Apr. 22/00	Tor.	CQF	Tor. 2	Ott. 1	Steve Thomas	14:47	Tor.
May 2/00	Pit.	CSF	Phi. 4	Pit. 3	Andy Delmore	11:01	Phi.
May 3/00	Det.	CSF	Col. 3	Det. 2	Chris Drury	10:21	Col.
May 4/00	Pit.	CSF	Phi. 2	Pit. 1	Keith Primeau	92:01	Phi.
May 23/00	Dal.	CF	Dal. 3	Col. 2	Joe Nieuwendyk	12:10	Dal.
Jun. 8/00	N.J.	F	Dal. 1	N.J. 0	Mike Modano	46:21	N.J.
Jun. 10/00	Dal.	F	N.J. 2	Dal. 1	Jason Arnott	28:20	N.J.
Apr. 11/01	Dal.	CQF	Dal. 2	Edm. 1	Jamie Langenbrunner	2:08	Dal.
Apr. 13/01	Ott.	CQF	Tor. 1	Ott. 0	Mats Sundin	10:49	Tor.
Apr. 14/01	Phi.	CQF	Buf. 4	Phi. 3	Jay McKee	18:02	Buf.
Apr. 15/01	Edm.	CQF	Dal. 3	Edm. 2	Benoit Hogue	19:48	Dal.
Apr. 16/01	Tor.	CQF	Tor. 3	Ott. 2	Cory Cross	2:16	Tor.
Apr. 16/01	Van.	CQF	Col. 4	Van. 3	Peter Forsberg	2:50	Col.
Apr. 17/01	Buf.	CQF	Buf. 4	Phi. 3	Curtis Brown	6:13	Buf.
Apr. 17/01	Edm.	CQF	Edm. 2	Dal. 1	Mike Comrie	17:19	Dal.
Apr. 18/01	Car.	CQF	Car. 3	N.J. 2	Rod Brind'Amour	:46	N.J.
Apr. 18/01	Pit.	CQF	Wsh. 4	Pit. 3	Jeff Halpern	4:01	Pit.
Apr. 18/01	L.A.	CQF	L.A. 4	Det. 3	Eric Belanger	2:36	L.A.
Apr. 19/01	Dal.	CQF	Dal. 4	Edm. 3	Kirk Muller	8:01	Dal.
Apr. 19/01	St.L.	CQF	St.L. 3	S.J. 2	Bryce Salvador	9:54	St.L.
Apr. 23/01	Pit.	CQF	Pit. 4	Wsh. 3	Martin Straka	13:04	Pit.
Apr. 23/01	L.A.	CQF	L.A. 3	Det. 2	Adam Deadmarsh	4:48	L.A.
Apr. 26/01	Col.	CSF	L.A. 4	Col. 3	Jaroslav Modry	14:23	Col.
Apr. 28/01	N.J.	CSF	N.J. 6	Tor. 5	Randy McKay	5:31	N.J.
May 1/01	Tor.	CSF	N.J. 3	Tor. 2	Brian Rafalski	7:00	N.J.
May 1/01	St.L.	CSF	St.L. 3	Dal. 2	Cory Stillman	29:26	St.L.
May 5/01	Buf.	CSF	Buf. 3	Pit. 2	Stu Barnes	8:34	Pit.
May 6/01	L.A.	CSF	L.A. 1	Col. 0	Glen Murray	22:41	Col.
May 8/01	Pit.	CSF	Pit. 3	Buf. 2	Martin Straka	11:29	Pit.
May 10/01	Buf.	CSF	Pit. 3	Buf. 2	Darius Kasparaitis	13:01	Pit.
May 16/01	St.L.	CF	St.L. 4	Col. 3	Scott Young	30:27	Col.
May 18/01	St.L.	CF	Col. 4	St.L. 3	Stephane Yelle	4:23	Col.
May 21/01	Col.	CF	Col. 2	St.L. 1	Joe Sakic	:24	Col.
Apr. 17/02	Phi.	CQF	Phi. 1	Ott. 0	Ruslan Fedotenko	7:47	Ott.
Apr. 17/02	Det.	CQF	Van. 4	Det. 3	Henrik Sedin	13:59	Det.
Apr. 19/02	Car.	CQF	Car. 2	N.J. 1	Bates Battaglia	15:26	Car.
Apr. 24/02	Car.	CQF	Car. 3	N.J. 2	Josef Vasicek	8:16	Car.
Apr. 25/02	Col.	CQF	L.A. 1	Col. 0	Craig Johnson	2:19	Col.
Apr. 26/02	Phi.	CQF	Ott. 2	Phi. 1	Martin Havlat	7:33	Ott.
May 4/02	Tor.	CSF	Tor. 3	Ott. 2	Gary Roberts	44:30	Tor.
May 7/02	Mtl.	CSF	Mtl. 2	Car. 1	Donald Audette	2:26	Car.
May 9/02	Mtl.	CSF	Car. 4	Mtl. 3	Niclas Wallin	3:14	Car.
May 13/02	S.J.	CSF	Col. 2	S.J. 1	Peter Forsberg	2:47	Col.
May 19/02	Car.	CF	Car. 2	Tor. 1	Niclas Wallin	13:42	Car.
May 20/02	Det.	CF	Col. 4	Det. 3	Chris Drury	2:17	Det.
May 21/02	Tor.	CF	Car. 2	Tor. 1	Jeff O'Neill	6:01	Car.
May 22/02	Col.	CF	Det. 2	Col. 1	Fredrik Olausson	12:44	Det.
May 27/02	Det.	CF	Col. 2	Det. 1	Peter Forsberg	6:24	Det.
May 28/02	Tor.	CF	Car. 2	Tor. 1	Martin Gelinas	8:05	Car.
Jun. 4/02	Det.	F	Car. 3	Det. 2	Ron Francis	:58	Det.
Jun. 8/02	Car.	F	Det. 3	Car. 2	Igor Larionov	54:47	Det.
Apr. 10/03	Det.	CQF	Ana. 2	Det. 1	Paul Kariya	43:18	Ana.
Apr. 14/03	NYI	CQF	Ott. 3	NYI 2	Todd White	22:25	Ott.
Apr. 14/03	Tor.	CQF	Tor. 4	Phi. 3	Tomas Kaberle	27:20	Phi.
Apr. 15/03	Wsh.	CQF	T.B. 4	Wsh. 3	Vincent Lecavalier	2:29	T.B.
Apr. 16/03	Tor.	CQF	Phi. 3	Tor. 2	Mark Recchi	53:54	Phi.
Apr. 16/03	Ana.	CQF	Ana. 3	Det. 2	Steve Rucchin	6:53	Ana.
Apr. 20/03	Wsh.	CQF	T.B. 2	Wsh. 1	Martin St. Louis	44:03	T.B.
Apr. 21/03	Tor.	CQF	Tor. 2	Phi. 1	Travis Green	30:51	Phi.
Apr. 21/03	Min.	CQF	Min. 3	Col. 2	Richard Park	4:22	Min.
Apr. 22/03	Col.	CQF	Min. 3	Col. 2	Andrew Brunette	3:25	Min.
Apr. 24/03	Dal.	CSF	Ana. 4	Dal. 3	Petr Sykora	80:48	Ana.
Apr. 25/03	Van.	CSF	Van. 4	Min. 3	Trent Klatt	3:42	Min.
Apr. 26/03	N.J.	CSF	N.J. 3	T.B. 2	Jamie Langenbrunner	2:09	N.J.
Apr. 26/03	Dal.	CSF	Ana. 3	Dal. 2	Mike Leclerc	1:44	Ana.
Apr. 29/03	Phi.	CSF	Ott. 3	Phi. 2	Wade Redden	6:43	Ott.
May 2/03	Min.	CSF	Van. 3	Min. 2	Brent Sopel	15:52	Min.
May 2/03	N.J.	CSF	N.J. 2	T.B. 1	Grant Marshall	51:12	N.J.
May 10/03	Min.	CF	Ana. 1	Min. 0	Petr Sykora	28:06	Ana.
May 10/03	Ott.	CF	Ott. 3	N.J. 2	Shaun Van Allen	3:08	N.J.
May 21/03	N.J.	CF	Ott. 2	N.J. 1	Chris Phillips	15:51	N.J.
May 31/03	Ana.	F	Ana. 3	N.J. 2	Ruslan Salei	6:59	N.J.
Jun. 2/03	Ana.	F	Ana. 1	N.J. 0	Steve Thomas	0:39	N.J.
Apr. 8/04	S.J.	CQF	S.J. 1	St.L. 0	Niko Dimitrakos	9:16	S.J.
Apr. 9/04	Bos.	CQF	Bos. 2	Mtl. 1	PatriceBergeron	1:26	Mtl.
Apr. 12/04	Dal.	CQF	Dal. 4	Col. 3	Steve Ott	2:11	Col.
Apr. 13/04	Mtl.	CQF	Bos. 4	Mtl. 3	Glen Murray	29:27	Mtl.
Apr. 14/04	Dal.	CQF	Col. 3	Dal. 2	Marek Svatos	25:21	Col.
Apr. 16/04	T.B.	CQF	T.B. 3	NYI 2	Martin St. Louis	4:07	T.B.
Apr. 17/04	Cgy.	CQF	Van. 5	Cgy 4	Brendan Morrison	42:28	Cgy.
Apr. 18/04	Ott.	CQF	Ott. 2	Tor. 1	Mike Fisher	21:47	Tor.
Apr. 19/04	Van.	CQF	Cgy. 3	Van. 2	Martin Gelinas	1:25	Cgy.
Apr. 22/04	Det.	CSF	Cgy. 2	Det. 1	Marcus Nilson	2:39	Cgy.
Apr. 27/04	Mtl.	CSF	T.B. 4	Mtl 3	Brad Richards	1:05	T.B.
Apr. 28/04	Col	CSF	Col. 1	S.J. 0	Joe Sakic	5:15	S.J.
May 1/04	S.J.	CSF	Col. 2	S.J. 1	Joe Sakic	1:54	S.J.
May 3/04	Cgy	CSF	Cgy. 1	Det. 0	Martin Gelinas	19:13	Cgy.
May 4/04	Phi.	CSF	Phi. 3	Tor. 2	Jeremy Roenick	7:39	Phi.
May 9/04	S.J.	CF	Cgy. 4	S.J. 3	Steve Montador	18:43	Cgy.
May 20/04	Phi.	CF	Phi. 5	T.B. 4	Simon Gagne	18:18	T.B.
Jun. 3/04	T.B.	F	Cgy. 3	T.B. 2	Oleg Saprykin	14:40	T.B.
Jun. 5/04	Cgy.	F	T.B. 3	Cgy. 2	Martin St. Louis	20:33	T.B.

NHL Playoff Coaching Records

Coach	Team	Games Coached	Wins	Losses	Ties	Playoff Years	Cup Wins	Career
Abel, Sid	Chicago	7	3	4	0	1		
	Detroit	69	29	40	0	8		
	Total	76	32	44	0	9		1952-76
Adams, Jack	Detroit	105	52	52	1	15	3	1927-47
Allen, Keith	Philadelphia	11	3	8	0	2		1967-69
Arbour, Al	St. Louis	11	4	7	0	1		
	NY Islanders	198	119	79	0	15	4	
	Total	209	123	86	0	16	4	1970-94
Babcock, Mike	Anaheim	21	15	6	0	1		2002-04
Barber, Bill	Philadelphia	11	3	8	0	2		2000-02
Berenson, Red	St. Louis	14	5	9	0	2		1979-82
Bergeron, Michel	Quebec	68	31	37	0	7		1980-90
Berry, Bob	Los Angeles	10	2	8	0	3		
	Montreal	8	2	6	0	2		
	St. Louis	15	7	8	0	2		
	Total	33	11	22	0	7		1978-94
Beverley, Nick	Toronto	6	2	4	0	1		1995-96
Blackburn, Don	Hartford	3	0	3	0	1		1979-81
Blair, Wren	Minnesota	14	7	7	0	1		1967-70
Blake, Toe	Montreal	119	82	37	0	13	8	1955-68
Boileau, Marc	Pittsburgh	9	5	4	0	1		1973-76
Boivin, Leo	St. Louis	3	1	2	0	1		1975-78
Boucher, Frank	NY Rangers	27	13	14	0	4	1	1939-54
Boucher, Georges	Mtl. Maroons	2	0	2	0	1		1930-50
Bowman, Scotty	St. Louis	52	26	26	0	4		
	Montreal	98	70	28	0	8	5	
	Buffalo	36	18	18	0	5		
	Pittsburgh	33	23	10	0	2	1	
	Detroit	134	86	48	0	9	3	
	Total	353	223	130	0	28	9	1967-02
Bowness, Rick	Boston	15	8	7	0	1		1988-04
Brooks, Herb	NY Rangers	24	12	12	0	3		
	New Jersey	5	1	4	0	1		
	Pittsburgh	11	6	5	0	1		
	Total	40	19	21	0	5		1981-00
Brophy, John	Toronto	19	9	10	0	2		1986-89
Burns, Charlie	Minnesota	6	2	4	0	1		1969-75
Burns, Pat	Montreal	56	30	26	0	4		
	Toronto	46	23	23	0	3		
	Boston	18	8	10	0	3		
	New Jersey	29	17	12	0	2	1	
	Total	149	78	71	0	11	1	1988-04
Campbell, Colin	NY Rangers	36	18	18	0	3		1994-98
Carpenter, Doug	Toronto	5	1	4	0	1		1984-91
Carroll, Dick	Toronto	7	4	3	0	1	1	1917-19
Cassidy, Bruce	Washington	6	2	4	0	1		2002-04
Cheevers, Gerry	Boston	34	15	19	0	4		1980-85
Cherry, Don	Boston	55	31	24	0	5		1974-80
Clancy, King	Toronto	14	2	12	0	3		1937-56
Clapper, Dit	Boston	25	8	17	0	4		1945-49
Cleghorn, Odie	Pittsburgh	4	1	2	1	2		1925-29
Cleghorn, Sprague	Mtl. Maroons	4	1	1	2	1		1931-32
Constantine, Kevin	San Jose	25	11	14	0	2		
	Pittsburgh	19	8	11	0	2		
	New Jersey	6	2	4	0	1		
	Total	50	21	29	0	5		1993-02
Crawford, Marc	Quebec	6	2	4	0	1		
	Colorado	46	29	17	0	3	1	
	Vancouver	31	12	19	0	4		
	Total	83	43	40	0	8	1	1994-03
Creighton, Fred	Atlanta	9	2	7	0	4		1974-80
Crisp, Terry	Calgary	37	22	15	0	3	1	
	Tampa Bay	6	2	4	0	1		
	Total	43	24	19	0	4	1	1987-98
Crozier, Joe	Buffalo	6	2	4	0	1		1971-81
Cunniff, John	New Jersey	6	2	4	0	1		1982-91
Curry, Alex	Ottawa	2	0	1	1	1		1925-26
Dandurand, Leo	Montreal	16	10	6	0	4	1	1921-35
Day, Hap	Toronto	80	49	31	0	9	5	1940-50
Demers, Jacques	St. Louis	33	16	17	0	3		
	Detroit	38	20	18	0	3		
	Montreal	27	19	8	0	2	1	
	Total	98	55	43	0	8	1	1979-99
Denneny, Cy	Boston	5	5	0	0	1	1	1928-33
Dudley, Rick	Buffalo	12	4	8	0	2		1989-04
Dugal, Jules	Montreal	3	1	2	0	1		1938-39
Duncan, Art	Toronto	2	0	1	1	1		1926-32
Dutton, Red	NY Americans	16	6	10	0	4		1935-42
Esposito, Phil	NY Rangers	10	2	8	0	2		1986-89
Evans, Jack	Hartford	16	8	8	0	2		1975-88
Ferguson, John	Winnipeg	9	0	3	0	1		1975-86
Francis, Bob	Phoenix	10	2	8	0	2		1999-04
Francis, Emile	NY Rangers	75	34	41	0	9		
	St. Louis	14	5	9	0	2		
	Total	89	39	50	0	11		1965-83
Ftorek, Robbie	Los Angeles	16	5	11	0	2		
	New Jersey	7	3	4	0	1		
	Boston	6	2	4	0	1		
	Total	29	10	19	0	4		1987-02
Gainey, Bob	Minnesota	30	17	13	0	2		
	Dallas	14	6	8	0	2		
	Total	44	23	21	0	4		1990-96
Geoffrion, Bernie	Atlanta	4	0	4	0	1		1968-80
Gerard, Eddie	Mtl. Maroons	25	11	9	5	5	1	1917-35
Gill, David	Ottawa	8	3	2	3	2	1	1926-29
Glover, Fred	Oakland	11	3	8	0	2		1968-74
Gordon, Jackie	Minnesota	25	11	14	0	3		1970-75
Goring, Butch	Boston	3	0	3	0	1		1985-01
Gorman, Tommy	NY Americans	2	0	1	1	1		
	Chicago	8	6	1	1	1		
	Mtl. Maroons	15	7	6	2	3	1	
	Total	25	13	8	4	5	2	1925-38
Gottselig, Johnny	Chicago	4	0	4	0	1		1944-48
Granato, Tony	Colorado	18	9	9	0	2		2002-04
Green, Pete	Ottawa	26	14	9	3	6	3	1919-25
Green, Ted	Edmonton	16	8	8	0	1		1991-94
Guidolin, Bep	Boston	21	11	10	0	2		1972-76
Harris, Ted	Minnesota	2	0	2	0	1		1975-78
Hart, Cecil	Montreal	37	16	17	4	8	2	1926-39
Hartley, Bob	Colorado	80	49	31	0	4	1	1998-04
Hartsburg, Craig	Chicago	16	8	8	0	2		
	Anaheim	4	0	4	0	1		
	Total	20	8	12	0	3		1995-01
Harvey, Doug	NY Rangers	6	2	4	0	1		1961-62
Hay, Don	Phoenix	7	3	4	0	1		1996-01
Henning, Lorne	Minnesota	5	2	3	0	1		1985-01
Hitchcock, Ken	Dallas	80	47	33	0	5	1	
	Philadelphia	31	17	14	0	2		
	Total	111	64	47	0	7	1	1995-04
Hlinka, Ivan	Pittsburgh	18	9	9	0	1		2000-02
Holmgren, Paul	Philadelphia	19	10	9	0	1		1988-96
Imlach, Punch	Toronto	92	44	48	0	11	4	1958-80
Inglis, Bill	Buffalo	3	1	2	0	1		1978-79
Irvin, Dick	Chicago	9	5	3	1	1		
	Toronto	66	33	32	1	9	1	
	Montreal	115	62	53	0	14	3	
	Total	190	100	88	2	24	4	1928-56
Ivan, Tommy	Detroit	67	36	31	0	7	3	1947-58
Johnson, Bob	Calgary	52	25	27	0	5		
	Pittsburgh	24	16	8	0	1	1	
	Total	76	41	35	0	6	1	1982-91
Johnson, Tom	Boston	22	15	7	0	2	1	1970-73
Johnston, Eddie	Chicago	7	3	4	0	1		
	Pittsburgh	46	22	24	0	5		
	Total	53	25	28	0	6		1979-97
Julien, Claude	Montreal	11	4	7	0	1		2002-04
Kasper, Steve	Boston	5	1	4	0	1		1995-97
Keenan, Mike	Philadelphia	57	32	25	0	4		
	Chicago	60	33	27	0	4		
	NY Rangers	23	16	7	0	1	1	
	St. Louis	20	10	10	0	2		
	Total	160	91	69	0	11	1	1984-04
Kelly, Pat	Colorado	2	0	2	0	1		1977-79
Kelly, Red	Los Angeles	18	7	11	0	2		
	Pittsburgh	14	6	8	0	2		
	Toronto	30	11	19	0	4		
	Total	62	24	38	0	8		1967-77
King, Dave	Calgary	20	8	12	0	3		1992-02
Kitchen, Mike	St. Louis	5	1	4	0	1		2003-04
Kromm, Bobby	Detroit	7	3	4	0	1		1977-80
Lalonde, Newsy	Montreal	16	7	6	3	4		
	Ottawa	2	0	1	1	1		
	Total	18	7	7	4	5		1917-35
Laviolette, Peter	NY Islanders	12	4	8	0	2		2001-04
Lemaire, Jacques	Montreal	27	15	12	0	2		
	New Jersey	56	34	22	0	4	1	
	Minnesota	18	8	10	0	1		
	Total	101	57	44	0	7	1	1983-04
Lewis, Dave	Detroit	16	6	10	0	2		1998-04
Ley, Rick	Hartford	13	5	8	0	2		
	Vancouver	11	4	7	0	1		
	Total	24	9	15	0	3		1989-96
Long, Barry	Winnipeg	11	3	8	0	2		1983-86
Loughlin, Clem	Chicago	4	1	2	1	2		1934-37
Low, Ron	Edmonton	28	10	18	0	3		1994-00
Lowe, Kevin	Edmonton	5	1	4	0	1		1999-00
MacLean, Doug	Florida	27	13	14	0	2		1995-04
MacNeil, Al	Montreal	20	12	8	0	1	1	
	Atlanta	4	1	3	0	1		
	Calgary	19	9	10	0	2		
	Total	43	22	21	0	4	1	1970-82
MacTavish, Craig	Edmonton	12	4	8	0	2		2000-04
Magnuson, Keith	Chicago	3	0	3	0	1		1980-82
Mahoney, Bill	Minnesota	16	7	9	0	1		1983-85
Maloney, Dan	Toronto	10	6	4	0	1		
	Winnipeg	15	5	10	0	2		
	Total	25	11	14	0	3		1984-89
Maloney, Phil	Vancouver	7	1	6	0	2		1973-77

Coach	Team	Games Coached	Wins	Losses	Ties	Playoff Year	Cup Wins	Career
Martin, Jacques	St. Louis	16	7	9	0	2		
	Ottawa	69	31	38	0	8		
	Total	85	38	47	0	10		1986-04
Maurice, Paul	Carolina	35	17	18	0	3		1995-04
McCammon, Bob	Philadelphia	10	1	9	0	3		
	Vancouver	7	3	4	0	1		
	Total	17	4	13	0	4		1978-91
McLellan, John	Toronto	11	3	8	0	2		1969-73
McVie, Tom	New Jersey	14	6	8	0	2		1975-92
Melrose, Barry	Los Angeles	24	13	11	0	1		1992-95
Milbury, Mike	Boston	40	23	17	0	2		1989-98
Muckler, John	Edmonton	40	25	15	0	2	1	
	Buffalo	27	11	16	0	4		
	Total	67	36	31	0	6	1	1968-00
Muldoon, Pete	Chicago	2	0	1	1	1		1926-27
Munro, Dunc	Mtl. Maroons	4	1	3	0	1		1929-31
Murdoch, Bob	Chicago	5	1	4	0	1		
	Winnipeg	7	3	4	0	1		
	Total	12	4	8	0	2		1987-91
Murphy, Mike	Los Angeles	5	1	4	0	1		1986-98
Murray, Andy	Los Angeles	24	10	14	0	3		1999-04
Murray, Bryan	Washington	53	24	29	0	7		
	Detroit	25	10	15	0	3		
	Total	78	34	44	0	10		1981-02
Murray, Terry	Washington	39	18	21	0	4		
	Philadelphia	46	28	18	0	3		
	Florida	4	0	4	0	1		
	Total	89	46	43	0	8		1989-01
Neale, Harry	Vancouver	14	3	11	0	4		1978-86
Neilson, Roger	Toronto	19	8	11	0	2		
	Buffalo	8	4	4	0	1		
	Vancouver	21	12	9	0	2		
	NY Rangers	29	13	16	0	3		
	Philadelphia	29	14	15	0	3		
	Total	106	51	55	0	11		1977-02
Nolan, Ted	Buffalo	12	5	7	0	1		1995-97
Nykoluk, Mike	Toronto	7	1	6	0	2		1980-84
O'Connell, Mike	Boston	5	1	4	0	1		2002-03
O'Donoghue, George	Toronto	7	4	2	1	1	1	1921-23
O'Reilly, Terry	Boston	37	17	19	1	3		1986-89
Oliver, Murray	Minnesota	13	5	8	0	2		1981-83
Paddock, John	Winnipeg	13	5	8	0	2		1991-95
Page, Pierre	Minnesota	12	4	8	0	2		
	Quebec	6	2	4	0	1		
	Calgary	4	0	4	0	1		
	Total	22	6	16	0	4		1988-98
Patrick, Craig	NY Rangers	17	7	10	0	2		
	Pittsburgh	5	1	4	0	1		
	Total	22	8	14	0	3		1980-97
Patrick, Frank	Boston	6	2	4	0	2		1934-36
Patrick, Lester	NY Rangers	65	32	26	7	12	2	1926-39
Patrick, Lynn	NY Rangers	12	7	5	0	1		
	Boston	28	9	18	1	4		
	Total	40	16	23	1	5		1948-76
Perron, Jean	Montreal	48	30	18	0	3	1	1985-89
Perry, Don	Los Angeles	10	4	6	0	1		1981-84
Pilous, Rudy	Chicago	41	19	22	0	5	1	1957-63
Plager, Barclay	St. Louis	4	1	3	0	1		1977-83
Pleau, Larry	Hartford	10	2	8	0	2		1980-89
Polano, Nick	Detroit	7	1	6	0	2		1982-85
Powers, Eddie	Toronto	2	0	2	0	1		1924-26
Primeau, Joe	Toronto	15	8	6	1	2	1	1950-53
Pronovost, Marcel	Buffalo	8	3	5	0	1		1977-79
Pulford, Bob	Los Angeles	26	10	16	0	4		
	Chicago	45	17	28	0	6		
	Total	71	27	44	0	10		1972-00
Quenneville, Joel	St. Louis	68	34	34	0	7		1996-04
Quinn, Pat	Philadelphia	39	22	17	0	3		
	Los Angeles	3	0	3	0	1		
	Vancouver	61	31	30	0	5		
	Toronto	80	41	39	0	6		
	Total	183	94	89	0	15		1978-04
Reay, Billy	Chicago	116	56	60	0	12		1957-77
Risebrough, Doug	Calgary	7	3	4	0	1		1990-92
Roberts, Jim	Hartford	7	3	4	0	1		1981-97
Robinson, Larry	Los Angeles	4	0	4	0	1		
	New Jersey	48	31	17	0	2	1	
	Total	52	31	21	0	3	1	1995-02
Ross, Art	Boston	65	27	33	5	11	1	1917-45
Ruel, Claude	Montreal	27	18	9	0	3	1	1968-81
Ruff, Lindy	Buffalo	54	32	22	0	4		1997-04
Sather, Glen	Edmonton	127	89	37	1	10	4	1979-04
Sator, Ted	NY Rangers	16	8	8	0	1		
	Buffalo	11	3	8	0	2		
	Total	27	11	16	0	3		1985-89
Schinkel, Ken	Pittsburgh	6	2	4	0	2		1972-77
Schmidt, Milt	Boston	34	15	19	0	4		1954-76
Schoenfeld, Jim	New Jersey	20	11	9	0	1		
	Washington	24	10	14	0	3		
	Phoenix	13	5	8	0	2		
	Total	57	26	31	0	6		1985-99
Shero, Fred	Philadelphia	83	48	35	0	6	2	
	NY Rangers	27	15	12	0	2		
	Total	110	63	47	0	8	2	1971-81
Simpson, Terry	NY Islanders	20	9	11	0	2		
	Winnipeg	6	2	4	0	1		
	Total	26	11	15	0	3		1986-96
Sinden, Harry	Boston	43	24	19	0	5	1	1966-85
Skinner, Jimmy	Detroit	26	14	12	0	3	1	1954-58
Smith, Alf	Ottawa	5	1	4	0	1		1918-19
Smith, Floyd	Buffalo	32	16	16	0	3		1971-80
Smythe, Conn	Toronto	4	2	2	0	1		1927-31
Sonmor, Glen	Minnesota	43	25	18	0	3		1978-87
Stasiuk, Vic	Philadelphia	4	0	4	0	1		1969-73
Stewart, Bill	Chicago	10	7	3	0	1	1	1937-39
Stewart, Ron	Los Angeles	2	0	2	0	1		1975-78
Stirling, Steve	NY Islanders	5	1	4	0	1		2003-04
Sullivan, Mike	Boston	7	3	4	0	1		2003-04
Sutter, Brian	St. Louis	41	20	21	0	4		
	Boston	22	7	15	0	3		
	Chicago	5	1	4	0	1		
	Total	68	28	40	0	8		1988-04
Sutter, Darryl	Chicago	26	11	15	0	3		
	San Jose	42	18	24	0	5		
	Calgary	26	15	11	0	1		
	Total	94	44	50	0	9		1992-04
Talbot, Jean-Guy	St. Louis	5	1	4	0	1		
	NY Rangers	3	1	2	0	1		
	Total	8	2	6	0	2		1972-78
Tessier, Orval	Chicago	18	9	9	0	2		1982-85
Therrien, Michel	Montreal	12	6	6	0	1		2000-02
Thompson, Paul	Chicago	19	7	12	0	4		1938-45
Tippett, Dave	Dallas	17	7	10	0	2		2002-04
Tobin, Bill	Chicago	4	1	2	1	2		1929-32
Tortorella, John	Tampa Bay	34	21	13	0	2	1	1999-04
Tremblay, Mario	Montreal	11	3	8	0	2		1995-97
Trotz, Barry	Nashville	6	2	4	0	1		1998-04
Ubriaco, Gene	Pittsburgh	11	7	4	0	1		1988-90
Vigneault, Alain	Montreal	10	4	6	0	1		1997-01
Watson, Phil	NY Rangers	16	4	12	0	3		1955-63
Watt, Tom	Winnipeg	7	1	6	0	2		
	Vancouver	3	0	3	0	1		
	Total	10	1	9	0	3		1981-92
Webster, Tom	Los Angeles	28	12	16	0	3		1986-92
Weiland, Cooney	Boston	17	10	7	0	2	1	1939-41
White, Bill	Chicago	2	0	2	0	1		1976-77
Wilson, Johnny	Pittsburgh	12	4	8	0	2		1969-80
Wilson, Ron	Anaheim	11	4	7	0	1		
	Washington	32	15	17	0	3		
	San Jose	17	10	7	0	1		
	Total	60	29	31	0	5		1993-04
Young, Garry	St. Louis	2	0	2	0	1		1972-76

Tampa Bay's John Tortorella (far left) and Calgary's Darryl Sutter (left) guided their teams to the Stanley Cup finals in 2004.

Penalty Shots in Stanley Cup Playoff Games

Date	Player	Goaltender	Scored		Final Score			Series
Mar. 25/37	Lionel Conacher, Mtl. Maroons	Tiny Thompson, Boston	No	Mtl. M.	0	at Bos.	4	QF
Apr. 15/37	Alex Shibicky, NY Rangers	Earl Robertson, Detroit	No	NYR	0	at Det.	3	F
Apr. 13/44	Virgil Johnson, Chicago	Bill Durnan, Montreal	No	Chi.	4	at Mtl.	5*	F
Apr. 9/68	Wayne Connelly, Minnesota	Terry Sawchuk, Los Angeles	Yes	L.A.	5	at Min.	7	QF
Apr. 27/68	Jim Roberts, St. Louis	Cesare Maniago, Minnesota	No	St.L.	4	at Min.	3	SF
May 16/71	Frank Mahovlich, Montreal	Tony Esposito, Chicago	No	Chi.	3	at Mtl.	4	F
May 7/75	Bill Barber, Philadelphia	Chico Resch, NY Islanders	No	Phi.	3	at NYI	4*	SF
Apr. 20/79	Mike Walton, Chicago	Chico Resch, NY Islanders	No	NYI	4	at Chi.	0	QF
Apr. 9/81	Peter McNab, Boston	Don Beaupre, Minnesota	No	Min.	5	at Bos.	4*	PR
Apr. 17/81	Anders Hedberg, NY Rangers	Mike Liut, St. Louis	Yes	NYR	6	at St.L.	4	QF
Apr. 9/83	Denis Potvin, NY Islanders	Pat Riggin, Washington	No	NYI	6	at Wsh.	5	DSF
Apr. 28/84	Wayne Gretzky, Edmonton	Don Beaupre, Minnesota	Yes	Edm.	8	at Min.	5	CF
May 1/84	Mats Naslund, Montreal	Billy Smith, NY Islanders	No	Mtl.	1	at NYI	3	CF
Apr. 14/85	Bob Carpenter, Washington	Billy Smith, NY Islanders	No	Wsh.	4	at NYI	6	DF
May 28/85	Ron Sutter, Philadelphia	Grant Fuhr, Edmonton	No	Phi.	3	at Edm.	3	F
May 30/85	Dave Poulin, Philadelphia	Grant Fuhr, Edmonton	No	Phi.	3	at Edm.	8	F
Apr. 9/88	John Tucker, Buffalo	Andy Moog, Boston	Yes	Bos.	2	at Buf.	6	DSF
Apr. 9/88	Petr Klima, Detroit	Allan Bester, Toronto	Yes	Det.	6	at Tor.	5	DSF
Apr. 8/89	Neal Broten, Minnesota	Greg Millen, St. Louis	Yes	St.L.	3	at Min.	3	DSF
Apr. 4/90	Al MacInnis, Calgary	Kelly Hrudey, Los Angeles	Yes	L.A.	5	at Cgy.	3	DSF
Apr. 5/90	Randy Wood, NY Islanders	Mike Richter, NY Rangers	No	NYI	1	at NYR	2	DSF
May 3/90	Kelly Miller, Washington	Andy Moog, Boston	No	Wsh.	3	at Bos.	5	CF
May 18/90	Petr Klima, Edmonton	Reggie Lemelin, Boston	No	Edm.	7	at Bos.	2	F
Apr. 6/91	Basil McRae, Minnesota	Ed Belfour, Chicago	Yes	Min.	2	at Chi.	5	DSF
Apr. 10/91	Steve Duchesne, Los Angeles	Kirk McLean, Vancouver	Yes	L.A.	6	at Van.	1	DSF
May 11/92	Jaromir Jagr, Pittsburgh	John Vanbiesbrouck, NYR	Yes	Pit.	3	at NYR	2	DF
May 13/92	Shawn McEachern, Pittsburgh	John Vanbiesbrouck, NYR	No	NYR	1	at Pit.	5	DF
June 7/94	Pavel Bure, Vancouver	Mike Richter, NYR	No	NYR	4	at Van.	1	F
May 9/95	Patrick Poulin, Chicago	Felix Potvin, Toronto	No	Tor.	3	at Chi.	0	CQF
May 10/95	Michal Pivonka, Washington	Tom Barrasso, Pittsburgh	No	Pit.	2	at Wsh.	6	CQF
Apr. 24/96	Joe Juneau, Washington	Ken Wregget, Pittsburgh	No	Pit.	3	at Wsh.	2**	CQF
May 11/97	Eric Lindros, Philadelphia	Steve Shields, Buffalo	Yes	Phi.	6	at Buf.	3	CSF
Apr. 23/98	Alexei Morozov, Pittsburgh	Andy Moog, Montreal	No	Mtl.	3	at Pit.	2**	CQF
Apr. 22/99	Mats Sundin, Toronto	John Vanbiesbrouck, Phi.	No	Phi.	3	at Tor.	0	CQF
May 29/99	Mats Sundin, Toronto	Dominik Hasek, Buffalo	Yes	Tor.	2	at Buf.	5	CF
Apr. 16/00	Eric Desjardins, Philadelphia	Dominik Hasek, Buffalo	No	Phi.	2	at Buf.	0	CQF
Apr. 11/01	Mark Recchi, Philadelphia	Dominik Hasek, Buffalo	No	Buf.	2	at Phi.	1	CQF
May 2/01	Martin Straka, Pittsburgh	Dominik Hasek, Buffalo	No	Buf.	5	at Pit.	2	CSF
May 12/01	Joe Sakic, Colorado	Roman Turek, St. Louis	Yes	St.L.	1	at Col.	4	CF
Apr. 21/02	Todd Bertuzzi, Vancouver	Dominik Hasek, Detroit	No	Det.	3	at Van.	1	CQF
Apr. 24/02	Shawn Bates, NY Islanders	Curtis Joseph, Toronto	Yes	Tor.	3	at NYI	4	CQF
Apr. 26/02	Mike Johnson, Phoenix	Evgeni Nabokov, San Jose	Yes	Phx.	1	at S.J.	4	CQF
Apr. 15/03	Dainius Zubrus, Washington	Nikolai Khabibulin, Tampa Bay	No	T.B.	4	at Wsh.	3	CQF
Apr. 21/03	Robert Reichel, Toronto	Roman Cechmanek, Philadelphia	No	Phi.	1	at Tor.	2	CQF
Apr. 7/04	Steve Sullivan, Nashville	Manny Legace, Detroit	No	Nsh.	1	at Det.	3	CQF

Vancouver's Brendan Morrison ended the longest game of the 2004 playoffs when he scored at 2:28 of the third overtime period as the Canucks beat Calgary 5-4 in game six of their Western Conference Quarterfinal series.

Overtime Record of Current Teams

(Listed by number of OT games played)

Team	Overall				Home				Last OT Game	Road				Last OT Game
	GP	W	L	T	GP	W	L	T		GP	W	L	T	
Montreal	125	70	53	2	59	37	21	1	Apr. 27/04	66	33	32	1	Apr. 9/04
Toronto	106	54	51	1	68	36	31	1	May 4/04	38	18	20	0	Apr. 18/04
Boston	100	40	57	3	46	21	24	1	Apr. 9/04	54	19	33	2	Apr. 13/04
Detroit	76	33	43	0	45	16	29	0	Apr. 22/04	31	17	14	0	May 3/04
NY Rangers	63	30	33	0	27	12	15	0	Apr. 22/97	36	18	18	0	May 11/97
Chicago	62	30	30	2	30	16	13	1	Apr. 20/97	32	14	17	1	May 2/96
Philadelphia	58	28	30	0	26	13	13	0	May 20/04	32	15	17	0	May 4/04
Dallas[1]	54	24	30	0	27	11	16	0	Apr. 14/04	27	13	14	0	May 1/01
St. Louis	50	27	23	0	26	20	6	0	May 18/01	24	7	14	0	Apr. 8/04
Colorado[2]	49	28	21	0	19	9	10	0	Apr. 22/03	30	19	11	0	Apr. 14/04
Buffalo	46	25	21	0	26	16	10	0	May 10/01	20	9	11	0	May 8/01
NY Islanders	40	29	11	0	18	14	4	0	Apr. 14/03	22	15	7	0	Apr. 16/04
Edmonton	38	21	17	0	21	11	10	0	Apr. 17/01	17	10	7	0	Apr. 19/01
Calgary[3]	37	16	21	0	17	5	12	0	Jun. 5/04	20	11	9	0	Jun. 3/04
Los Angeles	35	17	18	0	19	11	8	0	May 6/01	16	6	10	0	Apr. 25/02
Vancouver	35	17	18	0	15	6	9	0	Apr. 19/04	20	11	9	0	Apr. 17/04
New Jersey[4]	33	10	23	0	14	5	9	0	May 21/03	19	5	14	0	Jun. 2/03
Washington	31	14	17	0	12	5	7	0	Apr. 20/03	19	9	10	0	Apr. 23/01
Pittsburgh	28	15	13	0	18	10	8	0	May 8/01	10	5	5	0	May 10/01
Carolina[5]	23	14	9	0	14	9	5	0	Jun. 8/02	9	5	4	0	Jun. 4/02
Ottawa	16	9	7	0	6	4	2	0	Apr. 18/04	10	5	5	0	May 21/03
San Jose	13	4	9	0	8	2	6	0	May 9/04	5	2	3	0	Apr. 28/04
Phoenix[6]	12	5	7	0	8	3	5	0	May 4/99	4	2	2	0	Apr. 27/93
Anaheim	11	8	3	0	4	3	1	0	Jun. 2/03	7	5	2	0	May 10/03
Tampa Bay	11	7	4	0	3	2	1	0	Jun. 3/04	8	5	3	0	Jun. 5/04
Florida	5	2	3	0	3	1	2	0	Apr. 25/97	2	1	1	0	Apr. 22/97
Minnesota	5	2	3	0	3	1	2	0	May 10/03	2	1	1	0	Apr. 25/03

[1] Totals include those of Minnesota North Stars 1967-93.
[2] Totals include those of Quebec 1979-95.
[3] Totals include those of Atlanta Flames 1972-80.
[4] Totals include those of Kansas City and Colorado Rockies 1974-82.
[5] Totals include those of Hartford 1979-97.
[6] Totals include those of Winnipeg 1979-96.

Martin Gelinas' goal at 1:25 of overtime gave Calgary a 3-2 win over Vancouver in game seven of their first-round matchup. Gelinas also scored the series winner in overtime against Detroit in round two.

Ten Longest Overtime Games

Date	City	Series	Score					Scorer	Overtime	Series Winner
Mar. 24/36	Mtl.	SF	Det.	1		Mtl. M.	0	Mud Bruneteau	116:30	Det.
Apr. 3/33	Tor.	SF	Tor.	1		Bos.	0	Ken Doraty	104:46	Tor.
May 4/00	Pit.	CSF	Phi.	2		Pit.	1	Keith Primeau	92:01	Phi.
Apr. 24/03	Dal.	CSF	Ana.	4		Dal.	3	Petr Sykora	80:48	Ana.
Apr. 24/96	Wsh.	CQF	Pit.	3		Wsh.	2	Petr Nedved	79:15	Pit.
Mar. 23/43	Det.	SF	Tor.	3		Det.	2	Jack McLean	70:18	Det.
Mar. 28/30	Mtl.	SF	Mtl.	2		NYR	1	Gus Rivers	68:52	Mtl.
Apr. 18/87	Wsh.	DSF	NYI	3		Wsh.	2	Pat LaFontaine	68:47	NYI
Apr. 27/94	Buf.	CQF	Buf.	1		N.J.	0	Dave Hannan	65:43	N.J.
Mar. 27/51	Det.	SF	Mtl.	3		Det.	2	Maurice Richard	61:09	Mtl.

Key to Prospect, NHL Player and Goaltender Registers

Demographics: Position, shooting side (catching hand for goaltenders), height, weight, place and date of birth as well as draft information, if any, is located on this line.

Major Junior, NCAA, minor pro, senior European and NHL clubs form a permanent part of each player's data panel. If a player sees action with more than one club in any of the above categories, a separate line is included for each one.

Olympic Team statistics are also listed.

Player's NHL organization as of August 11, 2004. This includes players under contract, unsigned draft choices and other players on reserve lists. Free agents as of August 11, 2004 show a blank here.

The complete career data panels of players with NHL experience who announced their retirement before the start of the 2003-04 season are included in the 2003-04 Player Register. These newly-retired players also show a blank here.

Each NHL club's minor-pro affiliates are listed on page 7.

					Regular Season														Playoffs							
Season	Club	League	GP	G	A	Pts	PIM	PP	SH	GW	S	%	+/-	TF	F%	Min	GP	G	A	Pts	PIM	PP	SH	W	Min

RICHARDS, Brad   (RIH-chahrds, BRAD)   **T.B.**

Center. Shoots left. 6'1", 198 lbs.   Born, Murray Harbour, P.E.I., May 2, 1980. Tampa Bay's 2nd choice, 64th overall, in 1998 Entry Draft.

Season	Club	League	GP	G	A	Pts	PIM	PP	SH	GW	S	%	+/-	TF	F%	Min	GP	G	A	Pts	PIM	PP	SH	W	Min
1996-97	Notre Dame	SJHL	63	39	48	87	73	....	....	....	....	....	....	....	....	....									
1997-98	Rimouski Oceanic	QMJHL	68	33	82	115	44	....	....	....	....	....	....	....	....	....	19	8	24	32	2	....	....		....
1998-99	Rimouski Oceanic	QMJHL	59	39	92	131	55	....	....	....	....	....	....	....	....	....	11	9	12	21	6	....	....		....
99-2000	Rimouski Oceanic	QMJHL	63	*71	*115	*186	69	....	....	....	....	....	....	....	....	....	12	13	*24	*37	16	....	....		....
2000-01	Tampa Bay	NHL	82	21	41	62	14	7	0	3	179	11.7	–10	955	41.4	16:54	....	....	....	....	....	....	....		....
2001-02	Tampa Bay	NHL	82	20	42	62	13	5	0	0	251	8.0	–18	911	41.2	19:48	....	....	....	....	....	....	....		....
2002-03	Tampa Bay	NHL	80	17	57	74	24	4	0	2	277	6.1	3	1007	47.5	19:56	11	0	5	5	2	0	0	0	22:21
2003-04♦	Tampa Bay	NHL	82	26	53	79	12	5	1	6	244	10.7	14	1167	46.7	20:26	23	12	14	*26	4	7	0	7	23:28
	NHL Totals		326	84	193	277	63	21	1	11	951	8.8		4040	44.4	19:16	34	12		31	1	7	0	7	23:07

SJHL Rookie of the Year (1997) • QMJHL First All-Star Team (2000) • Canadian Major Junior First All-Star Team (2000) • Canadian Major Junior Player of the Year (2000) • Memorial Cup All-Star Team (2000) • Stafford Smythe Memorial Trophy (Memorial Cup MVP) (2000) • NHL All-Rookie Team (2001) • Lady Byng Trophy (2004) • Conn Smythe Trophy (2004)

Diamond (♦) indicates member of Stanley Cup-winning team.

All-Star Team selections and awards are listed below player's year-by-year data.

NHL All-Star Game appearances are listed above trade notes.

Asterisk (*) indicates league leader in this statistical category.

Trade and free agent signing dates are based on when the player's contract is filed with NHL Central Registry. This date often differs from the date when the club announces that it has made a trade or come to terms with a free agent.

All trades, free agent signings and other transactions involving NHL clubs are listed in chronological order. First draft selection for players who re-enter the NHL Entry Draft is noted here. Other special notes are also listed here. These are highlighted with a bullet (•).

Pronunciation of Player Names

United Press International phonetic style.

AY	long A as in mate
A	short A as in cat
AI	nasal A as on air
AH	short A as in father
AW	broad A as in talk
EE	long E as in meat
EH	short E as in get
UH	hollow E as in me
AY	French long E with acute accent as in Pathe
IH	middle E as in pretty
EW	EW dipthong as in few
IGH	long I as in time
EE	French long I as in machine
IH	short I as in pity
OH	long O as in note
AH	short O as in hot
AW	broad O as in fought
OI	OI dipthong as in noise
OO	long double OO as in fool
U	short double O as in foot
OW	OW dipthong as in how
EW	long U as in mule
OO	long U as in rule
U	middle U as in put
UH	short U as in shut or hurt
K	hard C as in cat
S	soft C as in cease
SH	soft CH as in machine
CH	hard CH or TCH as in catch
Z	hard S as in bells
S	soft S as in sun
G	hard G as in gang
J	soft G as in general
ZH	soft J as in French version of Joliet
KH	gutteral CH as in Scottish version of Loch

THIS **73**RD EDITION OF THE *NHL Official Guide & Record Book* is the sixth to include additional statistical categories for forwards and defensemen in the National Hockey League. These categories are, from left to right in the sample panel above, power-play goals (PP), shorthand goals (SH), game-winning goals (GW), shots on goal (S), percentage of shots that score (%), plus-minus rating (+/–), total faceoffs taken (TF), faceoff winning percentage (F%), and average time-on-ice per game played (Min).

To integrate this data, the Player Register has been is split into two sections. The Prospect Register presents data on players who have yet to play in the NHL. The NHL Player Register, containing more information and a photo of each player, lists all active players who have appeared in an NHL regular-season or playoff game at any time.

Goaltenders, whether prospects or active NHLers, are included in one register.

Registers (with their starting page) are presented in the following order: Prospects (267), NHL Players (339), Goaltenders (573), Retired Players (596) and Retired Goaltenders (630).

League abbreviations, page 337
Late additions to the Registers, page 338.

Some information is unavailable at press time. Readers are encouraged to contribute.
See page 5 for contact names and addresses.

2004-05 Prospect Register

Note: The 2004-05 Prospect Register lists forwards and defensemen only. Goaltenders are listed separately. The Prospect Register lists every player drafted in the first five rounds of the 2004 Entry Draft, players on NHL Reserve Lists and other players who have not yet played in the NHL. Trades and roster changes are current as of August 11, 2004.

Abbreviations: A – assists; **G** – goals; **GP** – games played; **PIM** – penalties in minutes; **TP** – total points; ***** – league-leading total.

NHL Player Register begins on page 339.

Goaltender Register begins on page 573.

League Abbreviations are listed on page 337.

AALTONEN, Juhamatti   (AL-toh-nehn, YOO-haw-MAH-tee)   ST.L.

Right wing. Shoots right. 5'11", 163 lbs.   Born, Ii, Finland, June 4, 1985.
(St. Louis' 12th choice, 284th overall, in 2003 Entry Draft).

				Regular Season					Playoffs			
Season	Club	League	GP	G	A	TP	PIM	GP	G	A	TP	PIM
2001-02	Karpat Oulu B	Finn-Jr.	23	9	11	20	28	2	0	0	0	0
2002-03	Karpat Oulu B	Finn-Jr.	33	9	16	25	8	1	0	0	0	7
	Karpat Oulu B	Finn-Jr.	2	5	1	6	6	....	....	....	....	....
	Karpat Oulu	Finland	1	0	0	0	0	....	....	....	....	....
2003-04	Karpat Oulu Jr.	Finn-Jr.	32	30	15	45	32	3	1	0	1	2
	Karpat Oulu	Finland	8	0	0	0	2	....	....	....	....	....

ADAMS, John   (A-duhms, JAWN)   BUF.

Defense. Shoots left. 6'2", 188 lbs.   Born, Orono, ME, December 21, 1982.
(Buffalo's 4th choice, 82nd overall, in 2002 Entry Draft).

				Regular Season					Playoffs			
Season	Club	League	GP	G	A	TP	PIM	GP	G	A	TP	PIM
99-2000	Breck Mustangs	Hi-School	25	6	30	36	....	....	....	....	....	....
2000-01	Breck Mustangs	Hi-School	25	13	29	42	....	....	....	....	....	....
2001-02	Boston College	H-East	25	0	5	5	20	....	....	....	....	....
2002-03	Boston College	H-East	34	2	5	7	22	....	....	....	....	....
2003-04	Boston College	H-East	42	3	7	10	26	....	....	....	....	....

ADDUONO, Jeremy   (uh-DOO-noh, JAIR-eh-mee)   BUF.

Right wing. Shoots right. 6', 182 lbs.   Born, Thunder Bay, Ont., August 4, 1978.
(Buffalo's 8th choice, 184th overall, in 1997 Entry Draft).

				Regular Season					Playoffs			
Season	Club	League	GP	G	A	TP	PIM	GP	G	A	TP	PIM
1994-95	Thunder Bay Flyers	USHL	40	11	10	21	8	....	....	....	....	....
1995-96	Sudbury Wolves	OHL	66	15	22	37	14	....	....	....	....	....
1996-97	Sudbury Wolves	OHL	66	29	40	69	24	....	....	....	....	....
1997-98	Sudbury Wolves	OHL	66	37	69	106	40	10	5	5	10	10
1998-99	Team Canada	Nat-Tm	44	10	18	28	10	....	....	....	....	....
99-2000	Rochester	AHL	51	23	22	45	20	21	6	11	17	2
2000-01	Rochester	AHL	76	24	30	54	53	4	1	0	1	4
2001-02	Rochester	AHL	79	15	20	35	38	1	1	0	1	0
2002-03	Bridgeport	AHL	54	13	13	26	14	9	2	5	7	2
2003-04	Kolner Haie	Germany	41	13	11	24	16	5	2	2	4	0

Signed as a free agent by **Kolner Haie** (Germany), September 1, 2003.

AHOSILTA, Marko   (ah-hoh-SIHL-tuh, MAHR-koh)   N.J.

Center. Shoots left. 5'8", 165 lbs.   Born, Kuopio, Finland, January 24, 1980.
(New Jersey's 11th choice, 227th overall, in 1998 Entry Draft).

				Regular Season					Playoffs			
Season	Club	League	GP	G	A	TP	PIM	GP	G	A	TP	PIM
1994-95	KalPa Kuopio-C	Finn-Jr.	13	4	6	10	10	....	....	....	....	....
1995-96	KalPa Kuopio Jr.	Finn-Jr.	12	4	8	12	10	....	....	....	....	....
1996-97	KalPa Kuopio Jr.	Finn-Jr.	35	15	21	36	36	5	2	0	2	2
1997-98	KalPa Kuopio Jr.	Finn-Jr.	14	14	13	27	10	....	....	....	....	....
	KalPa Kuopio	Finland	2	0	0	0	0	....	....	....	....	....
	Finland	WJC-18	6	4	3	7	10	....	....	....	....	....
1998-99	KalPa Kuopio	Finland	1	0	0	0	0	....	....	....	....	....
	KalPa Kuopio Jr.	Finn-Jr.	24	7	7	14	10	....	....	....	....	....
99-2000	KalPa Kuopio Jr.	Finn-Jr.	10	6	4	10	8	....	....	....	....	....
	KJT Jarvenpaa	Finland-2	30	19	5	24	10	....	....	....	....	....
2000-01					DID NOT PLAY							
2001-02	KalPa Kuopio	Finland-2	44	17	20	37	24	3	0	1	1	2
2002-03	KalPa Kuopio	Finland-2	39	23	22	45	32	4	0	1	1	2
2003-04	KalPa Kuopio	Finland-2	44	13	20	33	44	11	7	2	9	12
	Team Finland	Finland-2	4	0	0	0	4	....	....	....	....	....

AIKINS, Justin   (AY-kihns, JUHS-tihn)   CBJ

Center. Shoots left. 6', 176 lbs.   Born, Surrey, B.C., January 12, 1982.
(Columbus' 7th choice, 173rd overall, in 2001 Entry Draft).

				Regular Season					Playoffs			
Season	Club	League	GP	G	A	TP	PIM	GP	G	A	TP	PIM
1998-99	Langley Hornets	BCHL	52	6	21	27	16	....	....	....	....	....
99-2000	Langley Hornets	BCHL	59	29	38	67	46	....	....	....	....	....
2000-01	Langley Hornets	BCHL	59	30	61	91	47	....	....	....	....	....
2001-02	New Hampshire	H-East	29	4	4	8	6	....	....	....	....	....
2002-03	New Hampshire	H-East	42	4	18	22	20	....	....	....	....	....
2003-04	New Hampshire	H-East	41	10	31	41	26	....	....	....	....	....

AKKANEN, Karri   (ah-KAHN-uhn, KAH-ree)   T.B.

Center. Shoots right. 6'6", 227 lbs.   Born, Tampere, Finland, January 29, 1984.
(Tampa Bay's 6th choice, 174th overall, in 2002 Entry Draft).

				Regular Season					Playoffs			
Season	Club	League	GP	G	A	TP	PIM	GP	G	A	TP	PIM
2000-01	Ilves Tampere-B	Finn-Jr.	32	5	10	15	20	....	....	....	....	....
2001-02	Ilves Tampere-B	Finn-Jr.	15	6	6	12	30	4	0	1	1	4
	Ilves Tampere Jr.	Finn-Jr.	5	0	1	1	4	....	....	....	....	....
2002-03	Ilves Tampere	Finland	21	0	1	1	0	....	....	....	....	....
	Ilves Tampere-B	Finn-Jr.	11	1	6	7	65	....	....	....	....	....
	Ilves Tampere Jr.	Finn-Jr.	13	6	14	20	16	....	....	....	....	....
2003-04	Ilves Tampere Jr.	Finn-Jr.	4	0	1	1	22	....	....	....	....	....
	Tappara Jr.	Finn-Jr.	31	4	8	12	58	14	4	3	7	16

ALBERTS, Andrew   (AL-buhrts, AN-droo)   BOS.

Defense. Shoots left. 6'4", 218 lbs.   Born, Minneapolis, MN, June 30, 1981.
(Boston's 5th choice, 179th overall, in 2001 Entry Draft).

				Regular Season					Playoffs			
Season	Club	League	GP	G	A	TP	PIM	GP	G	A	TP	PIM
1998-99	Benide High	Hi-School	26	10	25	35	....	....	....	....	....	....
99-2000	Waterloo	USHL	49	2	2	4	55	4	0	0	0	12
2000-01	Waterloo	USHL	54	4	10	14	128	....	....	....	....	....
2001-02	Boston College	H-East	38	2	10	12	52	....	....	....	....	....
2002-03	Boston College	H-East	39	6	16	22	60	....	....	....	....	....
2003-04	Boston College	H-East	42	4	12	16	64	....	....	....	....	....

Hockey East Second All-Star Team (2004) • NCAA East First All-American Team (2004)

ALEN, Juha   (AL-ehn, YOO-haw)   ANA.

Defense. Shoots left. 6'3", 220 lbs.   Born, Tampere, Finland, October 25, 1981.
(Anaheim's 4th choice, 90th overall, in 2003 Entry Draft).

				Regular Season					Playoffs			
Season	Club	League	GP	G	A	TP	PIM	GP	G	A	TP	PIM
1998-99	KooVee Jr.	Finn-Jr.	36	6	7	13	42	....	....	....	....	....
99-2000	KooVee Jr.	Finn-Jr.	22	2	4	6	28	....	....	....	....	....
2000-01	Ilves Tampere Jr.	Finn-Jr.	42	2	12	14	62	....	....	....	....	....
2001-02	Soo Indians	NAHL	54	10	10	20	46	2	0	1	1	0
2002-03	Northern Michigan	CCHA	40	4	19	23	64	....	....	....	....	....
2003-04	Cincinnati	AHL	59	2	3	5	64	9	0	0	0	14

ALEXANDROV, Viktor   (al-ehx-AN-drawv, VIHK-tohr)   ST.L.

Left wing. Shoots left. 5'11", 183 lbs.   Born, Ust-Kamenogorsk, USSR, December 28, 1985.
(St. Louis' 3rd choice, 83rd overall, in 2004 Entry Draft).

				Regular Season					Playoffs			
Season	Club	League	GP	G	A	TP	PIM	GP	G	A	TP	PIM
2001-02	Ust-Kamenogorsk	Russia-2	45	12	17	29	48	2	0	1	1	2
2002-03	Yaroslavl	Russia	2	0	0	0	2	....	....	....	....	....
	Energiya Kemerovo	Russia-2	15	2	4	6	12	....	....	....	....	....
	Novokuznetsk	Russia	11	0	0	0	4	....	....	....	....	....
2003-04	Novokuznetsk	Russia	57	5	4	9	26	4	1	2	4	4

ALMTORP, Jonas   (AHLM-tohrp, YOH-nuhs)   EDM.

Center. Shoots left. 6'1", 190 lbs.   Born, Uppsala, Sweden, November 17, 1983.
(Edmonton's 7th choice, 111th overall, in 2002 Entry Draft).

				Regular Season					Playoffs			
Season	Club	League	GP	G	A	TP	PIM	GP	G	A	TP	PIM
99-2000	MoDo 18	Swede-Jr.	22	*19	12	31	*55	....	....	....	....	....
	MoDo Jr.	Swede-Jr.	7	1	0	1	0	....	....	....	....	....
2000-01	MoDo 18	Swede-Jr.	12	11	1	12	30	....	....	....	....	....
	MoDo Jr.	Swede-Jr.	27	19	7	26	38	7	6	1	7	10
2001-02	MoDo	Sweden	3	0	0	0	0	....	....	....	....	....
	MoDo Jr.	Swede-Jr.	37	26	18	44	102	2	1	1	2	4
2002-03	MoDo	Sweden	28	1	1	2	22	....	....	....	....	....
	MoDo	Swede-2	12	5	4	9	49	....	....	....	....	....
	MoDo Jr.	Swede-Jr.	5	2	2	4	....	....	....	....	....	....
2003-04	MoDo	Sweden	20	0	0	0	4	3	0	0	0	0
	IF Sundsvall	Swede-2	32	9	9	18	65	....	....	....	....	....
	MoDo Jr.	Swede-Jr.	3	0	0	0	14	....	....	....	....	....

ALTAREV, Dmitri (al-ta-REHV, dih-MEE-tree) NYI

Left wing. Shoots left. 6'3", 191 lbs. Born, Penza, USSR, August 12, 1980.
(NY Islanders' 8th choice, 264th overall, in 2000 Entry Draft).

			Regular Season					Playoffs				
Season	Club	League	GP	G	A	TP	PIM	GP	G	A	TP	PIM
1997-98	Dizelist Penza 2	Russia-3	57	15	8	23	83	....	....	....	....	....
1998-99	Dizelist Penza 2	Russia-4	35	4	3	7	30	....	....	....	....	....
	Dizelist Penza	Russia-2	6	2	0	2	8	....	....	....	....	....
99-2000	Dizelist Penza 2	Russia-3	44	10	8	18	25	....	....	....	....	....
2000-01	Nizhny Novgorod	Russia	36	1	2	3	26	....	....	....	....	....
2001-02	Niz. Novgorod 2	Russia-3	10	5	6	11	12	....	....	....	....	....
	Nizhny Novgorod	Russia	32	2	3	5	42	....	....	....	....	....
2002-03	Dizelist Penza	Russia-3	47	22	26	48	106	....	....	....	....	....
2003-04	Dizelist Penza	Russia-2	56	19	20	39	86	4	1	0	1	8

ANDERSON, R.J. (AN-duhr-suhn, AHR-JAY) PHI.

Defense. Shoots right. 5'11", 180 lbs. Born, Maple Wood, MN, July 16, 1986.
(Philadelphia's 2nd choice, 101st overall, in 2004 Entry Draft).

			Regular Season					Playoffs				
Season	Club	League	GP	G	A	TP	PIM	GP	G	A	TP	PIM
2002-03	Centennial	Hi-School	24	6	35	41	10	....	....	....	....	....
2003-04	Centennial	Hi-School	30	29	56	85	34	....	....	....	....	....
	Team Northeast	UMEHL	24	9	16	25	....	....	....	....	....	....

ANDERSSON, Johan (AN-duhr-suhn, YOH-hahn) CHI.

Center. Shoots left. 6'1", 201 lbs. Born, Motala, Sweden, May 18, 1984.
(Chicago's 6th choice, 181st overall, in 2003 Entry Draft).

			Regular Season					Playoffs				
Season	Club	League	GP	G	A	TP	PIM	GP	G	A	TP	PIM
2000-01	Troja/Ljungby	Swede-2	3	0	0	0	0	....	....	....	....	....
2001-02	Troja/Ljungby	Swede-2	42	2	0	2	10	5	2	0	2	2
2002-03	Troja/Ljungby	Swede-2	20	8	4	12	16	....	....	....	....	....
2003-04	Troja/Ljungby	Swede-2	43	13	11	24	94	....	....	....	....	....

ANDREWS, Bobby (AN-drooz, BAW-bee)

Center. Shoots left. 6'1", 200 lbs. Born, Birtle, Man., January 5, 1978.

			Regular Season					Playoffs				
Season	Club	League	GP	G	A	TP	PIM	GP	G	A	TP	PIM
1996-97	Cleveland	NAJHL	45	21	22	43	259	....	....	....	....	....
1997-98	Langley Thunder	BCHL	59	26	48	74	143	....	....	....	....	....
1998-99	Alaska-Fairbanks	CCHA	31	5	11	16	38	....	....	....	....	....
99-2000	Alaska-Fairbanks	CCHA	34	13	12	25	72	....	....	....	....	....
2000-01	Alaska-Fairbanks	CCHA	36	9	16	25	46	....	....	....	....	....
2001-02	Alaska-Fairbanks	CCHA	37	14	23	37	46	....	....	....	....	....
	Hartford Wolf Pack	AHL	1	0	0	0	0	7	0	0	0	2
2002-03	Hartford Wolf Pack	AHL	58	6	7	13	33	2	0	0	0	0
2003-04	Hartford Wolf Pack	AHL	49	9	11	20	26	....	....	....	....	....

CCHA Second All-Star Team (2002)

Signed as a free agent by **NY Rangers**, March 19, 2002.

ANDREWS, Daryl (AN-drooz, DAIR-ihl)

Defense. Shoots left. 6'3", 215 lbs. Born, Campbell River, B.C., April 27, 1977.
(New Jersey's 11th choice, 173rd overall, in 1996 Entry Draft).

			Regular Season					Playoffs				
Season	Club	League	GP	G	A	TP	PIM	GP	G	A	TP	PIM
1995-96	Melfort Mustangs	SJHL	55	2	12	14	51	....	....	....	....	....
1996-97	West. Michigan	CCHA	37	6	20	26	86	....	....	....	....	....
1997-98	West. Michigan	CCHA	36	3	0	3	81	....	....	....	....	....
1998-99	West. Michigan	CCHA	33	3	11	14	42	....	....	....	....	....
99-2000	West. Michigan	CCHA	36	3	16	19	52	....	....	....	....	....
	Albany River Rats	AHL	9	0	2	2	9	5	0	0	0	0
2000-01	Albany River Rats	AHL	80	2	8	10	49	....	....	....	....	....
2001-02	Albany River Rats	AHL	69	3	10	13	60	....	....	....	....	....
2002-03	Albany River Rats	AHL	75	3	6	9	52	....	....	....	....	....
2003-04	San Antonio	AHL	75	0	9	9	68	....	....	....	....	....

CCHA Rookie of the Year (1997)

ANGER, Niklas (AN-guhr, NIHK-lahs) MTL.

Right wing. Shoots left. 6'1", 185 lbs. Born, Gavle, Sweden, July 31, 1977.
(Montreal's 5th choice, 112th overall, in 1995 Entry Draft).

			Regular Season					Playoffs				
Season	Club	League	GP	G	A	TP	PIM	GP	G	A	TP	PIM
1993-94	Djurgarden Jr.	Swede-Jr.	2	0	0	0	0	....	....	....	....	....
1994-95	Djurgarden Jr.	Swede-Jr.	30	14	12	26	26	....	....	....	....	....
	Djurgarden	Sweden	1	0	0	0	0	....	....	....	....	....
1995-96	Djurgarden Jr.	Swede-Jr.	24	13	16	29	26	....	....	....	....	....
	Djurgarden	Sweden	10	0	0	0	2	....	....	....	....	....
1996-97	Djurgarden Jr.	Swede-Jr.	2	1	2	3	0	....	....	....	....	....
	Arlanda Mastra	Swede-2	16	5	9	14	6	....	....	....	....	....
	Linkopings HC	Swede-2	10	2	2	4	10	14	3	7	10	2
	Djurgarden	Sweden	4	0	0	0	0	....	....	....	....	....
1997-98	Djurgarden	Sweden	45	2	5	7	37	12	0	1	1	2
1998-99	AIK Solna Jr.	Swede-Jr.	1	0	0	0	0	....	....	....	....	....
	AIK Solna	Sweden	47	6	6	12	16	....	....	....	....	....
99-2000	AIK Solna	Sweden	50	11	13	24	14	....	....	....	....	....
2000-01	AIK Solna	Sweden	50	5	10	15	22	5	0	1	1	2
2001-02	AIK Solna	Sweden	50	12	20	32	16	....	....	....	....	....
2002-03	Brynas IF Gavle	Sweden	48	20	12	32	28	....	....	....	....	....
2003-04	Brynas IF Gavle	Sweden	50	11	15	26	26	....	....	....	....	....

ANSHAKOV, Sergei (an-sha-KAHV, SAIR-gay) PIT.

Left wing. Shoots left. 6'3", 179 lbs. Born, Moscow, USSR, January 13, 1984.
(Los Angeles' 2nd choice, 50th overall, in 2002 Entry Draft).

			Regular Season					Playoffs				
Season	Club	League	GP	G	A	TP	PIM	GP	G	A	TP	PIM
2000-01	Dyn. Moscow 18	Exhib.	6	7	1	8	2	....	....	....	....	....
2001-02	HC CSKA 2	Russia-3	3	3	1	4	0	....	....	....	....	....
	HC CSKA Moscow	Russia-2	46	20	12	22	10	....	....	....	....	....
2002-03	CSKA Moscow	Russia	25	1	2	3	4	....	....	....	....	....
2003-04	CSKA Moscow	Russia	33	3	2	5	12	....	....	....	....	....

Traded to **Pittsburgh** by **Los Angeles** with Martin Strbak for Martin Straka, November 30, 2003.

AQUINO, Anthony (a-KEE-noh, AN-thuh-nee) ATL.

Right wing. Shoots right. 5'10", 190 lbs. Born, Mississauga, Ont., August 1, 1982.
(Dallas' 3rd choice, 92nd overall, in 2001 Entry Draft).

			Regular Season					Playoffs				
Season	Club	League	GP	G	A	TP	PIM	GP	G	A	TP	PIM
1997-98	Mississauga	OPJHL	50	10	13	23	14	....	....	....	....	....
1998-99	Bramalea Blues	OPJHL	47	31	44	75	31	....	....	....	....	....
99-2000	Merrimack College	H-East	36	15	14	29	12	....	....	....	....	....
2000-01	Merrimack College	H-East	38	17	25	42	22	....	....	....	....	....
2001-02	Merrimack College	H-East	36	24	20	44	20	....	....	....	....	....
2002-03	Oshawa Generals	OHL	14	10	9	19	6	....	....	....	....	....
	Chicago Wolves	AHL	5	0	0	0	4	....	....	....	....	....
2003-04	Chicago Wolves	AHL	2	0	0	0	0	....	....	....	....	....
	Gwinnett	ECHL	62	27	26	53	34	8	1	2	3	0

Hockey East All-Rookie Team (2000) • Hockey East Second All-Star Team (2001)

• Left Merrimack (H-East) and signed as a free agent by **Oshawa** (OHL), September 25, 2002. • Ruled ineligible to play remainder of 2002-03 OHL season because of OHL overage restrictions, November 7, 2002. Rights traded to **Atlanta** by **Dallas** for Dallas' 6th round choice (previously acquired, Dallas selected Drew Bagnall) in 2003 Entry Draft and future considerations, March 11, 2003.

ARCHER, Andrew (AHR-chuhr, AN-droo) MTL.

Defense. Shoots right. 6'4", 212 lbs. Born, Calgary, Alta., May 15, 1983.
(Montreal's 7th choice, 203rd overall, in 2001 Entry Draft).

			Regular Season					Playoffs				
Season	Club	League	GP	G	A	TP	PIM	GP	G	A	TP	PIM
1998-99	Richmond Hill	OMHA	STATISTICS NOT AVAILABLE									
99-2000	Oshawa Generals	OHL	47	0	1	1	24	3	0	1	1	2
2000-01	Oshawa Generals	OHL	2	0	0	0	4	....	....	....	....	....
	Guelph Storm	OHL	50	0	2	2	59	4	0	0	0	4
2001-02	Guelph Storm	OHL	58	3	10	13	76	9	0	2	2	16
2002-03	Guelph Storm	OHL	65	2	16	18	138	11	2	2	4	18
2003-04	Hamilton Bulldogs	AHL	30	0	1	1	23	3	0	0	0	0
	Columbus	ECHL	6	0	1	1	19	....	....	....	....	....

• Missed majority of 2003-04 season recovering from hernia injury suffered in training camp, September 15, 2003.

ARMSTRONG, Colby (AHRM-stawng, KOHL-bee) PIT.

Right wing. Shoots right. 6'2", 195 lbs. Born, Lloydminster, Sask., November 23, 1982.
(Pittsburgh's 1st choice, 21st overall, in 2001 Entry Draft).

			Regular Season					Playoffs				
Season	Club	League	GP	G	A	TP	PIM	GP	G	A	TP	PIM
1998-99	Sask. Contacts	SMHL	33	21	19	40	103	....	....	....	....	....
	Red Deer Rebels	WHL	1	0	1	1	0	....	....	....	....	....
99-2000	Red Deer Rebels	WHL	68	13	25	38	122	2	0	1	1	11
2000-01	Red Deer Rebels	WHL	72	36	42	78	156	21	6	6	12	29
2001-02	Red Deer Rebels	WHL	64	27	41	68	115	23	6	10	16	32
2002-03	Wilkes-Barre	AHL	73	7	11	18	76	3	0	0	0	4
2003-04	Wilkes-Barre	AHL	67	10	17	27	71	24	3	1	4	45

ARTEMENKOV, Yuri (ahr-TUH-mehn-kahv, YOO-ree) CGY.

Right wing. Shoots left. 6'1", 174 lbs. Born, Moscow, USSR, February 3, 1984.
(Calgary's 4th choice, 112th overall, in 2002 Entry Draft).

			Regular Season					Playoffs				
Season	Club	League	GP	G	A	TP	PIM	GP	G	A	TP	PIM
99-2000	Team Russia	Nat-Tm	5	1	1	2	0	....	....	....	....	....
2000-01	Krylja Sovetov 2	Russia-3	2	0	0	0	4	....	....	....	....	....
2001-02	Krylja Sovetov 2	Russia-3	32	24	15	42	10	....	....	....	....	....
2002-03	Krylja Sovetov	Russia	3	0	0	0	0	....	....	....	....	....
	Krylja Sovetov 2	Russia-3	7	2	2	4	12	....	....	....	....	....
	Kirovo-Chepetsk	Russia-2	1	0	0	0	0	....	....	....	....	....
2003-04	Krylja Sovetov	Russia-2	27	3	1	4	6	....	....	....	....	....

ARTUKHIN, Evgeni (ahr-TYEW-khin, yehv-GEH-nee) T.B.

Right wing. Shoots left. 6'4", 215 lbs. Born, Moscow, USSR, April 4, 1983.
(Tampa Bay's 4th choice, 94th overall, in 2001 Entry Draft).

			Regular Season					Playoffs				
Season	Club	League	GP	G	A	TP	PIM	GP	G	A	TP	PIM
99-2000	Vityaz Podolsk 2	Russia-3	26	9	8	17	46	....	....	....	....	....
	Vityaz Podolsk	Russia-2	3	0	0	0	2	....	....	....	....	....
2000-01	Vityaz Podolsk	Russia	24	0	1	1	14	....	....	....	....	....
2001-02	Vityaz Podolsk 2	Russia-3	4	3	1	4	6	....	....	....	....	....
	Vityaz Podolsk	Russia-2	49	15	7	22	94	12	0	1	1	18
2002-03	Moncton Wildcats	QMJHL	53	13	27	40	204	6	1	2	3	29
2003-04	Hershey Bears	AHL	36	3	3	6	111	....	....	....	....	....
	Pensacola	ECHL	6	1	0	1	14	....	....	....	....	....

ASLUND, Calle (AZ-luhnd, KAL-ee) BUF.

Defense. Shoots left. 6'2", 198 lbs. Born, Haninge, Sweden, March 29, 1983.
(Buffalo's 6th choice, 234th overall, in 2001 Entry Draft).

			Regular Season					Playoffs				
Season	Club	League	GP	G	A	TP	PIM	GP	G	A	TP	PIM
99-2000	Huddinge IK 18	Swede-Jr.	17	1	5	6	48	....	....	....	....	....
2000-01	Huddinge IK 18	Swede-Jr.	8	1	3	4	30	....	....	....	....	....
	Huddinge IK Jr.	Swede-Jr.	7	0	1	1	14	....	....	....	....	....
2001-02	Huddinge IK Jr.	Swede-Jr.	27	1	6	7	66	....	....	....	....	....
	Huddinge IK	Swede-2	26	0	0	0	47	....	....	....	....	....
2002-03	Huddinge IK Jr.	Swede-Jr.	5	0	2	2	16	3	0	0	0	25
	Huddinge IK	Swede-2	37	3	3	6	66	2	0	0	0	6
2003-04	Huddinge	Swede-2	46	1	1	2	123	....	....	....	....	....
	Huddinge Jr.	Swede-Jr.	1	0	1	1	2	....	....	....	....	....

ATHERTON, P.J. (A-thur-tuhn, PEE-JAY) T.B.

Defense. Shoots right. 6'2", 208 lbs. Born, Edina, MN, August 16, 1982.
(Tampa Bay's 5th choice, 170th overall, in 2002 Entry Draft).

			Regular Season					Playoffs				
Season	Club	League	GP	G	A	TP	PIM	GP	G	A	TP	PIM
99-2000	Edina Hornets	Hi-School	38	7	15	22	....	....	....	....	....	....
	Cedar Rapids	USHL	5	0	1	1	4	....	....	....	....	....
2000-01	Cedar Rapids	USHL	43	4	9	13	99	4	2	0	2	10
2001-02	Cedar Rapids	USHL	51	7	22	29	101	8	0	0	0	14
2002-03	U. of Minnesota	WCHA	20	2	2	4	20	....	....	....	....	....
2003-04	U. of Minnesota	WCHA	28	0	2	2	36	....	....	....	....	....

ATYUSHOV, Vitali (a-tew-SHAWF, vih-TAL-ee) OTT.

Defense. Shoots left. 6'1", 205 lbs. Born, Penza, USSR, July 4, 1979.
(Ottawa's 8th choice, 276th overall, in 2002 Entry Draft).

			Regular Season					Playoffs				
Season	Club	League	GP	G	A	TP	PIM	GP	G	A	TP	PIM
1997-98	Krylja Sovetov	Russia	4	0	0	0	2	....	....	....	....	....
1998-99	Dizelist Penza 2	Russia-4	2	1	1	2	2	....	....	....	....	....
	Dizelist Penza	Russia-2	22	0	0	0	22	....	....	....	....	....
	Krylja Sovetov	Russia	17	1	0	1	20	....	....	....	....	....
	Krylja Sovetov	Russia-Q	21	0	5	5	50	....	....	....	....	....
99-2000	Perm	Russia	38	4	0	4	50	3	0	0	0	12
2000-01	Perm	Russia	44	3	9	12	32	....	....	....	....	....
2001-02	Perm	Russia	51	4	8	12	66	....	....	....	....	....
2002-03	Ak Bars Kazan	Russia	33	0	9	9	12	2	0	0	0	0
2003-04	Magnitogorsk	Russia	56	5	9	14	26	14	2	3	5	6

AUCOIN, Keith (oh-KOIN, KEETH)

Center. Shoots right. 5'9", 185 lbs. Born, Waltham, MA, November 6, 1978.

			Regular Season					Playoffs				
Season	Club	League	GP	G	A	TP	PIM	GP	G	A	TP	PIM
1996-97	Clemsford Lions	Hi-School	STATISTICS NOT AVAILABLE									
1997-98	Norwich University	ECAC-3	26	19	14	33	....	....	....	....	....	....
1998-99	Norwich University	ECAC-3	31	33	39	72	....	....	....	....	....	....
99-2000	Norwich University	ECAC-3	31	36	41	77	14	....	....	....	....	....
2000-01	Norwich University	ECAC-3	28	26	30	56	26	....	....	....	....	....
2001-02	Lowell	AHL	30	6	10	16	8	....	....	....	....	....
	Florida Everblades	ECHL	1	0	2	2	0	....	....	....	....	....
	BC Icemen	UHL	44	23	35	58	42	10	3	5	8	4
2002-03	Providence Bruins	AHL	78	25	49	74	71	4	0	1	1	6
2003-04	Cincinnati	AHL	80	18	30	48	64	9	0	3	3	4

ECAC-3 First All-Star Team (2000, 2001) • ECAC-3 Player of the Year (2000, 2001)

Signed as a free agent by **Lowell** (AHL), June 19, 2001. Signed as a free agent by **Providence** (AHL), August 2, 2002. Signed as a free agent by **Anaheim**, August 29, 2003.

BABY, Stephen (BAY-bee, STEE-vehn) ATL.

Right wing. Shoots right. 6'5", 230 lbs. Born, Chicago, IL, January 31, 1980.
(Atlanta's 8th choice, 188th overall, in 1999 Entry Draft).

			Regular Season					Playoffs				
Season	Club	League	GP	G	A	TP	PIM	GP	G	A	TP	PIM
1997-98	Green Bay	USHL	56	17	17	34	85	4	1	3	4	8
1998-99	Green Bay	USHL	55	23	24	47	83	6	1	1	2	4
99-2000	Cornell Big Red	ECAC	31	4	10	14	52	....	....	....	....	....
2000-01	Cornell Big Red	ECAC	32	8	20	28	47	....	....	....	....	....
2001-02	Cornell Big Red	ECAC	35	9	23	32	42	....	....	....	....	....
2002-03	Cornell Big Red	ECAC	36	8	*33	41	60	....	....	....	....	....
2003-04	Chicago Wolves	AHL	68	14	12	26	72	10	1	4	5	6

ECAC Second All-Star Team (2002, 2003) • NCAA East Second All-American Team (2003)

BACKER, Per (BAK-uhr, PAIR) DET.

Right wing. Shoots left. 6'1", 161 lbs. Born, Grums, Sweden, January 4, 1982.
(Detroit's 7th choice, 187th overall, in 2000 Entry Draft).

			Regular Season					Playoffs				
Season	Club	League	GP	G	A	TP	PIM	GP	G	A	TP	PIM
1998-99	Grums IK	Swede-2	17	1	1	2	4	....	....	....	....	....
99-2000	Grums IK	Swede-2	46	12	10	22	24	....	....	....	....	....
2000-01	Bofors IK	Swede-2	27	9	10	19	10	....	....	....	....	....
	Bofors IK	Swede-Q	14	11	5	16	6	....	....	....	....	....
2001-02	Farjestad	Sweden	47	4	8	12	12	10	5	1	6	10
2002-03	Farjestad	Sweden	49	11	16	27	46	12	1	1	2	12
2003-04	Farjestad	Sweden	49	7	6	13	24	17	0	0	0	8

BACKES, David (BA-kuhs, DAY-vihd) ST.L.

Center. Shoots right. 6'2", 200 lbs. Born, Blaine, MN, May 1, 1984.
(St. Louis' 2nd choice, 62nd overall, in 2003 Entry Draft).

			Regular Season					Playoffs				
Season	Club	League	GP	G	A	TP	PIM	GP	G	A	TP	PIM
99-2000	Spring Lake Park	Hi-School	24	17	20	37	....	....	....	....	....	....
2000-01	Spring Lake Park	Hi-School	24	29	46	75	....	....	....	....	....	....
2001-02	Chicago Steel	USHL	25	31	36	67	....	2	1	1	2	....
	Lincoln Stars	USHL	30	11	10	21	54	3	0	0	0	2
2002-03	Lincoln Stars	USHL	57	28	41	69	126	7	4	1	5	17
2003-04	Minnesota State	WCHA	39	16	21	37	66	....	....	....	....	....

USHL First All-Star Team (2003) • WCHA All-Rookie Team (2004)

BAGNALL, Drew (BAG-nuhl, DROO) FLA.

Defense. Shoots left. 6'3", 205 lbs. Born, Oakbank, Man., October 26, 1983.
(Dallas' 9th choice, 195th overall, in 2003 Entry Draft).

			Regular Season					Playoffs				
Season	Club	League	GP	G	A	TP	PIM	GP	G	A	TP	PIM
2000-01	Battlefords N'Stars	SJHL	58	7	20	27	205	....	....	....	....	....
2001-02	Battlefords N'Stars	SJHL	60	16	23	39	247	....	....	....	....	....
2002-03	Battlefords N'Stars	SJHL	55	17	46	63	248	4	0	1	1	4
2003-04	St. Lawrence	ECAC	40	5	13	18	61	....	....	....	....	....

Traded to **Florida** by **Dallas** with Dallas' 2nd round compensatory choice (later traded to Phoenix - Phoenix selected Enver Lisin) for Valeri Bure, March 8, 2004.

BAHEN, Chris (BAY-hehn, KRIHS) CAR.

Defense. Shoots left. 6', 180 lbs. Born, Montreal, Que., November 16, 1980.
(Colorado's 10th choice, 189th overall, in 2000 Entry Draft).

			Regular Season					Playoffs				
Season	Club	League	GP	G	A	TP	PIM	GP	G	A	TP	PIM
1994-95	Thornhill	OMHA	40	12	38	50	82	....	....	....	....	....
1995-96	Thornhill	OMHA	40	18	51	69	96	....	....	....	....	....
1996-97	Thornhill	OMHA	40	23	42	65	108	....	....	....	....	....
1997-98	Thornhill Rattlers	MTJHL	45	5	9	14	131	....	....	....	....	....
1998-99	Milton Merchants	OPJHL	32	3	14	17	20	....	....	....	....	....
99-2000	Clarkson Knights	ECAC	34	8	10	18	54	....	....	....	....	....
2000-01	Clarkson Knights	ECAC	34	3	7	10	45	....	....	....	....	....
2001-02	Clarkson Knights	ECAC	37	2	6	8	36	....	....	....	....	....
2002-03	Clarkson Knights	ECAC	34	3	14	17	45	....	....	....	....	....
2003-04	EV Landshut	German-2	35	3	5	8	48	12	1	5	6	6

ECAC All-Academic Team (2002)

Signed as a free agent by **EV Landshut** (German-2) with Colorado retaining NHL rights, August 21, 2003. Traded to **Carolina** by **Colorado** with Washington's 3rd round choice (previously acquired, Carolina selected Casey Borer) in 2004 Entry Draft for Bob Boughner, February 20, 2004.

BAHENSKY, Zdenek (ba-HEHN-skee, z'DEHN-ehk) NYR

Right wing. Shoots left. 6'2", 191 lbs. Born, Most, Czechoslovakia, January 3, 1986.
(NY Rangers' 7th choice, 73rd overall, in 2004 Entry Draft).

			Regular Season					Playoffs				
Season	Club	League	GP	G	A	TP	PIM	GP	G	A	TP	PIM
2001-02	Litvinov 18	Czech-Jr.	46	16	17	33	102	2	0	0	0	0
2002-03	Litvinov 18	Czech-Jr.	3	2	3	5	4	....	....	....	....	....
	Litvinov Jr.	Czech-Jr.	31	4	2	6	8	....	....	....	....	....
2003-04	Litvinov Jr.	Czech-Jr.	52	14	15	29	204	2	1	1	2	14

BAIER, Paul (BAI-uhr, PAWL) L.A.

Defense. Shoots right. 6'3", 212 lbs. Born, Summit, NJ, February 2, 1985.
(Los Angeles' 2nd choice, 95th overall, in 2004 Entry Draft).

			Regular Season					Playoffs				
Season	Club	League	GP	G	A	TP	PIM	GP	G	A	TP	PIM
2002-03	Deerfield Academy	Hi-School	25	2	15	17	24	....	....	....	....	....
2003-04	Deerfield Academy	Hi-School	23	6	4	10	22	....	....	....	....	....

• Signed Letter of Intent to attend **Brown University** (ECAC), June 6, 2004.

BAINES, Ajay (BAYNZ, AY-JAY) CHI.

Center. Shoots left. 5'10", 179 lbs. Born, Kamloops, B.C., March 25, 1978.

			Regular Season					Playoffs				
Season	Club	League	GP	G	A	TP	PIM	GP	G	A	TP	PIM
1994-95	Kamloops	BCAHA	52	45	79	124	139	....	....	....	....	....
1995-96	Kamloops Blazers	WHL	68	14	29	43	43	....	....	....	....	....
1996-97	Kamloops Blazers	WHL	70	32	43	75	106	5	4	1	5	6
1997-98	Kamloops Blazers	WHL	72	34	25	59	88	....	....	....	....	....
1998-99	Kamloops Blazers	WHL	72	33	32	65	145	15	7	6	13	20
99-2000	Greenville Grrrowl	ECHL	67	24	31	55	102	15	2	5	7	13
2000-01	Norfolk Admirals	AHL	73	18	18	36	92	9	0	1	1	2
2001-02	Norfolk Admirals	AHL	80	16	28	44	70	4	0	1	1	0
2002-03	Norfolk Admirals	AHL	74	8	14	22	108	9	2	1	3	18
2003-04	Norfolk Admirals	AHL	80	15	27	42	81	8	1	3	4	13

Signed as a free agent by **Chicago**, August 1, 2001.

BALAN, Scott (BAY-luhn, SKAWT) CHI.

Defense. Shoots right. 6'3", 195 lbs. Born, Medicine Hat, Alta., May 29, 1982.
(Chicago's 5th choice, 106th overall, in 2000 Entry Draft).

			Regular Season					Playoffs				
Season	Club	League	GP	G	A	TP	PIM	GP	G	A	TP	PIM
1997-98	Regina Chiefs	SMHL	56	6	25	31	139	....	....	....	....	....
	Regina Pats	WHL	1	0	1	1	0	....	....	....	....	....
1998-99	Regina Pats	WHL	63	1	8	9	42	....	....	....	....	....
99-2000	Regina Pats	WHL	67	3	11	14	157	7	0	1	1	17
2000-01	Regina Pats	WHL	42	2	5	7	69	....	....	....	....	....
	Saskatoon Blades	WHL	28	0	5	5	49	....	....	....	....	....
2001-02	Saskatoon Blades	WHL	27	1	10	11	40	....	....	....	....	....
2002-03	Roanoke Express	ECHL	44	1	9	10	63	4	0	0	0	2
	Norfolk Admirals	AHL	15	0	0	0	27	....	....	....	....	....
2003-04	Norfolk Admirals	AHL	23	0	1	1	35	....	....	....	....	....
	Florence Pride	ECHL	50	2	12	14	97	....	....	....	....	....

• Missed majority of 2001-02 season recovering from knee injury suffered in game vs. Saskatoon (WHL), December 18, 2001.

BALASTIK, Jaroslav (ba-LASH-tihk, YAHR-roh-slav) CBJ

Right wing. Shoots left. 6', 198 lbs. Born, Gottwaldov, Czech., November 28, 1979.
(Columbus' 9th choice, 184th overall, in 2002 Entry Draft).

			Regular Season					Playoffs				
Season	Club	League	GP	G	A	TP	PIM	GP	G	A	TP	PIM
1996-97	Zlin Jr.	Czech-Jr.	45	27	24	51	....	....	....	....	....	....
1997-98	Zlin Jr.	Czech-Jr.	36	21	35	56	....	7	2	3	5	....
	Zlin	Czech	6	0	2	2	....	....	....	....	....	....
1998-99	Zlin Jr.	Czech-Jr.	....	....	....	....	....	2	0	0	0	....
	Zlin	Czech	41	4	8	12	12	9	1	0	1	27
99-2000	Zlin Jr.	Czech-Jr.	4	5	5	10	2	....	....	....	....	....
	Zlin	Czech	48	7	10	17	0	4	0	1	1	2
2000-01	Zlin	Czech	52	8	17	25	32	6	1	1	2	6
2001-02	Zlin	Czech	50	25	19	44	32	11	3	5	8	14
2002-03	HC Hame Zlin	Czech	31	14	8	22	26	....	....	....	....	....
	HPK Hameenlinna	Finland	13	5	7	12	2	13	4	3	7	6
2003-04	HC Hame Zlin	Czech	51	*29	18	47	54	17	*9	9	*18	32

BALLANTYNE, Paul (BAL-uhn-tughn, PAWL) DET.

Defense. Shoots right. 6'3", 200 lbs. Born, Waterloo, Ont., July 16, 1982.
(Detroit's 8th choice, 196th overall, in 2000 Entry Draft).

			Regular Season					Playoffs				
Season	Club	League	GP	G	A	TP	PIM	GP	G	A	TP	PIM
1997-98	Waterloo Lions	OMHA	30	4	16	20	55	....	....	....	....	....
	Waterloo Siskins	OJHL-B	1	0	0	0	0	....	....	....	....	....
1998-99	Sault Ste. Marie	OHL	53	0	6	6	33	5	1	0	1	4
99-2000	Sault Ste. Marie	OHL	58	4	15	19	60	17	2	3	5	17
2000-01	Sault Ste. Marie	OHL	63	12	28	40	60	....	....	....	....	....
2001-02	Sault Ste. Marie	OHL	68	4	24	28	40	6	1	1	2	8
2002-03	Toledo Storm	ECHL	56	10	16	26	41	7	0	1	1	2
	Grand Rapids	AHL	7	0	0	0	8	....	....	....	....	....
2003-04	Grand Rapids	AHL	9	1	1	2	6	....	....	....	....	....
	Toledo Storm	ECHL	54	13	23	36	20	....	....	....	....	....
	Louisiana	ECHL	3	1	0	1	0	7	1	0	1	0

BALLARD, Keith (BAL-uhrd, KEETH) PHX.

Defense. Shoots left. 5'11", 202 lbs. Born, Baudette, MN, November 26, 1982.
(Buffalo's 1st choice, 11th overall, in 2002 Entry Draft).

			Regular Season					Playoffs				
Season	Club	League	GP	G	A	TP	PIM	GP	G	A	TP	PIM
99-2000	U.S. National U-18	USDP	58	12	21	33	....	....	....	....	....	....
2000-01	Omaha Lancers	USHL	56	22	29	51	168	10	1	6	7	8
2001-02	U. of Minnesota	WCHA	41	10	13	23	42	....	....	....	....	....
2002-03	U. of Minnesota	WCHA	41	12	29	41	78	....	....	....	....	....
2003-04	U. of Minnesota	WCHA	37	11	25	36	83	....	....	....	....	....

USHL First All-Star Team (2001) • WCHA All-Rookie Team (2002) • WCHA First All-Star Team (2003, 2004) • NCAA West First All-American Team (2004)

Traded to **Colorado** by **Buffalo** for Steve Reinprecht, July 3, 2003. Traded to **Phoenix** by **Colorado** with Derek Morris for Ossi Vaananen, Chris Gratton and Phoenix's 2nd round choice in 2005 Entry Draft, March 8, 2004.

BARANKA, Ivan (ba-RAN-kuh, IGH-vuhn) **NYR**

Defense. Shoots left. 6'2", 180 lbs. Born, Ilava, Czech., May 19, 1985.
(NY Rangers' 2nd choice, 50th overall, in 2003 Entry Draft).

			Regular Season					Playoffs				
Season	Club	League	GP	G	A	TP	PIM	GP	G	A	TP	PIM
2002-03	Dubnica Jr.	Slovak-Jr.	27	1	7	8	44	....	....	....	....	....
	Dubnica	Slovak-2	2	0	0	0	0	....	....	....	....	....
2003-04	Everett Silvertips	WHL	58	3	12	15	69	20	3	5	8	26

BARANOV, Konstantin (buh-RA-nawf, kawn-stuhn-TEEN) **PHI.**

Right wing. Shoots left. 6'2", 185 lbs. Born, Omsk, USSR, January 11, 1982.
(Philadelphia's 3rd choice, 126th overall, in 2002 Entry Draft).

			Regular Season					Playoffs				
Season	Club	League	GP	G	A	TP	PIM	GP	G	A	TP	PIM
1998-99	Omsk 2	Russia-4	23	18	8	26	40	....	....	....	....	....
	Avangard Omsk	Russia	1	0	0	0	0	2	0	0	0	0
99-2000	Omsk 2	Russia-3	33	15	8	23	46	....	....	....	....	....
	Avangard Omsk	Russia	1	0	0	0	2	....	....	....	....	....
2000-01	Kristall Saratov	Russia-2	26	6	9	15	26	....	....	....	....	....
	Ufa Salavat	Russia	8	1	0	1	4	....	....	....	....	....
2001-02	Avangard Omsk	Russia	5	0	0	0	6	....	....	....	....	....
	Mechel	Russia	6	1	2	3	2	....	....	....	....	....
	Lada Togliatti	Russia	20	2	4	6	18	3	0	2	2	0
2002-03	Avangard Omsk	Russia	6	0	1	1	2	....	....	....	....	....
	Ufa Salavat	Russia	11	2	2	4	0	....	....	....	....	....
	CSKA Moscow	Russia	14	4	1	5	10	....	....	....	....	....
	Avangard Omsk 2	Russia-3	3	4	6	10	2	....	....	....	....	....
2003-04	Avangard Omsk	Russia	51	6	10	16	50	11	2	2	4	6

BARARUK, David (BAIR-a-ruhk, DAY-vihd) **DAL.**

Center. Shoots left. 6', 175 lbs. Born, Moose Jaw, Sask., May 26, 1983.
(Dallas' 8th choice, 147th overall, in 2002 Entry Draft).

			Regular Season					Playoffs				
Season	Club	League	GP	G	A	TP	PIM	GP	G	A	TP	PIM
99-2000	Moose Jaw AAA	SMMHL	STATISTICS NOT AVAILABLE									
	Moose Jaw	WHL	21	0	2	2	0	2	0	0	0	0
2000-01	Moose Jaw	WHL	53	6	9	15	9	3	0	0	0	0
2001-02	Moose Jaw	WHL	72	33	29	62	31	12	3	2	5	0
2002-03	Moose Jaw	WHL	66	29	64	93	44	13	5	9	14	4
2003-04	Idaho Steelheads	ECHL	16	7	8	15	4	15	5	9	14	2
	Utah Grizzlies	AHL	52	5	7	12	4	....	....	....	....	....

WHL East Second All-Star Team (2003)

BARKER, Cam (BAR-kuhr, KAM) **CHI.**

Defense. Shoots left. 6'3", 213 lbs. Born, Winnipeg, Man., April 4, 1986.
(Chicago's 1st choice, 3rd overall, in 2004 Entry Draft).

			Regular Season					Playoffs				
Season	Club	League	GP	G	A	TP	PIM	GP	G	A	TP	PIM
2001-02	Cornwall Colts	OPJHL	72	6	23	29	132	....	....	....	....	....
	Medicine Hat	WHL	3	0	1	1	0	....	....	....	....	....
2002-03	Medicine Hat	WHL	64	10	37	47	79	11	3	4	7	17
2003-04	Medicine Hat	WHL	69	21	44	65	105	20	3	9	12	18

BARKUNOV, Alexander (bahr-koo-NAHF, al-ehx-AN-duhr) **CHI.**

Defense. Shoots right. 6'1", 199 lbs. Born, Novosibirsk, USSR, May 13, 1981.
(Chicago's 7th choice, 151st overall, in 2000 Entry Draft).

			Regular Season					Playoffs				
Season	Club	League	GP	G	A	TP	PIM	GP	G	A	TP	PIM
1996-97	Yaroslavl 2	Russia-3	1	0	0	0	0	....	....	....	....	....
1997-98	Torpedo Yaroslavl	Russia	20	1	1	2	6	....	....	....	....	....
1998-99	Yaroslavl 2	Russia-3	19	0	3	3	8	....	....	....	....	....
99-2000	Torpedo Yaroslavl	Russia	38	5	9	14	16	8	2	1	3	0
2000-01	Yaroslavl	Russia	34	5	1	6	10	2	0	0	0	2
2001-02	Yaroslavl 2	Russia-3	10	1	4	5	2	....	....	....	....	....
	Yaroslavl	Russia	15	0	0	0	2	....	....	....	....	....
	Amur Khabarovsk	Russia	7	0	0	0	0	....	....	....	....	....
2002-03	Perm	Russia	28	0	1	1	16	....	....	....	....	....
2003-04	Nizhny Novgorod	Russia	20	0	2	2	16	....	....	....	....	....
	Novogorod 2	Russia-3	STATISTICS NOT AVAILABLE									

BARRETT, Nathan (BAIR-uht, NAY-thun) **TOR.**

Center. Shoots left. 6', 189 lbs. Born, Vancouver, B.C., August 3, 1981.
(Vancouver's 6th choice, 241st overall, in 2000 Entry Draft).

			Regular Season					Playoffs				
Season	Club	League	GP	G	A	TP	PIM	GP	G	A	TP	PIM
1996-97	Langley Bantams	BCAHA	90	107	109	216	96	....	....	....	....	....
1997-98	Tri-City Americans	WHL	47	1	1	2	23	....	....	....	....	....
1998-99	Tri-City Americans	WHL	33	9	9	18	19	....	....	....	....	....
	Lethbridge	WHL	22	12	9	21	19	4	1	0	1	0
99-2000	Lethbridge	WHL	72	44	38	82	38	....	....	....	....	....
2000-01	Lethbridge	WHL	70	46	53	99	66	5	1	1	2	6
2001-02	Lethbridge	WHL	72	45	*62	*107	100	4	0	1	1	6
2002-03	St. John's	AHL	69	9	22	31	35	....	....	....	....	....
2003-04	St. John's	AHL	49	17	21	38	41	....	....	....	....	....

WHL East Second All-Star Team (2001) • WHL East First All-Star Team (2002)

Signed as a free agent by **Toronto**, July 31, 2002.

BARTHEL, Clayton (bahr-TEHL, KLAY-tuhn) **WSH.**

Defense. Shoots left. 6'2", 205 lbs. Born, Lahr, West Germany, April 2, 1986.
(Washington's 7th choice, 88th overall, in 2004 Entry Draft).

			Regular Season					Playoffs				
Season	Club	League	GP	G	A	TP	PIM	GP	G	A	TP	PIM
2001-02	Kelowna AA	BCAHA	40	13	15	28	....	....	....	....	....	....
2002-03	Seattle	WHL	62	1	8	9	48	15	1	1	2	10
2003-04	Seattle	WHL	72	3	14	17	125	....	....	....	....	....

BARTSCHI, Patrik (BAIRT-chee, PAT-rihk) **PIT.**

Center/Right wing. Shoots right. 6', 199 lbs. Born, Bulach, Switz., August 20, 1984.
(Pittsburgh's 8th choice, 202nd overall, in 2002 Entry Draft).

			Regular Season					Playoffs				
Season	Club	League	GP	G	A	TP	PIM	GP	G	A	TP	PIM
99-2000	Kloten Flyers Jr.	Swiss-Jr.	26	12	14	26	14	....	....	....	....	....
2000-01	Kloten Flyers Jr.	Swiss-Jr.	36	38	30	68	14	6	11	3	14	6
	EHC Kloten	Swiss	2	0	0	0	0	....	....	....	....	....
	HC Thurgau	Swiss-2	1	1	0	1	0	....	....	....	....	....
2001-02	Kloten Flyers Jr.	Swiss-Jr.	9	10	7	17	4	2	3	2	5	2
	Kloten Flyers	Swiss	24	4	4	8	8	11	2	2	4	2
2002-03	Kloten Flyers	Swiss	44	21	16	37	39	5	1	3	4	4
2003-04	Kloten Flyers	Swiss	40	12	24	36	6	....	....	....	....	....
	Kloten Flyers	Swiss-Q	1	0	0	0	0	....	....	....	....	....

BAUM, Dan (BAWM, DAN) **EDM.**

Center. Shoots left. 6'1", 189 lbs. Born, Biggar, Sask., June 4, 1983.
(Edmonton's 8th choice, 215th overall, in 2001 Entry Draft).

			Regular Season					Playoffs				
Season	Club	League	GP	G	A	TP	PIM	GP	G	A	TP	PIM
1998-99	Swift Current	SMHL	....	....	....	....	....	....	....	....	....	....
99-2000	Prince George	WHL	55	6	10	16	82	12	1	0	1	19
2000-01	Prince George	WHL	59	9	14	23	169	6	1	2	3	27
2001-02	Prince George	WHL	72	32	35	67	197	6	5	3	8	25
2002-03	Prince George	WHL	72	32	41	73	218	5	2	0	2	9
2003-04	Toronto	AHL	37	4	6	10	154	3	0	1	1	0
	Columbus	ECHL	3	0	0	0	7	....	....	....	....	....

BEAULIEU, Pierre-Olivier (BOI-loh, pee-AIR-oh-LIH-vee-ay) **DET.**

Defense. Shoots left. 6'4", 184 lbs. Born, St-Pierre Becquets, Que., February 24, 1984.
(Detroit's 8th choice, 260th overall, in 2002 Entry Draft).

			Regular Season					Playoffs				
Season	Club	League	GP	G	A	TP	PIM	GP	G	A	TP	PIM
99-2000	Cap-de-Madelaine	QAAA	38	3	5	8	28	....	....	....	....	....
2000-01	Montreal Rocket	QMJHL	61	3	8	11	31	....	....	....	....	....
2001-02	Montreal Rocket	QMJHL	31	4	3	7	21	....	....	....	....	....
	Quebec Remparts	QMJHL	31	0	4	4	44	9	0	0	0	6
2002-03	Quebec Remparts	QMJHL	20	3	2	5	29	....	....	....	....	....
	Victoriaville Tigres	QMJHL	22	0	5	5	12	3	0	0	0	6
2003-04	Victoriaville Tigres	QMJHL	30	1	6	7	37	....	....	....	....	....
	Halifax	QMJHL	32	3	12	15	40	....	....	....	....	....

BECKETT, Jason (Beh-keht, JAY-suhn) **MIN.**

Defense. Shoots right. 6'3", 218 lbs. Born, Lethbridge, Alta., July 23, 1980.
(Philadelphia's 2nd choice, 42nd overall, in 1998 Entry Draft).

			Regular Season					Playoffs				
Season	Club	League	GP	G	A	TP	PIM	GP	G	A	TP	PIM
1996-97	Lethbridge	AMHL	34	7	10	17	118	....	....	....	....	....
1997-98	Seattle	WHL	71	1	11	12	241	5	0	0	0	16
1998-99	Seattle	WHL	70	4	26	30	195	11	0	1	1	40
99-2000	Seattle	WHL	70	3	15	18	183	7	1	1	2	12
2000-01	Trenton Titans	ECHL	17	2	2	4	24	15	0	1	1	26
	Philadelphia	AHL	56	2	10	12	107	....	....	....	....	....
2001-02	Philadelphia	AHL	9	0	0	0	11	....	....	....	....	....
	Milwaukee	AHL	28	2	4	6	56	....	....	....	....	....
	Trenton Titans	ECHL	14	1	1	2	49	3	0	0	0	4
2002-03	Milwaukee	AHL	64	2	10	12	130	6	0	1	1	12
2003-04	Houston Aeros	AHL	72	4	7	11	168	2	0	0	0	7

Traded to **Nashville** by **Philadelphia** with Petr Hubacek for Yves Sarault, January 11, 2002. Signed as a free agent by **Minnesota**, August 6, 2003.

BELAK, Graham (BEE-lak, GRAY-ham) **NYI**

Left wing. Shoots left. 6'5", 230 lbs. Born, Saskatoon, Sask., August 1, 1979.
(Colorado's 2nd choice, 53rd overall, in 1997 Entry Draft).

			Regular Season					Playoffs				
Season	Club	League	GP	G	A	TP	PIM	GP	G	A	TP	PIM
1993-94	North Battleford	SMBHL	50	3	14	17	110	5	0	3	3	30
1994-95	North Battleford	SMBHL	48	10	20	30	152	....	....	....	....	....
1995-96	North Battleford	SJHL	55	3	14	17	110	....	....	....	....	....
1996-97	Edmonton Ice	WHL	61	3	5	8	251	....	....	....	....	....
1997-98	Edmonton Ice	WHL	47	5	5	10	168	....	....	....	....	....
	Hershey Bears	AHL	1	0	0	0	15	....	....	....	....	....
1998-99	Kootenay Ice	WHL	45	3	1	4	201	7	0	0	0	38
99-2000	Kootenay Ice	WHL	49	4	9	13	197	21	2	3	5	*61
2000-01	U. of Alberta	CWUAA	1	0	0	0	0	....	....	....	....	....
2001-02	Trenton Titans	ECHL	60	6	6	12	305	....	....	....	....	....
	Trenton Titans	ECHL	60	6	6	12	305	....	....	....	....	....
	Bridgeport	AHL	7	0	0	0	5	....	....	....	....	....
2002-03	Bridgeport	AHL	30	0	1	1	60	2	0	0	0	0
	Trenton Titans	ECHL	2	0	0	0	15	....	....	....	....	....
	Cincinnati	ECHL	40	1	0	1	157	....	....	....	....	....
2003-04	Bridgeport	AHL	72	1	2	3	220	7	0	1	1	29

BELL, Brendan (BEHL, BREHN-duhn) **TOR.**

Defense. Shoots left. 6'1", 205 lbs. Born, Ottawa, Ont., March 31, 1983.
(Toronto's 3rd choice, 65th overall, in 2001 Entry Draft).

			Regular Season					Playoffs				
Season	Club	League	GP	G	A	TP	PIM	GP	G	A	TP	PIM
1998-99	Ottawa Jr. Sens	OCJHL	54	7	20	27	46	....	....	....	....	....
99-2000	Ottawa 67's	OHL	48	1	32	33	34	5	0	1	1	4
2000-01	Ottawa 67's	OHL	68	7	32	39	59	20	1	11	12	22
2001-02	Ottawa 67's	OHL	67	10	36	46	56	13	2	5	7	25
2002-03	Ottawa 67's	OHL	55	14	39	53	46	23	8	19	27	25
2003-04	St. John's	AHL	74	7	18	25	72	....	....	....	....	....

OHL First All-Star Team (2003) • Canadian Major Junior First All-Star Team (2003) • Canadian Major Junior Defenseman of the Year (2003)

BELLAMY, Rob (BEHL-ah-mee, RAWB) **PHI.**

Right wing. Shoots right. 6', 190 lbs. Born, Providence, RI, May 30, 1985.
(Philadelphia's 1st choice, 92nd overall, in 2004 Entry Draft).

			Regular Season					Playoffs				
Season	Club	League	GP	G	A	TP	PIM	GP	G	A	TP	PIM
2002-03	Berkshire Bears	Hi-School	32	21	21	42	128	....	....	....	....	....
2003-04	New England	EJHL	36	19	21	40	95	....	....	....	....	....

• Signed Letter of Intent to attend **U. of Maine** (H-East), May 9, 2003.

BELLE, Shawn (BEHL, SHAWN) **DAL.**

Defense. Shoots left. 6'1", 220 lbs. Born, Edmonton, Alta., January 3, 1985.
(St. Louis' 1st choice, 30th overall, in 2003 Entry Draft).

			Regular Season					Playoffs				
Season	Club	League	GP	G	A	TP	PIM	GP	G	A	TP	PIM
99-2000	K of C Squires	AMBHL	34	7	20	27	36	....	....	....	....	....
2000-01	K of C Squires	AMBHL	39	18	30	48	69	....	....	....	....	....
	Regina Pats	WHL	4	0	3	3	0	....	....	....	....	....
	Tri City Americans	WHL	2	0	1	1	0	....	....	....	....	....
2001-02	Tri City Americans	WHL	64	1	17	18	51	5	2	1	3	2
2002-03	Tri-City Americans	WHL	66	7	14	21	79	....	....	....	....	....
2003-04	Tri-City Americans	WHL	55	9	20	29	68	11	3	5	8	15

Rights traded to **Dallas** by **St. Louis** for Jason Bacashihua, June 25, 2004.

BELLEMARE, Thomas (BEHL-mahr, TAW-muhs) CGY.

Right wing. Shoots right. 6'3", 236 lbs. Born, Shawinigan, Que., January 11, 1984.
(Calgary's 7th choice, 206th overall, in 2003 Entry Draft).

			Regular Season					Playoffs				
Season	Club	League	GP	G	A	TP	PIM	GP	G	A	TP	PIM
2002-03	Drummondville	QMJHL	67	5	3	8	474	....	....	....	....	....
2003-04	Drummondville	QMJHL	60	2	5	7	181	7	0	0	0	2

BELLISSIMO, Vince (behl-IHS-ih-moh, VIHNTS) FLA.

Center. Shoots right. 6', 199 lbs. Born, Toronto, Ont., December 14, 1982.
(Florida's 6th choice, 158th overall, in 2002 Entry Draft).

			Regular Season					Playoffs				
Season	Club	League	GP	G	A	TP	PIM	GP	G	A	TP	PIM
99-2000	St. Michael's B	OPJHL	47	30	29	59	31	....	....	....	....	....
2000-01	St. Michael's B	OPJHL	47	32	64	96	28	6	6	8	14	....
2001-02	Topeka	USHL	61	37	39	76	33	....	....	....	....	....
2002-03	Western Michigan	CCHA	37	19	17	36	18	....	....	....	....	....
2003-04	Western Michigan	CCHA	38	13	27	40	42	....	....	....	....	....

USHL First All-Star Team (2002) • USHL Top Forward (2002) • CCHA All-Rookie Team (2003)

BEMBRIDGE, Garrett (bem-BRIHDJ, GAHR-reht)

Right wing. Shoots right. 6', 180 lbs. Born, Melfort, Sask., July 6, 1981.
(Calgary's 8th choice, 207th overall, in 2001 Entry Draft).

			Regular Season					Playoffs				
Season	Club	League	GP	G	A	TP	PIM	GP	G	A	TP	PIM
1997-98	Saskatoon Blazers	SMHL	44	29	45	74	74	....	....	....	....	....
	Saskatoon Blades	WHL	6	1	1	2	0	1	0	0	0	0
1998-99	Saskatoon Blades	WHL	68	23	27	50	30	....	....	....	....	....
99-2000	Saskatoon Blades	WHL	72	27	31	58	41	11	5	5	10	2
2000-01	Saskatoon Blades	WHL	72	38	40	78	40	....	....	....	....	....
2001-02	Saint John Flames	AHL	66	9	12	21	22	....	....	....	....	....
2002-03	Saint John Flames	AHL	64	9	10	19	33	....	....	....	....	....
2003-04	Lowell	AHL	57	5	9	14	44	....	....	....	....	....
	Las Vegas	ECHL	13	4	3	7	12	2	0	0	0	0

• Re-entered NHL Entry Draft. Originally NY Rangers' 6th choice, 137th overall, in 1999 Entry Draft.

BERGFORS, Henrik (BAIRG-fohrz, HEHN-rihk) T.B.

Defense. Shoots right. 6'4", 227 lbs. Born, Stockholm, Sweden, May 15, 1982.
(Tampa Bay's 14th choice, 289th overall, in 2001 Entry Draft).

			Regular Season					Playoffs				
Season	Club	League	GP	G	A	TP	PIM	GP	G	A	TP	PIM
99-2000	AIK Solna-18	Swede-Jr.	19	1	1	2	55	....	....	....	....	....
	AIK Solna Jr.	Swede-Jr.	12	0	1	1	6	....	....	....	....	....
2000-01	Sodertalje SK Jr.	Swede-Jr.	14	1	0	1	16	....	....	....	....	....
2001-02	Sodertalje SK Jr.	Swede-Jr.	40	4	4	8	62	2	1	0	1	2
2002-03	Sodertalje SK	Sweden	8	0	0	0	0	....	....	....	....	....
	HC Orebro	Swede-2	18	0	0	0	60	....	....	....	....	....
	Sodertalje SK Jr.	Swede-Jr.	7	0	2	2	29	....	....	....	....	....
2003-04	Wichita Thunder	CHL	DID NOT PLAY – INJURED									

• Missed entire 2003-04 season recovering from shoulder injury suffered in pre-season game vs. Tulsa (CHL), September 10, 2003.

BERGGREN, Johan (BUHR-gruhn, YOH-han) DET.

Defense. Shoots left. 6'3", 176 lbs. Born, Vastra Amtevik, Sweden, May 18, 1984.
(Detroit's 4th choice, 131st overall, in 2002 Entry Draft).

			Regular Season					Playoffs				
Season	Club	League	GP	G	A	TP	PIM	GP	G	A	TP	PIM
2001-02	HC Sunne	Swede-3	25	1	7	8	22	....	....	....	....	....
2002-03	HC Sunne Jr.	Swede-Jr.	12	4	0	4	20	....	....	....	....	....
	HC Sunne	Swede-3	36	1	10	11	40	....	....	....	....	....
2003-04	Sodertalje SK	Sweden	43	0	1	1	20	....	....	....	....	....
	Sodertalje Jr.	Swede-Jr.	25	1	7	8	28	2	0	0	0	0

BERNIER, Marc-Andre (BAIRN-yay, MAHRK-AWN-dray) VAN.

Right wing. Shoots right. 6'4", 198 lbs. Born, Laval, Que., February 5, 1985.
(Vancouver's 2nd choice, 60th overall, in 2003 Entry Draft).

			Regular Season					Playoffs				
Season	Club	League	GP	G	A	TP	PIM	GP	G	A	TP	PIM
99-2000	Laval Laurentides	QAAA	15	2	3	5	10	9	1	0	1	2
2000-01	Laval Laurentides	QAAA	26	6	12	18	16	8	3	2	5	6
2001-02	Halifax	QMJHL	49	0	6	6	20	2	0	0	0	0
2002-03	Halifax	QMJHL	67	29	29	58	43	21	9	8	17	8
2003-04	Cape Breton	QMJHL	58	27	23	50	27	5	1	3	4	2

BERNIER, Steve (BAIRN-yay, STEEV) S.J.

Right wing. Shoots right. 6'2", 230 lbs. Born, Quebec City, Que., March 31, 1985.
(San Jose's 2nd choice, 16th overall, in 2003 Entry Draft).

			Regular Season					Playoffs				
Season	Club	League	GP	G	A	TP	PIM	GP	G	A	TP	PIM
1998-99	Quebec AA Aces	QAHA	28	33	23	56	24	....	....	....	....	....
99-2000	Quebec AA Aces	QAHA	26	12	23	35	42	....	....	....	....	....
2000-01	Ste-Foy	QAAA	39	17	35	52	48	16	9	17	26	8
2001-02	Moncton Wildcats	QMJHL	66	31	28	59	51	....	....	....	....	....
2002-03	Moncton Wildcats	QMJHL	71	49	52	101	90	2	1	0	1	2
2003-04	Moncton Wildcats	QMJHL	66	36	46	82	80	20	7	10	17	17

QMJHL All-Rookie Team (2002) • QMJHL Second All-Star Team (2003, 2004)

BERNIKOV, Ruslan (BAIR-nih-kahf, roos-LAHN) DAL.

Right wing. Shoots left. 6'3", 198 lbs. Born, Vidnoye, USSR, December 4, 1977.
(Dallas' 6th choice, 139th overall, in 2000 Entry Draft).

			Regular Season					Playoffs				
Season	Club	League	GP	G	A	TP	PIM	GP	G	A	TP	PIM
1996-97	Dyn. Moscow 2	Russia-3	32	11	4	15	20	....	....	....	....	....
	Dynamo Moscow	Russia	2	0	0	0	0	....	....	....	....	....
1997-98	Yekaterinburg 2	Russia-3	2	1	1	2	0	....	....	....	....	....
	Yekaterinburg	Russia	43	7	7	14	55	....	....	....	....	....
1998-99	Dynamo Moscow	Russia	6	0	1	1	2	....	....	....	....	....
	Krylja Sovetov	Russia	20	3	1	4	24	....	....	....	....	....
	CSKA Moscow	Russia	1	0	0	0	0	....	....	....	....	....
	Cherepovets	Russia	5	0	0	0	0	1	0	0	0	0
99-2000	Dynamo Moscow	Russia	6	2	1	3	2	....	....	....	....	....
	Amur Khabarovsk	Russia	14	3	6	9	10	5	3	1	4	2
2000-01	Amur Khabarovsk	Russia	33	1	4	5	40	....	....	....	....	....
2001-02	Amur Khabarovsk	Russia	38	7	10	17	20	....	....	....	....	....
2002-03	Krylja Sovetov	Russia	50	15	10	25	40	....	....	....	....	....
2003-04	Lada Togliatti	Russia	49	8	10	18	51	6	0	0	0	4

BERTI, Adam (BUHR-tee, A-duhm) CHI.

Left wing. Shoots left. 6'3", 193 lbs. Born, Scarborough, Ont., July 1, 1986.
(Chicago's 6th choice, 68th overall, in 2004 Entry Draft).

			Regular Season					Playoffs				
Season	Club	League	GP	G	A	TP	PIM	GP	G	A	TP	PIM
2001-02	Oshawa Electric	OMHA	STATISTICS NOT AVAILABLE									
2002-03	Oshawa Generals	OHL	15	3	3	6	12	....	....	....	....	....
2003-04	Oshawa Generals	OHL	66	17	29	46	44	7	0	2	2	4

BETTS, Kaleb (BEHTZ, KAHL-uhb) NSH.

Center. Shoots left. 5'10", 185 lbs. Born, Maple Ridge, B.C., January 10, 1983.
(Nashville's 6th choice, 235th overall, in 2002 Entry Draft).

			Regular Season					Playoffs				
Season	Club	League	GP	G	A	TP	PIM	GP	G	A	TP	PIM
2000-01	Chilliwack Chiefs	BCHL	58	17	20	37	79	....	....	....	....	....
2001-02	Chilliwack Chiefs	BCHL	54	35	37	72	92	....	....	....	....	....
2002-03	Nebraska-Omaha	CCHA	DID NOT PLAY – ACADEMICALLY INELIGIBLE									
2003-04	Nebraska-Omaha	CCHA	35	9	13	22	48	....	....	....	....	....

BEZRUKOV, Dmitri (behz-ROO-kahv, dih-MEE-tree) T.B.

Left wing. Shoots left. 6'3", 187 lbs. Born, Kazan, USSR, November 9, 1977.
(Tampa Bay's 11th choice, 259th overall, in 2001 Entry Draft).

			Regular Season					Playoffs				
Season	Club	League	GP	G	A	TP	PIM	GP	G	A	TP	PIM
1997-98	Nizhnekamsk 2	Russia-3	8	0	1	1	6	....	....	....	....	....
	Nizhnekamsk	Russia	14	5	3	8	4	....	....	....	....	....
1998-99	Nizhnekamsk 2	Russia-4	1	3	0	3	0	....	....	....	....	....
	Nizhnekamsk	Russia	39	4	6	10	18	3	1	0	1	2
99-2000	Nizhnekamsk 2	Russia-3	4	0	0	0	6	....	....	....	....	....
	Leninogorsk	Russia-2	8	2	1	3	8	....	....	....	....	....
	Nizhnekamsk	Russia	28	5	6	11	45	3	0	1	1	2
2000-01	Nizhnekamsk	Russia	35	7	10	17	54	4	0	2	2	2
2001-02	Nizhnekamsk	Russia	38	5	6	11	45	....	....	....	....	....
2002-03	Spartak Moscow	Russia	51	10	12	22	24	....	....	....	....	....
2003-04	Nizhnekamsk	Russia	17	1	3	4	10	....	....	....	....	....
	Cherepovets 2	Russia-3	12	7	10	17	20	....	....	....	....	....
	Cherepovets	Russia	8	0	0	0	0	....	....	....	....	....

BICKELL, Bryan (bih-KEHL, BRIGH-uhn) CHI.

Left wing. Shoots left. 6'3", 213 lbs. Born, Bowmanville, Ont., March 9, 1986.
(Chicago's 3rd choice, 41st overall, in 2004 Entry Draft).

			Regular Season					Playoffs				
Season	Club	League	GP	G	A	TP	PIM	GP	G	A	TP	PIM
2000-01	Tor. Red Wings	GTHL	68	24	26	50	20	5	3	1	4	4
2001-02	Tor. Red Wings	GTHL	65	31	41	72	76	2	2	2	4	0
2002-03	Ottawa 67's	OHL	50	7	10	17	4	20	5	3	8	12
2003-04	Ottawa 67's	OHL	59	20	16	36	76	7	3	0	3	11

BIEKSA, Kevin (BEEKS-ah, KEH-vihn) VAN.

Defense. Shoots right. 6'1", 190 lbs. Born, Grimsby, Ont., June 16, 1981.
(Vancouver's 4th choice, 151st overall, in 2001 Entry Draft).

			Regular Season					Playoffs				
Season	Club	League	GP	G	A	TP	PIM	GP	G	A	TP	PIM
1997-98	Burlington	OPJHL	27	0	3	3	10	....	....	....	....	....
1998-99	Burlington	OPJHL	49	8	29	37	83	....	....	....	....	....
99-2000	Burlington	OPJHL	49	6	27	33	139	....	....	....	....	....
2000-01	Bowling Green	CCHA	35	4	9	13	90	....	....	....	....	....
2001-02	Bowling Green	CCHA	40	5	10	15	68	....	....	....	....	....
2002-03	Bowling Green	CCHA	34	8	17	25	92	....	....	....	....	....
2003-04	Bowling Green	CCHA	38	7	15	22	66	....	....	....	....	....
	Manitoba Moose	AHL	4	0	2	2	2	....	....	....	....	....

BIRNER, Michal (BUHR-nuhr, MEE-khahl) ST.L.

Left wing. Shoots left. 6', 183 lbs. Born, Litomerice, Czechoslovakia, March 2, 1986.
(St. Louis' 4th choice, 116th overall, in 2004 Entry Draft).

			Regular Season					Playoffs				
Season	Club	League	GP	G	A	TP	PIM	GP	G	A	TP	PIM
2000-01	Slavia Praha 18	Czech-Jr.	48	16	24	40	20	7	0	1	1	6
2001-02	Slavia Praha 18	Czech-Jr.	46	24	34	58	28	21	1	0	1	0
2002-03	Slavia Praha 18	Czech-Jr.	5	5	6	11	14	5	4	3	7	20
	Slavia Praha Jr.	Czech-Jr.	31	4	8	12	10	3	1	0	1	2
2003-04	Slavia Praha Jr.	Czech-Jr.	55	25	35	60	112	2	0	1	1	4
	HC Slavia Praha	Czech	1	0	0	0	0	....	....	....	....	....

BISSONNETTE, Paul (bih-sawn-EHT, PAWL) PIT.

Defense. Shoots left. 6'3", 212 lbs. Born, Welland, Ont., March 11, 1985.
(Pittsburgh's 5th choice, 121st overall, in 2003 Entry Draft).

			Regular Season					Playoffs				
Season	Club	League	GP	G	A	TP	PIM	GP	G	A	TP	PIM
2000-01	Welland	OMHA	STATISTICS NOT AVAILABLE									
2001-02	North Bay	OHL	57	3	3	6	21	5	0	0	0	2
2002-03	Saginaw Spirit	OHL	67	7	16	23	57	....	....	....	....	....
2003-04	Saginaw Spirit	OHL	67	5	14	19	96	....	....	....	....	....

BITZ, Byron (BIHTZ, BRIGH-uhn) BOS.

Right wing. Shoots right. 6'3", 200 lbs. Born, Saskatoon, Sask., July 21, 1984.
(Boston's 4th choice, 107th overall, in 2003 Entry Draft).

			Regular Season					Playoffs				
Season	Club	League	GP	G	A	TP	PIM	GP	G	A	TP	PIM
2000-01	Saskatoon	SMBHL	40	17	35	52	....	....	....	....	....	....
2001-02	Saskatoon	SMHL	41	25	48	73	69	11	12	10	22	9
2002-03	Nanaimo Clippers	BCHL	58	27	46	73	59	....	....	....	....	....
2003-04	Cornell Big Red	ECAC	31	5	16	21	36	....	....	....	....	....

BJORK, Johan (b'YAWRK, YOH-han) OTT.

Defense. Shoots left. 6'1", 176 lbs. Born, Malmo, Sweden, August 28, 1984.
(Ottawa's 5th choice, 125th overall, in 2002 Entry Draft).

			Regular Season					Playoffs				
Season	Club	League	GP	G	A	TP	PIM	GP	G	A	TP	PIM
99-2000	Malmo IF-18	Swede-Jr.	8	0	1	1	8	....	....	....	....	....
2000-01	Malmo IF Jr.	Swede-Jr.	22	0	2	2	12	....	....	....	....	....
	Malmo IF-18	Swede-Jr.	3	0	0	0	8	....	....	....	....	....
2001-02	Malmo IF Jr.	Swede-Jr.	36	1	4	5	72	3	0	0	0	2
2002-03	Malmo	Sweden	21	0	0	0	6	....	....	....	....	....
	Malmo IF Jr.	Swede-Jr.	22	7	12	19	36	6	0	2	2	6
	IK Pantern	Swede-2	STATISTICS NOT AVAILABLE									
2003-04	Malmo Jr.	Swede-Jr.	16	4	5	9	6	3	0	0	0	0
	Malmo	Sweden	27	1	0	1	6	....	....	....	....	....

BLACK, Greg (BLAK, GREHG) ST.L.

Center. Shoots right. 6', 203 lbs. Born, Surrey, B.C., May 13, 1982.

			Regular Season					Playoffs				
Season	Club	League	GP	G	A	TP	PIM	GP	G	A	TP	PIM
1998-99	South Surrey	BCHL	STATISTICS NOT AVAILABLE									
	Seattle	WHL	2	0	0	0	0	....	....	....	....	....
99-2000	Seattle	WHL	63	8	7	15	114	7	0	1	1	14
2000-01	Seattle	WHL	59	9	11	20	178	....	....	....	....	....
2001-02	Seattle	WHL	63	27	18	45	205	11	5	2	7	37
2002-03	Seattle	WHL	71	36	27	63	203	8	5	5	10	14
2003-04	Worcester IceCats	AHL	39	4	5	9	129	10	0	0	0	10
	Peoria Rivermen	ECHL	15	5	2	7	69	....	....	....	....	....

Signed as a free agent by **St. Louis**, March 20, 2003.

BLAHO, Stefan (BLA-hoh, STEH-fan) NYI

Right wing. Shoots left. 6'1", 198 lbs. Born, Trencin, Czech., June 22, 1985.
(NY Islanders' 5th choice, 120th overall, in 2003 Entry Draft).

			Regular Season					Playoffs				
Season	Club	League	GP	G	A	TP	PIM	GP	G	A	TP	PIM
2002-03	Dukla Trencin Jr.	Slovak-Jr.	17	6	5	11	50	16	4	7	11	30
2003-04	Sudbury Wolves	OHL	51	8	8	16	58	6	1	2	3	2

BLANAR, Jan (BLAH-nuhr, YAHN) FLA.

Defense. Shoots left. 6'3", 185 lbs. Born, Trencin, Czech., June 6, 1983.
(Florida's 11th choice, 263rd overall, in 2001 Entry Draft).

			Regular Season					Playoffs				
Season	Club	League	GP	G	A	TP	PIM	GP	G	A	TP	PIM
1997-98	Dukla Trencin Jr.	Czech-Jr.	22	0	2	2	2	....	....	....	....	....
1998-99	Dukla Trencin Jr.	Czech-Jr.	45	2	8	10	20	....	....	....	....	....
99-2000	Dukla Trencin Jr.	Czech-Jr.	47	8	7	15	18	....	....	....	....	....
2000-01	Dukla Trencin Jr.	Slovak-Jr.	35	3	6	9	16	....	....	....	....	....
2001-02	Dukla Trencin Jr.	Slovak-Jr.	42	3	12	15	....	....	....	....	....	....
	Dukla Trencin	Slovakia	11	0	0	0	2	....	....	....	....	....
2002-03	Dukla Trencin Jr.	Slovak-Jr.	42	3	11	14	40	3	0	1	1	10
	Dukla Trencin	Slovakia	2	0	0	0	0	2	0	0	0	0
2003-04	Liptov. Mikulas	Slovakia	13	0	0	0	0	....	....	....	....	....
	Dubnica	Slovak-2	16	1	4	5	31	9	0	2	2	4

BLANSHAN, Cody (BLAHN-suhn, KOH-dee) NYI

Defense. Shoots left. 6'1", 200 lbs. Born, St. Paul, MN, February 14, 1984.
(NY Islanders' 8th choice, 238th overall, in 2003 Entry Draft).

			Regular Season					Playoffs				
Season	Club	League	GP	G	A	TP	PIM	GP	G	A	TP	PIM
2001-02	Sioux Falls	USHL	55	3	13	16	150	3	0	0	0	5
2002-03	Nebraska-Omaha	CCHA	38	0	5	5	*103	....	....	....	....	....
2003-04	Medicine Hat	WHL	70	4	7	11	88	20	2	3	5	30

• Left University of **Nebraska-Omaha** (CCHA) and signed as a free agent by **Medicine-Hat** (WHL), June 27, 2003.

BLATAK, Miroslav (BLAT-ak, MEER-oh-slav) DET.

Defense. Shoots left. 5'11", 172 lbs. Born, Gottwaldov, Czech., May 25, 1982.
(Detroit's 3rd choice, 129th overall, in 2001 Entry Draft).

			Regular Season					Playoffs				
Season	Club	League	GP	G	A	TP	PIM	GP	G	A	TP	PIM
99-2000	Vsetin 18	Czech-Jr.	30	0	0	0	12	....	....	....	....	....
	Vsetin Jr.	Czech-Jr.	12	0	2	2	10	....	....	....	....	....
2000-01	Vsetin 18	Czech-Jr.	33	7	8	15	56	....	....	....	....	....
	Vsetin Jr.	Czech-Jr.	12	2	4	6	54	7	0	6	6	6
	Zlin	Czech	8	0	2	2	0	6	0	0	0	0
2001-02	Dukla Jihlava Jr.	Czech-Jr.	3	0	0	0	0	....	....	....	....	....
	Zlin Jr.	Czech-Jr.	3	0	0	0	8	....	....	....	....	....
	HC Dukla Jihlava	Czech-2	1	0	0	0	0	2	0	0	0	0
	Zlin	Czech	39	4	7	11	18	11	1	2	3	8
2002-03	HC Hame Zlin	Czech	49	4	12	16	34	....	....	....	....	....
2003-04	HC Hame Zlin	Czech	50	5	10	15	34	17	3	3	6	10

BLINDENBACHER, Severin (blihn-duhn-BAH-khur, SEH-vuhr-ihn) PHX.

Defense. Shoots right. 5'11", 189 lbs. Born, Bulach, Switz., March 15, 1983.
(Phoenix's 9th choice, 273rd overall, in 2001 Entry Draft).

			Regular Season					Playoffs				
Season	Club	League	GP	G	A	TP	PIM	GP	G	A	TP	PIM
1998-99	Kloten Flyers Jr.	Swiss-Jr.	5	0	2	2	4	....	....	....	....	....
99-2000	Kloten Flyers Jr.	Swiss-Jr.	30	8	10	18	18	4	1	1	2	8
2000-01	EHC Kloten	Swiss	27	0	2	2	17	9	0	0	0	10
2001-02	Kloten Flyers	Swiss	38	1	3	4	22	10	0	2	2	10
	Kloten Flyers	Swiss-Jr.	....	....	....	....	....	1	0	1	1	2
2002-03	Kloten Flyers	Swiss	43	4	19	23	52	5	1	0	1	4
2003-04	Kloten Flyers	Swiss	34	4	10	14	58	....	....	....	....	....
	Kloten Flyers	Swiss-Q	8	2	3	5	2	....	....	....	....	....

BLOM, Stefan (BLAWM, STEH-fan) DET.

Defense. Shoots left. 6'2", 189 lbs. Born, Stockholm, Sweden, July 30, 1985.
(Detroit's 5th choice, 194th overall, in 2003 Entry Draft).

			Regular Season					Playoffs				
Season	Club	League	GP	G	A	TP	PIM	GP	G	A	TP	PIM
2002-03	Hammarby IF 18	Swede-Jr.	18	3	0	0	4	....	....	....	....	....
	Hammarby Jr.	Swede-Jr.	27	4	2	6	12	2	0	0	0	0
2003-04	Djurgarden Jr.	Swede-Jr.	33	2	5	7	16	....	....	....	....	....

BLOMDAHL, Patric (BLAWM-dahl, PAT-rihk) WSH.

Right wing. Shoots left. 6'1", 202 lbs. Born, Stockholm, Sweden, January 30, 1984.
(Washington's 13th choice, 272nd overall, in 2002 Entry Draft).

			Regular Season					Playoffs				
Season	Club	League	GP	G	A	TP	PIM	GP	G	A	TP	PIM
2000-01	AIK Solna 18	Swede-Jr.	9	5	1	6	35	....	....	....	....	....
2001-02	AIK Solna 18	Swede-Jr.	3	0	0	0	2	....	....	....	....	....
	AIK Solna Jr.	Swede-Jr.	20	7	6	13	18	....	....	....	....	....
2002-03	AIK Solna Jr.	Swede-Jr.	19	6	5	11	107	....	....	....	....	....
	AIK Solna	Swede-2	12	1	0	1	10	....	....	....	....	....
	AIK Solna	Swede-Q	9	0	1	1	4	7	1	0	1	4
2003-04	AIK Solna Jr.	Swede-Jr.	8	4	1	5	43	....	....	....	....	....
	AIK Solna	Swede-2	48	9	5	14	46	5	0	0	0	0

BOBROV, Viktor (bawb-RAWV, VIHK-tohr) CGY.

Center. Shoots left. 6'1", 176 lbs. Born, Novocheboksarsk, USSR, January 1, 1984.
(Calgary's 7th choice, 146th overall, in 2002 Entry Draft).

			Regular Season					Playoffs				
Season	Club	League	GP	G	A	TP	PIM	GP	G	A	TP	PIM
99-2000	Novogord	Russia-Jr.	6	6	1	7	0	....	....	....	....	....
2000-01	CSKA Moscow	Russia-Jr.	31	30	17	47	32	4	4	3	7	4
2001-02	HC CSKA 2	Russia-3	36	11	16	27	20	....	....	....	....	....
2002-03	Elemash Elektrosal	Russia-2	48	7	7	14	16	....	....	....	....	....
2003-04	Kristall Elektrostal	Russia-2	60	6	10	16	38	....	....	....	....	....

BOCHENSKI, Brandon (boh-CHEHN-skee, BRAN-duhn) OTT.

Right wing. Shoots right. 6', 180 lbs. Born, Blaine, MN, April 4, 1982.
(Ottawa's 9th choice, 223rd overall, in 2001 Entry Draft).

			Regular Season					Playoffs				
Season	Club	League	GP	G	A	TP	PIM	GP	G	A	TP	PIM
99-2000	Blaine Bengals	Hi-School	28	32	30	62	....	....	....	....	....	....
2000-01	Lincoln Stars	USHL	55	*47	33	80	22	11	5	7	12	4
2001-02	North Dakota	WCHA	36	17	15	32	34	....	....	....	....	....
2002-03	North Dakota	WCHA	43	35	27	62	42	....	....	....	....	....
2003-04	North Dakota	WCHA	41	27	33	60	40	....	....	....	....	....

USHL First All-Star Team (2001) • USHL Rookie of the Year (2001) • WCHA All-Rookie Team (2002) • WCHA Rookie of the Year (2002) • WCHA Second All-Star Team (2003) • WCHA First All-Star Team (2004) • NCAA West First All-American Team (2004)

BODIE, Troy (BOH-dee, TROI) EDM.

Right wing. Shoots right. 6'4", 213 lbs. Born, Portage La Prairie, Man., January 25, 1985.
(Edmonton's 12th choice, 278th overall, in 2003 Entry Draft).

			Regular Season					Playoffs				
Season	Club	League	GP	G	A	TP	PIM	GP	G	A	TP	PIM
2001-02	Central Plains	MMHL	40	22	21	43	10	....	....	....	....	....
2002-03	Kelowna Rockets	WHL	35	4	4	8	36	11	1	1	2	2
2003-04	Kelowna Rockets	WHL	71	8	12	20	112	17	7	3	10	6

BOHAC, Jan (BOH-hach, YAHN) OTT.

Center. Shoots left. 6'4", 201 lbs. Born, Tabor, Czech., February 3, 1982.
(Ottawa's 4th choice, 87th overall, in 2000 Entry Draft).

			Regular Season					Playoffs				
Season	Club	League	GP	G	A	TP	PIM	GP	G	A	TP	PIM
1997-98	HC Slavia Praha Jr.	Czech-Jr.	39	8	12	20	12	....	....	....	....	....
1998-99	HC Slavia Praha Jr.	Czech-Jr.	35	6	6	12	10	....	....	....	....	....
	HC Slavia Praha	Czech	2	0	0	0	0	....	....	....	....	....
99-2000	HC Slavia Praha Jr.	Czech-Jr.	22	7	8	15	6	7	0	1	1	4
	HC Slavia Praha	Czech	25	1	2	3	4	....	....	....	....	....
2000-01	HC Slavia Praha	Czech	19	2	0	2	0	2	0	0	0	0
	HC Banik Most	Czech-2	5	0	2	2	0	....	....	....	....	....
2001-02	Trinec Jr.	Czech-Jr.	2	0	1	1	0	....	....	....	....	....
	HC Ocelari Trinec	Czech	16	0	1	1	4	....	....	....	....	....
	HC Banik Most	Czech-3	5	0	2	2	0	....	....	....	....	....
	Liberec	Czech-2	10	0	2	2	0	2	0	0	0	0
2002-03	Usti nad Labem	Czech-2	8	0	1	1	2	....	....	....	....	....
	HC Sovan	Czech-2	8	0	1	1	2	....	....	....	....	....
2003-04	HC Briacon	France	15	4	7	11	2	4	1	1	2	0

BOIS, Danny (BOIZ, DA-nee) OTT.

Right wing. Shoots right. 6'1", 210 lbs. Born, Thunder Bay, Ont., June 1, 1983.
(Colorado's 2nd choice, 97th overall, in 2001 Entry Draft).

			Regular Season					Playoffs				
Season	Club	League	GP	G	A	TP	PIM	GP	G	A	TP	PIM
1998-99	Thunder Bay Kings	TBMHL	15	7	12	19	28	....	....	....	....	....
99-2000	Wellington Dukes	MTJHL	37	15	20	35	115	....	....	....	....	....
2000-01	London Knights	OHL	66	21	16	37	218	5	2	1	3	19
2001-02	London Knights	OHL	62	16	14	30	256	12	2	2	4	47
2002-03	London Knights	OHL	56	19	13	32	207	13	4	6	10	38
2003-04	London Knights	OHL	52	14	25	39	242	7	4	4	8	29

Signed as a free agent by **Ottawa**, April 30, 2004.

BOISVERT, Hugo (bwuh-VAIR, HEW-goh)

Center. Shoots left. 6', 200 lbs. Born, St-Eustache, Que., February 11, 1976.

			Regular Season					Playoffs				
Season	Club	League	GP	G	A	TP	PIM	GP	G	A	TP	PIM
1994-95	Cornwall Colts	OCJHL	27	13	19	32	26	....	....	....	....	....
1995-96	Cornwall Colts	OCJHL	54	40	90	130	102	15	15	20	35	44
1996-97	Ohio State	CCHA	38	11	27	38	44	....	....	....	....	....
1997-98	Ohio State	CCHA	42	23	*35	58	70	....	....	....	....	....
1998-99	Ohio State	CCHA	41	24	27	51	54	....	....	....	....	....
99-2000	Team Canada	Nat-Tm	39	10	14	24	12	....	....	....	....	....
2000-01	Orlando	IHL	68	6	12	18	41	16	4	5	9	23
2001-02	Grand Rapids	AHL	74	11	18	29	48	5	1	3	4	4
2002-03	Grand Rapids	AHL	78	18	13	31	68	15	5	1	6	10
2003-04	Grand Rapids	AHL	80	9	16	25	48	4	0	0	0	8

CCHA First All-Star Team (1998, 1999) • NCAA West First All-American Team (1998) • NCAA West Second All-American Team (1999)

Signed as a free agent by **Atlanta**, June 25, 1999.

BOLDUC, Alexandre (bohl-DUHK, ahl-ehx-AHN-druh) ST.L.

Center. Shoots left. 6'1", 178 lbs. Born, Montreal, Que., June 26, 1985.
(St. Louis' 6th choice, 127th overall, in 2003 Entry Draft).

			Regular Season					Playoffs				
Season	Club	League	GP	G	A	TP	PIM	GP	G	A	TP	PIM
2000-01	Notre Dame	SMHL	61	17	35	52	....	....	....	....	....	....
2001-02	Rouyn-Noranda	QMJHL	64	6	14	20	69	4	1	1	2	4
2002-03	Rouyn-Noranda	QMJHL	66	14	29	43	131	4	0	2	2	2
2003-04	Rouyn-Noranda	QMJHL	65	23	35	58	115	11	3	4	7	18

BOLDUC, Jean-Michel (bohl-DUHK, ZHAWN-mee-SHEHL) MIN.

Defense. Shoots left. 6'4", 190 lbs. Born, Portland, ME, February 27, 1985.
(Minnesota's 9th choice, 281st overall, in 2003 Entry Draft).

			Regular Season					Playoffs				
Season	Club	League	GP	G	A	TP	PIM	GP	G	A	TP	PIM
99-2000	Jonquiere Elites	QAAA	4	0	0	0	4	....	....	....	....	....
2000-01	Jonquiere Elites	QAAA	36	6	10	16	58	1	0	0	0	10
2001-02	Quebec Remparts	QMJHL	68	2	9	11	54	9	0	2	2	13
2002-03	Quebec Remparts	QMJHL	68	5	14	19	164	10	0	0	0	37
2003-04	Rimouski Oceanic	QMJHL	63	8	42	50	133	9	1	4	5	12

BOLF, Lukas (BAWLF, LOO-kahsh) PIT.

Defense. Shoots left. 6'1", 190 lbs. Born, Vrchlabi, Czech., February 20, 1985.
(Pittsburgh's 7th choice, 169th overall, in 2003 Entry Draft).

			Regular Season					Playoffs				
Season	Club	League	GP	G	A	TP	PIM	GP	G	A	TP	PIM
99-2000	Karlovy Vary Jr.	Czech-Jr.	43	2	7	9	57	....	....	....	....	....
2000-01	Sparta Praha 18	Czech-Jr.	42	4	13	17	54	....	....	....	....	....
2001-02	Hameenlinna B	Finn-Jr.	6	1	5	6	12	1	0	0	0	0
	Hameenlinna	Finn-Jr.	25	0	4	4	18	5	0	0	0	2
	Sparta Praha Jr.	Czech-Jr.	21	2	3	5	35	....	....	....	....	....
2002-03	Sparta Praha Jr.	Czech-Jr.	28	3	7	10	....	....	....	....	....	....
2003-04	Barrie Colts	OHL	56	2	18	20	42	12	0	2	2	26

BOLLAND, Dave (BOHL-uhnd, DAYV) CHI.

Center. Shoots right. 6', 168 lbs. Born, Toronto, Ont., June 5, 1986.
(Chicago's 2nd choice, 32nd overall, in 2004 Entry Draft).

			Regular Season					Playoffs				
Season	Club	League	GP	G	A	TP	PIM	GP	G	A	TP	PIM
2000-01	Tor. Red Wings	GTHL	95	79	67	146	....	....	....	....	....	....
2001-02	Tor. Red Wings	GTHL	36	35	35	70	40	....	....	....	....	....
2002-03	London Knights	OHL	64	7	10	17	21	14	2	1	3	2
2003-04	London Knights	OHL	65	37	30	67	58	15	3	10	13	18

BONDAREV, Arseny (BAWN-duh-rehv, ar-SEH-nee) N.J.

Left wing. Shoots left. 6', 185 lbs. Born, Tomichi, USSR, April 9, 1985.
(New Jersey's 7th choice, 292nd overall, in 2003 Entry Draft).

			Regular Season					Playoffs				
Season	Club	League	GP	G	A	TP	PIM	GP	G	A	TP	PIM
2001-02	Yaroslavl Jr.	Russia-Jr.	29	18	18	36	36	7	2	3	5	10
	Yaroslavl 2	Russia-3	11	0	1	1	4	....	....	....	....	....
2002-03	Yaroslavl 2	Russia-3		STATISTICS NOT AVAILABLE								
	Yaroslavl Jr.	Russia-Jr.	....	....	....	....	....	3	2	1	3	0
2003-04	Yaroslavl 2	Russia-3	56	14	12	26	96	....	....	....	....	....

BONNEAU, Jimmy (BAW-noh, JIHM-mee) MTL.

Left wing. Shoots left. 6'3", 224 lbs. Born, Baie-Comeau, Que., March 22, 1985.
(Montreal's 10th choice, 241st overall, in 2003 Entry Draft).

			Regular Season					Playoffs				
Season	Club	League	GP	G	A	TP	PIM	GP	G	A	TP	PIM
2000-01	Jonquiere Elites	QAAA	1	0	0	0	0	....	....	....	....	....
2001-02	Jonquiere Elites	QAAA	40	5	10	15	55	3	1	1	2	2
2002-03	Montreal Rocket	QMJHL	65	1	5	6	261	7	0	0	0	12
2003-04	PEI Rocket	QMJHL	70	7	12	19	263	11	1	0	1	12

BOOGAARD, Derek (BOO-gard, DAIR-ihk) MIN.

Left wing. Shoots right. 6'7", 250 lbs. Born, Saskatoon, Sask., June 23, 1982.
(Minnesota's 6th choice, 202nd overall, in 2001 Entry Draft).

			Regular Season					Playoffs				
Season	Club	League	GP	G	A	TP	PIM	GP	G	A	TP	PIM
1998-99	Regina Caps	SJHL	35	2	3	5	166	....	....	....	....	....
99-2000	Regina Pats	WHL	5	0	0	0	17	....	....	....	....	....
	Prince George	WHL	33	0	0	0	149	....	....	....	....	....
2000-01	Prince George	WHL	61	1	8	9	245	6	1	0	1	31
2001-02	Prince George	WHL	2	0	0	0	16	....	....	....	....	....
	Medicine Hat	WHL	46	1	8	9	178	....	....	....	....	....
2002-03	Medicine Hat	WHL	27	1	2	3	65	....	....	....	....	....
	Louisiana	ECHL	33	1	2	3	240	2	0	0	0	0
2003-04	Houston Aeros	AHL	53	0	4	4	207	2	0	1	1	16

• Released by **Medicine Hat** (WHL) and signed as a free agent by **Louisiana** (ECHL), December 13, 2002.

BOOTH, David (BOOTH, DAY-vihd) FLA.

Left wing. Shoots left. 6', 212 lbs. Born, Detroit, MI, November 24, 1984.
(Florida's 3rd choice, 53rd overall, in 2004 Entry Draft).

			Regular Season					Playoffs				
Season	Club	League	GP	G	A	TP	PIM	GP	G	A	TP	PIM
99-2000	Det. Honeybaked	MWEHL		STATISTICS NOT AVAILABLE								
2000-01	Det. Compuware	NAJHL	42	17	13	30	44	2	1	0	1	2
2001-02	U.S. National U-18	USDP	58	17	12	29	41	....	....	....	....	....
2002-03	Michigan State	CCHA	39	17	19	36	53	....	....	....	....	....
2003-04	Michigan State	CCHA	30	8	10	18	30	....	....	....	....	....

CCHA All-Rookie Team (2003)

BORDELEAU, Patrick (BOHR-duh-loh, PAT-rihk) MIN.

Left wing. Shoots left. 6'5", 195 lbs. Born, Montreal, Que., March 23, 1986.
(Minnesota's 6th choice, 114th overall, in 2004 Entry Draft).

			Regular Season					Playoffs				
Season	Club	League	GP	G	A	TP	PIM	GP	G	A	TP	PIM
2002-03	Gatineau Intrepide	QAAA	39	8	13	21	50	....	....	....	....	....
2003-04	Val-d'Or Foreurs	QMJHL	68	7	11	18	97	7	1	1	2	8

BORER, Casey (BOHR-uhr, KAY-see) CAR.

Defense. Shoots left. 6'2", 197 lbs. Born, Minneapolis, MN, July 28, 1985.
(Carolina's 3rd choice, 69th overall, in 2004 Entry Draft).

			Regular Season					Playoffs				
Season	Club	League	GP	G	A	TP	PIM	GP	G	A	TP	PIM
2001-02	Shat.-St. Mary's	Hi-School		STATISTICS NOT AVAILABLE								
2002-03	U.S. National U-18	USDP	56	3	4	7	46	....	....	....	....	....
2003-04	St. Cloud State	WCHA	31	0	8	8	18	....	....	....	....	....

BORNHAMMAR, David (BOHRN-ham-uhr, DAY-vihd) WSH.

Defense. Shoots left. 6', 180 lbs. Born, Lidingo, Sweden, June 15, 1981.
(Washington's 8th choice, 192nd overall, in 1999 Entry Draft).

			Regular Season					Playoffs				
Season	Club	League	GP	G	A	TP	PIM	GP	G	A	TP	PIM
1997-98	AIK Solna Jr.	Swede-Jr.	13	0	1	1	10	....	....	....	....	....
1998-99	AIK Solna Jr.	Swede-Jr.	33	5	5	10	30	....	....	....	....	....
99-2000	Kelowna Rockets	WHL	62	3	24	27	36	2	0	0	0	0
2000-01	AIK Solna Jr.	Swede-Jr.	10	0	3	3	37	....	....	....	....	....
	AIK Solna	Sweden	37	4	2	6	57	4	0	1	1	0
2001-02	AIK Solna	Sweden	48	1	6	7	34	....	....	....	....	....
	AIK Solna	Swede-Q	8	0	1	1	4	....	....	....	....	....
2002-03	AIK Solna	Swede-2	50	8	9	17	32	4	1	0	1	8
2003-04	Blue Devils Weiden	German-2	25	5	8	13	18	....	....	....	....	....

• Name when drafted was David Johannson.

BOURQUE, Chris (BOHRK, KRIHS) WSH.

Center. Shoots left. 5'7", 170 lbs. Born, Boston, MA, January 29, 1986.
(Washington's 4th choice, 33rd overall, in 2004 Entry Draft).

			Regular Season					Playoffs				
Season	Club	League	GP	G	A	TP	PIM	GP	G	A	TP	PIM
2002-03	Cushing Academy	Hi-School	28	31	26	57	49	....	....	....	....	....
2003-04	Cushing Academy	Hi-School	31	37	53	90	96	....	....	....	....	....

BOURQUE, Rene (BOHRK, reh-NAY) CHI.

Left wing. Shoots left. 6'2", 205 lbs. Born, Lac La Biche, Alta., December 10, 1981.

			Regular Season					Playoffs				
Season	Club	League	GP	G	A	TP	PIM	GP	G	A	TP	PIM
2000-01	U. of Wisconsin	WCHA	32	10	5	15	18	....	....	....	....	....
2001-02	U. of Wisconsin	WCHA	38	12	7	19	26	....	....	....	....	....
2002-03	U. of Wisconsin	WCHA	40	19	8	27	54	....	....	....	....	....
2003-04	U. of Wisconsin	WCHA	42	16	20	36	74	....	....	....	....	....

Signed as a free agent by **Chicago**, July 29, 2004.

BOYCHUK, Johnny (BOI-chuhk, JAW-nee) COL.

Defense. Shoots right. 6'2", 215 lbs. Born, Edmonton, Alta., January 19, 1984.
(Colorado's 2nd choice, 61st overall, in 2002 Entry Draft).

			Regular Season					Playoffs				
Season	Club	League	GP	G	A	TP	PIM	GP	G	A	TP	PIM
1998-99	Edm. Cycle	AMBHL	36	8	20	28	59	....	....	....	....	....
99-2000	Edm. Cycle	AMHL	35	6	17	23	59	....	....	....	....	....
2000-01	Calgary Hitmen	WHL	66	4	8	12	61	12	1	1	2	17
2001-02	Calgary Hitmen	WHL	70	8	32	40	85	7	1	1	2	6
2002-03	Calgary Hitmen	WHL	40	8	18	26	58	....	....	....	....	....
	Moose Jaw	WHL	27	5	17	22	32	13	2	6	8	29
2003-04	Moose Jaw	WHL	62	13	20	33	71	10	1	9	10	9

BOYD, Dustin (BOID, DUHS-tihn) CGY.

Center. Shoots left. 6', 186 lbs. Born, Winnipeg, Man., July 16, 1986.
(Calgary's 3rd choice, 98th overall, in 2004 Entry Draft).

			Regular Season					Playoffs				
Season	Club	League	GP	G	A	TP	PIM	GP	G	A	TP	PIM
2001-02	Winnipeg Warriors	MMHL	40	50	57	107	16	....	....	....	....	....
2002-03	Moose Jaw	WHL	63	11	17	28	15	13	0	3	3	2
2003-04	Moose Jaw	WHL	72	18	20	38	40	10	2	2	4	8

BOYLE, Brian (BOIL, BRIGH-uhn) L.A.

Center. Shoots left. 6'6", 222 lbs. Born, Dorchester, MA, December 18, 1984.
(Los Angeles' 2nd choice, 26th overall, in 2003 Entry Draft).

			Regular Season					Playoffs				
Season	Club	League	GP	G	A	TP	PIM	GP	G	A	TP	PIM
2000-01	St. Sebastian's	Hi-School	25	20	19	39	....	....	....	....	....	....
2001-02	St. Sebastian's	Hi-School	28	21	26	47	22	....	....	....	....	....
2002-03	St. Sebastian's	Hi-School	31	32	31	62	46	....	....	....	....	....
2003-04	Boston College	H-East	35	5	3	8	36	....	....	....	....	....

BRAXENHOLM, Per (BRAX-ehn-hohlm, PAIR) NYI

Defense. Shoots left. 6'3", 215 lbs. Born, Karlskrona, Sweden, October 31, 1983.
(NY Islanders' 7th choice, 283rd overall, in 2002 Entry Draft).

			Regular Season					Playoffs				
Season	Club	League	GP	G	A	TP	PIM	GP	G	A	TP	PIM
2001-02	Morrum GoIS IK	Swede-2	25	0	2	2	2	....	....	....	....	....
	Kallinge/Ronneby	Swede-2	1	1	0	1	4	....	....	....	....	....
2002-03	Morrum GoIS IK	Swede-2	37	1	1	2	8	2	0	0	0	0
2003-04	Morrum GoIS IK	Swede-2	27	1	0	1	18	....	....	....	....	....

BRENK, Jake (BREHNK, JAYK) EDM.

Center. Shoots right. 6'2", 187 lbs. Born, Detroit Lakes, MN, April 16, 1982.
(Edmonton's 6th choice, 154th overall, in 2001 Entry Draft).

			Regular Season					Playoffs				
Season	Club	League	GP	G	A	TP	PIM	GP	G	A	TP	PIM
99-2000	Breck Mustangs	Hi-School	28	18	23	41	....	....	....	....	....	....
2000-01	Breck Mustangs	Hi-School	22	28	30	58	22	....	....	....	....	....
2001-02	Minnesota State	WCHA	21	3	3	6	6	....	....	....	....	....
2002-03	Minnesota State	WCHA	36	3	9	12	38	....	....	....	....	....
2003-04	Minnesota State	WCHA	30	4	7	11	36	....	....	....	....	....

BRENT, Tim (BREHNT, TIHM) ANA.

Center. Shoots right. 6', 180 lbs. Born, Cambridge, Ont., March 10, 1984.
(Anaheim's 3rd choice, 75th overall, in 2004 Entry Draft).

			Regular Season					Playoffs				
Season	Club	League	GP	G	A	TP	PIM	GP	G	A	TP	PIM
99-2000	Cambridge	OJHL-B	40	19	16	35	42	....	....	....	....	....
2000-01	St. Michael's	OHL	64	9	19	28	31	18	2	8	10	6
2001-02	St. Michael's	OHL	61	19	40	59	52	14	7	12	19	20
2002-03	St. Michael's	OHL	60	24	42	66	74	19	7	17	24	14
2003-04	St. Michael's	OHL	53	26	41	67	105	18	4	13	17	24

• Re-entered NHL Entry Draft. Originally Anaheim's 2nd choice, 37th overall, in 2002 Entry Draft.

BRODZIAK, Kyle (brohd-ZEE-ak, KIGHL) EDM.

Center. Shoots right. 6'2", 198 lbs. Born, St. Paul, Alta., May 25, 1984.
(Edmonton's 9th choice, 214th overall, in 2003 Entry Draft).

			Regular Season					Playoffs				
Season	Club	League	GP	G	A	TP	PIM	GP	G	A	TP	PIM
99-2000	Ft. Saskatchewan	AMBHL	36	23	33	56	57	....	....	....	....	....
	Moose Jaw	WHL	2	0	0	0	0	....	....	....	....	....
2000-01	Moose Jaw	WHL	57	2	8	10	49	3	0	0	0	0
2001-02	Moose Jaw	WHL	72	8	12	20	56	12	0	3	3	11
2002-03	Moose Jaw	WHL	72	32	30	62	84	13	5	3	8	16
2003-04	Moose Jaw	WHL	70	39	54	93	58	10	5	4	9	10

WHL East First All-Star Team (2004)

BROOKBANK, Sheldon (BRUK-bank, SHEHL-dohn) ANA.

Defense. Shoots right. 6'2", 200 lbs. Born, Lanigan, Sask., October 3, 1980.

			Regular Season					Playoffs				
Season	Club	League	GP	G	A	TP	PIM	GP	G	A	TP	PIM
2000-01	Humboldt Broncos	SJHL	59	14	35	49	281	....	....	....	....	....
2001-02	Mississippi	ECHL	62	8	21	29	137	10	1	4	5	27
	Grand Rapids	AHL	6	0	1	1	24	....	....	....	....	....
2002-03	Grand Rapids	AHL	69	2	11	13	136	15	1	3	4	28
2003-04	Cincinnati	AHL	74	2	9	11	216	9	0	2	2	20

Signed as a free agent by **Anaheim**, July 21, 2003.

BROOKS, Alex (BROOKS, AL-ehx) **N.J.**

Defense. Shoots right. 6'1", 205 lbs. Born, Madison, WI, August 21, 1976.

			Regular Season					Playoffs				
Season	Club	League	GP	G	A	TP	PIM	GP	G	A	TP	PIM
1993-94	Madison Capitols	USHL	13	3	11	14	....	....	....	....	....	....
1994-95	Madison West	Hi-School	24	13	28	41	....	....	....	....	....	....
1995-96	Green Bay	USHL	46	3	22	25	....	....	....	....	....	....
1996-97	U. of Wisconsin	WCHA	DID NOT PLAY – INJURED									
1997-98	U. of Wisconsin	WCHA	40	1	4	5	72	....	....	....	....	....
1998-99	U. of Wisconsin	WCHA	37	0	3	3	73	....	....	....	....	....
99-2000	U. of Wisconsin	WCHA	41	4	10	14	78	....	....	....	....	....
2000-01	U. of Wisconsin	WCHA	41	3	16	19	76	....	....	....	....	....
2001-02	Jokerit Helsinki	Finland	53	1	3	4	109	12	0	0	0	11
2002-03	Albany River Rats	AHL	66	0	7	7	56	....	....	....	....	....
2003-04	Albany River Rats	AHL	77	2	6	8	100	....	....	....	....	....

• Missed entire 1996-97 season recovering from back injury suffered during off-season training, August, 1996. • Signed as a free agent by **New Jersey**, July 12, 2002.

BROS, Michal (BROHSH, MEE-khahl) **MIN.**

Center. Shoots right. 6'1", 195 lbs. Born, Olomouc, Czech., January 25, 1976.
(San Jose's 6th choice, 130th overall, in 1995 Entry Draft).

			Regular Season					Playoffs				
Season	Club	League	GP	G	A	TP	PIM	GP	G	A	TP	PIM
1994-95	HC Olomouc Jr.	Czech-Jr.	34	29	32	61	....	....	....	....	....	....
1995-96	HC Olomouc	Czech	35	8	11	19	....	4	2	0	2	....
1996-97	HC Olomouc	Czech	50	13	14	27	28	....	....	....	....	....
1997-98	HC Petra Vsetin	Czech	47	14	18	32	28	10	3	1	4	2
	HC Petra Vsetin	EuroHL	9	3	0	3	2	....	....	....	....	....
1998-99	HC Slovnaft Vsetin	Czech	42	10	18	28	18	12	1	3	4	....
99-2000	HC Sparta Praha	Czech	49	6	30	36	49	9	1	3	4	4
2000-01	HC Sparta Praha	Czech	27	3	13	16	22	13	4	6	10	8
2001-02	HC Sparta Praha	Czech	48	19	29	48	71	13	7	*11	*18	8
2002-03	HC Sparta Praha	Czech	40	13	17	30	90	10	2	4	6	8
2003-04	HC Sparta Praha	Czech	46	15	25	40	60	13	1	3	4	6

Selected by **Minnesota** from **San Jose** in Expansion Draft, June 23, 2000.

BROWN, Marc (BROWN, MAHRK)

Left wing. Shoots left. 6'1", 196 lbs. Born, White Rock, B.C., March 10, 1979.

			Regular Season					Playoffs				
Season	Club	League	GP	G	A	TP	PIM	GP	G	A	TP	PIM
1995-96	Abbotsford Pilots	PIJHL	35	20	15	35	15	....	....	....	....	....
1996-97	Spokane Chiefs	WHL	52	4	8	12	37	2	0	0	0	0
1997-98	Spokane Chiefs	WHL	41	10	15	25	35	....	....	....	....	....
	Prince Albert	WHL	23	6	8	14	21	....	....	....	....	....
1998-99	Prince Albert	WHL	72	35	45	80	47	14	12	6	18	6
99-2000	Worcester IceCats	AHL	72	13	11	24	24	17	3	1	4	0
2000-01	Worcester IceCats	AHL	34	9	10	19	27	10	0	1	1	6
2001-02	Worcester IceCats	AHL	74	30	25	55	42	3	2	2	4	0
2002-03	Worcester IceCats	AHL	58	13	15	28	24	....	....	....	....	....
2003-04	Worcester IceCats	AHL	65	14	20	34	34	7	0	1	1	0

Signed as a free agent by **St. Louis**, September 24, 1999. • Missed majority of 2000-01 season recovering from abdominal injury suffered in training camp, September 27, 2000.

BROWN, Mike (BROWN, MIGHK) **VAN.**

Right wing. Shoots right. 6', 210 lbs. Born, Northbrook, IL, June 24, 1985.
(Vancouver's 4th choice, 159th overall, in 2004 Entry Draft).

			Regular Season					Playoffs				
Season	Club	League	GP	G	A	TP	PIM	GP	G	A	TP	PIM
2000-01	Chicago Chill	USAHA	66	27	23	50	....	....	....	....	....	....
2001-02	U.S. National U-17	USDP	63	11	15	26	69	....	....	....	....	....
2002-03	U.S. National U-18	USDP	43	5	6	11	45	....	....	....	....	....
2003-04	U. of Michigan	CCHA	42	8	5	13	51	....	....	....	....	....

BROWN, Paul (BROWN, PAWL) **NSH.**

Right wing. Shoots right. 6'2", 184 lbs. Born, Edmonton, Alta., July 21, 1984.
(Nashville's 6th choice, 89th overall, in 2003 Entry Draft).

			Regular Season					Playoffs				
Season	Club	League	GP	G	A	TP	PIM	GP	G	A	TP	PIM
99-2000	Prince George	BCAHA	65	84	120	204	260	....	....	....	....	....
	Regina Pats	WHL	3	0	0	0	0	....	....	....	....	....
2000-01	Regina Pats	WHL	33	3	1	4	83	....	....	....	....	....
	Kamloops Blazers	WHL	30	6	11	17	118	2	0	0	0	4
2001-02	Kamloops Blazers	WHL	37	7	12	19	130	1	0	0	0	0
2002-03	Kamloops Blazers	WHL	67	21	36	57	231	6	3	0	3	20
2003-04	Kamloops Blazers	WHL	59	11	20	31	222	5	0	1	1	13

• Missed majority of 2001-02 season recovering from off-season ankle injury, August 20, 2001.

BROWNLEE, Chad (BROWN-lee, CHAD) **VAN.**

Defense. Shoots right. 6'2", 184 lbs. Born, Kelowna, B.C., July 12, 1984.
(Vancouver's 6th choice, 190th overall, in 2003 Entry Draft).

			Regular Season					Playoffs				
Season	Club	League	GP	G	A	TP	PIM	GP	G	A	TP	PIM
2001-02	Vernon Vipers	BCHL	55	6	12	18	62	....	....	....	....	....
2002-03	Vernon Vipers	BCHL	58	8	16	24	63	18	2	7	9	14
2003-04	Minnesota State	WCHA	35	2	1	3	44	....	....	....	....	....

BRUNELLE, Mathieu (broo-nehl, MA-tyew) **PHI.**

Left wing. Shoots left. 5'11", 180 lbs. Born, Warwick, Que., April 6, 1983.
(Philadelphia's 7th choice, 201st overall, in 2002 Entry Draft).

			Regular Season					Playoffs				
Season	Club	League	GP	G	A	TP	PIM	GP	G	A	TP	PIM
99-2000	Magog	QAAA	42	26	31	57	64	19	8	7	15	20
2000-01	Victoriaville Tigers	QMJHL	65	7	11	18	39	13	1	1	2	0
2001-02	Victoriaville Tigers	QMJHL	72	43	64	107	105	14	7	6	13	35
2002-03	Victoriaville Tigres	QMJHL	39	21	29	50	75	....	....	....	....	....
	Hull Olympiques	QMJHL	31	17	19	36	42	20	*22	16	38	20
2003-04	Philadelphia	AHL	7	0	1	1	2	....	....	....	....	....
	Trenton Titans	ECHL	64	26	30	56	100	....	....	....	....	....

BUCKLEY, Brendan (BUHK-lee, BREHN-duhn)

Defense. Shoots right. 6'1", 205 lbs. Born, Needham, MA, February 26, 1977.
(Anaheim's 3rd choice, 117th overall, in 1996 Entry Draft).

			Regular Season					Playoffs				
Season	Club	League	GP	G	A	TP	PIM	GP	G	A	TP	PIM
1994-95	Boston Jr. Bruins	Exhib.	48	22	43	65	164	....	....	....	....	....
1995-96	Boston College	H-East	34	0	4	4	72	....	....	....	....	....
1996-97	Boston College	H-East	38	2	6	8	90	....	....	....	....	....
1997-98	Boston College	H-East	41	1	12	13	69	....	....	....	....	....
1998-99	Boston College	H-East	43	1	13	14	75	....	....	....	....	....
99-2000	Cincinnati	AHL	4	0	0	0	6	....	....	....	....	....
	Quad City	UHL	61	1	10	11	73	9	1	0	1	10
2000-01	Wilkes-Barre	AHL	63	2	8	10	62	21	0	2	2	33
2001-02	Wilkes-Barre	AHL	80	1	19	20	116	....	....	....	....	....
2002-03	Wilkes-Barre	AHL	80	2	6	8	99	6	0	0	0	2
2003-04	Wilkes-Barre	AHL	45	2	4	6	61	....	....	....	....	....
	Syracuse Crunch	AHL	30	0	4	4	40	7	0	0	0	14

Signed as a free agent by **Pittsburgh**, September 28, 2000. Traded to **Columbus** by **Pittsburgh** for Pauli Levokari, February 10, 2004.

BULATOV, Alexei (boo-LA-tahf, al-EHX-ay) **NYR**

Right wing. Shoots left. 6'1", 185 lbs. Born, Sverdlovsk, USSR, January 24, 1978.
(NY Rangers' 11th choice, 254th overall, in 1999 Entry Draft).

			Regular Season					Playoffs				
Season	Club	League	GP	G	A	TP	PIM	GP	G	A	TP	PIM
1996-97	Yekaterinburg	Russia	20	2	4	6	2	....	....	....	....	....
	Yekaterinburg	Russia-Q	22	6	6	12	10	....	....	....	....	....
1997-98	Yekaterinburg	Russia	15	5	3	8	10	....	....	....	....	....
	Yekaterinburg	Russia-Q	22	7	6	13	14	....	....	....	....	....
1998-99	Yekaterinburg	Russia-2	47	21	16	37	24	....	....	....	....	....
99-2000	Cherepovets	Russia	9	1	0	1	0	....	....	....	....	....
	Ufa Salavat	Russia	6	0	3	3	2	....	....	....	....	....
	CSK VVS Samara	Russia	6	0	0	0	2	....	....	....	....	....
2000-01	Magnitogorsk	Russia	32	2	3	5	4	....	....	....	....	....
2001-02	Novokuznetsk	Russia	25	2	6	8	6	....	....	....	....	....
2002-03	Moskovik Kurgan	Russia-2	25	8	8	16	12	....	....	....	....	....
2003-04	Zauralje Kurgan	Russia-2	28	5	7	12	51	4	0	0	0	27

BUMAGIN, Yevgeny (boo-MA-gihn, yehv-GEH-nee) **DET.**

Center. Shoots left. 6', 170 lbs. Born, Belgorod, USSR, April 7, 1982.
(Detroit's 11th choice, 260th overall, in 2000 Entry Draft).

			Regular Season					Playoffs				
Season	Club	League	GP	G	A	TP	PIM	GP	G	A	TP	PIM
1997-98	Lada Togliatti 2	Russia-3	7	0	0	0	2	....	....	....	....	....
1998-99	Lada Togliatti 2	Russia-4	40	7	8	15	22	....	....	....	....	....
99-2000	Lada Togliatti 2	Russia-3	36	23	8	31	....	....	....	....	....	....
2000-01	CSK VVS Samara	Russia-2	13	1	0	1	10	....	....	....	....	....
2001-02	Dizelist Penza	Russia-2	40	2	0	2	0	....	....	....	....	....
2002-03	Motor Barnaul	Russia-2	41	4	3	7	14	....	....	....	....	....
2003-04	Karaganda	Russia-2	15	4	1	5	4	....	....	....	....	....

BURISH, Adam (BUHR-ish, A-duhm) **CHI.**

Right wing. Shoots right. 6'1", 189 lbs. Born, Madison, WI, January 6, 1983.
(Chicago's 9th choice, 282nd overall, in 2002 Entry Draft).

			Regular Season					Playoffs				
Season	Club	League	GP	G	A	TP	PIM	GP	G	A	TP	PIM
2000-01	Edgewood High	Hi-School	22	25	30	55	22	....	....	....	....	....
2001-02	Green Bay	USHL	61	24	33	57	122	1	0	0	0	0
2002-03	U. of Wisconsin	WCHA	19	0	6	6	32	....	....	....	....	....
2003-04	U. of Wisconsin	WCHA	43	6	13	19	63	....	....	....	....	....

BURKHALTER, Loic (buhrk-HAHL-tuhr, LOIK) **PHX.**

Center. Shoots left. 6', 202 lbs. Born, La Chaux-de-Fonds, Switz., February 11, 1980.
(Phoenix's 8th choice, 290th overall, in 2003 Entry Draft).

			Regular Season					Playoffs				
Season	Club	League	GP	G	A	TP	PIM	GP	G	A	TP	PIM
1996-97	Chaux-de-Fonds	Swiss	24	1	0	1	0	....	....	....	....	....
1997-98	Chaux-de-Fonds Jr.	Swiss-Jr.	4	4	2	6	16	....	....	....	....	....
	Chaux-de-Fonds	Swiss	36	3	4	7	8	12	1	0	1	2
1998-99	Chaux-de-Fonds	Swiss-2	38	19	29	48	28	12	4	8	12	10
99-2000	Rapperswil	Swiss	44	7	5	12	16	11	2	9	11	0
2000-01	Rapperswil	Swiss	31	7	5	12	20	4	1	1	2	0
2001-02	HC Ambri-Piotta	Switz	44	9	12	21	28	6	2	2	4	6
2002-03	HC Ambri-Piotta	Switz.	44	12	22	34	42	4	1	0	1	2
2003-04	HC Ambri-Piotta	Swiss	47	21	26	47	40	7	1	2	3	4

BUT, Anton (BOOT, AN-tawn) **T.B.**

Left wing. Shoots left. 6'1", 190 lbs. Born, Kharkov, USSR, July 3, 1980.
(New Jersey's 7th choice, 119th overall, in 1998 Entry Draft).

			Regular Season					Playoffs				
Season	Club	League	GP	G	A	TP	PIM	GP	G	A	TP	PIM
1995-96	Yaroslavl 2	CIS-2	60	30	12	42	10	....	....	....	....	....
1996-97	Yaroslavl 2	Russia-3	70	30	20	50	20	....	....	....	....	....
1997-98	Yaroslavl 2	Russia-2	48	12	5	17	28	....	....	....	....	....
1998-99	Yaroslavl 2	Russia-3	22	12	8	20	59	....	....	....	....	....
	Torpedo Yaroslavl	Russia	5	0	0	0	0	....	....	....	....	....
99-2000	Yaroslavl 2	Russia-3	1	0	0	0	2	....	....	....	....	....
	Torpedo Yaroslavl	Russia	26	2	5	7	16	8	2	1	3	0
2000-01	Yaroslavl	Russia	42	14	6	20	14	11	1	3	4	8
2001-02	Yaroslavl	Russia	48	14	11	25	14	6	0	1	1	2
2002-03	Yaroslavl	Russia	44	16	13	29	16	9	1	2	3	6
2003-04	Yaroslavl	Russia	51	11	10	21	24	3	0	0	0	0

Rights traded to **Tampa Bay** by **New Jersey** with Josef Boumedienne and Sascha Goc for Andrei Zyuzin, November 9, 2001.

BUTURLIN, Alexander (boo-tuhr-LIHN, AL-ehx-an-DEHR) **MTL.**

Right wing. Shoots left. 5'11", 182 lbs. Born, Moscow, USSR, September 3, 1981.
(Montreal's 1st choice, 39th overall, in 1999 Entry Draft).

			Regular Season					Playoffs				
Season	Club	League	GP	G	A	TP	PIM	GP	G	A	TP	PIM
1997-98	CSKA Moscow 2	Russia-3	50	12	15	27	46	....	....	....	....	....
	CSKA Moscow	Russia	2	0	0	0	0	....	....	....	....	....
1998-99	CSKA Moscow	Russia	16	1	0	1	6	3	1	0	1	2
99-2000	Sarnia Sting	OHL	57	20	27	47	46	7	4	2	6	12
2000-01	Sarnia Sting	OHL	57	28	37	65	27	4	3	1	4	0
2001-02	Ufa Salavat	Russia	32	3	3	6	42	....	....	....	....	....
2002-03	Lada Togliatti	Russia	49	6	14	20	71	10	3	0	3	4
2003-04	Lada Togliatti	Russia	53	7	13	20	78	6	0	1	1	4

BYERS, Dane (BIGH-uhrs, DAYN) NYR

Left wing. Shoots left. 6'2", 189 lbs. Born, Nipawin, Sask., February 21, 1986.
(NY Rangers' 4th choice, 48th overall, in 2004 Entry Draft).

			Regular Season					Playoffs				
Season	Club	League	GP	G	A	TP	PIM	GP	G	A	TP	PIM
2001-02	Prince Albert	SMMHL		STATISTICS NOT AVAILABLE								
2002-03	Prince Albert	WHL	49	8	6	14	46	....	....	....	....	....
2003-04	Prince Albert	WHL	51	9	8	17	134	6	1	2	3	17

BYFUGLIEN, Dustin (bigh-FEWG-lehn, DUHS-tihn) CHI.

Defense. Shoots right. 6'3", 275 lbs. Born, Minneapolis, MN, March 27, 1985.
(Chicago's 8th choice, 245th overall, in 2003 Entry Draft).

			Regular Season					Playoffs				
Season	Club	League	GP	G	A	TP	PIM	GP	G	A	TP	PIM
2001-02	Chicago Mission	MAHL	52	32	30	62	40	....	....	....	....	....
	Brandon	WHL	3	0	0	0	0	....	....	....	....	....
2002-03	Brandon	WHL	8	1	1	2	4	....	....	....	....	....
	Prince George	WHL	48	9	28	37	74	5	1	3	4	12
2003-04	Prince George	WHL	66	16	29	45	137	....	....	....	....	....

BYRNE, Trevor (BUHR-ne, TREH-vuhr) ST.L.

Defense. Shoots left. 6'3", 205 lbs. Born, Hingham, MA, May 7, 1980.
(St. Louis' 4th choice, 143rd overall, in 1999 Entry Draft).

			Regular Season					Playoffs				
Season	Club	League	GP	G	A	TP	PIM	GP	G	A	TP	PIM
1997-98	Deerfield Academy	Hi-School	25	5	14	19	16	....	....	....	....	....
1998-99	Deerfield Academy	Hi-School	25	9	19	28	22	....	....	....	....	....
99-2000	Dartmouth	ECAC	30	3	9	12	40	....	....	....	....	....
2000-01	Dartmouth	ECAC	34	5	21	26	52	....	....	....	....	....
2001-02	Dartmouth	ECAC	32	5	16	21	38	....	....	....	....	....
2002-03	Dartmouth	ECAC	34	8	16	24	28	....	....	....	....	....
2003-04	Worcester IceCats	AHL	63	7	13	20	22	9	2	2	4	2
	Peoria Rivermen	ECHL	6	0	0	0	0	....	....	....	....	....

ECAC Second All-Star Team (2001, 2002, 2003)

CALDWELL, Ryan (KAWLD-wehl, RIGH-uhn) NYI

Defense. Shoots left. 6'2", 174 lbs. Born, Deloraine, Man., June 15, 1981.
(NY Islanders' 7th choice, 202nd overall, in 2000 Entry Draft).

			Regular Season					Playoffs				
Season	Club	League	GP	G	A	TP	PIM	GP	G	A	TP	PIM
1998-99	Shat.-St. Mary's	Hi-School	29	24	55	79	22	....	....	....	....	....
99-2000	Thunder Bay Flyers	USHL	46	3	20	23	152	....	....	....	....	....
2000-01	U. of Denver	WCHA	36	3	20	23	76	....	....	....	....	....
2001-02	U. of Denver	WCHA	40	3	16	19	76	....	....	....	....	....
2002-03	U. of Denver	WCHA	38	5	14	19	58	....	....	....	....	....
2003-04	U. of Denver	WCHA	42	15	12	27	96	....	....	....	....	....

WCHA All-Rookie Team (2001) • WCHA Second All-Star Team (2004) • NCAA West First All-American Team (2004) • NCAA Championship All-Tournament Team (2004)

CALLAHAN, Joe (kal-AH-han, JOH) PHX.

Defense. Shoots right. 6'3", 219 lbs. Born, Brockton, MA, December 20, 1982.
(Phoenix's 4th choice, 70th overall, in 2002 Entry Draft).

			Regular Season					Playoffs				
Season	Club	League	GP	G	A	TP	PIM	GP	G	A	TP	PIM
2000-01	B.C. High Irish	Hi-School		STATISTICS NOT AVAILABLE								
2001-02	Yale University	ECAC	31	3	8	11	20	....	....	....	....	....
2002-03	Yale University	ECAC	32	2	11	13	38	....	....	....	....	....
2003-04	Yale University	ECAC	31	6	14	20	38	....	....	....	....	....
	Springfield Falcons	AHL	13	0	4	4	12	....	....	....	....	....

CALLAHAN, Ryan (kal-AH-han, RIGH-uhn) NYR

Right wing. Shoots right. 5'10", 175 lbs. Born, Rochester, NY, March 21, 1985.
(NY Rangers' 9th choice, 127th overall, in 2004 Entry Draft).

			Regular Season					Playoffs				
Season	Club	League	GP	G	A	TP	PIM	GP	G	A	TP	PIM
2002-03	Guelph Storm	OHL	59	14	17	31	47	11	0	3	3	2
2003-04	Guelph Storm	OHL	68	36	32	68	86	22	*13	8	21	20

CAMPBELL, Ed (KAM-behl, EHD)

Defense. Shoots left. 6'2", 204 lbs. Born, Worcester, MA, November 26, 1974.
(NY Rangers' 9th choice, 190th overall, in 1993 Entry Draft).

			Regular Season					Playoffs				
Season	Club	League	GP	G	A	TP	PIM	GP	G	A	TP	PIM
1992-93	Omaha Lancers	USHL	42	9	19	28	160	....	....	....	....	....
1993-94	U. Mass-Lowell	H-East	40	8	16	24	114	....	....	....	....	....
1994-95	U. Mass-Lowell	H-East	34	6	24	30	105	....	....	....	....	....
1995-96	U. Mass-Lowell	H-East	39	6	33	39	*107	....	....	....	....	....
1996-97	Binghamton	AHL	74	5	17	22	108	4	0	0	0	2
1997-98	Hartford Wolf Pack	AHL	9	0	1	1	9	14	0	2	2	33
	Fort Wayne	IHL	50	10	5	15	147	....	....	....	....	....
1998-99	Hartford Wolf Pack	AHL	18	0	3	3	24	7	0	3	3	14
	Fort Wayne	IHL	46	1	16	17	137	....	....	....	....	....
99-2000	Orlando	IHL	81	2	7	9	217	3	0	0	0	6
2000-01	Worcester IceCats	AHL	78	5	27	32	207	10	1	0	1	10
2001-02	Worcester IceCats	AHL	70	3	15	18	172	3	0	0	0	5
2002-03	Grand Rapids	AHL	80	0	12	12	140	15	0	1	1	22
2003-04	Providence Bruins	AHL	67	1	8	9	92	2	0	0	0	2

Signed as a free agent by **St. Louis**, July 1, 2001. Signed as a free agent by **Detroit**, August 5, 2002. Signed as a free agent by **Boston**, July 31, 2003.

CAMPBELL, Joe (KAM-behl, JOH) CGY.

Defense. Shoots left. 6'4", 172 lbs. Born, Duluth, MN, June 26, 1982.
(Calgary's 10th choice, 233rd overall, in 2001 Entry Draft).

			Regular Season					Playoffs				
Season	Club	League	GP	G	A	TP	PIM	GP	G	A	TP	PIM
2000-01	Des Moines	USHL	56	7	11	18	53	3	0	1	1	4
2001-02	U. of Wisconsin	WCHA	7	0	0	0	0	....	....	....	....	....
2002-03	U. of Wisconsin	WCHA	1	0	0	0	0	....	....	....	....	....
	Des Moines	USHL	34	3	15	18	60	....	....	....	....	....
2003-04	Wisc.-Superior	NCHA	13	0	3	3	10	....	....	....	....	....

• Left **U. of Wisconsin** (WCHA) and signed as a free agent with **Des Moines** (USHL), December 27, 2002.

CARCILLO, Daniel (KAR-sihl-oh, DAN-yuhl) PIT.

Left wing. Shoots left. 5'11", 202 lbs. Born, King City, Ont., January 28, 1985.
(Pittsburgh's 4th choice, 73rd overall, in 2003 Entry Draft).

			Regular Season					Playoffs				
Season	Club	League	GP	G	A	TP	PIM	GP	G	A	TP	PIM
2001-02	Milton Merchants	OJHL-B	47	15	16	31	162	....	....	....	....	....
2002-03	Sarnia Sting	OHL	68	29	37	66	157	6	0	4	4	14
2003-04	Sarnia Sting	OHL	61	30	29	59	148	4	1	2	3	12

CARKNER, Matt (KARK-nehr, MAT) S.J.

Defense. Shoots right. 6'4", 235 lbs. Born, Winchester, Ont., November 3, 1980.
(Montreal's 2nd choice, 58th overall, in 1999 Entry Draft).

			Regular Season					Playoffs				
Season	Club	League	GP	G	A	TP	PIM	GP	G	A	TP	PIM
1996-97	Winchester Hawks	OJHL-B	29	1	18	19	....	....	....	....	....	....
1997-98	Peterborough	OHL	57	0	6	6	121	4	0	0	0	2
1998-99	Peterborough	OHL	60	2	16	18	173	5	0	0	0	20
99-2000	Peterborough	OHL	62	3	13	16	177	5	0	1	1	6
2000-01	Peterborough	OHL	53	8	8	16	128	7	0	3	3	25
2001-02	Cleveland Barons	AHL	74	0	3	3	335	....	....	....	....	....
2002-03	Cleveland Barons	AHL	39	1	4	5	104	....	....	....	....	....
2003-04	Cleveland Barons	AHL	60	2	11	13	115	9	0	3	3	39

Signed as a free agent by **San Jose**, June 6, 2001. • Missed majority of 2002-03 season recovering from knee injury suffered in game vs. Utah (AHL), January 4, 2003.

CARLE, Matthew (KARL, MA-thew) S.J.

Defense. Shoots left. 6', 182 lbs. Born, Anchorage, AK, September 25, 1984.
(San Jose's 4th choice, 47th overall, in 2003 Entry Draft).

			Regular Season					Playoffs				
Season	Club	League	GP	G	A	TP	PIM	GP	G	A	TP	PIM
99-2000	Alaska All-Stars	AASHA	42	14	28	42	....	....	....	....	....	....
2000-01	U.S. National U-17	USDP	68	1	5	6	31	....	....	....	....	....
2001-02	U.S. National U-18	USDP	64	4	15	19	51	....	....	....	....	....
2002-03	River City Lancers	USHL	59	12	30	42	98	11	2	2	4	20
2003-04	U. of Denver	WCHA	30	5	20	25	33	....	....	....	....	....

USHL First All-Star Team (2003) • USHL Defenseman of the Year (2003) • WCHA All-Rookie Team (2004)

CARON, Ed (kahr-OHN, EHD) EDM.

Center. Shoots left. 6'2", 228 lbs. Born, Nashua, NH, April 30, 1982.
(Edmonton's 3rd choice, 52nd overall, in 2001 Entry Draft).

			Regular Season					Playoffs				
Season	Club	League	GP	G	A	TP	PIM	GP	G	A	TP	PIM
1998-99	Phillips Exeter	Hi-School	31	39	30	69	28	....	....	....	....	....
99-2000	Phillips Exeter	Hi-School	26	22	26	48	24	....	....	....	....	....
2000-01	Phillips Exeter	Hi-School	17	30	20	50	42	....	....	....	....	....
2001-02	New Hampshire	H-East	34	6	7	13	51	....	....	....	....	....
2002-03	Yale University	ECAC		DID NOT PLAY – TRANSFERRED COLLEGES								
2003-04	New Hampshire	H-East	35	5	1	6	61	....	....	....	....	....

• Left **New Hampshire** (H-East) and signed Letter of Intent to attend **Yale** (ECAC), April 26, 2002. • Left **Yale** (ECAC) and returned to **New Hampshire** (H-East), January 16, 2003.

CARSON, Brett (KAR-suhn, BREHT) CAR.

Defense. Shoots right. 6'4", 220 lbs. Born, Regina, Sask., November 29, 1985.
(Carolina's 4th choice, 109th overall, in 2004 Entry Draft).

			Regular Season					Playoffs				
Season	Club	League	GP	G	A	TP	PIM	GP	G	A	TP	PIM
99-2000	Pipestone Valley	SSMHL	8	0	0	0	0	....	....	....	....	....
2000-01	Pipestone Valley	SSMHL	31	5	17	22	20	....	....	....	....	....
2001-02	Yorkton Mallers	SMHL	41	16	37	53	32	....	....	....	....	....
	Moose Jaw	WHL	6	0	0	0	0	12	2	0	2	0
2002-03	Moose Jaw	WHL	28	1	4	5	28	....	....	....	....	....
	Calgary Hitmen	WHL	30	3	6	9	4	5	2	1	3	0
2003-04	Calgary Hitmen	WHL	71	5	27	32	49	7	0	0	0	6

CARTELLI, Mario (kar-TEHL-lee, MAHR-ee-oh) ATL.

Defense. Shoots right. 6'1", 200 lbs. Born, Karvina, Czech., November 16, 1979.
(Atlanta's 9th choice, 262nd overall, in 2001 Entry Draft).

			Regular Season					Playoffs				
Season	Club	League	GP	G	A	TP	PIM	GP	G	A	TP	PIM
1998-99	Trinec	Czech	34	1	1	2	14	8	2	1	3	4
99-2000	Trinec Jr.	Czech-Jr.	5	3	0	3	0	....	....	....	....	....
	HC Ocelari Trinec	Czech	42	7	4	11	14	4	0	0	0	0
2000-01	HC Ocelari Trinec	Czech	46	11	16	27	24	....	....	....	....	....
2001-02	HC Ocelari Trinec	Czech	20	0	1	1	12	....	....	....	....	....
	Kladno	Czech	24	3	8	11	14	....	....	....	....	....
	HC Prostejov	Czech-2	3	0	2	2	2	....	....	....	....	....
	Kladno	Czech-Q	5	0	1	1	16	....	....	....	....	....
2002-03	HC Ocelari Trinec	Czech	29	1	9	10	16	....	....	....	....	....
	Havirov	Czech	13	1	4	5	20	....	....	....	....	....
2003-04	Plzen	Czech	40	4	8	12	24	12	2	4	6	8

CARTER, Jeff (KAR-tuhr, JEHF) PHI.

Center. Shoots right. 6'3", 182 lbs. Born, London, Ont., January 1, 1985.
(Philadelphia's 1st choice, 11th overall, in 2003 Entry Draft).

			Regular Season					Playoffs				
Season	Club	League	GP	G	A	TP	PIM	GP	G	A	TP	PIM
2000-01	Strathroy Rockets	OJHL-B	49	27	20	47	10	....	....	....	....	....
2001-02	Sault Ste. Marie	OHL	63	18	17	35	12	4	0	0	0	2
2002-03	Sault Ste. Marie	OHL	61	35	36	71	55	4	0	2	2	2
2003-04	Sault Ste. Marie	OHL	57	36	30	66	26	....	....	....	....	....
	Philadelphia	AHL	....	....	....	....	....	12	4	1	5	0

OHL Second All-Star Team (2004)

CAVANAGH, Tom (KAV-a-NAW, TAWM) S.J.

Left wing. Shoots left. 5'10", 178 lbs. Born, Warwick, RI, March 24, 1982.
(San Jose's 6th choice, 182nd overall, in 2001 Entry Draft).

			Regular Season					Playoffs				
Season	Club	League	GP	G	A	TP	PIM	GP	G	A	TP	PIM
1997-98	Toll Gate Titans	Hi-School	15	5	17	22	6	4	2	8	10	4
1998-99	Toll Gate Titans	Hi-School	15	9	20	29	26	5	5	4	9	6
99-2000	Toll Gate Titans	Hi-School	18	25	29	*54	28	5	0	12	12	9
2000-01	Phillips Exeter	Hi-School	31	*42	40	82	34	....	....	....	....	....
2001-02	Harvard University	ECAC	34	8	17	25	4	....	....	....	....	....
2002-03	Harvard University	ECAC	34	14	13	27	31	....	....	....	....	....
2003-04	Harvard University	ECAC	36	16	20	36	26	....	....	....	....	....

CAVANAUGH, Dan (KAV-a-naw, DAN) MIN.

Center. Shoots right. 6'1", 190 lbs. Born, Springfield, MA, March 3, 1980.
(Calgary's 2nd choice, 38th overall, in 1999 Entry Draft).

			Regular Season					Playoffs				
Season	Club	League	GP	G	A	TP	PIM	GP	G	A	TP	PIM
1995-96	New England	EJHL	43	8	7	15	....	....	....	....	....	....
1996-97	New England	EJHL	56	23	46	69	....	....	....	....	....	....
1997-98	New England	EJHL	38	31	*47	*78	58	13	8	12	30	....
1998-99	Boston University	H-East	36	6	8	14	60	....	....	....	....	....
99-2000	Boston University	H-East	40	9	25	34	62	....	....	....	....	....
2000-01	Boston University	H-East	35	7	21	28	43	....	....	....	....	....
2001-02	Houston Aeros	AHL	70	3	16	19	41	5	0	0	0	0
2002-03	Houston Aeros	AHL	77	13	13	26	126	23	2	2	4	20
2003-04	Houston Aeros	AHL	73	16	23	39	94	2	0	1	1	2

Rights traded to **Minnesota** by **Calgary** with Calgary's 8th round choice (Jake Riddle) in 2001 Entry Draft for Mike Vernon, June 23, 2000.

CAVOSIE, Marc (kuh-VOI-see, MAHRK) MIN.

Center. Shoots left. 6', 173 lbs. Born, Albany, NY, August 6, 1981.
(Minnesota's 3rd choice, 99th overall, in 2000 Entry Draft).

			Regular Season					Playoffs				
Season	Club	League	GP	G	A	TP	PIM	GP	G	A	TP	PIM
1995-96	Albany	Hi-School	22	8	27	31	....	....	....	....	....	....
1996-97	Albany	Hi-School	28	26	45	71	....	....	....	....	....	....
1997-98	Albany	Hi-School	28	38	33	71	....	....	....	....	....	....
1998-99	Albany	Hi-School	28	23	20	43	32	....	....	....	....	....
99-2000	RPI Engineers	ECAC	29	11	17	28	10	....	....	....	....	....
2000-01	RPI Engineers	ECAC	28	13	16	29	47	....	....	....	....	....
2001-02	RPI Engineers	ECAC	36	23	*27	*50	44	....	....	....	....	....
2002-03	Houston Aeros	AHL	54	5	14	19	24	19	3	5	8	12
2003-04	Houston Aeros	AHL	75	10	21	31	37	2	1	0	1	0

ECAC First All-Star Team (2002) • ECAC Player of the Year (2002)

CEREDA, Luca (suh-REH-duh, LOO-ka) TOR.

Center. Shoots left. 6'2", 212 lbs. Born, Lugano, Switz., September 7, 1981.
(Toronto's 1st choice, 24th overall, in 1999 Entry Draft).

			Regular Season					Playoffs				
Season	Club	League	GP	G	A	TP	PIM	GP	G	A	TP	PIM
1996-97	HC Ambri-Piotta	Swiss	35	13	8	21	....	....	....	....	....	....
1997-98	HC Ambri-Piotta	Swiss	28	17	27	44	24	....	....	....	....	....
1998-99	Ambri Jr.	Swiss-Jr.	3	4	3	7	20	....	....	....	....	....
	HC Ambri-Piotta	Swiss	38	6	10	16	8	15	0	6	6	4
99-2000	HC Ambri-Piotta	Swiss	44	1	5	6	14	9	0	1	1	2
2000-01	Ottawa 67's	OHL		DID NOT PLAY								
2001-02	St. John's	AHL	71	5	8	13	23	11	2	1	3	10
2002-03	St. John's	AHL	68	7	18	25	26	....	....	....	....	....
2003-04	St. John's	AHL	22	0	2	2	8	....	....	....	....	....
	SC Bern	Swiss	9	1	3	4	22	15	4	0	4	4

• Missed entire 2000-01 season recovering from heart surgery, October 19, 2000. • Loaned to **SC Bern** (Swiss) by **Toronto**, January 21, 2004.

CHABADA, Martin (KHA-ba-da, MAHR-tehn) NYI

Left wing. Shoots right. 6'1", 203 lbs. Born, Prague, Czech., June 14, 1977.
(NY Islanders' 6th choice, 252nd overall, in 2002 Entry Draft).

			Regular Season					Playoffs				
Season	Club	League	GP	G	A	TP	PIM	GP	G	A	TP	PIM
1996-97	HC Sparta Praha	EuroHL	1	0	0	0	0	4	0	0	0	2
	HC Sparta Praha	Czech	16	1	2	3	4	4	0	1	1	2
1997-98	HC Sparta Praha	EuroHL	4	0	1	1	4	....	....	....	....	....
	HC Sparta Praha	Czech	40	7	12	19	57	11	1	0	1	4
1998-99	HC Sparta Praha	EuroHL	6	1	1	2	10	2	2	1	3	6
	HC Sparta Praha	Czech	39	3	9	12	14	1	0	0	0	0
99-2000	HC Sparta Praha	Czech	35	7	12	19	12	9	2	2	4	4
2000-01	HC Sparta Praha	Czech	43	9	10	19	36	12	0	0	0	8
2001-02	HC Sparta Praha	Czech	51	19	21	40	113	13	4	7	11	4
2002-03	Bridgeport	AHL	66	17	13	30	50	9	3	4	7	4
2003-04	Bridgeport	AHL	10	2	3	5	0	....	....	....	....	....
	HC Sparta Praha	Czech	31	8	18	26	65	13	7	3	10	22

Signed as a free agent by **Sparta Praha** (Czech), November 6, 2003.

CHARTIER, Christian (SHAR-tee-yay, KRIHS-t'yehn) TOR.

Defense. Shoots left. 6', 216 lbs. Born, Russell, Man., December 29, 1980.
(Edmonton's 8th choice, 199th overall, in 1999 Entry Draft).

			Regular Season					Playoffs				
Season	Club	League	GP	G	A	TP	PIM	GP	G	A	TP	PIM
1995-96	Yellowhead Chiefs	MMHL	36	8	23	31	68	....	....	....	....	....
1996-97	Saskatoon Blades	WHL	64	2	23	25	32	....	....	....	....	....
1997-98	Saskatoon Blades	WHL	68	8	33	41	43	6	0	3	3	12
1998-99	Saskatoon Blades	WHL	62	2	14	16	71	....	....	....	....	....
99-2000	Saskatoon Blades	WHL	11	2	2	4	4	....	....	....	....	....
	Prince George	WHL	57	16	36	52	60	13	4	9	13	12
2000-01	Prince George	WHL	63	12	56	68	99	6	1	4	5	6
2001-02	St. John's	AHL	65	5	10	15	18	11	0	4	4	4
2002-03	St. John's	AHL	67	4	22	26	48	....	....	....	....	....
2003-04	St. John's	AHL	62	3	14	17	34	....	....	....	....	....

WHL West Second All-Star Team (2000) • WHL West First All-Star Team (2001)

Signed as a free agent by **Toronto**, June 25, 2001.

CHERNOV, Artem (chair-NAHF, AR-tehm) DAL.

Center. Shoots left. 5'10", 176 lbs. Born, Novokuznetsk, USSR, April 28, 1982.
(Dallas' 7th choice, 162nd overall, in 2000 Entry Draft).

			Regular Season					Playoffs				
Season	Club	League	GP	G	A	TP	PIM	GP	G	A	TP	PIM
1997-98	Novokuznetsk 2	Russia-3	4	0	0	0	0	....	....	....	....	....
1998-99	Novokuznetsk 2	Russia-4	32	9	7	16	14	....	....	....	....	....
99-2000	Magnitogorsk	Russia	10	2	3	5	0	5	0	0	0	0
2000-01	Magnitogorsk	Russia	44	15	17	32	30	....	....	....	....	....
2001-02	Avangard Omsk	Russia	43	6	5	11	4	....	....	....	....	....
2002-03	Avangard Omsk	Russia	48	9	10	19	6	12	1	1	2	4
2003-04	Omsk 2	Russia-3		STATISTICS NOT AVAILABLE								

CHERNYKH, Dmitri (TCHAIR-nihk, dih-MEE-tree) NYI

Right wing. Shoots left. 6', 180 lbs. Born, Voskresensk, USSR, February 27, 1985.
(NY Islanders' 2nd choice, 48th overall, in 2003 Entry Draft).

			Regular Season					Playoffs				
Season	Club	League	GP	G	A	TP	PIM	GP	G	A	TP	PIM
2001-02	Voskresensk 2	Russia-3	28	9	6	15	32	....	....	....	....	....
	Voskresensk	Russia-2	7	0	0	0	2	....	....	....	....	....
2002-03	Voskresensk	Russia-2	29	5	4	9	29	....	....	....	....	....
	Voskresensk 2	Russia-3	1	0	0	0	18	....	....	....	....	....
2003-04	CSKA Moscow	Russia	27	2	2	4	0	....	....	....	....	....

CHIPCHURA, Kyle (chip-CHUHR-a, KIGHL) MTL.

Center. Shoots left. 6'3", 204 lbs. Born, Westlock, Alta., February 19, 1986.
(Montreal's 1st choice, 18th overall, in 2004 Entry Draft).

			Regular Season					Playoffs				
Season	Club	League	GP	G	A	TP	PIM	GP	G	A	TP	PIM
2000-01	Spruce Grove	AMBHL	36	26	34	60	48	....	....	....	....	....
2001-02	Ft. Saskatchewan	AMHL	33	15	36	51	78	17	16	20	36	....
2002-03	Prince Albert	WHL	63	9	21	30	89	....	....	....	....	....
2003-04	Prince Albert	WHL	64	15	33	48	118	6	2	4	6	12

CHRISTENSEN, Erik (KRIHS-tehn-suhn, AIR-ihk) PIT.

Center. Shoots left. 6'1", 191 lbs. Born, Edmonton, Alta., December 17, 1983.
(Pittsburgh's 3rd choice, 69th overall, in 2002 Entry Draft).

			Regular Season					Playoffs				
Season	Club	League	GP	G	A	TP	PIM	GP	G	A	TP	PIM
1998-99	Leduc Oil Kings	AMBHL	36	34	42	76	70	....	....	....	....	....
99-2000	Kamloops Blazers	WHL	66	9	5	14	41	4	0	0	0	2
2000-01	Kamloops Blazers	WHL	72	21	23	44	36	4	1	1	2	0
2001-02	Kamloops Blazers	WHL	70	22	36	58	68	4	0	0	0	4
2002-03	Kamloops Blazers	WHL	67	*54	54	*108	60	6	1	7	8	14
2003-04	Kamloops Blazers	WHL	29	10	14	24	40	....	....	....	....	....
	Brandon	WHL	34	17	21	38	20	11	8	4	12	8

WHL West First All-Star Team (2003)

CHUCKO, Kris (CHUH-koh, KRIHS) CGY.

Left wing. Shoots right. 6'2", 190 lbs. Born, Burnaby, B.C., March 13, 1986.
(Calgary's 1st choice, 24th overall, in 2004 Entry Draft).

			Regular Season					Playoffs				
Season	Club	League	GP	G	A	TP	PIM	GP	G	A	TP	PIM
2002-03	Salmon Arm	BCHL	59	14	19	33	80	11	5	3	8	12
2003-04	Salmon Arm	BCHL	53	32	55	87	161	14	10	9	19	36

• Signed Letter of Intent to attend **U. Of Minnesota** (WCHA), December 31, 2003.

CIZEK, Martin (CHEE-zhehk, MAHR-tehn) BUF.

Defense. Shoots left. 6'1", 188 lbs. Born, Beroun, Czech., May 17, 1984.
(Buffalo's 10th choice, 271st overall, in 2002 Entry Draft).

			Regular Season					Playoffs				
Season	Club	League	GP	G	A	TP	PIM	GP	G	A	TP	PIM
99-2000	HC Slavia Praha Jr.	Czech-Jr.	46	1	11	12	24	....	....	....	....	....
2000-01	HC Slavia Praha Jr.	Czech-Jr.	53	14	10	24	26	....	....	....	....	....
2001-02	HC Slavia Praha Jr.	Czech-Jr.	42	2	6	8	30	....	....	....	....	....
2002-03	Plymouth Whalers	OHL	58	2	7	9	40	18	1	1	2	6
2003-04	HC Kladno Jr.	Czech-Jr.	50	9	23	32	34	7	0	3	3	2
	HC Medvedi	Czech-2	8	0	0	0	2	1	0	0	0	0

CLOUTHIER, Brett (KLOO-tyay, BREHT) N.J.

Left wing. Shoots left. 6'5", 225 lbs. Born, Ottawa, Ont., June 9, 1981.
(New Jersey's 3rd choice, 50th overall, in 1999 Entry Draft).

			Regular Season					Playoffs				
Season	Club	League	GP	G	A	TP	PIM	GP	G	A	TP	PIM
1997-98	Kanata Valley	OCJHL	50	12	10	22	135	....	....	....	....	....
1998-99	Kingston	OHL	64	8	14	22	227	5	1	1	2	4
99-2000	Kingston	OHL	65	13	26	39	*266	5	2	0	2	17
2000-01	Kingston	OHL	68	28	29	57	165	4	1	0	1	10
2001-02	Albany River Rats	AHL	62	4	0	4	109	....	....	....	....	....
2002-03	Albany River Rats	AHL	74	6	7	13	220	....	....	....	....	....
2003-04	Albany River Rats	AHL	39	1	0	1	122	....	....	....	....	....
	Cincinnati	ECHL	12	3	3	6	14	....	....	....	....	....

CLOUTIER, David (KLOO-tyay, DAY-vihd) S.J.

Defense. Shoots right. 6'1", 200 lbs. Born, Quebec City, Que., December 17, 1981.

			Regular Season					Playoffs				
Season	Club	League	GP	G	A	TP	PIM	GP	G	A	TP	PIM
1997-98	Levis	QAAA	42	5	17	22	....	4	1	0	1	0
1998-99	Sherbrooke	QMJHL	46	2	2	4	39	4	0	0	0	2
99-2000	Montreal Rocket	QMJHL	33	2	7	9	36	....	....	....	....	....
	Val-d'Or Foreurs	QMJHL	30	5	8	13	24	....	....	....	....	....
2000-01	Val-d'Or Foreurs	QMJHL	72	14	20	34	200	21	3	9	12	36
2001-02	Val-d'Or Foreurs	QMJHL	38	16	16	32	123	....	....	....	....	....
	Cape Breton	QMJHL	22	9	17	26	60	16	7	15	22	24
2002-03	Cleveland Barons	AHL	80	10	17	27	90	....	....	....	....	....
2003-04	Cleveland Barons	AHL	50	2	9	11	49	1	0	0	0	0

Signed as a free agent by **San Jose**, July 10, 2002.

CLOWE, Ryan (KLOH, RIGH-uhn) S.J.

Right wing. Shoots right. 6'2", 215 lbs. Born, St. John's, Nfld., September 30, 1982.
(San Jose's 5th choice, 175th overall, in 2001 Entry Draft).

			Regular Season					Playoffs				
Season	Club	League	GP	G	A	TP	PIM	GP	G	A	TP	PIM
99-2000	St. John's	NFAHA		STATISTICS NOT AVAILABLE								
2000-01	Rimouski Oceanic	QMJHL	32	15	10	25	43	11	8	1	9	12
2001-02	Rimouski Oceanic	QMJHL	53	28	45	73	120	7	1	6	7	2
2002-03	Rimouski Oceanic	QMJHL	17	8	19	27	44	....	....	....	....	....
	Montreal Rocket	QMJHL	43	18	30	48	60	7	3	7	10	6
2003-04	Cleveland Barons	AHL	72	11	29	40	97	8	3	1	4	9

COBURN, Braydon (KOH-buhrn, BRAY-duhn) ATL.

Defense. Shoots left. 6'5", 220 lbs. Born, Calgary, Alta., February 27, 1985.
(Atlanta's 1st choice, 8th overall, in 2003 Entry Draft).

			Regular Season					Playoffs				
Season	Club	League	GP	G	A	TP	PIM	GP	G	A	TP	PIM
2000-01	Notre Dame	SMHL	32	3	19	22	70	....	....	....	....	....
	Portland	WHL	2	0	1	1	0	14	0	4	4	2
2001-02	Portland	WHL	68	4	33	37	100	7	1	1	2	9
2002-03	Portland	WHL	53	3	16	19	147	7	0	1	1	8
2003-04	Portland	WHL	55	10	20	30	92	5	0	1	1	10

WHL Rookie of the Year (2002) • WHL West First All-Star Team (2004)

COLBERT, Will (KOHL-buhrt, WIHL) **OTT.**

Defense. Shoots left. 6'3", 212 lbs. Born, Arnprior, Ont., February 6, 1985.
(Ottawa's 7th choice, 228th overall, in 2003 Entry Draft).

			Regular Season					Playoffs				
Season	**Club**	**League**	**GP**	**G**	**A**	**TP**	**PIM**	**GP**	**G**	**A**	**TP**	**PIM**
2001-02	Pembroke	COJHL	52	2	6	8	20	....	....	....	....	....
2002-03	Ottawa 67's	OHL	56	1	6	7	23	23	1	5	6	7
2003-04	Ottawa 67's	OHL	55	3	18	21	28	7	0	4	4	0

COLE, Phil (KOHL, FIHL) **N.J.**

Defense. Shoots left. 6'4", 205 lbs. Born, Winnipeg, Man., September 6, 1982.
(New Jersey's 8th choice, 125th overall, in 2000 Entry Draft).

			Regular Season					Playoffs				
Season	**Club**	**League**	**GP**	**G**	**A**	**TP**	**PIM**	**GP**	**G**	**A**	**TP**	**PIM**
1997-98	Winnipeg Sharks	MMHL	45	0	18	18	68	5	0	4	4	2
1998-99	Lethbridge	WHL	45	2	1	3	64	4	0	0	0	0
99-2000	Lethbridge	WHL	51	1	6	7	112	....	....	....	....	....
2000-01	Lethbridge	WHL	63	6	15	21	129	1	0	0	0	2
2001-02	Lethbridge	WHL	33	3	13	16	87	....	....	....	....	....
	Vancouver Giants	WHL	6	0	1	1	18	....	....	....	....	....
	Medicine Hat	WHL	15	1	5	6	49	....	....	....	....	....
2002-03	Columbus	ECHL	51	4	5	9	135	....	....	....	....	....
	Albany River Rats	AHL	4	0	0	0	6	....	....	....	....	....
2003-04	Albany River Rats	AHL	39	1	3	4	80	....	....	....	....	....
	Cincinnati	ECHL	12	1	0	1	33	....	....	....	....	....

COLLEY, Kevin **NYI**

Center. Shoots right. 5'10", 175 lbs. Born, New Haven, CT, January 4, 1979.

			Regular Season					Playoffs				
Season	**Club**	**League**	**GP**	**G**	**A**	**TP**	**PIM**	**GP**	**G**	**A**	**TP**	**PIM**
1996-97	Oshawa Generals	OHL	64	19	17	36	46	16	2	4	6	25
1997-98	Oshawa Generals	OHL	57	27	41	68	107	7	1	5	6	14
1998-99	Oshawa Generals	OHL	63	39	62	101	68	14	7	13	20	32
99-2000	Hartford Wolf Pack	AHL	5	0	0	0	2	....	....	....	....	....
	Charlotte	ECHL	5	2	1	3	10	....	....	....	....	....
	Dayton Bombers	ECHL	24	8	6	14	111	2	1	0	1	4
2000-01	Pensacola	ECHL	23	6	11	17	44	....	....	....	....	....
	New Orleans Brass	ECHL	23	11	8	19	27	8	1	1	2	12
2001-02	Atlantic City	ECHL	41	23	30	53	90	....	....	....	....	....
	Providence Bruins	AHL	4	0	1	1	27	....	....	....	....	....
	Rochester	AHL	25	3	4	7	70	2	0	1	1	0
2002-03	Atlantic City	ECHL	50	33	38	71	190	17	13	7	20	27
	Syracuse Crunch	AHL	16	2	3	5	6	....	....	....	....	....
	Worcester IceCats	AHL	6	1	1	2	27	....	....	....	....	....
2003-04	Bridgeport	AHL	78	12	19	31	122	3	1	0	1	12

Signed as a free agent by **NY Islanders**, June 10, 2004.

COLLINS, Dustin (KAWL-ihns, DUHS-tihn) **T.B.**

Center/Left wing. Shoots left. 6'3", 196 lbs. Born, Payson, AZ, February 28, 1985.
(Tampa Bay's 5th choice, 163rd overall, in 2004 Entry Draft).

			Regular Season					Playoffs				
Season	**Club**	**League**	**GP**	**G**	**A**	**TP**	**PIM**	**GP**	**G**	**A**	**TP**	**PIM**
2001-02	U.S. National U-17	USDP	63	6	10	16	38	....	....	....	....	....
2002-03	U.S. National U-18	USDP	53	6	11	17	31	....	....	....	....	....
2003-04	Northern Michigan	CCHA	37	1	5	6	30	....	....	....	....	....

COLLINS, Rob (KAW-lihns, RAWB) **NYI**

Center. Shoots right. 5'10", 174 lbs. Born, Kitchener, Ont., March 15, 1974.

			Regular Season					Playoffs				
Season	**Club**	**League**	**GP**	**G**	**A**	**TP**	**PIM**	**GP**	**G**	**A**	**TP**	**PIM**
1997-98	Elmira Sugar Kings	OJHL		STATISTICS NOT AVAILABLE								
1998-99	Ferris State	CCHA	36	3	9	12	14	....	....	....	....	....
99-2000	Ferris State	CCHA	38	11	20	31	39	....	....	....	....	....
2000-01	Ferris State	CCHA	35	15	17	32	23	....	....	....	....	....
2001-02	Ferris State	CCHA	36	15	33	48	30	....	....	....	....	....
	Grand Rapids	AHL	5	0	2	2	0	....	....	....	....	....
2002-03	Grand Rapids	AHL	73	11	20	31	16	15	3	8	11	10
2003-04	Bridgeport	AHL	75	9	23	32	42	7	3	5	8	10

CCHA First All-Star Team (2002) • NCAA West Second All-American Team (2002)

Signed as a free agent by **NY Islanders**, July, 2003.

COLLINS, Sean (KAW-lihns, SHAWN) **COL.**

Left wing. Shoots left. 5'9", 180 lbs. Born, Boston, MA, February 9, 1983.
(Colorado's 10th choice, 289th overall, in 2002 Entry Draft).

			Regular Season					Playoffs				
Season	**Club**	**League**	**GP**	**G**	**A**	**TP**	**PIM**	**GP**	**G**	**A**	**TP**	**PIM**
1997-98	Reading High	Hi-School	22	32	26	58	....	....	....	....	....	....
1998-99	Reading High	Hi-School	25	32	35	67	....	....	....	....	....	....
99-2000	Reading High	Hi-School	22	37	42	79	....	....	....	....	....	....
2000-01	Reading High	Hi-School	24	28	36	64	....	....	....	....	....	....
2001-02	New Hampshire	H-East	40	20	25	45	4	....	....	....	....	....
2002-03	New Hampshire	H-East	41	22	8	30	12	....	....	....	....	....
2003-04	New Hampshire	H-East	41	16	26	42	28	....	....	....	....	....

COLLITON, Jeremy (KAW-lih-tuhn, JAIR-eh-mee) **NYI**

Center. Shoots right. 6'2", 195 lbs. Born, Blackie, Alta., January 13, 1985.
(NY Islanders' 4th choice, 58th overall, in 2003 Entry Draft).

			Regular Season					Playoffs				
Season	**Club**	**League**	**GP**	**G**	**A**	**TP**	**PIM**	**GP**	**G**	**A**	**TP**	**PIM**
99-2000	Airdrie Express	AMHL	33	16	25	41	28	....	....	....	....	....
2000-01	Crows Nest Pass	AJHL	63	18	30	48	98	....	....	....	....	....
2001-02	Prince Albert	WHL	68	11	21	32	53	....	....	....	....	....
2002-03	Prince Albert	WHL	58	20	28	48	76	....	....	....	....	....
2003-04	Prince Albert	WHL	62	24	26	50	73	6	5	5	10	8

COMEAU, Blake (KOH-moh, BLAYK) **NYI**

Right wing. Shoots right. 6'1", 198 lbs. Born, Meadow Lake, Sask., February 18, 1986.
(NY Islanders' 2nd choice, 47th overall, in 2004 Entry Draft).

			Regular Season					Playoffs				
Season	**Club**	**League**	**GP**	**G**	**A**	**TP**	**PIM**	**GP**	**G**	**A**	**TP**	**PIM**
2001-02	Sask. Contacts	SMHL	42	27	33	60	72	....	....	....	....	....
	Kelowna Rockets	WHL	3	0	0	0	4	....	....	....	....	....
2002-03	Kelowna Rockets	WHL	54	5	18	23	77	19	2	1	3	20
2003-04	Kelowna Rockets	WHL	71	10	23	33	123	17	4	2	6	23

CONBOY, Tim (KAWN-boy, TIHM) **S.J.**

Defense. Shoots right. 6'1", 205 lbs. Born, Farmington, MN, March 22, 1982.
(San Jose's 6th choice, 217th overall, in 2002 Entry Draft).

			Regular Season					Playoffs				
Season	**Club**	**League**	**GP**	**G**	**A**	**TP**	**PIM**	**GP**	**G**	**A**	**TP**	**PIM**
99-2000	Brainerd High	Hi-School	22	20	26	46	....	....	....	....	....	....
2000-01	Rochester	USHL	51	5	9	14	256	....	....	....	....	....
2001-02	Rochester	USHL	14	1	6	7	65	....	....	....	....	....
	Topeka	USHL	29	4	15	19	128	....	....	....	....	....
2002-03	St. Cloud State	WCHA	31	3	12	15	48	....	....	....	....	....
2003-04	St. Cloud State	WCHA	32	5	5	10	68	....	....	....	....	....
	Cleveland Barons	AHL	....	....	....	....	....	3	0	3	3	4

CONNE, Flavien (KAW-neh, FLA-vee-ehn) **L.A.**

Center. Shoots left. 5'9", 176 lbs. Born, Geneva, Switz., April 1, 1980.
(Los Angeles' 10th choice, 250th overall, in 2000 Entry Draft).

			Regular Season					Playoffs				
Season	**Club**	**League**	**GP**	**G**	**A**	**TP**	**PIM**	**GP**	**G**	**A**	**TP**	**PIM**
1995-96	Geneva Jr.	Swiss-Jr.	22	39	27	56	32	....	....	....	....	....
1996-97	Geneva	Swiss-2	30	9	8	17	8	5	1	1	2	4
1997-98	Geneva Jr.	Swiss-Jr.	37	15	12	27	57	3	0	2	2	2
	Geneva	Swiss-2	9	11	6	17	12	....	....	....	....	....
	HC Ambri-Piotta	Swiss	1	0	0	0	0	....	....	....	....	....
1998-99	Fribourg Jr.	Swiss-Jr.	1	1	1	2	2	....	....	....	....	....
	Fribourg	Swiss	37	14	14	28	59	4	4	1	5	6
	Fribourg	EuroHL	3	0	0	0	0	....	....	....	....	....
99-2000	Fribourg	Swiss	44	19	22	41	38	4	0	1	1	0
2000-01	HC Lugano	Swiss	42	9	14	23	8	15	2	6	8	37
2001-02	HC Lugano	Swiss	44	12	13	25	20	5	1	1	2	0
	Switzerland	Olympics	1	0	0	0	0	....	....	....	....	....
2002-03	HC Lugano	Swiss	42	15	23	38	32	16	4	4	8	10
2003-04	HC Lugano	Swiss	32	11	13	24	18	16	8	4	12	12

COOK, Tim (KUK, TIHM) **OTT.**

Defense. Shoots right. 6'4", 190 lbs. Born, Montclair, NJ, March 13, 1984.
(Ottawa's 5th choice, 142nd overall, in 2003 Entry Draft).

			Regular Season					Playoffs				
Season	**Club**	**League**	**GP**	**G**	**A**	**TP**	**PIM**	**GP**	**G**	**A**	**TP**	**PIM**
2000-01	Hotchkiss High	Hi-School	22	2	10	12	22	....	....	....	....	....
2001-02	Omaha Lancers	USHL	42	2	4	6	39	5	0	1	1	2
2002-03	River City Lancers	USHL	59	3	12	15	62	10	0	2	2	18
2003-04	U. of Michigan	CCHA	24	0	2	2	28	....	....	....	....	....

COURCHAINE, Adam (KOOR-shayn, A-duhm) **MIN.**

Center. Shoots left. 5'10", 175 lbs. Born, Winnipeg, Man., May 23, 1984.
(Minnesota's 7th choice, 219th overall, in 2003 Entry Draft).

			Regular Season					Playoffs				
Season	**Club**	**League**	**GP**	**G**	**A**	**TP**	**PIM**	**GP**	**G**	**A**	**TP**	**PIM**
2000-01	Winnipeg Warriors	MMHL	50	77	42	119	40	....	....	....	....	....
2001-02	Medicine Hat	WHL	44	5	5	10	6	....	....	....	....	....
	Vancouver Giants	WHL	29	16	12	28	8	....	....	....	....	....
2002-03	Vancouver Giants	WHL	71	43	42	85	24	4	2	1	3	2
2003-04	Vancouver Giants	WHL	70	39	43	82	34	11	4	6	10	6

WHL West First All-Star Team (2004)

COX, Justin (KAWKS, JUHS-tihn)

Right wing. Shoots right. 6', 173 lbs. Born, Merritt, B.C., March 13, 1981.
(Dallas' 6th choice, 184th overall, in 1999 Entry Draft).

			Regular Season					Playoffs				
Season	**Club**	**League**	**GP**	**G**	**A**	**TP**	**PIM**	**GP**	**G**	**A**	**TP**	**PIM**
1996-97	Spruce Grove	AMHL	78	57	92	149	86	....	....	....	....	....
1997-98	Prince George	WHL	40	1	4	5	15	2	0	0	0	0
1998-99	Prince George	WHL	72	9	13	22	51	7	1	0	1	13
99-2000	Prince George	WHL	71	33	38	71	74	13	2	4	6	16
2000-01	Prince George	WHL	71	30	38	68	91	6	3	4	7	20
2001-02	Fort Worth	CHL	2	2	0	2	0	....	....	....	....	....
	Utah Grizzlies	AHL	74	10	7	17	53	5	0	1	1	0
2002-03	Utah Grizzlies	AHL	53	3	12	15	22	2	0	0	0	2
2003-04	Utah Grizzlies	AHL	78	12	11	23	65	....	....	....	....	....

CRABB, Joey (KRAB, JOH-ee) **NYR**

Right wing. Shoots right. 6'1", 179 lbs. Born, Anchorage, AK, April 3, 1983.
(NY Rangers' 7th choice, 226th overall, in 2002 Entry Draft).

			Regular Season					Playoffs				
Season	**Club**	**League**	**GP**	**G**	**A**	**TP**	**PIM**	**GP**	**G**	**A**	**TP**	**PIM**
99-2000	U.S. National U-17	USDP	55	13	10	23	69	....	....	....	....	....
2000-01	U.S. National U-18	USDP	60	12	13	25	40	....	....	....	....	....
2001-02	Green Bay	USHL	61	15	27	42	94	7	4	8	12	21
2002-03	Colorado College	WCHA	35	4	4	8	40	....	....	....	....	....
2003-04	Colorado College	WCHA	39	15	12	27	20	....	....	....	....	....

CRAIG, Ryan (KRAIG, RIGH-uhn) **T.B.**

Center. Shoots left. 6'1", 208 lbs. Born, Abbotsford, B.C., January 6, 1982.
(Tampa Bay's 10th choice, 255th overall, in 2002 Entry Draft).

			Regular Season					Playoffs				
Season	**Club**	**League**	**GP**	**G**	**A**	**TP**	**PIM**	**GP**	**G**	**A**	**TP**	**PIM**
1997-98	Abbotsford	BCAHA	80	118	120	238	110	....	....	....	....	....
	Brandon	WHL	1	0	0	0	0	....	....	....	....	....
1998-99	Brandon	WHL	54	11	12	23	46	5	0	0	0	4
99-2000	Brandon	WHL	65	17	19	36	40	....	....	....	....	....
2000-01	Brandon	WHL	70	38	33	71	49	6	3	0	3	7
2001-02	Brandon	WHL	52	29	35	64	52	19	11	10	21	13
2002-03	Brandon	WHL	60	42	32	74	69	17	5	8	13	29
2003-04	Hershey Bears	AHL	61	4	8	12	24	....	....	....	....	....
	Pensacola	ECHL	5	3	5	8	0	2	0	1	1	0

WHL East First All-Star Team (2003) • Canadian Major Junior Humanitarian Player of the Year (2003)

CRAMPTON, Steve (KRAMP-tuhn, STEE-vehn) **PIT.**

Right wing. Shoots right. 6'3", 205 lbs. Born, Winnipeg, Man., April 12, 1982.
(Pittsburgh's 8th choice, 248th overall, in 2000 Entry Draft).

			Regular Season					Playoffs				
Season	**Club**	**League**	**GP**	**G**	**A**	**TP**	**PIM**	**GP**	**G**	**A**	**TP**	**PIM**
1997-98	Winnipeg Sharks	MMHL	29	33	38	71	76	....	....	....	....	....
1998-99	Moose Jaw	WHL	52	7	5	12	31	9	1	1	2	4
99-2000	Moose Jaw	WHL	69	22	20	42	91	4	0	3	3	9
2000-01	Moose Jaw	WHL	72	26	33	59	153	4	1	2	3	6
2001-02	Moose Jaw	WHL	37	19	24	43	71	12	4	10	14	20
2002-03	Wheeling Nailers	ECHL	69	13	26	39	79	....	....	....	....	....
2003-04	Wheeling Nailers	ECHL	70	19	34	53	115	5	2	2	4	4

CROMBEEN, Brandon (KRAWM-been, BRAN-duhn) DAL.

Right wing. Shoots right. 6'2", 200 lbs. Born, Denver, CO, July 10, 1985.
(Dallas' 3rd choice, 54th overall, in 2003 Entry Draft).

			Regular Season					Playoffs				
Season	Club	League	GP	G	A	TP	PIM	GP	G	A	TP	PIM
2000-01	Newmarket	OPJHL	35	14	14	28	63	....	....	....	....	....
2001-02	Barrie Colts	OHL	60	12	13	25	118	20	1	1	2	31
2002-03	Barrie Colts	OHL	63	22	24	46	133	6	1	0	1	8
2003-04	Barrie Colts	OHL	62	21	29	50	154	12	5	7	12	35

CUDDIHY, Jimmy (KUH-dih-hee, JIHM-mee) DET.

Center. Shoots left. 6'3", 194 lbs. Born, Ottawa, Ont., April 22, 1984.
(Detroit's 6th choice, 197th overall, in 2002 Entry Draft).

			Regular Season					Playoffs				
Season	Club	League	GP	G	A	TP	PIM	GP	G	A	TP	PIM
99-2000	Gatineau	QAAA	41	14	13	27	24	....	....	....	....	....
2000-01	Shawinigan	QMJHL	61	5	11	16	46	10	0	0	0	0
2001-02	Shawinigan	QMJHL	56	9	18	27	69	10	0	1	1	8
2002-03	Shawinigan	QMJHL	66	14	40	54	96	9	1	13	14	10
2003-04	Shawinigan	QMJHL	64	20	37	57	54	9	0	6	6	10

CULL, Trent (KUHL, TREHNT)

Defense. Shoots left. 6'2", 215 lbs. Born, Brampton, Ont., September 27, 1973.

			Regular Season					Playoffs				
Season	Club	League	GP	G	A	TP	PIM	GP	G	A	TP	PIM
1988-89	Georgetown	OJHL-B	36	1	5	6	51	....	....	....	....	....
1989-90	Owen Sound	OHL	57	0	5	5	53	12	0	2	2	11
1990-91	Owen Sound	OHL	24	1	2	3	19	....	....	....	....	....
	Windsor Spitfires	OHL	33	1	6	7	34	11	0	0	0	8
1991-92	Windsor Spitfires	OHL	32	0	6	6	66	....	....	....	....	....
	Kingston	OHL	18	0	0	0	31	....	....	....	....	....
1992-93	Kingston	OHL	60	11	28	39	144	16	2	8	10	37
1993-94	Kingston	OHL	50	2	30	32	147	6	0	1	1	6
1994-95	St. John's	AHL	43	0	1	1	53	....	....	....	....	....
	Brantford Smoke	ColHL	4	0	0	0	14	....	....	....	....	....
1995-96	St. John's	AHL	46	2	1	3	118	4	0	0	0	6
1996-97	St. John's	AHL	75	4	5	9	219	8	0	1	1	18
1997-98	Houston Aeros	IHL	72	4	8	12	201	4	0	0	0	4
1998-99	Houston Aeros	IHL	72	2	14	16	232	19	0	2	2	34
99-2000	Springfield Falcons	AHL	28	0	2	2	74	....	....	....	....	....
	Houston Aeros	IHL	35	2	7	9	133	5	0	0	0	24
2000-01	Wilkes-Barre	AHL	71	11	15	26	166	21	3	2	5	28
2001-02	Houston Aeros	AHL	74	1	11	12	158	12	0	2	2	8
2002-03	Syracuse Crunch	AHL	40	0	8	8	115	....	....	....	....	....
2003-04	Syracuse Crunch	AHL	58	2	7	9	146	5	1	0	1	16

Signed as a free agent by **Toronto**, June 4, 1994. Signed as a free agent by **Phoenix**, August 26, 1999. Signed as a free agent by **Pittsburgh**, August 28, 2000. Signed as a free agent by **Minnesota**, July 13, 2001.

CULLEN, Joe (KUH-lehn, JOH) EDM.

Center. Shoots left. 6'1", 210 lbs. Born, Virginia, MN, February 14, 1981.
(Edmonton's 7th choice, 211th overall, in 2000 Entry Draft).

			Regular Season					Playoffs				
Season	Club	League	GP	G	A	TP	PIM	GP	G	A	TP	PIM
1997-98	Moorhead Spuds	Hi-School	23	18	18	36	....	....	....	....	....	....
1998-99	U.S. National U-17	USDP	52	11	15	26	33	....	....	....	....	....
99-2000	Colorado College	WCHA	29	4	6	10	30	....	....	....	....	....
2000-01	Colorado College	WCHA	34	8	12	20	38	....	....	....	....	....
2001-02	Colorado College	WCHA	43	9	12	21	42	....	....	....	....	....
2002-03	Colorado College	WCHA	42	20	15	35	56	....	....	....	....	....
2003-04	Toronto	AHL	69	14	16	30	30	3	0	0	0	2

CULLEN, Mark (KUH-lehn, MAHRK) MIN.

Center. Shoots left. 5'11", 175 lbs. Born, Moorhead, MN, October 28, 1978.

			Regular Season					Playoffs				
Season	Club	League	GP	G	A	TP	PIM	GP	G	A	TP	PIM
1996-97	Fargo High	Hi-School	30	20	45	65	....	....	....	....	....	....
1997-98	Fargo-Moorhead	USHL	30	17	37	54	16	4	3	0	3	25
1998-99	Colorado College	WCHA	42	8	25	33	22	....	....	....	....	....
99-2000	Colorado College	WCHA	37	11	20	31	22	....	....	....	....	....
2000-01	Colorado College	WCHA	31	20	33	53	26	....	....	....	....	....
2001-02	Colorado College	WCHA	43	14	36	50	14	....	....	....	....	....
2002-03	Houston Aeros	AHL	72	22	25	47	20	15	3	7	10	4
2003-04	Houston Aeros	AHL	53	10	18	28	28	2	0	0	0	0

USHL All-Rookie Team (1998) • USHL Rookie of the Year (1998) • WCHA First All-Star Team (2001, 2002) • NCAA West Second All-American Team (2001)

Signed as a free agent by **Minnesota**, April 8, 2002.

CUNNING, Cam (KUH-nihng, KAM) CGY.

Left wing. Shoots left. 6'1", 197 lbs. Born, Powell River, B.C., June 4, 1985.
(Calgary's 8th choice, 240th overall, in 2003 Entry Draft).

			Regular Season					Playoffs				
Season	Club	League	GP	G	A	TP	PIM	GP	G	A	TP	PIM
2001-02	Powell River	BCHL		STATISTICS NOT AVAILABLE								
2002-03	Kamloops Blazers	WHL	71	7	12	19	54	6	1	0	1	2
2003-04	Kamloops Blazers	WHL	65	14	13	27	62	5	1	1	2	10

CURRY, Sean (KUH-ree, SHAWN) CAR.

Defense. Shoots right. 6'4", 230 lbs. Born, Burnsville, MN, April 29, 1982.
(Carolina's 6th choice, 211th overall, in 2001 Entry Draft).

			Regular Season					Playoffs				
Season	Club	League	GP	G	A	TP	PIM	GP	G	A	TP	PIM
99-2000	Burnsville	Hi-School	23	8	18	26	....	....	....	....	....	....
2000-01	Tri-City Americans	WHL	72	5	12	17	113	....	....	....	....	....
2001-02	Tri-City Americans	WHL	36	6	6	12	84	....	....	....	....	....
	Medicine Hat	WHL	24	4	13	17	43	....	....	....	....	....
2002-03	Lowell	AHL	35	0	2	2	62	....	....	....	....	....
	Florida Everblades	ECHL	32	1	6	7	77	1	0	0	0	0
2003-04	Lowell	AHL	74	1	8	9	66	....	....	....	....	....

DALLMAN, Kevin (DAL-mahn, KEH-vihn) BOS.

Defense. Shoots right. 5'11", 195 lbs. Born, Niagara Falls, Ont., February 26, 1981.

			Regular Season					Playoffs				
Season	Club	League	GP	G	A	TP	PIM	GP	G	A	TP	PIM
1996-97	Niagrara Falls	OJHL-B	3	0	1	1	2	....	....	....	....	....
1997-98	Niagrara Falls	OJHL-B	47	13	25	38	42	....	....	....	....	....
1998-99	Guelph Storm	OHL	68	8	30	38	52	11	1	4	5	2
99-2000	Guelph Storm	OHL	67	13	46	59	38	6	0	2	2	11
2000-01	Guelph Storm	OHL	66	25	52	77	88	1	0	0	0	0
2001-02	Guelph Storm	OHL	67	23	63	86	68	9	8	8	16	22
2002-03	Providence Bruins	AHL	72	2	19	21	53	....	....	....	....	....
2003-04	Providence Bruins	AHL	65	6	23	29	44	2	0	0	0	0

Signed as a free agent by **Boston**, July 18, 2002.

D'AMOUR, Dominic (dah-MOHR, DOHM-ihn-ihk) TOR.

Defense. Shoots left. 6'3", 202 lbs. Born, La Salle, Que., January 28, 1984.
(Toronto's 4th choice, 88th overall, in 2002 Entry Draft).

			Regular Season					Playoffs				
Season	Club	League	GP	G	A	TP	PIM	GP	G	A	TP	PIM
99-2000	Charles-Lemoyne	QAAA	35	3	8	11	47	16	1	1	2	14
2000-01	Charles-Lemoyne	QAAA	11	1	4	5	36	....	....	....	....	....
	Rouyn-Noranda	QMJHL	18	0	0	0	10	....	....	....	....	....
2001-02	Hull Olympiques	QMJHL	68	5	5	10	225	12	0	3	3	32
2002-03	Hull Olympiques	QMJHL	65	5	25	30	211	17	2	3	5	51
2003-04	Gatineau	QMJHL	61	15	38	53	211	15	3	6	9	*41

DANIELSSON, Nicklas (DAN-yehl-suhn, NIHK-las) VAN.

Right wing. Shoots right. 6'1", 169 lbs. Born, Uppsala, Sweden, December 7, 1984.
(Vancouver's 5th choice, 160th overall, in 2003 Entry Draft).

			Regular Season					Playoffs				
Season	Club	League	GP	G	A	TP	PIM	GP	G	A	TP	PIM
2000-01	Vasteras Jr.	Swede-Jr.	9	6	8	14	12	....	....	....	....	....
	Vasteras IK	Swede-4	13	3	5	8	2	....	....	....	....	....
2001-02	Brynas IF Gavle Jr.	Swede-Jr.	42	15	14	29	74	....	....	....	....	....
2002-03	Brynas IF Gavle Jr.	Swede-Jr.	21	21	12	33	24	2	1	0	1	2
	Brynas IF Gavle	Sweden	26	0	4	4	10	....	....	....	....	....
	Brynas IF Gavle	Swede-Q	6	0	0	0	4	....	....	....	....	....
2003-04	Brynas IF Gavle	Sweden	47	6	0	6	22	....	....	....	....	....
	Brynas IF Gavle Jr.	Swede-Jr.	10	8	8	16	12	5	3	1	4	48
	Almtuna	Swede-2	4	1	1	2	6	....	....	....	....	....

DANILICS, Raimonds (da-NIH-likhs, RAY-mawndz) T.B.

Forward. Shoots right. 6'3", 180 lbs. Born, Riga, Latvia, July 17, 1985.
(Tampa Bay's 7th choice, 255th overall, in 2003 Entry Draft).

			Regular Season					Playoffs				
Season	Club	League	GP	G	A	TP	PIM	GP	G	A	TP	PIM
2000-01	Daugavpils Jr.	Latvia-Jr.	20	6	8	14	....	....	....	....	....	....
	Prizma Riga	Latvia	2	0	0	0	0	....	....	....	....	....
2001-02	Daugavpils Jr.	Latvia-Jr.	16	4	5	9	10	....	....	....	....	....
2002-03	Daugavpils Jr.	Latvia-Jr.	14	4	5	9	18	....	....	....	....	....
	Daugavpils Jr.	EEHL-B	18	7	15	22	29	....	....	....	....	....
2003-04	Lukko Rauma Jr.	Finn-Jr.	27	0	0	0	12	....	....	....	....	....

DARZINS, Lauris (DAHR-zihnzh, LOW-rihs) NSH.

Forward. Shoots right. 6'2", 176 lbs. Born, Riga, Latvia, January 28, 1985.
(Nashville's 13th choice, 268th overall, in 2003 Entry Draft).

			Regular Season					Playoffs				
Season	Club	League	GP	G	A	TP	PIM	GP	G	A	TP	PIM
2001-02	Lukko Rauma B	Finn-Jr.	7	4	1	5	4	....	....	....	....	....
	Lukko Rauma Jr.	Finn-Jr.	5	1	0	1	0	....	....	....	....	....
2002-03	Lukko Rauma B	Finn-Jr.	13	10	10	20	6	....	....	....	....	....
	Lukko Rauma Jr.	Finn-Jr.	13	6	4	10	6	....	....	....	....	....
2003-04	Lukko Rauma Jr.	Finn-Jr.	35	17	8	25	14	....	....	....	....	....

DAVIS, George (DAY-vihs, JOHRJ) ANA.

Right wing. Shoots right. 6'1", 240 lbs. Born, North Sydney, N.S., July 28, 1983.
(Anaheim's 5th choice, 140th overall, in 2002 Entry Draft).

			Regular Season					Playoffs				
Season	Club	League	GP	G	A	TP	PIM	GP	G	A	TP	PIM
2000-01	Cape Breton	QMJHL	44	0	1	1	196	5	0	0	0	14
2001-02	Cape Breton	QMJHL	46	4	1	5	274	16	1	2	3	18
2002-03	Cape Breton	QMJHL	43	5	8	13	182	....	....	....	....	....
	Halifax	QMJHL	25	0	2	2	89	25	1	3	4	32
2003-04	Halifax	QMJHL	46	2	10	12	155	....	....	....	....	....
	Cincinnati	AHL	7	0	0	0	9	....	....	....	....	....

DAWES, Nigel (DAWZ, NIGH-juhl) NYR

Left wing. Shoots left. 5'8", 170 lbs. Born, Winnipeg, Man., February 9, 1985.
(NY Rangers' 5th choice, 149th overall, in 2003 Entry Draft).

			Regular Season					Playoffs				
Season	Club	League	GP	G	A	TP	PIM	GP	G	A	TP	PIM
2000-01	Winnipeg Warriors	MMHL	36	55	41	96	74	....	....	....	....	....
2001-02	Kootenay Ice	WHL	54	15	19	34	14	22	9	6	15	8
2002-03	Kootenay Ice	WHL	72	47	45	92	54	11	4	8	12	6
2003-04	Kootenay Ice	WHL	56	47	23	70	31	4	1	2	3	10
	Hartford Wolf Pack	AHL	4	0	0	0	0	....	....	....	....	....

WHL West First All-Star Team (2004)

DAWSON, Aaron (DAW-suhn, AIR-ruhn) CAR.

Defense. Shoots left. 6'5", 220 lbs. Born, Terre Haute, IN, March 11, 1985.
(Carolina's 3rd choice, 102nd overall, in 2003 Entry Draft).

			Regular Season					Playoffs				
Season	Club	League	GP	G	A	TP	PIM	GP	G	A	TP	PIM
2001-02	Peterborough	OPJHL	41	9	20	29	79	....	....	....	....	....
	Peterborough	OHL	5	0	0	0	2	....	....	....	....	....
2002-03	Peterborough	OHL	65	1	8	9	76	7	0	0	0	8
2003-04	Peterborough	OHL	24	1	4	5	35	....	....	....	....	....

DeMARCHI, Matt   (dih-MAHR-shee, MAT)   N.J.

Defense. Shoots left. 6'3", 190 lbs. Born, Bemidji, MN, May 4, 1981.
(New Jersey's 4th choice, 57th overall, in 2000 Entry Draft).

Season	Club	League	GP	G	A	TP	PIM	GP	G	A	TP	PIM
1997-98	North Iowa	USHL	34	1	2	3	66	10	0	1	1	19
1998-99	North Iowa	USHL	53	4	14	18	131	....	....	....	....	....
99-2000	U. of Minnesota	WCHA	39	1	6	7	82	....	....	....	....	....
2000-01	U. of Minnesota	WCHA	39	4	9	13	*149	....	....	....	....	....
2001-02	U. of Minnesota	WCHA	36	3	8	11	112	....	....	....	....	....
2002-03	U. of Minnesota	WCHA	44	8	9	17	130	....	....	....	....	....
2003-04	Albany River Rats	AHL	52	4	10	14	78	....	....	....	....	....

NCAA Championship All-Tournament Team (2003)

DEMEN-WILLAUME, Richard   (deh-MEHN-WIHL-awm, RIH-kahrd)   COL.

Defense. Shoots left. 6'3", 196 lbs. Born, Asa, Sweden, January 28, 1986.
(Colorado's 4th choice, 154th overall, in 2004 Entry Draft).

Season	Club	League	GP	G	A	TP	PIM	GP	G	A	TP	PIM
2001-02	Vastra Frolunda 18	Swede-Jr.	13	2	2	4	14	3	1	0	1	2
	Vastra Frolunda Jr.	Swede-Jr.	1	0	0	0	0	....	....	....	....	....
2002-03	Vastra Frolunda 18	Swede-Jr.	22	0	6	6	14	5	0	1	1	6
	Vastra Frolunda Jr.	Swede-Jr.	1	0	0	0	2	7	1	2	3	4
2003-04	Vastra Frolunda Jr.	Swede-Jr.	35	6	7	13	22	....	....	....	....	....

DENISOV, Denis   (den-NEES-ahf, deh-NEES)   BUF.

Left wing. Shoots left. 6', 183 lbs. Born, Kalinin, USSR, December 31, 1981.
(Buffalo's 4th choice, 149th overall, in 2000 Entry Draft).

Season	Club	League	GP	G	A	TP	PIM	GP	G	A	TP	PIM
1997-98	HC CSKA Moscow	Russia	7	0	0	0	4	....	....	....	....	....
1998-99	HC CSKA Moscow	Russia-2	42	1	6	7	16	....	....	....	....	....
99-2000	HC CSKA Moscow	Russia-2	39	1	8	9	16	....	....	....	....	....
2000-01	HC CSKA Moscow	Russia-2	41	0	3	3	6	....	....	....	....	....
2001-02	Krylja Sovetov	Russia	47	3	4	7	37	....	....	....	....	....
	Krylja Sovetov 2	Russia-3	3	0	1	1	18	....	....	....	....	....
2002-03	Ufa Salavat	Russia	50	2	8	10	12	3	0	1	1	0
2003-04	Ak Bars Kazan	Russia	51	4	11	15	34	7	0	0	0	4

DESBIENS, Guillaume   (deh-BYEHN, gwee-AHM)   ATL.

Right wing. Shoots left. 6'2", 205 lbs. Born, Alma, Que., April 20, 1985.
(Atlanta's 3rd choice, 116th overall, in 2003 Entry Draft).

Season	Club	League	GP	G	A	TP	PIM	GP	G	A	TP	PIM
2001-02	Rouyn-Noranda	QMJHL	65	14	10	24	115	4	1	1	2	9
2002-03	Rouyn-Noranda	QMJHL	64	15	18	33	233	4	0	0	0	4
2003-04	Rouyn-Noranda	QMJHL	58	20	21	41	199	4	2	2	4	24

DESCHENES, Nick   (duh-SHAYN, NIHK)

Left wing. Shoots left. 6'3", 223 lbs. Born, Morinville, Alta., December 6, 1978.

Season	Club	League	GP	G	A	TP	PIM	GP	G	A	TP	PIM
1998-99	Fort Saskatchewan	AJHL	58	40	45	85	70	....	....	....	....	....
99-2000	Yale University	ECAC	29	6	9	15	15	....	....	....	....	....
2000-01	Yale University	ECAC	31	17	20	37	22	....	....	....	....	....
2001-02	Yale University	ECAC	23	5	11	16	4	....	....	....	....	....
2002-03	Yale University	ECAC	31	8	11	19	37	....	....	....	....	....
2003-04	Trenton Titans	ECHL	13	2	6	8	8	....	....	....	....	....
	Philadelphia	AHL	31	5	2	7	12	1	0	0	0	0

Signed as a free agent by **Philadelphia**, May 21, 2003.

DICAIRE, Gerard   (dih-KAIR, zhehr-AHR)   T.B.

Defense. Shoots left. 6'2", 190 lbs. Born, Faro, Yukon, September 14, 1982.
(Tampa Bay's 4th choice, 162nd overall, in 2002 Entry Draft).

Season	Club	League	GP	G	A	TP	PIM	GP	G	A	TP	PIM
1997-98	Tumble Ridge	NWJHL	34	15	28	43	63	....	....	....	....	....
1998-99	Prince George	BCHL	51	6	22	28	28	....	....	....	....	....
99-2000	Seattle	WHL	68	11	25	36	38	7	0	1	1	6
2000-01	Seattle	WHL	69	15	36	51	33	9	0	2	2	4
2001-02	Seattle	WHL	41	4	25	29	25	....	....	....	....	....
	Kootenay Ice	WHL	25	2	21	23	9	22	1	14	15	24
2002-03	Kootenay Ice	WHL	72	15	44	59	79	11	2	6	8	12
2003-04	Utah Grizzlies	AHL	53	2	7	9	36	....	....	....	....	....

• Re-entered NHL Entry Draft. Originally Buffalo's 2nd choice, 48th overall, in 2000 Entry Draft.
WHL West Second All-Star Team (2001, 2003)

DiCASMIRRO, Nate   (dee-CAZ-MIHR-oh, NAYT)   EDM.

Left wing. Shoots left. 5'11", 205 lbs. Born, Burnsville, MN, September 27, 1978.

Season	Club	League	GP	G	A	TP	PIM	GP	G	A	TP	PIM
1996-97	North Iowa	USHL	51	18	22	40	86	12	0	6	6	22
1997-98	North Iowa	USHL	52	29	45	74	118	11	5	5	10	34
1998-99	St. Cloud State	WCHA	34	6	8	14	46	....	....	....	....	....
99-2000	St. Cloud State	WCHA	40	19	24	43	26	....	....	....	....	....
2000-01	St. Cloud State	WCHA	32	9	20	29	26	....	....	....	....	....
2001-02	St. Cloud State	WCHA	41	17	33	50	58	....	....	....	....	....
	Hamilton Bulldogs	AHL	1	0	0	0	0	10	0	5	5	6
2002-03	Hamilton Bulldogs	AHL	49	5	12	17	22	16	2	1	3	8
2003-04	Toronto	AHL	71	17	18	35	37	2	0	1	1	0

USHL First All-Star Team (1998) • USHL MVP (1998) • WCHA Second All-Star Team (2002)
Signed as a free agent by **Edmonton**, May 28, 2002.

DISALVATORE, Jon   (dih-sal-vuh-TOH-ray, JAWN)   ST.L.

Right wing. Shoots right. 6'1", 200 lbs. Born, Bangor, ME, March 30, 1981.
(San Jose's 2nd choice, 104th overall, in 2000 Entry Draft).

Season	Club	League	GP	G	A	TP	PIM	GP	G	A	TP	PIM
1997-98	New England	EJHL	38	24	41	65	....	....	....	....	....	....
1998-99	New England	EJHL	48	44	76	*120	38	....	....	....	....	....
99-2000	Providence College	H-East	38	15	12	27	12	....	....	....	....	....
2000-01	Providence College	H-East	36	9	16	25	29	....	....	....	....	....
2001-02	Providence College	H-East	38	16	26	42	6	....	....	....	....	....
2002-03	Providence College	H-East	36	19	29	48	12	....	....	....	....	....
2003-04	Cleveland Barons	AHL	74	22	24	46	30	8	1	1	2	2

Signed as a free agent by **St. Louis**, June 30, 2004.

DIXON, Stephen   (DIHX-uhn, STEE-vehn)   PIT.

Center. Shoots left. 5'11", 188 lbs. Born, Halifax, N.S., September 7, 1985.
(Pittsburgh's 9th choice, 229th overall, in 2003 Entry Draft).

Season	Club	League	GP	G	A	TP	PIM	GP	G	A	TP	PIM
2001-02	Cape Breton	QMJHL	64	16	15	31	12	16	3	5	8	12
2002-03	Cape Breton	QMJHL	72	28	42	70	54	4	0	0	0	6
2003-04	Cape Breton	QMJHL	55	22	50	72	33	5	1	0	1	0

DOBRYSHKIN, Yuri   (doh-BRIHSH-kihn, yew-REE)   ATL.

Left wing. Shoots right. 6', 190 lbs. Born, Penza, USSR, July 19, 1979.
(Atlanta's 7th choice, 159th overall, in 1999 Entry Draft).

Season	Club	League	GP	G	A	TP	PIM	GP	G	A	TP	PIM
1996-97	Krylja Sovetov 2	Russia-3	35	13	5	18	42	....	....	....	....	....
	Krylja Sovetov 2	Russia	2	0	0	0	0	2	0	0	0	0
1997-98	Krylja Sovetov 2	Russia-3	26	12	5	17	68	....	....	....	....	....
	Krylja Sovetov	Russia	22	4	0	4	12	....	....	....	....	....
1998-99	Krylja Sovetov	Russia	50	11	5	16	86	....	....	....	....	....
99-2000	Ak Bars Kazan	Russia	27	6	9	15	24	17	2	0	2	10
2000-01	Ak Bars Kazan	Russia	40	10	5	15	32	4	2	0	2	2
2001-02	Ak Bars Kazan	Russia	38	9	8	17	22	11	0	2	2	6
2002-03	Cherepovets	Russia	49	19	7	26	82	12	5	2	7	12
2003-04	Cherepovets	Russia	53	11	7	18	75	....	....	....	....	....

DOELL, Kevin   (DOH-ehl, KEH-vihn)   ATL.

Center. Shoots left. 5'11", 190 lbs. Born, Saskatoon, Sask., July 15, 1979.

Season	Club	League	GP	G	A	TP	PIM	GP	G	A	TP	PIM
99-2000	U. of Denver	WCHA	40	8	15	23	18	....	....	....	....	....
2000-01	U. of Denver	WCHA	36	9	10	19	26	....	....	....	....	....
2001-02	U. of Denver	WCHA	41	20	23	43	28	....	....	....	....	....
2002-03	U. of Denver	WCHA	41	25	26	51	34	....	....	....	....	....
2003-04	Gwinnett	ECHL	63	33	41	74	88	13	1	6	7	12
	Chicago Wolves	AHL	8	1	1	2	6	1	0	0	0	0

ECHL All-Rookie Team (2004) • ECHL Rookie of the Year (2004)
Signed as a free agent by **Atlanta**, June 30, 2004.

DOHERTY, John   (DOH-her-tee, JAWN)   TOR.

Defense. Shoots right. 6'4", 213 lbs. Born, Malden, MA, March 25, 1984.
(Toronto's 1st choice, 57th overall, in 2003 Entry Draft).

Season	Club	League	GP	G	A	TP	PIM	GP	G	A	TP	PIM
2001-02	Phillips Andover	Hi-School	24	5	18	23	....	....	....	....	....	....
2002-03	Phillips Andover	Hi-School	24	12	12	24	40	....	....	....	....	....
	NH Jr. Monarchs	EJHL	11	1	4	5	36	....	....	....	....	....
2003-04	New Hampshire	H-East	16	1	2	3	6	....	....	....	....	....

DONALLY, Ryan   (DAWN-ah-lee, RIGH-uhn)   CGY.

Left wing. Shoots left. 6'4", 210 lbs. Born, Tecumseh, Ont., February 4, 1985.
(Calgary's 3rd choice, 97th overall, in 2003 Entry Draft).

Season	Club	League	GP	G	A	TP	PIM	GP	G	A	TP	PIM
2001-02	Windsor Spitfires	OHL	53	6	7	13	77	16	0	2	2	6
2002-03	Windsor Spitfires	OHL	65	11	15	26	108	7	0	1	1	8
2003-04	Windsor Spitfires	OHL	44	8	14	22	93	....	....	....	....	....

DONIKA, Mikhail   (DAW-nih-ka, mih-kigh-EHL)   DAL.

Defense. Shoots left. 6', 185 lbs. Born, Yaroslavl, USSR, May 15, 1979.
(Dallas' 11th choice, 272nd overall, in 1999 Entry Draft).

Season	Club	League	GP	G	A	TP	PIM	GP	G	A	TP	PIM
1996-97	Yaroslavl 2	Russia-3	15	3	5	8	6	....	....	....	....	....
	Torpedo Yaroslavl	Russia-2	19	1	2	3	32	2	0	0	0	0
1997-98	Yaroslavl 2	Russia-3	30	0	2	2	14	....	....	....	....	....
	Torpedo Yaroslavl	Russia	4	0	1	1	4	....	....	....	....	....
1998-99	Yaroslavl 2	Russia-3	4	0	1	1	4	....	....	....	....	....
	Torpedo Yaroslavl	Russia	37	0	1	1	10	....	....	....	....	....
99-2000	Torpedo Yaroslavl	Russia	35	0	1	1	22	10	0	0	0	4
2000-01	Dynamo Moscow	Russia	43	1	3	4	12	....	....	....	....	....
2001-02	Amur Khabarovsk	Russia	51	1	3	4	66	....	....	....	....	....
2002-03	Spartak Moscow	Russia	51	3	1	4	16	....	....	....	....	....
2003-04	Spartak Moscow	Russia-2	55	4	14	18	14	12	2	1	3	2

DORNIC, Ivan   (DOHR-nihch, ee-VAHN)   NYR

Center. Shoots right. 6', 183 lbs. Born, Bratislava, Czech., April 12, 1985.
(NY Rangers' 6th choice, 176th overall, in 2003 Entry Draft).

Season	Club	League	GP	G	A	TP	PIM	GP	G	A	TP	PIM
2001-02	Slov. Bratislava Jr.	Slovak-Jr.	17	7	7	14	33	....	....	....	....	....
2002-03	Slov. Bratislava Jr.	Slovak-Jr.	33	13	13	26	45	....	....	....	....	....
	Slov. Bratislava	Slovakia	3	1	0	1	0	....	....	....	....	....
2003-04	Portland	WHL	54	6	8	14	28	5	0	0	0	4

DOWELL, Jake   (DOW-uhl, JAYK)   CHI.

Center. Shoots left. 6', 202 lbs. Born, Eau Claire, WI, March 4, 1985.
(Chicago's 10th choice, 140th overall, in 2004 Entry Draft).

Season	Club	League	GP	G	A	TP	PIM	GP	G	A	TP	PIM
2000-01	Eau Claire Mem.	Hi-School	24	25	30	55	....	....	....	....	....	....
2001-02	U.S. National U-17	USDP	55	10	13	23	65	....	....	....	....	....
2002-03	U.S. National U-18	USDP	63	10	19	29	67	....	....	....	....	....
2003-04	U. of Wisconsin	WCHA	37	6	13	19	48	....	....	....	....	....

DOWN, Blaine   (DOWN, BLAYN)   NYI

Left wing. Shoots left. 5'11", 170 lbs. Born, Whitby, Ont., July 16, 1982.

Season	Club	League	GP	G	A	TP	PIM	GP	G	A	TP	PIM
1998-99	Oshawa	OPJHL	36	18	22	40	75	....	....	....	....	....
99-2000	Barrie Colts	OHL	43	17	22	39	49	22	10	6	16	18
2000-01	Barrie Colts	OHL	62	35	38	73	80	5	2	0	2	10
2001-02	Barrie Colts	OHL	63	25	36	61	92	20	15	10	25	34
2002-03	Bridgeport	AHL	54	8	13	21	30	9	0	0	0	21
2003-04	Bridgeport	AHL	51	6	13	19	34	4	0	1	1	6

Signed as a free agent by **NY Islanders**, August 13, 2002.

DROZDETSKY, Alexander — (drawz-DEHT-skee, al-ehx-AN-duhr) — PHI.

Right wing. Shoots left. 6', 180 lbs. Born, Moscow, USSR, November 10, 1981. .
(Philadelphia's 2nd choice, 94th overall, in 2000 Entry Draft).

Season	Club	League	GP	G	A	TP	PIM	GP	G	A	TP	PIM
1997-98	St. Petersburg 2	Russia-3	19	0	1	1	0					
1998-99	St. Petersburg 2	Russia-4	24	5	3	8	12					
99-2000	St. Petersburg 2	Russia-3	4	4	1	5	2					
	SKA St. Petersburg	Russia	32	2	0	2	10	4	0	0	0	0
2000-01	SKA St. Petersburg	Russia	42	6	7	13	74					
2001-02	CSKA Moscow	Russia	49	11	6	17	26					
2002-03	CSKA Moscow	Russia	46	14	13	27	30					
2003-04	Ak Bars Kazan	Russia	57	16	15	31	62	1	0	0	0	2

DUBEC, Marek — (DOO-behts, MAIR-ehk) — BUF.

Left wing. Shoots left. 6', 179 lbs. Born, Bratislava, Czech., February 26, 1982.
(Buffalo's 7th choice, 247th overall, in 2001 Entry Draft).

Season	Club	League	GP	G	A	TP	PIM	GP	G	A	TP	PIM
1996-97	Bratislava Jr.	Czech-Jr.	47	19	8	27	20					
1997-98	Bratislava Jr.	Czech-Jr.	40	17	18	35	59					
1998-99	Bratislava Jr.	Czech-Jr.	47	23	20	43	38					
99-2000	Bratislava Jr.	Czech-Jr.	36	16	10	26	61					
2000-01	Vsetin Jr.	Czech-Jr.	45	27	15	42	52	8	7	2	9	20
2001-02	Vsetin Jr.	Czech-Jr.	18	12	9	21	32					
	Vsetin	Czech	5	1	0	1	0	4	2	0	2	4
2002-03	Vsetin	Czech	22	2	4	6	24	4	0	0	0	2
	Vsetin Jr.	Czech-Jr.	8	6	6	12	24	5	1	0	1	12
	Slavia Trebec	Czech-2	16	3	2	5	24					
2003-04	HC Hame Zlin	Czech	5	0	1	1	2					
	HC Vsetin	Czech	41	7	6	13	73					
	HC Slezan Opava	Czech-2	3	0	1	1	2	1	0	0	0	4
	HC Sareza Ostrava	Czech-3										

DUBEN, Premysl — (DUH-behn, PREHM-uh-suhl) — NYR

Defense. Shoots left. 6'3", 220 lbs. Born, Jihlava, Czech., October 5, 1981.
(NY Rangers' 3rd choice, 112th overall, in 2000 Entry Draft).

Season	Club	League	GP	G	A	TP	PIM	GP	G	A	TP	PIM
1997-98	Dukla Jihlava Jr.	Czech-Jr.	25	1	6	7	34					
1998-99	Dukla Jihlava Jr.	Czech-Jr.	41	1	5	6	18					
99-2000	Dukla Jihlava Jr.	Czech-Jr.	27	4	2	6	36	14	0	1	1	4
	HC Dukla Jihlava	Czech-2	19	0	1	1	10					
2000-01	HC Dukla Jihlava	Czech-2	5	0	0	0	10					
	Baie-Comeau	QMJHL	32	0	8	8	36	9	1	0	1	12
2001-02	Dukla Jihlava Jr.	Czech-Jr.	13	0	5	5	20					
	HC Dukla Jihlava	Czech-2	33	0	1	1	36	6	0	0	0	0
2002-03	HC Dukla Jihlava	Czech-2	24	0	1	1	20	12	0	0	0	10
2003-04	Havlickuv Brod	Czech-3	12	0	1	1	12					
	HC Dukla Jihlava	Czech-2	20	0	0	0	47	10	0	0	0	16

DUBINSKY, Brandon — (DOO-bihn-skee, BRAN-duhn) — NYR

Center. Shoots left. 5'11", 180 lbs. Born, Anchorage, AK, April 29, 1986.
(NY Rangers' 6th choice, 60th overall, in 2004 Entry Draft).

Season	Club	League	GP	G	A	TP	PIM	GP	G	A	TP	PIM
2001-02	Alaska All-Stars	AASHA	37	14	24	38						
2002-03	Portland	WHL	44	8	18	26	35	7	2	2	4	10
2003-04	Portland	WHL	71	30	48	78	137	5	0	2	2	6

WHL West Second All-Star Team (2004)

DUDA, Radek — (DOO-duh, RA-dehk) — CGY.

Right wing. Shoots left. 6'1", 193 lbs. Born, Skolov, Czech., January 28, 1979.
(Calgary's 7th choice, 192nd overall, in 1998 Entry Draft).

Season	Club	League	GP	G	A	TP	PIM	GP	G	A	TP	PIM
1994-95	Sokolov Jr.	Czech-Jr.	36	67	37	104						
1995-96	Sparta Praha Jr.	Czech-Jr.	39	15	10	25						
1996-97	Sparta Praha Jr.	Czech-Jr.	21	9	14	23						
	Sokolov Jr.	Czech	1	0	0	0						
	HC Sparta Praha	Czech						1	0	0	0	0
1997-98	HC Sparta Praha	Czech	39	3	3	6	41	10	0	2	2	6
1998-99	Regina Pats	WHL	65	24	31	55	139					
99-2000	Lethbridge	WHL	69	42	64	106	193					
2000-01	HC Keramika Plzen	Czech	24	5	6	11	49					
	HC Sparta Praha	Czech	18	2	1	3	66					
2001-02	HC Keramika Plzen	Czech	49	17	18	35	156	6	1	5	6	18
2002-03	HC Keramika Plzen	Czech	13	5	8	13	47					
	HC Slavia Praha	Czech	31	12	15	27	105	17	7	3	10	40
2003-04	Ak Bars Kazan	Russia	41	6	9	15	58	3	1	1	2	2

DUPUIS, Philippe — (doo-PWEE, fihl-EEP) — CBJ

Center. Shoots right. 6', 192 lbs. Born, Laval, Que., April 24, 1985.
(Columbus' 5th choice, 104th overall, in 2003 Entry Draft).

Season	Club	League	GP	G	A	TP	PIM	GP	G	A	TP	PIM
2000-01	Laval-Laurentides	QAAA	46	16	27	43	74	8	1	5	6	30
2001-02	Hull Olympiques	QMJHL	67	7	14	21	59	12	6	5	11	14
2002-03	Hull Olympiques	QMJHL	68	22	34	56	89	20	2	4	6	22
2003-04	Gatineau	QMJHL	60	18	37	55	77	15	6	10	16	14

DVORAK, Petr — (duv-VOHR-ak, PEE-tuhr) — WSH.

Center. Shoots right. 6', 194 lbs. Born, Roznov, Czech., October 11, 1983.
(Washington's 8th choice, 118th overall, in 2002 Entry Draft).

Season	Club	League	GP	G	A	TP	PIM	GP	G	A	TP	PIM
99-2000	Havirov Jr.	Czech-Jr.	47	28	28	56	79					
2000-01	Havirov Jr.	Czech-Jr.	36	12	15	27	18					
	HC Femax Havirov	Czech	1	0	0	0	0					
2001-02	Havirov Jr.	Czech-Jr.	40	24	25	49	90					
	Sumperk	Czech-2	1	1	0	1	0					
	HC Femax Havirov	Czech	7	0	0	0	4					
2002-03	Regina Pats	WHL	64	16	23	39	30	5	2	1	3	2
2003-04	Havirov Jr.	Czech-Jr.	15	6	6	12	47					
	Havirov	Czech-2	26	5	4	9	22					

DWYER, Jeff — (DWIGH-uhr, JEHF) — ATL.

Defense. Shoots left. 6'1", 205 lbs. Born, Greenwich, CT, November 22, 1980.
(Atlanta's 8th choice, 178th overall, in 2000 Entry Draft).

Season	Club	League	GP	G	A	TP	PIM	GP	G	A	TP	PIM
1996-97	Choate-Rosemary	Hi-School	28	5	11	16						
1997-98	Choate-Rosemary	Hi-School	28	9	14	23						
1998-99	Choate-Rosemary	Hi-School	27	8	22	30						
99-2000	Choate-Rosemary	Hi-School	25	11	30	41	25					
2000-01	Yale University	ECAC	31	3	18	21	16					
2001-02	Yale University	ECAC	31	6	9	15	16					
2002-03	Yale University	ECAC	32	1	17	18	26					
2003-04	Yale University	ECAC	30	4	11	15	38					
	Chicago Wolves	AHL	11	0	0	0	0					

DWYER, Patrick — (DWIGH-uhr, PAT-rihk) — ATL.

Right wing. Shoots right. 5'11", 170 lbs. Born, Great Falls, MT, June 22, 1983.
(Atlanta's 3rd choice, 116th overall, in 2002 Entry Draft).

Season	Club	League	GP	G	A	TP	PIM	GP	G	A	TP	PIM
2000-01	Great Falls	NWJHL		33	57	90	106	12	10	12	22	
2001-02	West. Michigan	CCHA	38	17	19	36	20					
2002-03	West. Michigan	CCHA	33	9	10	19	20					
2003-04	West. Michigan	CCHA	35	13	13	26	22					

CCHA All-Rookie Team (2002) • CCHA Rookie of the Year (2002)

DYMENT, Chris — (DIGH-mehnt, KRIHS)

Defense. Shoots right. 6'3", 207 lbs. Born, Reading, MA, October 24, 1979.
(Montreal's 3rd choice, 97th overall, in 1999 Entry Draft).

Season	Club	League	GP	G	A	TP	PIM	GP	G	A	TP	PIM
1997-98	Reading High	Hi-School	22	22	22	44	15					
1998-99	Boston University	H-East	25	1	5	6	16					
99-2000	Boston University	H-East	42	11	20	31	42					
2000-01	Boston University	H-East	37	1	10	11	38					
2001-02	Boston University	H-East	37	7	18	25	24					
2002-03	Houston Aeros	AHL	40	2	3	5	64	17	0	1	1	8
2003-04	Houston Aeros	AHL	13	0	1	1	12					
	Springfield Falcons	AHL	23	0	1	1	16					

Hockey East First All-Star Team (2000) • NCAA East Second All-American Team (2000) • Hockey East Second All-Star Team (2002)

Traded to **Minnesota** by **Montreal** for Minnesota's 5th round choice (later traded to Calgary – Calgary selected Jiri Cetkovsky) in 2002 Entry Draft, May 25, 2002. Traded to **Phoenix** by **Minnesota** for Michael Schutte, December 9, 2003.

EAGER, Ben — (EE-guhr, BEHN) — PHI.

Left wing. Shoots left. 6'3", 215 lbs. Born, Ottawa, Ont., January 22, 1984.
(Phoenix's 2nd choice, 23rd overall, in 2002 Entry Draft).

Season	Club	League	GP	G	A	TP	PIM	GP	G	A	TP	PIM
99-2000	Ottawa Jr. Sens	OCJHL	50	8	11	19	119					
2000-01	Oshawa Generals	OHL	61	4	6	10	120					
2001-02	Oshawa Generals	OHL	63	14	23	37	255	5	0	1	1	13
2002-03	Oshawa Generals	OHL	58	16	24	40	216	8	0	4	4	8
2003-04	Oshawa Generals	OHL	61	25	27	52	204	7	2	3	5	31
	Philadelphia	NHL	5	0	0	0	0	3	0	1	1	8

Traded to **Philadelphia** by **Phoenix** with Sean Burke and Branko Radivojevic for Mike Comrie, February 9, 2004.

EAVES, Ben — (EEVZ, BEHN) — PIT.

Center. Shoots right. 5'8", 180 lbs. Born, Minneapolis, MN, March 27, 1982.
(Pittsburgh's 6th choice, 131st overall, in 2001 Entry Draft).

Season	Club	League	GP	G	A	TP	PIM	GP	G	A	TP	PIM
1998-99	Minnesota Selects	USAHA	71	68	88	156	12					
99-2000	Shat.-St. Mary's	Hi-School	57	47	71	118	16					
2000-01	Boston College	H-East	40	13	26	39	12					
2001-02	Boston College	H-East	23	13	26	39	12					
2002-03	Boston College	H-East	36	18	*39	*57	18					
2003-04	Boston College	H-East	26	9	25	34	4					

Hockey East Second All-Star Team (2002) • Hockey East First All-Star Team (2003) • Hockey East Player of the Year (2003) (co-winner - Michael Ayers) • NCAA East First All-American Team (2003)

EAVES, Patrick — (EEVZ, PAT-rihk) — OTT.

Right wing. Shoots right. 6', 185 lbs. Born, Calgary, Alta., May 1, 1984.
(Ottawa's 1st choice, 29th overall, in 2003 Entry Draft).

Season	Club	League	GP	G	A	TP	PIM	GP	G	A	TP	PIM
99-2000	Shat.-St. Mary's	Hi-School	50	23	24	47						
2000-01	U.S. National U-17	USDP	47	19	19	38	78					
	United States	Nt-Team	12	8	8	16	18					
2001-02	U.S. National U-18	USDP	49	25	28	53	142					
	United States	Nt-Team	11	6	12	18	47					
2002-03	Boston College	H-East	14	10	8	18	61					
2003-04	Boston College	H-East	34	18	23	41	66					

Hockey East Second All-Star Team (2004) • NCAA East Second All-American Team (2004)
• Missed majority of 2002-03 season recovering from neck injury suffered in game vs. Maine (H-East), December 7, 2002.

ECKERBLOM, Niklas — (EK-kuhr-blawm, NIHK-las) — MIN.

Center. Shoots left. 6'1", 196 lbs. Born, Vasterhaninge, Sweden, January 4, 1984.
(Minnesota's 7th choice, 204th overall, in 2002 Entry Draft).

Season	Club	League	GP	G	A	TP	PIM	GP	G	A	TP	PIM
99-2000	Djurgarden-18	Swede-Jr.	13	5	3	8	37					
2000-01				DID NOT PLAY								
2001-02	Djurgarden-18	Swede-Jr.	5	9	2	11	8					
	Djurgarden Jr.	Swede-Jr.	1	0	0	0	0					
2002-03	Djurgarden Jr.	Swede-Jr.	6	0	2	2	4					
	Djurgarden	Sweden	10	0	1	1	0	5	0	0	0	0
	Transunds IF	Swede-3	19	0	3	3	12					
2003-04	Djurgarden Jr.	Swede-Jr.	19	14	7	21	66	3	0	0	0	0
	Djurgarden	Sweden	38	0	0	0	8					
	Hammarby	Swede-2	1	0	0	0	0					

EDLER, Alexander (EHD-luhr, al-EHX-AN-duhr) VAN.

Defense. Shoots left. 6'3", 194 lbs. Born, Stockholm, Sweden, April 21, 1986.
(Vancouver's 2nd choice, 91st overall, in 2004 Entry Draft).

			Regular Season					Playoffs				
Season	**Club**	**League**	**GP**	**G**	**A**	**TP**	**PIM**	**GP**	**G**	**A**	**TP**	**PIM**
2001-02	Jamtland	Exhib.	8	0	1	1	2	....	....	....	....	....
2002-03	Jamtland	Exhib.	8	2	1	3	0	....	....	....	....	....
2003-04	Jamtland Jr.	Swede-Jr.	6	0	3	3	6	....	....	....	....	....
	Jamtland	Swede-3	24	3	6	9	20	....	....	....	....	....

EGENER, Mike (EHG-eh-nuhr, MIGHK) T.B.

Defense. Shoots left. 6'4", 195 lbs. Born, Lahr, West Germany, September 26, 1984.
(Tampa Bay's 1st choice, 34th overall, in 2003 Entry Draft).

			Regular Season					Playoffs				
Season	**Club**	**League**	**GP**	**G**	**A**	**TP**	**PIM**	**GP**	**G**	**A**	**TP**	**PIM**
99-2000	Calgary Bruins	CMHA	27	4	9	13	88	....	....	....	....	....
2000-01	Calgary Hitmen	WHL	52	1	0	1	91	6	0	0	0	5
2001-02	Calgary Hitmen	WHL	68	2	7	9	175	6	0	0	0	23
2002-03	Calgary Hitmen	WHL	40	2	8	10	210	3	1	0	1	8
2003-04	Calgary Hitmen	WHL	64	1	16	17	228	7	1	1	2	47

ELLIOTT, Brandon (EHL-lee-awt, BRAN-duhn) T.B.

Defense. Shoots left. 6'4", 225 lbs. Born, Orangeville, Ont., March 8, 1984.
(Tampa Bay's 4th choice, 158th overall, in 2004 Entry Draft).

			Regular Season					Playoffs				
Season	**Club**	**League**	**GP**	**G**	**A**	**TP**	**PIM**	**GP**	**G**	**A**	**TP**	**PIM**
2001-02	Orangeville	OJHL-B		STATISTICS NOT AVAILABLE								
	Mississauga	OHL	7	0	0	0	14	....	....	....	....	....
2002-03	Collingwood Blues	OPJHL		STATISTICS NOT AVAILABLE								
2003-04	Collingwood Blues	OPJHL	25	6	15	21	138	....	....	....	....	....
	Mississauga	OHL	30	0	4	4	89	13	0	0	0	32

ELOFSSON, Jonas (EHL-uhf-suhn, YOH-nuhs)

Defense. Shoots left. 6'1", 180 lbs. Born, Ulricehamn, Sweden, January 31, 1979.
(Edmonton's 4th choice, 94th overall, in 1997 Entry Draft).

			Regular Season					Playoffs				
Season	**Club**	**League**	**GP**	**G**	**A**	**TP**	**PIM**	**GP**	**G**	**A**	**TP**	**PIM**
1995-96	Farjestad Jr.	Swede-Jr.	26	6	11	17	18	....	....	....	....	....
1996-97	Farjestad	Sweden	3	0	0	0	0	5	0	1	1	0
	Farjestad	EuroHL	2	1	1	2	0	....	....	....	....	....
1997-98	Farjestad	Sweden	29	3	2	5	14	12	0	1	1	6
	Farjestad	EuroHL	7	1	1	2	4	....	....	....	....	....
1998-99	Farjestad	Sweden	40	2	7	9	18	4	0	0	0	0
	Farjestad	EuroHL	5	1	0	1	4	....	....	....	....	....
99-2000	Farjestad	Sweden	47	3	6	9	44	4	0	0	0	6
2000-01	HV 71 Jonkoping	Sweden	30	1	3	4	12	....	....	....	....	....
	TPS Turku	Finland	10	0	0	0	0	....	....	....	....	....
2001-02	Leksands IF	Sweden	30	8	20	28	12	....	....	....	....	....
	Leksands IF	Swede-Q	10	1	4	5	4	10	1	1	2	10
2002-03	Leksands IF	Sweden	46	6	3	9	26	5	0	0	0	8
2003-04	Leksands IF	Sweden	45	1	5	6	40	....	....	....	....	....

Traded to **Chicago** by **Edmonton** with Boris Mironov and Dean McAmmond for Chad Kilger, Daniel Cleary, Ethan Moreau and Christian Laflamme, March 20, 1999.

ELOMO, Teemu (eh-LOH-moh, TEE-moo) DAL.

Left wing. Shoots left. 5'11", 176 lbs. Born, Turku, Finland, January 13, 1979.
(Dallas' 5th choice, 132nd overall, in 1997 Entry Draft).

			Regular Season					Playoffs				
Season	**Club**	**League**	**GP**	**G**	**A**	**TP**	**PIM**	**GP**	**G**	**A**	**TP**	**PIM**
1993-94	TPS Turku-C	Finn-Jr.	34	7	25	32	56	....	....	....	....	....
1994-95	TPS Turku-C	Finn-Jr.	24	19	22	41	82	....	....	....	....	....
	TPS Turku-B	Finn-Jr.	8	5	2	7	12	2	1	0	1	0
1995-96	TPS Turku-B	Finn-Jr.	17	9	8	17	28	....	....	....	....	....
	TPS Turku Jr.	Finn-Jr.	2	0	0	0	0	....	....	....	....	....
	Kiekko-67 Turku	Finland-2	11	1	0	1	14	6	2	0	2	8
1996-97	TPS Turku Jr.	Finn-Jr.	9	6	2	8	16	....	....	....	....	....
	Kiekko-67 Turku	Finland-2	15	4	3	7	24	....	....	....	....	....
	TPS Turku	Finland	6	0	1	1	0	3	0	0	0	2
1997-98	TPS Turku	Finland	26	3	3	6	14	3	1	0	1	2
	TPS Turku	EuroHL	3	0	0	0	2	....	....	....	....	....
1998-99	TPS Turku	Finland	34	4	8	12	16	5	0	0	0	2
99-2000	TPS Turku	Finland	52	9	7	16	28	11	3	2	5	0
2000-01	TPS Turku	Finland	56	2	10	12	44	10	1	3	4	0
2001-02	Blues Espoo	Finland	49	12	14	26	66	3	0	0	0	14
2002-03	Blues Espoo	Finland	54	13	29	42	60	7	1	1	2	4
2003-04	Blues Espoo	Finland	55	11	12	23	34	9	5	1	6	14

ENEQVIST, Johan (EHN-uh-kvist, YOH-han) MTL.

Left wing. Shoots left. 6', 183 lbs. Born, Nacka, Sweden, January 21, 1982.
(Montreal's 5th choice, 109th overall, in 2000 Entry Draft).

			Regular Season					Playoffs				
Season	**Club**	**League**	**GP**	**G**	**A**	**TP**	**PIM**	**GP**	**G**	**A**	**TP**	**PIM**
99-2000	Leksands IF-18	Swede-Jr.	5	1	1	2	28	....	....	....	....	....
	Leksands IF Jr.	Swede-Jr.	36	10	13	23	36	2	0	0	0	0
2000-01	Leksands IF Jr.	Swede-Jr.	21	19	15	34	2	2	1	1	2	4
	Leksands IF	Sweden	2	0	0	0	0	....	....	....	....	....
2001-02	Leksands IF Jr.	Swede-Jr.	7	3	6	9	18	....	....	....	....	....
	Leksands IF	Sweden	45	3	7	10	24	....	....	....	....	....
2002-03	Leksands IF	Sweden	42	2	6	8	77	5	0	0	0	6
2003-04	Hammarby	Swede-2	53	11	20	31	38	....	....	....	....	....

ENGELLAND, Deryk (ehn-GUHL-uhnd, DEH-rihk) CGY.

Defense. Shoots right. 6'2", 205 lbs. Born, Edmonton, Alta., April 5, 1982.
(New Jersey's 11th choice, 194th overall, in 2000 Entry Draft).

			Regular Season					Playoffs				
Season	**Club**	**League**	**GP**	**G**	**A**	**TP**	**PIM**	**GP**	**G**	**A**	**TP**	**PIM**
1998-99	Moose Jaw	WHL	2	0	0	0	0	....	....	....	....	....
99-2000	Moose Jaw	WHL	55	0	5	5	62	4	0	0	0	0
2000-01	Moose Jaw	WHL	65	4	11	15	157	4	0	0	0	10
2001-02	Moose Jaw	WHL	56	7	10	17	102	12	0	2	2	27
2002-03	Moose Jaw	WHL	65	3	8	11	199	13	1	1	2	20
2003-04	Lowell	AHL	26	0	0	0	34	....	....	....	....	....
	Las Vegas	ECHL	35	2	11	13	63	2	0	0	0	0

Signed as a free agent by **Calgary**, July, 2003.

ENSTROM, Tobias (EHN-stuhm, toh-BEE-uhs) ATL.

Defense. Shoots left. 5'9", 175 lbs. Born, Nordingra, Sweden, November 5, 1984.
(Atlanta's 8th choice, 239th overall, in 2003 Entry Draft).

			Regular Season					Playoffs				
Season	**Club**	**League**	**GP**	**G**	**A**	**TP**	**PIM**	**GP**	**G**	**A**	**TP**	**PIM**
99-2000	MoDo 18	Swede-Jr.	3	0	0	0	0	....	....	....	....	....
2000-01	MoDo 18	Swede-Jr.	16	7	6	13	18	....	....	....	....	....
	MoDo Jr.	Swede-Jr.	1	0	0	0	0	....	....	....	....	....
2001-02	MoDo Jr.	Swede-Jr.	21	1	7	8	10	2	1	1	2	2
2002-03	MoDo Jr.	Swede-Jr.	7	4	6	10	31	....	....	....	....	....
	MoDo	Sweden	42	1	5	6	16	6	0	1	1	4
2003-04	MoDo	Sweden	33	1	4	5	6	6	1	1	2	2

ERICKSON, Mike (AIR-ihk-suhn, MIGHK) MIN.

Right wing. Shoots right. 6'2", 201 lbs. Born, Minneapolis, MN, April 12, 1983.
(Minnesota's 3rd choice, 72nd overall, in 2002 Entry Draft).

			Regular Season					Playoffs				
Season	**Club**	**League**	**GP**	**G**	**A**	**TP**	**PIM**	**GP**	**G**	**A**	**TP**	**PIM**
1998-99	Eden Prairie Eagles	Hi-School	23	24	18	42	....	....	....	....	....	....
99-2000	Eden Prairie Eagles	Hi-School	25	38	25	63	....	....	....	....	....	....
2000-01	Eden Prairie Eagles	Hi-School	22	24	26	50	....	....	....	....	....	....
	Des Moines	USHL	4	0	0	0	0	3	0	0	0	0
2001-02	U. of Minnesota	WCHA	9	1	2	3	2	....	....	....	....	....
2002-03	U. of Minnesota	WCHA	16	0	2	2	4	....	....	....	....	....
	Des Moines	USHL	28	12	18	30	10	4	1	3	4	0
2003-04	Des Moines	USHL	58	*37	24	61	23	3	1	2	3	0

• Missed majority of 2001-02 season recovering from foot injury suffered in game vs. U. of Minnesota-Duluth (WCHA), November 17, 2001. • Granted leave of absence by U. of Minnesota (WCHA), January 14, 2003. • Signed as a free agent by **Des Moines** (USHL), January 14, 2003. • Signed Letter of Intent to attend **Western Michigan University** (CCHA), October 29, 2003.

ERIKSSON, Loui (AIR-ihk-suhn, LOO-ee) DAL.

Left wing. Shoots left. 6'1", 183 lbs. Born, Goteborg, Sweden, July 17, 1985.
(Dallas' 1st choice, 33rd overall, in 2003 Entry Draft).

			Regular Season					Playoffs				
Season	**Club**	**League**	**GP**	**G**	**A**	**TP**	**PIM**	**GP**	**G**	**A**	**TP**	**PIM**
2000-01	V. Frolunda-18	Swede-Jr.	9	5	3	8	4	....	....	....	....	....
	V. Frolunda Jr.	Swede-Jr.	1	0	0	0	0	....	....	....	....	....
2001-02	V. Frolunda-18	Swede-Jr.	1	1	0	1	0	....	....	....	....	....
	V. Frolunda Jr.	Swede-Jr.	35	7	15	22	2	8	2	3	5	2
2002-03	V. Frolunda Jr.	Swede-Jr.	30	16	15	31	10	8	4	6	10	4
2003-04	Vastra Frolunda	Sweden	46	8	5	13	4	10	1	5	6	0

ERIKSSON, Tim (AIR-ihk-suhn, TIHM) L.A.

Center. Shoots left. 5'9", 161 lbs. Born, Sodertalje, Sweden, February 5, 1982.
(Los Angeles' 7th choice, 206th overall, in 2000 Entry Draft).

			Regular Season					Playoffs				
Season	**Club**	**League**	**GP**	**G**	**A**	**TP**	**PIM**	**GP**	**G**	**A**	**TP**	**PIM**
1997-98	Sodertalje SK Jr.	Swede-Jr.	11	7	12	19	10	....	....	....	....	....
1998-99	V. Frolunda Jr.	Swede-Jr.	29	7	8	15	6	....	....	....	....	....
99-2000	V. Frolunda Jr.	Swede-Jr.	36	16	25	41	82	....	....	....	....	....
2000-01	Hammarby	Swede-2	1	2	1	3	0	....	....	....	....	....
	Hammarby	Swede-2	38	9	22	31	10	14	2	4	6	8
2001-02	Hammarby	Swede-2	44	10	30	40	34	2	0	1	1	0
2002-03	Linkopings HC	Sweden	49	2	8	10	8	....	....	....	....	....
	Linkopings HC	Swede-Q	10	1	4	5	16	....	....	....	....	....
2003-04	Linkopings HC	Sweden	50	10	16	26	39	5	0	0	0	4

ESTRADA, Kevin (eh-STRA-duh, KEH-vihn) CAR.

Right wing. Shoots left. 5'11", 185 lbs. Born, Surrey, B.C., May 28, 1982.
(Carolina's 3rd choice, 91st overall, in 2001 Entry Draft).

			Regular Season					Playoffs				
Season	**Club**	**League**	**GP**	**G**	**A**	**TP**	**PIM**	**GP**	**G**	**A**	**TP**	**PIM**
1997-98	Chilliwack Chiefs	BCHL	35	1	5	6	17	....	....	....	....	....
1998-99	Chilliwack Chiefs	BCHL	58	13	29	42	58	....	....	....	....	....
99-2000	Chilliwack Chiefs	BCHL	45	9	20	29	29	30	6	27	33	14
2000-01	Chilliwack Chiefs	BCHL	59	34	*84	*118	65	....	....	....	....	....
2001-02	Michigan State	CCHA	40	4	7	11	24	....	....	....	....	....
2002-03	Michigan State	CCHA	35	7	4	11	16	....	....	....	....	....
2003-04	Michigan State	CCHA	34	6	10	16	43	....	....	....	....	....

EVANS, Blake (EH-vans, BLAYK) ST.L.

Center. Shoots right. 6'1", 210 lbs. Born, Smiley, Sask., July 2, 1980.
(Washington's 10th choice, 251st overall, in 1998 Entry Draft).

			Regular Season					Playoffs				
Season	**Club**	**League**	**GP**	**G**	**A**	**TP**	**PIM**	**GP**	**G**	**A**	**TP**	**PIM**
1995-96	Sask. Contacts	SMHL	41	15	23	38	84	....	....	....	....	....
1996-97	Spokane Chiefs	WHL	53	4	7	11	19	7	0	0	0	0
1997-98	Spokane Chiefs	WHL	16	6	5	11	29	....	....	....	....	....
	Tri-City Americans	WHL	57	13	29	42	102	....	....	....	....	....
1998-99	Tri-City Americans	WHL	72	18	29	47	131	12	0	4	4	16
99-2000	Tri-City Americans	WHL	72	27	43	70	110	4	1	0	1	6
2000-01	Tri-City Americans	WHL	40	28	31	59	70	....	....	....	....	....
	Regina Pats	WHL	27	24	19	43	50	6	6	2	8	8
2001-02	Peoria Rivermen	ECHL	43	17	20	37	26	....	....	....	....	....
	Worcester IceCats	AHL	28	4	5	9	18	3	0	0	0	2
2002-03	Worcester IceCats	AHL	78	13	21	34	79	3	0	0	0	0
2003-04	Worcester IceCats	AHL	80	21	23	44	91	10	2	3	5	10

WHL East Second All-Star Team (2001)

Signed as a free agent by **St. Louis**, April 11, 2001.

EVSEEV, Vladislav (yehv-SAY-ehv, VLA-dih-slav) BOS.

Left wing. Shoots left. 6'2", 200 lbs. Born, Moscow, USSR, September 10, 1984.
(Boston's 2nd choice, 56th overall, in 2002 Entry Draft).

			Regular Season					Playoffs				
Season	**Club**	**League**	**GP**	**G**	**A**	**TP**	**PIM**	**GP**	**G**	**A**	**TP**	**PIM**
99-2000	Moscow Dyno. Jr.	Russia-Jr.	5	2	3	5	6	....	....	....	....	....
	Moscow Dyno. 18	Russia-Jr.	6	5	2	7	2	....	....	....	....	....
2000-01	Dyno. Moscow Jr.	Russia-Jr.	6	5	2	7	2	....	....	....	....	....
2001-02	CSKA Moscow 2	Russia-3	8	2	1	3	2	....	....	....	....	....
	HC CSKA	Russia-2	15	2	5	7	10	....	....	....	....	....
	CSKA Moscow-18	Russia-Jr.	5	4	4	8	4	....	....	....	....	....
2002-03	Dynamo Moscow	Russia	22	1	1	2	2	1	0	0	0	0
2003-04	Vityaz Podolsk	Russia-2	8	1	2	3	2	7	0	0	0	2

EZHOV, Denis (YEHZH-awf, DEH-nihs) BUF.

Defense. Shoots left. 5'11", 200 lbs. Born, Togliatti, USSR, February 28, 1985.
(Buffalo's 5th choice, 114th overall, in 2003 Entry Draft).

			Regular Season					Playoffs				
Season	Club	League	GP	G	A	TP	PIM	GP	G	A	TP	PIM
99-2000	Lada Togliatti 2	Russia-3	4	0	0	0	4	....	....	....	....	....
2000-01	Lada Togliatti 2	Russia-3	STATISTICS NOT AVAILABLE									
2001-02	Lada Togliatti 2	Russia-3	STATISTICS NOT AVAILABLE									
	Lada Togliatti Jr.	Russia-Jr.	4	2	4	6	6	....	....	....	....	....
	Lada Togliatti	Russia	15	0	0	0	6	....	....	....	....	....
2002-03	Lada Togliatti 2	Russia-3	15	2	7	9	4	....	....	....	....	....
	CSK VVS Samara	Russia-2	9	0	1	1	8	....	....	....	....	....
	CSKA Moscow 18	Russia-Jr.	7	0	5	5	10	....	....	....	....	....
2003-04	Novokuznetsk	Russia	19	0	1	1	2	3	0	0	0	0
	CSKA Moscow 2	Russia-3	4	1	2	3	2	....	....	....	....	....

FABRY, Branislav (FA-bree, BRAN-ih-slav) BUF.

Left wing. Shoots left. 6', 185 lbs. Born, Bratislava, Czech., January 15, 1985.
(Buffalo's 2nd choice, 65th overall, in 2003 Entry Draft).

			Regular Season					Playoffs				
Season	Club	League	GP	G	A	TP	PIM	GP	G	A	TP	PIM
2000-01	Slov. Bratislava Jr.	Slovak-Jr.	47	22	25	47	....	....	....	....	....	....
2001-02	Slov. Bratislava Jr.	Slovak-Jr.	48	29	37	66	....	....	....	....	....	....
2002-03	Slov. Bratislava Jr.	Slovak-Jr.	32	12	15	27	84	....	....	....	....	....
	Slov. Bratislava	Slovakia	8	0	0	0	0	....	....	....	....	....
2003-04	Slov. Bratislava Jr.	Slovak-Jr.	4	5	2	7	14	....	....	....	....	....
	Slov. Bratislava	Slovakia	44	1	6	7	2	5	0	0	0	0

FALARDEAU, Lee (FAL-ahr-doh, LEE) NYR

Center. Shoots left. 6'4", 203 lbs. Born, Midland, MI, July 22, 1983.
(NY Rangers' 1st choice, 33rd overall, in 2002 Entry Draft).

			Regular Season					Playoffs				
Season	Club	League	GP	G	A	TP	PIM	GP	G	A	TP	PIM
99-2000	U.S. National U-17	USDP	61	9	14	23	....	....	....	....	....	....
2000-01	U.S. National U-18	USDP	61	10	21	31	26	....	....	....	....	....
2001-02	Michigan State	CCHA	34	4	10	14	24	....	....	....	....	....
2002-03	Michigan State	CCHA	39	9	6	15	39	....	....	....	....	....
2003-04	Michigan State	CCHA	35	5	5	10	28	....	....	....	....	....

FATA, Drew (FA-tuh, DROO) PIT.

Defense. Shoots left. 6'1", 220 lbs. Born, Sault Ste. Marie, Ont., July 28, 1983.
(Pittsburgh's 3rd choice, 86th overall, in 2001 Entry Draft).

			Regular Season					Playoffs				
Season	Club	League	GP	G	A	TP	PIM	GP	G	A	TP	PIM
1998-99	S.S. Marie AA	NOHA	46	4	16	20	55	....	....	....	....	....
99-2000	St. Michael's B	OPJHL	49	9	18	27	144	....	....	....	....	....
2000-01	St. Michael's	OHL	58	5	15	20	134	18	1	3	4	26
2001-02	St. Michael's	OHL	67	7	21	28	175	15	1	9	10	38
2002-03	St. Michael's	OHL	35	6	13	19	66	....	....	....	....	....
	Kingston	OHL	34	2	17	19	64	....	....	....	....	....
2003-04	Wilkes-Barre	AHL	23	1	2	3	26	....	....	....	....	....
	Wheeling Nailers	ECHL	28	6	10	16	61	4	0	0	0	8

FEDOROV, Yevgeny (FEH-duh-rahf, yehv-GEH-nee) L.A.

Center. Shoots left. 5'10", 187 lbs. Born, Sverdlovsk, USSR, November 11, 1980.
(Los Angeles' 6th choice, 201st overall, in 2000 Entry Draft).

			Regular Season					Playoffs				
Season	Club	League	GP	G	A	TP	PIM	GP	G	A	TP	PIM
1997-98	Krylja Sovetov 2	Russia-3	20	1	6	7	48	....	....	....	....	....
	Krylja Sovetov	Russia	32	1	0	1	12	....	....	....	....	....
1998-99	Krylja Sovetov	Russia	52	5	3	8	61	....	....	....	....	....
99-2000	Perm	Russia	37	5	5	10	20	3	0	1	1	4
2000-01	Perm	Russia	43	9	9	18	18	....	....	....	....	....
2001-02	Ak Bars Kazan	Russia	45	10	12	22	12	11	0	0	0	2
2002-03	Ak Bars Kazan	Russia	46	4	11	15	26	5	1	0	1	2
2003-04	Ak Bars Kazan	Russia	47	7	4	11	14	4	0	0	0	0

FEHR, Eric (FAIR, AIR-ihk) WSH.

Right wing. Shoots right. 6'3", 186 lbs. Born, Winkler, Man., September 7, 1985.
(Washington's 1st choice, 18th overall, in 2003 Entry Draft).

			Regular Season					Playoffs				
Season	Club	League	GP	G	A	TP	PIM	GP	G	A	TP	PIM
2000-01	Pembina	MMHL	36	45	13	58	30	....	....	....	....	....
	Brandon	WHL	4	0	0	0	0	....	....	....	....	....
2001-02	Brandon	WHL	63	11	16	27	29	12	1	1	2	0
2002-03	Brandon	WHL	70	26	29	55	76	17	4	8	12	26
2003-04	Brandon	WHL	71	50	34	84	129	7	5	0	5	16

FEMENELLA, Arthur (feh-meh-NEHL-uh, AHR-thuhr) T.B.

Defense. Shoots right. 6'7", 235 lbs. Born, Annandale, NJ, June 6, 1982.
(Tampa Bay's 7th choice, 188th overall, in 2001 Entry Draft).

			Regular Season					Playoffs				
Season	Club	League	GP	G	A	TP	PIM	GP	G	A	TP	PIM
1998-99	U.S. National U-17	USDP	51	0	2	2	135	....	....	....	....	....
99-2000	U.S. National U-17	USDP	54	0	8	8	156	....	....	....	....	....
	Sioux City	USHL	3	0	0	0	7	....	....	....	....	....
2000-01	Sioux City	USHL	52	1	1	2	*252	3	0	0	0	2
2001-02	Sioux City	USHL	56	1	10	11	215	12	0	1	1	32
2002-03	Sioux City	USHL	48	1	6	7	197	....	....	....	....	....
2003-04	U. of Vermont	ECAC	27	1	0	1	67	....	....	....	....	....

FERGUSON, Troy (fuhr-GUH-suhn, TROI) CAR.

Right wing. Shoots right. 5'10", 170 lbs. Born, Calgary, Alta., September 30, 1980.
(Carolina's 7th choice, 276th overall, in 2000 Entry Draft).

			Regular Season					Playoffs				
Season	Club	League	GP	G	A	TP	PIM	GP	G	A	TP	PIM
1996-97	Kitchener	OJHL-B	47	14	15	29	16	....	....	....	....	....
1997-98	U.S. National U-18	USDP	54	11	9	20	14	....	....	....	....	....
1998-99	U.S. National U-17	USDP	24	3	10	13	14	....	....	....	....	....
	U.S. National U-18	USDP	29	4	4	8	20	....	....	....	....	....
99-2000	Michigan State	CCHA	42	5	7	12	10	....	....	....	....	....
2000-01	Michigan State	CCHA	41	4	10	14	12	....	....	....	....	....
2001-02	Michigan State	CCHA	39	1	5	6	14	....	....	....	....	....
2002-03	Michigan State	CCHA	39	2	7	9	4	....	....	....	....	....
	Lowell	AHL	6	1	0	1	2	....	....	....	....	....
2003-04	DID NOT PLAY — ATTENDED MEDICAL SCHOOL											

FERLAND, Jonathan (fair-LAWN, JAWN-ah-thun) MTL.

Right wing. Shoots right. 6'2", 211 lbs. Born, Quebec City, Que., February 9, 1983.
(Montreal's 5th choice, 212th overall, in 2002 Entry Draft).

			Regular Season					Playoffs				
Season	Club	League	GP	G	A	TP	PIM	GP	G	A	TP	PIM
1998-99	Laval-Laurentides	QAAA	42	18	17	35	50	....	....	....	....	....
99-2000	Moncton Wildcats	QMJHL	52	3	6	9	21	11	0	1	1	0
2000-01	Acadie-Bathurst	QMJHL	70	17	11	28	135	13	0	4	4	47
2001-02	Acadie-Bathurst	QMJHL	55	28	46	74	104	10	2	10	12	8
2002-03	Acadie-Bathurst	QMJHL	68	45	44	89	94	11	4	5	9	16
2003-04	Hamilton Bulldogs	AHL	70	5	10	15	43	10	0	0	0	6

FERNHOLM, Daniel (FUHRN-hohlm, DAN-yehl) PIT.

Defense. Shoots left. 6'4", 218 lbs. Born, Stockholm, Sweden, December 20, 1983.
(Pittsburgh's 4th choice, 101st overall, in 2002 Entry Draft).

			Regular Season					Playoffs				
Season	Club	League	GP	G	A	TP	PIM	GP	G	A	TP	PIM
99-2000	Mora IK Jr.	Swede-Jr.	2	1	1	2	4	....	....	....	....	....
	Mora IK Jr.	Swede-Jr.	33	3	3	6	8	1	0	0	0	0
2000-01	Mora IK Jr.	Swede-Jr.	3	0	1	1	2	....	....	....	....	....
	Mora IK	Swede-2	2	0	0	0	0	....	....	....	....	....
2001-02	Djurgarden Jr.	Swede-Jr.	8	6	13	19	12	3	0	0	0	0
2002-03	Huddinge IK	Swede-2	39	6	10	16	20	2	1	0	1	0
	Huddinge IK Jr.	Swede-Jr.	1	0	0	0	2	....	....	....	....	....
2003-04	Djurgarden	Sweden	37	4	7	11	28	4	0	0	0	4
	Hammarby	Swede-2	15	1	3	4	6	....	....	....	....	....

FIEDLER, Jonas (FIHD-luhr, YOH-nahsh) CAR.

Right wing. Shoots right. 6'2", 180 lbs. Born, Jihlava, Czech., May 29, 1984.
(Carolina's 7th choice, 235th overall, in 2004 Entry Draft).

			Regular Season					Playoffs				
Season	Club	League	GP	G	A	TP	PIM	GP	G	A	TP	PIM
99-2000	Dukla Jihlava Jr.	Czech-Jr.	48	11	11	22	48	....	....	....	....	....
2000-01	Dukla Jihlava Jr.	Czech-Jr.	44	29	33	62	167	....	....	....	....	....
2001-02	Plymouth Whalers	OHL	68	8	12	20	27	6	0	1	1	4
2002-03	Plymouth Whalers	OHL	63	7	21	28	59	18	5	9	14	10
2003-04	Plymouth Whalers	OHL	63	18	28	46	83	9	1	6	7	16

• Re-entered NHL Entry Draft. Originally San Jose's 3rd choice, 86th overall, in 2002 Entry Draft.

FILEWICH, Jonathan (FIGHL-uh-which, JAWN-ah-thun) PIT.

Right wing. Shoots right. 6'2", 205 lbs. Born, Kelowna, B.C., October 2, 1984.
(Pittsburgh's 3rd choice, 70th overall, in 2003 Entry Draft).

			Regular Season					Playoffs				
Season	Club	League	GP	G	A	TP	PIM	GP	G	A	TP	PIM
1998-99	Sherwood Park	AMBHL	36	29	43	72	90	....	....	....	....	....
99-2000	Sherwood Park	AMHL	33	28	20	48	59	....	....	....	....	....
	Prince George	WHL	3	0	0	0	0	....	....	....	....	....
2000-01	Prince George	WHL	61	9	16	25	32	....	....	....	....	....
2001-02	Prince George	WHL	66	13	19	32	23	7	2	0	2	2
2002-03	Prince George	WHL	51	27	27	54	45	5	1	1	2	2
2003-04	Prince George	WHL	72	30	25	55	52	....	....	....	....	....

FILIPOWICZ, Jayme (fihl-ih-POW-its, JAY-mee)

Defense. Shoots left. 6'2", 215 lbs. Born, Arlington Heights, IL, June 15, 1976.

			Regular Season					Playoffs				
Season	Club	League	GP	G	A	TP	PIM	GP	G	A	TP	PIM
1993-94	Rochester	USHL	47	7	16	23	52	....	....	....	....	....
1994-95	Dubuque	USHL	35	4	10	14	....	....	....	....	....	....
1995-96	Dubuque	USHL	45	7	16	23	52	....	....	....	....	....
1996-97	New Hampshire	H-East	35	3	16	19	43	....	....	....	....	....
1997-98	New Hampshire	H-East	38	3	28	31	47	....	....	....	....	....
1998-99	New Hampshire	H-East	41	8	30	38	56	....	....	....	....	....
99-2000	Milwaukee	IHL	76	9	23	32	118	3	0	1	1	0
2000-01	Milwaukee	IHL	68	0	13	13	101	2	0	0	0	2
2001-02	Quebec Citadelles	AHL	63	0	7	7	107	1	0	0	0	2
2002-03	Saint John Flames	AHL	63	2	13	15	106	....	....	....	....	....
	Richmond	ECHL	20	1	8	9	36	....	....	....	....	....
2003-04	Hartford Wolf Pack	AHL	63	2	6	8	116	7	0	1	1	2

Hockey East First All-Star Team (1999) • NCAA East Second All-American Team (1999) • NCAA Championship All-Tournament Team (1999)

Signed as a free agent by **Nashville**, June 17, 1999.

FILPPULA, Valtteri (FIHL-poo-luh, VAL-tuhr-ee) DET.

Center. Shoots left. 5'11", 172 lbs. Born, Vantaa, Finland, March 20, 1984.
(Detroit's 3rd choice, 95th overall, in 2002 Entry Draft).

			Regular Season					Playoffs				
Season	Club	League	GP	G	A	TP	PIM	GP	G	A	TP	PIM
2000-01	Jokerit Helsinki-B	Finn-Jr.	31	18	29	47	4	....	....	....	....	....
	Jokerit Helsinki Jr.	Finn-Jr.	1	0	1	1	0	....	....	....	....	....
2001-02	Jokerit Helsinki-B	Finn-Jr.	1	0	1	1	0	....	....	....	....	....
	Jokerit Helsinki Jr.	Finn-Jr.	40	8	15	23	14	9	4	9	13	2
2002-03	Jokerit Helsinki Jr.	Finn-Jr.	35	16	37	53	39	11	4	10	14	4
2003-04	Jokerit Helsinki	Finland	49	5	13	18	6	....	....	....	....	....

FINGER, Jeff (FIHN-guhr, JEHF) COL.

Defense. Shoots left. 6'2", 195 lbs. Born, Hancock, MI, December 18, 1979.
(Colorado's 11th choice, 240th overall, in 1999 Entry Draft).

			Regular Season					Playoffs				
Season	Club	League	GP	G	A	TP	PIM	GP	G	A	TP	PIM
1997-98	Green Bay	USHL	51	5	9	14	208	4	0	0	0	18
1998-99	Green Bay	USHL	54	11	28	39	199	6	0	3	3	14
99-2000	Green Bay	USHL	55	13	35	48	15	14	3	11	14	40
2000-01	St. Cloud State	WCHA	41	4	5	9	84	....	....	....	....	....
2001-02	St. Cloud State	WCHA	42	6	20	26	105	....	....	....	....	....
2002-03	St. Cloud State	WCHA	24	5	8	13	46	....	....	....	....	....
2003-04	Hershey Bears	AHL	63	2	9	11	88	....	....	....	....	....
	Reading Royals	ECHL	10	2	5	7	24	....	....	....	....	....

FISTRIC, Mark (FIHST-rihc, MAHRK) DAL.

Defense. Shoots left. 6'2", 232 lbs. Born, Edmonton, Alta., June 1, 1986.
(Dallas' 1st choice, 28th overall, in 2004 Entry Draft).

			Regular Season					Playoffs				
Season	Club	League	GP	G	A	TP	PIM	GP	G	A	TP	PIM
2000-01	Edmonton MLAC	AMBHL	34	13	13	26	144	....	....	....	....	....
2001-02	Edmonton MLAC	AMHL	30	8	10	18	85	....	....	....	....	....
	Vancouver	WHL	4	0	2	2	0	....	....	....	....	....
2002-03	Vancouver Giants	WHL	63	2	7	9	81	4	0	0	0	8
2003-04	Vancouver Giants	WHL	72	1	11	12	192	11	0	2	2	10

FITZGERALD, Zack (fihtz-JAIR-uhld, ZAK) **ST.L.**

Defense. Shoots left. 6'2", 205 lbs. Born, Two Harbors, MN, June 16, 1985.
(St. Louis' 4th choice, 88th overall, in 2003 Entry Draft).

			Regular Season					Playoffs				
Season	Club	League	GP	G	A	TP	PIM	GP	G	A	TP	PIM
2000-01	Duluth East	Hi-School	26	1	7	8	44	....	....	....	....	....
2001-02	Seattle	WHL	61	3	7	10	214	10	0	2	2	19
2002-03	Seattle	WHL	64	8	14	22	232	15	0	4	4	33
2003-04	Seattle	WHL	58	4	15	19	163	....	....	....	....	....

FITZRANDOLPH, Colin (fihts-RAN-dawlf, KAW-lihn) **ATL.**

Center. Shoots left. 6'3", 220 lbs. Born, Canton, NY, April 23, 1982.
(Atlanta's 8th choice, 201st overall, in 2001 Entry Draft).

			Regular Season					Playoffs				
Season	Club	League	GP	G	A	TP	PIM	GP	G	A	TP	PIM
2000-01	Phillips Exeter	Hi-School	23	7	33	40	....	....	....	....	....	....
2001-02	St. Lawrence	ECAC	13	0	3	3	21	....	....	....	....	....
2002-03	St. Lawrence	ECAC	31	2	4	6	16	....	....	....	....	....
2003-04	St. Lawrence	ECAC	32	2	6	8	28	....	....	....	....	....

FLACHE, Paul (FLAK, PAWL) **ATL.**

Defense. Shoots right. 6'5", 220 lbs. Born, Toronto, Ont., March 4, 1982.
(Atlanta's 5th choice, 144th overall, in 2002 Entry Draft).

			Regular Season					Playoffs				
Season	Club	League	GP	G	A	TP	PIM	GP	G	A	TP	PIM
1998-99	Cobourg Cougars	OPJHL	41	1	6	7	50	....	....	....	....	....
99-2000	Brampton	OHL	54	1	0	1	59	6	0	0	0	8
2000-01	Brampton	OHL	68	8	16	24	100	9	1	1	2	18
2001-02	Brampton	OHL	68	9	35	44	148	....	....	....	....	....
2002-03	Greenville Grrrowl	ECHL	46	1	9	10	64	4	0	4	4	6
2003-04	Chicago Wolves	AHL	9	2	2	4	12	....	....	....	....	....
	Gwinnett	ECHL	62	3	15	18	114	10	2	2	4	4

• Re-entered NHL Entry Draft. Originally Edmonton's 5th choice, 152nd overall, in 2000 Entry Draft.

FLEISCHMANN, Tomas (FLIGHSH-muhn, TAW-mash) **WSH.**

Left wing. Shoots left. 6', 165 lbs. Born, Koprivnice, Czech., May 16, 1984.
(Detroit's 2nd choice, 63rd overall, in 2002 Entry Draft).

			Regular Season					Playoffs				
Season	Club	League	GP	G	A	TP	PIM	GP	G	A	TP	PIM
99-2000	HC Vitkovice Jr.	Czech-Jr.	46	9	13	22	6	....	....	....	....	....
2000-01	HC Vitkovice 18	Czech-Jr.	30	28	34	62	8	....	....	....	....	....
	HC Vitkovice Jr.	Czech-Jr.	21	4	9	13	8	....	....	....	....	....
2001-02	HC Vitkovice Jr.	Czech-Jr.	46	26	35	51	16	....	....	....	....	....
	TJ Novy Jicin	Czech-3	8	3	2	5	8	7	3	4	7	35
2002-03	Moose Jaw	WHL	65	21	50	71	36	12	4	11	15	6
2003-04	Moose Jaw	WHL	60	33	42	75	32	10	3	4	7	10

WHL East Second All-Star Team (2004)

Traded to **Washington** by **Detroit** with Detroit's 1st round choice (Mike Green) in 2004 Entry Draft and Detroit's 4th round choice in 2006 Entry Draft for Robert Lang, February 27, 2004.

FLOOD, Mark (FLUD, MAHRK) **MTL.**

Defense. Shoots right. 6'1", 189 lbs. Born, Charlottetown, PEI, September 29, 1984.
(Montreal's 8th choice, 188th overall, in 2003 Entry Draft).

			Regular Season					Playoffs				
Season	Club	League	GP	G	A	TP	PIM	GP	G	A	TP	PIM
2000-01	Charlottetown	PEIHA		STATISTICS NOT AVAILABLE								
	Charlottetown	MJrHL	11	0	2	2	2	....	....	....	....	....
2001-02	Peterborough	OHL	57	1	4	5	21	6	0	0	0	2
2002-03	Peterborough	OHL	68	5	24	29	18	7	1	2	3	0
2003-04	Peterborough	OHL	68	15	29	44	30	....	....	....	....	....

FLYNN, Rob (FLIHN, RAWB) **NYR**

Right wing. Shoots right. 6'2", 210 lbs. Born, Boston, MA, January 8, 1983.
(NY Rangers' 9th choice, 270th overall, in 2002 Entry Draft).

			Regular Season					Playoffs				
Season	Club	League	GP	G	A	TP	PIM	GP	G	A	TP	PIM
99-2000	Milton Academy	Hi-School	30	27	29	56	....	....	....	....	....	....
2000-01	U.S. National U-18	USDP	65	8	17	25	50	....	....	....	....	....
2001-02	Harvard University	ECAC	30	1	3	4	6	....	....	....	....	....
2002-03	Harvard University	ECAC	19	4	1	5	14	....	....	....	....	....
2003-04	Harvard University	ECAC	28	2	3	5	14	....	....	....	....	....

FOLEY, Patrick (FOH-lee, PAT-rihk) **PIT.**

Left wing. Shoots left. 6'1", 220 lbs. Born, Boston, MA, January 24, 1981.
(Pittsburgh's 6th choice, 185th overall, in 2000 Entry Draft).

			Regular Season					Playoffs				
Season	Club	League	GP	G	A	TP	PIM	GP	G	A	TP	PIM
1996-97	St. Sebastian's	Hi-School	23	11	12	23	....	....	....	....	....	....
1997-98	St. Sebastian's	Hi-School	25	17	24	41	....	....	....	....	....	....
	U.S. National U-18	USDP	8	3	3	6	8	....	....	....	....	....
1998-99	U.S. National U-17	USDP	52	7	9	16	146	....	....	....	....	....
99-2000	New Hampshire	H-East	30	3	7	10	61	....	....	....	....	....
2000-01	New Hampshire	H-East		DID NOT PLAY – INJURED								
2001-02	New Hampshire	H-East	35	8	4	12	58	....	....	....	....	....
2002-03	New Hampshire	H-East	39	8	10	18	38	....	....	....	....	....
2003-04	New Hampshire	H-East	39	4	3	7	44	....	....	....	....	....

• Missed entire 2000-01 season recovering from head injury suffered in game vs. U. Mass-Lowell (H-East), February 4, 2000.

FORD, Scott (FOHRD, SKAWT) **S.J.**

Defense. Shoots right. 6'3", 225 lbs. Born, Charlie Lake, B.C., December 24, 1979.

			Regular Season					Playoffs				
Season	Club	League	GP	G	A	TP	PIM	GP	G	A	TP	PIM
99-2000	Merritt	BCHL	42	1	14	15	90	....	....	....	....	....
2000-01	Brown University	ECAC	23	2	6	8	18	....	....	....	....	....
2001-02	Brown University	ECAC	31	1	6	7	38	....	....	....	....	....
2002-03	Brown University	ECAC	33	6	11	17	44	....	....	....	....	....
2003-04	Brown University	ECAC	31	6	9	15	30	....	....	....	....	....

Signed as a free agent by **San Jose**, June 27, 2004.

FORREST, J.D. (FOH-rehst, JAY-DEE) **CAR.**

Defense. Shoots left. 5'9", 170 lbs. Born, Auburn, NY, April 15, 1981.
(Carolina's 5th choice, 181st overall, in 2000 Entry Draft).

			Regular Season					Playoffs				
Season	Club	League	GP	G	A	TP	PIM	GP	G	A	TP	PIM
1997-98	U.S. National U-18	USDP	74	7	26	33	41	....	....	....	....	....
1998-99	U.S. National U-17	USDP	2	1	0	1	4	....	....	....	....	....
	U.S. National U-18	USDP	48	5	21	26	34	....	....	....	....	....
99-2000	U.S. National U-17	USDP	49	6	28	34	36	....	....	....	....	....
	U.S. National U-18	USDP	8	0	0	0	2	....	....	....	....	....
2000-01	Boston College	H-East	38	6	17	23	40	....	....	....	....	....
2001-02	Boston College	H-East	35	8	19	27	28	....	....	....	....	....
2002-03	Boston College	H-East	34	6	25	31	28	....	....	....	....	....
2003-04	Boston College	H-East	37	4	13	17	26	....	....	....	....	....

Hockey East Second All-Star Team (2003) • NCAA East Second All-American Team (2003)

Signed as a free agent by **SaiPa** (Finland), May 21, 2004.

FORSANDER, Johan (fohr-SAHN-duhr, YOH-hahn) **DET.**

Left wing. Shoots left. 6'1", 174 lbs. Born, Jonkoping, Sweden, April 28, 1978.
(Detroit's 3rd choice, 108th overall, in 1996 Entry Draft).

			Regular Season					Playoffs				
Season	Club	League	GP	G	A	TP	PIM	GP	G	A	TP	PIM
1994-95	HV 71 Jr.	Swede-Jr.	25	2	2	4	6	....	....	....	....	....
1995-96	HV 71 Jr.	Swede-Jr.	27	15	8	23	12	....	....	....	....	....
	HV 71 Jonkoping	Sweden	6	0	0	0	0	3	0	0	0	2
1996-97	HV 71 Jr.	Swede-Jr.	6	7	3	10	6	....	....	....	....	....
	HV 71 Jonkoping	Sweden	44	3	2	5	6	5	0	0	0	0
1997-98	HV 71 Jr.	Swede-Jr.	5	1	1	2	6	....	....	....	....	....
	HV 71 Jonkoping	Sweden	46	3	2	5	12	5	0	0	0	0
1998-99	HV 71 Jonkoping	Sweden	48	5	4	9	6	....	....	....	....	....
99-2000	HV 71 Jonkoping	Sweden	48	9	9	18	6	6	0	0	0	4
2000-01	HV 71 Jonkoping	Sweden		DID NOT PLAY – INJURED								
2001-02	Djurgarden	Sweden	48	5	6	11	16	5	0	0	0	4
2002-03	Djurgarden	Sweden	41	1	2	3	49	10	2	2	4	4
2003-04	AIK Solna	Swede-2	48	11	21	32	48	5	0	4	4	10

• Missed entire 2000-01 season recovering from foot injury suffered in training camp, September 2, 2000.

FORSTER, Beat (FOHRS-tuhr, BEE-at) **PHX.**

Defense. Shoots left. 6'1", 214 lbs. Born, Herisau, Switz., February 2, 1983.
(Phoenix's 4th choice, 78th overall, in 2001 Entry Draft).

			Regular Season					Playoffs				
Season	Club	League	GP	G	A	TP	PIM	GP	G	A	TP	PIM
99-2000	HC Davos Jr.	Swiss-Jr.	34	4	15	19	40	6	1	0	1	6
2000-01	HC Davos Jr.	Swiss-Jr.	27	6	7	13	44	....	....	....	....	....
	SC Herisau	Swiss-2	3	0	0	0	16	....	....	....	....	....
	HC Davos	Swiss	7	0	0	0	6	3	0	0	0	2
2001-02	HC Davos	Swiss-Jr.	4	2	2	4	12	....	....	....	....	....
	HC Davos	Swiss	33	1	3	4	51	16	0	1	1	2
2002-03	HC Davos	Swiss	30	1	4	5	24	17	0	1	1	16
2003-04	HC Davos	Swiss	44	3	8	11	34	6	0	0	0	36

FOSTER, Adrian (FAW-stuhr, AY-dree-uhn) **N.J.**

Center. Shoots left. 6', 205 lbs. Born, Lethbridge, Alta., January 15, 1982.
(New Jersey's 1st choice, 28th overall, in 2001 Entry Draft).

			Regular Season					Playoffs				
Season	Club	League	GP	G	A	TP	PIM	GP	G	A	TP	PIM
1997-98	Calgary Buffaloes	AMHL	36	26	54	80	50	9	3	14	17	18
1998-99	Calgary Canucks	AJHL	18	15	17	32	18	....	....	....	....	....
99-2000	Saskatoon Blades	WHL	7	1	2	3	6	....	....	....	....	....
2000-01	Saskatoon Blades	WHL	5	0	5	5	4	....	....	....	....	....
2001-02	Saskatoon Blades	WHL	13	9	3	12	18	....	....	....	....	....
	Brandon	WHL	14	5	10	15	23	15	4	11	15	14
2002-03	Albany River Rats	AHL	9	3	0	3	4	....	....	....	....	....
2003-04	Albany River Rats	AHL	44	8	13	21	25	....	....	....	....	....

• Missed majority of 1998-99 season recovering from ankle injury. • Missed majority of 1999-2000, 2000-01, 2001-02 and 2002-03 seasons recovering from abdominal injury, October, 1999.

FOY, Matt (FOI, MAT) **MIN.**

Right wing. Shoots right. 6'2", 219 lbs. Born, Oakville, Ont., May 18, 1983.
(Minnesota's 6th choice, 175th overall, in 2002 Entry Draft).

			Regular Season					Playoffs				
Season	Club	League	GP	G	A	TP	PIM	GP	G	A	TP	PIM
2000-01	Wexford Raiders	OPJHL	47	43	49	92	30	....	....	....	....	....
2001-02	Merrimack College	H-East	31	7	17	24	48	....	....	....	....	....
2002-03	Ottawa 67's	OHL	68	61	71	132	112	21	11	20	31	47
2003-04	Houston Aeros	AHL	51	11	13	24	74	1	0	0	0	0

OHL First All-Star Team (2003)

• Officially announced intention to withdraw from **Merrimack** (H-East) for academic reasons, May 30, 2002.

FRANSSON, Johan (FRAN-suhn, YOH-hahn) **DAL.**

Defense. Shoots left. 6'1", 183 lbs. Born, Kalix, Sweden, February 18, 1985.
(Dallas' 2nd choice, 34th overall, in 2004 Entry Draft).

			Regular Season					Playoffs				
Season	Club	League	GP	G	A	TP	PIM	GP	G	A	TP	PIM
2000-01	Kalix HF	Sweden-3	19	0	6	6	8	....	....	....	....	....
2001-02	Lulea HF 18	Swede-Jr.	5	2	0	2	0	....	....	....	....	....
	Lulea HF Jr.	Swede-Jr.	29	4	4	8	28	5	0	1	1	8
2002-03	Lulea HF Jr.	Swede-Jr.	24	2	4	6	67	....	....	....	....	....
	Lulea HF 18	Swede-Jr.	2	0	0	0	2	....	....	....	....	....
	Lulea HF	Sweden	3	0	0	0	0	....	....	....	....	....
2003-04	Lulea HF Jr.	Swede-Jr.	5	0	2	2	10	....	....	....	....	....
	Lulea HF	Sweden	44	3	3	6	28	2	0	0	0	4

FRANZEN, Johan (FRAN-zehn, YOH-hahn) **DET.**

Defense. Shoots left. 6'2", 207 lbs. Born, Landsbro, Sweden, December 23, 1979.
(Detroit's 1st choice, 97th overall, in 2004 Entry Draft).

			Regular Season					Playoffs				
Season	Club	League	GP	G	A	TP	PIM	GP	G	A	TP	PIM
2001-02	Linkopings HC	Sweden	36	2	6	8	64	....	....	....	....	....
2002-03	Linkopings HC	Sweden	37	2	4	6	14	....	....	....	....	....
2003-04	Linkopings HC	Sweden	49	12	18	30	26	5	0	1	1	8

FRASER, Colin (FRAY-zuhr, KAW-lihn) CHI.

Center. Shoots left. 6'1", 182 lbs. Born, Sicamous, B.C., January 28, 1985.
(Philadelphia's 3rd choice, 69th overall, in 2003 Entry Draft).

			Regular Season					Playoffs				
Season	Club	League	GP	G	A	TP	PIM	GP	G	A	TP	PIM
2000-01	Port Coquitlam	PIJHL	38	16	24	40	90	8	2	2	4	21
2001-02	Red Deer Rebels	WHL	67	11	31	42	126	23	2	1	3	39
2002-03	Red Deer Rebels	WHL	69	15	37	52	192	22	7	6	13	40
2003-04	Red Deer Rebels	WHL	70	24	29	53	174	19	5	9	14	24

Traded to **Chicago** by **Philadelphia** with Jim Vandermeer and Los Angeles' 2nd round choice (previously acquired, Chicago selected Bryan Bickell) in 2004 Entry Draft for Alex Zhamnov and Washington's 4th round choice (previously acquired, Philadelphia selected R.J. Anderson) in 2004 Entry Draft, February 19, 2004.

FRETTER, Colton (FREH-tuhr, KOHL-tuhn) ATL.

Center. Shoots right. 5'10", 190 lbs. Born, Harrow, Ont., March 12, 1982.
(Atlanta's 8th choice, 230th overall, in 2002 Entry Draft).

			Regular Season					Playoffs				
Season	Club	League	GP	G	A	TP	PIM	GP	G	A	TP	PIM
99-2000	Chatham Maroons	OJHL-B	40	12	22	34	34	....	....	....	....	....
2000-01	Chatham Maroons	OJHL-B	54	33	39	72	....	15	7	6	13	....
2001-02	Chatham Maroons	OJHL-B	52	51	53	104	62	15	5	3	8	2
2002-03	Michigan State	CCHA	35	7	15	22	36	....	....	....	....	....
2003-04	Michigan State	CCHA	39	6	11	17	22	....	....	....	....	....

FRIED, Robert (FREED, RAW-buhrt) FLA.

Right wing. Shoots right. 6'2", 210 lbs. Born, Philadelphia, PA, March 8, 1981.
(Florida's 2nd choice, 77th overall, in 2000 Entry Draft).

			Regular Season					Playoffs				
Season	Club	League	GP	G	A	TP	PIM	GP	G	A	TP	PIM
1998-99	Deerfield Academy	Hi-School	24	13	20	33	28	....	....	....	....	....
99-2000	Deerfield Academy	Hi-School	26	25	20	45	35	....	....	....	....	....
2000-01	Harvard University	ECAC	30	4	1	5	22	....	....	....	....	....
2001-02	Harvard University	ECAC	31	7	5	12	16	....	....	....	....	....
2002-03	Harvard University	ECAC	33	3	10	13	26	....	....	....	....	....
2003-04	Harvard University	ECAC	35	4	9	13	24	....	....	....	....	....

FROGREN, Jonas (FREW-grehn, YOH-nuhs) CGY.

Defense. Shoots left. 6'1", 190 lbs. Born, Falun, Sweden, August 28, 1980.
(Calgary's 8th choice, 206th overall, in 1998 Entry Draft).

			Regular Season					Playoffs				
Season	Club	League	GP	G	A	TP	PIM	GP	G	A	TP	PIM
1996-97	Farjestad Jr.	Swede-Jr.	20	2	7	9	4	....	....	....	....	....
1997-98	Farjestad Jr.	Swede-Jr.	28	5	6	11	12	2	1	0	1	0
1998-99	Farjestad Jr.	Swede-Jr.	28	10	8	18	16	6	0	2	2	10
	Farjestad	Sweden	22	0	0	0	2	....	....	....	....	....
	Farjestad	EuroHL	5	0	0	0	0	2	0	0	0	0
99-2000	Bofors IK	Swede-2	43	2	7	9	40	....	....	....	....	....
2000-01	Farjestad	Sweden	49	3	0	3	10	16	0	0	0	4
	Farjestad Jr.	Swede-Jr.	1	0	0	0	0	....	....	....	....	....
2001-02	Farjestad	Sweden	50	3	6	9	18	10	0	0	0	4
2002-03	Farjestad	Sweden	50	1	7	8	48	14	0	0	0	16
2003-04	Farjestad	Sweden	47	5	5	10	38	17	2	0	2	6

FUGERE, Nick (FOO-jhair, NIHK) NSH.

Left wing. Shoots left. 6'2", 225 lbs. Born, Shawinigan, Que., September 20, 1985.
(Nashville's 3rd choice, 107th overall, in 2004 Entry Draft).

			Regular Season					Playoffs				
Season	Club	League	GP	G	A	TP	PIM	GP	G	A	TP	PIM
2001-02	Hull Olympiques	QMJHL	65	7	2	9	180	12	2	1	3	70
2002-03	Hull Olympiques	QMJHL	60	15	9	24	247	19	3	3	6	28
2003-04	Gatineau	QMJHL	54	10	13	23	121	15	3	4	7	11

FUNK, Michael (FUHNK, MIGH-kuhl) BUF.

Defense. Shoots left. 6'4", 199 lbs. Born, Abbotsford, B.C., August 15, 1986.
(Buffalo's 2nd choice, 43rd overall, in 2004 Entry Draft).

			Regular Season					Playoffs				
Season	Club	League	GP	G	A	TP	PIM	GP	G	A	TP	PIM
2001-02	Abbotsford Hawks	BCAHA	72	9	24	33	84	....	....	....	....	....
2002-03	Portland	WHL	68	1	15	16	54	7	0	1	1	15
2003-04	Portland	WHL	71	3	25	28	86	5	0	1	1	6

FURRER, Philippe (FUHR-ruhr, fihl-EEP) NYR

Defense. Shoots left. 6'1", 187 lbs. Born, Bern, Switz., June 16, 1985.
(NY Rangers' 7th choice, 179th overall, in 2003 Entry Draft).

			Regular Season					Playoffs				
Season	Club	League	GP	G	A	TP	PIM	GP	G	A	TP	PIM
2000-01	SC Bern Jr.	Swiss-Jr.	....	....	....	....	....	3	0	0	0	0
2001-02	SC Bern Jr.	Swiss-Jr.	29	5	11	16	31	1	0	0	0	0
	SC Bern	Swiss	10	0	0	0	0	....	....	....	....	....
2002-03	SC Bern Jr.	Swiss-Jr.	11	1	11	12	12	....	....	....	....	....
	SC Bern	Swiss	27	0	1	1	6	13	0	0	0	2
2003-04	SC Bern	Swiss	DID NOT PLAY – INJURED									

• Missed entire 2003-04 season recovering from hip injury suffered during 2002-03 season.

GABINET, Mike (GA-bihn-AY, MIGHK) L.A.

Defense. Shoots left. 6'3", 180 lbs. Born, Edmonton, Alta., September 26, 1981.
(Los Angeles' 10th choice, 237th overall, in 2001 Entry Draft).

			Regular Season					Playoffs				
Season	Club	League	GP	G	A	TP	PIM	GP	G	A	TP	PIM
1998-99	Edmonton Leafs	AMHL	33	1	15	16	34	....	....	....	....	....
99-2000	Lloydminster	AJHL	56	4	25	29	30	9	2	4	6	4
2000-01	Nebraska-Omaha	CCHA	30	2	13	15	14	....	....	....	....	....
2001-02	Nebraska-Omaha	CCHA	21	0	4	4	8	....	....	....	....	....
2002-03	Nebraska-Omaha	CCHA	40	0	4	4	46	....	....	....	....	....
2003-04	Nebraska-Omaha	CCHA	39	4	20	24	70	....	....	....	....	....

GAJIC, Milan (GAY-jihk, MEE-lan) ATL.

Center. Shoots right. 6', 190 lbs. Born, Vancouver, B.C., January 6, 1981.
(Atlanta's 4th choice, 112th overall, in 2001 Entry Draft).

			Regular Season					Playoffs				
Season	Club	League	GP	G	A	TP	PIM	GP	G	A	TP	PIM
1997-98	Merritt	BCHL	51	6	14	20	....	....	....	....	....	....
1998-99	Burnaby Bulldogs	BCHL	56	29	30	59	41	....	....	....	....	....
99-2000	Burnaby Bulldogs	BCHL	56	34	47	81	42	....	....	....	....	....
2000-01	Burnaby Bulldogs	BCHL	50	46	52	98	84	....	....	....	....	....
2001-02	U. of Michigan	CCHA	39	9	13	22	22	....	....	....	....	....
2002-03	U. of Michigan	CCHA	38	11	10	21	38	....	....	....	....	....
2003-04	U. of Michigan	CCHA	40	13	20	33	32	....	....	....	....	....

GARLOCK, Ryan (GAHR-lawk, RIGH-uhn) CHI.

Center. Shoots left. 6'1", 197 lbs. Born, Iroquois Falls, Ont., April 24, 1986.
(Chicago's 4th choice, 45th overall, in 2004 Entry Draft).

			Regular Season					Playoffs				
Season	Club	League	GP	G	A	TP	PIM	GP	G	A	TP	PIM
2001-02	Timmons Rangers	NOBHL	34	*34	31	*65	62	....	....	....	....	....
2002-03	Guelph Storm	OHL	51	3	12	15	26	11	1	1	2	0
2003-04	Guelph Storm	OHL	36	16	18	34	32	....	....	....	....	....
	Windsor Spitfires	OHL	16	3	10	13	12	4	1	0	1	6

GELECH, Randall (GEH-lehkh, RAN-duhl) PHX.

Center. Shoots right. 6'3", 212 lbs. Born, Wynard, Sask., February 2, 1984.
(Phoenix's 5th choice, 208th overall, in 2003 Entry Draft).

			Regular Season					Playoffs				
Season	Club	League	GP	G	A	TP	PIM	GP	G	A	TP	PIM
99-2000	Naicam Bantams	BCAHA	STATISTICS NOT AVAILABLE									
2000-01	Kelowna Rockets	WHL	51	1	9	10	19	6	0	0	0	4
2001-02	Kelowna Rockets	WHL	48	6	2	8	33	15	2	1	3	15
2002-03	Kelowna Rockets	WHL	67	25	20	45	93	19	8	4	12	17
2003-04	Kelowna Rockets	WHL	71	30	19	49	117	17	10	4	14	22

Memorial Cup All-Star Team (2004)

GELLARD, Mike (GEHL-ahrd, MIGHK)

Left wing. Shoots left. 6'1", 193 lbs. Born, Markham, Ont., October 10, 1978.

			Regular Season					Playoffs				
Season	Club	League	GP	G	A	TP	PIM	GP	G	A	TP	PIM
1995-96	Thornhill Islanders	MTJHL	49	15	24	39	2	16	6	9	15	0
1996-97	Thornhill Islanders	MTJHL	43	29	37	66	4	9	3	10	13	0
1997-98	St. Lawrence	ECAC	31	4	6	10	18	....	....	....	....	....
1998-99	St. Lawrence	ECAC	39	10	11	21	22	....	....	....	....	....
99-2000	St. Lawrence	ECAC	36	14	22	36	36	....	....	....	....	....
2000-01	St. Lawrence	ECAC	37	19	*38	*57	14	....	....	....	....	....
2001-02			DID NOT PLAY									
2002-03	Providence Bruins	AHL	63	5	11	16	24	4	0	0	0	2
2003-04	Providence Bruins	AHL	33	2	1	3	16	....	....	....	....	....

ECAC First All-Star Team (2001)

Signed as a free agent by **Boston**, August 2, 2001. • Missed entire 2001-02 season recovering from viral infection diagnosed during training camp, September 20, 2001. • Missed majority of 2003-04 season recovering from head injury suffered in game vs. Manchester (AHL), January 23, 2004.

GENOVY, Jeff (jeh-NOH-vee, JEHF) CBJ

Left wing. Shoots left. 6'3", 191 lbs. Born, Kalamazoo, MI, December 4, 1982.
(Columbus' 4th choice, 96th overall, in 2002 Entry Draft).

			Regular Season					Playoffs				
Season	Club	League	GP	G	A	TP	PIM	GP	G	A	TP	PIM
1998-99	Soo Hawks	GLHL	43	10	10	20	39	....	....	....	....	....
99-2000	West. Michigan	MMHL	STATISTICS NOT AVAILABLE									
	Det. Compuware	NAJHL	9	0	3	3	2	2	0	0	0	0
2000-01	Sault Ste. Marie	NAJHL	54	12	14	26	26	8	0	1	1	4
2001-02	Des Moines	USHL	52	23	23	46	86	3	1	4	5	2
2002-03	Clarkson Knights	ECAC	34	5	8	13	45	....	....	....	....	....
2003-04	Clarkson Knights	ECAC	36	2	7	9	42	....	....	....	....	....

GENS, Matt (GEHZ, MAT) VAN.

Defense. Shoots right. 6', 180 lbs. Born, Detroit Lakes, MN, March 31, 1983.
(Vancouver's 11th choice, 278th overall, in 2002 Entry Draft).

			Regular Season					Playoffs				
Season	Club	League	GP	G	A	TP	PIM	GP	G	A	TP	PIM
99-2000	U.S. National U-17	USDP	54	4	9	13	46	....	....	....	....	....
2000-01	U.S. National U-18	USDP	57	14	13	27	50	....	....	....	....	....
2001-02	St. Cloud State	WCHA	40	6	17	23	28	....	....	....	....	....
2002-03	St. Cloud State	WCHA	36	4	10	14	30	....	....	....	....	....
2003-04	St. Cloud State	WCHA	30	3	7	10	22	....	....	....	....	....

WCHA All-Rookie Team (2002)

GERVAIS, Bruno (ZHUR-vay, BROO-noh) NYI

Defense. Shoots right. 6', 188 lbs. Born, Longueuil, Que., October 3, 1984.
(NY Islanders' 6th choice, 182nd overall, in 2003 Entry Draft).

			Regular Season					Playoffs				
Season	Club	League	GP	G	A	TP	PIM	GP	G	A	TP	PIM
99-2000	Antoine-Girouard	QAAA	6	0	0	0	0	4	0	0	0	0
2000-01	Antoine-Girouard	QAAA	40	8	27	35	46	7	4	2	6	8
2001-02	Acadie-Bathurst	QMJHL	65	4	12	16	42	16	3	1	4	8
2002-03	Acadie-Bathurst	QMJHL	72	22	28	50	73	11	3	5	8	14
2003-04	Acadie-Bathurst	QMJHL	23	4	6	10	28	....	....	....	....	....

QMJHL Second All-Star Team (2003)

Missed majority of 2003-04 season recovering from knee injury suffered during Team Canada Jr. training camp, December 12, 2003.

GETZLAF, Ryan (GEHTZ-laf, RIGH-uhn) ANA.

Center. Shoots right. 6'2", 205 lbs. Born, Regina, Sask., May 10, 1985.
(Anaheim's 1st choice, 19th overall, in 2003 Entry Draft).

			Regular Season					Playoffs				
Season	Club	League	GP	G	A	TP	PIM	GP	G	A	TP	PIM
2000-01	Regina Rangers	SBHL	41	33	41	74	189	....	....	....	....	....
	Regina P.C.	SMHL	8	4	3	7	8	....	....	....	....	....
2001-02	Calgary Hitmen	WHL	63	9	9	18	34	7	2	1	3	4
2002-03	Calgary Hitmen	WHL	70	29	39	68	121	5	1	1	2	6
2003-04	Calgary Hitmen	WHL	49	28	47	75	97	7	5	1	6	12

WHL East First All-Star Team (2004)

GIBBONS, Ryan (GIH-buhnz, RIGH-uhn) PHX.

Right wing. Shoots right. 6'4", 210 lbs. Born, N. Vancouver, B.C., January 1, 1985.
(Phoenix's 4th choice, 178th overall, in 2003 Entry Draft).

			Regular Season					Playoffs				
Season	Club	League	GP	G	A	TP	PIM	GP	G	A	TP	PIM
2000-01	Hollyburn Huskies	BCAHA	48	62	64	126	160	....	....	....	....	....
2001-02	Seattle	WHL	49	2	2	4	41	10	0	0	0	2
2002-03	Seattle	WHL	67	9	6	15	91	15	3	1	4	22
2003-04	Seattle	WHL	44	12	5	17	62	....	....	....	....	....

GIFFORD, Brian (GIH-fuhrd, BRIGH-uhn) **PIT.**

Center. Shoots left. 6'1", 173 lbs. Born, Fargo, ND, November 12, 1985.
(Pittsburgh's 5th choice, 85th overall, in 2004 Entry Draft).

			Regular Season					Playoffs				
Season	Club	League	GP	G	A	TP	PIM	GP	G	A	TP	PIM
2002-03	Moorhead Spuds	Hi-School	30	18	20	38	32	....	....	....	....	....
2003-04	Moorhead Spuds	Hi-School	26	19	37	56	26	....	....	....	....	....

GILBERT, Tom (GIHL-buhrt, TAWM) **EDM.**

Defense. Shoots right. 6'2", 190 lbs. Born, Minneapolis, MN, January 10, 1983.
(Colorado's 5th choice, 129th overall, in 2002 Entry Draft).

			Regular Season					Playoffs				
Season	Club	League	GP	G	A	TP	PIM	GP	G	A	TP	PIM
99-2000	Bloomington-Jeff.	Hi-School	18	7	18	25	....	....	....	....	....	....
2000-01	Bloomington-Jeff.	Hi-School	23	20	18	38	....	....	....	....	....	....
	Chicago Steel	USHL	1	0	0	0	0	....	....	....	....	....
2001-02	Chicago Steel	USHL	57	13	15	28	62	4	0	0	0	4
2002-03	U. of Wisconsin	WCHA	39	7	13	20	36	....	....	....	....	....
2003-04	U. of Wisconsin	WCHA	39	6	15	21	36	....	....	....	....	....

Traded to **Edmonton** by **Colorado** for Tommy Salo and Edmonton's 6th round choice in 2005 Entry Draft, March 8, 2004.

GILL, Aaron (GIHL, AIR-ruhn) **S.J.**

Center. Shoots right. 6', 180 lbs. Born, Rochester, MN, March 5, 1980.

			Regular Season					Playoffs				
Season	Club	League	GP	G	A	TP	PIM	GP	G	A	TP	PIM
1996-97	Shat.-St. Mary's	Hi-School	STATISTICS NOT AVAILABLE									
1997-98	Rochester	USHL	56	11	12	23	6	....	....	....	....	....
1998-99	Rochester	USHL	56	10	20	30	35	....	....	....	....	....
99-2000	Rochester	USHL	55	27	23	50	43	....	....	....	....	....
2000-01	Notre Dame	CCHA	38	11	15	26	37	....	....	....	....	....
2001-02	Notre Dame	CCHA	38	8	14	22	20	....	....	....	....	....
2002-03	Notre Dame	CCHA	38	13	12	25	14	....	....	....	....	....
2003-04	Notre Dame	CCHA	39	17	21	38	16	....	....	....	....	....
	Cleveland Barons	AHL	6	1	0	1	2	3	0	0	0	0

CCHA Second All-Star Team (2004)

Signed to a PTO (tryout) contract by **Cleveland** (AHL), April 2, 2004. Signed as a free agent by **San Jose**, April 23, 2004.

GILLIES, Trevor **NYR**

Left wing. Shoots left. 6'3", 210 lbs. Born, Cambridge, Ont., January 30, 1979.

			Regular Season					Playoffs				
Season	Club	League	GP	G	A	TP	PIM	GP	G	A	TP	PIM
1996-97	North Bay	OHL	26	0	3	3	72	....	....	....	....	....
1997-98	North Bay	OHL	2	0	0	0	4	....	....	....	....	....
	Sarnia Sting	OHL	17	0	1	1	33	....	....	....	....	....
	Oshawa Generals	OHL	45	1	2	3	184	7	0	1	1	12
1998-99	Oshawa Generals	OHL	66	6	9	15	270	11	0	2	2	28
99-2000	Mississippi	ECHL	53	0	6	6	202	....	....	....	....	....
	Lowell	AHL	8	0	0	0	38	....	....	....	....	....
2000-01	Greensboro	ECHL	63	1	6	7	303	....	....	....	....	....
	Worcester IceCats	AHL	....	....	....	....	....	6	0	0	0	24
2001-02	Augusta Lynx	ECHL	46	0	1	1	269	....	....	....	....	....
	Richmond	ECHL	18	0	1	1	51	....	....	....	....	....
	Providence Bruins	AHL	5	0	0	0	21	....	....	....	....	....
2002-03	Lowell	AHL	25	0	1	1	132	....	....	....	....	....
	Richmond	ECHL	6	0	0	0	20	....	....	....	....	....
	Peoria Rivermen	ECHL	24	0	1	1	180	....	....	....	....	....
2003-04	Springfield Falcons	AHL	61	2	1	3	277	....	....	....	....	....

Signed as a free agent by **NY Rangers**, July 20, 2004.

GIMAEV, Sergei (gih-MIGH-ehv, SAIR-gay) **OTT.**

Defense. Shoots left. 6'1", 183 lbs. Born, Moscow, USSR, February 16, 1984.
(Ottawa's 6th choice, 166th overall, in 2003 Entry Draft).

			Regular Season					Playoffs				
Season	Club	League	GP	G	A	TP	PIM	GP	G	A	TP	PIM
2001-02	CSKA Moscow 2	Russia-3	36	0	10	10	50	....	....	....	....	....
2002-03	Cherepovets	Russia	11	0	0	0	4	....	....	....	....	....
2003-04	Cherepovets	Russia	50	1	3	4	32	....	....	....	....	....

GIROUX, Alexandre (ZHIH-roo, al-ehx-AN-dreh) **NYR**

Center/Left wing. Shoots left. 6'3", 190 lbs. Born, Quebec City, Que., June 16, 1981.
(Ottawa's 9th choice, 213th overall, in 1999 Entry Draft).

			Regular Season					Playoffs				
Season	Club	League	GP	G	A	TP	PIM	GP	G	A	TP	PIM
1997-98	Ste-Foy	QAAA	42	28	30	58	96	....	....	....	....	....
1998-99	Hull Olympiques	QMJHL	67	15	22	37	124	22	2	2	4	8
99-2000	Hull Olympiques	QMJHL	72	52	47	99	117	15	12	6	18	30
2000-01	Hull Olympiques	QMJHL	38	31	32	63	62	....	....	....	....	....
	Rouyn-Noranda	QMJHL	25	13	14	27	56	9	2	6	8	22
2001-02	Grand Rapids	AHL	70	11	16	27	74	....	....	....	....	....
2002-03	Binghamton	AHL	67	19	16	35	101	10	1	0	1	10
2003-04	Binghamton	AHL	59	19	23	42	79	....	....	....	....	....
	Hartford Wolf Pack	AHL	16	6	3	9	13	16	3	4	7	28

Traded to **NY Rangers** by **Ottawa** with Karel Rachunek for Greg De Vries, March 9, 2004.

GLADSKIKH, Evgeny (glad-SKEEKH, ehv-GEH-nee) **VAN.**

Right wing. Shoots left. 6', 176 lbs. Born, Magnitogorsk, USSR, April 24, 1982.
(Vancouver's 3rd choice, 114th overall, in 2001 Entry Draft).

			Regular Season					Playoffs				
Season	Club	League	GP	G	A	TP	PIM	GP	G	A	TP	PIM
1998-99	Magnitogorsk 2	Russia-4	16	3	3	6	6	....	....	....	....	....
99-2000	Magnitogorsk 2	Russia-3	39	17	2	19	24	....	....	....	....	....
	Magnitogorsk	Russia	1	0	0	0	0	....	....	....	....	....
2000-01	Magnitogorsk 2	Russia-3	11	10	7	17	6	....	....	....	....	....
	Magnitogorsk	Russia	31	3	5	8	10	12	0	2	2	2
2001-02	Magnitogorsk	Russia	32	5	6	11	6	4	0	0	0	4
2002-03	Magnitogorsk	Russia	42	4	7	11	18	3	0	0	0	2
2003-04	Magnitogorsk	Russia	47	13	13	26	22	14	3	1	4	10

GLASS, Tanner (GLAS, TA-nuhr) **FLA.**

Forward. Shoots left. 6', 196 lbs. Born, Regina, Sask., November 29, 1983.
(Florida's 13th choice, 265th overall, in 2003 Entry Draft).

			Regular Season					Playoffs				
Season	Club	League	GP	G	A	TP	PIM	GP	G	A	TP	PIM
2000-01	Yorkton Mailers	SMHL	39	31	29	60	120	4	3	1	4	10
2001-02	Penticton Panthers	BCHL	57	11	28	39	171	....	....	....	....	....
2002-03	Penticton Panthers	BCHL	32	15	25	40	108	....	....	....	....	....
	Nanaimo Clippers	BCHL	18	8	14	22	46	....	....	....	....	....
2003-04	Dartmouth	ECAC	26	4	7	11	18	....	....	....	....	....

GLAZACHEV, Konstantin (GLAH-zuh-chehv, kawn-stuhn-TIHN) **NSH.**

Left wing. Shoots right. 6', 165 lbs. Born, Arkhangelsk, USSR, February 18, 1985.
(Nashville's 2nd choice, 35th overall, in 2003 Entry Draft).

			Regular Season					Playoffs				
Season	Club	League	GP	G	A	TP	PIM	GP	G	A	TP	PIM
2001-02	Yaroslavl 18	Russia-Jr.	30	22	21	43	38	....	....	....	....	....
	Yaroslavl 2	Russia-3	7	5	6	11	6	....	....	....	....	....
2002-03	Yaroslavl 2	Russia-3	STATISTICS NOT AVAILABLE									
	Yaroslavl	Russia	13	3	4	7	4	4	0	0	0	0
2003-04	Yaroslavl 2	Russia-3	9	6	5	11	8	....	....	....	....	....
	Yaroslavl	Russia	35	4	3	7	4	2	0	0	0	0

GLENCROSS, Curtis (GLEHN-kraws, KUHR-tis) **ANA.**

Center. Shoots left. 6'1", 190 lbs. Born, Kindersley, Sask., December 28, 1982.

			Regular Season					Playoffs				
Season	Club	League	GP	G	A	TP	PIM	GP	G	A	TP	PIM
2001-02	Brooks Bandits	AJHL	....	42	26	68	....	....	....	....	....	....
2002-03	Alaska Anchorage	WCHA	35	11	12	23	79	....	....	....	....	....
2003-04	Alaska-Anchorage	WCHA	37	21	13	34	79	....	....	....	....	....
	Cincinnati	AHL	7	2	1	3	6	9	1	6	7	10

Signed as a free agent by **Anaheim**, March 25, 2004.

GLOBKE, Rob (GLAWB-kee, RAWB) **FLA.**

Center. Shoots right. 6'2", 200 lbs. Born, Farmington, MI, October 24, 1982.
(Florida's 3rd choice, 40th overall, in 2002 Entry Draft).

			Regular Season					Playoffs				
Season	Club	League	GP	G	A	TP	PIM	GP	G	A	TP	PIM
1998-99	Det. Compuware	NAJHL	55	8	14	22	111	7	1	2	3	2
99-2000	U.S. National U-18	USDP	54	15	21	36	68	....	....	....	....	....
2000-01	U. of Notre Dame	CCHA	33	17	9	26	74	....	....	....	....	....
2001-02	U. of Notre Dame	CCHA	33	11	11	22	79	....	....	....	....	....
2002-03	U. of Notre Dame	CCHA	40	21	15	36	44	....	....	....	....	....
2003-04	U. of Notre Dame	CCHA	39	19	21	40	42	....	....	....	....	....

CCHA Second All-Star Team (2004)

GLOVER, Dan (GLUH-vuhr, DAN) **N.J.**

Defense. Shoots left. 6'2", 175 lbs. Born, Delburne, Alta., May 4, 1983.
(New Jersey's 10th choice, 250th overall, in 2002 Entry Draft).

			Regular Season					Playoffs				
Season	Club	League	GP	G	A	TP	PIM	GP	G	A	TP	PIM
2000-01	Red Deer Chiefs	AMHL	35	1	5	6	40	....	....	....	....	....
2001-02	Camrose Kodiacs	AJHL	55	1	10	11	110	....	....	....	....	....
2002-03	Camrose Kodiacs	AJHL	61	5	14	19	118	27	0	6	6	32
2003-04	Cornell Big Red	ECAC	23	1	2	3	20	....	....	....	....	....

GLUMAC, Mike (GLOO-kmak, MIGHK) **ST.L.**

Right wing. Shoots right. 6'2", 205 lbs. Born, Niagara Falls, Ont., April 5, 1980.

			Regular Season					Playoffs				
Season	Club	League	GP	G	A	TP	PIM	GP	G	A	TP	PIM
1997-98	Newmarket	OPJHL	36	16	16	32	57	....	....	....	....	....
1998-99	Miami University	CCHA	35	2	0	2	44	....	....	....	....	....
99-2000	Miami University	CCHA	36	8	5	13	52	....	....	....	....	....
2000-01	Miami University	CCHA	37	9	10	19	46	....	....	....	....	....
2001-02	Miami University	CCHA	36	15	8	23	28	....	....	....	....	....
2002-03	Pee Dee Pride	ECHL	69	37	32	69	49	....	....	....	....	....
	Cleveland Barons	AHL	2	0	0	0	0	....	....	....	....	....
2003-04	Worcester IceCats	AHL	80	28	24	52	74	10	3	3	6	11

ECHL All-Rookie Team (2003)

Signed as a free agent by **Pee Dee** (ECHL), August 28, 2002. Signed as a free agent by **Worcester** (AHL), October 6, 2003. Signed as a free agent by **St. Louis**, June 29, 2004.

GOERTZEN, Steve (GUHRT-sehn, STEEV) **CBJ**

Right wing. Shoots right. 6'1", 190 lbs. Born, Stony Plain, Alta., May 26, 1984.
(Columbus' 11th choice, 225th overall, in 2002 Entry Draft).

			Regular Season					Playoffs				
Season	Club	League	GP	G	A	TP	PIM	GP	G	A	TP	PIM
99-2000	Spruce Grove	AMBHL	36	16	17	33	30	....	....	....	....	....
2000-01	St. Albert Raiders	AMHL	34	11	19	30	70	....	....	....	....	....
	St. Albert Saints	AJHL	1	0	0	0	0	....	....	....	....	....
2001-02	Seattle	WHL	66	6	9	15	45	11	2	0	2	4
2002-03	Seattle	WHL	71	12	19	31	95	14	4	3	7	9
2003-04	Seattle	WHL	69	15	18	33	115	....	....	....	....	....
	Syracuse Crunch	AHL	8	0	3	3	4	1	0	0	0	0

GOLIGOSKI, Alex (goh-lih-GAW-skee, AL-ehx) **PIT.**

Defense. Shoots right. 5'11", 180 lbs. Born, Grand Rapids, MN, July 30, 1985.
(Pittsburgh's 3rd choice, 61st overall, in 2004 Entry Draft).

			Regular Season					Playoffs				
Season	Club	League	GP	G	A	TP	PIM	GP	G	A	TP	PIM
2002-03	Grand Rapids	Hi-School	28	14	20	34	22	....	....	....	....	....
2003-04	Grand Rapids	Hi-School	26	25	31	56	16	....	....	....	....	....
	Sioux Falls	USHL	10	0	2	2	6	....	....	....	....	....

GOLOVIN, Alexander (goh-loh-VEEN, al-ehx-AN-duhr) **CHI.**

Left wing. Shoots left. 5'11", 194 lbs. Born, Moscow, USSR, March 26, 1983.
(Chicago's 9th choice, 174th overall, in 2001 Entry Draft).

			Regular Season					Playoffs				
Season	Club	League	GP	G	A	TP	PIM	GP	G	A	TP	PIM
1998-99	Omsk 2	Russia-4	6	2	4	6	4	....	....	....	....	....
99-2000	Omsk 2	Russia-3	24	12	14	26	10	....	....	....	....	....
2000-01	Omsk 2	Russia-3	40	22	34	56	12	....	....	....	....	....
2001-02	Mostovik Kurgan	Russia-2	56	16	23	39	20	....	....	....	....	....
2002-03	Avangard Omsk	Russia	8	2	0	2	0	....	....	....	....	....
	Omsk 2	Russia-3	13	14	8	22	16	....	....	....	....	....
	Sibir Novosibirsk	Russia	20	4	3	7	4	....	....	....	....	....
2003-04	Avangard Omsk	Russia	27	2	2	4	4	....	....	....	....	....
	Omsk 2	Russia-3	24	15	15	30	4	....	....	....	....	....

GORBUNOV, Vladimir (gohr-buh-NAHF, vla-DIH-meer) NYI

Right wing. Shoots left. 6', 174 lbs. Born, Moscow, USSR, April 22, 1982.
(NY Islanders' 4th choice, 105th overall, in 2000 Entry Draft).

			Regular Season					Playoffs				
Season	Club	League	GP	G	A	TP	PIM	GP	G	A	TP	PIM
99-2000	HC CSKA	Russia-2	22	11	7	18	32	....	....	....	....	....
2000-01	HC CSKA	Russia-2	43	10	14	24	63	....	....	....	....	....
2001-02	HC CSKA	Russia-2	46	16	18	34	22	....	....	....	....	....
	CSKA Moscow 2	Russia-3	3	1	1	2	0	....	....	....	....	....
2002-03	CSKA Moscow	Russia	35	5	5	10	46	....	....	....	....	....
	CSKA Moscow 2	Russia-3	STATISTICS NOT AVAILABLE									
2003-04	CSKA Moscow	Russia	34	4	7	11	56	....	....	....	....	....

GORGES, Josh (GOHR-juhz, JAWSH) S.J.

Defense. Shoots left. 6'1", 190 lbs. Born, Kelowna, B.C., August 14, 1984.

			Regular Season					Playoffs				
Season	Club	League	GP	G	A	TP	PIM	GP	G	A	TP	PIM
2000-01	Kelowna Rockets	WHL	57	4	6	10	24	6	1	1	2	4
2001-02	Kelowna Rockets	WHL	72	7	34	41	74	15	1	7	8	8
2002-03	Kelowna Rockets	WHL	54	11	48	59	76	19	3	17	20	16
2003-04	Kelowna Rockets	WHL	62	11	31	42	38	17	2	13	15	6

WHL West First All-Star Team (2004) • Won George Parsons Trophy (Memorial Cup Tournament Most Sportsmanlike Player) (2004)

Signed as a free agent by **San Jose**, September 20, 2002.

GOROVIKOV, Konstantin (goh-roh-vih-KAHF, kawn-stehn-TEEN) OTT.

Left wing. Shoots left. 5'11", 172 lbs. Born, Novosibirsk, USSR, August 31, 1977.
(Ottawa's 10th choice, 269th overall, in 1999 Entry Draft).

			Regular Season					Playoffs				
Season	Club	League	GP	G	A	TP	PIM	GP	G	A	TP	PIM
1994-95	St. Petersburg 2	CIS-2	38	6	5	11	22	....	....	....	....	....
	SKA St. Petersburg	CIS	13	1	0	1	4	2	0	0	0	0
1995-96	St. Petersburg 2	CIS-2	3	2	0	2	0	....	....	....	....	....
	SKA St. Petersburg	CIS	45	2	4	6	18	2	0	0	0	0
1996-97	SKA St. Petersburg	Russia	37	4	2	6	20	....	....	....	....	....
1997-98	SKA St. Petersburg	Russia	44	6	12	18	22	....	....	....	....	....
1998-99	SKA St. Petersburg	Russia	42	12	7	19	14	....	....	....	....	....
99-2000	Grand Rapids	IHL	57	9	14	23	30	8	1	0	1	4
2000-01	Grand Rapids	IHL	68	7	19	26	48	....	....	....	....	....
2001-02	Ufa Salavat	Russia	51	13	18	31	32	....	....	....	....	....
2002-03	Ufa Salavat	Russia	48	10	5	15	44	3	0	1	1	0
2003-04	Cherepovets	Russia	50	7	9	16	26	....	....	....	....	....

GRABOVSKY, Mikhail (gra-BAWV-skee, mih-kigh-EHL) MTL.

Center. Shoots left. 5'11", 181 lbs. Born, Potsdam, East Germany, January 31, 1984.
(Montreal's 4th choice, 150th overall, in 2004 Entry Draft).

			Regular Season					Playoffs				
Season	Club	League	GP	G	A	TP	PIM	GP	G	A	TP	PIM
2001-02	HC Minsk	Belarus	26	10	7	17	16	....	....	....	....	....
2002-03	HC Minsk	Belarus	STATISTICS NOT AVAILABLE									
2003-04	Neftekhimik	Russia	45	6	11	17	26	5	0	0	0	4

GRACIK, Juraj (GRAH0chihk, YUH-righ) ATL.

Right wing. Shoots right. 6'3", 190 lbs. Born, Topolcany, Czechoslovakia, August 14, 1986.
(Atlanta's 5th choice, 142nd overall, in 2004 Entry Draft).

			Regular Season					Playoffs				
Season	Club	League	GP	G	A	TP	PIM	GP	G	A	TP	PIM
2002-03	Topolcany Jr.	Slovak-Jr.	24	10	7	17	28	....	....	....	....	....
2003-04	Topolcany Jr.	Slovak-Jr.	28	22	12	34	78	....	....	....	....	....
	Topolcany	Slovakia-2	28	16	8	24	8	4	1	0	1	0

GRAHAM, Bruce (GRAY-uhm, BROOS) NYR

Center. Shoots left. 6'6", 220 lbs. Born, Moncton, N.B., December 2, 1985.
(NY Rangers' 5th choice, 51st overall, in 2004 Entry Draft).

			Regular Season					Playoffs				
Season	Club	League	GP	G	A	TP	PIM	GP	G	A	TP	PIM
2001-02	Moncton Flyers	NBMML	STATISTICS NOT AVAILABLE									
	Moncton Wildcats	QMJHL	3	0	0	0	0	....	....	....	....	....
2002-03	Moncton Wildcats	QMJHL	66	15	13	28	80	6	0	2	2	0
2003-04	Moncton Wildcats	QMJHL	68	24	33	57	89	18	0	14	14	4

GRANATH, Elias (GRA-nuth, EHL-ee-ahs) DAL.

Defense. Shoots left. 6'1", 174 lbs. Born, Borlange, Sweden, September 6, 1985.
(Dallas' 10th choice, 196th overall, in 2003 Entry Draft).

			Regular Season					Playoffs				
Season	Club	League	GP	G	A	TP	PIM	GP	G	A	TP	PIM
2001-02	Leksands IF 18	Swede Jr.	11	0	1	1	8	4	0	0	0	2
	Leksands IF Jr.	Swede-Jr.	6	0	0	0	0	1	0	0	0	0
2002-03	Leksands IF Jr.	Swede-Jr.	29	0	4	4	49	....	....	....	....	....
	Leksands IF 18	Swede-Jr.	6	0	2	2	0	2	0	1	1	8
2003-04	Leksands IF Jr.	Swede-Jr.	25	4	4	8	34	....	....	....	....	....
	Leksands IF	Swede-Q	10	0	0	0	4	....	....	....	....	....

GRASBERG, Gustav (GRAHS-buhrg, GOO-stahv) NSH.

Center. Shoots left. 6', 193 lbs. Born, Furudal, Sweden, April 6, 1983.
(Nashville's 8th choice, 240th overall, in 2001 Entry Draft).

			Regular Season					Playoffs				
Season	Club	League	GP	G	A	TP	PIM	GP	G	A	TP	PIM
99-2000	Mora IK 18	Swede-Jr.	1	0	0	0	6	....	....	....	....	....
	Mora IK Jr.	Swede-Jr.	37	10	15	25	44	....	....	....	....	....
2000-01	Mora IK Jr.	Swede-Jr.	15	6	4	10	40	2	1	2	3	4
	Mora IK	Swede-2	12	1	0	1	4	....	....	....	....	....
	Mora IK 18	Swede-Jr.	7	3	4	7	12	7	1	2	3	10
2001-02	Mora IK Jr.	Swede-Jr.	1	0	0	0	8	....	....	....	....	....
	Mora IK	Swede-2	46	13	7	20	72	3	0	0	0	2
2002-03	Hammarby	Swede-2	28	5	7	12	62	....	....	....	....	....
	Hammarby Jr.	Swede-Jr.	8	4	4	8	14	....	....	....	....	....
	Hammarby	Swede-Q	10	0	0	0	25	4	0	0	0	2
2003-04	Bofors	Swede-2	46	2	6	8	66	5	0	0	0	0

GRATTON, Josh PHI.

Left wing. Shoots left. 6'2", 210 lbs. Born, Scarborough, Ont., September 9, 1982.

			Regular Season					Playoffs				
Season	Club	League	GP	G	A	TP	PIM	GP	G	A	TP	PIM
2000-01	Sudbury Wolves	OHL	44	5	13	18	110	9	1	1	2	25
2001-02	Sudbury Wolves	OHL	14	5	4	9	47	....	....	....	....	....
	Kingston	OHL	46	14	14	28	140	1	1	0	1	7
2002-03	Windsor Spitfires	OHL	62	26	30	56	192	6	2	1	3	8
2003-04	San Diego Gulls	ECHL	30	4	6	10	239	....	....	....	....	....
	Cincinnati	AHL	21	2	2	4	69	8	0	0	0	35

Signed as a free agent by **Philadelphia**, July 28, 2004.

GRAVEL, Mathieu (gruh-VEHL, MA-tyew) CBJ

Left wing. Shoots left. 6'4", 195 lbs. Born, Montreal, Que., October 19, 1984.
(Columbus' 9th choice, 233rd overall, in 2003 Entry Draft).

			Regular Season					Playoffs				
Season	Club	League	GP	G	A	TP	PIM	GP	G	A	TP	PIM
99-2000	Antoine-Girouard	QAAA	18	3	6	9	4	7	0	0	0	4
2000-01	Antoine-Girouard	QAAA	42	24	24	48	46	7	5	5	10	0
2001-02	Shawinigan	QMJHL	71	16	15	31	87	12	1	2	3	0
2002-03	Shawinigan	QMJHL	72	24	26	50	60	6	2	2	4	2
2003-04	Shawinigan	QMJHL	59	14	21	35	50	10	1	0	1	12

GRECO, Brady (GREH-koh, BRAY-dee) T.B.

Defense. Shoots right. 6'3", 198 lbs. Born, Bryan, OH, March 4, 1983.
(Tampa Bay's 8th choice, 256th overall, in 2003 Entry Draft).

			Regular Season					Playoffs				
Season	Club	League	GP	G	A	TP	PIM	GP	G	A	TP	PIM
1997/00	Edgewood	Hi-School	66	29	33	62	....	....	....	....	....	....
2000-01	Billings Bulls	AWJHL	STATISTICS NOT AVAILABLE									
2001-02	Michigan Tech	WCHA	24	1	9	10	28	....	....	....	....	....
2002-03	Chicago Steel	USHL	57	9	20	29	225	....	....	....	....	....
2003-04	Colorado College	WCHA	28	7	5	12	22	....	....	....	....	....

• Statistics for **Edgewood** (Hi-School) are career totals for 1997-2000 seasons

GREEN, Mike (GREEN, MIGHK) WSH.

Defense. Shoots right. 6'1", 198 lbs. Born, Calgary, Alta., October 12, 1985.
(Washington's 3rd choice, 29th overall, in 2004 Entry Draft).

			Regular Season					Playoffs				
Season	Club	League	GP	G	A	TP	PIM	GP	G	A	TP	PIM
2000-01	Calgary Northstars	AMHL	36	4	23	27	34	....	....	....	....	....
	Saskatoon Blades	WHL	7	0	2	2	0	....	....	....	....	....
2001-02	Saskatoon Blades	WHL	62	3	20	23	57	7	0	1	1	2
2002-03	Saskatoon Blades	WHL	72	6	36	42	70	6	0	2	2	6
2003-04	Saskatoon Blades	WHL	59	14	25	39	92	....	....	....	....	....

GREENE, Matt (GREEN, MAT) EDM.

Defense. Shoots right. 6'3", 223 lbs. Born, Grand Ledge, MI, May 13, 1983.
(Edmonton's 4th choice, 44th overall, in 2002 Entry Draft).

			Regular Season					Playoffs				
Season	Club	League	GP	G	A	TP	PIM	GP	G	A	TP	PIM
2000-01	U.S. National U-18	USDP	54	0	10	10	59	....	....	....	....	....
2001-02	Green Bay	USHL	55	4	20	24	150	7	0	1	1	31
2002-03	North Dakota	WCHA	39	0	4	4	*135	....	....	....	....	....
2003-04	North Dakota	WCHA	40	1	16	17	86	....	....	....	....	....

USHL Second All-Star Team (2002)

GRENZY, Michael (GREHN-zee, MIGH-kuhl) CHI.

Defense. Shoots left. 6'4", 199 lbs. Born, Niagara Falls, NY, February 6, 1984.
(Chicago's 9th choice, 275th overall, in 2003 Entry Draft).

			Regular Season					Playoffs				
Season	Club	League	GP	G	A	TP	PIM	GP	G	A	TP	PIM
99-2000	Toronto Marlies	MTHL	56	7	34	41	....	....	....	....	....	....
2000-01	U.S. National U-17	USDP	69	0	1	1	23	....	....	....	....	....
2001-02	U.S. National U-17	USDP	33	0	5	5	36	....	....	....	....	....
	U.S. National U-18	USDP	18	0	1	1	2	....	....	....	....	....
2002-03	Chicago Steel	USHL	51	3	13	16	48	....	....	....	....	....
2003-04	Clarkson Knights	ECAC	22	2	3	5	36	....	....	....	....	....

GRIGORENKO, Igor (grih-goh-REHN-koh, EE-gohr) DET.

Right wing. Shoots right. 5'10", 178 lbs. Born, Togliatti, USSR, April 9, 1983.
(Detroit's 1st choice, 62nd overall, in 2001 Entry Draft).

			Regular Season					Playoffs				
Season	Club	League	GP	G	A	TP	PIM	GP	G	A	TP	PIM
1998-99	Lada Togliatti 2	Russia-4	19	3	3	6	2	....	....	....	....	....
99-2000	Lada Togliatti 2	Russia-3	38	17	18	35	36	....	....	....	....	....
	Volga Jr.	Russia-Jr.	5	4	2	6	4	....	....	....	....	....
2000-01	Lada Togliatti 2	Russia-3	6	5	4	9	....	....	....	....	....	....
	CSK VVS Samara	Russia-2	39	10	10	20	....	....	....	....	....	....
	Lada Togliatti	Russia	....	....	....	....	....	5	1	0	1	4
2001-02	Lada Togliatti	Russia	41	8	9	17	58	4	1	0	1	2
2002-03	Lada Togliatti	Russia	47	19	11	30	82	10	1	*6	7	10
2003-04	Lada Togliatti 2	Russia-3	6	2	2	4	0	2	0	1	1	0
	Lada Togliatti	Russia	....	....	....	....	....	3	0	0	0	0

• Missed majority of 2003-04 season recovering from injuries suffered in automobile accident, May 16, 2003.

GROSSMAN, Nicklas (GROHS-man, NIH-kluhs) DAL.

Defense. Shoots left. 6'4", 187 lbs. Born, Stockholm, Sweden, January 22, 1985.
(Dallas' 4th choice, 56th overall, in 2004 Entry Draft).

			Regular Season					Playoffs				
Season	Club	League	GP	G	A	TP	PIM	GP	G	A	TP	PIM
2002-03	Sodertalje SK Jr.	Swede-Jr.	34	1	1	2	32	....	....	....	....	....
2003-04	Sodertalje SK Jr.	Swede-Jr.	33	1	2	3	32	2	0	0	0	0
	Sodertalje SK	Sweden	1	0	0	0	0	....	....	....	....	....

GROT, Denis (GROHT, DEH-nihs) VAN.

Defense. Shoots left. 6', 185 lbs. Born, Minsk, USSR, June 1, 1984.
(Vancouver's 2nd choice, 55th overall, in 2002 Entry Draft).

			Regular Season					Playoffs				
Season	Club	League	GP	G	A	TP	PIM	GP	G	A	TP	PIM
2000-01	Yaroslavl 2	Russia-3	34	5	1	6	10	....	....	....	....	....
	Russia	Nat-Tm	5	0	2	2	8	....	....	....	....	....
2001-02	Yaroslavl 2	Russia-3	14	1	0	1	10	....	....	....	....	....
	Elektrostal 2	Russia-3	3	0	1	1	2	....	....	....	....	....
	Elektrostal	Russia-2	33	1	1	2	42	....	....	....	....	....
2002-03	HC Lipetsk	Russia-2	27	4	4	8	28	....	....	....	....	....
2003-04	Yaroslavl	Russia	31	0	2	2	4	3	0	0	0	2

GROULX, Danny (GROO, DA-nee) DET.

Defense. Shoots left. 6', 205 lbs. Born, LaSalle, Que., June 23, 1981.

			Regular Season					Playoffs				
Season	Club	League	GP	G	A	TP	PIM	GP	G	A	TP	PIM
1996-97	Charles-Lemoyne	QAAA	40	2	26	28	....	15	3	15	18	....
1997-98	Val-d'Or Foreurs	QMJHL	63	4	16	20	61	19	1	4	5	18
1998-99	Val-d'Or Foreurs	QMJHL	36	3	26	29	55	....	....	....	....	....
	Acadie-Bathurst	QMJHL	36	2	15	17	51	18	0	2	2	6
99-2000	Victoriaville Tigres	QMJHL	66	12	55	67	131	6	0	4	4	14
2000-01	Victoriaville Tigres	QMJHL	72	16	71	87	164	13	2	19	21	46
2001-02	Victoriaville Tigres	QMJHL	68	29	83	112	165	22	9	*30	39	68
2002-03	Grand Rapids	AHL	71	3	7	10	52	7	0	1	1	7
2003-04	Grand Rapids	AHL	79	8	13	21	93	3	0	0	0	0

QMJHL First All-Star Team (2001, 2002) • Canadian Major Junior First All-Star Team (2002) • Memorial Cup All-Star Team (2002) • Memorial Cup MVP (2002)

Signed as a free agent by **Detroit**, August 12, 2002.

GUENETTE, Francois-Pierre (gwih-NEHT, frahn-SWUH-PEE-air) VAN.

Center. Shoots right. 6'1", 180 lbs. Born, Laval, Que., January 18, 1984.
(Vancouver's 7th choice, 222nd overall, in 2003 Entry Draft).

			Regular Season					Playoffs				
Season	Club	League	GP	G	A	TP	PIM	GP	G	A	TP	PIM
99-2000	Laval-Laurentide	QAAA	33	15	18	33	14	9	3	6	9	2
2000-01	Laval-Laurentide	QAAA	41	17	27	44	47	8	3	8	11	4
2001-02	Halifax	QMJHL	35	2	11	13	14	11	3	4	7	0
2002-03	Halifax	QMJHL	72	38	49	87	24	24	10	17	27	12
2003-04	Cape Breton	QMJHL	69	34	51	85	26	5	0	2	2	2

GUENIN, Nate (GEH-nihn, NAYT) NYR

Defense. Shoots right. 6'2", 191 lbs. Born, Sewickley, PA, December 10, 1982.
(NY Rangers' 3rd choice, 127th overall, in 2002 Entry Draft).

			Regular Season					Playoffs				
Season	Club	League	GP	G	A	TP	PIM	GP	G	A	TP	PIM
99-2000	Pittsburgh Hornets	AAHA	40	3	10	13	122	....	....	....	....	....
2000-01	Green Bay	USHL	54	2	11	13	70	4	1	1	2	6
2001-02	Green Bay	USHL	56	4	11	15	150	7	3	3	6	10
2002-03	Ohio State	CCHA	42	2	9	11	85	....	....	....	....	....
2003-04	Ohio State	CCHA	29	2	15	17	92	....	....	....	....	....

USHL All-Rookie Team (2001)

GUERIN, Marty (GAIR-ihn, MAHR-tee) L.A.

Right wing. Shoots right. 6'1", 190 lbs. Born, Manchester, NH, May 25, 1983.
(Los Angeles' 10th choice, 274th overall, in 2003 Entry Draft).

			Regular Season					Playoffs				
Season	Club	League	GP	G	A	TP	PIM	GP	G	A	TP	PIM
2000-01	Omaha Lancers	USHL	42	3	5	8	24	7	0	0	0	0
2001-02	Omaha Lancers	USHL	31	12	11	33	16	....	....	....	....	....
	Des Moines	USHL	7	2	1	3	2	....	....	....	....	....
2002-03	Des Moines	USHL	60	27	33	60	30	4	1	3	4	6
2003-04	Miami University	CCHA	41	14	19	33	18	....	....	....	....	....

Traded to **Des Moines** (USHL) by **Omaha** (USHL) for Ryan Bennett, January 14, 2002.

GUITE, Ben (GEE-tay, BEHN)

Right wing. Shoots right. 6'1", 205 lbs. Born, Montreal, Que., July 17, 1978.
(Montreal's 8th choice, 172nd overall, in 1997 Entry Draft).

			Regular Season					Playoffs				
Season	Club	League	GP	G	A	TP	PIM	GP	G	A	TP	PIM
1994-95	Lac St-Louis Lions	QAAA	40	9	12	21	....	4	0	0	0	0
1995-96	Capital District	Exhib.	STATISTICS NOT AVAILABLE									
1996-97	U. of Maine	H-East	34	7	7	14	21	....	....	....	....	....
1997-98	U. of Maine	H-East	32	6	12	18	20	....	....	....	....	....
1998-99	U. of Maine	H-East	40	12	16	28	30	....	....	....	....	....
99-2000	U. of Maine	H-East	40	22	14	36	36	....	....	....	....	....
2000-01	Tallahassee	ECHL	68	11	18	29	34	....	....	....	....	....
2001-02	Bridgeport	AHL	68	12	18	30	39	....	....	....	....	....
	Cincinnati	AHL	10	2	5	7	4	3	0	0	0	2
2002-03	Cincinnati	AHL	80	13	16	29	44	....	....	....	....	....
2003-04	Bridgeport	AHL	79	6	18	24	73	7	0	0	0	6

Signed as a free agent by **NY Islanders**, August, 2001. Traded to **Anaheim** by **NY Islanders** with the rights to Bjorn Mellin for Dave Roche, March 19, 2002. Signed as a free agent by **NY Rangers**, September 16, 2003. Signed as a free agent by **Bridgeport** (AHL), October 10, 2003.

GUSEV, Vladimir (GOO-sehv, vla-DIH-meer) CHI.

Defense. Shoots left. 6'2", 205 lbs. Born, Novosibirsk, USSR, November 24, 1982.
(Chicago's 6th choice, 115th overall, in 2001 Entry Draft).

			Regular Season					Playoffs				
Season	Club	League	GP	G	A	TP	PIM	GP	G	A	TP	PIM
99-2000	Novokuznetsk 2	Russia-3	21	1	0	1	52	....	....	....	....	....
	Magnitogorsk	Russia	....	....	....	....	....	3	0	0	0	0
2000-01	Amur Khabarovsk	Russia	1	0	0	0	0	....	....	....	....	....
	Sibir Novosibirsk 2	Russia-3	3	0	0	0	8	....	....	....	....	....
	Sibir Novosibirsk	Russia-2	1	0	0	0	0	....	....	....	....	....
	Omsk 2	Russia-3	4	1	0	1	4	....	....	....	....	....
2001-02	Sibir Novosibirsk	Russia-2	42	1	3	4	82	....	....	....	....	....
2002-03	Sibir Novosibirsk 2	Russia-3	28	6	12	18	42	....	....	....	....	....
2003-04	Florence Pride	ECHL	55	5	9	14	59	....	....	....	....	....
	Norfolk Admirals	AHL	10	0	1	1	10	....	....	....	....	....

GUSKOV, Alexander (goos-KAWF, ahl-ehx-AN-duhr) CBJ

Defense. Shoots left. 6'2", 202 lbs. Born, Gorky, USSR, November 26, 1976.
(Columbus' 8th choice, 200th overall, in 2003 Entry Draft).

			Regular Season					Playoffs				
Season	Club	League	GP	G	A	TP	PIM	GP	G	A	TP	PIM
1996-97	Motor Zavolzhje	Russia-2	32	3	3	6	20	....	....	....	....	....
1997-98	Motor Zavolzhje	Russia-2	24	2	4	6	26	....	....	....	....	....
	Lada Togliatti	Russia	10	0	1	1	8	....	....	....	....	....
1998-99	Chelyabinsk	Russia	11	2	0	2	4	....	....	....	....	....
	Lada Togliatti	Russia	30	1	3	4	10	5	0	0	0	4
99-2000	Nizhnekamsk	Russia	36	4	17	21	40	4	0	0	0	4
2000-01	Nizhnekamsk	Russia	43	4	9	13	24	4	0	0	0	0
2001-02	Yaroslavl	Russia	51	9	9	18	28	9	1	2	3	2
2002-03	Yaroslavl	Russia	48	10	17	27	32	10	1	1	2	6
2003-04	Yaroslavl	Russia	51	9	12	21	18	3	0	0	0	0

GUYER, Gino (GIGH-uhr, JEE-noh) DAL.

Center. Shoots left. 5'10", 184 lbs. Born, Grand Rapids, MN, October 14, 1983.
(Dallas' 7th choice, 165th overall, in 2003 Entry Draft).

			Regular Season					Playoffs				
Season	Club	League	GP	G	A	TP	PIM	GP	G	A	TP	PIM
2000-01	Lincoln Stars	USHL	5	2	2	4	2	10	3	5	8	0
2001-02	Greenway High	Hi-School	26	35	50	85	18	....	....	....	....	....
	Lincoln Stars	USHL	15	7	10	17	0	4	0	1	1	0
2002-03	U. of Minnesota	WCHA	41	13	16	29	10	....	....	....	....	....
2003-04	U. of Minnesota	WCHA	44	11	21	32	14	....	....	....	....	....

HAFNER, Peter (HAF-nuhr, PEE-tuhr) FLA.

Defense. Shoots right. 6'5", 195 lbs. Born, Summit, NJ, July 26, 1983.
(Florida's 10th choice, 232nd overall, in 2002 Entry Draft).

			Regular Season					Playoffs				
Season	Club	League	GP	G	A	TP	PIM	GP	G	A	TP	PIM
2000-01	Taft High School	Hi-School	24	1	9	10	12	....	....	....	....	....
2001-02	Taft High School	Hi-School	26	2	19	21	20	....	....	....	....	....
2002-03	Harvard University	ECAC	25	0	2	2	14	....	....	....	....	....
2003-04	Harvard University	ECAC	35	1	6	7	16	....	....	....	....	....

HAGGLUND, Johan (HAG-luhnd, YOH-hahn) T.B.

Center. Shoots left. 6'2", 212 lbs. Born, Ornskoldsvik, Sweden, June 9, 1982.
(Tampa Bay's 4th choice, 126th overall, in 2000 Entry Draft).

			Regular Season					Playoffs				
Season	Club	League	GP	G	A	TP	PIM	GP	G	A	TP	PIM
1998-99	MoDo Jr.	Swede-Jr.	28	16	22	38	52	....	....	....	....	....
99-2000	MoDo 18	Swede-Jr.	7	1	2	3	8	....	....	....	....	....
	MoDo Jr.	Swede-Jr.	35	7	10	17	75	2	1	0	1	0
2000-01	MoDo Jr.	Swede-Jr.	21	9	9	18	66	....	....	....	....	....
2001-02	Orebro IK	Swede-2	36	6	4	10	50	....	....	....	....	....
2002-03	Orebro IK	Swede-2	19	8	6	14	26	....	....	....	....	....
	Hammarby IF	Swede-2	7	1	1	2	6	....	....	....	....	....
	Hammarby IF	Swede-Q	14	1	4	5	2	9	1	1	2	6
2003-04	Hammarby IF	Swede-2	43	6	7	13	32	....	....	....	....	....

HAGOS, Yared (HA-gohs, YAIR-ehd) DAL.

Center. Shoots left. 6'1", 202 lbs. Born, Stockholm, Sweden, March 27, 1983.
(Dallas' 2nd choice, 70th overall, in 2001 Entry Draft).

			Regular Season					Playoffs				
Season	Club	League	GP	G	A	TP	PIM	GP	G	A	TP	PIM
1998-99	AIK Solna Jr.	Swede-Jr.	32	8	12	20	22	....	....	....	....	....
99-2000	AIK Solna 18	Swede-Jr.	13	4	6	10	6	....	....	....	....	....
	AIK Solna Jr.	Swede-Jr.	17	6	4	10	10	....	....	....	....	....
2000-01	AIK Solna Jr.	Swede-Jr.	24	8	13	21	46	2	2	1	3	2
	AIK Solna	Sweden	....	....	....	....	....	5	0	0	0	0
2001-02	AIK Solna Jr.	Swede-Jr.	1	0	3	3	2	1	0	2	2	0
	AIK Solna	Sweden	45	4	6	10	36	....	....	....	....	....
	AIK Solna	Swede-Q	9	0	0	0	12	....	....	....	....	....
2002-03	AIK Solna	Swede-2	49	10	22	32	67	4	0	1	1	2
	AIK Solna Jr.	Swede-Jr.	1	0	1	1	0	....	....	....	....	....
2003-04	Timra IK	Sweden	48	9	11	20	75	10	3	1	4	6

HAJEK, David (HIGH-ehk, DAV-vihd) CGY.

Defense. Shoots left. 5'11", 165 lbs. Born, Chomutov, Czech., June 13, 1980.
(Calgary's 8th choice, 239th overall, in 2000 Entry Draft).

			Regular Season					Playoffs				
Season	Club	League	GP	G	A	TP	PIM	GP	G	A	TP	PIM
1996-97	KLH Chomutov Jr.	Czech-Jr.	36	8	14	22	30	4	0	0	0	2
1997-98	KLH Chomutov Jr.	Czech-Jr.	36	3	9	12	18	....	....	....	....	....
1998-99	Melville	SJHL	25	10	19	29	....	....	....	....	....	....
	Spokane Chiefs	WHL	27	0	3	3	10	....	....	....	....	....
99-2000	KLH Chomutov Jr.	Czech-Jr.	7	1	5	6	14	....	....	....	....	....
	KLH Chomutov	Czech-2	28	1	5	6	14	12	1	3	4	10
2000-01	Kladno	Czech	40	1	1	2	66	....	....	....	....	....
2001-02	Kladno	Czech	48	0	7	7	16	5	0	1	1	4
2002-03	Kladno	Czech-2	4	0	0	0	0	....	....	....	....	....
	Hradec Kralove	Czech-2	4	0	1	1	4	....	....	....	....	....
	Hradec Kralove	Czech-Q	6	0	1	1	2	....	....	....	....	....
2003-04	Karlovy Vary	Czech	33	2	5	7	6	....	....	....	....	....
	KLH Chomutov	Czech-2	13	1	3	4	12	....	....	....	....	....

HAKEWILL, James (HAYK-wihl, JAYMZ) CGY.

Defense. Shoots left. 6'3", 205 lbs. Born, Wilmette, IL, June 7, 1982.
(Calgary's 6th choice, 145th overall, in 2001 Entry Draft).

			Regular Season					Playoffs				
Season	Club	League	GP	G	A	TP	PIM	GP	G	A	TP	PIM
99-2000	Westminster High	Hi-School	23	3	13	16	22	....	....	....	....	....
2000-01	Westminster High	Hi-School	23	4	15	19	30	....	....	....	....	....
2001-02	St. Lawrence	ECAC	30	2	2	4	18	....	....	....	....	....
2002-03	St. Lawrence	ECAC	34	1	3	4	61	....	....	....	....	....
2003-04	St. Lawrence	ECAC	31	1	2	3	37	....	....	....	....	....

HALVARDSSON, Johan (HAL-vahrds-sohn, YOH-hahn) NYI

Defense. Shoots left. 6'3", 198 lbs. Born, Jonkoping, Sweden, December 26, 1979.
(NY Islanders' 8th choice, 102nd overall, in 1999 Entry Draft).

			Regular Season					Playoffs				
Season	Club	League	GP	G	A	TP	PIM	GP	G	A	TP	PIM
1997-98	HV 71 Jr.	Swede-Jr.	28	5	5	10	65	....	....	....	....	....
1998-99	HV 71 Jonkoping	Sweden	17	1	2	3	33	....	....	....	....	....
99-2000	HV 71 Jonkoping	Sweden	46	0	3	3	75	5	0	0	0	8
2000-01	HV 71 Jonkoping	Sweden	33	0	0	0	24	....	....	....	....	....
2001-02	HV 71 Jonkoping	Sweden	3	0	0	0	0	....	....	....	....	....
2002-03	HV 71 Jonkoping	Sweden	39	0	1	1	14	7	0	0	0	0
2003-04	HV 71 Jonkoping	Sweden	11	0	4	4	39	17	1	3	4	41
	IK Oskarshamn	Swede-2	32	3	4	7	94	....	....	....	....	....

• Missed majority of 2001-02 season recovering from knee injury suffered in game vs. Sodertalje (Sweden), September 23, 2001.

HAMALAINEN, Ville (ha-muh-LAY-nuhn, VIHL-ee) CGY.

Left wing. Shoots left. 5'11", 178 lbs. Born, Lappeenranta, Finland, July 6, 1981.
(Calgary's 11th choice, 251st overall, in 2001 Entry Draft).

			Regular Season					Playoffs				
Season	Club	League	GP	G	A	TP	PIM	GP	G	A	TP	PIM
1997-98	SaiPa Jr.	Finn-Jr.	31	8	27	35	24	....	....	....	....	....
1998-99	SaiPa Jr.	Finn-Jr.	12	6	26	32	26	14	10	12	22	22
	SaiPa	Finland	12	1	0	1	8	....	....	....	....	....
99-2000	SaiPa	Finland	47	6	4	10	20	....	....	....	....	....
	KooKoo Kouvola	Finland-2	3	0	1	1	2	....	....	....	....	....
	SaiPa Jr.	Finn-Jr.	1	2	2	4	2	2	1	1	2	2
2000-01	SaiPa	Finland	42	0	4	4	10	....	....	....	....	....
	SaiPa Jr.	Finn-Jr.	1	1	1	2	0	....	....	....	....	....
2001-02	SaiPa	Finland	51	4	9	13	24	....	....	....	....	....
	SaiPa Jr.	Finn-Jr.	5	4	4	8	2	9	5	6	11	18
2002-03	FPS Forssa	Finland-2	13	4	8	12	6	....	....	....	....	....
	Tappara Tampere	Finland	35	1	2	3	6	6	0	0	0	2
2003-04	KalPa Kuopio	Finland-2	45	21	25	46	36	11	0	7	7	6

HAMILTON, Mike (HAM-ihl-tuhn, MIGHK) ATL.

Forward. Shoots left. 6'1", 200 lbs. Born, Vancouver, B.C., May 2, 1983.
(Atlanta's 6th choice, 175th overall, in 2003 Entry Draft).

			Regular Season					Playoffs				
Season	Club	League	GP	G	A	TP	PIM	GP	G	A	TP	PIM
99-2000	Peninsula Panthers	VIJHL	44	33	42	75	94	....	....	....	....	....
2000-01	Peninsula Panthers	VIJHL	19	15	20	35	106	....	....	....	....	....
	Victoria Salsa	BCHL	31	2	5	7	18	....	....	....	....	....
2001-02	Victoria Salsa	BCHL	13	5	2	7	14	....	....	....	....	....
	Merritt	BCHL	45	23	36	59	64	....	....	....	....	....
2002-03	Merritt	BCHL	56	42	51	95	133	....	....	....	....	....
2003-04	U. of Maine	H-East	29	7	6	13	40	....	....	....	....	....

HANNULA, Mika (HAH-noo-lah, MEE-kah) MIN.

Right wing. Shoots left. 5'11", 180 lbs. Born, Huddinge, Sweden, April 2, 1979.
(Minnesota's 10th choice, 269th overall, in 2002 Entry Draft).

			Regular Season					Playoffs				
Season	Club	League	GP	G	A	TP	PIM	GP	G	A	TP	PIM
1996-97	AIK Solna Jr.	Swede-Jr.	26	4	4	8	58	....	....	....	....	....
1997-98	Djurgarden Jr.	Swede-Jr.	14	10	6	16	22	2	1	1	2	0
	Lukko Rauma	Finn-Jr.	6	2	0	2	36	....	....	....	....	....
1998-99	Lidingo HC	Swede-2	32	10	0	10	47	....	....	....	....	....
99-2000	Hammarby	Swede-2	43	10	10	20	53	2	0	0	0	2
2000-01	Malmo IF Jr.	Swede-Jr.	1	1	1	2	0	....	....	....	....	....
	Malmo IF	Sweden	45	2	9	11	26	8	3	2	5	14
2001-02	Malmo IF	Sweden	41	10	7	17	14	5	2	1	3	0
2002-03	Malmo IF	Sweden	49	15	15	30	72	....	....	....	....	....
2003-04	Houston Aeros	AHL	67	9	18	27	59	....	....	....	....	....

HANNUS, Tommi (HA-nuhs, TAW-mee) L.A.

Left wing. Shoots right. 6', 180 lbs. Born, Vantaa, Finland, June 27, 1980.
(Los Angeles' 7th choice, 190th overall, in 1998 Entry Draft).

			Regular Season					Playoffs				
Season	Club	League	GP	G	A	TP	PIM	GP	G	A	TP	PIM
1994-95	TPS Turku C	Finn-Jr.	27	24	13	37	43	....	....	....	....	....
1995-96	TPS Turku C	Finn-Jr.	29	34	22	56	67	....	....	....	....	....
	TPS Turku B	Finn-Jr.	1	1	0	1	2	....	....	....	....	....
1996-97	TPS Turku Jr.	Finn-Jr.	27	7	7	14	6	....	....	....	....	....
	TPS Turku B	Finn-Jr.	18	7	7	14	6	6	4	2	6	10
1997-98	TPS Turku Jr.	Finn-Jr.	19	6	3	9	4	....	....	....	....	....
	TPS Turku B	Finn-Jr.	9	5	4	9	8	....	....	....	....	....
1998-99	TPS Turku Jr.	Finn-Jr.	8	5	4	9	22	....	....	....	....	....
	TuTo Turku	Finland-2	18	6	4	10	16	8	0	2	2	8
99-2000	TPS Turku Jr.	Finn-Jr.	3	4	3	7	6	....	....	....	....	....
	TuTo Turku	Finland-2	27	11	6	17	20	....	....	....	....	....
	Assat Pori	Finland	13	1	0	1	4	....	....	....	....	....
2000-01	TuTo Turku	Finland-2	29	9	8	17	16	11	*7	7	14	*24
2001-02	TPS Turku	Finland	47	4	2	6	6	3	1	0	1	0
2002-03	Jokerit Helsinki	Finland	31	1	0	1	25	....	....	....	....	....
	Kiekko-Vantaa	Finland-2	14	7	7	14	4	12	3	5	8	8
2003-04	Pelicans Lahti	Finland	55	15	4	19	20	....	....	....	....	....

HANSEN, Matthew (HAN-suhn, MA-thew) VAN.

Defense. Shoots left. 6'4", 198 lbs. Born, Winnipeg, Man., January 18, 1985.
(Vancouver's 10th choice, 285th overall, in 2003 Entry Draft).

			Regular Season					Playoffs				
Season	Club	League	GP	G	A	TP	PIM	GP	G	A	TP	PIM
2000-01	North Battleford	SMHL	72	23	33	56	45	....	....	....	....	....
	Seattle	WHL	2	0	0	0	0	....	....	....	....	....
2001-02	Seattle	WHL	44	3	1	4	10	11	0	0	0	2
2002-03	Seattle	WHL	51	3	18	21	24	15	0	5	5	2
2003-04	Seattle	WHL	60	4	22	26	27	....	....	....	....	....

HARANT, Tomas (HAH-rant, TAW-mahsh) NSH.

Defense. Shoots left. 6'3", 201 lbs. Born, Zilina, Czech., April 28, 1980.
(Nashville's 8th choice, 173rd overall, in 2000 Entry Draft).

			Regular Season					Playoffs				
Season	Club	League	GP	G	A	TP	PIM	GP	G	A	TP	PIM
1995-96	HK SKP Zilina Jr.	Slovak-Jr.	46	3	9	12	142	....	....	....	....	....
1996-97	HK SKP Zilina Jr.	Slovak-Jr.	44	1	4	5	18	....	....	....	....	....
1997-98	HK SKP Zilina Jr.	Slovak-Jr.	41	5	7	12	72	....	....	....	....	....
	HK SKP Zilina	Slovak-2	5	0	0	0	0	....	....	....	....	....
1998-99	HK SKP Zilina Jr.	Slovak-Jr.	33	1	6	7	108	....	....	....	....	....
99-2000	HK SKP Zilina	Slovak-2	26	0	3	3	34	....	....	....	....	....
2000-01	Trinec Jr.	Czech-Jr.	5	1	2	3	8	1	0	0	0	4
	HC Ocelari Trinec	Czech	15	1	2	3	14	....	....	....	....	....
2001-02	MsHK SKP Zilina	Slovakia	51	2	3	5	46	4	0	0	0	4
2002-03	Havirov	Czech	19	0	1	1	40	....	....	....	....	....
	MsHK SKP Zilina	Slovakia	28	2	3	5	86	4	1	0	1	24
2003-04	Dynamo Moscow	Russia	31	1	0	1	18	3	0	0	0	0

HARIKKALA, Jaakko (HAHR-ee-kuh-lah, YAH-koh) BOS.

Defense. Shoots left. 6'2", 215 lbs. Born, Kalanti, Finland, March 30, 1981.
(Boston's 4th choice, 118th overall, in 1999 Entry Draft).

			Regular Season					Playoffs				
Season	Club	League	GP	G	A	TP	PIM	GP	G	A	TP	PIM
1997-98	Jaa-Kotkat	Finland-3	5	0	2	2	8	....	....	....	....	....
	Jaa-Kotkat	Finland-2	45	2	6	8	65	....	....	....	....	....
1998-99	Lukko Rauma Jr.	Finn-Jr.	11	1	3	4	22	....	....	....	....	....
	Lukko Rauma	Finland	35	0	0	0	10	....	....	....	....	....
99-2000	Lukko Rauma	Finland	24	0	0	0	2	....	....	....	....	....
	Lukko Rauma Jr.	Finn-Jr.	19	1	8	9	40	7	1	1	2	31
2000-01	Lukko Rauma Jr.	Finn-Jr.	2	2	0	2	2	....	....	....	....	....
	Jaa-Kotkat	Finland-2	10	0	2	2	16	....	....	....	....	....
	Lukko Rauma	Finland	10	0	0	0	0	....	....	....	....	....
2001-02	Lukko Rauma	Finland	47	4	8	12	40	....	....	....	....	....
	Lukko Rauma Jr.	Finn-Jr.	3	0	1	1	0	....	....	....	....	....
2002-03	Lukko Rauma	Finland	54	7	6	13	48	....	....	....	....	....
2003-04	Lukko Rauma	Finland	55	4	4	8	26	4	0	0	0	0

HARRISON, Jay (HAIR-ih-suhn, JAY) TOR.

Defense. Shoots left. 6'4", 211 lbs. Born, Oshawa, Ont., November 3, 1982.
(Toronto's 4th choice, 82nd overall, in 2001 Entry Draft).

			Regular Season					Playoffs				
Season	Club	League	GP	G	A	TP	PIM	GP	G	A	TP	PIM
1997-98	Oshawa	OJHL-B	42	1	11	12	143	....	....	....	....	....
1998-99	Brampton	OHL	63	1	14	15	108	....	....	....	....	....
99-2000	Brampton	OHL	68	2	18	20	139	6	0	2	2	15
2000-01	Brampton	OHL	53	4	15	19	112	9	1	1	2	17
2001-02	Brampton	OHL	61	12	31	43	116	....	....	....	....	....
	St. John's	AHL	7	0	1	1	2	10	0	0	0	4
	Memphis	CHL	....	....	....	....	....	1	0	0	0	2
2002-03	St. John's	AHL	72	2	8	10	72	....	....	....	....	....
2003-04	St. John's	AHL	70	4	5	9	141	....	....	....	....	....

OHL All-Rookie Team (1999)

HARTSBURG, Chris (HAHRTZ-buhrg, KRIHS)

Right wing. Shoots right. 6', 200 lbs. Born, Edina, MN, May 30, 1980.
(New Jersey's 7th choice, 214th overall, in 1999 Entry Draft).

			Regular Season					Playoffs				
Season	Club	League	GP	G	A	TP	PIM	GP	G	A	TP	PIM
1995-96	Cambridge	OJHL-B	46	12	15	27	10	....	....	....	....	....
1996-97	Cambridge	OJHL-B	47	14	19	33	29	....	....	....	....	....
1997-98	Omaha Lancers	USHL	54	16	19	35	58	12	2	2	4	20
1998-99	Colorado College	WCHA	34	6	4	10	60	....	....	....	....	....
99-2000	Colorado College	WCHA	33	3	2	5	50	....	....	....	....	....
2000-01	Colorado College	WCHA	41	8	7	15	38	....	....	....	....	....
2001-02	Colorado College	WCHA	40	14	8	22	50	....	....	....	....	....
2002-03	Albany River Rats	AHL	40	7	3	10	22	....	....	....	....	....
2003-04	Albany River Rats	AHL	51	4	5	9	26	....	....	....	....	....

HARVEY, Kevin (HAHR-vee, KEH-vihn) CGY.

Left wing. Shoots left. 6'2", 175 lbs. Born, Branchton, Ont., September 14, 1984.
(Calgary's 9th choice, 270th overall, in 2003 Entry Draft).

			Regular Season					Playoffs				
Season	Club	League	GP	G	A	TP	PIM	GP	G	A	TP	PIM
2001-02	Kingston	OJHL-B	6	0	0	0	0	....	....	....	....	....
	Oakville Blades	OJHL-B	30	5	17	22	221	....	....	....	....	....
	Kingston	OHL	2	0	1	1	0	....	....	....	....	....
2002-03	Oakville Blades	OJHL-B	19	7	15	22	127	....	....	....	....	....
	Georgetown	OPJHL	16	4	9	13	34	....	....	....	....	....
2003-04	Owen Sound	OHL	59	8	8	16	159	7	1	1	2	2

HASKINS, Tyler (HA-skihns, TIGH-luhr) DET.

Center. Shoots right. 6'1", 177 lbs. Born, Cleveland, OH, May 26, 1986.
(Detroit's 4th choice, 162nd overall, in 2004 Entry Draft).

			Regular Season					Playoffs				
Season	Club	League	GP	G	A	TP	PIM	GP	G	A	TP	PIM
2001-02	Sioux City	USHL	46	3	8	11	20	12	1	0	1	15
2002-03	Guelph Storm	OHL	54	7	14	21	14	11	3	2	5	10
2003-04	Guelph Storm	OHL	9	1	3	4	2	....	....	....	....	....
	St. Michael's	OHL	54	17	24	41	30	18	5	4	9	10

HAVEL, Marian (HAH-vuhl, MAIR-ee-uhn) WSH.

Center/Left wing. Shoots left. 6', 180 lbs. Born, Jihlava, Czech., January 26, 1984.
(Washington's 10th choice, 179th overall, in 2002 Entry Draft).

			Regular Season					Playoffs				
Season	Club	League	GP	G	A	TP	PIM	GP	G	A	TP	PIM
99-2000	Dukla Jihlava Jr.	Czech-Jr.	50	35	22	57	70	....	....	....	....	....
	Sioux City	USHL	4	0	1	1	0	....	....	....	....	....
2000-01	Dukla Jihlava 18	Czech-Jr.	7	11	18	29	36	....	....	....	....	....
	Dukla Jihlava Jr.	Czech-Jr.	14	9	10	19	64	....	....	....	....	....
	HC Dukla Jihlava	Czech-2	26	2	2	4	14	....	....	....	....	....
2001-02	Vancouver Giants	WHL	67	17	16	33	83	....	....	....	....	....
2002-03	Vancouver Giants	WHL	5	1	2	3	12	....	....	....	....	....
	Swift Current	WHL	56	8	19	27	46	4	0	0	0	2
2003-04	Plzen	Czech	2	0	0	0	2	....	....	....	....	....
	HC Dukla Jihlava	Czech-2	31	3	3	6	8	15	2	1	3	8

HAVELKA, Petr (huh-VEHL-kah, PEE-tuhr) PIT.

Left wing. Shoots left. 6'2", 185 lbs. Born, Most, Czech., March 4, 1979.
(Pittsburgh's 6th choice, 152nd overall, in 1997 Entry Draft).

			Regular Season					Playoffs				
Season	Club	League	GP	G	A	TP	PIM	GP	G	A	TP	PIM
1995-96	Sparta Praha Jr.	Czech-Jr.	40	15	10	25	....	....	....	....	....	....
1996-97	Sparta Praha Jr.	Czech-Jr.	22	14	13	27	....	....	....	....	....	....
	HC Sparta Praha	Czech	....	....	....	....	....	1	0	0	0	0
1997-98	Sparta Praha Jr.	Czech-Jr.	DID NOT PLAY – INJURED									
1998-99	Sparta Praha Jr.	Czech-Jr.	5	7	3	10	....	4	1	1	2	....
	HC Velvana Kladno	Czech	5	0	0	0	0	....	....	....	....	....
99-2000	Sparta Praha Jr.	Czech-Jr.	2	1	0	1	0	....	....	....	....	....
	Beroun	Czech-2	5	2	4	6	29	....	....	....	....	....
	HC Velvana Kladno	Czech	6	1	2	3	2	....	....	....	....	....
	HC Sparta Praha	Czech	10	0	1	1	0	3	0	0	0	0
2000-01	Beroun	Czech-2	3	0	0	0	0	....	....	....	....	....
	HC Sparta Praha	Czech	....	....	....	....	....	7	1	0	1	2
2001-02	Sparta Praha Jr.	Czech-Jr.	2	1	0	1	0	....	....	....	....	....
	Usti nad Labem	Czech-3	2	0	0	0	2	....	....	....	....	....
	HC Sparta Praha	Czech	35	3	4	7	12	6	0	0	0	2
2002-03	HC Sparta Praha	Czech	47	10	6	16	38	8	1	3	4	0
2003-04	HC Sparta Praha	Czech	6	1	1	2	2	....	....	....	....	....
	HC Mlada Boleslav	Czech-2	3	1	2	3	2	....	....	....	....	....

HAVERN, Ned (HA-vuhrn, NEHD) DAL.

Left wing. Shoots left. 6'1", 190 lbs. Born, Boston, MA, October 1, 1982.
(Dallas' 12th choice, 273rd overall, in 2002 Entry Draft).

			Regular Season					Playoffs				
Season	Club	League	GP	G	A	TP	PIM	GP	G	A	TP	PIM
2000-01	Arlington High	Hi-School	STATISTICS NOT AVAILABLE									
2001-02	Boston College	H-East	38	6	6	12	10	....	....	....	....	....
2002-03	Boston College	H-East	36	4	8	12	10	....	....	....	....	....
2003-04	Boston College	H-East	37	8	3	11	24	....	....	....	....	....

HEALEY, Eric (HEE-lee, AIR-ihk)

Left wing. Shoots left. 5'11", 200 lbs. Born, Hull, MA, January 20, 1975.

			Regular Season					Playoffs				
Season	Club	League	GP	G	A	TP	PIM	GP	G	A	TP	PIM
1993-94	New England	NEJHL	37	61	76	137	....	....	....	....	....	....
1994-95	RPI Engineers	ECAC	37	13	11	24	35	....	....	....	....	....
1995-96	RPI Engineers	ECAC	35	18	22	40	57	....	....	....	....	....
1996-97	RPI Engineers	ECAC	36	30	26	56	63	....	....	....	....	....
1997-98	RPI Engineers	ECAC	35	21	27	48	42	....	....	....	....	....
1998-99	Saint John Flames	AHL	64	14	24	38	77	....	....	....	....	....
	Orlando	IHL	13	5	4	9	13	8	1	0	1	12
99-2000	Springfield Falcons	AHL	32	14	15	29	51	1	0	0	0	2
2000-01	Springfield Falcons	AHL	66	16	17	33	53	....	....	....	....	....
2001-02	Jackson Bandits	ECHL	2	1	1	2	0	....	....	....	....	....
	Manchester	AHL	65	24	34	58	45	5	2	2	4	8
2002-03	Manchester	AHL	75	*42	31	73	47	3	1	0	1	2
2003-04	Chicago Wolves	AHL	71	31	20	51	52	10	3	6	9	10

ECAC Second All-Star Team (1997) • NCAA East Second All-American Team (1997, 1998) • ECAC First All-Star Team (1998) • Fred Hunt Memorial Trophy (Sportsmanship – AHL) (2003) (co-winner - Chris Ferraro)

Signed as a free agent by **Calgary**, September 22, 1998. Signed as a free agent by **Phoenix**, July 26, 1999. Signed to try-out contract by **Manchester** (AHL), September 30, 2001. Signed as a free agent by **Atlanta**, August 12, 2003.

HECIMOVIC, John (heh-CHIH-moh-vihk, JAWN) FLA.

Right wing. Shoots right. 6'1", 210 lbs. Born, Sarnia, Ont., March 31, 1984.
(Florida's 12th choice, 264th overall, in 2003 Entry Draft).

			Regular Season					Playoffs				
Season	Club	League	GP	G	A	TP	PIM	GP	G	A	TP	PIM
99-2000	Kitchener	OMHL	55	14	33	47	26	....	....	....	....	....
2000-01	Sarnia Sting	OHL	62	6	11	17	27	4	0	0	0	5
2001-02	Sarnia Sting	OHL	65	30	19	49	64	5	1	3	4	2
2002-03	Sarnia Sting	OHL	60	30	32	62	112	6	4	2	6	6
2003-04	Sarnia Sting	OHL	68	30	32	62	98	5	2	3	5	6

HEDLUND, Andy OTT.

Defense. Shoots left. 6'3", 215 lbs. Born, Osseo, MN, May 16, 1978.

			Regular Season					Playoffs				
Season	Club	League	GP	G	A	TP	PIM	GP	G	A	TP	PIM
1997-98	Fargo-Moorhead	USHL	56	4	12	16	135	4	0	4	4	0
1998-99	Minnesota State	WCHA	34	1	2	3	34	....	....	....	....	....
99-2000	Minnesota State	WCHA	36	4	2	6	58	....	....	....	....	....
2000-01	Minnesota State	WCHA	38	6	6	12	64	....	....	....	....	....
2001-02	Minnesota State	WCHA	37	5	10	15	48	....	....	....	....	....
	Trenton Titans	ECHL	2	0	0	0	0	6	0	0	0	6
2002-03	Trenton Titans	ECHL	13	1	2	3	14	....	....	....	....	....
	Binghampton	AHL	59	1	7	8	48	10	0	0	0	0
2003-04	Binghampton	AHL	80	4	19	23	108	2	0	0	0	2

Signed as a free agent by **Trenton** (ECHL), March 28, 2002. Signed as a free agent by **Binghamton** (AHL), November 3, 2002. Signed as a free agent by **Ottawa**, December 18, 2003.

HEDMAN, Oscar (HEHD-man, AWS-kuhr) WSH.

Defense. Shoots left. 6', 209 lbs. Born, Ornskoldsvik, Sweden, April 21, 1986.
(Washington's 8th choice, 132nd overall, in 2004 Entry Draft).

			Regular Season					Playoffs				
Season	Club	League	GP	G	A	TP	PIM	GP	G	A	TP	PIM
2002-03	MoDo 18	Swede-Jr.	14	4	5	9	8	6	2	1	3	32
	MoDo Jr.	Swede-Jr.	5	0	1	1	2	....	....	....	....	....
2003-04	MoDo Jr.	Swede-Jr.	25	7	11	18	28	8	3	3	6	6
	MoDo 18	Swede-Jr.	3	3	1	4	2	2	0	3	3	0
	MoDo	Sweden	24	1	2	3	6	6	0	0	0	0

HEID, Chris (HIGHD, KRIHS) MIN.

Defense. Shoots left. 6'2", 205 lbs. Born, Langley, B.C., March 14, 1983.
(Minnesota's 3rd choice, 74th overall, in 2001 Entry Draft).

			Regular Season					Playoffs				
Season	Club	League	GP	G	A	TP	PIM	GP	G	A	TP	PIM
1998-99	Kamloops	BCAHA	58	26	34	60	65	....	....	....	....	....
	Spokane Chiefs	WHL	1	0	0	0	0	....	....	....	....	....
99-2000	Spokane Chiefs	WHL	44	1	7	8	25	6	0	0	0	4
2000-01	Spokane Chiefs	WHL	51	2	15	17	76	12	0	4	4	12
2001-02	Spokane Chiefs	WHL	69	7	28	35	56	11	1	4	5	8
2002-03	Spokane Chiefs	WHL	60	9	36	45	66	11	2	11	13	10
2003-04	Houston Aeros	AHL	58	3	10	13	35	....	....	....	....	....

HEJDA, Jan (HAY-dah, YAHN) BUF.

Defense. Shoots left. 6'3", 209 lbs. Born, Prague, Czech., June 18, 1978.
(Buffalo's 4th choice, 106th overall, in 2003 Entry Draft).

			Regular Season					Playoffs				
Season	Club	League	GP	G	A	TP	PIM	GP	G	A	TP	PIM
1997-98	HC Slavia Praha	Czech	44	2	5	7	51	5	0	0	0	6
1998-99	HC Slavia Praha	Czech	34	1	2	3	38	....	....	....	....	....
99-2000	HC Slavia Praha	Czech	26	1	2	3	14	....	....	....	....	....
	HC Femax Havirov	Czech	7	0	2	2	6	....	....	....	....	....
	HC Stadion Liberec	Czech-2	1	0	0	0	4	....	....	....	....	....
2000-01	HC Slavia Praha	Czech	38	2	6	8	70	11	3	0	3	12
	SK Kadan	Czech-2	8	1	0	1	6	....	....	....	....	....
2001-02	HC Slavia Praha	Czech	42	9	8	17	52	9	1	1	2	14
2002-03	HC Slavia Praha	Czech	52	6	11	17	44	17	5	8	13	12
2003-04	CSKA Moscow	Russia	60	1	5	6	26	....	....	....	....	....

HELBLING, Timo (HEHL-blihng, TEE-moh) T.B.

Defense. Shoots right. 6'3", 209 lbs. Born, Basel, Switz., July 21, 1981.
(Nashville's 11th choice, 162nd overall, in 1999 Entry Draft).

			Regular Season					Playoffs				
Season	Club	League	GP	G	A	TP	PIM	GP	G	A	TP	PIM
1997-98	HC Davos Jr.	Swiss-Jr.	34	6	6	12	38	....	....	....	....	....
1998-99	HC Davos Jr.	Swiss-Jr.	28	5	10	15	116	2	1	3	4	35
	HC Davos	Swiss	44	0	0	0	8	4	0	0	0	0
99-2000	HC Davos	Swiss	44	0	0	0	49	5	0	0	0	0
2000-01	Windsor Spitfires	OHL	54	7	14	21	90	7	0	2	2	11
	Milwaukee	IHL	....	....	....	....	....	1	0	0	0	0
2001-02	Milwaukee	AHL	67	2	6	8	59	....	....	....	....	....
2002-03	Milwaukee	AHL	23	0	1	1	37	....	....	....	....	....
	Toledo Storm	ECHL	35	3	8	11	75	7	0	1	1	2
2003-04	Milwaukee	AHL	37	0	2	2	46	....	....	....	....	....
	Utah Grizzlies	AHL	23	3	2	5	47	....	....	....	....	....

Traded to **Tampa Bay** by **Nashville** for Tampa Bay's 8th round choice (Pekka Rinne) in 2004 Entry Draft, February 25, 2004.

HELFENSTEIN, Sven (hehl-fehn-SHTIGHN, SVEHN) NYR

Left wing. Shoots right. 5'10", 176 lbs. Born, Winterthur, Switz., July 30, 1982.
(NY Rangers' 6th choice, 175th overall, in 2000 Entry Draft).

			Regular Season					Playoffs				
Season	Club	League	GP	G	A	TP	PIM	GP	G	A	TP	PIM
1997-98	Kloten Flyers Jr.	Swiss-Jr.	31	6	8	14	14	....	....	....	....	....
1998-99	Kloten Flyers Jr.	Swiss-Jr.	33	25	18	43	14	7	5	3	8	2
	EHC Kloten	Swiss	2	0	0	0	0	....	....	....	....	....
99-2000	EHC Kloten	Swiss	40	6	3	9	28	6	0	1	1	0
2000-01	Kloten Flyers Jr.	Swiss-Jr.	2	3	3	6	0	....	....	....	....	....
	EHC Kloten	Swiss	8	1	1	2	0	....	....	....	....	....
	La Chaux-de-Fonds	Swiss	23	2	8	10	6	12	1	3	4	6
	HC Thurgau	Swiss-2	4	2	1	3	8	....	....	....	....	....
2001-02	SC Bern	Swiss	35	2	10	12	39	6	0	0	0	4
	SC Bern Jr.	Swiss-Jr.	....	....	....	....	....	4	4	2	6	2
2002-03	SC Bern	Swiss	32	2	3	5	14	11	0	0	0	4
	EHC Biel	Swiss-2	11	3	4	7	12	....	....	....	....	....
2003-04	ZSC Lions Zurich	Swiss	38	5	8	13	6	13	2	1	3	6
	GCK Lions Zurich	Swiss-2	9	4	7	11	2	....	....	....	....	....

HELMINEN, Dwight (HEHL-mih-nehn, DWIGHT) NYR

Center. Shoots left. 6', 200 lbs. Born, Hancock, MI, June 22, 1983.
(Edmonton's 12th choice, 244th overall, in 2002 Entry Draft).

			Regular Season					Playoffs				
Season	Club	League	GP	G	A	TP	PIM	GP	G	A	TP	PIM
1998-99	Det, Compuware	MNHL	32	9	7	16	....	....	....	....	....	....
99-2000	U.S. National U-17	USDP	30	7	10	17	8	....	....	....	....	....
	U.S. National U-18	USDP	51	6	10	16	6	....	....	....	....	....
2000-01	U.S. National U-18	USDP	67	21	44	65	30	....	....	....	....	....
2001-02	U. of Michigan	CCHA	39	10	8	18	10	....	....	....	....	....
2002-03	U. of Michigan	CCHA	39	17	16	33	34	....	....	....	....	....
2003-04	U. of Michigan	CCHA	41	17	11	28	4	....	....	....	....	....

Traded to **NY Rangers** by **Edmonton** with Stephen Valiquette and Edmonton's 2nd round compensatory choice (Dane Byers) in 2004 Entry Draft and future considerations for Petr Nedved and Jussi Markkanen, March 3, 2004.

HEMINGWAY, Brett (HEH-mihng-way, BREHT) COL.

Right wing. Shoots right. 6'1", 185 lbs. Born, Yorkton, Sask., September 28, 1983.
(Colorado's 6th choice, 225th overall, in 2003 Entry Draft).

			Regular Season					Playoffs				
Season	Club	League	GP	G	A	TP	PIM	GP	G	A	TP	PIM
2000-01	Port Coquitlam	PIJHL	36	22	19	41	24	....	....	....	....	....
2001-02	Coquitlam Express	BCHL	60	45	39	84	31	....	....	....	....	....
2002-03	Coquitlam Express	BCHL	60	42	50	92	50	7	7	5	12	4
2003-04	New Hampshire	H-East	34	7	12	19	8	....	....	....	....	....

Hockey East All-Rookie Team (2004)

HEMINGWAY, Colin (HEH-mihng-way, CAW-lihn) ST.L.

Right wing. Shoots right. 6', 170 lbs. Born, Surrey, B.C., August 12, 1980.
(St. Louis' 7th choice, 221st overall, in 1999 Entry Draft).

			Regular Season					Playoffs				
Season	Club	League	GP	G	A	TP	PIM	GP	G	A	TP	PIM
1996-97	Port Coquitlam	PIJHL	34	23	24	47	52	....	....	....	....	....
1997-98	South Surrey	BCHL	58	12	16	28	46	....	....	....	....	....
1998-99	South Surrey	BCHL	59	40	64	104	52	....	....	....	....	....
99-2000	New Hampshire	H-East	22	3	5	8	6	....	....	....	....	....
2000-01	New Hampshire	H-East	37	9	18	27	16	....	....	....	....	....
2001-02	New Hampshire	H-East	40	*33	33	66	30	....	....	....	....	....
2002-03	New Hampshire	H-East	40	22	25	47	51	....	....	....	....	....
2003-04	Worcester IceCats	AHL	13	2	0	2	11	....	....	....	....	....
	Peoria Rivermen	ECHL	36	20	24	44	34	2	0	0	0	0

Hockey East First All-Star Team (2002) • Hockey East Second All-Star Team (2003) • NCAA East Second All-American Team (2003)

HENDRIKX, Trevor (HEHN-drihx, TREH-vuhr) CBJ

Defense. Shoots right. 6'2", 200 lbs. Born, Winchester, Ont., March 29, 1985.
(Columbus' 10th choice, 283rd overall, in 2003 Entry Draft).

			Regular Season					Playoffs				
Season	Club	League	GP	G	A	TP	PIM	GP	G	A	TP	PIM
2000-01	Gloucester	OPJHL	26	2	3	5	25	....	....	....	....	....
2001-02	Peterborough	OHL	46	1	3	4	37	5	0	0	0	4
2002-03	Peterborough	OHL	56	1	8	9	128	7	0	0	0	4
2003-04	Peterborough	OHL	63	8	24	32	208	....	....	....	....	....

HENKEL, Jim (HEHN-kehl, JIHM) CAR.

Center. Shoots left. 6'2", 180 lbs. Born, Red Bank, NJ, May 25, 1979.
(Los Angeles' 8th choice, 217th overall, in 1998 Entry Draft).

			Regular Season					Playoffs				
Season	Club	League	GP	G	A	TP	PIM	GP	G	A	TP	PIM
1997-98	New England	EJHL	37	34	37	71	....	11	7	17	24	....
1998-99	RPI Engineers	ECAC	20	0	4	4	14	....	....	....	....	....
99-2000	RPI Engineers	ECAC	34	2	5	7	28	....	....	....	....	....
2000-01	RPI Engineers	ECAC	34	11	19	30	44	....	....	....	....	....
2001-02	RPI Engineers	ECAC	35	9	15	24	22	....	....	....	....	....
2002-03	Atlantic City	ECHL	68	32	36	68	25	19	3	12	15	8
	Cleveland Barons	AHL	2	0	0	0	0	....	....	....	....	....
2003-04	Atlantic City	ECHL	22	14	11	25	15	2	0	2	2	0
	Grand Rapids	AHL	15	2	1	3	4	....	....	....	....	....
	Worcester IceCats	AHL	3	0	0	0	0	....	....	....	....	....
	Lowell	AHL	35	11	13	24	6	....	....	....	....	....
	Providence Bruins	AHL	....	....	....	....	....	1	0	1	1	0

Signed as a free agent by **Carolina**, July 26, 2004.

HENNESSY, Joshua (HEHN-eh-see, JAW-shoo-wuh) S.J.

Center. Shoots left. 6', 190 lbs. Born, Brockton, MA, February 7, 1985.
(San Jose's 3rd choice, 43rd overall, in 2003 Entry Draft).

			Regular Season					Playoffs				
Season	Club	League	GP	G	A	TP	PIM	GP	G	A	TP	PIM
2000-01	Milton Academy	Hi-School	28	20	30	50	20	....	....	....	....	....
2001-02	Quebec Remparts	QMJHL	70	20	20	40	24	9	3	9	12	8
2002-03	Quebec Remparts	QMJHL	72	33	51	84	44	11	6	9	15	10
2003-04	Quebec Remparts	QMJHL	59	40	42	82	55	....	....	....	....	....

HENNING, Petter (HEH-nihng, PEH-tehr) NYR

Right wing. Shoots left. 6', 209 lbs. Born, Ornskoldsvik, Sweden, September 15, 1980.
(NY Rangers' 10th choice, 251st overall, in 1999 Entry Draft).

			Regular Season					Playoffs				
Season	Club	League	GP	G	A	TP	PIM	GP	G	A	TP	PIM
1997-98	MoDo Jr.	Swede-Jr.	27	7	6	13	12	....	....	....	....	....
1998-99	MoDo Jr.	Swede-Jr.	38	10	10	20	74	....	....	....	....	....
	MoDo	Sweden	1	0	0	0	0	....	....	....	....	....
99-2000	Sodertalje SK Jr.	Swede-Jr.	3	1	0	1	0	....	....	....	....	....
	Skelleftea AIK	Swede-2	8	0	0	0	2	....	....	....	....	....
2000-01	Tingsryds AIF	Swede-2	40	3	5	8	18	3	0	0	0	6
2001-02	Tingsryds AIF	Swede-2	32	9	4	13	18	....	....	....	....	....
	Tingsryds AIF	Swede-Q	13	2	0	2	12	2	0	0	0	0
2002-03	Tingsryds AIF	Swede-3	40	13	19	32	....	....	....	....	....	....
2003-04	Tingsryds AIF	Swede-3	31	9	5	14	24	....	....	....	....	....

HENRICH, Adam (HEHN-rihch, A-duhm) T.B.

Left wing. Shoots left. 6'4", 220 lbs. Born, Thornhill, Ont., January 19, 1984.
(Tampa Bay's 1st choice, 60th overall, in 2002 Entry Draft).

			Regular Season					Playoffs				
Season	Club	League	GP	G	A	TP	PIM	GP	G	A	TP	PIM
99-2000	Don Mills Flyers	GTHL	54	30	52	82	86	....	....	....	....	....
2000-01	Brampton	OHL	48	5	4	9	27	9	0	0	0	6
2001-02	Brampton	OHL	66	33	30	63	92	....	....	....	....	....
2002-03	Brampton	OHL	63	31	33	64	84	11	4	1	5	25
2003-04	Brampton	OHL	65	29	29	58	146	12	5	1	6	24

HENRICH, Michael (HEHN-rihch, MIGH-kuhl)

Right wing. Shoots right. 6'2", 206 lbs. Born, Thornhill, Ont., March 3, 1980.
(Edmonton's 1st choice, 13th overall, in 1998 Entry Draft).

			Regular Season					Playoffs				
Season	Club	League	GP	G	A	TP	PIM	GP	G	A	TP	PIM
1995-96	Wexford Raiders	MTJHL	4	1	0	1	0	....	....	....	....	....
1996-97	Barrie Colts	OHL	52	9	15	24	19	9	0	5	5	0
1997-98	Barrie Colts	OHL	66	41	22	63	75	5	1	3	4	0
1998-99	Barrie Colts	OHL	62	38	33	71	42	12	0	2	2	4
99-2000	Barrie Colts	OHL	66	38	48	86	69	25	10	18	28	30
2000-01	Tallahassee	ECHL	6	1	1	2	0	....	....	....	....	....
	Hamilton Bulldogs	AHL	73	5	10	15	36	....	....	....	....	....
2001-02	Hamilton Bulldogs	AHL	67	14	24	38	24	9	2	2	4	2
2002-03	Hamilton Bulldogs	AHL	12	0	0	0	2	....	....	....	....	....
	Mora IK	Swede-2	12	3	1	4	16	....	....	....	....	....
	Hershey Bears	AHL	9	0	1	1	4	1	0	0	0	0
2003-04	Toronto	AHL	58	14	10	24	28	3	2	0	2	0

HILL, Ed (HIHL, EHD) CAR.

Defense. Shoots left. 6'3", 215 lbs. Born, Newburyport, MA, October 24, 1980.
(Nashville's 5th choice, 61st overall, in 1999 Entry Draft).

			Regular Season					Playoffs				
Season	Club	League	GP	G	A	TP	PIM	GP	G	A	TP	PIM
1996-97	Green Bay	USHL	61	4	11	15	36	17	0	1	1	14
1997-98	Green Bay	USHL	51	1	16	17	76	3	0	0	0	0
1998-99	Barrie Colts	OHL	53	7	17	24	42	12	0	2	2	8
99-2000	Barrie Colts	OHL	66	1	18	19	63	25	1	3	4	14
2000-01	Barrie Colts	OHL	60	3	19	22	104	5	0	1	1	2
2001-02	Florida Everblades	ECHL	34	2	12	14	22	....	....	....	....	....
	Lowell	AHL	37	0	0	0	37	5	0	1	1	12
2002-03	Lowell	AHL	29	1	3	4	30	....	....	....	....	....
	Florida Everblades	ECHL	16	1	5	6	10	1	0	0	0	0
2003-04	Lowell	AHL	26	0	2	2	16	....	....	....	....	....
	Florida Everblades	ECHL	3	0	0	0	9	....	....	....	....	....

Signed as a free agent by **Carolina**, July 16, 2002.

HINZ, Chad (HIHNZ, CHAD)

Center. Shoots right. 5'10", 190 lbs. Born, Saskatoon, Sask., March 21, 1979.
(Edmonton's 8th choice, 187th overall, in 1997 Entry Draft).

			Regular Season					Playoffs				
Season	Club	League	GP	G	A	TP	PIM	GP	G	A	TP	PIM
1994-95	Sask. Contacts	SMHL	29	25	21	46	41	....	....	....	....	....
1995-96	Moose Jaw	WHL	70	22	32	54	65	....	....	....	....	....
1996-97	Moose Jaw	WHL	72	37	47	84	47	12	4	1	5	11
1997-98	Moose Jaw	WHL	72	20	57	77	45	4	1	2	3	2
1998-99	Moose Jaw	WHL	71	42	*75	117	40	11	4	12	16	12
	Hamilton Bulldogs	AHL	3	0	0	0	2	....	....	....	....	....
99-2000	Hamilton Bulldogs	AHL	18	1	4	5	2	5	1	0	1	0
	Tallahassee	ECHL	49	15	25	40	35	....	....	....	....	....
2000-01	Hamilton Bulldogs	AHL	78	13	22	35	30	....	....	....	....	....
2001-02	Hamilton Bulldogs	AHL	71	6	13	19	27	15	2	8	10	8
2002-03	Hamilton Bulldogs	AHL	65	12	12	24	36	22	1	5	6	17
2003-04	Toronto	AHL	74	11	23	34	50	3	1	3	4	2

WHL East First All-Star Team (1999)

HIRSCHOVITS, Kim (HUHR-shoh-vihts, KIHM) NYR

Center. Shoots left. 6'1", 180 lbs. Born, Helsinki, Finland, May 9, 1982.
(NY Rangers' 6th choice, 194th overall, in 2002 Entry Draft).

			Regular Season					Playoffs				
Season	Club	League	GP	G	A	TP	PIM	GP	G	A	TP	PIM
1996-97	HIFK Helsinki C	Finn-Jr.	1	0	1	1	0	....	....	....	....	....
1997-98	HIFK Helsinki C	Finn-Jr.	35	20	31	51	46	....	....	....	....	....
1998-99	HIFK Helsinki B	Finn-Jr.	34	21	11	32	54	....	....	....	....	....
99-2000	HIFK Helsinki Jr.	Finn-Jr.	40	10	11	21	45	3	0	1	1	0
2000-01	HIFK Helsinki Jr.	Finn-Jr.	35	24	20	44	41	9	6	6	12	4
	HIFK Helsinki	Finland	2	0	0	0	0	....	....	....	....	....
2001-02	Chicago Steel	USHL	6	2	2	4	6	....	....	....	....	....
	HIFK Helsinki	Finland	45	6	10	16	24	....	....	....	....	....
	HIFK Helsinki Jr.	Finn-Jr.	5	4	7	11	8	4	3	6	9	0
	Jarvenpaa	Finland-2	3	1	2	3	6	....	....	....	....	....
2002-03	HIFK Helsinki	Finland	55	4	11	15	26	4	0	0	0	0
	KJT Jarvenpaa	Finland-2	3	1	2	3	6	....	....	....	....	....
2003-04	HIFK Helsinki	Finland	56	7	12	19	56	13	1	3	4	8

HOGEBOOM, Greg (HOH-guh-BOOM, GREHG) L.A.

Right wing. Shoots right. 6', 190 lbs. Born, Toronto, Ont., September 26, 1982.
(Los Angeles' 6th choice, 152nd overall, in 2002 Entry Draft).

			Regular Season					Playoffs				
Season	Club	League	GP	G	A	TP	PIM	GP	G	A	TP	PIM
1998-99	North York	GTHL		STATISTICS NOT AVAILABLE								
99-2000	Wexford Raiders	OPJHL	48	32	47	79	44	....	....	....	....	....
2000-01	Miami University	CCHA	38	8	5	13	20	....	....	....	....	....
2001-02	Miami University	CCHA	36	14	9	23	22	....	....	....	....	....
2002-03	Miami University	CCHA	41	24	18	42	16	....	....	....	....	....
2003-04	Miami University	CCHA	41	19	23	42	16	....	....	....	....	....
	Manchester	AHL	3	0	1	1	0	....	....	....	....	....

CCHA Second All-Star Team (2004)

HOGG, Kris (HAWG, KRIHS) CGY.

Left wing. Shoots left. 5'10", 172 lbs. Born, Salmon Arm, B.C., June 17, 1986.
(Calgary's 5th choice, 121st overall, in 2004 Entry Draft).

			Regular Season					Playoffs				
Season	Club	League	GP	G	A	TP	PIM	GP	G	A	TP	PIM
2002-03	Kamloops Blazers	WHL	58	5	2	7	12	5	1	0	1	0
2003-04	Kamloops Blazers	WHL	72	24	14	38	79	5	0	1	1	6

HOGGAN, Jeff (HOH-guhn, JEHF)

Right wing. Shoots right. 6', 200 lbs. Born, Hope, B.C., February 1, 1978.

			Regular Season					Playoffs				
Season	Club	League	GP	G	A	TP	PIM	GP	G	A	TP	PIM
1998-99	Powell River	BCHL		STATISTICS NOT AVAILABLE								
99-2000	Nebraska-Omaha	CCHA	34	16	9	25	82	....	....	....	....	....
2000-01	Nebraska-Omaha	CCHA	42	12	17	29	78	....	....	....	....	....
2001-02	Nebraska-Omaha	CCHA	41	24	21	45	92	....	....	....	....	....
	Houston Aeros	AHL	....	....	....	....	....	4	0	0	0	2
2002-03	Houston Aeros	AHL	65	6	5	11	45	14	1	2	3	23
2003-04	Houston Aeros	AHL	77	21	15	36	88	2	0	1	1	4

CCHA First All-Star Team (2002) • NCAA West Second All-American Team (2002)

Signed to a try-out contract by **Houston** (AHL), April 4, 2002. Signed as a free agent by **Minnesota**, August 20, 2002.

HOHENER, Martin (HOH-ehn-uhr, MAHR-tihn) NSH.

Defense. Shoots left. 6'1", 192 lbs. Born, Zurich, Switz., June 23, 1980.
(Nashville's 12th choice, 284th overall, in 2000 Entry Draft).

			Regular Season					Playoffs				
Season	Club	League	GP	G	A	TP	PIM	GP	G	A	TP	PIM
1996-97	Kloten Flyers Jr.	Swiss-Jr.	37	4	7	11	....	....	....	....	....	....
1997-98	Kloten Flyers Jr.	Swiss-Jr.	25	2	9	11	31	....	....	....	....	....
	EHC Bulach	Swiss-2	4	0	0	0	0	....	....	....	....	....
1998-99	Kloten Flyers Jr.	Swiss-Jr.	21	5	8	13	22	2	1	0	1	2
	EHC Kloten	Swiss	20	0	1	1	2	9	0	1	1	0
99-2000	EHC Kloten	Swiss	44	4	2	6	20	5	0	1	1	2
2000-01	EHC Kloten	Swiss	35	4	5	9	32	9	0	1	1	6
2001-02	Kloten Flyers	Swiss	44	4	12	16	12	9	0	1	1	2
	Switzerland	Olympics	4	0	0	0	0	....	....	....	....	....
2002-03	Kloten Flyers	Swiss	30	0	2	2	8	3	0	0	0	4
2003-04	Geneve	Swiss	39	7	12	19	16	12	0	3	3	8

HOLLWEG, Ryan (HOHL-wehg, RIGH-uhn) NYR

Center. Shoots left. 5'9", 201 lbs. Born, Downey, CA, April 23, 1983.
(NY Rangers' 10th choice, 238th overall, in 2001 Entry Draft).

			Regular Season					Playoffs				
Season	Club	League	GP	G	A	TP	PIM	GP	G	A	TP	PIM
1998-99	Langley Hornets	BCHL	58	14	40	54	187	....	....	....	....	....
	Grandview	PIJHL	41	23	27	50	135	....	....	....	....	....
99-2000	Medicine Hat	WHL	54	19	27	46	107	....	....	....	....	....
2000-01	Medicine Hat	WHL	65	19	39	58	125	....	....	....	....	....
2001-02	Medicine Hat	WHL	58	30	40	70	121	....	....	....	....	....
	Hartford Wolf Pack	AHL	8	1	1	2	2	9	0	2	2	19
2002-03	Medicine Hat	WHL	4	1	1	2	8	....	....	....	....	....
2003-04	Medicine Hat	WHL	52	25	32	57	117	20	6	9	15	22

HOLMQVIST, Andreas (HOHLM-kvihst, ahn-DRAY-uhs) T.B.

Defense. Shoots right. 6'4", 190 lbs. Born, Stockholm, Sweden, July 23, 1981.
(Tampa Bay's 3rd choice, 61st overall, in 2001 Entry Draft).

			Regular Season					Playoffs				
Season	Club	League	GP	G	A	TP	PIM	GP	G	A	TP	PIM
99-2000	Hammarby Jr.	Swede-Jr.	33	8	12	20	16	6	1	2	3	4
2000-01	Hammarby Jr.	Swede-Jr.	47	6	15	21	40	....	....	....	....	....
2001-02	Hammarby	Swede-2	42	11	13	24	97	....	....	....	....	....
2002-03	Linkopings HC	Sweden	43	4	9	13	28	....	....	....	....	....
	Linkopings HC	Swede-Q	10	0	0	0	4	....	....	....	....	....
2003-04	Pensacola	ECHL	63	4	33	37	16	5	0	4	4	0
	Hamilton Bulldogs	AHL	4	0	0	0	0	....	....	....	....	....

HOLTET, Marius (HOHL-teht, MAIR-ee-uhs) DAL.

Center. Shoots right. 6', 183 lbs. Born, Hamar, Norway, August 31, 1984.
(Dallas' 4th choice, 42nd overall, in 2002 Entry Draft).

			Regular Season					Playoffs				
Season	Club	League	GP	G	A	TP	PIM	GP	G	A	TP	PIM
2000-01	Farjestad 18	Swede-Jr.	5	3	1	4	16	....	....	....	....	....
	Farjestad Jr.	Swede-Jr.	18	2	2	4	18	....	....	....	....	....
2001-02	Farjestad Jr.	Swede-Jr.	37	12	7	19	70	....	....	....	....	....
2002-03	Skare BK	Swede-3		STATISTICS NOT AVAILABLE								
	Bofors IK	Swede-2	14	1	1	2	8	2	0	0	0	2
2003-04	Bofors	Swede-2	43	11	3	14	90	5	2	0	2	4

HOLUB, Jan (HOH-luhb, YAN) NYI

Defense. Shoots left. 6'3", 185 lbs. Born, Liberec, Czech., May 3, 1983.
(NY Islanders' 4th choice, 197th overall, in 2001 Entry Draft).

			Regular Season					Playoffs				
Season	Club	League	GP	G	A	TP	PIM	GP	G	A	TP	PIM
99-2000	HC Liberec Jr.	Czech-Jr.	2	0	0	0	0	....	....	....	....	....
	HC Liberec 18	Czech-Jr.	33	2	5	7	65	....	....	....	....	....
2000-01	HC Liberec Jr.	Czech-Jr.	43	0	6	6	42	....	....	....	....	....
2001-02	HC Liberec Jr.	Czech-Jr.	11	2	0	2	24	....	....	....	....	....
	Jablonec nad Nisou	Czech-3	3	0	0	0	2	....	....	....	....	....
	HC Tygri Liberec	Czech-3	30	1	3	4	22	12	0	0	0	2
2002-03	Liberec	Czech	21	2	2	4	4	....	....	....	....	....
	Liberec Jr.	Czech-Jr.	13	0	6	6	63	8	0	1	1	8
2003-04	Liberec	Czech	30	1	0	1	22	....	....	....	....	....
	Liberec Jr.	Czech-Jr.	1	0	1	1	0	....	....	....	....	....
	Beroun	Czech-2	17	2	3	5	26	....	....	....	....	....

HOOTON, Brock (HOO-tuhn, BRAWK) OTT.

Right wing. Shoots right. 6'2", 185 lbs. Born, Smithers, B.C., March 20, 1983.
(Ottawa's 6th choice, 150th overall, in 2002 Entry Draft).

			Regular Season					Playoffs				
Season	Club	League	GP	G	A	TP	PIM	GP	G	A	TP	PIM
1998-99	Smithers Selects	BCAHA	40	30	55	85	30	....	....	....	....	....
99-2000	Campbell River	VIJHL	40	8	17	25	8	....	....	....	....	....
2000-01	Quesnel	BCHL	60	11	26	37	....	....	....	....	....	....
2001-02	Quesnel	BCHL	60	34	50	84	33	....	....	....	....	....
2002-03	St. Cloud State	WCHA	26	1	6	7	14	....	....	....	....	....
2003-04	St. Cloud State	WCHA	35	5	10	15	4	....	....	....	....	....

HOPE, Joey (HOHP, JOH-ee) PHI.

Defense. Shoots right. 6', 180 lbs. Born, Anchorage, AK, January 1, 1982.

			Regular Season					Playoffs				
Season	Club	League	GP	G	A	TP	PIM	GP	G	A	TP	PIM
1998-99	U.S. National U-17	USDP	43	4	7	11	125	....	....	....	....	....
99-2000	U.S. National U-18	USDP	47	5	13	18	66	....	....	....	....	....
2000-01	Prince George	WHL	13	1	3	4	6	....	....	....	....	....
	Portland	WHL	56	6	24	30	103	13	1	7	8	10
2001-02	Portland	WHL	64	9	27	36	124	3	0	2	2	8
2002-03	Portland	WHL	54	12	27	39	142	....	....	....	....	....
2003-04	Philadelphia	AHL	48	0	4	4	32	9	0	1	1	6
	Trenton Titans	ECHL	4	0	2	2	0	....	....	....	....	....

Signed as a free agent by **Philadelphia**, July 14, 2003.

HOSPELT, Kai (HAWS-pehlt, KIGH) S.J.

Forward. Shoots left. 6'1", 187 lbs. Born, Cologne, Germany, August 23, 1985.
(San Jose's 8th choice, 216th overall, in 2003 Entry Draft).

			Regular Season					Playoffs				
Season	Club	League	GP	G	A	TP	PIM	GP	G	A	TP	PIM
2000-01	Kolner Haie Jr.	Ger.-Jr.	35	25	18	43	16	....	....	....	....	....
2001-02	Kolner Haie Jr.	Ger.-Jr.	40	51	55	106	10	5	6	2	8	4
2002-03	Kolner Haie Jr.	Ger.-Jr.	29	39	42	81	20	3	2	5	7	2
	Kolner Haie	Germany	21	0	2	2	0	6	0	1	1	0
2003-04	Kolner Haie	Germany	47	2	2	4	18	6	0	0	0	2

HRABAL, Josef (huh-RA-buhl, YOH-sehf) EDM.

Defense. Shoots left. 6'1", 176 lbs. Born, Prerov, Czech., August 17, 1985.
(Edmonton's 11th choice, 248th overall, in 2003 Entry Draft).

			Regular Season					Playoffs				
Season	Club	League	GP	G	A	TP	PIM	GP	G	A	TP	PIM
99-2000	HC Vsetin 16	Czech-Jr.	32	0	0	0	0	2	0	0	0	0
2000-01	HC Vsetin 16	Czech-Jr.	43	3	5	8	33	....	....	....	....	....
2001-02	HC Vsetin 16	Czech-Jr.	10	2	5	7	6	....	....	....	....	....
	HC Vsetin Jr.	Czech-Jr.	38	4	2	6	18	....	....	....	....	....
2002-03	HC Vsetin Jr.	Czech-Jr.	30	6	7	13	12	9	2	4	6	10
	HC Vsetin	Czech	6	0	0	0	4	....	....	....	....	....
2003-04	HC Vsetin	Czech	13	0	0	0	2	....	....	....	....	....
	HC Vsetin Jr.	Czech-Jr.	46	12	8	20	54	7	1	0	1	2

HRDEL, Zbynek (HUHR-duhl, ZBIGH-nek) T.B.

Center. Shoots right. 6'2", 194 lbs. Born, Pisek, Czech., August 19, 1985.
(Tampa Bay's 10th choice, 286th overall, in 2003 Entry Draft).

			Regular Season					Playoffs				
Season	Club	League	GP	G	A	TP	PIM	GP	G	A	TP	PIM
99-2000	HC Tabor 18	Czech-Jr.	13	6	6	12	10	....	....	....	....	....
2000-01	Sparta Praha 18	Czech-Jr.	46	11	11	22	22	....	....	....	....	....
2001-02	Sparta Praha 18	Czech-Jr.	31	24	19	43	42	6	4	3	7	2
2002-03	Rimouski Oceanic	QMJHL	65	10	14	24	131	....	....	....	....	....
2003-04	Rimouski Oceanic	QMJHL	54	15	31	46	41	9	4	6	10	4

HROMAS, Karel (huh-ROM-mahs, KAH-rehl) CHI.

Left wing. Shoots left. 6'2", 189 lbs. Born, Beroun, Czechoslovakia, January 27, 1986.
(Chicago's 8th choice, 123rd overall, in 2004 Entry Draft).

			Regular Season					Playoffs				
Season	Club	League	GP	G	A	TP	PIM	GP	G	A	TP	PIM
2000-01	Sparta Praha 18	Czech-Jr.	34	4	18	22	6	....	....	....	....	....
2001-02	Sparta Praha 18	Czech-Jr.	39	19	15	34	55	6	3	2	5	6
2002-03	Sparta Praha 18	Czech-Jr.	1	3	1	4	0	....	....	....	....	....
	Sparta Praha Jr.	Czech-Jr.	32	6	7	13	14	3	0	1	1	4
2003-04	Sparta Praha Jr.	Czech-Jr.	21	10	10	20	16	....	....	....	....	....
	HC Sparta Praha	Czech	13	0	0	0	0	2	0	0	0	0

HRUSKA, David (huhr-OOSH-kah, dah-VEED) OTT.

Right wing. Shoots right. 5'10", 206 lbs. Born, Sokolov, Czech., January 8, 1977.
(Ottawa's 6th choice, 131st overall, in 1995 Entry Draft).

			Regular Season					Playoffs				
Season	Club	League	GP	G	A	TP	PIM	GP	G	A	TP	PIM
1994-95	Sokolov	Czech-2	5	2	4	6	4	....	....	....	....	....
1995-96	Red Deer Rebels	WHL	28	14	14	28	6	....	....	....	....	....
	HC Petra Vsetin	Czech	5	1	0	1	....	1	0	0	0	0
1996-97	HC Petra Vsetin	Czech	20	4	2	6	4	6	2	4	6	0
	Sokolov	Czech-2	4	3	0	3	....	....	....	....	....	....
1997-98	HC Petra Vsetin	Czech	14	5	1	6	0	....	....	....	....	....
	HC Petra Vsetin	EuroHL	5	0	0	0	0	....	....	....	....	....
1998-99	HC Opava	Czech	4	1	0	1	0	....	....	....	....	....
99-2000	HC Karlovy Vary	Czech	43	17	10	27	8	....	....	....	....	....
2000-01	HC Karlovy Vary	Czech	50	14	5	19	12	....	....	....	....	....
2001-02	Litvinov	Czech	19	*14	3	17	0	....	....	....	....	....
	HC Femax Havirov	Czech	23	*17	12	29	2	....	....	....	....	....
	Kloten Flyers	Swiss	....	....	....	....	....	1	0	0	0	0
2002-03	HC Slavia Praha	Czech	37	13	13	26	10	15	2	2	4	0
2003-04	HC Slavia Praha	Czech	51	18	19	37	12	19	4	5	9	12

HUBL, Viktor (HEW-buhl, VIHK-tohr) WSH.

Left wing. Shoots left. 6', 183 lbs. Born, Chomutov, Czech., August 13, 1978.
(Washington's 10th choice, 284th overall, in 2001 Entry Draft).

			Regular Season					Playoffs				
Season	Club	League	GP	G	A	TP	PIM	GP	G	A	TP	PIM
1997-98	KLH Chomutov	Czech-2	50	18	17	35	....	....	....	....	....	....
1998-99	KLH Chomutov	Czech-2	5	2	1	3	....	....	....	....	....	....
	Litvinov	Czech	27	2	6	8	10	....	....	....	....	....
99-2000	KLH Chomutov	Czech-2	8	2	4	6	4	....	....	....	....	....
	Litvinov	Czech	36	6	9	15	16	....	....	....	....	....
2000-01	HC Slavia Praha	Czech	50	16	24	40	24	11	0	2	2	6
2001-02	HC Slavia Praha	Czech	48	11	14	25	34	8	0	1	1	6
2002-03	Litvinov	Czech	39	8	13	21	30	....	....	....	....	....
2003-04	Litvinov	Czech	52	9	17	26	24	....	....	....	....	....

HULT, Alexander (HUHLT, al-EHX-AN-duhr) S.J.

Center. Shoots left. 6'1", 200 lbs. Born, Falun, Sweden, November 19, 1984.
(San Jose's 9th choice, 236th overall, in 2003 Entry Draft).

			Regular Season					Playoffs				
Season	Club	League	GP	G	A	TP	PIM	GP	G	A	TP	PIM
2000-01	HV 71 18	Swede-Jr.	13	4	12	16	24	....	....	....	....	....
2001-02	HV 71 18	Swede-Jr.	1	0	0	0	2	....	....	....	....	....
	HV 71 Jr.	Swede-Jr.	35	11	7	18	87	....	....	....	....	....
	HV 71	Sweden	....	....	....	....	....	1	0	0	0	0
2002-03	HV 71 Jr.	Swede-Jr.	24	11	14	25	24	....	....	....	....	....
	HV 71 Jonkoping	Sweden	1	0	0	0	2	....	....	....	....	....
	Tranas AIF	Swede-2	5	1	0	1	0	....	....	....	....	....
2003-04	IK Oskarshamn	Swede-2	29	2	7	9	22	....	....	....	....	....
	HV 71 Jonkoping	Sweden	3	0	0	0	2	....	....	....	....	....
	Djurgarden Jr.	Swede-Jr.	11	6	10	16	16	....	....	....	....	....
	Djurgarden	Sweden	8	0	0	0	0	3	0	0	0	0

HULVA, Jakub (HUHL-vuh, YA-kuhb) BUF.

Right wing. Shoots left. 6', 172 lbs. Born, Opava, Czech., May 6, 1984.
(Buffalo's 5th choice, 108th overall, in 2002 Entry Draft).

			Regular Season					Playoffs				
Season	Club	League	GP	G	A	TP	PIM	GP	G	A	TP	PIM
99-2000	HC Vitkovice Jr.	Czech-Jr.	49	20	34	54	38	....	....	....	....	....
2000-01	HC Vitkovice 18	Czech-Jr.	30	28	40	68	22	....	....	....	....	....
	HC Vitkovice Jr.	Czech-Jr.	20	5	6	11	6	....	....	....	....	....
	HC Vitkovice	Czech	1	0	0	0	0	....	....	....	....	....
2001-02	HC Vitkovice Jr.	Czech-Jr.	45	25	24	49	36	....	....	....	....	....
	HC Opava	Czech-2	4	0	0	0	2	....	....	....	....	....
	HC Vitkovice	Czech	1	0	0	0	0	2	0	0	0	0
2002-03	HC Vitkovice Jr.	Czech-Jr.	28	13	16	29	28	1	0	3	3	2
	HC Opava	Czech-2	6	0	0	0	0	....	....	....	....	....
	HC Vitkovice	Czech	5	0	1	1	0	3	0	0	0	0
2003-04	HC Vitkovice Jr.	Czech-Jr.	13	11	7	18	28	....	....	....	....	....
	HC Slezan Opava	Czech-2	19	8	3	11	8	....	....	....	....	....
	HC Vitkovice	Czech	20	0	1	1	2	4	1	0	1	0

HUNTER, J.J. (HUHN-tuhr, JAY-JAY) EDM.

Right wing. Shoots left. 6'1", 185 lbs. Born, Shaunavon, Sask., July 6, 1980.

			Regular Season					Playoffs				
Season	Club	League	GP	G	A	TP	PIM	GP	G	A	TP	PIM
1998-99	Kelowna Rockets	WHL	66	18	32	50	61	6	1	2	3	2
99-2000	Kelowna Rockets	WHL	66	22	26	48	61	5	1	0	1	2
2000-01	Kelowna Rockets	WHL	12	1	5	6	4	....	....	....	....	....
	Prince Albert	WHL	58	28	17	45	40	....	....	....	....	....
2001-02	Columbus	ECHL	60	23	22	45	59	....	....	....	....	....
	Hamilton Bulldogs	AHL	1	0	0	0	0	1	0	0	0	0
2002-03	Hamilton Bulldogs	AHL	2	0	0	0	2	....	....	....	....	....
	Columbus	ECHL	70	17	36	53	82	....	....	....	....	....
2003-04	Toronto	AHL	56	12	16	28	53	3	1	1	2	2
	Columbus	ECHL	4	2	1	3	2	....	....	....	....	....

Signed as a free agent by **Edmonton**, August 19, 2002.

HUSKINS, Kent (HUHS-kihns, KEHNT)

Defense. Shoots left. 6'3", 215 lbs. Born, Ottawa, Ont., May 4, 1979.
(Chicago's 3rd choice, 156th overall, in 1998 Entry Draft).

			Regular Season					Playoffs				
Season	Club	League	GP	G	A	TP	PIM	GP	G	A	TP	PIM
1995-96	Kanata Valley	OCJHL	49	6	21	27	18	....	....	....	....	....
1996-97	Kanata Valley	OCJHL	53	11	36	47	89	....	....	....	....	....
1997-98	Clarkson Knights	ECAC	35	2	8	10	46	....	....	....	....	....
1998-99	Clarkson Knights	ECAC	37	5	11	16	28	....	....	....	....	....
99-2000	Clarkson Knights	ECAC	28	2	16	18	30	....	....	....	....	....
2000-01	Clarkson Knights	ECAC	35	6	28	34	22	....	....	....	....	....
2001-02	Norfolk Admirals	AHL	65	4	11	15	44	4	0	1	1	0
2002-03	Norfolk Admirals	AHL	80	5	22	27	48	9	2	2	4	4
2003-04	San Antonio	AHL	79	5	14	19	42	....	....	....	....	....

ECAC First All-Star Team (2000, 2001) • NCAA East First All-American Team (2001)

Signed as a free agent by **Florida**, August 14, 2003.

HUTCHINS, Michael (HUHCH-ihns, MIGH-kuhl) S.J.

Defense. Shoots left. 5'11", 185 lbs. Born, Wolfeboro, NH, October 27, 1982.
(San Jose's 7th choice, 288th overall, in 2002 Entry Draft).

			Regular Season					Playoffs				
Season	Club	League	GP	G	A	TP	PIM	GP	G	A	TP	PIM
99-2000	St. Paul's Prep	Hi-School	30	5	12	17	....	....	....	....	....	....
2000-01	St. Paul's Prep	Hi-School	27	8	27	35	36	....	....	....	....	....
2001-02	Des Moines	USHL	60	7	30	37	133	3	0	1	1	2
2002-03	New Hampshire	H-East	DID NOT PLAY – FRESHMAN									
2003-04	New Hampshire	H-East	22	1	0	1	34	....	....	....	....	....

HYNES, Shane (HIGHNZ, SHAYN) ANA.

Right wing. Shoots right. 6'3", 210 lbs. Born, Montreal, Que., November 7, 1983.
(Anaheim's 3rd choice, 86th overall, in 2003 Entry Draft).

			Regular Season					Playoffs				
Season	Club	League	GP	G	A	TP	PIM	GP	G	A	TP	PIM
99-2000	Calgary Flames	AMHL	30	8	12	20	20	....	....	....	....	....
2000-01	Calgary Flames	AMHL	28	18	21	38	76	....	....	....	....	....
2001-02	Nanaimo Clippers	BCHL	50	38	36	74	183	....	....	....	....	....
2002-03	Cornell Big Red	ECAC	32	11	9	20	36	....	....	....	....	....
2003-04	Cornell Big Red	ECAC	30	9	9	18	54	....	....	....	....	....

IGNATUSHKIN, Igor (ihg-nah-TOOSH-kihn, EE-gohr) WSH.

Center. Shoots left. 5'11", 175 lbs. Born, Elektrostal, USSR, April 7, 1984.
(Washington's 12th choice, 242nd overall, in 2002 Entry Draft).

			Regular Season					Playoffs				
Season	Club	League	GP	G	A	TP	PIM	GP	G	A	TP	PIM
99-2000	Kristal Elektrostal 2	Russia-3	5	0	0	0	0	....	....	....	....	....
2000-01	Team Center 84	Exhib.	5	1	1	2	0	....	....	....	....	....
2001-02	Elektrostal 2	Russia-3	6	2	3	5	6	....	....	....	....	....
	Elektrostal	Russia-2	46	1	4	5	20	....	....	....	....	....
	Elektrostal	Russia-Jr.	8	5	8	13	4	....	....	....	....	....
	Russia	WJC-18	8	2	9	11	2	....	....	....	....	....
2002-03	Elektrostal	Russia-2	36	9	10	19	8	....	....	....	....	....
2003-04	Kristall Elektrostal	Russia-2	49	6	2	8	22	....	....	....	....	....

IMMONEN, Jarkko (IH-moh-nihn, YAHR-koh) NYR

Center. Shoots right. 6', 202 lbs. Born, Rantasalmi, Finland, April 19, 1982.
(Toronto's 8th choice, 254th overall, in 2002 Entry Draft).

			Regular Season					Playoffs				
Season	Club	League	GP	G	A	TP	PIM	GP	G	A	TP	PIM
1997-98	SaPKo Jr.	Finn-Jr.	14	8	12	20	0	....	....	....	....	....
1998-99	SaPKo Savonlinna	Finland-2	36	2	2	4	6	....	....	....	....	....
	SaPKo Jr.	Finn-Jr.	12	6	10	16	34	....	....	....	....	....
99-2000	SaPKo Savonlinna	Finland-2	42	18	16	34	34	....	....	....	....	....
	SaPKo Jr.	Finn-Jr.	2	1	1	2	2	....	....	....	....	....
2000-01	TuTo Turku	Finland-2	41	20	20	40	22	11	5	7	12	10
	TuTo Turku Jr.	Finn-Jr.	1	0	1	1	2	1	0	0	0	6
2001-02	Assat Pori	Finland	44	0	2	2	6	....	....	....	....	....
	Assat Pori Jr.	Finn-Jr.	3	1	1	2	4	8	5	1	6	10
2002-03	JYP Jyvaskyla	Finland	56	10	23	33	34	7	1	1	2	8
2003-04	JYP Jyvaskyla	Finland	52	23	26	49	28	2	0	0	0	0

Traded to **NY Rangers** by **Toronto** with Maxim Kondratiev, Toronto's 1st round choice (later traded to Calgary - Calgary selected Kris Chucko) in 2004 Entry Draft and Toronto's 2nd round choice in 2005 Entry Draft for Brian Leetch and Edmonton's 4th round choice (previously acquired, Toronto selected Roman Kukumberg) in 2004 Entry Draft, March 3, 2004.

IRGL, Zbynek (UHR-guhl, ZBIH-nehk) NSH.

Center. Shoots right. 5'11", 183 lbs. Born, Vitkovice, Czech., November 29, 1980.
(Nashville's 9th choice, 197th overall, in 2000 Entry Draft).

			Regular Season					Playoffs				
Season	Club	League	GP	G	A	TP	PIM	GP	G	A	TP	PIM
1996-97	HC Vitkovice Jr.	Czech-Jr.	43	44	22	66	....	....	....	....	....	....
1997-98	HC Vitkovice Jr.	Czech-Jr.	37	17	10	27	....	....	....	....	....	....
1998-99	HC Vitkovice Jr.	Czech-Jr.	18	9	8	17	....	....	....	....	....	....
	HC Vitkovice	Czech	33	2	2	4	6	4	0	0	0	....
99-2000	HC Dukla Jihlava	Czech-2	1	0	0	0	0	....	....	....	....	....
	HC Vitkovice	Czech	47	7	5	12	10	....	....	....	....	....
2000-01	HC Vitkovice	Czech	37	0	1	1	8	4	0	0	0	0
	HC Slean Opava	Czech-2	9	3	2	5	2	....	....	....	....	....
	HC Vitkovice Jr.	Czech-Jr.	4	6	3	9	2	....	....	....	....	....
2001-02	HC Vitkovice	Czech	39	2	8	10	8	13	4	0	4	6
2002-03	HC Vitkovice	Czech	51	6	7	13	14	5	0	1	1	0
2003-04	HC Vitkovice	Czech	51	19	16	35	18	4	1	0	1	6

IRMEN, Danny (UHR-mehn, DA-nee) MIN.

Center. Shoots right. 6', 190 lbs. Born, Fargo, ND, September 6, 1984.
(Minnesota's 3rd choice, 78th overall, in 2003 Entry Draft).

			Regular Season					Playoffs				
Season	Club	League	GP	G	A	TP	PIM	GP	G	A	TP	PIM
2001-02	Lincoln Stars	USHL	61	17	36	53	....	....	....	....	....	....
2002-03	Lincoln Stars	USHL	45	21	34	55	78	10	8	6	14	17
2003-04	U. of Minnesota	WCHA	44	14	8	22	40	....	....	....	....	....

USHL 2nd All-Star Team (2003) • USHL Playoff MVP (2003)

ISAKOV, Evgeni (ih-SA-kawf, ehv-GEH-nee) PIT.

Right wing. Shoots left. 6'1", 196 lbs. Born, Krasnoyarsk, USSR, October 13, 1984.
(Pittsburgh's 6th choice, 161st overall, in 2003 Entry Draft).

			Regular Season					Playoffs				
Season	Club	League	GP	G	A	TP	PIM	GP	G	A	TP	PIM
99-2000	Rubin Tyumen 2	Russia-3	7	0	2	2	16	....	....	....	....	....
2000-01	Rubin Tyumen 2	Russia-3	....	....	....	....	....	....	....	....	....	....
	Gazovik Tyumen	Russia-3	11	1	1	2	12	....	....	....	....	....
2001-02	Gazovik Tyumen	Russia-2	19	2	2	4	2	....	....	....	....	....
	Elektrostal	Russia-2	29	3	2	5	24	....	....	....	....	....
	Elektrostal 2	Russia-3	11	3	3	6	43	....	....	....	....	....
2002-03	Cherepovets	Russia	36	0	3	3	12	1	0	0	0	0
2003-04	Cherepovets	Russia	38	3	2	5	18	....	....	....	....	....
	Cherepovets 2	Russia-3	14	4	8	12	48	....	....	....	....	....

IVANANS, Raitis (ih-VAH-nehns, RIGH-this) MTL.

Left wing. Shoots left. 6'3", 220 lbs. Born, Riga, Latvia, January 1, 1979.

			Regular Season					Playoffs				
Season	Club	League	GP	G	A	TP	PIM	GP	G	A	TP	PIM
1997-98	Flint Generals	UHL	18	0	1	1	20	....	....	....	....	....
1998-99	Macon Whoopee	CHL	16	1	1	2	20	....	....	....	....	....
	Tulsa Oilers	CHL	32	2	7	9	39	....	....	....	....	....
99-2000	Pensacola	ECHL	59	3	7	10	146	2	0	0	0	0
2000-01	New Haven	UHL	66	4	10	14	270	8	1	0	1	4
	Hershey Bears	AHL	2	0	0	0	0	....	....	....	....	....
2001-02	Toledo Storm	ECHL	16	2	2	4	59	....	....	....	....	....
	Baton Rouge	ECHL	40	4	5	9	180	....	....	....	....	....
2002-03	Milwaukee	AHL	17	0	0	0	38	1	0	0	0	15
	Rockford IceHogs	UHL	50	4	2	6	208	....	....	....	....	....
2003-04	Milwaukee	AHL	54	1	7	8	166	7	0	1	1	17
	Rockford IceHogs	UHL	1	0	0	0	0	....	....	....	....	....

Signed as a free agent by **Montreal**, July 16, 2004

IVANOV, Alexei (ih-van-AWF, al-EHX-ay) CHI.

Center. Shoots left. 5'9", 174 lbs. Born, Tynda, USSR, January 5, 1985.
(Chicago's 5th choice, 156th overall, in 2003 Entry Draft).

			Regular Season					Playoffs				
Season	Club	League	GP	G	A	TP	PIM	GP	G	A	TP	PIM
2001-02	Yaroslavl 2	Russia-3	26	9	10	19	16	....	....	....	....	....
	Polet	Russia-4	4	0	0	0	0	....	....	....	....	....
	Yaroslavl Jr.	Russia-Jr.	28	21	17	38	76	7	1	5	6	6
2002-03	Yaroslavl 2	Russia-3	STATISTICS NOT AVAILABLE									
	Yaroslavl Jr.	Russia-Jr.	6	5	3	8	0	....	....	....	....	....
2003-04	Ufa Salavat	Russia	3	0	0	0	0	....	....	....	....	....
	HC Rybinsk	Russia-2	12	0	2	2	8	....	....	....	....	....

JAAKOLA, Topi (YAH-koh-luh, TOH-pee) FLA.

Defense. Shoots left. 6'1", 185 lbs. Born, Oulu, Finland, November 15, 1983.
(Florida's 5th choice, 134th overall, in 2002 Entry Draft).

			Regular Season					Playoffs				
Season	Club	League	GP	G	A	TP	PIM	GP	G	A	TP	PIM
99-2000	Karpat Oulu Jr.	Finn-Jr.	36	5	12	17	71	5	1	1	2	4
2000-01	Karpat Oulu Jr.	Finn-Jr.	35	4	10	14	47	6	0	2	2	6
	Karpat Oulu	Finland	4	0	0	0	2	....	....	....	....	....
2001-02	Karpat Oulu Jr.	Finn-Jr.	3	0	0	0	2	2	1	0	1	4
	Karpat Oulu	Finland	44	0	4	4	18	4	0	0	0	4
2002-03	Karpat Oulu	Finland	52	2	2	4	18	15	0	0	0	8
2003-04	Karpat Oulu	Finland	52	0	4	4	12	14	0	1	1	6

JAASKELAINEN, Teemu (yas-keh-LIGH-nuhn, TEE-moo) CHI.

Defense. Shoots left. 6'1", 207 lbs. Born, Tampere, Finland, June 7, 1983.
(Chicago's 11th choice, 205th overall, in 2001 Entry Draft).

			Regular Season					Playoffs				
Season	Club	League	GP	G	A	TP	PIM	GP	G	A	TP	PIM
1998-99	Ilves Tampere C	Finn-Jr.	22	1	4	5	8	3	0	0	0	2
99-2000	Ilves Tampere B	Finn-Jr.	36	5	1	6	20	....	....	....	....	....
2000-01	Ilves Tampere B	Finn-Jr.	5	1	1	2	16	....	....	....	....	....
	Ilves Tampere Jr.	Finn-Jr.	41	4	1	5	30	....	....	....	....	....
2001-02	Ilves Tampere Jr.	Finn-Jr.	13	1	6	7	8	....	....	....	....	....
	Ilves Tampere	Finland	38	0	0	0	24	3	0	0	0	0
2002-03	Ilves Tampere	Finland	48	1	4	5	16	....	....	....	....	....
	Ilves Tampere Jr.	Finn-Jr.	7	3	4	7	4	....	....	....	....	....
2003-04	Ilves Tampere	Finland	44	6	3	9	14	7	0	0	0	0
	Ilves Tampere Jr.	Finn-Jr.	1	0	0	0	2	....	....	....	....	....

JACKSON, Todd (JAK-suhn, TAWD) DET.

Right wing. Shoots right. 5'11", 170 lbs. Born, Syracuse, NY, April 10, 1981.
(Detroit's 10th choice, 251st overall, in 2000 Entry Draft).

			Regular Season					Playoffs				
Season	Club	League	GP	G	A	TP	PIM	GP	G	A	TP	PIM
1998-99	U.S. National U-17	USDP	53	11	9	20	56	....	....	....	....	....
99-2000	U.S. National U-17	USDP	29	8	10	18	25	....	....	....	....	....
	U.S. National U-18	USDP	23	8	6	14	12	....	....	....	....	....
2000-01	U. of Maine	H-East	39	4	8	12	8	....	....	....	....	....
2001-02	U. of Maine	H-East	39	7	21	28	10	....	....	....	....	....
2002-03	U. of Maine	H-East	39	13	13	26	22	....	....	....	....	....
2003-04	U. of Maine	H-East	44	21	12	33	34	....	....	....	....	....

Hockey East Second All-Star Team (2004) • NCAA East Second All-American Team (2004)

JACQUES, Jean-Francois (ZHAWK, ZHAWN-fran-SWUH) EDM.

Left wing. Shoots left. 6'4", 217 lbs. Born, Terrebonne, Que., April 29, 1985.
(Edmonton's 3rd choice, 68th overall, in 2003 Entry Draft).

			Regular Season					Playoffs				
Season	Club	League	GP	G	A	TP	PIM	GP	G	A	TP	PIM
2000-01	Cap-d-Madeleine	QAAA	39	22	13	35	28	10	5	8	13	14
2001-02	Baie-Comeau	QMJHL	66	10	14	24	136	5	1	0	1	2
2002-03	Baie-Comeau	QMJHL	67	12	21	33	123	12	4	2	6	13
2003-04	Baie-Comeau	QMJHL	59	20	24	44	70	4	1	0	1	4

JAMES, Connor (JAYMZ, KAW-nuhr) L.A.

Right wing. Shoots right. 5'10", 168 lbs. Born, Calgary, Alta., August 25, 1982.
(Los Angeles' 11th choice, 279th overall, in 2002 Entry Draft).

			Regular Season					Playoffs				
Season	Club	League	GP	G	A	TP	PIM	GP	G	A	TP	PIM
1998-99	Calgary Buffaloes	AMHL	36	33	53	86	20	....	....	....	....	....
99-2000	Calgary Royals	AJHL	64	36	57	93	41	....	....	....	....	....
2000-01	U. of Denver	WCHA	38	8	19	27	14	....	....	....	....	....
2001-02	U. of Denver	WCHA	41	16	26	42	18	....	....	....	....	....
2002-03	U. of Denver	WCHA	41	20	23	43	12	....	....	....	....	....
2003-04	U. of Denver	WCHA	40	13	25	38	16	....	....	....	....	....

NCAA Championship All-Tournament Team (2004)

JAMINKI, Tommi (yah-MIHN-kee,TAW-mee) CHI.

Left wing. Shoots right. 6'2", 196 lbs. Born, Turku, Finland, February 11, 1983.
(Chicago's 8th choice, 142nd overall, in 2001 Entry Draft).

			Regular Season					Playoffs				
Season	Club	League	GP	G	A	TP	PIM	GP	G	A	TP	PIM
99-2000	KJT Kerawa Jr.	Finn-Jr.	35	9	10	19	106	....	....	....	....	....
2000-01	Blues Espoo Jr.	Finn-Jr.	36	6	6	12	16	....	....	....	....	....
2001-02	Blues Espoo Jr.	Finn-Jr.	31	9	7	16	66	2	0	0	0	2
	Blues Espoo	Finland	4	0	0	0	0	....	....	....	....	....
2002-03	Ilves Tampere	Finland	45	2	0	2	0	....	....	....	....	....
	Ilves Tampere Jr.	Finn-Jr.	10	5	3	8	25	10	10	4	14	2
2003-04	Ilves Tampere	Finland	51	3	3	6	6	7	1	0	1	2
	Ilves Tampere Jr.	Finn-Jr.	12	5	1	6	4	....	....	....	....	....

JAMTIN, Andreas (yahm-TEEN, ahn-DRAY-uhs) DET.

Right wing. Shoots left. 5'11", 185 lbs. Born, Stockholm, Sweden, May 4, 1983.
(Detroit's 4th choice, 157th overall, in 2001 Entry Draft).

			Regular Season					Playoffs				
Season	Club	League	GP	G	A	TP	PIM	GP	G	A	TP	PIM
1998-99	AIK Solna Jr.	Swede-Jr.	44	33	29	62	105	....	....	....	....	....
99-2000	Farjestad Jr.	Swede-Jr.	28	6	6	12	36	....	....	....	....	....
2000-01	Farjestad 18	Swede-Jr.	1	1	0	1	2	....	....	....	....	....
	Farjestad Jr.	Swede-Jr.	13	5	8	13	83	....	....	....	....	....
	Farjestad	Sweden	1	0	0	0	0	....	....	....	....	....
2001-02	AIK Solna	Sweden	42	2	3	5	55	....	....	....	....	....
	AIK Stockholm	Swede-2	12	12	15	27	61	1	2	2	4	2
	AIK Stockholm	Swede-Q	10	1	2	3	4	....	....	....	....	....
2002-03	AIK Stockholm	Swede-2	28	14	15	29	62	....	....	....	....	....
	AIK Stockholm	Swede-Q	14	7	3	10	65	14	4	3	7	18
2003-04	HV 71 Jonkoping	Sweden	39	5	13	18	105	16	3	3	6	*68

JANCEVSKI, Dan (jan-SEHV-skee, DAN) DAL.

Defense. Shoots left. 6'3", 212 lbs. Born, Windsor, Ont., June 15, 1981.
(Dallas' 2nd choice, 66th overall, in 1999 Entry Draft).

			Regular Season					Playoffs				
Season	Club	League	GP	G	A	TP	PIM	GP	G	A	TP	PIM
1995-96	Riverside Selects	OMHA	59	9	22	31	67	....	....	....	....	....
1996-97	Windsor Lions	OMHA	47	6	20	26	99	....	....	....	....	....
1997-98	Tecumseh	OJHL-B	49	3	11	14	145	....	....	....	....	....
1998-99	London Knights	OHL	68	2	12	14	115	25	1	7	8	24
99-2000	London Knights	OHL	59	8	15	23	138	....	....	....	....	....
2000-01	London Knights	OHL	39	4	23	27	95	....	....	....	....	....
	Sudbury Wolves	OHL	31	3	14	17	42	12	0	9	9	17
2001-02	Utah Grizzlies	AHL	77	0	13	13	147	5	0	0	0	4
2002-03	Utah Grizzlies	AHL	76	1	10	11	172	2	0	1	1	12
2003-04	Utah Grizzlies	AHL	80	5	17	22	171	....	....	....	....	....

JANSSEN, Cam (JAN-suhn, KAM) N.J.

Right wing. Shoots right. 5'11", 205 lbs. Born, St. Louis, MO, April 15, 1984.
(New Jersey's 6th choice, 117th overall, in 2002 Entry Draft).

			Regular Season					Playoffs				
Season	Club	League	GP	G	A	TP	PIM	GP	G	A	TP	PIM
2000-01	St. Louis Jr. Blues	NAJHL	45	1	2	3	244	....	....	....	....	....
2001-02	Windsor Spitfires	OHL	64	5	17	22	*268	10	0	0	0	13
2002-03	Windsor Spitfires	OHL	50	1	12	13	211	7	0	1	1	22
2003-04	Windsor Spitfires	OHL	35	4	9	13	144	....	....	....	....	....
	Guelph Storm	OHL	29	7	4	11	125	22	3	3	6	49

JARMAN, Kevin (JAR-muhn, KEH-vihn) **CBJ**

Left wing. Shoots left. 6', 184 lbs. Born, Toronto, Ont., March 12, 1985.
(Columbus' 4th choice, 103rd overall, in 2003 Entry Draft).

			Regular Season					Playoffs				
Season	Club	League	GP	G	A	TP	PIM	GP	G	A	TP	PIM
2001-02	Stouffville Spirit	OPJHL	44	20	13	33	53	....	....	....	....	....
2002-03	Stouffville Spirit	OPJHL	46	41	39	80	49	11	5	3	8	6
2003-04	Massachusetts	H-East	34	4	6	10	28	....	....	....	....	....

JARRETT, Cole (JAIR-reht, KOHL) **NYI**

Defense. Shoots left. 6', 195 lbs. Born, Sault Ste. Marie, Ont., January 4, 1983.
(Columbus' 6th choice, 141st overall, in 2001 Entry Draft).

			Regular Season					Playoffs				
Season	Club	League	GP	G	A	TP	PIM	GP	G	A	TP	PIM
1998-99	Waterloo Siskins	OJHL-B	44	6	10	16	43	4	2	2	4	5
99-2000	Plymouth Whalers	OHL	57	3	7	10	47	23	3	7	10	19
2000-01	Plymouth Whalers	OHL	60	12	36	48	98	19	6	12	18	29
2001-02	Plymouth Whalers	OHL	51	14	24	38	92	6	1	1	2	18
2002-03	Plymouth Whalers	OHL	58	14	41	55	138	14	5	6	11	29
2003-04	Bridgeport	AHL	59	2	14	16	38	....	....	....	....	....

Signed as a free agent by **NY Islanders**, September 9, 2003.

JENSEN, Joe (JEHN-suhn, JOH) **PIT.**

Center. Shoots left. 5'11", 180 lbs. Born, Maple Grove, MN, February 6, 1983.
(Pittsburgh's 10th choice, 232nd overall, in 2003 Entry Draft).

			Regular Season					Playoffs				
Season	Club	League	GP	G	A	TP	PIM	GP	G	A	TP	PIM
2000-01	Sioux City	USHL	56	14	20	34	59	8	2	4	6	12
2001-02	Sioux City	USHL	57	20	26	46	135	3	0	0	0	6
2002-03	St. Cloud State	WCHA	37	9	9	18	14	....	....	....	....	....
2003-04	St. Cloud State	WCHA	38	10	14	24	42	....	....	....	....	....

JESSIMAN, Hugh (JEHS-ih-muhn, HEW) **NYR**

Right wing. Shoots right. 6'5", 218 lbs. Born, New York, NY, March 28, 1984.
(NY Rangers' 1st choice, 12th overall, in 2003 Entry Draft).

			Regular Season					Playoffs				
Season	Club	League	GP	G	A	TP	PIM	GP	G	A	TP	PIM
2001-02	Brunswick Bruins	Hi-School	18	25	27	52	40	....	....	....	....	....
2002-03	Dartmouth	ECAC	34	23	24	47	48	....	....	....	....	....
2003-04	Dartmouth	ECAC	34	16	17	33	71	....	....	....	....	....

ECAC All-Rookie Team (2003) • ECAC Rookie of the Year (2003) • ECAC Second All-Star Team (2004)

JOHANSSON, Daniel (yoh-HAN-suhn, DAN-yehl) **L.A.**

Center. Shoots left. 5'11", 176 lbs. Born, Ornskoldsvik, Sweden, July 5, 1981.
(Los Angeles' 6th choice, 125th overall, in 1999 Entry Draft).

			Regular Season					Playoffs				
Season	Club	League	GP	G	A	TP	PIM	GP	G	A	TP	PIM
1997-98	MoDo Jr.	Swede-Jr.	6	0	0	0	0	....	....	....	....	....
1998-99	MoDo Jr.	Swede-Jr.	43	10	19	29	....	....	....	....	....	....
99-2000	MoDo Jr.	Swede-Jr.	35	11	21	32	34	....	....	....	....	....
	MoDo	EuroHL	2	0	0	0	0	....	....	....	....	....
2000-01	Bodens IK	Swede-2	36	4	3	7	10	4	0	0	0	0
2001-02	Bodens IK	Swede-2	37	2	3	5	10	....	....	....	....	....
	Vaxjo HC	Swede-3	8	2	5	7	6	....	....	....	....	....
2002-03	Vaxjo HC	Swede-3	44	6	18	24	....	....	....	....	....	....
2003-04	Vaxjo HC	Swede-2	46	6	8	14	6	5	0	0	0	0

JOHANSSON, Eric (joh-HAHN-suhn, AIR-ihk) **N.J.**

Center. Shoots left. 6', 195 lbs. Born, Edmonton, Alta., January 7, 1982.
(New Jersey's 8th choice, 187th overall, in 2002 Entry Draft).

			Regular Season					Playoffs				
Season	Club	League	GP	G	A	TP	PIM	GP	G	A	TP	PIM
1997-98	Edmonton CAC	AMHA	22	13	10	23	19	....	....	....	....	....
1998-99	Tri-City Americans	WHL	48	8	14	22	20	6	1	1	2	2
99-2000	Tri-City Americans	WHL	72	24	36	60	38	4	0	0	0	2
2000-01	Tri-City Americans	WHL	72	36	44	80	72	....	....	....	....	....
2001-02	Tri-City Americans	WHL	69	44	59	103	73	5	1	2	3	5
2002-03	Albany River Rats	AHL	66	7	9	16	24	....	....	....	....	....
2003-04	Albany River Rats	AHL	63	7	19	26	32	....	....	....	....	....

• Re-entered NHL Entry Draft. Originally Minnesota's 9th choice, 255th overall, in 2000 Entry Draft.

WHL West Second All-Star Team (2002)

JOHANSSON, Fredrik (yoh-HAHN-suhn, FREHD-rihk) **EDM.**

Center. Shoots left. 5'11", 180 lbs. Born, Munkedal, Sweden, February 27, 1984.
(Edmonton's 14th choice, 274th overall, in 2002 Entry Draft).

			Regular Season					Playoffs				
Season	Club	League	GP	G	A	TP	PIM	GP	G	A	TP	PIM
2000-01	V. Frolunda Jr.	Swede-Jr.	22	3	4	7	8	3	0	1	1	4
	V. Frolunda 18	Swede-Jr.	6	5	1	6	4	....	....	....	....	....
2001-02	V. Frolunda Jr.	Swede-Jr.	42	13	23	36	39	....	....	....	....	....
	V. Frolunda 18	Swede-Jr.	1	0	1	1	0	....	....	....	....	....
2002-03	V. Frolunda Jr.	Swede-Jr.	30	13	34	47	24	3	0	2	2	2
	Vastra Frolunda	Sweden	9	0	0	0	2	5	0	0	0	0
2003-04	Vastra Frolunda Jr.	Swede-Jr.	7	1	2	3	4	4	2	4	6	0
	Halmstad	Swede-2	1	0	0	0	0	....	....	....	....	....
	Vastra Frolunda	Sweden	48	1	3	4	6	10	0	0	0	0

JOHANSSON, Jonas (yoh-HAHN-suhn, YOH-nuhs) **WSH.**

Right wing. Shoots right. 6'1", 180 lbs. Born, Jonkoping, Sweden, March 18, 1984.
(Colorado's 1st choice, 28th overall, in 2002 Entry Draft).

			Regular Season					Playoffs				
Season	Club	League	GP	G	A	TP	PIM	GP	G	A	TP	PIM
99-2000	HV 71 Jr.	Swede-Jr.	9	6	3	9	2	2	0	0	0	4
	Smaland 16	Swede-Jr.	8	3	3	6	4	....	....	....	....	....
2000-01	HV 71 Jr.	Swede-Jr.	27	13	8	21	14	2	1	0	1	0
2001-02	HV 71 Jr.	Swede-Jr.	26	15	19	34	20	....	....	....	....	....
	HV 71 Jonkoping	Sweden	5	0	0	0	0	2	0	0	0	0
2002-03	Kamloops Blazers	WHL	26	10	25	35	8	6	1	2	3	4
2003-04	Kamloops Blazers	WHL	72	18	19	37	70	5	2	2	4	4

Traded to **Washington** by **Colorado** with Bates Battaglia for Steve Konowalchuk and Washington's 3rd round choice (later traded to Carolina – Carolina selected Casey Borer) in 2004 Entry Draft, October 22, 2003.

JOHANSSON, Mikael (yoh-HAHN-suhn), MIGH-kuhl) **DET.**

Center. Shoots left. 5'10", 176 lbs. Born, Arvika, Sweden, June 27, 1985.
(Detroit's 8th choice, 289th overall, in 2003 Entry Draft).

			Regular Season					Playoffs				
Season	Club	League	GP	G	A	TP	PIM	GP	G	A	TP	PIM
2001-02	Arvika HC	Swede-3	31	1	13	14	34	6	0	0	0	6
2002-03	Arvika HC	Swede-3	30	13	28	41	89	....	....	....	....	....
2003-04	Skare BK Karlstad	Swede-3	10	1	5	6	6	....	....	....	....	....

JOHNSON, Gregg (JAWN-suhn, GREHG) **OTT.**

Center. Shoots left. 5'11", 183 lbs. Born, Windsor, CT, June 18, 1982.
(Ottawa's 11th choice, 256th overall, in 2001 Entry Draft).

			Regular Season					Playoffs				
Season	Club	League	GP	G	A	TP	PIM	GP	G	A	TP	PIM
1997-98	New England	EJHL	40	13	24	37	....	....	....	....	....	....
1998-99	New England	EJHL	40	29	27	56	....	....	....	....	....	....
99-2000	New England	EJHL	40	40	69	109	....	....	....	....	....	....
2000-01	Boston University	H-East	35	5	5	10	20	....	....	....	....	....
2001-02	Boston University	H-East	33	5	18	23	34	....	....	....	....	....
2002-03	Boston University	H-East	24	1	4	5	18	....	....	....	....	....
2003-04	Boston University	H-East	33	3	6	9	38	....	....	....	....	....
	Binghamton	AHL	5	1	0	1	4	1	0	0	0	0

JOHNSON, Jonas (YAWN-suhn, YEW-nuhs) **ST.L.**

Center. Shoots left. 6'2", 185 lbs. Born, Gavle, Sweden, March 23, 1970.
(St. Louis' 7th choice, 221st overall, in 2002 Entry Draft).

			Regular Season					Playoffs				
Season	Club	League	GP	G	A	TP	PIM	GP	G	A	TP	PIM
1987-88	Stromsboro	Swede-2	13	4	3	7	0	....	....	....	....	....
1988-89	Stromsboro	Swede-2	27	5	3	8	10	....	....	....	....	....
1989-90	Stromsboro	Swede-2	24	13	6	19	8	2	1	1	2	0
1990-91	Bjorkloven	Swede-2	36	10	15	25	32	2	0	0	0	0
1991-92	Brynas IF Gavle	Sweden	36	6	9	15	8	5	3	0	3	0
1992-93	Brynas IF Gavle	Sweden	39	8	16	24	24	10	6	4	10	6
1993-94	Brynas IF Gavle	Sweden	39	11	16	27	14	7	2	1	3	8
1994-95	Brynas IF Gavle	Sweden	39	9	15	24	26	14	4	6	10	14
1995-96	Brynas IF Gavle	Sweden	22	11	6	17	12	....	....	....	....	....
	Brynas IF Gavle	Swede-Q	18	6	25	31	4	10	1	9	10	8
1996-97	Landshut	Germany	48	7	19	26	6	7	2	0	2	4
1997-98	Landshut	Germany	48	8	6	14	26	6	0	1	1	8
1998-99	Vastra Frolunda	Sweden	46	13	21	34	44	4	1	1	2	6
99-2000	Vastra Frolunda	Sweden	50	17	18	35	73	5	0	2	2	6
2000-01	Vastra Frolunda	Sweden	50	15	29	44	75	5	4	3	7	12
2001-02	Vastra Frolunda	Sweden	50	14	31	45	24	10	3	3	6	4
2002-03	Vastra Frolunda	Sweden	49	12	23	35	24	16	3	3	6	27
2003-04	Vastra Frolunda	Sweden	49	14	14	28	68	10	3	5	8	2

JOHNSON, Nick (JAWN-suhn, NIHK) **PIT.**

Right wing. Shoots right. 6'1", 183 lbs. Born, Calgary, Alta., December 24, 1985.
(Pittsburgh's 4th choice, 67th overall, in 2004 Entry Draft).

			Regular Season					Playoffs				
Season	Club	League	GP	G	A	TP	PIM	GP	G	A	TP	PIM
2002-03	St. Albert Saints	AJHL	60	21	30	51	10	....	....	....	....	....
2003-04	St. Albert Saints	AJHL	51	35	36	71	33	4	0	2	2	0

• Signed Letter of Intent to attend **Dartmouth** (ECAC), September 29, 2003.

JOHNSON, Tyler (JAWN-suhn, TIGH-luhr) **CGY.**

Center. Shoots right. 6'2", 173 lbs. Born, Edmonton, Alta., July 11, 1985.
(Calgary's 6th choice, 173rd overall, in 2003 Entry Draft).

			Regular Season					Playoffs				
Season	Club	League	GP	G	A	TP	PIM	GP	G	A	TP	PIM
2000-01	Leduc Oill Kings	AMHL	1	0	0	0	0	....	....	....	....	....
	Leduc Oil Barons	AMBHL	36	21	31	52	57	4	3	4	7	6
2001-02	Leduc Oil Kings	WHL	18	4	18	22	26	....	....	....	....	....
	Moose Jaw	WHL	24	2	1	3	11	10	0	0	0	2
2002-03	Moose Jaw	WHL	49	8	6	14	39	13	2	1	3	9
2003-04	Moose Jaw	WHL	22	2	2	4	12	....	....	....	....	....
	Red Deer Rebels	WHL	35	7	9	16	19	19	5	5	10	18

JOKILA, Janne (YOHK-ih-luh, YAH-nee) **CBJ**

Left wing. Shoots left. 5'9", 174 lbs. Born, Turku, Finland, April 22, 1982.
(Columbus' 7th choice, 200th overall, in 2000 Entry Draft).

			Regular Season					Playoffs				
Season	Club	League	GP	G	A	TP	PIM	GP	G	A	TP	PIM
1996-97	TPS Turku C	Finn-Jr.	30	25	17	42	24	6	*5	*5	*10	2
1997-98	TPS Turku B	Finn-Jr.	30	11	10	21	28	6	3	1	4	2
1998-99	TPS Turku Jr.	Finn-Jr.	36	17	15	32	77	....	....	....	....	....
99-2000	TPS Turku Jr.	Finn-Jr.	35	10	7	17	32	13	3	3	6	4
2000-01	TPS Turku Jr.	Finn-Jr.	22	15	15	30	30	2	0	1	1	4
	TPS Turku	Finland	2	0	0	0	0	....	....	....	....	....
	SaiPa	Finland	8	1	1	2	0	....	....	....	....	....
2001-02	TPS Turku	Finland	14	1	1	2	4	....	....	....	....	....
	SaiPa	Finland	12	0	0	0	2	....	....	....	....	....
	Lukko Rauma	Finland	14	0	1	1	18	....	....	....	....	....
2002-03	River City	USHL	45	15	17	32	57	7	1	5	6	4
2003-04	Dayton Bombers	ECHL	69	17	23	40	69	....	....	....	....	....
	Syracuse Crunch	AHL	7	0	0	0	0	....	....	....	....	....

JOKINEN, Jussi (YOH-kih-nihn, YOO-see) **DAL.**

Center. Shoots left. 5'11", 183 lbs. Born, Kalajoki, Finland, April 1, 1983.
(Dallas' 7th choice, 192nd overall, in 2001 Entry Draft).

			Regular Season					Playoffs				
Season	Club	League	GP	G	A	TP	PIM	GP	G	A	TP	PIM
1998-99	Karpat Oulu C	Finn-Jr.	27	29	34	63	12	....	....	....	....	....
99-2000	Karpat Oulu Jr.	Finn-Jr.	28	4	6	10	14	....	....	....	....	....
	Karpat Oulu B	Finn-Jr.	15	6	25	31	14	6	2	3	5	0
2000-01	Karpat Oulu B	Finn-Jr.	1	2	1	3	0	....	....	....	....	....
	Karpat Oulu Jr.	Finn-Jr.	41	18	31	49	69	6	2	2	4	0
2001-02	Karpat Oulu	Finland	54	10	6	16	34	4	1	0	1	0
	Karpat Oulu Jr.	Finn-Jr.	2	4	1	5	2	1	1	1	2	0
2002-03	Karpat Oulu	Finland	51	14	23	37	10	15	2	1	3	33
2003-04	Karpat Oulu	Finland	55	15	23	38	20	15	3	4	7	6

JONASEN, Marcus (YOH-nuh-suhn, MAHR-kuhs) NYR

Left wing. Shoots right. 6'4", 220 lbs. Born, Vasteras, Sweden, January 12, 1984.
(NY Rangers' 2nd choice, 81st overall, in 2002 Entry Draft).

			Regular Season					Playoffs				
Season	Club	League	GP	G	A	TP	PIM	GP	G	A	TP	PIM
2000-01	Vasteras IK Jr.	Swede-Jr.	3	2	1	3	0	....	....	....	....	....
	Vasteras IK	Sweden	13	3	5	8	6	....	....	....	....	....
2001-02	Vasteras IK Jr.	Swede-Jr.	3	0	0	0	4	....	....	....	....	....
	Vasteras IK	Swede-2	16	2	1	3	6	....	....	....	....	....
	Vasteras IK	Swede-Q	2	0	0	0	0	....	....	....	....	....
2002-03	Hammarby Jr.	Swede-Jr.	27	16	9	25	28	2	1	0	1	2
2003-04	Tri-City Americans	WHL	43	12	14	26	28	11	4	4	8	8

JONES, David (JOHNZ, DAY-vihd) COL.

Right wing. Shoots right. 6'3", 220 lbs. Born, Guelph, Ont., August 10, 1984.
(Colorado's 8th choice, 288th overall, in 2003 Entry Draft).

			Regular Season					Playoffs				
Season	Club	League	GP	G	A	TP	PIM	GP	G	A	TP	PIM
2000-01	PoCo Bucs	PIJHL	40	18	11	29	33	....	....	....	....	....
2001-02	Coquitlam Express	BCHL	59	19	32	51	62	....	....	....	....	....
2002-03	Coquitlam Express	BCHL	35	9	19	28	55	7	2	6	8	8
2003-04	Coquitlam Express	BCHL	53	33	60	93	78	7	3	6	9	4

JONES, Matt (JOHNZ, MAT) PHX.

Defense. Shoots left. 6', 214 lbs. Born, Downers Grove, IL, August 8, 1983.
(Phoenix's 5th choice, 80th overall, in 2002 Entry Draft).

			Regular Season					Playoffs				
Season	Club	League	GP	G	A	TP	PIM	GP	G	A	TP	PIM
99-2000	Green Bay	USHL	54	1	4	5	59	13	0	0	0	2
2000-01	Green Bay	USHL	52	3	10	13	58	4	0	0	0	2
2001-02	North Dakota	WCHA	37	2	5	7	20	....	....	....	....	....
2002-03	North Dakota	WCHA	39	1	6	7	26	....	....	....	....	....
2003-04	North Dakota	WCHA	41	7	14	21	40	....	....	....	....	....

WCHA Second All-Star Team (2004)

JONES, Ryan (JOHNZ, RIGH-uhn) MIN.

Right wing. Shoots right. 6'1", 200 lbs. Born, Chatham, Ont., June 14, 1984.
(Minnesota's 5th choice, 111th overall, in 2004 Entry Draft).

			Regular Season					Playoffs				
Season	Club	League	GP	G	A	TP	PIM	GP	G	A	TP	PIM
2002-03	Chatham Maroons	OJHL-B	38	12	11	23	42	....	....	....	....	....
2003-04	Chatham Maroons	OJHL-B	46	39	30	69	64	17	17	9	26	25

• Signed Letter of Intent to attend **Miami University** (CCHA), November 11, 2003.

JONSSON, Lars (YAWN-suhn, LARZ) BOS.

Defense. Shoots left. 6'1", 198 lbs. Born, Borlange, Sweden, January 2, 1982.
(Boston's 1st choice, 7th overall, in 2000 Entry Draft).

			Regular Season					Playoffs				
Season	Club	League	GP	G	A	TP	PIM	GP	G	A	TP	PIM
1998-99	Leksands IF Jr.	Swede-Jr.	40	4	8	12	42	....	....	....	....	....
99-2000	Leksands IF Jr.	Swede-Jr.	34	16	22	38	50	2	0	0	0	0
	Leksands IF	Sweden	5	0	0	0	4	....	....	....	....	....
2000-01	Leksands IF Jr.	Swede-Jr.	7	1	3	4	6	....	....	....	....	....
	Leksands IF	Sweden	31	2	1	3	12	....	....	....	....	....
2001-02	Leksands IF Jr.	Swede-Jr.	3	2	1	3	4	1	0	0	0	0
	Leksands IF	Swede-2	28	1	7	8	59	....	....	....	....	....
	Leksands IF	Swede-Q	12	1	7	8	35	8	0	2	2	6
2002-03	Leksands IF	Sweden	21	0	0	0	12	5	0	0	0	2
	IF Bjorkloven Umea	Swede-2	9	3	4	7	10	....	....	....	....	....
	IFK Arboga IK	Swede-2	4	0	0	0	4	....	....	....	....	....
2003-04	Leksands IF	Sweden	50	3	9	12	30	....	....	....	....	....
	Leksands IF	Swede-Q	4	1	0	1	2	....	....	....	....	....

JONSSON, Robin (YAWN-suhn, RAW-bihn) ST.L.

Defense. Shoots right. 6'2", 194 lbs. Born, Upplands Vasby, Sweden, December 10, 1983.
(St. Louis' 4th choice, 120th overall, in 2002 Entry Draft).

			Regular Season					Playoffs				
Season	Club	League	GP	G	A	TP	PIM	GP	G	A	TP	PIM
99-2000	Farjestad 18	Swede-Jr.	8	0	0	0	24	....	....	....	....	....
	Farjestad Jr.	Swede-Jr.	18	2	2	4	12	....	....	....	....	....
2000-01	Farjestad Jr.	Swede-Jr.	24	3	8	11	34	....	....	....	....	....
	Farjestad	Sweden	....	....	....	....	....	1	0	0	0	0
2001-02	Bofors IK	Swede-2	55	3	4	7	36	....	....	....	....	....
	Farjestad	Sweden	1	0	0	0	0	....	....	....	....	....
2002-03	Bofors IK	Swede-2	7	0	2	2	6	....	....	....	....	....
2003-04	Farjestad	Sweden	28	0	0	0	10	....	....	....	....	....
	Bofors	Swede-2	18	3	3	6	18	5	0	1	1	6

• Missed majority of 2002-03 season recovering from cancer surgery, October 30, 2002.

JORDE, Ryan (JOHR-dee, RIGH-uhn) BUF.

Defense. Shoots right. 6'3", 223 lbs. Born, Kelowna, B.C., March 23, 1982.
(Buffalo's 8th choice, 279th overall, in 2001 Entry Draft).

			Regular Season					Playoffs				
Season	Club	League	GP	G	A	TP	PIM	GP	G	A	TP	PIM
1997-98	Tri-City Americans	WHL	3	0	1	1	2	....	....	....	....	....
	Notre Dame	SMBHL	STATISTICS NOT AVAILABLE									
1998-99	Tri-City Americans	WHL	19	0	1	1	7	....	....	....	....	....
	Lethbridge	WHL	21	2	5	7	22	4	0	0	0	0
99-2000	Lethbridge	WHL	54	1	6	7	112	....	....	....	....	....
2000-01	Lethbridge	WHL	11	0	0	0	49	....	....	....	....	....
	Tri-City Americans	WHL	56	1	6	7	170	....	....	....	....	....
2001-02	Tri-City Americans	WHL	29	0	6	6	68	....	....	....	....	....
	Moose Jaw	WHL	23	0	4	4	62	8	0	1	1	2
2002-03	Rochester	AHL	70	0	2	2	136	....	....	....	....	....
2003-04	Rochester	AHL	18	0	1	1	30	....	....	....	....	....

• Spent majority of 2003-04 season as a healthy reserve.

JOSEPH, Shane (JOH-sehf, SHAYN) S.J.

Center. Shoots right. 5'9", 170 lbs. Born, Brooks, Alta., July 23, 1981.

			Regular Season					Playoffs				
Season	Club	League	GP	G	A	TP	PIM	GP	G	A	TP	PIM
1997-98	Medicine Hat	AMHL	35	23	34	57	20	....	....	....	....	....
1998-99	Bow Valley Eagles	AJHL	60	36	34	70	14	....	....	....	....	....
99-2000	Minnesota State	WCHA	5	0	0	0	0	....	....	....	....	....
2000-01	Minnesota State	WCHA	16	0	5	5	2	....	....	....	....	....
2001-02	Minnesota State	WCHA	38	20	11	31	0	....	....	....	....	....
2002-03	Minnesota State	WCHA	41	29	36	65	6	....	....	....	....	....
2003-04	Minnesota State	WCHA	39	19	24	43	2	....	....	....	....	....
	Cleveland Barons	AHL	12	4	5	9	0	9	5	4	9	0

WCHA First All-Star Team (2003) • NCAA West Second All-American Team (2003)

• Missed majority of 1999-2000 season recovering from knee injury suffered in game vs. St. Clouid State (WCHA), November 11, 1999. Signed to a PTO (professional tryout) contract by **Cleveland** (AHL), March 17, 2004. Signed as a free agent by **San Jose**, June 27, 2004.

JOUDREY, Andrew (JOO-dree, AN-droo) WSH.

Center. Shoots left. 5'11", 191 lbs. Born, Halifax, N.S., July 15, 1984.
(Washington's 5th choice, 249th overall, in 2003 Entry Draft).

			Regular Season					Playoffs				
Season	Club	League	GP	G	A	TP	PIM	GP	G	A	TP	PIM
2000-01	Dartmouth	NSMHL	82	51	70	121	....	....	....	....	....	....
2001-02	Notre Dame	SJHL	57	24	38	62	14	....	....	....	....	....
2002-03	Notre Dame	SJHL	53	27	51	78	16	....	....	....	....	....
2003-04	U. of Wisconsin	WCHA	42	7	15	22	2	....	....	....	....	....

JOUKOV, Mishail (ZHOO-kawv, mee-shigh-EHL) EDM.

Left wing. Shoots left. 6'3", 187 lbs. Born, Leningrad, USSR, January 3, 1985.
(Edmonton's 4th choice, 72nd overall, in 2003 Entry Draft).

			Regular Season					Playoffs				
Season	Club	League	GP	G	A	TP	PIM	GP	G	A	TP	PIM
2000-01	Mora IK Jr.	Swede-Jr.	28	9	14	23	6	9	2	4	6	0
2001-02	IFK Arboga IK	Swede-2	37	4	9	13	12	3	1	0	1	2
2002-03	IFK Arboga IK	Swede-2	41	9	14	23	30	3	3	1	4	0
2003-04	Vasteras	Swede-2	44	5	12	17	16	....	....	....	....	....
	HV 71 Jonkoping	Sweden	3	0	0	0	0	....	....	....	....	....

JUNTUNEN, Henrik (YUN-tuh-nehn, HEHN-rihk) L.A.

Right wing. Shoots right. 6'2", 185 lbs. Born, Goteborg, Sweden, April 24, 1983.
(Los Angeles' 5th choice, 83rd overall, in 2001 Entry Draft).

			Regular Season					Playoffs				
Season	Club	League	GP	G	A	TP	PIM	GP	G	A	TP	PIM
99-2000	Karpat Oulu Jr.	Finn-Jr.	34	16	7	23	18	5	0	0	0	2
2000-01	Karpat Oulu Jr.	Finn-Jr.	17	4	4	8	12	....	....	....	....	....
	Karpat Oulu	Finland	....	....	....	....	....	2	0	0	0	0
2001-02	Karpat Oulu Jr.	Finn-Jr.	34	19	11	30	42	3	1	1	2	0
	Karpat Oulu	Finland	13	0	0	0	2	....	....	....	....	....
2002-03	Karpat Oulu	Finland	50	5	4	9	30	15	2	0	2	4
	Karpat Oulu Jr.	Finn-Jr.	2	0	0	0	0	....	....	....	....	....
2003-04	Karpat Oulu	Finland	50	4	8	12	30	13	0	1	1	25

JURCINA, Milan (YEWR-chee-nah, MEE-lan) BOS.

Defense. Shoots right. 6'4", 198 lbs. Born, Liptovsky Mikulas, Czech., June 7, 1983.
(Boston's 7th choice, 241st overall, in 2001 Entry Draft).

			Regular Season					Playoffs				
Season	Club	League	GP	G	A	TP	PIM	GP	G	A	TP	PIM
1997-98	L. Mikulas Jr.	Slovak-Jr.	44	2	7	9	37	....	....	....	....	....
1998-99	L. Mikulas Jr.	Slovak-Jr.	1	0	0	0	0	....	....	....	....	....
99-2000	L. Mikulas Jr.	Slovak-Jr.	STATISTICS NOT AVAILABLE									
2000-01	Halifax	QMJHL	68	0	5	5	56	6	0	2	2	12
2001-02	Halifax	QMJHL	61	4	16	20	58	13	5	3	8	10
2002-03	Halifax	QMJHL	51	15	13	28	102	25	6	6	12	40
2003-04	Providence Bruins	AHL	73	5	12	17	52	2	0	1	1	2

KADEYKIN, Anton (ka-DAY-kihn, AN-tawn) N.J.

Defense. Shoots left. 6'3", 205 lbs. Born, Elektrostal, USSR, May 17, 1984.
(New Jersey's 1st choice, 51st overall, in 2002 Entry Draft).

			Regular Season					Playoffs				
Season	Club	League	GP	G	A	TP	PIM	GP	G	A	TP	PIM
99-2000	Elektrostal 2	Russia-3	5	0	0	0	0	....	....	....	....	....
2000-01	Elektrostal 2	Russia-3	3	0	1	1	2	....	....	....	....	....
	Russia	Exhib.	5	0	1	1	6	....	....	....	....	....
2001-02	Elektrostal 2	Russia-3	21	2	2	4	46	....	....	....	....	....
	Elektrostal	Russia-2	20	0	0	0	16	....	....	....	....	....
2002-03	Sarnia Sting	OHL	55	2	8	10	34	6	0	1	1	0
2003-04	Sarnia Sting	OHL	39	0	2	2	38	3	0	0	0	0

KADLEC, Petr (KAD-lehts, PEE-tuhr) FLA.

Defense. Shoots left. 5'11", 180 lbs. Born, Prague, Czech., January 5, 1977.
(Florida's 11th choice, 234th overall, in 2003 Entry Draft).

			Regular Season					Playoffs				
Season	Club	League	GP	G	A	TP	PIM	GP	G	A	TP	PIM
1995-96	HC Slavia Praha Jr.	Czech-Jr.	23	2	12	14	....	....	....	....	....	....
	HC Slavia Praha	Czech.	24	1	2	3	6	3	0	0	0	0
	HC Kralupy	Czech-2	4	0	1	1	4	....	....	....	....	....
1996-97	HC Slavia Praha	Czech.	39	0	4	4	18	....	....	....	....	....
	HC Medvedi	Czech-2	5	0	2	2	....	....	....	....	....	....
1997-98	HC Slavia Praha	Czech.	51	5	12	17	22	5	1	2	3	4
1998-99	HC Slavia Praha	Czech.	48	2	15	17	22	....	....	....	....	....
99-2000	HC Plzen	Czech-2	39	6	21	27	32	7	0	4	4	0
	HC Slavia Praha	Czech.	12	0	0	0	10	....	....	....	....	....
2000-01	HC Slavia Praha	Czech.	45	8	19	27	44	10	1	3	4	34
2001-02	HC Slavia Praha	Czech	52	5	25	30	63	9	0	3	3	14
2002-03	HC Slavia Praha	Czech	49	4	19	23	46	17	1	6	7	26
2003-04	HC Slavia Praha	Czech	36	3	18	21	34	17	2	5	7	14

KAHNBERG, Magnus (KAHN-buhrg, MAG-nuhs) CAR.

Left wing. Shoots left. 6'1", 185 lbs. Born, Kullered, Sweden, February 25, 1980.
(Carolina's 6th choice, 212th overall, in 2000 Entry Draft).

			Regular Season					Playoffs				
Season	Club	League	GP	G	A	TP	PIM	GP	G	A	TP	PIM
1997-98	V. Frolunda 18	Swede-Jr.	11	15	6	21	6	8	5	8	13	6
	V. Frolunda Jr.	Swede-Jr.	28	6	7	13	8	2	0	0	0	0
1998-99	V. Frolunda Jr.	Swede-Jr.	34	23	18	41	4	4	1	1	2	0
99-2000	V. Frolunda Jr.	Swede-Jr.	35	45	21	66	30	6	7	4	11	4
	Vastra Frolunda	Sweden	4	0	0	0	0	....	....	....	....	....
2000-01	V. Frolunda 18	Swede-Jr.	1	8	1	9	0	....	....	....	....	....
	V. Frolunda Jr.	Swede-Jr.	2	*2	1	3	2	....	....	....	....	....
	Vastra Frolunda	Sweden	50	8	6	14	6	5	0	0	0	2
2001-02	Vastra Frolunda	Sweden	50	14	11	25	24	10	5	0	5	2
2002-03	Vastra Frolunda	Sweden	50	14	20	34	22	15	2	6	8	12
2003-04	Vastra Frolunda	Sweden	50	*33	16	*49	20	10	5	2	7	10

KAIGORODOV, Alexei (kay-goh-ROH-dahv, al-EHX-ay) OTT.

Center. Shoots left. 6'1", 183 lbs. Born, Chelyabinsk, USSR, July 29, 1983.
(Ottawa's 2nd choice, 47th overall, in 2002 Entry Draft).

			Regular Season					Playoffs				
Season	Club	League	GP	G	A	TP	PIM	GP	G	A	TP	PIM
1998-99	Magnitogorsk 2	Russia-4	10	6	4	10	2	....	....	....	....	....
99-2000	Magnitogorsk 2	Russia-3	19	2	3	5	8	....	....	....	....	....
2000-01	Magnitogorsk 2	Russia-3	45	12	30	42	26	....	....	....	....	....
2001-02	Magnitogorsk	Russia	46	4	12	16	20	9	0	3	3	2
2002-03	Magnitogorsk	Russia	46	8	14	22	20	3	0	1	1	0
2003-04	Magnitogorsk	Russia	49	4	12	16	24	14	2	2	4	4

KAIP, Rylan (KAYP, RIH-luhn) ATL.

Center. Shoots right. 6', 180 lbs. Born, Wilcox, Sask., March 19, 1984.
(Atlanta's 9th choice, 269th overall, in 2003 Entry Draft).

			Regular Season					Playoffs				
Season	Club	League	GP	G	A	TP	PIM	GP	G	A	TP	PIM
2000-01	Notre Dame	SJHL	5	0	0	0	0	1	0	0	0	0
2001-02	Notre Dame	SJHL	61	14	18	32	77	....	....	....	....	....
2002-03	Notre Dame	SJHL	57	20	36	56	164	6	1	6	7	21
2003-04	Notre Dame	SJHL	54	30	36	66	133	4	1	1	2	6

KALTEVA, Mikko (KAL-tuh-vah, MEE-koh) COL.

Defense. Shoots left. 6'3", 190 lbs. Born, Hyvinkaa, Finland, May 25, 1984.
(Colorado's 4th choice, 107th overall, in 2002 Entry Draft).

			Regular Season					Playoffs				
Season	Club	League	GP	G	A	TP	PIM	GP	G	A	TP	PIM
2000-01	Jokerit-B Jr.	Finn-Jr.	11	1	4	5	6	6	3	1	4	2
	Jokerit Helsinki Jr.	Finn-Jr.	34	0	3	3	12	....	....	....	....	....
2001-02	Jokerit Helsinki Jr.	Finn-Jr.	29	5	3	8	10	1	0	0	0	0
	Jokerit-B Jr.	Finn-Jr.	....	....	....	....	....	8	2	2	4	0
2002-03	Jokerit-B Jr.	Finn-Jr.	34	7	8	15	30	10	2	4	6	4
2003-04	Jokerit Helsinki Jr.	Finn-Jr.	39	14	10	24	42	3	0	0	0	0
	Jokerit Helsinki	Finland	2	0	0	0	0	8	0	0	0	2

KANKAANPERA, Markus (kan-kahn-PEHR-a, MAHR-kus) VAN.

Defense. Shoots left. 6'1", 191 lbs. Born, Skelleftea, Sweden, April 27, 1980.
(Vancouver's 7th choice, 218th overall, in 1999 Entry Draft).

			Regular Season					Playoffs				
Season	Club	League	GP	G	A	TP	PIM	GP	G	A	TP	PIM
1995-96	JYP Jyvaskyla B	Finn-Jr.	9	1	1	2	4	....	....	....	....	....
1996-97	JYP Jyvaskyla Jr.	Finn-Jr.	33	3	5	8	83	....	....	....	....	....
1997-98	JYP Jyvaskyla B	Finn-Jr.	13	4	10	14	18	5	3	2	5	6
	JYP Jyvaskyla Jr.	Finn-Jr.	32	0	0	0	2	....	....	....	....	....
1998-99	JYP Jyvaskyla Jr.	Finn-Jr.	1	0	0	0	4	....	....	....	....	....
	JYP Jyvaskyla	Finland	50	0	2	2	85	3	0	0	0	0
99-2000	JYP Jyvaskyla Jr.	Finn-Jr.	3	1	1	2	2	3	0	1	1	6
	JYP Jyvaskyla	Finland	47	0	5	5	87	....	....	....	....	....
2000-01	JYP Jyvaskyla	Finland	53	5	4	9	60	....	....	....	....	....
2001-02	HPK Hameenlinna	Finland	51	4	3	7	80	8	0	0	0	10
2002-03	Jokerit Helsinki	Finland	52	1	4	5	94	10	1	2	3	6
2003-04	Jokerit Helsinki	Finland	55	6	6	12	101	8	1	1	2	8

KANKO, Petr (KAN-koh, PEE-tuhr) L.A.

Right wing. Shoots left. 5'9", 195 lbs. Born, Pribram, Czech., February 7, 1984.
(Los Angeles' 3rd choice, 66th overall, in 2002 Entry Draft).

			Regular Season					Playoffs				
Season	Club	League	GP	G	A	TP	PIM	GP	G	A	TP	PIM
2000-01	Sparta Praha Jr.	Czech-Jr.	43	27	10	37	80	....	....	....	....	....
	HC Sparta Praha	Czech	6	1	0	1	0	....	....	....	....	....
2001-02	Kitchener Rangers	OHL	61	28	32	60	54	4	0	2	2	0
2002-03	Kitchener Rangers	OHL	60	33	34	67	123	20	11	16	27	17
2003-04	Kitchener Rangers	OHL	55	26	42	68	97	5	2	2	4	10
	Manchester	AHL	6	1	3	4	0	6	1	3	4	2

KANTEE, Kevin (KAN-tee, KEH-vihn) CHI.

Defense. Shoots left. 6'2", 202 lbs. Born, Idaho Falls, ID, January 29, 1984.
(Chicago's 6th choice, 188th overall, in 2002 Entry Draft).

			Regular Season					Playoffs				
Season	Club	League	GP	G	A	TP	PIM	GP	G	A	TP	PIM
99-2000	Jokerit Helsinki Jr.	Finn-Jr.	13	0	2	2	6	....	....	....	....	....
	Jokerit Helsinki C	Finn-Jr.	9	2	8	10	8	6	2	1	3	44
2000-01	Jokerit Helsinki Jr.	Finn-Jr.	34	10	8	18	16	6	0	2	2	4
2001-02	Jokerit Helsinki Jr.	Finn-Jr.	34	2	7	9	16	1	0	0	0	0
	Jokerit Helsinki B	Finn-Jr.	1	2	0	2	12	5	2	1	3	....
2002-03	Jokerit Helsinki Jr.	Finn-Jr.	34	5	17	22	34	11	3	4	7	16
2003-04	Jokerit Helsinki Jr.	Finn-Jr.	26	1	17	18	38	3	0	0	0	0
	Jokerit Helsinki	Finland	19	0	1	1	4	6	0	1	1	2

KARLSSON, Gabriel (KARLS-suhn, ga-BREE-ehl) DAL.

Center. Shoots left. 6'1", 189 lbs. Born, Borlange, Sweden, January 22, 1980.
(Dallas' 3rd choice, 86th overall, in 1998 Entry Draft).

			Regular Season					Playoffs				
Season	Club	League	GP	G	A	TP	PIM	GP	G	A	TP	PIM
1996-97	HV 71 Jr.	Swede-Jr.	25	7	9	16	....	....	....	....	....	....
1997-98	HV 71 Jr.	Swede-Jr.	27	11	15	26	32	....	....	....	....	....
	HV 71 Jonkoping	Sweden	1	0	0	0	0	....	....	....	....	....
1998-99	HV 71 Jr.	Swede-Jr.	12	4	9	13	4	....	....	....	....	....
	HV 71 Jonkoping	Sweden	33	2	1	3	2	....	....	....	....	....
99-2000	HV 71 Jonkoping	Sweden	50	5	3	8	12	6	0	0	0	2
2000-01	Assat Pori	Finland	17	2	2	4	6	....	....	....	....	....
	Leksands IF	Sweden	35	9	8	17	10	....	....	....	....	....
2001-02	Sodertalje SK	Sweden	47	8	7	15	18	....	....	....	....	....
2002-03	Sodertalje SK	Sweden	39	4	3	7	12	....	....	....	....	....
	Sodertalje Jr.	Swede-Jr.	1	0	1	1	0	....	....	....	....	....
2003-04	Sodertalje SK	Sweden	50	7	10	17	65	....	....	....	....	....

KARLSSON, Jens (KARLS-suhn, YEHNZ) L.A.

Right wing. Shoots right. 6'3", 205 lbs. Born, Goteborg, Sweden, November 7, 1982.
(Los Angeles' 1st choice, 18th overall, in 2001 Entry Draft).

			Regular Season					Playoffs				
Season	Club	League	GP	G	A	TP	PIM	GP	G	A	TP	PIM
1997-98	V. Frolunda 16	Swede-Jr.	8	9	3	12	32	....	....	....	....	....
	V. Frolunda Jr.	Swede-Jr.	17	2	3	5	4	....	....	....	....	....
1998-99	V. Frolunda 18	Swede-Jr.	32	27	17	44	110	4	2	2	4	0
99-2000	V. Frolunda 18	Swede-Jr.	3	6	3	9	6	....	....	....	....	....
	V. Frolunda Jr.	Swede-Jr.	32	24	13	37	82	6	3	0	3	42
2000-01	V. Frolunda Jr.	Swede-Jr.	25	20	15	35	154	1	0	1	1	2
	Molndals IF	Swede-2	5	1	1	2	35	....	....	....	....	....
	Vastra Frolunda	Sweden	19	2	0	2	4	5	1	3	4	50
2001-02	Vastra Frolunda	Sweden	46	6	9	15	44	10	1	0	1	18
	V. Frolunda Jr.	Swede-Jr.	....	....	....	....	....	2	0	1	1	12
2002-03	Vastra Frolunda	Sweden	45	5	6	11	101	11	3	2	5	41
2003-04	Vastra Frolunda	Sweden	50	3	13	16	62	10	4	0	4	6

KARLSSON, Mattias (KARL-suhn, MA-tee-uhs) OTT.

Defense. Shoots left. 6'2", 192 lbs. Born, Stora, Sweden, April 15, 1985.
(Ottawa's 4th choice, 135th overall, in 2003 Entry Draft).

			Regular Season					Playoffs				
Season	Club	League	GP	G	A	TP	PIM	GP	G	A	TP	PIM
2001-02	Brynas IF Gavle 18	Swede-Jr.	5	2	1	3	6	....	....	....	....	....
	Brynas IF Gavle Jr.	Swede-Jr.	13	0	1	1	12	....	....	....	....	....
2002-03	Brynas IF Gavle Jr.	Swede-Jr.	27	11	6	17	93	2	0	0	0	4
	Brynas IF Gavle	Sweden	3	0	0	0	0	....	....	....	....	....
	Brynas IF Gavle	Swede-Q	3	0	0	0	0	....	....	....	....	....
2003-04	Brynas IF Gavle Jr.	Swede-Jr.	20	5	8	13	67	5	0	4	4	10
	Brynas IF Gavle	Sweden	39	0	0	0	6	....	....	....	....	....

KARSUMS, Martins (KAHR-suhmz, MAHR-tihnsh) BOS.

Right wing. Shoots right. 5'10", 179 lbs. Born, Riga, Latvia, February 26, 1986.
(Boston's 2nd choice, 64th overall, in 2004 Entry Draft).

			Regular Season					Playoffs				
Season	Club	League	GP	G	A	TP	PIM	GP	G	A	TP	PIM
2000-01	Prizma '83 Riga	Latvia-Jr.	2	0	0	0	0	....	....	....	....	....
	HK Lido Nafta Riga	Latvia-Jr.	18	8	6	14	....	....	....	....	....	....
2001-02	Prizma '83 Riga	EEHL-B	16	7	8	15	4	....	....	....	....	....
	Prizma '83 Riga	Latvia	6	4	1	5	4	....	....	....	....	....
2002-03	HK Riga 2000	EEHL	2	0	0	0	0	....	....	....	....	....
	Vilki Riga	Latvia	STATISTICS NOT AVAILABLE									
2003-04	Moncton Wildcats	QMJHL	60	30	23	53	76	20	8	9	17	14

QMJHL All-Rookie Team (2004)

KASPAR, Lukas (kas-PAHR, LOO-kahsh) S.J.

Right wing. Shoots left. 6'2", 198 lbs. Born, Most, Czechoslovakia, September 23, 1985.
(San Jose's 1st choice, 22nd overall, in 2004 Entry Draft).

			Regular Season					Playoffs				
Season	Club	League	GP	G	A	TP	PIM	GP	G	A	TP	PIM
2000-01	Litvinov 18	Czech-Jr.	48	27	19	46	64	6	2	3	5	0
2001-02	Litvinov 18	Czech-Jr.	48	35	41	76	143	2	1	1	2	0
2002-03	Litvinov Jr.	Czech-Jr.	26	14	14	28	40	....	....	....	....	....
	Litvinov	Czech	9	1	1	2	2	....	....	....	....	....
2003-04	Litvinov Jr.	Czech-Jr.	23	21	14	35	56	1	0	0	0	0
	Litvinov	Czech	37	4	2	6	10	....	....	....	....	....
	Usti nad Labem	Czech-2	1	1	0	1	0	....	....	....	....	....
	SK HC Banik Most	Czech-3	....	....	....	....	....	1	0	0	0	2

KASPARIK, Pavel (kas-PAHR-ihk, PAH-vehl) PHI.

Center. Shoots left. 6'2", 198 lbs. Born, Pisek, Czech., November 11, 1979.
(Philadelphia's 4th choice, 200th overall, in 1999 Entry Draft).

			Regular Season					Playoffs				
Season	Club	League	GP	G	A	TP	PIM	GP	G	A	TP	PIM
1996-97	IHC Pisek Jr.	Czech-Jr.	36	12	5	17	....	....	....	....	....	....
1997-98	IHC Pisek Jr.	Czech-Jr.	39	21	19	40	....	....	....	....	....	....
	IHC Pisek	Czech-2	15	3	3	6	....	....	....	....	....	....
1998-99	IHC Pisek Jr.	Czech-Jr.	7	2	3	5	....	....	....	....	....	....
	IHC Pisek	Czech-2	51	20	23	43	....	....	....	....	....	....
99-2000	IHC Pisek	Czech-2	24	6	9	15	....	....	....	....	....	....
	HC Femax Havirov	Czech	1	0	0	0	0	....	....	....	....	....
	HC Sparta Praha	Czech	22	1	1	2	0	....	....	....	....	....
2000-01	HC Karlovy Vary	Czech	29	1	2	3	20	....	....	....	....	....
	HC Sparta Praha	Czech	19	5	1	6	18	13	2	0	2	12
2001-02	HC Sparta Praha	Czech	50	14	11	25	10	13	2	0	2	4
2002-03	HC Sparta Praha	Czech	21	0	4	4	4	....	....	....	....	....
	Liberec	Czech	30	8	9	17	26	....	....	....	....	....
2003-04	Liberec	Czech	52	12	16	28	89	....	....	....	....	....

KAUPPINEN, Marko (KOW-pih-nehn, MAHR-koh) PHI.

Defense. Shoots left. 6', 178 lbs. Born, Mikkeli, Finland, March 23, 1979.
(Philadelphia's 7th choice, 214th overall, in 1997 Entry Draft).

			Regular Season					Playoffs				
Season	Club	League	GP	G	A	TP	PIM	GP	G	A	TP	PIM
1994-95	Jukurit Mikkeli C	Finn-Jr.	31	12	11	23	48	....	....	....	....	....
1995-96	Jukurit Mikkeli	Finland-3	19	1	5	6	10	3	0	0	0	0
1996-97	JYP Jyvaskyla Jr.	Finn-Jr.	29	2	3	5	14	7	0	0	0	29
	JYP Jyvaskyla B	Finn-Jr.	12	1	6	7	16	....	....	....	....	....
1997-98	JYP Jyvaskyla Jr.	Finn-Jr.	16	2	4	6	16	....	....	....	....	....
	Diskos Jyvaskyla	Finland-2	2	2	1	3	0	....	....	....	....	....
	JYP Jyvaskyla	Finland	33	2	6	8	26	....	....	....	....	....
1998-99	JYP Jyvaskyla Jr.	Finn-Jr.	3	2	1	3	6	....	....	....	....	....
	JYP Jyvaskyla	Finland	49	5	7	12	56	3	0	0	0	6
99-2000	Jokerit Helsinki Jr.	Finn-Jr.	5	0	3	3	8	1	1	0	1	4
	Jokerit Helsinki	Finland	47	4	9	13	16	10	1	3	4	2
2000-01	AIK Solna	Sweden	4	0	0	0	4	....	....	....	....	....
	Jokerit Helsinki	Finland	48	5	7	12	41	5	0	0	0	8
	Kiekko-Vanta	Finland-2	1	0	0	0	9	....	....	....	....	....
2001-02	TPS Turku	Finland	55	4	9	13	55	5	1	0	1	2
2002-03	TPS Turku	Finland	53	3	10	13	52	7	0	0	0	27
2003-04	TPS Turku	Finland	42	1	3	4	18	13	0	1	1	14

KAZIONOV, Dmitri (ka-zee-OH-nahv, dih-MEE-tree) T.B.

Center. Shoots left. 6'3", 185 lbs. Born, Moscow, USSR, May 13, 1984.
(Tampa Bay's 2nd choice, 100th overall, in 2002 Entry Draft).

			Regular Season					Playoffs				
Season	Club	League	GP	G	A	TP	PIM	GP	G	A	TP	PIM
99-2000	Dyn. Moscow 2	Russia-3	2	1	0	1	0	....	....	....	....	....
2000-01	THC Tver	Russia-2	33	1	1	2	6	....	....	....	....	....
2001-02	HC CSKA	Russia-2	2	0	1	1	0	....	....	....	....	....
	HC CSKA 2	Russia-3	10	1	0	1	4	....	....	....	....	....
	Lada Togliatti	Russia	3	0	0	0	0	....	....	....	....	....
	Lada Togliatti 2	Russia-3	16	10	9	19	0	....	....	....	....	....
2002-03	Lada Togliatti	Russia	5	0	1	1	4	....	....	....	....	....
	Lada Togliatti 2	Russia-3	34	14	13	27	26	....	....	....	....	....
2003-04	Lada Togliatti 2	Russia-3	5	3	2	5	0	4	0	0	0	0
	Lada Togliatti	Russia	47	5	5	10	34	5	0	0	0	4

KEITH, Duncan (KEETH, DUHN-kuhn) CHI.

Defense. Shoots left. 6', 182 lbs. Born, Winnipeg, Man., July 16, 1983.
(Chicago's 2nd choice, 54th overall, in 2002 Entry Draft).

			Regular Season					Playoffs				
Season	Club	League	GP	G	A	TP	PIM	GP	G	A	TP	PIM
1998-99	Penticton	BCAHA	44	51	57	108	45	....	....	....	....	....
99-2000	Penticton Panthers	BCHL	59	9	27	36	37	....	....	....	....	....
2000-01	Penticton Panthers	BCHL	60	18	64	82	61	9	4	6	10	18
2001-02	Michigan State	CCHA	41	3	12	15	18	....	....	....	....	....
2002-03	Michigan State	CCHA	15	3	6	9	8	....	....	....	....	....
	Kelowna Rockets	WHL	37	11	35	46	60	19	3	11	14	12
2003-04	Norfolk Admirals	AHL	75	7	18	25	44	8	1	1	2	6

• Left **Michigan State** (CCHA) and signed as a free agent by **Kelowna** (WHL), December 27, 2002.

KELL, Trevor (KEHL, TREH-vuhr) CHI.

Right wing. Shoots right. 5'11", 181 lbs. Born, Thunder Bay, Ont., June 23, 1986.
(Chicago's 9th choice, 131st overall, in 2004 Entry Draft).

			Regular Season					Playoffs				
Season	Club	League	GP	G	A	TP	PIM	GP	G	A	TP	PIM
2002-03	Wellington Dukes	OPJHL	42	13	17	30	24	....	....	....	....	....
2003-04	London Knights	OHL	62	9	14	23	48	15	7	8	15	14

KELLY, Regan (KEHL-lee, REE-guhn) TOR.

Defense. Shoots left. 6'2", 200 lbs. Born, Watrous, Sask., March 9, 1981.
(Philadelphia's 7th choice, 259th overall, in 2000 Entry Draft).

			Regular Season					Playoffs				
Season	Club	League	GP	G	A	TP	PIM	GP	G	A	TP	PIM
1997-98	Tisdale Trojans	SMHL	41	2	13	15	24	....	....	....	....	....
1998-99	Nipawin Hawks	SJHL	52	4	14	18	30	....	....	....	....	....
99-2000	Nipawin Hawks	SJHL	46	8	21	29	20	....	....	....	....	....
2000-01	Providence College	H-East	36	4	21	25	58	....	....	....	....	....
2001-02	Providence College	H-East	38	6	10	16	48	....	....	....	....	....
2002-03	St. John's	AHL	71	3	15	18	36	....	....	....	....	....
2003-04	St. John's	AHL	55	2	9	11	42	....	....	....	....	....

Hockey East All-Rookie Team (2001) • Hockey East All-Tournament Team (2001)

Rights traded to **Toronto** by **Philadelphia** for Chris McAllister, September 26, 2000.

KENNEDY, Tyler (KEH-nuh-dee, TIGH-luhr) PIT.

Center. Shoots right. 5'10", 183 lbs. Born, Sault Ste. Marie, Ont., July 15, 1986.
(Pittsburgh's 6th choice, 99th overall, in 2004 Entry Draft).

			Regular Season					Playoffs				
Season	Club	League	GP	G	A	TP	PIM	GP	G	A	TP	PIM
2001-02	Soo Thunder	NOBHA		STATISTICS NOT AVAILABLE								
2002-03	Sault Ste. Marie	OHL	61	5	10	15	28	4	0	0	0	0
2003-04	Sault Ste. Marie	OHL	63	16	26	42	28	....	....	....	....	....

KESA, Teemu (KEH-sah, TEE-moo) N.J.

Defense. Shoots right. 6'1", 190 lbs. Born, Helsinki, Finland, June 7, 1981.
(New Jersey's 5th choice, 100th overall, in 1999 Entry Draft).

			Regular Season					Playoffs				
Season	Club	League	GP	G	A	TP	PIM	GP	G	A	TP	PIM
1996-97	Tappara Jr.	Finn-Jr.	32	1	5	6	58	4	1	0	4	29
1997-98	Ilves Tampere-B	Finn-Jr.	33	8	1	9	78	....	....	....	....	....
1998-99	Ilves Tampere-B	Finn-Jr.	24	4	5	9	146	10	0	0	0	12
	Ilves Tampere Jr.	Finn-Jr.	6	0	1	1	10	....	....	....	....	....
99-2000	Ilves Tampere Jr.	Finn-Jr.	31	1	7	8	92	....	....	....	....	....
	Ilves Tampere	Finland	5	0	0	0	8	....	....	....	....	....
2000-01	Ilves Tampere Jr.	Finn-Jr.	4	1	0	1	4	....	....	....	....	....
	Sport Vassa	Finland-2	1	0	1	1	0	....	....	....	....	....
2001-02	Lukko Rauma	Finland	34	2	0	2	32	....	....	....	....	....
	Lukko Rauma Jr.	Finn-Jr.	3	0	4	4	4	....	....	....	....	....
2002-03	Lukko Rauma	Finland	37	1	0	1	22	....	....	....	....	....
2003-04	Lukko Rauma	Finland	49	2	2	4	62	....	....	....	....	....

KHOMITSKY, Vadim (khoh-MIHT-skee, va-DEEM) DAL.

Defense. Shoots left. 6'1", 185 lbs. Born, Voskresensk, USSR, July 21, 1982.
(Dallas' 5th choice, 123rd overall, in 2000 Entry Draft).

			Regular Season					Playoffs				
Season	Club	League	GP	G	A	TP	PIM	GP	G	A	TP	PIM
1998-99	Voskresensk	Russia	9	0	0	0	10	....	....	....	....	....
99-2000	Voskresensk	Russia-2	17	0	0	0	31	....	....	....	....	....
	HC CSKA	Russia-2	11	0	1	1	10	....	....	....	....	....
2000-01	HC CSKA	Russia-2	44	2	7	9	89	....	....	....	....	....
2001-02	HC CSKA	Russia-2	68	2	18	20	63	....	....	....	....	....
2002-03	CSKA Moscow	Russia	51	3	2	5	58	....	....	....	....	....
2003-04	CSKA Moscow	Russia	54	3	3	6	46	....	....	....	....	....

KHOMUTOV, Ivan (khoh-moo-TAWF, ee-VAHN) N.J.

Right wing. Shoots left. 6'3", 205 lbs. Born, Saratov, USSR, March 11, 1985.
(New Jersey's 3rd choice, 93rd overall, in 2003 Entry Draft).

			Regular Season					Playoffs				
Season	Club	League	GP	G	A	TP	PIM	GP	G	A	TP	PIM
2000-01	Dyn. Moscow 16	Rus-Jr.	5	2	4	6	4	....	....	....	....	....
2001-02	HC CSKA 2	Russia 3	30	11	8	19	14	....	....	....	....	....
	CSKA Moscow 18	Russia-Jr.	14	9	6	15	16	10	6	4	10	8
2002-03	Elektrostal	Russia 2	20	1	1	2	8	....	....	....	....	....
2003-04	London Knights	OHL	40	9	12	21	25	15	3	1	4	7

KINCH, Matt (KIHNCH, MATT) NYR

Defense. Shoots left. 6', 195 lbs. Born, Red Deer, Alta., February 17, 1980.
(Buffalo's 8th choice, 146th overall, in 1999 Entry Draft).

			Regular Season					Playoffs				
Season	Club	League	GP	G	A	TP	PIM	GP	G	A	TP	PIM
1995-96	Red Deer	AMHL	35	6	17	23	31	....	....	....	....	....
	Calgary Hitmen	WHL	1	0	1	1	2	....	....	....	....	....
1996-97	Calgary Hitmen	WHL	64	10	22	32	31	....	....	....	....	....
1997-98	Calgary Hitmen	WHL	55	7	24	31	13	18	3	2	5	4
1998-99	Calgary Hitmen	WHL	68	14	69	83	16	21	8	15	23	59
99-2000	Calgary Hitmen	WHL	62	14	61	75	24	13	2	12	14	8
2000-01	Calgary Hitmen	WHL	70	18	66	84	52	12	3	6	9	6
2001-02	Hartford Wolf Pack	AHL	40	1	7	8	4	....	....	....	....	....
	Charlotte	ECHL	26	3	12	15	13	5	3	2	5	0
2002-03	Hartford Wolf Pack	AHL	66	7	22	29	28	2	0	0	0	0
2003-04	Hartford Wolf Pack	AHL	67	1	19	20	38	1	0	0	0	0

WHL East First All-Star Team (1999, 2001) • Memorial Cup All-Star Team (1999) • WHL East Second All-Star Team (2000) • Canadian Major Junior First All-Star Team (2001)

Signed as a free agent by **NY Rangers**, June 26, 2001.

KING, D.J. (KIHNG, DEE-JAY) ST.L.

Center. Shoots left. 6'3", 205 lbs. Born, Meadow Lake, Sask., January 27, 1984.
(St. Louis' choice, 191st overall, in 2002 Entry Draft).

			Regular Season					Playoffs				
Season	Club	League	GP	G	A	TP	PIM	GP	G	A	TP	PIM
2000-01	Beardy's	SMHL	52	30	28	58	120	....	....	....	....	....
2001-02	Lethbridge	WHL	65	10	14	24	104	....	....	....	....	....
2002-03	Lethbridge	WHL	55	15	17	32	139	....	....	....	....	....
2003-04	Lethbridge	WHL	35	8	15	23	102	....	....	....	....	....
	Kelowna Rockets	WHL	28	5	2	7	80	17	1	6	7	16

KLEIN, Kevin (KLIGHN, KEH-vihn) NSH.

Defense. Shoots right. 6'1", 187 lbs. Born, Kitchener, Ont., December 13, 1984.
(Nashville's 3rd choice, 37th overall, in 2003 Entry Draft).

			Regular Season					Playoffs				
Season	Club	League	GP	G	A	TP	PIM	GP	G	A	TP	PIM
99-2000	Kitchener	OMHA	54	12	29	41	40	....	....	....	....	....
2000-01	St. Michael's	OHL	58	3	16	19	21	18	0	5	5	17
2001-02	St. Michael's	OHL	68	5	22	27	35	15	2	7	9	12
2002-03	St. Michael's	OHL	67	11	33	44	88	17	1	9	10	8
2003-04	St. Michael's	OHL	5	0	1	1	2	....	....	....	....	....
	Guelph Storm	OHL	46	6	23	29	40	22	10	11	21	12

KLEMA, David (KLEE-mah, DAY-vihd) PHX.

Center. Shoots left. 6', 178 lbs. Born, Roseau, MN, April 3, 1982.
(Phoenix's 5th choice, 148th overall, in 2001 Entry Draft).

			Regular Season					Playoffs				
Season	Club	League	GP	G	A	TP	PIM	GP	G	A	TP	PIM
1998-99	Roseau Rams	Hi-School	28	25	35	63	....	....	....	....	....	....
99-2000	Roseau Rams	Hi-School	28	16	31	47	8	....	....	....	....	....
	Fargo-Moorhead	USHL	6	0	2	2	4	....	....	....	....	....
	Des Moines	USHL	4	1	1	2	0	6	1	1	2	0
2000-01	Des Moines	USHL	56	13	40	53	58	3	1	0	1	0
2001-02	Boston University	H-East	38	6	11	17	4	....	....	....	....	....
2002-03	Boston University	H-East	28	5	8	13	14	....	....	....	....	....
2003-04	Boston University	H-East	26	4	10	14	14	....	....	....	....	....

KLEPIS, Jakub (KLEH-pihsh, YA-kuhb) WSH.

Center. Shoots right. 6', 200 lbs. Born, Prague, Czech., June 5, 1984.
(Ottawa's 1st choice, 16th overall, in 2002 Entry Draft).

			Regular Season					Playoffs				
Season	Club	League	GP	G	A	TP	PIM	GP	G	A	TP	PIM
99-2000	HC Slavia Praha Jr.	Czech-Jr.	48	14	26	40	30	....	....	....	....	....
2000-01	HC Slavia Praha Jr.	Czech-Jr.	52	21	25	46	82	....	....	....	....	....
2001-02	Portland	WHL	70	14	50	64	111	7	0	3	3	22
2002-03	HC Slavia Praha	Czech	38	2	6	8	22	4	0	0	0	6
	HC Slavia Praha Jr.	Czech-Jr.	11	4	5	9	59	3	0	3	3	4
2003-04	HC Slavia Praha	Czech	44	4	9	13	43	17	5	3	8	10

Traded to **Buffalo** by **Ottawa** for Vaclav Varada and Buffalo's 5th round choice (Tim Cook) in 2003 Entry Draft, February 25, 2003. Traded to **Washington** by **Buffalo** for Mike Grier, March 9, 2004.

KLUBERTANZ, Kyle (KLOO-buhr-tanz, KIGHL) ANA.

Defense. Shoots right. 6', 178 lbs. Born, Madison, WI, September 23, 1985.
(Anaheim's 3rd choice, 74th overall, in 2004 Entry Draft).

			Regular Season					Playoffs				
Season	Club	League	GP	G	A	TP	PIM	GP	G	A	TP	PIM
2002-03	Green Bay	USHL	60	8	26	34	73	....	....	....	....	....
2003-04	Green Bay	USHL	57	6	21	27	124	....	....	....	....	....

• Signed Letter of Intent to attend **U. of Wisconsin** (WCHA), March 12, 2003.

KLYAZMIN, Sergei (klee-YAZ-mihn, SAIR-gay) COL.

Left wing. Shoots left. 6'4", 200 lbs. Born, Moscow, USSR, January 3, 1982.
(Colorado's 6th choice, 92nd overall, in 2000 Entry Draft).

			Regular Season					Playoffs				
Season	Club	League	GP	G	A	TP	PIM	GP	G	A	TP	PIM
1998-99	Krylja Sovetov 2	Russia-4	21	1	4	5	14	....	....	....	....	....
99-2000	Dyn. Moscow 2	Russia-3	16	3	2	5	18	....	....	....	....	....
2000-01	Halifax	QMJHL	65	33	28	61	76	6	1	2	3	16
2001-02	Halifax	QMJHL	46	24	37	61	34	....	....	....	....	....
2002-03	Hershey Bears	AHL	8	0	0	0	2	....	....	....	....	....
2003-04			DID NOT PLAY – INJURED									

• Missed majority of 2001-02 and 2002-03 seasons and entire 2003-04 season recovering from knee injury suffered in game vs. Rimouski (QMJHL), January 20, 2002.

KNOEPFLI, Mike (NAWF-lee, MIGHK) TOR.

Left wing. Shoots left. 6'1", 185 lbs. Born, Georgetown, Ont., April 9, 1982.
(Toronto's 12th choice, 276th overall, in 2001 Entry Draft).

			Regular Season					Playoffs				
Season	Club	League	GP	G	A	TP	PIM	GP	G	A	TP	PIM
99-2000	Georgetown	OPJHL	48	37	47	84	75	....	....	....	....	....
2000-01	Georgetown	OPJHL	47	45	38	83	....	....	....	....	....	....
2001-02	Cornell Big Red	ECAC	34	4	11	15	14	....	....	....	....	....
2002-03	Cornell Big Red	ECAC	36	8	16	24	8	....	....	....	....	....
2003-04	Cornell Big Red	ECAC	32	8	16	24	12	....	....	....	....	....

KNOPP, Ben (KUH-nawp, BEHN) CBJ

Right wing. Shoots right. 6'1", 190 lbs. Born, Calgary, Alta., April 8, 1982.
(Columbus' 2nd choice, 69th overall, in 2000 Entry Draft).

			Regular Season					Playoffs				
Season	Club	League	GP	G	A	TP	PIM	GP	G	A	TP	PIM
1997-98	Calgary Buffaloes	AMHL	35	28	48	76	34	10	10	6	16	30
1998-99	Calgary Canucks	AJHL	55	37	45	82	161	6	6	6	12	6
99-2000	Moose Jaw	WHL	72	30	30	60	101	4	2	2	4	4
2000-01	Moose Jaw	WHL	58	22	34	56	105	4	0	0	0	11
2001-02	Moose Jaw	WHL	37	18	14	32	56	....	....	....	....	....
	Kamloops Blazers	WHL	41	26	25	51	63	4	0	1	1	4
2002-03	Dayton Bombers	ECHL	53	7	13	20	83	....	....	....	....	....
	Syracuse Crunch	AHL	12	1	1	2	2	....	....	....	....	....
2003-04	Syracuse Crunch	AHL	63	7	5	12	81	....	....	....	....	....

KNYAZEV, Igor (kuh-NYA-zhev, EE-gohr) PHX.

Defense. Shoots left. 6', 208 lbs. Born, Elektrostal, USSR, January 27, 1983.
(Carolina's 1st choice, 15th overall, in 2001 Entry Draft).

			Regular Season					Playoffs				
Season	Club	League	GP	G	A	TP	PIM	GP	G	A	TP	PIM
99-2000	Spartak Moscow 2	Russia-3	13	2	4	6	74	....	....	....	....	....
	Spartak Moscow	Russia-2	26	1	1	2	6	....	....	....	....	....
2000-01	Spartak Moscow	Russia-2	53	6	5	11	101	....	....	....	....	....
2001-02	Spartak Moscow	Russia	3	0	0	0	8	....	....	....	....	....
	Spartak Moscow 2	Russia-3	2	0	1	1	0	....	....	....	....	....
	Ak Bars Kazan	Russia	14	0	1	1	4	3	0	0	0	0
2002-03	Lowell	AHL	68	2	5	7	68	....	....	....	....	....
2003-04	Springfield Falcons	AHL	72	1	6	7	61	....	....	....	....	....

Traded to **Phoenix** by **Carolina** with David Tanabe for Danny Markov and future considerations (Edmonton's 3rd round choice (previously acquired, later traded to NY Rangers - NY Rangers selected Billy Ryan) in 2004 Entry Draft, June 26, 2004), June 21, 2003.

KOALSKA, Matt (KOHL-skuh, MAT)

Center. Shoots left. 6'1", 196 lbs. Born, St. Paul, MN, May 16, 1980.
(Nashville's 7th choice, 154th overall, in 2000 Entry Draft).

			Regular Season					Playoffs				
Season	Club	League	GP	G	A	TP	PIM	GP	G	A	TP	PIM
1998-99	Hill-Murray	Hi-School	26	20	50	70	18	....	....	....	....	....
99-2000	Twin Cities	USHL	57	24	34	58	19	13	5	5	10	4
2000-01	U. of Minnesota	WCHA	42	10	24	34	36	....	....	....	....	....
2001-02	U. of Minnesota	WCHA	44	10	23	33	34	....	....	....	....	....
2002-03	U. of Minnesota	WCHA	41	9	31	40	26	....	....	....	....	....
2003-04	U. of Minnesota	WCHA	44	13	26	39	44	....	....	....	....	....

KOCI, David (KOH-chee, DAY-vihd) PIT.

Defense. Shoots left. 6'6", 230 lbs. Born, Prague, Czech., May 12, 1981.
(Pittsburgh's 5th choice, 146th overall, in 2000 Entry Draft).

			Regular Season					Playoffs				
Season	Club	League	GP	G	A	TP	PIM	GP	G	A	TP	PIM
1997-98	Sparta Praha Jr.	Czech-Jr.	41	2	9	11	105	....	....	....	....	....
1998-99	Hvezda Praha Jr.	Czech-Jr.	22	1	3	4	36	....	....	....	....	....
	Sparta Praha Jr.	Czech-Jr.	7	0	0	0	4	....	....	....	....	....
99-2000	Sparta Praha Jr.	Czech-Jr.	47	0	6	6	124	....	....	....	....	....
2000-01	Prince George	WHL	70	2	7	9	155	6	0	0	0	20
2001-02	Wheeling Nailers	ECHL	33	2	4	6	105	....	....	....	....	....
	Wilkes-Barre	AHL	26	1	3	4	98	....	....	....	....	....
2002-03	Wheeling Nailers	ECHL	48	0	1	1	103	....	....	....	....	....
	Wilkes-Barre	AHL	9	0	0	0	4	....	....	....	....	....
2003-04	Wilkes-Barre	AHL	78	1	7	8	298	10	0	0	0	24

Signed as a free agent by **HC Liberec** (Czech), May 18, 2004.

KOIVISTO, Toni (KOI-vihs-toh, TOH-nee) FLA.

Left wing. Shoots left. 6', 180 lbs. Born, Ylitornio, Finland, November 5, 1982.
(Florida's 9th choice, 200th overall, in 2001 Entry Draft).

			Regular Season					Playoffs				
Season	Club	League	GP	G	A	TP	PIM	GP	G	A	TP	PIM
1997-98	Lukko Rauma-B	Finn-Jr.	10	10	4	14	0	....	....	....	....	....
1998-99	Lukko Rauma-B	Finn-Jr.	8	6	5	11	2	....	....	....	....	....
	Lukko Rauma Jr.	Finn-Jr.	24	5	2	7	8	....	....	....	....	....
99-2000	Lukko Rauma Jr.	Finn-Jr.	32	21	12	33	8	8	2	1	3	0
	Lukko Rauma	Finland	11	1	0	1	2	....	....	....	....	....
2000-01	Lukko Rauma	Finland	47	5	1	6	6	2	0	0	0	0
	Lukko Rauma Jr.	Finn-Jr.	16	9	15	24	6	1	0	0	0	0
	Jaa-Kotkat	Finland-2	2	0	0	0	0	....	....	....	....	....
2001-02	Lukko Rauma Jr.	Finn-Jr.	6	7	3	10	2	....	....	....	....	....
	Lukko Rauma	Finland	52	4	10	14	8	....	....	....	....	....
2002-03	Lukko Rauma	Finland	56	7	6	13	16	....	....	....	....	....
2003-04	Lukko Rauma	Finland	54	4	8	12	57	4	0	0	0	0

KOIVU, Mikko (KOI-voo, MEE-koh) MIN.

Center. Shoots left. 6'2", 205 lbs. Born, Turku, Finland, March 12, 1983.
(Minnesota's 1st choice, 6th overall, in 2001 Entry Draft).

			Regular Season					Playoffs				
Season	Club	League	GP	G	A	TP	PIM	GP	G	A	TP	PIM
1997-98	TPS Turku-C	Finn-Jr.	32	6	12	18	34	....	....	....	....	....
1998-99	TPS Turku-C	Finn-Jr.	30	17	42	59	26	5	2	*9	*11	25
99-2000	TPS Turku Jr.	Finn-Jr.	41	8	17	25	40	13	1	4	5	8
2000-01	TPS Turku Jr.	Finn-Jr.	26	9	36	45	26	4	2	2	4	8
	TPS Turku	Finland	21	0	1	1	2	....	....	....	....	....
2001-02	TPS Turku	Finland	48	4	3	7	34	8	0	3	3	4
	TPS Turku Jr.	Finn-Jr.	2	0	1	1	12	....	....	....	....	....
2002-03	TPS Turku	Finland	37	7	13	20	20	7	2	2	4	6
2003-04	TPS Turku	Finland	45	6	24	30	36	13	1	7	8	8

KOJEVNIKOV, Alexander (kuh-ZHEHV-nih-kahv, al-ehx-AN-duhr) CHI.

Left wing. Shoots left. 6'3", 199 lbs. Born, Moscow, USSR, April 12, 1984.
(Chicago's 3rd choice, 93rd overall, in 2002 Entry Draft).

			Regular Season					Playoffs				
Season	Club	League	GP	G	A	TP	PIM	GP	G	A	TP	PIM
2001-02	Krylja Sovetov 2	Russia-3	32	12	15	27	59	....	....	....	....	....
	Krylja Sovetov 18	Russia-Jr.	31	30	17	47	140	....	....	....	....	....
2002-03	Krylja Sovetov	Russia	5	0	0	0	4	....	....	....	....	....
	Krylia Sovetov 2	Russia-3	3	1	2	3	28	....	....	....	....	....
2003-04	Val d'Or Foreurs	QMJHL	19	10	4	14	22	....	....	....	....	....
	Quebec Remparts	QMJHL	16	3	4	7	16	4	0	2	2	4

KOKOREV, Dimitri (KOH-koh-rehf, DEH-mee-tree) CGY.

Defense. Shoots left. 6'3", 198 lbs. Born, Moscow, USSR, January 9, 1979.
(Calgary's 4th choice, 51st overall, in 1997 Entry Draft).

			Regular Season					Playoffs				
Season	Club	League	GP	G	A	TP	PIM	GP	G	A	TP	PIM
1996-97	Dyn. Moscow 2	Russia-3	27	2	4	6	24	....	....	....	....	....
	Dynamo Moscow	Russia	1	0	0	0	0	....	....	....	....	....
1997-98	Dynamo Moscow	Russia	24	1	2	3	20	....	....	....	....	....
1998-99	Dynamo Moscow	Russia	26	0	1	1	20	8	1	0	1	0
	Dyn. Moscow 2	Russia-3	14	0	2	2	20	....	....	....	....	....
99-2000	THC Tver	Russia-2	20	6	3	9	32	....	....	....	....	....
	Dynamo Moscow	Russia	22	0	1	1	14	1	0	0	0	0
2000-01	Dynamo Moscow	Russia	5	0	1	1	4	....	....	....	....	....
2001-02	CSKA Moscow 2	Russia-3	11	2	2	4	22	....	....	....	....	....
	CSKA Moscow	Russia	32	1	3	4	32	....	....	....	....	....
2002-03	Sibir Novosibirsk	Russia	26	0	1	1	59	....	....	....	....	....
2003-04	Spartak Moscow	Russia-2	15	0	0	0	10	....	....	....	....	....
	Kristall Elektrostal	Russia-2	10	0	1	1	16	....	....	....	....	....

KOLARIK, Tyler (koh-LAHR-ihk, TIGH-luhr) CBJ

Center. Shoots right. 5'10", 185 lbs. Born, Philadelphia, PA, January 26, 1981.
(Columbus' 5th choice, 150th overall, in 2000 Entry Draft).

			Regular Season					Playoffs				
Season	Club	League	GP	G	A	TP	PIM	GP	G	A	TP	PIM
99-2000	Deerfield Academy	Hi-School	26	31	22	53	8	....	....	....	....	....
	NY/Mid-Atlantic	MBHL	3	4	3	7	0	....	....	....	....	....
2000-01	Harvard University	ECAC	32	13	15	28	36	....	....	....	....	....
2001-02	Harvard University	ECAC	32	9	21	30	32	....	....	....	....	....
2002-03	Harvard University	ECAC	30	15	13	28	20	....	....	....	....	....
2003-04	Harvard University	ECAC	36	12	18	30	24	....	....	....	....	....

KOLESOV, Sergei (KOH-leh-sawf, SAIR-gay) DET.

Defense. Shoots left. 6'4", 187 lbs. Born, Novopolotsk, USSR, May 22, 1986.
(Detroit's 3rd choice, 151st overall, in 2004 Entry Draft).

			Regular Season					Playoffs				
Season	Club	League	GP	G	A	TP	PIM	GP	G	A	TP	PIM
2003-04	Dynamo Minsk	Belarus		STATISTICS NOT AVAILABLE								

KOLLAR, Tomas (koh-LAHR, TAW-mash) DET.

Left wing. Shoots left. 6'2", 211 lbs. Born, Stockholm, Sweden, April 20, 1982.
(Detroit's 6th choice, 226th overall, in 2003 Entry Draft).

			Regular Season					Playoffs				
Season	Club	League	GP	G	A	TP	PIM	GP	G	A	TP	PIM
99-2000	Hammarby IF Jr.	Swede-Jr.	42	10	15	25	52	....	....	....	....	....
2000-01	Hammarby IF Jr.	Swede-Jr.	8	2	4	6	12	....	....	....	....	....
	Hammarby IF	Swede-2	23	3	2	5	10	....	....	....	....	....
	Hammarby IF	Swede-Q	9	0	0	0	4	....	....	....	....	....
2001-02	Hammarby IF	Swede-2	46	9	9	18	24	2	3	0	3	2
	Hammarby IF Jr.	Swede-Jr.	3	0	3	3	6	2	1	0	1	0
2002-03	Hammarby IF	Swede-Q	13	3	1	4	10	8	2	4	6	8
	Hammarby IF	Swede-2	27	10	8	18	45	....	....	....	....	....
2003-04	Djurgarden	Sweden	50	6	8	14	22	4	0	0	0	0

KOLOZVARY, Ivan (KOH-lohzh-vah-ree, EE-vahn) TOR.

Center. Shoots left. 6', 169 lbs. Born, Ilava, Czech., February 16, 1983.
(Toronto's 9th choice, 198th overall, in 2001 Entry Draft).

			Regular Season					Playoffs				
Season	Club	League	GP	G	A	TP	PIM	GP	G	A	TP	PIM
1998-99	Dukla Trencin Jr.	Slovak-Jr.	46	13	24	37	12	....	....	....	....	....
99-2000	Dukla Trencin Jr.	Slovak-Jr.	51	10	27	37	14	....	....	....	....	....
2000-01	Dukla Trencin Jr.	Slovak-Jr.	39	13	10	23	14	....	....	....	....	....
	Dukla Trencin	Slovakia	14	0	0	0	2	7	0	2	2	2
2001-02	Dukla Trencin	Slovakia	31	1	5	6	2	5	1	1	2	0
2002-03	Dukla Trencin	Slovakia	48	6	11	17	28	12	2	2	4	4
2003-04	Dukla Trencin	Slovakia	48	5	11	16	14	4	0	0	0	2

KOLTSOV, Ivan (kohlt-SAHV, ee-VAHN) EDM.

Defense. Shoots left. 6'2", 182 lbs. Born, Cherepovets, USSR, March 7, 1984.
(Edmonton's 6th choice, 106th overall, in 2002 Entry Draft).

			Regular Season					Playoffs				
Season	Club	League	GP	G	A	TP	PIM	GP	G	A	TP	PIM
2001-02	Cherepovets 2	Russia-3	27	2	2	4	24	....	....	....	....	....
2002-03	Leninogorsk	Russia-2	1	0	1	1	2	....	....	....	....	....
	Cherepovets 2	Russia-3	34	4	7	11	26	....	....	....	....	....
2003-04	Cherepovets 2	Russia-3	14	2	2	4	20	....	....	....	....	....

KOLTSOV, Kirill (kohlt-SAHV, kih-RIHL) **VAN.**

Defense. Shoots left. 5'11", 183 lbs. Born, Chelyabinsk, USSR, February 1, 1983.
(Vancouver's 1st choice, 49th overall, in 2002 Entry Draft).

			Regular Season					Playoffs				
Season	Club	League	GP	G	A	TP	PIM	GP	G	A	TP	PIM
1997-98	California	CBHL		STATISTICS NOT AVAILABLE								
1998-99	Streetsville Derbys	OPJHL	20	5	7	12	4	....	....	....	....	....
99-2000	Omsk 2	Russia-3	27	0	7	7	30	....	....	....	....	....
	Avangard Omsk	Russia	2	0	0	0	0	....	....	....	....	....
2000-01	Avangard Omsk	Russia	39	0	1	1	20	16	1	3	4	12
2001-02	Avangard Omsk	Russia	41	1	5	6	34	11	1	0	1	8
2002-03	Avangard Omsk	Russia	45	4	8	12	54	12	1	3	4	8
2003-04	Manitoba Moose	AHL	74	7	25	32	62	....	....	....	....	....

KOLUSZ, Marcin (KOH-loosh, MART-sihn) **MIN.**

Right wing. Shoots left. 6'1", 180 lbs. Born, Limanowa, Poland, January 18, 1985.
(Minnesota's 4th choice, 157th overall, in 2003 Entry Draft).

			Regular Season					Playoffs				
Season	Club	League	GP	G	A	TP	PIM	GP	G	A	TP	PIM
2000-01	Nowy Targ	Poland	5	0	0	0	2	....	....	....	....	....
2001-02	Nowy Targ Jr.	Poland-Jr.	11	13	5	18	22	....	....	....	....	....
2002-03	Nowy Targ	Poland	30	2	4	6	10	2	0	0	0	0
2003-04	Vancouver Giants	WHL	64	6	12	18	19	6	1	0	1	0

KOMADOSKI, Neil (koh-mah-DAW-skee, NEEL) **OTT.**

Defense. Shoots left. 6'2", 215 lbs. Born, Chesterfield, MO, February 10, 1982.
(Ottawa's 3rd choice, 81st overall, in 2001 Entry Draft).

			Regular Season					Playoffs				
Season	Club	League	GP	G	A	TP	PIM	GP	G	A	TP	PIM
1997-98	Aurora Tigers	OPJHL	1	0	0	0	0	....	....	....	....	....
1998-99	USA National U-17	USDP	1	1	0	1	0	....	....	....	....	....
	USA National U-18	USDP	50	8	7	15	202	....	....	....	....	....
99-2000	USA National U-18	USDP	49	3	11	14	222	....	....	....	....	....
2000-01	U. of Notre Dame	CCHA	30	2	5	7	106	....	....	....	....	....
2001-02	U. of Notre Dame	CCHA	37	2	9	11	100	....	....	....	....	....
2002-03	U. of Notre Dame	CCHA	40	1	23	24	46	....	....	....	....	....
2003-04	U. of Notre Dame	CCHA	39	5	15	20	48	....	....	....	....	....
	Binghamton	AHL	3	0	0	0	2	1	0	0	0	0

KONSORADA, Tim (kawn-sohr-A-duh, TIHM) **CBJ**

Right wing. Shoots right. 6', 201 lbs. Born, Ft. Saskatchewan, Alta., March 21, 1984.
(Columbus' 8th choice, 168th overall, in 2002 Entry Draft).

			Regular Season					Playoffs				
Season	Club	League	GP	G	A	TP	PIM	GP	G	A	TP	PIM
1998-99	Fort Saskatchewan	ABHL	36	26	45	71	8	....	....	....	....	....
99-2000	Fort Saskatchewan	AMHL	34	11	23	34	6	....	....	....	....	....
	Brandon	WHL	5	1	2	3	0	....	....	....	....	....
2000-01	Brandon	WHL	67	9	14	23	33	5	2	3	5	11
2001-02	Brandon	WHL	71	17	28	45	36	19	2	11	13	8
2002-03	Brandon	WHL	72	22	48	70	74	17	4	10	14	19
2003-04	Brandon	WHL	25	3	18	21	23	11	2	5	7	8

KOPECKY, Milan (koh-PEHTS-kee, MEE-lan) **PHI.**

Left wing. Shoots left. 6', 180 lbs. Born, Kolin, Czech., May 11, 1981.
(Philadelphia's 8th choice, 287th overall, in 2000 Entry Draft).

			Regular Season					Playoffs				
Season	Club	League	GP	G	A	TP	PIM	GP	G	A	TP	PIM
1998-99	Sparta Praha Jr.	Czech-Jr.	49	14	21	35	....	....	....	....	....	....
99-2000	HC Slavia Praha Jr.	Czech-Jr.	36	17	7	24	24	7	5	3	8	0
	HC Slavia Praha	Czech	2	0	0	0	0	....	....	....	....	....
2000-01	HC Slavia Praha Jr.	Czech-Jr.	38	19	17	36	36	....	....	....	....	....
	SC Kalin	Czech-2	8	2	4	6	2	....	....	....	....	....
2001-02	HC Slavia Praha Jr.	Czech-Jr.	3	2	0	2	4	....	....	....	....	....
	Beroun	Czech-2	36	10	9	19	16	....	....	....	....	....
	HC Slavia Praha	Czech	....	....	....	....	....	1	0	0	0	0
2002-03	HC Slavia Praha	Czech	33	4	6	10	20	17	2	1	3	8
	Beroun	Czech-2	7	2	4	6	6	....	....	....	....	....
2003-04	HC Slavia Praha	Czech	49	5	6	11	20	19	3	0	3	12

KOPECKY, Tomas (koh-PEHTS-kee, TAW-mahsh) **DET.**

Center. Shoots left. 6'3", 187 lbs. Born, Ilava, Czech., February 5, 1982.
(Detroit's 2nd choice, 38th overall, in 2000 Entry Draft).

			Regular Season					Playoffs				
Season	Club	League	GP	G	A	TP	PIM	GP	G	A	TP	PIM
1997-98	Dukla Trencin Jr.	Slovak-Jr.	41	19	22	41	....	....	....	....	....	....
1998-99	Dukla Trencin Jr.	Slovak-Jr.	44	13	16	29	18	....	....	....	....	....
99-2000	Dukla Trencin Jr.	Slovak-Jr.	14	8	9	17	36	....	....	....	....	....
	Dukla Trencin	Slovakia	52	3	4	7	24	5	0	0	0	0
2000-01	Lethbridge	WHL	49	22	28	50	52	5	1	1	2	6
	Cincinnati	AHL	1	0	0	0	0	....	....	....	....	....
2001-02	Lethbridge	WHL	60	34	42	76	94	4	2	1	3	15
	Cincinnati	AHL	2	1	1	2	6	2	0	0	0	0
2002-03	Grand Rapids	AHL	70	17	21	38	32	14	0	0	0	6
2003-04	Grand Rapids	AHL	48	6	6	12	28	1	0	0	0	2

KOREIS, Jakub (KOHR-ays, YA-kuhb) **PHX.**

Center. Shoots left. 6'3", 213 lbs. Born, Plzen, Czech, June 26, 1984.
(Phoenix's 1st choice, 19th overall, in 2002 Entry Draft).

			Regular Season					Playoffs				
Season	Club	League	GP	G	A	TP	PIM	GP	G	A	TP	PIM
99-2000	Plzen 18	Czech-Jr.	41	21	22	43	44	....	....	....	....	....
	Plzen Jr.	Czech-Jr.	3	2	1	3	2	....	....	....	....	....
2000-01	Plzen 18	Czech-Jr.	9	7	10	17	28	....	....	....	....	....
	Plzen Jr.	Czech-Jr.	43	14	15	29	83	....	....	....	....	....
2001-02	Plzen Jr.	Czech-Jr.	23	14	14	28	38	....	....	....	....	....
	HC Keramika Plzen	Czech	20	3	0	3	10	....	....	....	....	....
2002-03	HC Keramika Plzen	Czech	23	1	6	7	8	....	....	....	....	....
	Plzen Jr.	Czech-Jr.	10	3	5	8	28	....	....	....	....	....
2003-04	Guelph Storm	OHL	48	11	28	39	85	22	8	10	18	24

KORNEEV, Konstantin (kor-NEE-ehv, kawn-stuhn-TIHN) **MTL.**

Defense. Shoots left. 5'11", 176 lbs. Born, Moscow, USSR, June 5, 1984.
(Montreal's 6th choice, 275th overall, in 2002 Entry Draft).

			Regular Season					Playoffs				
Season	Club	League	GP	G	A	TP	PIM	GP	G	A	TP	PIM
99-2000	Krylja Sovetov 2	Russia-3	1	0	0	0	0	....	....	....	....	....
2000-01	Russia Jr.	Exhib.	12	0	4	4	10	....	....	....	....	....
2001-02	Krylja Sovetov 2	Russia-3	26	9	19	28	44	....	....	....	....	....
	Krylja Sovetov	Russia	4	0	2	2	0	2	0	0	0	2
	Krylja Sovetov Jr.	Russia-Jr.	13	4	25	29	20	12	12	18	30	24
2002-03	Krylja Sovetov	Russia	49	2	8	10	28	....	....	....	....	....
2003-04	Ak Bars Kazan	Russia	55	1	4	5	8	8	0	1	1	2

KORPIKARI, Oskari (kohr-pih-KAH-ree, AWS-kahr-ee) **MTL.**

Defense. Shoots left. 6'2", 210 lbs. Born, Oulu, Finland, April 5, 1984.
(Montreal's 9th choice, 217th overall, in 2003 Entry Draft).

			Regular Season					Playoffs				
Season	Club	League	GP	G	A	TP	PIM	GP	G	A	TP	PIM
2001-02	Karpat Oulu 18	Finn-Jr.	22	7	3	10	16	2	0	0	0	0
	Karpat Oulu Jr.	Finn-Jr.	5	0	0	0	0	....	....	....	....	....
2002-03	Karpat Oulu Jr.	Finn-Jr.	23	3	7	10	8	2	0	0	0	0
	Karpat Oulu	Finland	23	0	1	1	4	15	0	0	0	6
2003-04	Karpat Oulu	Finland	35	0	1	1	14	7	0	0	0	2
	Karpat Oulu Jr.	Finn-Jr.	7	3	1	4	8	....	....	....	....	....

KORPIKOSKI, Lauri (kohr-pih-KAWS-kee, LOW-ree) **NYR**

Left wing. Shoots left. 6', 180 lbs. Born, Turku, Finland, July 28, 1986.
(NY Rangers' 2nd choice, 19th overall, in 2004 Entry Draft).

			Regular Season					Playoffs				
Season	Club	League	GP	G	A	TP	PIM	GP	G	A	TP	PIM
2002-03	TPS Turku Jr.	Finn-Jr.	21	7	4	11	10	....	....	....	....	....
2003-04	TPS Turku Jr.	Finn-Jr.	36	12	8	20	20	8	5	5	10	20

KORSUNOV, Vladimir (KOHR-suhn-ahv, vla-DIH-meer) **ANA.**

Defense. Shoots left. 6'2", 202 lbs. Born, Moscow, USSR, March 16, 1983.
(Anaheim's 5th choice, 105th overall, in 2001 Entry Draft).

			Regular Season					Playoffs				
Season	Club	League	GP	G	A	TP	PIM	GP	G	A	TP	PIM
99-2000	Spartak Moscow 2	Russia-3	22	1	11	12	60	....	....	....	....	....
2000-01	Spartak Moscow	Russia-2	10	0	0	0	2	....	....	....	....	....
2001-02	Spartak Moscow 2	Russia-3	2	1	0	1	8	....	....	....	....	....
	Spartak Moscow	Russia	40	0	3	3	28	....	....	....	....	....
2002-03	Spartak Moscow	Russia	42	1	4	5	50	....	....	....	....	....
2003-04	Spartak Moscow	Russia-2	56	1	8	9	66	5	1	0	1	6

KOSMACHEV, Dmitri (kaws-ma-CHEHV, dih-MEE-tree) **CBJ**

Defense. Shoots right. 6'3", 209 lbs. Born, Gorky, USSR, June 7, 1985.
(Columbus' 3rd choice, 71st overall, in 2003 Entry Draft).

			Regular Season					Playoffs				
Season	Club	League	GP	G	A	TP	PIM	GP	G	A	TP	PIM
2001-02	HC CSKA 2	Russia-3	6	1	0	1	2	....	....	....	....	....
	HC CSKA Moscow	Russia-2	49	0	1	1	12	....	....	....	....	....
2002-03	CSKA Moscow	Russia	27	0	0	0	2	....	....	....	....	....
2003-04	CSKA Moscow	Russia	34	0	2	2	12	....	....	....	....	....

KOSTITSYN, Andrei (kaws-TIHT-sihn, AWN-dray) **MTL.**

Wing. Shoots right. 6', 208 lbs. Born, Novopolosk, USSR, February 3, 1985.
(Montreal's 1st choice, 10th overall, in 2003 Entry Draft).

			Regular Season					Playoffs				
Season	Club	League	GP	G	A	TP	PIM	GP	G	A	TP	PIM
2000-01	Novopolotsk	Belarus	1	2	1	3	2	....	....	....	....	....
	Novopolotsk	EEHL	5	1	0	1	0	....	....	....	....	....
	Yunost Minsk	Belarus	3	1	4	5	8	....	....	....	....	....
	HC Vitebsk	Belarus	17	17	6	23	42	....	....	....	....	....
2001-02	Novopolotsk	Belarus	17	9	6	15	28	....	....	....	....	....
	Novopolotsk	EEHL	29	9	8	17	16	....	....	....	....	....
	Yunost Minsk	Belarus	6	2	0	2	8	....	....	....	....	....
2002-03	CSKA Moscow	Russia	6	0	0	0	2	....	....	....	....	....
	Voskresensk	Russia-2	2	1	1	2	0	....	....	....	....	....
	Yunost Minsk	Belarus	4	6	4	10	43	....	....	....	....	....
	CSKA Moscow 2	Russia-3	3	2	2	4	25	....	....	....	....	....
2003-04	CSKA Moscow 2	Russia-3		STATISTICS NOT AVAILABLE								
	CSKA Moscow	Russia	12	0	1	1	2	....	....	....	....	....
	Yunost Minsk	Belarus		STATISTICS NOT AVAILABLE								

KOUBA, Ladislav (KOH-bah, LA-dih-slahv) **PHX.**

Left wing. Shoots left. 6'2", 213 lbs. Born, Vimperk, Czech., September 10, 1983.
(Phoenix's 9th choice, 216th overall, in 2002 Entry Draft).

			Regular Season					Playoffs				
Season	Club	League	GP	G	A	TP	PIM	GP	G	A	TP	PIM
99-2000	Plzen Jr.	Czech-Jr.	34	28	20	48	....	....	....	....	....	....
2000-01	Red Deer Rebels	WHL	62	5	7	12	29	3	0	0	0	2
2001-02	Red Deer Rebels	WHL	62	16	14	30	33	23	5	3	8	6
2002-03	Red Deer Rebels	WHL	68	12	28	40	48	23	5	6	11	4
2003-04	Red Deer Rebels	WHL	25	2	10	12	23	19	4	2	6	8
	Springfield Falcons	AHL	3	0	0	0	2	....	....	....	....	....
	Adirondack	UHL	26	7	4	11	6	....	....	....	....	....

KOVAC, Kristian (KOH-vach, KRIHST-yan) **COL.**

Right wing. Shoots right. 6'2", 205 lbs. Born, Kosice, Czech., January 1, 1981.
(Colorado's 5th choice, 122nd overall, in 1999 Entry Draft).

			Regular Season					Playoffs				
Season	Club	League	GP	G	A	TP	PIM	GP	G	A	TP	PIM
1997-98	HC Kosice Jr.	Slovak-Jr.	47	22	11	33	103	....	....	....	....	....
1998-99	HC Kosice Jr.	Slovak-Jr.	39	30	20	50	73	2	1	0	1	2
	HC Kosice	Slovakia	6	0	0	0	2	....	....	....	....	....
99-2000	Victoriaville Tigres	QMJHL	65	11	18	29	50	5	0	0	0	4
2000-01	Victoriaville Tigres	QMJHL	51	10	20	30	38	13	2	3	5	4
2001-02	HC Kosice	Slovakia	26	5	9	14	10	11	0	0	0	4
2002-03	HC Kosice	Slovakia	48	6	8	14	54	7	1	0	1	2
2003-04	HC Kosice	Slovakia	38	11	12	23	12	....	....	....	....	....

KOZAK, Rick (KOH-zak, RIHK) **NYR**

Right wing. Shoots right. 6'2", 187 lbs. Born, Winnipeg, Man., August 19, 1985.
(Philadelphia's 7th choice, 95th overall, in 2003 Entry Draft).

			Regular Season					Playoffs				
Season	Club	League	GP	G	A	TP	PIM	GP	G	A	TP	PIM
2000-01	Norman	MMHL	31	17	27	44	166	....	....	....	....	....
2001-02	Swan Valley	MJHL	35	14	21	35	103	4	0	0	0	4
	Prince George	WHL	4	0	0	0	11	....	....	....	....	....
2002-03	Swan Valley	MJHL	25	17	20	37	99	....	....	....	....	....
	Brandon	WHL	38	9	6	15	87	16	6	5	11	51
2003-04	Brandon	WHL	25	5	3	8	83	....	....	....	....	....
	Kamloops Blazers	WHL	29	9	6	15	77	5	1	0	1	12
	Hartford Wolf Pack	AHL	2	0	1	1	0	....	....	....	....	....

Traded to **NY Rangers** by **Philadelphia** with Philadelphia's 2nd round choice in 2005 Entry Draft for Vladimir Malakhov, March 8, 2004.

KRACIK, Jaroslav (KRAH-chihk, YAHR-roh-slav) **CBJ**

Right wing. Shoots left. 6', 178 lbs. Born, Plzen, Czech., January 18, 1983.
(Columbus' 12th choice, 231st overall, in 2002 Entry Draft).

			Regular Season					Playoffs				
Season	**Club**	**League**	**GP**	**G**	**A**	**TP**	**PIM**	**GP**	**G**	**A**	**TP**	**PIM**
99-2000	Plzen 18	Czech-Jr.	45	31	36	67	28	....	....	....	....	....
	Plzen Jr.	Czech-Jr.	6	1	0	1	2	....	....	....	....	....
2000-01	Plzen Jr.	Czech-Jr.	47	20	28	48	16	....	....	....	....	....
2001-02	Plzen Jr.	Czech-Jr.	39	14	35	49	46	....	....	....	....	....
	HC Klatovy	Czech-3	6	5	3	8	0	....	....	....	....	....
	HC Keramika Plzen	Czech	4	0	1	1	0	2	0	0	0	0
2002-03	Plzen Jr.	Czech-Jr.	33	11	17	28	40	1	0	1	1	0
	HC Keramika Plzen	Czech	4	0	0	0	0	....	....	....	....	....
	Usti nad Labem	Czech-2	9	1	1	2	4	4	0	0	0	0
2003-04	Plzen Jr.	Czech-Jr.	46	32	47	79	107	....	....	....	....	....
	Plzen	Czech	19	2	2	4	18	12	0	6	6	2

KREJCI, David (KRIGH-chee, DAY-vihd) **BOS.**

Center. Shoots right. 5'11", 176 lbs. Born, Sternberk, Czech., April 28, 1986.
(Boston's 1st choice, 63rd overall, in 2004 Entry Draft).

			Regular Season					Playoffs				
Season	**Club**	**League**	**GP**	**G**	**A**	**TP**	**PIM**	**GP**	**G**	**A**	**TP**	**PIM**
2000-01	HC Olomouc 18	Czech-Jr.	26	2	6	8	4	3	1	1	2	0
2001-02	Trinec 18	Czech-Jr.	48	32	27	59	30	6	2	4	6	2
2002-03	Trinec 18	Czech-Jr.	22	12	24	36	42	....	....	....	....	....
	Trinec Jr. B	Czech-Jr.	12	4	5	9	2	12	5	5	10	8
2003-04	Kladno Jr.	Czech-Jr.	50	23	37	60	37	7	3	6	9	4

KREPS, Kamil (KREHPS, KA-mihl) **FLA.**

Center. Shoots right. 6'1", 190 lbs. Born, Litomerice, Czech., November 18, 1984.
(Florida's 3rd choice, 38th overall, in 2003 Entry Draft).

			Regular Season					Playoffs				
Season	**Club**	**League**	**GP**	**G**	**A**	**TP**	**PIM**	**GP**	**G**	**A**	**TP**	**PIM**
99-2000	Litvinov Jr.	Czech-Jr.	48	18	16	34	10	....	....	....	....	....
2000-01	Litvinov Jr.	Czech-Jr.	47	16	23	39	6	6	2	6	8	10
2001-02	Brampton	OHL	68	19	24	43	14	....	....	....	....	....
2002-03	Brampton	OHL	53	19	42	61	12	11	3	5	8	4
2003-04	Brampton	OHL	57	19	27	46	19	12	7	8	15	2

KRIKUNOV, Ilja (krih-koo-NAWF, IHL-yah) **VAN.**

Left wing. Shoots left. 5'11", 169 lbs. Born, Elektrostal, USSR, February 27, 1984.
(Vancouver's 8th choice, 223rd overall, in 2002 Entry Draft).

			Regular Season					Playoffs				
Season	**Club**	**League**	**GP**	**G**	**A**	**TP**	**PIM**	**GP**	**G**	**A**	**TP**	**PIM**
2000-01	Elektrostal 2	Russia-3	4	0	0	0	2	....	....	....	....	....
2001-02	Elektrostal 2	Russia-3	5	3	6	9	4	....	....	....	....	....
	Elektrostal	Russia-2	48	12	10	22	28	....	....	....	....	....
2002-03	Elektrostal	Russia-2	48	19	9	28	34	....	....	....	....	....
2003-04	Voskresensk	Russia	50	10	9	19	14	....	....	....	....	....

KRONVALL, Staffan (KRAWN-wahl, STAH-fuhn) **TOR.**

Defense. Shoots left. 6'3", 209 lbs. Born, Jarfalla, Sweden, September 10, 1982.
(Toronto's 9th choice, 285th overall, in 2002 Entry Draft).

			Regular Season					Playoffs				
Season	**Club**	**League**	**GP**	**G**	**A**	**TP**	**PIM**	**GP**	**G**	**A**	**TP**	**PIM**
99-2000	Huddinge IK Jr.	Swede-Jr.	34	2	0	2	38	....	....	....	....	....
	Huddinge IK 18	Swede-Jr.	7	0	3	3	0	....	....	....	....	....
2000-01	Huddinge IK Jr.	Swede-Jr.	23	6	1	7	16	....	....	....	....	....
	Huddinge IK	Swede-2	1	0	0	0	0	....	....	....	....	....
2001-02	Huddinge IK	Swede-2	42	4	7	11	30	....	....	....	....	....
	Huddinge IK Jr.	Swede-Jr.	1	0	0	0	0	4	2	1	3	27
2002-03	Djurgarden	Sweden	50	5	13	18	46	12	3	2	5	18
2003-04	Djurgarden	Sweden	44	1	5	6	54	4	0	1	1	2

KRUCHININ, Andrei (kroo-CHIHN-ihn, AWN-dray) **MTL.**

Defense. Shoots left. 5'11", 187 lbs. Born, Karaganda, USSR, May 18, 1978.
(Montreal's 7th choice, 189th overall, in 1998 Entry Draft).

			Regular Season					Playoffs				
Season	**Club**	**League**	**GP**	**G**	**A**	**TP**	**PIM**	**GP**	**G**	**A**	**TP**	**PIM**
1996-97	Lada Togliatti	Russia	19	0	1	1	8	11	0	0	0	0
1997-98	Lada Togliatti	Russia	43	0	4	4	73	....	....	....	....	....
1998-99	Lada Togliatti	Russia	41	1	4	5	56	6	0	1	1	2
99-2000	CSK VVS Samara	Russia	6	1	0	1	0	....	....	....	....	....
	Lada Togliatti	Russia	25	1	2	3	24	6	1	0	1	4
2000-01	Perm	Russia	14	1	3	4	10	....	....	....	....	....
	Lada Togliatti	Russia	14	0	2	2	12	3	0	0	0	0
2001-02	Avangard Omsk	Russia	21	0	0	0	6	....	....	....	....	....
	Nizhnekamsk	Russia	17	1	3	4	8	....	....	....	....	....
2002-03	Nizhnekamsk	Russia	30	1	6	7	16	....	....	....	....	....
2003-04	Nizhnekamsk	Russia	49	2	6	8	53	5	1	1	2	4

KRYUKOV, Artem (KREE-oo-kahf, AHR-tehm) **BUF.**

Center. Shoots left. 6'3", 180 lbs. Born, Novosibirsk, USSR, March 5, 1982.
(Buffalo's 1st choice, 15th overall, in 2000 Entry Draft).

			Regular Season					Playoffs				
Season	**Club**	**League**	**GP**	**G**	**A**	**TP**	**PIM**	**GP**	**G**	**A**	**TP**	**PIM**
1997-98	Torpedo Yaroslavl	Russia	7	0	0	0	2	....	....	....	....	....
1998-99	Yaroslavl 2	Russia-3	20	2	2	4	6	....	....	....	....	....
99-2000	Yaroslavl 2	Russia-3	14	1	1	2	12	....	....	....	....	....
	Torpedo Yaroslavl	Russia	3	0	0	0	4	....	....	....	....	....
2000-01	Yaroslavl 2	Russia-3	6	0	0	0	2	11	0	0	0	8
	SKA St. Petersburg	Russia	14	0	2	2	14	....	....	....	....	....
2001-02	Yaroslavl	Russia	15	1	3	4	10	6	1	0	1	8
2002-03	Sibir Novosibirsk	Russia	9	0	0	0	27	....	....	....	....	....
2003-04	Yaroslavl 2	Russia-3	30	5	4	9	26	....	....	....	....	....
	Yaroslavl	Russia	4	0	2	2	0	....	....	....	....	....

KUBISTA, Jan (KOO-bihsh-tuh, YAHN) **BOS.**

Right wing. Shoots left. 6', 189 lbs. Born, Kolin, Czech., April 12, 1984.
(Boston's 3rd choice, 130th overall, in 2002 Entry Draft).

			Regular Season					Playoffs				
Season	**Club**	**League**	**GP**	**G**	**A**	**TP**	**PIM**	**GP**	**G**	**A**	**TP**	**PIM**
99-2000	Pardubice-18	Czech-Jr.	44	16	18	34	10	....	....	....	....	....
	SC Kolin Jr.	Czech-Jr.	5	4	2	6	0	....	....	....	....	....
2000-01	Pardubice-18	Czech-Jr.	53	33	24	57	61	8	6	7	13	16
	Pardubice Jr.	Czech-Jr.	1	0	1	1	0	....	....	....	....	....
2001-02	Pardubice Jr.	Czech-Jr.	48	12	12	24	36	....	....	....	....	....
2002-03	Pardubice Jr.	Czech-Jr.	32	16	11	27	40	....	....	....	....	....
	Pardubice	Czech	9	1	1	2	0	....	....	....	....	....
	Hradec Kralove	Czech-2	2	0	0	0	0	....	....	....	....	....
2003-04	Pardubice	Czech	3	0	0	0	0	....	....	....	....	....
	Hradec Kralove	Czech-2	5	0	0	0	0	....	....	....	....	....
	Pardubice Jr.	Czech-Jr.	39	22	23	45	80	....	....	....	....	....

KUHTINOV, Roman (kukh-TEEN-nawv, ROH-muhn) **NYI**

Defense. Shoots right. 6'1", 207 lbs. Born, Belgorod, USSR, December 1, 1975.
(NY Islanders' 7th choice, 280th overall, in 2001 Entry Draft).

			Regular Season					Playoffs				
Season	**Club**	**League**	**GP**	**G**	**A**	**TP**	**PIM**	**GP**	**G**	**A**	**TP**	**PIM**
1997-98	Raichikhinsk	Russia-3	36	18	8	26	46	....	....	....	....	....
1998-99	Novokuznetsk	Russia	42	2	9	11	26	6	0	0	0	2
99-2000	Novokuznetsk	Russia	37	2	6	8	28	14	1	1	2	8
2000-01	Novokuznetsk	Russia	44	7	10	17	36	....	....	....	....	....
2001-02	Ufa Salavat	Russia	51	11	10	21	74	....	....	....	....	....
2002-03	Ufa Salavat	Russia	50	4	7	11	72	3	2	0	2	4
2003-04	Cherepovets	Russia	54	2	6	8	46	....	....	....	....	....

KUIPER, Nick (KIGH-puhr, NIHK) **CHI.**

Defense. Shoots right. 6'3", 215 lbs. Born, Beaconsfield, Que., February 12, 1982.

			Regular Season					Playoffs				
Season	**Club**	**League**	**GP**	**G**	**A**	**TP**	**PIM**	**GP**	**G**	**A**	**TP**	**PIM**
1998-99	Lac St-Louis Lions	QAAA	42	3	23	26	36	5	0	3	3	4
99-2000	Hawkesbury	COJHL	46	7	22	29	40	....	....	....	....	....
2000-01	Hawkesbury	COJHL	32	7	10	17	22	....	....	....	....	....
	Massachusetts	H-East	13	0	1	1	2	....	....	....	....	....
2001-02	Massachusetts	H-East	32	2	9	11	10	....	....	....	....	....
2002-03	Massachusetts	H-East	36	3	3	6	34	....	....	....	....	....
2003-04	Massachusetts	H-East	37	5	5	10	72	....	....	....	....	....

Signed as a free agent by **Chicago**, March 31, 2004.

KUKUMBERG, Roman (KOO-kuhm-buhrg, ROH-muhn) **TOR.**

Center. Shoots right. 6'1", 198 lbs. Born, Bratislava, Czechoslovakia, April 8, 1980.
(Toronto's 2nd choice, 113th overall, in 2004 Entry Draft).

			Regular Season					Playoffs				
Season	**Club**	**League**	**GP**	**G**	**A**	**TP**	**PIM**	**GP**	**G**	**A**	**TP**	**PIM**
2001-02	Dukla Trencin	Slovakia	46	12	9	21	20	4	0	0	0	2
2002-03	Dukla Trencin	Slovakia	53	18	18	36	60	12	6	5	11	12
2003-04	Dukla Trencin	Slovakia	51	16	20	36	93	11	4	8	12	14

KUTNY, Vladimir (KOOT-nee, vla-DIH-meer) **DET.**

Left wing. Shoots left. 6'4", 195 lbs. Born, Trencin, Czech., May 22, 1985.
(Detroit's 7th choice, 258th overall, in 2003 Entry Draft).

			Regular Season					Playoffs				
Season	**Club**	**League**	**GP**	**G**	**A**	**TP**	**PIM**	**GP**	**G**	**A**	**TP**	**PIM**
2001-02	HC Trencin Jr.	Slovak-Jr.	STATISTICS NOT AVAILABLE									
2002-03	Quebec Remparts	QMJHL	66	7	12	19	37	11	0	1	1	2
2003-04	Quebec Remparts	QMJHL	30	6	8	14	8	....	....	....	....	....
	Val-d'Or Foreurs	QMJHL	28	7	8	15	16	7	2	3	5	7

LAATIKAINEN, Arto (lah-tee-KIGH-nuhn, AHR-toh) **NYR**

Defense. Shoots left. 6', 187 lbs. Born, Espoo, Finland, May 24, 1980.
(NY Rangers' 8th choice, 197th overall, in 1999 Entry Draft).

			Regular Season					Playoffs				
Season	**Club**	**League**	**GP**	**G**	**A**	**TP**	**PIM**	**GP**	**G**	**A**	**TP**	**PIM**
1996-97	Kiekko Espoo Jr.	Finn-Jr.	34	2	9	11	34	....	....	....	....	....
	Kiekko Espoo B	Finn-Jr.	11	2	5	7	2	....	....	....	....	....
1997-98	Kiekko Espoo B	Finn-Jr.	7	2	1	3	6	....	....	....	....	....
	Kiekko Espoo Jr.	Finn-Jr.	35	7	9	16	24	5	2	0	2	2
1998-99	Blues Espoo Jr.	Finn-Jr.	3	0	1	1	4	1	1	1	2	0
	Blues Espoo	Finland	48	0	6	6	14	4	0	2	2	2
99-2000	Blues Espoo Jr.	Finn-Jr.	1	0	0	0	2	....	....	....	....	....
	Blues Espoo	Finland	51	6	5	11	12	4	1	0	1	4
2000-01	Blues Espoo	Finland	54	5	9	14	38	....	....	....	....	....
	KJT Jarvenpaa	Finland-2	1	1	1	2	0	....	....	....	....	....
2001-02	Blues Espoo	Finland	56	5	6	11	32	3	0	0	0	0
2002-03	Blues Espoo	Finland	51	1	8	9	24	7	0	3	3	4
2003-04	Blues Espoo	Finland	55	4	20	24	30	....	....	....	....	....

LADD, Andrew (LAD, AN-droo) **CAR.**

Left wing. Shoots left. 6'2", 200 lbs. Born, Maple Ridge, B.C., December 12, 1985.
(Carolina's 1st choice, 4th overall, in 2004 Entry Draft).

			Regular Season					Playoffs				
Season	**Club**	**League**	**GP**	**G**	**A**	**TP**	**PIM**	**GP**	**G**	**A**	**TP**	**PIM**
2000-01	Okanoghan Chiefs	BCAHA	6	4	8	12	10	....	....	....	....	....
2001-02	Port Coquitlam	BCAHA	50	50	41	91	49	....	....	....	....	....
	Vancouver	WHL	1	0	0	0	0	....	....	....	....	....
2002-03	Coquitlam Express	BCHL	58	15	40	55	61	....	....	....	....	....
2003-04	Calgary Hitmen	WHL	71	30	45	75	119	7	1	6	7	10

LAINE, Teemu (LIGH-neh, TEE-moo) **N.J.**

Right wing. Shoots left. 6'1", 200 lbs. Born, Helsinki, Finland, August 9, 1982.
(New Jersey's 2nd choice, 39th overall, in 2000 Entry Draft).

			Regular Season					Playoffs				
Season	**Club**	**League**	**GP**	**G**	**A**	**TP**	**PIM**	**GP**	**G**	**A**	**TP**	**PIM**
1997-98	Jokerit Helsinki B	Finn-Jr.	20	20	24	44	54	5	1	3	4	4
1998-99	Jokerit Helsinki Jr.	Finn-Jr.	29	20	17	37	83	6	0	2	2	6
99-2000	Jokerit Helsinki Jr.	Finn-Jr.	23	5	9	14	42	....	....	....	....	....
	Jokerit Helsinki	Finland	14	1	1	2	8	....	....	....	....	....
2000-01	Jokerit Helsinki Jr.	Finn-Jr.	4	1	2	3	18	1	0	0	0	0
	Kiekko Vantaa	Finland-2	18	2	4	6	30	....	....	....	....	....
	Jokerit Helsinki	Finland	25	3	2	5	10	5	1	0	1	2
2001-02	Jokerit Helsinki Jr.	Finn-Jr.	8	9	5	14	50	1	0	0	0	2
	Kiekko Vantaa	Finland-2	9	6	4	10	4	....	....	....	....	....
	Jokerit Helsinki	Finland	38	0	1	1	45	7	0	0	0	2
2002-03	Jokerit Helsinki	Finland	53	7	5	12	52	9	1	1	2	2
2003-04	Jokerit Helsinki	Finland	56	5	8	13	50	8	1	1	2	2

LAKOS, Andre (LA-kaws, AWN-dray) **CBJ**

Defense. Shoots right. 6'6", 230 lbs. Born, Vienna, Austria, July 29, 1979.
(New Jersey's 4th choice, 95th overall, in 1999 Entry Draft).

			Regular Season					Playoffs				
Season	Club	League	GP	G	A	TP	PIM	GP	G	A	TP	PIM
1995-96	Montreal-Bourassa	QAAA	40	2	13	15	68	....	....	....	....	....
1996-97	Shelburne Wolves	MTJHL	36	5	12	17	47	....	....	....	....	....
1997-98	St. Michael's	OHL	49	2	10	12	54	....	....	....	....	....
1998-99	Barrie Colts	OHL	62	4	23	27	40	12	3	3	6	8
99-2000	Albany River Rats	AHL	65	1	7	8	41	5	0	2	2	4
2000-01	Albany River Rats	AHL	51	1	20	21	29	....	....	....	....	....
2001-02	Albany River Rats	AHL	36	0	3	3	24	....	....	....	....	....
	Utah Grizzlies	AHL	26	0	1	1	28	1	0	0	0	0
	Austria	Olympics	4	0	0	0	6	....	....	....	....	....
2002-03	Augusta Lynx	ECHL	5	0	2	2	8	....	....	....	....	....
2003-04	Vienna	Austria	48	6	19	25	75	....	....	....	....	....

Traded to **Dallas** by **New Jersey** with future considerations for Valeri Kamensky, January 16, 2002. Signed as a free agent by **Columbus**, July 7, 2004.

LALIBERTE, David (lal-IH-buhr-tee, DAY-vihd) **PHI.**

Right wing. Shoots right. 6'1", 194 lbs. Born, St-Jean-Sur-Richelieu, Que., March 17, 1986.
(Philadelphia's 3rd choice, 124th overall, in 2004 Entry Draft).

			Regular Season					Playoffs				
Season	Club	League	GP	G	A	TP	PIM	GP	G	A	TP	PIM
2001-02	Antoine-Girouard	QAAA	41	21	21	42	14	15	8	9	17	6
2002-03	Montreal Rocket	QMJHL	66	15	14	29	10	6	3	0	3	2
2003-04	PEI Rocket	QMJHL	70	21	22	43	51	11	1	3	4	6

LALIBERTE, John (lal-IH-buhr-tee, JAWN) **VAN.**

Right wing. Shoots left. 6'1", 185 lbs. Born, Portland, ME, August 5, 1983.
(Vancouver's 5th choice, 114th overall, in 2002 Entry Draft).

			Regular Season					Playoffs				
Season	Club	League	GP	G	A	TP	PIM	GP	G	A	TP	PIM
99-2000	Exeter Eagles	Hi-School	32	37	40	77	60	....	....	....	....	....
2000-01	N.H. Jr. Monarchs	EJHL	53	33	42	75	42	....	....	....	....	....
2001-02	N.H. Jr. Monarchs	EJHL	35	39	44	*83	60	....	....	....	....	....
2002-03	Boston University	H-East	26	5	6	11	12	....	....	....	....	....
2003-04	Boston University	H-East	35	5	11	16	20	....	....	....	....	....

LAMBERT, Michael (lam-BAIR, MIGH-kuhl) **MTL.**

Left wing. Shoots left. 6'2", 200 lbs. Born, Trois-Rivieres, Que., March 10, 1984.
(Montreal's 3rd choice, 99th overall, in 2002 Entry Draft).

			Regular Season					Playoffs				
Season	Club	League	GP	G	A	TP	PIM	GP	G	A	TP	PIM
1998-99	Cap-d-Madeleine	QAAA	3	0	0	0	0	....	....	....	....	....
99-2000	Cap-d-Madeleine	QAAA	42	20	16	36	38	1	0	2	2	0
2000-01	Acadie-Bathurst	QMJHL	23	2	5	7	15	....	....	....	....	....
	Montreal Rocket	QMJHL	33	6	12	18	14	....	....	....	....	....
2001-02	Montreal Rocket	QMJHL	71	29	24	53	111	7	1	6	7	15
2002-03	Montreal Rocket	QMJHL	71	28	32	60	53	7	2	2	4	10
2003-04	PEI Rocket	QMJHL	67	42	42	84	53	11	6	7	13	6

LAMMERS, John (LA-muhrs, JAWN) **DAL.**

Left wing. Shoots left. 5'11", 184 lbs. Born, Bowmanville, Ont., January 29, 1986.
(Dallas' 5th choice, 86th overall, in 2004 Entry Draft).

			Regular Season					Playoffs				
Season	Club	League	GP	G	A	TP	PIM	GP	G	A	TP	PIM
2001-02	Langley	BCAHA	64	51	69	120	30	....	....	....	....	....
	Lethbridge	WHL	5	0	0	0	0	....	....	....	....	....
2002-03	Lethbridge	WHL	53	17	15	32	11	....	....	....	....	....
2003-04	Lethbridge	WHL	62	21	24	45	31	....	....	....	....	....

LANDOLT, Shaun (LAN-dohlt, SHAWN) **TOR.**

Right wing. Shoots right. 6'1", 202 lbs. Born, Abbotsford, B.C., October 2, 1984.
(Toronto's 6th choice, 237th overall, in 2003 Entry Draft).

			Regular Season					Playoffs				
Season	Club	League	GP	G	A	TP	PIM	GP	G	A	TP	PIM
2000-01	Moose Jaw	WHL	49	4	4	8	40	4	0	0	0	0
2001-02	Moose Jaw	WHL	27	8	7	15	56	8	0	0	0	10
2002-03	Moose Jaw	WHL	45	8	16	24	53	....	....	....	....	....
	Calgary Hitmen	WHL	30	7	9	16	18	5	0	1	1	6
2003-04	Calgary Hitmen	WHL	65	16	20	36	45	7	0	3	3	12

LANNON, Ryan (LA-nuhn, RIGH-uhn) **PIT.**

Defense. Shoots left. 6'2", 220 lbs. Born, Worcester, MA, December 14, 1982.
(Pittsburgh's 10th choice, 239th overall, in 2002 Entry Draft).

			Regular Season					Playoffs				
Season	Club	League	GP	G	A	TP	PIM	GP	G	A	TP	PIM
1998-99	Team USA	USDP-17	56	3	4	7	36	....	....	....	....	....
99-2000	Cushing Academy	Hi-School		STATISTICS NOT AVAILABLE								
2000-01	Cushing Academy	Hi-School		STATISTICS NOT AVAILABLE								
2001-02	Harvard University	ECAC	34	0	2	2	38	....	....	....	....	....
2002-03	Harvard University	ECAC	34	3	11	14	39	....	....	....	....	....
2003-04	Harvard University	ECAC	35	0	9	9	36	....	....	....	....	....

LAPIERRE, Maxim (la-PEE-air, MAX-ihm) **MTL.**

Center. Shoots right. 6'2", 201 lbs. Born, St. Leonard, Que., March 29, 1985.
(Montreal's 3rd choice, 61st overall, in 2003 Entry Draft).

			Regular Season					Playoffs				
Season	Club	League	GP	G	A	TP	PIM	GP	G	A	TP	PIM
2001-02	Cap-d-Madeleine	QAAAA	42	14	27	41	44	10	3	5	8	16
	Montreal Rocket	QMJHL	9	2	0	2	2	....	....	....	....	....
2002-03	Montreal Rocket	QMJHL	72	22	21	43	55	7	1	3	4	6
2003-04	PEI Rocket	QMJHL	67	25	36	61	138	11	7	2	9	14

LaROSE, Chad (lah-ROHZ, CHAD) **CAR.**

Right wing. Shoots right. 5'10", 173 lbs. Born, Fraser, MI, March 27, 1982.

			Regular Season					Playoffs				
Season	Club	League	GP	G	A	TP	PIM	GP	G	A	TP	PIM
99-2000	Sioux-Falls	USHL	54	29	26	55	28	3	0	1	1	0
2000-01	Sioux-Falls	USHL	24	11	22	33	50	....	....	....	....	....
	Plymouth Whalers	OHL	32	18	7	25	24	19	10	10	20	22
2001-02	PlymouthWhalers	OHL	53	32	27	59	40	6	3	4	7	16
2002-03	Plymouth Whalers	OHL	67	61	56	117	52	15	9	8	17	25
2003-04	Florida Everblades	ECHL	41	16	19	35	16	14	3	4	7	20
	Lowell	AHL	36	7	9	16	29	....	....	....	....	....

OHL Second All-Star Team (2003)

Signed as a free agent by **Carolina**, August 6, 2003.

LARRIVEE, Christian (la-ree-VAY, krihs-TYEH) **MTL.**

Center. Shoots left. 6'4", 207 lbs. Born, Gaspe, Que., August 25, 1982.
(Montreal's 6th choice, 114th overall, in 2000 Entry Draft).

			Regular Season					Playoffs				
Season	Club	League	GP	G	A	TP	PIM	GP	G	A	TP	PIM
1998-99	Jonquiere Elites	QAAA	42	26	36	62	10	....	....	....	....	....
99-2000	Chicoutimi	QMJHL	69	8	15	23	18	....	....	....	....	....
2000-01	Chicoutimi	QMJHL	72	32	48	80	46	7	3	1	4	4
2001-02	Chicoutimi	QMJHL	72	48	52	100	60	4	2	5	7	0
2002-03	Chicoutimi	QMJHL	50	18	40	58	49	....	....	....	....	....
2003-04	Columbus	ECHL	72	11	22	33	28	....	....	....	....	....

LAVRENTIEV, Anton (lahv-REHN-tee-yehv, AN-tawn) **NSH.**

Defense. Shoots right. 6'4", 196 lbs. Born, Kazan, USSR, August 25, 1983.
(Nashville's 7th choice, 178th overall, in 2001 Entry Draft).

			Regular Season					Playoffs				
Season	Club	League	GP	G	A	TP	PIM	GP	G	A	TP	PIM
2000-01	Ak Bars Kazan 2	Russia-3		STATISTICS NOT AVAILABLE								
2001-02	Sudbury Wolves	OHL	10	0	0	0	17	....	....	....	....	....
	Ak Bars Kazan 2	Russia-3		STATISTICS NOT AVAILABLE								
2002-03	Yuzhny Ural Orsk	Russia-3	13	0	1	1	14	....	....	....	....	....
2003-04	HC Rybinsk	Russia-2	31	2	1	3	49	....	....	....	....	....

LAWSON, Lucas (LAW-suhn, LOO-kuhs) **NYR**

Center. Shoots left. 6'1", 195 lbs. Born, Braeside, Ont., August 10, 1979.

			Regular Season					Playoffs				
Season	Club	League	GP	G	A	TP	PIM	GP	G	A	TP	PIM
1996-97	Arnprior Packers	OJHL-B		STATISTICS NOT AVAILABLE								
1997-98	Kanata Valley	COJHL		STATISTICS NOT AVAILABLE								
1998-99	Kanata Valley	COJHL	50	40	45	85	124	3	2	10	12	0
99-2000	U. of Maine	H-East	23	2	3	5	12	....	....	....	....	....
2000-01	U. of Maine	H-East	39	9	11	20	16	....	....	....	....	....
2001-02	U. of Maine	H-East	44	18	13	31	37	....	....	....	....	....
2002-03	U. of Maine	H-East	39	21	16	37	18	....	....	....	....	....
	Hartford Wolf Pack	AHL	....	....	....	....	....	2	0	0	0	0
2003-04	Charlotte	ECHL	26	11	13	24	10	....	....	....	....	....
	Hartford Wolf Pack	AHL	32	3	4	7	27	5	0	0	0	0

Hockey East Second All-Star Team (2003)

Signed as a free agent by **NY Rangers**, April 4, 2003.

LEBDA, Brett (LEHB-dah, BREHT) **DET.**

Defense. Shoots left. 5'11", 194 lbs. Born, Buffalo Grove, IL, January 15, 1982.

			Regular Season					Playoffs				
Season	Club	League	GP	G	A	TP	PIM	GP	G	A	TP	PIM
2000-01	U. of Notre Dame	CCHA	39	7	19	26	109	....	....	....	....	....
2001-02	U. of Notre Dame	CCHA	34	6	8	14	54	....	....	....	....	....
2002-03	U. of Notre Dame	CCHA	40	7	14	21	48	....	....	....	....	....
2003-04	U. of Notre Dame	CCHA	39	6	18	24	42	....	....	....	....	....
	Grand Rapids	AHL	6	0	1	1	0	4	0	0	0	2

CCHA All-Rookie Team (2001) • CCHA Second All-Star Team (2004)

Signed as a free agent by **Detroit**, April 1, 2004.

LEBLOND-LETOURNEAU, Pierre-Luc (leh-BLAWN-leh-TOOR-noh) **N.J.**

Left wing. Shoots left. 6'2", 210 lbs. Born, Levis, Que., June 4, 1985.
(New Jersey's 4th choice, 216th overall, in 2004 Entry Draft).

			Regular Season					Playoffs				
Season	Club	League	GP	G	A	TP	PIM	GP	G	A	TP	PIM
2003-04	Baie-Comeau	QMJHL	62	2	3	5	198	4	0	0	0	6

LEE, Carter (LEE, KAHR-tuhr) **S.J.**

Forward. Shoots right. 6'1", 190 lbs. Born, Toms River, NJ, July 2, 1984.
(San Jose's 11th choice, 276th overall, in 2003 Entry Draft).

			Regular Season					Playoffs				
Season	Club	League	GP	G	A	TP	PIM	GP	G	A	TP	PIM
2001-02	Canterbury High	Hi-School	34	10	9	19	45	....	....	....	....	....
2002-03	Canterbury High	Hi-School	35	38	22	60	40	....	....	....	....	....
2003-04	Canterbury High	Hi-School	30	19	26	45	40	....	....	....	....	....

Signed Letter of Intent to attend **Northeastern** (ECAC), November 20, 2003.

LEHMAN, Scott (LAY-man, SKAWT) **ATL.**

Defense. Shoots left. 6'1", 200 lbs. Born, Fort Mcmurray, Alta., January 5, 1986.
(Atlanta's 3rd choice, 76th overall, in 2004 Entry Draft).

			Regular Season					Playoffs				
Season	Club	League	GP	G	A	TP	PIM	GP	G	A	TP	PIM
2002-03	St. Michael's	OHL	53	3	10	13	50	19	1	3	4	34
2003-04	St. Michael's	OHL	66	5	27	32	189	18	2	2	4	38

LEHOUX, Yanick (luh-HOO, YAH-nihk) **L.A.**

Center. Shoots right. 6'1", 200 lbs. Born, Montreal, Que., April 8, 1982.
(Los Angeles' 3rd choice, 86th overall, in 2000 Entry Draft).

			Regular Season					Playoffs				
Season	Club	League	GP	G	A	TP	PIM	GP	G	A	TP	PIM
1997-98	Cap-d-Madeleine	QAAA	42	29	50	79	26	....	....	....	....	....
1998-99	Baie-Comeau	QMJHL	63	10	20	30	31	....	....	....	....	....
99-2000	Baie-Comeau	QMJHL	67	31	61	92	14	6	1	2	3	2
2000-01	Baie-Comeau	QMJHL	70	67	68	135	62	11	8	16	24	0
2001-02	Baie-Comeau	QMJHL	66	56	69	125	63	5	5	4	9	0
	Manchester	AHL	....	....	....	....	....	1	0	0	0	0
2002-03	Manchester	AHL	78	16	21	37	26	1	0	0	0	0
2003-04	Manchester	AHL	66	14	28	42	22	5	2	3	5	16

QMJHL Second All-Star Team (2002)

LEHTONEN, Mikko (LEHT-oh-nehn, MEE-koh) **NSH.**

Defense. Shoots left. 6'1", 194 lbs. Born, Oulu, Finland, June 12, 1979.
(Nashville's 9th choice, 271st overall, in 2001 Entry Draft).

			Regular Season					Playoffs				
Season	Club	League	GP	G	A	TP	PIM	GP	G	A	TP	PIM
1995-96	Karpat Oulu-B	Finn-Jr.	15	4	5	9	30	....	....	....	....	....
1996-97	Karpat Oulu Jr.	Finn-Jr.	35	6	19	25	82	....	....	....	....	....
1997-98	Karpat Oulu Jr.	Finn-Jr.	20	3	4	7	40	....	....	....	....	....
	Karpat Oulu-B	Finn-Jr.	11	5	7	12	31	....	....	....	....	....
1998-99	Karpat Oulu Jr.	Finn-Jr.	22	7	8	15	51	....	....	....	....	....
	Karpat Oulu	Finland-2	2	0	0	0	0	....	....	....	....	....
	Karpat Oulu-B	Finn-Jr.	13	6	14	20	14	....	....	....	....	....
99-2000	Karpat Oulu	Finland-2	45	5	10	15	26	6	0	0	0	4
2000-01	Karpat Oulu	Finland	54	6	9	15	58	9	0	3	3	4
2001-02	Karpat Oulu	Finland	55	8	11	19	32	4	1	1	2	4
2002-03	Karpat Oulu	Finland	55	5	12	17	50	15	3	1	4	22
2003-04	Karpat Oulu	Finland	53	5	13	18	62	12	2	4	6	8

LEHUN, Jonathan (leh-HOON, JAWN-ah-thuhn) **ST.L.**

Center. Shoots left. 6', 170 lbs. Born, Toronto, Ont., February 22, 1984.
(St. Louis' 9th choice, 189th overall, in 2003 Entry Draft).

			Regular Season					Playoffs				
Season	**Club**	**League**	**GP**	**G**	**A**	**TP**	**PIM**	**GP**	**G**	**A**	**TP**	**PIM**
2000-01	St. Michael's	OPJHL	40	15	20	35	....	....	....	....	....	....
2001-02	St. Michael's	OPJHL	47	34	42	76	57	....	....	....	....	....
2002-03	St. Cloud State	WCHA	35	8	8	16	18	....	....	....	....	....
2003-04	Owen Sound	OHL	58	13	24	37	14	5	1	2	3	4

Left **St. Cloud State** (WCHA) and signed by **Owen Sound** (OHL), June 21, 2003

LEPISTO, Sami (LEH-pihs-toh, SA-mee) **WSH.**

Defense. Shoots left. 6', 176 lbs. Born, Espoo, Finland, October 17, 1984.
(Washington's 6th choice, 66th overall, in 2004 Entry Draft).

			Regular Season					Playoffs				
Season	**Club**	**League**	**GP**	**G**	**A**	**TP**	**PIM**	**GP**	**G**	**A**	**TP**	**PIM**
2001-02	Jokerit Helsinki Jr.	Finn-Jr.	14	0	5	5	21	....	....	....	....	....
	Jokerit Jr. B	Finn-Jr.	20	8	14	22	36	8	4	8	12	12
2002-03	Jokerit Helsinki Jr.	Finn-Jr.	36	5	14	19	34	11	1	5	6	8
2003-04	Jokerit Helsinki	Finland	53	3	4	7	20	8	0	1	1	4

LESSARD, Junior (leh-SAHRD, JOO-nyuhr) **DAL.**

Right wing/Center. Shoots right. 6', 195 lbs. Born, St-Joseph-de-Beauce, Que., May 26, 1980.

			Regular Season					Playoffs				
Season	**Club**	**League**	**GP**	**G**	**A**	**TP**	**PIM**	**GP**	**G**	**A**	**TP**	**PIM**
99-2000	Portage Terriers	MJHL	60	60	48	108	61	....	....	....	....	....
2000-01	Minnesota-Duluth	WCHA	36	4	8	12	12	....	....	....	....	....
2001-02	Minnesota-Duluth	WCHA	39	17	13	30	50	....	....	....	....	....
2002-03	Minnesota-Duluth	WCHA	40	21	16	37	20	....	....	....	....	....
2003-04	Minnesota-Duluth	WCHA	45	*32	31	*63	34	....	....	....	....	....

WCHA First All-Star Team (2004) • WCHA Player of the Year (2004) • NCAA West First All-American Team (2004) • NCAA Championship All-Tournament Team (2004) • Hobey Baker Memorial Award (Top U.S. Collegiate Player) (2004)

Signed as a free agent by **Dallas**, April 15, 2004.

LEVESQUE, Willie (luh-VEHK, WIHL-lee)

Right wing. Shoots right. 6', 195 lbs. Born, Oak Bluffs, MA, January 22, 1980.
(San Jose's 3rd choice, 111th overall, in 1999 Entry Draft).

			Regular Season					Playoffs				
Season	**Club**	**League**	**GP**	**G**	**A**	**TP**	**PIM**	**GP**	**G**	**A**	**TP**	**PIM**
1997-98	U.S. National U-18	USDP	60	12	24	36	118	....	....	....	....	....
1998-99	Northeastern	H-East	34	12	10	22	38	....	....	....	....	....
99-2000	Northeastern	H-East	33	9	13	22	45	....	....	....	....	....
2000-01	Northeastern	H-East	35	13	16	29	62	....	....	....	....	....
2001-02	Northeastern	H-East	30	6	10	16	42	....	....	....	....	....
2002-03	Cleveland Barons	AHL	64	4	5	9	32	....	....	....	....	....
2003-04	Cleveland Barons	AHL	27	1	2	3	20	7	0	1	1	6
	Johnstown Chiefs	ECHL	31	5	6	11	27	....	....	....	....	....

Hockey East All-Rookie Team (1999)

LEVINSKI, Dimitri (leh-VIHN-skee, DEH-mih-TREE) **CHI.**

Left wing. Shoots left. 6'2", 193 lbs. Born, Ust-Kamenogorsk, USSR, June 23, 1981.
(Chicago's 2nd choice, 46th overall, in 1999 Entry Draft).

			Regular Season					Playoffs				
Season	**Club**	**League**	**GP**	**G**	**A**	**TP**	**PIM**	**GP**	**G**	**A**	**TP**	**PIM**
1996-97	Avangard Omsk 2	Russia-3	15	6	2	8	8	....	....	....	....	....
1997-98	Avangard Omsk 2	Russia-3	18	5	2	7	8	....	....	....	....	....
1998-99	Cherepovets 3	Russia-4	3	2	0	2	2	....	....	....	....	....
	Cherepovets 2	Russia-3	26	4	2	6	39	....	....	....	....	....
	Cherepovets	Russia	1	0	0	0	0	....	....	....	....	....
99-2000	SKA St. Petersburg	Russia	25	0	2	2	4	4	0	0	0	0
2000-01	Khabarovsk 2	Russia-3	22	0	2	2	2	....	....	....	....	....
	Amur Khabarovsk	Russia	19	0	2	2	2	....	....	....	....	....
2001-02	HC CSKA	Russia-2	49	6	2	8	28	....	....	....	....	....
2002-03	SKA St. Petersburg	Russia	21	0	1	1	4	....	....	....	....	....
	Voskresesnsk	Russia	STATISTICS NOT AVAILABLE									
2003-04	Voskresesnsk	Russia	39	7	4	11	4	....	....	....	....	....

LEVOKARI, Pauli (leh-voh-KAHR-ee, PAWL-ee)

Defense. Shoots left. 6'7", 260 lbs. Born, Luvia, Finland, April 7, 1979.
(Atlanta's 10th choice, 257th overall, in 2002 Entry Draft).

			Regular Season					Playoffs				
Season	**Club**	**League**	**GP**	**G**	**A**	**TP**	**PIM**	**GP**	**G**	**A**	**TP**	**PIM**
1993-94	Assat Pori-C	Finn-Jr.	32	1	2	3	50	....	....	....	....	....
1994-95	Assat Pori-C	Finn-Jr.	STATISTICS NOT AVAILABLE									
1995-96	Assat Pori-B	Finn-Jr.	28	5	6	11	42	....	....	....	....	....
	Assat Pori Jr.	Finn-Jr.	10	0	1	1	22	....	....	....	....	....
1996-97	Assat Pori Jr.	Finn-Jr.	35	3	8	11	78	4	0	0	0	10
	Assat Pori	Finland	1	0	0	0	0	....	....	....	....	....
1997-98	Assat Pori Jr.	Finn-Jr.	27	2	5	7	79	....	....	....	....	....
	Assat Pori	Finland	16	0	0	0	0	1	0	0	0	0
1998-99	Assat Pori Jr.	Finn-Jr.	19	4	3	7	68	....	....	....	....	....
	Assat Pori	Finland	27	0	2	2	8	....	....	....	....	....
99-2000	Assat Pori	Finland	51	3	2	5	80	....	....	....	....	....
2000-01	Assat Pori	Finland	12	1	0	1	12	....	....	....	....	....
	Jokerit Helsinki	Finland	10	0	0	0	6	....	....	....	....	....
	Kiekko-Vantaa	Finland-2	22	3	6	9	68	3	0	1	1	6
2001-02	HIFK Helsinki	Finland	29	3	5	8	86	....	....	....	....	....
2002-03	Chicago Wolves	AHL	6	0	1	1	12	....	....	....	....	....
	Greenville Grrrowl	ECHL	4	0	0	0	8	....	....	....	....	....
	Syracuse Crunch	AHL	45	4	6	10	88	....	....	....	....	....
2003-04	Syracuse Crunch	AHL	28	0	3	3	49	....	....	....	....	....
	Wilkes-Barre	AHL	27	3	4	7	54	3	0	0	0	2

Traded to **Columbus** by **Atlanta** with Tomi Kallio for Chris Nielsen and Petteri Nummelin, December 2, 2002. Traded to **Pittsburgh** by **Columbus** for Brendan Buckley, February 10, 2004.

LEWANDOWSKI, Eduard (luh-wan-DOW-skee, EHD-wahrd) **PHX.**

Left wing. Shoots left. 6'1", 205 lbs. Born, Krasnoturjinsk, USSR, May 3, 1980.
(Phoenix's 6th choice, 242nd overall, in 2003 Entry Draft).

			Regular Season					Playoffs				
Season	**Club**	**League**	**GP**	**G**	**A**	**TP**	**PIM**	**GP**	**G**	**A**	**TP**	**PIM**
1997-98	EC Wilhelmshaven	German-3	48	19	12	31	46	....	....	....	....	....
1998-99	EC Wilhelmshaven	German-3	49	35	21	56	96	....	....	....	....	....
99-2000	EC Wilhelmshaven	German-2	48	15	26	41	104	....	....	....	....	....
2000-01	EC Wilhelmshaven	German-2	47	22	30	52	97	....	....	....	....	....
2001-02	Eisbaren Berlin	Germany	59	7	15	22	57	4	0	0	0	2
2002-03	Kolner Haie	Germany	46	6	14	20	46	13	3	3	6	43
2003-04	Kolner Haie	Germany	52	16	17	33	85	5	1	2	3	16

LEWIS, Grant (LOO-ihs, GRANT) **ATL.**

Defense. Shoots right. 6'3", 190 lbs. Born, Pittsburgh, PA, January 20, 1985.
(Atlanta's 2nd choice, 40th overall, in 2004 Entry Draft).

			Regular Season					Playoffs				
Season	**Club**	**League**	**GP**	**G**	**A**	**TP**	**PIM**	**GP**	**G**	**A**	**TP**	**PIM**
2001-02	Pittsburgh Hornets	PHAA	STATISTICS NOT AVAILABLE									
2002-03	Pittsburgh Forge	NAJHL	50	2	7	9	59	....	....	....	....	....
2003-04	Dartmouth	ECAC	34	3	22	25	57	....	....	....	....	....

ECAC All-Rookie Team (2004) • ECAC First All-Star Team (2004)

LIFFITON, David (LIH-fih-tuhn, DAY-vihd) **NYR**

Defense. Shoots left. 6'2", 201 lbs. Born, Windsor, Ont., October 18, 1984.
(Colorado's 1st choice, 63rd overall, in 2003 Entry Draft).

			Regular Season					Playoffs				
Season	**Club**	**League**	**GP**	**G**	**A**	**TP**	**PIM**	**GP**	**G**	**A**	**TP**	**PIM**
2000-01	Aylmer Aces	OJHL-B	51	1	9	10	51	....	....	....	....	....
2001-02	Plymouth Whalers	OHL	62	3	9	12	65	6	0	0	0	0
2002-03	Plymouth Whalers	OHL	64	5	11	16	139	18	1	3	4	29
2003-04	Plymouth Whalers	OHL	44	2	9	11	85	9	0	0	0	12

Traded to **NY Rangers** by **Colorado** with Chris McAllister and Florida's 2nd round choice (previously acquired, later traded back to Florida – Florida selected David Shantz) in 2004 Entry Draft for Matthew Barnaby, and NY Rangers' 3rd round choice (Denis Parshin) in 2004 Entry Draft, March 8, 2004.

LINDSTROM, Andreas (LIHND-struhm, an-DRAY-uhs) **BOS.**

Right wing. Shoots left. 6'5", 210 lbs. Born, Lulea, Sweden, September 1, 1982.
(Boston's 12th choice, 279th overall, in 2000 Entry Draft).

			Regular Season					Playoffs				
Season	**Club**	**League**	**GP**	**G**	**A**	**TP**	**PIM**	**GP**	**G**	**A**	**TP**	**PIM**
99-2000	Lulea HF Jr.	Swede-Jr.	9	2	2	4	14	....	....	....	....	....
2000-01	Lulea HF Jr.	Swede-Jr.	21	8	6	14	18	....	....	....	....	....
	Lulea HF	Sweden	3	0	0	0	0	8	1	0	1	0
2001-02	Lulea HF Jr.	Swede-Jr.	17	5	4	9	40	2	1	0	1	6
	Lulea HF	Sweden	....	....	....	....	....	1	0	0	0	4
2002-03	Bodens IK	Swede-2	35	0	2	2	24	....	....	....	....	....
2003-04	Asploven	Swede-3	33	13	9	22	82	....	....	....	....	....

LINDSTROM, Joakim (LIHND-struhm, YOH-ah-kihm) **CBJ**

Center. Shoots left. 6', 187 lbs. Born, Skelleftea, Sweden, December 5, 1983.
(Columbus' 2nd choice, 41st overall, in 2002 Entry Draft).

			Regular Season					Playoffs				
Season	**Club**	**League**	**GP**	**G**	**A**	**TP**	**PIM**	**GP**	**G**	**A**	**TP**	**PIM**
99-2000	MoDo 18	Swede-Jr.	17	6	*14	20	32	....	....	....	....	....
	MoDo Jr.	Swede-Jr.	10	4	4	8	2	....	....	....	....	....
2000-01	MoDo Jr.	Swede-Jr.	12	7	14	21	46	4	2	3	5	24
	MoDo	Sweden	10	2	3	5	2	7	0	1	1	0
2001-02	MoDo Jr.	Swede-Jr.	10	9	6	15	67	....	....	....	....	....
	IF Troja-Ljungby	Swede-2	3	0	0	0	12	....	....	....	....	....
	MoDo	Sweden	42	4	3	7	20	14	3	5	8	8
2002-03	MoDo	Sweden	29	4	2	6	14	6	1	1	2	2
	MoDo Jr.	Swede-Jr.	2	5	1	6	8	....	....	....	....	....
	Ornskoldsviks SK	Swede-2	2	1	1	2	4	....	....	....	....	....
2003-04	MoDo	Sweden	15	0	2	2	0	....	....	....	....	....
	Sundsvall	Swede-2	2	0	5	5	0	....	....	....	....	....

LINDSTROM, Liam (LIHND-struhm, LEE-uhm) **PHX.**

Center. Shoots left. 6', 189 lbs. Born, Edmonton, Alta., January 12, 1985.
(Phoenix's 3rd choice, 115th overall, in 2003 Entry Draft).

			Regular Season					Playoffs				
Season	**Club**	**League**	**GP**	**G**	**A**	**TP**	**PIM**	**GP**	**G**	**A**	**TP**	**PIM**
2000-01	Mora IK 18	Swede-Jr.	14	3	4	7	14	....	....	....	....	....
	Mora IK Jr.	Swede-Jr.	1	0	0	0	2	1	0	0	0	0
2001-02	Mora IK 18	Swede-Jr.	2	2	0	2	0	1	1	0	1	4
	Mora IK Jr.	Swede-Jr.	25	5	8	13	12	....	....	....	....	....
2002-03	Mora IK 18	Swede-Jr.	4	3	1	4	8	....	....	....	....	....
	Mora IK Jr.	Swede-2	20	3	7	10	57	....	....	....	....	....
	Mora IK	Swede-2	13	0	0	0	0	....	....	....	....	....
	Mora IK	Swede-Q	1	0	0	0	0	....	....	....	....	....
2003-04	Sundsvall	Swede-2	26	0	0	0	4	2	0	0	0	0

LINDSTROM, Sanny (LIHND-struhm, SAN-nee) **COL.**

Defense. Shoots left. 6'2", 205 lbs. Born, Stockholm, Sweden, December 24, 1979.
(Colorado's 4th choice, 112th overall, in 1999 Entry Draft).

			Regular Season					Playoffs				
Season	**Club**	**League**	**GP**	**G**	**A**	**TP**	**PIM**	**GP**	**G**	**A**	**TP**	**PIM**
1997-98	Huddinge IK	Swede-2	32	6	6	12	46	....	....	....	....	....
1998-99	Huddinge IK	Swede-2	37	4	4	8	65	....	....	....	....	....
99-2000	Hershey Bears	AHL	42	1	2	3	57	....	....	....	....	....
	Baton Rouge	ECHL	11	1	2	3	16	....	....	....	....	....
2000-01	Hershey Bears	AHL	24	0	0	0	61	....	....	....	....	....
	Quad City	UHL	5	1	1	2	10	....	....	....	....	....
2001-02	Quad City	UHL	38	4	23	27	71	12	0	3	3	20
	Hershey Bears	AHL	2	0	0	0	0	....	....	....	....	....
2002-03	Timra IK	Sweden	39	1	1	2	81	9	0	1	1	0
2003-04	Timra IK	Sweden	48	1	3	4	91	10	2	0	2	24

• Missed majority of 2000-01 season recovering from knee injury suffered in practice, March 5, 2000.

LINHART, Tomas (LIHN-hart, TAW-mash) **MTL.**

Defense. Shoots left. 6'2", 209 lbs. Born, Pardubice, Czech., February 16, 1984.
(Montreal's 2nd choice, 45th overall, in 2002 Entry Draft).

			Regular Season					Playoffs				
Season	**Club**	**League**	**GP**	**G**	**A**	**TP**	**PIM**	**GP**	**G**	**A**	**TP**	**PIM**
99-2000	Pardubice 18	Czech-Jr.	45	2	8	10	83	....	....	....	....	....
2000-01	Pardubice 18	Czech-Jr.	23	5	7	12	82	....	....	....	....	....
	Pardubice Jr.	Czech-Jr.	29	1	6	7	12	4	0	0	0	0
2001-02	Pardubice Jr.	Czech-Jr.	38	2	4	6	28	....	....	....	....	....
	Sumperk	Czech-2	1	0	0	0	2	....	....	....	....	....
2002-03	Mississauga	OHL	27	0	2	2	12	....	....	....	....	....
	London Knights	OHL	28	0	2	2	18	1	0	0	0	0
2003-04	Pardubice Jr.	Czech-Jr.	24	3	6	9	67	....	....	....	....	....
	Hradec Kralove	Czech-2	24	1	1	2	12	3	0	0	0	0
	Pardubice	Czech	6	0	0	0	0	5	0	0	0	2

LISCAK, Robert **BOS.**

Center. Shoots left. 6', 192 lbs. Born, Skalica, Czech., April 4, 1978.

			Regular Season					Playoffs				
Season	Club	League	GP	G	A	TP	PIM	GP	G	A	TP	PIM
1995-96	HK Skalica Jr.	Slovak-Jr.	49	26	21	47	26	....	....	....	....	....
	HK Skalica	Slovakia-2	3	0	0	0	0	....	....	....	....	....
1996-97	HK Skalica	Slovakia-2	STATISTICS NOT AVAILABLE									
1997-98	Nipawain Hawks	SJHL	63	27	50	77	39	....	....	....	....	....
1998-99	Nipawin Hawks	SJHL	54	27	40	67	93	....	....	....	....	....
99-2000	U. of Maine	H-East	27	6	7	13	30	....	....	....	....	....
2000-01	U. of Maine	H-East	39	11	9	20	36	....	....	....	....	....
2001-02	U. of Maine	H-East	44	17	20	37	32	....	....	....	....	....
2002-03	U. of Maine	H-East	39	12	22	34	42	....	....	....	....	....
	Providence Bruins	AHL	....	....	....	....	....	1	0	0	0	0
2003-04	Providence Bruins	AHL	28	0	4	4	12	....	....	....	....	....
	Augusta Lynx	ECHL	12	0	4	4	10	....	....	....	....	....
	Trenton Titans	ECHL	18	5	6	11	23	....	....	....	....	....

Signed to PTO (Pro Tryout) contract by **Providence** (AHL), April 12, 2003. Signed as a free agent by **Boston**, July 28, 2003.

LISIN, Enver (LIH-sihn, EHN-vuhr) **PHX.**

Right wing. Shoots left. 6'2", 190 lbs. Born, Moscow, USSR, April 22, 1986.
(Phoenix's 3rd choice, 50th overall, in 2004 Entry Draft).

			Regular Season					Playoffs				
Season	Club	League	GP	G	A	TP	PIM	GP	G	A	TP	PIM
2001-02	Dyn. Moscow 2	Russia-3	6	3	0	3	14	....	....	....	....	....
2002-03	Dyn. Moscow 2	Russia-3	STATISTICS NOT AVAILABLE									
	Dyn. Moscow 17	Russia-Jr.	7	3	2	5	6	....	....	....	....	....
2003-04	Dyn. Moscow 2	Russia-3	STATISTICS NOT AVAILABLE									
	Kristall Saratov	Russia-2	35	10	6	16	30	4	1	0	1	0

LITVINENKO, Alexei (liht-vihn-EHN-koh, al-EHX-ay) **PHX.**

Defense. Shoots left. 6'4", 180 lbs. Born, Ust-Kamenogorsk, USSR, March 7, 1980.
(Phoenix's 9th choice, 262nd overall, in 1999 Entry Draft).

			Regular Season					Playoffs				
Season	Club	League	GP	G	A	TP	PIM	GP	G	A	TP	PIM
1997-98	Kamenogorsk 2	Russia-3	12	0	0	0	8	....	....	....	....	....
	Ust-Kamenogorsk	Russia-2	2	0	0	0	0	....	....	....	....	....
1998-99	Kamenogorsk 2	Russia-4	31	3	4	7	52	....	....	....	....	....
	Kamenogorsk 2	Russia-3	16	0	4	4	14	....	....	....	....	....
99-2000	Dynamo Moscow	Russia	7	0	0	0	4	....	....	....	....	....
2000-01	Dynamo Moscow	Russia	6	0	0	0	0	....	....	....	....	....
	Yekaterinburg	Russia	26	0	0	0	42	....	....	....	....	....
2001-02	Magnitogorsk	Russia	20	0	3	3	29	9	1	1	2	20
2002-03	Magnitogorsk	Russia	21	0	2	2	28	....	....	....	....	....
2003-04	Magnitogorsk	Russia	7	0	0	0	8	....	....	....	....	....
	Magnitogorsk 2	Russia-3	6	3	5	8	31	....	....	....	....	....

LOCKE, Corey (LAWK, KOHR-ee) **MTL.**

Center. Shoots left. 5'9", 175 lbs. Born, Toronto, Ont., May 8, 1984.
(Montreal's 5th choice, 113th overall, in 2003 Entry Draft).

			Regular Season					Playoffs				
Season	Club	League	GP	G	A	TP	PIM	GP	G	A	TP	PIM
2000-01	Newmarket	OPJHL	49	34	51	85	16	16	10	12	22	14
2001-02	Ottawa 67's	OHL	55	18	25	43	18	13	6	7	13	10
2002-03	Ottawa 67's	OHL	66	*63	*88	*151	83	23	*19	19	*38	30
2003-04	Ottawa 67's	OHL	65	*51	67	*118	82	7	7	3	10	10

OHL First All-Star Team (2003, 2004) • Canadian Major Junior First All-Star Team (2003, 2004) • OHL Player of the Year (2003, 2004) • Canadian Major Junior Player of the Year (2003)

LOJEK, Martin (LOI-yehk, MAHR-tehn) **FLA.**

Defense. Shoots right. 6'5", 220 lbs. Born, Brno, Czech., August 19, 1985.
(Florida's 5th choice, 105th overall, in 2003 Entry Draft).

			Regular Season					Playoffs				
Season	Club	League	GP	G	A	TP	PIM	GP	G	A	TP	PIM
2000-01	Pardubice Jr.	Czech-Jr.	48	2	2	4	42	7	0	0	0	6
2001-02	Pardubice Jr.	Czech-Jr.	40	2	4	6	24	7	1	0	1	2
2002-03	Brampton	OHL	65	1	13	14	47	11	0	1	1	6
2003-04	Brampton	OHL	68	3	17	20	37	12	0	4	4	2

LOUHIVAARA, Ossi (loo-hih-VAH-rah, AW-see) **OTT.**

Forward. Shoots right. 6', 179 lbs. Born, Kotka, Finland, August 21, 1983.
(Ottawa's 8th choice, 260th overall, in 2003 Entry Draft).

			Regular Season					Playoffs				
Season	Club	League	GP	G	A	TP	PIM	GP	G	A	TP	PIM
99-2000	Titaanit Kotka Jr.	Finn-Jr.	1	0	0	0	0	....	....	....	....	....
2000-01	Titaanit Kotka Jr.	Finn-Jr.	32	10	12	22	10	....	....	....	....	....
	Titaanit Kotka	Finland-2	....	....	....	....	....	2	1	2	3	2
2001-02	Titaanit Kotka Jr.	Finn-Jr.	34	13	14	27	10	3	1	1	2	0
2002-03	KooKoo Kouvola	Finland-2	44	20	15	35	20	9	1	3	4	4
2003-04	KooKoo Kouvola	Finland-2	41	13	17	30	4	9	1	1	2	2

LUCHKIN, Vladislav (LOOCH-kihn, VLA-dih-slav) **CHI.**

Center. Shoots left. 6'1", 185 lbs. Born, Cherepovets, USSR, February 3, 1982.
(Chicago's 11th choice, 225th overall, in 2000 Entry Draft).

			Regular Season					Playoffs				
Season	Club	League	GP	G	A	TP	PIM	GP	G	A	TP	PIM
1997-98	Cherepovets 2	Russia-3	23	2	5	7	12	....	....	....	....	....
1998-99	Cherepovets 2	Russia-3	25	6	4	10	8	....	....	....	....	....
	Cherepovets 3	Russia-4	8	1	3	4	10	....	....	....	....	....
99-2000	Cherepovets 2	Russia-3	30	23	10	33	36	....	....	....	....	....
2000-01	Cherepovets	Russia	28	2	3	5	10	6	2	0	2	4
2001-02	Cherepovets 2	Russia-3	6	5	6	11	0	....	....	....	....	....
	Cherepovets	Russia	27	4	6	10	12	....	....	....	....	....
2002-03	Cherepovets	Russia	2	0	0	0	2	....	....	....	....	....
	SKA St. Petersburg	Russia	4	0	0	0	0	....	....	....	....	....
	Cherepovets 2	Russia-3	12	3	9	12	88	....	....	....	....	....
2003-04	Perm	Russia-2	39	9	17	26	32	13	8	1	9	8

LUKACEVIC, Ned (loo-kuh-SAY-vihk, NEHD) **L.A.**

Left wing. Shoots left. 6', 185 lbs. Born, Podgorica, Serbia, February 11, 1986.
(Los Angeles' 3rd choice, 110th overall, in 2004 Entry Draft).

			Regular Season					Playoffs				
Season	Club	League	GP	G	A	TP	PIM	GP	G	A	TP	PIM
2000-01	Port Coquitlam	BAHA	60	42	48	90	....	....	....	....	....	....
2001-02	Port Coquitlam	BAHA	70	40	55	95	60	....	....	....	....	....
	Spokane Chiefs	WHL	1	1	0	1	0	....	....	....	....	....
2002-03	Spokane Chiefs	WHL	31	0	4	4	29	4	0	1	1	0
2003-04	Spokane Chiefs	WHL	72	19	14	33	65	4	1	1	2	2

LUKES, Frantisek (LOO-kehsh, FRAHN-tih-sehk) **PHX.**

Left wing. Shoots right. 5'9", 173 lbs. Born, Kadan, Czech., September 25, 1982.
(Phoenix's 8th choice, 243rd overall, in 2001 Entry Draft).

			Regular Season					Playoffs				
Season	Club	League	GP	G	A	TP	PIM	GP	G	A	TP	PIM
99-2000	Litvinov Jr.	Czech-Jr.	36	15	13	28	....	....	....	....	....	....
2000-01	St. Michael's	OHL	61	23	33	56	37	18	4	9	13	12
2001-02	St. Michael's	OHL	63	27	37	64	50	15	7	11	18	16
2002-03	St. Michael's	OHL	62	27	46	73	55	19	8	15	23	28
2003-04	Springfield Falcons	AHL	63	8	20	28	30	....	....	....	....	....

LUNDBERG, Eric (LUHND-buhrg, AIR-ihk) **COL.**

Defense. Shoots right. 6'3", 200 lbs. Born, Vernon, CT, April 13, 1983.
(Colorado's 3rd choice, 94th overall, in 2002 Entry Draft).

			Regular Season					Playoffs				
Season	Club	League	GP	G	A	TP	PIM	GP	G	A	TP	PIM
99-2000	New England	EJHL	36	8	36	42	106	....	....	....	....	....
2000-01	New England	EJHL	36	6	28	34	92	10	2	10	12	14
2001-02	Providence College	H-East	36	0	9	9	28	....	....	....	....	....
2002-03	Providence College	H-East	33	0	6	6	30	....	....	....	....	....
2003-04	Providence College	H-East	33	0	6	6	45	....	....	....	....	....

LUNDBOHM, Bryan (LUHND-bawm, BRIGH-uhn)

Right wing. Shoots left. 5'10", 184 lbs. Born, Roseau, MN, August 24, 1977.

			Regular Season					Playoffs				
Season	Club	League	GP	G	A	TP	PIM	GP	G	A	TP	PIM
1996-97	Lincoln Stars	USHL	52	13	33	45	33	14	8	4	12	33
1997-98	Lincoln Stars	USHL	55	26	38	64	10	9	2	7	9	0
1998-99	North Dakota	WCHA	32	2	9	11	4	....	....	....	....	....
99-2000	North Dakota	WCHA	44	22	22	44	14	....	....	....	....	....
2000-01	North Dakota	WCHA	46	*32	27	69	38	....	....	....	....	....
2001-02	Milwaukee	AHL	79	11	23	34	63	....	....	....	....	....
2002-03	Milwaukee	AHL	80	9	17	26	63	6	1	5	6	0
2003-04	Milwaukee	AHL	28	6	8	14	8	....	....	....	....	....

USHL First All-Star Team (1998) • WCHA First All-Star Team (2001) • NCAA West Second All-American Team (2001) • NCAA Championship All-Tournament Team (2001)

Signed as a free agent by **Nashville**, May 1, 2001. Signed as a free agent by **Milwaukee** (AHL), November 25, 2003. • Missed majority of 2003-04 season recovering from groin injury suffered in game vs. Philadelphia (AHL), January 31, 2004.

LUNDIN, Mike (LUHN-dihn, MIGHK) **T.B.**

Defense. Shoots left. 6'2", 180 lbs. Born, Burnsville, MN, September 24, 1984.
(Tampa Bay's 3rd choice, 102nd overall, in 2004 Entry Draft).

			Regular Season					Playoffs				
Season	Club	League	GP	G	A	TP	PIM	GP	G	A	TP	PIM
2002-03	Apple Valley	Hi-School	27	8	20	27	....	....	....	....	....	....
2003-04	U. of Maine	H-East	44	3	16	19	34	....	....	....	....	....

LUNDQVIST, Joel (LOOND-kvihst, JOHL) **DAL.**

Center. Shoots left. 6', 185 lbs. Born, Are, Sweden, March 2, 1982.
(Dallas' 3rd choice, 68th overall, in 2000 Entry Draft).

			Regular Season					Playoffs				
Season	Club	League	GP	G	A	TP	PIM	GP	G	A	TP	PIM
1997-98	Rogle Jr.	Swede-Jr.	59	36	40	76	....	....	....	....	....	....
1998-99	V. Frolunda 18	Swede-Jr.	32	26	38	64	37	4	3	1	4	2
99-2000	V. Frolunda 18	Swede-Jr.	4	2	4	6	4	....	....	....	....	....
	V. Frolunda Jr.	Swede-Jr.	25	7	12	19	2	6	2	3	5	2
2000-01	V. Frolunda Jr.	Swede-Jr.	18	14	27	41	12	....	....	....	....	....
	Molndals HS	Swede-2	26	18	13	31	22	....	....	....	....	....
	Vastra Frolunda	Sweden	9	0	0	0	0	....	....	....	....	....
2001-02	Vastra Frolunda	Sweden	46	12	14	26	28	10	1	3	4	8
	V. Frolunda Jr.	Swede-Jr.	....	....	....	....	....	1	0	0	0	0
2002-03	Vastra Frolunda	Sweden	50	17	20	37	113	16	6	3	9	12
2003-04	Vastra Frolunda	Sweden	49	9	14	23	48	10	2	2	4	8

LUNDQVIST, Stefan (LUHND-kvihst, STEH-fan) **NYR**

Right wing. Shoots left. 6'3", 209 lbs. Born, Gavle, Sweden, February 18, 1978.
(NY Rangers' 7th choice, 180th overall, in 1998 Entry Draft).

			Regular Season					Playoffs				
Season	Club	League	GP	G	A	TP	PIM	GP	G	A	TP	PIM
1994-95	Avesta BK	Swede-2	3	0	1	1	0	....	....	....	....	....
1995-96	Avesta BK	Swede-3	27	24	13	37	10	....	....	....	....	....
1996-97	Avesta BK	Swede-3	31	37	29	66	....	....	....	....	....	....
1997-98	Brynas IF Gavle jr.	Swede-Jr.	21	23	15	38	2	....	....	....	....	....
	Brynas IF Gavle	Sweden	27	2	2	4	0	1	0	0	0	0
1998-99	Brynas IF Gavle	Sweden	13	0	0	0	0	....	....	....	....	....
	Uppsala	Swede-2	15	7	8	15	0	....	....	....	....	....
	Mora IK	Swede-2	23	10	7	17	22	4	2	2	4	2
99-2000	Brynas IF Gavle	Sweden	48	6	4	10	12	11	1	0	1	0
	Brynas IF Gavle	EuroHL	6	1	1	2	2	....	....	....	....	....
2000-01	Skelleftea AIK	Swede-2	35	21	11	32	14	1	0	0	0	0
2001-02	Skelleftea AIK	Swede-2	40	28	14	42	20	5	1	0	1	4
2002-03	Vasteras	Swede-2	40	23	14	37	12	....	....	....	....	....
2003-04	Avesta BK	Swede-4	13	21	15	36	6	....	....	....	....	....

LUTTINEN, Arttu (LOO-tuh-nehn, AHR-too) **OTT.**

Left wing. Shoots left. 5'10", 205 lbs. Born, Helsinki, Finland, September 9, 1983.
(Ottawa's 3rd choice, 75th overall, in 2002 Entry Draft).

			Regular Season					Playoffs				
Season	Club	League	GP	G	A	TP	PIM	GP	G	A	TP	PIM
99-2000	HIFK Helsinki Jr.	Finn-Jr.	17	5	9	14	10	2	0	0	0	2
2000-01	HIFK Helsinki-B	Finn-Jr.	20	14	20	34	141	....	....	....	....	....
	HIFK Helsinki Jr.	Finn-Jr.	8	4	2	6	4	8	0	1	1	2
2001-02	HIFK Helsinki Jr.	Finn-Jr.	24	16	17	23	60	1	0	0	0	0
2002-03	HIFK Helsinki	Finland	41	4	4	8	10	1	0	0	0	0
	HIFK Helsinki Jr.	Finn-Jr.	10	8	9	17	52	8	4	6	10	20
2003-04	HIFK Helsinki	Finland	50	1	7	8	12	12	0	0	0	0

LYAMIN, Kirill (L'YAH-mihn, kih-RIHL) **OTT.**

Defense. Shoots left. 6'2", 208 lbs. Born, Moscow, USSR, January 13, 1986.
(Ottawa's 2nd choice, 58th overall, in 2004 Entry Draft).

			Regular Season					Playoffs				
Season	Club	League	GP	G	A	TP	PIM	GP	G	A	TP	PIM
2001-02	CSKA Moscow 18	Russia-Jr.	7	1	1	2	4	....	....	....	....	....
	Team Moscow 18	Exhib.	5	0	3	3	4	....	....	....	....	....
2002-03	CSKA Moscow 2	Russia-3	5	0	0	0	10	....	....	....	....	....
	CSKA Moscow 18	Russia-Jr.	6	0	2	2	4	....	....	....	....	....
	Team Moscow 18	Exhib.	5	0	0	0	6	....	....	....	....	....
2003-04	CSKA Moscow 2	Russia-3	STATISTICS NOT AVAILABLE									
	CSKA Moscow	Russia	28	0	3	3	12	....	....	....	....	....

LYNCH, Darren (LIHNCH, DAIR-uhn) CGY.

Right wing. Shoots right. 5'11", 175 lbs. Born, Regina, Sask., July 7, 1983.

			Regular Season					Playoffs				
Season	Club	League	GP	G	A	TP	PIM	GP	G	A	TP	PIM
1998-99	Reg. Pat Canadians	SMHL	44	33	30	63	20	....	....	....	....	....
	Lethbridge	WHL	1	0	0	0	2	....	....	....	....	....
99-2000	Lethbridge	WHL	50	3	5	8	19	....	....	....	....	....
2000-01	Lethbridge	WHL	27	4	4	8	9	5	0	1	1	14
2001-02	Vancouver Giants	WHL	72	30	31	61	51	....	....	....	....	....
2002-03	Vancouver Giants	WHL	70	29	53	82	44	4	0	0	0	6
2003-04	Vancouver Giants	WHL	71	22	37	59	51	11	5	4	9	6

Signed as a free agent by **Calgary**, September 27, 2002.

LYNCH, Paul (LIHNCH, PAWL) T.B.

Defense. Shoots left. 6'2", 195 lbs. Born, Salem, MA, April 23, 1982.
(Tampa Bay's 6th choice, 138th overall, in 2001 Entry Draft).

			Regular Season					Playoffs				
Season	Club	League	GP	G	A	TP	PIM	GP	G	A	TP	PIM
99-2000	Brooks High	Hi-School	23	21	25	46	34	....	....	....	....	....
2000-01	Valley Juniors	EJHL	21	3	4	7	143	....	....	....	....	....
2001-02	U. of Maine	H-East	22	2	4	6	24	....	....	....	....	....
2002-03	U. of Maine	H-East	10	0	3	3	6	....	....	....	....	....
2003-04	Massachusetts	H-East	DID NOT PLAY – TRANSFERRED COLLEGES									

Transferred from **U. of Maine** (H-East) to **U. Massachusetts** (H-East), September 10, 2003.

LYUBUSHIN, Mikhail (l'yoo-BOOSH-ihn, mih-kigh-EHL) L.A.

Defense. Shoots left. 6'1", 183 lbs. Born, Moscow, USSR, July 24, 1983.
(Los Angeles' 9th choice, 215th overall, in 2002 Entry Draft).

			Regular Season					Playoffs				
Season	Club	League	GP	G	A	TP	PIM	GP	G	A	TP	PIM
99-2000	Podolsk 2	Russia-3	24	2	2	4	69	....	....	....	....	....
2000-01	Krylja Sovetov	Russia-2	2	0	1	1	0	1	0	0	0	0
2001-02	Krylja Sovetov 2	Russia-3	20	3	6	9	24	....	....	....	....	....
	THC Tver	Russia-2	22	1	0	1	18	....	....	....	....	....
	Krylja Sovetov	Russia	13	0	1	1	14	3	0	0	0	0
2002-03	Krylja Sovetov	Russia	49	0	6	6	26	....	....	....	....	....
2003-04	Dynamo Moscow	Russia	38	1	2	3	18	2	0	0	0	2

MAATTA, Tero (MAH-tuh, TEH-roh) S.J.

Defense. Shoots left. 6'1", 220 lbs. Born, Vantaa, Finland, January 2, 1982.
(San Jose's 1st choice, 41st overall, in 2000 Entry Draft).

			Regular Season					Playoffs				
Season	Club	League	GP	G	A	TP	PIM	GP	G	A	TP	PIM
1996-97	Kiekko Vantaa-C	Finn-Jr.	20	2	6	8	6	....	....	....	....	....
	Haukat-C	Finn-Jr.	8	3	1	4	10	....	....	....	....	....
1997-98	Jokerit Helsinki-B	Finn-Jr.	28	4	7	11	10	2	0	0	0	2
1998-99	Jokerit Helsinki Jr.	Finn-Jr.	38	4	8	12	75	8	1	3	4	6
99-2000	Jokerit Helsinki-B	Finn-Jr.	13	4	10	14	24	1	0	0	0	25
	Jokerit Helsinki Jr.	Finn-Jr.	31	4	4	8	53	....	....	....	....	....
2000-01	Blues Espoo Jr.	Finn-Jr.	6	0	1	1	6	....	....	....	....	....
	KJT Jarvenpaa	Finland-2	6	0	3	3	31	....	....	....	....	....
	Blues Espoo	Finland	44	4	4	8	24	....	....	....	....	....
2001-02	Blues Espoo Jr.	Finn-Jr.	8	2	6	8	2	....	....	....	....	....
	Blues Espoo	Finland	51	4	6	10	65	3	0	0	0	0
2002-03	Assat Pori	Finland	7	0	0	0	29	....	....	....	....	....
	Blues Espoo	Finland	43	0	3	3	56	7	0	1	1	4
2003-04	Blues Espoo	Finland	56	1	14	15	41	9	0	1	1	8

MacARTHUR, Clarke (muh-KAR-thuhr, KLAHRK) BUF.

Left wing. Shoots left. 6', 180 lbs. Born, Lloydminster, Alta., April 6, 1985.
(Buffalo's 3rd choice, 74th overall, in 2003 Entry Draft).

			Regular Season					Playoffs				
Season	Club	League	GP	G	A	TP	PIM	GP	G	A	TP	PIM
99-2000	Lloydminster	CABHL	24	19	45	64	51	5	9	6	15	4
2000-01	Strathcona	AMBHL	38	36	63	99	44	8	6	2	8	10
2001-02	Drayton Valley	AJHL	61	22	40	62	33	16	5	8	13	34
2002-03	Medicine Hat	WHL	70	23	52	75	104	11	3	6	9	8
2003-04	Medicine Hat	WHL	62	35	40	75	93	20	8	10	18	16

Memorial Cup All-Star Team (2004)

MACHO, Michal (MA-khoh, MEE-khahl) S.J.

Center. Shoots right. 6'1", 170 lbs. Born, Martin, Czech., January 17, 1982.
(San Jose's 5th choice, 183rd overall, in 2000 Entry Draft).

			Regular Season					Playoffs				
Season	Club	League	GP	G	A	TP	PIM	GP	G	A	TP	PIM
1995-96	MHC Martin 18	Czech-Jr.	12	0	6	6	2	....	....	....	....	....
1996-97	MHC Martin 18	Czech-Jr.	52	43	44	87	50	....	....	....	....	....
1997-98	MHC Martin 18	Slovak-Jr.	46	41	54	95	58	....	....	....	....	....
	MHC Martin Jr.	Czech-Jr.	9	3	4	7	0	....	....	....	....	....
1998-99	King's Edge Hill	Hi-School	50	45	55	100	....	....	....	....	....	....
	MHC Martin Jr.	Czech-Jr.	2	2	3	5	0	....	....	....	....	....
99-2000	MHC Martin Jr.	Slovak-Jr.	30	38	44	82	....	....	....	....	....	....
	MHC Martin	Slovak-2	8	1	5	6	4	....	....	....	....	....
2000-01	MHC Martin	Slovakia	37	5	10	15	12	3	1	1	2	2
2001-02	MHC Martin	Slovakia	40	12	8	20	20	....	....	....	....	....
2002-03	Slov. Bratislava	Slovakia	51	5	4	9	26	12	1	0	1	0
2003-04	Slov. Bratislava	Slovakia	33	7	7	14	14	12	5	3	8	26

MacKENZIE, Aaron (muh-KEHN-zee, AIR-ruhn) ST.L.

Defense. Shoots left. 6', 193 lbs. Born, Terrace Bay, Ont., March 7, 1981.

			Regular Season					Playoffs				
Season	Club	League	GP	G	A	TP	PIM	GP	G	A	TP	PIM
1998-99	Thunder Bay Flyers	USHL	49	8	12	20	123	3	0	1	1	0
99-2000	U. of Denver	WCHA	40	1	9	10	56	....	....	....	....	....
2000-01	U. of Denver	WCHA	37	2	6	8	45	....	....	....	....	....
2001-02	U. of Denver	WCHA	39	5	18	23	30	....	....	....	....	....
2002-03	U. of Denver	WCHA	41	11	21	32	33	....	....	....	....	....
2003-04	Worcester IceCats	AHL	66	5	9	14	108	10	0	2	2	10

WCHA First All-Star Team (2003)

Signed as a free agent by **Worcester** (AHL), October 6, 2003. Signed as a free agent by **St. Louis**, June 29, 2004.

MacLEAN, Cail (mihk-LAYN, KAYL)

Right wing. Shoots right. 6', 205 lbs. Born, Middleton, N.S., September 30, 1976.

			Regular Season					Playoffs				
Season	Club	League	GP	G	A	TP	PIM	GP	G	A	TP	PIM
1993-94	Kingston	OHL	53	7	7	14	15	1	0	0	0	0
1994-95	Kingston	OHL	65	11	17	28	17	6	0	0	0	0
1995-96	Kingston	OHL	66	15	37	52	53	6	2	2	4	2
1996-97	Kingston	OHL	60	34	42	76	47	5	1	1	2	2
1997-98	Jacksonville	ECHL	66	30	35	65	44	....	....	....	....	....
	Cleveland	IHL	1	0	0	0	0	....	....	....	....	....
	Cincinnati	AHL	7	0	1	1	4	....	....	....	....	....
1998-99	Jacksonville	ECHL	40	29	28	57	14	....	....	....	....	....
	Indianapolis Ice	IHL	35	13	7	20	20	7	2	2	4	0
99-2000	Trenton Titans	ECHL	50	34	25	59	24	14	10	5	15	6
	Michigan K-Wings	IHL	14	0	3	3	6	....	....	....	....	....
	Lowell	AHL	5	0	1	1	0	....	....	....	....	....
	Philadelphia	AHL	3	0	0	0	0	....	....	....	....	....
2000-01	Trenton Titans	ECHL	49	28	17	45	26	19	13	4	17	10
	Grand Rapids	IHL	16	2	0	2	0	....	....	....	....	....
	Philadelphia	AHL	9	0	1	1	4	....	....	....	....	....
2001-02	Providence Bruins	AHL	9	1	0	1	0	....	....	....	....	....
	Hartford Wolf Pack	AHL	1	0	0	0	0	....	....	....	....	....
	Trenton Titans	ECHL	41	17	17	34	18	....	....	....	....	....
	Lowell	AHL	3	0	1	1	0	....	....	....	....	....
	Hershey Bears	AHL	21	4	6	10	4	6	0	0	0	0
2002-03	Hershey Bears	AHL	74	16	13	29	14	5	0	0	0	0
2003-04	Bridgeport	AHL	61	6	10	16	16	7	1	0	1	0

Signed as a free agent by **NY Islanders**, July 22, 2003.

MacMURCHY, Ryan (mak-MUHR-chee, RIGH-uhn) ST.L.

Right wing. Shoots right. 5'11", 190 lbs. Born, Regina, Sask., April 27, 1983.
(St. Louis' 9th choice, 284th overall, in 2002 Entry Draft).

			Regular Season					Playoffs				
Season	Club	League	GP	G	A	TP	PIM	GP	G	A	TP	PIM
1998-99	Regina Capitals	SMHL	40	18	15	33	....	....	....	....	....	....
99-2000	Regina Capitals	SMHL	38	23	44	67	....	....	....	....	....	....
2000-01	Vernon Vipers	BCHL	30	4	6	10	....	....	....	....	....	....
2001-02	Notre Dame	AJHL	61	32	52	84	63	11	2	5	7	13
2002-03	U. of Wisconsin	WCHA	39	10	14	24	69	....	....	....	....	....
2003-04	U. of Wisconsin	WCHA	43	15	13	28	95	....	....	....	....	....

MAKELA, Tuukka (MA-kuh-luh TUH-kuh) BOS.

Defense. Shoots left. 6'3", 202 lbs. Born, Helsinki, Finland, May 24, 1982.
(Boston's 5th choice, 66th overall, in 2000 Entry Draft).

			Regular Season					Playoffs				
Season	Club	League	GP	G	A	TP	PIM	GP	G	A	TP	PIM
1997-98	HIFK Helsinki Jr.	Finn-Jr.	5	0	0	0	4	....	....	....	....	....
1998-99	HIFK Helsinki Jr.	Finn-Jr.	32	1	1	2	20	3	0	1	1	0
99-2000	HIFK Helsinki Jr.	Finn-Jr.	36	2	5	7	22	2	0	0	0	0
2000-01	Montreal Rocket	QMJHL	9	2	1	3	14	....	....	....	....	....
2001-02	HPK-Jr.	Finn-Jr.	12	3	0	3	26	7	2	2	4	18
	HPK Hameenlinna	Finland	49	2	3	5	44	8	0	0	0	10
2002-03	HPK Hameenlinna	Finland	52	1	5	6	86	13	0	0	0	14
2003-04	HPK Hameenlinna	Finland	54	3	1	4	44	8	0	1	1	6

• Missed majority of 2000-01 season recovering from head injury suffered in game vs. Rouyn-Noranda (QMJHL), September 20, 2000.

MAKI, Tomi (MA-kee, TAW-mee) CGY.

Right wing. Shoots left. 5'11", 172 lbs. Born, Helsinki, Finland, August 19, 1983.
(Calgary's 4th choice, 108th overall, in 2001 Entry Draft).

			Regular Season					Playoffs				
Season	Club	League	GP	G	A	TP	PIM	GP	G	A	TP	PIM
1997-98	Jokerit Helsinki-C	Finn-Jr.	4	0	1	1	0	2	0	0	0	0
1998-99	Jokerit Helsinki-C	Finn-Jr.	32	20	22	42	40	....	....	....	....	....
99-2000	Jokerit Helsinki Jr.	Finn-Jr.	33	6	1	7	12	3	0	0	0	0
2000-01	Jokerit Helsinki-B	Finn-Jr.	10	4	9	13	4	6	4	3	7	0
	Jokerit Helsinki Jr.	Finn-Jr.	39	7	8	15	10	2	0	0	0	2
2001-02	Jokerit Helsinki Jr.	Finn-Jr.	29	12	13	25	12	1	0	0	0	2
	Kiekko Vantaa	Finland-2	5	0	0	0	0	....	....	....	....	....
	Jokerit Helsinki	Finland	8	0	1	1	2	....	....	....	....	....
2002-03	Jokerit Helsinki	Finland	18	2	2	4	4	1	0	0	0	0
	Jokerit Helsinki Jr.	Finn-Jr.	14	4	4	8	12	11	3	3	6	4
	Kiekko-Vantaa	Finland-2	5	0	0	0	0	....	....	....	....	....
2003-04	Jokerit Helsinki	Finland	50	5	5	10	14	8	0	0	0	0

MALENKYKH, Vladimir (MAH-lihn-keh, vla-DIH-meer) PIT.

Defense. Shoots left. 6'1", 190 lbs. Born, Togliatti, USSR, October 1, 1980.
(Pittsburgh's 7th choice, 157th overall, in 1999 Entry Draft).

			Regular Season					Playoffs				
Season	Club	League	GP	G	A	TP	PIM	GP	G	A	TP	PIM
1997-98	Lada Togliatti 2	Russia-3	39	6	4	10	112	....	....	....	....	....
1998-99	Lada Togliatti 2	Russia-4	38	6	3	9	68	....	....	....	....	....
	Lada Togliatti	Russia	9	0	0	0	2	....	....	....	....	....
99-2000	Lada Togliatti 2	Russia-3	34	7	9	16	98	....	....	....	....	....
	CSK VVS Samara	Russia	7	0	1	1	14	....	....	....	....	....
	Lada Togliatti	Russia	1	0	0	0	0	....	....	....	....	....
	CSK VVS Samara 2	Russia-3	1	0	1	1	2	....	....	....	....	....
2000-01	Lada Togliatti	Russia	25	1	1	2	14	5	0	0	0	26
2001-02	Lada Togliatti	Russia	47	5	4	9	88	4	0	0	0	2
2002-03	Lada Togliatti	Russia	30	3	1	4	36	10	0	0	0	6
2003-04	Lada Togliatti	Russia	44	2	4	6	42	3	0	0	0	0

MALKIN, Evgeni (MAHL-kihn, ehv-GEH-nee) PIT.

Center. Shoots left. 6'3", 186 lbs. Born, Magnitogorsk, USSR, July 31, 1986.
(Pittsburgh's 1st choice, 2nd overall, in 2004 Entry Draft).

			Regular Season					Playoffs				
Season	Club	League	GP	G	A	TP	PIM	GP	G	A	TP	PIM
2003-04	Magnitogorsk 2	Russia-3	2	1	0	1	8	....	....	....	....	....
	Magnitogorsk	Russia	34	3	9	12	12	....	....	....	....	....

MALMIVAARA, Olli (mal-MIH-vah-ruh, OH-lee) CHI.

Defense. Shoots left. 6'7", 220 lbs. Born, Kajaani, Finland, March 13, 1982.
(Chicago's 6th choice, 117th overall, in 2000 Entry Draft).

			Regular Season					Playoffs				
Season	Club	League	GP	G	A	TP	PIM	GP	G	A	TP	PIM
1998-99	Jokerit Helsinki-B	Finn-Jr.	35	1	8	9	10	7	0	0	0	2
99-2000	Jokerit Helsinki-B	Finn-Jr.	8	3	4	7	8	1	0	0	0	2
	Jokerit Helsinki Jr.	Finn-Jr.	27	3	3	6	12	12	0	2	2	2
2000-01	Jokerit Helsinki Jr.	Finn-Jr.	33	10	13	23	24	2	0	0	0	0
	Kiekko Vantaa	Finland-2	4	1	0	1	2	....	....	....	....	....
	Jokerit Helsinki	Finland	5	0	0	0	2	....	....	....	....	....
2001-02	Jokerit Helsinki Jr.	Finn-Jr.	2	0	1	1	0	....	....	....	....	....
	Jokerit Helsinki	Finland	53	0	6	6	16	11	0	0	0	2
2002-03	Jokerit Helsinki	Finland	42	1	0	1	22	5	0	0	0	0
	Kiekko Vantaa	Finland-2	2	1	1	2	2	....	....	....	....	....
2003-04	Jokerit Helsinki	Finland	25	1	0	1	2	....	....	....	....	....
	SaiPa	Finland	11	1	0	1	6	....	....	....	....	....

MALONEY, Brian (muh-LOH-nee, BRIGH-uhn) ATL.

Left wing. Shoots left. 6'1", 205 lbs. Born, Bassano, Alta., September 27, 1978.

			Regular Season					Playoffs				
Season	Club	League	GP	G	A	TP	PIM	GP	G	A	TP	PIM
1997-98	Old Grizzlys	AJHL	31	21	13	34	....	....	....	....	....	....
	Chilliwack	BCHL	27	4	12	16	36	....	....	....	....	....
1998-99	Chilliwack	BCHL	60	40	75	115	121	....	....	....	....	....
99-2000	Michigan State	CCHA	42	12	19	31	87	....	....	....	....	....
2000-01	Michigan State	CCHA	41	15	22	37	86	....	....	....	....	....
2001-02	Michigan State	CCHA	37	17	16	33	71	....	....	....	....	....
2002-03	Michigan State	CCHA	39	19	16	35	48	....	....	....	....	....
	Chicago Wolves	AHL	4	0	1	1	11	....	....	....	....	....
2003-04	Chicago Wolves	AHL	69	9	11	20	56	10	1	1	2	17

Signed as a free agent by **Atlanta**, April 2, 2003.

MANSON, Lane (MAN-suhn, LAYN) ATL.

Defense. Shoots left. 6'8", 265 lbs. Born, Watrous, Sask., February 14, 1984.
(Atlanta's 4th choice, 124th overall, in 2002 Entry Draft).

			Regular Season					Playoffs				
Season	Club	League	GP	G	A	TP	PIM	GP	G	A	TP	PIM
99-2000	North Battleford	SMBHL	41	7	12	19	110	....	....	....	....	....
2000-01	North Battleford	MMHL	40	14	12	26	180	....	....	....	....	....
2001-02	Moose Jaw	WHL	67	4	3	7	88	12	0	1	1	6
2002-03	Moose Jaw	WHL	66	0	5	5	192	13	0	0	0	12
2003-04	Moose Jaw	WHL	72	3	9	12	253	10	0	2	2	18

MANTYLA, Tuukka (man-TYEW-la, TOO-OO-kuh) L.A.

Defense. Shoots left. 5'9", 172 lbs. Born, Tampere, Finland, May 25, 1981.
(Los Angeles' 8th choice, 153rd overall, in 2001 Entry Draft).

			Regular Season					Playoffs				
Season	Club	League	GP	G	A	TP	PIM	GP	G	A	TP	PIM
1995-96	Tappara C	Finn-Jr.	32	2	2	4	28	....	....	....	....	....
1996-97	Tappara C	Finn-Jr.	32	12	25	37	52	4	1	2	3	4
	Tappara B	Finn-Jr.	2	0	0	0	2	....	....	....	....	....
1997-98	Tappara B	Finn-Jr.	31	2	23	25	49	....	....	....	....	....
	Tappara Jr.	Finn-Jr.	2	0	0	0	0	6	0	0	0	4
1998-99	Tappara B	Finn-Jr.	10	4	4	8	42	....	....	....	....	....
	Tappara Jr.	Finn-Jr.	34	5	13	18	42	....	....	....	....	....
99-2000	Tappara Jr.	Finn-Jr.	7	2	5	7	22	5	2	5	7	4
	Tappara Tampere	Finland	43	2	8	10	16	4	0	0	0	0
2000-01	Tappara Tampere	Finland	53	6	14	20	32	10	2	2	4	10
2001-02	Tappara Tampere	Finland	56	5	10	15	70	10	2	4	6	8
2002-03	Tappara Tampere	Finland	54	3	19	22	58	15	0	2	2	6
2003-04	Lulea HF	Sweden	43	6	10	16	67	5	0	0	0	2

MANTYMAA, Ville (man-T'YUH-mah, VIHL-ee) ANA.

Defense. Shoots right. 6'3", 183 lbs. Born, Seinajoki, Finland, March 8, 1985.
(Anaheim's 9th choice, 280th overall, in 2003 Entry Draft).

			Regular Season					Playoffs				
Season	Club	League	GP	G	A	TP	PIM	GP	G	A	TP	PIM
1998-99	S-Kiekko C	Finn-Jr.	3	0	0	0	2	....	....	....	....	....
99-2000	S-Kiekko C	Finn-Jr.	8	0	0	0	0	....	....	....	....	....
2000-01	Tapp. Tampere B	Finn-Jr.	2	0	0	0	0	....	....	....	....	....
	Tapp. Tampere C	Finn-Jr.	13	1	2	3	14	4	0	1	1	4
2001-02	Tapp. Tampere B	Finn-Jr.	1	0	0	0	2	....	....	....	....	....
	Tapp. Tampere Jr.	Finn-Jr.	32	4	2	6	24	....	....	....	....	....
2002-03	Tappara Tampere	Finland	8	0	0	0	0	1	0	0	0	0
	Tappara Tampere	Finland	8	0	0	0	0	1	0	0	0	0
2003-04	Pelicans Lahti	Finland	2	0	0	0	0	....	....	....	....	....
	Tappara Tampere	Finland	19	0	2	2	8	....	....	....	....	....
	Tappara Jr.	Finn-Jr.	21	1	7	8	14	14	0	3	3	8

MAREK, Jan (MAIR-ehk, YAHN) NYR

Center. Shoots right. 5'10", 178 lbs. Born, Jindrichuv Hradec, Czech., December 31, 1979.
(NY Rangers' 10th choice, 243rd overall, in 2003 Entry Draft).

			Regular Season					Playoffs				
Season	Club	League	GP	G	A	TP	PIM	GP	G	A	TP	PIM
1998-99	HC Trinec	Czech.	32	2	2	4	2	6	0	0	0	0
99-2000	HC Trinec Jr.	Czech-Jr.	6	5	5	10	10	1	0	0	0	0
	HC Opava	Czech-2	3	0	1	1	4	....	....	....	....	....
	HC Hradec	Czech-2	4	0	3	3	10	....	....	....	....	....
	HC Hradec	Czech-Q	2	0	1	1	12	....	....	....	....	....
	HC Trinec	Czech.	32	1	5	6	4	2	0	0	0	0
2000-01	HC Trinec	Czech.	38	7	4	11	2	....	....	....	....	....
2001-02	HC Ocelari Trinec	Czech.	52	13	27	40	44	6	1	3	4	6
2002-03	HC Ocelari Trinec	Czech	51	*32	30	62	42	12	6	4	10	22
2003-04	HC Sparta Praha	Czech	50	21	30	51	62	11	4	9	13	26

MARJAMAKI, Masi (mahr-juh-MA-kee, MAH-see) BOS.

Left wing. Shoots left. 6'2", 184 lbs. Born, Pori, Finland, January 16, 1985.
(Boston's 3rd choice, 66th overall, in 2003 Entry Draft).

			Regular Season					Playoffs				
Season	Club	League	GP	G	A	TP	PIM	GP	G	A	TP	PIM
2001-02	Assat Pori Jr.	Finn-Jr.	25	6	16	22	93	6	3	3	6	4
2002-03	Red Deer Rebels	WHL	65	15	20	35	56	23	1	2	3	20
2003-04	Red Deer Rebels	WHL	28	6	8	14	46	....	....	....	....	....
	Moose Jaw	WHL	35	15	10	25	57	10	1	3	4	15

MARS, Per (MAHRZ, PAIR) CBJ

Center. Shoots left. 6'3", 210 lbs. Born, Ostersund, Sweden, October 23, 1982.
(Columbus' 5th choice, 87th overall, in 2001 Entry Draft).

			Regular Season					Playoffs				
Season	Club	League	GP	G	A	TP	PIM	GP	G	A	TP	PIM
2000-01	Brynas IF Gavle jr.	Swede-Jr.	23	7	7	14	62	....	....	....	....	....
	Brynas IF Gavle	Sweden	6	0	0	0	0	2	0	0	0	0
2001-02	Brynas IF Gavle	Sweden	12	0	0	0	14	....	....	....	....	....
	Tierp HK	Swede-2	29	1	4	5	22	11	1	0	1	35
2002-03	Brynas IF Gavle	Sweden	7	0	0	0	2	....	....	....	....	....
	Lincoln Stars	USHL	42	9	9	18	60	9	1	2	3	14
2003-04	IF Bjorkloven Umea	Swede-2	46	4	1	5	67	....	....	....	....	....

MARSH, Tyson (MAHRSH, TIGH-suhn) TOR.

Defense. Shoots left. 6'1", 190 lbs. Born, Quesnel, B.C, June 20, 1984.

			Regular Season					Playoffs				
Season	Club	League	GP	G	A	TP	PIM	GP	G	A	TP	PIM
2000-01	Quesnel	BCHL	52	4	2	6	25	....	....	....	....	....
2001-02	Vancouver Giants	WHL	69	2	14	16	85	....	....	....	....	....
2002-03	Vancouver Giants	WHL	68	3	15	18	143	3	0	1	1	4
2003-04	Vancouver Giants	WHL	67	3	18	21	102	11	0	3	3	4

Signed as a free agent by **Toronto**, September 18, 2002.

MARTTINEN, Jyri (MAHR-tih-nehn, YUHR-ee) CGY.

Defense. Shoots left. 5'11", 190 lbs. Born, Tikkakoski, Finland, September 1, 1982.
(Calgary's 12th choice, 238th overall, in 2002 Entry Draft).

			Regular Season					Playoffs				
Season	Club	League	GP	G	A	TP	PIM	GP	G	A	TP	PIM
1997-98	JYP Jyvaskyla C	Finn-Jr.	22	2	3	5	34	....	....	....	....	....
1998-99	JYP Jyvaskyla B	Finn-Jr.	22	1	3	4	12	5	0	0	0	0
99-2000	JYP Jyvaskyla B	Finn-Jr.	14	7	4	11	22	....	....	....	....	....
	JyP Jyvaskyla	Finn-Jr.	3	0	0	0	2	....	....	....	....	....
2000-01	JYP Jyvaskyla Jr.	Finn-Jr.	40	2	8	10	73	6	1	1	2	6
	JYP Jyvaskyla	Finland	8	1	0	1	6	....	....	....	....	....
2001-02	JYP Jyvaskyla	Finland	50	1	4	5	67	....	....	....	....	....
	JYP Jyvaskyla Jr.	Finn-Jr.	5	0	2	2	2	1	0	0	0	0
2002-03	JYP Jyvaskyla	Finland	29	3	2	5	32	....	....	....	....	....
2003-04	JYP Jyvaskyla	Finland	54	6	13	19	115	2	0	0	0	2

MARTZ, Nathan (MAHRTZ, NAY-thun) NYR

Center. Shoots left. 6'3", 169 lbs. Born, Chilliwack, B.C., March 4, 1981.
(NY Rangers' 4th choice, 140th overall, in 2000 Entry Draft).

			Regular Season					Playoffs				
Season	Club	League	GP	G	A	TP	PIM	GP	G	A	TP	PIM
1997-98	Chilliwack Chiefs	BCHL	59	8	13	21	86	....	....	....	....	....
1998-99	Chilliwack Chiefs	BCHL	59	20	38	58	....	....	....	....	....	....
99-2000	Chilliwack Chiefs	BCHL	59	35	75	110	97	....	....	....	....	....
2000-01	New Hampshire	H-East	37	5	14	19	20	....	....	....	....	....
2001-02	New Hampshire	H-East	28	3	7	10	12	....	....	....	....	....
2002-03	New Hampshire	H-East	42	12	15	27	20	....	....	....	....	....
2003-04	New Hampshire	H-East	30	5	21	26	43	....	....	....	....	....

NCAA Championship All-Tournament Team (2003)

MASSEN, James (MA-suhn, JAYMS) N.J.

Right wing. Shoots right. 6'1", 228 lbs. Born, Bismarck, ND, January 13, 1982.
(New Jersey's 9th choice, 194th overall, in 2001 Entry Draft).

			Regular Season					Playoffs				
Season	Club	League	GP	G	A	TP	PIM	GP	G	A	TP	PIM
1998-99	Bismarck Bobcats	Hi-School	11	1	3	4	14	....	....	....	....	....
99-2000	Sioux Falls	USHL	53	16	17	33	25	3	0	0	0	2
2000-01	Sioux Falls	USHL	56	37	38	75	56	8	6	2	8	4
2001-02	North Dakota	WCHA	34	5	8	13	18	....	....	....	....	....
2002-03	North Dakota	WCHA	42	15	20	35	12	....	....	....	....	....
2003-04	North Dakota	WCHA	20	1	5	6	0	....	....	....	....	....

USHL First All-Star Team (2001)

MATEJOVSKY, Radek (ma-teh-YAHV-skee, ra-DEHK) NYI

Right wing. Shoots right. 6'1", 187 lbs. Born, Praha, Czech., November 17, 1977.
(NY Islanders' 9th choice, 250th overall, in 1998 Entry Draft).

			Regular Season					Playoffs				
Season	Club	League	GP	G	A	TP	PIM	GP	G	A	TP	PIM
1992-93	C. Budejovice Jr.	Czech-Jr.	25	38	24	62	....	....	....	....	....	....
1993-94	Slavia IPS Praha Jr.	Czech-Jr.	45	30	26	56	....	....	....	....	....	....
1994-95	HC Slavia Praha Jr.	Czech-Jr.	28	7	8	15	12	....	....	....	....	....
1995-96	HC Slavia Praha Jr.	Czech-Jr.	47	37	21	58	24	....	....	....	....	....
1996-97	HC Slavia Praha Jr.	Czech-Jr.	4	1	1	2	....	....	....	....	....	....
	H+S Beroun	Czech-2	12	3	1	4	18	....	....	....	....	....
	HC Slavia Praha	Czech	41	3	4	7	10	3	0	0	0	0
1997-98	HC Slavia Praha	Czech	52	9	4	13	24	3	0	0	0	0
1998-99	HC Dukla Jihlava	Czech	52	12	10	22	57	....	....	....	....	....
	HC Dukla Jihlava	Czech-Q	7	3	3	6	41	....	....	....	....	....
99-2000	HC Slavia Praha	Czech	25	4	3	7	22	....	....	....	....	....
	Pardubice	Czech	25	2	4	6	18	3	0	0	0	0
2000-01	HC Slavia Praha	Czech	39	6	8	14	63	11	1	2	3	18
2001-02	HC Slavia Praha	Czech	35	3	1	4	42	9	0	0	0	6
2002-03	HC Keramika Plzen	Czech	42	7	11	18	126	....	....	....	....	....
2003-04	Plzen	Czech	52	9	8	17	121	12	2	4	6	49

MAUNU, Mitch (MOW-MOW, MIHTCH) CHI.

Defense. Shoots left. 6'1", 205 lbs. Born, Thunder Bay, Ont., July 30, 1986.
(Chicago's 7th choice, 120th overall, in 2004 Entry Draft).

			Regular Season					Playoffs				
Season	Club	League	GP	G	A	TP	PIM	GP	G	A	TP	PIM
2002-03	Windsor Spitfires	OHL	62	4	15	19	25	7	0	1	1	0
2003-04	Windsor Spitfires	OHL	68	11	15	26	91	4	1	0	1	0

MAXIMENKO, Andrei (max-EE-mehn-koh, AWN-dray) DET.

Left wing. Shoots right. 5'11", 172 lbs. Born, Moscow, USSR, January 10, 1981.
(Detroit's 2nd choice, 149th overall, in 1999 Entry Draft).

			Regular Season					Playoffs				
Season	Club	League	GP	G	A	TP	PIM	GP	G	A	TP	PIM
1997-98	Krylja Sovetov 2	Russia-3	42	2	4	6	12	....	....	....	....	....
1998-99	Krylja Sovetov	Russia	28	1	2	3	24	....	....	....	....	....
99-2000	Krylja Sovetov 2	Russia-3	6	4	2	6	26	....	....	....	....	....
	Krylja Sovetov	Russia-2	39	6	7	13	41	....	....	....	....	....
2000-01	Krylja Sovetov	Russia-2	28	2	5	7	8	....	....	....	....	....
2001-02	THC Tver	Russia-2	20	3	7	10	6	....	....	....	....	....
	Krylja Sovetov 2	Russia-3	7	3	5	8	2	....	....	....	....	....
	Perm	Russia	9	0	1	1	2	....	....	....	....	....
2002-03	Kristall Saratov	Russia-2	47	12	12	24	36	....	....	....	....	....
2003-04	Krylja Sovetov	Russia-2	19	2	3	5	8	....	....	....	....	....

MAY, Scott (MAY, SKAWT) **TOR.**

Right wing. Shoots right. 5'9", 185 lbs. Born, Calgary, Alta., January 8, 1982.
(Toronto's 7th choice, 222nd overall, in 2002 Entry Draft).

			Regular Season					Playoffs				
Season	**Club**	**League**	**GP**	**G**	**A**	**TP**	**PIM**	**GP**	**G**	**A**	**TP**	**PIM**
99-2000	South Surrey	BCHL	54	42	42	84	....	....	....	....	....	....
2000-01	Ohio State	CCHA	37	9	9	18	26	....	....	....	....	....
2001-02	Ohio State	CCHA	40	12	18	30	42	*....	....	....	....	....
2002-03	Ohio State	CCHA	43	10	25	35	56	....	....	....	....	....
2003-04	Ohio State	CCHA	41	15	19	34	42	....	....	....	....	....
	St. John's	AHL	5	1	1	2	2	....	....	....	....	....

McASLAN, Sean (mihk-AZ-luhn, SHAWN) **EDM.**

Left wing. Shoots right. 6'1", 190 lbs. Born, Okotoks, Alta., January 12, 1980.

			Regular Season					Playoffs				
Season	**Club**	**League**	**GP**	**G**	**A**	**TP**	**PIM**	**GP**	**G**	**A**	**TP**	**PIM**
1996-97	Calgary Hitmen	WHL	26	2	3	5	22	....	....	....	....	....
1997-98	Calgary Hitmen	WHL	69	8	16	24	83	....	....	....	....	....
1998-99	Calgary Hitmen	WHL	71	7	16	23	110	21	2	1	3	18
99-2000	Calgary Hitmen	WHL	72	18	16	34	117	13	4	2	6	49
2000-01	Calgary Hitmen	WHL	51	21	32	53	137	12	3	5	8	29
2001-02	Columbus	ECHL	72	16	21	37	139	....	....	....	....	....
2002-03	Columbus	ECHL	53	15	17	32	132	....	....	....	....	....
	Hamilton Bulldogs	AHL	1	0	0	0	0	....	....	....	....	....
2003-04	Toronto	AHL	62	12	15	27	66	3	0	1	1	2

Signed as a free agent by **Edmonton**, March 14, 2001.

McCARTHY, Jeremiah (mih-KAHR-thee, jeh-rih-MIGH-uh)

Defense. Shoots left. 6', 210 lbs. Born, Boston, MA, March 1, 1976.

			Regular Season					Playoffs				
Season	**Club**	**League**	**GP**	**G**	**A**	**TP**	**PIM**	**GP**	**G**	**A**	**TP**	**PIM**
1994-95	Harvard Crimson	ECAC	25	3	5	8	4	....	....	....	....	....
1995-96	Harvard Crimson	ECAC	32	4	12	16	20	....	....	....	....	....
1996-97	Harvard Crimson	ECAC	32	4	9	13	22	....	....	....	....	....
1997-98	Harvard Crimson	ECAC	28	11	10	21	38	....	....	....	....	....
1998-99	Peoria Rivermen	ECHL	6	1	2	3	6	....	....	....	....	....
	Worcester IceCats	AHL	59	5	10	15	37	4	0	2	2	0
99-2000	Missouri	UHL	33	10	25	35	45	....	....	....	....	....
	Springfield Falcons	AHL	43	5	9	14	16	5	1	1	2	0
2000-01	Cincinnati	IHL	69	6	12	18	34	3	0	0	0	0
2001-02	Lowell	AHL	74	7	28	35	43	5	0	2	2	0
2002-03	Amur Khabarovsk	Russia	4	0		0	2	....	....	....	....	....
	Lowell	AHL	44	1	16	17	44	....	....	....	....	....
	Grand Rapids	AHL	11	0	1	1	2	12	0	1	1	6
2003-04	Springfield Falcons	AHL	79	7	15	22	26	....	....	....	....	....

Signed as a free agent by **Carolina**, August 21, 2000. Signed as a free agent by **Amur** (Russia), July 19, 2002. Traded to **Grand Rapids** (AHL) by **Lowell** (AHL) for Dustin Whitecotton and Rustyn Dolyny, March 13, 2003. Signed as a free agent by **Springfield** (AHL), September 11, 2003.

McCLEMENT, Jay (muh-KLEHM-ehnt, JAY) **ST.L.**

Center. Shoots left. 6'1", 193 lbs. Born, Kingston, Ont., March 2, 1983.
(St. Louis' 1st choice, 57th overall, in 2001 Entry Draft).

			Regular Season					Playoffs				
Season	**Club**	**League**	**GP**	**G**	**A**	**TP**	**PIM**	**GP**	**G**	**A**	**TP**	**PIM**
1997-98	Kingston	OPJHL	48	3	8	11	15	....	....	....	....	....
1998-99	Kingston	OPJHL	51	25	28	53	34	....	....	....	....	....
99-2000	Brampton	OHL	63	13	16	29	34	6	0	4	4	8
2000-01	Brampton	OHL	66	30	19	49	61	9	4	2	6	10
2001-02	Brampton	OHL	61	26	29	55	43	....	....	....	....	....
2002-03	Brampton	OHL	45	22	27	49	37	11	3	4	7	11
	Worcester IceCats	AHL	....	....	....	....	....	1	0	0	0	0
2003-04	Worcester IceCats	AHL	69	12	13	25	20	10	0	3	3	0

McCONNELL, Brian (mih-CAW-nuhl, BRIGH-uhn) **CGY.**

Center. Shoots left. 6'2", 190 lbs. Born, Boston, MA, February 1, 1983.
(Calgary's 2nd choice, 39th overall, in 2002 Entry Draft).

			Regular Season					Playoffs				
Season	**Club**	**League**	**GP**	**G**	**A**	**TP**	**PIM**	**GP**	**G**	**A**	**TP**	**PIM**
1998-99	Thayer Academy	Hi-School	23	12	27	39	....	....	....	....	....	....
99-2000	U.S. National U-17	USDP	48	8	11	19	76	....	....	....	....	....
2000-01	U.S. National U-18	USDP	62	19	25	44	143	....	....	....	....	....
2001-02	Boston University	H-East	38	11	15	26	68	....	....	....	....	....
2002-03	Boston University	H-East	34	11	14	25	70	....	....	....	....	....
2003-04	Boston University	H-East	37	11	5	16	68	....	....	....	....	....

McCUTCHEON, Mark (mih-KUH-chuhn, MAHRK) **COL.**

Center. Shoots right. 6', 177 lbs. Born, Ithaca, NY, May 21, 1984.
(Colorado's 3rd choice, 146th overall, in 2003 Entry Draft).

			Regular Season					Playoffs				
Season	**Club**	**League**	**GP**	**G**	**A**	**TP**	**PIM**	**GP**	**G**	**A**	**TP**	**PIM**
2001-02	New England	EJHL	36	24	26	50	84	....	....	....	....	....
2002-03	New England	EJHL	35	27	22	49	76	10	8	5	13	24
2003-04	Cornell Big Red	ECAC	32	0	4	4	12	....	....	....	....	....

McDONALD, Brent (muhk-DAW-nuhld, BREHNT) **CAR.**

Center. Shoots right. 5'11", 180 lbs. Born, Olds, Alta., October 7, 1979.
(Carolina's 10th choice, 239th overall, in 1998 Entry Draft).

			Regular Season					Playoffs				
Season	**Club**	**League**	**GP**	**G**	**A**	**TP**	**PIM**	**GP**	**G**	**A**	**TP**	**PIM**
1994-95	Red Deer Vipers	AMHL	26	16	24	40	55	....	....	....	....	....
1995-96	Red Deer Rebels	WHL	68	1	7	8	55	6	0	1	1	2
1996-97	Red Deer Rebels	WHL	69	11	17	28	94	16	4	3	7	38
1997-98	Red Deer Rebels	WHL	69	18	27	45	93	5	0	2	2	4
1998-99	Red Deer Rebels	WHL	38	17	18	35	64	....	....	....	....	....
	Prince George	WHL	34	13	13	26	40	7	1	1	2	18
99-2000	Prince George	WHL	7	1	3	4	6	....	....	....	....	....
	Spokane Chiefs	WHL	61	28	30	58	77	15	5	8	13	42
2000-01	Florida Everblades	ECHL	67	11	11	22	55	5	1	0	1	4
2001-02	Florida Everblades	ECHL	69	12	20	32	92	6	2	2	4	4
	Lowell	AHL	2	0	0	0	0	2	0	0	0	0
2002-03	Lowell	AHL	52	7	8	15	29	....	....	....	....	....
	Florida Everblades	ECHL	18	10	4	14	14	1	1	0	1	2
2003-04	Florida Everblades	ECHL	53	22	33	55	65	17	1	7	8	14

McDONALD, Colin (mihk-DAW-nuhld, KAW-lihn) **EDM.**

Right wing. Shoots right. 6'2", 190 lbs. Born, New Haven, CT, September 30, 1984.
(Edmonton's 2nd choice, 51st overall, in 2003 Entry Draft).

			Regular Season					Playoffs				
Season	**Club**	**League**	**GP**	**G**	**A**	**TP**	**PIM**	**GP**	**G**	**A**	**TP**	**PIM**
2001-02	New England	EJHL	39	16	20	36	50	....	....	....	....	....
2002-03	New England	EJHL	44	28	40	*68	59	....	....	....	....	....
2003-04	Providence College	H-East	37	10	6	16	47	....	....	....	....	....

Hockey East All-Rookie Team (2004)

McGRATH, Evan (muh-GRATH, EH-vuhn) **DET.**

Center. Shoots left. 5'11", 181 lbs. Born, Oakville, Ont., January 14, 1986.
(Detroit's 2nd choice, 128th overall, in 2004 Entry Draft).

			Regular Season					Playoffs				
Season	**Club**	**League**	**GP**	**G**	**A**	**TP**	**PIM**	**GP**	**G**	**A**	**TP**	**PIM**
2001-02	Oakville Blades	OPJHL	49	43	44	87	24	....	....	....	....	....
2002-03	Kitchener Rangers	OHL	64	16	31	47	40	21	6	2	8	6
2003-04	Kitchener Rangers	OHL	68	15	36	51	28	5	2	1	3	2

OHL All-Rookie Team (2003)

McGRATTAN, Brian (muhk-GRA-tuhn, BRIGH-uhn) **OTT.**

Right wing. Shoots right. 6'4", 225 lbs. Born, Hamilton, Ont., September 2, 1981.
(Los Angeles' 5th choice, 104th overall, in 1999 Entry Draft).

			Regular Season					Playoffs				
Season	**Club**	**League**	**GP**	**G**	**A**	**TP**	**PIM**	**GP**	**G**	**A**	**TP**	**PIM**
1997-98	Guelph Royals	OJHL-B	15	4	3	7	94	....	....	....	....	....
	Guelph Storm	OHL	25	3	2	5	11	....	....	....	....	....
1998-99	Guelph Storm	OHL	6	1	3	4	15	....	....	....	....	....
	Sudbury Wolves	OHL	53	7	10	17	153	4	0	0	0	8
99-2000	Sudbury Wolves	OHL	25	2	8	10	79	....	....	....	....	....
	Mississauga	OHL	42	9	13	22	166	....	....	....	....	....
2000-01	Mississauga	OHL	31	20	9	29	83	....	....	....	....	....
2001-02	Mississauga	OHL	7	2	3	5	16	....	....	....	....	....
	Owen Sound	OHL	2	0	0	0	0	....	....	....	....	....
	Oshawa Generals	OHL	25	10	5	15	72	....	....	....	....	....
	Sault Ste. Marie	OHL	26	8	7	15	71	6	2	0	2	20
2002-03	Binghamton	AHL	59	9	10	19	173	1	0	0	0	0
2003-04	Binghamton	AHL	66	9	11	20	327	1	0	0	0	0

Signed as a free agent by **Ottawa**, June 2, 2002.

McIVER, Nathan (mihk-IGH-vuhr, NAY-thun) **VAN.**

Defense. Shoots left. 6'2", 185 lbs. Born, Kinkora, PEI, January 6, 1985.
(Vancouver's 9th choice, 254th overall, in 2003 Entry Draft).

			Regular Season					Playoffs				
Season	**Club**	**League**	**GP**	**G**	**A**	**TP**	**PIM**	**GP**	**G**	**A**	**TP**	**PIM**
2001-02	Summerside	MJrHL	47	4	4	8	91	5	0	0	0	9
2002-03	St. Michael's	OHL	68	5	10	15	121	19	0	4	4	41
2003-04	St. Michael's	OHL	57	4	11	15	183	16	0	1	1	22

McKENZIE, Jim (MIHK-ehn-zee, JIHM) **OTT.**

Right wing. Shoots right. 6'1", 209 lbs. Born, St. Paul, MN, June 10, 1984.
(Ottawa's 7th choice, 141st overall, in 2004 Entry Draft).

			Regular Season					Playoffs				
Season	**Club**	**League**	**GP**	**G**	**A**	**TP**	**PIM**	**GP**	**G**	**A**	**TP**	**PIM**
2000-01	Hill-Murray	Hi-School	27	9	13	22	....	....	....	....	....	....
2001-02	Green Bay	USHL	17	1	2	3	34	....	....	....	....	....
	U.S. National U-18	USDP	19	7	11	18	23	....	....	....	....	....
2002-03	Sioux Falls	USHL	45	6	18	24	108	....	....	....	....	....
2003-04	Sioux Falls	USHL	59	26	38	64	168	....	....	....	....	....

Signed Letter of Intent to attend **Michigan State** (CCHA), February 10, 2004.

McLACHLAN, Darren (muhk-LAWK-luhn, DAIR-rehn) **PHX.**

Left wing. Shoots left. 6'1", 223 lbs. Born, Penticton, B.C., February 16, 1983.
(Boston's 2nd choice, 77th overall, in 2001 Entry Draft).

			Regular Season					Playoffs				
Season	**Club**	**League**	**GP**	**G**	**A**	**TP**	**PIM**	**GP**	**G**	**A**	**TP**	**PIM**
1998-99	Campbell River	VIJHL	31	15	25	40	212	....	....	....	....	....
	Seattle	WHL	2	0	1	1	7	....	....	....	....	....
99-2000	Seattle	WHL	54	5	1	6	175	7	0	0	0	9
2000-01	Seattle	WHL	42	10	9	19	161	9	1	3	4	18
2001-02	Seattle	WHL	51	15	16	31	153	10	1	0	1	20
2002-03	Seattle	WHL	66	17	43	60	195	5	1	0	1	11
2003-04	Adirondack	UHL	39	3	7	10	166	....	....	....	....	....
	Springfield Falcons	AHL	11	1	0	1	39	....	....	....	....	....

Rights traded to **Phoenix** by **Boston** for Phoenix's 5th round choice (Kris Versteeg) in 2004 Entry Draft, May 30, 2003.

McLEOD, Kiel (muk-KLOWD, KIGHL) **PHX.**

Center. Shoots right. 6'6", 240 lbs. Born, Ft. Saskatchewan, Alta., December 30, 1982.
(Columbus' 3rd choice, 53rd overall, in 2001 Entry Draft).

			Regular Season					Playoffs				
Season	**Club**	**League**	**GP**	**G**	**A**	**TP**	**PIM**	**GP**	**G**	**A**	**TP**	**PIM**
1997-98	North Delta	BCAHA	55	57	55	112	202	....	....	....	....	....
1998-99	Kelowna Rockets	WHL	55	12	15	27	48	6	0	1	1	2
99-2000	Kelowna Rockets	WHL	59	17	13	30	100	5	2	1	3	2
2000-01	Kelowna Rockets	WHL	65	38	28	66	94	4	4	1	5	8
2001-02	Kelowna Rockets	WHL	41	17	31	48	62	15	3	10	13	14
2002-03	Kelowna Rockets	WHL	68	39	51	90	163	8	5	5	10	4
2003-04	Springfield Falcons	AHL	77	7	11	18	71	....	....	....	....	....

WHL West Second All-Star Team (2003)

Signed as a free agent by **Phoenix**, June 9, 2003.

MEECH, Derek (MEECH, DAIR-ihk) **DET.**

Defense. Shoots left. 5'11", 182 lbs. Born, Winnipeg, Man., April 21, 1984.
(Detroit's 7th choice, 229th overall, in 2002 Entry Draft).

			Regular Season					Playoffs				
Season	**Club**	**League**	**GP**	**G**	**A**	**TP**	**PIM**	**GP**	**G**	**A**	**TP**	**PIM**
99-2000	Winnipeg Warriors	MMMHL	36	15	40	55	24	....	....	....	....	....
	Red Deer Rebels	WHL	5	1	0	1	2	....	....	....	....	....
2000-01	Red Deer Rebels	WHL	60	2	7	9	40	22	0	0	0	9
2001-02	Red Deer Rebels	WHL	71	8	19	27	33	13	1	1	2	6
2002-03	Red Deer Rebels	WHL	65	6	16	22	53	12	1	1	2	12
2003-04	Red Deer Rebels	WHL	62	10	28	38	40	19	4	7	11	10

WHL East Second All-Star Team (2004)

MEIDL, Vaclav (MAY-duhl, VAT-slav) NSH.

Center. Shoots left. 6'4", 198 lbs. Born, Prostejov, Czechoslovakia, May 27, 1986.
(Nashville's 2nd choice, 81st overall, in 2004 Entry Draft).

			Regular Season					Playoffs				
Season	Club	League	GP	G	A	TP	PIM	GP	G	A	TP	PIM
2001-02	Zlin 18	Czech-Jr.	7	1	0	1	2	....	....	....	....	....
	Trinec 18	Czech-Jr.	36	11	11	22	18	4	1	1	2	2
2002-03	Havirov	Czech	5	0	1	1	4	....	....	....	....	....
	Havirov 18	Czech-Jr.	13	10	13	23	30	....	....	....	....	....
	Havirov Jr.	Czech-Jr.	28	1	7	8	22	....	....	....	....	....
	Havirov	Czech	5	0	1	1	4	....	....	....	....	....
2003-04	Plymouth Whalers	OHL	67	14	28	42	108	9	0	3	3	4

MELANSON, Mathieu (muh-LAWN-suhn, MA-tyew) MIN.

Left wing. Shoots left. 6'1", 185 lbs. Born, Long Island, NY, August 31, 1985.
(Minnesota's 8th choice, 251st overall, in 2003 Entry Draft).

			Regular Season					Playoffs				
Season	Club	League	GP	G	A	TP	PIM	GP	G	A	TP	PIM
2001-02	Moncton	MAAA		STATISTICS NOT AVAILABLE								
2002-03	Chicoutimi	QMJHL	69	20	27	47	62	4	0	0	0	14
2003-04	Chicoutimi	QMJHL	35	10	17	27	40	....	....	....	....	....
	Quebec Remparts	QMJHL	29	9	11	20	6	5	0	0	0	2

MELIN, Bjorn (MEH-lihn, b-YOHRN) ANA.

Right wing. Shoots right. 6'1", 178 lbs. Born, Jonkoping, Sweden, July 4, 1981.
(NY Islanders' 11th choice, 163rd overall, in 1999 Entry Draft).

			Regular Season					Playoffs				
Season	Club	League	GP	G	A	TP	PIM	GP	G	A	TP	PIM
1997-98	HV 71 Jr.	Swede-Jr.	8	0	3	3	2	....	....	....	....	....
1998-99	HV 71 Jr.	Swede-Jr.	30	12	7	19	50	....	....	....	....	....
99-2000	HV 71 Jr.	Swede-Jr.	24	19	16	35	70	....	....	....	....	....
	HV 71 Jonkoping	Sweden	23	3	0	3	2	5	0	0	0	0
2000-01	HV 71 Jr.	Swede-Jr.	10	6	5	11	66	....	....	....	....	....
	HV 71 Jonkoping	Sweden	43	2	1	3	26	....	....	....	....	....
2001-02	HV 71 Jonkoping	Sweden	50	7	9	16	40	8	0	0	0	6
2002-03	HV 71 Jonkoping	Sweden	48	7	9	16	44	7	0	2	2	6
2003-04	HV 71 Jonkoping	Sweden	47	7	11	18	28	19	4	8	12	10

Rights traded to **Anaheim** by **NY Islanders** with Ben Guite for Dave Roche, March 19, 2002.

MESZAROS, Andrej (MEHT-zahr-ohsh, AWN-dray) OTT.

Defense. Shoots left. 6'2", 189 lbs. Born, Povazska Bystrica, Czech., October 13, 1985.
(Ottawa's 1st choice, 23rd overall, in 2004 Entry Draft).

			Regular Season					Playoffs				
Season	Club	League	GP	G	A	TP	PIM	GP	G	A	TP	PIM
2002-03	Dukla Trencin	Slovakia	23	0	1	1	4	....	....	....	....	....
	Dukla Trencin Jr.	Slovak-Jr.	33	6	10	16	12	....	....	....	....	....
2003-04	Dukla Trencin Jr.	Slovak-Jr.	5	2	2	4	0	....	....	....	....	....
	Dukla Trencin	Slovakia	44	3	3	6	8	14	3	1	4	2

METCALF, Peter (MEHT-kaf, PEE-tuhr)

Defense. Shoots left. 6', 200 lbs. Born, Steamboat Springs, CO, February 25, 1979.
(Toronto's 9th choice, 267th overall, in 1999 Entry Draft).

			Regular Season					Playoffs				
Season	Club	League	GP	G	A	TP	PIM	GP	G	A	TP	PIM
1997-98	Cushing Academy	Hi-School	25	18	48	66	....	....	....	....	....	....
1998-99	U. of Maine	H-East	33	6	17	23	34	....	....	....	....	....
99-2000	U. of Maine	H-East	40	4	17	21	56	....	....	....	....	....
2000-01	U. of Maine	H-East	31	5	9	14	44	....	....	....	....	....
2001-02	U. of Maine	H-East	44	9	41	50	66	....	....	....	....	....
2002-03	Providence Bruins	AHL	40	0	6	6	24	....	....	....	....	....
	Atlantic City	ECHL	18	2	11	13	48	19	4	6	10	25
2003-04	Trenton Titans	ECHL	25	2	15	17	43	....	....	....	....	....
	Providence Bruins	AHL	42	2	13	15	41	1	0	0	0	4

Hockey East First All-Star Team (2002) • NCAA Championship All-Tournament Team (2002)

Signed as a free agent by **Boston**, June 6, 2002.

METHOT, Francois (meh-TOH, FRAN-swaw)

Center. Shoots right. 6', 203 lbs. Born, Montreal, Que., April 26, 1978.
(Buffalo's 4th choice, 54th overall, in 1996 Entry Draft).

			Regular Season					Playoffs				
Season	Club	League	GP	G	A	TP	PIM	GP	G	A	TP	PIM
1993-94	Montreal-Bourassa	QAAA	44	17	38	55	....	4	3	1	4	4
1994-95	St-Hyacinthe Laser	QMJHL	60	14	38	52	22	5	0	1	1	0
1995-96	St-Hyacinthe Laser	QMJHL	68	32	62	94	22	12	6	6	12	4
1996-97	Rouyn-Noranda	QMJHL	47	21	30	51	22	....	....	....	....	....
	Shawinigan	QMJHL	18	8	17	25	2	7	2	6	8	2
1997-98	Shawinigan	QMJHL	36	23	42	65	10	6	1	3	4	5
1998-99	Rochester	AHL	58	5	8	13	8	9	0	1	1	0
99-2000	Rochester	AHL	80	14	18	32	20	21	2	4	6	16
2000-01	Rochester	AHL	79	22	33	55	35	4	1	3	4	0
2001-02	Rochester	AHL	59	17	17	34	28	2	1	0	1	0
2002-03	Rochester	AHL	58	19	34	53	22	3	0	4	4	0
2003-04	Portland Pirates	AHL	53	8	19	27	12	....	....	....	....	....

Signed as a free agent by **Washington**, August 19, 2003.

METHOT, Marc (meh-TOH, MAHRK) CBJ

Defense. Shoots left. 6'3", 196 lbs. Born, Ottawa, Ont., June 21, 1985.
(Columbus' 7th choice, 168th overall, in 2003 Entry Draft).

			Regular Season					Playoffs				
Season	Club	League	GP	G	A	TP	PIM	GP	G	A	TP	PIM
2001-02	Kanata Laser	OJHL	50	3	10	13	22	....	....	....	....	....
2002-03	London Knights	OHL	68	2	13	15	46	14	2	4	6	6
2003-04	London Knights	OHL	63	2	9	11	66	15	0	3	3	18

MEYER, Stefan (MAY-uhr, steh-FAN) FLA.

Left wing. Shoots left. 6'1", 194 lbs. Born, Medicine Hat, Alta., July 20, 1985.
(Florida's 4th choice, 55th overall, in 2003 Entry Draft).

			Regular Season					Playoffs				
Season	Club	League	GP	G	A	TP	PIM	GP	G	A	TP	PIM
2000-01	Notre Dame	SBHL	50	36	52	88	71	....	....	....	....	....
2001-02	Medicine Hat	WHL	67	18	22	40	48	....	....	....	....	....
2002-03	Medicine Hat	WHL	70	36	16	52	90	11	3	3	6	14
2003-04	Medicine Hat	WHL	72	34	41	75	69	19	7	10	17	27

MICKA, Tomas (MIHTSKA, TAW-mas) EDM.

Left wing. Shoots left. 6'2", 180 lbs. Born, Jihlava, Czech., June 7, 1983.
(Edmonton's 13th choice, 245th overall, in 2002 Entry Draft).

			Regular Season					Playoffs				
Season	Club	League	GP	G	A	TP	PIM	GP	G	A	TP	PIM
99-2000	HC Slavia Praha Jr.	Czech-Jr.	42	17	18	35	24	....	....	....	....	....
2000-01	HC Slavia Praha Jr.	Czech-Jr.	45	2	8	10	65	3	0	1	1	0
2001-02	HC Slavia Praha Jr.	Czech-Jr.	46	12	16	28	79	....	....	....	....	....
	HC Slavia Praha	Czech	1	0	0	0	0	....	....	....	....	....
2002-03	Havirov	Czech	23	1	0	1	12	....	....	....	....	....
	Havirov Jr.	Czech-Jr.	11	4	3	7	12	....	....	....	....	....
	Zdar nad Sazavou	Czech-2	4	1	0	1	2	....	....	....	....	....
2003-04	Columbus	ECHL	67	17	15	32	52	....	....	....	....	....

MIETTINEN, Tommi (mih-EHT-tih-nehn,TAW-mee) ANA.

Center. Shoots left. 5'10", 165 lbs. Born, Kuopio, Finland, December 3, 1975.
(Anaheim's 9th choice, 236th overall, in 1994 Entry Draft).

			Regular Season					Playoffs				
Season	Club	League	GP	G	A	TP	PIM	GP	G	A	TP	PIM
1991-92	KalPa Kuopio Jr.	Finn-Jr.	37	9	16	25	12	....	....	....	....	....
1992-93	KalPa Kuopio-B	Finn-Jr.	7	3	8	11	2	....	....	....	....	....
	KalPa Kuopio Jr.	Finn-Jr.	26	16	27	43	14	....	....	....	....	....
	KalPa Kuopio	Finland	14	0	0	0	0	....	....	....	....	....
1993-94	KalPa Kuopio Jr.	Finn-Jr.	9	5	9	14	10	....	....	....	....	....
	KalPa Kuopio	Finland	47	5	7	12	14	....	....	....	....	....
1994-95	KalPa Kuopio Jr.	Finn-Jr.	2	1	3	4	2	....	....	....	....	....
	KalPa Kuopio	Finland	48	13	16	29	26	3	1	1	2	2
1995-96	TPS Turku	Finland	36	3	10	13	10	10	2	1	3	29
1996-97	TPS Turku	Finland	41	6	15	21	6	12	3	4	7	8
	TPS Turku	EuroHL	6	2	2	4	2	4	1	1	2	0
1997-98	TPS Turku	Finland	42	8	6	14	26	4	0	0	0	0
	TPS Turku	EuroHL	3	0	0	0	2	....	....	....	....	....
1998-99	TPS Turku	Finland	54	10	17	27	26	10	4	4	8	0
99-2000	Ilves Tampere	Finland	54	13	20	33	24	....	....	....	....	....
2000-01	Ilves Tampere	Finland	55	10	20	30	38	9	0	1	1	4
2001-02	Ilves Tampere	Finland	55	11	31	42	36	3	0	0	0	2
2002-03	Brynas IF Gavle	Sweden	50	9	17	26	76	....	....	....	....	....
2003-04	Brynas IF Gavle	Sweden	50	13	21	34	56	....	....	....	....	....

MIKHAILISHIN, Alexander (mih-khigh-LIHSH-ihn) N.J.

Defense. Shoots left. 6'4", 210 lbs. Born, Neustrelitz, East Germany, February 24, 1986.
(New Jersey's 2nd choice, 155th overall, in 2004 Entry Draft).

			Regular Season					Playoffs				
Season	Club	League	GP	G	A	TP	PIM	GP	G	A	TP	PIM
2001-02	Spartak Moscow 2	Russia-3	15	0	0	0	2	....	....	....	....	....
2002-03	Spartak Moscow 2	Russia-3	7	1	1	2	4	....	....	....	....	....
2003-04	Spartak Moscow 2	Russia-3		STATISTICS NOT AVAILABLE								

MIKHAILOV, Konstantin (mih-KHIGH-lawv, kawn-stuhn-TEEN) VAN.

Center. Shoots left. 5'11", 174 lbs. Born, Moscow, USSR, February 12, 1983.
(Vancouver's 6th choice, 245th overall, in 2001 Entry Draft).

			Regular Season					Playoffs				
Season	Club	League	GP	G	A	TP	PIM	GP	G	A	TP	PIM
99-2000	Dyn. Moscow 2	Russia-3	14	3	2	5	14	....	....	....	....	....
2000-01	Nizhnekamsk	Russia	24	0	2	2	12	....	....	....	....	....
2001-02	Nizhnekamsk	Russia	38	3	6	9	10	....	....	....	....	....
2002-03	Dynamo Moscow	Russia	14	0	1	1	31	....	....	....	....	....
	Nizhnekamsk	Russia	15	1	1	2	6	....	....	....	....	....
2003-04	Sibir Novosibirsk	Russia	15	0	1	1	2	....	....	....	....	....

MIKHNOV, Alexei (MIHKH-nahf, al-EHX-ay) EDM.

Left wing. Shoots left. 6'5", 200 lbs. Born, Kiev, USSR, August 31, 1982.
(Edmonton's 1st choice, 17th overall, in 2000 Entry Draft).

			Regular Season					Playoffs				
Season	Club	League	GP	G	A	TP	PIM	GP	G	A	TP	PIM
1997-98	Torpedo Yaroslavl	Russia	6	0	0	0	0	....	....	....	....	....
1998-99	Yaroslavl 2	Russia-3	14	2	2	4	4	....	....	....	....	....
99-2000	Yaroslavl 2	Russia-3	53	24	17	41	10	....	....	....	....	....
2000-01	HC CSKA	Russia-2	4	0	0	0	2	....	....	....	....	....
	THC Tver	Russia-2	22	5	11	16	6	....	....	....	....	....
2001-02	DynamoMoscow2	Russia-3	8	8	6	14	0	....	....	....	....	....
	Dynamo Moscow	Russia	35	2	1	3	4	3	0	0	0	2
	Salavat Yulayev	Russia	1	0	0	0	0	....	....	....	....	....
2002-03	Sibir Novosibirsk	Russia	51	7	9	16	10	....	....	....	....	....
2003-04	Sibir Novosibirsk	Russia	58	14	8	22	22	....	....	....	....	....

MIKKOLA, Ilkka (mih-KOHLA, IHL-ka) MTL.

Defense. Shoots left. 6', 189 lbs. Born, Oulu, Finland, January 18, 1979.
(Montreal's 3rd choice, 65th overall, in 1997 Entry Draft).

			Regular Season					Playoffs				
Season	Club	League	GP	G	A	TP	PIM	GP	G	A	TP	PIM
1993-94	Karpat Oulu-C	Finn-Jr.	22	3	6	9	4	4	0	1	1	4
1994-95	Karpat Oulu-C	Finn-Jr.	31	17	27	44	24	3	0	0	0	8
1995-96	Karpat Oulu-B	Finn-Jr.	4	2	0	2	0	....	....	....	....	....
	Karpat Oulu Jr.	Finn-Jr.	21	2	3	5	20	....	....	....	....	....
	Karpat Oulu	Finland-2	10	0	4	4	29	2	0	0	0	2
1996-97	Karpat Oulu Jr.	Finn-Jr.	40	7	12	19	32	6	0	0	0	4
	Karpat Oulu B	Finn-Jr.	1	0	1	1	2	....	....	....	....	....
1997-98	Karpat Oulu Jr.	Finn-Jr.	8	4	2	6	10	....	....	....	....	....
	Karpat Oulu	Finland-2	27	7	2	9	34	....	....	....	....	....
1998-99	TPS Turku	Finland	42	1	3	4	41	10	1	0	1	6
99-2000	TPS Turku	Finland	54	2	6	8	48	11	0	0	0	6
	Karpat Oulu	EuroHL	5	0	2	2	4	4	0	0	0	4
2000-01	TPS Turku	Finland	37	3	6	9	22	10	0	1	1	4
2001-02	Jokerit Helsinki	Finland	55	3	2	5	14	12	1	3	4	6
2002-03	Jokerit Helsinki	Finland	38	4	10	14	8	10	0	1	1	10
2003-04	Karpat Oulu	Finland	52	3	13	16	22	15	0	2	2	8

MIKKONEN, Tuomas (mih-KOH-nehn, TWOH-muhs) DAL.

Left wing. Shoots left. 6'1", 183 lbs. Born, Jyvaskyla, Finland, March 25, 1983.
(Dallas' 11th choice, 243rd overall, in 2002 Entry Draft).

			Regular Season					Playoffs				
Season	Club	League	GP	G	A	TP	PIM	GP	G	A	TP	PIM
1998-99	JYP Jyvaskyla C	Finn-Jr.	18	3	4	7	20	....	....	....	....	....
99-2000	JYP Jyvaskyla Jr.	Finn-Jr.	3	0	0	0	2	....	....	....	....	....
	JYP Jyvaskyla B	Finn-Jr.	21	4	1	5	88	15	3	0	3	10
2000-01	JYP Jyvaskyla Jr.	Finn-Jr.	27	7	8	15	16	....	....	....	....	....
2001-02	JYP Jyvaskyla	Finland	12	1	2	3	12	....	....	....	....	....
	JYP Jyvaskyla Jr.	Finn-Jr.	17	5	9	14	47	4	0	2	2	0
2002-03	JYP Jyvaskyla	Finland	48	5	3	8	41	2	0	1	1	25
2003-04	JYP Jyvaskyla	Finland	43	5	3	8	8	2	0	0	0	0

MILLER, Andrew (MIHL-luhr, AN-droo) ANA.

Left wing. Shoots left. 6'2", 165 lbs. Born, Dover, NJ, February 17, 1984.
(Anaheim's 6th choice, 186th overall, in 2003 Entry Draft).

			Regular Season					Playoffs				
Season	Club	League	GP	G	A	TP	PIM	GP	G	A	TP	PIM
2000-01	Capital Centre	NAJHL	37	4	3	7	22	....	....	....	....	....
2001-02	Capital Centre	NAJHL	54	18	16	34	56	....	....	....	....	....
2002-03	Capital Centre	NAJHL	11	10	9	19	....	....	....	....	....	....
	River City Lancers	USHL	49	14	11	25	22	11	5	4	9	6
2003-04	Michigan State	CCHA	41	4	6	10	39	....	....	....	....	....

MILROY, Duncan (MIHL-roi, DUHN-can) MTL.

Right wing. Shoots right. 6', 197 lbs. Born, Edmonton, Alta., February 8, 1983.
(Montreal's 3rd choice, 37th overall, in 2001 Entry Draft).

			Regular Season					Playoffs				
Season	Club	League	GP	G	A	TP	PIM	GP	G	A	TP	PIM
1998-99	Edm. Leafs	AMHL	34	34	36	70	73	....	....	....	....	....
	Swift Current	WHL	3	0	0	0	0	....	....	....	....	....
99-2000	Swift Current	WHL	68	15	15	30	20	12	3	5	8	12
2000-01	Swift Current	WHL	68	38	54	92	51	19	9	12	21	6
2001-02	Swift Current	WHL	26	20	11	31	20	....	....	....	....	....
	Kootenay Ice	WHL	38	25	31	56	24	22	*17	*20	*37	26
2002-03	Kootenay Ice	WHL	61	34	44	78	40	11	5	3	8	8
2003-04	Hamilton Bulldogs	AHL	50	4	10	14	14	10	3	1	4	4

MINAKOV, Oleg (mih-nah-KAHV, OH-lehg) CHI.

Right wing. Shoots left. 6'3", 206 lbs. Born, Elektrostal, USSR, February 18, 1983.
(Chicago's 12th choice, 216th overall, in 2001 Entry Draft).

			Regular Season					Playoffs				
Season	Club	League	GP	G	A	TP	PIM	GP	G	A	TP	PIM
99-2000	Elektrostal 2	Russia-3	19	10	2	12	16	....	....	....	....	....
	Kristall Elektrostal	Russia	4	0	0	0	0	....	....	....	....	....
2000-01	Elektrostal	Russia-2	25	0	3	3	6	....	....	....	....	....
2001-02	Elektrostal 2	Russia-3	26	9	7	16	14	....	....	....	....	....
	Elektrostal	Russia-2	16	0	1	1	14	....	....	....	....	....
2002-03	Amur Khabarovsk	Russia	47	5	0	5	12	....	....	....	....	....
	Khabarovsk 2	Russia-3	3	2	1	3	0	....	....	....	....	....
2003-04	Amur Khabarovsk	Russia	24	3	0	3	24	....	....	....	....	....
	Khabarovsk 2	Russia-3	12	2	6	8	8	....	....	....	....	....

MIRNOV, Igor (mihr-NAWF, EE-gohr) OTT.

Left wing. Shoots left. 5'11", 191 lbs. Born, Chita, USSR, September 19, 1984.
(Ottawa's 2nd choice, 67th overall, in 2003 Entry Draft).

			Regular Season					Playoffs				
Season	Club	League	GP	G	A	TP	PIM	GP	G	A	TP	PIM
2001-02	Dyn. Moscow 2	Russia-3	30	33	17	50	34	....	....	....	....	....
	Dynamo Moscow	Russia	6	0	0	0	0	....	....	....	....	....
	Dynamo Jr.	Russia-Jr.	3	3	0	3	2	....	....	....	....	....
2002-03	Dynamo Moscow	Russia	50	3	7	10	49	5	0	0	0	2
2003-04	Dynamo Moscow	Russia	53	11	10	21	26	3	0	0	0	2

MISCHLER, Greg (MIH-schluhr, GREHG)

Center. Shoots left. 6'3", 174 lbs. Born, Holbrook, NY, September 15, 1978.
(Vancouver's 10th choice, 204th overall, in 1998 Entry Draft).

			Regular Season					Playoffs				
Season	Club	League	GP	G	A	TP	PIM	GP	G	A	TP	PIM
1997-98	Northeastern	H-East	39	7	13	20	22	....	....	....	....	....
1998-99	Northeastern	H-East	33	8	15	23	36	....	....	....	....	....
99-2000	Northeastern	H-East	34	9	14	23	22	....	....	....	....	....
2000-01	Northeastern	H-East	36	10	*32	42	34	....	....	....	....	....
2001-02	Cleveland Barons	AHL	65	10	14	24	71	....	....	....	....	....
2002-03	Cleveland Barons	AHL	67	12	12	24	64	....	....	....	....	....
2003-04	Reading Royals	ECHL	69	13	44	57	100	12	5	7	12	6

Signed as a free agent by **San Jose**, June 13, 2001.

MISHARIN, Grigory (mih-SHAHR-ihn, g'YOHR-gee) MIN.

Defense. Shoots left. 6', 198 lbs. Born, Yekaterinburg, USSR, May 11, 1985.
(Minnesota's 6th choice, 207th overall, in 2003 Entry Draft).

			Regular Season					Playoffs				
Season	Club	League	GP	G	A	TP	PIM	GP	G	A	TP	PIM
2001-02	Yekaterinburg	Russia-3	STATISTICS NOT AVAILABLE									
	Magnitogorsk Jr.	Russia-Jr.	STATISTICS NOT AVAILABLE									
2002-03	Yekaterinburg	Russia-2	28	1	3	4	16	....	....	....	....	....
2003-04	Saginaw Spirit	OHL	65	5	22	27	42	....	....	....	....	....

MITCHELL, John (MIH-chuhl, JAWN) TOR.

Center. Shoots left. 6'1", 182 lbs. Born, Oakville, Ont., January 22, 1985.
(Toronto's 4th choice, 158th overall, in 2003 Entry Draft).

			Regular Season					Playoffs				
Season	Club	League	GP	G	A	TP	PIM	GP	G	A	TP	PIM
2000-01	Waterloo Siskens	OPJHL	47	15	29	44	33	....	....	....	....	....
2001-02	Plymouth Whalers	OHL	62	9	9	18	23	6	1	0	1	4
2002-03	Plymouth Whalers	OHL	68	18	37	55	31	18	2	10	12	8
2003-04	Plymouth Whalers	OHL	65	28	54	82	45	9	6	6	12	6

MITCHELL, Torrey (MIH-chuhl, TOHR-ee) S.J.

Center. Shoots right. 5'11", 175 lbs. Born, Montreal, Que., January 30, 1985.
(San Jose's 3rd choice, 126th overall, in 2004 Entry Draft).

			Regular Season					Playoffs				
Season	Club	League	GP	G	A	TP	PIM	GP	G	A	TP	PIM
2002-03	Hotchkiss	Hi-School	26	19	30	49	33	....	....	....	....	....
2003-04	Hotchkiss	Hi-School	25	25	37	62	42	....	....	....	....	....

Signed Letter of Intent to attend **U. of Vermont** (ECAC), October 14, 2003.

MOJZIS, Tomas (MOI-shihsh, TAW-mash) VAN.

Defense. Shoots left. 6'1", 186 lbs. Born, Kolin, Czech., May 2, 1982.
(Toronto's 11th choice, 246th overall, in 2001 Entry Draft).

			Regular Season					Playoffs				
Season	Club	League	GP	G	A	TP	PIM	GP	G	A	TP	PIM
99-2000	Pardubice Jr.	Czech-Jr.	40	7	1	8	....	....	....	....	....	....
2000-01	Moose Jaw	WHL	72	11	25	36	115	4	0	1	1	8
2001-02	Moose Jaw	WHL	28	2	11	13	43	....	....	....	....	....
	Seattle	WHL	36	8	15	23	66	11	1	3	4	20
2002-03	Seattle	WHL	62	21	49	70	126	15	1	6	7	36
2003-04	Manitoba Moose	AHL	63	5	13	18	50	....	....	....	....	....

WHL West First All-Star Team (2003) • Canadian Major Junior First All-Star Team (2003)

Traded to **Vancouver** by **Toronto** for Brad Leeb, September 4, 2002.

MONDOU, Benoit (mawn-DOO, BEHN-wah) BOS.

Center. Shoots right. 5'10", 165 lbs. Born, Montreal, Que., May 3, 1985.
(Boston's 9th choice, 247th overall, in 2003 Entry Draft).

			Regular Season					Playoffs				
Season	Club	League	GP	G	A	TP	PIM	GP	G	A	TP	PIM
2000-01	Richelieu	Q-RHL	STATISTICS NOT AVAILABLE									
2001-02	Baie-Comeau	QMJHL	64	25	45	70	36	5	1	5	6	4
2002-03	Baie-Comeau	QMJHL	25	5	16	21	12	....	....	....	....	....
	Shawinigan	QMJHL	35	6	35	41	21	9	3	8	11	8
2003-04	Shawinigan	QMJHL	68	34	61	95	32	10	4	9	13	2

Canadian Major Junior Most Sportsmanlike Player of the Year (2004)

MONYCH, Lance (MOH-nihch, LANTS) PHX.

Right wing. Shoots right. 6'3", 194 lbs. Born, Red Deer, Alta., July 25, 1984.
(Phoenix's 6th choice, 97th overall, in 2002 Entry Draft).

			Regular Season					Playoffs				
Season	Club	League	GP	G	A	TP	PIM	GP	G	A	TP	PIM
99-2000	Brandon Hawks	MBHL	30	32	34	66	98	....	....	....	....	....
	Brandon	WHL	3	0	0	0	0	....	....	....	....	....
2000-01	Brandon	WHL	53	14	8	22	34	6	1	0	1	0
2001-02	Brandon	WHL	71	18	30	48	96	19	4	3	7	20
2002-03	Brandon	WHL	70	19	26	45	111	17	7	3	10	20
2003-04	Brandon	WHL	58	29	26	55	71	11	2	6	8	8

MOORE, Greg (MOOR, GREHG) NYR

Right wing. Shoots right. 6'1", 206 lbs. Born, Lisbon, ME, March 26, 1984.
(Calgary's 5th choice, 143rd overall, in 2003 Entry Draft).

			Regular Season					Playoffs				
Season	Club	League	GP	G	A	TP	PIM	GP	G	A	TP	PIM
99-2000	St. Dominic High	Hi-School	31	32	40	72	....	....	....	....	....	....
2000-01	U.S. National U-17	USDP	69	12	18	30	23	....	....	....	....	....
2001-02	U.S. National U-18	USDP	53	13	24	37	20	....	....	....	....	....
2002-03	U. of Maine	H-East	33	9	7	16	10	....	....	....	....	....
2003-04	U. of Maine	H-East	39	15	8	23	44	....	....	....	....	....

Traded to **NY Rangers** by **Calgary** with Jamie McLennan and Blair Betts for Chris Simon and NY Rangers' 7th round choice (Matt Schneider) in 2004 Entry Draft, March 6, 2004.

MORMINA, Joey (mohr-MEE-nah, JOH-ee) PHI.

Defense. Shoots left. 6'6", 220 lbs. Born, Montreal, Que., June 29, 1982.
(Philadelphia's 6th choice, 193rd overall, in 2002 Entry Draft).

			Regular Season					Playoffs				
Season	Club	League	GP	G	A	TP	PIM	GP	G	A	TP	PIM
2000-01	Holderness School	Hi-School	29	15	15	30	....	....	....	....	....	....
2001-02	Colgate University	ECAC	34	2	13	15	28	....	....	....	....	....
2002-03	Colgate University	ECAC	40	4	9	13	52	....	....	....	....	....
2003-04	Colgate University	ECAC	28	2	10	12	26	....	....	....	....	....

MORRIS, Mike (MOHR-his, MIGHK) S.J.

Right wing. Shoots right. 6'1", 182 lbs. Born, Dorchester, MA, July 14, 1983.
(San Jose's 1st choice, 27th overall, in 2002 Entry Draft).

			Regular Season					Playoffs				
Season	Club	League	GP	G	A	TP	PIM	GP	G	A	TP	PIM
2000-01	St. Sebastian's	Hi-School	28	20	28	48	18	....	....	....	....	....
2001-02	St. Sebastian's	Hi-School	31	29	29	58	26	....	....	....	....	....
2002-03	Northeastern	H-East	26	9	12	21	16	....	....	....	....	....
2003-04	Northeastern	H-East	34	10	20	30	14	....	....	....	....	....

MORRISON, Justin (MOHR-ih-suhn, JUHS-tihn) VAN.

Right wing. Shoots right. 6'3", 205 lbs. Born, Los Angeles, CA, September 10, 1979.
(Vancouver's 4th choice, 81st overall, in 1998 Entry Draft).

			Regular Season					Playoffs				
Season	Club	League	GP	G	A	TP	PIM	GP	G	A	TP	PIM
1996-97	Omaha Lancers	USHL	62	12	24	36	44	10	2	4	6	8
1997-98	Colorado College	WCHA	42	4	9	13	8	....	....	....	....	....
1998-99	Colorado College	WCHA	38	23	15	38	33	....	....	....	....	....
99-2000	Colorado College	WCHA	38	7	19	26	28	....	....	....	....	....
2000-01	Colorado College	WCHA	41	21	14	35	42	....	....	....	....	....
2001-02	Manitoba Moose	AHL	64	10	9	19	37	7	1	0	1	4
2002-03	Manitoba Moose	AHL	30	10	6	16	13	14	2	3	5	4
	Columbia Inferno	ECHL	40	20	35	55	39	2	0	0	0	4
2003-04	Manitoba Moose	AHL	66	18	18	36	27	....	....	....	....	....

MORROW, Thomas (MOHR-roh, TAW-muhs) BUF.

Defense. Shoots left. 6'6", 198 lbs. Born, St. Paul, MN, October 21, 1983.
(Buffalo's 6th choice, 150th overall, in 2003 Entry Draft).

			Regular Season					Playoffs				
Season	Club	League	GP	G	A	TP	PIM	GP	G	A	TP	PIM
2000-01	Hill-Murray	Hi-School	30	2	12	14	....	....	....	....	....	....
2001-02	Hill-Murray	Hi-School	31	3	27	39	....	....	....	....	....	....
2002-03	Tri-City Storm	USHL	23	1	3	4	64	....	....	....	....	....
	Des Moines	USHL	34	1	6	7	40	....	....	....	....	....
2003-04	Boston University	H-East	38	0	3	3	34	....	....	....	....	....

MOSOVSKY, Karel (moh-SAWV-skee, KA-rehl)

Left wing. Shoots right. 6'2", 198 lbs. Born, Piesk, Czech., August 22, 1981.
(Buffalo's 6th choice, 117th overall, in 1999 Entry Draft).

			Regular Season					Playoffs				
Season	Club	League	GP	G	A	TP	PIM	GP	G	A	TP	PIM
1997-98	C. Budejovice Jr.	Czech-Jr.	36	15	17	32	52	....	....	....	....	....
1998-99	Regina Pats	WHL	68	26	25	51	58	....	....	....	....	....
99-2000	Regina Pats	WHL	56	24	34	58	80	7	3	1	4	12
2000-01	Regina Pats	WHL	61	25	26	51	59	6	1	3	4	8
2001-02	Rochester	AHL	5	1	1	2	0	....	....	....	....	....
2002-03	Rochester	AHL	62	5	4	9	75	....	....	....	....	....
2003-04	Rochester	AHL	46	5	1	6	52	....	....	....	....	....

• Missed majority of 2001-02 season recovering from shoulder injury suffered in training camp, September 9, 2001.

MOSS, David (MAWS, DAY-vihd) CGY.

Left wing. Shoots left. 6'3", 185 lbs. Born, Dearborn, MI, December 28, 1981.
(Calgary's 9th choice, 220th overall, in 2001 Entry Draft).

			Regular Season					Playoffs				
Season	Club	League	GP	G	A	TP	PIM	GP	G	A	TP	PIM
99-2000	Catholic Central	Hi-School	28	18	20	28	20	....	....	....	....	....
2000-01	St. Louis Sting	NAJHL	9	2	2	4	2	....	....	....	....	....
	Cedar Rapids	USHL	51	20	18	38	14	4	0	1	1	2
2001-02	U. of Michigan	CCHA	43	4	9	13	10	....	....	....	....	....
2002-03	U. of Michigan	CCHA	43	14	17	31	37	....	....	....	....	....
2003-04	U. of Michigan	CCHA	38	8	12	20	18	....	....	....	....	....

MOULSON, Matt (MOWL-suhn, MAT) **PIT.**

Left wing. Shoots left. 6'1", 195 lbs. Born, North York, Ont., November 1, 1983.
(Pittsburgh's 11th choice, 263rd overall, in 2003 Entry Draft).

			Regular Season					Playoffs				
Season	Club	League	GP	G	A	TP	PIM	GP	G	A	TP	PIM
2001-02	Guelph	OJHL-B	42	56	46	102	80	....	....	....	....	....
2002-03	Cornell Big Red	ECAC	33	13	10	23	22	....	....	....	....	....
2003-04	Cornell Big Red	ECAC	32	18	17	35	37	....	....	....	....	....

MOZYAKIN, Sergei (mohz-YA-kihn, SAIR-gay) **CBJ**

Left wing. Shoots right. 5'10", 165 lbs. Born, Yaroslavl, USSR, March 30, 1981.
(Columbus' 13th choice, 263rd overall, in 2002 Entry Draft).

			Regular Season					Playoffs				
Season	Club	League	GP	G	A	TP	PIM	GP	G	A	TP	PIM
1998-99	Val d'Or Foreurs	QMJHL	4	0	1	1	2	....	....	....	....	....
99-2000	CSKA Moscow 2	Russia-3	6	9	3	12	6	....	....	....	....	....
	HC CSKA Moscow	Russia-2	44	23	25	48	10	....	....	....	....	....
2000-01	HC CSKA Moscow	Russia-2	37	22	28	50	18	....	....	....	....	....
	CSKA Moscow	Russia	9	0	2	2	0	....	....	....	....	....
2001-02	HC CSKA Moscow	Russia-2	54	34	30	64	10	12	9	12	21	4
2002-03	CSKA Moscow	Russia	33	12	15	27	18	....	....	....	....	....
2003-04	CSKA Moscow	Russia	45	21	19	40	6	....	....	....	....	....

MUKHACHEV, Andrei (moo-khah-CHEHV, AWN-dray) **NSH.**

Defense. Shoots left. 6'3", 196 lbs. Born, Sverdlovsk, USSR, July 21, 1980.
(Nashville's 11th choice, 210th overall, in 2003 Entry Draft).

			Regular Season					Playoffs				
Season	Club	League	GP	G	A	TP	PIM	GP	G	A	TP	PIM
1998-99	CSKA Moscow	Russia-2	38	0	2	2	30	....	....	....	....	....
99-2000	CSKA Moscow	Russia-2	40	2	9	11	44	....	....	....	....	....
2000-01	CSKA Moscow 2	Russia-3	8	1	5	6	18	....	....	....	....	....
	CSKA Moscow	Russia-2	40	2	9	11	44	....	....	....	....	....
2001-02	CSKA Moscow	Russia-2	39	3	9	12	28	12	2	5	7	10
2002-03	CSKA Moscow	Russia	50	3	7	10	30	....	....	....	....	....
2003-04	CSKA Moscow	Russia	38	2	4	6	28	....	....	....	....	....

MULICK, Robert (muhl-LIHK, RAW-buhrt)

Defense. Shoots right. 6'2", 210 lbs. Born, Toronto, Ont., October 23, 1979.
(San Jose's 8th choice, 185th overall, in 1998 Entry Draft).

			Regular Season					Playoffs				
Season	Club	League	GP	G	A	TP	PIM	GP	G	A	TP	PIM
1994-95	Mississauga Reps	MTHL	52	8	23	31	80	....	....	....	....	....
1995-96	Sault Ste. Marie	OHL	54	0	3	3	58	3	0	0	0	0
1996-97	Sault Ste. Marie	OHL	60	2	8	10	49	11	0	1	1	12
1997-98	Sault Ste. Marie	OHL	61	0	10	10	109	....	....	....	....	....
1998-99	Sault Ste. Marie	OHL	66	1	12	13	83	5	0	1	1	10
99-2000	Kentucky	AHL	52	0	0	0	52	9	0	0	0	10
2000-01	Kentucky	AHL	71	0	6	6	55	2	0	0	0	0
2001-02	Cleveland Barons	AHL	60	0	2	2	77	....	....	....	....	....
2002-03	Cleveland Barons	AHL	24	0	0	0	14	....	....	....	....	....
2003-04	Cleveland Barons	AHL	63	1	5	6	26	3	0	0	0	2

Missed majority of 2002-03 season recovering from thigh injury suffered in game vs. Hamilton (AHL), December 6, 2002.

MURATOV, Yevgeny (muhr-A-tahf, ehv-GEH-nee) **EDM.**

Left wing. Shoots right. 5'10", 178 lbs. Born, Nizhny Tagil, USSR, January 28, 1981.
(Edmonton's 10th choice, 274th overall, in 2000 Entry Draft).

			Regular Season					Playoffs				
Season	Club	League	GP	G	A	TP	PIM	GP	G	A	TP	PIM
1997-98	Nizhnekamsk 2	Russia-3	39	7	7	14	2	....	....	....	....	....
1998-99	Nizhnekamsk 2	Russia-4	37	26	9	35	32	....	....	....	....	....
	Nizhnekamsk	Russia	4	0	0	0	0	3	1	0	1	2
99-2000	Nizhnekamsk	Russia	29	9	7	16	2	....	....	....	....	....
	Ak Bars Kazan	Russia	8	2	2	4	2	9	0	0	0	2
2000-01	Nizhnekamsk	Russia	42	9	8	17	14	4	0	0	0	0
2001-02	Nizhnekamsk	Russia	45	5	13	18	4	....	....	....	....	....
2002-03	Nizhnekamsk	Russia	51	10	11	21	41	....	....	....	....	....
2003-04	Nizhnekamsk	Russia	20	1	6	7	8	....	....	....	....	....

MURPHY, Mark (MUHR-fee, MAHRK) **PHI.**

Left wing. Shoots right. 5'11", 200 lbs. Born, Stoughton, MA, August 6, 1976.
(Toronto's 6th choice, 197th overall, in 1995 Entry Draft).

			Regular Season					Playoffs				
Season	Club	League	GP	G	A	TP	PIM	GP	G	A	TP	PIM
1994-95	Stratford Cullitons	OJHL-B	47	52	56	108	64	....	....	....	....	....
1995-96	Stratford Cullitons	OJHL-B	1	0	0	0	0	....	....	....	....	....
	RPI Engineers	ECAC	32	1	1	2	50	....	....	....	....	....
1996-97	RPI Engineers	ECAC	34	9	18	27	56	....	....	....	....	....
1997-98	RPI Engineers	ECAC	35	8	27	35	63	....	....	....	....	....
1998-99	RPI Engineers	ECAC	37	11	30	41	76	....	....	....	....	....
99-2000	Wilkes-Barre	AHL	38	11	22	33	35	....	....	....	....	....
	Trenton Titans	ECHL	37	21	18	39	60	12	2	8	10	17
	Philadelphia	AHL	....	....	....	....	....	2	0	0	0	0
2000-01	Portland Pirates	AHL	76	29	41	70	92	3	2	0	2	2
2001-02	Portland Pirates	AHL	77	20	37	57	56	....	....	....	....	....
2002-03	Portland Pirates	AHL	55	18	24	42	84	3	0	1	1	2
2003-04	Philadelphia	AHL	80	16	22	38	104	12	5	4	9	0

Signed as a free agent by **Washington**, July 13, 2000. Signed as a free agent by **Philadelphia**, July 24, 2003.

MURPHY, Patrick (MUHR-fee, PAT-rihk) **EDM.**

Left wing. Shoots left. 6'1", 195 lbs. Born, Van Nuys, CA, July 24, 1983.
(Edmonton's 11th choice, 211th overall, in 2002 Entry Draft).

			Regular Season					Playoffs				
Season	Club	League	GP	G	A	TP	PIM	GP	G	A	TP	PIM
2000-01	Newmarket	OPJHL	40	13	18	31	95	....	....	....	....	....
2001-02	Newmarket	OPJHL	48	11	21	32	99	....	....	....	....	....
2002-03	Northern Michigan	CCHA	22	1	2	3	26	....	....	....	....	....
2003-04	Northern Michigan	CCHA	35	5	3	8	50	....	....	....	....	....

MURPHY, Ryan (MUHR-fee, RIGH-yan) **N.J.**

Left wing. Shoots left. 6'1", 210 lbs. Born, Van Nuys, CA, March 21, 1979.
(Carolina's 4th choice, 113th overall, in 1999 Entry Draft).

			Regular Season					Playoffs				
Season	Club	League	GP	G	A	TP	PIM	GP	G	A	TP	PIM
1995-96	Thornhill Islanders	MTJHL	32	13	16	29	49	1	0	0	0	0
1996-97	Thornhill Islanders	MTJHL	41	22	32	54	36	12	7	8	15	....
1997-98	Bowling Green	CCHA	36	3	9	12	27	....	....	....	....	....
1998-99	Bowling Green	CCHA	34	10	23	33	38	....	....	....	....	....
99-2000	Bowling Green	CCHA	36	9	10	19	63	....	....	....	....	....
2000-01	Bowling Green	CCHA	38	23	15	38	22	....	....	....	....	....
2001-02	Florida Everblades	ECHL	66	13	18	31	38	6	1	2	3	4
2002-03	Florida Everblades	ECHL	58	28	17	45	47	1	0	0	0	0
	Lowell	AHL	12	1	2	3	4	....	....	....	....	....
2003-04	Albany River Rats	AHL	71	10	9	19	28	....	....	....	....	....

Signed as a free agent by **New Jersey**, July 30, 2003.

MURRAY, Andrew (MUHR-ree, AN-droo) **CBJ**

Center. Shoots left. 6'2", 210 lbs. Born, Selkirk, Man., November 6, 1981.
(Columbus' 11th choice, 242nd overall, in 2001 Entry Draft).

			Regular Season					Playoffs				
Season	Club	League	GP	G	A	TP	PIM	GP	G	A	TP	PIM
99-2000	Selkirk Steelers	MJHL	63	29	48	77	....	....	....	....	....	....
2000-01	Selkirk Steelers	MJHL	64	46	56	102	72	5	3	0	3	6
2001-02	Bemidji State	CHA	35	15	15	30	22	....	....	....	....	....
2002-03	Bemidji State	CHA	36	9	18	27	38	....	....	....	....	....
2003-04	Bemidji State	CHA	25	6	14	20	41	....	....	....	....	....

CHA All-Rookie Team (2002)

MURRAY, Brady (MUHR-ree, BRAY-dee) **L.A.**

Center. Shoots left. 5'9", 165 lbs. Born, Brandon, Man., August 17, 1984.
(Los Angeles' 6th choice, 152nd overall, in 2003 Entry Draft).

			Regular Season					Playoffs				
Season	Club	League	GP	G	A	TP	PIM	GP	G	A	TP	PIM
2001-02	Shat.-St. Mary's	Hi-School	60	58	92	150	50	....	....	....	....	....
2002-03	Salmon Arm	BCHL	59	42	59	101	30	....	....	....	....	....
2003-04	North Dakota	WCHA	37	19	27	46	32	....	....	....	....	....

WCHA All-Rookie Team (2004) • WCHA Rookie of the Year (2004)

MURRAY, Doug (MUHR-ree, DUHG) **S.J.**

Defense. Shoots left. 6'3", 245 lbs. Born, Bromma, Sweden, March 12, 1980.
(San Jose's 6th choice, 241st overall, in 1999 Entry Draft).

			Regular Season					Playoffs				
Season	Club	League	GP	G	A	TP	PIM	GP	G	A	TP	PIM
1998-99	NY Apple Core	MJBHL	60	17	47	64	62	....	....	....	....	....
99-2000	Cornell Big Red	ECAC	32	3	6	9	38	....	....	....	....	....
2000-01	Cornell Big Red	ECAC	25	5	13	18	39	....	....	....	....	....
2001-02	Cornell Big Red	ECAC	35	11	21	32	67	....	....	....	....	....
2002-03	Cornell Big Red	ECAC	35	5	20	25	30	....	....	....	....	....
2003-04	Cleveland Barons	AHL	72	10	12	22	75	9	3	0	3	37

ECAC First All-Star Team (2002, 2003) • NCAA East First All-American Team (2003)

NASBY, Bret (NAZ-bee, BREHT) **FLA.**

Defense. Shoots right. 6'3", 188 lbs. Born, Grimsby, Ont., March 22, 1986.
(Florida's 5th choice, 152nd overall, in 2004 Entry Draft).

			Regular Season					Playoffs				
Season	Club	League	GP	G	A	TP	PIM	GP	G	A	TP	PIM
2002-03	Grimsby	OJHL-C	53	6	14	20	63	....	....	....	....	....
2003-04	Oshawa Generals	OHL	56	0	7	7	41	7	0	3	3	6

NASLUND, Fredrik (NAZ-luhnd, FREHD-uhr-ihk) **DAL.**

Left wing. Shoots right. 6'4", 211 lbs. Born, Bromma, Sweden, February 11, 1986.
(Dallas' 6th choice, 104th overall, in 2004 Entry Draft).

			Regular Season					Playoffs				
Season	Club	League	GP	G	A	TP	PIM	GP	G	A	TP	PIM
2002-03	Vasteras Jr.	Swede-Jr.	34	12	9	21	8	....	....	....	....	....
2003-04	Vasteras Jr.	Swede-Jr.	17	13	15	28	6	3	0	1	1	4
	Vasteras	Swede-2	32	2	4	6	0	....	....	....	....	....

NAUROV, Alexander (naw-OO-rawf, ahl-ehx-AN-duhr) **DAL.**

Right wing. Shoots left. 5'11", 191 lbs. Born, Saratov, USSR, March 4, 1985.
(Dallas' 5th choice, 134th overall, in 2003 Entry Draft).

			Regular Season					Playoffs				
Season	Club	League	GP	G	A	TP	PIM	GP	G	A	TP	PIM
99-2000	Yaroslavl 16	Russia-Jr.	....	....	....	....	....	6	1	2	3	4
2000-01	Yaroslavl 18	Russia-Jr.	29	13	14	27	40	7	2	4	6	2
2001-02	Yaroslavl Jr.	Russia-Jr.	36	15	18	33	42	....	....	....	....	....
	Yaroslavl 2	Russia-3	12	0	0	0	16	....	....	....	....	....
2002-03	Yaroslavl Jr.	Russia-Jr.	4	3	0	3	0	....	....	....	....	....
	Yaroslavl 2	Russia-3	9	3	7	10	0	....	....	....	....	....
2003-04	Yaroslavl 2	Russia-3	24	9	5	14	73	....	....	....	....	....

NEILSON, Eric (NEEHL-sohn, AIR-ihk) **L.A.**

Right wing. Shoots right. 6'1", 201 lbs. Born, Fredericton, N.B., August 18, 1984.
(Los Angeles' 4th choice, 143rd overall, in 2004 Entry Draft).

			Regular Season					Playoffs				
Season	Club	League	GP	G	A	TP	PIM	GP	G	A	TP	PIM
2001-02	Rimouski Oceanic	QMJHL	48	0	2	2	130	4	0	0	0	25
2002-03	Rimouski Oceanic	QMJHL	53	2	9	11	341	....	....	....	....	....
2003-04	Rimouski Oceanic	QMJHL	50	4	11	15	194	9	0	0	0	28

NEMEC, Ondrej (NEH-mehts, AWN-dray) **PIT.**

Defense. Shoots right. 6'1", 196 lbs. Born, Trebic, Czech., April 18, 1984.
(Pittsburgh's 2nd choice, 35th overall, in 2002 Entry Draft).

			Regular Season					Playoffs				
Season	Club	League	GP	G	A	TP	PIM	GP	G	A	TP	PIM
1998-99	Trebic Jr.	Czech-Jr.	31	18	13	31	....	....	....	....	....	....
99-2000	Vsetin Jr.	Czech-Jr.	5	0	2	2	4	....	....	....	....	....
	Vsetin 18	Czech-Jr.	48	6	18	24	62	....	....	....	....	....
2000-01	Vsetin Jr.	Czech-Jr.	42	10	12	22	77	....	....	....	....	....
	Vsetin 18	Czech-Jr.	8	3	7	10	20	....	....	....	....	....
2001-02	Vsetin Jr.	Czech-Jr.	8	4	7	11	47	....	....	....	....	....
	Trebic	Czech-2	9	1	0	1	18	....	....	....	....	....
	Vsetin	Czech	44	5	3	8	79	....	....	....	....	....
2002-03	Vsetin	Czech	39	2	7	9	40	4	0	0	0	2
	Trebic	Czech-2	2	0	0	0	6	....	....	....	....	....
2003-04	HC Vsetin	Czech	42	2	4	6	30	....	....	....	....	....
	SK Trebic	Czech-2	2	0	0	0	2	....	....	....	....	....
	Wilkes-Barre	AHL	7	1	2	3	2	7	0	1	1	6

NEPRYAYEV, Ivan (neh-pree-YIGH-ehv, IGH-van) **WSH.**

Center. Shoots left. 6'1", 180 lbs. Born, Yaroslavl, USSR, February 4, 1982.
(Washington's 5th choice, 163rd overall, in 2000 Entry Draft).

			Regular Season					Playoffs				
Season	Club	League	GP	G	A	TP	PIM	GP	G	A	TP	PIM
1997-98	Torpedo Yaroslavl	Russia	6	0	0	0	0	....	....	....	....	....
1998-99	Yaroslavl 2	Russia-3	15	1	0	1	0	....	....	....	....	....
99-2000	Yaroslavl 2	Russia-3	40	8	14	22	....	....	....	....	....	....
2000-01	Yaroslavl	Russia	10	0	0	0	2	....	....	....	....	....
2001-02	Yaroslavl 2	Russia-3	2	1	0	1	18	....	....	....	....	....
	Yaroslavl	Russia	36	3	8	11	28	....	....	....	....	....
2002-03	Yaroslavl	Russia	26	3	6	9	12	6	1	0	1	0
2003-04	Yaroslavl 2	Russia-3	13	5	10	15	12	....	....	....	....	....

NEWBURY, Kris (new-BUHR-ee, KRIHS)

Center. Shoots left. 5'10", 200 lbs. Born, Brampton, Ont., February 19, 1982.
(San Jose's 4th choice, 139th overall, in 2002 Entry Draft).

			Regular Season					Playoffs				
Season	Club	League	GP	G	A	TP	PIM	GP	G	A	TP	PIM
1996-97	Brampton Capitals	OPJHL	28	9	4	13	36	....	....	....	....	....
1997-98	Brampton Capitals	OPJHL	46	11	21	32	161	....	....	....	....	....
1998-99	Belleville Bulls	OHL	51	6	8	14	89	....	....	....	....	....
99-2000	Belleville Bulls	OHL	34	6	18	24	72	....	....	....	....	....
	Sarnia Sting	OHL	27	6	8	14	44	7	0	3	3	16
2000-01	Sarnia Sting	OHL	64	28	30	58	126	4	1	3	4	20
2001-02	Sarnia Sting	OHL	66	42	62	104	141	5	1	3	4	15
2002-03	Sarnia Sting	OHL	64	34	58	92	149	6	4	4	8	16
2003-04	St. John's	AHL	72	5	15	20	153	....	....	....	....	....

Signed as a free agent by **St. John's** (AHL), October 2, 2003.

NEWMAN, Jared (NOO-muhn, JAIR-ehd) **CAR.**

Defense. Shoots right. 6'2", 201 lbs. Born, Detroit, MI, March 7, 1982.
(Carolina's 4th choice, 110th overall, in 2000 Entry Draft).

			Regular Season					Playoffs				
Season	Club	League	GP	G	A	TP	PIM	GP	G	A	TP	PIM
1997-98	Det. Compuware	NAJHL	49	1	4	5	69	....	....	....	....	....
1998-99	Plymouth Whalers	OHL	66	2	15	17	57	11	1	2	3	9
99-2000	Plymouth Whalers	OHL	50	1	15	16	123	23	0	5	5	34
2000-01	Plymouth Whalers	OHL	34	0	4	4	114	6	0	3	3	26
2001-02	Plymouth Whalers	OHL	60	2	14	16	106	6	0	1	1	8
2002-03	Florida Everblades	ECHL	29	1	1	2	82	....	....	....	....	....
2003-04	Lowell	AHL	8	0	1	1	2	....	....	....	....	....
	Florida Everblades	ECHL	42	2	7	9	87	17	2	3	5	14

NICKERSON, Matt (NIH-kuhr-suhn, MAT) **DAL.**

Defense. Shoots right. 6'4", 230 lbs. Born, New Haven, CT, January 11, 1985.
(Dallas' 4th choice, 99th overall, in 2003 Entry Draft).

			Regular Season					Playoffs				
Season	Club	League	GP	G	A	TP	PIM	GP	G	A	TP	PIM
2000-01	Victoria Salsa	BCHL	....	....	....	....	196	....	....	....	....	....
2001-02	Texas Tornado	NAHL	47	1	12	13	97	6	0	0	0	6
2002-03	Texas Tornado	NAHL	47	6	23	29	277	6	0	1	1	*18
2003-04	Clarkson Knights	ECAC	38	5	9	14	*179	....	....	....	....	....

NIELSEN, Frans (NEEL-sehn, FRAHNS) **NYI**

Center. Shoots left. 5'11", 172 lbs. Born, Herning, Denmark, April 24, 1984.
(NY Islanders' 2nd choice, 87th overall, in 2002 Entry Draft).

			Regular Season					Playoffs				
Season	Club	League	GP	G	A	TP	PIM	GP	G	A	TP	PIM
99-2000	Herning IK Jr.	Denmark	36	18	16	34	6	....	....	....	....	....
2000-01	Herning IK	Denmark	38	18	19	37	6	....	....	....	....	....
2001-02	Malmo IF	Sweden	20	0	1	1	0	....	....	....	....	....
	Malmo IF Jr.	Swede-Jr.	29	15	27	42	8	7	3	7	10	2
2002-03	Malmo	Sweden	47	3	6	9	10	....	....	....	....	....
	Malmo IF Jr.	Swede-Jr.	2	1	3	4	0	....	....	....	....	....
2003-04	Malmo	Sweden	50	9	7	16	28	....	....	....	....	....
	Malmo	Swede-Q	10	3	5	8	2	....	....	....	....	....

NIINIMAKI, Jesse (NIH-nee-ma-kee, JEH-see) **EDM.**

Center. Shoots left. 6'2", 183 lbs. Born, Tampere, Finland, August 19, 1983.
(Edmonton's 1st choice, 15th overall, in 2002 Entry Draft).

			Regular Season					Playoffs				
Season	Club	League	GP	G	A	TP	PIM	GP	G	A	TP	PIM
1998-99	Tappara-C	Finn-Jr.	22	7	22	29	18	4	0	2	2	2
99-2000	Ilves Tampere Jr.	Finn-Jr.	14	0	5	5	6	....	....	....	....	....
2000-01	Ilves Tampere 18	Finn-Jr.	16	3	5	8	40	....	....	....	....	....
	Ilves Tampere Jr.	Finn-Jr.	18	2	4	6	6	....	....	....	....	....
2001-02	Ilves Tampere Jr.	Finn-Jr.	27	9	23	32	54	....	....	....	....	....
	Ilves Tampere	Finland	16	2	4	6	4	3	0	0	0	0
2002-03	Ilves Tampere	Finland	41	4	13	17	12	....	....	....	....	....
	Ilves Tampere Jr.	Finn-Jr.	9	2	7	9	4	....	....	....	....	....
	Sport Vaasa	Finland-2	2	0	1	1	10	....	....	....	....	....
2003-04	Ilves Tampere	Finland	10	3	3	6	2	....	....	....	....	....

NIKITIN, Nikita (nih-KEE-tihn, nih-KEE-tuh) **ST.L.**

Defense. Shoots left. 6'3", 178 lbs. Born, Omsk, USSR, June 16, 1986.
(St. Louis' 5th choice, 136th overall, in 2004 Entry Draft).

			Regular Season					Playoffs				
Season	Club	League	GP	G	A	TP	PIM	GP	G	A	TP	PIM
2002-03	Omsk 2	Russia-3	34	3	7	10	4	....	....	....	....	....
	Omsk 17	Russia-Jr.	7	0	1	1	2	....	....	....	....	....
2003-04	Omsk 2	Russia-3	34	3	8	11	22	....	....	....	....	....

NIKOLOV, Angel (NIH-koh-lohv, AYN-jehl) **S.J.**

Defense. Shoots left. 6'2", 205 lbs. Born, Most, Czech., November 18, 1975.
(San Jose's 2nd choice, 37th overall, in 1994 Entry Draft).

			Regular Season					Playoffs				
Season	Club	League	GP	G	A	TP	PIM	GP	G	A	TP	PIM
1993-94	Litvinov	Czech	10	2	2	4	....	3	0	0	0	....
1994-95	Litvinov	Czech	41	1	4	5	18	4	0	0	0	27
1995-96	Litvinov	Czech	40	1	7	8	....	10	0	1	1	....
	Litvinov	EuroHL	6	0	1	1	0	2	0	0	0	2
1996-97	Litvinov	Czech	47	0	9	9	44	....	....	....	....	....
1997-98	Litvinov	Czech	51	1	4	5	53	4	0	3	3	27
1998-99	Litvinov	Czech	51	5	12	17	54	....	....	....	....	....
	Litvinov	EuroHL	5	1	0	1	2	....	....	....	....	....
99-2000	Litvinov	Czech	51	6	15	21	32	7	1	2	3	2
2000-01	Litvinov	Czech	48	5	11	16	85	6	0	1	1	6
2001-02	JYP Jyvaskyla	Finland	53	4	16	20	56	....	....	....	....	....
2002-03	JYP Jyvaskyla	Finland	46	2	11	13	54	7	0	3	3	6
2003-04	Novokuznetsk	Russia	57	2	6	8	61	4	0	0	0	2

NIKULIN, Alexander (nih-KOO-lihn, al-EHX-AN-duhr) **OTT.**

Center. Shoots left. 6'1", 195 lbs. Born, Moscow, USSR, August 25, 1985.
(Ottawa's 6th choice, 122nd overall, in 2004 Entry Draft).

			Regular Season					Playoffs				
Season	Club	League	GP	G	A	TP	PIM	GP	G	A	TP	PIM
2002-03	CSKA Moscow 2	Russia-3	46	22	14	36	....	....	....	....	....	....
2003-04	CSKA Moscow 2	Russia-3	47	21	20	41	46	....	....	....	....	....

NIKULIN, Ilja (nih-KOO-lihn, ihl-YUH) **ATL.**

Defense. Shoots left. 6'3", 210 lbs. Born, Moscow, USSR, March 12, 1982.
(Atlanta's 2nd choice, 31st overall, in 2000 Entry Draft).

			Regular Season					Playoffs				
Season	Club	League	GP	G	A	TP	PIM	GP	G	A	TP	PIM
1998-99	Dyn. Moscow 2	Russia-3	23	0	2	2	18	....	....	....	....	....
99-2000	Dyn. Moscow 2	Russia-3	4	2	1	3	10	....	....	....	....	....
	THC Tver	Russia-2	39	3	6	9	84	....	....	....	....	....
2000-01	Dynamo Moscow	Russia	44	0	4	4	61	....	....	....	....	....
2001-02	Dyn. Moscow 2	Russia-3	2	0	1	1	2	....	....	....	....	....
	Dynamo Moscow	Russia	47	2	1	3	44	3	0	0	0	0
2002-03	Dynamo Moscow	Russia	40	1	4	5	46	5	0	1	1	4
2003-04	Dynamo Moscow	Russia	54	1	5	6	56	3	0	0	0	2

NILSSON, Magnus (NIHL-suhn, MAG-nuhs) **DET.**

Right wing. Shoots left. 6'1", 187 lbs. Born, Finspang, Sweden, February 1, 1978.
(Detroit's 5th choice, 144th overall, in 1996 Entry Draft).

			Regular Season					Playoffs				
Season	Club	League	GP	G	A	TP	PIM	GP	G	A	TP	PIM
1995-96	Vita Hasten	Swede-2	28	3	3	6	16	....	....	....	....	....
1996-97	Malmo IF Jr.	Swede-Jr.	14	10	9	19	45	....	....	....	....	....
	Malmo IF	Sweden	12	0	0	0	0	....	....	....	....	....
1997-98	Malmo IF	Sweden	45	6	1	7	6	....	....	....	....	....
1998-99	Malmo IF	Sweden	42	0	0	0	10	4	0	0	0	0
99-2000	Malmo IF	Sweden	44	5	5	10	63	6	0	0	0	25
2000-01	Louisiana	ECHL	68	13	11	24	66	11	3	2	5	8
2001-02	Toledo Storm	ECHL	57	15	20	35	63	....	....	....	....	....
2002-03	Lulea HF	Sweden	47	9	5	14	72	4	0	2	2	2
2003-04	Lulea HF	Sweden	49	10	9	19	60	3	0	0	0	27

NILSSON, Mattias (NIHL-suhn, MA-tee-uhs) **NSH.**

Defense. Shoots left. 6'3", 195 lbs. Born, Ornskoldsvik, Sweden, February 6, 1982.
(Nashville's 3rd choice, 72nd overall, in 2000 Entry Draft).

			Regular Season					Playoffs				
Season	Club	League	GP	G	A	TP	PIM	GP	G	A	TP	PIM
1997-98	MoDo Jr.	Swede-Jr.	40	20	14	34	34	....	....	....	....	....
1998-99	MoDo Jr.	Swede-Jr.	30	7	7	14	26	....	....	....	....	....
99-2000	MoDo Jr.	Swede-Jr.	33	5	5	10	56	2	0	0	0	0
	MoDo-18	Swede-Jr.	7	0	2	2	10	....	....	....	....	....
2000-01	MoDo Jr.	Swede-Jr.	18	2	3	5	62	....	....	....	....	....
2001-02	Hammarby Jr.	Swede-Jr.	25	3	8	11	40	....	....	....	....	....
	Hammarby	Swede-2	20	0	1	1	18	2	1	0	1	0
2002-03	Hammarby	Swede-2	38	2	6	8	26	....	....	....	....	....
	Hammarby Jr.	Swede-Jr.	2	1	0	1	2	....	....	....	....	....
2003-04	IF Vallentuna BK	Swede-2	7	0	0	0	16	....	....	....	....	....
	Vallentuna	Swede-Q	7	0	0	0	16	....	....	....	....	....
	Hammarby Jr.	Swede-Jr.	7	0	0	0	10	....	....	....	....	....
	Hammarby IF	Swede-2	25	2	5	7	22	....	....	....	....	....
	Hammarby IF	Swede-Q	4	0	0	0	0	9	0	1	1	4

NILSSON, Robert (NIHL-suhn, RAW-buhrt) **NYI**

Center. Shoots left. 5'11", 176 lbs. Born, Calgary, Alta., January 10, 1985.
(NY Islanders' 1st choice, 15th overall, in 2003 Entry Draft).

			Regular Season					Playoffs				
Season	Club	League	GP	G	A	TP	PIM	GP	G	A	TP	PIM
2000-01	Leksands IF Jr.	Swede-Jr.	23	14	28	42	26	2	0	0	0	2
	Leksands IF-18	Swede-Jr.	4	6	3	9	6	2	0	2	2	2
2001-02	Leksands IF Jr.	Swede-Jr.	21	13	18	31	24	5	0	5	5	8
	Leksands IF	Swede-2	14	1	4	5	8	....	....	....	....	....
2002-03	Leksands IF	Sweden	41	8	13	21	10	5	0	1	1	2
	Leksands IF Jr.	Swede-Jr.	....	....	....	....	....	2	1	1	2	2
2003-04	Leksands IF Jr.	Swede-Jr.	4	2	8	10	4	....	....	....	....	....
	Leksands IF	Sweden	34	2	4	6	6	....	....	....	....	....
	Fribourg	Swiss	7	1	3	4	2	4	1	0	1	2

NISKALA, Janne (NIHS-kah-lah, YAH-nee) **NSH.**

Defense. Shoots left. 6', 187 lbs. Born, Rauma, Finland, September 22, 1981.
(Nashville's 5th choice, 147th overall, in 2004 Entry Draft).

			Regular Season					Playoffs				
Season	Club	League	GP	G	A	TP	PIM	GP	G	A	TP	PIM
2001-02	Lukko Rauma	Finland	55	7	13	20	81	....	....	....	....	....
2002-03	Lukko Rauma	Finland	46	4	5	9	40	....	....	....	....	....
2003-04	Lukko Rauma	Finland	55	21	15	36	73	4	0	0	0	16

NITTEL, Ahren (NIH-tuhl, AH-rehn) **N.J.**

Left wing. Shoots left. 6'3", 225 lbs. Born, Waterloo, Ont., December 6, 1983.
(New Jersey's 5th choice, 85th overall, in 2002 Entry Draft).

			Regular Season					Playoffs				
Season	Club	League	GP	G	A	TP	PIM	GP	G	A	TP	PIM
99-2000	Streetsville Derbys	OPJHL	11	1	5	6	10	....	....	....	....	....
2000-01	Windsor Spitfires	OHL	46	6	4	10	56	7	3	1	4	16
2001-02	Windsor Spitfires	OHL	52	19	11	30	100	9	4	1	5	23
2002-03	Windsor Spitfires	OHL	22	5	4	9	30	....	....	....	....	....
	Oshawa Generals	OHL	20	15	7	22	25	13	5	2	7	10
2003-04	Albany River Rats	AHL	42	4	3	7	24	....	....	....	....	....
	Adirondack	UHL	2	1	0	1	0	....	....	....	....	....

NOKELAINEN, Petteri (noh-kuh-LAY-nehn, PEH-tuh-ree) **NYI**

Center. Shoots right. 6'1", 187 lbs. Born, Imatra, Finland, January 16, 1986.
(NY Islanders' 1st choice, 16th overall, in 2004 Entry Draft).

			Regular Season					Playoffs				
Season	Club	League	GP	G	A	TP	PIM	GP	G	A	TP	PIM
2001-02	SaiPa Jr. C	Finn-Jr.	14	18	8	26	18	2	0	1	1	0
	SaiPa Jr. B	Finn-Jr.	6	2	1	3	14	....	....	....	....	....
2002-03	SaiPa	Finland	2	1	0	1	2	....	....	....	....	....
	SaiPa Jr. B	Finn-Jr.	10	3	8	11	18	....	....	....	....	....
	SaiPa Jr.	Finn-Jr.	28	7	4	11	28	3	1	0	1	4
	SaiPa	Finland	2	1	0	1	2	....	....	....	....	....
2003-04	SaiPa	Finland	40	4	4	8	16	....	....	....	....	....
	SaiPa Jr.	Finn-Jr.	10	5	3	8	4	4	0	1	1	0

NOLAN, Brandon (NOH-lan, BRAN-duhn) VAN.

Center. Shoots left. 6', 180 lbs. Born, Sault Ste. Marie, Ont., July 18, 1983.
(Vancouver's 3rd choice, 111th overall, in 2003 Entry Draft).

			Regular Season					Playoffs				
Season	Club	League	GP	G	A	TP	PIM	GP	G	A	TP	PIM
99-2000	St. Catharines	OJHL-B	47	18	13	31	10	....	....	....	....	....
2000-01	Oshawa Generals	OHL	52	15	23	38	21	....	....	....	....	....
2001-02	Oshawa Generals	OHL	57	30	28	58	78	5	2	4	6	4
2002-03	Oshawa Generals	OHL	68	36	52	88	57	13	10	7	17	4
2003-04	Manitoba Moose	AHL	48	7	10	17	18	....	....	....	....	....
	Columbia Inferno	ECHL	19	5	10	15	38	3	0	1	1	17

• Re-entered NHL Entry Draft. Originally New Jersey's 6th choice, 72nd overall, in 2001 Entry Draft.

OHL Second All-Star Team (2003)

NORDGREN, Niklas (NORHD-grehn, NIHK-las) CAR.

Left wing. Shoots right. 5'11", 185 lbs. Born, Ornskoldsvik, Sweden, June 28, 1979.
(Carolina's 7th choice, 195th overall, in 1997 Entry Draft).

			Regular Season					Playoffs				
Season	Club	League	GP	G	A	TP	PIM	GP	G	A	TP	PIM
1995-96	MoDo 18	Swede-Jr.	30	37	27	64	....	....	....	....	....	....
1996-97	MoDo Jr.	Swede-Jr.	22	14	6	20	....	....	....	....	....	....
	MoDo	Sweden	5	0	0	0	0	....	....	....	....	....
1997-98	MoDo Jr.	Swede-Jr.	28	15	15	30	52	....	....	....	....	....
1998-99	MoDo	Sweden	7	0	0	0	2	....	....	....	....	....
	MoDo Jr.	Swede-Jr.	22	7	4	11	22	3	2	1	3	0
99-2000	IF Sundsvall	Swede-2	27	21	11	32	58	....	....	....	....	....
	MoDo	EuroHL	1	0	0	0	0	1	0	0	0	0
2000-01	IF Sundsvall	Swede-2	35	22	19	41	45	....	....	....	....	....
2001-02	Timra IK Jr.	Swede-Jr.	1	1	1	2	0	....	....	....	....	....
	Timra IK	Sweden	49	8	6	14	16	....	....	....	....	....
	Timra IK	Swede-Q	10	3	3	5	4	....	....	....	....	....
2002-03	Timra IK	Sweden	47	20	23	43	40	10	1	4	5	4
2003-04	Timra IK	Sweden	46	13	15	28	44	10	4	1	5	32

NORDQVIST, Jonas (NAWRD-kvihst, YOH-nuhs) CHI.

Center. Shoots left. 6'3", 202 lbs. Born, Leksand, Sweden, April 26, 1982.
(Chicago's 3rd choice, 49th overall, in 2000 Entry Draft).

			Regular Season					Playoffs				
Season	Club	League	GP	G	A	TP	PIM	GP	G	A	TP	PIM
1997-98	Leksands IF Jr.	Swede-Jr.	42	26	35	61	....	....	....	....	....	....
1998-99	Leksands IF Jr.	Swede-Jr.	32	14	25	39	....	....	....	....	....	....
99-2000	Leksands IF Jr.	Swede-Jr.	34	15	24	39	32	2	0	0	0	2
	Leksands IF	Sweden	3	0	0	0	0	....	....	....	....	....
	Leksands IF 18	Swede-Jr.	2	0	2	2	0	4	3	5	8	0
2000-01	Leksands IF Jr.	Swede-Jr.	10	6	13	19	6	5	1	6	7	2
	Leksands IF	Sweden	42	3	4	7	4	....	....	....	....	....
2001-02	Leksands IF Jr.	Swede-Jr.	8	14	7	21	6	1	0	1	1	0
	Leksands IF	Swede-2	40	8	7	15	16	....	....	....	....	....
2002-03	Rogle	Swede-2	27	12	19	32	4	....	....	....	....	....
	Rogle	Swede-Q	14	4	2	6	4	10	2	1	3	4
2003-04	Lulea HF	Sweden	47	13	11	24	18	3	0	0	0	2

NOVAK, Filip (NOH-vak, FIH-lihp) FLA.

Defense. Shoots left. 6'1", 185 lbs. Born, Ceske Budejovice, Czech., May 7, 1982.
(NY Rangers' 1st choice, 64th overall, in 2000 Entry Draft).

			Regular Season					Playoffs				
Season	Club	League	GP	G	A	TP	PIM	GP	G	A	TP	PIM
1998-99	C. Budejovice Jr.	Czech-Jr.	68	8	10	18	34	....	....	....	....	....
99-2000	Regina Pats	WHL	47	7	32	39	70	7	1	4	5	5
2000-01	Regina Pats	WHL	64	17	50	67	75	6	1	4	5	6
2001-02	Regina Pats	WHL	60	12	46	58	125	6	2	2	4	19
2002-03	San Antonio	AHL	57	10	17	27	79	1	0	0	0	0
2003-04			DID NOT PLAY – INJURED									

WHL East Second All-Star Team (2001) • WHL East First All-Star Team (2002) • AHL All-Rookie Team (2003)

Traded to **Florida** by **NY Rangers** with Igor Ulanov, NY Rangers' 1st (later traded to Calgary – Calgary selected Eric Nystrom) and 2nd (Rob Globke) round choices in 2002 Entry Draft and NY Rangers' 4th round choice (later traded to Atlanta – Atlanta selected Guillaume Desbiens) in 2003 Entry Draft for Pavel Bure and Florida's 2nd round choice (Lee Falardeau) in 2002 Entry Draft, March 18, 2002. • Missed entire 2003-04 season recovering from ankle injury suffered in training camp, September 17, 2003.

NOVAK, Zbynek (NOH-vahk, z'BIHN-nehk) WSH.

Left wing. Shoots left. 6'2", 194 lbs. Born, Kutna Hora, Czech., July 23, 1983.
(Washington's 5th choice, 191st overall, in 2001 Entry Draft).

			Regular Season					Playoffs				
Season	Club	League	GP	G	A	TP	PIM	GP	G	A	TP	PIM
99-2000	HC Slavia Praha Jr.	Czech-Jr.	15	1	2	3	8	2	1	0	1	0
	HC Slavia Praha 18	Czech-Jr.	31	14	12	26	12	....	....	....	....	....
2000-01	HC Slavia Praha Jr.	Czech-Jr.	44	10	8	18	24	3	1	0	1	2
2001-02	HC Slavia Praha 18	Czech-Jr.	3	1	0	1	2	....	....	....	....	....
	HC Slavia Praha Jr.	Czech-Jr.	23	11	12	23	8	....	....	....	....	....
	HC Slavia Praha	Czech	27	0	1	1	2	....	....	....	....	....
	HC Brod	Czech-3	5	0	2	2	0	2	1	0	1	2
2002-03	Beroun	Czech-2	30	4	7	11	14	....	....	....	....	....
	HC Slavia Praha	Czech	10	1	0	1	0	6	0	0	0	0
	HC Slavia Praha Jr.	Czech-Jr.	3	1	1	2	2	2	1	0	1	4
2003-04	Plzen Jr.	Czech-Jr.	34	13	18	31	36	....	....	....	....	....
	HC Havirov	Czech-2	5	0	0	0	4	....	....	....	....	....
	Havirov Jr.	Czech-Jr.	6	0	0	0	6	....	....	....	....	....

NOVOTNY, Jiri (NOH-vaht-nee, YOO-ree) BUF.

Center. Shoots right. 6'2", 194 lbs. Born, Pelhrimov, Czech., August 12, 1983.
(Buffalo's 1st choice, 22nd overall, in 2001 Entry Draft).

			Regular Season					Playoffs				
Season	Club	League	GP	G	A	TP	PIM	GP	G	A	TP	PIM
99-2000	C. Budejovice Jr.	Czech-Jr.	36	11	10	21	6	....	....	....	....	....
	C. Budejovice 18	Czech-Jr.	11	5	7	12	4	....	....	....	....	....
	HC Slezan Opava	Czech-2	17	2	2	4	6	....	....	....	....	....
2000-01	C. Budejovice Jr.	Czech-Jr.	33	10	10	20	....	....	....	....	....	....
	SHC Hradec	Czech-3	1	0	0	0	0	....	....	....	....	....
2001-02	C. Budejovice Jr.	Czech-Jr.	7	4	4	8	4	....	....	....	....	....
	Jindrichuv Hradec	Czech-3	3	1	3	4	0	....	....	....	....	....
	Ceske Budejovice	Czech	41	8	6	14	6	....	....	....	....	....
2002-03	Rochester	AHL	43	2	9	11	14	3	0	1	1	10
2003-04	Rochester	AHL	48	1	14	15	16	13	0	1	1	10

NOWAK, Brett (NOH-wak, BREHT)

Center. Shoots left. 6'2", 192 lbs. Born, New Haven, CT, May 20, 1981.
(Boston's 7th choice, 102nd overall, in 2000 Entry Draft).

			Regular Season					Playoffs				
Season	Club	League	GP	G	A	TP	PIM	GP	G	A	TP	PIM
1997-98	Hotchkiss High	Hi-School	21	24	42	66	42	....	....	....	....	....
1998-99	Hotchkiss High	Hi-School	20	21	36	57	6	....	....	....	....	....
99-2000	Harvard Crimson	ECAC	26	6	11	17	20	....	....	....	....	....
2000-01	Harvard Crimson	ECAC	24	7	9	16	26	....	....	....	....	....
2001-02	Harvard Crimson	ECAC	33	14	17	31	50	....	....	....	....	....
2002-03	Harvard Crimson	ECAC	33	12	29	41	57	....	....	....	....	....
2003-04	Providence Bruins	AHL	55	3	10	13	37	1	1	0	1	2

ECAC Second All-Star Team (2002)

NUSSLI, Thomas (NEWS-lee, TAW-muhs) VAN.

Right wing. Shoots left. 6'2", 207 lbs. Born, Nesskin, Switz., March 12, 1982.
(Vancouver's 10th choice, 277th overall, in 2002 Entry Draft).

			Regular Season					Playoffs				
Season	Club	League	GP	G	A	TP	PIM	GP	G	A	TP	PIM
1998-99	HC Herisau Jr.	Swiss-Jr.	33	30	15	45	24	....	....	....	....	....
	SC Herisau	Swiss-2	5	1	0	1	0	3	1	0	1	0
99-2000	EV Zug	Swiss	2	0	0	0	0	....	....	....	....	....
	EV Zug Jr.	Swiss-Jr.	33	14	18	32	99	2	1	1	2	8
	EV Zug	Swiss	2	0	0	0	0	....	....	....	....	....
2000-01	EHC Basel	Swiss-2	6	1	2	3	6	....	....	....	....	....
	EV Zug Jr.	Swiss-Jr.	9	7	7	14	30	....	....	....	....	....
	EV Zug	Swiss	34	6	2	8	10	4	0	0	0	2
2001-02	EV Zug Jr.	Swiss-Jr.	1	0	1	1	0	....	....	....	....	....
	EV Zug	Swiss	19	2	2	4	8	....	....	....	....	....
	EHC Basel	Swiss-2	15	3	1	4	70	....	....	....	....	....
	Rapperswil	Swiss-2	....	....	....	....	....	5	1	1	2	2
2002-03	Rapperswil	Swiss	40	6	5	11	43	6	0	0	0	4
2003-04	Rapperswil	Swiss	37	6	6	12	18	....	....	....	....	....
	Rapperswil	Swiss-Q	6	0	0	0	0	....	....	....	....	....

NYSTROM, Eric (NIGH-stuhm, AIR-ihk) CGY.

Left wing. Shoots left. 6'1", 195 lbs. Born, Syosset, NY, February 14, 1983.
(Calgary's 1st choice, 10th overall, in 2002 Entry Draft).

			Regular Season					Playoffs				
Season	Club	League	GP	G	A	TP	PIM	GP	G	A	TP	PIM
1998-99	Nassau Lions	NYAHA	STATISTICS NOT AVAILABLE									
99-2000	U.S. National U-17	USDP	55	7	16	23	57	....	....	....	....	....
2000-01	U.S. National U-18	USDP	66	15	17	32	102	....	....	....	....	....
2001-02	U. of Michigan	CCHA	40	18	13	31	42	....	....	....	....	....
2002-03	U. of Michigan	CCHA	39	15	11	26	24	....	....	....	....	....
2003-04	U. of Michigan	CCHA	43	10	12	22	50	....	....	....	....	....

CCHA All-Rookie Team (2002)

O'BRIEN, Doug (oh-BRIGH-uhn, DUHG) T.B.

Defense. Shoots left. 6'1", 200 lbs. Born, St. John's, Nfld., February 16, 1984.
(Tampa Bay's 4th choice, 192nd overall, in 2003 Entry Draft).

			Regular Season					Playoffs				
Season	Club	League	GP	G	A	TP	PIM	GP	G	A	TP	PIM
99-2000	St. John's AAA	NAHA	STATISTICS NOT AVAILABLE									
2000-01	Hull Olympiques	QMJHL	47	1	6	7	16	5	0	1	1	0
2001-02	Hull Olympiques	QMJHL	46	1	5	6	36	12	0	0	0	14
2002-03	Hull Olympiques	QMJHL	71	10	34	44	102	19	3	12	15	18
2003-04	Gatineau	QMJHL	66	17	46	63	146	15	1	8	9	16

QMJHL First All-Star Team (2004) • Memorial Cup All-Star Team (2004) • Won Ed Chynoweth Trophy (Memorial Cup Tournament Leading Scorer) (2004)

O'BRIEN, Shane (oh-BRIGH-uhn, SHAYN) ANA.

Defense. Shoots left. 6'2", 235 lbs. Born, Port Hope, Ont., August 9, 1983.
(Anaheim's 8th choice, 250th overall, in 2003 Entry Draft).

			Regular Season					Playoffs				
Season	Club	League	GP	G	A	TP	PIM	GP	G	A	TP	PIM
99-2000	Port Hope	OJHL	47	6	27	33	110	....	....	....	....	....
2000-01	Kingston	OHL	61	2	12	14	89	4	0	1	1	6
2001-02	Kingston	OHL	67	10	23	33	132	1	0	0	0	2
2002-03	Kingston	OHL	28	8	15	23	100	....	....	....	....	....
	St. Michael's	OHL	34	8	11	19	108	19	4	10	14	*79
2003-04	Cincinnati	AHL	60	2	8	10	163	9	0	2	2	20

O'BYRNE, Ryan (oh-BUHRN, RIGH-uhn) MTL.

Defense. Shoots right. 6'5", 223 lbs. Born, Victoria, B.C., July 19, 1984.
(Montreal's 4th choice, 79th overall, in 2003 Entry Draft).

			Regular Season					Playoffs				
Season	Club	League	GP	G	A	TP	PIM	GP	G	A	TP	PIM
2001-02	Victoria Salsa	BCHL	52	2	9	11	91	....	....	....	....	....
2002-03	Victoria Salsa	BCHL	32	3	6	9	94	....	....	....	....	....
	Nanaimo Clippers	BCHL	9	2	4	6	24	....	....	....	....	....
2003-04	Cornell Big Red	ECAC	31	0	2	2	71	....	....	....	....	....

ODUYA, John (oh-DOO-yuh, JAWN) WSH.

Defense. Shoots left. 6', 200 lbs. Born, Stockholm, Sweden, October 1, 1981.
(Washington's 6th choice, 221st overall, in 2001 Entry Draft).

			Regular Season					Playoffs				
Season	Club	League	GP	G	A	TP	PIM	GP	G	A	TP	PIM
1996-97	Hammarby Jr.	Swede-Jr.	13	0	0	0	....	....	....	....	....	....
1997-98	Hammarby Jr.	Swede-Jr.	26	3	11	14	70	....	....	....	....	....
1998-99	Hammarby Jr.	Swede-Jr.	38	14	31	45	45	....	....	....	....	....
99-2000	Hammarby Jr.	Swede-Jr.	32	3	18	21	48	6	1	2	3	4
	Hammarby	Swede-2	1	0	0	0	0	1	0	0	0	0
2000-01	Moncton Wildcats	QMJHL	44	11	38	49	147	....	....	....	....	....
	Victoriaville Tigres	QMJHL	24	3	16	19	112	13	4	9	13	10
2001-02	Hammarby	Swede-2	46	11	14	25	66	2	1	0	1	4
2002-03	Hammarby	Swede-2	48	15	25	40	200	....	....	....	....	....
	Hammarby	Swede-Q	....	....	....	....	....	10	7	5	12	38
2003-04	Djurgardens IF	Sweden	42	4	4	8	*173	4	0	0	0	6

OGORODNIKOV, Sergei (oh-goh-RAWD-nee-kawf, SAIR-gay) NYI

Center. Shoots left. 6', 178 lbs. Born, Irkutsk, USSR, January 21, 1986.
(NY Islanders' 3rd choice, 82nd overall, in 2004 Entry Draft).

			Regular Season					Playoffs				
Season	Club	League	GP	G	A	TP	PIM	GP	G	A	TP	PIM
2002-03	Dyn. Moscow 2	Russia-3	STATISTICS NOT AVAILABLE									
	Dyn. Moscow 17	Russia-Jr.	7	4	3	7	8	....	....	....	....	....
2003-04	Dyn. Moscow 2	Russia-3	STATISTICS NOT AVAILABLE									
	THC Tver	Russia-2	21	8	3	11	14	....	....	....	....	....

O'HANLEY, Brian (oh-HAN-lee, BRIGH-uhn) **S.J.**

Defense. Shoots left. 6', 177 lbs. Born, Quincy, MA, December 18, 1984.
(San Jose's 10th choice, 267th overall, in 2003 Entry Draft).

			Regular Season					Playoffs				
Season	Club	League	GP	G	A	TP	PIM	GP	G	A	TP	PIM
2001-02	Boston College HS	Hi-School	24	22	13	35	20	....	....	....	....	....
2002-03	Boston College HS	Hi-School	23	22	21	43	12	....	....	....	....	....
2003-04	Salisbury School	Hi-School	26	11	28	39	....	....	....	....	....	....

• Signed Letter of Intent to attend **Boston College** (H-East), April 11, 2003.

OLAFSON, Mark (OH-lahf-suhn, MAHRK) **WSH.**

Right wing. Shoots right. 6'1", 209 lbs. Born, Winnipeg, Man., March 22, 1985.
(Washington's 6th choice, 279th overall, in 2003 Entry Draft).

			Regular Season					Playoffs				
Season	Club	League	GP	G	A	TP	PIM	GP	G	A	TP	PIM
2000-01	Wpg. Hawks	WWHA	29	25	30	55	72	....	....	....	....	....
2001-02	St. James	MJHL	59	31	32	63	61	....	....	....	....	....
2002-03	Kelowna Rockets	WHL	50	4	8	12	109	19	2	4	6	20
2003-04	Lethbridge	WHL	26	1	5	6	20	....	....	....	....	....
	Kelowna Rockets	WHL	41	5	10	15	64	....	....	....	....	....

OLESZ, Rostislav (OH-lehsh, RAHS-tih-slav) **FLA.**

Center. Shoots left. 6'1", 207 lbs. Born, Bilovec, Czechoslovakia, October 10, 1985.
(Florida's 1st choice, 7th overall, in 2004 Entry Draft).

			Regular Season					Playoffs				
Season	Club	League	GP	G	A	TP	PIM	GP	G	A	TP	PIM
99-2000	HC Vitkovice 16	Czech-Jr.	48	23	20	43	56	3	1	0	1	2
2000-01	HC Vitkovice 16	Czech-Jr.	31	42	27	69	57	2	2	3	5	0
	HC Vitkovice Jr.	Czech-Jr.	15	10	3	13	14	....	....	....	....	....
	HC Vitkovice	Czech	3	0	1	1	0	....	....	....	....	....
2001-02	HC Vitkovice 16	Czech-Jr.	2	2	0	2	0	....	....	....	....	....
	HC Vitkovice	Czech	11	1	2	3	0	....	....	....	....	....
	HC Vitkovice Jr.	Czech-Jr.	34	19	20	39	81	2	0	0	0	2
	HC Vitkovice	Czech	11	1	2	3	0	....	....	....	....	....
2002-03	HC Vitkovice	Czech	40	6	3	9	41	5	0	0	0	2
	HC Vitkovice Jr.	Czech-Jr.	7	1	1	2	12	....	....	....	....	....
	HC Slezan Opava	Czech-2	1	0	0	0	0	....	....	....	....	....
	HC Dukla Jihlava	Czech-2	2	1	0	1	0	1	0	0	0	0
	HC Vitkovice	Czech	40	6	3	9	41	5	0	0	0	2
2003-04	HC Vitkovice Jr.	Czech-Jr.	3	2	0	2	0	....	....	....	....	....
	HC Vitkovice	Czech	35	1	11	12	10	6	2	1	3	4

OLSON, Glenn (OHL-suhn, GLEHN) **S.J.**

Left wing. Shoots left. 6'4", 230 lbs. Born, Fort McNeil, B.C., May 1, 1984.

			Regular Season					Playoffs				
Season	Club	League	GP	G	A	TP	PIM	GP	G	A	TP	PIM
2002-03	Cowichan Valley	BCHL	41	1	4	5	168	....	....	....	....	....
2003-04	Kootenay Ice	WHL	41	2	1	3	126	4	0	0	0	8

Signed as a free agent by **San Jose**, September 18, 2003.

OLSSON, Kalle (OHL-suhn, KAL-ay) **EDM.**

Right wing. Shoots left. 6', 183 lbs. Born, Munkedal, Sweden, January 31, 1985.
(Edmonton's 6th choice, 147th overall, in 2003 Entry Draft).

			Regular Season					Playoffs				
Season	Club	League	GP	G	A	TP	PIM	GP	G	A	TP	PIM
2000-01	Lysekils HK Viking	Sweden-4	30	5	5	10	12	....	....	....	....	....
2001-02	Vastra Frolunda Jr.	Swede-Jr.	35	10	10	20	10	8	1	5	6	4
2002-03	Vastra Frolunda Jr.	Swede-Jr.	30	22	13	35	18	6	4	3	7	4
2003-04	Vastra Frolunda Jr.	Swede-Jr.	30	13	13	26	28	5	2	1	3	2
	Vastra Frolunda	Sweden	4	1	0	1	0	2	0	0	0	0

OLVECKY, Peter (ohl-VEH-tskee, PEE-tuhr) **MIN.**

Center. Shoots left. 6'2", 185 lbs. Born, Trencin, Czech., October 11, 1985.
(Minnesota's 3rd choice, 78th overall, in 2004 Entry Draft).

			Regular Season					Playoffs				
Season	Club	League	GP	G	A	TP	PIM	GP	G	A	TP	PIM
2003-04	Dukla Trencin Jr.	Slov-Jr.	40	16	20	36	74	2	0	0	0	12
	Dukla Trencin	Slovakia	16	0	0	0	18	....	....	....	....	....
	Dukla Trencin B	Slov-2	2	0	0	0	0	....	....	....	....	....

OLVER, Darin (AWL-vuhr, DAIR-uhn) **NYR**

Center. Shoots left. 6', 165 lbs. Born, Burnaby, B.C., March 5, 1985.
(NY Rangers' 3rd choice, 36th overall, in 2004 Entry Draft).

			Regular Season					Playoffs				
Season	Club	League	GP	G	A	TP	PIM	GP	G	A	TP	PIM
2002-03	Chilliwack Chiefs	BCHL	59	34	55	89	57	....	....	....	....	....
2003-04	Northern Michigan	CCHA	41	13	21	34	26	....	....	....	....	....

ONDRUS, Ben (AWN-druhs, BEHN) **TOR.**

Left wing. Shoots right. 6', 185 lbs. Born, Sherwood Park, Alta., June 25, 1982.

			Regular Season					Playoffs				
Season	Club	League	GP	G	A	TP	PIM	GP	G	A	TP	PIM
1997-98	Sherwood Park	AMBHL	....	....	....	....	....	....	....	....	....	....
1998-99	Swift Current	WHL	46	4	4	8	58	6	0	1	1	8
99-2000	Swift Current	WHL	67	14	15	29	138	12	1	0	1	22
2000-01	Swift Current	WHL	69	13	17	30	151	....	....	....	....	....
2001-02	Swift Current	WHL	67	30	41	71	153	12	4	3	7	18
2002-03	Swift Current	WHL	67	33	36	69	98	3	0	1	1	11
	Idaho	WCHL	4	0	3	3	0	5	0	1	1	6
2003-04	St. John's	AHL	60	6	11	17	102	....	....	....	....	....

Signed as a free agent by **Idaho** (WCHL), March 23, 2003. Signed as a free agent by **St. John's** (AHL), September 1, 2003. Signed as a fee agent by **Toronto**, May 27, 2004.

O'NEILL, Wes (oh-NEEL, WEHS) **NYI**

Defense. Shoots left. 6'4", 200 lbs. Born, Windsor, Ont., March 3, 1986.
(NY Islanders' 4th choice, 115th overall, in 2004 Entry Draft).

			Regular Season					Playoffs				
Season	Club	League	GP	G	A	TP	PIM	GP	G	A	TP	PIM
2000-01	Chatham Maroons	OJHL-B	51	6	9	15	50	....	....	....	....	....
2001-02	Chatham Maroons	OJHL-B	51	9	36	45	....	....	....	....	....	....
2002-03	Green Bay	USHL	50	2	15	17	79	....	....	....	....	....
2003-04	Notre Dame	CCHA	39	2	10	12	28	....	....	....	....	....

OREKHOVSKY, Oleg (oh-reh-KHOHV-skee, OH-lehg) **MIN.**

Defense. Shoots right. 6', 180 lbs. Born, Krasnoyarsk, USSR, November 3, 1977.
(Washington's 11th choice, 206th overall, in 1996 Entry Draft).

			Regular Season					Playoffs				
Season	Club	League	GP	G	A	TP	PIM	GP	G	A	TP	PIM
1994-95	Dynamo Moscow	CIS	30	0	1	1	18	....	....	....	....	....
1995-96	Dynamo Moscow	CIS	22	1	2	3	14	8	0	0	0	6
1996-97	Dynamo Moscow	Russia	32	4	2	6	16	4	2	1	3	2
1997-98	Dynamo Moscow	EuroHL	7	2	1	3	12	....	....	....	....	....
	Dynamo Moscow	Russia	40	4	5	9	34	....	....	....	....	....
1998-99	Dynamo Moscow	EuroHL	3	1	1	2	2	6	0	0	0	6
	Dynamo Moscow	Russia	42	1	1	2	22	16	1	2	3	6
99-2000	Dynamo Moscow	EuroHL	6	1	0	1	2	....	....	....	....	....
	Dynamo Moscow	Russia	37	3	6	9	38	15	1	0	1	4
2000-01	Dynamo Moscow	Russia	40	2	4	6	44	....	....	....	....	....
2001-02	Dynamo Moscow	Russia	50	2	15	17	50	3	1	0	1	2
2002-03	Dynamo Moscow	Russia	38	1	4	5	20	5	0	1	1	4
2003-04	Avangard Omsk	Russia	45	2	4	6	38	11	0	0	0	2

Selected by **Minnesota** from **Washington** in Expansion Draft, June 23, 2000.

ORESKOVICH, Victor (oh-rehs-KOH-vihvh, VIHK-tohr) **COL.**

Right wing. Shoots right. 6'2", 216 lbs. Born, Whitby, Ont., August 15, 1986.
(Colorado's 2nd choice, 55th overall, in 2004 Entry Draft).

			Regular Season					Playoffs				
Season	Club	League	GP	G	A	TP	PIM	GP	G	A	TP	PIM
2002-03	Milton IceHawks	OPJHL	49	28	46	74	51	....	....	....	....	....
2003-04	Green Bay	USHL	58	11	26	37	33	....	....	....	....	....

Signed Letter of Intent to attend **Notre Dame** (CCHA), May 5, 2003.

ORLOV, Maxim (ohr-LAHF, max-EEM) **WSH.**

Center. Shoots left. 6', 176 lbs. Born, Moscow, USSR, March 31, 1981.
(Washington's 9th choice, 219th overall, in 1999 Entry Draft).

			Regular Season					Playoffs				
Season	Club	League	GP	G	A	TP	PIM	GP	G	A	TP	PIM
1998-99	CSKA Moscow	Russia	2	0	0	0	2	1	0	0	0	0
99-2000	CSKA Moscow	Russia	25	0	0	0	2	2	0	0	0	2
2000-01	CSKA Moscow	Russia	41	5	4	9	14	....	....	....	....	....
2001-02	CSKA Moscow 2	Russia-3	7	7	4	11	4	....	....	....	....	....
	CSKA Moscow	Russia	35	3	5	8	14	....	....	....	....	....
2002-03	MGU-Pingviny	Russia-3	2	0	0	0	0	....	....	....	....	....
	Leninogorsk	Russia-2	25	3	8	11	24	....	....	....	....	....
2003-04	Leninogorsk	Russia-2	35	5	9	14	39	2	0	0	0	0

O'SULLIVAN, Patrick (oh-SUHL-ih-van, PAT-rihk) **MIN.**

Center. Shoots left. 5'11", 190 lbs. Born, Winston Salem, NC, February 1, 1985.
(Minnesota's 2nd choice, 56th overall, in 2003 Entry Draft).

			Regular Season					Playoffs				
Season	Club	League	GP	G	A	TP	PIM	GP	G	A	TP	PIM
99-2000	Strathroy Rockets	OJHL-B	45	6	13	19	53	....	....	....	....	....
2000-01	U.S. National U-17	USDP	64	30	45	75	69	....	....	....	....	....
2001-02	Mississauga	OHL	68	34	58	92	61	....	....	....	....	....
	U.S. National U-18	USDP	1	1	0	1	2	....	....	....	....	....
2002-03	Mississauga	OHL	56	40	41	81	57	5	2	9	11	18
2003-04	Mississauga	OHL	53	43	39	82	32	24	12	11	23	16

OTTOSSON, Kristofer (AW-toh-suhn, KRIHS-tuh-fuhr) **NYI**

Right wing. Shoots left. 5'10", 187 lbs. Born, Stockholm, Sweden, January 9, 1976.
(NY Islanders' 6th choice, 148th overall, in 2000 Entry Draft).

			Regular Season					Playoffs				
Season	Club	League	GP	G	A	TP	PIM	GP	G	A	TP	PIM
1993-94	Djurgarden Jr.	Swede-Jr.	13	3	6	9	4	....	....	....	....	....
1994-95	Djurgarden Jr.	Swede-Jr.	15	8	23	31	2	....	....	....	....	....
	Djurgarden	Sweden	30	0	0	0	2	3	0	0	0	0
1995-96	Djurgarden Jr.	Swede-Jr.	15	5	12	17	4	....	....	....	....	....
	Djurgarden	Sweden	32	1	0	1	2	2	0	0	0	0
1996-97	Djurgarden Jr.	Swede-Jr.	2	1	1	2	0	....	....	....	....	....
	Arlanda Mastra	Swede-2	6	6	0	6	0	....	....	....	....	....
	Djurgarden	Sweden	20	0	0	0	2	....	....	....	....	....
	Huddinge IK	Swede-2	13	1	3	4	2	2	0	1	1	0
1997-98	Huddinge IK	Swede-2	16	10	13	23	6	14	7	7	14	8
1998-99	Huddinge IK	Swede-2	27	12	17	29	14	14	3	2	5	2
	Djurgarden	EuroHL	1	0	0	0	0	....	....	....	....	....
99-2000	Djurgarden	Sweden	47	25	15	40	12	13	7	2	9	2
2000-01	Djurgarden	Sweden	46	17	24	41	14	14	*7	4	11	4
2001-02	Djurgarden	Sweden	41	13	8	21	12	4	0	0	0	0
2002-03	Djurgarden	Sweden	46	19	19	38	30	12	1	4	5	0
2003-04	Djurgarden	Sweden	50	7	12	19	16	4	0	1	1	4

OUELLET, Michel (oo-LEHT, mee-SHEHL) **PIT.**

Right wing. Shoots right. 6', 201 lbs. Born, Rimouski, Que., March 5, 1982.
(Pittsburgh's 4th choice, 124th overall, in 2000 Entry Draft).

			Regular Season					Playoffs				
Season	Club	League	GP	G	A	TP	PIM	GP	G	A	TP	PIM
1997-98	Jonquiere Elites	QAAA	33	20	32	52	52	....	....	....	....	....
1998-99	Rimouski Oceanic	QMJHL	28	7	13	20	10	11	0	1	1	6
99-2000	Rimouski Oceanic	QMJHL	72	36	53	89	38	14	4	5	9	14
2000-01	Rimouski Oceanic	QMJHL	63	42	50	92	50	11	6	7	13	8
2001-02	Rimouski Oceanic	QMJHL	61	40	58	98	66	7	3	6	9	4
2002-03	Wheeling Nailers	ECHL	55	20	26	46	40	....	....	....	....	....
	Wilkes-Barre	AHL	4	0	2	2	0	....	....	....	....	....
2003-04	Wilkes-Barre	AHL	79	30	19	49	34	22	2	10	12	6

AHL All-Rookie Team (2004)

OULAHEN, Ryan (OO-la-hehn, RIGH-uhn) **DET.**

Center. Shoots left. 6'1", 180 lbs. Born, Newmarket, Ont., March 26, 1985.
(Detroit's 3rd choice, 164th overall, in 2003 Entry Draft).

			Regular Season					Playoffs				
Season	Club	League	GP	G	A	TP	PIM	GP	G	A	TP	PIM
2000-01	Wexford Raiders	OMHA	66	38	58	96	18	....	....	....	....	....
2001-02	Newmarket	OPJHL	48	18	17	35	4	....	....	....	....	....
2002-03	Brampton	OHL	61	21	22	43	6	11	2	1	3	2
2003-04	Brampton	OHL	57	17	18	35	26	12	3	7	10	6

OVECHKIN, Alexander (oh-VEHCH-kihn, al-EHX-AN-duhr) **WSH.**

Left wing. Shoots right. 6'2", 212 lbs. Born, Moscow, USSR, September 17, 1985.
(Washington's 1st choice, 1st overall, in 2004 Entry Draft).

			Regular Season					Playoffs				
Season	Club	League	GP	G	A	TP	PIM	GP	G	A	TP	PIM
2001-02	Dyn. Moscow 2	Russia-3	19	18	8	26	20	....	....	....	....	....
	Dynamo Moscow	Russia	22	2	2	4	4	3	0	0	0	0
2002-03	Dynamo Moscow	Russia	40	8	7	15	28	5	0	0	0	2
2003-04	Dynamo Moscow	Russia	53	13	11	24	40	3	0	0	0	2

OYSTRICK, Nathan (OI-strihk, NAY-thun) **ATL.**

Defense. Shoots left. 6', 195 lbs. Born, Regina, Sask., December 17, 1982.
(Atlanta's 7th choice, 198th overall, in 2002 Entry Draft).

			Regular Season					Playoffs				
Season	Club	League	GP	G	A	TP	PIM	GP	G	A	TP	PIM
99-2000	Reg. Pat Canadiens	SMHL	43	6	22	28	214	....	....	....	....	....
2000-01	South Surrey	BCHL		STATISTICS NOT AVAILABLE								
2001-02	South Surrey	BCHL	50	15	42	57	142	....	....	....	....	....
2002-03	Northern Michigan	CCHA	34	2	10	12	26	....	....	....	....	....
2003-04	Northern Michigan	CCHA	39	8	20	28	98	....	....	....	....	....

CCHA Second All-Star Team (2004)

PACKARD, Dennis (PA-kuhrd, DEH-nihs) **T.B.**

Left wing. Shoots left. 6'5", 215 lbs. Born, St. Catherines, Ont., February 9, 1982.
(Tampa Bay's 8th choice, 219th overall, in 2001 Entry Draft).

			Regular Season					Playoffs				
Season	Club	League	GP	G	A	TP	PIM	GP	G	A	TP	PIM
99-2000	U.S. National U-18	USDP	55	11	14	25	85	....	....	....	....	....
2000-01	Harvard University	ECAC	33	4	4	8	28	....	....	....	....	....
2001-02	Harvard University	ECAC	32	9	10	19	34	....	....	....	....	....
2002-03	Harvard University	ECAC	30	8	8	16	32	....	....	....	....	....
2003-04	Harvard University	ECAC	36	11	11	22	16	....	....	....	....	....

PADDOCK, Cam (PA-dawk, KAM) **PIT.**

Center. Shoots right. 6'1", 191 lbs. Born, Vancouver, B.C., March 22, 1983.
(Pittsburgh's 6th choice, 137th overall, in 2002 Entry Draft).

			Regular Season					Playoffs				
Season	Club	League	GP	G	A	TP	PIM	GP	G	A	TP	PIM
99-2000	Kelowna Rockets	WHL	46	5	5	10	42	5	0	0	0	0
2000-01	Kelowna Rockets	WHL	72	14	10	24	110	6	0	0	0	4
2001-02	Kelowna Rockets	WHL	72	38	35	73	122	15	8	6	14	35
2002-03	Kelowna Rockets	WHL	71	33	26	59	107	19	11	8	19	18
2003-04	Kelowna Rockets	WHL	62	17	22	39	86	16	3	4	7	22
	Wilkes-Barre	AHL	1	0	0	0	2	....	....	....	....	....

PAETSCH, Nathan (PASH, NAY-thuhn) **BUF.**

Defense. Shoots left. 6', 195 lbs. Born, Humboldt, Sask., March 30, 1983.
(Buffalo's 8th choice, 202nd overall, in 2003 Entry Draft).

			Regular Season					Playoffs				
Season	Club	League	GP	G	A	TP	PIM	GP	G	A	TP	PIM
1998-99	Tisdale Trojans	SMHL	74	20	55	75	120	....	....	....	....	....
	Moose Jaw	WHL	2	0	0	0	0	....	....	....	....	....
99-2000	Moose Jaw	WHL	68	9	35	44	49	4	0	1	1	0
2000-01	Moose Jaw	WHL	70	8	54	62	118	4	1	2	3	6
2001-02	Moose Jaw	WHL	59	16	36	52	86	12	0	4	4	16
2002-03	Moose Jaw	WHL	59	15	39	54	81	13	3	10	13	6
2003-04	Rochester	AHL	54	5	5	10	49	16	1	1	2	28

• Re-entered NHL Entry Draft. Originally Washington's 1st choice, 58th overall, in 2001 Entry Draft.

WHL East Second All-Star Team (2003)

PAILLE, Dan (PIGH-yay, DAN) **BUF.**

Left wing. Shoots left. 6', 200 lbs. Born, Welland, Ont., April 15, 1984.
(Buffalo's 2nd choice, 20th overall, in 2002 Entry Draft).

			Regular Season					Playoffs				
Season	Club	League	GP	G	A	TP	PIM	GP	G	A	TP	PIM
99-2000	Welland Cougars	OJHL-B	42	14	17	31	19	16	16	16	32	....
2000-01	Guelph Storm	OHL	64	22	31	53	57	4	2	0	2	2
2001-02	Guelph Storm	OHL	62	27	30	57	54	9	5	2	7	9
2002-03	Guelph Storm	OHL	54	30	27	57	28	11	8	6	14	6
2003-04	Guelph Storm	OHL	59	37	43	80	63	22	9	9	18	14

PAINCHAUD, Chad (PAYN-show, CHAD) **ATL.**

Left wing. Shoots left. 5'11", 175 lbs. Born, Mississauga, Ont., May 27, 1986.
(Atlanta's 4th choice, 106th overall, in 2004 Entry Draft).

			Regular Season					Playoffs				
Season	Club	League	GP	G	A	TP	PIM	GP	G	A	TP	PIM
2002-03	Mississauga Reps	GTHL	52	47	47	94	....	....	....	....	....	....
2003-04	Mississauga	OHL	68	17	25	42	25	24	4	6	10	23

PANOV, Konstantin (PAN-ahv, KAWN-stan-tihn) **NSH.**

Left wing. Shoots left. 6', 195 lbs. Born, Chelyabinsk, USSR, June 29, 1980.
(Nashville's 10th choice, 131st overall, in 1999 Entry Draft).

			Regular Season					Playoffs				
Season	Club	League	GP	G	A	TP	PIM	GP	G	A	TP	PIM
1996-97	Chelyabinsk 2	Russia-3	25	18	30	48	22	....	....	....	....	....
1997-98	Yunior-T Kurgan	Russia-3	20	7	3	10	6	....	....	....	....	....
	Chelyabinsk	Russia	6	2	0	2	4	2	0	0	0	0
1998-99	Kamloops Blazers	WHL	62	33	30	63	62	13	5	3	8	10
99-2000	Kamloops Blazers	WHL	64	43	30	73	47	....	....	....	....	....
2000-01	Kamloops Blazers	WHL	69	44	56	100	54	4	1	0	1	2
2001-02	Milwaukee	AHL	15	1	5	6	2	....	....	....	....	....
2002-03	Milwaukee	AHL	67	11	20	31	30	2	0	0	0	0
	Toledo Storm	ECHL	2	1	0	1	0	....	....	....	....	....
2003-04	Khabarovsk 2	Russia-3	8	8	6	14	5	....	....	....	....	....
	Amur Khabarovsk	Russia	29	0	1	1	10	....	....	....	....	....

WHL West Second All-Star Team (2000) • WHL West First All-Star Team (2001)

PANZER, Jeff (PAN-zuhr, JEHF) **ST.L.**

Center. Shoots left. 5'7", 160 lbs. Born, Grand Forks, ND, April 7, 1978.

			Regular Season					Playoffs				
Season	Club	League	GP	G	A	TP	PIM	GP	G	A	TP	PIM
1996-97	Fargo-Moorhead	USHL	49	30	40	70	52	6	3	7	10	0
1997-98	North Dakota	WCHA	37	14	23	37	18	....	....	....	....	....
1998-99	North Dakota	WCHA	37	21	26	47	14	....	....	....	....	....
99-2000	North Dakota	WCHA	44	19	*44	63	16	....	....	....	....	....
2000-01	North Dakota	WCHA	46	26	*55	*81	28	....	....	....	....	....
2001-02	Worcester IceCats	AHL	70	26	27	53	29	3	0	2	2	0
2002-03	Worcester IceCats	AHL	80	22	32	54	36	3	1	1	2	0
2003-04	Worcester IceCats	AHL	60	14	25	39	20	10	1	4	5	4

WCHA Second All-Star Team (1999) • WCHA First All-Star Team (2000, 2001) • NCAA West First All-American Team (2000, 2001)

Signed as a free agent by **St. Louis**, April 30, 2001.

PARENTEAU, Pierre (pair-ehn-TOH, PEE-air) **ANA.**

Center. Shoots right. 5'11", 195 lbs. Born, Hull, Que., March 24, 1983.
(Anaheim's 11th choice, 264th overall, in 2001 Entry Draft).

			Regular Season					Playoffs				
Season	Club	League	GP	G	A	TP	PIM	GP	G	A	TP	PIM
99-2000	Charles-Lemoyne	QAAA	40	25	40	65	18	16	4	9	13	8
2000-01	Moncton Wildcats	QMJHL	45	10	19	29	38	....	....	....	....	....
	Chicoutimi	QMJHL	28	10	13	23	14	7	4	7	11	2
2001-02	Chicoutimi	QMJHL	68	51	67	118	120	4	3	1	4	10
2002-03	Chicoutimi	QMJHL	31	20	35	55	56	....	....	....	....	....
	Sherbrooke	QMJHL	28	13	35	48	84	12	8	11	19	6
2003-04	Cincinnati	AHL	66	14	16	30	20	7	1	2	3	6

PARISE, Zach (pah-REE-say, ZAK) **N.J.**

Center. Shoots left. 5'11", 185 lbs. Born, Minneapolis, MN, July 28, 1984.
(New Jersey's 1st choice, 17th overall, in 2003 Entry Draft).

			Regular Season					Playoffs				
Season	Club	League	GP	G	A	TP	PIM	GP	G	A	TP	PIM
2000-01	Shat.-St. Mary's	Hi-School	58	69	93	162	....	....	....	....	....	....
2001-02	Shat.-St. Mary's	Hi-School	67	77	101	178	58	....	....	....	....	....
	U.S. National U-18	USDP	12	7	7	14	6	....	....	....	....	....
2002-03	North Dakota	WCHA	39	26	35	61	34	....	....	....	....	....
2003-04	North Dakota	WCHA	37	23	32	55	24	....	....	....	....	....

WCHA All-Rookie Team (2003) • WCHA First All-Star Team (2004) • NCAA West First All-American Team (2004)

PAROULEK, Martin (PAHR-oh-lehk, MAHR-tihn) **CBJ**

Right wing. Shoots right. 6', 193 lbs. Born, Uherske Hradiste, Czech., November 4, 1979.
(Columbus' 9th choice, 278th overall, in 2000 Entry Draft).

			Regular Season					Playoffs				
Season	Club	League	GP	G	A	TP	PIM	GP	G	A	TP	PIM
1998-99	Vsetin Jr.	Czech-Jr.	45	25	19	44	....	....	....	....	....	....
	HC Slovnaft Vsetin	Czech	11	1	1	2	....	7	0	1	1	0
99-2000	HC Slovnaft Vsetin	Czech	48	11	14	25	24	8	1	1	2	4
2000-01	Sumperk	Czech-2	14	0	1	1	27	....	....	....	....	....
	HC Slovnaft Vsetin	Czech	28	10	4	14	16	14	3	3	6	10
2001-02	Syracuse Crunch	AHL	59	11	14	25	31	9	1	1	2	4
2002-03	Syracuse Crunch	AHL	9	0	1	1	6	....	....	....	....	....
	HC Sparta Praha	Czech	16	1	4	5	16	9	1	1	2	8
2003-04	HC Sparta Praha	Czech	17	2	1	3	4	....	....	....	....	....
	Plzen	Czech	19	7	10	17	16	12	1	3	4	12

• Released by **Syracuse** (AHL) and signed as a free agent by **Sparta Praha** (Czech) with Columbus retaining NHL rights, January 13, 2003.

PARROS, George (PAIR-ohs, JOHRJ) **L.A.**

Right wing. Shoots right. 6'4", 210 lbs. Born, Washington, PA, December 29, 1979.
(Los Angeles' 9th choice, 222nd overall, in 1999 Entry Draft).

			Regular Season					Playoffs				
Season	Club	League	GP	G	A	TP	PIM	GP	G	A	TP	PIM
1996-97	Delbarton Wave	Hi-School	14	15	8	23	....	....	....	....	....	....
1997-98	Delbarton Wave	Hi-School	15	22	17	39	....	....	....	....	....	....
1998-99	Chicago Freeze	NAJHL	54	30	20	50	126	....	....	....	....	....
99-2000	Princeton	ECAC	27	4	2	6	14	....	....	....	....	....
2000-01	Princeton	ECAC	31	7	10	17	38	....	....	....	....	....
2001-02	Princeton	ECAC	31	9	13	22	36	....	....	....	....	....
2002-03	Princeton	ECAC	22	0	7	7	29	....	....	....	....	....
	Manchester	AHL	9	0	1	1	7	....	....	....	....	....
2003-04	Manchester	AHL	57	3	6	9	126	5	0	0	0	4

PARSHIN, Denis (PAHR-shihn, DEH-nihs **COL.**

Right wing. Shoots left. 5'9", 146 lbs. Born, Rybinsk, USSR, February 1, 1986.
(Colorado's 3rd choice, 72nd overall, in 2004 Entry Draft).

			Regular Season					Playoffs				
Season	Club	League	GP	G	A	TP	PIM	GP	G	A	TP	PIM
2002-03	CSKA Moscow 2	Russia-3	4	1	0	1	2	....	....	....	....	....
	CSKA Moscow 18	Russia-Jr.	7	4	3	7	6	....	....	....	....	....
2003-04	CSKA Moscow	Russia	27	2	4	6	4	....	....	....	....	....
	CSKA Moscow 2	Russia-3		STATISTICS NOT AVAILABLE								

PAUKOVICH, Geoff (paw-KOH-vihch, JEHF) **EDM.**

Left wing. Shoots left. 6'4", 208 lbs. Born, Englewood, CO, April 24, 1986.
(Edmonton's 4th choice, 57th overall, in 2004 Entry Draft).

			Regular Season					Playoffs				
Season	Club	League	GP	G	A	TP	PIM	GP	G	A	TP	PIM
2002-03	Tri City Storm	USHL	31	1	3	4	29	....	....	....	....	....
2003-04	U.S. National U-18	USDP	55	10	11	21	77	....	....	....	....	....

Signed Letter of Intent to attend **U. of Denver** (WCHA), June 30, 2002.

PECKER, Cory (PEH-kuhr, KOH-ree) **ANA.**

Center. Shoots right. 6', 195 lbs. Born, Montreal, Que., March 20, 1981.
(Calgary's 7th choice, 166th overall, in 1999 Entry Draft).

			Regular Season					Playoffs				
Season	**Club**	**League**	**GP**	**G**	**A**	**TP**	**PIM**	**GP**	**G**	**A**	**TP**	**PIM**
1995-96	Lac St-Louis Lions	QAAA	5	0	0	0	0	....	....	....	....	....
1996-97	Lac St-Louis Lions	QAAA	40	30	40	70	....	7	4	2	6	....
1997-98	Sault Ste. Marie	OHL	29	3	4	7	15	....	....	....	....	....
1998-99	Sault Ste. Marie	OHL	68	25	34	59	24	5	1	2	3	2
99-2000	Sault Ste. Marie	OHL	65	33	36	69	38	12	6	8	14	8
2000-01	Sault Ste. Marie	OHL	31	24	16	40	37	....	....	....	....	....
	Erie Otters	OHL	30	17	22	39	32	15	14	9	23	16
2001-02	Erie Otters	OHL	56	*53	46	99	108	21	*25	17	*42	36
2002-03	Cincinnati	AHL	77	20	13	33	66	....	....	....	....	....
2003-04	Cincinnati	AHL	54	6	10	16	32	....	....	....	....	....
	Binghamton	AHL	14	3	5	8	27	1	0	0	0	0

OHL Second All-Star Team (2001) • OHL First All-Star Team (2002) • Memorial Cup All-Star Team (2002)

• Missed majority of 1997-98 season after being diagnosed with Chron's Disease. Signed as a free agent by **Anaheim**, July 8, 2002.

PEMBERTON, James (PEHM-buhr-tuhn, JAYMZ) **FLA.**

Defense. Shoots right. 6'4", 215 lbs. Born, Providence, RI, October 2, 1983.
(Florida's 6th choice, 124th overall, in 2003 Entry Draft).

			Regular Season					Playoffs				
Season	**Club**	**League**	**GP**	**G**	**A**	**TP**	**PIM**	**GP**	**G**	**A**	**TP**	**PIM**
1998-99	Mount St. Charles	Hi-School	15	0	1	1	6	6	0	1	1	4
99-2000	Mount St. Charles	Hi-School	18	2	11	13	10	6	0	7	7	0
2000-01	Mount St. Charles	Hi-School	18	5	14	19	8	5	1	8	9	6
2001-02	New England	EJHL	32	9	13	22	59	13	8	5	13	10
2002-03	Providence College	H-East	33	2	9	11	18	....	....	....	....	....
2003-04	Providence College	H-East	37	0	8	8	30	....	....	....	....	....

PENNER, Dustin (PEH-nuhr, DUHS-tihn) **ANA.**

Left wing. Shoots left. 6'4", 240 lbs. Born, Winkler, Man., September 28, 1982.

			Regular Season					Playoffs				
Season	**Club**	**League**	**GP**	**G**	**A**	**TP**	**PIM**	**GP**	**G**	**A**	**TP**	**PIM**
2001-02	MSU - Bottineau	NJCAA	23	20	12	32	30	....	....	....	....	....
2002-03	U. of Maine	H-East		DID NOT PLAY – FRESHMAN								
2003-04	U. of Maine	H-East	43	11	12	23	52	....	....	....	....	....

NCAA Championship All-Tournament Team (2004)

Signed as a free agent by **Anaheim**, May 12, 2004.

PEREZHOGIN, Alexander (pehr-eh-ZHO-ghin, al-ehx-AN-duhr) **MTL.**

Left wing. Shoots left. 6', 185 lbs. Born, Ust-Kamenogorsk, USSR, August 10, 1983.
(Montreal's 2nd choice, 25th overall, in 2001 Entry Draft).

			Regular Season					Playoffs				
Season	**Club**	**League**	**GP**	**G**	**A**	**TP**	**PIM**	**GP**	**G**	**A**	**TP**	**PIM**
1998-99	Avangard Omsk 2	Russia-4	4	0	1	1	0	....	....	....	....	....
	Avangard Omsk	Russia	22	12	11	23	12	....	....	....	....	....
99-2000	Avangard Omsk 2	Russia-3	22	12	11	23	12	....	....	....	....	....
	Avangard Omsk	Russia	1	0	0	0	0	....	....	....	....	....
2000-01	Omsk Jr.	Russia-Jr.	6	1	5	6	4	....	....	....	....	....
	Avangard Omsk 2	Russia-3	41	47	24	71	40	....	....	....	....	....
	Avangard Omsk	Russia	....	....	....	....	....	1	0	0	0	0
2001-02	Avangard Omsk	Russia	4	1	0	1	4	....	....	....	....	....
	Mostovik Kurgan	Russia-2	19	14	10	24	10	....	....	....	....	....
2002-03	Avangard Omsk	Russia	48	15	6	21	28	8	0	2	2	4
2003-04	Hamilton Bulldogs	AHL	77	23	27	50	52	5	3	3	6	16

PERIARD, Michel (pair-EE-ahr, mee-SHEHL) **FLA.**

Defense. Shoots left. 5'11", 183 lbs. Born, Montreal, Que., November 10, 1979.
(Ottawa's 8th choice, 188th overall, in 1998 Entry Draft).

			Regular Season					Playoffs				
Season	**Club**	**League**	**GP**	**G**	**A**	**TP**	**PIM**	**GP**	**G**	**A**	**TP**	**PIM**
1996-97	Charles-Lemoyne	QAAA	40	8	15	23	64	15	7	20	27	....
1997-98	Shawinigan	QMJHL	68	14	30	44	64	5	0	0	0	18
1998-99	Shawinigan	QMJHL	64	14	40	54	90	6	1	2	3	4
99-2000	Rimouski Oceanic	QMJHL	70	25	75	100	58	14	5	17	22	16
2000-01	Port Huron	UHL	23	1	8	9	30	....	....	....	....	....
	Rockford IceHogs	UHL	31	3	14	17	20	....	....	....	....	....
	Louisville Panthers	AHL	7	0	1	1	0	....	....	....	....	....
2001-02	Macon Whoopee	ECHL	72	4	19	23	26	....	....	....	....	....
2002-03	San Antonio	AHL	10	3	5	8	6	....	....	....	....	....
	Laredo Bucks	CHL	50	18	35	53	26	9	3	5	8	4
2003-04	San Antonio	AHL	77	9	23	32	30	....	....	....	....	....

QMJHL First All-Star Team (2000) • Canadian Major Junior First All-Star Team (2000) • Memorial Cup All-Star Team (2000)

Signed as a free agent by **Florida**, August 1, 2000.

PERREAULT, Joel (PAIR-oh, JOHL) **ANA.**

Right wing. Shoots right. 6'1", 203 lbs. Born, Montreal, Que., April 6, 1983.
(Anaheim's 7th choice, 137th overall, in 2001 Entry Draft).

			Regular Season					Playoffs				
Season	**Club**	**League**	**GP**	**G**	**A**	**TP**	**PIM**	**GP**	**G**	**A**	**TP**	**PIM**
99-2000	Antoine-Girouard	QAAA	19	4	7	11	6	....	....	....	....	....
2000-01	Baie-Comeau	QMJHL	68	10	14	24	46	11	1	1	2	10
2001-02	Baie-Comeau	QMJHL	57	18	44	62	96	5	2	0	2	6
2002-03	Baie-Comeau	QMJHL	70	51	65	*116	93	12	3	7	10	14
2003-04	Cincinnati	AHL	65	14	14	28	38	9	1	1	2	2

QMJHL First All-Star Team (2003) • Canadian Major Junior First All-Star Team (2003)

PERRY, Corey (PAIR-ee, KOHR-ee) **ANA.**

Right wing. Shoots right. 6'2", 195 lbs. Born, Peterborough, Ont., May 16, 1985.
(Anaheim's 2nd choice, 28th overall, in 2003 Entry Draft).

			Regular Season					Playoffs				
Season	**Club**	**League**	**GP**	**G**	**A**	**TP**	**PIM**	**GP**	**G**	**A**	**TP**	**PIM**
2000-01	Peterborough	OMHA	64	69	46	115	20	3	3	0	3	0
2001-02	London Knights	OHL	67	28	31	59	56	12	2	3	5	30
2002-03	London Knights	OHL	67	25	53	78	145	14	7	16	23	27
2003-04	London Knights	OHL	66	40	*73	113	98	15	7	15	22	20
	Cincinnati	AHL	....	....	....	....	....	3	1	1	2	4

OHL First All-Star Team (2004)

PERSSON, Kristofer (PAIR-suhn, KRIHS-toh-fuhr) **CGY.**

Right wing. Shoots left. 6'3", 194 lbs. Born, Umea, Sweden, January 14, 1984.
(Calgary's 8th choice, 159th overall, in 2002 Entry Draft).

			Regular Season					Playoffs				
Season	**Club**	**League**	**GP**	**G**	**A**	**TP**	**PIM**	**GP**	**G**	**A**	**TP**	**PIM**
99-2000	Bjorkloven Jr.	Swede-Jr.	8	4	1	5	2	....	....	....	....	....
	Team Sweden-16	Nat-Tm	3	1	0	1	0	....	....	....	....	....
2000-01	MoDo Jr.	Swede-Jr.	16	8	3	11	4	6	1	0	1	2
2001-02	MoDo Jr.	Swede-Jr.	26	9	7	16	2	3	2	0	2	0
2002-03	MoDo Jr.	Swede-Jr.	24	16	12	28	10	....	....	....	....	....
	Ornskoldsviks SK	Swede-2	20	4	5	9	8	....	....	....	....	....
2003-04	IF Bjorkloven Umea	Swede-2	30	5	1	6	12	....	....	....	....	....

PERVYSHIN, Andrei (pair-VIHSH-ihn, AWN-dray) **ST.L.**

Defense. Shoots left. 5'8", 156 lbs. Born, Arkhangelsk, USSR, February 2, 1985.
(St. Louis' 11th choice, 253rd overall, in 2003 Entry Draft).

			Regular Season					Playoffs				
Season	**Club**	**League**	**GP**	**G**	**A**	**TP**	**PIM**	**GP**	**G**	**A**	**TP**	**PIM**
2001-02	Yaroslavl 2	Russia-3	21	2	6	8	14	....	....	....	....	....
	Yaroslavl Jr.	Russia-Jr.	30	7	19	26	42	7	2	5	7	4
2002-03	Yaroslavl 2	Russia-3		STATISTICS NOT AVAILABLE								
	Yaroslavl	Russia	9	0	1	1	0	2	0	0	0	0
	Yaroslavl Jr.	Russia-Jr.	....	....	....	....	....	2	2	1	3	0
2003-04	Spartak Moscow	Russia-2	59	3	6	9	14	13	0	1	1	4

PESTUNOV, Dmitri (pehs-too-NAWF, dih-MEE-tree) **PHX.**

Center. Shoots left. 5'9", 196 lbs. Born, Ust-Kamenogorsk, USSR, January 22, 1985.
(Phoenix's 2nd choice, 80th overall, in 2003 Entry Draft).

			Regular Season					Playoffs				
Season	**Club**	**League**	**GP**	**G**	**A**	**TP**	**PIM**	**GP**	**G**	**A**	**TP**	**PIM**
2001-02	Magnitogorsk 2	Russia-3		STATISTICS NOT AVAILABLE								
	Magnitogorsk Jr.	Russia-Jr.	7	3	8	11	14	....	....	....	....	....
2002-03	Magnitogorsk 18	Russia-Jr.	2	2	5	7	0	....	....	....	....	....
	Magnitogorsk	Russia	32	4	0	4	0	....	....	....	....	....
2003-04	Magnitogorsk	Russia	51	6	7	13	40	14	0	3	3	25
	Magnitogorsk Jr.	Russia-Jr.	6	3	15	18	2	3	0	2	2	4

PETER, Emanuel (PEE-tuhr, ih-MAN-yew-ehl) **CGY.**

Center. Shoots left. 6', 198 lbs. Born, Nieder Uzwil, Switz., June 9, 1984.
(Calgary's 6th choice, 142nd overall, in 2002 Entry Draft).

			Regular Season					Playoffs				
Season	**Club**	**League**	**GP**	**G**	**A**	**TP**	**PIM**	**GP**	**G**	**A**	**TP**	**PIM**
99-2000	SC Herisau-Jr.	Swiss-Jr.	18	2	12	14	....	....	....	....	....	....
2000-01	Uzwil Jr.	Swiss-Jr.	26	6	20	26	14	1	0	0	0	0
	EHC Uzwil Hawks	Swiss-3	18	2	10	12	....	....	....	....	....	....
2001-02	Kloten Flyers	Swiss	39	1	7	8	14	3	0	0	0	0
	Kloten Flyers Jr.	Swiss-Jr.	4	1	2	3	4	3	1	0	1	4
2002-03	Kloten Flyers	Swiss	43	0	10	10	42	5	0	0	0	4
2003-04	Kloten Flyers	Swiss	45	3	6	9	16	....	....	....	....	....
	Kloten Flyers	Swiss-Q	1	0	1	1	0	....	....	....	....	....

PETIOT, Richard (PEH-tee-awt, RIH-chuhrd) **L.A.**

Defense. Shoots left. 6'2", 190 lbs. Born, Daysland, Alta., August 20, 1982.
(Los Angeles' 6th choice, 116th overall, in 2001 Entry Draft).

			Regular Season					Playoffs				
Season	**Club**	**League**	**GP**	**G**	**A**	**TP**	**PIM**	**GP**	**G**	**A**	**TP**	**PIM**
2000-01	Camrose Kodiacs	AJHL	55	8	16	24	81	8	2	1	3	8
2001-02	Colorado College	WCHA	39	4	6	10	35	....	....	....	....	....
2002-03	Colorado College	WCHA	38	1	6	7	86	....	....	....	....	....
2003-04	Colorado College	WCHA	39	3	5	8	61	....	....	....	....	....

AJHL All-Rookie Team (2001) • AJHL South Second All-Star Team (2001)

PETRASEK, David (PEH-truh-sehk, DAY-vihd) **DET.**

Defense. Shoots right. 6', 187 lbs. Born, Jonkoping, Sweden, February 1, 1976.
(Detroit's 10th choice, 226th overall, in 1998 Entry Draft).

			Regular Season					Playoffs				
Season	**Club**	**League**	**GP**	**G**	**A**	**TP**	**PIM**	**GP**	**G**	**A**	**TP**	**PIM**
1993-94	HV 71 Jr.	Swede-Jr.	14	3	3	6	26	....	....	....	....	....
1994-95	HV 71 Jr.	Swede-Jr.	19	8	9	17	55	....	....	....	....	....
	HV 71 Jonkoping	Sweden	30	0	1	1	6	11	0	0	0	0
1995-96	HV 71 Jr.	Swede-Jr.	12	1	5	6	16	....	....	....	....	....
	HV 71 Jonkoping	Sweden	36	0	1	1	14	1	0	0	0	0
1996-97	HV 71 Jr.	Swede-Jr.	3	0	0	0	....	....	....	....	....	....
	HV 71 Jonkoping	Sweden	49	2	4	6	14	5	0	0	0	4
1997-98	HV 71 Jonkoping	Sweden	43	6	7	13	80	5	2	2	4	14
1998-99	HV 71 Jonkoping	Sweden	45	3	4	7	48	....	....	....	....	....
99-2000	HV 71 Jonkoping	Sweden	46	4	6	10	54	5	1	1	2	41
2000-01	Malmo IF	Sweden	47	7	7	14	74	9	1	1	2	8
2001-02	Malmo IF	Sweden	47	2	9	11	48	2	1	0	1	2
2002-03	Malmo IF	Sweden	50	7	6	13	72	....	....	....	....	....
2003-04	Malmo IF	Sweden	49	8	16	24	123	....	....	....	....	....
	Malmo IF	Swede-Q	10	2	0	2	16	....	....	....	....	....

PETRE, Henrik (PEH-truh, HEHN-rihk) **WSH.**

Defense. Shoots left. 6'1", 187 lbs. Born, Stockholm, Sweden, April 9, 1979.
(Washington's 5th choice, 143rd overall, in 1997 Entry Draft).

			Regular Season					Playoffs				
Season	**Club**	**League**	**GP**	**G**	**A**	**TP**	**PIM**	**GP**	**G**	**A**	**TP**	**PIM**
1995-96	Djurgarden Jr.	Swede-Jr.	21	6	4	10	8	....	....	....	....	....
1996-97	Djurgarden Jr.	Swede-Jr.	20	7	6	13	....	....	....	....	....	....
1997-98	Huddinge IK	Swede-2	30	4	4	8	30	....	....	....	....	....
	Djurgarden	Sweden	3	0	0	0	0	....	....	....	....	....
1998-99	Huddinge IK	Swede-2	14	0	1	1	20	....	....	....	....	....
	Djurgarden	Sweden	9	0	0	0	10	....	....	....	....	....
99-2000	Brynas IF Gavle	Sweden	47	3	3	6	73	11	1	0	1	12
	Brynas IF Gavle	EuroHL	5	0	2	2	4	....	....	....	....	....
2000-01	Brynas IF Gavle	Sweden	27	2	3	5	20	4	0	1	1	27
2001-02	Brynas IF Gavle	Sweden	24	2	1	3	49	4	0	0	0	4
2002-03	Brynas IF Gavle	Sweden	47	1	5	6	32	....	....	....	....	....
	Brynas IF Gavle	Swede-Q	10	1	1	2	10	....	....	....	....	....
2003-04	Brynas IF Gavle	Sweden	10	0	1	1	6	....	....	....	....	....
	Mora IK	Swede-2	2	1	0	1	4	....	....	....	....	....

PETROCHININ, Evgeny (peht-roh-CHIH-nihn, ehv-GEH-nee) CBJ

Defense. Shoots left. 6'2", 190 lbs. Born, Murmansk, USSR, February 7, 1976.
(Dallas' 5th choice, 150th overall, in 1994 Entry Draft).

			Regular Season					Playoffs				
Season	Club	League	GP	G	A	TP	PIM	GP	G	A	TP	PIM
1993-94	Spartak Moscow	CIS	2	0	0	0	0	....	....	....	....	....
1994-95	Spartak Moscow	CIS	45	0	2	2	14	....	....	....	....	....
1995-96	Spartak Moscow	CIS	50	5	17	22	18	5	3	0	3	0
1996-97	Spartak Moscow	Russia	32	5	6	11	52	....	....	....	....	....
1997-98	Spartak Moscow	Russia	46	12	6	18	100	....	....	....	....	....
1998-99	Spartak Moscow	Russia	21	4	6	10	14	....	....	....	....	....
	Ak Bars Kazan	Russia	6	0	2	2	2	9	1	1	2	24
99-2000	Magnitogorsk	Russia	33	7	10	17	38	14	2	1	3	26
2000-01	Cherepovets	Russia	40	8	7	15	38	9	2	0	2	40
2001-02	Cherepovets	Russia	35	35	2	8	10	1	0	0	0	0
2002-03	Cherepovets	Russia	29	3	6	9	14	10	1	0	1	0
2003-04	Cherepovets 2	Russia-3	1	0	2	2	0	....	....	....	....	....

Rights traded to **Columbus** by **Dallas** for Kirk Muller, September 28, 2001.

PETRUIC, Neil (peh-TROO-ihk, NEEL) OTT.

Defense. Shoots left. 6'1", 180 lbs. Born, Regina, Sask., July 30, 1982.
(Ottawa's 10th choice, 235th overall, in 2001 Entry Draft).

			Regular Season					Playoffs				
Season	Club	League	GP	G	A	TP	PIM	GP	G	A	TP	PIM
99-2000	Kindersley Klippers	SJHL	68	5	25	30	....	....	....	....	....	....
2000-01	Kindersley Klippers	SJHL	68	18	24	42	123	....	....	....	....	....
2001-02	Minnesota-Duluth	WCHA	40	3	6	9	54	....	....	....	....	....
2002-03	Minnesota-Duluth	WCHA	40	6	8	14	78	....	....	....	....	....
2003-04	Minnesota-Duluth	WCHA	45	4	10	14	56	....	....	....	....	....

SJHL First All-Star Team (2001)

PETTERSTROM, Pontus (PEH-tuhr-stawm, PAWN-tuhs) NYR

Left wing. Shoots left. 6', 174 lbs. Born, Nybro, Sweden, April 21, 1982.
(NY Rangers' 8th choice, 226th overall, in 2001 Entry Draft).

			Regular Season					Playoffs				
Season	Club	League	GP	G	A	TP	PIM	GP	G	A	TP	PIM
99-2000	Leksands IF 18	Swede-Jr.	7	1	2	3	4	....	....	....	....	....
	Leksands IF Jr.	Swede-Jr.	37	13	10	23	26	2	0	0	0	4
2000-01	Tingsryds AIF	Swede-2	24	6	5	11	24	....	....	....	....	....
	Tingsryds AIF	Swede-Q	14	2	0	2	0	3	0	2	2	2
2001-02	Tingsryds AIF	Swede-2	41	8	7	15	0	....	....	....	....	....
2002-03	Skelleftea	Swede-2	26	9	5	14	12	....	....	....	....	....
	Skelleftea	Swede-Q	12	6	0	6	6	8	2	1	3	4
2003-04	Skelleftea	Swede-2	39	12	17	29	18	....	....	....	....	....
	Skelleftea	Swede-Q	7	1	1	2	2	....	....	....	....	....

PHANEUF, Dion (fah-NOOF, DEE-awn) CGY.

Defense. Shoots left. 6'2", 205 lbs. Born, Edmonton, Alta., April 10, 1985.
(Calgary's 1st choice, 9th overall, in 2003 Entry Draft).

			Regular Season					Playoffs				
Season	Club	League	GP	G	A	TP	PIM	GP	G	A	TP	PIM
2000-01	Southgate Lions	AMBHL	35	15	50	65	208	4	3	4	7	15
2001-02	Red Deer Rebels	WHL	67	5	12	17	170	21	0	2	2	14
2002-03	Red Deer Rebels	WHL	71	16	14	30	185	23	7	7	14	34
2003-04	Red Deer Rebels	WHL	62	19	24	43	126	19	2	9	11	30

WHL East First All-Star Team (2004) • WHL Defenseman of the Year (2004) • Canadian Major Junior First All-Star Team (2004)

PICARD, Alexandre (pee-KAR, al-ehx-AHN-druh CBJ

Left wing. Shoots left. 6'2", 190 lbs. Born, Les Saules, Que., October 9, 1985.
(Columbus' 1st choice, 8th overall, in 2004 Entry Draft).

			Regular Season					Playoffs				
Season	Club	League	GP	G	A	TP	PIM	GP	G	A	TP	PIM
2000-01	St-Francois	QAAA	5	1	1	2	0	....	....	....	....	....
2001-02	St-Francois	QAAA	41	21	30	51	48	8	2	7	9	8
	Sherbrooke	QMJHL	6	0	3	3	0	....	....	....	....	....
2002-03	Sherbrooke	QMJHL	66	14	15	29	41	12	4	0	4	10
2003-04	Lewiston	QMJHL	69	39	41	80	88	7	7	4	11	6

QMJHL Second All-Star Team (2004)

PICARD, Alexandre (pee-KAR, ahl-ehx-AHN-druh) PHI.

Defense. Shoots left. 6'2", 214 lbs. Born, Gatineau, Que., July 5, 1985.
(Philadelphia's 5th choice, 85th overall, in 2003 Entry Draft).

			Regular Season					Playoffs				
Season	Club	League	GP	G	A	TP	PIM	GP	G	A	TP	PIM
2000-01	Gatineau Intrepide	QAAA	42	6	15	21	38	11	0	1	1	8
2001-02	Halifax	QMJHL	59	2	12	14	28	13	2	3	5	6
2002-03	Halifax	QMJHL	71	4	30	34	64	25	1	5	6	14
2003-04	Cape Breton	QMJHL	57	10	26	36	44	5	0	0	0	0

PIISPANEN, Arsi (pihz-PAH-nehn, AHR-see) CBJ

Right wing. Shoots right. 6'3", 163 lbs. Born, Jyvaskyla, Finland, July 23, 1985.
(Columbus' 6th choice, 138th overall, in 2003 Entry Draft).

			Regular Season					Playoffs				
Season	Club	League	GP	G	A	TP	PIM	GP	G	A	TP	PIM
2000-01	Jokerit Helsinki B	Finn-Jr.	3	0	2	2	0	....	....	....	....	....
2001-02	Jokerit Helsinki Jr.	Finn-Jr.	26	7	19	26	8	8	4	3	7	12
	Jokerit Helsinki Jr.	Finn-Jr.	1	0	0	0	0	....	....	....	....	....
2002-03	Jokerit Helsinki Jr.	Finn-Jr.	41	20	15	35	10	13	3	5	8	2
2003-04	Jokerit Helsinki Jr.	Finn-Jr.	36	5	25	30	12	10	3	3	6	2
	Jokerit Helsinki	Finland	5	0	0	0	0	4	0	0	0	0

PIKKARAINEN, Ilkka (pih-kar-AY-nihn, IHL-kah) N.J.

Right wing. Shoots right. 6'2", 200 lbs. Born, Sonkajarvi, Finland, April 19, 1981.
(New Jersey's 9th choice, 218th overall, in 2002 Entry Draft).

			Regular Season					Playoffs				
Season	Club	League	GP	G	A	TP	PIM	GP	G	A	TP	PIM
1998-99	HIFK Helsinki Jr.	Finn-Jr.	37	12	13	25	38	2	1	0	1	27
99-2000	HIFK Helsinki Jr.	Finn-Jr.	28	3	2	5	14	3	1	1	2	2
2000-01	HIFK Helsinki Jr.	Finn-Jr.	38	27	31	58	186	9	2	5	7	26
	HIFK Helsinki	Finland	4	0	0	0	8	2	0	0	0	0
2001-02	HIFK Helsinki	Finland	54	9	9	18	111	....	....	....	....	....
2002-03	HIFK Helsinki	Finland	47	11	12	23	40	....	....	....	....	....
2003-04	Albany River Rats	AHL	63	8	10	18	118	....	....	....	....	....

PINEAULT, Adam (pih-NOH, A-duhm) CBJ

Right wing. Shoots right. 6'1", 193 lbs. Born, Holyoke, MA, May 23, 1986.
(Columbus' 2nd choice, 46th overall, in 2004 Entry Draft).

			Regular Season					Playoffs				
Season	Club	League	GP	G	A	TP	PIM	GP	G	A	TP	PIM
2000-01	Boston Jr. Bruins	EJHL	57	30	35	65	56	....	....	....	....	....
2001-02	U.S. National U-17	USDP	58	16	8	24	25	....	....	....	....	....
2002-03	U.S. National U-17	USDP	52	18	19	37	89	....	....	....	....	....
	U.S. National U-18	USDP	4	4	3	7	6	....	....	....	....	....
2003-04	Boston College	H-East	30	4	4	8	32	....	....	....	....	....

PISELLINI, Gino (pih-sehl-EE-nee, JEE-noh) PHI.

Right wing. Shoots right. 6', 210 lbs. Born, Melrose Park, IL, August 5, 1986.
(Philadelphia's 5th choice, 149th overall, in 2004 Entry Draft).

			Regular Season					Playoffs				
Season	Club	League	GP	G	A	TP	PIM	GP	G	A	TP	PIM
2002-03	Team Ilinois	MWEHL		STATISTICS NOT AVAILABLE								
2003-04	Plymouth Whalers	OHL	68	15	15	30	214	9	0	3	3	23

PLATIL, Jan (PLA-tihl, YAN) OTT.

Defense. Shoots left. 6'2", 195 lbs. Born, Kladno, Czech., February 9, 1983.
(Ottawa's 8th choice, 218th overall, in 2001 Entry Draft).

			Regular Season					Playoffs				
Season	Club	League	GP	G	A	TP	PIM	GP	G	A	TP	PIM
1998-99	Kladno Jr.	Czech-Jr.	46	8	12	20	....	....	....	....	....	....
99-2000	Kladno Jr.	Czech-Jr.	39	5	6	11	....	....	....	....	....	....
2000-01	Barrie Colts	OHL	60	6	18	24	114	5	0	0	0	12
2001-02	Barrie Colts	OHL	68	13	34	47	136	20	1	5	6	51
2002-03	Barrie Colts	OHL	61	15	36	51	163	6	1	5	6	8
2003-04	Binghamton	AHL	66	1	3	4	142	....	....	....	....	....

PLATONOV, Denis (PLAH-tah-nahv, DIHN-ihs) NSH.

Right wing. Shoots left. 6'3", 202 lbs. Born, Saratov, USSR, November 6, 1981.
(Nashville's 4th choice, 75th overall, in 2001 Entry Draft).

			Regular Season					Playoffs				
Season	Club	League	GP	G	A	TP	PIM	GP	G	A	TP	PIM
1997-98	Kristall Saratov 2	Russia-3	20	4	2	6	34	....	....	....	....	....
1998-99	Kristall Saratov	Russia-2	14	1	0	1	61	....	....	....	....	....
99-2000	Kristall Saratov 2	Russia-3	5	0	0	0	37	....	....	....	....	....
	Kristall Saratov	Russia-2	32	9	4	13	60	....	....	....	....	....
2000-01	Kristall Saratov	Russia-2	51	14	6	20	75	....	....	....	....	....
2001-02	Kristall Saratov	Russia-2	50	18	14	32	96	....	....	....	....	....
2002-03	Ak Bars Kazan	Russia	47	8	9	17	49	5	0	0	0	2
2003-04	Milwaukee	AHL	3	0	0	0	0	....	....	....	....	....
	Ak Bars Kazan	Russia	28	5	3	8	18	8	1	0	1	2
	AK Bars Kazan 2	Russia-3		STATISTICS NOT AVAILABLE								

Assigned to **Ak Bars Kazan** (Russia) by **Nashville**, October 29, 2003.

PLATT, Jason (PLAT, JAY-suhn) EDM.

Defense. Shoots left. 6'1", 210 lbs. Born, San Francisco, CA, April 29, 1981.
(Edmonton's 9th choice, 247th overall, in 2000 Entry Draft).

			Regular Season					Playoffs				
Season	Club	League	GP	G	A	TP	PIM	GP	G	A	TP	PIM
1998-99	Omaha Lancers	USHL	56	2	9	11	65	11	0	0	0	8
99-2000	Omaha Lancers	USHL	49	1	6	7	65	4	0	0	0	9
2000-01	Providence College	H-East	26	0	2	2	12	....	....	....	....	....
2001-02	Providence College	H-East	36	2	5	7	60	....	....	....	....	....
2002-03	Providence College	H-East	30	1	7	8	41	....	....	....	....	....
2003-04	Providence College	H-East	34	2	5	7	36	....	....	....	....	....
	Toronto	AHL	1	0	0	0	0	....	....	....	....	....

PLEHANOV, Andrei (pleh-HA-nawf, AWN-dray) CBJ

Defense. Shoots right. 6'1", 187 lbs. Born, Nizhnekamsk, USSR, July 12, 1986.
(Columbus' 5th choice, 96th overall, in 2004 Entry Draft).

			Regular Season					Playoffs				
Season	Club	League	GP	G	A	TP	PIM	GP	G	A	TP	PIM
2003-04	Nizhnekamsk 2	Russia-3		STATISTICS NOT AVAILABLE								

PLIHAL, Tomas (PLEE-hahl, TAW-mahsh) S.J.

Center. Shoots left. 6'1", 195 lbs. Born, Frydlant v Cechach, Czech., March 28, 1983.
(San Jose's 4th choice, 140th overall, in 2001 Entry Draft).

			Regular Season					Playoffs				
Season	Club	League	GP	G	A	TP	PIM	GP	G	A	TP	PIM
99-2000	HC Liberec 18	Czech-Jr.	38	22	14	36	....	....	....	....	....	....
	HC Liberec Jr.	Czech-Jr.	2	0	0	0	0	....	....	....	....	....
2000-01	HC Liberec 18	Czech-Jr.	18	3	5	8	....	....	....	....	....	....
	HC Liberec Jr.	Czech-Jr.	33	16	12	28	....	....	....	....	....	....
2001-02	Kootenay Ice	WHL	72	32	54	86	28	22	4	10	14	14
2002-03	Kootenay Ice	WHL	67	35	42	77	113	11	2	4	6	18
2003-04	Cleveland Barons	AHL	51	4	12	16	16	6	0	3	3	2

PODLESAK, Martin (PAWD-leh-shahk, MAHR-tihn) PHX.

Center. Shoots left. 6'6", 219 lbs. Born, Melnik, Czech., September 26, 1982.
(Phoenix's 3rd choice, 45th overall, in 2001 Entry Draft).

			Regular Season					Playoffs				
Season	Club	League	GP	G	A	TP	PIM	GP	G	A	TP	PIM
99-2000	Sparta Praha Jr.	Czech-Jr.	24	6	5	11	....	11	6	2	8	....
2000-01	Tri-City Americans	WHL	39	13	13	26	36	....	....	....	....	....
	Lethbridge	WHL	21	8	6	14	23	3	1	1	2	2
2001-02	Lethbridge	WHL	34	14	20	34	33	....	....	....	....	....
2002-03	Springfield Falcons	AHL	3	0	0	0	4	....	....	....	....	....
2003-04	Springfield Falcons	AHL	57	5	9	14	21	....	....	....	....	....

• Missed majority of 2002-03 season recovering from head injury suffered in game vs. Manchester (AHL), October 23, 2002.

POHANKA, Igor (poh-HAHN-kah, EE-gohr) ANA.

Center. Shoots left. 6'2", 210 lbs. Born, Piestany, Czech., July 5, 1983.
(New Jersey's 2nd choice, 44th overall, in 2001 Entry Draft).

			Regular Season					Playoffs				
Season	Club	League	GP	G	A	TP	PIM	GP	G	A	TP	PIM
1996-97	HK Piestany	Slovak-Jr.	3	1	3	4	4	....	....	....	....	....
1997-98	S. Bratislava Jr.	Slovak-Jr.	40	19	22	41	6	....	....	....	....	....
1998-99	S. Bratislava Jr.	Czech-Jr.	40	14	21	35	36	....	....	....	....	....
99-2000	S. Bratislava Jr.	Slovak-Jr.	57	36	41	77	62	....	....	....	....	....
2000-01	Prince Albert	WHL	70	16	33	49	24	....	....	....	....	....
2001-02	Prince Albert	WHL	58	25	43	68	18	....	....	....	....	....
2002-03	Prince Albert	WHL	56	25	31	56	28	....	....	....	....	....
2003-04	Cincinnati	AHL	42	5	6	11	6	4	0	0	0	0
	San Diego Gulls	ECHL	11	1	5	6	10	3	0	2	2	0

Traded to **Anaheim** by **New Jersey** with Petr Sykora, Mike Commodore and Jean-Francois Damphousse for Jeff Friesen, Oleg Tverdovsky and Maxim Balmochnykh, July 6, 2002.

POHL, Petr (PAWL, PEE-tuhr) CBJ

Right wing. Shoots right. 5'11", 185 lbs. Born, Prostejov, Czechoslovakia, August 28, 1986.
(Columbus' 6th choice, 133rd overall, in 2004 Entry Draft).

			Regular Season					Playoffs				
Season	Club	League	GP	G	A	TP	PIM	GP	G	A	TP	PIM
2001-02	HC Vitkovice 18	Czech-Jr.	38	34	19	53	65	2	1	0	1	4
	HC Vitkovice Jr.	Czech-Jr.	10	0	2	2	2	....	....	....	....	....
2002-03	HC Vitkovice Jr.	Czech-Jr.	36	13	22	35	30	2	1	0	1	6
2003-04	Gatineau	QMJHL	70	23	27	50	16	8	0	2	2	2

POLAK, Vojtech (POH-lahk, VOI-tehk) DAL.

Left wing. Shoots left. 5'11", 180 lbs. Born, Ostrov nad Ohri, Czech., June 27, 1985.
(Dallas' 2nd choice, 36th overall, in 2003 Entry Draft).

			Regular Season					Playoffs				
Season	Club	League	GP	G	A	TP	PIM	GP	G	A	TP	PIM
99-2000	Karlovy Vary Jr.	Czech-Jr.	49	17	23	40	48	....	....	....	....	....
2000-01	Karlovy Vary Jr.	Czech-Jr.	47	36	33	69	38	....	....	....	....	....
	Karlovy Vary	Czech	2	0	0	0	0	....	....	....	....	....
2001-02	Karlovy Vary Jr.	Czech-Jr.	37	11	14	25	26	....	....	....	....	....
	Karlovy Vary	Czech	9	1	1	2	2	....	....	....	....	....
2002-03	Karlovy Vary	Czech	41	7	9	16	51	....	....	....	....	....
	Karlovy Vary Jr.	Czech-Jr.	6	3	7	10	18	....	....	....	....	....
2003-04	HC Sparta Praha	Czech	1	1	0	1	0	....	....	....	....	....
	Karlovy Vary	Czech	44	0	8	8	42	....	....	....	....	....
	Karlovy Vary Jr.	Czech-Jr.	5	8	4	12	2	....	....	....	....	....

POLASKI, Scott (poh-LAHZ-kee, SKAWT) PHX.

Right wing. Shoots right. 6'2", 182 lbs. Born, Colorado Springs, CO, August 4, 1982.
(Phoenix's 6th choice, 180th overall, in 2001 Entry Draft).

			Regular Season					Playoffs				
Season	Club	League	GP	G	A	TP	PIM	GP	G	A	TP	PIM
1998-99	Pikes Point Selects	AAHA	60	40	46	86	....	....	....	....	....	....
99-2000	Sioux City	USHL	58	15	22	37	46	5	3	6	9	0
2000-01	Sioux City	USHL	51	18	26	44	65	3	0	1	1	0
2001-02	Colorado College	WCHA	38	4	12	16	28	....	....	....	....	....
2002-03	Colorado College	WCHA	42	4	6	10	24	....	....	....	....	....
2003-04	Colorado College	WCHA	39	9	12	21	22	....	....	....	....	....

POLCIK, Peter (POHL-chihk, PEE-tuhr) WSH.

Right wing. Shoots left. 6'4", 190 lbs. Born, Nitra, Czech., July 23, 1983.
(Washington's 8th choice, 254th overall, in 2001 Entry Draft).

			Regular Season					Playoffs				
Season	Club	League	GP	G	A	TP	PIM	GP	G	A	TP	PIM
1998-99	MHC Nitra Jr.	Slovak-Jr.	35	13	16	29	14	....	....	....	....	....
99-2000	MHC Nitra Jr.	Slovak-Jr.	40	26	20	46	82	....	....	....	....	....
2000-01	MHC Nitra Jr.	Slovak-Jr.	42	8	10	18	32	....	....	....	....	....
2001-02	Montreal Rocket	QMJHL	70	9	12	21	35	2	0	0	0	0
2002-03	MHC Nitra Jr.	Slovak-Jr.	45	20	21	41	53	2	1	0	1	2
	HKM Nitra	Slovak-2	18	3	1	4	2	....	....	....	....	....
2003-04	HKm Nitra	Slovakia	4	0	0	0	0	....	....	....	....	....
	Usti nad Labem	Czech-2	3	0	0	0	4	....	....	....	....	....
	HC Dukla Senica	Slovakia-2	10	2	5	7	14	4	0	0	0	2

POLUSHIN, Alexander (puh-LOOSH-ihn, al-ehx-AN-duhr) T.B.

Center. Shoots left. 6'3", 200 lbs. Born, Kirovo-Chepetsk, USSR, May 8, 1983.
(Tampa Bay's 2nd choice, 47th overall, in 2001 Entry Draft).

			Regular Season					Playoffs				
Season	Club	League	GP	G	A	TP	PIM	GP	G	A	TP	PIM
99-2000	Dyn. Moscow 2	Russia-3	18	4	3	7	14	....	....	....	....	....
	Spartak Moscow	Russia-2	14	1	0	1	2	....	....	....	....	....
2000-01	THC Tver	Russia-2	38	10	5	15	10	....	....	....	....	....
2001-02	HC CSKA	Russia-2	55	28	21	49	18	....	....	....	....	....
2002-03	CSKA Moscow	Russia	47	5	6	11	22	....	....	....	....	....
2003-04	CSKA Moscow	Russia	13	5	2	7	4	....	....	....	....	....

PORTER, Chris (POHR-tuhr, KRIHS) CHI.

Center. Shoots left. 6'1", 203 lbs. Born, Toronto, Ont., May 29, 1984.
(Chicago's 10th choice, 282nd overall, in 2003 Entry Draft).

			Regular Season					Playoffs				
Season	Club	League	GP	G	A	TP	PIM	GP	G	A	TP	PIM
2001-02	Shat.-St. Mary's	Hi-School	75	10	25	35	32	....	....	....	....	....
2002-03	Lincoln Stars	USHL	59	13	22	35	74	10	4	3	7	10
2003-04	North Dakota	WCHA	41	10	15	25	46	....	....	....	....	....

PORTER, Kevin (POHR-tuhr, KEH-vihn) PHX.

Left wing. Shoots left. 5'11", 194 lbs. Born, Detroit, MI, March 12, 1986.
(Phoenix's 5th choice, 119th overall, in 2004 Entry Draft).

			Regular Season					Playoffs				
Season	Club	League	GP	G	A	TP	PIM	GP	G	A	TP	PIM
2002-03	U.S. National U-17	USDP	59	28	20	48	25	....	....	....	....	....
	U.S. National U-18	USDP	13	1	2	3	2	....	....	....	....	....
2003-04	U.S. National U-18	USDP	55	8	29	37	30	....	....	....	....	....

POTTER, Corey (PAW-tuhr, KOHR-ee) NYR

Defense. Shoots right. 6'2", 183 lbs. Born, Lansing, MI, January 5, 1984.
(NY Rangers' 4th choice, 122nd overall, in 2003 Entry Draft).

			Regular Season					Playoffs				
Season	Club	League	GP	G	A	TP	PIM	GP	G	A	TP	PIM
99-2000	Det. Honey Baked	MWEHL	58	10	38	48	....	....	....	....	....	....
2000-01	U.S. National U-17	USDP	66	4	4	8	26	....	....	....	....	....
2001-02	U.S. National U-18	USDP	61	6	11	17	65	....	....	....	....	....
2002-03	Michigan State	CCHA	35	4	4	8	30	....	....	....	....	....
2003-04	Michigan State	CCHA	38	0	8	8	63	....	....	....	....	....

POTULNY, Grant (puh-TUHL-nee, GRANT) OTT.

Center. Shoots left. 6'3", 205 lbs. Born, Grand Forks, ND, March 4, 1980.
(Ottawa's 7th choice, 157th overall, in 2000 Entry Draft).

			Regular Season					Playoffs				
Season	Club	League	GP	G	A	TP	PIM	GP	G	A	TP	PIM
1998-99	Lincoln Stars	USHL	46	7	11	18	76	10	2	1	3	7
99-2000	Lincoln Stars	USHL	56	25	30	55	85	10	3	4	7	4
2000-01	U. of Minnesota	WCHA	42	22	11	33	38	....	....	....	....	....
2001-02	U. of Minnesota	WCHA	43	15	19	34	38	....	....	....	....	....
2002-03	U. of Minnesota	WCHA	23	15	8	23	12	....	....	....	....	....
2003-04	U. of Minnesota	WCHA	38	16	10	26	28	....	....	....	....	....
	Binghamton	AHL	3	0	1	1	0	2	0	0	0	0

NCAA Championship All-Tournament Team (2002) • NCAA Championship Tournament MVP (2002)

POTULNY, Ryan (poh-TOOL-nee, RIGH-uhn) PHI.

Center. Shoots left. 6', 190 lbs. Born, Grand Forks, ND, September 5, 1984.
(Philadelphia's 6th choice, 87th overall, in 2003 Entry Draft).

			Regular Season					Playoffs				
Season	Club	League	GP	G	A	TP	PIM	GP	G	A	TP	PIM
2000-01	Grand Forks High	Hi-School	STATISTICS NOT AVAILABLE									
2001-02	Lincoln Stars	USHL	60	23	34	57	65	4	0	1	1	2
2002-03	Lincoln Stars	USHL	54	35	*43	*78	18	10	6	*11	*17	8
2003-04	U. of Minnesota	WCHA	15	6	8	14	10	....	....	....	....	....

USHL First All-Star Team (2003) • USHL Player of the Year (2003) • USA Junior Player of the Year (2003)

Missed majority of 2003-04 season recovering from knee injury suffered in game vs. North Dakota (WCHA), November 7, 2003.

POULIOT, Marc-Antoine (poo-YOH, MAHRK-AN-twahn) EDM.

Center. Shoots right. 6'1", 195 lbs. Born, Quebec City, Que., May 22, 1985.
(Edmonton's 1st choice, 22nd overall, in 2003 Entry Draft).

			Regular Season					Playoffs				
Season	Club	League	GP	G	A	TP	PIM	GP	G	A	TP	PIM
2000-01	Ste-Foy Governors	QAAA	38	16	39	55	52	16	8	12	20	16
2001-02	Rimouski Oceanic	QMJHL	28	9	14	23	32	5	0	0	0	4
2002-03	Rimouski Oceanic	QMJHL	65	32	41	73	100	....	....	....	....	....
2003-04	Rimouski Oceanic	QMJHL	42	25	33	58	62	9	5	7	12	12

PRESTBERG, Pelle (PREHST-buhrg, PEHL-lee) ANA.

Left wing. Shoots left. 5'10", 170 lbs. Born, Jonkoping, Sweden, February 5, 1975.
(Anaheim's 7th choice, 233rd overall, in 1998 Entry Draft).

			Regular Season					Playoffs				
Season	Club	League	GP	G	A	TP	PIM	GP	G	A	TP	PIM
1990-91	IFK Munkfors	Swede-3	3	0	3	3	....	....	....	....	....	....
1991-92	IFK Munkfors	Swede-3	26	6	10	16	18	....	....	....	....	....
1992-93	IFK Munkfors	Swede-3	36	8	8	16	20	....	....	....	....	....
1993-94	Sunne IK	Swede-2	32	8	6	14	16	....	....	....	....	....
1994-95	IFK Munkfors	Swede-3	27	13	9	22	44	....	....	....	....	....
1995-96	IFK Munkfors	Swede-3	30	20	11	31	32	....	....	....	....	....
1996-97	IFK Munkfors	Swede-3	32	28	10	38	50	....	....	....	....	....
1997-98	Farjestad	Sweden	45	29	15	44	22	12	*9	2	11	8
1998-99	Farjestad	Sweden	48	18	15	33	28	4	0	1	1	4
99-2000	Farjestad	Sweden	48	13	9	22	26	7	1	1	2	18
2000-01	Vastra Frolunda	Sweden	50	14	9	23	18	5	0	0	0	8
2001-02	Vastra Frolunda	Sweden	50	14	11	25	28	10	5	0	5	12
2002-03	Farjestad	Sweden	45	12	6	18	26	14	5	1	6	8
2003-04	Farjestad	Sweden	50	22	23	45	50	12	2	1	3	2

PREUCIL, Petr (PREE-oo-chihl, PEE-tuhr) NYR

Center. Shoots left. 6'1", 168 lbs. Born, Most, Czech., January 21, 1983.
(NY Rangers' 7th choice, 206th overall, in 2001 Entry Draft).

			Regular Season					Playoffs				
Season	Club	League	GP	G	A	TP	PIM	GP	G	A	TP	PIM
99-2000	Litvinov Jr.	Czech-Jr.	23	7	4	11	....	....	....	....	....	....
2000-01	Quebec Remparts	QMJHL	70	12	35	47	121	4	1	0	1	11
2001-02	Quebec Remparts	QMJHL	57	14	20	34	116	9	2	3	5	24
2002-03	Drummondville	QMJHL	32	14	19	33	46	....	....	....	....	....
	Baie-Comeau	QMJHL	26	3	9	12	55	12	7	4	11	35
2003-04	Baie-Comeau	QMJHL	27	8	17	25	56	....	....	....	....	....
	Rouyn-Noranda	QMJHL	21	3	11	14	27	11	4	7	11	29

PRINTZ, David (PRIHNTS, DAY-vihd) PHI.

Defense. Shoots left. 6'5", 220 lbs. Born, Stockholm, Sweden, July 24, 1980.
(Philadelphia's 9th choice, 225th overall, in 2001 Entry Draft).

			Regular Season					Playoffs				
Season	Club	League	GP	G	A	TP	PIM	GP	G	A	TP	PIM
1996-97	AIK Solna Jr.	Swede-Jr.	1	0	0	0	0	....	....	....	....	....
1997-98	AIK Solna Jr.	Swede-Jr.	8	0	0	0	6	....	....	....	....	....
1998-99	AIK Solna Jr.	Swede-Jr.	23	1	0	1	14	....	....	....	....	....
99-2000	AIK Solna Jr.	Swede-Jr.	36	8	4	12	53	....	....	....	....	....
2000-01	Great Falls	AWHL	54	13	23	36	93	13	3	5	8	16
2001-02	AIK Solna Jr.	Swede-Jr.	8	2	3	5	20	....	....	....	....	....
	AIK Solna	Sweden	37	3	2	5	59	....	....	....	....	....
	AIK Solna	Swede-Q	10	0	0	0	12	....	....	....	....	....
2002-03	HPK Hameenlinna	Finland	17	1	0	1	10	....	....	....	....	....
	Ilves Tampere	Finland	25	1	2	3	10	....	....	....	....	....
2003-04	AIK Solna	Swede-2	51	2	9	11	60	5	2	0	2	4

PRUCHA, Petr (PROO-khah, PEE-tuhr) NYR

Right wing. Shoots right. 5'10", 161 lbs. Born, Chrudim, Czech., September 14, 1982.
(NY Rangers' 8th choice, 240th overall, in 2002 Entry Draft).

			Regular Season					Playoffs				
Season	Club	League	GP	G	A	TP	PIM	GP	G	A	TP	PIM
99-2000	HC Chrudim Jr.	Czech-Jr.	43	35	27	62	62	....	....	....	....	....
2000-01	Pardubice Jr.	Czech	54	39	22	61	18	....	....	....	....	....
2001-02	Pardubice Jr.	Czech	28	38	28	66	18	3	2	6	8	0
	Sumperk	Czech-2	8	6	4	10	0	....	....	....	....	....
	Sumperk	Czech-Q	5	5	3	8	0	....	....	....	....	....
	Pardubice	Czech	20	1	1	2	2	5	0	0	0	0
2002-03	Pardubice	Czech	49	7	9	16	12	17	2	6	8	8
	Pardubice Jr.	Czech	4	5	4	9	25	....	....	....	....	....
	HC Kralove	Czech-2	11	3	5	8	35	....	....	....	....	....
2003-04	HC Kralove	Czech-2	3	1	0	1	25	....	....	....	....	....
	Pardubice	Czech	48	11	13	24	24	7	4	3	7	2

PRUST, Brandon (PROOST, BRAN-duhn) CGY.

Center/Left wing. Shoots left. 5'11", 191 lbs. Born, London, Ont., March 16, 1984.
(Calgary's 2nd choice, 70th overall, in 2004 Entry Draft).

			Regular Season					Playoffs				
Season	Club	League	GP	G	A	TP	PIM	GP	G	A	TP	PIM
2001-02	London Nationals	OJHL-B	52	17	35	52	38	....	....	....	....	....
2002-03	London Knights	OHL	65	12	17	29	94	14	2	1	3	21
2003-04	London Knights	OHL	64	19	33	52	269	15	7	13	20	33

PSURNY, Roman (P'SHUHR-nee, ROH-muhn) NYR

Left wing. Shoots left. 6'1", 163 lbs. Born, Gottwaldov, Czechoslovakia, February 23, 1986.
(NY Rangers' 10th choice, 135th overall, in 2004 Entry Draft).

			Regular Season					Playoffs				
Season	Club	League	GP	G	A	TP	PIM	GP	G	A	TP	PIM
2001-02	Zlin 18	Czech-Jr.	42	19	36	55	57	6	3	3	6	6
2002-03	HC Hame Zlin 18	Czech-Jr.	22	17	27	44	20	3	1	1	2	4
	HC Hame Zlin Jr.	Czech-Jr.	15	3	7	10	0	....	....	....	....	....
2003-04	HC Hame Zlin Jr.	Czech-Jr.	52	18	33	51	104	5	0	0	0	2
	HC Hame Zlin	Czech	9	0	0	0	0	....	....	....	....	....

PUDLICK, Michael (PUHD-lihk, MIGH-kuhl)

Defense. Shoots left. 6'3", 190 lbs. Born, Blaine, MN, February 24, 1978.

			Regular Season					Playoffs				
Season	Club	League	GP	G	A	TP	PIM	GP	G	A	TP	PIM
1995-96	Blaine Bengals	Hi-School	25	9	30	39	....	....	....	....	....	....
1996-97	Twin Cities	USHL	49	10	19	29	93	5	0	2	2	4
1997-98	Twin Cities	USHL	50	3	14	17	138	....	....	....	....	....
1998-99	St. Cloud State	WCHA	37	13	12	25	74	....	....	....	....	....
99-2000	St. Cloud State	WCHA	40	8	22	30	65	....	....	....	....	....
2000-01	Lowell	AHL	57	7	13	20	39	4	0	1	1	2
2001-02	Manchester	AHL	64	9	6	15	42	3	0	0	0	6
2002-03	Manchester	AHL	68	7	17	24	52	1	0	0	0	0
2003-04	Portland Pirates	AHL	69	9	15	24	60	3	2	1	3	2

WCHA First All-Star Team (2000) • NCAA West Second All-American Team (2000)

Signed as a free agent by **Los Angeles**, April 5, 2000.

PULLIAINEN, Tuukka (poo-le-AY-nehn, TOO-kuh) L.A.

Right wing. Shoots left. 5'11", 176 lbs. Born, Turku, Finland, August 25, 1984.
(Los Angeles' 10th choice, 248th overall, in 2002 Entry Draft).

			Regular Season					Playoffs				
Season	Club	League	GP	G	A	TP	PIM	GP	G	A	TP	PIM
2000-01	TuTu Turku Jr.	Finn-Jr.	37	3	11	14	8	1	1	1	2	0
2001-02	TuTu Turku	Finland-2	41	11	8	19	8	2	0	1	1	25
	TuTu Turku Jr.	Finn-Jr.	3	0	2	2	0	1	0	0	0	2
2002-03	TuTu Turku	Finland-2	42	15	17	32	12	....	....	....	....	....
2003-04	TPS Turku	Finland	2	0	0	0	0	....	....	....	....	....
	TPS Turku Jr.	Finn-Jr.	1	0	0	0	0	....	....	....	....	....
	TuTo Turku	Finland-2	44	6	25	31	12	....	....	....	....	....

PUNCOCHAR, Petr (POON-choh-hahr, PEE-tuhr) CHI.

Defense. Shoots right. 6'1", 215 lbs. Born, Tabor, Czech., June 8, 1983.
(Chicago's 10th choice, 186th overall, in 2001 Entry Draft).

			Regular Season					Playoffs				
Season	Club	League	GP	G	A	TP	PIM	GP	G	A	TP	PIM
1998-99	C. Budejovice Jr.	Czech-Jr.	45	6	12	18	20	....	....	....	....	....
99-2000	C. Budejovice Jr.	Czech-Jr.	18	1	3	4	4	....	....	....	....	....
	Karlovy Vary Jr.	Czech-Jr.	23	1	1	2	4	2	0	0	0	2
	HC Karlovy Vary	Czech	1	0	0	0	0	....	....	....	....	....
2000-01	Karlovy Vary Jr.	Czech-Jr.	35	8	5	13	14	....	....	....	....	....
	HC Karlovy Vary	Czech	8	1	0	1	4	....	....	....	....	....
	HC Banik Most	Czech-3	1	0	0	0	0	....	....	....	....	....
2001-02	Karlovy Vary Jr.	Czech-Jr.	5	0	0	0	6	....	....	....	....	....
	HC Banik	Czech-3	7	2	1	3	0	....	....	....	....	....
	HC Karlovy Vary	Czech	32	0	2	2	36	....	....	....	....	....
2002-03	Karlovy Vary	Czech	17	0	3	3	16	....	....	....	....	....
	Karlovy Vary Jr.	Czech-Jr.	15	5	4	9	8	....	....	....	....	....
	KLH Chomutov	Czech-2	5	0	1	1	2	....	....	....	....	....
	Havirov	Czech	9	0	0	0	2	....	....	....	....	....
	Havirov	Czech-Q	....	....	....	....	....	4	0	0	0	2
2003-04	Znojmo	Czech	4	0	0	0	0	....	....	....	....	....
	Karlovy Vary	Czech	1	0	0	0	2	....	....	....	....	....
	Karlovy Vary Jr.	Czech-Jr.	2	0	0	0	0	....	....	....	....	....
	SK Kadan	Czech-2	20	3	0	3	14	....	....	....	....	....
	HC Dukla Jihlava	Czech-2	14	0	0	0	14	16	1	4	5	12

PUSHKAREV, Konstantin (puhsh-kar-EHV, kawn-stuhn-TIHN) L.A.

Right wing. Shoots left. 6', 169 lbs. Born, Ust-Kamenogorsk, USSR, February 12, 1985.
(Los Angeles' 4th choice, 44th overall, in 2003 Entry Draft).

			Regular Season					Playoffs				
Season	Club	League	GP	G	A	TP	PIM	GP	G	A	TP	PIM
2002-03	Kamenogorsk 2	Russia 3		Statistics not available								
	Ust-Kamenogorsk	Russia 2	4	0	0	0	4	....	....	....	....	....
2003-04	Avangard Omsk	Russia	5	1	0	1	0	....	....	....	....	....
	Omsk 2	Russia-3	34	17	11	28	64	....	....	....	....	....

QUINCEY, Kyle (KWIHN-see, KIGHL) DET.

Defense. Shoots left. 6'1", 194 lbs. Born, Kitchener, Ont., August 12, 1985.
(Detroit's 2nd choice, 132nd overall, in 2003 Entry Draft).

			Regular Season					Playoffs				
Season	Club	League	GP	G	A	TP	PIM	GP	G	A	TP	PIM
2001-02	Mississauga	OPJHL	27	5	14	19	31	....	....	....	....	....
2002-03	London Knights	OHL	66	6	12	18	77	14	3	4	7	11
2003-04	London Knights	OHL	3	0	2	2	4	....	....	....	....	....
	Mississauga	OHL	61	14	23	37	135	24	3	13	16	32

RACHUNEK, Ivan (ra-KHOO-nuhk, EE-vahn) T.B.

Left wing. Shoots left. 5'9", 180 lbs. Born, Gottwaldov, Czech., July 6, 1981.
(Tampa Bay's 8th choice, 187th overall, in 1999 Entry Draft).

			Regular Season					Playoffs				
Season	Club	League	GP	G	A	TP	PIM	GP	G	A	TP	PIM
1997-98	Zlin Jr.	Czech-Jr.	48	15	25	40	172	....	....	....	....	....
1998-99	Zlin Jr.	Czech-Jr.	40	37	22	59	70	....	....	....	....	....
	HC ZPS-Barum Zlin	Czech	5	0	0	0	0	....	....	....	....	....
99-2000	Zlin	Czech	5	0	1	1	2	....	....	....	....	....
	Zlin Jr.	Czech-Jr.	3	0	7	7	4	....	....	....	....	....
	Windsor Spitfires	OHL	15	2	2	4	21	....	....	....	....	....
2000-01	Zlin	Czech	50	8	9	17	95	6	1	0	1	8
2001-02	Zlin	Czech	48	9	11	20	143	11	3	4	7	6
2002-03	HC Hame Zlin	Czech	48	9	16	25	52	....	....	....	....	....
2003-04	Ceske Budejovice	Czech	5	0	2	2	0	....	....	....	....	....

RADULOV, Alexander (rah-DOO-lahf, al-EHX-AN-duhr) NSH.

Left wing. Shoots left. 6'1", 185 lbs. Born, Nizhy Tagil, USSR, July 5, 1986.
(Nashville's 1st choice, 15th overall, in 2004 Entry Draft).

			Regular Season					Playoffs				
Season	Club	League	GP	G	A	TP	PIM	GP	G	A	TP	PIM
2002-03	Dyn. Moscow 2	Russia-3		Statistics not available								
	Dyn. Moscow 17	Russia-Jr.	6	4	6	10	26	....	....	....	....	....
2003-04	Dynamo Moscow	Russia	1	0	0	0	2	....	....	....	....	....
	Dyn. Moscow 2	Russia-3		Statistics not available								
	THC Tver	Russia-2	42	15	16	31	102	....	....	....	....	....

RADUNSKE, Brock (ra-DOON-skee, BRAWK) EDM.

Left wing. Shoots left. 6'4", 196 lbs. Born, Kitchener, Ont., April 5, 1983.
(Edmonton's 5th choice, 79th overall, in 2002 Entry Draft).

			Regular Season					Playoffs				
Season	Club	League	GP	G	A	TP	PIM	GP	G	A	TP	PIM
99-2000	Aurora Tigers	OPJHL	42	6	14	20	23	4	4	8	12	2
2000-01	Newmarket	OPJHL	48	30	39	69	65	....	....	....	....	....
2001-02	Michigan State	CCHA	41	4	9	13	28	....	....	....	....	....
2002-03	Michigan State	CCHA	36	11	18	29	30	....	....	....	....	....
2003-04	Michigan State	CCHA	42	12	10	22	60	....	....	....	....	....

RAJAMAKI, Erkki (righ-ya-MA-kee, UHR-kee) ST.L.

Left wing. Shoots left. 6'2", 205 lbs. Born, Vantaa, Finland, October 30, 1978.
(Tampa Bay's 9th choice, 216th overall, in 1999 Entry Draft).

			Regular Season					Playoffs				
Season	Club	League	GP	G	A	TP	PIM	GP	G	A	TP	PIM
1993-94	Vantaa HT C	Finn-Jr.	10	0	1	1	0	....	....	....	....	....
1994-95	Kiekko Vantaa Jr.	Finn-Jr.	2	0	0	0	0	....	....	....	....	....
1995-96	Kiekko Vantaa Jr.	Finn-Jr.		Did not play – injured								
1996-97	Kiekko Vantaa B	Finn-Jr.	33	14	19	33	32	....	....	....	....	....
1997-98	HIFK Helsinki Jr.	Finn-Jr.	14	1	2	3	2	....	....	....	....	....
	Kiekko Vantaa B	Finn-Jr.	....	....	....	....	....	10	3	0	3	2
1998-99	HIFK Helsinki B	Finn-Jr.	14	2	2	4	8	....	....	....	....	....
	HIFK Helsinki	Finland	14	0	0	0	2	....	....	....	....	....
	HIFK Helsinki Jr.	Finn-Jr.	....	....	....	....	....	13	7	3	10	45
99-2000	Colgate	ECAC	31	1	6	7	20	....	....	....	....	....
2000-01	Newcastle Jesters	Britain	11	1	0	1	0	....	....	....	....	....
	FoPS Forssa	Finland-2	4	1	3	4	0	....	....	....	....	....
	HIFK Helsinki	Finland	50	1	2	3	10	5	0	0	0	2
2001-02	HPK Hameenlinna	Finland	56	12	7	19	75	8	1	2	3	2
2002-03	HPK Hameenlinna	Finland	40	4	3	7	100	10	1	0	1	36
2003-04	Ilves Tampere	Finland	43	12	6	18	89	5	0	0	0	0

Traded to **St. Louis** by **Tampa Bay** for St. Louis' 8th round choice (Justin Keller) in 2004 Entry Draft, October 27, 2003.

RAKHMATULLIN, Ashkat (rahkh-ma-TOO-lihn, ahs-KHAHT) MIN.

Left wing. Shoots left. 5'11", 165 lbs. Born, Ufa, USSR, May 31, 1978.
(Hartford's 10th choice, 231st overall, in 1996 Entry Draft).

			Regular Season					Playoffs				
Season	Club	League	GP	G	A	TP	PIM	GP	G	A	TP	PIM
1996-97	Ufa Salavat	Russia	28	1	3	4	8	3	0	0	0	0
1997-98	Ufa Salavat	Russia	14	0	1	1	6	....	....	....	....	....
1998-99	Asheville Smoke	UHL	31	6	10	16	23	4	1	0	1	0
	Fayetteville Force	CHL	4	0	0	0	4	....	....	....	....	....
	Florida Everblades	ECHL	6	0	1	1	2	....	....	....	....	....
99-2000	Ufa Salavat	Russia	34	5	8	13	14	....	....	....	....	....
2000-01	Ufa Salavat	Russia	44	7	15	22	22	....	....	....	....	....
2001-02	SKA St. Petersburg	Russia	30	7	7	14	14	....	....	....	....	....
2002-03	Sibir Novosibirsk	Russia	11	1	1	2	4	....	....	....	....	....
	Krylja Sovetov	Russia	19	2	1	3	16	....	....	....	....	....
2003-04	Almetievsk	Russia-2	52	11	19	30	72	....	....	....	....	....

Rights transferred to **Carolina** after **Hartford** franchise relocated, June 25, 1997. Traded to **Minnesota** by **Carolina** with Carolina's 3rd round choice (later traded to NY Rangers – NY Rangers selected Garth Murray) in 2001 Entry Draft and Carolina's compensatory 5th round choice (Armands Berzins) in 2002 Entry Draft for Scott Pellerin, March 1, 2001.

RAMHOLT, Tim (RAM-hohlt, TIHM) CGY.

Defense. Shoots left. 6'1", 194 lbs. Born, Zurich, Switz., November 2, 1984.
(Calgary's 2nd choice, 39th overall, in 2003 Entry Draft).

			Regular Season					Playoffs				
Season	Club	League	GP	G	A	TP	PIM	GP	G	A	TP	PIM
99-2000	Grasshopper Jr.	Swiss-Jr.	35	2	9	11	26	4	0	2	2	4
	Grasshopper	Swiss-2	2	0	0	0	0	....	....	....	....	....
2000-01	GC SCK Lions	Swiss-2	37	0	2	2	38	3	0	0	0	4
	GC SCK Lions Jr.	Swiss-Jr.	17	3	6	9	10	....	....	....	....	....
2001-02	ZSC Lions Zurich	Swiss	37	3	0	3	14	17	0	3	3	2
	GCK Zurich Jr.	Swiss-Jr.	5	2	2	4	4	....	....	....	....	....
	GCK Zurich	Swiss-2	3	0	0	0	0	....	....	....	....	....
2002-03	ZSC Lions Zurich	Swiss	30	2	0	2	12	9	0	1	1	0
	GCK Lions Zurich	Swiss-2	12	0	4	4	6	....	....	....	....	....
2003-04	Cape Breton	QMJHL	51	9	27	36	26	5	0	1	1	4

RANGER, Paul (RAIN-juhr, PAWL) T.B.

Defense. Shoots left. 6'2", 210 lbs. Born, Whitby, Ont., September 12, 1984.
(Tampa Bay's choice, 183rd overall, in 2002 Entry Draft).

			Regular Season					Playoffs				
Season	Club	League	GP	G	A	TP	PIM	GP	G	A	TP	PIM
99-2000	Whitby AA	OMHA		Statistics not available								
2000-01	Oshawa Generals	OHL	32	0	1	1	2	....	....	....	....	....
2001-02	Oshawa Generals	OHL	62	0	9	9	49	5	0	0	0	4
2002-03	Oshawa Generals	OHL	68	10	28	38	70	13	0	3	3	10
2003-04	Oshawa Generals	OHL	62	12	31	43	72	7	0	1	1	10

RAWLYK, Rory (RAW-lihk, ROHR-ee) NYR

Defense. Shoots right. 6'3", 175 lbs. Born, Edmonton, Alta., September 9, 1983.

			Regular Season					Playoffs				
Season	Club	League	GP	G	A	TP	PIM	GP	G	A	TP	PIM
1998-99	Edm. Maple Leafs	AMBHL	36	6	18	24	58	....	....	....	....	....
99-2000	Edm. United Cycle	AMHL	28	3	14	17	34	....	....	....	....	....
2000-01	Camrose Kodiaks	AJHL	24	3	6	9	16	16	1	5	6	32
	Medicine Hat	WHL	17	0	1	1	6	....	....	....	....	....
2001-02	Medicine Hat	WHL	40	2	9	11	59	....	....	....	....	....
	Vancouver Giants	WHL	28	3	7	10	21	....	....	....	....	....
2002-03	Vancouver Giants	WHL	4	1	1	2	8	....	....	....	....	....
	Prince Albert	WHL	28	6	9	15	16	....	....	....	....	....
	Red Deer Rebels	WHL	20	4	5	9	16	23	2	9	11	30
2003-04	Hartford Wolf Pack	AHL	5	1	0	1	2	....	....	....	....	....
	Charlotte	ECHL	67	9	23	32	24	....	....	....	....	....

Signed as a free agent by **NY Rangers**, September 15, 2001.

READY, Ryan (REH-dee, RIGH-yan)

Left wing. Shoots left. 6'2", 195 lbs. Born, Peterborough, Ont., November 7, 1978.
(Calgary's 8th choice, 100th overall, in 1997 Entry Draft).

			Regular Season					Playoffs				
Season	**Club**	**League**	**GP**	**G**	**A**	**TP**	**PIM**	**GP**	**G**	**A**	**TP**	**PIM**
1994-95	Peterborough	OPJHL	48	20	33	53	65	....	....	....	....	....
1995-96	Belleville Bulls	OHL	63	5	13	18	54	10	0	2	2	2
1996-97	Belleville Bulls	OHL	66	23	24	47	102	6	1	3	4	4
1997-98	Belleville Bulls	OHL	66	33	39	72	80	10	5	2	7	12
1998-99	Belleville Bulls	OHL	63	33	59	92	73	21	10	28	38	22
99-2000	Syracuse Crunch	AHL	70	4	12	16	59	2	0	0	0	0
2000-01	Kansas City Blades	IHL	67	10	15	25	75	....	....	....	....	....
2001-02	Manitoba Moose	AHL	72	23	32	55	73	7	5	1	6	4
2002-03	Manitoba Moose	AHL	68	24	26	50	52	14	2	5	7	2
2003-04	Manitoba Moose	AHL	64	7	18	25	55	....	....	....	....	....
	Worcester IceCats	AHL	16	2	5	7	10	10	1	2	3	10

OHL First All-Star Team (1999)

Signed as a free agent by **Vancouver**, June 16, 1999. Traded to **St. Louis** by **Vancouver** for Sergei Varlamov, March 9, 2004.

REDDOX, Liam (REH-dawks, LEE-uhm) EDM.

Left wing. Shoots left. 5'9", 179 lbs. Born, East York, Ont., January 27, 1986.
(Edmonton's 5th choice, 112th overall, in 2004 Entry Draft).

			Regular Season					Playoffs				
Season	**Club**	**League**	**GP**	**G**	**A**	**TP**	**PIM**	**GP**	**G**	**A**	**TP**	**PIM**
2002-03	Wellington Dukes	OPJHL	45	32	32	64	29	....	....	....	....	....
	Peterborough	OHL	4	0	0	0	0	....	....	....	....	....
2003-04	Peterborough	OHL	68	31	33	64	24	....	....	....	....	....

OHL All-Rookie Team (2004)

REDENBACH, Tyler (REH-dehn-bak, TIGH-luhr) PHX.

Center. Shoots left. 5'11", 191 lbs. Born, Regina, Sask., September 25, 1984.
(Phoenix's 1st choice, 77th overall, in 2003 Entry Draft).

			Regular Season					Playoffs				
Season	**Club**	**League**	**GP**	**G**	**A**	**TP**	**PIM**	**GP**	**G**	**A**	**TP**	**PIM**
2000-01	North Kamloops	BCAHA	49	60	66	126	22	....	....	....	....	....
2001-02	Prince George	WHL	65	3	18	21	30	7	0	1	1	2
2002-03	Prince George	WHL	36	8	34	42	29	....	....	....	....	....
	Swift Current	WHL	24	9	17	26	6	4	0	4	4	4
2003-04	Swift Current	WHL	71	31	*74	*105	52	5	1	1	2	14

WHL East Second All-Star Team (2004)

REDIKER, Frank (REH-dih-kuhr, FRANK) BOS.

Defense. Shoots left. 6'1", 200 lbs. Born, Sterling Heights, MI, March 15, 1985.
(Boston's 5th choice, 118th overall, in 2003 Entry Draft).

			Regular Season					Playoffs				
Season	**Club**	**League**	**GP**	**G**	**A**	**TP**	**PIM**	**GP**	**G**	**A**	**TP**	**PIM**
2000-01	Det. Compuware	NAJHL	39	3	7	10	131	3	0	0	0	8
2001-02	Windsor Spitfires	OHL	59	9	13	22	170	8	0	0	0	22
2002-03	Windsor Spitfires	OHL	51	8	8	16	120	7	0	2	2	10
2003-04	Windsor Spitfires	OHL	1	0	1	1	2	....	....	....	....	....
	London Knights	OHL	24	3	6	9	43	....	....	....	....	....

Missed majority of 2003-04 season recovering from shoulder (off-season surgery) and knee (March 6, 2004 vs. Guelph) injuries.

REDLIHS, Jekabs (REHD-lihs, YEH-kabs) CBJ

Defense. Shoots left. 6'2", 185 lbs. Born, Riga, Latvia, March 29, 1982.
(Columbus' 6th choice, 119th overall, in 2002 Entry Draft).

			Regular Season					Playoffs				
Season	**Club**	**League**	**GP**	**G**	**A**	**TP**	**PIM**	**GP**	**G**	**A**	**TP**	**PIM**
1998-99	Dynamo Riga 18	Latvia-Jr.		STATISTICS NOT AVAILABLE								
99-2000	HC Essamika Jr.	EEHL	16	1	4	5	6	....	....	....	....	....
	Metalurgs Liepaja	Latvia	1	0	0	0	0	....	....	....	....	....
	Metalurgs Liepaja	EEHL	11	0	0	0	2	....	....	....	....	....
2000-01	Metalurgs Liepaja	EEHL	31	1	3	4	....	....	....	....	....	....
	Metalurgs Liepaja	Latvia	23	4	5	9	....	....	....	....	....	....
2001-02	NY Apple Core	EJHL	38	3	16	19	24	....	....	....	....	....
2002-03	Boston University	H-East	40	4	12	16	12	....	....	....	....	....
2003-04	Boston University	H-East	23	2	4	6	53	....	....	....	....	....

Hockey East All-Rookie Team (2003)

REDLIHS, Krisjanis (REHD-lihs, krihs-JA-nihs) N.J.

Defense. Shoots left. 6'3", 190 lbs. Born, Riga, Latvia, January 15, 1981.
(New Jersey's 7th choice, 154th overall, in 2002 Entry Draft).

			Regular Season					Playoffs				
Season	**Club**	**League**	**GP**	**G**	**A**	**TP**	**PIM**	**GP**	**G**	**A**	**TP**	**PIM**
1998-99	Dynamo Riga 18	Latvia-Jr.		STATISTICS NOT AVAILABLE								
99-2000	Metalurgs Liepaja	EEHL	12	1	3	4	0	....	....	....	....	....
2000-01	Metalurgs Liepaja	EEHL	27	2	2	4	....	....	....	....	....	....
	Metalurgs Liepaja	Latvia	22	1	6	7	....	....	....	....	....	....
2001-02	Metalurgs Liepaja	EEHL	32	0	2	2	....	11	1	1	2	....
	Metalurgs Liepaja	Latvia	13	0	6	6	4	3	2	2	4	0
2002-03	Albany River Rats	AHL	61	1	9	10	20	....	....	....	....	....
2003-04	Albany River Rats	AHL	66	9	10	19	16	....	....	....	....	....

REESE, Dylan (REES, DIH-luhn) NYR

Defense. Shoots right. 6', 195 lbs. Born, Pittsburgh, PA, August 29, 1984.
(NY Rangers' 9th choice, 209th overall, in 2003 Entry Draft).

			Regular Season					Playoffs				
Season	**Club**	**League**	**GP**	**G**	**A**	**TP**	**PIM**	**GP**	**G**	**A**	**TP**	**PIM**
2000-01	Pittsburgh Hornets	MWEHL	66	14	42	66	....	....	....	....	....	....
2001-02	Pittsburgh Forge	NAHL	48	7	16	23	70	7	0	2	2	4
2002-03	Pittsburgh Forge	NAHL	56	11	30	41	98	5	2	3	5	6
2003-04	Harvard University	ECAC	21	1	4	5	18	....	....	....	....	....

REGIER, Steve (reh-GEER, STEEV) NYI

Left wing. Shoots left. 6'4", 194 lbs. Born, Edmonton, Alta., August 31, 1984.
(NY Islanders' 5th choice, 148th overall, in 2004 Entry Draft).

			Regular Season					Playoffs				
Season	**Club**	**League**	**GP**	**G**	**A**	**TP**	**PIM**	**GP**	**G**	**A**	**TP**	**PIM**
2000-01	Leduc Oil Kings	AMHL	35	22	39	61	135	....	....	....	....	....
2001-02	Medicine Hat	WHL	59	1	4	5	31	....	....	....	....	....
2002-03	Medicine Hat	WHL	61	11	10	21	114	11	2	2	4	20
2003-04	Medicine Hat	WHL	72	25	35	60	111	18	5	11	16	20

REGIN JENSEN, Peter (REE-gihn-JEHN-sehn, PEE-tuhr) OTT.

Center. Shoots left. 6'1", 174 lbs. Born, Herning, Denmark, April 16, 1986.
(Ottawa's 4th choice, 87th overall, in 2004 Entry Draft).

			Regular Season					Playoffs				
Season	**Club**	**League**	**GP**	**G**	**A**	**TP**	**PIM**	**GP**	**G**	**A**	**TP**	**PIM**
2002-03	Herning IK	Denmark	24	0	1	1	4	10	1	3	4	4
2003-04	Herning IK	Denmark	33	9	11	20	14	....	....	....	....	....

REHAK, Denis (REH-hahk, DEH-nihs NYI

Defense. Shoots left. 6'2", 196 lbs. Born, Trencin, Czech., May 14, 1985.
(NY Islanders' 7th choice, 212th overall, in 2003 Entry Draft).

			Regular Season					Playoffs				
Season	**Club**	**League**	**GP**	**G**	**A**	**TP**	**PIM**	**GP**	**G**	**A**	**TP**	**PIM**
2002-03	Trencin Jr.	Slovak-Jr.	24	0	1	1	8	....	....	....	....	....
2003-04	Prince George	WHL	25	0	3	3	12	....	....	....	....	....
	Dukla Trencin B	Slovak-2	3	1	0	1	4	....	....	....	....	....

REID, Darren (REED, DAIR-uhn) T.B.

Right wing. Shoots right. 6'2", 190 lbs. Born, Lac La Biche, Alta., May 8, 1983.
(Tampa Bay's 11th choice, 256th overall, in 2002 Entry Draft).

			Regular Season					Playoffs				
Season	**Club**	**League**	**GP**	**G**	**A**	**TP**	**PIM**	**GP**	**G**	**A**	**TP**	**PIM**
2000-01	Drayton Valley	AJHL	55	8	18	26	116	....	....	....	....	....
2001-02	Drayton Valley	AJHL	31	9	12	21	195	....	....	....	....	....
	Medicine Hat	WHL	37	8	9	17	70	....	....	....	....	....
2002-03	Medicine Hat	WHL	63	14	30	44	163	11	5	0	5	19
2003-04	Medicine Hat	WHL	67	33	48	81	194	20	*13	8	21	31

REITZ, Erik (RIGHTZ, AIR-ihk) MIN.

Defense. Shoots right. 6'1", 210 lbs. Born, Detroit, MI, July 29, 1982.
(Minnesota's 5th choice, 170th overall, in 2000 Entry Draft).

			Regular Season					Playoffs				
Season	**Club**	**League**	**GP**	**G**	**A**	**TP**	**PIM**	**GP**	**G**	**A**	**TP**	**PIM**
1998-99	Leamington Flyers	OJHL-B	50	5	10	15	80	....	....	....	....	....
99-2000	Barrie Colts	OHL	63	2	10	12	85	25	0	5	5	44
2000-01	Barrie Colts	OHL	68	5	21	26	178	5	1	0	1	21
2001-02	Barrie Colts	OHL	61	13	27	40	153	20	4	16	20	40
2002-03	Houston Aeros	AHL	62	6	13	19	112	11	0	3	3	31
2003-04	Houston Aeros	AHL	69	5	19	24	148	2	0	0	0	0

Memorial Cup All-Star Team (2000) • OHL First All-Star Team (2002)

REYNOLDS, Peter (REH-nolds, PEE-tuhr) CAR.

Defense. Shoots right. 6'3", 200 lbs. Born, Waterloo, Ont., April 27, 1981.
(Carolina's 8th choice, 274th overall, in 2001 Entry Draft).

			Regular Season					Playoffs				
Season	**Club**	**League**	**GP**	**G**	**A**	**TP**	**PIM**	**GP**	**G**	**A**	**TP**	**PIM**
1996-97	Caledon	MTJHL	45	1	10	11	69	....	....	....	....	....
1997-98	London Knights	OHL	55	0	8	8	30	16	0	0	0	10
1998-99	London Knights	OHL	59	2	25	27	55	23	2	3	5	24
99-2000	North Bay	OHL	61	3	29	32	53	6	1	3	4	10
2000-01	North Bay	OHL	58	2	27	29	85	4	0	1	1	7
	St. John's	AHL	2	0	0	0	0	1	0	0	0	0
2001-02	Lowell	AHL	45	1	2	3	38	....	....	....	....	....
	Florida Everblades	ECHL	7	0	0	0	10	....	....	....	....	....
2002-03	Florida Everblades	ECHL	66	1	9	10	111	1	0	0	0	0
2003-04	Lowell	AHL	5	0	0	0	0	....	....	....	....	....
	Florida Everblades	ECHL	34	3	2	5	51	....	....	....	....	....
	Augusta Lynx	ECHL	4	1	0	1	4	....	....	....	....	....

• Re-entered NHL Entry Draft. Originally Toronto's 2nd choice, 60th overall, in 1999 Entry Draft.
Traded to **Augusta** (ECHL) by **Florida** (ECHL) for the rights to Chris Thompson, January 14, 2004.

RIAZANTSEV, Alexander (ree-ZAHNT-sehv, al-ehx-AN-duhr) WSH.

Defense. Shoots right. 6', 210 lbs. Born, Moscow, USSR, March 15, 1980.
(Colorado's 10th choice, 167th overall, in 1998 Entry Draft).

			Regular Season					Playoffs				
Season	**Club**	**League**	**GP**	**G**	**A**	**TP**	**PIM**	**GP**	**G**	**A**	**TP**	**PIM**
1996-97	Spartak Moscow 2	Russia-3	18	0	0	0	8	....	....	....	....	....
	Spartak Moscow	Russia	20	1	2	3	4	....	....	....	....	....
1997-98	Spartak Moscow 2	Russia-3	31	3	8	11	26	....	....	....	....	....
	Victoriaville Tigres	QMJHL	22	6	9	15	14	4	0	0	0	0
1998-99	Victoriaville Tigres	QMJHL	64	17	40	57	57	6	0	3	3	10
	Hershey Bears	AHL	2	0	0	0	0	....	....	....	....	....
99-2000	Victoriaville Tigres	QMJHL	48	17	45	62	45	6	2	5	7	20
	Hershey Bears	AHL	2	0	1	1	2	6	1	1	2	0
2000-01	Hershey Bears	AHL	66	5	18	23	26	11	0	0	0	2
2001-02	Hershey Bears	AHL	76	5	19	24	28	5	0	1	1	4
2002-03	Hershey Bears	AHL	57	5	10	15	65	....	....	....	....	....
	Milwaukee	AHL	14	3	4	7	9	5	0	4	4	2
2003-04	Yaroslavl 2	Russia-3	1	0	0	0	0	....	....	....	....	....
	Yaroslavl	Russia-2	41	3	8	11	60	....	....	....	....	....

Traded to **Nashville** by **Colorado** for Nashville's 7th round choice (Linus Videll) in 2003 Entry Draft, March 11, 2003. Traded to **Washington** by **Nashville** for Mike Farrell, July 14, 2003.

RICHARDS, Mike (RIH-chahrds, MIGHK) PHI.

Center. Shoots left. 5'11", 185 lbs. Born, Kenora, Ont., February 11, 1985.
(Philadelphia's 2nd choice, 24th overall, in 2003 Entry Draft).

			Regular Season					Playoffs				
Season	**Club**	**League**	**GP**	**G**	**A**	**TP**	**PIM**	**GP**	**G**	**A**	**TP**	**PIM**
2000-01	Kenora Stars	NOHA	85	76	73	149	20	....	....	....	....	....
2001-02	Kitchener Rangers	OHL	65	20	38	58	52	4	0	1	1	6
2002-03	Kitchener Rangers	OHL	67	37	50	87	99	21	9	18	27	24
2003-04	Kitchener Rangers	OHL	58	36	53	89	82	1	0	0	0	0

Memorial Cup All-Star Team (2003)

RICHARDSON, Brad (RIH-chard-suhn, BRAD) COL.

Center. Shoots left. 5'11", 178 lbs. Born, Belleville, Ont., February 4, 1985.
(Colorado's 4th choice, 163rd overall, in 2003 Entry Draft).

			Regular Season					Playoffs				
Season	**Club**	**League**	**GP**	**G**	**A**	**TP**	**PIM**	**GP**	**G**	**A**	**TP**	**PIM**
2000-01	Quinte Red Devils	OMHA		STATISTICS NOT AVAILABLE								
2001-02	Owen Sound	OHL	58	12	21	33	20	....	....	....	....	....
2002-03	Owen Sound	OHL	67	27	40	67	54	4	1	1	2	10
2003-04	Owen Sound	OHL	15	7	9	16	4	....	....	....	....	....

RICHMOND, Danny (RIHCH-muhnd, DA-nee) **CAR.**

Defense. Shoots left. 6', 175 lbs. Born, Chicago, IL, August 1, 1984.
(Carolina's 2nd choice, 31st overall, in 2003 Entry Draft).

			Regular Season					Playoffs				
Season	Club	League	GP	G	A	TP	PIM	GP	G	A	TP	PIM
2000-01	Team Illinois	MWEHL	79	25	40	65	....	....	....	....	....	....
2001-02	Chicago Steel	USHL	56	8	45	53	129	4	0	4	4	20
2002-03	U. of Michigan	CCHA	43	3	19	22	48	....	....	....	....	....
2003-04	London Knights	OHL	59	13	22	35	92	15	5	6	11	10

USHL All-Rookie Team (2002) • USHL First All-Star Team (2002) • USHL Rookie of the Year (2002) • CCHA All-Rookie Team (2003)

Left **U. of Michigan** (CCHA) and signed with **Guelph** (OHL), June 6, 2003.

RICHTER, Martin (RIHKH-tuhr, MAHR-tihn) **NYR**

Defense. Shoots right. 6'1", 196 lbs. Born, Prostejov, Czech., June 2, 1977.
(NY Rangers' 9th choice, 269th overall, in 2000 Entry Draft).

			Regular Season					Playoffs				
Season	Club	League	GP	G	A	TP	PIM	GP	G	A	TP	PIM
1995-96	HC Olomouc	Czech	3	0	0	0	0	1	0	0	0	0
1996-97	HC Olomouc	Czech	27	1	0	1	26	....	....	....	....	....
1997-98	HC Karlovy Vary	Czech	42	1	2	3	32	....	....	....	....	....
1998-99	HC Karlovy Vary	Czech	51	3	6	9	44	....	....	....	....	....
99-2000	HC Karlovy Vary	Czech	24	0	5	5	18	....	....	....	....	....
	SaiPa	Finland	26	1	3	4	54	....	....	....	....	....
2000-01	SaiPa	Finland	41	4	5	9	80	....	....	....	....	....
	Hartford Wolf Pack	AHL	1	0	0	0	0	....	....	....	....	....
2001-02	Hartford Wolf Pack	AHL	29	1	1	2	36	....	....	....	....	....
	HC Sparta Praha	Czech	8	0	0	0	14	13	0	0	0	10
2002-03	HC Sparta Praha	Czech	34	2	7	9	77	8	0	0	0	10
2003-04	HC Sparta Praha	Czech	16	2	2	4	16	....	....	....	....	....
	CSKA Moscow	Russia	14	0	0	0	33	....	....	....	....	....

RIDDLE, Troy (RIH-duhl, TROI) **ST.L.**

Center. Shoots right. 6', 172 lbs. Born, Minneapolis, MN, August 24, 1981.
(St. Louis' 5th choice, 129th overall, in 2000 Entry Draft).

			Regular Season					Playoffs				
Season	Club	League	GP	G	A	TP	PIM	GP	G	A	TP	PIM
1997-98	St. Margaret's	Hi-School	29	33	35	68	....	....	....	....	....	....
1998-99	St. Margaret's	Hi-School	29	54	45	99	....	....	....	....	....	....
99-2000	Des Moines	USHL	53	36	30	66	95	8	2	2	4	31
2000-01	U. of Minnesota	WCHA	38	16	14	30	49	....	....	....	....	....
2001-02	U. of Minnesota	WCHA	44	16	31	47	46	....	....	....	....	....
2002-03	U. of Minnesota	WCHA	45	26	26	52	50	....	....	....	....	....
2003-04	U. of Minnesota	WCHA	44	24	25	49	52	....	....	....	....	....

USHL Second All-Star Team (2000) • USHL Rookie of the Year (2000)

ROACH, Andy (ROHCH, AN-dee) **ST.L.**

Defense. Shoots right. 5'11", 181 lbs. Born, Mattawan, MI, August 22, 1973.

			Regular Season					Playoffs				
Season	Club	League	GP	G	A	TP	PIM	GP	G	A	TP	PIM
1991-92	Waterloo	USHL	45	12	16	28	6	....	....	....	....	....
1992-93	Waterloo	USHL	42	13	17	30	22	....	....	....	....	....
1993-94	Ferris State	CCHA	32	4	15	19	18	....	....	....	....	....
1994-95	Ferris State	CCHA	36	11	19	30	26	....	....	....	....	....
1995-96	Ferris State	CCHA	33	15	19	34	44	....	....	....	....	....
1996-97	Ferris State	CCHA	37	12	34	46	18	....	....	....	....	....
1997-98	San Antonio	IHL	67	8	16	24	30	....	....	....	....	....
1998-99	Long Beach	IHL	41	5	21	26	34	....	....	....	....	....
	Utah Grizzlies	IHL	44	7	10	17	18	....	....	....	....	....
99-2000	Krefeld Penguins	German	55	19	22	41	40	4	0	0	0	2
2000-01	Adler Mannheim	German	59	7	13	20	32	12	2	2	4	6
2001-02	Adler Mannheim	German	60	9	21	30	16	12	1	5	6	8
2002-03	Adler Mannheim	German	49	18	16	34	16	8	4	5	9	4
2003-04	Adler Mannheim	German	46	11	21	32	26	6	2	0	2	6

Signed as a free agent by **St. Louis**, June 30, 2004.

ROBERTSON, Josh (RAW-buhrt-suhn, JAWSH) **WSH.**

Center. Shoots right. 5'11", 186 lbs. Born, Whitman, MA, August 25, 1984.
(Washington's 4th choice, 155th overall, in 2003 Entry Draft).

			Regular Season					Playoffs				
Season	Club	League	GP	G	A	TP	PIM	GP	G	A	TP	PIM
2000-01	Whitman-Hanson	Hi-School	28	30	28	58	....	....	....	....	....	....
2001-02	Whitman-Hanson	Hi-School	30	50	55	105	....	....	....	....	....	....
2002-03	Proctor Academy	Hi-School	34	37	44	81	....	....	....	....	....	....
2003-04	Proctor Academy	Hi-School	20	23	37	60	....	....	....	....	....	....

• Signed Letter of Intent to attend **Northeastern** (ECAC), April 1, 2003.

ROBINSON, Brent (RAW-bihn-suhn, BREHNT) **PHI.**

Left wing. Shoots left. 6'1", 195 lbs. Born, Pointe Claire, Que., March 10, 1981.

			Regular Season					Playoffs				
Season	Club	League	GP	G	A	TP	PIM	GP	G	A	TP	PIM
1997-98	Lac St-Louis Lions	QAAA	42	23	33	56	....	5	2	4	6	....
1998/00	Hotchkiss	Hi-School	52	41	49	90	....	....	....	....	....	....
2000-01	Brown University	ECAC	23	1	7	8	2	....	....	....	....	....
2001-02	Brown University	ECAC	31	9	13	22	4	....	....	....	....	....
2002-03	Brown University	ECAC	35	15	23	38	18	....	....	....	....	....
2003-04	Brown University	ECAC	31	13	18	31	10	....	....	....	....	....
	Hamilton Bulldogs	AHL	5	0	0	0	0	....	....	....	....	....

Signed to a PTO (tryout) contract by **Hamilton** (AHL), March 25, 2004. Signed as a free agent by **Philadelphia**, June 23, 2004.

ROBINSON, Darcy (RAW-bihn-suhn, DAHR-see) **PIT.**

Defense. Shoots right. 6'3", 235 lbs. Born, Kamloops, B.C., May 3, 1981.
(Pittsburgh's 10th choice, 233rd overall, in 1999 Entry Draft).

			Regular Season					Playoffs				
Season	Club	League	GP	G	A	TP	PIM	GP	G	A	TP	PIM
1996-97	Kamloops	BCAHA	59	18	42	60	188	....	....	....	....	....
1997-98	Saskatoon Blades	WHL	62	1	2	3	84	4	0	0	0	2
1998-99	Saskatoon Blades	WHL	48	3	6	9	86	....	....	....	....	....
99-2000	Saskatoon Blades	WHL	59	5	9	14	91	10	1	3	4	13
2000-01	Saskatoon Blades	WHL	41	2	6	8	80	....	....	....	....	....
	Red Deer Rebels	WHL	30	1	5	6	70	20	1	1	2	20
2001-02	Wheeling Nailers	ECHL	10	2	3	5	43	....	....	....	....	....
	Wilkes-Barre	AHL	40	0	5	5	35	....	....	....	....	....
2002-03	Wilkes-Barre	AHL	48	1	7	8	89	6	1	0	1	5
	Wheeling Nailers	ECHL	1	0	1	1	0	....	....	....	....	....
2003-04	Wilkes-Barre	AHL	57	2	6	8	64	1	0	0	0	0

ROBINSON, Jody **NYI**

Defense. Shoots left. 6'2", 205 lbs. Born, New Haven, CT, September 23, 1978.

			Regular Season					Playoffs				
Season	Club	League	GP	G	A	TP	PIM	GP	G	A	TP	PIM
1997-98	Mercyhurst	MAAC	27	3	5	8	0	....	....	....	....	....
1998-99	Mercyhurst	MAAC	25	2	11	13	0	....	....	....	....	....
99-2000	Mercyhurst	MAAC	36	5	14	19	24	....	....	....	....	....
2000-01	Mercyhurst	MAAC	35	3	15	18	28	....	....	....	....	....
2001-02	Elmira Jackals	UHL	72	3	8	11	82	14	0	3	3	6
2002-03	Elmira Jackals	UHL	43	2	9	11	56	....	....	....	....	....
	Rochester	AHL	9	0	1	1	8	....	....	....	....	....
	Bridgeport	AHL	28	0	3	3	24	1	0	0	0	10
2003-04	Bridgeport	AHL	73	1	6	7	86	7	1	1	2	6

Signed as a free agent by **NY Islanders**, July 2, 2003.

ROCHE, Ken (ROHCH, KEHN) **NYR**

Center. Shoots left. 5'11", 185 lbs. Born, Boston, MA, January 2, 1984.
(NY Rangers' 3rd choice, 75th overall, in 2003 Entry Draft).

			Regular Season					Playoffs				
Season	Club	League	GP	G	A	TP	PIM	GP	G	A	TP	PIM
2000-01	St. Sebastian's	Hi-School	31	20	18	38	....	....	....	....	....	....
2001-02	St. Sebastian's	Hi-School	31	27	33	60	....	....	....	....	....	....
2002-03	St. Sebastian's	Hi-School	29	25	28	53	16	....	....	....	....	....
2003-04	Boston University	H-East	38	9	9	18	14	....	....	....	....	....

RODMAN, Marcel (RAWD-muhn, mahr-SEHL) **BOS.**

Right wing. Shoots right. 6'1", 183 lbs. Born, Jesenice, Yugoslavia, September 25, 1981.
(Boston's 8th choice, 282nd overall, in 2001 Entry Draft).

			Regular Season					Playoffs				
Season	Club	League	GP	G	A	TP	PIM	GP	G	A	TP	PIM
1997-98	Acroni Jesenice Jr.	Sloven.-Jr.	44	29	44	73	14	....	....	....	....	....
1998-99	Pickering Panthers	OPJHL	37	30	21	51	8	....	....	....	....	....
99-2000	Peterborough	OHL	61	17	20	37	16	5	1	2	3	0
2000-01	Peterborough	OHL	61	36	35	71	14	7	4	2	6	2
2001-02	Acroni Jesenice	EEHL	7	4	2	6	4	....	....	....	....	....
	Acroni Jesenice	Slovenia	9	12	6	18	4	....	....	....	....	....
2002-03	EHC Graz	Austria	44	22	25	47	22	....	....	....	....	....
2003-04	Krefeld Pinguine	Germany	52	3	9	12	18	....	....	....	....	....

ROGERS, Andy (RAW-juhrs, AN-dee) **T.B.**

Defense. Shoots left. 6'5", 206 lbs. Born, Calgary, Alta., August 25, 1986.
(Tampa Bay's 1st choice, 30th overall, in 2004 Entry Draft).

			Regular Season					Playoffs				
Season	Club	League	GP	G	A	TP	PIM	GP	G	A	TP	PIM
2000-01	Calgary AA Gold	CMHA	32	2	7	9	32	....	....	....	....	....
2001-02	Calgary AAA Gold	CBHL	30	1	13	14	80	....	....	....	....	....
2002-03	Calgary Hitmen	WHL	25	0	3	3	17	....	....	....	....	....
2003-04	Calgary Hitmen	WHL	64	1	3	4	89	7	0	0	0	11

ROGERS, Brandon (RAW-juhrs, BRAN-duhn) **ANA.**

Defense. Shoots right. 6'1", 190 lbs. Born, Rochester, NH, February 27, 1982.
(Anaheim's 6th choice, 118th overall, in 2001 Entry Draft).

			Regular Season					Playoffs				
Season	Club	League	GP	G	A	TP	PIM	GP	G	A	TP	PIM
1998-99	Hotchkiss Bearcats	Hi-School	22	8	13	21	....	....	....	....	....	....
99-2000	Hotchkiss High	Hi-School	25	9	12	21	35	....	....	....	....	....
2000-01	Hotchkiss High	Hi-School	22	10	13	23	45	....	....	....	....	....
2001-02	U. of Michigan	CCHA	32	2	1	3	30	....	....	....	....	....
2002-03	U. of Michigan	CCHA	43	4	21	25	65	....	....	....	....	....
2003-04	U. of Michigan	CCHA	43	7	16	23	46	....	....	....	....	....

CCHA Second All-Star Team (2004)

ROHLFS, David (ROHLFS, DAY-vihd) **EDM.**

Right wing. Shoots right. 6'3", 219 lbs. Born, Ann Arbor, MI, June 4, 1984.
(Edmonton's 7th choice, 154th overall, in 2003 Entry Draft).

			Regular Season					Playoffs				
Season	Club	League	GP	G	A	TP	PIM	GP	G	A	TP	PIM
2000-01	Detroit	MWEHL	70	35	21	56	....	....	....	....	....	....
	Det. Compuware	NAJHL	4	0	1	1	0	....	....	....	....	....
2001-02	Det. Compuware	NAJHL	60	13	10	23	36	....	....	....	....	....
2002-03	Det. Compuware	NAHL	53	30	14	44	36	5	2	1	3	8
2003-04	U. of Michigan	CCHA	43	7	6	13	26	....	....	....	....	....

ROME, Aaron (ROHM, AIR-uhn) **ANA.**

Defense. Shoots left. 6'1", 225 lbs. Born, Nesbitt, Man., September 27, 1983.
(Los Angeles' 4th choice, 104th overall, in 2002 Entry Draft).

			Regular Season					Playoffs				
Season	Club	League	GP	G	A	TP	PIM	GP	G	A	TP	PIM
1998-99	Sask. Contacts	SMHL	STATISTICS NOT AVAILABLE									
	Saskatoon Blades	WHL	1	0	0	0	0	....	....	....	....	....
99-2000	Saskatoon Blades	WHL	47	0	6	6	22	1	0	0	0	0
2000-01	Saskatoon Blades	WHL	3	0	0	0	2	....	....	....	....	....
	Kootenay Ice	WHL	53	2	8	10	43	11	1	3	4	6
2001-02	Kootenay Ice	WHL	33	4	13	17	55	....	....	....	....	....
	Swift Current	WHL	37	3	11	14	113	10	1	4	5	23
2002-03	Swift Current	WHL	61	12	44	56	201	4	1	0	1	20
2003-04	Swift Current	WHL	41	7	26	33	122	....	....	....	....	....
	Moose Jaw	WHL	28	3	16	19	88	8	0	6	6	17

WHL East Second All-Star Team (2004)

Signed as a free agent by **Anaheim**, June 7, 2004.

ROME, Ashton (ROHM, ASH-tuhn) **BOS.**

Right wing. Shoots right. 6', 193 lbs. Born, Nesbitt, Man., December 31, 1985.
(Boston's 3rd choice, 108th overall, in 2004 Entry Draft).

			Regular Season					Playoffs				
Season	Club	League	GP	G	A	TP	PIM	GP	G	A	TP	PIM
2002-03	Moose Jaw	WHL	61	5	10	15	103	13	1	1	2	6
2003-04	Moose Jaw	WHL	72	15	22	37	139	10	6	2	8	18

ROMY , Kevin (ROH-mee, KEH-vihn) **PHI.**

Center. Shoots left. 5'11", 180 lbs. Born, La Chaux-de-Fonds, Switz., January 31, 1985.
(Philadelphia's 8th choice, 108th overall, in 2003 Entry Draft).

			Regular Season					Playoffs				
Season	Club	League	GP	G	A	TP	PIM	GP	G	A	TP	PIM
2000-01	Chaux-de-Fonds Jr.	Swiss-Jr.	24	28	16	44	42	....	....	....	....	....
	La Chaux-de-Fonds	Swiss	17	0	0	0	0	2	0	0	0	0
2001-02	La Chaux-de-Fonds	Swiss-2	35	10	13	23	16	10	5	5	10	6
	Chaux-de-Fonds Jr.	Swiss-Jr.	1	0	0	0	0	....	....	....	....	....
2002-03	Geneve	Swiss	35	2	2	4	18	6	0	0	0	2
	La Chaux-de-Fonds	Swiss-2	1	0	0	0	0	....	....	....	....	....
2003-04	Geneve	Swiss	39	6	7	13	10	12	1	2	3	6

ROONEEM, Mark (ROO-neem, MAHRK) **MIN.**

Left wing. Shoots left. 6'2", 185 lbs. Born, Hinton, Alta., January 9, 1983.
(Los Angeles' 5th choice, 115th overall, in 2002 Entry Draft).

			Regular Season					Playoffs				
Season	Club	League	GP	G	A	TP	PIM	GP	G	A	TP	PIM
1998-99	Spruce Grove	AMBHL	36	32	30	62	183	....	....	....	....	....
99-2000	Kamloops Blazers	WHL	50	3	8	11	39	4	0	0	0	4
2000-01	Kamloops Blazers	WHL	62	8	9	17	77	4	1	0	1	8
2001-02	Kamloops Blazers	WHL	69	18	23	41	77	4	0	0	0	10
2002-03	Kamloops Blazers	WHL	40	9	6	15	60	....	....	....	....	....
	Calgary Hitmen	WHL	31	2	8	10	43	5	0	2	2	0
2003-04	Calgary Hitmen	WHL	52	22	18	40	61	7	1	2	3	4

Signed as a free agent by **Minnesota**, June 4, 2004.

RORABECK, Ryan (rawr-AH-behk, RIGH-uhn) **CAR.**

Center. Shoots left. 6'1", 173 lbs. Born, Oshawa, Ont., February 27, 1985.
(Carolina's 9th choice, 262nd overall, in 2003 Entry Draft).

			Regular Season					Playoffs				
Season	Club	League	GP	G	A	TP	PIM	GP	G	A	TP	PIM
2001-02	St. Michael's	OHL	61	8	6	14	10	9	0	0	0	4
2002-03	St. Michael's	OHL	55	11	19	30	20	19	4	9	13	10
2003-04	St. Michael's	OHL	64	14	34	48	54	18	3	4	7	10

ROSEHILL, Jay (ROHZ-hihl, JAY) **T.B.**

Defense. Shoots left. 6'3", 195 lbs. Born, Olds, Alta., July 16, 1985.
(Tampa Bay's 6th choice, 227th overall, in 2003 Entry Draft).

			Regular Season					Playoffs				
Season	Club	League	GP	G	A	TP	PIM	GP	G	A	TP	PIM
2002-03	Olds Grizzlys	AJHL	59	1	4	5	219	....	....	....	....	....
2003-04	Olds Grizzlys	AJHL	42	4	12	16	172	14	2	2	4	....

ROULEAU, Alexandre (ROO-loh, al-ehx-AHN-druh) **PIT.**

Defense. Shoots left. 6'1", 192 lbs. Born, Mont-Laurier, Que., July 29, 1983.
(Pittsburgh's 4th choice, 96th overall, in 2001 Entry Draft).

			Regular Season					Playoffs				
Season	Club	League	GP	G	A	TP	PIM	GP	G	A	TP	PIM
1998-99	Amos Forestiers	QAAA	41	7	6	13	144	....	....	....	....	....
99-2000	Amos Forestiers	QAAA	25	5	10	15	114	....	....	....	....	....
	Val-d'Or Foreurs	QMJHL	41	3	3	6	39	....	....	....	....	....
2000-01	Val-d'Or Foreurs	QMJHL	70	8	17	25	124	21	1	0	1	46
2001-02	Val-d'Or Foreurs	QMJHL	69	14	25	39	174	7	0	2	2	16
2002-03	Val-d'Or Foreurs	QMJHL	31	7	12	19	92	....	....	....	....	....
	Quebec Remparts	QMJHL	24	9	17	26	74	11	2	4	6	23
2003-04	Wilkes-Barre	AHL	14	0	2	2	16	....	....	....	....	....
	Wheeling Nailers	ECHL	30	3	1	4	38	5	0	1	1	6

QMJHL Second All-Star Team (2003)

ROUSSIN, Dany (roo-SEH, DA-nee) **FLA.**

Center. Shoots left. 6'1", 190 lbs. Born, Quebec City, Que., January 9, 1985.
(Florida's 10th choice, 223rd overall, in 2003 Entry Draft).

			Regular Season					Playoffs				
Season	Club	League	GP	G	A	TP	PIM	GP	G	A	TP	PIM
2000-01	Ste-Foy Governors	QAAA	38	27	27	54	42	16	8	13	21	16
2001-02	Sherbrooke	QMJHL	66	10	14	24	38	....	....	....	....	....
2002-03	Sherbrooke	QMJHL	33	8	8	16	18	....	....	....	....	....
	Rimouski Oceanic	QMJHL	38	12	26	38	69	....	....	....	....	....
2003-04	Rimouski Oceanic	QMJHL	66	*59	58	117	70	9	2	10	12	12

QMJHL First All-Star Team (2004)

ROY, Jimmy (ROI, JIHM-mee)

Center. Shoots right. 5'11", 170 lbs. Born, Sioux Lookout, Ont., September 22, 1975.
(Dallas' 7th choice, 254th overall, in 1994 Entry Draft).

			Regular Season					Playoffs				
Season	Club	League	GP	G	A	TP	PIM	GP	G	A	TP	PIM
1993-94	Thunder Bay Flyers	USHL	46	21	33	54	101	....	....	....	....	....
1994-95	Michigan Tech	WCHA	38	5	11	16	62	....	....	....	....	....
1995-96	Michigan Tech	WCHA	42	17	17	34	84	....	....	....	....	....
1996-97	Team Canada	Nat-Tm	55	10	17	27	82	....	....	....	....	....
1997-98	Manitoba Moose	IHL	61	8	10	18	133	3	0	0	0	6
1998-99	Manitoba Moose	IHL	78	10	16	26	185	5	0	1	1	6
99-2000	Manitoba Moose	IHL	74	12	9	21	187	1	0	0	0	16
2000-01	Manitoba Moose	IHL	77	18	13	31	150	12	1	1	2	22
2001-02	Manitoba Moose	AHL	73	16	22	38	167	7	2	0	2	28
2002-03	Manitoba Moose	AHL	50	5	10	15	95	14	4	4	8	27
2003-04	Manitoba Moose	AHL	78	13	16	29	186	....	....	....	....	....

ROY, Marc-Andre (WAH, MAHRK-AWN-dray) **VAN.**

Left wing. Shoots left. 6'2", 220 lbs. Born, Montreal, Que., October 27, 1983.
(Vancouver's 7th choice, 214th overall, in 2002 Entry Draft).

			Regular Season					Playoffs				
Season	Club	League	GP	G	A	TP	PIM	GP	G	A	TP	PIM
99-2000	Magog	QAAA	2	0	0	0	0	....	....	....	....	....
2000-01	Magog	QAAA	39	5	19	24	40	17	1	5	6	20
	Baie-Comeau	QMJHL	5	0	0	0	5	....	....	....	....	....
2001-02	Baie-Comeau	QMJHL	58	0	1	1	432	5	0	0	0	0
2002-03	Baie-Comeau	QMJHL	68	2	3	5	*653	6	0	0	0	25
2003-04	Columbia Inferno	ECHL	50	1	1	2	153	....	....	....	....	....

ROY, Mathieu (WAH, MA-tyew) **EDM.**

Defense. Shoots right. 6'2", 214 lbs. Born, St-Georges, Que., August 10, 1983.
(Edmonton's 10th choice, 215th overall, in 2003 Entry Draft).

			Regular Season					Playoffs				
Season	Club	League	GP	G	A	TP	PIM	GP	G	A	TP	PIM
1998-99	Levis	QAAA	11	4	1	5	16	....	....	....	....	....
99-2000	Levis	QAAA	24	3	4	7	88	6	1	1	2	22
	Val d'Or Foreurs	QMJHL	48	1	4	5	66	....	....	....	....	....
2000-01	Val d'Or Foreurs	QMJHL	30	0	7	7	60	17	0	0	0	4
	Val d'Or Foreurs	M-Cup	....	....	....	....	....	5	0	0	0	0
2001-02	Val-d'Or Foreurs	QMJHL	53	7	26	33	103	7	0	2	2	19
2002-03	Val-d'Or Foreurs	QMJHL	52	11	21	32	164	7	1	0	1	8
2003-04	Toronto	AHL	30	0	2	2	46	....	....	....	....	....
	Columbus	ECHL	10	1	2	3	13	....	....	....	....	....

ROZAKOV, Roman (roh-zah-KAWF, ROH-muhn) **CGY.**

Defense. Shoots left. 6'1", 198 lbs. Born, Murmansk, USSR, March 29, 1981.
(Calgary's 4th choice, 106th overall, in 1999 Entry Draft).

			Regular Season					Playoffs				
Season	Club	League	GP	G	A	TP	PIM	GP	G	A	TP	PIM
1997-98	Lada Togliatti 2	Russia-3	36	0	2	2	43	....	....	....	....	....
1998-99	Lada Togliatti 2	Russia-4	30	0	0	0	14	....	....	....	....	....
99-2000	Lada Togliatti 2	Russia-3	11	1	2	3	16	....	....	....	....	....
	CSK VSV Samara 2	Russia-3	2	0	2	2	8	....	....	....	....	....
	Krylja Sovetov	Russia-2	23	0	1	1	41	....	....	....	....	....
	CSK VSV Samara 2	Russia-2	2	0	0	0	0	....	....	....	....	....
2000-01	Magnitogorsk	Russia	21	0	1	1	10	....	....	....	....	....
2001-02	CSK VVS Samara	Russia-2	5	0	0	0	0	....	....	....	....	....
	CSKA Moscow	Russia	16	1	1	2	8	....	....	....	....	....
2002-03	Lada Togliatti	Russia	4	0	0	0	0	....	....	....	....	....
	Cherepovets	Russia	17	1	0	1	18	2	0	0	0	0
2003-04	Lowell	AHL	2	0	0	0	4	....	....	....	....	....
	Cherepovets	Russia	16	0	1	1	34	....	....	....	....	....

Assigned to **Cherepovets** (Russia) by **Calgary**, October 20, 2003.

RUDENKO, Konstantin (roo-DEHN-koh, KOHN-stan-tihn) **PHI.**

Left wing. Shoots right. 5'11", 180 lbs. Born, Ust-Kamenogorsk, USSR, July 23, 1981.
(Philadelphia's 3rd choice, 160th overall, in 1999 Entry Draft).

			Regular Season					Playoffs				
Season	Club	League	GP	G	A	TP	PIM	GP	G	A	TP	PIM
1997-98	Omsk 2	Russia-3	22	7	8	15	4	....	....	....	....	....
1998-99	Cherepovets	Russia	28	15	9	24	67	....	....	....	....	....
	Cherepovets 2	Russia-3	3	0	1	1	4	....	....	....	....	....
99-2000	St. Petersburg 2	Russia-3	7	2	4	6	2	....	....	....	....	....
	SKA St. Petersburg	Russia	19	1	1	2	10	1	0	0	0	0
2000-01	Yaroslavl	Russia	18	2	3	5	28	9	2	1	3	8
2001-02	Yaroslavl 2	Russia-3	2	1	1	2	2	....	....	....	....	....
	Yaroslavl	Russia	8	0	2	2	12	1	0	0	0	0
2002-03	Yaroslavl	Russia	20	3	4	7	20	2	0	0	0	0
2003-04	Yaroslavl 2	Russia-3	4	4	2	6	4	....	....	....	....	....
	Yaroslavl	Russia	43	10	12	22	18	3	0	0	0	0

RUGGERI, Rosario (ROO-gee-AIR-ee, roh-ZAHR-ee-oh) **PHI.**

Defense. Shoots left. 6'1", 202 lbs. Born, Montreal, Que., June 8, 1984.
(Philadelphia's 2nd choice, 105th overall, in 2002 Entry Draft).

			Regular Season					Playoffs				
Season	Club	League	GP	G	A	TP	PIM	GP	G	A	TP	PIM
99-2000	Lac St-Louis Lions	QAAA	40	0	7	7	70	....	....	....	....	....
2000-01	Lac St-Louis Lions	QAAA	24	6	11	17	117	5	1	3	4	4
	Montreal Rocket	QMJHL	9	0	0	0	8	....	....	....	....	....
2001-02	Chicoutimi	QMJHL	60	2	15	17	131	4	1	1	2	10
2002-03	Chicoutimi	QMJHL	70	10	37	47	64	3	0	0	0	21
2003-04	Chicoutimi	QMJHL	65	12	36	48	98	18	2	2	4	28

RULLIER, Joe (ROO-yay, JOH) **L.A.**

Defense. Shoots right. 6'3", 211 lbs. Born, Montreal, Que., January 28, 1980.
(Los Angeles' 5th choice, 133rd overall, in 1998 Entry Draft).

			Regular Season					Playoffs				
Season	Club	League	GP	G	A	TP	PIM	GP	G	A	TP	PIM
1996-97	Montreal-Bourassa	QAAA	24	5	10	15	....	....	....	....	....	....
	Rimouski Oceanic	QMJHL	23	0	3	3	87	4	0	0	0	11
1997-98	Rimouski Oceanic	QMJHL	55	1	10	11	176	16	1	4	5	34
1998-99	Rimouski Oceanic	QMJHL	54	7	32	39	202	11	2	3	5	26
99-2000	Rimouski Oceanic	QMJHL	49	3	32	35	161	14	1	8	9	34
2000-01	Lowell	AHL	63	1	1	2	162	4	0	1	1	2
2001-02	Manchester	AHL	62	2	2	4	133	3	0	0	0	5
2002-03	Manchester	AHL	62	3	6	9	166	3	0	0	0	2
2003-04	Manchester	AHL	73	3	12	15	186	6	0	0	0	4

RUZICKA, Stefan (roo-ZHEECH-kuh, STEH-fan) **PHI.**

Left wing. Shoots right. 5'11", 189 lbs. Born, Nitra, Czech., February 17, 1985.
(Philadelphia's 4th choice, 81st overall, in 2003 Entry Draft).

			Regular Season					Playoffs				
Season	Club	League	GP	G	A	TP	PIM	GP	G	A	TP	PIM
2000-01	MHC Nitra Jr.	Slovak-Jr.	38	30	15	45	....	....	....	....	....	....
2001-02	MHC Nitra Jr.	Slovak-Jr.	29	27	25	52	....	....	....	....	....	....
	MHC Nitra	Slovak	19	0	5	5	29	....	....	....	....	....
2002-03	HKm Nitra Jr.	Slovak-Jr.	30	18	22	40	64	....	....	....	....	....
	HKm Nitra	Slovak-2	17	5	7	12	4	....	....	....	....	....
2003-04	Owen Sound	OHL	62	34	38	72	63	7	1	6	7	8
	Philadelphia	AHL	2	0	0	0	0	3	1	0	1	2

OHL All-Rookie Team (2004) • OHL Second All-Star Team (2004)

RYABYKIN, Dmitri (ryah-BEE-kihn, dih-MEE-tree) **CGY.**

Defense. Shoots right. 6'1", 203 lbs. Born, Chirchik, USSR, March 24, 1976.
(Calgary's 2nd choice, 45th overall, in 1994 Entry Draft).

			Regular Season					Playoffs				
Season	Club	League	GP	G	A	TP	PIM	GP	G	A	TP	PIM
1994-95	Dynamo Moscow	CIS	48	0	0	0	12	11	0	2	2	0
1995-96	Dynamo Moscow	CIS	47	3	1	4	49	13	1	1	2	6
1996-97	Dynamo Moscow	Russia	34	1	10	11	12	4	0	0	0	8
1997-98	Dynamo Moscow	Russia	34	1	4	5	16	....	....	....	....	....
	Dynamo Moscow	EuroHL	7	1	1	2	6	....	....	....	....	....
1998-99	Avangard Omsk	Russia	40	3	10	13	42	5	0	0	0	42
99-2000	Avangard Omsk	Russia	36	5	10	15	42	8	3	2	5	2
2000-01	Avangard Omsk	Russia	43	3	8	11	101	16	3	4	7	16
2001-02	Avangard Omsk	Russia	17	4	7	11	60	11	4	3	7	6
2002-03	Avangard Omsk	Russia	51	7	18	25	113	12	1	2	3	33
2003-04	Avangard Omsk	Russia	57	8	12	20	94	11	1	4	5	4

RYAN, Billy (RIGH-uhn, BIHL-lee) **NYR**

Center. Shoots left. 6'1", 175 lbs. Born, Boston, MA, October 23, 1985.
(NY Rangers' 8th choice, 80th overall, in 2004 Entry Draft).

			Regular Season					Playoffs				
Season	Club	League	GP	G	A	TP	PIM	GP	G	A	TP	PIM
2002-03	Cushing Academy	Hi-School	29	14	33	47	10	....	....	....	....	....
2003-04	Cushing Academy	Hi-School	37	35	55	90	40	....	....	....	....	....

Signed Letter of Intent to attend **U. of Maine** (H-East), March 23, 2004.

RYAN, Michael (RIGH-uhn, MIGH-kuhl) **BUF.**

Center. Shoots left. 6'1", 180 lbs. Born, Boston, MA, May 16, 1980.
(Dallas' 1st choice, 32nd overall, in 1999 Entry Draft).

			Regular Season					Playoffs				
Season	Club	League	GP	G	A	TP	PIM	GP	G	A	TP	PIM
1997-98	Boston College HS	Hi-School	23	22	14	36	28	....	....	....	....	....
1998-99	Boston College HS	Hi-School	21	20	24	44	22	....	....	....	....	....
99-2000	Northeastern	H-East	32	4	9	13	47	....	....	....	....	....
2000-01	Northeastern	H-East	33	17	12	29	52	....	....	....	....	....
2001-02	Northeastern	H-East	36	24	15	39	54	....	....	....	....	....
2002-03	Northeastern	H-East	34	18	14	32	30	....	....	....	....	....
2003-04	Rochester	AHL	45	3	9	12	31	....	....	....	....	....

Traded to **Buffalo** by **Dallas** with Dallas's 2nd round choice (Branislav Fabry) in 2003 Entry Draft for Stu Barnes, March 10, 2003.

RYAN, Prestin (RIGH-uhn, PREH-stuhn) **CBJ**

Defense. Shoots left. 6', 192 lbs. Born, Arcola, Sask., June 29, 1980.

			Regular Season					Playoffs				
Season	Club	League	GP	G	A	TP	PIM	GP	G	A	TP	PIM
99-2000	Estevan Bruins	SJHL		STATISTICS NOT AVAILABLE								
2000-01	U. of Maine	H-East		DID NOT PLAY – FRESHMAN								
2001-02	U. of Maine	H-East	39	6	9	15	*91	....	....	....	....	....
2002-03	U. of Maine	H-East	37	1	8	9	*120	....	....	....	....	....
2003-04	U. of Maine	H-East	43	4	18	22	*148	....	....	....	....	....
	Syracuse Crunch	AHL	....	....	....	....	....	3	0	0	0	2

Hockey East Second All-Star Team (2004) • NCAA East Second All-American Team (2004) • NCAA Championship All-Tournament Team (2004)

Signed as a free agent by **Columbus**, April 12, 2004.

RYBIN, Maxim (ray-bihn, max-EEM) **ANA.**

Left wing. Shoots right. 5'8", 182 lbs. Born, Zhukovsky, USSR, June 15, 1981.
(Anaheim's 4th choice, 141st overall, in 1999 Entry Draft).

			Regular Season					Playoffs				
Season	Club	League	GP	G	A	TP	PIM	GP	G	A	TP	PIM
1996-97	Spartak Moscow 2	Russia-3	5	0	0	0	4	....	....	....	....	....
	Spartak Moscow	Russia	6	0	0	0	0	....	....	....	....	....
1997-98	Spartak Moscow 2	Russia-3	25	13	5	18	26	....	....	....	....	....
	Spartak Moscow	Russia	5	0	0	0	2	....	....	....	....	....
1998-99	Spartak Moscow	Russia	53	15	12	27	83	....	....	....	....	....
99-2000	Sarnia Sting	OHL	66	29	27	56	47	7	4	1	5	2
2000-01	Sarnia Sting	OHL	67	34	36	70	60	4	0	3	3	2
2001-02	Ufa Salavat	Russia	41	6	4	10	30	....	....	....	....	....
2002-03	Cherepovets	Russia	3	0	1	1	2	....	....	....	....	....
	Spartak Moscow	Russia	29	9	4	13	65	....	....	....	....	....
2003-04	Cherepovets	Russia	53	14	14	28	24	....	....	....	....	....
	Cherepovets 2	Russia-3	3	2	2	4	2	....	....	....	....	....

RYZNAR, Jason (RIHZ-nuhr, JAY-suhn) **N.J.**

Left wing. Shoots left. 6'3", 205 lbs. Born, Anchorage, AK, February 19, 1983.
(New Jersey's 3rd choice, 64th overall, in 2002 Entry Draft).

			Regular Season					Playoffs				
Season	Club	League	GP	G	A	TP	PIM	GP	G	A	TP	PIM
1998-99	Alaska All-Stars	AAHA		STATISTICS NOT AVAILABLE								
99-2000	U.S. National U-17	USDP	52	5	10	15	22	....	....	....	....	....
2000-01	U.S. National U-18	USDP	66	15	17	32	102	....	....	....	....	....
2001-02	U. of Michigan	CCHA	40	9	7	16	22	....	....	....	....	....
2002-03	U. of Michigan	CCHA	34	7	9	16	24	....	....	....	....	....
2003-04	U. of Michigan	CCHA	36	6	11	17	28	....	....	....	....	....

SAARINEN, Pasi (SAH-rih-nehn, PA-see) **S.J.**

Defense. Shoots right. 5'11", 194 lbs. Born, Tampere, Finland, April 17, 1977.
(San Jose's 7th choice, 256th overall, in 2000 Entry Draft).

			Regular Season					Playoffs				
Season	Club	League	GP	G	A	TP	PIM	GP	G	A	TP	PIM
1993-94	Ilves Tampere Jr.	Finn-Jr.	34	5	4	9	24	6	1	2	3	4
1994-95	Ilves Tampere Jr.	Finn-Jr.	24	4	5	9	55	....	....	....	....	....
	Ilves Tampere	Finland	1	0	0	0	0	....	....	....	....	....
1995-96	Ilves Tampere	Finn-Jr.	8	2	2	4	24	....	....	....	....	....
	KooVee Tampere	Finland-2	7	1	1	2	22	....	....	....	....	....
	Ilves Tampere	Finland	7	0	1	1	10	....	....	....	....	....
1996-97	Ilves Tampere Jr.	Finn-Jr.	9	3	3	6	22	....	....	....	....	....
	Ilves Tampere	Finland	44	4	3	7	83	6	1	0	1	10
1997-98	Ilves Tampere	Finland	36	11	8	19	73	....	....	....	....	....
1998-99	Ilves Tampere	Finland	45	2	8	10	56	4	1	0	1	8
	Ilves Tampere	EuroHL	....	....	....	....	....	6	2	0	2	6
99-2000	Ilves Tampere	Finland	50	9	19	28	79	3	0	0	0	26
2000-01	Jokerit Helsinki	Finland	52	6	9	15	79	5	2	0	2	4
2001-02	Jokerit Helsinki	Finland	32	0	0	0	48	10	0	2	2	0
2002-03	HIFK Helsinki	Finland	53	2	3	5	53	2	0	0	0	2
2003-04	HIFK Helsinki	Finland	52	8	7	15	42	13	3	4	7	14

SAGAT, Martin (SHA-gat, MAHR-tehn) **TOR.**

Left wing. Shoots right. 6'3", 191 lbs. Born, Handlova, Czech., November 11, 1984.
(Toronto's 2nd choice, 91st overall, in 2003 Entry Draft).

			Regular Season					Playoffs				
Season	Club	League	GP	G	A	TP	PIM	GP	G	A	TP	PIM
2002-03	Dukla Trencin Jr.	Slovak-Jr.	37	18	20	38	49	3	1	3	4	4
	Dukla Trencin	Slovakia	17	0	0	0	0	2	0	0	0	0
2003-04	Kootenay Ice	WHL	57	11	32	43	39	4	0	2	2	2

SAINOMAA, Teemu (SIGH-noh-muh, TEE-moo) **OTT.**

Left wing. Shoots left. 6'3", 202 lbs. Born, Helsinki, Finland, May 15, 1981.
(Ottawa's 3rd choice, 62nd overall, in 1999 Entry Draft).

			Regular Season					Playoffs				
Season	Club	League	GP	G	A	TP	PIM	GP	G	A	TP	PIM
1997-98	Jokerit Helsinki-B	Finn-Jr.	12	3	5	8	8	3	1	1	2	6
1998-99	Jokerit Helsinki Jr.	Finn-Jr.	11	4	5	9	0	....	....	....	....	....
99-2000	Jokerit Helsinki Jr.	Finn-Jr.	30	6	7	13	59	11	6	2	8	20
	Jokerit Helsinki	Finland	6	0	0	0	0	....	....	....	....	....
2000-01	Jokerit Helsinki Jr.	Finn-Jr.	24	17	8	25	37	1	0	1	1	0
	Jokerit Helsinki	Finland	28	1	3	4	2	4	0	1	1	0
2001-02	Jokerit Helsinki Jr.	Finn-Jr.	6	2	2	4	27	....	....	....	....	....
	Kiekko Vantaa	Finland-2	1	0	0	0	0	....	....	....	....	....
	Jokerit Helsinki	Finland	44	1	4	5	4	1	0	0	0	0
2002-03	Pelicans Lahti	Finland	51	2	3	5	10	....	....	....	....	....
2003-04	Kiekko-Vantaa	Finland-2	40	3	10	13	24	5	0	1	1	12

ST. JACQUES, Chris (SAINT ZHAWK, KRIHS) **TOR.**

Center. Shoots right. 5'8", 181 lbs. Born, Edmonton, Alta., January 22, 1983.

			Regular Season					Playoffs				
Season	Club	League	GP	G	A	TP	PIM	GP	G	A	TP	PIM
99-2000	Medicine Hat	WHL	61	21	18	39	65	....	....	....	....	....
2000-01	Medicine Hat	WHL	70	37	36	73	84	....	....	....	....	....
2001-02	Medicine Hat	WHL	45	30	38	68	50	....	....	....	....	....
2002-03	Medicine Hat	WHL	70	31	*65	96	78	11	2	14	16	17
2003-04	Medicine Hat	WHL	64	33	59	92	80	20	12	*15	*27	18

Signed as a free agent by **Toronto**, June 2, 2004.

SALMONSSON, Johannes (sal-MUHN-suhn, yoh-HA-nuhs) **PIT.**

Left wing. Shoots left. 6'2", 183 lbs. Born, Uppsala, Sweden, February 7, 1986.
(Pittsburgh's 2nd choice, 31st overall, in 2004 Entry Draft).

			Regular Season					Playoffs				
Season	Club	League	GP	G	A	TP	PIM	GP	G	A	TP	PIM
2002-03	Almtuna	Swede-2	26	10	14	24	4	....	....	....	....	....
	Almtuna	Swede-Q	8	2	4	6	14	....	....	....	....	....
2003-04	Djurgarden Jr.	Swede-Jr.	6	4	9	13	6	....	....	....	....	....
	Djurgarden	Sweden	25	0	3	3	4	....	....	....	....	....
	Almtuna	Swede-2	2	0	0	0	0	....	....	....	....	....

SALONEN, Pasi (SAH-loh-nehn, PA-see) **WSH.**

Left wing. Shoots left. 5'11", 187 lbs. Born, Vierumaki, Finland, December 18, 1985.
(Washington's 9th choice, 138th overall, in 2004 Entry Draft).

			Regular Season					Playoffs				
Season	Club	League	GP	G	A	TP	PIM	GP	G	A	TP	PIM
2002-03	HIFK Helsinki Jr.	Finn-Jr.	32	16	11	27	10	10	8	3	11	2
2003-04	HIFK Helsinki Jr.	Finn-Jr.	30	12	10	22	60	9	4	4	8	8
	HIFK Helsinki	Finland	3	0	0	0	0	....	....	....	....	....
	Team Finland Jr.	Finn-2	3	0	0	0	0	....	....	....	....	....

SAMOILOV, Igor (sam-OI-lawf, EE-gohr) **PHX.**

Defense. Shoots left. 5'11", 195 lbs. Born, Moscow, USSR, January 23, 1982.
(Phoenix's 6th choice, 217th overall, in 2000 Entry Draft).

			Regular Season					Playoffs				
Season	Club	League	GP	G	A	TP	PIM	GP	G	A	TP	PIM
1998-99	Yaroslavl 2	Russia-3	16	0	1	1	6	....	....	....	....	....
99-2000	Yaroslavl 2	Russia-3	40	1	3	4	50	....	....	....	....	....
2000-01	SKA St. Petersburg	Russia	40	0	2	2	22	....	....	....	....	....
2001-02	Cherepovets	Russia	35	1	2	3	14	4	0	0	0	2
2002-03	Cherepovets	Russia	5	0	0	0	14	....	....	....	....	....
	Cherepovets	Russia-3		STATISTICS NOT AVAILABLE								
2003-04	Kristall Elektrostal	Russia-2	16	2	5	7	16	....	....	....	....	....
	Leninogorsk	Russia-2	8	0	1	1	4	....	....	....	....	....
	HC Rybinsk	Russia-2	25	0	5	5	12	....	....	....	....	....

SANDSTROM, Jan (SAND-struhm, YAN) **ANA.**

Defense. Shoots left. 6', 190 lbs. Born, Pitea, Sweden, January 24, 1978.
(Anaheim's 5th choice, 173rd overall, in 1999 Entry Draft).

			Regular Season					Playoffs				
Season	Club	League	GP	G	A	TP	PIM	GP	G	A	TP	PIM
1994-95	Pitea HC	Swede-2	12	1	0	1	4	....	....	....	....	....
1995-96	Pitea HC	Swede-2	29	1	11	12	18	....	....	....	....	....
1996-97	Pitea HC	Swede-2	28	3	4	7	28	....	....	....	....	....
1997-98	AIK Solna	Sweden	38	0	2	2	16	....	....	....	....	....
1998-99	AIK Solna	Sweden	47	2	7	9	18	....	....	....	....	....
99-2000	AIK Solna	Sweden	49	2	6	8	22	....	....	....	....	....
2000-01	Skelleftea AIK	Swede-2	22	0	5	5	14	....	....	....	....	....
	AIK Solna	Sweden	18	1	3	4	10	....	....	....	....	....
2001-02	Lulea HF	Sweden	41	2	4	6	12	5	0	2	2	2
2002-03	Lulea HF	Sweden	48	3	5	8	36	4	1	0	1	6
2003-04	Lulea HF	Sweden	49	1	10	11	20	5	0	1	1	2

SANNITZ, Raffaele (ZAH-nihts, ra-FIGH-ehl-lay) **CBJ**

Center. Shoots left. 6'1", 187 lbs. Born, Mendrisio, Switz., May 18, 1983.
(Columbus' 9th choice, 204th overall, in 2001 Entry Draft).

			Regular Season					Playoffs				
Season	Club	League	GP	G	A	TP	PIM	GP	G	A	TP	PIM
1997-98	HC Lugano Jr.	Swiss-Jr.	33	7	12	19	54	....	....	....	....	....
1998-99	HC Lugano Jr.	Swiss-Jr.	38	5	12	17	62	....	....	....	....	....
	HC Lugano	Swiss	8	0	1	1	0	....	....	....	....	....
99-2000	HC Lugano Jr.	Swiss-Jr.	33	13	16	29	47	....	....	....	....	....
	HC Lugano	Swiss	1	0	0	0	2	....	....	....	....	....
2000-01	HC Sierre	Swiss-2	2	0	0	0	0	....	....	....	....	....
	HC Lugano Jr.	Swiss-Jr.	35	22	30	52	152	2	0	0	0	0
	HC Lugano	Swiss	13	1	0	1	0	2	0	0	0	0
2001-02	HC Lugano Jr.	Swiss-Jr.	14	14	13	27	18	3	3	2	5	4
	HC Lugano	Swiss	38	3	4	7	37	12	1	1	2	2
2002-03	HC Lugano	Swiss	14	1	1	2	37	....	....	....	....	....
2003-04	HC Lugano	Swiss	48	7	9	16	20	16	2	1	3	8
	EHC Chur	Swiss-2	2	2	1	3	2	....	....	....	....	....

• Missed majority of 2002-03 season recovering from shoulder injury suffered in game vs. Kloten (Swiss), October 12, 2002.

SARAUER, Andrew (suh-ROW-uhr, AN-droo) **VAN.**

Left wing. Shoots left. 6'4", 194 lbs. Born, Saskatoon, Sask., November 17, 1984.
(Vancouver's 3rd choice, 125th overall, in 2004 Entry Draft).

			Regular Season					Playoffs				
Season	Club	League	GP	G	A	TP	PIM	GP	G	A	TP	PIM
2002-03	Victoria Salsa	BCHL	57	11	17	28	73	....	....	....	....	....
2003-04	Langley Hornets	BCHL	57	43	32	75	71	....	....	....	....	....

Signed Letter of Intent to attend **Northern Michigan** (WCHA), February 17, 2004.

SAUNDERS, Nathan (SAWN-duhrs, NAY-thun) **ANA.**

Defense. Shoots right. 6'4", 215 lbs. Born, Charlottetown, PEI, April 25, 1985.
(Anaheim's 5th choice, 119th overall, in 2003 Entry Draft).

			Regular Season					Playoffs				
Season	**Club**	**League**	**GP**	**G**	**A**	**TP**	**PIM**	**GP**	**G**	**A**	**TP**	**PIM**
2000-01	Sherwood Park	PEIHA	STATISTICS NOT AVAILABLE									
2001-02	Moncton Wildcats	QMJHL	54	4	11	15	88	....	....	....	....	....
2002-03	Moncton Wildcats	QMJHL	69	1	13	14	241	6	2	3	5	12
2003-04	Moncton Wildcats	QMJHL	68	4	26	30	267	20	1	1	2	34

SAVIELS, Agris (sah-VEE-ehls, AG-rihs) **COL.**

Defense. Shoots left. 6'1", 210 lbs. Born, Riga, Latvia, January 15, 1982.
(Colorado's 4th choice, 63rd overall, in 2000 Entry Draft).

			Regular Season					Playoffs				
Season	**Club**	**League**	**GP**	**G**	**A**	**TP**	**PIM**	**GP**	**G**	**A**	**TP**	**PIM**
1996-97	Dynamo Riga	Lat.-Jr.	15	1	2	3	4	....	....	....	....	....
	HK Lido-Nafta	Latvia	40	4	15	19	40	....	....	....	....	....
1997-98	Dynamo Riga	Lat.-Jr.	15	1	2	3	4	....	....	....	....	....
	HK Lido-Nafta	Latvia	40	7	21	28	30	....	....	....	....	....
1998-99	Notre Dame	SMBHL	18	6	9	15	25	....	....	....	....	....
	Notre Dame	SJHL	30	6	13	19	....	....	....	....	....	....
99-2000	Owen Sound	OHL	65	7	25	32	56	....	....	....	....	....
2000-01	Owen Sound	OHL	68	14	37	51	46	5	0	1	1	2
2001-02	Owen Sound	OHL	60	5	27	32	37	....	....	....	....	....
2002-03	Hershey Bears	AHL	43	0	3	3	33	3	0	0	0	0
	Reading Royals	ECHL	8	1	0	1	4	....	....	....	....	....
2003-04	Hershey Bears	AHL	67	2	5	7	39	....	....	....	....	....

SAWADA, Raymond (suh-WAW-duh, RAY-mawnd) **DAL.**

Right wing. Shoots right. 6'2", 195 lbs. Born, Richmond, B.C., February 19, 1985.
(Dallas' 3rd choice, 52nd overall, in 2004 Entry Draft).

			Regular Season					Playoffs				
Season	**Club**	**League**	**GP**	**G**	**A**	**TP**	**PIM**	**GP**	**G**	**A**	**TP**	**PIM**
2002-03	Richmond	PIJHL	36	7	17	24	155	....	....	....	....	....
2003-04	Nanaimo Clippers	BCHL	54	20	32	52	93	25	6	16	22	22

Signed Letter of Intent to attend **Cornell** (H-East), August 22, 2003.

SAWYER, Jean-Claude (SOI-uhr, ZHAWN-KLOHD) **MIN.**

Defense. Shoots left. 6'2", 194 lbs. Born, Saint John, N.B., August 12, 1986.
(Minnesota's 8th choice, 161st overall, in 2004 Entry Draft).

			Regular Season					Playoffs				
Season	**Club**	**League**	**GP**	**G**	**A**	**TP**	**PIM**	**GP**	**G**	**A**	**TP**	**PIM**
2002-03	Cape Breton	QMJHL	31	3	2	5	44	3	0	0	0	2
2003-04	Cape Breton	QMJHL	56	5	13	18	48	2	0	0	0	2

SCHAFER, Evan (SHAY-fuhr, EH-vuhn) **FLA.**

Defense. Shoots right. 6'2", 221 lbs. Born, Mankota, Sask., October 9, 1985.
(Florida's 4th choice, 105th overall, in 2004 Entry Draft).

			Regular Season					Playoffs				
Season	**Club**	**League**	**GP**	**G**	**A**	**TP**	**PIM**	**GP**	**G**	**A**	**TP**	**PIM**
2001-02	Sask. Contacts	SMHL	47	9	22	31	49	....	....	....	....	....
2002-03	Prince Albert	WHL	53	0	1	1	76	....	....	....	....	....
2003-04	Prince Albert	WHL	71	3	6	9	190	6	0	0	0	14

SCHAUER, Stefan (SHOW-uhr, SHTEH-fuhn) **OTT.**

Defense. Shoots left. 6'1", 185 lbs. Born, Schongau, West Germany, January 12, 1983.
(Ottawa's 6th choice, 162nd overall, in 2001 Entry Draft).

			Regular Season					Playoffs				
Season	**Club**	**League**	**GP**	**G**	**A**	**TP**	**PIM**	**GP**	**G**	**A**	**TP**	**PIM**
99-2000	Riessersee-16	Ger.-Jr.	14	4	8	12	85	....	....	....	....	....
	Riessersee Jr.	Ger.-Jr.	30	7	14	21	82	....	....	....	....	....
	Riessersee	German-3	3	0	0	0	0	....	....	....	....	....
2000-01	Riessersee Jr.	Ger.-Jr.	11	1	7	8	24	....	....	....	....	....
	Riessersee	German-3	39	1	2	3	12	5	0	1	1	0
2001-02	Riessersee	German-2	46	2	18	20	46	8	0	2	2	18
2002-03	Kolner Haie	Germany	28	0	1	1	12	15	1	0	1	2
	EV Duisburg	German-2	23	1	4	5	10	....	....	....	....	....
2003-04	EV Duisberg	German-2	8	0	0	0	10	....	....	....	....	....
	Kolner Haie	Germany	45	1	1	2	41	5	0	0	0	4

SCHEFFELMAIER, Brett (sch-EHFEHL-mai-uhr, BREHT) **ST.L.**

Defense. Shoots right. 6'5", 214 lbs. Born, Coronation, Alta., March 31, 1981.
(St. Louis' 5th choice, 190th overall, in 2001 Entry Draft).

			Regular Season					Playoffs				
Season	**Club**	**League**	**GP**	**G**	**A**	**TP**	**PIM**	**GP**	**G**	**A**	**TP**	**PIM**
1997-98	Red Deer	AMHL	13	0	4	4	36	....	....	....	....	....
	Medicine Hat	WHL	25	0	1	1	69	....	....	....	....	....
1998-99	Medicine Hat	WHL	69	3	10	13	252	....	....	....	....	....
99-2000	Medicine Hat	WHL	71	1	9	10	281	....	....	....	....	....
2000-01	Medicine Hat	WHL	62	3	10	13	279	....	....	....	....	....
2001-02	Medicine Hat	WHL	45	4	6	10	180	....	....	....	....	....
2002-03	Worcester IceCats	AHL	54	0	2	2	143	3	0	0	0	7
2003-04	Worcester IceCats	AHL	23	0	1	1	56	3	0	0	0	0
	Peoria Rivermen	ECHL	10	1	2	3	21	....	....	....	....	....

• Re-entered NHL Entry Draft. Originally Tampa Bay's 3rd choice, 75th overall, in 1999 Entry Draft.
• Missed majority of 2003-04 season recovering from hand injury suffered in training camp, September 27, 2003.

SCHELL, Brad (SHEHL, BRAD) **ATL.**

Center. Shoots left. 6'1", 180 lbs. Born, Scott, Sask., August 5, 1984.
(Atlanta's 6th choice, 167th overall, in 2002 Entry Draft).

			Regular Season					Playoffs				
Season	**Club**	**League**	**GP**	**G**	**A**	**TP**	**PIM**	**GP**	**G**	**A**	**TP**	**PIM**
99-2000	North Battleford	SMHL	62	38	42	80	28	....	....	....	....	....
	Spokane Chiefs	WHL	1	0	0	0	0	....	....	....	....	....
2000-01	Spokane Chiefs	WHL	60	7	6	13	10	12	0	2	2	2
2001-02	Spokane Chiefs	WHL	70	20	36	56	16	11	0	8	8	6
2002-03	Spokane Chiefs	WHL	37	8	13	21	26	10	0	5	5	2
2003-04	Spokane Chiefs	WHL	71	35	57	92	47	4	1	0	1	0

WHL West Second All-Star Team (2004)

Missed majority of 2002-03 season recovering from off-season back surgery.

SCHEVJEV, Maxim (shehv-YAWF-yehv, MAX-ihm) **BUF.**

Center. Shoots left. 6', 178 lbs. Born, Noginsk, USSR, July 5, 1984.
(Buffalo's 7th choice, 178th overall, in 2002 Entry Draft).

			Regular Season					Playoffs				
Season	**Club**	**League**	**GP**	**G**	**A**	**TP**	**PIM**	**GP**	**G**	**A**	**TP**	**PIM**
99-2000	Elektrostal 2	Russia-3	11	0	1	1	2	....	....	....	....	....
2000-01	Elektrosta	Russia-2	7	0	0	0	6	....	....	....	....	....
2001-02	Elektrostal 2	Russia-3	6	1	2	3	2	....	....	....	....	....
	Elektrostal	Russia-2	49	6	9	15	34	....	....	....	....	....
2002-03	Amur Khabarovsk	Russia	21	0	0	0	10	....	....	....	....	....
	Amur 2	Russia-3	5	2	1	3	4	....	....	....	....	....
2003-04	Kristall Elektrostal	Russia-2	26	4	5	9	20	....	....	....	....	....
	Voskresensk	Russia	18	1	0	1	2	....	....	....	....	....

SCHNEIDER, Andy (SHNIGH-duhr, AN-dee) **PIT.**

Defense. Shoots left. 6'1", 215 lbs. Born, Grand Forks, ND, July 31, 1981.
(Pittsburgh's 7th choice, 156th overall, in 2001 Entry Draft).

			Regular Season					Playoffs				
Season	**Club**	**League**	**GP**	**G**	**A**	**TP**	**PIM**	**GP**	**G**	**A**	**TP**	**PIM**
1998-99	Lincoln Stars	USHL	9	0	4	4	8	4	0	0	0	2
99-2000	Lincoln Stars	USHL	46	7	10	17	102	10	6	4	10	27
2000-01	Lincoln Stars	USHL	54	12	24	36	134	....	....	....	....	....
2001-02	North Dakota	WCHA	35	3	11	14	65	....	....	....	....	....
2002-03	North Dakota	WCHA	43	11	30	41	52	....	....	....	....	....
2003-04	North Dakota	WCHA	39	2	10	12	54	....	....	....	....	....

SCHREMP, Rob (SHREHMP, RAWB) **EDM.**

Center. Shoots left. 5'11", 197 lbs. Born, Syracuse, NY, July 1, 1986.
(Edmonton's 2nd choice, 25th overall, in 2004 Entry Draft).

			Regular Season					Playoffs				
Season	**Club**	**League**	**GP**	**G**	**A**	**TP**	**PIM**	**GP**	**G**	**A**	**TP**	**PIM**
2000-01	Syracuse Jrs.	OPJHL	49	32	46	78	....	....	....	....	....	....
2001-02	Syracuse Jrs.	OPJHL	47	41	47	88	93	1	1	2	3	0
2002-03	Mississauga	OHL	65	26	48	74	25	2	1	0	1	0
2003-04	Mississauga	OHL	3	2	4	6	0	....	....	....	....	....
	U.S. National U-18	USDP	2	0	0	0	8	....	....	....	....	....
	London Knights	OHL	60	28	41	69	18	15	7	6	13	2

OHL All-Rookie Team (2003) • OHL Rookie of the Year (2003)

SCHUBERT, Christoph (SHOO-buhrt, KRIHS-tawf) **OTT.**

Defense. Shoots left. 6'2", 210 lbs. Born, Munich, West Germany, February 5, 1982.
(Ottawa's 5th choice, 127th overall, in 2001 Entry Draft).

			Regular Season					Playoffs				
Season	**Club**	**League**	**GP**	**G**	**A**	**TP**	**PIM**	**GP**	**G**	**A**	**TP**	**PIM**
1998-99	EV Landshut Jr.	Ger.-Jr.	28	15	20	35	77	....	....	....	....	....
99-2000	EV Landshut Jr.	Ger.-Jr.	11	14	11	25	51	....	....	....	....	....
	EV Landshut	German-3	55	7	5	12	68	....	....	....	....	....
2000-01	Munchen Barons	Germany	55	6	3	9	80	10	0	2	2	27
2001-02	Munchen Barons	Germany	50	5	11	16	125	9	3	4	7	32
2002-03	Binghamton	AHL	70	2	8	10	102	8	0	1	1	2
2003-04	Binghamton	AHL	70	2	10	12	69	1	0	0	0	0

SCHULTZ, Jeff (SHUHLTZ, JEHF) **WSH.**

Defense. Shoots left. 6'6", 212 lbs. Born, Calgary, Alta., February 25, 1986.
(Washington's 2nd choice, 27th overall, in 2004 Entry Draft).

			Regular Season					Playoffs				
Season	**Club**	**League**	**GP**	**G**	**A**	**TP**	**PIM**	**GP**	**G**	**A**	**TP**	**PIM**
2000-01	Calgary Hawks	CBHA	27	7	8	15	20	....	....	....	....	....
2001-02	Calgary Rangers	CBHL	27	5	18	23	42	....	....	....	....	....
2002-03	Calgary Hitmen	WHL	50	2	1	3	4	4	0	0	0	0
2003-04	Calgary Hitmen	WHL	72	11	24	35	33	7	1	1	2	0

SCHUTTE, Michael (SHOOT, MIGH-kuhl)

Defense. Shoots left. 6'2", 199 lbs. Born, Burlington, Ont., July 28, 1979.

			Regular Season					Playoffs				
Season	**Club**	**League**	**GP**	**G**	**A**	**TP**	**PIM**	**GP**	**G**	**A**	**TP**	**PIM**
1998-99	Burlington	OPJHL	47	26	44	70	38	....	....	....	....	....
99-2000	U. of Maine	H-East	23	2	7	9	14	....	....	....	....	....
2000-01	U. of Maine	H-East	38	15	10	25	20	....	....	....	....	....
2001-02	U. of Maine	H-East	39	13	18	31	31	....	....	....	....	....
2002-03	Springfield Falcons	AHL	48	5	11	16	27	....	....	....	....	....
	Lowell	AHL	13	2	5	7	8	....	....	....	....	....
2003-04	Springfield Falcons	AHL	12	2	2	4	10	....	....	....	....	....
	Houston Aeros	AHL	36	3	0	3	20	1	0	1	1	0

NCAA Championship All-Tournament Team (2002)

Signed as a free agent by **Phoenix**, May 30, 2002. Traded to **Minnesota** by **Phoenix** for Chris Dyment, December 9, 2003.

SEABROOK, Brent (SEE-bruk, BREHNT) **CHI.**

Defense. Shoots right. 6'3", 215 lbs. Born, Richmond, B.C., April 20, 1985.
(Chicago's 1st choice, 14th overall, in 2003 Entry Draft).

			Regular Season					Playoffs				
Season	**Club**	**League**	**GP**	**G**	**A**	**TP**	**PIM**	**GP**	**G**	**A**	**TP**	**PIM**
2000-01	Delta Ice Hawks	PIJHL	54	16	26	42	55	....	....	....	....	....
	Lethbridge	WHL	4	0	0	0	0	....	....	....	....	....
2001-02	Lethbridge	WHL	67	6	33	39	70	4	1	1	2	2
2002-03	Lethbridge	WHL	69	9	33	42	113	....	....	....	....	....
2003-04	Lethbridge	WHL	61	12	29	41	107	....	....	....	....	....

SEDOV, Pavel (se-DAHF, PAH-vehl) **T.B.**

Right wing. Shoots left. 6'3", 200 lbs. Born, Voskresensk, USSR, January 12, 1982.
(Tampa Bay's 5th choice, 161st overall, in 2000 Entry Draft).

			Regular Season					Playoffs				
Season	**Club**	**League**	**GP**	**G**	**A**	**TP**	**PIM**	**GP**	**G**	**A**	**TP**	**PIM**
99-2000	Voskresensk	Russia-2	10	0	0	0	2	....	....	....	....	....
	Voskresensk 2	Russia-3	21	5	5	-10	26	....	....	....	....	....
2000-01	Voskresensk	Russia-2	38	2	1	3	10	....	....	....	....	....
2001-02	Voskresensk 2	Russia-3	12	4	1	5	0	....	....	....	....	....
	Voskresensk	Russia-2	18	3	1	4	0	....	....	....	....	....
2002-03	Voskresensk	Russia-2	25	1	5	6	6	....	....	....	....	....
	Voskresensk 2	Russia-3	7	2	4	6	4	....	....	....	....	....
2003-04	THC Tver	Russia-2	26	2	6	8	6	....	....	....	....	....
	Voskresensk	Russia	10	1	0	1	2	....	....	....	....	....
	Voskresensk	Russia-3	STATISTICS NOT AVAILABLE									

SEELEY, Richard (SEE-lee, RIH-chuhrd) **L.A.**

Defense. Shoots left. 6'2", 205 lbs. Born, Powell River, B.C., April 30, 1979.
(Los Angeles' 6th choice, 137th overall, in 1997 Entry Draft).

			Regular Season					Playoffs				
Season	Club	League	GP	G	A	TP	PIM	GP	G	A	TP	PIM
1995-96	Powell River	BCJHL	44	1	8	9	42	....	....	....	....	....
1996-97	Lethbridge	WHL	3	0	0	0	11	....	....	....	....	....
	Prince Albert	WHL	18	0	1	1	9	4	0	0	0	2
1997-98	Prince Albert	WHL	65	8	21	29	114	....	....	....	....	....
1998-99	Prince Albert	WHL	61	10	48	58	110	14	1	11	12	14
99-2000	Lowell	AHL	36	5	1	6	37	....	....	....	....	....
2000-01	Lowell	AHL	55	2	8	10	102	....	....	....	....	....
	Trenton Titans	ECHL	9	0	2	2	18	....	....	....	....	....
2001-02	Manchester	AHL	61	2	10	12	78	5	0	0	0	6
2002-03	Manchester	AHL	69	4	14	18	127	3	0	1	1	0
2003-04	Manchester	AHL	56	2	9	11	80	6	0	0	0	0

SEGAL, Brandon (SEE-guhl, BRAN-duhn) **NSH.**

Right wing. Shoots right. 6'3", 214 lbs. Born, Richmond, B.C., July 12, 1983.
(Nashville's 2nd choice, 102nd overall, in 2002 Entry Draft).

			Regular Season					Playoffs				
Season	Club	League	GP	G	A	TP	PIM	GP	G	A	TP	PIM
99-2000	Calgary Hitmen	WHL	44	2	6	8	76	13	1	1	2	13
	Delta Ice Hawks	PIJHL	....	....	....	....	....	3	0	1	1	2
2000-01	Calgary Hitmen	WHL	72	16	11	27	103	12	1	1	2	17
2001-02	Calgary Hitmen	WHL	71	43	40	83	122	7	1	4	5	16
2002-03	Calgary Hitmen	WHL	71	31	27	58	104	5	2	2	4	4
2003-04	Milwaukee	AHL	44	11	10	21	54	13	2	1	3	21

SEIKOLA, Markus (SAY-koh-la, MAHR-kuhs) **TOR.**

Defense. Shoots right. 6'1", 194 lbs. Born, Laitila, Finland, June 5, 1982.
(Toronto's 7th choice, 209th overall, in 2000 Entry Draft).

			Regular Season					Playoffs				
Season	Club	League	GP	G	A	TP	PIM	GP	G	A	TP	PIM
1996-97	TPS Turku-C	Finn-Jr.	4	1	0	1	4	1	0	0	0	0
1997-98	TPS Turku Jr.	Finn-Jr.	2	0	0	0	0	1	0	0	0	2
1998-99	TPS Turku Jr.	Finn-Jr.	36	2	10	12	24	....	....	....	....	....
99-2000	TPS Turku-B	Finn-Jr.	9	2	1	3	6	....	....	....	....	....
2000-01	TPS Turku Jr.	Finn-Jr.	26	13	7	20	6	3	1	0	1	0
	TPS Turku	Finland	23	1	0	1	16	....	....	....	....	....
2001-02	TPS Turku	Finland	51	4	4	8	20	7	1	1	2	12
	TPS Turku Jr.	Finn-Jr.	1	0	1	1	2	2	1	0	1	2
2002-03	TPS Turku	Finland	56	5	4	9	36	7	1	0	1	2
2003-04	TPS Turku	Finland	46	3	6	9	12	13	0	1	1	6

SEITSONEN, Aki (SIGHT-soh-nehn, AH-kee) **CGY.**

Center. Shoots right. 6'3", 206 lbs. Born, Riihimaki, Finland, February 5, 1986.
(Calgary's 4th choice, 118th overall, in 2004 Entry Draft).

			Regular Season					Playoffs				
Season	Club	League	GP	G	A	TP	PIM	GP	G	A	TP	PIM
2001-02	Ahmat C	Finn-Jr.	14	15	16	31	10	6	5	3	8	4
2002-03	HPK-B Jr.	Finn-Jr.	28	15	18	33	6	2	1	1	2	0
	HPK Jr.	Finn-Jr.	1	1	0	1	0	....	....	....	....	....
2003-04	Prince Albert	WHL	71	16	24	40	18	5	0	0	0	0

SEKERA, Andrej (SEH-kuhr-ah, AWN-dray) **BUF.**

Defense. Shoots left. 6', 191 lbs. Born, Bojnice, Czechoslovakia, June 8, 1986.
(Buffalo's 3rd choice, 71st overall, in 2004 Entry Draft).

			Regular Season					Playoffs				
Season	Club	League	GP	G	A	TP	PIM	GP	G	A	TP	PIM
2001-02	Dukla Trencin Jr.	Slovak-Jr.	52	5	10	15	10	....	....	....	....	....
2002-03	Dukla Trencin Jr.	Slovak-Jr.	48	9	15	24	20	....	....	....	....	....
2003-04	Dukla Trencin Jr.	Slovak-Jr.	42	5	12	17	40	2	0	1	1	4
	Dukla Trencin	Slovakia	3	0	0	0	2	....	....	....	....	....
	Dukla Trencin B	Slovak-2	5	0	0	0	0	....	....	....	....	....

SELUYANOV, Alexander (sehl-oo-YA-nahf, al-ehx-AN-duhr) **DET.**

Defense. Shoots right. 5'11", 172 lbs. Born, Ufa, USSR, March 24, 1982.
(Detroit's 5th choice, 128th overall, in 2000 Entry Draft).

			Regular Season					Playoffs				
Season	Club	League	GP	G	A	TP	PIM	GP	G	A	TP	PIM
1997-98	Novoil Ufa	Russia-3	19	0	1	1	8	....	....	....	....	....
1998-99	Novoil Ufa	Russia-4	20	3	3	6	8	....	....	....	....	....
99-2000	Ufa 2	Russia-3	18	3	4	7	10	....	....	....	....	....
	Ufa Salavat	Russia	13	1	2	3	4	....	....	....	....	....
2000-01	Ufa Salavat	Russia	30	0	3	3	10	....	....	....	....	....
2001-02	CSK VVS Samara	Russia-2	30	2	7	9	58	....	....	....	....	....
	Lada Togliatti	Russia	6	0	0	0	0	....	....	....	....	....
2002-03	Lada Togliatti	Russia	26	2	4	6	12	4	0	0	0	4
	CSK VVS Samara	Russia-2	16	4	4	8	34	....	....	....	....	....
2003-04	Lada Togliatti 2	Russia-3	5	0	1	1	10	4	2	0	2	6
	Lada Togliatti	Russia	43	1	3	4	20	2	0	0	0	0

SEMENOV, Dmitri (seh-MEH-nahv, dih-MEE-tree) **DET.**

Right wing. Shoots left. 5'10", 178 lbs. Born, Moscow, USSR, April 19, 1982.
(Detroit's 4th choice, 127th overall, in 2000 Entry Draft).

			Regular Season					Playoffs				
Season	Club	League	GP	G	A	TP	PIM	GP	G	A	TP	PIM
1997-98	Dynamo Moscow	Russia	13	2	1	3	2	....	....	....	....	....
1998-99	DynamoMoscow2	Russia-3	26	14	4	18	16	....	....	....	....	....
99-2000	THC Tver	Russia-2	16	4	2	6	63	....	....	....	....	....
2000-01	Dynamo Moscow	Russia	12	0	0	0	8	....	....	....	....	....
	Yekaterinburg	Russia	24	0	0	0	18	....	....	....	....	....
2001-02	DynamoMoscow2	Russia-3	6	5	2	7	6	....	....	....	....	....
	Yekaterinburg	Russia-2	6	1	2	3	2	....	....	....	....	....
	Dynamo Moscow	Russia	25	2	1	3	8	....	....	....	....	....
2002-03	Spartak Moscow	Russia	6	0	0	0	4	....	....	....	....	....
	THC Tver	Russia-2	16	1	2	3	22	....	....	....	....	....
2003-04	Krylja Sovetov	Russia-2	44	3	4	7	44	....	....	....	....	....

SEMIN, Dmitri (SEH-min, dih-MEE-tree) **ST.L.**

Center. Shoots left. 5'10", 185 lbs. Born, Moscow, USSR, August 14, 1983.
(St. Louis' 4th choice, 159th overall, in 2001 Entry Draft).

			Regular Season					Playoffs				
Season	Club	League	GP	G	A	TP	PIM	GP	G	A	TP	PIM
99-2000	Spartak Moscow 2	Russia-3	27	9	10	19	10	....	....	....	....	....
	Spartak Moscow	Russia-2	1	0	0	0	0	....	....	....	....	....
2000-01	Spartak Moscow	Russia-2	21	6	3	9	4	11	2	3	5	4
2001-02	Spartak Moscow 2	Russia-3	4	5	0	5	4	....	....	....	....	....
	Spartak Moscow	Russia	44	2	6	8	14	....	....	....	....	....
2002-03	Spartak Moscow	Russia	51	9	13	22	30	....	....	....	....	....
2003-04	Spartak Moscow	Russia-2	60	15	23	38	34	13	2	2	4	2

SERSEN, Michal (suhr-SEHN, MEE-khahl) **PIT.**

Defense. Shoots left. 6'1", 200 lbs. Born, Celnica, Czechoslovakia, December 28, 1985.
(Pittsburgh's 7th choice, 130th overall, in 2004 Entry Draft).

			Regular Season					Playoffs				
Season	Club	League	GP	G	A	TP	PIM	GP	G	A	TP	PIM
2002-03	Bratislava Jr.	Slovak-Jr.	33	5	4	9	51	....	....	....	....	....
	Slov. Bratislava	Slovakia	17	0	0	0	0	....	....	....	....	....
2003-04	Rimouski Oceanic	QMJHL	45	7	18	25	30	9	1	5	6	6

SERTICH, Andrew (SUHR-tihch, AN-droo) **PIT.**

Left wing. Shoots left. 6', 175 lbs. Born, Coleraine, MN, May 6, 1983.
(Pittsburgh's 5th choice, 136th overall, in 2002 Entry Draft).

			Regular Season					Playoffs				
Season	Club	League	GP	G	A	TP	PIM	GP	G	A	TP	PIM
1998/00	Greenway Raiders	Hi-School	47	39	58	97	....	....	....	....	....	....
2000-01	Greenway Raiders	Hi-School	31	35	45	80	14	....	....	....	....	....
2001-02	Greenway Raiders	Hi-School	26	24	48	72	35	....	....	....	....	....
	Sioux Falls	USHL	13	2	4	6	0	2	0	0	0	2
2002-03	U. of Minnesota	WCHA	44	5	9	14	12	....	....	....	....	....
2003-04	U. of Minnesota	WCHA	43	8	14	22	14	....	....	....	....	....

SETZINGER, Oliver (SEHT-zihn-guhr, AW-lih-vuhr) **NSH.**

Center. Shoots left. 6', 189 lbs. Born, Horn, Austria, July 11, 1983.
(Nashville's 5th choice, 76th overall, in 2001 Entry Draft).

			Regular Season					Playoffs				
Season	Club	League	GP	G	A	TP	PIM	GP	G	A	TP	PIM
1998-99	Wiener EV Jr.	Austria-Jr.	30	25	27	52	30	....	....	....	....	....
99-2000	Ilves Tampere Jr.	Finn-Jr.	35	6	4	10	65	....	....	....	....	....
	Ilves Tampere-B	Finn-Jr.	18	16	9	25	38	....	....	....	....	....
	Ilves Tampere	Finland	1	0	0	0	2	....	....	....	....	....
	Ilves Tampere	Finland-2	18	16	9	25	38	....	....	....	....	....
2000-01	Ilves Tampere Jr.	Finn-Jr.	31	8	12	20	74	....	....	....	....	....
	Ilves Tampere	Finland	14	0	1	1	10	....	....	....	....	....
2001-02	Ilves Tampere Jr.	Finn-Jr.	1	0	0	0	2	....	....	....	....	....
	Ilves Tampere	Finland	10	1	0	1	4	....	....	....	....	....
	Sport Vaasa	Finland-2	8	5	2	7	6	....	....	....	....	....
	Austria	Olympics	4	1	0	1	2	....	....	....	....	....
	EHC Linz	Austria	8	6	7	13	4	13	4	14	18	14
2002-03	Pelicans Lahti	Finland	56	7	14	21	54	....	....	....	....	....
2003-04	Pelicans Lahti	Finland	20	2	4	6	22	....	....	....	....	....
	KalPa Kuopio	Finland-2	8	4	7	11	20	....	....	....	....	....
	HPK Hameenlinna	Finland	14	6	3	9	10	8	4	2	6	4

SEYDOUX, Philippe (SAY-doo, fihl-EEP) **OTT.**

Defense. Shoots left. 6'2", 185 lbs. Born, Bern, Switz., February 23, 1985.
(Ottawa's 3rd choice, 100th overall, in 2003 Entry Draft).

			Regular Season					Playoffs				
Season	Club	League	GP	G	A	TP	PIM	GP	G	A	TP	PIM
2000-01	SC Bern Jr.	Swiss-Jr.	30	1	3	4	8	4	1	2	0	6
2001-02	SC Bern Jr.	Swiss-Jr.	35	8	17	25	94	7	3	5	0	24
	SC Bern	Swiss	7	0	0	0	0	2	0	0	0	0
2002-03	Kloten Flyers Jr.	Swiss-Jr.	14	2	10	12	50	....	....	....	....	....
	Kloten Flyers	Swiss	14	0	1	1	4	5	0	0	0	6
2003-04	Kloten Flyers	Swiss	24	2	3	5	20	....	....	....	....	....
	Kloten Flyers	Swiss-Q	8	1	3	4	2	....	....	....	....	....

SHADILOV, Igor (sha-DEE-lahf, EE-gor) **WSH.**

Defense. Shoots left. 6'2", 189 lbs. Born, Moscow, USSR, June 7, 1980.
(Washington's 10th choice, 249th overall, in 1999 Entry Draft).

			Regular Season					Playoffs				
Season	Club	League	GP	G	A	TP	PIM	GP	G	A	TP	PIM
1996-97	Dyno. Moscow Jr.	Russia-Jr.	30	3	7	10	30	....	....	....	....	....
1997-98	Dynamo Moscow	Russia	38	1	0	1	6	....	....	....	....	....
1998-99	Dynamo Moscow	Russia	28	2	9	11	15	....	....	....	....	....
	Dynamo Moscow	Russia	2	0	0	0	0	....	....	....	....	....
	Krylja Sovetov	Russia	9	0	0	0	0	....	....	....	....	....
99-2000	THC Tver	Russia-2	14	0	3	3	6	....	....	....	....	....
	Dynamo Moscow	Russia	26	0	2	2	8	16	0	0	0	2
2000-01	Dynamo Moscow	Russia	34	1	5	6	12	....	....	....	....	....
2001-02	Cherepovets	Russia	33	7	3	10	10	4	0	0	0	2
2002-03	Cherepovets	Russia	32	3	3	6	28	12	1	3	4	4
2003-04	Dynamo Moscow	Russia	56	4	8	12	16	3	0	1	1	2

SHAFIGULIN, Grigory (sha-fih-GOO-lihn, grih-GOH-ree) **NSH.**

Center. Shoots left. 6'2", 185 lbs. Born, Chelyabinsk, USSR, January 13, 1985.
(Nashville's 8th choice, 98th overall, in 2003 Entry Draft).

			Regular Season					Playoffs				
Season	Club	League	GP	G	A	TP	PIM	GP	G	A	TP	PIM
2000-01	Chelyabinsk Jr.	Russia-Jr.	6	3	2	5	8	....	....	....	....	....
2001-02	Yaroslavl 2	Russia-3	19	2	2	4	12	....	....	....	....	....
2002-03	Yaroslavl Jr.	Russia-Jr.	33	18	12	30	46	7	0	4	4	31
	Yaroslavl 2	Russia-3	19	2	2	4	12	....	....	....	....	....
	Yaroslavl	Russia	11	0	1	1	4	8	0	0	0	4
2003-04	Yaroslavl 2	Russia-3	11	3	8	11	22	....	....	....	....	....
	Yaroslavl	Russia	29	3	0	3	4	2	0	0	0	0

SHARROW, Jim (SHA-row, JIHM) **ATL.**

Defense. Shoots right. 6'2", 180 lbs. Born, Framingham, MA, January 31, 1985.
(Atlanta's 2nd choice, 110th overall, in 2003 Entry Draft).

			Regular Season					Playoffs				
Season	Club	League	GP	G	A	TP	PIM	GP	G	A	TP	PIM
2000-01	Cardigan Mtn.	Hi-School		STATISTICS NOT AVAILABLE								
2001-02	U.S. National U-17	USDP	61	5	16	21	30	....	....	....	....	....
2002-03	Halifax	QMJHL	70	2	14	16	54	25	2	4	6	24
2003-04	Halifax	QMJHL	52	12	26	38	67	....	....	....	....	....

QMJHL All-Rookie Team (2003)

SHASBY, Matt (SHAS-bee, MAT) **MTL.**

Defense. Shoots left. 6'2", 196 lbs. Born, Sioux Falls, SD, July 2, 1980.
(Montreal's 7th choice, 150th overall, in 1999 Entry Draft).

			Regular Season					Playoffs				
Season	Club	League	GP	G	A	TP	PIM	GP	G	A	TP	PIM
1997-98	Lincoln Stars	USHL	43	1	15	16	30	8	0	0	0	2
1998-99	Lincoln Stars	USHL	17	1	4	5	10	....	....	....	....	....
	Des Moines	USHL	32	3	18	21	24	11	0	1	1	12
99-2000	Alaska-Anchorage	WCHA	32	1	8	9	36	....	....	....	....	....
2000-01	Alaska-Anchorage	WCHA	35	4	14	18	32	....	....	....	....	....
2001-02	Alaska-Anchorage	WCHA	35	7	20	27	72	....	....	....	....	....
2002-03	Alaska-Anchorage	WCHA	25	0	11	11	18	....	....	....	....	....
2003-04	Columbus	ECHL	66	8	20	28	34	....	....	....	....	....

WCHA Second All-Star Team (2002)

SHASTIN, Yegor (SHAS-tihn, yeh-GOHR) **CGY.**

Left wing. Shoots left. 5'9", 172 lbs. Born, Kiev, USSR, September 10, 1982.
(Calgary's 5th choice, 124th overall, in 2001 Entry Draft).

			Regular Season					Playoffs				
Season	**Club**	**League**	**GP**	**G**	**A**	**TP**	**PIM**	**GP**	**G**	**A**	**TP**	**PIM**
1997-98	Omsk 2	Russia-3	4	0	1	1	0	....	....	....	....	....
1998-99	Omsk 2	Russia-4	19	11	17	28	30	....	....	....	....	....
	Avangard Omsk	Russia	4	0	0	0	0	4	0	1	1	0
99-2000	Omsk 2	Russia-3	11	6	5	11	20	....	....	....	....	....
	Avangard Omsk	Russia	26	2	4	6	20	7	3	1	4	16
2000-01	Omsk 2	Russia-3	14	13	9	22	62	....	....	....	....	....
	Avangard Omsk	Russia	35	3	11	14	59	9	1	0	1	18
2001-02	Avangard Omsk	Russia	26	2	5	7	10	11	1	0	1	8
2002-03	HC Ambri-Piotta	Swiss	44	2	3	5	18	3	1	0	1	2
	HC Sierre	Swiss-2	2	1	0	1	0	....	....	....	....	....
2003-04	Sibir Novosibirsk	Russia	57	7	5	12	28	....	....	....	....	....

SHEFER, Andrei (SHEH-fuhr, AN-dray) **L.A.**

Left wing. Shoots left. 6'1", 194 lbs. Born, Yekaterinburg, USSR, July 26, 1981.
(Los Angeles' 1st choice, 43rd overall, in 1999 Entry Draft).

			Regular Season					Playoffs				
Season	**Club**	**League**	**GP**	**G**	**A**	**TP**	**PIM**	**GP**	**G**	**A**	**TP**	**PIM**
1997-98	Yekaterinburg 2	Russia-3	16	3	3	6	18	....	....	....	....	....
1998-99	Cherepovets 3	Russia-4	6	2	2	4	18	....	....	....	....	....
	Cherepovets 2	Russia-3	21	6	5	11	20	....	....	....	....	....
	Cherepovets	Russia	8	1	0	1	4	....	....	....	....	....
99-2000	Halifax	QMJHL	72	34	42	76	30	10	0	5	5	4
2000-01	SKA St. Petersburg	Russia	11	6	1	7	4	....	....	....	....	....
	Cherepovets	Russia	20	1	1	2	10	6	1	0	1	0
2001-02	Cherepovets 2	Russia-3	3	1	2	3	2	....	....	....	....	....
	Cherepovets	Russia	8	0	0	0	6	....	....	....	....	....
	SKA St. Petersburg	Russia	28	4	4	8	10	....	....	....	....	....
2002-03	Cherepovets	Russia	37	2	4	6	10	10	0	0	0	0
	Cherepovets 2	Russia-2	3	1	2	3	2	....	....	....	....	....
2003-04	Cherepovets	Russia	55	4	6	10	46	....	....	....	....	....

SHEMETOV, Sergei (shuh-MEH-tawf, SAIR-gay) **COL.**

Left wing. Shoots left. 6'1", 185 lbs. Born, Yaroslavl, USSR, September 3, 1984.
(Colorado's 9th choice, 258th overall, in 2002 Entry Draft).

			Regular Season					Playoffs				
Season	**Club**	**League**	**GP**	**G**	**A**	**TP**	**PIM**	**GP**	**G**	**A**	**TP**	**PIM**
2000-01	Yaroslavl 2	Russia-3	30	7	0	7	24	....	....	....	....	....
2001-02	Yaroslavl 2	Russia-3	17	3	4	7	42	....	....	....	....	....
	Elektrostal 2	Russia-3	3	0	0	0	8	....	....	....	....	....
	Elektrostal	Russia-2	15	1	1	2	26	....	....	....	....	....
2002-03	HC Voronezh	Russia-2	13	0	1	1	35	....	....	....	....	....
2003-04	Nizhnekamsk	Russia	10	0	0	0	2	....	....	....	....	....
	Gazovik Tyumen	Russia-2	10	0	0	0	8	....	....	....	....	....
	Spartak Moscow	Russia-2	56	16	31	47	71	....	....	....	....	....

SHINKAR, Alexander (shihn-KAHR, al-ehx-AN-duhr) **TOR.**

Right wing. Shoots left. 6', 176 lbs. Born, Ufa, USSR, July 3, 1981.
(Toronto's 9th choice, 254th overall, in 2000 Entry Draft).

			Regular Season					Playoffs				
Season	**Club**	**League**	**GP**	**G**	**A**	**TP**	**PIM**	**GP**	**G**	**A**	**TP**	**PIM**
1997-98	Novoil Ufa	Russia-3	22	6	2	8	4	....	....	....	....	....
1998-99	Cherepovets 2	Russia-3	25	7	2	9	8	....	....	....	....	....
	Cherepovets 3	Russia-4	8	0	4	4	4	....	....	....	....	....
99-2000	Cherepovets	Russia	18	1	1	2	2	8	0	0	0	0
2000-01	SKA St. Petersburg	Russia	43	7	4	11	50	....	....	....	....	....
2001-02	Ufa Salavat	Russia	27	3	3	6	8	....	....	....	....	....
	SKA St. Petersburg	Russia	18	3	4	7	10	....	....	....	....	....
2002-03	Cherepovets	Russia	32	3	1	4	12	11	0	1	1	6
2003-04	Ufa Salavat	Russia	15	2	0	2	16	....	....	....	....	....
	SKA St. Petersburg	Russia	12	4	1	5	0	....	....	....	....	....

SHKOTOV, Alexei (SHKOH-tahv, al-EHX-ay) **ST.L.**

Right wing. Shoots left. 5'11", 161 lbs. Born, Elektrostal, USSR, June 22, 1984.
(St. Louis' 1st choice, 48th overall, in 2002 Entry Draft).

			Regular Season					Playoffs				
Season	**Club**	**League**	**GP**	**G**	**A**	**TP**	**PIM**	**GP**	**G**	**A**	**TP**	**PIM**
2000-01	Elektrostal 2	Russia-3	2	0	0	0	0	....	....	....	....	....
2001-02	Elektrostal 2	Russia-3	4	4	5	9	2	....	....	....	....	....
	Elektrostal	Russia-2	52	17	9	26	40	....	....	....	....	....
2002-03	CSKA Moscow	Russia	33	5	1	6	20	....	....	....	....	....
2003-04	Moncton Wildcats	QMJHL	7	2	4	6	2	....	....	....	....	....
	Quebec Remparts	QMJHL	36	25	36	61	24	5	3	1	4	4

SIDORENKO, Kirill (sih-dohr-EHN-koh, KIH-rihl) **DAL.**

Center. Shoots left. 6'3", 187 lbs. Born, Omsk, USSR, March 30, 1983.
(Dallas' 9th choice, 180th overall, in 2002 Entry Draft).

			Regular Season					Playoffs				
Season	**Club**	**League**	**GP**	**G**	**A**	**TP**	**PIM**	**GP**	**G**	**A**	**TP**	**PIM**
1998-99	Omsk 2	Russia-4	2	0	0	0	2	....	....	....	....	....
99-2000	Omsk 2	Russia-3	26	2	11	13	14	....	....	....	....	....
2000-01	Omsk 2	Russia-3	30	8	7	15	44	....	....	....	....	....
2001-02	Mostovik Kurgan	Russia-2	50	11	6	17	64	....	....	....	....	....
2002-03	Sibir Novosibirsk	Russia	8	1	1	2	2	....	....	....	....	....
2003-04	Energiya Kemerovo	Russia-2	14	1	1	2	6	....	....	....	....	....
	Zauralje Kurgan	Russia-2	32	3	3	6	6	4	0	0	0	27

SIDYAKIN, Andrei (sihd-YA-kihn, AN-dray) **MTL.**

Right wing. Shoots left. 5'11", 169 lbs. Born, Ufa, USSR, January 20, 1979.
(Montreal's 10th choice, 202nd overall, in 1997 Entry Draft).

			Regular Season					Playoffs				
Season	**Club**	**League**	**GP**	**G**	**A**	**TP**	**PIM**	**GP**	**G**	**A**	**TP**	**PIM**
1994-95	Ufa Salavat	CIS	7	0	1	1	0	....	....	....	....	....
1995-96	Ufa Salavat	CIS	25	1	0	1	4	3	0	0	0	2
1996-97	Ufa Salavat	Russia	29	3	5	8	4	....	....	....	....	....
1997-98	Ufa Salavat	Russia	42	5	4	9	32	....	....	....	....	....
1998-99	Ufa Salavat	Russia	36	6	4	10	14	2	0	0	0	2
99-2000	Ufa Salavat	Russia	38	7	2	9	32	....	....	....	....	....
2000-01	Ufa Salavat	Russia	44	10	13	23	42	....	....	....	....	....
2001-02	Ufa Salavat	Russia	43	9	7	16	20	....	....	....	....	....
2002-03	Cherepovets	Russia	38	8	8	16	20	2	0	0	0	4
2003-04	Cherepovets	Russia-3	4	2	3	5	0	....	....	....	....	....
	Cherepovets	Russia	19	1	2	3	12	....	....	....	....	....
	Ufa Salavat	Russia	29	8	8	16	28	....	....	....	....	....

SINDEL, Jakub (SHIHN-dehl, YA-kuhb) **CHI.**

Center. Shoots right. 6', 172 lbs. Born, Jihlava, Czechoslovakia, January 24, 1986.
(Chicago's 5th choice, 54th overall, in 2004 Entry Draft).

			Regular Season					Playoffs				
Season	**Club**	**League**	**GP**	**G**	**A**	**TP**	**PIM**	**GP**	**G**	**A**	**TP**	**PIM**
99-2000	Slavia Praha 18	Czech-Jr.	32	10	6	16	6	....	....	....	....	....
2000-01	Slavia Praha 18	Czech-Jr.	26	12	15	27	2	6	1	0	1	0
2001-02	Slavia Praha 18	Czech-Jr.	34	32	14	46	34	2	0	1	1	2
	Slavia Praha Jr.	Czech-Jr.	14	7	4	11	10	....	....	....	....	....
2002-03	Slavia Praha Jr.	Czech-Jr.	35	12	11	23	39	2	0	1	1	0
2003-04	Sparta Praha Jr.	Czech-Jr.	13	8	14	22	4	....	....	....	....	....
	Sparta Praha	Czech	34	5	1	6	14	13	1	1	2	2
	Dukla Jihlava	Czech-2	1	0	0	0	0	....	....	....	....	....

SIPOTZ, Brian (SIHP-awtz, BRIGH-uhn) **ATL.**

Defense. Shoots right. 6'7", 250 lbs. Born, South Bend, IN, September 16, 1981.
(Atlanta's 3rd choice, 100th overall, in 2001 Entry Draft).

			Regular Season					Playoffs				
Season	**Club**	**League**	**GP**	**G**	**A**	**TP**	**PIM**	**GP**	**G**	**A**	**TP**	**PIM**
99-2000	Culver Academy	Hi-School	45	14	22	36	56	....	....	....	....	....
2000-01	Miami University	CCHA	32	0	1	1	48	....	....	....	....	....
2001-02	Miami University	CCHA	25	0	1	1	28	....	....	....	....	....
2002-03	Miami University	CCHA	26	0	0	0	24	....	....	....	....	....
2003-04	Miami University	CCHA	36	0	3	3	39	....	....	....	....	....

SKINNER, Brett (SKIH-nuhr, BREHT) **VAN.**

Defense. Shoots left. 6'1", 170 lbs. Born, Brandon, Man., June 28, 1983.
(Vancouver's 3rd choice, 68th overall, in 2002 Entry Draft).

			Regular Season					Playoffs				
Season	**Club**	**League**	**GP**	**G**	**A**	**TP**	**PIM**	**GP**	**G**	**A**	**TP**	**PIM**
1998-99	Brandon Kings	MMBHL	29	3	18	21	20	....	....	....	....	....
99-2000	Brandon Kings	MMHL	40	8	27	35	48	....	....	....	....	....
2000-01	Trail Smoke Eaters	BCHL	59	11	24	35	43	....	....	....	....	....
2001-02	Des Moines	USHL	44	9	38	47	25	3	0	1	1	0
2002-03	U. of Denver	WCHA	37	4	13	17	27	....	....	....	....	....
2003-04	U. of Denver	WCHA	44	7	23	30	32	....	....	....	....	....

USHL First All-Star Team (2002) • USHL Defenseman of the Year (2002)

SKLADANY, Frantisek (sklah-DAH-nee, FRAN-tih-shehk) **COL.**

Left wing. Shoots left. 6', 185 lbs. Born, Martin, Czech., April 22, 1982.
(Colorado's 4th choice, 143rd overall, in 2001 Entry Draft).

			Regular Season					Playoffs				
Season	**Club**	**League**	**GP**	**G**	**A**	**TP**	**PIM**	**GP**	**G**	**A**	**TP**	**PIM**
1995-96	Martin Jr.	Slovak-Jr.	8	2	1	3	2	....	....	....	....	....
1996-97	Martin Jr.	Slovak-Jr.	46	29	28	57	18	....	....	....	....	....
1997-98	Martin Jr.	Slovak-Jr.	53	46	37	83	18	....	....	....	....	....
1998-99	Martin Jr.	Slovak-Jr.	10	2	4	6	4	....	....	....	....	....
	Martin	Slovakia	1	0	0	0	0	....	....	....	....	....
99-2000	Martin Jr.	Slovak-Jr.	3	2	3	5	0	....	....	....	....	....
	Martin	Slovak-2	13	1	4	5	2	....	....	....	....	....
2000-01	Boston University	H-East	35	4	5	9	4	....	....	....	....	....
2001-02	Boston University	H-East	33	13	13	26	23	....	....	....	....	....
2002-03	Boston University	H-East	41	14	21	35	34	....	....	....	....	....
2003-04	Boston University	H-East	37	3	21	24	16	....	....	....	....	....

SKLENAR, Jaroslav (SKLEH-nahr, YAHR-oh-slav) **TOR.**

Right wing. Shoots right. 6', 167 lbs. Born, Ivancice, Czech., November 22, 1982.
(Toronto's 8th choice, 183rd overall, in 2001 Entry Draft).

			Regular Season					Playoffs				
Season	**Club**	**League**	**GP**	**G**	**A**	**TP**	**PIM**	**GP**	**G**	**A**	**TP**	**PIM**
99-2000	Trinec Jr.	Czech-Jr.	32	5	6	11	2	....	....	....	....	....
2000-01	HC Ytong Brno Jr.	Czech-Jr.	26	10	11	21	22	....	....	....	....	....
	HC Ytong Brno	Czech-3	21	4	4	8	6	....	....	....	....	....
2001-02	Znojmo	Czech	4	0	0	0	2	....	....	....	....	....
	HC Ytong Brno	Czech-2	5	0	0	0	4	....	....	....	....	....
	Rosice	Czech-2	8	3	1	4	0	....	....	....	....	....
	Ottawa 67's	OHL	4	1	0	1	0	....	....	....	....	....
2002-03	HK 36 Skalica	Slovakia	13	0	0	0	0	....	....	....	....	....
	Znojmo	Czech	10	0	0	0	0	....	....	....	....	....
	Trebic	Czech-2	8	0	1	1	2	....	....	....	....	....
	HC Hvezda Brno	Czech-2	1	0	0	0	0	....	....	....	....	....
2003-04	HC Velka Bites	Czech-3	34	9	10	19	49	....	....	....	....	....

SKOLNEY, Wade (SKOHL-nee, WAYD) **PHI.**

Defense. Shoots right. 6', 197 lbs. Born, Wynyard, Sask., June 24, 1981.

			Regular Season					Playoffs				
Season	**Club**	**League**	**GP**	**G**	**A**	**TP**	**PIM**	**GP**	**G**	**A**	**TP**	**PIM**
1996-97	Niacam	SBHL	54	33	70	103	193	....	....	....	....	....
	Brandon	WHL	1	0	0	0	0	....	....	....	....	....
1997-98	Brandon	WHL	42	1	11	12	49	3	0	0	0	0
1998-99	Brandon	WHL	39	3	10	13	60	5	0	1	1	16
99-2000	Brandon	WHL	13	0	2	2	23	....	....	....	....	....
2000-01	Brandon	WHL	28	2	9	11	37	....	....	....	....	....
2001-02	Brandon	WHL	50	4	12	16	179	19	2	7	9	56
2002-03	Philadelphia	AHL	68	2	7	9	102	....	....	....	....	....
2003-04	Philadelphia	AHL	56	1	8	9	106	12	0	0	0	23

Signed as a free agent by **Philadelphia**, May 20, 2002.

SKOOG, Simon (SKOOG, SEE-muhn) **ST.L.**

Defense. Shoots left. 6'2", 218 lbs. Born, Solvesborg, Sweden, February 17, 1983.
(St. Louis' 8th choice, 283rd overall, in 2001 Entry Draft).

			Regular Season					Playoffs				
Season	**Club**	**League**	**GP**	**G**	**A**	**TP**	**PIM**	**GP**	**G**	**A**	**TP**	**PIM**
99-2000	Malmo IF Jr.	Swede-Jr.	4	0	0	0	0	....	....	....	....	....
2000-01	Morrums GoIS IK	Swede-2	27	0	1	1	12	....	....	....	....	....
2001-02	Morrums GoIS IK	Swede-2	53	3	8	11	46	....	....	....	....	....
2002-03	Morrums GoIS IK	Swede-2	39	2	4	6	38	2	0	1	1	4
2003-04	HV 71 Jr.	Swede-Jr.	1	1	0	1	0	....	....	....	....	....
	HV 71 Jonkoping	Sweden	49	6	2	8	47	19	0	1	1	2

SLATER, Jim (SLAY-tuhr, JIHM) ATL.

Center. Shoots left. 6', 190 lbs. Born, Petoskey, MI, December 9, 1982.
(Atlanta's 2nd choice, 30th overall, in 2002 Entry Draft).

			Regular Season					Playoffs				
Season	Club	League	GP	G	A	TP	PIM	GP	G	A	TP	PIM
1998-99	Cleveland Barons	NAJHL	50	13	20	33	58	2	0	0	0	2
99-2000	Cleveland Barons	NAJHL	56	35	50	85	129	3	1	3	4	4
2000-01	Cleveland Barons	NAJHL	48	27	37	64	122	6	6	6	12	6
2001-02	Michigan State	CCHA	37	11	21	32	50	....	....	....	....	....
2002-03	Michigan State	CCHA	37	18	26	44	26	....	....	....	....	....
2003-04	Michigan State	CCHA	42	19	29	*48	38	....	....	....	....	....

CCHA All-Rookie Team (2002) • CCHA First All-Star Team (2003, 2004) • NCAA West Second All-American Team (2004)

SLOAN, Tyler (SLOHN, TIGH-luhr)

Defense. Shoots left. 6'4", 190 lbs. Born, Calgary, Alta., March 15, 1981.

			Regular Season					Playoffs				
Season	Club	League	GP	G	A	TP	PIM	GP	G	A	TP	PIM
1997-98	Calgary Buffaloes	AMHL	36	2	11	13	24	10	0	4	4	2
1998-99	Calgary Royals	AJHL	STATISTICS NOT AVAILABLE									
99-2000	Calgary Royals	AJHL	45	5	26	31	80	....	....	....	....	....
2000-01	Kamloops Blazers	WHL	70	5	28	33	146	4	0	0	0	4
2001-02	Kamloops Blazers	WHL	70	3	29	32	89	4	0	0	0	15
	Syracuse Crunch	AHL	2	0	0	0	5	....	....	....	....	....
2002-03	Syracuse Crunch	AHL	39	2	1	3	46	....	....	....	....	....
	Dayton Bombers	ECHL	14	1	2	3	22	....	....	....	....	....
2003-04	Syracuse Crunch	AHL	69	2	4	6	50	7	0	0	0	8

Signed as a free agent by **Columbus**, September 24, 2000.

SLOVAK, Tomas (SLOHW-vahk, TAW-mawsh) COL.

Defense. Shoots right. 6'1", 203 lbs. Born, Kosice, Czech., April 5, 1983.
(Nashville's 3rd choice, 42nd overall, in 2001 Entry Draft).

			Regular Season					Playoffs				
Season	Club	League	GP	G	A	TP	PIM	GP	G	A	TP	PIM
1997-98	HC Kosice Jr.	Slovak-Jr.	47	1	6	7	24	....	....	....	....	....
1998-99	HC Kosice Jr.	Slovak-Jr.	45	6	14	20	65	....	....	....	....	....
99-2000	HC Kosice Jr.	Slovak-Jr.	55	16	28	44	117	....	....	....	....	....
	HC Kosice	Slovakia	2	0	0	0	0	....	....	....	....	....
2000-01	HC Kosice	Slovakia	43	5	5	10	28	3	1	0	1	2
2001-02	Kelowna Rockets	WHL	53	2	24	26	41	15	0	0	0	8
2002-03	Kelowna Rockets	WHL	65	18	53	71	86	19	2	*20	22	26
2003-04	Hershey Bears	AHL	42	3	8	11	16	....	....	....	....	....
	Reading Royals	ECHL	20	3	7	10	32	....	....	....	....	....

WHL West First All-Star Team (2003)

Traded to **Colorado** by **Nashville** for Sergei Soin, June 21, 2003.

SMABY, Matt (SMA-bee, MAT) T.B.

Defense. Shoots left. 6'5", 202 lbs. Born, Minneapolis, MN, October 14, 1984.
(Tampa Bay's 2nd choice, 41st overall, in 2003 Entry Draft).

			Regular Season					Playoffs				
Season	Club	League	GP	G	A	TP	PIM	GP	G	A	TP	PIM
2001-02	Shat.-St. Mary's	Hi-School	65	7	18	25	134	....	....	....	....	....
2002-03	Shat.-St. Mary's	Hi-School	57	3	20	23	114	....	....	....	....	....
2003-04	North Dakota	WCHA	39	1	6	7	81	....	....	....	....	....

SMID, Ladislav (SHMIHD, LA-dih-slahv) ANA.

Defense. Shoots left. 6'3", 200 lbs. Born, Frydlant V Cechach, Czech., February 1, 1986.
(Anaheim's 1st choice, 9th overall, in 2004 Entry Draft).

			Regular Season					Playoffs				
Season	Club	League	GP	G	A	TP	PIM	GP	G	A	TP	PIM
99-2000	Liberec 16	Czech-Jr.	29	0	2	2	12	....	....	....	....	....
2000-01	Liberec 16	Czech-Jr.	47	0	9	9	24	....	....	....	....	....
2001-02	Liberec 16	Czech-Jr.	26	5	7	12	82	....	....	....	....	....
	Liberec Jr.	Czech-Jr.	17	1	3	3	10	....	....	....	....	....
2002-03	Liberec Jr.	Czech-Jr.	32	1	14	15	12	8	2	1	3	31
	Liberec	Czech	4	0	0	0	0	....	....	....	....	....
2003-04	Liberec Jr.	Czech-Jr.	14	4	10	14	38	2	1	0	1	6
	Liberec	Czech	45	1	1	2	51	....	....	....	....	....
	Beroun	Czech-2	....	....	....	....	....	3	1	1	2	4

SMITH, Jeff (SMIHTH, JEHF) PHI.

Left wing. Shoots left. 6'6", 212 lbs. Born, Regina, Sask., January 2, 1981.

			Regular Season					Playoffs				
Season	Club	League	GP	G	A	TP	PIM	GP	G	A	TP	PIM
1998-99	Reg. Pat Cdns.	SMHL	35	28	19	47	71	....	....	....	....	....
	Red Deer Rebels	WHL	25	0	0	0	0	....	....	....	....	....
99-2000	Red Deer Rebels	WHL	63	9	6	15	74	....	....	....	....	....
2000-01	Red Deer Rebels	WHL	72	22	11	33	187	....	....	....	....	....
2001-02	Red Deer Rebels	WHL	69	9	15	24	236	23	6	6	12	30
2002-03	Trenton Titans	ECHL	35	1	7	8	103	1	0	0	0	4
	Philadelphia	AHL	11	1	0	1	22	....	....	....	....	....
2003-04	Trenton Titans	ECHL	47	7	5	12	174	....	....	....	....	....
	Philadelphia	AHL	5	0	0	0	0	....	....	....	....	....

Signed as a free agent by **Philadelphia**, August 20, 2002.

SMITH, Jordan (SMIHTH, JOHN-dan) ANA.

Defense. Shoots right. 6'1", 220 lbs. Born, Sault Ste. Marie, Ont., November 4, 1985.
(Anaheim's 2nd choice, 39th overall, in 2004 Entry Draft).

			Regular Season					Playoffs				
Season	Club	League	GP	G	A	TP	PIM	GP	G	A	TP	PIM
2001-02	Soo Thunderbirds	NOJHL	8	1	2	3	12	....	....	....	....	....
	Sault Ste. Marie	OHL	19	0	0	0	25	2	0	0	0	2
2002-03	Sault Ste. Marie	OHL	60	2	8	10	107	4	0	0	0	6
2003-04	Sault Ste. Marie	OHL	68	6	20	26	140	....	....	....	....	....

SMITH, Kenny (SMIHTH, KEHN-nee) EDM.

Defense. Shoots right. 6'2", 209 lbs. Born, Stoneham, MA, December 31, 1981.
(Edmonton's 4th choice, 84th overall, in 2001 Entry Draft).

			Regular Season					Playoffs				
Season	Club	League	GP	G	A	TP	PIM	GP	G	A	TP	PIM
1998-99	U.S. National U-17	USDP	29	2	5	7	32	....	....	....	....	....
99-2000	U.S. National U-18	USDP	27	4	6	10	77	....	....	....	....	....
2000-01	Harvard University	ECAC	21	0	2	2	37	....	....	....	....	....
2001-02	Harvard Universtiy	ECAC	33	3	10	13	48	....	....	....	....	....
2002-03	Harvard University	ECAC	33	4	11	15	52	....	....	....	....	....
2003-04	Harvard University	ECAC	34	4	7	11	44	....	....	....	....	....

SMITH, Tim (SMIHTH, TIHM) VAN.

Center. Shoots left. 5'9", 160 lbs. Born, Whitecourt, Alta., July 21, 1981.
(Vancouver's 7th choice, 272nd overall, in 2000 Entry Draft).

			Regular Season					Playoffs				
Season	Club	League	GP	G	A	TP	PIM	GP	G	A	TP	PIM
1997-98	Lebret Eagles	SJHL	36	6	7	13	12	....	....	....	....	....
1998-99	Spokane Chiefs	WHL	57	5	20	25	21	....	....	....	....	....
99-2000	Spokane Chiefs	WHL	71	26	70	96	65	15	7	7	14	32
2000-01	Spokane Chiefs	WHL	38	19	37	56	65	....	....	....	....	....
	Swift Current	WHL	30	12	22	34	38	19	10	14	24	38
2001-02	Swift Current	WHL	67	28	47	75	123	12	7	6	13	20
2002-03	Columbia Inferno	ECHL	68	22	37	59	44	17	5	11	16	16
	Manitoba Moose	AHL	3	0	0	0	0	....	....	....	....	....
2003-04	Columbia Inferno	ECHL	69	33	*62	*95	112	4	1	3	4	8
	Manitoba Moose	AHL	1	0	0	0	0	....	....	....	....	....

ECHL First All-Star Team (2004)

SOCHOR, Jan (soh-KHAWR, YAN) TOR.

Left wing. Shoots right. 6', 198 lbs. Born, Usti nad Labem, Czech., January 17, 1980.
(Toronto's 6th choice, 161st overall, in 1999 Entry Draft).

			Regular Season					Playoffs				
Season	Club	League	GP	G	A	TP	PIM	GP	G	A	TP	PIM
1996-97	HC Slavia Praha Jr.	Czech-Jr.	26	11	12	23	....	....	....	....	....	....
1997-98	HC Slavia Praha Jr.	Czech-Jr.	33	26	12	38	....	....	....	....	....	....
	HC Slavia Praha	Czech	14	1	1	2	2	1	0	0	0	0
1998-99	HC Slavia Praha Jr.	Czech-Jr.	7	2	1	3	2	....	....	....	....	....
	HC Slavia Praha	Czech	47	10	10	20	14	....	....	....	....	....
99-2000	HC Slavia Praha Jr.	Czech-Jr.	12	5	5	10	6	....	....	....	....	....
	HC Slavia Praha	Czech	39	7	11	18	37	....	....	....	....	....
	Slovan Labem	Czech-2	6	2	3	5	8	....	....	....	....	....
2000-01	Vsetin Jr.	Czech-Jr.	8	5	3	8	0	....	....	....	....	....
	HC Slovnaft Vsetin	Czech	41	5	4	9	28	3	0	0	0	0
2001-02	HC Vsetin	Czech	27	4	0	4	8	....	....	....	....	....
2002-03	HC Vsetin	Czech	17	2	0	2	10	....	....	....	....	....
	SK Kaden	Czech-2	18	4	6	10	10	....	....	....	....	....
2003-04	FPS Forssa	Finland-2	26	5	8	13	26	....	....	....	....	....
	HC Prostejov	Czech-2	5	1	1	2	2	....	....	....	....	....
	HC Vsetin	Czech	5	1	0	1	0	....	....	....	....	....

SODERBERG, Anders (SOH-dehr-buhrg, AN-duhrs) BOS.

Right wing. Shoots right. 5'6", 161 lbs. Born, Ornskoldsvik, Sweden, October 7, 1975.
(Boston's 10th choice, 234th overall, in 1996 Entry Draft).

			Regular Season					Playoffs				
Season	Club	League	GP	G	A	TP	PIM	GP	G	A	TP	PIM
1992-93	MoDo Jr.	Swede-Jr.	13	6	12	18	2	....	....	....	....	....
	MoDo	Sweden	1	0	0	0	0	....	....	....	....	....
1993-94	MoDo Jr.	Swede-Jr.	9	8	5	13	10	....	....	....	....	....
	MoDo	Sweden	19	0	0	0	2	9	0	0	0	0
1994-95	MoDo	Sweden	38	9	14	23	2	....	....	....	....	....
1995-96	MoDo	Sweden	40	10	18	28	10	8	3	3	6	0
1996-97	MoDo	Sweden	39	9	13	22	16	....	....	....	....	....
1997-98	MoDo	Sweden	44	15	10	25	4	9	5	1	6	2
1998-99	MoDo	Sweden	49	6	15	21	18	13	3	6	9	4
99-2000	MoDo	Sweden	43	15	10	25	18	9	1	2	3	0
2000-01	MoDo	Sweden	42	11	4	15	12	6	1	6	7	0
2001-02	MoDo	Sweden	30	6	9	15	6	11	0	0	0	0
2002-03	MoDo	Sweden	49	10	19	29	4	6	0	3	3	0
2003-04	MoDo	Sweden	47	6	12	18	8	6	3	2	5	0

SODERBERG, Carl (SOH-dehr-buhrg, KARL) ST.L.

Center. Shoots left. 6'3", 198 lbs. Born, Malmo, Sweden, October 12, 1985.
(St. Louis' 2nd choice, 49th overall, in 2004 Entry Draft).

			Regular Season					Playoffs				
Season	Club	League	GP	G	A	TP	PIM	GP	G	A	TP	PIM
2000-01	Skane	Exhib.	8	1	2	3	2	....	....	....	....	....
	Malmo IF 18	Swede-Jr.	3	1	1	2	0	....	....	....	....	....
2001-02	Malmo IF 18	Swede-Jr.	13	9	20	29	18	....	....	....	....	....
	Malmo IF Jr.	Swede-Jr.	4	0	2	2	2	7	0	2	2	4
2002-03	Malmo 18	Swede-Jr.	4	6	3	9	25	....	....	....	....	....
	Malmo Jr.	Swede-Jr.	28	17	18	35	22	6	2	4	6	8
2003-04	Malmo Jr.	Swede-Jr.	27	23	25	48	30	6	1	2	3	10
	Malmo	Sweden	24	1	1	2	8	....	....	....	....	....
	Malmo	Swede-Q	8	1	1	2	4	....	....	....	....	....

SODERSTROM, Christian (SAW-duhr-struhm, KRIHS-tyehn) DET.

Left wing. Shoots left. 6'1", 176 lbs. Born, Sundsvall, Sweden, October 13, 1980.
(Detroit's 9th choice, 262nd overall, in 2002 Entry Draft).

			Regular Season					Playoffs				
Season	Club	League	GP	G	A	TP	PIM	GP	G	A	TP	PIM
1997-98	Timra IK Jr.	Swede-Jr.	27	7	10	17	22	....	....	....	....	....
1998-99	Timra IK Jr.	Swede-Jr.	STATISTICS NOT AVAILABLE									
	Timra IK	Swede-2	3	0	1	1	2	....	....	....	....	....
99-2000	Timra IK Jr.	Swede-Jr.	3	4	3	7	0	....	....	....	....	....
	Timra IK	Swede-2	29	5	3	8	2	....	....	....	....	....
	Timra IK	Swede-Q	14	3	3	6	2	10	1	0	1	2
2000-01	Timra IK	Sweden	46	6	6	12	16	....	....	....	....	....
2001-02	Timra IK	Sweden	48	8	8	16	16	....	....	....	....	....
	Timra IK	Swede-Q	....	....	....	....	....	9	0	1	1	4
2002-03	Timra IK	Sweden	44	5	10	15	6	10	1	2	3	2
2003-04	Timra IK	Sweden	48	7	6	13	62	10	1	1	2	4

SOIN, Sergei (SOY-ihn, SAIR-gay) NSH.

Center/Left wing. Shoots left. 6', 175 lbs. Born, Moscow, USSR, March 31, 1982.
(Colorado's 3rd choice, 50th overall, in 2000 Entry Draft).

			Regular Season					Playoffs				
Season	Club	League	GP	G	A	TP	PIM	GP	G	A	TP	PIM
1997-98	Krylja Sovetov 2	Russia-3	2	0	0	0	0	....	....	....	....	....
1998-99	Krylja Sovetov	Russia	34	1	4	5	12	....	....	....	....	....
99-2000	Krylja Sovetov 2	Russia-3	8	2	3	5	12	....	....	....	....	....
	Krylja Sovetov	Russia-2	32	8	8	16	28	14	0	2	2	6
2000-01	Krylja Sovetov 2	Russia-3	8	2	3	5	12	....	....	....	....	....
	Krylja Sovetov	Russia-2	19	6	3	9	8	11	2	2	4	2
2001-02	Krylja Sovetov 2	Russia-3	5	2	6	8	20	....	....	....	....	....
	Krylja Sovetov	Russia	41	5	7	12	8	....	....	....	....	....
2002-03	Krylja Sovetov	Russia	49	8	6	14	40	....	....	....	....	....
2003-04	CSKA Moscow	Russia	49	1	6	7	32	....	....	....	....	....

Traded to **Nashville** by **Colorado** for Tomas Slovak, June 21, 2003.

SOMERVUORI, Eero (soh-muhr-VOH-ree, AIR-oh) T.B.

Right wing. Shoots right. 5'10", 185 lbs. Born, Jarvenpaa, Finland, February 7, 1979.
(Tampa Bay's 9th choice, 170th overall, in 1997 Entry Draft).

			Regular Season					Playoffs				
Season	Club	League	GP	G	A	TP	PIM	GP	G	A	TP	PIM
1993-94	Jokerit Helsinki-C	Finn-Jr.	29	23	31	54	16	....	....	....	....	....
1994-95	Jokerit Helsinki-C	Finn-Jr.	17	23	16	39	8	6	7	3	10	2
	Jokerit Helsinki-B	Finn-Jr.	15	8	10	18	4	....	....	....	....	....
	Jokerit Helsinki Jr.	Finn-Jr.	10	1	1	2	2	1	0	1	1	0
1995-96	Jokerit Helsinki Jr.	Finn-Jr.	28	14	12	26	10	9	4	1	5	4
	Jokerit Helsinki-B	Finn-Jr.	13	10	13	23	6	....	....	....	....	....
	Haukat Jarvenpaa	Finland-2	1	0	0	0	0	....	....	....	....	....
	Jokerit Helsinki	Finland	6	1	2	3	0	....	....	....	....	....
1996-97	Jokerit Helsinki Jr.	Finn-Jr.	28	20	19	39	30	5	3	0	3	4
	Jokerit Helsinki	Finland	35	1	1	2	2	5	0	0	0	0
	Jokerit Helsinki	EuroHL	3	0	0	0	0	2	2	0	0	0
1997-98	Jokerit Helsinki	Finland	42	3	7	10	12	8	2	1	3	6
	Jokerit Helsinki	EuroHL	5	0	0	0	0	....	....	....	....	....
	Jokerit Helsinki Jr.	Finn-Jr.	14	4	8	12	2	....	....	....	....	....
1998-99	Jokerit Helsinki	Finland	50	7	8	15	24	3	1	0	1	6
	Jokerit Helsinki	EuroHL	6	0	0	0	0	1	0	0	0	0
	Jokerit Helsinki Jr.	Finn-Jr.	4	1	1	2	2	4	3	0	3	2
99-2000	Jokerit Helsinki	Finland	54	6	6	12	10	11	1	0	1	0
2000-01	HPK Hameenlinna	Finland	56	14	6	20	35	....	....	....	....	....
2001-02	HPK Hameenlinna	Finland	56	25	23	48	34	8	2	2	4	6
2002-03	HPK Hameenlinna	Finland	56	21	24	45	42	13	2	3	5	0
2003-04	Hamilton Bulldogs	AHL	79	19	14	33	14	10	2	3	5	0

SOUCY, J.F. (SOO-cee, JAY-EHF) T.B.

Center. Shoots left. 6'3", 180 lbs. Born, Riviere Du Loup, Que., March 25, 1983.
(Tampa Bay's 10th choice, 252nd overall, in 2001 Entry Draft).

			Regular Season					Playoffs				
Season	Club	League	GP	G	A	TP	PIM	GP	G	A	TP	PIM
1998-99	Levis	QAAA	42	6	17	23	82	....	....	....	....	....
99-2000	Val-d'Or Foreurs	QMJHL	55	1	4	5	9	....	....	....	....	....
2000-01	Val-d'Or Foreurs	QMJHL	38	3	4	7	57	....	....	....	....	....
	Montreal Rocket	QMJHL	27	3	8	11	37	....	....	....	....	....
2001-02	Montreal Rocket	QMJHL	49	8	13	21	94	7	0	2	2	8
2002-03	Montreal Rocket	QMJHL	65	24	31	55	168	7	0	2	2	24
2003-04	Pensacola	ECHL	57	10	10	20	199	5	0	0	0	23
	Hershey Bears	AHL	12	2	2	4	29	....	....	....	....	....

SOUTHERN, Dirk (SUH-thuhrn, DUHRK) ANA.

Center. Shoots right. 6', 177 lbs. Born, Winnipeg, Man., August 9, 1983.
(Anaheim's 7th choice, 218th overall, in 2003 Entry Draft).

			Regular Season					Playoffs				
Season	Club	League	GP	G	A	TP	PIM	GP	G	A	TP	PIM
2000-01	Winnipeg Saints	MJHL	STATISTICS NOT AVAILABLE									
2001-02	Lincoln Stars	USHL	60	22	36	58	46	4	1	1	2	2
2002-03	Northern Michigan	CCHA	41	11	22	33	55	....	....	....	....	....
2003-04	Northern Michigan	CCHA	37	10	15	25	32	....	....	....	....	....

CCHA All-Rookie Team (2003)

SPANG, Dan (SPANG, DAN) S.J.

Defense. Shoots left. 6', 205 lbs. Born, Winchester, MA, August 18, 1983.
(San Jose's 2nd choice, 52nd overall, in 2002 Entry Draft).

			Regular Season					Playoffs				
Season	Club	League	GP	G	A	TP	PIM	GP	G	A	TP	PIM
2000-01	Winchester High	Hi-School	24	8	37	45	14	....	....	....	....	....
2001-02	Winchester High	Hi-School	6	9	8	17	14	....	....	....	....	....
2002-03	Boston University	H-East	27	3	6	9	14	....	....	....	....	....
2003-04	Boston University	H-East	38	5	9	14	12	....	....	....	....	....

• Missed majority of 2001-02 season recovering from head injuries suffered in automobile accident, October 2001.

SPENCER, Steve (SPEHN-suhr, STEEV) N.J.

Defense. Shoots left. 6'3", 220 lbs. Born, Regina, Sask., June 16, 1982.
(Nashville's 8th choice, 266th overall, in 2002 Entry Draft).

			Regular Season					Playoffs				
Season	Club	League	GP	G	A	TP	PIM	GP	G	A	TP	PIM
2000-01	La Ronge	SJHL	48	3	6	9	176	....	....	....	....	....
2001-02	Swift Current	WHL	65	1	4	5	226	11	0	0	0	36
2002-03	Swift Current	WHL	72	2	2	4	187	4	0	0	0	17
2003-04	South Carolina	ECHL	35	0	5	5	119	7	0	0	0	13

• Missed majority of 2003-04 season recovering from wrist injury suffered in game vs. Augusta (ECHL), December 20, 2003. Signed as a free agent by **New Jersey**, July 27, 2004.

SPRUKTS, Janis (SPRUKTS, YAN-ish) FLA.

Center. Shoots left. 6'3", 224 lbs. Born, Riga, Latvia, January 31, 1982.
(Florida's 7th choice, 234th overall, in 2000 Entry Draft).

			Regular Season					Playoffs				
Season	Club	League	GP	G	A	TP	PIM	GP	G	A	TP	PIM
99-2000	Lukko Rauma Jr.	Finn-Jr.	26	2	5	7	6	3	0	0	0	0
	Essamika Jr.	EEHL-2	2	4	4	8	0	....	....	....	....	....
2000-01	Lukko Rauma Jr.	Finn-Jr.	36	15	22	37	24	3	0	0	0	0
	Lukko Rauma	Finland	9	0	0	0	2	....	....	....	....	....
2001-02	Acadie-Bathurst	QMJHL	63	35	44	79	46	16	14	8	22	12
	Sport Vassa	Finland-2	21	5	6	11	8	....	....	....	....	....
2002-03	Sport Vassa	Finland-2	21	5	6	11	8	....	....	....	....	....
	Acadie-Bathurst	QMJHL	30	9	29	38	12	11	3	5	8	0
2003-04	ASK Ogre	Latvia	5	2	4	6	0	....	....	....	....	....
	Odense IK	Denmark	2	0	1	1	2	....	....	....	....	....

• Released by **Sport Vassa** (Finland-2) and returned to **Acadie-Bathurst** (QMJHL), January 3, 2003.

SPRUNGER, Julien (SRUHN-guhr, JEW-lee-ehn) MIN.

Right wing. Shoots right. 6'4", 197 lbs. Born, Fribourg, Switzerland, January 4, 1986.
(Minnesota's 7th choice, 117th overall, in 2004 Entry Draft).

			Regular Season					Playoffs				
Season	Club	League	GP	G	A	TP	PIM	GP	G	A	TP	PIM
2002-03	Fribourg	Swiss	2	0	0	0	0	....	....	....	....	....
	Fribourg Jr.	Swiss-Jr.	24	21	19	40	32	....	....	....	....	....
	HC Dudingen	Swiss-3	9	7	1	8	....	2	1	1	2	....
2003-04	Fribourg	Swiss	42	2	3	5	14	4	0	0	0	4

STAAL, Kim (STAHL, KIHM) MTL.

Center. Shoots right. 6', 185 lbs. Born, Herlev, Denmark, March 10, 1978.
(Montreal's 4th choice, 92nd overall, in 1996 Entry Draft).

			Regular Season					Playoffs				
Season	Club	League	GP	G	A	TP	PIM	GP	G	A	TP	PIM
1994-95	Malmo IF Jr.	Swede-Jr.	17	4	2	6	4	....	....	....	....	....
1995-96	Malmo IF Jr.	Swede-Jr.	30	24	20	44	14	....	....	....	....	....
1996-97	Malmo IF Jr.	Swede-Jr.	3	6	4	10	2	....	....	....	....	....
	Malmo IF	Sweden	4	0	1	1	2	....	....	....	....	....
1997-98	Malmo IF Jr.	Swede-Jr.	20	13	11	24	36	....	....	....	....	....
	Malmo IF	Sweden	13	0	1	1	1	....	....	....	....	....
1998-99	Malmo IF	Sweden	48	1	5	6	14	4	0	0	0	0
99-2000	Malmo IF	Sweden	50	14	10	24	24	6	1	1	2	4
2000-01	Malmo IF	Sweden	48	16	15	31	32	9	4	2	6	4
2001-02	MoDo	Sweden	49	14	23	37	16	12	3	7	10	2
2002-03	MoDo	Sweden	14	4	5	9	4	6	1	0	1	0
	Ornskoldviks SK	Swede-2	2	3	0	3	0	....	....	....	....	....
2003-04	Malmo	Sweden	45	15	8	23	14	....	....	....	....	....
	Malmo	Swede-Q	10	7	7	14	4	....	....	....	....	....

STAFFORD, Drew (STA-fuhrd, DROO) BUF.

Right wing. Shoots right. 6'1", 202 lbs. Born, Milwaukee, WI, October 30, 1985.
(Buffalo's 1st choice, 13th overall, in 2004 Entry Draft).

			Regular Season					Playoffs				
Season	Club	League	GP	G	A	TP	PIM	GP	G	A	TP	PIM
2000-01	Shat.-St. Mary's	Hi-School	STATISTICS NOT AVAILABLE									
2001-02	Shat.-St. Mary's	Hi-School	45	35	53	88	30	....	....	....	....	....
2002-03	Shat.-St. Mary's	Hi-School	65	49	67	116	....	....	....	....	....	....
2003-04	North Dakota	WCHA	36	11	21	32	30	....	....	....	....	....

STAFFORD, Garrett (STA-fuhrd, GAIR-reht) S.J.

Defense. Shoots right. 6', 190 lbs. Born, Los Angeles, CA, January 28, 1980.

			Regular Season					Playoffs				
Season	Club	League	GP	G	A	TP	PIM	GP	G	A	TP	PIM
1996-97	Des Moines	USHL	37	1	10	11	40	5	0	0	0	0
1997-98	Des Moines	USHL	53	6	17	23	89	12	1	3	4	42
1998-99	Des Moines	USHL	56	8	33	41	54	13	2	2	4	18
99-2000	New Hampshire	H-East	38	3	9	12	28	....	....	....	....	....
2000-01	New Hampshire	H-East	37	5	21	26	44	....	....	....	....	....
2001-02	New Hampshire	H-East	36	5	22	27	42	....	....	....	....	....
2002-03	New Hampshire	H-East	23	1	15	16	24	....	....	....	....	....
2003-04	Cleveland Barons	AHL	73	12	34	46	71	6	0	0	0	6

AHL All-Rookie Team (2004) • AHL Second All-Star Team (2004)

Signed as a free agent by **Cleveland** (AHL), October 10, 2003. Signed as a free agent by **San Jose**, December 9, 2003.

STALS, Juris (STAHLS, YOO-rihs) NYR

Left wing. Shoots left. 6'3", 187 lbs. Born, Riga, Latvia, August 4, 1982.
(NY Rangers' 11th choice, 269th overall, in 2001 Entry Draft).

			Regular Season					Playoffs				
Season	Club	League	GP	G	A	TP	PIM	GP	G	A	TP	PIM
99-2000	Lukko Rauma Jr.	Finn-Jr.	2	1	0	1	2	....	....	....	....	....
2000-01	Lukko Rauma Jr.	Finn-Jr.	45	23	22	45	26	3	1	0	1	0
2001-02	Sarnia Sting	OHL	60	23	22	45	12	5	0	1	1	2
2002-03	Sport Vassa	Finland-2	23	3	3	6	16	....	....	....	....	....
	Owen Sound	OHL	25	8	15	23	14	4	0	4	4	4
	Hartford Wolf Pack	AHL	2	0	1	1	0	....	....	....	....	....
2003-04	Hartford Wolf Pack	AHL	62	4	14	18	24	1	0	0	0	0

STASTNY, Yan (STAS-nee, YAHN) BOS.

Center. Shoots left. 5'11", 175 lbs. Born, Quebec City, Que., September 30, 1982.
(Boston's 6th choice, 259th overall, in 2002 Entry Draft).

			Regular Season					Playoffs				
Season	Club	League	GP	G	A	TP	PIM	GP	G	A	TP	PIM
99-2000	St. Louis Sting	NAJHL	45	12	23	35	77	....	....	....	....	....
2000-01	St. Louis Sting	NAJHL	6	0	2	2	23	....	....	....	....	....
	Omaha Lancers	USHL	44	17	14	31	101	11	6	6	12	12
2001-02	Notre Dame	CCHA	33	6	11	17	38	....	....	....	....	....
2002-03	Notre Dame	CCHA	39	14	9	23	44	....	....	....	....	....
2003-04	Nurnberg	Germany	44	9	20	29	83	6	0	1	1	6

Signed as a free agent by **Nurenburg** (Germany), September 18, 2003.

STASYUK, Denis (stah-S'YUHK, DEH-nihs) FLA.

Center. Shoots left. 6'1", 165 lbs. Born, Novokuznetsk, USSR, September 2, 1985.
(Florida's 9th choice, 171st overall, in 2003 Entry Draft).

			Regular Season					Playoffs				
Season	Club	League	GP	G	A	TP	PIM	GP	G	A	TP	PIM
2002-03	Novokuznetsk 2	Russia-3	STATISTICS NOT AVAILABLE									
	Novokuznetsk	Russia	11	1	0	1	0	....	....	....	....	....
	Novokuznetsk 17	Rus-Jr.	5	1	2	3	4	....	....	....	....	....
2003-04	Novokuznetsk	Russia	5	0	0	0	0	....	....	....	....	....
	Novokuznetsk 2	Russia-3	STATISTICS NOT AVAILABLE									

STECKEL, Dave (STEH-kuhl, DAYV) L.A.

Center. Shoots left. 6'5", 200 lbs. Born, Westbend, WI, March 15, 1982.
(Los Angeles' 2nd choice, 30th overall, in 2001 Entry Draft).

			Regular Season					Playoffs				
Season	Club	League	GP	G	A	TP	PIM	GP	G	A	TP	PIM
1998-99	U.S. National U-17	USDP	51	3	14	17	18	....	....	....	....	....
	U.S. National U-18	USDP	2	0	0	0	2	....	....	....	....	....
99-2000	U.S. National U-18	USDP	52	13	13	26	94	....	....	....	....	....
2000-01	Ohio State	CCHA	33	17	18	35	80	....	....	....	....	....
2001-02	Ohio State	CCHA	36	6	16	22	75	....	....	....	....	....
2002-03	Ohio State	CCHA	36	10	8	18	50	....	....	....	....	....
2003-04	Ohio State	CCHA	41	17	13	30	44	....	....	....	....	....

CCHA All-Rookie Team (2001)

STEEN, Alexander (STEEN, al-ehx-AN-duhr) TOR.

Center. Shoots left. 5'11", 183 lbs. Born, Winnipeg, Man., March 1, 1984.
(Toronto's 1st choice, 24th overall, in 2002 Entry Draft).

			Regular Season					Playoffs				
Season	Club	League	GP	G	A	TP	PIM	GP	G	A	TP	PIM
99-2000	Goteborg Jr.	Swede-Jr.	8	5	7	12	0	....	....	....	....	....
	V. Frolunda-18	Swede-Jr.	14	3	5	8	16	....	....	....	....	....
2000-01	V. Frolunda Jr.	Swede-Jr.	23	11	12	23	15	3	1	0	1	2
	V. Frolunda-18	Swede-Jr.	6	3	3	6	9	....	....	....	....	....
2001-02	V. Frolunda Jr.	Swede-Jr.	23	21	17	38	47	2	1	1	2	2
	Vastra Frolunda	Sweden	26	0	3	3	14	10	1	2	3	0
2002-03	Vastra Frolunda	Sweden	45	5	10	15	18	16	2	3	5	4
	V. Frolunda Jr.	Swede-Jr.	2	0	2	2	0	....	....	....	....	....
2003-04	Vastra Frolunda	Sweden	48	10	14	24	50	10	4	6	10	14

STEEN, Calle (STEEN, CAL-lee) DET.

Right wing. Shoots left. 5'11", 198 lbs. Born, Stockholm, Sweden, May 16, 1980.
(Detroit's 6th choice, 142nd overall, in 1998 Entry Draft).

			Regular Season					Playoffs				
Season	Club	League	GP	G	A	TP	PIM	GP	G	A	TP	PIM
1995-96	Hammarby Jr.	Swede-Jr.	5	0	0	0	0	....	....	....	....	....
1996-97	Hammarby Jr.	Swede-Jr.	24	4	9	13	....	....	....	....	....	....
1997-98	Hammarby	Swede-2	21	1	3	4	22	....	....	....	....	....
1998-99	Hammarby	Swede-2	33	4	16	20	28	5	0	2	2	6
99-2000	Mora IK	Swede-2	32	4	4	8	48	9	0	2	2	10
2000-01	Bofors IK	Swede-2	31	4	7	11	69	....	....	....	....	....
	JYP Jyvaskyla	Finland	5	0	0	0	0	....	....	....	....	....
2001-02	Bofors IK	Swede-2	53	12	22	34	78	6	2	2	4	12
2002-03	Bofors IK	Swede-2	27	12	17	29	71	....	....	....	....	....
	Bofors IK	Swede-Q	6	2	3	5	41	....	....	....	....	....
	Farjestad	Sweden	11	0	2	2	2	12	1	5	6	12
2003-04	Farjestad	Sweden	43	2	10	12	42	15	2	3	5	41
	Bofors IK	Swede-2	4	1	2	3	4	....	....	....	....	....

STEEVES, Ryan (STEEVZ, RIGH-uhn) COL.

Center/Left wing. Shoots left. 6', 195 lbs. Born, Ottawa, Ont., December 31, 1982.
(Colorado's 8th choice, 227th overall, in 2002 Entry Draft).

			Regular Season					Playoffs				
Season	Club	League	GP	G	A	TP	PIM	GP	G	A	TP	PIM
1998-99	Ottawa Jr. Sens	OCJHL	51	17	12	29	45	....	....	....	....	....
99-2000	Ottawa Jr. Sens	OCJHL	55	36	39	75	87	....	....	....	....	....
2000-01	Yale University	ECAC	23	3	2	5	10	....	....	....	....	....
2001-02	Yale University	ECAC	31	9	13	22	20	....	....	....	....	....
2002-03	Yale University	ECAC	32	15	23	38	36	....	....	....	....	....
2003-04	Yale University	ECAC	31	10	16	26	44	....	....	....	....	....

STEHLIK, Richard (SHTEH-lihk, RIH-chuhrd) NSH.

Defense. Shoots left. 6'4", 245 lbs. Born, Skalica, Czech., June 22, 1984.
(Nashville's 5th choice, 76th overall, in 2003 Entry Draft).

			Regular Season					Playoffs				
Season	Club	League	GP	G	A	TP	PIM	GP	G	A	TP	PIM
99-2000	HK 36 Skalica Jr.	Slovak-Jr.	50	10	5	15	....	....	....	....	....	....
2000-01	HK 36 Skalica	Slovak	45	1	1	2	14	3	0	0	0	2
2001-02	HK 36 Skalica	Slovak	35	1	0	1	12	....	....	....	....	....
2002-03	Sherbrooke	QMJHL	43	8	16	24	105	12	1	5	6	20
2003-04	Lewiston	QMJHL	44	11	25	36	109	7	0	1	1	12

STEMPNIAK, Lee (STEHMP-nee-ak, LEE) ST.L.

Right wing. Shoots right. 6', 190 lbs. Born, Buffalo, NY, February 4, 1983.
(St. Louis' 7th choice, 148th overall, in 2003 Entry Draft).

			Regular Season					Playoffs				
Season	Club	League	GP	G	A	TP	PIM	GP	G	A	TP	PIM
2000-01	Buffalo Lightning	OPJHL	48	34	51	86	36	....	....	....	....	....
2001-02	Dartmouth	ECAC	32	12	9	21	8	....	....	....	....	....
2002-03	Dartmouth	ECAC	34	21	28	49	32	....	....	....	....	....
2003-04	Dartmouth	ECAC	34	16	22	38	42	....	....	....	....	....

ECAC First All-Star Team (2004) • NCAA East First All-American Team (2004)

STEPHENSON, Logan (STEE-vehn-suhn, LOH-guhn) PHX.

Defense. Shoots left. 6'2", 185 lbs. Born, Saskatoon, Sask., February 19, 1986.
(Phoenix's 2nd choice, 35th overall, in 2004 Entry Draft).

			Regular Season					Playoffs				
Season	Club	League	GP	G	A	TP	PIM	GP	G	A	TP	PIM
2001-02	Notre Dame	SMHL	37	4	2	6	74	....	....	....	....	....
	Tri-City Americans	WHL	....	....	....	....	....	3	0	0	0	0
2002-03	Tri-City Americans	WHL	50	0	6	6	121	....	....	....	....	....
2003-04	Tri-City Americans	WHL	69	3	8	11	112	11	1	1	2	10

STEPHENSON, Shay (STEE-vehn-suhn, SHAY) CAR.

Left wing. Shoots left. 6'4", 200 lbs. Born, Outlook, Sask., September 13, 1983.
(Carolina's 7th choice, 198th overall, in 2003 Entry Draft).

			Regular Season					Playoffs				
Season	Club	League	GP	G	A	TP	PIM	GP	G	A	TP	PIM
99-2000	Notre Dame	SMHL	42	23	7	30	46	....	....	....	....	....
2000-01	Red Deer Rebels	WHL	44	1	4	5	30	22	0	0	0	15
2001-02	Red Deer Rebels	WHL	59	9	10	19	55	23	0	3	3	14
2002-03	Red Deer Rebels	WHL	67	17	15	32	84	23	6	5	11	33
2003-04	Red Deer Rebels	WHL	60	11	19	30	34	19	5	7	12	16

• Re-entered NHL Entry Draft. Originally Edmonton's 11th choice, 278th overall, in 2001 Entry Draft.

STEPP, Joel (STEHP, JOHL) ANA.

Center. Shoots left. 6', 215 lbs. Born, Estevan, Sask., February 11, 1983.
(Anaheim's 3rd choice, 69th overall, in 2001 Entry Draft).

			Regular Season					Playoffs				
Season	Club	League	GP	G	A	TP	PIM	GP	G	A	TP	PIM
1998-99	Estevan	SMBHL	60	65	70	135	120	....	....	....	....	....
	Red Deer Rebels	WHL	2	0	0	0	0	....	....	....	....	....
99-2000	Red Deer Rebels	WHL	65	11	13	24	59	4	1	0	1	8
2000-01	Red Deer Rebels	WHL	70	24	13	37	89	22	6	3	9	24
2001-02	Red Deer Rebels	WHL	70	27	26	53	59	23	11	11	22	24
2002-03	Red Deer Rebels	WHL	24	4	11	15	18	23	6	7	13	26
2003-04	Cincinnati	AHL	65	7	7	14	28	9	1	1	2	2

• Missed majority of 2002-03 season recovering from wrist surgery, September 12, 2002.

STERLING, Brett (STUHR-lihng, BRET) ATL.

Left wing. Shoots left. 5'7", 175 lbs. Born, Los Angeles, CA, April 24, 1984.
(Atlanta's 5th choice, 145th overall, in 2003 Entry Draft).

			Regular Season					Playoffs				
Season	Club	League	GP	G	A	TP	PIM	GP	G	A	TP	PIM
99-2000	L.A. Jr. Kings	SCAHA	35	45	25	70	....	....	....	....	....	....
2000-01	U.S. National U-17	USDP	60	26	36	62	66	....	....	....	....	....
2001-02	U.S. National U-18	USDP	50	29	19	48	36	....	....	....	....	....
2002-03	Colorado College	WCHA	36	27	11	38	30	....	....	....	....	....
2003-04	Colorado College	WCHA	30	16	12	28	40	....	....	....	....	....

WCHA All-Rookie Team (2003)

STEVENSON, Grant (STEE-vehn-suhn, GRANT) S.J.

Center. Shoots right. 5'11", 170 lbs. Born, Spruce Grove, Alta., October 15, 1981.

			Regular Season					Playoffs				
Season	Club	League	GP	G	A	TP	PIM	GP	G	A	TP	PIM
1998-99	Spruce Grove	RAMHL	26	15	32	47	90	8	10	10	20	30
99-2000	Bonnyville	AJHL	63	20	38	58	....	....	....	....	....	....
2000-01	Grand Prairie	AJHL	53	24	49	73	62	15	7	2	9	38
2001-02	Minnesota State	WCHA	38	8	8	16	36	....	....	....	....	....
2002-03	Minnesota State	WCHA	38	27	36	63	38	....	....	....	....	....
2003-04	Cleveland Barons	AHL	71	13	26	39	45	9	0	7	7	6

WCHA First All-Star Team (2003) • NCAA West Second All-American Team (2003)

Signed as a free agent by **San Jose**, April 18, 2003.

STEWART, Anthony (STEW-ahrt, AN-toh-nee) FLA.

Center. Shoots right. 6'1", 225 lbs. Born, Lasalle, Que., January 5, 1985.
(Florida's 2nd choice, 25th overall, in 2003 Entry Draft).

			Regular Season					Playoffs				
Season	Club	League	GP	G	A	TP	PIM	GP	G	A	TP	PIM
2000-01	North York	MTHL	34	30	70	100	....	....	....	....	....	....
2001-02	Kingston	OHL	65	19	24	43	12	1	0	0	0	0
2002-03	Kingston	OHL	68	32	38	70	47	....	....	....	....	....
2003-04	Kingston	OHL	53	35	23	58	76	5	3	4	7	7

STEWART, Danny (STEW-ahrt, DA-nee) MTL.

Left wing. Shoots left. 6', 178 lbs. Born, Charlottetown, PEI, April 23, 1985.
(Montreal's 6th choice, 123rd overall, in 2003 Entry Draft).

			Regular Season					Playoffs				
Season	Club	League	GP	G	A	TP	PIM	GP	G	A	TP	PIM
2001-02	Rimouski Oceanic	QMJHL	63	9	6	15	71	4	0	0	0	0
2002-03	Rimouski Oceanic	QMJHL	65	19	21	40	144	....	....	....	....	....
2003-04	Rimouski Oceanic	QMJHL	69	25	42	67	80	9	3	1	4	6

STOKES, Ryan (STOHKS, RIGH-uhn) MIN.

Defense. Shoots left. 6'4", 220 lbs. Born, Sarnia, Ont., June 23, 1983.

			Regular Season					Playoffs				
Season	Club	League	GP	G	A	TP	PIM	GP	G	A	TP	PIM
2001-02	Barrie Colts	OHL	53	0	5	5	31	20	0	0	0	16
2002-03	Mississauga	OHL	59	2	7	9	139	5	0	1	1	22
2003-04	Mississauga	OHL	66	4	20	24	179	24	2	9	11	74

Signed as a free agent by **Minnesota**, May 25, 2004.

STONE, Ryan (STOHN, RIGH-uhn) PIT.

Center. Shoots left. 6'2", 200 lbs. Born, Calgary, Alta., March 20, 1985.
(Pittsburgh's 2nd choice, 32nd overall, in 2003 Entry Draft).

			Regular Season					Playoffs				
Season	Club	League	GP	G	A	TP	PIM	GP	G	A	TP	PIM
2000-01	Cgy. North Stars	AMHL	34	37	28	55	90	....	....	....	....	....
2001-02	Brandon	WHL	65	11	27	38	128	19	0	3	3	39
2002-03	Brandon	WHL	54	14	31	45	158	12	4	2	6	20
2003-04	Brandon	WHL	50	20	38	58	125	11	1	3	4	24

STONER, Clayton (STOH-nuhr, KLAY-tuhn) MIN.

Defense. Shoots left. 6'3", 225 lbs. Born, Port Mcneil, B.C., February 19, 1985.
(Minnesota's 4th choice, 79th overall, in 2004 Entry Draft).

			Regular Season					Playoffs				
Season	Club	League	GP	G	A	TP	PIM	GP	G	A	TP	PIM
2000-01	Campbell River	VIJHL	47	4	16	20	57	....	....	....	....	....
2001-02	Campbell River	VIJHL	42	12	35	47	199	....	....	....	....	....
2002-03	Tri-City Americans	WHL	58	4	12	16	85	....	....	....	....	....
2003-04	Tri-City Americans	WHL	71	7	24	31	109	11	1	1	2	8

STONKUS, Alexei (STAWN-kuhs, al-EHX-ay) NYI

Defense. Shoots left. 5'11", 175 lbs. Born, Yaroslavl, USSR, May 6, 1984.
(NY Islanders' 4th choice, 189th overall, in 2002 Entry Draft).

			Regular Season					Playoffs				
Season	Club	League	GP	G	A	TP	PIM	GP	G	A	TP	PIM
2000-01	Russia Jr,	Exhib.	8	1	1	2	14	....	....	....	....	....
	Yaroslavl Jr.	Russia-Jr.	....	....	....	....	....	6	0	0	0	2
2001-02	Yaroslavl 2	Russia-3	12	3	3	6	8	....	....	....	....	....
	Elektrostal 2	Russia-3	4	1	0	1	6	....	....	....	....	....
	Elektrostal	Russia-2	31	1	3	4	26	....	....	....	....	....
2002-03	Yaroslavl	Russia	11	0	0	0	2	....	....	....	....	....
2003-04	Yaroslavl	Russia	2	0	0	0	0	....	....	....	....	....

STORTINI, Zachery (stohr-TEE-nee, ZA-kuh-ree) EDM.

Right wing. Shoots right. 6'3", 216 lbs. Born, Elliot Lake, Ont., September 11, 1985.
(Edmonton's 5th choice, 94th overall, in 2003 Entry Draft).

			Regular Season					Playoffs				
Season	Club	League	GP	G	A	TP	PIM	GP	G	A	TP	PIM
2000-01	Newmarket	OPJHL	34	3	10	13	68	....	....	....	....	....
2001-02	Sudbury Wolves	OHL	65	8	6	14	187	5	1	0	1	24
2002-03	Sudbury Wolves	OHL	62	13	16	29	222	....	....	....	....	....
2003-04	Sudbury Wolves	OHL	62	21	16	37	151	7	1	1	2	14
	Toronto	AHL	2	0	0	0	7	3	0	0	0	4

STRACHAN, Tyson (STRAWN, TIGH-suhn) CAR.

Defense. Shoots right. 6'3", 205 lbs. Born, Melfort, Sask., October 30, 1984.
(Carolina's 6th choice, 137th overall, in 2003 Entry Draft).

			Regular Season					Playoffs				
Season	Club	League	GP	G	A	TP	PIM	GP	G	A	TP	PIM
2001-02	Tisdale	SMHL	42	5	18	23	70	....	....	....	....	....
	Melville	SJHL	2	0	0	0	0	....	....	....	....	....
2002-03	Vernon Vipers	BCHL	56	6	22	28	99	....	....	....	....	....
2003-04	Ohio State	CCHA	30	2	5	7	8	....	....	....	....	....

STREIT, Martin (STREET, MAHR-tihn) CBJ

Right wing. Shoots right. 6'2", 202 lbs. Born, Vyskov, Czech., February 2, 1977.
(Philadelphia's 7th choice, 178th overall, in 1995 Entry Draft).

			Regular Season					Playoffs				
Season	Club	League	GP	G	A	TP	PIM	GP	G	A	TP	PIM
1995-96	HC Olomouc Jr.	Czech-Jr.	19	10	6	16	....	....	....	....	....	....
	HC Olomouc	Czech	10	0	0	0	....	....	....	....	....	....
1996-97	HC Olomouc	Czech	18	1	2	3	14	....	....	....	....	....
1997-98	HC Karlovy Vary	Czech	48	5	13	18	24	....	....	....	....	....
1998-99	HC Karlovy Vary	Czech	48	9	4	13	34	....	....	....	....	....
99-2000	HC Karlovy Vary	Czech	18	0	2	2	20	....	....	....	....	....
	HC Vitkovice	Czech	31	3	6	9	28	....	....	....	....	....
2000-01	HC Karlovy Vary	Czech	14	0	1	1	12	....	....	....	....	....
	HC Femax Havirov	Czech	11	0	0	0	6	....	....	....	....	....
2001-02	Vsetin	Czech	35	3	4	7	65	....	....	....	....	....
2002-03	Vsetin	Czech	47	8	5	13	48	4	0	0	0	2
2003-04	HC Prostejov	Czech-2	45	5	7	12	67	....	....	....	....	....

Selected by **Columbus** from **Philadelphia** in Expansion Draft, June 23, 2000.

STUART, Colin (STEW-ahrt, CAW-lihn) ATL.

Center. Shoots left. 6'1", 195 lbs. Born, Rochester, MN, July 8, 1982.
(Atlanta's 5th choice, 135th overall, in 2001 Entry Draft).

			Regular Season					Playoffs				
Season	Club	League	GP	G	A	TP	PIM	GP	G	A	TP	PIM
1998-99	Lourdes High	Hi-School	23	22	32	54	....	....	....	....	....	....
99-2000	Lincoln Stars	USHL	53	18	19	37	38	9	1	3	4	2
2000-01	Colorado College	WCHA	41	2	7	9	26	....	....	....	....	....
2001-02	Colorado College	WCHA	43	13	9	22	34	....	....	....	....	....
2002-03	Colorado College	WCHA	42	13	11	24	56	....	....	....	....	....
2003-04	Colorado College	WCHA	30	10	12	22	38	....	....	....	....	....

STUART, Mark (STEW-ahrt, MAHRK) BOS.

Defense. Shoots left. 6'1", 209 lbs. Born, Rochester, MN, April 27, 1984.
(Boston's 1st choice, 21st overall, in 2003 Entry Draft).

			Regular Season					Playoffs				
Season	Club	League	GP	G	A	TP	PIM	GP	G	A	TP	PIM
99-2000	Lourdes High	Hi-School	28	19	22	41	....	....	....	....	....	....
2000-01	U.S. National U-17	USDP	64	3	16	19	120	....	....	....	....	....
2001-02	U.S. National U-18	USDP	61	9	11	20	25	....	....	....	....	....
	United States	Nt-Team	15	3	4	7	51	....	....	....	....	....
2002-03	Colorado College	WCHA	38	3	17	20	81	....	....	....	....	....
2003-04	Colorado College	WCHA	37	4	11	15	100	....	....	....	....	....

WCHA All-Rookie Team (2003)

STUSSI, Rene (SHTOO-see, REH-nay) ANA.

Center. Shoots right. 5'11", 183 lbs. Born, Muri, Switz., December 13, 1978.
(Anaheim's 7th choice, 209th overall, in 1997 Entry Draft).

			Regular Season					Playoffs				
Season	Club	League	GP	G	A	TP	PIM	GP	G	A	TP	PIM
1995-96	HC Thurgau	Swiss-2	34	2	4	6	10	7	3	0	3	2
1996-97	HC Thurgau	Swiss-2	42	20	31	51	24	8	5	4	9	4
1997-98	Kloten Flyers Jr.	Swiss-Jr.	1	5	0	5	0	....	....	....	....	....
	EHC Bulach	Swiss-2	4	3	5	8	20	....	....	....	....	....
	EHC Kloten	Swiss	38	9	8	17	10	7	1	0	1	4
1998-99	EHC Kloten	Swiss	36	5	5	10	14	....	....	....	....	....
	ZSC Lions Zurich	Swiss	7	1	1	2	6	7	1	1	2	4
99-2000	EV Zug	Swiss	45	7	5	12	13	9	0	1	1	0
2000-01	EHC Chur	Swiss	36	7	7	14	26	11	1	1	2	26
2001-02	EHC Chur	Swiss	21	3	2	5	2	....	....	....	....	....
	EHC Basel	Swiss-2	16	11	11	22	2	....	....	....	....	....
	HC Ajoie	Swiss-2	....	....	....	....	....	8	6	4	10	0
2002-03	EHC Basel	Swiss-2	38	22	26	48	8	15	6	12	18	8
2003-04	EHC Basel	Swiss	45	6	10	16	18	....	....	....	....	....
	EHC Basel	Swiss-Q	8	1	0	1	2	....	....	....	....	....

SUBBOTIN, Dmitri (soo-BOH-tihn, dih-MEE-tree) CBJ

Left wing. Shoots left. 6'1", 183 lbs. Born, Tomsk, USSR, October 20, 1977.
(NY Rangers' 3rd choice, 76th overall, in 1996 Entry Draft).

			Regular Season					Playoffs				
Season	Club	League	GP	G	A	TP	PIM	GP	G	A	TP	PIM
1993-94	Yekaterinburg	CIS	12	0	3	3	4	....	....	....	....	....
1994-95	Yekaterinburg	CIS	52	9	6	15	75	2	0	0	0	2
1995-96	CSKA Moscow	CIS	41	6	5	11	62	3	0	0	0	0
1996-97	HC CSKA	Russia-2	8	1	0	1	8	....	....	....	....	....
	HC CSKA	Russia	17	5	3	8	22	2	0	0	0	2
1997-98	HC CSKA	Russia	16	1	1	2	47	....	....	....	....	....
1998-99	Dynamo Moscow	Russia	1	0	1	1	0	....	....	....	....	....
	Lada Togliatti	Russia	31	8	3	11	47	7	0	0	0	4
99-2000	Lada Togliatti	Russia	27	10	4	14	26	7	1	1	2	4
	Lada Togliatti 2	Russia-3	2	0	1	1	0	....	....	....	....	....
2000-01	Dynamo Moscow	Russia	39	11	15	26	48	....	....	....	....	....
2001-02	Magnitogorsk	Russia	38	8	3	11	18	9	0	2	2	10
2002-03	Cherepovets	Russia	10	0	1	1	31	....	....	....	....	....
	CSKA Moscow	Russia	20	3	9	12	6	....	....	....	....	....
2003-04	CSKA Moscow	Russia	20	0	3	3	14	....	....	....	....	....
	Avangard Omsk	Russia	26	6	6	12	36	11	2	3	5	6

Selected by **Columbus** from **NY Rangers** in Expansion Draft, June 23, 2000.

SULLIVAN, Mike (SUHL-ih-vuhn, MIGHK) L.A.

Center. Shoots left. 6'4", 190 lbs. Born, Scarborough, Ont., September 14, 1984.
(Los Angeles' 9th choice, 244th overall, in 2003 Entry Draft).

			Regular Season					Playoffs				
Season	Club	League	GP	G	A	TP	PIM	GP	G	A	TP	PIM
2001-02	Uxbridge Bruins	OJHL-C	42	22	27	49	20	....	....	....	....	....
2002-03	Stouffville Spirit	OPJHL	42	24	39	64	14	....	....	....	....	....
2003-04	Clarkson Knights	ECAC	40	8	11	19	14	....	....	....	....	....

SULLIVAN, Sean (SUHL-ih-vuhn, SHAWN) PHX.

Defense. Shoots left. 6', 180 lbs. Born, Boston, MA, March 29, 1984.
(Phoenix's 7th choice, 272nd overall, in 2003 Entry Draft).

			Regular Season					Playoffs				
Season	Club	League	GP	G	A	TP	PIM	GP	G	A	TP	PIM
2001-02	St. Sebastian's	Hi-School	31	3	11	14	4	....	....	....	....	....
2002-03	St. Sebastian's	Hi-School	41	9	30	39	59	....	....	....	....	....
2003-04	Boston University	H-East	36	2	5	7	14	....	....	....	....	....

SULZER, Alexander (ZUHLT-suhr, ahl-ehx-AN-duhr) NSH.

Defense. Shoots left. 6'1", 204 lbs. Born, Kaufbeuren, West Germany, May 30, 1984.
(Nashville's 7th choice, 92nd overall, in 2003 Entry Draft).

			Regular Season					Playoffs				
Season	Club	League	GP	G	A	TP	PIM	GP	G	A	TP	PIM
2000-01	ESV Kaufbeuren	German-3	38	3	6	9	20	....	....	....	....	....
	Kaufbeuren Jr.	Ger-Jr.	1	0	2	2	2	....	....	....	....	....
2001-02	ESV Kaufbeuren	German-3	19	1	9	10	14	....	....	....	....	....
	Kaufbeuren Jr.	Ger-Jr.	1	0	0	0	4	....	....	....	....	....
2002-03	ESV Kaufbeuren	German-2	26	5	3	8	38	1	0	1	1	4
	Hamburg Freezers	Germany	18	0	1	1	18	5	0	0	0	12
2003-04	DEG Metro Stars	Germany	46	4	1	5	56	4	0	0	0	8

SUNDIN, Andreas (suhn-DEEN, an-DRAY-uhs DET.

Left wing. Shoots left. 6', 185 lbs. Born, Linkoping, Sweden, March 15, 1984.
(Detroit's 4th choice, 170th overall, in 2003 Entry Draft).

			Regular Season					Playoffs				
Season	Club	League	GP	G	A	TP	PIM	GP	G	A	TP	PIM
99-2000	Linkopings-18	Swede-Jr.	3	2	1	3	2	....	....	....	....	....
2000-01	Linkopings Jr.	Swede-Jr.	STATISTICS NOT AVAILABLE									
2001-02	Linkopings Jr.	Swede-Jr.	19	31	13	44	8	....	....	....	....	....
2002-03	Linkopings Jr.	Swede-Jr.	4	4	3	7	6	....	....	....	....	....
	Linkopings HC	Sweden	8	0	1	1	0	....	....	....	....	....
	Linkopings HC	Swede-Q	7	1	0	1	0	....	....	....	....	....
2003-04	Linkopings HC Jr.	Swede-Jr.	22	16	16	32	14	....	....	....	....	....
	Vasteras	Swede-2	13	4	5	9	0	....	....	....	....	....
	Linkopings HC	Sweden	28	0	0	0	0	5	0	0	0	0

SUTER, Ryan (SOO-tuhr, RIGH-uhn) NSH.

Defense. Shoots left. 6'1", 183 lbs. Born, Madison, WI, January 21, 1985.
(Nashville's 1st choice, 7th overall, in 2003 Entry Draft).

			Regular Season					Playoffs				
Season	Club	League	GP	G	A	TP	PIM	GP	G	A	TP	PIM
2000-01	Culver Academy	Hi-School	26	13	32	45	....	....	....	....	....	....
2001-02	U.S. National U-17	USDP	43	4	21	25	96	....	....	....	....	....
	U.S. National U-18	USDP	27	4	10	14	6	....	....	....	....	....
2002-03	U.S. National U-18	USDP	51	9	22	31	136	....	....	....	....	....
2003-04	U. of Wisconsin	WCHA	39	3	16	19	93	....	....	....	....	....

WCHA All-Rookie Team (2004)

SVAGROVSKY, David (shva-GRAWF-skee, DAY-vihd) COL.

Right wing. Shoots right. 6'3", 205 lbs. Born, Prague, Czech., December 21, 1984.
(Colorado's 2nd choice, 131st overall, in 2003 Entry Draft).

			Regular Season					Playoffs				
Season	Club	League	GP	G	A	TP	PIM	GP	G	A	TP	PIM
99-2000	HC Slavia Praha Jr.	Czech-Jr.	31	1	3	4	12	....	....	....	....	....
2000-01	HC Slavia Praha Jr.	Czech-Jr.	48	20	29	49	82	7	5	1	6	10
2001-02	HC Slavia Praha Jr.	Czech-Jr.	44	7	6	13	38	....	....	....	....	....
2002-03	Seattle	WHL	68	17	25	42	47	15	4	6	10	12
2003-04	Seattle	WHL	52	6	11	17	42	....	....	....	....	....

SVENSK, Mikael (SVEHNSK, mih-KIGH-ehl) EDM.

Defense. Shoots right. 6'2", 191 lbs. Born, Gällstad, Sweden, February 28, 1983.
(Edmonton's 7th choice, 185th overall, in 2001 Entry Draft).

			Regular Season					Playoffs				
Season	Club	League	GP	G	A	TP	PIM	GP	G	A	TP	PIM
99-2000	V. Frolunda-18	Swede-Jr.	18	2	6	8	6	2	0	0	0	2
	V. Frolunda Jr.	Swede-Jr.	10	1	1	2	12	2	0	0	0	0
2000-01	V. Frolunda-18	Swede-Jr.	6	0	1	1	4	3	0	1	1	2
	V. Frolunda Jr.	Swede-Jr.	15	1	0	1	4	....	....	....	....	....
2001-02	V. Frolunda Jr.	Swede-Jr.	34	4	1	5	16	5	1	0	1	2
2002-03	Vastra Frolunda	Sweden	17	0	0	0	0	3	0	0	0	0
	V. Frolunda Jr.	Swede-Jr.	25	1	3	4	10	6	1	0	1	4
2003-04	Halmstad	Swede-2	45	2	2	4	18	....	....	....	....	....

SVENSSON, Jimmie (SVEHN-sohn, JIH-mee) DET.

Center. Shoots left. 6'1", 183 lbs. Born, Vasteras, Sweden, February 25, 1982.
(Detroit's 9th choice, 228th overall, in 2000 Entry Draft).

			Regular Season					Playoffs				
Season	Club	League	GP	G	A	TP	PIM	GP	G	A	TP	PIM
99-2000	Vasteras IK-18	Swede-Jr.	5	1	3	4	20	....	....	....	....	....
	Vasteras IK Jr.	Swede-Jr.	29	10	2	12	121	....	....	....	....	....
2000-01	Malmo IF Jr.	Swede-Jr.	23	3	1	4	74	....	....	....	....	....
2001-02	Malmo IF Jr.	Swede-Jr.	38	18	10	28	105	5	0	1	1	10
2002-03	IF Troja Ljungby	Swede-2	52	13	8	21	139	....	....	....	....	....
2003-04	Malmo	Sweden	31	2	0	2	6	....	....	....	....	....
	Malmo Jr.	Swede-Jr.	7	1	2	3	4	....	....	....	....	....
	IF Troja Ljungby	Swede-2	14	7	2	9	24	....	....	....	....	....

SWANSON, Jeremy (SWAWN-suhn, JAIR-eh-mee) FLA.

Defense. Shoots left. 6', 199 lbs. Born, Nipigon, Ont., June 21, 1984.
(Florida's choice, 169th overall, in 2002 Entry Draft).

			Regular Season					Playoffs				
Season	Club	League	GP	G	A	TP	PIM	GP	G	A	TP	PIM
99-2000	Thunder Bay Kings	TBMHA	48	8	16	24	19	....	....	....	....	....
2000-01	Sault Ste. Marie	OHL	54	1	6	7	60	....	....	....	....	....
2001-02	Barrie Colts	OHL	67	8	16	24	78	20	1	4	5	12
2002-03	Barrie Colts	OHL	68	7	34	41	129	....	....	....	....	....
2003-04	Barrie Colts	OHL	66	6	28	34	120	12	0	5	5	16

OHL Second All-Star Team (2004)

TALBOT, Maxime (TAL-buht, MAX-eem) PIT.

Center. Shoots left. 5'11", 176 lbs. Born, Lemoyne, Que., February 11, 1984.
(Pittsburgh's 9th choice, 234th overall, in 2002 Entry Draft).

			Regular Season					Playoffs				
Season	Club	League	GP	G	A	TP	PIM	GP	G	A	TP	PIM
99-2000	Antoine-Girouard	QAAA	42	19	21	40	32	7	3	6	9	0
2000-01	Rouyn-Noranda	QMJHL	40	9	15	24	78	....	....	....	....	....
	Hull Olympiques	QMJHL	24	6	7	13	60	5	1	0	1	2
2001-02	Hull Olympiques	QMJHL	65	24	36	60	174	12	4	6	10	51
2002-03	Hull Olympiques	QMJHL	69	46	58	104	130	20	14	*30	*44	33
2003-04	Gatineau	QMJHL	51	25	73	98	41	15	*11	*16	*27	0

QMJHL Second All-Star Team (2003, 2004)

TALLACKSON, Barry (TAL-ak-suhn, BAIR-ee) **N.J.**

Right wing. Shoots right. 6'4", 196 lbs. Born, Grafton, ND, April 14, 1983.
(New Jersey's 2nd choice, 53rd overall, in 2002 Entry Draft).

				Regular Season					Playoffs			
Season	**Club**	**League**	**GP**	**G**	**A**	**TP**	**PIM**	**GP**	**G**	**A**	**TP**	**PIM**
99-2000	U.S. National U-17	USDP	53	14	6	20	90	....	....	....	....	....
2000-01	U.S. National U-18	USDP	63	23	24	47	77	....	....	....	....	....
2001-02	U. of Minnesota	WCHA	44	13	10	23	44	....	....	....	....	....
2002-03	U. of Minnesota	WCHA	32	9	14	23	18	....	....	....	....	....
2003-04	U. of Minnesota	WCHA	44	10	15	25	46	....	....	....	....	....

TAMBELLINI, Jeff (tam-buh-LEE-nee, JEHF) **L.A.**

Left wing. Shoots left. 5'11", 186 lbs. Born, Calgary, Alta., April 13, 1984.
(Los Angeles' 3rd choice, 27th overall, in 2003 Entry Draft).

				Regular Season					Playoffs			
Season	**Club**	**League**	**GP**	**G**	**A**	**TP**	**PIM**	**GP**	**G**	**A**	**TP**	**PIM**
99-2000	Poco Buckeroos	PIJHL	41	30	34	64	....	....	....	....	....	....
2000-01	Chilliwack Chiefs	BCHL	54	21	30	51	13	....	....	....	....	....
2001-02	Chilliwack Chiefs	BCHL	34	46	71	117	23	29	27	27	54	....
2002-03	U. of Michigan	CCHA	43	26	19	45	24	....	....	....	....	....
2003-04	U. of Michigan	CCHA	39	15	12	27	18	....	....	....	....	....

CCHA All-Rookie Team (2003) • CCHA Second All-Star Team (2003) • CCHA Rookie of the Year (2003)

TARATUKHIN, Andrei (tahr-a-TOO-khin, AN-dray) **CGY.**

Center. Shoots left. 6', 198 lbs. Born, Omsk, USSR, February 22, 1983.
(Calgary's 2nd choice, 41st overall, in 2001 Entry Draft).

				Regular Season					Playoffs			
Season	**Club**	**League**	**GP**	**G**	**A**	**TP**	**PIM**	**GP**	**G**	**A**	**TP**	**PIM**
99-2000	Omsk 2	Russia-3	27	10	6	16	16	....	....	....	....	....
	Avangard Omsk	Russia	....	....	....	....	....	1	1	0	1	0
2000-01	Omsk 2	Russia-3	41	19	28	47	69	....	....	....	....	....
2001-02	Mostovik Kurgan	Russia-2	44	13	22	35	30	....	....	....	....	....
	Yaroslavl 2	Russia-3	5	5	2	7	12	....	....	....	....	....
2002-03	Avangard Omsk	Russia	21	0	1	1	4	7	1	0	1	18
	Omsk 2	Russia-3	15	4	13	17	20	....	....	....	....	....
2003-04	Avangard Omsk	Russia	8	0	0	0	4	....	....	....	....	....
	Omsk 2	Russia-3	9	6	5	11	6	....	....	....	....	....
	Mechel	Russia-2	15	3	12	15	12	12	1	4	5	6

TARDIF, Jamie (tahr-DIHF, JAY-mee) **CGY.**

Right wing. Shoots right. 6', 207 lbs. Born, Welland, Ont., January 23, 1985.
(Calgary's 4th choice, 112th overall, in 2003 Entry Draft).

				Regular Season					Playoffs			
Season	**Club**	**League**	**GP**	**G**	**A**	**TP**	**PIM**	**GP**	**G**	**A**	**TP**	**PIM**
2000-01	Welland Cougars	OJHL-B	STATISTICS NOT AVAILABLE									
2001-02	Peterborough	OHL	64	22	22	44	30	6	0	1	1	2
2002-03	Peterborough	OHL	68	31	29	60	32	7	3	4	7	0
2003-04	Peterborough	OHL	64	25	28	53	56	....	....	....	....	....

TARKIR, Zach (TAHR-kihr, ZAK) **N.J.**

Defense. Shoots right. 6', 180 lbs. Born, Fresno, CA, June 28, 1984.
(New Jersey's 4th choice, 167th overall, in 2003 Entry Draft).

				Regular Season					Playoffs			
Season	**Club**	**League**	**GP**	**G**	**A**	**TP**	**PIM**	**GP**	**G**	**A**	**TP**	**PIM**
2001-02	Great Falls	AWHL	24	3	5	8	....	8	0	3	3	....
2002-03	Chilliwack Chiefs	BCHL	53	5	28	33	86	....	....	....	....	....
2003-04	Northern Michigan	CCHA	36	2	3	5	40	....	....	....	....	....

TARNASKY, Nick (tahr-NAS-kee, NIHK) **T.B.**

Center. Shoots left. 6'2", 218 lbs. Born, Rocky Mtn. House, Alta., November 25, 1984.
(Tampa Bay's 11th choice, 287th overall, in 2003 Entry Draft).

				Regular Season					Playoffs			
Season	**Club**	**League**	**GP**	**G**	**A**	**TP**	**PIM**	**GP**	**G**	**A**	**TP**	**PIM**
99-2000	Leduc Oil Kings	AMBHL	36	21	11	32	59	....	....	....	....	....
2000-01	Leduc Oil Kings	AMHL	35	39	29	68	95	....	....	....	....	....
2001-02	Drayton Valley	AJHL	20	7	4	11	10	....	....	....	....	....
	Vancouver Giants	WHL	10	1	0	1	5	....	....	....	....	....
2002-03	Kelowna Rockets	WHL	39	4	12	16	39	....	....	....	....	....
	Lethbridge	WHL	30	5	8	13	45	....	....	....	....	....
2003-04	Lethbridge	WHL	71	26	23	49	108	....	....	....	....	....

TARVAINEN, Jussi (tahr-VIGH-nehn, YU-see) **EDM.**

Right wing. Shoots right. 6'3", 215 lbs. Born, Lahti, Finland, May 31, 1976.
(Edmonton's 7th choice, 95th overall, in 1994 Entry Draft).

				Regular Season					Playoffs			
Season	**Club**	**League**	**GP**	**G**	**A**	**TP**	**PIM**	**GP**	**G**	**A**	**TP**	**PIM**
1991-92	KalPa Kuopio-C	Finn-Jr.	3	0	3	3	4	....	....	....	....	....
1992-93	KalPa Kuopio-B	Finn-Jr.	18	13	9	22	38	....	....	....	....	....
	KalPa Kuopio Jr.	Finn-Jr.	17	3	6	9	35	....	....	....	....	....
1993-94	KalPa Kuopio Jr.	Finn-Jr.	16	9	14	23	12	....	....	....	....	....
	Junkkarit	Finland-2	1	0	0	0	0	....	....	....	....	....
	KalPa Kuopio	Finland	42	3	4	7	20	....	....	....	....	....
1994-95	KalPa Kuopio Jr.	Finn-Jr.	3	4	0	4	2	....	....	....	....	....
	KalPa Kuopio	Finland	45	10	7	17	34	3	0	0	0	2
1995-96	KalPa Kuopio Jr.	Finn-Jr.	3	2	3	5	10	7	3	4	7	12
	KalPa Kuopio	Finland	47	8	11	19	50	....	....	....	....	....
1996-97	KalPa Kuopio	Finland	49	14	26	40	62	....	....	....	....	....
	KalPa Kuopio Jr.	Finn-Jr.	....	....	....	....	....	1	0	0	0	2
	KalPa Kuopio	Finland-2	....	....	....	....	....	6	4	3	7	4
1997-98	JYP Jyvaskyla	Finland	43	12	26	38	59	....	....	....	....	....
1998-99	JYP Jyvaskyla	Finland	54	17	24	41	84	3	0	0	0	8
99-2000	Tappara Tampere	Finland	52	20	27	47	91	4	1	0	1	2
2000-01	Tappara Tampere	Finland	56	23	32	55	36	10	*8	2	10	2
2001-02	Tappara Tampere	Finland	56	24	26	50	42	10	4	3	7	0
2002-03	Tappara Tampere	Finland	56	14	21	35	24	15	*7	2	9	4
2003-04	Linkopings HC	Sweden	48	20	15	35	26	5	0	0	0	10

TATARINOV, Alexander (ta-TAHR-ee-nahf, al-ehx-AN-duhr) **PHX.**

Right wing. Shoots left. 5'11", 176 lbs. Born, Sverdlovsk, USSR, April 14, 1982.
(Phoenix's 2nd choice, 53rd overall, in 2000 Entry Draft).

				Regular Season					Playoffs			
Season	**Club**	**League**	**GP**	**G**	**A**	**TP**	**PIM**	**GP**	**G**	**A**	**TP**	**PIM**
1998-99	Yaroslavl 2	Russia-3	32	11	10	21	89	....	....	....	....	....
	Spartak Moscow	Russia	3	0	0	0	0	....	....	....	....	....
99-2000	Yaroslavl 2	Russia-3	35	12	12	24	36	....	....	....	....	....
2000-01	Kristall Saratov	Russia-2	24	3	3	6	8	....	....	....	....	....
	Yaroslavl	Russia	2	0	1	1	0	1	0	0	0	0
2001-02	Yaroslavl	Russia	21	4	3	7	8	....	....	....	....	....
	Amur Khabarovsk	Russia	11	0	0	0	0	....	....	....	....	....
	Yaroslavl 2	Russia-3	5	5	2	7	12	....	....	....	....	....
2002-03	Perm	Russia	31	6	5	11	16	....	....	....	....	....
2003-04	Spartak Moscow	Russia-2	43	8	11	19	14	9	2	5	7	2

TATICEK, Petr (TA-tih-chehk, PEE-tuhr) **FLA.**

Center. Shoots left. 6'3", 195 lbs. Born, Rakovnik, Czech., September 22, 1983.
(Florida's 2nd choice, 9th overall, in 2002 Entry Draft).

				Regular Season					Playoffs			
Season	**Club**	**League**	**GP**	**G**	**A**	**TP**	**PIM**	**GP**	**G**	**A**	**TP**	**PIM**
1998-99	Kladno-18	Czech-Jr.	42	24	17	41	....	....	....	....	....	....
99-2000	Kladno Jr.	Czech-Jr.	48	11	16	27	26	....	....	....	....	....
	HC Velvana Kladno	Czech	4	0	0	0	4	....	....	....	....	....
2000-01	Kladno Jr.	Czech-Jr.	30	7	12	19	54	....	....	....	....	....
	Kladno	Czech	3	0	0	0	0	....	....	....	....	....
2001-02	Sault Ste. Marie	OHL	60	21	42	63	32	6	3	3	6	4
2002-03	Sault Ste. Marie	OHL	54	12	45	57	44	4	1	0	1	0
2003-04	San Antonio	AHL	63	4	15	19	6	....	....	....	....	....

TAYLOR, Jake (TAY-luhr, JAIK) **NYR**

Defense. Shoots right. 6'4", 220 lbs. Born, Rochester, MN, August 1, 1983.
(NY Rangers' 5th choice, 177th overall, in 2002 Entry Draft).

				Regular Season					Playoffs			
Season	**Club**	**League**	**GP**	**G**	**A**	**TP**	**PIM**	**GP**	**G**	**A**	**TP**	**PIM**
2000-01	Rochester High	Hi-School	29	9	15	24	34	....	....	....	....	....
	Green Bay	USHL	5	0	0	0	8	....	....	....	....	....
2001-02	Green Bay	USHL	56	1	2	3	147	7	0	0	0	11
2002-03	Green Bay	USHL	60	8	8	16	160	....	....	....	....	....
2003-04	U. of Minnesota	WCHA	39	2	6	8	68	....	....	....	....	....

TERESCHENKO, Alexei (teh-REH-shehn-koh, al-EHX-ay) **DAL.**

Center. Shoots left. 5'11", 176 lbs. Born, Mozhaisk, USSR, December 16, 1980.
(Dallas' 4th choice, 91st overall, in 2000 Entry Draft).

				Regular Season					Playoffs			
Season	**Club**	**League**	**GP**	**G**	**A**	**TP**	**PIM**	**GP**	**G**	**A**	**TP**	**PIM**
1996-97	Dyn. Moscow 2	Russia-3	9	0	0	0	2	....	....	....	....	....
1997-98	Dynamo Moscow	Russia	26	6	7	13	30	....	....	....	....	....
1998-99	Dyn. Moscow 2	Russia-3	28	4	17	21	20	....	....	....	....	....
	THC Tver	Russia-2	12	3	4	7	4	....	....	....	....	....
	Dynamo Moscow	Russia	1	0	1	1	0	2	0	0	0	0
99-2000	Dynamo Moscow	Russia	27	1	1	2	10	17	1	1	2	8
2000-01	Dynamo Moscow	Russia	39	3	2	5	18	....	....	....	....	....
2001-02	Yaroslavl 2	Russia-3	1	0	0	0	0	....	....	....	....	....
	Dynamo Moscow	Russia	40	3	6	9	20	3	0	0	0	0
2002-03	Dynamo Moscow	Russia	40	7	9	16	14	5	1	0	1	2
2003-04	Dynamo Moscow	Russia	47	8	12	20	26	3	0	0	0	4

TERNAVSKY, Artem (tuhr-NAV-skee, ahr-TEHM) **WSH.**

Defense. Shoots left. 6'3", 213 lbs. Born, Magnitogorsk, USSR, June 2, 1983.
(Washington's 4th choice, 160th overall, in 2001 Entry Draft).

				Regular Season					Playoffs			
Season	**Club**	**League**	**GP**	**G**	**A**	**TP**	**PIM**	**GP**	**G**	**A**	**TP**	**PIM**
99-2000	CSKA Moscow Jr.	Russia-Jr.	2	0	1	1	0	....	....	....	....	....
	HC CSKA 2	Russia-3	25	0	4	4	42	....	....	....	....	....
2000-01	Sherbrooke	QMJHL	65	3	15	18	143	....	....	....	....	....
2001-02	Mostovik Kurgan	Russia-2	25	0	0	0	46	....	....	....	....	....
2002-03	Sibir Novosibirsk	Russia	42	1	1	2	20	....	....	....	....	....
2003-04	Ufa Salavat	Russia	12	0	0	0	4	....	....	....	....	....
	Magnitogorsk 2	Russia-3	7	1	0	1	0	....	....	....	....	....

TESLYUK, Roman (tehs-L'YUHK, ROH-muhn) **EDM.**

Defense. Shoots right. 6'1", 195 lbs. Born, Severomorsk, USSR, January 21, 1986.
(Edmonton's 3rd choice, 44th overall, in 2004 Entry Draft).

				Regular Season					Playoffs			
Season	**Club**	**League**	**GP**	**G**	**A**	**TP**	**PIM**	**GP**	**G**	**A**	**TP**	**PIM**
2001-02	HC CSKA Jr.	Russia-Jr.	STATISTICS NOT AVAILABLE									
	HC CSKA 2	Russia-3	1	0	0	0	4	....	....	....	....	....
2002-03	CSKA Moscow Jr.	Russia-3	6	4	4	8	2	....	....	....	....	....
	CSKA Moscow 2	Russia-3	6	0	2	2	6	....	....	....	....	....
2003-04	Kamloops Blazers	WHL	70	5	9	14	118	5	0	1	1	2

THELEN, A.J. (THAY-lehn, AY-JAY) **MIN.**

Defense. Shoots left. 6'3", 210 lbs. Born, Shakopee, Minn., March 11, 1986.
(Minnesota's 1st choice, 12th overall, in 2004 Entry Draft).

				Regular Season					Playoffs			
Season	**Club**	**League**	**GP**	**G**	**A**	**TP**	**PIM**	**GP**	**G**	**A**	**TP**	**PIM**
2000-01	Shat.-St. Mary's	Hi-School	40	22	17	39	....	....	....	....	....	....
2001-02	Shat.-St. Mary's	Hi-School	62	20	33	53	....	....	....	....	....	....
2002-03	U.S. National U-17	USDP	64	6	8	14	80	....	....	....	....	....
	U.S. National U-18	USDP	3	0	0	0	0	....	....	....	....	....
2003-04	Michigan State	CCHA	41	11	18	29	50	....	....	....	....	....

CCHA All-Rookie Team (2004) • CCHA First All-Star Team (2004) • NCAA West Second All-American Team (2004)

THINEL, Marc-Andre (tih-nehl, MAHRK-AWN-dray) **MTL.**

Right wing. Shoots left. 6', 178 lbs. Born, St-Jerome, Que., March 24, 1981.
(Montreal's 6th choice, 145th overall, in 1999 Entry Draft).

				Regular Season					Playoffs			
Season	**Club**	**League**	**GP**	**G**	**A**	**TP**	**PIM**	**GP**	**G**	**A**	**TP**	**PIM**
1996-97	Laval Laurentide	QAAA	40	12	10	22	....	13	0	5	5	....
1997-98	Victoriaville Tigres	QMJHL	58	7	10	17	20	6	0	3	3	4
1998-99	Victoriaville Tigres	QMJHL	66	45	58	103	16	6	5	3	8	4
99-2000	Victoriaville Tigres	QMJHL	71	59	73	132	55	6	5	6	11	18
2000-01	Victoriaville Tigres	QMJHL	70	62	88	150	101	13	12	13	25	18
2001-02	Quebec Citadelles	AHL	73	6	4	10	8	2	0	0	0	0
2002-03	Utah Grizzlies	AHL	44	5	15	20	10	2	0	0	0	0
	Lexington	ECHL	27	14	14	28	6	....	....	....	....	....
2003-04	Columbus	ECHL	47	17	25	42	32	....	....	....	....	....
	Hamilton Bulldogs	AHL	14	1	1	2	2	10	1	0	1	6

QMJHL First All-Star Team (2000) • QMJHL Second All-Star Team (2001)

THOMPSON, Nate (TAWM-suhn, NAYT) **BOS.**

Center. Shoots left. 6', 190 lbs. Born, Anchorage, AK, October 5, 1984.
(Boston's 8th choice, 183rd overall, in 2003 Entry Draft).

			Regular Season					Playoffs				
Season	Club	League	GP	G	A	TP	PIM	GP	G	A	TP	PIM
2000-01	Alaska All-Stars	AASHL		STATISTICS NOT AVAILABLE								
2001-02	Seattle	WHL	69	13	26	39	42	11	1	3	4	13
2002-03	Seattle	WHL	61	10	24	34	48	15	5	4	9	6
2003-04	Seattle	WHL	65	13	23	36	24	....	....	....	....	....

THORBURN, Chris (THOHR-buhrn, KRIHS) **BUF.**

Center. Shoots right. 6'3", 207 lbs. Born, Sault Ste. Marie, Ont., June 3, 1983.
(Buffalo's 3rd choice, 50th overall, in 2001 Entry Draft).

			Regular Season					Playoffs				
Season	Club	League	GP	G	A	TP	PIM	GP	G	A	TP	PIM
1998-99	Elliot Lake Vikings	NOJHA	40	21	12	33	28	....	....	....	....	....
99-2000	North Bay	OHL	56	12	8	20	33	6	0	2	2	0
2000-01	North Bay	OHL	66	22	32	54	64	4	0	1	1	9
2001-02	North Bay	OHL	67	15	43	58	112	5	1	2	3	8
2002-03	Saginaw Spirit	OHL	37	19	19	38	68	....	....	....	....	....
	Plymouth Whalers	OHL	27	11	22	33	56	18	11	9	20	10
2003-04	Rochester	AHL	58	6	16	22	77	16	3	2	5	18

TIMONEN, Jussi (TEEM-oh-nehn, YU-see) **PHI.**

Defense. Shoots left. 6', 200 lbs. Born, Kuopio, Finland, June 29, 1983.
(Philadelphia's 3rd choice, 146th overall, in 2001 Entry Draft).

			Regular Season					Playoffs				
Season	Club	League	GP	G	A	TP	PIM	GP	G	A	TP	PIM
99-2000	KalPa Kuopio Jr.	Finn-Jr.	33	4	2	6	16	4	0	0	0	4
2000-01	Kalpa Kuopio-B	Finn-Jr.	38	6	7	13	22	....	....	....	....	....
	KalPa Kuopio Jr.	Finn-Jr.	1	0	1	1	0	....	....	....	....	....
2001-02	KalPa Kuopio Jr.	Finn-Jr.	10	1	1	2	10	....	....	....	....	....
	Kalpa Kuopio	Finland-2	41	3	8	11	10	8	0	2	2	0
2002-03	TPS Turku	Finland	39	1	0	1	10	7	0	2	2	4
	TuTu Turku	Finland-2	3	0	0	0	0	....	....	....	....	....
2003-04	TPS Turku	Finland	20	0	0	0	4	....	....	....	....	....
	Jukurit Mikkeli	Finland-2	25	7	9	16	10	13	0	4	4	0

TKACHENKO, Ivan (t'kuh-CHEHN-koh, ee-VAHN) **CBJ**

Left wing. Shoots left. 5'10", 183 lbs. Born, Yaroslavl, USSR, November 9, 1979.
(Columbus' 5th choice, 98th overall, in 2002 Entry Draft).

			Regular Season					Playoffs				
Season	Club	League	GP	G	A	TP	PIM	GP	G	A	TP	PIM
1997-98	Yaroslavl 2	Russia-2		STATISTICS NOT AVAILABLE								
	Torpedo Yaroslavl	Russia	....	....	....	....	....	1	0	0	0	0
1998-99	Yaroslavl 2	Russia-3	28	15	13	28	26	....	....	....	....	....
99-2000	Yaroslavl 2	Russia-3	1	1	0	1	0	....	....	....	....	....
	Motor Zavolzhje	Russia-2	43	15	14	29	22	....	....	....	....	....
	Nizhnekamsk 2	Russia-3	8	6	3	9	24	....	....	....	....	....
	Nizhnekamsk	Russia	5	1	0	1	0	4	0	1	1	0
2000-01	Nizhnekamsk	Russia	28	2	2	4	14	4	0	1	1	0
2001-02	Yaroslavl 2	Russia-3	1	0	1	1	2	....	....	....	....	....
	Yaroslavl	Russia	44	13	20	33	57	9	5	2	7	4
2002-03	Yaroslavl	Russia	44	11	6	17	57	10	2	3	5	6
2003-04	Yaroslavl	Russia	56	7	11	18	22	3	0	0	0	0

TOBIN, Mark (TOH-bihn, MAHRK) **T.B.**

Left wing. Shoots left. 6'3", 204 lbs. Born, St. John's, Nfld., November 26, 1985.
(Tampa Bay's 2nd choice, 65th overall, in 2004 Entry Draft).

			Regular Season					Playoffs				
Season	Club	League	GP	G	A	TP	PIM	GP	G	A	TP	PIM
2002-03	Rimouski Oceanic	QMJHL	68	8	8	16	176	....	....	....	....	....
2003-04	Rimouski Oceanic	QMJHL	69	22	16	38	112	9	4	1	5	12

TOFFEY, John (TAW-fee, JAWN) **T.B.**

Center. Shoots left. 6'3", 215 lbs. Born, Barnstable, MA, November 26, 1982.
(Tampa Bay's 13th choice, 287th overall, in 2002 Entry Draft).

			Regular Season					Playoffs				
Season	Club	League	GP	G	A	TP	PIM	GP	G	A	TP	PIM
1997/00	St. Sebastian's	Hi-School	65	29	27	56	....	....	....	....	....	....
2000-01	St. Sebastian's	Hi-School	22	22	24	46	....	....	....	....	....	....
2001-02	Ohio State	CCHA	24	2	3	5	4	....	....	....	....	....
2002-03	Walpole Stars	EJHL	19	7	8	15	10	....	....	....	....	....
2003-04	Massachusetts	H-East	20	2	3	5	16	....	....	....	....	....

TOLKUNOV, Dmitri (tohl-ku-NAWF, di-MEE-tree) **FLA.**

Defense. Shoots right. 6'2", 200 lbs. Born, Kiev, USSR, May 5, 1979.

			Regular Season					Playoffs				
Season	Club	League	GP	G	A	TP	PIM	GP	G	A	TP	PIM
1996-97	Hull Olympiques	QMJHL	34	3	8	11	99	....	....	....	....	....
	Beauport Harfangs	QMJHL	27	3	7	10	18	4	0	1	1	4
1997-98	Quebec Remparts	QMJHL	66	10	25	35	81	14	3	9	12	22
1998-99	Quebec Rafales	QMJHL	69	11	57	68	110	13	2	7	9	22
99-2000	Cleveland	IHL	65	3	12	15	54	8	0	0	0	2
2000-01	Norfolk Admirals	AHL	78	5	18	23	93	9	0	1	1	4
2001-02	Norfolk Admirals	AHL	51	1	18	19	20	4	0	0	0	2
2002-03	Norfolk Admirals	AHL	47	1	17	18	39	....	....	....	....	....
2003-04	Yaroslavl 2	Russia-3	14	4	3	7	11	....	....	....	....	....
	Yaroslavl	Russia	6	0	0	0	4	....	....	....	....	....
	Amur Khabarovsk	Russia	27	1	2	3	28	....	....	....	....	....

QMJHL Second All-Star Team (1999)

Signed as a free agent by **Chicago**, October 8, 1998. Traded to **Florida** by **Chicago** for NY Islanders' 9th round choice (previously acquired by Florida – later traded to San Jose – San Jose selected Carter Lee) in 2003 Entry Draft, June 21, 2003. Signed as a free agent by **Yaroslavl** (Russia), September 8, 2003, with **Florida** retaining NHL rights.

TOLLEFSEN, Ole-Kristian (TOHL-uhf-suhn, OH-lay-KRIHS-tyahn) **CBJ**

Defense. Shoots left. 6'2", 200 lbs. Born, Oslo, Norway, March 29, 1984.
(Columbus' 3rd choice, 65th overall, in 2002 Entry Draft).

			Regular Season					Playoffs				
Season	Club	League	GP	G	A	TP	PIM	GP	G	A	TP	PIM
2000-01	Lillehammer IK	Norway	4	0	0	0	2	....	....	....	....	....
2001-02	Lillehammer IK	Norway	37	1	5	6	63	6	1	1	2	10
	Lillehammer IK	Nor-Jr.	....	....	....	....	....	1	0	2	2	4
2002-03	Brandon	WHL	43	6	14	20	73	17	0	2	2	38
2003-04	Brandon	WHL	53	3	27	30	94	11	0	4	4	15

TOLSA, Jari (TOHL-suh, YA-ree) **DET.**

Center. Shoots left. 6', 172 lbs. Born, Goteborg, Sweden, April 20, 1981.
(Detroit's 1st choice, 120th overall, in 1999 Entry Draft).

			Regular Season					Playoffs				
Season	Club	League	GP	G	A	TP	PIM	GP	G	A	TP	PIM
1997-98	V. Frolunda Jr.	Swede-Jr.	26	18	25	43	30	....	....	....	....	....
1998-99	V. Frolunda Jr.	Swede-Jr.	35	16	21	37	51	4	1	3	4	2
99-2000	V. Frolunda Jr.	Swede-Jr.	33	12	47	59	43	6	3	8	11	4
	Vastra Frolunda	Sweden	10	0	0	0	0	....	....	....	....	....
2000-01	V. Frolunda Jr.	Swede-Jr.	11	4	6	10	8	2	2	4	6	4
	Molndals HK	Swede-2	1	0	2	2	0	....	....	....	....	....
	Vastra Frolunda	Sweden	42	2	5	7	18	5	0	0	0	0
2001-02	Vastra Frolunda	Sweden	48	8	16	24	18	10	0	0	0	4
2002-03	Vastra Frolunda	Sweden	43	9	14	23	24	16	4	1	5	8
2003-04	Vastra Frolunda	Sweden	50	8	20	28	36	10	2	4	6	4

TOMANEK, Roman (toh-MA-nehk, ROH-muhn) **PHX.**

Right wing. Shoots right. 6'1", 176 lbs. Born, Povazka Bystrica, Czech., January 28, 1986.
(Phoenix's 4th choice, 103rd overall, in 2004 Entry Draft).

			Regular Season					Playoffs				
Season	Club	League	GP	G	A	TP	PIM	GP	G	A	TP	PIM
2003-04	Pov. Bystrica 18	Slovak-Jr.	10	14	10	24	31	....	....	....	....	....
	Pov. Bystrica Jr.	Slovak-Jr.	16	22	13	35	86	....	....	....	....	....
	Pov. Bystrica	Slovak-2	29	11	9	20	30	....	....	....	....	....

TOMICA, Marek (TAW-miht-suh, MAIR-ehk) **DAL.**

Left wing. Shoots left. 6', 178 lbs. Born, Prague, Czech., January 1, 1981.
(Dallas' 10th choice, 285th overall, in 2001 Entry Draft).

			Regular Season					Playoffs				
Season	Club	League	GP	G	A	TP	PIM	GP	G	A	TP	PIM
1996-97	Dukla Jihlava	Czech-18	22	3	4	7	....	....	....	....	....	....
1997-98	Dukla Jihlava	Czech-18	36	24	28	52	....	....	....	....	....	....
1998-99	Dukla Jihlava	Czech-Jr.		STATISTICS NOT AVAILABLE								
99-2000	HC Slavia Praha Jr.	Czech-Jr.	41	13	8	21	16	7	2	3	5	0
	HC Slavia Praha	Czech	13	0	0	0	2	....	....	....	....	....
2000-01	HC Slavia Praha Jr.	Czech-Jr.	5	2	2	4	4	....	....	....	....	....
	Beroun	Czech-2	8	0	2	2	2	....	....	....	....	....
	HC Mlada Boleslav	Czech-3	2	0	0	0	6	....	....	....	....	....
	HC Slavia Praha	Czech	37	3	9	12	8	11	0	0	0	0
2001-02	HC Slavia Praha	Czech	49	6	8	14	14	8	0	0	0	4
	HC Slavia Praha Jr.	Czech-Jr.	5	2	3	5	0	....	....	....	....	....
2002-03	HC Slavia Praha	Czech	32	1	3	4	14	13	0	1	1	10
2003-04	HC Slavia Praha	Czech	48	3	9	12	20	19	4	2	6	10

TOPOL, Sergei (TOH-puhl, SAIR-gay) **VAN.**

Forward. Shoots left. 6'1", 183 lbs. Born, Omsk, USSR, February 15, 1985.
(Vancouver's 8th choice, 252nd overall, in 2003 Entry Draft).

			Regular Season					Playoffs				
Season	Club	League	GP	G	A	TP	PIM	GP	G	A	TP	PIM
2002-03	Omsk 2	Russia-3	45	16	5	21	18	....	....	....	....	....
2003-04	Avangard Omsk	Russia	9	0	0	0	2	....	....	....	....	....
	Omsk 2	Russia-3	39	25	14	39	10	....	....	....	....	....

TRATTNIG, Matthias (TRAT-nihg, MAH-tee-uhs) **CBJ**

Center. Shoots left. 6'1", 208 lbs. Born, Graz, Austria, April 22, 1979.
(Chicago's 2nd choice, 94th overall, in 1998 Entry Draft).

			Regular Season					Playoffs				
Season	Club	League	GP	G	A	TP	PIM	GP	G	A	TP	PIM
1995-96	EC Graz	Austria	17	0	1	1	0	....	....	....	....	....
1996-97	Capital District	NYJHL	51	30	54	84	64	....	....	....	....	....
1997-98	U. of Maine	H-East	34	8	9	17	30	....	....	....	....	....
1998-99	U. of Maine	H-East	39	5	5	10	32	....	....	....	....	....
99-2000	U. of Maine	H-East	39	8	11	19	26	....	....	....	....	....
2000-01	U. of Maine	H-East	37	11	13	24	51	....	....	....	....	....
2001-02	Djurgarden	Sweden	44	4	5	9	26	5	0	0	0	0
	Austria	Olympics	4	1	1	2	2	....	....	....	....	....
2002-03	Djurgarden	Sweden	48	7	5	12	67	12	3	2	5	16
2003-04	Kassel Huskies	Germany	52	12	19	31	72	....	....	....	....	....

Signed as a free agent by **Columbus**, July 7, 2004.

TRAVIS, Dan (TRA-vihs, DAN) **FLA.**

Right wing. Shoots right. 6'3", 220 lbs. Born, Concord, NH, November 26, 1983.
(Florida's 7th choice, 141st overall, in 2003 Entry Draft).

			Regular Season					Playoffs				
Season	Club	League	GP	G	A	TP	PIM	GP	G	A	TP	PIM
2000-01	Bishop Guerdin	Hi-School	24	29	27	56	....	....	....	....	....	....
2001-02	Deerfield Academy	Hi-School	23	14	18	32	30	....	....	....	....	....
2002-03	Deerfield Academy	Hi-School	25	16	27	43	30	....	....	....	....	....
2003-04	New Hampshire	H-East	14	2	4	6	2	....	....	....	....	....

TREILLE, Yorick (TRAYL, YOH-rihk)

Right wing. Shoots right. 6'3", 213 lbs. Born, Cannes, France, July 15, 1980.
(Chicago's 7th choice, 195th overall, in 1999 Entry Draft).

			Regular Season					Playoffs				
Season	Club	League	GP	G	A	TP	PIM	GP	G	A	TP	PIM
1997-98	Notre Dame	SJHL	54	18	28	46	42	....	....	....	....	....
1998-99	U. Mass-Lowell	H-East	30	6	5	11	24	....	....	....	....	....
99-2000	U. Mass-Lowell	H-East	33	10	12	22	34	....	....	....	....	....
2000-01	U. Mass-Lowell	H-East	31	10	14	24	35	....	....	....	....	....
2001-02	U. Mass-Lowell	H-East	30	10	16	26	24	....	....	....	....	....
2002-03	Norfolk Admirals	AHL	27	3	2	5	25	....	....	....	....	....
	HIFK Helsinki	Finland	5	0	1	1	4	....	....	....	....	....
2003-04	Norfolk Admirals	AHL	74	12	12	24	54	8	2	0	2	4

TREMBLAY, Jonathan (TRAHM-blay, JAWN-ah-thuhn) **S.J.**

Right wing. Shoots right. 6'3", 240 lbs. Born, Fauquier, Ont., March 3, 1984.
(San Jose's 6th choice, 201st overall, in 2003 Entry Draft).

			Regular Season					Playoffs				
Season	Club	League	GP	G	A	TP	PIM	GP	G	A	TP	PIM
2001-02	Timmons Majors	GNML		STATISTICS NOT AVAILABLE								
	Acadie-Bathurst	QMJHL	2	0	0	0	5	1	0	0	0	0
2002-03	Acadie-Bathurst	QMJHL	62	0	1	1	232	9	0	0	0	45
2003-04	Acadie-Bathurst	QMJHL	60	3	0	3	*316	....	....	....	....	....

TROJOVSKY, Matej (troh-YAWV-skee, MAH-tehzh) CAR.

Defense. Shoots left. 6'5", 220 lbs. Born, Plzen, Czech., October 12, 1984.
(Carolina's 5th choice, 130th overall, in 2003 Entry Draft).

			Regular Season					Playoffs				
Season	Club	League	GP	G	A	TP	PIM	GP	G	A	TP	PIM
99-2000	Plzen Jr.	Czech-Jr.	36	2	13	15	58	5	0	1	1	2
2000-01	Lincoln Stars	USHL	17	1	0	1	29	....	....	....	....	....
2001-02	Regina Pats	WHL	67	3	10	13	154	6	0	1	1	18
2002-03	Regina Pats	WHL	70	3	6	9	229	5	0	0	0	6
2003-04	Swift Current	WHL	61	3	6	9	201	3	0	0	0	10

TROLIGA, Tomas (TROH-lih-guh, TAW-mash) ST.L.

Center. Shoots right. 6'4", 200 lbs. Born, Presov, Czech., April 24, 1984.
(St. Louis' 3rd choice, 89th overall, in 2002 Entry Draft).

			Regular Season					Playoffs				
Season	Club	League	GP	G	A	TP	PIM	GP	G	A	TP	PIM
99-2000	HK VTJ Presov Jr.	Slovak-Jr.	39	6	1	7	56	....	....	....	....	....
2000-01	HK VTJ Presov Jr.	Slovak-Jr.	30	14	16	30	108	....	....	....	....	....
	HK VTJ Presov	Slovak-2	7	1	0	1	8	....	....	....	....	....
2001-02	Nova Ves Jr.	Slovak-Jr.		STATISTICS NOT AVAILABLE								
	Spisska Nova Ves	Slovak-2	11	2	5	7	0	....	....	....	....	....
2002-03	HC Kosice	Slovakia	29	1	1	2	16	....	....	....	....	....
	MHC Martin	Slovakia	11	1	2	3	18	4	0	0	0	6
2003-04	Calgary Hitmen	WHL	59	11	23	34	103	7	0	1	1	16

TRUBACHEV, Yuri (troo-bah-CHEHV, YOO-ree) CGY.

Center. Shoots left. 5'9", 187 lbs. Born, Cherepovets, USSR, March 9, 1983.
(Calgary's 7th choice, 164th overall, in 2001 Entry Draft).

			Regular Season					Playoffs				
Season	Club	League	GP	G	A	TP	PIM	GP	G	A	TP	PIM
1997-98	Cherepovets 2	Russia-3	1	0	0	0	0	....	....	....	....	....
1998-99	Cherepovets 3	Russia-4	9	5	1	6	0	....	....	....	....	....
	Cherepovets 2	Russia-3	2	0	0	0	0	....	....	....	....	....
99-2000	Cherepovets 2	Russia-3	42	13	19	32	76	....	....	....	....	....
2000-01	SKA St. Petersburg	Russia	34	6	5	11	24	....	....	....	....	....
2001-02	Cherepovets 2	Russia-3	5	3	3	6	2	....	....	....	....	....
	Cherepovets	Russia	32	2	1	3	6	4	0	2	2	0
2002-03	Cherepovets	Russia	48	5	7	12	26	12	1	2	3	6
2003-04	Cherepovets	Russia	59	8	10	18	50	....	....	....	....	....

TUKIO, Arto (TOO-kee-oh, AHR-toh) NYI

Defense. Shoots left. 5'10", 176 lbs. Born, Tampere, Finland, April 4, 1981.
(NY Islanders' 3rd choice, 101st overall, in 2000 Entry Draft).

			Regular Season					Playoffs				
Season	Club	League	GP	G	A	TP	PIM	GP	G	A	TP	PIM
1995-96	Ilves Tampere C	Finn-Jr.	28	3	5	8	20	....	....	....	....	....
1996-97	Ilves Tampere C	Finn-Jr.	6	1	3	4	4	....	....	....	....	....
	Ilves Tampere B	Finn-Jr.	20	0	2	2	6	1	1	0	1	0
1997-98	Ilves Tampere B	Finn-Jr.	39	7	7	14	64	....	....	....	....	....
	Ilves Tampere Jr.	Finn-Jr.	....	....	....	....	....	4	1	0	1	4
1998-99	Ilves Tampere B	Finn-Jr.	10	1	5	6	18	....	....	....	....	....
	Ilves Tampere Jr.	Finn-Jr.	18	1	4	5	12	10	0	0	0	2
99-2000	Ilves Tampere Jr.	Finn-Jr.	11	2	1	3	24	....	....	....	....	....
	Hermes Kokkola	Finland-2	1	0	0	0	0	....	....	....	....	....
	Ilves Tampere	Finland	42	2	1	3	20	3	0	0	0	0
2000-01	Ilves Tampere Jr.	Finn-Jr.	3	1	1	2	0	....	....	....	....	....
	Ilves Tampere	Finland	43	5	10	15	26	7	2	1	3	4
2001-02	Ilves Tampere	Finland	47	8	9	17	28	3	0	1	1	0
2002-03	Jokerit Helsinki	Finland	49	6	10	16	26	9	0	1	1	4
2003-04	Jokerit Helsinki	Finland	54	4	12	16	10	....	....	....	....	....

TUKONEN, Lauri (too-KOH-nehn, LOW-ree) L.A.

Right wing. Shoots right. 6'2", 200 lbs. Born, Hyvinkaa, Finland, September 1, 1986.
(Los Angeles' 1st choice, 11th overall, in 2004 Entry Draft).

			Regular Season					Playoffs				
Season	Club	League	GP	G	A	TP	PIM	GP	G	A	TP	PIM
2001-02	Ahmat Jr. C	Finn-Jr.	5	4	6	10	2	5	3	5	8	2
	Ahmat Jr.	Finn-Jr.	2	4	0	4	2	....	....	....	....	....
	Ahmat Hyvinkaa	Finland-2	24	7	4	11	6	....	....	....	....	....
2002-03	Ahmat Jr.	Finn-Jr.	3	3	1	4	2	1	0	0	0	0
	Ahmat Hyvinkaa	Finland-2	12	2	2	4	2	....	....	....	....	....
	Blues Espoo Jr.	Finn-Jr.	17	6	6	12	18	5	0	0	0	10
2003-04	Blues Espoo	Finland	35	3	3	6	16	7	0	0	0	0
	Blues Espoo Jr.	Finn-Jr.	14	14	9	23	4	....	....	....	....	....

TUMA, Martin (TOO-ma, MAHR-tehn) FLA.

Defense. Shoots left. 6'4", 209 lbs. Born, Most, Czech., September 14, 1985.
(Florida's 8th choice, 162nd overall, in 2003 Entry Draft).

			Regular Season					Playoffs				
Season	Club	League	GP	G	A	TP	PIM	GP	G	A	TP	PIM
2000-01	Litvinov Jr.	Czech-Jr.	45	4	12	16	62	6	0	3	3	8
2001-02	Litvinov Jr.	Czech-Jr.	39	2	1	3	104	2	0	0	0	0
	Litvinov	Czech	1	0	0	0	2	....	....	....	....	....
2002-03	Litvinov Jr.	Czech-Jr.	34	1	3	4	123	....	....	....	....	....
2003-04	Sault Ste. Marie	OHL	57	0	5	5	48	....	....	....	....	....

TUNIK, Yevgeny (TOO-nihk, yehv-GEH-nee) NYI

Center. Shoots left. 6'2", 198 lbs. Born, Kraskovo, USSR, November 17, 1984.
(NY Islanders' 3rd choice, 53rd overall, in 2003 Entry Draft).

			Regular Season					Playoffs				
Season	Club	League	GP	G	A	TP	PIM	GP	G	A	TP	PIM
99-2000	Elektrostal 2	Russia-3	3	0	0	0	4	....	....	....	....	....
2000-01	Elektrostal	Russia-2	8	2	0	2	2	....	....	....	....	....
2001-02	Elektrostal 2	Russia-3	14	13	6	19	18	....	....	....	....	....
	Elektrostal	Russia-2	22	5	0	5	8	....	....	....	....	....
2002-03	Elektrostal	Russia-2	42	14	10	24	24	....	....	....	....	....
	Elektrostal 2	Russia-3	1	0	0	0	0	....	....	....	....	....
2003-04	St. Petersburg 2	Russia-3	9	6	5	11	54	1	0	0	0	2
	SKA St. Petersburg	Russia	32	3	1	4	26	....	....	....	....	....

TUOKKO, Marco (too-OH-koh, MAHR-koh) DAL.

Center. Shoots left. 6', 185 lbs. Born, Raisio, Finland, March 27, 1979.
(Dallas' 9th choice, 219th overall, in 2000 Entry Draft).

			Regular Season					Playoffs				
Season	Club	League	GP	G	A	TP	PIM	GP	G	A	TP	PIM
1995-96	TPS Turku B	Finn-Jr.	31	9	13	22	49	3	1	0	1	0
	Kiekko-67 Turku	Finland-2	1	0	0	0	0	....	....	....	....	....
1996-97	TPS Turku B	Finn-Jr.	5	1	3	4	0	6	1	6	7	4
	TPS Turku Jr.	Finn-Jr.	30	8	7	15	32	....	....	....	....	....
	Kiekko-67 Turku	Finland-2	6	3	1	4	31	....	....	....	....	....
1997-98	TPS Turku Jr.	Finn-Jr.	26	5	13	18	77	7	1	4	5	14
1998-99	TPS Turku Jr.	Finn-Jr.	1	0	0	0	0	....	....	....	....	....
	TPS Turku	Finland	48	5	4	9	24	10	0	1	1	10
99-2000	TPS Turku	Finland	54	10	10	20	73	11	2	2	4	6
2000-01	TPS Turku	Finland	53	5	11	16	54	10	2	2	4	16
2001-02	TPS Turku	Finland	42	2	9	11	69	8	1	1	2	4
2002-03	TPS Turku	Finland	41	5	4	9	42	7	1	1	2	2
2003-04	TPS Turku	Finland	54	8	9	17	55	13	4	1	5	4

TURON, David (TUHR-awn, DAY-vihd) TOR.

Defense. Shoots right. 6'3", 202 lbs. Born, Havirov, Czech., October 4, 1983.
(Toronto's 5th choice, 122nd overall, in 2002 Entry Draft).

			Regular Season					Playoffs				
Season	Club	League	GP	G	A	TP	PIM	GP	G	A	TP	PIM
99-2000	SK Karvina Jr.	Czech-Jr.	2	0	0	0	0	....	....	....	....	....
	Havirov Jr.	Czech-Jr.	41	14	11	25	54	....	....	....	....	....
2000-01	Havirov Jr.	Czech-Jr.	43	12	7	19	26	....	....	....	....	....
	HC Femax Havirov	Czech	4	0	0	0	4	....	....	....	....	....
2001-02	Havirov Jr.	Czech-Jr.	41	5	11	16	75	....	....	....	....	....
	HC Femax Havirov	Czech	14	0	1	1	10	....	....	....	....	....
2002-03	Portland	WHL	36	3	6	9	38	7	0	2	2	0
2003-04	St. John's	AHL	11	0	1	1	2	....	....	....	....	....
	Memphis	CHL	42	8	7	15	57	....	....	....	....	....

• Missed majority of 2002-03 season recovering from shoulder injury suffered in training camp, September 26, 2002.

UCHEVATOV, Victor (oo-cheh-VA-tawf, VIHK-tohr) FLA.

Defense. Shoots left. 6'4", 225 lbs. Born, Angarsk, USSR, February 10, 1983.
(New Jersey's 4th choice, 60th overall, in 2001 Entry Draft).

			Regular Season					Playoffs				
Season	Club	League	GP	G	A	TP	PIM	GP	G	A	TP	PIM
2000-01	Yaroslavl 2	Russia-3	28	1	1	2	74	....	....	....	....	....
2001-02	Albany River Rats	AHL	64	0	2	2	50	....	....	....	....	....
2002-03	Albany River Rats	AHL	55	0	2	2	27	....	....	....	....	....
2003-04	Albany River Rats	AHL	52	0	3	3	46	....	....	....	....	....
	San Antonio	AHL	22	3	4	7	6	....	....	....	....	....

Traded to **Florida** by **New Jersey** with Christian Berglund for Viktor Kozlov, March 1, 2004.

UJCIK, Viktor (OOY-chehk, VIHK-tohr) MTL.

Right wing. Shoots left. 5'11", 194 lbs. Born, Jihlava, Czech., May 24, 1972.
(Montreal's 8th choice, 266th overall, in 2001 Entry Draft).

			Regular Season					Playoffs				
Season	Club	League	GP	G	A	TP	PIM	GP	G	A	TP	PIM
1990-91	Dukla Jihlava	Czech	2	0	0	0	0	....	....	....	....	....
1991-92	Dukla Jihlava	Czech	35	10	9	19	32	8	3	4	7	0
1992-93	Dukla Jihlava	Czech	30	16	16	32	....	....	....	....	....	....
1993-94	HC Dukla Jihlava	Czech	44	17	30	47	....	4	3	3	6	....
1994-95	HC Dukla Jihlava	Czech	42	20	16	36	65	2	1	2	3	2
1995-96	HC Slavia Praha	Czech	39	*37	19	56	59	7	8	4	12	6
1996-97	HC Slavia Praha	Czech	40	26	21	47	41	3	1	1	2	2
1997-98	HC Slavia Praha	Czech	17	13	8	21	12	....	....	....	....	....
	HC Zele. Trinec	Czech	31	21	22	43	63	13	8	10	18	4
1998-99	HC Zele. Trinec	Czech	44	20	23	43	55	10	4	4	8	18
99-2000	HC Ocelari Trinec	Czech	42	14	20	34	32	4	1	0	1	28
2000-01	HC Ocelari Trinec	Czech	31	8	12	20	20	....	....	....	....	....
	HC Slavia Praha	Czech	19	9	9	18	8	11	8	8	16	10
2001-02	HC Slavia Praha	Czech	52	25	23	48	51	9	3	0	3	6
2002-03	HC Keramika Plzen	Czech	23	12	5	17	41	....	....	....	....	....
	HC Sparta Praha	Czech	26	11	6	17	14	10	3	5	8	6
2003-04	HC Sparta Praha	Czech	19	11	7	18	6	13	0	2	2	18
	Dukla Jihlava	Czech-2	4	4	0	4	4	....	....	....	....	....

UMBERGER, R.J. (UHM-buhr-guhr, AHR-JAY) PHI.

Center. Shoots left. 6'2", 200 lbs. Born, Pittsburgh, PA, May 3, 1982.
(Vancouver's 1st choice, 16th overall, in 2001 Entry Draft).

			Regular Season					Playoffs				
Season	Club	League	GP	G	A	TP	PIM	GP	G	A	TP	PIM
1997-98	Plum Mustangs	Hi-School	26	*60	*56	*116	....	....	....	....	....	....
1998-99	U.S. National U-17	USDP	50	29	29	58	....	....	....	....	....	....
99-2000	U.S. National U-18	USDP	57	33	35	68	20	....	....	....	....	....
2000-01	Ohio State	CCHA	32	14	23	37	18	....	....	....	....	....
2001-02	Ohio State	CCHA	37	18	21	39	31	....	....	....	....	....
2002-03	Ohio State	CCHA	43	26	27	53	16	....	....	....	....	....
2003-04				DID NOT PLAY								

CCHA All-Rookie Team (2001) • CCHA Rookie of the Year (2001) • CCHA First All-Star Team (2003) • NCAA West Second All-American Team (2003)

• Missed entire 2003-04 season due to a contract dispute. Traded to **NY Rangers** by **Vancouver** with Martin Grenier for Martin Rucinsky, March 9, 2004. Signed as a free agent by **Philadelphia**, June 16, 2004.

UMICEVIC, Dragan (oo-mih-CHAY-vihk, DRA-guhn) EDM.

Left wing. Shoots right. 6', 191 lbs. Born, Köping, Sweden, October 9, 1984.
(Edmonton's 8th choice, 184th overall, in 2003 Entry Draft).

			Regular Season					Playoffs				
Season	Club	League	GP	G	A	TP	PIM	GP	G	A	TP	PIM
99-2000	Koping HC	Swede-3		STATISTICS NOT AVAILABLE				....	....	....	....	....
2000-01	Sodertalje SK 18	Swede-Jr.	16	8	5	13	49	....	....	....	....	....
	Sodertalje SK Jr.	Swede-Jr.	1	0	0	0	0	....	....	....	....	....
2001-02	Sodertalje SK Jr.	Swede-Jr.	36	20	31	51	41	....	....	....	....	....
	Sodertalje SK	Sweden	3	1	0	1	0	....	....	....	....	....
2002-03	Sodertalje SK	Sweden	22	2	3	5	4	....	....	....	....	....
	Sodertalje SK Jr.	Swede-Jr.	24	19	14	33	28	....	....	....	....	....
2003-04	Sodertalje SK Jr.	Swede-Jr.	9	3	5	8	24	....	....	....	....	....
	IF Bjorkloven	Swede-2	21	8	8	16	45	....	....	....	....	....
	Sodertalje SK	Sweden	8	0	0	0	0	....	....	....	....	....

UPPER, Dmitri (OO-puhr, dih-MEE-tree) NYI

Center. Shoots right. 6'1", 185 lbs. Born, Ust-Kamenogorsk, USSR, July 27, 1978.
(NY Islanders' 5th choice, 136th overall, in 2000 Entry Draft).

			Regular Season					Playoffs				
Season	Club	League	GP	G	A	TP	PIM	GP	G	A	TP	PIM
1997-98	Ust-Kamenogorsk	Russia-2	47	16	12	28	44	....	....	....	....	....
1998-99	Ust-Kamenog. 2	Russia-4	29	10	11	21	44	....	....	....	....	....
	Nizhny Novgorod	Russia-2	11	4	10	14	16	17	6	6	12	49
99-2000	Nizhny Novgorod	Russia	36	14	6	20	50	5	1	1	2	4
2000-01	Nizhny Novgorod	Russia	6	0	2	2	4	....	....	....	....	....
	Ak Bars Kazan	Russia	31	7	4	11	6	1	0	0	0	0
2001-02	Spartak Moscow	Russia	51	16	9	25	74	....	....	....	....	....
2002-03	Spartak Moscow	Russia	43	7	13	20	63	....	....	....	....	....
2003-04	CSKA Moscow	Russia	58	10	9	19	48	....	....	....	....	....

URQUHART, Cory (UHRK-hahrt, KOHR-ee) MTL.

Center. Shoots left. 6'3", 200 lbs. Born, Halifax, N.S., October 1, 1984.
(Montreal's 2nd choice, 40th overall, in 2003 Entry Draft).

			Regular Season					Playoffs				
Season	Club	League	GP	G	A	TP	PIM	GP	G	A	TP	PIM
1997-98	East Hants	NSBHL	60	35	46	81	24	....	....	....	....	....
1998-99	East Hants	NSBHL	62	54	60	114	74	....	....	....	....	....
99-2000	Dalhousie	NSMHL	21	15	14	29	12	....	....	....	....	....
2000-01	Quebec Remparts	QMJHL	60	25	24	49	32	2	0	0	0	2
2001-02	Quebec Remparts	QMJHL	36	8	10	18	4	....	....	....	....	....
	Montreal Rocket	QMJHL	34	9	9	18	6	7	3	2	5	0
2002-03	Montreal Rocket	QMJHL	71	35	43	78	28	7	9	6	15	6
2003-04	PEI Rocket	QMJHL	67	35	44	79	52	10	6	7	13	14

USTRNUL, Libor (OOS-tuhr-nuhl, LEE-bohr) ATL.

Defense. Shoots left. 6'5", 235 lbs. Born, Sternberk, Czech., February 20, 1982.
(Atlanta's 3rd choice, 42nd overall, in 2000 Entry Draft).

			Regular Season					Playoffs				
Season	Club	League	GP	G	A	TP	PIM	GP	G	A	TP	PIM
1997-98	HC Olomouc Jr.	Czech-Jr.	45	2	11	13	54	....	....	....	....	....
1998-99	Thunder Bay Flyers	USHL	52	2	5	7	65	18	1	4	5	95
99-2000	Plymouth Whalers	OHL	68	0	15	15	208	23	0	3	3	29
2000-01	Plymouth Whalers	OHL	35	3	13	16	66	19	1	4	5	19
2001-02	Plymouth Whalers	OHL	43	1	8	9	84	2	0	0	0	6
	Chicago Wolves	AHL	1	0	0	0	0	1	0	0	0	5
2002-03	Chicago Wolves	AHL	40	1	1	2	94	6	0	0	0	0
2003-04	Chicago Wolves	AHL	46	1	1	2	68	4	0	1	1	13

UTKIN, Dmitri (OOT-kihn, dih-MEE-tree) BOS.

Left wing. Shoots left. 6', 169 lbs. Born, Yaroslavl, USSR, June 10, 1984.
(Boston's 5th choice, 228th overall, in 2002 Entry Draft).

			Regular Season					Playoffs				
Season	Club	League	GP	G	A	TP	PIM	GP	G	A	TP	PIM
2000-01	Yaroslavl 2	Russia-3	49	12	1	13	10	....	....	....	....	....
2001-02	Yaroslavl 2	Russia-3	32	15	7	22	33	....	....	....	....	....
	Yaroslavl-18	Russia-Jr.	....	....	....	....	....	7	4	9	13	0
	Yaroslavl Jr.	Russia-Jr.	....	....	....	....	....	6	3	3	6	4
2002-03	Yaroslavl	Russia	4	0	1	1	0	....	....	....	....	....
2003-04	Spartak Moscow	Russia-2	57	10	10	20	8	13	3	3	6	2

VAINIO, Niko (VAY-nee-oh, NEE-koh) DAL.

Defense. Shoots left. 6'1", 180 lbs. Born, Helsinki, Finland, January 24, 1985.
(Dallas' 11th choice, 259th overall, in 2003 Entry Draft).

			Regular Season					Playoffs				
Season	Club	League	GP	G	A	TP	PIM	GP	G	A	TP	PIM
2000-01	Jokerit Helsinki B	Finn-Jr.	15	0	1	1	8	....	....	....	....	....
2001-02	Jokerit Helsinki B	Finn-Jr.	26	8	9	17	18	8	0	3	3	6
2002-03	Jokerit Helsinki B	Finn-Jr.	7	2	6	8	8	....	....	....	....	....
	Jokerit Helsinki Jr.	Finn-Jr.	35	1	1	2	8	11	0	0	0	2
2003-04	Jokerit Helsinki Jr.	Finn-Jr.	17	1	0	1	26	....	....	....	....	....

VALABIK, Boris (vuh-LA-bihk, BOHR-ihs) ATL.

Defense. Shoots left. 6'7", 230 lbs. Born, Nitra, Czechoslovakia, February 14, 1986.
(Atlanta's 1st choice, 10th overall, in 2004 Entry Draft).

			Regular Season					Playoffs				
Season	Club	League	GP	G	A	TP	PIM	GP	G	A	TP	PIM
2002-03	HKm Nitra Jr.	Slovak-Jr.	46	2	12	14	145	....	....	....	....	....
2003-04	Kitchener Rangers	OHL	68	3	13	16	278	5	0	0	0	8

OHL All-Rookie Team (2004) • Canadian Major Junior All-Rookie Team (2004)

VALCAK, Patrik (VAHL-chahk, PAT-rihk) BOS.

Center. Shoots left. 6'1", 185 lbs. Born, Ostrava, Czech., December 16, 1984.
(Boston's 6th choice, 129th overall, in 2003 Entry Draft).

			Regular Season					Playoffs				
Season	Club	League	GP	G	A	TP	PIM	GP	G	A	TP	PIM
2000-01	Sareza Ostrava Jr.	Czech-Jr.	44	13	16	29	34	....	....	....	....	....
2001-02	Sareza Ostrava Jr.	Czech-Jr.	45	9	16	25	44	....	....	....	....	....
2002-03	Sareza Ostrava Jr.	Czech-Jr.	38	14	18	32	131	....	....	....	....	....
2003-04	Lethbridge	WHL	35	2	9	11	28	....	....	....	....	....
	Kelowna Rockets	WHL	22	0	1	1	13	11	0	0	0	6

VALDIX, Andreas (VAHL-dihx, an-DRAY-uhs) WSH.

Left wing. Shoots left. 5'11", 170 lbs. Born, Malmo, Sweden, December 6, 1984.
(Washington's 3rd choice, 109th overall, in 2003 Entry Draft).

			Regular Season					Playoffs				
Season	Club	League	GP	G	A	TP	PIM	GP	G	A	TP	PIM
99-2000	Malmo IF Jr.	Swede-Jr.	14	3	7	10	39	....	....	....	....	....
2000-01	Malmo IF 18	Swede-Jr.	6	2	2	4	12	....	....	....	....	....
	Malmo IF Jr.	Swede-Jr.	19	3	3	6	8	3	2	2	4	4
2001-02	Malmo Jr.	Swede-Jr.	39	13	13	26	86	7	0	3	3	6
	Malmo IF	Sweden	1	0	0	0	0	....	....	....	....	....
2002-03	Malmo Jr.	Swede-Jr.	11	10	12	22	16	6	2	5	7	8
	Malmo	Sweden	39	2	0	2	10	....	....	....	....	....
2003-04	Malmo Jr.	Swede-Jr.	9	4	3	7	4	....	....	....	....	....
	Malmo	Sweden	47	2	3	5	8	....	....	....	....	....

VALETTE, Craig (va-LEHT, KRAIG) S.J.

Center. Shoots left. 6', 190 lbs. Born, Shellbrook, Sask., October 7, 1982.

			Regular Season					Playoffs				
Season	Club	League	GP	G	A	TP	PIM	GP	G	A	TP	PIM
1998-99	Sask. Contacts	SMHL	36	19	22	41	....	....	....	....	....	....
99-2000	Saskatoon Blades	WHL	47	2	1	3	25	3	0	0	0	0
2000-01	Saskatoon Blades	WHL	24	2	0	2	19	....	....	....	....	....
	Portland	WHL	39	8	6	14	39	16	0	2	2	27
2001-02	Portland	WHL	67	8	14	22	160	7	2	1	3	6
2002-03	Portland	WHL	71	30	26	56	192	7	5	4	9	18
2003-04	Cleveland Barons	AHL	56	6	10	16	77	5	0	0	0	2

Signed as a free agent by **San Jose**, April 4, 2003.

VALTONEN, Tomek (VAL-tuh-nehn, Toh-MEHK) DET.

Left wing. Shoots left. 6'1", 198 lbs. Born, Piotrkow Trybunalski, Poland, January 8, 1980.
(Detroit's 3rd choice, 56th overall, in 1998 Entry Draft).

			Regular Season					Playoffs				
Season	Club	League	GP	G	A	TP	PIM	GP	G	A	TP	PIM
1995-96	Ilves Tampere-C	Finn-Jr.	9	3	3	6	24	....	....	....	....	....
	Ilves Tampere-B	Finn-Jr.	11	7	7	14	28	....	....	....	....	....
	Ilves Tampere Jr.	Finn-Jr.	....	....	....	....	....	1	0	0	0	0
1996-97	Ilves Tampere-B	Finn-Jr.	26	10	9	19	82	3	0	1	1	6
	Ilves Tampere Jr.	Finn-Jr.	1	0	0	0	0	....	....	....	....	....
1997-98	JoKP Joensuu Jr.	Finn-Jr.	3	0	0	0	12	....	....	....	....	....
	JoKP Joensuu	Finland-2	6	1	2	3	39	....	....	....	....	....
	Ilves Tampere Jr.	Finn-Jr.	13	3	2	5	36	....	....	....	....	....
	Ilves Tampere	Finland	19	1	0	1	14	3	0	0	0	0
	Ilves Tampere-B	Finn-Jr.	....	....	....	....	....	7	0	2	2	16
1998-99	Plymouth Whalers	OHL	43	8	16	24	53	7	1	0	1	0
99-2000	Jokerit Helsinki	Finland	41	0	3	3	63	9	1	0	1	8
2000-01	Jokerit Helsinki	Finland	45	3	2	5	138	3	0	0	0	0
2001-02	Jokerit Helsinki	Finland	55	4	4	8	65	11	2	1	3	2
2002-03	Jokerit Helsinki	Finland	51	5	9	14	38	10	1	1	2	4
2003-04	Jokerit Helsinki	Finland	53	15	16	31	78	8	1	3	4	8

VAN DER GULIK, David (VAN-DUHR-GOO-lihk, DAY-vihd) CGY.

Right wing. Shoots left. 5'11", 175 lbs. Born, Abbotsford, B.C., April 20, 1983.
(Calgary's 10th choice, 206th overall, in 2002 Entry Draft).

			Regular Season					Playoffs				
Season	Club	League	GP	G	A	TP	PIM	GP	G	A	TP	PIM
99-2000	Chilliwack Chiefs	BCHL	41	35	46	81	....	....	....	....	....	....
2000-01	Chilliwack Chiefs	BCHL	60	42	38	80	....	....	....	....	....	....
2001-02	Chilliwack Chiefs	BCHL	56	38	62	100	90	13	8	11	19	....
2002-03	Boston University	H-East	40	10	10	20	56	....	....	....	....	....
2003-04	Boston University	H-East	35	13	7	20	74	....	....	....	....	....

Hockey East All-Rookie Team (2003)

VANDERMEER, Peter (VAN-duhr-meer, PEE-tuhr) DET.

Left wing. Shoots left. 6', 210 lbs. Born, Carolina, Alta., October 14, 1975.

			Regular Season					Playoffs				
Season	Club	League	GP	G	A	TP	PIM	GP	G	A	TP	PIM
1992-93	Red Deer	AMHL	34	26	30	56	172	....	....	....	....	....
	Red Deer Rebels	WHL	2	0	0	0	2	....	....	....	....	....
1993-94	Red Deer Rebels	WHL	54	4	9	13	170	....	....	....	....	....
1994-95	Red Deer Rebels	WHL	61	16	16	32	218	....	....	....	....	....
1995-96	Red Deer Rebels	WHL	63	21	40	61	207	....	....	....	....	....
1996-97	Columbus Chill	ECHL	30	6	11	17	195	7	2	1	3	26
1997-98	Columbus Chill	ECHL	20	4	7	11	78	....	....	....	....	....
	Richmond	ECHL	18	2	5	7	165	....	....	....	....	....
	Rochester	AHL	30	4	2	6	140	4	1	0	1	13
1998-99	Binghamton	UHL	62	15	21	36	*390	5	2	2	4	0
	Rochester	AHL	2	1	0	1	16	16	1	0	1	38
99-2000	Richmond	ECHL	58	31	25	56	*457	3	0	1	1	20
	Wilkes-Barre	AHL	4	0	0	0	7	....	....	....	....	....
	Providence Bruins	AHL	....	....	....	....	....	9	0	3	3	2
2000-01	Providence Bruins	AHL	62	19	18	37	240	4	0	0	0	16
2001-02	Trenton Titans	ECHL	2	0	1	1	2	....	....	....	....	....
	Philadelphia	AHL	61	5	1	6	313	5	0	0	0	8
2002-03	Philadelphia	AHL	77	5	8	13	335	....	....	....	....	....
2003-04	Philadelphia	AHL	71	5	8	13	*398	12	1	0	1	29

Signed as a free agent by **Philadelphia**, July 6, 2001. Signed as a free agent by **Detroit**, July, 2004.

VANEK, Thomas (VAH-nehk, TAW-muhs) BUF.

Left wing. Shoots right. 6'2", 208 lbs. Born, Vienna, Austria, January 19, 1984.
(Buffalo's 1st choice, 5th overall, in 2003 Entry Draft).

			Regular Season					Playoffs				
Season	Club	League	GP	G	A	TP	PIM	GP	G	A	TP	PIM
99-2000	Sioux Falls	USHL	35	15	18	33	12	3	0	1	1	0
2000-01	Sioux Falls	USHL	20	19	10	29	15	8	5	4	9	2
2001-02	Sioux Falls	USHL	53	46	45	91	54	3	0	0	0	9
2002-03	U. of Minnesota	WCHA	45	31	31	62	60	....	....	....	....	....
2003-04	U. of Minnesota	WCHA	38	26	25	51	72	....	....	....	....	....

USHL First All-Star Team (2002) • USHL MVP (2002) • WCHA All-Rookie Team (2003) • WCHA Second All-Star Team (2003, 2004) • WCHA Rookie of the Year (2003) • NCAA Championship All-Tournament Team (2003) • NCAA Tournament MVP (2003) • NCAA West Second All-American Team (2004)

VANNELLI, Michael (vuh-NEHL-ee, MIGH-kuhl) ATL.

Defense. Shoots right. 6'2", 190 lbs. Born, St. Paul, MN, October 2, 1983.
(Atlanta's 4th choice, 136th overall, in 2003 Entry Draft).

			Regular Season					Playoffs				
Season	Club	League	GP	G	A	TP	PIM	GP	G	A	TP	PIM
2001-02	Cretin-Durham	Hi-School	28	0	5	5	16	....	....	....	....	....
	Sioux Falls	USHL	37	0	5	5	24	....	....	....	....	....
2002-03	Sioux Falls	USHL	60	13	34	47	88	....	....	....	....	....
2003-04	U. of Minnesota	WCHA	27	2	9	11	10	....	....	....	....	....

USHL First All-Star Team (2003)

VAN OENE, Darren (van OH-uhn, DAIR-rehn)

Left wing. Shoots left. 6'4", 216 lbs. Born, Edmonton, Alta., January 18, 1978.
(Buffalo's 3rd choice, 33rd overall, in 1996 Entry Draft).

			Regular Season					Playoffs				
Season	Club	League	GP	G	A	TP	PIM	GP	G	A	TP	PIM
1993-94	Edmonton SSAC	AMHL	34	15	16	31	121	....	....	....	....	....
1994-95	Brandon	WHL	58	5	13	18	106	18	1	1	2	34
1995-96	Brandon	WHL	47	10	18	28	126	18	1	6	7	*78
1996-97	Brandon	WHL	56	21	27	48	139	6	2	3	5	19
1997-98	Brandon	WHL	51	23	24	47	161	18	6	8	14	51
1998-99	Rochester	AHL	73	11	20	31	143	12	2	4	6	8
99-2000	Rochester	AHL	80	20	18	38	153	21	1	3	4	24
2000-01	Rochester	AHL	64	10	12	22	147	4	1	0	1	4
2001-02	Rochester	AHL	52	8	6	14	73	2	0	0	0	4
2002-03	Providence Bruins	AHL	78	11	17	28	109	4	0	0	0	21
2003-04	Providence Bruins	AHL	72	9	16	25	111	2	0	0	0	0

Signed as a free agent by **Boston**, July 29, 2002.

VAS, Janos (VAHSH, YAH-nohsh) DAL.

Left wing. Shoots left. 6'1", 183 lbs. Born, Dunaferr, Hungary, January 29, 1984.
(Dallas' 2nd choice, 32nd overall, in 2002 Entry Draft).

			Regular Season					Playoffs				
Season	Club	League	GP	G	A	TP	PIM	GP	G	A	TP	PIM
99-2000	Dunaferr SE	Hungary	2	2	0	0	0	....	....	....	....	....
2000-01	Malmo IF Jr.	Swede-Jr.	23	4	4	8	12	....	....	....	....	....
	Malmo IF 18	Swede-Jr.	3	2	0	2	4	....	....	....	....	....
2001-02	Malmo IF Jr.	Swede-Jr.	36	15	19	34	52	7	8	2	10	4
2002-03	Malmo IF Jr.	Swede-Jr.	17	5	12	17	14	....	....	....	....	....
	IK Pantern	Swede-2	STATISTICS NOT AVAILABLE									
	IF Troja/Ljunby	Swede-2	17	2	2	4	20	....	....	....	....	....
	Malmo	Sweden	14	1	0	1	2	....	....	....	....	....
2003-04	Malmo Jr.	Swede-Jr.	15	5	3	8	14	8	5	2	7	33
	Malmo	Sweden	6	0	0	0	0	....	....	....	....	....
	IK Pantern	Swede-3	3	0	2	2	....	....	....	....	....	....
	Malmo	Swede-Q	1	0	0	0	0	....	....	....	....	....

VAVRA, Josef (VAHV-rah, YOH-zuhf) OTT.

Left wing. Shoots left. 6', 199 lbs. Born, Valasske Mezirici, Czech., March 17, 1984.
(Ottawa's 7th choice, 246th overall, in 2002 Entry Draft).

			Regular Season					Playoffs				
Season	Club	League	GP	G	A	TP	PIM	GP	G	A	TP	PIM
99-2000	HC Vsetin 16	Czech-Jr.	50	25	21	46	90	....	....	....	....	....
2000-01	HC Vsetin 16	Czech-Jr.	32	22	33	55	99	....	....	....	....	....
	Vsetin Jr.	Czech-Jr.	11	0	2	2	2	....	....	....	....	....
2001-02	Vsetin Jr.	Czech-Jr.	35	3	12	15	39	....	....	....	....	....
2002-03	Tri-City Americans	WHL	37	2	5	7	26	....	....	....	....	....
2003-04	Kootenay Ice	WHL	18	2	4	6	24	....	....	....	....	....
	HC Vsetin	Czech	4	0	0	0	0	....	....	....	....	....

• Missed majority of 2002-03 season recovering from knee injury suffered in game vs. Portland (WHL), November 6, 2002.

VENALAINEN, Sami (veh-na-LIGH-nehn, SA-mee) PHX.

Right wing. Shoots right. 5'11", 183 lbs. Born, Kangasala, Finland, October 14, 1981.
(Phoenix's 7th choice, 249th overall, in 2000 Entry Draft).

			Regular Season					Playoffs				
Season	Club	League	GP	G	A	TP	PIM	GP	G	A	TP	PIM
1996-97	Tappara C	Finn-Jr.	32	21	17	38	31	4	2	1	3	0
1997-98	Tappara C	Finn-Jr.	2	2	0	2	6	6	4	5	9	6
	Tappara B	Finn-Jr.	33	18	7	25	12	....	....	....	....	....
1998-99	Tappara B	Finn-Jr.	31	27	17	44	45	....	....	....	....	....
	Tappara Jr.	Finn-Jr.	10	3	2	5	29	....	....	....	....	....
99-2000	Tappara Jr.	Finn-Jr.	37	8	9	17	18	....	....	....	....	....
2000-01	Tappara Jr.	Finn-Jr.	21	6	13	19	12	9	3	1	4	0
	Tappara Tampere	Finland	36	0	1	1	2	1	0	0	0	0
2001-02	Tappara Tampere	Finland	56	5	8	13	24	10	0	1	1	8
2002-03	Tappara Tampere	Finland	55	5	9	14	48	13	0	0	0	10
2003-04	Tappara Tampere	Finland	56	18	15	33	22	3	1	0	1	0

VERSTEEG, Kris (vuhr-STEEG, KRIHS) BOS.

Right wing. Shoots right. 5'9", 159 lbs. Born, Lethbridge, Alta., May 13, 1986.
(Boston's 4th choice, 134th overall, in 2004 Entry Draft).

			Regular Season					Playoffs				
Season	Club	League	GP	G	A	TP	PIM	GP	G	A	TP	PIM
2002-03	Lethbridge	WHL	57	8	10	18	32	....	....	....	....	....
2003-04	Lethbridge	WHL	68	16	33	49	85	....	....	....	....	....

VIDELL, Linus (vih-DEHL, LIH-nuhs) COL.

Left wing. Shoots left. 6'3", 214 lbs. Born, Skarpnack, Sweden, May 5, 1985.
(Colorado's 5th choice, 204th overall, in 2003 Entry Draft).

			Regular Season					Playoffs				
Season	Club	League	GP	G	A	TP	PIM	GP	G	A	TP	PIM
2000-01	AIK Solna 16	Swede-Jr.	8	12	2	14	....	....	....	....	....	....
2001-02	AIK Solna 18	Swede-Jr.	14	12	5	17	12	4	7	1	8	....
2002-03	Brynas IF Jr.	Swede-Jr.	19	4	7	11	4	....	....	....	....	....
	Sodertalje SK 18	Swede-Jr.	1	0	0	0	2	....	....	....	....	....
	Sodertalje SK Jr.	Swede-Jr.	9	4	2	6	0	3	0	1	1	0
2003-04	Sodertalje SK Jr.	Swede-Jr.	27	20	15	35	6	2	0	0	0	0
	Sodertalje SK	Sweden	23	0	2	2	0	....	....	....	....	....

VIHKO, Joonas (VIH-koh, YOO-nuhs) ANA.

Center. Shoots right. 5'9", 172 lbs. Born, Helsinki, Finland, April 6, 1981.
(Anaheim's 4th choice, 103rd overall, in 2002 Entry Draft).

			Regular Season					Playoffs				
Season	Club	League	GP	G	A	TP	PIM	GP	G	A	TP	PIM
1998-99	HIFK Helsinki Jr.	Finn-Jr.	32	15	14	29	10	3	1	1	2	0
99-2000	HIFK Helsinki Jr.	Finn-Jr.	38	12	15	27	36	3	0	0	0	0
2000-01	HIFK Helsinki Jr.	Finn-Jr.	27	23	17	40	85	7	5	2	7	18
	HIFK Helsinki	Finland	3	0	0	0	2	....	....	....	....	....
2001-02	HIFK Helsinki	Finland	48	13	11	24	89	....	....	....	....	....
	HIFK Helsinki Jr.	Finn-Jr.	....	....	....	....	....	2	0	2	2	4
2002-03	HIFK Helsinki	Finland	50	14	11	25	20	1	0	0	0	2
2003-04	HIFK Helsinki	Finland	52	9	8	17	56	13	3	5	8	6

VIITANEN, Mikko (vee-EE-tan-ehn, MEE-koh) COL.

Defense. Shoots left. 6'3", 220 lbs. Born, Rajamaki, Finland, February 18, 1982.
(Colorado's 6th choice, 149th overall, in 2001 Entry Draft).

			Regular Season					Playoffs				
Season	Club	League	GP	G	A	TP	PIM	GP	G	A	TP	PIM
1998-99	HPK-B	Finn-Jr.	36	3	6	9	40	....	....	....	....	....
	HPK Jr.	Finn-Jr.	1	0	0	0	0	....	....	....	....	....
99-2000	Chicago Freeze	NAJHL	53	4	6	10	126	....	....	....	....	....
2000-01	Ahmat Jr.	Finn-Jr.	9	3	4	7	41	....	....	....	....	....
	Ahmat Hyvinkaa	Finland-2	41	3	9	12	66	3	0	0	0	0
2001-02	Blues Espoo Jr.	Finn-Jr.	10	1	3	4	16	....	....	....	....	....
	Blues Espoo	Finland	3	0	0	0	6	....	....	....	....	....
	Jukurit Mikkeli	Finland-2	21	0	3	3	26	....	....	....	....	....
2002-03	KJT Jarvenpaa	Finland-2	9	0	1	1	56	....	....	....	....	....
	Blues Espoo	Finland	1	0	0	0	0	....	....	....	....	....
2003-04	Hershey Bears	AHL	20	1	1	2	14	....	....	....	....	....
	Reading Royals	ECHL	47	0	4	4	21	13	0	1	1	8

VIKINGSTAD, Tore (VIH-kihng-stahd, TOO-reh) ST.L.

Left wing. Shoots left. 6'4", 204 lbs. Born, Stavenger, Norway, October 8, 1975.
(St. Louis' 5th choice, 180th overall, in 1999 Entry Draft).

			Regular Season					Playoffs				
Season	Club	League	GP	G	A	TP	PIM	GP	G	A	TP	PIM
1993-94	Viking	Norway	2	0	0	0	0	....	....	....	....	....
1994-95	Viking	Norway	28	5	3	8	8	4	1	2	3	2
1995-96	Viking	Norway	27	12	11	23	....	....	....	....	....	....
1996-97	Stjernen	Norway	42	23	35	58	20	....	....	....	....	....
1997-98	Stjernen	Norway	42	26	31	57	18	....	....	....	....	....
1998-99	Farjestad	Sweden	49	9	11	20	18	4	2	3	5	0
	Farjestad	EuroHL	6	1	1	2	10	....	....	....	....	....
99-2000	Farjestad	Sweden	47	8	19	27	26	7	3	0	3	6
2000-01	Leksands IF	Sweden	41	10	15	25	24	....	....	....	....	....
	Leksands IF	Swede-Q	9	3	3	6	16	....	....	....	....	....
2001-02	DEG Metro Stars	Germany	58	18	30	48	6	....	....	....	....	....
2002-03	DEG Metro Stars	Germany	45	13	18	31	40	5	1	0	1	0
2003-04	DEG Metro Stars	Germany	50	9	21	30	38	4	1	2	3	2

VISHNYAKOV, Albert (vihsh-nyeh-KAWF, al-BAIRT) T.B.

Wing. Shoots right. 6', 185 lbs. Born, Almyetevsk, USSR, December 30, 1983.
(Tampa Bay's 9th choice, 273rd overall, in 2003 Entry Draft).

			Regular Season					Playoffs				
Season	Club	League	GP	G	A	TP	PIM	GP	G	A	TP	PIM
99-2000	Almetjevsk 2	Russia-3	41	11	5	16	68	....	....	....	....	....
2000-01	Almetjevsk	Russia-2	29	0	0	0	2	....	....	....	....	....
2001-02	Ak Bars Kazan	Russia	9	0	1	1	2	....	....	....	....	....
	Nizhny Novgorod	Russia	6	1	0	1	0	....	....	....	....	....
	Nizhny Novgorod 2	Russia-3	4	2	2	4	10	....	....	....	....	....
2002-03	Ak Bars Kazan	Russia	47	7	6	13	47	5	1	0	1	0
2003-04	Nizhnekamsk	Russia	10	2	3	5	10	....	....	....	....	....
	Ak Bars Kazan 2	Russia-3	STATISTICS NOT AVAILABLE									
	Ak Bars Kazan	Russia	10	1	1	2	8	....	....	....	....	....

VLCEK, Ladislav (vuhl-CHEHK, LA-dih-slahv) DAL.

Right wing. Shoots left. 5'11", 184 lbs. Born, Kladno, Czech., September 26, 1981.
(Dallas' 8th choice, 192nd overall, in 2000 Entry Draft).

			Regular Season					Playoffs				
Season	Club	League	GP	G	A	TP	PIM	GP	G	A	TP	PIM
1998-99	Kladno Jr.	Czech-Jr.	46	13	27	40	....	....	....	....	....	....
	HC Velvana Kladno	Czech	4	0	1	1	0	....	....	....	....	....
99-2000	Kladno Jr.	Czech-Jr.	34	16	15	31	16	....	....	....	....	....
	HC CKD Slany	Czech-3	4	3	0	3	0	....	....	....	....	....
	Kralupy	Czech-3	1	0	1	1	0	5	2	2	4	4
	HC Velvana Kladno	Czech	21	3	2	5	4	....	....	....	....	....
2000-01	Kladno	Czech	45	6	10	16	22	....	....	....	....	....
2001-02	Kladno	Czech	20	3	1	4	14	....	....	....	....	....
	HC Ocelari Trinec	Czech	28	3	6	9	18	6	1	0	1	2
2002-03	HC Hame Zlin	Czech	13	2	1	3	0	....	....	....	....	....
	Karlovy Vary	Czech	12	1	0	1	2	....	....	....	....	....
	Beroun	Czech-2	12	3	3	6	12	....	....	....	....	....
	Beroun	Czech-Q	6	0	2	2	2	....	....	....	....	....
2003-04	IHC Pisek	Czech-2	5	1	0	1	0	....	....	....	....	....
	HC Rabat Kladno	Czech	9	1	1	2	2	....	....	....	....	....
	KLH Chomutov	Czech-2	7	2	0	2	0	2	0	0	0	0

VOCE, Tony (VOHS, TOH-nee) PHI.

Center. Shoots left. 5'8", 185 lbs. Born, Philadelphia, PA, October 30, 1980.

			Regular Season					Playoffs				
Season	Club	League	GP	G	A	TP	PIM	GP	G	A	TP	PIM
99-2000	Lawrence Acad.	Hi-School	STATISTICS NOT AVAILABLE									
2000-01	Boston College	H-East	42	12	14	26	40	....	....	....	....	....
2001-02	Boston College	H-East	38	26	22	48	65	....	....	....	....	....
2002-03	Boston College	H-East	37	*23	23	46	56	....	....	....	....	....
2003-04	Boston College	H-East	42	*29	18	47	48	....	....	....	....	....

Hockey East First All-Star Team (2002, 2004) • NCAA East First All-American Team (2004)

Signed as a free agent by **Philadelphia**, July 13, 2004.

VODRAZKA, Jan (voh-DRAZ-kuh, YAHN)

Defense. Shoots left. 6'1", 200 lbs. Born, Plzen, Czech., November 10, 1976.

			Regular Season					Playoffs				
Season	Club	League	GP	G	A	TP	PIM	GP	G	A	TP	PIM
1994-95	HC Plzen Jr.	Czech-Jr.	STATISTICS NOT AVAILABLE									
1995-96	Detroit Whalers	OHL	47	5	11	16	117	17	2	3	5	29
1996-97	Detroit Whalers	OHL	61	7	21	28	238	5	0	1	1	17
	Richmond	ECHL	4	0	0	0	12	7	0	1	1	36
1997-98	Milwaukee	IHL	10	0	0	0	32	....	....	....	....	....
	Madison Monsters	UHL	55	3	15	18	224	6	1	1	2	36
1998-99	Pee Dee Pride	ECHL	64	8	12	20	262	13	0	0	0	56
99-2000	Kansas City Blades	IHL	66	2	8	10	280	....	....	....	....	....
2000-01	Kansas City Blades	IHL	65	3	11	14	227	....	....	....	....	....
	Kentucky	AHL	6	0	0	0	31	....	....	....	....	....
2001-02	Florida Everblades	ECHL	4	0	0	0	6	....	....	....	....	....
	Lowell	AHL	49	1	3	4	152	5	0	0	0	2
2002-03	Saint John Flames	AHL	80	1	4	5	169	....	....	....	....	....
2003-04	Houston Aeros	AHL	54	1	7	8	82	2	0	0	0	4

Signed as a free agent by **Milwaukee** (IHL), October 5, 1997. Signed as a free agent by **Kansas City** (IHL), September 15, 1999. Signed as a free agent by **Lowell** (AHL), August 10, 2001. Signed as a free agent by **Calgary**, September 9, 2002. Signed as a free agent by **Minnesota**, October 22, 2003.

VOLKOV, Igor (VOHL-kawf, EE-gohr) **NYI**

Right wing. Shoots left. 6', 189 lbs. Born, Ufa, USSR, January 24, 1983.
(NY Islanders' 9th choice, 246th overall, in 2003 Entry Draft).

			Regular Season					Playoffs				
Season	Club	League	GP	G	A	TP	PIM	GP	G	A	TP	PIM
2000-01	Ufa Salavat	Russia	30	1	1	2	4	....	....	....	....	....
2001-02	Ufa Salavat	Russia	43	3	1	4	8	....	....	....	....	....
2002-03	Ufa Salavat	Russia	41	9	5	14	32	3	1	0	1	4
2003-04	Ufa Salavat	Russia	45	11	13	24	38	....	....	....	....	....

VOLKOV, Konstantin (VOHL-kawf, kawn-stuhn-TIHN) **TOR.**

Right wing. Shoots left. 6', 174 lbs. Born, Kolpino, USSR, February 7, 1985.
(Toronto's 3rd choice, 125th overall, in 2003 Entry Draft).

			Regular Season					Playoffs				
Season	Club	League	GP	G	A	TP	PIM	GP	G	A	TP	PIM
2000-01	St. Petersburg	Russia-2	2	0	1	1	0	....	....	....	....	....
2001-02	Dyn. Moscow 2	Russia-3	21	3	7	10	10	....	....	....	....	....
2002-03	Dyn. Moscow 2	Russia-3	29	13	17	30	2	....	....	....	....	....
	Dyn. Moscow Jr.	Russia-Jr.	29	15	22	37	2	4	4	7	11	16
2003-04	THC Tver	Russia-2	18	0	6	6	6	....	....	....	....	....
	CSK VVS Samara	Russia-2	22	6	6	12	16	....	....	....	....	....
	Lada Togliatti 2	Russia-3	10	2	7	9	10	11	0	10	10	4

VOLOSHENKO, Roman (voh-loh-SHEHN-koh, ROH-muhn) **MIN.**

Left wing. Shoots right. 6'1", 189 lbs. Born, Brest, USSR, May 12, 1986.
(Minnesota's 2nd choice, 42nd overall, in 2004 Entry Draft).

			Regular Season					Playoffs				
Season	Club	League	GP	G	A	TP	PIM	GP	G	A	TP	PIM
2001-02	Krylja Sovetov 2	Russia-3	8	2	3	5	0	....	....	....	....	....
2002-03	Krylja Sovetov	Russia	5	0	1	1	2	....	....	....	....	....
	Krylja Sovetov 2	Russia-3	6	3	1	4	2	....	....	....	....	....
2003-04	Krylja Sovetov	Russia-2	46	7	8	15	40	4	1	1	2	4

VONDRKA, Michal (VOHND-rah-ka, MEE-khahl) **BUF.**

Left wing. Shoots right. 6', 178 lbs. Born, Ceske Budejovice, Czech., May 17, 1983.
(Buffalo's 5th choice, 155th overall, in 2001 Entry Draft).

			Regular Season					Playoffs				
Season	Club	League	GP	G	A	TP	PIM	GP	G	A	TP	PIM
1998-99	C. Budejovice 18	Czech-Jr.	50	28	15	43	....	....	....	....	....	....
99-2000	C. Budejovice Jr.	Czech-Jr.	31	12	7	19	16	....	....	....	....	....
2000-01	C. Budejovice Jr.	Czech-Jr.	37	9	14	23	37	....	....	....	....	....
	Ceske Budejovice	Czech	8	1	0	1	2	....	....	....	....	....
	Hradec Kralove	Czech-2	1	0	1	1	2	....	....	....	....	....
2001-02	C. Budejovice Jr.	Czech-Jr.	14	3	9	12	8	....	....	....	....	....
	IHC Pisek	Czech-2	2	1	0	1	0	....	....	....	....	....
	Ceske Budejovice	Czech	33	1	1	2	2	....	....	....	....	....
2002-03	Ceske Budejovice	Czech	27	1	3	4	4	3	0	0	0	0
	C. Budejovice Jr.	Czech-Jr.	7	4	1	5	4	....	....	....	....	....
	IHC Pisek	Czech-2	20	4	2	6	39	3	1	0	1	0
2003-04	Ceske Budejovice	Czech	8	1	0	1	0	....	....	....	....	....
	HC Slavia Praha	Czech	37	6	7	13	8	19	2	1	3	4

VOROBIEV, Dmitri (voh-roh-BEE-ehf, dih-MEE-tree **TOR.**

Defense. Shoots left. 6'1", 211 lbs. Born, Togliatti, USSR, October 18, 1985.
(Toronto's 3rd choice, 157th overall, in 2004 Entry Draft).

			Regular Season					Playoffs				
Season	Club	League	GP	G	A	TP	PIM	GP	G	A	TP	PIM
2002-03	Lada Togliatti 2	Russia-3	31	3	5	8	12	....	....	....	....	....
	Lada Togliatti 17	Russia-Jr.	7	2	3	5	14	....	....	....	....	....
2003-04	Lada Togliatti 2	Russia-3	10	1	1	2	4	....	....	....	....	....
	Lada Togliatti	Russia	23	1	0	1	12	4	0	0	0	4

VOROS, Aaron (VOH-ruhs, AIR-uhn) **N.J.**

Center. Shoots left. 6'4", 190 lbs. Born, Vancouver, B.C., July 2, 1981.
(New Jersey's 10th choice, 229th overall, in 2001 Entry Draft).

			Regular Season					Playoffs				
Season	Club	League	GP	G	A	TP	PIM	GP	G	A	TP	PIM
99-2000	Victoria Salsa	BCHL	58	14	21	35	285	....	....	....	....	....
2000-01	Victoria Salsa	BCHL	57	34	34	68	196	30	16	15	31	....
2001-02	Alaska-Fairbanks	CCHA	37	18	12	30	*101	....	....	....	....	....
2002-03	Alaska-Fairbanks	CCHA	16	2	5	7	42	....	....	....	....	....
2003-04	Alaska-Fairbanks	CCHA	36	16	8	24	*132	....	....	....	....	....
	Albany River Rats	AHL	9	2	1	3	14	....	....	....	....	....

CCHA All-Rookie Team (2002)

Missed majority of 2002-03 season recovering from leg surgery, January 30, 2003.

VOROSHNIN, Pavel (vo-rohsh-NIHN, PAH-vehl) **BUF.**

Defense. Shoots left. 6'3", 175 lbs. Born, Chelyabinsk, USSR, March 23, 1984.
(Buffalo's 7th choice, 172nd overall, in 2003 Entry Draft).

			Regular Season					Playoffs				
Season	Club	League	GP	G	A	TP	PIM	GP	G	A	TP	PIM
2001-02	Chelyabinsk	Russia-2	32	0	2	2	10	....	....	....	....	....
2002-03	Mississauga	OHL	68	9	27	36	81	1	0	0	0	2
2003-04	Mississauga	OHL	18	0	4	4	6	....	....	....	....	....
	Owen Sound	OHL	40	3	18	21	36	7	0	2	2	4

VOSTRIKOV, Artem (VAWS-trih-kawv, ahr-TEHM) **CBJ**

Center. Shoots left. 6'1", 175 lbs. Born, Togliatti, USSR, March 23, 1983.
(Columbus' 8th choice, 187th overall, in 2001 Entry Draft).

			Regular Season					Playoffs				
Season	Club	League	GP	G	A	TP	PIM	GP	G	A	TP	PIM
99-2000	Lada Togliatti 2	Russia-3	26	2	1	3	4	....	....	....	....	....
2000-01	Lada Togliatti 2	Russia-3	3	1	0	1	2	1	0	0	0	0
2001-02	Lada Togliatti	Russia	12	1	1	2	0	....	....	....	....	....
	CSK VVS Samara	Russia-2	17	1	4	5	36	6	0	0	0	4
2002-03	Spartak Moscow	Russia	20	2	3	5	0	....	....	....	....	....
2003-04	Krylja Sovetov	Russia-2	49	10	15	25	64	4	1	1	2	4

VRANA, Petr (vuh-RA-nuh, PEE-tuhr) **N.J.**

Left wing. Shoots left. 5'10", 175 lbs. Born, Sternberk, Czech., March 29, 1985.
(New Jersey's 2nd choice, 42nd overall, in 2003 Entry Draft).

			Regular Season					Playoffs				
Season	Club	League	GP	G	A	TP	PIM	GP	G	A	TP	PIM
99-2000	HC Olomouc 16	Czech-Jr.	43	12	18	30	24	....	....	....	....	....
2000-01	HC Olomouc 16	Czech-Jr.	41	38	48	86	32	3	1	3	4	6
2001-02	Havirov 16	Czech-Jr.	6	10	9	19	....	....	....	....	....	....
	Havirov Jr.	Czech-Jr.	38	11	12	23	....	....	....	....	....	....
	HC Femax Havirov	Czech	6	0	0	0	4	....	....	....	....	....
2002-03	Halifax	QMJHL	72	37	46	83	32	24	5	15	20	12
2003-04	Halifax	QMJHL	48	13	25	38	56	....	....	....	....	....

QMJHL All-Rookie Team (2003) • QMJHL Rookie of the Year (2003)

VYDARENY, Rene (vih-DAH-reh-nay, REH-nay) **MTL.**

Defense. Shoots left. 6'1", 198 lbs. Born, Bratislava, Czech., May 6, 1981.
(Vancouver's 3rd choice, 69th overall, in 1999 Entry Draft).

			Regular Season					Playoffs				
Season	Club	League	GP	G	A	TP	PIM	GP	G	A	TP	PIM
1997-98	S. Bratislava Jr.	Slovak-Jr.	50	5	14	19	26	....	....	....	....	....
1998-99	S. Bratislava Jr.	Slovak-Jr.	42	4	7	11	65	2	0	0	0	2
	HK Kabat Trnava	Slovak-2	20	1	6	7	6	....	....	....	....	....
99-2000	Rimouski Oceanic	QMJHL	51	7	23	30	41	14	2	2	4	20
2000-01	Kansas City Blades	IHL	39	0	1	1	25	....	....	....	....	....
2001-02	Manitoba Moose	AHL	61	3	11	14	15	7	0	2	2	4
	Columbia Inferno	ECHL	10	2	1	3	9	....	....	....	....	....
2002-03	Manitoba Moose	AHL	71	2	8	10	46	14	0	2	2	16
2003-04	Manitoba Moose	AHL	50	2	10	12	16	....	....	....	....	....
	Hamilton Bulldogs	AHL	13	0	3	3	2	10	0	1	1	9

• Missed majority of 2000-01 season due to dispute over ownership of playing rights between **Vancouver** and **HC Bratislava** (Slovakia), November 28, 2000. Traded to **Montreal** by **Vancouver** for Sylvain Blouin, March 9, 2004.

WALLIN, Viktor (WAHL-in, VIHK-tohr) **ANA.**

Defense. Shoots left. 6'3", 200 lbs. Born, Jonkoping, Sweden, January 17, 1980.
(Anaheim's 3rd choice, 112th overall, in 1998 Entry Draft).

			Regular Season					Playoffs				
Season	Club	League	GP	G	A	TP	PIM	GP	G	A	TP	PIM
1996-97	HV 71 Jr.	Swede-Jr.	16	1	2	3	....	....	....	....	....	....
1997-98	HV 71 Jr.	Swede-Jr.	28	9	15	24	42	....	....	....	....	....
1998-99	HV 71 Jonkoping	Sweden	23	0	0	0	4	....	....	....	....	....
99-2000	HV 71 Jr.	Swede-Jr.	6	3	1	4	2	....	....	....	....	....
	HV 71 Jonkoping	Sweden	43	2	2	4	16	6	1	1	2	4
2000-01	HV 71 Jonkoping	Sweden	5	0	1	1	2	....	....	....	....	....
2001-02	Timra IK	Sweden	35	0	3	3	18	....	....	....	....	....
	Timra IK	Swede-Q	10	0	1	1	9	....	....	....	....	....
2002-03	AIK Solna	Swede-2	50	3	15	18	34	4	0	0	0	4
2003-04	AIK Solna	Swede-2	46	7	14	21	32	5	1	1	2	2
	AIK Solna	Swede-Q	10	1	0	1	2	....	....	....	....	....

WALSH, Brendan (WAHLSH, BREHN-duhn)

Right wing. Shoots right. 5'9", 181 lbs. Born, Dorchester, MA, October 22, 1974.

			Regular Season					Playoffs				
Season	Club	League	GP	G	A	TP	PIM	GP	G	A	TP	PIM
1993-94	Omaha Lancers	USHL	31	9	20	29	187	....	....	....	....	....
1994-95	Omaha Lancers	USHL	56	20	36	56	198	....	....	....	....	....
1995-96	Boston University	H-East	38	8	16	24	90	....	....	....	....	....
1996-97	Boston University	H-East	27	5	8	13	83	....	....	....	....	....
1997-98	U. of Maine	H-East	DID NOT PLAY – TRANSFERRED COLLEGES									
1998-99	U. of Maine	H-East	30	7	13	20	58	....	....	....	....	....
99-2000	U. of Maine	H-East	39	9	21	30	*106	....	....	....	....	....
2000-01	Jackson Bandits	ECHL	25	3	6	9	179	....	....	....	....	....
	Cleveland	IHL	10	1	1	2	45	4	0	0	0	11
2001-02	Wheeling Nailers	ECHL	29	7	15	22	168	....	....	....	....	....
	Wilkes-Barre	AHL	29	2	2	4	184	....	....	....	....	....
2002-03	San Antonio	AHL	48	2	5	7	202	3	0	1	1	0
	Atlantic City	ECHL	6	0	2	2	40	....	....	....	....	....
2003-04	Providence Bruins	AHL	52	10	7	17	281	2	0	0	0	14

Signed as a free agent by **Minnesota**, May 18, 2000.

WALSH, Mike (WAHLSH, MIGHK) **NYR**

Left wing. Shoots left. 6'2", 194 lbs. Born, Royal Oak, MI, March 4, 1983.
(NY Rangers' 4th choice, 143rd overall, in 2002 Entry Draft).

			Regular Season					Playoffs				
Season	Club	League	GP	G	A	TP	PIM	GP	G	A	TP	PIM
2000-01	Det. Compuware	NAJHL	50	10	12	22	59	3	1	0	1	4
2001-02	Det. Compuware	NAJHL	53	25	25	49	69	6	4	2	6	8
2002-03	U. of Notre Dame	CCHA	23	1	1	2	14	....	....	....	....	....
2003-04	U. of Notre Dame	CCHA	39	12	13	25	46	....	....	....	....	....

WALSH, Tom (WAHLSH, TAWM) **S.J.**

Defense. Shoots left. 6', 190 lbs. Born, Arlington, MA, April 22, 1983.
(San Jose's 5th choice, 163rd overall, in 2002 Entry Draft).

			Regular Season					Playoffs				
Season	Club	League	GP	G	A	TP	PIM	GP	G	A	TP	PIM
2000-01	Deerfield Academy	Hi-School	23	10	26	36	25	....	....	....	....	....
2001-02	Deerfield Academy	Hi-School	21	3	18	21	8	....	....	....	....	....
2002-03	Harvard University	ECAC	32	1	6	7	30	....	....	....	....	....
2003-04	Harvard University	ECAC	24	1	4	5	24	....	....	....	....	....

WALTER, Ben (WAHL-tuhr, BEHN) **BOS.**

Center. Shoots left. 6'1", 195 lbs. Born, Beaconsfield, Que., May 11, 1984.
(Boston's 5th choice, 160th overall, in 2004 Entry Draft).

			Regular Season					Playoffs				
Season	Club	League	GP	G	A	TP	PIM	GP	G	A	TP	PIM
2000-01	Langley Hornets	BCHL	50	8	22	30	19	....	....	....	....	....
2001-02	Langley Hornets	BCHL	50	29	47	76	29	....	....	....	....	....
2002-03	U. Mass-Lowell	H-East	35	5	12	17	12	....	....	....	....	....
2003-04	U. Mass-Lowell	H-East	36	18	16	34	18	....	....	....	....	....

WATHIER, Francis (waw-TEE-ay, FRAN-sihs) **DAL.**

Left wing. Shoots left. 6'3", 198 lbs. Born, St Isidore, Ont., December 7, 1984.
(Dallas' 8th choice, 185th overall, in 2003 Entry Draft).

			Regular Season					Playoffs				
Season	Club	League	GP	G	A	TP	PIM	GP	G	A	TP	PIM
2001-02	Hull Olympiques	QMJHL	63	1	3	4	68	12	1	2	3	30
2002-03	Hull Olympiques	QMJHL	72	9	18	27	143	20	1	6	7	20
2003-04	Gatineau	QMJHL	51	9	16	25	127	15	0	2	2	23

WATSON, Greg (WAWT-suhn, GREHG) **OTT.**

Center. Shoots left. 6', 205 lbs. Born, Eastend, Sask., March 2, 1983.
(Florida's 3rd choice, 34th overall, in 2001 Entry Draft).

			Regular Season					Playoffs				
Season	**Club**	**League**	**GP**	**G**	**A**	**TP**	**PIM**	**GP**	**G**	**A**	**TP**	**PIM**
1998-99	Calgary Buffaloes	AMHL	71	23	23	46	120	....	....	....	....	....
	Prince Albert	WHL	2	0	0	0	5	....	....	....	....	....
99-2000	Prince Albert	WHL	67	10	5	15	63	6	0	2	2	2
2000-01	Prince Albert	WHL	71	22	28	50	72	....	....	....	....	....
2001-02	Prince Albert	WHL	51	22	30	52	88	....	....	....	....	....
2002-03	Prince Albert	WHL	39	11	15	26	58	....	....	....	....	....
	Brandon	WHL	30	6	14	20	37	17	3	8	11	12
2003-04	Binghamton	AHL	69	4	7	11	72	2	0	0	0	2

Traded to **Ottawa** by **Florida** with Billy Thompson for Jani Hurme, October 1, 2002.

WAUGH, Geoff (WAW, JEHF) **DAL.**

Defense. Shoots right. 6'3", 210 lbs. Born, Winnipeg, Man., August 25, 1983.
(Dallas' 6th choice, 78th overall, in 2002 Entry Draft).

			Regular Season					Playoffs				
Season	**Club**	**League**	**GP**	**G**	**A**	**TP**	**PIM**	**GP**	**G**	**A**	**TP**	**PIM**
2000-01	Kindersley Klippers	SJHL	57	2	5	7	74	....	....	....	....	....
2001-02	Kindersley Klippers	SJHL	59	4	21	25	125	18	0	8	8	59
2002-03	Northern Michigan	CCHA	39	0	7	7	41	....	....	....	....	....
2003-04	Northern Michigan	CCHA	41	2	13	15	72	....	....	....	....	....

WEBER, Shea (WEH-buhr, SHAY) **NSH.**

Defense. Shoots right. 6'3", 195 lbs. Born, Sicamous, B.C., August 14, 1985.
(Nashville's 4th choice, 49th overall, in 2003 Entry Draft).

			Regular Season					Playoffs				
Season	**Club**	**League**	**GP**	**G**	**A**	**TP**	**PIM**	**GP**	**G**	**A**	**TP**	**PIM**
2001-02	Sicamous Eagles	KIJHL	47	9	33	42	87	....	....	....	....	....
	Kelowna Rockets	WHL	5	0	0	0	0	....	....	....	....	....
2002-03	Kelowna Rockets	WHL	70	2	16	18	167	19	1	4	5	26
2003-04	Kelowna Rockets	WHL	60	12	20	32	126	17	3	14	17	16

WHL West Second All-Star Team (2004) • Memorial Cup All-Star Team (2004)

WELCH, Dan (WEHLCH, DAN) **L.A.**

Right wing. Shoots right. 5'10", 199 lbs. Born, Lansing, MI, February 23, 1981.
(Los Angeles' 9th choice, 245th overall, in 2000 Entry Draft).

			Regular Season					Playoffs				
Season	**Club**	**League**	**GP**	**G**	**A**	**TP**	**PIM**	**GP**	**G**	**A**	**TP**	**PIM**
1996/99	Hastings Huskies	Hi-School	90	76	123	199	....	....	....	....	....	....
99-2000	U. of Minnesota	WCHA	36	6	8	14	31	....	....	....	....	....
2000-01	Omaha Lancers	USHL	52	30	27	57	103	12	9	13	22	20
2001-02	U. of Minnesota	WCHA	19	4	7	11	12	....	....	....	....	....
	Omaha Lancers	USHL	7	4	2	6	8	....	....	....	....	....
2002-03	U. of Minnesota	WCHA	18	5	5	10	12	....	....	....	....	....
	Manchester	AHL	42	3	9	12	22	3	0	0	0	0
2003-04	Manchester	AHL	31	6	6	12	18	1	0	0	0	0

• Statistics for **Hastings** (Hi-School) are career totals for 1996-1999 seasons. • Ruled academically ineligible to play 2000-01 WCHA season by U. of Minnesota (WCHA). • Dismissed from U. of Minnesota (WCHA) hockey program for academic violations, January 3, 2003.

WELCH, Noah (WEHLCH, NOH-ah) **PIT.**

Defense. Shoots left. 6'4", 212 lbs. Born, Brighton, MA, August 26, 1982.
(Pittsburgh's 2nd choice, 54th overall, in 2001 Entry Draft).

			Regular Season					Playoffs				
Season	**Club**	**League**	**GP**	**G**	**A**	**TP**	**PIM**	**GP**	**G**	**A**	**TP**	**PIM**
99-2000	St. Sebastian's	Hi-School	26	4	11	15	35	....	....	....	....	....
	Eastern-Mass	MBAHL	4	0	3	3	6	....	....	....	....	....
2000-01	St. Sebastian's	Hi-School	30	11	20	31	37	....	....	....	....	....
2001-02	Harvard University	ECAC	27	5	6	11	56	....	....	....	....	....
2002-03	Harvard University	ECAC	34	6	22	28	70	....	....	....	....	....
2003-04	Harvard University	ECAC	34	6	13	19	58	....	....	....	....	....

ECAC All-Rookie Team (2002) • ECAC Second All-Star Team (2002, 2003) • NCAA East Second All-American Team (2003)

WELLAR, Patrick (WEHL-uhr, PAT-rihk) **ST.L.**

Defense. Shoots left. 6'3", 210 lbs. Born, Carrot River, Sask., December 4, 1983.
(Washington's 5th choice, 77th overall, in 2002 Entry Draft).

			Regular Season					Playoffs				
Season	**Club**	**League**	**GP**	**G**	**A**	**TP**	**PIM**	**GP**	**G**	**A**	**TP**	**PIM**
99-2000	Sask. Contacts	SMHL	44	5	15	20	120	....	....	....	....	....
	Portland	WHL	1	0	0	0	0	....	....	....	....	....
2000-01	Portland	WHL	57	2	7	9	65	10	0	1	1	13
2001-02	Portland	WHL	61	3	10	13	125	7	0	2	2	4
2002-03	Portland	WHL	11	1	4	5	31	....	....	....	....	....
	Calgary Hitmen	WHL	49	3	11	14	88	5	0	0	0	15
2003-04	Calgary Hitmen	WHL	68	7	10	17	132	7	1	1	2	10

Signed as a free agent by **St. Louis**, June 30, 2004.

WELLER, Craig (WEHL-uhr, KRAIG) **NYR**

Defense. Shoots right. 6'3", 195 lbs. Born, Calgary, Alta., January 17, 1981.
(St. Louis' 6th choice, 167th overall, in 2000 Entry Draft).

			Regular Season					Playoffs				
Season	**Club**	**League**	**GP**	**G**	**A**	**TP**	**PIM**	**GP**	**G**	**A**	**TP**	**PIM**
1997-98	Calgary Flames	AMHL	33	2	10	12	65	3	0	1	1	2
1998-99	Calgary Canucks	AJHL	49	4	14	18	80	13	0	1	1	10
99-2000	Calgary Canucks	AJHL	53	3	14	17	100	4	0	0	0	4
2000-01	U. Minn-Duluth	WCHA	6	0	1	1	0	....	....	....	....	....
	Kootenay Ice	WHL	30	1	5	6	40	11	0	2	2	26
2001-02	Kootenay Ice	WHL	69	5	13	18	127	22	3	7	10	27
2002-03	Hartford Wolf Pack	AHL	11	0	0	0	8	2	0	0	0	0
	Charlotte	ECHL	48	3	11	14	84	....	....	....	....	....
2003-04	Hartford Wolf Pack	AHL	68	5	9	14	86	16	2	2	4	30

WHL West Second All-Star Team (2002)

• Left **Minnesota-Duluth** (WCHA) and signed as a free agent by **Kootenay** (WHL), January 7, 2001. Signed as a free agent by **NY Rangers**, July 11, 2002.

WELLER, Shawn (WEHL-uhr, SHAWN) **OTT.**

Left wing. Shoots left. 6'1", 188 lbs. Born, Glens Falls, NY, July 8, 1986.
(Ottawa's 3rd choice, 77th overall, in 2004 Entry Draft).

			Regular Season					Playoffs				
Season	**Club**	**League**	**GP**	**G**	**A**	**TP**	**PIM**	**GP**	**G**	**A**	**TP**	**PIM**
2001-02	South Glen Falls	Hi-School	25	32	21	53	....	....	....	....	....	....
2002-03	Capital District	EJHL	STATISTICS NOT AVAILABLE									
2003-04	Capital District	EJHL	37	18	25	43	110	3	3	3	6	6
	Capital District	Exhib.	30	16	19	35	78	....	....	....	....	....

WENNERBERG, Mattias (VEH-nuhr-buhrg, MA-tee-uhs) **CHI.**

Center. Shoots left. 5'11", 191 lbs. Born, Uma, Sweden, August 6, 1981.
(Chicago's 6th choice, 194th overall, in 1999 Entry Draft).

			Regular Season					Playoffs				
Season	**Club**	**League**	**GP**	**G**	**A**	**TP**	**PIM**	**GP**	**G**	**A**	**TP**	**PIM**
1996-97	Vilhelmina HC	Swede-4	20	7	12	19	14	....	....	....	....	....
1997-98	MoDo Jr.	Swede-Jr.	30	10	17	27	....	....	....	....	....	....
1998-99	MoDo Jr.	Swede-Jr.	43	13	12	25	....	....	....	....	....	....
99-2000	MoDo Jr.	Swede-Jr.	32	14	6	20	102	....	....	....	....	....
2000-01	Bodens IK	Swede-2	34	9	4	13	36	....	....	....	....	....
2001-02	IF Bjorkloven Umea	Swede-2	21	8	10	18	43	....	....	....	....	....
	MoDo	Sweden	24	2	2	4	16	13	4	4	8	*39
2002-03	MoDo	Sweden	50	17	8	25	30	6	0	0	0	2
2003-04	MoDo	Sweden	50	4	3	7	34	14	3	5	8	4

WERNER, Steve (WUHR-nuhr, STEEV) **WSH.**

Right wing. Shoots right. 6', 197 lbs. Born, Washington, DC, August 8, 1984.
(Washington's 2nd choice, 83rd overall, in 2003 Entry Draft).

			Regular Season					Playoffs				
Season	**Club**	**League**	**GP**	**G**	**A**	**TP**	**PIM**	**GP**	**G**	**A**	**TP**	**PIM**
99-2000	Wsh. Jr. Capitals	MetroHL	42	32	45	77	....	....	....	....	....	....
2000-01	U.S. National U-17	USDP	69	12	23	35	26	....	....	....	....	....
2001-02	U.S. National U-18	USDP	54	16	20	36	42	....	....	....	....	....
2002-03	Massachusetts	H-East	37	16	22	38	4	....	....	....	....	....
2003-04	Massachusetts	H-East	33	7	17	24	18	....	....	....	....	....

Hockey East All-Rookie Team (2003)

WHARTON, Kyle (WAWR-tuhn, KIGHL) **CBJ**

Defense. Shoots left. 6'2", 185 lbs. Born, Ottawa, Ont., March 3, 1986.
(Columbus' 3rd choice, 59th overall, in 2004 Entry Draft).

			Regular Season					Playoffs				
Season	**Club**	**League**	**GP**	**G**	**A**	**TP**	**PIM**	**GP**	**G**	**A**	**TP**	**PIM**
2001-02	Ottawa Valley	OMHA	34	18	24	42	....	....	....	....	....	....
2002-03	Ottawa 67's	OHL	39	3	5	8	16	....	....	....	....	....
2003-04	Ottawa 67's	OHL	43	4	10	14	50	7	2	3	5	4

WHEELER, Blake (WEE-luhr, BLAYK) **PHX.**

Right wing. Shoots right. 6'5", 200 lbs. Born, Robbinsdale, MN, August 31, 1986.
(Phoenix's 1st choice, 5th overall, in 2004 Entry Draft).

			Regular Season					Playoffs				
Season	**Club**	**League**	**GP**	**G**	**A**	**TP**	**PIM**	**GP**	**G**	**A**	**TP**	**PIM**
2002-03	Breck Mustangs	Hi-School	26	15	27	42	....	....	....	....	....	....
2003-04	Team Northwest	UMEHL	24	5	6	11	....	....	....	....	....	....
	Breck Mustangs	Hi-School	27	39	50	89	34	3	6	5	11	0

Signed Letter of Intent to attend **University of Minnesota** (WCHA), April 4, 2004.

WHITE, Ian (WIGHT, EE-uhn) **TOR.**

Defense. Shoots right. 5'10", 185 lbs. Born, Winnipeg, Man., June 4, 1984.
(Toronto's 6th choice, 191st overall, in 2002 Entry Draft).

			Regular Season					Playoffs				
Season	**Club**	**League**	**GP**	**G**	**A**	**TP**	**PIM**	**GP**	**G**	**A**	**TP**	**PIM**
99-2000	Eastman Selects	MAHA	32	29	33	62	36	....	....	....	....	....
2000-01	Swift Current	WHL	69	12	31	43	24	....	....	....	....	....
2001-02	Swift Current	WHL	70	32	47	79	40	12	4	5	9	12
2002-03	Swift Current	WHL	64	24	44	68	44	4	0	4	4	0
2003-04	Swift Current	WHL	43	9	23	32	32	5	1	3	4	8
	St. John's	AHL	8	0	4	4	2	....	....	....	....	....

WHL East Second All-Star Team (2002) • WHL East First All-Star Team (2003)

WHITNEY, Ryan (WIHT-nee, RIGH-uhn) **PIT.**

Defense. Shoots left. 6'4", 202 lbs. Born, Boston, MA, February 19, 1983.
(Pittsburgh's 1st choice, 5th overall, in 2002 Entry Draft).

			Regular Season					Playoffs				
Season	**Club**	**League**	**GP**	**G**	**A**	**TP**	**PIM**	**GP**	**G**	**A**	**TP**	**PIM**
99-2000	Thayer Academy	Hi-School	22	5	33	38	....	....	....	....	....	....
2000-01	U.S. National U-17	USDP	60	9	31	40	86	....	....	....	....	....
2001-02	Boston University	H-East	35	4	17	21	46	....	....	....	....	....
2002-03	Boston University	H-East	34	3	10	13	48	....	....	....	....	....
2003-04	Boston University	H-East	38	9	16	25	56	....	....	....	....	....
	Wilkes-Barre	AHL	....	....	....	....	....	20	1	9	10	6

Hockey East All-Rookie Team (2002)

WICHSER, Adrian (WIH-shuhr, A-dree-uhn) **FLA.**

Center. Shoots left. 6', 180 lbs. Born, Winterthur, Switz., March 18, 1980.
(Florida's 9th choice, 231st overall, in 1998 Entry Draft).

			Regular Season					Playoffs				
Season	**Club**	**League**	**GP**	**G**	**A**	**TP**	**PIM**	**GP**	**G**	**A**	**TP**	**PIM**
1997-98	EHC Kloten	Swiss	35	6	5	11	31	7	0	1	1	8
1998-99	EHC Kloten	Swiss	40	11	14	25	14	9	7	0	7	8
	Kloten Flyers Jr.	Swiss-Jr.	....	....	....	....	....	1	1	2	3	2
99-2000	EHC Kloten	Swiss	33	8	15	23	12	6	2	1	3	0
2000-01	EHC Kloten	Swiss	31	9	9	18	12	9	2	3	5	0
2001-02	Kloten Flyers	Swiss	41	18	27	45	16	11	4	4	8	2
2002-03	HC Lugano	Swiss	44	*26	17	43	4	15	2	2	4	2
2003-04	HC Lugano	Swiss	47	17	20	37	16	16	6	7	13	4

WICK, Roman (WIHK, ROH-muhn) **OTT.**

Right wing. Shoots left. 6'1", 187 lbs. Born, Kloten, Switzerland, December 30, 1985.
(Ottawa's 8th choice, 156th overall, in 2004 Entry Draft).

			Regular Season					Playoffs				
Season	**Club**	**League**	**GP**	**G**	**A**	**TP**	**PIM**	**GP**	**G**	**A**	**TP**	**PIM**
2000-01	EHC Kloten Jr.	Swiss-Jr.	26	4	1	5	6	5	1	0	1	2
2001-02	Kloten Flyers Jr.	Swiss-Jr.	34	19	27	46	32	8	1	2	3	4
2002-03	Kloten Flyers	Swiss	9	1	0	1	4	1	0	0	0	0
	Kloten Flyers Jr.	Swiss-Jr.	28	29	22	51	68	2	0	1	1	0
2003-04	Kloten Flyers	Swiss	20	1	1	2	6	....	....	....	....	....
	Kloten Flyers	Swiss-Q	7	3	1	4	0	....	....	....	....	....
	GCK Lions Zurich	Swiss-2	6	4	0	4	6	....	....	....	....	....

WIDEMAN, Dennis (WIGHD-muhn, DEH-nihs) **ST.L.**

Defense. Shoots right. 6', 200 lbs. Born, Kitchener, Ont., March 20, 1983.
(Buffalo's 9th choice, 241st overall, in 2002 Entry Draft).

			Regular Season					Playoffs				
Season	Club	League	GP	G	A	TP	PIM	GP	G	A	TP	PIM
1998-99	Elmira Sugar Kings	OJHL-B	47	18	30	48	142	....	....	....	....	....
99-2000	Sudbury Wolves	OHL	63	10	26	36	64	12	1	2	3	22
2000-01	Sudbury Wolves	OHL	25	7	11	18	37	....	....	....	....	....
	London Knights	OHL	24	8	8	16	38	5	0	4	4	6
2001-02	London Knights	OHL	65	27	42	69	141	12	4	9	13	26
2002-03	London Knights	OHL	55	20	27	47	83	14	6	6	12	10
2003-04	London Knights	OHL	60	24	41	65	85	15	7	10	17	17

OHL First All-Star Team (2004)

Signed as a free agent by **St. Louis**, June 30, 2004.

WIDING, Daniel (VEE-dihng, DAN-yehl) **NSH.**

Right wing. Shoots right. 6'1", 197 lbs. Born, Gavle, Sweden, April 13, 1982.
(Nashville's 2nd choice, 36th overall, in 2000 Entry Draft).

			Regular Season					Playoffs				
Season	Club	League	GP	G	A	TP	PIM	GP	G	A	TP	PIM
99-2000	Leksands IF-18	Swede-Jr.	6	2	1	3	20	....	....	....	....	....
	Leksands IF Jr.	Swede-Jr.	34	15	12	27	65	2	1	0	1	4
	Leksands IF	Sweden	3	0	0	0	2	....	....	....	....	....
2000-01	Leksands IF Jr.	Swede-Jr.	6	2	3	5	31	....	....	....	....	....
	Leksands IF	Sweden	40	6	5	11	18	....	....	....	....	....
2001-02	Leksands IF Jr.	Swede-Jr.	3	2	6	8	2	....	....	....	....	....
	Leksands IF	Swede-2	55	12	12	24	92	....	....	....	....	....
2002-03	Leksands IF	Sweden	47	2	2	4	8	5	0	0	0	2
	Leksands IF Jr.	Swede-Jr.	2	0	1	1	4	....	....	....	....	....
2003-04	Pelicans Lahti	Finland	54	6	7	13	62	....	....	....	....	....

WILFORD, Marty (WIHL-fohrd, MAHR-tee) **CHI.**

Defense. Shoots left. 6'1", 212 lbs. Born, Cobourg, Ont., April 17, 1977.
(Chicago's 7th choice, 149th overall, in 1995 Entry Draft).

			Regular Season					Playoffs				
Season	Club	League	GP	G	A	TP	PIM	GP	G	A	TP	PIM
1993-94	Peterborough	OPJHL	40	3	19	22	*107	....	....	....	....	....
1994-95	Oshawa Generals	OHL	63	1	6	7	95	7	1	1	2	4
1995-96	Oshawa Generals	OHL	65	3	24	27	107	5	0	1	1	4
1996-97	Oshawa Generals	OHL	62	19	43	62	126	16	2	18	20	28
1997-98	Columbus Chill	ECHL	46	8	27	35	123	....	....	....	....	....
	Indianapolis Ice	IHL	26	0	4	4	16	....	....	....	....	....
1998-99	Indianapolis Ice	IHL	80	3	13	16	116	7	0	1	1	16
99-2000	Cleveland	IHL	7	0	3	3	24	....	....	....	....	....
	Houston Aeros	IHL	45	0	9	9	30	11	2	2	4	18
2000-01	Norfolk Admirals	AHL	80	7	41	48	102	9	1	5	6	8
2001-02	St. John's	AHL	60	4	21	25	70	....	....	....	....	....
	Milwaukee	AHL	8	1	3	4	12	....	....	....	....	....
	Hartford Wolf Pack	AHL	9	0	2	2	2	10	3	3	6	4
2002-03	Norfolk Admirals	AHL	80	13	35	48	87	9	0	3	3	16
2003-04	Norfolk Admirals	AHL	80	5	35	40	67	8	0	3	3	18

OHL Second All-Star Team (1997)

Traded to **Toronto** by **Chicago** for Shawn Thornton, September 30, 2001. Traded to **Nashville** by **Toronto** with D.J. Smith for Marc Moro, March 1, 2002. Signed as a free agent by **Chicago**, July 8, 2003.

WILLIAMS, Jeremy (WIHL-yuhms, JAIR-eh-mee) **TOR.**

Center. Shoots right. 5'11", 184 lbs. Born, Regina, Sask., January 26, 1984.
(Toronto's 5th choice, 220th overall, in 2003 Entry Draft).

			Regular Season					Playoffs				
Season	Club	League	GP	G	A	TP	PIM	GP	G	A	TP	PIM
2001-02	Swift Current	SMMHL	24	18	23	41	64	....	....	....	....	....
	Swift Current	WHL	32	6	7	13	30	12	1	0	1	4
2002-03	Swift Current	WHL	72	41	52	93	117	4	1	0	1	6
2003-04	St. John's	AHL	4	0	2	2	0	....	....	....	....	....
	Swift Current	WHL	68	*52	49	101	82	5	2	1	3	12

WHL East First All-Star Team (2004) • Canadian Major Junior First All-Star Team (2004)

WINCHESTER, Brad (WIHN-chehst-uhr, BRAD) **EDM.**

Left wing. Shoots left. 6'5", 215 lbs. Born, Madison, WI, March 1, 1981.
(Edmonton's 2nd choice, 35th overall, in 2000 Entry Draft).

			Regular Season					Playoffs				
Season	Club	League	GP	G	A	TP	PIM	GP	G	A	TP	PIM
1997-98	U.S. National U-18	USDP	74	22	23	45	162	....	....	....	....	....
1998-99	U.S. National U-18	USDP	65	21	23	44	103	....	....	....	....	....
99-2000	U. of Wisconsin	WCHA	33	9	9	18	48	....	....	....	....	....
2000-01	U. of Wisconsin	WCHA	41	7	9	16	71	....	....	....	....	....
2001-02	U. of Wisconsin	WCHA	38	14	20	34	38	....	....	....	....	....
2002-03	U. of Wisconsin	WCHA	38	10	6	16	58	....	....	....	....	....
2003-04	Toronto	AHL	65	13	6	19	85	3	0	0	0	2

WISNIEWSKI, James (wihs-NEHV-skee, JAYMS) **CHI.**

Defense. Shoots right. 6', 206 lbs. Born, Canton, MI, February 21, 1984.
(Chicago's 5th choice, 156th overall, in 2002 Entry Draft).

			Regular Season					Playoffs				
Season	Club	League	GP	G	A	TP	PIM	GP	G	A	TP	PIM
99-2000	Det. Compuware	NAJHL	50	5	11	16	67	5	0	3	3	4
2000-01	Plymouth Whalers	OHL	53	6	23	29	72	19	3	10	13	34
2001-02	Plymouth Whalers	OHL	62	11	25	36	100	6	1	2	3	6
2002-03	Plymouth Whalers	OHL	52	18	34	52	60	18	2	10	12	14
2003-04	Plymouth Whalers	OHL	50	17	53	70	63	9	3	7	10	8

OHL First All-Star Team (2004) • OHL Defenseman of the Year (2004) • Canadian Major Junior First All-Star Team (2004) • Canadian Major Junior Defenseman of the Year (2004)

WOLSKI, Wojtek (WOHL-skee, VOI-tehk) **COL.**

Left wing. Shoots left. 6'3", 200 lbs. Born, Zabrze, Poland, February 24, 1986.
(Colorado's 1st choice, 21st overall, in 2004 Entry Draft).

			Regular Season					Playoffs				
Season	Club	League	GP	G	A	TP	PIM	GP	G	A	TP	PIM
2001-02	St. Michael's	OPJHL	33	16	33	49	40	....	....	....	....	....
2002-03	Brampton	OHL	64	25	32	57	26	11	5	0	5	6
2003-04	Brampton	OHL	66	29	41	70	30	12	5	3	8	8

OHL First All-Star Team (2004)

WOOD, Dustin (WUD, DUHS-tihn) **PHX.**

Defense. Shoots left. 6', 185 lbs. Born, Scarborough, Ont., May 21, 1981.

			Regular Season					Playoffs				
Season	Club	League	GP	G	A	TP	PIM	GP	G	A	TP	PIM
1998-99	Peterborough	OHL	62	1	8	9	14	5	0	0	0	0
99-2000	Peterborough	OHL	66	2	13	15	29	5	0	1	1	0
2000-01	Peterborough	OHL	64	5	20	25	41	7	0	3	3	11
2001-02	Peterborough	OHL	68	13	38	51	57	6	2	1	3	4
2002-03	Trenton Titans	ECHL	63	4	23	27	28	3	0	1	1	2
	Bridgeport	AHL	6	0	0	0	2	....	....	....	....	....
2003-04	Springfield Falcons	AHL	75	2	6	8	22	....	....	....	....	....
	Adirondack	UHL	1	0	0	0	0	....	....	....	....	....

Signed as a free agent by **Phoenix**, June 2, 2004.

WOOD, Stephen (WUD, STEE-vehn) **PHI.**

Defense. Shoots right. 6'3", 210 lbs. Born, Sudbury, MA, August 18, 1981.

			Regular Season					Playoffs				
Season	Club	League	GP	G	A	TP	PIM	GP	G	A	TP	PIM
99-2000	Lawrence	Hi-School	STATISTICS NOT AVAILABLE									
2000-01	Providence College	H-East	36	3	4	7	68	....	....	....	....	....
2001-02	Providence College	H-East	36	5	18	23	78	....	....	....	....	....
2002-03	Providence College	H-East	34	9	20	29	48	....	....	....	....	....
2003-04	Providence College	H-East	37	11	18	29	66	....	....	....	....	....
	Philadelphia	AHL	4	0	0	0	0	....	....	....	....	....

Hockey East Second All-Star Team (2003) • Hockey East First All-Star Team (2004) • NCAA East Second All-American Team (2004)

Signed as a free agent by **Philadelphia**, March 21, 2004.

WOODFORD, Mike (WUD-fohrd, MIGHK) **FLA.**

Right wing. Shoots right. 5'11", 185 lbs. Born, Boston, MA, October 4, 1981.
(Florida's 6th choice, 117th overall, in 2001 Entry Draft).

			Regular Season					Playoffs				
Season	Club	League	GP	G	A	TP	PIM	GP	G	A	TP	PIM
99-2000	Cushing Academy	Hi-School	31	35	35	70	60	....	....	....	....	....
2000-01	Cushing Academy	Hi-School	36	34	39	73	68	....	....	....	....	....
2001-02	U. of Michigan	CCHA	43	8	11	19	46	....	....	....	....	....
2002-03	U. of Michigan	CCHA	37	5	12	17	73	....	....	....	....	....
2003-04	U. of Michigan	CCHA	40	1	5	6	53	....	....	....	....	....

WOYWITKA, Jeff (WOI-wiht-ka, JEHF) **EDM.**

Defense. Shoots left. 6'2", 209 lbs. Born, Vermilion, Alta., September 1, 1983.
(Philadelphia's 1st choice, 27th overall, in 2001 Entry Draft).

			Regular Season					Playoffs				
Season	Club	League	GP	G	A	TP	PIM	GP	G	A	TP	PIM
1998-99	Wainwright	AAHA	26	7	15	22	60	....	....	....	....	....
99-2000	Red Deer Rebels	WHL	67	4	12	16	40	4	0	3	3	2
2000-01	Red Deer Rebels	WHL	72	7	28	35	113	22	2	8	10	25
2001-02	Red Deer Rebels	WHL	72	14	23	37	109	23	2	10	12	22
2002-03	Red Deer Rebels	WHL	57	16	36	52	65	23	1	9	10	25
2003-04	Philadelphia	AHL	29	0	6	6	51	....	....	....	....	....
	Toronto	AHL	53	4	18	22	41	3	0	0	0	2

WHL East Second All-Star Team (2002) • WHL East First All-Star Team (2003)

Traded to **Edmonton** by **Philadelphia** with Philadelphia's 1st round choice (Rob Schremp) in 2004 Entry Draft and Philadelphia's 3rd round choice in 2005 Entry Draft for Mike Comrie, December 16, 2003.

WOZNIEWSKI, Andy (wuhz-NYOO-skee, AN-dee) **TOR.**

Defense. Shoots left. 6'4", 220 lbs. Born, Buffalo Grove, IL, May 25, 1980.

			Regular Season					Playoffs				
Season	Club	League	GP	G	A	TP	PIM	GP	G	A	TP	PIM
99-2000	U. Mass-Lowell	H-East	17	1	1	2	8	....	....	....	....	....
2000-01	Texas Tornados	NAJHL	54	10	34	44	98	8	2	7	9	12
2001-02	U. of Wisconsin	WCHA	39	3	13	16	54	....	....	....	....	....
2002-03	U. of Wisconsin	WCHA	33	1	7	8	47	....	....	....	....	....
2003-04	U. of Wisconsin	WCHA	43	6	8	14	*104	....	....	....	....	....
	St. John's	AHL	3	0	1	1	0	....	....	....	....	....

Signed as a free agent by **Toronto**, May 27, 2004.

WYMAN, James (WIGH-muhn, JAYMZ) **MTL.**

Right wing. Shoots right. 6'1", 195 lbs. Born, Edina, MN, February 27, 1986.
(Montreal's 3rd choice, 100th overall, in 2004 Entry Draft).

			Regular Season					Playoffs				
Season	Club	League	GP	G	A	TP	PIM	GP	G	A	TP	PIM
2001-02	Blake Bears	Hi-School	26	7	5	12	....	....	....	....	....	....
2002-03	Blake Bears	Hi-School	28	17	23	40	12	....	....	....	....	....
2003-04	Team Southwest	UMEHL	24	8	8	16	....	....	....	....	....	....
	Blake Bears	Hi-School	27	31	24	55	4	....	....	....	....	....

YACBOSKI, Darryl (yak-BAW-skee, DAIR-ihl) **COL.**

Defense. Shoots left. 6'3", 216 lbs. Born, N. Vancouver, B.C., January 13, 1985.
(Colorado's 7th choice, 257th overall, in 2003 Entry Draft).

			Regular Season					Playoffs				
Season	Club	League	GP	G	A	TP	PIM	GP	G	A	TP	PIM
2000-01	Langley AA Eagles	BCAHA	STATISTICS NOT AVAILABLE									
2001-02	Regina Pats	WHL	33	0	4	4	26	....	....	....	....	....
2002-03	Regina Pats	WHL	37	2	3	5	63	....	....	....	....	....
2003-04	Regina Pats	WHL	11	0	0	0	18	....	....	....	....	....
	Calgary Hitmen	WHL	53	4	4	8	97	7	0	0	0	10

YACHMENEV, Denis (YATCH-muh-nehv, DEH-nihs) **FLA.**

Left wing. Shoots left. 6'1", 185 lbs. Born, Chelyabinsk, USSR, June 4, 1984.
(Florida's 9th choice, 200th overall, in 2002 Entry Draft).

			Regular Season					Playoffs				
Season	Club	League	GP	G	A	TP	PIM	GP	G	A	TP	PIM
2000-01	Chelyabinsk 2	Russia-3	36	40	27	67	....	....	....	....	....	....
2001-02	North Bay	OHL	65	17	12	29	32	5	2	0	2	0
2002-03	Saginaw Spirit	OHL	68	17	28	45	69	....	....	....	....	....
2003-04	Avangard Omsk 2	Russia-3	13	12	4	16	10	....	....	....	....	....
	Amur Khabarovsk	Russia	25	0	1	1	4	....	....	....	....	....

YEMELIN, Alexei (yeh-MUH-lehn, al-EXH-ay) **MTL.**

Defense. Shoots left. 6', 187 lbs. Born, Kuibyshev, USSR, April 25, 1986.
(Montreal's 2nd choice, 84th overall, in 2004 Entry Draft).

			Regular Season					Playoffs				
Season	Club	League	GP	G	A	TP	PIM	GP	G	A	TP	PIM
2002-03	Lada Togliatti 2	Russia-3	31	1	1	2	20	....	....	....	....	....
	Lada Togliatti 17	Russia-Jr.	7	1	2	3	6	....	....	....	....	....
2003-04	Lada Togliatti 2	Russia-3	2	0	0	0	10	....	....	....	....	....
	CSK VVS Samara	Russia-2	52	2	4	6	180	1	0	0	0	18

YOUNG, Bryan (YUHNG, BRIGH-uhn) **EDM.**

Defense. Shoots left. 6'1", 191 lbs. Born, Ennismore, Ont., August 6, 1986.
(Edmonton's 6th choice, 146th overall, in 2004 Entry Draft).

			Regular Season					Playoffs				
Season	**Club**	**League**	**GP**	**G**	**A**	**TP**	**PIM**	**GP**	**G**	**A**	**TP**	**PIM**
2002-03	Lindsay Muskies	OPJHL	47	1	9	10	56	....	....	....	....	....
	Peterborough	OHL	2	0	0	0	0	....	....	....	....	....
2003-04	Peterborough	OHL	60	0	8	8	63	....	....	....	....	....

YTFELDT, David (YOOT-fehld, DAY-vihd) **VAN.**

Defense. Shoots left. 6'1", 187 lbs. Born, Ornskoldsvik, Sweden, September 29, 1979.
(Vancouver's 6th choice, 136th overall, in 1998 Entry Draft).

			Regular Season					Playoffs				
Season	**Club**	**League**	**GP**	**G**	**A**	**TP**	**PIM**	**GP**	**G**	**A**	**TP**	**PIM**
1996-97	Leksands IF Jr.	Swede-Jr.	25	3	5	8		....	....	....	....	....
1997-98	Leksands IF Jr.	Swede-Jr.	28	13	10	23	101	....	....	....	....	....
	Leksands IF	Sweden	10	0	0	0	2	....	....	....	....	....
1998-99	Leksands IF	Sweden	39	0	4	4	65	4	0	1	1	4
99-2000	Leksands IF	Sweden	50	3	9	12	72	....	....	....	....	....
2000-01	V. Frolunda Jr.	Swede-Jr.	2	2	1	3	0	....	....	....	....	....
	JYP Jyvaskyla	Finland	11	0	4	4	26	....	....	....	....	....
	Vastra Frolunda	Sweden	9	0	1	1	8	5	0	1	1	4
2001-02	Linkopings HC	Sweden	8	0	0	0	4	....	....	....	....	....
2002-03	Nykoping	Swede-2	15	5	6	11	30	....	....	....	....	....
2003-04	IFK Stromsund	Sweden-4		DID NOT PLAY – INJURED								

• Name when drafted was David Jonsson.

YUNKOV, Mikhail (yuhn-KAWF, mih-kigh-EHL) **WSH.**

Center. Shoots left. 6', 180 lbs. Born, Voskresensk, USSR, February 16, 1986.
(Washington's 5th choice, 62nd overall, in 2004 Entry Draft).

			Regular Season					Playoffs				
Season	**Club**	**League**	**GP**	**G**	**A**	**TP**	**PIM**	**GP**	**G**	**A**	**TP**	**PIM**
2001-02	Krylja Sovetov 2	Russia-3	4	0	1	1	0	....	....	....	....	....
	Krylya Sovetov 18	Russia-Jr.	28	11	23	34	44	....	....	....	....	....
2002-03	Krylja Sovetov 2	Russia-3	3	0	1	1	0	....	....	....	....	....
	Krylja Sovetov	Russia	7	1	0	1	2	....	....	....	....	....
	Krylya Sovetov 18	Russia-Jr.	47	20	37	57	26	....	....	....	....	....
2003-04	Krylja Sovetov	Russia-2	38	5	10	15	12	4	0	1	1	0
	Krylja Sovetov 2	Russia-3		STATISTICS NOT AVAILABLE								

ZAINULLIN, Ruslan (zihj-NOO-luhn, roos-LAHN) **CGY.**

Right wing. Shoots left. 6'2", 202 lbs. Born, Kazan, USSR, February 14, 1982.
(Tampa Bay's 2nd choice, 34th overall, in 2000 Entry Draft).

			Regular Season					Playoffs				
Season	**Club**	**League**	**GP**	**G**	**A**	**TP**	**PIM**	**GP**	**G**	**A**	**TP**	**PIM**
1997-98	Ak Bars Kazan 2	Russia-3	27	0	1	1	2	....	....	....	....	....
1998-99	Ak Bars Kazan 2	Russia-4	36	13	8	21	22	....	....	....	....	....
99-2000	Ak Bars Kazan 2	Russia-3	12	13	6	19	....	....	....	....	....	....
	Ak Bars Kazan	Russia	14	1	1	2	4	....	....	....	....	....
2000-01	Ak Bars Kazan	Russia	29	1	3	4	14	1	0	0	0	0
2001-02	Ak Bars Kazan	Russia	21	0	2	2	8	3	0	0	0	2
2002-03	Ak Bars Kazan	Russia	4	0	1	1	2	....	....	....	....	....
	Nizhnekamsk	Russia	13	1	1	2	8	....	....	....	....	....
2003-04	Dynamo Moscow	Russia	47	3	5	8	30	3	0	0	0	0

Traded to **Phoenix** by **Tampa Bay** with Mike Johnson, Paul Mara and NY Islanders' 2nd round choice (previously acquired, Phoenix selected Matthew Spiller) in 2001 Entry Draft for Nikolai Khabibulin and Stan Neckar, March 5, 2001. Rights traded to **Atlanta** by **Phoenix** with Kirill Safronov and Phoenix's 4th round choice (Patrick Dwyer) in 2002 Entry Draft for Darcy Hordichuk and Atlanta's 4th (Lance Monych) and 5th (John Zeiler) round choices in 2002 Entry Draft, March 19, 2002. Traded to **Calgary** by **Atlanta** for Marc Savard, November 15, 2002.

ZAJAC, Travis (ZAY-jak, TRA-vihs) **N.J.**

Center. Shoots right. 6'2", 205 lbs. Born, Winnipeg, Man., May 13, 1985.
(New Jersey's 1st choice, 20th overall, in 2004 Entry Draft).

			Regular Season					Playoffs				
Season	**Club**	**League**	**GP**	**G**	**A**	**TP**	**PIM**	**GP**	**G**	**A**	**TP**	**PIM**
2002-03	Salmon Arm	BCHL	59	16	36	52	27	11	2	4	6	6
2003-04	Salmon Arm	BCHL	59	43	69	112	110	14	10	13	23	10

Signed Letter of Intent to attend **North Dakota** (WCHA), November 25, 2003.

ZAKHAROV, Konstantin (za-KHAHR-awv, kawn-stuhn-TIHN) **ST.L.**

Left wing. Shoots right. 6'1", 185 lbs. Born, Minsk, USSR, May 2, 1985.
(St. Louis' 5th choice, 101st overall, in 2003 Entry Draft).

			Regular Season					Playoffs				
Season	**Club**	**League**	**GP**	**G**	**A**	**TP**	**PIM**	**GP**	**G**	**A**	**TP**	**PIM**
2000-01	Yunost Minsk	Belarus	19	11	7	18	40	....	....	....	....	....
2001-02	Yunost Minsk	Belarus	16	7	5	12	39	....	....	....	....	....
2002-03	HC Gomel	Belarus	19	8	19	27	18	....	....	....	....	....
	HC Gomel	EEHL	14	2	4	6	10	....	....	....	....	....
	Yunost Minsk	Belarus	17	18	19	37	34	....	....	....	....	....
2003-04	Moncton Wildcats	QMJHL	55	33	16	49	63	20	7	9	16	18

ZALEWSKI, Steven (zuh-LOO-skee, STEE-vehn) **S.J.**

Center. Shoots left. 6', 185 lbs. Born, Utica, NY, August 20, 1986.
(San Jose's 5th choice, 153rd overall, in 2004 Entry Draft).

			Regular Season					Playoffs				
Season	**Club**	**League**	**GP**	**G**	**A**	**TP**	**PIM**	**GP**	**G**	**A**	**TP**	**PIM**
2002-03	New Hartford Prep	Hi-School		STATISTICS NOT AVAILABLE								
2003-04	Northwood	Hi-School	40	32	34	66	22	....	....	....	....	....

ZANON, Greg (ZA-nuhn, GREHG) **NSH.**

Defense. Shoots left. 5'11", 190 lbs. Born, Burnaby, B.C., June 5, 1980.
(Ottawa's 6th choice, 156th overall, in 2000 Entry Draft).

			Regular Season					Playoffs				
Season	**Club**	**League**	**GP**	**G**	**A**	**TP**	**PIM**	**GP**	**G**	**A**	**TP**	**PIM**
1995-96	Burnaby Beavers	BCAHA	49	16	27	43	142	....	....	....	....	....
1996-97	Victoria Salsa	BCHL	53	4	13	17	124	....	....	....	....	....
1997-98	Victoria Salsa	BCHL	59	11	21	32	108	7	0	2	2	10
1998-99	South Surrey	BCHL	59	17	54	71	154	....	....	....	....	....
99-2000	Nebraska-Omaha	CCHA	42	3	26	29	56	....	....	....	....	....
2000-01	Nebraska-Omaha	CCHA	39	12	16	28	64	....	....	....	....	....
2001-02	Nebraska-Omaha	CCHA	41	9	16	25	54	....	....	....	....	....
2002-03	Nebraska-Omaha	CCHA	32	6	19	25	44	....	....	....	....	....
2003-04	Milwaukee	AHL	62	4	12	16	59	22	2	6	8	31

CCHA First All-Star Team (2001) • NCAA West Second All-American Team (2001, 2002) • CCHA Second All-Star Team (2002)

Signed as a free agent by **Nashville**, July 9, 2004.

ZARB, Chris (ZAHRB, KRIHS) **PHI.**

Defense. Shoots right. 6'4", 176 lbs. Born, San Diego, CA, January 11, 1985.
(Philadelphia's 4th choice, 144th overall, in 2004 Entry Draft).

			Regular Season					Playoffs				
Season	**Club**	**League**	**GP**	**G**	**A**	**TP**	**PIM**	**GP**	**G**	**A**	**TP**	**PIM**
2002-03	Det. Little Caesar's	MWEHL	60	15	35	50	60	....	....	....	....	....
2003-04	Tri-City Storm	USHL	43	4	20	24	78	11	0	4	4	17

ZEILER, John (ZIGH-luhr, JAWN) **PHX.**

Right wing. Shoots right. 6', 193 lbs. Born, Pittsburgh, PA, November 21, 1982.
(Phoenix's 7th choice, 132nd overall, in 2002 Entry Draft).

			Regular Season					Playoffs				
Season	**Club**	**League**	**GP**	**G**	**A**	**TP**	**PIM**	**GP**	**G**	**A**	**TP**	**PIM**
99-2000	Pittsburgh Hornets	PAHA	27	17	15	32	94	....	....	....	....	....
2000-01	Sioux City	USHL	56	8	20	28	45	2	0	0	0	26
2001-02	Sioux City	USHL	60	23	27	50	116	12	2	3	5	25
2002-03	St. Lawrence	ECAC	37	10	17	27	28	....	....	....	....	....
2003-04	St. Lawrence	ECAC	41	8	*28	36	42	....	....	....	....	....

ECAC All-Rookie Team (2003)

ZHVACHKIN, Leonid (ZNVAHCH-kihn, lay-oh-NEED) **NYR**

Defense. Shoots left. 6'3", 189 lbs. Born, Tula, USSR, February 24, 1983.
(NY Rangers' 9th choice, 230th overall, in 2001 Entry Draft).

			Regular Season					Playoffs				
Season	**Club**	**League**	**GP**	**G**	**A**	**TP**	**PIM**	**GP**	**G**	**A**	**TP**	**PIM**
99-2000	HC CSKA 2	Russia-3	9	0	1	1	12	....	....	....	....	....
2000-01	Vityaz Podolsk 2	Russia-3		STATISTICS NOT AVAILABLE								
2001-02	Guelph Storm	OHL	62	2	2	4	58	9	0	0	0	5
2002-03	Guelph Storm	OHL	25	0	2	2	34	....	....	....	....	....
	Barrie Colts	OHL	31	0	1	1	35	6	0	0	0	6
2003-04	Krylja Sovetov	Russia-2	18	0	0	0	36	....	....	....	....	....
	Krylja Sovetov 2	Russia-3		STATISTICS NOT AVAILABLE								

ZIB, Lukas (ZIHB, LOO-kahsh) **EDM.**

Defense. Shoots right. 6'1", 200 lbs. Born, Ceske Budejovice, Czech., February 24, 1977.
(Edmonton's 3rd choice, 57th overall, in 1995 Entry Draft).

			Regular Season					Playoffs				
Season	**Club**	**League**	**GP**	**G**	**A**	**TP**	**PIM**	**GP**	**G**	**A**	**TP**	**PIM**
1994-95	Ceske Budejovice	Czech	13	2	0	2	16	9	1	0	1	6
1995-96	C. Budejovice Jr.	Czech-Jr.	11	5	1	6	....	....	....	....	....	....
	Ceske Budejovice	Czech	10	1	0	1	....	2	0	0	0	....
1996-97	Ceske Budejovice	Czech	13	0	0	0	4	2	0	0	0	0
1997-98	Ceske Budejovice	Czech	47	5	6	11	22	....	....	....	....	....
1998-99	Ceske Budejovice	Czech	24	1	4	5	18	....	....	....	....	....
99-2000	Ceske Budejovice	Czech	38	3	6	9	10	1	0	0	0	0
2000-01	Ceske Budejovice	Czech	22	2	3	5	16	....	....	....	....	....
	Continental Zlin	Czech	19	4	3	7	8	....	....	....	....	....
2001-02	HC Karlovy Vary	Czech	36	4	10	14	20	....	....	....	....	....
	Blues Espoo	Finland	5	0	0	0	2	....	....	....	....	....
2002-03	Schwenningen	Germany	49	3	11	14	52	6	1	2	3	6
	Schwenningen	German-Q	6	1	2	3	6	....	....	....	....	....
2003-04	Nizhny Novgorod	Russia	47	8	5	13	44	....	....	....	....	....
	Molot Perm	Russia-2	9	5	7	12	20	11	1	2	3	12

ZIMAKOV, Sergei (zih-MAH-kahv, SAIR-gay) **WSH.**

Defense. Shoots left. 6'1", 194 lbs. Born, Moscow, USSR, January 15, 1978.
(Washington's 4th choice, 58th overall, in 1996 Entry Draft).

			Regular Season					Playoffs				
Season	**Club**	**League**	**GP**	**G**	**A**	**TP**	**PIM**	**GP**	**G**	**A**	**TP**	**PIM**
1994-95	Omaha Lancers	USHL	48	14	46	60	22	....	....	....	....	....
1995-96	Krylja Sovetov	CIS	49	2	7	9	36	....	....	....	....	....
1996-97	Krylja Sovetov	Russia	39	4	3	7	57	2	0	0	0	0
1997-98	Krylja Sovetov	Russia	42	4	1	5	48	....	....	....	....	....
1998-99	Ak Bars Kazan	Russia	28	1	0	1	6	8	0	1	1	6
99-2000	Perm	Russia	31	1	2	3	34	3	0	1	1	0
2000-01	CSKA Moscow 2	Russia-3	3	2	2	4	2	....	....	....	....	....
	CSKA Moscow	Russia	26	1	5	6	28	....	....	....	....	....
2001-02	CSKA Moscow	Russia	42	3	10	13	74	....	....	....	....	....
2002-03	Yulayev Ufa	Russia	11	0	0	0	8	....	....	....	....	....
	Yulayev Ufa 2			STATISTICS NOT AVAILABLE								
2003-04	Spartak Moscow	Russia-2	60	11	17	28	38	12	0	1	1	10

ZINGONI, Peter (zihn-GOH-nee, PEE-tuhr) **CBJ**

Center. Shoots left. 6', 180 lbs. Born, Bridgeport, CT, April 28, 1981.
(Columbus' 8th choice, 231st overall, in 2000 Entry Draft).

			Regular Season					Playoffs				
Season	**Club**	**League**	**GP**	**G**	**A**	**TP**	**PIM**	**GP**	**G**	**A**	**TP**	**PIM**
1998-99	New England	EJHL	40	26	22	48	....	....	....	....	....	....
99-2000	New England	EJHL	40	39	38	77	85	3	1	1	2	0
2000-01	Providence College	H-East	28	2	6	8	38	....	....	....	....	....
2001-02	Providence College	H-East	31	7	10	17	27	....	....	....	....	....
2002-03	Providence College	H-East	32	12	13	25	26	....	....	....	....	....
2003-04	Providence College	H-East	36	13	19	32	54	....	....	....	....	....
	Syracuse Crunch	AHL	5	2	2	4	0	....	....	....	....	....

ZOTKIN, Alexei (ZOHT-kihn, al-EHX-ay) **CHI.**

Left wing. Shoots left. 6', 200 lbs. Born, Magnitogorsk, USSR, February 5, 1982.
(Chicago's 7th choice, 119th overall, in 2001 Entry Draft).

			Regular Season					Playoffs				
Season	**Club**	**League**	**GP**	**G**	**A**	**TP**	**PIM**	**GP**	**G**	**A**	**TP**	**PIM**
1997-98	Magnitogorsk 2	Russia-3	2	0	1	1	2	....	....	....	....	....
1998-99	Magnitogorsk 2	Russia-4	23	5	1	6	20	....	....	....	....	....
99-2000	Magnitogorsk 2	Russia-3	38	22	27	49	86	....	....	....	....	....
	Magnitogorsk	Russia	1	0	0	0	0	....	....	....	....	....
2000-01	Magnitogorsk 2	Russia-3	5	6	2	8	26	....	....	....	....	....
	Magnitogorsk	Russia	40	2	3	5	34	12	1	1	2	20
2001-02	Magnitogorsk	Russia	25	3	0	3	10	8	0	1	1	2
2002-03	Magnitogorsk	Russia	35	3	3	6	38	....	....	....	....	....
2003-04	Magnitogorsk	Russia	9	1	2	3	2	....	....	....	....	....
	Magnitogorsk 2	Russia-3	5	5	2	7	16	....	....	....	....	....

League Abbreviations

AAHA	Alberta Amateur Hockey Association
AAHL	Alaska Amateur Hockey League
ACHA	American Collegiate Hockey Association
ACHL	Atlantic Coast Hockey League
AFHL	American Frontier Hockey League
AHL	American Hockey League
AJHL	Alberta Junior Hockey Leagues
Alpenliga	Alpenliga (Austria, Italy, Slovenia 1994-1999)
AMBHL	Alberta Major Bantam Hockey League
AMHL	Alberta Midget AAA Hockey League
AUAA	Atlantic University Athletic Association
AWHL	American West Hockey League
BCAHA	British Columbia Amateur Hockey Association
BCHL	British Columbia (Junior) Hockey League (also BCJHL)
CCHA	Central Collegiate Hockey Association
CEGEP	Quebec College Prep
CHA	College Hockey America
CHL	Central Hockey League
CIS	Commonwealth of Independent States
CIS	Canadian Interuniversity Sport
ColHL	Colonial Hockey League
CSHL	Central States Hockey League
CWUAA	Canadian Western University Athletic Association
ECAC	Eastern College Athletic Conference
ECHL	East Coast Hockey League
EEHL	Eastern European Hockey League
EJHL	Eastern Junior Hockey League
EuroHL	European Hockey League
Exhib.	Exhibition Games, Series or Season
G.N.	Great Northern
GPAC	Great Plains Athletic Conference
GTHL	Greater Toronto Hockey League
H-East	Hockey East
HJHL	Heritage Junior Hockey League
Hi-School	High School (also H.S.)
IEL	Internationale Eishockey Liga
IHL	International Hockey League
IJHL	Interstate Junior Hockey League
KIDHL	Kootenay International Junior B Hockey League
LCJHL	Little Caesar's Junior Hockey League
MAAC	Metro Atlantic Athletic Conference
MAHA	Manitoba Amateur Hockey Association
MBHL	Metropolitan Boston Hockey League
MEHL	Midwest Elite Hockey League
MIAC	Minnesota Intercollegiate Athletic Conference
MJHL	Manitoba Junior Hockey League
MJrHL	Maritime Junior Major Hockey League
MMHL	Manitoba Midget AAA Hockey League
MNHL	Michigan National Hockey League
MTJHL	Metropolitan Toronto Junior Hockey League
MTHL	Metro Toronto Hockey League
NAHL	North American Hockey League (Tier I Junior)
NAJHL	North American Junior Hockey League
Nat-Team	National Team (also Nt.-Team)
NBAHA	New Brunswick Amateur Hockey Association
NCAA	National Collegiate Athletic Association
NEJHL	New England Junior Hockey League
NFAHA	Newfoundland Amateur Hockey Association
NHL	National Hockey League
NOHA	Northern Ontario Hockey Association
NOJHL	Northern Ontario Junior Hockey League
NSMHL	Nova Scotia Midget AAA Hockey League
OCJHL	Ontario Central Junior A Hockey League
OHL	Ontario Hockey League
OJHL-B	Ontario Junior B Hockey Leagues
OMHA	Ontario Minor Hockey Association
OMJHL	Ontario Major Junior Hockey League
OPJHL	Ontario Provincial Junior A Hockey League
OUAA	Ontario Universities Athletic Association
QAAA	Quebec Amateur Athletic Association
QAHA	Quebec Amateur Hockey Association
QJHL	Quebec Junior Hockey League
QMJHL	Quebec Major Junior Hockey League
PCJHL	Pacific Coast Junior Hockey League
PIJHL	Pacific International Junior Hockey League
RAMHL	Rural Alberta Midget Hockey League
RMJHL	Rocky Mountain Junior Hockey League
SAHA	Saskatchewan Amateur Hockey Association
SBHL	Saskatchewan Bantam Hockey League
SIJHL	Superior International Junior Hockey League
SJHL	Saskatchewan Junior Hockey League
SMHL	Saskatchewan Midget AAA Hockey League
SSJHL	Southern Saskatchewan Junior B Hockey League
SunHL	Sunshine Hockey League
TBAHA	Thunder Bay Amateur Hockey Association
TBJHL	Thunder Bay Junior Hockey League
TBMHL	Thunder Bay Midget Hockey League
UHL	United Hockey League
USAHA	United States Amateur Hockey Association
USDP	United States National Development Program
USHL	United States (Junior A) Hockey League
VIJHL	Vancouver Island Junior Hockey League
WCHA	Western Collegiate Hockey Association
WCHL	West Coast Hockey League
WHA	World Hockey Association
WHL	Western Hockey League
WNYHA	Western New York Hockey Association
WPHL	Western Professional Hockey League
WSJHL	Western States Junior Hockey League

Late Additions to Player Register

ELLIS, Matt   (EH-lihs, MAT)   DET.
Left wing. Shoots left. 6' 1", 190 lbs.   Born, Welland, Ont., August 31, 1981.

				Regular Season					Playoffs			
Season	Club	League	GP	G	A	TP	PIM	GP	G	A	TP	PIM
1998-99	St. Michael's	OHL	47	10	8	18	6	....	....	....	....	....
99-2000	St. Michael's	OHL	59	15	20	35	20	....	....	....	....	....
2000-01	St. Michael's	OHL	68	21	24	45	19	18	4	8	12	6
2001-02	St. Michael's	OHL	66	38	51	89	20	15	8	6	14	6
2002-03	Toledo	ECHL	71	27	32	59	34	7	3	5	8	0
2003-04	Grand Rapids	AHL	64	5	10	15	23	4	0	0	0	2

Signed as a free agent by **Detroit**, May 10, 2002.

GERMYN, Carsen   (JUHR-mihn, KAHR-sehn)   CGY.
Right wing. Shoots right. 5' 10", 185 lbs.   Born, Campbell River, B.C., February 22, 1985.

				Regular Season					Playoffs			
Season	Club	League	GP	G	A	TP	PIM	GP	G	A	TP	PIM
1998-99	Kelowna	WHL	59	6	10	16	61	5	0	0	0	2
99-2000	Kelowna	WHL	71	16	29	45	111	5	3	3	6	4
2000-01	Kelowna	WHL	71	35	52	87	102	6	2	6	8	10
2001-02	Kelowna	WHL	23	19	18	28	43	....	....	....	....	....
	Red Deer	WHL	37	23	25	48	83	23	4	12	16	24
2002-03	Red Deer	WHL	63	26	33	59	108	23	4	9	13	25
2003-04	Norfolk	AHL	77	11	16	27	104	6	1	0	1	2

Signed as a free agent by **Calgary**, July 6, 2004.

GIORDANO, Mark   (jee-ohr-DAN-oh, MAHRK)   CGY.
Defense. Shoots left. 6', 203 lbs.   Born, Toronto, Ont., May 10, 1983.

				Regular Season					Playoffs			
Season	Club	League	GP	G	A	TP	PIM	GP	G	A	TP	PIM
2002-03	Owen Sound	OHL	71	27	32	59	34	7	3	5	8	0
2003-04	Owen Sound	OHL	64	5	10	15	23	4	0	0	0	2

Signed as a free agent by **Calgary**, July 6, 2004.

HEINTZ, Davin   (HIGHNTZ, DAH-vihn)   CGY.
Left wing. Shoots left. 6'4", 213 lbs.   Born, Luseland, Sask., June 20, 1983.

				Regular Season					Playoffs			
Season	Club	League	GP	G	A	TP	PIM	GP	G	A	TP	PIM
99-2000	Saskatoon	WHL	28	3	1	4	4	11	0	3	3	5
2000-01	Saskatoon	WHL	67	5	8	13	6	....	....	....	....	....
2001-02	Saskatoon	WHL	63	16	23	39	71	7	0	1	1	7
2002-03	Swift Current	WHL	51	14	9	23	36	4	1	1	2	6
2003-04	Swift Current	WHL	62	24	26	50	47	5	1	0	1	6

Signed as a free agent by **Calgary**, July 6, 2004.

MacDONALD, Joey   (mihk-DAWN-uhld, JOH-ee)   DET.
Goaltender. Catches left. 5' 10", 170 lbs.   Born, Halifax, N.S., February 7, 1980.

					Regular Season						Playoffs				
Season	Club	League	GP	W	L	T	Mins	GA	SO	Avg	GP	W	L	Mins	GA	SO	Avg
1997-98	Halifax	QMJHL	17	3	12	0	816	54	0	3.97	3	1	2	140	15	0	6.43
1998-99	Peterborough	OHL	47	22	15	2	2483	123	3	2.97	3	0	2	145	13	0	5.38
99-2000	Peterborough	OHL	48	20	15	6	2641	125	2	2.84	5	5	4	280	16	1	3.43
2000-01	Peterborough	OHL	57	25	21	7	3284	161	1	2.94	7	3	4	425	18	0	2.54
2001-02	Toledo	ECHL	38	12	15	7	2084	100	1	2.88	...	...	...	...	...	...	...
2002-03	Grand Rapids	AHL	25	14	6	0	1337	49	3	2.20	1	0	0	8	1	0	7.95
2003-04	Grand Rapids	AHL	39	22	12	3	2249	74	6	1.97	1	0	1	40	4	0	6.04

Signed as a free agent by **Detroit**, December 21, 2001.

NILSON, Patrik   (nihl-SUHN, PA-trihk)   CGY.
Center. Shoots right. 6', 180 lbs.   Born, Baltsa, Sweden, May 18, 1981.

				Regular Season					Playoffs			
Season	Club	League	GP	G	A	TP	PIM	GP	G	A	TP	PIM
99-2000	Djurgardens	Sweden	6	0	0	0	2	...	...	...	...	...
	Huddinge	Swe.-2	25	11	6	17	38	...	...	...	...	...
2000-01	Djurgardens	Sweden	24	1	0	1	4	...	...	...	...	...
	Djurgardens Jr.	Swe.-Jr.	10	5	6	11	18	...	...	...	...	...
2001-02	Mora	Swe.-2	42	6	19	25	71	...	...	...	...	...
2002-03	Mora	Swe.-2	35	9	9	18	12	...	...	...	...	...
2003-04	Laredo	CHL	60	27	38	65	62	15	8	2	10	12
	San Antonio	AHL	3	0	0	0	0	...	...	...	...	...

Signed as a free agent by **Calgary**, July 6, 2004.

REGEHR, RICHIE   (reh-GEER, RIH-chee)   CGY.
Defense. Shoots right. 6', 190 lbs.   Born, Rosthern, Sask., January 17, 1983.

				Regular Season					Playoffs			
Season	Club	League	GP	G	A	TP	PIM	GP	G	A	TP	PIM
99-2000	Kelowna	WHL	50	6	8	14	22	5	0	1	1	0
2000-01	Kelowna	WHL	71	10	27	37	68	6	0	1	1	4
2001-02	Portland	WHL	52	8	36	44	62	7	2	2	4	8
2002-03	Portland	WHL	67	16	45	61	115	7	2	2	4	8
2003-04	Portland	WHL	65	9	34	43	88	5	0	1	1	6

Signed as a free agent by **Calgary**, July 6, 2004.

RYAN, Matt   (RIGH-uhn, MAT)   L.A.
Center. Shoots left. 6', 185 lbs.   Born, Born: Sharon, Ont., November 12, 1983.

				Regular Season					Playoffs			
Season	Club	League	GP	G	A	TP	PIM	GP	G	A	TP	PIM
2001-02	Niagara Univ.	CHA	32	7	12	19	32	...	...	...	...	...
2002-03	Guelph	OHL	48	14	11	25	34	11	2	7	9	0
2003-04	Guelph	OHL	68	42	35	77	63	22	8	11	19	24

Signed as a free agent by **Los Angeles**, August 2, 2004.

TAYLOR, Justin   (TAY-luhr, JUHS-tihn)   CGY.
Left wing. Shoots left. 6'4", 200 lbs.   Born, Edmonton, Alta., January 1, 1983.

				Regular Season					Playoffs			
Season	Club	League	GP	G	A	TP	PIM	GP	G	A	TP	PIM
2002-03	Medicine Hat	WHL	39	1	5	6	11	...	...	...	...	...
2003-04	Red Deer	WHL	57	16	22	38	39	19	6	10	16	13

Signed as a free agent by **Calgary**, July 6, 2004.

FREE AGENT SIGNINGS

CAMPBELL, Jim signed as a free agent by NY Islanders, August 11, 2004.

SEELEY, Richard signed as a free agent by NY Islanders, August 13, 2004.

TRADES

PROSPAL, Vaclav traded to Tampa Bay by Anaheim for Tampa Bay's 2nd round choice in the 2005 Entry Draft, August 16, 2004.

2004-05 NHL Player Register

Note: The 2004-05 NHL Player Register lists forwards and defensemen only. Goaltenders are listed separately. The NHL Player Register lists every skater who played in the NHL in 2003-04 plus additional players with NHL experience. Trades and roster changes are current as of August 11, 2004.

Abbreviations: A – assists; **F%** – faceoff winning percentage; **G** – goals; **GP** – games played; **GT** – game-tying goals scored; **GW** – game-winning goals scored; **Min** – average time on ice; **PIM** – penalties in minutes; **+/–** – plus/minus rating; **PP** – powerplay goals scored; **Pts** – points; **S** – shots on goal; **S%** – shooting percentage; **SH** – shorthand goal scored; **TF** – Total faceoffs taken; ***** – league-leading total; **♦** – member of Stanley Cup-winning team.

Prospect Register begins on page 267.
Goaltender Register begins on page 573.
League abbreviations are listed on page 337.

						Regular Season														Playoffs					
Season	Club	League	GP	G	A	Pts	PIM	PP	SH	GW	S	%	+/-	TF	F%	Min	GP	G	A	Pts	PIM	PP	SH	GW	Min

ABID, Ramzi   (a-BIHD, RAM-zee)   **PIT.**

Left wing. Shoots left. 6'2", 210 lbs.   Born, Montreal, Que., March 24, 1980. Phoenix's 3rd choice, 85th overall, in 2000 Entry Draft.

Season	Club	League	GP	G	A	Pts	PIM	PP	SH	GW	S	%	+/-	TF	F%	Min	GP	G	A	Pts	PIM	PP	SH	GW	Min
1995-96	Richelieu Riverains	QAAA	42	10	14	24	18	....	....	....	....	....	....	....	....	....	4	1	2	3	2	....	....	....	....
1996-97	Chicoutimi	QMJHL	65	13	24	37	141	....	....	....	....	....	....	....	....	....	21	2	12	14	28	....	....	....	....
1997-98	Chicoutimi	QMJHL	68	50	*85	*135	266	....	....	....	....	....	....	....	....	....	6	3	4	7	10	....	....	....	....
1998-99	Chicoutimi	QMJHL	21	11	15	26	97	....	....	....	....	....	....	....	....	....	....	....	....	....	....	....	....	....	....
	Acadie-Bathurst	QMJHL	24	14	22	36	102	....	....	....	....	....	....	....	....	....	23	14	20	34	*84	....	....	....	....
99-2000	Acadie-Bathurst	QMJHL	13	10	11	21	61	....	....	....	....	....	....	....	....	....	....	....	....	....	....	....	....	....	....
	Halifax	QMJHL	59	57	80	137	148	....	....	....	....	....	....	....	....	....	10	10	13	23	18	....	....	....	....
2000-01	Springfield	AHL	17	6	4	10	38	....	....	....	....	....	....	....	....	....	....	....	....	....	....	....	....	....	....
2001-02	Springfield	AHL	66	18	25	43	214	....	....	....	....	....	....	....	....	....	....	....	....	....	....	....	....	....	....
2002-03	**Phoenix**	**NHL**	**30**	**10**	**8**	**18**	**30**	4	0	3	52	19.2	1	1100.0		12:30	....	....	....	....	....	....	....	....	....
	Springfield	AHL	27	15	10	25	50	....	....	....	....	....	....	....	....	....	....	....	....	....	....	....	....	....	....
	Pittsburgh	**NHL**	**3**	**0**	**0**	**0**	**2**	0	0	0	7	0.0	–5	1	0.0	17:33	....	....	....	....	....	....	....	....	....
2003-04	**Pittsburgh**	**NHL**	**16**	**3**	**2**	**5**	**27**	2	0	1	35	8.6	–5	2	0.0	12:56	....	....	....	....	....	....	....	....	....
	NHL Totals		**49**	**13**	**10**	**23**	**59**	6	0	4	94	13.8		4	25.0	12:57	....	....	....	....	....	....	....	....	....

• Re-entered NHL Entry Draft. Originally Colorado's 5th choice, 28th overall, in 1998 Entry Draft.
QMJHL First All-Star Team (1998, 2000) • Jean Beliveau Trophy (QMJHL Leading Scorer) (1998) • Michel Briere Trophy (QMJHL MVP) (1998) • Canadian Major Junior First All-Star Team (2000) • Ed Chynoweth Trophy (Memorial Cup Leading Scorer) (2000)
• Missed majority of 2000-01 season recovering from wrist injury suffered in game vs. Louisville (AHL), October 27, 2000. Traded to **Pittsburgh** by **Phoenix** with Dan Focht and Guillaume Lefebvre for Jan Hrdina and Francois Leroux, March 11, 2003. • Missed majority of 2003-04 season recovering from knee injury suffered in game vs. Edmonton, December 6, 2003.

ADAMS, Craig   (A-duhms, KRAYG)   **CAR.**

Right wing. Shoots right. 6', 200 lbs.   Born, Seria, Brunei, April 26, 1977. Hartford's 9th choice, 223rd overall, in 1996 Entry Draft.

Season	Club	League	GP	G	A	Pts	PIM	PP	SH	GW	S	%	+/-	TF	F%	Min	GP	G	A	Pts	PIM	PP	SH	GW	Min
1994-95	Calgary Canucks	AJHL					STATISTICS NOT AVAILABLE																			
1995-96	Harvard Crimson	ECAC	34	8	9	17	56	....	....	....	....	....	....	....	....	....	....	....	....	....	....	....	....	....	....
1996-97	Harvard Crimson	ECAC	32	6	4	10	36	....	....	....	....	....	....	....	....	....	....	....	....	....	....	....	....	....	....
1997-98	Harvard Crimson	ECAC	12	6	6	12	12	....	....	....	....	....	....	....	....	....	....	....	....	....	....	....	....	....	....
1998-99	Harvard Crimson	ECAC	31	9	14	23	53	....	....	....	....	....	....	....	....	....	....	....	....	....	....	....	....	....	....
99-2000	Cincinnati	IHL	73	12	12	24	124	....	....	....	....	....	....	....	....	....	8	0	1	1	14	....	....	....	....
2000-01	**Carolina**	**NHL**	**44**	**1**	**0**	**1**	**20**	0	0	0	15	6.7	–7	4	25.0	4:30	3	0	0	0	0	0	0	0	3:45
	Cincinnati	IHL	4	0	1	1	9	....	....	....	....	....	....	....	....	....	1	0	0	0	2	....	....	....	....
2001-02	**Carolina**	**NHL**	**33**	**0**	**1**	**1**	**38**	0	0	0	17	0.0	2	9	33.3	5:54	1	0	0	0	0	0	0	0	7:41
	Lowell	AHL	22	5	4	9	51	....	....	....	....	....	....	....	....	....	....	....	....	....	....	....	....	....	....
2002-03	**Carolina**	**NHL**	**81**	**6**	**12**	**18**	**71**	0	1	0	107	5.6	–11	20	35.0	12:12	....	....	....	....	....	....	....	....	....
2003-04	**Carolina**	**NHL**	**80**	**7**	**10**	**17**	**69**	0	1	0	110	6.4	–5	20	45.0	13:41	....	....	....	....	....	....	....	....	....
	NHL Totals		**238**	**14**	**23**	**37**	**198**	1	1	1	249	5.6		53	37.7	10:24	4	0	0	0	0	0	0	0	4:44

Rights transferred to **Carolina** after **Hartford** franchise relocated, June 25, 1997. • Missed majority of 1997-98 season recovering from shoulder injury suffered in game vs. University of Wisconsin (WCHA), December 27, 1997.

ADAMS, Kevyn   (A-duhms, KEH-vihn)   **CAR.**

Center. Shoots right. 6'1", 195 lbs.   Born, Washington, DC, October 8, 1974. Boston's 1st choice, 25th overall, in 1993 Entry Draft.

Season	Club	League	GP	G	A	Pts	PIM	PP	SH	GW	S	%	+/-	TF	F%	Min	GP	G	A	Pts	PIM	PP	SH	GW	Min
1990-91	Niagara Scenics	NAJHL	55	17	20	37	24	....	....	....	....	....	....	....	....	....	....	....	....	....	....	....	....	....	....
1991-92	Niagara Scenics	NAJHL	40	25	33	58	51	....	....	....	....	....	....	....	....	....	....	....	....	....	....	....	....	....	....
1992-93	Miami-Ohio	CCHA	40	17	15	32	18	....	....	....	....	....	....	....	....	....	....	....	....	....	....	....	....	....	....
1993-94	Miami-Ohio	CCHA	36	15	28	43	24	....	....	....	....	....	....	....	....	....	....	....	....	....	....	....	....	....	....
1994-95	Miami-Ohio	CCHA	38	20	29	49	30	....	....	....	....	....	....	....	....	....	....	....	....	....	....	....	....	....	....
1995-96	Miami-Ohio	CCHA	36	17	30	47	30	....	....	....	....	....	....	....	....	....	....	....	....	....	....	....	....	....	....
1996-97	Grand Rapids	IHL	82	22	25	47	47	....	....	....	....	....	....	....	....	....	5	1	1	2	4	....	....	....	....
1997-98	**Toronto**	**NHL**	**5**	**0**	**0**	**0**	**7**	0	0	0	3	0.0	0	....	....	....	....	....	....	....	....	....	....	....	....
	St. John's	AHL	59	17	20	37	99	....	....	....	....	....	....	....	....	....	4	0	0	0	4	....	....	....	....
1998-99	**Toronto**	**NHL**	**1**	**0**	**0**	**0**	**0**	0	0	0	1	0.0	0	9	44.4	7:56	7	0	2	2	14	0	0	0	11:18
	St. John's	AHL	80	15	35	50	85	....	....	....	....	....	....	....	....	....	5	2	0	2	4	....	....	....	....
99-2000	**Toronto**	**NHL**	**52**	**5**	**8**	**13**	**39**	0	0	1	70	7.1	–7	604	56.5	12:23	12	1	0	1	7	0	1	0	11:06
	St. John's	AHL	23	6	11	17	24	....	....	....	....	....	....	....	....	....	....	....	....	....	....	....	....	....	....
2000-01	**Columbus**	**NHL**	**66**	**8**	**12**	**20**	**52**	0	0	1	84	9.5	–4	1152	57.4	15:18	....	....	....	....	....	....	....	....	....
	Florida	**NHL**	**12**	**3**	**6**	**9**	**2**	0	0	2	21	14.3	7	198	47.5	17:25	....	....	....	....	....	....	....	....	....
2001-02	**Florida**	**NHL**	**44**	**4**	**8**	**12**	**28**	0	0	1	71	5.6	–3	572	57.9	13:21	....	....	....	....	....	....	....	....	....
	Carolina	**NHL**	**33**	**2**	**3**	**5**	**15**	0	0	1	37	5.4	–2	187	58.8	9:05	23	1	0	1	4	0	0	0	7:29
2002-03	**Carolina**	**NHL**	**77**	**9**	**9**	**18**	**57**	0	0	0	169	5.3	–8	1018	53.1	14:39	....	....	....	....	....	....	....	....	....
2003-04	**Carolina**	**NHL**	**73**	**10**	**12**	**22**	**43**	0	5	1	141	7.1	6	722	51.9	13:17	....	....	....	....	....	....	....	....	....
	NHL Totals		**363**	**41**	**58**	**99**	**243**	0	5	6	597	6.9		4462	55.0	13:34	42	2	2	4	25	0	1	0	9:09

CCHA Second All-Star Team (1995)
Signed as a free agent by **Toronto**, August 7, 1997. Selected by **Columbus** from **Toronto** in Expansion Draft, June 23, 2000. Traded to **Florida** by **Columbus** with Columbus's 4th round choice (Mike Woodford) in 2001 Entry Draft for Ray Whitney and future considerations, March 13, 2001. Traded to **Carolina** by **Florida** with Bret Hedican and Tomas Malec for Sandis Ozolinsh and Byron Ritchie, January 16, 2002.

Regular Season (GP–Min) | Playoffs (GP–Min)

AFANASENKOV, Dmitry

(a-fahn-A-sehn-kahv, dih-MEE-tree) **T.B.**

Left wing. Shoots right. 6'2", 200 lbs. Born, Arkhangelsk, USSR, May 12, 1980. Tampa Bay's 3rd choice, 72nd overall, in 1998 Entry Draft.

Season	Club	League	GP	G	A	Pts	PIM	PP	SH	GW	S	%	+/-	TF	F%	Min	GP	G	A	Pts	PIM	PP	SH	GW	Min
1995-96	Yaroslavl Jr.	CIS-Jr.	35	28	16	44	8	....	....	....	....	....	....	....	....	....	....	....	....	....	....	....	....	....	....
	Yaroslavl 2	CIS-2	25	10	5	15	10	....	....	....	....	....	....	....	....	....	....	....	....	....	....	....	....	....	....
1996-97	Yaroslavl 2	Russia-3	45	20	15	35	14	....	....	....	....	....	....	....	....	....	....	....	....	....	....	....	....	....	....
1997-98	Yaroslavl 2	Russia-2	48	14	7	21	20	....	....	....	....	....	....	....	....	....	....	....	....	....	....	....	....	....	....
1998-99	Moncton Wildcats	QMJHL	15	5	5	10	12	....	....	....	....	....	....	....	....	....	....	....	....	....	....	....	....	....	....
	Sherbrooke	QMJHL	51	23	30	53	22	....	....	....	....	....	....	....	....	....	13	10	6	16	6	....	....	....	....
99-2000	Sherbrooke	QMJHL	60	56	43	99	70	....	....	....	....	....	....	....	....	....	5	3	2	5	4	....	....	....	....
2000-01	**Tampa Bay**	**NHL**	**9**	**1**	**1**	**2**	**4**	**0**	**0**	**0**	**8**	**12.5**	**1**	**7**	**28.6**	**11:24**	....	....	....	....	....	....	....	....	....
	Detroit Vipers	IHL	65	15	22	37	26	....	....	....	....	....	....	....	....	....	....	....	....	....	....	....	....	....	....
2001-02	**Tampa Bay**	**NHL**	**5**	**0**	**0**	**0**	**0**	**0**	**0**	**0**	**1**	**0.0**	**–1**	**0**	**0.0**	**4:54**	....	....	....	....	....	....	....	....	....
	Springfield	AHL	28	4	5	9	4	....	....	....	....	....	....	....	....	....	....	....	....	....	....	....	....	....	....
	Grand Rapids	AHL	18	1	2	3	2	....	....	....	....	....	....	....	....	....	....	....	....	....	....	....	....	....	....
2002-03	Springfield	AHL	41	4	9	13	25	....	....	....	....	....	....	....	....	....	....	....	....	....	....	....	....	....	....
	Kloten Flyers	Swiss	....	....	....	....	....	....	....	....	....	....	....	....	....	....	5	1	1	2	0	....	....	....	....
2003-04♦	**Tampa Bay**	**NHL**	**71**	**6**	**10**	**16**	**12**	**0**	**0**	**1**	**98**	**6.1**	**–4**	**2**	**0.0**	**12:21**	**23**	**1**	**2**	**3**	**6**	**0**	**0**	**0**	**13:06**
	NHL Totals		**85**	**7**	**11**	**18**	**16**	**0**	**0**	**1**	**107**	**6.5**		**9**	**22.2**	**11:49**	**23**	**1**	**2**	**3**	**6**	**0**	**0**	**0**	**13:06**

• Assigned to **Kloten** (Swiss) by **Tampa Bay**, February 19, 2003.

AFINOGENOV, Maxim

(ah-fihn-ah-GEHN-ahf, mahx-EEM) **BUF.**

Right wing. Shoots left. 6', 190 lbs. Born, Moscow, USSR, September 4, 1979. Buffalo's 3rd choice, 69th overall, in 1997 Entry Draft.

Season	Club	League	GP	G	A	Pts	PIM	PP	SH	GW	S	%	+/-	TF	F%	Min	GP	G	A	Pts	PIM	PP	SH	GW	Min
1996-97	Dynamo Moscow	Russia	29	6	5	11	10	....	....	....	....	....	....	....	....	....	4	0	2	2	0	....	....	....	....
	Dynamo Moscow	EuroHL	3	0	0	0	0	....	....	....	....	....	....	....	....	....	3	1	0	1	4	....	....	....	....
1997-98	Dynamo Moscow	Russia	35	10	5	15	53	....	....	....	....	....	....	....	....	....	....	....	....	....	....	....	....	....	....
	Dynamo Moscow	EuroHL	6	3	1	4	27	....	....	....	....	....	....	....	....	....	....	....	....	....	....	....	....	....	....
1998-99	Dynamo Moscow	Russia	38	8	13	21	24	....	....	....	....	....	....	....	....	....	16	*10	6	*16	14	....	....	....	....
	Dynamo Moscow	EuroHL	5	3	5	8	29	....	....	....	....	....	....	....	....	....	4	2	1	3	27	....	....	....	....
99-2000	**Buffalo**	**NHL**	**65**	**16**	**18**	**34**	**41**	**2**	**0**	**2**	**128**	**12.5**	**–4**	**0**	**0.0**	**13:09**	**5**	**0**	**1**	**1**	**2**	**0**	**0**	**0**	**12:53**
	Rochester	AHL	15	6	12	18	8	....	....	....	....	....	....	....	....	....	8	3	1	4	4	....	....	....	....
2000-01	**Buffalo**	**NHL**	**78**	**14**	**22**	**36**	**40**	**3**	**0**	**5**	**190**	**7.4**	**1**	**2**	**0.0**	**14:32**	**11**	**2**	**3**	**5**	**4**	**0**	**0**	**0**	**10:56**
2001-02	**Buffalo**	**NHL**	**81**	**21**	**19**	**40**	**69**	**3**	**1**	**0**	**234**	**9.0**	**–9**	**1**	**100.0**	**15:22**	....	....	....	....	....	....	....	....	....
	Russia	Olympics	6	2	2	4	4	....	....	....	....	....	....	....	....	....	....	....	....	....	....	....	....	....	....
2002-03	**Buffalo**	**NHL**	**35**	**5**	**6**	**11**	**21**	**2**	**0**	**2**	**77**	**6.5**	**–12**	**4**	**50.0**	**13:24**	....	....	....	....	....	....	....	....	....
2003-04	**Buffalo**	**NHL**	**73**	**17**	**14**	**31**	**57**	**3**	**0**	**4**	**148**	**11.5**	**–4**	**9**	**22.2**	**13:46**	....	....	....	....	....	....	....	....	....
	NHL Totals		**332**	**73**	**79**	**152**	**228**	**13**	**1**	**13**	**777**	**9.4**		**16**	**31.3**	**14:11**	**16**	**2**	**4**	**6**	**6**	**0**	**0**	**0**	**11:32**

• Missed majority of 2002-03 season recovering from head injury suffered in training camp, October 8, 2002.

AITKEN, Johnathan

(ATE-kin, JAWN-uh-thuhn) **VAN.**

Defense. Shoots left. 6'4", 230 lbs. Born, Edmonton, Alta., May 24, 1978. Boston's 1st choice, 8th overall, in 1996 Entry Draft.

Season	Club	League	GP	G	A	Pts	PIM	PP	SH	GW	S	%	+/-	TF	F%	Min	GP	G	A	Pts	PIM	PP	SH	GW	Min
1993-94	Sherwood Park	AMHL	31	4	9	13	54	....	....	....	....	....	....	....	....	....	....	....	....	....	....	....	....	....	....
1994-95	Medicine Hat	WHL	53	0	5	5	71	....	....	....	....	....	....	....	....	....	5	0	0	0	0	....	....	....	....
1995-96	Medicine Hat	WHL	71	6	14	20	131	....	....	....	....	....	....	....	....	....	5	1	0	1	6	....	....	....	....
1996-97	Brandon	WHL	65	4	18	22	211	....	....	....	....	....	....	....	....	....	6	0	0	0	4	....	....	....	....
1997-98	Brandon	WHL	69	9	25	34	183	....	....	....	....	....	....	....	....	....	18	0	8	8	67	....	....	....	....
1998-99	Providence Bruins	AHL	65	2	9	11	92	....	....	....	....	....	....	....	....	....	13	0	0	0	17	....	....	....	....
99-2000	**Boston**	**NHL**	**3**	**0**	**0**	**0**	**0**	**0**	**0**	**0**	**2**	**0.0**	**–3**	**0**	**0.0**	**18:57**	....	....	....	....	....	....	....	....	....
	Providence Bruins	AHL	70	2	12	14	121	....	....	....	....	....	....	....	....	....	11	1	0	1	26	....	....	....	....
2000-01	HC Sparta Praha	Czech	24	0	3	3	62	....	....	....	....	....	....	....	....	....	....	....	....	....	....	....	....	....	....
2001-02	Norfolk Admirals	AHL	28	0	1	1	43	....	....	....	....	....	....	....	....	....	4	0	0	0	2	....	....	....	....
	Jackson Bandits	ECHL	43	1	9	10	141	....	....	....	....	....	....	....	....	....	....	....	....	....	....	....	....	....	....
2002-03	Norfolk Admirals	AHL	80	1	7	8	207	....	....	....	....	....	....	....	....	....	9	2	1	3	18	....	....	....	....
2003-04	**Chicago**	**NHL**	**41**	**0**	**1**	**1**	**70**	**0**	**0**	**0**	**37**	**0.0**	**–9**	**0**	**0.0**	**17:15**	....	....	....	....	....	....	....	....	....
	Norfolk Admirals	AHL	40	1	4	5	97	....	....	....	....	....	....	....	....	....	8	1	4	5	27	....	....	....	....
	NHL Totals		**44**	**0**	**1**	**1**	**70**	**0**	**0**	**0**	**39**	**0.0**		**0**	**0.0**	**17:22**	....	....	....	....	....	....	....	....	....

WHL East Second All-Star Team (1998)

Signed as a free agent by **Norfolk** (AHL), September 6, 2001. Signed as a free agent by **Chicago**, May 22, 2002. Signed as a free agent by **Vancouver**, July 7, 2004.

ALBELIN, Tommy

(AHL-buh-leen,TAW-mee)

Defense. Shoots left. 6'2", 195 lbs. Born, Stockholm, Sweden, May 21, 1964. Quebec's 7th choice, 158th overall, in 1983 Entry Draft.

Season	Club	League	GP	G	A	Pts	PIM	PP	SH	GW	S	%	+/-	TF	F%	Min	GP	G	A	Pts	PIM	PP	SH	GW	Min
1980-81	Stocksunds IF	Swede-3	18	6	1	7	....	....	....	....	....	....	....	....	....	....	....	....	....	....	....	....	....	....	....
1981-82	Stocksunds IF	Swede-3	22	6	2	8	....	....	....	....	....	....	....	....	....	....	....	....	....	....	....	....	....	....	....
1982-83	Djurgarden	Sweden	19	2	5	7	4	....	....	....	....	....	....	....	....	....	6	1	0	1	2	....	....	....	....
1983-84	Djurgarden	Sweden	30	9	5	14	26	....	....	....	....	....	....	....	....	....	4	0	1	1	2	....	....	....	....
1984-85	Djurgarden	Sweden	32	9	8	17	22	....	....	....	....	....	....	....	....	....	8	2	1	3	4	....	....	....	....
1985-86	Djurgarden	Sweden	35	4	8	12	26	....	....	....	....	....	....	....	....	....	....	....	....	....	....	....	....	....	....
1986-87	Djurgarden	Sweden	33	7	5	12	49	....	....	....	....	....	....	....	....	....	2	0	0	0	0	....	....	....	....
1987-88	**Quebec**	**NHL**	**60**	**3**	**23**	**26**	**47**	**0**	**0**	**0**	**98**	**3.1**	**–7**	....	....	....	....	....	....	....	....	....	....	....	....
1988-89	**Quebec**	**NHL**	**14**	**2**	**4**	**6**	**27**	**1**	**0**	**1**	**16**	**12.5**	**–6**	....	....	....	....	....	....	....	....	....	....	....	....
	Halifax Citadels	AHL	8	2	5	7	4	....	....	....	....	....	....	....	....	....	....	....	....	....	....	....	....	....	....
	New Jersey	**NHL**	**46**	**7**	**24**	**31**	**40**	**1**	**1**	**1**	**82**	**8.5**	**18**	....	....	....	....	....	....	....	....	....	....	....	....
1989-90	**New Jersey**	**NHL**	**68**	**6**	**23**	**29**	**63**	**4**	**0**	**0**	**125**	**4.8**	**–1**	....	....	....	....	....	....	....	....	....	....	....	....
1990-91	**New Jersey**	**NHL**	**47**	**2**	**12**	**14**	**44**	**1**	**0**	**0**	**66**	**3.0**	**1**	....	....	....	**3**	**0**	**1**	**1**	**2**	**0**	**0**	**0**	....
	Utica Devils	AHL	14	4	2	6	10	....	....	....	....	....	....	....	....	....	....	....	....	....	....	....	....	....	....
1991-92	**New Jersey**	**NHL**	**19**	**0**	**4**	**4**	**4**	**0**	**0**	**0**	**18**	**0.0**	**7**	....	....	....	**1**	**1**	**1**	**2**	**0**	**0**	**0**	**0**	....
	Utica Devils	AHL	11	4	6	10	4	....	....	....	....	....	....	....	....	....	....	....	....	....	....	....	....	....	....
1992-93	**New Jersey**	**NHL**	**36**	**1**	**5**	**6**	**14**	**1**	**0**	**1**	**33**	**3.0**	**0**	....	....	....	**5**	**2**	**0**	**2**	**0**	**1**	**0**	**1**	....
1993-94	**New Jersey**	**NHL**	**62**	**2**	**17**	**19**	**36**	**1**	**0**	**1**	**62**	**3.2**	**20**	....	....	....	**20**	**2**	**5**	**7**	**14**	**1**	**0**	**1**	....
	Albany River Rats	AHL	4	0	2	2	17	....	....	....	....	....	....	....	....	....	....	....	....	....	....	....	....	....	....
1994-95♦	**New Jersey**	**NHL**	**48**	**5**	**10**	**15**	**20**	**2**	**0**	**0**	**60**	**8.3**	**9**	....	....	....	**20**	**1**	**7**	**8**	**2**	**0**	**0**	**0**	....
1995-96	**New Jersey**	**NHL**	**53**	**1**	**12**	**13**	**14**	**0**	**0**	**0**	**90**	**1.1**	**0**	....	....	....	....	....	....	....	....	....	....	....	....
	Calgary	**NHL**	**20**	**0**	**1**	**1**	**4**	**0**	**0**	**0**	**31**	**0.0**	**1**	....	....	....	**4**	**0**	**0**	**0**	**0**	**0**	**0**	**0**	....
1996-97	**Calgary**	**NHL**	**72**	**4**	**11**	**15**	**14**	**2**	**0**	**0**	**103**	**3.9**	**–8**	....	....	....	....	....	....	....	....	....	....	....	....
1997-98	**Calgary**	**NHL**	**69**	**2**	**17**	**19**	**32**	**1**	**0**	**2**	**88**	**2.3**	**9**	....	....	....	....	....	....	....	....	....	....	....	....
	Sweden	Olympics	3	0	0	0	4	....	....	....	....	....	....	....	....	....	....	....	....	....	....	....	....	....	....
1998-99	**Calgary**	**NHL**	**60**	**1**	**5**	**6**	**8**	**0**	**0**	**0**	**54**	**1.9**	**–11**	**1**	**0.0**	**19:08**	....	....	....	....	....	....	....	....	....
99-2000	**Calgary**	**NHL**	**41**	**4**	**6**	**10**	**12**	**1**	**1**	**1**	**37**	**10.8**	**–3**	**0**	**0.0**	**21:35**	....	....	....	....	....	....	....	....	....
2000-01	**Calgary**	**NHL**	**77**	**1**	**19**	**20**	**22**	**1**	**0**	**0**	**69**	**1.4**	**2**	**0**	**0.0**	**20:53**	....	....	....	....	....	....	....	....	....
2001-02	**New Jersey**	**NHL**	**42**	**1**	**3**	**4**	**4**	**0**	**0**	**1**	**33**	**3.0**	**0**	**0**	**0.0**	**13:20**	**6**	**0**	**0**	**0**	**0**	**0**	**0**	**0**	**14:11**
2002-03♦	**New Jersey**	**NHL**	**37**	**1**	**6**	**7**	**6**	**0**	**1**	**0**	**30**	**3.3**	**10**	**0**	**0.0**	**15:13**	**16**	**1**	**0**	**1**	**2**	**0**	**0**	**0**	**14:18**
	Albany River Rats	AHL	5	0	2	2	2	....	....	....	....	....	....	....	....	....	....	....	....	....	....	....	....	....	....
2003-04	**New Jersey**	**NHL**	**45**	**1**	**3**	**4**	**4**	**0**	**0**	**0**	**27**	**3.7**	**7**	**0**	**0.0**	**14:48**	**4**	**0**	**1**	**1**	**0**	**0**	**0**	**0**	**13:13**
	NHL Totals		**916**	**44**	**205**	**249**	**415**	**16**	**3**	**8**	**1122**	**3.9**		**1**	**0.0**	**17:59**	**79**	**7**	**15**	**22**	**20**	**2**	**0**	**2**	**14:06**

Traded to **New Jersey** by **Quebec** for New Jersey's 4th round choice (Niklas Andersson) in 1989 Entry Draft, December 12, 1988. Traded to **Calgary** by **New Jersey** with Cale Hulse and Jocelyn Lemieux for Phil Housley and Dan Keczmer, February 26, 1996. Signed as a free agent by **New Jersey**, July 9, 2001.

ALEXEEV, Nikita

(uh-LEHX-ee-ehv, nih-KEE-tuh) **T.B.**

Right wing. Shoots left. 6'5", 225 lbs. Born, Murmansk, USSR, December 27, 1981. Tampa Bay's 1st choice, 8th overall, in 2000 Entry Draft.

Season	Club	League	GP	G	A	Pts	PIM	PP	SH	GW	S	%	+/-	TF	F%	Min	GP	G	A	Pts	PIM	PP	SH	GW	Min
1996-97	Krylja Sovetov Jr.	Russia-Jr.	45	4	6	10	8	....	....	....	....	....	....	....	....	....	....	....	....	....	....	....	....	....	....
1997-98	Krylja Sovetov 2	Russia-3	61	11	4	15	36	....	....	....	....	....	....	....	....	....	....	....	....	....	....	....	....	....	....
1998-99	Erie Otters	OHL	61	17	18	35	14	....	....	....	....	....	....	....	....	....	5	1	1	2	4	....	....	....	....
99-2000	Erie Otters	OHL	64	24	29	53	42	....	....	....	....	....	....	....	....	....	13	4	3	7	6	....	....	....	....
2000-01	Erie Otters	OHL	64	31	41	72	45	....	....	....	....	....	....	....	....	....	12	7	7	14	12	....	....	....	....
2001-02	**Tampa Bay**	**NHL**	**44**	**4**	**4**	**8**	**8**	**1**	**0**	**1**	**47**	**8.5**	**–9**	**0**	**0.0**	**11:26**	....	....	....	....	....	....	....	....	....
	Springfield	AHL	35	5	9	14	16	....	....	....	....	....	....	....	....	....	....	....	....	....	....	....	....	....	....

Season	Club	League	GP	G	A	Pts	PIM	PP	SH	GW	S	%	+/-	TF	F%	Min	GP	G	A	Pts	PIM	PP	SH	GW	Min
			Regular Season														Playoffs								
2002-03	Tampa Bay	NHL	37	4	2	6	8	1	0	1	52	7.7	–6	3	33.3	11:31	11	1	0	1	0	0	0	0	10:12
	Springfield	AHL	36	7	5	12	8	....	....	....	....	....	....	....	....	....	....	....	....	....	....	....	....	....	....
2003-04	Hershey Bears	AHL	14	0	1	1	8	....	....	....	....	....	....	....	....	....	....	....	....	....	....	....	....	....	....
	NHL Totals		81	8	6	14	16	2	0	2	99	8.1		3	33.3	11:28	11	1	0	1	0	0	0	0	10:12

• Missed majority of 2003-04 season recovering from shoulder injury suffered in game vs. Philadelphia (AHL) on November 2, 2003.

ALFREDSSON, Daniel

(AHL-frehd-suhn, DAN-yehl) **OTT.**

Right wing. Shoots right. 5'11", 199 lbs. Born, Goteborg, Sweden, December 11, 1972. Ottawa's 5th choice, 133rd overall, in 1994 Entry Draft.

Season	Club	League	GP	G	A	Pts	PIM	PP	SH	GW	S	%	+/-	TF	F%	Min	GP	G	A	Pts	PIM	PP	SH	GW	Min
1990-91	IF Molndal	Swede-2	3	0	0	0	2	....	....	....	....	....	....	....	....	....	....	....	....	....	....	....	....	....	....
1991-92	IF Molndal	Swede-2	32	12	8	20	43	....	....	....	....	....	....	....	....	....	8	4	4	8	4	....	....	....	....
1992-93	Vastra Frolunda	Sweden	20	1	5	6	8	....	....	....	....	....	....	....	....	....	....	....	....	....	....	....	....	....	....
1993-94	Vastra Frolunda	Sweden	39	20	10	30	18	....	....	....	....	....	....	....	....	....	....	....	....	....	....	....	....	....	....
1994-95	Vastra Frolunda	Sweden	22	7	11	18	22	....	....	....	....	....	....	....	....	....	4	1	1	2	....	....	....	....	....
1995-96	Ottawa	NHL	82	26	35	61	28	8	2	3	212	12.3	–18	....	....	....	....	....	....	....	....	....	....	....	....
1996-97	Ottawa	NHL	76	24	47	71	30	11	1	1	247	9.7	5	....	....	....	7	5	2	7	6	3	0	2	....
1997-98	Ottawa	NHL	55	17	28	45	18	7	0	7	149	11.4	7	....	....	....	11	7	2	9	20	2	1	1	....
	Sweden	Olympics	4	2	3	5	2	....	....	....	....	....	....	....	....	....	....	....	....	....	....	....	....	....	....
1998-99	Ottawa	NHL	58	11	22	33	14	3	0	5	163	6.7	8	7	57.1	17:22	4	1	2	3	4	1	0	0	22:23
99-2000	Ottawa	NHL	57	21	38	59	28	4	2	0	164	12.8	11	3	66.7	18:45	6	1	3	4	2	1	0	0	20:22
2000-01	Ottawa	NHL	68	24	46	70	30	10	0	3	206	11.7	11	8	50.0	18:47	4	1	0	1	2	0	0	0	21:20
2001-02	Ottawa	NHL	78	37	34	71	45	9	1	4	243	15.2	3	30	30.0	20:19	12	7	6	13	4	3	0	3	21:43
	Sweden	Olympics	4	1	4	5	2	....	....	....	....	....	....	....	....	....	....	....	....	....	....	....	....	....	....
2002-03	Ottawa	NHL	78	27	51	78	42	9	0	6	240	11.3	15	40	40.0	19:32	18	4	4	8	12	4	0	1	18:00
2003-04	Ottawa	NHL	77	32	48	80	24	9	0	5	230	13.9	12	33	24.2	19:24	7	1	2	3	2	0	0	0	20:03
	NHL Totals		629	219	349	568	259	70	6	34	1854	11.8		121	35.5	19:07	69	27	21	48	52	14	1	7	20:02

NHL All-Rookie Team (1996) • Calder Memorial Trophy (1996)
Played in NHL All-Star Game (1996, 1997, 1998, 2004)

ALLEN, Bobby

(AHL-lehn, BAW-bee) **N.J.**

Defense. Shoots left. 6'1", 205 lbs. Born, Braintree, MA, November 14, 1978. Boston's 2nd choice, 52nd overall, in 1998 Entry Draft.

Season	Club	League	GP	G	A	Pts	PIM	PP	SH	GW	S	%	+/-	TF	F%	Min	GP	G	A	Pts	PIM	PP	SH	GW	Min
1996-97	Cushing Academy	Hi-School	36	11	33	44	28	....	....	....	....	....	....	....	....	....	....	....	....	....	....	....	....	....	....
1997-98	Boston College	H-East	40	7	21	28	49	....	....	....	....	....	....	....	....	....	....	....	....	....	....	....	....	....	....
1998-99	Boston College	H-East	43	9	23	32	34	....	....	....	....	....	....	....	....	....	....	....	....	....	....	....	....	....	....
99-2000	Boston College	H-East	42	4	23	27	40	....	....	....	....	....	....	....	....	....	....	....	....	....	....	....	....	....	....
2000-01	Boston College	H-East	42	5	18	23	28	....	....	....	....	....	....	....	....	....	....	....	....	....	....	....	....	....	....
2001-02	Providence Bruins	AHL	49	5	10	15	18	....	....	....	....	....	....	....	....	....	....	....	....	....	....	....	....	....	....
	Hamilton	AHL	10	1	6	7	0	....	....	....	....	....	....	....	....	....	14	0	3	3	6	....	....	....	....
2002-03	Edmonton	NHL	1	0	0	0	0	0	0	0	0	0.0	0	0	0.0	2:53	....	....	....	....	....	....	....	....	....
	Hamilton	AHL	56	1	12	13	24	....	....	....	....	....	....	....	....	....	23	0	5	5	10	....	....	....	....
2003-04	Toronto	AHL	56	5	10	15	18	....	....	....	....	....	....	....	....	....	3	0	2	2	4	....	....	....	....
	NHL Totals		1	0	0	0	0	0	0	0	0	0.0		0	0.0	2:53	....	....	....	....	....	....	....	....	....

Hockey East Second All-Star Team (2000) • Hockey East First All-Star Team (2001) • NCAA East First All-American Team (2001)
Traded to **Edmonton** by **Boston** for Sean Brown, March 19, 2002. Signed as a free agent by **New Jersey**, July 22, 2004.

ALLEN, Bryan

(AHL-lehn, BRIGH-uhn) **VAN.**

Defense. Shoots left. 6'4", 220 lbs. Born, Kingston, Ont., August 21, 1980. Vancouver's 1st choice, 4th overall, in 1998 Entry Draft.

Season	Club	League	GP	G	A	Pts	PIM	PP	SH	GW	S	%	+/-	TF	F%	Min	GP	G	A	Pts	PIM	PP	SH	GW	Min
1995-96	Ernestown Jets	OJHL-C	36	1	16	17	71	....	....	....	....	....	....	....	....	....	....	....	....	....	....	....	....	....	....
1996-97	Oshawa Generals	OHL	60	2	4	6	76	....	....	....	....	....	....	....	....	....	18	1	3	4	26	....	....	....	....
1997-98	Oshawa Generals	OHL	48	6	13	19	126	....	....	....	....	....	....	....	....	....	5	0	5	5	18	....	....	....	....
1998-99	Oshawa Generals	OHL	37	7	15	22	77	....	....	....	....	....	....	....	....	....	15	0	3	3	26	....	....	....	....
99-2000	Oshawa Generals	OHL	3	0	2	2	12	....	....	....	....	....	....	....	....	....	3	0	0	0	13	....	....	....	....
	Syracuse Crunch	AHL	9	1	1	2	11	....	....	....	....	....	....	....	....	....	2	0	0	0	2	....	....	....	....
2000-01	Vancouver	NHL	6	0	0	0	0	0	0	0	2	0.0	0	0	0.0	9:20	2	0	0	0	2	0	0	0	13:47
	Kansas City	IHL	75	5	20	25	99	....	....	....	....	....	....	....	....	....	....	....	....	....	....	....	....	....	....
2001-02	Vancouver	NHL	11	0	0	0	6	0	0	0	4	0.0	1	0	0.0	10:47	....	....	....	....	....	....	....	....	....
	Manitoba Moose	AHL	68	7	18	25	121	....	....	....	....	....	....	....	....	....	5	0	1	1	8	....	....	....	....
2002-03	Vancouver	NHL	48	5	3	8	73	0	0	1	43	11.6	8	0	0.0	12:56	1	0	0	0	2	0	0	0	10:35
	Manitoba Moose	AHL	7	0	1	1	4	....	....	....	....	....	....	....	....	....	....	....	....	....	....	....	....	....	....
2003-04	Vancouver	NHL	74	2	5	7	94	0	0	0	70	2.9	–10	0	0.0	16:51	4	0	0	0	2	0	0	0	14:37
	NHL Totals		139	7	8	15	173	0	0	1	119	5.9		0	0.0	14:42	7	0	0	0	6	0	0	0	13:48

OHL First All-Star Team (1999)
• Missed majority of 1999-2000 season recovering from knee injury suffered in training camp, September 21, 1999.

ALLISON, Jamie

(AL-lih-suhn, JAY-mee) **NSH.**

Defense. Shoots left. 6'1", 200 lbs. Born, Lindsay, Ont., May 13, 1975. Calgary's 2nd choice, 44th overall, in 1993 Entry Draft.

Season	Club	League	GP	G	A	Pts	PIM	PP	SH	GW	S	%	+/-	TF	F%	Min	GP	G	A	Pts	PIM	PP	SH	GW	Min
1990-91	Waterloo Siskins	OJHL-B	38	3	8	11	91	....	....	....	....	....	....	....	....	....	....	....	....	....	....	....	....	....	....
1991-92	Windsor Spitfires	OHL	59	4	8	12	70	....	....	....	....	....	....	....	....	....	4	1	1	2	2	....	....	....	....
1992-93	Detroit	OHL	61	0	13	13	64	....	....	....	....	....	....	....	....	....	15	2	5	7	23	....	....	....	....
1993-94	Detroit	OHL	40	2	22	24	69	....	....	....	....	....	....	....	....	....	17	2	9	11	35	....	....	....	....
1994-95	Detroit	OHL	50	1	14	15	119	....	....	....	....	....	....	....	....	....	18	2	7	9	35	....	....	....	....
	Calgary	NHL	1	0	0	0	0	0	0	0	0	0.0	0	....	....	....	....	....	....	....	....	....	....	....	....
1995-96	Saint John Flames	AHL	71	3	16	19	223	....	....	....	....	....	....	....	....	....	14	0	2	2	16	....	....	....	....
1996-97	Calgary	NHL	20	0	0	0	35	0	0	0	8	0.0	–4	....	....	....	....	....	....	....	....	....	....	....	....
	Saint John Flames	AHL	46	3	6	9	139	....	....	....	....	....	....	....	....	....	5	0	1	1	4	....	....	....	....
1997-98	Calgary	NHL	43	3	8	11	104	0	0	1	27	11.1	3	....	....	....	....	....	....	....	....	....	....	....	....
	Saint John Flames	AHL	16	0	5	5	49	....	....	....	....	....	....	....	....	....	....	....	....	....	....	....	....	....	....
1998-99	Saint John Flames	AHL	5	0	0	0	23	....	....	....	....	....	....	....	....	....	....	....	....	....	....	....	....	....	....
	Chicago	NHL	39	2	2	4	62	0	0	0	24	8.3	0	0	0.0	14:01	....	....	....	....	....	....	....	....	....
	Indianapolis Ice	IHL	3	1	0	1	10	....	....	....	....	....	....	....	....	....	....	....	....	....	....	....	....	....	....
99-2000	Chicago	NHL	59	1	3	4	102	0	0	0	24	4.2	–5	0	0.0	14:14	....	....	....	....	....	....	....	....	....
2000-01	Chicago	NHL	44	1	3	4	53	0	0	0	16	6.3	7	1	100.0	14:33	....	....	....	....	....	....	....	....	....
2001-02	Calgary	NHL	37	0	2	2	24	0	0	0	14	0.0	–3	2	0.0	7:44	....	....	....	....	....	....	....	....	....
	Columbus	NHL	7	0	0	0	28	0	0	0	2	0.0	–4	0	0.0	11:23	....	....	....	....	....	....	....	....	....
2002-03	Columbus	NHL	48	0	1	1	99	0	0	0	23	0.0	–15	1	100.0	11:57	....	....	....	....	....	....	....	....	....
2003-04	Nashville	NHL	47	0	3	3	76	0	0	0	19	0.0	–7	0	0.0	13:04	....	....	....	....	....	....	....	....	....
	NHL Totals		345	7	22	29	583	0	0	1	157	4.5		4	50.0	12:45	....	....	....	....	....	....	....	....	....

Traded to **Chicago** by **Calgary** with Marty McInnis and Erik Andersson for Jeff Shantz and Steve Dubinsky, October 27, 1998. Claimed by **Calgary** from **Chicago** in Waiver Draft, September 28, 2001.
Traded to **Columbus** by **Calgary** for Blake Sloan, March 19, 2002. Signed as a free agent by **Nashville**, September 10, 2003.

ALLISON, Jason

(AL-lih-suhn, JAY-suhn)

Center. Shoots right. 6'3", 215 lbs. Born, North York, Ont., May 29, 1975. Washington's 2nd choice, 17th overall, in 1993 Entry Draft.

Season	Club	League	GP	G	A	Pts	PIM	PP	SH	GW	S	%	+/-	TF	F%	Min	GP	G	A	Pts	PIM	PP	SH	GW	Min
1990-91	North York	MTJHL	63	53	41	94	....	....	....	....	....	....	....	....	....	....	....	....	....	....	....	....	....	....	....
1991-92	London Knights	OHL	65	11	19	30	15	....	....	....	....	....	....	....	....	....	7	0	0	0	0	....	....	....	....
1992-93	London Knights	OHL	66	42	76	118	50	....	....	....	....	....	....	....	....	....	12	7	13	20	8	....	....	....	....
1993-94	London Knights	OHL	56	55	87	*142	68	....	....	....	....	....	....	....	....	....	5	2	13	15	13	....	....	....	....
	Washington	NHL	2	0	1	1	0	0	0	0	5	0.0	1	....	....	....	....	....	....	....	....	....	....	....	....
	Portland Pirates	AHL	....	....	....	....	....	....	....	....	....	....	....	....	....	....	6	2	1	3	0	....	....	....	....
1994-95	London Knights	OHL	15	15	21	36	43	....	....	....	....	....	....	....	....	....	....	....	....	....	....	....	....	....	....
	Washington	NHL	12	2	1	3	6	2	0	0	9	22.2	–3	....	....	....	....	....	....	....	....	....	....	....	....
	Portland Pirates	AHL	8	5	4	9	2	....	....	....	....	....	....	....	....	....	7	3	8	11	2	....	....	....	....
1995-96	Washington	NHL	19	0	3	3	2	0	0	0	18	0.0	–3	....	....	....	....	....	....	....	....	....	....	....	....
	Portland Pirates	AHL	57	28	41	69	42	....	....	....	....	....	....	....	....	....	6	1	6	7	9	....	....	....	....

			Regular Season														Playoffs								
Season	Club	League	GP	G	A	Pts	PIM	PP	SH	GW	S	%	+/-	TF	F%	Min	GP	G	A	Pts	PIM	PP	SH	GW	Min
1996-97	Washington	NHL	53	5	17	22	25	1	0	1	71	7.0	–3	....	....	....	....	....	....	....	....	....	....	....	....
	Boston	NHL	19	3	9	12	9	1	0	0	28	10.7	–3	....	....	....	....	....	....	....	....	....	....	....	....
1997-98	Boston	NHL	81	33	50	83	60	5	0	8	158	20.9	33	....	....	....	6	2	6	8	4	1	0	0	....
1998-99	Boston	NHL	82	23	53	76	68	5	1	3	158	14.6	5	1760	52.2	22:23	12	2	9	11	6	1	0	0	25:36
99-2000	Boston	NHL	37	10	18	28	20	3	0	1	66	15.2	5	100	60.0	21:33	....	....	....	....	....	....	....	....	....
2000-01	Boston	NHL	82	36	59	95	85	11	3	6	185	19.5	–8	1897	51.9	23:21	....	....	....	....	....	....	....	....	....
2001-02	Los Angeles	NHL	73	19	55	74	68	5	0	2	139	13.7	2	1698	54.5	21:47	7	3	3	6	4	0	0	1	22:26
2002-03	Los Angeles	NHL	26	6	22	28	22	2	0	3	46	13.0	9	538	50.9	21:36	....	....	....	....	....	....	....	....	....
2003-04	Los Angeles	NHL	DID NOT PLAY – INJURED																						
	NHL Totals		486	137	288	425	365	35	4	24	883	15.5		5993	52.8	22:20	25	7	18	25	14	2	0	1	24:26

OHL First All-Star Team (1994) • OHL MVP (1994) • Canadian Major Junior First All-Star Team (1994) • Canadian Major Junior Player of the Year (1994)

Played in NHL All-Star Game (2001)

Traded to **Boston** by **Washington** with Jim Carey, Anson Carter and Washington's 3rd round choice (Lee Goren) in 1997 Entry Draft for Bill Ranford, Adam Oates and Rick Tocchet, March 1, 1997. • Missed majority of 1999-2000 season recovering from thumb injury suffered in game vs. NY Islanders, January 8, 2000. Traded to **Los Angeles** by **Boston** with Mikko Eloranta for Jozef Stumpel and Glen Murray, October 24, 2001. • Missed majority of 2002-03 season and entire 2003-04 season recovering from knee (October 29, 2002 vs. Atlanta) and hip (January 25, 2003 vs. New Jersey) injuries.

AMONTE, Tony

(uh-MAHN-tee, TOH-nee) **PHI.**

Right wing. Shoots left. 6', 200 lbs. Born, Hingham, MA, August 2, 1970. NY Rangers' 3rd choice, 68th overall, in 1988 Entry Draft.

Season	Club	League	GP	G	A	Pts	PIM	PP	SH	GW	S	%	+/-	TF	F%	Min	GP	G	A	Pts	PIM	PP	SH	GW	Min
1986-87	Thayer Academy	Hi-School	25	25	32	57	....	....	....	....	....	....	....	....	....	....	....	....	....	....	....	....	....	....	....
1987-88	Thayer Academy	Hi-School	28	30	38	68	....	....	....	....	....	....	....	....	....	....	....	....	....	....	....	....	....	....	....
1988-89	Thayer Academy	Hi-School	25	35	38	73	....	....	....	....	....	....	....	....	....	....	....	....	....	....	....	....	....	....	....
1989-90	Boston University	H-East	41	25	33	58	52	....	....	....	....	....	....	....	....	....	....	....	....	....	....	....	....	....	....
1990-91	Boston University	H-East	38	31	37	68	82	....	....	....	....	....	....	....	....	....	....	....	....	....	....	....	....	....	....
	NY Rangers	NHL	....	....	....	....	....	....	....	....	....	....	....	....	....	....	2	0	2	2	2	0	0	0	....
1991-92	NY Rangers	NHL	79	35	34	69	55	9	0	4	234	15.0	12	....	....	....	13	3	6	9	2	2	0	0	....
1992-93	NY Rangers	NHL	83	33	43	76	49	13	0	4	270	12.2	0	....	....	....	....	....	....	....	....	....	....	....	....
1993-94	NY Rangers	NHL	72	16	22	38	31	3	0	4	179	8.9	5	....	....	....	....	....	....	....	....	....	....	....	....
	Chicago	NHL	7	1	3	4	6	1	0	0	16	6.3	–5	....	....	....	6	4	2	6	4	1	0	1	....
1994-95	HC Fassa	Euroliga	14	22	16	38	10	....	....	....	....	....	....	....	....	....	....	....	....	....	....	....	....	....	....
	HC Fassa	EuroHL	2	5	1	6	0	....	....	....	....	....	....	....	....	....	....	....	....	....	....	....	....	....	....
	Chicago	NHL	48	15	20	35	41	6	1	3	105	14.3	7	....	....	....	16	3	3	6	10	0	0	0	....
1995-96	Chicago	NHL	81	31	32	63	62	5	4	5	216	14.4	10	....	....	....	7	2	4	6	6	1	0	0	....
1996-97	Chicago	NHL	81	41	36	77	64	9	2	4	266	15.4	35	....	....	....	6	4	2	6	8	0	0	0	....
1997-98	Chicago	NHL	82	31	42	73	66	7	3	5	296	10.5	21	....	....	....	....	....	....	....	....	....	....	....	....
	United States	Olympics	4	0	1	1	4	....	....	....	....	....	....	....	....	....	....	....	....	....	....	....	....	....	....
1998-99	Chicago	NHL	82	44	31	75	60	14	3	8	256	17.2	0	8	12.5	22:12	....	....	....	....	....	....	....	....	....
99-2000	Chicago	NHL	82	43	41	84	48	11	5	2	260	16.5	10	22	22.7	21:54	....	....	....	....	....	....	....	....	....
2000-01	Chicago	NHL	82	35	29	64	54	9	1	3	256	13.7	–22	27	40.7	22:09	....	....	....	....	....	....	....	....	....
2001-02	Chicago	NHL	82	27	39	66	67	6	1	4	232	11.6	11	30	43.3	21:18	5	0	1	1	4	0	0	0	18:43
	United States	Olympics	6	2	2	4	0	....	....	....	....	....	....	....	....	....	....	....	....	....	....	....	....	....	....
2002-03	Phoenix	NHL	59	13	23	36	26	6	0	3	170	7.6	–12	53	35.9	19:27	....	....	....	....	....	....	....	....	....
	Philadelphia	NHL	13	7	8	15	2	1	1	2	37	18.9	12	3	33.3	17:39	13	1	6	7	4	0	0	0	19:16
2003-04	Philadelphia	NHL	80	20	33	53	38	4	0	3	173	11.6	13	8	37.5	15:14	18	3	5	8	6	2	0	0	14:41
	NHL Totals		1013	392	436	828	669	104	21	54	2966	13.2		151	35.1	20:22	86	20	31	51	46	6	0	1	16:54

Hockey East Second All-Star Team (1991) • NCAA Championship All-Tournament Team (1991) • NHL All-Rookie Team (1992)

Played in NHL All-Star Game (1997, 1998, 1999, 2000, 2001)

• Missed majority of 1985-86 season recovering from knee injury, October, 1985. Traded to **Chicago** by **NY Rangers** with the rights to Matt Oates for Stephane Matteau and Brian Noonan, March 21, 1994. Signed as a free agent by **Phoenix**, July 12, 2002. Traded to **Philadelphia** by **Phoenix** for Guillaume Lefebvre, Atlanta's 3rd round choice (previously acquired, Phoenix selected Tyler Redenbach) in 2003 Entry Draft and Philadelphia's 2nd round choice (later traded to NY Rangers – NY Rangers selected Brandon Dubinsky) in 2004 Entry Draft, March 10, 2003.

ANDREYCHUK, Dave

(AN-druh-chuhk, DAYV) **T.B.**

Left wing. Shoots right. 6'4", 220 lbs. Born, Hamilton, Ont., September 29, 1963. Buffalo's 3rd choice, 16th overall, in 1982 Entry Draft.

Season	Club	League	GP	G	A	Pts	PIM	PP	SH	GW	S	%	+/-	TF	F%	Min	GP	G	A	Pts	PIM	PP	SH	GW	Min
1979-80	Hamilton Hawks	OMHA	21	25	24	49	....	....	....	....	....	....	....	....	....	....	....	....	....	....	....	....	....	....	....
1980-81	Oshawa Generals	OMJHL	67	22	22	44	80	....	....	....	....	....	....	....	....	....	10	3	2	5	20	....	....	....	....
1981-82	Oshawa Generals	OHL	67	57	43	100	71	....	....	....	....	....	....	....	....	....	3	1	4	5	16	....	....	....	....
1982-83	Oshawa Generals	OHL	14	8	24	32	6	....	....	....	....	....	....	....	....	....	....	....	....	....	....	....	....	....	....
	Buffalo	NHL	43	14	23	37	16	3	0	1	66	21.2	6	....	....	....	4	1	0	1	4	0	0	0	....
1983-84	Buffalo	NHL	78	38	42	80	42	10	0	7	178	21.3	20	....	....	....	2	0	1	1	2	0	0	0	....
1984-85	Buffalo	NHL	64	31	30	61	54	14	0	2	153	20.3	–4	....	....	....	5	4	2	6	4	0	0	2	....
1985-86	Buffalo	NHL	80	36	51	87	61	12	0	3	225	16.0	3	....	....	....	....	....	....	....	....	....	....	....	....
1986-87	Buffalo	NHL	77	25	48	73	46	13	0	2	255	9.8	2	....	....	....	....	....	....	....	....	....	....	....	....
1987-88	Buffalo	NHL	80	30	48	78	112	15	0	5	253	11.9	1	....	....	....	6	2	4	6	0	1	0	0	....
1988-89	Buffalo	NHL	56	28	24	52	40	7	0	3	145	19.3	0	....	....	....	5	0	3	3	0	0	0	0	....
1989-90	Buffalo	NHL	73	40	42	82	42	18	0	3	206	19.4	6	....	....	....	6	2	5	7	2	1	0	0	....
1990-91	Buffalo	NHL	80	36	33	69	32	13	0	4	234	15.4	11	....	....	....	6	2	2	4	8	1	0	0	....
1991-92	Buffalo	NHL	80	41	50	91	71	28	0	2	337	12.2	–9	....	....	....	7	1	3	4	12	0	0	0	....
1992-93	Buffalo	NHL	52	29	32	61	48	20	0	2	171	17.0	–8	....	....	....	....	....	....	....	....	....	....	....	....
	Toronto	NHL	31	25	13	38	8	12	0	2	139	18.0	12	....	....	....	21	12	7	19	35	4	0	3	....
1993-94	Toronto	NHL	83	53	46	99	98	21	5	8	333	15.9	22	....	....	....	18	5	5	10	16	3	1	0	....
1994-95	Toronto	NHL	48	22	16	38	34	8	0	2	168	13.1	–7	....	....	....	7	3	2	5	25	2	0	0	....
1995-96	Toronto	NHL	61	20	24	44	54	12	2	3	200	10.0	–11	....	....	....	....	....	....	....	....	....	....	....	....
	New Jersey	NHL	15	8	5	13	10	2	0	0	41	19.5	2	....	....	....	....	....	....	....	....	....	....	....	....
1996-97	New Jersey	NHL	82	27	34	61	48	4	1	2	233	11.6	38	....	....	....	1	0	0	0	0	0	0	0	....
1997-98	New Jersey	NHL	75	14	34	48	26	4	0	2	180	7.8	19	....	....	....	6	1	0	1	4	1	0	0	....
1998-99	New Jersey	NHL	52	15	13	28	20	4	0	3	110	13.6	1	9	44.4	15:32	4	2	0	2	4	0	0	0	10:40
99-2000	Boston	NHL	63	19	14	33	28	7	0	2	192	9.9	–11	446	52.0	19:50	....	....	....	....	....	....	....	....	....
	Colorado	NHL	14	1	2	3	2	1	0	1	41	2.4	–9	15	60.0	17:16	17	3	2	5	18	2	0	0	16:22
2000-01	Buffalo	NHL	74	20	13	33	32	8	0	4	119	16.8	0	187	49.7	12:00	13	1	2	3	4	1	0	0	11:04
2001-02	Tampa Bay	NHL	82	21	17	38	109	9	1	5	161	13.0	–12	1393	53.0	16:26	....	....	....	....	....	....	....	....	....
2002-03	Tampa Bay	NHL	72	20	14	34	34	15	0	3	170	11.8	–12	1117	58.4	16:27	11	3	3	6	10	1	0	1	21:23
2003-04♦	Tampa Bay	NHL	82	21	18	39	42	10	0	5	165	12.7	–9	1475	57.8	17:06	23	1	13	14	14	0	0	0	18:51
	NHL Totals		1597	634	686	1320	1109	270	9	76	4475	14.2		4642	55.6	16:13	162	43	54	97	162	17	1	6	16:40

Played in NHL All-Star Game (1990, 1994)

Traded to **Toronto** by **Buffalo** with Daren Puppa and Buffalo's 1st round choice (Kenny Jonsson) in 1993 Entry Draft for Grant Fuhr and Toronto's 5th round choice (Kevin Popp) in 1995 Entry Draft, February 2, 1993. Traded to **New Jersey** by **Toronto** for New Jersey's 2nd round choice (Marek Posmyk) in 1996 Entry Draft and New Jersey's 3rd round choice (later traded back to New Jersey – New Jersey selected Andre Lakos) in 1999 Entry Draft, March 13, 1996. Signed as a free agent by **Boston**, July 29, 1999. Traded to **Colorado** by **Boston** with Raymond Bourque for Brian Rolston, Martin Grenier, Samuel Pahlsson and New Jersey's 1st round choice (previously acquired, Boston selected Martin Samuelsson) in 2000 Entry Draft, March 6, 2000. Signed as a free agent by **Buffalo**, July 13, 2000. Signed as a free agent by **Tampa Bay**, July 13, 2001.

ANGELSTAD, Mel

(AN-gehl-stahd, MEHL)

Left wing. Shoots left. 6'2", 214 lbs. Born, Saskatoon, Sask., October 31, 1972.

Season	Club	League	GP	G	A	Pts	PIM	PP	SH	GW	S	%	+/-	TF	F%	Min	GP	G	A	Pts	PIM	PP	SH	GW	Min
1988-89	Allan Legionnaires	MAHA	35	15	23	38	256	....	....	....	....	....	....	....	....	....	....	....	....	....	....	....	....	....	....
1989-90	Warman Valley	MJHL	38	1	5	6	411	....	....	....	....	....	....	....	....	....	....	....	....	....	....	....	....	....	....
1990-91	Flin Flon Bombers	MJHL	62	6	11	17	463	....	....	....	....	....	....	....	....	....	....	....	....	....	....	....	....	....	....
1991-92	Dauphin Kings	MJHL	44	8	29	37	*296	....	....	....	....	....	....	....	....	....	....	....	....	....	....	....	....	....	....
1992-93	Thunder Bay	ColHL	45	2	5	7	256	....	....	....	....	....	....	....	....	....	5	0	0	0	10	....	....	....	....
	Nashville Knights	ECHL	1	0	0	0	14	....	....	....	....	....	....	....	....	....	....	....	....	....	....	....	....	....	....
1993-94	Thunder Bay	ColHL	58	1	20	21	374	....	....	....	....	....	....	....	....	....	9	1	2	3	65	....	....	....	....
	P.E.I. Senators	AHL	1	0	0	0	5	....	....	....	....	....	....	....	....	....	....	....	....	....	....	....	....	....	....
1994-95	Thunder Bay	ColHL	46	0	8	8	317	....	....	....	....	....	....	....	....	....	7	0	3	3	62	....	....	....	....
	P.E.I. Senators	AHL	3	0	0	0	16	....	....	....	....	....	....	....	....	....	....	....	....	....	....	....	....	....	....
1995-96	Thunder Bay	ColHL	51	3	3	6	335	....	....	....	....	....	....	....	....	....	16	0	6	6	94	....	....	....	....
	Phoenix	IHL	5	0	0	0	43	....	....	....	....	....	....	....	....	....	....	....	....	....	....	....	....	....	....
1996-97	Thunder Bay	ColHL	66	10	21	31	422	....	....	....	....	....	....	....	....	....	7	0	1	1	21	....	....	....	....
1997-98	Fort Worth	WPHL	19	1	6	7	102	....	....	....	....	....	....	....	....	....	....	....	....	....	....	....	....	....	....
	Las Vegas	IHL	3	0	0	0	5	....	....	....	....	....	....	....	....	....	....	....	....	....	....	....	....	....	....
	Orlando	IHL	63	1	3	4	321	....	....	....	....	....	....	....	....	....	8	0	0	0	29	....	....	....	....

			Regular Season														Playoffs								
Season	Club	League	GP	G	A	Pts	PIM	PP	SH	GW	S	%	+/-	TF	F%	Min	GP	G	A	Pts	PIM	PP	SH	GW	Min
1998-99	Michigan	IHL	78	3	5	8	421	....	....	....	....	....	....	....	....	....	5	1	0	1	16	....	....	....	....
99-2000	Michigan	IHL	33	3	4	7	144	....	....	....	....	....	....	....	....	....	....	....	....	....	....	....	....	....	....
2000-01	Manitoba Moose	IHL	67	1	5	6	232	....	....	....	....	....	....	....	....	....	8	0	0	0	26	....	....	....	....
2001-02	Portland Pirates	AHL	53	1	7	8	212	....	....	....	....	....	....	....	....	....	....	....	....	....	....	....	....	....	....
2002-03	Portland Pirates	AHL	57	5	2	7	139	....	....	....	....	....	....	....	....	....	3	0	0	0	6	....	....	....	....
2003-04	Portland Pirates	AHL	53	0	1	1	118	....	....	....	....	....	....	....	....	....	....	....	....	....	....	....	....	....	....
	Washington	**NHL**	**2**	**0**	**0**	**0**	**2**	**0**	**0**	**0**	**1**	**0.0**	**0**	**0**	**0.0**	**13:00**	....	....	....	....	....	....	....	....	....
	NHL Totals		**2**	**0**	**0**	**0**	**2**	**0**	**0**	**0**	**1**	**0.0**		**0**	**0.0**	**13:00**	....	....	....	....	....	....	....	....	....

Signed as a free agent by **Dallas**, July 29, 1998. Signed as a free agent by **Portland** (AHL), July 30, 2003. Signed as a free agent by **Washington**, April 3, 2004.

ANTROPOV, Nik

(an-TROH-pahv, NIHK) **TOR.**

Center. Shoots left. 6'6", 220 lbs. Born, Vost, USSR, February 18, 1980. Toronto's 1st choice, 10th overall, in 1998 Entry Draft.

			Regular Season														Playoffs								
Season	Club	League	GP	G	A	Pts	PIM	PP	SH	GW	S	%	+/-	TF	F%	Min	GP	G	A	Pts	PIM	PP	SH	GW	Min
1995-96	Ust-Kamenog. Jr.	CIS-Jr.	20	18	20	38	30	....	....	....	....	....	....	....	....	....	....	....	....	....	....	....	....	....	....
1996-97	Ust-Kamenogorsk	Russia-2	8	2	1	3	6	....	....	....	....	....	....	....	....	....	....	....	....	....	....	....	....	....	....
1997-98	Ust-Kamenogorsk	Russia-2	42	15	24	39	62	....	....	....	....	....	....	....	....	....	....	....	....	....	....	....	....	....	....
1998-99	Dynamo Moscow	Russia	30	5	9	14	30	....	....	....	....	....	....	....	....	....	11	0	1	1	4	....	....	....	....
99-2000	**Toronto**	**NHL**	**66**	**12**	**18**	**30**	**41**	**0**	**0**	**2**	**89**	**13.5**	**14**	**501**	**46.3**	**12:48**	**3**	**0**	**0**	**0**	**4**	**0**	**0**	**0**	**10:14**
	St. John's	AHL	2	0	0	0	4	....	....	....	....	....	....	....	....	....	....	....	....	....	....	....	....	....	....
2000-01	**Toronto**	**NHL**	**52**	**6**	**11**	**17**	**30**	**0**	**0**	**1**	**71**	**8.5**	**5**	**431**	**44.3**	**10:02**	**9**	**2**	**1**	**3**	**12**	**1**	**0**	**1**	**11:04**
2001-02	**Toronto**	**NHL**	**11**	**1**	**1**	**2**	**4**	**0**	**0**	**0**	**12**	**8.3**	**–1**	**31**	**38.7**	**8:57**	....	....	....	....	....	....	....	....	....
	St. John's	AHL	34	11	24	35	47	....	....	....	....	....	....	....	....	....	....	....	....	....	....	....	....	....	....
2002-03	**Toronto**	**NHL**	**72**	**16**	**29**	**45**	**124**	**2**	**1**	**6**	**102**	**15.7**	**11**	**621**	**40.1**	**15:00**	**3**	**0**	**0**	**0**	**0**	**0**	**0**	**0**	**19:17**
2003-04	**Toronto**	**NHL**	**62**	**13**	**18**	**31**	**62**	**1**	**1**	**2**	**89**	**14.6**	**7**	**309**	**40.8**	**15:18**	**13**	**0**	**2**	**2**	**18**	**0**	**0**	**0**	**15:56**
	NHL Totals		**263**	**48**	**77**	**125**	**261**	**3**	**2**	**11**	**363**	**13.2**		**1893**	**42.8**	**13:17**	**28**	**2**	**3**	**5**	**34**	**1**	**0**	**1**	**14:07**

ARKHIPOV, Denis

(AHR-kih-pahv, DEH-nihs) **NSH.**

Center. Shoots left. 6'3", 214 lbs. Born, Kazan, USSR, May 19, 1979. Nashville's 2nd choice, 60th overall, in 1998 Entry Draft.

			Regular Season														Playoffs								
Season	Club	League	GP	G	A	Pts	PIM	PP	SH	GW	S	%	+/-	TF	F%	Min	GP	G	A	Pts	PIM	PP	SH	GW	Min
1994-95	Ak Bars Kazan Jr.	CIS-Jr.	40	20	12	32	10	....	....	....	....	....	....	....	....	....	....	....	....	....	....	....	....	....	....
1995-96	Ak Bars Kazan Jr.	CIS-Jr.	40	15	8	23	30	....	....	....	....	....	....	....	....	....	....	....	....	....	....	....	....	....	....
	Ak Bars Kazan	CIS	15	10	8	18	10	....	....	....	....	....	....	....	....	....	....	....	....	....	....	....	....	....	....
1996-97	Ak Bars Kazan 2	Russia-3	50	17	23	40	20	....	....	....	....	....	....	....	....	....	....	....	....	....	....	....	....	....	....
	Ak Bars Kazan	Russia	1	1	0	1	0	....	....	....	....	....	....	....	....	....	....	....	....	....	....	....	....	....	....
1997-98	Ak Bars Kazan	Russia	29	2	2	4	2	....	....	....	....	....	....	....	....	....	....	....	....	....	....	....	....	....	....
1998-99	Ak Bars Kazan	Russia	34	12	1	13	22	....	....	....	....	....	....	....	....	....	9	2	3	5	6	....	....	....	....
	Ak Bars Kazan	EuroHL	4	0	0	0	0	....	....	....	....	....	....	....	....	....	1	0	0	0	0	....	....	....	....
99-2000	Ak Bars Kazan	Russia	32	7	9	16	14	....	....	....	....	....	....	....	....	....	18	5	5	10	6	....	....	....	....
2000-01	**Nashville**	**NHL**	**40**	**6**	**7**	**13**	**4**	**0**	**0**	**0**	**42**	**14.3**	**0**	**299**	**43.8**	**9:56**	....	....	....	....	....	....	....	....	....
	Milwaukee	IHL	40	9	8	17	11	....	....	....	....	....	....	....	....	....	....	....	....	....	....	....	....	....	....
2001-02	**Nashville**	**NHL**	**82**	**20**	**22**	**42**	**16**	**7**	**0**	**6**	**118**	**16.9**	**–18**	**1108**	**44.8**	**15:43**	....	....	....	....	....	....	....	....	....
2002-03	**Nashville**	**NHL**	**79**	**11**	**24**	**35**	**32**	**3**	**0**	**1**	**148**	**7.4**	**–18**	**1069**	**46.7**	**15:09**	....	....	....	....	....	....	....	....	....
2003-04	**Nashville**	**NHL**	**72**	**9**	**12**	**21**	**22**	**3**	**0**	**3**	**91**	**9.9**	**–2**	**926**	**44.7**	**13:58**	....	....	....	....	....	....	....	....	....
	NHL Totals		**273**	**46**	**65**	**111**	**74**	**13**	**0**	**10**	**399**	**11.5**		**3402**	**45.3**	**14:15**	....	....	....	....	....	....	....	....	....

ARMSTRONG, Chris

(ahrm-STRAWNG, KRIHS)

Defense. Shoots left. 6', 205 lbs. Born, Regina, Sask., June 26, 1975. Florida's 3rd choice, 57th overall, in 1993 Entry Draft.

			Regular Season														Playoffs								
Season	Club	League	GP	G	A	Pts	PIM	PP	SH	GW	S	%	+/-	TF	F%	Min	GP	G	A	Pts	PIM	PP	SH	GW	Min
1990-91	Whitewood	SMHL	40	25	30	55	40	....	....	....	....	....	....	....	....	....	....	....	....	....	....	....	....	....	....
1991-92	Moose Jaw	WHL	43	2	7	9	19	....	....	....	....	....	....	....	....	....	4	0	0	0	0	....	....	....	....
1992-93	Moose Jaw	WHL	67	9	35	44	104	....	....	....	....	....	....	....	....	....	....	....	....	....	....	....	....	....	....
1993-94	Moose Jaw	WHL	64	13	55	68	54	....	....	....	....	....	....	....	....	....	....	....	....	....	....	....	....	....	....
	Cincinnati	IHL	1	0	0	0	0	....	....	....	....	....	....	....	....	....	10	1	3	4	2	....	....	....	....
1994-95	Moose Jaw	WHL	66	17	54	71	61	....	....	....	....	....	....	....	....	....	10	2	12	14	22	....	....	....	....
	Cincinnati	IHL	....	....	....	....	....	....	....	....	....	....	....	....	....	....	9	1	3	4	10	....	....	....	....
1995-96	Carolina	AHL	78	9	33	42	65	....	....	....	....	....	....	....	....	....	....	....	....	....	....	....	....	....	....
1996-97	Carolina	AHL	66	9	23	32	38	....	....	....	....	....	....	....	....	....	....	....	....	....	....	....	....	....	....
1997-98	Fort Wayne	IHL	79	8	36	44	66	....	....	....	....	....	....	....	....	....	4	0	2	2	4	....	....	....	....
1998-99	Milwaukee	IHL	5	0	3	3	4	....	....	....	....	....	....	....	....	....	....	....	....	....	....	....	....	....	....
	Hershey Bears	AHL	65	12	32	44	30	....	....	....	....	....	....	....	....	....	5	0	1	1	0	....	....	....	....
99-2000	Kentucky	AHL	78	9	48	57	77	....	....	....	....	....	....	....	....	....	9	1	5	6	4	....	....	....	....
2000-01	**Minnesota**	**NHL**	**3**	**0**	**0**	**0**	**0**	**0**	**0**	**0**	**4**	**0.0**	**–3**	**0**	**0.0**	**18:06**	....	....	....	....	....	....	....	....	....
	Cleveland	IHL	77	9	32	41	42	....	....	....	....	....	....	....	....	....	4	0	2	2	2	....	....	....	....
2001-02	Bridgeport	AHL	80	10	38	48	49	....	....	....	....	....	....	....	....	....	20	3	8	11	4	....	....	....	....
2002-03	Augsburg	Germany	22	3	16	19	32	....	....	....	....	....	....	....	....	....	....	....	....	....	....	....	....	....	....
	EV Zug	Swiss	21	0	7	7	45	....	....	....	....	....	....	....	....	....	....	....	....	....	....	....	....	....	....
2003-04	**Anaheim**	**NHL**	**4**	**0**	**1**	**1**	**0**	**0**	**0**	**0**	**8**	**0.0**	**–1**	**0**	**0.0**	**12:32**	....	....	....	....	....	....	....	....	....
	Cincinnati	AHL	70	9	37	46	48	....	....	....	....	....	....	....	....	....	9	1	3	4	2	....	....	....	....
	NHL Totals		**7**	**0**	**1**	**1**	**0**	**0**	**0**	**0**	**12**	**0.0**		**0**	**0.0**	**14:55**	....	....	....	....	....	....	....	....	....

WHL East First All-Star Team (1994) • Canadian Major Junior Second All-Star Team (1994) • WHL East Second All-Star Team (1995)

Claimed by **Nashville** from **Florida** in Expansion Draft, June 26, 1998. Signed as a free agent by **San Jose**, September 2, 1999. Selected by **Minnesota** from **San Jose** in Expansion Draft, June 23, 2000. Signed as a free agent by **NY Islanders**, August 8, 2001. Signed as a free agent by **EV Zug** (Swiss), June 14, 2002. Signed as a free agent by **Anaheim**, June 26, 2003. Signed as a free agent by **ERC Ingolstadt** (Germany), April 4, 2004.

ARMSTRONG, Derek

(ahrm-STRAWNG, DAIR-ihk) **L.A.**

Center. Shoots right. 6', 195 lbs. Born, Ottawa, Ont., April 23, 1973. NY Islanders' 5th choice, 128th overall, in 1992 Entry Draft.

			Regular Season														Playoffs								
Season	Club	League	GP	G	A	Pts	PIM	PP	SH	GW	S	%	+/-	TF	F%	Min	GP	G	A	Pts	PIM	PP	SH	GW	Min
1989-90	Hawkesbury	OCJHL	48	8	10	18	30	....	....	....	....	....	....	....	....	....	....	....	....	....	....	....	....	....	....
1990-91	Hawkesbury	OCJHL	54	27	45	72	49	....	....	....	....	....	....	....	....	....	....	....	....	....	....	....	....	....	....
	Sudbury Wolves	OHL	2	0	2	2	0	....	....	....	....	....	....	....	....	....	....	....	....	....	....	....	....	....	....
1991-92	Sudbury Wolves	OHL	66	31	54	85	22	....	....	....	....	....	....	....	....	....	9	2	2	4	2	....	....	....	....
1992-93	Sudbury Wolves	OHL	66	44	62	106	56	....	....	....	....	....	....	....	....	....	14	9	10	19	26	....	....	....	....
1993-94	**NY Islanders**	**NHL**	**1**	**0**	**0**	**0**	**0**	**0**	**0**	**0**	**2**	**0.0**	**0**	....	....	....	....	....	....	....	....	....	....	....	....
	Salt Lake	IHL	76	23	35	58	61	....	....	....	....	....	....	....	....	....	....	....	....	....	....	....	....	....	....
1994-95	Denver Grizzlies	IHL	59	13	18	31	65	....	....	....	....	....	....	....	....	....	6	0	2	2	0	....	....	....	....
1995-96	**NY Islanders**	**NHL**	**19**	**1**	**3**	**4**	**14**	**0**	**0**	**0**	**23**	**4.3**	**–6**	....	....	....	....	....	....	....	....	....	....	....	....
	Worcester IceCats	AHL	51	11	15	26	33	....	....	....	....	....	....	....	....	....	4	2	1	3	0	....	....	....	....
1996-97	**NY Islanders**	**NHL**	**50**	**6**	**7**	**13**	**33**	**0**	**0**	**2**	**36**	**16.7**	**–8**	....	....	....	....	....	....	....	....	....	....	....	....
	Utah Grizzlies	IHL	17	4	8	12	10	....	....	....	....	....	....	....	....	....	6	0	4	4	4	....	....	....	....
1997-98	**Ottawa**	**NHL**	**9**	**2**	**0**	**2**	**9**	**0**	**0**	**1**	**8**	**25.0**	**1**	....	....	....	....	....	....	....	....	....	....	....	....
	Detroit Vipers	IHL	10	0	1	1	2	....	....	....	....	....	....	....	....	....	....	....	....	....	....	....	....	....	....
	Hartford	AHL	54	16	30	46	40	....	....	....	....	....	....	....	....	....	15	2	6	8	22	....	....	....	....
1998-99	**NY Rangers**	**NHL**	**3**	**0**	**0**	**0**	**0**	**0**	**0**	**0**	**1**	**0.0**	**0**	**0**	**0.0**	**2:50**	....	....	....	....	....	....	....	....	....
	Hartford	AHL	59	29	51	80	73	....	....	....	....	....	....	....	....	....	7	5	4	9	10	....	....	....	....
99-2000	**NY Rangers**	**NHL**	**1**	**0**	**0**	**0**	**0**	**0**	**0**	**0**	**1**	**0.0**	**0**	**3**	**33.3**	**3:10**	....	....	....	....	....	....	....	....	....
	Hartford	AHL	77	28	54	82	101	....	....	....	....	....	....	....	....	....	23	7	16	23	24	....	....	....	....
2000-01	**NY Rangers**	**NHL**	**3**	**0**	**0**	**0**	**0**	**0**	**0**	**0**	**6**	**0.0**	**0**	**30**	**50.0**	**11:22**	....	....	....	....	....	....	....	....	....
	Hartford	AHL	75	32	*69	*101	73	....	....	....	....	....	....	....	....	....	5	0	6	6	6	....	....	....	....
2001-02	SC Bern	Swiss	44	17	36	53	62	....	....	....	....	....	....	....	....	....	6	3	5	8	8	....	....	....	....
2002-03	**Los Angeles**	**NHL**	**66**	**12**	**26**	**38**	**30**	**2**	**0**	**1**	**106**	**11.3**	**5**	**708**	**50.0**	**15:40**	....	....	....	....	....	....	....	....	....
	Manchester	AHL	2	3	0	3	4	....	....	....	....	....	....	....	....	....	....	....	....	....	....	....	....	....	....
2003-04	**Los Angeles**	**NHL**	**57**	**14**	**21**	**35**	**33**	**5**	**0**	**1**	**101**	**13.9**	**4**	**912**	**52.0**	**17:00**	....	....	....	....	....	....	....	....	....
	NHL Totals		**209**	**35**	**57**	**92**	**119**	**7**	**0**	**5**	**284**	**12.3**		**1653**	**51.1**	**15:46**	....	....	....	....	....	....	....	....	....

AHL Second All-Star Team (2000) • AHL First All-Star Team (2001) • John P. Sollenberger Trophy (Top Scorer – AHL) (2001) • Les Cunningham Award (MVP – AHL) (2001)

Signed as a free agent by **Ottawa**, July 28, 1997. Loaned to **Hartford** (AHL) by **Ottawa**, October 28, 1997. Signed as a free agent by **NY Rangers**, August 10, 1998. Signed as a free agent by **SC Bern** (Swiss) with NY Rangers retaining NHL rights, July 18, 2001. Traded to **Los Angeles** by **NY Rangers** for Los Angeles' 6th round choice (Chris Holt) in 2003 Entry Draft, July 16, 2002.

ARNASON, Tyler
(AHR-na-suhn, TIGH-luhr) **CHI.**

Center. Shoots left. 5'11", 192 lbs. Born, Oklahoma City, OK, March 16, 1979. Chicago's 6th choice, 183rd overall, in 1998 Entry Draft.

Season	Club	League	GP	G	A	Pts	PIM	PP	SH	GW	S	%	+/-	TF	F%	Min	Playoffs GP	G	A	Pts	PIM	PP	SH	GW	Min
1996-97	Winnipeg South	MJHL	50	35	50	85	15	....	....	....	....	....	....	....	....	....	6	3	3	6	18	....	....	....	....
1997-98	Fargo-Moorhead	USHL	52	37	45	82	16	....	....	....	....	....	....	....	....	....	4	1	1	2	2	....	....	....	....
1998-99	St. Cloud State	WCHA	38	14	17	31	16	....	....	....	....	....	....	....	....	....	....	....	....	....	....	....	....	....	....
99-2000	St. Cloud State	WCHA	39	19	30	49	18	....	....	....	....	....	....	....	....	....	....	....	....	....	....	....	....	....	....
2000-01	St. Cloud State	WCHA	41	28	28	56	14	....	....	....	....	....	....	....	....	....	....	....	....	....	....	....	....	....	....
2001-02	**Chicago**	**NHL**	**21**	**3**	**1**	**4**	**4**	**0**	**0**	**0**	**19**	**15.8**	**–3**	**112**	**41.1**	**9:28**	**3**	**0**	**0**	**0**	**0**	**0**	**0**	**0**	**7:43**
	Norfolk Admirals	AHL	60	26	30	56	42	....	....	....	....	....	....	....	....	....	....	....	....	....	....	....	....	....	....
2002-03	**Chicago**	**NHL**	**82**	**19**	**20**	**39**	**20**	**3**	**0**	**6**	**178**	**10.7**	**7**	**626**	**40.3**	**14:30**	....	....	....	....	....	....	....	....	....
2003-04	**Chicago**	**NHL**	**82**	**22**	**33**	**55**	**16**	**6**	**0**	**2**	**222**	**9.9**	**–13**	**904**	**43.1**	**16:34**	....	....	....	....	....	....	....	....	....
	NHL Totals		**185**	**44**	**54**	**98**	**40**	**9**	**0**	**8**	**419**	**10.5**		**1642**	**41.9**	**14:51**	**3**	**0**	**0**	**0**	**0**	**0**	**0**	**0**	**7:43**

USHL First All-Star Team (1998) • WCHA All-Rookie Team (1999) • WCHA Second All-Star Team (2000) • AHL All-Rookie Team (2002) • Dudley "Red" Garrett Memorial Trophy (Top Rookie – AHL) (2002) • NHL All-Rookie Team (2003)

ARNOTT, Jason
(AHR-niht, JAY-suhn) **DAL.**

Center. Shoots right. 6'4", 220 lbs. Born, Collingwood, Ont., October 11, 1974. Edmonton's 1st choice, 7th overall, in 1993 Entry Draft.

Season	Club	League	GP	G	A	Pts	PIM	PP	SH	GW	S	%	+/-	TF	F%	Min	Playoffs GP	G	A	Pts	PIM	PP	SH	GW	Min
1989-90	Stayner Siskins	OJHL-C	34	21	31	52	12	....	....	....	....	....	....	....	....	....	....	....	....	....	....	....	....	....	....
1990-91	Lindsay Bears	OJHL-B	42	17	44	61	10	....	....	....	....	....	....	....	....	....	8	9	8	17	6	....	....	....	....
1991-92	Oshawa Generals	OHL	57	9	15	24	12	....	....	....	....	....	....	....	....	....	....	....	....	....	....	....	....	....	....
1992-93	Oshawa Generals	OHL	56	41	57	98	74	....	....	....	....	....	....	....	....	....	13	9	9	18	20	....	....	....	....
1993-94	**Edmonton**	**NHL**	**78**	**33**	**35**	**68**	**104**	**10**	**0**	**4**	**194**	**17.0**	**1**	....	....	....	....	....	....	....	....	....	....	....	....
1994-95	**Edmonton**	**NHL**	**42**	**15**	**22**	**37**	**128**	**7**	**0**	**1**	**156**	**9.6**	**–14**	....	....	....	....	....	....	....	....	....	....	....	....
1995-96	**Edmonton**	**NHL**	**64**	**28**	**31**	**59**	**87**	**8**	**0**	**5**	**244**	**11.5**	**–6**	....	....	....	....	....	....	....	....	....	....	....	....
1996-97	**Edmonton**	**NHL**	**67**	**19**	**38**	**57**	**92**	**10**	**1**	**2**	**248**	**7.7**	**–21**	....	....	....	**12**	**3**	**6**	**9**	**18**	**1**	**0**	**0**	....
1997-98	**Edmonton**	**NHL**	**35**	**5**	**13**	**18**	**78**	**1**	**0**	**0**	**100**	**5.0**	**–16**	....	....	....	....	....	....	....	....	....	....	....	....
	New Jersey	**NHL**	**35**	**5**	**10**	**15**	**21**	**3**	**0**	**2**	**99**	**5.1**	**–8**	....	....	....	**5**	**0**	**2**	**2**	**0**	**0**	**0**	**0**	....
1998-99	**New Jersey**	**NHL**	**74**	**27**	**27**	**54**	**79**	**8**	**0**	**3**	**200**	**13.5**	**10**	**872**	**49.3**	**15:24**	**7**	**2**	**2**	**4**	**4**	**1**	**0**	**0**	**16:48**
99-2000♦	**New Jersey**	**NHL**	**76**	**22**	**34**	**56**	**51**	**7**	**0**	**4**	**244**	**9.0**	**22**	**1172**	**46.9**	**17:05**	**23**	**8**	**12**	**20**	**18**	**3**	**0**	**1**	**16:29**
2000-01	**New Jersey**	**NHL**	**54**	**21**	**34**	**55**	**75**	**8**	**0**	**3**	**138**	**15.2**	**23**	**760**	**49.6**	**16:12**	**23**	**8**	**7**	**15**	**16**	**5**	**0**	**0**	**15:49**
2001-02	**New Jersey**	**NHL**	**63**	**22**	**19**	**41**	**59**	**8**	**0**	**1**	**169**	**13.0**	**3**	**934**	**47.8**	**17:13**	....	....	....	....	....	....	....	....	....
	Dallas	**NHL**	**10**	**3**	**1**	**4**	**6**	**2**	**0**	**2**	**28**	**10.7**	**–1**	**77**	**52.0**	**18:13**	....	....	....	....	....	....	....	....	....
2002-03	**Dallas**	**NHL**	**72**	**23**	**24**	**47**	**51**	**7**	**0**	**6**	**169**	**13.6**	**9**	**1130**	**53.3**	**16:12**	**11**	**3**	**2**	**5**	**6**	**1**	**0**	**0**	**15:35**
2003-04	**Dallas**	**NHL**	**73**	**21**	**36**	**57**	**66**	**5**	**0**	**5**	**143**	**14.7**	**23**	**1203**	**53.0**	**17:00**	**5**	**1**	**1**	**2**	**2**	**1**	**0**	**0**	**17:23**
	NHL Totals		**743**	**244**	**324**	**568**	**897**	**84**	**1**	**38**	**2132**	**11.4**		**6148**	**50.1**	**16:33**	**86**	**25**	**32**	**57**	**64**	**12**	**0**	**1**	**16:13**

NHL All-Rookie Team (1994)

Played in NHL All-Star Game (1997)

Traded to **New Jersey** by **Edmonton** with Bryan Muir for Valeri Zelepukin and Bill Guerin, January 4, 1998. Traded to **Dallas** by **New Jersey** with Randy McKay and New Jersey's 1st round choice (later traded to Columbus – later traded to Buffalo – Buffalo selected Dan Paille) in 2002 Entry Draft for Joe Nieuwendyk and Jamie Langenbrunner, March 19, 2002.

ARVEDSON, Magnus
(AHR-vehd-suhn, MAG-nuhs)

Left wing. Shoots left. 6'2", 198 lbs. Born, Karlstad, Sweden, November 25, 1971. Ottawa's 4th choice, 119th overall, in 1997 Entry Draft.

Season	Club	League	GP	G	A	Pts	PIM	PP	SH	GW	S	%	+/-	TF	F%	Min	Playoffs GP	G	A	Pts	PIM	PP	SH	GW	Min
1990-91	Orebro IK	Swede-2	29	7	11	18	12	....	....	....	....	....	....	....	....	....	2	0	1	1	2	....	....	....	....
1991-92	Orebro IK	Swede-2	32	12	21	33	30	....	....	....	....	....	....	....	....	....	7	4	4	8	4	....	....	....	....
1992-93	Orebro IK	Swede-2	36	11	18	29	34	....	....	....	....	....	....	....	....	....	6	2	1	3	0	....	....	....	....
1993-94	Farjestad	Sweden	16	1	7	8	10	....	....	....	....	....	....	....	....	....	....	....	....	....	....	....	....	....	....
	Farjestad	Swede-2	18	4	2	6	20	....	....	....	....	....	....	....	....	....	3	2	0	2	0	....	....	....	....
1994-95	Farjestad Jr.	Swede-Jr.	1	0	0	0	0	....	....	....	....	....	....	....	....	....	....	....	....	....	....	....	....	....	....
	Farjestad	Sweden	36	1	6	7	45	....	....	....	....	....	....	....	....	....	4	0	0	0	6	....	....	....	....
1995-96	Farjestad	Sweden	40	10	14	24	40	....	....	....	....	....	....	....	....	....	8	0	3	3	10	....	....	....	....
1996-97	Farjestad	Sweden	48	13	11	24	36	....	....	....	....	....	....	....	....	....	14	4	7	11	8	....	....	....	....
	Farjestad	EuroHL	5	1	0	1	2	....	....	....	....	....	....	....	....	....	2	0	1	1	2	....	....	....	....
1997-98	**Ottawa**	**NHL**	**61**	**11**	**15**	**26**	**36**	**0**	**1**	**0**	**90**	**12.2**	**2**	....	....	....	**11**	**0**	**1**	**1**	**6**	**0**	**0**	**0**	....
1998-99	**Ottawa**	**NHL**	**80**	**21**	**26**	**47**	**50**	**0**	**4**	**6**	**136**	**15.4**	**33**	**25**	**20.0**	**17:08**	**3**	**0**	**1**	**1**	**2**	**0**	**0**	**0**	**21:32**
99-2000	**Ottawa**	**NHL**	**47**	**15**	**13**	**28**	**36**	**1**	**1**	**4**	**91**	**16.5**	**4**	**11**	**45.5**	**18:04**	**6**	**0**	**0**	**0**	**6**	**0**	**0**	**0**	**17:25**
2000-01	**Ottawa**	**NHL**	**51**	**17**	**16**	**33**	**24**	**1**	**2**	**4**	**79**	**21.5**	**23**	**7**	**28.6**	**16:01**	**2**	**0**	**0**	**0**	**0**	**0**	**0**	**0**	**16:20**
2001-02	**Ottawa**	**NHL**	**74**	**12**	**27**	**39**	**35**	**0**	**0**	**1**	**121**	**9.9**	**27**	**8**	**37.5**	**17:44**	**12**	**2**	**1**	**3**	**4**	**0**	**0**	**0**	**17:00**
	Sweden	Olympics	4	0	0	0	0	....	....	....	....	....	....	....	....	....	....	....	....	....	....	....	....	....	....
2002-03	**Ottawa**	**NHL**	**80**	**16**	**21**	**37**	**48**	**2**	**0**	**4**	**138**	**11.6**	**13**	**30**	**36.7**	**17:54**	**18**	**1**	**5**	**6**	**16**	**0**	**0**	**0**	**15:35**
2003-04	**Vancouver**	**NHL**	**41**	**8**	**7**	**15**	**12**	**2**	**0**	**4**	**54**	**14.8**	**7**	**15**	**20.0**	**14:30**	....	....	....	....	....	....	....	....	....
	NHL Totals		**434**	**100**	**125**	**225**	**241**	**6**	**8**	**23**	**709**	**14.1**		**96**	**30.2**	**17:06**	**52**	**3**	**8**	**11**	**34**	**0**	**0**	**0**	**16:44**

Signed as a free agent by **Vancouver**, September 10, 2003. • Missed majority of 2003-04 season recovering from knee injury suffered in game vs. Washington, January 31, 2004.

ASHAM, Arron
(ASH-uhm, AIR-ruhn) **NYI**

Right wing. Shoots right. 5'11", 209 lbs. Born, Portage La Prairie, Man., April 13, 1978. Montreal's 3rd choice, 71st overall, in 1996 Entry Draft.

Season	Club	League	GP	G	A	Pts	PIM	PP	SH	GW	S	%	+/-	TF	F%	Min	Playoffs GP	G	A	Pts	PIM	PP	SH	GW	Min
1993-94	Portage	MAHA	21	18	19	37	82	....	....	....	....	....	....	....	....	....	....	....	....	....	....	....	....	....	....
1994-95	Red Deer Rebels	WHL	62	11	16	27	126	....	....	....	....	....	....	....	....	....	....	....	....	....	....	....	....	....	....
1995-96	Red Deer Rebels	WHL	70	32	45	77	174	....	....	....	....	....	....	....	....	....	10	6	3	9	20	....	....	....	....
1996-97	Red Deer Rebels	WHL	67	45	51	96	149	....	....	....	....	....	....	....	....	....	16	12	14	26	36	....	....	....	....
1997-98	Red Deer Rebels	WHL	67	43	49	92	153	....	....	....	....	....	....	....	....	....	5	0	2	2	8	....	....	....	....
	Fredericton	AHL	2	1	1	2	0	....	....	....	....	....	....	....	....	....	2	0	1	1	0	....	....	....	....
1998-99	**Montreal**	**NHL**	**7**	**0**	**0**	**0**	**0**	**0**	**0**	**0**	**5**	**0.0**	**–4**	**0**	**0.0**	**7:27**	....	....	....	....	....	....	....	....	....
	Fredericton	AHL	60	16	18	34	118	....	....	....	....	....	....	....	....	....	13	8	6	14	11	....	....	....	....
99-2000	**Montreal**	**NHL**	**33**	**4**	**2**	**6**	**24**	**0**	**1**	**1**	**29**	**13.8**	**–7**	**1**	**0.0**	**10:14**	....	....	....	....	....	....	....	....	....
	Quebec Citadelles	AHL	13	4	5	9	32	....	....	....	....	....	....	....	....	....	2	0	0	0	2	....	....	....	....
2000-01	**Montreal**	**NHL**	**46**	**2**	**3**	**5**	**59**	**0**	**0**	**0**	**32**	**6.3**	**–9**	**3**	**100.0**	**8:28**	....	....	....	....	....	....	....	....	....
	Quebec Citadelles	AHL	15	7	9	16	51	....	....	....	....	....	....	....	....	....	7	1	2	3	2	....	....	....	....
2001-02	**Montreal**	**NHL**	**35**	**5**	**4**	**9**	**55**	**0**	**0**	**0**	**30**	**16.7**	**7**	**4**	**25.0**	**8:13**	**3**	**0**	**1**	**1**	**0**	**0**	**0**	**0**	**5:39**
	Quebec Citadelles	AHL	24	9	14	23	35	....	....	....	....	....	....	....	....	....	....	....	....	....	....	....	....	....	....
2002-03	**NY Islanders**	**NHL**	**78**	**15**	**19**	**34**	**57**	**4**	**0**	**1**	**114**	**13.2**	**1**	**17**	**41.2**	**12:13**	**5**	**0**	**0**	**0**	**16**	**0**	**0**	**0**	**15:09**
2003-04	**NY Islanders**	**NHL**	**79**	**12**	**12**	**24**	**92**	**1**	**0**	**0**	**108**	**11.1**	**–12**	**23**	**34.8**	**13:13**	**5**	**0**	**1**	**1**	**4**	**0**	**0**	**0**	**8:44**
	NHL Totals		**278**	**38**	**40**	**78**	**287**	**5**	**1**	**2**	**318**	**11.9**		**48**	**39.6**	**11:01**	**13**	**0**	**2**	**2**	**20**	**0**	**0**	**0**	**10:29**

Traded to **NY Islanders** by **Montreal** with Montreal's 5th round choice (Marcus Paulsson) in 2002 Entry Draft for Mariusz Czerkawski, June 22, 2002.

AUBIN, Serge
(oh-BEHN, SAIRZH) **ATL.**

Left wing. Shoots left. 6'1", 200 lbs. Born, Val-d'Or, Que., February 15, 1975. Pittsburgh's 9th choice, 161st overall, in 1994 Entry Draft.

Season	Club	League	GP	G	A	Pts	PIM	PP	SH	GW	S	%	+/-	TF	F%	Min	Playoffs GP	G	A	Pts	PIM	PP	SH	GW	Min
1990-91	Abitibi Forestiers	QAAA	27	2	4	6	10	....	....	....	....	....	....	....	....	....	....	....	....	....	....	....	....	....	....
1991-92	Abitibi Forestiers	QAAA	42	28	32	60	36	....	....	....	....	....	....	....	....	....	1	0	1	1	0	....	....	....	....
1992-93	Drummondville	QMJHL	65	16	34	50	30	....	....	....	....	....	....	....	....	....	8	0	1	1	16	....	....	....	....
1993-94	Granby Bisons	QMJHL	63	42	32	74	80	....	....	....	....	....	....	....	....	....	7	2	3	5	8	....	....	....	....
1994-95	Granby Bisons	QMJHL	60	37	73	110	55	....	....	....	....	....	....	....	....	....	11	8	15	23	4	....	....	....	....
1995-96	Hampton Roads	ECHL	62	24	62	86	74	....	....	....	....	....	....	....	....	....	3	1	4	5	10	....	....	....	....
	Cleveland	IHL	2	0	0	0	0	....	....	....	....	....	....	....	....	....	2	0	0	0	0	....	....	....	....
1996-97	Cleveland	IHL	57	9	16	25	38	....	....	....	....	....	....	....	....	....	2	0	0	0	0	....	....	....	....
1997-98	Syracuse Crunch	AHL	55	6	14	20	57	....	....	....	....	....	....	....	....	....	....	....	....	....	....	....	....	....	....
	Hershey Bears	AHL	5	2	1	3	0	....	....	....	....	....	....	....	....	....	7	1	3	4	6	....	....	....	....
1998-99	Hershey Bears	AHL	64	30	39	69	58	....	....	....	....	....	....	....	....	....	3	0	1	1	2	....	....	....	....
	Colorado	**NHL**	**1**	**0**	**0**	**0**	**0**	**0**	**0**	**0**	**1**	**0.0**	**0**	**1**	**0.0**	**4:16**	....	....	....	....	....	....	....	....	....
99-2000	**Colorado**	**NHL**	**15**	**2**	**1**	**3**	**6**	**0**	**0**	**1**	**14**	**14.3**	**1**	**79**	**50.6**	**6:37**	**17**	**0**	**1**	**1**	**6**	**0**	**0**	**0**	**5:06**
	Hershey Bears	AHL	58	42	38	80	56	....	....	....	....	....	....	....	....	....	....	....	....	....	....	....	....	....	....
2000-01	**Columbus**	**NHL**	**81**	**13**	**17**	**30**	**107**	**0**	**0**	**2**	**110**	**11.8**	**–20**	**1346**	**51.3**	**16:20**	....	....	....	....	....	....	....	....	....
2001-02	**Columbus**	**NHL**	**71**	**8**	**8**	**16**	**32**	**1**	**0**	**1**	**86**	**9.3**	**–20**	**780**	**50.5**	**15:30**	....	....	....	....	....	....	....	....	....

			Regular Season														Playoffs								
Season	Club	League	GP	G	A	Pts	PIM	PP	SH	GW	S	%	+/-	TF	F%	Min	GP	G	A	Pts	PIM	PP	SH	GW	Min
2002-03	**Colorado**	**NHL**	66	4	6	10	64	0	0	1	62	6.5	−2	613	50.2	11:58	5	0	0	0	4	0	0	0	5:25
2003-04	**Atlanta**	**NHL**	66	10	15	25	73	1	0	2	97	10.3	0	668	49.1	16:00	....	....	....	....	....	....	....	....	....
	NHL Totals		300	37	47	84	282	2	0	7	370	10.0		3487	50.5	14:34	22	0	1	1	10	0	0	0	5:10

AHL First All-Star Team (2000)

Signed as a free agent by **Hershey** (AHL), July 24, 1998. Signed as a free agent by **Colorado**, December 22, 1998. Signed as a free agent by **Columbus**, July 11, 2000. Signed as a free agent by **Colorado**, August 27, 2002. Claimed by **Atlanta** from **Colorado** in Waiver Draft, October 3, 2003.

AUCOIN, Adrian

(oh-KOIN, AY-dree-an) **NYI**

Defense. Shoots right. 6'2", 214 lbs. Born, Ottawa, Ont., July 3, 1973. Vancouver's 7th choice, 117th overall, in 1992 Entry Draft.

Season	Club	League	GP	G	A	Pts	PIM	PP	SH	GW	S	%	+/-	TF	F%	Min	GP	G	A	Pts	PIM	PP	SH	GW	Min
1989-90	Nepean Raiders	OCJHL	54	2	14	16	95	....	....	....	....	....	....	....	....	....	4	0	1	1	....	....	....	....	....
1990-91	Nepean Raiders	OCJHL	56	17	33	50	125	....	....	....	....	....	....	....	....	....	....	....	....	....	....	....	....	....	....
1991-92	Boston University	H-East	32	2	10	12	60	....	....	....	....	....	....	....	....	....	....	....	....	....	....	....	....	....	....
1992-93	Team Canada	Nat-Tm	42	8	10	18	71	....	....	....	....	....	....	....	....	....	....	....	....	....	....	....	....	....	....
1993-94	Team Canada	Nat-Tm	59	5	12	17	80	....	....	....	....	....	....	....	....	....	....	....	....	....	....	....	....	....	....
	Canada	Olympics	4	0	0	0	2	....	....	....	....	....	....	....	....	....	....	....	....	....	....	....	....	....	....
	Hamilton	AHL	13	1	2	3	19	....	....	....	....	....	....	....	....	....	4	0	2	2	6	....	....	....	....
1994-95	Syracuse Crunch	AHL	71	13	18	31	52	....	....	....	....	....	....	....	....	....	....	....	....	....	....	....	....	....	....
	Vancouver	**NHL**	1	1	0	1	0	0	0	0	2	50.0	1	....	....	....	4	1	0	1	0	1	0	0	....
1995-96	**Vancouver**	**NHL**	49	4	14	18	34	2	0	0	85	4.7	8	....	....	....	6	0	0	0	2	0	0	0	....
	Syracuse Crunch	AHL	29	5	13	18	47	....	....	....	....	....	....	....	....	....	....	....	....	....	....	....	....	....	....
1996-97	**Vancouver**	**NHL**	70	5	16	21	63	1	0	0	116	4.3	0	....	....	....	....	....	....	....	....	....	....	....	....
1997-98	**Vancouver**	**NHL**	35	3	3	6	21	1	0	1	44	6.8	−4	....	....	....	....	....	....	....	....	....	....	....	....
1998-99	**Vancouver**	**NHL**	82	23	11	34	77	18	2	3	174	13.2	−14	1	100.0	23:52	....	....	....	....	....	....	....	....	....
99-2000	**Vancouver**	**NHL**	57	10	14	24	30	4	0	1	126	7.9	7	0	0.0	23:06	....	....	....	....	....	....	....	....	....
2000-01	**Vancouver**	**NHL**	47	3	13	16	20	1	0	0	99	3.0	13	0	0.0	18:21	....	....	....	....	....	....	....	....	....
	Tampa Bay	**NHL**	26	1	11	12	25	1	0	0	60	1.7	−8	0	0.0	23:34	....	....	....	....	....	....	....	....	....
2001-02	**NY Islanders**	**NHL**	81	12	22	34	62	7	0	1	232	5.2	23	0	0.0	28:54	7	2	5	7	4	2	0	0	32:19
2002-03	**NY Islanders**	**NHL**	73	8	27	35	70	5	0	1	175	4.6	−5	0	0.0	29:01	5	1	2	3	4	0	0	0	31:43
2003-04	**NY Islanders**	**NHL**	81	13	31	44	54	4	0	2	213	6.1	29	0	0.0	26:38	5	0	0	0	6	0	0	0	28:21
	NHL Totals		602	83	162	245	456	44	2	9	1326	6.3		1	100.0	25:25	27	4	7	11	16	3	0	0	30:58

Played in NHL All-Star Game (2004)

• Missed majority of 1997-98 season recovering from ankle (October 4, 1997 vs. Anaheim) and groin (November 1, 1997 vs. Pittsburgh) injuries. Traded to **Tampa Bay** by **Vancouver** with Vancouver's 2nd round choice (Alexander Polushin) in 2001 Entry Draft for Dan Cloutier, February 7, 2001. Traded to **NY Islanders** by **Tampa Bay** with Alexander Kharitonov for Mathieu Biron and NY Islanders' 2nd round choice (later traded to Washington – later traded to Vancouver – Vancouver selected Denis Grot) in 2002 Entry Draft, June 22, 2001.

AUDETTE, Donald

(aw-DEHT, DAW-nohld)

Right wing. Shoots right. 5'8", 190 lbs. Born, Laval, Que., September 23, 1969. Buffalo's 8th choice, 183rd overall, in 1989 Entry Draft.

Season	Club	League	GP	G	A	Pts	PIM	PP	SH	GW	S	%	+/-	TF	F%	Min	GP	G	A	Pts	PIM	PP	SH	GW	Min
1985-86	Laval Laurentide	QAAA	41	32	38	70	51	....	....	....	....	....	....	....	....	....	8	5	9	14	10	....	....	....	....
1986-87	Laval Titan	QMJHL	66	17	22	39	36	....	....	....	....	....	....	....	....	....	14	2	6	8	10	....	....	....	....
1987-88	Laval Titan	QMJHL	63	48	61	109	56	....	....	....	....	....	....	....	....	....	14	7	12	19	20	....	....	....	....
1988-89	Laval Titan	QMJHL	70	76	85	161	123	....	....	....	....	....	....	....	....	....	17	17	12	29	43	....	....	....	....
1989-90	Rochester	AHL	70	42	46	88	78	....	....	....	....	....	....	....	....	....	15	9	8	17	29	....	....	....	....
	Buffalo	**NHL**	....	....	....	....	....	....	....	....	....	....	....	....	....	....	2	0	0	0	0	0	0	0	....
1990-91	**Buffalo**	**NHL**	8	4	3	7	4	2	0	1	17	23.5	−1	....	....	....	....	....	....	....	....	....	....	....	....
	Rochester	AHL	5	4	0	4	2	....	....	....	....	....	....	....	....	....	....	....	....	....	....	....	....	....	....
1991-92	**Buffalo**	**NHL**	63	31	17	48	75	5	0	6	153	20.3	−1	....	....	....	....	....	....	....	....	....	....	....	....
1992-93	**Buffalo**	**NHL**	44	12	7	19	51	2	0	0	92	13.0	−8	....	....	....	8	2	2	4	6	0	0	0	....
	Rochester	AHL	6	8	4	12	10	....	....	....	....	....	....	....	....	....	....	....	....	....	....	....	....	....	....
1993-94	**Buffalo**	**NHL**	77	29	30	59	41	16	1	4	207	14.0	2	....	....	....	7	0	1	1	6	0	0	0	....
1994-95	**Buffalo**	**NHL**	46	24	13	37	27	13	0	7	124	19.4	−3	....	....	....	5	1	1	2	4	1	0	0	....
1995-96	**Buffalo**	**NHL**	23	12	13	25	18	8	0	1	92	13.0	0	....	....	....	....	....	....	....	....	....	....	....	....
1996-97	**Buffalo**	**NHL**	73	28	22	50	48	8	0	5	182	15.4	−6	....	....	....	11	4	5	9	6	3	0	0	....
1997-98	**Buffalo**	**NHL**	75	24	20	44	59	10	0	5	198	12.1	10	....	....	....	15	5	8	13	10	3	0	2	....
1998-99	**Los Angeles**	**NHL**	49	18	18	36	51	6	0	2	152	11.8	7	4	50.0	16:50	....	....	....	....	....	....	....	....	....
99-2000	**Los Angeles**	**NHL**	49	12	20	32	45	1	0	3	112	10.7	6	4	50.0	14:56	....	....	....	....	....	....	....	....	....
	Atlanta	**NHL**	14	7	4	11	12	0	1	1	50	14.0	−4	0	0.0	21:35	....	....	....	....	....	....	....	....	....
2000-01	**Atlanta**	**NHL**	64	32	39	71	64	13	1	2	187	17.1	−3	7	57.1	20:18	....	....	....	....	....	....	....	....	....
	Buffalo	**NHL**	12	2	6	8	12	1	0	1	38	5.3	1	1	0.0	17:25	13	3	6	9	4	0	0	0	17:06
2001-02	**Dallas**	**NHL**	20	4	8	12	12	3	0	2	49	8.2	2	2	50.0	12:26	....	....	....	....	....	....	....	....	....
	Montreal	**NHL**	13	1	5	6	8	0	0	1	33	3.0	1	1	100.0	17:42	12	6	4	10	10	2	0	2	15:32
2002-03	**Montreal**	**NHL**	54	11	12	23	19	4	0	4	118	9.3	−7	6	33.3	15:30	....	....	....	....	....	....	....	....	....
	Hamilton	AHL	11	5	5	10	8	....	....	....	....	....	....	....	....	....	....	....	....	....	....	....	....	....	....
2003-04	**Montreal**	**NHL**	23	3	5	8	16	0	0	0	41	7.3	−4	4	50.0	13:28	....	....	....	....	....	....	....	....	....
	Florida	**NHL**	28	6	7	13	22	5	0	0	66	9.1	−9	4	50.0	16:02	....	....	....	....	....	....	....	....	....
	NHL Totals		735	260	249	509	584	97	3	45	1911	13.6		33	48.5	16:41	73	21	27	48	46	9	0	4	16:21

QMJHL First All-Star Team (1989) • AHL First All-Star Team (1990) • Dudley "Red" Garret Memorial Trophy (Top Rookie – AHL) (1990)

Played in NHL ALL-Star Game (2001)

• Missed majority of 1990-91 season recovering from knee injury suffered in game vs. Edmonton, November 16, 1990. • Missed majority of 1995-96 season recovering from knee injury suffered in training camp, September 23, 1995. Traded to **Los Angeles** by **Buffalo** for Los Angeles' 2nd round choice (Milan Bartovic) in 1999 Entry Draft, December 18, 1998. Traded to **Atlanta** by **Los Angeles** with Frantisek Kaberle for Kelly Buchberger and Nelson Emerson, March 13, 2000. Traded to **Buffalo** by **Atlanta** for the rights to Kamil Piros and Buffalo's 4th round choice (later traded to St. Louis – St. Louis selected Igor Valeyev) in 2001 Entry Draft, March 13, 2001. Signed as a free agent by **Dallas**, July 2, 2001. Traded to **Montreal** by **Dallas** with Shaun Van Allen for Martin Rucinsky and Benoit Brunet, November 21, 2001. • Missed majority of 2001-02 season recovering from wrist injury suffered in game vs. NY Rangers, December 1, 2001. Signed as a free agent by **Florida**, January 15, 2004, following release by Montreal,

AULIN, Jared

(AW-lihn, JAIR-ehd) **WSH.**

Center/Right wing. Shoots right. 6', 192 lbs. Born, Calgary, Alta., March 15, 1982. Colorado's 2nd choice, 47th overall, in 2000 Entry Draft.

Season	Club	League	GP	G	A	Pts	PIM	PP	SH	GW	S	%	+/-	TF	F%	Min	GP	G	A	Pts	PIM	PP	SH	GW	Min
1997-98	Airdrie Xtreme	AAHA	55	42	61	103	60	....	....	....	....	....	....	....	....	....	....	....	....	....	....	....	....	....	....
	Kamloops Blazers	WHL	2	0	0	0	0	....	....	....	....	....	....	....	....	....	....	....	....	....	....	....	....	....	....
1998-99	Kamloops Blazers	WHL	55	7	19	26	23	....	....	....	....	....	....	....	....	....	13	1	3	4	2	....	....	....	....
99-2000	Kamloops Blazers	WHL	57	17	38	55	70	....	....	....	....	....	....	....	....	....	4	0	1	1	6	....	....	....	....
2000-01	Kamloops Blazers	WHL	70	31	*77	108	62	....	....	....	....	....	....	....	....	....	4	0	2	2	0	....	....	....	....
2001-02	Kamloops Blazers	WHL	46	33	34	67	80	....	....	....	....	....	....	....	....	....	4	1	2	3	2	....	....	....	....
2002-03	**Los Angeles**	**NHL**	17	2	2	4	0	1	0	0	21	9.5	−3	92	41.3	9:55	....	....	....	....	....	....	....	....	....
	Manchester	AHL	44	12	32	44	21	....	....	....	....	....	....	....	....	....	3	0	4	4	0	....	....	....	....
2003-04	Portland Pirates	AHL	10	2	1	3	4	....	....	....	....	....	....	....	....	....	6	1	1	2	4	....	....	....	....
	NHL Totals		17	2	2	4	0	1	0	0	21	9.5		92	41.3	9:55	....	....	....	....	....	....	....	....	....

WHL West First All-Star Team (2001, 2002)

Traded to **Los Angeles** by **Colorado** to complete transaction that sent Rob Blake and Steve Reinprecht to Colorado (February 21, 2001), March 22, 2001. • Missed majopriy of 2003-04 season recovering from shoulder injury suffered in training camp, September 4, 2003. Traded to **Washington** by **Los Angeles** for Anson Carter, March 8, 2004.

AVERY, Sean

(AY-vuhr-ee, SHAWN) **L.A.**

Center. Shoots left. 5'10", 185 lbs. Born, Pickering, Ont., April 10, 1980.

Season	Club	League	GP	G	A	Pts	PIM	PP	SH	GW	S	%	+/-	TF	F%	Min	GP	G	A	Pts	PIM	PP	SH	GW	Min
1995-96	Markham	OMHA	70	34	81	115	180	....	....	....	....	....	....	....	....	....	....	....	....	....	....	....	....	....	....
	Markham Waxers	OJHL	1	0	0	0	4	....	....	....	....	....	....	....	....	....	....	....	....	....	....	....	....	....	....
1996-97	Owen Sound	OHL	58	10	21	31	86	....	....	....	....	....	....	....	....	....	4	1	0	1	4	....	....	....	....
1997-98	Owen Sound	OHL	47	13	41	54	105	....	....	....	....	....	....	....	....	....	....	....	....	....	....	....	....	....	....
1998-99	Owen Sound	OHL	28	22	23	45	70	....	....	....	....	....	....	....	....	....	....	....	....	....	....	....	....	....	....
	Kingston	OHL	33	14	25	39	88	....	....	....	....	....	....	....	....	....	5	1	3	4	13	....	....	....	....
99-2000	Kingston	OHL	55	28	56	84	215	....	....	....	....	....	....	....	....	....	5	2	2	4	26	....	....	....	....
2000-01	Cincinnati	AHL	58	8	15	23	304	....	....	....	....	....	....	....	....	....	4	1	0	1	19	....	....	....	....
2001-02	**Detroit**	**NHL**	36	2	2	4	68	0	0	1	30	6.7	1	299	51.8	7:51	....	....	....	....	....	....	....	....	....
	Cincinnati	AHL	36	14	7	21	106	....	....	....	....	....	....	....	....	....	....	....	....	....	....	....	....	....	....

			Regular Season														Playoffs								
Season	Club	League	GP	G	A	Pts	PIM	PP	SH	GW	S	%	+/-	TF	F%	Min	GP	G	A	Pts	PIM	PP	SH	GW	Min
2002-03	Detroit	NHL	39	5	6	11	120	0	0	2	40	12.5	7	224	58.0	7:03	....	....	....	....	....	....	....	....	....
	Grand Rapids	AHL	15	6	6	12	82	....	....	....	....	....	....	....	....	....	....	....	....	....	....	....	....	....	....
	Los Angeles	NHL	12	1	3	4	33	0	0	0	19	5.3	0	49	46.9	13:50	....	....	....	....	....	....	....	....	....
	Manchester	AHL	....	....	....	....	....	....	....	....	....	....	....	....	....	....	3	2	1	3	8	....	....	....	....
2003-04	Los Angeles	NHL	76	9	19	28	*261	0	0	2	125	7.2	2	124	54.8	11:41	....	....	....	....	....	....	....	....	....
	NHL Totals		163	17	30	47	482	0	0	5	214	7.9		696	54.0	9:54	....	....	....	....	....	....	....	....	....

Signed as a free agent by **Detroit**, September 21, 1999. Traded to **Los Angeles** by **Detroit** with Maxim Kuznetsov, Detroit's 1st round choice (Jeff Tambellini) in 2003 Entry Draft and Detroit's 2nd round choice (later traded to Boston – Boston selected Martins Karsums) in 2004 Entry Draft for Mathieu Schneider, March 11, 2003.

AXELSSON, P.J.

(AHX-ehl-suhn, PEE-JAY) **BOS.**

Left wing. Shoots left. 6'1", 184 lbs. Born, Kungalv, Sweden, February 26, 1975. Boston's 7th choice, 177th overall, in 1995 Entry Draft.

			Regular Season														Playoffs								
Season	Club	League	GP	G	A	Pts	PIM	PP	SH	GW	S	%	+/-	TF	F%	Min	GP	G	A	Pts	PIM	PP	SH	GW	Min
1992-93	V. Frolunda Jr.	Swede-Jr.	16	9	5	14	12	....	....	....	....	....	....	....	....	....	....	....	....	....	....	....	....	....	....
	Vastra Frolunda	Sweden	1	0	0	0	0	....	....	....	....	....	....	....	....	....	....	....	....	....	....	....	....	....	....
1993-94	Vastra Frolunda	Sweden	11	0	0	0	4	....	....	....	....	....	....	....	....	....	4	0	0	0	0	....	....	....	....
1994-95	V. Frolunda Jr.	Swede-Jr.	19	16	9	25	22	....	....	....	....	....	....	....	....	....	....	....	....	....	....	....	....	....	....
	Vastra Frolunda	Sweden	11	2	1	3	6	....	....	....	....	....	....	....	....	....	5	0	0	0	0	....	....	....	....
1995-96	Vastra Frolunda	Sweden	36	15	5	20	10	....	....	....	....	....	....	....	....	....	13	3	0	3	10	....	....	....	....
1996-97	Vastra Frolunda	Sweden	50	19	15	34	34	....	....	....	....	....	....	....	....	....	3	0	2	2	0	....	....	....	....
	Vastra Frolunda	EuroHL	3	1	1	2	0	....	....	....	....	....	....	....	....	....	3	0	0	0	2	....	....	....	....
1997-98	Boston	NHL	82	8	19	27	38	2	0	1	144	5.6	–14	....	....	....	6	1	0	1	0	0	0	0	....
1998-99	Boston	NHL	77	7	10	17	18	0	0	2	146	4.8	–14	8	75.0	16:38	12	1	1	2	4	0	0	0	15:11
99-2000	Boston	NHL	81	10	16	26	24	0	0	4	186	5.4	1	22	27.3	16:43	....	....	....	....	....	....	....	....	....
2000-01	Boston	NHL	81	8	15	23	27	0	0	2	146	5.5	–12	41	36.6	12:30	....	....	....	....	....	....	....	....	....
2001-02	Boston	NHL	78	7	17	24	16	0	2	0	127	5.5	6	17	35.3	14:42	6	2	1	3	6	0	1	1	16:48
	Sweden	Olympics	4	0	0	0	2	....	....	....	....	....	....	....	....	....	....	....	....	....	....	....	....	....	....
2002-03	Boston	NHL	66	17	19	36	24	2	2	1	122	13.9	8	17	23.5	16:37	5	0	0	0	6	0	0	0	13:23
2003-04	Boston	NHL	68	6	14	20	42	0	0	1	107	5.6	2	13	15.4	16:19	7	0	0	0	4	0	0	0	14:43
	NHL Totals		533	63	110	173	189	4	4	11	978	6.4		118	33.1	15:31	36	4	2	6	20	0	1	1	15:06

BABCHUK, Anton

(bab-CHUHK, AN-tawn) **CHI.**

Defense. Shoots right. 6'5", 202 lbs. Born, Kiev, USSR, May 6, 1984. Chicago's 1st choice, 21st overall, in 2002 Entry Draft.

			Regular Season														Playoffs								
Season	Club	League	GP	G	A	Pts	PIM	PP	SH	GW	S	%	+/-	TF	F%	Min	GP	G	A	Pts	PIM	PP	SH	GW	Min
99-2000	Elektrostal 18	Russia-Jr.	5	0	0	0	18	....	....	....	....	....	....	....	....	....	....	....	....	....	....	....	....	....	....
	Elektrostal Jr.	Russia-Jr.	6	0	0	0	8	....	....	....	....	....	....	....	....	....	....	....	....	....	....	....	....	....	....
	Elektrostal 2	Russia-3	18	0	1	1	18	....	....	....	....	....	....	....	....	....	....	....	....	....	....	....	....	....	....
2000-01	Elektrostal	Russia-2	7	0	0	0	12	....	....	....	....	....	....	....	....	....	....	....	....	....	....	....	....	....	....
	Team Russia 17	Nat-Tm	15	1	3	4	12	....	....	....	....	....	....	....	....	....	....	....	....	....	....	....	....	....	....
2001-02	Elektrostal	Russia-2	40	7	8	15	90	....	....	....	....	....	....	....	....	....	....	....	....	....	....	....	....	....	....
	Elektrostal 2	Russia-3	3	0	0	0	8	....	....	....	....	....	....	....	....	....	....	....	....	....	....	....	....	....	....
2002-03	Ak Bars Kazan	Russia	10	0	0	0	4	....	....	....	....	....	....	....	....	....	....	....	....	....	....	....	....	....	....
	St. Petersburg	Russia	20	3	0	3	10	....	....	....	....	....	....	....	....	....	....	....	....	....	....	....	....	....	....
	St. Petersburg	Russia-2	1	1	0	1	0	....	....	....	....	....	....	....	....	....	....	....	....	....	....	....	....	....	....
2003-04	Chicago	NHL	5	0	2	2	2	0	0	0	11	0.0	–1	0	0.0	12:43	....	....	....	....	....	....	....	....	....
	Norfolk Admirals	AHL	73	8	14	22	89	....	....	....	....	....	....	....	....	....	8	0	2	2	6	....	....	....	....
	NHL Totals		5	0	2	2	2	0	0	0	11	0.0		0	0.0	12:43	....	....	....	....	....	....	....	....	....

BACKMAN, Christian

(BAK-man, KRIH-stan) **ST.L.**

Defense. Shoots left. 6'4", 198 lbs. Born, Alingsas, Sweden, April 28, 1980. St. Louis' 1st choice, 24th overall, in 1998 Entry Draft.

			Regular Season														Playoffs								
Season	Club	League	GP	G	A	Pts	PIM	PP	SH	GW	S	%	+/-	TF	F%	Min	GP	G	A	Pts	PIM	PP	SH	GW	Min
1996-97	V. Frolunda Jr.	Swede-Jr.	26	2	5	7	16	....	....	....	....	....	....	....	....	....	....	....	....	....	....	....	....	....	....
1997-98	V. Frolunda 18	Swede-Jr.	4	4	1	5	2	....	....	....	....	....	....	....	....	....	5	2	2	4	2	....	....	....	....
	V. Frolunda Jr.	Swede-Jr.	28	5	14	19	12	....	....	....	....	....	....	....	....	....	2	0	1	1	4	....	....	....	....
1998-99	V. Frolunda Jr.	Swede-Jr.	4	0	2	2	4	....	....	....	....	....	....	....	....	....	....	....	....	....	....	....	....	....	....
	Vastra Frolunda	Sweden	49	0	4	4	4	....	....	....	....	....	....	....	....	....	4	0	0	0	0	....	....	....	....
99-2000	V. Frolunda Jr.	Swede-Jr.	5	1	1	2	0	....	....	....	....	....	....	....	....	....	3	1	1	2	0	....	....	....	....
	Gislaveds IK	Swede-2	21	5	2	7	8	....	....	....	....	....	....	....	....	....	....	....	....	....	....	....	....	....	....
	Vastra Frolunda	Sweden	27	1	0	1	14	....	....	....	....	....	....	....	....	....	5	0	0	0	0	....	....	....	....
2000-01	Vastra Frolunda	Sweden	50	1	10	11	32	....	....	....	....	....	....	....	....	....	3	0	2	2	2	....	....	....	....
2001-02	Vastra Frolunda	Sweden	44	7	4	11	38	....	....	....	....	....	....	....	....	....	10	0	0	0	8	....	....	....	....
2002-03	St. Louis	NHL	4	0	0	0	0	0	0	0	4	0.0	–3	0	0.0	12:22	....	....	....	....	....	....	....	....	....
	Worcester IceCats	AHL	72	8	19	27	66	....	....	....	....	....	....	....	....	....	3	0	1	1	5	....	....	....	....
2003-04	St. Louis	NHL	66	5	13	18	16	1	0	0	92	5.4	3	0	0.0	19:20	5	0	2	2	4	0	0	0	23:06
	Worcester IceCats	AHL	4	1	2	3	2	....	....	....	....	....	....	....	....	....	....	....	....	....	....	....	....	....	....
	NHL Totals		70	5	13	18	16	1	0	0	96	5.2		0	0.0	18:56	5	0	2	2	4	0	0	0	23:06

BALA, Chris

(BA-la, KRIHS) **COL.**

Left wing. Shoots left. 6'1", 196 lbs. Born, Alexandria, VA, September 24, 1978. Ottawa's 3rd choice, 58th overall, in 1998 Entry Draft.

			Regular Season														Playoffs								
Season	Club	League	GP	G	A	Pts	PIM	PP	SH	GW	S	%	+/-	TF	F%	Min	GP	G	A	Pts	PIM	PP	SH	GW	Min
1996-97	Hill-Murray	Hi-School	23	28	33	61	36	....	....	....	....	....	....	....	....	....	....	....	....	....	....	....	....	....	....
1997-98	Harvard Crimson	ECAC	33	16	14	30	23	....	....	....	....	....	....	....	....	....	....	....	....	....	....	....	....	....	....
1998-99	Harvard Crimson	ECAC	28	5	10	15	16	....	....	....	....	....	....	....	....	....	....	....	....	....	....	....	....	....	....
99-2000	Harvard Crimson	ECAC	30	10	14	24	18	....	....	....	....	....	....	....	....	....	....	....	....	....	....	....	....	....	....
2000-01	Harvard Crimson	ECAC	32	14	16	30	24	....	....	....	....	....	....	....	....	....	....	....	....	....	....	....	....	....	....
2001-02	Ottawa	NHL	6	0	1	1	0	0	0	0	2	0.0	1	0	0.0	5:43	....	....	....	....	....	....	....	....	....
	Grand Rapids	AHL	70	21	16	37	9	....	....	....	....	....	....	....	....	....	4	0	1	1	0	....	....	....	....
2002-03	Binghamton	AHL	51	6	18	24	20	....	....	....	....	....	....	....	....	....	14	2	5	7	4	....	....	....	....
2003-04	Houston Aeros	AHL	61	11	7	18	18	....	....	....	....	....	....	....	....	....	....	....	....	....	....	....	....	....	....
	Hershey Bears	AHL	13	4	2	6	0	....	....	....	....	....	....	....	....	....	....	....	....	....	....	....	....	....	....
	NHL Totals		6	0	1	1	0	0	0	0	2	0.0		0	0.0	5:43	....	....	....	....	....	....	....	....	....

Traded to **Nashville** by **Ottawa** for Peter Smrek, June 26, 2003. Traded to **Minnesota** by **Nashville** for Curtis Murphy, June 26, 2003. Traded to **Colorado** by **Minnesota** for Jordan Krestanovich, March 9, 2004.

BALEJ, Jozef

(BAH-lay, YOH-zehf) **NYR**

Right wing. Shoots right. 6'1", 187 lbs. Born, Myjava, Czech., February 22, 1982. Montreal's 3rd choice, 78th overall, in 2000 Entry Draft.

			Regular Season														Playoffs								
Season	Club	League	GP	G	A	Pts	PIM	PP	SH	GW	S	%	+/-	TF	F%	Min	GP	G	A	Pts	PIM	PP	SH	GW	Min
1996-97	Dukla Trencin Jr.	Slovak-Jr.	51	31	25	56	36	....	....	....	....	....	....	....	....	....	....	....	....	....	....	....	....	....	....
1997-98	Dukla Trencin Jr.	Slovak-Jr.	52	57	40	97	60	....	....	....	....	....	....	....	....	....	....	....	....	....	....	....	....	....	....
1998-99	Thunder Bay	USHL	38	8	7	15	9	....	....	....	....	....	....	....	....	....	....	....	....	....	....	....	....	....	....
	Rochester	USHL	17	0	1	1	2	....	....	....	....	....	....	....	....	....	....	....	....	....	....	....	....	....	....
99-2000	Portland	WHL	65	22	23	45	33	....	....	....	....	....	....	....	....	....	....	....	....	....	....	....	....	....	....
2000-01	Portland	WHL	46	32	21	53	18	....	....	....	....	....	....	....	....	....	16	9	6	15	6	....	....	....	....
2001-02	Portland	WHL	65	51	41	92	52	....	....	....	....	....	....	....	....	....	7	0	2	2	6	....	....	....	....
2002-03	Hamilton	AHL	56	5	15	20	29	....	....	....	....	....	....	....	....	....	....	....	....	....	....	....	....	....	....
2003-04	Montreal	NHL	4	0	0	0	0	0	0	0	4	0.0	–1	2	50.0	12:38	....	....	....	....	....	....	....	....	....
	Hamilton	AHL	55	25	33	58	32	....	....	....	....	....	....	....	....	....	....	....	....	....	....	....	....	....	....
	NY Rangers	NHL	13	1	4	5	4	0	0	0	25	4.0	0	1	0.0	13:06	....	....	....	....	....	....	....	....	....
	Hartford	AHL	5	1	3	4	21	....	....	....	....	....	....	....	....	....	16	9	7	16	10	....	....	....	....
	NHL Totals		17	1	4	5	4	0	0	0	29	3.4		3	33.3	12:59	....	....	....	....	....	....	....	....	....

WHL West First All-Star Team (2002)

Traded to **NY Rangers** by **Montreal** with Montreal's 2nd round choice (Bruce Graham) in 2004 Entry Draft for Alex Kovalev, March 2, 2004.

BALMOCHNYKH, Maxim
(bahl-MAWCH-nihky, mahx-EEM)

Left wing. Shoots left. 6'1", 210 lbs. Born, Lipetsk, USSR, March 7, 1979. Anaheim's 2nd choice, 45th overall, in 1997 Entry Draft.

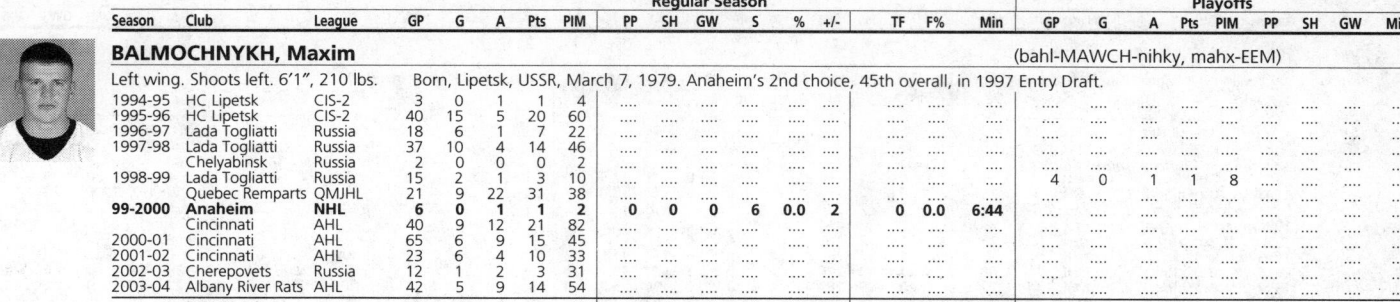

			Regular Season														Playoffs								
Season	Club	League	GP	G	A	Pts	PIM	PP	SH	GW	S	%	+/-	TF	F%	Min	GP	G	A	Pts	PIM	PP	SH	GW	Min
1994-95	HC Lipetsk	CIS-2	3	0	1	1	4	....	....	....	....	....	....	....	....	....	....	....	....	....	....	....	....	....	....
1995-96	HC Lipetsk	CIS-2	40	15	5	20	60	....	....	....	....	....	....	....	....	....	....	....	....	....	....	....	....	....	....
1996-97	Lada Togliatti	Russia	18	6	1	7	22	....	....	....	....	....	....	....	....	....	....	....	....	....	....	....	....	....	....
1997-98	Lada Togliatti	Russia	37	10	4	14	46	....	....	....	....	....	....	....	....	....	....	....	....	....	....	....	....	....	....
	Chelyabinsk	Russia	2	0	0	0	2	....	....	....	....	....	....	....	....	....	....	....	....	....	....	....	....	....	....
1998-99	Lada Togliatti	Russia	15	2	1	3	10	....	....	....	....	....	....	....	....	....	4	0	1	1	8	....	....	....	....
	Quebec Remparts	QMJHL	21	9	22	31	38	....	....	....	....	....	....	....	....	....	....	....	....	....	....	....	....	....	....
99-2000	**Anaheim**	**NHL**	**6**	**0**	**1**	**1**	**2**	**0**	**0**	**0**	**6**	**0.0**	**2**	**0**	**0.0**	**6:44**	....	....	....	....	....	....	....	....	....
	Cincinnati	AHL	40	9	12	21	82	....	....	....	....	....	....	....	....	....	....	....	....	....	....	....	....	....	....
2000-01	Cincinnati	AHL	65	6	9	15	45	....	....	....	....	....	....	....	....	....	....	....	....	....	....	....	....	....	....
2001-02	Cincinnati	AHL	23	6	4	10	33	....	....	....	....	....	....	....	....	....	....	....	....	....	....	....	....	....	....
2002-03	Cherepovets	Russia	12	1	2	3	31	....	....	....	....	....	....	....	....	....	....	....	....	....	....	....	....	....	....
2003-04	Albany River Rats	AHL	42	5	9	14	54	....	....	....	....	....	....	....	....	....	....	....	....	....	....	....	....	....	....
	NHL Totals		**6**	**0**	**1**	**1**	**2**	**0**	**0**	**0**	**6**	**0.0**		**0**	**0.0**	**6:44**	....	....	....	....	....	....	....	....	....

Traded to **New Jersey** by **Anaheim** with Jeff Friesen and Oleg Tverdovsky for Petr Sykora, Mike Commodore, Jean-Francois Damphousse and Igor Pohanka, July 6, 2002.

BANCROFT, Steve
(BAN-crawft, STEEV)

Defense. Shoots left. 6'1", 214 lbs. Born, Toronto, Ont., October 6, 1970. Toronto's 3rd choice, 21st overall, in 1989 Entry Draft.

Season	Club	League	GP	G	A	Pts	PIM	PP	SH	GW	S	%	+/-	TF	F%	Min	GP	G	A	Pts	PIM	PP	SH	GW	Min
1985-86	Madoc	OJHL-C	7	1	0	1	21	....	....	....	....	....	....	....	....	....	....	....	....	....	....	....	....	....	....
	Trenton Bobcats	OJHL-B	16	1	5	6	16	....	....	....	....	....	....	....	....	....	....	....	....	....	....	....	....	....	....
1986-87	St. Catharines	OJHL-B	11	5	8	13	20	....	....	....	....	....	....	....	....	....	....	....	....	....	....	....	....	....	....
	Trenton Bobcats	OJHL-B	13	2	3	5	45	....	....	....	....	....	....	....	....	....	....	....	....	....	....	....	....	....	....
1987-88	Belleville Bulls	OHL	56	1	8	9	42	....	....	....	....	....	....	....	....	....	....	....	....	....	....	....	....	....	....
1988-89	Belleville Bulls	OHL	66	7	30	37	99	....	....	....	....	....	....	....	....	....	5	0	2	2	10	....	....	....	....
1989-90	Belleville Bulls	OHL	53	10	33	43	135	....	....	....	....	....	....	....	....	....	11	3	9	12	38	....	....	....	....
1990-91	Newmarket Saints	AHL	9	0	3	3	22	....	....	....	....	....	....	....	....	....	....	....	....	....	....	....	....	....	....
	Maine Mariners	AHL	53	2	12	14	46	....	....	....	....	....	....	....	....	....	2	0	0	0	2	....	....	....	....
1991-92	Maine Mariners	AHL	26	1	3	4	45	....	....	....	....	....	....	....	....	....	....	....	....	....	....	....	....	....	....
	Indianapolis Ice	IHL	36	8	23	31	49	....	....	....	....	....	....	....	....	....	....	....	....	....	....	....	....	....	....
1992-93	**Chicago**	**NHL**	**1**	**0**	**0**	**0**	**0**	**0**	**0**	**0**	**0**	**0.0**	**0**	....	....	....	....	....	....	....	....	....	....	....	....
	Indianapolis Ice	IHL	53	10	35	45	138	....	....	....	....	....	....	....	....	....	....	....	....	....	....	....	....	....	....
	Moncton Hawks	AHL	21	3	13	16	16	....	....	....	....	....	....	....	....	....	5	0	0	0	16	....	....	....	....
1993-94	Cleveland	IHL	33	2	12	14	58	....	....	....	....	....	....	....	....	....	....	....	....	....	....	....	....	....	....
1994-95	Detroit Vipers	IHL	6	1	3	4	0	....	....	....	....	....	....	....	....	....	....	....	....	....	....	....	....	....	....
	Fort Wayne	IHL	50	7	17	24	100	....	....	....	....	....	....	....	....	....	....	....	....	....	....	....	....	....	....
	St. John's	AHL	4	2	0	2	2	....	....	....	....	....	....	....	....	....	5	0	3	3	8	....	....	....	....
1995-96	Los Angeles	IHL	15	3	10	13	22	....	....	....	....	....	....	....	....	....	....	....	....	....	....	....	....	....	....
	Chicago Wolves	IHL	64	9	41	50	91	....	....	....	....	....	....	....	....	....	9	1	7	8	22	....	....	....	....
1996-97	Chicago Wolves	IHL	39	6	10	16	66	....	....	....	....	....	....	....	....	....	....	....	....	....	....	....	....	....	....
	Las Vegas	IHL	36	9	28	37	64	....	....	....	....	....	....	....	....	....	3	0	0	0	2	....	....	....	....
1997-98	Las Vegas	IHL	70	15	44	59	148	....	....	....	....	....	....	....	....	....	....	....	....	....	....	....	....	....	....
	Saint John Flames	AHL	9	0	4	4	12	....	....	....	....	....	....	....	....	....	19	2	11	13	30	....	....	....	....
1998-99	Saint John Flames	AHL	8	1	4	5	22	....	....	....	....	....	....	....	....	....	....	....	....	....	....	....	....	....	....
	Providence Bruins	AHL	62	7	34	41	78	....	....	....	....	....	....	....	....	....	15	0	6	6	28	....	....	....	....
99-2000	Cincinnati	IHL	39	6	14	20	37	....	....	....	....	....	....	....	....	....	....	....	....	....	....	....	....	....	....
	Houston Aeros	IHL	37	2	18	20	47	....	....	....	....	....	....	....	....	....	10	2	6	8	40	....	....	....	....
2000-01	Kentucky	AHL	80	23	50	73	162	....	....	....	....	....	....	....	....	....	3	0	2	2	8	....	....	....	....
2001-02	**San Jose**	**NHL**	**5**	**0**	**1**	**1**	**2**	**0**	**0**	**0**	**5**	**0.0**	**−2**	**0**	**0.0**	**10:24**	....	....	....	....	....	....	....	....	....
	Cleveland Barons	AHL	72	6	38	44	226	....	....	....	....	....	....	....	....	....	....	....	....	....	....	....	....	....	....
2002-03	Worcester IceCats	AHL	21	4	6	10	32	....	....	....	....	....	....	....	....	....	....	....	....	....	....	....	....	....	....
	Binghamton	AHL	29	1	11	12	40	....	....	....	....	....	....	....	....	....	14	0	0	0	12	....	....	....	....
2003-04	Binghamton	AHL	77	7	16	23	131	....	....	....	....	....	....	....	....	....	2	0	0	0	2	....	....	....	....
	NHL Totals		**6**	**0**	**1**	**1**	**2**	**0**	**0**	**0**	**5**	**0.0**		**0**	**0.0**	**10:24**	....	....	....	....	....	....	....	....	....

AHL First All-Star Team (2001)

Traded to **Boston** by **Toronto** for Rob Cimetta, November 9, 1990. Traded to **Chicago** by **Boston** with Boston's 11th round choice (later traded to Winnipeg – Winnipeg selected Russ Hewson) in 1993 Entry Draft for Chicago's 11th round choice (Evgeny Pavlov) in 1992 Entry Draft, January 8, 1992. Traded to **Winnipeg** by **Chicago** with future considerations for Troy Murray, February 21, 1993. Claimed by **Florida** from **Winnipeg** in Expansion Draft, June 24, 1993. Signed as a free agent by **Pittsburgh**, August 2, 1993. Signed as a free agent by **Los Angeles** (IHL), August 30, 1995. Signed as a free agent by **Carolina**, August 4, 1999. Traded to **Houston** (IHL) by **Cincinnati** (IHL) for Brian Felsner with Carolina retaining his NHL rights, January 19, 2000. Signed as a free agent by **San Jose**, August 10, 2000. Signed as a free agent by **St. Louis**, July 16, 2002. Signed as a free agent by **Binghamton** (AHL), November 14, 2003.

BANHAM, Frank
(BAN-ham, FRANK)

Right wing. Shoots right. 6', 190 lbs. Born, Calahoo, Alta., April 14, 1975. Washington's 4th choice, 147th overall, in 1993 Entry Draft.

Season	Club	League	GP	G	A	Pts	PIM	PP	SH	GW	S	%	+/-	TF	F%	Min	GP	G	A	Pts	PIM	PP	SH	GW	Min
1991-92	Fernie Ghostriders	RMJHL	47	45	45	90	120	....	....	....	....	....	....	....	....	....	....	....	....	....	....	....	....	....	....
1992-93	Saskatoon Blades	WHL	71	29	33	62	55	....	....	....	....	....	....	....	....	....	9	2	7	9	8	....	....	....	....
1993-94	Saskatoon Blades	WHL	65	28	39	67	99	....	....	....	....	....	....	....	....	....	16	8	11	19	36	....	....	....	....
1994-95	Saskatoon Blades	WHL	70	50	39	89	63	....	....	....	....	....	....	....	....	....	8	2	6	8	12	....	....	....	....
1995-96	Saskatoon Blades	WHL	72	*83	69	152	116	....	....	....	....	....	....	....	....	....	4	6	0	6	2	....	....	....	....
	Baltimore Bandits	AHL	9	1	4	5	0	....	....	....	....	....	....	....	....	....	7	1	1	2	2	....	....	....	....
1996-97	**Anaheim**	**NHL**	**3**	**0**	**0**	**0**	**0**	**0**	**0**	**0**	**1**	**0.0**	**−2**	....	....	....	....	....	....	....	....	....	....	....	....
	Baltimore Bandits	AHL	21	11	13	24	4	....	....	....	....	....	....	....	....	....	....	....	....	....	....	....	....	....	....
1997-98	**Anaheim**	**NHL**	**21**	**9**	**2**	**11**	**12**	**1**	**0**	**0**	**43**	**20.9**	**−6**	....	....	....	....	....	....	....	....	....	....	....	....
	Cincinnati	AHL	35	7	8	15	39	....	....	....	....	....	....	....	....	....	....	....	....	....	....	....	....	....	....
1998-99	Cincinnati	AHL	66	22	27	49	20	....	....	....	....	....	....	....	....	....	3	0	1	1	0	....	....	....	....
99-2000	**Anaheim**	**NHL**	**3**	**0**	**0**	**0**	**2**	**0**	**0**	**0**	**4**	**0.0**	**0**	**5**	**40.0**	**6:47**	....	....	....	....	....	....	....	....	....
	Cincinnati	AHL	72	19	22	41	58	....	....	....	....	....	....	....	....	....	....	....	....	....	....	....	....	....	....
2000-01	Blues Espoo	Finland	56	24	27	51	70	....	....	....	....	....	....	....	....	....	....	....	....	....	....	....	....	....	....
2001-02	Jokerit Helsinki	Finland	52	22	16	38	38	....	....	....	....	....	....	....	....	....	12	*8	1	9	22	....	....	....	....
2002-03	Jokerit Helsinki	Finland	17	3	4	7	12	....	....	....	....	....	....	....	....	....	....	....	....	....	....	....	....	....	....
	Phoenix	**NHL**	**5**	**0**	**0**	**0**	**2**	**0**	**0**	**0**	**5**	**0.0**	**−1**	**1**	**0.0**	**7:52**	....	....	....	....	....	....	....	....	....
	Springfield	AHL	62	23	17	40	36	....	....	....	....	....	....	....	....	....	6	2	1	3	2	....	....	....	....
2003-04	Springfield	AHL	39	6	8	14	18	....	....	....	....	....	....	....	....	....	....	....	....	....	....	....	....	....	....
	Dynamo Moscow	Russia	6	1	1	2	8	....	....	....	....	....	....	....	....	....	....	....	....	....	....	....	....	....	....
	NHL Totals		**32**	**9**	**2**	**11**	**16**	**1**	**0**	**0**	**53**	**17.0**		**6**	**33.3**	**7:27**	....	....	....	....	....	....	....	....	....

WHL East First All-Star Team (1996)

Signed as a free agent by **Anaheim**, January 27, 1996. Signed as a free agent by **Jokerit Helsinki** (Finland), April 24, 2001. Signed as a free agent by **Phoenix**, November 7, 2002. Signed as a free agent by **Dynamo Moscow** (Russia), February 13, 2004.

BARINKA, Michal
(ba-RIHN-kuh, MIGH-kuhl) **CHI.**

Defense. Shoots left. 6'3", 217 lbs. Born, Vyskov, Czech., June 12, 1984. Chicago's 3rd choice, 59th overall, in 2003 Entry Draft.

Season	Club	League	GP	G	A	Pts	PIM	PP	SH	GW	S	%	+/-	TF	F%	Min	GP	G	A	Pts	PIM	PP	SH	GW	Min
99-2000	HC Budejovice 18	Czech-Jr.	48	1	12	13	26	....	....	....	....	....	....	....	....	....	6	0	2	2	4	....	....	....	....
2000-01	HC Budejovice Jr.	Czech-Jr.	26	1	8	9	14	....	....	....	....	....	....	....	....	....	3	0	0	0	0	....	....	....	....
	HC Budejovice 18	Czech-Jr.	7	0	1	1	6	....	....	....	....	....	....	....	....	....	....	....	....	....	....	....	....	....	....
2001-02	HC Budejovice Jr.	Czech-Jr.	31	3	13	16	60	....	....	....	....	....	....	....	....	....	7	3	4	7	35	....	....	....	....
	Ceske Budejovice	Czech	3	0	0	0	0	....	....	....	....	....	....	....	....	....	....	....	....	....	....	....	....	....	....
2002-03	HC Budejovice Jr.	Czech-Jr.	14	1	5	6	34	....	....	....	....	....	....	....	....	....	....	....	....	....	....	....	....	....	....
	Ceske Budejovice	Czech	31	0	1	1	14	....	....	....	....	....	....	....	....	....	4	0	0	0	2	....	....	....	....
2003-04	**Chicago**	**NHL**	**9**	**0**	**1**	**1**	**6**	**0**	**0**	**0**	**15**	**0.0**	**−5**	**0**	**0.0**	**13:48**	....	....	....	....	....	....	....	....	....
	Norfolk Admirals	AHL	40	4	2	6	80	....	....	....	....	....	....	....	....	....	....	....	....	....	....	....	....	....	....
	NHL Totals		**9**	**0**	**1**	**1**	**6**	**0**	**0**	**0**	**15**	**0.0**		**0**	**0.0**	**13:48**	....	....	....	....	....	....	....	....	....

BARNABY, Matthew
(BAHR-na-BEE, MA-thew) **CHI.**

Right wing. Shoots left. 6', 189 lbs. Born, Ottawa, Ont., May 4, 1973. Buffalo's 5th choice, 83rd overall, in 1992 Entry Draft.

			Regular Season														Playoffs								
Season	Club	League	GP	G	A	Pts	PIM	PP	SH	GW	S	%	+/-	TF	F%	Min	GP	G	A	Pts	PIM	PP	SH	GW	Min
1989-90	Hull Frontaliers	QAHA	50	43	50	93	149	....	....	....	....	....	....	....	....	....	....	....	....	....	....	....	....	....	....
	L'Outaouais	QAAA	2	0	0	0	0	....	....	....	....	....	....	....	....	....	....	....	....	....	....	....	....	....	....
1990-91	Beauport	QMJHL	52	9	5	14	262	....	....	....	....	....	....	....	....	....	....	....	....	....	....	....	....	....	....
1991-92	Beauport	QMJHL	63	29	37	66	*476	....	....	....	....	....	....	....	....	....	....	....	....	....	....	....	....	....	....
1992-93	Victoriaville Tigres	QMJHL	65	44	67	111	*448	....	....	....	....	....	....	....	....	....	6	2	4	6	44	....	....	....	....
	Buffalo	**NHL**	**2**	**1**	**0**	**1**	**10**	**1**	**0**	**0**	**8**	**12.5**	**0**	....	....	....	**1**	**0**	**1**	**1**	**4**	**0**	**0**	**0**	....
1993-94	**Buffalo**	**NHL**	**35**	**2**	**4**	**6**	**106**	**1**	**0**	**0**	**13**	**15.4**	**–7**	....	....	....	**3**	**0**	**0**	**0**	**17**	**0**	**0**	**0**	....
	Rochester	AHL	42	10	32	42	153	....	....	....	....	....	....	....	....	....	....	....	....	....	....	....	....	....	....
1994-95	Rochester	AHL	56	21	29	50	274	....	....	....	....	....	....	....	....	....	....	....	....	....	....	....	....	....	....
	Buffalo	**NHL**	**23**	**1**	**1**	**2**	**116**	**0**	**0**	**0**	**27**	**3.7**	**–2**	....	....	....	....	....	....	....	....	....	....	....	....
1995-96	**Buffalo**	**NHL**	**73**	**15**	**16**	**31**	***335**	**0**	**0**	**0**	**131**	**11.5**	**–2**	....	....	....	....	....	....	....	....	....	....	....	....
1996-97	**Buffalo**	**NHL**	**68**	**19**	**24**	**43**	**249**	**2**	**0**	**1**	**121**	**15.7**	**16**	....	....	....	**8**	**0**	**4**	**4**	**36**	**0**	**0**	**0**	....
1997-98	**Buffalo**	**NHL**	**72**	**5**	**20**	**25**	**289**	**0**	**0**	**2**	**96**	**5.2**	**8**	....	....	....	**15**	**7**	**6**	**13**	**22**	**3**	**0**	**1**	....
1998-99	**Buffalo**	**NHL**	**44**	**4**	**14**	**18**	**143**	**0**	**0**	**3**	**52**	**7.7**	**–2**	**6**	**16.7**	**13:56**	....	....	....	....	....	....	....	....	....
	Pittsburgh	**NHL**	**18**	**2**	**2**	**4**	**34**	**1**	**0**	**0**	**27**	**7.4**	**–10**	**3**	**66.7**	**13:33**	**13**	**0**	**0**	**0**	**35**	**0**	**0**	**0**	**10:27**
99-2000	**Pittsburgh**	**NHL**	**64**	**12**	**12**	**24**	**197**	**0**	**0**	**3**	**80**	**15.0**	**3**	**75**	**44.0**	**12:38**	**11**	**0**	**2**	**2**	**29**	**0**	**0**	**0**	**13:41**
2000-01	**Pittsburgh**	**NHL**	**47**	**1**	**4**	**5**	***168**	**0**	**0**	**0**	**38**	**2.6**	**–7**	**15**	**33.3**	**7:49**	....	....	....	....	....	....	....	....	....
	Tampa Bay	**NHL**	**29**	**4**	**4**	**8**	***97**	**1**	**0**	**0**	**29**	**13.8**	**–3**	**1**	**100.0**	**12:34**	....	....	....	....	....	....	....	....	....
2001-02	**Tampa Bay**	**NHL**	**29**	**0**	**0**	**0**	**70**	**0**	**0**	**0**	**13**	**0.0**	**–7**	**1**	**0.0**	**7:54**	....	....	....	....	....	....	....	....	....
	NY Rangers	**NHL**	**48**	**8**	**13**	**21**	**144**	**0**	**0**	**1**	**56**	**14.3**	**–3**	**12**	**33.3**	**11:24**	....	....	....	....	....	....	....	....	....
2002-03	**NY Rangers**	**NHL**	**79**	**14**	**22**	**36**	**142**	**1**	**0**	**1**	**104**	**13.5**	**9**	**5**	**40.0**	**13:00**	....	....	....	....	....	....	....	....	....
2003-04	**NY Rangers**	**NHL**	**69**	**12**	**20**	**32**	**120**	**0**	**0**	**1**	**80**	**15.0**	**15**	**23**	**43.5**	**11:49**	....	....	....	....	....	....	....	....	....
	Colorado	**NHL**	**13**	**4**	**5**	**9**	**37**	**1**	**0**	**2**	**24**	**16.7**	**3**	**1**	**100.0**	**15:25**	**11**	**0**	**2**	**2**	**27**	**0**	**0**	**0**	**12:22**
	NHL Totals		**713**	**104**	**161**	**265**	**2257**	**8**	**0**	**14**	**899**	**11.6**		**142**	**41.5**	**11:51**	**62**	**7**	**15**	**22**	**170**	**3**	**0**	**1**	**12:04**

Traded to **Pittsburgh** by **Buffalo** for Stu Barnes, March 11, 1999. Traded to **Tampa Bay** by **Pittsburgh** for Wayne Primeau, February 1, 2001. Traded to **NY Rangers** by **Tampa Bay** for Zdeno Ciger, December 12, 2001. Traded to **Colorado** by **NY Rangers** with NY Rangers' 3rd round choice (Denis Parshin) in 2004 Entry Draft for Chris McAllister, David Liffiton and Florida's 2nd round choice (previously acquired, later traded back to Florida – Florida selected David Shantz) in 2004 Entry Draft, March 8, 2004. Signed as a free agent by **Chicago**, July 2, 2004.

BARNES, Ryan
(BAHR-nz, RIGH-uhn) **DET.**

Left wing. Shoots left. 6'1", 201 lbs. Born, Dunnville, Ont., January 30, 1980. Detroit's 2nd choice, 55th overall, in 1998 Entry Draft.

Season	Club	League	GP	G	A	Pts	PIM	PP	SH	GW	S	%	+/-	TF	F%	Min	GP	G	A	Pts	PIM	PP	SH	GW	Min
1996-97	Quinte Hawks	MTJHL	46	15	19	34	245	....	....	....	....	....	....	....	....	....	....	....	....	....	....	....	....	....	....
1997-98	Sudbury Wolves	OHL	46	13	18	31	111	....	....	....	....	....	....	....	....	....	10	0	2	2	24	....	....	....	....
1998-99	Sudbury Wolves	OHL	8	2	0	2	23	....	....	....	....	....	....	....	....	....	....	....	....	....	....	....	....	....	....
	St. Michael's	OHL	31	11	14	25	*215	....	....	....	....	....	....	....	....	....	....	....	....	....	....	....	....	....	....
	Barrie Colts	OHL	24	16	14	30	*161	....	....	....	....	....	....	....	....	....	12	2	4	6	40	....	....	....	....
99-2000	Barrie Colts	OHL	31	17	12	29	98	....	....	....	....	....	....	....	....	....	25	7	7	14	49	....	....	....	....
2000-01	Cincinnati	AHL	1	0	0	0	7	....	....	....	....	....	....	....	....	....	....	....	....	....	....	....	....	....	....
	Toledo Storm	ECHL	16	2	4	6	31	....	....	....	....	....	....	....	....	....	....	....	....	....	....	....	....	....	....
2001-02	Toledo Storm	ECHL	1	1	0	1	0	....	....	....	....	....	....	....	....	....	....	....	....	....	....	....	....	....	....
	Cincinnati	AHL	46	2	3	5	152	....	....	....	....	....	....	....	....	....	....	....	....	....	....	....	....	....	....
2002-03	Grand Rapids	AHL	73	5	6	11	151	....	....	....	....	....	....	....	....	....	15	1	1	2	17	....	....	....	....
2003-04	**Detroit**	**NHL**	**2**	**0**	**0**	**0**	**0**	**0**	**0**	**0**	**0**	**0.0**	**0**	**0**	**0.0**	**2:22**	....	....	....	....	....	....	....	....	....
	Grand Rapids	AHL	69	6	13	19	175	....	....	....	....	....	....	....	....	....	4	0	0	0	7	....	....	....	....
	NHL Totals		**2**	**0**	**0**	**0**	**0**	**0**	**0**	**0**	**0**	**0.0**		**0**	**0.0**	**2:22**	....	....	....	....	....	....	....	....	....

• Missed majority of 2000-01 season recovering from head injury suffered in training camp, September, 2000.

BARNES, Stu
(BAHRNZ, STEW) **DAL.**

Center. Shoots right. 5'11", 180 lbs. Born, Spruce Grove, Alta., December 25, 1970. Winnipeg's 1st choice, 4th overall, in 1989 Entry Draft.

Season	Club	League	GP	G	A	Pts	PIM	PP	SH	GW	S	%	+/-	TF	F%	Min	GP	G	A	Pts	PIM	PP	SH	GW	Min
1986-87	St. Albert Saints	AJHL	53	41	34	*75	103	....	....	....	....	....	....	....	....	....	19	7	15	22	....	....	....	....	....
1987-88	New Westminster	WHL	71	37	64	101	88	....	....	....	....	....	....	....	....	....	5	2	3	5	6	....	....	....	....
1988-89	Tri-City	WHL	70	59	82	141	117	....	....	....	....	....	....	....	....	....	7	6	5	11	10	....	....	....	....
1989-90	Tri-City	WHL	63	52	92	144	165	....	....	....	....	....	....	....	....	....	7	1	5	6	26	....	....	....	....
1990-91	Team Canada	Nat-Tm	53	22	27	49	68	....	....	....	....	....	....	....	....	....	....	....	....	....	....	....	....	....	....
1991-92	**Winnipeg**	**NHL**	**46**	**8**	**9**	**17**	**26**	**4**	**0**	**0**	**75**	**10.7**	**–2**	....	....	....	....	....	....	....	....	....	....	....	....
	Moncton Hawks	AHL	30	13	19	32	10	....	....	....	....	....	....	....	....	....	11	3	9	12	6	....	....	....	....
1992-93	**Winnipeg**	**NHL**	**38**	**12**	**10**	**22**	**10**	**3**	**0**	**3**	**73**	**16.4**	**–3**	....	....	....	**6**	**1**	**3**	**4**	**2**	**0**	**0**	**0**	....
	Moncton Hawks	AHL	42	23	31	54	58	....	....	....	....	....	....	....	....	....	....	....	....	....	....	....	....	....	....
1993-94	**Winnipeg**	**NHL**	**18**	**5**	**4**	**9**	**8**	**2**	**0**	**0**	**24**	**20.8**	**–1**	....	....	....	....	....	....	....	....	....	....	....	....
	Florida	**NHL**	**59**	**18**	**20**	**38**	**30**	**6**	**1**	**3**	**148**	**12.2**	**5**	....	....	....	....	....	....	....	....	....	....	....	....
1994-95	**Florida**	**NHL**	**41**	**10**	**19**	**29**	**8**	**1**	**0**	**2**	**93**	**10.8**	**7**	....	....	....	....	....	....	....	....	....	....	....	....
1995-96	**Florida**	**NHL**	**72**	**19**	**25**	**44**	**46**	**8**	**0**	**5**	**158**	**12.0**	**–12**	....	....	....	**22**	**6**	**10**	**16**	**4**	**2**	**0**	**2**	....
1996-97	**Florida**	**NHL**	**19**	**2**	**8**	**10**	**10**	**1**	**0**	**0**	**44**	**4.5**	**–3**	....	....	....	....	....	....	....	....	....	....	....	....
	Pittsburgh	**NHL**	**62**	**17**	**22**	**39**	**16**	**4**	**0**	**3**	**132**	**12.9**	**–20**	....	....	....	**5**	**0**	**1**	**1**	**0**	**0**	**0**	**0**	....
1997-98	**Pittsburgh**	**NHL**	**78**	**30**	**35**	**65**	**30**	**15**	**1**	**5**	**196**	**15.3**	**15**	....	....	....	**6**	**3**	**3**	**6**	**2**	**0**	**0**	**1**	....
1998-99	**Pittsburgh**	**NHL**	**64**	**20**	**12**	**32**	**20**	**13**	**0**	**3**	**155**	**12.9**	**–12**	**720**	**51.9**	**17:52**	....	....	....	....	....	....	....	....	....
	Buffalo	**NHL**	**17**	**0**	**4**	**4**	**10**	**0**	**0**	**0**	**25**	**0.0**	**1**	**236**	**51.3**	**18:20**	**21**	**7**	**3**	**10**	**6**	**4**	**0**	**1**	**14:40**
99-2000	**Buffalo**	**NHL**	**82**	**20**	**25**	**45**	**16**	**8**	**2**	**2**	**137**	**14.6**	**–3**	**778**	**48.5**	**17:23**	**5**	**3**	**0**	**3**	**2**	**2**	**0**	**1**	**17:02**
2000-01	**Buffalo**	**NHL**	**75**	**19**	**24**	**43**	**26**	**3**	**2**	**5**	**160**	**11.9**	**–2**	**1470**	**48.3**	**19:06**	**13**	**4**	**4**	**8**	**2**	**2**	**0**	**2**	**18:30**
2001-02	**Buffalo**	**NHL**	**68**	**17**	**31**	**48**	**26**	**5**	**0**	**4**	**127**	**13.4**	**6**	**984**	**47.2**	**18:35**	....	....	....	....	....	....	....	....	....
2002-03	**Buffalo**	**NHL**	**68**	**11**	**21**	**32**	**20**	**2**	**1**	**2**	**124**	**8.9**	**–13**	**923**	**49.0**	**18:29**	....	....	....	....	....	....	....	....	....
	Dallas	**NHL**	**13**	**2**	**5**	**7**	**8**	**2**	**0**	**1**	**25**	**8.0**	**2**	**76**	**44.7**	**17:23**	**12**	**2**	**3**	**5**	**0**	**0**	**0**	**2**	**19:06**
2003-04	**Dallas**	**NHL**	**77**	**11**	**18**	**29**	**18**	**0**	**1**	**4**	**135**	**8.1**	**7**	**879**	**52.9**	**18:05**	**5**	**0**	**0**	**0**	**0**	**0**	**0**	**0**	**14:59**
	NHL Totals		**897**	**221**	**292**	**513**	**328**	**77**	**8**	**42**	**1831**	**12.1**		**6066**	**49.4**	**18:13**	**95**	**26**	**27**	**53**	**18**	**10**	**0**	**9**	**16:45**

WHL West Second All-Star Team (1988, 1989) • WHL Rookie of the Year (1988) • WHL MVP (1989)

Traded to **Florida** by **Winnipeg** with St. Louis' 6th round choice (previously acquired, later traded to Edmonton – later traded back to Winnipeg – Winnipeg selected Chris Kibermanis) in 1994 Entry Draft for Randy Gilhen, November 25, 1993. Traded to **Pittsburgh** by **Florida** with Jason Woolley for Chris Wells, November 19, 1996. Traded to **Buffalo** by **Pittsburgh** for Matthew Barnaby, March 11, 1999. Traded to **Dallas** by **Buffalo** for Michael Ryan and Dallas's 2nd round choice (Branislav Fabry) in 2003 Entry Draft, March 10, 2003.

BARNEY, Scott
(BAHR-nee, SKAWT) **L.A.**

Center. Shoots right. 6'4", 208 lbs. Born, Oshawa, Ont., March 27, 1979. Los Angeles' 3rd choice, 29th overall, in 1997 Entry Draft.

Season	Club	League	GP	G	A	Pts	PIM	PP	SH	GW	S	%	+/-	TF	F%	Min	GP	G	A	Pts	PIM	PP	SH	GW	Min
1994-95	North York	MTJHL	41	16	19	35	88	....	....	....	....	....	....	....	....	....	....	....	....	....	....	....	....	....	....
1995-96	Peterborough	OHL	60	22	24	46	52	....	....	....	....	....	....	....	....	....	24	6	8	14	38	....	....	....	....
1996-97	Peterborough	OHL	64	21	33	54	110	....	....	....	....	....	....	....	....	....	9	0	3	3	16	....	....	....	....
1997-98	Peterborough	OHL	62	44	32	76	60	....	....	....	....	....	....	....	....	....	4	1	0	1	6	....	....	....	....
1998-99	Peterborough	OHL	44	41	26	67	80	....	....	....	....	....	....	....	....	....	5	4	1	5	4	....	....	....	....
	Springfield	AHL	5	0	0	0	2	....	....	....	....	....	....	....	....	....	1	0	0	0	2	....	....	....	....
99-2000			DID NOT PLAY – INJURED																						
2000-01			DID NOT PLAY – INJURED																						
2001-02			DID NOT PLAY – INJURED																						
2002-03	**Los Angeles**	**NHL**	**5**	**0**	**0**	**0**	**0**	**0**	**0**	**0**	**5**	**0.0**	**–1**	**0**	**0.0**	**9:04**	....	....	....	....	....	....	....	....	....
	Manchester	AHL	57	13	5	18	74	....	....	....	....	....	....	....	....	....	....	....	....	....	....	....	....	....	....
2003-04	**Los Angeles**	**NHL**	**19**	**5**	**6**	**11**	**4**	**2**	**0**	**0**	**31**	**16.1**	**3**	**7**	**14.3**	**11:12**	....	....	....	....	....	....	....	....	....
	Manchester	AHL	44	20	14	34	28	....	....	....	....	....	....	....	....	....	6	2	3	5	8	....	....	....	....
	NHL Totals		**24**	**5**	**6**	**11**	**4**	**2**	**0**	**0**	**36**	**13.9**		**7**	**14.3**	**10:46**	....	....	....	....	....	....	....	....	....

• Missed entire 1999-2000, 2000-01 and 2001-02 seasons recovering from back injury suffered in training camp, September 28, 1999.

BARON, Murray

(BAIR-uhn, MUHR-ray)

Defense. Shoots left. 6'3", 215 lbs. Born, Prince George, B.C., June 1, 1967. Philadelphia's 7th choice, 167th overall, in 1986 Entry Draft.

			Regular Season													Playoffs								
Season	Club	League	GP	G	A	Pts	PIM	PP	SH	GW	S	%	+/-	TF	F%	Min	GP	G	A	Pts	PIM	PP	SH	GW	Min
1984-85	Vernon Lakers	BCJHL	37	5	9	14	93	....	....	....	....	....	....	....	....	....	13	5	6	11	107	....	....	....	....
1985-86	Vernon Lakers	BCJHL	46	12	32	44	179	....	....	....	....	....	....	....	....	....	7	1	2	3	13	....	....	....	....
1986-87	North Dakota	WCHA	41	4	10	14	62	....	....	....	....	....	....	....	....	....	....	....	....	....	....	....	....	....	....
1987-88	North Dakota	WCHA	41	1	10	11	95	....	....	....	....	....	....	....	....	....	....	....	....	....	....	....	....	....	....
1988-89	North Dakota	WCHA	40	2	6	8	92	....	....	....	....	....	....	....	....	....	....	....	....	....	....	....	....	....	....
	Hershey Bears	AHL	9	0	3	3	8	....	....	....	....	....	....	....	....	....	....	....	....	....	....	....	....	....	....
1989-90	Philadelphia	NHL	16	2	2	4	12	0	0	0	18	11.1	-1	....	....	....	....	....	....	....	....	....	....	....	....
	Hershey Bears	AHL	50	0	10	10	101	....	....	....	....	....	....	....	....	....	....	....	....	....	....	....	....	....	....
1990-91	Philadelphia	NHL	67	8	8	16	74	3	0	1	86	9.3	-3	....	....	....	....	....	....	....	....	....	....	....	....
	Hershey Bears	AHL	6	2	3	5	0	....	....	....	....	....	....	....	....	....	....	....	....	....	....	....	....	....	....
1991-92	St. Louis	NHL	67	3	8	11	94	0	0	0	55	5.5	-3	....	....	....	2	0	0	0	2	0	0	0	....
1992-93	St. Louis	NHL	53	2	2	4	59	0	0	1	42	4.8	-5	....	....	....	11	0	0	0	12	0	0	0	....
1993-94	St. Louis	NHL	77	5	9	14	123	0	0	0	73	6.8	-14	....	....	....	4	0	0	0	10	0	0	0	....
1994-95	St. Louis	NHL	39	0	5	5	93	0	0	0	28	0.0	9	....	....	....	7	1	1	2	2	0	0	0	....
1995-96	St. Louis	NHL	82	2	9	11	190	0	0	0	86	2.3	3	....	....	....	13	1	0	1	20	0	1	0	....
1996-97	St. Louis	NHL	11	0	2	2	11	0	0	0	7	0.0	-4	....	....	....	....	....	....	....	....	....	....	....	....
	Montreal	NHL	60	1	5	6	107	0	0	0	52	1.9	-16	....	....	....	....	....	....	....	....	....	....	....	....
	Phoenix	NHL	8	0	0	0	4	0	0	0	5	0.0	0	....	....	....	1	0	0	0	0	0	0	0	....
1997-98	Phoenix	NHL	45	1	5	6	106	0	0	0	23	4.3	-10	....	....	....	6	0	2	2	6	0	0	0	....
1998-99	Vancouver	NHL	81	2	6	8	115	0	0	0	53	3.8	-23	0	0.0	18:14	....	....	....	....	....	....	....	....	....
99-2000	Vancouver	NHL	81	2	10	12	67	0	0	0	48	4.2	8	2	50.0	21:36	....	....	....	....	....	....	....	....	....
2000-01	Vancouver	NHL	82	3	8	11	63	0	0	1	56	5.4	-13	3	66.7	19:24	4	0	0	0	0	0	0	0	22:16
2001-02	Vancouver	NHL	61	1	6	7	68	0	0	0	38	2.6	8	2	50.0	16:57	6	0	1	1	10	0	0	0	12:30
2002-03	Vancouver	NHL	78	2	4	6	62	0	0	0	34	5.9	13	0	0.0	17:01	14	0	4	4	10	0	0	0	17:34
2003-04	St. Louis	NHL	80	1	5	6	61	0	0	0	57	1.8	-6	0	0.0	19:14	5	0	0	0	6	0	0	0	18:55
	NHL Totals		988	35	94	129	1309	3	0	3	761	4.6		7	57.1	18:50	73	2	8	10	78	0	1	0	17:24

Traded to **St. Louis** by **Philadelphia** with Ron Sutter for Dan Quinn and Rod Brind'Amour, September 22, 1991. Traded to **Montreal** by **St. Louis** with Shayne Corson and St. Louis' 5th round choice (Gennady Razin) in 1997 Entry Draft for Pierre Turgeon, Rory Fitzpatrick and Craig Conroy, October 29, 1996. Traded to **Phoenix** by **Montreal** with Chris Murray for Dave Manson, March 18, 1997. Signed as a free agent by **Vancouver**, July 14, 1998. Signed as a free agent by **St. Louis**, September 5, 2003.

BARTECKO, Lubos

(bahr-TESHK-oh, LOO-bohsh)

Left wing. Shoots left. 5'11", 200 lbs. Born, Kezmarok, Czech., July 14, 1976.

Season	Club	League	GP	G	A	Pts	PIM	PP	SH	GW	S	%	+/-	TF	F%	Min	GP	G	A	Pts	PIM	PP	SH	GW	Min
1994-95	HK SKP Poprad	Slovakia	3	1	0	1	0	....	....	....	....	....	....	....	....	....	....	....	....	....	....	....	....	....	....
1995-96	Chicoutimi	QMJHL	70	32	41	73	50	....	....	....	....	....	....	....	....	....	17	8	15	23	10	....	....	....	....
1996-97	Drummondville	QMJHL	58	40	51	91	49	....	....	....	....	....	....	....	....	....	8	1	8	9	4	....	....	....	....
1997-98	Worcester IceCats	AHL	34	10	12	22	24	....	....	....	....	....	....	....	....	....	10	4	2	6	2	....	....	....	....
1998-99	HC SKP Poprad	Slovakia	1	1	0	1	0	....	....	....	....	....	....	....	....	....	....	....	....	....	....	....	....	....	....
	St. Louis	NHL	32	5	11	16	6	0	0	1	37	13.5	4	0	0.0	13:13	5	0	0	0	2	0	0	0	13:29
	Worcester IceCats	AHL	49	14	24	38	22	....	....	....	....	....	....	....	....	....	....	....	....	....	....	....	....	....	....
99-2000	St. Louis	NHL	67	16	23	39	51	3	0	3	75	21.3	24	10	50.0	13:33	7	1	1	2	0	0	0	0	12:02
	Worcester IceCats	AHL	12	4	7	11	4	....	....	....	....	....	....	....	....	....	....	....	....	....	....	....	....	....	....
2000-01	St. Louis	NHL	50	5	8	13	12	0	0	3	51	9.8	-1	2	50.0	10:25	....	....	....	....	....	....	....	....	....
2001-02	Atlanta	NHL	71	13	14	27	30	1	0	0	96	13.5	-15	4	25.0	14:28	....	....	....	....	....	....	....	....	....
	Slovakia	Olympics	4	0	1	1	0	....	....	....	....	....	....	....	....	....	....	....	....	....	....	....	....	....	....
2002-03	Atlanta	NHL	37	7	9	16	8	0	0	1	54	13.0	3	6	100.0	12:31	....	....	....	....	....	....	....	....	....
2003-04	HC Sparta Praha	Czech	25	12	8	20	45	....	....	....	....	....	....	....	....	....	13	2	4	6	26	....	....	....	....
	NHL Totals		257	46	65	111	107	4	0	8	313	14.7		22	59.1	13:00	12	1	1	2	2	0	0	0	12:39

Signed as a free agent by **St. Louis**, October 3, 1997. Traded to **Atlanta** by **St. Louis** for Buffalo's 4th round choice (previously acquired, St. Louis selected Igor Valeyev) in 2001 Entry Draft, June 23, 2001. • Missed majority of 2002-03 season recovering from wrist (November 2, 2002 vs. Florida) and groin (January 13, 2003 vs. Philadelphia) injuries. Signed as a free agent by **HC Sparta Praha** (Czech), November 2, 2003.

BARTOVIC, Milan

(BAHR-tuh-vihch, MIH-lan) **BUF.**

Right wing. Shoots left. 5'11", 192 lbs. Born, Trencin, Czech., April 9, 1981. Buffalo's 2nd choice, 35th overall, in 1999 Entry Draft.

Season	Club	League	GP	G	A	Pts	PIM	PP	SH	GW	S	%	+/-	TF	F%	Min	GP	G	A	Pts	PIM	PP	SH	GW	Min
1997-98	Dukla Trencin Jr.	Slovak-Jr.	26	2	6	8	27	....	....	....	....	....	....	....	....	....	....	....	....	....	....	....	....	....	....
1998-99	Dukla Trencin Jr.	Slovak-Jr.	46	36	35	71	62	....	....	....	....	....	....	....	....	....	6	9	3	12	10	....	....	....	....
99-2000	Tri-City	WHL	18	8	9	17	12	....	....	....	....	....	....	....	....	....	....	....	....	....	....	....	....	....	....
	Brandon	WHL	38	18	22	40	28	....	....	....	....	....	....	....	....	....	....	....	....	....	....	....	....	....	....
2000-01	Brandon	WHL	34	15	25	40	40	....	....	....	....	....	....	....	....	....	6	1	2	3	8	....	....	....	....
	Rochester	AHL	2	1	1	2	0	....	....	....	....	....	....	....	....	....	4	0	1	1	2	....	....	....	....
2001-02	Rochester	AHL	73	15	11	26	56	....	....	....	....	....	....	....	....	....	2	0	0	0	0	....	....	....	....
2002-03	Buffalo	NHL	3	1	0	1	0	0	0	0	5	20.0	0	1	100.0	9:52	....	....	....	....	....	....	....	....	....
	Rochester	AHL	74	18	10	28	84	....	....	....	....	....	....	....	....	....	3	0	0	0	0	....	....	....	....
2003-04	Buffalo	NHL	23	1	8	9	18	0	0	0	30	3.3	1	2	100.0	12:53	....	....	....	....	....	....	....	....	....
	Rochester	AHL	52	18	11	29	52	....	....	....	....	....	....	....	....	....	2	0	0	0	2	....	....	....	....
	NHL Totals		26	2	8	10	18	0	0	0	35	5.7		3	100.0	12:32	....	....	....	....	....	....	....	....	....

• Missed majority of 2000-01 season recovering from shoulder injury suffered in game vs. Red Deer (WHL), October 10, 2000.

BATES, Shawn

(BAYTS, SHAWN) **NYI**

Center. Shoots right. 6', 205 lbs. Born, Melrose, MA, April 3, 1975. Boston's 4th choice, 103rd overall, in 1993 Entry Draft.

Season	Club	League	GP	G	A	Pts	PIM	PP	SH	GW	S	%	+/-	TF	F%	Min	GP	G	A	Pts	PIM	PP	SH	GW	Min
1990-91	Medford	Hi-School	22	18	43	61	6	....	....	....	....	....	....	....	....	....	....	....	....	....	....	....	....	....	....
1991-92	Medford	Hi-School	22	38	41	79	10	....	....	....	....	....	....	....	....	....	....	....	....	....	....	....	....	....	....
1992-93	Medford	Hi-School	25	49	46	95	20	....	....	....	....	....	....	....	....	....	....	....	....	....	....	....	....	....	....
1993-94	Boston University	H-East	41	10	19	29	24	....	....	....	....	....	....	....	....	....	....	....	....	....	....	....	....	....	....
1994-95	Boston University	H-East	38	18	12	30	48	....	....	....	....	....	....	....	....	....	....	....	....	....	....	....	....	....	....
1995-96	Boston University	H-East	40	28	22	50	54	....	....	....	....	....	....	....	....	....	....	....	....	....	....	....	....	....	....
1996-97	Boston University	H-East	41	17	18	35	64	....	....	....	....	....	....	....	....	....	....	....	....	....	....	....	....	....	....
1997-98	Boston	NHL	13	2	0	2	2	0	0	0	12	16.7	-3	....	....	....	....	....	....	....	....	....	....	....	....
	Providence Bruins	AHL	50	15	19	34	22	....	....	....	....	....	....	....	....	....	....	....	....	....	....	....	....	....	....
1998-99	Boston	NHL	33	5	4	9	2	0	0	0	30	16.7	3	178	51.1	8:35	12	0	0	0	4	0	0	0	5:12
	Providence Bruins	AHL	37	25	21	46	39	....	....	....	....	....	....	....	....	....	....	....	....	....	....	....	....	....	....
99-2000	Boston	NHL	44	5	7	12	14	0	0	1	65	7.7	-17	460	47.0	10:52	....	....	....	....	....	....	....	....	....
2000-01	Boston	NHL	45	2	3	5	26	0	0	0	59	3.4	-12	413	50.6	9:19	....	....	....	....	....	....	....	....	....
	Providence Bruins	AHL	11	5	8	13	12	....	....	....	....	....	....	....	....	....	8	2	6	8	8	....	....	....	....
2001-02	NY Islanders	NHL	71	17	35	52	30	1	4	4	150	11.3	18	306	49.4	18:45	7	2	4	6	11	1	0	1	20:27
2002-03	NY Islanders	NHL	74	13	29	42	52	1	6	1	126	10.3	-9	398	57.0	18:26	5	1	0	1	0	1	0	0	18:36
2003-04	NY Islanders	NHL	69	9	23	32	46	0	1	1	115	7.8	-8	603	55.9	18:26	5	0	0	0	4	0	0	0	17:14
	NHL Totals		349	53	101	154	172	2	11	7	557	9.5		2358	52.2	15:19	29	3	4	7	19	2	0	1	13:16

NCAA Championship All-Tournament Team (1995)

Signed as a free agent by **NY Islanders**, July 8, 2001.

BATTAGLIA, Bates

(buh-TAG-lee-ah, BAYTS)

Left wing. Shoots left. 6'2", 205 lbs. Born, Chicago, IL, December 13, 1975. Anaheim's 6th choice, 132nd overall, in 1994 Entry Draft.

Season	Club	League	GP	G	A	Pts	PIM	PP	SH	GW	S	%	+/-	TF	F%	Min	GP	G	A	Pts	PIM	PP	SH	GW	Min
1992-93	Team Illinois	MEHL	60	42	42	84	68	....	....	....	....	....	....	....	....	....	....	....	....	....	....	....	....	....	....
1993-94	Caledon	MTJHL	44	15	33	48	104	....	....	....	....	....	....	....	....	....	....	....	....	....	....	....	....	....	....
1994-95	Lake Superior	CCHA	38	6	14	20	34	....	....	....	....	....	....	....	....	....	....	....	....	....	....	....	....	....	....
1995-96	Lake Superior	CCHA	40	13	22	35	48	....	....	....	....	....	....	....	....	....	....	....	....	....	....	....	....	....	....
1996-97	Lake Superior	CCHA	38	12	27	39	80	....	....	....	....	....	....	....	....	....	....	....	....	....	....	....	....	....	....
1997-98	Carolina	NHL	33	2	4	6	10	0	0	1	21	9.5	-1	....	....	....	....	....	....	....	....	....	....	....	....
	New Haven	AHL	48	15	21	36	48	....	....	....	....	....	....	....	....	....	1	0	0	0	0	....	....	....	....
1998-99	Carolina	NHL	60	7	11	18	97	0	0	0	52	13.5	7	144	39.6	9:53	6	0	3	3	8	0	0	0	15:22
99-2000	Carolina	NHL	77	16	18	34	39	3	0	3	86	18.6	20	23	26.1	15:12	....	....	....	....	....	....	....	....	....
2000-01	Carolina	NHL	80	12	15	27	76	2	0	3	133	9.0	-14	5	60.0	14:28	6	0	2	2	2	0	0	0	11:25
2001-02	Carolina	NHL	82	21	25	46	44	5	1	2	167	12.6	-6	12	33.3	19:05	23	5	9	14	14	1	0	1	20:42

			Regular Season														Playoffs								
Season	Club	League	GP	G	A	Pts	PIM	PP	SH	GW	S	%	+/-	TF	F%	Min	GP	G	A	Pts	PIM	PP	SH	GW	Min
2002-03	Carolina	NHL	70	5	14	19	90	0	1	1	96	5.2	–17	16	25.0	18:39	....	....	....	....	....	....	....	....	....
	Colorado	NHL	13	1	5	6	10	1	0	1	27	3.7	–2	3	0.0	15:19	7	0	2	2	4	0	0	0	14:39
2003-04	Colorado	NHL	4	0	1	1	4	0	0	0	1	0.0	–1	1	100.0	11:04	....	....	....	....	....	....	....	....	....
	Washington	NHL	66	4	6	10	38	0	0	1	69	5.8	–23	116	32.8	13:37	....	....	....	....	....	....	....	....	....
	NHL Totals		485	68	99	167	408	11	2	12	652	10.4		320	35.3	15:20	42	5	16	21	28	1	0	1	17:36

Traded to **Hartford** by **Anaheim** with Anaheim's 4th round choice (Josef Vasicek) in 1998 Entry Draft for Mark Janssens, March 18, 1997. Rights transferred to **Carolina** after **Hartford** franchise relocated, June 25, 1997. Traded to **Colorado** by **Carolina** for Radim Vrbata, March 11, 2003. Traded to **Washington** by **Colorado** with Jonas Johansson for Steve Konowalchuk and Washington's 3rd round choice (later traded to Carolina – Carolina selected Casey Borer) in 2004 Entry Draft, October 22, 2003.

BAUMGARTNER, Nolan

(BAWM-gahrt-nuhr, NOH-lan) **VAN.**

Defense. Shoots right. 6'2", 205 lbs. Born, Calgary, Alta., March 23, 1976. Washington's 1st choice, 10th overall, in 1994 Entry Draft.

Season	Club	League	GP	G	A	Pts	PIM	PP	SH	GW	S	%	+/-	TF	F%	Min	GP	G	A	Pts	PIM	PP	SH	GW	Min
1991-92	Calgary Flames	AMHL	39	11	29	40	40	....	....	....	....	....	....	....	....	....	....	....	....	....	....	....	....	....	....
1992-93	Kamloops Blazers	WHL	43	0	5	5	30	....	....	....	....	....	....	....	....	....	11	1	1	2	0	....	....	....	....
1993-94	Kamloops Blazers	WHL	69	13	42	55	109	....	....	....	....	....	....	....	....	....	19	3	14	17	33	....	....	....	....
1994-95	Kamloops Blazers	WHL	62	8	36	44	71	....	....	....	....	....	....	....	....	....	21	4	13	17	16	....	....	....	....
1995-96	Kamloops Blazers	WHL	28	13	15	28	45	....	....	....	....	....	....	....	....	....	16	1	9	10	26	....	....	....	....
	Washington	NHL	1	0	0	0	0	0	0	0	0	0.0	–1	....	....	....	1	0	0	0	10	0	0	0	....
1996-97	Portland Pirates	AHL	8	2	2	4	4	....	....	....	....	....	....	....	....	....	....	....	....	....	....	....	....	....	....
1997-98	Washington	NHL	4	0	1	1	0	0	0	0	4	0.0	0	....	....	....	....	....	....	....	....	....	....	....	....
	Portland Pirates	AHL	70	2	24	26	70	....	....	....	....	....	....	....	....	....	10	1	4	5	10	....	....	....	....
1998-99	Washington	NHL	5	0	0	0	0	0	0	0	1	0.0	–3	0	0.0	8:41	....	....	....	....	....	....	....	....	....
	Portland Pirates	AHL	38	5	14	19	62	....	....	....	....	....	....	....	....	....	....	....	....	....	....	....	....	....	....
99-2000	Washington	NHL	8	0	1	1	2	0	0	0	6	0.0	1	0	0.0	10:31	....	....	....	....	....	....	....	....	....
	Portland Pirates	AHL	71	5	18	23	56	....	....	....	....	....	....	....	....	....	4	1	2	3	10	....	....	....	....
2000-01	Chicago	NHL	8	0	0	0	6	0	0	0	7	0.0	–4	2	50.0	12:40	....	....	....	....	....	....	....	....	....
	Norfolk Admirals	AHL	63	5	28	33	75	....	....	....	....	....	....	....	....	....	9	2	3	5	11	....	....	....	....
2001-02	Norfolk Admirals	AHL	76	10	24	34	72	....	....	....	....	....	....	....	....	....	4	0	1	1	2	....	....	....	....
2002-03	Vancouver	NHL	8	1	2	3	4	1	0	0	7	14.3	4	0	0.0	11:36	2	0	0	0	0	0	0	0	11:06
	Manitoba Moose	AHL	59	8	31	39	82	....	....	....	....	....	....	....	....	....	1	0	0	0	4	....	....	....	....
2003-04	Pittsburgh	NHL	5	0	0	0	2	0	0	0	6	0.0	–7	0	0.0	19:20	....	....	....	....	....	....	....	....	....
	Vancouver	NHL	9	0	3	3	2	0	0	0	9	0.0	3	0	0.0	11:52	....	....	....	....	....	....	....	....	....
	Manitoba Moose	AHL	55	6	21	27	101	....	....	....	....	....	....	....	....	....	....	....	....	....	....	....	....	....	....
	NHL Totals		48	1	7	8	16	1	0	0	40	2.5		2	50.0	12:13	3	0	0	0	10	0	0	0	11:06

Memorial Cup All-Star Team (1994, 1995) • WHL West First All-Star Team (1995, 1996) • Canadian Major Junior First All-Star Team (1995) • Canadian Major Junior Defenseman of the Year (1995)

Traded to **Chicago** by **Washington** for Remi Royer, July 20, 2000. Signed as a free agent by **Vancouver**, July 11, 2002. Claimed by **Pittsburgh** from **Vancouver** in Waiver Draft, October 3, 2003. Claimed on waivers by **Vancouver** from **Pittsburgh**, November 1, 2003. Signed as a free agent by **Frankfurt** (Germany), April 25, 2004.

BAYDA, Ryan

(BAY-duh, RIGH-uhn) **CAR.**

Left wing. Shoots left. 5'11", 185 lbs. Born, Saskatoon, Sask., December 9, 1980. Carolina's 2nd choice, 80th overall, in 2000 Entry Draft.

Season	Club	League	GP	G	A	Pts	PIM	PP	SH	GW	S	%	+/-	TF	F%	Min	GP	G	A	Pts	PIM	PP	SH	GW	Min
1995-96	Saskatoon Flyers	SMHL	60	85	74	159	85	....	....	....	....	....	....	....	....	....	....	....	....	....	....	....	....	....	....
1996-97	Sask. Contacts	SMHL	44	22	23	45	18	....	....	....	....	....	....	....	....	....	....	....	....	....	....	....	....	....	....
1997-98	Sask. Contacts	SMHL	41	29	49	78	103	....	....	....	....	....	....	....	....	....	....	....	....	....	....	....	....	....	....
1998-99	Vernon Vipers	BCHL	45	24	58	82	15	....	....	....	....	....	....	....	....	....	....	....	....	....	....	....	....	....	....
99-2000	North Dakota	WCHA	44	17	23	40	30	....	....	....	....	....	....	....	....	....	....	....	....	....	....	....	....	....	....
2000-01	North Dakota	WCHA	46	25	34	59	48	....	....	....	....	....	....	....	....	....	....	....	....	....	....	....	....	....	....
2001-02	North Dakota	WCHA	37	19	28	47	52	....	....	....	....	....	....	....	....	....	....	....	....	....	....	....	....	....	....
	Lowell	AHL	3	1	1	2	0	....	....	....	....	....	....	....	....	....	5	3	0	3	0	....	....	....	....
2002-03	Carolina	NHL	25	4	10	14	16	0	0	1	49	8.2	–5	2	100.0	17:15	....	....	....	....	....	....	....	....	....
	Lowell	AHL	53	11	32	43	32	....	....	....	....	....	....	....	....	....	....	....	....	....	....	....	....	....	....
2003-04	Carolina	NHL	44	3	3	6	22	0	0	1	65	4.6	–14	4	0.0	10:57	....	....	....	....	....	....	....	....	....
	Lowell	AHL	34	7	15	22	28	....	....	....	....	....	....	....	....	....	....	....	....	....	....	....	....	....	....
	NHL Totals		69	7	13	20	38	0	0	2	114	6.1		6	33.3	13:14	....	....	....	....	....	....	....	....	....

BCHL Rookie of the Year (1999) • WCHA All-Rookie Team (2000) • WCHA Second All-Star Team (2001, 2002)

BEAUCHEMIN, Francois

(boh-sheh-MEH, frahn-SWUH) **MTL.**

Defense. Shoots left. 6', 214 lbs. Born, Sorel, Que., June 4, 1980. Montreal's 3rd choice, 75th overall, in 1998 Entry Draft.

Season	Club	League	GP	G	A	Pts	PIM	PP	SH	GW	S	%	+/-	TF	F%	Min	GP	G	A	Pts	PIM	PP	SH	GW	Min
1995-96	Richelieu Riverains	QAAA	40	9	23	32	59	....	....	....	....	....	....	....	....	....	....	....	....	....	....	....	....	....	....
1996-97	Laval Titan	QMJHL	66	7	21	28	132	....	....	....	....	....	....	....	....	....	3	0	0	0	2	....	....	....	....
1997-98	Laval Titan	QMJHL	70	12	35	47	132	....	....	....	....	....	....	....	....	....	16	1	3	4	23	....	....	....	....
1998-99	Acadie-Bathurst	QMJHL	31	4	17	21	53	....	....	....	....	....	....	....	....	....	23	2	16	18	55	....	....	....	....
99-2000	Acadie-Bathurst	QMJHL	38	11	36	47	64	....	....	....	....	....	....	....	....	....	....	....	....	....	....	....	....	....	....
	Moncton Wildcats	QMJHL	33	8	31	39	35	....	....	....	....	....	....	....	....	....	16	2	11	13	14	....	....	....	....
2000-01	Quebec Citadelles	AHL	56	3	6	9	44	....	....	....	....	....	....	....	....	....	....	....	....	....	....	....	....	....	....
2001-02	Quebec Citadelles	AHL	56	8	11	19	88	....	....	....	....	....	....	....	....	....	3	0	1	1	0	....	....	....	....
	Mississippi	ECHL	7	1	3	4	2	....	....	....	....	....	....	....	....	....	....	....	....	....	....	....	....	....	....
2002-03	Montreal	NHL	1	0	0	0	0	0	0	0	1	0.0	–1	0	0.0	17:11	....	....	....	....	....	....	....	....	....
	Hamilton	AHL	75	7	21	28	92	....	....	....	....	....	....	....	....	....	23	1	9	10	16	....	....	....	....
2003-04	Hamilton	AHL	77	9	27	36	57	....	....	....	....	....	....	....	....	....	10	2	4	6	18	....	....	....	....
	NHL Totals		1	0	0	0	0	0	0	0	1	0.0		0	0.0	17:11	....	....	....	....	....	....	....	....	....

QMJHL All-Rookie Team (1997) • QMJHL Second All-Star Team (2000)

BEAUDOIN, Eric

(boh-DWEH, AIR-ihk) **FLA.**

Left wing. Shoots left. 6'5", 210 lbs. Born, Ottawa, Ont., May 3, 1980. Tampa Bay's 4th choice, 92nd overall, in 1998 Entry Draft.

Season	Club	League	GP	G	A	Pts	PIM	PP	SH	GW	S	%	+/-	TF	F%	Min	GP	G	A	Pts	PIM	PP	SH	GW	Min
1996-97	Ottawa Jr. Sens	OCJHL	54	12	19	31	55	....	....	....	....	....	....	....	....	....	....	....	....	....	....	....	....	....	....
1997-98	Guelph Storm	OHL	62	9	13	22	43	....	....	....	....	....	....	....	....	....	12	3	2	5	4	....	....	....	....
1998-99	Guelph Storm	OHL	66	28	43	71	79	....	....	....	....	....	....	....	....	....	11	5	3	8	12	....	....	....	....
99-2000	Guelph Storm	OHL	68	38	34	72	126	....	....	....	....	....	....	....	....	....	6	3	0	3	2	....	....	....	....
2000-01	Louisville Panthers	AHL	71	15	10	25	78	....	....	....	....	....	....	....	....	....	....	....	....	....	....	....	....	....	....
2001-02	Florida	NHL	8	1	3	4	4	0	0	1	11	9.1	–2	1	0.0	17:27	....	....	....	....	....	....	....	....	....
	Utah Grizzlies	AHL	44	5	16	21	83	....	....	....	....	....	....	....	....	....	....	....	....	....	....	....	....	....	....
2002-03	Florida	NHL	15	0	1	1	25	0	0	0	11	0.0	–7	27	29.6	9:52	....	....	....	....	....	....	....	....	....
	San Antonio	AHL	41	14	23	37	36	....	....	....	....	....	....	....	....	....	3	1	0	1	0	....	....	....	....
2003-04	Florida	NHL	30	2	4	6	12	0	0	0	30	6.7	–6	13	30.8	10:19	....	....	....	....	....	....	....	....	....
	San Antonio	AHL	38	20	22	42	45	....	....	....	....	....	....	....	....	....	....	....	....	....	....	....	....	....	....
	NHL Totals		53	3	8	11	41	0	0	1	52	5.8		41	29.3	11:16	....	....	....	....	....	....	....	....	....

Traded to **Florida** by **Tampa Bay** for Florida's 7th round choice (Marek Priechodsky) in 2000 Entry Draft, June 1, 2000.

BEDNAR, Jaroslav

(BEHD-nahr, YA-roh-slahv)

Right wing. Shoots right. 6', 198 lbs. Born, Prague, Czech., November 8, 1976. Los Angeles' 4th choice, 51st overall, in 2001 Entry Draft.

Season	Club	League	GP	G	A	Pts	PIM	PP	SH	GW	S	%	+/-	TF	F%	Min	GP	G	A	Pts	PIM	PP	SH	GW	Min
1994-95	HC Slavia Praha	Czech	20	6	7	13	4	....	....	....	....	....	....	....	....	....	3	0	0	0	0	....	....	....	....
1995-96	HC Slavia Praha	Czech	20	3	1	4	6	....	....	....	....	....	....	....	....	....	3	0	0	0	0	....	....	....	....
1996-97	HC Slavia Praha	Czech	45	18	12	30	18	....	....	....	....	....	....	....	....	....	....	....	....	....	....	....	....	....	....
1997-98	HC Slavia Praha	Czech	14	2	5	7	6	....	....	....	....	....	....	....	....	....	....	....	....	....	....	....	....	....	....
	Plzen	Czech	34	26	15	41	16	....	....	....	....	....	....	....	....	....	5	2	4	6	4	....	....	....	....
	Plzen	EuroHL	....	....	....	....	....	....	....	....	....	....	....	....	....	....	5	4	2	6	4	....	....	....	....
1998-99	HC Sparta Praha	Czech	52	23	14	37	30	....	....	....	....	....	....	....	....	....	8	5	2	7	0	....	....	....	....
99-2000	JYP Jyvaskyla	Finland	53	34	28	62	56	....	....	....	....	....	....	....	....	....	....	....	....	....	....	....	....	....	....
2000-01	HIFK Helsinki	Finland	56	*32	28	60	51	....	....	....	....	....	....	....	....	....	5	3	1	4	0	....	....	....	....
2001-02	Los Angeles	NHL	22	4	2	6	8	1	0	2	20	20.0	–4	2	50.0	10:42	3	0	0	0	0	0	0	0	11:48
	Manchester	AHL	48	16	21	37	16	....	....	....	....	....	....	....	....	....	....	....	....	....	....	....	....	....	....
2002-03	Los Angeles	NHL	15	0	9	9	4	0	0	0	29	0.0	3	7	57.1	14:00	....	....	....	....	....	....	....	....	....
	Florida	NHL	52	5	13	18	14	2	0	1	66	7.6	–2	42	42.9	14:09	....	....	....	....	....	....	....	....	....

			Regular Season														Playoffs								
Season	Club	League	GP	G	A	Pts	PIM	PP	SH	GW	S	%	+/-	TF	F%	Min	GP	G	A	Pts	PIM	PP	SH	GW	Min
2003-04	**Florida**	**NHL**	**13**	**1**	**1**	**2**	**4**	**0**	**0**	**0**	**19**	**5.3**	**2**	**41**	**43.9**	**13:02**									
	San Antonio	AHL	2	2	1	3	0																		
	Avangard Omsk	Russia	29	10	5	15	34										11	2	0	2	2				
	NHL Totals		**102**	**10**	**25**	**35**	**30**	**3**	**0**	**3**	**134**	**7.5**		**92**	**44.6**	**13:15**	**3**	**0**	**0**	**0**	**0**	**0**	**0**	**0**	**11:48**

Traded to **Florida** by **Los Angeles** with Andreas Lilja for Dmitry Yushkevich and NY Islanders' 5th round choice (previously acquired, Los Angeles selected Brady Murray) in 2003 Entry Draft, November 26, 2002. Signed as a free agent by **Avangard Omsk** (Russia), December 11, 2003.

BEECH, Kris

(BEECH, KRIHS) **PIT.**

Center. Shoots left. 6'2", 208 lbs. Born, Salmon Arm, B.C., February 5, 1981. Washington's 1st choice, 7th overall, in 1999 Entry Draft.

1996-97	Sicamous Eagles	KIJHL	49	34	36	70	80																		
	Calgary Hitmen	WHL	8	1	1	2	0																		
1997-98	Calgary Hitmen	WHL	58	10	25	35	24										12	4	5	9	32				
1998-99	Calgary Hitmen	WHL	68	26	41	67	103										6	1	4	5	8				
99-2000	Calgary Hitmen	WHL	66	32	54	86	99										5	3	5	8	16				
2000-01	**Washington**	**NHL**	**4**	**0**	**0**	**0**	**2**	**0**	**0**	**0**	**0**	**0.0**	**−2**	**25**	**36.0**	**7:29**									
	Calgary Hitmen	WHL	40	22	44	66	103										10	2	8	10	26				
2001-02	**Pittsburgh**	**NHL**	**79**	**10**	**15**	**25**	**45**	**2**	**0**	**0**	**126**	**7.9**	**−25**	**604**	**45.2**	**13:33**									
2002-03	**Pittsburgh**	**NHL**	**12**	**0**	**1**	**1**	**6**	**0**	**0**	**0**	**6**	**0.0**	**−3**	**96**	**42.7**	**10:34**									
	Wilkes-Barre	AHL	50	19	24	43	76										5	1	1	2	0				
2003-04	**Pittsburgh**	**NHL**	**4**	**0**	**1**	**1**	**6**	**0**	**0**	**0**	**6**	**0.0**	**0**	**45**	**40.0**	**12:32**									
	Wilkes-Barre	AHL	53	20	25	45	97										22	9	6	15	22				
	NHL Totals		**99**	**10**	**17**	**27**	**59**	**2**	**0**	**0**	**138**	**7.2**		**770**	**44.3**	**12:55**									

Returned to **Calgary** (WHL) by **Washington**, October 24, 2000. Traded to **Pittsburgh** by **Washington** with Michal Sivek, Ross Lupaschuk and future considerations for Jaromir Jagr and Frantisek Kucera, July 11, 2001.

BEGIN, Steve

(bay-ZHIN, STEEV) **MTL.**

Center. Shoots left. 5'11", 195 lbs. Born, Trois-Rivieres, Que., June 14, 1978. Calgary's 3rd choice, 40th overall, in 1996 Entry Draft.

1993-94	Cap-d-Madelaine	QAAA	8	0	1	1	6										2	0	0	0	0				
1994-95	Cap-d-Madelaine	QAAA	35	9	15	24	48										3	0	0	0	2				
1995-96	Val-d'Or Foreurs	QMJHL	64	13	23	36	218										13	1	3	4	33				
1996-97	Val-d'Or Foreurs	QMJHL	58	13	33	46	229										10	0	3	3	8				
	Saint John Flames	AHL															4	0	2	2	6				
1997-98	**Calgary**	**NHL**	**5**	**0**	**0**	**0**	**23**	**0**	**0**	**0**	**2**	**0.0**	**0**												
	Val-d'Or Foreurs	QMJHL	35	18	17	35	73										15	2	12	14	34				
1998-99	Saint John Flames	AHL	73	11	9	20	156										7	2	0	2	18				
99-2000	**Calgary**	**NHL**	**13**	**1**	**1**	**2**	**18**	**0**	**0**	**0**	**3**	**33.3**	**−3**	**19**	**47.4**	**7:13**									
	Saint John Flames	AHL	47	13	12	25	99																		
2000-01	**Calgary**	**NHL**	**4**	**0**	**0**	**0**	**21**	**0**	**0**	**0**	**3**	**0.0**	**0**	**0**	**0.0**	**6:04**									
	Saint John Flames	AHL	58	14	14	28	109										19	10	7	17	18				
2001-02	**Calgary**	**NHL**	**51**	**7**	**5**	**12**	**79**	**1**	**0**	**0**	**65**	**10.8**	**−3**	**129**	**53.5**	**9:25**									
2002-03	**Calgary**	**NHL**	**50**	**3**	**1**	**4**	**51**	**0**	**0**	**1**	**59**	**5.1**	**−7**	**50**	**60.0**	**9:13**									
2003-04	**Montreal**	**NHL**	**52**	**10**	**5**	**15**	**41**	**0**	**1**	**1**	**91**	**11.0**	**6**	**436**	**48.6**	**12:32**	**9**	**0**	**1**	**1**	**10**	**0**	**0**	**0**	**12:26**
	NHL Totals		**175**	**21**	**12**	**33**	**233**	**1**	**1**	**2**	**223**	**9.4**		**634**	**50.5**	**10:04**	**9**	**0**	**1**	**1**	**10**	**0**	**0**	**0**	**12:26**

Jack A. Butterfield Trophy (Playoff MVP – AHL) (2001)

Traded to **Buffalo** by **Calgary** with Chris Drury for Steve Reinprecht and Rhett Warrener, July 3, 2003. Claimed by **Montreal** from **Buffalo** in Waiver Draft, October 3, 2003.

BEKAR, Derek

(BEH-kahr, DAIR-ihk)

Left wing. Shoots left. 6'3", 197 lbs. Born, Burnaby, B.C., September 15, 1975. St. Louis' 7th choice, 205th overall, in 1995 Entry Draft.

1992-93	Notre Dame	SMHL	29	25	24	49	68																		
1993-94	Notre Dame	SJHL	62	20	31	51	77																		
1994-95	Powell River	BCJHL	46	33	29	62	35																		
1995-96	New Hampshire	H-East	34	15	18	33	4																		
1996-97	New Hampshire	H-East	39	18	21	39	34																		
1997-98	New Hampshire	H-East	35	32	28	60	46																		
1998-99	Worcester IceCats	AHL	51	16	20	36	6										4	0	0	0	0				
99-2000	**St. Louis**	**NHL**	**1**	**0**	**0**	**0**	**0**	**0**	**0**	**0**	**0**	**0.0**	**0**	**0**	**0.0**	**5:14**									
	Worcester IceCats	AHL	71	21	19	40	26										7	0	3	3	2				
2000-01	Worcester IceCats	AHL	18	5	2	7	10																		
	Portland Pirates	AHL	58	19	16	35	49										3	0	0	0	0				
2001-02	Manchester	AHL	74	27	20	47	42										5	1	4	5	2				
2002-03	**Los Angeles**	**NHL**	**6**	**0**	**0**	**0**	**4**	**0**	**0**	**0**	**4**	**0.0**	**−1**	**1**	**0.0**	**7:29**									
	Manchester	AHL	51	19	19	38	49										3	0	0	0	2				
2003-04	**NY Islanders**	**NHL**	**4**	**0**	**0**	**0**	**2**	**0**	**0**	**0**	**3**	**0.0**	**0**	**7**	**0.0**	**5:35**									
	Bridgeport	AHL	76	24	11	35	57										3	2	2	4	0				
	NHL Totals		**11**	**0**	**0**	**0**	**6**	**0**	**0**	**0**	**7**	**0.0**		**8**	**0.0**	**6:35**									

Hockey East Second All-Star Team (1998)

Traded to **Washington** by **St. Louis** for Mike Peluso, November 29, 2000. Signed as a free agent by **Los Angeles**, September 25, 2001. Signed as a free agent by **NY Islanders**, September 10, 2003.

BELAK, Wade

(BEE-lak, WAYD) **TOR.**

Defense/Right wing. Shoots right. 6'5", 221 lbs. Born, Saskatoon, Sask., July 3, 1976. Quebec's 1st choice, 12th overall, in 1994 Entry Draft.

1991-92	North Battleford	SMBHL	57	6	20	26	186																		
1992-93	North Battleford	SJHL	50	5	15	20	146																		
	Saskatoon Blades	WHL	7	0	0	0	23										7	0	0	0	0				
1993-94	Saskatoon Blades	WHL	69	4	13	17	226										16	2	2	4	43				
1994-95	Saskatoon Blades	WHL	72	4	14	18	290										9	0	0	0	36				
	Cornwall Aces	AHL															11	1	2	3	40				
1995-96	Saskatoon Blades	WHL	63	3	15	18	207										4	0	0	0	9				
	Cornwall Aces	AHL	5	0	0	0	18										2	0	0	0	2				
1996-97	**Colorado**	**NHL**	**5**	**0**	**0**	**0**	**11**	**0**	**0**	**0**	**1**	**0.0**	**−1**												
	Hershey Bears	AHL	65	1	7	8	320										16	0	1	1	61				
1997-98	**Colorado**	**NHL**	**8**	**1**	**1**	**2**	**27**	**0**	**0**	**1**	**2**	**50.0**	**−3**												
	Hershey Bears	AHL	11	0	0	0	30																		
1998-99	**Colorado**	**NHL**	**22**	**0**	**0**	**0**	**71**	**0**	**0**	**0**	**5**	**0.0**	**−2**	**0**	**0.0**	**6:48**									
	Hershey Bears	AHL	17	0	1	1	49																		
	Calgary	**NHL**	**9**	**0**	**1**	**1**	**23**	**0**	**0**	**0**	**2**	**0.0**	**3**	**0**	**0.0**	**10:46**									
	Saint John Flames	AHL	12	0	2	2	43										6	0	1	1	23				
99-2000	**Calgary**	**NHL**	**40**	**0**	**2**	**2**	**122**	**0**	**0**	**0**	**11**	**0.0**	**−4**	**1**	**0.0**	**7:33**									
2000-01	**Calgary**	**NHL**	**23**	**0**	**0**	**0**	**79**	**0**	**0**	**0**	**8**	**0.0**	**−2**	**0**	**0.0**	**6:54**									
	Toronto	**NHL**	**16**	**1**	**1**	**2**	**31**	**0**	**0**	**0**	**8**	**12.5**	**−4**	**0**	**0.0**	**13:38**									
2001-02	**Toronto**	**NHL**	**63**	**1**	**3**	**4**	**142**	**0**	**0**	**0**	**47**	**2.1**	**2**	**0**	**0.0**	**9:14**	**16**	**1**	**0**	**1**	**18**	**0**	**0**	**0**	**7:28**
2002-03	**Toronto**	**NHL**	**55**	**3**	**6**	**9**	**196**	**0**	**0**	**0**	**33**	**9.1**	**−2**	**0**	**0.0**	**10:50**	**2**	**0**	**0**	**0**	**4**	**0**	**0**	**0**	**8:22**
2003-04	**Toronto**	**NHL**	**34**	**1**	**1**	**2**	**109**	**0**	**0**	**0**	**15**	**6.7**	**0**	**0**	**0.0**	**7:00**	**4**	**0**	**0**	**0**	**14**	**0**	**0**	**0**	**9:59**
	NHL Totals		**275**	**7**	**15**	**22**	**811**	**0**	**0**	**1**	**132**	**5.3**		**1**	**0.0**	**8:56**	**22**	**1**	**0**	**1**	**36**	**0**	**0**	**0**	**8:00**

Rights transferred to **Colorado** after **Quebec** franchise relocated, June 21, 1995. Traded to **Calgary** by **Colorado** with Rene Corbet, Robyn Regehr and Colorado's 2nd round compensatory choice (Jarret Stoll) in 2000 Entry Draft for Theoren Fleury and Chris Dingman, February 28, 1999. • Missed majority of 1999-2000 and 2000-01 seasons recovering from shoulder injury suffered in game vs. Colorado, February 10, 2000. Claimed on waivers by **Toronto** from **Calgary**, February 16, 2001. • Missed majority of 2003-04 season recovering from abdomen (November 20, 2003 vs. Edmonton) and knee (January 6, 2004 vs. Nashville) injuries.

BELANGER, Eric
(buh-LAWN-zhay, AIR-ihk) **L.A.**

Center. Shoots left. 6', 185 lbs. Born, Sherbrooke, Que., December 16, 1977. Los Angeles' 5th choice, 96th overall, in 1996 Entry Draft.

			Regular Season														Playoffs								
Season	Club	League	GP	G	A	Pts	PIM	PP	SH	GW	S	%	+/-	TF	F%	Min	GP	G	A	Pts	PIM	PP	SH	GW	Min
1993-94	Magog	QAAA	32	19	24	43	24	....	....	....	....	....	....	....	....	....	13	5	6	11	36	....	....	....	....
1994-95	Beauport	QMJHL	71	12	28	40	24	....	....	....	....	....	....	....	....	....	18	5	9	14	25	....	....	....	....
1995-96	Beauport	QMJHL	59	35	48	83	18	....	....	....	....	....	....	....	....	....	20	13	14	27	6	....	....	....	....
1996-97	Beauport	QMJHL	31	13	37	50	30	....	....	....	....	....	....	....	....	....	....	....	....	....	....	....	....	....	....
	Rimouski Oceanic	QMJHL	31	26	41	67	36	....	....	....	....	....	....	....	....	....	4	2	3	5	10	....	....	....	....
1997-98	Fredericton	AHL	56	17	34	51	28	....	....	....	....	....	....	....	....	....	4	2	1	3	2	....	....	....	....
1998-99	Springfield	AHL	33	8	18	26	10	....	....	....	....	....	....	....	....	....	3	0	1	1	2	....	....	....	....
	Long Beach	IHL	1	0	0	0	0	....	....	....	....	....	....	....	....	....	....	....	....	....	....	....	....	....	....
99-2000	Lowell	AHL	65	15	25	40	20	....	....	....	....	....	....	....	....	....	7	3	3	6	2	....	....	....	....
	Mohawk Valley	UHL	3	0	0	0	0	....	....	....	....	....	....	....	....	....	....	....	....	....	....	....	....	....	....
2000-01	**Los Angeles**	**NHL**	**62**	**9**	**12**	**21**	**16**	**1**	**2**	**1**	**80**	**11.3**	**14**	**849**	**56.4**	**13:25**	**13**	**1**	**4**	**5**	**2**	**0**	**0**	**1**	**13:47**
	Lowell	AHL	13	8	10	18	4	....	....	....	....	....	....	....	....	....	....	....	....	....	....	....	....	....	....
2001-02	**Los Angeles**	**NHL**	**53**	**8**	**16**	**24**	**21**	**2**	**1**	**1**	**67**	**11.9**	**2**	**882**	**57.7**	**14:33**	**7**	**0**	**0**	**0**	**4**	**0**	**0**	**0**	**12:57**
2002-03	**Los Angeles**	**NHL**	**62**	**16**	**19**	**35**	**26**	**0**	**3**	**1**	**114**	**14.0**	**–5**	**1143**	**51.8**	**17:42**	....	....	....	....	....	....	....	....	....
2003-04	**Los Angeles**	**NHL**	**81**	**13**	**20**	**33**	**44**	**0**	**1**	**2**	**132**	**9.8**	**–16**	**1418**	**53.7**	**17:01**	....	....	....	....	....	....	....	....	....
	NHL Totals		**258**	**46**	**67**	**113**	**107**	**3**	**7**	**5**	**393**	**11.7**		**4292**	**54.5**	**15:48**	**20**	**1**	**4**	**5**	**6**	**0**	**0**	**1**	**13:30**

BELANGER, Ken
(buh-LAWN-zhay, KEHN)

Left wing. Shoots left. 6'4", 225 lbs. Born, Sault Ste. Marie, Ont., May 14, 1974. Hartford's 7th choice, 153rd overall, in 1992 Entry Draft.

Season	Club	League	GP	G	A	Pts	PIM	PP	SH	GW	S	%	+/-	TF	F%	Min	GP	G	A	Pts	PIM	PP	SH	GW	Min
1990-91	Soo Legion	NOHA	43	24	29	53	169	....	....	....	....	....	....	....	....	....	....	....	....	....	....	....	....	....	....
1991-92	Ottawa 67's	OHL	51	4	4	8	174	....	....	....	....	....	....	....	....	....	11	0	0	0	24	....	....	....	....
1992-93	Ottawa 67's	OHL	34	6	12	18	139	....	....	....	....	....	....	....	....	....	....	....	....	....	....	....	....	....	....
	Guelph Storm	OHL	29	10	14	24	86	....	....	....	....	....	....	....	....	....	5	2	1	3	14	....	....	....	....
1993-94	Guelph Storm	OHL	55	11	22	33	185	....	....	....	....	....	....	....	....	....	9	2	3	5	30	....	....	....	....
1994-95	St. John's	AHL	47	5	5	10	246	....	....	....	....	....	....	....	....	....	4	0	0	0	30	....	....	....	....
	Toronto	**NHL**	**3**	**0**	**0**	**0**	**9**	**0**	**0**	**0**	**1**	**0.0**	**0**	....	....	....	....	....	....	....	....	....	....	....	....
1995-96	St. John's	AHL	40	16	14	30	222	....	....	....	....	....	....	....	....	....	....	....	....	....	....	....	....	....	....
	NY Islanders	**NHL**	**7**	**0**	**0**	**0**	**27**	**0**	**0**	**0**	**0**	**0.0**	**–2**	....	....	....	....	....	....	....	....	....	....	....	....
1996-97	**NY Islanders**	**NHL**	**18**	**0**	**2**	**2**	**102**	**0**	**0**	**0**	**5**	**0.0**	**–1**	....	....	....	....	....	....	....	....	....	....	....	....
	Kentucky	AHL	38	10	12	22	164	....	....	....	....	....	....	....	....	....	4	0	1	1	27	....	....	....	....
1997-98	**NY Islanders**	**NHL**	**37**	**3**	**1**	**4**	**101**	**0**	**0**	**1**	**10**	**30.0**	**1**	....	....	....	....	....	....	....	....	....	....	....	....
1998-99	**NY Islanders**	**NHL**	**9**	**1**	**1**	**2**	**30**	**0**	**0**	**0**	**3**	**33.3**	**1**	**0**	**0.0**	**5:05**	....	....	....	....	....	....	....	....	....
	Boston	**NHL**	**45**	**1**	**4**	**5**	**152**	**0**	**0**	**0**	**16**	**6.3**	**–2**	**1**	**0.0**	**4:38**	**12**	**1**	**0**	**1**	**16**	**0**	**0**	**0**	**5:11**
99-2000	**Boston**	**NHL**	**37**	**2**	**2**	**4**	**44**	**0**	**0**	**0**	**20**	**10.0**	**–4**	**1**	**0.0**	**5:17**	....	....	....	....	....	....	....	....	....
2000-01	**Boston**	**NHL**	**40**	**2**	**2**	**4**	**121**	**0**	**0**	**1**	**35**	**5.7**	**–6**	**1**	**100.0**	**7:06**	....	....	....	....	....	....	....	....	....
	Providence Bruins	AHL	10	1	4	5	47	....	....	....	....	....	....	....	....	....	2	0	0	0	4	....	....	....	....
2001-02	**Los Angeles**	**NHL**	**43**	**2**	**0**	**2**	**85**	**0**	**0**	**0**	**22**	**9.1**	**–5**	**0**	**0.0**	**4:22**	....	....	....	....	....	....	....	....	....
2002-03	**Los Angeles**	**NHL**	**4**	**0**	**0**	**0**	**17**	**0**	**0**	**0**	**0**	**0.0**	**0**	**0**	**0.0**	**4:03**	....	....	....	....	....	....	....	....	....
2003-04	**Los Angeles**	**NHL**	DID NOT PLAY – INJURED																						
	NHL Totals		**243**	**11**	**12**	**23**	**688**	**0**	**0**	**2**	**112**	**9.8**		**3**	**33.3**	**5:16**	**12**	**1**	**0**	**1**	**16**	**0**	**0**	**0**	**5:11**

Traded to **Toronto** by **Hartford** for Toronto's 9th round choice (Matt Ball) in 1994 Entry Draft, March 18, 1994. Traded to **NY Islanders** by **Toronto** with Damian Rhodes for future considerations (Kirk Muller and Don Beaupre, January 23, 1996), January 23, 1996. Traded to **Boston** by **NY Islanders** for Ted Donato, November 7, 1998. • Missed majority of 1999-2000 season recovering from head injury suffered in game vs. Toronto, November 11, 1999. Signed as a free agent by **Los Angeles**, July 2, 2001. • Missed majority of 2002-03 season and entire 2003-04 season recovering from head injury suffered in game vs. San Jose, November 5, 2002.

BELL, Mark
(BEHL, MAHRK) **CHI.**

Center. Shoots left. 6'4", 205 lbs. Born, St. Paul's, Ont., August 5, 1980. Chicago's 1st choice, 8th overall, in 1998 Entry Draft.

Season	Club	League	GP	G	A	Pts	PIM	PP	SH	GW	S	%	+/-	TF	F%	Min	GP	G	A	Pts	PIM	PP	SH	GW	Min
1995-96	Stratford Cullitons	OJHL-B	47	8	15	23	32	....	....	....	....	....	....	....	....	....	....	....	....	....	....	....	....	....	....
1996-97	Ottawa 67's	OHL	65	8	12	20	40	....	....	....	....	....	....	....	....	....	24	4	7	11	13	....	....	....	....
1997-98	Ottawa 67's	OHL	55	34	26	60	87	....	....	....	....	....	....	....	....	....	13	6	5	11	14	....	....	....	....
1998-99	Ottawa 67's	OHL	44	29	26	55	69	....	....	....	....	....	....	....	....	....	9	6	5	11	8	....	....	....	....
99-2000	Ottawa 67's	OHL	48	34	38	72	95	....	....	....	....	....	....	....	....	....	2	0	1	1	0	....	....	....	....
2000-01	**Chicago**	**NHL**	**13**	**0**	**1**	**1**	**4**	**0**	**0**	**0**	**14**	**0.0**	**0**	**141**	**48.9**	**12:00**	....	....	....	....	....	....	....	....	....
	Norfolk Admirals	AHL	61	15	27	42	126	....	....	....	....	....	....	....	....	....	9	4	3	7	10	....	....	....	....
2001-02	**Chicago**	**NHL**	**80**	**12**	**16**	**28**	**124**	**1**	**0**	**1**	**120**	**10.0**	**–6**	**47**	**42.6**	**12:39**	**5**	**0**	**0**	**0**	**8**	**0**	**0**	**0**	**9:18**
2002-03	**Chicago**	**NHL**	**82**	**14**	**15**	**29**	**113**	**0**	**2**	**0**	**127**	**11.0**	**0**	**377**	**52.5**	**14:04**	....	....	....	....	....	....	....	....	....
2003-04	**Chicago**	**NHL**	**82**	**21**	**24**	**45**	**106**	**2**	**0**	**1**	**202**	**10.4**	**–14**	**387**	**48.3**	**17:37**	....	....	....	....	....	....	....	....	....
	NHL Totals		**257**	**47**	**56**	**103**	**347**	**3**	**2**	**2**	**463**	**10.2**		**952**	**49.8**	**14:39**	**5**	**0**	**0**	**0**	**8**	**0**	**0**	**0**	**9:18**

BELLEFEUILLE, Blake
(BEHL-fay, BLAYK)

Center. Shoots right. 5'10", 208 lbs. Born, Framingham, MA, December 27, 1977.

Season	Club	League	GP	G	A	Pts	PIM	PP	SH	GW	S	%	+/-	TF	F%	Min	GP	G	A	Pts	PIM	PP	SH	GW	Min
1994-95	Framingham	Hi-School	30	42	50	92	....	....	....	....	....	....	....	....	....	....	....	....	....	....	....	....	....	....	....
1995-96	Framingham	Hi-School	30	31	60	91	....	....	....	....	....	....	....	....	....	....	....	....	....	....	....	....	....	....	....
1996-97	Boston College	H-East	34	16	19	35	20	....	....	....	....	....	....	....	....	....	....	....	....	....	....	....	....	....	....
1997-98	Boston College	H-East	41	19	20	39	35	....	....	....	....	....	....	....	....	....	....	....	....	....	....	....	....	....	....
1998-99	Boston College	H-East	43	24	25	49	80	....	....	....	....	....	....	....	....	....	....	....	....	....	....	....	....	....	....
99-2000	Boston College	H-East	39	18	31	49	28	....	....	....	....	....	....	....	....	....	....	....	....	....	....	....	....	....	....
2000-01	Syracuse Crunch	AHL	50	5	5	10	18	....	....	....	....	....	....	....	....	....	5	0	0	0	0	....	....	....	....
2001-02	**Columbus**	**NHL**	**2**	**0**	**1**	**1**	**0**	**0**	**0**	**0**	**2**	**0.0**	**1**	**15**	**60.0**	**8:21**	....	....	....	....	....	....	....	....	....
	Syracuse Crunch	AHL	75	11	19	30	33	....	....	....	....	....	....	....	....	....	4	2	0	2	0	....	....	....	....
2002-03	**Columbus**	**NHL**	**3**	**0**	**0**	**0**	**0**	**0**	**0**	**0**	**0**	**0.0**	**0**	**17**	**64.7**	**7:01**	....	....	....	....	....	....	....	....	....
	Syracuse Crunch	AHL	63	12	19	31	44	....	....	....	....	....	....	....	....	....	....	....	....	....	....	....	....	....	....
2003-04	Providence Bruins	AHL	7	1	0	1	2	....	....	....	....	....	....	....	....	....	....	....	....	....	....	....	....	....	....
	Norfolk Admirals	AHL	59	4	8	12	17	....	....	....	....	....	....	....	....	....	5	1	1	2	0	....	....	....	....
	NHL Totals		**5**	**0**	**1**	**1**	**0**	**0**	**0**	**0**	**2**	**0.0**		**32**	**62.5**	**7:33**	....	....	....	....	....	....	....	....	....

Hockey East Second All-Star Team (2000)

Signed as a free agent by **Columbus**, May 26, 2000. Signed to a tryout (PTO) contract by **Providence** (AHL), October 10, 2003. Signed to a PTO (tryout) contract by **Norfolk** (AHL), November 6, 2003, following release by Providence (AHL).

BERARD, Bryan
(buh-RAHRD, BRIGH-uhn) **CHI.**

Defense. Shoots left. 6'2", 220 lbs. Born, Woonsocket, RI, March 5, 1977. Ottawa's 1st choice, 1st overall, in 1995 Entry Draft.

Season	Club	League	GP	G	A	Pts	PIM	PP	SH	GW	S	%	+/-	TF	F%	Min	GP	G	A	Pts	PIM	PP	SH	GW	Min
1991-92	Mount St. Charles	Hi-School	15	3	15	18	4	....	....	....	....	....	....	....	....	....	....	....	....	....	....	....	....	....	....
1992-93	Mount St. Charles	Hi-School	15	8	12	20	18	....	....	....	....	....	....	....	....	....	....	....	....	....	....	....	....	....	....
1993-94	Mount St. Charles	Hi-School	15	11	26	37	4.5	....	....	....	....	....	....	....	....	....	4	3	3	6	6	....	....	....	....
1994-95	Detroit	OHL	58	20	55	75	97	....	....	....	....	....	....	....	....	....	21	4	20	24	38	....	....	....	....
1995-96	Detroit	OHL	56	31	58	89	116	....	....	....	....	....	....	....	....	....	17	7	18	25	41	....	....	....	....
1996-97	**NY Islanders**	**NHL**	**82**	**8**	**40**	**48**	**86**	**3**	**0**	**1**	**172**	**4.7**	**1**	....	....	....	....	....	....	....	....	....	....	....	....
1997-98	**NY Islanders**	**NHL**	**75**	**14**	**32**	**46**	**59**	**8**	**1**	**2**	**192**	**7.3**	**–32**	....	....	....	....	....	....	....	....	....	....	....	....
	United States	Olympics	2	0	0	0	0	....	....	....	....	....	....	....	....	....	....	....	....	....	....	....	....	....	....
1998-99	**NY Islanders**	**NHL**	**31**	**4**	**11**	**15**	**26**	**2**	**0**	**3**	**72**	**5.6**	**–6**	**0**	**0.0**	**24:45**	....	....	....	....	....	....	....	....	....
	Toronto	**NHL**	**38**	**5**	**14**	**19**	**22**	**2**	**0**	**2**	**63**	**7.9**	**7**	**0**	**0.0**	**22:38**	**17**	**1**	**8**	**9**	**8**	**1**	**0**	**0**	**21:11**
99-2000	**Toronto**	**NHL**	**64**	**3**	**27**	**30**	**42**	**1**	**0**	**0**	**98**	**3.1**	**11**	**0**	**0.0**	**19:34**	....	....	....	....	....	....	....	....	....
2000-01	**Toronto**	**NHL**	DID NOT PLAY – INJURED																						
2001-02	**NY Rangers**	**NHL**	**82**	**2**	**21**	**23**	**60**	**0**	**0**	**0**	**132**	**1.5**	**–1**	**0**	**0.0**	**19:38**	....	....	....	....	....	....	....	....	....
2002-03	**Boston**	**NHL**	**80**	**10**	**28**	**38**	**64**	**4**	**0**	**1**	**205**	**4.9**	**–4**	**0**	**0.0**	**21:21**	**3**	**1**	**0**	**1**	**2**	**0**	**0**	**0**	**21:50**
2003-04	**Chicago**	**NHL**	**58**	**13**	**34**	**47**	**53**	**6**	**0**	**0**	**203**	**6.4**	**–24**	**0**	**0.0**	**21:46**	....	....	....	....	....	....	....	....	....
	NHL Totals		**510**	**59**	**207**	**266**	**412**	**26**	**1**	**9**	**1137**	**5.2**		**0**	**0.0**	**21:08**	**20**	**2**	**8**	**10**	**10**	**1**	**0**	**0**	**21:17**

OHL All-Rookie Team (1995) • OHL First All-Star Team (1995, 1996) • OHL Rookie of the Year (1995) • Canadian Major Junior First All-Star Team (1995, 1996) • Canadian Major Junior Rookie of the Year (1995) • Canadian Major Junior Defenseman of the Year (1996) • NHL All-Rookie Team (1997) • Calder Memorial Trophy (1997) • Bill Masterton Memorial Trophy (2004)

Traded to **NY Islanders** by **Ottawa** with Don Beaupre and Martin Straka for Damian Rhodes and Wade Redden, January 23, 1996. Traded to **Toronto** by **NY Islanders** with NY Islanders' 6th round choice (Jan Sochor) in 1999 Entry Draft for Felix Potvin and Toronto's 6th round choice (later traded to Tampa Bay – Tampa Bay selected Fedor Fedorov) in 1999 Entry Draft, January 9, 1999. • Missed remainder of 1999-2000 season and entire 2000-01 season recovering from eye injury suffered in game vs. Ottawa, March 11, 2000. Signed as a free agent by **NY Rangers**, October 5, 2001. Signed as a free agent by **Boston**, August 13, 2002. Signed as a free agent by **Chicago**, October 31, 2003.

Season	Club	League	Regular Season GP	G	A	Pts	PIM	PP	SH	GW	S	%	+/-	TF	F%	Min	Playoffs GP	G	A	Pts	PIM	PP	SH	GW	Min

BEREHOWSKY, Drake

(beh-reh-HOW-skee, DRAYK)

Defense. Shoots right. 6'2", 225 lbs. Born, Toronto, Ont., January 3, 1972. Toronto's 1st choice, 10th overall, in 1990 Entry Draft.

Season	Club	League	GP	G	A	Pts	PIM	PP	SH	GW	S	%	+/-	TF	F%	Min	GP	G	A	Pts	PIM	PP	SH	GW	Min
1987-88	Barrie Colts	OJHL-B	40	10	36	46	81	....	....	....	....	....	....	....	....	....	....	....	....	....	....	....	....	....	....
1988-89	Kingston Raiders	OHL	63	7	39	46	85	....	....	....	....	....	....	....	....	....	....	....	....	....	....	....	....	....	....
1989-90	Kingston	OHL	9	3	11	14	28	....	....	....	....	....	....	....	....	....	....	....	....	....	....	....	....	....	....
1990-91	**Toronto**	**NHL**	**8**	**0**	**1**	**1**	**25**	**0**	**0**	**0**	**4**	**0.0**	**–6**	....	....	....	....	....	....	....	....	....	....	....	....
	Kingston	OHL	13	5	13	18	38	....	....	....	....	....	....	....	....	....	....	....	....	....	....	....	....	....	....
	North Bay	OHL	26	7	23	30	51	....	....	....	....	....	....	....	....	....	10	2	7	9	21	....	....	....	....
1991-92	North Bay	OHL	62	19	63	82	147	....	....	....	....	....	....	....	....	....	21	7	24	31	22	....	....	....	....
	Toronto	**NHL**	**1**	**0**	**0**	**0**	**0**	**0**	**0**	**0**	**0**	**0.0**	**0**	....	....	....	....	....	....	....	....	....	....	....	....
	St. John's	AHL	....	....	....	....	....	....	....	....	....	....	....	....	....	....	6	0	5	5	21	....	....	....	....
1992-93	**Toronto**	**NHL**	**41**	**4**	**15**	**19**	**61**	**1**	**0**	**1**	**41**	**9.8**	**1**	....	....	....	....	....	....	....	....	....	....	....	....
	St. John's	AHL	28	10	17	27	38	....	....	....	....	....	....	....	....	....	....	....	....	....	....	....	....	....	....
1993-94	**Toronto**	**NHL**	**49**	**2**	**8**	**10**	**63**	**2**	**0**	**2**	**29**	**6.9**	**–3**	....	....	....	....	....	....	....	....	....	....	....	....
	St. John's	AHL	18	3	12	15	40	....	....	....	....	....	....	....	....	....	....	....	....	....	....	....	....	....	....
1994-95	**Toronto**	**NHL**	**25**	**0**	**2**	**2**	**15**	**0**	**0**	**0**	**12**	**0.0**	**–10**	....	....	....	....	....	....	....	....	....	....	....	....
	Pittsburgh	**NHL**	**4**	**0**	**0**	**0**	**13**	**0**	**0**	**0**	**2**	**0.0**	**1**	....	....	....	**1**	**0**	**0**	**0**	**0**	**0**	**0**	**0**	....
1995-96	**Pittsburgh**	**NHL**	**1**	**0**	**0**	**0**	**0**	**0**	**0**	**0**	**0**	**0.0**	**1**	....	....	....	....	....	....	....	....	....	....	....	....
	Cleveland	IHL	74	6	28	34	141	....	....	....	....	....	....	....	....	....	3	0	3	3	6	....	....	....	....
1996-97	Carolina	AHL	49	2	15	17	55	....	....	....	....	....	....	....	....	....	....	....	....	....	....	....	....	....	....
	San Antonio	IHL	16	3	4	7	36	....	....	....	....	....	....	....	....	....	....	....	....	....	....	....	....	....	....
1997-98	**Edmonton**	**NHL**	**67**	**1**	**6**	**7**	**169**	**1**	**0**	**1**	**58**	**1.7**	**1**	....	....	....	**12**	**1**	**2**	**3**	**14**	**0**	**0**	**1**	....
	Hamilton	AHL	8	2	0	2	21	....	....	....	....	....	....	....	....	....	....	....	....	....	....	....	....	....	....
1998-99	**Nashville**	**NHL**	**74**	**2**	**15**	**17**	**140**	**0**	**0**	**0**	**79**	**2.5**	**–9**	**1**	**100.0**	**21:43**	....	....	....	....	....	....	....	....	....
99-2000	**Nashville**	**NHL**	**79**	**12**	**20**	**32**	**87**	**5**	**0**	**1**	**102**	**11.8**	**–4**	**0**	**0.0**	**22:39**	....	....	....	....	....	....	....	....	....
2000-01	**Nashville**	**NHL**	**66**	**6**	**18**	**24**	**100**	**3**	**0**	**1**	**94**	**6.4**	**–9**	**1**	**0.0**	**21:38**	....	....	....	....	....	....	....	....	....
	Vancouver	**NHL**	**14**	**1**	**1**	**2**	**21**	**1**	**0**	**0**	**13**	**7.7**	**0**	**0**	**0.0**	**17:10**	**4**	**0**	**0**	**0**	**12**	**0**	**0**	**0**	**14:20**
2001-02	**Vancouver**	**NHL**	**25**	**1**	**2**	**3**	**18**	**0**	**0**	**1**	**15**	**6.7**	**–5**	**1**	**0.0**	**13:28**	....	....	....	....	....	....	....	....	....
	Phoenix	**NHL**	**32**	**1**	**4**	**5**	**42**	**0**	**0**	**0**	**23**	**4.3**	**5**	**0**	**0.0**	**12:20**	**5**	**0**	**1**	**1**	**4**	**0**	**0**	**0**	**13:00**
2002-03	**Phoenix**	**NHL**	**7**	**1**	**2**	**3**	**27**	**0**	**0**	**0**	**8**	**12.5**	**0**	**0**	**0.0**	**10:52**	....	....	....	....	....	....	....	....	....
	Springfield	AHL	2	0	0	0	0	....	....	....	....	....	....	....	....	....	....	....	....	....	....	....	....	....	....
2003-04	**Pittsburgh**	**NHL**	**47**	**5**	**16**	**21**	**50**	**3**	**0**	**0**	**62**	**8.1**	**–16**	**0**	**0.0**	**21:13**	....	....	....	....	....	....	....	....	....
	Toronto	**NHL**	**9**	**1**	**2**	**3**	**17**	**0**	**0**	**0**	**8**	**12.5**	**5**	**0**	**0.0**	**16:17**	....	....	....	....	....	....	....	....	....
	NHL Totals		**549**	**37**	**112**	**149**	**848**	**16**	**0**	**7**	**550**	**6.7**		**3**	**33.3**	**19:52**	**22**	**1**	**3**	**4**	**30**	**0**	**0**	**1**	**13:36**

OHL First All-Star Team (1992) • Canadian Major Junior Defenseman of the Year (1992)

Traded to **Pittsburgh** by **Toronto** for Grant Jennings, April 7, 1995. Signed as a free agent by **Edmonton**, September 30, 1997. Traded to **Nashville** by **Edmonton** with Eric Fichaud and Greg de Vries for Mikhail Shtalenkov and Jim Dowd, October 1, 1998. Traded to **Vancouver** by **Nashville** for Atlanta's 2nd round choice (previously acquired, Nashville selected Timofei Shishkanov) in 2001 Entry Draft, March 9, 2001. Traded to **Phoenix** by **Vancouver** with Denis Pederson for Todd Warriner, Trevor Letowski, Tyler Bouck and Phoenix's 3rd round choice (later traded back to Phoenix – Phoenix selected Dimitri Pestunov) in 2003 Entry Draft, December 28, 2001. • Missed majority of 2002-03 season recovering from knee injury suffered in training camp, September 24, 2002. Signed as a free agent by **Pittsburgh**, August, 29, 2003. Traded to **Toronto** by **Pittsburgh** for Ric Jackman, February 11, 2004.

BERENZWEIG, Bubba

(BAIR-ehn-zwighg, BUH-buh)

Defense. Shoots left. 6'1", 217 lbs. Born, Arlington Heights, IL, August 8, 1977. NY Islanders' 5th choice, 109th overall, in 1996 Entry Draft.

Season	Club	League	GP	G	A	Pts	PIM	PP	SH	GW	S	%	+/-	TF	F%	Min	GP	G	A	Pts	PIM	PP	SH	GW	Min
1992-93	Loomis-Chaffee	Hi-School	22	5	13	18	....	....	....	....	....	....	....	....	....	....	....	....	....	....	....	....	....	....	....
1993-94	Loomis-Chaffee	Hi-School	22	12	27	39	....	....	....	....	....	....	....	....	....	....	....	....	....	....	....	....	....	....	....
1994-95	Loomis-Chaffee	Hi-School	23	19	23	42	10	....	....	....	....	....	....	....	....	....	....	....	....	....	....	....	....	....	....
1995-96	U. of Michigan	CCHA	42	4	8	12	4	....	....	....	....	....	....	....	....	....	....	....	....	....	....	....	....	....	....
1996-97	U. of Michigan	CCHA	38	7	12	19	49	....	....	....	....	....	....	....	....	....	....	....	....	....	....	....	....	....	....
1997-98	U. of Michigan	CCHA	45	8	11	19	32	....	....	....	....	....	....	....	....	....	....	....	....	....	....	....	....	....	....
1998-99	U. of Michigan	CCHA	42	7	24	31	38	....	....	....	....	....	....	....	....	....	....	....	....	....	....	....	....	....	....
99-2000	**Nashville**	**NHL**	**2**	**0**	**0**	**0**	**0**	**0**	**0**	**0**	**3**	**0.0**	**–1**	**0**	**0.0**	**17:31**	....	....	....	....	....	....	....	....	....
	Milwaukee	IHL	79	4	23	27	48	....	....	....	....	....	....	....	....	....	3	1	2	3	0	....	....	....	....
2000-01	**Nashville**	**NHL**	**5**	**0**	**0**	**0**	**0**	**0**	**0**	**0**	**0**	**0.0**	**0**	**0**	**0.0**	**11:57**	....	....	....	....	....	....	....	....	....
	Milwaukee	IHL	72	10	26	36	38	....	....	....	....	....	....	....	....	....	5	0	4	4	4	....	....	....	....
2001-02	**Nashville**	**NHL**	**26**	**3**	**7**	**10**	**14**	**0**	**0**	**1**	**27**	**11.1**	**–3**	**1**	**0.0**	**13:45**	....	....	....	....	....	....	....	....	....
	Milwaukee	AHL	23	2	5	7	23	....	....	....	....	....	....	....	....	....	....	....	....	....	....	....	....	....	....
2002-03	**Nashville**	**NHL**	**4**	**0**	**0**	**0**	**0**	**0**	**0**	**0**	**5**	**0.0**	**0**	**0**	**0.0**	**17:47**	....	....	....	....	....	....	....	....	....
	Milwaukee	AHL	48	6	11	17	26	....	....	....	....	....	....	....	....	....	....	....	....	....	....	....	....	....	....
	Utah Grizzlies	AHL	26	6	11	17	4	....	....	....	....	....	....	....	....	....	....	....	....	....	....	....	....	....	....
2003-04	Utah Grizzlies	AHL	21	4	3	7	2	....	....	....	....	....	....	....	....	....	....	....	....	....	....	....	....	....	....
	NHL Totals		**37**	**3**	**7**	**10**	**14**	**0**	**0**	**1**	**35**	**8.6**		**1**	**0.0**	**14:08**	....	....	....	....	....	....	....	....	....

CCHA Second All-Star Team (1998) • NCAA Championship All-Tournament Team (1998) • Ken McKenzie Trophy (Outstanding U.S.- Born Player – IHL) (2000) • IHL Second All-Star Team (2001)

Traded to **Nashville** by **NY Islanders** for Nashville's 4th round choice (Johan Halvardsson) in 1999 Entry Draft, April 14, 1999. Traded to **Dallas** by **Nashvlle** with future considerations for Jon Sim, February 17, 2003. Suspended by **Dallas** for violating terms of contract, December 3, 2003.

BERG, Aki

(BUHRG, AH-kee) **TOR.**

Defense. Shoots left. 6'3", 213 lbs. Born, Turku, Finland, July 28, 1977. Los Angeles' 1st choice, 3rd overall, in 1995 Entry Draft.

Season	Club	League	GP	G	A	Pts	PIM	PP	SH	GW	S	%	+/-	TF	F%	Min	GP	G	A	Pts	PIM	PP	SH	GW	Min
1992-93	TPS Turku Jr.	Finn-Jr.	39	18	24	42	24	....	....	....	....	....	....	....	....	....	....	....	....	....	....	....	....	....	....
1993-94	TPS Turku Jr.	Finn-Jr.	21	3	11	14	24	....	....	....	....	....	....	....	....	....	7	0	0	0	10	....	....	....	....
	Kiekko-67 Turku	Finland-2	12	1	1	2	16	....	....	....	....	....	....	....	....	....	....	....	....	....	....	....	....	....	....
	TPS Turku	Finland	6	0	3	3	4	....	....	....	....	....	....	....	....	....	....	....	....	....	....	....	....	....	....
1994-95	TPS Turku Jr.	Finn-Jr.	8	1	0	1	30	....	....	....	....	....	....	....	....	....	....	....	....	....	....	....	....	....	....
	Kiekko-67 Turku	Finland-2	21	3	9	12	24	....	....	....	....	....	....	....	....	....	7	0	0	0	10	....	....	....	....
	TPS Turku	Finland	5	0	0	0	4	....	....	....	....	....	....	....	....	....	....	....	....	....	....	....	....	....	....
1995-96	**Los Angeles**	**NHL**	**51**	**0**	**7**	**7**	**29**	**0**	**0**	**0**	**56**	**0.0**	**–13**	....	....	....	....	....	....	....	....	....	....	....	....
	Phoenix	IHL	20	0	3	3	18	....	....	....	....	....	....	....	....	....	2	0	0	0	4	....	....	....	....
1996-97	**Los Angeles**	**NHL**	**41**	**2**	**6**	**8**	**24**	**2**	**0**	**0**	**65**	**3.1**	**–9**	....	....	....	....	....	....	....	....	....	....	....	....
	Phoenix	IHL	23	1	3	4	21	....	....	....	....	....	....	....	....	....	....	....	....	....	....	....	....	....	....
1997-98	**Los Angeles**	**NHL**	**72**	**0**	**8**	**8**	**61**	**0**	**0**	**0**	**58**	**0.0**	**3**	....	....	....	**4**	**0**	**3**	**3**	**0**	**0**	**0**	**0**	....
	Finland	Olympics	6	0	0	0	6	....	....	....	....	....	....	....	....	....	....	....	....	....	....	....	....	....	....
1998-99	TPS Turku	Finland	48	8	7	15	137	....	....	....	....	....	....	....	....	....	9	1	1	2	45	....	....	....	....
99-2000	**Los Angeles**	**NHL**	**70**	**3**	**13**	**16**	**45**	**0**	**0**	**0**	**70**	**4.3**	**–1**	**0**	**0.0**	**16:39**	**2**	**0**	**0**	**0**	**2**	**0**	**0**	**0**	**15:03**
2000-01	**Los Angeles**	**NHL**	**47**	**0**	**4**	**4**	**43**	**0**	**0**	**0**	**31**	**0.0**	**3**	**0**	**0.0**	**14:54**	....	....	....	....	....	....	....	....	....
	Toronto	**NHL**	**12**	**3**	**0**	**3**	**2**	**3**	**0**	**1**	**12**	**25.0**	**–6**	**0**	**0.0**	**18:13**	**11**	**0**	**2**	**2**	**4**	**0**	**0**	**0**	**16:31**
2001-02	**Toronto**	**NHL**	**81**	**1**	**10**	**11**	**46**	**0**	**0**	**0**	**66**	**1.5**	**14**	**1**	**100.0**	**18:43**	**20**	**0**	**1**	**1**	**37**	**0**	**0**	**0**	**18:25**
	Finland	Olympics	4	1	0	1	2	....	....	....	....	....	....	....	....	....	....	....	....	....	....	....	....	....	....
2002-03	**Toronto**	**NHL**	**78**	**4**	**7**	**11**	**28**	**0**	**0**	**2**	**49**	**8.2**	**3**	**0**	**0.0**	**15:02**	**7**	**1**	**1**	**2**	**2**	**0**	**0**	**0**	**19:45**
2003-04	**Toronto**	**NHL**	**79**	**2**	**7**	**9**	**40**	**0**	**0**	**0**	**69**	**2.9**	**–1**	**1**	**0.0**	**18:18**	**10**	**0**	**0**	**0**	**2**	**0**	**0**	**0**	**14:52**
	NHL Totals		**531**	**15**	**62**	**77**	**318**	**5**	**0**	**3**	**476**	**3.2**		**2**	**50.0**	**16:57**	**54**	**1**	**7**	**8**	**47**	**0**	**0**	**0**	**17:20**

Traded to **Toronto** by **Los Angeles** for Adam Mair and Toronto's 2nd round choice (Mike Cammalleri) in 2001 Entry Draft, March 13, 2001.

BERGENHEIM, Sean

(BUHR-gehn-highm, SHAWN) **NYI**

Center. Shoots left. 5'11", 194 lbs. Born, Helsinki, Finland, February 8, 1984. NY Islanders' 1st choice, 22nd overall, in 2002 Entry Draft.

Season	Club	League	GP	G	A	Pts	PIM	PP	SH	GW	S	%	+/-	TF	F%	Min	GP	G	A	Pts	PIM	PP	SH	GW	Min
1997-98	Jokerit Jr. C	Finn-Jr.	12	3	3	6	6	....	....	....	....	....	....	....	....	....	5	0	0	0	0	....	....	....	....
1998-99	Jokerit Jr. C	Finn-Jr.	20	9	9	18	30	....	....	....	....	....	....	....	....	....	....	....	....	....	....	....	....	....	....
99-2000	Jokerit Helsinki Jr.	Finn-Jr.	30	22	11	33	34	....	....	....	....	....	....	....	....	....	3	1	0	1	0	....	....	....	....
	Jokerit Jr. B	Finn-Jr.	17	10	8	18	14	....	....	....	....	....	....	....	....	....	3	1	0	1	2	....	....	....	....
	Jokerit Jr. C	Finn-Jr.	5	7	4	11	49	....	....	....	....	....	....	....	....	....	5	9	2	11	2	....	....	....	....
2000-01	Jokerit Helsinki Jr.	Finn-Jr.	19	7	4	11	30	....	....	....	....	....	....	....	....	....	8	9	5	14	12	....	....	....	....
	Jokerit Jr. B	Finn-Jr.	1	1	0	1	4	....	....	....	....	....	....	....	....	....	2	0	0	0	2	....	....	....	....
2001-02	Jokerit Helsinki	Finland	28	2	2	4	4	....	....	....	....	....	....	....	....	....	....	....	....	....	....	....	....	....	....
	Jokerit Helsinki Jr.	Finn-Jr.	23	11	19	30	36	....	....	....	....	....	....	....	....	....	6	6	2	8	20	....	....	....	....
	Kiekko Vantaa	Finland-2	4	0	0	0	52	....	....	....	....	....	....	....	....	....	....	....	....	....	....	....	....	....	....
	Jokerit Jr. B	Finn-Jr.	....	....	....	....	....	....	....	....	....	....	....	....	....	....	5	6	2	8	18	....	....	....	....
2002-03	Jokerit Helsinki	Finland	38	3	3	6	4	....	....	....	....	....	....	....	....	....	2	0	0	0	0	....	....	....	....

			Regular Season														Playoffs								
Season	Club	League	GP	G	A	Pts	PIM	PP	SH	GW	S	%	+/-	TF	F%	Min	GP	G	A	Pts	PIM	PP	SH	GW	Min
2003-04	Jokerit Helsinki	Finland	20	2	2	4	18	....	....	....	....	....	....	....	....	....	3	1	1	2	0	....	....	....	....
	NY Islanders	NHL	18	1	1	2	4	0	1	0	12	8.3	–4	2	50.0	8:55	....	....	....	....	....	....	....	....	....
	Bridgeport	AHL	....	....	....	....	....	....	....	....	....	....	....	....	....	....	7	2	3	5	10	....	....	....	....
	NHL Totals		18	1	1	2	4	0	1	0	12	8.3		2	50.0	8:55	....	....	....	....	....	....	....	....	....

BERGERON, Marc-Andre

(BAIR-zhur-uhn, MAHRK-AWN-dray) **EDM.**

Defense. Shoots left. 5'10", 197 lbs. Born, St-Louis-de-France, Que., October 13, 1980.

Season	Club	League	GP	G	A	Pts	PIM	PP	SH	GW	S	%	+/-	TF	F%	Min	GP	G	A	Pts	PIM	PP	SH	GW	Min
1996-97	Cap-d-Madelaine	QAAA	4	0	1	1	0	....	....	....	....	....	....	....	....	....	2	0	0	0	0	....	....	....	....
1997-98	Baie-Comeau	QMJHL	40	6	14	20	48	....	....	....	....	....	....	....	....	....	....	....	....	....	....	....	....	....	....
1998-99	Baie-Comeau	QMJHL	46	8	14	22	57	....	....	....	....	....	....	....	....	....	....	....	....	....	....	....	....	....	....
	Shawinigan	QMJHL	24	6	7	13	66	....	....	....	....	....	....	....	....	....	5	2	2	4	24	....	....	....	....
99-2000	Shawinigan	QMJHL	70	24	50	74	173	....	....	....	....	....	....	....	....	....	13	4	7	11	45	....	....	....	....
2000-01	Shawinigan	QMJHL	69	42	59	101	185	....	....	....	....	....	....	....	....	....	10	4	11	15	24	....	....	....	....
2001-02	Hamilton	AHL	50	2	13	15	61	....	....	....	....	....	....	....	....	....	9	1	4	5	8	....	....	....	....
2002-03	**Edmonton**	**NHL**	**5**	**1**	**1**	**2**	**9**	**0**	**0**	**0**	**5**	**20.0**	**2**	**0**	**0.0**	**16:30**	**1**	**0**	**1**	**1**	**0**	**0**	**0**	**0**	**19:20**
	Hamilton	AHL	66	8	31	39	73	....	....	....	....	....	....	....	....	....	20	0	7	7	25	....	....	....	....
2003-04	**Edmonton**	**NHL**	**54**	**9**	**17**	**26**	**26**	**3**	**0**	**0**	**105**	**8.6**	**13**	**0**	**0.0**	**17:39**	....	....	....	....	....	....	....	....	....
	Toronto	AHL	17	4	3	7	23	....	....	....	....	....	....	....	....	....	....	....	....	....	....	....	....	....	....
	NHL Totals		**59**	**10**	**18**	**28**	**35**	**3**	**0**	**0**	**110**	**9.1**		**0**	**0.0**	**17:33**	**1**	**0**	**1**	**1**	**0**	**0**	**0**	**0**	**19:20**

QMJHL First All-Star Team (2001) • Canadian Major Junior First All-Star Team (2001) • Canadian Major Junior Defenseman of the Year (2001) • AHL Second All-Star Team (2003)
Signed as a free agent by **Edmonton**, July 20, 2001.

BERGERON, Patrice

(BAIR-zhuhr-uhn, pa-TREEZ) **BOS.**

Center. Shoots right. 6', 186 lbs. Born, Ancienne-Lorette, Que., July 24, 1985. Boston's 2nd choice, 45th overall, in 2003 Entry Draft.

Season	Club	League	GP	G	A	Pts	PIM	PP	SH	GW	S	%	+/-	TF	F%	Min	GP	G	A	Pts	PIM	PP	SH	GW	Min
2000-01	Ste-Foy	QAAA	5	1	2	3	0	....	....	....	....	....	....	....	....	....	....	....	....	....	....	....	....	....	....
2001-02	St-Francois	QAAA	38	25	37	62	18	....	....	....	....	....	....	....	....	....	8	6	4	10	10	....	....	....	....
	Acadie-Bathurst	QMJHL	4	0	1	1	0	....	....	....	....	....	....	....	....	....	....	....	....	....	....	....	....	....	....
2002-03	Acadie-Bathurst	QMJHL	70	23	50	73	62	....	....	....	....	....	....	....	....	....	11	6	9	15	6	....	....	....	....
2003-04	**Boston**	**NHL**	**71**	**16**	**23**	**39**	**22**	**7**	**0**	**2**	**133**	**12.0**	**5**	**699**	**49.4**	**16:21**	**7**	**1**	**3**	**4**	**0**	**0**	**0**	**1**	**17:13**
	NHL Totals		**71**	**16**	**23**	**39**	**22**	**7**	**0**	**2**	**133**	**12.0**		**699**	**49.4**	**16:21**	**7**	**1**	**3**	**4**	**0**	**0**	**0**	**1**	**17:13**

BERGEVIN, Marc

(BUHR-zheh-vihn, MAHRK)

Defense. Shoots left. 6'1", 209 lbs. Born, Montreal, Que., August 11, 1965. Chicago's 3rd choice, 60th overall, in 1983 Entry Draft.

Season	Club	League	GP	G	A	Pts	PIM	PP	SH	GW	S	%	+/-	TF	F%	Min	GP	G	A	Pts	PIM	PP	SH	GW	Min
1981-82	Mtl-Concordia	QAAA	44	10	20	30	54	....	....	....	....	....	....	....	....	....	5	0	2	2	4	....	....	....	....
1982-83	Chicoutimi	QMJHL	64	3	27	30	113	....	....	....	....	....	....	....	....	....	....	....	....	....	....	....	....	....	....
1983-84	Chicoutimi	QMJHL	70	10	35	45	125	....	....	....	....	....	....	....	....	....	....	....	....	....	....	....	....	....	....
	Springfield	AHL	7	0	1	1	2	....	....	....	....	....	....	....	....	....	....	....	....	....	....	....	....	....	....
1984-85	**Chicago**	**NHL**	**60**	**0**	**6**	**6**	**54**	**0**	**0**	**0**	**41**	**0.0**	**–9**	....	....	....	**6**	**0**	**3**	**3**	**2**	**0**	**0**	**0**	....
	Springfield	AHL	....	....	....	....	....	....	....	....	....	....	....	....	....	....	4	0	0	0	0	....	....	....	....
1985-86	**Chicago**	**NHL**	**71**	**7**	**7**	**14**	**60**	**0**	**0**	**1**	**50**	**14.0**	**0**	....	....	....	**3**	**0**	**0**	**0**	**0**	**0**	**0**	**0**	....
1986-87	**Chicago**	**NHL**	**66**	**4**	**10**	**14**	**66**	**0**	**0**	**0**	**56**	**7.1**	**4**	....	....	....	**3**	**1**	**0**	**1**	**2**	**0**	**0**	**0**	....
1987-88	**Chicago**	**NHL**	**58**	**1**	**6**	**7**	**85**	**0**	**0**	**0**	**51**	**2.0**	**–19**	....	....	....	....	....	....	....	....	....	....	....	....
	Saginaw Hawks	IHL	10	2	7	9	20	....	....	....	....	....	....	....	....	....	....	....	....	....	....	....	....	....	....
1988-89	**Chicago**	**NHL**	**11**	**0**	**0**	**0**	**18**	**0**	**0**	**0**	**9**	**0.0**	**–3**	....	....	....	....	....	....	....	....	....	....	....	....
	NY Islanders	**NHL**	**58**	**2**	**13**	**15**	**62**	**1**	**0**	**0**	**56**	**3.6**	**2**	....	....	....	....	....	....	....	....	....	....	....	....
1989-90	**NY Islanders**	**NHL**	**18**	**0**	**4**	**4**	**30**	**0**	**0**	**0**	**12**	**0.0**	**–8**	....	....	....	....	....	....	....	....	....	....	....	....
	Springfield	AHL	47	7	16	23	66	....	....	....	....	....	....	....	....	....	17	2	11	13	16	....	....	....	....
1990-91	Capital District	AHL	7	0	5	5	6	....	....	....	....	....	....	....	....	....	....	....	....	....	....	....	....	....	....
	Hartford	**NHL**	**4**	**0**	**0**	**0**	**4**	**0**	**0**	**0**	**2**	**0.0**	**–3**	....	....	....	....	....	....	....	....	....	....	....	....
	Springfield	AHL	58	4	23	27	85	....	....	....	....	....	....	....	....	....	18	0	7	7	26	....	....	....	....
1991-92	**Hartford**	**NHL**	**75**	**7**	**17**	**24**	**64**	**4**	**1**	**1**	**96**	**7.3**	**–13**	....	....	....	**5**	**0**	**0**	**0**	**2**	**0**	**0**	**0**	....
1992-93	**Tampa Bay**	**NHL**	**78**	**2**	**12**	**14**	**66**	**0**	**0**	**0**	**69**	**2.9**	**–16**	....	....	....	....	....	....	....	....	....	....	....	....
1993-94	**Tampa Bay**	**NHL**	**83**	**1**	**15**	**16**	**87**	**0**	**0**	**1**	**76**	**1.3**	**–5**	....	....	....	....	....	....	....	....	....	....	....	....
1994-95	**Tampa Bay**	**NHL**	**44**	**2**	**4**	**6**	**51**	**0**	**1**	**0**	**32**	**6.3**	**–6**	....	....	....	....	....	....	....	....	....	....	....	....
1995-96	**Detroit**	**NHL**	**70**	**1**	**9**	**10**	**33**	**0**	**0**	**0**	**26**	**3.8**	**7**	....	....	....	**17**	**1**	**0**	**1**	**14**	**1**	**0**	**0**	....
1996-97	**St. Louis**	**NHL**	**82**	**0**	**4**	**4**	**53**	**0**	**0**	**0**	**30**	**0.0**	**–9**	....	....	....	**6**	**1**	**0**	**1**	**8**	**0**	**0**	**0**	....
1997-98	**St. Louis**	**NHL**	**81**	**3**	**7**	**10**	**90**	**0**	**0**	**0**	**40**	**7.5**	**–2**	....	....	....	**10**	**0**	**1**	**1**	**8**	**0**	**0**	**0**	....
1998-99	**St. Louis**	**NHL**	**52**	**1**	**1**	**2**	**99**	**0**	**0**	**0**	**40**	**2.5**	**–14**	**0**	**0.0**	**16:09**	....	....	....	....	....	....	....	....	....
99-2000	**St. Louis**	**NHL**	**81**	**1**	**8**	**9**	**75**	**0**	**0**	**0**	**54**	**1.9**	**27**	**0**	**0.0**	**21:16**	**7**	**0**	**1**	**1**	**6**	**0**	**0**	**0**	**19:05**
2000-01	**St. Louis**	**NHL**	**2**	**0**	**0**	**0**	**0**	**0**	**0**	**0**	**1**	**0.0**	**1**	**0**	**0.0**	**14:51**	....	....	....	....	....	....	....	....	....
	Pittsburgh	**NHL**	**36**	**1**	**4**	**5**	**26**	**0**	**0**	**0**	**11**	**9.1**	**5**	**0**	**0.0**	**16:57**	**12**	**0**	**1**	**1**	**2**	**0**	**0**	**0**	**18:22**
2001-02	**St. Louis**	**NHL**	**30**	**0**	**3**	**3**	**2**	**0**	**0**	**0**	**13**	**0.0**	**6**	**0**	**0.0**	**12:15**	**7**	**0**	**0**	**0**	**4**	**0**	**0**	**0**	**14:36**
	Worcester IceCats	AHL	2	0	0	0	0	....	....	....	....	....	....	....	....	....	....	....	....	....	....	....	....	....	....
2002-03	**Pittsburgh**	**NHL**	**69**	**2**	**5**	**7**	**36**	**0**	**0**	**0**	**27**	**7.4**	**–9**	**0**	**0.0**	**18:46**	....	....	....	....	....	....	....	....	....
	Tampa Bay	**NHL**	**1**	**0**	**0**	**0**	**0**	**0**	**0**	**0**	**0**	**0.0**	**–2**	**0**	**0.0**	**18:26**	....	....	....	....	....	....	....	....	....
2003-04	**Pittsburgh**	**NHL**	**52**	**1**	**8**	**9**	**27**	**0**	**0**	**0**	**23**	**4.3**	**–8**	**0**	**0.0**	**17:01**	....	....	....	....	....	....	....	....	....
	Vancouver	**NHL**	**9**	**0**	**2**	**2**	**2**	**0**	**0**	**0**	**7**	**0.0**	**2**	**0**	**0.0**	**10:19**	**3**	**0**	**0**	**0**	**2**	**0**	**0**	**0**	**8:41**
	NHL Totals		**1191**	**36**	**145**	**181**	**1090**	**5**	**2**	**3**	**822**	**4.4**		**0**	**0.0**	**17:39**	**79**	**3**	**6**	**9**	**50**	**1**	**0**	**0**	**16:37**

Traded to **NY Islanders** by **Chicago** with Gary Nylund for Steve Konroyd and Bob Bassen, November 25, 1988. Traded to **Hartford** by **NY Islanders** for Hartford's 5th round choice (Ryan Duthie) in 1992 Entry Draft, October 30, 1990. Signed as a free agent by **Tampa Bay**, July 9, 1992. Traded to **Detroit** by **Tampa Bay** with Ben Hankinson for Shawn Burr and Detroit's 3rd round choice (later traded to Boston – Boston selected Jason Doyle) in 1996 Entry Draft, August 17, 1995. Signed as a free agent by **St. Louis**, July 31, 1996. Traded to **Pittsburgh** by **St. Louis** for Dan Trebil, December 28, 2000.
• Missed majority of 2000-01 season recovering from thumb (October 5, 2000 vs. Phoenix) and knee (February 23, 2001 vs. Detroit) injuries. Signed as a free agent by **St. Louis**, November 6, 2001. Signed as a free agent by **Pittsburgh**, July 18, 2002. Traded to **Tampa Bay** by **Pittsburgh** for Brian Holzinger, March 11, 2003. Traded to **Pittsburgh** by **Tampa Bay** for NY Rangers' 9th round choice (previously acquired, Tampa Bay selected Albert Vishnyakov) in 2003 Entry Draft, May 12, 2003. Traded to **Vancouver** by **Pittsburgh** for Vancouver's 7th round choice (Jordan Morrison) in 2004 Entry Draft, March 9, 2004.

BERGLUND, Christian

(BUHRG-luhnd, KRIH-stan) **FLA.**

Left wing. Shoots left. 5'11", 190 lbs. Born, Orebro, Sweden, March 12, 1980. New Jersey's 3rd choice, 37th overall, in 1998 Entry Draft.

Season	Club	League	GP	G	A	Pts	PIM	PP	SH	GW	S	%	+/-	TF	F%	Min	GP	G	A	Pts	PIM	PP	SH	GW	Min
1994-95	Kariskoga IK	Swede-4	20	14	13	27	....	....	....	....	....	....	....	....	....	....	....	....	....	....	....	....	....	....	....
1995-96	Kristinehamn SK	Swede-3	23	8	8	16	12	....	....	....	....	....	....	....	....	....	....	....	....	....	....	....	....	....	....
1996-97	Farjestad Jr.	Swede-Jr.	21	2	3	5	24	....	....	....	....	....	....	....	....	....	....	....	....	....	....	....	....	....	....
1997-98	Farjestad Jr.	Swede-Jr.	29	23	19	42	88	....	....	....	....	....	....	....	....	....	2	0	0	0	0	....	....	....	....
	Farjestad	Sweden	1	0	0	0	0	....	....	....	....	....	....	....	....	....	....	....	....	....	....	....	....	....	....
1998-99	Farjestad Jr.	Swede-Jr.	5	3	4	7	22	....	....	....	....	....	....	....	....	....	....	....	....	....	....	....	....	....	....
	Farjestad	Sweden	37	2	4	6	37	....	....	....	....	....	....	....	....	....	4	1	0	1	4	....	....	....	....
99-2000	Farjestad Jr.	Swede-Jr.	5	3	5	8	8	....	....	....	....	....	....	....	....	....	....	....	....	....	....	....	....	....	....
	Bofors IK	Swede-2	6	2	0	2	12	....	....	....	....	....	....	....	....	....	....	....	....	....	....	....	....	....	....
	Farjestad	Sweden	43	8	6	14	44	....	....	....	....	....	....	....	....	....	7	2	1	3	10	....	....	....	....
2000-01	Farjestad	Sweden	49	17	20	37	*142	....	....	....	....	....	....	....	....	....	16	7	7	14	22	....	....	....	....
2001-02	**New Jersey**	**NHL**	**15**	**2**	**7**	**9**	**8**	**0**	**0**	**0**	**22**	**9.1**	**–3**	**2**	**50.0**	**12:26**	**3**	**0**	**0**	**0**	**2**	**0**	**0**	**0**	**11:31**
	Albany River Rats	AHL	60	21	26	47	69	....	....	....	....	....	....	....	....	....	....	....	....	....	....	....	....	....	....
2002-03	**New Jersey**	**NHL**	**38**	**4**	**5**	**9**	**20**	**0**	**0**	**0**	**50**	**8.0**	**3**	**11**	**9.1**	**10:11**	....	....	....	....	....	....	....	....	....
	Albany River Rats	AHL	26	6	14	20	57	....	....	....	....	....	....	....	....	....	....	....	....	....	....	....	....	....	....
2003-04	**New Jersey**	**NHL**	**23**	**2**	**3**	**5**	**4**	**0**	**0**	**0**	**33**	**6.1**	**–4**	**2**	**50.0**	**11:22**	....	....	....	....	....	....	....	....	....
	Florida	**NHL**	**10**	**3**	**1**	**4**	**10**	**0**	**0**	**0**	**17**	**17.6**	**–2**	**14**	**28.6**	**12:01**	....	....	....	....	....	....	....	....	....
	NHL Totals		**86**	**11**	**16**	**27**	**42**	**0**	**0**	**0**	**122**	**9.0**		**29**	**24.1**	**11:06**	**3**	**0**	**0**	**0**	**2**	**0**	**0**	**0**	**11:31**

• Missed majority of 2003-04 season recovering from hip injury suffered in game vs. Philadelphia, December 12, 2003. Traded to **Florida** by **New Jersey** with Victor Uchevatov for Viktor Kozlov, March 1, 2004.

BERRY, Rick

(BAIR-ree, RIHK)

Defense. Shoots left. 6'2", 210 lbs. Born, Birtle, Man., November 4, 1978. Colorado's 3rd choice, 55th overall, in 1997 Entry Draft.

			Regular Season														Playoffs								
Season	Club	League	GP	G	A	Pts	PIM	PP	SH	GW	S	%	+/-	TF	F%	Min	GP	G	A	Pts	PIM	PP	SH	GW	Min
1994-95	Yellowhead Pass	MMHL	33	12	19	31	90	....	....	....	....	....	....	....	....	....	....	....	....	....	....	....	....	....	....
1995-96	Seattle	WHL	59	4	9	13	103	....	....	....	....	....	....	....	....	....	1	0	0	0	0	....	....	....	....
1996-97	Seattle	WHL	72	12	21	33	125	....	....	....	....	....	....	....	....	....	15	3	7	10	23	....	....	....	....
1997-98	Seattle	WHL	37	5	12	17	100	....	....	....	....	....	....	....	....	....	....	....	....	....	....	....	....	....	....
	Spokane Chiefs	WHL	22	4	9	13	31	....	....	....	....	....	....	....	....	....	17	1	4	5	26	....	....	....	....
1998-99	Hershey Bears	AHL	62	2	6	8	153	....	....	....	....	....	....	....	....	....	....	....	....	....	....	....	....	....	....
99-2000	Hershey Bears	AHL	64	9	16	25	148	....	....	....	....	....	....	....	....	....	13	2	3	5	24	....	....	....	....
2000-01	Colorado	NHL	19	0	4	4	38	0	0	0	10	0.0	5	0	0.0	12:08	....	....	....	....	....	....	....	....	....
	Hershey Bears	AHL	48	6	17	23	87	....	....	....	....	....	....	....	....	....	12	2	2	4	18	....	....	....	....
2001-02	Colorado	NHL	57	0	0	0	60	0	0	0	29	0.0	1	0	0.0	9:29	....	....	....	....	....	....	....	....	....
	Pittsburgh	NHL	13	0	2	2	21	0	0	0	20	0.0	-4	0	0.0	19:39	....	....	....	....	....	....	....	....	....
2002-03	Washington	NHL	43	2	1	3	87	0	0	1	40	5.0	-3	0	0.0	12:58	....	....	....	....	....	....	....	....	....
2003-04	Washington	NHL	65	0	6	6	108	0	0	0	43	0.0	-5	2	50.0	12:11	....	....	....	....	....	....	....	....	....
	Portland Pirates	AHL	10	2	1	3	12	....	....	....	....	....	....	....	....	....	....	....	....	....	....	....	....	....	....
	NHL Totals		197	2	13	15	314	0	0	1	142	1.4		2	50.0	12:04	....	....	....	....	....	....	....	....	....

Traded to **Pittsburgh** by **Colorado** with Ville Nieminen for Darius Kasparaitis, March 19, 2002. Claimed by **Washington** from **Pittsburgh** in Waiver Draft, October 4, 2002.

BERTUZZI, Todd

(buhr-TOO-zee, TAWD) **VAN.**

Right wing. Shoots left. 6'3", 245 lbs. Born, Sudbury, Ont., February 2, 1975. NY Islanders' 1st choice, 23rd overall, in 1993 Entry Draft.

			Regular Season														Playoffs								
Season	Club	League	GP	G	A	Pts	PIM	PP	SH	GW	S	%	+/-	TF	F%	Min	GP	G	A	Pts	PIM	PP	SH	GW	Min
1990-91	Sudbury Legion	NOHA	48	25	46	71	247	....	....	....	....	....	....	....	....	....	....	....	....	....	....	....	....	....	....
	Sud. Cub Wolves	NOJHA	3	3	2	5	10	....	....	....	....	....	....	....	....	....	....	....	....	....	....	....	....	....	....
1991-92	Guelph Storm	OHL	47	7	14	21	145	....	....	....	....	....	....	....	....	....	....	....	....	....	....	....	....	....	....
1992-93	Guelph Storm	OHL	59	27	32	59	164	....	....	....	....	....	....	....	....	....	5	2	2	4	6	....	....	....	....
1993-94	Guelph Storm	OHL	61	28	54	82	165	....	....	....	....	....	....	....	....	....	9	2	6	8	30	....	....	....	....
1994-95	Guelph Storm	OHL	62	54	65	119	58	....	....	....	....	....	....	....	....	....	14	*15	18	33	41	....	....	....	....
1995-96	NY Islanders	NHL	76	18	21	39	83	4	0	2	127	14.2	-14	....	....	....	....	....	....	....	....	....	....	....	....
1996-97	NY Islanders	NHL	64	10	13	23	68	3	0	1	79	12.7	-3	....	....	....	....	....	....	....	....	....	....	....	....
	Utah Grizzlies	IHL	13	5	5	10	16	....	....	....	....	....	....	....	....	....	....	....	....	....	....	....	....	....	....
1997-98	NY Islanders	NHL	52	7	11	18	58	1	0	1	63	11.1	-19	....	....	....	....	....	....	....	....	....	....	....	....
	Vancouver	NHL	22	6	9	15	63	1	1	1	39	15.4	2	....	....	....	....	....	....	....	....	....	....	....	....
1998-99	Vancouver	NHL	32	8	8	16	44	1	0	3	72	11.1	-6	191	43.5	18:28	....	....	....	....	....	....	....	....	....
99-2000	Vancouver	NHL	80	25	25	50	126	4	0	2	173	14.5	-2	476	46.6	15:24	....	....	....	....	....	....	....	....	....
2000-01	Vancouver	NHL	79	25	30	55	93	14	0	3	203	12.3	-18	84	45.2	17:13	4	2	2	4	8	0	0	0	19:01
2001-02	Vancouver	NHL	72	36	49	85	110	14	0	3	203	17.7	21	151	49.0	19:40	6	2	2	4	14	1	0	0	21:50
2002-03	Vancouver	NHL	82	46	51	97	144	25	0	7	243	18.9	2	208	47.1	20:34	14	2	4	6	*60	0	0	0	21:05
2003-04	Vancouver	NHL	69	17	43	60	122	8	0	2	156	10.9	21	111	45.1	21:00	....	....	....	....	....	....	....	....	....
	NHL Totals		628	198	260	458	911	75	1	25	1358	14.6		1221	46.3	18:41	24	6	8	14	82	1	0	0	20:55

OHL Second All-Star team (1995) • NHL First All-Star Team (2003)

Played in NHL All-Star Game (2003, 2004)

Traded to **Vancouver** by **NY Islanders** with Bryan McCabe and NY Islanders' 3rd round choice (Jarkko Ruutu) in 1998 Entry Draft for Trevor Linden, February 6, 1998. • Missed majority of 1998-99 season recovering from leg injury suffered in game vs. Washington, November 1, 1998.

BETTS, Blair

(BEHTS, BLAIR) **NYR**

Center. Shoots left. 6'1", 200 lbs. Born, Edmonton, Alta., February 16, 1980. Calgary's 2nd choice, 33rd overall, in 1998 Entry Draft.

			Regular Season														Playoffs								
Season	Club	League	GP	G	A	Pts	PIM	PP	SH	GW	S	%	+/-	TF	F%	Min	GP	G	A	Pts	PIM	PP	SH	GW	Min
1995-96	Sherwood Park	AMHL	34	22	19	41	69	....	....	....	....	....	....	....	....	....	....	....	....	....	....	....	....	....	....
1996-97	Prince George	WHL	58	12	18	30	19	....	....	....	....	....	....	....	....	....	15	2	2	4	6	....	....	....	....
1997-98	Prince George	WHL	71	35	41	76	38	....	....	....	....	....	....	....	....	....	11	4	6	10	8	....	....	....	....
1998-99	Prince George	WHL	42	20	22	42	39	....	....	....	....	....	....	....	....	....	7	3	2	5	8	....	....	....	....
99-2000	Prince George	WHL	44	24	35	59	38	....	....	....	....	....	....	....	....	....	13	11	11	22	6	....	....	....	....
2000-01	Saint John Flames	AHL	75	13	15	28	28	....	....	....	....	....	....	....	....	....	19	2	3	5	4	....	....	....	....
2001-02	Calgary	NHL	6	1	0	1	2	0	0	1	4	25.0	-1	39	48.7	7:05	....	....	....	....	....	....	....	....	....
	Saint John Flames	AHL	67	20	29	49	10	....	....	....	....	....	....	....	....	....	....	....	....	....	....	....	....	....	....
2002-03	Calgary	NHL	9	1	3	4	0	0	0	0	16	6.3	3	71	53.5	11:33	....	....	....	....	....	....	....	....	....
	Saint John Flames	AHL	19	6	7	13	6	....	....	....	....	....	....	....	....	....	....	....	....	....	....	....	....	....	....
2003-04	Calgary	NHL	20	1	2	3	10	1	0	1	21	4.8	-1	248	54.0	12:46	....	....	....	....	....	....	....	....	....
	NHL Totals		35	3	5	8	12	1	0	2	41	7.3		358	53.4	11:29	....	....	....	....	....	....	....	....	....

• Missed majority of 2002-03 season recovering from shoulder injury suffered in training camp, September 27, 2002. • Missed majority of 2003-04 season recovering from shoulder injury suffered in game vs. Chicago, November 22, 2003. Traded to **NY Rangers** by **Calgary** with Jamie McLennan and Greg Moore for Chris Simon and NY Rangers' 7th round choice (Matt Schneider) in 2004 Entry Draft, March 6, 2004.

BEZINA, Goran

(BEH-zee-nuh, GOH-ran)

Defense. Shoots left. 6'2", 215 lbs. Born, Split, Yugoslavia, March 21, 1980. Phoenix's 8th choice, 234th overall, in 1999 Entry Draft.

			Regular Season														Playoffs								
Season	Club	League	GP	G	A	Pts	PIM	PP	SH	GW	S	%	+/-	TF	F%	Min	GP	G	A	Pts	PIM	PP	SH	GW	Min
1998-99	Fribourg Jr.	Swiss-Jr.	22	11	6	17	64	....	....	....	....	....	....	....	....	....	....	....	....	....	....	....	....	....	....
	Fribourg	EuroHL	6	0	0	0	0	....	....	....	....	....	....	....	....	....	....	....	....	....	....	....	....	....	....
	Fribourg	Swiss	38	0	0	0	14	....	....	....	....	....	....	....	....	....	4	0	0	0	2	....	....	....	....
99-2000	Fribourg Jr.	Swiss-Jr.	2	0	1	1	16	....	....	....	....	....	....	....	....	....	2	1	1	2	8	....	....	....	....
	Fribourg	Swiss	44	3	6	9	10	....	....	....	....	....	....	....	....	....	4	0	0	0	6	....	....	....	....
	EHC Visp	Swiss-2	2	0	0	0	2	....	....	....	....	....	....	....	....	....	....	....	....	....	....	....	....	....	....
2000-01	Fribourg	Swiss	44	10	10	20	44	....	....	....	....	....	....	....	....	....	5	1	1	2	12	....	....	....	....
2001-02	Springfield	AHL	66	2	11	13	50	....	....	....	....	....	....	....	....	....	....	....	....	....	....	....	....	....	....
2002-03	Springfield	AHL	64	3	4	7	27	....	....	....	....	....	....	....	....	....	6	0	1	1	0	....	....	....	....
2003-04	Phoenix	NHL	3	0	0	0	2	0	0	0	0	0.0	-1	0	0.0	5:17	....	....	....	....	....	....	....	....	....
	Springfield	AHL	74	11	10	21	65	....	....	....	....	....	....	....	....	....	....	....	....	....	....	....	....	....	....
	NHL Totals		3	0	0	0	2	0	0	0	0	0.0		0	0.0	5:17	....	....	....	....	....	....	....	....	....

Signed as a free agent by **HC Geneve-Servette** (Swiss), May 18, 2004.

BICEK, Jiri

(bee-SEHK, YEH-ree) **N.J.**

Right wing. Shoots left. 5'10", 190 lbs. Born, Kosice, Czech., December 3, 1978. New Jersey's 4th choice, 131st overall, in 1997 Entry Draft.

			Regular Season														Playoffs								
Season	Club	League	GP	G	A	Pts	PIM	PP	SH	GW	S	%	+/-	TF	F%	Min	GP	G	A	Pts	PIM	PP	SH	GW	Min
1994-95	HC Kosice Jr.	Slovak-Jr.	42	38	36	74	18	....	....	....	....	....	....	....	....	....	....	....	....	....	....	....	....	....	....
1995-96	HC Kosice	Slovakia	30	10	15	25	16	....	....	....	....	....	....	....	....	....	9	2	4	6	0	....	....	....	....
1996-97	HC Kosice	Slovakia	44	11	14	25	20	....	....	....	....	....	....	....	....	....	7	1	3	4	....	....	....	....	....
1997-98	Albany River Rats	AHL	50	10	10	20	22	....	....	....	....	....	....	....	....	....	13	1	6	7	4	....	....	....	....
1998-99	Albany River Rats	AHL	79	15	45	60	102	....	....	....	....	....	....	....	....	....	5	2	2	4	2	....	....	....	....
99-2000	Albany River Rats	AHL	80	7	36	43	51	....	....	....	....	....	....	....	....	....	4	0	2	2	0	....	....	....	....
2000-01	New Jersey	NHL	5	1	0	1	4	0	0	0	10	10.0	0	0	0.0	13:04	....	....	....	....	....	....	....	....	....
	Albany River Rats	AHL	73	12	29	41	73	....	....	....	....	....	....	....	....	....	....	....	....	....	....	....	....	....	....
2001-02	New Jersey	NHL	1	0	0	0	0	0	0	0	2	0.0	-1	0	0.0	13:10	....	....	....	....	....	....	....	....	....
	Albany River Rats	AHL	62	15	19	34	45	....	....	....	....	....	....	....	....	....	....	....	....	....	....	....	....	....	....
2002-03♦	New Jersey	NHL	44	5	6	11	25	1	0	1	63	7.9	7	3	0.0	11:48	5	0	0	0	0	0	0	0	8:10
	Albany River Rats	AHL	24	4	10	14	28	....	....	....	....	....	....	....	....	....	....	....	....	....	....	....	....	....	....
2003-04	New Jersey	NHL	12	0	1	1	0	0	0	0	10	0.0	0	1	0.0	9:55	2	0	0	0	0	0	0	0	12:26
	Albany River Rats	AHL	55	12	18	30	37	....	....	....	....	....	....	....	....	....	....	....	....	....	....	....	....	....	....
	NHL Totals		62	6	7	13	29	1	0	1	85	7.1		4	0.0	11:34	7	0	0	0	0	0	0	0	9:23

BIRON, Mathieu (BEE-rawn, MA-tyew) **FLA.**

Defense. Shoots right. 6'6", 220 lbs. Born, Lac-St-Charles, Que., April 29, 1980. Los Angeles' 1st choice, 21st overall, in 1998 Entry Draft.

			Regular Season														Playoffs								
Season	Club	League	GP	G	A	Pts	PIM	PP	SH	GW	S	%	+/-	TF	F%	Min	GP	G	A	Pts	PIM	PP	SH	GW	Min
1996-97	Ste-Foy	QAAA	40	4	22	26	49	....	....	....	....	....	....	....	....	....	10	3	4	7	....	....	....	....	....
1997-98	Shawinigan	QMJHL	59	8	28	36	60	....	....	....	....	....	....	....	....	....	6	0	1	1	10	....	....	....	....
1998-99	Shawinigan	QMJHL	69	13	32	45	116	....	....	....	....	....	....	....	....	....	6	0	2	2	6	....	....	....	....
99-2000	**NY Islanders**	**NHL**	**60**	**4**	**4**	**8**	**38**	**2**	**0**	**2**	**70**	**5.7**	**–13**	**2**	**0.0**	**15:02**	....	....	....	....	....	....	....	....	....
2000-01	**NY Islanders**	**NHL**	**14**	**0**	**1**	**1**	**12**	**0**	**0**	**0**	**10**	**0.0**	**2**	**0**	**0.0**	**12:21**	....	....	....	....	....	....	....	....	....
	Lowell	AHL	22	1	3	4	17	....	....	....	....	....	....	....	....	....	....	....	....	....	....	....	....	....	....
	Springfield	AHL	34	0	6	6	18	....	....	....	....	....	....	....	....	....	....	....	....	....	....	....	....	....	....
2001-02	**Tampa Bay**	**NHL**	**36**	**0**	**0**	**0**	**12**	**0**	**0**	**0**	**35**	**0.0**	**–16**	**0**	**0.0**	**14:47**	....	....	....	....	....	....	....	....	....
	Springfield	AHL	35	4	9	13	16	....	....	....	....	....	....	....	....	....	....	....	....	....	....	....	....	....	....
2002-03	**Florida**	**NHL**	**34**	**1**	**8**	**9**	**14**	**0**	**1**	**0**	**52**	**1.9**	**–18**	**0**	**0.0**	**21:08**	....	....	....	....	....	....	....	....	....
	San Antonio	AHL	43	3	8	11	58	....	....	....	....	....	....	....	....	....	....	....	....	....	....	....	....	....	....
2003-04	**Florida**	**NHL**	**57**	**3**	**10**	**13**	**51**	**0**	**0**	**1**	**75**	**4.0**	**–13**	**0**	**0.0**	**18:13**	....	....	....	....	....	....	....	....	....
	NHL Totals		**201**	**8**	**23**	**31**	**127**	**2**	**1**	**3**	**242**	**3.3**		**2**	**0.0**	**16:44**	....	....	....	....	....	....	....	....	....

Traded to **NY Islanders** by **Los Angeles** with Olli Jokinen, Josh Green and Los Angeles' 1st round choice (Taylor Pyatt) in 1999 Entry Draft for Ziggy Palffy, Brian Smolinski, Marcel Cousineau and New Jersey's 4th round choice (previously acquired, Los Angeles selected Daniel Johansson) in 1999 Entry Draft, June 20, 1999. Traded to **Tampa Bay** by **NY Islanders** with NY Islanders' 2nd round choice (later traded to Washington – later traded to Vancouver – Vancouver selected Denis Grot) in 2002 Entry Draft for Adrian Aucoin and Alexander Kharitonov, June 22, 2001. Claimed by **Columbus** from **Tampa Bay** in Waiver Draft, October 4, 2002. Traded to **Florida** by **Columbus** for Petr Tenkrat, October 4, 2002.

BISHAI, Mike (BIHSH-igh, MIGHK) **EDM.**

Center. Shoots left. 5'11", 185 lbs. Born, Edmonton, Alta., May 30, 1979.

			Regular Season														Playoffs								
Season	Club	League	GP	G	A	Pts	PIM	PP	SH	GW	S	%	+/-	TF	F%	Min	GP	G	A	Pts	PIM	PP	SH	GW	Min
1996-97	South Surrey	BCHL	38	6	13	19	10	....	....	....	....	....	....	....	....	....	....	....	....	....	....	....	....	....	....
1997-98	South Surrey	BCHL	47	48	52	100	36	....	....	....	....	....	....	....	....	....	....	....	....	....	....	....	....	....	....
1998-99	West. Michigan	CCHA	26	0	3	3	20	....	....	....	....	....	....	....	....	....	....	....	....	....	....	....	....	....	....
99-2000	West. Michigan	CCHA	35	18	19	37	52	....	....	....	....	....	....	....	....	....	....	....	....	....	....	....	....	....	....
2000-01	West. Michigan	CCHA	37	23	*45	*68	37	....	....	....	....	....	....	....	....	....	....	....	....	....	....	....	....	....	....
2001-02	West. Michigan	CCHA	34	10	27	37	28	....	....	....	....	....	....	....	....	....	....	....	....	....	....	....	....	....	....
	Hamilton	AHL	3	0	0	0	0	....	....	....	....	....	....	....	....	....	....	....	....	....	....	....	....	....	....
2002-03	Hamilton	AHL	27	7	5	12	11	....	....	....	....	....	....	....	....	....	6	2	1	3	2	....	....	....	....
	Columbus	ECHL	25	12	17	29	24	....	....	....	....	....	....	....	....	....	....	....	....	....	....	....	....	....	....
2003-04	**Edmonton**	**NHL**	**14**	**0**	**2**	**2**	**19**	**0**	**0**	**0**	**14**	**0.0**	**0**	**113**	**41.6**	**9:09**	....	....	....	....	....	....	....	....	....
	Toronto	AHL	48	11	22	33	18	....	....	....	....	....	....	....	....	....	3	0	0	0	4	....	....	....	....
	NHL Totals		**14**	**0**	**2**	**2**	**19**	**0**	**0**	**0**	**14**	**0.0**		**113**	**41.6**	**9:09**	....	....	....	....	....	....	....	....	....

CCHA Second All-Star Team (2001) • NCAA West Second All-American Team (2001)

Signed as a free agent by **Edmonton**, May 28, 2002.

BLAKE, Jason (BLAYK, JAY-suhn) **NYI**

Center. Shoots left. 5'10", 180 lbs. Born, Moorhead, MN, September 2, 1973.

			Regular Season														Playoffs								
Season	Club	League	GP	G	A	Pts	PIM	PP	SH	GW	S	%	+/-	TF	F%	Min	GP	G	A	Pts	PIM	PP	SH	GW	Min
1991-92	Moorhead Spuds	Hi-School	25	30	30	60	....	....	....	....	....	....	....	....	....	....	....	....	....	....	....	....	....	....	....
1992-93	Waterloo	USHL	45	24	27	51	107	....	....	....	....	....	....	....	....	....	....	....	....	....	....	....	....	....	....
1993-94	Waterloo	USHL	47	50	50	100	76	....	....	....	....	....	....	....	....	....	....	....	....	....	....	....	....	....	....
1994-95	Ferris State	CCHA	36	16	16	32	46	....	....	....	....	....	....	....	....	....	....	....	....	....	....	....	....	....	....
1995-96	North Dakota	CCHA	DID NOT PLAY – TRANSFERRED COLLEGES																						
1996-97	North Dakota	WCHA	43	19	32	51	44	....	....	....	....	....	....	....	....	....	....	....	....	....	....	....	....	....	....
1997-98	North Dakota	WCHA	38	24	27	51	62	....	....	....	....	....	....	....	....	....	....	....	....	....	....	....	....	....	....
1998-99	North Dakota	WCHA	38	*28	*41	*69	49	....	....	....	....	....	....	....	....	....	....	....	....	....	....	....	....	....	....
	Los Angeles	**NHL**	**1**	**1**	**0**	**1**	**0**	**0**	**0**	**0**	**5**	**20.0**	**1**	**14**	**35.7**	**17:13**	....	....	....	....	....	....	....	....	....
	Orlando	IHL	5	3	5	8	6	....	....	....	....	....	....	....	....	....	13	3	4	7	20	....	....	....	....
99-2000	**Los Angeles**	**NHL**	**64**	**5**	**18**	**23**	**26**	**0**	**0**	**1**	**131**	**3.8**	**4**	**269**	**43.9**	**11:17**	**3**	**0**	**0**	**0**	**0**	**0**	**0**	**0**	**9:35**
	Long Beach	IHL	7	3	6	9	2	....	....	....	....	....	....	....	....	....	....	....	....	....	....	....	....	....	....
2000-01	**Los Angeles**	**NHL**	**17**	**1**	**3**	**4**	**10**	**0**	**0**	**0**	**27**	**3.7**	**–8**	**13**	**61.5**	**10:03**	....	....	....	....	....	....	....	....	....
	Lowell	AHL	2	0	1	1	2	....	....	....	....	....	....	....	....	....	....	....	....	....	....	....	....	....	....
	NY Islanders	**NHL**	**30**	**4**	**8**	**12**	**24**	**1**	**1**	**0**	**73**	**5.5**	**–12**	**118**	**44.1**	**15:43**	....	....	....	....	....	....	....	....	....
2001-02	**NY Islanders**	**NHL**	**82**	**8**	**10**	**18**	**36**	**0**	**0**	**1**	**136**	**5.9**	**–11**	**23**	**43.5**	**12:54**	**7**	**0**	**1**	**1**	**13**	**0**	**0**	**0**	**12:13**
2002-03	**NY Islanders**	**NHL**	**81**	**25**	**30**	**55**	**58**	**3**	**1**	**4**	**253**	**9.9**	**16**	**22**	**18.2**	**17:38**	**5**	**0**	**1**	**1**	**2**	**0**	**0**	**0**	**19:39**
2003-04	**NY Islanders**	**NHL**	**75**	**22**	**25**	**47**	**56**	**1**	**4**	**3**	**243**	**9.1**	**11**	**70**	**41.4**	**18:49**	**4**	**2**	**0**	**2**	**2**	**0**	**0**	**0**	**18:09**
	NHL Totals		**350**	**66**	**94**	**160**	**210**	**5**	**6**	**9**	**868**	**7.6**		**529**	**42.7**	**15:05**	**19**	**2**	**2**	**4**	**17**	**0**	**0**	**0**	**15:00**

WCHA First All-Star Team (1997, 1998, 1999) • NCAA West Second All-American Team (1998) • WCHA Player of the Year (1999) • NCAA West First All-American Team (1999)

Signed as a free agent by **Los Angeles**, April 20, 1999. Traded to **NY Islanders** by **Los Angeles** for NY Islanders' 5th round choice (Joel Andresen) in 2002 Entry Draft, January 3, 2001.

BLAKE, Rob (BLAYK, RAWB) **COL.**

Defense. Shoots right. 6'4", 225 lbs. Born, Simcoe, Ont., December 10, 1969. Los Angeles' 4th choice, 70th overall, in 1988 Entry Draft.

			Regular Season														Playoffs								
Season	Club	League	GP	G	A	Pts	PIM	PP	SH	GW	S	%	+/-	TF	F%	Min	GP	G	A	Pts	PIM	PP	SH	GW	Min
1985-86	Brantford Classics	OJHL-B	39	3	13	16	43	....	....	....	....	....	....	....	....	....	....	....	....	....	....	....	....	....	....
1986-87	Stratford Cullitons	OJHL-B	31	11	20	31	115	....	....	....	....	....	....	....	....	....	....	....	....	....	....	....	....	....	....
1987-88	Bowling Green	CCHA	43	5	8	13	88	....	....	....	....	....	....	....	....	....	....	....	....	....	....	....	....	....	....
1988-89	Bowling Green	CCHA	46	11	21	32	140	....	....	....	....	....	....	....	....	....	....	....	....	....	....	....	....	....	....
1989-90	Bowling Green	CCHA	42	23	36	59	140	....	....	....	....	....	....	....	....	....	....	....	....	....	....	....	....	....	....
	Los Angeles	**NHL**	**4**	**0**	**0**	**0**	**4**	**0**	**0**	**0**	**3**	**0.0**	**0**	....	....	....	**8**	**1**	**3**	**4**	**4**	**1**	**0**	**0**	....
1990-91	**Los Angeles**	**NHL**	**75**	**12**	**34**	**46**	**125**	**9**	**0**	**2**	**150**	**8.0**	**3**	....	....	....	**12**	**1**	**4**	**5**	**26**	**1**	**0**	**0**	....
1991-92	**Los Angeles**	**NHL**	**57**	**7**	**13**	**20**	**102**	**5**	**0**	**0**	**131**	**5.3**	**–5**	....	....	....	**6**	**2**	**1**	**3**	**12**	**0**	**0**	**0**	....
1992-93	**Los Angeles**	**NHL**	**76**	**16**	**43**	**59**	**152**	**10**	**0**	**4**	**243**	**6.6**	**18**	....	....	....	**23**	**4**	**6**	**10**	**46**	**1**	**1**	**0**	....
1993-94	**Los Angeles**	**NHL**	**84**	**20**	**48**	**68**	**137**	**7**	**0**	**6**	**304**	**6.6**	**–7**	....	....	....	....	....	....	....	....	....	....	....	....
1994-95	**Los Angeles**	**NHL**	**24**	**4**	**7**	**11**	**38**	**4**	**0**	**1**	**76**	**5.3**	**–16**	....	....	....	....	....	....	....	....	....	....	....	....
1995-96	**Los Angeles**	**NHL**	**6**	**1**	**2**	**3**	**8**	**0**	**0**	**0**	**13**	**7.7**	**0**	....	....	....	....	....	....	....	....	....	....	....	....
1996-97	**Los Angeles**	**NHL**	**62**	**8**	**23**	**31**	**82**	**4**	**0**	**1**	**169**	**4.7**	**–28**	....	....	....	....	....	....	....	....	....	....	....	....
1997-98	**Los Angeles**	**NHL**	**81**	**23**	**27**	**50**	**94**	**11**	**0**	**4**	**261**	**8.8**	**–3**	....	....	....	**4**	**0**	**0**	**0**	**6**	**0**	**0**	**0**	....
	Canada	Olympics	6	1	1	2	2	....	....	....	....	....	....	....	....	....	....	....	....	....	....	....	....	....	....
1998-99	**Los Angeles**	**NHL**	**62**	**12**	**23**	**35**	**128**	**5**	**1**	**2**	**216**	**5.6**	**–7**	**0**	**0.0**	**24:52**	....	....	....	....	....	....	....	....	....
99-2000	**Los Angeles**	**NHL**	**77**	**18**	**39**	**57**	**112**	**12**	**0**	**5**	**327**	**5.5**	**10**	**0**	**0.0**	**28:30**	**4**	**0**	**2**	**2**	**4**	**0**	**0**	**0**	**30:10**
2000-01	**Los Angeles**	**NHL**	**54**	**17**	**32**	**49**	**69**	**9**	**0**	**1**	**223**	**7.6**	**–8**	**0**	**0.0**	**28:11**	....	....	....	....	....	....	....	....	....
	♦ **Colorado**	**NHL**	**13**	**2**	**8**	**10**	**8**	**1**	**0**	**1**	**44**	**4.5**	**11**	**0**	**0.0**	**26:03**	**23**	**6**	**13**	**19**	**16**	**3**	**0**	**0**	**29:26**
2001-02	**Colorado**	**NHL**	**75**	**16**	**40**	**56**	**58**	**10**	**0**	**2**	**229**	**7.0**	**16**	**0**	**0.0**	**27:35**	**20**	**6**	**6**	**12**	**16**	**1**	**0**	**0**	**26:38**
	Canada	Olympics	6	1	2	3	2	....	....	....	....	....	....	....	....	....	....	....	....	....	....	....	....	....	....
2002-03	**Colorado**	**NHL**	**79**	**17**	**28**	**45**	**57**	**8**	**2**	**3**	**269**	**6.3**	**20**	**0**	**0.0**	**26:21**	**7**	**1**	**2**	**3**	**8**	**0**	**0**	**0**	**27:28**
2003-04	**Colorado**	**NHL**	**74**	**13**	**33**	**46**	**61**	**8**	**0**	**3**	**242**	**5.4**	**6**	**1**	**0.0**	**24:23**	**9**	**0**	**5**	**5**	**6**	**0**	**0**	**0**	**20:17**
	NHL Totals		**903**	**186**	**400**	**586**	**1235**	**103**	**3**	**35**	**2900**	**6.4**		**1**	**0.0**	**26:37**	**116**	**21**	**42**	**63**	**144**	**7**	**1**	**0**	**27:04**

CCHA Second All-Star Team (1989) • CCHA First All-Star Team (1990) • NCAA West First All-American Team (1990) • NHL All-Rookie Team (1991) • NHL First All-Star Team (1998) • James Norris Memorial Trophy (1998) • NHL Second All-Star Team (2000, 2001, 2002)

Played in NHL All-Star Game (1994, 1999, 2000, 2001, 2002, 2003, 2004)

• Missed majority of 1995-96 season recovering from knee injury suffered in game vs. Washington, October 20, 1995. Traded to **Colorado** by **Los Angeles** with Steve Reinprecht for Adam Deadmarsh, Aaron Miller, a player to be named later (Jared Aulin, March 22, 2001), Colorado's 1st round choices in 2001 (Dave Steckel) and 2003 (Brian Boyle) Entry Drafts, February 21, 2001.

BLATNY, Zdenek (BLAT-nee, z'DEHN-ehk)

Left wing. Shoots left. 6'1", 190 lbs. Born, Brno, Czech., January 14, 1981. Atlanta's 3rd choice, 68th overall, in 1999 Entry Draft.

			Regular Season														Playoffs								
Season	Club	League	GP	G	A	Pts	PIM	PP	SH	GW	S	%	+/-	TF	F%	Min	GP	G	A	Pts	PIM	PP	SH	GW	Min
1997-98	Kometa Brno Jr.	Czech-Jr.	42	22	21	43	40	....	....	....	....	....	....	....	....	....	....	....	....	....	....	....	....	....	....
1998-99	Seattle	WHL	44	18	15	33	25	....	....	....	....	....	....	....	....	....	11	4	0	4	24	....	....	....	....
99-2000	Seattle	WHL	7	4	5	9	12	....	....	....	....	....	....	....	....	....	....	....	....	....	....	....	....	....	....
	Kootenay Ice	WHL	61	43	39	82	119	....	....	....	....	....	....	....	....	....	21	10	*17	27	46	....	....	....	....
2000-01	Kootenay Ice	WHL	58	37	48	85	120	....	....	....	....	....	....	....	....	....	11	8	10	18	24	....	....	....	....
2001-02	Chicago Wolves	AHL	41	4	3	7	30	....	....	....	....	....	....	....	....	....	3	2	0	2	0	....	....	....	....
	Greenville	ECHL	12	5	5	10	17	....	....	....	....	....	....	....	....	....	9	2	8	10	14	....	....	....	....

			Regular Season														Playoffs								
Season	Club	League	GP	G	A	Pts	PIM	PP	SH	GW	S	%	+/-	TF	F%	Min	GP	G	A	Pts	PIM	PP	SH	GW	Min
2002-03	**Atlanta**	**NHL**	**4**	**0**	**0**	**0**	**0**	**0**	**0**	**0**	**2**	**0.0**	**–1**	**0**	**0.0**	**10:31**	....	....	....	....	....	....	....	....	....
	Chicago Wolves	AHL	72	12	9	21	62	....	....	....	....	....	....	....	....	....	9	0	2	2	20	....	....	....	....
2003-04	**Atlanta**	**NHL**	**16**	**3**	**0**	**3**	**6**	**0**	**0**	**0**	**17**	**17.6**	**0**	**13**	**38.5**	**10:27**	....	....	....	....	....	....	....	....	....
	Chicago Wolves	AHL	61	11	23	34	115	....	....	....	....	....	....	....	....	....	10	0	4	4	24	....	....	....	....
	NHL Totals		**20**	**3**	**0**	**3**	**6**	**0**	**0**	**0**	**19**	**15.8**		**13**	**38.5**	**10:28**	....	....	....	....	....	....	....	....	....

WHL East Second All-Star Team (2000)

BLOUIN, Sylvain

(bluh-WHEN, SIHL-veh)

Left wing. Shoots left. 6'2", 215 lbs. Born, Montreal, Que., May 21, 1974. NY Rangers' 5th choice, 104th overall, in 1994 Entry Draft.

1991-92	Laval Titan	QMJHL	28	0	0	0	23	....	....	....	....	....	....	....	....	....	9	0	0	0	35	....	....	....	....
1992-93	Laval Titan	QMJHL	68	0	10	10	373	....	....	....	....	....	....	....	....	....	13	1	0	1	*66	....	....	....	....
1993-94	Laval Titan	QMJHL	62	18	22	40	*492	....	....	....	....	....	....	....	....	....	21	4	13	17	*177	....	....	....	....
1994-95	Chicago Wolves	IHL	1	0	0	0	2	....	....	....	....	....	....	....	....	....	....	....	....	....	....	....	....	....	....
	Charlotte	ECHL	50	5	7	12	280	....	....	....	....	....	....	....	....	....	3	0	0	0	6	....	....	....	....
	Binghamton	AHL	10	1	0	1	46	....	....	....	....	....	....	....	....	....	2	0	0	0	24	....	....	....	....
1995-96	Binghamton	AHL	71	5	8	13	*352	....	....	....	....	....	....	....	....	....	4	0	3	3	4	....	....	....	....
1996-97	**NY Rangers**	**NHL**	**6**	**0**	**0**	**0**	**18**	**0**	**0**	**0**	**1**	**0.0**	**–1**	....	....	....	....	....	....	....	....	....	....	....	....
	Binghamton	AHL	62	13	17	30	301	....	....	....	....	....	....	....	....	....	4	2	1	3	16	....	....	....	....
1997-98	**NY Rangers**	**NHL**	**1**	**0**	**0**	**0**	**5**	**0**	**0**	**0**	**0**	**0.0**	**0**	....	....	....	....	....	....	....	....	....	....	....	....
	Hartford	AHL	53	8	9	17	286	....	....	....	....	....	....	....	....	....	9	0	1	1	63	....	....	....	....
1998-99	**Montreal**	**NHL**	**5**	**0**	**0**	**0**	**19**	**0**	**0**	**0**	**1**	**0.0**	**0**	**0**	**0.0**	**3:37**	....	....	....	....	....	....	....	....	....
	Fredericton	AHL	67	6	10	16	333	....	....	....	....	....	....	....	....	....	15	2	0	2	*87	....	....	....	....
99-2000	Worcester IceCats	AHL	70	16	18	34	337	....	....	....	....	....	....	....	....	....	8	3	5	8	30	....	....	....	....
2000-01	**Minnesota**	**NHL**	**41**	**3**	**2**	**5**	**117**	**0**	**0**	**0**	**37**	**8.1**	**–5**	**2**	**100.0**	**9:54**	....	....	....	....	....	....	....	....	....
2001-02	**Minnesota**	**NHL**	**43**	**0**	**2**	**2**	**130**	**0**	**0**	**0**	**28**	**0.0**	**–11**	**0**	**0.0**	**9:51**	....	....	....	....	....	....	....	....	....
2002-03	**Minnesota**	**NHL**	**2**	**0**	**0**	**0**	**4**	**0**	**0**	**0**	**1**	**0.0**	**0**	**1**	**0.0**	**7:38**	....	....	....	....	....	....	....	....	....
	Montreal	**NHL**	**17**	**0**	**0**	**0**	**43**	**0**	**0**	**0**	**3**	**0.0**	**–3**	**0**	**0.0**	**3:36**	....	....	....	....	....	....	....	....	....
	Hamilton	AHL	19	2	4	6	39	....	....	....	....	....	....	....	....	....	11	1	1	2	28	....	....	....	....
2003-04	Hamilton	AHL	29	2	1	3	75	....	....	....	....	....	....	....	....	....	....	....	....	....	....	....	....	....	....
	Manitoba Moose	AHL	11	1	0	1	22	....	....	....	....	....	....	....	....	....	....	....	....	....	....	....	....	....	....
	NHL Totals		**115**	**3**	**4**	**7**	**336**	**0**	**0**	**0**	**71**	**4.2**		**3**	**66.7**	**8:34**	....	....	....	....	....	....	....	....	....

Traded to **Montreal** by **NY Rangers** with NY Rangers' 6th round choice (later traded to Phoenix – Phoenix selected Erik Lewerstrom) in 1999 Entry Draft for Peter Popovic, June 30, 1998. Signed as a free agent by **St. Louis**, August 25, 1999. Signed as a free agent by **Montreal**, July 7, 2000. Claimed by **Minnesota** from **Montreal** in Waiver Draft, September 29, 2000. • Missed majority of 2000-01 season recovering from shoulder injury suffered in game vs. Chicago, December 7, 2000. Traded to **Montreal** by **Minnesota** for Montreal's 7th round choice (Grigory Misharin) in 2003 Entry Draft, October 31, 2002. • Missed majority of 2003-04 season recovering from shoulder injury suffered in pre-season game vs. Toronto, September 23, 2003. Traded to **Vancouver** by **Montreal** for Rene Vydareny, March 9, 2004.

BOGUNIECKI, Eric

(BOH-guhn-ih-kee, AIR-ihk) **ST.L.**

Center. Shoots right. 5'8", 192 lbs. Born, New Haven, CT, May 6, 1975. St. Louis' 6th choice, 193rd overall, in 1993 Entry Draft.

1992-93	Westminster High	Hi-School	24	30	24	54	55	....	....	....	....	....	....	....	....	....	....	....	....	....	....	....	....	....	....
1993-94	New Hampshire	H-East	40	17	16	33	66	....	....	....	....	....	....	....	....	....	....	....	....	....	....	....	....	....	....
1994-95	New Hampshire	H-East	34	12	16	28	62	....	....	....	....	....	....	....	....	....	....	....	....	....	....	....	....	....	....
1995-96	New Hampshire	H-East	32	23	28	51	46	....	....	....	....	....	....	....	....	....	....	....	....	....	....	....	....	....	....
1996-97	New Hampshire	H-East	36	26	31	57	58	....	....	....	....	....	....	....	....	....	....	....	....	....	....	....	....	....	....
1997-98	Dayton Bombers	ECHL	26	19	18	37	36	....	....	....	....	....	....	....	....	....	....	....	....	....	....	....	....	....	....
	Fort Wayne	IHL	35	4	8	12	29	....	....	....	....	....	....	....	....	....	4	1	2	3	10	....	....	....	....
1998-99	Fort Wayne	IHL	72	32	34	66	100	....	....	....	....	....	....	....	....	....	2	0	1	1	2	....	....	....	....
99-2000	**Florida**	**NHL**	**4**	**0**	**0**	**0**	**2**	**0**	**0**	**0**	**5**	**0.0**	**–1**	**25**	**36.0**	**8:35**	....	....	....	....	....	....	....	....	....
	Louisville Panthers	AHL	57	33	42	75	148	....	....	....	....	....	....	....	....	....	4	3	2	5	20	....	....	....	....
2000-01	Louisville Panthers	AHL	28	13	12	25	56	....	....	....	....	....	....	....	....	....	....	....	....	....	....	....	....	....	....
	St. Louis	**NHL**	**1**	**0**	**0**	**0**	**0**	**0**	**0**	**0**	**1**	**0.0**	**–1**	**0**	**0.0**	**13:44**	....	....	....	....	....	....	....	....	....
	Worcester IceCats	AHL	45	17	28	45	100	....	....	....	....	....	....	....	....	....	9	3	2	5	10	....	....	....	....
2001-02	**St. Louis**	**NHL**	**8**	**0**	**1**	**1**	**4**	**0**	**0**	**0**	**10**	**0.0**	**–2**	**21**	**38.1**	**11:42**	**1**	**0**	**1**	**1**	**0**	**0**	**0**	**0**	**8:01**
	Worcester IceCats	AHL	63	*38	46	84	181	....	....	....	....	....	....	....	....	....	3	2	0	2	4	....	....	....	....
2002-03	**St. Louis**	**NHL**	**80**	**22**	**27**	**49**	**38**	**3**	**1**	**5**	**117**	**18.8**	**22**	**5**	**40.0**	**14:00**	**7**	**1**	**2**	**3**	**2**	**1**	**0**	**0**	**13:09**
2003-04	**St. Louis**	**NHL**	**27**	**6**	**4**	**10**	**20**	**2**	**0**	**2**	**40**	**15.0**	**–1**	**1**	**0.0**	**14:42**	**1**	**0**	**0**	**0**	**0**	**0**	**0**	**0**	**12:52**
	Worcester IceCats	AHL	3	0	1	1	0	....	....	....	....	....	....	....	....	....	....	....	....	....	....	....	....	....	....
	NHL Totals		**120**	**28**	**32**	**60**	**64**	**5**	**1**	**7**	**173**	**16.2**		**52**	**36.5**	**13:50**	**9**	**1**	**3**	**4**	**2**	**1**	**0**	**0**	**12:33**

Hockey East Second All-Star Team (1997) • AHL First All-Star Team (2002) • Les Cunningham Plaque (MVP – AHL) (2002)

Signed as a free agent by **Florida**, July 7, 1999. Traded to **St. Louis** by **Florida** for Andrei Podkonicky, December 17, 2000. • Missed majority of 2003-04 season recovering from shoulder (September 23, 2003 in training camp) and head (February 28, 2004 vs. Vancouver) injuries.

BOILEAU, Patrick

(BWOI-loh, PAT-rihk)

Defense. Shoots right. 6', 202 lbs. Born, Montreal, Que., February 22, 1975. Washington's 3rd choice, 69th overall, in 1993 Entry Draft.

1990-91	Laval Laurentide	QAAA	3	0	1	1	0	....	....	....	....	....	....	....	....	....	....	....	....	....	....	....	....	....	....
1991-92	Laval Laurentide	QAAA	42	9	36	45	94	....	....	....	....	....	....	....	....	....	12	3	5	8	10	....	....	....	....
1992-93	Laval Titan	QMJHL	69	4	19	23	73	....	....	....	....	....	....	....	....	....	13	1	2	3	10	....	....	....	....
1993-94	Laval Titan	QMJHL	64	13	57	70	56	....	....	....	....	....	....	....	....	....	21	1	7	8	24	....	....	....	....
1994-95	Laval Titan	QMJHL	38	8	25	33	46	....	....	....	....	....	....	....	....	....	20	4	16	20	24	....	....	....	....
1995-96	Portland Pirates	AHL	78	10	28	38	41	....	....	....	....	....	....	....	....	....	19	1	3	4	12	....	....	....	....
1996-97	**Washington**	**NHL**	**1**	**0**	**0**	**0**	**0**	**0**	**0**	**0**	**0**	**0.0**	**0**	....	....	....	....	....	....	....	....	....	....	....	....
	Portland Pirates	AHL	67	16	28	44	63	....	....	....	....	....	....	....	....	....	5	1	1	2	4	....	....	....	....
1997-98	Portland Pirates	AHL	47	6	21	27	53	....	....	....	....	....	....	....	....	....	10	0	1	1	8	....	....	....	....
1998-99	**Washington**	**NHL**	**4**	**0**	**1**	**1**	**2**	**0**	**0**	**0**	**7**	**0.0**	**–4**	**0**	**0.0**	**15:56**	....	....	....	....	....	....	....	....	....
	Portland Pirates	AHL	52	6	18	24	52	....	....	....	....	....	....	....	....	....	....	....	....	....	....	....	....	....	....
	Indianapolis Ice	IHL	29	8	13	21	27	....	....	....	....	....	....	....	....	....	4	0	1	1	2	....	....	....	....
99-2000	Portland Pirates	AHL	63	2	15	17	61	....	....	....	....	....	....	....	....	....	4	0	0	0	4	....	....	....	....
2000-01	Portland Pirates	AHL	77	6	14	20	50	....	....	....	....	....	....	....	....	....	3	0	0	0	8	....	....	....	....
2001-02	**Washington**	**NHL**	**2**	**0**	**0**	**0**	**2**	**0**	**0**	**0**	**0**	**0.0**	**–1**	**0**	**0.0**	**11:52**	....	....	....	....	....	....	....	....	....
	Portland Pirates	AHL	75	17	19	36	43	....	....	....	....	....	....	....	....	....	....	....	....	....	....	....	....	....	....
2002-03	**Detroit**	**NHL**	**25**	**2**	**6**	**8**	**14**	**0**	**0**	**1**	**18**	**11.1**	**8**	**0**	**0.0**	**13:58**	....	....	....	....	....	....	....	....	....
	Grand Rapids	AHL	23	2	11	13	39	....	....	....	....	....	....	....	....	....	....	....	....	....	....	....	....	....	....
2003-04	**Pittsburgh**	**NHL**	**16**	**3**	**4**	**7**	**8**	**3**	**0**	**0**	**41**	**7.3**	**–16**	**0**	**0.0**	**19:52**	....	....	....	....	....	....	....	....	....
	Wilkes-Barre	AHL	51	6	29	35	43	....	....	....	....	....	....	....	....	....	24	3	9	12	24	....	....	....	....
	NHL Totals		**48**	**5**	**11**	**16**	**26**	**3**	**0**	**1**	**66**	**7.6**		**0**	**0.0**	**16:03**	....	....	....	....	....	....	....	....	....

Canadian Major Junior Scholastic Player of the Year (1994)

Loaned to **Indianapolis** (IHL) by **Washington** (Portland-AHL), February 4, 1999. Signed as a free agent by **Detroit**, August 5, 2002. Signed as a free agent by **Pittsburgh**, August 28, 2003. Signed as a free agent by **HC Lausanne** (Swiss), May 13, 2004.

BOMBARDIR, Brad

(bawm-bahr-DEER, BRAD)

Defense. Shoots left. 6'1", 205 lbs. Born, Powell River, B.C., May 5, 1972. New Jersey's 5th choice, 56th overall, in 1990 Entry Draft.

1988-89	Powell River	BCJHL	30	6	5	11	24	....	....	....	....	....	....	....	....	....	6	0	0	0	0	....	....	....	....
1989-90	Powell River	BCJHL	60	10	35	45	93	....	....	....	....	....	....	....	....	....	8	2	3	5	4	....	....	....	....
1990-91	North Dakota	WCHA	33	3	6	9	18	....	....	....	....	....	....	....	....	....	....	....	....	....	....	....	....	....	....
1991-92	North Dakota	WCHA	35	3	14	17	54	....	....	....	....	....	....	....	....	....	....	....	....	....	....	....	....	....	....
1992-93	North Dakota	WCHA	38	8	15	23	34	....	....	....	....	....	....	....	....	....	....	....	....	....	....	....	....	....	....
1993-94	North Dakota	WCHA	38	5	17	22	38	....	....	....	....	....	....	....	....	....	....	....	....	....	....	....	....	....	....
1994-95	Albany River Rats	AHL	77	5	22	27	22	....	....	....	....	....	....	....	....	....	14	0	3	3	6	....	....	....	....
1995-96	Albany River Rats	AHL	80	6	25	31	63	....	....	....	....	....	....	....	....	....	3	0	1	1	4	....	....	....	....
1996-97	Albany River Rats	AHL	32	0	8	8	6	....	....	....	....	....	....	....	....	....	16	1	3	4	8	....	....	....	....
1997-98	**New Jersey**	**NHL**	**43**	**1**	**5**	**6**	**8**	**0**	**0**	**0**	**16**	**6.3**	**11**	....	....	....	....	....	....	....	....	....	....	....	....
	Albany River Rats	AHL	5	0	0	0	0	....	....	....	....	....	....	....	....	....	....	....	....	....	....	....	....	....	....
1998-99	**New Jersey**	**NHL**	**56**	**1**	**7**	**8**	**16**	**0**	**0**	**0**	**47**	**2.1**	**–4**	**1**	**0.0**	**15:03**	**5**	**0**	**0**	**0**	**0**	**0**	**0**	**0**	**16:03**
99-2000♦	**New Jersey**	**NHL**	**32**	**3**	**1**	**4**	**6**	**0**	**0**	**0**	**24**	**12.5**	**–6**	**0**	**0.0**	**15:54**	**1**	**0**	**0**	**0**	**0**	**0**	**0**	**0**	**18:55**
2000-01	**Minnesota**	**NHL**	**70**	**0**	**15**	**15**	**42**	**0**	**0**	**0**	**81**	**0.0**	**–6**	**1**	**0.0**	**20:50**	....	....	....	....	....	....	....	....	....
2001-02	**Minnesota**	**NHL**	**28**	**1**	**2**	**3**	**14**	**1**	**0**	**0**	**24**	**4.2**	**–6**	**0**	**0.0**	**20:33**	....	....	....	....	....	....	....	....	....

			Regular Season														Playoffs								
Season	Club	League	GP	G	A	Pts	PIM	PP	SH	GW	S	%	+/-	TF	F%	Min	GP	G	A	Pts	PIM	PP	SH	GW	Min
2002-03	Minnesota	NHL	58	1	14	15	16	1	0	0	55	1.8	15	0	0.0	22:01	4	0	0	0	0	0	0	0	14:52
2003-04	Minnesota	NHL	56	1	2	3	21	0	0	1	38	2.6	–10	0	0.0	20:14	....	....	....	....	....	....	....	....	....
	Nashville	NHL	13	0	0	0	4	0	0	0	9	0.0	1	0	0.0	19:03	6	0	1	1	2	0	0	0	19:38
	NHL Totals		356	8	46	54	127	2	0	1	294	2.7		2	0.0	19:18	16	0	1	1	2	0	0	0	17:17

AHL Second All-Star Team (1996)

• Missed majority of 1999-2000 season recovering from esophagus injury suffered in game vs. Philadelphia, October 30, 1999. Traded to **Minnesota** by **New Jersey** for Chris Terreri and Minnesota's 9th round choice (later traded to Tampa Bay – Tampa Bay selected Thomas Ziegler) in 2000 Entry Draft, June 23, 2000. • Missed majority of 2001-02 season recovering from ankle injury suffered in game vs. San Jose, October 16, 2001. Traded to **Nashville** by **Minnesota** with Sergei Zholtok for Buffalo's 3rd round choice (previously acquired, Minnesota selected Clayton Stoner) in 2004 Entry Draft and Nashville's 4th round choice (Patrick Bordeleau) in 2004 Entry Draft, March 5, 2004.

BONDRA, Peter

(BAWN-druh, PEE-tuhr)

Right wing. Shoots left. 6', 200 lbs. Born, Luck, USSR, February 7, 1968. Washington's 9th choice, 156th overall, in 1990 Entry Draft.

1986-87	VSZ Kosice	Czech	32	4	5	9	24	....	....	....	....	....	....	....	....	....	....	....	....	....	....	....	....	....	....
1987-88	VSZ Kosice	Czech	45	27	11	38	20	....	....	....	....	....	....	....	....	....	....	....	....	....	....	....	....	....	....
1988-89	VSZ Kosice	Czech	40	30	10	40	20	....	....	....	....	....	....	....	....	....	....	....	....	....	....	....	....	....	....
1989-90	VSZ Kosice	Czech	44	29	17	46	....	....	....	....	....	....	....	....	....	....	5	7	2	9	....	....	....	....	....
1990-91	Washington	NHL	54	12	16	28	47	4	0	1	95	12.6	–10	....	....	....	4	0	1	1	2	0	0	0	....
1991-92	Washington	NHL	71	28	28	56	42	4	0	3	158	17.7	16	....	....	....	7	6	2	8	4	1	0	0	....
1992-93	Washington	NHL	83	37	48	85	70	10	0	7	239	15.5	8	....	....	....	6	0	6	6	0	0	0	0	....
1993-94	Washington	NHL	69	24	19	43	40	4	0	2	200	12.0	22	....	....	....	9	2	4	6	4	0	0	1	....
1994-95	HC Kosice	Slovakia	2	1	0	1	0	....	....	....	....	....	....	....	....	....	....	....	....	....	....	....	....	....	....
	Washington	NHL	47	*34	9	43	24	12	6	3	177	19.2	9	....	....	....	7	5	3	8	10	2	0	1	....
1995-96	Detroit Vipers	IHL	7	8	1	9	0	....	....	....	....	....	....	....	....	....	....	....	....	....	....	....	....	....	....
	Washington	NHL	67	52	28	80	40	11	4	7	322	16.1	18	....	....	....	6	3	2	5	8	2	0	1	....
1996-97	Washington	NHL	77	46	31	77	72	10	4	3	314	14.6	7	....	....	....	....	....	....	....	....	....	....	....	....
1997-98	Washington	NHL	76	*52	26	78	44	11	5	13	284	18.3	14	....	....	....	17	7	5	12	12	3	0	2	....
	Slovakia	Olympics	2	1	0	1	25	....	....	....	....	....	....	....	....	....	....	....	....	....	....	....	....	....	....
1998-99	Washington	NHL	66	31	24	55	56	6	3	5	284	10.9	–1	1	0.0	20:35	....	....	....	....	....	....	....	....	....
99-2000	Washington	NHL	62	21	17	38	30	5	3	5	187	11.2	5	2	50.0	18:48	5	1	1	2	4	1	0	0	17:30
2000-01	Washington	NHL	82	45	36	81	60	22	4	8	305	14.8	8	2	50.0	20:48	6	2	0	2	2	2	0	1	24:55
2001-02	Washington	NHL	77	39	31	70	80	17	1	8	333	11.7	–2	2	50.0	21:43	....	....	....	....	....	....	....	....	....
2002-03	Washington	NHL	76	30	26	56	52	9	2	4	256	11.7	–3	13	30.8	18:53	6	4	2	6	8	2	0	0	22:39
2003-04	Washington	NHL	54	21	14	35	22	12	0	4	136	15.4	–17	2	50.0	18:43	....	....	....	....	....	....	....	....	....
	Ottawa	NHL	23	5	9	14	16	2	0	1	52	9.6	1	4	0.0	18:21	7	0	0	0	6	0	0	0	16:36
	NHL Totals		984	477	362	839	695	139	32	74	3342	14.3		26	30.8	19:56	80	30	26	56	60	13	0	6	20:23

Played in NHL All-Star Game (1993, 1996, 1997, 1998, 1999)

Traded to **Ottawa** by **Washington** for Brooks Laich, Ottawa's 2nd round choice in 2005 Entry Draft and future considerations, February 18, 2004.

BONK, Radek

(BOHNK, RA-dehk) **MTL.**

Center. Shoots left. 6'3", 220 lbs. Born, Krnov, Czech., January 9, 1976. Ottawa's 1st choice, 3rd overall, in 1994 Entry Draft.

1990-91	Slezan Opava Jr.	Czech-Jr.	35	47	42	89	25	....	....	....	....	....	....	....	....	....	....	....	....	....	....	....	....	....	....
1991-92	AC ZPS Zlin Jr.	Czech-Jr.	45	47	36	83	30	....	....	....	....	....	....	....	....	....	....	....	....	....	....	....	....	....	....
1992-93	AC ZPS Zlin	Czech	30	5	5	10	10	....	....	....	....	....	....	....	....	....	....	....	....	....	....	....	....	....	....
1993-94	Las Vegas	IHL	76	42	45	87	208	....	....	....	....	....	....	....	....	....	5	1	2	3	10	....	....	....	....
1994-95	Las Vegas	IHL	33	7	13	20	62	....	....	....	....	....	....	....	....	....	....	....	....	....	....	....	....	....	....
	Ottawa	NHL	42	3	8	11	28	1	0	0	40	7.5	–5	....	....	....	....	....	....	....	....	....	....	....	....
	P.E.I. Senators	AHL	....	....	....	....	....	....	....	....	....	....	....	....	....	....	1	0	0	0	0	....	....	....	....
1995-96	Ottawa	NHL	76	16	19	35	36	5	0	1	161	9.9	–5	....	....	....	....	....	....	....	....	....	....	....	....
1996-97	Ottawa	NHL	53	5	13	18	14	0	1	0	82	6.1	–4	....	....	....	7	0	1	1	4	0	0	0	....
1997-98	Ottawa	NHL	65	7	9	16	16	1	0	0	93	7.5	–13	....	....	....	5	0	0	0	2	0	0	0	....
1998-99	Ottawa	NHL	81	16	16	32	48	0	1	6	110	14.5	15	1184	50.1	13:44	4	0	0	0	6	0	0	0	16:16
99-2000	Pardubice	Czech	3	1	0	1	4	....	....	....	....	....	....	....	....	....	....	....	....	....	....	....	....	....	....
	Ottawa	NHL	80	23	37	60	53	10	0	5	167	13.8	–2	1654	52.0	18:14	6	0	0	0	8	0	0	0	15:37
2000-01	Ottawa	NHL	74	23	36	59	52	5	2	3	139	16.5	27	1506	51.2	18:16	2	0	0	0	2	0	0	0	14:32
2001-02	Ottawa	NHL	82	25	45	70	52	6	2	5	170	14.7	3	1530	51.0	17:57	12	3	7	10	6	2	0	1	18:53
2002-03	Ottawa	NHL	70	22	32	54	36	11	0	4	146	15.1	6	1218	46.2	17:32	18	6	5	11	10	2	0	0	17:43
2003-04	Ottawa	NHL	66	12	32	44	66	6	0	1	98	12.2	2	1184	44.9	17:38	7	0	2	2	0	0	0	0	18:29
	NHL Totals		689	152	247	399	401	45	6	25	1206	12.6		8276	49.5	17:11	61	9	15	24	38	4	0	1	17:36

Garry F. Longman Memorial Trophy (Top Rookie – IHL) (1994)

Played in NHL All-Star Game (2000, 2001)

Traded to **Los Angeles** by **Ottawa** for Los Angeles' 3rd round choice (Shawn Weller) in 2004 Entry Draft, June 26, 2004. Traded to **Montreal** by **Los Angeles** with Cristobal Huet for Mathieu Garon and San Jose's 3rd round choice (previously acquired, Los Angeles selected Paul Baier) in 2004 Entry Draft, June 26, 2004.

BONNI, Ryan

(baw-NEE, RIGH-uhn)

Defense. Shoots left. 6'4", 190 lbs. Born, Winnipeg, Man., February 18, 1979. Vancouver's 2nd choice, 34th overall, in 1997 Entry Draft.

1994-95	Winnipeg Sharks	MMHL	24	3	19	22	59	....	....	....	....	....	....	....	....	....	....	....	....	....	....	....	....	....	....
1995-96	Saskatoon Blades	WHL	63	1	7	8	78	....	....	....	....	....	....	....	....	....	3	0	0	0	0	....	....	....	....
1996-97	Saskatoon Blades	WHL	69	11	19	30	219	....	....	....	....	....	....	....	....	....	....	....	....	....	....	....	....	....	....
1997-98	Saskatoon Blades	WHL	42	5	14	19	100	....	....	....	....	....	....	....	....	....	....	....	....	....	....	....	....	....	....
1998-99	Saskatoon Blades	WHL	51	6	26	32	211	....	....	....	....	....	....	....	....	....	....	....	....	....	....	....	....	....	....
	Red Deer Rebels	WHL	20	3	10	13	41	....	....	....	....	....	....	....	....	....	9	0	4	4	25	....	....	....	....
99-2000	Vancouver	NHL	3	0	0	0	0	0	0	0	1	0.0	–1	0	0.0	9:37	....	....	....	....	....	....	....	....	....
	Syracuse Crunch	AHL	71	5	13	18	125	....	....	....	....	....	....	....	....	....	2	0	1	1	2	....	....	....	....
2000-01	Kansas City	IHL	80	2	9	11	127	....	....	....	....	....	....	....	....	....	....	....	....	....	....	....	....	....	....
2001-02	Manitoba Moose	AHL	11	0	1	1	33	....	....	....	....	....	....	....	....	....	2	0	0	0	2	....	....	....	....
	Columbia Inferno	ECHL	46	3	18	21	128	....	....	....	....	....	....	....	....	....	4	0	4	4	10	....	....	....	....
2002-03	St. John's	AHL	61	1	8	9	86	....	....	....	....	....	....	....	....	....	....	....	....	....	....	....	....	....	....
2003-04	Greensboro	ECHL	15	1	7	8	49	....	....	....	....	....	....	....	....	....	....	....	....	....	....	....	....	....	....
	Grand Rapids	AHL	54	1	6	7	98	....	....	....	....	....	....	....	....	....	4	0	0	0	8	....	....	....	....
	NHL Totals		3	0	0	0	0	0	0	0	1	0.0		0	0.0	9:37	....	....	....	....	....	....	....	....	....

Traded to **Toronto** by **Vancouver** for Toronto's 8th round choice (Sergei Topol) in 2003 Entry Draft, June 25, 2002. Signed as a free agent by **Greensboro** (ECHL), October, 2003. Signed as a free agent by **Grand Rapids** (AHL), December 11, 2003.

BONVIE, Dennis

(BOHN-vee, DEHN-his) **COL.**

Right wing. Shoots right. 5'11", 205 lbs. Born, Antigonish, N.S., July 23, 1973.

1989-90	Antigonish	NSMHL	50	15	30	45	52	....	....	....	....	....	....	....	....	....	....	....	....	....	....	....	....	....	....
1990-91	Antigonish	MJrHL	40	1	8	9	347	....	....	....	....	....	....	....	....	....	....	....	....	....	....	....	....	....	....
1991-92	Kitchener Rangers	OHL	7	1	1	2	23	....	....	....	....	....	....	....	....	....	....	....	....	....	....	....	....	....	....
	North Bay	OHL	49	0	12	12	261	....	....	....	....	....	....	....	....	....	21	0	1	1	91	....	....	....	....
1992-93	North Bay	OHL	64	3	21	24	*316	....	....	....	....	....	....	....	....	....	5	0	0	0	34	....	....	....	....
1993-94	Cape Breton	AHL	63	1	10	11	278	....	....	....	....	....	....	....	....	....	4	0	0	0	11	....	....	....	....
1994-95	Cape Breton	AHL	74	5	15	20	422	....	....	....	....	....	....	....	....	....	....	....	....	....	....	....	....	....	....
	Edmonton	NHL	2	0	0	0	0	0	0	0	0	0.0	0	....	....	....	....	....	....	....	....	....	....	....	....
1995-96	Edmonton	NHL	8	0	0	0	47	0	0	0	0	0.0	–3	....	....	....	....	....	....	....	....	....	....	....	....
	Cape Breton	AHL	38	13	14	27	269	....	....	....	....	....	....	....	....	....	....	....	....	....	....	....	....	....	....
1996-97	Hamilton	AHL	73	9	20	29	*522	....	....	....	....	....	....	....	....	....	22	3	11	14	*91	....	....	....	....
1997-98	Edmonton	NHL	4	0	0	0	27	0	0	0	0	0.0	0	....	....	....	....	....	....	....	....	....	....	....	....
	Hamilton	AHL	57	11	19	30	295	....	....	....	....	....	....	....	....	....	9	0	5	5	18	....	....	....	....
1998-99	Chicago	NHL	11	0	0	0	44	0	0	0	1	0.0	–4	0	0.0	3:59	....	....	....	....	....	....	....	....	....
	Portland Pirates	AHL	3	1	0	1	16	....	....	....	....	....	....	....	....	....	....	....	....	....	....	....	....	....	....
	Philadelphia	AHL	37	4	10	14	158	....	....	....	....	....	....	....	....	....	14	3	3	6	26	....	....	....	....
99-2000	Pittsburgh	NHL	28	0	0	0	80	0	0	0	6	0.0	–2	0	0.0	3:14	....	....	....	....	....	....	....	....	....
	Wilkes-Barre	AHL	42	5	26	31	243	....	....	....	....	....	....	....	....	....	....	....	....	....	....	....	....	....	....
2000-01	Pittsburgh	NHL	3	0	0	0	0	0	0	0	1	0.0	–1	0	0.0	3:30	....	....	....	....	....	....	....	....	....
	Wilkes-Barre	AHL	65	5	18	23	221	....	....	....	....	....	....	....	....	....	21	0	4	4	35	....	....	....	....

Season	Club	League	GP	G	A	Pts	PIM	PP	SH	GW	S	%	+/-	TF	F%	Min	GP	G	A	Pts	PIM	PP	SH	GW	Min
			Regular Season														Playoffs								
2001-02	**Boston**	**NHL**	**23**	**1**	**2**	**3**	**84**	**0**	**0**	**0**	**5**	**20.0**	**3**	**0**	**0.0**	**5:05**	**1**	**0**	**0**	**0**	**0**	**0**	**0**	**0**	**3:07**
	Providence Bruins	AHL	55	8	8	16	290	....	....	....	....	....	....	....	....	....	....	....	....	....	....	....	....	....	....
2002-03	**Ottawa**	**NHL**	**12**	**0**	**0**	**0**	**29**	**0**	**0**	**0**	**3**	**0.0**	**–1**	**0**	**0.0**	**3:05**	....	....	....	....	....	....	....	....	....
	Binghamton	AHL	51	7	3	10	311	....	....	....	....	....	....	....	....	....	14	2	4	6	*85	....	....	....	....
2003-04	Binghamton	AHL	29	2	4	6	137	....	....	....	....	....	....	....	....	....	....	....	....	....	....	....	....	....	....
	Colorado	**NHL**	**1**	**0**	**0**	**0**	**0**	**0**	**0**	**0**	**1**	**0.0**	**0**	**0**	**0.0**	**7:01**	....	....	....	....	....	....	....	....	....
	Hershey Bears	AHL	30	3	6	9	154	....	....	....	....	....	....	....	....	....	....	....	....	....	....	....	....	....	....
	NHL Totals		**92**	**1**	**2**	**3**	**311**	**0**	**0**	**0**	**17**	**5.9**		**0**	**0.0**	**3:55**	**1**	**0**	**0**	**0**	**0**	**0**	**0**	**0**	**3:07**

Signed as a free agent by **Edmonton**, August 25, 1994. Claimed by **Chicago** from **Edmonton** in Waiver Draft, October 5, 1998. Traded to **Philadelphia** by **Chicago** for Frank Bialowas, January 8, 1999. Signed as a free agent by **Pittsburgh**, September 20, 1999. Signed as a free agent by **Boston**, October 5, 2001. Signed as a free agent by **Ottawa**, August 26, 2002. Traded to **Colorado** by **Ottawa** for Charlie Stephens, January 23, 2004.

BOOTLAND, Darryl

(BOOT-land, DAIR-ihl) **DET.**

Right wing. Shoots right. 6'1", 194 lbs. Born, Toronto, Ont., November 2, 1981. Colorado's 12th choice, 252nd overall, in 2000 Entry Draft.

Season	Club	League	GP	G	A	Pts	PIM	PP	SH	GW	S	%	+/-	TF	F%	Min	GP	G	A	Pts	PIM	PP	SH	GW	Min
1997-98	Orangeville	OJHL-B	44	22	26	48	177	....	....	....	....	....	....	....	....	....	....	....	....	....	....	....	....	....	....
1998-99	Barrie Colts	OHL	38	18	11	29	89	....	....	....	....	....	....	....	....	....	....	....	....	....	....	....	....	....	....
	St. Michael's	OHL	28	12	6	18	80	....	....	....	....	....	....	....	....	....	....	....	....	....	....	....	....	....	....
99-2000	St. Michael's	OHL	65	24	30	54	166	....	....	....	....	....	....	....	....	....	....	....	....	....	....	....	....	....	....
2000-01	St. Michael's	OHL	56	32	33	65	136	....	....	....	....	....	....	....	....	....	11	3	1	4	20	....	....	....	....
2001-02	St. Michael's	OHL	61	41	56	97	137	....	....	....	....	....	....	....	....	....	15	8	10	18	50	....	....	....	....
2002-03	Grand Rapids	AHL	16	1	4	5	41	....	....	....	....	....	....	....	....	....	15	3	2	5	46	....	....	....	....
	Toledo Storm	ECHL	54	17	19	36	322	....	....	....	....	....	....	....	....	....	....	....	....	....	....	....	....	....	....
2003-04	**Detroit**	**NHL**	**22**	**1**	**1**	**2**	**74**	**0**	**0**	**1**	**13**	**7.7**	**–3**	**1**	**100.0**	**6:07**	....	....	....	....	....	....	....	....	....
	Grand Rapids	AHL	54	12	2	14	175	....	....	....	....	....	....	....	....	....	4	0	1	1	2	....	....	....	....
	NHL Totals		**22**	**1**	**1**	**2**	**74**	**0**	**0**	**1**	**13**	**7.7**		**1**	**100.0**	**6:07**	....	....	....	....	....	....	....	....	....

Signed as a free agent by **Detroit**, July 25, 2002.

BOTTERILL, Jason

(BOH-tuhr-ihl, JAY-suhn)

Left wing. Shoots left. 6'4", 220 lbs. Born, Edmonton, Alta., May 19, 1976. Dallas' 1st choice, 20th overall, in 1994 Entry Draft.

Season	Club	League	GP	G	A	Pts	PIM	PP	SH	GW	S	%	+/-	TF	F%	Min	GP	G	A	Pts	PIM	PP	SH	GW	Min
1992-93	St. Paul's Prep	Hi-School	22	22	26	48	....	....	....	....	....	....	....	....	....	....	....	....	....	....	....	....	....	....	....
1993-94	U. of Michigan	CCHA	36	20	19	39	94	....	....	....	....	....	....	....	....	....	....	....	....	....	....	....	....	....	....
1994-95	U. of Michigan	CCHA	34	14	14	28	117	....	....	....	....	....	....	....	....	....	....	....	....	....	....	....	....	....	....
1995-96	U. of Michigan	CCHA	37	*32	25	57	*143	....	....	....	....	....	....	....	....	....	....	....	....	....	....	....	....	....	....
1996-97	U. of Michigan	CCHA	42	*37	24	61	129	....	....	....	....	....	....	....	....	....	....	....	....	....	....	....	....	....	....
1997-98	**Dallas**	**NHL**	**4**	**0**	**0**	**0**	**19**	**0**	**0**	**0**	**2**	**0.0**	**–1**	....	....	....	....	....	....	....	....	....	....	....	....
	Michigan	IHL	50	11	11	22	82	....	....	....	....	....	....	....	....	....	4	0	0	0	5	....	....	....	....
1998-99	**Dallas**	**NHL**	**17**	**0**	**0**	**0**	**23**	**0**	**0**	**0**	**8**	**0.0**	**–2**	**0**	**0.0**	**8:19**	....	....	....	....	....	....	....	....	....
	Michigan	IHL	56	13	25	38	106	....	....	....	....	....	....	....	....	....	5	2	1	3	4	....	....	....	....
99-2000	**Atlanta**	**NHL**	**25**	**1**	**4**	**5**	**17**	**0**	**0**	**1**	**17**	**5.9**	**–7**	**2**	**50.0**	**11:16**	....	....	....	....	....	....	....	....	....
	Orlando	IHL	17	7	8	15	27	....	....	....	....	....	....	....	....	....	....	....	....	....	....	....	....	....	....
	Calgary	**NHL**	**2**	**0**	**0**	**0**	**0**	**0**	**0**	**0**	**2**	**0.0**	**–4**	**0**	**0.0**	**8:00**	....	....	....	....	....	....	....	....	....
	Saint John Flames	AHL	21	3	4	7	39	....	....	....	....	....	....	....	....	....	3	0	0	0	19	....	....	....	....
2000-01	Saint John Flames	AHL	60	13	20	33	101	....	....	....	....	....	....	....	....	....	19	2	7	9	30	....	....	....	....
2001-02	**Calgary**	**NHL**	**4**	**1**	**0**	**1**	**2**	**1**	**0**	**1**	**4**	**25.0**	**–3**	**0**	**0.0**	**9:26**	....	....	....	....	....	....	....	....	....
	Saint John Flames	AHL	71	21	21	42	121	....	....	....	....	....	....	....	....	....	....	....	....	....	....	....	....	....	....
2002-03	**Buffalo**	**NHL**	**17**	**1**	**4**	**5**	**14**	**1**	**0**	**0**	**20**	**5.0**	**1**	**5**	**40.0**	**10:48**	....	....	....	....	....	....	....	....	....
	Rochester	AHL	64	37	22	59	105	....	....	....	....	....	....	....	....	....	3	1	1	2	21	....	....	....	....
2003-04	**Buffalo**	**NHL**	**19**	**2**	**1**	**3**	**14**	**1**	**0**	**0**	**20**	**10.0**	**0**	**4**	**25.0**	**11:24**	....	....	....	....	....	....	....	....	....
	Rochester	AHL	46	16	17	33	68	....	....	....	....	....	....	....	....	....	16	5	10	15	19	....	....	....	....
	NHL Totals		**88**	**5**	**9**	**14**	**89**	**3**	**0**	**2**	**73**	**6.8**		**11**	**36.4**	**10:27**	....	....	....	....	....	....	....	....	....

CCHA Second All-Star Team (1996) • NCAA West Second All-American Team (1997)

Traded to **Atlanta** by **Dallas** for Jamie Pushor, July 15, 1999. Traded to **Calgary** by **Atlanta** with Darryl Shannon for Hnat Domenichelli and Dmitri Vlasenkov, February 11, 2000. Signed as a free agent by **Buffalo**, August 12, 2002.

BOUCHARD, Joel

(BOO-shahrd, JOHL)

Defense. Shoots left. 6'1", 209 lbs. Born, Montreal, Que., January 23, 1974. Calgary's 7th choice, 129th overall, in 1992 Entry Draft.

Season	Club	League	GP	G	A	Pts	PIM	PP	SH	GW	S	%	+/-	TF	F%	Min	GP	G	A	Pts	PIM	PP	SH	GW	Min
1989-90	Mtl-Bourassa	QAAA	41	7	17	24	10	....	....	....	....	....	....	....	....	....	1	1	0	1	0	....	....	....	....
1990-91	Longueuil	QMJHL	53	3	19	22	34	....	....	....	....	....	....	....	....	....	8	1	0	1	11	....	....	....	....
1991-92	Verdun	QMJHL	70	9	20	29	55	....	....	....	....	....	....	....	....	....	19	1	7	8	20	....	....	....	....
1992-93	Verdun	QMJHL	60	10	49	59	126	....	....	....	....	....	....	....	....	....	4	0	2	2	4	....	....	....	....
1993-94	Verdun	QMJHL	60	15	55	70	62	....	....	....	....	....	....	....	....	....	4	1	0	1	6	....	....	....	....
	Saint John Flames	AHL	1	0	0	0	0	....	....	....	....	....	....	....	....	....	2	0	0	0	0	....	....	....	....
1994-95	Saint John Flames	AHL	77	6	25	31	63	....	....	....	....	....	....	....	....	....	5	1	0	1	4	....	....	....	....
	Calgary	**NHL**	**2**	**0**	**0**	**0**	**0**	**0**	**0**	**0**	**0**	**0.0**	**0**	....	....	....	....	....	....	....	....	....	....	....	....
1995-96	**Calgary**	**NHL**	**4**	**0**	**0**	**0**	**4**	**0**	**0**	**0**	**0**	**0.0**	**0**	....	....	....	....	....	....	....	....	....	....	....	....
	Saint John Flames	AHL	74	8	25	33	104	....	....	....	....	....	....	....	....	....	16	1	4	5	10	....	....	....	....
1996-97	**Calgary**	**NHL**	**76**	**4**	**5**	**9**	**49**	**0**	**1**	**0**	**61**	**6.6**	**–23**	....	....	....	....	....	....	....	....	....	....	....	....
1997-98	**Calgary**	**NHL**	**44**	**5**	**7**	**12**	**57**	**0**	**1**	**1**	**51**	**9.8**	**0**	....	....	....	....	....	....	....	....	....	....	....	....
	Saint John Flames	AHL	3	2	1	3	6	....	....	....	....	....	....	....	....	....	....	....	....	....	....	....	....	....	....
1998-99	**Nashville**	**NHL**	**64**	**4**	**11**	**15**	**60**	**0**	**0**	**0**	**78**	**5.1**	**–10**	**0**	**0.0**	**22:34**	....	....	....	....	....	....	....	....	....
99-2000	**Nashville**	**NHL**	**52**	**1**	**4**	**5**	**23**	**0**	**0**	**0**	**60**	**1.7**	**–11**	**0**	**0.0**	**18:41**	....	....	....	....	....	....	....	....	....
	Dallas	**NHL**	**2**	**0**	**0**	**0**	**2**	**0**	**0**	**0**	**1**	**0.0**	**1**	**0**	**0.0**	**9:45**	....	....	....	....	....	....	....	....	....
2000-01	**Phoenix**	**NHL**	**32**	**1**	**2**	**3**	**22**	**0**	**0**	**0**	**26**	**3.8**	**–8**	**0**	**0.0**	**14:28**	....	....	....	....	....	....	....	....	....
	Grand Rapids	IHL	19	3	9	12	8	....	....	....	....	....	....	....	....	....	....	....	....	....	....	....	....	....	....
2001-02	**New Jersey**	**NHL**	**1**	**0**	**1**	**1**	**0**	**0**	**0**	**0**	**0**	**0.0**	**1**	**0**	**0.0**	**19:26**	....	....	....	....	....	....	....	....	....
	Albany River Rats	AHL	70	9	22	31	28	....	....	....	....	....	....	....	....	....	....	....	....	....	....	....	....	....	....
2002-03	**NY Rangers**	**NHL**	**27**	**5**	**7**	**12**	**14**	**1**	**0**	**2**	**41**	**12.2**	**6**	**0**	**0.0**	**20:07**	....	....	....	....	....	....	....	....	....
	Hartford	AHL	22	6	14	20	22	....	....	....	....	....	....	....	....	....	....	....	....	....	....	....	....	....	....
	Pittsburgh	**NHL**	**7**	**0**	**1**	**1**	**0**	**0**	**0**	**0**	**6**	**0.0**	**–6**	**0**	**0.0**	**21:49**	....	....	....	....	....	....	....	....	....
2003-04	**NY Rangers**	**NHL**	**28**	**1**	**7**	**8**	**10**	**0**	**0**	**0**	**34**	**2.9**	**2**	**0**	**0.0**	**16:42**	....	....	....	....	....	....	....	....	....
	NHL Totals		**339**	**21**	**45**	**66**	**241**	**1**	**2**	**3**	**358**	**5.9**		**0**	**0.0**	**19:10**	....	....	....	....	....	....	....	....	....

QMJHL First All-Star Team (1994)

Claimed by **Nashville** from **Calgary** in Expansion Draft, June 26, 1998. Claimed on waivers by **Dallas** from **Nashville**, March 14, 2000. Signed as a free agent by **Phoenix**, August 31, 2000. Signed as a free agent by **New Jersey**, October 25, 2001. Signed as a free agent by **NY Rangers**, August 5, 2002. Traded to **Pittsburgh** by **NY Rangers** with Richard Lintner, Rico Fata , Mikael Samuelsson and future considerations for Mike Wilson, Alex Kovalev, Janne Laukkanen and Dan LaCouture, February 10, 2003. Signed as a free agent by **Buffalo**, July 14, 2003. Claimed by **NY Rangers** from **Buffalo** in Waiver Draft, October 3, 2003. • Spent majority of 2003-04 season as a healthy reserve.

BOUCHARD, Pierre-Marc

(BOO-shahrd, PEE-air- MAHRK) **MIN.**

Center. Shoots left. 5'10", 165 lbs. Born, Sherbrooke, Que., April 27, 1984. Minnesota's 1st choice, 8th overall, in 2002 Entry Draft.

Season	Club	League	GP	G	A	Pts	PIM	PP	SH	GW	S	%	+/-	TF	F%	Min	GP	G	A	Pts	PIM	PP	SH	GW	Min
1998-99	Mtl.-Bourassa	QAHA	28	23	41	64	....	....	....	....	....	....	....	....	....	....	....	....	....	....	....	....	....	....	....
99-2000	Charles-Lemoyne	QAAA	42	28	*45	*74	20	....	....	....	....	....	....	....	....	....	9	4	8	12	6	....	....	....	....
2000-01	Chicoutimi	QMJHL	67	38	57	95	20	....	....	....	....	....	....	....	....	....	6	5	8	13	0	....	....	....	....
2001-02	Chicoutimi	QMJHL	69	46	*94	*140	54	....	....	....	....	....	....	....	....	....	4	2	3	5	4	....	....	....	....
2002-03	**Minnesota**	**NHL**	**50**	**7**	**13**	**20**	**18**	**5**	**0**	**1**	**53**	**13.2**	**1**	**474**	**40.7**	**13:16**	**5**	**0**	**1**	**1**	**2**	**0**	**0**	**0**	**13:15**
2003-04	**Minnesota**	**NHL**	**61**	**4**	**18**	**22**	**22**	**2**	**0**	**0**	**60**	**6.7**	**–7**	**60**	**50.0**	**14:00**	....	....	....	....	....	....	....	....	....
	NHL Totals		**111**	**11**	**31**	**42**	**40**	**7**	**0**	**1**	**113**	**9.7**		**534**	**41.8**	**13:40**	**5**	**0**	**1**	**1**	**2**	**0**	**0**	**0**	**13:15**

QMJHL Rookie of the Year (2001) • QMJHL First All-Star Team (2002) • Canadian Major Junior First All-Star Team (2002) • Canadian Major Junior Player of the Year (2002)

BOUCHER, Philippe (boo-SHAY, fihl-EEP) DAL.

Defense. Shoots right. 6'3", 221 lbs. Born, Ste-Apollinaire, Que., March 24, 1973. Buffalo's 1st choice, 13th overall, in 1991 Entry Draft.

			Regular Season														Playoffs								
Season	Club	League	GP	G	A	Pts	PIM	PP	SH	GW	S	%	+/-	TF	F%	Min	GP	G	A	Pts	PIM	PP	SH	GW	Min
1988-89	Ste-Foy	QAAA	5	0	0	0	2																		
1989-90	Ste-Foy	QAAA	42	26	60	86	76										12	6	*19	25	16				
1990-91	Granby Bisons	QMJHL	69	21	46	67	92																		
1991-92	Granby Bisons	QMJHL	49	22	37	59	47																		
	Laval Titan	QMJHL	16	7	11	18	36										10	5	6	11	8				
1992-93	Laval Titan	QMJHL	16	12	15	27	37										13	6	15	21	12				
	Buffalo	NHL	18	0	4	4	14	0	0	0	28	0.0	1												
	Rochester	AHL	5	4	3	7	8										3	0	1	1	2				
1993-94	Buffalo	NHL	38	6	8	14	29	4	0	1	67	9.0	–1				7	1	1	2	2	1	0	0	
	Rochester	AHL	31	10	22	32	51																		
1994-95	Rochester	AHL	43	14	27	41	26																		
	Buffalo	NHL	9	1	4	5	0	0	0	0	15	6.7	6												
	Los Angeles	NHL	6	1	0	1	4	0	0	0	15	6.7	–3												
1995-96	Los Angeles	NHL	53	7	16	23	31	5	0	1	145	4.8	–26												
	Phoenix	IHL	10	4	3	7	4																		
1996-97	Los Angeles	NHL	60	7	18	25	25	2	0	1	159	4.4	0												
1997-98	Los Angeles	NHL	45	6	10	16	49	1	0	0	80	7.5	6												
	Long Beach	IHL	2	0	1	1	4																		
1998-99	Los Angeles	NHL	45	2	6	8	32	1	0	0	87	2.3	–12	0	0.0	17:51									
99-2000	Los Angeles	NHL	1	0	0	0	0	0	0	0	3	0.0	0	0	0.0	17:04									
	Long Beach	IHL	14	4	11	15	8										6	0	9	9	8				
2000-01	Los Angeles	NHL	22	2	4	6	20	2	0	0	40	5.0	4	0	0.0	18:25	13	0	1	1	2	0	0	0	15:48
	Manitoba Moose	IHL	45	10	22	32	39																		
2001-02	Los Angeles	NHL	80	7	23	30	94	4	0	2	198	3.5	0	0	0.0	21:36	5	0	1	1	2	0	0	0	19:31
2002-03	Dallas	NHL	80	7	20	27	94	1	1	3	137	5.1	28	1	0.0	20:29	11	1	2	3	11	0	0	0	21:28
2003-04	Dallas	NHL	70	8	16	24	64	2	0	2	134	6.0	15	0	0.0	22:24	5	1	0	1	6	0	0	0	23:57
	NHL Totals		527	54	129	183	456	22	1	10	1108	4.9		1	0.0	20:40	41	3	5	8	23	1	0	0	19:23

QMJHL Second All-Star Team (1991, 1992) • QMJHL Defensive Rookie of the Year (1991) • Canadian Major Junior Rookie of the Year (1991)

Traded to **Los Angeles** by **Buffalo** with Denis Tsygurov and Grant Fuhr for Alexei Zhitnik, Robb Stauber, Charlie Huddy and Los Angeles' 5th round choice (Marian Menhart) in 1995 Entry Draft, February 14, 1995. • Missed majority of 1999-2000 season recovering from foot injury suffered in training camp, September, 1999. Signed as a free agent by **Dallas**, July 2, 2002.

BOUCK, Tyler (BOWK, TIGH-luhr) VAN.

Center. Shoots left. 6', 196 lbs. Born, Camrose, Alta., January 13, 1980. Dallas' 2nd choice, 57th overall, in 1998 Entry Draft.

Season	Club	League	GP	G	A	Pts	PIM	PP	SH	GW	S	%	+/-	TF	F%	Min	GP	G	A	Pts	PIM	PP	SH	GW	Min
1995-96	Sherwood Park	AMHL	22	10	21	31	58																		
1996-97	Prince George	WHL	12	0	2	2	11																		
1997-98	Prince George	WHL	65	11	26	37	90										11	1	0	1	21				
1998-99	Prince George	WHL	56	22	25	47	178										2	0	2	2	10				
99-2000	Prince George	WHL	57	30	33	63	183										13	6	13	19	36				
2000-01	Dallas	NHL	48	2	5	7	29	0	0	1	41	4.9	–3	1	0.0	8:59	1	0	0	0	0	0	0	0	9:02
	Utah Grizzlies	IHL	24	2	6	8	39																		
2001-02	Phoenix	NHL	7	0	0	0	4	0	0	0	3	0.0	–1	0	0.0	6:54									
	Springfield	AHL	21	1	2	3	33																		
	Manitoba Moose	AHL	20	4	4	8	25																		
2002-03	Manitoba Moose	AHL	76	10	28	38	103										14	2	2	4	10				
2003-04	Vancouver	NHL	18	1	2	3	23	0	1	0	12	8.3	–4	0	0.0	9:18	1	0	0	0	0	0	0	0	5:15
	Manitoba Moose	AHL	49	11	14	25	100																		
	NHL Totals		73	3	7	10	56	0	1	1	56	5.4		1	0.0	8:52	2	0	0	0	0	0	0	0	7:08

WHL West First All-Star Team (2000)

Traded to **Phoenix** by **Dallas** for Jyrki Lumme, June 23, 2001. Traded to **Vancouver** by **Phoenix** with Todd Warriner, Trevor Letowski and Phoenix's 3rd round choice (later traded back to Phoenix – Phoenix selected Dimitri Pestunov) in 2003 Entry Draft for Drake Berehowsky and Denis Pederson, December 28, 2001.

BOUGHNER, Bob (BOOG-nuhr, BAWB) COL.

Defense. Shoots right. 6', 203 lbs. Born, Windsor, Ont., March 8, 1971. Detroit's 2nd choice, 32nd overall, in 1989 Entry Draft.

Season	Club	League	GP	G	A	Pts	PIM	PP	SH	GW	S	%	+/-	TF	F%	Min	GP	G	A	Pts	PIM	PP	SH	GW	Min
1986-87	Belle River	OJHL-C	37	3	11	14	88																		
1987-88	St. Mary's Lincolns	OJHL-B	36	4	18	22	177																		
1988-89	Sault Ste. Marie	OHL	64	6	15	21	182																		
1989-90	Sault Ste. Marie	OHL	49	7	23	30	122																		
1990-91	Sault Ste. Marie	OHL	64	13	33	46	156										14	2	9	11	35				
1991-92	Toledo Storm	ECHL	28	3	10	13	79										5	2	0	2	15				
	Adirondack	AHL	1	0	0	0	7																		
1992-93	Adirondack	AHL	69	1	16	17	190																		
1993-94	Adirondack	AHL	72	8	14	22	292										10	1	1	2	18				
1994-95	Cincinnati	IHL	81	2	14	16	192										10	0	0	0	18				
1995-96	Carolina	AHL	46	2	15	17	127																		
	Buffalo	NHL	31	0	1	1	104	0	0	0	14	0.0	3												
1996-97	Buffalo	NHL	77	1	7	8	225	0	0	0	34	2.9	12				11	0	1	1	9	0	0	0	
1997-98	Buffalo	NHL	69	1	3	4	165	0	0	0	26	3.8	5				14	0	4	4	15	0	0	0	
1998-99	Nashville	NHL	79	3	10	13	137	0	0	1	59	5.1	–6	0	0.0	18:31									
99-2000	Nashville	NHL	62	2	4	6	97	0	0	0	32	6.3	–13	0	0.0	17:20									
	Pittsburgh	NHL	11	1	0	1	69	1	0	1	8	12.5	2	0	0.0	17:05	11	0	2	2	15	0	0	0	18:40
2000-01	Pittsburgh	NHL	58	1	3	4	147	0	0	0	46	2.2	18	0	0.0	16:30	18	0	1	1	22	0	0	0	17:08
2001-02	Calgary	NHL	79	2	4	6	170	0	0	0	58	3.4	9	0	0.0	18:43									
2002-03	Calgary	NHL	69	3	14	17	126	0	0	1	62	4.8	5	0	0.0	19:51									
2003-04	Carolina	NHL	43	0	5	5	80	0	0	0	26	0.0	–9	0	0.0	14:47									
	Colorado	NHL	11	0	0	0	8	0	0	0	8	0.0	–1	0	0.0	13:26	11	0	4	4	6	0	0	0	15:39
	NHL Totals		589	14	51	65	1328	1	0	3	373	3.8		0	0.0	17:45	65	0	12	12	67	0	0	0	17:09

Signed as a free agent by **Florida**, July 25, 1994. Traded to **Buffalo** by **Florida** for Buffalo's 3rd round choice (Chris Allen) in 1996 Entry Draft, February 1, 1996. Claimed by **Nashville** from **Buffalo** in Expansion Draft, June 26, 1998. Traded to **Pittsburgh** by **Nashville** for Pavel Skrbek, March 13, 2000. Signed as a free agent by **Calgary**, July 2, 2001. Traded to **Carolina** by **Calgary** for New Jersey's 4th round choice (previously acquired, Calgary selected Kristopher Hogg) in 2004 Entry Draft and future considerations, July 16, 2003. Traded to **Colorado** by **Carolina** for Chris Bahen and Washington's 3rd round choice (previously acquired, Carolina selected Casey Borer) in 2004 Entry Draft, February 20, 2004.

BOUILLON, Francis (BOO-liawn, FRAN-sihs) MTL.

Defense. Shoots left. 5'8", 196 lbs. Born, New York, NY, October 17, 1975.

Season	Club	League	GP	G	A	Pts	PIM	PP	SH	GW	S	%	+/-	TF	F%	Min	GP	G	A	Pts	PIM	PP	SH	GW	Min
1991-92	Mtl-Bourassa	QAAA	42	2	5	7	28										9	1	0	1	6				
1992-93	Laval Titan	QMJHL	46	0	7	7	45																		
1993-94	Laval Titan	QMJHL	68	3	15	18	129										19	2	9	11	48				
1994-95	Laval Titan	QMJHL	72	8	25	33	115										20	3	11	14	21				
1995-96	Granby	QMJHL	68	11	35	46	156										21	2	12	14	30				
1996-97	Wheeling Nailers	ECHL	69	10	32	42	77										3	0	2	2	10				
1997-98	Quebec Rafales	IHL	71	8	27	35	76																		
1998-99	Fredericton	AHL	79	19	36	55	174										5	2	1	3	0				
99-2000	Montreal	NHL	74	3	13	16	38	2	0	1	76	3.9	–7	1	0.0	15:52									
2000-01	Montreal	NHL	29	0	6	6	26	0	0	0	24	0.0	3	0	0.0	13:24									
	Quebec Citadelles	AHL	4	0	0	0	0																		
2001-02	Montreal	NHL	28	0	5	5	33	0	0	0	24	0.0	–5	0	0.0	18:47									
	Quebec Citadelles	AHL	38	8	14	22	30																		
2002-03	Nashville	NHL	4	0	0	0	2	0	0	0	0	0.0	–1	0	0.0	12:52									
	Montreal	NHL	20	3	1	4	2	0	1	0	30	10.0	–1	0	0.0	20:24									
	Hamilton	AHL	29	1	12	13	31																		
2003-04	Montreal	NHL	73	2	16	18	70	0	0	0	86	2.3	1	0	0.0	19:39	11	0	0	0	7	0	0	0	18:00
	NHL Totals		228	8	41	49	171	2	1	1	240	3.3		1	0.0	17:28	11	0	0	0	7	0	0	0	18:00

Signed as a free agent by **Montreal**, August 18, 1998. • Missed majority of 2000-01 season recovering from ankle injury suffered in game vs. Calgary, December 31, 2000. Claimed by **Nashville** from **Montreal** in Waiver Draft, October 4, 2002. Claimed on waivers by **Montreal** from **Nashville**, October 25, 2002.

BOULERICE, Jesse

(BOO-luhr-ighs, JEHS-see) **CAR.**

Right wing. Shoots right. 6'2", 203 lbs. Born, Plattsburgh, NY, August 10, 1978. Philadelphia's 4th choice, 133rd overall, in 1996 Entry Draft.

			Regular Season														Playoffs								
Season	Club	League	GP	G	A	Pts	PIM	PP	SH	GW	S	%	+/-	TF	F%	Min	GP	G	A	Pts	PIM	PP	SH	GW	Min
1994-95	Hawkesbury	OCJHL	46	1	8	9	160	....	....	....	....	....	....	....	....	....	....	....	....	....	....	....	....	....	....
1995-96	Detroit	OHL	64	2	5	7	150	....	....	....	....	....	....	....	....	....	16	0	0	0	12	....	....	....	....
1996-97	Detroit	OHL	33	10	14	24	209	....	....	....	....	....	....	....	....	....	....	....	....	....	....	....	....	....	....
1997-98	Plymouth Whalers	OHL	53	20	23	43	170	....	....	....	....	....	....	....	....	....	13	2	4	6	35	....	....	....	....
1998-99	Philadelphia	AHL	24	1	2	3	82	....	....	....	....	....	....	....	....	....	....	....	....	....	....	....	....	....	....
	New Orleans	ECHL	12	0	1	1	38	....	....	....	....	....	....	....	....	....	....	....	....	....	....	....	....	....	....
99-2000	Philadelphia	AHL	40	3	4	7	85	....	....	....	....	....	....	....	....	....	4	0	2	2	4	....	....	....	....
	Trenton Titans	ECHL	25	8	8	16	90	....	....	....	....	....	....	....	....	....	....	....	....	....	....	....	....	....	....
2000-01	Philadelphia	AHL	60	3	4	7	256	....	....	....	....	....	....	....	....	....	10	1	1	2	28	....	....	....	....
2001-02	**Philadelphia**	**NHL**	**3**	**0**	**0**	**0**	**5**	**0**	**0**	**0**	**1**	**0.0**	**–1**	**0**	**0.0**	**4:18**	....	....	....	....	....	....	....	....	....
	Philadelphia	AHL	41	2	5	7	204	....	....	....	....	....	....	....	....	....	....	....	....	....	....	....	....	....	....
	Lowell	AHL	15	2	4	6	80	....	....	....	....	....	....	....	....	....	5	0	2	2	6	....	....	....	....
2002-03	**Carolina**	**NHL**	**48**	**2**	**1**	**3**	**108**	**0**	**0**	**0**	**12**	**16.7**	**–2**	**0**	**0.0**	**3:54**	....	....	....	....	....	....	....	....	....
2003-04	**Carolina**	**NHL**	**76**	**6**	**1**	**7**	**127**	**0**	**0**	**0**	**46**	**13.0**	**–5**	**0**	**0.0**	**6:32**	....	....	....	....	....	....	....	....	....
	NHL Totals		**127**	**8**	**2**	**10**	**240**	**0**	**0**	**0**	**59**	**13.6**		**0**	**0.0**	**5:29**	....	....	....	....	....	....	....	....	....

Traded to **Carolina** by **Philadelphia** for Greg Koehler, February 13, 2002.

BOULTON, Eric

(BOHL-tuhn, AIR-ihk) **BUF.**

Left wing. Shoots left. 6', 222 lbs. Born, Halifax, N.S., August 17, 1976. NY Rangers' 12th choice, 234th overall, in 1994 Entry Draft.

Season	Club	League	GP	G	A	Pts	PIM	PP	SH	GW	S	%	+/-	TF	F%	Min	GP	G	A	Pts	PIM	PP	SH	GW	Min
1992-93	Cole Harbour	MJrHL	44	12	15	27	212	....	....	....	....	....	....	....	....	....	....	....	....	....	....	....	....	....	....
1993-94	Oshawa Generals	OHL	45	4	3	7	149	....	....	....	....	....	....	....	....	....	5	0	0	0	16	....	....	....	....
1994-95	Oshawa Generals	OHL	27	7	5	12	125	....	....	....	....	....	....	....	....	....	....	....	....	....	....	....	....	....	....
	Sarnia Sting	OHL	24	3	7	10	134	....	....	....	....	....	....	....	....	....	4	0	1	1	10	....	....	....	....
1995-96	Sarnia Sting	OHL	66	14	29	43	243	....	....	....	....	....	....	....	....	....	9	0	3	3	29	....	....	....	....
1996-97	Binghamton	AHL	23	2	3	5	67	....	....	....	....	....	....	....	....	....	3	0	0	0	4	....	....	....	....
	Charlotte	ECHL	44	14	11	25	325	....	....	....	....	....	....	....	....	....	3	0	1	1	6	....	....	....	....
1997-98	Charlotte	ECHL	53	11	16	27	202	....	....	....	....	....	....	....	....	....	4	1	0	1	0	....	....	....	....
	Fort Wayne	IHL	8	0	2	2	42	....	....	....	....	....	....	....	....	....	....	....	....	....	....	....	....	....	....
1998-99	Kentucky	AHL	34	3	3	6	154	....	....	....	....	....	....	....	....	....	10	0	1	1	36	....	....	....	....
	Florida Everblades	ECHL	26	9	13	22	143	....	....	....	....	....	....	....	....	....	....	....	....	....	....	....	....	....	....
	Houston Aeros	IHL	7	1	0	1	41	....	....	....	....	....	....	....	....	....	....	....	....	....	....	....	....	....	....
99-2000	Rochester	AHL	76	2	2	4	276	....	....	....	....	....	....	....	....	....	18	2	1	3	53	....	....	....	....
2000-01	**Buffalo**	**NHL**	**35**	**1**	**2**	**3**	**94**	**0**	**0**	**0**	**20**	**5.0**	**–1**	**2**	**0.0**	**5:42**	....	....	....	....	....	....	....	....	....
2001-02	**Buffalo**	**NHL**	**35**	**2**	**3**	**5**	**129**	**0**	**0**	**1**	**21**	**9.5**	**–1**	**0**	**0.0**	**6:08**	....	....	....	....	....	....	....	....	....
2002-03	**Buffalo**	**NHL**	**58**	**1**	**5**	**6**	**178**	**0**	**0**	**0**	**33**	**3.0**	**1**	**6**	**33.3**	**6:35**	....	....	....	....	....	....	....	....	....
2003-04	**Buffalo**	**NHL**	**44**	**1**	**2**	**3**	**110**	**0**	**0**	**0**	**20**	**5.0**	**–2**	**1**	**0.0**	**4:52**	....	....	....	....	....	....	....	....	....
	NHL Totals		**172**	**5**	**12**	**17**	**511**	**0**	**0**	**1**	**94**	**5.3**		**9**	**22.2**	**5:52**	....	....	....	....	....	....	....	....	....

Signed as a free agent by **Buffalo**, September 14, 1999.

BOUMEDIENNE, Josef

(BOO-mih-dyehn, JOH-sehf) **WSH.**

Defense. Shoots left. 6'2", 205 lbs. Born, Stockholm, Sweden, January 12, 1978. New Jersey's 7th choice, 91st overall, in 1996 Entry Draft.

Season	Club	League	GP	G	A	Pts	PIM	PP	SH	GW	S	%	+/-	TF	F%	Min	GP	G	A	Pts	PIM	PP	SH	GW	Min
1994-95	Huddinge IK Jr.	Swede-Jr.	10	0	2	2	57	....	....	....	....	....	....	....	....	....	....	....	....	....	....	....	....	....	....
1995-96	Huddinge IK Jr.	Swede-Jr.	25	2	4	6	66	....	....	....	....	....	....	....	....	....	....	....	....	....	....	....	....	....	....
	Huddinge IK	Swede-2	7	0	0	0	14	....	....	....	....	....	....	....	....	....	....	....	....	....	....	....	....	....	....
1996-97	Sodertalje SK	Sweden	32	1	1	2	32	....	....	....	....	....	....	....	....	....	....	....	....	....	....	....	....	....	....
1997-98	Sodertalje SK	Sweden	26	3	3	6	28	....	....	....	....	....	....	....	....	....	....	....	....	....	....	....	....	....	....
1998-99	Tappara Tampere	Finland	51	6	8	14	119	....	....	....	....	....	....	....	....	....	....	....	....	....	....	....	....	....	....
99-2000	Tappara Tampere	Finland	50	8	24	32	160	....	....	....	....	....	....	....	....	....	4	1	2	3	10	....	....	....	....
2000-01	Albany River Rats	AHL	79	8	28	36	117	....	....	....	....	....	....	....	....	....	....	....	....	....	....	....	....	....	....
2001-02	**New Jersey**	**NHL**	**1**	**1**	**0**	**1**	**2**	**0**	**0**	**0**	**1**	**100.0**	**–1**	**0**	**0.0**	**20:23**	....	....	....	....	....	....	....	....	....
	Albany River Rats	AHL	9	0	3	3	10	....	....	....	....	....	....	....	....	....	....	....	....	....	....	....	....	....	....
	Tampa Bay	**NHL**	**3**	**0**	**0**	**0**	**4**	**0**	**0**	**0**	**0**	**0.0**	**–1**	**0**	**0.0**	**10:58**	....	....	....	....	....	....	....	....	....
	Springfield	AHL	53	7	25	32	57	....	....	....	....	....	....	....	....	....	....	....	....	....	....	....	....	....	....
2002-03	Binghamton	AHL	26	2	15	17	62	....	....	....	....	....	....	....	....	....	....	....	....	....	....	....	....	....	....
	Washington	**NHL**	**6**	**1**	**0**	**1**	**0**	**0**	**0**	**1**	**7**	**14.3**	**–1**	**0**	**0.0**	**19:33**	....	....	....	....	....	....	....	....	....
	Portland Pirates	AHL	44	8	22	30	77	....	....	....	....	....	....	....	....	....	....	....	....	....	....	....	....	....	....
2003-04	**Washington**	**NHL**	**37**	**2**	**12**	**14**	**30**	**2**	**0**	**0**	**44**	**4.5**	**–10**	**0**	**0.0**	**23:02**	....	....	....	....	....	....	....	....	....
	Portland Pirates	AHL	13	1	8	9	10	....	....	....	....	....	....	....	....	....	....	....	....	....	....	....	....	....	....
	NHL Totals		**47**	**4**	**12**	**16**	**36**	**2**	**0**	**1**	**52**	**7.7**		**0**	**0.0**	**21:46**	....	....	....	....	....	....	....	....	....

Traded to **Tampa Bay** by **New Jersey** with Sascha Goc and the rights to Anton But for Andrei Zyuzin, November 9, 2001. Traded to **Ottawa** by **Tampa Bay** for Ottawa's 7th round choice (Fredrik Norrena) in 2002 Entry Draft, June 23, 2002. Traded to **Washington** by **Ottawa** for Dean Melanson, December 16, 2002.

BOUWMEESTER, Jay

(BOW-mee-stuhr, JAY) **FLA.**

Defense. Shoots left. 6'4", 210 lbs. Born, Edmonton, Alta., September 27, 1983. Florida's 1st choice, 3rd overall, in 2002 Entry Draft.

Season	Club	League	GP	G	A	Pts	PIM	PP	SH	GW	S	%	+/-	TF	F%	Min	GP	G	A	Pts	PIM	PP	SH	GW	Min
1998-99	Edmonton SSAC	AMHL	32	14	29	43	36	....	....	....	....	....	....	....	....	....	....	....	....	....	....	....	....	....	....
	Medicine Hat	WHL	8	2	1	3	2	....	....	....	....	....	....	....	....	....	....	....	....	....	....	....	....	....	....
99-2000	Medicine Hat	WHL	64	13	21	34	26	....	....	....	....	....	....	....	....	....	....	....	....	....	....	....	....	....	....
2000-01	Medicine Hat	WHL	61	14	39	53	44	....	....	....	....	....	....	....	....	....	....	....	....	....	....	....	....	....	....
2001-02	Medicine Hat	WHL	61	11	50	61	42	....	....	....	....	....	....	....	....	....	....	....	....	....	....	....	....	....	....
2002-03	**Florida**	**NHL**	**82**	**4**	**12**	**16**	**14**	**2**	**0**	**0**	**110**	**3.6**	**–29**	**0**	**0.0**	**20:09**	....	....	....	....	....	....	....	....	....
2003-04	**Florida**	**NHL**	**61**	**2**	**18**	**20**	**30**	**0**	**0**	**0**	**85**	**2.4**	**–15**	**0**	**0.0**	**23:02**	....	....	....	....	....	....	....	....	....
	San Antonio	AHL	2	0	1	1	2	....	....	....	....	....	....	....	....	....	....	....	....	....	....	....	....	....	....
	NHL Totals		**143**	**6**	**30**	**36**	**44**	**2**	**0**	**0**	**195**	**3.1**		**0**	**0.0**	**21:23**	....	....	....	....	....	....	....	....	....

WHL East First All-Star Team (2002) • NHL All-Rookie Team (2003)

BOYES, Brad

(BOIZ, BRAD) **BOS.**

Center. Shoots right. 6'1", 195 lbs. Born, Mississauga, Ont., April 17, 1982. Toronto's 1st choice, 24th overall, in 2000 Entry Draft.

Season	Club	League	GP	G	A	Pts	PIM	PP	SH	GW	S	%	+/-	TF	F%	Min	GP	G	A	Pts	PIM	PP	SH	GW	Min
1997-98	Mississauga Reps	MTHL	44	27	50	77	....	....	....	....	....	....	....	....	....	....	....	....	....	....	....	....	....	....	....
1998-99	Erie Otters	OHL	59	24	36	60	30	....	....	....	....	....	....	....	....	....	5	1	2	3	10	....	....	....	....
99-2000	Erie Otters	OHL	68	36	46	82	38	....	....	....	....	....	....	....	....	....	13	6	8	14	10	....	....	....	....
2000-01	Erie Otters	OHL	59	45	45	90	42	....	....	....	....	....	....	....	....	....	15	10	13	23	8	....	....	....	....
2001-02	Erie Otters	OHL	47	36	41	77	42	....	....	....	....	....	....	....	....	....	21	22	*19	41	27	....	....	....	....
2002-03	St. John's	AHL	65	23	28	51	45	....	....	....	....	....	....	....	....	....	....	....	....	....	....	....	....	....	....
	Cleveland Barons	AHL	15	7	6	13	21	....	....	....	....	....	....	....	....	....	....	....	....	....	....	....	....	....	....
2003-04	**San Jose**	**NHL**	**1**	**0**	**0**	**0**	**2**	**0**	**0**	**0**	**0**	**0.0**	**–2**	**0**	**0.0**	**13:03**	....	....	....	....	....	....	....	....	....
	Cleveland Barons	AHL	61	25	35	60	38	....	....	....	....	....	....	....	....	....	....	....	....	....	....	....	....	....	....
	Providence Bruins	AHL	17	6	6	12	13	....	....	....	....	....	....	....	....	....	2	1	0	1	0	....	....	....	....
	NHL Totals		**1**	**0**	**0**	**0**	**2**	**0**	**0**	**0**	**0**	**0.0**		**0**	**0.0**	**13:03**	....	....	....	....	....	....	....	....	....

Canadian Major Junior Scholastic Player of the Year (2000) • OHL Second All-Star Team (2001) • OHL First All-Star Team (2002) • AHL All-Rookie Team (2003) • AHL Second All-Star Team (2004)

Traded to **San Jose** by **Toronto** with Alyn McCauley and Toronto's 1st round choice (later traded to Boston – Boston selected Mark Stuart) in 2003 Entry Draft for Owen Nolan, March 5, 2003. Traded to **Boston** by **San Jose** for Jeff Jillson, March 9, 2004.

BOYLE, Dan

(BOIL, DAN) **T.B.**

Defense. Shoots right. 5'11", 190 lbs. Born, Ottawa, Ont., July 12, 1976.

Season	Club	League	GP	G	A	Pts	PIM	PP	SH	GW	S	%	+/-	TF	F%	Min	GP	G	A	Pts	PIM	PP	SH	GW	Min
1992-93	Gloucester	OCJHL	55	22	51	73	60	....	....	....	....	....	....	....	....	....	....	....	....	....	....	....	....	....	....
1993-94	Gloucester	OCJHL	53	27	54	81	155	....	....	....	....	....	....	....	....	....	....	....	....	....	....	....	....	....	....
1994-95	Miami-Ohio	CCHA	35	8	18	26	24	....	....	....	....	....	....	....	....	....	....	....	....	....	....	....	....	....	....
1995-96	Miami-Ohio	CCHA	36	7	20	27	70	....	....	....	....	....	....	....	....	....	....	....	....	....	....	....	....	....	....
1996-97	Miami-Ohio	CCHA	40	11	43	54	52	....	....	....	....	....	....	....	....	....	....	....	....	....	....	....	....	....	....
1997-98	Miami-Ohio	CCHA	37	14	26	40	58	....	....	....	....	....	....	....	....	....	....	....	....	....	....	....	....	....	....

			Regular Season														Playoffs								
Season	Club	League	GP	G	A	Pts	PIM	PP	SH	GW	S	%	+/-	TF	F%	Min	GP	G	A	Pts	PIM	PP	SH	GW	Min
1998-99	**Florida**	**NHL**	**22**	**3**	**5**	**8**	**6**	**1**	**0**	**1**	**31**	**9.7**	**0**	**1**	**100.0**	**18:50**	....	....	....	....	....	....	....	....	....
	Kentucky	AHL	53	8	34	42	87	....	....	....	....	....	....	....	....	....	12	3	5	8	16	....	....	....	....
99-2000	**Florida**	**NHL**	**13**	**0**	**3**	**3**	**4**	**0**	**0**	**0**	**9**	**0.0**	**–2**	**0**	**0.0**	**16:57**	....	....	....	....	....	....	....	....	....
	Louisville Panthers	AHL	58	14	38	52	75	....	....	....	....	....	....	....	....	....	4	0	2	2	8	....	....	....	....
2000-01	**Florida**	**NHL**	**69**	**4**	**18**	**22**	**28**	**1**	**0**	**0**	**83**	**4.8**	**–14**	**0**	**0.0**	**16:56**	....	....	....	....	....	....	....	....	....
	Louisville Panthers	AHL	6	0	5	5	12	....	....	....	....	....	....	....	....	....	....	....	....	....	....	....	....	....	....
2001-02	**Florida**	**NHL**	**25**	**3**	**3**	**6**	**12**	**1**	**0**	**0**	**31**	**9.7**	**–1**	**2**	**50.0**	**15:40**	....	....	....	....	....	....	....	....	....
	Tampa Bay	**NHL**	**41**	**5**	**15**	**20**	**27**	**2**	**0**	**1**	**68**	**7.4**	**–15**	**0**	**0.0**	**22:28**	....	....	....	....	....	....	....	....	....
2002-03	**Tampa Bay**	**NHL**	**77**	**13**	**40**	**53**	**44**	**8**	**0**	**1**	**136**	**9.6**	**9**	**2**	**0.0**	**24:31**	**11**	**0**	**7**	**7**	**6**	**0**	**0**	**0**	**27:45**
2003-04♦	**Tampa Bay**	**NHL**	**78**	**9**	**30**	**39**	**60**	**3**	**0**	**2**	**137**	**6.6**	**23**	**0**	**0.0**	**22:46**	**23**	**2**	**8**	**10**	**16**	**1**	**0**	**0**	**21:27**
	NHL Totals		**325**	**37**	**114**	**151**	**181**	**16**	**0**	**5**	**495**	**7.5**		**5**	**40.0**	**20:52**	**34**	**2**	**15**	**17**	**22**	**1**	**0**	**0**	**23:29**

CCHA First All-Star Team (1997, 1998) • NCAA West First All-American Team (1997, 1998) • AHL Second All-Star Team (1999, 2000)
Signed as a free agent by **Florida**, March 30, 1998. Traded to **Tampa Bay** by **Florida** for Tampa Bay's 5th round choice (Martin Tuma) in 2003 Entry Draft, January 7, 2002.

BOYNTON, Nick

(BOIN-tuhn, NIHK) **BOS.**

Defense. Shoots right. 6'2", 210 lbs. Born, Nobleton, Ont., January 14, 1979. Boston's 1st choice, 21st overall, in 1999 Entry Draft.

Season	Club	League	GP	G	A	Pts	PIM	PP	SH	GW	S	%	+/-	TF	F%	Min	GP	G	A	Pts	PIM	PP	SH	GW	Min
1993-94	Caledon	MTJHL	4	0	1	1	0	....	....	....	....	....	....	....	....	....	....	....	....	....	....	....	....	....	....
1994-95	Caledon	MTJHL	44	10	35	45	139	....	....	....	....	....	....	....	....	....	....	....	....	....	....	....	....	....	....
1995-96	Ottawa 67's	OHL	64	10	14	24	90	....	....	....	....	....	....	....	....	....	4	0	3	3	10	....	....	....	....
1996-97	Ottawa 67's	OHL	63	13	51	64	143	....	....	....	....	....	....	....	....	....	24	4	*24	28	38	....	....	....	....
1997-98	Ottawa 67's	OHL	40	7	31	38	94	....	....	....	....	....	....	....	....	....	13	0	4	4	24	....	....	....	....
1998-99	Ottawa 67's	OHL	51	11	48	59	83	....	....	....	....	....	....	....	....	....	9	1	9	10	18	....	....	....	....
99-2000	**Boston**	**NHL**	**5**	**0**	**0**	**0**	**0**	**0**	**0**	**0**	**6**	**0.0**	**–5**	**0**	**0.0**	**21:21**	....	....	....	....	....	....	....	....	....
	Providence Bruins	AHL	53	5	14	19	66	....	....	....	....	....	....	....	....	....	12	1	0	1	6	....	....	....	....
2000-01	**Boston**	**NHL**	**1**	**0**	**0**	**0**	**0**	**0**	**0**	**0**	**1**	**0.0**	**–1**	**0**	**0.0**	**14:27**	....	....	....	....	....	....	....	....	....
	Providence Bruins	AHL	78	6	27	33	105	....	....	....	....	....	....	....	....	....	17	0	2	2	35	....	....	....	....
2001-02	**Boston**	**NHL**	**80**	**4**	**14**	**18**	**107**	**0**	**0**	**1**	**136**	**2.9**	**18**	**0**	**0.0**	**18:30**	**6**	**1**	**2**	**3**	**8**	**0**	**0**	**0**	**21:30**
2002-03	**Boston**	**NHL**	**78**	**7**	**17**	**24**	**99**	**0**	**1**	**2**	**160**	**4.4**	**8**	**1**	**0.0**	**22:41**	**5**	**0**	**1**	**1**	**4**	**0**	**0**	**0**	**23:22**
2003-04	**Boston**	**NHL**	**81**	**6**	**24**	**30**	**98**	**1**	**1**	**1**	**178**	**3.4**	**17**	**0**	**0.0**	**22:32**	**7**	**0**	**2**	**2**	**2**	**0**	**0**	**0**	**24:44**
	NHL Totals		**245**	**17**	**55**	**72**	**304**	**1**	**2**	**4**	**481**	**3.5**		**1**	**0.0**	**21:13**	**18**	**1**	**5**	**6**	**14**	**0**	**0**	**0**	**23:16**

• Re-entered NHL Entry Draft. Originally Washington's 1st choice, 9th overall, in 1997 Entry Draft.
OHL All-Rookie Team (1996) • Memorial Cup All-Star Team (1999) • Stafford Smythe Memorial Trophy (Memorial Cup MVP) (1999) • NHL All-Rookie Team (2002)
Played in NHL All-Star Game (2004)

BRADLEY, Matt

(BRAD-lee, MAT) **PIT.**

Right wing. Shoots right. 6'3", 199 lbs. Born, Stittsville, Ont., June 13, 1978. San Jose's 4th choice, 102nd overall, in 1996 Entry Draft.

Season	Club	League	GP	G	A	Pts	PIM	PP	SH	GW	S	%	+/-	TF	F%	Min	GP	G	A	Pts	PIM	PP	SH	GW	Min
1994-95	Cumberland	OCJHL	49	13	20	33	18	....	....	....	....	....	....	....	....	....	....	....	....	....	....	....	....	....	....
1995-96	Kingston	OHL	55	10	14	24	17	....	....	....	....	....	....	....	....	....	6	0	1	1	6	....	....	....	....
1996-97	Kingston	OHL	65	24	24	48	41	....	....	....	....	....	....	....	....	....	5	0	4	4	2	....	....	....	....
	Kentucky	AHL	1	0	1	1	0	....	....	....	....	....	....	....	....	....	....	....	....	....	....	....	....	....	....
1997-98	Kingston	OHL	55	33	50	83	24	....	....	....	....	....	....	....	....	....	8	3	4	7	7	....	....	....	....
1998-99	Kentucky	AHL	79	23	20	43	57	....	....	....	....	....	....	....	....	....	10	1	4	5	4	....	....	....	....
99-2000	Kentucky	AHL	80	22	19	41	81	....	....	....	....	....	....	....	....	....	9	6	3	9	9	....	....	....	....
2000-01	**San Jose**	**NHL**	**21**	**1**	**1**	**2**	**19**	**0**	**0**	**0**	**16**	**6.3**	**0**	**0**	**0.0**	**6:58**	....	....	....	....	....	....	....	....	....
	Kentucky	AHL	22	5	8	13	16	....	....	....	....	....	....	....	....	....	1	1	0	1	5	....	....	....	....
2001-02	**San Jose**	**NHL**	**54**	**9**	**13**	**22**	**43**	**0**	**0**	**2**	**63**	**14.3**	**22**	**2**	**0.0**	**8:27**	**10**	**0**	**0**	**0**	**0**	**0**	**0**	**0**	**5:16**
2002-03	**San Jose**	**NHL**	**46**	**2**	**3**	**5**	**37**	**0**	**0**	**0**	**21**	**9.5**	**–1**	**1**	**0.0**	**7:54**	....	....	....	....	....	....	....	....	....
2003-04	**Pittsburgh**	**NHL**	**82**	**7**	**9**	**16**	**65**	**0**	**0**	**1**	**85**	**8.2**	**–27**	**29**	**41.4**	**12:48**	....	....	....	....	....	....	....	....	....
	NHL Totals		**203**	**19**	**26**	**45**	**164**	**0**	**0**	**3**	**185**	**10.3**		**32**	**37.5**	**9:56**	**10**	**0**	**0**	**0**	**0**	**0**	**0**	**0**	**5:16**

William Hanley Award (Most Gentlemanly Player – OHL) (1998)
Traded to **Pittsburgh** by **San Jose** for Wayne Primeau, March 11, 2003.

BRANDNER, Christoph

(BRAND-nuhr, KRIH-stahf) **MIN.**

Left wing. Shoots left. 6'4", 224 lbs. Born, Bruck an der Mur, Austria, July 5, 1975. Minnesota's 8th choice, 237th overall, in 2002 Entry Draft.

Season	Club	League	GP	G	A	Pts	PIM	PP	SH	GW	S	%	+/-	TF	F%	Min	GP	G	A	Pts	PIM	PP	SH	GW	Min
1997-98	Klagenfurter AC	Austria	27	12	7	19	18	....	....	....	....	....	....	....	....	....	....	....	....	....	....	....	....	....	....
	Klagenfurter AC	Alpenliga	STATISTICS NOT AVAILABLE					....	....	....	....	....	....	....	....	....	....	....	....	....	....	....	....	....	....
1998-99	Klagenfurter AC	Austria	21	8	8	16	6	....	....	....	....	....	....	....	....	....	....	....	....	....	....	....	....	....	....
	Klagenfurter AC	Alpenliga	33	23	10	33	16	....	....	....	....	....	....	....	....	....	....	....	....	....	....	....	....	....	....
99-2000	Klagenfurter AC	IEL	34	29	19	48	30	....	....	....	....	....	....	....	....	....	....	....	....	....	....	....	....	....	....
	Klagenfurter AC	Austria	16	8	3	11	20	....	....	....	....	....	....	....	....	....	....	....	....	....	....	....	....	....	....
2000-01	Klagenfurter AC	Austria	6	6	2	8	4	....	....	....	....	....	....	....	....	....	....	....	....	....	....	....	....	....	....
	Krefeld Pinguine	Germany	59	24	24	48	34	....	....	....	....	....	....	....	....	....	....	....	....	....	....	....	....	....	....
2001-02	Krefeld Pinguine	Germany	50	30	25	55	20	....	....	....	....	....	....	....	....	....	3	1	0	1	4	....	....	....	....
	Austria	Olympics	4	0	1	1	2	....	....	....	....	....	....	....	....	....	....	....	....	....	....	....	....	....	....
2002-03	Krefeld Pinguine	Germany	49	*28	17	45	26	....	....	....	....	....	....	....	....	....	14	9	9	18	8	....	....	....	....
2003-04	**Minnesota**	**NHL**	**35**	**4**	**5**	**9**	**8**	**1**	**0**	**0**	**50**	**8.0**	**–2**	**4**	**50.0**	**13:20**	....	....	....	....	....	....	....	....	....
	Houston Aeros	AHL	37	7	7	14	18	....	....	....	....	....	....	....	....	....	2	1	0	1	0	....	....	....	....
	NHL Totals		**35**	**4**	**5**	**9**	**8**	**1**	**0**	**0**	**50**	**8.0**		**4**	**50.0**	**13:20**	....	....	....	....	....	....	....	....	....

BRASHEAR, Donald

(bra-SHEER, DAWN-ohld) **PHI.**

Left wing. Shoots left. 6'2", 235 lbs. Born, Bedford, IN, January 7, 1972.

Season	Club	League	GP	G	A	Pts	PIM	PP	SH	GW	S	%	+/-	TF	F%	Min	GP	G	A	Pts	PIM	PP	SH	GW	Min
1988-89	Ste-Foy	QAAA	10	1	2	3	10	....	....	....	....	....	....	....	....	....	....	....	....	....	....	....	....	....	....
1989-90	Longueuil	QMJHL	64	12	14	26	169	....	....	....	....	....	....	....	....	....	7	0	0	0	11	....	....	....	....
1990-91	Longueuil	QMJHL	68	12	26	38	195	....	....	....	....	....	....	....	....	....	8	0	3	3	33	....	....	....	....
1991-92	Verdun	QMJHL	65	18	24	42	283	....	....	....	....	....	....	....	....	....	18	4	2	6	98	....	....	....	....
1992-93	Fredericton	AHL	76	11	3	14	261	....	....	....	....	....	....	....	....	....	5	0	0	0	8	....	....	....	....
1993-94	**Montreal**	**NHL**	**14**	**2**	**2**	**4**	**34**	**0**	**0**	**0**	**15**	**13.3**	**0**	....	....	....	**2**	**0**	**0**	**0**	**0**	**0**	**0**	**0**	....
	Fredericton	AHL	62	38	28	66	250	....	....	....	....	....	....	....	....	....	....	....	....	....	....	....	....	....	....
1994-95	Fredericton	AHL	29	10	9	19	182	....	....	....	....	....	....	....	....	....	17	7	5	12	77	....	....	....	....
	Montreal	**NHL**	**20**	**1**	**1**	**2**	**63**	**0**	**0**	**1**	**10**	**10.0**	**–5**	....	....	....	....	....	....	....	....	....	....	....	....
1995-96	**Montreal**	**NHL**	**67**	**0**	**4**	**4**	**223**	**0**	**0**	**0**	**25**	**0.0**	**–10**	....	....	....	**6**	**0**	**0**	**0**	**2**	**0**	**0**	**0**	....
1996-97	**Montreal**	**NHL**	**10**	**0**	**0**	**0**	**38**	**0**	**0**	**0**	**6**	**0.0**	**–2**	....	....	....	....	....	....	....	....	....	....	....	....
	Vancouver	**NHL**	**59**	**8**	**5**	**13**	**207**	**0**	**0**	**2**	**55**	**14.5**	**–6**	....	....	....	....	....	....	....	....	....	....	....	....
1997-98	**Vancouver**	**NHL**	**77**	**9**	**9**	**18**	***372**	**0**	**0**	**1**	**64**	**14.1**	**–9**	....	....	....	....	....	....	....	....	....	....	....	....
1998-99	**Vancouver**	**NHL**	**82**	**8**	**10**	**18**	**209**	**2**	**0**	**1**	**112**	**7.1**	**–25**	**6**	**16.7**	**13:25**	....	....	....	....	....	....	....	....	....
99-2000	**Vancouver**	**NHL**	**60**	**11**	**2**	**13**	**136**	**1**	**0**	**3**	**83**	**13.3**	**–9**	**11**	**36.4**	**13:07**	....	....	....	....	....	....	....	....	....
2000-01	**Vancouver**	**NHL**	**79**	**9**	**19**	**28**	**145**	**0**	**0**	**1**	**127**	**7.1**	**0**	**6**	**16.7**	**13:27**	**4**	**0**	**0**	**0**	**0**	**0**	**0**	**0**	**14:47**
2001-02	**Vancouver**	**NHL**	**31**	**5**	**8**	**13**	**90**	**1**	**0**	**0**	**45**	**11.1**	**–8**	**4**	**25.0**	**13:58**	....	....	....	....	....	....	....	....	....
	Philadelphia	**NHL**	**50**	**4**	**15**	**19**	**109**	**0**	**0**	**2**	**62**	**6.5**	**0**	**1**	**0.0**	**13:00**	**5**	**0**	**0**	**0**	**19**	**0**	**0**	**0**	**9:55**
2002-03	**Philadelphia**	**NHL**	**80**	**8**	**17**	**25**	**161**	**0**	**0**	**1**	**99**	**8.1**	**5**	**27**	**33.3**	**13:23**	**13**	**1**	**2**	**3**	**21**	**0**	**0**	**0**	**11:09**
2003-04	**Philadelphia**	**NHL**	**64**	**6**	**7**	**13**	**212**	**0**	**0**	**0**	**72**	**8.3**	**–1**	**18**	**38.9**	**11:02**	**18**	**1**	**3**	**4**	**61**	**1**	**0**	**0**	**8:56**
	NHL Totals		**693**	**71**	**99**	**170**	**1999**	**4**	**0**	**12**	**775**	**9.2**		**73**	**31.5**	**13:02**	**48**	**2**	**5**	**7**	**103**	**1**	**0**	**0**	**10:21**

Signed as a free agent by **Montreal**, July 28, 1992. Traded to **Vancouver** by **Montreal** for Jassen Cullimore, November 13, 1996. Traded to **Philadelphia** by **Vancouver** with Vancouver's 6th round choice (later traded to Columbus – Columbus selected Jaroslav Balastik) in 2002 Entry Draft for Jan Hlavac and Tampa Bay's 3rd round choice (previously acquired, Vancouver selected Brett Skinner) in 2002 Entry Draft, December 17, 2001.

BRENDL, Pavel

(BREHN-duhl, PAH-vehl) **CAR.**

Right wing. Shoots right. 6'1", 206 lbs. Born, Opocno, Czech., March 23, 1981. NY Rangers' 1st choice, 4th overall, in 1999 Entry Draft.

Season	Club	League	GP	G	A	Pts	PIM	PP	SH	GW	S	%	+/-	TF	F%	Min	GP	G	A	Pts	PIM	PP	SH	GW	Min
1996-97	HC Olomouc Jr.	Czech-Jr.	40	35	17	52	....	....	....	....	....	....	....	....	....	....	....	....	....	....	....	....	....	....	....
1997-98	HC Olomouc Jr.	Czech-Jr.	38	29	23	52	....	....	....	....	....	....	....	....	....	....	....	....	....	....	....	....	....	....	....
	HC Olomouc	Czech-2	12	1	1	2	....	....	....	....	....	....	....	....	....	....	....	....	....	....	....	....	....	....	....
1998-99	Calgary Hitmen	WHL	68	*73	61	*134	40	....	....	....	....	....	....	....	....	....	20	*21	*25	*46	18	....	....	....	....
99-2000	Calgary Hitmen	WHL	61	*59	52	111	94	....	....	....	....	....	....	....	....	....	10	7	12	19	8	....	....	....	....
	Hartford	AHL	....	....	....	....	....	....	....	....	....	....	....	....	....	....	2	0	0	0	0	....	....	....	....

			Regular Season														Playoffs								
Season	Club	League	GP	G	A	Pts	PIM	PP	SH	GW	S	%	+/-	TF	F%	Min	GP	G	A	Pts	PIM	PP	SH	GW	Min
2000-01	Calgary Hitmen	WHL	49	40	35	75	66	....	....	....	....	....	....	....	....	....	10	7	6	13	6	....	....	....	....
2001-02	**Philadelphia**	**NHL**	**8**	**1**	**0**	**1**	**2**	**0**	**0**	**0**	**6**	**16.7**	**–1**	**21**	**19.1**	**8:59**	**2**	**0**	**0**	**0**	**0**	**0**	**0**	**0**	**11:28**
	Philadelphia	AHL	64	15	22	37	22	....	....	....	....	....	....	....	....	....	5	4	1	5	0	....	....	....	....
2002-03	**Philadelphia**	**NHL**	**42**	**5**	**7**	**12**	**4**	**1**	**0**	**1**	**80**	**6.3**	**8**	**9**	**22.2**	**10:19**	....	....	....	....	....	....	....	....	....
	Carolina	**NHL**	**8**	**0**	**1**	**1**	**2**	**0**	**0**	**0**	**14**	**0.0**	**–3**	**2**	**50.0**	**15:05**	....	....	....	....	....	....	....	....	....
2003-04	**Carolina**	**NHL**	**18**	**5**	**3**	**8**	**8**	**1**	**0**	**1**	**27**	**18.5**	**0**	**1**	**0.0**	**14:48**	....	....	....	....	....	....	....	....	....
	Lowell	AHL	33	17	16	33	34	....	....	....	....	....	....	....	....	....	....	....	....	....	....	....	....	....	....
	NHL Totals		**76**	**11**	**11**	**22**	**16**	**2**	**0**	**2**	**127**	**8.7**		**33**	**21.2**	**11:45**	**2**	**0**	**0**	**0**	**0**	**0**	**0**	**0**	**11:28**

WHL East First All-Star Team (1999) • Canadian Major Junior First All-Star Team (1999) • Canadian Major Junior Rookie of the Year (1999) • Memorial Cup All-Star Team (1999) • WHL East Second All-Star Team (2000)

Traded to **Philadelphia** by **NY Rangers** with Jan Hlavac, Kim Johnsson and NY Rangers' 3rd round choice (Stefan Ruzicka) in 2003 Entry Draft for Eric Lindros, August 20, 2001. Traded to **Carolina** by **Philadelphia** with Bruno St. Jacques for Sami Kapanen and Ryan Bast, February 7, 2003.

BRENNAN, Kip

(BREHN-nan, KIHP) **ATL.**

Left wing. Shoots left. 6'4", 230 lbs. Born, Kingston, Ont., August 27, 1980. Los Angeles' 4th choice, 103rd overall, in 1998 Entry Draft.

Season	Club	League	GP	G	A	Pts	PIM	PP	SH	GW	S	%	+/-	TF	F%	Min	GP	G	A	Pts	PIM	PP	SH	GW	Min
1995-96	St. Michael's B	MTJHL	40	0	11	11	155	....	....	....	....	....	....	....	....	....	....	....	....	....	....	....	....	....	....
1996-97	Windsor Spitfires	OHL	42	0	10	10	156	....	....	....	....	....	....	....	....	....	5	0	1	1	16	....	....	....	....
1997-98	Windsor Spitfires	OHL	24	0	7	7	103	....	....	....	....	....	....	....	....	....	....	....	....	....	....	....	....	....	....
	Sudbury Wolves	OHL	24	0	3	3	85	....	....	....	....	....	....	....	....	....	....	....	....	....	....	....	....	....	....
1998-99	Sudbury Wolves	OHL	38	9	12	21	160	....	....	....	....	....	....	....	....	....	....	....	....	....	....	....	....	....	....
99-2000	Sudbury Wolves	OHL	55	16	16	32	228	....	....	....	....	....	....	....	....	....	12	3	3	6	67	....	....	....	....
2000-01	Lowell	AHL	23	2	3	5	117	....	....	....	....	....	....	....	....	....	....	....	....	....	....	....	....	....	....
	Sudbury Wolves	OHL	27	7	14	21	94	....	....	....	....	....	....	....	....	....	12	5	6	11	*92	....	....	....	....
2001-02	**Los Angeles**	**NHL**	**4**	**0**	**0**	**0**	**22**	**0**	**0**	**0**	**0**	**0.0**	**1**	**0**	**0.0**	**4:40**	....	....	....	....	....	....	....	....	....
	Manchester	AHL	44	4	1	5	269	....	....	....	....	....	....	....	....	....	4	0	1	1	26	....	....	....	....
2002-03	Manchester	AHL	35	3	2	5	195	....	....	....	....	....	....	....	....	....	3	0	0	0	0	....	....	....	....
	Los Angeles	**NHL**	**19**	**0**	**0**	**0**	**57**	**0**	**0**	**0**	**6**	**0.0**	**0**	**2**	**0.0**	**4:52**	....	....	....	....	....	....	....	....	....
2003-04	**Los Angeles**	**NHL**	**18**	**1**	**0**	**1**	**79**	**0**	**0**	**0**	**6**	**16.7**	**–1**	**0**	**0.0**	**5:01**	....	....	....	....	....	....	....	....	....
	Manchester	AHL	2	0	0	0	6	....	....	....	....	....	....	....	....	....	....	....	....	....	....	....	....	....	....
	Atlanta	**NHL**	**5**	**0**	**0**	**0**	**17**	**0**	**0**	**0**	**2**	**0.0**	**0**	**0**	**0.0**	**3:37**	....	....	....	....	....	....	....	....	....
	NHL Totals		**46**	**1**	**0**	**1**	**175**	**0**	**0**	**0**	**14**	**7.1**		**2**	**0.0**	**4:46**	....	....	....	....	....	....	....	....	....

Traded to **Atlanta** by **Los Angeles** for Jeff Cowan, March 9, 2004. • Spent majority 2003-04 season as a healthy reserve.

BRENNAN, Rich

(BREHN-nan, RIHCH)

Defense. Shoots right. 6'2", 200 lbs. Born, Schenectady, NY, November 26, 1972. Quebec's 3rd choice, 46th overall, in 1991 Entry Draft.

Season	Club	League	GP	G	A	Pts	PIM	PP	SH	GW	S	%	+/-	TF	F%	Min	GP	G	A	Pts	PIM	PP	SH	GW	Min
1988-89	Albany	Hi-School	25	17	30	47	57	....	....	....	....	....	....	....	....	....	....	....	....	....	....	....	....	....	....
1989-90	Tabor Academy	Hi-School	33	12	14	26	68	....	....	....	....	....	....	....	....	....	....	....	....	....	....	....	....	....	....
1990-91	Tabor Academy	Hi-School	34	13	37	50	91	....	....	....	....	....	....	....	....	....	....	....	....	....	....	....	....	....	....
1991-92	Boston University	H-East	30	4	13	17	50	....	....	....	....	....	....	....	....	....	....	....	....	....	....	....	....	....	....
1992-93	Boston University	H-East	40	9	11	20	68	....	....	....	....	....	....	....	....	....	....	....	....	....	....	....	....	....	....
1993-94	Boston University	H-East	41	8	27	35	82	....	....	....	....	....	....	....	....	....	....	....	....	....	....	....	....	....	....
1994-95	Boston University	H-East	31	5	22	27	56	....	....	....	....	....	....	....	....	....	....	....	....	....	....	....	....	....	....
1995-96	Brantford Smoke	ColHL	5	1	2	3	2	....	....	....	....	....	....	....	....	....	....	....	....	....	....	....	....	....	....
	Cornwall Aces	AHL	36	4	8	12	61	....	....	....	....	....	....	....	....	....	7	0	0	0	6	....	....	....	....
1996-97	**Colorado**	**NHL**	**2**	**0**	**0**	**0**	**0**	**0**	**0**	**0**	**0**	**0.0**	**0**	....	....	....	....	....	....	....	....	....	....	....	....
	Hershey Bears	AHL	74	11	45	56	88	....	....	....	....	....	....	....	....	....	23	2	*16	18	22	....	....	....	....
1997-98	**San Jose**	**NHL**	**11**	**1**	**2**	**3**	**2**	**1**	**0**	**0**	**24**	**4.2**	**–4**	....	....	....	....	....	....	....	....	....	....	....	....
	Kentucky	AHL	42	11	17	28	71	....	....	....	....	....	....	....	....	....	....	....	....	....	....	....	....	....	....
	Hartford	AHL	9	2	4	6	12	....	....	....	....	....	....	....	....	....	15	4	5	9	14	....	....	....	....
1998-99	**NY Rangers**	**NHL**	**24**	**1**	**3**	**4**	**23**	**0**	**0**	**0**	**36**	**2.8**	**–4**	**0**	**0.0**	**13:02**	....	....	....	....	....	....	....	....	....
	Hartford	AHL	47	4	24	28	42	....	....	....	....	....	....	....	....	....	....	....	....	....	....	....	....	....	....
99-2000	Lowell	AHL	67	15	30	45	110	....	....	....	....	....	....	....	....	....	7	1	5	6	0	....	....	....	....
2000-01	**Los Angeles**	**NHL**	**2**	**0**	**0**	**0**	**0**	**0**	**0**	**0**	**1**	**0.0**	**–3**	**0**	**0.0**	**14:44**	....	....	....	....	....	....	....	....	....
	Lowell	AHL	69	10	31	41	146	....	....	....	....	....	....	....	....	....	....	....	....	....	....	....	....	....	....
2001-02	**Nashville**	**NHL**	**4**	**0**	**0**	**0**	**2**	**0**	**0**	**0**	**0**	**0.0**	**0**	**0**	**0.0**	**14:31**	....	....	....	....	....	....	....	....	....
	Milwaukee	AHL	23	4	8	12	27	....	....	....	....	....	....	....	....	....	....	....	....	....	....	....	....	....	....
	Manchester	AHL	16	2	5	7	6	....	....	....	....	....	....	....	....	....	5	1	1	2	16	....	....	....	....
2002-03	**Boston**	**NHL**	**7**	**0**	**1**	**1**	**6**	**0**	**0**	**0**	**12**	**0.0**	**3**	**0**	**0.0**	**13:37**	....	....	....	....	....	....	....	....	....
	Providence Bruins	AHL	41	3	29	32	51	....	....	....	....	....	....	....	....	....	....	....	....	....	....	....	....	....	....
2003-04	Providence Bruins	AHL	56	12	15	27	47	....	....	....	....	....	....	....	....	....	2	0	1	1	2	....	....	....	....
	NHL Totals		**50**	**2**	**6**	**8**	**33**	**1**	**0**	**0**	**73**	**2.7**		**0**	**0.0**	**13:24**	....	....	....	....	....	....	....	....	....

Hockey East First All-Star Team (1994) • NCAA East Second All-American Team (1994)

Rights transferred to **Colorado** after **Quebec** franchise relocated, June 21, 1995. Signed as a free agent by **San Jose**, July 9, 1997. Traded to **NY Rangers** by **San Jose** for Jason Muzzatti, March 24, 1998. Signed as a free agent by **Nashville**, September 23, 1999. Claimed by **Los Angeles** from **Nashville** in Waiver Draft, September 27, 1999. Signed as a free agent by **Nashville**, August 8, 2001. Traded to **Los Angeles** by **Nashville** for Brett Hauer, December 19, 2001. Signed as a free agent by **Boston**, July 18, 2002.

BREWER, Eric

(BREW-uhr, AIR-ihk) **EDM.**

Defense. Shoots left. 6'4", 225 lbs. Born, Vernon, B.C., April 17, 1979. NY Islanders' 2nd choice, 5th overall, in 1997 Entry Draft.

Season	Club	League	GP	G	A	Pts	PIM	PP	SH	GW	S	%	+/-	TF	F%	Min	GP	G	A	Pts	PIM	PP	SH	GW	Min
1994-95	Kamloops	BCAHA	40	19	19	38	62	....	....	....	....	....	....	....	....	....	....	....	....	....	....	....	....	....	....
1995-96	Prince George	WHL	63	4	10	14	25	....	....	....	....	....	....	....	....	....	....	....	....	....	....	....	....	....	....
1996-97	Prince George	WHL	71	5	24	29	81	....	....	....	....	....	....	....	....	....	15	2	4	6	16	....	....	....	....
1997-98	Prince George	WHL	34	5	28	33	45	....	....	....	....	....	....	....	....	....	11	4	2	6	19	....	....	....	....
1998-99	**NY Islanders**	**NHL**	**63**	**5**	**6**	**11**	**32**	**2**	**0**	**0**	**63**	**7.9**	**–14**	**0**	**0.0**	**15:28**	....	....	....	....	....	....	....	....	....
99-2000	**NY Islanders**	**NHL**	**26**	**0**	**2**	**2**	**20**	**0**	**0**	**0**	**30**	**0.0**	**–11**	**0**	**0.0**	**18:33**	....	....	....	....	....	....	....	....	....
	Lowell	AHL	25	2	2	4	26	....	....	....	....	....	....	....	....	....	7	0	0	0	0	....	....	....	....
2000-01	**Edmonton**	**NHL**	**77**	**7**	**14**	**21**	**53**	**2**	**0**	**2**	**91**	**7.7**	**15**	**0**	**0.0**	**18:31**	**6**	**1**	**5**	**6**	**2**	**1**	**0**	**0**	**28:12**
2001-02	**Edmonton**	**NHL**	**81**	**7**	**18**	**25**	**45**	**6**	**0**	**2**	**165**	**4.2**	**–5**	**0**	**0.0**	**23:56**	....	....	....	....	....	....	....	....	....
	Canada	Olympics	6	2	0	2	0	....	....	....	....	....	....	....	....	....	....	....	....	....	....	....	....	....	....
2002-03	**Edmonton**	**NHL**	**80**	**8**	**21**	**29**	**45**	**1**	**0**	**1**	**147**	**5.4**	**–11**	**1**	**100.0**	**24:56**	**6**	**1**	**3**	**4**	**6**	**0**	**0**	**0**	**25:31**
2003-04	**Edmonton**	**NHL**	**77**	**7**	**18**	**25**	**67**	**3**	**0**	**1**	**135**	**5.2**	**–6**	**0**	**0.0**	**24:40**	....	....	....	....	....	....	....	....	....
	NHL Totals		**404**	**34**	**79**	**113**	**262**	**14**	**0**	**6**	**631**	**5.4**		**1**	**100.0**	**21:34**	**12**	**2**	**8**	**10**	**8**	**1**	**0**	**0**	**26:51**

WHL West Second All-Star Team (1998)

Played in NHL All-Star Game (2003)

Traded to **Edmonton** by **NY Islanders** with Josh Green and NY Islanders' 2nd round choice (Brad Winchester) in 2000 Entry Draft for Roman Hamrlik, June 24, 2000.

BRIERE, Daniel

(bree-AIR, DAN-yehl) **BUF.**

Center. Shoots right. 5'10", 178 lbs. Born, Gatineau, Que., October 6, 1977. Phoenix's 2nd choice, 24th overall, in 1996 Entry Draft.

Season	Club	League	GP	G	A	Pts	PIM	PP	SH	GW	S	%	+/-	TF	F%	Min	GP	G	A	Pts	PIM	PP	SH	GW	Min
1992-93	Abitibi Regents	QAAA	42	24	30	54	28	....	....	....	....	....	....	....	....	....	3	0	3	3	8	....	....	....	....
1993-94	Gatineau	QAAA	44	56	47	103	56	....	....	....	....	....	....	....	....	....	....	....	....	....	....	....	....	....	....
1994-95	Drummondville	QMJHL	72	51	72	123	54	....	....	....	....	....	....	....	....	....	4	2	3	5	2	....	....	....	....
1995-96	Drummondville	QMJHL	67	*67	*96	*163	84	....	....	....	....	....	....	....	....	....	6	6	12	18	8	....	....	....	....
1996-97	Drummondville	QMJHL	59	52	78	130	94	....	....	....	....	....	....	....	....	....	8	7	7	14	14	....	....	....	....
1997-98	**Phoenix**	**NHL**	**5**	**1**	**0**	**1**	**2**	**0**	**0**	**0**	**4**	**25.0**	**1**	....	....	....	....	....	....	....	....	....	....	....	....
	Springfield	AHL	68	36	56	92	42	....	....	....	....	....	....	....	....	....	4	1	2	3	4	....	....	....	....
1998-99	**Phoenix**	**NHL**	**64**	**8**	**14**	**22**	**30**	**2**	**0**	**2**	**90**	**8.9**	**–3**	**484**	**47.5**	**11:13**	....	....	....	....	....	....	....	....	....
	Las Vegas	IHL	1	1	1	2	0	....	....	....	....	....	....	....	....	....	....	....	....	....	....	....	....	....	....
	Springfield	AHL	13	2	6	8	20	....	....	....	....	....	....	....	....	....	3	0	1	1	2	....	....	....	....
99-2000	**Phoenix**	**NHL**	**13**	**1**	**1**	**2**	**0**	**0**	**0**	**0**	**9**	**11.1**	**0**	**65**	**49.2**	**7:41**	**1**	**0**	**0**	**0**	**0**	**0**	**0**	**0**	**6:16**
	Springfield	AHL	58	29	42	71	56	....	....	....	....	....	....	....	....	....	....	....	....	....	....	....	....	....	....
2000-01	**Phoenix**	**NHL**	**30**	**11**	**4**	**15**	**12**	**9**	**0**	**1**	**43**	**25.6**	**–2**	**210**	**50.0**	**10:50**	....	....	....	....	....	....	....	....	....
	Springfield	AHL	30	21	25	46	30	....	....	....	....	....	....	....	....	....	....	....	....	....	....	....	....	....	....
2001-02	**Phoenix**	**NHL**	**78**	**32**	**28**	**60**	**52**	**12**	**0**	**5**	**149**	**21.5**	**6**	**951**	**51.8**	**15:44**	**5**	**2**	**1**	**3**	**2**	**1**	**0**	**1**	**16:25**

			Regular Season														Playoffs								
Season	Club	League	GP	G	A	Pts	PIM	PP	SH	GW	S	%	+/-	TF	F%	Min	GP	G	A	Pts	PIM	PP	SH	GW	Min
2002-03	Phoenix	NHL	68	17	29	46	50	4	0	3	142	12.0	–21	1108	52.5	17:02	....	....	....	....	....	....	....	....	....
	Buffalo	NHL	14	7	5	12	12	5	0	1	39	17.9	1	206	50.0	17:49	....	....	....	....	....	....	....	....	....
2003-04	Buffalo	NHL	82	28	37	65	70	11	0	3	194	14.4	–7	1066	47.1	18:20	....	....	....	....	....	....	....	....	....
	NHL Totals		354	105	118	223	228	43	0	15	670	15.7		4090	50.0	15:08	6	2	1	3	2	1	0	1	14:43

QMJHL All-Rookie Team (1995) • QMJHL Offensive Rookie of the Year (1995) • QMJHL Second All-Star Team (1996, 1997) • AHL First All-Star Team (1998) • Dudley "Red" Garrett Memorial Trophy (Top Rookie – AHL) (1998)

Traded to **Buffalo** by **Phoenix** with Phoenix's 3rd round choice (Andrej Sekera) in 2004 Entry Draft for Chris Gratton and Buffalo's 4th round choice (later traded to Edmonton – Edmonton selected Liam Reddox) in 2004 Entry Draft, March 10, 2003.

BRIGLEY, Travis

(BRIH-glee, TRA-vihs)

Left wing. Shoots left. 6', 205 lbs. Born, Coronation, Alta., June 16, 1977. Calgary's 2nd choice, 39th overall, in 1996 Entry Draft.

Season	Club	League	GP	G	A	Pts	PIM	PP	SH	GW	S	%	+/-	TF	F%	Min	GP	G	A	Pts	PIM	PP	SH	GW	Min
1992-93	Leduc Oil Barons	AMHL	32	36	24	60	56	....	....	....	....	....	....	....	....	....	....	....	....	....	....	....	....	....	....
1993-94	Leduc Oil Barons	AMHL	34	29	44	73	141	....	....	....	....	....	....	....	....	....	....	....	....	....	....	....	....	....	....
	Lethbridge	WHL	1	0	0	0	0	....	....	....	....	....	....	....	....	....	....	....	....	....	....	....	....	....	....
1994-95	Lethbridge	WHL	64	14	18	32	14	....	....	....	....	....	....	....	....	....	....	....	....	....	....	....	....	....	....
1995-96	Lethbridge	WHL	69	34	43	77	94	....	....	....	....	....	....	....	....	....	4	2	3	5	8	....	....	....	....
1996-97	Lethbridge	WHL	71	43	47	90	56	....	....	....	....	....	....	....	....	....	19	9	9	18	31	....	....	....	....
1997-98	Calgary	NHL	2	0	0	0	2	0	0	0	1	0.0	0	....	....	....	....	....	....	....	....	....	....	....	....
	Saint John Flames	AHL	79	17	15	32	28	....	....	....	....	....	....	....	....	....	8	0	0	0	0	....	....	....	....
1998-99	Saint John Flames	AHL	74	15	35	50	48	....	....	....	....	....	....	....	....	....	7	3	1	4	2	....	....	....	....
99-2000	Calgary	NHL	17	0	2	2	4	0	0	0	17	0.0	–6	2	0.0	14:14	....	....	....	....	....	....	....	....	....
	Saint John Flames	AHL	9	3	1	4	4	....	....	....	....	....	....	....	....	....	....	....	....	....	....	....	....	....	....
	Detroit Vipers	IHL	29	6	10	16	24	....	....	....	....	....	....	....	....	....	....	....	....	....	....	....	....	....	....
	Philadelphia	AHL	15	2	2	4	15	....	....	....	....	....	....	....	....	....	5	1	0	1	4	....	....	....	....
2000-01	Knoxville Speed	UHL	4	2	4	6	4	....	....	....	....	....	....	....	....	....	....	....	....	....	....	....	....	....	....
	Cardiff Devils	Britain	12	5	9	14	6	....	....	....	....	....	....	....	....	....	....	....	....	....	....	....	....	....	....
	Louisville Panthers	AHL	49	14	21	35	34	....	....	....	....	....	....	....	....	....	....	....	....	....	....	....	....	....	....
2001-02	Macon Whoopee	ECHL	8	4	3	7	2	....	....	....	....	....	....	....	....	....	....	....	....	....	....	....	....	....	....
	Cincinnati	AHL	70	22	21	43	40	....	....	....	....	....	....	....	....	....	3	2	0	2	0	....	....	....	....
2002-03	Cincinnati	AHL	64	18	27	45	58	....	....	....	....	....	....	....	....	....	....	....	....	....	....	....	....	....	....
	Hershey Bears	AHL	13	3	5	8	4	....	....	....	....	....	....	....	....	....	5	1	2	3	2	....	....	....	....
2003-04	Colorado	NHL	36	3	4	7	10	1	0	0	39	7.7	0	198	43.4	11:52	....	....	....	....	....	....	....	....	....
	Hershey Bears	AHL	18	6	6	12	8	....	....	....	....	....	....	....	....	....	....	....	....	....	....	....	....	....	....
	NHL Totals		55	3	6	9	16	1	0	0	57	5.3		200	43.0	12:38	....	....	....	....	....	....	....	....	....

Traded to **Philadelphia** by **Calgary** with Calgary's 6th round choice (Andrei Razin) in 2001 Entry Draft for Marc Bureau, March 6, 2000. Signed as a free agent by **Cardiff** (Britain), November 3, 2000. Signed as a free agent by **Florida**, December 16, 2000. Signed as a free agent by **Anaheim**, January 22, 2002. Traded to **Colorado** by **Anaheim** for future considerations, August 12, 2003.

BRIMANIS, Aris

(brih-MAN-ihs, AR-ihs) **ST.L.**

Defense. Shoots right. 6'3", 215 lbs. Born, Cleveland, OH, March 14, 1972. Philadelphia's 3rd choice, 86th overall, in 1991 Entry Draft.

Season	Club	League	GP	G	A	Pts	PIM	PP	SH	GW	S	%	+/-	TF	F%	Min	GP	G	A	Pts	PIM	PP	SH	GW	Min
1988-89	Culver Eagles	Hi-School	38	10	13	23	24	....	....	....	....	....	....	....	....	....	....	....	....	....	....	....	....	....	....
1989-90	Culver Eagles	Hi-School	37	15	10	25	52	....	....	....	....	....	....	....	....	....	....	....	....	....	....	....	....	....	....
1990-91	Bowling Green	CCHA	38	3	6	9	42	....	....	....	....	....	....	....	....	....	....	....	....	....	....	....	....	....	....
1991-92	Bowling Green	CCHA	32	2	9	11	38	....	....	....	....	....	....	....	....	....	....	....	....	....	....	....	....	....	....
1992-93	Brandon	WHL	71	8	50	58	110	....	....	....	....	....	....	....	....	....	4	2	1	3	7	....	....	....	....
1993-94	Philadelphia	NHL	1	0	0	0	0	0	0	0	1	0.0	–1	....	....	....	....	....	....	....	....	....	....	....	....
	Hershey Bears	AHL	75	8	15	23	65	....	....	....	....	....	....	....	....	....	11	2	3	5	12	....	....	....	....
1994-95	Hershey Bears	AHL	76	8	17	25	68	....	....	....	....	....	....	....	....	....	6	1	1	2	14	....	....	....	....
1995-96	Philadelphia	NHL	17	0	2	2	12	0	0	0	11	0.0	–1	....	....	....	....	....	....	....	....	....	....	....	....
	Hershey Bears	AHL	54	9	22	31	64	....	....	....	....	....	....	....	....	....	5	1	2	3	4	....	....	....	....
1996-97	Philadelphia	NHL	3	0	1	1	0	0	0	0	1	0.0	0	....	....	....	....	....	....	....	....	....	....	....	....
	Philadelphia	AHL	65	14	18	32	69	....	....	....	....	....	....	....	....	....	10	2	2	4	13	....	....	....	....
1997-98	Philadelphia	AHL	30	1	11	12	26	....	....	....	....	....	....	....	....	....	....	....	....	....	....	....	....	....	....
	Michigan	IHL	35	3	9	12	24	....	....	....	....	....	....	....	....	....	4	1	0	1	4	....	....	....	....
1998-99	Grand Rapids	IHL	66	16	21	37	70	....	....	....	....	....	....	....	....	....	....	....	....	....	....	....	....	....	....
	Fredericton	AHL	8	2	4	6	6	....	....	....	....	....	....	....	....	....	15	3	10	13	18	....	....	....	....
99-2000	NY Islanders	NHL	18	2	1	3	6	2	0	0	16	12.5	–5	1	0.0	20:00	....	....	....	....	....	....	....	....	....
	Kansas City	IHL	46	5	17	22	28	....	....	....	....	....	....	....	....	....	....	....	....	....	....	....	....	....	....
	Providence Bruins	AHL	7	0	2	2	2	....	....	....	....	....	....	....	....	....	14	3	4	7	10	....	....	....	....
2000-01	NY Islanders	NHL	56	0	8	8	26	0	0	0	66	0.0	–12	0	0.0	15:36	....	....	....	....	....	....	....	....	....
	Chicago Wolves	IHL	20	2	2	4	14	....	....	....	....	....	....	....	....	....	16	3	1	4	8	....	....	....	....
2001-02	Anaheim	NHL	5	0	0	0	9	0	0	0	2	0.0	–1	0	0.0	9:31	....	....	....	....	....	....	....	....	....
	Cincinnati	AHL	72	2	9	11	44	....	....	....	....	....	....	....	....	....	3	1	0	1	0	....	....	....	....
2002-03	Worcester IceCats	AHL	38	8	13	21	51	....	....	....	....	....	....	....	....	....	3	0	0	0	2	....	....	....	....
2003-04	St. Louis	NHL	13	0	0	0	4	0	0	0	3	0.0	0	1	100.0	12:02	....	....	....	....	....	....	....	....	....
	Worcester IceCats	AHL	65	4	15	19	56	....	....	....	....	....	....	....	....	....	10	1	0	1	6	....	....	....	....
	NHL Totals		113	2	12	14	57	2	0	0	100	2.0		2	50.0	15:37	....	....	....	....	....	....	....	....	....

Signed as a free agent by **NY Islanders**, August 16, 1999. Loaned to **Providence** (AHL) by **NY Islanders**, March 14, 2000. Signed as a free agent by **Anaheim**, August 1, 2001. Signed as a free agent by **St. Louis**, August 15, 2002. • Missed majority of 2002-03 season recovering from leg injury suffered in game vs. Utah (AHL), December 20, 2002.

BRIND'AMOUR, Rod

(BRIHND-uh-MOHR, RAWD) **CAR.**

Center. Shoots left. 6'1", 200 lbs. Born, Ottawa, Ont., August 9, 1970. St. Louis' 1st choice, 9th overall, in 1988 Entry Draft.

Season	Club	League	GP	G	A	Pts	PIM	PP	SH	GW	S	%	+/-	TF	F%	Min	GP	G	A	Pts	PIM	PP	SH	GW	Min
1986-87	Notre Dame	SMHL	33	38	50	88	66	....	....	....	....	....	....	....	....	....	....	....	....	....	....	....	....	....	....
1987-88	Notre Dame	SJHL	56	46	61	107	136	....	....	....	....	....	....	....	....	....	....	....	....	....	....	....	....	....	....
1988-89	Michigan State	CCHA	42	27	32	59	63	....	....	....	....	....	....	....	....	....	....	....	....	....	....	....	....	....	....
	St. Louis	NHL	....	....	....	....	....	....	....	....	....	....	....	....	....	....	5	2	0	2	4	0	0	0	....
1989-90	St. Louis	NHL	79	26	35	61	46	10	0	1	160	16.3	23	....	....	....	12	5	8	13	6	1	0	0	....
1990-91	St. Louis	NHL	78	17	32	49	93	4	0	3	169	10.1	2	....	....	....	13	2	5	7	10	1	0	0	....
1991-92	Philadelphia	NHL	80	33	44	77	100	8	4	5	202	16.3	–3	....	....	....	....	....	....	....	....	....	....	....	....
1992-93	Philadelphia	NHL	81	37	49	86	89	13	4	4	206	18.0	–8	....	....	....	....	....	....	....	....	....	....	....	....
1993-94	Philadelphia	NHL	84	35	62	97	85	14	1	4	230	15.2	–9	....	....	....	....	....	....	....	....	....	....	....	....
1994-95	Philadelphia	NHL	48	12	27	39	33	4	1	2	86	14.0	–4	....	....	....	15	6	9	15	8	2	1	1	....
1995-96	Philadelphia	NHL	82	26	61	87	110	4	4	5	213	12.2	20	....	....	....	12	2	5	7	6	1	0	0	....
1996-97	Philadelphia	NHL	82	27	32	59	41	8	2	3	205	13.2	2	....	....	....	19	*13	8	21	10	4	2	1	....
1997-98	Philadelphia	NHL	82	36	38	74	54	10	2	8	205	17.6	–2	....	....	....	5	2	2	4	7	0	0	0	....
	Canada	Olympics	6	1	2	3	0	....	....	....	....	....	....	....	....	....	....	....	....	....	....	....	....	....	....
1998-99	Philadelphia	NHL	82	24	50	74	47	10	0	3	191	12.6	3	1773	56.5	21:29	6	1	3	4	0	0	0	0	25:08
99-2000	Philadelphia	NHL	12	5	3	8	4	4	0	0	26	19.2	–1	291	60.5	20:50	....	....	....	....	....	....	....	....	....
	Carolina	NHL	33	4	10	14	22	0	1	1	61	6.6	–12	704	55.5	20:35	....	....	....	....	....	....	....	....	....
2000-01	Carolina	NHL	79	20	36	56	47	5	1	5	163	12.3	–7	1907	60.4	22:07	6	1	3	4	6	0	0	1	23:27
2001-02	Carolina	NHL	81	23	32	55	40	5	2	5	162	14.2	3	2058	59.2	22:07	23	4	8	12	16	2	1	1	24:52
2002-03	Carolina	NHL	48	14	23	37	37	7	1	0	110	12.7	–9	1242	56.5	23:46	....	....	....	....	....	....	....	....	....
2003-04	Carolina	NHL	78	12	26	38	28	1	0	1	141	8.5	0	1817	61.1	21:23	....	....	....	....	....	....	....	....	....
	NHL Totals		1109	351	560	911	876	107	23	50	2530	13.9		9792	58.7	21:53	116	38	51	89	73	11	4	4	24:41

CCHA Rookie of the Year (1989) • NHL All-Rookie Team (1990)

Played in NHL All-Star Game (1992)

Traded to **Philadelphia** by **St. Louis** with Dan Quinn for Ron Sutter and Murray Baron, September 22, 1991. Traded to **Carolina** by **Philadelphia** with Jean-Marc Pelletier and Philadelphia's 2nd round choice (later traded to Colorado – Colorado selected Agris Saviels) in 2000 Entry Draft for Keith Primeau and Carolina's 5th round choice (later traded to NY Islanders – NY Islanders selected Kristofer Ottosson) in 2000 Entry Draft, January 23, 2000.

Season	Club	League	GP	G	A	Pts	PIM	PP	SH	GW	S	%	+/-	TF	F%	Min	GP	G	A	Pts	PIM	PP	SH	GW	Min
			Regular Season														Playoffs								

BRISEBOIS, Patrice

(BREES-bwah, pa-TREEZ) **MTL.**

Defense. Shoots right. 6'2", 203 lbs. Born, Montreal, Que., January 27, 1971. Montreal's 2nd choice, 30th overall, in 1989 Entry Draft.

Season	Club	League	GP	G	A	Pts	PIM	PP	SH	GW	S	%	+/-	TF	F%	Min	GP	G	A	Pts	PIM	PP	SH	GW	Min
1986-87	Mtl-Bourassa	QAAA	39	15	19	34	66	....	....	....	....	....	....	....	....	....	....	....	....	....	....	....	....	....	....
1987-88	Laval Titan	QMJHL	48	10	34	44	95	....	....	....	....	....	....	....	....	....	6	0	2	2	2	....	....	....	....
1988-89	Laval Titan	QMJHL	50	20	45	65	95	....	....	....	....	....	....	....	....	....	17	8	14	22	45	....	....	....	....
1989-90	Laval Titan	QMJHL	56	18	70	88	108	....	....	....	....	....	....	....	....	....	13	7	9	16	26	....	....	....	....
1990-91	Drummondville	QMJHL	54	17	44	61	72	....	....	....	....	....	....	....	....	....	14	6	18	24	49	....	....	....	....
	Montreal	**NHL**	**10**	**0**	**2**	**2**	**4**	**0**	**0**	**0**	**11**	**0.0**	**1**	....	....	....	....	....	....	....	....	....	....	....	....
1991-92	**Montreal**	**NHL**	**26**	**2**	**8**	**10**	**20**	**0**	**0**	**1**	**37**	**5.4**	**9**	....	....	....	**11**	**2**	**4**	**6**	**6**	**1**	**0**	**1**	....
	Fredericton	AHL	53	12	27	39	51	....	....	....	....	....	....	....	....	....	....	....	....	....	....	....	....	....	....
1992-93 ♦	**Montreal**	**NHL**	**70**	**10**	**21**	**31**	**79**	**4**	**0**	**2**	**123**	**8.1**	**6**	....	....	....	**20**	**0**	**4**	**4**	**18**	**0**	**0**	**0**	....
1993-94	**Montreal**	**NHL**	**53**	**2**	**21**	**23**	**63**	**1**	**0**	**0**	**71**	**2.8**	**5**	....	....	....	**7**	**0**	**4**	**4**	**6**	**0**	**0**	**0**	....
1994-95	**Montreal**	**NHL**	**35**	**4**	**8**	**12**	**26**	**0**	**0**	**2**	**67**	**6.0**	**−2**	....	....	....	....	....	....	....	....	....	....	....	....
1995-96	**Montreal**	**NHL**	**69**	**9**	**27**	**36**	**65**	**3**	**0**	**1**	**127**	**7.1**	**10**	....	....	....	**6**	**1**	**2**	**3**	**6**	**0**	**0**	**0**	....
1996-97	**Montreal**	**NHL**	**49**	**2**	**13**	**15**	**24**	**0**	**0**	**1**	**72**	**2.8**	**−7**	....	....	....	**3**	**1**	**1**	**2**	**24**	**0**	**0**	**1**	....
1997-98	**Montreal**	**NHL**	**79**	**10**	**27**	**37**	**67**	**5**	**0**	**1**	**125**	**8.0**	**16**	....	....	....	**10**	**1**	**0**	**1**	**0**	**0**	**0**	**0**	....
1998-99	**Montreal**	**NHL**	**54**	**3**	**9**	**12**	**28**	**1**	**0**	**1**	**90**	**3.3**	**−8**	**0**	**0.0**	**22:26**	....	....	....	....	....	....	....	....	....
99-2000	**Montreal**	**NHL**	**54**	**10**	**25**	**35**	**18**	**5**	**0**	**2**	**88**	**11.4**	**−1**	**0**	**0.0**	**23:14**	....	....	....	....	....	....	....	....	....
2000-01	**Montreal**	**NHL**	**77**	**15**	**21**	**36**	**28**	**11**	**0**	**4**	**178**	**8.4**	**−31**	**1**	**100.0**	**24:43**	....	....	....	....	....	....	....	....	....
2001-02	**Montreal**	**NHL**	**71**	**4**	**29**	**33**	**25**	**2**	**1**	**1**	**95**	**4.2**	**9**	**0**	**0.0**	**23:53**	**10**	**1**	**1**	**2**	**2**	**0**	**0**	**0**	**22:05**
2002-03	**Montreal**	**NHL**	**73**	**4**	**25**	**29**	**32**	**1**	**0**	**1**	**105**	**3.8**	**−14**	**0**	**0.0**	**23:23**	....	....	....	....	....	....	....	....	....
2003-04	**Montreal**	**NHL**	**71**	**4**	**27**	**31**	**22**	**2**	**0**	**0**	**96**	**4.2**	**17**	**0**	**0.0**	**21:20**	**11**	**2**	**1**	**3**	**4**	**1**	**0**	**0**	**22:30**
	NHL Totals		**791**	**79**	**263**	**342**	**501**	**35**	**1**	**17**	**1285**	**6.1**		**1**	**100.0**	**23:13**	**78**	**8**	**17**	**25**	**66**	**2**	**0**	**2**	**22:18**

QMJHL Second All-Star Team (1990) • QMJHL First All-Star Team (1991) • Canadian Major Junior Defenseman of the Year (1991) • Memorial Cup All-Star Team (1991)

BROOKBANK, Wade

(BRUK-bank, WAYD) **VAN.**

Defense. Shoots left. 6'4", 225 lbs. Born, Lanigan, Sask., September 29, 1977.

Season	Club	League	GP	G	A	Pts	PIM	PP	SH	GW	S	%	+/-	TF	F%	Min	GP	G	A	Pts	PIM	PP	SH	GW	Min
1997-98	Melville	SJHL	58	8	21	29	330	....	....	....	....	....	....	....	....	....	....	....	....	....	....	....	....	....	....
	Anchorage Aces	WCHL	7	0	0	0	46	....	....	....	....	....	....	....	....	....	4	0	0	0	20	....	....	....	....
1998-99	Anchorage Aces	WCHL	56	0	4	4	337	....	....	....	....	....	....	....	....	....	....	....	....	....	....	....	....	....	....
99-2000	Oklahoma City	CHL	68	3	9	12	354	....	....	....	....	....	....	....	....	....	7	1	1	2	29	....	....	....	....
2000-01	Orlando	IHL	29	0	1	1	122	....	....	....	....	....	....	....	....	....	4	0	0	0	6	....	....	....	....
	Oklahoma City	CHL	46	1	13	14	267	....	....	....	....	....	....	....	....	....	5	0	0	0	24	....	....	....	....
2001-02	Grand Rapids	AHL	73	1	6	7	337	....	....	....	....	....	....	....	....	....	3	0	1	1	14	....	....	....	....
2002-03	Binghamton	AHL	8	0	0	0	28	....	....	....	....	....	....	....	....	....	....	....	....	....	....	....	....	....	....
2003-04	**Nashville**	**NHL**	**9**	**0**	**0**	**0**	**38**	**0**	**0**	**0**	**1**	**0.0**	**−4**	**0**	**0.0**	**3:28**	....	....	....	....	....	....	....	....	....
	Milwaukee	AHL	6	0	0	0	6	....	....	....	....	....	....	....	....	....	....	....	....	....	....	....	....	....	....
	Binghamton	AHL	4	0	0	0	31	....	....	....	....	....	....	....	....	....	....	....	....	....	....	....	....	....	....
	Vancouver	**NHL**	**20**	**2**	**0**	**2**	**95**	**0**	**0**	**1**	**6**	**33.3**	**3**	**0**	**0.0**	**3:50**	....	....	....	....	....	....	....	....	....
	Manitoba Moose	AHL	4	0	0	0	12	....	....	....	....	....	....	....	....	....	....	....	....	....	....	....	....	....	....
	NHL Totals		**29**	**2**	**0**	**2**	**133**	**0**	**0**	**1**	**7**	**28.6**		**0**	**0.0**	**3:43**	....	....	....	....	....	....	....	....	....

Signed as a free agent by **Orlando** (IHL), September 1, 2000. Signed as a free agent by **Ottawa**, July 27, 2001. • Missed majority of 2002-03 season recovering from knee injury suffered in game vs. Wilkes-Barre (AHL), November 2, 2002. Claimed by **Nashville** from **Ottawa** in Waiver Draft, October 3, 2003. Traded to **Vancouver** by **Nashville** for future considerations, December 17, 2003. Claimed on waivers by **Ottawa** from **Vancouver**, December 19, 2003. Traded to **Florida** by **Ottawa** for future considerations, December 29, 2003. Claimed on waivers by **Vancouver** from **Florida**, January 3, 2004.

BROWN, Brad

(BROWN, BRAD) **BUF.**

Defense. Shoots right. 6'4", 220 lbs. Born, Baie Verte, Nfld., December 27, 1975. Montreal's 1st choice, 18th overall, in 1994 Entry Draft.

Season	Club	League	GP	G	A	Pts	PIM	PP	SH	GW	S	%	+/-	TF	F%	Min	GP	G	A	Pts	PIM	PP	SH	GW	Min
1990-91	Tor. Red Wings	MTHL	80	15	45	60	105	....	....	....	....	....	....	....	....	....	....	....	....	....	....	....	....	....	....
	St. Michael's B	OJHL-B	2	0	0	0	0	....	....	....	....	....	....	....	....	....	....	....	....	....	....	....	....	....	....
1991-92	North Bay	OHL	49	2	9	11	170	....	....	....	....	....	....	....	....	....	18	0	6	6	43	....	....	....	....
1992-93	North Bay	OHL	61	4	9	13	228	....	....	....	....	....	....	....	....	....	2	0	2	2	13	....	....	....	....
1993-94	North Bay	OHL	66	8	24	32	196	....	....	....	....	....	....	....	....	....	18	3	12	15	33	....	....	....	....
1994-95	North Bay	OHL	64	8	38	46	172	....	....	....	....	....	....	....	....	....	6	1	4	5	8	....	....	....	....
1995-96	Barrie Colts	OHL	27	3	13	16	82	....	....	....	....	....	....	....	....	....	....	....	....	....	....	....	....	....	....
	Fredericton	AHL	38	0	3	3	148	....	....	....	....	....	....	....	....	....	10	2	1	3	6	....	....	....	....
1996-97	**Montreal**	**NHL**	**8**	**0**	**0**	**0**	**22**	**0**	**0**	**0**	**0**	**0.0**	**−1**	....	....	....	....	....	....	....	....	....	....	....	....
	Fredericton	AHL	64	3	7	10	368	....	....	....	....	....	....	....	....	....	....	....	....	....	....	....	....	....	....
1997-98	Fredericton	AHL	64	1	8	9	297	....	....	....	....	....	....	....	....	....	4	0	0	0	29	....	....	....	....
1998-99	**Montreal**	**NHL**	**5**	**0**	**0**	**0**	**21**	**0**	**0**	**0**	**0**	**0.0**	**0**	**0**	**0.0**	**6:02**	....	....	....	....	....	....	....	....	....
	Chicago	**NHL**	**61**	**1**	**7**	**8**	**184**	**0**	**0**	**0**	**26**	**3.8**	**−4**	**0**	**0.0**	**15:08**	....	....	....	....	....	....	....	....	....
99-2000	**Chicago**	**NHL**	**57**	**0**	**9**	**9**	**134**	**0**	**0**	**0**	**15**	**0.0**	**−1**	**0**	**0.0**	**14:12**	....	....	....	....	....	....	....	....	....
2000-01	**NY Rangers**	**NHL**	**48**	**1**	**3**	**4**	**107**	**0**	**0**	**0**	**14**	**7.1**	**0**	**0**	**0.0**	**14:31**	....	....	....	....	....	....	....	....	....
2001-02	**Minnesota**	**NHL**	**51**	**0**	**4**	**4**	**123**	**0**	**0**	**0**	**23**	**0.0**	**−11**	**0**	**0.0**	**15:54**	....	....	....	....	....	....	....	....	....
2002-03	**Minnesota**	**NHL**	**57**	**0**	**1**	**1**	**90**	**0**	**0**	**0**	**10**	**0.0**	**−1**	**0**	**0.0**	**9:14**	**11**	**0**	**0**	**0**	**16**	**0**	**0**	**0**	**8:23**
2003-04	**Minnesota**	**NHL**	**30**	**0**	**1**	**1**	**54**	**0**	**0**	**0**	**14**	**0.0**	**−1**	**0**	**0.0**	**9:41**	....	....	....	....	....	....	....	....	....
	Buffalo	**NHL**	**13**	**0**	**2**	**2**	**12**	**0**	**0**	**0**	**6**	**0.0**	**3**	**0**	**0.0**	**16:33**	....	....	....	....	....	....	....	....	....
	NHL Totals		**330**	**2**	**27**	**29**	**747**	**0**	**0**	**0**	**108**	**1.9**		**0**	**0.0**	**13:22**	**11**	**0**	**0**	**0**	**16**	**0**	**0**	**0**	**8:23**

OHL All-Rookie Team (1992)

Traded to **Chicago** by **Montreal** with Jocelyn Thibault and Dave Manson for Jeff Hackett, Eric Weinrich, Alain Nasreddine and Tampa Bay's 4th round choice (previously acquired, Montreal selected Chris Dyment) in 1999 Entry Draft, November 16, 1998. Traded to **NY Rangers** by **Chicago** with Michal Grosek for future considerations, October 5, 2000. Signed as a free agent by **Minnesota**, July 31, 2001. Traded to **Buffalo** by **Minnesota** with Minnesota's 6th round choice in 2005 Entry Draft for a 4th round choice in 2005 Entry Draft, March 8, 2004.

BROWN, Curtis

(BROWN, KUHR-tihs) **CHI.**

Center/Left wing. Shoots left. 6', 196 lbs. Born, Unity, Sask., February 12, 1976. Buffalo's 2nd choice, 43rd overall, in 1994 Entry Draft.

Season	Club	League	GP	G	A	Pts	PIM	PP	SH	GW	S	%	+/-	TF	F%	Min	GP	G	A	Pts	PIM	PP	SH	GW	Min
1990-91	Unity Bantams	SBHL	60	93	104	197	55	....	....	....	....	....	....	....	....	....	....	....	....	....	....	....	....	....	....
1991-92	Moose Jaw	SMHL	36	35	30	65	44	....	....	....	....	....	....	....	....	....	....	....	....	....	....	....	....	....	....
1992-93	Moose Jaw	WHL	71	13	16	29	30	....	....	....	....	....	....	....	....	....	....	....	....	....	....	....	....	....	....
1993-94	Moose Jaw	WHL	72	27	38	65	82	....	....	....	....	....	....	....	....	....	....	....	....	....	....	....	....	....	....
1994-95	Moose Jaw	WHL	70	51	53	104	63	....	....	....	....	....	....	....	....	....	10	8	7	15	20	....	....	....	....
	Buffalo	**NHL**	**1**	**1**	**1**	**2**	**2**	**0**	**0**	**0**	**4**	**25.0**	**2**	....	....	....	....	....	....	....	....	....	....	....	....
1995-96	Moose Jaw	WHL	25	20	18	38	30	....	....	....	....	....	....	....	....	....	....	....	....	....	....	....	....	....	....
	Prince Albert	WHL	19	12	21	33	8	....	....	....	....	....	....	....	....	....	18	10	15	25	18	....	....	....	....
	Buffalo	**NHL**	**4**	**0**	**0**	**0**	**0**	**0**	**0**	**0**	**1**	**0.0**	**0**	....	....	....	....	....	....	....	....	....	....	....	....
	Rochester	AHL	....	....	....	....	....	....	....	....	....	....	....	....	....	....	12	0	1	1	2	....	....	....	....
1996-97	**Buffalo**	**NHL**	**28**	**4**	**3**	**7**	**18**	**0**	**0**	**1**	**31**	**12.9**	**4**	....	....	....	....	....	....	....	....	....	....	....	....
	Rochester	AHL	51	22	21	43	30	....	....	....	....	....	....	....	....	....	10	4	6	10	4	....	....	....	....
1997-98	**Buffalo**	**NHL**	**63**	**12**	**12**	**24**	**34**	**1**	**1**	**2**	**91**	**13.2**	**11**	....	....	....	**13**	**1**	**2**	**3**	**10**	**1**	**0**	**0**	....
1998-99	**Buffalo**	**NHL**	**78**	**16**	**31**	**47**	**56**	**5**	**1**	**3**	**128**	**12.5**	**23**	**1198**	**45.0**	**17:30**	**21**	**7**	**6**	**13**	**10**	**3**	**0**	**3**	**18:51**
99-2000	**Buffalo**	**NHL**	**74**	**22**	**29**	**51**	**42**	**5**	**0**	**4**	**149**	**14.8**	**19**	**1318**	**48.6**	**18:11**	**5**	**1**	**3**	**4**	**6**	**1**	**0**	**0**	**17:11**
2000-01	**Buffalo**	**NHL**	**70**	**10**	**22**	**32**	**34**	**2**	**1**	**0**	**105**	**9.5**	**15**	**1159**	**50.4**	**16:34**	**13**	**5**	**0**	**5**	**8**	**0**	**2**	**1**	**18:14**
2001-02	**Buffalo**	**NHL**	**82**	**20**	**17**	**37**	**32**	**4**	**1**	**5**	**171**	**11.7**	**−4**	**1608**	**49.0**	**17:48**	....	....	....	....	....	....	....	....	....
2002-03	**Buffalo**	**NHL**	**74**	**15**	**16**	**31**	**40**	**3**	**4**	**4**	**144**	**10.4**	**4**	**1387**	**49.5**	**16:53**	....	....	....	....	....	....	....	....	....
2003-04	**Buffalo**	**NHL**	**68**	**9**	**12**	**21**	**30**	**2**	**1**	**2**	**117**	**7.7**	**2**	**1182**	**51.5**	**16:36**	....	....	....	....	....	....	....	....	....
	San Jose	**NHL**	**12**	**2**	**2**	**4**	**6**	**0**	**0**	**0**	**21**	**9.5**	**1**	**105**	**47.6**	**16:26**	**17**	**0**	**2**	**2**	**18**	**0**	**0**	**0**	**14:37**
	NHL Totals		**554**	**111**	**145**	**256**	**294**	**22**	**9**	**21**	**962**	**11.5**		**7957**	**49.0**	**17:16**	**69**	**14**	**13**	**27**	**52**	**5**	**2**	**4**	**17:16**

WHL East First All-Star Team (1995) • WHL East Second All-Star Team (1996)

Traded to **San Jose** by **Buffalo** with Andy Delmore for Jeff Jillson and San Jose's 9th round choice in 2005 Entry Draft, March 9, 2004. Signed as a free agent by **Chicago**, July 2, 2004.

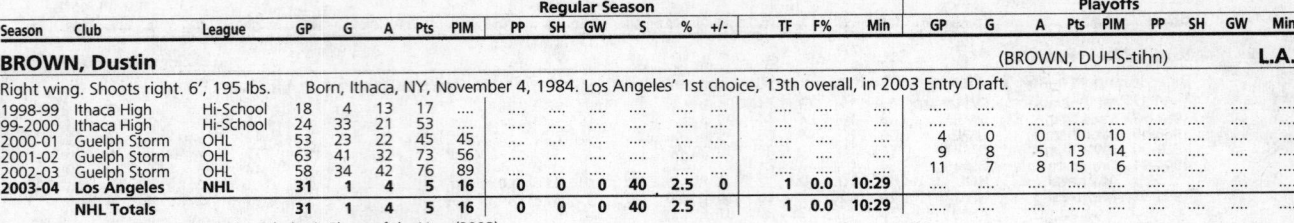

BROWN, Dustin

(BROWN, DUHS-tihn) **L.A.**

Right wing. Shoots right. 6', 195 lbs. Born, Ithaca, NY, November 4, 1984. Los Angeles' 1st choice, 13th overall, in 2003 Entry Draft.

			Regular Season														Playoffs								
Season	Club	League	GP	G	A	Pts	PIM	PP	SH	GW	S	%	+/-	TF	F%	Min	GP	G	A	Pts	PIM	PP	SH	GW	Min
1998-99	Ithaca High	Hi-School	18	4	13	17	....	....	....	....	....	....	....	....	....	....	....	....	....	....	....	....	....	....	....
99-2000	Ithaca High	Hi-School	24	33	21	53	....	....	....	....	....	....	....	....	....	....	....	....	....	....	....	....	....	....	....
2000-01	Guelph Storm	OHL	53	23	22	45	45	....	....	....	....	....	....	....	....	....	4	0	0	0	10	....	....	....	....
2001-02	Guelph Storm	OHL	63	41	32	73	56	....	....	....	....	....	....	....	....	....	9	8	5	13	14	....	....	....	....
2002-03	Guelph Storm	OHL	58	34	42	76	89	....	....	....	....	....	....	....	....	....	11	7	8	15	6	....	....	....	....
2003-04	**Los Angeles**	**NHL**	**31**	**1**	**4**	**5**	**16**	**0**	**0**	**0**	**40**	**2.5**	**0**	**1**	**0.0**	**10:29**	....	....	....	....	....	....	....	....	....
	NHL Totals		**31**	**1**	**4**	**5**	**16**	**0**	**0**	**0**	**40**	**2.5**		**1**	**0.0**	**10:29**	....	....	....	....	....	....	....	....	....

OHL All-Rookie Team (2001) • Canadian Major Junior Scholastic Player of the Year (2003)

• Missed majority of 2003-04 season recovering from ankle injury suffered in game vs. Chicago, November 29, 2003.

BROWN, Mike

(BROWN, MIGHK)

Left wing. Shoots left. 6'5", 185 lbs. Born, Surrey, B.C., April 27, 1979. Florida's 1st choice, 20th overall, in 1997 Entry Draft.

Season	Club	League	GP	G	A	Pts	PIM	PP	SH	GW	S	%	+/-	TF	F%	Min	GP	G	A	Pts	PIM	PP	SH	GW	Min
1993-94	Penticton	BCJHL	50	52	48	100	100	....	....	....	....	....	....	....	....	....	....	....	....	....	....	....	....	....	....
1994-95	Merritt	BCJHL	45	3	4	7	145	....	....	....	....	....	....	....	....	....	....	....	....	....	....	....	....	....	....
1995-96	Red Deer Rebels	WHL	62	4	5	9	125	....	....	....	....	....	....	....	....	....	10	0	0	0	18	....	....	....	....
1996-97	Red Deer Rebels	WHL	70	19	13	32	243	....	....	....	....	....	....	....	....	....	16	1	2	3	47	....	....	....	....
1997-98	Kamloops Blazers	WHL	72	23	33	56	305	....	....	....	....	....	....	....	....	....	7	2	1	3	22	....	....	....	....
1998-99	Kamloops Blazers	WHL	69	28	16	44	*285	....	....	....	....	....	....	....	....	....	15	3	7	10	*68	....	....	....	....
99-2000	Syracuse Crunch	AHL	71	13	18	31	284	....	....	....	....	....	....	....	....	....	4	0	0	0	0	....	....	....	....
2000-01	**Vancouver**	**NHL**	**1**	**0**	**0**	**0**	**5**	**0**	**0**	**0**	**1**	**0.0**	**0**	**0**	**0.0**	**4:48**	....	....	....	....	....	....	....	....	....
	Kansas City	IHL	78	14	13	27	214	....	....	....	....	....	....	....	....	....	....	....	....	....	....	....	....	....	....
2001-02	**Vancouver**	**NHL**	**15**	**0**	**0**	**0**	**72**	**0**	**0**	**0**	**2**	**0.0**	**1**	**0**	**0.0**	**3:29**	....	....	....	....	....	....	....	....	....
	Manitoba Moose	AHL	31	7	9	16	155	....	....	....	....	....	....	....	....	....	6	0	1	1	16	....	....	....	....
2002-03	**Anaheim**	**NHL**	**16**	**1**	**1**	**2**	**44**	**0**	**0**	**1**	**8**	**12.5**	**0**	**0**	**0.0**	**0:00**	....	....	....	....	....	....	....	....	....
	Cincinnati	AHL	27	3	3	6	85	....	....	....	....	....	....	....	....	....	....	....	....	....	....	....	....	....	....
2003-04	St. John's	AHL	21	3	3	6	74	....	....	....	....	....	....	....	....	....	....	....	....	....	....	....	....	....	....
	Binghamton	AHL	38	4	7	11	131	....	....	....	....	....	....	....	....	....	....	....	....	....	....	....	....	....	....
	NHL Totals		**32**	**1**	**1**	**2**	**121**	**0**	**0**	**1**	**11**	**9.1**		**0**	**0.0**	**1:47**	....	....	....	....	....	....	....	....	....

Traded to **Vancouver** by **Florida** with Ed Jovanovski, Dave Gagner, Kevin Weekes and Florida's 1st round choice (Nathan Smith) in 2000 Entry Draft for Pavel Bure, Bret Hedican, Brad Ference and Vancouver's 3rd round choice (Robert Fried) in 2000 Entry Draft, January 17, 1999. Claimed on waivers by **Anaheim** from **Vancouver**, October 11, 2002. Signed as a free agent by **St. John's** (AHL), October 11, 2003. Signed as a free agent by **Binghampton** (AHL), January 8, 2004.

BROWN, Sean

(BROWN, SHAWN) **N.J.**

Defense. Shoots left. 6'3", 215 lbs. Born, Oshawa, Ont., November 5, 1976. Boston's 2nd choice, 21st overall, in 1995 Entry Draft.

Season	Club	League	GP	G	A	Pts	PIM	PP	SH	GW	S	%	+/-	TF	F%	Min	GP	G	A	Pts	PIM	PP	SH	GW	Min
1992-93	Oshawa	OJHL-B	15	0	1	1	9	....	....	....	....	....	....	....	....	....	....	....	....	....	....	....	....	....	....
1993-94	Wellington Dukes	MTJHL	32	5	14	19	165	....	....	....	....	....	....	....	....	....	....	....	....	....	....	....	....	....	....
	Belleville Bulls	OHL	28	1	2	3	53	....	....	....	....	....	....	....	....	....	8	0	0	0	17	....	....	....	....
1994-95	Belleville Bulls	OHL	58	2	16	18	200	....	....	....	....	....	....	....	....	....	16	4	2	6	*67	....	....	....	....
1995-96	Belleville Bulls	OHL	37	10	23	33	150	....	....	....	....	....	....	....	....	....	....	....	....	....	....	....	....	....	....
	Sarnia Sting	OHL	26	8	17	25	112	....	....	....	....	....	....	....	....	....	10	1	0	1	38	....	....	....	....
1996-97	**Edmonton**	**NHL**	**5**	**0**	**0**	**0**	**4**	**0**	**0**	**0**	**2**	**0.0**	**–1**	....	....	....	....	....	....	....	....	....	....	....	....
	Hamilton	AHL	61	1	7	8	238	....	....	....	....	....	....	....	....	....	19	1	0	1	47	....	....	....	....
1997-98	**Edmonton**	**NHL**	**18**	**0**	**1**	**1**	**43**	**0**	**0**	**0**	**9**	**0.0**	**–1**	....	....	....	....	....	....	....	....	....	....	....	....
	Hamilton	AHL	43	4	6	10	166	....	....	....	....	....	....	....	....	....	6	0	2	2	38	....	....	....	....
1998-99	**Edmonton**	**NHL**	**51**	**0**	**7**	**7**	**188**	**0**	**0**	**0**	**27**	**0.0**	**1**	**0**	**0.0**	**12:14**	**1**	**0**	**0**	**0**	**10**	**0**	**0**	**0**	**7:33**
99-2000	**Edmonton**	**NHL**	**72**	**4**	**8**	**12**	**192**	**0**	**0**	**2**	**36**	**11.1**	**1**	**0**	**0.0**	**12:41**	**3**	**0**	**0**	**0**	**23**	**0**	**0**	**0**	**6:12**
2000-01	**Edmonton**	**NHL**	**62**	**2**	**3**	**5**	**110**	**0**	**0**	**0**	**30**	**6.7**	**2**	**0**	**0.0**	**11:07**	....	....	....	....	....	....	....	....	....
2001-02	**Edmonton**	**NHL**	**61**	**6**	**4**	**10**	**127**	**3**	**0**	**1**	**58**	**10.3**	**8**	**0**	**0.0**	**12:36**	....	....	....	....	....	....	....	....	....
	Boston	**NHL**	**12**	**0**	**1**	**1**	**47**	**0**	**0**	**0**	**6**	**0.0**	**–1**	**0**	**0.0**	**16:22**	**4**	**0**	**0**	**0**	**2**	**0**	**0**	**0**	**5:49**
2002-03	**Boston**	**NHL**	**69**	**1**	**5**	**6**	**117**	**0**	**0**	**0**	**39**	**2.6**	**–6**	**2**	**50.0**	**6:26**	....	....	....	....	....	....	....	....	....
2003-04	**New Jersey**	**NHL**	**39**	**0**	**3**	**3**	**44**	**0**	**0**	**0**	**25**	**0.0**	**5**	**0**	**0.0**	**13:56**	**1**	**0**	**0**	**0**	**2**	**0**	**0**	**0**	**11:20**
	Albany River Rats	AHL	21	1	6	7	56	....	....	....	....	....	....	....	....	....	....	....	....	....	....	....	....	....	....
	NHL Totals		**389**	**13**	**32**	**45**	**872**	**3**	**0**	**3**	**232**	**5.6**		**2**	**50.0**	**11:25**	**9**	**0**	**0**	**0**	**37**	**0**	**0**	**0**	**6:45**

OHL Second All-Star Team (1996)

Rights traded to **Edmonton** by **Boston** with Mariusz Czerkawski and Boston's 1st round choice (Matthieu Descoteaux) in 1996 Entry Draft for Bill Ranford, January 11, 1996. Traded to **Boston** by **Edmonton** for Bobby Allen, March 19, 2002. Signed as a free agent by **New Jersey**, July 24, 2003.

BRULE, Steve

(broo-LAY, STEEV)

Right wing. Shoots right. 6', 200 lbs. Born, Montreal, Que., January 15, 1975. New Jersey's 6th choice, 143rd overall, in 1993 Entry Draft.

Season	Club	League	GP	G	A	Pts	PIM	PP	SH	GW	S	%	+/-	TF	F%	Min	GP	G	A	Pts	PIM	PP	SH	GW	Min
1990-91	L'est Cantonniers	QAHA	32	25	30	55	20	....	....	....	....	....	....	....	....	....	....	....	....	....	....	....	....	....	....
1991-92	Mtl-Bourassa	QAAA	40	33	37	70	46	....	....	....	....	....	....	....	....	....	9	9	7	16	10	....	....	....	....
1992-93	St-Jean Lynx	QMJHL	70	33	47	80	46	....	....	....	....	....	....	....	....	....	4	0	0	0	9	....	....	....	....
1993-94	St-Jean Lynx	QMJHL	66	41	64	105	46	....	....	....	....	....	....	....	....	....	5	2	1	3	0	....	....	....	....
1994-95	St-Jean Lynx	QMJHL	69	44	64	108	42	....	....	....	....	....	....	....	....	....	7	3	4	7	8	....	....	....	....
	Albany River Rats	AHL	3	1	4	5	0	....	....	....	....	....	....	....	....	....	14	9	5	14	4	....	....	....	....
1995-96	Albany River Rats	AHL	80	30	21	51	37	....	....	....	....	....	....	....	....	....	4	0	0	0	17	....	....	....	....
1996-97	Albany River Rats	AHL	79	28	48	76	27	....	....	....	....	....	....	....	....	....	16	7	7	14	12	....	....	....	....
1997-98	Albany River Rats	AHL	80	34	43	77	34	....	....	....	....	....	....	....	....	....	13	8	3	11	4	....	....	....	....
1998-99	Albany River Rats	AHL	78	32	52	84	35	....	....	....	....	....	....	....	....	....	5	3	1	4	4	....	....	....	....
99-2000	Albany River Rats	AHL	75	30	46	76	18	....	....	....	....	....	....	....	....	....	5	1	2	3	0	....	....	....	....
	♦ New Jersey	**NHL**	....	....	....	....	....	....	....	....	....	....	....	....	....	....	**1**	**0**	**0**	**0**	**0**	**0**	**0**	**0**	**13:00**
2000-01	Manitoba Moose	IHL	78	21	48	69	22	....	....	....	....	....	....	....	....	....	13	3	10	13	12	....	....	....	....
2001-02	Cincinnati	AHL	77	21	42	63	50	....	....	....	....	....	....	....	....	....	3	0	1	1	0	....	....	....	....
2002-03	**Colorado**	**NHL**	**2**	**0**	**0**	**0**	**0**	**0**	**0**	**0**	**2**	**0.0**	**0**	**0**	**0.0**	**9:06**	....	....	....	....	....	....	....	....	....
	Hershey Bears	AHL	49	18	19	37	30	....	....	....	....	....	....	....	....	....	5	4	0	4	8	....	....	....	....
2003-04	Hershey Bears	AHL	79	29	29	58	82	....	....	....	....	....	....	....	....	....	....	....	....	....	....	....	....	....	....
	NHL Totals		**2**	**0**	**0**	**0**	**0**	**0**	**0**	**0**	**2**	**0.0**		**0**	**0.0**	**9:06**	**1**	**0**	**0**	**0**	**0**	**0**	**0**	**0**	**13:00**

QMJHL All-Rookie Team (1993) • QMJHL Offensive Rookie of the Year (1993) • QMJHL Second All-Star Team (1995)

Signed as a free agent by **Detroit**, July 20, 2000. Signed as a free agent by **Colorado**, July 22, 2002.

BRUNETTE, Andrew

(broo-NEHT, AN-droo) **MIN.**

Left wing. Shoots left. 6'1", 210 lbs. Born, Sudbury, Ont., August 24, 1973. Washington's 6th choice, 174th overall, in 1993 Entry Draft.

Season	Club	League	GP	G	A	Pts	PIM	PP	SH	GW	S	%	+/-	TF	F%	Min	GP	G	A	Pts	PIM	PP	SH	GW	Min
1989-90	Rayside-Balfour	NOHA	32	38	*65	*103	....	....	....	....	....	....	....	....	....	....	....	....	....	....	....	....	....	....	....
	Rayside-Balfour	NOJHA	4	1	1	2	0	....	....	....	....	....	....	....	....	....	....	....	....	....	....	....	....	....	....
1990-91	Owen Sound	OHL	63	15	20	35	15	....	....	....	....	....	....	....	....	....	....	....	....	....	....	....	....	....	....
1991-92	Owen Sound	OHL	66	51	47	98	42	....	....	....	....	....	....	....	....	....	5	5	0	5	8	....	....	....	....
1992-93	Owen Sound	OHL	66	*62	*100	*162	91	....	....	....	....	....	....	....	....	....	8	8	6	14	16	....	....	....	....
1993-94	Portland Pirates	AHL	23	9	11	20	10	....	....	....	....	....	....	....	....	....	2	0	1	1	0	....	....	....	....
	Providence Bruins	AHL	3	0	0	0	0	....	....	....	....	....	....	....	....	....	....	....	....	....	....	....	....	....	....
	Hampton Roads	ECHL	20	12	18	30	32	....	....	....	....	....	....	....	....	....	7	7	6	13	18	....	....	....	....
1994-95	Portland Pirates	AHL	79	30	50	80	53	....	....	....	....	....	....	....	....	....	7	3	3	6	10	....	....	....	....
1995-96	**Washington**	**NHL**	**11**	**3**	**3**	**6**	**0**	**0**	**0**	**1**	**16**	**18.8**	**5**	....	....	....	**6**	**1**	**3**	**4**	**0**	**0**	**0**	**0**	....
	Portland Pirates	AHL	69	28	66	94	125	....	....	....	....	....	....	....	....	....	20	11	18	29	15	....	....	....	....
1996-97	**Washington**	**NHL**	**23**	**4**	**7**	**11**	**12**	**2**	**0**	**0**	**23**	**17.4**	**–3**	....	....	....	....	....	....	....	....	....	....	....	....
	Portland Pirates	AHL	50	22	51	73	48	....	....	....	....	....	....	....	....	....	5	1	2	3	0	....	....	....	....
1997-98	**Washington**	**NHL**	**28**	**11**	**12**	**23**	**12**	**4**	**0**	**2**	**42**	**26.2**	**2**	....	....	....	....	....	....	....	....	....	....	....	....
	Portland Pirates	AHL	43	21	46	67	64	....	....	....	....	....	....	....	....	....	10	1	11	12	12	....	....	....	....
1998-99	**Nashville**	**NHL**	**77**	**11**	**20**	**31**	**26**	**7**	**0**	**1**	**65**	**16.9**	**–10**	**8**	**50.0**	**13:13**	....	....	....	....	....	....	....	....	....
99-2000	**Atlanta**	**NHL**	**81**	**23**	**27**	**50**	**30**	**9**	**0**	**2**	**107**	**21.5**	**–32**	**8**	**25.0**	**15:42**	....	....	....	....	....	....	....	....	....
2000-01	**Atlanta**	**NHL**	**77**	**15**	**44**	**59**	**26**	**6**	**0**	**4**	**104**	**14.4**	**–5**	**11**	**54.6**	**16:58**	....	....	....	....	....	....	....	....	....
2001-02	**Minnesota**	**NHL**	**81**	**21**	**48**	**69**	**18**	**10**	**0**	**2**	**106**	**19.8**	**–4**	**111**	**58.6**	**16:02**	....	....	....	....	....	....	....	....	....

			Regular Season														Playoffs								
Season	Club	League	GP	G	A	Pts	PIM	PP	SH	GW	S	%	+/-	TF	F%	Min	GP	G	A	Pts	PIM	PP	SH	GW	Min
2002-03	Minnesota	NHL	82	18	28	46	30	9	0	2	97	18.6	–10	59	44.1	14:29	18	7	6	13	4	4	0	1	15:00
2003-04	Minnesota	NHL	82	15	34	49	12	7	0	3	90	16.7	3	49	46.9	15:32	....	....	....	....	....	....	....	....	....
	NHL Totals		542	121	223	344	166	54	0	17	650	18.6		246	51.2	15:19	24	8	9	17	4	4	0	1	15:00

OHL First All-Star Team (1993) • Canadian Major Junior Second All-Star Team (1993) • AHL Second All-Star Team (1995)

Claimed by **Nashville** from **Washington** in Expansion Draft, June 26, 1998. Traded to **Atlanta** by **Nashville** for Atlanta's 5th round choice (Matt Hendricks) in 2000 Entry Draft, June 21, 1999. Signed as a free agent by **Minnesota**, July 17, 2001.

BRYLIN, Sergei

(BRIH-lin, SAIR-gay) **N.J.**

Center. Shoots left. 5'10", 190 lbs. Born, Moscow, USSR, January 13, 1974. New Jersey's 2nd choice, 42nd overall, in 1992 Entry Draft.

Season	Club	League	GP	G	A	Pts	PIM	PP	SH	GW	S	%	+/-	TF	F%	Min	GP	G	A	Pts	PIM	PP	SH	GW	Min
1991-92	CSKA Moscow	CIS	44	1	6	7	4	....	....	....	....	....	....	....	....	....	....	....	....	....	....	....	....	....	....
1992-93	CSKA Moscow	CIS	42	5	4	9	36	....	....	....	....	....	....	....	....	....	....	....	....	....	....	....	....	....	....
1993-94	CSKA Moscow	CIS	39	4	6	10	36	....	....	....	....	....	....	....	....	....	3	1	0	1	2	....	....	....	....
	Russian Penguins	IHL	13	4	5	9	18	....	....	....	....	....	....	....	....	....	....	....	....	....	....	....	....	....	....
1994-95	Albany River Rats	AHL	63	19	35	54	78	....	....	....	....	....	....	....	....	....	....	....	....	....	....	....	....	....	....
♦	New Jersey	NHL	26	6	8	14	8	0	0	0	41	14.6	12	....	....	....	12	1	2	3	4	0	0	0	....
1995-96	New Jersey	NHL	50	4	5	9	26	0	0	1	51	7.8	–2	....	....	....	....	....	....	....	....	....	....	....	....
1996-97	New Jersey	NHL	29	2	2	4	20	0	0	0	34	5.9	–13	....	....	....	....	....	....	....	....	....	....	....	....
	Albany River Rats	AHL	43	17	24	41	38	....	....	....	....	....	....	....	....	....	16	4	8	12	12	....	....	....	....
1997-98	New Jersey	NHL	18	2	3	5	0	0	0	0	20	10.0	4	....	....	....	....	....	....	....	....	....	....	....	....
	Albany River Rats	AHL	44	21	22	43	60	....	....	....	....	....	....	....	....	....	....	....	....	....	....	....	....	....	....
1998-99	New Jersey	NHL	47	5	10	15	28	3	0	1	51	9.8	8	184	50.5	12:55	5	3	1	4	4	1	0	1	18:21
99-2000♦	New Jersey	NHL	64	9	11	20	20	1	0	1	84	10.7	0	72	41.7	13:23	17	3	5	8	0	0	0	0	13:02
2000-01	New Jersey	NHL	75	23	29	52	24	3	1	0	130	17.7	25	43	44.2	15:31	20	3	4	7	6	1	0	1	13:07
2001-02	New Jersey	NHL	76	16	28	44	10	5	0	3	133	12.0	21	17	47.1	17:11	6	0	2	2	2	0	0	0	19:05
2002-03♦	New Jersey	NHL	52	11	8	19	16	3	1	1	86	12.8	–2	90	32.2	16:11	19	1	3	4	8	0	0	1	17:03
2003-04	New Jersey	NHL	82	14	19	33	20	7	0	1	98	14.3	10	695	46.6	16:25	5	0	0	0	0	0	0	0	15:02
	NHL Totals		519	92	123	215	172	22	2	8	728	12.6		1101	45.7	15:27	84	11	17	28	24	2	0	3	15:08

BUCHBERGER, Kelly

(BUK-buhr-guhr, KEHL-lee)

Right wing. Shoots left. 6'2", 210 lbs. Born, Langenburg, Sask., December 2, 1966. Edmonton's 8th choice, 188th overall, in 1985 Entry Draft.

Season	Club	League	GP	G	A	Pts	PIM	PP	SH	GW	S	%	+/-	TF	F%	Min	GP	G	A	Pts	PIM	PP	SH	GW	Min
1983-84	Melville	SJHL	60	14	11	25	139	....	....	....	....	....	....	....	....	....	....	....	....	....	....	....	....	....	....
1984-85	Moose Jaw	WHL	51	12	17	29	114	....	....	....	....	....	....	....	....	....	....	....	....	....	....	....	....	....	....
1985-86	Moose Jaw	WHL	72	14	22	36	206	....	....	....	....	....	....	....	....	....	13	11	4	15	37	....	....	....	....
1986-87	Nova Scotia Oilers	AHL	70	12	20	32	257	....	....	....	....	....	....	....	....	....	5	0	1	1	23	....	....	....	....
♦	Edmonton	NHL	....	....	....	....	....	....	....	....	....	....	....	....	....	....	3	0	1	1	5	0	0	0	....
1987-88	Edmonton	NHL	19	1	0	1	81	0	0	0	10	10.0	–1	....	....	....	....	....	....	....	....	....	....	....	....
	Nova Scotia Oilers	AHL	49	21	23	44	206	....	....	....	....	....	....	....	....	....	2	0	0	0	11	....	....	....	....
1988-89	Edmonton	NHL	66	5	9	14	234	1	0	1	57	8.8	–14	....	....	....	....	....	....	....	....	....	....	....	....
1989-90♦	Edmonton	NHL	55	2	6	8	168	0	0	2	35	5.7	–8	....	....	....	19	0	5	5	13	0	0	0	....
1990-91	Edmonton	NHL	64	3	1	4	160	0	0	2	54	5.6	–6	....	....	....	12	2	1	3	25	0	0	0	....
1991-92	Edmonton	NHL	79	20	24	44	157	0	4	3	90	22.2	9	....	....	....	16	1	4	5	32	0	0	0	....
1992-93	Edmonton	NHL	83	12	18	30	133	1	2	3	92	13.0	–27	....	....	....	....	....	....	....	....	....	....	....	....
1993-94	Edmonton	NHL	84	3	18	21	199	0	0	0	93	3.2	–20	....	....	....	....	....	....	....	....	....	....	....	....
1994-95	Edmonton	NHL	48	7	17	24	82	2	1	5	73	9.6	0	....	....	....	....	....	....	....	....	....	....	....	....
1995-96	Edmonton	NHL	82	11	14	25	184	0	2	3	119	9.2	–20	....	....	....	....	....	....	....	....	....	....	....	....
1996-97	Edmonton	NHL	81	8	30	38	159	0	0	3	78	10.3	4	....	....	....	12	5	2	7	16	0	0	1	....
1997-98	Edmonton	NHL	82	6	17	23	122	1	1	1	86	7.0	–10	....	....	....	12	1	2	3	25	0	0	0	....
1998-99	Edmonton	NHL	52	4	4	8	68	0	2	1	29	13.8	–6	23	26.1	11:49	4	0	0	0	0	0	0	0	10:06
99-2000	Atlanta	NHL	68	5	12	17	139	0	0	0	56	8.9	–34	577	45.6	16:21	....	....	....	....	....	....	....	....	....
	Los Angeles	NHL	13	2	1	3	13	0	0	0	20	10.0	–2	6	16.7	14:43	4	0	0	0	4	0	0	0	8:56
2000-01	Los Angeles	NHL	82	6	14	20	75	0	0	1	66	9.1	–10	155	40.7	14:26	8	1	0	1	2	0	0	0	9:58
2001-02	Los Angeles	NHL	74	6	7	13	105	0	0	1	39	15.4	–13	126	41.3	10:21	7	0	0	0	7	0	0	0	8:48
2002-03	Phoenix	NHL	79	3	9	12	109	0	1	0	32	9.4	0	784	43.1	9:59	....	....	....	....	....	....	....	....	....
2003-04	Pittsburgh	NHL	71	1	3	4	109	0	0	0	34	2.9	–19	64	45.3	10:21	....	....	....	....	....	....	....	....	....
	NHL Totals		1182	105	204	309	2297	5	13	26	1063	9.9		1735	43.3	12:17	97	10	15	25	129	0	0	1	9:27

Claimed by **Atlanta** from **Edmonton** in Expansion Draft, June 25, 1999. Traded to **Los Angeles** by **Atlanta** with Nelson Emerson for Donald Audette and Frantisek Kaberle, March 13, 2000. Signed as a free agent by **Phoenix**, July 7, 2002. Signed as a free agent by **Pittsburgh**, July 31, 2003.

BULIS, Jan

(BOO-lihs, YAHN) **MTL.**

Center. Shoots left. 6'1", 208 lbs. Born, Pardubice, Czech., March 18, 1978. Washington's 3rd choice, 43rd overall, in 1996 Entry Draft.

Season	Club	League	GP	G	A	Pts	PIM	PP	SH	GW	S	%	+/-	TF	F%	Min	GP	G	A	Pts	PIM	PP	SH	GW	Min
1993-94	HC Pardubice Jr.	Czech-Jr.	25	16	11	27	....	....	....	....	....	....	....	....	....	....	....	....	....	....	....	....	....	....	....
1994-95	Kelowna Spartans	BCJHL	51	23	25	48	36	....	....	....	....	....	....	....	....	....	17	7	9	16	0	....	....	....	....
1995-96	Barrie Colts	OHL	59	29	30	59	22	....	....	....	....	....	....	....	....	....	7	2	3	5	2	....	....	....	....
1996-97	Barrie Colts	OHL	64	42	61	103	42	....	....	....	....	....	....	....	....	....	9	3	7	10	10	....	....	....	....
1997-98	Kingston	OHL	2	0	1	1	0	....	....	....	....	....	....	....	....	....	12	8	10	18	12	....	....	....	....
	Washington	NHL	48	5	11	16	18	0	0	0	37	13.5	–5	....	....	....	....	....	....	....	....	....	....	....	....
	Portland Pirates	AHL	3	1	4	5	12	....	....	....	....	....	....	....	....	....	....	....	....	....	....	....	....	....	....
1998-99	Washington	NHL	38	7	16	23	6	3	0	3	57	12.3	3	599	48.9	14:27	....	....	....	....	....	....	....	....	....
	Cincinnati	IHL	10	2	2	4	14	....	....	....	....	....	....	....	....	....	....	....	....	....	....	....	....	....	....
99-2000	Washington	NHL	56	9	22	31	30	0	0	1	92	9.8	7	609	45.5	13:55	....	....	....	....	....	....	....	....	....
2000-01	Washington	NHL	39	5	13	18	26	1	0	0	41	12.2	0	224	46.9	11:53	....	....	....	....	....	....	....	....	....
	Portland Pirates	AHL	4	0	2	2	0	....	....	....	....	....	....	....	....	....	....	....	....	....	....	....	....	....	....
	Montreal	NHL	12	0	5	5	0	0	0	0	20	0.0	–1	230	48.3	18:25	....	....	....	....	....	....	....	....	....
2001-02	Montreal	NHL	53	9	10	19	8	1	0	3	87	10.3	–2	156	43.0	13:34	6	0	0	0	6	0	0	0	12:25
2002-03	Montreal	NHL	82	16	24	40	30	0	0	2	160	10.0	9	153	42.5	15:42	....	....	....	....	....	....	....	....	....
2003-04	Montreal	NHL	72	13	17	30	30	1	1	4	147	8.8	–8	103	46.6	17:07	11	1	1	2	4	0	0	0	17:23
	NHL Totals		400	64	118	182	148	6	1	13	641	10.0		2074	46.6	14:55	17	1	1	2	10	0	0	0	15:38

Traded to **Montreal** by **Washington** with Richard Zednik and Washington's 1st round choice (Alexander Perezhogin) in 2001 Entry Draft for Trevor Linden, Dainius Zubrus and New Jersey's 2nd round choice (previously acquired, later traded to Tampa Bay – Tampa Bay selected Andreas Holmqvist) in 2001 Entry Draft, March 13, 2001.

BURE, Valeri

(boo-RAY, VAL-uhr-ee)

Right wing. Shoots right. 5'10", 185 lbs. Born, Moscow, USSR, June 13, 1974. Montreal's 2nd choice, 33rd overall, in 1992 Entry Draft.

Season	Club	League	GP	G	A	Pts	PIM	PP	SH	GW	S	%	+/-	TF	F%	Min	GP	G	A	Pts	PIM	PP	SH	GW	Min
1990-91	CSKA Moscow	USSR	3	0	0	0	0	....	....	....	....	....	....	....	....	....	....	....	....	....	....	....	....	....	....
1991-92	Spokane Chiefs	WHL	53	27	22	49	78	....	....	....	....	....	....	....	....	....	10	11	6	17	10	....	....	....	....
1992-93	Spokane Chiefs	WHL	66	68	79	147	49	....	....	....	....	....	....	....	....	....	9	6	11	17	14	....	....	....	....
1993-94	Spokane Chiefs	WHL	59	40	62	102	48	....	....	....	....	....	....	....	....	....	3	5	3	8	2	....	....	....	....
1994-95	Fredericton	AHL	45	23	25	48	32	....	....	....	....	....	....	....	....	....	....	....	....	....	....	....	....	....	....
	Montreal	NHL	24	3	1	4	6	0	0	1	39	7.7	–1	....	....	....	....	....	....	....	....	....	....	....	....
1995-96	Montreal	NHL	77	22	20	42	28	5	0	1	143	15.4	10	....	....	....	6	0	1	1	6	0	0	0	....
1996-97	Montreal	NHL	64	14	21	35	6	4	0	2	131	10.7	4	....	....	....	5	0	1	1	2	0	0	0	....
1997-98	Montreal	NHL	50	7	22	29	33	2	0	1	134	5.2	–5	....	....	....	....	....	....	....	....	....	....	....	....
	Calgary	NHL	16	5	4	9	2	0	0	1	45	11.1	0	....	....	....	....	....	....	....	....	....	....	....	....
	Russia	Olympics	6	1	0	1	0	....	....	....	....	....	....	....	....	....	....	....	....	....	....	....	....	....	....
1998-99	Calgary	NHL	80	26	27	53	22	7	0	4	260	10.0	0	15	40.0	16:11	....	....	....	....	....	....	....	....	....
99-2000	Calgary	NHL	82	35	40	75	50	13	0	6	308	11.4	–7	8	25.0	20:58	....	....	....	....	....	....	....	....	....
2000-01	Calgary	NHL	78	27	28	55	26	16	0	2	276	9.8	–21	9	11.1	19:01	....	....	....	....	....	....	....	....	....
2001-02	Florida	NHL	31	8	10	18	12	2	0	1	100	8.0	–3	30	33.3	18:36	....	....	....	....	....	....	....	....	....
	Russia	Olympics	6	1	0	1	2	....	....	....	....	....	....	....	....	....	....	....	....	....	....	....	....	....	....
2002-03	Florida	NHL	46	5	21	26	10	3	0	2	150	3.3	–11	19	31.6	18:38	....	....	....	....	....	....	....	....	....
	St. Louis	NHL	5	0	2	2	0	0	0	0	11	0.0	–2	0	0.0	15:11	6	0	2	2	8	0	0	0	11:14

Season	Club	League	Regular Season GP	G	A	Pts	PIM	PP	SH	GW	S	%	+/-	TF	F%	Min	Playoffs GP	G	A	Pts	PIM	PP	SH	GW	Min
2003-04	**Florida**	**NHL**	**55**	**20**	**25**	**45**	**20**	**8**	**0**	**4**	**175**	**11.4**	**0**	**29**	**41.4**	**19:13**	....	....	....	....	....	....	....	....	....
	Dallas	**NHL**	**13**	**2**	**5**	**7**	**6**	**0**	**0**	**0**	**34**	**5.9**	**3**	**2**	**0.0**	**17:51**	**5**	**0**	**3**	**3**	**0**	**0**	**0**	**0**	**17:13**
	NHL Totals		**621**	**174**	**226**	**400**	**221**	**60**	**0**	**25**	**1806**	**9.6**		**112**	**33.0**	**18:42**	**22**	**0**	**7**	**7**	**16**	**0**	**0**	**0**	**13:57**

WHL West First All-Star Team (1993) • WHL West Second All-Star Team (1994)

Played in NHL All-Star Game (2000)

Traded to **Calgary** by **Montreal** with Montreal's 4th round choice (Shaun Sutter) in 1998 Entry Draft for Jonas Hoglund and Zarley Zalapski, February 1, 1998. Traded to **Florida** by **Calgary** with Jason Wiemer for Rob Niedermayer and Philadelphia's 2nd round choice (previously acquired, Calgary selected Andrei Medvedev) in 2001 Entry Draft, June 24, 2001. • Missed majority of 2001-02 season recovering from knee injury suffered in game vs. Vancouver, October 16, 2001. Traded to **St. Louis** by **Florida** with Florida's 5th round choice (Nikita Nikitin) in 2004 Entry Draft for Mike Van Ryn, March 11, 2003. Claimed on waivers by **Florida**, June 25, 2003. Traded to **Dallas** by **Florida** for Drew Bagnall and Dallas' 2nd round compensatory choice (later traded to Phoenix - Phoenix selected Enver Lisin) in 2004 Entry Draft, March 8, 2004.

BURNETT, Garrett

(buhr-NEHT, GAIR-eht) **ANA.**

Left wing. Shoots left. 6'3", 230 lbs. Born, Coquitlam, B.C., September 23, 1975.

Season	Club	League	GP	G	A	Pts	PIM	PP	SH	GW	S	%	+/-	TF	F%	Min	GP	G	A	Pts	PIM	PP	SH	GW	Min
1993-94	Trail	RJHL	26	2	1	3	248	....	....	....	....	....	....	....	....	....	....	....	....	....	....	....	....	....	....
1994-95	Sault Ste. Marie	OHL	14	0	1	1	78	....	....	....	....	....	....	....	....	....	....	....	....	....	....	....	....	....	....
	Kitchener Rangers	OHL	22	0	1	1	74	....	....	....	....	....	....	....	....	....	3	0	1	1	23	....	....	....	....
1995-96	Utica Blizzard	ColHL	15	0	1	1	78	....	....	....	....	....	....	....	....	....	....	....	....	....	....	....	....	....	....
	Oklahoma City	CHL	3	0	0	0	20	....	....	....	....	....	....	....	....	....	....	....	....	....	....	....	....	....	....
	Tulsa Oilers	CHL	6	1	0	1	94	....	....	....	....	....	....	....	....	....	....	....	....	....	....	....	....	....	....
	Nashville Knights	ECHL	3	0	0	0	22	....	....	....	....	....	....	....	....	....	....	....	....	....	....	....	....	....	....
	Jacksonville	ECHL	8	0	1	1	38	....	....	....	....	....	....	....	....	....	1	0	0	0	0	....	....	....	....
1996-97	Knoxville	ECHL	50	5	11	16	321	....	....	....	....	....	....	....	....	....	....	....	....	....	....	....	....	....	....
1997-98	Johnstown Chiefs	ECHL	34	1	1	2	331	....	....	....	....	....	....	....	....	....	....	....	....	....	....	....	....	....	....
	Philadelphia	AHL	14	1	2	3	129	....	....	....	....	....	....	....	....	....	....	....	....	....	....	....	....	....	....
1998-99	Kentucky	AHL	31	1	0	1	186	....	....	....	....	....	....	....	....	....	....	....	....	....	....	....	....	....	....
99-2000	Kentucky	AHL	58	3	3	6	*506	....	....	....	....	....	....	....	....	....	4	0	0	0	31	....	....	....	....
2000-01	Cleveland	IHL	54	2	4	6	250	....	....	....	....	....	....	....	....	....	....	....	....	....	....	....	....	....	....
2001-02	New Haven	UHL	4	1	0	1	40	....	....	....	....	....	....	....	....	....	....	....	....	....	....	....	....	....	....
	Cincinnati	AHL	32	1	0	1	175	....	....	....	....	....	....	....	....	....	....	....	....	....	....	....	....	....	....
2002-03	Hartford	AHL	62	6	1	7	*346	....	....	....	....	....	....	....	....	....	1	0	0	0	2	....	....	....	....
2003-04	**Anaheim**	**NHL**	**39**	**1**	**2**	**3**	**184**	**0**	**0**	**0**	**24**	**4.2**	**0**	**1**	**0.0**	**3:36**	....	....	....	....	....	....	....	....	....
	NHL Totals		**39**	**1**	**2**	**3**	**184**	**0**	**0**	**0**	**24**	**4.2**		**1**	**0.0**	**3:36**	....	....	....	....	....	....	....	....	....

Signed as a free agent by **San Jose**, July 2, 1998. • Missed majority of 2001-02 season recovering from knee injury suffered in game vs. New Haven (AHL), January 15, 2002. Signed as a free agent by **Hartford** (AHL), August 22, 2002. Signed as a free agent by **Anaheim**, July 25, 2003. • Spent majority of 2003-04 season as a healthy reserve.

BURNS, Brent

(BUHRNZ, BREHNT) **MIN.**

Defense. Shoots right. 6'4", 200 lbs. Born, Ajax, Ont., March 9, 1985. Minnesota's 1st choice, 20th overall, in 2003 Entry Draft.

Season	Club	League	GP	G	A	Pts	PIM	PP	SH	GW	S	%	+/-	TF	F%	Min	GP	G	A	Pts	PIM	PP	SH	GW	Min
2000-01	North York	MTHL	46	4	7	11	16	....	....	....	....	....	....	....	....	....	....	....	....	....	....	....	....	....	....
2001-02	Couchiching	OPJHL	68	15	25	40	14	....	....	....	....	....	....	....	....	....	....	....	....	....	....	....	....	....	....
2002-03	Brampton	OHL	68	15	25	40	14	....	....	....	....	....	....	....	....	....	11	5	6	11	6	....	....	....	....
2003-04	**Minnesota**	**NHL**	**36**	**1**	**5**	**6**	**12**	**0**	**0**	**0**	**34**	**2.9**	**–10**	**7**	**28.6**	**13:29**	....	....	....	....	....	....	....	....	....
	Houston Aeros	AHL	1	0	1	1	2	....	....	....	....	....	....	....	....	....	....	....	....	....	....	....	....	....	....
	NHL Totals		**36**	**1**	**5**	**6**	**12**	**0**	**0**	**0**	**34**	**2.9**		**7**	**28.6**	**13:29**	....	....	....	....	....	....	....	....	....

• Spent majority of 2003-04 season on assignment to Team Canada and as a healthy reserve.

BUTENSCHON, Sven

(BUH-tehn-shohn, SVEHN) **NYI**

Defense. Shoots left. 6'4", 215 lbs. Born, Itzehoe, West Germany, March 22, 1976. Pittsburgh's 3rd choice, 57th overall, in 1994 Entry Draft.

Season	Club	League	GP	G	A	Pts	PIM	PP	SH	GW	S	%	+/-	TF	F%	Min	GP	G	A	Pts	PIM	PP	SH	GW	Min
1991-92	Eastman Selects	MMHL	36	2	10	12	110	....	....	....	....	....	....	....	....	....	....	....	....	....	....	....	....	....	....
1992-93	Eastman Selects	MMHL	35	14	22	36	101	....	....	....	....	....	....	....	....	....	....	....	....	....	....	....	....	....	....
1993-94	Brandon	WHL	70	3	19	22	51	....	....	....	....	....	....	....	....	....	4	0	0	0	6	....	....	....	....
1994-95	Brandon	WHL	21	1	5	6	44	....	....	....	....	....	....	....	....	....	18	1	2	3	11	....	....	....	....
1995-96	Brandon	WHL	70	4	37	41	99	....	....	....	....	....	....	....	....	....	19	1	12	13	18	....	....	....	....
1996-97	Cleveland	IHL	75	3	12	15	68	....	....	....	....	....	....	....	....	....	10	0	1	1	4	....	....	....	....
1997-98	**Pittsburgh**	**NHL**	**8**	**0**	**0**	**0**	**6**	**0**	**0**	**0**	**4**	**0.0**	**–1**	....	....	....	....	....	....	....	....	....	....	....	....
	Syracuse Crunch	AHL	65	14	23	37	66	....	....	....	....	....	....	....	....	....	5	1	2	3	0	....	....	....	....
1998-99	**Pittsburgh**	**NHL**	**17**	**0**	**0**	**0**	**6**	**0**	**0**	**0**	**8**	**0.0**	**–7**	**0**	**0.0**	**13:08**	....	....	....	....	....	....	....	....	....
	Houston Aeros	IHL	57	1	4	5	81	....	....	....	....	....	....	....	....	....	....	....	....	....	....	....	....	....	....
99-2000	**Pittsburgh**	**NHL**	**3**	**0**	**0**	**0**	**0**	**0**	**0**	**0**	**2**	**0.0**	**3**	**0**	**0.0**	**16:25**	....	....	....	....	....	....	....	....	....
	Wilkes-Barre	AHL	75	19	21	40	101	....	....	....	....	....	....	....	....	....	....	....	....	....	....	....	....	....	....
2000-01	**Pittsburgh**	**NHL**	**5**	**0**	**1**	**1**	**2**	**0**	**0**	**0**	**6**	**0.0**	**1**	**0**	**0.0**	**17:51**	....	....	....	....	....	....	....	....	....
	Wilkes-Barre	AHL	55	7	28	35	85	....	....	....	....	....	....	....	....	....	....	....	....	....	....	....	....	....	....
	Edmonton	**NHL**	**7**	**1**	**1**	**2**	**2**	**0**	**0**	**0**	**3**	**33.3**	**2**	**0**	**0.0**	**11:07**	....	....	....	....	....	....	....	....	....
2001-02	**Edmonton**	**NHL**	**14**	**0**	**0**	**0**	**4**	**0**	**0**	**0**	**8**	**0.0**	**0**	**0**	**0.0**	**9:39**	....	....	....	....	....	....	....	....	....
	Hamilton	AHL	61	9	35	44	88	....	....	....	....	....	....	....	....	....	....	....	....	....	....	....	....	....	....
2002-03	**NY Islanders**	**NHL**	**37**	**0**	**4**	**4**	**26**	**0**	**0**	**0**	**19**	**0.0**	**–6**	**0**	**0.0**	**12:26**	....	....	....	....	....	....	....	....	....
	Bridgeport	AHL	36	3	13	16	58	....	....	....	....	....	....	....	....	....	9	3	6	9	6	....	....	....	....
2003-04	**NY Islanders**	**NHL**	**41**	**1**	**6**	**7**	**30**	**0**	**0**	**0**	**17**	**5.9**	**–3**	**0**	**0.0**	**11:15**	**4**	**0**	**0**	**0**	**0**	**0**	**0**	**0**	**7:42**
	Bridgeport	AHL	5	0	1	1	4	....	....	....	....	....	....	....	....	....	....	....	....	....	....	....	....	....	....
	NHL Totals		**132**	**2**	**12**	**14**	**76**	**0**	**0**	**0**	**67**	**3.0**		**0**	**0.0**	**12:04**	**4**	**0**	**0**	**0**	**0**	**0**	**0**	**0**	**7:42**

Traded to **Edmonton** by **Pittsburgh** for Dan LaCouture, March 13, 2001. Signed as a free agent by **Florida**, July 9, 2002. Traded to **NY Islanders** by **Florida** for Juraj Kolnik and NY Islanders' 9th round choice (later traded to San Jose – San Jose selected Carter Lee) in 2003 Entry Draft, October 11, 2003.

BUZEK, Petr

(BOO-zehk, PEE-tuhr)

Defense. Shoots left. 6'1", 220 lbs. Born, Jihlava, Czech., April 26, 1977. Dallas' 3rd choice, 63rd overall, in 1995 Entry Draft.

Season	Club	League	GP	G	A	Pts	PIM	PP	SH	GW	S	%	+/-	TF	F%	Min	GP	G	A	Pts	PIM	PP	SH	GW	Min
1993-94	Dukla Jihlava Jr.	Czech-Jr.	3	0	0	0	....	....	....	....	....	....	....	....	....	....	....	....	....	....	....	....	....	....	....
1994-95	HC Dukla Jihlava	Czech	43	2	5	7	47	....	....	....	....	....	....	....	....	....	2	0	0	0	2	....	....	....	....
1995-96	Michigan	IHL	DID NOT PLAY – INJURED																						
1996-97	Michigan	IHL	67	4	6	10	48	....	....	....	....	....	....	....	....	....	....	....	....	....	....	....	....	....	....
1997-98	**Dallas**	**NHL**	**2**	**0**	**0**	**0**	**2**	**0**	**0**	**0**	**0**	**0.0**	**1**	....	....	....	....	....	....	....	....	....	....	....	....
	Michigan	IHL	60	10	15	25	58	....	....	....	....	....	....	....	....	....	2	0	1	1	17	....	....	....	....
1998-99	**Dallas**	**NHL**	**2**	**0**	**0**	**0**	**2**	**0**	**0**	**0**	**0**	**0.0**	**0**	**0**	**0.0**	**13:50**	....	....	....	....	....	....	....	....	....
	Michigan	IHL	74	5	14	19	68	....	....	....	....	....	....	....	....	....	5	0	0	0	10	....	....	....	....
99-2000	**Atlanta**	**NHL**	**63**	**5**	**14**	**19**	**41**	**3**	**0**	**0**	**90**	**5.6**	**–22**	**0**	**0.0**	**18:24**	....	....	....	....	....	....	....	....	....
2000-01	**Atlanta**	**NHL**	**5**	**0**	**0**	**0**	**8**	**0**	**0**	**0**	**11**	**0.0**	**2**	**0**	**0.0**	**17:26**	....	....	....	....	....	....	....	....	....
2001-02	**Atlanta**	**NHL**	**9**	**0**	**0**	**0**	**13**	**0**	**0**	**0**	**2**	**0.0**	**–4**	**0**	**0.0**	**15:58**	....	....	....	....	....	....	....	....	....
	Chicago Wolves	AHL	4	0	1	1	2	....	....	....	....	....	....	....	....	....	....	....	....	....	....	....	....	....	....
	Calgary	**NHL**	**32**	**1**	**3**	**4**	**14**	**0**	**0**	**0**	**34**	**2.9**	**4**	**0**	**0.0**	**17:12**	....	....	....	....	....	....	....	....	....
2002-03	**Calgary**	**NHL**	**44**	**3**	**5**	**8**	**14**	**3**	**0**	**0**	**48**	**6.3**	**–6**	**0**	**0.0**	**14:22**	....	....	....	....	....	....	....	....	....
2003-04	HC Sparta Praha	Czech	5	0	0	0	10	....	....	....	....	....	....	....	....	....	....	....	....	....	....	....	....	....	....
	NHL Totals		**157**	**9**	**22**	**31**	**94**	**6**	**0**	**0**	**185**	**4.9**		**0**	**0.0**	**16:47**	....	....	....	....	....	....	....	....	....

Played in NHL All-Star Game (2000)

• Missed entire 1995-96 season recovering from injuries suffered in automobile accident, July, 1995. Claimed by **Atlanta** from **Dallas** in Expansion Draft, June 25, 1999. • Missed majority of 2000-01 season recovering from neck injury suffered in game vs. Anaheim, October 17, 2000. Traded to **Calgary** by **Atlanta** with Atlanta's 6th round choice (Adam Pardy) in 2004 Entry Draft for Jeff Cowan and the rights to Kurtis Foster, December 18, 2001. Loaned to **HC Sparta Praha** (Czech) by **Calgary**, October 20, 2003.

BYKOV, Dmitri

(BEE-kawv, dih-MEE-tree)

Defense. Shoots left. 5'10", 169 lbs. Born, Izhevsk, USSR, May 5, 1977. Detroit's 6th choice, 258th overall, in 2001 Entry Draft.

Season	Club	League	GP	G	A	Pts	PIM	PP	SH	GW	S	%	+/-	TF	F%	Min	GP	G	A	Pts	PIM	PP	SH	GW	Min
1995-96	CSK VVS Samara	CIS	50	1	2	3	39	....	....	....	....	....	....	....	....	....	....	....	....	....	....	....	....	....	....
1996-97	CSK VVS Samara	Russia	44	1	6	7	20	....	....	....	....	....	....	....	....	....	2	0	0	0	2	....	....	....	....
1997-98	Lada Togliatti	Russia	9	0	1	1	4	....	....	....	....	....	....	....	....	....	....	....	....	....	....	....	....	....	....
	CSK VVS Samara	Russia	27	0	5	5	14	....	....	....	....	....	....	....	....	....	....	....	....	....	....	....	....	....	....
	Yaroslavl	Russia	10	1	2	3	6	....	....	....	....	....	....	....	....	....	7	0	1	1	10	....	....	....	....
1998-99	Lada Togliatti	Russia	39	0	6	6	24	....	....	....	....	....	....	....	....	....	7	1	0	1	8	....	....	....	....
	CSK VVS Samara	Russia	2	0	0	0	0	....	....	....	....	....	....	....	....	....	....	....	....	....	....	....	....	....	....

			Regular Season														Playoffs								
Season	**Club**	**League**	**GP**	**G**	**A**	**Pts**	**PIM**	**PP**	**SH**	**GW**	**S**	**%**	**+/-**	**TF**	**F%**	**Min**	**GP**	**G**	**A**	**Pts**	**PIM**	**PP**	**SH**	**GW**	**Min**
99-2000	Ak Bars Kazan	Russia	35	3	8	11	18	....	....	....	....	....	....	....	....	....	18	0	2	2	8	....	....	....	....
	Ak Bars Kazan 2	Russia-3	3	0	1	1	4	....	....	....	....	....	....	....	....	....	....	....	....	....	....	....	....	....	....
2000-01	Ak Bars Kazan	Russia	39	3	8	11	28	....	....	....	....	....	....	....	....	....	4	0	1	1	4	....	....	....	....
2001-02	Ak Bars Kazan	Russia	44	1	1	2	38	....	....	....	....	....	....	....	....	....	11	0	0	0	4	....	....	....	....
2002-03	**Detroit**	**NHL**	**71**	**2**	**10**	**12**	**43**	**1**	**0**	**0**	**58**	**3.4**	**1**	**2**	**100.0**	**18:22**	**4**	**0**	**0**	**0**	**0**	**0**	**0**	**0**	**11:14**
2003-04	Ak Bars Kazan	Russia	55	5	11	16	46	....	....	....	....	....	....	....	....	....	8	2	1	3	10	....	....	....	....
	NHL Totals		**71**	**2**	**10**	**12**	**43**	**1**	**0**	**0**	**58**	**3.4**		**2**	**100.0**	**18:22**	**4**	**0**	**0**	**0**	**0**	**0**	**0**	**0**	**11:14**

Signed as a free agent by **Ak Bars Kazan** (Russia), June 18, 2003.

BYLSMA, Dan

(BIGHL-zmah, DAN)

Right wing. Shoots left. 6'2", 212 lbs. Born, Grand Haven, MI, September 19, 1970. Winnipeg's 7th choice, 109th overall, in 1989 Entry Draft.

1986-87	Oakville Blades	OJHL-B	10	4	9	13	21	....	....	....	....	....	....	....	....	....	....	....	....	....	....	....	....	....	....
	St. Mary's Lincolns	OJHL-B	27	14	28	42	21	....	....	....	....	....	....	....	....	....	....	....	....	....	....	....	....	....	....
1987-88	St. Mary's Lincolns	OJHL-B	40	30	39	69	33	....	....	....	....	....	....	....	....	....	8	8	18	26	....	....	....	....	....
1988-89	Bowling Green	CCHA	32	3	7	10	10	....	....	....	....	....	....	....	....	....	....	....	....	....	....	....	....	....	....
1989-90	Bowling Green	CCHA	44	13	17	30	30	....	....	....	....	....	....	....	....	....	....	....	....	....	....	....	....	....	....
1990-91	Bowling Green	CCHA	40	9	12	21	48	....	....	....	....	....	....	....	....	....	....	....	....	....	....	....	....	....	....
1991-92	Bowling Green	CCHA	34	11	14	25	24	....	....	....	....	....	....	....	....	....	....	....	....	....	....	....	....	....	....
1992-93	Greensboro	ECHL	60	25	35	60	66	....	....	....	....	....	....	....	....	....	1	0	1	1	10	....	....	....	....
	Rochester	AHL	2	0	1	1	0	....	....	....	....	....	....	....	....	....	....	....	....	....	....	....	....	....	....
1993-94	Greensboro	ECHL	25	14	16	30	52	....	....	....	....	....	....	....	....	....	....	....	....	....	....	....	....	....	....
	Albany River Rats	AHL	3	0	1	1	2	....	....	....	....	....	....	....	....	....	....	....	....	....	....	....	....	....	....
	Moncton Hawks	AHL	50	12	16	28	25	....	....	....	....	....	....	....	....	....	21	3	4	7	31	....	....	....	....
1994-95	Phoenix	IHL	81	19	23	42	41	....	....	....	....	....	....	....	....	....	9	4	4	8	4	....	....	....	....
1995-96	**Los Angeles**	**NHL**	**4**	**0**	**0**	**0**	**0**	**0**	**0**	**0**	**6**	**0.0**	**0**	....	....	....	....	....	....	....	....	....	....	....	....
	Phoenix	IHL	78	22	20	42	48	....	....	....	....	....	....	....	....	....	4	1	0	1	2	....	....	....	....
1996-97	**Los Angeles**	**NHL**	**79**	**3**	**6**	**9**	**32**	**0**	**0**	**0**	**86**	**3.5**	**–15**	....	....	....	....	....	....	....	....	....	....	....	....
1997-98	**Los Angeles**	**NHL**	**65**	**3**	**9**	**12**	**33**	**0**	**0**	**0**	**57**	**5.3**	**9**	....	....	....	**2**	**0**	**0**	**0**	**0**	**0**	**0**	**0**	....
	Long Beach	IHL	8	2	3	5	0	....	....	....	....	....	....	....	....	....	....	....	....	....	....	....	....	....	....
1998-99	**Los Angeles**	**NHL**	**8**	**0**	**0**	**0**	**2**	**0**	**0**	**0**	**3**	**0.0**	**–1**	**0**	**0.0**	**9:51**	....	....	....	....	....	....	....	....	....
	Springfield	AHL	2	0	2	2	2	....	....	....	....	....	....	....	....	....	....	....	....	....	....	....	....	....	....
	Long Beach	IHL	58	10	8	18	53	....	....	....	....	....	....	....	....	....	4	0	0	0	8	....	....	....	....
99-2000	**Los Angeles**	**NHL**	**64**	**3**	**6**	**9**	**55**	**0**	**1**	**0**	**43**	**7.0**	**–2**	**62**	**43.6**	**10:23**	**3**	**0**	**0**	**0**	**0**	**0**	**0**	**0**	**10:21**
	Long Beach	IHL	6	0	3	3	2	....	....	....	....	....	....	....	....	....	....	....	....	....	....	....	....	....	....
	Lowell	AHL	2	1	1	2	2	....	....	....	....	....	....	....	....	....	....	....	....	....	....	....	....	....	....
2000-01	**Anaheim**	**NHL**	**82**	**1**	**9**	**10**	**22**	**0**	**0**	**0**	**50**	**2.0**	**–12**	**10**	**50.0**	**11:45**	....	....	....	....	....	....	....	....	....
2001-02	**Anaheim**	**NHL**	**77**	**8**	**9**	**17**	**28**	**0**	**1**	**2**	**72**	**11.1**	**5**	**257**	**42.4**	**11:36**	....	....	....	....	....	....	....	....	....
2002-03	**Anaheim**	**NHL**	**39**	**1**	**4**	**5**	**12**	**0**	**0**	**0**	**23**	**4.3**	**–1**	**28**	**53.6**	**9:29**	**11**	**0**	**1**	**1**	**2**	**0**	**0**	**0**	**9:44**
2003-04	**Anaheim**	**NHL**	**11**	**0**	**0**	**0**	**0**	**0**	**0**	**0**	**6**	**0.0**	**–3**	**13**	**53.9**	**7:04**	....	....	....	....	....	....	....	....	....
	Cincinnati	AHL	36	3	3	6	53	....	....	....	....	....	....	....	....	....	8	1	1	2	4	....	....	....	....
	NHL Totals		**429**	**19**	**43**	**62**	**184**	**0**	**2**	**2**	**346**	**5.5**		**370**	**44.1**	**10:51**	**16**	**0**	**1**	**1**	**2**	**0**	**0**	**0**	**9:52**

Signed as a free agent by **Los Angeles**, July 7, 1994. Signed as a free agent by **Anaheim**, July 13, 2000. • Missed majority of 2002-03 season recovering from knee (January 28, 2003 vs. San Jose) and head (February 9, 2003 vs. Carolina) injuries.

CAIRNS, Eric

(KAIRNZ, AIR-ihk) **FLA.**

Defense. Shoots left. 6'6", 230 lbs. Born, Oakville, Ont., June 27, 1974. NY Rangers' 3rd choice, 72nd overall, in 1992 Entry Draft.

1990-91	Burlington	OJHL-B	37	5	16	21	120	....	....	....	....	....	....	....	....	....	....	....	....	....	....	....	....	....	....
1991-92	Detroit	OHL	64	1	11	12	237	....	....	....	....	....	....	....	....	....	7	0	0	0	31	....	....	....	....
1992-93	Detroit	OHL	64	3	13	16	194	....	....	....	....	....	....	....	....	....	15	0	3	3	24	....	....	....	....
1993-94	Detroit	OHL	59	7	35	42	204	....	....	....	....	....	....	....	....	....	17	0	4	4	46	....	....	....	....
1994-95	Birmingham Bulls	ECHL	11	1	3	4	49	....	....	....	....	....	....	....	....	....	....	....	....	....	....	....	....	....	....
	Binghamton	AHL	27	0	3	3	134	....	....	....	....	....	....	....	....	....	9	1	1	2	28	....	....	....	....
1995-96	Binghamton	AHL	46	1	13	14	192	....	....	....	....	....	....	....	....	....	4	0	0	0	37	....	....	....	....
	Charlotte	ECHL	6	0	1	1	34	....	....	....	....	....	....	....	....	....	....	....	....	....	....	....	....	....	....
1996-97	**NY Rangers**	**NHL**	**40**	**0**	**1**	**1**	**147**	**0**	**0**	**0**	**17**	**0.0**	**–7**	....	....	....	**3**	**0**	**0**	**0**	**0**	**0**	**0**	**0**	....
	Binghamton	AHL	10	1	1	2	96	....	....	....	....	....	....	....	....	....	....	....	....	....	....	....	....	....	....
1997-98	**NY Rangers**	**NHL**	**39**	**0**	**3**	**3**	**92**	**0**	**0**	**0**	**17**	**0.0**	**–3**	....	....	....	....	....	....	....	....	....	....	....	....
	Hartford	AHL	7	1	2	3	43	....	....	....	....	....	....	....	....	....	....	....	....	....	....	....	....	....	....
1998-99	Hartford	AHL	11	0	2	2	49	....	....	....	....	....	....	....	....	....	....	....	....	....	....	....	....	....	....
	NY Islanders	**NHL**	**9**	**0**	**3**	**3**	**23**	**0**	**0**	**0**	**2**	**0.0**	**1**	**0**	**0.0**	**10:15**	....	....	....	....	....	....	....	....	....
	Lowell	AHL	24	0	0	0	91	....	....	....	....	....	....	....	....	....	3	1	0	1	32	....	....	....	....
99-2000	**NY Islanders**	**NHL**	**67**	**2**	**7**	**9**	**196**	**0**	**0**	**0**	**55**	**3.6**	**–5**	**0**	**0.0**	**17:43**	....	....	....	....	....	....	....	....	....
	Providence Bruins	AHL	4	1	1	2	14	....	....	....	....	....	....	....	....	....	....	....	....	....	....	....	....	....	....
2000-01	**NY Islanders**	**NHL**	**45**	**2**	**2**	**4**	**106**	**0**	**0**	**0**	**21**	**9.5**	**–18**	**1**	**0.0**	**16:24**	....	....	....	....	....	....	....	....	....
2001-02	**NY Islanders**	**NHL**	**74**	**2**	**5**	**7**	**176**	**0**	**0**	**1**	**34**	**5.9**	**–2**	**0**	**0.0**	**11:09**	**7**	**0**	**0**	**0**	**15**	**0**	**0**	**0**	**13:54**
2002-03	**NY Islanders**	**NHL**	**60**	**1**	**4**	**5**	**124**	**0**	**0**	**0**	**31**	**3.2**	**–7**	**0**	**0.0**	**11:50**	**5**	**0**	**0**	**0**	**13**	**0**	**0**	**0**	**6:02**
2003-04	**NY Islanders**	**NHL**	**72**	**2**	**6**	**8**	**189**	**0**	**0**	**0**	**24**	**8.3**	**–5**	**0**	**0.0**	**11:44**	**1**	**0**	**0**	**0**	**0**	**0**	**0**	**0**	**3:53**
	NHL Totals		**406**	**9**	**31**	**40**	**1053**	**0**	**0**	**1**	**201**	**4.5**		**1**	**0.0**	**13:27**	**16**	**0**	**0**	**0**	**28**	**0**	**0**	**0**	**10:06**

Claimed on waivers by **NY Islanders** from **NY Rangers**, December 22, 1998. Signed as a free agent by **Florida**, July 5, 2004.

CAJANEK, Petr

(chuh-YA-nihk, PEE-tuhr) **ST.L.**

Right wing. Shoots left. 5'11", 176 lbs. Born, Gottwaldov, Czech., August 18, 1975. St. Louis' 6th choice, 253rd overall, in 2001 Entry Draft.

1993-94	AC ZPS Zlin	Czech	34	5	4	9	....	....	....	....	....	....	....	....	....	....	3	0	0	0	....	....	....	....	....
1994-95	AC ZPS Zlin	Czech	35	7	9	16	8	....	....	....	....	....	....	....	....	....	12	2	6	8	4	....	....	....	....
1995-96	AC ZPS Zlin	Czech	36	8	11	19	32	....	....	....	....	....	....	....	....	....	8	2	6	8	8	....	....	....	....
1996-97	AC ZPS Zlin	Czech	50	9	30	39	46	....	....	....	....	....	....	....	....	....	....	....	....	....	....	....	....	....	....
1997-98	Zlin	Czech	46	19	27	46	117	....	....	....	....	....	....	....	....	....	....	....	....	....	....	....	....	....	....
1998-99	Zlin	Czech	49	15	33	48	123	....	....	....	....	....	....	....	....	....	11	5	7	12	12	....	....	....	....
99-2000	Zlin	Czech	50	23	34	57	66	....	....	....	....	....	....	....	....	....	4	1	0	1	0	....	....	....	....
2000-01	Zlin	Czech	52	18	31	49	105	....	....	....	....	....	....	....	....	....	6	0	4	4	22	....	....	....	....
2001-02	Zlin	Czech	49	20	44	64	64	....	....	....	....	....	....	....	....	....	11	5	7	12	10	....	....	....	....
	Czech Republic	Olympics	4	0	0	0	0	....	....	....	....	....	....	....	....	....	....	....	....	....	....	....	....	....	....
2002-03	**St. Louis**	**NHL**	**51**	**9**	**29**	**38**	**20**	**2**	**2**	**1**	**90**	**10.0**	**16**	**793**	**48.4**	**15:56**	**2**	**0**	**0**	**0**	**2**	**0**	**0**	**0**	**11:07**
2003-04	**St. Louis**	**NHL**	**70**	**12**	**14**	**26**	**16**	**3**	**0**	**4**	**126**	**9.5**	**12**	**1000**	**47.6**	**17:48**	**5**	**0**	**2**	**2**	**2**	**0**	**0**	**0**	**19:27**
	NHL Totals		**121**	**21**	**43**	**64**	**36**	**5**	**2**	**5**	**216**	**9.7**		**1793**	**48.0**	**17:01**	**7**	**0**	**2**	**2**	**4**	**0**	**0**	**0**	**17:04**

CALDER, Kyle

(KAWL-dehr, KIGHL) **CHI.**

Left wing. Shoots left. 5'11", 176 lbs. Born, Mannville, Alta., January 5, 1979. Chicago's 7th choice, 130th overall, in 1997 Entry Draft.

1994-95	Leduc Oil Barons	AMHL	27	25	32	57	22	....	....	....	....	....	....	....	....	....	....	....	....	....	....	....	....	....	....
1995-96	Regina Pats	WHL	27	1	7	8	10	....	....	....	....	....	....	....	....	....	11	0	0	0	0	....	....	....	....
1996-97	Regina Pats	WHL	62	25	34	59	17	....	....	....	....	....	....	....	....	....	5	3	0	3	6	....	....	....	....
1997-98	Regina Pats	WHL	62	27	50	77	58	....	....	....	....	....	....	....	....	....	2	0	1	1	0	....	....	....	....
1998-99	Regina Pats	WHL	34	23	28	51	29	....	....	....	....	....	....	....	....	....	....	....	....	....	....	....	....	....	....
	Kamloops Blazers	WHL	27	19	18	37	30	....	....	....	....	....	....	....	....	....	15	6	10	16	6	....	....	....	....
99-2000	**Chicago**	**NHL**	**8**	**1**	**1**	**2**	**2**	**0**	**0**	**0**	**5**	**20.0**	**–3**	**2**	**0.0**	**9:59**	....	....	....	....	....	....	....	....	....
	Cleveland	IHL	74	14	22	36	43	....	....	....	....	....	....	....	....	....	9	2	2	4	14	....	....	....	....
2000-01	**Chicago**	**NHL**	**43**	**5**	**10**	**15**	**14**	**0**	**0**	**1**	**63**	**7.9**	**–4**	**2**	**0.0**	**12:43**	....	....	....	....	....	....	....	....	....
	Norfolk Admirals	AHL	37	12	15	27	21	....	....	....	....	....	....	....	....	....	9	2	6	8	2	....	....	....	....
2001-02	**Chicago**	**NHL**	**81**	**17**	**36**	**53**	**47**	**6**	**0**	**3**	**133**	**12.8**	**8**	**0**	**0.0**	**16:33**	**5**	**2**	**0**	**2**	**2**	**1**	**0**	**0**	**16:45**
2002-03	**Chicago**	**NHL**	**82**	**15**	**27**	**42**	**40**	**7**	**0**	**2**	**164**	**9.1**	**–6**	**4**	**25.0**	**16:43**	....	....	....	....	....	....	....	....	....
2003-04	**Chicago**	**NHL**	**66**	**21**	**18**	**39**	**29**	**10**	**0**	**1**	**144**	**14.6**	**–18**	**13**	**30.8**	**17:08**	....	....	....	....	....	....	....	....	....
	NHL Totals		**280**	**59**	**92**	**151**	**132**	**23**	**0**	**7**	**509**	**11.6**		**21**	**23.8**	**15:58**	**5**	**2**	**0**	**2**	**2**	**1**	**0**	**0**	**16:45**

CAMMALLERI, Michael

(kam-UH-LAIR-ee, MIGH-kuhl) **L.A.**

Center. Shoots left. 5'9", 180 lbs. Born, Richmond Hill, Ont., June 8, 1982. Los Angeles' 3rd choice, 49th overall, in 2001 Entry Draft.

			Regular Season														Playoffs								
Season	Club	League	GP	G	A	Pts	PIM	PP	SH	GW	S	%	+/-	TF	F%	Min	GP	G	A	Pts	PIM	PP	SH	GW	Min
1997-98	Bramalea Blues	OPJHL	46	36	52	88	30	....	....	....	....	....	....	....	....	....	....	....	....	....	....	....	....	....	....
1998-99	Bramalea Blues	OPJHL	41	31	72	103	51	....	....	....	....	....	....	....	....	....	....	....	....	....	....	....	....	....	....
99-2000	U. of Michigan	CCHA	39	13	13	26	32	....	....	....	....	....	....	....	....	....	....	....	....	....	....	....	....	....	....
2000-01	U. of Michigan	CCHA	42	*29	32	61	24	....	....	....	....	....	....	....	....	....	....	....	....	....	....	....	....	....	....
2001-02	U. of Michigan	CCHA	29	23	21	44	28	....	....	....	....	....	....	....	....	....	....	....	....	....	....	....	....	....	....
2002-03	**Los Angeles**	**NHL**	**28**	**5**	**3**	**8**	**22**	**2**	**0**	**2**	**40**	**12.5**	**-4**	**253**	**51.4**	**14:05**	....	....	....	....	....	....	....	....	....
	Manchester	AHL	13	5	15	20	12	....	....	....	....	....	....	....	....	....	....	....	....	....	....	....	....	....	....
2003-04	**Los Angeles**	**NHL**	**31**	**9**	**6**	**15**	**20**	**2**	**0**	**2**	**53**	**17.0**	**1**	**280**	**53.6**	**13:18**	....	....	....	....	....	....	....	....	....
	Manchester	AHL	41	20	19	39	28	....	....	....	....	....	....	....	....	....	1	0	1	1	0	....	....	....	....
	NHL Totals		**59**	**14**	**9**	**23**	**42**	**4**	**0**	**4**	**93**	**15.1**		**533**	**52.5**	**13:40**	....	....	....	....	....	....	....	....	....

CCHA First All-Star Team (2001) • NCAA West Second All-American Team (2001) • CCHA Second All-Star Team (2002) • NCAA West First All-American Team (2002)
• Missed majority of 2002-03 season recovering from head injury suffered in game vs. San Jose, January 28, 2003.

CAMPBELL, Brian

(KAM-behl, BRIGH-uhn) **BUF.**

Defense. Shoots left. 6', 190 lbs. Born, Strathroy, Ont., May 23, 1979. Buffalo's 7th choice, 156th overall, in 1997 Entry Draft.

Season	Club	League	GP	G	A	Pts	PIM	PP	SH	GW	S	%	+/-	TF	F%	Min	GP	G	A	Pts	PIM	PP	SH	GW	Min
1994-95	Petrolia Oil Barons	OJHL-B	49	11	27	38	43	....	....	....	....	....	....	....	....	....	....	....	....	....	....	....	....	....	....
1995-96	Ottawa 67's	OHL	66	5	22	27	23	....	....	....	....	....	....	....	....	....	4	0	1	1	2	....	....	....	....
1996-97	Ottawa 67's	OHL	66	7	36	43	12	....	....	....	....	....	....	....	....	....	24	2	11	13	8	....	....	....	....
1997-98	Ottawa 67's	OHL	66	14	39	53	31	....	....	....	....	....	....	....	....	....	13	1	14	15	0	....	....	....	....
1998-99	Ottawa 67's	OHL	62	12	75	87	27	....	....	....	....	....	....	....	....	....	9	2	10	12	6	....	....	....	....
	Rochester	AHL	....	....	....	....	....	....	....	....	....	....	....	....	....	....	2	0	0	0	0	....	....	....	....
99-2000	**Buffalo**	**NHL**	**12**	**1**	**4**	**5**	**4**	**0**	**0**	**0**	**10**	**10.0**	**-2**	**0**	**0.0**	**15:48**	....	....	....	....	....	....	....	....	....
	Rochester	AHL	67	2	24	26	22	....	....	....	....	....	....	....	....	....	21	0	3	3	0	....	....	....	....
2000-01	**Buffalo**	**NHL**	**8**	**0**	**0**	**0**	**2**	**0**	**0**	**0**	**7**	**0.0**	**-2**	**0**	**0.0**	**15:40**	....	....	....	....	....	....	....	....	....
	Rochester	AHL	65	7	25	32	24	....	....	....	....	....	....	....	....	....	4	0	1	1	0	....	....	....	....
2001-02	**Buffalo**	**NHL**	**29**	**3**	**3**	**6**	**12**	**0**	**0**	**0**	**30**	**10.0**	**0**	**1**	**0.0**	**15:18**	....	....	....	....	....	....	....	....	....
	Rochester	AHL	45	2	35	37	13	....	....	....	....	....	....	....	....	....	....	....	....	....	....	....	....	....	....
2002-03	**Buffalo**	**NHL**	**65**	**2**	**17**	**19**	**20**	**0**	**0**	**1**	**90**	**2.2**	**-8**	**1**	**0.0**	**18:40**	....	....	....	....	....	....	....	....	....
2003-04	**Buffalo**	**NHL**	**53**	**3**	**8**	**11**	**12**	**0**	**0**	**0**	**45**	**6.7**	**-8**	**0**	**0.0**	**16:02**	....	....	....	....	....	....	....	....	....
	NHL Totals		**167**	**9**	**32**	**41**	**50**	**0**	**0**	**1**	**182**	**4.9**		**2**	**0.0**	**16:54**	....	....	....	....	....	....	....	....	....

OHL First All-Star Team (1999) • OHL MVP (1999) • Canadian Major Junior First All-Star Team (1999) • Canadian Major Junior Player of the Year (1999) • George Parsons Trophy (Memorial Cup Most Sportsmanlike Player) (1999)

CAMPBELL, Gregory

(KAM-behl, GREH-goh-ree) **FLA.**

Left wing. Shoots left. 6', 191 lbs. Born, London, Ont., December 17, 1983. Florida's 4th choice, 67th overall, in 2002 Entry Draft.

Season	Club	League	GP	G	A	Pts	PIM	PP	SH	GW	S	%	+/-	TF	F%	Min	GP	G	A	Pts	PIM	PP	SH	GW	Min
1998-99	Aylmer Aces	OJHL-B	49	5	9	14	44	....	....	....	....	....	....	....	....	....	....	....	....	....	....	....	....	....	....
99-2000	St. Thomas Stars	OJHL-B	51	12	8	20	51	....	....	....	....	....	....	....	....	....	....	....	....	....	....	....	....	....	....
2000-01	Plymouth Whalers	OHL	65	2	12	14	40	....	....	....	....	....	....	....	....	....	10	0	0	0	7	....	....	....	....
2001-02	Plymouth Whalers	OHL	65	17	36	53	105	....	....	....	....	....	....	....	....	....	6	0	2	2	13	....	....	....	....
2002-03	Kitchener Rangers	OHL	55	23	33	56	116	....	....	....	....	....	....	....	....	....	21	15	4	19	34	....	....	....	....
2003-04	**Florida**	**NHL**	**2**	**0**	**0**	**0**	**5**	**0**	**0**	**0**	**0**	**0.0**	**-1**	**1**	**0.0**	**9:09**	....	....	....	....	....	....	....	....	....
	San Antonio	AHL	76	13	16	29	73	....	....	....	....	....	....	....	....	....	....	....	....	....	....	....	....	....	....
	NHL Totals		**2**	**0**	**0**	**0**	**5**	**0**	**0**	**0**	**0**	**0.0**		**1**	**0.0**	**9:09**	....	....	....	....	....	....	....	....	....

Memorial Cup All-Star Team (2003) • Ed Chynoweth Trophy (Memorial Cup Tournament Leading Scorer) (2003)

CAMPBELL, Jim

(KAM-behl, JIHM)

Right wing. Shoots right. 6'2", 205 lbs. Born, Worcester, MA, April 3, 1973. Montreal's 2nd choice, 28th overall, in 1991 Entry Draft.

Season	Club	League	GP	G	A	Pts	PIM	PP	SH	GW	S	%	+/-	TF	F%	Min	GP	G	A	Pts	PIM	PP	SH	GW	Min
1988-89	Northfield Prep	Hi-School	12	12	8	20	6	....	....	....	....	....	....	....	....	....	....	....	....	....	....	....	....	....	....
1989-90	Northfield Prep	Hi-School	8	14	7	21	8	....	....	....	....	....	....	....	....	....	....	....	....	....	....	....	....	....	....
1990-91	Lawrence Prep	Hi-School	26	36	47	83	26	....	....	....	....	....	....	....	....	....	....	....	....	....	....	....	....	....	....
1991-92	Hull Olympiques	QMJHL	64	41	44	85	51	....	....	....	....	....	....	....	....	....	6	7	3	10	8	....	....	....	....
1992-93	Hull Olympiques	QMJHL	50	42	29	71	66	....	....	....	....	....	....	....	....	....	8	11	4	15	43	....	....	....	....
1993-94	Team USA	Nat-Tm	56	24	33	57	59	....	....	....	....	....	....	....	....	....	....	....	....	....	....	....	....	....	....
	United States	Olympics	8	0	0	0	6	....	....	....	....	....	....	....	....	....	....	....	....	....	....	....	....	....	....
	Fredericton	AHL	19	6	17	23	6	....	....	....	....	....	....	....	....	....	....	....	....	....	....	....	....	....	....
1994-95	Fredericton	AHL	77	27	24	51	103	....	....	....	....	....	....	....	....	....	12	0	7	7	8	....	....	....	....
1995-96	Fredericton	AHL	44	28	23	51	24	....	....	....	....	....	....	....	....	....	....	....	....	....	....	....	....	....	....
	Anaheim	**NHL**	**16**	**2**	**3**	**5**	**36**	**1**	**0**	**0**	**25**	**8.0**	**0**	....	....	....	....	....	....	....	....	....	....	....	....
	Baltimore Bandits	AHL	16	13	7	20	8	....	....	....	....	....	....	....	....	....	12	7	5	12	10	....	....	....	....
1996-97	**St. Louis**	**NHL**	**68**	**23**	**20**	**43**	**68**	**5**	**0**	**6**	**169**	**13.6**	**3**	....	....	....	**4**	**1**	**0**	**1**	**6**	**1**	**0**	**0**	....
1997-98	**St. Louis**	**NHL**	**76**	**22**	**19**	**41**	**55**	**7**	**0**	**6**	**147**	**15.0**	**0**	....	....	....	**10**	**7**	**3**	**10**	**12**	**4**	**0**	**2**	....
1998-99	**St. Louis**	**NHL**	**55**	**4**	**21**	**25**	**41**	**1**	**0**	**0**	**99**	**4.0**	**-8**	**7**	**42.9**	**13:34**	....	....	....	....	....	....	....	....	....
99-2000	Manitoba Moose	IHL	10	1	3	4	10	....	....	....	....	....	....	....	....	....	....	....	....	....	....	....	....	....	....
	St. Louis	**NHL**	**2**	**0**	**0**	**0**	**9**	**0**	**0**	**0**	**6**	**0.0**	**0**	**0**	**0.0**	**15:17**	....	....	....	....	....	....	....	....	....
	Worcester IceCats	AHL	66	31	34	65	88	....	....	....	....	....	....	....	....	....	9	1	2	3	6	....	....	....	....
2000-01	**Montreal**	**NHL**	**57**	**9**	**11**	**20**	**53**	**6**	**0**	**1**	**81**	**11.1**	**-3**	**14**	**42.9**	**10:19**	....	....	....	....	....	....	....	....	....
	Quebec Citadelles	AHL	3	5	0	5	6	....	....	....	....	....	....	....	....	....	....	....	....	....	....	....	....	....	....
2001-02	**Chicago**	**NHL**	**9**	**1**	**1**	**2**	**4**	**0**	**0**	**0**	**12**	**8.3**	**-3**	**1**	**0.0**	**13:21**	....	....	....	....	....	....	....	....	....
	Norfolk Admirals	AHL	44	11	14	25	26	....	....	....	....	....	....	....	....	....	4	3	1	4	2	....	....	....	....
2002-03	San Antonio	AHL	64	16	37	53	55	....	....	....	....	....	....	....	....	....	1	0	0	0	0	....	....	....	....
	Florida	**NHL**	**1**	**0**	**0**	**0**	**0**	**0**	**0**	**0**	**3**	**0.0**	**0**	**1**	**0.0**	**8:56**	....	....	....	....	....	....	....	....	....
2003-04	Chicago Wolves	AHL	41	10	13	23	41	....	....	....	....	....	....	....	....	....	....	....	....	....	....	....	....	....	....
	Nizhnekamsk	Russia	2	0	0	0	2	....	....	....	....	....	....	....	....	....	....	....	....	....	....	....	....	....	....
	NHL Totals		**284**	**61**	**75**	**136**	**266**	**20**	**0**	**13**	**542**	**11.3**		**23**	**39.1**	**12:03**	**14**	**8**	**3**	**11**	**18**	**5**	**0**	**2**	....

NHL All-Rookie Team (1997)

Traded to **Anaheim** by **Montreal** for Robert Dirk, January 21, 1996. Signed as a free agent by **St. Louis**, July 11, 1996. Loaned to **Manitoba** (IHL) by **St. Louis**, October 4, 1999 and recalled November 1, 1999. Signed as a free agent by **Montreal**, August 21, 2000. Signed as a free agent by **Chicago**, November 19, 2001. Signed as a free agent by **Florida**, July 19, 2002. Signed as a free agent by **Chicago** (AHL), December 10, 2003.

CARNEY, Keith

(KAHRN-nee, KEETH) **ANA.**

Defense. Shoots left. 6'2", 211 lbs. Born, Providence, RI, February 3, 1970. Buffalo's 3rd choice, 76th overall, in 1988 Entry Draft.

Season	Club	League	GP	G	A	Pts	PIM	PP	SH	GW	S	%	+/-	TF	F%	Min	GP	G	A	Pts	PIM	PP	SH	GW	Min
1987-88	Mount St. Charles	Hi-School	23	12	43	55	....	....	....	....	....	....	....	....	....	....	....	....	....	....	....	....	....	....	....
1988-89	U. of Maine	H-East	40	4	22	26	24	....	....	....	....	....	....	....	....	....	....	....	....	....	....	....	....	....	....
1989-90	U. of Maine	H-East	41	3	41	44	43	....	....	....	....	....	....	....	....	....	....	....	....	....	....	....	....	....	....
1990-91	U. of Maine	H-East	40	7	49	56	38	....	....	....	....	....	....	....	....	....	....	....	....	....	....	....	....	....	....
1991-92	Team USA	Nat-Tm	49	2	17	19	16	....	....	....	....	....	....	....	....	....	....	....	....	....	....	....	....	....	....
	Buffalo	**NHL**	**14**	**1**	**2**	**3**	**18**	**1**	**0**	**0**	**17**	**5.9**	**-3**	....	....	....	**7**	**0**	**3**	**3**	**0**	**0**	**0**	**0**	....
	Rochester	AHL	24	1	10	11	2	....	....	....	....	....	....	....	....	....	2	0	2	2	0	....	....	....	....
1992-93	**Buffalo**	**NHL**	**30**	**2**	**4**	**6**	**55**	**0**	**0**	**1**	**26**	**7.7**	**3**	....	....	....	**8**	**0**	**3**	**3**	**6**	**0**	**0**	**0**	....
	Rochester	AHL	41	5	21	26	32	....	....	....	....	....	....	....	....	....	....	....	....	....	....	....	....	....	....
1993-94	**Buffalo**	**NHL**	**7**	**1**	**3**	**4**	**4**	**0**	**0**	**0**	**6**	**16.7**	**-1**	....	....	....	....	....	....	....	....	....	....	....	....
	Chicago	**NHL**	**30**	**3**	**5**	**8**	**35**	**0**	**0**	**0**	**31**	**9.7**	**15**	....	....	....	**6**	**0**	**1**	**1**	**4**	**0**	**0**	**0**	....
	Indianapolis Ice	IHL	28	0	14	14	20	....	....	....	....	....	....	....	....	....	....	....	....	....	....	....	....	....	....
1994-95	**Chicago**	**NHL**	**18**	**1**	**0**	**1**	**11**	**0**	**0**	**1**	**14**	**7.1**	**-1**	....	....	....	**4**	**0**	**1**	**1**	**0**	**0**	**0**	**0**	....
1995-96	**Chicago**	**NHL**	**82**	**5**	**14**	**19**	**94**	**1**	**0**	**1**	**69**	**7.2**	**31**	....	....	....	**10**	**0**	**3**	**3**	**4**	**0**	**0**	**0**	....
1996-97	**Chicago**	**NHL**	**81**	**3**	**15**	**18**	**62**	**0**	**0**	**1**	**77**	**3.9**	**26**	....	....	....	**6**	**1**	**1**	**2**	**2**	**0**	**0**	**0**	....
1997-98	**Chicago**	**NHL**	**60**	**2**	**13**	**15**	**73**	**0**	**1**	**0**	**53**	**3.8**	**-7**	....	....	....	....	....	....	....	....	....	....	....	....
	United States	Olympics	4	0	0	0	2	....	....	....	....	....	....	....	....	....	....	....	....	....	....	....	....	....	....
	Phoenix	**NHL**	**20**	**1**	**6**	**7**	**18**	**1**	**0**	**0**	**18**	**5.6**	**5**	....	....	....	**6**	**0**	**0**	**0**	**4**	**0**	**0**	**0**	....
1998-99	**Phoenix**	**NHL**	**82**	**2**	**14**	**16**	**62**	**0**	**2**	**0**	**62**	**3.2**	**15**	**0**	**0.0**	**22:46**	**7**	**1**	**2**	**3**	**10**	**0**	**0**	**0**	**23:59**
99-2000	**Phoenix**	**NHL**	**82**	**4**	**20**	**24**	**87**	**0**	**0**	**1**	**73**	**5.5**	**11**	**0**	**0.0**	**21:12**	**5**	**0**	**0**	**0**	**17**	**0**	**0**	**0**	**22:38**
2000-01	**Phoenix**	**NHL**	**82**	**2**	**14**	**16**	**86**	**0**	**0**	**0**	**65**	**3.1**	**15**	**0**	**0.0**	**20:53**	....	....	....	....	....	....	....	....	....
2001-02	**Anaheim**	**NHL**	**60**	**5**	**9**	**14**	**30**	**0**	**0**	**1**	**66**	**7.6**	**14**	**0**	**0.0**	**20:47**	....	....	....	....	....	....	....	....	....

Season	Club	League	GP	G	A	Pts	PIM	PP	SH	GW	S	%	+/-	TF	F%	Min	GP	G	A	Pts	PIM	PP	SH	GW	Min
			Regular Season														Playoffs								
2002-03	**Anaheim**	**NHL**	**81**	**4**	**18**	**22**	**65**	**0**	**0**	**1**	**87**	**4.6**	**8**	**0**	**0.0**	**0:00**	**21**	**0**	**4**	**4**	**16**	**0**	**0**	**0**	
2003-04	**Anaheim**	**NHL**	**69**	**2**	**5**	**7**	**42**	**1**	**0**	**0**	**58**	**3.4**	**-5**	**0**	**0.0**	**21:43**									
	NHL Totals		**798**	**38**	**142**	**180**	**742**	**4**	**3**	**7**	**722**	**5.3**		**0**	**0.0**	**17:41**	**80**	**2**	**18**	**20**	**63**	**0**	**0**	**0**	**23:25**

Hockey East Second All-Star Team (1990) • NCAA East Second All-American Team (1990) • Hockey East First All-Star Team (1991) • NCAA East First All-American Team (1991)

Traded to **Chicago** by **Buffalo** with Buffalo's 6th round choice (Marc Magliarditi) in 1995 Entry Draft for Craig Muni and Chicago's 5th round choice (Daniel Bienvenue) in 1995 Entry Draft, October 26, 1993. Traded to **Phoenix** by **Chicago** with Jim Cummins for Chad Kilger and Jayson More, March 4, 1998. Traded to **Anaheim** by **Phoenix** for Calgary's 2nd round choice (previously acquired, later traded back to Calgary – Calgary selected Andrei Taratukhin) in 2001 Entry Draft, June 19, 2001.

CARTER, Anson

(KAHR-tuhr, AN-sohn)

Right wing. Shoots right. 6'1", 200 lbs. Born, Toronto, Ont., June 6, 1974. Quebec's 11th choice, 220th overall, in 1992 Entry Draft.

Season	Club	League	GP	G	A	Pts	PIM	PP	SH	GW	S	%	+/-	TF	F%	Min	GP	G	A	Pts	PIM	PP	SH	GW	Min
1989-90	Don Mills	MTHL	40	15	47	62	105																		
1990-91	Don Mills	MTHL	67	69	73	142	43																		
1991-92	Wexford Raiders	MTJHL	42	18	22	40	24																		
1992-93	Michigan State	CCHA	34	15	7	22	20																		
1993-94	Michigan State	CCHA	39	30	24	54	36																		
1994-95	Michigan State	CCHA	39	34	17	51	40																		
1995-96	Michigan State	CCHA	42	23	20	43	36																		
1996-97	**Washington**	**NHL**	**19**	**3**	**2**	**5**	**7**	**1**	**0**	**1**	**28**	**10.7**	**0**												
	Portland Pirates	AHL	27	19	19	38	11																		
	Boston	**NHL**	**19**	**8**	**5**	**13**	**2**	**1**	**1**	**1**	**51**	**15.7**	**-7**												
1997-98	**Boston**	**NHL**	**78**	**16**	**27**	**43**	**31**	**6**	**0**	**4**	**179**	**8.9**	**7**				**6**	**1**	**1**	**2**	**0**	**0**	**0**	**0**	
1998-99	Utah Grizzlies	IHL	6	1	1	2	0																		
	Boston	**NHL**	**55**	**24**	**16**	**40**	**22**	**6**	**0**	**6**	**123**	**19.5**	**7**	**172**	**43.0**	**18:44**	**12**	**4**	**3**	**7**	**0**	**1**	**0**	**1**	**21:31**
99-2000	**Boston**	**NHL**	**59**	**22**	**25**	**47**	**14**	**4**	**0**	**1**	**144**	**15.3**	**8**	**793**	**48.2**	**20:31**									
2000-01	**Edmonton**	**NHL**	**61**	**16**	**26**	**42**	**23**	**7**	**1**	**4**	**102**	**15.7**	**1**	**80**	**47.5**	**18:13**	**6**	**3**	**1**	**4**	**4**	**1**	**0**	**1**	**19:42**
2001-02	**Edmonton**	**NHL**	**82**	**28**	**32**	**60**	**25**	**12**	**0**	**6**	**181**	**15.5**	**3**	**316**	**46.5**	**19:18**									
2002-03	**Edmonton**	**NHL**	**68**	**25**	**30**	**55**	**20**	**10**	**0**	**1**	**176**	**14.2**	**-11**	**217**	**43.8**	**19:39**									
	NY Rangers	**NHL**	**11**	**1**	**4**	**5**	**6**	**0**	**0**	**0**	**17**	**5.9**	**0**	**5**	**20.0**	**17:49**									
2003-04	**NY Rangers**	**NHL**	**43**	**10**	**7**	**17**	**14**	**4**	**1**	**2**	**63**	**15.9**	**-12**	**21**	**28.6**	**15:35**									
	Washington	**NHL**	**19**	**5**	**5**	**10**	**6**	**2**	**0**	**2**	**33**	**15.2**	**2**	**9**	**44.4**	**19:33**									
	Los Angeles	**NHL**	**15**	**0**	**1**	**1**	**0**	**0**	**0**	**0**	**18**	**0.0**	**-5**	**58**	**29.3**	**16:43**									
	NHL Totals		**529**	**158**	**180**	**338**	**170**	**53**	**3**	**28**	**1115**	**14.2**		**1671**	**45.7**	**18:47**	**24**	**8**	**5**	**13**	**4**	**2**	**0**	**2**	**20:54**

CCHA First All-Star Team (1994, 1995) • NCAA West Second All-American Team (1995) • CCHA Second All-Star Team (1996)

Rights transferred to **Colorado** after **Quebec** franchise relocated, June 21, 1995. Traded to **Washington** by **Colorado** for Washington's 4th round choice (Ben Storey) in 1996 Entry Draft, April 3, 1996. Traded to **Boston** by **Washington** with Jim Carey, Jason Allison and Washington's 3rd round choice (Lee Goren) in 1997 Entry Draft for Bill Ranford, Adam Oates and Rick Tocchet, March 1, 1997. Signed as a free agent by **Utah** (IHL) with Boston retaining NHL rights, October 20, 1998. Traded to **Edmonton** by **Boston** with Boston's 1st (Ales Hemsky) and 2nd (Doug Lynch) round choices in 2001 Entry Draft for Bill Guerin and future considerations, November 15, 2000. Traded to **NY Rangers** by **Edmonton** with Ales Pisa for Radek Dvorak and Cory Cross, March 11, 2003. Traded to **Washington** by **NY Rangers** for Jaromir Jagr, January 23, 2004. Traded to **Los Angeles** by **Washington** for Jared Aulin, March 8, 2004.

CASSELS, Andrew

(KAS-uhls, AN-droo) **CBJ**

Center. Shoots left. 6'1", 185 lbs. Born, Bramalea, Ont., July 23, 1969. Montreal's 1st choice, 17th overall, in 1987 Entry Draft.

Season	Club	League	GP	G	A	Pts	PIM	PP	SH	GW	S	%	+/-	TF	F%	Min	GP	G	A	Pts	PIM	PP	SH	GW	Min
1985-86	Bramalea Blues	OPJHL	33	18	25	43	26																		
1986-87	Ottawa 67's	OHL	66	26	66	92	28										11	5	9	14	7				
1987-88	Ottawa 67's	OHL	61	48	*103	*151	39										16	8	*24	*32	13				
1988-89	Ottawa 67's	OHL	56	37	97	134	66										12	5	10	15	10				
1989-90	**Montreal**	**NHL**	**6**	**2**	**0**	**2**	**2**	**0**	**0**	**1**	**5**	**40.0**	**1**												
	Sherbrooke	AHL	55	22	45	67	25										12	2	11	13	6				
1990-91	**Montreal**	**NHL**	**54**	**6**	**19**	**25**	**20**	**1**	**0**	**3**	**55**	**10.9**	**2**				**8**	**0**	**2**	**2**	**2**	**0**	**0**	**0**	
1991-92	**Hartford**	**NHL**	**67**	**11**	**30**	**41**	**18**	**2**	**2**	**3**	**99**	**11.1**	**3**				**7**	**2**	**4**	**6**	**6**	**1**	**0**	**0**	
1992-93	**Hartford**	**NHL**	**84**	**21**	**64**	**85**	**62**	**8**	**3**	**1**	**134**	**15.7**	**-11**												
1993-94	**Hartford**	**NHL**	**79**	**16**	**42**	**58**	**37**	**8**	**1**	**3**	**126**	**12.7**	**-21**												
1994-95	**Hartford**	**NHL**	**46**	**7**	**30**	**37**	**18**	**1**	**0**	**1**	**74**	**9.5**	**-3**												
1995-96	**Hartford**	**NHL**	**81**	**20**	**43**	**63**	**39**	**6**	**0**	**1**	**135**	**14.8**	**8**												
1996-97	**Hartford**	**NHL**	**81**	**22**	**44**	**66**	**46**	**8**	**0**	**2**	**142**	**15.5**	**-16**												
1997-98	**Calgary**	**NHL**	**81**	**17**	**27**	**44**	**32**	**6**	**1**	**2**	**138**	**12.3**	**-7**												
1998-99	**Calgary**	**NHL**	**70**	**12**	**25**	**37**	**18**	**4**	**1**	**3**	**97**	**12.4**	**-12**	**1322**	**51.1**	**18:58**									
99-2000	**Vancouver**	**NHL**	**79**	**17**	**45**	**62**	**16**	**6**	**0**	**1**	**109**	**15.6**	**8**	**1127**	**48.3**	**19:19**									
2000-01	**Vancouver**	**NHL**	**66**	**12**	**44**	**56**	**10**	**2**	**0**	**1**	**104**	**11.5**	**1**	**1164**	**49.9**	**19:22**									
2001-02	**Vancouver**	**NHL**	**53**	**11**	**39**	**50**	**22**	**7**	**0**	**1**	**64**	**17.2**	**5**	**866**	**50.4**	**17:27**	**6**	**2**	**1**	**3**	**0**	**1**	**0**	**0**	**16:55**
2002-03	**Columbus**	**NHL**	**79**	**20**	**48**	**68**	**30**	**9**	**1**	**5**	**113**	**17.7**	**-4**	**1649**	**48.8**	**19:52**									
2003-04	**Columbus**	**NHL**	**58**	**6**	**20**	**26**	**26**	**2**	**0**	**0**	**91**	**6.6**	**-24**	**1205**	**45.1**	**19:18**									
	NHL Totals		**984**	**200**	**520**	**720**	**396**	**70**	**9**	**28**	**1486**	**13.5**		**7333**	**48.9**	**19:07**	**21**	**4**	**7**	**11**	**8**	**2**	**0**	**0**	**16:55**

OHL Rookie of the Year (1987) • OHL First All-Star Team (1988,1989) • OHL MVP (1988)

Traded to **Hartford** by **Montreal** for Hartford's 2nd round choice (Valeri Bure) in 1992 Entry Draft, September 17, 1991. Transferred to **Carolina** after **Hartford** franchise relocated, June 25, 1997. Traded to **Calgary** by **Carolina** with Jean-Sebastien Giguere for Gary Roberts and Trevor Kidd, August 25, 1997. Signed as a free agent by **Vancouver**, August 19, 1999. Signed as a free agent by **Columbus**, August 15, 2002.

CHARA, Zdeno

(CHAH-rah, ZDEH-noh) **OTT.**

Defense. Shoots left. 6'9", 260 lbs. Born, Trencin, Czech., March 18, 1977. NY Islanders' 3rd choice, 56th overall, in 1996 Entry Draft.

Season	Club	League	GP	G	A	Pts	PIM	PP	SH	GW	S	%	+/-	TF	F%	Min	GP	G	A	Pts	PIM	PP	SH	GW	Min
1994-95	Dukla Trencin B	Slovak-Jr.	30	22	22	44	113																		
	Dukla Trencin Jr.	Slovak-Jr.	2	0	0	0	0																		
1995-96	Dukla Trencin Jr.	Slovak-Jr.	22	1	13	14	80																		
	HK VTJ Piestany	Slovak-2	10	1	3	4	10																		
	Sparta Praha Jr.	Czech-Jr.	15	1	2	3	42																		
	HC Sparta Praha	Czech	1	0	0	0	0																		
1996-97	Prince George	WHL	49	3	19	22	120										15	1	7	8	45				
1997-98	**NY Islanders**	**NHL**	**25**	**0**	**1**	**1**	**50**	**0**	**0**	**0**	**10**	**0.0**	**1**												
	Kentucky	AHL	48	4	9	13	125										1	0	0	0	4				
1998-99	**NY Islanders**	**NHL**	**59**	**2**	**6**	**8**	**83**	**0**	**1**	**0**	**56**	**3.6**	**-8**	**0**	**0.0**	**18:54**									
	Lowell	AHL	23	2	2	4	47																		
99-2000	**NY Islanders**	**NHL**	**65**	**2**	**9**	**11**	**57**	**0**	**0**	**1**	**47**	**4.3**	**-27**	**0**	**0.0**	**22:52**									
2000-01	**NY Islanders**	**NHL**	**82**	**2**	**7**	**9**	**157**	**0**	**1**	**0**	**83**	**2.4**	**-27**	**0**	**0.0**	**22:20**									
2001-02	Dukla Trencin	Slovakia	8	2	2	4	32																		
	Ottawa	**NHL**	**75**	**10**	**13**	**23**	**156**	**4**	**1**	**2**	**105**	**9.5**	**30**	**0**	**0.0**	**22:16**	**10**	**0**	**1**	**1**	**12**	**0**	**0**	**0**	**26:07**
2002-03	**Ottawa**	**NHL**	**74**	**9**	**30**	**39**	**116**	**3**	**0**	**2**	**168**	**5.4**	**29**	**0**	**0.0**	**24:57**	**18**	**1**	**6**	**7**	**14**	**0**	**0**	**0**	**25:07**
2003-04	**Ottawa**	**NHL**	**79**	**16**	**25**	**41**	**147**	**7**	**0**	**3**	**185**	**8.6**	**33**	**0**	**0.0**	**24:38**	**7**	**1**	**1**	**2**	**8**	**0**	**0**	**0**	**24:38**
	NHL Totals		**459**	**41**	**91**	**132**	**766**	**14**	**3**	**8**	**654**	**6.3**		**0**	**0.0**	**22:48**	**35**	**2**	**8**	**10**	**34**	**0**	**0**	**0**	**25:18**

NHL First All-Star Team (2004)

Played in NHL All-Star Game (2003)

Traded to **Ottawa** by **NY Islanders** with Bill Muckalt and NY Islanders' 1st round choice (Jason Spezza) in 2001 Entry Draft for Alexei Yashin, June 23, 2001.

CHARTRAND, Brad

(SHAR-trand, BRAD)

Center. Shoots left. 5'11", 185 lbs. Born, Winnipeg, Man., December 14, 1974.

Season	Club	League	GP	G	A	Pts	PIM	PP	SH	GW	S	%	+/-	TF	F%	Min	GP	G	A	Pts	PIM	PP	SH	GW	Min
1988-89	Winnipeg Hawks	MMHL	24	30	50	80	40																		
1989-90	Winnipeg Hawks	MMHL	24	26	55	81	40																		
1990-91	Winnipeg Hawks	MMHL	34	26	45	71	40																		
1991-92	St. James	MJHL	45	24	25	49	32																		
1992-93	Cornell Big Red	ECAC	26	10	6	16	16																		
1993-94	Cornell Big Red	ECAC	30	4	14	18	48																		
1994-95	Cornell Big Red	ECAC	28	9	9	18	10																		
1995-96	Cornell Big Red	ECAC	34	24	19	43	16																		
1996-97	Team Canada	Nat-Tm	54	10	14	24	42																		
1997-98	Team Canada	Nat-Tm	60	24	30	54	47																		
	Rapperswil	Swiss	8	2	3	5	4																		
1998-99	St. John's	AHL	64	16	14	30	48										5	0	2	2	2				

			Regular Season														Playoffs								
Season	Club	League	GP	G	A	Pts	PIM	PP	SH	GW	S	%	+/-	TF	F%	Min	GP	G	A	Pts	PIM	PP	SH	GW	Min
99-2000	**Los Angeles**	**NHL**	**50**	**6**	**6**	**12**	**17**	**0**	**1**	**3**	**51**	**11.8**	**4**	**62**	**53.2**	**11:03**	**4**	**0**	**0**	**0**	**6**	**0**	**0**	**0**	**8:09**
	Lowell	AHL	16	5	10	15	8	....	....	....	....	....	....	....	....	....	....	....	....	....	....	....	....	....	....
	Long Beach	IHL	1	0	0	0	0	....	....	....	....	....	....	....	....	....	3	0	0	0	0	....	....	....	....
2000-01	**Los Angeles**	**NHL**	**4**	**1**	**0**	**1**	**2**	**0**	**0**	**1**	**6**	**16.7**	**–2**	**0**	**0.0**	**11:37**	....	....	....	....	....	....	....	....	....
	Lowell	AHL	72	17	34	51	44	....	....	....	....	....	....	....	....	....	4	0	1	1	8	....	....	....	....
2001-02	**Los Angeles**	**NHL**	**46**	**7**	**9**	**16**	**40**	**0**	**0**	**1**	**49**	**14.3**	**5**	**481**	**53.2**	**12:05**	**7**	**1**	**1**	**2**	**2**	**0**	**0**	**1**	**11:07**
	Manchester	AHL	22	10	12	22	31	....	....	....	....	....	....	....	....	....	....	....	....	....	....	....	....	....	....
2002-03	**Los Angeles**	**NHL**	**62**	**8**	**6**	**14**	**33**	**0**	**1**	**2**	**64**	**12.5**	**–10**	**623**	**51.4**	**12:14**	....	....	....	....	....	....	....	....	....
2003-04	**Los Angeles**	**NHL**	**53**	**3**	**4**	**7**	**30**	**0**	**1**	**0**	**63**	**4.8**	**–3**	**290**	**54.1**	**11:36**	....	....	....	....	....	....	....	....	....
	NHL Totals		**215**	**25**	**25**	**50**	**122**	**0**	**3**	**7**	**233**	**10.7**		**1456**	**52.6**	**11:46**	**11**	**1**	**1**	**2**	**8**	**0**	**0**	**1**	**10:03**

Signed as a free agent by **Los Angeles**, July 15, 1999.

CHEECHOO, Jonathan

(CHEE-choo, JAWN-ah-thuhn) **S.J.**

Right wing. Shoots right. 6'1", 190 lbs. Born, Moose Factory, Ont., July 15, 1980. San Jose's 2nd choice, 29th overall, in 1998 Entry Draft.

1996-97	Kitchener	OJHL-B	43	35	41	76	33	....	....	....	....	....	....	....	....	....	....	....	....	....	....	....	....	....	....
1997-98	Belleville Bulls	OHL	64	31	45	76	62	....	....	....	....	....	....	....	....	....	10	4	2	6	10	....	....	....	....
1998-99	Belleville Bulls	OHL	63	35	47	82	74	....	....	....	....	....	....	....	....	....	21	15	15	30	27	....	....	....	....
99-2000	Belleville Bulls	OHL	66	45	46	91	102	....	....	....	....	....	....	....	....	....	16	5	12	17	16	....	....	....	....
2000-01	Kentucky	AHL	75	32	34	66	63	....	....	....	....	....	....	....	....	....	3	0	0	0	0	....	....	....	....
2001-02	Cleveland Barons	AHL	53	21	25	46	54	....	....	....	....	....	....	....	....	....	....	....	....	....	....	....	....	....	....
2002-03	**San Jose**	**NHL**	**66**	**9**	**7**	**16**	**39**	**0**	**0**	**3**	**94**	**9.6**	**–5**	**8**	**37.5**	**10:43**	....	....	....	....	....	....	....	....	....
	Cleveland Barons	AHL	9	3	4	7	16	....	....	....	....	....	....	....	....	....	....	....	....	....	....	....	....	....	....
2003-04	**San Jose**	**NHL**	**81**	**28**	**19**	**47**	**33**	**8**	**0**	**9**	**175**	**16.0**	**5**	**7**	**14.3**	**16:12**	**17**	**4**	**6**	**10**	**10**	**1**	**0**	**0**	**17:37**
	NHL Totals		**147**	**37**	**26**	**63**	**72**	**8**	**0**	**12**	**269**	**13.8**		**15**	**26.7**	**13:44**	**17**	**4**	**6**	**10**	**10**	**1**	**0**	**0**	**17:37**

OHL All-Rookie Team (1998)

CHELIOS, Chris

(CHELL-EE-ohs, KRIHS) **DET.**

Defense. Shoots right. 6'1", 190 lbs. Born, Chicago, IL, January 25, 1962. Montreal's 5th choice, 40th overall, in 1981 Entry Draft.

1979-80	Moose Jaw	SJHL	53	12	31	43	118	....	....	....	....	....	....	....	....	....	....	....	....	....	....	....	....	....	....
1980-81	Moose Jaw	SJHL	54	23	64	87	175	....	....	....	....	....	....	....	....	....	....	....	....	....	....	....	....	....	....
1981-82	U. of Wisconsin	WCHA	43	6	43	49	50	....	....	....	....	....	....	....	....	....	....	....	....	....	....	....	....	....	....
1982-83	U. of Wisconsin	WCHA	26	9	17	26	50	....	....	....	....	....	....	....	....	....	....	....	....	....	....	....	....	....	....
1983-84	Team USA	Nat-Tm	60	14	35	49	58	....	....	....	....	....	....	....	....	....	....	....	....	....	....	....	....	....	....
	United States	Olympics	6	0	4	4	8	....	....	....	....	....	....	....	....	....	....	....	....	....	....	....	....	....	....
	Montreal	**NHL**	**12**	**0**	**2**	**2**	**12**	**0**	**0**	**0**	**23**	**0.0**	**–5**	....	....	....	**15**	**1**	**9**	**10**	**17**	**1**	**0**	**0**	....
1984-85	**Montreal**	**NHL**	**74**	**9**	**55**	**64**	**87**	**2**	**1**	**0**	**199**	**4.5**	**11**	....	....	....	**9**	**2**	**8**	**10**	**17**	**2**	**0**	**0**	....
1985-86 ♦	**Montreal**	**NHL**	**41**	**8**	**26**	**34**	**67**	**2**	**0**	**0**	**101**	**7.9**	**4**	....	....	....	**20**	**2**	**9**	**11**	**49**	**1**	**0**	**0**	....
1986-87	**Montreal**	**NHL**	**71**	**11**	**33**	**44**	**124**	**6**	**0**	**2**	**141**	**7.8**	**–5**	....	....	....	**17**	**4**	**9**	**13**	**38**	**2**	**1**	**0**	....
1987-88	**Montreal**	**NHL**	**71**	**20**	**41**	**61**	**172**	**10**	**1**	**5**	**199**	**10.1**	**14**	....	....	....	**11**	**3**	**1**	**4**	**29**	**1**	**0**	**0**	....
1988-89	**Montreal**	**NHL**	**80**	**15**	**58**	**73**	**185**	**8**	**0**	**6**	**206**	**7.3**	**35**	....	....	....	**21**	**4**	**15**	**19**	**28**	**1**	**0**	**2**	....
1989-90	**Montreal**	**NHL**	**53**	**9**	**22**	**31**	**136**	**1**	**2**	**1**	**123**	**7.3**	**20**	....	....	....	**5**	**0**	**1**	**1**	**8**	**0**	**0**	**0**	....
1990-91	**Chicago**	**NHL**	**77**	**12**	**52**	**64**	**192**	**5**	**2**	**2**	**187**	**6.4**	**23**	....	....	....	**6**	**1**	**7**	**8**	**46**	**1**	**0**	**0**	....
1991-92	**Chicago**	**NHL**	**80**	**9**	**47**	**56**	**245**	**2**	**2**	**2**	**239**	**3.8**	**24**	....	....	....	**18**	**6**	**15**	**21**	**37**	**3**	**0**	**1**	....
1992-93	**Chicago**	**NHL**	**84**	**15**	**58**	**73**	**282**	**8**	**0**	**2**	**290**	**5.2**	**14**	....	....	....	**4**	**0**	**2**	**2**	**14**	**0**	**0**	**0**	....
1993-94	**Chicago**	**NHL**	**76**	**16**	**44**	**60**	**212**	**7**	**1**	**2**	**219**	**7.3**	**12**	....	....	....	**6**	**1**	**1**	**2**	**8**	**1**	**0**	**0**	....
1994-95	EHC Biel-Bienne	Swiss	3	0	3	3	4	....	....	....	....	....	....	....	....	....	....	....	....	....	....	....	....	....	....
	Chicago	**NHL**	**48**	**5**	**33**	**38**	**72**	**3**	**1**	**0**	**166**	**3.0**	**17**	....	....	....	**16**	**4**	**7**	**11**	**12**	**0**	**1**	**3**	....
1995-96	**Chicago**	**NHL**	**81**	**14**	**58**	**72**	**140**	**7**	**0**	**3**	**219**	**6.4**	**25**	....	....	....	**9**	**0**	**3**	**3**	**8**	**0**	**0**	**0**	....
1996-97	**Chicago**	**NHL**	**72**	**10**	**38**	**48**	**112**	**2**	**0**	**2**	**194**	**5.2**	**16**	....	....	....	**6**	**0**	**1**	**1**	**8**	**0**	**0**	**0**	....
1997-98	**Chicago**	**NHL**	**81**	**3**	**39**	**42**	**151**	**1**	**0**	**0**	**205**	**1.5**	**–7**	....	....	....	....	....	....	....	....	....	....	....	....
	United States	Olympics	4	2	0	2	2	....	....	....	....	....	....	....	....	....	....	....	....	....	....	....	....	....	....
1998-99	**Chicago**	**NHL**	**65**	**8**	**26**	**34**	**89**	**2**	**1**	**0**	**172**	**4.7**	**–4**	**4**	**25.0**	**27:19**	....	....	....	....	....	....	....	....	....
	Detroit	**NHL**	**10**	**1**	**1**	**2**	**4**	**1**	**0**	**1**	**15**	**6.7**	**5**	**0**	**0.0**	**22:21**	**10**	**0**	**4**	**4**	**14**	**0**	**0**	**0**	**27:15**
99-2000	**Detroit**	**NHL**	**81**	**3**	**31**	**34**	**103**	**0**	**0**	**0**	**135**	**2.2**	**48**	**0**	**0.0**	**25:16**	**9**	**0**	**1**	**1**	**8**	**0**	**0**	**0**	**24:06**
2000-01	**Detroit**	**NHL**	**24**	**0**	**3**	**3**	**45**	**0**	**0**	**0**	**26**	**0.0**	**4**	**0**	**0.0**	**22:51**	**5**	**1**	**0**	**1**	**2**	**0**	**0**	**0**	**19:41**
2001-02 ♦	**Detroit**	**NHL**	**79**	**6**	**33**	**39**	**126**	**1**	**0**	**1**	**128**	**4.7**	**40**	**0**	**0.0**	**25:18**	**23**	**1**	**13**	**14**	**44**	**1**	**0**	**0**	**26:22**
	United States	Olympics	6	1	0	1	4	....	....	....	....	....	....	....	....	....	....	....	....	....	....	....	....	....	....
2002-03	**Detroit**	**NHL**	**66**	**2**	**17**	**19**	**78**	**0**	**1**	**1**	**92**	**2.2**	**4**	**0**	**0.0**	**24:15**	**4**	**0**	**0**	**0**	**2**	**0**	**0**	**0**	**25:43**
2003-04	**Detroit**	**NHL**	**69**	**2**	**19**	**21**	**61**	**0**	**0**	**0**	**113**	**1.8**	**12**	**0**	**0.0**	**21:21**	**8**	**0**	**1**	**1**	**4**	**0**	**0**	**0**	**21:13**
	NHL Totals		**1395**	**178**	**736**	**914**	**2695**	**68**	**12**	**30**	**3392**	**5.2**		**4**	**25.0**	**24:32**	**222**	**30**	**107**	**137**	**393**	**14**	**2**	**6**	**24:52**

WCHA Second All-Star Team (1983) • NCAA Championship All-Tournament Team (1983) • NHL All-Rookie Team (1985) • NHL First All-Star Team (1989, 1993, 1995, 1996, 2002) • James Norris Memorial Trophy (1989, 1993, 1996) • NHL Second All-Star Team (1991, 1997) • Bud Light Plus/Minus Award (2002)

Played in NHL All-Star Game (1985, 1990, 1991, 1992, 1993, 1994, 1996, 1997, 1998, 2000, 2002)

Traded to **Chicago** by **Montreal** with Montreal's 2nd round choice (Michael Pomichter) in 1991 Entry Draft for Denis Savard, June 29, 1990. Traded to **Detroit** by **Chicago** for Anders Eriksson and Detroit's 1st round choices in 1999 (Steve McCarthy) and 2001 (Adam Munro) Entry Drafts, March 23, 1999. • Missed majority of 2000-01 season recovering from knee injury suffered in game vs. Dallas, November 17, 2000.

CHIMERA, Jason

(chihm-AIR-a, JAY-suhn) **PHX.**

Left wing. Shoots left. 6'2", 206 lbs. Born, Edmonton, Alta., May 2, 1979. Edmonton's 5th choice, 121st overall, in 1997 Entry Draft.

1994-95	Edmonton Pats	AMHL	33	27	31	58	42	....	....	....	....	....	....	....	....	....	....	....	....	....	....	....	....	....	....
1995-96	Edmonton Pats	AMHL	34	23	24	47	44	....	....	....	....	....	....	....	....	....	....	....	....	....	....	....	....	....	....
1996-97	Medicine Hat	WHL	71	16	23	39	64	....	....	....	....	....	....	....	....	....	4	0	1	1	4	....	....	....	....
1997-98	Medicine Hat	WHL	72	34	32	66	93	....	....	....	....	....	....	....	....	....	....	....	....	....	....	....	....	....	....
	Hamilton	AHL	4	0	0	0	8	....	....	....	....	....	....	....	....	....	....	....	....	....	....	....	....	....	....
1998-99	Medicine Hat	WHL	37	18	22	40	84	....	....	....	....	....	....	....	....	....	....	....	....	....	....	....	....	....	....
	Brandon	WHL	21	14	12	26	32	....	....	....	....	....	....	....	....	....	5	4	1	5	8	....	....	....	....
99-2000	Hamilton	AHL	78	15	13	28	77	....	....	....	....	....	....	....	....	....	10	0	2	2	12	....	....	....	....
2000-01	**Edmonton**	**NHL**	**1**	**0**	**0**	**0**	**0**	**0**	**0**	**0**	**0**	**0.0**	**0**	**0**	**0.0**	**6:58**	....	....	....	....	....	....	....	....	....
	Hamilton	AHL	78	29	25	54	93	....	....	....	....	....	....	....	....	....	....	....	....	....	....	....	....	....	....
2001-02	**Edmonton**	**NHL**	**3**	**1**	**0**	**1**	**0**	**0**	**0**	**0**	**3**	**33.3**	**–3**	**0**	**0.0**	**12:44**	....	....	....	....	....	....	....	....	....
	Hamilton	AHL	77	26	51	77	158	....	....	....	....	....	....	....	....	....	15	4	6	10	10	....	....	....	....
2002-03	**Edmonton**	**NHL**	**66**	**14**	**9**	**23**	**36**	**0**	**1**	**4**	**90**	**15.6**	**–2**	**11**	**54.6**	**10:46**	**2**	**0**	**2**	**2**	**0**	**0**	**0**	**0**	**10:55**
2003-04	**Edmonton**	**NHL**	**60**	**4**	**8**	**12**	**57**	**0**	**0**	**1**	**79**	**5.1**	**–1**	**22**	**31.8**	**10:07**	....	....	....	....	....	....	....	....	....
	NHL Totals		**130**	**19**	**17**	**36**	**93**	**0**	**1**	**5**	**172**	**11.0**		**33**	**39.4**	**10:29**	**2**	**0**	**2**	**2**	**0**	**0**	**0**	**0**	**10:54**

AHL First All-Star Team (2002)

Traded to **Phoenix** by **Edmonton** with Edmonton's 3rd round choice (later transferred to Carolina – later traded to NY Rangers – NY Rangers selected Billy Ryan) in 2004 Entry Draft for New Jersey's 2nd round choice (previously acquired, Edmonton selected Geoff Paukovich) in 2004 Entry Draft and Buffalo's 4th round choice (previously acquired, Edmonton selected Liam Reddox) in 2004 Entry Draft, June 26, 2004.

CHISTOV, Stanislav

(chihs-TAHV, STAHN-ihs-lahv) **ANA.**

Left wing. Shoots right. 5'10", 193 lbs. Born, Chelyabinsk, USSR, April 17, 1983. Anaheim's 1st choice, 5th overall, in 2001 Entry Draft.

1998-99	Chelyabinsk 2	Russia-4	1	0	0	0	0	....	....	....	....	....	....	....	....	....	....	....	....	....	....	....	....	....	....
	Georgetown	OPJHL	14	10	7	17	21	....	....	....	....	....	....	....	....	....	....	....	....	....	....	....	....	....	....
99-2000	Omsk Jr.	Russia-Jr.	5	4	3	7	8	....	....	....	....	....	....	....	....	....	....	....	....	....	....	....	....	....	....
	Omsk 2	Russia-3	18	12	4	16	24	....	....	....	....	....	....	....	....	....	....	....	....	....	....	....	....	....	....
	Novokuznetsk	Russia	9	7	4	11	18	....	....	....	....	....	....	....	....	....	....	....	....	....	....	....	....	....	....
	Avangard Omsk	Russia	3	1	0	1	2	....	....	....	....	....	....	....	....	....	....	....	....	....	....	....	....	....	....
2000-01	Omsk 2	Russia-3	8	5	4	9	2	....	....	....	....	....	....	....	....	....	....	....	....	....	....	....	....	....	....
	Avangard Omsk	Russia	24	4	8	12	12	....	....	....	....	....	....	....	....	....	5	0	0	0	2	....	....	....	....
2001-02	Avangard Omsk	Russia	9	0	0	0	4	....	....	....	....	....	....	....	....	....	....	....	....	....	....	....	....	....	....
	CSKA Moscow 2	Russia-3	1	1	2	3	0	....	....	....	....	....	....	....	....	....	....	....	....	....	....	....	....	....	....
2002-03	**Anaheim**	**NHL**	**79**	**12**	**18**	**30**	**54**	**3**	**0**	**2**	**114**	**10.5**	**4**	**3**	**0.0**	**13:35**	**21**	**4**	**2**	**6**	**8**	**0**	**0**	**1**	**13:22**
2003-04	**Anaheim**	**NHL**	**56**	**2**	**16**	**18**	**26**	**2**	**0**	**0**	**70**	**2.9**	**–16**	**4**	**0.0**	**12:20**	....	....	....	....	....	....	....	....	....
	Cincinnati	AHL	23	5	8	13	45	....	....	....	....	....	....	....	....	....	9	6	2	8	4	....	....	....	....
	NHL Totals		**135**	**14**	**34**	**48**	**80**	**5**	**0**	**2**	**184**	**7.6**		**7**	**0.0**	**13:04**	**21**	**4**	**2**	**6**	**8**	**0**	**0**	**1**	**13:22**

			Regular Season														Playoffs								
Season	Club	League	GP	G	A	Pts	PIM	PP	SH	GW	S	%	+/-	TF	F%	Min	GP	G	A	Pts	PIM	PP	SH	GW	Min

CHOUINARD, Eric

(shwee-NAHR, AIR-ihk)

Left wing. Shoots left. 6'3", 215 lbs. Born, Atlanta, GA, July 8, 1980. Montreal's 1st choice, 16th overall, in 1998 Entry Draft.

Season	Club	League	GP	G	A	Pts	PIM	PP	SH	GW	S	%	+/-	TF	F%	Min	GP	G	A	Pts	PIM	PP	SH	GW	Min
1995-96	Magog	QAHA	22	12	14	26	12	....	....	....	....	....	....	....	....	....	....	....	....	....	....	....	....	....	....
	Ste-Foy	QAAA	17	2	5	7	....	....	....	....	....	....	....	....	....	....	15	7	12	19	12	....	....	....	....
1996-97	Ste-Foy	QAAA	40	29	41	70	40	....	....	....	....	....	....	....	....	....	10	14	9	23	....	....	....	....	....
1997-98	Quebec Remparts	QMJHL	68	41	42	83	18	....	....	....	....	....	....	....	....	....	14	7	10	17	6	....	....	....	....
1998-99	Quebec Remparts	QMJHL	62	50	59	109	56	....	....	....	....	....	....	....	....	....	13	8	10	18	8	....	....	....	....
	Fredericton	AHL	....	....	....	....	....	....	....	....	....	....	....	....	....	....	6	3	2	5	0	....	....	....	....
99-2000	Quebec Remparts	QMJHL	50	57	47	104	105	....	....	....	....	....	....	....	....	....	11	14	4	18	8	....	....	....	....
2000-01	**Montreal**	**NHL**	**13**	**1**	**3**	**4**	**0**	**1**	**0**	**0**	**11**	**9.1**	**0**	**31**	**54.8**	**10:59**	....	....	....	....	....	....	....	....	....
	Quebec Citadelles	AHL	48	12	21	33	6	....	....	....	....	....	....	....	....	....	9	2	0	2	2	....	....	....	....
2001-02	Quebec Citadelles	AHL	65	19	23	42	18	....	....	....	....	....	....	....	....	....	2	0	0	0	0	....	....	....	....
2002-03	Utah Grizzlies	AHL	32	12	12	24	16	....	....	....	....	....	....	....	....	....	....	....	....	....	....	....	....	....	....
	Philadelphia	**NHL**	**28**	**4**	**4**	**8**	**8**	**1**	**0**	**0**	**45**	**8.9**	**2**	**12**	**33.3**	**9:38**	....	....	....	....	....	....	....	....	....
2003-04	**Philadelphia**	**NHL**	**17**	**3**	**0**	**3**	**0**	**0**	**0**	**0**	**15**	**20.0**	**–3**	**24**	**50.0**	**7:59**	....	....	....	....	....	....	....	....	....
	Philadelphia	AHL	1	0	0	0	0	....	....	....	....	....	....	....	....	....	....	....	....	....	....	....	....	....	....
	Minnesota	**NHL**	**31**	**3**	**4**	**7**	**6**	**0**	**0**	**1**	**45**	**6.7**	**–7**	**261**	**44.8**	**13:36**	....	....	....	....	....	....	....	....	....
	NHL Totals		**89**	**11**	**11**	**22**	**14**	**2**	**0**	**1**	**116**	**9.5**		**328**	**45.7**	**10:54**	....	....	....	....	....	....	....	....	....

Traded to **Philadelphia** by **Montreal** for Philadelphia's 2nd round choice (Maxim Lapierre) in 2003 Entry Draft, January 29, 2003. Traded to **Minnesota** by **Philadelphia** for Minnesota's 5th round choice (Chris Zarb) in 2004 Entry Draft, December 17, 2003.

CHOUINARD, Marc

(shwee-NAHR, MAHRK) **MIN.**

Center. Shoots right. 6'5", 218 lbs. Born, Charlesbourg, Que., May 6, 1977. Winnipeg's 2nd choice, 32nd overall, in 1995 Entry Draft.

Season	Club	League	GP	G	A	Pts	PIM	PP	SH	GW	S	%	+/-	TF	F%	Min	GP	G	A	Pts	PIM	PP	SH	GW	Min
1992-93	Beaubourg Selects	QAHA	28	26	45	71	42	....	....	....	....	....	....	....	....	....	....	....	....	....	....	....	....	....	....
	Ste-Foy	QAAA	3	1	1	2	2	....	....	....	....	....	....	....	....	....	....	....	....	....	....	....	....	....	....
1993-94	Beauport	QMJHL	62	11	19	30	23	....	....	....	....	....	....	....	....	....	13	2	5	7	2	....	....	....	....
1994-95	Beauport	QMJHL	68	24	40	64	32	....	....	....	....	....	....	....	....	....	18	1	6	7	4	....	....	....	....
1995-96	Beauport	QMJHL	30	14	21	35	19	....	....	....	....	....	....	....	....	....	....	....	....	....	....	....	....	....	....
	Halifax	QMJHL	24	6	12	18	17	....	....	....	....	....	....	....	....	....	6	2	1	3	2	....	....	....	....
1996-97	Halifax	QMJHL	63	24	49	73	74	....	....	....	....	....	....	....	....	....	18	9	16	25	12	....	....	....	....
1997-98	Cincinnati	AHL	8	1	2	3	4	....	....	....	....	....	....	....	....	....	....	....	....	....	....	....	....	....	....
1998-99	Cincinnati	AHL	69	7	8	15	20	....	....	....	....	....	....	....	....	....	3	0	0	0	4	....	....	....	....
99-2000	Cincinnati	AHL	70	17	16	33	29	....	....	....	....	....	....	....	....	....	....	....	....	....	....	....	....	....	....
2000-01	**Anaheim**	**NHL**	**44**	**3**	**4**	**7**	**12**	**0**	**0**	**1**	**26**	**11.5**	**–5**	**414**	**60.9**	**7:50**	....	....	....	....	....	....	....	....	....
	Cincinnati	AHL	32	10	9	19	4	....	....	....	....	....	....	....	....	....	....	....	....	....	....	....	....	....	....
2001-02	**Anaheim**	**NHL**	**45**	**4**	**5**	**9**	**10**	**0**	**0**	**0**	**40**	**10.0**	**2**	**581**	**54.9**	**10:36**	....	....	....	....	....	....	....	....	....
2002-03	**Anaheim**	**NHL**	**70**	**3**	**4**	**7**	**40**	**0**	**1**	**0**	**52**	**5.8**	**–9**	**662**	**54.5**	**9:25**	**15**	**1**	**0**	**1**	**0**	**0**	**0**	**0**	**7:16**
2003-04	**Minnesota**	**NHL**	**45**	**11**	**10**	**21**	**17**	**3**	**1**	**2**	**70**	**15.7**	**4**	**809**	**53.7**	**15:58**	....	....	....	....	....	....	....	....	....
	NHL Totals		**204**	**21**	**23**	**44**	**79**	**3**	**2**	**3**	**188**	**11.2**		**2466**	**55.4**	**10:47**	**15**	**1**	**0**	**1**	**0**	**0**	**0**	**0**	**7:16**

Traded to **Anaheim** by **Winnipeg** with Teemu Selanne and Winnipeg's 4th round choice (later traded to Toronto – later traded to Montreal – Montreal selected Kim Staal) in 1996 Entry Draft for Chad Kilger, Oleg Tverdovsky and Anaheim's 3rd round choice (Per-Anton Lundstrom) in 1996 Entry Draft, February 7, 1996. Signed as a free agent by **Minnesota**, July 28, 2003.

CHRISTIE, Ryan

(KRIHS-tee, RIGH-yuhn)

Left wing. Shoots left. 6'3", 200 lbs. Born, Beamsville, Ont., July 3, 1978. Dallas' 4th choice, 112th overall, in 1996 Entry Draft.

Season	Club	League	GP	G	A	Pts	PIM	PP	SH	GW	S	%	+/-	TF	F%	Min	GP	G	A	Pts	PIM	PP	SH	GW	Min
1994-95	St. Catharines	OJHL-B	40	10	11	21	96	....	....	....	....	....	....	....	....	....	....	....	....	....	....	....	....	....	....
1995-96	Owen Sound	OHL	66	29	17	46	93	....	....	....	....	....	....	....	....	....	6	1	1	2	0	....	....	....	....
1996-97	Owen Sound	OHL	66	23	29	52	136	....	....	....	....	....	....	....	....	....	4	1	1	2	8	....	....	....	....
1997-98	Owen Sound	OHL	66	39	41	80	208	....	....	....	....	....	....	....	....	....	11	3	5	8	13	....	....	....	....
1998-99	Michigan	IHL	48	4	5	9	74	....	....	....	....	....	....	....	....	....	3	1	1	2	2	....	....	....	....
99-2000	**Dallas**	**NHL**	**5**	**0**	**0**	**0**	**0**	**0**	**0**	**0**	**1**	**0.0**	**–1**	**0**	**0.0**	**2:29**	....	....	....	....	....	....	....	....	....
	Michigan	IHL	76	24	25	49	140	....	....	....	....	....	....	....	....	....	....	....	....	....	....	....	....	....	....
2000-01	Utah Grizzlies	IHL	69	22	16	38	88	....	....	....	....	....	....	....	....	....	....	....	....	....	....	....	....	....	....
2001-02	**Calgary**	**NHL**	**2**	**0**	**0**	**0**	**0**	**0**	**0**	**0**	**0**	**0.0**	**–1**	**0**	**0.0**	**6:10**	....	....	....	....	....	....	....	....	....
	Saint John Flames	AHL	77	21	18	39	61	....	....	....	....	....	....	....	....	....	....	....	....	....	....	....	....	....	....
2002-03	Saint John Flames	AHL	67	10	14	24	84	....	....	....	....	....	....	....	....	....	....	....	....	....	....	....	....	....	....
2003-04	Las Vegas	ECHL	60	16	11	27	142	....	....	....	....	....	....	....	....	....	4	3	1	4	2	....	....	....	....
	Toronto	AHL	3	0	0	0	0	....	....	....	....	....	....	....	....	....	....	....	....	....	....	....	....	....	....
	NHL Totals		**7**	**0**	**0**	**0**	**0**	**0**	**0**	**0**	**1**	**0.0**		**0**	**0.0**	**3:32**	....	....	....	....	....	....	....	....	....

Signed as a free agent by **Calgary**, July 1, 2001. Signed as a free agent by **Las Vegas** (ECHL), October 20, 2003. Signed to a tryout (PTO) contract by **Toronto** (AHL), February 22, 2004.

CHUBAROV, Artem

(choo-BAH-rahf, AHR-tehm) **VAN.**

Center. Shoots left. 6'1", 189 lbs. Born, Gorky, USSR, December 12, 1979. Vancouver's 2nd choice, 31st overall, in 1998 Entry Draft.

Season	Club	League	GP	G	A	Pts	PIM	PP	SH	GW	S	%	+/-	TF	F%	Min	GP	G	A	Pts	PIM	PP	SH	GW	Min
1994-95	Niz. Novgorod Jr.	CIS-Jr.	60	20	30	50	20	....	....	....	....	....	....	....	....	....	....	....	....	....	....	....	....	....	....
1995-96	Niz. Novgorod Jr.	CIS-Jr.	60	22	25	47	20	....	....	....	....	....	....	....	....	....	....	....	....	....	....	....	....	....	....
1996-97	Niz. Novgorod 2	Russia-3	40	24	5	29	16	....	....	....	....	....	....	....	....	....	....	....	....	....	....	....	....	....	....
	Nizhny Novgorod	Russia	15	1	1	2	8	....	....	....	....	....	....	....	....	....	....	....	....	....	....	....	....	....	....
1997-98	Dynamo Moscow	Russia	30	1	4	5	4	....	....	....	....	....	....	....	....	....	....	....	....	....	....	....	....	....	....
1998-99	Dynamo Moscow	Russia	34	8	2	10	10	....	....	....	....	....	....	....	....	....	12	0	0	0	4	....	....	....	....
99-2000	**Vancouver**	**NHL**	**49**	**1**	**8**	**9**	**10**	**0**	**0**	**1**	**53**	**1.9**	**–4**	**488**	**48.0**	**11:43**	....	....	....	....	....	....	....	....	....
	Syracuse Crunch	AHL	14	7	6	13	4	....	....	....	....	....	....	....	....	....	1	0	0	0	0	....	....	....	....
2000-01	**Vancouver**	**NHL**	**1**	**0**	**0**	**0**	**0**	**0**	**0**	**0**	**0**	**0.0**	**–1**	**17**	**52.9**	**15:08**	....	....	....	....	....	....	....	....	....
	Kansas City	IHL	10	7	4	11	12	....	....	....	....	....	....	....	....	....	....	....	....	....	....	....	....	....	....
2001-02	**Vancouver**	**NHL**	**51**	**5**	**5**	**10**	**10**	**0**	**0**	**3**	**73**	**6.8**	**–3**	**517**	**53.6**	**12:37**	**6**	**0**	**1**	**1**	**0**	**0**	**0**	**0**	**14:44**
	Manitoba Moose	AHL	19	7	12	19	4	....	....	....	....	....	....	....	....	....	....	....	....	....	....	....	....	....	....
2002-03	**Vancouver**	**NHL**	**62**	**7**	**13**	**20**	**6**	**1**	**0**	**1**	**78**	**9.0**	**4**	**862**	**50.8**	**14:21**	**14**	**0**	**2**	**2**	**4**	**0**	**0**	**0**	**14:56**
2003-04	**Vancouver**	**NHL**	**65**	**12**	**7**	**19**	**14**	**1**	**1**	**3**	**93**	**12.9**	**1**	**963**	**53.3**	**14:05**	**7**	**0**	**1**	**1**	**0**	**0**	**0**	**0**	**19:07**
	NHL Totals		**228**	**25**	**33**	**58**	**40**	**2**	**1**	**8**	**297**	**8.4**		**2847**	**51.7**	**13:19**	**27**	**0**	**4**	**4**	**4**	**0**	**0**	**0**	**15:59**

• Missed majority of 2000-01 season recovering from shoulder injury suffered in game vs. Manitoba (IHL), November 15, 2000.

CIBAK, Martin

(TSEE-bak, MAHR-tihn) **T.B.**

Center. Shoots left. 6'1", 195 lbs. Born, Liptovsky Mikulas, Czech., May 17, 1980. Tampa Bay's 11th choice, 252nd overall, in 1998 Entry Draft.

Season	Club	League	GP	G	A	Pts	PIM	PP	SH	GW	S	%	+/-	TF	F%	Min	GP	G	A	Pts	PIM	PP	SH	GW	Min
1995-96	L. Mikulas Jr.	Slovak-Jr.	48	38	35	73	....	....	....	....	....	....	....	....	....	....	....	....	....	....	....	....	....	....	....
1996-97	L. Mikulas Jr.	Slovak-Jr.	45	22	18	40	....	....	....	....	....	....	....	....	....	....	....	....	....	....	....	....	....	....	....
1997-98	L. Mikulas Jr.	Slovak-Jr.	42	31	21	52	....	....	....	....	....	....	....	....	....	....	....	....	....	....	....	....	....	....	....
	Liptov. Mikulas	Slovakia	28	1	3	4	10	....	....	....	....	....	....	....	....	....	....	....	....	....	....	....	....	....	....
1998-99	Medicine Hat	WHL	66	21	26	47	72	....	....	....	....	....	....	....	....	....	....	....	....	....	....	....	....	....	....
99-2000	Medicine Hat	WHL	58	16	29	45	77	....	....	....	....	....	....	....	....	....	....	....	....	....	....	....	....	....	....
2000-01	Detroit Vipers	IHL	79	10	28	38	88	....	....	....	....	....	....	....	....	....	....	....	....	....	....	....	....	....	....
2001-02	**Tampa Bay**	**NHL**	**26**	**1**	**5**	**6**	**8**	**0**	**0**	**0**	**22**	**4.5**	**–6**	**85**	**34.1**	**11:08**	....	....	....	....	....	....	....	....	....
	Springfield	AHL	52	5	9	14	44	....	....	....	....	....	....	....	....	....	....	....	....	....	....	....	....	....	....
2002-03	Springfield	AHL	62	5	15	20	78	....	....	....	....	....	....	....	....	....	6	1	2	3	4	....	....	....	....
2003-04♦	**Tampa Bay**	**NHL**	**63**	**2**	**7**	**9**	**30**	**0**	**0**	**0**	**44**	**4.5**	**–1**	**321**	**45.2**	**7:35**	**6**	**0**	**1**	**1**	**0**	**0**	**0**	**0**	**7:35**
	Hershey Bears	AHL	1	0	0	0	2	....	....	....	....	....	....	....	....	....	....	....	....	....	....	....	....	....	....
	NHL Totals		**89**	**3**	**12**	**15**	**38**	**0**	**0**	**0**	**66**	**4.5**		**406**	**42.9**	**8:37**	**6**	**0**	**1**	**1**	**0**	**0**	**0**	**0**	**7:35**

CIERNIK, Ivan

(CHAIR-nihk, ee-VAHN)

Right wing. Shoots left. 6'1", 234 lbs. Born, Levice, Czech., October 30, 1977. Ottawa's 6th choice, 216th overall, in 1996 Entry Draft.

Season	Club	League	GP	G	A	Pts	PIM	PP	SH	GW	S	%	+/-	TF	F%	Min	GP	G	A	Pts	PIM	PP	SH	GW	Min
1994-95	HC Nitra Jr.	Slovak-Jr.	30	22	15	37	36	....	....	....	....	....	....	....	....	....	....	....	....	....	....	....	....	....	....
	HC Nitra	Slovakia	7	1	0	1	2	....	....	....	....	....	....	....	....	....	....	....	....	....	....	....	....	....	....
1995-96	HC Nitra	Slovakia	35	9	7	16	36	....	....	....	....	....	....	....	....	....	8	3	3	6	....	....	....	....	....
1996-97	HC Nitra	Slovakia	41	11	19	30	....	....	....	....	....	....	....	....	....	....	....	....	....	....	....	....	....	....	....
1997-98	**Ottawa**	**NHL**	**2**	**0**	**0**	**0**	**0**	**0**	**0**	**0**	**0**	**0.0**	**0**	....	....	....	....	....	....	....	....	....	....	....	....
	Worcester IceCats	AHL	53	9	12	21	38	....	....	....	....	....	....	....	....	....	1	0	0	0	2	....	....	....	....

			Regular Season														Playoffs								
Season	Club	League	GP	G	A	Pts	PIM	PP	SH	GW	S	%	+/-	TF	F%	Min	GP	G	A	Pts	PIM	PP	SH	GW	Min
1998-99	Adirondack	AHL	21	1	4	5	4	....	....	....	....	....	....	....	....	....	....	....	....	....	....	....	....	....	....
	Cincinnati	AHL	32	10	3	13	10	....	....	....	....	....	....	....	....	....	2	0	0	0	2	....	....	....	....
99-2000	Grand Rapids	IHL	66	13	12	25	64	....	....	....	....	....	....	....	....	....	6	0	6	6	2	....	....	....	....
2000-01	**Ottawa**	**NHL**	**4**	**2**	**0**	**2**	**2**	**0**	**0**	**0**	**7**	**28.6**	**2**	**0**	**0.0**	**7:41**	....	....	....	....	....	....	....	....	....
	Grand Rapids	IHL	66	27	38	65	53	....	....	....	....	....	....	....	....	....	10	5	6	11	26	....	....	....	....
2001-02	**Ottawa**	**NHL**	**23**	**1**	**2**	**3**	**4**	**0**	**0**	**0**	**18**	**5.6**	**0**	**7**	**71.4**	**7:51**	....	....	....	....	....	....	....	....	....
	Grand Rapids	AHL	2	2	1	3	0	....	....	....	....	....	....	....	....	....	....	....	....	....	....	....	....	....	....
	Washington	**NHL**	**6**	**0**	**1**	**1**	**2**	**0**	**0**	**0**	**5**	**0.0**	**0**	**0**	**0.0**	**9:15**	....	....	....	....	....	....	....	....	....
	Portland Pirates	AHL	26	10	5	15	28	....	....	....	....	....	....	....	....	....	....	....	....	....	....	....	....	....	....
2002-03	**Washington**	**NHL**	**47**	**8**	**10**	**18**	**24**	**0**	**0**	**2**	**61**	**13.1**	**6**	**9**	**33.3**	**11:48**	**2**	**0**	**1**	**1**	**6**	**0**	**0**	**0**	**9:09**
	Portland Pirates	AHL	13	4	6	10	6	....	....	....	....	....	....	....	....	....	....	....	....	....	....	....	....	....	....
2003-04	**Washington**	**NHL**	**7**	**1**	**1**	**2**	**0**	**0**	**0**	**0**	**8**	**12.5**	**1**	**0**	**0.0**	**9:38**	....	....	....	....	....	....	....	....	....
	Portland Pirates	AHL	54	10	21	31	43	....	....	....	....	....	....	....	....	....	7	2	1	3	10	....	....	....	....
	NHL Totals		**89**	**12**	**14**	**26**	**32**	**0**	**0**	**2**	**99**	**12.1**		**16**	**50.0**	**10:13**	**2**	**0**	**1**	**1**	**6**	**0**	**0**	**0**	**9:09**

Loaned to **Cincinnati** (AHL) by **Ottawa** with Ratislav Pavlikovsky and Erich Goldmann, January 12, 1999. Claimed on waivers by **Washington** from **Ottawa**, January 19, 2002. Signed as a free agent by **EHC Wolfsberg** (Germany), May 4, 2004.

CLARK, Brett

(KLAHRK, BREHT) **COL.**

Defense. Shoots left. 6'1", 195 lbs. Born, Wapella, Sask., December 23, 1976. Montreal's 7th choice, 154th overall, in 1996 Entry Draft.

			Regular Season														Playoffs								
Season	Club	League	GP	G	A	Pts	PIM	PP	SH	GW	S	%	+/-	TF	F%	Min	GP	G	A	Pts	PIM	PP	SH	GW	Min
1994-95	Melville	SJHL	62	19	32	51	77	....	....	....	....	....	....	....	....	....	....	....	....	....	....	....	....	....	....
1995-96	U. of Maine	H-East	39	7	31	38	22	....	....	....	....	....	....	....	....	....	....	....	....	....	....	....	....	....	....
1996-97	Team Canada	Nat-Tm	57	6	21	27	52	....	....	....	....	....	....	....	....	....	....	....	....	....	....	....	....	....	....
1997-98	**Montreal**	**NHL**	**41**	**1**	**0**	**1**	**20**	**0**	**0**	**0**	**26**	**3.8**	**–3**	....	....	....	....	....	....	....	....	....	....	....	....
	Fredericton	AHL	20	0	6	6	6	....	....	....	....	....	....	....	....	....	4	0	1	1	17	....	....	....	....
1998-99	**Montreal**	**NHL**	**61**	**2**	**2**	**4**	**16**	**0**	**0**	**0**	**36**	**5.6**	**–3**	**0**	**0.0**	**13:11**	....	....	....	....	....	....	....	....	....
	Fredericton	AHL	3	1	0	1	0	....	....	....	....	....	....	....	....	....	....	....	....	....	....	....	....	....	....
99-2000	**Atlanta**	**NHL**	**14**	**0**	**1**	**1**	**4**	**0**	**0**	**0**	**13**	**0.0**	**–12**	**0**	**0.0**	**16:51**	....	....	....	....	....	....	....	....	....
	Orlando	IHL	63	9	17	26	31	....	....	....	....	....	....	....	....	....	6	0	1	1	0	....	....	....	....
2000-01	**Atlanta**	**NHL**	**28**	**1**	**2**	**3**	**14**	**0**	**0**	**0**	**35**	**2.9**	**–12**	**0**	**0.0**	**18:02**	....	....	....	....	....	....	....	....	....
	Orlando	IHL	43	2	9	11	32	....	....	....	....	....	....	....	....	....	15	1	6	7	2	....	....	....	....
2001-02	Chicago Wolves	AHL	42	3	17	20	18	....	....	....	....	....	....	....	....	....	....	....	....	....	....	....	....	....	....
	Atlanta	**NHL**	**2**	**0**	**0**	**0**	**0**	**0**	**0**	**0**	**0**	**0.0**	**–3**	**1**	**100.0**	**15:32**	....	....	....	....	....	....	....	....	....
	Hershey Bears	AHL	32	7	9	16	12	....	....	....	....	....	....	....	....	....	8	0	2	2	6	....	....	....	....
2002-03	Hershey Bears	AHL	80	8	27	35	26	....	....	....	....	....	....	....	....	....	5	0	4	4	4	....	....	....	....
2003-04	**Colorado**	**NHL**	**12**	**1**	**1**	**2**	**6**	**0**	**0**	**0**	**14**	**7.1**	**3**	**0**	**0.0**	**10:26**	....	....	....	....	....	....	....	....	....
	Hershey Bears	AHL	64	11	21	32	37	....	....	....	....	....	....	....	....	....	....	....	....	....	....	....	....	....	....
	NHL Totals		**158**	**5**	**6**	**11**	**60**	**0**	**0**	**0**	**124**	**4.0**		**1**	**100.0**	**14:32**	....	....	....	....	....	....	....	....	....

Claimed by **Atlanta** from **Montreal** in Expansion Draft, June 25, 1999. Traded to **Colorado** by **Atlanta** for Frederic Cassivi, January 24, 2002.

CLARK, Chris

(KLAHRK, KRIHS) **CGY.**

Right wing. Shoots right. 6', 200 lbs. Born, South Windsor, CT, March 8, 1976. Calgary's 3rd choice, 77th overall, in 1994 Entry Draft.

			Regular Season														Playoffs								
Season	Club	League	GP	G	A	Pts	PIM	PP	SH	GW	S	%	+/-	TF	F%	Min	GP	G	A	Pts	PIM	PP	SH	GW	Min
1990-91	South Windsor	Hi-School	23	16	15	31	24	....	....	....	....	....	....	....	....	....	....	....	....	....	....	....	....	....	....
1991-92	Springfield	NEJHL	49	21	29	50	56	....	....	....	....	....	....	....	....	....	....	....	....	....	....	....	....	....	....
1992-93	Springfield	NEJHL	43	17	60	77	120	....	....	....	....	....	....	....	....	....	....	....	....	....	....	....	....	....	....
1993-94	Springfield	NEJHL	35	31	26	57	185	....	....	....	....	....	....	....	....	....	....	....	....	....	....	....	....	....	....
1994-95	Clarkson Knights	ECAC	32	12	11	23	92	....	....	....	....	....	....	....	....	....	....	....	....	....	....	....	....	....	....
1995-96	Clarkson Knights	ECAC	38	10	8	18	108	....	....	....	....	....	....	....	....	....	....	....	....	....	....	....	....	....	....
1996-97	Clarkson Knights	ECAC	37	23	25	48	*86	....	....	....	....	....	....	....	....	....	....	....	....	....	....	....	....	....	....
1997-98	Clarkson Knights	ECAC	35	18	21	39	*106	....	....	....	....	....	....	....	....	....	....	....	....	....	....	....	....	....	....
1998-99	Saint John Flames	AHL	73	13	27	40	123	....	....	....	....	....	....	....	....	....	7	2	4	6	15	....	....	....	....
99-2000	**Calgary**	**NHL**	**22**	**0**	**1**	**1**	**14**	**0**	**0**	**0**	**17**	**0.0**	**–3**	**0**	**0.0**	**9:02**	....	....	....	....	....	....	....	....	....
	Saint John Flames	AHL	48	16	17	33	134	....	....	....	....	....	....	....	....	....	....	....	....	....	....	....	....	....	....
2000-01	**Calgary**	**NHL**	**29**	**5**	**1**	**6**	**38**	**1**	**0**	**0**	**43**	**11.6**	**0**	**3**	**33.3**	**11:56**	....	....	....	....	....	....	....	....	....
	Saint John Flames	AHL	48	18	17	35	131	....	....	....	....	....	....	....	....	....	18	4	10	14	49	....	....	....	....
2001-02	**Calgary**	**NHL**	**64**	**10**	**7**	**17**	**79**	**2**	**1**	**4**	**109**	**9.2**	**–12**	**21**	**33.3**	**13:57**	....	....	....	....	....	....	....	....	....
2002-03	**Calgary**	**NHL**	**81**	**10**	**12**	**22**	**126**	**2**	**0**	**2**	**156**	**6.4**	**–11**	**40**	**32.5**	**14:24**	....	....	....	....	....	....	....	....	....
2003-04	**Calgary**	**NHL**	**82**	**10**	**15**	**25**	**106**	**4**	**0**	**2**	**137**	**7.3**	**–3**	**97**	**36.1**	**14:05**	**26**	**3**	**3**	**6**	**30**	**1**	**0**	**0**	**14:34**
	NHL Totals		**278**	**35**	**36**	**71**	**363**	**9**	**1**	**8**	**462**	**7.6**		**161**	**34.8**	**13:31**	**26**	**3**	**3**	**6**	**30**	**1**	**0**	**0**	**14:34**

ECAC Second All-Star Team (1998)

CLARKE, Noah

(KLAHRK, NOH-uh) **L.A.**

Left wing. Shoots left. 5'9", 185 lbs. Born, LaVerne, CA, June 11, 1979. Los Angeles' 10th choice, 250th overall, in 1999 Entry Draft.

			Regular Season														Playoffs								
Season	Club	League	GP	G	A	Pts	PIM	PP	SH	GW	S	%	+/-	TF	F%	Min	GP	G	A	Pts	PIM	PP	SH	GW	Min
1996-97	Shat.-St. Mary's	Hi-School	30	33	44	77	....	....	....	....	....	....	....	....	....	....	....	....	....	....	....	....	....	....	....
1997-98	Des Moines	USHL	54	19	30	49	29	....	....	....	....	....	....	....	....	....	12	2	9	11	23	....	....	....	....
1998-99	Des Moines	USHL	52	31	32	63	47	....	....	....	....	....	....	....	....	....	13	8	2	10	16	....	....	....	....
99-2000	Colorado College	WCHA	39	17	20	37	30	....	....	....	....	....	....	....	....	....	....	....	....	....	....	....	....	....	....
2000-01	Colorado College	WCHA	41	12	20	32	22	....	....	....	....	....	....	....	....	....	....	....	....	....	....	....	....	....	....
2001-02	Colorado College	WCHA	42	13	24	37	32	....	....	....	....	....	....	....	....	....	....	....	....	....	....	....	....	....	....
2002-03	Colorado College	WCHA	42	21	*49	70	15	....	....	....	....	....	....	....	....	....	....	....	....	....	....	....	....	....	....
	Manchester	AHL	3	1	1	2	0	....	....	....	....	....	....	....	....	....	....	....	....	....	....	....	....	....	....
2003-04	**Los Angeles**	**NHL**	**2**	**0**	**1**	**1**	**0**	**0**	**0**	**0**	**3**	**0.0**	**1**	**0**	**0.0**	**9:39**	....	....	....	....	....	....	....	....	....
	Manchester	AHL	71	25	26	51	24	....	....	....	....	....	....	....	....	....	6	3	1	4	4	....	....	....	....
	NHL Totals		**2**	**0**	**1**	**1**	**0**	**0**	**0**	**0**	**3**	**0.0**		**0**	**0.0**	**9:39**	....	....	....	....	....	....	....	....	....

USHL All-Rookie Team (1998) • USHL First All-Star Team (1999) • Curt Hammer Award (Most Gentlemanly Player – USHL) (1999) • WCHA All-Rookie Team (2000) • WCHA Second All-Star Team (2003) • NCAA West First All-American Team (2003) • AHL All-Rookie Team (2004)

CLASSEN, Greg

(KLAW-sihn, GREHG)

Center. Shoots left. 6'1", 200 lbs. Born, Aylsham, Sask., August 24, 1977.

			Regular Season														Playoffs								
Season	Club	League	GP	G	A	Pts	PIM	PP	SH	GW	S	%	+/-	TF	F%	Min	GP	G	A	Pts	PIM	PP	SH	GW	Min
1997-98	Nipawin Hawks	SJHL	59	32	50	82	50	....	....	....	....	....	....	....	....	....	14	8	13	21	6	....	....	....	....
1998-99	Merrimack	H-East	36	14	11	25	28	....	....	....	....	....	....	....	....	....	....	....	....	....	....	....	....	....	....
99-2000	Merrimack	H-East	36	14	16	30	16	....	....	....	....	....	....	....	....	....	....	....	....	....	....	....	....	....	....
	Milwaukee	IHL	11	1	0	1	2	....	....	....	....	....	....	....	....	....	2	0	0	0	2	....	....	....	....
2000-01	**Nashville**	**NHL**	**27**	**2**	**4**	**6**	**14**	**1**	**0**	**0**	**18**	**11.1**	**–4**	**195**	**42.1**	**10:16**	....	....	....	....	....	....	....	....	....
	Milwaukee	IHL	23	5	10	15	31	....	....	....	....	....	....	....	....	....	5	0	0	0	0	....	....	....	....
2001-02	**Nashville**	**NHL**	**55**	**5**	**6**	**11**	**30**	**0**	**1**	**0**	**32**	**15.6**	**1**	**389**	**43.2**	**10:09**	....	....	....	....	....	....	....	....	....
	Milwaukee	AHL	8	2	4	6	12	....	....	....	....	....	....	....	....	....	....	....	....	....	....	....	....	....	....
2002-03	**Nashville**	**NHL**	**8**	**0**	**0**	**0**	**4**	**0**	**0**	**0**	**2**	**0.0**	**–3**	**65**	**52.3**	**10:02**	....	....	....	....	....	....	....	....	....
	Milwaukee	AHL	72	20	28	48	61	....	....	....	....	....	....	....	....	....	6	1	1	2	4	....	....	....	....
2003-04	Milwaukee	AHL	68	18	29	47	95	....	....	....	....	....	....	....	....	....	20	4	3	7	12	....	....	....	....
	NHL Totals		**90**	**7**	**10**	**17**	**48**	**1**	**1**	**0**	**52**	**13.5**		**649**	**43.8**	**10:10**	....	....	....	....	....	....	....	....	....

Hockey East All-Rookie Team (1999)

Signed as a free agent by **Nashville**, March 27, 2000. Signed as a free agent by **Assat Pori**, (Finland), July 25, 2004.

CLEARY, Daniel

(KLIH-ree, DAN-yehl) **PHX.**

Right wing. Shoots left. 6', 211 lbs. Born, Carbonear, Nfld., December 18, 1978. Chicago's 1st choice, 13th overall, in 1997 Entry Draft.

			Regular Season														Playoffs								
Season	Club	League	GP	G	A	Pts	PIM	PP	SH	GW	S	%	+/-	TF	F%	Min	GP	G	A	Pts	PIM	PP	SH	GW	Min
1993-94	Kingston	MTJHL	41	18	28	46	33	....	....	....	....	....	....	....	....	....	2	0	1	1	0	....	....	....	....
1994-95	Belleville Bulls	OHL	62	26	55	81	62	....	....	....	....	....	....	....	....	....	16	7	10	17	23	....	....	....	....
1995-96	Belleville Bulls	OHL	64	53	62	115	74	....	....	....	....	....	....	....	....	....	14	10	17	27	40	....	....	....	....
1996-97	Belleville Bulls	OHL	64	32	48	80	88	....	....	....	....	....	....	....	....	....	6	3	4	7	6	....	....	....	....
1997-98	Belleville Bulls	OHL	30	16	31	47	14	....	....	....	....	....	....	....	....	....	10	6	*17	*23	10	....	....	....	....
	Chicago	**NHL**	**6**	**0**	**0**	**0**	**0**	**0**	**0**	**0**	**4**	**0.0**	**–2**	....	....	....	....	....	....	....	....	....	....	....	....
	Indianapolis Ice	IHL	4	2	1	3	6	....	....	....	....	....	....	....	....	....	....	....	....	....	....	....	....	....	....

			Regular Season														Playoffs								
Season	Club	League	GP	G	A	Pts	PIM	PP	SH	GW	S	%	+/-	TF	F%	Min	GP	G	A	Pts	PIM	PP	SH	GW	Min
1998-99	Chicago	NHL	35	4	5	9	24	0	0	0	49	8.2	–1	13	46.2	14:21	....	....	....	....	....	....	....	....	....
	Portland Pirates	AHL	30	9	17	26	74	....	....	....	....	....	....	....	....	....	....	....	....	....	....	....	....	....	....
	Hamilton	AHL	9	0	1	1	7	....	....	....	....	....	....	....	....	....	3	0	0	0	0	....	....	....	....
99-2000	Edmonton	NHL	17	3	2	5	8	0	0	1	18	16.7	–1	1	100.0	9:44	4	0	1	1	2	0	0	0	8:40
	Hamilton	AHL	58	22	52	74	108	....	....	....	....	....	....	....	....	....	5	2	3	5	18	....	....	....	....
2000-01	Edmonton	NHL	81	14	21	35	37	2	0	2	107	13.1	5	13	23.1	12:58	6	1	1	2	8	1	0	0	14:09
2001-02	Edmonton	NHL	65	10	19	29	51	2	1	1	75	13.3	–1	5	60.0	12:43	....	....	....	....	....	....	....	....	....
2002-03	Edmonton	NHL	57	4	13	17	31	0	0	1	89	4.5	5	5	40.0	11:58	....	....	....	....	....	....	....	....	....
2003-04	Phoenix	NHL	68	6	11	17	42	0	3	0	83	7.2	–8	51	39.2	13:12	....	....	....	....	....	....	....	....	....
	NHL Totals		329	41	71	112	193	4	4	5	425	9.6		88	39.8	12:46	10	1	2	3	10	1	0	0	11:57

OHL All-Rookie Team (1995) • OHL First All-Star Team (1996, 1997) • AHL Second All-Star Team (2000)

Traded to **Edmonton** by **Chicago** with Chad Kilger, Ethan Moreau and Christian Laflamme for Boris Mironov, Dean McAmmond and Jonas Elofsson, March 20, 1999. Signed as a free agent by **Phoenix**, July 15, 2003.

CLYMER, Ben

(KLIH-mehr, BEHN)

Left wing. Shoots right. 6'1", 199 lbs. Born, Bloomington, MN, April 11, 1978. Boston's 3rd choice, 27th overall, in 1997 Entry Draft.

1993-94	Jefferson Jaguars	Hi-School	23	3	7	10	20	....	....	....	....	....	....	....	....	....	....	....	....	....	....	....	....	....	....
1994-95	Jefferson Jaguars	Hi-School	28	11	22	33	36	....	....	....	....	....	....	....	....	....	....	....	....	....	....	....	....	....	....
1995-96	Jefferson Jaguars	Hi-School	18	12	34	46	34	....	....	....	....	....	....	....	....	....	5	0	6	6	6	....	....	....	....
1996-97	U. of Minnesota	WCHA	29	7	13	20	64	....	....	....	....	....	....	....	....	....	....	....	....	....	....	....	....	....	....
1997-98	U. of Minnesota	WCHA	1	0	0	0	2	....	....	....	....	....	....	....	....	....	....	....	....	....	....	....	....	....	....
1998-99	Seattle	WHL	70	12	44	56	93	....	....	....	....	....	....	....	....	....	11	1	5	6	12	....	....	....	....
99-2000	Tampa Bay	NHL	60	2	6	8	87	2	0	0	98	2.0	–26	3	66.7	19:37	....	....	....	....	....	....	....	....	....
	Detroit Vipers	IHL	19	1	9	10	30	....	....	....	....	....	....	....	....	....	....	....	....	....	....	....	....	....	....
2000-01	Tampa Bay	NHL	23	5	1	6	21	3	0	0	25	20.0	–7	8	25.0	13:03	....	....	....	....	....	....	....	....	....
	Detroit Vipers	IHL	53	5	8	13	88	....	....	....	....	....	....	....	....	....	....	....	....	....	....	....	....	....	....
2001-02	Tampa Bay	NHL	81	14	20	34	36	4	0	2	151	9.3	–10	14	28.6	17:26	....	....	....	....	....	....	....	....	....
2002-03	Tampa Bay	NHL	65	6	12	18	57	1	0	1	103	5.8	–2	15	0.0	13:39	11	0	2	2	6	0	0	0	13:30
2003-04♦	Tampa Bay	NHL	66	2	8	10	50	0	0	0	96	2.1	5	25	28.0	9:48	5	0	0	0	0	0	0	0	7:46
	NHL Totals		295	29	47	76	251	10	0	3	473	6.1		65	23.1	15:00	16	0	2	2	6	0	0	0	11:42

• Missed majority of 1997-98 season recovering from shoulder injury suffered in game vs. U. of Michigan (CCHA), October 10, 1997. Signed as a free agent by **Tampa Bay**, October 2, 1999.

COLAIACOVO, Carlo

(koh-lee-A-KOH-voh, KAR-loh) **TOR.**

Defense. Shoots left. 6'1", 188 lbs. Born, Toronto, Ont., January 27, 1983. Toronto's 1st choice, 17th overall, in 2001 Entry Draft.

1998-99	Mississauga Reps	GTHL	44	10	12	23	28	....	....	....	....	....	....	....	....	....	....	....	....	....	....	....	....	....	....
99-2000	Erie Otters	OHL	52	4	18	22	12	....	....	....	....	....	....	....	....	....	13	2	4	6	9	....	....	....	....
2000-01	Erie Otters	OHL	62	12	27	39	59	....	....	....	....	....	....	....	....	....	14	4	7	11	16	....	....	....	....
2001-02	Erie Otters	OHL	60	13	27	40	49	....	....	....	....	....	....	....	....	....	21	7	10	17	20	....	....	....	....
2002-03	Toronto	NHL	2	0	1	1	0	0	0	0	1	0.0	0	0	0.0	13:43	....	....	....	....	....	....	....	....	....
	Erie Otters	OHL	35	14	21	35	12	....	....	....	....	....	....	....	....	....	....	....	....	....	....	....	....	....	....
2003-04	Toronto	NHL	2	0	1	1	2	0	0	0	0	0.0	1	0	0.0	13:56	....	....	....	....	....	....	....	....	....
	St. John's	AHL	62	6	25	31	50	....	....	....	....	....	....	....	....	....	....	....	....	....	....	....	....	....	....
	NHL Totals		4	0	2	2	2	0	0	0	1	0.0		0	0.0	13:49	....	....	....	....	....	....	....	....	....

OHL Second All-Star Team (2002, 2003)

• Returned to **Erie** (OHL) by **Toronto**, November 10, 2002.

COLE, Erik

(KOHL, AIR-ihk) **CAR.**

Left wing. Shoots left. 6'2", 200 lbs. Born, Oswego, NY, November 6, 1978. Carolina's 3rd choice, 71st overall, in 1998 Entry Draft.

1995-96	Oswego	Hi-School	40	49	41	90	....	....	....	....	....	....	....	....	....	....	....	....	....	....	....	....	....	....	....
1996-97	Des Moines	USHL	48	30	34	64	140	....	....	....	....	....	....	....	....	....	5	2	0	2	6	....	....	....	....
1997-98	Clarkson Knights	ECAC	34	11	20	31	55	....	....	....	....	....	....	....	....	....	....	....	....	....	....	....	....	....	....
1998-99	Clarkson Knights	ECAC	36	*22	20	42	50	....	....	....	....	....	....	....	....	....	....	....	....	....	....	....	....	....	....
99-2000	Clarkson Knights	ECAC	33	19	11	30	46	....	....	....	....	....	....	....	....	....	....	....	....	....	....	....	....	....	....
	Cincinnati	IHL	9	4	3	7	2	....	....	....	....	....	....	....	....	....	7	1	1	2	2	....	....	....	....
2000-01	Cincinnati	IHL	69	23	20	43	28	....	....	....	....	....	....	....	....	....	5	1	0	1	2	....	....	....	....
2001-02	Carolina	NHL	81	16	24	40	35	3	0	2	159	10.1	–10	17	47.1	16:04	23	6	3	9	30	1	0	1	18:27
2002-03	Carolina	NHL	53	14	13	27	72	6	2	3	125	11.2	1	56	39.3	17:08	....	....	....	....	....	....	....	....	....
2003-04	Carolina	NHL	80	18	24	42	93	2	2	3	172	10.5	–4	15	46.7	18:06	....	....	....	....	....	....	....	....	....
	NHL Totals		214	48	61	109	200	11	4	8	456	10.5		88	42.0	17:05	23	6	3	9	30	1	0	1	18:27

ECAC Rookie of the Year (1998) (co-winner - Willie Mitchell) • ECAC First All-Star Team (1999) • NCAA East Second All-American Team (1999) • ECAC Second All-Star Team (2000)

COMMODORE, Mike

(KAWM-uh-dohr, MIGHK) **CGY.**

Defense. Shoots right. 6'4", 230 lbs. Born, Fort Saskatchewan, Alta., November 7, 1979. New Jersey's 2nd choice, 42nd overall, in 1999 Entry Draft.

1996-97	Ft. Saskatchewan	AJHL	51	3	8	11	244	....	....	....	....	....	....	....	....	....	....	....	....	....	....	....	....	....	....
1997-98	North Dakota	WCHA	29	0	5	5	74	....	....	....	....	....	....	....	....	....	....	....	....	....	....	....	....	....	....
1998-99	North Dakota	WCHA	39	5	8	13	154	....	....	....	....	....	....	....	....	....	....	....	....	....	....	....	....	....	....
99-2000	North Dakota	WCHA	38	5	7	12	*154	....	....	....	....	....	....	....	....	....	....	....	....	....	....	....	....	....	....
2000-01	New Jersey	NHL	20	1	4	5	14	0	0	0	11	9.1	5	0	0.0	12:46	....	....	....	....	....	....	....	....	....
	Albany River Rats	AHL	41	2	5	7	59	....	....	....	....	....	....	....	....	....	....	....	....	....	....	....	....	....	....
2001-02	New Jersey	NHL	37	0	1	1	30	0	0	0	22	0.0	–12	0	0.0	12:37	....	....	....	....	....	....	....	....	....
	Albany River Rats	AHL	14	0	3	3	31	....	....	....	....	....	....	....	....	....	....	....	....	....	....	....	....	....	....
2002-03	Cincinnati	AHL	61	2	9	11	210	....	....	....	....	....	....	....	....	....	....	....	....	....	....	....	....	....	....
	Calgary	NHL	6	0	1	1	19	0	0	0	5	0.0	2	0	0.0	11:35	....	....	....	....	....	....	....	....	....
	Saint John Flames	AHL	7	0	3	3	18	....	....	....	....	....	....	....	....	....	....	....	....	....	....	....	....	....	....
2003-04	Calgary	NHL	12	0	0	0	25	0	0	0	10	0.0	–4	0	0.0	15:17	20	0	2	2	19	0	0	0	11:34
	Lowell	AHL	37	5	11	16	75	....	....	....	....	....	....	....	....	....	....	....	....	....	....	....	....	....	....
	NHL Totals		75	1	6	7	88	0	0	0	48	2.1		0	0.0	13:00	20	0	2	2	19	0	0	0	11:34

NCAA Championship All-Tournament Team (2000)

Traded to **Anaheim** by **New Jersey** with Petr Sykora, Jean-Francois Damphousse and Igor Pohanka for Jeff Friesen, Oleg Tverdovsky and Maxim Balmochnykh, July 6, 2002. Traded to **Calgary** by **Anaheim** with Jean-Francois Damphousse for Rob Niedermayer, March 11, 2003.

COMRIE, Mike

(KAWM-ree, MIGHK) **PHX.**

Center. Shoots left. 5'9", 185 lbs. Born, Edmonton, Alta., September 11, 1980. Edmonton's 5th choice, 91st overall, in 1999 Entry Draft.

1995-96	Edmonton SSAC	AMHL	33	51	52	103	....	....	....	....	....	....	....	....	....	....	....	....	....	....	....	....	....	....	....
1996-97	St. Albert Saints	AJHL	63	37	41	78	44	....	....	....	....	....	....	....	....	....	....	....	....	....	....	....	....	....	....
1997-98	St. Albert Saints	AJHL	58	*60	*78	*138	134	....	....	....	....	....	....	....	....	....	19	*24	*24	*48	51	....	....	....	....
1998-99	U. of Michigan	CCHA	42	19	25	44	38	....	....	....	....	....	....	....	....	....	....	....	....	....	....	....	....	....	....
99-2000	U. of Michigan	CCHA	40	24	35	59	95	....	....	....	....	....	....	....	....	....	....	....	....	....	....	....	....	....	....
2000-01	Kootenay Ice	WHL	37	39	40	79	79	....	....	....	....	....	....	....	....	....	....	....	....	....	....	....	....	....	....
	Edmonton	NHL	41	8	14	22	14	3	0	1	62	12.9	6	372	43.3	11:23	6	1	2	3	0	1	0	1	15:00
2001-02	Edmonton	NHL	82	33	27	60	45	8	0	5	170	19.4	16	1198	47.3	17:32	....	....	....	....	....	....	....	....	....
2002-03	Edmonton	NHL	69	20	31	51	90	8	0	6	170	11.8	–18	1069	47.1	17:51	6	1	0	1	10	0	0	0	13:07
2003-04	Philadelphia	NHL	21	4	5	9	12	0	0	1	36	11.1	2	165	50.9	12:51	....	....	....	....	....	....	....	....	....
	Phoenix	NHL	28	8	7	15	16	1	1	1	65	12.3	–8	304	50.3	17:50	....	....	....	....	....	....	....	....	....
	NHL Totals		241	73	84	157	177	20	1	14	503	14.5		3108	47.2	16:12	12	2	2	4	10	1	0	1	14:03

CCHA All-Rookie Team (1999) • CCHA First All-Star Team (1999) • CCHA Rookie of the Year (1999) • CCHA First All-Star Team (2000) • NCAA West Second All-American Team (2000)

• Left **University of Michigan** (CCHA) and signed as a free agent by **Kootenay** (WHL), August 23, 2000. • Left **Kootenay** (WHL) and signed with **Edmonton**, December 30, 2000. Traded to **Philadelphia** by **Edmonton** for Jeff Woywitka, Philadelphia's 1st round choice (Rob Schremp) in 2004 Entry Draft and Philadelphia's 3rd round choice in 2005 Entry Draft, December 16, 2003. Traded to **Phoenix** by **Philadelphia** for Sean Burke, Branko Radivojevic and Ben Eager, February 9, 2004.

CONNOLLY, Tim
(KAHN-noh-lee, TIHM) **BUF.**

Center. Shoots right. 6'1", 182 lbs. Born, Syracuse, NY, May 7, 1981. NY Islanders' 1st choice, 5th overall, in 1999 Entry Draft.

			Regular Season														Playoffs								
Season	Club	League	GP	G	A	Pts	PIM	PP	SH	GW	S	%	+/-	TF	F%	Min	GP	G	A	Pts	PIM	PP	SH	GW	Min
1996-97	Syracuse	MTJHL	50	42	62	104	34	....	....	....	....	....	....	....	....	....	....	....	....	....	....	....	....	....	....
1997-98	Erie Otters	OHL	59	30	32	62	32	....	....	....	....	....	....	....	....	....	7	1	6	7	6	....	....	....	....
1998-99	Erie Otters	OHL	46	34	34	68	50	....	....	....	....	....	....	....	....	....	....	....	....	....	....	....	....	....	....
99-2000	**NY Islanders**	**NHL**	**81**	**14**	**20**	**34**	**44**	**2**	**1**	**1**	**114**	**12.3**	**-25**	**786**	**36.3**	**16:18**	....	....	....	....	....	....	....	....	....
2000-01	**NY Islanders**	**NHL**	**82**	**10**	**31**	**41**	**42**	**5**	**0**	**0**	**171**	**5.8**	**-14**	**989**	**41.7**	**20:02**	....	....	....	....	....	....	....	....	....
2001-02	**Buffalo**	**NHL**	**82**	**10**	**35**	**45**	**34**	**3**	**0**	**3**	**126**	**7.9**	**4**	**1074**	**39.6**	**16:58**	....	....	....	....	....	....	....	....	....
2002-03	**Buffalo**	**NHL**	**80**	**12**	**13**	**25**	**32**	**6**	**0**	**2**	**159**	**7.5**	**-28**	**845**	**42.8**	**16:00**	....	....	....	....	....	....	....	....	....
2003-04	**Buffalo**	**NHL**	DID NOT PLAY – INJURED																						
	NHL Totals		**325**	**46**	**99**	**145**	**152**	**16**	**1**	**6**	**570**	**8.1**		**3694**	**40.2**	**17:20**	....	....	....	....	....	....	....	....	....

Traded to **Buffalo** by **NY Islanders** with Taylor Pyatt for Michael Peca, June 24, 2001. • Missed entire 2003-04 season recovering from head injury suffered in pre-season game vs. Chicago, October 2, 2003.

CONROY, Craig
(KAWN-roi, KRAYG) **L.A.**

Center. Shoots right. 6'2", 197 lbs. Born, Potsdam, NY, September 4, 1971. Montreal's 7th choice, 123rd overall, in 1990 Entry Draft.

Season	Club	League	GP	G	A	Pts	PIM	PP	SH	GW	S	%	+/-	TF	F%	Min	GP	G	A	Pts	PIM	PP	SH	GW	Min
1989-90	Northfield Prep	Hi-School	31	33	43	76	....	....	....	....	....	....	....	....	....	....	....	....	....	....	....	....	....	....	....
1990-91	Clarkson Knights	ECAC	40	8	21	29	24	....	....	....	....	....	....	....	....	....	....	....	....	....	....	....	....	....	....
1991-92	Clarkson Knights	ECAC	31	19	17	36	36	....	....	....	....	....	....	....	....	....	....	....	....	....	....	....	....	....	....
1992-93	Clarkson Knights	ECAC	35	10	23	33	26	....	....	....	....	....	....	....	....	....	....	....	....	....	....	....	....	....	....
1993-94	Clarkson Knights	ECAC	34	26	*40	*66	46	....	....	....	....	....	....	....	....	....	....	....	....	....	....	....	....	....	....
1994-95	Fredericton	AHL	55	26	18	44	29	....	....	....	....	....	....	....	....	....	11	7	3	10	6	....	....	....	....
	Montreal	**NHL**	**6**	**1**	**0**	**1**	**0**	**0**	**0**	**0**	**4**	**25.0**	**-1**	....	....	....	....	....	....	....	....	....	....	....	....
1995-96	**Montreal**	**NHL**	**7**	**0**	**0**	**0**	**2**	**0**	**0**	**0**	**1**	**0.0**	**-4**	....	....	....	....	....	....	....	....	....	....	....	....
	Fredericton	AHL	67	31	38	69	65	....	....	....	....	....	....	....	....	....	10	5	7	12	6	....	....	....	....
1996-97	Fredericton	AHL	9	10	6	16	10	....	....	....	....	....	....	....	....	....	....	....	....	....	....	....	....	....	....
	St. Louis	**NHL**	**61**	**6**	**11**	**17**	**43**	**0**	**0**	**1**	**74**	**8.1**	**0**	....	....	....	**6**	**0**	**0**	**0**	**8**	**0**	**0**	**0**	....
	Worcester IceCats	AHL	5	5	6	11	2	....	....	....	....	....	....	....	....	....	....	....	....	....	....	....	....	....	....
1997-98	**St. Louis**	**NHL**	**81**	**14**	**29**	**43**	**46**	**0**	**3**	**1**	**118**	**11.9**	**20**	....	....	....	**10**	**1**	**2**	**3**	**8**	**0**	**0**	**1**	....
1998-99	**St. Louis**	**NHL**	**69**	**14**	**25**	**39**	**38**	**0**	**1**	**1**	**134**	**10.4**	**14**	**1190**	**54.6**	**16:39**	**13**	**2**	**1**	**3**	**6**	**0**	**0**	**0**	**15:09**
99-2000	**St. Louis**	**NHL**	**79**	**12**	**15**	**27**	**36**	**1**	**2**	**3**	**98**	**12.2**	**5**	**1339**	**53.6**	**14:48**	**7**	**0**	**2**	**2**	**2**	**0**	**0**	**0**	**13:13**
2000-01	**St. Louis**	**NHL**	**69**	**11**	**14**	**25**	**46**	**0**	**3**	**2**	**101**	**10.9**	**2**	**729**	**55.1**	**14:01**	....	....	....	....	....	....	....	....	....
	Calgary	**NHL**	**14**	**3**	**4**	**7**	**14**	**0**	**1**	**0**	**32**	**9.4**	**0**	**264**	**52.7**	**18:08**	....	....	....	....	....	....	....	....	....
2001-02	**Calgary**	**NHL**	**81**	**27**	**48**	**75**	**32**	**7**	**2**	**4**	**146**	**18.5**	**24**	**1654**	**54.3**	**20:56**	....	....	....	....	....	....	....	....	....
2002-03	**Calgary**	**NHL**	**79**	**22**	**37**	**59**	**36**	**5**	**0**	**2**	**143**	**15.4**	**-4**	**1579**	**57.0**	**19:47**	....	....	....	....	....	....	....	....	....
2003-04	**Calgary**	**NHL**	**63**	**8**	**39**	**47**	**44**	**2**	**0**	**0**	**112**	**7.1**	**13**	**1402**	**53.9**	**19:13**	**26**	**6**	**11**	**17**	**12**	**2**	**0**	**1**	**20:23**
	NHL Totals		**609**	**118**	**222**	**340**	**337**	**15**	**12**	**14**	**963**	**12.3**		**8157**	**54.7**	**17:38**	**62**	**9**	**16**	**25**	**36**	**2**	**0**	**2**	**17:48**

ECAC First All-Star Team (1994) • NCAA East First All-American Team (1994) • NCAA Final Four All-Tournament Team (1994)

Traded to **St. Louis** by **Montreal** with Pierre Turgeon and Rory Fitzpatrick for Murray Baron, Shayne Corson and St. Louis' 5th round choice (Gennady Razin) in 1997 Entry Draft, October 29, 1996. Traded to **Calgary** by **St. Louis** with St. Louis' 7th round choice (David Moss) in 2001 Entry Draft for Cory Stillman, March 13, 2001. Signed as a free agent by **Los Angeles**, July 6, 2004.

COOKE, Matt
(KUK, MAT) **VAN.**

Center. Shoots left. 5'11", 205 lbs. Born, Belleville, Ont., September 7, 1978. Vancouver's 8th choice, 144th overall, in 1997 Entry Draft.

Season	Club	League	GP	G	A	Pts	PIM	PP	SH	GW	S	%	+/-	TF	F%	Min	GP	G	A	Pts	PIM	PP	SH	GW	Min
1994-95	Wellington Dukes	MTJHL	46	9	23	32	62	....	....	....	....	....	....	....	....	....	....	....	....	....	....	....	....	....	....
1995-96	Windsor Spitfires	OHL	61	8	11	19	102	....	....	....	....	....	....	....	....	....	7	1	3	4	6	....	....	....	....
1996-97	Windsor Spitfires	OHL	65	45	50	95	146	....	....	....	....	....	....	....	....	....	5	5	5	10	10	....	....	....	....
1997-98	Windsor Spitfires	OHL	23	14	19	33	50	....	....	....	....	....	....	....	....	....	....	....	....	....	....	....	....	....	....
	Kingston	OHL	25	8	13	21	49	....	....	....	....	....	....	....	....	....	12	8	8	16	20	....	....	....	....
1998-99	**Vancouver**	**NHL**	**30**	**0**	**2**	**2**	**27**	**0**	**0**	**0**	**22**	**0.0**	**-12**	**189**	**40.2**	**8:07**	....	....	....	....	....	....	....	....	....
	Syracuse Crunch	AHL	37	15	18	33	119	....	....	....	....	....	....	....	....	....	....	....	....	....	....	....	....	....	....
99-2000	**Vancouver**	**NHL**	**51**	**5**	**7**	**12**	**39**	**0**	**1**	**1**	**58**	**8.6**	**3**	**71**	**39.4**	**11:48**	....	....	....	....	....	....	....	....	....
	Syracuse Crunch	AHL	18	5	8	13	27	....	....	....	....	....	....	....	....	....	....	....	....	....	....	....	....	....	....
2000-01	**Vancouver**	**NHL**	**81**	**14**	**13**	**27**	**94**	**0**	**2**	**0**	**121**	**11.6**	**5**	**321**	**43.0**	**14:35**	**4**	**0**	**0**	**0**	**4**	**0**	**0**	**0**	**12:04**
2001-02	**Vancouver**	**NHL**	**82**	**13**	**20**	**33**	**111**	**1**	**0**	**2**	**103**	**12.6**	**4**	**28**	**32.1**	**14:03**	**6**	**3**	**2**	**5**	**0**	**1**	**0**	**0**	**15:09**
2002-03	**Vancouver**	**NHL**	**82**	**15**	**27**	**42**	**82**	**1**	**4**	**0**	**118**	**12.7**	**21**	**31**	**35.5**	**13:24**	**14**	**2**	**1**	**3**	**12**	**0**	**0**	**0**	**14:06**
2003-04	**Vancouver**	**NHL**	**53**	**11**	**12**	**23**	**73**	**1**	**1**	**4**	**79**	**13.9**	**5**	**34**	**52.9**	**14:06**	**7**	**3**	**1**	**4**	**12**	**0**	**0**	**1**	**18:23**
	NHL Totals		**379**	**58**	**81**	**139**	**426**	**3**	**8**	**7**	**501**	**11.6**		**674**	**41.5**	**13:15**	**31**	**8**	**4**	**12**	**28**	**1**	**0**	**1**	**15:01**

CORAZZINI, Carl
(koh-ra-ZEE-nee, KAHRL)

Center. Shoots right. 5'10", 182 lbs. Born, Framingham, MA, April 21, 1979.

Season	Club	League	GP	G	A	Pts	PIM	PP	SH	GW	S	%	+/-	TF	F%	Min	GP	G	A	Pts	PIM	PP	SH	GW	Min
1996-97	St. Sebastian's	Hi-School	25	29	31	60	....	....	....	....	....	....	....	....	....	....	....	....	....	....	....	....	....	....	....
1997-98	Boston University	H-East	36	9	6	15	4	....	....	....	....	....	....	....	....	....	....	....	....	....	....	....	....	....	....
1998-99	Boston University	H-East	37	15	9	24	12	....	....	....	....	....	....	....	....	....	....	....	....	....	....	....	....	....	....
99-2000	Boston University	H-East	42	22	20	42	44	....	....	....	....	....	....	....	....	....	....	....	....	....	....	....	....	....	....
2000-01	Boston University	H-East	35	16	20	36	48	....	....	....	....	....	....	....	....	....	....	....	....	....	....	....	....	....	....
2001-02	Providence Bruins	AHL	61	7	8	15	10	....	....	....	....	....	....	....	....	....	....	....	....	....	....	....	....	....	....
2002-03	Providence Bruins	AHL	33	7	6	13	4	....	....	....	....	....	....	....	....	....	4	0	0	0	0	....	....	....	....
	Atlantic City	ECHL	27	13	8	21	14	....	....	....	....	....	....	....	....	....	....	....	....	....	....	....	....	....	....
2003-04	**Boston**	**NHL**	**12**	**2**	**0**	**2**	**0**	**0**	**1**	**0**	**16**	**12.5**	**2**	**6**	**33.3**	**10:41**	....	....	....	....	....	....	....	....	....
	Providence Bruins	AHL	62	16	9	25	6	....	....	....	....	....	....	....	....	....	2	1	0	1	2	....	....	....	....
	NHL Totals		**12**	**2**	**0**	**2**	**0**	**0**	**1**	**0**	**16**	**12.5**		**6**	**33.3**	**10:41**	....	....	....	....	....	....	....	....	....

Hockey East All-Rookie Team (1998) • Hockey East First All-Star Team (2001) • NCAA East Second All-American Team (2001)

Signed as a free agent by **Boston**, August 8, 2001.

CORSO, Daniel
(KOHR-soh, DAN-yehl)

Center. Shoots left. 5'10", 187 lbs. Born, Montreal, Que., April 3, 1978. St. Louis' 6th choice, 169th overall, in 1996 Entry Draft.

Season	Club	League	GP	G	A	Pts	PIM	PP	SH	GW	S	%	+/-	TF	F%	Min	GP	G	A	Pts	PIM	PP	SH	GW	Min
1993-94	Magog	QAAA	36	17	22	39	....	....	....	....	....	....	....	....	....	....	12	10	12	22	....	....	....	....	....
1994-95	Victoriaville Tigres	QMJHL	65	27	26	53	6	....	....	....	....	....	....	....	....	....	4	2	5	7	2	....	....	....	....
1995-96	Victoriaville Tigres	QMJHL	65	49	65	114	77	....	....	....	....	....	....	....	....	....	12	6	7	13	4	....	....	....	....
1996-97	Victoriaville Tigres	QMJHL	54	51	68	119	50	....	....	....	....	....	....	....	....	....	....	....	....	....	....	....	....	....	....
1997-98	Victoriaville Tigres	QMJHL	35	24	51	75	20	....	....	....	....	....	....	....	....	....	3	1	1	2	2	....	....	....	....
1998-99	Worcester IceCats	AHL	63	14	14	28	26	....	....	....	....	....	....	....	....	....	....	....	....	....	....	....	....	....	....
99-2000	Worcester IceCats	AHL	71	21	34	55	19	....	....	....	....	....	....	....	....	....	9	2	3	5	10	....	....	....	....
2000-01	**St. Louis**	**NHL**	**28**	**10**	**3**	**13**	**14**	**5**	**0**	**4**	**42**	**23.8**	**0**	**296**	**56.1**	**13:56**	**12**	**0**	**1**	**1**	**0**	**0**	**0**	**0**	**8:52**
	Worcester IceCats	AHL	52	19	37	56	47	....	....	....	....	....	....	....	....	....	....	....	....	....	....	....	....	....	....
2001-02	**St. Louis**	**NHL**	**41**	**4**	**7**	**11**	**6**	**1**	**0**	**2**	**25**	**16.0**	**3**	**423**	**54.9**	**11:13**	**2**	**0**	**0**	**0**	**0**	**0**	**0**	**0**	**8:51**
2002-03	**St. Louis**	**NHL**	**1**	**0**	**0**	**0**	**0**	**0**	**0**	**0**	**0**	**0.0**	**-1**	**8**	**50.0**	**7:44**	....	....	....	....	....	....	....	....	....
	Worcester IceCats	AHL	1	0	0	0	0	....	....	....	....	....	....	....	....	....	....	....	....	....	....	....	....	....	....
2003-04	Binghamton	AHL	32	7	11	18	16	....	....	....	....	....	....	....	....	....	....	....	....	....	....	....	....	....	....
	Atlanta	**NHL**	**7**	**0**	**1**	**1**	**0**	**0**	**0**	**0**	**2**	**0.0**	**-2**	**105**	**47.6**	**12:59**	....	....	....	....	....	....	....	....	....
	Chicago Wolves	AHL	29	8	18	26	15	....	....	....	....	....	....	....	....	....	10	1	5	6	0	....	....	....	....
	NHL Totals		**77**	**14**	**11**	**25**	**20**	**6**	**0**	**6**	**69**	**20.3**		**832**	**54.3**	**12:19**	**14**	**0**	**1**	**1**	**0**	**0**	**0**	**0**	**8:52**

QMJHL All-Rookie Team (1995) • QMJHL First All-Star Team (1997) • QMJHL MVP (1997)

• Spent majority of 2001-02 season on practice roster, October 22, 2001. • Missed majority of 2002-03 season recovering from shoulder injury suffered in game vs. Anaheim, October 10, 2003. Signed as a free agent by **Ottawa**, September 2, 2003. Traded to **Atlanta** by **Ottawa** for Brad Tapper, January 6, 2004.

CORSON, Shayne

(KOHR-sohn, SHAYN) **DAL.**

Left wing. Shoots left. 6'1", 202 lbs. Born, Barrie, Ont., August 13, 1966. Montreal's 2nd choice, 8th overall, in 1984 Entry Draft.

			Regular Season														Playoffs								
Season	Club	League	GP	G	A	Pts	PIM	PP	SH	GW	S	%	+/-	TF	F%	Min	GP	G	A	Pts	PIM	PP	SH	GW	Min
1982-83	Barrie Colts	OJHL-B	23	13	29	42	87	....	....	....	....	....	....	....	....	....	....	....	....	....	....	....	....	....	....
1983-84	Brantford	OHL	66	25	46	71	165	....	....	....	....	....	....	....	....	....	6	4	1	5	26	....	....	....	....
1984-85	Hamilton	OHL	54	27	63	90	154	....	....	....	....	....	....	....	....	....	11	3	7	10	19	....	....	....	....
1985-86	Hamilton	OHL	47	41	57	98	153	....	....	....	....	....	....	....	....	....	....	....	....	....	....	....	....	....	....
	Montreal	**NHL**	**3**	**0**	**0**	**0**	**2**	**0**	**0**	**0**	**1**	**0.0**	**-3**	....	....	....	....	....	....	....	....	....	....	....	....
1986-87	**Montreal**	**NHL**	**55**	**12**	**11**	**23**	**144**	**0**	**1**	**3**	**69**	**17.4**	**10**	....	....	....	**17**	**6**	**5**	**11**	**30**	**1**	**1**	**1**	....
1987-88	**Montreal**	**NHL**	**71**	**12**	**27**	**39**	**152**	**2**	**0**	**2**	**90**	**13.3**	**22**	....	....	....	**3**	**1**	**0**	**1**	**12**	**0**	**0**	**0**	....
1988-89	**Montreal**	**NHL**	**80**	**26**	**24**	**50**	**193**	**10**	**0**	**3**	**133**	**19.5**	**-1**	....	....	....	**21**	**4**	**5**	**9**	**65**	**2**	**0**	**2**	....
1989-90	**Montreal**	**NHL**	**76**	**31**	**44**	**75**	**144**	**7**	**0**	**6**	**192**	**16.1**	**33**	....	....	....	**11**	**2**	**8**	**10**	**20**	**0**	**0**	**0**	....
1990-91	**Montreal**	**NHL**	**71**	**23**	**24**	**47**	**138**	**7**	**0**	**2**	**164**	**14.0**	**9**	....	....	....	**13**	**9**	**6**	**15**	**36**	**4**	**1**	**3**	....
1991-92	**Montreal**	**NHL**	**64**	**17**	**36**	**53**	**118**	**3**	**0**	**2**	**165**	**10.3**	**15**	....	....	....	**10**	**2**	**5**	**7**	**15**	**0**	**0**	**0**	....
1992-93	**Edmonton**	**NHL**	**80**	**16**	**31**	**47**	**209**	**9**	**2**	**1**	**164**	**9.8**	**-19**	....	....	....	....	....	....	....	....	....	....	....	....
1993-94	**Edmonton**	**NHL**	**64**	**25**	**29**	**54**	**118**	**11**	**0**	**3**	**171**	**14.6**	**-8**	....	....	....	....	....	....	....	....	....	....	....	....
1994-95	**Edmonton**	**NHL**	**48**	**12**	**24**	**36**	**86**	**2**	**0**	**1**	**131**	**9.2**	**-17**	....	....	....	....	....	....	....	....	....	....	....	....
1995-96	**St. Louis**	**NHL**	**77**	**18**	**28**	**46**	**192**	**13**	**0**	**0**	**150**	**12.0**	**3**	....	....	....	**13**	**8**	**6**	**14**	**22**	**6**	**1**	**1**	....
1996-97	**St. Louis**	**NHL**	**11**	**2**	**1**	**3**	**24**	**1**	**0**	**0**	**19**	**10.5**	**-4**	....	....	....	....	....	....	....	....	....	....	....	....
	Montreal	**NHL**	**47**	**6**	**15**	**21**	**80**	**2**	**0**	**2**	**96**	**6.3**	**-5**	....	....	....	**5**	**1**	**0**	**1**	**4**	**0**	**1**	**0**	....
1997-98	**Montreal**	**NHL**	**62**	**21**	**34**	**55**	**108**	**14**	**1**	**1**	**142**	**14.8**	**2**	....	....	....	**10**	**3**	**6**	**9**	**26**	**1**	**0**	**1**	....
	Canada	Olympics	6	1	1	2	2	....	....	....	....	....	....	....	....	....	....	....	....	....	....	....	....	....	....
1998-99	**Montreal**	**NHL**	**63**	**12**	**20**	**32**	**147**	**7**	**0**	**4**	**142**	**8.5**	**-10**	**184**	**45.1**	**20:42**	....	....	....	....	....	....	....	....	....
99-2000	**Montreal**	**NHL**	**70**	**8**	**20**	**28**	**115**	**2**	**0**	**1**	**121**	**6.6**	**-2**	**445**	**43.4**	**19:05**	....	....	....	....	....	....	....	....	....
2000-01	**Toronto**	**NHL**	**77**	**8**	**18**	**26**	**189**	**0**	**0**	**2**	**102**	**7.8**	**1**	**602**	**48.8**	**15:50**	**11**	**1**	**1**	**2**	**14**	**0**	**0**	**0**	**18:59**
2001-02	**Toronto**	**NHL**	**74**	**12**	**21**	**33**	**120**	**0**	**1**	**1**	**111**	**10.8**	**11**	**598**	**45.5**	**17:04**	**19**	**1**	**6**	**7**	**33**	**0**	**0**	**0**	**21:04**
2002-03	**Toronto**	**NHL**	**46**	**7**	**8**	**15**	**49**	**0**	**0**	**0**	**69**	**10.1**	**-5**	**202**	**44.6**	**15:02**	**2**	**0**	**0**	**0**	**2**	**0**	**0**	**0**	**9:42**
2003-04	**Dallas**	**NHL**	**17**	**5**	**5**	**10**	**29**	**0**	**1**	**1**	**21**	**23.8**	**12**	**23**	**43.5**	**13:31**	**5**	**0**	**1**	**1**	**12**	**0**	**0**	**0**	**13:56**
	NHL Totals		**1156**	**273**	**420**	**693**	**2357**	**90**	**6**	**35**	**2253**	**12.1**		**2054**	**45.9**	**17:25**	**140**	**38**	**49**	**87**	**291**	**14**	**4**	**8**	**18:52**

Played in NHL All-Star Game (1990, 1994, 1998)

Traded to **Edmonton** by **Montreal** with Brent Gilchrist and Vladimir Vujtek for Vincent Damphousse and Edmonton's 4th round choice (Adam Wiesel) in 1993 Entry Draft, August 27, 1992. Signed as a free agent by **St. Louis**, July 28, 1995. Traded to **Montreal** by **St. Louis** with Murray Baron and St. Louis' 5th round choice (Gennady Razin) in 1997 Entry Draft for Pierre Turgeon, Rory Fitzpatrick and Craig Conroy, October 29, 1996. Signed as a free agent by **Toronto**, July 4, 2000. • Officially announced retirement, April 15, 2003. Signed as a free agent by **Dallas**, February 18, 2004.

CORVO, Joe

(KOHR-voh, JOH-sehf) **L.A.**

Defense. Shoots right. 6'1", 205 lbs. Born, Oak Park, IL, June 20, 1977. Los Angeles' 4th choice, 83rd overall, in 1997 Entry Draft.

Season	Club	League	GP	G	A	Pts	PIM	PP	SH	GW	S	%	+/-	TF	F%	Min	GP	G	A	Pts	PIM	PP	SH	GW	Min
1995-96	West. Michigan	CCHA	41	5	25	30	38	....	....	....	....	....	....	....	....	....	....	....	....	....	....	....	....	....	....
1996-97	West. Michigan	CCHA	32	12	21	33	85	....	....	....	....	....	....	....	....	....	....	....	....	....	....	....	....	....	....
1997-98	West. Michigan	CCHA	32	5	12	17	93	....	....	....	....	....	....	....	....	....	....	....	....	....	....	....	....	....	....
1998-99	Springfield	AHL	50	5	15	20	32	....	....	....	....	....	....	....	....	....	....	....	....	....	....	....	....	....	....
	Hampton Roads	ECHL	5	0	0	0	15	....	....	....	....	....	....	....	....	....	4	0	1	1	0	....	....	....	....
99-2000			DID NOT PLAY																						
2000-01	Lowell	AHL	77	10	23	33	31	....	....	....	....	....	....	....	....	....	4	3	1	4	0	....	....	....	....
2001-02	Manchester	AHL	80	13	37	50	30	....	....	....	....	....	....	....	....	....	5	0	5	5	0	....	....	....	....
2002-03	**Los Angeles**	**NHL**	**50**	**5**	**7**	**12**	**14**	**2**	**0**	**0**	**84**	**6.0**	**2**	**0**	**0.0**	**18:37**	....	....	....	....	....	....	....	....	....
	Manchester	AHL	26	8	18	26	8	....	....	....	....	....	....	....	....	....	3	0	0	0	0	....	....	....	....
2003-04	**Los Angeles**	**NHL**	**72**	**8**	**17**	**25**	**36**	**0**	**0**	**3**	**150**	**5.3**	**7**	**1**	**0.0**	**21:08**	....	....	....	....	....	....	....	....	....
	NHL Totals		**122**	**13**	**24**	**37**	**50**	**2**	**0**	**3**	**234**	**5.6**		**1**	**0.0**	**20:06**	....	....	....	....	....	....	....	....	....

CCHA All-Rookie Team (1996) • CCHA Second All-Star Team (1997)

• Missed entire 1999-2000 season after failing to come to contract terms with **Los Angeles.**

COWAN, Jeff

(KOW-an, JEHF) **L.A.**

Left wing. Shoots left. 6'2", 210 lbs. Born, Scarborough, Ont., September 27, 1976.

Season	Club	League	GP	G	A	Pts	PIM	PP	SH	GW	S	%	+/-	TF	F%	Min	GP	G	A	Pts	PIM	PP	SH	GW	Min
1992-93	Guelph Platers	OJHL-B	45	8	8	16	22	....	....	....	....	....	....	....	....	....	....	....	....	....	....	....	....	....	....
1993-94	Guelph Platers	OJHL-B	43	30	26	56	96	....	....	....	....	....	....	....	....	....	....	....	....	....	....	....	....	....	....
	Guelph Storm	OHL	17	1	0	1	5	....	....	....	....	....	....	....	....	....	....	....	....	....	....	....	....	....	....
1994-95	Guelph Storm	OHL	51	10	7	17	14	....	....	....	....	....	....	....	....	....	14	1	1	2	0	....	....	....	....
1995-96	Barrie Colts	OHL	66	38	14	52	29	....	....	....	....	....	....	....	....	....	5	1	2	3	6	....	....	....	....
1996-97	Saint John Flames	AHL	22	5	5	10	8	....	....	....	....	....	....	....	....	....	....	....	....	....	....	....	....	....	....
	Roanoke Express	ECHL	47	21	13	34	42	....	....	....	....	....	....	....	....	....	....	....	....	....	....	....	....	....	....
1997-98	Saint John Flames	AHL	69	15	13	28	23	....	....	....	....	....	....	....	....	....	13	4	1	5	14	....	....	....	....
1998-99	Saint John Flames	AHL	71	7	12	19	117	....	....	....	....	....	....	....	....	....	4	0	1	1	10	....	....	....	....
99-2000	**Calgary**	**NHL**	**13**	**4**	**1**	**5**	**16**	**0**	**0**	**0**	**26**	**15.4**	**2**	**0**	**0.0**	**10:22**	....	....	....	....	....	....	....	....	....
	Saint John Flames	AHL	47	15	10	25	77	....	....	....	....	....	....	....	....	....	....	....	....	....	....	....	....	....	....
2000-01	**Calgary**	**NHL**	**51**	**9**	**4**	**13**	**74**	**2**	**0**	**1**	**48**	**18.8**	**-8**	**5**	**20.0**	**9:06**	....	....	....	....	....	....	....	....	....
2001-02	**Calgary**	**NHL**	**19**	**1**	**0**	**1**	**40**	**0**	**0**	**1**	**13**	**7.7**	**-3**	**2**	**50.0**	**7:44**	....	....	....	....	....	....	....	....	....
	Atlanta	**NHL**	**38**	**4**	**1**	**5**	**50**	**0**	**0**	**1**	**51**	**7.8**	**-11**	**5**	**20.0**	**12:27**	....	....	....	....	....	....	....	....	....
2002-03	**Atlanta**	**NHL**	**66**	**3**	**5**	**8**	**115**	**0**	**0**	**0**	**52**	**5.8**	**-15**	**10**	**30.0**	**8:24**	....	....	....	....	....	....	....	....	....
2003-04	**Atlanta**	**NHL**	**58**	**9**	**15**	**24**	**68**	**1**	**0**	**1**	**74**	**12.2**	**2**	**9**	**22.2**	**10:04**	....	....	....	....	....	....	....	....	....
	Los Angeles	**NHL**	**13**	**2**	**1**	**3**	**24**	**1**	**0**	**0**	**15**	**13.3**	**-1**	**2**	**50.0**	**11:43**	....	....	....	....	....	....	....	....	....
	NHL Totals		**258**	**32**	**27**	**59**	**387**	**4**	**0**	**4**	**279**	**11.5**		**33**	**27.3**	**9:44**	....	....	....	....	....	....	....	....	....

Signed as a free agent by **Calgary**, October 2, 1995. Traded to **Atlanta** by **Calgary** with the rights to Kurtis Foster for Petr Buzek and Atlanta's 6th round choice (Adam Pardy) in 2004 Entry Draft, December 18, 2001. Traded to **Los Angeles** by **Atlanta** for Kip Brennan, March 9, 2004.

CROSS, Cory

(KRAWS, KOHR-ee) **EDM.**

Defense. Shoots left. 6'5", 225 lbs. Born, Lloydminster, Alta., January 3, 1971. Tampa Bay's 1st choice, 1st overall, in 1992 Supplemental Draft.

Season	Club	League	GP	G	A	Pts	PIM	PP	SH	GW	S	%	+/-	TF	F%	Min	GP	G	A	Pts	PIM	PP	SH	GW	Min
1990-91	U. of Alberta	CWUAA	20	2	5	7	16	....	....	....	....	....	....	....	....	....	....	....	....	....	....	....	....	....	....
1991-92	U. of Alberta	CWUAA	41	4	11	15	82	....	....	....	....	....	....	....	....	....	....	....	....	....	....	....	....	....	....
1992-93	U. of Alberta	CWUAA	43	11	28	39	107	....	....	....	....	....	....	....	....	....	....	....	....	....	....	....	....	....	....
	Atlanta Knights	IHL	7	0	1	1	2	....	....	....	....	....	....	....	....	....	4	0	0	0	6	....	....	....	....
1993-94	**Tampa Bay**	**NHL**	**5**	**0**	**0**	**0**	**6**	**0**	**0**	**0**	**5**	**0.0**	**-3**	....	....	....	....	....	....	....	....	....	....	....	....
	Atlanta Knights	IHL	70	4	14	18	72	....	....	....	....	....	....	....	....	....	9	1	2	3	14	....	....	....	....
1994-95	Atlanta Knights	IHL	41	5	10	15	67	....	....	....	....	....	....	....	....	....	....	....	....	....	....	....	....	....	....
	Tampa Bay	**NHL**	**43**	**1**	**5**	**6**	**41**	**0**	**0**	**1**	**35**	**2.9**	**-6**	....	....	....	....	....	....	....	....	....	....	....	....
1995-96	**Tampa Bay**	**NHL**	**75**	**2**	**14**	**16**	**66**	**0**	**0**	**0**	**57**	**3.5**	**4**	....	....	....	**6**	**0**	**0**	**0**	**22**	**0**	**0**	**0**	....
1996-97	**Tampa Bay**	**NHL**	**72**	**4**	**5**	**9**	**95**	**0**	**0**	**2**	**75**	**5.3**	**6**	....	....	....	....	....	....	....	....	....	....	....	....
1997-98	**Tampa Bay**	**NHL**	**74**	**3**	**6**	**9**	**77**	**0**	**1**	**0**	**72**	**4.2**	**-24**	....	....	....	....	....	....	....	....	....	....	....	....
1998-99	**Tampa Bay**	**NHL**	**67**	**2**	**16**	**18**	**92**	**0**	**0**	**0**	**96**	**2.1**	**-25**	**0**	**0.0**	**22:38**	....	....	....	....	....	....	....	....	....
99-2000	**Toronto**	**NHL**	**71**	**4**	**11**	**15**	**64**	**0**	**0**	**1**	**60**	**6.7**	**13**	**0**	**0.0**	**15:59**	**12**	**0**	**2**	**2**	**2**	**0**	**0**	**0**	**15:21**
2000-01	**Toronto**	**NHL**	**41**	**3**	**5**	**8**	**50**	**1**	**0**	**1**	**34**	**8.8**	**7**	**0**	**0.0**	**18:00**	**11**	**2**	**1**	**3**	**10**	**0**	**0**	**1**	**16:05**
2001-02	**Toronto**	**NHL**	**50**	**3**	**9**	**12**	**54**	**0**	**0**	**1**	**39**	**7.7**	**11**	**0**	**0.0**	**15:18**	**12**	**0**	**0**	**0**	**8**	**0**	**0**	**0**	**17:00**
2002-03	**NY Rangers**	**NHL**	**26**	**0**	**4**	**4**	**16**	**0**	**0**	**0**	**18**	**0.0**	**13**	**1**	**0.0**	**17:12**	....	....	....	....	....	....	....	....	....
	Hartford	AHL	2	0	0	0	2	....	....	....	....	....	....	....	....	....	....	....	....	....	....	....	....	....	....
	Edmonton	**NHL**	**11**	**2**	**3**	**5**	**8**	**1**	**0**	**1**	**11**	**18.2**	**3**	**0**	**0.0**	**17:51**	**6**	**0**	**1**	**1**	**20**	**0**	**0**	**0**	**20:37**
2003-04	**Edmonton**	**NHL**	**68**	**7**	**14**	**21**	**56**	**1**	**1**	**1**	**83**	**8.4**	**9**	**0**	**0.0**	**19:14**	....	....	....	....	....	....	....	....	....
	NHL Totals		**603**	**31**	**92**	**123**	**625**	**3**	**1**	**8**	**585**	**5.3**		**1**	**0.0**	**18:17**	**47**	**2**	**4**	**6**	**62**	**0**	**0**	**1**	**16:48**

Traded to **Toronto** by **Tampa Bay** with Tampa Bay's 7th round choice (Ivan Kolozvary) in 2001 Entry Draft for Fredrik Modin, October 1, 1999. Signed as a free agent by **NY Rangers**, December 17, 2002. Traded to **Edmonton** by **NY Rangers** with Radek Dvorak for Anson Carter and Ales Pisa, March 11, 2003.

CULLEN, David (KUH-lehn, DAY-vihd)

Defense. Shoots right. 6'2", 209 lbs. Born, St. Catharines, Ont., December 30, 1976.

			Regular Season														Playoffs								
Season	Club	League	GP	G	A	Pts	PIM	PP	SH	GW	S	%	+/-	TF	F%	Min	GP	G	A	Pts	PIM	PP	SH	GW	Min
1992-93	Thorold	OJHL-B	34	4	6	10	28	....	....	....	....	....	....	....	....	....	....	....	....	....	....	....	....	....	....
1993-94	Thorold	OJHL-B	40	10	35	45	26	....	....	....	....	....	....	....	....	....	....	....	....	....	....	....	....	....	....
1994-95	Thorold	OJHL-B	36	16	30	46	12	....	....	....	....	....	....	....	....	....	....	....	....	....	....	....	....	....	....
1995-96	U. of Maine	H-East	34	2	4	6	22	....	....	....	....	....	....	....	....	....	....	....	....	....	....	....	....	....	....
1996-97	U. of Maine	H-East	35	5	25	30	8	....	....	....	....	....	....	....	....	....	....	....	....	....	....	....	....	....	....
1997-98	U. of Maine	H-East	36	10	27	37	24	....	....	....	....	....	....	....	....	....	....	....	....	....	....	....	....	....	....
1998-99	U. of Maine	H-East	41	11	33	44	24	....	....	....	....	....	....	....	....	....	....	....	....	....	....	....	....	....	....
99-2000	Springfield	AHL	78	10	21	31	57	....	....	....	....	....	....	....	....	....	2	0	0	0	2	....	....	....	....
2000-01	Springfield	AHL	69	13	29	42	40	....	....	....	....	....	....	....	....	....	....	....	....	....	....	....	....	....	....
	Phoenix	**NHL**	**2**	**0**	**0**	**0**	**0**	**0**	**0**	**0**	**0**	**0.0**	**1**	**0**	**0.0**	**12:25**	....	....	....	....	....	....	....	....	....
2001-02	**Phoenix**	**NHL**	**14**	**0**	**0**	**0**	**6**	**0**	**0**	**0**	**3**	**0.0**	**–5**	**0**	**0.0**	**12:21**	....	....	....	....	....	....	....	....	....
	Springfield	AHL	15	1	4	5	4	....	....	....	....	....	....	....	....	....	....	....	....	....	....	....	....	....	....
	Minnesota	**NHL**	**3**	**0**	**0**	**0**	**0**	**0**	**0**	**0**	**0**	**0.0**	**–3**	**0**	**0.0**	**14:02**	....	....	....	....	....	....	....	....	....
	Houston Aeros	AHL	38	5	15	20	4	....	....	....	....	....	....	....	....	....	13	0	6	6	6	....	....	....	....
2002-03	Houston Aeros	AHL	72	2	27	29	42	....	....	....	....	....	....	....	....	....	23	3	4	7	14	....	....	....	....
2003-04	Rochester	AHL	75	12	35	47	26	....	....	....	....	....	....	....	....	....	16	1	4	5	6	....	....	....	....
	NHL Totals		**19**	**0**	**0**	**0**	**6**	**0**	**0**	**0**	**3**	**0.0**		**0**	**0.0**	**12:37**	....	....	....	....	....	....	....	....	....

Hockey East First All-Star Team (1999) • NCAA East First All-American Team (1999) • NCAA Championship All-Tournament Team (1999)

Signed as a free agent by **Phoenix**, April 16, 1999. Traded to **Minnesota** by **Phoenix** for Sebastien Bordeleau, January 4, 2002. Signed as a free agent by **Buffalo**, July 28, 2003.

CULLEN, Matt (KUH-lehn, MAT) CAR.

Center. Shoots left. 6'2", 199 lbs. Born, Virginia, MN, November 2, 1976. Anaheim's 2nd choice, 35th overall, in 1996 Entry Draft.

			Regular Season														Playoffs								
Season	Club	League	GP	G	A	Pts	PIM	PP	SH	GW	S	%	+/-	TF	F%	Min	GP	G	A	Pts	PIM	PP	SH	GW	Min
1994-95	Moorhead Spuds	Hi-School	28	47	42	89	78	....	....	....	....	....	....	....	....	....	....	....	....	....	....	....	....	....	....
1995-96	St. Cloud State	WCHA	39	12	29	41	28	....	....	....	....	....	....	....	....	....	....	....	....	....	....	....	....	....	....
1996-97	St. Cloud State	WCHA	36	15	30	45	70	....	....	....	....	....	....	....	....	....	....	....	....	....	....	....	....	....	....
	Baltimore Bandits	AHL	6	3	3	6	7	....	....	....	....	....	....	....	....	....	3	0	2	2	0	....	....	....	....
1997-98	**Anaheim**	**NHL**	**61**	**6**	**21**	**27**	**23**	**2**	**0**	**0**	**75**	**8.0**	**–4**	....	....	....	....	....	....	....	....	....	....	....	....
	Cincinnati	AHL	18	15	12	27	2	....	....	....	....	....	....	....	....	....	....	....	....	....	....	....	....	....	....
1998-99	**Anaheim**	**NHL**	**75**	**11**	**14**	**25**	**47**	**5**	**1**	**1**	**112**	**9.8**	**–12**	**1047**	**47.7**	**15:31**	**4**	**0**	**0**	**0**	**0**	**0**	**0**	**0**	**15:30**
	Cincinnati	AHL	3	1	2	3	8	....	....	....	....	....	....	....	....	....	....	....	....	....	....	....	....	....	....
99-2000	**Anaheim**	**NHL**	**80**	**13**	**26**	**39**	**24**	**1**	**0**	**1**	**137**	**9.5**	**5**	**1247**	**44.6**	**16:54**	....	....	....	....	....	....	....	....	....
2000-01	**Anaheim**	**NHL**	**82**	**10**	**30**	**40**	**38**	**4**	**0**	**1**	**159**	**6.3**	**–23**	**1478**	**48.0**	**18:15**	....	....	....	....	....	....	....	....	....
2001-02	**Anaheim**	**NHL**	**79**	**18**	**30**	**48**	**24**	**3**	**1**	**4**	**164**	**11.0**	**–1**	**1283**	**51.4**	**17:01**	....	....	....	....	....	....	....	....	....
2002-03	**Anaheim**	**NHL**	**50**	**7**	**14**	**21**	**12**	**1**	**0**	**1**	**77**	**9.1**	**–4**	**271**	**50.6**	**14:18**	....	....	....	....	....	....	....	....	....
	Florida	**NHL**	**30**	**6**	**6**	**12**	**22**	**2**	**1**	**1**	**54**	**11.1**	**–4**	**423**	**47.3**	**14:43**	....	....	....	....	....	....	....	....	....
2003-04	**Florida**	**NHL**	**56**	**6**	**13**	**19**	**24**	**1**	**0**	**2**	**75**	**8.0**	**–2**	**735**	**50.6**	**14:12**	....	....	....	....	....	....	....	....	....
	NHL Totals		**513**	**77**	**154**	**231**	**214**	**19**	**3**	**11**	**853**	**9.0**		**6484**	**48.3**	**16:10**	**4**	**0**	**0**	**0**	**0**	**0**	**0**	**0**	**15:30**

WCHA Second All-Star Team (1997)

Traded to **Florida** by **Anaheim** with Pavel Trnka and Anaheim's 4th round choice (James Pemberton) in 2003 Entry Draft for Sandis Ozolinsh and Lance Ward, January 30, 2003. Signed as a free agent by **Carolina**, August 5, 2004.

CULLIMORE, Jassen (KUHL-ih-mohr, JAY-sehn) CHI.

Defense. Shoots left. 6'5", 244 lbs. Born, Simcoe, Ont., December 4, 1972. Vancouver's 2nd choice, 29th overall, in 1991 Entry Draft.

			Regular Season														Playoffs								
Season	Club	League	GP	G	A	Pts	PIM	PP	SH	GW	S	%	+/-	TF	F%	Min	GP	G	A	Pts	PIM	PP	SH	GW	Min
1986-87	Caledonia	OJHL-C	18	2	0	2	9	....	....	....	....	....	....	....	....	....	....	....	....	....	....	....	....	....	....
1987-88	Simcoe Rams	OJHL-C	35	11	14	25	92	....	....	....	....	....	....	....	....	....	....	....	....	....	....	....	....	....	....
1988-89	Peterboro B's	OJHL-B	29	11	17	28	88	....	....	....	....	....	....	....	....	....	....	....	....	....	....	....	....	....	....
	Peterborough	OHL	20	2	1	3	6	....	....	....	....	....	....	....	....	....	....	....	....	....	....	....	....	....	....
1989-90	Peterborough	OHL	59	2	6	8	61	....	....	....	....	....	....	....	....	....	11	0	2	2	8	....	....	....	....
1990-91	Peterborough	OHL	62	8	16	24	74	....	....	....	....	....	....	....	....	....	4	1	0	1	7	....	....	....	....
1991-92	Peterborough	OHL	54	9	37	46	65	....	....	....	....	....	....	....	....	....	10	3	6	9	8	....	....	....	....
1992-93	Hamilton	AHL	56	5	7	12	60	....	....	....	....	....	....	....	....	....	....	....	....	....	....	....	....	....	....
1993-94	Hamilton	AHL	71	8	20	28	86	....	....	....	....	....	....	....	....	....	3	0	1	1	2	....	....	....	....
1994-95	Syracuse Crunch	AHL	33	2	7	9	66	....	....	....	....	....	....	....	....	....	....	....	....	....	....	....	....	....	....
	Vancouver	**NHL**	**34**	**1**	**2**	**3**	**39**	**0**	**0**	**0**	**30**	**3.3**	**–2**	....	....	....	**11**	**0**	**0**	**0**	**12**	**0**	**0**	**0**	....
1995-96	**Vancouver**	**NHL**	**27**	**1**	**1**	**2**	**21**	**0**	**0**	**1**	**12**	**8.3**	**4**	....	....	....	....	....	....	....	....	....	....	....	....
1996-97	**Vancouver**	**NHL**	**3**	**0**	**0**	**0**	**2**	**0**	**0**	**0**	**2**	**0.0**	**–2**	....	....	....	....	....	....	....	....	....	....	....	....
	Montreal	**NHL**	**49**	**2**	**6**	**8**	**42**	**0**	**1**	**1**	**52**	**3.8**	**4**	....	....	....	**2**	**0**	**0**	**0**	**2**	**0**	**0**	**0**	....
1997-98	**Montreal**	**NHL**	**3**	**0**	**0**	**0**	**4**	**0**	**0**	**0**	**1**	**0.0**	**0**	....	....	....	....	....	....	....	....	....	....	....	....
	Fredericton	AHL	5	1	0	1	8	....	....	....	....	....	....	....	....	....	....	....	....	....	....	....	....	....	....
	Tampa Bay	**NHL**	**25**	**1**	**2**	**3**	**22**	**1**	**0**	**0**	**17**	**5.9**	**–4**	....	....	....	....	....	....	....	....	....	....	....	....
1998-99	**Tampa Bay**	**NHL**	**78**	**5**	**12**	**17**	**81**	**1**	**1**	**1**	**73**	**6.8**	**–22**	**0**	**0.0**	**20:14**	....	....	....	....	....	....	....	....	....
99-2000	Providence Bruins	AHL	16	5	10	15	31	....	....	....	....	....	....	....	....	....	....	....	....	....	....	....	....	....	....
	Tampa Bay	**NHL**	**46**	**1**	**1**	**2**	**66**	**0**	**0**	**0**	**23**	**4.3**	**–12**	**2**	**0.0**	**15:38**	....	....	....	....	....	....	....	....	....
2000-01	**Tampa Bay**	**NHL**	**74**	**1**	**6**	**7**	**80**	**0**	**0**	**0**	**56**	**1.8**	**–6**	**0**	**0.0**	**19:43**	....	....	....	....	....	....	....	....	....
2001-02	**Tampa Bay**	**NHL**	**78**	**4**	**9**	**13**	**58**	**0**	**0**	**1**	**84**	**4.8**	**–1**	**0**	**0.0**	**20:07**	....	....	....	....	....	....	....	....	....
2002-03	**Tampa Bay**	**NHL**	**28**	**1**	**3**	**4**	**31**	**0**	**0**	**0**	**23**	**4.3**	**3**	**0**	**0.0**	**18:25**	**11**	**1**	**1**	**2**	**4**	**0**	**0**	**0**	**22:11**
2003-04♦	**Tampa Bay**	**NHL**	**79**	**2**	**5**	**7**	**58**	**0**	**0**	**1**	**78**	**2.6**	**8**	**0**	**0.0**	**19:02**	**11**	**0**	**2**	**2**	**6**	**0**	**0**	**0**	**15:15**
	NHL Totals		**524**	**19**	**47**	**66**	**504**	**2**	**2**	**5**	**451**	**4.2**		**2**	**0.0**	**19:10**	**35**	**1**	**3**	**4**	**24**	**0**	**0**	**0**	**18:43**

OHL Second All-Star Team (1992)

Traded to **Montreal** by **Vancouver** for Donald Brashear, November 13, 1996. Claimed on waivers by **Tampa Bay** from **Montreal**, January 22, 1998. Loaned to **Providence** (AHL) by **Tampa Bay**, October 1, 1999. • Missed majority of 2002-03 season recovering from elbow injury suffered in game vs. Vancouver, November 29, 2002. Signed as a free agent by **Chicago**, July 22, 2004.

CUMMINS, Jim (KUH-mihns, JIHM)

Right wing. Shoots right. 6'2", 212 lbs. Born, Dearborn, MI, May 17, 1970. NY Rangers' 5th choice, 67th overall, in 1989 Entry Draft.

			Regular Season														Playoffs								
Season	Club	League	GP	G	A	Pts	PIM	PP	SH	GW	S	%	+/-	TF	F%	Min	GP	G	A	Pts	PIM	PP	SH	GW	Min
1987-88	Det. Compuware	NAJHL	31	11	15	26	146	....	....	....	....	....	....	....	....	....	....	....	....	....	....	....	....	....	....
1988-89	Michigan State	CCHA	30	3	8	11	98	....	....	....	....	....	....	....	....	....	....	....	....	....	....	....	....	....	....
1989-90	Michigan State	CCHA	41	8	7	15	94	....	....	....	....	....	....	....	....	....	....	....	....	....	....	....	....	....	....
1990-91	Michigan State	CCHA	34	9	6	15	110	....	....	....	....	....	....	....	....	....	....	....	....	....	....	....	....	....	....
1991-92	**Detroit**	**NHL**	**1**	**0**	**0**	**0**	**7**	**0**	**0**	**0**	**0**	**0.0**	**0**	....	....	....	....	....	....	....	....	....	....	....	....
	Adirondack	AHL	65	7	13	20	338	....	....	....	....	....	....	....	....	....	5	0	0	0	19	....	....	....	....
1992-93	**Detroit**	**NHL**	**7**	**1**	**1**	**2**	**58**	**0**	**0**	**0**	**5**	**20.0**	**0**	....	....	....	....	....	....	....	....	....	....	....	....
	Adirondack	AHL	43	16	4	20	179	....	....	....	....	....	....	....	....	....	9	3	1	4	4	....	....	....	....
1993-94	**Philadelphia**	**NHL**	**22**	**1**	**2**	**3**	**71**	**0**	**0**	**0**	**17**	**5.9**	**0**	....	....	....	....	....	....	....	....	....	....	....	....
	Hershey Bears	AHL	17	6	6	12	70	....	....	....	....	....	....	....	....	....	....	....	....	....	....	....	....	....	....
	Tampa Bay	**NHL**	**4**	**0**	**0**	**0**	**13**	**0**	**0**	**0**	**3**	**0.0**	**–1**	....	....	....	....	....	....	....	....	....	....	....	....
	Atlanta Knights	IHL	7	4	5	9	14	....	....	....	....	....	....	....	....	....	13	1	2	3	90	....	....	....	....
1994-95	**Tampa Bay**	**NHL**	**10**	**1**	**0**	**1**	**41**	**0**	**0**	**1**	**3**	**33.3**	**–3**	....	....	....	....	....	....	....	....	....	....	....	....
	Chicago	**NHL**	**27**	**3**	**1**	**4**	**117**	**0**	**0**	**0**	**20**	**15.0**	**–3**	....	....	....	**14**	**1**	**1**	**2**	**4**	**0**	**0**	**1**	....
1995-96	**Chicago**	**NHL**	**52**	**2**	**4**	**6**	**180**	**0**	**0**	**2**	**34**	**5.9**	**–1**	....	....	....	**10**	**0**	**0**	**0**	**2**	**0**	**0**	**0**	....
1996-97	**Chicago**	**NHL**	**65**	**6**	**6**	**12**	**199**	**0**	**0**	**0**	**61**	**9.8**	**4**	....	....	....	**6**	**0**	**0**	**0**	**24**	**0**	**0**	**0**	....
1997-98	**Chicago**	**NHL**	**55**	**0**	**2**	**2**	**178**	**0**	**0**	**0**	**33**	**0.0**	**–9**	....	....	....	....	....	....	....	....	....	....	....	....
	Phoenix	**NHL**	**20**	**0**	**0**	**0**	**47**	**0**	**0**	**0**	**10**	**0.0**	**–7**	....	....	....	**3**	**0**	**0**	**0**	**4**	**0**	**0**	**0**	....
1998-99	**Phoenix**	**NHL**	**55**	**1**	**7**	**8**	**190**	**0**	**0**	**0**	**26**	**3.8**	**3**	**0**	**0.0**	**7:07**	**3**	**0**	**1**	**1**	**0**	**0**	**0**	**0**	**4:27**
99-2000	**Montreal**	**NHL**	**47**	**3**	**5**	**8**	**92**	**0**	**0**	**0**	**33**	**9.1**	**–5**	**4**	**25.0**	**8:58**	....	....	....	....	....	....	....	....	....
2000-01	**Anaheim**	**NHL**	**79**	**5**	**6**	**11**	**167**	**0**	**0**	**1**	**45**	**11.1**	**–11**	**7**	**28.6**	**7:14**	....	....	....	....	....	....	....	....	....
2001-02	**Anaheim**	**NHL**	**2**	**0**	**0**	**0**	**0**	**0**	**0**	**0**	**0**	**0.0**	**–1**	**0**	**0.0**	**7:27**	....	....	....	....	....	....	....	....	....
	Cincinnati	AHL	11	1	4	5	39	....	....	....	....	....	....	....	....	....	....	....	....	....	....	....	....	....	....
	NY Islanders	**NHL**	**10**	**0**	**0**	**0**	**31**	**0**	**0**	**0**	**3**	**0.0**	**–5**	**1**	**100.0**	**4:26**	**1**	**0**	**0**	**0**	**9**	**0**	**0**	**0**	**6:15**

			Regular Season														Playoffs								
Season	Club	League	GP	G	A	Pts	PIM	PP	SH	GW	S	%	+/-	TF	F%	Min	GP	G	A	Pts	PIM	PP	SH	GW	Min
2002-03			OUT OF HOCKEY – RETIRED																						
2003-04	**Colorado**	**NHL**	**55**	**1**	**2**	**3**	**147**	**0**	**0**	**1**	**25**	**4.0**	**–5**	**30**	**33.3**	**5:50**	....	....	....	....	....	....	....	....	....
	NHL Totals		**511**	**24**	**36**	**60**	**1538**	**0**	**0**	**5**	**318**	**7.5**		**42**	**33.3**	**7:07**	**37**	**1**	**2**	**3**	**43**	**0**	**0**	**1**	**4:54**

Traded to **Detroit** by **NY Rangers** with Kevin Miller and Dennis Vial for Joe Kocur and Per Djoos, March 5, 1991. Traded to **Philadelphia** by **Detroit** with Philadelphia's 4th round choice (previously acquired, later traded to Boston – Boston selected Charles Paquette) in 1993 Entry Draft for Greg Johnson and Philadelphia's 5th round choice (Frederic Deschenes) in 1994 Entry Draft, June 20, 1993. Traded to **Tampa Bay** by **Philadelphia** with Philadelphia's 4th round choice (later traded back to Philadelphia – Philadelphia selected Radovan Somik) in 1995 Entry Draft for Rob DiMaio, March 18, 1994. Traded to **Chicago** by **Tampa Bay** with Tom Tilley and Jeff Buchanan for Paul Ysebaert and Rich Sutter, February 22, 1995. Traded to **Phoenix** by **Chicago** with Keith Carney for Chad Kilger and Jayson More, March 4, 1998. Traded to **Montreal** by **Phoenix** for NY Rangers' 6th round choice (previously acquired, Phoenix selected Erik Lewerstrom) in 1999 Entry Draft, June 26, 1999. Signed as a free agent by **Anaheim**, July 5, 2000. Traded to **NY Islanders** by **Anaheim** for Dave Roche, January 14, 2002. • Officially announced retirement July 2, 2002. Signed as a free agent by **Colorado**, September 26, 2003.

CUTTA, Jakub (KOO-tuh, YA-kuhb) WSH.

Defense. Shoots left. 6'3", 210 lbs. Born, Jablonec nad Nisou, Czech., December 29, 1981. Washington's 3rd choice, 61st overall, in 2000 Entry Draft.

Season	Club	League	GP	G	A	Pts	PIM	PP	SH	GW	S	%	+/-	TF	F%	Min	GP	G	A	Pts	PIM	PP	SH	GW	Min
1997-98	HC Liberec Jr.	Czech-Jr.	29	3	13	16	70	....	....	....	....	....	....	....	....	....	....	....	....	....	....	....	....	....	....
1998-99	Swift Current	WHL	59	3	3	6	63	....	....	....	....	....	....	....	....	....	....	....	....	....	....	....	....	....	....
99-2000	Swift Current	WHL	71	2	12	14	114	....	....	....	....	....	....	....	....	....	12	0	2	2	24	....	....	....	....
2000-01	**Washington**	**NHL**	**3**	**0**	**0**	**0**	**0**	**0**	**0**	**0**	**1**	**0.0**	**–1**	**0**	**0.0**	**11:33**	....	....	....	....	....	....	....	....	....
	Swift Current	WHL	47	5	8	13	102	....	....	....	....	....	....	....	....	....	16	1	3	4	32	....	....	....	....
2001-02	**Washington**	**NHL**	**2**	**0**	**0**	**0**	**0**	**0**	**0**	**0**	**2**	**0.0**	**–3**	**0**	**0.0**	**16:02**	....	....	....	....	....	....	....	....	....
	Portland Pirates	AHL	56	1	3	4	69	....	....	....	....	....	....	....	....	....	....	....	....	....	....	....	....	....	....
2002-03	Portland Pirates	AHL	66	3	12	15	106	....	....	....	....	....	....	....	....	....	3	0	0	0	2	....	....	....	....
2003-04	**Washington**	**NHL**	**3**	**0**	**0**	**0**	**0**	**0**	**0**	**0**	**1**	**0.0**	**–1**	**0**	**0.0**	**13:54**	....	....	....	....	....	....	....	....	....
	Portland Pirates	AHL	59	1	5	6	58	....	....	....	....	....	....	....	....	....	7	2	0	2	7	....	....	....	....
	NHL Totals		**8**	**0**	**0**	**0**	**0**	**0**	**0**	**0**	**4**	**0.0**		**0**	**0.0**	**13:33**	....	....	....	....	....	....	....	....	....

CZERKAWSKI, Mariusz (chehr-KAWV-skee, MAIR-ee-UHZ)

Right wing. Shoots left. 6', 200 lbs. Born, Radomsko, Poland, April 13, 1972. Boston's 5th choice, 106th overall, in 1991 Entry Draft.

Season	Club	League	GP	G	A	Pts	PIM	PP	SH	GW	S	%	+/-	TF	F%	Min	GP	G	A	Pts	PIM	PP	SH	GW	Min
1990-91	GKS Tychy	Poland	24	25	15	40	....	....	....	....	....	....	....	....	....	....	....	....	....	....	....	....	....	....	....
1991-92	Djurgarden	Sweden	39	8	5	13	4	....	....	....	....	....	....	....	....	....	3	0	0	0	2	....	....	....	....
	Poland	Olympics	5	0	1	1	4	....	....	....	....	....	....	....	....	....	....	....	....	....	....	....	....	....	....
1992-93	Hammarby	Swede-2	32	*39	30	*69	74	....	....	....	....	....	....	....	....	....	13	*16	7	*23	34	....	....	....	....
1993-94	Djurgarden	Sweden	39	13	21	34	20	....	....	....	....	....	....	....	....	....	6	3	1	4	2	....	....	....	....
	Boston	**NHL**	**4**	**2**	**1**	**3**	**0**	**1**	**0**	**0**	**11**	**18.2**	**–2**	....	....	....	**13**	**3**	**3**	**6**	**4**	**1**	**0**	**0**	....
1994-95	Kiekko Espoo	Finland	7	9	3	12	10	....	....	....	....	....	....	....	....	....	....	....	....	....	....	....	....	....	....
	Boston	**NHL**	**47**	**12**	**14**	**26**	**31**	**1**	**0**	**2**	**126**	**9.5**	**4**	....	....	....	**5**	**1**	**0**	**1**	**0**	**0**	**0**	**0**	....
1995-96	**Boston**	**NHL**	**33**	**5**	**6**	**11**	**10**	**1**	**0**	**0**	**63**	**7.9**	**–11**	....	....	....	....	....	....	....	....	....	....	....	....
	Edmonton	**NHL**	**37**	**12**	**17**	**29**	**8**	**2**	**0**	**1**	**79**	**15.2**	**7**	....	....	....	....	....	....	....	....	....	....	....	....
1996-97	**Edmonton**	**NHL**	**76**	**26**	**21**	**47**	**16**	**4**	**0**	**3**	**182**	**14.3**	**0**	....	....	....	**12**	**2**	**1**	**3**	**10**	**0**	**0**	**0**	....
1997-98	**NY Islanders**	**NHL**	**68**	**12**	**13**	**25**	**23**	**2**	**0**	**1**	**136**	**8.8**	**11**	....	....	....	....	....	....	....	....	....	....	....	....
1998-99	**NY Islanders**	**NHL**	**78**	**21**	**17**	**38**	**14**	**4**	**0**	**1**	**205**	**10.2**	**–10**	**2**	**0.0**	**14:18**	....	....	....	....	....	....	....	....	....
99-2000	**NY Islanders**	**NHL**	**79**	**35**	**35**	**70**	**34**	**16**	**0**	**4**	**276**	**12.7**	**–16**	**4**	**25.0**	**17:45**	....	....	....	....	....	....	....	....	....
2000-01	**NY Islanders**	**NHL**	**82**	**30**	**32**	**62**	**48**	**10**	**1**	**0**	**287**	**10.5**	**–24**	**8**	**50.0**	**18:44**	....	....	....	....	....	....	....	....	....
2001-02	**NY Islanders**	**NHL**	**82**	**22**	**29**	**51**	**48**	**6**	**0**	**6**	**169**	**13.0**	**–8**	**10**	**10.0**	**15:58**	**7**	**2**	**2**	**4**	**4**	**1**	**0**	**0**	**12:58**
2002-03	**Montreal**	**NHL**	**43**	**5**	**9**	**14**	**16**	**1**	**0**	**0**	**77**	**6.5**	**–7**	**2**	**0.0**	**13:10**	....	....	....	....	....	....	....	....	....
	Hamilton	AHL	20	8	12	20	12	....	....	....	....	....	....	....	....	....	6	1	3	4	6	....	....	....	....
2003-04	**NY Islanders**	**NHL**	**81**	**25**	**24**	**49**	**16**	**9**	**0**	**2**	**157**	**15.9**	**8**	**6**	**16.7**	**13:02**	**5**	**0**	**1**	**1**	**0**	**0**	**0**	**0**	**10:43**
	NHL Totals		**710**	**207**	**218**	**425**	**264**	**57**	**1**	**20**	**1768**	**11.7**		**32**	**21.9**	**15:42**	**42**	**8**	**7**	**15**	**18**	**2**	**0**	**0**	**12:02**

Played in NHL All-Star Game (2000)

Traded to **Edmonton** by **Boston** with Sean Brown and Boston's 1st round choice (Matthieu Descoteaux) in 1996 Entry Draft for Bill Ranford, January 11, 1996. Traded to **NY Islanders** by **Edmonton** for Dan LaCouture, August 25, 1997. Traded to **Montreal** by **NY Islanders** for Arron Asham and Montreal's 5th round choice (Marcus Paulsson) in 2002 Entry Draft, June 22, 2002. Signed as a free agent by **NY Islanders**, July 17, 2003.

DACKELL, Andreas (DA-kuhl, an-DRAY-uhs)

Right wing. Shoots right. 5'11", 194 lbs. Born, Gavle, Sweden, December 29, 1972. Ottawa's 3rd choice, 136th overall, in 1996 Entry Draft.

Season	Club	League	GP	G	A	Pts	PIM	PP	SH	GW	S	%	+/-	TF	F%	Min	GP	G	A	Pts	PIM	PP	SH	GW	Min
1990-91	Brynas IF Gavle	Sweden	3	0	1	1	2	....	....	....	....	....	....	....	....	....	....	....	....	....	....	....	....	....	....
1991-92	Brynas IF Gavle Jr.	Swede-Jr.	26	17	24	41	42	....	....	....	....	....	....	....	....	....	2	3	1	4	2	....	....	....	....
	Brynas IF Gavle	Sweden	4	0	0	0	2	....	....	....	....	....	....	....	....	....	2	0	1	1	4	....	....	....	....
1992-93	Brynas IF Gavle	Sweden	40	12	15	27	12	....	....	....	....	....	....	....	....	....	10	4	5	9	2	....	....	....	....
1993-94	Brynas IF Gavle	Sweden	38	12	17	29	47	....	....	....	....	....	....	....	....	....	7	2	2	4	8	....	....	....	....
	Sweden	Olympics	4	0	0	0	0	....	....	....	....	....	....	....	....	....	....	....	....	....	....	....	....	....	....
1994-95	Brynas IF Gavle	Sweden	39	17	16	33	34	....	....	....	....	....	....	....	....	....	14	3	3	6	14	....	....	....	....
1995-96	Brynas IF Gavle	Sweden	40	25	22	47	79	....	....	....	....	....	....	....	....	....	10	9	6	15	12	....	....	....	....
1996-97	**Ottawa**	**NHL**	**79**	**12**	**19**	**31**	**8**	**2**	**0**	**3**	**79**	**15.2**	**–6**	....	....	....	**7**	**1**	**0**	**1**	**0**	**0**	**0**	**0**	....
1997-98	**Ottawa**	**NHL**	**82**	**15**	**18**	**33**	**24**	**3**	**2**	**2**	**130**	**11.5**	**–11**	....	....	....	**11**	**1**	**1**	**2**	**2**	**1**	**0**	**0**	....
1998-99	**Ottawa**	**NHL**	**77**	**15**	**35**	**50**	**30**	**6**	**0**	**3**	**107**	**14.0**	**9**	**5**	**40.0**	**17:18**	**4**	**0**	**1**	**1**	**0**	**0**	**0**	**0**	**18:49**
99-2000	**Ottawa**	**NHL**	**82**	**10**	**25**	**35**	**18**	**0**	**0**	**1**	**99**	**10.1**	**5**	**1**	**100.0**	**16:17**	**6**	**2**	**1**	**3**	**2**	**0**	**0**	**1**	**18:14**
2000-01	**Ottawa**	**NHL**	**81**	**13**	**18**	**31**	**24**	**1**	**0**	**3**	**72**	**18.1**	**7**	**13**	**15.4**	**14:02**	**4**	**0**	**0**	**0**	**0**	**0**	**0**	**0**	**12:19**
2001-02	**Montreal**	**NHL**	**79**	**15**	**18**	**33**	**24**	**2**	**3**	**2**	**83**	**18.1**	**–3**	**16**	**31.3**	**17:14**	**12**	**1**	**2**	**3**	**6**	**0**	**0**	**0**	**16:21**
2002-03	**Montreal**	**NHL**	**73**	**7**	**18**	**25**	**24**	**0**	**0**	**1**	**74**	**9.5**	**–5**	**18**	**27.8**	**14:53**	....	....	....	....	....	....	....	....	....
2003-04	**Montreal**	**NHL**	**60**	**4**	**8**	**12**	**10**	**0**	**0**	**0**	**50**	**8.0**	**8**	**16**	**25.0**	**15:21**	....	....	....	....	....	....	....	....	....
	NHL Totals		**613**	**91**	**159**	**250**	**162**	**14**	**5**	**15**	**694**	**13.1**		**69**	**27.5**	**15:52**	**44**	**5**	**5**	**10**	**10**	**1**	**0**	**1**	**16:33**

Traded to **Montreal** by **Ottawa** for Montreal's 8th round choice (Neil Petruic) in 2001 Entry Draft, June 24, 2001. Signed as a free agent by **Brynas** (Sweden), May 14, 2004.

DAGENAIS, Pierre (da-ZHUH-nay, PEE-air) MTL.

Right wing. Shoots left. 6'4", 217 lbs. Born, Blainville, Que., March 4, 1978. New Jersey's 6th choice, 105th overall, in 1998 Entry Draft.

Season	Club	League	GP	G	A	Pts	PIM	PP	SH	GW	S	%	+/-	TF	F%	Min	GP	G	A	Pts	PIM	PP	SH	GW	Min
1994-95	Laval Laurentide	QAAA	34	28	14	42	68	....	....	....	....	....	....	....	....	....	13	10	9	19	32	....	....	....	....
1995-96	Moncton Alpines	QMJHL	67	43	25	68	59	....	....	....	....	....	....	....	....	....	....	....	....	....	....	....	....	....	....
1996-97	Moncton Wildcats	QMJHL	6	4	2	6	0	....	....	....	....	....	....	....	....	....	....	....	....	....	....	....	....	....	....
	Laval Titan	QMJHL	37	16	14	30	40	....	....	....	....	....	....	....	....	....	....	....	....	....	....	....	....	....	....
	Rouyn-Noranda	QMJHL	27	21	8	29	22	....	....	....	....	....	....	....	....	....	....	....	....	....	....	....	....	....	....
1997-98	Rouyn-Noranda	QMJHL	60	*66	67	133	50	....	....	....	....	....	....	....	....	....	6	6	2	8	2	....	....	....	....
1998-99	Albany River Rats	AHL	69	17	13	30	37	....	....	....	....	....	....	....	....	....	4	0	0	0	0	....	....	....	....
99-2000	Albany River Rats	AHL	80	35	30	65	47	....	....	....	....	....	....	....	....	....	5	1	0	1	14	....	....	....	....
2000-01	**New Jersey**	**NHL**	**9**	**3**	**2**	**5**	**6**	**1**	**0**	**1**	**20**	**15.0**	**1**	**8**	**37.5**	**12:22**	....	....	....	....	....	....	....	....	....
	Albany River Rats	AHL	69	34	28	62	52	....	....	....	....	....	....	....	....	....	....	....	....	....	....	....	....	....	....
2001-02	**New Jersey**	**NHL**	**16**	**3**	**3**	**6**	**4**	**1**	**0**	**1**	**30**	**10.0**	**–5**	**5**	**40.0**	**10:54**	....	....	....	....	....	....	....	....	....
	Albany River Rats	AHL	6	0	2	2	2	....	....	....	....	....	....	....	....	....	....	....	....	....	....	....	....	....	....
	Florida	**NHL**	**26**	**7**	**1**	**8**	**4**	**2**	**0**	**0**	**47**	**14.9**	**–5**	**4**	**75.0**	**11:04**	....	....	....	....	....	....	....	....	....
	Utah Grizzlies	AHL	4	1	1	2	2	....	....	....	....	....	....	....	....	....	....	....	....	....	....	....	....	....	....
2002-03	**Florida**	**NHL**	**9**	**0**	**0**	**0**	**4**	**0**	**0**	**0**	**5**	**0.0**	**–1**	**0**	**0.0**	**6:01**	....	....	....	....	....	....	....	....	....
	San Antonio	AHL	49	21	14	35	28	....	....	....	....	....	....	....	....	....	3	2	0	2	2	....	....	....	....
2003-04	**Montreal**	**NHL**	**50**	**17**	**10**	**27**	**24**	**4**	**0**	**3**	**149**	**11.4**	**15**	**121**	**42.2**	**13:53**	**8**	**0**	**1**	**1**	**6**	**0**	**0**	**0**	**12:06**
	Hamilton	AHL	20	12	9	21	19	....	....	....	....	....	....	....	....	....	....	....	....	....	....	....	....	....	....
	NHL Totals		**110**	**30**	**16**	**46**	**42**	**8**	**0**	**5**	**251**	**12.0**		**138**	**42.8**	**12:01**	**8**	**0**	**1**	**1**	**6**	**0**	**0**	**0**	**12:06**

• Re-entered NHL Entry Draft. Originally New Jersey's 4th choice, 47th overall, in 1996 Entry Draft.

QMJHL All-Rookie Team (1996) • QMJHL Second All-Star Team (1998) • AHL Second All-Star Team (2001)

Claimed on waivers by **Florida** from **New Jersey**, January 12, 2002. Signed as a free agent by **Montreal**, July 4, 2003.

			Regular Season														Playoffs								
Season	Club	League	GP	G	A	Pts	PIM	PP	SH	GW	S	%	+/-	TF	F%	Min	GP	G	A	Pts	PIM	PP	SH	GW	Min

DAIGLE, Alexandre
(DAYG, al-ehx-AHN-druh) **MIN.**

Center. Shoots left. 6', 195 lbs. Born, Montreal, Que., February 7, 1975. Ottawa's 1st choice, 1st overall, in 1993 Entry Draft.

Season	Club	League	GP	G	A	Pts	PIM	PP	SH	GW	S	%	+/-	TF	F%	Min	GP	G	A	Pts	PIM	PP	SH	GW	Min
1990-91	Laval Laurentide	QAAA	42	*50	*60	*110	98	....	....	....	....	....	....	....	....	....	13	5	9	14	23	....	....	....	....
1991-92	Victoriaville Tigres	QMJHL	66	35	75	110	63	....	....	....	....	....	....	....	....	....	....	....	....	....	....	....	....	....	....
1992-93	Victoriaville Tigres	QMJHL	53	45	92	137	85	....	....	....	....	....	....	....	....	....	6	5	6	11	4	....	....	....	....
1993-94	**Ottawa**	**NHL**	**84**	**20**	**31**	**51**	**40**	**4**	**0**	**2**	**168**	**11.9**	**–45**	....	....	....	....	....	....	....	....	....	....	....	....
1994-95	Victoriaville Tigres	QMJHL	18	14	20	34	16	....	....	....	....	....	....	....	....	....	....	....	....	....	....	....	....	....	....
	Ottawa	**NHL**	**47**	**16**	**21**	**37**	**14**	**4**	**1**	**2**	**105**	**15.2**	**–22**	....	....	....	....	....	....	....	....	....	....	....	....
1995-96	**Ottawa**	**NHL**	**50**	**5**	**12**	**17**	**24**	**1**	**0**	**0**	**77**	**6.5**	**–30**	....	....	....	....	....	....	....	....	....	....	....	....
1996-97	**Ottawa**	**NHL**	**82**	**26**	**25**	**51**	**33**	**4**	**0**	**5**	**203**	**12.8**	**–33**	....	....	....	**7**	**0**	**0**	**0**	**2**	**0**	**0**	**0**	....
1997-98	**Ottawa**	**NHL**	**38**	**7**	**9**	**16**	**8**	**4**	**0**	**2**	**68**	**10.3**	**–7**	....	....	....	....	....	....	....	....	....	....	....	....
	Philadelphia	**NHL**	**37**	**9**	**17**	**26**	**6**	**4**	**0**	**3**	**78**	**11.5**	**–1**	....	....	....	**5**	**0**	**2**	**2**	**0**	**0**	**0**	**0**	....
1998-99	**Philadelphia**	**NHL**	**31**	**3**	**2**	**5**	**2**	**1**	**0**	**1**	**26**	**11.5**	**–1**	**53**	**39.6**	**7:59**	....	....	....	....	....	....	....	....	....
	Tampa Bay	**NHL**	**32**	**6**	**6**	**12**	**2**	**3**	**0**	**0**	**56**	**10.7**	**–12**	**4**	**50.0**	**13:59**	....	....	....	....	....	....	....	....	....
99-2000	**NY Rangers**	**NHL**	**58**	**8**	**18**	**26**	**23**	**1**	**0**	**1**	**52**	**15.4**	**–5**	**339**	**53.1**	**10:59**	....	....	....	....	....	....	....	....	....
	Hartford	AHL	16	6	13	19	4	....	....	....	....	....	....	....	....	....	....	....	....	....	....	....	....	....	....
2000-01			OUT OF HOCKEY – RETIRED																						
2001-02			OUT OF HOCKEY – RETIRED																						
2002-03	**Pittsburgh**	**NHL**	**33**	**4**	**3**	**7**	**8**	**1**	**0**	**0**	**48**	**8.3**	**–10**	**24**	**33.3**	**10:57**	....	....	....	....	....	....	....	....	....
	Wilkes-Barre	AHL	40	9	29	38	18	....	....	....	....	....	....	....	....	....	4	0	1	1	0	....	....	....	....
2003-04	**Minnesota**	**NHL**	**78**	**20**	**31**	**51**	**14**	**6**	**0**	**3**	**145**	**13.8**	**–4**	**72**	**51.4**	**15:10**	....	....	....	....	....	....	....	....	....
	NHL Totals		**570**	**124**	**175**	**299**	**174**	**33**	**1**	**19**	**1026**	**12.1**		**492**	**50.4**	**12:24**	**12**	**0**	**2**	**2**	**2**	**0**	**0**	**0**	....

QMJHL Second All-Star Team (1992) • QMJHL Offensive Rookie of the Year (1992) • Canadian Major Junior Rookie of the Year (1992) • QMJHL First All-Star Team (1993)

Traded to **Philadelphia** by **Ottawa** for Vaclav Prospal, Pat Falloon and Dallas' 2nd round choice (previously acquired, Ottawa selected Chris Bala) in 1998 Entry Draft, January 17, 1998. Traded to **Edmonton** by **Philadelphia** for Andrei Kovalenko, January 29, 1999. Traded to **Tampa Bay** by **Edmonton** for Alexander Selivanov, January 29, 1999. Traded to **NY Rangers** by **Tampa Bay** for cash, October 3, 1999. Signed as a free agent by **Pittsburgh**, August 13, 2002. Signed as a free agent by **Minnesota**, September 30, 2003.

DALEY, Trevor
(DAY-lee, TREH-vuhr) **DAL.**

Defense. Shoots left. 5'9", 197 lbs. Born, Toronto, Ont., October 9, 1983. Dallas' 5th choice, 43rd overall, in 2002 Entry Draft.

Season	Club	League	GP	G	A	Pts	PIM	PP	SH	GW	S	%	+/-	TF	F%	Min	GP	G	A	Pts	PIM	PP	SH	GW	Min
1998-99	Vaughan Vipers	OPJHL	44	10	36	46	79	....	....	....	....	....	....	....	....	....	....	....	....	....	....	....	....	....	....
99-2000	Sault Ste. Marie	OHL	54	16	30	46	77	....	....	....	....	....	....	....	....	....	15	3	7	10	12	....	....	....	....
2000-01	Sault Ste. Marie	OHL	58	14	27	41	105	....	....	....	....	....	....	....	....	....	....	....	....	....	....	....	....	....	....
2001-02	Sault Ste. Marie	OHL	47	9	39	48	38	....	....	....	....	....	....	....	....	....	6	2	2	4	4	....	....	....	....
2002-03	Sault Ste. Marie	OHL	57	20	33	53	128	....	....	....	....	....	....	....	....	....	1	0	0	0	2	....	....	....	....
2003-04	**Dallas**	**NHL**	**27**	**1**	**5**	**6**	**14**	**1**	**0**	**0**	**34**	**2.9**	**–6**	**0**	**0.0**	**16:02**	**1**	**0**	**0**	**0**	**0**	**0**	**0**	**0**	**10:21**
	Utah Grizzlies	AHL	40	8	6	14	76	....	....	....	....	....	....	....	....	....	....	....	....	....	....	....	....	....	....
	NHL Totals		**27**	**1**	**5**	**6**	**14**	**1**	**0**	**0**	**34**	**2.9**		**0**	**0.0**	**16:02**	**1**	**0**	**0**	**0**	**0**	**0**	**0**	**0**	**10:21**

DAMPHOUSSE, Vincent
(DAHM-fooz, VIHN-sihnt) **S.J.**

Center. Shoots left. 6'1", 200 lbs. Born, Montreal, Que., December 17, 1967. Toronto's 1st choice, 6th overall, in 1986 Entry Draft.

Season	Club	League	GP	G	A	Pts	PIM	PP	SH	GW	S	%	+/-	TF	F%	Min	GP	G	A	Pts	PIM	PP	SH	GW	Min
1982-83	Mtl-Bourassa	QAAA	48	33	45	78	22	....	....	....	....	....	....	....	....	....	10	4	4	8	12	....	....	....	....
1983-84	Laval Voisins	QMJHL	66	29	36	65	25	....	....	....	....	....	....	....	....	....	....	....	....	....	....	....	....	....	....
1984-85	Laval Voisins	QMJHL	68	35	68	103	62	....	....	....	....	....	....	....	....	....	....	....	....	....	....	....	....	....	....
1985-86	Laval Titan	QMJHL	69	45	110	155	70	....	....	....	....	....	....	....	....	....	14	9	27	36	12	....	....	....	....
1986-87	**Toronto**	**NHL**	**80**	**21**	**25**	**46**	**26**	**4**	**0**	**1**	**142**	**14.8**	**–6**	....	....	....	**12**	**1**	**5**	**6**	**8**	**1**	**0**	**0**	....
1987-88	**Toronto**	**NHL**	**75**	**12**	**36**	**48**	**40**	**1**	**0**	**2**	**111**	**10.8**	**2**	....	....	....	**6**	**0**	**1**	**1**	**10**	**0**	**0**	**0**	....
1988-89	**Toronto**	**NHL**	**80**	**26**	**42**	**68**	**75**	**6**	**0**	**4**	**190**	**13.7**	**–8**	....	....	....	....	....	....	....	....	....	....	....	....
1989-90	**Toronto**	**NHL**	**80**	**33**	**61**	**94**	**56**	**9**	**0**	**5**	**229**	**14.4**	**2**	....	....	....	**5**	**0**	**2**	**2**	**2**	**0**	**0**	**0**	....
1990-91	**Toronto**	**NHL**	**79**	**26**	**47**	**73**	**65**	**10**	**1**	**4**	**247**	**10.5**	**–31**	....	....	....	....	....	....	....	....	....	....	....	....
1991-92	**Edmonton**	**NHL**	**80**	**38**	**51**	**89**	**53**	**12**	**1**	**8**	**247**	**15.4**	**10**	....	....	....	**16**	**6**	**8**	**14**	**8**	**1**	**0**	**0**	....
1992-93◆	**Montreal**	**NHL**	**84**	**39**	**58**	**97**	**98**	**9**	**3**	**8**	**287**	**13.6**	**5**	....	....	....	**20**	**11**	**12**	**23**	**16**	**5**	**0**	**3**	....
1993-94	**Montreal**	**NHL**	**84**	**40**	**51**	**91**	**75**	**13**	**0**	**10**	**274**	**14.6**	**0**	....	....	....	**7**	**1**	**2**	**3**	**8**	**0**	**0**	**0**	....
1994-95	Ratingen	Germany	11	5	7	12	24	....	....	....	....	....	....	....	....	....	....	....	....	....	....	....	....	....	....
	Montreal	**NHL**	**48**	**10**	**30**	**40**	**42**	**4**	**0**	**4**	**123**	**8.1**	**15**	....	....	....	....	....	....	....	....	....	....	....	....
1995-96	**Montreal**	**NHL**	**80**	**38**	**56**	**94**	**158**	**11**	**4**	**3**	**254**	**15.0**	**5**	....	....	....	**6**	**4**	**4**	**8**	**0**	**0**	**1**	**2**	....
1996-97	**Montreal**	**NHL**	**82**	**27**	**54**	**81**	**82**	**7**	**2**	**3**	**244**	**11.1**	**–6**	....	....	....	**5**	**0**	**0**	**0**	**2**	**0**	**0**	**0**	....
1997-98	**Montreal**	**NHL**	**76**	**18**	**41**	**59**	**58**	**2**	**1**	**5**	**164**	**11.0**	**14**	....	....	....	**10**	**3**	**6**	**9**	**22**	**1**	**0**	**0**	....
1998-99	**Montreal**	**NHL**	**65**	**12**	**24**	**36**	**46**	**3**	**2**	**2**	**147**	**8.2**	**–7**	**1425**	**48.4**	**20:27**	....	....	....	....	....	....	....	....	....
	San Jose	**NHL**	**12**	**7**	**6**	**13**	**4**	**3**	**0**	**1**	**43**	**16.3**	**3**	**230**	**51.3**	**19:21**	**6**	**3**	**2**	**5**	**6**	**0**	**2**	**0**	**22:58**
99-2000	**San Jose**	**NHL**	**82**	**21**	**49**	**70**	**58**	**3**	**1**	**1**	**204**	**10.3**	**4**	**1642**	**49.0**	**20:26**	**12**	**1**	**7**	**8**	**16**	**1**	**0**	**0**	**22:14**
2000-01	**San Jose**	**NHL**	**45**	**9**	**37**	**46**	**62**	**4**	**0**	**3**	**101**	**8.9**	**17**	**1027**	**52.7**	**20:49**	**6**	**2**	**1**	**3**	**14**	**0**	**1**	**0**	**20:22**
2001-02	**San Jose**	**NHL**	**82**	**20**	**38**	**58**	**60**	**7**	**2**	**4**	**172**	**11.6**	**8**	**1690**	**49.9**	**19:38**	**12**	**2**	**6**	**8**	**12**	**1**	**0**	**0**	**19:14**
2002-03	**San Jose**	**NHL**	**82**	**23**	**38**	**61**	**66**	**15**	**0**	**6**	**176**	**13.1**	**–13**	**1301**	**51.7**	**19:09**	....	....	....	....	....	....	....	....	....
2003-04	**San Jose**	**NHL**	**82**	**12**	**29**	**41**	**66**	**7**	**0**	**4**	**156**	**7.7**	**–5**	**764**	**52.6**	**17:09**	**17**	**7**	**7**	**14**	**20**	**3**	**0**	**3**	**18:53**
	NHL Totals		**1378**	**432**	**773**	**1205**	**1190**	**130**	**17**	**78**	**3511**	**12.3**		**8079**	**50.4**	**19:28**	**140**	**41**	**63**	**104**	**144**	**13**	**4**	**8**	**20:21**

QMJHL Second All-Star Team (1986)

Played in NHL All-Star Game (1991, 1992, 2002)

Traded to **Edmonton** by **Toronto** with Peter Ing, Scott Thornton and Luke Richardson for Grant Fuhr, Glenn Anderson and Craig Berube, September 19, 1991. Traded to **Montreal** by **Edmonton** with Edmonton's 4th round choice (Adam Wiesel) in 1993 Entry Draft for Shayne Corson, Brent Gilchrist and Vladimir Vujtek, August 27, 1992. Traded to **San Jose** by **Montreal** for Phoenix's 5th round choice (previously acquired, Montreal selected Marc-Andre Thinel) in 1999 Entry Draft, San Jose's 1st round choice (Marcel Hossa) in 2000 Entry Draft and 2nd round choice (later traded to Columbus – Columbus selected Kiel McLeod) in 2001 Entry Draft, March 23, 1999.

DANDENAULT, Mathieu
(DAHN-deh-noh, MA-tyew) **DET.**

Right wing/Defense. Shoots right. 6', 200 lbs. Born, Sherbrooke, Que., February 3, 1976. Detroit's 2nd choice, 49th overall, in 1994 Entry Draft.

Season	Club	League	GP	G	A	Pts	PIM	PP	SH	GW	S	%	+/-	TF	F%	Min	GP	G	A	Pts	PIM	PP	SH	GW	Min
1990-91	Gloucester	OMHA	44	52	50	102	30	....	....	....	....	....	....	....	....	....	....	....	....	....	....	....	....	....	....
1991-92	Vanier Voyageurs	OCJHL	33	27	31	58	20	....	....	....	....	....	....	....	....	....	....	....	....	....	....	....	....	....	....
	Gloucester	OCJHL	6	3	4	7	0	....	....	....	....	....	....	....	....	....	....	....	....	....	....	....	....	....	....
1992-93	Gloucester	OCJHL	55	11	26	37	64	....	....	....	....	....	....	....	....	....	....	....	....	....	....	....	....	....	....
1993-94	Sherbrooke	QMJHL	67	17	36	53	67	....	....	....	....	....	....	....	....	....	12	4	10	14	12	....	....	....	....
1994-95	Sherbrooke	QMJHL	67	37	70	107	76	....	....	....	....	....	....	....	....	....	7	1	7	8	10	....	....	....	....
1995-96	**Detroit**	**NHL**	**34**	**5**	**7**	**12**	**6**	**1**	**0**	**0**	**32**	**15.6**	**6**	....	....	....	....	....	....	....	....	....	....	....	....
	Adirondack	AHL	4	0	0	0	0	....	....	....	....	....	....	....	....	....	....	....	....	....	....	....	....	....	....
1996-97◆	**Detroit**	**NHL**	**65**	**3**	**9**	**12**	**28**	**0**	**0**	**0**	**81**	**3.7**	**–10**	....	....	....	....	....	....	....	....	....	....	....	....
1997-98◆	**Detroit**	**NHL**	**68**	**5**	**12**	**17**	**43**	**0**	**0**	**0**	**75**	**6.7**	**5**	....	....	....	**3**	**1**	**0**	**1**	**0**	**1**	**0**	**0**	....
1998-99	**Detroit**	**NHL**	**75**	**4**	**10**	**14**	**59**	**0**	**0**	**0**	**94**	**4.3**	**17**	**3**	**0.0**	**15:10**	**10**	**0**	**1**	**1**	**0**	**0**	**0**	**0**	**11:51**
99-2000	**Detroit**	**NHL**	**81**	**6**	**12**	**18**	**20**	**0**	**0**	**0**	**98**	**6.1**	**–12**	**1**	**100.0**	**12:10**	**6**	**0**	**0**	**0**	**2**	**0**	**0**	**0**	**8:31**
2000-01	**Detroit**	**NHL**	**73**	**10**	**15**	**25**	**38**	**2**	**0**	**2**	**95**	**10.5**	**11**	**0**	**0.0**	**16:06**	**6**	**0**	**1**	**1**	**0**	**0**	**0**	**0**	**14:11**
2001-02◆	**Detroit**	**NHL**	**81**	**8**	**12**	**20**	**44**	**2**	**0**	**3**	**97**	**8.2**	**–5**	**1**	**0.0**	**16:43**	**23**	**1**	**2**	**3**	**8**	**0**	**1**	**0**	**13:29**
2002-03	**Detroit**	**NHL**	**74**	**4**	**15**	**19**	**64**	**1**	**0**	**0**	**74**	**5.4**	**25**	**0**	**0.0**	**19:08**	**4**	**0**	**0**	**0**	**2**	**0**	**0**	**0**	**25:51**
2003-04	**Detroit**	**NHL**	**65**	**3**	**9**	**12**	**40**	**0**	**1**	**0**	**68**	**4.4**	**9**	**1**	**0.0**	**13:47**	**12**	**1**	**1**	**2**	**6**	**0**	**0**	**1**	**13:33**
	NHL Totals		**616**	**48**	**101**	**149**	**342**	**6**	**1**	**5**	**714**	**6.7**		**6**	**16.7**	**15:31**	**64**	**3**	**5**	**8**	**18**	**1**	**1**	**1**	**13:37**

DANTON, Mike
(DAHN-tuhn, MIGHK)

Center. Shoots right. 5'9", 190 lbs. Born, Brampton, Ont., October 21, 1980. New Jersey's 8th choice, 135th overall, in 2000 Entry Draft.

Season	Club	League	GP	G	A	Pts	PIM	PP	SH	GW	S	%	+/-	TF	F%	Min	GP	G	A	Pts	PIM	PP	SH	GW	Min
1996-97	Quinte Hawks	MTJHL	35	10	18	28	281	....	....	....	....	....	....	....	....	....	....	....	....	....	....	....	....	....	....
1997-98	Sarnia Sting	OHL	12	6	1	7	37	....	....	....	....	....	....	....	....	....	....	....	....	....	....	....	....	....	....
	St. Michael's	OHL	18	4	6	10	77	....	....	....	....	....	....	....	....	....	....	....	....	....	....	....	....	....	....
1998-99	St. Michael's	OHL	27	18	22	40	116	....	....	....	....	....	....	....	....	....	....	....	....	....	....	....	....	....	....
	Barrie Colts	OHL	26	15	20	35	62	....	....	....	....	....	....	....	....	....	9	6	5	11	38	....	....	....	....
99-2000	Barrie Colts	OHL	58	34	53	87	203	....	....	....	....	....	....	....	....	....	25	7	16	23	*107	....	....	....	....
2000-01	**New Jersey**	**NHL**	**2**	**0**	**0**	**0**	**6**	**0**	**0**	**0**	**3**	**0.0**	**0**	**6**	**50.0**	**7:52**	....	....	....	....	....	....	....	....	....
	Albany River Rats	AHL	69	19	15	34	195	....	....	....	....	....	....	....	....	....	....	....	....	....	....	....	....	....	....

Season	Club	League	GP	G	A	Pts	PIM	PP	SH	GW	S	%	+/-	TF	F%	Min	GP	G	A	Pts	PIM	PP	SH	GW	Min
			Regular Season														Playoffs								
2001-02	Albany River Rats	AHL	DID NOT PLAY – SUSPENDED																						
2002-03	**New Jersey**	**NHL**	**17**	**2**	**0**	**2**	**35**	**0**	**0**	**0**	**18**	**11.1**	**0**	**111**	**39.6**	**8:59**	....	....	....	....	....	....	....	....	....
2003-04	**St. Louis**	**NHL**	**68**	**7**	**5**	**12**	**141**	**0**	**1**	**0**	**72**	**9.7**	**–8**	**32**	**28.1**	**11:57**	**5**	**1**	**0**	**1**	**2**	**0**	**0**	**0**	**7:25**
	NHL Totals		**87**	**9**	**5**	**14**	**182**	**0**	**1**	**0**	**93**	**9.7**		**149**	**37.6**	**11:16**	**5**	**1**	**0**	**1**	**2**	**0**	**0**	**0**	**7:25**

• Legally changed last name from **Jefferson** to **Danton**, July 25, 2002.

• Suspended for 2001-02 season by New Jersey for refusing to report to Albany (AHL), October 2, 2001. • Missed majority of 2002-03 season after being suspended by New Jersey for refusing to report to Albany (AHL), December 3, 2002. Traded to **St. Louis** by **New Jersey** with New Jersey's 3rd round choice (Konstantin Zakharov) in 2003 Entry Draft for St. Louis's 3rd round choice (Ivan Khomutov) in 2003 Entry Draft, June 21, 2003.

DARBY, Craig

(DAHR-bee, KRAYG) **T.B.**

Center. Shoots right. 6'4", 205 lbs. Born, Oneida, NY, September 26, 1972. Montreal's 3rd choice, 43rd overall, in 1991 Entry Draft.

Season	Club	League	GP	G	A	Pts	PIM	PP	SH	GW	S	%	+/-	TF	F%	Min	GP	G	A	Pts	PIM	PP	SH	GW	Min
1987-88	Albany	Hi-School	29	11	27	38	....	....	....	....	....	....	....	....	....	....	....	....	....	....	....	....	....	....	....
1988-89	Albany	Hi-School	29	36	40	*76	....	....	....	....	....	....	....	....	....	....	....	....	....	....	....	....	....	....	....
1989-90	Albany	Hi-School	29	32	53	85	....	....	....	....	....	....	....	....	....	....	....	....	....	....	....	....	....	....	....
1990-91	Albany	Hi-School	29	33	61	*94	....	....	....	....	....	....	....	....	....	....	4	8	1	9	....	....	....	....	....
1991-92	Providence	H-East	35	17	24	41	47	....	....	....	....	....	....	....	....	....	....	....	....	....	....	....	....	....	....
1992-93	Providence	H-East	35	11	21	32	62	....	....	....	....	....	....	....	....	....	....	....	....	....	....	....	....	....	....
1993-94	Fredericton	AHL	66	23	33	56	51	....	....	....	....	....	....	....	....	....	....	....	....	....	....	....	....	....	....
1994-95	Fredericton	AHL	64	21	47	68	82	....	....	....	....	....	....	....	....	....	....	....	....	....	....	....	....	....	....
	Montreal	**NHL**	**10**	**0**	**2**	**2**	**0**	**0**	**0**	**0**	**4**	**0.0**	**–5**	....	....	....	....	....	....	....	....	....	....	....	....
	NY Islanders	**NHL**	**3**	**0**	**0**	**0**	**0**	**0**	**0**	**0**	**1**	**0.0**	**–1**	....	....	....	....	....	....	....	....	....	....	....	....
1995-96	**NY Islanders**	**NHL**	**10**	**0**	**2**	**2**	**0**	**0**	**0**	**0**	**1**	**0.0**	**–1**	....	....	....	....	....	....	....	....	....	....	....	....
	Worcester IceCats	AHL	68	22	28	50	47	....	....	....	....	....	....	....	....	....	4	1	1	2	2	....	....	....	....
1996-97	**Philadelphia**	**NHL**	**9**	**1**	**4**	**5**	**2**	**0**	**1**	**0**	**13**	**7.7**	**2**	....	....	....	....	....	....	....	....	....	....	....	....
	Philadelphia	AHL	59	26	33	59	24	....	....	....	....	....	....	....	....	....	10	3	6	9	0	....	....	....	....
1997-98	**Philadelphia**	**NHL**	**3**	**1**	**0**	**1**	**0**	**0**	**0**	**0**	**3**	**33.3**	**0**	....	....	....	....	....	....	....	....	....	....	....	....
	Philadelphia	AHL	77	*42	45	87	34	....	....	....	....	....	....	....	....	....	20	5	9	14	4	....	....	....	....
1998-99	Milwaukee	IHL	81	32	22	54	33	....	....	....	....	....	....	....	....	....	2	3	0	3	0	....	....	....	....
99-2000	**Montreal**	**NHL**	**76**	**7**	**10**	**17**	**14**	**0**	**1**	**2**	**90**	**7.8**	**–14**	**1068**	**48.3**	**13:45**	....	....	....	....	....	....	....	....	....
2000-01	**Montreal**	**NHL**	**78**	**12**	**16**	**28**	**16**	**0**	**1**	**0**	**97**	**12.4**	**–17**	**1214**	**46.9**	**15:53**	....	....	....	....	....	....	....	....	....
2001-02	**Montreal**	**NHL**	**2**	**0**	**0**	**0**	**0**	**0**	**0**	**0**	**0**	**0.0**	**0**	**10**	**30.0**	**5:20**	....	....	....	....	....	....	....	....	....
	Quebec Citadelles	AHL	66	16	55	71	18	....	....	....	....	....	....	....	....	....	3	2	1	3	0	....	....	....	....
2002-03	**New Jersey**	**NHL**	**3**	**0**	**1**	**1**	**0**	**0**	**0**	**0**	**1**	**0.0**	**–1**	**21**	**47.6**	**10:36**	....	....	....	....	....	....	....	....	....
	Albany River Rats	AHL	76	23	51	74	42	....	....	....	....	....	....	....	....	....	....	....	....	....	....	....	....	....	....
2003-04	**New Jersey**	**NHL**	**2**	**0**	**0**	**0**	**0**	**0**	**0**	**0**	**0**	**0.0**	**–1**	**17**	**58.8**	**7:06**	....	....	....	....	....	....	....	....	....
	Albany River Rats	AHL	77	21	48	69	44	....	....	....	....	....	....	....	....	....	....	....	....	....	....	....	....	....	....
	NHL Totals		**196**	**21**	**35**	**56**	**32**	**0**	**3**	**2**	**210**	**10.0**		**2330**	**47.6**	**14:32**	....	....	....	....	....	....	....	....	....

Hockey East Rookie of the Year (1992) (co-winner - Ian Moran) • AHL First All-Star Team (1998) • AHL Second All-Star Team (2003)

Traded to **NY Islanders** by **Montreal** with Kirk Muller and Mathieu Schneider for Pierre Turgeon and Vladimir Malakhov, April 5, 1995. Claimed on waivers by **Philadelphia** from **NY Islanders**, June 4, 1996. Claimed by **Nashville** from **Philadelphia** in Expansion Draft, June 26, 1998. Signed as a free agent by **Montreal**, August 4, 1999. Signed as a free agent by **New Jersey**, July 12, 2002. Signed as a free agent by **Tampa Bay**, July 19, 2004.

DARCHE, Mathieu

(DAHRSH, MA-thew) **COL.**

Left wing. Shoots left. 6'1", 210 lbs. Born, St. Laurent, Que., November 26, 1976.

Season	Club	League	GP	G	A	Pts	PIM	PP	SH	GW	S	%	+/-	TF	F%	Min	GP	G	A	Pts	PIM	PP	SH	GW	Min
1995-96	Choate-Rosemary	Hi-School	STATISTICS NOT AVAILABLE																						
1996-97	McGill Redmen	OUAA	23	1	2	3	27	....	....	....	....	....	....	....	....	....	....	....	....	....	....	....	....	....	....
1997-98	McGill Redmen	OUAA	40	28	17	45	69	....	....	....	....	....	....	....	....	....	....	....	....	....	....	....	....	....	....
1998-99	McGill Redmen	OUAA	32	16	24	40	60	....	....	....	....	....	....	....	....	....	....	....	....	....	....	....	....	....	....
99-2000	McGill Redmen	OUAA	33	31	41	*72	38	....	....	....	....	....	....	....	....	....	5	2	8	10	16	....	....	....	....
2000-01	**Columbus**	**NHL**	**9**	**0**	**0**	**0**	**0**	**0**	**0**	**0**	**9**	**0.0**	**–4**	**1**	**0.0**	**10:07**	....	....	....	....	....	....	....	....	....
	Syracuse Crunch	AHL	66	16	24	40	21	....	....	....	....	....	....	....	....	....	5	0	1	1	4	....	....	....	....
2001-02	**Columbus**	**NHL**	**14**	**1**	**1**	**2**	**6**	**0**	**0**	**0**	**15**	**6.7**	**–5**	**3**	**33.3**	**9:49**	....	....	....	....	....	....	....	....	....
	Syracuse Crunch	AHL	63	22	23	45	26	....	....	....	....	....	....	....	....	....	10	2	5	7	2	....	....	....	....
2002-03	**Columbus**	**NHL**	**1**	**0**	**0**	**0**	**0**	**0**	**0**	**0**	**0**	**0.0**	**–1**	**0**	**0.0**	**6:57**	....	....	....	....	....	....	....	....	....
	Syracuse Crunch	AHL	76	32	32	64	38	....	....	....	....	....	....	....	....	....	....	....	....	....	....	....	....	....	....
2003-04	**Nashville**	**NHL**	**2**	**0**	**0**	**0**	**0**	**0**	**0**	**0**	**1**	**0.0**	**–1**	**0**	**0.0**	**6:39**	....	....	....	....	....	....	....	....	....
	Milwaukee	AHL	76	28	31	59	41	....	....	....	....	....	....	....	....	....	22	6	8	14	8	....	....	....	....
	NHL Totals		**26**	**1**	**1**	**2**	**6**	**0**	**0**	**0**	**25**	**4.0**		**4**	**25.0**	**9:34**	....	....	....	....	....	....	....	....	....

• Played CIAU Football (1996-97) • OUAA East Second All-Star Team (1998) • OUAA East First All-Star Team (1999) • OUAA First All-Star Team (2000) • CIAU All-Canadian Team (2000)

Signed as a free agent by **Columbus**, May 16, 2000. Signed as a free agent by **Nashville**, September 10, 2003. Signed as a free agent by **Colorado**, July 26, 2004.

DATSYUK, Pavel

(daht-SOOK, PAH-vehl) **DET.**

Center. Shoots left. 5'11", 180 lbs. Born, Sverdlovsk, USSR, July 20, 1978. Detroit's 8th choice, 171st overall, in 1998 Entry Draft.

Season	Club	League	GP	G	A	Pts	PIM	PP	SH	GW	S	%	+/-	TF	F%	Min	GP	G	A	Pts	PIM	PP	SH	GW	Min
1996-97	Yekaterinburg 2	Russia-3	18	2	2	4	4	....	....	....	....	....	....	....	....	....	....	....	....	....	....	....	....	....	....
	Yekaterinburg	Russia	36	12	10	22	12	....	....	....	....	....	....	....	....	....	....	....	....	....	....	....	....	....	....
1997-98	Yekaterinburg	Russia	24	3	5	8	4	....	....	....	....	....	....	....	....	....	....	....	....	....	....	....	....	....	....
	Yekaterinburg	Russia	22	7	8	15	4	....	....	....	....	....	....	....	....	....	....	....	....	....	....	....	....	....	....
1998-99	Yekaterinburg 2	Russia-4	10	14	14	28	4	....	....	....	....	....	....	....	....	....	....	....	....	....	....	....	....	....	....
	Yekaterinburg	Russia-2	35	21	23	44	14	....	....	....	....	....	....	....	....	....	9	3	7	10	10	....	....	....	....
99-2000	Yekaterinburg	Russia	15	1	3	4	4	....	....	....	....	....	....	....	....	....	....	....	....	....	....	....	....	....	....
2000-01	Ak Bars Kazan	Russia	42	9	18	27	10	....	....	....	....	....	....	....	....	....	4	0	1	1	2	....	....	....	....
2001-02♦	**Detroit**	**NHL**	**70**	**11**	**24**	**35**	**4**	**2**	**0**	**1**	**79**	**13.9**	**4**	**794**	**47.7**	**13:39**	**21**	**3**	**3**	**6**	**2**	**1**	**0**	**1**	**10:40**
	Russia	Olympics	6	1	2	3	0	....	....	....	....	....	....	....	....	....	....	....	....	....	....	....	....	....	....
2002-03	**Detroit**	**NHL**	**64**	**12**	**39**	**51**	**16**	**1**	**0**	**1**	**82**	**14.6**	**20**	**778**	**48.2**	**15:28**	**4**	**0**	**0**	**0**	**0**	**0**	**0**	**0**	**18:48**
2003-04	**Detroit**	**NHL**	**75**	**30**	**38**	**68**	**35**	**8**	**1**	**4**	**136**	**22.1**	**–2**	**1314**	**54.0**	**18:16**	**12**	**0**	**6**	**6**	**2**	**0**	**0**	**0**	**17:23**
	NHL Totals		**209**	**53**	**101**	**154**	**55**	**11**	**1**	**6**	**297**	**17.8**		**2886**	**50.7**	**15:52**	**37**	**3**	**9**	**12**	**4**	**1**	**0**	**1**	**13:44**

Played in NHL All-Star Game (2004)

• Spent majority of 1999-2000 season on **Ak Bars Kazan** (Russia) reserve squad.

DAVIDSON, Matt

(DAY-vihd-SOHN, MAT)

Right wing. Shoots right. 6'3", 196 lbs. Born, Flin Flon, Man., August 9, 1977. Buffalo's 5th choice, 94th overall, in 1995 Entry Draft.

Season	Club	League	GP	G	A	Pts	PIM	PP	SH	GW	S	%	+/-	TF	F%	Min	GP	G	A	Pts	PIM	PP	SH	GW	Min
1992-93	Sask. Contacts	SMHL	36	14	18	32	36	....	....	....	....	....	....	....	....	....	....	....	....	....	....	....	....	....	....
1993-94	Portland	WHL	59	4	12	16	18	....	....	....	....	....	....	....	....	....	10	0	0	0	4	....	....	....	....
1994-95	Portland	WHL	72	17	20	37	51	....	....	....	....	....	....	....	....	....	9	1	3	4	0	....	....	....	....
1995-96	Portland	WHL	70	24	26	50	96	....	....	....	....	....	....	....	....	....	7	2	2	4	2	....	....	....	....
1996-97	Portland	WHL	72	44	27	71	47	....	....	....	....	....	....	....	....	....	6	0	1	1	2	....	....	....	....
1997-98	Rochester	AHL	72	15	12	27	12	....	....	....	....	....	....	....	....	....	3	1	0	1	2	....	....	....	....
1998-99	Rochester	AHL	80	26	15	41	44	....	....	....	....	....	....	....	....	....	18	2	1	3	6	....	....	....	....
99-2000	Rochester	AHL	80	12	20	32	30	....	....	....	....	....	....	....	....	....	19	4	2	6	8	....	....	....	....
2000-01	**Columbus**	**NHL**	**5**	**0**	**0**	**0**	**0**	**0**	**0**	**0**	**2**	**0.0**	**2**	**0**	**0.0**	**7:14**	....	....	....	....	....	....	....	....	....
	Syracuse Crunch	AHL	72	14	11	25	24	....	....	....	....	....	....	....	....	....	5	1	2	3	2	....	....	....	....
2001-02	**Columbus**	**NHL**	**17**	**1**	**2**	**3**	**10**	**0**	**0**	**0**	**18**	**5.6**	**–11**	**7**	**0.0**	**14:34**	....	....	....	....	....	....	....	....	....
	Syracuse Crunch	AHL	47	9	11	20	64	....	....	....	....	....	....	....	....	....	8	1	3	4	4	....	....	....	....
2002-03	**Columbus**	**NHL**	**34**	**4**	**5**	**9**	**18**	**0**	**0**	**0**	**28**	**14.3**	**–12**	**7**	**28.6**	**11:49**	....	....	....	....	....	....	....	....	....
	Syracuse Crunch	AHL	48	18	16	34	26	....	....	....	....	....	....	....	....	....	....	....	....	....	....	....	....	....	....
2003-04	Lowell	AHL	66	14	28	42	36	....	....	....	....	....	....	....	....	....	....	....	....	....	....	....	....	....	....
	NHL Totals		**56**	**5**	**7**	**12**	**28**	**0**	**0**	**0**	**48**	**10.4**		**14**	**14.3**	**12:14**	....	....	....	....	....	....	....	....	....

Traded to **Columbus** by **Buffalo** with Jean-Luc Grand-Pierre, San Jose's 5th round choice (previously acquired, Columbus selected Tyler Kolarik) in 2000 Entry Draft and Buffalo's 5th round choice (later traded to Calgary – later traded to Detroit – Detroit selected Andreas Jamtin) in 2001 Entry Draft to complete Expansion Draft agreement which had Columbus select Geoff Sanderson and Dwayne Roloson from Buffalo, June 23, 2000. Signed as a free agent by **Calgary**, July 15, 2003.

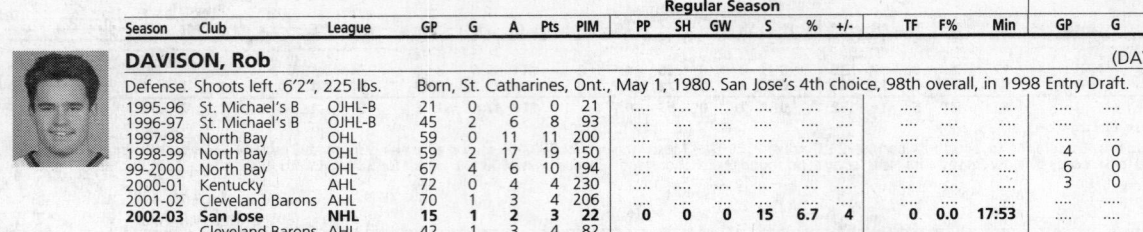

DAVISON, Rob

(DAY-vihs-ohn, RAWB) **S.J.**

Defense. Shoots left. 6'2", 225 lbs. Born, St. Catharines, Ont., May 1, 1980. San Jose's 4th choice, 98th overall, in 1998 Entry Draft.

Season	Club	League	GP	G	A	Pts	PIM	PP	SH	GW	S	%	+/-	TF	F%	Min	Playoffs GP	G	A	Pts	PIM	PP	SH	GW	Min
1995-96	St. Michael's B	OJHL-B	21	0	0	0	21	....	....	....	....	....	....	....	....	....	....	....	....	....	....	....	....	....	....
1996-97	St. Michael's B	OJHL-B	45	2	6	8	93	....	....	....	....	....	....	....	....	....	....	....	....	....	....	....	....	....	....
1997-98	North Bay	OHL	59	0	11	11	200	....	....	....	....	....	....	....	....	....	....	....	....	....	....	....	....	....	....
1998-99	North Bay	OHL	59	2	17	19	150	....	....	....	....	....	....	....	....	....	4	0	1	1	12	....	....	....	....
99-2000	North Bay	OHL	67	4	6	10	194	....	....	....	....	....	....	....	....	....	6	0	1	1	8	....	....	....	....
2000-01	Kentucky	AHL	72	0	4	4	230	....	....	....	....	....	....	....	....	....	3	0	0	0	0	....	....	....	....
2001-02	Cleveland Barons	AHL	70	1	3	4	206	....	....	....	....	....	....	....	....	....	....	....	....	....	....	....	....	....	....
2002-03	**San Jose**	**NHL**	**15**	**1**	**2**	**3**	**22**	**0**	**0**	**0**	**15**	**6.7**	**4**	**0**	**0.0**	**17:53**	....	....	....	....	....	....	....	....	....
	Cleveland Barons	AHL	42	1	3	4	82	....	....	....	....	....	....	....	....	....	....	....	....	....	....	....	....	....	....
2003-04	**San Jose**	**NHL**	**55**	**0**	**3**	**3**	**92**	**0**	**0**	**0**	**33**	**0.0**	**–3**	**0**	**0.0**	**14:22**	**5**	**0**	**2**	**2**	**4**	**0**	**0**	**0**	**9:01**
	NHL Totals		**70**	**1**	**5**	**6**	**114**	**0**	**0**	**0**	**48**	**2.1**		**0**	**0.0**	**15:08**	**5**	**0**	**2**	**2**	**4**	**0**	**0**	**0**	**9:01**

DAW, Jeff

(DAW, JEHF)

Center. Shoots right. 6'3", 190 lbs. Born, Carlisle, Ont., February 28, 1972.

Season	Club	League	GP	G	A	Pts	PIM	PP	SH	GW	S	%	+/-	TF	F%	Min	Playoffs GP	G	A	Pts	PIM	PP	SH	GW	Min
1989-90	Milton Merchants	OPJHL	42	19	29	48	2	....	....	....	....	....	....	....	....	....	....	....	....	....	....	....	....	....	....
1990-91	Milton Merchants	OPJHL	34	21	41	62	22	....	....	....	....	....	....	....	....	....	....	....	....	....	....	....	....	....	....
1991-92	Milton Merchants	OPJHL	41	33	33	66	20	....	....	....	....	....	....	....	....	....	....	....	....	....	....	....	....	....	....
1992-93	U. Mass-Lowell	H-East	37	12	18	30	14	....	....	....	....	....	....	....	....	....	....	....	....	....	....	....	....	....	....
1993-94	U. Mass-Lowell	H-East	40	6	12	18	12	....	....	....	....	....	....	....	....	....	....	....	....	....	....	....	....	....	....
1994-95	U. Mass-Lowell	H-East	40	27	15	42	24	....	....	....	....	....	....	....	....	....	....	....	....	....	....	....	....	....	....
1995-96	U. Mass-Lowell	H-East	40	23	28	51	10	....	....	....	....	....	....	....	....	....	....	....	....	....	....	....	....	....	....
1996-97	Wheeling Nailers	ECHL	13	3	8	11	26	....	....	....	....	....	....	....	....	....	....	....	....	....	....	....	....	....	....
	Hamilton	AHL	56	11	8	19	39	....	....	....	....	....	....	....	....	....	19	4	5	9	0	....	....	....	....
1997-98	Hamilton	AHL	79	28	35	63	20	....	....	....	....	....	....	....	....	....	9	6	3	9	0	....	....	....	....
1998-99	Hamilton	AHL	66	18	29	47	10	....	....	....	....	....	....	....	....	....	11	0	3	3	4	....	....	....	....
99-2000	Cleveland	IHL	9	4	1	5	2	....	....	....	....	....	....	....	....	....	....	....	....	....	....	....	....	....	....
	Houston Aeros	IHL	44	9	8	17	12	....	....	....	....	....	....	....	....	....	....	....	....	....	....	....	....	....	....
	Lowell	AHL	10	0	5	5	4	....	....	....	....	....	....	....	....	....	7	1	2	3	6	....	....	....	....
2000-01	Lowell	AHL	65	28	28	56	33	....	....	....	....	....	....	....	....	....	3	0	1	1	2	....	....	....	....
	Cleveland	IHL	8	2	3	5	2	....	....	....	....	....	....	....	....	....	....	....	....	....	....	....	....	....	....
2001-02	**Colorado**	**NHL**	**1**	**0**	**1**	**1**	**0**	**0**	**0**	**0**	**2**	**0.0**	**0**	**0**	**0.0**	**12:34**	....	....	....	....	....	....	....	....	....
	Hershey Bears	AHL	79	26	25	51	22	....	....	....	....	....	....	....	....	....	8	1	1	2	4	....	....	....	....
2002-03	Lowell	AHL	51	14	16	30	18	....	....	....	....	....	....	....	....	....	....	....	....	....	....	....	....	....	....
	Springfield	AHL	12	2	4	6	2	....	....	....	....	....	....	....	....	....	6	0	2	2	2	....	....	....	....
2003-04	St. John's	AHL	67	10	23	33	17	....	....	....	....	....	....	....	....	....	....	....	....	....	....	....	....	....	....
	NHL Totals		**1**	**0**	**1**	**1**	**0**	**0**	**0**	**0**	**2**	**0.0**		**0**	**0.0**	**12:34**	....	....	....	....	....	....	....	....	....

Signed as a free agent by **Edmonton**, August 1, 1996. Signed as a free agent by **Chicago**, July 22, 1999. Traded to **Lowell** (AHL) by **Houston** (IHL) with Chicago retaining NHL rights for David Hymovitz, March 17, 2000. Selected by **Minnesota** from **Chicago** in Expansion Draft, June 23, 2000. Signed as a free agent by **Colorado**, July 23, 2001. Signed as a free agent by **Carolina**, August 27, 2002. Traded to **Toronto** by **Carolina** for future considerations, May 29, 2003.

DAZÉ, Eric

(dah-ZAY, AIR-ihk) **CHI.**

Right wing. Shoots left. 6'6", 235 lbs. Born, Montreal, Que., July 2, 1975. Chicago's 5th choice, 90th overall, in 1993 Entry Draft.

Season	Club	League	GP	G	A	Pts	PIM	PP	SH	GW	S	%	+/-	TF	F%	Min	Playoffs GP	G	A	Pts	PIM	PP	SH	GW	Min
1990-91	Laval Laurentide	QAHA	30	25	20	45	30	....	....	....	....	....	....	....	....	....	....	....	....	....	....	....	....	....	....
1991-92	Laval Laurentide	QAAA	35	30	29	59	40	....	....	....	....	....	....	....	....	....	12	8	10	18	8	....	....	....	....
1992-93	Beauport	QMJHL	68	19	36	55	24	....	....	....	....	....	....	....	....	....	....	....	....	....	....	....	....	....	....
1993-94	Beauport	QMJHL	66	59	48	107	31	....	....	....	....	....	....	....	....	....	15	16	8	24	2	....	....	....	....
1994-95	Beauport	QMJHL	57	54	45	99	20	....	....	....	....	....	....	....	....	....	16	9	12	21	23	....	....	....	....
	Chicago	**NHL**	**4**	**1**	**1**	**2**	**2**	**0**	**0**	**0**	**1**	**100.0**	**2**	....	....	....	**16**	**0**	**1**	**1**	**4**	**0**	**0**	**0**	....
1995-96	**Chicago**	**NHL**	**80**	**30**	**23**	**53**	**18**	**2**	**0**	**2**	**167**	**18.0**	**16**	....	....	....	**10**	**3**	**5**	**8**	**0**	**0**	**0**	**1**	....
1996-97	**Chicago**	**NHL**	**71**	**22**	**19**	**41**	**16**	**11**	**0**	**4**	**176**	**12.5**	**–4**	....	....	....	**6**	**2**	**1**	**3**	**2**	**0**	**0**	**0**	....
1997-98	**Chicago**	**NHL**	**80**	**31**	**11**	**42**	**22**	**10**	**0**	**7**	**216**	**14.4**	**4**	....	....	....	....	....	....	....	....	....	....	....	....
1998-99	**Chicago**	**NHL**	**72**	**22**	**20**	**42**	**22**	**8**	**0**	**2**	**189**	**11.6**	**–13**	**4**	**0.0**	**16:16**	....	....	....	....	....	....	....	....	....
99-2000	**Chicago**	**NHL**	**59**	**23**	**13**	**36**	**28**	**6**	**0**	**1**	**143**	**16.1**	**–16**	**9**	**22.2**	**16:15**	....	....	....	....	....	....	....	....	....
2000-01	**Chicago**	**NHL**	**79**	**33**	**24**	**57**	**16**	**9**	**1**	**8**	**205**	**16.1**	**1**	**3**	**33.3**	**17:45**	....	....	....	....	....	....	....	....	....
2001-02	**Chicago**	**NHL**	**82**	**38**	**32**	**70**	**36**	**12**	**0**	**5**	**264**	**14.4**	**17**	**5**	**0.0**	**17:07**	**5**	**0**	**0**	**0**	**2**	**0**	**0**	**0**	**17:12**
2002-03	**Chicago**	**NHL**	**54**	**22**	**22**	**44**	**14**	**3**	**0**	**5**	**170**	**12.9**	**10**	**4**	**25.0**	**16:17**	....	....	....	....	....	....	....	....	....
2003-04	**Chicago**	**NHL**	**19**	**4**	**7**	**11**	**0**	**1**	**0**	**0**	**76**	**5.3**	**–7**	**1**	**0.0**	**18:56**	....	....	....	....	....	....	....	....	....
	NHL Totals		**600**	**226**	**172**	**398**	**174**	**62**	**1**	**34**	**1607**	**14.1**		**26**	**15.4**	**16:55**	**37**	**5**	**7**	**12**	**8**	**0**	**0**	**1**	**17:12**

QMJHL First All-Star Team (1994, 1995) • Canadian Major Junior Most Sportsmanlike Player of the Year (1995) • NHL All-Rookie Team (1996)

Played in NHL All-Star Game (2002)

• Missed majority of 2003-04 season recovering from back injury suffered in game vs. Los Angeles, October 16, 2003.

DEADMARSH, Adam

(DEHD-mahrsh, A-duhm)

Right wing. Shoots right. 6', 205 lbs. Born, Trail, B.C., May 10, 1975. Quebec's 2nd choice, 14th overall, in 1993 Entry Draft.

Season	Club	League	GP	G	A	Pts	PIM	PP	SH	GW	S	%	+/-	TF	F%	Min	Playoffs GP	G	A	Pts	PIM	PP	SH	GW	Min
1990-91	Beaver Valley	KIJHL	35	28	44	72	95	....	....	....	....	....	....	....	....	....	....	....	....	....	....	....	....	....	....
1991-92	Portland	WHL	68	30	30	60	81	....	....	....	....	....	....	....	....	....	6	3	3	6	13	....	....	....	....
1992-93	Portland	WHL	58	33	36	69	126	....	....	....	....	....	....	....	....	....	16	7	8	15	29	....	....	....	....
1993-94	Portland	WHL	65	43	56	99	212	....	....	....	....	....	....	....	....	....	10	9	8	17	33	....	....	....	....
1994-95	Portland	WHL	29	28	20	48	129	....	....	....	....	....	....	....	....	....	....	....	....	....	....	....	....	....	....
	Quebec	**NHL**	**48**	**9**	**8**	**17**	**56**	**0**	**0**	**0**	**48**	**18.8**	**16**	....	....	....	**6**	**0**	**1**	**1**	**0**	**0**	**0**	**0**	....
1995-96♦	**Colorado**	**NHL**	**78**	**21**	**27**	**48**	**142**	**3**	**0**	**2**	**151**	**13.9**	**20**	....	....	....	**22**	**5**	**12**	**17**	**25**	**1**	**0**	**0**	....
1996-97	**Colorado**	**NHL**	**78**	**33**	**27**	**60**	**136**	**10**	**3**	**4**	**198**	**16.7**	**8**	....	....	....	**17**	**3**	**6**	**9**	**24**	**1**	**0**	**1**	....
1997-98	**Colorado**	**NHL**	**73**	**22**	**21**	**43**	**125**	**10**	**0**	**6**	**187**	**11.8**	**0**	....	....	....	**7**	**2**	**0**	**2**	**4**	**1**	**0**	**0**	....
	United States	Olympics	4	1	0	1	2	....	....	....	....	....	....	....	....	....	....	....	....	....	....	....	....	....	....
1998-99	**Colorado**	**NHL**	**66**	**22**	**27**	**49**	**99**	**10**	**0**	**3**	**152**	**14.5**	**–2**	**621**	**45.9**	**20:46**	**19**	**8**	**4**	**12**	**20**	**3**	**0**	**0**	**18:51**
99-2000	**Colorado**	**NHL**	**71**	**18**	**27**	**45**	**106**	**5**	**0**	**4**	**153**	**11.8**	**–10**	**430**	**46.5**	**20:27**	**17**	**4**	**11**	**15**	**21**	**1**	**0**	**1**	**18:47**
2000-01	**Colorado**	**NHL**	**39**	**13**	**13**	**26**	**59**	**7**	**0**	**2**	**86**	**15.1**	**–2**	**56**	**55.4**	**17:38**	....	....	....	....	....	....	....	....	....
	Los Angeles	**NHL**	**18**	**4**	**2**	**6**	**4**	**0**	**0**	**0**	**40**	**10.0**	**3**	**21**	**57.1**	**18:47**	**13**	**3**	**3**	**6**	**4**	**0**	**0**	**2**	**20:09**
2001-02	**Los Angeles**	**NHL**	**76**	**29**	**33**	**62**	**71**	**12**	**0**	**5**	**139**	**20.9**	**8**	**60**	**38.3**	**19:17**	**4**	**1**	**3**	**4**	**2**	**0**	**0**	**0**	**18:51**
	United States	Olympics	6	1	1	2	2	....	....	....	....	....	....	....	....	....	....	....	....	....	....	....	....	....	....
2002-03	**Los Angeles**	**NHL**	**20**	**13**	**4**	**17**	**21**	**4**	**0**	**1**	**55**	**23.6**	**2**	**26**	**46.2**	**19:18**	....	....	....	....	....	....	....	....	....
2003-04	**Los Angeles**	**NHL**	DID NOT PLAY – INJURED																						
	NHL Totals		**567**	**184**	**189**	**373**	**819**	**61**	**3**	**27**	**1209**	**15.2**		**1214**	**46.4**	**19:39**	**105**	**26**	**40**	**66**	**100**	**7**	**0**	**4**	**19:09**

Transferred to **Colorado** after **Quebec** franchise relocated, June 21, 1995. Traded to **Los Angeles** by **Colorado** with Aaron Miller, a player to be named later (Jared Aulin, March 22, 2001), Colorado's 1st round choice (Dave Steckel) in 2001 Entry Draft and Colorado's 1st round choice (Brian Boyle) in 2003 Entry Draft for Rob Blake and Steve Reinprecht, February 21, 2001. • Missed majority of 2002-03 season and entire 2003-04 season recovering from head injury suffered in game vs. Phoenix, December 15, 2002.

DEFAUW, Brad

(duh-FOU, BRAD) **CAR.**

Left wing. Shoots left. 6'2", 220 lbs. Born, Edina, MN, November 10, 1977. Carolina's 2nd choice, 28th overall, in 1997 Entry Draft.

Season	Club	League	GP	G	A	Pts	PIM	PP	SH	GW	S	%	+/-	TF	F%	Min	Playoffs GP	G	A	Pts	PIM	PP	SH	GW	Min
1995-96	Apple Valley	Hi-School	28	21	34	55	14	....	....	....	....	....	....	....	....	....	....	....	....	....	....	....	....	....	....
1996-97	North Dakota	WCHA	37	7	6	13	39	....	....	....	....	....	....	....	....	....	....	....	....	....	....	....	....	....	....
1997-98	North Dakota	WCHA	36	9	11	20	34	....	....	....	....	....	....	....	....	....	....	....	....	....	....	....	....	....	....
1998-99	North Dakota	WCHA	34	11	12	23	64	....	....	....	....	....	....	....	....	....	....	....	....	....	....	....	....	....	....
99-2000	North Dakota	WCHA	43	13	9	22	52	....	....	....	....	....	....	....	....	....	....	....	....	....	....	....	....	....	....
2000-01	Cincinnati	IHL	82	20	31	51	39	....	....	....	....	....	....	....	....	....	4	2	0	2	8	....	....	....	....
2001-02	Lowell	AHL	63	17	21	38	29	....	....	....	....	....	....	....	....	....	5	2	1	3	6	....	....	....	....
2002-03	**Carolina**	**NHL**	**9**	**3**	**0**	**3**	**2**	**1**	**0**	**1**	**19**	**15.8**	**–2**	**0**	**0.0**	**13:45**	....	....	....	....	....	....	....	....	....
	Lowell	AHL	61	11	12	23	48	....	....	....	....	....	....	....	....	....	....	....	....	....	....	....	....	....	....
2003-04	Lowell	AHL	30	4	3	7	6	....	....	....	....	....	....	....	....	....	....	....	....	....	....	....	....	....	....
	NHL Totals		**9**	**3**	**0**	**3**	**2**	**1**	**0**	**1**	**19**	**15.8**		**0**	**0.0**	**13:45**	....	....	....	....	....	....	....	....	....

• Missed majority of 2003-04 season recovering from elbow injury suffered in game vs. Los Angeles, March 15, 2003.

DELMORE, Andy
(DEHL-mohr, AN-dee)

Defense. Shoots right. 6'1", 200 lbs. Born, LaSalle, Ont., December 26, 1976.

			Regular Season														Playoffs								
Season	Club	League	GP	G	A	Pts	PIM	PP	SH	GW	S	%	+/-	TF	F%	Min	GP	G	A	Pts	PIM	PP	SH	GW	Min
1992-93	Chatham	OJHL-B	47	4	21	25	38	....	....	....	....	....	....	....	....	....	....	....	....	....	....	....	....	....	....
1993-94	North Bay	OHL	45	2	7	9	33	....	....	....	....	....	....	....	....	....	17	0	0	0	2	....	....	....	....
1994-95	North Bay	OHL	40	2	14	16	21	....	....	....	....	....	....	....	....	....	....	....	....	....	....	....	....	....	....
	Sarnia Sting	OHL	27	5	13	18	27	....	....	....	....	....	....	....	....	....	3	0	0	0	2	....	....	....	....
1995-96	Sarnia Sting	OHL	64	21	38	59	45	....	....	....	....	....	....	....	....	....	10	3	7	10	2	....	....	....	....
1996-97	Sarnia Sting	OHL	64	18	60	78	39	....	....	....	....	....	....	....	....	....	12	2	10	12	10	....	....	....	....
	Fredericton	AHL	4	0	1	1	0	....	....	....	....	....	....	....	....	....	....	....	....	....	....	....	....	....	....
1997-98	Philadelphia	AHL	73	9	30	39	46	....	....	....	....	....	....	....	....	....	18	4	4	8	21	....	....	....	....
1998-99	**Philadelphia**	**NHL**	**2**	**0**	**1**	**1**	**0**	**0**	**0**	**0**	**2**	**0.0**	**-1**	**0**	**0.0**	**20:42**	....	....	....	....	....	....	....	....	....
	Philadelphia	AHL	70	5	18	23	51	....	....	....	....	....	....	....	....	....	15	1	4	5	6	....	....	....	....
99-2000	**Philadelphia**	**NHL**	**27**	**2**	**5**	**7**	**8**	**0**	**0**	**1**	**55**	**3.6**	**-1**	**0**	**0.0**	**17:17**	**18**	**5**	**2**	**7**	**14**	**1**	**0**	**1**	**17:33**
	Philadelphia	AHL	39	12	14	26	31	....	....	....	....	....	....	....	....	....	....	....	....	....	....	....	....	....	....
2000-01	**Philadelphia**	**NHL**	**66**	**5**	**9**	**14**	**16**	**2**	**0**	**0**	**119**	**4.2**	**2**	**0**	**0.0**	**17:39**	**2**	**1**	**0**	**1**	**2**	**0**	**0**	**1**	**15:20**
2001-02	**Nashville**	**NHL**	**73**	**16**	**22**	**38**	**22**	**11**	**0**	**3**	**175**	**9.1**	**-13**	**0**	**0.0**	**19:40**	....	....	....	....	....	....	....	....	....
2002-03	**Nashville**	**NHL**	**71**	**18**	**16**	**34**	**28**	**14**	**0**	**6**	**149**	**12.1**	**-17**	**0**	**0.0**	**17:05**	....	....	....	....	....	....	....	....	....
2003-04	**Buffalo**	**NHL**	**37**	**2**	**5**	**7**	**29**	**2**	**0**	**0**	**40**	**5.0**	**-5**	**0**	**0.0**	**15:11**	....	....	....	....	....	....	....	....	....
	Rochester	AHL	8	0	2	2	2	....	....	....	....	....	....	....	....	....	....	....	....	....	....	....	....	....	....
	NHL Totals		**276**	**43**	**58**	**101**	**103**	**29**	**0**	**10**	**540**	**8.0**		**0**	**0.0**	**17:41**	**20**	**6**	**2**	**8**	**16**	**1**	**0**	**2**	**17:19**

OHL First All-Star Team (1997)

Signed as a free agent by **Philadelphia**, June 9, 1997. Traded to **Nashville** by **Philadelphia** for Nashville's 3rd round choice (later traded to Phoenix – Phoenix selected Joe Callahan) in 2002 Entry Draft, July 31, 2001. Traded to **Buffalo** by **Nashville** for Buffalo's 3rd round choice (later traded to Minnesota – Minnesota selected Clayton Stoner) in 2004 Entry Draft, June 27, 2003. Traded to **San Jose** by **Buffalo** with Curtis Brown for Jeff Jillson and San Jose's 9th round choice in 2005 Entry Draft, March 9, 2004. Traded to **Boston** by **San Jose** for future considerations, March 9, 2004.

DEMITRA, Pavol
(deh-MEET-rah, PAH-vohl)

Left wing. Shoots left. 6', 206 lbs. Born, Dubnica, Czech., November 29, 1974. Ottawa's 9th choice, 227th overall, in 1993 Entry Draft.

			Regular Season														Playoffs								
Season	Club	League	GP	G	A	Pts	PIM	PP	SH	GW	S	%	+/-	TF	F%	Min	GP	G	A	Pts	PIM	PP	SH	GW	Min
1991-92	Dubnica	Czech-2	28	13	10	23	12	....	....	....	....	....	....	....	....	....	....	....	....	....	....	....	....	....	....
1992-93	CAPEH Dubnica	Czech-2	4	3	0	3		....	....	....	....	....	....	....	....	....	....	....	....	....	....	....	....	....	....
	Dukla Trencin	Czech	46	11	17	28	0	....	....	....	....	....	....	....	....	....	....	....	....	....	....	....	....	....	....
1993-94	**Ottawa**	**NHL**	**12**	**1**	**1**	**2**	**4**	**1**	**0**	**0**	**10**	**10.0**	**-7**	....	....	....	....	....	....	....	....	....	....	....	....
	P.E.I. Senators	AHL	41	18	23	41	8	....	....	....	....	....	....	....	....	....	....	....	....	....	....	....	....	....	....
1994-95	P.E.I. Senators	AHL	61	26	48	74	23	....	....	....	....	....	....	....	....	....	5	0	7	7	0	....	....	....	....
	Ottawa	**NHL**	**16**	**4**	**3**	**7**	**0**	**1**	**0**	**0**	**21**	**19.0**	**-4**	....	....	....	....	....	....	....	....	....	....	....	....
1995-96	**Ottawa**	**NHL**	**31**	**7**	**10**	**17**	**6**	**2**	**0**	**1**	**66**	**10.6**	**-3**	....	....	....	....	....	....	....	....	....	....	....	....
	P.E.I. Senators	AHL	48	28	53	81	44	....	....	....	....	....	....	....	....	....	....	....	....	....	....	....	....	....	....
1996-97	Dukla Trencin	Slovakia	1	1	1	2		....	....	....	....	....	....	....	....	....	....	....	....	....	....	....	....	....	....
	Las Vegas	IHL	22	8	13	21	10	....	....	....	....	....	....	....	....	....	....	....	....	....	....	....	....	....	....
	St. Louis	**NHL**	**8**	**3**	**0**	**3**	**2**	**2**	**0**	**1**	**15**	**20.0**	**0**	....	....	....	**6**	**1**	**3**	**4**	**6**	**0**	**0**	**0**	....
	Grand Rapids	IHL	42	20	30	50	24	....	....	....	....	....	....	....	....	....	....	....	....	....	....	....	....	....	....
1997-98	**St. Louis**	**NHL**	**61**	**22**	**30**	**52**	**22**	**4**	**4**	**6**	**147**	**15.0**	**11**	....	....	....	**10**	**3**	**3**	**6**	**2**	**0**	**0**	**0**	....
1998-99	**St. Louis**	**NHL**	**82**	**37**	**52**	**89**	**16**	**14**	**0**	**10**	**259**	**14.3**	**13**	**250**	**44.0**	**20:10**	**13**	**5**	**4**	**9**	**4**	**3**	**0**	**1**	**19:10**
99-2000	**St. Louis**	**NHL**	**71**	**28**	**47**	**75**	**8**	**8**	**0**	**4**	**241**	**11.6**	**34**	**41**	**39.0**	**19:13**	....	....	....	....	....	....	....	....	....
2000-01	**St. Louis**	**NHL**	**44**	**20**	**25**	**45**	**16**	**5**	**0**	**5**	**124**	**16.1**	**27**	**8**	**37.5**	**18:03**	**15**	**2**	**4**	**6**	**2**	**0**	**0**	**1**	**18:13**
2001-02	**St. Louis**	**NHL**	**82**	**35**	**43**	**78**	**46**	**11**	**0**	**10**	**212**	**16.5**	**13**	**1224**	**48.1**	**19:11**	**10**	**4**	**7**	**11**	**6**	**2**	**1**	**1**	**19:45**
	Slovakia	Olympics	2	1	2	3	2	....	....	....	....	....	....	....	....	....	....	....	....	....	....	....	....	....	....
2002-03	**St. Louis**	**NHL**	**78**	**36**	**57**	**93**	**32**	**11**	**0**	**4**	**205**	**17.6**	**0**	**1253**	**46.1**	**19:47**	**7**	**2**	**4**	**6**	**2**	**1**	**0**	**0**	**18:20**
2003-04	**St. Louis**	**NHL**	**68**	**23**	**35**	**58**	**18**	**8**	**0**	**5**	**179**	**12.8**	**1**	**770**	**47.3**	**20:30**	**5**	**1**	**0**	**1**	**4**	**0**	**0**	**0**	**18:07**
	NHL Totals		**553**	**216**	**303**	**519**	**170**	**67**	**4**	**46**	**1479**	**14.6**		**3546**	**46.8**	**19:35**	**66**	**18**	**25**	**43**	**26**	**6**	**1**	**3**	**18:47**

Lady Byng Trophy (2000)

Played in NHL All-Star Game (1999, 2000, 2002)

Traded to **St. Louis** by **Ottawa** for Christer Olsson, November 27, 1996.

DEMPSEY, Nathan
(DEHMP-see, NAY-thun) **L.A.**

Defense. Shoots right. 6', 190 lbs. Born, Spruce Grove, Alta., July 14, 1974. Toronto's 12th choice, 245th overall, in 1992 Entry Draft.

			Regular Season														Playoffs								
Season	Club	League	GP	G	A	Pts	PIM	PP	SH	GW	S	%	+/-	TF	F%	Min	GP	G	A	Pts	PIM	PP	SH	GW	Min
1990-91	St. Albert Saints	AMHL	34	11	20	31	73	....	....	....	....	....	....	....	....	....	....	....	....	....	....	....	....	....	....
1991-92	Regina Pats	WHL	70	4	22	26	72	....	....	....	....	....	....	....	....	....	....	....	....	....	....	....	....	....	....
1992-93	Regina Pats	WHL	72	12	29	41	95	....	....	....	....	....	....	....	....	....	13	3	8	11	14	....	....	....	....
	St. John's	AHL	....	....	....	....	....	....	....	....	....	....	....	....	....	....	2	0	0	0	0	....	....	....	....
1993-94	Regina Pats	WHL	56	14	36	50	100	....	....	....	....	....	....	....	....	....	4	0	0	0	4	....	....	....	....
1994-95	St. John's	AHL	74	7	30	37	91	....	....	....	....	....	....	....	....	....	5	1	0	1	11	....	....	....	....
1995-96	St. John's	AHL	73	5	15	20	103	....	....	....	....	....	....	....	....	....	4	1	0	1	9	....	....	....	....
1996-97	**Toronto**	**NHL**	**14**	**1**	**1**	**2**	**2**	**0**	**0**	**0**	**11**	**9.1**	**-2**	....	....	....	....	....	....	....	....	....	....	....	....
	St. John's	AHL	52	8	18	26	108	....	....	....	....	....	....	....	....	....	6	1	0	1	4	....	....	....	....
1997-98	St. John's	AHL	68	12	16	28	85	....	....	....	....	....	....	....	....	....	4	0	0	0	0	....	....	....	....
1998-99	St. John's	AHL	67	2	29	31	70	....	....	....	....	....	....	....	....	....	5	0	1	1	2	....	....	....	....
99-2000	**Toronto**	**NHL**	**6**	**0**	**2**	**2**	**2**	**0**	**0**	**0**	**3**	**0.0**	**2**	**1**	**0.0**	**13:40**	....	....	....	....	....	....	....	....	....
	St. John's	AHL	44	15	12	27	40	....	....	....	....	....	....	....	....	....	....	....	....	....	....	....	....	....	....
2000-01	**Toronto**	**NHL**	**25**	**1**	**9**	**10**	**4**	**1**	**0**	**0**	**31**	**3.2**	**13**	**0**	**0.0**	**15:53**	....	....	....	....	....	....	....	....	....
	St. John's	AHL	55	11	28	39	60	....	....	....	....	....	....	....	....	....	4	0	4	4	8	....	....	....	....
2001-02	**Toronto**	**NHL**	**3**	**0**	**0**	**0**	**0**	**0**	**0**	**0**	**3**	**0.0**	**1**	**0**	**0.0**	**14:00**	**6**	**0**	**2**	**2**	**0**	**0**	**0**	**0**	**14:31**
	St. John's	AHL	75	13	48	61	66	....	....	....	....	....	....	....	....	....	11	1	5	6	8	....	....	....	....
2002-03	**Chicago**	**NHL**	**67**	**5**	**23**	**28**	**26**	**1**	**0**	**2**	**124**	**4.0**	**-7**	**0**	**0.0**	**20:55**	....	....	....	....	....	....	....	....	....
2003-04	**Chicago**	**NHL**	**58**	**8**	**17**	**25**	**30**	**2**	**0**	**1**	**155**	**5.2**	**-5**	**1**	**0.0**	**23:48**	....	....	....	....	....	....	....	....	....
	Los Angeles	**NHL**	**17**	**4**	**3**	**7**	**2**	**1**	**0**	**0**	**28**	**14.3**	**-7**	**0**	**0.0**	**20:23**	....	....	....	....	....	....	....	....	....
	NHL Totals		**190**	**19**	**55**	**74**	**66**	**5**	**0**	**3**	**355**	**5.4**		**2**	**0.0**	**20:44**	**6**	**0**	**2**	**2**	**0**	**0**	**0**	**0**	**14:30**

WHL East Second All-Star Team (1994) • AHL Second All-Star Team (2002) • Fred Hunt Memorial Trophy (Sportsmanship – AHL) (2002)

Signed as a free agent by **Chicago**, July 12, 2002. Traded to **Los Angeles** by **Chicago** for Los Angeles' 5th round choice in 2005 Entry Draft and future considerations, March 2, 2004.

DESJARDINS, Eric
(deh-ZHAHR-dai, AIR-ihk) **PHI.**

Defense. Shoots right. 6'1", 205 lbs. Born, Rouyn, Que., June 14, 1969. Montreal's 3rd choice, 38th overall, in 1987 Entry Draft.

			Regular Season														Playoffs								
Season	Club	League	GP	G	A	Pts	PIM	PP	SH	GW	S	%	+/-	TF	F%	Min	GP	G	A	Pts	PIM	PP	SH	GW	Min
1985-86	Laval Laurentide	QAAA	42	6	30	36	54	....	....	....	....	....	....	....	....	....	8	2	10	12	14	....	....	....	....
1986-87	Granby Bisons	QMJHL	66	14	24	38	178	....	....	....	....	....	....	....	....	....	8	3	2	5	10	....	....	....	....
1987-88	Granby Bisons	QMJHL	62	18	49	67	138	....	....	....	....	....	....	....	....	....	5	0	3	3	10	....	....	....	....
	Sherbrooke	AHL	3	0	0	0	6	....	....	....	....	....	....	....	....	....	4	0	2	2	2	....	....	....	....
1988-89	**Montreal**	**NHL**	**36**	**2**	**12**	**14**	**26**	**1**	**0**	**0**	**39**	**5.1**	**9**	....	....	....	**14**	**1**	**1**	**2**	**6**	**1**	**0**	**0**	....
1989-90	**Montreal**	**NHL**	**55**	**3**	**13**	**16**	**51**	**1**	**0**	**0**	**48**	**6.3**	**1**	....	....	....	**6**	**0**	**0**	**0**	**10**	**0**	**0**	**0**	....
1990-91	**Montreal**	**NHL**	**62**	**7**	**18**	**25**	**27**	**0**	**0**	**1**	**114**	**6.1**	**7**	....	....	....	**13**	**1**	**4**	**5**	**8**	**1**	**0**	**0**	....
1991-92	**Montreal**	**NHL**	**77**	**6**	**32**	**38**	**50**	**4**	**0**	**2**	**141**	**4.3**	**17**	....	....	....	**11**	**3**	**3**	**6**	**4**	**1**	**0**	**0**	....
1992-93♦	**Montreal**	**NHL**	**82**	**13**	**32**	**45**	**98**	**7**	**0**	**1**	**163**	**8.0**	**20**	....	....	....	**20**	**4**	**10**	**14**	**23**	**1**	**0**	**1**	....
1993-94	**Montreal**	**NHL**	**84**	**12**	**23**	**35**	**97**	**6**	**1**	**3**	**193**	**6.2**	**-1**	....	....	....	**7**	**0**	**2**	**2**	**4**	**0**	**0**	**0**	....
1994-95	**Montreal**	**NHL**	**9**	**0**	**6**	**6**	**2**	**0**	**0**	**0**	**14**	**0.0**	**2**	....	....	....	....	....	....	....	....	....	....	....	....
	Philadelphia	**NHL**	**34**	**5**	**18**	**23**	**12**	**1**	**0**	**1**	**79**	**6.3**	**10**	....	....	....	**15**	**4**	**4**	**8**	**10**	**1**	**0**	**2**	....
1995-96	**Philadelphia**	**NHL**	**80**	**7**	**40**	**47**	**45**	**5**	**0**	**2**	**184**	**3.8**	**19**	....	....	....	**12**	**0**	**6**	**6**	**2**	**0**	**0**	**0**	....
1996-97	**Philadelphia**	**NHL**	**82**	**12**	**34**	**46**	**50**	**5**	**1**	**1**	**183**	**6.6**	**25**	....	....	....	**19**	**2**	**8**	**10**	**12**	**0**	**0**	**0**	....
1997-98	**Philadelphia**	**NHL**	**77**	**6**	**27**	**33**	**36**	**2**	**1**	**0**	**150**	**4.0**	**11**	....	....	....	**5**	**0**	**1**	**1**	**0**	**0**	**0**	**0**	....
	Canada	Olympics	6	0	0	0	2	....	....	....	....	....	....	....	....	....	....	....	....	....	....	....	....	....	....
1998-99	**Philadelphia**	**NHL**	**68**	**15**	**36**	**51**	**38**	**6**	**0**	**2**	**190**	**7.9**	**18**	**0**	**0.0**	**25:48**	**6**	**2**	**2**	**4**	**4**	**1**	**0**	**1**	**26:40**
99-2000	**Philadelphia**	**NHL**	**81**	**14**	**41**	**55**	**32**	**8**	**0**	**4**	**207**	**6.8**	**20**	**1**	**0.0**	**27:01**	**18**	**2**	**10**	**12**	**2**	**1**	**0**	**1**	**28:00**
2000-01	**Philadelphia**	**NHL**	**79**	**15**	**33**	**48**	**50**	**6**	**1**	**4**	**187**	**8.0**	**-3**	**3**	**100.0**	**26:27**	**6**	**1**	**1**	**2**	**0**	**0**	**0**	**0**	**27:49**
2001-02	**Philadelphia**	**NHL**	**65**	**6**	**19**	**25**	**24**	**2**	**1**	**0**	**117**	**5.1**	**-1**	**2**	**0.0**	**22:12**	**5**	**0**	**1**	**1**	**2**	**0**	**0**	**0**	**22:30**

			Regular Season														Playoffs								
Season	Club	League	GP	G	A	Pts	PIM	PP	SH	GW	S	%	+/-	TF	F%	Min	GP	G	A	Pts	PIM	PP	SH	GW	Min
2002-03	**Philadelphia**	**NHL**	**79**	**8**	**24**	**32**	**35**	**1**	**0**	**2**	**197**	**4.1**	**30**	**0**	**0.0**	**22:55**	**5**	**2**	**1**	**3**	**0**	**0**	**0**	**0**	**27:38**
2003-04	**Philadelphia**	**NHL**	**48**	**1**	**11**	**12**	**28**	**0**	**0**	**0**	**92**	**1.1**	**11**	**1**	**0.0**	**22:29**	....	....	....	....	....	....	....	....	....
	NHL Totals		**1098**	**132**	**419**	**551**	**701**	**55**	**5**	**23**	**2298**	**5.7**		**7**	**42.9**	**24:41**	**162**	**22**	**54**	**76**	**87**	**7**	**0**	**5**	**27:02**

QMJHL Second All-Star Team (1987) • QMJHL First All-Star Team (1988) • NHL Second All-Star Team (1999, 2000)

Played in NHL All-Star Game (1992, 1996, 2000)

Traded to **Philadelphia** by **Montreal** with Gilbert Dionne and John LeClair for Mark Recchi and Philadelphia's 3rd round choice (Martin Hohenberger) in 1995 Entry Draft, February 9, 1995.

DEVEREAUX, Boyd

(DEH-vuhr-oh, BOID) **PHX.**

Center. Shoots left. 6'2", 195 lbs. Born, Seaforth, Ont., April 16, 1978. Edmonton's 1st choice, 6th overall, in 1996 Entry Draft.

1992-93	Seaforth Sailors	OJHL-D	34	7	20	27	13	....	....	....	....	....	....	....	....	....	....	....	....	....	....	....	....	....	....
1993-94	Stratford Cullitons	OJHL-B	46	12	27	39	8	....	....	....	....	....	....	....	....	....	....	....	....	....	....	....	....	....	....
1994-95	Stratford Cullitons	OJHL-B	45	31	74	105	21	....	....	....	....	....	....	....	....	....	....	....	....	....	....	....	....	....	....
1995-96	Kitchener Rangers	OHL	66	20	38	58	35	....	....	....	....	....	....	....	....	....	12	3	7	10	4	....	....	....	....
1996-97	Kitchener Rangers	OHL	54	28	41	69	37	....	....	....	....	....	....	....	....	....	13	4	11	15	8	....	....	....	....
	Hamilton	AHL	....	....	....	....	....	....	....	....	....	....	....	....	....	....	1	0	1	1	0	....	....	....	....
1997-98	**Edmonton**	**NHL**	**38**	**1**	**4**	**5**	**6**	**0**	**0**	**0**	**27**	**3.7**	**–5**	....	....	....	....	....	....	....	....	....	....	....	....
	Hamilton	AHL	14	5	6	11	6	....	....	....	....	....	....	....	....	....	9	1	1	2	8	....	....	....	....
1998-99	**Edmonton**	**NHL**	**61**	**6**	**8**	**14**	**23**	**0**	**1**	**4**	**39**	**15.4**	**2**	**409**	**42.8**	**10:09**	**1**	**0**	**0**	**0**	**0**	**0**	**0**	**0**	**32:46**
	Hamilton	AHL	7	4	6	10	2	....	....	....	....	....	....	....	....	....	8	0	3	3	4	....	....	....	....
99-2000	**Edmonton**	**NHL**	**76**	**8**	**19**	**27**	**20**	**0**	**1**	**2**	**108**	**7.4**	**7**	**241**	**34.9**	**12:36**	....	....	....	....	....	....	....	....	....
2000-01	**Detroit**	**NHL**	**55**	**5**	**6**	**11**	**14**	**0**	**0**	**0**	**66**	**7.6**	**1**	**124**	**37.1**	**10:08**	**2**	**0**	**0**	**0**	**0**	**0**	**0**	**0**	**10:39**
2001-02♦	**Detroit**	**NHL**	**79**	**9**	**16**	**25**	**24**	**0**	**0**	**2**	**116**	**7.8**	**9**	**12**	**33.3**	**11:30**	**21**	**2**	**4**	**6**	**4**	**0**	**0**	**0**	**10:58**
2002-03	**Detroit**	**NHL**	**61**	**3**	**9**	**12**	**16**	**0**	**0**	**1**	**72**	**4.2**	**4**	**7**	**42.9**	**9:26**	....	....	....	....	....	....	....	....	....
2003-04	**Detroit**	**NHL**	**61**	**6**	**9**	**15**	**20**	**0**	**0**	**2**	**62**	**9.7**	**–1**	**14**	**50.0**	**9:58**	**3**	**1**	**0**	**1**	**0**	**0**	**0**	**0**	**6:36**
	NHL Totals		**431**	**38**	**71**	**109**	**123**	**0**	**2**	**11**	**490**	**7.8**		**807**	**39.5**	**10:45**	**27**	**3**	**4**	**7**	**4**	**0**	**0**	**0**	**11:16**

Canadian Major Junior Scholastic Player of the Year (1996)

Signed as a free agent by **Detroit**, August 23, 2000. Signed as a free agent by **Phoenix**, July 5, 2004.

de VRIES, Greg

(deh-VREES, GREHG) **OTT.**

Defense. Shoots left. 6'3", 215 lbs. Born, Sundridge, Ont., January 4, 1973.

1988-89	Cortina Astros	OMHA	35	28	40	68	....	....	....	....	....	....	....	....	....	....	....	....	....	....	....	....	....	....	....
1989-90	Aurora Eagles	OJHL	42	1	16	17	32	....	....	....	....	....	....	....	....	....	....	....	....	....	....	....	....	....	....
1990-91	Stratford Cullitons	OJHL-B	40	8	32	40	120	....	....	....	....	....	....	....	....	....	3	2	1	3	20	....	....	....	....
1991-92	Thorold Eagles	OJHL-B	3	0	0	0	0	....	....	....	....	....	....	....	....	....	....	....	....	....	....	....	....	....	....
	Bowling Green	CCHA	24	0	3	3	20	....	....	....	....	....	....	....	....	....	....	....	....	....	....	....	....	....	....
1992-93	Niagara Falls	OHL	62	3	23	26	86	....	....	....	....	....	....	....	....	....	4	0	1	1	6	....	....	....	....
1993-94	Niagara Falls	OHL	64	5	40	45	135	....	....	....	....	....	....	....	....	....	....	....	....	....	....	....	....	....	....
	Cape Breton	AHL	9	0	0	0	11	....	....	....	....	....	....	....	....	....	1	0	0	0	0	....	....	....	....
1994-95	Cape Breton	AHL	77	5	19	24	68	....	....	....	....	....	....	....	....	....	....	....	....	....	....	....	....	....	....
1995-96	**Edmonton**	**NHL**	**13**	**1**	**1**	**2**	**12**	**0**	**0**	**0**	**8**	**12.5**	**–2**	....	....	....	....	....	....	....	....	....	....	....	....
	Cape Breton	AHL	58	9	30	39	174	....	....	....	....	....	....	....	....	....	....	....	....	....	....	....	....	....	....
1996-97	**Edmonton**	**NHL**	**37**	**0**	**4**	**4**	**52**	**0**	**0**	**0**	**31**	**0.0**	**–2**	....	....	....	**12**	**0**	**1**	**1**	**8**	**0**	**0**	**0**	....
	Hamilton	AHL	34	4	14	18	26	....	....	....	....	....	....	....	....	....	....	....	....	....	....	....	....	....	....
1997-98	**Edmonton**	**NHL**	**65**	**7**	**4**	**11**	**80**	**1**	**0**	**0**	**53**	**13.2**	**–17**	....	....	....	**7**	**0**	**0**	**0**	**21**	**0**	**0**	**0**	....
1998-99	**Nashville**	**NHL**	**6**	**0**	**0**	**0**	**4**	**0**	**0**	**0**	**1**	**1.0**	**–4**	**0**	**0.0**	**18:11**	....	....	....	....	....	....	....	....	....
	Colorado	**NHL**	**67**	**1**	**3**	**4**	**60**	**0**	**0**	**0**	**56**	**56.0**	**–3**	**1**	**100.0**	**16:23**	**19**	**0**	**2**	**2**	**22**	**0**	**0**	**0**	**12:09**
99-2000	**Colorado**	**NHL**	**69**	**2**	**7**	**9**	**73**	**0**	**0**	**0**	**40**	**5.0**	**–7**	**0**	**0.0**	**14:59**	**5**	**0**	**0**	**0**	**4**	**0**	**0**	**0**	**8:09**
2000-01♦	**Colorado**	**NHL**	**79**	**5**	**12**	**17**	**51**	**0**	**0**	**0**	**76**	**6.6**	**23**	**0**	**0.0**	**17:06**	**23**	**0**	**1**	**1**	**20**	**0**	**0**	**0**	**14:17**
2001-02	**Colorado**	**NHL**	**82**	**8**	**12**	**20**	**57**	**1**	**1**	**3**	**148**	**5.4**	**18**	**1**	**0.0**	**23:03**	**21**	**4**	**9**	**13**	**2**	**0**	**0**	**1**	**24:12**
2002-03	**Colorado**	**NHL**	**82**	**6**	**26**	**32**	**70**	**0**	**0**	**2**	**112**	**5.4**	**15**	**1**	**100.0**	**22:15**	**7**	**2**	**0**	**2**	**0**	**0**	**0**	**0**	**22:11**
2003-04	**NY Rangers**	**NHL**	**53**	**3**	**12**	**15**	**37**	**0**	**0**	**0**	**58**	**5.2**	**12**	**0**	**0.0**	**19:01**	....	....	....	....	....	....	....	....	....
	Ottawa	**NHL**	**13**	**0**	**1**	**1**	**6**	**0**	**0**	**0**	**12**	**0.0**	**0**	**0**	**0.0**	**17:51**	**7**	**0**	**1**	**1**	**8**	**0**	**0**	**0**	**17:51**
	NHL Totals		**566**	**33**	**82**	**115**	**502**	**2**	**1**	**5**	**595**	**5.5**		**3**	**66.7**	**18:57**	**101**	**6**	**14**	**20**	**85**	**0**	**0**	**1**	**16:56**

Signed as a free agent by **Edmonton**, March 20, 1994. Traded to **Nashville** by **Edmonton** with Eric Fichaud and Drake Berehowsky for Mikhail Shtalenkov and Jim Dowd, October 1, 1998. Traded to **Colorado** by **Nashville** for Colorado's 2nd round choice (Ed Hill) in 1999 Entry Draft, October 24, 1998. Signed as a free agent by **NY Rangers**, July 14, 2003. Traded to **Ottawa** by **NY Rangers** for Karel Rachunek and Alexandre Giroux, March 9, 2004.

DiMAIO, Rob

(duh-MIGH-oh, RAWB) **DAL.**

Right wing. Shoots right. 5'10", 190 lbs. Born, Calgary, Alta., February 19, 1968. NY Islanders' 6th choice, 118th overall, in 1987 Entry Draft.

1984-85	Kamloops Blazers	WHL	55	9	18	27	29	....	....	....	....	....	....	....	....	....	7	1	3	4	2	....	....	....	....
1985-86	Kamloops Blazers	WHL	6	1	0	1	0	....	....	....	....	....	....	....	....	....	....	....	....	....	....	....	....	....	....
	Medicine Hat	WHL	55	20	30	50	82	....	....	....	....	....	....	....	....	....	22	6	6	12	39	....	....	....	....
1986-87	Medicine Hat	WHL	70	27	43	70	130	....	....	....	....	....	....	....	....	....	20	7	11	18	46	....	....	....	....
1987-88	Medicine Hat	WHL	54	47	43	90	120	....	....	....	....	....	....	....	....	....	14	12	19	*31	59	....	....	....	....
1988-89	**NY Islanders**	**NHL**	**16**	**1**	**0**	**1**	**30**	**0**	**0**	**1**	**16**	**6.3**	**–6**	....	....	....	....	....	....	....	....	....	....	....	....
	Springfield	AHL	40	13	18	31	67	....	....	....	....	....	....	....	....	....	....	....	....	....	....	....	....	....	....
1989-90	**NY Islanders**	**NHL**	**7**	**0**	**0**	**0**	**2**	**0**	**0**	**0**	**2**	**0.0**	**0**	....	....	....	**1**	**1**	**0**	**1**	**4**	**0**	**0**	**0**	....
	Springfield	AHL	54	25	27	52	69	....	....	....	....	....	....	....	....	....	16	4	7	11	45	....	....	....	....
1990-91	**NY Islanders**	**NHL**	**1**	**0**	**0**	**0**	**0**	**0**	**0**	**0**	**0**	**0.0**	**0**	....	....	....	....	....	....	....	....	....	....	....	....
	Capital District	AHL	12	3	4	7	22	....	....	....	....	....	....	....	....	....	....	....	....	....	....	....	....	....	....
1991-92	**NY Islanders**	**NHL**	**50**	**5**	**2**	**7**	**43**	**0**	**2**	**0**	**43**	**11.6**	**–23**	....	....	....	....	....	....	....	....	....	....	....	....
1992-93	**Tampa Bay**	**NHL**	**54**	**9**	**15**	**24**	**62**	**2**	**0**	**0**	**75**	**12.0**	**0**	....	....	....	....	....	....	....	....	....	....	....	....
1993-94	**Tampa Bay**	**NHL**	**39**	**8**	**7**	**15**	**40**	**2**	**0**	**1**	**51**	**15.7**	**–5**	....	....	....	....	....	....	....	....	....	....	....	....
	Philadelphia	**NHL**	**14**	**3**	**5**	**8**	**6**	**0**	**0**	**1**	**30**	**10.0**	**1**	....	....	....	....	....	....	....	....	....	....	....	....
1994-95	**Philadelphia**	**NHL**	**36**	**3**	**1**	**4**	**53**	**0**	**0**	**0**	**34**	**8.8**	**8**	....	....	....	**15**	**2**	**4**	**6**	**4**	**0**	**1**	**1**	....
1995-96	**Philadelphia**	**NHL**	**59**	**6**	**15**	**21**	**58**	**1**	**1**	**0**	**49**	**12.2**	**0**	....	....	....	**3**	**0**	**0**	**0**	**0**	**0**	**0**	**0**	....
1996-97	**Boston**	**NHL**	**72**	**13**	**15**	**28**	**82**	**0**	**3**	**2**	**152**	**8.6**	**–21**	....	....	....	....	....	....	....	....	....	....	....	....
1997-98	**Boston**	**NHL**	**79**	**10**	**17**	**27**	**82**	**0**	**0**	**4**	**112**	**8.9**	**–13**	....	....	....	**6**	**1**	**0**	**1**	**8**	**0**	**0**	**0**	....
1998-99	**Boston**	**NHL**	**71**	**7**	**14**	**21**	**95**	**1**	**0**	**0**	**121**	**5.8**	**–14**	**83**	**45.8**	**16:41**	**12**	**2**	**0**	**2**	**8**	**0**	**0**	**1**	**16:50**
99-2000	**Boston**	**NHL**	**50**	**5**	**16**	**21**	**42**	**0**	**0**	**0**	**93**	**5.4**	**–1**	**278**	**44.2**	**16:47**	....	....	....	....	....	....	....	....	....
	NY Rangers	**NHL**	**12**	**1**	**3**	**4**	**8**	**0**	**0**	**0**	**18**	**5.6**	**–8**	**1**	**0.0**	**15:30**	....	....	....	....	....	....	....	....	....
2000-01	**Carolina**	**NHL**	**74**	**6**	**18**	**24**	**54**	**0**	**2**	**1**	**99**	**6.1**	**–14**	**46**	**43.5**	**14:58**	**6**	**0**	**0**	**0**	**4**	**0**	**0**	**0**	**14:30**
2001-02	Utah Grizzlies	AHL	3	1	1	2	0	....	....	....	....	....	....	....	....	....	....	....	....	....	....	....	....	....	....
	Dallas	**NHL**	**61**	**6**	**6**	**12**	**25**	**0**	**2**	**2**	**63**	**9.5**	**–2**	**76**	**44.7**	**10:52**	....	....	....	....	....	....	....	....	....
2002-03	**Dallas**	**NHL**	**69**	**10**	**9**	**19**	**76**	**0**	**0**	**2**	**81**	**12.3**	**18**	**49**	**44.9**	**12:58**	**12**	**1**	**4**	**5**	**10**	**0**	**0**	**0**	**15:50**
2003-04	**Dallas**	**NHL**	**69**	**9**	**15**	**24**	**52**	**0**	**1**	**1**	**76**	**11.8**	**2**	**21**	**38.1**	**12:58**	**5**	**0**	**1**	**1**	**2**	**0**	**0**	**0**	**10:28**
	NHL Totals		**833**	**102**	**158**	**260**	**810**	**6**	**11**	**15**	**1115**	**9.1**		**554**	**44.2**	**14:13**	**60**	**7**	**9**	**16**	**40**	**0**	**1**	**2**	**15:11**

Stafford Smythe Memorial Trophy (Memorial Cup MVP) (1988)

Claimed by **Tampa Bay** from **NY Islanders** in Expansion Draft, June 18, 1992. Traded to **Philadelphia** by **Tampa Bay** for Jim Cummins and Philadelphia's 4th round choice (later traded back to Philadelphia – Philadelphia selected Radovan Somik) in 1995 Entry Draft, March 18, 1994. Claimed by **San Jose** from **Philadelphia** in Waiver Draft, September 30, 1996. Traded to **Boston** by **San Jose** for Boston's 5th round choice (Adam Nittel) in 1997 Entry Draft, September 30, 1996. Traded to **NY Rangers** by **Boston** for Mike Knuble, March 10, 2000. Traded to **Carolina** by **NY Rangers** with Darren Langdon for Sandy McCarthy and Carolina's 4th round choice (Bryce Lampman) in 2001 Entry Draft, August 4, 2000. Signed as a free agent by **Dallas**, July 1, 2001.

DIMITRAKOS, Niko

(DIH-mih-tra-kohs, NEEK-oh) **S.J.**

Right wing. Shoots right. 5'10", 205 lbs. Born, Sommerville, MA, May 21, 1979. San Jose's 4th choice, 155th overall, in 1999 Entry Draft.

1994-95	Matignon	Hi-School	23	10	12	22	....	....	....	....	....	....	....	....	....	....	....	....	....	....	....	....	....	....	....
1995-96	Matignon	Hi-School	25	12	28	40	....	....	....	....	....	....	....	....	....	....	....	....	....	....	....	....	....	....	....
1996-97	Matignon	Hi-School	25	23	32	55	....	....	....	....	....	....	....	....	....	....	....	....	....	....	....	....	....	....	....
1997-98	Avon Old Farms	Hi-School	26	27	28	55	....	....	....	....	....	....	....	....	....	....	....	....	....	....	....	....	....	....	....
1998-99	U. of Maine	H-East	35	8	19	27	33	....	....	....	....	....	....	....	....	....	....	....	....	....	....	....	....	....	....
99-2000	U. of Maine	H-East	32	11	16	27	16	....	....	....	....	....	....	....	....	....	....	....	....	....	....	....	....	....	....
2000-01	U. of Maine	H-East	29	11	14	25	43	....	....	....	....	....	....	....	....	....	....	....	....	....	....	....	....	....	....
2001-02	U. of Maine	H-East	43	20	31	51	44	....	....	....	....	....	....	....	....	....	....	....	....	....	....	....	....	....	....
2002-03	**San Jose**	**NHL**	**21**	**6**	**7**	**13**	**8**	**3**	**0**	**0**	**34**	**17.6**	**–7**	**2**	**50.0**	**14:15**	....	....	....	....	....	....	....	....	....
	Cleveland Barons	AHL	55	15	29	44	30	....	....	....	....	....	....	....	....	....	....	....	....	....	....	....	....	....	....

			Regular Season														Playoffs								
Season	Club	League	GP	G	A	Pts	PIM	PP	SH	GW	S	%	+/-	TF	F%	Min	GP	G	A	Pts	PIM	PP	SH	GW	Min
2003-04	**San Jose**	**NHL**	**68**	**9**	**15**	**24**	**49**	**2**	**0**	**4**	**116**	**7.8**	**6**	**4**	**50.0**	**13:20**	**15**	**1**	**8**	**9**	**8**	**0**	**0**	**1**	**14:31**
	Cleveland Barons	AHL	7	4	4	8	4	....	....	....	....	....	....	....	....	....	....	....	....	....	....	....	....	....	....
	NHL Totals		**89**	**15**	**22**	**37**	**57**	**5**	**0**	**4**	**150**	**10.0**		**6**	**50.0**	**13:33**	**15**	**1**	**8**	**9**	**8**	**0**	**0**	**1**	**14:31**

NCAA Championship All-Tournament Team (1999) • Hockey East Second All-Star Team (2002)

DINGMAN, Chris

(DIHNG-man, KRIHS) **T.B.**

Left wing. Shoots left. 6'4", 235 lbs. Born, Edmonton, Alta., July 6, 1976. Calgary's 1st choice, 19th overall, in 1994 Entry Draft.

Season	Club	League	GP	G	A	Pts	PIM	PP	SH	GW	S	%	+/-	TF	F%	Min	GP	G	A	Pts	PIM	PP	SH	GW	Min
1991-92	Edm. Mercurys	AMHL	36	23	18	41	72	....	....	....	....	....	....	....	....	....	....	....	....	....	....	....	....	....	....
1992-93	Brandon	WHL	50	10	17	27	64	....	....	....	....	....	....	....	....	....	4	0	0	0	0	....	....	....	....
1993-94	Brandon	WHL	45	21	20	41	77	....	....	....	....	....	....	....	....	....	13	1	7	8	39	....	....	....	....
1994-95	Brandon	WHL	66	40	43	83	201	....	....	....	....	....	....	....	....	....	3	1	0	1	9	....	....	....	....
1995-96	Brandon	WHL	40	16	29	45	109	....	....	....	....	....	....	....	....	....	19	12	11	23	60	....	....	....	....
	Saint John Flames	AHL	....	....	....	....	....	....	....	....	....	....	....	....	....	....	1	0	0	0	0	....	....	....	....
1996-97	Saint John Flames	AHL	71	5	6	11	195	....	....	....	....	....	....	....	....	....	....	....	....	....	....	....	....	....	....
1997-98	**Calgary**	**NHL**	**70**	**3**	**3**	**6**	**149**	**1**	**0**	**0**	**47**	**6.4**	**-11**	....	....	....	....	....	....	....	....	....	....	....	....
1998-99	**Calgary**	**NHL**	**2**	**0**	**0**	**0**	**17**	**0**	**0**	**0**	**1**	**0.0**	**-2**	**0**	**0.0**	**8:11**	....	....	....	....	....	....	....	....	....
	Saint John Flames	AHL	50	5	7	12	140	....	....	....	....	....	....	....	....	....	....	....	....	....	....	....	....	....	....
	Colorado	**NHL**	**1**	**0**	**0**	**0**	**7**	**0**	**0**	**0**	**0**	**0.0**	**0**	**0**	**0.0**	**0:30**	....	....	....	....	....	....	....	....	....
	Hershey Bears	AHL	17	1	3	4	102	....	....	....	....	....	....	....	....	....	5	0	2	2	6	....	....	....	....
99-2000	**Colorado**	**NHL**	**68**	**8**	**3**	**11**	**132**	**2**	**0**	**1**	**54**	**14.8**	**-2**	**2**	**0.0**	**6:29**	....	....	....	....	....	....	....	....	....
2000-01♦	**Colorado**	**NHL**	**41**	**1**	**1**	**2**	**108**	**0**	**0**	**0**	**33**	**3.0**	**-3**	**0**	**0.0**	**6:26**	**16**	**0**	**4**	**4**	**14**	**0**	**0**	**0**	**6:18**
2001-02	**Carolina**	**NHL**	**30**	**0**	**1**	**1**	**77**	**0**	**0**	**0**	**17**	**0.0**	**-2**	**2**	**100.0**	**6:54**	....	....	....	....	....	....	....	....	....
	Tampa Bay	**NHL**	**14**	**0**	**4**	**4**	**26**	**0**	**0**	**0**	**24**	**0.0**	**-8**	**0**	**0.0**	**10:43**	....	....	....	....	....	....	....	....	....
2002-03	**Tampa Bay**	**NHL**	**51**	**2**	**1**	**3**	**91**	**0**	**0**	**0**	**41**	**4.9**	**-11**	**3**	**33.3**	**9:34**	**10**	**1**	**0**	**1**	**4**	**0**	**0**	**0**	**12:45**
2003-04♦	**Tampa Bay**	**NHL**	**74**	**1**	**5**	**6**	**140**	**0**	**0**	**0**	**65**	**1.5**	**-9**	**20**	**30.0**	**8:16**	**23**	**1**	**1**	**2**	**63**	**0**	**0**	**0**	**5:58**
	NHL Totals		**351**	**15**	**18**	**33**	**747**	**3**	**0**	**1**	**282**	**5.3**		**27**	**33.3**	**7:45**	**49**	**2**	**5**	**7**	**81**	**0**	**0**	**0**	**7:28**

Traded to **Colorado** by **Calgary** with Theoren Fleury for Rene Corbet, Wade Belak, Robyn Regehr and Colorado's 2nd round compensatory choice (Jarret Stoll) in 2000 Entry Draft, February 28, 1999. • Missed majority of 2000-01 season recovering from knee injury suffered in game vs. Ottawa, November 15, 2000. Traded to **Carolina** by **Colorado** for Carolina's 5th round choice (Mikko Viitanen) in 2001 Entry Draft, June 24, 2001. Traded to **Tampa Bay** by **Carolina** with Shane Willis for Kevin Weekes, March 5, 2002.

DiPENTA, Joe

(DIH-pehn-tah, JOH)

Defense. Shoots left. 6'2", 235 lbs. Born, Barrie, Ont., February 25, 1979. Florida's 2nd choice, 61st overall, in 1998 Entry Draft.

Season	Club	League	GP	G	A	Pts	PIM	PP	SH	GW	S	%	+/-	TF	F%	Min	GP	G	A	Pts	PIM	PP	SH	GW	Min
1996-97	Smiths Falls Bears	OCJHL	54	13	22	35	92	....	....	....	....	....	....	....	....	....	....	....	....	....	....	....	....	....	....
1997-98	Boston University	H-East	38	2	16	18	50	....	....	....	....	....	....	....	....	....	....	....	....	....	....	....	....	....	....
1998-99	Boston University	H-East	36	2	15	17	72	....	....	....	....	....	....	....	....	....	....	....	....	....	....	....	....	....	....
99-2000	Halifax	QMJHL	63	13	43	56	83	....	....	....	....	....	....	....	....	....	10	3	4	7	26	....	....	....	....
2000-01	Philadelphia	AHL	71	3	5	8	65	....	....	....	....	....	....	....	....	....	10	1	2	3	15	....	....	....	....
2001-02	Philadelphia	AHL	61	2	4	6	71	....	....	....	....	....	....	....	....	....	....	....	....	....	....	....	....	....	....
	Chicago Wolves	AHL	15	0	2	2	15	....	....	....	....	....	....	....	....	....	25	1	3	4	22	....	....	....	....
2002-03	**Atlanta**	**NHL**	**3**	**1**	**1**	**2**	**0**	**0**	**0**	**0**	**2**	**50.0**	**3**	**0**	**0.0**	**15:47**	....	....	....	....	....	....	....	....	....
	Chicago Wolves	AHL	76	2	17	19	107	....	....	....	....	....	....	....	....	....	9	0	1	1	7	....	....	....	....
2003-04	Chicago Wolves	AHL	73	0	6	6	105	....	....	....	....	....	....	....	....	....	10	1	0	1	13	....	....	....	....
	NHL Totals		**3**	**1**	**1**	**2**	**0**	**0**	**0**	**0**	**2**	**50.0**		**0**	**0.0**	**15:47**	....	....	....	....	....	....	....	....	....

• Left **Boston U.** (H-East) and signed with **Halifax** (QMJHL), May 2, 1999. Signed as a free agent by **Philadelphia**, July 12, 2000. Traded to **Atlanta** by **Philadelphia** for Jarrod Skalde, March 5, 2002.

DOAN, Shane

(DOHN, SHAYN) **PHX.**

Right wing. Shoots right. 6'2", 216 lbs. Born, Halkirk, Alta., October 10, 1976. Winnipeg's 1st choice, 7th overall, in 1995 Entry Draft.

Season	Club	League	GP	G	A	Pts	PIM	PP	SH	GW	S	%	+/-	TF	F%	Min	GP	G	A	Pts	PIM	PP	SH	GW	Min
1991-92	Killam Selects	AAHA	56	80	84	164	74	....	....	....	....	....	....	....	....	....	....	....	....	....	....	....	....	....	....
1992-93	Kamloops Blazers	WHL	51	7	12	19	65	....	....	....	....	....	....	....	....	....	13	0	1	1	8	....	....	....	....
1993-94	Kamloops Blazers	WHL	52	24	24	48	88	....	....	....	....	....	....	....	....	....	....	....	....	....	....	....	....	....	....
1994-95	Kamloops Blazers	WHL	71	37	57	94	106	....	....	....	....	....	....	....	....	....	21	6	10	16	16	....	....	....	....
1995-96	**Winnipeg**	**NHL**	**74**	**7**	**10**	**17**	**101**	**1**	**0**	**3**	**106**	**6.6**	**-9**	....	....	....	**6**	**0**	**0**	**0**	**6**	**0**	**0**	**0**	....
1996-97	**Phoenix**	**NHL**	**63**	**4**	**8**	**12**	**49**	**0**	**0**	**0**	**100**	**4.0**	**-3**	....	....	....	**4**	**0**	**0**	**0**	**2**	**0**	**0**	**0**	....
1997-98	**Phoenix**	**NHL**	**33**	**5**	**6**	**11**	**35**	**0**	**0**	**3**	**42**	**11.9**	**-3**	....	....	....	**6**	**1**	**0**	**1**	**6**	**0**	**0**	**0**	....
	Springfield	AHL	39	21	21	42	64	....	....	....	....	....	....	....	....	....	....	....	....	....	....	....	....	....	....
1998-99	**Phoenix**	**NHL**	**79**	**6**	**16**	**22**	**54**	**0**	**0**	**0**	**156**	**3.8**	**-5**	**6**	**16.7**	**12:42**	**7**	**2**	**2**	**4**	**6**	**0**	**0**	**2**	**17:58**
99-2000	**Phoenix**	**NHL**	**81**	**26**	**25**	**51**	**66**	**1**	**1**	**4**	**221**	**11.8**	**6**	**25**	**36.0**	**16:51**	**4**	**1**	**2**	**3**	**8**	**1**	**0**	**0**	**18:11**
2000-01	**Phoenix**	**NHL**	**76**	**26**	**37**	**63**	**89**	**6**	**1**	**6**	**220**	**11.8**	**0**	**15**	**40.0**	**19:32**	....	....	....	....	....	....	....	....	....
2001-02	**Phoenix**	**NHL**	**81**	**20**	**29**	**49**	**61**	**6**	**0**	**2**	**205**	**9.8**	**11**	**52**	**44.2**	**18:10**	**5**	**2**	**2**	**4**	**6**	**0**	**0**	**0**	**17:21**
2002-03	**Phoenix**	**NHL**	**82**	**21**	**37**	**58**	**86**	**7**	**0**	**2**	**225**	**9.3**	**3**	**623**	**39.8**	**18:47**	....	....	....	....	....	....	....	....	....
2003-04	**Phoenix**	**NHL**	**79**	**27**	**41**	**68**	**47**	**9**	**2**	**1**	**254**	**10.6**	**-11**	**55**	**40.0**	**21:46**	....	....	....	....	....	....	....	....	....
	NHL Totals		**648**	**142**	**209**	**351**	**588**	**30**	**4**	**21**	**1529**	**9.3**		**776**	**39.8**	**17:58**	**32**	**6**	**6**	**12**	**34**	**1**	**0**	**2**	**17:49**

Memorial Cup All-Star Team (1995) • Stafford Smythe Memorial Trophy (Memorial Cup MVP) (1995)

Played in NHL All-Star Game (2004)

Transferred to **Phoenix** after **Winnipeg** franchise relocated, July 1, 1996.

DOIG, Jason

(DOIG, JAY-suhn) **WSH.**

Defense. Shoots right. 6'3", 230 lbs. Born, Montreal, Que., January 29, 1977. Winnipeg's 3rd choice, 34th overall, in 1995 Entry Draft.

Season	Club	League	GP	G	A	Pts	PIM	PP	SH	GW	S	%	+/-	TF	F%	Min	GP	G	A	Pts	PIM	PP	SH	GW	Min
1990-91	North Shore	QAHA	31	30	33	63	53	....	....	....	....	....	....	....	....	....	....	....	....	....	....	....	....	....	....
1991-92	North Shore	QAHA	29	11	11	22	20	....	....	....	....	....	....	....	....	....	....	....	....	....	....	....	....	....	....
1992-93	Lac St-Louis Lions	QAAA	35	11	16	27	40	....	....	....	....	....	....	....	....	....	7	5	5	10	16	....	....	....	....
1993-94	St-Jean Lynx	QMJHL	63	8	17	25	65	....	....	....	....	....	....	....	....	....	5	0	2	2	2	....	....	....	....
1994-95	Laval Titan	QMJHL	55	13	42	55	259	....	....	....	....	....	....	....	....	....	20	4	13	17	39	....	....	....	....
1995-96	Laval Titan	QMJHL	5	3	6	9	20	....	....	....	....	....	....	....	....	....	....	....	....	....	....	....	....	....	....
	Granby	QMJHL	24	4	30	34	91	....	....	....	....	....	....	....	....	....	20	10	22	32	*110	....	....	....	....
	Winnipeg	**NHL**	**15**	**1**	**1**	**2**	**28**	**0**	**0**	**0**	**7**	**14.3**	**-2**	....	....	....	....	....	....	....	....	....	....	....	....
	Springfield	AHL	5	0	0	0	28	....	....	....	....	....	....	....	....	....	....	....	....	....	....	....	....	....	....
1996-97	Granby	QMJHL	39	14	33	47	211	....	....	....	....	....	....	....	....	....	5	0	4	4	27	....	....	....	....
	Las Vegas	IHL	6	0	1	1	19	....	....	....	....	....	....	....	....	....	....	....	....	....	....	....	....	....	....
	Springfield	AHL	5	0	3	3	2	....	....	....	....	....	....	....	....	....	17	1	4	5	37	....	....	....	....
1997-98	**Phoenix**	**NHL**	**4**	**0**	**1**	**1**	**12**	**0**	**0**	**0**	**1**	**0.0**	**-4**	....	....	....	....	....	....	....	....	....	....	....	....
	Springfield	AHL	46	2	25	27	153	....	....	....	....	....	....	....	....	....	3	0	0	0	2	....	....	....	....
1998-99	**Phoenix**	**NHL**	**9**	**0**	**1**	**1**	**10**	**0**	**0**	**0**	**0**	**0.0**	**2**	**0**	**0.0**	**5:08**	....	....	....	....	....	....	....	....	....
	Springfield	AHL	32	3	5	8	67	....	....	....	....	....	....	....	....	....	....	....	....	....	....	....	....	....	....
	Hartford	AHL	8	1	4	5	40	....	....	....	....	....	....	....	....	....	7	1	1	2	39	....	....	....	....
99-2000	**NY Rangers**	**NHL**	**7**	**0**	**1**	**1**	**22**	**0**	**0**	**0**	**3**	**0.0**	**-2**	**0**	**0.0**	**8:50**	....	....	....	....	....	....	....	....	....
	Hartford	AHL	27	3	11	14	70	....	....	....	....	....	....	....	....	....	21	1	5	6	20	....	....	....	....
2000-01	**NY Rangers**	**NHL**	**3**	**0**	**0**	**0**	**0**	**0**	**0**	**0**	**1**	**0.0**	**0**	**0**	**0.0**	**6:35**	....	....	....	....	....	....	....	....	....
	Hartford	AHL	52	4	20	24	178	....	....	....	....	....	....	....	....	....	5	0	1	1	4	....	....	....	....
2001-02	Grand Rapids	AHL	57	1	17	18	103	....	....	....	....	....	....	....	....	....	5	0	0	0	18	....	....	....	....
2002-03	**Washington**	**NHL**	**55**	**3**	**5**	**8**	**108**	**0**	**0**	**1**	**41**	**7.3**	**-3**	**1**	**0.0**	**14:11**	**6**	**0**	**1**	**1**	**6**	**0**	**0**	**0**	**16:52**
	Portland Pirates	AHL	21	1	4	5	66	....	....	....	....	....	....	....	....	....	....	....	....	....	....	....	....	....	....
2003-04	**Washington**	**NHL**	**65**	**2**	**9**	**11**	**105**	**0**	**0**	**0**	**59**	**3.4**	**-12**	**0**	**0.0**	**19:09**	....	....	....	....	....	....	....	....	....
	NHL Totals		**158**	**6**	**18**	**24**	**285**	**0**	**0**	**1**	**112**	**5.4**		**1**	**0.0**	**15:29**	**6**	**0**	**1**	**1**	**6**	**0**	**0**	**0**	**16:52**

QMJHL All-Rookie Team (1994) • Memorial Cup All-Star Team (1996)

Transferred to **Phoenix** after **Winnipeg** franchise relocated, July 1, 1996. Traded to **NY Rangers** by **Phoenix** with Phoenix's 6th round choice (Jay Dardis) in 1999 Entry Draft for Stan Neckar, March 23, 1999. Traded to **Ottawa** by **NY Rangers** with Jeff Ulmer for Sean Gagnon, June 29, 2001. Signed as free agent by **Washington**, September 12, 2002.

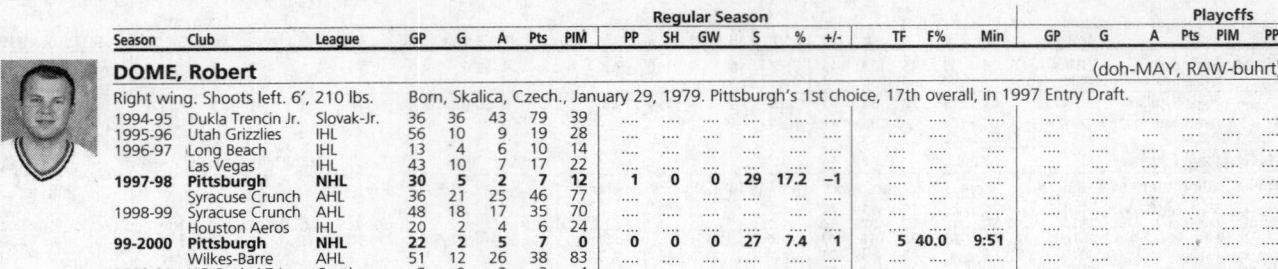

DOME, Robert

(doh-MAY, RAW-buhrt)

Right wing. Shoots left. 6', 210 lbs. Born, Skalica, Czech., January 29, 1979. Pittsburgh's 1st choice, 17th overall, in 1997 Entry Draft.

			Regular Season														Playoffs								
Season	Club	League	GP	G	A	Pts	PIM	PP	SH	GW	S	%	+/-	TF	F%	Min	GP	G	A	Pts	PIM	PP	SH	GW	Min
1994-95	Dukla Trencin Jr.	Slovak-Jr.	36	36	43	79	39	....	....	....	....	....	....	....	....	....	....	....	....	....	....	....	....	....	....
1995-96	Utah Grizzlies	IHL	56	10	9	19	28	....	....	....	....	....	....	....	....	....	....	....	....	....	....	....	....	....	....
1996-97	Long Beach	IHL	13	4	6	10	14	....	....	....	....	....	....	....	....	....	....	....	....	....	....	....	....	....	....
	Las Vegas	IHL	43	10	7	17	22	....	....	....	....	....	....	....	....	....	....	....	....	....	....	....	....	....	....
1997-98	**Pittsburgh**	**NHL**	**30**	**5**	**2**	**7**	**12**	**1**	**0**	**0**	**29**	**17.2**	**–1**	....	....	....	....	....	....	....	....	....	....	....	....
	Syracuse Crunch	AHL	36	21	25	46	77	....	....	....	....	....	....	....	....	....	....	....	....	....	....	....	....	....	....
1998-99	Syracuse Crunch	AHL	48	18	17	35	70	....	....	....	....	....	....	....	....	....	....	....	....	....	....	....	....	....	....
	Houston Aeros	IHL	20	2	4	6	24	....	....	....	....	....	....	....	....	....	....	....	....	....	....	....	....	....	....
99-2000	**Pittsburgh**	**NHL**	**22**	**2**	**5**	**7**	**0**	**0**	**0**	**0**	**27**	**7.4**	**1**	**5**	**40.0**	**9:51**	....	....	....	....	....	....	....	....	....
	Wilkes-Barre	AHL	51	12	26	38	83	....	....	....	....	....	....	....	....	....	....	....	....	....	....	....	....	....	....
2000-01	HC Ocelari Trinec	Czech	5	0	3	3	4	....	....	....	....	....	....	....	....	....	....	....	....	....	....	....	....	....	....
	Kladno	Czech	29	9	12	21	57	....	....	....	....	....	....	....	....	....	....	....	....	....	....	....	....	....	....
2001-02	Wilkes-Barre	AHL	39	9	8	17	53	....	....	....	....	....	....	....	....	....	....	....	....	....	....	....	....	....	....
2002-03	**Calgary**	**NHL**	**1**	**0**	**0**	**0**	**0**	**0**	**0**	**0**	**1**	**0.0**	**0**	**0**	**0.0**	**8:16**	....	....	....	....	....	....	....	....	....
	Saint John Flames	AHL	56	27	29	56	41	....	....	....	....	....	....	....	....	....	....	....	....	....	....	....	....	....	....
2003-04	Lowell	AHL	13	5	7	12	19	....	....	....	....	....	....	....	....	....	....	....	....	....	....	....	....	....	....
	Sodertalje SK	Sweden	28	10	19	29	8	....	....	....	....	....	....	....	....	....	....	....	....	....	....	....	....	....	....
	NHL Totals		**53**	**7**	**7**	**14**	**12**	**1**	**0**	**0**	**57**	**12.3**		**5**	**40.0**	**9:47**	....	....	....	....	....	....	....	....	....

• Missed majority of 2001-02 season recovering from heel injury suffered during off-season training, July 10, 2001. Signed as a free agent by **Calgary**, July 17, 2002. Assigned to **Sodertalje** (Sweden) by **Calgary**, November 19, 2003.

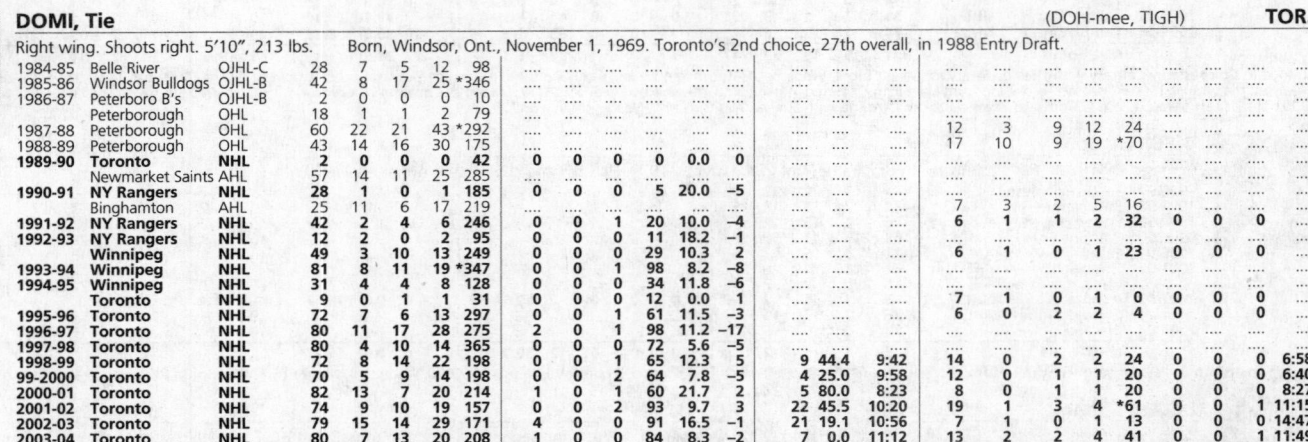

DOMI, Tie

(DOH-mee, TIGH) **TOR.**

Right wing. Shoots right. 5'10", 213 lbs. Born, Windsor, Ont., November 1, 1969. Toronto's 2nd choice, 27th overall, in 1988 Entry Draft.

Season	Club	League	GP	G	A	Pts	PIM	PP	SH	GW	S	%	+/-	TF	F%	Min	GP	G	A	Pts	PIM	PP	SH	GW	Min
1984-85	Belle River	OJHL-C	28	7	5	12	98	....	....	....	....	....	....	....	....	....	....	....	....	....	....	....	....	....	....
1985-86	Windsor Bulldogs	OJHL-B	42	8	17	25	*346	....	....	....	....	....	....	....	....	....	....	....	....	....	....	....	....	....	....
1986-87	Peterboro B's	OJHL-B	2	0	0	0	10	....	....	....	....	....	....	....	....	....	....	....	....	....	....	....	....	....	....
	Peterborough	OHL	18	1	1	2	79	....	....	....	....	....	....	....	....	....	....	....	....	....	....	....	....	....	....
1987-88	Peterborough	OHL	60	22	21	43	*292	....	....	....	....	....	....	....	....	....	12	3	9	12	24	....	....	....	....
1988-89	Peterborough	OHL	43	14	16	30	175	....	....	....	....	....	....	....	....	....	17	10	9	19	*70	....	....	....	....
1989-90	**Toronto**	**NHL**	**2**	**0**	**0**	**0**	**42**	**0**	**0**	**0**	**0**	**0.0**	**0**	....	....	....	....	....	....	....	....	....	....	....	....
	Newmarket Saints	AHL	57	14	11	25	285	....	....	....	....	....	....	....	....	....	....	....	....	....	....	....	....	....	....
1990-91	**NY Rangers**	**NHL**	**28**	**1**	**0**	**1**	**185**	**0**	**0**	**0**	**5**	**20.0**	**–5**	....	....	....	....	....	....	....	....	....	....	....	....
	Binghamton	AHL	25	11	6	17	219	....	....	....	....	....	....	....	....	....	7	3	2	5	16	....	....	....	....
1991-92	**NY Rangers**	**NHL**	**42**	**2**	**4**	**6**	**246**	**0**	**0**	**1**	**20**	**10.0**	**–4**	....	....	....	**6**	**1**	**1**	**2**	**32**	**0**	**0**	**0**	....
1992-93	**NY Rangers**	**NHL**	**12**	**2**	**0**	**2**	**95**	**0**	**0**	**0**	**11**	**18.2**	**–1**	....	....	....	....	....	....	....	....	....	....	....	....
	Winnipeg	**NHL**	**49**	**3**	**10**	**13**	**249**	**0**	**0**	**0**	**29**	**10.3**	**2**	....	....	....	**6**	**1**	**0**	**1**	**23**	**0**	**0**	**0**	....
1993-94	**Winnipeg**	**NHL**	**81**	**8**	**11**	**19**	***347**	**0**	**0**	**1**	**98**	**8.2**	**–8**	....	....	....	....	....	....	....	....	....	....	....	....
1994-95	**Winnipeg**	**NHL**	**31**	**4**	**4**	**8**	**128**	**0**	**0**	**0**	**34**	**11.8**	**–6**	....	....	....	....	....	....	....	....	....	....	....	....
	Toronto	**NHL**	**9**	**0**	**1**	**1**	**31**	**0**	**0**	**0**	**12**	**0.0**	**1**	....	....	....	**7**	**1**	**0**	**1**	**0**	**0**	**0**	**0**	....
1995-96	**Toronto**	**NHL**	**72**	**7**	**6**	**13**	**297**	**0**	**0**	**1**	**61**	**11.5**	**–3**	....	....	....	**6**	**0**	**2**	**2**	**4**	**0**	**0**	**0**	....
1996-97	**Toronto**	**NHL**	**80**	**11**	**17**	**28**	**275**	**2**	**0**	**1**	**98**	**11.2**	**–17**	....	....	....	....	....	....	....	....	....	....	....	....
1997-98	**Toronto**	**NHL**	**80**	**4**	**10**	**14**	**365**	**0**	**0**	**0**	**72**	**5.6**	**–5**	....	....	....	....	....	....	....	....	....	....	....	....
1998-99	**Toronto**	**NHL**	**72**	**8**	**14**	**22**	**198**	**0**	**0**	**1**	**65**	**12.3**	**5**	**9**	**44.4**	**9:42**	**14**	**0**	**2**	**2**	**24**	**0**	**0**	**0**	**6:58**
99-2000	**Toronto**	**NHL**	**70**	**5**	**9**	**14**	**198**	**0**	**0**	**2**	**64**	**7.8**	**–5**	**4**	**25.0**	**9:58**	**12**	**0**	**1**	**1**	**20**	**0**	**0**	**0**	**6:40**
2000-01	**Toronto**	**NHL**	**82**	**13**	**7**	**20**	**214**	**1**	**0**	**1**	**60**	**21.7**	**2**	**5**	**80.0**	**8:23**	**8**	**0**	**1**	**1**	**20**	**0**	**0**	**0**	**8:27**
2001-02	**Toronto**	**NHL**	**74**	**9**	**10**	**19**	**157**	**0**	**0**	**2**	**93**	**9.7**	**3**	**22**	**45.5**	**10:20**	**19**	**1**	**3**	**4**	***61**	**0**	**0**	**1**	**11:15**
2002-03	**Toronto**	**NHL**	**79**	**15**	**14**	**29**	**171**	**4**	**0**	**0**	**91**	**16.5**	**–1**	**21**	**19.1**	**10:56**	**7**	**1**	**0**	**1**	**13**	**0**	**0**	**0**	**14:47**
2003-04	**Toronto**	**NHL**	**80**	**7**	**13**	**20**	**208**	**1**	**0**	**0**	**84**	**8.3**	**–2**	**7**	**0.0**	**11:12**	**13**	**2**	**2**	**4**	**41**	**0**	**0**	**1**	**11:49**
	NHL Totals		**943**	**99**	**130**	**229**	**3406**	**8**	**0**	**10**	**897**	**11.0**		**68**	**33.8**	**10:05**	**98**	**7**	**12**	**19**	**238**	**0**	**0**	**2**	**9:49**

Traded to **NY Rangers** by **Toronto** with Mark LaForest for Greg Johnston, June 28, 1990. Traded to **Winnipeg** by **NY Rangers** with Kris King for Ed Olczyk, December 28, 1992. Traded to **Toronto** by **Winnipeg** for Mike Eastwood and Toronto's 3rd round choice (Brad Isbister) in 1995 Entry Draft, April 7, 1995. Traded to **Nashville** by **Toronto** for Nashville's 8th round choice (Shaun Landolt) in 2003 Entry Draft, June 30, 2002. Signed as a free agent by **Toronto**, July 14, 2002.

DONATO, Ted

(duh-NAH-toh, TEHD)

Left wing. Shoots left. 5'10", 180 lbs. Born, Boston, MA, April 28, 1969. Boston's 6th choice, 98th overall, in 1987 Entry Draft.

Season	Club	League	GP	G	A	Pts	PIM	PP	SH	GW	S	%	+/-	TF	F%	Min	GP	G	A	Pts	PIM	PP	SH	GW	Min
1986-87	Catholic Memorial	Hi-School	22	29	34	63	30	....	....	....	....	....	....	....	....	....	....	....	....	....	....	....	....	....	....
1987-88	Harvard Crimson	ECAC	28	12	14	26	24	....	....	....	....	....	....	....	....	....	....	....	....	....	....	....	....	....	....
1988-89	Harvard Crimson	ECAC	34	14	37	51	30	....	....	....	....	....	....	....	....	....	....	....	....	....	....	....	....	....	....
1989-90	Harvard Crimson	ECAC	16	5	6	11	34	....	....	....	....	....	....	....	....	....	....	....	....	....	....	....	....	....	....
1990-91	Harvard Crimson	ECAC	27	19	*37	56	26	....	....	....	....	....	....	....	....	....	....	....	....	....	....	....	....	....	....
1991-92	Team USA	Nat-Tm	52	11	22	33	24	....	....	....	....	....	....	....	....	....	....	....	....	....	....	....	....	....	....
	United States	Olympics	8	4	3	7	8	....	....	....	....	....	....	....	....	....	....	....	....	....	....	....	....	....	....
	Boston	**NHL**	**10**	**1**	**2**	**3**	**8**	**0**	**0**	**0**	**13**	**7.7**	**–1**	....	....	....	**15**	**3**	**4**	**7**	**4**	**0**	**0**	**1**	....
1992-93	**Boston**	**NHL**	**82**	**15**	**20**	**35**	**61**	**3**	**2**	**5**	**118**	**12.7**	**2**	....	....	....	**4**	**0**	**1**	**1**	**0**	**0**	**0**	**0**	....
1993-94	**Boston**	**NHL**	**84**	**22**	**32**	**54**	**59**	**9**	**2**	**1**	**158**	**13.9**	**0**	....	....	....	**13**	**4**	**2**	**6**	**10**	**2**	**0**	**1**	....
1994-95	TuTo Turku	Finland	14	5	5	10	47	....	....	....	....	....	....	....	....	....	....	....	....	....	....	....	....	....	....
	Boston	**NHL**	**47**	**10**	**10**	**20**	**10**	**1**	**0**	**1**	**71**	**14.1**	**3**	....	....	....	**5**	**0**	**0**	**0**	**4**	**0**	**0**	**0**	....
1995-96	**Boston**	**NHL**	**82**	**23**	**26**	**49**	**46**	**7**	**0**	**1**	**152**	**15.1**	**6**	....	....	....	**5**	**1**	**2**	**3**	**2**	**1**	**0**	**0**	....
1996-97	**Boston**	**NHL**	**67**	**25**	**26**	**51**	**37**	**6**	**2**	**2**	**172**	**14.5**	**–9**	....	....	....	....	....	....	....	....	....	....	....	....
1997-98	**Boston**	**NHL**	**79**	**16**	**23**	**39**	**54**	**3**	**0**	**5**	**129**	**12.4**	**6**	....	....	....	**5**	**0**	**0**	**0**	**2**	**0**	**0**	**0**	....
1998-99	**Boston**	**NHL**	**14**	**1**	**3**	**4**	**4**	**0**	**0**	**0**	**22**	**4.5**	**0**	**18**	**44.4**	**15:21**	....	....	....	....	....	....	....	....	....
	NY Islanders	**NHL**	**55**	**7**	**11**	**18**	**27**	**2**	**0**	**0**	**68**	**10.3**	**–10**	**142**	**45.8**	**12:09**	....	....	....	....	....	....	....	....	....
	Ottawa	**NHL**	**13**	**3**	**2**	**5**	**10**	**1**	**0**	**0**	**16**	**18.8**	**2**	**4**	**25.0**	**11:10**	**1**	**0**	**0**	**0**	**0**	**0**	**0**	**0**	**5:38**
99-2000	**Anaheim**	**NHL**	**81**	**11**	**19**	**30**	**26**	**2**	**0**	**3**	**138**	**8.0**	**–3**	**212**	**41.5**	**14:35**	....	....	....	....	....	....	....	....	....
2000-01	**Dallas**	**NHL**	**65**	**8**	**17**	**25**	**26**	**1**	**0**	**3**	**71**	**11.3**	**6**	**16**	**37.5**	**10:13**	**8**	**0**	**1**	**1**	**0**	**0**	**0**	**0**	**10:25**
2001-02	**NY Islanders**	**NHL**	**1**	**0**	**0**	**0**	**0**	**0**	**0**	**0**	**1**	**0.0**	**–1**	**0**	**0.0**	**7:55**	....	....	....	....	....	....	....	....	....
	Bridgeport	AHL	1	0	0	0	0	....	....	....	....	....	....	....	....	....	....	....	....	....	....	....	....	....	....
	St. Louis	**NHL**	**2**	**0**	**0**	**0**	**2**	**0**	**0**	**0**	**0**	**0.0**	**–2**	**15**	**53.3**	**9:17**	....	....	....	....	....	....	....	....	....
	Los Angeles	**NHL**	**2**	**0**	**0**	**0**	**2**	**0**	**0**	**0**	**1**	**0.0**	**–2**	**10**	**20.0**	**7:20**	....	....	....	....	....	....	....	....	....
	Manchester	AHL	36	18	25	43	19	....	....	....	....	....	....	....	....	....	5	1	3	4	0	....	....	....	....
2002-03	**NY Rangers**	**NHL**	**49**	**2**	**1**	**3**	**6**	**0**	**0**	**0**	**30**	**6.7**	**–1**	**290**	**47.9**	**8:33**	....	....	....	....	....	....	....	....	....
	Hartford	AHL	18	8	12	20	14	....	....	....	....	....	....	....	....	....	....	....	....	....	....	....	....	....	....
2003-04	**Boston**	**NHL**	**63**	**6**	**5**	**11**	**18**	**0**	**3**	**1**	**35**	**17.1**	**2**	**206**	**49.0**	**9:16**	**2**	**0**	**0**	**0**	**0**	**0**	**0**	**0**	**5:32**
	Providence Bruins	AHL	15	3	9	12	24	....	....	....	....	....	....	....	....	....	....	....	....	....	....	....	....	....	....
	NHL Totals		**796**	**150**	**197**	**347**	**396**	**35**	**9**	**22**	**1195**	**12.6**		**913**	**45.8**	**11:21**	**58**	**8**	**10**	**18**	**22**	**3**	**0**	**2**	**9:05**

NCAA Championship All-Tournament Team (1989) • NCAA Championship Tournament MVP (1989) • ECAC First All-Star Team (1991)

Traded to **NY Islanders** by **Boston** for Ken Belanger, November 7, 1998. Traded to **Ottawa** by **NY Islanders** for Ottawa's 4th round choice (later traded to Phoenix – Phoenix selected Preston Mizzi) in 1999 Entry Draft, March 20, 1999. Traded to **Anaheim** by **Ottawa** with the rights to Antti-Jussi Niemi for Patrick Lalime, June 18, 1999. Signed as a free agent agent by **Dallas**, August 17, 2000. Signed as a free agent by **NY Islanders**, January 16, 2002. Claimed on waivers by **Los Angeles** from **NY Islanders**, January 28, 2002. Claimed on waivers by **St. Louis** from **Los Angeles**, March 6, 2002. Claimed on waivers by **Los Angeles** from **St. Louis**, March 19, 2002. • Missed majority of 2001-02 season recovering from shoulder injury suffered in game vs. St. John's (AHL), January 9, 2002. Signed as a free agent by **NY Rangers**, July 8, 2002. Signed as a free agent by **Boston,** July 22, 2003.

DONOVAN, Shean

(DAW-nuh-vuhn, SHAWN) **CGY.**

Right wing. Shoots right. 6'2", 200 lbs. Born, Timmins, Ont., January 22, 1975. San Jose's 2nd choice, 28th overall, in 1993 Entry Draft.

Season	Club	League	GP	G	A	Pts	PIM	PP	SH	GW	S	%	+/-	TF	F%	Min	GP	G	A	Pts	PIM	PP	SH	GW	Min
1990-91	Kanata Valley	OCJHL	44	8	5	13	8	....	....	....	....	....	....	....	....	....	....	....	....	....	....	....	....	....	....
1991-92	Ottawa 67's	OHL	58	11	8	19	14	....	....	....	....	....	....	....	....	....	11	1	0	1	5	....	....	....	....
1992-93	Ottawa 67's	OHL	66	29	23	52	33	....	....	....	....	....	....	....	....	....	....	....	....	....	....	....	....	....	....
1993-94	Ottawa 67's	OHL	62	35	49	84	63	....	....	....	....	....	....	....	....	....	17	10	11	21	14	....	....	....	....
1994-95	Ottawa 67's	OHL	29	22	19	41	41	....	....	....	....	....	....	....	....	....	....	....	....	....	....	....	....	....	....
	San Jose	**NHL**	**14**	**0**	**0**	**0**	**6**	**0**	**0**	**0**	**13**	**0.0**	**–6**	....	....	....	**7**	**0**	**1**	**1**	**6**	**0**	**0**	**0**	....
	Kansas City	IHL	5	0	2	2	7	....	....	....	....	....	....	....	....	....	14	5	3	8	23	....	....	....	....
1995-96	**San Jose**	**NHL**	**74**	**13**	**8**	**21**	**39**	**0**	**1**	**2**	**73**	**17.8**	**–17**	....	....	....	....	....	....	....	....	....	....	....	....
	Kansas City	IHL	4	0	0	0	8	....	....	....	....	....	....	....	....	....	5	0	0	0	8	....	....	....	....
1996-97	**San Jose**	**NHL**	**73**	**9**	**6**	**15**	**42**	**0**	**1**	**0**	**115**	**7.8**	**–18**	....	....	....	....	....	....	....	....	....	....	....	....
	Kentucky	AHL	3	1	3	4	18	....	....	....	....	....	....	....	....	....	....	....	....	....	....	....	....	....	....

			Regular Season														Playoffs								
Season	Club	League	GP	G	A	Pts	PIM	PP	SH	GW	S	%	+/-	TF	F%	Min	GP	G	A	Pts	PIM	PP	SH	GW	Min
1997-98	San Jose	NHL	20	3	3	6	22	0	0	0	24	12.5	3	....	....	....	....	....	....	....	....	....	....	....	....
	Colorado	NHL	47	5	7	12	48	0	0	0	57	8.8	3	....	....	....	....	....	....	....	....	....	....	....	....
1998-99	Colorado	NHL	68	7	12	19	37	1	0	1	81	8.6	4	9	22.2	8:46	5	0	0	0	2	0	0	0	4:55
99-2000	Colorado	NHL	18	1	0	1	8	0	0	0	13	7.7	–4	1	0.0	5:20	....	....	....	....	....	....	....	....	....
	Atlanta	NHL	33	4	7	11	18	1	0	1	53	7.5	–13	22	31.8	14:19	....	....	....	....	....	....	....	....	....
2000-01	Atlanta	NHL	63	12	11	23	47	1	3	1	93	12.9	–14	218	45.9	14:03	....	....	....	....	....	....	....	....	....
2001-02	Atlanta	NHL	48	6	6	12	40	1	0	2	64	9.4	–16	12	50.0	13:30	....	....	....	....	....	....	....	....	....
	Pittsburgh	NHL	13	2	1	3	4	0	0	0	18	11.1	–5	4	0.0	14:34	....	....	....	....	....	....	....	....	....
2002-03	Pittsburgh	NHL	52	4	5	9	30	0	1	0	66	6.1	–6	37	24.3	13:01	....	....	....	....	....	....	....	....	....
	Calgary	NHL	13	1	2	3	7	0	0	1	22	4.5	–2	3	66.7	15:39	....	....	....	....	....	....	....	....	....
2003-04	Calgary	NHL	82	18	24	42	72	3	3	8	138	13.0	14	53	39.6	14:55	24	5	5	10	23	0	0	2	15:27
	NHL Totals		618	85	92	177	420	7	9	16	830	10.2		359	40.9	12:48	36	5	6	11	31	0	0	2	13:38

Traded to **Colorado** by **San Jose** with San Jose's 1st round choice (Alex Tanguay) in 1998 Entry Draft for Mike Ricci and Colorado's 2nd round choice (later traded to Buffalo – Buffalo selected Jaroslav Kristek), in 1998 Entry Draft, November 21, 1997. Traded to **Atlanta** by **Colorado** for Rick Tabaracci, December 8, 1999. Claimed on waivers by **Pittsburgh** from **Atlanta**, March 15, 2002. Traded to **Calgary** by **Pittsburgh** for Micki Dupont and Mathias Johansson, March 11, 2003.

DOULL, Doug

(DOOL, DUHG)

Left wing. Shoots left. 6'2", 216 lbs. Born, Green Bay, N.S., May 31, 1974.

Season	Club	League	GP	G	A	Pts	PIM	PP	SH	GW	S	%	+/-	TF	F%	Min	GP	G	A	Pts	PIM	PP	SH	GW	Min
1990-91	Wexford Raiders	MTHL	39	22	36	58	141	....	....	....	....	....	....	....	....	....	....	....	....	....	....	....	....	....	....
1991-92	Belleville Bulls	OHL	62	6	11	17	123	....	....	....	....	....	....	....	....	....	....	....	....	....	....	....	....	....	....
1992-93	Belleville Bulls	OHL	65	19	37	56	143	....	....	....	....	....	....	....	....	....	....	....	....	....	....	....	....	....	....
1993-94	Belleville Bulls	OHL	62	13	24	37	143	....	....	....	....	....	....	....	....	....	....	....	....	....	....	....	....	....	....
1994-95	Belleville Bulls	OHL	29	7	12	19	71	....	....	....	....	....	....	....	....	....	16	2	13	15	39	....	....	....	....
1995-96	St. Mary's Huskies	AUAA	11	4	4	8	54	....	....	....	....	....	....	....	....	....	....	....	....	....	....	....	....	....	....
1996-97	St. Mary's Huskies	AUAA	18	3	10	13	138	....	....	....	....	....	....	....	....	....	....	....	....	....	....	....	....	....	....
1997-98	St. Mary's Huskies	AUAA	25	4	11	15	227	....	....	....	....	....	....	....	....	....	....	....	....	....	....	....	....	....	....
1998-99	Michigan	IHL	55	4	11	15	227	....	....	....	....	....	....	....	....	....	3	1	1	2	4	....	....	....	....
99-2000	Detroit Vipers	IHL	17	0	2	2	69	....	....	....	....	....	....	....	....	....	....	....	....	....	....	....	....	....	....
	Manitoba Moose	IHL	45	4	4	8	184	....	....	....	....	....	....	....	....	....	2	0	0	0	2	....	....	....	....
2000-01	Manchester Storm	Britain	15	1	6	7	51	....	....	....	....	....	....	....	....	....	....	....	....	....	....	....	....	....	....
	Saint John Flames	AHL	49	3	10	13	167	....	....	....	....	....	....	....	....	....	16	0	1	1	32	....	....	....	....
2001-02	St. John's	AHL	36	5	8	13	166	....	....	....	....	....	....	....	....	....	9	0	1	1	17	....	....	....	....
2002-03	St. John's	AHL	70	15	10	25	257	....	....	....	....	....	....	....	....	....	....	....	....	....	....	....	....	....	....
2003-04	Boston	NHL	35	0	1	1	132	0	0	0	4	0.0	2	0	0.0	2:50	....	....	....	....	....	....	....	....	....
	Providence Bruins	AHL	22	1	0	1	98	....	....	....	....	....	....	....	....	....	....	....	....	....	....	....	....	....	....
	NHL Totals		35	0	1	1	132	0	0	0	4	0.0		0	0.0	2:50									

Signed as a free agent by **Manchester** (Britain), August 15, 2000. Signed to a 25-game tryout contract by **Saint John** (AHL) after securing release from **Manchester** (Britain), December 19, 2000. Signed as a free agent by **Saint John** (AHL), February 18, 2001. Signed as a free agent by **Toronto**, July 25, 2001. • Missed majority of 2001-02 season recovering from ankle injury suffered in game vs. Manitoba (AHL), October 19, 2001. Signed as a free agent by **Boston**, July 28, 2003.

DOWD, Jim

(DOWD, JIHM)

Center. Shoots right. 6'1", 190 lbs. Born, Brick, NJ, December 25, 1968. New Jersey's 7th choice, 149th overall, in 1987 Entry Draft.

Season	Club	League	GP	G	A	Pts	PIM	PP	SH	GW	S	%	+/-	TF	F%	Min	GP	G	A	Pts	PIM	PP	SH	GW	Min
1983-84	Brick High	Hi-School	20	19	30	49	....	....	....	....	....	....	....	....	....	....	....	....	....	....	....	....	....	....	....
1984-85	Brick High	Hi-School	24	58	55	113	....	....	....	....	....	....	....	....	....	....	....	....	....	....	....	....	....	....	....
1985-86	Brick High	Hi-School	24	47	51	98	....	....	....	....	....	....	....	....	....	....	....	....	....	....	....	....	....	....	....
1986-87	Brick High	Hi-School	24	22	33	55	....	....	....	....	....	....	....	....	....	....	....	....	....	....	....	....	....	....	....
1987-88	Lake Superior	CCHA	45	18	27	45	16	....	....	....	....	....	....	....	....	....	....	....	....	....	....	....	....	....	....
1988-89	Lake Superior	CCHA	46	24	35	59	40	....	....	....	....	....	....	....	....	....	....	....	....	....	....	....	....	....	....
1989-90	Lake Superior	CCHA	46	25	*67	92	30	....	....	....	....	....	....	....	....	....	....	....	....	....	....	....	....	....	....
1990-91	Lake Superior	CCHA	44	24	*54	*78	53	....	....	....	....	....	....	....	....	....	....	....	....	....	....	....	....	....	....
1991-92	New Jersey	NHL	1	0	0	0	0	0	0	0	0	0.0	0	....	....	....	....	....	....	....	....	....	....	....	....
	Utica Devils	AHL	78	17	42	59	47	....	....	....	....	....	....	....	....	....	4	2	2	4	4	....	....	....	....
1992-93	New Jersey	NHL	1	0	0	0	0	0	0	0	1	0.0	–1	....	....	....	....	....	....	....	....	....	....	....	....
	Utica Devils	AHL	78	27	45	72	62	....	....	....	....	....	....	....	....	....	5	1	7	8	10	....	....	....	....
1993-94	New Jersey	NHL	15	5	10	15	0	2	0	0	26	19.2	8	....	....	....	19	2	6	8	8	0	0	0	....
	Albany River Rats	AHL	58	26	37	63	76	....	....	....	....	....	....	....	....	....	....	....	....	....	....	....	....	....	....
1994-95♦	New Jersey	NHL	10	1	4	5	0	1	0	0	14	7.1	–5	....	....	....	11	2	1	3	8	0	0	1	....
1995-96	New Jersey	NHL	28	4	9	13	17	0	0	0	41	9.8	–1	....	....	....	....	....	....	....	....	....	....	....	....
	Vancouver	NHL	38	1	6	7	6	0	0	0	35	2.9	–8	....	....	....	1	0	0	0	0	0	0	0	....
1996-97	NY Islanders	NHL	3	0	0	0	0	0	0	0	0	0.0	–1	....	....	....	....	....	....	....	....	....	....	....	....
	Utah Grizzlies	IHL	48	10	21	31	27	....	....	....	....	....	....	....	....	....	....	....	....	....	....	....	....	....	....
	Saint John Flames	AHL	24	5	11	16	18	....	....	....	....	....	....	....	....	....	5	1	2	3	0	....	....	....	....
1997-98	Calgary	NHL	48	6	8	14	12	0	1	0	58	10.3	10	....	....	....	....	....	....	....	....	....	....	....	....
	Saint John Flames	AHL	35	8	30	38	20	....	....	....	....	....	....	....	....	....	19	3	13	16	10	....	....	....	....
1998-99	Edmonton	NHL	1	0	0	0	0	0	0	0	1	0.0	0	7	14.3	9:47	....	....	....	....	....	....	....	....	....
	Hamilton	AHL	51	15	29	44	82	....	....	....	....	....	....	....	....	....	11	3	6	9	8	....	....	....	....
99-2000	Edmonton	NHL	69	5	18	23	45	2	0	1	103	4.9	10	720	54.0	13:08	5	2	1	3	4	0	0	0	15:22
2000-01	Minnesota	NHL	68	7	22	29	80	0	0	0	92	7.6	–6	1154	50.7	17:50	....	....	....	....	....	....	....	....	....
2001-02	Minnesota	NHL	82	13	30	43	54	5	0	1	111	11.7	–14	1243	52.9	15:34	....	....	....	....	....	....	....	....	....
2002-03	Minnesota	NHL	78	8	17	25	31	3	1	2	78	10.3	–1	930	47.9	13:03	15	0	2	2	0	0	0	0	12:58
2003-04	Minnesota	NHL	55	4	20	24	38	2	0	2	41	9.8	6	712	48.5	14:07	....	....	....	....	....	....	....	....	....
	Montreal	NHL	14	3	2	5	6	0	1	0	13	23.1	6	167	47.3	13:30	11	0	2	2	2	0	0	0	15:34
	NHL Totals		511	57	146	203	289	15	3	6	614	9.3		4933	50.7	14:41	62	6	12	18	22	0	0	1	14:17

CCHA Second All-Star Team (1990) • NCAA West Second All-American Team (1990) • CCHA First All-Star Team (1991) • CCHA Player of the Year (1991) • NCAA West First All-American Team (1991)

• Missed majority of 1994-95 season recovering from shoulder injury suffered in game vs. Quebec, February 2, 1995. Traded to **Hartford** by **New Jersey** with New Jersey's 2nd round choice (later traded to Calgary – Calgary selected Dmitri Kokorev) in 1997 Entry Draft for Jocelyn Lemieux and Hartford's 2nd round choice (later traded to Dallas – Dallas selected John Erskine) in 1998 Entry Draft, December 19, 1995. Traded to **Vancouver** by **Hartford** with Frantisek Kucera and Hartford's 2nd round choice (Ryan Bonni) in 1997 Entry Draft for Jeff Brown and Vancouver's 3rd round choice (later traded to Calgary – Calgary selected Paul Manning) in 1998 Entry Draft, December 19, 1995. Claimed by **NY Islanders** from **Vancouver** in Waiver Draft, September 30, 1996. Signed as a free agent by **Calgary**, August, 1997. Traded to **Nashville** by **Calgary** for future considerations, June 26, 1998. Traded to **Edmonton** by **Nashville** with Mikhail Shtalenkov for Eric Fichaud, Drake Berehowsky and Greg de Vries, October 1, 1998. Selected by **Minnesota** from **Edmonton** in Expansion Draft, June 23, 2000. Traded to **Montreal** by **Minnesota** for Montreal's 4th round choice (Julien Sprunger) in 2004 Entry Draft, March 4, 2004.

DOWNEY, Aaron

(DOW-nee, AIR-ruhn) **DAL.**

Right wing. Shoots right. 6'1", 216 lbs. Born, Shelburne, Ont., August 27, 1974.

Season	Club	League	GP	G	A	Pts	PIM	PP	SH	GW	S	%	+/-	TF	F%	Min	GP	G	A	Pts	PIM	PP	SH	GW	Min
1990-91	Grand Valley	OJHL-C	27	6	8	14	57	....	....	....	....	....	....	....	....	....	....	....	....	....	....	....	....	....	....
1991-92	Collingwood	OJHL-B	40	9	8	17	111	....	....	....	....	....	....	....	....	....	....	....	....	....	....	....	....	....	....
1992-93	Guelph Storm	OHL	53	3	3	6	88	....	....	....	....	....	....	....	....	....	5	1	0	1	0	....	....	....	....
1993-94	Cole Harbour	NSMHL	35	8	20	28	210	....	....	....	....	....	....	....	....	....	....	....	....	....	....	....	....	....	....
1994-95	Cole Harbour	NSMHL	40	10	31	41	320	....	....	....	....	....	....	....	....	....	....	....	....	....	....	....	....	....	....
1995-96	Hampton Roads	ECHL	65	12	11	23	354	....	....	....	....	....	....	....	....	....	....	....	....	....	....	....	....	....	....
1996-97	Manitoba Moose	IHL	2	0	0	0	17	....	....	....	....	....	....	....	....	....	....	....	....	....	....	....	....	....	....
	Portland Pirates	AHL	3	0	0	0	19	....	....	....	....	....	....	....	....	....	....	....	....	....	....	....	....	....	....
	Hampton Roads	ECHL	64	8	8	16	338	....	....	....	....	....	....	....	....	....	9	0	3	3	26	....	....	....	....
1997-98	Providence Bruins	AHL	78	5	10	15	*407	....	....	....	....	....	....	....	....	....	....	....	....	....	....	....	....	....	....
1998-99	Providence Bruins	AHL	75	10	12	22	*401	....	....	....	....	....	....	....	....	....	19	1	1	2	46	....	....	....	....
99-2000	Boston	NHL	1	0	0	0	0	0	0	0	0	0.0	0	0	0.0	8:31	....	....	....	....	....	....	....	....	....
	Providence Bruins	AHL	47	6	4	10	221	....	....	....	....	....	....	....	....	....	14	1	0	1	24	....	....	....	....
2000-01	Chicago	NHL	3	0	0	0	6	0	0	0	2	0.0	–1	0	0.0	5:30	....	....	....	....	....	....	....	....	....
	Norfolk Admirals	AHL	67	6	15	21	234	....	....	....	....	....	....	....	....	....	9	0	0	0	4	....	....	....	....
2001-02	Chicago	NHL	36	1	0	1	76	0	0	1	10	10.0	–2	0	0.0	5:06	4	0	0	0	8	0	0	0	6:29
	Norfolk Admirals	AHL	12	0	2	2	21	....	....	....	....	....	....	....	....	....	....	....	....	....	....	....	....	....	....
2002-03	Dallas	NHL	43	1	1	2	69	0	0	0	14	7.1	1	0	0.0	4:47	....	....	....	....	....	....	....	....	....
2003-04	Dallas	NHL	37	1	1	2	77	0	0	1	11	9.1	2	0	0.0	4:30	....	....	....	....	....	....	....	....	....
	NHL Totals		120	3	2	5	228	0	0	2	37	8.1		0	0.0	4:50	4	0	0	0	8	0	0	0	6:29

Signed as a free agent by **Boston**, January 20, 1998. Signed as a free agent by **Chicago**, August 13, 2000. Signed as a free agent by **Dallas**, July 3, 2002. • Spent majority of 2003-04 season as a healthy reserve.

DRAKE, Dallas

(DRAYK, DAL-uhs) **ST.L.**

Right wing. Shoots left. 6'1", 190 lbs. Born, Trail, B.C., February 4, 1969. Detroit's 6th choice, 116th overall, in 1989 Entry Draft.

			Regular Season														Playoffs								
Season	Club	League	GP	G	A	Pts	PIM	PP	SH	GW	S	%	+/-	TF	F%	Min	GP	G	A	Pts	PIM	PP	SH	GW	Min
1984-85	Rossland	KIJHL	30	13	37	50	....	....	....	....	....	....	....	....	....	....	....	....	....	....	....	....	....	....	....
1985-86	Rossland	KIJHL	41	53	73	126	....	....	....	....	....	....	....	....	....	....	....	....	....	....	....	....	....	....	....
1986-87	Rossland	KIJHL	40	55	80	135	....	....	....	....	....	....	....	....	....	....	....	....	....	....	....	....	....	....	....
1987-88	Vernon Lakers	BCJHL	47	39	85	124	50	....	....	....	....	....	....	....	....	....	11	9	17	26	30	....	....	....	....
1988-89	North. Michigan	WCHA	38	17	22	39	22	....	....	....	....	....	....	....	....	....	7	1	2	3	4	....	....	....	....
1989-90	North. Michigan	WCHA	36	13	24	37	42	....	....	....	....	....	....	....	....	....	....	....	....	....	....	....	....	....	....
1990-91	North. Michigan	WCHA	44	22	36	58	89	....	....	....	....	....	....	....	....	....	....	....	....	....	....	....	....	....	....
1991-92	North. Michigan	WCHA	38	*39	41	*80	46	....	....	....	....	....	....	....	....	....	....	....	....	....	....	....	....	....	....
1992-93	**Detroit**	**NHL**	**72**	**18**	**26**	**44**	**93**	**3**	**2**	**5**	**89**	**20.2**	**15**	....	....	....	**7**	**3**	**3**	**6**	**6**	**1**	**0**	**0**	....
1993-94	**Detroit**	**NHL**	**47**	**10**	**22**	**32**	**37**	**0**	**1**	**2**	**78**	**12.8**	**5**	....	....	....	....	....	....	....	....	....	....	....	....
	Adirondack	AHL	1	2	0	2	0	....	....	....	....	....	....	....	....	....	....	....	....	....	....	....	....	....	....
	Winnipeg	**NHL**	**15**	**3**	**5**	**8**	**12**	**1**	**1**	**1**	**34**	**8.8**	**–6**	....	....	....	....	....	....	....	....	....	....	....	....
1994-95	**Winnipeg**	**NHL**	**43**	**8**	**18**	**26**	**30**	**0**	**0**	**1**	**66**	**12.1**	**–6**	....	....	....	....	....	....	....	....	....	....	....	....
1995-96	**Winnipeg**	**NHL**	**69**	**19**	**20**	**39**	**36**	**4**	**4**	**2**	**121**	**15.7**	**–7**	....	....	....	**3**	**0**	**0**	**0**	**0**	**0**	**0**	**0**	....
1996-97	**Phoenix**	**NHL**	**63**	**17**	**19**	**36**	**52**	**5**	**1**	**1**	**113**	**15.0**	**–11**	....	....	....	**7**	**0**	**1**	**1**	**2**	**0**	**0**	**0**	....
1997-98	**Phoenix**	**NHL**	**60**	**11**	**29**	**40**	**71**	**3**	**0**	**2**	**112**	**9.8**	**17**	....	....	....	**4**	**0**	**1**	**1**	**2**	**0**	**0**	**0**	....
1998-99	**Phoenix**	**NHL**	**53**	**9**	**22**	**31**	**65**	**0**	**0**	**3**	**105**	**8.6**	**17**	**5**	**60.0**	**15:38**	**7**	**4**	**3**	**7**	**4**	**2**	**0**	**1**	**19:51**
99-2000	**Phoenix**	**NHL**	**79**	**15**	**30**	**45**	**62**	**0**	**2**	**5**	**127**	**11.8**	**11**	**4**	**25.0**	**15:48**	**5**	**0**	**1**	**1**	**4**	**0**	**0**	**0**	**15:30**
2000-01	**St. Louis**	**NHL**	**82**	**12**	**29**	**41**	**71**	**2**	**0**	**3**	**142**	**8.5**	**18**	**11**	**45.5**	**14:44**	**15**	**4**	**2**	**6**	**16**	**0**	**1**	**1**	**14:08**
2001-02	**St. Louis**	**NHL**	**80**	**11**	**15**	**26**	**87**	**1**	**3**	**2**	**116**	**9.5**	**8**	**92**	**32.6**	**13:26**	**8**	**0**	**0**	**0**	**8**	**0**	**0**	**0**	**11:59**
2002-03	**St. Louis**	**NHL**	**80**	**20**	**10**	**30**	**66**	**4**	**1**	**2**	**113**	**17.7**	**–7**	**56**	**39.3**	**14:48**	**7**	**1**	**4**	**5**	**23**	**0**	**0**	**1**	**13:04**
2003-04	**St. Louis**	**NHL**	**79**	**13**	**22**	**35**	**65**	**3**	**2**	**1**	**121**	**10.7**	**10**	**92**	**45.7**	**16:57**	**5**	**1**	**1**	**2**	**2**	**0**	**0**	**1**	**16:45**
	NHL Totals		**822**	**166**	**267**	**433**	**747**	**26**	**17**	**30**	**1337**	**12.4**		**260**	**39.6**	**15:12**	**68**	**13**	**16**	**29**	**67**	**3**	**1**	**4**	**14:53**

WCHA First All-Star Team (1992) • NCAA West First All-American Team (1992)

Traded to **Winnipeg** by **Detroit** with Tim Cheveldae for Bob Essensa and Sergei Bautin, March 8, 1994. Transferred to **Phoenix** after **Winnipeg** franchise relocated, July 1, 1996. Selected by **Minnesota** from **Phoenix** in Expansion Draft, June 23, 2000. Signed as a free agent by **St. Louis**, July 1, 2000.

DRAPER, Kris

(DRAY-puhr, KRIHS) **DET.**

Center. Shoots left. 5'11", 190 lbs. Born, Toronto, Ont., May 24, 1971. Winnipeg's 4th choice, 62nd overall, in 1989 Entry Draft.

Season	Club	League	GP	G	A	Pts	PIM	PP	SH	GW	S	%	+/-	TF	F%	Min	GP	G	A	Pts	PIM	PP	SH	GW	Min
1987-88	Don Mills	MTHL	40	35	32	67	46	....	....	....	....	....	....	....	....	....	....	....	....	....	....	....	....	....	....
1988-89	Team Canada	Nat-Tm	60	11	15	26	16	....	....	....	....	....	....	....	....	....	....	....	....	....	....	....	....	....	....
1989-90	Team Canada	Nat-Tm	61	12	22	34	44	....	....	....	....	....	....	....	....	....	....	....	....	....	....	....	....	....	....
1990-91	Ottawa 67's	OHL	39	19	42	61	35	....	....	....	....	....	....	....	....	....	17	8	11	19	20	....	....	....	....
	Winnipeg	**NHL**	**3**	**1**	**0**	**1**	**5**	**0**	**0**	**0**	**1**	**100.0**	**0**	....	....	....	....	....	....	....	....	....	....	....	....
	Moncton Hawks	AHL	7	2	1	3	2	....	....	....	....	....	....	....	....	....	....	....	....	....	....	....	....	....	....
1991-92	**Winnipeg**	**NHL**	**10**	**2**	**0**	**2**	**2**	**0**	**0**	**0**	**19**	**10.5**	**0**	....	....	....	**2**	**0**	**0**	**0**	**0**	**0**	**0**	**0**	....
	Moncton Hawks	AHL	61	11	18	29	113	....	....	....	....	....	....	....	....	....	4	0	1	1	6	....	....	....	....
1992-93	**Winnipeg**	**NHL**	**7**	**0**	**0**	**0**	**2**	**0**	**0**	**0**	**5**	**0.0**	**–6**	....	....	....	....	....	....	....	....	....	....	....	....
	Moncton Hawks	AHL	67	12	23	35	40	....	....	....	....	....	....	....	....	....	5	2	2	4	18	....	....	....	....
1993-94	**Detroit**	**NHL**	**39**	**5**	**8**	**13**	**31**	**0**	**1**	**0**	**55**	**9.1**	**11**	....	....	....	**7**	**2**	**2**	**4**	**4**	**0**	**1**	**0**	....
	Adirondack	AHL	46	20	23	43	49	....	....	....	....	....	....	....	....	....	....	....	....	....	....	....	....	....	....
1994-95	**Detroit**	**NHL**	**36**	**2**	**6**	**8**	**22**	**0**	**0**	**0**	**44**	**4.5**	**1**	....	....	....	**18**	**4**	**1**	**5**	**12**	**0**	**1**	**1**	....
1995-96	**Detroit**	**NHL**	**52**	**7**	**9**	**16**	**32**	**0**	**1**	**0**	**51**	**13.7**	**2**	....	....	....	**18**	**4**	**2**	**6**	**18**	**0**	**1**	**0**	....
1996-97♦	**Detroit**	**NHL**	**76**	**8**	**5**	**13**	**73**	**1**	**0**	**1**	**85**	**9.4**	**–11**	....	....	....	**20**	**2**	**4**	**6**	**12**	**0**	**1**	**0**	....
1997-98♦	**Detroit**	**NHL**	**64**	**13**	**10**	**23**	**45**	**1**	**0**	**4**	**96**	**13.5**	**5**	....	....	....	**19**	**1**	**3**	**4**	**12**	**0**	**0**	**1**	....
1998-99	**Detroit**	**NHL**	**80**	**4**	**14**	**18**	**79**	**0**	**1**	**1**	**78**	**5.1**	**2**	**887**	**54.6**	**12:43**	**10**	**0**	**1**	**1**	**6**	**0**	**0**	**0**	**11:35**
99-2000	**Detroit**	**NHL**	**51**	**5**	**7**	**12**	**28**	**0**	**0**	**3**	**76**	**6.6**	**3**	**380**	**57.6**	**13:33**	**9**	**2**	**0**	**2**	**6**	**0**	**0**	**0**	**12:26**
2000-01	**Detroit**	**NHL**	**75**	**8**	**17**	**25**	**38**	**0**	**1**	**1**	**123**	**6.5**	**17**	**997**	**56.5**	**13:26**	**6**	**0**	**1**	**1**	**2**	**0**	**0**	**0**	**16:08**
2001-02♦	**Detroit**	**NHL**	**82**	**15**	**15**	**30**	**56**	**0**	**2**	**3**	**137**	**10.9**	**26**	**756**	**53.2**	**15:35**	**23**	**2**	**3**	**5**	**20**	**0**	**0**	**0**	**17:00**
2002-03	**Detroit**	**NHL**	**82**	**14**	**21**	**35**	**82**	**0**	**1**	**2**	**142**	**9.9**	**6**	**1059**	**56.9**	**16:12**	**4**	**0**	**0**	**0**	**4**	**0**	**0**	**0**	**17:29**
2003-04	**Detroit**	**NHL**	**67**	**24**	**16**	**40**	**31**	**2**	**5**	**1**	**149**	**16.1**	**22**	**1058**	**56.9**	**17:44**	**12**	**1**	**3**	**4**	**6**	**0**	**0**	**0**	**18:29**
	NHL Totals		**724**	**108**	**128**	**236**	**526**	**4**	**12**	**16**	**1061**	**10.2**		**5137**	**55.9**	**14:54**	**148**	**18**	**20**	**38**	**102**	**0**	**4**	**2**	**15:44**

Frank J. Selke Trophy (2004)

Traded to **Detroit** by **Winnipeg** for future considerations, June 30, 1993.

DRUKEN, Harold

(DROO-kehn, HAIR-ohld) **TOR.**

Center. Shoots left. 6', 200 lbs. Born, St. John's, Nfld., January 26, 1979. Vancouver's 3rd choice, 36th overall, in 1997 Entry Draft.

Season	Club	League	GP	G	A	Pts	PIM	PP	SH	GW	S	%	+/-	TF	F%	Min	GP	G	A	Pts	PIM	PP	SH	GW	Min
1995-96	Noble-Greenough	Hi-School	30	37	28	65	28	....	....	....	....	....	....	....	....	....	....	....	....	....	....	....	....	....	....
1996-97	Detroit	OHL	63	27	31	58	14	....	....	....	....	....	....	....	....	....	5	3	2	5	0	....	....	....	....
1997-98	Plymouth Whalers	OHL	64	38	44	82	12	....	....	....	....	....	....	....	....	....	15	9	11	20	4	....	....	....	....
1998-99	Plymouth Whalers	OHL	60	*58	45	103	34	....	....	....	....	....	....	....	....	....	11	9	12	21	14	....	....	....	....
99-2000	**Vancouver**	**NHL**	**33**	**7**	**9**	**16**	**10**	**2**	**0**	**0**	**69**	**10.1**	**14**	**307**	**47.9**	**13:01**	....	....	....	....	....	....	....	....	....
	Syracuse Crunch	AHL	47	20	25	45	32	....	....	....	....	....	....	....	....	....	4	1	2	3	6	....	....	....	....
2000-01	**Vancouver**	**NHL**	**55**	**15**	**15**	**30**	**14**	**6**	**0**	**3**	**82**	**18.3**	**2**	**598**	**43.8**	**11:59**	**4**	**0**	**1**	**1**	**0**	**0**	**0**	**0**	**13:44**
	Kansas City	IHL	15	5	9	14	20	....	....	....	....	....	....	....	....	....	....	....	....	....	....	....	....	....	....
2001-02	**Vancouver**	**NHL**	**27**	**4**	**4**	**8**	**6**	**1**	**0**	**2**	**33**	**12.1**	**–1**	**269**	**54.7**	**11:09**	....	....	....	....	....	....	....	....	....
	Manitoba Moose	AHL	11	2	9	11	4	....	....	....	....	....	....	....	....	....	....	....	....	....	....	....	....	....	....
2002-03	**Vancouver**	**NHL**	**3**	**1**	**1**	**2**	**0**	**0**	**0**	**0**	**3**	**33.3**	**–1**	**21**	**47.6**	**8:48**	....	....	....	....	....	....	....	....	....
	Carolina	**NHL**	**10**	**0**	**1**	**1**	**2**	**0**	**0**	**0**	**3**	**0.0**	**–1**	**31**	**41.9**	**4:03**	....	....	....	....	....	....	....	....	....
	Toronto	**NHL**	**5**	**0**	**2**	**2**	**2**	**0**	**0**	**0**	**8**	**0.0**	**1**	**25**	**44.0**	**12:50**	....	....	....	....	....	....	....	....	....
	St. John's	AHL	6	0	3	3	2	....	....	....	....	....	....	....	....	....	....	....	....	....	....	....	....	....	....
	Carolina	**NHL**	**4**	**0**	**0**	**0**	**0**	**0**	**0**	**0**	**2**	**0.0**	**0**	**8**	**75.0**	**3:52**	....	....	....	....	....	....	....	....	....
	Lowell	AHL	24	8	10	18	8	....	....	....	....	....	....	....	....	....	....	....	....	....	....	....	....	....	....
2003-04	**Toronto**	**NHL**	**9**	**0**	**4**	**4**	**2**	**0**	**0**	**0**	**19**	**0.0**	**4**	**3**	**33.3**	**10:48**	....	....	....	....	....	....	....	....	....
	St. John's	AHL	57	26	25	51	31	....	....	....	....	....	....	....	....	....	....	....	....	....	....	....	....	....	....
	NHL Totals		**146**	**27**	**36**	**63**	**36**	**9**	**0**	**5**	**219**	**12.3**		**1262**	**47.3**	**11:11**	**4**	**0**	**1**	**1**	**0**	**0**	**0**	**0**	**13:43**

OHL All-Rookie Team (1997) • OHL Second All-Star Team (1999)

Missed majority of 2001-02 season recovering from ankle injury suffered in game vs. Dallas, December 2, 2001. Traded to **Carolina** by **Vancouver** with Jan Hlavac for Darren Langdon and Marek Malik, November 1, 2002. Claimed on waivers by **Toronto** from **Carolina**, December 11, 2002. Claimed on waivers by **Carolina** from **Toronto**, January 17, 2003. Traded to **Toronto** by **Carolina** for Allan Rourke, May 29, 2003.

DRURY, Chris

(DROO-ree, KRIHS) **BUF.**

Center. Shoots right. 5'10", 180 lbs. Born, Trumbull, CT, August 20, 1976. Quebec's 5th choice, 72nd overall, in 1994 Entry Draft.

Season	Club	League	GP	G	A	Pts	PIM	PP	SH	GW	S	%	+/-	TF	F%	Min	GP	G	A	Pts	PIM	PP	SH	GW	Min
1991-92	Fairfield Prep	Hi-School	25	22	27	49	....	....	....	....	....	....	....	....	....	....	....	....	....	....	....	....	....	....	....
1992-93	Fairfield Prep	Hi-School	24	25	32	57	15	....	....	....	....	....	....	....	....	....	....	....	....	....	....	....	....	....	....
1993-94	Fairfield Prep	Hi-School	24	37	18	55	....	....	....	....	....	....	....	....	....	....	....	....	....	....	....	....	....	....	....
1994-95	Boston University	H-East	39	12	15	27	38	....	....	....	....	....	....	....	....	....	....	....	....	....	....	....	....	....	....
1995-96	Boston University	H-East	37	35	33	*68	46	....	....	....	....	....	....	....	....	....	....	....	....	....	....	....	....	....	....
1996-97	Boston University	H-East	41	*38	24	62	64	....	....	....	....	....	....	....	....	....	....	....	....	....	....	....	....	....	....
1997-98	Boston University	H-East	38	28	29	57	88	....	....	....	....	....	....	....	....	....	....	....	....	....	....	....	....	....	....
1998-99	**Colorado**	**NHL**	**79**	**20**	**24**	**44**	**62**	**6**	**0**	**3**	**138**	**14.5**	**9**	**418**	**46.9**	**13:15**	**19**	**6**	**2**	**8**	**4**	**0**	**0**	**4**	**11:28**
99-2000	**Colorado**	**NHL**	**82**	**20**	**47**	**67**	**42**	**7**	**0**	**2**	**213**	**9.4**	**8**	**1321**	**53.1**	**18:33**	**17**	**4**	**10**	**14**	**4**	**1**	**0**	**2**	**18:30**
2000-01♦	**Colorado**	**NHL**	**71**	**24**	**41**	**65**	**47**	**11**	**0**	**5**	**204**	**11.8**	**6**	**552**	**55.1**	**18:03**	**23**	**11**	**5**	**16**	**4**	**2**	**0**	**2**	**19:06**
2001-02	**Colorado**	**NHL**	**82**	**21**	**25**	**46**	**38**	**5**	**0**	**6**	**236**	**8.9**	**1**	**1139**	**53.2**	**17:57**	**21**	**5**	**7**	**12**	**10**	**1**	**0**	**3**	**17:01**
	United States	Olympics	6	0	0	0	0	....	....	....	....	....	....	....	....	....	....	....	....	....	....	....	....	....	....
2002-03	**Calgary**	**NHL**	**80**	**23**	**30**	**53**	**33**	**5**	**1**	**5**	**224**	**10.3**	**–9**	**942**	**53.8**	**18:33**	....	....	....	....	....	....	....	....	....
2003-04	**Buffalo**	**NHL**	**76**	**18**	**35**	**53**	**68**	**5**	**1**	**2**	**152**	**11.8**	**8**	**1491**	**54.9**	**18:04**	....	....	....	....	....	....	....	....	....
	NHL Totals		**470**	**126**	**202**	**328**	**290**	**39**	**2**	**23**	**1167**	**10.8**		**5863**	**53.4**	**17:24**	**80**	**26**	**24**	**50**	**22**	**4**	**0**	**11**	**16:37**

Hockey East Second All-Star Team (1996, 1997) • NCAA East Second All-American Team (1996) • Hockey East Player of the Year (1997, 1998) • NCAA East First All-American Team (1997, 1998) • NCAA Championship All-Tournament Team (1997) • Hockey East First All-Star Team (1998) • Hobey Baker Memorial Award (Top U.S. Collegiate Player) (1998) • NHL All-Rookie Team (1999) • Calder Memorial Trophy (1999)

Rights transferred to **Colorado** after **Quebec** franchise relocated, June 21, 1995. Traded to **Calgary** by **Colorado** with Stephane Yelle for Derek Morris, Jeff Shantz and Dean McAmmond, October 1, 2002. Traded to **Buffalo** by **Calgary** with Steve Begin for Steve Reinprecht and Rhett Warrener, July 3, 2003.

			Regular Season														Playoffs								
Season	Club	League	GP	G	A	Pts	PIM	PP	SH	GW	S	%	+/-	TF	F%	Min	GP	G	A	Pts	PIM	PP	SH	GW	Min

DUMONT, J.P.

(DOO-mawnt, JAY-pee) **BUF.**

Right wing. Shoots left. 6'1", 205 lbs. Born, Montreal, Que., April 1, 1978. NY Islanders' 1st choice, 3rd overall, in 1996 Entry Draft.

Season	Club	League	GP	G	A	Pts	PIM	PP	SH	GW	S	%	+/-	TF	F%	Min	GP	G	A	Pts	PIM	PP	SH	GW	Min
1993-94	Mtl-Bourassa	QAAA	44	27	20	47	44										4	2	3	5	4				
1994-95	Mtl-Bourassa	QAAA	10	2	7	9	12																		
	Val-d'Or Foreurs	QMJHL	48	5	14	19	24																		
1995-96	Val-d'Or Foreurs	QMJHL	66	48	57	105	109										13	12	8	20	22				
1996-97	Val-d'Or Foreurs	QMJHL	62	44	64	108	86										13	9	7	16	12				
1997-98	Val-d'Or Foreurs	QMJHL	55	57	42	99	63										19	31	15	46	18				
1998-99	**Chicago**	**NHL**	**25**	**9**	**6**	**15**	**10**	**0**	**0**	**2**	**42**	**21.4**	**7**	**10**	**50.0**	**14:14**									
	Portland Pirates	AHL	50	32	14	46	39																		
	Chicago Wolves	IHL															10	4	1	5	6				
99-2000	**Chicago**	**NHL**	**47**	**10**	**8**	**18**	**18**	**0**	**0**	**1**	**86**	**11.6**	**–6**	**12**	**33.3**	**12:54**									
	Cleveland	IHL	7	5	2	7	8																		
	Rochester	AHL	13	7	10	17	18										21	14	7	21	32				
2000-01	**Buffalo**	**NHL**	**79**	**23**	**28**	**51**	**54**	**9**	**0**	**5**	**156**	**14.7**	**1**	**3**	**33.3**	**15:01**	**13**	**4**	**3**	**7**	**8**	**0**	**0**	**0**	**14:32**
2001-02	**Buffalo**	**NHL**	**76**	**23**	**21**	**44**	**42**	**7**	**0**	**3**	**154**	**14.9**	**–10**	**4**	**50.0**	**15:14**									
2002-03	**Buffalo**	**NHL**	**76**	**14**	**21**	**35**	**44**	**2**	**0**	**2**	**135**	**10.4**	**–14**	**15**	**20.0**	**15:04**									
2003-04	**Buffalo**	**NHL**	**77**	**22**	**31**	**53**	**40**	**10**	**0**	**1**	**156**	**14.1**	**–9**	**32**	**43.8**	**17:00**									
	NHL Totals		**380**	**101**	**115**	**216**	**208**	**28**	**0**	**14**	**729**	**13.9**		**76**	**38.2**	**15:09**	**13**	**4**	**3**	**7**	**8**	**0**	**0**	**0**	**14:32**

QMJHL Second All-Star Team (1997)

Rights traded to **Chicago** by **NY Islanders** with Chicago's 5th round choice (later traded to Philadelphia – Philadelphia selected Francis Belanger) in 1998 Entry Draft for Dmitri Nabokov, May 30, 1998. Traded to **Buffalo** by **Chicago** with Doug Gilmour for Michal Grosek, March 10, 2000.

DUPUIS, Pascal

(doo-PWEE, pas-KAL) **MIN.**

Left wing. Shoots left. 6', 196 lbs. Born, Laval, Que., April 7, 1979.

Season	Club	League	GP	G	A	Pts	PIM	PP	SH	GW	S	%	+/-	TF	F%	Min	GP	G	A	Pts	PIM	PP	SH	GW	Min
1995-96	Laval Laurentide	QAAA	41	10	15	25											14	11	11	22					
1996-97	Rouyn-Noranda	QMJHL	44	9	15	24	20																		
1997-98	Rouyn-Noranda	QMJHL	39	9	17	26	36																		
	Shawinigan	QMJHL	28	7	13	20	10										6	2	0	2	4				
1998-99	Shawinigan	QMJHL	57	30	42	72	118										6	1	8	9	18				
99-2000	Shawinigan	QMJHL	61	50	55	105	99										13	*15	7	22	4				
2000-01	**Minnesota**	**NHL**	**4**	**1**	**0**	**1**	**4**	**1**	**0**	**0**	**8**	**12.5**	**0**	**0**	**0.0**	**15:36**									
	Cleveland	IHL	70	19	24	43	37										4	0	0	0	0				
2001-02	**Minnesota**	**NHL**	**76**	**15**	**12**	**27**	**16**	**3**	**2**	**0**	**154**	**9.7**	**–10**	**40**	**32.5**	**15:08**									
2002-03	**Minnesota**	**NHL**	**80**	**20**	**28**	**48**	**44**	**6**	**0**	**4**	**183**	**10.9**	**17**	**186**	**40.9**	**17:30**	**16**	**4**	**4**	**8**	**8**	**2**	**0**	**1**	**16:58**
2003-04	**Minnesota**	**NHL**	**59**	**11**	**15**	**26**	**20**	**2**	**0**	**1**	**127**	**8.7**	**5**	**129**	**45.7**	**15:48**									
	NHL Totals		**219**	**47**	**55**	**102**	**84**	**12**	**2**	**5**	**472**	**10.0**		**355**	**41.7**	**16:11**	**16**	**4**	**4**	**8**	**8**	**2**	**0**	**1**	**16:58**

Signed as a free agent by **Minnesota**, August 18, 2000.

DUSABLON, Benoit

(doo-sah-BLAW, BEHN-wah)

Center. Shoots left. 6'1", 207 lbs. Born, Ste Anne de la Perad, Que., August 1, 1979.

Season	Club	League	GP	G	A	Pts	PIM	PP	SH	GW	S	%	+/-	TF	F%	Min	GP	G	A	Pts	PIM	PP	SH	GW	Min
1995-96	Cap-d-Madelaine	QAAA	43	19	31	50	71																		
1996-97	Halifax	QMJHL	61	7	7	14	181																		
1997-98	Halifax	QMJHL	7	1	0	1	7																		
	Val d'Or Foreurs	QMJHL	57	14	11	25	56										19	2	9	11	33				
1998-99	Val d'Or Foreurs	QMJHL	67	42	74	116	63										6	2	6	8	4				
99-2000	Val d'Or Foreurs	QMJHL	41	29	53	82	45																		
	Halifax	QMJHL	31	18	35	53	18										10	6	7	13	12				
2000-01	Johnstown Chiefs	ECHL	11	2	3	5	4																		
	Tallahassee	ECHL	49	21	29	50	33																		
2001-02	Charlotte	ECHL	19	12	13	25	2																		
	Hartford	AHL	38	8	15	23	16										9	1	2	3	4				
2002-03	Hartford	AHL	50	8	16	24	41										1	0	0	0	0				
2003-04	**NY Rangers**	**NHL**	**3**	**0**	**0**	**0**	**2**	**0**	**0**	**0**	**3**	**0.0**	**–1**	**21**	**42.9**	**8:19**									
	Hartford	AHL	35	10	14	24	18										16	2	5	7	6				
	Charlotte	ECHL	19	10	10	20	10																		
	NHL Totals		**3**	**0**	**0**	**0**	**2**	**0**	**0**	**0**	**3**	**0.0**		**21**	**42.9**	**8:19**									

Signed as a free agent by **NY Rangers**, October 1, 2001.

DVORAK, Radek

(duh-VOHR-ak, RA-dehk) **EDM.**

Right wing. Shoots right. 6'2", 200 lbs. Born, Tabor, Czech., March 9, 1977. Florida's 1st choice, 10th overall, in 1995 Entry Draft.

Season	Club	League	GP	G	A	Pts	PIM	PP	SH	GW	S	%	+/-	TF	F%	Min	GP	G	A	Pts	PIM	PP	SH	GW	Min
1992-93	C. Budejovice Jr.	Czech-Jr.	35	44	46	90																			
1993-94	C. Budejovice Jr.	Czech-Jr.	20	17	18	35																			
	Ceske Budejovice	Czech	8	0	0	0	0																		
1994-95	Ceske Budejovice	Czech	10	3	5	8	2										9	5	1	6					
1995-96	**Florida**	**NHL**	**77**	**13**	**14**	**27**	**20**	**0**	**0**	**4**	**126**	**10.3**	**5**				**16**	**1**	**3**	**4**	**0**	**0**	**0**	**0**	
1996-97	**Florida**	**NHL**	**78**	**18**	**21**	**39**	**30**	**2**	**0**	**1**	**139**	**12.9**	**–2**				**3**	**0**	**0**	**0**	**0**	**0**	**0**	**0**	
1997-98	**Florida**	**NHL**	**64**	**12**	**24**	**36**	**33**	**2**	**3**	**0**	**112**	**10.7**	**–1**												
1998-99	**Florida**	**NHL**	**82**	**19**	**24**	**43**	**29**	**0**	**4**	**0**	**182**	**10.4**	**7**	**98**	**46.9**	**16:13**									
99-2000	**Florida**	**NHL**	**35**	**7**	**10**	**17**	**6**	**0**	**0**	**1**	**67**	**10.4**	**5**	**16**	**37.5**	**15:25**									
	NY Rangers	**NHL**	**46**	**11**	**22**	**33**	**10**	**2**	**1**	**0**	**90**	**12.2**	**0**	**34**	**35.3**	**18:24**									
2000-01	**NY Rangers**	**NHL**	**82**	**31**	**36**	**67**	**20**	**5**	**2**	**3**	**230**	**13.5**	**9**	**20**	**30.0**	**19:04**									
2001-02	**NY Rangers**	**NHL**	**65**	**17**	**20**	**37**	**14**	**3**	**3**	**1**	**210**	**8.1**	**–20**	**5**	**0.0**	**19:44**									
	Czech Republic	Olympics	4	0	0	0	0																		
2002-03	**NY Rangers**	**NHL**	**63**	**6**	**21**	**27**	**16**	**2**	**0**	**0**	**134**	**4.5**	**–3**	**9**	**44.4**	**15:42**									
	Edmonton	**NHL**	**12**	**4**	**4**	**8**	**14**	**1**	**0**	**0**	**32**	**12.5**	**–3**	**1**	**0.0**	**16:07**	**4**	**1**	**0**	**1**	**0**	**0**	**0**	**1**	**15:05**
2003-04	**Edmonton**	**NHL**	**78**	**15**	**35**	**50**	**26**	**6**	**0**	**0**	**188**	**8.0**	**18**	**24**	**29.2**	**16:56**									
	NHL Totals		**682**	**153**	**231**	**384**	**218**	**23**	**13**	**10**	**1510**	**10.1**		**207**	**39.1**	**17:25**	**23**	**2**	**3**	**5**	**0**	**0**	**0**	**1**	**15:05**

Traded to **San Jose** by **Florida** for Mike Vernon and San Jose's 3rd round choice (Sean O'Connor) in 2000 Entry Draft, December 30, 1999. Traded to **NY Rangers** by **San Jose** for Todd Harvey and NY Rangers' 4th round choice (Dimitri Patzold) in 2001 Entry Draft, December 30, 1999. Traded to **Edmonton** by **NY Rangers** with Cory Cross for Anson Carter and Ales Pisa, March 11, 2003.

DWYER, Gordie

(DWIGH-uhr, GOHR-dee) **CAR.**

Left wing. Shoots left. 6'3", 215 lbs. Born, Dalhousie, N.B., January 25, 1978. Montreal's 5th choice, 152nd overall, in 1998 Entry Draft.

Season	Club	League	GP	G	A	Pts	PIM	PP	SH	GW	S	%	+/-	TF	F%	Min	GP	G	A	Pts	PIM	PP	SH	GW	Min
1993-94	Magog	QAAA	42	7	15	22	62										4	2	1	3	0				
1994-95	Hull Olympiques	QMJHL	57	3	7	10	204										17	1	3	4	54				
1995-96	Hull Olympiques	QMJHL	25	5	9	14	199																		
	Laval Titan	QMJHL	22	5	17	22	72																		
	Beauport	QMJHL	22	4	9	13	87										20	3	5	8	104				
1996-97	Drummondville	QMJHL	66	21	48	69	393										8	6	1	7	39				
1997-98	Quebec Remparts	QMJHL	59	18	27	45	365										14	4	9	13	67				
1998-99	Fredericton	AHL	14	0	0	0	46																		
	New Orleans	ECHL	36	1	3	4	163										11	0	0	0	27				
99-2000	Quebec Citadelles	AHL	7	0	0	0	37																		
	Tampa Bay	**NHL**	**24**	**0**	**1**	**1**	**135**	**0**	**0**	**0**	**7**	**0.0**	**–6**	**0**	**0.0**	**4:57**									
	Detroit Vipers	IHL	27	0	2	2	147																		
2000-01	**Tampa Bay**	**NHL**	**28**	**0**	**1**	**1**	**96**	**0**	**0**	**0**	**12**	**0.0**	**–7**	**2**	**50.0**	**5:47**									
	Detroit Vipers	IHL	24	2	3	5	169																		
2001-02	**Tampa Bay**	**NHL**	**26**	**0**	**2**	**2**	**60**	**0**	**0**	**0**	**6**	**0.0**	**–4**	**0**	**0.0**	**5:05**									
	Springfield	AHL	17	1	3	4	80																		
2002-03	**NY Rangers**	**NHL**	**17**	**0**	**1**	**1**	**50**	**0**	**0**	**0**	**8**	**0.0**	**–1**	**1**	**0.0**	**6:28**									
	Hartford	AHL	15	3	2	5	117																		
	Montreal	**NHL**	**11**	**0**	**0**	**0**	**46**	**0**	**0**	**0**	**2**	**0.0**	**–2**	**2**	**50.0**	**7:33**									

			Regular Season														Playoffs								
Season	Club	League	GP	G	A	Pts	PIM	PP	SH	GW	S	%	+/-	TF	F%	Min	GP	G	A	Pts	PIM	PP	SH	GW	Min
2003-04	**Montreal**	**NHL**	**2**	**0**	**0**	**0**	**7**	**0**	**0**	**0**	**0**	**0.0**	**0**	**0**	**0.0**	**5:55**	....	....	....	....	....	....	....	....	....
	Hamilton	AHL	55	6	6	12	110	....	....	....	....	....	....	....	....	....	6	0	0	0	15	....	....	....	....
•	**NHL Totals**		**108**	**0**	**5**	**5**	**394**	**0**	**0**	**0**	**35**	**0.0**		**5**	**40.0**	**5:43**	....	....	....	....	....	....	....	....	....

• Re-entered NHL Entry Draft. Originally St. Louis' 2nd choice, 67th overall, in 1996 Entry Draft.

Traded to **Tampa Bay** by **Montreal** for Mike McBain, November 26, 1999. Traded to **NY Rangers** by **Tampa Bay** for Boyd Kane, October 10, 2002. Claimed on waivers by **Montreal** from **NY Rangers**, February 21, 2003. Signed as a free agent by **Carolina**, August 11, 2004.

DYKHUIS, Karl

(DIGH-kowz, KAHRL) **MTL.**

Defense. Shoots left. 6'3", 209 lbs. Born, Sept-Iles, Que., July 8, 1972. Chicago's 1st choice, 16th overall, in 1990 Entry Draft.

Season	Club	League	GP	G	A	Pts	PIM	PP	SH	GW	S	%	+/-	TF	F%	Min	GP	G	A	Pts	PIM	PP	SH	GW	Min
1987-88	Lac St-Jean	QAAA	37	2	12	14	....	....	....	....	....	....	....	....	....	....	2	0	1	1	2	....	....	....	....
1988-89	Hull Olympiques	QMJHL	63	2	29	31	59	....	....	....	....	....	....	....	....	....	9	1	9	10	6	....	....	....	....
1989-90	Hull Olympiques	QMJHL	69	10	46	56	119	....	....	....	....	....	....	....	....	....	11	2	5	7	2	....	....	....	....
1990-91	Team Canada	Nat-Tm	37	2	9	11	16	....	....	....	....	....	....	....	....	....	....	....	....	....	....	....	....	....	....
	Longueuil	QMJHL	3	1	4	5	6	....	....	....	....	....	....	....	....	....	8	2	5	7	6	....	....	....	....
1991-92	Team Canada	Nat-Tm	19	1	2	3	16	....	....	....	....	....	....	....	....	....	....	....	....	....	....	....	....	....	....
	Verdun	QMJHL	29	5	19	24	55	....	....	....	....	....	....	....	....	....	17	0	12	12	14	....	....	....	....
	Chicago	**NHL**	**6**	**1**	**3**	**4**	**4**	**1**	**0**	**0**	**12**	**8.3**	**–1**	....	....	....	....	....	....	....	....	....	....	....	....
1992-93	**Chicago**	**NHL**	**12**	**0**	**5**	**5**	**0**	**0**	**0**	**0**	**10**	**0.0**	**2**	....	....	....	....	....	....	....	....	....	....	....	....
	Indianapolis Ice	IHL	59	5	18	23	76	....	....	....	....	....	....	....	....	....	5	1	1	2	8	....	....	....	....
1993-94	Indianapolis Ice	IHL	73	7	25	32	132	....	....	....	....	....	....	....	....	....	....	....	....	....	....	....	....	....	....
1994-95	Indianapolis Ice	IHL	52	2	21	23	63	....	....	....	....	....	....	....	....	....	....	....	....	....	....	....	....	....	....
	Philadelphia	**NHL**	**33**	**2**	**6**	**8**	**37**	**1**	**0**	**1**	**46**	**4.3**	**7**	....	....	....	**15**	**4**	**4**	**8**	**14**	**2**	**0**	**2**	....
	Hershey Bears	AHL	1	0	0	0	0	....	....	....	....	....	....	....	....	....	....	....	....	....	....	....	....	....	....
1995-96	**Philadelphia**	**NHL**	**82**	**5**	**15**	**20**	**101**	**1**	**0**	**0**	**104**	**4.8**	**12**	....	....	....	**12**	**2**	**2**	**4**	**22**	**1**	**0**	**0**	....
1996-97	**Philadelphia**	**NHL**	**62**	**4**	**15**	**19**	**35**	**2**	**0**	**1**	**101**	**4.0**	**6**	....	....	....	**18**	**0**	**3**	**3**	**2**	**0**	**0**	**0**	....
1997-98	**Tampa Bay**	**NHL**	**78**	**5**	**9**	**14**	**110**	**0**	**1**	**0**	**91**	**5.5**	**–8**	....	....	....	....	....	....	....	....	....	....	....	....
1998-99	**Tampa Bay**	**NHL**	**33**	**2**	**1**	**3**	**18**	**0**	**0**	**0**	**27**	**7.4**	**–21**	**0**	**0.0**	**20:14**	....	....	....	....	....	....	....	....	....
	Philadelphia	**NHL**	**45**	**2**	**4**	**6**	**32**	**1**	**0**	**0**	**61**	**3.3**	**–2**	**0**	**0.0**	**18:15**	**5**	**1**	**0**	**1**	**4**	**0**	**0**	**0**	**18:05**
99-2000	**Philadelphia**	**NHL**	**5**	**0**	**1**	**1**	**6**	**0**	**0**	**0**	**5**	**0.0**	**–2**	**0**	**0.0**	**14:54**	....	....	....	....	....	....	....	....	....
	Montreal	**NHL**	**67**	**7**	**12**	**19**	**40**	**3**	**1**	**0**	**64**	**10.9**	**–3**	**0**	**0.0**	**19:53**	....	....	....	....	....	....	....	....	....
2000-01	**Montreal**	**NHL**	**67**	**8**	**9**	**17**	**44**	**2**	**0**	**1**	**66**	**12.1**	**9**	**4**	**100.0**	**15:40**	....	....	....	....	....	....	....	....	....
2001-02	**Montreal**	**NHL**	**80**	**5**	**7**	**12**	**32**	**0**	**0**	**1**	**85**	**5.9**	**16**	**0**	**0.0**	**19:54**	**12**	**1**	**1**	**2**	**8**	**0**	**0**	**0**	**18:39**
2002-03	**Montreal**	**NHL**	**65**	**1**	**4**	**5**	**34**	**0**	**0**	**0**	**24**	**4.2**	**–5**	**1**	**0.0**	**15:00**	....	....	....	....	....	....	....	....	....
2003-04	**Montreal**	**NHL**	**9**	**0**	**0**	**0**	**2**	**0**	**0**	**0**	**6**	**0.0**	**–2**	**1**	**0.0**	**13:02**	....	....	....	....	....	....	....	....	....
	Hamilton	AHL	54	5	17	22	61	....	....	....	....	....	....	....	....	....	5	1	0	1	8	....	....	....	....
	NHL Totals		**644**	**42**	**91**	**133**	**495**	**11**	**2**	**4**	**702**	**6.0**		**6**	**66.7**	**17:52**	**62**	**8**	**10**	**18**	**50**	**3**	**0**	**2**	**18:29**

QMJHL All-Rookie Team (1989) • QMJHL Defensive Rookie of the Year (1989) • QMJHL First All-Star Team (1990)

Traded to **Philadelphia** by **Chicago** for Bob Wilkie and Philadelphia's 5th round choice (Kyle Calder) in 1997 Entry Draft, February 16, 1995. Traded to **Tampa Bay** by **Philadelphia** with Mikael Renberg for Philadelphia's 1st round choices (previously acquired) in 1998 (Simon Gagne), 1999 (Maxime Ouellet), 2000 (Justin Williams) and 2001 (later traded to Ottawa – Ottawa selected Tim Gleason) Entry Drafts, August 20, 1997. Traded to **Philadelphia** by **Tampa Bay** for Petr Svoboda, December 28, 1998. Traded to **Montreal** by **Philadelphia** for cash, October 20, 1999.

EAKINS, Dallas

(EE-kins, DAL-las)

Defense. Shoots left. 6'2", 195 lbs. Born, Dade City, FL, February 27, 1967. Washington's 11th choice, 208th overall, in 1985 Entry Draft.

Season	Club	League	GP	G	A	Pts	PIM	PP	SH	GW	S	%	+/-	TF	F%	Min	GP	G	A	Pts	PIM	PP	SH	GW	Min
1983-84	Peterboro AA	OMHA	29	7	20	27	67	....	....	....	....	....	....	....	....	....	....	....	....	....	....	....	....	....	....
	Peterborough	OJHL-B	5	0	3	3	4	....	....	....	....	....	....	....	....	....	....	....	....	....	....	....	....	....	....
1984-85	Peterborough	OHL	48	0	8	8	96	....	....	....	....	....	....	....	....	....	7	0	0	0	18	....	....	....	....
1985-86	Peterborough	OHL	60	6	16	22	134	....	....	....	....	....	....	....	....	....	16	0	1	1	30	....	....	....	....
1986-87	Peterborough	OHL	54	3	11	14	145	....	....	....	....	....	....	....	....	....	12	1	4	5	37	....	....	....	....
1987-88	Peterborough	OHL	64	11	27	38	129	....	....	....	....	....	....	....	....	....	12	3	12	15	16	....	....	....	....
1988-89	Baltimore	AHL	62	0	10	10	139	....	....	....	....	....	....	....	....	....	....	....	....	....	....	....	....	....	....
1989-90	Moncton Hawks	AHL	75	2	11	13	189	....	....	....	....	....	....	....	....	....	....	....	....	....	....	....	....	....	....
1990-91	Moncton Hawks	AHL	75	1	12	13	132	....	....	....	....	....	....	....	....	....	9	0	1	1	44	....	....	....	....
1991-92	Moncton Hawks	AHL	67	3	13	16	136	....	....	....	....	....	....	....	....	....	11	2	1	3	16	....	....	....	....
1992-93	**Winnipeg**	**NHL**	**14**	**0**	**2**	**2**	**38**	**0**	**0**	**0**	**9**	**0.0**	**2**	....	....	....	....	....	....	....	....	....	....	....	....
	Moncton Hawks	AHL	55	4	6	10	132	....	....	....	....	....	....	....	....	....	....	....	....	....	....	....	....	....	....
1993-94	**Florida**	**NHL**	**1**	**0**	**0**	**0**	**0**	**0**	**0**	**0**	**2**	**0.0**	**0**	....	....	....	....	....	....	....	....	....	....	....	....
	Cincinnati	IHL	80	1	18	19	143	....	....	....	....	....	....	....	....	....	8	0	1	1	41	....	....	....	....
1994-95	Cincinnati	IHL	59	6	12	18	69	....	....	....	....	....	....	....	....	....	....	....	....	....	....	....	....	....	....
	Florida	**NHL**	**17**	**0**	**1**	**1**	**35**	**0**	**0**	**0**	**3**	**0.0**	**2**	....	....	....	....	....	....	....	....	....	....	....	....
1995-96	**St. Louis**	**NHL**	**16**	**0**	**1**	**1**	**34**	**0**	**0**	**0**	**6**	**0.0**	**–2**	....	....	....	....	....	....	....	....	....	....	....	....
	Worcester IceCats	AHL	4	0	0	0	12	....	....	....	....	....	....	....	....	....	....	....	....	....	....	....	....	....	....
	Winnipeg	**NHL**	**2**	**0**	**0**	**0**	**0**	**0**	**0**	**0**	**0**	**0.0**	**1**	....	....	....	....	....	....	....	....	....	....	....	....
1996-97	**Phoenix**	**NHL**	**4**	**0**	**0**	**0**	**10**	**0**	**0**	**0**	**2**	**0.0**	**–3**	....	....	....	....	....	....	....	....	....	....	....	....
	Springfield	AHL	38	6	7	13	63	....	....	....	....	....	....	....	....	....	....	....	....	....	....	....	....	....	....
	NY Rangers	**NHL**	**3**	**0**	**0**	**0**	**6**	**0**	**0**	**0**	**2**	**0.0**	**–1**	....	....	....	**4**	**0**	**0**	**0**	**4**	**0**	**0**	**0**	....
	Binghamton	AHL	19	1	7	8	15	....	....	....	....	....	....	....	....	....	....	....	....	....	....	....	....	....	....
1997-98	**Florida**	**NHL**	**23**	**0**	**1**	**1**	**44**	**0**	**0**	**0**	**16**	**0.0**	**1**	....	....	....	....	....	....	....	....	....	....	....	....
	New Haven	AHL	4	0	1	1	7	....	....	....	....	....	....	....	....	....	....	....	....	....	....	....	....	....	....
1998-99	**Toronto**	**NHL**	**18**	**0**	**2**	**2**	**24**	**0**	**0**	**0**	**11**	**0.0**	**3**	**0**	**0.0**	**16:28**	**1**	**0**	**0**	**0**	**0**	**0**	**0**	**0**	**2:28**
	Chicago Wolves	IHL	2	0	0	0	0	....	....	....	....	....	....	....	....	....	....	....	....	....	....	....	....	....	....
	St. John's	AHL	20	3	7	10	16	....	....	....	....	....	....	....	....	....	5	0	1	1	6	....	....	....	....
99-2000	**NY Islanders**	**NHL**	**2**	**0**	**1**	**1**	**2**	**0**	**0**	**0**	**4**	**0.0**	**3**	**0**	**0.0**	**21:28**	....	....	....	....	....	....	....	....	....
	Chicago Wolves	IHL	68	5	26	31	99	....	....	....	....	....	....	....	....	....	16	1	4	5	16	....	....	....	....
2000-01	**Calgary**	**NHL**	**17**	**0**	**1**	**1**	**11**	**0**	**0**	**0**	**4**	**0.0**	**–1**	**0**	**0.0**	**12:18**	....	....	....	....	....	....	....	....	....
	Chicago Wolves	IHL	64	3	16	19	49	....	....	....	....	....	....	....	....	....	14	0	0	0	24	....	....	....	....
2001-02	**Calgary**	**NHL**	**3**	**0**	**0**	**0**	**4**	**0**	**0**	**0**	**0**	**0.0**	**1**	**0**	**0.0**	**14:21**	....	....	....	....	....	....	....	....	....
	Chicago Wolves	AHL	54	2	15	17	58	....	....	....	....	....	....	....	....	....	25	0	6	6	53	....	....	....	....
2002-03	Chicago Wolves	AHL	72	4	11	15	84	....	....	....	....	....	....	....	....	....	9	1	0	1	31	....	....	....	....
2003-04	Manitoba Moose	AHL	64	1	7	8	68	....	....	....	....	....	....	....	....	....	....	....	....	....	....	....	....	....	....
	NHL Totals		**120**	**0**	**9**	**9**	**208**	**0**	**0**	**0**	**59**	**0.0**		**0**	**0.0**	**14:47**	**5**	**0**	**0**	**0**	**4**	**0**	**0**	**0**	**2:28**

IHL Second All-Star Team (2000)

Signed as a free agent by **Winnipeg**, October 17, 1989. Signed as a free agent by **Florida**, July 8, 1993. Traded to **St. Louis** by **Florida** for St. Louis' 4th round choice (Ivan Novoseltsev) in 1997 Entry Draft, September 28, 1995. Claimed on waivers by **Winnipeg** from **St. Louis**, March 20, 1996. Transferred to **Phoenix** after **Winnipeg** franchise relocated, July 1, 1996. Traded to **NY Rangers** by **Phoenix** with Mike Eastwood for Jayson More, February 6, 1997. Signed as a free agent by **Florida**, July 30, 1997. Signed as a free agent by **Toronto**, July 28, 1998. Signed as a free agent by **NY Islanders**, August 12, 1999. Traded to **Chicago** by **NY Islanders** for future considerations, March 3, 2000. Signed as a free agent by **Calgary**, July 27, 2000. Signed as a free agent by **Atlanta**, July 23, 2002. Signed as a free agent by **Vancouver**, August 6, 2003.

EASTWOOD, Mike

(EEST-wuhd, MIGHK) **PIT.**

Center. Shoots right. 6'3", 216 lbs. Born, Ottawa, Ont., July 1, 1967. Toronto's 5th choice, 91st overall, in 1987 Entry Draft.

Season	Club	League	GP	G	A	Pts	PIM	PP	SH	GW	S	%	+/-	TF	F%	Min	GP	G	A	Pts	PIM	PP	SH	GW	Min
1984-85	Nepean Raiders	OCJHL	46	10	13	23	18	....	....	....	....	....	....	....	....	....	....	....	....	....	....	....	....	....	....
1985-86	Nepean Raiders	OCJHL	7	4	2	6	6	....	....	....	....	....	....	....	....	....	....	....	....	....	....	....	....	....	....
1986-87	Pembroke	OCJHL	54	58	45	103	62	....	....	....	....	....	....	....	....	....	23	36	11	47	32	....	....	....	....
1987-88	West. Michigan	CCHA	42	5	8	13	14	....	....	....	....	....	....	....	....	....	....	....	....	....	....	....	....	....	....
1988-89	West. Michigan	CCHA	40	10	13	23	87	....	....	....	....	....	....	....	....	....	....	....	....	....	....	....	....	....	....
1989-90	West. Michigan	CCHA	40	25	27	52	36	....	....	....	....	....	....	....	....	....	....	....	....	....	....	....	....	....	....
1990-91	West. Michigan	CCHA	42	29	32	61	84	....	....	....	....	....	....	....	....	....	....	....	....	....	....	....	....	....	....
1991-92	**Toronto**	**NHL**	**9**	**0**	**2**	**2**	**4**	**0**	**0**	**0**	**6**	**0.0**	**–4**	....	....	....	....	....	....	....	....	....	....	....	....
	St. John's	AHL	61	18	25	43	28	....	....	....	....	....	....	....	....	....	16	9	10	19	16	....	....	....	....
1992-93	**Toronto**	**NHL**	**12**	**1**	**6**	**7**	**21**	**0**	**0**	**0**	**11**	**9.1**	**–2**	....	....	....	**10**	**1**	**2**	**3**	**8**	**0**	**0**	**0**	....
	St. John's	AHL	60	24	35	59	32	....	....	....	....	....	....	....	....	....	....	....	....	....	....	....	....	....	....
1993-94	**Toronto**	**NHL**	**54**	**8**	**10**	**18**	**28**	**1**	**0**	**2**	**41**	**19.5**	**2**	....	....	....	**18**	**3**	**2**	**5**	**12**	**1**	**0**	**1**	....
1994-95	**Toronto**	**NHL**	**36**	**5**	**5**	**10**	**32**	**0**	**0**	**0**	**38**	**13.2**	**–12**	....	....	....	....	....	....	....	....	....	....	....	....
	Winnipeg	**NHL**	**13**	**3**	**6**	**9**	**4**	**0**	**0**	**0**	**17**	**17.6**	**3**	....	....	....	....	....	....	....	....	....	....	....	....
1995-96	**Winnipeg**	**NHL**	**80**	**14**	**14**	**28**	**20**	**2**	**0**	**3**	**94**	**14.9**	**–14**	....	....	....	**6**	**0**	**1**	**1**	**2**	**0**	**0**	**0**	....
1996-97	**Phoenix**	**NHL**	**33**	**1**	**3**	**4**	**4**	**0**	**0**	**0**	**22**	**4.5**	**–3**	....	....	....	....	....	....	....	....	....	....	....	....
	NY Rangers	**NHL**	**27**	**1**	**7**	**8**	**10**	**0**	**0**	**0**	**22**	**4.5**	**2**	....	....	....	**15**	**1**	**2**	**3**	**22**	**0**	**0**	**0**	....
1997-98	**NY Rangers**	**NHL**	**48**	**5**	**5**	**10**	**16**	**0**	**0**	**0**	**34**	**14.7**	**–2**	....	....	....	....	....	....	....	....	....	....	....	....
	St. Louis	**NHL**	**10**	**1**	**0**	**1**	**6**	**0**	**0**	**1**	**4**	**25.0**	**0**	....	....	....	**3**	**1**	**0**	**1**	**0**	**0**	**0**	**1**	....

Season	Club	League	GP	G	A	Pts	PIM	PP	SH	GW	S	%	+/-	TF	F%	Min	GP	G	A	Pts	PIM	PP	SH	GW	Min
			Regular Season														Playoffs								
1998-99	St. Louis	NHL	82	9	21	30	36	0	0	0	76	11.8	6	1235	56.6	14:59	13	1	1	2	6	0	0	0	16:02
99-2000	St. Louis	NHL	79	19	15	34	32	1	3	3	83	22.9	5	872	52.2	15:08	7	1	1	2	6	0	0	0	13:28
2000-01	St. Louis	NHL	77	6	17	23	28	0	2	1	51	11.8	4	1230	53.4	14:08	15	0	2	2	2	0	0	0	15:13
2001-02	St. Louis	NHL	71	7	10	17	41	0	0	2	60	11.7	–2	1110	53.8	12:55	10	0	0	0	6	0	0	0	15:32
2002-03	St. Louis	NHL	17	1	3	4	8	1	0	0	7	14.3	1	203	42.9	10:44	....	....	....	....	....	....	....	....	....
	Chicago	NHL	53	2	10	12	24	0	0	0	32	6.3	–6	713	53.3	12:54	....	....	....	....	....	....	....	....	....
2003-04	Pittsburgh	NHL	82	4	15	19	40	0	0	1	55	7.3	–18	1401	51.5	14:09	....	....	....	....	....	....	....	....	....
	NHL Totals		783	87	149	236	354	5	5	13	653	13.3		6764	53.2	14:00	97	8	11	19	64	1	0	2	15:15

CCHA Second All-Star Team (1991)

Traded to **Winnipeg** by **Toronto** with Toronto's 3rd round choice (Brad Isbister) in 1995 Entry Draft for Tie Domi, April 7, 1995. Transferred to **Phoenix** after **Winnipeg** franchise relocated, July 1, 1996. Traded to **NY Rangers** by **Phoenix** with Dallas Eakins for Jayson More, February 6, 1997. Traded to **St. Louis** by **NY Rangers** for Harry York, March 24, 1998. Claimed on waivers by **Chicago** from **St. Louis**, December 11, 2002. Signed as a free agent by **Pittsburgh**, July 31, 2003.

EATON, Mark

(EE-tohn, MAHRK) **NSH.**

Defense. Shoots left. 6'2", 208 lbs. Born, Wilmington, DE, May 6, 1977.

Season	Club	League	GP	G	A	Pts	PIM	PP	SH	GW	S	%	+/-	TF	F%	Min	GP	G	A	Pts	PIM	PP	SH	GW	Min
1995-96	Waterloo	USHL	50	4	21	25	....	....	....	....	....	....	....	....	....	....	....	....	....	....	....	....	....	....	....
1996-97	Waterloo	USHL	50	6	32	38	62	....	....	....	....	....	....	....	....	....	....	....	....	....	....	....	....	....	....
1997-98	U. of Notre Dame	CCHA	41	12	17	29	32	....	....	....	....	....	....	....	....	....	....	....	....	....	....	....	....	....	....
1998-99	Philadelphia	AHL	74	9	27	36	38	....	....	....	....	....	....	....	....	....	16	4	8	12	0	....	....	....	....
99-2000	Philadelphia	NHL	27	1	1	2	8	0	0	1	25	4.0	1	0	0.0	18:17	7	0	0	0	0	0	0	0	13:36
	Philadelphia	AHL	47	9	17	26	6	....	....	....	....	....	....	....	....	....	....	....	....	....	....	....	....	....	....
2000-01	Nashville	NHL	34	3	8	11	14	1	0	1	32	9.4	7	0	0.0	17:13	....	....	....	....	....	....	....	....	....
	Milwaukee	IHL	34	3	12	15	27	....	....	....	....	....	....	....	....	....	....	....	....	....	....	....	....	....	....
2001-02	Nashville	NHL	58	3	5	8	24	0	0	0	52	5.8	–12	0	0.0	17:12	....	....	....	....	....	....	....	....	....
2002-03	Nashville	NHL	50	2	7	9	22	0	0	0	52	3.8	1	0	0.0	15:45	....	....	....	....	....	....	....	....	....
	Milwaukee	AHL	3	1	0	1	2	....	....	....	....	....	....	....	....	....	....	....	....	....	....	....	....	....	....
2003-04	Nashville	NHL	75	4	9	13	26	0	0	1	82	4.9	16	0	0.0	20:56	6	0	0	0	2	0	0	0	19:51
	NHL Totals		244	13	30	43	94	1	0	3	243	5.3		0	0.0	18:10	13	0	0	0	2	0	0	0	16:29

USHL Second All-Star Team (1997) • Curt Hammer Award (Most Gentlemanly Player – USHL) (1997) • CCHA Rookie of the Year (1998)

Signed as a free agent by **Philadelphia**, August 4, 1998. Traded to **Nashville** by **Philadelphia** for Detroit's 3rd round choice (previously acquired, Philadelphia selected Patrick Sharp) in 2001 Entry Draft, September 29, 2000.

EHRHOFF, Christian

(AIR-hawf, KRIHS-tyehn) **S.J.**

Defense. Shoots left. 6'2", 195 lbs. Born, Moers, West Germany, July 6, 1982. San Jose's 2nd choice, 106th overall, in 2001 Entry Draft.

Season	Club	League	GP	G	A	Pts	PIM	PP	SH	GW	S	%	+/-	TF	F%	Min	GP	G	A	Pts	PIM	PP	SH	GW	Min
1998-99	Krefeld Jr.	German-Jr.	22	10	14	24	46	....	....	....	....	....	....	....	....	....	....	....	....	....	....	....	....	....	....
99-2000	Duisburger SC	German-3	41	3	12	15	50	....	....	....	....	....	....	....	....	....	....	....	....	....	....	....	....	....	....
	Krefeld Pinguine	Germany	9	1	0	1	6	....	....	....	....	....	....	....	....	....	3	0	0	0	0	....	....	....	....
2000-01	Duisburger SC	German-3	6	1	2	3	12	....	....	....	....	....	....	....	....	....	....	....	....	....	....	....	....	....	....
	Krefeld Pinguine	Germany	58	3	11	14	73	....	....	....	....	....	....	....	....	....	....	....	....	....	....	....	....	....	....
2001-02	Krefeld Pinguine	Germany	46	7	17	24	81	....	....	....	....	....	....	....	....	....	3	0	0	0	2	....	....	....	....
	Germany	Olympics	7	0	0	0	8	....	....	....	....	....	....	....	....	....	....	....	....	....	....	....	....	....	....
2002-03	Krefeld Pinguine	Germany	48	10	17	27	54	....	....	....	....	....	....	....	....	....	14	3	6	9	24	....	....	....	....
2003-04	San Jose	NHL	41	1	11	12	14	0	0	1	58	1.7	4	0	0.0	15:23	....	....	....	....	....	....	....	....	....
	Cleveland Barons	AHL	27	4	10	14	43	....	....	....	....	....	....	....	....	....	9	2	6	8	11	....	....	....	....
	NHL Totals		41	1	11	12	14	0	0	1	58	1.7		0	0.0	15:23	....	....	....	....	....	....	....	....	....

EKMAN, Nils

(EHK-mahn, NIHLS) **S.J.**

Left wing. Shoots left. 6', 185 lbs. Born, Stockholm, Sweden, March 11, 1976. Calgary's 6th choice, 107th overall, in 1994 Entry Draft.

Season	Club	League	GP	G	A	Pts	PIM	PP	SH	GW	S	%	+/-	TF	F%	Min	GP	G	A	Pts	PIM	PP	SH	GW	Min
1993-94	Hammarby Jr.	Swede-Jr.	11	4	5	9	14	....	....	....	....	....	....	....	....	....	....	....	....	....	....	....	....	....	....
	Hammarby	Swede-2	18	7	2	9	4	....	....	....	....	....	....	....	....	....	....	....	....	....	....	....	....	....	....
1994-95	Hammarby Jr.	Swede-Jr.	2	2	1	3	0	....	....	....	....	....	....	....	....	....	....	....	....	....	....	....	....	....	....
	Hammarby	Swede-2	32	10	8	18	18	....	....	....	....	....	....	....	....	....	....	....	....	....	....	....	....	....	....
1995-96	Hammarby	Swede-2	26	9	7	16	53	....	....	....	....	....	....	....	....	....	1	0	0	0	0	....	....	....	....
1996-97	Kiekko Espoo	Finland	50	24	19	43	60	....	....	....	....	....	....	....	....	....	4	2	0	2	4	....	....	....	....
1997-98	Kiekko Espoo	Finland	43	14	14	28	86	....	....	....	....	....	....	....	....	....	7	2	2	4	27	....	....	....	....
	Saint John Flames	AHL	....	....	....	....	....	....	....	....	....	....	....	....	....	....	1	0	0	0	2	....	....	....	....
1998-99	Blues Espoo	Finland	52	20	14	34	96	....	....	....	....	....	....	....	....	....	3	1	1	2	6	....	....	....	....
99-2000	Detroit Vipers	IHL	10	7	2	9	8	....	....	....	....	....	....	....	....	....	....	....	....	....	....	....	....	....	....
	Tampa Bay	NHL	28	2	2	4	36	1	0	0	42	4.8	–8	3	0.0	11:12	....	....	....	....	....	....	....	....	....
	Long Beach	IHL	27	11	12	23	26	....	....	....	....	....	....	....	....	....	5	3	3	6	4	....	....	....	....
2000-01	Tampa Bay	NHL	43	9	11	20	40	2	1	1	72	12.5	–15	16	37.5	15:45	....	....	....	....	....	....	....	....	....
	Detroit Vipers	IHL	33	22	14	36	63	....	....	....	....	....	....	....	....	....	....	....	....	....	....	....	....	....	....
2001-02	Djurgarden	Sweden	38	16	15	31	57	....	....	....	....	....	....	....	....	....	4	1	0	1	32	....	....	....	....
2002-03	Hartford	AHL	57	30	36	66	73	....	....	....	....	....	....	....	....	....	2	0	2	2	4	....	....	....	....
2003-04	San Jose	NHL	82	22	33	55	34	1	4	5	147	15.0	30	23	21.7	14:54	16	0	3	3	8	0	0	0	13:02
	NHL Totals		153	33	46	79	110	4	5	6	261	12.6		42	26.2	14:28	16	0	3	3	8	0	0	0	13:02

Garry F. Longman Memorial Trophy (Top Rookie – IHL) (2000)

Traded to **Tampa Bay** by **Calgary** with Calgary's 4th round choice (later traded to NY Islanders – NY Islanders selected Vladimir Gorbunov) in 2000 Entry Draft for Andreas Johansson, November 20, 1999. Traded to **NY Rangers** by **Tampa Bay** with Kyle Freadrich for Tim Taylor, June 30, 2001. Traded to **San Jose** by **NY Rangers** for Chad Wiseman, August 12, 2003.

ELIAS, Patrik

(ehl-EE-ahsh, PA-trihk) **N.J.**

Center. Shoots left. 6'1", 195 lbs. Born, Trebic, Czech., April 13, 1976. New Jersey's 2nd choice, 51st overall, in 1994 Entry Draft.

Season	Club	League	GP	G	A	Pts	PIM	PP	SH	GW	S	%	+/-	TF	F%	Min	GP	G	A	Pts	PIM	PP	SH	GW	Min
1992-93	Poldi Kladno	Czech	2	0	0	0	....	....	....	....	....	....	....	....	....	....	....	....	....	....	....	....	....	....	....
1993-94	HC Kladno	Czech	15	1	2	3	....	....	....	....	....	....	....	....	....	....	11	2	2	4	....	....	....	....	....
1994-95	HC Kladno	Czech	28	4	3	7	37	....	....	....	....	....	....	....	....	....	7	1	2	3	12	....	....	....	....
1995-96	New Jersey	NHL	1	0	0	0	0	0	0	0	2	0.0	–1	....	....	....	....	....	....	....	....	....	....	....	....
	Albany River Rats	AHL	74	27	36	63	83	....	....	....	....	....	....	....	....	....	4	1	1	2	2	....	....	....	....
1996-97	New Jersey	NHL	17	2	3	5	2	0	0	0	23	8.7	–4	....	....	....	8	2	3	5	4	1	0	0	....
	Albany River Rats	AHL	57	24	43	67	76	....	....	....	....	....	....	....	....	....	6	1	2	3	8	....	....	....	....
1997-98	New Jersey	NHL	74	18	19	37	28	5	0	6	147	12.2	18	....	....	....	4	0	1	1	0	0	0	0	....
	Albany River Rats	AHL	3	3	0	3	2	....	....	....	....	....	....	....	....	....	....	....	....	....	....	....	....	....	....
1998-99	New Jersey	NHL	74	17	33	50	34	3	0	2	157	10.8	19	99	38.4	15:50	7	0	5	5	6	0	0	0	18:07
99-2000	Trebic	Czech-2	2	2	1	3	2	....	....	....	....	....	....	....	....	....	....	....	....	....	....	....	....	....	....
	Pardubice	Czech	5	1	4	5	31	....	....	....	....	....	....	....	....	....	....	....	....	....	....	....	....	....	....
	◆ New Jersey	NHL	72	35	37	72	58	9	0	9	183	19.1	16	134	45.5	17:28	23	7	*13	20	9	2	1	1	17:44
2000-01	New Jersey	NHL	82	40	56	96	51	8	3	6	220	18.2	45	155	41.3	18:44	25	9	14	23	10	3	1	2	18:14
2001-02	New Jersey	NHL	75	29	32	61	36	8	1	8	199	14.6	4	128	45.3	18:57	6	2	4	6	6	2	0	0	20:33
	Czech Republic	Olympics	4	1	1	2	0	....	....	....	....	....	....	....	....	....	....	....	....	....	....	....	....	....	....
2002-03◆	New Jersey	NHL	81	28	29	57	22	6	0	4	255	11.0	17	427	43.8	18:05	24	5	8	13	26	2	0	2	17:14
2003-04	New Jersey	NHL	82	38	43	81	44	9	3	9	300	12.7	26	49	36.7	18:46	5	3	2	5	2	1	0	1	18:59
	NHL Totals		558	207	252	459	275	48	7	44	1486	13.9		992	42.9	18:00	102	28	50	78	63	11	2	6	18:02

NHL All-Rookie Team (1998) • NHL First All-Star Team (2001) • Bud Light Plus/Minus Award (2001) (tied with Joe Sakic)

Played in NHL All-Star Game (2000, 2002)

ELLISON, Matt

(EHL-ih-suhn, MAT) **CHI.**

Right wing. Shoots right. 6', 192 lbs. Born, Duncan, B.C., December 8, 1983. Chicago's 4th choice, 128th overall, in 2002 Entry Draft.

Season	Club	League	GP	G	A	Pts	PIM	PP	SH	GW	S	%	+/-	TF	F%	Min	GP	G	A	Pts	PIM	PP	SH	GW	Min
1997-98	Cowichan Valley	BCAHA	24	27	31	58	10	....	....	....	....	....	....	....	....	....	....	....	....	....	....	....	....	....	....
1998-99	Kerry Park	VIJHL	38	40	47	87	110	....	....	....	....	....	....	....	....	....	....	....	....	....	....	....	....	....	....
99-2000	Cowichan	BCHL	60	11	23	34	95	....	....	....	....	....	....	....	....	....	....	....	....	....	....	....	....	....	....
2000-01	Cowichan	BCHL	60	22	44	66	102	....	....	....	....	....	....	....	....	....	....	....	....	....	....	....	....	....	....
2001-02	Cowichan	BCHL	60	42	*75	*117	76	....	....	....	....	....	....	....	....	....	10	5	6	11	8	....	....	....	....
2002-03	Red Deer Rebels	WHL	72	40	56	96	80	....	....	....	....	....	....	....	....	....	22	7	13	20	28	....	....	....	....

			Regular Season														Playoffs								
Season	Club	League	GP	G	A	Pts	PIM	PP	SH	GW	S	%	+/-	TF	F%	Min	GP	G	A	Pts	PIM	PP	SH	GW	Min
2003-04	**Chicago**	**NHL**	**10**	**0**	**1**	**1**	**0**	**0**	**0**	**0**	**4**	**0.0**	**-3**	**46**	**39.1**	**12:40**	....	....	....	....	....	....	....	....	....
	Norfolk Admirals	AHL	71	14	21	35	115	....	....	....	....	....	....	....	....	....	7	0	1	1	4	....	....	....	....
	NHL Totals		**10**	**0**	**1**	**1**	**0**	**0**	**0**	**0**	**4**	**0.0**		**46**	**39.1**	**12:40**	....	....	....	....	....	....	....	....	....

WHL East Second All-Star Team (2003) • Canadian Major Junior Rookie of the Year (2003)

ELORANTA, Mikko

(ehl-oh-RAN-tuh, MEE-koh)

Left wing. Shoots left. 6', 190 lbs. Born, Turku, Finland, August 24, 1972. Boston's 9th choice, 247th overall, in 1999 Entry Draft.

Season	Club	League	GP	G	A	Pts	PIM	PP	SH	GW	S	%	+/-	TF	F%	Min	GP	G	A	Pts	PIM	PP	SH	GW	Min
1989-90	TPS Turku Jr.	Finn-Jr.	2	0	0	0	0	....	....	....	....	....	....	....	....	....	....	....	....	....	....	....	....	....	....
1990-91	TPS Turku Jr.	Finn-Jr.	35	8	8	16	18	....	....	....	....	....	....	....	....	....	....	....	....	....	....	....	....	....	....
1991-92	TPS Turku Jr.	Finn-Jr.	19	3	1	4	8	....	....	....	....	....	....	....	....	....	8	0	0	0	0	....	....	....	....
1992-93	TPS Turku Jr.	Finn-Jr.	31	11	6	17	20	....	....	....	....	....	....	....	....	....	6	0	4	4	6	....	....	....	....
1993-94	Kiekko-67 Turku	Finland-2	45	3	4	7	24	....	....	....	....	....	....	....	....	....	....	....	....	....	....	....	....	....	....
1994-95	Kiekko-67 Turku	Finland-2	47	18	14	32	52	....	....	....	....	....	....	....	....	....	3	3	0	3	4	....	....	....	....
1995-96	Kiekko-67 Turku	Finland-2	8	6	7	13	2	....	....	....	....	....	....	....	....	....	....	....	....	....	....	....	....	....	....
	Ilves Tampere	Finland	43	18	15	33	86	....	....	....	....	....	....	....	....	....	3	0	2	2	2	....	....	....	....
1996-97	TPS Turku	Finland	31	6	15	21	52	....	....	....	....	....	....	....	....	....	10	5	2	7	6	....	....	....	....
	TPS Turku	EuroHL	6	3	1	4	6	....	....	....	....	....	....	....	....	....	1	0	0	0	0	....	....	....	....
1997-98	TPS Turku	Finland	46	23	14	37	82	....	....	....	....	....	....	....	....	....	2	0	0	0	8	....	....	....	....
	TPS Turku	EuroHL	3	1	0	1	12	....	....	....	....	....	....	....	....	....	....	....	....	....	....	....	....	....	....
1998-99	TPS Turku	Finland	52	19	21	40	103	....	....	....	....	....	....	....	....	....	10	1	6	7	26	....	....	....	....
99-2000	**Boston**	**NHL**	**50**	**6**	**12**	**18**	**36**	**1**	**0**	**0**	**59**	**10.2**	**-10**	**77**	**35.1**	**12:18**	....	....	....	....	....	....	....	....	....
2000-01	**Boston**	**NHL**	**62**	**12**	**11**	**23**	**38**	**1**	**1**	**2**	**89**	**13.5**	**2**	**82**	**23.2**	**10:26**	....	....	....	....	....	....	....	....	....
2001-02	**Boston**	**NHL**	**6**	**0**	**0**	**0**	**2**	**0**	**0**	**0**	**15**	**0.0**	**-1**	**8**	**25.0**	**16:12**	....	....	....	....	....	....	....	....	....
	Los Angeles	**NHL**	**71**	**9**	**9**	**18**	**54**	**1**	**0**	**2**	**121**	**7.4**	**0**	**1**	**100.0**	**11:27**	**7**	**1**	**1**	**2**	**2**	**0**	**0**	**0**	**12:02**
	Finland	Olympics	4	2	0	2	2	....	....	....	....	....	....	....	....	....	....	....	....	....	....	....	....	....	....
2002-03	**Los Angeles**	**NHL**	**75**	**5**	**12**	**17**	**56**	**1**	**0**	**1**	**96**	**5.2**	**-15**	**14**	**42.9**	**12:50**	....	....	....	....	....	....	....	....	....
2003-04	TPS Turku	Finland	54	23	19	42	87	....	....	....	....	....	....	....	....	....	6	0	1	1	39	....	....	....	....
	NHL Totals		**264**	**32**	**44**	**76**	**186**	**4**	**1**	**5**	**380**	**8.4**		**182**	**30.2**	**11:52**	**7**	**1**	**1**	**2**	**2**	**0**	**0**	**0**	**12:02**

Traded to **Los Angeles** by **Boston** with Jason Allison for Jozef Stumpel and Glen Murray, October 24, 2001. Signed as a free agent by **TPS Turku** (Finland), September 3, 2003.

EMINGER, Steve

(EH-mihn-juhr, STEEV) **WSH.**

Defense. Shoots right. 6'2", 203 lbs. Born, Woodbridge, Ont., October 31, 1983. Washington's 1st choice, 12th overall, in 2002 Entry Draft.

Season	Club	League	GP	G	A	Pts	PIM	PP	SH	GW	S	%	+/-	TF	F%	Min	GP	G	A	Pts	PIM	PP	SH	GW	Min
1998-99	Bramalea Blues	OPJHL	47	6	9	15	81	....	....	....	....	....	....	....	....	....	....	....	....	....	....	....	....	....	....
99-2000	Kitchener Rangers	OHL	50	2	14	16	74	....	....	....	....	....	....	....	....	....	5	0	0	0	0	....	....	....	....
2000-01	Kitchener Rangers	OHL	54	6	26	32	66	....	....	....	....	....	....	....	....	....	....	....	....	....	....	....	....	....	....
2001-02	Kitchener Rangers	OHL	64	19	39	58	93	....	....	....	....	....	....	....	....	....	4	0	2	2	10	....	....	....	....
2002-03	**Washington**	**NHL**	**17**	**0**	**2**	**2**	**24**	**0**	**0**	**0**	**6**	**0.0**	**-3**	**0**	**0.0**	**10:08**	....	....	....	....	....	....	....	....	....
	Kitchener Rangers	OHL	23	2	27	29	40	....	....	....	....	....	....	....	....	....	21	3	8	11	44	....	....	....	....
2003-04	**Washington**	**NHL**	**41**	**0**	**4**	**4**	**45**	**0**	**0**	**0**	**12**	**0.0**	**-11**	**0**	**0.0**	**17:32**	....	....	....	....	....	....	....	....	....
	Portland Pirates	AHL	41	0	4	4	40	....	....	....	....	....	....	....	....	....	7	0	1	1	2	....	....	....	....
	NHL Totals		**58**	**0**	**6**	**6**	**69**	**0**	**0**	**0**	**18**	**0.0**		**0**	**0.0**	**15:22**	....	....	....	....	....	....	....	....	....

OHL Second All-Star Team (2002, 2003) • Memorial Cup All-Star Team (2003)

Returned to **Kitchener** (OHL) by **Washington**, January 2, 2003.

ENDICOTT, Shane

(ehn-DIH-kawt, SHAYN) **PIT.**

Center. Shoots left. 6'3", 214 lbs. Born, Saskatoon, Sask., December 21, 1981. Pittsburgh's 2nd choice, 52nd overall, in 2000 Entry Draft.

Season	Club	League	GP	G	A	Pts	PIM	PP	SH	GW	S	%	+/-	TF	F%	Min	GP	G	A	Pts	PIM	PP	SH	GW	Min
1997-98	Sask. Contacts	SMHL	43	31	32	63	42	....	....	....	....	....	....	....	....	....	....	....	....	....	....	....	....	....	....
	Seattle	WHL	....	....	....	....	....	....	....	....	....	....	....	....	....	....	5	0	0	0	0	....	....	....	....
1998-99	Seattle	WHL	72	13	26	39	27	....	....	....	....	....	....	....	....	....	11	0	1	1	0	....	....	....	....
99-2000	Seattle	WHL	70	23	32	55	62	....	....	....	....	....	....	....	....	....	7	1	6	7	6	....	....	....	....
2000-01	Seattle	WHL	72	36	43	79	86	....	....	....	....	....	....	....	....	....	9	4	5	9	12	....	....	....	....
2001-02	**Pittsburgh**	**NHL**	**4**	**0**	**1**	**1**	**4**	**0**	**0**	**0**	**2**	**0.0**	**-1**	**18**	**33.3**	**8:28**	....	....	....	....	....	....	....	....	....
	Wilkes-Barre	AHL	63	19	20	39	46	....	....	....	....	....	....	....	....	....	....	....	....	....	....	....	....	....	....
2002-03	Wilkes-Barre	AHL	74	13	26	39	68	....	....	....	....	....	....	....	....	....	6	0	2	2	4	....	....	....	....
2003-04	Wilkes-Barre	AHL	79	17	22	39	68	....	....	....	....	....	....	....	....	....	24	8	4	12	26	....	....	....	....
	NHL Totals		**4**	**0**	**1**	**1**	**4**	**0**	**0**	**0**	**2**	**0.0**		**18**	**33.3**	**8:28**	....	....	....	....	....	....	....	....	....

ERAT, Martin

(EE-rat, mahr-TIHN) **NSH.**

Left wing. Shoots left. 6', 195 lbs. Born, Trebic, Czech., August 29, 1981. Nashville's 12th choice, 191st overall, in 1999 Entry Draft.

Season	Club	League	GP	G	A	Pts	PIM	PP	SH	GW	S	%	+/-	TF	F%	Min	GP	G	A	Pts	PIM	PP	SH	GW	Min
1997-98	Zlin Jr.	Czech-Jr.	46	35	30	65	....	....	....	....	....	....	....	....	....	....	....	....	....	....	....	....	....	....	....
1998-99	Zlin Jr.	Czech-Jr.	35	21	23	44	....	....	....	....	....	....	....	....	....	....	....	....	....	....	....	....	....	....	....
	Zlin	Czech	5	0	0	0	2	....	....	....	....	....	....	....	....	....	....	....	....	....	....	....	....	....	....
99-2000	Saskatoon Blades	WHL	66	27	26	53	82	....	....	....	....	....	....	....	....	....	11	4	8	12	16	....	....	....	....
2000-01	Saskatoon Blades	WHL	31	19	35	54	48	....	....	....	....	....	....	....	....	....	....	....	....	....	....	....	....	....	....
	Red Deer Rebels	WHL	17	4	24	28	24	....	....	....	....	....	....	....	....	....	22	*15	*21	*36	32	....	....	....	....
2001-02	**Nashville**	**NHL**	**80**	**9**	**24**	**33**	**32**	**2**	**0**	**2**	**84**	**10.7**	**-11**	**3**	**66.7**	**13:10**	....	....	....	....	....	....	....	....	....
2002-03	**Nashville**	**NHL**	**27**	**1**	**7**	**8**	**14**	**1**	**0**	**0**	**39**	**2.6**	**-9**	**1**	**0.0**	**12:47**	....	....	....	....	....	....	....	....	....
	Milwaukee	AHL	45	10	22	32	41	....	....	....	....	....	....	....	....	....	6	5	4	9	4	....	....	....	....
2003-04	**Nashville**	**NHL**	**76**	**16**	**33**	**49**	**38**	**4**	**0**	**2**	**137**	**11.7**	**10**	**31**	**29.0**	**15:00**	**6**	**0**	**1**	**1**	**6**	**0**	**0**	**0**	**14:09**
	NHL Totals		**183**	**26**	**64**	**90**	**84**	**7**	**0**	**4**	**260**	**10.0**		**35**	**31.4**	**13:52**	**6**	**0**	**1**	**1**	**6**	**0**	**0**	**0**	**14:09**

ERIKSSON, Anders

(AIR-ihk-suhn, AND-uhrs)

Defense. Shoots left. 6'2", 220 lbs. Born, Bollnas, Sweden, January 9, 1975. Detroit's 1st choice, 22nd overall, in 1993 Entry Draft.

Season	Club	League	GP	G	A	Pts	PIM	PP	SH	GW	S	%	+/-	TF	F%	Min	GP	G	A	Pts	PIM	PP	SH	GW	Min
1992-93	MoDo Jr.	Swede-Jr.	10	5	3	8	14	....	....	....	....	....	....	....	....	....	....	....	....	....	....	....	....	....	....
	MoDo	Sweden	20	0	2	2	2	....	....	....	....	....	....	....	....	....	1	0	0	0	0	....	....	....	....
1993-94	MoDo Jr.	Swede-Jr.	3	1	2	3	34	....	....	....	....	....	....	....	....	....	....	....	....	....	....	....	....	....	....
	MoDo	Sweden	38	2	8	10	42	....	....	....	....	....	....	....	....	....	11	0	0	0	8	....	....	....	....
1994-95	MoDo	Sweden	39	3	6	9	54	....	....	....	....	....	....	....	....	....	....	....	....	....	....	....	....	....	....
1995-96	**Detroit**	**NHL**	**1**	**0**	**0**	**0**	**2**	**0**	**0**	**0**	**0**	**0.0**	**1**	....	....	....	**3**	**0**	**0**	**0**	**0**	**0**	**0**	**0**	....
	Adirondack	AHL	75	6	36	42	64	....	....	....	....	....	....	....	....	....	3	0	0	0	0	....	....	....	....
1996-97	**Detroit**	**NHL**	**23**	**0**	**6**	**6**	**10**	**0**	**0**	**0**	**27**	**0.0**	**5**	....	....	....	....	....	....	....	....	....	....	....	....
	Adirondack	AHL	44	3	25	28	36	....	....	....	....	....	....	....	....	....	4	0	1	1	4	....	....	....	....
1997-98♦	**Detroit**	**NHL**	**66**	**7**	**14**	**21**	**32**	**1**	**0**	**2**	**91**	**7.7**	**21**	....	....	....	**18**	**0**	**5**	**5**	**16**	**0**	**0**	**0**	....
1998-99	**Detroit**	**NHL**	**61**	**2**	**10**	**12**	**34**	**0**	**0**	**1**	**67**	**3.0**	**5**	**0**	**0.0**	**15:54**	....	....	....	....	....	....	....	....	....
	Chicago	**NHL**	**11**	**0**	**8**	**8**	**0**	**0**	**0**	**0**	**12**	**0.0**	**6**	**0**	**0.0**	**22:51**	....	....	....	....	....	....	....	....	....
99-2000	**Chicago**	**NHL**	**73**	**3**	**25**	**28**	**20**	**0**	**0**	**1**	**86**	**3.5**	**4**	**1**	**100.0**	**21:03**	....	....	....	....	....	....	....	....	....
2000-01	**Chicago**	**NHL**	**13**	**2**	**3**	**5**	**2**	**1**	**0**	**0**	**19**	**10.5**	**-4**	**0**	**0.0**	**21:20**	....	....	....	....	....	....	....	....	....
	Florida	**NHL**	**60**	**0**	**21**	**21**	**28**	**0**	**0**	**0**	**80**	**0.0**	**2**	**1**	**0.0**	**21:02**	....	....	....	....	....	....	....	....	....
2001-02	**Toronto**	**NHL**	**34**	**0**	**2**	**2**	**12**	**0**	**0**	**0**	**31**	**0.0**	**-1**	**0**	**0.0**	**15:55**	**10**	**0**	**0**	**0**	**0**	**0**	**0**	**0**	**17:24**
	St. John's	AHL	25	4	6	10	14	....	....	....	....	....	....	....	....	....	11	0	5	5	6	....	....	....	....
2002-03	**Toronto**	**NHL**	**4**	**0**	**0**	**0**	**0**	**0**	**0**	**0**	**7**	**0.0**	**1**	**0**	**0.0**	**19:02**	....	....	....	....	....	....	....	....	....
	St. John's	AHL	72	5	34	39	133	....	....	....	....	....	....	....	....	....	....	....	....	....	....	....	....	....	....
2003-04	**Columbus**	**NHL**	**66**	**7**	**20**	**27**	**18**	**2**	**0**	**1**	**84**	**8.3**	**-6**	**0**	**0.0**	**20:42**	....	....	....	....	....	....	....	....	....
	Syracuse Crunch	AHL	9	1	3	4	12	....	....	....	....	....	....	....	....	....	....	....	....	....	....	....	....	....	....
	NHL Totals		**412**	**21**	**109**	**130**	**158**	**4**	**0**	**5**	**504**	**4.2**		**2**	**50.0**	**19:30**	**31**	**0**	**5**	**5**	**16**	**0**	**0**	**0**	**17:24**

Traded to **Chicago** by **Detroit** with Detroit's 1st round choices in 1999 (Steve McCarthy) and 2001 (Adam Munro) Entry Drafts for Chris Chelios, March 23, 1999. Traded to **Florida** by **Chicago** for Jaroslav Spacek, November 6, 2000. Signed as a free agent by **Toronto**, July 9, 2001. Signed as a free agent by **Columbus**, October 10, 2003.

ERSKINE, John

(AIR-skign, JAWN) **DAL.**

Defense. Shoots left. 6'4", 215 lbs. Born, Kingston, Ont., June 26, 1980. Dallas' 1st choice, 39th overall, in 1998 Entry Draft.

Season	Club	League	Regular Season GP	G	A	Pts	PIM	PP	SH	GW	S	%	+/-	TF	F%	Min	Playoffs GP	G	A	Pts	PIM	PP	SH	GW	Min
1996-97	Quinte Hawks	MTJHL	48	4	16	20	241	....	....	....	....	....	....	....	....	....	....	....	....	....	....	....	....	....	....
1997-98	London Knights	OHL	55	0	9	9	205	....	....	....	....	....	....	....	....	....	16	0	5	5	25	....	....	....	....
1998-99	London Knights	OHL	57	8	12	20	208	....	....	....	....	....	....	....	....	....	25	5	10	15	38	....	....	....	....
99-2000	London Knights	OHL	58	12	31	43	177	....	....	....	....	....	....	....	....	....	....	....	....	....	....	....	....	....	....
2000-01	Utah Grizzlies	IHL	77	1	8	9	284	....	....	....	....	....	....	....	....	....	....	....	....	....	....	....	....	....	....
2001-02	**Dallas**	**NHL**	**33**	**0**	**1**	**1**	**62**	**0**	**0**	**0**	**16**	**0.0**	**–8**	**0**	**0.0**	**10:44**	....	....	....	....	....	....	....	....	....
	Utah Grizzlies	AHL	39	2	6	8	118	....	....	....	....	....	....	....	....	....	3	0	0	0	10	....	....	....	....
2002-03	Utah Grizzlies	AHL	52	2	8	10	274	....	....	....	....	....	....	....	....	....	1	0	1	1	15	....	....	....	....
	Dallas	**NHL**	**16**	**2**	**0**	**2**	**29**	**0**	**0**	**0**	**12**	**16.7**	**1**	**0**	**0.0**	**10:45**	....	....	....	....	....	....	....	....	....
2003-04	**Dallas**	**NHL**	**32**	**0**	**1**	**1**	**84**	**0**	**0**	**0**	**23**	**0.0**	**–9**	**0**	**0.0**	**12:36**	....	....	....	....	....	....	....	....	....
	Utah Grizzlies	AHL	5	0	0	0	18	....	....	....	....	....	....	....	....	....	....	....	....	....	....	....	....	....	....
	NHL Totals		**81**	**2**	**2**	**4**	**175**	**0**	**0**	**0**	**51**	**3.9**		**0**	**0.0**	**11:29**	....	....	....	....	....	....	....	....	....

OHL First All-Star Team (2000)

• Missed majority of 2003-04 season recovering from ankle (December 27, 2003 vs. Columbus) and hernia (January 24, 2004 vs. St. Louis) injuries.

EVANS, Brennan

(EH-vans, BREHN-nan) **CGY.**

Defense. Shoots left. 6'3", 205 lbs. Born, North Battleford, Sask., January 6, 1982.

Season	Club	League	Regular Season GP	G	A	Pts	PIM	PP	SH	GW	S	%	+/-	TF	F%	Min	Playoffs GP	G	A	Pts	PIM	PP	SH	GW	Min
1996-97	Camrose Bulldogs	SBHL	STATISTICS NOT AVAILABLE																						
1997-98	Leduc Oil Kings	AJHL	STATISTICS NOT AVAILABLE																						
1998-99	Camrose Kodiaks	AJHL	47	1	6	7	98	....	....	....	....	....	....	....	....	....	5	0	2	2	0	....	....	....	....
	Seattle	WHL	....	....	....	....	....	....	....	....	....	....	....	....	....	....	1	0	0	0	0	....	....	....	....
99-2000	Seattle	WHL	52	1	2	3	40	....	....	....	....	....	....	....	....	....	1	0	0	0	0	....	....	....	....
2000-01	Seattle	WHL	11	1	0	1	25	....	....	....	....	....	....	....	....	....	....	....	....	....	....	....	....	....	....
	Kootenay Ice	WHL	55	2	7	9	105	....	....	....	....	....	....	....	....	....	11	0	0	0	25	....	....	....	....
2001-02	Kootenay Ice	WHL	72	2	3	5	121	....	....	....	....	....	....	....	....	....	22	0	6	6	38	....	....	....	....
2002-03	Kootenay Ice	WHL	67	6	17	23	182	....	....	....	....	....	....	....	....	....	11	1	1	2	24	....	....	....	....
2003-04	**Calgary**	**NHL**	....	....	....	....	....	....	....	....	....	....	....	....	....	....	**2**	**0**	**0**	**0**	**0**	**0**	**0**	**0**	**2:52**
	Lowell	AHL	64	1	9	10	65	....	....	....	....	....	....	....	....	....	....	....	....	....	....	....	....	....	....
	NHL Totals		....	....	....	....	....	....	....	....	....	....	....	....	....	....	**2**	**0**	**0**	**0**	**0**	**0**	**0**	**0**	**2:52**

Signed as a free agent by **Calgary**, September 30, 2003.

EXELBY, Garnet

(EHX-uhl-bee, GAHR-neht) **ATL.**

Defense. Shoots left. 6'1", 215 lbs. Born, Ste. Anne, Man., August 16, 1981. Atlanta's 9th choice, 217th overall, in 1999 Entry Draft.

Season	Club	League	Regular Season GP	G	A	Pts	PIM	PP	SH	GW	S	%	+/-	TF	F%	Min	Playoffs GP	G	A	Pts	PIM	PP	SH	GW	Min
1997-98	Winnipeg South	MJHL	46	5	11	16	110	....	....	....	....	....	....	....	....	....	....	....	....	....	....	....	....	....	....
1998-99	Saskatoon Blades	WHL	61	5	3	8	91	....	....	....	....	....	....	....	....	....	....	....	....	....	....	....	....	....	....
99-2000	Saskatoon Blades	WHL	63	1	8	9	79	....	....	....	....	....	....	....	....	....	11	0	2	2	21	....	....	....	....
2000-01	Saskatoon Blades	WHL	43	5	10	15	110	....	....	....	....	....	....	....	....	....	....	....	....	....	....	....	....	....	....
	Regina Pats	WHL	22	2	8	10	51	....	....	....	....	....	....	....	....	....	6	0	2	2	2	....	....	....	....
2001-02	Chicago Wolves	AHL	75	3	4	7	257	....	....	....	....	....	....	....	....	....	25	0	4	4	49	....	....	....	....
2002-03	**Atlanta**	**NHL**	**15**	**0**	**2**	**2**	**41**	**0**	**0**	**0**	**9**	**0.0**	**0**	**0**	**0.0**	**18:04**	....	....	....	....	....	....	....	....	....
	Chicago Wolves	AHL	53	3	6	9	140	....	....	....	....	....	....	....	....	....	9	0	1	1	27	....	....	....	....
2003-04	**Atlanta**	**NHL**	**71**	**1**	**9**	**10**	**134**	**0**	**0**	**0**	**42**	**2.4**	**–10**	**0**	**0.0**	**19:32**	....	....	....	....	....	....	....	....	....
	NHL Totals		**86**	**1**	**11**	**12**	**175**	**0**	**0**	**0**	**51**	**2.0**		**0**	**0.0**	**19:17**	....	....	....	....	....	....	....	....	....

FAHEY, Jim

(FA-hee, JIHM) **S.J.**

Defense. Shoots right. 6', 205 lbs. Born, Boston, MA, May 11, 1979. San Jose's 9th choice, 212th overall, in 1998 Entry Draft.

Season	Club	League	Regular Season GP	G	A	Pts	PIM	PP	SH	GW	S	%	+/-	TF	F%	Min	Playoffs GP	G	A	Pts	PIM	PP	SH	GW	Min
1997-98	Catholic Memorial	Hi-School	24	12	32	44	28	....	....	....	....	....	....	....	....	....	....	....	....	....	....	....	....	....	....
1998-99	Northeastern	H-East	32	5	13	18	34	....	....	....	....	....	....	....	....	....	....	....	....	....	....	....	....	....	....
99-2000	Northeastern	H-East	36	3	17	20	62	....	....	....	....	....	....	....	....	....	....	....	....	....	....	....	....	....	....
2000-01	Northeastern	H-East	36	4	23	27	48	....	....	....	....	....	....	....	....	....	....	....	....	....	....	....	....	....	....
2001-02	Northeastern	H-East	39	14	32	46	50	....	....	....	....	....	....	....	....	....	....	....	....	....	....	....	....	....	....
2002-03	**San Jose**	**NHL**	**43**	**1**	**19**	**20**	**33**	**0**	**0**	**0**	**66**	**1.5**	**–3**	**1**	**100.0**	**18:20**	....	....	....	....	....	....	....	....	....
	Cleveland Barons	AHL	25	3	14	17	42	....	....	....	....	....	....	....	....	....	....	....	....	....	....	....	....	....	....
2003-04	**San Jose**	**NHL**	**15**	**0**	**2**	**2**	**18**	**0**	**0**	**0**	**19**	**0.0**	**–2**	**0**	**0.0**	**16:54**	**2**	**0**	**0**	**0**	**0**	**0**	**0**	**0**	**4:41**
	Cleveland Barons	AHL	32	1	18	19	64	....	....	....	....	....	....	....	....	....	....	....	....	....	....	....	....	....	....
	NHL Totals		**58**	**1**	**21**	**22**	**51**	**0**	**0**	**0**	**85**	**1.2**		**1**	**100.0**	**17:58**	**2**	**0**	**0**	**0**	**0**	**0**	**0**	**0**	**4:41**

Hockey East Second All-Star Team (2001) • Hockey East First All-Star Team (2002)

FARRELL, Mike

(FAIR-uhl, MIGHK)

Right wing. Shoots right. 6', 222 lbs. Born, Edina, MN, October 20, 1978. Washington's 9th choice, 220th overall, in 1998 Entry Draft.

Season	Club	League	Regular Season GP	G	A	Pts	PIM	PP	SH	GW	S	%	+/-	TF	F%	Min	Playoffs GP	G	A	Pts	PIM	PP	SH	GW	Min
1996-97	Culver Eagles	Hi-School	STATISTICS NOT AVAILABLE																						
1997-98	Providence	H-East	33	5	8	13	32	....	....	....	....	....	....	....	....	....	....	....	....	....	....	....	....	....	....
1998-99	Providence	H-East	29	3	12	15	51	....	....	....	....	....	....	....	....	....	....	....	....	....	....	....	....	....	....
99-2000	Providence	H-East	36	3	6	9	71	....	....	....	....	....	....	....	....	....	....	....	....	....	....	....	....	....	....
	Portland Pirates	AHL	7	2	0	2	0	....	....	....	....	....	....	....	....	....	4	0	1	1	0	....	....	....	....
2000-01	Portland Pirates	AHL	79	6	18	24	61	....	....	....	....	....	....	....	....	....	3	0	2	2	2	....	....	....	....
2001-02	**Washington**	**NHL**	**8**	**0**	**0**	**0**	**0**	**0**	**0**	**0**	**1**	**0.0**	**–1**	**0**	**0.0**	**5:35**	....	....	....	....	....	....	....	....	....
	Portland Pirates	AHL	61	12	15	27	62	....	....	....	....	....	....	....	....	....	....	....	....	....	....	....	....	....	....
2002-03	**Washington**	**NHL**	**4**	**0**	**0**	**0**	**2**	**0**	**0**	**0**	**2**	**0.0**	**1**	**0**	**0.0**	**2:48**	....	....	....	....	....	....	....	....	....
	Portland Pirates	AHL	68	12	12	24	107	....	....	....	....	....	....	....	....	....	3	0	1	1	0	....	....	....	....
2003-04	**Nashville**	**NHL**	**1**	**0**	**0**	**0**	**0**	**0**	**0**	**0**	**0**	**0.0**	**0**	**0**	**0.0**	**5:08**	....	....	....	....	....	....	....	....	....
	Milwaukee	AHL	49	10	8	18	66	....	....	....	....	....	....	....	....	....	19	1	1	2	13	....	....	....	....
	NHL Totals		**13**	**0**	**0**	**0**	**2**	**0**	**0**	**0**	**3**	**0.0**		**0**	**0.0**	**4:42**	....	....	....	....	....	....	....	....	....

Traded to **Nashville** by **Washington** for Alexander Riazantsev, July 14, 2003.

FAST, Brad

(FAST, BRAD) **CAR.**

Defense. Shoots left. 6', 185 lbs. Born, Fort St. John, B.C., February 21, 1980. Carolina's 2nd choice, 84th overall, in 1999 Entry Draft.

Season	Club	League	Regular Season GP	G	A	Pts	PIM	PP	SH	GW	S	%	+/-	TF	F%	Min	Playoffs GP	G	A	Pts	PIM	PP	SH	GW	Min
1994-95	Fort St. John	BCAHA	40	9	26	35	40	....	....	....	....	....	....	....	....	....	....	....	....	....	....	....	....	....	....
1995-96	Fort St. John	BCAHA	60	53	52	105	70	....	....	....	....	....	....	....	....	....	....	....	....	....	....	....	....	....	....
1996-97	Prince George	BCHL	49	3	7	10	19	....	....	....	....	....	....	....	....	....	....	....	....	....	....	....	....	....	....
1997-98	Prince George	BCHL	59	10	33	43	22	....	....	....	....	....	....	....	....	....	....	....	....	....	....	....	....	....	....
1998-99	Prince George	BCHL	59	27	46	73	....	....	....	....	....	....	....	....	....	....	....	....	....	....	....	....	....	....	....
99-2000	Michigan State	CCHA	42	5	9	14	20	....	....	....	....	....	....	....	....	....	....	....	....	....	....	....	....	....	....
2000-01	Michigan State	CCHA	42	4	24	28	16	....	....	....	....	....	....	....	....	....	....	....	....	....	....	....	....	....	....
2001-02	Michigan State	CCHA	41	10	16	26	26	....	....	....	....	....	....	....	....	....	....	....	....	....	....	....	....	....	....
2002-03	Michigan State	CCHA	39	11	35	46	28	....	....	....	....	....	....	....	....	....	....	....	....	....	....	....	....	....	....
	Lowell	AHL	7	0	1	1	12	....	....	....	....	....	....	....	....	....	....	....	....	....	....	....	....	....	....
2003-04	**Carolina**	**NHL**	**1**	**1**	**0**	**1**	**0**	**0**	**0**	**0**	**4**	**25.0**	**1**	**0**	**0.0**	**21:24**	....	....	....	....	....	....	....	....	....
	Lowell	AHL	79	10	25	35	35	....	....	....	....	....	....	....	....	....	....	....	....	....	....	....	....	....	....
	NHL Totals		**1**	**1**	**0**	**1**	**0**	**0**	**0**	**0**	**4**	**25.0**		**0**	**0.0**	**21:24**	....	....	....	....	....	....	....	....	....

CCHA First All-Star Team (2003) • NCAA West Second All-American Team (2003)

• One of only three players (Rolly Huard, Dean Morton) to score a goal in his only NHL game.

			Regular Season														Playoffs								
Season	Club	League	GP	G	A	Pts	PIM	PP	SH	GW	S	%	+/-	TF	F%	Min	GP	G	A	Pts	PIM	PP	SH	GW	Min

FATA, Rico

(FA-tuh, REE-koh) **PIT.**

Right wing. Shoots left. 6', 205 lbs. Born, Sault Ste. Marie, Ont., February 12, 1980. Calgary's 1st choice, 6th overall, in 1998 Entry Draft.

Season	Club	League	GP	G	A	Pts	PIM	PP	SH	GW	S	%	+/-	TF	F%	Min	GP	G	A	Pts	PIM	PP	SH	GW	Min
1994-95	Soo Legion	NOHA	51	52	51	103	....	....	....	....	....	....	....	....	....	....	....	....	....	....	....	....	....	....	....
1995-96	Sault Ste. Marie	OHL	62	11	15	26	52	....	....	....	....	....	....	....	....	....	4	0	0	0	0	....	....	....	....
1996-97	London Knights	OHL	59	19	34	53	76	....	....	....	....	....	....	....	....	....	....	....	....	....	....	....	....	....	....
1997-98	London Knights	OHL	64	43	33	76	110	....	....	....	....	....	....	....	....	....	16	9	5	14	*49	....	....	....	....
1998-99	**Calgary**	**NHL**	**20**	**0**	**1**	**1**	**4**	**0**	**0**	**0**	**13**	**0.0**	**0**	**2**	**50.0**	**7:36**	....	....	....	....	....	....	....	....	....
	London Knights	OHL	23	15	18	33	41	....	....	....	....	....	....	....	....	....	25	10	12	22	42	....	....	....	....
99-2000	**Calgary**	**NHL**	**2**	**0**	**0**	**0**	**0**	**0**	**0**	**0**	**0**	**0.0**	**–1**	**0**	**0.0**	**10:06**	....	....	....	....	....	....	....	....	....
	Saint John Flames	AHL	76	29	29	58	65	....	....	....	....	....	....	....	....	....	3	0	0	0	4	....	....	....	....
2000-01	**Calgary**	**NHL**	**5**	**0**	**0**	**0**	**6**	**0**	**0**	**0**	**6**	**0.0**	**–3**	**0**	**0.0**	**9:25**	....	....	....	....	....	....	....	....	....
	Saint John Flames	AHL	70	23	29	52	129	....	....	....	....	....	....	....	....	....	19	2	3	5	22	....	....	....	....
2001-02	**NY Rangers**	**NHL**	**10**	**0**	**0**	**0**	**0**	**0**	**0**	**0**	**8**	**0.0**	**–2**	**55**	**47.3**	**8:31**	....	....	....	....	....	....	....	....	....
	Hartford	AHL	61	35	36	71	36	....	....	....	....	....	....	....	....	....	10	2	5	7	4	....	....	....	....
2002-03	**NY Rangers**	**NHL**	**36**	**2**	**4**	**6**	**6**	**0**	**0**	**0**	**30**	**6.7**	**–1**	**30**	**50.0**	**7:16**	....	....	....	....	....	....	....	....	....
	Hartford	AHL	9	8	6	14	6	....	....	....	....	....	....	....	....	....	....	....	....	....	....	....	....	....	....
	Pittsburgh	**NHL**	**27**	**5**	**8**	**13**	**10**	**0**	**0**	**0**	**49**	**10.2**	**–6**	**87**	**49.4**	**17:46**	....	....	....	....	....	....	....	....	....
2003-04	**Pittsburgh**	**NHL**	**73**	**16**	**18**	**34**	**54**	**6**	**2**	**1**	**163**	**9.8**	**–46**	**1205**	**47.1**	**17:58**	....	....	....	....	....	....	....	....	....
	NHL Totals		**173**	**23**	**31**	**54**	**80**	**6**	**2**	**1**	**269**	**8.6**		**1379**	**47.4**	**13:38**	....	....	....	....	....	....	....	....	....

AHL Second All-Star Team (2002)

• Returned to **London** (OHL) by **Calgary** following WJC-A tournament, January 10, 1999. Claimed on waivers by **NY Rangers** from **Calgary**, October 3, 2001. Traded to **Pittsburgh** by **NY Rangers** with Joel Bouchard, Richard Lintner, Mikael Samuelsson and future considerations for Mike Wilson, Alex Kovalev, Janne Laukkanen and Dan LaCouture, February 10, 2003.

FEDOROV, Fedor

(FEH-duh-rahf, feh-DUHR) **VAN.**

Center. Shoots left. 6'3", 230 lbs. Born, Appatity, USSR, June 11, 1981. Vancouver's 2nd choice, 66th overall, in 2001 Entry Draft.

Season	Club	League	GP	G	A	Pts	PIM	PP	SH	GW	S	%	+/-	TF	F%	Min	GP	G	A	Pts	PIM	PP	SH	GW	Min
1997-98	Det. Caesars	MNHL	13	3	7	10	18	....	....	....	....	....	....	....	....	....	....	....	....	....	....	....	....	....	....
1998-99	Port Huron	UHL	42	2	5	7	20	....	....	....	....	....	....	....	....	....	....	....	....	....	....	....	....	....	....
99-2000	Windsor Spitfires	OHL	60	7	10	17	115	....	....	....	....	....	....	....	....	....	12	1	0	1	4	....	....	....	....
2000-01	Sudbury Wolves	OHL	67	33	45	78	88	....	....	....	....	....	....	....	....	....	12	4	6	10	36	....	....	....	....
2001-02	Manitoba Moose	AHL	8	2	1	3	6	....	....	....	....	....	....	....	....	....	....	....	....	....	....	....	....	....	....
	Columbia Inferno	ECHL	2	0	2	2	0	....	....	....	....	....	....	....	....	....	....	....	....	....	....	....	....	....	....
2002-03	**Vancouver**	**NHL**	**7**	**0**	**1**	**1**	**4**	**0**	**0**	**0**	**2**	**0.0**	**0**	**26**	**46.2**	**9:10**	....	....	....	....	....	....	....	....	....
	Manitoba Moose	AHL	50	10	13	23	61	....	....	....	....	....	....	....	....	....	3	1	2	3	0	....	....	....	....
2003-04	**Vancouver**	**NHL**	**8**	**0**	**1**	**1**	**4**	**0**	**0**	**0**	**10**	**0.0**	**0**	**4**	**50.0**	**10:59**	....	....	....	....	....	....	....	....	....
	Manitoba Moose	AHL	58	23	16	39	52	....	....	....	....	....	....	....	....	....	....	....	....	....	....	....	....	....	....
	NHL Totals		**15**	**0**	**2**	**2**	**8**	**0**	**0**	**0**	**12**	**0.0**		**30**	**46.7**	**10:08**	....	....	....	....	....	....	....	....	....

• Re-entered NHL Entry Draft. Originally Tampa Bay's 7th choice, 182nd overall, in 1999 Entry Draft.

Signed as an underage free agent by **Detroit** (IHL), August 5, 1998. Released by **Detroit** (IHL), September 30, 1998. Signed as an underage free agent by **Port Huron** (UHL), October 1, 1998. • Missed majority of 2001-02 season recovering from eye injury suffered in game vs. Macon (ECHL), November 17, 2001.

FEDOROV, Sergei

(FEH-duh-rahf, SAIR-gay) **ANA.**

Center. Shoots left. 6'2", 205 lbs. Born, Pskov, USSR, December 13, 1969. Detroit's 4th choice, 74th overall, in 1989 Entry Draft.

Season	Club	League	GP	G	A	Pts	PIM	PP	SH	GW	S	%	+/-	TF	F%	Min	GP	G	A	Pts	PIM	PP	SH	GW	Min
1985-86	Dynamo Minsk	USSR-2	15	6	1	7	10	....	....	....	....	....	....	....	....	....	....	....	....	....	....	....	....	....	....
1986-87	CSKA Moscow	USSR	29	6	6	12	12	....	....	....	....	....	....	....	....	....	....	....	....	....	....	....	....	....	....
1987-88	CSKA Moscow	USSR	48	7	9	16	20	....	....	....	....	....	....	....	....	....	....	....	....	....	....	....	....	....	....
1988-89	CSKA Moscow	USSR	44	9	8	17	35	....	....	....	....	....	....	....	....	....	....	....	....	....	....	....	....	....	....
1989-90	CSKA Moscow	USSR	48	19	10	29	22	....	....	....	....	....	....	....	....	....	....	....	....	....	....	....	....	....	....
1990-91	**Detroit**	**NHL**	**77**	**31**	**48**	**79**	**66**	**11**	**3**	**5**	**259**	**12.0**	**11**	....	....	....	**7**	**1**	**5**	**6**	**4**	**0**	**0**	**1**	....
1991-92	**Detroit**	**NHL**	**80**	**32**	**54**	**86**	**72**	**7**	**2**	**5**	**249**	**12.9**	**26**	....	....	....	**11**	**5**	**5**	**10**	**8**	**1**	**2**	**1**	....
1992-93	**Detroit**	**NHL**	**73**	**34**	**53**	**87**	**72**	**13**	**4**	**3**	**217**	**15.7**	**33**	....	....	....	**7**	**3**	**6**	**9**	**23**	**1**	**1**	**0**	....
1993-94	**Detroit**	**NHL**	**82**	**56**	**64**	**120**	**34**	**13**	**4**	**10**	**337**	**16.6**	**48**	....	....	....	**7**	**1**	**7**	**8**	**6**	**0**	**0**	**0**	....
1994-95	**Detroit**	**NHL**	**42**	**20**	**30**	**50**	**24**	**7**	**3**	**5**	**147**	**13.6**	**6**	....	....	....	**17**	**7**	***17**	***24**	**6**	**3**	**0**	**0**	....
1995-96	**Detroit**	**NHL**	**78**	**39**	**68**	**107**	**48**	**11**	**3**	**11**	**306**	**12.7**	**49**	....	....	....	**19**	**2**	***18**	**20**	**10**	**0**	**0**	**2**	....
1996-97♦	**Detroit**	**NHL**	**74**	**30**	**33**	**63**	**30**	**9**	**2**	**4**	**273**	**11.0**	**29**	....	....	....	**20**	**8**	**12**	**20**	**12**	**3**	**0**	**4**	....
1997-98	Russia	Olympics	6	1	5	6	8	....	....	....	....	....	....	....	....	....	....	....	....	....	....	....	....	....	....
	♦ Detroit	**NHL**	**21**	**6**	**11**	**17**	**25**	**2**	**0**	**2**	**68**	**8.8**	**10**	....	....	....	**22**	***10**	**10**	**20**	**12**	**2**	**1**	**1**	....
1998-99	**Detroit**	**NHL**	**77**	**26**	**37**	**63**	**66**	**6**	**2**	**3**	**224**	**11.6**	**9**	**1414**	**51.7**	**19:21**	**10**	**1**	**8**	**9**	**8**	**0**	**0**	**0**	**19:54**
99-2000	**Detroit**	**NHL**	**68**	**27**	**35**	**62**	**22**	**4**	**4**	**7**	**263**	**10.3**	**8**	**1274**	**53.8**	**20:05**	**9**	**4**	**4**	**8**	**4**	**2**	**0**	**1**	**20:48**
2000-01	**Detroit**	**NHL**	**75**	**32**	**37**	**69**	**40**	**14**	**2**	**7**	**268**	**11.9**	**12**	**1601**	**55.8**	**21:05**	**6**	**2**	**5**	**7**	**0**	**1**	**0**	**1**	**22:19**
2001-02♦	**Detroit**	**NHL**	**81**	**31**	**37**	**68**	**36**	**10**	**0**	**6**	**256**	**12.1**	**20**	**1160**	**51.7**	**19:33**	**23**	**5**	**14**	**19**	**20**	**2**	**1**	**0**	**22:20**
	Russia	Olympics	6	2	2	4	4	....	....	....	....	....	....	....	....	....	....	....	....	....	....	....	....	....	....
2002-03	**Detroit**	**NHL**	**80**	**36**	**47**	**83**	**52**	**10**	**2**	**11**	**281**	**12.8**	**15**	**1580**	**53.4**	**21:11**	**4**	**1**	**2**	**3**	**0**	**0**	**0**	**0**	**22:07**
2003-04	**Anaheim**	**NHL**	**80**	**31**	**34**	**65**	**42**	**9**	**2**	**6**	**268**	**11.6**	**–5**	**1558**	**56.6**	**21:05**	....	....	....	....	....	....	....	....	....
	NHL Totals		**988**	**431**	**588**	**1019**	**629**	**126**	**33**	**85**	**3416**	**12.6**		**8587**	**54.0**	**20:24**	**162**	**50**	**113**	**163**	**113**	**15**	**5**	**11**	**21:35**

NHL All-Rookie Team (1991) • NHL First All-Star Team (1994) • Frank J. Selke Trophy (1994, 1996) • Lester B. Pearson Award (1994) • Hart Trophy (1994)

Played in NHL All-Star Game (1992, 1994, 1996, 2001, 2002, 2003)

• Missed majority of 1997-98 season after failing to come to contract terms with **Detroit**. Signed as a free agent by **Anaheim**, July 19, 2003.

FEDORUK, Todd

(FEH-duh-ruhk, TAWD) **PHI.**

Left wing. Shoots left. 6'2", 235 lbs. Born, Redwater, Alta., February 13, 1979. Philadelphia's 6th choice, 164th overall, in 1997 Entry Draft.

Season	Club	League	GP	G	A	Pts	PIM	PP	SH	GW	S	%	+/-	TF	F%	Min	GP	G	A	Pts	PIM	PP	SH	GW	Min
1994-95	Ft. Saskatchewan	AMHL	STATISTICS NOT AVAILABLE																						
1995-96	Kelowna Rockets	WHL	44	1	1	2	83	....	....	....	....	....	....	....	....	....	4	0	0	0	6	....	....	....	....
1996-97	Kelowna Rockets	WHL	31	1	5	6	87	....	....	....	....	....	....	....	....	....	6	0	0	0	13	....	....	....	....
1997-98	Kelowna Rockets	WHL	31	3	5	8	120	....	....	....	....	....	....	....	....	....	....	....	....	....	....	....	....	....	....
	Regina Pats	WHL	21	4	3	7	80	....	....	....	....	....	....	....	....	....	9	1	2	3	23	....	....	....	....
1998-99	Regina Pats	WHL	39	12	12	24	107	....	....	....	....	....	....	....	....	....	....	....	....	....	....	....	....	....	....
	Prince Albert	WHL	28	6	4	10	75	....	....	....	....	....	....	....	....	....	13	1	6	7	49	....	....	....	....
99-2000	Trenton Titans	ECHL	18	2	5	7	118	....	....	....	....	....	....	....	....	....	....	....	....	....	....	....	....	....	....
	Philadelphia	AHL	19	1	2	3	40	....	....	....	....	....	....	....	....	....	5	0	1	1	2	....	....	....	....
2000-01	**Philadelphia**	**NHL**	**53**	**5**	**5**	**10**	**109**	**0**	**0**	**0**	**28**	**17.9**	**0**	**0**	**0.0**	**7:02**	**2**	**0**	**0**	**0**	**20**	**0**	**0**	**0**	**5:57**
	Philadelphia	AHL	14	0	1	1	49	....	....	....	....	....	....	....	....	....	....	....	....	....	....	....	....	....	....
2001-02	**Philadelphia**	**NHL**	**55**	**3**	**4**	**7**	**141**	**0**	**0**	**0**	**21**	**14.3**	**–2**	**5**	**0.0**	**6:21**	**3**	**0**	**0**	**0**	**0**	**0**	**0**	**0**	**2:46**
	Philadelphia	AHL	7	0	1	1	54	....	....	....	....	....	....	....	....	....	....	....	....	....	....	....	....	....	....
2002-03	**Philadelphia**	**NHL**	**63**	**1**	**5**	**6**	**105**	**0**	**0**	**0**	**33**	**3.0**	**1**	**1**	**0.0**	**6:30**	**1**	**0**	**0**	**0**	**0**	**0**	**0**	**0**	**4:52**
2003-04	**Philadelphia**	**NHL**	**49**	**1**	**4**	**5**	**136**	**0**	**0**	**1**	**33**	**3.0**	**–4**	**0**	**0.0**	**6:47**	**1**	**0**	**0**	**0**	**2**	**0**	**0**	**0**	**6:42**
	Philadelphia	AHL	2	0	2	2	2	....	....	....	....	....	....	....	....	....	....	....	....	....	....	....	....	....	....
	NHL Totals		**220**	**10**	**18**	**28**	**491**	**0**	**0**	**1**	**115**	**8.7**		**6**	**0.0**	**6:39**	**7**	**0**	**0**	**0**	**22**	**0**	**0**	**0**	**4:32**

FEDOTENKO, Ruslan

(feh-doh-TEHN-koh, roos-LAHN) **T.B.**

Left wing. Shoots left. 6'2", 195 lbs. Born, Kiev, Ukraine, January 18, 1979.

Season	Club	League	GP	G	A	Pts	PIM	PP	SH	GW	S	%	+/-	TF	F%	Min	GP	G	A	Pts	PIM	PP	SH	GW	Min
1995-96	SHVSM Kiev	EEHL	33	9	11	20	12	....	....	....	....	....	....	....	....	....	....	....	....	....	....	....	....	....	....
	Sokol Kiev	Russia-2	2	0	0	0	0	....	....	....	....	....	....	....	....	....	....	....	....	....	....	....	....	....	....
1996-97	TPS Turku B	Finn-Jr.	3	3	2	5	2	....	....	....	....	....	....	....	....	....	....	....	....	....	....	....	....	....	....
	TPS Turku Jr.	Finn-Jr.	11	1	1	2	2	....	....	....	....	....	....	....	....	....	....	....	....	....	....	....	....	....	....
	Kiekko-67	Finland-2	22	4	3	7	16	....	....	....	....	....	....	....	....	....	....	....	....	....	....	....	....	....	....
	Kiekko Turku	Finland-3	....	....	....	....	....	....	....	....	....	....	....	....	....	....	3	1	0	1	2	....	....	....	....
1997-98	Melfort Mustangs	SJHL	68	35	31	66	55	....	....	....	....	....	....	....	....	....	....	....	....	....	....	....	....	....	....
1998-99	Sioux City	USHL	55	43	34	77	139	....	....	....	....	....	....	....	....	....	5	5	1	6	9	....	....	....	....
99-2000	Trenton Titans	ECHL	8	5	3	8	9	....	....	....	....	....	....	....	....	....	....	....	....	....	....	....	....	....	....
	Philadelphia	AHL	67	16	34	50	42	....	....	....	....	....	....	....	....	....	2	0	0	0	0	....	....	....	....
2000-01	**Philadelphia**	**NHL**	**74**	**16**	**20**	**36**	**72**	**3**	**0**	**4**	**119**	**13.4**	**8**	**7**	**71.4**	**14:38**	**6**	**0**	**1**	**1**	**4**	**0**	**0**	**0**	**11:18**
	Philadelphia	AHL	8	1	0	1	8	....	....	....	....	....	....	....	....	....	....	....	....	....	....	....	....	....	....
2001-02	**Philadelphia**	**NHL**	**78**	**17**	**9**	**26**	**43**	**0**	**1**	**3**	**121**	**14.0**	**15**	**41**	**43.9**	**13:56**	**5**	**1**	**0**	**1**	**2**	**0**	**0**	**1**	**14:11**
	Ukraine	Olympics	1	1	0	1	4	....	....	....	....	....	....	....	....	....	....	....	....	....	....	....	....	....	....

			Regular Season														Playoffs								
Season	Club	League	GP	G	A	Pts	PIM	PP	SH	GW	S	%	+/-	TF	F%	Min	GP	G	A	Pts	PIM	PP	SH	GW	Min
2002-03	**Tampa Bay**	**NHL**	**76**	**19**	**13**	**32**	**44**	**6**	**0**	**6**	**114**	**16.7**	**–7**	**90**	**48.9**	**16:01**	**11**	**0**	**1**	**1**	**2**	**0**	**0**	**0**	**13:58**
2003-04♦	**Tampa Bay**	**NHL**	**77**	**17**	**22**	**39**	**30**	**0**	**0**	**3**	**116**	**14.7**	**14**	**58**	**55.2**	**14:39**	**22**	**12**	**2**	**14**	**14**	**5**	**0**	**3**	**16:40**
	NHL Totals		**305**	**69**	**64**	**133**	**189**	**9**	**1**	**16**	**470**	**14.7**		**196**	**50.5**	**14:48**	**44**	**13**	**4**	**17**	**22**	**5**	**0**	**4**	**14:59**

Signed as a free agent by **Philadelphia**, August 3, 1999. Traded to **Tampa Bay** by **Philadelphia** with Tampa Bay's 2nd round choice (previously acquired, later traded to Dallas – Dallas selected Tobias Stephan) in 2002 Entry Draft and Phoenix's 2nd round choice (previously acquired, later traded to San Jose – San Jose selected Dan Spang) in 2002 Entry Draft for Tampa Bay's 1st round choice (Joni Pitkanen) in 2002 Entry Draft, June 21, 2002.

FERENCE, Andrew

(FAIR-ehns, AN-droo) **CGY.**

Defense. Shoots left. 5'10", 196 lbs. Born, Edmonton, Alta., March 17, 1979. Pittsburgh's 8th choice, 208th overall, in 1997 Entry Draft.

Season	Club	League	GP	G	A	Pts	PIM	PP	SH	GW	S	%	+/-	TF	F%	Min	GP	G	A	Pts	PIM	PP	SH	GW	Min
1994-95	Sherwood Park	AMHL	31	4	14	18	74	....	....	....	....	....	....	....	....	....	....	....	....	....	....	....	....	....	....
	Portland	WHL	2	0	0	0	4	....	....	....	....	....	....	....	....	....	....	....	....	....	....	....	....	....	....
1995-96	Portland	WHL	72	9	31	40	159	....	....	....	....	....	....	....	....	....	7	1	3	4	12	....	....	....	....
1996-97	Portland	WHL	72	12	32	44	163	....	....	....	....	....	....	....	....	....	6	1	2	3	12	....	....	....	....
1997-98	Portland	WHL	72	11	57	68	142	....	....	....	....	....	....	....	....	....	16	2	18	20	28	....	....	....	....
1998-99	Portland	WHL	40	11	21	32	104	....	....	....	....	....	....	....	....	....	4	1	4	5	10	....	....	....	....
	Kansas City	IHL	5	1	2	3	4	....	....	....	....	....	....	....	....	....	3	0	0	0	9	....	....	....	....
99-2000	**Pittsburgh**	**NHL**	**30**	**2**	**4**	**6**	**20**	**0**	**0**	**1**	**26**	**7.7**	**3**	**0**	**0.0**	**16:19**	....	....	....	....	....	....	....	....	....
	Wilkes-Barre	AHL	44	8	20	28	58	....	....	....	....	....	....	....	....	....	....	....	....	....	....	....	....	....	....
2000-01	**Pittsburgh**	**NHL**	**36**	**4**	**11**	**15**	**28**	**1**	**0**	**1**	**47**	**8.5**	**6**	**0**	**0.0**	**18:51**	**18**	**3**	**7**	**10**	**16**	**1**	**0**	**1**	**22:02**
	Wilkes-Barre	AHL	43	6	18	24	95	....	....	....	....	....	....	....	....	....	3	1	0	1	12	....	....	....	....
2001-02	**Pittsburgh**	**NHL**	**75**	**4**	**7**	**11**	**73**	**1**	**0**	**0**	**82**	**4.9**	**–12**	**2**	**0.0**	**18:34**	....	....	....	....	....	....	....	....	....
2002-03	**Pittsburgh**	**NHL**	**22**	**1**	**3**	**4**	**36**	**1**	**0**	**0**	**22**	**4.5**	**–16**	**1**	**100.0**	**19:33**	....	....	....	....	....	....	....	....	....
	Wilkes-Barre	AHL	1	0	0	0	2	....	....	....	....	....	....	....	....	....	....	....	....	....	....	....	....	....	....
	Calgary	**NHL**	**16**	**0**	**4**	**4**	**6**	**0**	**0**	**0**	**17**	**0.0**	**1**	**0**	**0.0**	**17:38**	....	....	....	....	....	....	....	....	....
2003-04	**Calgary**	**NHL**	**72**	**4**	**12**	**16**	**53**	**1**	**0**	**0**	**86**	**4.7**	**5**	**0**	**0.0**	**18:40**	**26**	**0**	**3**	**3**	**25**	**0**	**0**	**0**	**24:13**
	NHL Totals		**251**	**15**	**41**	**56**	**216**	**4**	**0**	**2**	**280**	**5.4**		**3**	**33.3**	**18:24**	**44**	**3**	**10**	**13**	**41**	**1**	**0**	**1**	**23:19**

WHL West First All-Star Team (1998) • WHL West Second All-Star Team (1999)

• Missed majority of 2002-03 season recovering from groin (November 18, 2002 vs. Montreal) and ankle (March 20, 2003 vs. Los Angeles) injuries. Traded to **Calgary** by **Pittsburgh** for Calgary's 3rd round choice (Brian Gifford) in 2004 Entry Draft, February 9, 2003.

FERENCE, Brad

(FAIR-ehns, BRAD) **PHX.**

Defense. Shoots right. 6'3", 218 lbs. Born, Calgary, Alta., April 2, 1979. Vancouver's 1st choice, 10th overall, in 1997 Entry Draft.

Season	Club	League	GP	G	A	Pts	PIM	PP	SH	GW	S	%	+/-	TF	F%	Min	GP	G	A	Pts	PIM	PP	SH	GW	Min
1994-95	Calgary Royals	ABHL	60	19	47	66	220	....	....	....	....	....	....	....	....	....	....	....	....	....	....	....	....	....	....
1995-96	Calgary Royals	ABHL	22	7	21	28	140	....	....	....	....	....	....	....	....	....	....	....	....	....	....	....	....	....	....
	Spokane Chiefs	WHL	5	0	2	2	18	....	....	....	....	....	....	....	....	....	....	....	....	....	....	....	....	....	....
1996-97	Spokane Chiefs	WHL	67	6	20	26	324	....	....	....	....	....	....	....	....	....	9	0	4	4	21	....	....	....	....
1997-98	Spokane Chiefs	WHL	54	9	30	39	213	....	....	....	....	....	....	....	....	....	18	0	7	7	59	....	....	....	....
1998-99	Spokane Chiefs	WHL	31	3	22	25	125	....	....	....	....	....	....	....	....	....	....	....	....	....	....	....	....	....	....
	Tri-City	WHL	20	6	15	21	116	....	....	....	....	....	....	....	....	....	12	1	9	10	63	....	....	....	....
99-2000	**Florida**	**NHL**	**13**	**0**	**2**	**2**	**46**	**0**	**0**	**0**	**10**	**0.0**	**2**	**0**	**0.0**	**13:40**	....	....	....	....	....	....	....	....	....
	Louisville Panthers	AHL	58	2	7	9	231	....	....	....	....	....	....	....	....	....	2	0	0	0	2	....	....	....	....
2000-01	**Florida**	**NHL**	**14**	**0**	**1**	**1**	**14**	**0**	**0**	**0**	**5**	**0.0**	**–10**	**0**	**0.0**	**13:03**	....	....	....	....	....	....	....	....	....
	Louisville Panthers	AHL	52	3	21	24	200	....	....	....	....	....	....	....	....	....	....	....	....	....	....	....	....	....	....
2001-02	**Florida**	**NHL**	**80**	**2**	**15**	**17**	**254**	**0**	**0**	**0**	**65**	**3.1**	**–13**	**1**	**0.0**	**19:44**	....	....	....	....	....	....	....	....	....
2002-03	**Florida**	**NHL**	**60**	**2**	**6**	**8**	**118**	**0**	**0**	**0**	**41**	**4.9**	**2**	**0**	**0.0**	**15:58**	....	....	....	....	....	....	....	....	....
	Phoenix	**NHL**	**15**	**0**	**1**	**1**	**28**	**0**	**0**	**0**	**8**	**0.0**	**–5**	**0**	**0.0**	**16:33**	....	....	....	....	....	....	....	....	....
2003-04	**Phoenix**	**NHL**	**63**	**0**	**5**	**5**	**103**	**0**	**0**	**0**	**39**	**0.0**	**–19**	**0**	**0.0**	**14:03**	....	....	....	....	....	....	....	....	....
	NHL Totals		**245**	**4**	**30**	**34**	**563**	**0**	**0**	**0**	**168**	**2.4**		**1**	**0.0**	**16:27**	....	....	....	....	....	....	....	....	....

Memorial Cup All-Star Team (1998)

Traded to **Florida** by **Vancouver** with Pavel Bure, Bret Hedican and Vancouver's 3rd round choice (Robert Fried) in 2000 Entry Draft for Ed Jovanovski, Dave Gagner, Mike Brown, Kevin Weekes and Florida's 1st round choice (Nathan Smith) in 2000 Entry Draft, January 17, 1999. Traded to **Phoenix** by **Florida** for Darcy Hordichuk and Phoenix's 2nd round choice (later traded to Tampa Bay – Tampa Bay selected Matt Smaby) in 2003 Entry Draft, March 8, 2003.

FERGUSON, Scott

(fuhr-GUH-sohn, SKAWT)

Defense. Shoots left. 6'1", 195 lbs. Born, Camrose, Alta., January 6, 1973.

Season	Club	League	GP	G	A	Pts	PIM	PP	SH	GW	S	%	+/-	TF	F%	Min	GP	G	A	Pts	PIM	PP	SH	GW	Min
1990-91	Sherwood Park	AJHL	32	2	9	11	91	....	....	....	....	....	....	....	....	....	....	....	....	....	....	....	....	....	....
	Kamloops Blazers	WHL	4	0	0	0	0	....	....	....	....	....	....	....	....	....	....	....	....	....	....	....	....	....	....
1991-92	Kamloops Blazers	WHL	62	4	10	14	138	....	....	....	....	....	....	....	....	....	12	0	2	2	21	....	....	....	....
1992-93	Kamloops Blazers	WHL	71	4	19	23	206	....	....	....	....	....	....	....	....	....	13	0	2	2	24	....	....	....	....
1993-94	Kamloops Blazers	WHL	68	5	49	54	180	....	....	....	....	....	....	....	....	....	19	5	11	16	48	....	....	....	....
1994-95	Cape Breton	AHL	58	4	6	10	103	....	....	....	....	....	....	....	....	....	....	....	....	....	....	....	....	....	....
	Wheeling	ECHL	5	1	5	6	16	....	....	....	....	....	....	....	....	....	....	....	....	....	....	....	....	....	....
1995-96	Cape Breton	AHL	80	5	16	21	196	....	....	....	....	....	....	....	....	....	....	....	....	....	....	....	....	....	....
1996-97	Hamilton	AHL	74	6	14	20	115	....	....	....	....	....	....	....	....	....	21	5	7	12	59	....	....	....	....
1997-98	**Edmonton**	**NHL**	**1**	**0**	**0**	**0**	**0**	**0**	**0**	**0**	**0**	**0.0**	**1**	....	....	....	....	....	....	....	....	....	....	....	....
	Hamilton	AHL	77	7	17	24	150	....	....	....	....	....	....	....	....	....	9	0	3	3	16	....	....	....	....
1998-99	**Anaheim**	**NHL**	**2**	**0**	**1**	**1**	**0**	**0**	**0**	**0**	**1**	**0.0**	**0**	**0**	**0.0**	**15:09**	....	....	....	....	....	....	....	....	....
	Cincinnati	AHL	78	4	31	35	59	....	....	....	....	....	....	....	....	....	3	0	0	0	4	....	....	....	....
99-2000	Cincinnati	AHL	77	7	25	32	166	....	....	....	....	....	....	....	....	....	....	....	....	....	....	....	....	....	....
2000-01	**Edmonton**	**NHL**	**20**	**0**	**1**	**1**	**13**	**0**	**0**	**0**	**8**	**0.0**	**2**	**0**	**0.0**	**10:55**	**6**	**0**	**0**	**0**	**0**	**0**	**0**	**0**	**8:21**
	Hamilton	AHL	42	3	18	21	79	....	....	....	....	....	....	....	....	....	....	....	....	....	....	....	....	....	....
2001-02	**Edmonton**	**NHL**	**50**	**3**	**2**	**5**	**75**	**0**	**0**	**0**	**27**	**11.1**	**11**	**0**	**0.0**	**13:40**	....	....	....	....	....	....	....	....	....
2002-03	**Edmonton**	**NHL**	**78**	**3**	**5**	**8**	**120**	**0**	**0**	**0**	**45**	**6.7**	**11**	**1**	**100.0**	**0:00**	**5**	**0**	**0**	**0**	**8**	**0**	**0**	**0**	....
2003-04	**Edmonton**	**NHL**	**52**	**1**	**5**	**6**	**80**	**0**	**0**	**1**	**38**	**2.6**	**–5**	**0**	**0.0**	**13:21**	....	....	....	....	....	....	....	....	....
	NHL Totals		**203**	**7**	**14**	**21**	**288**	**0**	**0**	**1**	**119**	**5.9**		**1**	**0.0**	**8:03**	**11**	**0**	**0**	**0**	**8**	**0**	**0**	**0**	**8:21**

WHL West Second All-Star Team (1994)

Signed as a free agent by **Edmonton**, June 2, 1994. Traded to **Ottawa** by **Edmonton** for Frantisek Musil, March 9, 1998. Signed as a free agent by **Anaheim**, July 27, 1998. Signed as a free agent by **Edmonton**, July 5, 2000.

FERRARO, Chris

(fuh-RAHR-oh, KRIHS)

Center. Shoots right. 5'9", 175 lbs. Born, Port Jefferson, NY, January 24, 1973. NY Rangers' 4th choice, 85th overall, in 1992 Entry Draft.

Season	Club	League	GP	G	A	Pts	PIM	PP	SH	GW	S	%	+/-	TF	F%	Min	GP	G	A	Pts	PIM	PP	SH	GW	Min
1990-91	Dubuque	USHL	45	53	44	97	84	....	....	....	....	....	....	....	....	....	8	3	9	12	12	....	....	....	....
1991-92	Dubuque	USHL	20	30	19	49	52	....	....	....	....	....	....	....	....	....	....	....	....	....	....	....	....	....	....
	Waterloo	USHL	18	19	31	50	54	....	....	....	....	....	....	....	....	....	4	5	6	11	14	....	....	....	....
1992-93	U. of Maine	H-East	39	25	26	51	46	....	....	....	....	....	....	....	....	....	....	....	....	....	....	....	....	....	....
1993-94	U. of Maine	H-East	4	0	1	1	8	....	....	....	....	....	....	....	....	....	....	....	....	....	....	....	....	....	....
	Team USA	Nat-Tm	48	8	34	42	58	....	....	....	....	....	....	....	....	....	....	....	....	....	....	....	....	....	....
1994-95	Atlanta Knights	IHL	54	13	14	27	72	....	....	....	....	....	....	....	....	....	....	....	....	....	....	....	....	....	....
	Binghamton	AHL	13	6	4	10	38	....	....	....	....	....	....	....	....	....	10	2	3	5	16	....	....	....	....
1995-96	**NY Rangers**	**NHL**	**2**	**1**	**0**	**1**	**0**	**1**	**0**	**0**	**4**	**25.0**	**–3**	....	....	....	....	....	....	....	....	....	....	....	....
	Binghamton	AHL	77	32	67	99	208	....	....	....	....	....	....	....	....	....	4	4	2	6	13	....	....	....	....
1996-97	**NY Rangers**	**NHL**	**12**	**1**	**1**	**2**	**6**	**0**	**0**	**0**	**23**	**4.3**	**1**	....	....	....	....	....	....	....	....	....	....	....	....
	Binghamton	AHL	53	29	34	63	94	....	....	....	....	....	....	....	....	....	....	....	....	....	....	....	....	....	....
1997-98	**Pittsburgh**	**NHL**	**46**	**3**	**4**	**7**	**43**	**0**	**0**	**0**	**42**	**7.1**	**–2**	....	....	....	....	....	....	....	....	....	....	....	....
1998-99	**Edmonton**	**NHL**	**2**	**1**	**0**	**1**	**0**	**0**	**0**	**0**	**1**	**100.0**	**1**	**19**	**52.6**	**8:33**	....	....	....	....	....	....	....	....	....
	Hamilton	AHL	72	35	41	76	104	....	....	....	....	....	....	....	....	....	11	8	5	13	20	....	....	....	....
99-2000	**NY Islanders**	**NHL**	**11**	**1**	**3**	**4**	**8**	**0**	**0**	**0**	**15**	**6.7**	**1**	**92**	**50.0**	**9:30**	....	....	....	....	....	....	....	....	....
	Providence Bruins	AHL	21	9	9	18	32	....	....	....	....	....	....	....	....	....	....	....	....	....	....	....	....	....	....
	Chicago Wolves	IHL	25	7	18	25	40	....	....	....	....	....	....	....	....	....	16	5	8	13	14	....	....	....	....
2000-01	Albany River Rats	AHL	74	24	42	66	111	....	....	....	....	....	....	....	....	....	....	....	....	....	....	....	....	....	....
2001-02	**Washington**	**NHL**	**1**	**0**	**1**	**1**	**0**	**0**	**0**	**0**	**4**	**0.0**	**0**	**2**	**0.0**	**15:17**	....	....	....	....	....	....	....	....	....
	Portland Pirates	AHL	2	1	1	2	6	....	....	....	....	....	....	....	....	....	....	....	....	....	....	....	....	....	....

			Regular Season														Playoffs								
Season	**Club**	**League**	**GP**	**G**	**A**	**Pts**	**PIM**	**PP**	**SH**	**GW**	**S**	**%**	**+/-**	**TF**	**F%**	**Min**	**GP**	**G**	**A**	**Pts**	**PIM**	**PP**	**SH**	**GW**	**Min**
2002-03	Portland Pirates	AHL	57	19	32	51	121										3	0	1	1	6				
2003-04	Springfield	AHL	64	14	24	38	137																		
	NHL Totals		**74**	**7**	**9**	**16**	**57**	**1**	**0**	**0**	**89**	**7.9**		**113**	**49.6**	**9:47**									

Fred Hunt Memorial Trophy (Sportsmanship – AHL) (2003) (co-winner - Eric Healey)

Claimed on waivers by **Pittsburgh** from **NY Rangers**, October 1, 1997. Signed as a free agent by **Edmonton**, August 13, 1998. Signed as a free agent by **NY Islanders**, July 22, 1999. Signed as a free agent by **New Jersey**, July 20, 2000. Traded to **Washington** by **New Jersey** for future considerations, August 22, 2001. • Missed majority of 2001-02 season after being granted personal leave of absence by Washington, October 15, 2001. Signed as a free agent by **Phoenix**, July 17, 2003.

FERRARO, Peter

(fuh-RAHR-oh, PEE-tuhr)

Left wing. Shoots right. 5'10", 180 lbs. Born, Port Jefferson, NY, January 24, 1973. NY Rangers' 1st choice, 24th overall, in 1992 Entry Draft.

Season	Club	League	GP	G	A	Pts	PIM	PP	SH	GW	S	%	+/-	TF	F%	Min	GP	G	A	Pts	PIM	PP	SH	GW	Min
1990-91	Dubuque	USHL	29	21	31	52	83										8	7	5	12	10				
1991-92	Dubuque	USHL	21	25	25	50	92																		
	Waterloo	USHL	21	23	28	51	76										4	8	5	13	16				
1992-93	U. of Maine	H-East	36	18	32	50	106																		
1993-94	U. of Maine	H-East	4	3	6	9	16																		
	Team USA	Nat-Tm	60	30	34	64	87																		
	United States	Olympics	8	6	0	6	6																		
1994-95	Atlanta Knights	IHL	61	15	24	39	118																		
	Binghamton	AHL	12	2	6	8	67										11	4	3	7	51				
1995-96	**NY Rangers**	**NHL**	**5**	**0**	**1**	**1**	**0**	**0**	**0**	**0**	**6**	**0.0**	**–5**												
	Binghamton	AHL	68	48	53	101	157										4	1	6	7	22				
1996-97	**NY Rangers**	**NHL**	**2**	**0**	**0**	**0**	**0**	**0**	**0**	**0**	**3**	**0.0**	**0**				**2**	**0**	**0**	**0**	**0**	**0**	**0**	**0**	
	Binghamton	AHL	75	38	39	77	171										4	3	1	4	18				
1997-98	**Pittsburgh**	**NHL**	**29**	**3**	**4**	**7**	**12**	**0**	**0**	**0**	**34**	**8.8**	**–2**												
	NY Rangers	**NHL**	**1**	**0**	**0**	**0**	**2**	**0**	**0**	**0**	**3**	**0.0**	**–2**												
	Hartford	AHL	36	17	23	40	54										15	8	6	14	59				
1998-99	**Boston**	**NHL**	**46**	**6**	**8**	**14**	**44**	**1**	**0**	**1**	**61**	**9.8**	**10**	**70**	**37.1**	**10:12**									
	Providence Bruins	AHL	16	15	10	25	14										19	9	12	21	38				
99-2000	**Boston**	**NHL**	**5**	**0**	**1**	**1**	**0**	**0**	**0**	**0**	**3**	**0.0**	**–1**	**19**	**47.4**	**8:11**									
	Providence Bruins	AHL	48	21	25	46	98										13	5	7	12	14				
2000-01	Providence Bruins	AHL	78	26	45	71	109										17	4	5	9	34				
2001-02	**Washington**	**NHL**	**4**	**0**	**1**	**1**	**0**	**0**	**0**	**0**	**3**	**0.0**	**–1**	**0**	**0.0**	**12:54**									
	Portland Pirates	AHL	67	21	37	58	119																		
2002-03	Portland Pirates	AHL	59	22	41	63	123										3	0	2	2	16				
2003-04	Springfield	AHL	64	19	31	50	100																		
	NHL Totals		**92**	**9**	**15**	**24**	**58**	**1**	**0**	**1**	**113**	**8.0**		**89**	**39.3**	**10:13**	**2**	**0**	**0**	**0**	**0**	**0**	**0**	**0**	

AHL First All-Star Team (1996) • Jack A. Butterfield Trophy (Playoff MVP – AHL) (1999)

Claimed on waivers by **Pittsburgh** from **NY Rangers**, October 1, 1997. Claimed on waivers by **NY Rangers** from **Pittsburgh**, January 9, 1998. Signed as a free agent by **Boston**, August 5, 1998. Claimed by **Atlanta** from **Boston** in Expansion Draft, June 25, 1999. Traded to **Boston** by **Atlanta** for Randy Robitaille, June 25, 1999. Signed as a free agent by **Washington**, August 1, 2001. Signed as a free agent by **Phoenix**, July 17, 2003.

FIBIGER, Jesse

(feh-BEH-gehr, JEH-see) **OTT.**

Defense. Shoots left. 6'3", 210 lbs. Born, Victoria, B.C., April 4, 1978. Anaheim's 5th choice, 178th overall, in 1998 Entry Draft.

Season	Club	League	GP	G	A	Pts	PIM	PP	SH	GW	S	%	+/-	TF	F%	Min	GP	G	A	Pts	PIM	PP	SH	GW	Min
1996-97	Victoria Salsa	BCHL	53	6	18	24	88																		
1997-98	U. Minn-Duluth	WCHA	40	3	6	9	82																		
1998-99	U. Minn-Duluth	WCHA	36	4	16	20	61																		
99-2000	U. Minn-Duluth	WCHA	37	4	6	10	83																		
2000-01	U. Minn-Duluth	WCHA	37	0	8	8	56																		
2001-02	Cleveland Barons	AHL	79	6	12	18	94																		
2002-03	**San Jose**	**NHL**	**16**	**0**	**0**	**0**	**2**	**0**	**0**	**0**	**2**	**0.0**	**–5**	**0**	**0.0**	**6:05**									
	Cleveland Barons	AHL	59	3	11	14	63																		
2003-04	Cleveland Barons	AHL	55	5	12	17	39										9	0	2	2	8				
	NHL Totals		**16**	**0**	**0**	**0**	**2**	**0**	**0**	**0**	**2**	**0.0**		**0**	**0.0**	**6:05**									

Signed as a free agent by **San Jose**, August 15, 2001. Signed as a free agent by **Ottawa**, August 11, 2004.

FIDDLER, Vernon

(FIHD-luhr, VUHR-nuhn) **NSH.**

Center. Shoots left. 5'11", 197 lbs. Born, Edmonton, Alta., May 9, 1980.

Season	Club	League	GP	G	A	Pts	PIM	PP	SH	GW	S	%	+/-	TF	F%	Min	GP	G	A	Pts	PIM	PP	SH	GW	Min
1997-98	Kelowna Rockets	WHL	65	10	11	21	31										7	0	1	1	4				
1998-99	Kelowna Rockets	WHL	68	22	21	43	82										6	2	0	2	8				
99-2000	Kelowna Rockets	WHL	64	20	28	48	60										5	1	3	4	4				
2000-01	Kelowna Rockets	WHL	3	0	2	2	0																		
	Medicine Hat	WHL	67	33	38	71	100																		
	Arkansas	ECHL	3	0	1	1	2										5	3	0	3	5				
2001-02	Roanoke Express	ECHL	44	27	28	55	71																		
	Norfolk Admirals	AHL	38	8	5	13	28										4	1	3	4	2				
2002-03	**Nashville**	**NHL**	**19**	**4**	**2**	**6**	**14**	**0**	**0**	**1**	**20**	**20.0**	**2**	**171**	**53.8**	**9:40**									
	Milwaukee	AHL	54	8	16	24	70										6	1	2	3	14				
2003-04	**Nashville**	**NHL**	**17**	**0**	**0**	**0**	**23**	**0**	**0**	**0**	**8**	**0.0**	**–6**	**123**	**49.6**	**8:06**									
	Milwaukee	AHL	47	9	15	24	72										22	5	3	8	36				
	NHL Totals		**36**	**4**	**2**	**6**	**37**	**0**	**0**	**1**	**28**	**14.3**		**294**	**52.0**	**8:56**									

ECHL All-Rookie Team (2002)

Signed as a free agent by **Arkansas** (ECHL), March 31, 2001. Traded to **Roanoke** (ECHL) by **Arkansas** (ECHL) for Calvin Elfring, August 11, 2001. Signed as a free agent by **Nashville**, May 6, 2002.

FINLEY, Jeff

(FIHN-lee, JEHF)

Defense. Shoots left. 6'2", 205 lbs. Born, Edmonton, Alta., April 14, 1967. NY Islanders' 4th choice, 55th overall, in 1985 Entry Draft.

Season	Club	League	GP	G	A	Pts	PIM	PP	SH	GW	S	%	+/-	TF	F%	Min	GP	G	A	Pts	PIM	PP	SH	GW	Min
1983-84	Summerland	BCJHL	49	0	21	21	14																		
	Portland	WHL	5	0	0	0	5										5	0	1	1	4				
1984-85	Portland	WHL	69	6	44	50	57										6	1	2	3	2				
1985-86	Portland	WHL	70	11	59	70	83										15	1	7	8	16				
1986-87	Portland	WHL	72	13	53	66	113										20	1	*21	22	27				
1987-88	**NY Islanders**	**NHL**	**10**	**0**	**5**	**5**	**15**	**0**	**0**	**0**	**9**	**0.0**	**5**				**1**	**0**	**0**	**0**	**2**	**0**	**0**	**0**	
	Springfield	AHL	52	5	18	23	50																		
1988-89	**NY Islanders**	**NHL**	**4**	**0**	**0**	**0**	**6**	**0**	**0**	**0**	**1**	**0.0**	**1**												
	Springfield	AHL	65	3	16	19	55																		
1989-90	**NY Islanders**	**NHL**	**11**	**0**	**1**	**1**	**0**	**0**	**0**	**0**	**7**	**0.0**	**0**				**5**	**0**	**2**	**2**	**2**	**0**	**0**	**0**	
	Springfield	AHL	57	1	15	16	41										13	1	4	5	23				
1990-91	**NY Islanders**	**NHL**	**11**	**0**	**0**	**0**	**4**	**0**	**0**	**0**	**0**	**0.0**	**–1**												
	Capital District	AHL	67	10	34	44	34																		
1991-92	**NY Islanders**	**NHL**	**51**	**1**	**10**	**11**	**26**	**0**	**0**	**0**	**25**	**4.0**	**–6**												
	Capital District	AHL	20	1	9	10	6																		
1992-93	Capital District	AHL	61	6	29	35	34										4	0	1	1	0				
1993-94	**Philadelphia**	**NHL**	**55**	**1**	**8**	**9**	**24**	**0**	**0**	**0**	**43**	**2.3**	**16**												
1994-95	Hershey Bears	AHL	36	2	9	11	33										6	0	1	1	8				
1995-96	**Winnipeg**	**NHL**	**65**	**1**	**5**	**6**	**81**	**0**	**0**	**0**	**27**	**3.7**	**–2**				**6**	**0**	**0**	**0**	**4**	**0**	**0**	**0**	
	Springfield	AHL	14	3	12	15	22																		
1996-97	**Phoenix**	**NHL**	**65**	**3**	**7**	**10**	**40**	**1**	**0**	**1**	**38**	**7.9**	**–8**				**1**	**0**	**0**	**0**	**2**	**0**	**0**	**0**	
1997-98	**NY Rangers**	**NHL**	**63**	**1**	**6**	**7**	**55**	**0**	**0**	**0**	**32**	**3.1**	**–3**												
1998-99	**NY Rangers**	**NHL**	**2**	**0**	**0**	**0**	**0**	**0**	**0**	**0**	**0**	**0.0**	**–1**	**0**	**0.0**	**11:40**									
	Hartford	AHL	42	2	10	12	28																		
	St. Louis	**NHL**	**30**	**1**	**2**	**3**	**20**	**0**	**0**	**0**	**16**	**6.3**	**12**	**0**	**0.0**	**17:36**	**13**	**1**	**2**	**3**	**8**	**0**	**0**	**1**	**20:10**
99-2000	**St. Louis**	**NHL**	**74**	**2**	**8**	**10**	**38**	**0**	**0**	**2**	**31**	**6.5**	**26**	**1**	**100.0**	**17:49**	**7**	**0**	**2**	**2**	**4**	**0**	**0**	**0**	**17:21**
2000-01	**St. Louis**	**NHL**	**72**	**2**	**8**	**10**	**38**	**0**	**0**	**0**	**35**	**5.7**	**7**	**1**	**0.0**	**18:53**	**2**	**0**	**0**	**0**	**0**	**0**	**0**	**0**	**3:25**
2001-02	**St. Louis**	**NHL**	**78**	**0**	**6**	**6**	**30**	**0**	**0**	**0**	**39**	**0.0**	**12**	**0**	**0.0**	**18:31**	**10**	**0**	**0**	**0**	**8**	**0**	**0**	**0**	**18:02**

			Regular Season														Playoffs								
Season	Club	League	GP	G	A	Pts	PIM	PP	SH	GW	S	%	+/-	TF	F%	Min	GP	G	A	Pts	PIM	PP	SH	GW	Min
2002-03	St. Louis	NHL	64	1	3	4	46	0	0	1	30	3.3	–2	0	0.0	15:37	6	0	0	0	6	0	0	0	15:11
2003-04	St. Louis	NHL	53	0	1	1	34	0	0	0	25	0.0	–9	0	0.0	17:05	1	0	0	0	2	0	0	0	12:14
	NHL Totals		**708**	**13**	**70**	**83**	**457**	**1**	**0**	**4**	**358**	**3.6**		**2**	**50.0**	**17:38**	**52**	**1**	**6**	**7**	**38**	**0**	**0**	**1**	**17:17**

Rights traded to **Ottawa** by **NY Islanders** for Chris Luongo, June 30, 1993. Signed as a free agent by **Philadelphia**, July 30, 1993. Traded to **Winnipeg** by **Philadelphia** for Russ Romaniuk, June 27, 1995. Transferred to **Phoenix** after **Winnipeg** franchise relocated, July 1, 1996. Signed as a free agent by **NY Rangers**, August 18, 1997. Traded to **St. Louis** by **NY Rangers** with Geoff Smith for future considerations (Chris Kenady, February 22, 1999), February 13, 1999.

FISCHER, Jiri

(FIH-shuhr, YIH-ree) **DET.**

Defense. Shoots left. 6'5", 225 lbs. Born, Horovice, Czech., July 31, 1980. Detroit's 1st choice, 25th overall, in 1998 Entry Draft.

Season	Club	League	GP	G	A	Pts	PIM	PP	SH	GW	S	%	+/-	TF	F%	Min	GP	G	A	Pts	PIM	PP	SH	GW	Min
1995-96	Kladno Jr.	Czech-Jr.	39	6	10	16	....	....	....	....	....	....	....	....	....	....	....	....	....	....	....	....	....	....	....
1996-97	Kladno Jr.	Czech-Jr.	38	7	21	28	....	....	....	....	....	....	....	....	....	....	....	....	....	....	....	....	....	....	....
1997-98	Hull Olympiques	QMJHL	70	3	19	22	112	....	....	....	....	....	....	....	....	....	11	1	4	5	16	....	....	....	....
1998-99	Hull Olympiques	QMJHL	65	22	56	78	141	....	....	....	....	....	....	....	....	....	23	6	17	23	44	....	....	....	....
99-2000	**Detroit**	**NHL**	**52**	**0**	**8**	**8**	**45**	**0**	**0**	**0**	**41**	**0.0**	**1**	**0**	**0.0**	**10:51**	....	....	....	....	....	....	....	....	....
	Cincinnati	AHL	7	0	2	2	10	....	....	....	....	....	....	....	....	....	....	....	....	....	....	....	....	....	....
2000-01	**Detroit**	**NHL**	**55**	**1**	**8**	**9**	**59**	**0**	**0**	**0**	**64**	**1.6**	**3**	**0**	**0.0**	**16:46**	**5**	**0**	**0**	**0**	**9**	**0**	**0**	**0**	**16:25**
	Cincinnati	AHL	18	2	6	8	22	....	....	....	....	....	....	....	....	....	....	....	....	....	....	....	....	....	....
2001-02◆	**Detroit**	**NHL**	**80**	**2**	**8**	**10**	**67**	**0**	**0**	**1**	**103**	**1.9**	**17**	**0**	**0.0**	**17:10**	**22**	**3**	**3**	**6**	**30**	**0**	**0**	**1**	**19:41**
2002-03	**Detroit**	**NHL**	**15**	**1**	**5**	**6**	**16**	**0**	**0**	**0**	**19**	**5.3**	**0**	**0**	**0.0**	**21:24**	....	....	....	....	....	....	....	....	....
2003-04	**Detroit**	**NHL**	**81**	**4**	**15**	**19**	**75**	**1**	**0**	**0**	**115**	**3.5**	**0**	**0**	**0.0**	**18:30**	**11**	**1**	**0**	**1**	**16**	**0**	**0**	**0**	**11:29**
	NHL Totals		**283**	**8**	**44**	**52**	**262**	**1**	**0**	**1**	**342**	**2.3**		**0**	**0.0**	**16:32**	**38**	**4**	**3**	**7**	**55**	**0**	**0**	**1**	**16:53**

QMJHL First All-Star Team (1999)

• Missed majority of 2002-03 season recovering from knee injury suffered in game vs. Nashville, November 12, 2002.

FISHER, Mike

(FIH-shuhr, MIGHK) **OTT.**

Center. Shoots right. 6'1", 200 lbs. Born, Peterborough, Ont., June 5, 1980. Ottawa's 2nd choice, 44th overall, in 1998 Entry Draft.

Season	Club	League	GP	G	A	Pts	PIM	PP	SH	GW	S	%	+/-	TF	F%	Min	GP	G	A	Pts	PIM	PP	SH	GW	Min
1996-97	Peterborough	OPJHL	51	26	30	56	35	....	....	....	....	....	....	....	....	....	....	....	....	....	....	....	....	....	....
1997-98	Sudbury Wolves	OHL	66	24	25	49	65	....	....	....	....	....	....	....	....	....	9	2	2	4	13	....	....	....	....
1998-99	Sudbury Wolves	OHL	68	41	65	106	55	....	....	....	....	....	....	....	....	....	4	2	1	3	4	....	....	....	....
99-2000	**Ottawa**	**NHL**	**32**	**4**	**5**	**9**	**15**	**0**	**0**	**1**	**49**	**8.2**	**–6**	**356**	**47.8**	**12:57**	....	....	....	....	....	....	....	....	....
2000-01	**Ottawa**	**NHL**	**60**	**7**	**12**	**19**	**46**	**0**	**0**	**3**	**83**	**8.4**	**–1**	**709**	**50.2**	**11:38**	**4**	**0**	**1**	**1**	**4**	**0**	**0**	**0**	**13:41**
2001-02	**Ottawa**	**NHL**	**58**	**15**	**9**	**24**	**55**	**0**	**3**	**4**	**123**	**12.2**	**8**	**848**	**48.7**	**14:05**	**10**	**2**	**1**	**3**	**0**	**0**	**0**	**0**	**16:17**
2002-03	**Ottawa**	**NHL**	**74**	**18**	**20**	**38**	**54**	**5**	**1**	**3**	**142**	**12.7**	**13**	**1077**	**48.1**	**15:59**	**18**	**2**	**2**	**4**	**16**	**0**	**1**	**1**	**16:58**
2003-04	**Ottawa**	**NHL**	**24**	**4**	**6**	**10**	**39**	**1**	**0**	**0**	**47**	**8.5**	**–3**	**357**	**42.0**	**17:26**	**7**	**1**	**0**	**1**	**4**	**0**	**0**	**1**	**16:11**
	NHL Totals		**248**	**48**	**52**	**100**	**209**	**6**	**4**	**11**	**444**	**10.8**		**3347**	**48.0**	**14:14**	**39**	**5**	**4**	**9**	**24**	**0**	**1**	**2**	**16:19**

• Missed majority of 1999-2000 season recovering from knee injury suffered in game vs. Boston, December 30, 1999. • Missed majority of 2003-04 season recovering from elbow injury suffered in practice, October 4, 2003,

FITZGERALD, Tom

(fihtz-JAIR-uhld, TAWM) **BOS.**

Right wing. Shoots right. 6', 190 lbs. Born, Billerica, MA, August 28, 1968. NY Islanders' 1st choice, 17th overall, in 1986 Entry Draft.

Season	Club	League	GP	G	A	Pts	PIM	PP	SH	GW	S	%	+/-	TF	F%	Min	GP	G	A	Pts	PIM	PP	SH	GW	Min
1984-85	Austin Mustangs	Hi-School	18	20	21	41	....	....	....	....	....	....	....	....	....	....	....	....	....	....	....	....	....	....	....
1985-86	Austin Mustangs	Hi-School	24	35	38	73	....	....	....	....	....	....	....	....	....	....	....	....	....	....	....	....	....	....	....
1986-87	Providence	H-East	27	8	14	22	22	....	....	....	....	....	....	....	....	....	....	....	....	....	....	....	....	....	....
1987-88	Providence	H-East	36	19	15	34	50	....	....	....	....	....	....	....	....	....	....	....	....	....	....	....	....	....	....
1988-89	**NY Islanders**	**NHL**	**23**	**3**	**5**	**8**	**10**	**0**	**0**	**1**	**24**	**12.5**	**1**	....	....	....	....	....	....	....	....	....	....	....	....
	Springfield	AHL	61	24	18	42	43	....	....	....	....	....	....	....	....	....	....	....	....	....	....	....	....	....	....
1989-90	**NY Islanders**	**NHL**	**19**	**2**	**5**	**7**	**4**	**0**	**0**	**1**	**24**	**8.3**	**–3**	....	....	....	**4**	**1**	**0**	**1**	**4**	**0**	**0**	**0**	....
	Springfield	AHL	53	30	23	53	32	....	....	....	....	....	....	....	....	....	14	2	9	11	13	....	....	....	....
1990-91	**NY Islanders**	**NHL**	**41**	**5**	**5**	**10**	**24**	**0**	**0**	**2**	**60**	**8.3**	**–9**	....	....	....	....	....	....	....	....	....	....	....	....
	Capital District	AHL	27	7	7	14	50	....	....	....	....	....	....	....	....	....	....	....	....	....	....	....	....	....	....
1991-92	**NY Islanders**	**NHL**	**45**	**6**	**11**	**17**	**28**	**0**	**2**	**2**	**71**	**8.5**	**–3**	....	....	....	....	....	....	....	....	....	....	....	....
	Capital District	AHL	4	1	1	2	4	....	....	....	....	....	....	....	....	....	....	....	....	....	....	....	....	....	....
1992-93	**NY Islanders**	**NHL**	**77**	**9**	**18**	**27**	**34**	**0**	**3**	**1**	**83**	**10.8**	**–2**	....	....	....	**18**	**2**	**5**	**7**	**18**	**0**	**0**	**0**	....
1993-94	**Florida**	**NHL**	**83**	**18**	**14**	**32**	**54**	**0**	**3**	**1**	**144**	**12.5**	**–3**	....	....	....	....	....	....	....	....	....	....	....	....
1994-95	**Florida**	**NHL**	**48**	**3**	**13**	**16**	**31**	**0**	**0**	**0**	**78**	**3.8**	**–3**	....	....	....	....	....	....	....	....	....	....	....	....
1995-96	**Florida**	**NHL**	**82**	**13**	**21**	**34**	**75**	**1**	**6**	**2**	**141**	**9.2**	**–3**	....	....	....	**22**	**4**	**4**	**8**	**34**	**0**	**0**	**2**	....
1996-97	**Florida**	**NHL**	**71**	**10**	**14**	**24**	**64**	**0**	**2**	**1**	**135**	**7.4**	**7**	....	....	....	**5**	**0**	**1**	**1**	**0**	**0**	**0**	**0**	....
1997-98	**Florida**	**NHL**	**69**	**10**	**5**	**15**	**57**	**0**	**1**	**1**	**105**	**9.5**	**–4**	....	....	....	....	....	....	....	....	....	....	....	....
	Colorado	**NHL**	**11**	**2**	**1**	**3**	**22**	**0**	**1**	**0**	**14**	**14.3**	**0**	....	....	....	**7**	**0**	**1**	**1**	**20**	**0**	**0**	**0**	....
1998-99	**Nashville**	**NHL**	**80**	**13**	**19**	**32**	**48**	**0**	**0**	**1**	**180**	**7.2**	**–18**	**155**	**52.3**	**17:17**	....	....	....	....	....	....	....	....	....
99-2000	**Nashville**	**NHL**	**82**	**13**	**9**	**22**	**66**	**0**	**3**	**1**	**119**	**10.9**	**–18**	**264**	**51.9**	**13:57**	....	....	....	....	....	....	....	....	....
2000-01	**Nashville**	**NHL**	**82**	**9**	**9**	**18**	**71**	**0**	**2**	**2**	**135**	**6.7**	**–5**	**458**	**54.6**	**14:58**	....	....	....	....	....	....	....	....	....
2001-02	**Nashville**	**NHL**	**63**	**7**	**9**	**16**	**33**	**0**	**1**	**0**	**101**	**6.9**	**–4**	**525**	**48.4**	**14:15**	....	....	....	....	....	....	....	....	....
	Chicago	**NHL**	**15**	**1**	**3**	**4**	**6**	**0**	**1**	**0**	**24**	**4.2**	**–3**	**110**	**50.0**	**16:16**	**5**	**0**	**0**	**0**	**4**	**0**	**0**	**0**	**15:15**
2002-03	**Toronto**	**NHL**	**66**	**4**	**13**	**17**	**57**	**0**	**0**	**0**	**89**	**4.5**	**10**	**90**	**50.0**	**12:07**	**7**	**0**	**1**	**1**	**4**	**0**	**0**	**0**	**18:11**
2003-04	**Toronto**	**NHL**	**69**	**7**	**10**	**17**	**52**	**1**	**0**	**1**	**81**	**8.6**	**–2**	**300**	**53.0**	**12:23**	**10**	**0**	**0**	**0**	**6**	**0**	**0**	**0**	**13:26**
	NHL Totals		**1026**	**135**	**184**	**319**	**736**	**2**	**25**	**17**	**1608**	**8.4**		**1902**	**51.6**	**14:20**	**78**	**7**	**12**	**19**	**90**	**0**	**0**	**2**	**15:22**

Claimed by **Florida** from **NY Islanders** in Expansion Draft, June 24, 1993. Traded to **Colorado** by **Florida** for the rights to Mark Parrish and Anaheim's 3rd round choice (previously acquired, Florida selected Lance Ward) in 1998 Entry Draft, March 24, 1998. Signed as a free agent by **Nashville**, July 6, 1998. Traded to **Chicago** by **Nashville** for Chicago's 4th round choice (later traded to Anaheim – Anaheim selected Nathan Saunders) in 2003 Entry Draft and future considerations, March 13, 2002. Signed as a free agent by **Toronto**, July 17, 2002. Signed as a free agent by **Boston**, July 28, 2004.

FITZPATRICK, Rory

(FIHTZ-pa-trihk, ROHR-ee) **BUF.**

Defense. Shoots right. 6'2", 215 lbs. Born, Rochester, NY, January 11, 1975. Montreal's 2nd choice, 47th overall, in 1993 Entry Draft.

Season	Club	League	GP	G	A	Pts	PIM	PP	SH	GW	S	%	+/-	TF	F%	Min	GP	G	A	Pts	PIM	PP	SH	GW	Min
1990-91	Rochester	NAJHL	40	0	5	5	....	....	....	....	....	....	....	....	....	....	....	....	....	....	....	....	....	....	....
1991-92	Rochester	NAJHL	28	8	28	36	141	....	....	....	....	....	....	....	....	....	....	....	....	....	....	....	....	....	....
1992-93	Sudbury Wolves	OHL	58	4	20	24	68	....	....	....	....	....	....	....	....	....	14	0	0	0	17	....	....	....	....
1993-94	Sudbury Wolves	OHL	65	12	34	46	112	....	....	....	....	....	....	....	....	....	10	2	5	7	10	....	....	....	....
1994-95	Sudbury Wolves	OHL	56	12	36	48	72	....	....	....	....	....	....	....	....	....	18	3	15	18	21	....	....	....	....
	Fredericton	AHL	....	....	....	....	....	....	....	....	....	....	....	....	....	....	10	1	2	3	5	....	....	....	....
1995-96	**Montreal**	**NHL**	**42**	**0**	**2**	**2**	**18**	**0**	**0**	**0**	**31**	**0.0**	**–7**	....	....	....	**6**	**1**	**1**	**2**	**0**	**0**	**0**	**0**	....
	Fredericton	AHL	18	4	6	10	36	....	....	....	....	....	....	....	....	....	....	....	....	....	....	....	....	....	....
1996-97	**Montreal**	**NHL**	**6**	**0**	**1**	**1**	**6**	**0**	**0**	**0**	**5**	**0.0**	**–2**	....	....	....	....	....	....	....	....	....	....	....	....
	St. Louis	**NHL**	**2**	**0**	**0**	**0**	**2**	**0**	**0**	**0**	**1**	**0.0**	**–2**	....	....	....	....	....	....	....	....	....	....	....	....
	Worcester IceCats	AHL	49	4	13	17	78	....	....	....	....	....	....	....	....	....	5	1	2	3	0	....	....	....	....
1997-98	Worcester IceCats	AHL	62	8	22	30	111	....	....	....	....	....	....	....	....	....	11	0	3	3	26	....	....	....	....
1998-99	**St. Louis**	**NHL**	**1**	**0**	**0**	**0**	**2**	**0**	**0**	**0**	**0**	**0.0**	**–3**	**0**	**0.0**	**4:49**	....	....	....	....	....	....	....	....	....
	Worcester IceCats	AHL	53	5	16	21	82	....	....	....	....	....	....	....	....	....	4	0	1	1	17	....	....	....	....
99-2000	Worcester IceCats	AHL	28	0	5	5	48	....	....	....	....	....	....	....	....	....	....	....	....	....	....	....	....	....	....
	Milwaukee	IHL	27	2	1	3	27	....	....	....	....	....	....	....	....	....	3	0	2	2	2	....	....	....	....
2000-01	**Nashville**	**NHL**	**2**	**0**	**0**	**0**	**2**	**0**	**0**	**0**	**0**	**0.0**	**–2**	**0**	**0.0**	**9:47**	....	....	....	....	....	....	....	....	....
	Milwaukee	IHL	22	0	2	2	32	....	....	....	....	....	....	....	....	....	....	....	....	....	....	....	....	....	....
	Hamilton	AHL	34	3	17	20	29	....	....	....	....	....	....	....	....	....	....	....	....	....	....	....	....	....	....
2001-02	**Buffalo**	**NHL**	**5**	**0**	**0**	**0**	**4**	**0**	**0**	**0**	**2**	**0.0**	**–2**	**0**	**0.0**	**11:54**	....	....	....	....	....	....	....	....	....
	Rochester	AHL	60	4	8	12	83	....	....	....	....	....	....	....	....	....	2	0	1	1	0	....	....	....	....
2002-03	**Buffalo**	**NHL**	**36**	**1**	**3**	**4**	**16**	**0**	**0**	**0**	**29**	**3.4**	**–7**	**0**	**0.0**	**17:02**	....	....	....	....	....	....	....	....	....
	Rochester	AHL	41	5	11	16	65	....	....	....	....	....	....	....	....	....	....	....	....	....	....	....	....	....	....
2003-04	**Buffalo**	**NHL**	**60**	**4**	**7**	**11**	**44**	**2**	**0**	**2**	**78**	**5.1**	**–5**	**1**	**100.0**	**19:02**	....	....	....	....	....	....	....	....	....
	NHL Totals		**154**	**5**	**13**	**18**	**94**	**2**	**0**	**2**	**146**	**3.4**		**1**	**100.0**	**17:41**	**6**	**1**	**1**	**2**	**0**	**0**	**0**	**0**	....

OHL All-Rookie Team (1993)

Traded to **St. Louis** by **Montreal** with Pierre Turgeon and Craig Conroy for Murray Baron, Shayne Corson and St. Louis' 5th round choice (Gennady Razin) in 1997 Entry Draft, October 29, 1996. Claimed by **Boston** from **St. Louis** in Waiver Draft, October 5, 1998. Claimed on waivers by **St. Louis** from **Boston**, October 7, 1998. Traded to **Nashville** by **St. Louis** for Dan Keczmer, February 9, 2000. Traded to **Edmonton** by **Nashville** for future considerations, January 12, 2001. Signed as a free agent by **Buffalo**, August 14, 2001.

FLINN, Ryan
(FLIHN, RIGH-yan) **L.A.**

Left wing. Shoots left. 6'5", 248 lbs. Born, Halifax, N.S., April 20, 1980. New Jersey's 8th choice, 143rd overall, in 1998 Entry Draft.

			Regular Season														Playoffs								
Season	Club	League	GP	G	A	Pts	PIM	PP	SH	GW	S	%	+/-	TF	F%	Min	GP	G	A	Pts	PIM	PP	SH	GW	Min
1996-97	Laval Titan	QMJHL	23	3	2	5	56	....	....	....	....	....	....	....	....	....	2	0	0	0	0	....	....	....	....
1997-98	Laval Titan	QMJHL	59	4	12	16	217	....	....	....	....	....	....	....	....	....	15	1	0	1	63	....	....	....	....
1998-99	Acadie-Bathurst	QMJHL	44	3	4	7	195	....	....	....	....	....	....	....	....	....	23	2	0	2	37	....	....	....	....
99-2000	Halifax	QMJHL	67	14	19	33	365	....	....	....	....	....	....	....	....	....	....	....	....	....	....	....	....	....	....
2000-01	Cape Breton	QMJHL	57	16	17	33	280	....	....	....	....	....	....	....	....	....	9	1	1	2	43	....	....	....	....
2001-02	Reading Royals	ECHL	20	1	3	4	130	....	....	....	....	....	....	....	....	....	....	....	....	....	....	....	....	....	....
	Los Angeles	**NHL**	**10**	**0**	**0**	**0**	**51**	**0**	**0**	**0**	**2**	**0.0**	**0**	**0**	**0.0**	**3:29**	....	....	....	....	....	....	....	....	....
	Manchester	AHL	37	0	1	1	113	....	....	....	....	....	....	....	....	....	1	0	0	0	0	....	....	....	....
2002-03	**Los Angeles**	**NHL**	**19**	**1**	**0**	**1**	**28**	**0**	**0**	**0**	**13**	**7.7**	**0**	**0**	**0.0**	**5:28**	....	....	....	....	....	....	....	....	....
	Manchester	AHL	27	2	2	4	95	....	....	....	....	....	....	....	....	....	....	....	....	....	....	....	....	....	....
2003-04	Manchester	AHL	59	3	5	8	164	....	....	....	....	....	....	....	....	....	6	0	0	0	4	....	....	....	....
	NHL Totals		**29**	**1**	**0**	**1**	**79**	**0**	**0**	**0**	**15**	**6.7**		**0**	**0.0**	**4:47**	....	....	....	....	....	....	....	....	....

Signed as a free agent by **Los Angeles**, January 8, 2002.

FOCHT, Dan
(FOHKT, DAN)

Defense. Shoots left. 6'6", 234 lbs. Born, Regina, Sask., December 31, 1977. Phoenix's 1st choice, 11th overall, in 1996 Entry Draft.

Season	Club	League	GP	G	A	Pts	PIM	PP	SH	GW	S	%	+/-	TF	F%	Min	GP	G	A	Pts	PIM	PP	SH	GW	Min
1994-95	Saskatoon Blazers	SMHL	33	6	12	18	98	....	....	....	....	....	....	....	....	....	....	....	....	....	....	....	....	....	....
1995-96	Tri-City	WHL	63	6	12	18	161	....	....	....	....	....	....	....	....	....	11	1	1	2	23	....	....	....	....
1996-97	Tri-City	WHL	28	0	5	5	92	....	....	....	....	....	....	....	....	....	....	....	....	....	....	....	....	....	....
	Regina Pats	WHL	22	2	2	4	59	....	....	....	....	....	....	....	....	....	5	0	2	2	8	....	....	....	....
	Springfield	AHL	1	0	0	0	2	....	....	....	....	....	....	....	....	....	....	....	....	....	....	....	....	....	....
1997-98	Springfield	AHL	61	2	5	7	125	....	....	....	....	....	....	....	....	....	3	0	0	0	4	....	....	....	....
1998-99	Mississippi	ECHL	2	0	0	0	6	....	....	....	....	....	....	....	....	....	....	....	....	....	....	....	....	....	....
	Springfield	AHL	30	0	2	2	58	....	....	....	....	....	....	....	....	....	3	1	0	1	10	....	....	....	....
99-2000	Jokerit Helsinki	Finland	2	0	0	0	0	....	....	....	....	....	....	....	....	....	....	....	....	....	....	....	....	....	....
	Mississippi	ECHL	4	0	1	1	0	....	....	....	....	....	....	....	....	....	....	....	....	....	....	....	....	....	....
	Springfield	AHL	44	2	9	11	86	....	....	....	....	....	....	....	....	....	5	0	1	1	2	....	....	....	....
2000-01	Springfield	AHL	69	0	6	6	156	....	....	....	....	....	....	....	....	....	....	....	....	....	....	....	....	....	....
2001-02	**Phoenix**	**NHL**	**8**	**0**	**0**	**0**	**11**	**0**	**0**	**0**	**5**	**0.0**	**0**	**0**	**0.0**	**12:25**	**1**	**0**	**1**	**1**	**0**	**0**	**0**	**0**	**8:20**
	Springfield	AHL	56	2	8	10	134	....	....	....	....	....	....	....	....	....	....	....	....	....	....	....	....	....	....
2002-03	**Phoenix**	**NHL**	**10**	**0**	**0**	**0**	**10**	**0**	**0**	**0**	**1**	**0.0**	**–2**	**0**	**0.0**	**8:40**	....	....	....	....	....	....	....	....	....
	Springfield	AHL	37	2	7	9	80	....	....	....	....	....	....	....	....	....	....	....	....	....	....	....	....	....	....
	Pittsburgh	**NHL**	**12**	**0**	**3**	**3**	**19**	**0**	**0**	**0**	**11**	**0.0**	**–7**	**1**	**0.0**	**18:14**	....	....	....	....	....	....	....	....	....
2003-04	**Pittsburgh**	**NHL**	**52**	**2**	**3**	**5**	**105**	**0**	**0**	**0**	**56**	**3.6**	**–23**	**0**	**0.0**	**16:36**	....	....	....	....	....	....	....	....	....
	NHL Totals		**82**	**2**	**6**	**8**	**145**	**0**	**0**	**0**	**73**	**2.7**		**1**	**0.0**	**15:28**	**1**	**0**	**1**	**1**	**0**	**0**	**0**	**0**	**8:20**

Traded to **Pittsburgh** by **Phoenix** with Ramzi Abid and Guillaume Lefebvre for Jan Hrdina and Francois Leroux, March 11, 2003.

FOOTE, Adam
(FUT, A-duhm) **COL.**

Defense. Shoots right. 6'2", 215 lbs. Born, Toronto, Ont., July 10, 1971. Quebec's 2nd choice, 22nd overall, in 1989 Entry Draft.

Season	Club	League	GP	G	A	Pts	PIM	PP	SH	GW	S	%	+/-	TF	F%	Min	GP	G	A	Pts	PIM	PP	SH	GW	Min
1987-88	Whitby Midgets	OMHA	65	25	43	68	108	....	....	....	....	....	....	....	....	....	....	....	....	....	....	....	....	....	....
1988-89	Sault Ste. Marie	OHL	66	7	32	39	120	....	....	....	....	....	....	....	....	....	....	....	....	....	....	....	....	....	....
1989-90	Sault Ste. Marie	OHL	61	12	43	55	199	....	....	....	....	....	....	....	....	....	....	....	....	....	....	....	....	....	....
1990-91	Sault Ste. Marie	OHL	59	18	51	69	93	....	....	....	....	....	....	....	....	....	14	5	12	17	28	....	....	....	....
1991-92	**Quebec**	**NHL**	**46**	**2**	**5**	**7**	**44**	**0**	**0**	**0**	**55**	**3.6**	**–4**	....	....	....	....	....	....	....	....	....	....	....	....
	Halifax Citadels	AHL	6	0	1	1	2	....	....	....	....	....	....	....	....	....	....	....	....	....	....	....	....	....	....
1992-93	**Quebec**	**NHL**	**81**	**4**	**12**	**16**	**168**	**0**	**1**	**0**	**54**	**7.4**	**6**	....	....	....	**6**	**0**	**1**	**1**	**2**	**0**	**0**	**0**	....
1993-94	**Quebec**	**NHL**	**45**	**2**	**6**	**8**	**67**	**0**	**0**	**0**	**42**	**4.8**	**3**	....	....	....	....	....	....	....	....	....	....	....	....
1994-95	**Quebec**	**NHL**	**35**	**0**	**7**	**7**	**52**	**0**	**0**	**0**	**24**	**0.0**	**17**	....	....	....	**6**	**0**	**1**	**1**	**14**	**0**	**0**	**0**	....
1995-96 ◆	**Colorado**	**NHL**	**73**	**5**	**11**	**16**	**88**	**1**	**0**	**1**	**49**	**10.2**	**27**	....	....	....	**22**	**1**	**3**	**4**	**36**	**0**	**0**	**0**	....
1996-97	**Colorado**	**NHL**	**78**	**2**	**19**	**21**	**135**	**0**	**0**	**0**	**60**	**3.3**	**16**	....	....	....	**17**	**0**	**4**	**4**	**62**	**0**	**0**	**0**	....
1997-98	**Colorado**	**NHL**	**77**	**3**	**14**	**17**	**124**	**0**	**0**	**1**	**64**	**4.7**	**–3**	....	....	....	**7**	**0**	**0**	**0**	**23**	**0**	**0**	**0**	....
	Canada	Olympics	6	0	1	1	4	....	....	....	....	....	....	....	....	....	....	....	....	....	....	....	....	....	....
1998-99	**Colorado**	**NHL**	**64**	**5**	**16**	**21**	**92**	**3**	**0**	**0**	**83**	**6.0**	**20**	**0**	**0.0**	**24:50**	**19**	**2**	**3**	**5**	**24**	**1**	**0**	**0**	**28:34**
99-2000	**Colorado**	**NHL**	**59**	**5**	**13**	**18**	**98**	**1**	**0**	**2**	**63**	**7.9**	**5**	**0**	**0.0**	**25:51**	**16**	**0**	**7**	**7**	**28**	**0**	**0**	**0**	**26:05**
2000-01 ◆	**Colorado**	**NHL**	**35**	**3**	**12**	**15**	**42**	**1**	**1**	**1**	**59**	**5.1**	**6**	**0**	**0.0**	**25:22**	**23**	**3**	**4**	**7**	***47**	**1**	**0**	**1**	**28:22**
2001-02	**Colorado**	**NHL**	**55**	**5**	**22**	**27**	**55**	**1**	**1**	**0**	**85**	**5.9**	**7**	**0**	**0.0**	**25:59**	**21**	**1**	**6**	**7**	**28**	**0**	**0**	**0**	**27:46**
	Canada	Olympics	6	1	0	1	2	....	....	....	....	....	....	....	....	....	....	....	....	....	....	....	....	....	....
2002-03	**Colorado**	**NHL**	**78**	**11**	**20**	**31**	**88**	**3**	**0**	**2**	**106**	**10.4**	**30**	**0**	**0.0**	**25:43**	**6**	**0**	**1**	**1**	**8**	**0**	**0**	**0**	**24:12**
2003-04	**Colorado**	**NHL**	**73**	**8**	**22**	**30**	**87**	**5**	**0**	**1**	**105**	**7.6**	**13**	**0**	**0.0**	**24:03**	**11**	**0**	**4**	**4**	**10**	**0**	**0**	**0**	**25:06**
	NHL Totals		**799**	**55**	**179**	**234**	**1140**	**15**	**3**	**8**	**849**	**6.5**		**0**	**0.0**	**25:15**	**154**	**7**	**34**	**41**	**282**	**2**	**0**	**1**	**27:15**

OHL First All-Star Team (1991)

Transferred to **Colorado** after **Quebec** franchise relocated, June 21, 1995. • Missed majority of 2000-01 season recovering from shoulder injury suffered in game vs. Carolina, January 6, 2001.

FORBES, Colin
(FOHRBS, COHL-ihn) **CAR.**

Center. Shoots left. 6'3", 205 lbs. Born, New Westminster, B.C., February 16, 1976. Philadelphia's 5th choice, 166th overall, in 1994 Entry Draft.

Season	Club	League	GP	G	A	Pts	PIM	PP	SH	GW	S	%	+/-	TF	F%	Min	GP	G	A	Pts	PIM	PP	SH	GW	Min
1993-94	Sherwood Park	AJHL	47	18	22	40	76	....	....	....	....	....	....	....	....	....	....	....	....	....	....	....	....	....	....
1994-95	Portland	WHL	72	24	31	55	108	....	....	....	....	....	....	....	....	....	9	1	3	4	10	....	....	....	....
1995-96	Portland	WHL	72	33	44	77	137	....	....	....	....	....	....	....	....	....	7	2	5	7	14	....	....	....	....
	Hershey Bears	AHL	2	1	0	1	2	....	....	....	....	....	....	....	....	....	4	0	2	2	2	....	....	....	....
1996-97	**Philadelphia**	**NHL**	**3**	**1**	**0**	**1**	**0**	**0**	**0**	**0**	**3**	**33.3**	**0**	....	....	....	**3**	**0**	**0**	**0**	**0**	**0**	**0**	**0**	....
	Philadelphia	AHL	74	21	28	49	108	....	....	....	....	....	....	....	....	....	10	5	5	10	33	....	....	....	....
1997-98	**Philadelphia**	**NHL**	**63**	**12**	**7**	**19**	**59**	**2**	**0**	**2**	**93**	**12.9**	**2**	....	....	....	**5**	**0**	**0**	**0**	**2**	**0**	**0**	**0**	....
	Philadelphia	AHL	13	7	4	11	22	....	....	....	....	....	....	....	....	....	....	....	....	....	....	....	....	....	....
1998-99	**Philadelphia**	**NHL**	**66**	**9**	**7**	**16**	**51**	**0**	**0**	**4**	**92**	**9.8**	**0**	**2**	**50.0**	**12:35**	....	....	....	....	....	....	....	....	....
	Tampa Bay	**NHL**	**14**	**3**	**1**	**4**	**10**	**0**	**1**	**0**	**25**	**12.0**	**–5**	**0**	**0.0**	**17:30**	....	....	....	....	....	....	....	....	....
99-2000	**Tampa Bay**	**NHL**	**8**	**0**	**0**	**0**	**18**	**0**	**0**	**0**	**3**	**0.0**	**–4**	**1**	**0.0**	**8:53**	....	....	....	....	....	....	....	....	....
	Ottawa	**NHL**	**45**	**2**	**5**	**7**	**12**	**0**	**0**	**0**	**54**	**3.7**	**–1**	**82**	**47.6**	**8:34**	**5**	**1**	**0**	**1**	**14**	**0**	**0**	**0**	**6:48**
2000-01	**Ottawa**	**NHL**	**39**	**0**	**1**	**1**	**31**	**0**	**0**	**0**	**26**	**0.0**	**–3**	**10**	**40.0**	**6:10**	....	....	....	....	....	....	....	....	....
	NY Rangers	**NHL**	**19**	**1**	**4**	**5**	**15**	**0**	**0**	**0**	**20**	**5.0**	**–3**	**1**	**0.0**	**7:52**	....	....	....	....	....	....	....	....	....
2001-02	Utah Grizzlies	AHL	4	0	0	0	21	....	....	....	....	....	....	....	....	....	....	....	....	....	....	....	....	....	....
	Washington	**NHL**	**38**	**5**	**3**	**8**	**15**	**0**	**1**	**1**	**49**	**10.2**	**–2**	**253**	**44.7**	**11:01**	....	....	....	....	....	....	....	....	....
	Portland Pirates	AHL	14	4	5	9	18	....	....	....	....	....	....	....	....	....	....	....	....	....	....	....	....	....	....
2002-03	**Washington**	**NHL**	**5**	**0**	**0**	**0**	**0**	**0**	**0**	**0**	**3**	**0.0**	**–2**	**12**	**50.0**	**9:38**	....	....	....	....	....	....	....	....	....
	Portland Pirates	AHL	69	22	38	60	73	....	....	....	....	....	....	....	....	....	3	2	2	4	4	....	....	....	....
2003-04	**Washington**	**NHL**	**2**	**0**	**0**	**0**	**0**	**0**	**0**	**0**	**2**	**0.0**	**0**	**3**	**33.3**	**8:53**	....	....	....	....	....	....	....	....	....
	Portland Pirates	AHL	69	16	32	48	59	....	....	....	....	....	....	....	....	....	7	0	6	6	16	....	....	....	....
	NHL Totals		**302**	**33**	**28**	**61**	**211**	**2**	**2**	**7**	**370**	**8.9**		**364**	**45.1**	**10:12**	**13**	**1**	**0**	**1**	**16**	**0**	**0**	**0**	**6:48**

Traded to **Tampa Bay** by **Philadelphia** with Philadelphia's 4th round choice (Michal Lanicek) in 1999 Entry Draft for Mikael Andersson and Sandy McCarthy, March 20, 1999. Traded to **Ottawa** by **Tampa Bay** for Bruce Gardiner, November 11, 1999. Traded to **NY Rangers** by **Ottawa** for Eric Lacroix, March 1, 2001. Signed as a free agent by **Washington**, January 8, 2002. Signed as a free agent by **Hershey** (AHL), September 11, 2003. Signed as a free agent by **Portland** (AHL), October 14, 2003. Signed as a free agent by **Washington**, November 4, 2003. Signed as a free agent by **Carolina**, August 11, 2004.

FORSBERG, Peter
(FOHRS-buhrg, PEE-tuhr) **COL.**

Center. Shoots left. 6', 205 lbs. Born, Ornskoldsvik, Sweden, July 20, 1973. Philadelphia's 1st choice, 6th overall, in 1991 Entry Draft.

Season	Club	League	GP	G	A	Pts	PIM	PP	SH	GW	S	%	+/-	TF	F%	Min	GP	G	A	Pts	PIM	PP	SH	GW	Min
1989-90	MoDo Jr.	Swede-Jr.	30	15	12	27	42	....	....	....	....	....	....	....	....	....	....	....	....	....	....	....	....	....	....
	MoDo	Sweden	1	0	1	1	4	....	....	....	....	....	....	....	....	....	....	....	....	....	....	....	....	....	....
1990-91	MoDo Jr.	Swede-Jr.	39	38	64	102	56	....	....	....	....	....	....	....	....	....	....	....	....	....	....	....	....	....	....
	MoDo	Sweden	23	7	10	17	22	....	....	....	....	....	....	....	....	....	....	....	....	....	....	....	....	....	....
1991-92	MoDo	Sweden	39	9	18	27	78	....	....	....	....	....	....	....	....	....	....	....	....	....	....	....	....	....	....
1992-93	MoDo Jr.	Swede-Jr.	2	0	3	3	4	....	....	....	....	....	....	....	....	....	....	....	....	....	....	....	....	....	....
	MoDo	Sweden	39	23	24	47	92	....	....	....	....	....	....	....	....	....	3	4	1	5	0	....	....	....	....
1993-94	MoDo	Sweden	39	18	26	44	82	....	....	....	....	....	....	....	....	....	11	9	7	16	14	....	....	....	....
	Sweden	Olympics	8	2	6	8	6	....	....	....	....	....	....	....	....	....	....	....	....	....	....	....	....	....	....

Season	Club	League	GP	G	A	Pts	PIM	PP	SH	GW	S	%	+/-	TF	F%	Min	GP	G	A	Pts	PIM	PP	SH	GW	Min
			Regular Season														Playoffs								
1994-95	MoDo	Sweden	11	5	9	14	20	....	....	....	....	....	....	....	....	....	....	....	....	....	....	....	....	....	....
	Quebec	**NHL**	**47**	**15**	**35**	**50**	**16**	**3**	**0**	**3**	**86**	**17.4**	**17**	....	....	....	**6**	**2**	**4**	**6**	**4**	**1**	**0**	**0**	....
1995-96◆	**Colorado**	**NHL**	**82**	**30**	**86**	**116**	**47**	**7**	**3**	**3**	**217**	**13.8**	**26**	....	....	....	**22**	**10**	**11**	**21**	**18**	**3**	**0**	**1**	....
1996-97	**Colorado**	**NHL**	**65**	**28**	**58**	**86**	**73**	**5**	**4**	**4**	**188**	**14.9**	**31**	....	....	....	**14**	**5**	**12**	**17**	**10**	**3**	**0**	**0**	....
1997-98	**Colorado**	**NHL**	**72**	**25**	**66**	**91**	**94**	**7**	**3**	**7**	**202**	**12.4**	**6**	....	....	....	**7**	**6**	**5**	**11**	**12**	**2**	**0**	**0**	....
	Sweden	Olympics	4	1	4	5	6	....	....	....	....	....	....	....	....	....	....	....	....	....	....	....	....	....	....
1998-99	**Colorado**	**NHL**	**78**	**30**	**67**	**97**	**108**	**9**	**2**	**7**	**217**	**13.8**	**27**	**895**	**54.4**	**23:29**	**19**	**8**	**16**	***24**	**31**	**1**	**1**	**0**	**21:39**
99-2000	**Colorado**	**NHL**	**49**	**14**	**37**	**51**	**52**	**3**	**0**	**2**	**105**	**13.3**	**9**	**519**	**46.6**	**20:55**	**16**	**7**	**8**	**15**	**12**	**2**	**1**	**4**	**20:59**
2000-01◆	**Colorado**	**NHL**	**73**	**27**	**62**	**89**	**54**	**12**	**2**	**5**	**178**	**15.2**	**23**	**755**	**46.6**	**20:48**	**11**	**4**	**10**	**14**	**6**	**1**	**0**	**2**	**21:55**
2001-02	**Colorado**	**NHL**	....	....	....	....	....	....	....	....	....	....	....	....	....	....	**20**	**9**	***18**	***27**	**20**	**0**	**0**	**4**	**18:10**
2002-03	**Colorado**	**NHL**	**75**	**29**	***77**	***106**	**70**	**8**	**0**	**2**	**166**	**17.5**	**52**	**709**	**47.0**	**19:20**	**7**	**2**	**6**	**8**	**6**	**1**	**0**	**0**	**20:01**
2003-04	**Colorado**	**NHL**	**39**	**18**	**37**	**55**	**30**	**3**	**1**	**5**	**85**	**21.2**	**16**	**549**	**42.3**	**19:12**	**11**	**4**	**7**	**11**	**12**	**1**	**0**	**1**	**19:02**
	NHL Totals		**580**	**216**	**525**	**741**	**544**	**57**	**15**	**38**	**1444**	**15.0**		**3427**	**48.0**	**20:56**	**133**	**57**	**97**	**154**	**131**	**15**	**2**	**12**	**20:15**

NHL All-Rookie Team (1995) • Calder Memorial Trophy (1995) • NHL First All-Star Team (1998, 1999, 2003) • Bud Light Plus/Minus Award (2003) (tied with Milan Hejduk) • Art Ross Trophy (2003) • Hart Trophy (2003)

Played in NHL All-Star Game (1996, 1998, 1999, 2001, 2003)

Traded to **Quebec** by **Philadelphia** with Steve Duchesne, Kerry Huffman, Mike Ricci, Ron Hextall, Philadelphia's 1st round choice (Jocelyn Thibault) in 1993 Entry Draft, $15,000,000 and future considerations (Chris Simon and Philadelphia's 1st round choice (later traded to Toronto – later traded to Washington – Washington selected Nolan Baumgartner) in 1994 Entry Draft, July 21, 1992) for Eric Lindros, June 30, 1992. Transferred to **Colorado** after **Quebec** franchise relocated, June 21, 1995. • Missed entire 2001-02 regular season recovering from spleen injury suffered in game vs. Los Angeles, May 9, 2001 and ankle injury suffered in practice, January 10, 2002. • Missed majority of 2003-04 season recovering from groin (October 28, 2003 vs. Calgary) and hip (February 16, 2004 vs. Vancouver) injuries.

FORTIN, Jean-Francois

(fohr-TEHN, ZHAWN-fran-SWUH)

Defense. Shoots right. 6'2", 205 lbs. Born, Laval, Que., March 15, 1979. Washington's 2nd choice, 35th overall, in 1997 Entry Draft.

1993-94	Laval Laurentide	QAHA	31	8	20	28	32	....	....	....	....	....	....	....	....	....	....	....	....	....	....	....	....	....	....
1994-95	Abitibi Forestiers	QAAA	44	2	14	16	34	....	....	....	....	....	....	....	....	....	10	2	2	4	....	....	....	....	....
1995-96	Sherbrooke	QMJHL	69	7	15	22	40	....	....	....	....	....	....	....	....	....	7	2	6	8	2	....	....	....	....
1996-97	Sherbrooke	QMJHL	59	7	30	37	89	....	....	....	....	....	....	....	....	....	2	0	1	1	14	....	....	....	....
1997-98	Sherbrooke	QMJHL	55	12	25	37	37	....	....	....	....	....	....	....	....	....	....	....	....	....	....	....	....	....	....
1998-99	Sherbrooke	QMJHL	64	17	33	50	78	....	....	....	....	....	....	....	....	....	12	5	13	18	20	....	....	....	....
99-2000	Portland Pirates	AHL	43	3	5	8	44	....	....	....	....	....	....	....	....	....	2	0	0	0	0	....	....	....	....
	Hampton Roads	ECHL	7	0	2	2	0	....	....	....	....	....	....	....	....	....	....	....	....	....	....	....	....	....	....
2000-01	Richmond	ECHL	15	0	4	4	2	....	....	....	....	....	....	....	....	....	....	....	....	....	....	....	....	....	....
	Portland Pirates	AHL	32	1	7	8	22	....	....	....	....	....	....	....	....	....	1	0	0	0	0	....	....	....	....
2001-02	**Washington**	**NHL**	**36**	**1**	**3**	**4**	**20**	**0**	**0**	**0**	**24**	**4.2**	**–1**	**1**	**100.0**	**19:25**	....	....	....	....	....	....	....	....	....
	Portland Pirates	AHL	44	4	9	13	20	....	....	....	....	....	....	....	....	....	....	....	....	....	....	....	....	....	....
2002-03	**Washington**	**NHL**	**33**	**0**	**1**	**1**	**22**	**0**	**0**	**0**	**20**	**0.0**	**–3**	**0**	**0.0**	**15:14**	....	....	....	....	....	....	....	....	....
	Portland Pirates	AHL	10	2	1	3	17	....	....	....	....	....	....	....	....	....	....	....	....	....	....	....	....	....	....
2003-04	**Washington**	**NHL**	**2**	**0**	**0**	**0**	**0**	**0**	**0**	**0**	**0**	**0.0**	**0**	**0**	**0.0**	**7:57**	....	....	....	....	....	....	....	....	....
	Portland Pirates	AHL	4	0	1	1	6	....	....	....	....	....	....	....	....	....	....	....	....	....	....	....	....	....	....
	NHL Totals		**71**	**1**	**4**	**5**	**42**	**0**	**0**	**0**	**44**	**2.3**		**1**	**100.0**	**17:09**	....	....	....	....	....	....	....	....	....

• Missed majority of 2003-04 season recovering from back injury suffered in game vs.St. John's (AHL), October 24, 2003.

FOSTER, Kurtis

(FAW-stuhr, KUHR-this) **ANA.**

Defense. Shoots right. 6'5", 235 lbs. Born, Carp, Ont., November 24, 1981. Calgary's 2nd choice, 40th overall, in 2000 Entry Draft.

1996-97	Ottawa Valley	ODMHA	36	7	18	25	88	....	....	....	....	....	....	....	....	....	....	....	....	....	....	....	....	....	....
1997-98	Peterborough	OHL	39	1	1	2	45	....	....	....	....	....	....	....	....	....	4	0	0	0	2	....	....	....	....
1998-99	Peterborough	OHL	54	2	13	15	59	....	....	....	....	....	....	....	....	....	5	0	0	0	6	....	....	....	....
99-2000	Peterborough	OHL	68	6	18	24	116	....	....	....	....	....	....	....	....	....	5	1	2	3	4	....	....	....	....
2000-01	Peterborough	OHL	62	17	24	41	78	....	....	....	....	....	....	....	....	....	7	1	1	2	10	....	....	....	....
2001-02	Peterborough	OHL	33	10	4	14	58	....	....	....	....	....	....	....	....	....	....	....	....	....	....	....	....	....	....
	Chicago Wolves	AHL	39	6	9	15	59	....	....	....	....	....	....	....	....	....	14	1	1	2	21	....	....	....	....
2002-03	**Atlanta**	**NHL**	**2**	**0**	**0**	**0**	**0**	**0**	**0**	**0**	**1**	**0.0**	**–2**	**0**	**0.0**	**11:06**	....	....	....	....	....	....	....	....	....
	Chicago Wolves	AHL	75	15	27	42	159	....	....	....	....	....	....	....	....	....	9	1	3	4	14	....	....	....	....
2003-04	**Atlanta**	**NHL**	**3**	**0**	**1**	**1**	**0**	**0**	**0**	**0**	**1**	**0.0**	**0**	**0**	**0.0**	**6:58**	....	....	....	....	....	....	....	....	....
	Chicago Wolves	AHL	67	11	19	30	95	....	....	....	....	....	....	....	....	....	10	0	3	3	12	....	....	....	....
	NHL Totals		**5**	**0**	**1**	**1**	**0**	**0**	**0**	**0**	**2**	**0.0**		**0**	**0.0**	**8:37**	....	....	....	....	....	....	....	....	....

Rights traded to **Atlanta** by **Calgary** with Jeff Cowan for Petr Buzek and Atlanta's 6th round choice (Adam Pardy) in 2004 Entry Draft, December 18, 2001. Traded to **Anaheim** by **Atlanta** for Niclas Havelid, June 26, 2004.

FRANCIS, Ron

(FRAN-sihs, RAWN)

Center. Shoots left. 6'3", 200 lbs. Born, Sault Ste. Marie, Ont., March 1, 1963. Hartford's 1st choice, 4th overall, in 1981 Entry Draft.

1979-80	Soo Legion	NOHA	45	57	92	149	....	....	....	....	....	....	....	....	....	....	....	....	....	....	....	....	....	....	....
1980-81	Sault Ste. Marie	OMJHL	64	26	43	69	33	....	....	....	....	....	....	....	....	....	19	7	8	15	34	....	....	....	....
1981-82	Sault Ste. Marie	OHL	25	18	30	48	46	....	....	....	....	....	....	....	....	....	....	....	....	....	....	....	....	....	....
	Hartford	**NHL**	**59**	**25**	**43**	**68**	**51**	**12**	**0**	**1**	**163**	**15.3**	**–13**	....	....	....	....	....	....	....	....	....	....	....	....
1982-83	**Hartford**	**NHL**	**79**	**31**	**59**	**90**	**60**	**4**	**2**	**4**	**212**	**14.6**	**–25**	....	....	....	....	....	....	....	....	....	....	....	....
1983-84	**Hartford**	**NHL**	**72**	**23**	**60**	**83**	**45**	**5**	**0**	**5**	**202**	**11.4**	**–10**	....	....	....	....	....	....	....	....	....	....	....	....
1984-85	**Hartford**	**NHL**	**80**	**24**	**57**	**81**	**66**	**4**	**0**	**1**	**195**	**12.3**	**–23**	....	....	....	....	....	....	....	....	....	....	....	....
1985-86	**Hartford**	**NHL**	**53**	**24**	**53**	**77**	**24**	**7**	**1**	**4**	**120**	**20.0**	**8**	....	....	....	**10**	**1**	**2**	**3**	**4**	**0**	**0**	**0**	....
1986-87	**Hartford**	**NHL**	**75**	**30**	**63**	**93**	**45**	**7**	**0**	**7**	**189**	**15.9**	**10**	....	....	....	**6**	**2**	**2**	**4**	**6**	**1**	**0**	**0**	....
1987-88	**Hartford**	**NHL**	**80**	**25**	**50**	**75**	**87**	**11**	**1**	**3**	**172**	**14.5**	**–8**	....	....	....	**6**	**2**	**5**	**7**	**2**	**1**	**0**	**0**	....
1988-89	**Hartford**	**NHL**	**69**	**29**	**48**	**77**	**36**	**8**	**0**	**4**	**156**	**18.6**	**4**	....	....	....	**4**	**0**	**2**	**2**	**0**	**0**	**0**	**0**	....
1989-90	**Hartford**	**NHL**	**80**	**32**	**69**	**101**	**73**	**15**	**1**	**5**	**170**	**18.8**	**13**	....	....	....	**7**	**3**	**3**	**6**	**8**	**1**	**0**	**0**	....
1990-91	**Hartford**	**NHL**	**67**	**21**	**55**	**76**	**51**	**10**	**1**	**6**	**149**	**14.1**	**–2**	....	....	....	....	....	....	....	....	....	....	....	....
	◆ **Pittsburgh**	**NHL**	**14**	**2**	**9**	**11**	**21**	**0**	**0**	**1**	**25**	**8.0**	**0**	....	....	....	**24**	**7**	**10**	**17**	**24**	**0**	**0**	**4**	....
1991-92◆	**Pittsburgh**	**NHL**	**70**	**21**	**33**	**54**	**30**	**5**	**1**	**2**	**121**	**17.4**	**–7**	....	....	....	**21**	**8**	***19**	**27**	**6**	**2**	**0**	**2**	....
1992-93	**Pittsburgh**	**NHL**	**84**	**24**	**76**	**100**	**68**	**9**	**2**	**4**	**215**	**11.2**	**6**	....	....	....	**12**	**6**	**11**	**17**	**19**	**1**	**0**	**1**	....
1993-94	**Pittsburgh**	**NHL**	**82**	**27**	**66**	**93**	**62**	**8**	**0**	**2**	**216**	**12.5**	**–3**	....	....	....	**6**	**0**	**2**	**2**	**6**	**0**	**0**	**0**	....
1994-95	**Pittsburgh**	**NHL**	**44**	**11**	***48**	**59**	**18**	**3**	**0**	**1**	**94**	**11.7**	**30**	....	....	....	**12**	**6**	**13**	**19**	**4**	**2**	**0**	**0**	....
1995-96	**Pittsburgh**	**NHL**	**77**	**27**	***92**	**119**	**56**	**12**	**1**	**4**	**158**	**17.1**	**25**	....	....	....	**11**	**3**	**6**	**9**	**4**	**2**	**0**	**1**	....
1996-97	**Pittsburgh**	**NHL**	**81**	**27**	**63**	**90**	**20**	**10**	**1**	**2**	**183**	**14.8**	**7**	....	....	....	**5**	**1**	**2**	**3**	**2**	**1**	**0**	**0**	....
1997-98	**Pittsburgh**	**NHL**	**81**	**25**	**62**	**87**	**20**	**7**	**0**	**5**	**189**	**13.2**	**12**	....	....	....	**6**	**1**	**5**	**6**	**2**	**0**	**0**	**0**	....
1998-99	**Carolina**	**NHL**	**82**	**21**	**31**	**52**	**34**	**8**	**0**	**2**	**133**	**15.8**	**–2**	**1589**	**51.5**	**21:55**	**3**	**0**	**1**	**1**	**0**	**0**	**0**	**0**	**16:27**
99-2000	**Carolina**	**NHL**	**78**	**23**	**50**	**73**	**18**	**7**	**0**	**4**	**150**	**15.3**	**10**	**1566**	**53.3**	**21:58**	....	....	....	....	....	....	....	....	....
2000-01	**Carolina**	**NHL**	**82**	**15**	**50**	**65**	**32**	**7**	**0**	**4**	**130**	**11.5**	**–15**	**1271**	**57.5**	**20:15**	**3**	**0**	**0**	**0**	**0**	**0**	**0**	**0**	**13:21**
2001-02	**Carolina**	**NHL**	**80**	**27**	**50**	**77**	**18**	**14**	**0**	**5**	**165**	**16.4**	**4**	**1136**	**58.9**	**20:41**	**23**	**6**	**10**	**16**	**6**	**4**	**0**	**3**	**21:03**
2002-03	**Carolina**	**NHL**	**82**	**22**	**35**	**57**	**30**	**8**	**1**	**1**	**156**	**14.1**	**–22**	**880**	**52.5**	**19:56**	....	....	....	....	....	....	....	....	....
2003-04	**Carolina**	**NHL**	**68**	**10**	**20**	**30**	**14**	**5**	**0**	**1**	**79**	**12.7**	**–12**	**773**	**56.1**	**16:12**	....	....	....	....	....	....	....	....	....
	Toronto	**NHL**	**12**	**3**	**7**	**10**	**0**	**2**	**0**	**1**	**12**	**25.0**	**3**	**131**	**56.5**	**13:44**	**12**	**0**	**4**	**4**	**2**	**0**	**0**	**0**	**15:28**
	NHL Totals		**1731**	**549**	**1249**	**1798**	**979**	**188**	**12**	**79**	**3754**	**14.6**		**7346**	**54.8**	**20:06**	**171**	**46**	**97**	**143**	**95**	**15**	**0**	**11**	**18:31**

Alka-Seltzer Plus Award (1995) • Frank J. Selke Trophy (1995) • Lady Byng Trophy (1995, 1998, 2002) • King Clancy Memorial Trophy (2002)

Played in NHL All-Star Game (1983, 1985, 1990, 1996)

Traded to **Pittsburgh** by **Hartford** with Grant Jennings and Ulf Samuelsson for John Cullen, Jeff Parker and Zarley Zalapski, March 4, 1991. Signed as a free agent by **Carolina**, July 13, 1998. Traded to **Toronto** by **Carolina** for Toronto's 4th round choice in 2005 Entry Draft, March 9, 2004.

FRIESEN, Jeff

(FREE-zuhn, JEHF) **N.J.**

Left wing. Shoots left. 6'1", 205 lbs. Born, Meadow Lake, Sask., August 5, 1976. San Jose's 1st choice, 11th overall, in 1994 Entry Draft.

1991-92	Sask. Contacts	SMHL	35	37	51	88	75	....	....	....	....	....	....	....	....	....	....	....	....	....	....	....	....	....	....
	Regina Pats	WHL	4	3	1	4	2	....	....	....	....	....	....	....	....	....	....	....	....	....	....	....	....	....	....
1992-93	Regina Pats	WHL	70	45	38	83	23	....	....	....	....	....	....	....	....	....	13	7	10	17	8	....	....	....	....
1993-94	Regina Pats	WHL	66	51	67	118	48	....	....	....	....	....	....	....	....	....	4	3	2	5	2	....	....	....	....
1994-95	Regina Pats	WHL	25	21	23	44	22	....	....	....	....	....	....	....	....	....	....	....	....	....	....	....	....	....	....
	San Jose	**NHL**	**48**	**15**	**10**	**25**	**14**	**5**	**1**	**2**	**86**	**17.4**	**–8**	....	....	....	**11**	**1**	**5**	**6**	**4**	**0**	**0**	**0**	....
1995-96	**San Jose**	**NHL**	**79**	**15**	**31**	**46**	**42**	**2**	**0**	**0**	**123**	**12.2**	**–19**	....	....	....	....	....	....	....	....	....	....	....	....

			Regular Season														Playoffs								
Season	**Club**	**League**	**GP**	**G**	**A**	**Pts**	**PIM**	**PP**	**SH**	**GW**	**S**	**%**	**+/-**	**TF**	**F%**	**Min**	**GP**	**G**	**A**	**Pts**	**PIM**	**PP**	**SH**	**GW**	**Min**
1996-97	**San Jose**	**NHL**	**82**	**28**	**34**	**62**	**75**	**6**	**2**	**5**	**200**	**14.0**	**–8**	....	....	....	....	....	....	....	....	....	....	....	....
1997-98	**San Jose**	**NHL**	**79**	**31**	**32**	**63**	**40**	**7**	**6**	**7**	**186**	**16.7**	**8**	....	....	....	**6**	**0**	**1**	**1**	**2**	**0**	**0**	**0**	....
1998-99	**San Jose**	**NHL**	**78**	**22**	**35**	**57**	**42**	**10**	**1**	**3**	**215**	**10.2**	**3**	**24**	**33.3**	**19:25**	**6**	**2**	**2**	**4**	**14**	**1**	**0**	**0**	**22:22**
99-2000	**San Jose**	**NHL**	**82**	**26**	**35**	**61**	**47**	**11**	**3**	**7**	**191**	**13.6**	**–2**	**3**	**66.7**	**19:48**	**11**	**2**	**2**	**4**	**10**	**0**	**0**	**0**	**17:21**
2000-01	**San Jose**	**NHL**	**64**	**12**	**24**	**36**	**56**	**2**	**0**	**1**	**120**	**10.0**	**7**	**7**	**28.6**	**18:51**	....	....	....	....	....	....	....	....	....
	Anaheim	**NHL**	**15**	**2**	**10**	**12**	**10**	**2**	**0**	**0**	**29**	**6.9**	**–2**	**43**	**55.8**	**21:28**	....	....	....	....	....	....	....	....	....
2001-02	**Anaheim**	**NHL**	**81**	**17**	**26**	**43**	**44**	**1**	**1**	**0**	**161**	**10.6**	**–1**	**45**	**48.9**	**17:59**	....	....	....	....	....	....	....	....	....
2002-03 ♦	**New Jersey**	**NHL**	**81**	**23**	**28**	**51**	**26**	**3**	**0**	**4**	**179**	**12.8**	**23**	**11**	**45.5**	**15:33**	**24**	**10**	**4**	**14**	**6**	**1**	**0**	**4**	**16:02**
2003-04	**New Jersey**	**NHL**	**81**	**17**	**20**	**37**	**26**	**5**	**0**	**4**	**177**	**9.6**	**8**	**31**	**45.2**	**15:08**	**5**	**0**	**0**	**0**	**4**	**0**	**0**	**0**	**12:55**
	NHL Totals		**770**	**208**	**285**	**493**	**422**	**54**	**14**	**33**	**1667**	**12.5**		**164**	**47.0**	**17:52**	**63**	**15**	**14**	**29**	**40**	**2**	**0**	**4**	**16:50**

WHL Rookie of the Year (1993) • Canadian Major Junior Rookie of the Year (1993) • NHL All-Rookie Team (1995)

Traded to **Anaheim** by **San Jose** with Steve Shields and San Jose's 2nd round choice (later traded to Dallas – Dallas selected Vojtech Polak) in 2003 Entry Draft for Teemu Selanne, March 5, 2001. Traded to **New Jersey** by **Anaheim** with Oleg Tverdovsky and Maxim Balmochnykh for Petr Sykora, Mike Commodore, Jean-Francois Damphousse and Igor Pohanka, July 6, 2002.

FRITSCHE, Dan (FRIHCH, DAN) CBJ

Center. Shoots right. 6'1", 198 lbs. Born, Cleveland, OH, July 13, 1985. Columbus' 2nd choice, 46th overall, in 2003 Entry Draft.

Season	Club	League	GP	G	A	Pts	PIM	PP	SH	GW	S	%	+/-	TF	F%	Min	GP	G	A	Pts	PIM	PP	SH	GW	Min
2000-01	Cleveland Barons	NAJHL	49	23	29	52	47	....	....	....	....	....	....	....	....	....	1	1	1	2	0	....	....	....	....
2001-02	Sarnia Sting	OHL	17	5	13	18	20	....	....	....	....	....	....	....	....	....	....	....	....	....	....	....	....	....	....
2002-03	Sarnia Sting	OHL	61	32	39	71	79	....	....	....	....	....	....	....	....	....	5	2	2	4	4	....	....	....	....
2003-04	**Columbus**	**NHL**	**19**	**1**	**0**	**1**	**12**	**0**	**0**	**0**	**19**	**5.3**	**–5**	**139**	**38.1**	**8:24**	....	....	....	....	....	....	....	....	....
	Sarnia Sting	OHL	27	16	13	29	26	....	....	....	....	....	....	....	....	....	5	1	5	6	0	....	....	....	....
	Syracuse Crunch	AHL	4	2	0	2	0	....	....	....	....	....	....	....	....	....	4	0	1	1	4	....	....	....	....
	NHL Totals		**19**	**1**	**0**	**1**	**12**	**0**	**0**	**0**	**19**	**5.3**		**139**	**38.1**	**8:24**	....	....	....	....	....	....	....	....	....

• Missed majority of 2001-02 season recovering from shoulder surgery, December 12, 2001. • Returned to **Sarnia** (OHL) by **Columbus**, January 7, 2004.

FROLOV, Alexander (froh-LAHF, al-ehx-AN-duhr) L.A.

Left wing. Shoots right. 6'3", 210 lbs. Born, Moscow, USSR, June 19, 1982. Los Angeles' 1st choice, 20th overall, in 2000 Entry Draft.

Season	Club	League	GP	G	A	Pts	PIM	PP	SH	GW	S	%	+/-	TF	F%	Min	GP	G	A	Pts	PIM	PP	SH	GW	Min
1998-99	Spartak Moscow	Russia	1	0	0	0	0	....	....	....	....	....	....	....	....	....	....	....	....	....	....	....	....	....	....
99-2000	Yaroslavl 2	Russia-3	36	27	13	40	30	....	....	....	....	....	....	....	....	....	....	....	....	....	....	....	....	....	....
2000-01	Spartak Moscow	Russia-2	44	20	19	39	8	....	....	....	....	....	....	....	....	....	....	....	....	....	....	....	....	....	....
2001-02	Krylja Sovetov 2	Russia-3	2	0	0	0	4	....	....	....	....	....	....	....	....	....	....	....	....	....	....	....	....	....	....
	Krylja Sovetov	Russia	43	18	12	30	16	....	....	....	....	....	....	....	....	....	3	1	0	1	0	....	....	....	....
2002-03	**Los Angeles**	**NHL**	**79**	**14**	**17**	**31**	**34**	**1**	**0**	**3**	**141**	**9.9**	**12**	**9**	**22.2**	**14:23**	....	....	....	....	....	....	....	....	....
2003-04	Nizhny Novgorod	Russia	1	0	0	0	0	....	....	....	....	....	....	....	....	....	....	....	....	....	....	....	....	....	....
	Los Angeles	**NHL**	**77**	**24**	**24**	**48**	**24**	**5**	**2**	**3**	**168**	**14.3**	**8**	**34**	**32.4**	**17:13**	....	....	....	....	....	....	....	....	....
	NHL Totals		**156**	**38**	**41**	**79**	**58**	**6**	**2**	**6**	**309**	**12.3**		**43**	**30.2**	**15:47**	....	....	....	....	....	....	....	....	....

FUSSEY, Owen (FOO-see, OH-when) WSH.

Right wing. Shoots left. 6', 195 lbs. Born, Winnipeg, Man., April 2, 1983. Washington's 2nd choice, 90th overall, in 2001 Entry Draft.

Season	Club	League	GP	G	A	Pts	PIM	PP	SH	GW	S	%	+/-	TF	F%	Min	GP	G	A	Pts	PIM	PP	SH	GW	Min
1998-99	Wpg. Warriors	MMHL	40	38	33	71	24	....	....	....	....	....	....	....	....	....	....	....	....	....	....	....	....	....	....
99-2000	Calgary Hitmen	WHL	51	7	6	13	35	....	....	....	....	....	....	....	....	....	12	3	4	7	2	....	....	....	....
2000-01	Calgary Hitmen	WHL	48	15	10	25	33	....	....	....	....	....	....	....	....	....	12	2	1	3	6	....	....	....	....
2001-02	Calgary Hitmen	WHL	72	43	27	70	61	....	....	....	....	....	....	....	....	....	7	3	1	4	4	....	....	....	....
2002-03	Calgary Hitmen	WHL	39	17	18	35	31	....	....	....	....	....	....	....	....	....	....	....	....	....	....	....	....	....	....
	Moose Jaw	WHL	27	24	12	36	20	....	....	....	....	....	....	....	....	....	13	6	6	12	10	....	....	....	....
2003-04	**Washington**	**NHL**	**4**	**0**	**1**	**1**	**0**	**0**	**0**	**0**	**6**	**0.0**	**–1**	**0**	**0.0**	**8:16**	....	....	....	....	....	....	....	....	....
	Portland Pirates	AHL	69	6	7	13	23	....	....	....	....	....	....	....	....	....	7	0	0	0	5	....	....	....	....
	NHL Totals		**4**	**0**	**1**	**1**	**0**	**0**	**0**	**0**	**6**	**0.0**		**0**	**0.0**	**8:16**	....	....	....	....	....	....	....	....	....

GABORIK, Marian (GA-bohr-ihk, MAIR-ee-uhn) MIN.

Right wing. Shoots left. 6'1", 190 lbs. Born, Trencin, Czech., February 14, 1982. Minnesota's 1st choice, 3rd overall, in 2000 Entry Draft.

Season	Club	League	GP	G	A	Pts	PIM	PP	SH	GW	S	%	+/-	TF	F%	Min	GP	G	A	Pts	PIM	PP	SH	GW	Min
1997-98	Dukla Trencin Jr.	Slovak-Jr.	36	37	22	59	28	....	....	....	....	....	....	....	....	....	....	....	....	....	....	....	....	....	....
	Dukla Trencin	Slovakia	1	1	0	1	0	....	....	....	....	....	....	....	....	....	....	....	....	....	....	....	....	....	....
1998-99	Dukla Trencin	Slovakia	33	11	9	20	6	....	....	....	....	....	....	....	....	....	3	1	0	1	2	....	....	....	....
99-2000	Dukla Trencin	Slovakia	50	25	21	46	34	....	....	....	....	....	....	....	....	....	5	1	2	3	2	....	....	....	....
2000-01	**Minnesota**	**NHL**	**71**	**18**	**18**	**36**	**32**	**6**	**0**	**3**	**179**	**10.1**	**–6**	**3**	**33.3**	**15:26**	....	....	....	....	....	....	....	....	....
2001-02	**Minnesota**	**NHL**	**78**	**30**	**37**	**67**	**34**	**10**	**0**	**4**	**221**	**13.6**	**0**	**4**	**25.0**	**16:47**	....	....	....	....	....	....	....	....	....
2002-03	**Minnesota**	**NHL**	**81**	**30**	**35**	**65**	**46**	**5**	**1**	**8**	**280**	**10.7**	**12**	**16**	**25.0**	**17:24**	**18**	**9**	**8**	**17**	**6**	**4**	**0**	**0**	**18:12**
2003-04	Dukla Trencin	Slovakia	9	10	3	13	10	....	....	....	....	....	....	....	....	....	....	....	....	....	....	....	....	....	....
	Minnesota	**NHL**	**65**	**18**	**22**	**40**	**20**	**3**	**0**	**4**	**220**	**8.2**	**10**	**11**	**45.5**	**18:17**	....	....	....	....	....	....	....	....	....
	NHL Totals		**295**	**96**	**112**	**208**	**132**	**24**	**1**	**19**	**900**	**10.7**		**34**	**32.4**	**16:57**	**18**	**9**	**8**	**17**	**6**	**4**	**0**	**0**	**18:12**

Played in NHL All-Star Game (2003)

GAGNE, Simon (GAH-nyay, see-MOHN) PHI.

Left wing. Shoots left. 6', 190 lbs. Born, Ste-Foy, Que., February 29, 1980. Philadelphia's 1st choice, 22nd overall, in 1998 Entry Draft.

Season	Club	League	GP	G	A	Pts	PIM	PP	SH	GW	S	%	+/-	TF	F%	Min	GP	G	A	Pts	PIM	PP	SH	GW	Min
1995-96	Ste-Foy	QAAA	27	13	9	22	18	....	....	....	....	....	....	....	....	....	15	7	8	15	8	....	....	....	....
1996-97	Beauport	QMJHL	51	9	22	31	49	....	....	....	....	....	....	....	....	....	....	....	....	....	....	....	....	....	....
1997-98	Quebec Remparts	QMJHL	53	30	39	69	26	....	....	....	....	....	....	....	....	....	12	11	5	16	23	....	....	....	....
1998-99	Quebec Remparts	QMJHL	61	50	*70	*120	42	....	....	....	....	....	....	....	....	....	13	9	8	17	4	....	....	....	....
99-2000	**Philadelphia**	**NHL**	**80**	**20**	**28**	**48**	**22**	**8**	**1**	**4**	**159**	**12.6**	**11**	**443**	**42.2**	**14:59**	**17**	**5**	**5**	**10**	**2**	**2**	**0**	**1**	**16:46**
2000-01	**Philadelphia**	**NHL**	**69**	**27**	**32**	**59**	**18**	**6**	**0**	**7**	**191**	**14.1**	**24**	**21**	**28.6**	**18:05**	**6**	**3**	**0**	**3**	**0**	**2**	**0**	**0**	**19:09**
2001-02	**Philadelphia**	**NHL**	**79**	**33**	**33**	**66**	**32**	**4**	**1**	**7**	**199**	**16.6**	**31**	**6**	**83.3**	**18:09**	**5**	**0**	**0**	**0**	**2**	**0**	**0**	**0**	**19:16**
	Canada	Olympics	6	1	3	4	0	....	....	....	....	....	....	....	....	....	....	....	....	....	....	....	....	....	....
2002-03	**Philadelphia**	**NHL**	**46**	**9**	**18**	**27**	**16**	**1**	**1**	**3**	**115**	**7.8**	**20**	**70**	**42.9**	**17:24**	**13**	**4**	**1**	**5**	**6**	**0**	**1**	**1**	**18:13**
2003-04	**Philadelphia**	**NHL**	**80**	**24**	**21**	**45**	**29**	**6**	**0**	**6**	**211**	**11.4**	**12**	**104**	**39.4**	**16:27**	**18**	**5**	**4**	**9**	**12**	**0**	**0**	**1**	**16:48**
	NHL Totals		**354**	**113**	**132**	**245**	**117**	**25**	**3**	**27**	**875**	**12.9**		**644**	**41.8**	**16:56**	**59**	**17**	**10**	**27**	**22**	**4**	**1**	**3**	**17:33**

QMJHL Second All-Star Team (1999) • NHL All-Rookie Team (2000)
Played in NHL ALL-Star Game (2001)

GAINEY, Steve (GAY-nee, STEEV)

Left wing. Shoots left. 6'1", 192 lbs. Born, Montreal, Que., January 26, 1979. Dallas' 3rd choice, 77th overall, in 1997 Entry Draft.

Season	Club	League	GP	G	A	Pts	PIM	PP	SH	GW	S	%	+/-	TF	F%	Min	GP	G	A	Pts	PIM	PP	SH	GW	Min
1995-96	Kamloops Blazers	WHL	49	1	4	5	40	....	....	....	....	....	....	....	....	....	3	0	0	0	0	....	....	....	....
1996-97	Kamloops Blazers	WHL	60	9	18	27	60	....	....	....	....	....	....	....	....	....	2	0	0	0	9	....	....	....	....
1997-98	Kamloops Blazers	WHL	68	21	34	55	93	....	....	....	....	....	....	....	....	....	7	1	7	8	15	....	....	....	....
1998-99	Kamloops Blazers	WHL	68	30	34	64	155	....	....	....	....	....	....	....	....	....	15	5	4	9	38	....	....	....	....
99-2000	Fort Wayne	UHL	1	0	0	0	0	....	....	....	....	....	....	....	....	....	....	....	....	....	....	....	....	....	....
	Michigan	IHL	58	8	10	18	41	....	....	....	....	....	....	....	....	....	....	....	....	....	....	....	....	....	....
2000-01	**Dallas**	**NHL**	**1**	**0**	**0**	**0**	**0**	**0**	**0**	**0**	**0**	**0.0**	**0**	**0**	**0.0**	**2:21**	....	....	....	....	....	....	....	....	....
	Utah Grizzlies	IHL	61	7	7	14	167	....	....	....	....	....	....	....	....	....	....	....	....	....	....	....	....	....	....
2001-02	**Dallas**	**NHL**	**5**	**0**	**1**	**1**	**7**	**0**	**0**	**0**	**1**	**0.0**	**–1**	**0**	**0.0**	**7:24**	....	....	....	....	....	....	....	....	....
	Utah Grizzlies	AHL	58	16	18	34	87	....	....	....	....	....	....	....	....	....	....	....	....	....	....	....	....	....	....
2002-03	Utah Grizzlies	AHL	68	9	17	26	106	....	....	....	....	....	....	....	....	....	2	0	0	0	11	....	....	....	....
2003-04	**Dallas**	**NHL**	**7**	**0**	**0**	**0**	**7**	**0**	**0**	**0**	**0**	**0.0**	**1**	**0**	**0.0**	**5:27**	....	....	....	....	....	....	....	....	....
	Utah Grizzlies	AHL	45	7	8	15	74	....	....	....	....	....	....	....	....	....	....	....	....	....	....	....	....	....	....
	Philadelphia	AHL	27	2	7	9	27	....	....	....	....	....	....	....	....	....	11	0	1	1	14	....	....	....	....
	NHL Totals		**13**	**0**	**1**	**1**	**14**	**0**	**0**	**0**	**1**	**0.0**		**0**	**0.0**	**5:58**	....	....	....	....	....	....	....	....	....

Traded to **Philadelphia** by **Dallas** for Mike Siklenka, February 16, 2004.

GAMACHE, Simon

(ga-MOHSH, see-MOHN) **NSH.**

Center. Shoots left. 5'9", 185 lbs. Born, Thetford Mines, Que., January 3, 1981. Atlanta's 14th choice, 290th overall, in 2000 Entry Draft.

			Regular Season														Playoffs								
Season	Club	League	GP	G	A	Pts	PIM	PP	SH	GW	S	%	+/-	TF	F%	Min	GP	G	A	Pts	PIM	PP	SH	GW	Min
1997-98	Levis-Lauzon	QAAA	42	28	26	54	....	....	....	....	....	....	....	....	....	....	4	1	1	2	....	....	....	....	....
1998-99	Val-d'Or Foreurs	QMJHL	70	19	43	62	54	....	....	....	....	....	....	....	....	....	6	1	2	3	4	....	....	....	....
99-2000	Val-d'Or Foreurs	QMJHL	72	64	79	143	74	....	....	....	....	....	....	....	....	....	....	....	....	....	....	....	....	....	....
2000-01	Val-d'Or Foreurs	QMJHL	72	*74	*110	*184	70	....	....	....	....	....	....	....	....	....	21	*22	*35	*57	18	....	....	....	....
2001-02	Chicago Wolves	AHL	26	2	4	6	11	....	....	....	....	....	....	....	....	....	....	....	....	....	....	....	....	....	....
	Greenville	ECHL	31	19	19	38	35	....	....	....	....	....	....	....	....	....	17	*15	9	*24	22	....	....	....	....
2002-03	**Atlanta**	**NHL**	**2**	**0**	**0**	**0**	**2**	**0**	**0**	**0**	**3**	**0.0**	**–1**	**0**	**0.0**	**12:37**	....	....	....	....	....	....	....	....	....
	Chicago Wolves	AHL	76	35	42	77	37	....	....	....	....	....	....	....	....	....	9	7	2	9	4	....	....	....	....
2003-04	**Atlanta**	**NHL**	**2**	**0**	**1**	**1**	**0**	**0**	**0**	**0**	**1**	**0.0**	**0**	**0**	**0.0**	**6:39**	....	....	....	....	....	....	....	....	....
	Chicago Wolves	AHL	16	5	6	11	4	....	....	....	....	....	....	....	....	....	....	....	....	....	....	....	....	....	....
	Nashville	**NHL**	**7**	**1**	**0**	**1**	**0**	**1**	**0**	**0**	**4**	**25.0**	**–3**	**18**	**55.6**	**7:35**	....	....	....	....	....	....	....	....	....
	Milwaukee	AHL	52	18	27	45	26	....	....	....	....	....	....	....	....	....	22	6	*18	24	14	....	....	....	....
	NHL Totals		**11**	**1**	**1**	**2**	**2**	**1**	**0**	**0**	**8**	**12.5**		**18**	**55.6**	**8:20**	....	....	....	....	....	....	....	....	....

Canadian Major Junior Second All-Star Team (2000) • QMJHL First All-Star Team (2001) • Michel Briere Trophy (MVP – QMJHL) (2001) • Canadian Major Junior First All-Star Team (2001) • Canadian Major Junior Player of the Year (2001) • Sheetrock CHL Top Scorer Award (2001) • Memorial Cup All-Star Team (2001) • Ed Chynoweth Trophy (Memorial Cup Leading Scorer) (2001) • ECHL All-Rookie Team (2002) • ECHL Playoff MVP (2002) (co-winner - Tyrone Garner)

Traded to **Nashville** by **Atlanta** with Kirill Safronov for Ben Simon and Tomas Kloucek, December 2, 2003.

GAUSTAD, Paul

(GAW-stad, PAWL) **BUF.**

Center. Shoots left. 6'4", 217 lbs. Born, Fargo, ND, February 3, 1982. Buffalo's 6th choice, 220th overall, in 2000 Entry Draft.

			Regular Season														Playoffs								
Season	Club	League	GP	G	A	Pts	PIM	PP	SH	GW	S	%	+/-	TF	F%	Min	GP	G	A	Pts	PIM	PP	SH	GW	Min
1998-99	Portland Hawks	USAHA	45	47	53	100	81	....	....	....	....	....	....	....	....	....	....	....	....	....	....	....	....	....	....
99-2000	Portland	WHL	56	6	8	14	110	....	....	....	....	....	....	....	....	....	....	....	....	....	....	....	....	....	....
2000-01	Portland	WHL	70	11	30	41	168	....	....	....	....	....	....	....	....	....	16	10	6	16	59	....	....	....	....
2001-02	Portland	WHL	72	36	44	80	202	....	....	....	....	....	....	....	....	....	6	3	1	4	16	....	....	....	....
2002-03	**Buffalo**	**NHL**	**1**	**0**	**0**	**0**	**0**	**0**	**0**	**0**	**0**	**0.0**	**0**	**7**	**42.9**	**5:48**	....	....	....	....	....	....	....	....	....
	Rochester	AHL	80	14	39	53	137	....	....	....	....	....	....	....	....	....	3	0	0	0	4	....	....	....	....
2003-04	Rochester	AHL	78	9	22	31	169	....	....	....	....	....	....	....	....	....	16	3	10	13	30	....	....	....	....
	NHL Totals		**1**	**0**	**0**	**0**	**0**	**0**	**0**	**0**	**0**	**0.0**		**7**	**42.9**	**5:48**	....	....	....	....	....	....	....	....	....

GAUTHIER, Denis

(GOH-tyay, DEH-nihs) **CGY.**

Defense. Shoots left. 6'2", 224 lbs. Born, Montreal, Que., October 1, 1976. Calgary's 1st choice, 20th overall, in 1995 Entry Draft.

			Regular Season														Playoffs								
Season	Club	League	GP	G	A	Pts	PIM	PP	SH	GW	S	%	+/-	TF	F%	Min	GP	G	A	Pts	PIM	PP	SH	GW	Min
1991-92	Richelieu AA	QAHA	STATISTICS NOT AVAILABLE																						
1992-93	Drummondville	QMJHL	61	1	7	8	136	....	....	....	....	....	....	....	....	....	10	0	5	5	40	....	....	....	....
1993-94	Drummondville	QMJHL	60	0	7	7	176	....	....	....	....	....	....	....	....	....	9	2	0	2	41	....	....	....	....
1994-95	Drummondville	QMJHL	64	9	31	40	190	....	....	....	....	....	....	....	....	....	4	0	5	5	12	....	....	....	....
1995-96	Drummondville	QMJHL	53	25	49	74	140	....	....	....	....	....	....	....	....	....	6	4	4	8	32	....	....	....	....
	Saint John Flames	AHL	5	2	0	2	8	....	....	....	....	....	....	....	....	....	16	1	6	7	20	....	....	....	....
1996-97	Saint John Flames	AHL	73	3	28	31	74	....	....	....	....	....	....	....	....	....	5	0	0	0	6	....	....	....	....
1997-98	**Calgary**	**NHL**	**10**	**0**	**0**	**0**	**16**	**0**	**0**	**0**	**3**	**0.0**	**–5**	....	....	....	....	....	....	....	....	....	....	....	....
	Saint John Flames	AHL	68	4	20	24	154	....	....	....	....	....	....	....	....	....	21	0	4	4	83	....	....	....	....
1998-99	**Calgary**	**NHL**	**55**	**3**	**4**	**7**	**68**	**0**	**0**	**0**	**40**	**7.5**	**3**	**0**	**0.0**	**12:41**	....	....	....	....	....	....	....	....	....
	Saint John Flames	AHL	16	0	3	3	31	....	....	....	....	....	....	....	....	....	....	....	....	....	....	....	....	....	....
99-2000	**Calgary**	**NHL**	**39**	**1**	**1**	**2**	**50**	**0**	**0**	**0**	**29**	**3.4**	**–4**	**0**	**0.0**	**19:21**	....	....	....	....	....	....	....	....	....
2000-01	**Calgary**	**NHL**	**62**	**2**	**6**	**8**	**78**	**0**	**0**	**0**	**33**	**6.1**	**3**	**0**	**0.0**	**16:37**	....	....	....	....	....	....	....	....	....
2001-02	**Calgary**	**NHL**	**66**	**5**	**8**	**13**	**91**	**0**	**1**	**2**	**76**	**6.6**	**9**	**0**	**0.0**	**19:19**	....	....	....	....	....	....	....	....	....
2002-03	**Calgary**	**NHL**	**72**	**1**	**11**	**12**	**99**	**0**	**0**	**1**	**50**	**2.0**	**5**	**0**	**0.0**	**19:52**	....	....	....	....	....	....	....	....	....
2003-04	**Calgary**	**NHL**	**80**	**1**	**15**	**16**	**113**	**0**	**0**	**0**	**90**	**1.1**	**4**	**0**	**0.0**	**18:43**	**6**	**0**	**1**	**1**	**4**	**0**	**0**	**0**	**18:33**
	NHL Totals		**384**	**13**	**45**	**58**	**515**	**0**	**1**	**3**	**321**	**4.0**		**0**	**0.0**	**17:53**	**6**	**0**	**1**	**1**	**4**	**0**	**0**	**0**	**18:33**

QMJHL First All-Star Team (1996) • Canadian Major Junior First All-Star Team (1996)

• Missed majority of 1999-2000 season recovering from hip injury suffered in game vs. St. Louis, February 1, 2000.

GAVEY, Aaron

(GAY-vee, AIR-ruhn)

Center. Shoots left. 6'2", 189 lbs. Born, Sudbury, Ont., February 22, 1974. Tampa Bay's 4th choice, 74th overall, in 1992 Entry Draft.

			Regular Season														Playoffs								
Season	Club	League	GP	G	A	Pts	PIM	PP	SH	GW	S	%	+/-	TF	F%	Min	GP	G	A	Pts	PIM	PP	SH	GW	Min
1990-91	Peterborough	OPJHL	42	26	30	56	68	....	....	....	....	....	....	....	....	....	....	....	....	....	....	....	....	....	....
1991-92	Sault Ste. Marie	OHL	48	7	11	18	27	....	....	....	....	....	....	....	....	....	19	5	1	6	10	....	....	....	....
1992-93	Sault Ste. Marie	OHL	62	45	39	84	116	....	....	....	....	....	....	....	....	....	18	5	9	14	36	....	....	....	....
1993-94	Sault Ste. Marie	OHL	60	42	60	102	116	....	....	....	....	....	....	....	....	....	14	11	10	21	22	....	....	....	....
1994-95	Atlanta Knights	IHL	66	18	17	35	85	....	....	....	....	....	....	....	....	....	5	0	1	1	9	....	....	....	....
1995-96	**Tampa Bay**	**NHL**	**73**	**8**	**4**	**12**	**56**	**1**	**1**	**2**	**65**	**12.3**	**–6**	....	....	....	**6**	**0**	**0**	**0**	**4**	**0**	**0**	**0**	....
1996-97	**Tampa Bay**	**NHL**	**16**	**1**	**2**	**3**	**12**	**0**	**0**	**0**	**8**	**12.5**	**–1**	....	....	....	....	....	....	....	....	....	....	....	....
	Calgary	**NHL**	**41**	**7**	**9**	**16**	**34**	**3**	**0**	**1**	**54**	**13.0**	**–11**	....	....	....	....	....	....	....	....	....	....	....	....
1997-98	**Calgary**	**NHL**	**26**	**2**	**3**	**5**	**24**	**0**	**0**	**1**	**27**	**7.4**	**–5**	....	....	....	....	....	....	....	....	....	....	....	....
	Saint John Flames	AHL	8	4	3	7	28	....	....	....	....	....	....	....	....	....	....	....	....	....	....	....	....	....	....
1998-99	**Dallas**	**NHL**	**7**	**0**	**0**	**0**	**10**	**0**	**0**	**0**	**4**	**0.0**	**–1**	**43**	**48.8**	**8:09**	....	....	....	....	....	....	....	....	....
	Michigan	IHL	67	24	33	57	128	....	....	....	....	....	....	....	....	....	5	2	3	5	4	....	....	....	....
99-2000	**Dallas**	**NHL**	**41**	**7**	**6**	**13**	**44**	**1**	**0**	**2**	**39**	**17.9**	**0**	**263**	**51.7**	**9:55**	**13**	**1**	**2**	**3**	**10**	**0**	**0**	**1**	**6:09**
	Michigan	IHL	28	14	15	29	73	....	....	....	....	....	....	....	....	....	....	....	....	....	....	....	....	....	....
2000-01	**Minnesota**	**NHL**	**75**	**10**	**14**	**24**	**52**	**1**	**0**	**2**	**100**	**10.0**	**–8**	**584**	**43.5**	**14:00**	....	....	....	....	....	....	....	....	....
2001-02	**Minnesota**	**NHL**	**71**	**6**	**11**	**17**	**38**	**1**	**0**	**0**	**75**	**8.0**	**–21**	**254**	**42.5**	**11:55**	....	....	....	....	....	....	....	....	....
2002-03	**Toronto**	**NHL**	**5**	**0**	**1**	**1**	**0**	**0**	**0**	**0**	**8**	**0.0**	**1**	**31**	**48.4**	**11:19**	....	....	....	....	....	....	....	....	....
	St. John's	AHL	70	14	29	43	83	....	....	....	....	....	....	....	....	....	....	....	....	....	....	....	....	....	....
2003-04	St. John's	AHL	75	22	45	67	100	....	....	....	....	....	....	....	....	....	....	....	....	....	....	....	....	....	....
	NHL Totals		**355**	**41**	**50**	**91**	**270**	**7**	**1**	**8**	**380**	**10.8**		**1175**	**45.4**	**12:08**	**19**	**1**	**2**	**3**	**14**	**0**	**0**	**1**	**6:09**

Traded to **Calgary** by **Tampa Bay** for Rick Tabaracci, November 19, 1996. Traded to **Dallas** by **Calgary** for Bob Bassen, July 14, 1998. Traded to **Minnesota** by **Dallas** with Pavel Patera, Dallas' 8th round choice (Eric Johansson) in 2000 Entry Draft and Minnesota's 4th round choice (previously acquired, later traded to Los Angeles – Los Angeles selected Aaron Rome) in 2002 Entry Draft for Brad Lukowich and Minnesota's 3rd (Yared Hagos) and 9th (Dale Sullivan) round choices in 2001 Entry Draft, June 25, 2000. Signed as a free agent by **Toronto**, July 24, 2002.

GELINAS, Martin

(ZHEHL-in-nuh, MAHR-tihn) **CGY.**

Left wing. Shoots left. 5'11", 195 lbs. Born, Shawinigan, Que., June 5, 1970. Los Angeles' 1st choice, 7th overall, in 1988 Entry Draft.

			Regular Season														Playoffs								
Season	Club	League	GP	G	A	Pts	PIM	PP	SH	GW	S	%	+/-	TF	F%	Min	GP	G	A	Pts	PIM	PP	SH	GW	Min
1985-86	Noranda Aces	NOHA	5	1	1	2	0	....	....	....	....	....	....	....	....	....	....	....	....	....	....	....	....	....	....
1986-87	L'est Cantonniers	QAAA	41	36	42	78	36	....	....	....	....	....	....	....	....	....	7	7	5	12	2	....	....	....	....
1987-88	Hull Olympiques	QMJHL	65	63	68	131	74	....	....	....	....	....	....	....	....	....	17	15	18	33	32	....	....	....	....
1988-89	Hull Olympiques	QMJHL	41	38	39	77	31	....	....	....	....	....	....	....	....	....	9	5	4	9	14	....	....	....	....
	Edmonton	**NHL**	**6**	**1**	**2**	**3**	**0**	**0**	**0**	**0**	**14**	**7.1**	**–1**	....	....	....	....	....	....	....	....	....	....	....	....
1989-90♦	**Edmonton**	**NHL**	**46**	**17**	**8**	**25**	**30**	**5**	**0**	**2**	**71**	**23.9**	**0**	....	....	....	**20**	**2**	**3**	**5**	**6**	**0**	**0**	**0**	....
1990-91	**Edmonton**	**NHL**	**73**	**20**	**20**	**40**	**34**	**4**	**0**	**2**	**124**	**16.1**	**–7**	....	....	....	**18**	**3**	**6**	**9**	**25**	**0**	**0**	**1**	....
1991-92	**Edmonton**	**NHL**	**68**	**11**	**18**	**29**	**62**	**1**	**0**	**0**	**94**	**11.7**	**14**	....	....	....	**15**	**1**	**3**	**4**	**10**	**0**	**0**	**0**	....
1992-93	**Edmonton**	**NHL**	**65**	**11**	**12**	**23**	**30**	**0**	**0**	**1**	**93**	**11.8**	**3**	....	....	....	....	....	....	....	....	....	....	....	....
1993-94	**Quebec**	**NHL**	**31**	**6**	**6**	**12**	**8**	**0**	**0**	**0**	**53**	**11.3**	**–2**	....	....	....	....	....	....	....	....	....	....	....	....
	Vancouver	**NHL**	**33**	**8**	**8**	**16**	**26**	**3**	**0**	**1**	**54**	**14.8**	**–6**	....	....	....	**24**	**5**	**4**	**9**	**14**	**2**	**0**	**1**	....
1994-95	**Vancouver**	**NHL**	**46**	**13**	**10**	**23**	**36**	**1**	**0**	**4**	**75**	**17.3**	**8**	....	....	....	**3**	**0**	**1**	**1**	**0**	**0**	**0**	**0**	....
1995-96	**Vancouver**	**NHL**	**81**	**30**	**26**	**56**	**59**	**3**	**4**	**5**	**181**	**16.6**	**8**	....	....	....	**6**	**1**	**1**	**2**	**12**	**1**	**0**	**0**	....
1996-97	**Vancouver**	**NHL**	**74**	**35**	**33**	**68**	**42**	**6**	**1**	**3**	**177**	**19.8**	**6**	....	....	....	....	....	....	....	....	....	....	....	....
1997-98	**Vancouver**	**NHL**	**24**	**4**	**4**	**8**	**10**	**1**	**1**	**1**	**49**	**8.2**	**–6**	....	....	....	....	....	....	....	....	....	....	....	....
	Carolina	**NHL**	**40**	**12**	**14**	**26**	**30**	**2**	**1**	**4**	**98**	**12.2**	**1**	....	....	....	....	....	....	....	....	....	....	....	....
1998-99	**Carolina**	**NHL**	**76**	**13**	**15**	**28**	**67**	**0**	**0**	**2**	**111**	**11.7**	**3**	**6**	**50.0**	**13:13**	**6**	**0**	**3**	**3**	**2**	**0**	**0**	**0**	**19:33**
99-2000	**Carolina**	**NHL**	**81**	**14**	**16**	**30**	**40**	**3**	**0**	**0**	**139**	**10.1**	**–10**	**5**	**40.0**	**13:39**	....	....	....	....	....	....	....	....	....
2000-01	**Carolina**	**NHL**	**79**	**23**	**29**	**52**	**59**	**6**	**1**	**4**	**170**	**13.5**	**–4**	**6**	**0.0**	**17:54**	**6**	**0**	**1**	**1**	**6**	**0**	**0**	**0**	**17:51**
2001-02	**Carolina**	**NHL**	**72**	**13**	**16**	**29**	**30**	**3**	**0**	**1**	**121**	**10.7**	**–1**	**13**	**23.1**	**16:05**	**23**	**3**	**4**	**7**	**10**	**0**	**0**	**1**	**14:16**

			Regular Season														Playoffs								
Season	Club	League	GP	G	A	Pts	PIM	PP	SH	GW	S	%	+/-	TF	F%	Min	GP	G	A	Pts	PIM	PP	SH	GW	Min
2002-03	**Calgary**	**NHL**	81	21	31	52	51	6	0	3	152	13.8	–3	96	51.0	16:33	....	....	....	....	....	....	....	....	....
2003-04	**Calgary**	**NHL**	76	17	18	35	70	5	0	3	139	12.2	10	27	48.2	14:50	26	8	7	15	35	2	0	3	15:58
	NHL Totals		1052	269	286	555	684	49	8	36	1915	14.0		153	45.8	15:23	147	23	33	56	120	5	0	6	15:51

QMJHL First All-Star Team (1988) • QMJHL Offensive Rookie of the Year (1988) • Canadian Major Junior Rookie of the Year (1988) • George Parsons Trophy (Memorial Cup Most Sportsmanlike Player) (1988)

Traded to **Edmonton** by **Los Angeles** with Jimmy Carson and Los Angeles' 1st round choices in 1989 (later traded to New Jersey – New Jersey selected Jason Miller), 1991 (Martin Rucinsky) and 1993 (Nick Stajduhar) Entry Drafts and cash for Wayne Gretzky, Mike Krushelnyski and Marty McSorley, August 9, 1988. Traded to **Quebec** by **Edmonton** with Edmonton's 6th round choice (Nicholas Checco) in 1993 Entry Draft for Scott Pearson, June 20, 1993. Claimed on waivers by **Vancouver** from **Quebec**, January 15, 1994. Traded to **Carolina** by **Vancouver** with Kirk McLean for Sean Burke, Geoff Sanderson and Enrico Ciccone, January 3, 1998. Signed as a free agent by **Calgary**, July 2, 2002.

GERNANDER, Ken
(guhr-NAN-duhr, KEHN) **NYR**

Right wing. Shoots left. 5'10", 175 lbs. Born, Coleraine, MN, June 30, 1969. Winnipeg's 4th choice, 96th overall, in 1987 Entry Draft.

Season	Club	League	GP	G	A	Pts	PIM	PP	SH	GW	S	%	+/-	TF	F%	Min	GP	G	A	Pts	PIM	PP	SH	GW	Min
1985-86	Greenway Raiders	Hi-School	23	14	23	37	....	....	....	....	....	....	....	....	....	....	....	....	....	....	....	....	....	....	....
1986-87	Greenway Raiders	Hi-School	26	35	34	69	....	....	....	....	....	....	....	....	....	....	....	....	....	....	....	....	....	....	....
1987-88	U. of Minnesota	WCHA	44	14	14	28	14	....	....	....	....	....	....	....	....	....	....	....	....	....	....	....	....	....	....
1988-89	U. of Minnesota	WCHA	44	9	11	20	2	....	....	....	....	....	....	....	....	....	....	....	....	....	....	....	....	....	....
1989-90	U. of Minnesota	WCHA	44	32	17	49	24	....	....	....	....	....	....	....	....	....	....	....	....	....	....	....	....	....	....
1990-91	U. of Minnesota	WCHA	44	23	20	43	24	....	....	....	....	....	....	....	....	....	....	....	....	....	....	....	....	....	....
1991-92	Fort Wayne	IHL	13	7	6	13	2	....	....	....	....	....	....	....	....	....	....	....	....	....	....	....	....	....	....
	Moncton Hawks	AHL	43	8	18	26	9	....	....	....	....	....	....	....	....	....	8	1	1	2	2	....	....	....	....
1992-93	Moncton Hawks	AHL	71	18	29	47	20	....	....	....	....	....	....	....	....	....	5	1	4	5	0	....	....	....	....
1993-94	Moncton Hawks	AHL	71	22	25	47	12	....	....	....	....	....	....	....	....	....	19	6	1	7	0	....	....	....	....
1994-95	Binghamton	AHL	80	28	25	53	24	....	....	....	....	....	....	....	....	....	11	2	2	4	6	....	....	....	....
1995-96	**NY Rangers**	**NHL**	10	2	3	5	4	2	0	0	10	20.0	–3	....	....	....	6	0	0	0	0	0	0	0	....
	Binghamton	AHL	63	44	29	73	38	....	....	....	....	....	....	....	....	....	....	....	....	....	....	....	....	....	....
1996-97	Binghamton	AHL	46	13	18	31	30	....	....	....	....	....	....	....	....	....	2	0	1	1	0	....	....	....	....
	NY Rangers	**NHL**	....	....	....	....	....	....	....	....	....	....	....	....	....	....	9	0	0	0	0	0	0	0	....
1997-98	Hartford	AHL	80	35	28	63	26	....	....	....	....	....	....	....	....	....	12	5	6	11	4	....	....	....	....
1998-99	Hartford	AHL	70	23	26	49	32	....	....	....	....	....	....	....	....	....	7	1	2	3	2	....	....	....	....
99-2000	Hartford	AHL	79	28	29	57	24	....	....	....	....	....	....	....	....	....	23	5	5	10	0	....	....	....	....
2000-01	Hartford	AHL	80	22	27	49	39	....	....	....	....	....	....	....	....	....	2	0	0	0	0	....	....	....	....
2001-02	Hartford	AHL	75	18	31	49	19	....	....	....	....	....	....	....	....	....	10	1	3	4	4	....	....	....	....
2002-03	Hartford	AHL	72	17	19	36	22	....	....	....	....	....	....	....	....	....	2	0	0	0	0	....	....	....	....
2003-04	**NY Rangers**	**NHL**	2	0	0	0	2	0	0	0	0	0.0	–1	0	0.0	6:38	....	....	....	....	....	....	....	....	....
	Hartford	AHL	77	12	19	31	28	....	....	....	....	....	....	....	....	....	16	3	4	7	2	....	....	....	....
	NHL Totals		12	2	3	5	6	2	0	0	10	20.0		0	0.0	6:38	15	0	0	0	0	0	0	0	....

Fred Hunt Memorial Trophy (Sportsmanship – AHL) (1996, 2004)

Signed as a free agent by **NY Rangers**, July 4, 1994.

GILL, Hal
(GIHL, HAL) **BOS.**

Defense. Shoots left. 6'7", 250 lbs. Born, Concord, MA, April 6, 1975. Boston's 8th choice, 207th overall, in 1993 Entry Draft.

Season	Club	League	GP	G	A	Pts	PIM	PP	SH	GW	S	%	+/-	TF	F%	Min	GP	G	A	Pts	PIM	PP	SH	GW	Min
1992-93	Nashoba High	Hi-School	20	25	25	50	....	....	....	....	....	....	....	....	....	....	....	....	....	....	....	....	....	....	....
1993-94	Providence	H-East	31	1	2	3	26	....	....	....	....	....	....	....	....	....	....	....	....	....	....	....	....	....	....
1994-95	Providence	H-East	26	1	3	4	22	....	....	....	....	....	....	....	....	....	....	....	....	....	....	....	....	....	....
1995-96	Providence	H-East	39	5	12	17	54	....	....	....	....	....	....	....	....	....	....	....	....	....	....	....	....	....	....
1996-97	Providence	H-East	35	5	16	21	52	....	....	....	....	....	....	....	....	....	....	....	....	....	....	....	....	....	....
1997-98	**Boston**	**NHL**	68	2	4	6	47	0	0	0	56	3.6	4	....	....	....	6	0	0	0	4	0	0	0	....
	Providence Bruins	AHL	4	1	0	1	23	....	....	....	....	....	....	....	....	....	....	....	....	....	....	....	....	....	....
1998-99	**Boston**	**NHL**	80	3	7	10	63	0	0	2	102	2.9	–10	1	100.0	20:54	12	0	0	0	14	0	0	0	20:41
99-2000	**Boston**	**NHL**	81	3	9	12	51	0	0	0	120	2.5	0	0	0.0	17:15	....	....	....	....	....	....	....	....	....
2000-01	**Boston**	**NHL**	80	1	10	11	71	0	0	0	79	1.3	–2	0	0.0	18:21	....	....	....	....	....	....	....	....	....
2001-02	**Boston**	**NHL**	79	4	18	22	77	0	0	0	137	2.9	16	0	0.0	24:13	6	0	1	1	2	0	0	0	23:04
2002-03	**Boston**	**NHL**	76	4	13	17	56	0	0	0	114	3.5	21	0	0.0	20:42	5	0	0	0	4	0	0	0	20:19
2003-04	**Boston**	**NHL**	82	2	7	9	99	0	0	0	104	1.9	16	0	0.0	18:24	7	0	1	1	4	0	0	0	19:03
	NHL Totals		546	19	68	87	464	0	0	2	712	2.7		1	100.0	19:57	36	0	2	2	28	0	0	0	20:43

GIONTA, Brian
(jee-OHN-tuh, BRIGH-uhn) **N.J.**

Right wing. Shoots right. 5'7", 175 lbs. Born, Rochester, NY, January 18, 1979. New Jersey's 4th choice, 82nd overall, in 1998 Entry Draft.

Season	Club	League	GP	G	A	Pts	PIM	PP	SH	GW	S	%	+/-	TF	F%	Min	GP	G	A	Pts	PIM	PP	SH	GW	Min
1994-95	Rochester	NEJHL	28	*52	37	*89	....	....	....	....	....	....	....	....	....	....	....	....	....	....	....	....	....	....	....
1995-96	Niagara Scenics	MTJHL	51	47	44	91	59	....	....	....	....	....	....	....	....	....	....	....	....	....	....	....	....	....	....
1996-97	Niagara Scenics	MTJHL	50	57	70	127	101	....	....	....	....	....	....	....	....	....	6	6	11	17	21	....	....	....	....
1997-98	Boston College	H-East	40	30	32	62	44	....	....	....	....	....	....	....	....	....	....	....	....	....	....	....	....	....	....
1998-99	Boston College	H-East	39	27	33	60	46	....	....	....	....	....	....	....	....	....	....	....	....	....	....	....	....	....	....
99-2000	Boston College	H-East	42	*33	23	56	66	....	....	....	....	....	....	....	....	....	....	....	....	....	....	....	....	....	....
2000-01	Boston College	H-East	43	*33	21	*54	47	....	....	....	....	....	....	....	....	....	....	....	....	....	....	....	....	....	....
2001-02	**New Jersey**	**NHL**	33	4	7	11	8	0	0	0	58	6.9	10	36	44.4	13:25	6	2	2	4	0	0	1	2	17:08
	Albany River Rats	AHL	37	9	16	25	18	....	....	....	....	....	....	....	....	....	....	....	....	....	....	....	....	....	....
2002-03♦	**New Jersey**	**NHL**	58	12	13	25	23	2	0	3	129	9.3	5	14	57.1	14:48	24	1	8	9	6	0	0	0	14:31
2003-04	**New Jersey**	**NHL**	75	21	8	29	36	0	0	8	174	12.1	19	60	58.3	14:44	5	2	3	5	0	1	0	0	15:41
	NHL Totals		166	37	28	65	67	2	0	11	361	10.2		110	53.6	14:29	35	5	13	18	6	1	1	2	15:08

Hockey East Rookie of the Year (1998) • Hockey East Second All-Star Team (1998) • NCAA East Second All-American Team (1998) • Hockey East First All-Star Team (1999, 2000, 2001) • NCAA East First All-American Team (1999, 2000, 2001) • Hockey East Player of the Year (2001) • Walter Brown Award (New England's Outstanding American-born College player) (2001) (co-winner - Ty Conklin)

GIRARD, Jonathan
(zhih-RAHR, JAWN-ah-thuhn) **BOS.**

Defense. Shoots right. 5'11", 201 lbs. Born, Joliette, Que., May 27, 1980. Boston's 1st choice, 48th overall, in 1998 Entry Draft.

Season	Club	League	GP	G	A	Pts	PIM	PP	SH	GW	S	%	+/-	TF	F%	Min	GP	G	A	Pts	PIM	PP	SH	GW	Min
1995-96	Laval Laurentide	QAAA	39	11	22	33	44	....	....	....	....	....	....	....	....	....	16	4	11	15	16	....	....	....	....
1996-97	Laval Titan	QMJHL	39	11	23	34	13	....	....	....	....	....	....	....	....	....	3	0	3	3	0	....	....	....	....
1997-98	Laval Titan	QMJHL	64	20	47	67	44	....	....	....	....	....	....	....	....	....	16	2	16	18	13	....	....	....	....
1998-99	Acadie-Bathurst	QMJHL	50	9	58	67	60	....	....	....	....	....	....	....	....	....	23	13	18	31	22	....	....	....	....
	Boston	**NHL**	3	0	0	0	0	0	0	0	3	0.0	1	0	0.0	9:28	....	....	....	....	....	....	....	....	....
99-2000	**Boston**	**NHL**	23	1	2	3	2	0	0	0	17	5.9	–1	0	0.0	9:32	....	....	....	....	....	....	....	....	....
	Moncton Wildcats	QMJHL	26	10	25	35	36	....	....	....	....	....	....	....	....	....	16	3	15	18	36	....	....	....	....
	Providence Bruins	AHL	5	0	1	1	0	....	....	....	....	....	....	....	....	....	....	....	....	....	....	....	....	....	....
2000-01	**Boston**	**NHL**	31	3	13	16	14	2	0	1	42	7.1	2	0	0.0	16:32	....	....	....	....	....	....	....	....	....
	Providence Bruins	AHL	39	3	21	24	6	....	....	....	....	....	....	....	....	....	17	0	5	5	4	....	....	....	....
2001-02	**Boston**	**NHL**	20	0	3	3	9	0	0	0	28	0.0	0	0	0.0	14:43	1	0	0	0	2	0	0	0	10:06
	Providence Bruins	AHL	59	6	31	37	36	....	....	....	....	....	....	....	....	....	2	0	0	0	2	....	....	....	....
2002-03	**Boston**	**NHL**	73	6	16	22	21	2	0	2	123	4.9	4	0	0.0	20:50	2	0	1	1	0	0	0	0	16:40
2003-04	**Boston**	**NHL**	DID NOT PLAY – INJURED																						
	NHL Totals		150	10	34	44	46	4	0	3	213	4.7		0	0.0	17:10	3	0	1	1	2	0	0	0	14:28

QMJHL All-Rookie Team (1997) • QMJHL Second All-Star Team (1998) • QMJHL First All-Star Team (1999, 2000)

• Missed entire 2003-04 season recovering from pelvis injury suffered in automobile accident, July 24, 2003.

GIROUX, Raymond
(zhih-ROO, ray-MAWN) **MIN.**

Defense. Shoots left. 6'1", 190 lbs. Born, North Bay, Ont., July 20, 1976. Philadelphia's 7th choice, 202nd overall, in 1994 Entry Draft.

Season	Club	League	GP	G	A	Pts	PIM	PP	SH	GW	S	%	+/-	TF	F%	Min	GP	G	A	Pts	PIM	PP	SH	GW	Min
1992-93	Powassan Hawks	NOJHA	45	8	18	26	117	....	....	....	....	....	....	....	....	....	....	....	....	....	....	....	....	....	....
1993-94	Powassan Hawks	NOJHA	36	10	40	50	42	....	....	....	....	....	....	....	....	....	....	....	....	....	....	....	....	....	....
1994-95	Yale Bulldogs	ECAC	27	1	3	4	8	....	....	....	....	....	....	....	....	....	....	....	....	....	....	....	....	....	....
1995-96	Yale Bulldogs	ECAC	30	3	16	19	36	....	....	....	....	....	....	....	....	....	....	....	....	....	....	....	....	....	....
1996-97	Yale Bulldogs	ECAC	32	9	12	21	38	....	....	....	....	....	....	....	....	....	....	....	....	....	....	....	....	....	....
1997-98	Yale Bulldogs	ECAC	35	9	*30	39	62	....	....	....	....	....	....	....	....	....	....	....	....	....	....	....	....	....	....
1998-99	Lowell	AHL	59	13	19	32	92	....	....	....	....	....	....	....	....	....	3	1	1	2	0	....	....	....	....
99-2000	**NY Islanders**	**NHL**	14	0	9	9	10	0	0	0	24	0.0	0	9	22.2	14:40	....	....	....	....	....	....	....	....	....
	Lowell	AHL	49	12	21	33	34	....	....	....	....	....	....	....	....	....	7	0	0	0	2	....	....	....	....

Season	Club	League	Regular Season														Playoffs								
			GP	G	A	Pts	PIM	PP	SH	GW	S	%	+/-	TF	F%	Min	GP	G	A	Pts	PIM	PP	SH	GW	Min
2000-01	HIFK Helsinki	Finland	22	3	9	12	34																		
	AIK Solna	Sweden	9	0	1	1	16																		
	Jokerit Helsinki	Finland	24	4	9	13	16										5	0	0	0	0				
2001-02	**NY Islanders**	**NHL**	**2**	**0**	**0**	**0**	**2**	**0**	**0**	**0**	**2**	**0.0**	**–1**	**0**	**0.0**	**12:18**									
	Bridgeport	AHL	79	13	40	53	73										19	1	7	8	20				
2002-03	**New Jersey**	**NHL**	**11**	**0**	**1**	**1**	**6**	**0**	**0**	**0**	**20**	**0.0**	**–2**	**0**	**0.0**	**18:18**									
	Albany River Rats	AHL	67	11	38	49	49																		
2003-04	**New Jersey**	**NHL**	**11**	**0**	**3**	**3**	**4**	**0**	**0**	**0**	**17**	**0.0**	**–3**	**0**	**0.0**	**20:55**	**4**	**0**	**0**	**0**	**0**	**0**	**0**	**0**	**15:15**
	Albany River Rats	AHL	65	11	17	28	34																		
	NHL Totals		**38**	**0**	**13**	**13**	**22**	**0**	**0**	**0**	**63**	**0.0**		**9**	**22.2**	**17:24**	**4**	**0**	**0**	**0**	**0**	**0**	**0**	**0**	**15:15**

ECAC First All-Star Team (1998) • NCAA East First All-American Team (1998) • AHL First All-Star Team (2003)

Rights traded to **NY Islanders** by **Philadelphia** for NY Islanders' 6th round choice (later traded to Montreal – Montreal selected Scott Selig) in 2000 Entry Draft, August 25, 1998. Signed as a free agent by **New Jersey**, July 12, 2002. Signed as a free agent by **Minnesota**, July 7, 2004.

GLEASON, Tim

(GLEE-suhn, TIHM) **L.A.**

Defense. Shoots left. 6'1", 202 lbs. Born, Southfield, MI, January 29, 1983. Ottawa's 2nd choice, 23rd overall, in 2001 Entry Draft.

Season	Club	League	GP	G	A	Pts	PIM	PP	SH	GW	S	%	+/-	TF	F%	Min	GP	G	A	Pts	PIM	PP	SH	GW	Min
1998-99	Leamington Flyers	OJHL-B	52	5	26	31	76																		
99-2000	Windsor Spitfires	OHL	55	5	13	18	101										12	2	4	6	14				
2000-01	Windsor Spitfires	OHL	47	8	28	36	124										9	1	2	3	23				
2001-02	Windsor Spitfires	OHL	67	17	42	59	109										16	7	13	20	40				
2002-03	Windsor Spitfires	OHL	45	7	31	38	75										7	5	2	7	17				
2003-04	**Los Angeles**	**NHL**	**47**	**0**	**7**	**7**	**21**	**0**	**0**	**0**	**45**	**0.0**	**1**	**0**	**0.0**	**14:59**									
	Manchester	AHL	22	0	8	8	19										6	0	1	1	4				
	NHL Totals		**47**	**0**	**7**	**7**	**21**	**0**	**0**	**0**	**45**	**0.0**		**0**	**0.0**	**14:59**									

Rights traded to **Los Angeles** by **Ottawa** with future considerations for Bryan Smolinski, March 11, 2003.

GOC, Marcel

(GAWCH, mahr-SEHL) **S.J.**

Center. Shoots left. 6', 195 lbs. Born, Calw, West Germany, August 24, 1983. San Jose's 1st choice, 20th overall, in 2001 Entry Draft.

Season	Club	League	GP	G	A	Pts	PIM	PP	SH	GW	S	%	+/-	TF	F%	Min	GP	G	A	Pts	PIM	PP	SH	GW	Min
1998-99	Schwenningen Jr.	German-Jr.	12	23	10	33	12																		
99-2000	Schwenningen	Germany	51	0	3	3	4										11	1	1	2	2				
2000-01	Schwenningen	Germany	58	13	28	41	12																		
2001-02	Schwenningen	Germany	45	8	9	17	24																		
	Adler Mannheim	Germany	8	0	2	2	0																		
2002-03	Adler Mannheim	Germany	36	6	14	20	16										8	1	2	3	0				
2003-04	Cleveland Barons	AHL	78	16	21	37	24																		
	San Jose	**NHL**															**5**	**1**	**1**	**2**	**0**	**0**	**0**	**1**	**7:08**
	NHL Totals																**5**	**1**	**1**	**2**	**0**	**0**	**0**	**1**	**7:08**

GOC, Sascha

(GAWCH, SA-shah) **T.B.**

Defense. Shoots right. 6'2", 225 lbs. Born, Calw, West Germany, April 14, 1979. New Jersey's 5th choice, 159th overall, in 1997 Entry Draft.

Season	Club	League	GP	G	A	Pts	PIM	PP	SH	GW	S	%	+/-	TF	F%	Min	GP	G	A	Pts	PIM	PP	SH	GW	Min
1994-95	Schwenningen Jr.	German-Jr.	14	5	1	6	10																		
1995-96	Schwenningen Jr.	German-Jr.	11	3	6	9	77																		
	Schwenningen	Germany	1	0	0	0	0																		
1996-97	Schwenningen Jr.	German-Jr.	1	1	1	2	2																		
	Schwenningen	Germany	41	3	1	4	28										5	0	0	0	0				
1997-98	Schwenningen	Germany	49	5	5	10	45																		
	Schwenningen Jr.	German-Jr.	4	1	3	4	8																		
1998-99	Albany River Rats	AHL	55	1	12	13	24										2	0	0	0	0				
99-2000	Albany River Rats	AHL	64	9	22	31	35										5	2	0	2	6				
2000-01	**New Jersey**	**NHL**	**11**	**0**	**0**	**0**	**4**	**0**	**0**	**0**	**7**	**0.0**	**7**	**0**	**0.0**	**13:37**									
	Albany River Rats	AHL	55	10	29	39	49																		
2001-02	**New Jersey**	**NHL**	**2**	**0**	**0**	**0**	**0**	**0**	**0**	**0**	**2**	**0.0**	**–2**	**0**	**0.0**	**19:21**									
	Albany River Rats	AHL	10	0	5	5	12																		
	Tampa Bay	**NHL**	**9**	**0**	**0**	**0**	**0**	**0**	**0**	**0**	**2**	**0.0**	**0**	**0**	**0.0**	**5:32**									
	Springfield	AHL	36	3	9	12	30																		
2002-03	Adler Mannheim	Germany	49	1	3	4	87										7	1	0	1	*41				
2003-04	Adler Mannheim	Germany	46	5	12	17	58										3	0	0	0	0				
	NHL Totals		**22**	**0**	**0**	**0**	**4**	**0**	**0**	**0**	**11**	**0.0**		**0**	**0.0**	**10:50**									

Traded to **Tampa Bay** by **New Jersey** with Josef Boumedienne and the rights to Anton But for Andrei Zyuzin, November 9, 2001. Signed as a free agent by **Adler Mannheim** (Germany), April 23, 2002.

GODARD, Eric

(GAW-duhrd, AIR-ihk) **NYI**

Right wing. Shoots right. 6'4", 227 lbs. Born, Vernon, B.C., March 7, 1980.

Season	Club	League	GP	G	A	Pts	PIM	PP	SH	GW	S	%	+/-	TF	F%	Min	GP	G	A	Pts	PIM	PP	SH	GW	Min
1997-98	Lethbridge	WHL	7	0	0	0	26										2	0	0	0	0				
1998-99	Lethbridge	WHL	66	2	5	7	213										4	0	0	0	14				
99-2000	Lethbridge	WHL	60	3	5	8	*310																		
	Louisville Panthers	AHL	4	0	1	1	16																		
2000-01	Louisville Panthers	AHL	45	0	0	0	132																		
2001-02	Bridgeport	AHL	67	1	4	5	198										20	0	4	4	30				
2002-03	**NY Islanders**	**NHL**	**19**	**0**	**0**	**0**	**48**	**0**	**0**	**0**	**6**	**0.0**	**–3**	**0**	**0.0**	**4:32**	**2**	**0**	**1**	**1**	**4**	**0**	**0**	**0**	**1:09**
	Bridgeport	AHL	46	2	2	4	199										6	0	0	0	16				
2003-04	**NY Islanders**	**NHL**	**31**	**0**	**1**	**1**	**97**	**0**	**0**	**0**	**5**	**0.0**	**–2**	**1**	**0.0**	**3:46**									
	Bridgeport	AHL	7	0	0	0	13																		
	NHL Totals		**50**	**0**	**1**	**1**	**145**	**0**	**0**	**0**	**11**	**0.0**		**1**	**0.0**	**4:03**	**2**	**0**	**1**	**1**	**4**	**0**	**0**	**0**	**1:09**

Signed as a free agent by **Florida**, September 24, 1999. Traded to **NY Islanders** by **Florida** for Florida's 3rd round choice (previously acquired, Florida selected Gregory Campbell) in 2002 Entry Draft, June 22, 2002. • Spent majority of 2003-04 season as a healthy reserve.

GOMEZ, Scott

(GOH-mehz, SKAWT) **N.J.**

Center. Shoots left. 5'11", 200 lbs. Born, Anchorage, AK, December 23, 1979. New Jersey's 2nd choice, 27th overall, in 1998 Entry Draft.

Season	Club	League	GP	G	A	Pts	PIM	PP	SH	GW	S	%	+/-	TF	F%	Min	GP	G	A	Pts	PIM	PP	SH	GW	Min
1994-95	East High	Hi-School	28	30	48	78																			
1995-96	East High	Hi-School	27	*56	49	*101																			
	Anchorage	AAHL	40	*70	*67	*137	44																		
1996-97	South Surrey	BCHL	56	48	76	124	94										21	18	23	41	57				
1997-98	Tri-City	WHL	45	12	37	49	57																		
1998-99	Tri-City	WHL	58	30	*78	108	55										10	6	13	19	31				
99-2000♦	**New Jersey**	**NHL**	**82**	**19**	**51**	**70**	**78**	**7**	**0**	**1**	**204**	**9.3**	**14**	**341**	**44.6**	**16:21**	**23**	**4**	**6**	**10**	**4**	**1**	**0**	**2**	**14:08**
2000-01	**New Jersey**	**NHL**	**76**	**14**	**49**	**63**	**46**	**2**	**0**	**4**	**155**	**9.0**	**–1**	**1010**	**44.6**	**15:46**	**25**	**5**	**9**	**14**	**24**	**0**	**0**	**0**	**16:06**
2001-02	**New Jersey**	**NHL**	**76**	**10**	**38**	**48**	**36**	**1**	**0**	**1**	**156**	**6.4**	**–4**	**628**	**48.7**	**16:46**									
2002-03♦	**New Jersey**	**NHL**	**80**	**13**	**42**	**55**	**48**	**2**	**0**	**4**	**205**	**6.3**	**17**	**864**	**47.5**	**16:01**	**24**	**3**	**9**	**12**	**2**	**0**	**0**	**0**	**13:45**
2003-04	**New Jersey**	**NHL**	**80**	**14**	***56**	**70**	**70**	**3**	**0**	**1**	**189**	**7.4**	**18**	**1129**	**46.2**	**16:00**	**5**	**0**	**6**	**6**	**0**	**0**	**0**	**0**	**17:14**
	NHL Totals		**394**	**70**	**236**	**306**	**278**	**15**	**0**	**11**	**909**	**7.7**		**3972**	**46.3**	**16:11**	**77**	**12**	**30**	**42**	**30**	**1**	**0**	**2**	**14:51**

WHL West First All-Star Team (1999) • NHL All-Rookie Team (2000) • Calder Memorial Trophy (2000)

Played in NHL All-Star Game (2000)

GONCHAR, Sergei

(gohn-CHAR, SAIR-gay) **BOS.**

Defense. Shoots left. 6'2", 215 lbs. Born, Chelyabinsk, USSR, April 13, 1974. Washington's 1st choice, 14th overall, in 1992 Entry Draft.

Season	Club	League	GP	G	A	Pts	PIM	PP	SH	GW	S	%	+/-	TF	F%	Min	GP	G	A	Pts	PIM	PP	SH	GW	Min
1991-92	Chelyabinsk	CIS	31	1	0	1	6																		
1992-93	Dynamo Moscow	CIS	31	1	3	4	70										10	0	0	0	12				
1993-94	Dynamo Moscow	CIS	44	4	5	9	36										10	0	3	3	14				
	Portland Pirates	AHL															2	0	0	0	0				
1994-95	Portland Pirates	AHL	61	10	32	42	67																		
	Washington	**NHL**	**31**	**2**	**5**	**7**	**22**	**0**	**0**	**0**	**38**	**5.3**	**4**				**7**	**2**	**2**	**4**	**2**	**0**	**0**	**1**	
1995-96	**Washington**	**NHL**	**78**	**15**	**26**	**41**	**60**	**4**	**0**	**4**	**139**	**10.8**	**25**				**6**	**2**	**4**	**6**	**4**	**1**	**0**	**0**	

			Regular Season													Playoffs								
Season	Club	League	GP	G	A	Pts	PIM	PP	SH	GW	S	%	+/-	TF	F%	Min	GP	G	A	Pts	PIM	PP	SH	GW	Min
1996-97	**Washington**	**NHL**	**57**	**13**	**17**	**30**	**36**	**3**	**0**	**3**	**129**	**10.1**	**-11**	....	....	....	....	....	....	....	....	....	....	....	....
1997-98	Lada Togliatti	Russia	7	3	2	5	4	....	....	....	....	....	....	....	....	....	....	....	....	....	....	....	....	....	....
	Lada Togliatti	EuroHL	1	1	0	1	2	....	....	....	....	....	....	....	....	....	....	....	....	....	....	....	....	....	....
	Washington	**NHL**	**72**	**5**	**16**	**21**	**66**	**2**	**0**	**0**	**134**	**3.7**	**2**	....	....	....	**21**	**7**	**4**	**11**	**30**	**3**	**1**	**2**	....
	Russia	Olympics	6	0	2	2	0	....	....	....	....	....	....	....	....	....	....	....	....	....	....	....	....	....	....
1998-99	**Washington**	**NHL**	**53**	**21**	**10**	**31**	**57**	**13**	**1**	**3**	**180**	**11.7**	**1**	**0**	**0.0**	**23:55**	....	....	....	....	....	....	....	....	....
99-2000	**Washington**	**NHL**	**73**	**18**	**36**	**54**	**52**	**5**	**0**	**3**	**181**	**9.9**	**26**	**0**	**0.0**	**21:46**	**5**	**1**	**0**	**1**	**6**	**0**	**0**	**0**	**19:58**
2000-01	**Washington**	**NHL**	**76**	**19**	**38**	**57**	**70**	**8**	**0**	**2**	**241**	**7.9**	**12**	**1**	**100.0**	**22:26**	**6**	**1**	**3**	**4**	**2**	**1**	**0**	**0**	**19:45**
2001-02	**Washington**	**NHL**	**76**	**26**	**33**	**59**	**58**	**7**	**0**	**2**	**216**	**12.0**	**-1**	**1**	**100.0**	**23:51**	....	....	....	....	....	....	....	....	....
	Russia	Olympics	6	0	0	0	2	....	....	....	....	....	....	....	....	....	....	....	....	....	....	....	....	....	....
2002-03	**Washington**	**NHL**	**82**	**18**	**49**	**67**	**52**	**7**	**0**	**2**	**224**	**8.0**	**13**	**0**	**0.0**	**26:35**	**6**	**0**	**5**	**5**	**4**	**0**	**0**	**0**	**29:00**
2003-04	**Washington**	**NHL**	**56**	**7**	**42**	**49**	**44**	**4**	**0**	**0**	**127**	**5.5**	**-20**	**0**	**0.0**	**27:57**	....	....	....	....	....	....	....	....	....
	Boston	**NHL**	**15**	**4**	**5**	**9**	**12**	**2**	**0**	**0**	**34**	**11.8**	**6**	**0**	**0.0**	**25:32**	**7**	**1**	**4**	**5**	**4**	**1**	**0**	**1**	**27:51**
	NHL Totals		**669**	**148**	**277**	**425**	**529**	**55**	**1**	**19**	**1643**	**9.0**		**2**	**100.0**	**24:22**	**58**	**14**	**22**	**36**	**52**	**6**	**1**	**4**	**24:28**

NHL Second All-Star Team (2002, 2003)
Played in NHL All-Star Game (2001, 2002, 2003)
Traded to **Boston** by **Washington** for Shaonne Morrisonn and Boston's 1st (Jeff Schultz) and 2nd (Michail Yunkov) round choices in 2004 Entry Draft, March 3, 2004.

GORDON, Boyd

(GOHR-duhn, BOYD) **WSH.**

Right wing. Shoots right. 6', 198 lbs. Born, Unity, Sask., October 19, 1983. Washington's 3rd choice, 17th overall, in 2002 Entry Draft.

Season	Club	League	GP	G	A	Pts	PIM	PP	SH	GW	S	%	+/-	TF	F%	Min	GP	G	A	Pts	PIM	PP	SH	GW	Min
1997-98	Regina Flyers	SMHA	60	70	102	172	53	....	....	....	....	....	....	....	....	....	....	....	....	....	....	....	....	....	....
1998-99	Regina Rangers	SMBHL	60	70	102	172	53	....	....	....	....	....	....	....	....	....	....	....	....	....	....	....	....	....	....
99-2000	Red Deer Rebels	WHL	66	10	26	36	24	....	....	....	....	....	....	....	....	....	4	0	1	1	16	....	....	....	....
2000-01	Red Deer Rebels	WHL	72	12	27	39	39	....	....	....	....	....	....	....	....	....	22	3	6	9	2	....	....	....	....
2001-02	Red Deer Rebels	WHL	66	22	29	51	19	....	....	....	....	....	....	....	....	....	23	10	12	22	8	....	....	....	....
2002-03	Red Deer Rebels	WHL	56	33	48	81	28	....	....	....	....	....	....	....	....	....	23	8	12	20	14	....	....	....	....
2003-04	**Washington**	**NHL**	**41**	**1**	**5**	**6**	**8**	**0**	**0**	**0**	**42**	**2.4**	**-9**	**328**	**43.0**	**13:11**	....	....	....	....	....	....	....	....	....
	Portland Pirates	AHL	43	5	17	22	16	....	....	....	....	....	....	....	....	....	7	2	1	3	0	....	....	....	....
	NHL Totals		**41**	**1**	**5**	**6**	**8**	**0**	**0**	**0**	**42**	**2.4**		**328**	**43.0**	**13:11**	....	....	....	....	....	....	....	....	....

WHL East First All-Star Team (2003)

GOREN, Lee

(GOH-rehn, LEE) **VAN.**

Right wing. Shoots right. 6'3", 205 lbs. Born, Winnipeg, Man., December 26, 1977. Boston's 5th choice, 63rd overall, in 1997 Entry Draft.

Season	Club	League	GP	G	A	Pts	PIM	PP	SH	GW	S	%	+/-	TF	F%	Min	GP	G	A	Pts	PIM	PP	SH	GW	Min
1994-95	Wpg. Warriors	MMHL	31	19	31	50	50	....	....	....	....	....	....	....	....	....	....	....	....	....	....	....	....	....	....
1995-96	Minot Top Guns	SJHL	56	25	35	61	....	....	....	....	....	....	....	....	....	....	12	5	20	25	....	....	....	....	....
	Saskatoon Blades	WHL	2	0	0	0	2	....	....	....	....	....	....	....	....	....	....	....	....	....	....	....	....	....	....
1996-97	North Dakota	WCHA	DID NOT PLAY – FRESHMAN																						
1997-98	North Dakota	WCHA	29	3	13	16	26	....	....	....	....	....	....	....	....	....	....	....	....	....	....	....	....	....	....
1998-99	North Dakota	WCHA	38	26	19	45	20	....	....	....	....	....	....	....	....	....	....	....	....	....	....	....	....	....	....
99-2000	North Dakota	WCHA	44	*34	29	63	42	....	....	....	....	....	....	....	....	....	....	....	....	....	....	....	....	....	....
2000-01	**Boston**	**NHL**	**21**	**2**	**0**	**2**	**7**	**1**	**0**	**0**	**9**	**22.2**	**-3**	**21**	**38.1**	**4:24**	....	....	....	....	....	....	....	....	....
	Providence Bruins	AHL	54	15	18	33	72	....	....	....	....	....	....	....	....	....	17	5	2	7	11	....	....	....	....
2001-02	Providence Bruins	AHL	71	11	26	37	121	....	....	....	....	....	....	....	....	....	2	0	0	0	0	....	....	....	....
2002-03	**Boston**	**NHL**	**14**	**2**	**1**	**3**	**7**	**2**	**0**	**0**	**15**	**13.3**	**-2**	**0**	**0.0**	**8:15**	**5**	**0**	**0**	**0**	**5**	**0**	**0**	**0**	**6:29**
	Providence Bruins	AHL	65	32	37	69	106	....	....	....	....	....	....	....	....	....	3	0	1	1	0	....	....	....	....
2003-04	**Florida**	**NHL**	**2**	**0**	**1**	**1**	**0**	**0**	**0**	**0**	**1**	**0.0**	**-4**	**1**	**100.0**	**13:20**	....	....	....	....	....	....	....	....	....
	San Antonio	AHL	65	27	22	49	72	....	....	....	....	....	....	....	....	....	....	....	....	....	....	....	....	....	....
	NHL Totals		**37**	**4**	**2**	**6**	**14**	**3**	**0**	**0**	**25**	**16.0**		**22**	**40.9**	**6:20**	**5**	**0**	**0**	**0**	**5**	**0**	**0**	**0**	**6:29**

WCHA Second All-Star Team (2000) • NCAA West Second All-American Team (2000) • NCAA Championship All-Tournament Team (2000) • NCAA Championship Tournament MVP (2000)
• Ruled ineligible to play during 1996-97 season by NCAA due to appearance with **Saskatoon** (WHL) in 1995-96 season. Signed as a free agent by **Florida**, July 24, 2003. Signed as a free agent by **Vancouver**, July 7, 2004.

GRAND-PIERRE, Jean-Luc

(GRAHN pee-AIR, ZHAHN-LOOK)

Defense. Shoots right. 6'3", 223 lbs. Born, Montreal, Que., February 2, 1977. St. Louis' 6th choice, 179th overall, in 1995 Entry Draft.

Season	Club	League	GP	G	A	Pts	PIM	PP	SH	GW	S	%	+/-	TF	F%	Min	GP	G	A	Pts	PIM	PP	SH	GW	Min
1992-93	Lac St-Louis Lions	QAAA	1	0	0	0	2	....	....	....	....	....	....	....	....	....	....	....	....	....	....	....	....	....	....
1993-94	Beauport	QMJHL	46	1	4	5	27	....	....	....	....	....	....	....	....	....	1	0	0	0	0	....	....	....	....
1994-95	Val-d'Or Foreurs	QMJHL	59	10	13	23	126	....	....	....	....	....	....	....	....	....	....	....	....	....	....	....	....	....	....
1995-96	Val-d'Or Foreurs	QMJHL	67	13	21	34	209	....	....	....	....	....	....	....	....	....	13	1	4	5	47	....	....	....	....
1996-97	Val-d'Or Foreurs	QMJHL	58	9	24	33	186	....	....	....	....	....	....	....	....	....	13	5	8	13	46	....	....	....	....
1997-98	Rochester	AHL	75	4	6	10	211	....	....	....	....	....	....	....	....	....	4	0	0	0	2	....	....	....	....
1998-99	**Buffalo**	**NHL**	**16**	**0**	**1**	**1**	**17**	**0**	**0**	**0**	**11**	**0.0**	**0**	**0**	**0.0**	**13:36**	....	....	....	....	....	....	....	....	....
	Rochester	AHL	55	5	4	9	90	....	....	....	....	....	....	....	....	....	....	....	....	....	....	....	....	....	....
99-2000	**Buffalo**	**NHL**	**11**	**0**	**0**	**0**	**15**	**0**	**0**	**0**	**11**	**0.0**	**-1**	**0**	**0.0**	**15:11**	**4**	**0**	**0**	**0**	**4**	**0**	**0**	**0**	**17:34**
	Rochester	AHL	62	5	8	13	124	....	....	....	....	....	....	....	....	....	17	0	1	1	40	....	....	....	....
2000-01	**Columbus**	**NHL**	**64**	**1**	**4**	**5**	**73**	**0**	**0**	**0**	**33**	**3.0**	**-6**	**0**	**0.0**	**12:51**	....	....	....	....	....	....	....	....	....
2001-02	**Columbus**	**NHL**	**81**	**2**	**6**	**8**	**90**	**0**	**0**	**0**	**62**	**3.2**	**-28**	**3**	**0.0**	**15:20**	....	....	....	....	....	....	....	....	....
2002-03	**Columbus**	**NHL**	**41**	**1**	**0**	**1**	**64**	**0**	**0**	**0**	**32**	**3.1**	**-6**	**0**	**0.0**	**13:38**	....	....	....	....	....	....	....	....	....
	Syracuse Crunch	AHL	2	1	0	1	6	....	....	....	....	....	....	....	....	....	....	....	....	....	....	....	....	....	....
2003-04	**Columbus**	**NHL**	**16**	**0**	**0**	**0**	**12**	**0**	**0**	**0**	**15**	**0.0**	**-3**	**2**	**100.0**	**7:25**	....	....	....	....	....	....	....	....	....
	Atlanta	**NHL**	**27**	**2**	**2**	**4**	**26**	**0**	**1**	**0**	**19**	**10.5**	**-7**	**1**	**0.0**	**15:25**	....	....	....	....	....	....	....	....	....
	Washington	**NHL**	**13**	**1**	**0**	**1**	**14**	**0**	**0**	**0**	**19**	**5.3**	**-2**	**2**	**0.0**	**11:34**	....	....	....	....	....	....	....	....	....
	NHL Totals		**269**	**7**	**13**	**20**	**311**	**0**	**1**	**0**	**202**	**3.5**		**8**	**25.0**	**13:44**	**4**	**0**	**0**	**0**	**4**	**0**	**0**	**0**	**17:34**

Traded to **Buffalo** by **St. Louis** with Ottawa's 2nd round choice (previously acquired, Buffalo selected Cory Sarich) in 1996 Entry Draft and St. Louis' 3rd round choice (Maxim Afinogenov) in 1997 Entry Draft for Yuri Khmylev and Buffalo's 8th round choice (Andrei Podkonicky) in 1996 Entry Draft, March 20, 1996. Traded to **Columbus** by **Buffalo** with Matt Davidson, San Jose's 5th round choice (previously acquired, Columbus selected Tyler Kolarik) in 2000 Entry Draft and Buffalo's 5th round choice (later traded to Calgary – later traded to Detroit – Detroit selected Andreas Jamtin) in 2001 Entry Draft to complete Expansion Draft agreement which had Columbus select Geoff Sanderson and Dwayne Roloson from Buffalo, June 23, 2000. Traded to **Atlanta** by **Columbus** for future considerations, December 31, 2003. Claimed on waivers by **Washington** from **Atlanta**, March 9, 2004.

GRATTON, Benoit

(grah-TOHN, BEHN-wah)

Center. Shoots left. 5'11", 194 lbs. Born, Montreal, Que., December 28, 1976. Washington's 6th choice, 105th overall, in 1995 Entry Draft.

Season	Club	League	GP	G	A	Pts	PIM	PP	SH	GW	S	%	+/-	TF	F%	Min	GP	G	A	Pts	PIM	PP	SH	GW	Min
1992-93	Laval Laurentide	QAAA	40	19	38	57	74	....	....	....	....	....	....	....	....	....	13	1	9	10	27	....	....	....	....
1993-94	Laval Titan	QMJHL	51	9	14	23	70	....	....	....	....	....	....	....	....	....	20	2	1	3	19	....	....	....	....
1994-95	Laval Titan	QMJHL	71	30	58	88	199	....	....	....	....	....	....	....	....	....	20	8	*21	29	42	....	....	....	....
1995-96	Laval Titan	QMJHL	38	21	39	60	130	....	....	....	....	....	....	....	....	....	....	....	....	....	....	....	....	....	....
	Granby	QMJHL	27	12	46	58	97	....	....	....	....	....	....	....	....	....	21	13	26	39	68	....	....	....	....
1996-97	Portland Pirates	AHL	76	6	40	46	140	....	....	....	....	....	....	....	....	....	5	2	1	3	14	....	....	....	....
1997-98	**Washington**	**NHL**	**6**	**0**	**1**	**1**	**6**	**0**	**0**	**0**	**5**	**0.0**	**1**	....	....	....	....	....	....	....	....	....	....	....	....
	Portland Pirates	AHL	58	19	31	50	137	....	....	....	....	....	....	....	....	....	8	4	2	6	24	....	....	....	....
1998-99	**Washington**	**NHL**	**16**	**4**	**3**	**7**	**16**	**0**	**0**	**0**	**24**	**16.7**	**-1**	**136**	**54.4**	**13:28**	....	....	....	....	....	....	....	....	....
	Portland Pirates	AHL	64	18	42	60	135	....	....	....	....	....	....	....	....	....	....	....	....	....	....	....	....	....	....
99-2000	**Calgary**	**NHL**	**10**	**0**	**2**	**2**	**10**	**0**	**0**	**0**	**4**	**0.0**	**1**	**68**	**63.2**	**8:15**	....	....	....	....	....	....	....	....	....
	Saint John Flames	AHL	65	17	49	66	137	....	....	....	....	....	....	....	....	....	3	0	1	1	4	....	....	....	....
2000-01	**Calgary**	**NHL**	**14**	**1**	**3**	**4**	**14**	**0**	**0**	**0**	**13**	**7.7**	**0**	**105**	**63.8**	**9:11**	....	....	....	....	....	....	....	....	....
	Saint John Flames	AHL	53	10	36	46	153	....	....	....	....	....	....	....	....	....	....	....	....	....	....	....	....	....	....
2001-02	**Montreal**	**NHL**	**8**	**1**	**0**	**1**	**8**	**0**	**0**	**0**	**8**	**12.5**	**-1**	**98**	**63.3**	**9:51**	....	....	....	....	....	....	....	....	....
	Quebec Citadelles	AHL	35	10	19	29	70	....	....	....	....	....	....	....	....	....	3	2	3	5	10	....	....	....	....
2002-03	Hamilton	AHL	43	21	39	60	78	....	....	....	....	....	....	....	....	....	22	2	*15	17	73	....	....	....	....
2003-04	**Montreal**	**NHL**	**4**	**0**	**1**	**1**	**4**	**0**	**0**	**0**	**3**	**0.0**	**0**	**31**	**54.8**	**9:44**	....	....	....	....	....	....	....	....	....
	Hamilton	AHL	50	18	33	51	119	....	....	....	....	....	....	....	....	....	10	1	2	3	*67	....	....	....	....
	NHL Totals		**58**	**6**	**10**	**16**	**58**	**0**	**0**	**0**	**57**	**10.5**		**438**	**60.0**	**10:28**	....	....	....	....	....	....	....	....	....

Traded to **Calgary** by **Washington** for Steve Shirreffs, August 18, 1999. Claimed on waivers by **Montreal** from **Calgary**, April 11, 2001.

GRATTON, Chris
(GRA-tuhn, KRIHS) **COL.**

Center. Shoots left. 6'4", 225 lbs. Born, Brantford, Ont., July 5, 1975. Tampa Bay's 1st choice, 3rd overall, in 1993 Entry Draft.

			Regular Season														Playoffs								
Season	Club	League	GP	G	A	Pts	PIM	PP	SH	GW	S	%	+/-	TF	F%	Min	GP	G	A	Pts	PIM	PP	SH	GW	Min
1989-90	Brantford Classics	OJHL-B	1	0	2	2	2	....	....	....	....	....	....	....	....	....	....	....	....	....	....	....	....	....	....
1990-91	Brantford Classics	OJHL-B	31	30	30	60	28	....	....	....	....	....	....	....	....	....	....	....	....	....	....	....	....	....	....
1991-92	Kingston	OHL	62	27	39	66	37	....	....	....	....	....	....	....	....	....	....	....	....	....	....	....	....	....	....
1992-93	Kingston	OHL	58	55	54	109	125	....	....	....	....	....	....	....	....	....	16	11	18	29	42	....	....	....	....
1993-94	**Tampa Bay**	**NHL**	**84**	**13**	**29**	**42**	**123**	**5**	**1**	**2**	**161**	**8.1**	**-25**	....	....	....	....	....	....	....	....	....	....	....	....
1994-95	**Tampa Bay**	**NHL**	**46**	**7**	**20**	**27**	**89**	**2**	**0**	**0**	**91**	**7.7**	**-2**	....	....	....	....	....	....	....	....	....	....	....	....
1995-96	**Tampa Bay**	**NHL**	**82**	**17**	**21**	**38**	**105**	**7**	**0**	**3**	**183**	**9.3**	**-13**	....	....	....	**6**	**0**	**2**	**2**	**27**	**0**	**0**	**0**	....
1996-97	**Tampa Bay**	**NHL**	**82**	**30**	**32**	**62**	**201**	**9**	**0**	**4**	**230**	**13.0**	**-28**	....	....	....	....	....	....	....	....	....	....	....	....
1997-98	**Philadelphia**	**NHL**	**82**	**22**	**40**	**62**	**159**	**5**	**0**	**2**	**182**	**12.1**	**11**	....	....	....	**5**	**2**	**0**	**2**	**10**	**0**	**0**	**0**	....
1998-99	**Philadelphia**	**NHL**	**26**	**1**	**7**	**8**	**41**	**0**	**0**	**0**	**54**	**1.9**	**-8**	38	42.1	14:25	....	....	....	....	....	....	....	....	....
	Tampa Bay	**NHL**	**52**	**7**	**19**	**26**	**102**	**1**	**0**	**1**	**127**	**5.5**	**-20**	1032	53.9	18:20	....	....	....	....	....	....	....	....	....
99-2000	**Tampa Bay**	**NHL**	**58**	**14**	**27**	**41**	**121**	**4**	**0**	**1**	**168**	**8.3**	**-24**	1341	55.9	20:03	....	....	....	....	....	....	....	....	....
	Buffalo	**NHL**	**14**	**1**	**7**	**8**	**15**	**0**	**0**	**0**	**34**	**2.9**	**1**	256	54.3	16:40	**5**	**0**	**1**	**1**	**4**	**0**	**0**	**0**	**14:56**
2000-01	**Buffalo**	**NHL**	**82**	**19**	**21**	**40**	**102**	**5**	**0**	**5**	**156**	**12.2**	**0**	1161	57.3	14:37	**13**	**6**	**4**	**10**	**14**	**2**	**0**	**1**	**12:33**
2001-02	**Buffalo**	**NHL**	**82**	**15**	**24**	**39**	**75**	**1**	**0**	**5**	**139**	**10.8**	**0**	1297	53.8	14:57	....	....	....	....	....	....	....	....	....
2002-03	**Buffalo**	**NHL**	**66**	**15**	**29**	**44**	**86**	**4**	**0**	**2**	**187**	**8.0**	**-5**	1099	58.9	16:26	....	....	....	....	....	....	....	....	....
	Phoenix	**NHL**	**14**	**0**	**1**	**1**	**21**	**0**	**0**	**0**	**28**	**0.0**	**-11**	231	57.1	17:12	....	....	....	....	....	....	....	....	....
2003-04	**Phoenix**	**NHL**	**68**	**11**	**18**	**29**	**93**	**3**	**0**	**1**	**122**	**9.0**	**-19**	1090	55.3	14:40	....	....	....	....	....	....	....	....	....
	Colorado	**NHL**	**13**	**2**	**1**	**3**	**18**	**0**	**0**	**0**	**28**	**7.1**	**1**	252	57.5	16:55	**11**	**0**	**0**	**0**	**27**	**0**	**0**	**0**	**12:14**
	NHL Totals		**851**	**174**	**296**	**470**	**1351**	**46**	**1**	**26**	**1890**	**9.2**		**7797**	**55.8**	**16:12**	**40**	**8**	**7**	**15**	**82**	**2**	**0**	**1**	**12:50**

OHL All-Rookie Team (1992) • OHL Rookie of the Year (1992)

Signed as a free agent by **Philadelphia**, August 14, 1997. Traded to **Tampa Bay** by **Philadelphia** with Mike Sillinger for Mikael Renberg and Daymond Langkow, December 12, 1998. Traded to **Buffalo** by **Tampa Bay** with Tampa Bay's 2nd round choice (Derek Roy) in 2001 Entry Draft for Cory Sarich, Wayne Primeau, Brian Holzinger and Buffalo's 3rd round choice (Alexander Kharitonov) in 2000 Entry Draft, March 9, 2000. Traded to **Phoenix** by **Buffalo** with Buffalo's 4th round choice (later traded to Edmonton – Edmonton selected Liam Reddox) in 2004 Entry Draft for Daniel Briere and Phoenix's 3rd round choice (Andrej Sekera) in 2004 Entry Draft, March 10, 2003. Traded to **Colorado** by **Phoenix** with Ossi Vaananen and Phoenix's 2nd round choice in 2005 Entry Draft for Derek Morris and Keith Ballard, March 8, 2004.

GREBESHKOV, Denis
(greh-behsh-KAHV, DEH-nihs) **L.A.**

Defense. Shoots left. 6'1", 200 lbs. Born, Yaroslavl, USSR, October 11, 1983. Los Angeles' 1st choice, 18th overall, in 2002 Entry Draft.

Season	Club	League	GP	G	A	Pts	PIM	PP	SH	GW	S	%	+/-	TF	F%	Min	GP	G	A	Pts	PIM	PP	SH	GW	Min
99-2000	Yaroslavl 2	Russia-3	42	2	1	3	12	....	....	....	....	....	....	....	....	....	6	0	0	0	2	....	....	....	....
2000-01	Yaroslavl 2	Russia-3	34	7	2	9	20	....	....	....	....	....	....	....	....	....	....	....	....	....	....	....	....	....	....
2001-02	Yaroslavl 2	Russia-3	7	1	1	2	2	....	....	....	....	....	....	....	....	....	....	....	....	....	....	....	....	....	....
	Yaroslavl	Russia	27	1	2	3	10	....	....	....	....	....	....	....	....	....	....	....	....	....	....	....	....	....	....
2002-03	Yaroslavl	Russia	48	0	7	7	26	....	....	....	....	....	....	....	....	....	10	0	1	1	2	....	....	....	....
2003-04	**Los Angeles**	**NHL**	**4**	**0**	**1**	**1**	**0**	**0**	**0**	**0**	**5**	**0.0**	**-4**	0	0.0	18:29	....	....	....	....	....	....	....	....	....
	Manchester	AHL	43	2	7	9	34	....	....	....	....	....	....	....	....	....	6	0	1	1	6	....	....	....	....
	NHL Totals		**4**	**0**	**1**	**1**	**0**	**0**	**0**	**0**	**5**	**0.0**		**0**	**0.0**	**18:29**	....	....	....	....	....	....	....	....	....

GREEN, Josh
(GREEN, JAWSH)

Left wing. Shoots left. 6'4", 212 lbs. Born, Camrose, Alta., November 16, 1977. Los Angeles' 1st choice, 30th overall, in 1996 Entry Draft.

Season	Club	League	GP	G	A	Pts	PIM	PP	SH	GW	S	%	+/-	TF	F%	Min	GP	G	A	Pts	PIM	PP	SH	GW	Min
1992-93	Camrose Kodiacs	ABHL	60	55	45	100	80	....	....	....	....	....	....	....	....	....	....	....	....	....	....	....	....	....	....
1993-94	Medicine Hat	WHL	63	22	22	44	43	....	....	....	....	....	....	....	....	....	3	0	0	0	4	....	....	....	....
1994-95	Medicine Hat	WHL	68	32	23	55	64	....	....	....	....	....	....	....	....	....	5	5	1	6	2	....	....	....	....
1995-96	Medicine Hat	WHL	46	18	25	43	55	....	....	....	....	....	....	....	....	....	5	2	2	4	4	....	....	....	....
1996-97	Medicine Hat	WHL	51	25	32	57	61	....	....	....	....	....	....	....	....	....	....	....	....	....	....	....	....	....	....
	Swift Current	WHL	23	10	15	25	33	....	....	....	....	....	....	....	....	....	10	9	7	16	19	....	....	....	....
1997-98	Swift Current	WHL	5	9	1	10	9	....	....	....	....	....	....	....	....	....	....	....	....	....	....	....	....	....	....
	Portland	WHL	26	26	18	44	27	....	....	....	....	....	....	....	....	....	....	....	....	....	....	....	....	....	....
	Fredericton	AHL	43	16	15	31	14	....	....	....	....	....	....	....	....	....	4	1	3	4	6	....	....	....	....
1998-99	**Los Angeles**	**NHL**	**27**	**1**	**3**	**4**	**8**	**1**	**0**	**0**	**35**	**2.9**	**-5**	2	50.0	11:44	....	....	....	....	....	....	....	....	....
	Springfield	AHL	41	15	15	30	29	....	....	....	....	....	....	....	....	....	....	....	....	....	....	....	....	....	....
99-2000	**NY Islanders**	**NHL**	**49**	**12**	**14**	**26**	**41**	**2**	**0**	**3**	**109**	**11.0**	**-7**	12	50.0	13:36	....	....	....	....	....	....	....	....	....
	Lowell	AHL	17	6	2	8	19	....	....	....	....	....	....	....	....	....	....	....	....	....	....	....	....	....	....
2000-01	Hamilton	AHL	2	2	0	2	2	....	....	....	....	....	....	....	....	....	....	....	....	....	....	....	....	....	....
	Edmonton	**NHL**	....	....	....	....	....	....	....	....	....	....	....	....	....	....	**3**	**0**	**0**	**0**	**0**	**0**	**0**	**0**	**7:55**
2001-02	**Edmonton**	**NHL**	**61**	**10**	**5**	**15**	**52**	**1**	**0**	**1**	**78**	**12.8**	**9**	18	38.9	10:05	....	....	....	....	....	....	....	....	....
2002-03	**Edmonton**	**NHL**	**20**	**0**	**2**	**2**	**12**	**0**	**0**	**0**	**20**	**0.0**	**-3**	5	0.0	10:22	....	....	....	....	....	....	....	....	....
	NY Rangers	**NHL**	**4**	**0**	**0**	**0**	**2**	**0**	**0**	**0**	**3**	**0.0**	**-1**	0	0.0	9:06	....	....	....	....	....	....	....	....	....
	Washington	**NHL**	**21**	**1**	**2**	**3**	**7**	**0**	**0**	**0**	**20**	**5.0**	**1**	3	0.0	8:07	....	....	....	....	....	....	....	....	....
2003-04	**Calgary**	**NHL**	**36**	**2**	**4**	**6**	**24**	**0**	**0**	**0**	**47**	**4.3**	**-3**	39	30.8	11:18	....	....	....	....	....	....	....	....	....
	Lowell	AHL	22	6	9	15	46	....	....	....	....	....	....	....	....	....	....	....	....	....	....	....	....	....	....
	NY Rangers	**NHL**	**14**	**3**	**2**	**5**	**8**	**0**	**0**	**1**	**29**	**10.3**	**0**	9	55.6	14:16	....	....	....	....	....	....	....	....	....
	NHL Totals		**232**	**29**	**32**	**61**	**154**	**4**	**0**	**5**	**341**	**8.5**		**88**	**35.2**	**11:17**	**3**	**0**	**0**	**0**	**0**	**0**	**0**	**0**	**7:55**

Traded to **NY Islanders** by **Los Angeles** with Olli Jokinen, Mathieu Biron and Los Angeles' 1st round choice (Taylor Pyatt) in 1999 Entry Draft for Ziggy Palffy, Brian Smolinski, Marcel Cousineau and New Jersey's 4th round choice (previously acquired, Los Angeles selected Daniel Johansson) in 1999 Entry Draft, June 20, 1999. Traded to **Edmonton** by **NY Islanders** with Eric Brewer and NY Islanders' 2nd round choice (Brad Winchester) in 2000 Entry Draft for Roman Hamrlik, June 24, 2000. • Missed majority of 2000-01 season recovering from shoulder injury suffered in game vs. Detroit, October 10, 2000. Traded to **NY Rangers** by **Edmonton** for future considerations, December 12, 2002. Claimed on waivers by **Washington** from **NY Rangers**, January 15, 2003. Signed as a free agent by **Calgary**, July 17, 2003. Claimed on waivers by **NY Rangers** from **Calgary**, March 6, 2004.

GREEN, Mike
(GREEN, MIGHK)

Center. Shoots right. 5'11", 192 lbs. Born, Calgary, Alta., August 23, 1979.

Season	Club	League	GP	G	A	Pts	PIM	PP	SH	GW	S	%	+/-	TF	F%	Min	GP	G	A	Pts	PIM	PP	SH	GW	Min
1996-97	Cgy. North Stars	AMHL	35	34	27	61	78	....	....	....	....	....	....	....	....	....	....	....	....	....	....	....	....	....	....
	Edmonton Ice	WHL	7	0	2	2	0	....	....	....	....	....	....	....	....	....	....	....	....	....	....	....	....	....	....
1997-98	Edmonton Ice	WHL	71	15	26	41	16	....	....	....	....	....	....	....	....	....	....	....	....	....	....	....	....	....	....
1998-99	Kootenay Ice	WHL	71	35	45	80	37	....	....	....	....	....	....	....	....	....	7	2	2	4	4	....	....	....	....
99-2000	Kootenay Ice	WHL	69	43	49	92	63	....	....	....	....	....	....	....	....	....	21	9	16	25	20	....	....	....	....
2000-01	Port Huron	UHL	11	1	5	6	6	....	....	....	....	....	....	....	....	....	....	....	....	....	....	....	....	....	....
	Louisville Panthers	AHL	24	2	1	3	4	....	....	....	....	....	....	....	....	....	....	....	....	....	....	....	....	....	....
	Knoxville Speed	UHL	48	18	24	42	35	....	....	....	....	....	....	....	....	....	1	0	0	0	0	....	....	....	....
2001-02	Macon Whoopee	ECHL	54	27	35	62	18	....	....	....	....	....	....	....	....	....	....	....	....	....	....	....	....	....	....
	Cincinnati	AHL	22	2	9	11	4	....	....	....	....	....	....	....	....	....	3	0	0	0	0	....	....	....	....
2002-03	San Antonio	AHL	80	26	34	60	25	....	....	....	....	....	....	....	....	....	3	0	2	2	0	....	....	....	....
2003-04	**Florida**	**NHL**	**11**	**0**	**1**	**1**	**2**	**0**	**0**	**0**	**7**	**0.0**	**0**	42	47.6	8:16	....	....	....	....	....	....	....	....	....
	San Antonio	AHL	45	12	23	35	16	....	....	....	....	....	....	....	....	....	....	....	....	....	....	....	....	....	....
	NY Rangers	**NHL**	**13**	**1**	**2**	**3**	**2**	**0**	**0**	**0**	**13**	**7.7**	**0**	98	39.8	9:53	....	....	....	....	....	....	....	....	....
	NHL Totals		**24**	**1**	**3**	**4**	**4**	**0**	**0**	**0**	**20**	**5.0**		**140**	**42.1**	**9:08**	....	....	....	....	....	....	....	....	....

WHL East Second All-Star Team (2000)

Signed as a free agent by **Florida**, April 7, 2000. Claimed on waivers by **NY Rangers** from **Florida**, March 9, 2004.

GREEN, Travis
(GREEN, TRA-vihs)

Center. Shoots right. 6'2", 200 lbs. Born, Castlegar, B.C., December 20, 1970. NY Islanders' 2nd choice, 23rd overall, in 1989 Entry Draft.

Season	Club	League	GP	G	A	Pts	PIM	PP	SH	GW	S	%	+/-	TF	F%	Min	GP	G	A	Pts	PIM	PP	SH	GW	Min
1985-86	Castlegar Rebels	KIJHL	35	30	40	70	41	....	....	....	....	....	....	....	....	....	....	....	....	....	....	....	....	....	....
1986-87	Spokane Chiefs	WHL	64	8	17	25	27	....	....	....	....	....	....	....	....	....	3	0	0	0	0	....	....	....	....
1987-88	Spokane Chiefs	WHL	72	33	54	87	42	....	....	....	....	....	....	....	....	....	15	10	10	20	13	....	....	....	....
1988-89	Spokane Chiefs	WHL	75	51	51	102	79	....	....	....	....	....	....	....	....	....	....	....	....	....	....	....	....	....	....
1989-90	Spokane Chiefs	WHL	50	45	44	89	80	....	....	....	....	....	....	....	....	....	....	....	....	....	....	....	....	....	....
	Medicine Hat	WHL	25	15	24	39	19	....	....	....	....	....	....	....	....	....	3	0	0	0	2	....	....	....	....
1990-91	Capital District	AHL	73	21	34	55	26	....	....	....	....	....	....	....	....	....	....	....	....	....	....	....	....	....	....
1991-92	Capital District	AHL	71	23	27	50	10	....	....	....	....	....	....	....	....	....	7	0	4	4	21	....	....	....	....
1992-93	**NY Islanders**	**NHL**	**61**	**7**	**18**	**25**	**43**	**1**	**0**	**0**	**115**	**6.1**	**4**	....	....	....	**12**	**3**	**1**	**4**	**6**	**0**	**0**	**0**	....
	Capital District	AHL	20	12	11	23	39	....	....	....	....	....	....	....	....	....	....	....	....	....	....	....	....	....	....
1993-94	**NY Islanders**	**NHL**	**83**	**18**	**22**	**40**	**44**	**1**	**0**	**2**	**164**	**11.0**	**16**	....	....	....	**4**	**0**	**0**	**0**	**2**	**0**	**0**	**0**	....
1994-95	**NY Islanders**	**NHL**	**42**	**5**	**7**	**12**	**25**	**0**	**0**	**0**	**59**	**8.5**	**-10**	....	....	....	....	....	....	....	....	....	....	....	....

			Regular Season														Playoffs								
Season	Club	League	GP	G	A	Pts	PIM	PP	SH	GW	S	%	+/-	TF	F%	Min	GP	G	A	Pts	PIM	PP	SH	GW	Min
1995-96	NY Islanders	NHL	69	25	45	70	42	14	1	2	186	13.4	–20	....	....	....	....	....	....	....	....	....	....	....	....
1996-97	NY Islanders	NHL	79	23	41	64	38	10	0	3	177	13.0	–5	....	....	....	....	....	....	....	....	....	....	....	....
1997-98	NY Islanders	NHL	54	14	12	26	66	8	0	2	99	14.1	–19	....	....	....	....	....	....	....	....	....	....	....	....
	Anaheim	NHL	22	5	11	16	16	1	0	0	42	11.9	–10	....	....	....	....	....	....	....	....	....	....	....	....
1998-99	Anaheim	NHL	79	13	17	30	81	3	1	2	165	7.9	–7	1325	52.8	17:17	4	0	1	1	4	0	0	0	15:02
99-2000	Phoenix	NHL	78	25	21	46	45	6	0	2	157	15.9	–4	1322	55.6	16:36	5	2	1	3	2	0	0	0	17:23
2000-01	Phoenix	NHL	69	13	15	28	63	3	0	0	113	11.5	–11	1135	54.9	16:05	....	....	....	....	....	....	....	....	....
2001-02	Toronto	NHL	82	11	23	34	61	3	0	2	119	9.2	13	647	54.1	14:32	20	3	6	9	34	0	0	1	20:34
2002-03	Toronto	NHL	75	12	12	24	67	2	1	3	86	14.0	2	802	53.5	12:57	4	2	1	3	4	0	1	1	18:08
2003-04	Boston	NHL	64	11	5	16	67	2	0	2	104	10.6	–6	845	55.6	15:17	7	0	1	1	8	0	0	0	15:37
	NHL Totals		**857**	**182**	**249**	**431**	**658**	**54**	**3**	**20**	**1586**	**11.5**		**6076**	**54.4**	**15:28**	**56**	**10**	**11**	**21**	**60**	**0**	**1**	**2**	**18:30**

Traded to **Anaheim** by **NY Islanders** with Doug Houda and Tony Tuzzolino for Joe Sacco, J.J. Daigneault and Mark Janssens, February 6, 1998. Traded to **Phoenix** by **Anaheim** with Anaheim's 1st round choice (Scott Kelman) in 1999 Entry Draft for Oleg Tverdovsky, June 26, 1999. Traded to **Toronto** by **Phoenix** with Robert Reichel and Craig Mills for Danny Markov, June 12, 2001. Claimed by **Columbus** from **Toronto** in Waiver Draft, October 3, 2003. Traded to **Boston** by **Columbus** for Boston's 6th round choice (Lennart Petrell) in 2004 Entry Draft, October 3, 2003.

GRENIER, Martin

(GREH-nyay, MAHR-tihn) **NYR**

Defense. Shoots left. 6'5", 245 lbs. Born, Laval, Que., November 2, 1980. Colorado's 2nd choice, 45th overall, in 1999 Entry Draft.

1996-97	Laval Laurentide	QAAA	34	3	16	19	117	....	....	....	....	....	....	....	....	....	13	0	4	4	....	....	....	....	....
1997-98	Quebec Remparts	QMJHL	61	4	11	15	202	....	....	....	....	....	....	....	....	....	14	0	2	2	36	....	....	....	....
1998-99	Quebec Remparts	QMJHL	60	7	18	25	*479	....	....	....	....	....	....	....	....	....	13	0	4	4	29	....	....	....	....
99-2000	Quebec Remparts	QMJHL	67	11	35	46	302	....	....	....	....	....	....	....	....	....	7	1	4	5	27	....	....	....	....
2000-01	Quebec Remparts	QMJHL	26	5	16	21	82	....	....	....	....	....	....	....	....	....	....	....	....	....	....	....	....	....	....
	Victoriaville Tigres	QMJHL	28	9	19	28	108	....	....	....	....	....	....	....	....	....	13	2	8	10	51	....	....	....	....
2001-02	**Phoenix**	**NHL**	**5**	**0**	**0**	**0**	**5**	**0**	**0**	**0**	**1**	**0.0**	**0**	**1**	**100.0**	**5:56**	....	....	....	....	....	....	....	....	....
	Springfield	AHL	69	2	6	8	241	....	....	....	....	....	....	....	....	....	....	....	....	....	....	....	....	....	....
2002-03	**Phoenix**	**NHL**	**3**	**0**	**0**	**0**	**0**	**0**	**0**	**0**	**0**	**0.0**	**–1**	**0**	**0.0**	**6:11**	....	....	....	....	....	....	....	....	....
	Springfield	AHL	73	2	10	12	232	....	....	....	....	....	....	....	....	....	6	0	1	1	12	....	....	....	....
2003-04	**Vancouver**	**NHL**	**7**	**1**	**0**	**1**	**9**	**0**	**0**	**0**	**6**	**16.7**	**3**	**0**	**0.0**	**6:50**	....	....	....	....	....	....	....	....	....
	Manitoba Moose	AHL	38	5	4	9	145	....	....	....	....	....	....	....	....	....	....	....	....	....	....	....	....	....	....
	Hartford	AHL	12	0	2	2	105	....	....	....	....	....	....	....	....	....	9	0	1	1	32	....	....	....	....
	NHL Totals		**15**	**1**	**0**	**1**	**14**	**0**	**0**	**0**	**7**	**14.3**		**1**	**100.0**	**6:24**	....	....	....	....	....	....	....	....	....

Traded to **Boston** by **Colorado** with Brian Rolston, Samuel Pahlsson and New Jersey's 1st round choice (previously acquired, Boston selected Martin Samuelsson) in 2000 Entry Draft for Raymond Bourque and Dave Andreychuk, March 6, 2000. Signed as a free agent by **Phoenix**, June 27, 2001. Traded to **Vancouver** by **Phoenix** for Bryan Helmer, July 25, 2003. Traded to **NY Rangers** by **Vancouver** with R.J. Umberger for Martin Rucinsky, March 9, 2004.

GRIER, Mike

(GREER, MIGHK) **BUF.**

Right wing. Shoots right. 6'1", 227 lbs. Born, Detroit, MI, January 5, 1975. St. Louis' 7th choice, 219th overall, in 1993 Entry Draft.

1992-93	St. Sebastian's	Hi-School	22	16	27	43	32	....	....	....	....	....	....	....	....	....	....	....	....	....	....	....	....	....	....
1993-94	Boston University	H-East	39	9	9	18	56	....	....	....	....	....	....	....	....	....	....	....	....	....	....	....	....	....	....
1994-95	Boston University	H-East	37	*29	26	55	85	....	....	....	....	....	....	....	....	....	....	....	....	....	....	....	....	....	....
1995-96	Boston University	H-East	38	21	25	46	82	....	....	....	....	....	....	....	....	....	....	....	....	....	....	....	....	....	....
1996-97	**Edmonton**	**NHL**	**79**	**15**	**17**	**32**	**45**	**4**	**0**	**2**	**89**	**16.9**	**7**	....	....	....	**12**	**3**	**1**	**4**	**4**	**1**	**0**	**1**	....
1997-98	**Edmonton**	**NHL**	**66**	**9**	**6**	**15**	**73**	**1**	**0**	**1**	**90**	**10.0**	**–3**	....	....	....	**12**	**2**	**2**	**4**	**13**	**0**	**0**	**1**	....
1998-99	**Edmonton**	**NHL**	**82**	**20**	**24**	**44**	**54**	**3**	**2**	**1**	**143**	**14.0**	**5**	**34**	**20.6**	**15:57**	**4**	**1**	**1**	**2**	**6**	**0**	**0**	**0**	**23:26**
99-2000	**Edmonton**	**NHL**	**65**	**9**	**22**	**31**	**68**	**0**	**3**	**2**	**115**	**7.8**	**9**	**32**	**46.8**	**15:45**	....	....	....	....	....	....	....	....	....
2000-01	**Edmonton**	**NHL**	**74**	**20**	**16**	**36**	**20**	**2**	**3**	**2**	**124**	**16.1**	**11**	**36**	**38.9**	**16:44**	**6**	**0**	**0**	**0**	**8**	**0**	**0**	**0**	**21:23**
2001-02	**Edmonton**	**NHL**	**82**	**8**	**17**	**25**	**32**	**0**	**2**	**3**	**112**	**7.1**	**1**	**38**	**47.4**	**15:01**	....	....	....	....	....	....	....	....	....
2002-03	**Washington**	**NHL**	**82**	**15**	**17**	**32**	**36**	**2**	**2**	**2**	**133**	**11.3**	**–14**	**98**	**43.9**	**17:48**	**6**	**1**	**1**	**2**	**2**	**0**	**0**	**0**	**17:59**
2003-04	**Washington**	**NHL**	**68**	**8**	**12**	**20**	**32**	**1**	**1**	**0**	**115**	**7.0**	**–19**	**54**	**44.4**	**17:25**	....	....	....	....	....	....	....	....	....
	Buffalo	**NHL**	**14**	**1**	**8**	**9**	**4**	**0**	**0**	**0**	**18**	**5.6**	**10**	**11**	**63.6**	**17:29**	....	....	....	....	....	....	....	....	....
	NHL Totals		**612**	**105**	**139**	**244**	**364**	**13**	**13**	**13**	**939**	**11.2**		**303**	**42.2**	**16:28**	**40**	**7**	**5**	**12**	**33**	**1**	**0**	**2**	**20:37**

Hockey East First All-Star Team (1995) • NCAA East First All-American Team (1995)

Rights traded to **Edmonton** by **St. Louis** with Curtis Joseph for St. Louis' 1st round choices in 1996 (previously acquired, St. Louis selected Marty Reasoner) and 1997 (previously acquired, later traded to Los Angeles – Los Angeles selected Matt Zultek) Entry Drafts, August 4, 1995. Traded to **Washington** by **Edmonton** for Washington's 2nd round choice (later traded to NY Islanders – NY Islanders selected Evgeni Tunik) in 2003 Entry Draft and Vancouver's 3rd round choice (previously acquired, Edmonton selected Zachery Stortini) in 2003 Entry Draft, October 7, 2002. Traded to **Buffalo** by **Washington** for Jakub Klepis, March 9, 2004.

GROSEK, Michal

(GROH-shehk, MIGH-kuhl)

Left wing. Shoots right. 6'2", 207 lbs. Born, Vyskov, Czech., June 1, 1975. Winnipeg's 7th choice, 145th overall, in 1993 Entry Draft.

1992-93	AC ZPS Zlin	Czech	17	1	3	4	....	....	....	....	....	....	....	....	....	....	....	....	....	....	....	....	....	....	....
1993-94	Tacoma Rockets	WHL	30	25	20	45	106	....	....	....	....	....	....	....	....	....	7	2	2	4	30	....	....	....	....
	Winnipeg	**NHL**	**3**	**1**	**0**	**1**	**0**	**0**	**0**	**0**	**4**	**25.0**	**–1**	....	....	....	....	....	....	....	....	....	....	....	....
	Moncton Hawks	AHL	20	1	2	3	47	....	....	....	....	....	....	....	....	....	2	0	0	0	0	....	....	....	....
1994-95	Springfield	AHL	45	10	22	32	98	....	....	....	....	....	....	....	....	....	....	....	....	....	....	....	....	....	....
	Winnipeg	**NHL**	**24**	**2**	**2**	**4**	**21**	**0**	**0**	**1**	**27**	**7.4**	**–3**	....	....	....	....	....	....	....	....	....	....	....	....
1995-96	**Winnipeg**	**NHL**	**1**	**0**	**0**	**0**	**0**	**0**	**0**	**0**	**1**	**0.0**	**–1**	....	....	....	....	....	....	....	....	....	....	....	....
	Springfield	AHL	39	16	19	35	68	....	....	....	....	....	....	....	....	....	....	....	....	....	....	....	....	....	....
	Buffalo	**NHL**	**22**	**6**	**4**	**10**	**31**	**2**	**0**	**1**	**33**	**18.2**	**0**	....	....	....	....	....	....	....	....	....	....	....	....
1996-97	**Buffalo**	**NHL**	**82**	**15**	**21**	**36**	**71**	**1**	**0**	**2**	**117**	**12.8**	**25**	....	....	....	**12**	**3**	**3**	**6**	**8**	**0**	**0**	**0**	....
1997-98	**Buffalo**	**NHL**	**67**	**10**	**20**	**30**	**60**	**2**	**0**	**1**	**114**	**8.8**	**9**	....	....	....	**15**	**6**	**4**	**10**	**28**	**2**	**0**	**3**	....
1998-99	**Buffalo**	**NHL**	**76**	**20**	**30**	**50**	**102**	**4**	**0**	**3**	**140**	**14.3**	**21**	**5**	**60.0**	**17:14**	**13**	**0**	**4**	**4**	**28**	**0**	**0**	**0**	**11:51**
99-2000	**Buffalo**	**NHL**	**61**	**11**	**23**	**34**	**35**	**2**	**0**	**2**	**96**	**11.5**	**12**	**8**	**25.0**	**16:17**	....	....	....	....	....	....	....	....	....
	Chicago	**NHL**	**14**	**2**	**4**	**6**	**12**	**1**	**0**	**0**	**18**	**11.1**	**–1**	**1**	**0.0**	**13:06**	....	....	....	....	....	....	....	....	....
2000-01	**NY Rangers**	**NHL**	**65**	**9**	**11**	**20**	**61**	**2**	**0**	**0**	**84**	**10.7**	**–10**	**14**	**28.6**	**11:05**	....	....	....	....	....	....	....	....	....
	Hartford	AHL	12	8	7	15	12	....	....	....	....	....	....	....	....	....	....	....	....	....	....	....	....	....	....
2001-02	**NY Rangers**	**NHL**	**15**	**3**	**2**	**5**	**12**	**0**	**0**	**0**	**23**	**13.0**	**–3**	**2**	**0.0**	**12:24**	....	....	....	....	....	....	....	....	....
	Hartford	AHL	48	14	30	44	167	....	....	....	....	....	....	....	....	....	....	....	....	....	....	....	....	....	....
2002-03	**Boston**	**NHL**	**63**	**2**	**18**	**20**	**71**	**0**	**0**	**1**	**74**	**2.7**	**2**	**95**	**43.2**	**10:43**	**5**	**0**	**0**	**0**	**13**	**0**	**0**	**0**	**6:12**
2003-04	**Boston**	**NHL**	**33**	**3**	**2**	**5**	**33**	**0**	**0**	**0**	**24**	**12.5**	**1**	**82**	**51.2**	**6:14**	....	....	....	....	....	....	....	....	....
	NHL Totals		**526**	**84**	**137**	**221**	**509**	**14**	**0**	**11**	**755**	**11.1**		**207**	**44.4**	**13:04**	**45**	**9**	**11**	**20**	**77**	**2**	**0**	**3**	**10:17**

Traded to **Buffalo** by **Winnipeg** with Darryl Shannon for Craig Muni, February 15, 1996. Traded to **Chicago** by **Buffalo** for Doug Gilmour, J.P. Dumont and future considerations, March 10, 2000. Traded to **NY Rangers** by **Chicago** with Brad Brown for future considerations, October 5, 2000. Signed as a free agent by **Boston**, July 16, 2002. • Missed majority of 2003-04 season recovering from head injury suffered in game vs. Detroit, January 10, 2004.

GRUDEN, John

(GROO-duhn, JAWN)

Defense. Shoots left. 6', 203 lbs. Born, Virginia, MN, June 4, 1970. Boston's 7th choice, 168th overall, in 1990 Entry Draft.

1989-90	Waterloo	USHL	47	7	39	46	35	....	....	....	....	....	....	....	....	....	....	....	....	....	....	....	....	....	....
1990-91	Ferris State	CCHA	37	4	11	15	27	....	....	....	....	....	....	....	....	....	....	....	....	....	....	....	....	....	....
1991-92	Ferris State	CCHA	37	9	14	23	24	....	....	....	....	....	....	....	....	....	....	....	....	....	....	....	....	....	....
1992-93	Ferris State	CCHA	41	16	14	30	58	....	....	....	....	....	....	....	....	....	....	....	....	....	....	....	....	....	....
1993-94	Ferris State	CCHA	38	11	25	36	52	....	....	....	....	....	....	....	....	....	....	....	....	....	....	....	....	....	....
	Boston	**NHL**	**7**	**0**	**1**	**1**	**2**	**0**	**0**	**0**	**8**	**0.0**	**–3**	....	....	....	....	....	....	....	....	....	....	....	....
1994-95	**Boston**	**NHL**	**38**	**0**	**6**	**6**	**22**	**0**	**0**	**0**	**30**	**0.0**	**3**	....	....	....	....	....	....	....	....	....	....	....	....
	Providence Bruins	AHL	1	0	1	1	0	....	....	....	....	....	....	....	....	....	....	....	....	....	....	....	....	....	....
1995-96	**Boston**	**NHL**	**14**	**0**	**0**	**0**	**4**	**0**	**0**	**0**	**12**	**0.0**	**–3**	....	....	....	**3**	**0**	**1**	**1**	**0**	**0**	**0**	**0**	....
	Providence Bruins	AHL	39	5	19	24	29	....	....	....	....	....	....	....	....	....	....	....	....	....	....	....	....	....	....
1996-97	Providence Bruins	AHL	78	18	27	45	52	....	....	....	....	....	....	....	....	....	10	3	6	9	4	....	....	....	....
1997-98	Detroit Vipers	IHL	76	13	42	55	74	....	....	....	....	....	....	....	....	....	21	1	8	9	14	....	....	....	....
1998-99	**Ottawa**	**NHL**	**13**	**0**	**1**	**1**	**8**	**0**	**0**	**0**	**10**	**0.0**	**0**	**0**	**0.0**	**13:07**	....	....	....	....	....	....	....	....	....
	Detroit Vipers	IHL	59	10	28	38	52	....	....	....	....	....	....	....	....	....	10	0	1	1	6	....	....	....	....
99-2000	**Ottawa**	**NHL**	**9**	**0**	**0**	**0**	**4**	**0**	**0**	**0**	**3**	**0.0**	**0**	**0**	**0.0**	**16:29**	....	....	....	....	....	....	....	....	....
	Grand Rapids	IHL	50	5	17	22	24	....	....	....	....	....	....	....	....	....	12	1	4	5	8	....	....	....	....
2000-01	Grand Rapids	IHL	34	2	6	8	18	....	....	....	....	....	....	....	....	....	10	1	4	5	8	....	....	....	....
2001-02	Grand Rapids	AHL	57	3	14	17	48	....	....	....	....	....	....	....	....	....	5	1	0	1	2	....	....	....	....

								Regular Season									Playoffs								
Season	**Club**	**League**	**GP**	**G**	**A**	**Pts**	**PIM**	**PP**	**SH**	**GW**	**S**	**%**	**+/-**	**TF**	**F%**	**Min**	**GP**	**G**	**A**	**Pts**	**PIM**	**PP**	**SH**	**GW**	**Min**
2002-03	Eisbaren Berlin	Germany	38	6	25	31	34	....	....	....	....	....	....	....	....	....	9	2	6	8	4	....	....	....	....
2003-04	**Washington**	**NHL**	**11**	**1**	**0**	**1**	**6**	**0**	**0**	**1**	**7**	**14.3**	**–1**	**0**	**0.0**	**13:18**	....	....	....	....	....	....	....	....	....
	NHL Totals		**92**	**1**	**8**	**9**	**46**	**0**	**0**	**1**	**70**	**1.4**		**0**	**0.0**	**14:06**	**3**	**0**	**1**	**1**	**0**	**0**	**0**	**0**	....

CCHA First All-Star Team (1994) • NCAA West First All-American Team (1994) • IHL Second All-Star Team (1998) • AHL First All-Star Team (2002)

Signed as a free agent by **Ottawa**, August 7, 1998. • Missed majority of 2000-01 season recovering from shoulder injury suffered in training camp, October 1, 2000. Signed as a free agent by **Eisbaren Berlin** (Germany), May 3, 2002. Signed as a free agent by **Washington**, July 18, 2003. • Missed majority of 2003-04 season recovering from head injury suffered in game vs. Los Angeles, November 10, 2003.

GUERIN, Bill

(GAIR-ihn, BIHL) **DAL.**

Right wing. Shoots right. 6'2", 210 lbs. Born, Worcester, MA, November 9, 1970. New Jersey's 1st choice, 5th overall, in 1989 Entry Draft.

Season	Club	League	GP	G	A	Pts	PIM	PP	SH	GW	S	%	+/-	TF	F%	Min	GP	G	A	Pts	PIM	PP	SH	GW	Min
1985-86	Springfield	NEJHL	48	26	19	45	71	....	....	....	....	....	....	....	....	....	....	....	....	....	....	....	....	....	....
1986-87	Springfield	NEJHL	32	34	20	54	40	....	....	....	....	....	....	....	....	....	....	....	....	....	....	....	....	....	....
1987-88	Springfield	NEJHL	38	31	44	75	146	....	....	....	....	....	....	....	....	....	....	....	....	....	....	....	....	....	....
1988-89	Springfield	NEJHL	31	32	35	67	90	....	....	....	....	....	....	....	....	....	....	....	....	....	....	....	....	....	....
1989-90	Boston College	H-East	39	14	11	25	54	....	....	....	....	....	....	....	....	....	....	....	....	....	....	....	....	....	....
1990-91	Boston College	H-East	38	26	19	45	102	....	....	....	....	....	....	....	....	....	....	....	....	....	....	....	....	....	....
1991-92	Team USA	Nat-Tm	46	12	15	27	67	....	....	....	....	....	....	....	....	....	....	....	....	....	....	....	....	....	....
	New Jersey	**NHL**	**5**	**0**	**1**	**1**	**9**	**0**	**0**	**0**	**8**	**0.0**	**1**	....	....	....	**6**	**3**	**0**	**3**	**4**	**0**	**0**	**0**	....
	Utica Devils	AHL	22	13	10	23	6	....	....	....	....	....	....	....	....	....	4	1	3	4	14	....	....	....	....
1992-93	**New Jersey**	**NHL**	**65**	**14**	**20**	**34**	**63**	**0**	**0**	**2**	**123**	**11.4**	**14**	....	....	....	**5**	**1**	**1**	**2**	**4**	**0**	**0**	**0**	....
	Utica Devils	AHL	18	10	7	17	47	....	....	....	....	....	....	....	....	....	....	....	....	....	....	....	....	....	....
1993-94	**New Jersey**	**NHL**	**81**	**25**	**19**	**44**	**101**	**2**	**0**	**3**	**195**	**12.8**	**14**	....	....	....	**17**	**2**	**1**	**3**	**35**	**0**	**0**	**1**	....
1994-95♦	**New Jersey**	**NHL**	**48**	**12**	**13**	**25**	**72**	**4**	**0**	**3**	**96**	**12.5**	**6**	....	....	....	**20**	**3**	**8**	**11**	**30**	**1**	**0**	**0**	....
1995-96	**New Jersey**	**NHL**	**80**	**23**	**30**	**53**	**116**	**8**	**0**	**6**	**216**	**10.6**	**7**	....	....	....	....	....	....	....	....	....	....	....	....
1996-97	**New Jersey**	**NHL**	**82**	**29**	**18**	**47**	**95**	**7**	**0**	**9**	**177**	**16.4**	**–2**	....	....	....	**8**	**2**	**1**	**3**	**18**	**1**	**0**	**1**	....
1997-98	**New Jersey**	**NHL**	**19**	**5**	**5**	**10**	**13**	**1**	**0**	**2**	**48**	**10.4**	**0**	....	....	....	....	....	....	....	....	....	....	....	....
	Edmonton	**NHL**	**40**	**13**	**16**	**29**	**80**	**8**	**0**	**2**	**130**	**10.0**	**1**	....	....	....	**12**	**7**	**1**	**8**	**17**	**4**	**0**	**0**	....
	United States	Olympics	4	0	3	3	2	....	....	....	....	....	....	....	....	....	....	....	....	....	....	....	....	....	....
1998-99	**Edmonton**	**NHL**	**80**	**30**	**34**	**64**	**133**	**13**	**0**	**2**	**261**	**11.5**	**7**	**74**	**40.5**	**19:42**	**3**	**0**	**2**	**2**	**2**	**0**	**0**	**0**	**26:14**
99-2000	**Edmonton**	**NHL**	**70**	**24**	**22**	**46**	**123**	**11**	**0**	**2**	**188**	**12.8**	**4**	**13**	**46.2**	**18:01**	**5**	**3**	**2**	**5**	**9**	**1**	**0**	**0**	**17:55**
2000-01	**Edmonton**	**NHL**	**21**	**12**	**10**	**22**	**18**	**4**	**0**	**1**	**64**	**18.8**	**11**	**0**	**0.0**	**19:49**	....	....	....	....	....	....	....	....	....
	Boston	**NHL**	**64**	**28**	**35**	**63**	**122**	**7**	**1**	**4**	**225**	**12.4**	**–4**	**36**	**41.7**	**22:43**	....	....	....	....	....	....	....	....	....
2001-02	**Boston**	**NHL**	**78**	**41**	**25**	**66**	**91**	**10**	**1**	**7**	**355**	**11.5**	**–1**	**17**	**52.9**	**20:45**	**6**	**4**	**2**	**6**	**6**	**3**	**0**	**0**	**21:17**
	United States	Olympics	6	4	0	4	4	....	....	....	....	....	....	....	....	....	....	....	....	....	....	....	....	....	....
2002-03	**Dallas**	**NHL**	**64**	**25**	**25**	**50**	**113**	**11**	**0**	**2**	**229**	**10.9**	**5**	**20**	**25.0**	**18:33**	**4**	**0**	**0**	**0**	**4**	**0**	**0**	**0**	**8:34**
2003-04	**Dallas**	**NHL**	**82**	**34**	**35**	**69**	**109**	**9**	**0**	**10**	**263**	**12.9**	**14**	**16**	**18.8**	**18:42**	**5**	**0**	**1**	**1**	**4**	**0**	**0**	**0**	**20:09**
	NHL Totals		**879**	**315**	**308**	**623**	**1258**	**95**	**2**	**55**	**2578**	**12.2**		**176**	**38.6**	**19:42**	**91**	**25**	**19**	**44**	**133**	**10**	**0**	**2**	**18:44**

NHL Second All-Star Team (2002)

Played in NHL All-Star Game (2001, 2003, 2004)

Traded to **Edmonton** by **New Jersey** with Valeri Zelepukin for Jason Arnott and Bryan Muir, January 4, 1998. Traded to **Boston** by **Edmonton** for Anson Carter, Boston's 1st (Ales Hemsky) and 2nd (Doug Lynch) round choices in 2001 Entry Draft and future considerations, November 15, 2000. Signed as a free agent by **Dallas**, July 3, 2002.

GUOLLA, Steve

(GUH-wah-lah, STEEV)

Center. Shoots left. 6', 190 lbs. Born, Scarborough, Ont., March 15, 1973. Ottawa's 1st choice, 3rd overall, in 1994 Supplemental Draft.

Season	Club	League	GP	G	A	Pts	PIM	PP	SH	GW	S	%	+/-	TF	F%	Min	GP	G	A	Pts	PIM	PP	SH	GW	Min
1988-89	Tor. Red Wings	MTHL	25	14	20	34	....	....	....	....	....	....	....	....	....	....	....	....	....	....	....	....	....	....	....
1989-90	Tor. Red Wings	MTHL	40	42	47	89	....	....	....	....	....	....	....	....	....	....	....	....	....	....	....	....	....	....	....
1990-91	Wexford Raiders	MTJHL	44	34	44	78	34	....	....	....	....	....	....	....	....	....	12	12	16	28	....	....	....	....	....
1991-92	Michigan State	CCHA	33	4	9	13	8	....	....	....	....	....	....	....	....	....	....	....	....	....	....	....	....	....	....
1992-93	Michigan State	CCHA	39	19	35	54	6	....	....	....	....	....	....	....	....	....	....	....	....	....	....	....	....	....	....
1993-94	Michigan State	CCHA	41	23	46	69	16	....	....	....	....	....	....	....	....	....	....	....	....	....	....	....	....	....	....
1994-95	Michigan State	CCHA	40	16	35	51	16	....	....	....	....	....	....	....	....	....	....	....	....	....	....	....	....	....	....
1995-96	P.E.I. Senators	AHL	72	32	48	80	28	....	....	....	....	....	....	....	....	....	3	0	0	0	0	....	....	....	....
1996-97	**San Jose**	**NHL**	**43**	**13**	**8**	**21**	**14**	**2**	**0**	**1**	**81**	**16.0**	**–10**	....	....	....	....	....	....	....	....	....	....	....	....
	Kentucky	AHL	34	22	22	44	10	....	....	....	....	....	....	....	....	....	4	2	1	3	0	....	....	....	....
1997-98	**San Jose**	**NHL**	**7**	**1**	**1**	**2**	**0**	**0**	**0**	**0**	**9**	**11.1**	**–2**	....	....	....	....	....	....	....	....	....	....	....	....
	Kentucky	AHL	69	37	63	100	45	....	....	....	....	....	....	....	....	....	3	0	0	0	0	....	....	....	....
1998-99	**San Jose**	**NHL**	**14**	**2**	**2**	**4**	**6**	**0**	**0**	**1**	**22**	**9.1**	**3**	**172**	**36.6**	**13:54**	....	....	....	....	....	....	....	....	....
	Kentucky	AHL	53	29	47	76	33	....	....	....	....	....	....	....	....	....	....	....	....	....	....	....	....	....	....
99-2000	**Tampa Bay**	**NHL**	**46**	**6**	**10**	**16**	**11**	**2**	**0**	**0**	**52**	**11.5**	**2**	**155**	**45.8**	**11:26**	....	....	....	....	....	....	....	....	....
	Atlanta	**NHL**	**20**	**4**	**9**	**13**	**4**	**2**	**0**	**0**	**34**	**11.8**	**–13**	**345**	**42.6**	**17:47**	....	....	....	....	....	....	....	....	....
2000-01	**Atlanta**	**NHL**	**63**	**12**	**16**	**28**	**23**	**2**	**0**	**3**	**96**	**12.5**	**–6**	**859**	**47.7**	**14:41**	....	....	....	....	....	....	....	....	....
2001-02	Albany River Rats	AHL	68	25	35	60	27	....	....	....	....	....	....	....	....	....	....	....	....	....	....	....	....	....	....
2002-03	**New Jersey**	**NHL**	**12**	**2**	**0**	**2**	**2**	**0**	**0**	**0**	**6**	**33.3**	**1**	**61**	**41.0**	**8:00**	....	....	....	....	....	....	....	....	....
	Albany River Rats	AHL	22	11	17	28	4	....	....	....	....	....	....	....	....	....	....	....	....	....	....	....	....	....	....
2003-04	Albany River Rats	AHL	7	2	3	5	0	....	....	....	....	....	....	....	....	....	....	....	....	....	....	....	....	....	....
	NHL Totals		**205**	**40**	**46**	**86**	**60**	**8**	**0**	**5**	**300**	**13.3**		**1592**	**45.0**	**13:32**	....	....	....	....	....	....	....	....	....

CCHA Second All-Star Team (1994) • NCAA West Second All-American Team (1994) • AHL Second All-Star Team (1998, 1999) • Les Cunningham Award (MVP – AHL) (1998)

Signed as a free agent by **San Jose**, August 22, 1996. Traded to **Tampa Bay** by **San Jose** with Bill Houlder, Shawn Burr and Andrei Zyuzin for Niklas Sundstrom and NY Rangers' 3rd round choice (previously acquired, later traded to Chicago – Chicago selected Igor Radulov) in 2000 Entry Draft, August 4, 1999. Claimed on waivers by **Atlanta** from **Tampa Bay**, March 1, 2000. Signed as a free agent by **New Jersey**, October 21, 2001. • Missed majority of 2002-03 and 2003-04 seasons recovering from back injury suffered in game vs. NY Islanders, November 27, 2002. Signed as a free agent by **Kloten** (Swiss), April 22, 2004.

HAAKANA, Kari

(HA-kuh-nuh, KAH-ree) **EDM.**

Defense. Shoots left. 6'1", 222 lbs. Born, Outokumpu, Finland, November 8, 1973. Edmonton's 9th choice, 248th overall, in 2001 Entry Draft.

Season	Club	League	GP	G	A	Pts	PIM	PP	SH	GW	S	%	+/-	TF	F%	Min	GP	G	A	Pts	PIM	PP	SH	GW	Min
1990-91	Kiekko Espoo Jr.	Finn-Jr.	36	3	3	6	34	....	....	....	....	....	....	....	....	....	....	....	....	....	....	....	....	....	....
	Kiekko Espoo	Finland-2	4	0	1	1	0	....	....	....	....	....	....	....	....	....	....	....	....	....	....	....	....	....	....
1991-92	Kiekko Espoo Jr.	Finn-Jr.	26	0	4	4	34	....	....	....	....	....	....	....	....	....	....	....	....	....	....	....	....	....	....
1992-93	Lukko Rauma Jr.	Finn-Jr.	36	4	16	20	60	....	....	....	....	....	....	....	....	....	....	....	....	....	....	....	....	....	....
	Lukko Rauma	Finland	4	0	0	0	0	....	....	....	....	....	....	....	....	....	....	....	....	....	....	....	....	....	....
1993-94	Kiekko Espoo Jr.	Finn-Jr.	5	0	2	2	2	....	....	....	....	....	....	....	....	....	....	....	....	....	....	....	....	....	....
	Kiekko Espoo	Finland	47	3	2	5	40	....	....	....	....	....	....	....	....	....	....	....	....	....	....	....	....	....	....
1994-95	Kiekko Espoo	Finland	48	4	3	7	54	....	....	....	....	....	....	....	....	....	4	0	0	0	0	....	....	....	....
1995-96	Kiekko Espoo	Finland	45	1	7	8	48	....	....	....	....	....	....	....	....	....	....	....	....	....	....	....	....	....	....
1996-97	Kiekko Espoo	Finland	48	0	12	12	69	....	....	....	....	....	....	....	....	....	....	....	....	....	....	....	....	....	....
1997-98	Kiekko Espoo	Finland	47	4	1	5	59	....	....	....	....	....	....	....	....	....	8	0	1	1	6	....	....	....	....
1998-99	Rosenheim	Germany	51	1	9	10	58	....	....	....	....	....	....	....	....	....	....	....	....	....	....	....	....	....	....
99-2000	Rosenheim	Germany	51	3	5	8	46	....	....	....	....	....	....	....	....	....	10	1	4	5	28	....	....	....	....
2000-01	Jokerit Helsinki	Finland	52	2	8	10	98	....	....	....	....	....	....	....	....	....	5	0	0	0	2	....	....	....	....
2001-02	Hamilton	AHL	6	0	2	2	25	....	....	....	....	....	....	....	....	....	....	....	....	....	....	....	....	....	....
	Jokerit Helsinki	Finland	36	0	3	3	40	....	....	....	....	....	....	....	....	....	12	2	2	4	2	....	....	....	....
2002-03	**Edmonton**	**NHL**	**13**	**0**	**0**	**0**	**4**	**0**	**0**	**0**	**2**	**0.0**	**–2**	**0**	**0.0**	**7:55**	....	....	....	....	....	....	....	....	....
	Hamilton	AHL	12	0	4	4	12	....	....	....	....	....	....	....	....	....	14	1	2	3	6	....	....	....	....
2003-04	MoDo	Sweden	31	1	3	4	50	....	....	....	....	....	....	....	....	....	6	0	0	0	12	....	....	....	....
	NHL Totals		**13**	**0**	**0**	**0**	**4**	**0**	**0**	**0**	**2**	**0.0**		**0**	**0.0**	**7:55**	....	....	....	....	....	....	....	....	....

• Missed majority of 2002-03 season recovering from rib injury suffered in game vs. Vancouver, December 26, 2002. Signed as a free agent by **MoDo** (Sweden), August 25, 2003.

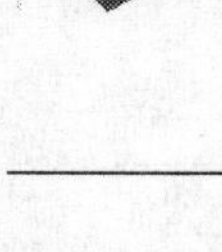

HAGMAN, Niklas

(HAG-muhn, NIHK-las) **FLA.**

Left wing. Shoots left. 6', 200 lbs. Born, Espoo, Finland, December 5, 1979. Florida's 3rd choice, 70th overall, in 1999 Entry Draft.

Season	Club	League	GP	G	A	Pts	PIM	PP	SH	GW	S	%	+/-	TF	F%	Min	GP	G	A	Pts	PIM	PP	SH	GW	Min
1994-95	HIFK Helsinki C	Finn-Jr.	28	30	15	45	40	....	....	....	....	....	....	....	....	....	4	2	0	2	6	....	....	....	....
1995-96	HIFK Helsinki B	Finn-Jr.	26	12	21	33	32	....	....	....	....	....	....	....	....	....	4	3	0	3	2	....	....	....	....
	HIFK Helsinki Jr.	Finn-Jr.	12	3	1	4	0	....	....	....	....	....	....	....	....	....	....	....	....	....	....	....	....	....	....
1996-97	HIFK Helsinki Jr.	Finn-Jr.	30	13	12	25	30	....	....	....	....	....	....	....	....	....	4	1	1	2	0	....	....	....	....
1997-98	HIFK Helsinki Jr.	Finn-Jr.	26	9	5	14	16	....	....	....	....	....	....	....	....	....	....	....	....	....	....	....	....	....	....
	HIFK Helsinki	Finland	8	1	0	1	0	....	....	....	....	....	....	....	....	....	....	....	....	....	....	....	....	....	....
	HIFK Helsinki B	Finn-Jr.	1	0	1	1	0	....	....	....	....	....	....	....	....	....	....	....	....	....	....	....	....	....	....

								Regular Season									Playoffs								
Season	Club	League	GP	G	A	Pts	PIM	PP	SH	GW	S	%	+/-	TF	F%	Min	GP	G	A	Pts	PIM	PP	SH	GW	Min
1998-99	HIFK Helsinki Jr.	Finn-Jr.	14	4	9	13	43	....	....	....	....	....	....	....	....	....	....	....	....	....	....	....	....	....	....
	HIFK Helsinki	Finland	17	1	1	2	14	....	....	....	....	....	....	....	....	....	....	....	....	....	....	....	....	....	....
	HIFK Helsinki	EuroHL	1	0	1	1	0	....	....	....	....	....	....	....	....	....	....	....	....	....	....	....	....	....	....
	Blues Espoo	Finland	14	1	1	2	2	....	....	....	....	....	....	....	....	....	4	1	0	1	0	....	....	....	....
99-2000	Karpat Oulu	Finland-2	41	17	18	35	12	....	....	....	....	....	....	....	....	....	7	4	2	6	....	....	....	....	....
2000-01	Karpat Oulu	Finland	56	28	18	46	32	....	....	....	....	....	....	....	....	....	8	3	1	4	0	....	....	....	....
2001-02	**Florida**	**NHL**	**78**	**10**	**18**	**28**	**8**	**0**	**1**	**2**	**134**	**7.5**	**–6**	**32**	**28.1**	**13:50**	....	....	....	....	....	....	....	....	....
	Finland	Olympics	4	1	2	3	0	....	....	....	....	....	....	....	....	....	....	....	....	....	....	....	....	....	....
2002-03	**Florida**	**NHL**	**80**	**8**	**15**	**23**	**20**	**2**	**0**	**0**	**132**	**6.1**	**–8**	**17**	**11.8**	**13:31**	....	....	....	....	....	....	....	....	....
2003-04	**Florida**	**NHL**	**75**	**10**	**13**	**23**	**22**	**0**	**1**	**2**	**122**	**8.2**	**–5**	**19**	**21.1**	**14:47**	....	....	....	....	....	....	....	....	....
	NHL Totals		**233**	**28**	**46**	**74**	**50**	**2**	**2**	**4**	**388**	**7.2**		**68**	**22.1**	**14:02**	....	....	....	....	....	....	....	....	....

HAHL, Riku

(HAHL, REE-koo) **COL.**

Center. Shoots left. 6'1", 205 lbs. Born, Hameenlinna, Finland, November 1, 1980. Colorado's 9th choice, 183rd overall, in 1999 Entry Draft.

Season	Club	League	GP	G	A	Pts	PIM	PP	SH	GW	S	%	+/-	TF	F%	Min	GP	G	A	Pts	PIM	PP	SH	GW	Min
1995-96	HPK C	Finn-Jr.	32	18	30	48	28	....	....	....	....	....	....	....	....	....	....	....	....	....	....	....	....	....	....
1996-97	HPK B	Finn-Jr.	32	19	24	43	22	....	....	....	....	....	....	....	....	....	....	....	....	....	....	....	....	....	....
	HPK Jr.	Finn-Jr.	2	0	1	1	2	....	....	....	....	....	....	....	....	....	6	2	0	2	2	....	....	....	....
1997-98	HPK B	Finn-Jr.	10	5	14	19	6	....	....	....	....	....	....	....	....	....	....	....	....	....	....	....	....	....	....
	HPK Jr.	Finn-Jr.	35	13	6	19	12	....	....	....	....	....	....	....	....	....	....	....	....	....	....	....	....	....	....
1998-99	HPK Jr.	Finn-Jr.	6	0	2	2	6	....	....	....	....	....	....	....	....	....	....	....	....	....	....	....	....	....	....
	HPK Hameenlinna	Finland	28	0	1	1	0	....	....	....	....	....	....	....	....	....	8	0	0	0	2	....	....	....	....
99-2000	HPK Jr.	Finn-Jr.	12	1	6	7	8	....	....	....	....	....	....	....	....	....	9	5	4	9	16	....	....	....	....
	HPK Hameenlinna	Finland	50	4	3	7	18	....	....	....	....	....	....	....	....	....	8	0	0	0	2	....	....	....	....
2000-01	HPK Jr.	Finn-Jr.	2	1	3	4	0	....	....	....	....	....	....	....	....	....	....	....	....	....	....	....	....	....	....
	HPK Hameenlinna	Finland	55	3	9	12	32	....	....	....	....	....	....	....	....	....	....	....	....	....	....	....	....	....	....
2001-02	**Colorado**	**NHL**	**22**	**2**	**3**	**5**	**14**	**0**	**0**	**1**	**17**	**11.8**	**1**	**94**	**35.1**	**9:26**	**21**	**1**	**2**	**3**	**0**	**0**	**0**	**0**	**7:31**
	Hershey Bears	AHL	52	6	17	23	16	....	....	....	....	....	....	....	....	....	....	....	....	....	....	....	....	....	....
2002-03	**Colorado**	**NHL**	**42**	**3**	**4**	**7**	**12**	**0**	**0**	**0**	**61**	**4.9**	**3**	**69**	**37.7**	**11:03**	**6**	**0**	**2**	**2**	**2**	**0**	**0**	**0**	**13:49**
	Hershey Bears	AHL	28	7	7	14	17	....	....	....	....	....	....	....	....	....	....	....	....	....	....	....	....	....	....
2003-04	**Colorado**	**NHL**	**28**	**0**	**1**	**1**	**12**	**0**	**0**	**0**	**40**	**0.0**	**–7**	**107**	**41.1**	**12:17**	**7**	**1**	**0**	**1**	**2**	**0**	**0**	**0**	**12:08**
	NHL Totals		**92**	**5**	**8**	**13**	**38**	**0**	**0**	**1**	**118**	**4.2**		**270**	**38.1**	**11:02**	**34**	**2**	**4**	**6**	**4**	**0**	**0**	**0**	**9:35**

• Missed majority of 2003-04 season recovering from shoulder injury suffered in game vs. Edmonton, October 23, 2003.

HAINSEY, Ron

(HAYN-zee, RAWN) **MTL.**

Defense. Shoots left. 6'3", 211 lbs. Born, Bolton, CT, March 24, 1981. Montreal's 1st choice, 13th overall, in 2000 Entry Draft.

Season	Club	League	GP	G	A	Pts	PIM	PP	SH	GW	S	%	+/-	TF	F%	Min	GP	G	A	Pts	PIM	PP	SH	GW	Min
1997-98	U.S. National U-18	USDP	66	6	15	21	44	....	....	....	....	....	....	....	....	....	....	....	....	....	....	....	....	....	....
1998-99	U.S. National U-18	USDP	48	5	12	17	45	....	....	....	....	....	....	....	....	....	....	....	....	....	....	....	....	....	....
99-2000	U. Mass-Lowell	H-East	30	3	8	11	20	....	....	....	....	....	....	....	....	....	....	....	....	....	....	....	....	....	....
2000-01	U. Mass-Lowell	H-East	33	10	26	36	51	....	....	....	....	....	....	....	....	....	....	....	....	....	....	....	....	....	....
	Quebec Citadelles	AHL	4	1	0	1	0	....	....	....	....	....	....	....	....	....	1	0	0	0	0	....	....	....	....
2001-02	Quebec Citadelles	AHL	63	7	24	31	26	....	....	....	....	....	....	....	....	....	3	0	0	0	0	....	....	....	....
2002-03	**Montreal**	**NHL**	**21**	**0**	**0**	**0**	**2**	**0**	**0**	**0**	**12**	**0.0**	**–1**	**0**	**0.0**	**12:25**	....	....	....	....	....	....	....	....	....
	Hamilton	AHL	33	2	11	13	26	....	....	....	....	....	....	....	....	....	23	1	10	11	20	....	....	....	....
2003-04	**Montreal**	**NHL**	**11**	**1**	**1**	**2**	**4**	**0**	**0**	**0**	**11**	**9.1**	**3**	**0**	**0.0**	**13:15**	....	....	....	....	....	....	....	....	....
	Hamilton	AHL	54	7	24	31	35	....	....	....	....	....	....	....	....	....	10	0	5	5	6	....	....	....	....
	NHL Totals		**32**	**1**	**1**	**2**	**6**	**0**	**0**	**0**	**23**	**4.3**		**0**	**0.0**	**12:42**	....	....	....	....	....	....	....	....	....

Hockey East First All-Star Team (2001) • NCAA East Second All-American Team (2001) • AHL All-Rookie Team (2002)

HAJT, Chris

(HIGHT, KRIHS)

Defense. Shoots left. 6'3", 206 lbs. Born, Saskatoon, Sask., July 5, 1978. Edmonton's 3rd choice, 32nd overall, in 1996 Entry Draft.

Season	Club	League	GP	G	A	Pts	PIM	PP	SH	GW	S	%	+/-	TF	F%	Min	GP	G	A	Pts	PIM	PP	SH	GW	Min
1993-94	Amherst Knights	WNYHA	38	8	20	28	16	....	....	....	....	....	....	....	....	....	....	....	....	....	....	....	....	....	....
1994-95	Guelph Storm	OHL	57	1	7	8	35	....	....	....	....	....	....	....	....	....	14	0	2	2	9	....	....	....	....
1995-96	Guelph Storm	OHL	63	8	27	35	69	....	....	....	....	....	....	....	....	....	16	0	6	6	13	....	....	....	....
1996-97	Guelph Storm	OHL	58	11	15	26	62	....	....	....	....	....	....	....	....	....	18	0	8	8	25	....	....	....	....
1997-98	Guelph Storm	OHL	44	2	21	23	46	....	....	....	....	....	....	....	....	....	12	1	5	6	11	....	....	....	....
1998-99	Hamilton	AHL	64	0	4	4	36	....	....	....	....	....	....	....	....	....	....	....	....	....	....	....	....	....	....
99-2000	Hamilton	AHL	54	0	8	8	30	....	....	....	....	....	....	....	....	....	10	0	2	2	0	....	....	....	....
2000-01	**Edmonton**	**NHL**	**1**	**0**	**0**	**0**	**0**	**0**	**0**	**0**	**0**	**0.0**	**–1**	**0**	**0.0**	**7:38**	....	....	....	....	....	....	....	....	....
	Hamilton	AHL	70	0	10	10	48	....	....	....	....	....	....	....	....	....	....	....	....	....	....	....	....	....	....
2001-02	Hamilton	AHL	39	2	3	5	34	....	....	....	....	....	....	....	....	....	15	1	2	3	8	....	....	....	....
2002-03	Portland Pirates	AHL	71	11	15	26	61	....	....	....	....	....	....	....	....	....	1	0	0	0	2	....	....	....	....
2003-04	**Washington**	**NHL**	**5**	**0**	**0**	**0**	**2**	**0**	**0**	**0**	**1**	**0.0**	**0**	**0**	**0.0**	**10:44**	....	....	....	....	....	....	....	....	....
	Portland Pirates	AHL	66	3	13	16	53	....	....	....	....	....	....	....	....	....	7	1	2	3	8	....	....	....	....
	NHL Totals		**6**	**0**	**0**	**0**	**2**	**0**	**0**	**0**	**1**	**0.0**		**0**	**0.0**	**10:13**	....	....	....	....	....	....	....	....	....

OHL Second All-Star Team (1998)

Signed as a free agent by **Washington**, July 23, 2002.

HALE, David

(HAYL, DAY-vihd) **N.J.**

Defense. Shoots left. 6'1", 215 lbs. Born, Colorado Springs, CO, June 18, 1981. New Jersey's 1st choice, 22nd overall, in 2000 Entry Draft.

Season	Club	League	GP	G	A	Pts	PIM	PP	SH	GW	S	%	+/-	TF	F%	Min	GP	G	A	Pts	PIM	PP	SH	GW	Min
1997-98	Colorado North	Hi-School	25	11	33	44	154	....	....	....	....	....	....	....	....	....	....	....	....	....	....	....	....	....	....
1998-99	Sioux City	USHL	56	3	15	18	127	....	....	....	....	....	....	....	....	....	5	0	0	0	18	....	....	....	....
99-2000	Sioux City	USHL	54	6	18	24	187	....	....	....	....	....	....	....	....	....	5	0	2	2	6	....	....	....	....
2000-01	North Dakota	WCHA	44	4	5	9	79	....	....	....	....	....	....	....	....	....	....	....	....	....	....	....	....	....	....
2001-02	North Dakota	WCHA	34	4	5	9	63	....	....	....	....	....	....	....	....	....	....	....	....	....	....	....	....	....	....
2002-03	North Dakota	WCHA	26	2	6	8	49	....	....	....	....	....	....	....	....	....	....	....	....	....	....	....	....	....	....
2003-04	**New Jersey**	**NHL**	**65**	**0**	**4**	**4**	**72**	**0**	**0**	**0**	**45**	**0.0**	**12**	**0**	**0.0**	**15:01**	**1**	**0**	**0**	**0**	**0**	**0**	**0**	**0**	**8:59**
	NHL Totals		**65**	**0**	**4**	**4**	**72**	**0**	**0**	**0**	**45**	**0.0**		**0**	**0.0**	**15:01**	**1**	**0**	**0**	**0**	**0**	**0**	**0**	**0**	**8:59**

USHL First All-Star Team (2000)

HALL, Adam

(HAWL, A-duhm) **NSH.**

Right wing. Shoots right. 6'3", 205 lbs. Born, Kalamazoo, MI, August 14, 1980. Nashville's 3rd choice, 52nd overall, in 1999 Entry Draft.

Season	Club	League	GP	G	A	Pts	PIM	PP	SH	GW	S	%	+/-	TF	F%	Min	GP	G	A	Pts	PIM	PP	SH	GW	Min
1996-97	Bramalea Blues	OPJHL	43	9	14	23	92	....	....	....	....	....	....	....	....	....	....	....	....	....	....	....	....	....	....
1997-98	U.S. National U-18	USDP	71	42	23	65	63	....	....	....	....	....	....	....	....	....	....	....	....	....	....	....	....	....	....
1998-99	Michigan State	CCHA	36	16	7	23	74	....	....	....	....	....	....	....	....	....	....	....	....	....	....	....	....	....	....
99-2000	Michigan State	CCHA	40	*26	13	39	38	....	....	....	....	....	....	....	....	....	....	....	....	....	....	....	....	....	....
2000-01	Michigan State	CCHA	42	18	12	30	42	....	....	....	....	....	....	....	....	....	....	....	....	....	....	....	....	....	....
2001-02	Michigan State	CCHA	41	19	15	34	36	....	....	....	....	....	....	....	....	....	....	....	....	....	....	....	....	....	....
	Nashville	**NHL**	**1**	**0**	**1**	**1**	**0**	**0**	**0**	**0**	**2**	**0.0**	**0**	**0**	**0.0**	**14:04**	....	....	....	....	....	....	....	....	....
	Milwaukee	AHL	6	2	2	4	4	....	....	....	....	....	....	....	....	....	....	....	....	....	....	....	....	....	....
2002-03	Milwaukee	AHL	1	0	0	0	2	....	....	....	....	....	....	....	....	....	....	....	....	....	....	....	....	....	....
	Nashville	**NHL**	**79**	**16**	**12**	**28**	**31**	**8**	**0**	**2**	**146**	**11.0**	**–8**	**17**	**52.9**	**14:09**	....	....	....	....	....	....	....	....	....
2003-04	**Nashville**	**NHL**	**79**	**13**	**14**	**27**	**37**	**6**	**0**	**1**	**151**	**8.6**	**–8**	**348**	**56.3**	**16:14**	**6**	**2**	**1**	**3**	**2**	**0**	**0**	**1**	**18:29**
	NHL Totals		**159**	**29**	**27**	**56**	**68**	**14**	**0**	**3**	**299**	**9.7**		**365**	**56.2**	**15:11**	**6**	**2**	**1**	**3**	**2**	**0**	**0**	**1**	**18:29**

CCHA Second All-Star Team (2000)

HALPERN, Jeff
(HAL-pehrn, JEHF) **WSH.**

Center. Shoots right. 6', 198 lbs. Born, Potomac, MD, May 3, 1976.

Season	Club	League	GP	G	A	Pts	PIM	PP	SH	GW	S	%	+/-	TF	F%	Min	GP	G	A	Pts	PIM	PP	SH	GW	Min
			Regular Season														Playoffs								
1994-95	Stratford Cullitons	OJHL-B	44	29	54	83	43	....	....	....	....	....	....	....	....	....	....	....	....	....	....	....	....	....	....
1995-96	Princeton	ECAC	29	3	11	14	30	....	....	....	....	....	....	....	....	....	....	....	....	....	....	....	....	....	....
1996-97	Princeton	ECAC	33	7	24	31	35	....	....	....	....	....	....	....	....	....	....	....	....	....	....	....	....	....	....
1997-98	Princeton	ECAC	36	*28	25	*53	46	....	....	....	....	....	....	....	....	....	....	....	....	....	....	....	....	....	....
1998-99	Princeton	ECAC	33	*22	22	44	32	....	....	....	....	....	....	....	....	....	....	....	....	....	....	....	....	....	....
	Portland Pirates	AHL	6	2	1	3	4	....	....	....	....	....	....	....	....	....	....	....	....	....	....	....	....	....	....
99-2000	**Washington**	**NHL**	**79**	**18**	**11**	**29**	**39**	**4**	**4**	**1**	**108**	**16.7**	**21**	**812**	**51.1**	**13:14**	**5**	**2**	**1**	**3**	**0**	**1**	**0**	**1**	**15:16**
2000-01	**Washington**	**NHL**	**80**	**21**	**21**	**42**	**60**	**2**	**1**	**5**	**110**	**19.1**	**13**	**1293**	**52.4**	**16:08**	**6**	**2**	**3**	**5**	**17**	**1**	**0**	**1**	**20:01**
2001-02	**Washington**	**NHL**	**48**	**5**	**14**	**19**	**29**	**0**	**0**	**4**	**74**	**6.8**	**–9**	**661**	**56.0**	**15:19**	....	....	....	....	....	....	....	....	....
2002-03	**Washington**	**NHL**	**82**	**13**	**21**	**34**	**88**	**1**	**2**	**2**	**126**	**10.3**	**6**	**1492**	**54.1**	**17:25**	**6**	**0**	**1**	**1**	**2**	**0**	**0**	**0**	**19:59**
2003-04	**Washington**	**NHL**	**79**	**19**	**27**	**46**	**56**	**7**	**0**	**2**	**114**	**16.7**	**–21**	**1509**	**54.3**	**19:03**	....	....	....	....	....	....	....	....	....
	NHL Totals		**368**	**76**	**94**	**170**	**272**	**14**	**7**	**14**	**532**	**14.3**		**5767**	**53.5**	**16:19**	**17**	**4**	**5**	**9**	**19**	**2**	**0**	**2**	**18:37**

ECAC Second All-Star Team (1998, 1999)

Signed as a free agent by **Washington**, March 29, 1999.

HAMEL, Denis
(ha-MEHL, deh-NEE) **OTT.**

Left wing. Shoots left. 6'1", 201 lbs. Born, Lachute, Que., May 10, 1977. St. Louis' 5th choice, 153rd overall, in 1995 Entry Draft.

Season	Club	League	GP	G	A	Pts	PIM	PP	SH	GW	S	%	+/-	TF	F%	Min	GP	G	A	Pts	PIM	PP	SH	GW	Min
1992-93	Lachute Regents	QAAA	32	18	24	42	....	....	....	....	....	....	....	....	....	....	....	....	....	....	....	....	....	....	....
1993-94	Lac St-Louis Lions	QAAA	28	10	11	21	50	....	....	....	....	....	....	....	....	....	....	....	....	....	....	....	....	....	....
	Abitibi Forestiers	QAAA	15	5	7	12	29	....	....	....	....	....	....	....	....	....	5	0	3	3	16	....	....	....	....
1994-95	Chicoutimi	QMJHL	66	15	12	27	155	....	....	....	....	....	....	....	....	....	12	2	0	2	27	....	....	....	....
1995-96	Chicoutimi	QMJHL	65	40	49	89	199	....	....	....	....	....	....	....	....	....	17	10	14	24	64	....	....	....	....
1996-97	Chicoutimi	QMJHL	70	50	50	100	357	....	....	....	....	....	....	....	....	....	20	15	10	25	58	....	....	....	....
1997-98	Rochester	AHL	74	10	15	25	98	....	....	....	....	....	....	....	....	....	4	1	2	3	0	....	....	....	....
1998-99	Rochester	AHL	74	16	17	33	121	....	....	....	....	....	....	....	....	....	20	3	4	7	10	....	....	....	....
99-2000	**Buffalo**	**NHL**	**3**	**1**	**0**	**1**	**0**	**0**	**0**	**0**	**3**	**33.3**	**–1**	**0**	**0.0**	**9:45**	....	....	....	....	....	....	....	....	....
	Rochester	AHL	76	34	24	58	122	....	....	....	....	....	....	....	....	....	21	6	7	13	49	....	....	....	....
2000-01	**Buffalo**	**NHL**	**41**	**8**	**3**	**11**	**22**	**1**	**1**	**3**	**55**	**14.5**	**–2**	**171**	**33.9**	**10:58**	....	....	....	....	....	....	....	....	....
2001-02	**Buffalo**	**NHL**	**61**	**2**	**6**	**8**	**28**	**0**	**0**	**0**	**80**	**2.5**	**–1**	**94**	**39.4**	**11:00**	....	....	....	....	....	....	....	....	....
2002-03	**Buffalo**	**NHL**	**25**	**2**	**0**	**2**	**17**	**0**	**0**	**1**	**41**	**4.9**	**–4**	**4**	**25.0**	**12:40**	....	....	....	....	....	....	....	....	....
	Rochester	AHL	48	27	20	47	64	....	....	....	....	....	....	....	....	....	3	3	2	5	4	....	....	....	....
2003-04	**Ottawa**	**NHL**	**5**	**0**	**0**	**0**	**0**	**0**	**0**	**0**	**6**	**0.0**	**–3**	**1**	**100.0**	**6:16**	....	....	....	....	....	....	....	....	....
	Binghamton	AHL	78	29	38	67	116	....	....	....	....	....	....	....	....	....	2	0	0	0	2	....	....	....	....
	NHL Totals		**135**	**13**	**9**	**22**	**67**	**1**	**1**	**4**	**185**	**7.0**		**270**	**35.9**	**11:06**	....	....	....	....	....	....	....	....	....

QMJHL All-Rookie Team (1995) • AHL First All-Star Team (2004)

Traded to **Buffalo** by **St. Louis** for Charlie Huddy and Buffalo's 7th round choice (Daniel Corso) in 1996 Entry Draft, March 19, 1996. • Missed majority of 2000-01 season recovering from knee injury suffered in game vs. NY Islanders, January 27, 2001. Signed as a free agent by **Ottawa**, July 5, 2003. Claimed by **Washington** from **Ottawa** in Waiver Draft, October 3, 2003. Traded to **Ottawa** by **Washington** for future considerations, October 5, 2003.

HAMHUIS, Dan
(HAM-yoos, DAN) **NSH.**

Defense. Shoots left. 6', 205 lbs. Born, Smithers, B.C., December 13, 1982. Nashville's 1st choice, 12th overall, in 2001 Entry Draft.

Season	Club	League	GP	G	A	Pts	PIM	PP	SH	GW	S	%	+/-	TF	F%	Min	GP	G	A	Pts	PIM	PP	SH	GW	Min
1997-98	Smithers A's	BCAHA	59	59	72	131	59	....	....	....	....	....	....	....	....	....	....	....	....	....	....	....	....	....	....
1998-99	Prince George	WHL	56	1	3	4	45	....	....	....	....	....	....	....	....	....	7	1	2	3	8	....	....	....	....
99-2000	Prince George	WHL	70	10	23	33	140	....	....	....	....	....	....	....	....	....	13	2	3	5	35	....	....	....	....
2000-01	Prince George	WHL	62	13	47	60	125	....	....	....	....	....	....	....	....	....	6	2	3	5	15	....	....	....	....
2001-02	Prince George	WHL	59	10	50	60	135	....	....	....	....	....	....	....	....	....	7	0	5	5	16	....	....	....	....
2002-03	Milwaukee	AHL	68	6	21	27	81	....	....	....	....	....	....	....	....	....	6	0	3	3	2	....	....	....	....
2003-04	**Nashville**	**NHL**	**80**	**7**	**19**	**26**	**57**	**2**	**0**	**4**	**115**	**6.1**	**–12**	**0**	**0.0**	**22:08**	**6**	**0**	**2**	**2**	**6**	**0**	**0**	**0**	**20:29**
	NHL Totals		**80**	**7**	**19**	**26**	**57**	**2**	**0**	**4**	**115**	**6.1**		**0**	**0.0**	**22:08**	**6**	**0**	**2**	**2**	**6**	**0**	**0**	**0**	**20:29**

WHL West First All-Star Team (2001, 2002) • WHL Player of the Year (2002) • Canadian Major Junior First All-Star Team (2002) • Canadian Major Junior Defenseman of the Year (2002)

HAMILTON, Jeff
(HAM-ihl-tuhn, JEHF) **NYI**

Center. Shoots right. 5'10", 180 lbs. Born, Englewood, OH, September 4, 1977.

Season	Club	League	GP	G	A	Pts	PIM	PP	SH	GW	S	%	+/-	TF	F%	Min	GP	G	A	Pts	PIM	PP	SH	GW	Min
1995-96	Avon Old Farms	Hi-School	24	29	23	52	....	....	....	....	....	....	....	....	....	....	....	....	....	....	....	....	....	....	....
1996-97	Yale University	ECAC	31	10	13	23	26	....	....	....	....	....	....	....	....	....	....	....	....	....	....	....	....	....	....
1997-98	Yale University	ECAC	33	27	20	47	28	....	....	....	....	....	....	....	....	....	....	....	....	....	....	....	....	....	....
1998-99	Yale University	ECAC	30	20	28	48	51	....	....	....	....	....	....	....	....	....	....	....	....	....	....	....	....	....	....
99-2000	Yale University	ECAC	2	0	1	1	0	....	....	....	....	....	....	....	....	....	....	....	....	....	....	....	....	....	....
2000-01	Yale University	ECAC	31	23	32	55	39	....	....	....	....	....	....	....	....	....	....	....	....	....	....	....	....	....	....
2001-02	Karpat Oulu	Finland	39	18	15	33	16	....	....	....	....	....	....	....	....	....	3	0	0	0	0	....	....	....	....
2002-03	Bridgeport	AHL	67	22	16	38	35	....	....	....	....	....	....	....	....	....	9	3	3	6	0	....	....	....	....
2003-04	**NY Islanders**	**NHL**	**1**	**0**	**0**	**0**	**0**	**0**	**0**	**0**	**1**	**0.0**	**0**	**0**	**0.0**	**10:00**	....	....	....	....	....	....	....	....	....
	Bridgeport	AHL	67	*43	25	68	26	....	....	....	....	....	....	....	....	....	7	4	0	4	4	....	....	....	....
	NHL Totals		**1**	**0**	**0**	**0**	**0**	**0**	**0**	**0**	**1**	**0.0**		**0**	**0.0**	**10:00**	....	....	....	....	....	....	....	....	....

ECAC All-Rookie Team (1997) • ECAC First All-Star Team (1998, 1999, 2001) • Ivy League First All-Star Team (1998, 1999, 2001) • NCAA East Second All-American Team (1998, 1999) • NCAA East First All-American Team (2001) • Ivy League Player of the Year (2001) • AHL First All-Star Team (2004) • Willie Marshall Award (Top Goal-scorer - AHL) (2004)

• Missed majority of 1999-2000 season recovering from abdominal injury originally suffered in game vs. U. of Michigan (CCHA), October 30, 1999. Signed as a free agent by **Karpat** (Finland), October 4, 2001. Signed as a free agent by **NY Islanders**, August 6, 2002.

HAMRLIK, Roman
(HAHM-reh-lik, ROH-muhn) **NYI**

Defense. Shoots left. 6'2", 200 lbs. Born, Zlin, Czech., April 12, 1974. Tampa Bay's 1st choice, 1st overall, in 1992 Entry Draft.

Season	Club	League	GP	G	A	Pts	PIM	PP	SH	GW	S	%	+/-	TF	F%	Min	GP	G	A	Pts	PIM	PP	SH	GW	Min
1990-91	AC ZPS Zlin	Czech	14	2	2	4	18	....	....	....	....	....	....	....	....	....	....	....	....	....	....	....	....	....	....
1991-92	AC ZPS Zlin	Czech	34	5	5	10	50	....	....	....	....	....	....	....	....	....	....	....	....	....	....	....	....	....	....
1992-93	**Tampa Bay**	**NHL**	**67**	**6**	**15**	**21**	**71**	**1**	**0**	**1**	**113**	**5.3**	**–21**	....	....	....	....	....	....	....	....	....	....	....	....
	Atlanta Knights	IHL	2	1	1	2	2	....	....	....	....	....	....	....	....	....	....	....	....	....	....	....	....	....	....
1993-94	**Tampa Bay**	**NHL**	**64**	**3**	**18**	**21**	**135**	**0**	**0**	**0**	**158**	**1.9**	**–14**	....	....	....	....	....	....	....	....	....	....	....	....
1994-95	AC ZPS Zlin	Czech	2	1	0	1	10	....	....	....	....	....	....	....	....	....	....	....	....	....	....	....	....	....	....
	Tampa Bay	**NHL**	**48**	**12**	**11**	**23**	**86**	**7**	**1**	**2**	**134**	**9.0**	**–18**	....	....	....	....	....	....	....	....	....	....	....	....
1995-96	**Tampa Bay**	**NHL**	**82**	**16**	**49**	**65**	**103**	**12**	**0**	**2**	**281**	**5.7**	**–24**	....	....	....	**5**	**0**	**1**	**1**	**4**	**0**	**0**	**0**	....
1996-97	**Tampa Bay**	**NHL**	**79**	**12**	**28**	**40**	**57**	**6**	**0**	**0**	**238**	**5.0**	**–29**	....	....	....	....	....	....	....	....	....	....	....	....
1997-98	**Tampa Bay**	**NHL**	**37**	**3**	**12**	**15**	**22**	**1**	**0**	**0**	**86**	**3.5**	**–18**	....	....	....	....	....	....	....	....	....	....	....	....
	Edmonton	**NHL**	**41**	**6**	**20**	**26**	**48**	**4**	**1**	**3**	**112**	**5.4**	**3**	....	....	....	**12**	**0**	**6**	**6**	**12**	**0**	**0**	**0**	....
	Czech Republic	Olympics	6	1	0	1	2	....	....	....	....	....	....	....	....	....	....	....	....	....	....	....	....	....	....
1998-99	**Edmonton**	**NHL**	**75**	**8**	**24**	**32**	**70**	**3**	**0**	**0**	**172**	**4.7**	**9**	**0**	**0.0**	**23:49**	**3**	**0**	**0**	**0**	**2**	**0**	**0**	**0**	**16:23**
99-2000	Zlin	Czech	6	0	3	3	4	....	....	....	....	....	....	....	....	....	....	....	....	....	....	....	....	....	....
	Edmonton	**NHL**	**80**	**8**	**37**	**45**	**68**	**5**	**0**	**0**	**180**	**4.4**	**1**	**0**	**0.0**	**25:18**	**5**	**0**	**1**	**1**	**4**	**0**	**0**	**0**	**24:44**
2000-01	**NY Islanders**	**NHL**	**76**	**16**	**30**	**46**	**92**	**5**	**1**	**4**	**232**	**6.9**	**–20**	**1**	**100.0**	**25:12**	....	....	....	....	....	....	....	....	....
2001-02	**NY Islanders**	**NHL**	**70**	**11**	**26**	**37**	**78**	**4**	**1**	**1**	**169**	**6.5**	**7**	**1**	**0.0**	**25:32**	**7**	**1**	**6**	**7**	**6**	**0**	**0**	**0**	**29:09**
	Czech Republic	Olympics	4	0	1	1	2	....	....	....	....	....	....	....	....	....	....	....	....	....	....	....	....	....	....
2002-03	**NY Islanders**	**NHL**	**73**	**9**	**32**	**41**	**87**	**3**	**0**	**2**	**151**	**6.0**	**21**	**0**	**0.0**	**26:34**	**5**	**0**	**2**	**2**	**2**	**0**	**0**	**0**	**29:24**
2003-04	**NY Islanders**	**NHL**	**81**	**7**	**22**	**29**	**68**	**2**	**0**	**2**	**182**	**3.8**	**2**	**0**	**0.0**	**24:35**	**5**	**0**	**1**	**1**	**2**	**0**	**0**	**0**	**25:30**
	NHL Totals		**873**	**117**	**324**	**441**	**985**	**53**	**4**	**17**	**2208**	**5.3**		**2**	**50.0**	**25:09**	**42**	**1**	**17**	**18**	**32**	**0**	**0**	**0**	**26:03**

Played in NHL All-Star Game (1996, 1999, 2003)

Traded to **Edmonton** by **Tampa Bay** with Paul Comrie for Bryan Marchment, Steve Kelly and Jason Bonsignore, December 30, 1997. Traded to **NY Islanders** by **Edmonton** for Eric Brewer, Josh Green and NY Islanders' 2nd round choice (Brad Winchester) in 2000 Entry Draft, June 24, 2000.

			Regular Season														Playoffs								
Season	Club	League	GP	G	A	Pts	PIM	PP	SH	GW	S	%	+/-	TF	F%	Min	GP	G	A	Pts	PIM	PP	SH	GW	Min

HANDZUS, Michal

(HAHND-zuhs, MIGH-kuhl) **PHI.**

Center. Shoots left. 6'5", 217 lbs. Born, Banska Bystrica, Czech., March 11, 1977. St. Louis' 3rd choice, 101st overall, in 1995 Entry Draft.

Season	Club	League	GP	G	A	Pts	PIM	PP	SH	GW	S	%	+/-	TF	F%	Min	GP	G	A	Pts	PIM	PP	SH	GW	Min
1993-94	B. Bystrica Jr.	Slovak-Jr.	40	23	36	59	....	....	....	....	....	....	....	....	....	....	....	....	....	....	....	....	....	....	....
1994-95	Banska Bystrica	Slovak-2	22	15	14	29	10	....	....	....	....	....	....	....	....	....	....	....	....	....	....	....	....	....	....
1995-96	Banska Bystrica	Slovakia	19	3	1	4	8	....	....	....	....	....	....	....	....	....	....	....	....	....	....	....	....	....	....
1996-97	HC SKP PS Poprad	Slovakia	44	15	18	33	....	....	....	....	....	....	....	....	....	....	....	....	....	....	....	....	....	....	....
1997-98	Worcester IceCats	AHL	69	27	36	63	54	....	....	....	....	....	....	....	....	....	11	2	6	8	10	....	....	....	....
1998-99	**St. Louis**	**NHL**	**66**	**4**	**12**	**16**	**30**	**0**	**0**	**0**	**78**	**5.1**	**-9**	**794**	**49.9**	**14:48**	**11**	**0**	**2**	**2**	**8**	**0**	**0**	**0**	**16:52**
99-2000	**St. Louis**	**NHL**	**81**	**25**	**28**	**53**	**44**	**3**	**4**	**5**	**166**	**15.1**	**19**	**1243**	**51.5**	**17:43**	**7**	**0**	**3**	**3**	**6**	**0**	**0**	**0**	**16:35**
2000-01	**St. Louis**	**NHL**	**36**	**10**	**14**	**24**	**12**	**3**	**2**	**2**	**58**	**17.2**	**11**	**581**	**50.6**	**18:00**	....	....	....	....	....	....	....	....	....
	Phoenix	**NHL**	**10**	**4**	**4**	**8**	**21**	**0**	**1**	**0**	**14**	**28.6**	**5**	**111**	**60.4**	**15:26**	....	....	....	....	....	....	....	....	....
2001-02	**Phoenix**	**NHL**	**79**	**15**	**30**	**45**	**34**	**3**	**1**	**1**	**94**	**16.0**	**-8**	**1227**	**48.7**	**16:09**	**5**	**0**	**0**	**0**	**2**	**0**	**0**	**0**	**15:01**
	Slovakia	Olympics	2	1	0	1	6	....	....	....	....	....	....	....	....	....	....	....	....	....	....	....	....	....	....
2002-03	**Philadelphia**	**NHL**	**82**	**23**	**21**	**44**	**46**	**1**	**1**	**9**	**133**	**17.3**	**13**	**1350**	**52.3**	**17:33**	**13**	**2**	**6**	**8**	**6**	**0**	**0**	**1**	**18:23**
2003-04	**Philadelphia**	**NHL**	**82**	**20**	**38**	**58**	**82**	**7**	**1**	**2**	**135**	**14.8**	**18**	**1457**	**49.9**	**18:43**	**18**	**5**	**5**	**10**	**10**	**0**	**0**	**0**	**18:33**
	NHL Totals		**436**	**101**	**147**	**248**	**269**	**17**	**10**	**19**	**678**	**14.9**		**6763**	**50.7**	**17:07**	**54**	**7**	**16**	**23**	**32**	**0**	**0**	**1**	**17:35**

Traded to **Phoenix** by **St. Louis** with Ladislav Nagy, the rights to Jeff Taffe and St. Louis' 1st round choice (Ben Eager) in 2002 Entry Draft for Keith Tkachuk, March 13, 2001. Traded to **Philadelphia** by **Phoenix** with Robert Esche for Brian Boucher and Nashville's 3rd round choice (previously acquired, Phoenix selected Joe Callahan) in 2002 Entry Draft, June 12, 2002.

HANKINSON, Casey

(HAN-kihn-suhn, KAY-see)

Left wing. Shoots left. 6'1", 187 lbs. Born, Edina, MN, May 8, 1976. Chicago's 9th choice, 201st overall, in 1995 Entry Draft.

Season	Club	League	GP	G	A	Pts	PIM	PP	SH	GW	S	%	+/-	TF	F%	Min	GP	G	A	Pts	PIM	PP	SH	GW	Min
1992-93	Edina Hornets	Hi-School	25	20	26	46	....	....	....	....	....	....	....	....	....	....	....	....	....	....	....	....	....	....	....
1993-94	Edina Hornets	Hi-School	24	21	20	41	50	....	....	....	....	....	....	....	....	....	....	....	....	....	....	....	....	....	....
1994-95	U. of Minnesota	WCHA	33	7	1	8	86	....	....	....	....	....	....	....	....	....	....	....	....	....	....	....	....	....	....
1995-96	U. of Minnesota	WCHA	39	16	19	35	101	....	....	....	....	....	....	....	....	....	....	....	....	....	....	....	....	....	....
1996-97	U. of Minnesota	WCHA	42	17	24	41	79	....	....	....	....	....	....	....	....	....	....	....	....	....	....	....	....	....	....
1997-98	U. of Minnesota	WCHA	35	10	12	22	81	....	....	....	....	....	....	....	....	....	....	....	....	....	....	....	....	....	....
1998-99	Portland Pirates	AHL	72	10	13	23	106	....	....	....	....	....	....	....	....	....	....	....	....	....	....	....	....	....	....
99-2000	Cleveland	IHL	82	7	22	29	140	....	....	....	....	....	....	....	....	....	2	0	0	0	2	....	....	....	....
2000-01	**Chicago**	**NHL**	**11**	**0**	**1**	**1**	**9**	**0**	**0**	**0**	**15**	**0.0**	**-3**	**0**	**0.0**	**9:46**	....	....	....	....	....	....	....	....	....
	Norfolk Admirals	AHL	69	30	21	51	74	....	....	....	....	....	....	....	....	....	9	5	4	9	2	....	....	....	....
2001-02	**Chicago**	**NHL**	**3**	**0**	**0**	**0**	**0**	**0**	**0**	**0**	**1**	**0.0**	**-2**	**6**	**33.3**	**8:38**	....	....	....	....	....	....	....	....	....
	Norfolk Admirals	AHL	72	19	30	49	85	....	....	....	....	....	....	....	....	....	4	1	2	3	0	....	....	....	....
2002-03	Norfolk Admirals	AHL	78	27	28	55	59	....	....	....	....	....	....	....	....	....	9	4	3	7	10	....	....	....	....
2003-04	**Anaheim**	**NHL**	**4**	**0**	**0**	**0**	**4**	**0**	**0**	**0**	**0**	**0.0**	**0**	**1**	**100.0**	**6:20**	....	....	....	....	....	....	....	....	....
	Cincinnati	AHL	78	15	23	38	123	....	....	....	....	....	....	....	....	....	9	4	1	5	10	....	....	....	....
	NHL Totals		**18**	**0**	**1**	**1**	**13**	**0**	**0**	**0**	**16**	**0.0**		**7**	**42.9**	**8:49**	....	....	....	....	....	....	....	....	....

Signed as a free agent by **Anaheim**, July 25, 2003.

HANNAN, Scott

(HAN-nan, SKAWT) **S.J.**

Defense. Shoots left. 6'1", 220 lbs. Born, Richmond, B.C., January 23, 1979. San Jose's 2nd choice, 23rd overall, in 1997 Entry Draft.

Season	Club	League	GP	G	A	Pts	PIM	PP	SH	GW	S	%	+/-	TF	F%	Min	GP	G	A	Pts	PIM	PP	SH	GW	Min
1994-95	Surrey Wolves	BCAHA	70	54	54	108	200	....	....	....	....	....	....	....	....	....	....	....	....	....	....	....	....	....	....
	Tacoma Rockets	WHL	2	0	0	0	0	....	....	....	....	....	....	....	....	....	....	....	....	....	....	....	....	....	....
1995-96	Kelowna Rockets	WHL	69	4	5	9	76	....	....	....	....	....	....	....	....	....	6	0	1	1	4	....	....	....	....
1996-97	Kelowna Rockets	WHL	70	17	26	43	101	....	....	....	....	....	....	....	....	....	6	0	0	0	8	....	....	....	....
1997-98	Kelowna Rockets	WHL	47	10	30	40	70	....	....	....	....	....	....	....	....	....	7	2	7	9	14	....	....	....	....
1998-99	**San Jose**	**NHL**	**5**	**0**	**2**	**2**	**6**	**0**	**0**	**0**	**4**	**0.0**	**0**	**0**	**0.0**	**7:15**	....	....	....	....	....	....	....	....	....
	Kelowna Rockets	WHL	47	15	30	45	92	....	....	....	....	....	....	....	....	....	6	1	2	3	14	....	....	....	....
	Kentucky	AHL	2	0	0	0	2	....	....	....	....	....	....	....	....	....	12	0	2	2	10	....	....	....	....
99-2000	**San Jose**	**NHL**	**30**	**1**	**2**	**3**	**10**	**0**	**0**	**0**	**28**	**3.6**	**7**	**1**	**0.0**	**17:09**	**1**	**0**	**1**	**1**	**0**	**0**	**0**	**0**	**18:14**
	Kentucky	AHL	41	5	12	17	40	....	....	....	....	....	....	....	....	....	....	....	....	....	....	....	....	....	....
2000-01	**San Jose**	**NHL**	**75**	**3**	**14**	**17**	**51**	**0**	**0**	**1**	**96**	**3.1**	**10**	**0**	**0.0**	**19:02**	**6**	**0**	**1**	**1**	**6**	**0**	**0**	**0**	**25:10**
2001-02	**San Jose**	**NHL**	**75**	**2**	**12**	**14**	**57**	**0**	**0**	**1**	**68**	**2.9**	**10**	**1**	**100.0**	**20:19**	**12**	**0**	**2**	**2**	**12**	**0**	**0**	**0**	**20:46**
2002-03	**San Jose**	**NHL**	**81**	**3**	**19**	**22**	**61**	**1**	**0**	**0**	**103**	**2.9**	**0**	**3**	**33.3**	**24:16**	....	....	....	....	....	....	....	....	....
2003-04	**San Jose**	**NHL**	**82**	**6**	**15**	**21**	**48**	**0**	**0**	**0**	**114**	**5.3**	**10**	**0**	**0.0**	**23:41**	**17**	**1**	**5**	**6**	**22**	**1**	**0**	**1**	**26:38**
	NHL Totals		**348**	**15**	**64**	**79**	**233**	**1**	**0**	**2**	**413**	**3.6**		**5**	**40.0**	**21:17**	**36**	**1**	**9**	**10**	**40**	**1**	**0**	**1**	**24:12**

WHL West First All-Star Team (1999)

HANSEN, Tavis

(HAN-suhn, TA-vihs)

Right wing. Shoots right. 6'1", 205 lbs. Born, Prince Albert, Sask., June 17, 1975. Winnipeg's 3rd choice, 58th overall, in 1994 Entry Draft.

Season	Club	League	GP	G	A	Pts	PIM	PP	SH	GW	S	%	+/-	TF	F%	Min	GP	G	A	Pts	PIM	PP	SH	GW	Min
1992-93	Shellbrook	SMHL	42	42	63	105	107	....	....	....	....	....	....	....	....	....	....	....	....	....	....	....	....	....	....
1993-94	Tacoma Rockets	WHL	71	23	31	54	122	....	....	....	....	....	....	....	....	....	8	1	3	4	17	....	....	....	....
1994-95	Tacoma Rockets	WHL	71	32	41	73	142	....	....	....	....	....	....	....	....	....	4	1	1	2	8	....	....	....	....
	Winnipeg	**NHL**	**1**	**0**	**0**	**0**	**0**	**0**	**0**	**0**	**0**	**0.0**	**0**	....	....	....	....	....	....	....	....	....	....	....	....
1995-96	Springfield	AHL	67	6	16	22	85	....	....	....	....	....	....	....	....	....	5	1	2	3	2	....	....	....	....
1996-97	**Phoenix**	**NHL**	**1**	**0**	**0**	**0**	**0**	**0**	**0**	**0**	**0**	**0.0**	**0**	....	....	....	....	....	....	....	....	....	....	....	....
	Springfield	AHL	12	3	1	4	23	....	....	....	....	....	....	....	....	....	....	....	....	....	....	....	....	....	....
1997-98	Springfield	AHL	73	20	14	34	70	....	....	....	....	....	....	....	....	....	4	1	2	3	18	....	....	....	....
1998-99	**Phoenix**	**NHL**	**20**	**2**	**1**	**3**	**12**	**0**	**0**	**0**	**14**	**14.3**	**-4**	**5**	**80.0**	**8:07**	**2**	**0**	**0**	**0**	**0**	**0**	**0**	**0**	**3:45**
	Springfield	AHL	63	23	11	34	85	....	....	....	....	....	....	....	....	....	3	0	1	1	5	....	....	....	....
99-2000	**Phoenix**	**NHL**	**5**	**0**	**0**	**0**	**0**	**0**	**0**	**0**	**2**	**0.0**	**0**	**0**	**0.0**	**4:17**	....	....	....	....	....	....	....	....	....
	Springfield	AHL	59	21	27	48	164	....	....	....	....	....	....	....	....	....	5	2	1	3	4	....	....	....	....
2000-01	**Phoenix**	**NHL**	**7**	**0**	**0**	**0**	**4**	**0**	**0**	**0**	**2**	**0.0**	**-1**	**1**	**100.0**	**5:05**	....	....	....	....	....	....	....	....	....
	Springfield	AHL	24	6	10	16	81	....	....	....	....	....	....	....	....	....	....	....	....	....	....	....	....	....	....
2001-02	Hershey Bears	AHL	35	9	6	15	50	....	....	....	....	....	....	....	....	....	8	0	3	3	8	....	....	....	....
2002-03	Cleveland Barons	AHL	80	23	21	44	81	....	....	....	....	....	....	....	....	....	....	....	....	....	....	....	....	....	....
2003-04	Cleveland Barons	AHL	77	17	17	34	118	....	....	....	....	....	....	....	....	....	9	5	2	7	13	....	....	....	....
	NHL Totals		**34**	**2**	**1**	**3**	**16**	**0**	**0**	**0**	**18**	**11.1**		**6**	**83.3**	**6:51**	**2**	**0**	**0**	**0**	**0**	**0**	**0**	**0**	**3:45**

Transferred to **Phoenix** after **Winnipeg** franchise relocated, July 1, 1996. • Missed majority of 2000-01 and 2001-02 seasons recovering from arm injury suffered in game vs. Hershey (AHL), February 3, 2001. Signed as a free agent by **Hershey** (AHL), January 16, 2002. Signed as a free agent by **San Jose**, September 5, 2002.

HARTIGAN, Mark

(HAHR-tih-guhn, MAHRK) **CBJ**

Center. Shoots left. 6', 205 lbs. Born, Fort St. John, B.C., October 15, 1977.

Season	Club	League	GP	G	A	Pts	PIM	PP	SH	GW	S	%	+/-	TF	F%	Min	GP	G	A	Pts	PIM	PP	SH	GW	Min
1996-97	Weyburn	SJHL	52	44	32	76	....	....	....	....	....	....	....	....	....	....	....	....	....	....	....	....	....	....	....
1997-98	Weyburn	SJHL	62	*59	46	*105	81	....	....	....	....	....	....	....	....	....	23	17	21	38	10	....	....	....	....
1998-99	St. Cloud State	WCHA	DID NOT PLAY – FRESHMAN																						
99-2000	St. Cloud State	WCHA	37	22	20	42	24	....	....	....	....	....	....	....	....	....	....	....	....	....	....	....	....	....	....
2000-01	St. Cloud State	WCHA	40	27	21	48	20	....	....	....	....	....	....	....	....	....	....	....	....	....	....	....	....	....	....
2001-02	St. Cloud State	WCHA	42	*37	38	75	42	....	....	....	....	....	....	....	....	....	....	....	....	....	....	....	....	....	....
	Atlanta	**NHL**	**2**	**0**	**0**	**0**	**2**	**0**	**0**	**0**	**3**	**0.0**	**-2**	**18**	**38.9**	**13:16**	....	....	....	....	....	....	....	....	....
2002-03	**Atlanta**	**NHL**	**23**	**5**	**2**	**7**	**6**	**1**	**0**	**0**	**25**	**20.0**	**-8**	**220**	**47.3**	**10:52**	....	....	....	....	....	....	....	....	....
	Chicago Wolves	AHL	55	15	31	46	43	....	....	....	....	....	....	....	....	....	9	1	2	3	10	....	....	....	....
2003-04	**Columbus**	**NHL**	**9**	**1**	**3**	**4**	**6**	**1**	**0**	**0**	**15**	**6.7**	**-2**	**138**	**40.6**	**16:19**	....	....	....	....	....	....	....	....	....
	Syracuse Crunch	AHL	69	23	23	46	86	....	....	....	....	....	....	....	....	....	7	1	4	5	8	....	....	....	....
	NHL Totals		**34**	**6**	**5**	**11**	**14**	**2**	**0**	**0**	**43**	**14.0**		**376**	**44.4**	**12:27**	....	....	....	....	....	....	....	....	....

WCHA First All-Star Team (2002) • WCHA Player of the Year (2002)

Signed as a free agent by **Atlanta**, March 27, 2002. Signed as a free agent by **Columbus**, July 15, 2003.

HARTNELL, Scott
(HAHRT-nuhl, SKAWT) **NSH.**

Left wing. Shoots left. 6'2", 205 lbs. Born, Regina, Sask., April 18, 1982. Nashville's 1st choice, 6th overall, in 2000 Entry Draft.

			Regular Season														Playoffs								
Season	Club	League	GP	G	A	Pts	PIM	PP	SH	GW	S	%	+/-	TF	F%	Min	GP	G	A	Pts	PIM	PP	SH	GW	Min
1997-98	Lloydminster	AJHL	56	9	25	34	82	....	....	....	....	....	....	....	....	....	4	2	1	3	8	....	....	....	....
	Prince Albert	WHL	1	0	1	1	2	....	....	....	....	....	....	....	....	....	....	....	....	....	....	....	....	....	....
1998-99	Prince Albert	WHL	65	10	34	44	104	....	....	....	....	....	....	....	....	....	14	0	5	5	22	....	....	....	....
99-2000	Prince Albert	WHL	62	27	55	82	124	....	....	....	....	....	....	....	....	....	6	3	2	5	6	....	....	....	....
2000-01	**Nashville**	**NHL**	**75**	**2**	**14**	**16**	**48**	**0**	**0**	**0**	**92**	**2.2**	**-8**	**3**	**33.3**	**10:54**	....	....	....	....	....	....	....	....	....
2001-02	**Nashville**	**NHL**	**75**	**14**	**27**	**41**	**111**	**3**	**0**	**4**	**162**	**8.6**	**5**	**12**	**25.0**	**16:58**	....	....	....	....	....	....	....	....	....
2002-03	**Nashville**	**NHL**	**82**	**12**	**22**	**34**	**101**	**2**	**0**	**2**	**221**	**5.4**	**-3**	**23**	**30.4**	**15:17**	....	....	....	....	....	....	....	....	....
2003-04	**Nashville**	**NHL**	**59**	**18**	**15**	**33**	**87**	**5**	**0**	**3**	**154**	**11.7**	**-5**	**48**	**37.5**	**16:16**	**6**	**1**	**2**	**3**	**2**	**0**	**0**	**0**	**15:37**
	NHL Totals		**291**	**46**	**78**	**124**	**347**	**10**	**0**	**9**	**629**	**7.3**		**86**	**33.7**	**14:47**	**6**	**1**	**2**	**3**	**2**	**0**	**0**	**0**	**15:37**

HARVEY, Todd
(HAHR-vee, TAWD) **S.J.**

Right wing/Center. Shoots right. 6', 210 lbs. Born, Hamilton, Ont., February 17, 1975. Dallas' 1st choice, 9th overall, in 1993 Entry Draft.

			Regular Season														Playoffs								
Season	Club	League	GP	G	A	Pts	PIM	PP	SH	GW	S	%	+/-	TF	F%	Min	GP	G	A	Pts	PIM	PP	SH	GW	Min
1989-90	Cambridge	OJHL-B	41	35	27	62	213	....	....	....	....	....	....	....	....	....	....	....	....	....	....	....	....	....	....
1990-91	Cambridge	OJHL-B	35	32	39	71	174	....	....	....	....	....	....	....	....	....	....	....	....	....	....	....	....	....	....
1991-92	Detroit	OHL	58	21	43	64	141	....	....	....	....	....	....	....	....	....	7	3	5	8	30	....	....	....	....
1992-93	Detroit	OHL	55	50	50	100	83	....	....	....	....	....	....	....	....	....	15	9	12	21	39	....	....	....	....
1993-94	Detroit	OHL	49	34	51	85	75	....	....	....	....	....	....	....	....	....	17	10	12	22	26	....	....	....	....
1994-95	Detroit	OHL	11	8	14	22	12	....	....	....	....	....	....	....	....	....	....	....	....	....	....	....	....	....	....
	Dallas	**NHL**	**40**	**11**	**9**	**20**	**67**	**2**	**0**	**1**	**64**	**17.2**	**-3**	....	....	....	**5**	**0**	**0**	**0**	**8**	**0**	**0**	**0**	....
1995-96	**Dallas**	**NHL**	**69**	**9**	**20**	**29**	**136**	**3**	**0**	**1**	**101**	**8.9**	**-13**	....	....	....	....	....	....	....	....	....	....	....	....
	Michigan	IHL	5	1	3	4	8	....	....	....	....	....	....	....	....	....	....	....	....	....	....	....	....	....	....
1996-97	**Dallas**	**NHL**	**71**	**9**	**22**	**31**	**142**	**1**	**0**	**2**	**99**	**9.1**	**19**	....	....	....	**7**	**0**	**1**	**1**	**10**	**0**	**0**	**0**	....
1997-98	**Dallas**	**NHL**	**59**	**9**	**10**	**19**	**104**	**0**	**0**	**1**	**88**	**10.2**	**5**	....	....	....	....	....	....	....	....	....	....	....	....
1998-99	**NY Rangers**	**NHL**	**37**	**11**	**17**	**28**	**72**	**6**	**0**	**2**	**58**	**19.0**	**-1**	**175**	**50.3**	**17:19**	....	....	....	....	....	....	....	....	....
99-2000	**NY Rangers**	**NHL**	**31**	**3**	**3**	**6**	**62**	**0**	**0**	**0**	**31**	**9.7**	**-9**	**173**	**49.1**	**12:21**	....	....	....	....	....	....	....	....	....
	San Jose	**NHL**	**40**	**8**	**4**	**12**	**78**	**2**	**0**	**0**	**59**	**13.6**	**-2**	**44**	**43.2**	**12:55**	**12**	**1**	**0**	**1**	**8**	**1**	**0**	**0**	**10:47**
2000-01	**San Jose**	**NHL**	**69**	**10**	**11**	**21**	**72**	**1**	**0**	**2**	**66**	**15.2**	**6**	**98**	**40.8**	**11:05**	**6**	**0**	**0**	**0**	**8**	**0**	**0**	**0**	**6:59**
2001-02	**San Jose**	**NHL**	**69**	**9**	**13**	**22**	**73**	**0**	**0**	**1**	**66**	**13.6**	**16**	**223**	**48.4**	**9:47**	**12**	**0**	**2**	**2**	**12**	**0**	**0**	**0**	**7:32**
2002-03	**San Jose**	**NHL**	**76**	**3**	**16**	**19**	**74**	**0**	**0**	**0**	**64**	**4.7**	**5**	**119**	**44.5**	**9:57**	....	....	....	....	....	....	....	....	....
2003-04	**San Jose**	**NHL**	**47**	**4**	**5**	**9**	**38**	**0**	**0**	**0**	**51**	**7.8**	**3**	**29**	**44.8**	**9:46**	**16**	**1**	**2**	**3**	**2**	**0**	**0**	**0**	**10:30**
	Cleveland Barons	AHL	13	6	1	7	29	....	....	....	....	....	....	....	....	....	....	....	....	....	....	....	....	....	....
	NHL Totals		**608**	**86**	**130**	**216**	**918**	**15**	**0**	**10**	**747**	**11.5**		**861**	**47.2**	**11:22**	**58**	**2**	**5**	**7**	**48**	**1**	**0**	**0**	**9:21**

OHL All-Rookie Team (1992)

Traded to **NY Rangers** by **Dallas** with Bob Errey and Dallas' 4th round choice (Boyd Kane) in 1998 Entry Draft for Brian Skrudland, Mike Keane and NY Rangers' 6th round choice (Pavel Patera) in 1998 Entry Draft, March 24, 1998. Traded to **San Jose** by **NY Rangers** with NY Rangers' 4th round choice (Dimitri Patzold) in 2001 Entry Draft for Radek Dvorak, December 30, 1999.

HATCHER, Derian
(HAT-chuhr, DAIR-ee-an) **DET.**

Defense. Shoots left. 6'5", 235 lbs. Born, Sterling Hts., MI, June 4, 1972. Minnesota's 1st choice, 8th overall, in 1990 Entry Draft.

			Regular Season														Playoffs								
Season	Club	League	GP	G	A	Pts	PIM	PP	SH	GW	S	%	+/-	TF	F%	Min	GP	G	A	Pts	PIM	PP	SH	GW	Min
1987-88	Detroit GPD	MNHL	25	5	13	18	52	....	....	....	....	....	....	....	....	....	....	....	....	....	....	....	....	....	....
1988-89	Detroit GPD	MNHL	51	19	35	54	100	....	....	....	....	....	....	....	....	....	....	....	....	....	....	....	....	....	....
1989-90	North Bay	OHL	64	14	38	52	81	....	....	....	....	....	....	....	....	....	5	2	3	5	8	....	....	....	....
1990-91	North Bay	OHL	64	13	49	62	163	....	....	....	....	....	....	....	....	....	10	2	10	12	28	....	....	....	....
1991-92	**Minnesota**	**NHL**	**43**	**8**	**4**	**12**	**88**	**0**	**0**	**2**	**51**	**15.7**	**7**	....	....	....	**5**	**0**	**2**	**2**	**8**	**0**	**0**	**0**	....
1992-93	**Minnesota**	**NHL**	**67**	**4**	**15**	**19**	**178**	**0**	**0**	**1**	**73**	**5.5**	**-27**	....	....	....	....	....	....	....	....	....	....	....	....
	Kalamazoo Wings	IHL	2	1	2	3	21	....	....	....	....	....	....	....	....	....	....	....	....	....	....	....	....	....	....
1993-94	**Dallas**	**NHL**	**83**	**12**	**19**	**31**	**211**	**2**	**1**	**2**	**132**	**9.1**	**19**	....	....	....	**9**	**0**	**2**	**2**	**14**	**0**	**0**	**0**	....
1994-95	**Dallas**	**NHL**	**43**	**5**	**11**	**16**	**105**	**2**	**0**	**2**	**74**	**6.8**	**3**	....	....	....	....	....	....	....	....	....	....	....	....
1995-96	**Dallas**	**NHL**	**79**	**8**	**23**	**31**	**129**	**2**	**0**	**1**	**125**	**6.4**	**-12**	....	....	....	....	....	....	....	....	....	....	....	....
1996-97	**Dallas**	**NHL**	**63**	**3**	**19**	**22**	**97**	**0**	**0**	**0**	**96**	**3.1**	**8**	....	....	....	**7**	**0**	**2**	**2**	**20**	**0**	**0**	**0**	....
1997-98	**Dallas**	**NHL**	**70**	**6**	**25**	**31**	**132**	**3**	**0**	**2**	**74**	**8.1**	**9**	....	....	....	**17**	**3**	**3**	**6**	**39**	**2**	**0**	**0**	....
	United States	Olympics	4	0	0	0	0	....	....	....	....	....	....	....	....	....	....	....	....	....	....	....	....	....	....
1998-99 ♦	**Dallas**	**NHL**	**80**	**9**	**21**	**30**	**102**	**3**	**0**	**2**	**125**	**7.2**	**21**	**0**	**0.0**	**24:44**	**18**	**1**	**6**	**7**	**24**	**0**	**0**	**0**	**29:06**
99-2000	**Dallas**	**NHL**	**57**	**2**	**22**	**24**	**68**	**0**	**0**	**0**	**90**	**2.2**	**6**	**0**	**0.0**	**27:33**	**23**	**1**	**3**	**4**	**29**	**0**	**0**	**0**	**27:40**
2000-01	**Dallas**	**NHL**	**80**	**2**	**21**	**23**	**77**	**1**	**0**	**2**	**97**	**2.1**	**5**	**0**	**0.0**	**25:53**	**10**	**0**	**1**	**1**	**16**	**0**	**0**	**0**	**28:53**
2001-02	**Dallas**	**NHL**	**80**	**4**	**21**	**25**	**87**	**1**	**0**	**0**	**111**	**3.6**	**12**	**0**	**0.0**	**26:40**	....	....	....	....	....	....	....	....	....
2002-03	**Dallas**	**NHL**	**82**	**8**	**22**	**30**	**106**	**1**	**1**	**2**	**159**	**5.0**	**37**	**0**	**0.0**	**25:51**	**11**	**1**	**2**	**3**	**33**	**0**	**0**	**0**	**30:02**
2003-04	**Detroit**	**NHL**	**15**	**0**	**4**	**4**	**8**	**0**	**0**	**0**	**18**	**0.0**	**4**	**0**	**0.0**	**19:38**	**12**	**0**	**1**	**1**	**15**	**0**	**0**	**0**	**22:54**
	NHL Totals		**842**	**71**	**227**	**298**	**1388**	**15**	**2**	**16**	**1225**	**5.8**		**0**	**0.0**	**25:48**	**112**	**6**	**22**	**28**	**198**	**2**	**0**	**0**	**27:45**

NHL Second All-Star Team (2003)

Played in NHL All-Star Game (1997)

Transferred to **Dallas** after **Minnesota** franchise relocated, June 9, 1993. Signed as a free agent by **Detroit**, July 3, 2003. • Missed majority of 2003-04 season recovering from knee injury suffered in game vs. Vancouver, October 16, 2003.

HAVELID, Niclas
(HAHV-lihd, NIH-kluhs) **ATL.**

Defense. Shoots left. 6', 200 lbs. Born, Stockholm, Sweden, April 12, 1973. Anaheim's 2nd choice, 83rd overall, in 1999 Entry Draft.

			Regular Season														Playoffs								
Season	Club	League	GP	G	A	Pts	PIM	PP	SH	GW	S	%	+/-	TF	F%	Min	GP	G	A	Pts	PIM	PP	SH	GW	Min
1988-89	Enkopings SK	Swede-3	7	0	1	1	0	....	....	....	....	....	....	....	....	....	....	....	....	....	....	....	....	....	....
1989-90	Enkopings SK	Swede-3	24	1	2	3	28	....	....	....	....	....	....	....	....	....	....	....	....	....	....	....	....	....	....
1990-91	RA-73	Swede-2	30	2	3	5	22	....	....	....	....	....	....	....	....	....	....	....	....	....	....	....	....	....	....
1991-92	AIK Solna	Sweden	10	0	0	0	2	....	....	....	....	....	....	....	....	....	....	....	....	....	....	....	....	....	....
1992-93	AIK Solna	Sweden	30	1	2	3	22	....	....	....	....	....	....	....	....	....	3	0	0	0	2	....	....	....	....
1993-94	AIK Solna	Swede-2	22	3	9	12	14	....	....	....	....	....	....	....	....	....	....	....	....	....	....	....	....	....	....
1994-95	AIK Solna	Swede-2	40	3	7	10	38	....	....	....	....	....	....	....	....	....	....	....	....	....	....	....	....	....	....
1995-96	AIK Solna	Sweden	40	5	6	11	30	....	....	....	....	....	....	....	....	....	....	....	....	....	....	....	....	....	....
1996-97	AIK Solna	Sweden	49	3	6	9	42	....	....	....	....	....	....	....	....	....	7	1	2	3	8	....	....	....	....
1997-98	AIK Solna	Sweden	43	8	4	12	42	....	....	....	....	....	....	....	....	....	10	1	3	4	39	....	....	....	....
1998-99	Malmo IF	Sweden	50	10	12	22	42	....	....	....	....	....	....	....	....	....	8	0	4	4	10	....	....	....	....
99-2000	**Anaheim**	**NHL**	**50**	**2**	**7**	**9**	**20**	**0**	**0**	**2**	**70**	**2.9**	**0**	**1**	**0.0**	**19:10**	....	....	....	....	....	....	....	....	....
	Cincinnati	AHL	2	0	0	0	0	....	....	....	....	....	....	....	....	....	....	....	....	....	....	....	....	....	....
2000-01	**Anaheim**	**NHL**	**47**	**4**	**10**	**14**	**34**	**2**	**0**	**1**	**69**	**5.8**	**-6**	**4**	**0.0**	**21:51**	....	....	....	....	....	....	....	....	....
2001-02	**Anaheim**	**NHL**	**52**	**1**	**2**	**3**	**40**	**0**	**0**	**0**	**45**	**2.2**	**-13**	**1**	**0.0**	**17:01**	....	....	....	....	....	....	....	....	....
2002-03	**Anaheim**	**NHL**	**82**	**11**	**22**	**33**	**30**	**4**	**0**	**5**	**169**	**6.5**	**5**	**3**	**0.0**	**22:30**	**21**	**0**	**4**	**4**	**2**	**0**	**0**	**0**	**25:41**
2003-04	**Anaheim**	**NHL**	**79**	**6**	**20**	**26**	**28**	**5**	**0**	**3**	**122**	**4.9**	**-28**	**0**	**0.0**	**22:39**	....	....	....	....	....	....	....	....	....
	NHL Totals		**310**	**24**	**61**	**85**	**152**	**11**	**0**	**11**	**475**	**5.1**		**9**	**0.0**	**20:59**	**21**	**0**	**4**	**4**	**2**	**0**	**0**	**0**	**25:41**

Traded to **Atlanta** by **Anaheim** for Kurtis Foster, June 26, 2004.

HAVLAT, Martin
(HAHV-lat, MAHR-tihn) **OTT.**

Left wing. Shoots left. 6'1", 190 lbs. Born, Mlada Boleslav, Czech., April 19, 1981. Ottawa's 1st choice, 26th overall, in 1999 Entry Draft.

			Regular Season														Playoffs								
Season	Club	League	GP	G	A	Pts	PIM	PP	SH	GW	S	%	+/-	TF	F%	Min	GP	G	A	Pts	PIM	PP	SH	GW	Min
1997-98	Ytong Brno Jr.	Czech-Jr.	32	38	29	67	....	....	....	....	....	....	....	....	....	....	....	....	....	....	....	....	....	....	....
1998-99	Trinec Jr.	Czech-Jr.	31	28	23	51	....	....	....	....	....	....	....	....	....	....	....	....	....	....	....	....	....	....	....
	Trinec	Czech	24	2	3	5	4	....	....	....	....	....	....	....	....	....	8	0	0	0	....	....	....	....	....
99-2000	HC Ocelari Trinec	Czech	46	13	29	42	42	....	....	....	....	....	....	....	....	....	4	0	2	2	8	....	....	....	....
2000-01	**Ottawa**	**NHL**	**73**	**19**	**23**	**42**	**20**	**7**	**0**	**5**	**133**	**14.3**	**8**	**40**	**30.0**	**13:47**	**4**	**0**	**0**	**0**	**2**	**0**	**0**	**0**	**14:04**
2001-02	**Ottawa**	**NHL**	**72**	**22**	**28**	**50**	**66**	**9**	**0**	**6**	**145**	**15.2**	**-7**	**15**	**40.0**	**14:46**	**12**	**2**	**5**	**7**	**14**	**2**	**0**	**2**	**16:19**
	Czech Republic	Olympics	4	3	1	4	27	....	....	....	....	....	....	....	....	....	....	....	....	....	....	....	....	....	....
2002-03	**Ottawa**	**NHL**	**67**	**24**	**35**	**59**	**30**	**9**	**0**	**4**	**179**	**13.4**	**20**	**7**	**14.3**	**16:27**	**18**	**5**	**6**	**11**	**14**	**1**	**0**	**2**	**16:27**
2003-04	HC Sparta Praha	Czech	5	1	3	4	8	....	....	....	....	....	....	....	....	....	....	....	....	....	....	....	....	....	....
	Ottawa	**NHL**	**68**	**31**	**37**	**68**	**46**	**13**	**0**	**7**	**175**	**17.7**	**12**	**11**	**36.4**	**16:44**	**7**	**0**	**3**	**3**	**2**	**0**	**0**	**0**	**16:10**
	NHL Totals		**280**	**96**	**123**	**219**	**162**	**38**	**0**	**22**	**632**	**15.2**		**73**	**31.5**	**15:23**	**41**	**7**	**14**	**21**	**32**	**3**	**0**	**4**	**16:08**

NHL All-Rookie Team (2001)

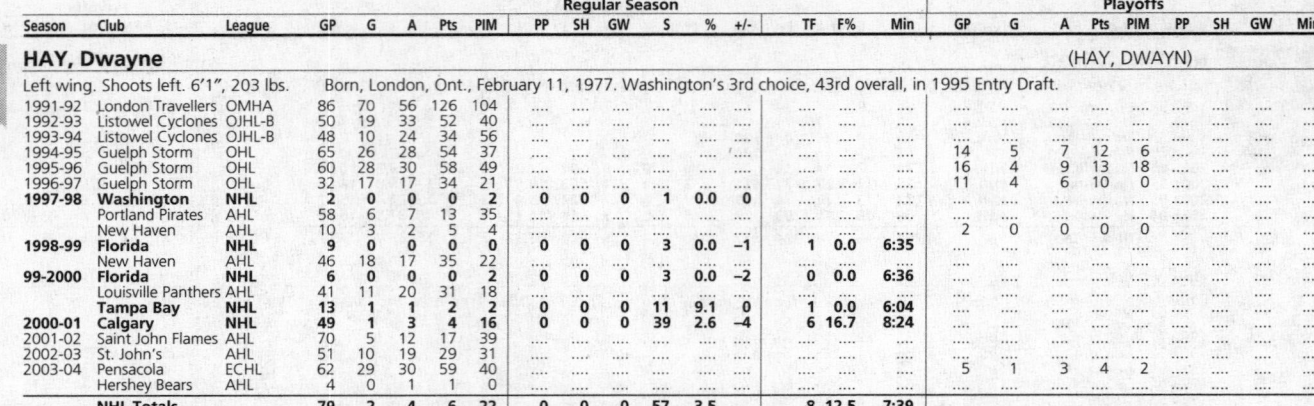

HAY, Dwayne
(HAY, DWAYN)

Left wing. Shoots left. 6'1", 203 lbs. Born, London, Ont., February 11, 1977. Washington's 3rd choice, 43rd overall, in 1995 Entry Draft.

			Regular Season														Playoffs								
Season	Club	League	GP	G	A	Pts	PIM	PP	SH	GW	S	%	+/-	TF	F%	Min	GP	G	A	Pts	PIM	PP	SH	GW	Min
1991-92	London Travellers	OMHA	86	70	56	126	104	....	....	....	....	....	....	....	....	....	....	....	....	....	....	....	....	....	....
1992-93	Listowel Cyclones	OJHL-B	50	19	33	52	40	....	....	....	....	....	....	....	....	....	....	....	....	....	....	....	....	....	....
1993-94	Listowel Cyclones	OJHL-B	48	10	24	34	56	....	....	....	....	....	....	....	....	....	....	....	....	....	....	....	....	....	....
1994-95	Guelph Storm	OHL	65	26	28	54	37	....	....	....	....	....	....	....	....	....	14	5	7	12	6	....	....	....	....
1995-96	Guelph Storm	OHL	60	28	30	58	49	....	....	....	....	....	....	....	....	....	16	4	9	13	18	....	....	....	....
1996-97	Guelph Storm	OHL	32	17	17	34	21	....	....	....	....	....	....	....	....	....	11	4	6	10	0	....	....	....	....
1997-98	**Washington**	**NHL**	**2**	**0**	**0**	**0**	**2**	**0**	**0**	**0**	**1**	**0.0**	**0**	....	....	....	....	....	....	....	....	....	....	....	....
	Portland Pirates	AHL	58	6	7	13	35	....	....	....	....	....	....	....	....	....	....	....	....	....	....	....	....	....	....
	New Haven	AHL	10	3	2	5	4	....	....	....	....	....	....	....	....	....	2	0	0	0	0	....	....	....	....
1998-99	**Florida**	**NHL**	**9**	**0**	**0**	**0**	**0**	**0**	**0**	**0**	**3**	**0.0**	**–1**	**1**	**0.0**	**6:35**	....	....	....	....	....	....	....	....	....
	New Haven	AHL	46	18	17	35	22	....	....	....	....	....	....	....	....	....	....	....	....	....	....	....	....	....	....
99-2000	**Florida**	**NHL**	**6**	**0**	**0**	**0**	**2**	**0**	**0**	**0**	**3**	**0.0**	**–2**	**0**	**0.0**	**6:36**	....	....	....	....	....	....	....	....	....
	Louisville Panthers	AHL	41	11	20	31	18	....	....	....	....	....	....	....	....	....	....	....	....	....	....	....	....	....	....
	Tampa Bay	**NHL**	**13**	**1**	**1**	**2**	**2**	**0**	**0**	**0**	**11**	**9.1**	**0**	**1**	**0.0**	**6:04**	....	....	....	....	....	....	....	....	....
2000-01	**Calgary**	**NHL**	**49**	**1**	**3**	**4**	**16**	**0**	**0**	**0**	**39**	**2.6**	**–4**	**6**	**16.7**	**8:24**	....	....	....	....	....	....	....	....	....
2001-02	Saint John Flames	AHL	70	5	12	17	39	....	....	....	....	....	....	....	....	....	....	....	....	....	....	....	....	....	....
2002-03	St. John's	AHL	51	10	19	29	31	....	....	....	....	....	....	....	....	....	....	....	....	....	....	....	....	....	....
2003-04	Pensacola	ECHL	62	29	30	59	40	....	....	....	....	....	....	....	....	....	5	1	3	4	2	....	....	....	....
	Hershey Bears	AHL	4	0	1	1	0	....	....	....	....	....	....	....	....	....	....	....	....	....	....	....	....	....	....
	NHL Totals		**79**	**2**	**4**	**6**	**22**	**0**	**0**	**0**	**57**	**3.5**		**8**	**12.5**	**7:39**	....	....	....	....	....	....	....	....	....

Traded to **Florida** by **Washington** with future considerations for Esa Tikkanen, March 9, 1998. Traded to **Tampa Bay** by **Florida** with Ryan Johnson for Mike Sillinger, March 14, 2000. Claimed on waivers by **Calgary** from **Tampa Bay**, October 3, 2000. Signed as a free agent by **Toronto**, November 30, 2002. Signed as a free agent by **Tampa Bay**, October 21, 2003.

HAYDAR, Darren
(HAY-duhr, DAIR-ehn) **NSH.**

Right wing. Shoots left. 5'9", 170 lbs. Born, Toronto, Ont., October 22, 1979. Nashville's 14th choice, 248th overall, in 1999 Entry Draft.

			Regular Season														Playoffs								
Season	Club	League	GP	G	A	Pts	PIM	PP	SH	GW	S	%	+/-	TF	F%	Min	GP	G	A	Pts	PIM	PP	SH	GW	Min
1995-96	Milton Merchants	OPJHL	6	1	2	3	4	....	....	....	....	....	....	....	....	....	....	....	....	....	....	....	....	....	....
1996-97	Milton Merchants	OPJHL	51	32	68	100	68	....	....	....	....	....	....	....	....	....	....	....	....	....	....	....	....	....	....
1997-98	Milton Merchants	OPJHL	51	*71	*69	*140	65	....	....	....	....	....	....	....	....	....	....	....	....	....	....	....	....	....	....
1998-99	New Hampshire	H-East	41	31	30	61	34	....	....	....	....	....	....	....	....	....	....	....	....	....	....	....	....	....	....
99-2000	New Hampshire	H-East	38	22	19	41	42	....	....	....	....	....	....	....	....	....	....	....	....	....	....	....	....	....	....
2000-01	New Hampshire	H-East	39	18	23	41	38	....	....	....	....	....	....	....	....	....	....	....	....	....	....	....	....	....	....
2001-02	New Hampshire	H-East	40	31	*45	*76	28	....	....	....	....	....	....	....	....	....	....	....	....	....	....	....	....	....	....
2002-03	**Nashville**	**NHL**	**2**	**0**	**0**	**0**	**0**	**0**	**0**	**0**	**1**	**0.0**	**–1**	**0**	**0.0**	**8:54**	....	....	....	....	....	....	....	....	....
	Milwaukee	AHL	75	29	46	75	36	....	....	....	....	....	....	....	....	....	6	1	4	5	2	....	....	....	....
2003-04	Milwaukee	AHL	79	22	37	59	35	....	....	....	....	....	....	....	....	....	22	11	15	26	10	....	....	....	....
	NHL Totals		**2**	**0**	**0**	**0**	**0**	**0**	**0**	**0**	**1**	**0.0**		**0**	**0.0**	**8:54**	....	....	....	....	....	....	....	....	....

Hockey East Second All-Star Team (1999, 2000) • Hockey East Rookie of the Year (1999) • Hockey East First All-Star Team (2002) • AHL All-Rookie Team (2003) • Dudley "Red" Garrett Memorial Trophy (Top Rookie – AHL) (2003)

HEALEY, Paul
(HEE-lee, PAWL)

Left wing. Shoots right. 6'2", 198 lbs. Born, Edmonton, Alta., March 20, 1975. Philadelphia's 7th choice, 192nd overall, in 1993 Entry Draft.

			Regular Season														Playoffs								
Season	Club	League	GP	G	A	Pts	PIM	PP	SH	GW	S	%	+/-	TF	F%	Min	GP	G	A	Pts	PIM	PP	SH	GW	Min
1991-92	Ft. Saskatchewan	AJHL	52	11	19	30	40	....	....	....	....	....	....	....	....	....	....	....	....	....	....	....	....	....	....
1992-93	Prince Albert	WHL	72	12	20	32	66	....	....	....	....	....	....	....	....	....	....	....	....	....	....	....	....	....	....
1993-94	Prince Albert	WHL	63	23	26	49	70	....	....	....	....	....	....	....	....	....	....	....	....	....	....	....	....	....	....
1994-95	Prince Albert	WHL	71	43	50	93	67	....	....	....	....	....	....	....	....	....	12	3	4	7	2	....	....	....	....
1995-96	Hershey Bears	AHL	60	7	15	22	35	....	....	....	....	....	....	....	....	....	....	....	....	....	....	....	....	....	....
1996-97	**Philadelphia**	**NHL**	**2**	**0**	**0**	**0**	**0**	**0**	**0**	**0**	**0**	**0.0**	**0**	....	....	....	....	....	....	....	....	....	....	....	....
	Philadelphia	AHL	64	21	19	40	56	....	....	....	....	....	....	....	....	....	10	4	1	5	10	....	....	....	....
1997-98	**Philadelphia**	**NHL**	**4**	**0**	**0**	**0**	**12**	**0**	**0**	**0**	**0**	**0.0**	**0**	....	....	....	....	....	....	....	....	....	....	....	....
	Philadelphia	AHL	71	34	18	52	48	....	....	....	....	....	....	....	....	....	20	6	2	8	4	....	....	....	....
1998-99	Philadelphia	AHL	72	26	20	46	39	....	....	....	....	....	....	....	....	....	15	4	6	10	11	....	....	....	....
99-2000	Milwaukee	IHL	76	21	18	39	28	....	....	....	....	....	....	....	....	....	3	1	2	3	0	....	....	....	....
2000-01	Hamilton	AHL	79	39	32	71	34	....	....	....	....	....	....	....	....	....	....	....	....	....	....	....	....	....	....
2001-02	**Toronto**	**NHL**	**21**	**3**	**7**	**10**	**2**	**0**	**0**	**0**	**29**	**10.3**	**7**	**5**	**60.0**	**11:03**	**18**	**0**	**1**	**1**	**2**	**0**	**0**	**0**	**9:01**
	St. John's	AHL	58	27	29	56	30	....	....	....	....	....	....	....	....	....	2	1	1	2	8	....	....	....	....
2002-03	**Toronto**	**NHL**	**44**	**3**	**7**	**10**	**16**	**1**	**0**	**0**	**43**	**7.0**	**8**	**13**	**38.5**	**12:00**	**4**	**0**	**1**	**1**	**2**	**0**	**0**	**0**	**9:14**
	St. John's	AHL	17	6	10	16	12	....	....	....	....	....	....	....	....	....	....	....	....	....	....	....	....	....	....
2003-04	**NY Rangers**	**NHL**	**4**	**0**	**0**	**0**	**0**	**0**	**0**	**0**	**0**	**0.0**	**0**	**1**	**0.0**	**4:50**	....	....	....	....	....	....	....	....	....
	Hartford	AHL	50	11	10	21	37	....	....	....	....	....	....	....	....	....	....	....	....	....	....	....	....	....	....
	San Antonio	AHL	18	5	5	10	20	....	....	....	....	....	....	....	....	....	....	....	....	....	....	....	....	....	....
	NHL Totals		**75**	**6**	**14**	**20**	**30**	**1**	**0**	**0**	**72**	**8.3**		**19**	**42.1**	**11:18**	**22**	**0**	**2**	**2**	**4**	**0**	**0**	**0**	**9:03**

WHL East Second All-Star Team (1995)

Traded to **Nashville** by **Philadelphia** for Matt Henderson, September 27, 1999. Signed as a free agent by **Edmonton**, August 31, 2000. Signed as a free agent by **Toronto**, July 24, 2001. Signed as a free agent by **NY Rangers**, July 28, 2003. Traded to **Florida** by **NY Rangers** for Jeff Paul, March 9, 2004.

HEATLEY, Dany
(HEET-lee, DA-nee) **ATL.**

Right wing. Shoots left. 6'3", 215 lbs. Born, Freiburg, West Germany, January 21, 1981. Atlanta's 1st choice, 2nd overall, in 2000 Entry Draft.

			Regular Season														Playoffs								
Season	Club	League	GP	G	A	Pts	PIM	PP	SH	GW	S	%	+/-	TF	F%	Min	GP	G	A	Pts	PIM	PP	SH	GW	Min
1996-97	Calgary Blazers	AMHL	25	30	42	72	26	....	....	....	....	....	....	....	....	....	....	....	....	....	....	....	....	....	....
1997-98	Calgary Buffaloes	AMHL	36	39	42	*81	34	....	....	....	....	....	....	....	....	....	10	10	12	*22	30	....	....	....	....
1998-99	Calgary Canucks	AJHL	60	*70	56	*126	91	....	....	....	....	....	....	....	....	....	13	*22	13	*35	6	....	....	....	....
99-2000	U. of Wisconsin	WCHA	38	28	28	56	32	....	....	....	....	....	....	....	....	....	....	....	....	....	....	....	....	....	....
2000-01	U. of Wisconsin	WCHA	39	24	33	57	74	....	....	....	....	....	....	....	....	....	....	....	....	....	....	....	....	....	....
2001-02	**Atlanta**	**NHL**	**82**	**26**	**41**	**67**	**56**	**7**	**0**	**4**	**202**	**12.9**	**–19**	**116**	**32.8**	**19:53**	....	....	....	....	....	....	....	....	....
2002-03	**Atlanta**	**NHL**	**77**	**41**	**48**	**89**	**58**	**19**	**1**	**6**	**252**	**16.3**	**–8**	**49**	**36.7**	**21:57**	....	....	....	....	....	....	....	....	....
2003-04	**Atlanta**	**NHL**	**31**	**13**	**12**	**25**	**18**	**5**	**0**	**3**	**83**	**15.7**	**–8**	**41**	**24.4**	**19:53**	....	....	....	....	....	....	....	....	....
	NHL Totals		**190**	**80**	**101**	**181**	**132**	**31**	**1**	**13**	**537**	**14.9**		**206**	**32.0**	**20:43**	....	....	....	....	....	....	....	....	....

WCHA First All-Star Team (2000) • WCHA Rookie of the Year (2000) • NCAA West Second All-American Team (2000) • WCHA Second All-Star Team (2001) • NCAA West First All-American Team (2001) • NHL All-Rookie Team (2002) • Calder Memorial Trophy (2002)

Played in NHL All-Star Game (2003)

• Missed majority of 2003-04 season recovering from injuries suffered in automobile accident, September 29, 2003.

HECHT, Jochen
(HEHKHT, YOH-khehn) **BUF.**

Left wing. Shoots left. 6'1", 200 lbs. Born, Mannheim, West Germany, June 21, 1977. St. Louis' 1st choice, 49th overall, in 1995 Entry Draft.

			Regular Season														Playoffs								
Season	Club	League	GP	G	A	Pts	PIM	PP	SH	GW	S	%	+/-	TF	F%	Min	GP	G	A	Pts	PIM	PP	SH	GW	Min
1993-94	Mannheim Jr.	German-Jr.	28	27	13	40	103	....	....	....	....	....	....	....	....	....	....	....	....	....	....	....	....	....	....
1994-95	Adler Mannheim	Germany	43	11	12	23	68	....	....	....	....	....	....	....	....	....	10	5	4	9	12	....	....	....	....
1995-96	Adler Mannheim	Germany	44	12	16	28	68	....	....	....	....	....	....	....	....	....	8	3	2	5	6	....	....	....	....
1996-97	Adler Mannheim	Germany	46	21	21	42	36	....	....	....	....	....	....	....	....	....	9	3	3	6	4	....	....	....	....
1997-98	Adler Mannheim	Germany	44	7	19	26	42	....	....	....	....	....	....	....	....	....	10	1	1	2	14	....	....	....	....
	Adler Mannheim	EuroHL	5	0	4	4	8	....	....	....	....	....	....	....	....	....	....	....	....	....	....	....	....	....	....
	Germany	Olympics	4	1	0	1	6	....	....	....	....	....	....	....	....	....	....	....	....	....	....	....	....	....	....
1998-99	**St. Louis**	**NHL**	**3**	**0**	**0**	**0**	**0**	**0**	**0**	**0**	**4**	**0.0**	**–2**	**19**	**21.1**	**13:16**	**5**	**2**	**0**	**2**	**0**	**0**	**0**	**0**	**16:40**
	Worcester IceCats	AHL	74	21	35	56	48	....	....	....	....	....	....	....	....	....	4	1	1	2	2	....	....	....	....
99-2000	**St. Louis**	**NHL**	**63**	**13**	**21**	**34**	**28**	**5**	**0**	**1**	**140**	**9.3**	**20**	**75**	**49.3**	**15:25**	**7**	**4**	**6**	**10**	**2**	**1**	**0**	**1**	**17:02**
2000-01	**St. Louis**	**NHL**	**72**	**19**	**25**	**44**	**48**	**8**	**3**	**1**	**208**	**9.1**	**11**	**160**	**43.8**	**17:56**	**15**	**2**	**4**	**6**	**4**	**0**	**0**	**0**	**17:19**
2001-02	**Edmonton**	**NHL**	**82**	**16**	**24**	**40**	**60**	**5**	**0**	**3**	**211**	**7.6**	**4**	**26**	**53.9**	**15:00**	....	....	....	....	....	....	....	....	....
	Germany	Olympics	4	1	1	2	2	....	....	....	....	....	....	....	....	....	....	....	....	....	....	....	....	....	....
2002-03	**Buffalo**	**NHL**	**49**	**10**	**16**	**26**	**30**	**2**	**0**	**2**	**145**	**6.9**	**4**	**33**	**30.3**	**17:55**	....	....	....	....	....	....	....	....	....
2003-04	**Buffalo**	**NHL**	**64**	**15**	**37**	**52**	**49**	**2**	**1**	**0**	**174**	**8.6**	**17**	**141**	**43.3**	**19:00**	....	....	....	....	....	....	....	....	....
	NHL Totals		**333**	**73**	**123**	**196**	**215**	**22**	**4**	**7**	**882**	**8.3**		**454**	**43.2**	**16:54**	**27**	**8**	**10**	**18**	**6**	**1**	**0**	**1**	**17:07**

Traded to **Edmonton** by **St. Louis** with Marty Reasoner and Jan Horacek for Doug Weight and Michel Riesen, July 1, 2001. Traded to **Buffalo** by **Edmonton** for Atlanta's 2nd round choice (previously acquired, Edmonton selected Jeff Deslauriers) in 2002 Entry Draft and Nashville's 2nd round choice (previously acquired, Edmonton selected Jarret Stoll) in 2002 Entry Draft, June 22, 2002.

HEDICAN, Bret
(HEH-dih-kan, BREHT) **CAR.**

Defense. Shoots left. 6'2", 205 lbs. Born, St. Paul, MN, August 10, 1970. St. Louis' 10th choice, 198th overall, in 1988 Entry Draft.

			Regular Season														Playoffs								
Season	Club	League	GP	G	A	Pts	PIM	PP	SH	GW	S	%	+/-	TF	F%	Min	GP	G	A	Pts	PIM	PP	SH	GW	Min
1987-88	North St. Paul	Hi-School	23	15	19	34	16	....	....	....	....	....	....	....	....	....	....	....	....	....	....	....	....	....	....
1988-89	St. Cloud State	NCAA-3	28	5	3	8	28	....	....	....	....	....	....	....	....	....	....	....	....	....	....	....	....	....	....
1989-90	St. Cloud State	NCAA-3	36	4	17	21	37	....	....	....	....	....	....	....	....	....	....	....	....	....	....	....	....	....	....
1990-91	St. Cloud State	WCHA	41	21	26	47	26	....	....	....	....	....	....	....	....	....	....	....	....	....	....	....	....	....	....
1991-92	Team USA	Nat-Tm	54	1	8	9	59	....	....	....	....	....	....	....	....	....	....	....	....	....	....	....	....	....	....
	United States	Olympics	8	0	0	0	4	....	....	....	....	....	....	....	....	....	....	....	....	....	....	....	....	....	....
	St. Louis	**NHL**	**4**	**1**	**0**	**1**	**0**	**0**	**0**	**0**	**1**	**100.0**	**1**	....	....	....	**5**	**0**	**0**	**0**	**0**	**0**	**0**	**0**	....
1992-93	**St. Louis**	**NHL**	**42**	**0**	**8**	**8**	**30**	**0**	**0**	**0**	**40**	**0.0**	**–2**	....	....	....	**10**	**0**	**0**	**0**	**14**	**0**	**0**	**0**	....
	Peoria Rivermen	IHL	19	0	8	8	10	....	....	....	....	....	....	....	....	....	....	....	....	....	....	....	....	....	....
1993-94	**St. Louis**	**NHL**	**61**	**0**	**11**	**11**	**64**	**0**	**0**	**0**	**78**	**0.0**	**–8**	....	....	....	....	....	....	....	....	....	....	....	....
	Vancouver	**NHL**	**8**	**0**	**1**	**1**	**0**	**0**	**0**	**0**	**10**	**0.0**	**1**	....	....	....	**24**	**1**	**6**	**7**	**16**	**0**	**0**	**0**	....
1994-95	**Vancouver**	**NHL**	**45**	**2**	**11**	**13**	**34**	**0**	**0**	**0**	**56**	**3.6**	**–3**	....	....	....	**11**	**0**	**2**	**2**	**6**	**0**	**0**	**0**	....
1995-96	**Vancouver**	**NHL**	**77**	**6**	**23**	**29**	**83**	**1**	**0**	**0**	**113**	**5.3**	**8**	....	....	....	**6**	**0**	**1**	**1**	**10**	**0**	**0**	**0**	....
1996-97	**Vancouver**	**NHL**	**67**	**4**	**15**	**19**	**51**	**2**	**0**	**1**	**93**	**4.3**	**–3**	....	....	....	....	....	....	....	....	....	....	....	....
1997-98	**Vancouver**	**NHL**	**71**	**3**	**24**	**27**	**79**	**1**	**0**	**0**	**84**	**3.6**	**3**	....	....	....	....	....	....	....	....	....	....	....	....
1998-99	**Vancouver**	**NHL**	**42**	**2**	**11**	**13**	**34**	**0**	**2**	**0**	**52**	**3.8**	**7**	**0**	**0.0**	**18:40**	....	....	....	....	....	....	....	....	....
	Florida	**NHL**	**25**	**3**	**7**	**10**	**17**	**0**	**0**	**1**	**38**	**7.9**	**–2**	**0**	**0.0**	**22:24**	....	....	....	....	....	....	....	....	....
99-2000	**Florida**	**NHL**	**76**	**6**	**19**	**25**	**68**	**2**	**0**	**1**	**58**	**10.3**	**4**	**0**	**0.0**	**19:36**	**4**	**0**	**0**	**0**	**0**	**0**	**0**	**0**	**20:42**
2000-01	**Florida**	**NHL**	**70**	**5**	**15**	**20**	**72**	**4**	**0**	**1**	**104**	**4.8**	**–7**	**0**	**0.0**	**21:49**	....	....	....	....	....	....	....	....	....
2001-02	**Florida**	**NHL**	**31**	**3**	**7**	**10**	**12**	**0**	**0**	**0**	**46**	**6.5**	**–4**	**0**	**0.0**	**24:27**	....	....	....	....	....	....	....	....	....
	Carolina	**NHL**	**26**	**2**	**4**	**6**	**10**	**0**	**0**	**1**	**39**	**5.1**	**3**	**0**	**0.0**	**22:56**	**23**	**1**	**4**	**5**	**20**	**0**	**0**	**0**	**23:52**
2002-03	**Carolina**	**NHL**	**72**	**3**	**14**	**17**	**75**	**1**	**0**	**1**	**113**	**2.7**	**–24**	**0**	**0.0**	**23:02**	....	....	....	....	....	....	....	....	....
2003-04	**Carolina**	**NHL**	**81**	**7**	**17**	**24**	**64**	**2**	**0**	**3**	**112**	**6.3**	**–10**	**0**	**0.0**	**22:35**	....	....	....	....	....	....	....	....	....
	NHL Totals		**798**	**47**	**187**	**234**	**693**	**13**	**2**	**9**	**1037**	**4.5**		**0**	**0.0**	**21:45**	**83**	**2**	**13**	**15**	**66**	**0**	**0**	**0**	**23:24**

WCHA First All-Star Team (1991)

Traded to **Vancouver** by **St. Louis** with Jeff Brown and Nathan LaFayette for Craig Janney, March 21, 1994. Traded to **Florida** by **Vancouver** with Pavel Bure, Brad Ference and Vancouver's 3rd round choice (Robert Fried) in 2000 Entry Draft for Ed Jovanovski, Dave Gagner, Mike Brown, Kevin Weekes and Florida's 1st round choice (Nathan Smith) in 2000 Entry Draft, January 17, 1999. Traded to **Carolina** by **Florida** with Kevyn Adams, Tomas Malec for Sandis Ozolinsh and Byron Ritchie, January 16, 2002.

HEDIN, Pierre
(heh-DEEN, PEE-air) **TOR.**

Defense. Shoots left. 6'1", 198 lbs. Born, Ornskoldsvik, Sweden, February 19, 1978. Toronto's 8th choice, 239th overall, in 1999 Entry Draft.

Season	Club	League	GP	G	A	Pts	PIM	PP	SH	GW	S	%	+/-	TF	F%	Min	GP	G	A	Pts	PIM	PP	SH	GW	Min
1994-95	MoDo Jr.	Swede-Jr.	21	0	3	3	20	....	....	....	....	....	....	....	....	....	....	....	....	....	....	....	....	....	....
1995-96	MoDo Jr.	Swede-Jr.	29	6	8	14	34	....	....	....	....	....	....	....	....	....	....	....	....	....	....	....	....	....	....
1996-97	MoDo	Sweden	19	1	2	3	6	....	....	....	....	....	....	....	....	....	....	....	....	....	....	....	....	....	....
1997-98	MoDo Jr.	Swede-Jr.	7	1	6	7	10	....	....	....	....	....	....	....	....	....	....	....	....	....	....	....	....	....	....
	MoDo	Sweden	29	2	1	3	26	....	....	....	....	....	....	....	....	....	9	1	1	2	4	....	....	....	....
1998-99	MoDo	Sweden	41	6	5	11	28	....	....	....	....	....	....	....	....	....	13	1	1	2	12	....	....	....	....
99-2000	MoDo	Sweden	48	9	5	14	36	....	....	....	....	....	....	....	....	....	13	0	2	2	8	....	....	....	....
2000-01	MoDo	Sweden	46	5	8	13	59	....	....	....	....	....	....	....	....	....	7	3	0	3	4	....	....	....	....
2001-02	MoDo	Sweden	39	7	9	16	20	....	....	....	....	....	....	....	....	....	14	*8	2	10	10	....	....	....	....
2002-03	MoDo	Sweden	46	8	14	22	32	....	....	....	....	....	....	....	....	....	6	0	1	1	4	....	....	....	....
2003-04	**Toronto**	**NHL**	**3**	**0**	**1**	**1**	**0**	**0**	**0**	**0**	**4**	**0.0**	**–1**	**0**	**0.0**	**19:20**	....	....	....	....	....	....	....	....	....
	St. John's	AHL	62	5	19	24	52	....	....	....	....	....	....	....	....	....	....	....	....	....	....	....	....	....	....
	NHL Totals		**3**	**0**	**1**	**1**	**0**	**0**	**0**	**0**	**4**	**0.0**		**0**	**0.0**	**19:20**	....	....	....	....	....	....	....	....	....

HEDSTROM, Jonathan
(HEHD-struhm, JAWN-ah-thuhn) **ANA.**

Right wing. Shoots left. 6', 200 lbs. Born, Skelleftea, Sweden, December 27, 1977. Toronto's 8th choice, 221st overall, in 1997 Entry Draft.

Season	Club	League	GP	G	A	Pts	PIM	PP	SH	GW	S	%	+/-	TF	F%	Min	GP	G	A	Pts	PIM	PP	SH	GW	Min
1995-96	Skelleftea AIK	Swede-2	7	0	0	0	0	....	....	....	....	....	....	....	....	....	....	....	....	....	....	....	....	....	....
1996-97	Skelleftea AIK Jr.	Swede-Jr.	9	4	4	8	....	....	....	....	....	....	....	....	....	....	....	....	....	....	....	....	....	....	....
	Skelleftea AIK	Swede-2	12	1	1	2	10	....	....	....	....	....	....	....	....	....	6	0	0	0	2	....	....	....	....
1997-98	Skelleftea AIK Jr.	Swede-Jr.	1	0	0	0	2	....	....	....	....	....	....	....	....	....	....	....	....	....	....	....	....	....	....
	Skelleftea AIK	Swede-2	16	2	3	5	....	....	....	....	....	....	....	....	....	....	....	....	....	....	....	....	....	....	....
1998-99	Skelleftea AIK	Swede-2	36	15	28	43	74	....	....	....	....	....	....	....	....	....	....	....	....	....	....	....	....	....	....
99-2000	Lulea HF	Sweden	48	9	17	26	46	....	....	....	....	....	....	....	....	....	9	2	1	3	12	....	....	....	....
2000-01	Lulea HF	Sweden	46	9	19	28	68	....	....	....	....	....	....	....	....	....	12	1	6	7	16	....	....	....	....
2001-02	Lulea HF	Sweden	47	11	7	18	38	....	....	....	....	....	....	....	....	....	4	2	1	3	6	....	....	....	....
2002-03	**Anaheim**	**NHL**	**4**	**0**	**0**	**0**	**0**	**0**	**0**	**0**	**3**	**0.0**	**–1**	**1**	**0.0**	**7:51**	....	....	....	....	....	....	....	....	....
	Cincinnati	AHL	50	14	21	35	62	....	....	....	....	....	....	....	....	....	....	....	....	....	....	....	....	....	....
2003-04	Djurgarden	Sweden	48	12	22	34	94	....	....	....	....	....	....	....	....	....	3	0	2	2	12	....	....	....	....
	NHL Totals		**4**	**0**	**0**	**0**	**0**	**0**	**0**	**0**	**3**	**0.0**		**1**	**0.0**	**7:51**	....	....	....	....	....	....	....	....	....

Rights traded to **Anaheim** by **Toronto** for Anaheim's 6th (Vadim Sozinov) and 7th (Markus Seikola) round choices in 2000 Entry Draft, June 25, 2000. Signed as a free agent by **Djurgarden** (Sweden), September 1, 2003

HEEREMA, Jeff
(HEER-eh-muh, JEHF)

Right wing. Shoots right. 6'1", 190 lbs. Born, Thunder Bay, Ont., January 17, 1980. Carolina's 1st choice, 11th overall, in 1998 Entry Draft.

Season	Club	League	GP	G	A	Pts	PIM	PP	SH	GW	S	%	+/-	TF	F%	Min	GP	G	A	Pts	PIM	PP	SH	GW	Min
1996-97	T. Bay Kings	TBMHL	54	42	29	71	112	....	....	....	....	....	....	....	....	....	....	....	....	....	....	....	....	....	....
1997-98	Sarnia Sting	OHL	63	32	40	72	88	....	....	....	....	....	....	....	....	....	5	4	1	5	10	....	....	....	....
1998-99	Sarnia Sting	OHL	62	31	39	70	113	....	....	....	....	....	....	....	....	....	6	5	1	6	0	....	....	....	....
99-2000	Sarnia Sting	OHL	67	36	41	77	62	....	....	....	....	....	....	....	....	....	7	4	2	6	10	....	....	....	....
2000-01	Cincinnati	IHL	73	17	16	33	42	....	....	....	....	....	....	....	....	....	4	0	0	0	0	....	....	....	....
2001-02	Lowell	AHL	76	33	37	70	90	....	....	....	....	....	....	....	....	....	5	2	3	5	2	....	....	....	....
2002-03	**Carolina**	**NHL**	**10**	**3**	**0**	**3**	**2**	**1**	**0**	**0**	**16**	**18.8**	**–2**	**0**	**0.0**	**9:37**	....	....	....	....	....	....	....	....	....
	Lowell	AHL	36	15	17	32	25	....	....	....	....	....	....	....	....	....	....	....	....	....	....	....	....	....	....
2003-04	**St. Louis**	**NHL**	**22**	**1**	**2**	**3**	**4**	**0**	**0**	**1**	**28**	**3.6**	**–5**	**2**	**50.0**	**10:26**	....	....	....	....	....	....	....	....	....
	Worcester IceCats	AHL	1	0	0	0	2	....	....	....	....	....	....	....	....	....	....	....	....	....	....	....	....	....	....
	Hartford	AHL	41	12	15	27	25	....	....	....	....	....	....	....	....	....	4	0	0	0	9	....	....	....	....
	NHL Totals		**32**	**4**	**2**	**6**	**6**	**1**	**0**	**1**	**44**	**9.1**		**2**	**50.0**	**10:11**	....	....	....	....	....	....	....	....	....

Claimed on waivers by **NY Rangers** from **Carolina**, September 30, 2003. Claimed by **St. Louis** from **NY Rangers** in Waiver Draft, October 3, 2003. Claimed on waivers by **NY Rangers** from **St. Louis**, January 10, 2004.

HEINS, Shawn
(HIGHNS, SHAWN)

Defense. Shoots left. 6'4", 210 lbs. Born, Eganville, Ont., December 24, 1973.

Season	Club	League	GP	G	A	Pts	PIM	PP	SH	GW	S	%	+/-	TF	F%	Min	GP	G	A	Pts	PIM	PP	SH	GW	Min
1991-92	Peterborough	OHL	49	1	1	2	73	....	....	....	....	....	....	....	....	....	7	0	0	0	5	....	....	....	....
1992-93	Peterborough	OHL	5	0	0	0	10	....	....	....	....	....	....	....	....	....	....	....	....	....	....	....	....	....	....
	Windsor Spitfires	OHL	53	7	10	17	107	....	....	....	....	....	....	....	....	....	....	....	....	....	....	....	....	....	....
1993-94	Renfrew	NOJHA	32	16	34	50	250	....	....	....	....	....	....	....	....	....	....	....	....	....	....	....	....	....	....
1994-95	Renfrew	NOJHA	35	30	49	79	188	....	....	....	....	....	....	....	....	....	....	....	....	....	....	....	....	....	....
1995-96	Mobile Mysticks	ECHL	62	7	20	27	152	....	....	....	....	....	....	....	....	....	....	....	....	....	....	....	....	....	....
	Cape Breton	AHL	1	0	0	0	0	....	....	....	....	....	....	....	....	....	....	....	....	....	....	....	....	....	....
1996-97	Mobile Mysticks	ECHL	56	6	17	23	253	....	....	....	....	....	....	....	....	....	3	0	2	2	2	....	....	....	....
	Kansas City	IHL	6	0	0	0	9	....	....	....	....	....	....	....	....	....	....	....	....	....	....	....	....	....	....
1997-98	Kansas City	IHL	82	22	28	50	303	....	....	....	....	....	....	....	....	....	11	1	0	1	49	....	....	....	....
1998-99	Team Canada	Nat-Tm	36	5	16	21	66	....	....	....	....	....	....	....	....	....	....	....	....	....	....	....	....	....	....
	San Jose	**NHL**	**5**	**0**	**0**	**0**	**13**	**0**	**0**	**0**	**4**	**0.0**	**0**	**0**	**0.0**	**13:38**	....	....	....	....	....	....	....	....	....
	Kentucky	AHL	18	2	2	4	108	....	....	....	....	....	....	....	....	....	12	2	7	9	10	....	....	....	....
99-2000	**San Jose**	**NHL**	**1**	**0**	**0**	**0**	**2**	**0**	**0**	**0**	**1**	**0.0**	**–1**	**0**	**0.0**	**10:57**	....	....	....	....	....	....	....	....	....
	Kentucky	AHL	69	11	52	63	238	....	....	....	....	....	....	....	....	....	9	3	3	6	44	....	....	....	....
2000-01	**San Jose**	**NHL**	**38**	**3**	**4**	**7**	**57**	**2**	**0**	**0**	**45**	**6.7**	**2**	**0**	**0.0**	**10:15**	**2**	**0**	**0**	**0**	**0**	**0**	**0**	**0**	**7:31**
2001-02	**San Jose**	**NHL**	**17**	**0**	**2**	**2**	**24**	**0**	**0**	**0**	**20**	**0.0**	**1**	**0**	**0.0**	**9:46**	....	....	....	....	....	....	....	....	....
2002-03	**San Jose**	**NHL**	**20**	**0**	**1**	**1**	**9**	**0**	**0**	**0**	**10**	**0.0**	**–2**	**0**	**0.0**	**8:32**	....	....	....	....	....	....	....	....	....
	Pittsburgh	**NHL**	**27**	**1**	**1**	**2**	**33**	**0**	**0**	**1**	**28**	**3.6**	**–2**	**0**	**0.0**	**19:11**	....	....	....	....	....	....	....	....	....

			Regular Season														Playoffs								
Season	Club	League	GP	G	A	Pts	PIM	PP	SH	GW	S	%	+/-	TF	F%	Min	GP	G	A	Pts	PIM	PP	SH	GW	Min
2003-04	**Atlanta**	**NHL**	**17**	**0**	**4**	**4**	**16**	**0**	**0**	**0**	**17**	**0.0**	**–1**	**0**	**0.0**	**13:53**	....	....	....	....	....	....	....	....	....
	Chicago Wolves	AHL	58	12	19	31	120	....	....	....	....	....	....	....	....	....	10	1	5	6	44	....	....	....	....
	NHL Totals		**125**	**4**	**12**	**16**	**154**	**2**	**0**	**1**	**125**	**3.2**		**0**	**0.0**	**12:28**	**2**	**0**	**0**	**0**	**0**	**0**	**0**	**0**	**7:31**

AHL First All-Star Team (2000)

Signed as a free agent by **San Jose**, January 5, 1997. • Missed majority of 2000-01 season recovering from head injury suffered in game vs. Chicago, February 14, 2001. • Missed majority of 2001-02 season recovering from knee (December 4, 2001 vs. Calgary) and jaw (January 19, 2002 vs. Colorado) injuries. Traded to **Pittsburgh** by **San Jose** for Pittsburgh's 5th round choice (Patrick Ehelechner) in 2003 Entry Draft, February 9, 2003. Signed as a free agent by **Atlanta**, September 10, 2003. Claimed on waivers by **NY Rangers** from **Atlanta**, September 30, 2003. Claimed by **Atlanta** from **NY Rangers** in Waiver Draft, October 3, 2003.

HEISTEN, Barrett

(HIGH-stehn, BAIR-reht)

Left wing. Shoots left. 6'1", 200 lbs. Born, Anchorage, AK, March 19, 1980. Buffalo's 1st choice, 20th overall, in 1999 Entry Draft.

Season	Club	League	GP	G	A	Pts	PIM	PP	SH	GW	S	%	+/-	TF	F%	Min	GP	G	A	Pts	PIM	PP	SH	GW	Min
1996-97	Anchorage	AAHL	39	35	29	64	....	....	....	....	....	....	....	....	....	....	....	....	....	....	....	....	....	....	....
1997-98	U.S. National U-18	USDP	50	11	26	37	245	....	....	....	....	....	....	....	....	....	....	....	....	....	....	....	....	....	....
1998-99	U. of Maine	H-East	34	12	16	28	72	....	....	....	....	....	....	....	....	....	....	....	....	....	....	....	....	....	....
99-2000	U. of Maine	H-East	37	13	24	37	86	....	....	....	....	....	....	....	....	....	....	....	....	....	....	....	....	....	....
2000-01	Seattle	WHL	58	20	57	77	61	....	....	....	....	....	....	....	....	....	9	2	6	8	20	....	....	....	....
2001-02	**NY Rangers**	**NHL**	**10**	**0**	**0**	**0**	**2**	**0**	**0**	**0**	**7**	**0.0**	**–4**	**7**	**28.6**	**7:36**	....	....	....	....	....	....	....	....	....
	Hartford	AHL	49	9	9	18	60	....	....	....	....	....	....	....	....	....	....	....	....	....	....	....	....	....	....
	Utah Grizzlies	AHL	12	5	1	6	14	....	....	....	....	....	....	....	....	....	5	1	0	1	4	....	....	....	....
2002-03	Utah Grizzlies	AHL	58	10	10	20	47	....	....	....	....	....	....	....	....	....	2	0	0	0	4	....	....	....	....
2003-04	Utah Grizzlies	AHL	73	4	13	17	98	....	....	....	....	....	....	....	....	....	....	....	....	....	....	....	....	....	....
	NHL Totals		**10**	**0**	**0**	**0**	**2**	**0**	**0**	**0**	**7**	**0.0**		**7**	**28.6**	**7:36**	....	....	....	....	....	....	....	....	....

• Left **University of Maine** (H-East) and signed with **Seattle** (WHL), August 7, 2000. Signed as a free agent by **NY Rangers**, June 16, 2001. Traded to **Dallas** by **NY Rangers** with Manny Malhotra for Martin Rucinsky and Roman Lyashenko, March 12, 2002.

HEJDUK, Milan

(HAY-dook, MEE-lan) **COL.**

Right wing. Shoots right. 5'11", 185 lbs. Born, Usti-nad-Labem, Czech., February 14, 1976. Quebec's 6th choice, 87th overall, in 1994 Entry Draft.

Season	Club	League	GP	G	A	Pts	PIM	PP	SH	GW	S	%	+/-	TF	F%	Min	GP	G	A	Pts	PIM	PP	SH	GW	Min
1993-94	HC Pardubice	Czech	22	6	3	9	....	....	....	....	....	....	....	....	....	....	10	5	1	6	....	....	....	....	....
1994-95	HC Pardubice	Czech	43	11	13	24	6	....	....	....	....	....	....	....	....	....	6	3	1	4	0	....	....	....	....
1995-96	Pardubice	Czech	37	13	7	20	....	....	....	....	....	....	....	....	....	....	....	....	....	....	....	....	....	....	....
1996-97	Pardubice	Czech	51	27	11	38	10	....	....	....	....	....	....	....	....	....	10	6	0	6	27	....	....	....	....
1997-98	Pardubice	Czech	48	26	19	45	20	....	....	....	....	....	....	....	....	....	3	0	0	0	2	....	....	....	....
	Czech Republic	Olympics	4	0	0	0	2	....	....	....	....	....	....	....	....	....	....	....	....	....	....	....	....	....	....
1998-99	**Colorado**	**NHL**	**82**	**14**	**34**	**48**	**26**	**4**	**0**	**5**	**178**	**7.9**	**8**	**2**	**50.0**	**15:45**	**16**	**6**	**6**	**12**	**4**	**1**	**0**	**3**	**15:53**
99-2000	**Colorado**	**NHL**	**82**	**36**	**36**	**72**	**16**	**13**	**0**	**9**	**228**	**15.8**	**14**	**3**	**100.0**	**19:58**	**17**	**5**	**4**	**9**	**6**	**3**	**0**	**1**	**19:56**
2000-01♦	**Colorado**	**NHL**	**80**	**41**	**38**	**79**	**36**	**12**	**1**	**9**	**213**	**19.2**	**32**	**3**	**33.3**	**19:52**	**23**	**7**	***16**	**23**	**6**	**4**	**0**	**1**	**21:33**
2001-02	**Colorado**	**NHL**	**62**	**21**	**23**	**44**	**24**	**7**	**1**	**5**	**139**	**15.1**	**0**	**5**	**40.0**	**20:11**	**16**	**3**	**3**	**6**	**4**	**1**	**0**	**0**	**18:24**
	Czech Republic	Olympics	4	1	0	1	0	....	....	....	....	....	....	....	....	....	....	....	....	....	....	....	....	....	....
2002-03	**Colorado**	**NHL**	**82**	***50**	**48**	**98**	**32**	**18**	**0**	**4**	**244**	**20.5**	**52**	**43**	**44.2**	**19:50**	**7**	**2**	**2**	**4**	**2**	**1**	**0**	**0**	**20:42**
2003-04	**Colorado**	**NHL**	**82**	**35**	**40**	**75**	**20**	**16**	**0**	**6**	**237**	**14.8**	**19**	**69**	**47.8**	**18:46**	**11**	**5**	**2**	**7**	**0**	**2**	**0**	**0**	**18:40**
	NHL Totals		**470**	**197**	**219**	**416**	**154**	**70**	**2**	**38**	**1239**	**15.9**		**125**	**47.2**	**19:01**	**90**	**28**	**33**	**61**	**22**	**12**	**0**	**5**	**19:16**

NHL All-Rookie Team (1999) • NHL Second All-Star Team (2003) • Bud Light Plus/Minus Award (2003) (tied with Peter Forsberg) • Maurice "Rocket" Richard Trophy (2003)

Played in NHL All-Star Game (2000, 2001)

Rights transferred to **Colorado** after **Quebec** franchise relocated, June 21, 1995.

HELMER, Bryan

(HEHL-muhr, BRIGH-uhn) **DET.**

Defense. Shoots right. 6'1", 200 lbs. Born, Sault Ste. Marie, Ont., July 15, 1972.

Season	Club	League	GP	G	A	Pts	PIM	PP	SH	GW	S	%	+/-	TF	F%	Min	GP	G	A	Pts	PIM	PP	SH	GW	Min
1989-90	Wellington Dukes	MTJHL	44	4	20	24	204	....	....	....	....	....	....	....	....	....	....	....	....	....	....	....	....	....	....
	Belleville Bulls	OHL	6	0	1	1	0	....	....	....	....	....	....	....	....	....	....	....	....	....	....	....	....	....	....
1990-91	Wellington Dukes	MTJHL	50	11	14	25	109	....	....	....	....	....	....	....	....	....	....	....	....	....	....	....	....	....	....
1991-92	Wellington Dukes	MTJHL	42	17	31	48	66	....	....	....	....	....	....	....	....	....	3	2	1	3	0	....	....	....	....
1992-93	Wellington Dukes	MTJHL	48	21	54	75	84	....	....	....	....	....	....	....	....	....	9	4	8	12	22	....	....	....	....
1993-94	Albany River Rats	AHL	65	4	19	23	79	....	....	....	....	....	....	....	....	....	5	0	0	0	9	....	....	....	....
1994-95	Albany River Rats	AHL	77	7	36	43	101	....	....	....	....	....	....	....	....	....	7	1	0	1	0	....	....	....	....
1995-96	Albany River Rats	AHL	80	14	30	44	107	....	....	....	....	....	....	....	....	....	4	2	0	2	6	....	....	....	....
1996-97	Albany River Rats	AHL	77	12	27	39	113	....	....	....	....	....	....	....	....	....	16	1	7	8	10	....	....	....	....
1997-98	Albany River Rats	AHL	80	14	49	63	101	....	....	....	....	....	....	....	....	....	13	4	9	13	18	....	....	....	....
1998-99	**Phoenix**	**NHL**	**11**	**0**	**0**	**0**	**23**	**0**	**0**	**0**	**11**	**0.0**	**2**	**0**	**0.0**	**7:43**	....	....	....	....	....	....	....	....	....
	Las Vegas	IHL	8	1	3	4	28	....	....	....	....	....	....	....	....	....	....	....	....	....	....	....	....	....	....
	St. Louis	**NHL**	**29**	**0**	**4**	**4**	**19**	**0**	**0**	**0**	**38**	**0.0**	**3**	**1**	**100.0**	**19:08**	....	....	....	....	....	....	....	....	....
	Worcester IceCats	AHL	16	7	8	15	18	....	....	....	....	....	....	....	....	....	4	0	0	0	12	....	....	....	....
99-2000	**St. Louis**	**NHL**	**15**	**1**	**1**	**2**	**10**	**1**	**0**	**1**	**19**	**5.3**	**–3**	**0**	**0.0**	**16:15**	....	....	....	....	....	....	....	....	....
	Worcester IceCats	AHL	54	10	25	35	124	....	....	....	....	....	....	....	....	....	9	1	4	5	10	....	....	....	....
2000-01	**Vancouver**	**NHL**	**20**	**2**	**4**	**6**	**18**	**0**	**0**	**0**	**28**	**7.1**	**0**	**0**	**0.0**	**16:51**	....	....	....	....	....	....	....	....	....
	Kansas City	IHL	42	4	15	19	76	....	....	....	....	....	....	....	....	....	....	....	....	....	....	....	....	....	....
2001-02	**Vancouver**	**NHL**	**40**	**5**	**5**	**10**	**53**	**2**	**0**	**1**	**43**	**11.6**	**10**	**0**	**0.0**	**12:04**	**6**	**0**	**0**	**0**	**0**	**0**	**0**	**0**	**9:09**
	Manitoba Moose	AHL	34	6	18	24	69	....	....	....	....	....	....	....	....	....	....	....	....	....	....	....	....	....	....
2002-03	**Vancouver**	**NHL**	**2**	**0**	**0**	**0**	**0**	**0**	**0**	**0**	**2**	**0.0**	**1**	**0**	**0.0**	**13:24**	....	....	....	....	....	....	....	....	....
	Manitoba Moose	AHL	60	7	24	31	82	....	....	....	....	....	....	....	....	....	14	0	4	4	20	....	....	....	....
2003-04	**Phoenix**	**NHL**	**17**	**0**	**1**	**1**	**10**	**0**	**0**	**0**	**10**	**0.0**	**–5**	**0**	**0.0**	**12:46**	....	....	....	....	....	....	....	....	....
	Springfield	AHL	9	1	6	7	6	....	....	....	....	....	....	....	....	....	....	....	....	....	....	....	....	....	....
	NHL Totals		**134**	**8**	**15**	**23**	**133**	**3**	**0**	**2**	**151**	**5.3**		**1**	**100.0**	**14:32**	**6**	**0**	**0**	**0**	**0**	**0**	**0**	**0**	**9:09**

AHL First All-Star Team (1998)

Signed as a free agent by **New Jersey**, July 10, 1994. Signed as a free agent by **Phoenix**, July 17, 1998. Claimed on waivers by **St. Louis** from **Phoenix**, December 19, 1998. Signed as a free agent by **Vancouver**, August 21, 2000. Traded to **Phoenix** by **Vancouver** for Martin Grenier, July 25, 2003. • Missed majority of 2003-04 season recovering from shoulder injury suffered in training camp, Septrmber 29, 2003. Signed as a free agent by **Detroit**, July, 2004.

HEMSKY, Ales

(HEHM-skee, ahl-EHSH) **EDM.**

Right wing. Shoots right. 6', 192 lbs. Born, Pardubice, Czech., August 13, 1983. Edmonton's 1st choice, 13th overall, in 2001 Entry Draft.

Season	Club	League	GP	G	A	Pts	PIM	PP	SH	GW	S	%	+/-	TF	F%	Min	GP	G	A	Pts	PIM	PP	SH	GW	Min
99-2000	Pardubice Jr.	Czech-Jr.	45	20	36	56	54	....	....	....	....	....	....	....	....	....	7	4	14	18	36	....	....	....	....
	Pardubice	Czech	4	0	1	1	0	....	....	....	....	....	....	....	....	....	....	....	....	....	....	....	....	....	....
2000-01	Hull Olympiques	QMJHL	68	36	64	100	67	....	....	....	....	....	....	....	....	....	5	2	3	5	2	....	....	....	....
2001-02	Hull Olympiques	QMJHL	53	27	70	97	86	....	....	....	....	....	....	....	....	....	10	6	10	16	6	....	....	....	....
2002-03	**Edmonton**	**NHL**	**59**	**6**	**24**	**30**	**14**	**0**	**0**	**1**	**50**	**12.0**	**5**	**3**	**33.3**	**12:04**	**6**	**0**	**0**	**0**	**0**	**0**	**0**	**0**	**12:46**
2003-04	**Edmonton**	**NHL**	**71**	**12**	**22**	**34**	**14**	**4**	**0**	**3**	**87**	**13.8**	**–7**	**3**	**33.3**	**14:26**	....	....	....	....	....	....	....	....	....
	NHL Totals		**130**	**18**	**46**	**64**	**28**	**4**	**0**	**4**	**137**	**13.1**		**6**	**33.3**	**13:22**	**6**	**0**	**0**	**0**	**0**	**0**	**0**	**0**	**12:46**

QMJHL Second All-Star Team (2002)

HENDERSON, Jay

(HEHN-duhr-SOHN, JAY)

Left wing. Shoots left. 5'11", 190 lbs. Born, Edmonton, Alta., September 17, 1978. Boston's 12th choice, 246th overall, in 1997 Entry Draft.

Season	Club	League	GP	G	A	Pts	PIM	PP	SH	GW	S	%	+/-	TF	F%	Min	GP	G	A	Pts	PIM	PP	SH	GW	Min
1993-94	Sherwood Park	AMBHL	31	12	21	33	36	....	....	....	....	....	....	....	....	....	....	....	....	....	....	....	....	....	....
1994-95	Red Deer Rebels	WHL	54	3	9	12	80	....	....	....	....	....	....	....	....	....	....	....	....	....	....	....	....	....	....
1995-96	Red Deer Rebels	WHL	71	15	13	28	139	....	....	....	....	....	....	....	....	....	10	1	1	2	11	....	....	....	....
1996-97	Edmonton Ice	WHL	66	28	32	60	127	....	....	....	....	....	....	....	....	....	....	....	....	....	....	....	....	....	....
1997-98	Edmonton Ice	WHL	72	49	45	94	130	....	....	....	....	....	....	....	....	....	....	....	....	....	....	....	....	....	....
	Providence Bruins	AHL	11	3	1	4	11	....	....	....	....	....	....	....	....	....	....	....	....	....	....	....	....	....	....
1998-99	**Boston**	**NHL**	**4**	**0**	**0**	**0**	**2**	**0**	**0**	**0**	**4**	**0.0**	**–1**	**0**	**0.0**	**5:39**	....	....	....	....	....	....	....	....	....
	Providence Bruins	AHL	55	7	9	16	172	....	....	....	....	....	....	....	....	....	2	0	0	0	2	....	....	....	....
99-2000	**Boston**	**NHL**	**16**	**1**	**3**	**4**	**9**	**0**	**0**	**0**	**18**	**5.6**	**1**	**2**	**0.0**	**5:22**	....	....	....	....	....	....	....	....	....
	Providence Bruins	AHL	60	18	27	45	200	....	....	....	....	....	....	....	....	....	14	1	2	3	16	....	....	....	....
2000-01	**Boston**	**NHL**	**13**	**0**	**0**	**0**	**26**	**0**	**0**	**0**	**12**	**0.0**	**–1**	**3**	**100.0**	**6:58**	....	....	....	....	....	....	....	....	....
	Providence Bruins	AHL	41	9	7	16	121	....	....	....	....	....	....	....	....	....	1	0	0	0	2	....	....	....	....

			Regular Season														Playoffs								
Season	Club	League	GP	G	A	Pts	PIM	PP	SH	GW	S	%	+/-	TF	F%	Min	GP	G	A	Pts	PIM	PP	SH	GW	Min
2001-02	Boston	NHL	DID NOT PLAY – INJURED																						
2002-03	Providence Bruins	AHL	39	7	13	20	152																		
	Hartford	AHL	14	3	4	7	27																		
	Houston Aeros	AHL	22	7	4	11	65										23	2	2	4	25				
2003-04	Milwaukee	AHL	70	15	16	31	122										18	1	3	4	55				
	NHL Totals		33	1	3	4	37	0	0	0	34	2.9		5	60.0	6:02									

• Missed entire 2001-02 season recovering from knee injury suffered in pre-season game vs. Detroit, September 21, 2001. Traded to **NY Rangers** by **Boston** for Boston's 9th round choice (later traded to San Jose - San Jose selected Brian Mahoney-Wilson) in 2004 Entry Draft, January 17, 2003. Traded to **Minnesota** by **NY Rangers** for Cory Larose, February 20, 2003. Signed as a free agent by **Milwaukee** (AHL), September 3, 2003.

HENDRICKSON, Darby
(HEHN-drihk-SOHN, DAHR-bee) **COL.**

Center. Shoots left. 6'1", 195 lbs. Born, Richfield, MN, August 28, 1972. Toronto's 3rd choice, 73rd overall, in 1990 Entry Draft.

Season	Club	League	GP	G	A	Pts	PIM	PP	SH	GW	S	%	+/-	TF	F%	Min	GP	G	A	Pts	PIM	PP	SH	GW	Min
1987-88	Richfield Spartans	Hi-School	22	12	9	21	10																		
1988-89	Richfield Spartans	Hi-School	22	22	20	42	12																		
1989-90	Richfield Spartans	Hi-School	24	23	27	50	49																		
1990-91	Richfield Spartans	Hi-School	27	32	29	61																			
1991-92	U. of Minnesota	WCHA	41	25	28	53	61																		
1992-93	U. of Minnesota	WCHA	31	12	15	27	35																		
1993-94	Team USA	Nat-Tm	59	12	16	28	30																		
	United States	Olympics	8	0	0	0	6																		
	Toronto	NHL															2	0	0	0	0	0	0	0	
	St. John's	AHL	6	4	1	5	4										3	1	1	2	0				
1994-95	St. John's	AHL	59	16	20	36	48																		
	Toronto	NHL	8	0	1	1	4	0	0	0	4	0.0	0												
1995-96	Toronto	NHL	46	6	6	12	47	0	0	0	43	14.0	–2												
	NY Islanders	NHL	16	1	4	5	33	0	0	1	30	3.3	–6												
1996-97	Toronto	NHL	64	11	6	17	47	0	1	0	105	10.5	–20												
	St. John's	AHL	12	5	4	9	21																		
1997-98	Toronto	NHL	80	8	4	12	67	0	0	0	115	7.0	–20												
1998-99	Toronto	NHL	35	2	3	5	30	0	0	0	34	5.9	–4	278	46.0	10:16									
	Vancouver	NHL	27	2	2	4	22	1	0	0	36	5.6	–15	427	46.8	17:15									
99-2000	Vancouver	NHL	40	5	4	9	14	0	1	1	39	12.8	–3	407	46.2	11:32									
	Syracuse Crunch	AHL	20	5	8	13	16																		
2000-01	Minnesota	NHL	72	18	11	29	36	3	1	1	114	15.8	1	1119	45.2	15:50									
2001-02	Minnesota	NHL	68	9	15	24	50	2	2	1	79	11.4	–22	1206	47.7	16:43									
2002-03	Minnesota	NHL	28	1	5	6	8	0	0	0	34	2.9	–3	413	48.4	15:16	17	2	3	5	4	0	0	1	16:58
2003-04	Minnesota	NHL	14	1	0	1	6	0	0	0	14	7.1	–7	170	47.1	14:12									
	Houston Aeros	AHL	31	4	5	9	19																		
	Colorado	NHL	20	1	3	4	6	0	0	0	21	4.8	–8	255	57.7	12:51	6	1	0	1	2	0	0	0	11:51
	NHL Totals		518	65	64	129	370	6	5	4	668	9.7		4275	47.3	14:38	25	3	3	6	6	0	0	1	15:38

WCHA Rookie of the Year (1992)

Traded to **NY Islanders** by **Toronto** with Sean Haggerty, Kenny Jonsson and Toronto's 1st round choice (Roberto Luongo) in 1997 Entry Draft for Wendel Clark, Mathieu Schneider and D.J. Smith, March 13, 1996. Traded to **Toronto** by **NY Islanders** for Toronto's 5th round choice (Jiri Dopita) in 1998 Entry Draft, October 11, 1996. Traded to **Vancouver** by **Toronto** for Chris McAllister, February 16, 1999. Selected by **Minnesota** from **Vancouver** in Expansion Draft, June 23, 2000. • Missed majority of 2002-03 season recovering from arm injury suffered in training camp, September 24, 2002. Traded to **Colorado** by **Minnesota** with Minnesota's 8th round choice (Brandon Yip) in 2004 Entry Draft for Colorado's 4th round choice in 2005 Entry Draft, February 25, 2004.

HENRY, Alex
(HEHN-ree, AL-ehx) **MIN.**

Defense. Shoots left. 6'5", 220 lbs. Born, Elliot Lake, Ont., October 18, 1979. Edmonton's 2nd choice, 67th overall, in 1998 Entry Draft.

Season	Club	League	GP	G	A	Pts	PIM	PP	SH	GW	S	%	+/-	TF	F%	Min	GP	G	A	Pts	PIM	PP	SH	GW	Min
1995-96	Timmins Majors	NOHA	30	4	11	15	6																		
	Timmins	NOJHA	2	0	0	0	0																		
1996-97	London Knights	OHL	61	1	10	11	65																		
1997-98	London Knights	OHL	62	5	9	14	97										16	0	3	3	14				
1998-99	London Knights	OHL	68	5	23	28	105										25	3	10	13	22				
99-2000	Hamilton	AHL	60	1	0	1	69																		
2000-01	Hamilton	AHL	56	2	3	5	87																		
2001-02	Hamilton	AHL	69	4	8	12	143										15	1	2	3	16				
2002-03	Edmonton	NHL	3	0	0	0	0	0	0	0	0	0.0	–1	0	0.0	7:02									
	Washington	NHL	38	0	0	0	80	0	0	0	8	0.0	–4	1	0.0	3:39									
	Portland Pirates	AHL	3	0	1	1	0																		
2003-04	Minnesota	NHL	71	2	4	6	106	0	0	0	37	5.4	4	2	0.0	14:53									
	NHL Totals		112	2	4	6	186	0	0	0	45	4.4		3	0.0	10:52									

Claimed on waivers by **Washington** from **Edmonton**, October 24, 2002. Claimed on waivers by **Minnesota** from **Washington**, October 9, 2003.

HENRY, Burke
(HEHN-ree, BUHRK)

Defense. Shoots left. 6'3", 206 lbs. Born, Ste. Rose, Man., January 21, 1979. NY Rangers' 3rd choice, 73rd overall, in 1997 Entry Draft.

Season	Club	League	GP	G	A	Pts	PIM	PP	SH	GW	S	%	+/-	TF	F%	Min	GP	G	A	Pts	PIM	PP	SH	GW	Min
1995-96	Brandon	WHL	50	6	11	17	58										19	0	4	4	19				
1996-97	Brandon	WHL	55	6	25	31	81										6	1	3	4	4				
1997-98	Brandon	WHL	72	18	65	83	153										18	3	16	19	37				
1998-99	Brandon	WHL	68	18	58	76	151										5	1	6	7	9				
99-2000	Hartford	AHL	64	3	12	15	47										5	0	0	0	2				
2000-01	Hartford	AHL	80	8	30	38	133										5	0	0	0	2				
2001-02	Saint John Flames	AHL	58	0	17	17	92																		
2002-03	Norfolk Admirals	AHL	60	6	22	28	121										9	1	2	3	9				
	Chicago	NHL	16	0	2	2	9	0	0	0	25	0.0	–13	0	0.0	18:32									
2003-04	Chicago	NHL	23	2	4	6	24	0	0	0	31	6.5	0	0	0.0	17:02									
	Norfolk Admirals	AHL	53	1	8	9	70										8	0	1	1	4				
	NHL Totals		39	2	6	8	33	0	0	0	56	3.6		0	0.0	17:39									

WHL East First All-Star Team (1998) • WHL East Second All-Star Team (1999)

Traded to **Calgary** by **NY Rangers** for Chris St. Croix, June 23, 2001. Signed to a PTO (tryout) contract by **Norfolk** (AHL), October 9, 2002. Signed as a free agent by **Norfolk** (AHL), October 23, 2002. Signed as a free agent by **Chicago**, December 11, 2002.

HERPERGER, Chris
(HUHR-puhr-GEHR, KRIHS)

Center. Shoots left. 6', 190 lbs. Born, Esterhazy, Sask., February 24, 1974. Philadelphia's 9th choice, 223rd overall, in 1992 Entry Draft.

Season	Club	League	GP	G	A	Pts	PIM	PP	SH	GW	S	%	+/-	TF	F%	Min	GP	G	A	Pts	PIM	PP	SH	GW	Min
1990-91	Swift Current	SMHL	STATISTICS NOT AVAILABLE																						
	Swift Current	WHL	10	0	1	1	5																		
1991-92	Swift Current	WHL	72	14	19	33	44										8	0	1	1	9				
1992-93	Swift Current	WHL	20	9	7	16	31																		
	Seattle	WHL	46	20	11	31	30										5	1	1	2	6				
1993-94	Seattle	WHL	71	44	51	95	110										9	12	10	22	12				
1994-95	Seattle	WHL	59	49	52	101	106										4	4	0	4	6				
	Hershey Bears	AHL	4	0	0	0	0																		
1995-96	Hershey Bears	AHL	46	8	12	20	36																		
	Baltimore Bandits	AHL	21	2	3	5	17										9	2	3	5	6				
1996-97	Baltimore Bandits	AHL	67	19	22	41	88										3	0	0	0	0				
1997-98	Team Canada	Nat-Tm	63	20	30	50	102																		
1998-99	Indianapolis Ice	IHL	79	19	29	48	81										7	0	4	4	4				
99-2000	Chicago	NHL	9	0	0	0	5	0	0	0	2	0.0	–2	52	55.8	7:39									
	Cleveland	IHL	73	22	26	48	122										9	3	3	6	8				
2000-01	Chicago	NHL	61	10	15	25	20	0	1	3	76	13.2	0	678	56.2	13:07									
	Norfolk Admirals	AHL	9	1	4	5	9																		
2001-02	Ottawa	NHL	72	4	9	13	43	0	0	0	81	4.9	4	769	49.3	11:19									

			Regular Season														Playoffs								
Season	Club	League	GP	G	A	Pts	PIM	PP	SH	GW	S	%	+/-	TF	F%	Min	GP	G	A	Pts	PIM	PP	SH	GW	Min
2002-03	**Atlanta**	**NHL**	**27**	**4**	**1**	**5**	**7**	**0**	**0**	**0**	**26**	**15.4**	**–11**	**187**	**44.4**	**12:30**									
	Chicago Wolves	AHL	7	1	1	2	14																		
	Manitoba Moose	AHL	15	6	6	12	12																		
2003-04	Krefeld Pinguine	Germany	38	10	16	26	50																		
	NHL Totals		**169**	**18**	**25**	**43**	**75**	**0**	**1**	**3**	**185**	**9.7**		**1686**	**51.7**	**11:58**									

WHL West Second All-Star Team (1995)

Traded to **Anaheim** by **Philadelphia** with Winnipeg/Phoenix's 7th round choice (previously acquired, Anaheim selected Tony Mohagen) in 1997 Entry Draft for Bob Corkum, February 6, 1996. Signed as a free agent by **Chicago**, September 2, 1998. Signed as a free agent by **Ottawa**, July 13, 2001. Signed as a free agent by **Atlanta**, August 1, 2002. Traded to **Vancouver** by **Atlanta** with Chris Nielsen for Jeff Farkas, January 20, 2003. Signed as a free agent by **Krefeld** (Germany), June 13, 2003.

HERR, Matt (HUHR, MAT)

Center. Shoots left. 6'2", 204 lbs. Born, Hackensack, NJ, May 26, 1976. Washington's 4th choice, 93rd overall, in 1994 Entry Draft.

1990-91	Hotchkiss High	Hi-School	26	9	5	14																			
1991-92	Hotchkiss High	Hi-School	25	17	16	33																			
1992-93	Hotchkiss High	Hi-School	24	48	30	78																			
1993-94	Hotchkiss High	Hi-School	24	28	19	47																			
1994-95	U. of Michigan	CCHA	37	11	8	19	51										3	1	0	1	4				
1995-96	U. of Michigan	CCHA	40	18	13	31	55										7	0	4	4	0				
1996-97	U. of Michigan	CCHA	43	29	23	52	67										6	2	2	4	8				
1997-98	U. of Michigan	CCHA	31	14	17	31	62																		
•1998-99	**Washington**	**NHL**	**30**	**2**	**2**	**4**	**8**	**1**	**0**	**0**	**40**	**5.0**	**–7**	**176**	**52.8**	**11:05**									
	Portland Pirates	AHL	46	15	14	29	29																		
99-2000	Portland Pirates	AHL	77	22	21	43	51										4	1	1	2	4				
2000-01	**Washington**	**NHL**	**22**	**2**	**3**	**5**	**17**	**0**	**0**	**1**	**20**	**10.0**	**3**	**2**	**100.0**	**8:09**									
	Portland Pirates	AHL	40	21	13	34	58																		
	Philadelphia	AHL	11	2	4	6	18										9	2	1	3	8				
2001-02	**Florida**	**NHL**	**3**	**0**	**0**	**0**	**0**	**0**	**0**	**0**	**1**	**0.0**	**–2**	**15**	**53.3**	**6:27**									
	Hershey Bears	AHL	61	18	16	34	68										7	1	2	3	15				
2002-03	**Boston**	**NHL**	**3**	**0**	**0**	**0**	**0**	**0**	**0**	**0**	**1**	**0.0**	**0**	**8**	**50.0**	**8:17**									
	Providence Bruins	AHL	77	34	38	72	146										4	0	1	1	12				
2003-04	Providence Bruins	AHL	71	18	26	44	108										2	0	1	1	0				
	NHL Totals		**58**	**4**	**5**	**9**	**25**	**1**	**0**	**1**	**62**	**6.5**		**201**	**53.2**	**9:35**									

AHL First All-Star Team (2003)

Traded to **Philadelphia** by **Washington** for Dean Melanson, March 13, 2001. Signed as a free agent by **Florida**, August 21, 2001. Signed as a free agent by **Boston**, July 18, 2002.

HIGGINS, Christopher (HIH-gihns, KRIHS-toh-fuhr) MTL.

Center. Shoots left. 5'11", 192 lbs. Born, Smithtown, NY, June 2, 1983. Montreal's 1st choice, 14th overall, in 2002 Entry Draft.

99-2000	Avon Old Farms	Hi-School	27	19	20	39	10																		
2000-01	Avon Old Farms	Hi-School	24	22	14	36	29																		
2001-02	Yale University	ECAC	27	14	17	31	32																		
2002-03	Yale University	ECAC	28	20	21	41	41																		
2003-04	**Montreal**	**NHL**	**2**	**0**	**0**	**0**	**0**	**0**	**0**	**0**	**0**	**0.0**	**0**	**9**	**22.2**	**6:18**									
	Hamilton	AHL	67	21	27	48	18										10	3	2	5	0				
	NHL Totals		**2**	**0**	**0**	**0**	**0**	**0**	**0**	**0**	**0**	**0.0**		**9**	**22.2**	**6:18**									

ECAC All-Rookie Team (2002) • ECAC Second All-Star Team (2002) • ECAC Rookie of the Year (2002) • ECAC First All-Star Team (2003) • ECAC Player of the Year (2003) (co-winner - David LeNeveu) • NCAA East First All-American Team (2003)

HILBERT, Andy (HIHL-buhrt, AN-dee) BOS.

Center/Left wing. Shoots left. 5'11", 194 lbs. Born, Lansing, MI, February 6, 1981. Boston's 3rd choice, 37th overall, in 2000 Entry Draft.

1997-98	U.S. National 18	USDP	75	34	30	64	148																		
1998-99	U.S. National 18	USDP	46	23	35	58	140																		
99-2000	U. of Michigan	CCHA	35	17	15	32	39																		
2000-01	U. of Michigan	CCHA	42	26	38	64	72																		
2001-02	**Boston**	**NHL**	**6**	**1**	**0**	**1**	**2**	**0**	**0**	**0**	**11**	**9.1**	**–2**	**4**	**50.0**	**11:34**									
	Providence Bruins	AHL	72	26	27	53	74										2	0	0	0	2				
2002-03	**Boston**	**NHL**	**14**	**0**	**3**	**3**	**7**	**0**	**0**	**0**	**22**	**0.0**	**–1**	**34**	**44.1**	**11:30**									
	Providence Bruins	AHL	64	35	35	70	119										4	0	1	1	4				
2003-04	**Boston**	**NHL**	**18**	**2**	**0**	**2**	**9**	**0**	**0**	**0**	**27**	**7.4**	**1**	**11**	**54.6**	**8:57**	**5**	**1**	**0**	**1**	**0**	**0**	**0**	**0**	**5:32**
	Providence Bruins	AHL	19	3	5	8	20																		
	NHL Totals		**38**	**3**	**3**	**6**	**18**	**0**	**0**	**0**	**60**	**5.0**		**49**	**46.9**	**10:18**	**5**	**1**	**0**	**1**	**0**	**0**	**0**	**0**	**5:32**

CCHA First All-Star Team (2001) • NCAA West First All-American Team (2001) • AHL All-Rookie Team (2002)

• Missed majority of 2003-04 season recovering from groin injury suffered in pre-season game vs. Detroit, September 15, 2003.

HILL, Sean (HIHL, SHAWN) FLA.

Defense. Shoots right. 6', 205 lbs. Born, Duluth, MN, February 14, 1970. Montreal's 9th choice, 167th overall, in 1988 Entry Draft.

1986-87	Lakefield Chiefs	OJHL-C	3	1	1	2	14																		
1987-88	East Duluth	Hi-School	24	10	17	27																			
1988-89	U. of Wisconsin	WCHA	45	2	23	25	69																		
1989-90	U. of Wisconsin	WCHA	42	14	39	53	78																		
1990-91	U. of Wisconsin	WCHA	37	19	32	51	122																		
	Montreal	**NHL**															**1**	**0**	**0**	**0**	**0**	**0**	**0**	**0**	
	Fredericton	AHL															3	0	2	2	2				
1991-92	Fredericton	AHL	42	7	20	27	65										7	1	3	4	6				
	Team USA	Nat-Tm	12	4	3	7	16																		
	United States	Olympics	8	2	0	2	6																		
	Montreal	**NHL**															**4**	**1**	**0**	**1**	**2**	**0**	**0**	**0**	
1992-93♦	**Montreal**	**NHL**	**31**	**2**	**6**	**8**	**54**	**1**	**0**	**1**	**37**	**5.4**	**–5**				**3**	**0**	**0**	**0**	**4**	**0**	**0**	**0**	
	Fredericton	AHL	6	1	3	4	10																		
1993-94	**Anaheim**	**NHL**	**68**	**7**	**20**	**27**	**78**	**2**	**1**	**1**	**165**	**4.2**	**–12**												
1994-95	**Ottawa**	**NHL**	**45**	**1**	**14**	**15**	**30**	**0**	**0**	**0**	**107**	**0.9**	**–11**												
1995-96	**Ottawa**	**NHL**	**80**	**7**	**14**	**21**	**94**	**2**	**0**	**2**	**157**	**4.5**	**–26**												
1996-97	**Ottawa**	**NHL**	**5**	**0**	**0**	**0**	**4**	**0**	**0**	**0**	**9**	**0.0**	**1**												
1997-98	**Ottawa**	**NHL**	**13**	**1**	**1**	**2**	**6**	**0**	**0**	**0**	**16**	**6.3**	**–3**												
	Carolina	**NHL**	**42**	**0**	**5**	**5**	**48**	**0**	**0**	**0**	**37**	**0.0**	**–2**												
1998-99	**Carolina**	**NHL**	**54**	**0**	**10**	**10**	**48**	**0**	**0**	**0**	**44**	**0.0**	**9**	**0**	**0.0**	**19:02**									
99-2000	**Carolina**	**NHL**	**62**	**13**	**31**	**44**	**59**	**8**	**0**	**2**	**150**	**8.7**	**3**	**1**	**0.0**	**24:31**									
2000-01	**St. Louis**	**NHL**	**48**	**1**	**10**	**11**	**51**	**0**	**0**	**0**	**47**	**2.1**	**5**	**1**	**0.0**	**17:23**	**15**	**0**	**1**	**1**	**12**	**0**	**0**	**0**	**13:46**
2001-02	**St. Louis**	**NHL**	**23**	**0**	**3**	**3**	**28**	**0**	**0**	**0**	**29**	**0.0**	**1**	**0**	**0.0**	**15:56**									
	Carolina	**NHL**	**49**	**7**	**23**	**30**	**61**	**4**	**0**	**2**	**116**	**6.0**	**–1**	**1**	**0.0**	**23:58**	**23**	**4**	**4**	**8**	**20**	**4**	**0**	**1**	**25:55**
2002-03	**Carolina**	**NHL**	**82**	**5**	**24**	**29**	**141**	**1**	**0**	**0**	**188**	**2.7**	**4**	**1**	**0.0**	**24:21**									
2003-04	**Carolina**	**NHL**	**80**	**13**	**26**	**39**	**84**	**6**	**0**	**1**	**228**	**5.7**	**–2**	**2**	**50.0**	**25:24**									
	NHL Totals		**682**	**57**	**187**	**244**	**786**	**24**	**1**	**9**	**1330**	**4.3**		**6**	**16.7**	**22:30**	**46**	**5**	**5**	**10**	**38**	**4**	**0**	**1**	**21:07**

WCHA Second All-Star Team (1990, 1991) • NCAA West Second All-American Team (1991)

Claimed by **Anaheim** from **Montreal** in Expansion Draft, June 24, 1993. Traded to **Ottawa** by **Anaheim** with Anaheim's 9th round choice (Frederic Cassivi) in 1994 Entry Draft for Ottawa's 3rd round choice (later traded to Tampa Bay – Tampa Bay selected Vadim Epanchintsev) in 1994 Entry Draft, June 29, 1994. • Missed remainder of 1996-97 season recovering from knee injury suffered in game vs. New Jersey, October 18, 1996. Traded to **Carolina** by **Ottawa** for Chris Murray, November 18, 1997. Signed as a free agent by **St. Louis**, July 1, 2000. Traded to **Carolina** by **St. Louis** for Steve Halko and Carolina's 4th round choice (later traded to Atlanta – Atlanta selected Lane Manson) in 2002 Entry Draft, December 5, 2001. Signed as a free agent by **Florida**, July 15, 2004.

			Regular Season														Playoffs								
Season	Club	League	GP	G	A	Pts	PIM	PP	SH	GW	S	%	+/-	TF	F%	Min	GP	G	A	Pts	PIM	PP	SH	GW	Min

HINOTE, Dan

(HIGH-noht, DAN) **COL.**

Right wing. Shoots right. 6', 190 lbs. Born, Leesburg, FL, January 30, 1977. Colorado's 9th choice, 167th overall, in 1996 Entry Draft.

1993-94	Elk River Elks	Hi-School	STATISTICS NOT AVAILABLE																						
1994-95	Army	NCAA	33	20	24	44	20	....	....	....	....	....	....	....	....	....	....	....	....	....	....	....	....	....	....
1995-96	Army	NCAA	34	21	24	45	22	....	....	....	....	....	....	....	....	....	....	....	....	....	....	....	....	....	....
1996-97	Oshawa Generals	OHL	60	15	13	28	58	....	....	....	....	....	....	....	....	....	18	4	5	9	8	....	....	....	....
1997-98	Oshawa Generals	OHL	35	12	15	27	39	....	....	....	....	....	....	....	....	....	5	2	2	4	7	....	....	....	....
	Hershey Bears	AHL	24	1	4	5	25	....	....	....	....	....	....	....	....	....	....	....	....	....	....	....	....	....	....
1998-99	Hershey Bears	AHL	65	4	16	20	95	....	....	....	....	....	....	....	....	....	5	3	1	4	6	....	....	....	....
99-2000	**Colorado**	**NHL**	**27**	**1**	**3**	**4**	**10**	**0**	**0**	**0**	**14**	**7.1**	**0**	**132**	**51.5**	**7:51**	....	....	....	....	....	....	....	....	....
	Hershey Bears	AHL	55	28	31	59	96	....	....	....	....	....	....	....	....	....	14	4	5	9	19	....	....	....	....
2000-01♦	**Colorado**	**NHL**	**76**	**5**	**10**	**15**	**51**	**1**	**0**	**1**	**69**	**7.2**	**1**	**506**	**49.8**	**10:21**	**23**	**2**	**4**	**6**	**21**	**0**	**0**	**0**	**8:22**
2001-02	**Colorado**	**NHL**	**58**	**6**	**6**	**12**	**39**	**0**	**1**	**3**	**75**	**8.0**	**8**	**267**	**51.3**	**12:27**	**19**	**1**	**2**	**3**	**9**	**0**	**0**	**0**	**10:46**
2002-03	**Colorado**	**NHL**	**60**	**6**	**4**	**10**	**49**	**0**	**0**	**3**	**65**	**9.2**	**4**	**218**	**46.8**	**10:36**	**7**	**1**	**2**	**3**	**2**	**0**	**0**	**0**	**14:19**
2003-04	**Colorado**	**NHL**	**59**	**4**	**7**	**11**	**57**	**0**	**2**	**0**	**53**	**7.5**	**–6**	**151**	**48.3**	**12:42**	**11**	**1**	**0**	**1**	**0**	**0**	**1**	**0**	**13:04**
	NHL Totals		**280**	**22**	**30**	**52**	**206**	**1**	**3**	**7**	**276**	**8.0**		**1274**	**49.6**	**11:06**	**60**	**5**	**8**	**13**	**32**	**0**	**1**	**0**	**10:41**

HLAVAC, Jan

(huh-LAH-vahch, YAHN)

Left wing. Shoots left. 6', 185 lbs. Born, Prague, Czech., September 20, 1976. NY Islanders' 2nd choice, 28th overall, in 1995 Entry Draft.

1993-94	Sparta Praha Jr.	Czech-Jr.	27	12	15	27	....	....	....	....	....	....	....	....	....	....	....	....	....	....	....	....	....	....	....
	HC Sparta Praha	Czech	9	1	1	2	....	....	....	....	....	....	....	....	....	....	....	....	....	....	....	....	....	....	....
1994-95	HC Sparta Praha	Czech	38	7	6	13	18	....	....	....	....	....	....	....	....	....	5	0	2	2	0	....	....	....	....
1995-96	HC Sparta Praha	Czech	34	8	5	13	....	....	....	....	....	....	....	....	....	....	12	1	2	3	....	....	....	....	....
1996-97	HC Sparta Praha	Czech	38	8	13	21	24	....	....	....	....	....	....	....	....	....	10	5	2	7	2	....	....	....	....
	HC Sparta Praha	EuroHL	3	4	0	4	6	....	....	....	....	....	....	....	....	....	....	....	....	....	....	....	....	....	....
1997-98	HC Sparta Praha	Czech	48	17	30	47	40	....	....	....	....	....	....	....	....	....	5	1	0	1	2	....	....	....	....
	HC Sparta Praha	EuroHL	5	0	3	3	4	....	....	....	....	....	....	....	....	....	....	....	....	....	....	....	....	....	....
1998-99	HC Sparta Praha	Czech	49	*33	20	53	52	....	....	....	....	....	....	....	....	....	6	1	3	4	....	....	....	....	....
	HC Sparta Praha	EuroHL	5	4	2	6	0	....	....	....	....	....	....	....	....	....	1	1	1	2	0	....	....	....	....
99-2000	**NY Rangers**	**NHL**	**67**	**19**	**23**	**42**	**16**	**6**	**0**	**2**	**134**	**14.2**	**3**	**6**	**33.3**	**15:09**	....	....	....	....	....	....	....	....	....
	Hartford	AHL	3	1	0	1	0	....	....	....	....	....	....	....	....	....	....	....	....	....	....	....	....	....	....
2000-01	**NY Rangers**	**NHL**	**79**	**28**	**36**	**64**	**20**	**5**	**0**	**6**	**195**	**14.4**	**3**	**0**	**0.0**	**16:38**	....	....	....	....	....	....	....	....	....
2001-02	**Philadelphia**	**NHL**	**31**	**7**	**3**	**10**	**8**	**0**	**0**	**1**	**62**	**11.3**	**5**	**0**	**0.0**	**12:36**	....	....	....	....	....	....	....	....	....
	Vancouver	**NHL**	**46**	**9**	**12**	**21**	**10**	**1**	**0**	**2**	**70**	**12.9**	**4**	**2**	**100.0**	**14:46**	**5**	**0**	**1**	**1**	**0**	**0**	**0**	**0**	**9:38**
2002-03	**Vancouver**	**NHL**	**9**	**1**	**1**	**2**	**6**	**0**	**0**	**0**	**7**	**14.3**	**–1**	**0**	**0.0**	**10:51**	....	....	....	....	....	....	....	....	....
	Carolina	**NHL**	**52**	**9**	**15**	**24**	**22**	**6**	**0**	**1**	**116**	**7.8**	**–9**	**21**	**38.1**	**17:10**	....	....	....	....	....	....	....	....	....
2003-04	**NY Rangers**	**NHL**	**72**	**5**	**21**	**26**	**16**	**2**	**0**	**0**	**125**	**4.0**	**–8**	**7**	**42.9**	**13:52**	....	....	....	....	....	....	....	....	....
	NHL Totals		**356**	**78**	**111**	**189**	**98**	**20**	**0**	**12**	**709**	**11.0**		**36**	**41.7**	**15:08**	**5**	**0**	**1**	**1**	**0**	**0**	**0**	**0**	**9:38**

Traded to **Calgary** by **NY Islanders** for Jorgen Jonsson, July 14, 1998. Rights traded to **NY Rangers** by **Calgary** with Calgary's 1st (Jamie Lundmark) and 3rd (later traded back to Calgary – Calgary selected Craig Andersson) round choices in 1999 Entry Draft for Marc Savard and NY Rangers' 1st round choice (Oleg Saprykin) in 1999 Entry Draft, June 26, 1999. Traded to **Philadelphia** by **NY Rangers** with Kim Johnsson, Pavel Brendl and NY Rangers' 3rd round choice (Stefan Ruzicka) in 2003 Entry Draft for Eric Lindros, August 20, 2001. Traded to **Vancouver** by **Philadelphia** with Tampa Bay's 3rd round choice (previously acquired, Vancouver selected Brett Skinner) in 2002 Entry Draft for Donald Brashear and Vancouver's 6th round choice (later traded to Columbus – Columbus selected Jaroslav Balastik) in 2002 Entry Draft, December 17, 2001. Traded to **Carolina** by **Vancouver** with Harold Druken for Darren Langdon and Marek Malik, November 1, 2002. Signed as a free agent by **NY Rangers**, August 28, 2003.

HNIDY, Shane

(NIGH-dee, SHAYN) **NSH.**

Defense. Shoots right. 6'2", 204 lbs. Born, Neepawa, Man., November 8, 1975. Buffalo's 7th choice, 173rd overall, in 1994 Entry Draft.

1990-91	Yellowhead Pass	MMHL	36	9	11	20	92	....	....	....	....	....	....	....	....	....	....	....	....	....	....	....	....	....	....
1991-92	Swift Current	WHL	56	1	3	4	11	....	....	....	....	....	....	....	....	....	4	0	0	0	0	....	....	....	....
1992-93	Swift Current	WHL	45	5	12	17	62	....	....	....	....	....	....	....	....	....	....	....	....	....	....	....	....	....	....
	Prince Albert	WHL	27	2	10	12	43	....	....	....	....	....	....	....	....	....	....	....	....	....	....	....	....	....	....
1993-94	Prince Albert	WHL	69	7	26	33	113	....	....	....	....	....	....	....	....	....	....	....	....	....	....	....	....	....	....
1994-95	Prince Albert	WHL	72	5	29	34	169	....	....	....	....	....	....	....	....	....	15	4	7	11	29	....	....	....	....
1995-96	Prince Albert	WHL	58	11	42	53	100	....	....	....	....	....	....	....	....	....	18	4	11	15	34	....	....	....	....
1996-97	Baton Rouge	ECHL	21	3	10	13	50	....	....	....	....	....	....	....	....	....	....	....	....	....	....	....	....	....	....
	Saint John Flames	AHL	44	2	12	14	112	....	....	....	....	....	....	....	....	....	....	....	....	....	....	....	....	....	....
1997-98	Grand Rapids	IHL	77	6	12	18	210	....	....	....	....	....	....	....	....	....	3	0	2	2	23	....	....	....	....
1998-99	Adirondack	AHL	68	9	20	29	121	....	....	....	....	....	....	....	....	....	3	0	1	1	0	....	....	....	....
99-2000	Cincinnati	AHL	68	9	19	28	153	....	....	....	....	....	....	....	....	....	....	....	....	....	....	....	....	....	....
2000-01	**Ottawa**	**NHL**	**52**	**3**	**2**	**5**	**84**	**0**	**0**	**1**	**47**	**6.4**	**8**	**0**	**0.0**	**13:05**	**1**	**0**	**0**	**0**	**0**	**0**	**0**	**0**	**13:23**
	Grand Rapids	IHL	2	0	0	0	2	....	....	....	....	....	....	....	....	....	....	....	....	....	....	....	....	....	....
2001-02	**Ottawa**	**NHL**	**33**	**1**	**1**	**2**	**57**	**0**	**0**	**0**	**34**	**2.9**	**–10**	**0**	**0.0**	**16:56**	**12**	**1**	**1**	**2**	**12**	**0**	**0**	**0**	**16:00**
2002-03	**Ottawa**	**NHL**	**67**	**0**	**8**	**8**	**130**	**0**	**0**	**0**	**58**	**0.0**	**–1**	**1**	**0.0**	**13:55**	**1**	**0**	**0**	**0**	**0**	**0**	**0**	**0**	**9:38**
2003-04	**Ottawa**	**NHL**	**37**	**0**	**5**	**5**	**72**	**0**	**0**	**0**	**16**	**0.0**	**2**	**0**	**0.0**	**11:19**	....	....	....	....	....	....	....	....	....
	Nashville	**NHL**	**9**	**0**	**2**	**2**	**10**	**0**	**0**	**0**	**12**	**0.0**	**3**	**0**	**0.0**	**18:11**	**5**	**0**	**0**	**0**	**6**	**0**	**0**	**0**	**12:31**
	NHL Totals		**198**	**4**	**18**	**22**	**353**	**0**	**0**	**1**	**167**	**2.4**		**1**	**0.0**	**13:54**	**19**	**1**	**1**	**2**	**18**	**0**	**0**	**0**	**14:37**

Signed as a free agent by **Detroit**, August 6, 1998. Traded to **Ottawa** by **Detroit** for Ottawa's 8th round choice (Todd Jackson) in 2000 Entry Draft, June 25, 2000. • Missed majority of 2001-02 season recovering from ankle injury suffered in game vs. Boston, December 26, 2001. Traded to **Nashville** by **Ottawa** for Colorado's 3rd round choice (previously acquired, Ottawa selected Peter Regin Jensen) in 2004 Entry Draft, March 9, 2004.

HOLDEN, Josh

(HOHL-dehn, JAWSH)

Center. Shoots left. 6', 190 lbs. Born, Calgary, Alta., January 18, 1978. Vancouver's 1st choice, 12th overall, in 1996 Entry Draft.

1993-94	Calgary Buffaloes	AMHL	34	14	15	29	82	....	....	....	....	....	....	....	....	....	....	....	....	....	....	....	....	....	....
1994-95	Regina Pats	WHL	62	20	23	43	45	....	....	....	....	....	....	....	....	....	4	3	1	4	0	....	....	....	....
1995-96	Regina Pats	WHL	70	57	55	112	105	....	....	....	....	....	....	....	....	....	11	4	5	9	23	....	....	....	....
1996-97	Regina Pats	WHL	58	49	49	98	148	....	....	....	....	....	....	....	....	....	5	3	2	5	10	....	....	....	....
1997-98	Regina Pats	WHL	56	41	58	99	134	....	....	....	....	....	....	....	....	....	2	2	2	4	10	....	....	....	....
1998-99	**Vancouver**	**NHL**	**30**	**2**	**4**	**6**	**10**	**1**	**0**	**0**	**44**	**4.5**	**–10**	**269**	**39.0**	**12:44**	....	....	....	....	....	....	....	....	....
	Syracuse Crunch	AHL	38	14	15	29	48	....	....	....	....	....	....	....	....	....	....	....	....	....	....	....	....	....	....
99-2000	**Vancouver**	**NHL**	**6**	**1**	**5**	**6**	**2**	**0**	**0**	**0**	**5**	**20.0**	**2**	**42**	**42.9**	**10:25**	....	....	....	....	....	....	....	....	....
	Syracuse Crunch	AHL	45	19	32	51	113	....	....	....	....	....	....	....	....	....	4	1	0	1	10	....	....	....	....
2000-01	**Vancouver**	**NHL**	**10**	**1**	**0**	**1**	**0**	**0**	**0**	**0**	**12**	**8.3**	**0**	**85**	**35.3**	**9:27**	....	....	....	....	....	....	....	....	....
	Kansas City	IHL	60	27	26	53	136	....	....	....	....	....	....	....	....	....	....	....	....	....	....	....	....	....	....
2001-02	**Carolina**	**NHL**	**8**	**0**	**0**	**0**	**2**	**0**	**0**	**0**	**3**	**0.0**	**0**	**41**	**41.5**	**5:17**	....	....	....	....	....	....	....	....	....
	Manitoba Moose	AHL	68	16	17	33	187	....	....	....	....	....	....	....	....	....	7	1	1	2	4	....	....	....	....
2002-03	**Toronto**	**NHL**	**5**	**1**	**0**	**1**	**2**	**0**	**0**	**0**	**6**	**16.7**	**–2**	**0**	**0.0**	**8:06**	....	....	....	....	....	....	....	....	....
	St. John's	AHL	65	24	29	53	123	....	....	....	....	....	....	....	....	....	....	....	....	....	....	....	....	....	....
2003-04	**Toronto**	**NHL**	**1**	**0**	**0**	**0**	**0**	**0**	**0**	**0**	**0**	**0.0**	**0**	**0**	**0.0**	**10:32**	....	....	....	....	....	....	....	....	....
	St. John's	AHL	52	22	33	55	106	....	....	....	....	....	....	....	....	....	....	....	....	....	....	....	....	....	....
	NHL Totals		**60**	**5**	**9**	**14**	**16**	**1**	**0**	**0**	**70**	**7.1**		**437**	**38.9**	**10:32**	....	....	....	....	....	....	....	....	....

WHL East Second All-Star Team (1998)

Claimed by **Carolina** from **Vancouver** in Waiver Draft, September 28, 2001. Claimed on waivers by **Vancouver** from **Carolina**, October 25, 2001. Traded to **Toronto** by **Vancouver** for Jeff Farkas, June 23, 2002.

HOLIK, Bobby

(HOH-leek, BAWB-ee) **NYR**

Center. Shoots right. 6'4", 230 lbs. Born, Jihlava, Czech., January 1, 1971. Hartford's 1st choice, 10th overall, in 1989 Entry Draft.

1987-88	Dukla Jihlava	Czech	31	5	9	14	16	....	....	....	....	....	....	....	....	....	....	....	....	....	....	....	....	....	....
1988-89	Dukla Jihlava	Czech	24	7	10	17	32	....	....	....	....	....	....	....	....	....	....	....	....	....	....	....	....	....	....
1989-90	Dukla Jihlava	Czech	42	15	26	41	....	....	....	....	....	....	....	....	....	....	....	....	....	....	....	....	....	....	....
1990-91	**Hartford**	**NHL**	**78**	**21**	**22**	**43**	**113**	**8**	**0**	**3**	**173**	**12.1**	**–3**	....	....	....	**6**	**0**	**0**	**0**	**7**	**0**	**0**	**0**	....
1991-92	**Hartford**	**NHL**	**76**	**21**	**24**	**45**	**44**	**1**	**0**	**2**	**207**	**10.1**	**4**	....	....	....	**7**	**0**	**1**	**1**	**6**	**0**	**0**	**0**	....
1992-93	**New Jersey**	**NHL**	**61**	**20**	**19**	**39**	**76**	**7**	**0**	**4**	**180**	**11.1**	**–6**	....	....	....	**5**	**1**	**1**	**2**	**6**	**0**	**0**	**0**	....
	Utica Devils	AHL	1	0	0	0	2	....	....	....	....	....	....	....	....	....	....	....	....	....	....	....	....	....	....
1993-94	**New Jersey**	**NHL**	**70**	**13**	**20**	**33**	**72**	**2**	**0**	**3**	**130**	**10.0**	**28**	....	....	....	**20**	**0**	**3**	**3**	**6**	**0**	**0**	**0**	....
1994-95♦	**New Jersey**	**NHL**	**48**	**10**	**10**	**20**	**18**	**0**	**0**	**2**	**84**	**11.9**	**9**	....	....	....	**20**	**4**	**4**	**8**	**22**	**2**	**0**	**1**	....
1995-96	**New Jersey**	**NHL**	**63**	**13**	**17**	**30**	**58**	**1**	**0**	**1**	**157**	**8.3**	**9**	....	....	....	....	....	....	....	....	....	....	....	....

			Regular Season														Playoffs								
Season	Club	League	GP	G	A	Pts	PIM	PP	SH	GW	S	%	+/-	TF	F%	Min	GP	G	A	Pts	PIM	PP	SH	GW	Min
1996-97	New Jersey	NHL	82	23	39	62	54	5	0	6	192	12.0	24	....	....	....	10	2	3	5	4	1	0	0	....
1997-98	New Jersey	NHL	82	29	36	65	100	8	0	8	238	12.2	23	....	....	....	5	0	0	0	8	0	0	0	....
1998-99	New Jersey	NHL	78	27	37	64	119	5	0	8	253	10.7	16	1350	53.6	17:34	7	0	7	7	6	0	0	0	18:14
99-2000 ♦	New Jersey	NHL	79	23	23	46	106	7	0	4	257	8.9	7	1390	55.6	16:53	23	3	7	10	14	0	0	1	17:29
2000-01	New Jersey	NHL	80	15	35	50	97	3	0	3	206	7.3	19	1365	56.0	15:49	25	6	10	16	37	1	0	3	16:05
2001-02	New Jersey	NHL	81	25	29	54	97	6	0	3	270	9.3	7	1594	54.5	17:42	6	4	1	5	2	1	0	0	17:53
2002-03	NY Rangers	NHL	64	16	19	35	52	3	0	2	213	7.5	–1	1390	58.2	18:07	....	....	....	....	....	....	....	....	....
2003-04	NY Rangers	NHL	82	25	31	56	96	8	0	4	225	11.1	4	1664	54.2	18:34	....	....	....	....	....	....	....	....	....
	NHL Totals		1024	281	361	642	1102	64	0	53	2785	10.1		8753	55.3	17:25	134	20	37	57	118	5	0	5	17:02

Played in NHL All-Star Game (1998, 1999)

Traded to **New Jersey** by **Hartford** with Hartford's 2nd round choice (Jay Pandolfo) in 1993 Entry Draft for Sean Burke and Eric Weinrich, August 28, 1992. Signed as a free agent by **NY Rangers**, July 1, 2002.

HOLLAND, Jason

(HAWL-land, JAY-suhn) **L.A.**

Defense. Shoots right. 6'3", 219 lbs. Born, Morinville, Alta., April 30, 1976. NY Islanders' 2nd choice, 38th overall, in 1994 Entry Draft.

Season	Club	League	GP	G	A	Pts	PIM	PP	SH	GW	S	%	+/-	TF	F%	Min	GP	G	A	Pts	PIM	PP	SH	GW	Min
1991-92	St. Albert Raiders	AMHL	38	9	29	38	94	....	....	....	....	....	....	....	....	....	....	....	....	....	....	....	....	....	....
1992-93	St. Albert Raiders	AMHL	31	11	25	36	36	....	....	....	....	....	....	....	....	....	....	....	....	....	....	....	....	....	....
	Kamloops Blazers	WHL	4	0	0	0	2	....	....	....	....	....	....	....	....	....	....	....	....	....	....	....	....	....	....
1993-94	Kamloops Blazers	WHL	59	14	15	29	80	....	....	....	....	....	....	....	....	....	18	2	3	5	4	....	....	....	....
1994-95	Kamloops Blazers	WHL	71	9	32	41	65	....	....	....	....	....	....	....	....	....	21	2	7	9	9	....	....	....	....
1995-96	Kamloops Blazers	WHL	63	24	33	57	98	....	....	....	....	....	....	....	....	....	16	4	9	13	22	....	....	....	....
1996-97	NY Islanders	NHL	4	1	0	1	0	0	0	0	3	33.3	1	....	....	....	....	....	....	....	....	....	....	....	....
	Kentucky	AHL	72	14	25	39	46	....	....	....	....	....	....	....	....	....	4	0	2	2	0	....	....	....	....
1997-98	NY Islanders	NHL	8	0	0	0	4	0	0	0	6	0.0	–4	....	....	....	....	....	....	....	....	....	....	....	....
	Kentucky	AHL	50	10	16	26	29	....	....	....	....	....	....	....	....	....	....	....	....	....	....	....	....	....	....
	Rochester	AHL	9	0	4	4	10	....	....	....	....	....	....	....	....	....	4	0	3	3	4	....	....	....	....
1998-99	Buffalo	NHL	3	0	0	0	8	0	0	0	2	0.0	–1	0	0.0	10:58	....	....	....	....	....	....	....	....	....
	Rochester	AHL	74	4	25	29	36	....	....	....	....	....	....	....	....	....	20	2	5	7	8	....	....	....	....
99-2000	Buffalo	NHL	9	0	1	1	0	0	0	0	8	0.0	0	0	0.0	15:31	1	0	0	0	0	0	0	0	15:41
	Rochester	AHL	54	3	15	18	24	....	....	....	....	....	....	....	....	....	12	1	0	1	2	....	....	....	....
2000-01	Rochester	AHL	63	4	19	23	45	....	....	....	....	....	....	....	....	....	4	1	0	1	0	....	....	....	....
2001-02	Los Angeles	NHL	3	0	0	0	0	0	0	0	1	0.0	–1	0	0.0	15:50	....	....	....	....	....	....	....	....	....
	Manchester	AHL	65	9	18	27	39	....	....	....	....	....	....	....	....	....	5	1	0	1	5	....	....	....	....
2002-03	Los Angeles	NHL	2	0	1	1	0	0	0	0	0	0.0	1	0	0.0	13:31	....	....	....	....	....	....	....	....	....
	Manchester	AHL	67	4	27	31	53	....	....	....	....	....	....	....	....	....	3	0	0	0	0	....	....	....	....
2003-04	Los Angeles	NHL	52	3	3	6	24	0	0	1	64	4.7	5	0	0.0	17:41	....	....	....	....	....	....	....	....	....
	NHL Totals		81	4	5	9	36	0	0	1	84	4.8		0	0.0	16:54	1	0	0	0	0	0	0	0	15:41

WHL West First All-Star Team (1996)

Traded to **Buffalo** by **NY Islanders** with Paul Kruse for Jason Dawe, March 24, 1998. Signed as a free agent by **Los Angeles**, August 23, 2001.

HOLMQVIST, Mikael

(HOHLM-kvihst, MIGH-kuhl) **ANA.**

Center. Shoots left. 6'3", 205 lbs. Born, Stockholm, Sweden, June 8, 1979. Anaheim's 1st choice, 18th overall, in 1997 Entry Draft.

Season	Club	League	GP	G	A	Pts	PIM	PP	SH	GW	S	%	+/-	TF	F%	Min	GP	G	A	Pts	PIM	PP	SH	GW	Min
1995-96	Djurgarden Jr.	Swede-Jr.	24	7	2	9	4	....	....	....	....	....	....	....	....	....	....	....	....	....	....	....	....	....	....
1996-97	Djurgarden Jr.	Swede-Jr.	39	29	35	64	110	....	....	....	....	....	....	....	....	....	....	....	....	....	....	....	....	....	....
	Djurgarden	Sweden	9	0	0	0	0	....	....	....	....	....	....	....	....	....	....	....	....	....	....	....	....	....	....
1997-98	Farjestad	Sweden	41	2	3	5	6	....	....	....	....	....	....	....	....	....	7	0	0	0	0	....	....	....	....
	Farjestad	EuroHL	5	2	2	4	2	....	....	....	....	....	....	....	....	....	....	....	....	....	....	....	....	....	....
1998-99	Farjestad Jr.	Swede-Jr.	2	2	2	4	2	....	....	....	....	....	....	....	....	....	....	....	....	....	....	....	....	....	....
	Farjestad	EuroHL	3	0	0	0	0	....	....	....	....	....	....	....	....	....	1	0	0	0	0	....	....	....	....
	Farjestad	Sweden	15	0	0	0	6	....	....	....	....	....	....	....	....	....	....	....	....	....	....	....	....	....	....
	Hammarby	Swede-2	3	2	0	2	0	....	....	....	....	....	....	....	....	....	....	....	....	....	....	....	....	....	....
99-2000	TPS Turku	Finland	54	12	3	15	14	....	....	....	....	....	....	....	....	....	11	2	3	5	4	....	....	....	....
2000-01	TPS Turku	Finland	46	4	5	9	8	....	....	....	....	....	....	....	....	....	10	1	3	4	2	....	....	....	....
2001-02	TPS Turku	Finland	56	9	13	22	16	....	....	....	....	....	....	....	....	....	8	1	0	1	12	....	....	....	....
2002-03	TPS Turku	Finland	56	15	25	40	36	....	....	....	....	....	....	....	....	....	7	0	0	0	4	....	....	....	....
2003-04	Anaheim	NHL	21	2	0	2	25	0	0	0	18	11.1	–6	16	31.3	8:24	....	....	....	....	....	....	....	....	....
	Cincinnati	AHL	24	7	7	14	20	....	....	....	....	....	....	....	....	....	....	....	....	....	....	....	....	....	....
	NHL Totals		21	2	0	2	25	0	0	0	18	11.1		16	31.3	8:24	....	....	....	....	....	....	....	....	....

HOLMSTROM, Tomas

(HOHLM-struhm, TAW-mas) **DET.**

Left wing. Shoots left. 6', 200 lbs. Born, Pitea, Sweden, January 23, 1973. Detroit's 9th choice, 257th overall, in 1994 Entry Draft.

Season	Club	League	GP	G	A	Pts	PIM	PP	SH	GW	S	%	+/-	TF	F%	Min	GP	G	A	Pts	PIM	PP	SH	GW	Min
1989-90	Pitea HC	Swede-2	9	1	0	1	4	....	....	....	....	....	....	....	....	....	....	....	....	....	....	....	....	....	....
1990-91	Pitea HC	Swede-2	26	5	4	9	16	....	....	....	....	....	....	....	....	....	....	....	....	....	....	....	....	....	....
1991-92	Pitea HC	Swede-2	31	15	12	27	44	....	....	....	....	....	....	....	....	....	....	....	....	....	....	....	....	....	....
1992-93	Pitea HC	Swede-2	32	17	15	32	30	....	....	....	....	....	....	....	....	....	....	....	....	....	....	....	....	....	....
1993-94	Bodens IK	Swede-2	34	23	16	39	86	....	....	....	....	....	....	....	....	....	9	3	3	6	24	....	....	....	....
1994-95	Lulea HF	Sweden	40	14	14	28	56	....	....	....	....	....	....	....	....	....	8	1	2	3	20	....	....	....	....
1995-96	Lulea HF	Sweden	34	12	11	23	78	....	....	....	....	....	....	....	....	....	11	6	2	8	22	....	....	....	....
1996-97 ♦	Detroit	NHL	47	6	3	9	33	3	0	0	53	11.3	–10	....	....	....	1	0	0	0	0	0	0	0	....
	Adirondack	AHL	6	3	1	4	7	....	....	....	....	....	....	....	....	....	....	....	....	....	....	....	....	....	....
1997-98 ♦	Detroit	NHL	57	5	17	22	44	1	0	1	48	10.4	6	....	....	....	22	7	12	19	16	2	0	0	....
1998-99	Detroit	NHL	82	13	21	34	69	5	0	4	100	13.0	–11	0	0.0	12:22	10	4	3	7	4	2	0	1	12:32
99-2000	Detroit	NHL	72	13	22	35	43	4	0	1	71	18.3	4	0	0.0	12:06	9	3	1	4	16	1	0	1	11:42
2000-01	Detroit	NHL	73	16	24	40	40	9	0	2	74	21.6	–12	2	50.0	11:41	6	1	3	4	8	1	0	0	14:23
2001-02 ♦	Detroit	NHL	69	8	18	26	58	6	0	1	79	10.1	–12	2	0.0	12:23	23	8	3	11	8	3	0	2	11:31
	Sweden	Olympics	4	1	0	1	0	....	....	....	....	....	....	....	....	....	....	....	....	....	....	....	....	....	....
2002-03	Detroit	NHL	74	20	20	40	62	12	0	2	109	18.3	11	2	0.0	12:28	4	1	1	2	4	1	0	0	14:37
2003-04	Detroit	NHL	67	15	15	30	38	6	0	0	74	20.3	8	3	0.0	12:23	12	2	2	4	10	1	0	1	11:27
	NHL Totals		541	96	140	236	387	46	0	11	608	15.8		9	11.1	12:14	87	26	25	51	66	11	0	5	12:09

HOLZINGER, Brian

(HOHL-zihn-guhr, BRIGH-uhn)

Center. Shoots right. 5'11", 186 lbs. Born, Parma, OH, October 10, 1972. Buffalo's 7th choice, 124th overall, in 1991 Entry Draft.

Season	Club	League	GP	G	A	Pts	PIM	PP	SH	GW	S	%	+/-	TF	F%	Min	GP	G	A	Pts	PIM	PP	SH	GW	Min
1988-89	Padua High	Hi-School	35	73	65	138	....	....	....	....	....	....	....	....	....	....	....	....	....	....	....	....	....	....	....
1989-90	Det. Compuware	NAJHL	44	36	37	73	....	....	....	....	....	....	....	....	....	....	....	....	....	....	....	....	....	....	....
1990-91	Det. Compuware	NAJHL	37	45	41	86	16	....	....	....	....	....	....	....	....	....	....	....	....	....	....	....	....	....	....
1991-92	Bowling Green	CCHA	30	14	8	22	36	....	....	....	....	....	....	....	....	....	....	....	....	....	....	....	....	....	....
1992-93	Bowling Green	CCHA	41	31	26	57	44	....	....	....	....	....	....	....	....	....	....	....	....	....	....	....	....	....	....
1993-94	Bowling Green	CCHA	38	22	15	37	24	....	....	....	....	....	....	....	....	....	....	....	....	....	....	....	....	....	....
1994-95	Bowling Green	CCHA	38	35	33	68	42	....	....	....	....	....	....	....	....	....	....	....	....	....	....	....	....	....	....
	Buffalo	NHL	4	0	3	3	0	0	0	0	3	0.0	2	....	....	....	4	2	1	3	2	1	0	0	....
1995-96	Buffalo	NHL	58	10	10	20	37	5	0	1	71	14.1	–21	....	....	....	....	....	....	....	....	....	....	....	....
	Rochester	AHL	17	10	11	21	14	....	....	....	....	....	....	....	....	....	19	10	14	24	10	....	....	....	....
1996-97	Buffalo	NHL	81	22	29	51	54	2	2	6	142	15.5	9	....	....	....	12	2	5	7	8	0	1	0	....
1997-98	Buffalo	NHL	69	14	21	35	36	4	2	1	116	12.1	–2	....	....	....	15	4	7	11	18	1	1	0	....
1998-99	Buffalo	NHL	81	17	17	34	45	5	0	2	143	11.9	2	852	50.4	16:31	21	3	5	8	33	1	0	0	15:50
99-2000	Buffalo	NHL	59	7	17	24	30	0	1	2	81	8.6	4	839	45.7	14:38	....	....	....	....	....	....	....	....	....
	Tampa Bay	NHL	14	3	3	6	21	1	1	0	23	13.0	–7	119	46.2	16:10	....	....	....	....	....	....	....	....	....
2000-01	Tampa Bay	NHL	70	11	25	36	64	3	0	2	87	12.6	–9	775	47.4	16:03	....	....	....	....	....	....	....	....	....
2001-02	Tampa Bay	NHL	23	1	2	3	4	0	0	0	20	5.0	–4	54	55.6	9:19	....	....	....	....	....	....	....	....	....
2002-03	Tampa Bay	NHL	5	0	1	1	2	0	0	0	3	0.0	1	26	34.6	9:08	....	....	....	....	....	....	....	....	....
	Springfield	AHL	28	6	20	26	16	....	....	....	....	....	....	....	....	....	....	....	....	....	....	....	....	....	....
	Pittsburgh	NHL	9	1	2	3	6	0	0	0	20	5.0	–6	161	47.8	16:24	....	....	....	....	....	....	....	....	....

			Regular Season														Playoffs								
Season	Club	League	GP	G	A	Pts	PIM	PP	SH	GW	S	%	+/-	TF	F%	Min	GP	G	A	Pts	PIM	PP	SH	GW	Min
2003-04	**Pittsburgh**	**NHL**	**61**	**6**	**15**	**21**	**38**	**1**	**1**	**1**	**82**	**7.3**	**–27**	**994**	**47.7**	**16:50**	....	....	....	....	....	....	....	....	....
	Columbus	**NHL**	**13**	**1**	**0**	**1**	**2**	**0**	**0**	**0**	**14**	**7.1**	**–4**	**155**	**54.8**	**15:17**	....	....	....	....	....	....	....	....	....
	NHL Totals		**547**	**93**	**145**	**238**	**339**	**21**	**7**	**15**	**805**	**11.6**		**3975**	**48.0**	**15:29**	**52**	**11**	**18**	**29**	**61**	**3**	**2**	**0**	**15:50**

CCHA Second All-Star Team (1993) • CCHA First All-Star Team (1995) • CCHA Player of the Year (1995) • NCAA West First All-American Team (1995) • Hobey Baker Memorial Award (Top U.S. Collegiate Player) (1995)

Traded to **Tampa Bay** by **Buffalo** with Cory Sarich, Wayne Primeau and Buffalo's 3rd round choice (Alexander Kharitonov) in 2000 Entry Draft for Chris Gratton and Tampa Bay's 2nd round choice (Derek Roy) in 2001 Entry Draft, March 9, 2000. • Missed majority of 2001-02 season recovering from shoulder injury suffered in game vs. Florida, October 7, 2001. Traded to **Pittsburgh** by **Tampa Bay** for Marc Bergevin, March 11, 2003. Traded to **Columbus** by **Pittsburgh** for Lasse Pirjeta, March 9, 2004.

HORCOFF, Shawn

(HOHR-cuhf, SHAWN) **EDM.**

Center. Shoots left. 6'1", 204 lbs. Born, Trail, B.C., September 17, 1978. Edmonton's 3rd choice, 99th overall, in 1998 Entry Draft.

1994-95	Trail Smokies	RMJHL	47	50	46	96	26	....	....	....	....	....	....	....	....	....	....	....	....	....	....	....	....	....	....
1995-96	Chilliwack Chiefs	BCHL	58	49	96	*145	44	....	....	....	....	....	....	....	....	....	9	5	19	24	12	....	....	....	....
1996-97	Michigan State	CCHA	40	10	13	23	20	....	....	....	....	....	....	....	....	....	....	....	....	....	....	....	....	....	....
1997-98	Michigan State	CCHA	34	14	13	27	50	....	....	....	....	....	....	....	....	....	....	....	....	....	....	....	....	....	....
1998-99	Michigan State	CCHA	39	12	25	37	70	....	....	....	....	....	....	....	....	....	....	....	....	....	....	....	....	....	....
99-2000	Michigan State	CCHA	42	14	*51	*65	50	....	....	....	....	....	....	....	....	....	....	....	....	....	....	....	....	....	....
2000-01	**Edmonton**	**NHL**	**49**	**9**	**7**	**16**	**10**	**0**	**0**	**2**	**42**	**21.4**	**8**	**122**	**41.8**	**9:14**	**5**	**0**	**0**	**0**	**0**	**0**	**0**	**0**	**6:31**
	Hamilton	AHL	24	10	18	28	19	....	....	....	....	....	....	....	....	....	....	....	....	....	....	....	....	....	....
2001-02	**Edmonton**	**NHL**	**61**	**8**	**14**	**22**	**18**	**0**	**0**	**0**	**57**	**14.0**	**3**	**454**	**46.3**	**11:20**	....	....	....	....	....	....	....	....	....
	Hamilton	AHL	2	1	2	3	6	....	....	....	....	....	....	....	....	....	....	....	....	....	....	....	....	....	....
2002-03	**Edmonton**	**NHL**	**78**	**12**	**21**	**33**	**55**	**2**	**0**	**3**	**98**	**12.2**	**10**	**301**	**42.9**	**13:30**	**6**	**3**	**1**	**4**	**6**	**0**	**0**	**1**	**15:27**
2003-04	**Edmonton**	**NHL**	**80**	**15**	**25**	**40**	**73**	**0**	**2**	**3**	**110**	**13.6**	**0**	**1378**	**50.7**	**17:31**	....	....	....	....	....	....	....	....	....
	NHL Totals		**268**	**44**	**67**	**111**	**156**	**2**	**2**	**8**	**307**	**14.3**		**2255**	**48.2**	**13:25**	**11**	**3**	**1**	**4**	**6**	**0**	**0**	**1**	**11:23**

CCHA First All-Star Team (2000) • CCHA Player of the Year (2000) • NCAA West First All-American Team (2000)

HORDICHUK, Darcy

(HOHR-dih-chuhk, DAHR-see) **FLA.**

Left wing. Shoots left. 6'1", 215 lbs. Born, Kamsack, Sask., August 10, 1980. Atlanta's 9th choice, 180th overall, in 2000 Entry Draft.

1996-97	Yorkton Mallers	SMHL	57	6	15	21	230	....	....	....	....	....	....	....	....	....	....	....	....	....	....	....	....	....	....
	Calgary Hitmen	WHL	3	0	0	0	2	....	....	....	....	....	....	....	....	....	....	....	....	....	....	....	....	....	....
1997-98	Dauphin Kings	MJHL	58	12	21	33	279	....	....	....	....	....	....	....	....	....	....	....	....	....	....	....	....	....	....
1998-99	Saskatoon Blades	WHL	66	3	2	5	246	....	....	....	....	....	....	....	....	....	....	....	....	....	....	....	....	....	....
99-2000	Saskatoon Blades	WHL	63	6	8	14	269	....	....	....	....	....	....	....	....	....	11	4	2	6	43	....	....	....	....
2000-01	**Atlanta**	**NHL**	**11**	**0**	**0**	**0**	**38**	**0**	**0**	**0**	**6**	**0.0**	**–3**	**0**	**0.0**	**7:18**	....	....	....	....	....	....	....	....	....
	Orlando	IHL	69	7	3	10	*369	....	....	....	....	....	....	....	....	....	16	3	3	6	*41	....	....	....	....
2001-02	**Atlanta**	**NHL**	**33**	**1**	**1**	**2**	**127**	**0**	**0**	**0**	**8**	**12.5**	**–5**	**4**	**25.0**	**6:03**	....	....	....	....	....	....	....	....	....
	Chicago Wolves	AHL	34	5	4	9	127	....	....	....	....	....	....	....	....	....	....	....	....	....	....	....	....	....	....
	Phoenix	**NHL**	**1**	**0**	**0**	**0**	**14**	**0**	**0**	**0**	**0**	**0.0**	**0**	**0**	**0.0**	**7:18**	....	....	....	....	....	....	....	....	....
2002-03	**Phoenix**	**NHL**	**25**	**0**	**0**	**0**	**82**	**0**	**0**	**0**	**5**	**0.0**	**–1**	**0**	**0.0**	**4:47**	....	....	....	....	....	....	....	....	....
	Springfield	AHL	22	1	3	4	38	....	....	....	....	....	....	....	....	....	....	....	....	....	....	....	....	....	....
	Florida	**NHL**	**3**	**0**	**0**	**0**	**15**	**0**	**0**	**0**	**2**	**0.0**	**–1**	**0**	**0.0**	**9:45**	....	....	....	....	....	....	....	....	....
2003-04	**Florida**	**NHL**	**57**	**3**	**1**	**4**	**158**	**0**	**0**	**1**	**27**	**11.1**	**–10**	**4**	**50.0**	**6:46**	....	....	....	....	....	....	....	....	....
	NHL Totals		**130**	**4**	**2**	**6**	**434**	**0**	**0**	**1**	**48**	**8.3**		**8**	**37.5**	**6:19**	....	....	....	....	....	....	....	....	....

Traded to **Phoenix** by **Atlanta** with Atlanta's 4th (Lance Monych) and 5th (John Zeiler) round choices in 2002 Entry Draft for Kiril Safronov, the rights to Ruslan Zainullin and Phoenix's 4th round choice (Patrick Dwyer) in 2002 Entry Draft, March 19, 2002. Traded to **Florida** by **Phoenix** with Phoenix's 2nd round choice (later traded to Tampa Bay – Tampa Bay selected Matt Smaby) in 2003 Entry Draft for Brad Ference, March 8, 2003.

HORTON, Nathan

(HOHR-tohn, NAY-thun) **FLA.**

Center. Shoots right. 6'2", 201 lbs. Born, Welland, Ont., May 29, 1985. Florida's 1st choice, 3rd overall, in 2003 Entry Draft.

2000-01	Thorold	OJHL-B	41	16	31	47	75	....	....	....	....	....	....	....	....	....	....	....	....	....	....	....	....	....	....
2001-02	Oshawa Generals	OHL	64	31	36	67	84	....	....	....	....	....	....	....	....	....	5	1	2	3	10	....	....	....	....
2002-03	Oshawa Generals	OHL	54	33	35	68	111	....	....	....	....	....	....	....	....	....	13	9	6	15	10	....	....	....	....
2003-04	**Florida**	**NHL**	**55**	**14**	**8**	**22**	**57**	**6**	**1**	**0**	**81**	**17.3**	**–5**	**270**	**41.9**	**13:20**	....	....	....	....	....	....	....	....	....
	NHL Totals		**55**	**14**	**8**	**22**	**57**	**6**	**1**	**0**	**81**	**17.3**		**270**	**41.9**	**13:20**	....	....	....	....	....	....	....	....	....

OHL All-Rookie Team (2002)

HOSSA, Marcel

(HOH-sah, MAHR-sehl) **MTL.**

Left wing. Shoots left. 6'2", 215 lbs. Born, Ilava, Czech., October 12, 1981. Montreal's 2nd choice, 16th overall, in 2000 Entry Draft.

1996-97	Dukla Trencin Jr.	Slovak-Jr.	45	30	21	51	30	....	....	....	....	....	....	....	....	....	....	....	....	....	....	....	....	....	....
1997-98	Dukla Trencin Jr.	Slovak-Jr.	39	11	38	49	44	....	....	....	....	....	....	....	....	....	....	....	....	....	....	....	....	....	....
1998-99	Portland	WHL	70	7	14	21	66	....	....	....	....	....	....	....	....	....	2	0	0	0	2	....	....	....	....
99-2000	Portland	WHL	60	24	29	53	58	....	....	....	....	....	....	....	....	....	....	....	....	....	....	....	....	....	....
2000-01	Portland	WHL	58	34	56	90	58	....	....	....	....	....	....	....	....	....	16	5	7	12	14	....	....	....	....
2001-02	**Montreal**	**NHL**	**10**	**3**	**1**	**4**	**2**	**0**	**0**	**0**	**20**	**15.0**	**2**	**0**	**0.0**	**11:09**	....	....	....	....	....	....	....	....	....
	Quebec Citadelles	AHL	50	17	15	32	24	....	....	....	....	....	....	....	....	....	3	0	0	0	4	....	....	....	....
2002-03	**Montreal**	**NHL**	**34**	**6**	**7**	**13**	**14**	**2**	**0**	**1**	**51**	**11.8**	**3**	**4**	**50.0**	**13:58**	....	....	....	....	....	....	....	....	....
	Hamilton	AHL	37	19	13	32	18	....	....	....	....	....	....	....	....	....	21	4	7	11	12	....	....	....	....
2003-04	**Montreal**	**NHL**	**15**	**1**	**1**	**2**	**8**	**0**	**0**	**0**	**19**	**5.3**	**–3**	**5**	**40.0**	**14:50**	....	....	....	....	....	....	....	....	....
	Hamilton	AHL	57	18	22	40	45	....	....	....	....	....	....	....	....	....	10	2	3	5	8	....	....	....	....
	NHL Totals		**59**	**10**	**9**	**19**	**24**	**2**	**0**	**1**	**90**	**11.1**		**9**	**44.4**	**13:43**	....	....	....	....	....	....	....	....	....

WHL West Second All-Star Team (2001)

HOSSA, Marian

(HOH-sah, MAIR-ee-uhn) **OTT.**

Right wing. Shoots left. 6'1", 208 lbs. Born, Stara Lubovna, Czech., January 12, 1979. Ottawa's 1st choice, 12th overall, in 1997 Entry Draft.

1995-96	Dukla Trencin Jr.	Slovak-Jr.	53	42	49	91	26	....	....	....	....	....	....	....	....	....	....	....	....	....	....	....	....	....	....
1996-97	Dukla Trencin	Slovakia	46	25	19	44	33	....	....	....	....	....	....	....	....	....	7	5	5	10	....	....	....	....	....
1997-98	Portland	WHL	53	45	40	85	50	....	....	....	....	....	....	....	....	....	16	13	6	19	6	....	....	....	....
	Ottawa	**NHL**	**7**	**0**	**1**	**1**	**0**	**0**	**0**	**0**	**10**	**0.0**	**–1**	....	....	....	....	....	....	....	....	....	....	....	....
1998-99	**Ottawa**	**NHL**	**60**	**15**	**15**	**30**	**37**	**1**	**0**	**2**	**124**	**12.1**	**18**	**4**	**25.0**	**13:59**	**4**	**0**	**2**	**2**	**4**	**0**	**0**	**0**	**16:46**
99-2000	**Ottawa**	**NHL**	**78**	**29**	**27**	**56**	**32**	**5**	**0**	**4**	**240**	**12.1**	**5**	**7**	**57.1**	**17:12**	**6**	**0**	**0**	**0**	**2**	**0**	**0**	**0**	**15:22**
2000-01	**Ottawa**	**NHL**	**81**	**32**	**43**	**75**	**44**	**11**	**2**	**7**	**249**	**12.9**	**19**	**14**	**42.9**	**18:01**	**4**	**1**	**1**	**2**	**4**	**0**	**0**	**0**	**19:01**
2001-02	Dukla Trencin	Slovakia	8	3	4	7	16	....	....	....	....	....	....	....	....	....	....	....	....	....	....	....	....	....	....
	Ottawa	**NHL**	**80**	**31**	**35**	**66**	**50**	**9**	**1**	**4**	**278**	**11.2**	**11**	**12**	**33.3**	**18:29**	**12**	**4**	**6**	**10**	**2**	**1**	**0**	**0**	**19:04**
	Slovakia	Olympics	2	4	2	6	0	....	....	....	....	....	....	....	....	....	....	....	....	....	....	....	....	....	....
2002-03	**Ottawa**	**NHL**	**80**	**45**	**35**	**80**	**34**	**14**	**0**	**10**	**229**	**19.7**	**8**	**19**	**36.8**	**18:31**	**18**	**5**	**11**	**16**	**6**	**3**	**0**	**1**	**18:41**
2003-04	**Ottawa**	**NHL**	**81**	**36**	**46**	**82**	**46**	**14**	**1**	**5**	**233**	**15.5**	**4**	**25**	**40.0**	**18:37**	**7**	**3**	**1**	**4**	**0**	**1**	**0**	**2**	**21:24**
	NHL Totals		**467**	**188**	**202**	**390**	**243**	**54**	**4**	**32**	**1363**	**13.8**		**81**	**39.5**	**17:38**	**51**	**13**	**21**	**34**	**18**	**5**	**0**	**3**	**18:38**

WHL West First All-Star Team (1998) • Canadian Major Junior First All-Star Team (1998) • Memorial Cup All-Star Team (1998) • NHL All-Rookie Team (1999)

Played in NHL All-Star Game (2001, 2003)

HRDINA, Jan

(huhr-DEE-nah, YAN) **N.J.**

Center. Shoots right. 6', 205 lbs. Born, Hradec Kralove, Czech., February 5, 1976. Pittsburgh's 4th choice, 128th overall, in 1995 Entry Draft.

1993-94	H. Kralove Jr.	Czech-Jr.	10	1	6	7	0	....	....	....	....	....	....	....	....	....	....	....	....	....	....	....	....	....	....
	Hradec Kralove	Czech	23	1	5	6	....	....	....	....	....	....	....	....	....	....	4	0	1	1	....	....	....	....	....
1994-95	Seattle	WHL	69	41	59	100	79	....	....	....	....	....	....	....	....	....	4	0	1	1	8	....	....	....	....
1995-96	Seattle	WHL	30	19	28	47	37	....	....	....	....	....	....	....	....	....	....	....	....	....	....	....	....	....	....
	Spokane Chiefs	WHL	18	10	16	26	25	....	....	....	....	....	....	....	....	....	18	5	14	19	49	....	....	....	....
1996-97	Cleveland	IHL	68	23	31	54	82	....	....	....	....	....	....	....	....	....	13	1	2	3	8	....	....	....	....
1997-98	Syracuse Crunch	AHL	72	20	24	44	82	....	....	....	....	....	....	....	....	....	5	1	3	4	10	....	....	....	....
1998-99	**Pittsburgh**	**NHL**	**82**	**13**	**29**	**42**	**40**	**3**	**0**	**2**	**94**	**13.8**	**–2**	**1461**	**56.7**	**16:26**	**13**	**4**	**1**	**5**	**12**	**1**	**0**	**1**	**21:03**
99-2000	**Pittsburgh**	**NHL**	**70**	**13**	**33**	**46**	**43**	**3**	**0**	**1**	**84**	**15.5**	**13**	**1392**	**53.7**	**18:47**	**9**	**4**	**8**	**12**	**2**	**1**	**0**	**0**	**22:04**
2000-01	**Pittsburgh**	**NHL**	**78**	**15**	**28**	**43**	**48**	**3**	**0**	**1**	**89**	**16.9**	**19**	**1067**	**53.8**	**15:56**	**18**	**2**	**5**	**7**	**8**	**0**	**0**	**0**	**15:04**

			Regular Season														Playoffs								
Season	Club	League	GP	G	A	Pts	PIM	PP	SH	GW	S	%	+/-	TF	F%	Min	GP	G	A	Pts	PIM	PP	SH	GW	Min
2001-02	**Pittsburgh**	**NHL**	**79**	**24**	**33**	**57**	**50**	**6**	**0**	**6**	**115**	**20.9**	**−7**	**667**	**50.4**	**19:51**	....	....	....	....	....	....	....	....	....
	Czech Republic	Olympics	4	0	0	0	0	....	....	....	....	....	....	....	....	....	....	....	....	....	....	....	....	....	....
2002-03	**Pittsburgh**	**NHL**	**57**	**14**	**25**	**39**	**34**	**11**	**0**	**4**	**84**	**16.7**	**1**	**984**	**56.0**	**19:45**	....	....	....	....	....	....	....	....	....
	Phoenix	**NHL**	**4**	**0**	**4**	**4**	**8**	**0**	**0**	**0**	**2**	**0.0**	**3**	**70**	**60.0**	**18:12**	....	....	....	....	....	....	....	....	....
2003-04	**Phoenix**	**NHL**	**55**	**11**	**15**	**26**	**30**	**5**	**0**	**1**	**62**	**17.7**	**−10**	**677**	**50.7**	**17:57**	....	....	....	....	....	....	....	....	....
	New Jersey	**NHL**	**13**	**1**	**6**	**7**	**10**	**0**	**0**	**0**	**11**	**9.1**	**4**	**148**	**55.4**	**12:51**	**5**	**2**	**0**	**2**	**2**	**0**	**0**	**0**	**13:22**
	NHL Totals		**438**	**91**	**173**	**264**	**263**	**31**	**0**	**15**	**541**	**16.8**		**6466**	**54.2**	**17:52**	**45**	**12**	**14**	**26**	**24**	**2**	**0**	**1**	**18:00**

Traded to **Phoenix** by **Pittsburgh** with Francois Leroux for Ramzi Abid, Dan Focht and Guillaume Lefebvre, March 11, 2003. Traded to **New Jersey** by **Phoenix** for Mike Rupp and New Jersey's 2nd round choice (later traded to Edmonton – Edmonton selected Geoff Paukovich) in 2004 Entry Draft, March 5, 2004.

HRKAC, Tony

(HUHR-kuhz, TOH-nee) **NSH.**

Center. Shoots left. 5'10", 190 lbs. Born, Thunder Bay, Ont., July 7, 1966. St. Louis' 2nd choice, 32nd overall, in 1984 Entry Draft.

Season	Club	League	GP	G	A	Pts	PIM	PP	SH	GW	S	%	+/-	TF	F%	Min	GP	G	A	Pts	PIM	PP	SH	GW	Min
1983-84	Orillia Travelways	OPJHL	42	*52	54	*106	20	....	....	....	....	....	....	....	....	....	....	....	....	....	....	....	....	....	....
1984-85	North Dakota	WCHA	36	18	36	54	16	....	....	....	....	....	....	....	....	....	....	....	....	....	....	....	....	....	....
1985-86	Team Canada	Nat-Tm	62	19	30	49	36	....	....	....	....	....	....	....	....	....	....	....	....	....	....	....	....	....	....
1986-87	North Dakota	WCHA	48	46	70	116	48	....	....	....	....	....	....	....	....	....	....	....	....	....	....	....	....	....	....
	St. Louis	**NHL**	....	....	....	....	....	....	....	....	....	....	....	....	....	....	**3**	**0**	**0**	**0**	**0**	**0**	**0**	**0**	....
1987-88	**St. Louis**	**NHL**	**67**	**11**	**37**	**48**	**22**	**2**	**1**	**3**	**86**	**12.8**	**5**	....	....	....	**10**	**6**	**1**	**7**	**4**	**3**	**1**	**1**	....
1988-89	**St. Louis**	**NHL**	**70**	**17**	**28**	**45**	**8**	**5**	**0**	**1**	**133**	**12.8**	**−10**	....	....	....	**4**	**1**	**1**	**2**	**0**	**0**	**0**	**1**	....
1989-90	**St. Louis**	**NHL**	**28**	**5**	**12**	**17**	**8**	**1**	**0**	**0**	**41**	**12.2**	**1**	....	....	....	....	....	....	....	....	....	....	....	....
	Quebec	**NHL**	**22**	**4**	**8**	**12**	**2**	**2**	**0**	**0**	**29**	**13.8**	**−5**	....	....	....	....	....	....	....	....	....	....	....	....
	Halifax Citadels	AHL	20	12	21	33	4	....	....	....	....	....	....	....	....	....	6	5	9	14	4	....	....	....	....
1990-91	**Quebec**	**NHL**	**70**	**16**	**32**	**48**	**16**	**6**	**0**	**0**	**122**	**13.1**	**−22**	....	....	....	....	....	....	....	....	....	....	....	....
	Halifax Citadels	AHL	3	4	1	5	2	....	....	....	....	....	....	....	....	....	....	....	....	....	....	....	....	....	....
1991-92	**San Jose**	**NHL**	**22**	**2**	**10**	**12**	**4**	**0**	**0**	**0**	**31**	**6.5**	**−2**	....	....	....	....	....	....	....	....	....	....	....	....
	Chicago	**NHL**	**18**	**1**	**2**	**3**	**6**	**0**	**0**	**0**	**22**	**4.5**	**4**	....	....	....	**3**	**0**	**0**	**0**	**2**	**0**	**0**	**0**	....
1992-93	Indianapolis Ice	IHL	80	45	*87	*132	70	....	....	....	....	....	....	....	....	....	5	0	2	2	2	....	....	....	....
1993-94	**St. Louis**	**NHL**	**36**	**6**	**5**	**11**	**8**	**1**	**1**	**1**	**43**	**14.0**	**−11**	....	....	....	**4**	**0**	**0**	**0**	**0**	**0**	**0**	**0**	....
	Peoria Rivermen	IHL	45	30	51	81	25	....	....	....	....	....	....	....	....	....	1	1	2	3	0	....	....	....	....
1994-95	Milwaukee	IHL	71	24	67	91	26	....	....	....	....	....	....	....	....	....	15	4	9	13	16	....	....	....	....
1995-96	Milwaukee	IHL	43	14	28	42	18	....	....	....	....	....	....	....	....	....	5	1	3	4	4	....	....	....	....
1996-97	Milwaukee	IHL	81	27	61	88	20	....	....	....	....	....	....	....	....	....	3	1	1	2	2	....	....	....	....
1997-98	**Dallas**	**NHL**	**13**	**5**	**3**	**8**	**0**	**3**	**0**	**0**	**14**	**35.7**	**0**	....	....	....	....	....	....	....	....	....	....	....	....
	Michigan	IHL	20	7	15	22	6	....	....	....	....	....	....	....	....	....	....	....	....	....	....	....	....	....	....
	Edmonton	**NHL**	**36**	**8**	**11**	**19**	**10**	**4**	**0**	**1**	**43**	**18.6**	**3**	....	....	....	**12**	**0**	**3**	**3**	**2**	**0**	**0**	**0**	....
1998-99♦	**Dallas**	**NHL**	**69**	**13**	**14**	**27**	**26**	**2**	**0**	**2**	**67**	**19.4**	**2**	**666**	**48.0**	**12:02**	**5**	**0**	**2**	**2**	**4**	**0**	**0**	**0**	**9:15**
99-2000	**NY Islanders**	**NHL**	**7**	**0**	**2**	**2**	**0**	**0**	**0**	**0**	**2**	**0.0**	**−1**	**34**	**35.3**	**11:22**	....	....	....	....	....	....	....	....	....
	Anaheim	**NHL**	**60**	**4**	**7**	**11**	**8**	**1**	**0**	**0**	**37**	**10.8**	**−2**	**536**	**50.8**	**9:04**	....	....	....	....	....	....	....	....	....
2000-01	**Anaheim**	**NHL**	**80**	**13**	**25**	**38**	**29**	**0**	**0**	**1**	**88**	**14.8**	**0**	**1072**	**50.7**	**13:46**	....	....	....	....	....	....	....	....	....
2001-02	**Atlanta**	**NHL**	**80**	**18**	**26**	**44**	**12**	**5**	**1**	**2**	**101**	**17.8**	**−12**	**935**	**47.5**	**17:29**	....	....	....	....	....	....	....	....	....
2002-03	**Atlanta**	**NHL**	**80**	**9**	**17**	**26**	**14**	**2**	**0**	**2**	**86**	**10.5**	**−16**	**1125**	**44.6**	**16:06**	....	....	....	....	....	....	....	....	....
2003-04	Milwaukee	AHL	68	20	39	59	20	....	....	....	....	....	....	....	....	....	22	8	12	20	8	....	....	....	....
	NHL Totals		**758**	**132**	**239**	**371**	**173**	**34**	**3**	**13**	**945**	**14.0**		**4368**	**47.9**	**13:56**	**41**	**7**	**7**	**14**	**12**	**3**	**1**	**2**	**9:15**

WCHA First All-Star Team (1987) • WCHA Player of the Year (1987) • NCAA West First All-American Team (1987) • NCAA Championship All-Tournament Team (1987) • NCAA Championship Tournament MVP (1987) • Hobey Baker Memorial Award (Top U.S. Collegiate Player) (1987) • James Gatschene Memorial Trophy (MVP – IHL) (1993) • IHL First All-Star Team (1993) • Leo P. Lamoureux Memorial Trophy (Top Scorer – IHL) (1993) • James Gatschene Memorial Trophy (MVP – IHL) (1993)

Traded to **Quebec** by **St. Louis** with Greg Millen for Jeff Brown, December 13, 1989. Traded to **San Jose** by **Quebec** for Greg Paslawski, May 31, 1991. Traded to **Chicago** by **San Jose** for Chicago's 6th round choice (Fredrik Oduya) in 1993 Entry Draft, February 7, 1992. Signed as a free agent by **St. Louis**, July 30, 1993. Signed as a free agent by **Dallas**, August 12, 1997. Claimed on waivers by **Edmonton** from **Dallas**, January 6, 1998. Traded to **Pittsburgh** by **Edmonton** with Bobby Dollas for Josef Beranek, June 16, 1998. Claimed by **Nashville** from **Pittsburgh** in Expansion Draft, June 26, 1998. Traded to **Dallas** by **Nashville** for future considerations, July 9, 1998. Signed as a free agent by **NY Islanders**, July 29, 1999. Traded to **Anaheim** by **NY Islanders** with Dean Malkoc for Ted Drury, October 29, 1999. Signed as a free agent by **Atlanta**, July 25, 2001. Signed as a free agent by **Nashville**, November 4, 2003.

HUBACEK, Petr

(HOO-buh-chehk, PEE-tuhr) **NSH.**

Center. Shoots right. 6'2", 183 lbs. Born, Brno, Czech., September 2, 1979. Philadelphia's 11th choice, 243rd overall, in 1998 Entry Draft.

Season	Club	League	GP	G	A	Pts	PIM	PP	SH	GW	S	%	+/-	TF	F%	Min	GP	G	A	Pts	PIM	PP	SH	GW	Min
1997-98	Kometa Brno Jr.	Czech-Jr.	17	9	5	14	....	....	....	....	....	....	....	....	....	....	....	....	....	....	....	....	....	....	....
	HC Kometa Brno	Czech-2	48	6	10	16	....	....	....	....	....	....	....	....	....	....	....	....	....	....	....	....	....	....	....
1998-99	HC Vitkovice	Czech	25	0	4	4	2	....	....	....	....	....	....	....	....	....	4	0	0	0	....	....	....	....	....
99-2000	HC Vitkovice	Czech	48	11	12	23	81	....	....	....	....	....	....	....	....	....	....	....	....	....	....	....	....	....	....
2000-01	**Philadelphia**	**NHL**	**6**	**1**	**0**	**1**	**2**	**0**	**0**	**0**	**5**	**20.0**	**−1**	**39**	**25.6**	**11:20**	....	....	....	....	....	....	....	....	....
	Philadelphia	AHL	62	3	9	12	29	....	....	....	....	....	....	....	....	....	9	0	1	1	6	....	....	....	....
2001-02	Philadelphia	AHL	22	1	6	7	8	....	....	....	....	....	....	....	....	....	....	....	....	....	....	....	....	....	....
	Milwaukee	AHL	14	2	0	2	0	....	....	....	....	....	....	....	....	....	....	....	....	....	....	....	....	....	....
2002-03	HC Hame Zlin	Czech	44	4	15	19	14	....	....	....	....	....	....	....	....	....	....	....	....	....	....	....	....	....	....
	HC Vitkovice	Czech	7	1	4	5	10	....	....	....	....	....	....	....	....	....	6	1	0	1	16	....	....	....	....
2003-04	HC Vitkovice	Czech	46	7	14	21	26	....	....	....	....	....	....	....	....	....	6	1	0	1	*53	....	....	....	....
	NHL Totals		**6**	**1**	**0**	**1**	**2**	**0**	**0**	**0**	**5**	**20.0**		**39**	**25.6**	**11:20**	....	....	....	....	....	....	....	....	....

Traded to **Nashville** by **Philadelphia** with Jason Beckett for Yves Sarault, January 11, 2002. Signed as a free agent by **HC Hame Zlin** (Czech) with Nashville retaining NHL rights, August 4, 2002.

HUDLER, Jiri

(HUHD-luhr, YIH-ree) **DET.**

Center. Shoots left. 5'9", 178 lbs. Born, Olomouc, Czech., January 4, 1984. Detroit's 1st choice, 58th overall, in 2002 Entry Draft.

Season	Club	League	GP	G	A	Pts	PIM	PP	SH	GW	S	%	+/-	TF	F%	Min	GP	G	A	Pts	PIM	PP	SH	GW	Min
1998-99	Vsetin 18	Czech-Jr.	46	57	57	114	....	....	....	....	....	....	....	....	....	....	....	....	....	....	....	....	....	....	....
99-2000	Vsetin Jr.	Czech-Jr.	53	29	31	60	75	....	....	....	....	....	....	....	....	....	....	....	....	....	....	....	....	....	....
	Vsetin	Czech	2	0	1	1	0	....	....	....	....	....	....	....	....	....	....	....	....	....	....	....	....	....	....
2000-01	Vsetin Jr.	Czech-Jr.	16	8	14	22	16	....	....	....	....	....	....	....	....	....	....	....	....	....	....	....	....	....	....
	HC Slovnaft Vsetin	Czech	22	1	4	5	10	....	....	....	....	....	....	....	....	....	....	....	....	....	....	....	....	....	....
	HC Femax Havirov	Czech	15	5	1	6	12	....	....	....	....	....	....	....	....	....	....	....	....	....	....	....	....	....	....
2001-02	Vsetin	Czech	46	15	31	46	54	....	....	....	....	....	....	....	....	....	....	....	....	....	....	....	....	....	....
	Liberec	Czech-2	13	9	7	16	10	....	....	....	....	....	....	....	....	....	....	....	....	....	....	....	....	....	....
	HC Olomouc	Czech-3	1	0	2	2	4	....	....	....	....	....	....	....	....	....	....	....	....	....	....	....	....	....	....
2002-03	Vsetin	Czech	30	19	27	46	22	....	....	....	....	....	....	....	....	....	....	....	....	....	....	....	....	....	....
	Ak Bars Kazan	Russia	11	1	5	6	12	....	....	....	....	....	....	....	....	....	1	0	0	0	0	....	....	....	....
2003-04	**Detroit**	**NHL**	**12**	**1**	**2**	**3**	**10**	**1**	**0**	**0**	**8**	**12.5**	**−1**	**50**	**30.0**	**8:09**	....	....	....	....	....	....	....	....	....
	Grand Rapids	AHL	57	17	32	49	46	....	....	....	....	....	....	....	....	....	4	1	5	6	2	....	....	....	....
	NHL Totals		**12**	**1**	**2**	**3**	**10**	**1**	**0**	**0**	**8**	**12.5**		**50**	**30.0**	**8:09**	....	....	....	....	....	....	....	....	....

HULBIG, Joe

(HUHL-bihg, JOH)

Left wing. Shoots left. 6'4", 215 lbs. Born, Norwood, MA, September 29, 1973. Edmonton's 1st choice, 13th overall, in 1992 Entry Draft.

Season	Club	League	GP	G	A	Pts	PIM	PP	SH	GW	S	%	+/-	TF	F%	Min	GP	G	A	Pts	PIM	PP	SH	GW	Min
1989-90	St. Sebastian's	Hi-School	30	13	12	25	....	....	....	....	....	....	....	....	....	....	....	....	....	....	....	....	....	....	....
1990-91	St. Sebastian's	Hi-School	30	23	19	42	....	....	....	....	....	....	....	....	....	....	....	....	....	....	....	....	....	....	....
1991-92	St. Sebastian's	Hi-School	17	19	24	43	30	....	....	....	....	....	....	....	....	....	....	....	....	....	....	....	....	....	....
1992-93	Providence	H-East	26	3	13	16	22	....	....	....	....	....	....	....	....	....	....	....	....	....	....	....	....	....	....
1993-94	Providence	H-East	28	6	4	10	36	....	....	....	....	....	....	....	....	....	....	....	....	....	....	....	....	....	....
1994-95	Providence	H-East	37	14	21	35	36	....	....	....	....	....	....	....	....	....	....	....	....	....	....	....	....	....	....
1995-96	Providence	H-East	31	14	22	36	56	....	....	....	....	....	....	....	....	....	....	....	....	....	....	....	....	....	....
1996-97	**Edmonton**	**NHL**	**6**	**0**	**0**	**0**	**0**	**0**	**0**	**0**	**4**	**0.0**	**−1**	....	....	....	**6**	**0**	**1**	**1**	**2**	**0**	**0**	**0**	....
	Hamilton	AHL	73	18	28	46	59	....	....	....	....	....	....	....	....	....	16	6	10	16	6	....	....	....	....
1997-98	**Edmonton**	**NHL**	**17**	**2**	**2**	**4**	**2**	**0**	**0**	**1**	**8**	**25.0**	**−1**	....	....	....	....	....	....	....	....	....	....	....	....
	Hamilton	AHL	46	15	16	31	52	....	....	....	....	....	....	....	....	....	3	0	1	1	2	....	....	....	....
1998-99	**Edmonton**	**NHL**	**1**	**0**	**0**	**0**	**2**	**0**	**0**	**0**	**2**	**0.0**	**1**	**0**	**0.0**	**8:20**	....	....	....	....	....	....	....	....	....
	Hamilton	AHL	76	22	24	46	68	....	....	....	....	....	....	....	....	....	11	4	2	6	18	....	....	....	....
99-2000	**Boston**	**NHL**	**24**	**2**	**2**	**4**	**8**	**0**	**0**	**0**	**15**	**13.3**	**−8**	**2**	**0.0**	**8:18**	....	....	....	....	....	....	....	....	....
	Providence Bruins	AHL	15	4	5	9	17	....	....	....	....	....	....	....	....	....	....	....	....	....	....	....	....	....	....
2000-01	**Boston**	**NHL**	**7**	**0**	**0**	**0**	**4**	**0**	**0**	**0**	**0**	**0.0**	**−3**	**0**	**0.0**	**5:28**	....	....	....	....	....	....	....	....	....
	Providence Bruins	AHL	36	4	11	15	19	....	....	....	....	....	....	....	....	....	15	2	2	4	20	....	....	....	....
2001-02	Providence Bruins	AHL	54	8	10	18	41	....	....	....	....	....	....	....	....	....	....	....	....	....	....	....	....	....	....
	Worcester IceCats	AHL	7	0	3	3	2	....	....	....	....	....	....	....	....	....	3	1	0	1	7	....	....	....	....

			Regular Season														Playoffs								
Season	Club	League	GP	G	A	Pts	PIM	PP	SH	GW	S	%	+/-	TF	F%	Min	GP	G	A	Pts	PIM	PP	SH	GW	Min
2002-03	Albany River Rats	AHL	35	11	9	20	20	....	....	....	....	....	....	....	....	....	....	....	....	....	....	....	....	....	....
2003-04	Albany River Rats	AHL	64	21	24	45	60	....	....	....	....	....	....	....	....	....	....	....	....	....	....	....	....	....	....
	NHL Totals		**55**	**4**	**4**	**8**	**16**	**0**	**0**	**1**	**29**	**13.8**		**2**	**0.0**	**7:41**	**6**	**0**	**1**	**1**	**2**	**0**	**0**	**0**	....

Signed as a free agent by **Boston**, July 23, 1999. • Missed majority of 2000-01 season recovering from head injury suffered in game vs. Ottawa, November 9, 2000. Signed as a free agent by **New Jersey**, October 1, 2002.

HULL, Brett

(HUHL, BREHT) **PHX.**

Right wing. Shoots right. 5'11", 203 lbs. Born, Belleville, Ont., August 9, 1964. Calgary's 6th choice, 117th overall, in 1984 Entry Draft.

Season	Club	League	GP	G	A	Pts	PIM	PP	SH	GW	S	%	+/-	TF	F%	Min	GP	G	A	Pts	PIM	PP	SH	GW	Min
1982-83	Penticton Knights	BCJHL	50	48	56	104	27	....	....	....	....	....	....	....	....	....	....	....	....	....	....	....	....	....	....
1983-84	Penticton Knights	BCJHL	56	*105	83	*188	20	....	....	....	....	....	....	....	....	....	....	....	....	....	....	....	....	....	....
1984-85	U. Minn-Duluth	WCHA	48	32	28	60	24	....	....	....	....	....	....	....	....	....	....	....	....	....	....	....	....	....	....
1985-86	U. Minn-Duluth	WCHA	42	52	32	84	46	....	....	....	....	....	....	....	....	....	....	....	....	....	....	....	....	....	....
	Calgary	**NHL**	....	....	....	....	....	....	....	....	....	....	....	....	....	....	**2**	**0**	**0**	**0**	**0**	**0**	**0**	**0**	....
1986-87	**Calgary**	**NHL**	**5**	**1**	**0**	**1**	**0**	**0**	**0**	**1**	**5**	**20.0**	**–1**	....	....	....	**4**	**2**	**1**	**3**	**0**	**0**	**0**	**0**	....
	Moncton	AHL	67	50	42	92	16	....	....	....	....	....	....	....	....	....	3	2	2	4	2	....	....	....	....
1987-88	**Calgary**	**NHL**	**52**	**26**	**24**	**50**	**12**	**4**	**0**	**3**	**153**	**17.0**	**10**	....	....	....	....	....	....	....	....	....	....	....	....
	St. Louis	**NHL**	**13**	**6**	**8**	**14**	**4**	**2**	**0**	**0**	**58**	**10.3**	**4**	....	....	....	**10**	**7**	**2**	**9**	**4**	**4**	**0**	**3**	....
1988-89	**St. Louis**	**NHL**	**78**	**41**	**43**	**84**	**33**	**16**	**0**	**6**	**305**	**13.4**	**–17**	....	....	....	**10**	**5**	**5**	**10**	**6**	**1**	**0**	**2**	....
1989-90	**St. Louis**	**NHL**	**80**	***72**	**41**	**113**	**24**	**27**	**0**	**12**	**385**	**18.7**	**–1**	....	....	....	**12**	**13**	**8**	**21**	**17**	**7**	**0**	**3**	....
1990-91	**St. Louis**	**NHL**	**78**	***86**	**45**	**131**	**22**	**29**	**0**	**11**	**389**	**22.1**	**23**	....	....	....	**13**	**11**	**8**	**19**	**4**	**3**	**0**	**2**	....
1991-92	**St. Louis**	**NHL**	**73**	***70**	**39**	**109**	**48**	**20**	**5**	**9**	**408**	**17.2**	**–2**	....	....	....	**6**	**4**	**4**	**8**	**4**	**1**	**1**	**1**	....
1992-93	**St. Louis**	**NHL**	**80**	**54**	**47**	**101**	**41**	**29**	**0**	**2**	**390**	**13.8**	**–27**	....	....	....	**11**	**8**	**5**	**13**	**2**	**5**	**0**	**2**	....
1993-94	**St. Louis**	**NHL**	**81**	**57**	**40**	**97**	**38**	**25**	**3**	**6**	**392**	**14.5**	**–3**	....	....	....	**4**	**2**	**1**	**3**	**0**	**1**	**0**	**0**	....
1994-95	**St. Louis**	**NHL**	**48**	**29**	**21**	**50**	**10**	**9**	**3**	**6**	**200**	**14.5**	**13**	....	....	....	**7**	**6**	**2**	**8**	**0**	**2**	**0**	**0**	....
1995-96	**St. Louis**	**NHL**	**70**	**43**	**40**	**83**	**30**	**16**	**5**	**6**	**327**	**13.1**	**4**	....	....	....	**13**	**6**	**5**	**11**	**10**	**2**	**1**	**1**	....
1996-97	**St. Louis**	**NHL**	**77**	**42**	**40**	**82**	**10**	**12**	**2**	**6**	**302**	**13.9**	**–9**	....	....	....	**6**	**2**	**7**	**9**	**2**	**0**	**0**	**0**	....
1997-98	**St. Louis**	**NHL**	**66**	**27**	**45**	**72**	**26**	**10**	**0**	**6**	**211**	**12.8**	**–1**	....	....	....	**10**	**3**	**3**	**6**	**2**	**1**	**0**	**1**	....
	United States	Olympics	4	2	1	3	0	....	....	....	....	....	....	....	....	....	....	....	....	....	....	....	....	....	....
1998-99♦	**Dallas**	**NHL**	**60**	**32**	**26**	**58**	**30**	**15**	**0**	**11**	**192**	**16.7**	**19**	**12**	**50.0**	**17:24**	**22**	**8**	**7**	**15**	**4**	**3**	**0**	**2**	**18:29**
99-2000	**Dallas**	**NHL**	**79**	**24**	**35**	**59**	**43**	**11**	**0**	**3**	**223**	**10.8**	**–21**	**10**	**40.0**	**18:37**	**23**	***11**	***13**	***24**	**4**	**3**	**0**	**4**	**19:59**
2000-01	**Dallas**	**NHL**	**79**	**39**	**40**	**79**	**18**	**11**	**0**	**8**	**219**	**17.8**	**10**	**10**	**30.0**	**17:53**	**10**	**2**	**5**	**7**	**6**	**1**	**0**	**0**	**20:10**
2001-02♦	**Detroit**	**NHL**	**82**	**30**	**33**	**63**	**35**	**7**	**1**	**4**	**247**	**12.1**	**18**	**5**	**20.0**	**18:49**	**23**	***10**	**8**	**18**	**4**	**3**	**2**	**2**	**17:54**
	United States	Olympics	6	3	5	8	6	....	....	....	....	....	....	....	....	....	....	....	....	....	....	....	....	....	....
2002-03	**Detroit**	**NHL**	**82**	**37**	**39**	**76**	**22**	**12**	**1**	**4**	**262**	**14.1**	**11**	**18**	**38.9**	**18:07**	**4**	**0**	**1**	**1**	**0**	**0**	**0**	**0**	**20:17**
2003-04	**Detroit**	**NHL**	**81**	**25**	**43**	**68**	**12**	**10**	**0**	**6**	**200**	**12.5**	**–4**	**7**	**42.9**	**16:54**	**12**	**3**	**2**	**5**	**4**	**1**	**0**	**1**	**15:15**
	NHL Totals		**1264**	**741**	**649**	**1390**	**458**	**265**	**20**	**110**	**4868**	**15.2**		**62**	**38.7**	**17:59**	**202**	**103**	**87**	**190**	**73**	**38**	**4**	**24**	**18:33**

WCHA Freshman of the Year (1985) • WCHA First All-Star Team (1986) • AHL First All-Star Team (1987) • Dudley "Red" Garrett Memorial Trophy (Top Rookie – AHL) (1987) • NHL First All-Star Team (1990, 1991, 1992) • Dodge Ram Tough Award (1990, 1991) • Lady Byng Trophy (1990) • ProSet/NHL Player of the Year Award (1991) • Lester B. Pearson Award (1991) • Hart Memorial Trophy (1991)

Played in NHL All-Star Game (1989, 1990, 1992, 1993, 1994, 1996, 1997, 2001)

Traded to **St. Louis** by **Calgary** with Steve Bozek for Rob Ramage and Rick Wamsley, March 7, 1988. Signed as a free agent by **Dallas**, July 3, 1998. Signed as a free agent by **Detroit**, August 22, 2001. Signed as a free agent by **Phoenix**, August 6, 2004.

HULL, Jody

(HUHL, JOH-dee)

Right wing. Shoots right. 6'2", 195 lbs. Born, Petrolia, Ont., February 2, 1969. Hartford's 1st choice, 18th overall, in 1987 Entry Draft.

Season	Club	League	GP	G	A	Pts	PIM	PP	SH	GW	S	%	+/-	TF	F%	Min	GP	G	A	Pts	PIM	PP	SH	GW	Min
1984-85	Cambridge	OJHL-B	38	13	17	30	39	....	....	....	....	....	....	....	....	....	....	....	....	....	....	....	....	....	....
1985-86	Peterborough	OHL	61	20	22	42	29	....	....	....	....	....	....	....	....	....	16	1	5	6	4	....	....	....	....
1986-87	Peterborough	OHL	49	18	34	52	22	....	....	....	....	....	....	....	....	....	12	4	9	13	14	....	....	....	....
1987-88	Peterborough	OHL	60	50	44	94	33	....	....	....	....	....	....	....	....	....	12	10	8	18	8	....	....	....	....
1988-89	**Hartford**	**NHL**	**60**	**16**	**18**	**34**	**10**	**6**	**0**	**2**	**82**	**19.5**	**6**	....	....	....	**1**	**0**	**0**	**0**	**2**	**0**	**0**	**0**	....
1989-90	**Hartford**	**NHL**	**38**	**7**	**10**	**17**	**21**	**2**	**0**	**0**	**46**	**15.2**	**–6**	....	....	....	**5**	**0**	**1**	**1**	**2**	**0**	**0**	**0**	....
	Binghamton	AHL	21	7	10	17	6	....	....	....	....	....	....	....	....	....	....	....	....	....	....	....	....	....	....
1990-91	**NY Rangers**	**NHL**	**47**	**5**	**8**	**13**	**10**	**0**	**0**	**0**	**57**	**8.8**	**2**	....	....	....	....	....	....	....	....	....	....	....	....
1991-92	**NY Rangers**	**NHL**	**3**	**0**	**0**	**0**	**2**	**0**	**0**	**0**	**4**	**0.0**	**–4**	....	....	....	....	....	....	....	....	....	....	....	....
	Binghamton	AHL	69	34	31	65	28	....	....	....	....	....	....	....	....	....	11	5	2	7	4	....	....	....	....
1992-93	**Ottawa**	**NHL**	**69**	**13**	**21**	**34**	**14**	**5**	**1**	**0**	**134**	**9.7**	**–24**	....	....	....	....	....	....	....	....	....	....	....	....
1993-94	**Florida**	**NHL**	**69**	**13**	**13**	**26**	**8**	**0**	**1**	**5**	**100**	**13.0**	**6**	....	....	....	....	....	....	....	....	....	....	....	....
1994-95	**Florida**	**NHL**	**46**	**11**	**8**	**19**	**8**	**0**	**0**	**4**	**63**	**17.5**	**–1**	....	....	....	....	....	....	....	....	....	....	....	....
1995-96	**Florida**	**NHL**	**78**	**20**	**17**	**37**	**25**	**2**	**0**	**3**	**120**	**16.7**	**5**	....	....	....	**14**	**3**	**2**	**5**	**0**	**0**	**0**	**0**	....
1996-97	**Florida**	**NHL**	**67**	**10**	**6**	**16**	**4**	**0**	**1**	**2**	**92**	**10.9**	**1**	....	....	....	**5**	**0**	**0**	**0**	**0**	**0**	**0**	**0**	....
1997-98	**Florida**	**NHL**	**21**	**2**	**0**	**2**	**4**	**0**	**1**	**0**	**23**	**8.7**	**1**	....	....	....	....	....	....	....	....	....	....	....	....
	Tampa Bay	**NHL**	**28**	**2**	**4**	**6**	**4**	**0**	**0**	**2**	**28**	**7.1**	**2**	....	....	....	....	....	....	....	....	....	....	....	....
1998-99	**Philadelphia**	**NHL**	**72**	**3**	**11**	**14**	**12**	**0**	**0**	**1**	**73**	**4.1**	**–2**	**15**	**53.3**	**12:59**	**6**	**0**	**0**	**0**	**4**	**0**	**0**	**0**	**15:38**
99-2000	Orlando	IHL	1	0	0	0	0	....	....	....	....	....	....	....	....	....	....	....	....	....	....	....	....	....	....
	Philadelphia	**NHL**	**67**	**10**	**3**	**13**	**4**	**0**	**2**	**2**	**63**	**15.9**	**8**	**36**	**41.7**	**11:58**	**18**	**0**	**1**	**1**	**0**	**0**	**0**	**0**	**14:20**
2000-01	**Philadelphia**	**NHL**	**71**	**7**	**8**	**15**	**10**	**0**	**2**	**2**	**78**	**9.0**	**–1**	**83**	**36.1**	**13:13**	**6**	**0**	**0**	**0**	**4**	**0**	**0**	**0**	**13:04**
2001-02	**Ottawa**	**NHL**	**24**	**2**	**2**	**4**	**6**	**0**	**0**	**1**	**12**	**16.7**	**0**	**10**	**30.0**	**10:10**	**12**	**1**	**1**	**2**	**2**	**0**	**0**	**0**	**11:06**
	Grand Rapids	AHL	3	2	1	3	2	....	....	....	....	....	....	....	....	....	....	....	....	....	....	....	....	....	....
2002-03	**Ottawa**	**NHL**	**70**	**3**	**8**	**11**	**14**	**0**	**0**	**1**	**42**	**7.1**	**–3**	**38**	**26.3**	**10:32**	**2**	**0**	**0**	**0**	**0**	**0**	**0**	**0**	**8:17**
2003-04	Binghamton	AHL	32	1	9	10	6	....	....	....	....	....	....	....	....	....	2	0	0	0	0	....	....	....	....
	Ottawa	**NHL**	**1**	**0**	**0**	**0**	**0**	**0**	**0**	**0**	**0**	**0.0**	**0**	**0**	**0.0**	**2:51**	....	....	....	....	....	....	....	....	....
	NHL Totals		**831**	**124**	**137**	**261**	**156**	**15**	**8**	**25**	**1017**	**12.2**		**182**	**36.3**	**12:00**	**69**	**4**	**5**	**9**	**14**	**0**	**0**	**0**	**13:11**

OHL Second All-Star Team (1988)

Traded to **NY Rangers** by **Hartford** for Carey Wilson and NY Rangers' 3rd round choice (Michael Nylander) in the 1991 Entry Draft, July 9, 1990. Traded to **Ottawa** by **NY Rangers** for future considerations, July 28, 1992. Signed as a free agent by **Florida**, August 10, 1993. Traded to **Tampa Bay** by **Florida** with Mark Fitzpatrick for Dino Ciccarelli and Jeff Norton, January 15, 1998. Signed as a free agent by **Philadelphia**, October 7, 1998. Claimed by **Atlanta** from **Philadelphia** in Expansion Draft, June 25, 1999. Traded to **Philadelphia** by **Atlanta** for cash, October 15, 1999. Signed as a free agent by **Ottawa**, January 24, 2002. • Named Player/Coach by Binghamton (AHL), July 3, 2003.

HULSE, Cale

(HUHLS, KAYL) **PHX.**

Defense. Shoots right. 6'3", 220 lbs. Born, Edmonton, Alta., November 10, 1973. New Jersey's 3rd choice, 66th overall, in 1992 Entry Draft.

Season	Club	League	GP	G	A	Pts	PIM	PP	SH	GW	S	%	+/-	TF	F%	Min	GP	G	A	Pts	PIM	PP	SH	GW	Min
1990-91	Calgary Royals	AJHL	49	3	23	26	220	....	....	....	....	....	....	....	....	....	....	....	....	....	....	....	....	....	....
1991-92	Portland	WHL	70	4	18	22	230	....	....	....	....	....	....	....	....	....	6	0	2	2	27	....	....	....	....
1992-93	Portland	WHL	72	10	26	36	284	....	....	....	....	....	....	....	....	....	16	4	4	8	65	....	....	....	....
1993-94	Albany River Rats	AHL	79	7	14	21	186	....	....	....	....	....	....	....	....	....	5	0	3	3	11	....	....	....	....
1994-95	Albany River Rats	AHL	77	5	13	18	215	....	....	....	....	....	....	....	....	....	12	1	1	2	17	....	....	....	....
1995-96	**New Jersey**	**NHL**	**8**	**0**	**0**	**0**	**15**	**0**	**0**	**0**	**5**	**0.0**	**–2**	....	....	....	....	....	....	....	....	....	....	....	....
	Albany River Rats	AHL	42	4	23	27	107	....	....	....	....	....	....	....	....	....	....	....	....	....	....	....	....	....	....
	Calgary	**NHL**	**3**	**0**	**0**	**0**	**5**	**0**	**0**	**0**	**4**	**0.0**	**3**	....	....	....	**1**	**0**	**0**	**0**	**0**	**0**	**0**	**0**	....
	Saint John Flames	AHL	13	2	7	9	39	....	....	....	....	....	....	....	....	....	....	....	....	....	....	....	....	....	....
1996-97	**Calgary**	**NHL**	**63**	**1**	**6**	**7**	**91**	**0**	**1**	**0**	**58**	**1.7**	**–2**	....	....	....	....	....	....	....	....	....	....	....	....
1997-98	**Calgary**	**NHL**	**79**	**5**	**22**	**27**	**169**	**1**	**1**	**0**	**117**	**4.3**	**1**	....	....	....	....	....	....	....	....	....	....	....	....
1998-99	**Calgary**	**NHL**	**73**	**3**	**9**	**12**	**117**	**0**	**0**	**0**	**83**	**3.6**	**–8**	**1**	**0.0**	**16:38**	....	....	....	....	....	....	....	....	....
99-2000	**Calgary**	**NHL**	**47**	**1**	**6**	**7**	**47**	**0**	**0**	**0**	**41**	**2.4**	**–11**	**1**	**100.0**	**12:38**	....	....	....	....	....	....	....	....	....
2000-01	**Nashville**	**NHL**	**82**	**1**	**7**	**8**	**128**	**0**	**0**	**1**	**93**	**1.1**	**–5**	**0**	**0.0**	**20:05**	....	....	....	....	....	....	....	....	....
2001-02	**Nashville**	**NHL**	**63**	**0**	**2**	**2**	**121**	**0**	**0**	**0**	**70**	**0.0**	**–18**	**0**	**0.0**	**18:51**	....	....	....	....	....	....	....	....	....
2002-03	**Nashville**	**NHL**	**80**	**2**	**6**	**8**	**121**	**0**	**0**	**1**	**82**	**2.4**	**–11**	**0**	**0.0**	**19:05**	....	....	....	....	....	....	....	....	....
2003-04	**Phoenix**	**NHL**	**82**	**3**	**17**	**20**	**123**	**1**	**0**	**0**	**115**	**2.6**	**–4**	**0**	**0.0**	**21:28**	....	....	....	....	....	....	....	....	....
	NHL Totals		**580**	**16**	**75**	**91**	**937**	**2**	**2**	**2**	**668**	**2.4**		**2**	**50.0**	**18:34**	**1**	**0**	**0**	**0**	**0**	**0**	**0**	**0**	....

Traded to **Calgary** by **New Jersey** with Tommy Albelin and Jocelyn Lemieux for Phil Housley and Dan Keczmer, February 26, 1996. Traded to **Nashville** by **Calgary** with Calgary's 3rd round choice (Denis Platonov) in 2001 Entry Draft for Sergei Krivokrasov, March 14, 2000. Signed as a free agent by **Phoenix**, July 10, 2003.

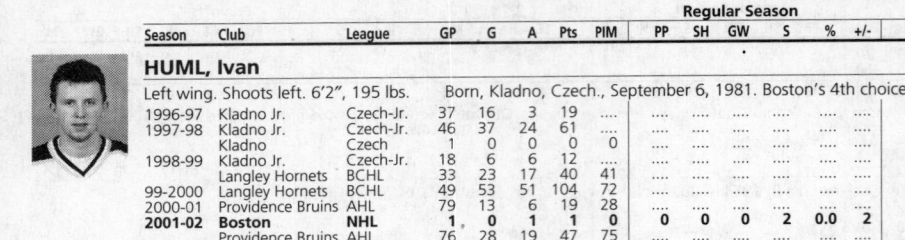

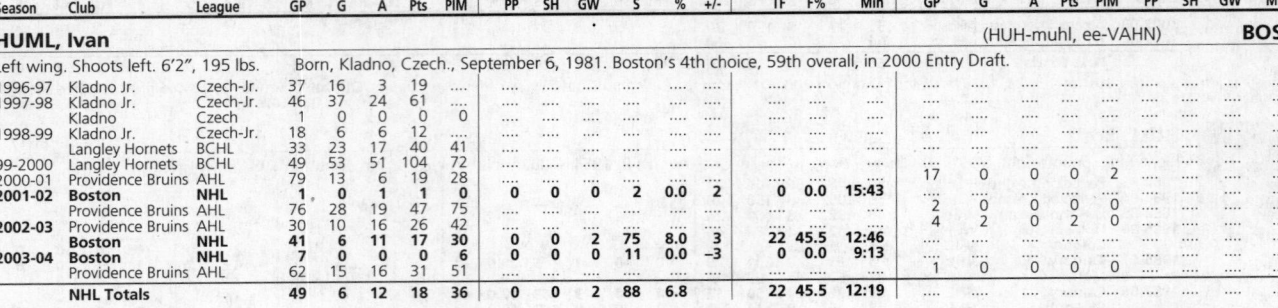

HUML, Ivan

(HUH-muhl, ee-VAHN) **BOS.**

Left wing. Shoots left. 6'2", 195 lbs. Born, Kladno, Czech., September 6, 1981. Boston's 4th choice, 59th overall, in 2000 Entry Draft.

			Regular Season														Playoffs								
Season	Club	League	GP	G	A	Pts	PIM	PP	SH	GW	S	%	+/-	TF	F%	Min	GP	G	A	Pts	PIM	PP	SH	GW	Min
1996-97	Kladno Jr.	Czech-Jr.	37	16	3	19	....	....	....	....	....	....	....	....	....	....	....	....	....	....	....	....	....	....	....
1997-98	Kladno Jr.	Czech-Jr.	46	37	24	61	....	....	....	....	....	....	....	....	....	....	....	....	....	....	....	....	....	....	....
	Kladno	Czech	1	0	0	0	0	....	....	....	....	....	....	....	....	....	....	....	....	....	....	....	....	....	....
1998-99	Kladno Jr.	Czech-Jr.	18	6	6	12	....	....	....	....	....	....	....	....	....	....	....	....	....	....	....	....	....	....	....
	Langley Hornets	BCHL	33	23	17	40	41	....	....	....	....	....	....	....	....	....	....	....	....	....	....	....	....	....	....
99-2000	Langley Hornets	BCHL	49	53	51	104	72	....	....	....	....	....	....	....	....	....	....	....	....	....	....	....	....	....	....
2000-01	Providence Bruins	AHL	79	13	6	19	28	....	....	....	....	....	....	....	....	....	17	0	0	0	2	....	....	....	....
2001-02	**Boston**	**NHL**	**1**	**0**	**1**	**1**	**0**	**0**	**0**	**0**	**2**	**0.0**	**2**	**0**	**0.0**	**15:43**	....	....	....	....	....	....	....	....	....
	Providence Bruins	AHL	76	28	19	47	75	....	....	....	....	....	....	....	....	....	2	0	0	0	0	....	....	....	....
2002-03	Providence Bruins	AHL	30	10	16	26	42	....	....	....	....	....	....	....	....	....	4	2	0	2	0	....	....	....	....
	Boston	**NHL**	**41**	**6**	**11**	**17**	**30**	**0**	**0**	**2**	**75**	**8.0**	**3**	**22**	**45.5**	**12:46**	....	....	....	....	....	....	....	....	....
2003-04	**Boston**	**NHL**	**7**	**0**	**0**	**0**	**6**	**0**	**0**	**0**	**11**	**0.0**	**–3**	**0**	**0.0**	**9:13**	....	....	....	....	....	....	....	....	....
	Providence Bruins	AHL	62	15	16	31	51	....	....	....	....	....	....	....	....	....	1	0	0	0	0	....	....	....	....
	NHL Totals		**49**	**6**	**12**	**18**	**36**	**0**	**0**	**2**	**88**	**6.8**		**22**	**45.5**	**12:19**	....	....	....	....	....	....	....	....	....

HUNTER, Trent

(HUHN-tuhr, TREHNT) **NYI**

Right wing. Shoots right. 6'3", 191 lbs. Born, Red Deer, Alta., July 5, 1980. Anaheim's 4th choice, 150th overall, in 1998 Entry Draft.

Season	Club	League	GP	G	A	Pts	PIM	PP	SH	GW	S	%	+/-	TF	F%	Min	GP	G	A	Pts	PIM	PP	SH	GW	Min
1996-97	Red Deer	AMHL	42	30	25	55	50	....	....	....	....	....	....	....	....	....	....	....	....	....	....	....	....	....	....
1997-98	Prince George	WHL	60	13	14	27	34	....	....	....	....	....	....	....	....	....	8	1	0	1	4	....	....	....	....
1998-99	Prince George	WHL	50	18	20	38	34	....	....	....	....	....	....	....	....	....	7	2	5	7	2	....	....	....	....
99-2000	Prince George	WHL	67	46	49	95	47	....	....	....	....	....	....	....	....	....	13	7	15	22	6	....	....	....	....
2000-01	Springfield	AHL	57	18	17	35	14	....	....	....	....	....	....	....	....	....	....	....	....	....	....	....	....	....	....
2001-02	Bridgeport	AHL	80	30	35	65	30	....	....	....	....	....	....	....	....	....	17	8	11	19	6	....	....	....	....
	NY Islanders	**NHL**	....	....	....	....	....	....	....	....	....	....	....	....	....	....	**4**	**1**	**1**	**2**	**2**	**0**	**0**	**0**	**11:13**
2002-03	**NY Islanders**	**NHL**	**8**	**0**	**4**	**4**	**4**	**0**	**0**	**0**	**19**	**0.0**	**5**	**1**	**0.0**	**12:13**	....	....	....	....	....	....	....	....	....
	Bridgeport	AHL	70	30	41	71	39	....	....	....	....	....	....	....	....	....	9	7	4	11	10	....	....	....	....
2003-04	**NY Islanders**	**NHL**	**77**	**25**	**26**	**51**	**16**	**4**	**0**	**7**	**187**	**13.4**	**23**	**19**	**36.8**	**15:39**	**5**	**0**	**0**	**0**	**4**	**0**	**0**	**0**	**11:38**
	NHL Totals		**85**	**25**	**30**	**55**	**20**	**4**	**0**	**7**	**206**	**12.1**		**20**	**35.0**	**15:19**	**9**	**1**	**1**	**2**	**6**	**0**	**0**	**0**	**11:27**

WHL West First All-Star Team (2000) • NHL All-Rookie Team (2004)

Traded to **NY Islanders** by **Anaheim** for Columbus' 4th round choice (previously acquired, Anaheim selected Jonas Ronnqvist) in 2000 Entry Draft, May 23, 2000.

HUSELIUS, Kristian

(hoo-SAY-lee-oos, KRIHST-yan) **FLA.**

Left wing. Shoots left. 6'1", 190 lbs. Born, Osterhaninge, Sweden, November 10, 1978. Florida's 2nd choice, 47th overall, in 1997 Entry Draft.

Season	Club	League	GP	G	A	Pts	PIM	PP	SH	GW	S	%	+/-	TF	F%	Min	GP	G	A	Pts	PIM	PP	SH	GW	Min
1994-95	Hammarby Jr.	Swede-Jr.	17	6	2	8	2	....	....	....	....	....	....	....	....	....	....	....	....	....	....	....	....	....	....
1995-96	Hammarby Jr.	Swede-Jr.	25	13	8	21	14	....	....	....	....	....	....	....	....	....	....	....	....	....	....	....	....	....	....
	Hammarby	Swede-2	6	1	0	1	0	....	....	....	....	....	....	....	....	....	....	....	....	....	....	....	....	....	....
1996-97	Farjestad	Sweden	13	2	0	2	4	....	....	....	....	....	....	....	....	....	5	1	0	1	0	....	....	....	....
1997-98	Farjestad	Sweden	34	2	1	3	2	....	....	....	....	....	....	....	....	....	11	0	0	0	0	....	....	....	....
	Farjestad	EuroHL	5	2	3	5	0	....	....	....	....	....	....	....	....	....	....	....	....	....	....	....	....	....	....
1998-99	Farjestad	Sweden	28	4	4	8	4	....	....	....	....	....	....	....	....	....	....	....	....	....	....	....	....	....	....
	Farjestad	EuroHL	6	2	2	4	8	....	....	....	....	....	....	....	....	....	1	0	0	0	0	....	....	....	....
	Vastra Frolunda	Sweden	20	2	2	4	2	....	....	....	....	....	....	....	....	....	4	1	0	1	0	....	....	....	....
99-2000	Vastra Frolunda	Sweden	50	21	23	44	20	....	....	....	....	....	....	....	....	....	5	2	2	4	8	....	....	....	....
2000-01	Vastra Frolunda	Sweden	49	*32	*35	*67	26	....	....	....	....	....	....	....	....	....	5	4	5	9	14	....	....	....	....
2001-02	**Florida**	**NHL**	**79**	**23**	**22**	**45**	**14**	**6**	**1**	**3**	**169**	**13.6**	**–4**	**14**	**21.4**	**16:55**	....	....	....	....	....	....	....	....	....
2002-03	**Florida**	**NHL**	**78**	**20**	**23**	**43**	**20**	**3**	**0**	**3**	**187**	**10.7**	**–6**	**6**	**33.3**	**17:20**	....	....	....	....	....	....	....	....	....
2003-04	**Florida**	**NHL**	**76**	**10**	**21**	**31**	**24**	**2**	**0**	**2**	**168**	**6.0**	**–6**	**185**	**37.8**	**14:14**	....	....	....	....	....	....	....	....	....
	NHL Totals		**233**	**53**	**66**	**119**	**58**	**11**	**1**	**8**	**524**	**10.1**		**205**	**36.6**	**16:11**	....	....	....	....	....	....	....	....	....

NHL All-Rookie Team (2002)

HUSSEY, Matt

(HUH-see, MAT) **PIT.**

Center. Shoots left. 6'2", 215 lbs. Born, New Haven, CT, May 28, 1979. Pittsburgh's 10th choice, 254th overall, in 1998 Entry Draft.

Season	Club	League	GP	G	A	Pts	PIM	PP	SH	GW	S	%	+/-	TF	F%	Min	GP	G	A	Pts	PIM	PP	SH	GW	Min
1996-97	Wayzata High	Hi-School	48	34	31	65	....	....	....	....	....	....	....	....	....	....	....	....	....	....	....	....	....	....	....
1997-98	Avon Old Farms	Hi-School	26	26	23	49	20	....	....	....	....	....	....	....	....	....	....	....	....	....	....	....	....	....	....
1998-99	U. of Wisconsin	WCHA	37	10	5	15	18	....	....	....	....	....	....	....	....	....	....	....	....	....	....	....	....	....	....
99-2000	U. of Wisconsin	WCHA	35	5	11	16	8	....	....	....	....	....	....	....	....	....	....	....	....	....	....	....	....	....	....
2000-01	U. of Wisconsin	WCHA	40	9	11	20	24	....	....	....	....	....	....	....	....	....	....	....	....	....	....	....	....	....	....
2001-02	U. of Wisconsin	WCHA	39	18	15	33	16	....	....	....	....	....	....	....	....	....	....	....	....	....	....	....	....	....	....
2002-03	Wilkes-Barre	AHL	69	12	11	23	28	....	....	....	....	....	....	....	....	....	2	0	0	0	0	....	....	....	....
2003-04	**Pittsburgh**	**NHL**	**3**	**2**	**1**	**3**	**0**	**2**	**0**	**0**	**8**	**25.0**	**–1**	**0**	**0.0**	**13:35**	....	....	....	....	....	....	....	....	....
	Wilkes-Barre	AHL	55	2	1	3	6	....	....	....	....	....	....	....	....	....	6	2	2	4	0	....	....	....	....
	NHL Totals		**3**	**2**	**1**	**3**	**0**	**2**	**0**	**0**	**8**	**25.0**		**0**	**0.0**	**13:35**	....	....	....	....	....	....	....	....	....

HUTCHINSON, Andrew

(HUHT-chihn-suhn, AN-droo) **NSH.**

Defense. Shoots right. 6'2", 204 lbs. Born, Evanston, IL, March 24, 1980. Nashville's 4th choice, 54th overall, in 1999 Entry Draft.

Season	Club	League	GP	G	A	Pts	PIM	PP	SH	GW	S	%	+/-	TF	F%	Min	GP	G	A	Pts	PIM	PP	SH	GW	Min
1996-97	Det. Caesars	MNHL	82	15	41	56	....	....	....	....	....	....	....	....	....	....	....	....	....	....	....	....	....	....	....
1997-98	U.S. National U-18	USDP	59	7	21	28	53	....	....	....	....	....	....	....	....	....	....	....	....	....	....	....	....	....	....
1998-99	Michigan State	CCHA	37	3	12	15	26	....	....	....	....	....	....	....	....	....	....	....	....	....	....	....	....	....	....
99-2000	Michigan State	CCHA	42	5	12	17	64	....	....	....	....	....	....	....	....	....	....	....	....	....	....	....	....	....	....
2000-01	Michigan State	CCHA	42	5	19	24	46	....	....	....	....	....	....	....	....	....	....	....	....	....	....	....	....	....	....
2001-02	Michigan State	CCHA	39	6	16	22	24	....	....	....	....	....	....	....	....	....	....	....	....	....	....	....	....	....	....
	Milwaukee	AHL	5	0	1	1	0	....	....	....	....	....	....	....	....	....	....	....	....	....	....	....	....	....	....
2002-03	Toledo Storm	ECHL	10	2	5	7	4	....	....	....	....	....	....	....	....	....	....	....	....	....	....	....	....	....	....
	Milwaukee	AHL	63	9	17	26	40	....	....	....	....	....	....	....	....	....	3	1	0	1	0	....	....	....	....
2003-04	**Nashville**	**NHL**	**18**	**4**	**4**	**8**	**4**	**2**	**0**	**1**	**24**	**16.7**	**1**	**0**	**0.0**	**16:43**	....	....	....	....	....	....	....	....	....
	Milwaukee	AHL	46	12	12	24	39	....	....	....	....	....	....	....	....	....	22	5	11	16	33	....	....	....	....
	NHL Totals		**18**	**4**	**4**	**8**	**4**	**2**	**0**	**1**	**24**	**16.7**		**0**	**0.0**	**16:43**	....	....	....	....	....	....	....	....	....

CCHA Second All-Star Team (2001, 2002) • NCAA West Second All-American Team (2002)

HYVONEN, Hannes

(HOO-voh-nuhn, HAH-nuhs) **CBJ**

Right wing. Shoots right. 6'2", 200 lbs. Born, Oulu, Finland, August 29, 1975. San Jose's 7th choice, 257th overall, in 1999 Entry Draft.

Season	Club	League	GP	G	A	Pts	PIM	PP	SH	GW	S	%	+/-	TF	F%	Min	GP	G	A	Pts	PIM	PP	SH	GW	Min
1993-94	Karpat Oulu Jr.	Finn-Jr.	35	15	13	28	26	....	....	....	....	....	....	....	....	....	3	0	0	0	0	....	....	....	....
	Karpat Oulu	Finland-2	3	3	1	4	2	....	....	....	....	....	....	....	....	....	....	....	....	....	....	....	....	....	....
1994-95	TPS Turku Jr.	Finn-Jr.	10	8	2	10	64	....	....	....	....	....	....	....	....	....	....	....	....	....	....	....	....	....	....
	Kiekko-67 Jr.	Finn-Jr.	1	1	0	1	0	....	....	....	....	....	....	....	....	....	....	....	....	....	....	....	....	....	....
	Kiekko-67 Turku	Finland-2	16	4	2	6	10	....	....	....	....	....	....	....	....	....	....	....	....	....	....	....	....	....	....
	TPS Turku	Finland	9	4	3	7	16	....	....	....	....	....	....	....	....	....	5	0	0	0	7	....	....	....	....
1995-96	Kiekko-67 Turku	Finland-2	2	1	0	1	8	....	....	....	....	....	....	....	....	....	....	....	....	....	....	....	....	....	....
	TPS Turku	Finland	30	11	5	16	49	....	....	....	....	....	....	....	....	....	7	0	1	1	28	....	....	....	....
1996-97	TPS Turku	Finland	41	10	5	15	48	....	....	....	....	....	....	....	....	....	10	4	2	6	14	....	....	....	....
1997-98	TPS Turku	Finland	29	2	6	8	71	....	....	....	....	....	....	....	....	....	2	0	0	0	0	....	....	....	....
1998-99	Blues Espoo	Finland	52	23	18	41	74	....	....	....	....	....	....	....	....	....	4	2	1	3	2	....	....	....	....
99-2000	Blues Espoo	Finland	18	5	2	7	*89	....	....	....	....	....	....	....	....	....	....	....	....	....	....	....	....	....	....
	HIFK Helsinki	Finland	22	2	2	4	*100	....	....	....	....	....	....	....	....	....	9	4	0	4	8	....	....	....	....
2000-01	HIFK Helsinki	Finland	56	14	12	26	34	....	....	....	....	....	....	....	....	....	5	0	0	0	8	....	....	....	....
2001-02	**San Jose**	**NHL**	**6**	**0**	**0**	**0**	**0**	**0**	**0**	**0**	**4**	**0.0**	**–2**	**0**	**0.0**	**5:40**	....	....	....	....	....	....	....	....	....
	Cleveland Barons	AHL	67	24	18	42	136	....	....	....	....	....	....	....	....	....	....	....	....	....	....	....	....	....	....

								Regular Season									Playoffs								
Season	Club	League	GP	G	A	Pts	PIM	PP	SH	GW	S	%	+/-	TF	F%	Min	GP	G	A	Pts	PIM	PP	SH	GW	Min
2002-03	**Columbus**	**NHL**	**36**	**4**	**5**	**9**	**22**	**0**	**0**	**0**	**48**	**8.3**	**–11**	**8**	**25.0**	**10:02**	....	....	....	....	....	....	....	....	....
	Farjestad	Sweden	10	11	0	11	12	....	....	....	....	....	....	....	....	....	14	5	0	5	41	....	....	....	....
2003-04	Farjestad	Sweden	47	15	13	28	98	....	....	....	....	....	....	....	....	....	17	7	5	12	43	....	....	....	....
	NHL Totals		**42**	**4**	**5**	**9**	**22**	**0**	**0**	**0**	**52**	**7.7**		**8**	**25.0**	**9:25**	....	....	....	....	....	....	....	....	....

Traded to **Florida** by **San Jose** for Florida's 7th round choice (Jonathon Tremblay) in 2003 Entry Draft, July 16, 2002. Claimed on waivers by **Columbus** from **Florida**, October 5, 2002. • Loaned to **Farjestad** (Sweden) by **Columbus**, January 25, 2003.

IGINLA, Jarome

(ih-GIHN-lah, jah-ROHM) **CGY.**

Right wing. Shoots right. 6'1", 208 lbs. Born, Edmonton, Alta., July 1, 1977. Dallas' 1st choice, 11th overall, in 1995 Entry Draft.

Season	Club	League	GP	G	A	Pts	PIM	PP	SH	GW	S	%	+/-	TF	F%	Min	GP	G	A	Pts	PIM	PP	SH	GW	Min
1991-92	St. Albert Raiders	AMHL	36	26	30	56	22	....	....	....	....	....	....	....	....	....	....	....	....	....	....	....	....	....	....
1992-93	St. Albert Raiders	AMHL	36	34	53	*87	20	....	....	....	....	....	....	....	....	....	....	....	....	....	....	....	....	....	....
1993-94	Kamloops Blazers	WHL	48	6	23	29	33	....	....	....	....	....	....	....	....	....	19	3	6	9	10	....	....	....	....
1994-95	Kamloops Blazers	WHL	72	33	38	71	111	....	....	....	....	....	....	....	....	....	21	7	11	18	34	....	....	....	....
1995-96	Kamloops Blazers	WHL	63	63	73	136	120	....	....	....	....	....	....	....	....	....	16	16	13	29	44	....	....	....	....
	Calgary	**NHL**	....	....	....	....	....	....	....	....	....	....	....	....	....	....	**2**	**1**	**1**	**2**	**0**	**0**	**0**	**0**	....
1996-97	**Calgary**	**NHL**	**82**	**21**	**29**	**50**	**37**	**8**	**1**	**3**	**169**	**12.4**	**–4**	....	....	....	....	....	....	....	....	....	....	....	....
1997-98	**Calgary**	**NHL**	**70**	**13**	**19**	**32**	**29**	**0**	**2**	**1**	**154**	**8.4**	**–10**	....	....	....	....	....	....	....	....	....	....	....	....
1998-99	**Calgary**	**NHL**	**82**	**28**	**23**	**51**	**58**	**7**	**0**	**4**	**211**	**13.3**	**1**	**111**	**51.4**	**16:30**	....	....	....	....	....	....	....	....	....
99-2000	**Calgary**	**NHL**	**77**	**29**	**34**	**63**	**26**	**12**	**0**	**4**	**256**	**11.3**	**0**	**278**	**52.9**	**18:24**	....	....	....	....	....	....	....	....	....
2000-01	**Calgary**	**NHL**	**77**	**31**	**40**	**71**	**62**	**10**	**0**	**4**	**229**	**13.5**	**–2**	**638**	**51.7**	**19:58**	....	....	....	....	....	....	....	....	....
2001-02	**Calgary**	**NHL**	**82**	***52**	**44**	***96**	**77**	**16**	**1**	**7**	**311**	**16.7**	**27**	**308**	**55.2**	**22:22**	....	....	....	....	....	....	....	....	....
	Canada	Olympics	6	3	1	4	0	....	....	....	....	....	....	....	....	....	....	....	....	....	....	....	....	....	....
2002-03	**Calgary**	**NHL**	**75**	**35**	**32**	**67**	**49**	**11**	**3**	**6**	**316**	**11.1**	**–10**	**90**	**43.3**	**21:26**	....	....	....	....	....	....	....	....	....
2003-04	**Calgary**	**NHL**	**81**	***41**	**32**	**73**	**84**	**8**	**4**	**10**	**265**	**15.5**	**21**	**305**	**54.4**	**21:18**	**26**	***13**	**9**	**22**	**45**	**4**	**2**	**3**	**23:18**
	NHL Totals		**626**	**250**	**253**	**503**	**422**	**72**	**11**	**39**	**1911**	**13.1**		**1730**	**52.5**	**19:59**	**28**	**14**	**10**	**24**	**45**	**4**	**2**	**3**	**23:18**

George Parsons Trophy (Memorial Cup Most Sportsmanlike Player) (1995) • WHL West First All-Star Team (1996) • Canadian Major Junior First All-Star Team (1996) • NHL All-Rookie Team (1997) • NHL First All-Star Team (2002) • Maurice "Rocket" Richard Trophy (2002) • Art Ross Trophy (2002) • Lester B. Pearson Award (2002) • NHL Second All-Star Team (2004) • King Clancy Memorial Trophy (2004) • Maurice "Rocket" Richard Trophy (2004) (tied with Ilya Kovalchuk and Rick Nash)

Played in NHL All-Star Game (2002, 2003, 2004)

Traded to **Calgary** by **Dallas** with Corey Millen for Joe Nieuwendyk, December 19, 1995.

ISBISTER, Brad

(IHZ-bihs-tuhr, BRAD) **EDM.**

Left wing. Shoots right. 6'4", 231 lbs. Born, Edmonton, Alta., May 7, 1977. Winnipeg's 4th choice, 67th overall, in 1995 Entry Draft.

Season	Club	League	GP	G	A	Pts	PIM	PP	SH	GW	S	%	+/-	TF	F%	Min	GP	G	A	Pts	PIM	PP	SH	GW	Min
1992-93	Calgary Canucks	ABHL	35	24	25	49	74	....	....	....	....	....	....	....	....	....	....	....	....	....	....	....	....	....	....
1993-94	Portland	WHL	64	7	10	17	45	....	....	....	....	....	....	....	....	....	10	0	2	2	0	....	....	....	....
1994-95	Portland	WHL	67	16	20	36	123	....	....	....	....	....	....	....	....	....	....	....	....	....	....	....	....	....	....
1995-96	Portland	WHL	71	45	44	89	184	....	....	....	....	....	....	....	....	....	7	2	4	6	20	....	....	....	....
1996-97	Portland	WHL	24	15	18	33	45	....	....	....	....	....	....	....	....	....	6	2	1	3	16	....	....	....	....
	Springfield	AHL	7	3	1	4	14	....	....	....	....	....	....	....	....	....	9	1	2	3	10	....	....	....	....
1997-98	**Phoenix**	**NHL**	**66**	**9**	**8**	**17**	**102**	**1**	**0**	**1**	**115**	**7.8**	**4**	....	....	....	**5**	**0**	**0**	**0**	**2**	**0**	**0**	**0**	....
	Springfield	AHL	9	8	2	10	36	....	....	....	....	....	....	....	....	....	....	....	....	....	....	....	....	....	....
1998-99	**Phoenix**	**NHL**	**32**	**4**	**4**	**8**	**46**	**0**	**0**	**2**	**48**	**8.3**	**1**	**3**	**0.0**	**11:33**	....	....	....	....	....	....	....	....	....
	Springfield	AHL	4	1	1	2	12	....	....	....	....	....	....	....	....	....	....	....	....	....	....	....	....	....	....
	Las Vegas	IHL	2	0	0	0	9	....	....	....	....	....	....	....	....	....	....	....	....	....	....	....	....	....	....
99-2000	**NY Islanders**	**NHL**	**64**	**22**	**20**	**42**	**100**	**9**	**0**	**1**	**135**	**16.3**	**–18**	**55**	**54.6**	**16:58**	....	....	....	....	....	....	....	....	....
2000-01	**NY Islanders**	**NHL**	**51**	**18**	**14**	**32**	**59**	**7**	**1**	**4**	**129**	**14.0**	**–19**	**255**	**45.9**	**19:26**	....	....	....	....	....	....	....	....	....
2001-02	**NY Islanders**	**NHL**	**79**	**17**	**21**	**38**	**113**	**4**	**0**	**2**	**142**	**12.0**	**1**	**71**	**45.1**	**15:18**	**3**	**1**	**1**	**2**	**17**	**1**	**0**	**1**	**12:33**
2002-03	**NY Islanders**	**NHL**	**53**	**10**	**13**	**23**	**34**	**2**	**0**	**2**	**90**	**11.1**	**–9**	**13**	**46.2**	**13:54**	....	....	....	....	....	....	....	....	....
	Edmonton	**NHL**	**13**	**3**	**2**	**5**	**9**	**0**	**0**	**1**	**29**	**10.3**	**0**	**10**	**50.0**	**13:14**	**6**	**0**	**1**	**1**	**12**	**0**	**0**	**0**	**10:04**
2003-04	**Edmonton**	**NHL**	**51**	**10**	**8**	**18**	**54**	**1**	**0**	**2**	**80**	**12.5**	**–2**	**55**	**56.4**	**12:46**	....	....	....	....	....	....	....	....	....
	NHL Totals		**409**	**93**	**90**	**183**	**517**	**24**	**1**	**15**	**768**	**12.1**		**462**	**47.8**	**15:12**	**14**	**1**	**2**	**3**	**31**	**1**	**0**	**1**	**10:54**

WHL West Second All-Star Team (1997)

Rights transferred to **Phoenix** after **Winnipeg** franchise relocated, July 1, 1996. Traded to **NY Islanders** by **Phoenix** with Phoenix's 3rd round choice (Brian Collins) in 1999 Entry Draft for Robert Reichel, NY Islanders' 3rd round choice (Jason Jaspers) in 1999 Entry Draft and Ottawa's 4th round choice (previously acquired, Phoenix selected Preston Mizzi) in 1999 Entry Draft, March 20, 1999. Traded to **Edmonton** by **NY Islanders** with Raffi Torres for Janne Niinimaa and Washington's 2nd round choice (previously acquired, NY Islanders selected Evgeni Tunik) in 2003 Entry Draft , March 11, 2003.

JACKMAN, Barret

(JAK-man, BAIR-reht) **ST.L.**

Defense. Shoots left. 6'1", 197 lbs. Born, Trail, B.C., March 5, 1981. St. Louis' 1st choice, 17th overall, in 1999 Entry Draft.

Season	Club	League	GP	G	A	Pts	PIM	PP	SH	GW	S	%	+/-	TF	F%	Min	GP	G	A	Pts	PIM	PP	SH	GW	Min
1996-97	Beaver Valley	VIJHL	32	22	25	47	180	....	....	....	....	....	....	....	....	....	....	....	....	....	....	....	....	....	....
1997-98	Regina Pats	WHL	68	2	11	13	224	....	....	....	....	....	....	....	....	....	9	0	3	3	32	....	....	....	....
1998-99	Regina Pats	WHL	70	8	36	44	259	....	....	....	....	....	....	....	....	....	....	....	....	....	....	....	....	....	....
99-2000	Regina Pats	WHL	53	9	37	46	175	....	....	....	....	....	....	....	....	....	6	1	1	2	19	....	....	....	....
	Worcester IceCats	AHL	....	....	....	....	....	....	....	....	....	....	....	....	....	....	2	0	0	0	13	....	....	....	....
2000-01	Regina Pats	WHL	43	9	27	36	138	....	....	....	....	....	....	....	....	....	6	0	3	3	8	....	....	....	....
2001-02	**St. Louis**	**NHL**	**1**	**0**	**0**	**0**	**0**	**0**	**0**	**0**	**1**	**0.0**	**0**	**0**	**0.0**	**18:56**	**1**	**0**	**0**	**0**	**2**	**0**	**0**	**0**	**18:24**
	Worcester IceCats	AHL	75	2	12	14	266	....	....	....	....	....	....	....	....	....	3	0	1	1	4	....	....	....	....
2002-03	**St. Louis**	**NHL**	**82**	**3**	**16**	**19**	**190**	**0**	**0**	**0**	**66**	**4.5**	**23**	**0**	**0.0**	**20:03**	**7**	**0**	**0**	**0**	**14**	**0**	**0**	**0**	**21:59**
2003-04	**St. Louis**	**NHL**	**15**	**1**	**2**	**3**	**41**	**0**	**0**	**0**	**11**	**9.1**	**–1**	**0**	**0.0**	**18:16**	....	....	....	....	....	....	....	....	....
	NHL Totals		**98**	**4**	**18**	**22**	**231**	**0**	**0**	**0**	**78**	**5.1**		**0**	**0.0**	**19:46**	**8**	**0**	**0**	**0**	**16**	**0**	**0**	**0**	**21:32**

WHL East Second All-Star Team (2000) • AHL All-Rookie Team (2002) • NHL All-Rookie Team (2003) • Calder Memorial Trophy (2003)

• Missed majority of 2003-04 season recovering from shoulder injury suffered in game vs. Vancouver, October 22, 2003.

JACKMAN, Ric

(JAK-man, RIHK) **PIT.**

Defense. Shoots right. 6'2", 197 lbs. Born, Toronto, Ont., June 28, 1978. Dallas' 1st choice, 5th overall, in 1996 Entry Draft.

Season	Club	League	GP	G	A	Pts	PIM	PP	SH	GW	S	%	+/-	TF	F%	Min	GP	G	A	Pts	PIM	PP	SH	GW	Min
1993-94	Mississauga Sens	MTHL	81	35	53	88	156	....	....	....	....	....	....	....	....	....	....	....	....	....	....	....	....	....	....
1994-95	Mississauga Sens	MTHL	53	20	37	57	120	....	....	....	....	....	....	....	....	....	....	....	....	....	....	....	....	....	....
	Richmond Hill	OJHL	10	2	9	11	16	....	....	....	....	....	....	....	....	....	....	....	....	....	....	....	....	....	....
1995-96	Sault Ste. Marie	OHL	66	13	29	42	97	....	....	....	....	....	....	....	....	....	4	1	0	1	15	....	....	....	....
1996-97	Sault Ste. Marie	OHL	53	13	34	47	116	....	....	....	....	....	....	....	....	....	10	2	6	8	24	....	....	....	....
1997-98	Sault Ste. Marie	OHL	60	33	40	73	111	....	....	....	....	....	....	....	....	....	....	....	....	....	....	....	....	....	....
	Michigan	IHL	14	1	5	6	10	....	....	....	....	....	....	....	....	....	4	0	0	0	10	....	....	....	....
1998-99	Michigan	IHL	71	13	17	30	106	....	....	....	....	....	....	....	....	....	5	0	4	4	6	....	....	....	....
99-2000	**Dallas**	**NHL**	**22**	**1**	**2**	**3**	**6**	**1**	**0**	**0**	**16**	**6.3**	**–1**	**0**	**0.0**	**8:06**	....	....	....	....	....	....	....	....	....
	Michigan	IHL	50	3	16	19	51	....	....	....	....	....	....	....	....	....	....	....	....	....	....	....	....	....	....
2000-01	**Dallas**	**NHL**	**16**	**0**	**0**	**0**	**18**	**0**	**0**	**0**	**10**	**0.0**	**–6**	**0**	**0.0**	**8:51**	....	....	....	....	....	....	....	....	....
	Utah Grizzlies	IHL	57	9	19	28	24	....	....	....	....	....	....	....	....	....	....	....	....	....	....	....	....	....	....
2001-02	**Boston**	**NHL**	**2**	**0**	**0**	**0**	**2**	**0**	**0**	**0**	**4**	**0.0**	**–1**	**0**	**0.0**	**13:26**	....	....	....	....	....	....	....	....	....
	Providence Bruins	AHL	9	0	1	1	8	....	....	....	....	....	....	....	....	....	2	0	0	0	2	....	....	....	....
2002-03	**Toronto**	**NHL**	**42**	**0**	**2**	**2**	**41**	**0**	**0**	**0**	**35**	**0.0**	**–10**	**0**	**0.0**	**13:59**	....	....	....	....	....	....	....	....	....
	St. John's	AHL	8	2	6	8	24	....	....	....	....	....	....	....	....	....	....	....	....	....	....	....	....	....	....
2003-04	**Toronto**	**NHL**	**29**	**2**	**4**	**6**	**13**	**1**	**0**	**1**	**35**	**5.7**	**–11**	**0**	**0.0**	**18:00**	....	....	....	....	....	....	....	....	....
	Pittsburgh	**NHL**	**25**	**7**	**17**	**24**	**14**	**6**	**0**	**1**	**56**	**12.5**	**–5**	**0**	**0.0**	**24:14**	....	....	....	....	....	....	....	....	....
	NHL Totals		**136**	**10**	**25**	**35**	**94**	**8**	**0**	**2**	**156**	**6.4**		**0**	**0.0**	**15:10**	....	....	....	....	....	....	....	....	....

OHL All-Rookie Team (1996) • OHL Second All-Star Team (1998)

Traded to **Boston** by **Dallas** for Cameron Mann, June 23, 2001. • Missed majority of 2001-02 season recovering from shoulder injury suffered in game vs. St. Louis, October 21, 2001. Traded to **Toronto** by **Boston** for the rights to Kris Vernarsky, May 13, 2002. Traded to **Pittsburgh** by **Toronto** for Drake Berehowsky, February 11, 2004.

JACKMAN, Tim

(JAK-man, TIHM) **CBJ**

Right wing. Shoots right. 6'4", 210 lbs. Born, Minot, ND, November 14, 1981. Columbus' 2nd choice, 38th overall, in 2001 Entry Draft.

			Regular Season														Playoffs								
Season	Club	League	GP	G	A	Pts	PIM	PP	SH	GW	S	%	+/-	TF	F%	Min	GP	G	A	Pts	PIM	PP	SH	GW	Min
1998-99	Park Center High	Hi-School	22	22	22	44	....	....	....	....	....	....	....	....	....	....	....	....	....	....	....	....	....	....	....
99-2000	Park Center High	Hi-School	19	34	22	56	....	....	....	....	....	....	....	....	....	....	....	....	....	....	....	....	....	....	....
	Twin Cities	USHL	25	11	9	20	58	....	....	....	....	....	....	....	....	....	13	8	5	13	12	....	....	....	....
2000-01	Minnesota State	WCHA	37	11	14	25	92	....	....	....	....	....	....	....	....	....	....	....	....	....	....	....	....	....	....
2001-02	Minnesota State	WCHA	36	14	14	28	86	....	....	....	....	....	....	....	....	....	....	....	....	....	....	....	....	....	....
2002-03	Syracuse Crunch	AHL	77	9	7	16	48	....	....	....	....	....	....	....	....	....	....	....	....	....	....	....	....	....	....
2003-04	**Columbus**	**NHL**	**19**	**1**	**2**	**3**	**16**	**0**	**0**	**0**	**18**	**5.6**	**−7**	**1**	**100.0**	**9:56**	....	....	....	....	....	....	....	....	....
	Syracuse Crunch	AHL	64	23	13	36	61	....	....	....	....	....	....	....	....	....	7	2	3	5	12	....	....	....	....
	NHL Totals		**19**	**1**	**2**	**3**	**16**	**0**	**0**	**0**	**18**	**5.6**		**1**	**100.0**	**9:56**	....	....	....	....	....	....	....	....	....

JAGR, Jaromir

(YAH-guhr, YAIR-oh-MEER) **NYR**

Right wing. Shoots left. 6'2", 234 lbs. Born, Kladno, Czech., February 15, 1972. Pittsburgh's 1st choice, 5th overall, in 1990 Entry Draft.

Season	Club	League	GP	G	A	Pts	PIM	PP	SH	GW	S	%	+/-	TF	F%	Min	GP	G	A	Pts	PIM	PP	SH	GW	Min
1984-85	Kladno Jr.	Czech-Jr.	34	24	17	41	....	....	....	....	....	....	....	....	....	....	....	....	....	....	....	....	....	....	....
1985-86	Kladno Jr.	Czech-Jr.	36	41	29	70	....	....	....	....	....	....	....	....	....	....	....	....	....	....	....	....	....	....	....
1986-87	Kladno Jr.	Czech-Jr.	30	35	35	70	....	....	....	....	....	....	....	....	....	....	....	....	....	....	....	....	....	....	....
1987-88	Kladno Jr.	Czech-Jr.	35	57	27	84	....	....	....	....	....	....	....	....	....	....	....	....	....	....	....	....	....	....	....
1988-89	Kladno	Czech	29	3	3	6	4	....	....	....	....	....	....	....	....	....	10	5	7	12	0	....	....	....	....
1989-90	Poldi Kladno	Czech	42	22	28	50	....	....	....	....	....	....	....	....	....	....	9	*8	2	10	....	....	....	....	....
1990-91♦	**Pittsburgh**	**NHL**	**80**	**27**	**30**	**57**	**42**	**7**	**0**	**4**	**136**	**19.9**	**−4**	....	....	....	**24**	**3**	**10**	**13**	**6**	**1**	**0**	**1**	....
1991-92♦	**Pittsburgh**	**NHL**	**70**	**32**	**37**	**69**	**34**	**4**	**0**	**4**	**194**	**16.5**	**12**	....	....	....	**21**	**11**	**13**	**24**	**6**	**2**	**0**	**4**	....
1992-93	**Pittsburgh**	**NHL**	**81**	**34**	**60**	**94**	**61**	**10**	**1**	**9**	**242**	**14.0**	**30**	....	....	....	**12**	**5**	**4**	**9**	**23**	**1**	**0**	**1**	....
1993-94	**Pittsburgh**	**NHL**	**80**	**32**	**67**	**99**	**61**	**9**	**0**	**6**	**298**	**10.7**	**15**	....	....	....	**6**	**2**	**4**	**6**	**16**	**0**	**0**	**1**	....
1994-95	HC Kladno	Czech	11	8	14	22	10	....	....	....	....	....	....	....	....	....	....	....	....	....	....	....	....	....	....
	HC Bolzano	Euroliga	5	8	8	16	4	....	....	....	....	....	....	....	....	....	....	....	....	....	....	....	....	....	....
	HC Bolzano	Italy	1	0	0	0	0	....	....	....	....	....	....	....	....	....	....	....	....	....	....	....	....	....	....
	EHC Schalke	German-3	1	1	10	11	0	....	....	....	....	....	....	....	....	....	....	....	....	....	....	....	....	....	....
	Pittsburgh	**NHL**	**48**	**32**	**38**	***70**	**37**	**8**	**3**	**7**	**192**	**16.7**	**23**	....	....	....	**12**	**10**	**5**	**15**	**6**	**2**	**1**	**1**	....
1995-96	**Pittsburgh**	**NHL**	**82**	**62**	**87**	**149**	**96**	**20**	**1**	**12**	**403**	**15.4**	**31**	....	....	....	**18**	**11**	**12**	**23**	**18**	**5**	**1**	**1**	....
1996-97	**Pittsburgh**	**NHL**	**63**	**47**	**48**	**95**	**40**	**11**	**2**	**6**	**234**	**20.1**	**22**	....	....	....	**5**	**4**	**4**	**8**	**4**	**2**	**0**	**0**	....
1997-98	**Pittsburgh**	**NHL**	**77**	**35**	***67**	***102**	**64**	**7**	**0**	**8**	**262**	**13.4**	**17**	....	....	....	**6**	**4**	**5**	**9**	**2**	**1**	**0**	**0**	....
	Czech Republic	Olympics	6	1	4	5	2	....	....	....	....	....	....	....	....	....	....	....	....	....	....	....	....	....	....
1998-99	**Pittsburgh**	**NHL**	**81**	**44**	***83**	***127**	**66**	**10**	**1**	**7**	**343**	**12.8**	**17**	**4**	**50.0**	**25:51**	**9**	**5**	**7**	**12**	**16**	**1**	**0**	**1**	**25:32**
99-2000	**Pittsburgh**	**NHL**	**63**	**42**	**54**	***96**	**50**	**10**	**0**	**5**	**290**	**14.5**	**25**	**9**	**22.2**	**23:12**	**11**	**8**	**8**	**16**	**6**	**2**	**0**	**4**	**24:32**
2000-01	**Pittsburgh**	**NHL**	**81**	**52**	***69**	***121**	**42**	**14**	**1**	**10**	**317**	**16.4**	**19**	**2**	**0.0**	**23:19**	**16**	**2**	**10**	**12**	**18**	**2**	**0**	**0**	**22:15**
2001-02	**Washington**	**NHL**	**69**	**31**	**48**	**79**	**30**	**10**	**0**	**3**	**197**	**15.7**	**0**	**2**	**50.0**	**21:43**	....	....	....	....	....	....	....	....	....
	Czech Republic	Olympics	4	2	3	5	4	....	....	....	....	....	....	....	....	....	....	....	....	....	....	....	....	....	....
2002-03	**Washington**	**NHL**	**75**	**36**	**41**	**77**	**38**	**13**	**2**	**9**	**290**	**12.4**	**5**	**5**	**20.0**	**21:18**	**6**	**2**	**5**	**7**	**2**	**1**	**0**	**0**	**25:13**
2003-04	**Washington**	**NHL**	**46**	**16**	**29**	**45**	**26**	**6**	**0**	**1**	**159**	**10.1**	**−4**	**1**	**0.0**	**21:05**	....	....	....	....	....	....	....	....	....
	NY Rangers	**NHL**	**31**	**15**	**14**	**29**	**12**	**4**	**0**	**2**	**98**	**15.3**	**−1**	**0**	**0.0**	**20:45**	....	....	....	....	....	....	....	....	....
	NHL Totals		**1027**	**537**	**772**	**1309**	**699**	**143**	**11**	**93**	**3655**	**14.7**		**23**	**26.1**	**22:46**	**146**	**67**	**87**	**154**	**123**	**20**	**2**	**14**	**23:59**

NHL All-Rookie Team (1991) • NHL First All-Star Team (1995, 1996, 1998, 1999, 2000, 2001) • Art Ross Trophy (1995, 1998, 1999, 2000, 2001) • NHL Second All-Star Team (1997) • Lester B. Pearson Award (1999, 2000) • Hart Trophy (1999)

Played in NHL All-Star Game (1992, 1993, 1996, 1998, 1999, 2000, 2002, 2003, 2004)

Traded to **Washington** by **Pittsburgh** with Frantisek Kucera for Kris Beech, Michal Sivek, Ross Lupaschuk and future considerations, July 11, 2001. Traded to **NY Rangers** by **Washington** for Anson Carter, January 23, 2003.

JAKOPIN, John

(JA-koh-pihn, JAWN)

Defense. Shoots right. 6'5", 239 lbs. Born, Toronto, Ont., May 16, 1975. Detroit's 4th choice, 97th overall, in 1993 Entry Draft.

Season	Club	League	GP	G	A	Pts	PIM	PP	SH	GW	S	%	+/-	TF	F%	Min	GP	G	A	Pts	PIM	PP	SH	GW	Min
1992-93	St. Michael's B	MTJHL	45	9	21	30	42	....	....	....	....	....	....	....	....	....	13	3	2	5	4	....	....	....	....
1993-94	Merrimack	H-East	36	2	8	10	64	....	....	....	....	....	....	....	....	....	....	....	....	....	....	....	....	....	....
1994-95	Merrimack	H-East	37	4	10	14	42	....	....	....	....	....	....	....	....	....	....	....	....	....	....	....	....	....	....
1995-96	Merrimack	H-East	32	10	15	25	68	....	....	....	....	....	....	....	....	....	....	....	....	....	....	....	....	....	....
1996-97	Merrimack	H-East	31	4	12	16	68	....	....	....	....	....	....	....	....	....	....	....	....	....	....	....	....	....	....
	Adirondack	AHL	3	0	0	0	9	....	....	....	....	....	....	....	....	....	....	....	....	....	....	....	....	....	....
1997-98	**Florida**	**NHL**	**2**	**0**	**0**	**0**	**4**	**0**	**0**	**0**	**1**	**0.0**	**−3**	....	....	....	....	....	....	....	....	....	....	....	....
	New Haven	AHL	60	2	18	20	151	....	....	....	....	....	....	....	....	....	3	0	0	0	0	....	....	....	....
1998-99	**Florida**	**NHL**	**3**	**0**	**0**	**0**	**0**	**0**	**0**	**0**	**0**	**0.0**	**−1**	**0**	**0.0**	**13:32**	....	....	....	....	....	....	....	....	....
	New Haven	AHL	60	2	7	9	154	....	....	....	....	....	....	....	....	....	....	....	....	....	....	....	....	....	....
99-2000	**Florida**	**NHL**	**17**	**0**	**0**	**0**	**26**	**0**	**0**	**0**	**1**	**0.0**	**−2**	**0**	**0.0**	**11:58**	....	....	....	....	....	....	....	....	....
	Louisville Panthers	AHL	23	4	6	10	47	....	....	....	....	....	....	....	....	....	....	....	....	....	....	....	....	....	....
2000-01	**Florida**	**NHL**	**60**	**1**	**2**	**3**	**62**	**0**	**0**	**0**	**23**	**4.3**	**−4**	**2**	**50.0**	**12:54**	....	....	....	....	....	....	....	....	....
	Louisville Panthers	AHL	8	0	1	1	21	....	....	....	....	....	....	....	....	....	....	....	....	....	....	....	....	....	....
2001-02	**Pittsburgh**	**NHL**	**19**	**0**	**4**	**4**	**42**	**0**	**0**	**0**	**3**	**0.0**	**2**	**0**	**0.0**	**8:16**	....	....	....	....	....	....	....	....	....
	Wilkes-Barre	AHL	30	3	5	8	90	....	....	....	....	....	....	....	....	....	....	....	....	....	....	....	....	....	....
2002-03	**San Jose**	**NHL**	**12**	**0**	**0**	**0**	**11**	**0**	**0**	**0**	**3**	**0.0**	**0**	**0**	**0.0**	**8:11**	....	....	....	....	....	....	....	....	....
	Cleveland Barons	AHL	18	0	4	4	27	....	....	....	....	....	....	....	....	....	....	....	....	....	....	....	....	....	....
2003-04	Hartford	AHL	42	3	4	7	99	....	....	....	....	....	....	....	....	....	....	....	....	....	....	....	....	....	....
	Binghamton	AHL	11	1	0	1	4	....	....	....	....	....	....	....	....	....	2	0	0	0	2	....	....	....	....
	NHL Totals		**113**	**1**	**6**	**7**	**145**	**0**	**0**	**0**	**31**	**3.2**		**2**	**50.0**	**11:28**	....	....	....	....	....	....	....	....	....

Signed as a free agent by **Florida**, May 14, 1997. • Missed majority of 1999-2000 season recovering from groin injury suffered in game vs. Carolina, February 1, 2000. Claimed on waivers by **Pittsburgh** from **Florida**, October 3, 2001. Signed as a free agent by **San Jose**, September 5, 2002. • Missed majority of 2002-03 season recovering from head injury suffered in game vs. Milwaukee (AHL), November 30, 2002. Signed as a free agent by **NY Rangers**, August 21, 2003. Loaned to **Binghamton** (AHL) by **NY Rangers**, March 12, 2004.

JANIK, Doug

(JAN-nihk, DUHG) **BUF.**

Defense. Shoots left. 6'2", 209 lbs. Born, Agawam, MA, March 26, 1980. Buffalo's 3rd choice, 55th overall, in 1999 Entry Draft.

Season	Club	League	GP	G	A	Pts	PIM	PP	SH	GW	S	%	+/-	TF	F%	Min	GP	G	A	Pts	PIM	PP	SH	GW	Min
1995-96	Springfield	NEJHL	48	16	38	54	....	....	....	....	....	....	....	....	....	....	....	....	....	....	....	....	....	....	....
1996-97	Springfield	NEJHL	39	12	24	36	22	....	....	....	....	....	....	....	....	....	11	5	9	14	10	....	....	....	....
1997-98	U.S. National U-18	USDP	65	8	26	34	105	....	....	....	....	....	....	....	....	....	....	....	....	....	....	....	....	....	....
1998-99	U. of Maine	H-East	35	3	13	16	44	....	....	....	....	....	....	....	....	....	....	....	....	....	....	....	....	....	....
99-2000	U. of Maine	H-East	36	6	14	20	54	....	....	....	....	....	....	....	....	....	....	....	....	....	....	....	....	....	....
2000-01	U. of Maine	H-East	39	3	15	18	52	....	....	....	....	....	....	....	....	....	....	....	....	....	....	....	....	....	....
2001-02	Rochester	AHL	80	6	17	23	100	....	....	....	....	....	....	....	....	....	2	0	0	0	0	....	....	....	....
2002-03	**Buffalo**	**NHL**	**6**	**0**	**0**	**0**	**2**	**0**	**0**	**0**	**1**	**0.0**	**1**	**0**	**0.0**	**7:42**	....	....	....	....	....	....	....	....	....
	Rochester	AHL	75	3	13	16	120	....	....	....	....	....	....	....	....	....	3	0	0	0	6	....	....	....	....
2003-04	**Buffalo**	**NHL**	**4**	**0**	**0**	**0**	**19**	**0**	**0**	**0**	**3**	**0.0**	**0**	**0**	**0.0**	**8:26**	....	....	....	....	....	....	....	....	....
	Rochester	AHL	74	2	14	16	109	....	....	....	....	....	....	....	....	....	16	1	2	3	22	....	....	....	....
	NHL Totals		**10**	**0**	**0**	**0**	**21**	**0**	**0**	**0**	**4**	**0.0**		**0**	**0.0**	**8:00**	....	....	....	....	....	....	....	....	....

JARDINE, Ryan

(JAHR-dighn, RIGH-yan) **FLA.**

Left wing. Shoots left. 6', 210 lbs. Born, Ottawa, Ont., March 15, 1980. Florida's 4th choice, 89th overall, in 1998 Entry Draft.

Season	Club	League	GP	G	A	Pts	PIM	PP	SH	GW	S	%	+/-	TF	F%	Min	GP	G	A	Pts	PIM	PP	SH	GW	Min
1996-97	Kanata Valley	OCJHL	52	30	27	57	76	....	....	....	....	....	....	....	....	....	....	....	....	....	....	....	....	....	....
1997-98	Sault Ste. Marie	OHL	65	28	32	60	16	....	....	....	....	....	....	....	....	....	....	....	....	....	....	....	....	....	....
1998-99	Sault Ste. Marie	OHL	68	27	34	61	56	....	....	....	....	....	....	....	....	....	5	0	1	1	6	....	....	....	....
99-2000	Sault Ste. Marie	OHL	65	43	34	77	58	....	....	....	....	....	....	....	....	....	17	11	8	19	16	....	....	....	....
2000-01	Louisville Panthers	AHL	77	12	14	26	38	....	....	....	....	....	....	....	....	....	....	....	....	....	....	....	....	....	....
2001-02	**Florida**	**NHL**	**8**	**0**	**2**	**2**	**2**	**0**	**0**	**0**	**6**	**0.0**	**0**	**2**	**100.0**	**8:55**	....	....	....	....	....	....	....	....	....
	Utah Grizzlies	AHL	64	16	16	32	56	....	....	....	....	....	....	....	....	....	4	1	1	2	0	....	....	....	....
2002-03	San Antonio	AHL	64	14	17	31	37	....	....	....	....	....	....	....	....	....	3	1	0	1	0	....	....	....	....
2003-04	San Antonio	AHL	22	6	1	7	12	....	....	....	....	....	....	....	....	....	....	....	....	....	....	....	....	....	....
	NHL Totals		**8**	**0**	**2**	**2**	**2**	**0**	**0**	**0**	**6**	**0.0**		**2**	**100.0**	**8:55**	....	....	....	....	....	....	....	....	....

OHL All-Rookie Team (1998)

• Missed majority of 2003-04 season recovering from knee injury suffered in game vs. Milwaukee (AHL), November 7, 2003.

JASPERS, Jason

(JAS-puhrs, JAY-suhn) **PHX.**

Center. Shoots left. 5'11", 207 lbs. Born, Thunder Bay, Ont., April 8, 1981. Phoenix's 4th choice, 71st overall, in 1999 Entry Draft.

			Regular Season														Playoffs								
Season	Club	League	GP	G	A	Pts	PIM	PP	SH	GW	S	%	+/-	TF	F%	Min	GP	G	A	Pts	PIM	PP	SH	GW	Min
1996-97	Thunder Bay	TBAHA	70	51	69	120	67	....	....	....	....	....	....	....	....	....	....	....	....	....	....	....	....	....	....
1997-98	Thunder Bay	TBAHA	72	45	75	120	90	....	....	....	....	....	....	....	....	....	....	....	....	....	....	....	....	....	....
1998-99	Sudbury Wolves	OHL	68	28	33	61	81	....	....	....	....	....	....	....	....	....	4	2	1	3	13	....	....	....	....
99-2000	Sudbury Wolves	OHL	68	46	61	107	107	....	....	....	....	....	....	....	....	....	12	4	6	10	27	....	....	....	....
2000-01	Sudbury Wolves	OHL	63	42	42	84	77	....	....	....	....	....	....	....	....	....	12	3	16	19	18	....	....	....	....
2001-02	**Phoenix**	**NHL**	**4**	**0**	**1**	**1**	**4**	**0**	**0**	**0**	**1**	**0.0**	**–1**	**14**	**35.7**	**8:07**	....	....	....	....	....	....	....	....	....
	Springfield	AHL	71	25	23	48	55	....	....	....	....	....	....	....	....	....	....	....	....	....	....	....	....	....	....
2002-03	**Phoenix**	**NHL**	**2**	**0**	**0**	**0**	**0**	**0**	**0**	**0**	**0**	**0.0**	**–1**	**14**	**57.1**	**7:17**	....	....	....	....	....	....	....	....	....
	Springfield	AHL	63	4	15	19	57	....	....	....	....	....	....	....	....	....	6	0	0	0	4	....	....	....	....
2003-04	**Phoenix**	**NHL**	**3**	**0**	**0**	**0**	**2**	**0**	**0**	**0**	**3**	**0.0**	**–1**	**19**	**57.9**	**11:24**	....	....	....	....	....	....	....	....	....
	Springfield	AHL	58	16	22	38	56	....	....	....	....	....	....	....	....	....	....	....	....	....	....	....	....	....	....
	NHL Totals		**9**	**0**	**1**	**1**	**6**	**0**	**0**	**0**	**4**	**0.0**		**47**	**51.1**	**9:01**	....	....	....	....	....	....	....	....	....

OHL Second All-Star Team (2000)

JILLSON, Jeff

(JIHL-sohn, JEHF) **BUF.**

Defense. Shoots right. 6'3", 220 lbs. Born, North Smithfield, RI, July 24, 1980. San Jose's 1st choice, 14th overall, in 1999 Entry Draft.

			Regular Season														Playoffs								
Season	Club	League	GP	G	A	Pts	PIM	PP	SH	GW	S	%	+/-	TF	F%	Min	GP	G	A	Pts	PIM	PP	SH	GW	Min
1995-96	Mount St. Charles	Hi-School	15	8	7	15	15	....	....	....	....	....	....	....	....	....	5	1	1	2	4	....	....	....	....
1996-97	Mount St. Charles	Hi-School	15	16	14	30	20	....	....	....	....	....	....	....	....	....	4	0	4	4	6	....	....	....	....
1997-98	Mount St. Charles	Hi-School	15	10	13	23	32	....	....	....	....	....	....	....	....	....	5	4	5	9	6	....	....	....	....
1998-99	U. of Michigan	CCHA	38	5	19	24	71	....	....	....	....	....	....	....	....	....	....	....	....	....	....	....	....	....	....
99-2000	U. of Michigan	CCHA	38	8	26	34	115	....	....	....	....	....	....	....	....	....	....	....	....	....	....	....	....	....	....
2000-01	U. of Michigan	CCHA	43	10	20	30	74	....	....	....	....	....	....	....	....	....	....	....	....	....	....	....	....	....	....
2001-02	**San Jose**	**NHL**	**48**	**5**	**13**	**18**	**29**	**3**	**0**	**2**	**47**	**10.6**	**2**	**0**	**0.0**	**14:36**	**4**	**0**	**0**	**0**	**0**	**0**	**0**	**0**	**5:45**
	Cleveland Barons	AHL	27	2	13	15	45	....	....	....	....	....	....	....	....	....	....	....	....	....	....	....	....	....	....
2002-03	**San Jose**	**NHL**	**26**	**0**	**6**	**6**	**9**	**0**	**0**	**0**	**22**	**0.0**	**–7**	**0**	**0.0**	**13:45**	....	....	....	....	....	....	....	....	....
	Cleveland Barons	AHL	19	3	5	8	12	....	....	....	....	....	....	....	....	....	....	....	....	....	....	....	....	....	....
	Providence Bruins	AHL	30	4	11	15	26	....	....	....	....	....	....	....	....	....	4	0	2	2	8	....	....	....	....
2003-04	**Boston**	**NHL**	**50**	**4**	**10**	**14**	**35**	**1**	**0**	**1**	**80**	**5.0**	**–1**	**0**	**0.0**	**17:53**	....	....	....	....	....	....	....	....	....
	Buffalo	**NHL**	**14**	**0**	**3**	**3**	**19**	**0**	**0**	**0**	**35**	**0.0**	**–3**	**0**	**0.0**	**18:21**	....	....	....	....	....	....	....	....	....
	NHL Totals		**138**	**9**	**32**	**41**	**92**	**4**	**0**	**3**	**184**	**4.9**		**0**	**0.0**	**16:01**	**4**	**0**	**0**	**0**	**0**	**0**	**0**	**0**	**5:45**

CCHA All-Rookie Team (1999) • CCHA First All-Star Team (2000, 2001) • NCAA West First All-American Team (2000) • NCAA West Second All-American Team (2001)

Traded to **Boston** by **San Jose** with Jeff Hackett for Kyle McLaren and Boston's 4th round choice (Torrey Mitchell) in 2004 Entry Draft, January 23, 2003. Traded to **San Jose** by **Boston** for Brad Boyes, March 9, 2004. Traded to **Buffalo** by **San Jose** with San Jose's 9th round choice in 2005 Entry Draft for Curtis Brown and Andy Delmore, March 9, 2004.

JOHANSSON, Andreas

(yoh-HAHN-suhn, ahn-DRAY-uhs)

Center. Shoots left. 6', 202 lbs. Born, Hofors, Sweden, May 19, 1973. NY Islanders' 7th choice, 136th overall, in 1991 Entry Draft.

			Regular Season														Playoffs								
Season	Club	League	GP	G	A	Pts	PIM	PP	SH	GW	S	%	+/-	TF	F%	Min	GP	G	A	Pts	PIM	PP	SH	GW	Min
1987-88	Bofors IK	Swede-3	1	0	0	0	0	....	....	....	....	....	....	....	....	....	....	....	....	....	....	....	....	....	....
1988-89	Bofors IK	Swede-3	28	19	11	30	....	....	....	....	....	....	....	....	....	....	....	....	....	....	....	....	....	....	....
1989-90	Falu IF	Swede-2	21	3	1	4	14	....	....	....	....	....	....	....	....	....	....	....	....	....	....	....	....	....	....
1990-91	Falu IF	Swede-2	31	12	10	22	38	....	....	....	....	....	....	....	....	....	....	....	....	....	....	....	....	....	....
1991-92	Farjestad	Sweden	30	3	1	4	10	....	....	....	....	....	....	....	....	....	6	0	0	0	4	....	....	....	....
1992-93	Farjestad	Sweden	38	4	7	11	38	....	....	....	....	....	....	....	....	....	2	0	0	0	0	....	....	....	....
1993-94	Farjestad	Sweden	37	11	16	27	24	....	....	....	....	....	....	....	....	....	3	1	4	5	2	....	....	....	....
1994-95	Farjestad	Sweden	36	9	10	19	42	....	....	....	....	....	....	....	....	....	4	0	0	0	10	....	....	....	....
1995-96	**NY Islanders**	**NHL**	**3**	**0**	**1**	**1**	**0**	**0**	**0**	**0**	**6**	**0.0**	**1**	....	....	....	....	....	....	....	....	....	....	....	....
	Worcester IceCats	AHL	29	5	5	10	32	....	....	....	....	....	....	....	....	....	....	....	....	....	....	....	....	....	....
	Utah Grizzlies	IHL	22	4	13	17	28	....	....	....	....	....	....	....	....	....	12	0	5	5	6	....	....	....	....
1996-97	**NY Islanders**	**NHL**	**15**	**2**	**2**	**4**	**0**	**1**	**0**	**0**	**21**	**9.5**	**–6**	....	....	....	....	....	....	....	....	....	....	....	....
	Pittsburgh	**NHL**	**27**	**2**	**7**	**9**	**20**	**0**	**0**	**0**	**38**	**5.3**	**–6**	....	....	....	....	....	....	....	....	....	....	....	....
	Cleveland	IHL	10	2	4	6	42	....	....	....	....	....	....	....	....	....	11	1	5	6	8	....	....	....	....
1997-98	**Pittsburgh**	**NHL**	**50**	**5**	**10**	**15**	**20**	**0**	**1**	**0**	**49**	**10.2**	**4**	....	....	....	**1**	**0**	**0**	**0**	**0**	**0**	**0**	**0**	....
	Sweden	Olympics	3	0	0	0	2	....	....	....	....	....	....	....	....	....	....	....	....	....	....	....	....	....	....
1998-99	**Ottawa**	**NHL**	**69**	**21**	**16**	**37**	**34**	**7**	**0**	**6**	**144**	**14.6**	**1**	**9**	**22.2**	**14:39**	**2**	**0**	**0**	**0**	**0**	**0**	**0**	**0**	**14:13**
99-2000	**Tampa Bay**	**NHL**	**12**	**2**	**3**	**5**	**8**	**0**	**0**	**0**	**11**	**18.2**	**1**	**0**	**0.0**	**10:50**	....	....	....	....	....	....	....	....	....
	Calgary	**NHL**	**28**	**3**	**7**	**10**	**14**	**1**	**0**	**0**	**47**	**6.4**	**–3**	**5**	**20.0**	**13:33**	....	....	....	....	....	....	....	....	....
2000-01	SC Bern	Swiss	40	15	29	44	94	....	....	....	....	....	....	....	....	....	7	5	4	9	0	....	....	....	....
2001-02	**NY Rangers**	**NHL**	**70**	**14**	**10**	**24**	**46**	**3**	**0**	**1**	**108**	**13.0**	**6**	**299**	**43.1**	**16:19**	....	....	....	....	....	....	....	....	....
2002-03	**Nashville**	**NHL**	**56**	**20**	**17**	**37**	**22**	**10**	**0**	**0**	**124**	**16.1**	**–4**	**14**	**50.0**	**16:46**	....	....	....	....	....	....	....	....	....
2003-04	**Nashville**	**NHL**	**47**	**12**	**15**	**27**	**26**	**3**	**1**	**1**	**108**	**11.1**	**–2**	**140**	**38.6**	**15:48**	**6**	**0**	**0**	**0**	**0**	**0**	**0**	**0**	**15:17**
	Milwaukee	AHL	1	0	0	0	2	....	....	....	....	....	....	....	....	....	....	....	....	....	....	....	....	....	....
	NHL Totals		**377**	**81**	**88**	**169**	**190**	**25**	**2**	**8**	**656**	**12.3**		**467**	**41.3**	**15:24**	**9**	**0**	**0**	**0**	**0**	**0**	**0**	**0**	**15:01**

Traded to **Pittsburgh** by **NY Islanders** with Darius Kasparaitis for Bryan Smolinski, November 17, 1996. Signed as a free agent by **Ottawa**, September 29, 1998. Traded to **Tampa Bay** by **Ottawa** for Rob Zamuner and Tampa Bay's 2nd round choice (later traded to Philadelphia – later traded back to Tampa Bay – later traded to Dallas – Dallas selected Tobias Stephan) in 2002 Entry Draft, June 29, 1999. Traded to **Calgary** by **Tampa Bay** for Nils Ekman and Calgary's 4th round choice (later traded to NY Islanders – NY Islanders selected Vladimir Gorbunov) in 2000 Entry Draft, November 13, 1999. • Missed majority of 1999-2000 season recovering from back injury suffered in game vs. Vancouver, January 2, 2000. Claimed by **NY Rangers** from **Calgary** in Waiver Draft, September 29, 2000. Signed as a free agent by **Nashville**, September 6, 2002.

JOHANSSON, Calle

(yoh-HAHN-suhn, KAL-ee)

Defense. Shoots left. 5'11", 203 lbs. Born, Goteborg, Sweden, February 14, 1967. Buffalo's 1st choice, 14th overall, in 1985 Entry Draft.

			Regular Season														Playoffs								
Season	Club	League	GP	G	A	Pts	PIM	PP	SH	GW	S	%	+/-	TF	F%	Min	GP	G	A	Pts	PIM	PP	SH	GW	Min
1981-82	KBA-67	Swede-3	27	3	3	6	....	....	....	....	....	....	....	....	....	....	....	....	....	....	....	....	....	....	....
1982-83	KBA-67	Swede-3	29	12	11	23	....	....	....	....	....	....	....	....	....	....	....	....	....	....	....	....	....	....	....
1983-84	Vastra Frolunda	Sweden	28	4	4	8	10	....	....	....	....	....	....	....	....	....	....	....	....	....	....	....	....	....	....
1984-85	Vastra Frolunda	Swede-2	30	8	13	21	16	....	....	....	....	....	....	....	....	....	....	....	....	....	....	....	....	....	....
1985-86	Bjorkloven	Sweden	17	1	2	3	4	....	....	....	....	....	....	....	....	....	....	....	....	....	....	....	....	....	....
1986-87	Bjorkloven	Sweden	30	2	13	15	20	....	....	....	....	....	....	....	....	....	6	1	3	4	6	....	....	....	....
1987-88	**Buffalo**	**NHL**	**71**	**4**	**38**	**42**	**37**	**2**	**0**	**0**	**93**	**4.3**	**12**	....	....	....	**6**	**0**	**1**	**1**	**0**	**0**	**0**	**0**	....
1988-89	**Buffalo**	**NHL**	**47**	**2**	**11**	**13**	**33**	**0**	**0**	**1**	**53**	**3.8**	**–7**	....	....	....	....	....	....	....	....	....	....	....	....
	Washington	**NHL**	**12**	**1**	**7**	**8**	**4**	**1**	**0**	**0**	**22**	**4.5**	**1**	....	....	....	**6**	**1**	**2**	**3**	**0**	**1**	**0**	**0**	....
1989-90	**Washington**	**NHL**	**70**	**8**	**31**	**39**	**25**	**4**	**0**	**2**	**103**	**7.8**	**7**	....	....	....	**15**	**1**	**6**	**7**	**4**	**0**	**0**	**0**	....
1990-91	**Washington**	**NHL**	**80**	**11**	**41**	**52**	**23**	**2**	**1**	**2**	**128**	**8.6**	**–2**	....	....	....	**10**	**2**	**7**	**9**	**8**	**1**	**0**	**0**	....
1991-92	**Washington**	**NHL**	**80**	**14**	**42**	**56**	**49**	**5**	**2**	**2**	**119**	**11.8**	**2**	....	....	....	**7**	**0**	**5**	**5**	**4**	**0**	**0**	**0**	....
1992-93	**Washington**	**NHL**	**77**	**7**	**38**	**45**	**56**	**6**	**0**	**1**	**133**	**5.3**	**3**	....	....	....	**6**	**0**	**5**	**5**	**4**	**0**	**0**	**0**	....
1993-94	**Washington**	**NHL**	**84**	**9**	**33**	**42**	**59**	**4**	**0**	**1**	**141**	**6.4**	**3**	....	....	....	**6**	**1**	**3**	**4**	**4**	**0**	**0**	**1**	....
1994-95	EHC Kloten	Swiss	5	1	2	3	8	....	....	....	....	....	....	....	....	....	....	....	....	....	....	....	....	....	....
	Washington	**NHL**	**46**	**5**	**26**	**31**	**35**	**4**	**0**	**2**	**112**	**4.5**	**–6**	....	....	....	**7**	**3**	**1**	**4**	**0**	**1**	**0**	**0**	....
1995-96	**Washington**	**NHL**	**78**	**10**	**25**	**35**	**50**	**4**	**0**	**0**	**182**	**5.5**	**13**	....	....	....	....	....	....	....	....	....	....	....	....
1996-97	**Washington**	**NHL**	**65**	**6**	**11**	**17**	**16**	**2**	**0**	**0**	**133**	**4.5**	**–2**	....	....	....	....	....	....	....	....	....	....	....	....
1997-98	**Washington**	**NHL**	**73**	**15**	**20**	**35**	**30**	**10**	**1**	**1**	**163**	**9.2**	**–11**	....	....	....	**21**	**2**	**8**	**10**	**16**	**0**	**0**	**0**	....
	Sweden	Olympics	4	0	0	0	2	....	....	....	....	....	....	....	....	....	....	....	....	....	....	....	....	....	....
1998-99	**Washington**	**NHL**	**67**	**8**	**21**	**29**	**22**	**2**	**0**	**2**	**145**	**5.5**	**10**	**0**	**0.0**	**23:58**	....	....	....	....	....	....	....	....	....
99-2000	**Washington**	**NHL**	**82**	**7**	**25**	**32**	**24**	**1**	**0**	**3**	**138**	**5.1**	**13**	**0**	**0.0**	**23:55**	**5**	**1**	**2**	**3**	**0**	**1**	**0**	**0**	**25:42**
2000-01	**Washington**	**NHL**	**76**	**7**	**29**	**36**	**26**	**5**	**0**	**0**	**154**	**4.5**	**11**	**0**	**0.0**	**23:44**	**6**	**1**	**2**	**3**	**2**	**0**	**0**	**0**	**23:41**
2001-02	**Washington**	**NHL**	**11**	**2**	**0**	**2**	**8**	**0**	**0**	**1**	**18**	**11.1**	**–4**	**0**	**0.0**	**21:14**	....	....	....	....	....	....	....	....	....
2002-03	**Washington**	**NHL**	**82**	**3**	**12**	**15**	**22**	**1**	**0**	**0**	**77**	**3.9**	**9**	**1**	**0.0**	**21:45**	**6**	**0**	**1**	**1**	**0**	**0**	**0**	**0**	**19:15**
2003-04	**Toronto**	**NHL**	**8**	**0**	**6**	**6**	**8**	**0**	**0**	**0**	**8**	**0.0**	**5**	**0**	**0.0**	**17:28**	**4**	**0**	**0**	**0**	**2**	**0**	**0**	**0**	**12:11**
	NHL Totals		**1109**	**119**	**416**	**535**	**519**	**53**	**4**	**17**	**1922**	**6.2**		**1**	**0.0**	**23:05**	**105**	**12**	**43**	**55**	**44**	**4**	**0**	**1**	**20:42**

NHL All-Rookie Team (1988)

Traded to **Washington** by **Buffalo** with Buffalo's 2nd round choice (Byron Dafoe) in 1989 Entry Draft for Clint Malarchuk, Grant Ledyard and Washington's 6th round choice (Brian Holzinger) in 1991 Entry Draft, March 7, 1989. • Missed majority of 2001-02 season recovering from rotator cuff injury suffered in game vs. Atlanta, November 10, 2001. • Officially announced retirement, August 7, 2003. Signed as a free agent by **Toronto**, March 9, 2004.

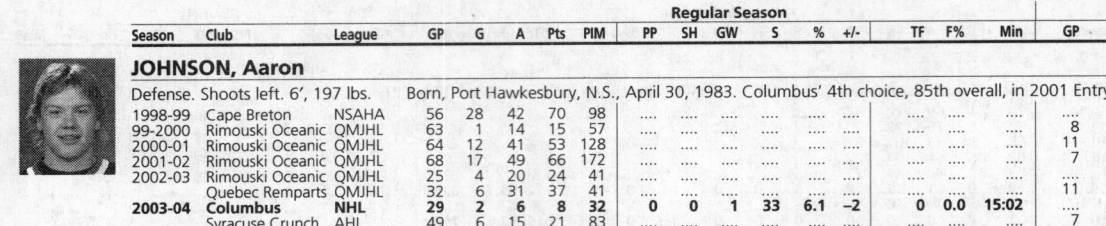

			Regular Season														Playoffs								
Season	Club	League	GP	G	A	Pts	PIM	PP	SH	GW	S	%	+/-	TF	F%	Min	GP	G	A	Pts	PIM	PP	SH	GW	Min

JOHNSON, Aaron
(JAWN-suhn, AIR-ruhn) **CBJ**

Defense. Shoots left. 6', 197 lbs. Born, Port Hawkesbury, N.S., April 30, 1983. Columbus' 4th choice, 85th overall, in 2001 Entry Draft.

Season	Club	League	GP	G	A	Pts	PIM	PP	SH	GW	S	%	+/-	TF	F%	Min	GP	G	A	Pts	PIM	PP	SH	GW	Min
1998-99	Cape Breton	NSAHA	56	28	42	70	98	....	....	....	....	....	....	....	....	....	....	....	....	....	....	....	....	....	....
99-2000	Rimouski Oceanic	QMJHL	63	1	14	15	57	....	....	....	....	....	....	....	....	....	8	0	0	0	0	....	....	....	....
2000-01	Rimouski Oceanic	QMJHL	64	12	41	53	128	....	....	....	....	....	....	....	....	....	11	2	4	6	35	....	....	....	....
2001-02	Rimouski Oceanic	QMJHL	68	17	49	66	172	....	....	....	....	....	....	....	....	....	7	1	2	3	12	....	....	....	....
2002-03	Rimouski Oceanic	QMJHL	25	4	20	24	41	....	....	....	....	....	....	....	....	....	....	....	....	....	....	....	....	....	....
	Quebec Remparts	QMJHL	32	6	31	37	41	....	....	....	....	....	....	....	....	....	11	4	4	8	25	....	....	....	....
2003-04	**Columbus**	**NHL**	**29**	**2**	**6**	**8**	**32**	**0**	**0**	**1**	**33**	**6.1**	**–2**	**0**	**0.0**	**15:02**	....	....	....	....	....	....	....	....	....
	Syracuse Crunch	AHL	49	6	15	21	83	....	....	....	....	....	....	....	....	....	7	2	3	5	27	....	....	....	....
	NHL Totals		**29**	**2**	**6**	**8**	**32**	**0**	**0**	**1**	**33**	**6.1**		**0**	**0.0**	**15:02**	....	....	....	....	....	....	....	....	....

JOHNSON, Craig
(JAWN-suhn, KRAYG)

Left wing. Shoots left. 6'2", 200 lbs. Born, St. Paul, MN, March 18, 1972. St. Louis' 1st choice, 33rd overall, in 1990 Entry Draft.

Season	Club	League	GP	G	A	Pts	PIM	PP	SH	GW	S	%	+/-	TF	F%	Min	GP	G	A	Pts	PIM	PP	SH	GW	Min
1987-88	Hill-Murray	Hi-School	28	14	20	34	4	....	....	....	....	....	....	....	....	....	....	....	....	....	....	....	....	....	....
1988-89	Hill-Murray	Hi-School	24	22	30	52	10	....	....	....	....	....	....	....	....	....	....	....	....	....	....	....	....	....	....
1989-90	Hill-Murray	Hi-School	23	15	36	51	0	....	....	....	....	....	....	....	....	....	....	....	....	....	....	....	....	....	....
1990-91	U. of Minnesota	WCHA	33	13	18	31	34	....	....	....	....	....	....	....	....	....	....	....	....	....	....	....	....	....	....
1991-92	U. of Minnesota	WCHA	41	17	38	55	66	....	....	....	....	....	....	....	....	....	....	....	....	....	....	....	....	....	....
1992-93	U. of Minnesota	WCHA	42	22	24	46	70	....	....	....	....	....	....	....	....	....	....	....	....	....	....	....	....	....	....
	Jacksonville	SunHL	23	2	9	11	38	....	....	....	....	....	....	....	....	....	....	....	....	....	....	....	....	....	....
1993-94	Team USA	Nat-Tm	54	25	26	51	64	....	....	....	....	....	....	....	....	....	....	....	....	....	....	....	....	....	....
	United States	Olympics	8	0	4	4	4	....	....	....	....	....	....	....	....	....	....	....	....	....	....	....	....	....	....
1994-95	**St. Louis**	**NHL**	**15**	**3**	**3**	**6**	**6**	**0**	**0**	**0**	**19**	**15.8**	**4**	....	....	....	**1**	**0**	**0**	**0**	**2**	**0**	**0**	**0**	....
	Peoria Rivermen	IHL	16	2	6	8	25	....	....	....	....	....	....	....	....	....	9	0	4	4	10	....	....	....	....
1995-96	**St. Louis**	**NHL**	**49**	**8**	**7**	**15**	**30**	**1**	**0**	**0**	**69**	**11.6**	**–4**	....	....	....	....	....	....	....	....	....	....	....	....
	Worcester IceCats	AHL	5	3	0	3	2	....	....	....	....	....	....	....	....	....	....	....	....	....	....	....	....	....	....
	Los Angeles	**NHL**	**11**	**5**	**4**	**9**	**6**	**3**	**0**	**0**	**28**	**17.9**	**–4**	....	....	....	....	....	....	....	....	....	....	....	....
1996-97	**Los Angeles**	**NHL**	**31**	**4**	**3**	**7**	**26**	**1**	**0**	**0**	**30**	**13.3**	**–7**	....	....	....	....	....	....	....	....	....	....	....	....
1997-98	**Los Angeles**	**NHL**	**74**	**17**	**21**	**38**	**42**	**6**	**0**	**2**	**125**	**13.6**	**9**	....	....	....	**4**	**1**	**0**	**1**	**4**	**0**	**0**	**0**	....
1998-99	**Los Angeles**	**NHL**	**69**	**7**	**12**	**19**	**32**	**2**	**0**	**2**	**94**	**7.4**	**–12**	**2**	**50.0**	**12:02**	....	....	....	....	....	....	....	....	....
99-2000	**Los Angeles**	**NHL**	**76**	**9**	**14**	**23**	**28**	**1**	**0**	**1**	**106**	**8.5**	**–10**	**9**	**55.6**	**13:56**	**4**	**1**	**0**	**1**	**2**	**0**	**0**	**0**	**11:28**
2000-01	**Los Angeles**	**NHL**	**26**	**4**	**5**	**9**	**16**	**0**	**0**	**0**	**36**	**11.1**	**0**	**2**	**100.0**	**10:40**	....	....	....	....	....	....	....	....	....
2001-02	**Los Angeles**	**NHL**	**72**	**13**	**14**	**27**	**24**	**4**	**1**	**3**	**102**	**12.7**	**14**	**11**	**36.4**	**14:15**	**7**	**1**	**2**	**3**	**2**	**0**	**0**	**1**	**14:00**
2002-03	**Los Angeles**	**NHL**	**70**	**3**	**6**	**9**	**22**	**0**	**0**	**0**	**87**	**3.4**	**–13**	**28**	**32.1**	**14:05**	....	....	....	....	....	....	....	....	....
2003-04	**Anaheim**	**NHL**	**39**	**1**	**2**	**3**	**14**	**0**	**0**	**0**	**45**	**2.2**	**–4**	**62**	**62.9**	**10:43**	....	....	....	....	....	....	....	....	....
	Toronto	**NHL**	**10**	**1**	**1**	**2**	**6**	**0**	**0**	**0**	**12**	**8.3**	**0**	**16**	**56.3**	**13:03**	....	....	....	....	....	....	....	....	....
	Washington	**NHL**	**15**	**0**	**6**	**6**	**8**	**0**	**0**	**0**	**20**	**0.0**	**–6**	**26**	**34.6**	**16:53**	....	....	....	....	....	....	....	....	....
	NHL Totals		**557**	**75**	**98**	**173**	**260**	**18**	**1**	**8**	**773**	**9.7**		**156**	**50.0**	**13:13**	**16**	**3**	**2**	**5**	**10**	**0**	**0**	**1**	**13:05**

Traded to **Los Angeles** by **St. Louis** with Patrice Tardif, Roman Vopat, St. Louis' 5th round choice (Peter Hogan) in 1996 Entry Draft and St. Louis' 1st round choice (Matt Zultek) in 1997 Entry Draft for Wayne Gretzky, February 27, 1996. • Missed majority of 2000-01 season recovering from ankle injury suffered in game vs. San Jose, December 26, 2000. Signed as a free agent by **Anaheim**, September 9, 2003. Claimed on waivers by **Toronto** from **Anaheim**, January 10, 2004. Claimed on waivers by **Washington** from **Toronto**, March 5, 2004.

JOHNSON, Greg
(JAWN-suhn, GREHG) **NSH.**

Center. Shoots left. 5'11", 200 lbs. Born, Thunder Bay, Ont., March 16, 1971. Philadelphia's 1st choice, 33rd overall, in 1989 Entry Draft.

Season	Club	League	GP	G	A	Pts	PIM	PP	SH	GW	S	%	+/-	TF	F%	Min	GP	G	A	Pts	PIM	PP	SH	GW	Min
1988-89	Thunder Bay	USHL	47	32	64	96	4	....	....	....	....	....	....	....	....	....	12	5	13	18	0	....	....	....	....
1989-90	North Dakota	WCHA	44	17	38	55	11	....	....	....	....	....	....	....	....	....	....	....	....	....	....	....	....	....	....
1990-91	North Dakota	WCHA	38	18	*61	79	6	....	....	....	....	....	....	....	....	....	....	....	....	....	....	....	....	....	....
1991-92	North Dakota	WCHA	39	20	*54	74	8	....	....	....	....	....	....	....	....	....	....	....	....	....	....	....	....	....	....
1992-93	North Dakota	WCHA	34	19	45	64	18	....	....	....	....	....	....	....	....	....	....	....	....	....	....	....	....	....	....
	Team Canada	Nat-Tm	23	6	14	20	2	....	....	....	....	....	....	....	....	....	....	....	....	....	....	....	....	....	....
1993-94	**Detroit**	**NHL**	**52**	**6**	**11**	**17**	**22**	**1**	**1**	**0**	**48**	**12.5**	**–7**	....	....	....	**7**	**2**	**2**	**4**	**2**	**1**	**0**	**0**	....
	Adirondack	AHL	3	2	4	6	0	....	....	....	....	....	....	....	....	....	4	0	4	4	2	....	....	....	....
	Canada	Olympics	8	0	3	3	0	....	....	....	....	....	....	....	....	....	....	....	....	....	....	....	....	....	....
1994-95	**Detroit**	**NHL**	**22**	**3**	**5**	**8**	**14**	**2**	**0**	**0**	**32**	**9.4**	**1**	....	....	....	**1**	**0**	**0**	**0**	**0**	**0**	**0**	**0**	....
1995-96	**Detroit**	**NHL**	**60**	**18**	**22**	**40**	**30**	**5**	**0**	**2**	**87**	**20.7**	**6**	....	....	....	**13**	**3**	**1**	**4**	**8**	**0**	**0**	**0**	....
1996-97	**Detroit**	**NHL**	**43**	**6**	**10**	**16**	**12**	**0**	**0**	**0**	**56**	**10.7**	**–5**	....	....	....	....	....	....	....	....	....	....	....	....
	Pittsburgh	**NHL**	**32**	**7**	**9**	**16**	**14**	**1**	**0**	**0**	**52**	**13.5**	**–13**	....	....	....	**5**	**1**	**0**	**1**	**2**	**0**	**0**	**0**	....
1997-98	**Pittsburgh**	**NHL**	**5**	**1**	**0**	**1**	**2**	**0**	**0**	**0**	**4**	**25.0**	**0**	....	....	....	....	....	....	....	....	....	....	....	....
	Chicago	**NHL**	**69**	**11**	**22**	**33**	**38**	**4**	**0**	**3**	**85**	**12.9**	**–2**	....	....	....	....	....	....	....	....	....	....	....	....
1998-99	**Nashville**	**NHL**	**68**	**16**	**34**	**50**	**24**	**2**	**3**	**0**	**120**	**13.3**	**–8**	**1441**	**53.6**	**19:26**	....	....	....	....	....	....	....	....	....
99-2000	**Nashville**	**NHL**	**82**	**11**	**33**	**44**	**40**	**2**	**0**	**1**	**133**	**8.3**	**–15**	**1684**	**50.8**	**19:13**	....	....	....	....	....	....	....	....	....
2000-01	**Nashville**	**NHL**	**82**	**15**	**17**	**32**	**46**	**1**	**0**	**4**	**97**	**15.5**	**–6**	**1583**	**51.8**	**17:49**	....	....	....	....	....	....	....	....	....
2001-02	**Nashville**	**NHL**	**82**	**18**	**26**	**44**	**38**	**3**	**0**	**2**	**145**	**12.4**	**–14**	**1764**	**51.8**	**19:34**	....	....	....	....	....	....	....	....	....
2002-03	**Nashville**	**NHL**	**38**	**8**	**9**	**17**	**22**	**0**	**0**	**0**	**55**	**14.5**	**7**	**753**	**52.1**	**17:11**	....	....	....	....	....	....	....	....	....
2003-04	**Nashville**	**NHL**	**82**	**14**	**18**	**32**	**33**	**1**	**4**	**4**	**100**	**14.0**	**–21**	**1607**	**55.1**	**17:38**	**6**	**1**	**2**	**3**	**0**	**0**	**0**	**0**	**17:48**
	NHL Totals		**717**	**134**	**216**	**350**	**335**	**22**	**8**	**16**	**1014**	**13.2**		**8832**	**52.5**	**18:35**	**32**	**7**	**5**	**12**	**12**	**1**	**0**	**0**	**17:48**

WCHA First All-Star Team (1991, 1992, 1993) • NCAA West First All-American Team (1991, 1993) • NCAA West Second All-American Team (1992)

Traded to **Detroit** by **Philadelphia** with Philadelphia's 5th round choice (Frederic Deschenes) in 1994 Entry Draft for Jim Cummins and Philadelphia's 4th round choice (previously acquired, later traded to Boston – Boston selected Charles Paquette) in 1993 Entry Draft, June 20, 1993. Traded to **Pittsburgh** by **Detroit** for Tomas Sandstrom, January 27, 1997. Traded to **Chicago** by **Pittsburgh** for Tuomas Gronman, October 27, 1997. Claimed by **Nashville** from **Chicago** in Expansion Draft, June 26, 1998. Missed majority of 2002-03 season recovering from head injury suffered in game vs. Vancouver, October 21, 2002.

JOHNSON, Matt
(JAWN-suhn, MAT) **MIN.**

Left wing. Shoots left. 6'5", 235 lbs. Born, Welland, Ont., November 23, 1975. Los Angeles' 2nd choice, 33rd overall, in 1994 Entry Draft.

Season	Club	League	GP	G	A	Pts	PIM	PP	SH	GW	S	%	+/-	TF	F%	Min	GP	G	A	Pts	PIM	PP	SH	GW	Min
1991-92	Welland Aerostars	OJHL-B	38	6	19	25	214	....	....	....	....	....	....	....	....	....	....	....	....	....	....	....	....	....	....
	Ajax Axemen	MTJHL	1	0	0	0	0	....	....	....	....	....	....	....	....	....	....	....	....	....	....	....	....	....	....
1992-93	Peterborough	OHL	66	8	17	25	211	....	....	....	....	....	....	....	....	....	16	1	1	2	56	....	....	....	....
1993-94	Peterborough	OHL	50	13	24	37	233	....	....	....	....	....	....	....	....	....	....	....	....	....	....	....	....	....	....
1994-95	Peterborough	OHL	14	1	2	3	43	....	....	....	....	....	....	....	....	....	....	....	....	....	....	....	....	....	....
	Los Angeles	**NHL**	**14**	**1**	**0**	**1**	**102**	**0**	**0**	**0**	**4**	**25.0**	**0**	....	....	....	....	....	....	....	....	....	....	....	....
1995-96	**Los Angeles**	**NHL**	**1**	**0**	**0**	**0**	**5**	**0**	**0**	**0**	**1**	**0.0**	**0**	....	....	....	....	....	....	....	....	....	....	....	....
	Phoenix	IHL	29	4	4	8	87	....	....	....	....	....	....	....	....	....	....	....	....	....	....	....	....	....	....
1996-97	**Los Angeles**	**NHL**	**52**	**1**	**3**	**4**	**194**	**0**	**0**	**0**	**20**	**5.0**	**–4**	....	....	....	....	....	....	....	....	....	....	....	....
1997-98	**Los Angeles**	**NHL**	**66**	**2**	**4**	**6**	**249**	**0**	**0**	**0**	**18**	**11.1**	**–8**	....	....	....	**4**	**0**	**0**	**0**	**6**	**0**	**0**	**0**	....
1998-99	**Los Angeles**	**NHL**	**49**	**2**	**1**	**3**	**131**	**0**	**0**	**0**	**14**	**14.3**	**–5**	**1**	**0.0**	**5:55**	....	....	....	....	....	....	....	....	....
99-2000	**Atlanta**	**NHL**	**64**	**2**	**5**	**7**	**144**	**0**	**0**	**0**	**54**	**3.7**	**–11**	**1**	**100.0**	**8:25**	....	....	....	....	....	....	....	....	....
2000-01	**Minnesota**	**NHL**	**50**	**1**	**1**	**2**	**137**	**0**	**0**	**0**	**21**	**4.8**	**–6**	**1**	**100.0**	**7:43**	....	....	....	....	....	....	....	....	....
2001-02	**Minnesota**	**NHL**	**60**	**4**	**0**	**4**	**183**	**0**	**0**	**1**	**23**	**17.4**	**–13**	**1**	**100.0**	**7:23**	....	....	....	....	....	....	....	....	....
2002-03	**Minnesota**	**NHL**	**60**	**3**	**5**	**8**	**201**	**0**	**0**	**1**	**24**	**12.5**	**–8**	**5**	**40.0**	**7:24**	**12**	**0**	**0**	**0**	**25**	**0**	**0**	**0**	**6:39**
2003-04	**Minnesota**	**NHL**	**57**	**7**	**1**	**8**	**177**	**0**	**0**	**1**	**21**	**33.3**	**4**	**3**	**33.3**	**6:27**	....	....	....	....	....	....	....	....	....
	NHL Totals		**473**	**23**	**20**	**43**	**1523**	**0**	**0**	**3**	**200**	**11.5**		**12**	**50.0**	**7:16**	**16**	**0**	**0**	**0**	**31**	**0**	**0**	**0**	**6:39**

OHL All-Rookie Team (1993)

Claimed by **Atlanta** from **Los Angeles** in Expansion Draft, June 25, 1999. Traded to **Minnesota** by **Atlanta** for San Jose's 3rd round choice (previously acquired, later traded to Pittsburgh – later traded to Columbus – Columbus selected Aaron Johnson) in 2001 Entry Draft, September 29, 2000.

JOHNSON, Mike
(JAWN-suhn, MIGHK) **PHX.**

Right wing. Shoots right. 6'2", 201 lbs. Born, Scarborough, Ont., October 3, 1974.

Season	Club	League	GP	G	A	Pts	PIM	PP	SH	GW	S	%	+/-	TF	F%	Min	GP	G	A	Pts	PIM	PP	SH	GW	Min
1991-92	Hillcrest Summits	MTHL	45	43	66	109		....	....	....	....	....	....	....	....	....	20	10	19	29		....	....	....	....
1992-93	Aurora Eagles	MTJHL	48	25	40	65	18	....	....	....	....	....	....	....	....	....	7	7	15	22		....	....	....	....
1993-94	Bowling Green	CCHA	38	6	14	20	18	....	....	....	....	....	....	....	....	....	....	....	....	....	....	....	....	....	....
1994-95	Bowling Green	CCHA	37	16	33	49	35	....	....	....	....	....	....	....	....	....	....	....	....	....	....	....	....	....	....
1995-96	Bowling Green	CCHA	30	12	19	31	22	....	....	....	....	....	....	....	....	....	....	....	....	....	....	....	....	....	....
1996-97	Bowling Green	CCHA	38	30	32	62	46	....	....	....	....	....	....	....	....	....	....	....	....	....	....	....	....	....	....
	Toronto	**NHL**	**13**	**2**	**2**	**4**	**4**	**0**	**1**	**1**	**27**	**7.4**	**–2**												

			Regular Season														Playoffs								
Season	Club	League	GP	G	A	Pts	PIM	PP	SH	GW	S	%	+/-	TF	F%	Min	GP	G	A	Pts	PIM	PP	SH	GW	Min
1997-98	Toronto	NHL	82	15	32	47	24	5	0	0	143	10.5	–4	....	....	....	....	....	....	....	....	....	....	....	....
1998-99	Toronto	NHL	79	20	24	44	35	5	3	2	149	13.4	13	15	53.3	16:16	17	3	2	5	4	0	0	1	16:28
99-2000	Toronto	NHL	52	11	14	25	23	2	1	3	89	12.4	8	2	50.0	15:22	....	....	....	....	....	....	....	....	....
	Tampa Bay	NHL	28	10	12	22	4	4	0	0	43	23.3	–2	5	60.0	20:33	....	....	....	....	....	....	....	....	....
2000-01	Tampa Bay	NHL	64	11	27	38	38	3	1	0	107	10.3	–10	2	0.0	18:13	....	....	....	....	....	....	....	....	....
	Phoenix	NHL	12	2	3	5	4	1	0	0	17	11.8	0	0	0.0	12:12	....	....	....	....	....	....	....	....	....
2001-02	Phoenix	NHL	57	5	22	27	28	1	2	0	73	6.8	14	13	30.8	15:49	5	1	1	2	6	0	0	0	14:45
2002-03	Phoenix	NHL	82	23	40	63	47	8	0	3	178	12.9	9	34	50.0	19:39	....	....	....	....	....	....	....	....	....
2003-04	Phoenix	NHL	11	1	9	10	10	1	0	0	17	5.9	–1	2	50.0	19:50	....	....	....	....	....	....	....	....	....
	NHL Totals		480	100	185	285	217	30	8	9	843	11.9		73	46.6	17:25	22	4	3	7	10	0	0	1	16:05

NHL All-Rookie Team (1998)

Signed as a free agent by **Toronto**, March 16, 1997. Traded to **Tampa Bay** by **Toronto** with Marek Posmyk, Toronto's 5th (Pavel Sedov) and 6th (Aaron Gionet) round choices in 2000 Entry Draft and future considerations for Darcy Tucker, Tampa Bay's 4th round choice (Miguel Delisle) in 2000 Entry Draft and future considerations, February 9, 2000. Traded to **Phoenix** by **Tampa Bay** with Paul Mara, Ruslan Zainullin and NY Islanders' 2nd round choice (previously acquired, Phoenix selected Matthew Spiller) in 2001 Entry Draft for Nikolai Khabibulin and Stan Neckar, March 5, 2001. • Missed majority of 2003-04 season recovering from shoulder injury suffered in game vs. Los Angeles, Novembeer 1, 2003.

JOHNSON, Ryan

(JAWN-suhn, RIGH-yuhn) **ST.L.**

Center. Shoots left. 6'1", 200 lbs. Born, Thunder Bay, Ont., June 14, 1976. Florida's 4th choice, 36th overall, in 1994 Entry Draft.

Season	Club	League	GP	G	A	Pts	PIM	PP	SH	GW	S	%	+/-	TF	F%	Min	GP	G	A	Pts	PIM	PP	SH	GW	Min
1992-93	Thunder Bay	TBAHA	60	25	33	58	....	....	....	....	....	....	....	....	....	....	....	....	....	....	....	....	....	....	....
1993-94	Thunder Bay	USHL	48	14	36	50	28	....	....	....	....	....	....	....	....	....	....	....	....	....	....	....	....	....	....
1994-95	North Dakota	WCHA	38	6	22	28	39	....	....	....	....	....	....	....	....	....	....	....	....	....	....	....	....	....	....
1995-96	North Dakota	WCHA	21	2	17	19	14	....	....	....	....	....	....	....	....	....	....	....	....	....	....	....	....	....	....
	Team Canada	Nat-Tm	28	5	12	17	14	....	....	....	....	....	....	....	....	....	....	....	....	....	....	....	....	....	....
1996-97	Carolina	AHL	79	18	24	42	28	....	....	....	....	....	....	....	....	....	....	....	....	....	....	....	....	....	....
1997-98	Florida	NHL	10	0	2	2	0	0	0	0	6	0.0	–4	....	....	....	....	....	....	....	....	....	....	....	....
	New Haven	AHL	64	19	48	67	12	....	....	....	....	....	....	....	....	....	3	0	1	1	0	....	....	....	....
1998-99	Florida	NHL	1	1	0	1	0	0	0	0	1	100.0	0	16	37.5	15:26	....	....	....	....	....	....	....	....	....
	New Haven	AHL	37	8	19	27	18	....	....	....	....	....	....	....	....	....	....	....	....	....	....	....	....	....	....
99-2000	Florida	NHL	66	4	12	16	14	0	0	0	44	9.1	1	684	51.8	11:47	....	....	....	....	....	....	....	....	....
	Tampa Bay	NHL	14	0	2	2	2	0	0	0	5	0.0	–9	117	53.0	11:02	....	....	....	....	....	....	....	....	....
2000-01	Tampa Bay	NHL	80	7	14	21	44	1	0	0	71	9.9	–20	951	48.9	15:47	....	....	....	....	....	....	....	....	....
2001-02	Florida	NHL	29	1	3	4	10	0	0	0	24	4.2	–5	336	47.9	13:00	....	....	....	....	....	....	....	....	....
2002-03	Florida	NHL	58	2	5	7	26	0	0	0	54	3.7	–13	689	48.0	10:40	....	....	....	....	....	....	....	....	....
	St. Louis	NHL	17	0	0	0	12	0	0	0	13	0.0	0	180	51.7	10:34	6	0	2	2	6	0	0	0	8:14
2003-04	St. Louis	NHL	69	4	7	11	8	0	1	1	36	11.1	–2	537	53.6	9:54	3	0	0	0	0	0	0	0	6:11
	NHL Totals		344	19	45	64	116	1	1	1	254	7.5		3510	50.1	12:11	9	0	2	2	6	0	0	0	7:33

Traded to **Tampa Bay** by **Florida** with Dwayne Hay for Mike Sillinger, March 14, 2000. Traded to **Florida** by **Tampa Bay** with Tampa Bay's 6th round choice (later traded back to Tampa Bay – Tampa Bay selected Doug O'Brien) in 2003 Entry Draft for Vaclav Prospal, July 10, 2001. • Missed majority of 2001-02 season recovering from head injury suffered in game vs. St. Louis, December 22, 2001. Claimed on waivers by **St. Louis** from **Florida**, February 19, 2003.

JOHNSSON, Kim

(YAWN-suhn, KIHM) **PHI.**

Defense. Shoots left. 6'1", 205 lbs. Born, Malmo, Sweden, March 16, 1976. NY Rangers' 15th choice, 286th overall, in 1994 Entry Draft.

Season	Club	League	GP	G	A	Pts	PIM	PP	SH	GW	S	%	+/-	TF	F%	Min	GP	G	A	Pts	PIM	PP	SH	GW	Min
1993-94	Malmo IF Jr.	Swede-Jr.	14	5	3	8	14	....	....	....	....	....	....	....	....	....	....	....	....	....	....	....	....	....	....
	Malmo IF	Sweden	2	0	0	0	0	....	....	....	....	....	....	....	....	....	....	....	....	....	....	....	....	....	....
1994-95	Malmo IF Jr.	Swede-Jr.	29	6	15	21	40	....	....	....	....	....	....	....	....	....	....	....	....	....	....	....	....	....	....
	Malmo IF	Sweden	13	0	0	0	4	....	....	....	....	....	....	....	....	....	1	0	0	0	0	....	....	....	....
1995-96	Malmo IF	Sweden	38	2	0	2	30	....	....	....	....	....	....	....	....	....	4	0	1	1	8	....	....	....	....
1996-97	Malmo IF	Sweden	49	4	9	13	42	....	....	....	....	....	....	....	....	....	4	0	0	0	2	....	....	....	....
1997-98	Malmo IF	Sweden	45	5	9	14	29	....	....	....	....	....	....	....	....	....	....	....	....	....	....	....	....	....	....
1998-99	Malmo IF	Sweden	49	9	8	17	76	....	....	....	....	....	....	....	....	....	8	2	3	5	12	....	....	....	....
99-2000	NY Rangers	NHL	76	6	15	21	46	1	0	1	101	5.9	–13	0	0.0	18:06	....	....	....	....	....	....	....	....	....
2000-01	NY Rangers	NHL	75	5	21	26	40	4	0	0	104	4.8	–3	0	0.0	21:16	....	....	....	....	....	....	....	....	....
2001-02	Philadelphia	NHL	82	11	30	41	42	5	0	1	150	7.3	12	0	0.0	23:02	5	0	0	0	2	0	0	0	22:48
	Sweden	Olympics	4	1	1	2	0	....	....	....	....	....	....	....	....	....	....	....	....	....	....	....	....	....	....
2002-03	Philadelphia	NHL	82	10	29	39	38	5	0	2	159	6.3	11	0	0.0	24:05	13	0	3	3	8	0	0	0	26:07
2003-04	Philadelphia	NHL	80	13	29	42	26	4	0	3	189	6.9	16	0	0.0	24:27	15	2	6	8	8	0	0	1	26:11
	NHL Totals		395	45	124	169	192	19	0	7	703	6.4		0	0.0	22:15	33	2	9	11	18	0	0	1	25:39

Traded to **Philadelphia** by **NY Rangers** with Jan Hlavac, Pavel Brendl and NY Rangers' 3rd round choice (Stefan Ruzicka) in 2003 Entry Draft for Eric Lindros, August 20, 2001.

JOKELA, Mikko

(YOH-kih-lah, MIH-koh) **VAN.**

Defense. Shoots right. 6'1", 210 lbs. Born, Lappeenranta, Finland, March 4, 1980. New Jersey's 5th choice, 96th overall, in 1998 Entry Draft.

Season	Club	League	GP	G	A	Pts	PIM	PP	SH	GW	S	%	+/-	TF	F%	Min	GP	G	A	Pts	PIM	PP	SH	GW	Min
1994-95	KalPa Kuopio C	Finn-Jr.	29	7	12	19	36	....	....	....	....	....	....	....	....	....	....	....	....	....	....	....	....	....	....
1995-96	KalPa Kuopio C	Finn-Jr.	23	10	19	29	103	....	....	....	....	....	....	....	....	....	6	3	5	8	4	....	....	....	....
	KalPa Kuopio B	Finn-Jr.	9	2	1	3	20	....	....	....	....	....	....	....	....	....	....	....	....	....	....	....	....	....	....
	KalPa Kuopio Jr.	Finn-Jr.	11	2	1	3	20	....	....	....	....	....	....	....	....	....	....	....	....	....	....	....	....	....	....
1996-97	KalPa Kuopio B	Finn-Jr.	11	3	2	5	8	....	....	....	....	....	....	....	....	....	5	1	1	2	4	....	....	....	....
	KalPa Kuopio Jr.	Finn-Jr.	22	2	4	6	4	....	....	....	....	....	....	....	....	....	....	....	....	....	....	....	....	....	....
	KalPa Kuopio B	Finn-Jr.	....	....	....	....	....	....	....	....	....	....	....	....	....	....	12	0	1	1	14	....	....	....	....
1997-98	HIFK Helsinki Jr.	Finn-Jr.	22	2	5	7	14	....	....	....	....	....	....	....	....	....	....	....	....	....	....	....	....	....	....
	Hermes Kokkola	Finland-2	6	0	1	1	2	....	....	....	....	....	....	....	....	....	....	....	....	....	....	....	....	....	....
	HIFK Helsinki	Finland	16	0	0	0	0	....	....	....	....	....	....	....	....	....	....	....	....	....	....	....	....	....	....
1998-99	KalPa Kuopio Jr.	Finn-Jr.	1	0	1	1	2	....	....	....	....	....	....	....	....	....	....	....	....	....	....	....	....	....	....
	KalPa Kuopio	Finland	42	1	2	3	18	....	....	....	....	....	....	....	....	....	....	....	....	....	....	....	....	....	....
	HIFK Helsinki	Finland	3	0	0	0	2	....	....	....	....	....	....	....	....	....	....	....	....	....	....	....	....	....	....
	KalPa Kuopio	Finland-2	....	....	....	....	....	....	....	....	....	....	....	....	....	....	6	0	0	0	2	....	....	....	....
99-2000	SaiPa	Finland	48	0	5	5	50	....	....	....	....	....	....	....	....	....	....	....	....	....	....	....	....	....	....
	SaiPa Jr.	Finn-Jr.	....	....	....	....	....	....	....	....	....	....	....	....	....	....	1	0	0	0	0	....	....	....	....
2000-01	SaiPa Jr.	Finn-Jr.	4	2	2	4	2	....	....	....	....	....	....	....	....	....	3	0	0	0	2	....	....	....	....
	KooKoo Kouvola	Finland-2	5	3	0	3	0	....	....	....	....	....	....	....	....	....	....	....	....	....	....	....	....	....	....
	SaiPa	Finland	50	1	0	1	24	....	....	....	....	....	....	....	....	....	....	....	....	....	....	....	....	....	....
2001-02	Albany River Rats	AHL	56	5	13	18	28	....	....	....	....	....	....	....	....	....	....	....	....	....	....	....	....	....	....
2002-03	Albany River Rats	AHL	44	8	11	19	35	....	....	....	....	....	....	....	....	....	....	....	....	....	....	....	....	....	....
	Vancouver	NHL	1	0	0	0	0	0	0	0	3	0.0	0	0	0.0	5:09	....	....	....	....	....	....	....	....	....
	Manitoba Moose	AHL	32	3	7	10	17	....	....	....	....	....	....	....	....	....	14	1	4	5	2	....	....	....	....
2003-04	Manitoba Moose	AHL	78	5	10	15	52	....	....	....	....	....	....	....	....	....	....	....	....	....	....	....	....	....	....
	NHL Totals		1	0	0	0	0	0	0	0	3	0.0		0	0.0	5:09	....	....	....	....	....	....	....	....	....

Traded to **Vancouver** by **New Jersey** for Steve Kariya, January 24, 2003. Signed as a free agent by **HPK Hameenlinna** (Finland), April 17, 2004.

JOKINEN, Olli

(YOH-kih-nihn, OH-lee) **FLA.**

Center. Shoots left. 6'3", 205 lbs. Born, Kuopio, Finland, December 5, 1978. Los Angeles' 1st choice, 3rd overall, in 1997 Entry Draft.

Season	Club	League	GP	G	A	Pts	PIM	PP	SH	GW	S	%	+/-	TF	F%	Min	GP	G	A	Pts	PIM	PP	SH	GW	Min
1992-93	KalPa Kuopio C	Finn-Jr.	14	8	3	11	12	....	....	....	....	....	....	....	....	....	....	....	....	....	....	....	....	....	....
1993-94	KalPa Kuopio C	Finn-Jr.	31	27	25	52	62	....	....	....	....	....	....	....	....	....	....	....	....	....	....	....	....	....	....
1994-95	KalPa Kuopio B	Finn-Jr.	12	9	14	23	46	....	....	....	....	....	....	....	....	....	....	....	....	....	....	....	....	....	....
	KalPa Kuopio Jr.	Finn-Jr.	6	0	1	1	6	....	....	....	....	....	....	....	....	....	....	....	....	....	....	....	....	....	....
1995-96	KalPa Kuopio Jr.	Finn-Jr.	25	20	14	34	47	....	....	....	....	....	....	....	....	....	7	4	4	8	20	....	....	....	....
	KalPa Kuopio	Finland	15	1	1	2	2	....	....	....	....	....	....	....	....	....	....	....	....	....	....	....	....	....	....
1996-97	HIFK Helsinki Jr.	Finn-Jr.	2	1	0	1	6	....	....	....	....	....	....	....	....	....	....	....	....	....	....	....	....	....	....
	HIFK Helsinki	Finland	50	14	27	41	88	....	....	....	....	....	....	....	....	....	....	....	....	....	....	....	....	....	....
1997-98	Los Angeles	NHL	8	0	0	0	6	0	0	0	12	0.0	–5	....	....	....	....	....	....	....	....	....	....	....	....
	HIFK Helsinki	Finland	30	11	28	39	8	....	....	....	....	....	....	....	....	....	9	*7	2	9	2	....	....	....	....
1998-99	Los Angeles	NHL	66	9	12	21	44	3	1	1	87	10.3	–10	779	43.9	14:42	....	....	....	....	....	....	....	....	....
	Springfield	AHL	9	3	6	9	6	....	....	....	....	....	....	....	....	....	....	....	....	....	....	....	....	....	....
99-2000	NY Islanders	NHL	82	11	10	21	80	1	2	3	138	8.0	0	841	46.1	16:15	....	....	....	....	....	....	....	....	....
2000-01	Florida	NHL	78	6	10	16	106	0	0	0	121	5.0	–22	638	42.3	13:23	....	....	....	....	....	....	....	....	....
2001-02	Florida	NHL	80	9	20	29	98	3	1	0	153	5.9	–16	1222	45.2	18:05	....	....	....	....	....	....	....	....	....
	Finland	Olympics	4	2	1	3	0	....	....	....	....	....	....	....	....	....	....	....	....	....	....	....	....	....	....

			Regular Season														Playoffs								
Season	Club	League	GP	G	A	Pts	PIM	PP	SH	GW	S	%	+/-	TF	F%	Min	GP	G	A	Pts	PIM	PP	SH	GW	Min
2002-03	Florida	NHL	81	36	29	65	79	13	3	6	240	15.0	-17	1925	46.7	22:02	....	....	....	....	....	....	....	....	....
2003-04	Florida	NHL	82	26	32	58	81	8	2	8	280	9.3	-16	1986	47.1	22:35	....	....	....	....	....	....	....	....	....
	NHL Totals		477	97	113	210	494	28	9	18	1031	9.4		7391	45.8	17:58	....	....	....	....	....	....	....	....	....

Played in NHL All-Star Game (2003)

Traded to **NY Islanders** by **Los Angeles** with Josh Green, Mathieu Biron and Los Angeles' 1st round choice (Taylor Pyatt) in 1999 Entry Draft for Ziggy Palffy, Bryan Smolinski, Marcel Cousineau and New Jersey's 4th round choice (previously acquired, Los Angeles selected Daniel Johansson) in 1999 Entry Draft, June 20, 1999. Traded to **Florida** by **NY Islanders** with Roberto Luongo for Mark Parrish and Oleg Kvasha, June 24, 2000.

JONES, Randy
(JOHNZ, RAN-dee) **PHI.**

Defense. Shoots left. 6'2", 200 lbs. Born, Quispamsis, N.B., July 23, 1981.

Season	Club	League	GP	G	A	Pts	PIM	PP	SH	GW	S	%	+/-	TF	F%	Min	GP	G	A	Pts	PIM	PP	SH	GW	Min
99-2000	Cobourg Cougars	OPJHL	STATISTICS NOT AVAILABLE																						
2000-01	Cobourg Cougars	OPJHL	28	15	21	36	46	....	....	....	....	....	....	....	....	....	....	....	....	....	....	....	....	....	....
2001-02	Clarkson	ECAC	34	9	11	20	32	....	....	....	....	....	....	....	....	....	....	....	....	....	....	....	....	....	....
2002-03	Clarkson	ECAC	33	13	20	33	65	....	....	....	....	....	....	....	....	....	....	....	....	....	....	....	....	....	....
2003-04	**Philadelphia**	**NHL**	**5**	**0**	**0**	**0**	**0**	**0**	**0**	**0**	**5**	**0.0**	**1**	**0**	**0.0**	**12:00**	....	....	....	....	....	....	....	....	....
	Philadelphia	AHL	55	8	24	32	63	....	....	....	....	....	....	....	....	....	12	0	1	1	17	....	....	....	....
	NHL Totals		**5**	**0**	**0**	**0**	**0**	**0**	**0**	**0**	**5**	**0.0**		**0**	**0.0**	**12:00**	....	....	....	....	....	....	....	....	....

ECAC First All-Star Team (2003)

Signed as a free agent by **Philadelphia**, July 24, 2003.

JONES, Ty
(JOHNZ, TIGH) **FLA.**

Right wing. Shoots right. 6'3", 218 lbs. Born, Richland, WA, February 22, 1979. Chicago's 2nd choice, 16th overall, in 1997 Entry Draft.

Season	Club	League	GP	G	A	Pts	PIM	PP	SH	GW	S	%	+/-	TF	F%	Min	GP	G	A	Pts	PIM	PP	SH	GW	Min
1993-94	Alaska All-Stars	AAHL	64	84	104	188	126	....	....	....	....	....	....	....	....	....	....	....	....	....	....	....	....	....	....
1994-95	Alaska All-Stars	AAHL	42	33	35	68	98	....	....	....	....	....	....	....	....	....	....	....	....	....	....	....	....	....	....
1995-96	Spokane Chiefs	WHL	34	1	0	1	77	....	....	....	....	....	....	....	....	....	3	0	0	0	6	....	....	....	....
1996-97	Spokane Chiefs	WHL	67	20	34	54	202	....	....	....	....	....	....	....	....	....	9	2	4	6	10	....	....	....	....
1997-98	Spokane Chiefs	WHL	60	36	48	84	161	....	....	....	....	....	....	....	....	....	18	2	14	16	35	....	....	....	....
1998-99	Spokane Chiefs	WHL	26	15	12	27	98	....	....	....	....	....	....	....	....	....	....	....	....	....	....	....	....	....	....
	Kamloops Blazers	WHL	20	3	16	19	84	....	....	....	....	....	....	....	....	....	14	5	3	8	22	....	....	....	....
	Chicago	**NHL**	**8**	**0**	**0**	**0**	**12**	**0**	**0**	**0**	**3**	**0.0**	**-1**	**0**	**0.0**	**7:53**	....	....	....	....	....	....	....	....	....
99-2000	Cleveland	IHL	10	1	1	2	34	....	....	....	....	....	....	....	....	....	....	....	....	....	....	....	....	....	....
	Florida Everblades	ECHL	48	11	26	37	81	....	....	....	....	....	....	....	....	....	5	1	1	2	17	....	....	....	....
2000-01	Norfolk Admirals	AHL	64	11	17	28	114	....	....	....	....	....	....	....	....	....	....	....	....	....	....	....	....	....	....
2001-02	Norfolk Admirals	AHL	55	6	14	20	172	....	....	....	....	....	....	....	....	....	4	0	0	0	2	....	....	....	....
2002-03	Anchorage Aces	WCHL	12	1	7	8	49	....	....	....	....	....	....	....	....	....	....	....	....	....	....	....	....	....	....
2003-04	Norfolk Admirals	AHL	37	4	5	9	93	....	....	....	....	....	....	....	....	....	....	....	....	....	....	....	....	....	....
	Florida	**NHL**	**6**	**0**	**0**	**0**	**7**	**0**	**0**	**0**	**1**	**0.0**	**0**	**0**	**0.0**	**3:05**	....	....	....	....	....	....	....	....	....
	San Antonio	AHL	2	0	0	0	2	....	....	....	....	....	....	....	....	....	....	....	....	....	....	....	....	....	....
	NHL Totals		**14**	**0**	**0**	**0**	**19**	**0**	**0**	**0**	**4**	**0.0**		**0**	**0.0**	**5:50**	....	....	....	....	....	....	....	....	....

• Missed majority of 2002-03 season recovering from shoulder injury suffered during off-season training, July 15, 2002. Signed as a free agent by **Anchorage** (WCHL), February 21, 2003 with Chicago retaining NHL rights. Traded to **Florida** by **Chicago** for future considerations, March 2, 2004.

JONSSON, Hans
(YAWN-suhn, HANS)

Defense. Shoots left. 6'1", 205 lbs. Born, Jarved, Sweden, August 2, 1973. Pittsburgh's 11th choice, 286th overall, in 1993 Entry Draft.

Season	Club	League	GP	G	A	Pts	PIM	PP	SH	GW	S	%	+/-	TF	F%	Min	GP	G	A	Pts	PIM	PP	SH	GW	Min
1991-92	Hasums IF	Swede-2	13	4	6	10	10	....	....	....	....	....	....	....	....	....	....	....	....	....	....	....	....	....	....
	MoDo	Sweden	6	0	1	1	4	....	....	....	....	....	....	....	....	....	....	....	....	....	....	....	....	....	....
1992-93	MoDo	Sweden	40	2	2	4	24	....	....	....	....	....	....	....	....	....	3	0	1	1	2	....	....	....	....
1993-94	MoDo	Sweden	23	4	1	5	18	....	....	....	....	....	....	....	....	....	10	0	1	1	12	....	....	....	....
1994-95	MoDo	Sweden	39	4	6	10	30	....	....	....	....	....	....	....	....	....	....	....	....	....	....	....	....	....	....
1995-96	MoDo	Sweden	36	10	6	16	30	....	....	....	....	....	....	....	....	....	8	2	1	3	24	....	....	....	....
1996-97	MoDo	Sweden	27	7	5	12	18	....	....	....	....	....	....	....	....	....	....	....	....	....	....	....	....	....	....
1997-98	MoDo	Sweden	40	8	6	14	40	....	....	....	....	....	....	....	....	....	8	1	1	2	12	....	....	....	....
1998-99	MoDo	Sweden	41	3	4	7	40	....	....	....	....	....	....	....	....	....	13	2	4	6	22	....	....	....	....
99-2000	**Pittsburgh**	**NHL**	**68**	**3**	**11**	**14**	**12**	**0**	**1**	**1**	**49**	**6.1**	**-5**	**0**	**0.0**	**18:34**	**11**	**0**	**1**	**1**	**6**	**0**	**0**	**0**	**23:16**
2000-01	**Pittsburgh**	**NHL**	**58**	**4**	**18**	**22**	**22**	**2**	**0**	**0**	**44**	**9.1**	**11**	**0**	**0.0**	**18:27**	**16**	**0**	**0**	**0**	**8**	**0**	**0**	**0**	**17:11**
2001-02	**Pittsburgh**	**NHL**	**53**	**2**	**5**	**7**	**22**	**2**	**0**	**0**	**37**	**5.4**	**-12**	**0**	**0.0**	**18:12**	....	....	....	....	....	....	....	....	....
2002-03	**Pittsburgh**	**NHL**	**63**	**1**	**4**	**5**	**36**	**0**	**0**	**0**	**40**	**2.5**	**-23**	**2**	**0.0**	**17:04**	....	....	....	....	....	....	....	....	....
2003-04	MoDo	Sweden	28	4	5	9	38	....	....	....	....	....	....	....	....	....	6	0	1	1	24	....	....	....	....
	NHL Totals		**242**	**10**	**38**	**48**	**92**	**4**	**1**	**1**	**170**	**5.9**		**2**	**0.0**	**18:04**	**27**	**0**	**1**	**1**	**14**	**0**	**0**	**0**	**19:39**

Signed as a free agent by **MoDo** (Sweden), September 26, 2003.

JONSSON, Kenny
(YAWN-suhn, KEHN-nee) **NYI**

Defense. Shoots left. 6'3", 217 lbs. Born, Angelholm, Sweden, October 6, 1974. Toronto's 1st choice, 12th overall, in 1993 Entry Draft.

Season	Club	League	GP	G	A	Pts	PIM	PP	SH	GW	S	%	+/-	TF	F%	Min	GP	G	A	Pts	PIM	PP	SH	GW	Min
1991-92	Rogle	Swede-2	30	4	11	15	24	....	....	....	....	....	....	....	....	....	5	0	0	0	0	....	....	....	....
1992-93	Rogle Jr.	Swede-Jr.	2	1	2	3	25	....	....	....	....	....	....	....	....	....	....	....	....	....	....	....	....	....	....
	Rogle	Sweden	39	3	10	13	42	....	....	....	....	....	....	....	....	....	....	....	....	....	....	....	....	....	....
1993-94	Rogle	Sweden	36	4	13	17	40	....	....	....	....	....	....	....	....	....	3	1	1	2	2	....	....	....	....
	Sweden	Olympics	3	1	0	1	0	....	....	....	....	....	....	....	....	....	....	....	....	....	....	....	....	....	....
1994-95	Rogle	Sweden	8	3	1	4	20	....	....	....	....	....	....	....	....	....	....	....	....	....	....	....	....	....	....
	St. John's	AHL	10	2	5	7	2	....	....	....	....	....	....	....	....	....	....	....	....	....	....	....	....	....	....
	Toronto	**NHL**	**39**	**2**	**7**	**9**	**16**	**0**	**0**	**1**	**50**	**4.0**	**-8**	....	....	....	**4**	**0**	**0**	**0**	**0**	**0**	**0**	**0**	....
1995-96	**Toronto**	**NHL**	**50**	**4**	**22**	**26**	**22**	**3**	**0**	**1**	**90**	**4.4**	**12**	....	....	....	....	....	....	....	....	....	....	....	....
	NY Islanders	**NHL**	**16**	**0**	**4**	**4**	**10**	**0**	**0**	**0**	**40**	**0.0**	**-5**	....	....	....	....	....	....	....	....	....	....	....	....
1996-97	**NY Islanders**	**NHL**	**81**	**3**	**18**	**21**	**24**	**1**	**0**	**0**	**92**	**3.3**	**10**	....	....	....	....	....	....	....	....	....	....	....	....
1997-98	**NY Islanders**	**NHL**	**81**	**14**	**26**	**40**	**58**	**6**	**0**	**2**	**108**	**13.0**	**-2**	....	....	....	....	....	....	....	....	....	....	....	....
1998-99	**NY Islanders**	**NHL**	**63**	**8**	**18**	**26**	**34**	**6**	**0**	**0**	**91**	**8.8**	**-18**	**0**	**0.0**	**24:59**	....	....	....	....	....	....	....	....	....
99-2000	**NY Islanders**	**NHL**	**65**	**1**	**24**	**25**	**32**	**1**	**0**	**0**	**84**	**1.2**	**-15**	**0**	**0.0**	**24:29**	....	....	....	....	....	....	....	....	....
2000-01	**NY Islanders**	**NHL**	**65**	**8**	**21**	**29**	**30**	**5**	**0**	**0**	**91**	**8.8**	**-22**	**0**	**0.0**	**24:04**	....	....	....	....	....	....	....	....	....
2001-02	**NY Islanders**	**NHL**	**76**	**10**	**22**	**32**	**26**	**2**	**1**	**0**	**107**	**9.3**	**15**	**2**	**0.0**	**25:34**	**5**	**1**	**2**	**3**	**4**	**1**	**0**	**0**	**23:48**
	Sweden	Olympics	3	1	0	1	2	....	....	....	....	....	....	....	....	....	....	....	....	....	....	....	....	....	....
2002-03	**NY Islanders**	**NHL**	**71**	**8**	**18**	**26**	**24**	**3**	**1**	**0**	**108**	**7.4**	**-8**	**6**	**50.0**	**23:12**	**5**	**0**	**1**	**1**	**0**	**0**	**0**	**0**	**28:46**
2003-04	**NY Islanders**	**NHL**	**79**	**5**	**24**	**29**	**22**	**3**	**0**	**2**	**106**	**4.7**	**25**	**0**	**0.0**	**22:56**	**5**	**0**	**0**	**0**	**2**	**0**	**0**	**0**	**21:58**
	NHL Totals		**686**	**63**	**204**	**267**	**298**	**30**	**2**	**6**	**967**	**6.5**		**8**	**37.5**	**24:11**	**19**	**1**	**3**	**4**	**6**	**1**	**0**	**0**	**24:51**

NHL All-Rookie Team (1995)

Traded to **NY Islanders** by **Toronto** with Sean Haggerty, Darby Hendrickson and Toronto's 1st round choice (Roberto Luongo) in 1997 Entry Draft for Wendel Clark, Mathieu Schneider and D.J. Smith, March 13, 1996.

JOVANOVSKI, Ed
(joh-van-OHV-skee, EHD) **VAN.**

Defense. Shoots left. 6'2", 210 lbs. Born, Windsor, Ont., June 26, 1976. Florida's 1st choice, 1st overall, in 1994 Entry Draft.

Season	Club	League	GP	G	A	Pts	PIM	PP	SH	GW	S	%	+/-	TF	F%	Min	GP	G	A	Pts	PIM	PP	SH	GW	Min
1991-92	Windsor	OMHA	50	25	40	65	88	....	....	....	....	....	....	....	....	....	....	....	....	....	....	....	....	....	....
1992-93	Windsor Bulldogs	OJHL-B	48	7	46	53	88	....	....	....	....	....	....	....	....	....	....	....	....	....	....	....	....	....	....
1993-94	Windsor Spitfires	OHL	62	15	36	51	221	....	....	....	....	....	....	....	....	....	4	0	0	0	15	....	....	....	....
1994-95	Windsor Spitfires	OHL	50	23	42	65	198	....	....	....	....	....	....	....	....	....	9	2	7	9	39	....	....	....	....
1995-96	**Florida**	**NHL**	**70**	**10**	**11**	**21**	**137**	**2**	**0**	**2**	**116**	**8.6**	**-3**	....	....	....	**22**	**1**	**8**	**9**	**52**	**0**	**0**	**0**	....
1996-97	**Florida**	**NHL**	**61**	**7**	**16**	**23**	**172**	**3**	**0**	**1**	**80**	**8.8**	**-1**	....	....	....	**5**	**0**	**0**	**0**	**4**	**0**	**0**	**0**	....
1997-98	**Florida**	**NHL**	**81**	**9**	**14**	**23**	**158**	**2**	**1**	**3**	**142**	**6.3**	**-12**	....	....	....	....	....	....	....	....	....	....	....	....
1998-99	**Florida**	**NHL**	**41**	**3**	**13**	**16**	**82**	**1**	**0**	**1**	**68**	**4.4**	**-4**	**0**	**0.0**	**22:35**	....	....	....	....	....	....	....	....	....
	Vancouver	**NHL**	**31**	**2**	**9**	**11**	**44**	**0**	**0**	**0**	**41**	**4.9**	**-5**	**0**	**0.0**	**21:16**	....	....	....	....	....	....	....	....	....
99-2000	**Vancouver**	**NHL**	**75**	**5**	**21**	**26**	**54**	**1**	**0**	**1**	**109**	**4.6**	**-3**	**0**	**0.0**	**24:03**	....	....	....	....	....	....	....	....	....
2000-01	**Vancouver**	**NHL**	**79**	**12**	**35**	**47**	**102**	**4**	**0**	**2**	**193**	**6.2**	**-1**	**0**	**0.0**	**24:57**	**4**	**1**	**1**	**2**	**0**	**0**	**0**	**0**	**25:54**
2001-02	**Vancouver**	**NHL**	**82**	**17**	**31**	**48**	**101**	**7**	**1**	**3**	**202**	**8.4**	**-7**	**0**	**0.0**	**25:11**	**6**	**1**	**4**	**5**	**8**	**1**	**0**	**0**	**25:48**
	Canada	Olympics	6	0	3	3	4	....	....	....	....	....	....	....	....	....	....	....	....	....	....	....	....	....	....

			Regular Season														Playoffs								
Season	Club	League	GP	G	A	Pts	PIM	PP	SH	GW	S	%	+/-	TF	F%	Min	GP	G	A	Pts	PIM	PP	SH	GW	Min
2002-03	Vancouver	NHL	67	6	40	46	113	2	0	1	145	4.1	19	0	0.0	24:15	14	7	1	8	22	4	1	2	23:40
2003-04	Vancouver	NHL	56	7	16	23	64	2	0	1	143	4.9	2	0	0.0	23:11	7	0	4	4	6	0	0	0	26:36
	NHL Totals		643	78	206	284	1027	24	2	15	1239	6.3		0	0.0	24:01	58	10	18	28	92	5	1	2	25:02

OHL All-Rookie Team (1994) • OHL Second All-Star Team (1994) • OHL First All-Star Team (1995) • NHL All-Rookie Team (1996)
Played in NHL All-Star Game (2001, 2002, 2003)
Traded to **Vancouver** by **Florida** with Dave Gagner, Mike Brown, Kevin Weekes and Florida's 1st round choice (Nathan Smith) in 2000 Entry Draft for Pavel Bure, Bret Hedican, Brad Ference and Vancouver's 3rd round choice (Robert Fried) in 2000 Entry Draft, January 17, 1999.

JUNEAU, Joe

(ZHOO-noh, JOH)

Center. Shoots left. 6', 195 lbs. Born, Pont-Rouge, Que., January 5, 1968. Boston's 3rd choice, 81st overall, in 1988 Entry Draft.

Season	Club	League	GP	G	A	Pts	PIM	PP	SH	GW	S	%	+/-	TF	F%	Min	GP	G	A	Pts	PIM	PP	SH	GW	Min
1983-84	Ste-Foy	QAAA	30	3	7	10	24	....	....	....	....	....	....	....	....	....	12	3	11	14	4	....	....	....	....
1984-85	Ste-Foy	QAAA	41	25	46	71	60	....	....	....	....	....	....	....	....	....	13	9	15	24	20	....	....	....	....
1985-86	Levis-Lauzon	CEGEP	STATISTICS NOT AVAILABLE																						
1986-87	Levis-Lauzon	CEGEP	38	27	57	84	....	....	....	....	....	....	....	....	....	....	....	....	....	....	....	....	....	....	....
1987-88	RPI Engineers	ECAC	31	16	29	45	18	....	....	....	....	....	....	....	....	....	....	....	....	....	....	....	....	....	....
1988-89	RPI Engineers	ECAC	30	12	23	35	40	....	....	....	....	....	....	....	....	....	....	....	....	....	....	....	....	....	....
1989-90	RPI Engineers	ECAC	34	18	*52	*70	31	....	....	....	....	....	....	....	....	....	....	....	....	....	....	....	....	....	....
1990-91	RPI Engineers	ECAC	29	23	40	63	68	....	....	....	....	....	....	....	....	....	....	....	....	....	....	....	....	....	....
1991-92	Team Canada	Nat-Tm	60	20	49	69	35	....	....	....	....	....	....	....	....	....	....	....	....	....	....	....	....	....	....
	Canada	Olympics	8	6	*9	*15	4	....	....	....	....	....	....	....	....	....	....	....	....	....	....	....	....	....	....
	Boston	**NHL**	**14**	**5**	**14**	**19**	**4**	**2**	**0**	**0**	**38**	**13.2**	**6**	....	....	....	**15**	**4**	**8**	**12**	**21**	**2**	**0**	**0**	....
1992-93	**Boston**	**NHL**	**84**	**32**	**70**	**102**	**33**	**9**	**0**	**3**	**229**	**14.0**	**23**	....	....	....	**4**	**2**	**4**	**6**	**6**	**2**	**0**	**0**	....
1993-94	**Boston**	**NHL**	**63**	**14**	**58**	**72**	**35**	**4**	**0**	**2**	**142**	**9.9**	**11**	....	....	....	....	....	....	....	....	....	....	....	....
	Washington	**NHL**	**11**	**5**	**8**	**13**	**6**	**2**	**0**	**0**	**22**	**22.7**	**0**	....	....	....	**11**	**4**	**5**	**9**	**6**	**2**	**0**	**1**	....
1994-95	**Washington**	**NHL**	**44**	**5**	**38**	**43**	**8**	**3**	**0**	**0**	**70**	**7.1**	**–1**	....	....	....	**7**	**2**	**6**	**8**	**2**	**0**	**0**	**0**	....
1995-96	**Washington**	**NHL**	**80**	**14**	**50**	**64**	**30**	**7**	**2**	**2**	**176**	**8.0**	**–3**	....	....	....	**5**	**0**	**7**	**7**	**6**	**0**	**0**	**0**	....
1996-97	**Washington**	**NHL**	**58**	**15**	**27**	**42**	**8**	**9**	**1**	**3**	**124**	**12.1**	**–11**	....	....	....	....	....	....	....	....	....	....	....	....
1997-98	**Washington**	**NHL**	**56**	**9**	**22**	**31**	**26**	**4**	**1**	**1**	**87**	**10.3**	**–8**	....	....	....	**21**	**7**	**10**	**17**	**8**	**1**	**1**	**4**	....
1998-99	**Washington**	**NHL**	**63**	**14**	**27**	**41**	**20**	**2**	**1**	**3**	**142**	**9.9**	**–3**	**437**	**48.1**	**19:28**	....	....	....	....	....	....	....	....	....
	Buffalo	**NHL**	**9**	**1**	**1**	**2**	**2**	**0**	**0**	**0**	**8**	**12.5**	**–1**	**8**	**12.5**	**17:11**	**20**	**3**	**8**	**11**	**10**	**0**	**1**	**0**	**16:51**
99-2000	**Ottawa**	**NHL**	**65**	**13**	**24**	**37**	**22**	**2**	**0**	**2**	**126**	**10.3**	**3**	**830**	**51.6**	**18:28**	**6**	**2**	**1**	**3**	**0**	**0**	**0**	**0**	**18:21**
2000-01	**Phoenix**	**NHL**	**69**	**10**	**23**	**33**	**28**	**5**	**0**	**3**	**100**	**10.0**	**–2**	**210**	**50.5**	**17:25**	....	....	....	....	....	....	....	....	....
2001-02	**Montreal**	**NHL**	**70**	**8**	**28**	**36**	**10**	**1**	**0**	**1**	**96**	**8.3**	**–3**	**1337**	**48.6**	**18:37**	**12**	**1**	**4**	**5**	**6**	**0**	**0**	**0**	**19:15**
2002-03	**Montreal**	**NHL**	**72**	**6**	**16**	**22**	**20**	**0**	**0**	**2**	**88**	**6.8**	**–10**	**1235**	**52.4**	**16:46**	....	....	....	....	....	....	....	....	....
2003-04	**Montreal**	**NHL**	**70**	**5**	**10**	**15**	**20**	**2**	**1**	**1**	**76**	**6.6**	**–4**	**994**	**50.9**	**15:47**	**11**	**0**	**1**	**1**	**4**	**0**	**0**	**0**	**10:53**
	NHL Totals		**828**	**156**	**416**	**572**	**272**	**52**	**6**	**23**	**1524**	**10.2**		**5051**	**50.4**	**17:42**	**112**	**25**	**54**	**79**	**69**	**7**	**2**	**5**	**16:17**

NCAA East First All-American Team (1990) • ECAC Second All-Star Team (1991) • NCAA East Second All-American Team (1991) • NHL All-Rookie Team (1993)
Traded to **Washington** by **Boston** for Al Iafrate, March 21, 1994. Traded to **Buffalo** by **Washington** with Washington's 3rd round choice (Tim Preston) in 1999 Entry Draft for Alexei Tezikov and Buffalo's 4th round compensatory choice (later traded to Calgary – Calgary selected Levente Szuper) in 2000 Entry Draft, March 22, 1999. Signed as a free agent by **Ottawa**, October 25, 1999. Selected by **Minnesota** from **Ottawa** in Expansion Draft, June 23, 2000. Traded to **Phoenix** by **Minnesota** for the rights to Rickard Wallin, June 23, 2000. Traded to **Montreal** by **Phoenix** for future considerations, June 15, 2001. • Officially announced retirement, May 1, 2004.

KABERLE, Frantisek

(KA-buhr-lay, FRAN-tih-sehk) **CAR.**

Defense. Shoots left. 6'1", 190 lbs. Born, Kladno, Czech., November 8, 1973. Los Angeles' 3rd choice, 76th overall, in 1999 Entry Draft.

Season	Club	League	GP	G	A	Pts	PIM	PP	SH	GW	S	%	+/-	TF	F%	Min	GP	G	A	Pts	PIM	PP	SH	GW	Min
1991-92	Poldi Kladno	Czech	37	1	4	5	8	....	....	....	....	....	....	....	....	....	8	0	1	1	0	....	....	....	....
1992-93	Poldi Kladno	Czech	40	4	5	9	....	....	....	....	....	....	....	....	....	....	9	2	4	6	....	....	....	....	....
1993-94	HC Kladno	Czech	41	4	16	20	....	....	....	....	....	....	....	....	....	....	11	1	1	2	....	....	....	....	....
1994-95	HC Kladno	Czech	40	7	17	24	20	....	....	....	....	....	....	....	....	....	8	0	3	3	12	....	....	....	....
1995-96	MoDo	Sweden	40	5	7	12	34	....	....	....	....	....	....	....	....	....	8	0	1	1	0	....	....	....	....
1996-97	MoDo	Sweden	50	3	11	14	28	....	....	....	....	....	....	....	....	....	....	....	....	....	....	....	....	....	....
1997-98	MoDo	Sweden	46	5	4	9	22	....	....	....	....	....	....	....	....	....	9	1	1	2	4	....	....	....	....
1998-99	MoDo	Sweden	45	15	18	33	4	....	....	....	....	....	....	....	....	....	13	2	5	7	8	....	....	....	....
99-2000	**Los Angeles**	**NHL**	**37**	**0**	**9**	**9**	**4**	**0**	**0**	**0**	**41**	**0.0**	**3**	**0**	**0.0**	**17:04**	....	....	....	....	....	....	....	....	....
	Long Beach	IHL	18	2	8	10	8	....	....	....	....	....	....	....	....	....	....	....	....	....	....	....	....	....	....
	Atlanta	**NHL**	**14**	**1**	**6**	**7**	**6**	**0**	**1**	**0**	**35**	**2.9**	**–13**	**0**	**0.0**	**24:39**	....	....	....	....	....	....	....	....	....
	Lowell	AHL	4	0	2	2	0	....	....	....	....	....	....	....	....	....	....	....	....	....	....	....	....	....	....
2000-01	**Atlanta**	**NHL**	**51**	**4**	**11**	**15**	**18**	**1**	**0**	**1**	**99**	**4.0**	**11**	**1**	**0.0**	**22:17**	....	....	....	....	....	....	....	....	....
2001-02	**Atlanta**	**NHL**	**61**	**5**	**20**	**25**	**24**	**1**	**0**	**0**	**82**	**6.1**	**–11**	**0**	**0.0**	**21:35**	....	....	....	....	....	....	....	....	....
2002-03	**Atlanta**	**NHL**	**79**	**7**	**19**	**26**	**32**	**3**	**1**	**2**	**105**	**6.7**	**–19**	**0**	**0.0**	**21:57**	....	....	....	....	....	....	....	....	....
2003-04	**Atlanta**	**NHL**	**67**	**3**	**26**	**29**	**30**	**2**	**0**	**1**	**94**	**3.2**	**2**	**2**	**50.0**	**23:20**	....	....	....	....	....	....	....	....	....
	NHL Totals		**309**	**20**	**91**	**111**	**114**	**7**	**2**	**4**	**456**	**4.4**		**3**	**33.3**	**21:46**	....	....	....	....	....	....	....	....	....

Traded to **Atlanta** by **Los Angeles** with Donald Audette for Kelly Buchberger and Nelson Emerson, March 13, 2000. Signed as a free agent by **Carolina**, July 15, 2004.

KABERLE, Tomas

(KA-buhr-lay, TAW-mas) **TOR.**

Defense. Shoots left. 6'1", 198 lbs. Born, Rakovnik, Czech., March 2, 1978. Toronto's 13th choice, 204th overall, in 1996 Entry Draft.

Season	Club	League	GP	G	A	Pts	PIM	PP	SH	GW	S	%	+/-	TF	F%	Min	GP	G	A	Pts	PIM	PP	SH	GW	Min
1994-95	HC Kladno Jr.	Czech-Jr.	37	7	10	17	....	....	....	....	....	....	....	....	....	....	....	....	....	....	....	....	....	....	....
	HC Kladno	Czech	4	0	1	1	0	....	....	....	....	....	....	....	....	....	....	....	....	....	....	....	....	....	....
1995-96	Kladno Jr.	Czech-Jr.	23	6	13	19	....	....	....	....	....	....	....	....	....	....	....	....	....	....	....	....	....	....	....
	HC Poldi Kladno	Czech	23	0	1	1	2	....	....	....	....	....	....	....	....	....	2	0	0	0	0	....	....	....	....
1996-97	HC Poldi Kladno	Czech	49	0	5	5	26	....	....	....	....	....	....	....	....	....	3	0	0	0	0	....	....	....	....
1997-98	Kladno	Czech	47	4	19	23	12	....	....	....	....	....	....	....	....	....	....	....	....	....	....	....	....	....	....
	St. John's	AHL	2	0	0	0	0	....	....	....	....	....	....	....	....	....	....	....	....	....	....	....	....	....	....
1998-99	**Toronto**	**NHL**	**57**	**4**	**18**	**22**	**12**	**0**	**0**	**2**	**71**	**5.6**	**3**	**0**	**0.0**	**18:42**	**14**	**0**	**3**	**3**	**2**	**0**	**0**	**0**	**17:10**
99-2000	**Toronto**	**NHL**	**82**	**7**	**33**	**40**	**24**	**2**	**0**	**0**	**82**	**8.5**	**3**	**0**	**0.0**	**22:55**	**12**	**1**	**4**	**5**	**0**	**0**	**0**	**1**	**23:01**
2000-01	**Toronto**	**NHL**	**82**	**6**	**39**	**45**	**24**	**0**	**0**	**1**	**96**	**6.3**	**10**	**2**	**0.0**	**22:41**	**11**	**1**	**3**	**4**	**0**	**0**	**0**	**1**	**21:33**
2001-02	Kladno	Czech	9	1	7	8	4	....	....	....	....	....	....	....	....	....	....	....	....	....	....	....	....	....	....
	Toronto	**NHL**	**69**	**10**	**29**	**39**	**2**	**5**	**0**	**3**	**85**	**11.8**	**5**	**2**	**100.0**	**25:00**	**20**	**2**	**8**	**10**	**16**	**0**	**0**	**0**	**28:40**
	Czech Republic	Olympics	4	0	1	1	2	....	....	....	....	....	....	....	....	....	....	....	....	....	....	....	....	....	....
2002-03	**Toronto**	**NHL**	**82**	**11**	**36**	**47**	**30**	**4**	**1**	**2**	**119**	**9.2**	**20**	**3**	**66.7**	**24:50**	**7**	**2**	**1**	**3**	**0**	**1**	**0**	**1**	**30:04**
2003-04	**Toronto**	**NHL**	**71**	**3**	**28**	**31**	**18**	**0**	**0**	**1**	**88**	**3.4**	**16**	**2**	**0.0**	**23:12**	**13**	**0**	**3**	**3**	**6**	**0**	**0**	**0**	**20:16**
	NHL Totals		**443**	**41**	**183**	**224**	**110**	**11**	**1**	**9**	**541**	**7.6**		**9**	**44.4**	**23:03**	**77**	**6**	**22**	**28**	**24**	**1**	**0**	**3**	**23:23**

Played in NHL All-Star Game (2002)
Signed as a restricted free agent by **Kladno** (Czech) with **Toronto** retaining NHL rights, September 29, 2001.

KALININ, Dmitri

(kah-LIHN-ihn, DIH-mih-TREE) **BUF.**

Defense. Shoots left. 6'3", 215 lbs. Born, Chelyabinsk, USSR, July 22, 1980. Buffalo's 1st choice, 18th overall, in 1998 Entry Draft.

Season	Club	League	GP	G	A	Pts	PIM	PP	SH	GW	S	%	+/-	TF	F%	Min	GP	G	A	Pts	PIM	PP	SH	GW	Min
1995-96	Chelyabinsk Jr.	CIS-Jr.	30	10	10	20	60	....	....	....	....	....	....	....	....	....	....	....	....	....	....	....	....	....	....
	Chelyabinsk	CIS	20	0	3	3	10	....	....	....	....	....	....	....	....	....	....	....	....	....	....	....	....	....	....
1996-97	Chelyabinsk 2	Russia-3	20	0	0	0	10	....	....	....	....	....	....	....	....	....	....	....	....	....	....	....	....	....	....
	Chelyabinsk	Russia	2	0	0	0	0	....	....	....	....	....	....	....	....	....	....	....	....	....	....	....	....	....	....
1997-98	Chelyabinsk	Russia	26	0	2	2	24	....	....	....	....	....	....	....	....	....	2	0	0	0	0	....	....	....	....
1998-99	Moncton Wildcats	QMJHL	39	7	18	25	44	....	....	....	....	....	....	....	....	....	4	1	1	2	0	....	....	....	....
	Rochester	AHL	3	0	1	1	14	....	....	....	....	....	....	....	....	....	7	0	0	0	6	....	....	....	....
99-2000	**Buffalo**	**NHL**	**4**	**0**	**0**	**0**	**4**	**0**	**0**	**0**	**3**	**0.0**	**0**	**0**	**0.0**	**16:53**	....	....	....	....	....	....	....	....	....
	Rochester	AHL	75	2	19	21	52	....	....	....	....	....	....	....	....	....	21	2	9	11	8	....	....	....	....
2000-01	**Buffalo**	**NHL**	**79**	**4**	**18**	**22**	**38**	**2**	**0**	**0**	**88**	**4.5**	**–2**	**1**	**100.0**	**19:50**	**13**	**0**	**2**	**2**	**4**	**0**	**0**	**0**	**20:05**
2001-02	**Buffalo**	**NHL**	**58**	**2**	**11**	**13**	**26**	**0**	**0**	**0**	**67**	**3.0**	**–6**	**0**	**0.0**	**18:03**	....	....	....	....	....	....	....	....	....
2002-03	**Buffalo**	**NHL**	**65**	**8**	**13**	**21**	**57**	**3**	**1**	**0**	**83**	**9.6**	**–7**	**0**	**0.0**	**21:41**	....	....	....	....	....	....	....	....	....
	Rochester	AHL	1	0	0	0	0	....	....	....	....	....	....	....	....	....	....	....	....	....	....	....	....	....	....
2003-04	**Buffalo**	**NHL**	**77**	**10**	**24**	**34**	**42**	**2**	**1**	**4**	**118**	**8.5**	**0**	**0**	**0.0**	**23:06**	....	....	....	....	....	....	....	....	....
	NHL Totals		**283**	**24**	**66**	**90**	**167**	**7**	**2**	**4**	**359**	**6.7**		**1**	**100.0**	**20:44**	**13**	**0**	**2**	**2**	**4**	**0**	**0**	**0**	**20:05**

KANE, Boyd

(KAYN, BOIYD) **PHI.**

Left wing. Shoots left. 6'2", 218 lbs. Born, Swift Current, Sask., April 18, 1978. NY Rangers' 4th choice, 114th overall, in 1998 Entry Draft.

Season	Club	League	Regular Season GP	G	A	Pts	PIM	PP	SH	GW	S	%	+/-	TF	F%	Min	Playoffs GP	G	A	Pts	PIM	PP	SH	GW	Min
1994-95	Regina Pats	WHL	25	6	5	11	6										4	0	0	0	0				
1995-96	Regina Pats	WHL	72	21	42	63	155										11	5	7	12	12				
1996-97	Regina Pats	WHL	66	25	50	75	154										5	1	1	2	15				
1997-98	Regina Pats	WHL	68	48	45	93	133										9	5	7	12	29				
1998-99	Hartford	AHL	56	3	5	8	23																		
	Charlotte	ECHL	12	5	6	11	14																		
99-2000	Charlotte	ECHL	47	10	19	29	110																		
	Hartford	AHL	8	0	0	0	9																		
	Binghamton	UHL	3	0	2	2	4										1	0	0	0	0				
2000-01	Charlotte	ECHL	12	9	8	17	6																		
	Hartford	AHL	56	11	17	28	81										5	2	0	2	2				
2001-02	Hartford	AHL	78	17	22	39	193										10	1	2	3	50				
2002-03	Springfield	AHL	72	15	22	37	121										6	3	1	4	8				
2003-04	**Philadelphia**	**NHL**	**7**	**0**	**0**	**0**	**7**	**0**	**0**	**0**	**6**	**0.0**	**–4**	**3**	**33.3**	**9:56**									
	Philadelphia	AHL	73	13	22	35	177										12	0	1	1	39				
	NHL Totals		**7**	**0**	**0**	**0**	**7**	**0**	**0**	**0**	**6**	**0.0**		**3**	**33.3**	**9:56**									

• Re-entered NHL Entry Draft. Originally Pittsburgh's 3rd choice, 72nd overall, in 1996 Entry Draft.
Traded to **Tampa Bay** by **NY Rangers** for Gordie Dwyer, October 10, 2002. Signed as a free agent by **Philadelphia**, July 14, 2003.

KAPANEN, Niko

(KA-pah-nehn, NEE-KOH) **DAL.**

Center. Shoots left. 5'9", 180 lbs. Born, Hattula, Finland, April 29, 1978. Dallas' 5th choice, 173rd overall, in 1998 Entry Draft.

Season	Club	League	Regular Season GP	G	A	Pts	PIM	PP	SH	GW	S	%	+/-	TF	F%	Min	Playoffs GP	G	A	Pts	PIM	PP	SH	GW	Min
1992-93	HPK C	Finn-Jr.	14	14	6	20	2																		
1993-94	HPK C	Finn-Jr.	2	0	1	1	0																		
	HPK Jr.	Finn-Jr.	31	17	33	50	34																		
1994-95	HPK B	Finn-Jr.	37	19	44	63	40																		
1995-96	HPK B	Finn-Jr.	10	6	6	12	8																		
	HPK Jr.	Finn-Jr.	26	15	22	37	34																		
	HPK Hameenlinna	Finland	7	1	0	1	0																		
1996-97	HPK Jr.	Finn-Jr.	5	1	7	8	2										2	0	1	1	2				
	HPK Hameenlinna	Finland	41	6	9	15	12										10	4	5	9	2				
	HPK Hameenlinna	EuroHL	6	3	0	3	4										1	0	0	0	0				
1997-98	HPK Jr.	Finn-Jr.	2	1	1	2	0																		
	HPK Hameenlinna	Finland	48	8	18	26	44																		
1998-99	HPK Hameenlinna	Finland	53	14	29	43	49										8	3	4	7	4				
99-2000	HPK Hameenlinna	Finland	53	20	28	48	40										8	1	9	10	4				
2000-01	TPS Turku	Finland	56	11	21	32	20										10	2	1	3	4				
2001-02	**Dallas**	**NHL**	**9**	**0**	**1**	**1**	**2**	**0**	**0**	**0**	**3**	**0.0**	**–1**	**59**	**40.7**	**9:44**									
	Utah Grizzlies	AHL	59	13	28	41	40										5	2	1	3	0				
2002-03	**Dallas**	**NHL**	**82**	**5**	**29**	**34**	**44**	**0**	**1**	**1**	**80**	**6.3**	**25**	**1111**	**47.5**	**14:39**	**12**	**4**	**3**	**7**	**12**	**0**	**1**	**0**	**16:03**
2003-04	**Dallas**	**NHL**	**67**	**1**	**5**	**6**	**16**	**0**	**0**	**0**	**57**	**1.8**	**–15**	**619**	**47.7**	**11:30**	**1**	**1**	**0**	**1**	**0**	**0**	**0**	**0**	**6:51**
	NHL Totals		**158**	**6**	**35**	**41**	**62**	**0**	**1**	**1**	**140**	**4.3**		**1789**	**47.3**	**13:02**	**13**	**5**	**3**	**8**	**12**	**0**	**1**	**0**	**15:21**

KAPANEN, Sami

(KA-pah-nehn, SA-mee) **PHI.**

Right wing. Shoots left. 5'10", 185 lbs. Born, Vantaa, Finland, June 14, 1973. Hartford's 4th choice, 87th overall, in 1995 Entry Draft.

Season	Club	League	Regular Season GP	G	A	Pts	PIM	PP	SH	GW	S	%	+/-	TF	F%	Min	Playoffs GP	G	A	Pts	PIM	PP	SH	GW	Min
1989-90	KalPa Kuopio Jr.	Finn-Jr.	30	14	13	27	4																		
1990-91	KalPa Kuopio Jr.	Finn-Jr.	31	9	27	36	10																		
	KalPa Kuopio	Finland	14	1	2	3	2										8	2	1	3	2				
1991-92	KalPa Kuopio Jr.	Finn-Jr.	8	1	3	4	12																		
	KalPa Kuopio	Finland	42	15	10	25	8																		
1992-93	KalPa Kuopio Jr.	Finn-Jr.	7	11	14	25	2																		
	KalPa Kuopio	Finland	37	4	17	21	12																		
1993-94	KalPa Kuopio	Finland	48	23	32	55	16																		
	Finland	Olympics	8	1	0	1	2																		
1994-95	HIFK Helsinki	Finland	49	14	28	42	42										3	0	0	0	0				
1995-96	**Hartford**	**NHL**	**35**	**5**	**4**	**9**	**6**	**0**	**0**	**0**	**46**	**10.9**	**0**												
	Springfield	AHL	28	14	17	31	4										3	1	2	3	0				
1996-97	**Hartford**	**NHL**	**45**	**13**	**12**	**25**	**2**	**3**	**0**	**2**	**82**	**15.9**	**6**												
1997-98	**Carolina**	**NHL**	**81**	**26**	**37**	**63**	**16**	**4**	**0**	**5**	**190**	**13.7**	**9**												
	Finland	Olympics	6	0	1	1	0																		
1998-99	**Carolina**	**NHL**	**81**	**24**	**35**	**59**	**10**	**5**	**0**	**7**	**254**	**9.4**	**–1**	**10**	**50.0**	**19:25**	**5**	**1**	**1**	**2**	**0**	**0**	**0**	**0**	**19:09**
99-2000	**Carolina**	**NHL**	**76**	**24**	**24**	**48**	**12**	**7**	**0**	**5**	**229**	**10.5**	**10**	**2**	**50.0**	**19:53**									
2000-01	**Carolina**	**NHL**	**82**	**20**	**37**	**57**	**24**	**7**	**0**	**4**	**223**	**9.0**	**–12**	**6**	**16.7**	**18:56**	**6**	**2**	**3**	**5**	**0**	**1**	**0**	**0**	**20:13**
2001-02	**Carolina**	**NHL**	**77**	**27**	**42**	**69**	**23**	**11**	**0**	**4**	**248**	**10.9**	**9**	**7**	**14.3**	**20:38**	**23**	**1**	**8**	**9**	**6**	**0**	**0**	**0**	**20:03**
	Finland	Olympics	4	1	2	3	4																		
2002-03	**Carolina**	**NHL**	**43**	**6**	**12**	**18**	**12**	**3**	**0**	**1**	**108**	**5.6**	**–17**	**16**	**31.3**	**18:37**									
	Philadelphia	**NHL**	**28**	**4**	**9**	**13**	**6**	**2**	**0**	**1**	**81**	**4.9**	**–1**	**5**	**40.0**	**19:21**	**13**	**4**	**3**	**7**	**6**	**2**	**0**	**0**	**20:12**
2003-04	**Philadelphia**	**NHL**	**74**	**12**	**18**	**30**	**14**	**0**	**1**	**2**	**149**	**8.1**	**9**	**18**	**44.4**	**16:31**	**18**	**3**	**7**	**10**	**6**	**0**	**1**	**1**	**17:41**
	NHL Totals		**622**	**161**	**230**	**391**	**125**	**42**	**1**	**31**	**1610**	**10.0**		**64**	**35.9**	**19:04**	**65**	**11**	**22**	**33**	**18**	**3**	**1**	**1**	**19:22**

Played in NHL All-Star Game (2000, 2002)
Transferred to **Carolina** after **Hartford** franchise relocated, June 25, 1997. Traded to **Philadelphia** by **Carolina** with Ryan Bast for Pavel Brendl and Bruno St. Jacques, February 7, 2003.

KARIYA, Paul

(kah-REE-ah, PAWL)

Left wing. Shoots left. 5'10", 176 lbs. Born, Vancouver, B.C., October 16, 1974. Anaheim's 1st choice, 4th overall, in 1993 Entry Draft.

Season	Club	League	Regular Season GP	G	A	Pts	PIM	PP	SH	GW	S	%	+/-	TF	F%	Min	Playoffs GP	G	A	Pts	PIM	PP	SH	GW	Min
1990-91	Penticton	BCJHL	54	45	67	112	8																		
1991-92	Penticton	BCJHL	40	46	86	132	18																		
1992-93	U. of Maine	H-East	39	25	*75	*100	12																		
1993-94	U. of Maine	H-East	12	8	16	24	4																		
	Team Canada	Nat-Tm	23	7	34	41	2																		
	Canada	Olympics	8	3	4	7	2																		
1994-95	**Anaheim**	**NHL**	**47**	**18**	**21**	**39**	**4**	**7**	**1**	**3**	**134**	**13.4**	**–17**												
1995-96	**Anaheim**	**NHL**	**82**	**50**	**58**	**108**	**20**	**20**	**3**	**9**	**349**	**14.3**	**9**												
1996-97	**Anaheim**	**NHL**	**69**	**44**	**55**	**99**	**6**	**15**	**3**	**10**	**340**	**12.9**	**36**				**11**	**7**	**6**	**13**	**4**	**4**	**0**	**1**	
1997-98	**Anaheim**	**NHL**	**22**	**17**	**14**	**31**	**23**	**3**	**0**	**2**	**103**	**16.5**	**12**												
1998-99	**Anaheim**	**NHL**	**82**	**39**	**62**	**101**	**40**	**11**	**2**	**4**	**429**	**9.1**	**17**	**91**	**48.4**	**25:32**	**3**	**1**	**3**	**4**	**0**	**0**	**0**	**0**	**26:03**
99-2000	**Anaheim**	**NHL**	**74**	**42**	**44**	**86**	**24**	**11**	**3**	**3**	**324**	**13.0**	**22**	**99**	**39.4**	**24:22**									
2000-01	**Anaheim**	**NHL**	**66**	**33**	**34**	**67**	**20**	**18**	**3**	**3**	**230**	**14.3**	**–9**	**149**	**44.3**	**23:02**									
2001-02	**Anaheim**	**NHL**	**82**	**32**	**25**	**57**	**28**	**11**	**0**	**8**	**289**	**11.1**	**–15**	**94**	**41.5**	**22:13**									
	Canada	Olympics	6	3	1	4	0																		
2002-03	**Anaheim**	**NHL**	**82**	**25**	**56**	**81**	**48**	**11**	**1**	**2**	**257**	**9.7**	**–3**	**39**	**30.8**	**20:17**	**21**	**6**	**6**	**12**	**6**	**0**	**0**	**1**	**21:15**
2003-04	**Colorado**	**NHL**	**51**	**11**	**25**	**36**	**22**	**5**	**1**	**1**	**110**	**10.0**	**–5**	**18**	**27.8**	**18:37**	**1**	**0**	**1**	**1**	**0**	**0**	**0**	**0**	**16:00**
	NHL Totals		**657**	**311**	**394**	**705**	**235**	**112**	**17**	**45**	**2565**	**12.1**		**490**	**41.8**	**22:33**	**36**	**14**	**16**	**30**	**10**	**4**	**0**	**2**	**21:37**

Hockey East First All-Star Team (1993) • Hockey East Rookie of the Year (1993) • Hockey East Player of the Year (1993) • NCAA East First All-American Team (1993) • NCAA Championship All-Tournament Team (1993) • Hobey Baker Memorial Award (Top U.S. Collegiate Player) (1993) • NHL All-Rookie Team (1995) • Lady Byng Trophy (1996, 1997) • NHL First All-Star Team (1996, 1997, 1999) • NHL Second All-Star Team (2000, 2003)
Played in NHL All-Star Game (1996, 1997, 1999, 2000, 2001, 2002, 2003)
• Missed majority of 1997-98 season after failing to come to contract terms with **Anaheim** and recovering from head injury suffered in game vs. San Jose, February 1, 1998. Signed as a free agent by **Colorado**, July 3, 2003.

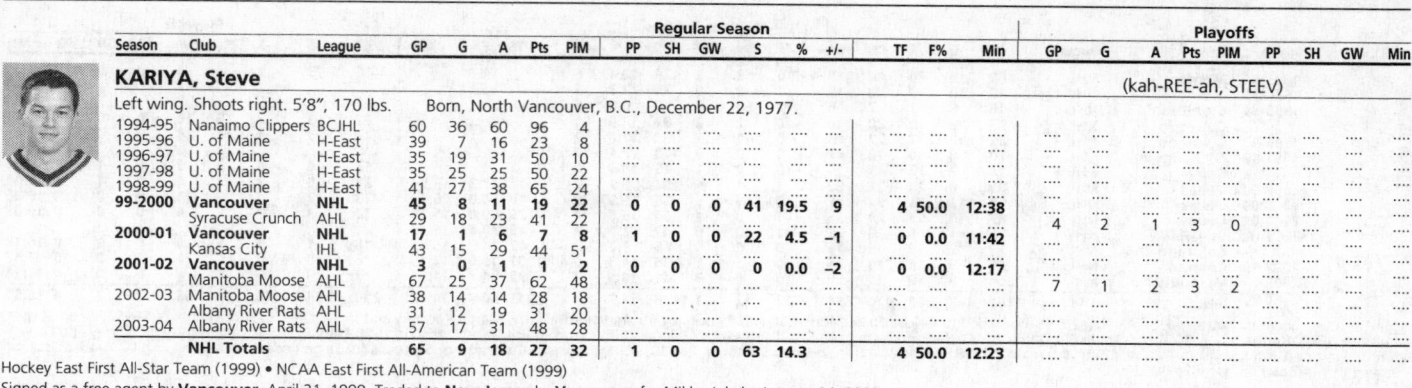

KARIYA, Steve

(kah-REE-ah, STEEV)

Left wing. Shoots right. 5'8", 170 lbs. Born, North Vancouver, B.C., December 22, 1977.

Season	Club	League	GP	G	A	Pts	PIM	PP	SH	GW	S	%	+/-	TF	F%	Min	Playoffs GP	G	A	Pts	PIM	PP	SH	GW	Min
1994-95	Nanaimo Clippers	BCJHL	60	36	60	96	4	....	....	....	....	....	....	....	....	....	....	....	....	....	....	....	....	....	....
1995-96	U. of Maine	H-East	39	7	16	23	8	....	....	....	....	....	....	....	....	....	....	....	....	....	....	....	....	....	....
1996-97	U. of Maine	H-East	35	19	31	50	10	....	....	....	....	....	....	....	....	....	....	....	....	....	....	....	....	....	....
1997-98	U. of Maine	H-East	35	25	25	50	22	....	....	....	....	....	....	....	....	....	....	....	....	....	....	....	....	....	....
1998-99	U. of Maine	H-East	41	27	38	65	24	....	....	....	....	....	....	....	....	....	....	....	....	....	....	....	....	....	....
99-2000	**Vancouver**	**NHL**	**45**	**8**	**11**	**19**	**22**	**0**	**0**	**0**	**41**	**19.5**	**9**	**4**	**50.0**	**12:38**	....	....	....	....	....	....	....	....	....
	Syracuse Crunch	AHL	29	18	23	41	22	....	....	....	....	....	....	....	....	....	4	2	1	3	0	....	....	....	....
2000-01	**Vancouver**	**NHL**	**17**	**1**	**6**	**7**	**8**	**1**	**0**	**0**	**22**	**4.5**	**–1**	**0**	**0.0**	**11:42**	....	....	....	....	....	....	....	....	....
	Kansas City	IHL	43	15	29	44	51	....	....	....	....	....	....	....	....	....	....	....	....	....	....	....	....	....	....
2001-02	**Vancouver**	**NHL**	**3**	**0**	**1**	**1**	**2**	**0**	**0**	**0**	**0**	**0.0**	**–2**	**0**	**0.0**	**12:17**	....	....	....	....	....	....	....	....	....
	Manitoba Moose	AHL	67	25	37	62	48	....	....	....	....	....	....	....	....	....	7	1	2	3	2	....	....	....	....
2002-03	Manitoba Moose	AHL	38	14	14	28	18	....	....	....	....	....	....	....	....	....	....	....	....	....	....	....	....	....	....
	Albany River Rats	AHL	31	12	19	31	20	....	....	....	....	....	....	....	....	....	....	....	....	....	....	....	....	....	....
2003-04	Albany River Rats	AHL	57	17	31	48	28	....	....	....	....	....	....	....	....	....	....	....	....	....	....	....	....	....	....
	NHL Totals		**65**	**9**	**18**	**27**	**32**	**1**	**0**	**0**	**63**	**14.3**		**4**	**50.0**	**12:23**	....	....	....	....	....	....	....	....	....

Hockey East First All-Star Team (1999) • NCAA East First All-American Team (1999)

Signed as a free agent by **Vancouver**, April 21, 1999. Traded to **New Jersey** by **Vancouver** for Mikko Jokela, January 24, 2003.

KARPOVTSEV, Alexander

(kar-POHV-tzehv, al-ehx-AN-duhr) **FLA.**

Defense. Shoots right. 6'3", 221 lbs. Born, Moscow, USSR, April 7, 1970. Quebec's 7th choice, 158th overall, in 1990 Entry Draft.

Season	Club	League	GP	G	A	Pts	PIM	PP	SH	GW	S	%	+/-	TF	F%	Min	Playoffs GP	G	A	Pts	PIM	PP	SH	GW	Min
1989-90	Dynamo Moscow	USSR	35	1	1	2	27	....	....	....	....	....	....	....	....	....	....	....	....	....	....	....	....	....	....
1990-91	Dynamo Moscow	USSR	40	0	5	5	15	....	....	....	....	....	....	....	....	....	....	....	....	....	....	....	....	....	....
1991-92	Dynamo Moscow	CIS	35	4	2	6	26	....	....	....	....	....	....	....	....	....	....	....	....	....	....	....	....	....	....
1992-93	Dynamo Moscow	CIS	36	3	11	14	100	....	....	....	....	....	....	....	....	....	7	2	1	3	0	....	....	....	....
1993-94◆	**NY Rangers**	**NHL**	**67**	**3**	**15**	**18**	**58**	**1**	**0**	**1**	**78**	**3.8**	**12**	....	....	....	**17**	**0**	**4**	**4**	**12**	**0**	**0**	**0**	....
1994-95	Dynamo Moscow	CIS	13	0	2	2	10	....	....	....	....	....	....	....	....	....	....	....	....	....	....	....	....	....	....
	NY Rangers	**NHL**	**47**	**4**	**8**	**12**	**30**	**1**	**0**	**1**	**82**	**4.9**	**–4**	....	....	....	**8**	**1**	**0**	**1**	**0**	**0**	**0**	**0**	....
1995-96	**NY Rangers**	**NHL**	**40**	**2**	**16**	**18**	**26**	**1**	**0**	**1**	**71**	**2.8**	**12**	....	....	....	**6**	**0**	**1**	**1**	**4**	**0**	**0**	**0**	....
1996-97	**NY Rangers**	**NHL**	**77**	**9**	**29**	**38**	**59**	**6**	**1**	**0**	**84**	**10.7**	**1**	....	....	....	**13**	**1**	**3**	**4**	**20**	**1**	**0**	**0**	....
1997-98	**NY Rangers**	**NHL**	**47**	**3**	**7**	**10**	**38**	**1**	**0**	**1**	**46**	**6.5**	**–1**	....	....	....	....	....	....	....	....	....	....	....	....
1998-99	**NY Rangers**	**NHL**	**2**	**1**	**0**	**1**	**0**	**0**	**0**	**0**	**4**	**25.0**	**1**	**0**	**0.0**	**22:38**	....	....	....	....	....	....	....	....	....
	Toronto	**NHL**	**56**	**2**	**25**	**27**	**52**	**1**	**0**	**1**	**61**	**3.3**	**38**	**0**	**0.0**	**20:58**	**14**	**1**	**3**	**4**	**12**	**1**	**0**	**0**	**19:44**
99-2000	**Toronto**	**NHL**	**69**	**3**	**14**	**17**	**54**	**3**	**0**	**0**	**51**	**5.9**	**9**	**2**	**0.0**	**20:14**	**11**	**0**	**3**	**3**	**4**	**0**	**0**	**0**	**21:04**
2000-01	Dynamo Moscow	Russia	5	0	1	1	0	....	....	....	....	....	....	....	....	....	....	....	....	....	....	....	....	....	....
	Chicago	**NHL**	**53**	**2**	**13**	**15**	**39**	**1**	**0**	**0**	**52**	**3.8**	**–4**	**0**	**0.0**	**20:28**	....	....	....	....	....	....	....	....	....
2001-02	**Chicago**	**NHL**	**65**	**1**	**9**	**10**	**40**	**0**	**1**	**0**	**40**	**2.5**	**10**	**3**	**33.3**	**20:40**	**5**	**1**	**0**	**1**	**0**	**0**	**0**	**1**	**20:53**
2002-03	**Chicago**	**NHL**	**40**	**4**	**10**	**14**	**12**	**3**	**0**	**1**	**36**	**11.1**	**–8**	**0**	**0.0**	**21:40**	....	....	....	....	....	....	....	....	....
2003-04	**Chicago**	**NHL**	**24**	**0**	**7**	**7**	**14**	**0**	**0**	**0**	**31**	**0.0**	**–17**	**0**	**0.0**	**19:56**	....	....	....	....	....	....	....	....	....
	NY Islanders	**NHL**	**3**	**0**	**1**	**1**	**4**	**0**	**0**	**0**	**3**	**0.0**	**1**	**0**	**0.0**	**10:54**	....	....	....	....	....	....	....	....	....
	NHL Totals		**590**	**34**	**154**	**188**	**426**	**18**	**2**	**6**	**639**	**5.3**		**5**	**20.0**	**20:35**	**74**	**4**	**14**	**18**	**52**	**2**	**0**	**1**	**20:25**

Traded to **NY Rangers** by **Quebec** for Mike Hurlbut, September 7, 1993. Traded to **Toronto** by **NY Rangers** with NY Rangers' 4th round choice (Mirko Murovic) in 1999 Entry Draft for Mathieu Schneider, October 14, 1998. Traded to **Chicago** by **Toronto** with Toronto's 4th round choice (Vladimir Gusev) in 2001 Entry Draft for Bryan McCabe, October 2, 2000. • Missed majority of 2002-03 season recovering from ankle (November 5, 2002 vs. Detroit) and cheekbone (February 20, 2003 vs. Phoenix) injuries. • Missed majority of 2003-04 season recovering from ankle injury suffered in game vs. San Jose, November 26, 2003. Traded to **NY Islanders** by **Chicago** for NY Islanders' 4th round choice in 2005 Entry Draft, March 9, 2004. Signed as a free agent by **Florida**, July 14, 2004.

KASPARAITIS, Darius

(KAZ-puhr-IGH-tihz, DAIR-ee-uhs) **NYR**

Defense. Shoots left. 5'11", 212 lbs. Born, Elektrenai, USSR, October 16, 1972. NY Islanders' 1st choice, 5th overall, in 1992 Entry Draft.

Season	Club	League	GP	G	A	Pts	PIM	PP	SH	GW	S	%	+/-	TF	F%	Min	Playoffs GP	G	A	Pts	PIM	PP	SH	GW	Min
1988-89	Dynamo Moscow	USSR	3	0	0	0	0	....	....	....	....	....	....	....	....	....	....	....	....	....	....	....	....	....	....
1989-90	Dynamo Moscow	USSR	1	0	0	0	0	....	....	....	....	....	....	....	....	....	....	....	....	....	....	....	....	....	....
1990-91	Dynamo Moscow	USSR	17	0	1	1	10	....	....	....	....	....	....	....	....	....	....	....	....	....	....	....	....	....	....
1991-92	Dynamo Moscow	CIS	31	2	10	12	14	....	....	....	....	....	....	....	....	....	....	....	....	....	....	....	....	....	....
1992-93	Dynamo Moscow	CIS	7	1	3	4	8	....	....	....	....	....	....	....	....	....	....	....	....	....	....	....	....	....	....
	NY Islanders	**NHL**	**79**	**4**	**17**	**21**	**166**	**0**	**0**	**0**	**92**	**4.3**	**15**	....	....	....	**18**	**0**	**5**	**5**	**31**	**0**	**0**	**0**	....
1993-94	**NY Islanders**	**NHL**	**76**	**1**	**10**	**11**	**142**	**0**	**0**	**0**	**81**	**1.2**	**–6**	....	....	....	**4**	**0**	**0**	**0**	**8**	**0**	**0**	**0**	....
1994-95	**NY Islanders**	**NHL**	**13**	**0**	**1**	**1**	**22**	**0**	**0**	**0**	**8**	**0.0**	**–11**	....	....	....	....	....	....	....	....	....	....	....	....
1995-96	**NY Islanders**	**NHL**	**46**	**1**	**7**	**8**	**93**	**0**	**0**	**0**	**34**	**2.9**	**–12**	....	....	....	....	....	....	....	....	....	....	....	....
1996-97	**NY Islanders**	**NHL**	**18**	**0**	**5**	**5**	**16**	**0**	**0**	**0**	**12**	**0.0**	**–7**	....	....	....	....	....	....	....	....	....	....	....	....
	Pittsburgh	**NHL**	**57**	**2**	**16**	**18**	**84**	**0**	**0**	**0**	**46**	**4.3**	**24**	....	....	....	**5**	**0**	**0**	**0**	**6**	**0**	**0**	**0**	....
1997-98	**Pittsburgh**	**NHL**	**81**	**4**	**8**	**12**	**127**	**0**	**2**	**0**	**71**	**5.6**	**3**	....	....	....	**5**	**0**	**0**	**0**	**8**	**0**	**0**	**0**	....
	Russia	Olympics	6	0	2	2	6	....	....	....	....	....	....	....	....	....	....	....	....	....	....	....	....	....	....
1998-99	**Pittsburgh**	**NHL**	**48**	**1**	**4**	**5**	**70**	**0**	**0**	**0**	**32**	**3.1**	**12**	**0**	**0.0**	**16:01**	....	....	....	....	....	....	....	....	....
99-2000	**Pittsburgh**	**NHL**	**73**	**3**	**12**	**15**	**146**	**1**	**0**	**1**	**76**	**3.9**	**–12**	**0**	**0.0**	**18:07**	**11**	**1**	**1**	**2**	**10**	**0**	**0**	**0**	**21:39**
2000-01	**Pittsburgh**	**NHL**	**77**	**3**	**16**	**19**	**111**	**1**	**0**	**0**	**81**	**3.7**	**11**	**0**	**0.0**	**19:14**	**17**	**1**	**1**	**2**	**26**	**0**	**0**	**1**	**19:52**
2001-02	**Pittsburgh**	**NHL**	**69**	**2**	**12**	**14**	**123**	**0**	**0**	**0**	**75**	**2.7**	**–1**	**1**	**0.0**	**20:32**	....	....	....	....	....	....	....	....	....
	Russia	Olympics	6	1	0	1	4	....	....	....	....	....	....	....	....	....	....	....	....	....	....	....	....	....	....
	Colorado	**NHL**	**11**	**0**	**0**	**0**	**19**	**0**	**0**	**0**	**6**	**0.0**	**1**	**0**	**0.0**	**19:44**	**21**	**0**	**3**	**3**	**18**	**0**	**0**	**0**	**20:46**
2002-03	**NY Rangers**	**NHL**	**80**	**3**	**11**	**14**	**85**	**0**	**0**	**1**	**84**	**3.6**	**5**	**0**	**0.0**	**18:54**	....	....	....	....	....	....	....	....	....
2003-04	**NY Rangers**	**NHL**	**44**	**1**	**9**	**10**	**48**	**0**	**0**	**0**	**29**	**3.4**	**11**	**0**	**0.0**	**16:23**	....	....	....	....	....	....	....	....	....
	NHL Totals		**772**	**25**	**128**	**153**	**1252**	**2**	**2**	**2**	**727**	**3.4**		**1**	**0.0**	**18:30**	**81**	**2**	**10**	**12**	**107**	**0**	**0**	**1**	**20:39**

Traded to **Pittsburgh** by **NY Islanders** with Andreas Johansson for Bryan Smolinski, November 17, 1996. Traded to **Colorado** by **Pittsburgh** for Ville Niemenen and Rick Berry, March 19, 2002. Signed as a free agent by **NY Rangers**, July 2, 2002.

KAVANAGH, Pat

(KA-vuh-naw, PAT) **OTT.**

Right wing. Shoots right. 6'3", 192 lbs. Born, Ottawa, Ont., March 14, 1979. Philadelphia's 2nd choice, 50th overall, in 1997 Entry Draft.

Season	Club	League	GP	G	A	Pts	PIM	PP	SH	GW	S	%	+/-	TF	F%	Min	Playoffs GP	G	A	Pts	PIM	PP	SH	GW	Min
1995-96	Kanata Valley	OCJHL	54	19	16	35	99	....	....	....	....	....	....	....	....	....	....	....	....	....	....	....	....	....	....
1996-97	Peterborough	OHL	43	6	8	14	53	....	....	....	....	....	....	....	....	....	11	1	1	2	12	....	....	....	....
1997-98	Peterborough	OHL	66	10	16	26	85	....	....	....	....	....	....	....	....	....	4	1	0	1	6	....	....	....	....
1998-99	Peterborough	OHL	68	26	43	69	118	....	....	....	....	....	....	....	....	....	5	0	5	5	10	....	....	....	....
99-2000	Syracuse Crunch	AHL	68	12	8	20	56	....	....	....	....	....	....	....	....	....	4	0	0	0	0	....	....	....	....
2000-01	Kansas City	IHL	78	26	15	41	86	....	....	....	....	....	....	....	....	....	....	....	....	....	....	....	....	....	....
	Vancouver	**NHL**	....	....	....	....	....	....	....	....	....	....	....	....	....	....	**3**	**0**	**0**	**0**	**2**	**0**	**0**	**0**	**8:27**
2001-02	Manitoba Moose	AHL	70	13	19	32	100	....	....	....	....	....	....	....	....	....	7	1	0	1	6	....	....	....	....
2002-03	Manitoba Moose	AHL	63	15	15	30	96	....	....	....	....	....	....	....	....	....	14	7	4	11	20	....	....	....	....
	Vancouver	**NHL**	**3**	**1**	**0**	**1**	**2**	**0**	**0**	**1**	**4**	**25.0**	**2**	**27**	**37.0**	**10:23**	....	....	....	....	....	....	....	....	....
2003-04	**Vancouver**	**NHL**	**3**	**1**	**0**	**1**	**0**	**0**	**0**	**0**	**1**	**100.0**	**0**	**21**	**52.4**	**7:58**	....	....	....	....	....	....	....	....	....
	Manitoba Moose	AHL	73	23	22	45	69	....	....	....	....	....	....	....	....	....	....	....	....	....	....	....	....	....	....
	NHL Totals		**6**	**2**	**0**	**2**	**2**	**0**	**0**	**1**	**5**	**40.0**		**48**	**43.8**	**9:11**	**3**	**0**	**0**	**0**	**2**	**0**	**0**	**0**	**8:27**

Traded to **Vancouver** by **Philadelphia** for Vancouver's 6th round choice (Konstantin Rudenko) in 1999 Entry Draft, June 1, 1999. Signed as a free agent by **Ottawa**, July 27, 2004.

KEANE, Mike

(KEEN, MIGHK)

Right wing. Shoots right. 5'10", 185 lbs. Born, Winnipeg, Man., May 29, 1967.

Season	Club	League	GP	G	A	Pts	PIM	PP	SH	GW	S	%	+/-	TF	F%	Min	Playoffs GP	G	A	Pts	PIM	PP	SH	GW	Min
1983-84	Wpg. Monarchs	MMHL	21	17	19	36	59	....	....	....	....	....	....	....	....	....	....	....	....	....	....	....	....	....	....
	Winnipeg	WHL	1	0	0	0	0	....	....	....	....	....	....	....	....	....	....	....	....	....	....	....	....	....	....
1984-85	Moose Jaw	WHL	65	17	26	43	141	....	....	....	....	....	....	....	....	....	....	....	....	....	....	....	....	....	....
1985-86	Moose Jaw	WHL	67	34	49	83	162	....	....	....	....	....	....	....	....	....	13	6	8	14	9	....	....	....	....
1986-87	Moose Jaw	WHL	53	25	45	70	107	....	....	....	....	....	....	....	....	....	9	3	9	12	11	....	....	....	....
	Sherbrooke	AHL	....	....	....	....	....	....	....	....	....	....	....	....	....	....	9	2	2	4	16	....	....	....	....
1987-88	Sherbrooke	AHL	78	25	43	68	70	....	....	....	....	....	....	....	....	....	6	1	1	2	18	....	....	....	....
1988-89	**Montreal**	**NHL**	**69**	**16**	**19**	**35**	**69**	**5**	**0**	**1**	**90**	**17.8**	**9**	....	....	....	**21**	**4**	**3**	**7**	**17**	**2**	**0**	**0**	....
1989-90	**Montreal**	**NHL**	**74**	**9**	**15**	**24**	**78**	**1**	**0**	**1**	**92**	**9.8**	**0**	....	....	....	**11**	**0**	**1**	**1**	**8**	**0**	**0**	**0**	....
1990-91	**Montreal**	**NHL**	**73**	**13**	**23**	**36**	**50**	**2**	**1**	**2**	**109**	**11.9**	**6**	....	....	....	**12**	**3**	**2**	**5**	**6**	**0**	**0**	**0**	....
1991-92	**Montreal**	**NHL**	**67**	**11**	**30**	**41**	**64**	**2**	**0**	**2**	**116**	**9.5**	**16**	....	....	....	**8**	**1**	**1**	**2**	**16**	**0**	**0**	**0**	....
1992-93◆	**Montreal**	**NHL**	**77**	**15**	**45**	**60**	**95**	**0**	**0**	**1**	**120**	**12.5**	**29**	....	....	....	**19**	**2**	**13**	**15**	**6**	**0**	**0**	**0**	....

			Regular Season														Playoffs								
Season	Club	League	GP	G	A	Pts	PIM	PP	SH	GW	S	%	+/-	TF	F%	Min	GP	G	A	Pts	PIM	PP	SH	GW	Min
1993-94	Montreal	NHL	80	16	30	46	119	6	2	2	129	12.4	6	....	....	....	6	3	1	4	4	0	0	0	....
1994-95	Montreal	NHL	48	10	10	20	15	1	0	0	75	13.3	5	....	....	....	....	....	....	....	....	....	....	....	....
1995-96	Montreal	NHL	18	0	7	7	6	0	0	0	17	0.0	–6	....	....	....	....	....	....	....	....	....	....	....	....
	♦ Colorado	NHL	55	10	10	20	40	0	2	2	67	14.9	1	....	....	....	22	3	2	5	16	0	0	1	....
1996-97	Colorado	NHL	81	10	17	27	63	0	1	1	91	11.0	2	....	....	....	17	3	1	4	24	0	0	1	....
1997-98	NY Rangers	NHL	70	8	10	18	47	2	0	0	113	7.1	–12	....	....	....	....	....	....	....	....	....	....	....	....
	Dallas	NHL	13	2	3	5	5	0	0	1	15	13.3	0	....	....	....	17	4	4	8	0	0	1	1	....
1998-99♦	Dallas	NHL	81	6	23	29	62	1	1	1	106	5.7	–2	11	27.3	13:57	23	5	2	7	6	0	1	1	18:02
99-2000	Dallas	NHL	81	13	21	34	41	0	4	3	85	15.3	9	10	50.0	16:10	23	2	4	6	14	0	0	0	16:20
2000-01	Dallas	NHL	67	10	14	24	35	1	0	1	64	15.6	4	25	60.0	15:28	10	3	2	5	4	0	0	0	16:08
2001-02	St. Louis	NHL	56	4	6	10	22	1	0	0	47	8.5	–2	49	30.6	14:19	....	....	....	....	....	....	....	....	....
	Colorado	NHL	22	2	5	7	16	0	0	0	26	7.7	–2	42	31.0	16:55	18	1	4	5	8	0	0	0	16:18
2002-03	Colorado	NHL	65	5	5	10	34	0	1	1	35	14.3	0	102	19.6	12:15	6	0	0	0	2	0	0	0	7:57
2003-04	Vancouver	NHL	64	8	9	17	20	0	0	2	41	19.5	7	72	34.7	11:11	7	0	0	0	4	0	0	0	12:18
	NHL Totals		**1161**	**168**	**302**	**470**	**881**	**22**	**12**	**21**	**1438**	**11.7**		**311**	**30.9**	**14:08**	**220**	**34**	**40**	**74**	**135**	**2**	**2**	**4**	**15:51**

Signed as a free agent by **Montreal**, September 25, 1985. Traded to **Colorado** by **Montreal** with Patrick Roy for Andrei Kovalenko, Martin Rucinsky and Jocelyn Thibault, December 6, 1995. Signed as a free agent by **NY Rangers**, July 30, 1997. Traded to **Dallas** by **NY Rangers** with Brian Skrudland and NY Rangers' 6th round choice (Pavel Patera) in 1998 Entry Draft for Todd Harvey, Bob Errey and Dallas' 4th round choice (Boyd Kane) in 1998 Entry Draft, March 24, 1998. Signed as a free agent by **St. Louis**, July 10, 2001. Traded to **Colorado** by **St. Louis** for Shjon Podein, February 11, 2002. Signed as a free agent by **Vancouver**, October 10, 2003.

KEEFE, Sheldon

(KEEF, SHEHL-duhn) **PHX.**

Right wing. Shoots right. 5'11", 185 lbs. Born, Brampton, Ont., September 17, 1980. Tampa Bay's 1st choice, 47th overall, in 1999 Entry Draft.

Season	Club	League	GP	G	A	Pts	PIM	PP	SH	GW	S	%	+/-	TF	F%	Min	GP	G	A	Pts	PIM	PP	SH	GW	Min
1995-96	Tor. Young Nats	MTHL	45	66	71	137	....	....	....	....	....	....	....	....	....	....	....	....	....	....	....	....	....	....	....
1996-97	Quinte Hawks	MTJHL	44	21	23	44	41	....	....	....	....	....	....	....	....	....	....	....	....	....	....	....	....	....	....
	Bramalea Blues	OPJHL	8	0	3	3	4	....	....	....	....	....	....	....	....	....	....	....	....	....	....	....	....	....	....
1997-98	Caledon	MTJHL	43	41	40	81	117	....	....	....	....	....	....	....	....	....	13	15	8	23	....	....	....	....	....
1998-99	St. Michael's	OHL	38	37	37	74	80	....	....	....	....	....	....	....	....	....	....	....	....	....	....	....	....	....	....
	Barrie Colts	OHL	28	14	28	42	60	....	....	....	....	....	....	....	....	....	10	5	5	10	31	....	....	....	....
99-2000	Barrie Colts	OHL	66	48	*73	*121	95	....	....	....	....	....	....	....	....	....	25	10	13	23	41	....	....	....	....
2000-01	Tampa Bay	NHL	49	4	0	4	38	0	0	0	32	12.5	–13	1	0.0	8:00	....	....	....	....	....	....	....	....	....
	Detroit Vipers	IHL	13	7	5	12	23	....	....	....	....	....	....	....	....	....	....	....	....	....	....	....	....	....	....
2001-02	Tampa Bay	NHL	39	6	7	13	16	0	0	1	52	11.5	–11	70	45.7	13:00	....	....	....	....	....	....	....	....	....
	Springfield	AHL	24	9	9	18	26	....	....	....	....	....	....	....	....	....	....	....	....	....	....	....	....	....	....
2002-03	Tampa Bay	NHL	37	2	5	7	24	0	0	0	51	3.9	–1	32	43.8	10:15	....	....	....	....	....	....	....	....	....
	Springfield	AHL	33	16	15	31	28	....	....	....	....	....	....	....	....	....	6	0	0	0	4	....	....	....	....
2003-04	Hershey Bears	AHL	59	16	16	32	82	....	....	....	....	....	....	....	....	....	....	....	....	....	....	....	....	....	....
	NHL Totals		**125**	**12**	**12**	**24**	**78**	**0**	**0**	**1**	**135**	**8.9**		**103**	**44.7**	**10:14**	....	....	....	....	....	....	....	....	....

OHL All-Rookie Team (1999) • OHL Rookie of the Year (1999) • OHL Second All-Star Team (2000) • Eddie Powers Memorial Trophy (Top Scorer – OHL) (2000) • Canadian Major Junior First All-Star Team (2000) • Memorial Cup All-Star Team (2000)

Claimed by **NY Rangers** from **Tampa Bay** in Waiver Draft, October 3, 2003. Claimed on waivers by **Tampa Bay** from **NY Rangers**, October 24, 2003. Signed as a free agent by **Phoenix**, July 12, 2004.

KEITH, Matt

(KEETH, MAT) **CHI.**

Right wing. Shoots right. 6'2", 200 lbs. Born, Edmonton, Alta., April 11, 1983. Chicago's 3rd choice, 59th overall, in 2001 Entry Draft.

Season	Club	League	GP	G	A	Pts	PIM	PP	SH	GW	S	%	+/-	TF	F%	Min	GP	G	A	Pts	PIM	PP	SH	GW	Min
1998-99	Banff Icemen	HJHL	STATISTICS NOT AVAILABLE																						
	Spokane Chiefs	WHL	7	1	0	1	4	....	....	....	....	....	....	....	....	....	....	....	....	....	....	....	....	....	....
99-2000	Spokane Chiefs	WHL	39	1	3	4	37	....	....	....	....	....	....	....	....	....	15	1	2	3	11	....	....	....	....
2000-01	Spokane Chiefs	WHL	33	13	14	27	63	....	....	....	....	....	....	....	....	....	12	1	3	4	14	....	....	....	....
2001-02	Spokane Chiefs	WHL	68	34	33	67	71	....	....	....	....	....	....	....	....	....	11	5	5	10	16	....	....	....	....
2002-03	Spokane Chiefs	WHL	7	2	2	4	11	....	....	....	....	....	....	....	....	....	....	....	....	....	....	....	....	....	....
	Red Deer Rebels	WHL	49	25	26	51	32	....	....	....	....	....	....	....	....	....	23	6	7	13	30	....	....	....	....
2003-04	Chicago	NHL	20	2	3	5	10	1	0	0	21	9.5	–5	2	100.0	11:58	....	....	....	....	....	....	....	....	....
	Norfolk Admirals	AHL	66	13	13	26	57	....	....	....	....	....	....	....	....	....	8	1	2	3	10	....	....	....	....
	NHL Totals		**20**	**2**	**3**	**5**	**10**	**1**	**0**	**0**	**21**	**9.5**		**2**	**100.0**	**11:58**	....	....	....	....	....	....	....	....	....

• Missed majority of 2000-01 season recovering from shoulder injury suffered in game vs. Tri-City (WHL), September 22, 2000.

KELLY, Chris

(KEHL-lee, KRIHS) **OTT.**

Center/Left wing. Shoots left. 6', 190 lbs. Born, Toronto, Ont., November 11, 1980. Ottawa's 4th choice, 94th overall, in 1999 Entry Draft.

Season	Club	League	GP	G	A	Pts	PIM	PP	SH	GW	S	%	+/-	TF	F%	Min	GP	G	A	Pts	PIM	PP	SH	GW	Min
1995-96	Toronto Marlies	MTHL	42	25	45	70	25	....	....	....	....	....	....	....	....	....	....	....	....	....	....	....	....	....	....
1996-97	Aurora Tigers	OPJHL	49	14	20	34	11	....	....	....	....	....	....	....	....	....	....	....	....	....	....	....	....	....	....
1997-98	London Knights	OHL	54	15	14	29	4	....	....	....	....	....	....	....	....	....	16	4	5	9	12	....	....	....	....
1998-99	London Knights	OHL	68	36	41	77	60	....	....	....	....	....	....	....	....	....	25	9	17	26	22	....	....	....	....
99-2000	London Knights	OHL	63	29	43	72	57	....	....	....	....	....	....	....	....	....	....	....	....	....	....	....	....	....	....
2000-01	London Knights	OHL	31	21	34	55	46	....	....	....	....	....	....	....	....	....	....	....	....	....	....	....	....	....	....
	Sudbury Wolves	OHL	19	5	16	21	17	....	....	....	....	....	....	....	....	....	12	11	5	16	14	....	....	....	....
2001-02	Muskegon Fury	UHL	4	1	2	3	0	....	....	....	....	....	....	....	....	....	....	....	....	....	....	....	....	....	....
	Grand Rapids	AHL	31	3	3	6	20	....	....	....	....	....	....	....	....	....	5	1	1	2	5	....	....	....	....
2002-03	Binghamton	AHL	77	17	14	31	73	....	....	....	....	....	....	....	....	....	14	2	3	5	8	....	....	....	....
2003-04	Ottawa	NHL	4	0	0	0	0	0	0	0	4	0.0	–2	5	40.0	9:29	....	....	....	....	....	....	....	....	....
	Binghamton	AHL	54	15	19	34	40	....	....	....	....	....	....	....	....	....	2	0	0	0	4	....	....	....	....
	NHL Totals		**4**	**0**	**0**	**0**	**0**	**0**	**0**	**0**	**4**	**0.0**		**5**	**40.0**	**9:29**	....	....	....	....	....	....	....	....	....

KELLY, Steve

(KEHL-lee, STEEV)

Center. Shoots left. 6'2", 205 lbs. Born, Vancouver, B.C., October 26, 1976. Edmonton's 1st choice, 6th overall, in 1995 Entry Draft.

Season	Club	League	GP	G	A	Pts	PIM	PP	SH	GW	S	%	+/-	TF	F%	Min	GP	G	A	Pts	PIM	PP	SH	GW	Min
1991-92	Westbank	BCAHA	30	25	60	85	75	....	....	....	....	....	....	....	....	....	....	....	....	....	....	....	....	....	....
1992-93	Prince Albert	WHL	65	11	9	20	75	....	....	....	....	....	....	....	....	....	....	....	....	....	....	....	....	....	....
1993-94	Prince Albert	WHL	65	19	42	61	106	....	....	....	....	....	....	....	....	....	....	....	....	....	....	....	....	....	....
1994-95	Prince Albert	WHL	68	31	41	72	153	....	....	....	....	....	....	....	....	....	15	7	9	16	35	....	....	....	....
1995-96	Prince Albert	WHL	70	27	74	101	203	....	....	....	....	....	....	....	....	....	18	13	18	31	47	....	....	....	....
1996-97	Edmonton	NHL	8	1	0	1	6	0	0	1	6	16.7	–1	....	....	....	6	0	0	0	2	0	0	0	....
	Hamilton	AHL	48	9	29	38	111	....	....	....	....	....	....	....	....	....	11	3	3	6	24	....	....	....	....
1997-98	Edmonton	NHL	19	0	2	2	8	0	0	0	5	0.0	–4	....	....	....	....	....	....	....	....	....	....	....	....
	Hamilton	AHL	11	2	8	10	18	....	....	....	....	....	....	....	....	....	....	....	....	....	....	....	....	....	....
	Tampa Bay	NHL	24	2	1	3	15	1	0	0	17	11.8	–9	....	....	....	....	....	....	....	....	....	....	....	....
	Milwaukee	IHL	5	0	1	1	19	....	....	....	....	....	....	....	....	....	....	....	....	....	....	....	....	....	....
	Cleveland	IHL	5	1	1	2	29	....	....	....	....	....	....	....	....	....	1	0	1	1	0	....	....	....	....
1998-99	Tampa Bay	NHL	34	1	3	4	27	0	0	1	15	6.7	–15	11	54.5	10:51	....	....	....	....	....	....	....	....	....
	Cleveland	IHL	18	6	7	13	36	....	....	....	....	....	....	....	....	....	....	....	....	....	....	....	....	....	....
99-2000	Detroit Vipers	IHL	1	0	0	0	4	....	....	....	....	....	....	....	....	....	....	....	....	....	....	....	....	....	....
	♦ New Jersey	NHL	1	0	0	0	0	0	0	0	0	0.0	0	0	0.0	4:28	10	0	0	0	4	0	0	0	11:32
	Albany River Rats	AHL	76	21	36	57	131	....	....	....	....	....	....	....	....	....	3	1	1	2	2	....	....	....	....
2000-01	New Jersey	NHL	24	2	2	4	21	0	0	0	18	11.1	0	87	48.3	9:58	....	....	....	....	....	....	....	....	....
	Los Angeles	NHL	11	1	0	1	4	0	0	0	4	25.0	0	51	39.2	6:44	8	0	0	0	2	0	0	0	5:23
2001-02	Los Angeles	NHL	8	0	1	1	2	0	0	0	0	0.0	–1	44	36.4	6:52	1	0	0	0	0	0	0	0	5:54
	Manchester	AHL	49	10	21	31	88	....	....	....	....	....	....	....	....	....	5	1	8	9	4	....	....	....	....
2002-03	Los Angeles	NHL	15	2	3	5	0	0	0	1	14	14.3	–6	133	42.9	12:29	....	....	....	....	....	....	....	....	....
	Manchester	AHL	54	19	44	63	144	....	....	....	....	....	....	....	....	....	3	0	1	1	0	....	....	....	....
2003-04	Los Angeles	NHL	3	0	0	0	0	0	0	0	5	0.0	0	30	43.3	10:30	....	....	....	....	....	....	....	....	....
	Manchester	AHL	59	21	49	70	117	....	....	....	....	....	....	....	....	....	1	0	0	0	2	....	....	....	....
	NHL Totals		**147**	**9**	**12**	**21**	**83**	**1**	**0**	**3**	**84**	**10.7**		**356**	**43.3**	**10:00**	**25**	**0**	**0**	**0**	**8**	**0**	**0**	**0**	**8:39**

Traded to **Tampa Bay** by **Edmonton** with Bryan Marchment and Jason Bonsignore for Roman Hamrlik and Paul Comrie, December 30, 1997. Traded to **New Jersey** by **Tampa Bay** for New Jersey's 7th round choice (Brian Eklund) in 2000 Entry Draft, October 7, 1999. Traded to **Los Angeles** by **New Jersey** to complete transaction that sent Bob Corkum to New Jersey (February 23, 2001), February 27, 2001. • Spent majority of 2000-01 season with New Jersey and Los Angeles as a healthy reserve. Signed as a free agent by **Mannheim** (Germany), May 4, 2004.

			Regular Season														Playoffs								
Season	Club	League	GP	G	A	Pts	PIM	PP	SH	GW	S	%	+/-	TF	F%	Min	GP	G	A	Pts	PIM	PP	SH	GW	Min

KESLER, Ryan

(KEHZ-luhr, RIGH-uhn) **VAN.**

Center. Shoots right. 6'1", 195 lbs. Born, Detroit, MI, August 31, 1984. Vancouver's 1st choice, 23rd overall, in 2003 Entry Draft.

Season	Club	League	GP	G	A	Pts	PIM	PP	SH	GW	S	%	+/-	TF	F%	Min	GP	G	A	Pts	PIM	PP	SH	GW	Min
99-2000	Det. Honey Baked	MWEHL	72	44	73	117	....	....	....	....	....	....	....	....	....	....	....	....	....	....	....	....	....	....	....
2000-01	U.S. National U-18	USDP	82	15	41	56	64	....	....	....	....	....	....	....	....	....	....	....	....	....	....	....	....	....	....
2001-02	U.S. National U-18	USDP	69	21	44	65	37	....	....	....	....	....	....	....	....	....	....	....	....	....	....	....	....	....	....
2002-03	Ohio State	CCHA	40	11	20	31	44	....	....	....	....	....	....	....	....	....	....	....	....	....	....	....	....	....	....
2003-04	**Vancouver**	**NHL**	**28**	**2**	**3**	**5**	**16**	**0**	**0**	**0**	**23**	**8.7**	**–2**	**194**	**40.2**	**10:42**	....	....	....	....	....	....	....	....	....
	Manitoba Moose	AHL	33	3	8	11	29	....	....	....	....	....	....	....	....	....	....	....	....	....	....	....	....	....	....
	NHL Totals		**28**	**2**	**3**	**5**	**16**	**0**	**0**	**0**	**23**	**8.7**		**194**	**40.2**	**10:42**	....	....	....	....	....	....	....	....	....

KHAVANOV, Alexander

(khuh-VAN-ahf, al-ehx-AN-duhr) **ST.L.**

Defense. Shoots left. 6'2", 205 lbs. Born, Moscow, USSR, January 30, 1972. St. Louis' 8th choice, 232nd overall, in 1999 Entry Draft.

Season	Club	League	GP	G	A	Pts	PIM	PP	SH	GW	S	%	+/-	TF	F%	Min	GP	G	A	Pts	PIM	PP	SH	GW	Min
1992-93	Birmingham Bulls	ECHL	19	0	3	3	14	....	....	....	....	....	....	....	....	....	....	....	....	....	....	....	....	....	....
	Raleigh Icecaps	ECHL	17	0	6	6	8	....	....	....	....	....	....	....	....	....	....	....	....	....	....	....	....	....	....
1993-94	St. Petersburg	CIS	41	1	2	3	24	....	....	....	....	....	....	....	....	....	....	....	....	....	....	....	....	....	....
1994-95	St. Petersburg	CIS	49	7	0	7	32	....	....	....	....	....	....	....	....	....	3	0	0	0	0	....	....	....	....
1995-96	St. Petersburg	CIS	32	1	5	6	41	....	....	....	....	....	....	....	....	....	....	....	....	....	....	....	....	....	....
	HPK Hameenlinna	Finland	16	0	2	2	4	....	....	....	....	....	....	....	....	....	9	0	0	0	0	....	....	....	....
1996-97	Cherepovets	Russia	39	3	8	11	56	....	....	....	....	....	....	....	....	....	3	1	0	1	4	....	....	....	....
1997-98	Cherepovets	Russia	44	3	5	8	46	....	....	....	....	....	....	....	....	....	....	....	....	....	....	....	....	....	....
1998-99	Dynamo Moscow	Russia	40	2	7	9	14	....	....	....	....	....	....	....	....	....	16	1	5	6	35	....	....	....	....
	Dynamo Moscow	EuroHL	5	0	1	1	2	....	....	....	....	....	....	....	....	....	6	0	0	0	4	....	....	....	....
99-2000	Dynamo Moscow	Russia	38	5	12	17	49	....	....	....	....	....	....	....	....	....	17	0	3	3	4	....	....	....	....
	Dynamo Moscow	EuroHL	6	2	0	2	0	....	....	....	....	....	....	....	....	....	....	....	....	....	....	....	....	....	....
2000-01	**St. Louis**	**NHL**	**74**	**7**	**16**	**23**	**52**	**2**	**0**	**0**	**92**	**7.6**	**16**	**0**	**0.0**	**20:54**	**15**	**3**	**2**	**5**	**14**	**1**	**0**	**0**	**21:16**
2001-02	**St. Louis**	**NHL**	**81**	**3**	**21**	**24**	**55**	**0**	**0**	**0**	**87**	**3.4**	**9**	**0**	**0.0**	**17:13**	**4**	**0**	**0**	**0**	**2**	**0**	**0**	**0**	**15:08**
2002-03	**St. Louis**	**NHL**	**81**	**8**	**25**	**33**	**48**	**2**	**1**	**2**	**90**	**8.9**	**–1**	**2**	**50.0**	**21:57**	**7**	**2**	**3**	**5**	**2**	**1**	**0**	**0**	**19:05**
2003-04	**St. Louis**	**NHL**	**48**	**3**	**7**	**10**	**18**	**2**	**0**	**0**	**62**	**4.8**	**2**	**1**	**0.0**	**19:20**	....	....	....	....	....	....	....	....	....
	NHL Totals		**284**	**21**	**69**	**90**	**173**	**6**	**1**	**2**	**331**	**6.3**		**3**	**33.3**	**19:53**	**26**	**5**	**5**	**10**	**18**	**2**	**0**	**0**	**19:44**

KILGER, Chad

(KIHL-guhr, CHAD) **TOR.**

Left wing. Shoots left. 6'4", 224 lbs. Born, Cornwall, Ont., November 27, 1976. Anaheim's 1st choice, 4th overall, in 1995 Entry Draft.

Season	Club	League	GP	G	A	Pts	PIM	PP	SH	GW	S	%	+/-	TF	F%	Min	GP	G	A	Pts	PIM	PP	SH	GW	Min
1992-93	Cornwall Colts	OCJHL	55	30	36	66	26	....	....	....	....	....	....	....	....	....	6	0	0	0	0	....	....	....	....
1993-94	Kingston	OHL	66	17	35	52	23	....	....	....	....	....	....	....	....	....	6	7	2	9	8	....	....	....	....
1994-95	Kingston	OHL	65	42	53	95	95	....	....	....	....	....	....	....	....	....	6	5	2	7	10	....	....	....	....
1995-96	**Anaheim**	**NHL**	**45**	**5**	**7**	**12**	**22**	**0**	**0**	**1**	**38**	**13.2**	**–2**	....	....	....	....	....	....	....	....	....	....	....	....
	Winnipeg	**NHL**	**29**	**2**	**3**	**5**	**12**	**0**	**0**	**0**	**19**	**10.5**	**–2**	....	....	....	**4**	**1**	**0**	**1**	**0**	**0**	**0**	**1**	....
1996-97	**Phoenix**	**NHL**	**24**	**4**	**3**	**7**	**13**	**1**	**0**	**0**	**30**	**13.3**	**–5**	....	....	....	....	....	....	....	....	....	....	....	....
	Springfield	AHL	52	17	28	45	36	....	....	....	....	....	....	....	....	....	16	5	7	12	56	....	....	....	....
1997-98	**Phoenix**	**NHL**	**10**	**0**	**1**	**1**	**4**	**0**	**0**	**0**	**9**	**0.0**	**–2**	....	....	....	....	....	....	....	....	....	....	....	....
	Springfield	AHL	35	14	14	28	33	....	....	....	....	....	....	....	....	....	....	....	....	....	....	....	....	....	....
	Chicago	**NHL**	**22**	**3**	**8**	**11**	**6**	**2**	**0**	**1**	**23**	**13.0**	**2**	....	....	....	....	....	....	....	....	....	....	....	....
1998-99	**Chicago**	**NHL**	**64**	**14**	**11**	**25**	**30**	**2**	**1**	**1**	**68**	**20.6**	**–1**	**488**	**56.6**	**14:03**	....	....	....	....	....	....	....	....	....
	Edmonton	**NHL**	**13**	**1**	**1**	**2**	**4**	**0**	**0**	**0**	**13**	**7.7**	**–3**	**82**	**53.7**	**11:22**	**4**	**0**	**0**	**0**	**4**	**0**	**0**	**0**	**12:59**
99-2000	**Edmonton**	**NHL**	**40**	**3**	**2**	**5**	**18**	**0**	**0**	**0**	**32**	**9.4**	**–6**	**269**	**48.0**	**8:33**	**3**	**0**	**0**	**0**	**0**	**0**	**0**	**0**	**8:01**
	Hamilton	AHL	7	4	2	6	4	....	....	....	....	....	....	....	....	....	....	....	....	....	....	....	....	....	....
2000-01	**Edmonton**	**NHL**	**34**	**5**	**2**	**7**	**17**	**1**	**0**	**0**	**28**	**17.9**	**–7**	**391**	**53.5**	**8:18**	....	....	....	....	....	....	....	....	....
	Montreal	**NHL**	**43**	**9**	**16**	**25**	**34**	**1**	**1**	**1**	**75**	**12.0**	**–1**	**319**	**52.4**	**17:57**	....	....	....	....	....	....	....	....	....
2001-02	**Montreal**	**NHL**	**75**	**8**	**15**	**23**	**27**	**0**	**1**	**2**	**87**	**9.2**	**–7**	**357**	**53.8**	**13:14**	**12**	**0**	**1**	**1**	**9**	**0**	**0**	**0**	**14:00**
2002-03	**Montreal**	**NHL**	**60**	**9**	**7**	**16**	**21**	**0**	**0**	**1**	**60**	**15.0**	**–4**	**208**	**46.6**	**10:42**	....	....	....	....	....	....	....	....	....
2003-04	**Montreal**	**NHL**	**36**	**2**	**2**	**4**	**14**	**0**	**0**	**0**	**29**	**6.9**	**2**	**95**	**48.4**	**10:26**	....	....	....	....	....	....	....	....	....
	Hamilton	AHL	2	1	0	1	0	....	....	....	....	....	....	....	....	....	....	....	....	....	....	....	....	....	....
	Toronto	**NHL**	**5**	**1**	**1**	**2**	**2**	**0**	**0**	**1**	**6**	**16.7**	**2**	**2**	**0.0**	**12:14**	**13**	**2**	**1**	**3**	**0**	**0**	**0**	**0**	**11:41**
	NHL Totals		**500**	**66**	**79**	**145**	**224**	**7**	**3**	**8**	**517**	**12.8**		**2211**	**52.5**	**12:12**	**36**	**3**	**2**	**5**	**13**	**0**	**0**	**1**	**12:22**

Traded to **Winnipeg** by **Anaheim** with Oleg Tverdovsky and Anaheim's 3rd round choice (Per-Anton Lundstrom) in 1996 Entry Draft for Teemu Selanne, Marc Chouinard and Winnipeg's 4th round choice (later traded to Toronto – later traded to Montreal – Montreal selected Kim Staal) in 1996 Entry Draft, February 7, 1996. Transferred to **Phoenix** after **Winnipeg** franchise relocated, July 1, 1996. Traded to **Chicago** by **Phoenix** with Jayson More for Keith Carney and Jim Cummins, March 4, 1998. Traded to **Edmonton** by **Chicago** with Daniel Cleary, Ethan Moreau and Christian Laflamme for Boris Mironov, Dean McAmmond and Jonas Elofsson, March 20, 1999. Traded to **Montreal** by **Edmonton** for Sergei Zholtok, December 18, 2000. Claimed on waivers by **Toronto** from **Montreal**, March 9, 2004.

KING, Jason

(KIHNG, JAY-suhn) **VAN.**

Center. Shoots left. 6'1", 195 lbs. Born, Corner Brook, Nfld., September 14, 1981. Vancouver's 5th choice, 212th overall, in 2001 Entry Draft.

Season	Club	League	GP	G	A	Pts	PIM	PP	SH	GW	S	%	+/-	TF	F%	Min	GP	G	A	Pts	PIM	PP	SH	GW	Min
99-2000	Halifax	QMJHL	53	3	7	10	8	....	....	....	....	....	....	....	....	....	10	0	0	0	2	....	....	....	....
2000-01	Halifax	QMJHL	72	48	41	89	78	....	....	....	....	....	....	....	....	....	6	3	2	5	16	....	....	....	....
2001-02	Halifax	QMJHL	61	*63	36	99	39	....	....	....	....	....	....	....	....	....	13	9	8	17	13	....	....	....	....
2002-03	**Vancouver**	**NHL**	**8**	**0**	**2**	**2**	**0**	**0**	**0**	**0**	**12**	**0.0**	**0**	**0**	**0.0**	**11:17**	....	....	....	....	....	....	....	....	....
	Manitoba Moose	AHL	67	20	20	40	15	....	....	....	....	....	....	....	....	....	14	4	3	7	14	....	....	....	....
2003-04	**Vancouver**	**NHL**	**47**	**12**	**9**	**21**	**8**	**6**	**0**	**1**	**107**	**11.2**	**0**	**3**	**66.7**	**12:43**	**1**	**0**	**0**	**0**	**0**	**0**	**0**	**0**	**6:21**
	Manitoba Moose	AHL	29	12	11	23	6	....	....	....	....	....	....	....	....	....	....	....	....	....	....	....	....	....	....
	NHL Totals		**55**	**12**	**11**	**23**	**8**	**6**	**0**	**1**	**119**	**10.1**		**3**	**66.7**	**12:30**	**1**	**0**	**0**	**0**	**0**	**0**	**0**	**0**	**6:21**

QMJHL Second All-Star Team (2001)

KLATT, Trent

(KLAT, TREHNT) **L.A.**

Right wing. Shoots right. 6'1", 210 lbs. Born, Robbinsdale, MN, January 30, 1971. Washington's 5th choice, 82nd overall, in 1989 Entry Draft.

Season	Club	League	GP	G	A	Pts	PIM	PP	SH	GW	S	%	+/-	TF	F%	Min	GP	G	A	Pts	PIM	PP	SH	GW	Min
1986-87	Osseo Orioles	Hi-School	22	9	27	36	....	....	....	....	....	....	....	....	....	....	....	....	....	....	....	....	....	....	....
1987-88	Osseo Orioles	Hi-School	22	19	17	36	....	....	....	....	....	....	....	....	....	....	....	....	....	....	....	....	....	....	....
1988-89	Osseo Orioles	Hi-School	22	24	39	63	....	....	....	....	....	....	....	....	....	....	....	....	....	....	....	....	....	....	....
1989-90	U. of Minnesota	WCHA	38	22	14	36	16	....	....	....	....	....	....	....	....	....	....	....	....	....	....	....	....	....	....
1990-91	U. of Minnesota	WCHA	39	16	28	44	58	....	....	....	....	....	....	....	....	....	....	....	....	....	....	....	....	....	....
1991-92	U. of Minnesota	WCHA	41	27	36	63	76	....	....	....	....	....	....	....	....	....	....	....	....	....	....	....	....	....	....
	Minnesota	**NHL**	**1**	**0**	**0**	**0**	**0**	**0**	**0**	**0**	**1**	**0.0**	**0**	....	....	....	**6**	**0**	**0**	**0**	**2**	**0**	**0**	**0**	....
1992-93	**Minnesota**	**NHL**	**47**	**4**	**19**	**23**	**38**	**1**	**0**	**0**	**69**	**5.8**	**2**	....	....	....	....	....	....	....	....	....	....	....	....
	Kalamazoo Wings	IHL	31	8	11	19	18	....	....	....	....	....	....	....	....	....	....	....	....	....	....	....	....	....	....
1993-94	**Dallas**	**NHL**	**61**	**14**	**24**	**38**	**30**	**3**	**0**	**2**	**86**	**16.3**	**13**	....	....	....	**9**	**2**	**1**	**3**	**4**	**1**	**0**	**0**	....
	Kalamazoo Wings	IHL	6	3	2	5	4	....	....	....	....	....	....	....	....	....	....	....	....	....	....	....	....	....	....
1994-95	**Dallas**	**NHL**	**47**	**12**	**10**	**22**	**26**	**5**	**0**	**3**	**91**	**13.2**	**–2**	....	....	....	**5**	**1**	**0**	**1**	**0**	**1**	**0**	**0**	....
1995-96	**Dallas**	**NHL**	**22**	**4**	**4**	**8**	**23**	**0**	**0**	**1**	**37**	**10.8**	**0**	....	....	....	....	....	....	....	....	....	....	....	....
	Michigan	IHL	2	1	2	3	5	....	....	....	....	....	....	....	....	....	....	....	....	....	....	....	....	....	....
	Philadelphia	**NHL**	**49**	**3**	**8**	**11**	**21**	**0**	**0**	**1**	**64**	**4.7**	**2**	....	....	....	**12**	**4**	**1**	**5**	**0**	**0**	**0**	**0**	....
1996-97	**Philadelphia**	**NHL**	**76**	**24**	**21**	**45**	**20**	**5**	**5**	**5**	**131**	**18.3**	**9**	....	....	....	**19**	**4**	**3**	**7**	**12**	**0**	**0**	**2**	....
1997-98	**Philadelphia**	**NHL**	**82**	**14**	**28**	**42**	**16**	**5**	**0**	**3**	**143**	**9.8**	**2**	....	....	....	**5**	**0**	**0**	**0**	**0**	**0**	**0**	**0**	....
1998-99	**Philadelphia**	**NHL**	**2**	**0**	**0**	**0**	**0**	**0**	**0**	**0**	**2**	**0.0**	**0**	**0**	**0.0**	**11:11**	....	....	....	....	....	....	....	....	....
	Vancouver	**NHL**	**73**	**4**	**10**	**14**	**12**	**0**	**0**	**0**	**58**	**6.9**	**–3**	**37**	**32.4**	**11:21**	....	....	....	....	....	....	....	....	....
99-2000	**Vancouver**	**NHL**	**47**	**10**	**10**	**20**	**26**	**8**	**0**	**0**	**100**	**10.0**	**–8**	**19**	**63.2**	**16:04**	....	....	....	....	....	....	....	....	....
	Syracuse Crunch	AHL	24	13	10	23	6	....	....	....	....	....	....	....	....	....	....	....	....	....	....	....	....	....	....
2000-01	**Vancouver**	**NHL**	**77**	**13**	**20**	**33**	**31**	**3**	**0**	**1**	**140**	**9.3**	**8**	**75**	**50.7**	**13:33**	**4**	**3**	**0**	**3**	**0**	**2**	**0**	**0**	**15:54**
2001-02	**Vancouver**	**NHL**	**34**	**8**	**7**	**15**	**10**	**2**	**1**	**3**	**67**	**11.9**	**9**	**101**	**54.5**	**15:27**	....	....	....	....	....	....	....	....	....
2002-03	**Vancouver**	**NHL**	**82**	**16**	**13**	**29**	**8**	**3**	**0**	**2**	**127**	**12.6**	**10**	**47**	**40.4**	**12:25**	**14**	**2**	**4**	**6**	**2**	**2**	**0**	**1**	**12:42**
2003-04	**Los Angeles**	**NHL**	**82**	**17**	**26**	**43**	**46**	**6**	**0**	**2**	**160**	**10.6**	**2**	**96**	**46.9**	**16:15**	....	....	....	....	....	....	....	....	....
	NHL Totals		**782**	**143**	**200**	**343**	**307**	**41**	**6**	**23**	**1276**	**11.2**		**375**	**48.3**	**13:55**	**74**	**16**	**9**	**25**	**20**	**6**	**0**	**3**	**13:25**

Minnesota High School Player of the Year (1989)

Traded to **Minnesota** by **Washington** with Steve Maltais for Shawn Chambers, June 21, 1991. Transferred to **Dallas** after **Minnesota** franchise relocated, June 9, 1993. Traded to **Philadelphia** by **Dallas** for Brent Fedyk, December 13, 1995. Traded to **Vancouver** by **Philadelphia** for Vancouver's 6th round choice (later traded to Atlanta – Atlanta selected Jeff Dwyer) in 2000 Entry Draft, October 19, 1998. • Missed majority of 2001-02 season recovering from abdominal injury suffered in game vs. Ottawa, November 20, 2001. Signed as a free agent by **Los Angeles**, July 7, 2003.

KLEE, Ken

(KLEE, KEHN) **TOR.**

Defense. Shoots right. 6', 210 lbs. Born, Indianapolis, IN, April 24, 1971. Washington's 11th choice, 177th overall, in 1990 Entry Draft.

			Regular Season														Playoffs								
Season	Club	League	GP	G	A	Pts	PIM	PP	SH	GW	S	%	+/-	TF	F%	Min	GP	G	A	Pts	PIM	PP	SH	GW	Min
1988-89	St. Michael's B	OJHL-B	40	9	23	32	64	....	....	....	....	....	....	....	....	....	27	5	12	17	54	....	....	....	....
1989-90	Bowling Green	CCHA	39	0	5	5	52	....	....	....	....	....	....	....	....	....	....	....	....	....	....	....	....	....	....
1990-91	Bowling Green	CCHA	37	7	28	35	50	....	....	....	....	....	....	....	....	....	....	....	....	....	....	....	....	....	....
1991-92	Bowling Green	CCHA	10	0	1	1	14	....	....	....	....	....	....	....	....	....	....	....	....	....	....	....	....	....	....
1992-93	Baltimore	AHL	77	4	14	18	93	....	....	....	....	....	....	....	....	....	7	0	1	1	15	....	....	....	....
1993-94	Portland Pirates	AHL	65	2	9	11	87	....	....	....	....	....	....	....	....	....	17	1	2	3	14	....	....	....	....
1994-95	Portland Pirates	AHL	49	5	7	12	89	....	....	....	....	....	....	....	....	....	....	....	....	....	....	....	....	....	....
	Washington	**NHL**	**23**	**3**	**1**	**4**	**41**	**0**	**0**	**0**	**18**	**16.7**	**2**	....	....	....	**7**	**0**	**0**	**0**	**4**	**0**	**0**	**0**	....
1995-96	**Washington**	**NHL**	**66**	**8**	**3**	**11**	**60**	**0**	**1**	**2**	**76**	**10.5**	**–1**	....	....	....	**1**	**0**	**0**	**0**	**0**	**0**	**0**	**0**	....
1996-97	**Washington**	**NHL**	**80**	**3**	**8**	**11**	**115**	**0**	**0**	**2**	**108**	**2.8**	**–5**	....	....	....	....	....	....	....	....	....	....	....	....
1997-98	**Washington**	**NHL**	**51**	**4**	**2**	**6**	**46**	**0**	**0**	**1**	**44**	**9.1**	**–3**	....	....	....	**9**	**1**	**0**	**1**	**10**	**0**	**0**	**0**	....
1998-99	**Washington**	**NHL**	**78**	**7**	**13**	**20**	**80**	**0**	**0**	**1**	**132**	**5.3**	**–9**	**0**	**0.0**	**19:07**	....	....	....	....	....	....	....	....	....
99-2000	**Washington**	**NHL**	**80**	**7**	**13**	**20**	**79**	**0**	**0**	**2**	**113**	**6.2**	**8**	**0**	**0.0**	**20:29**	**5**	**0**	**1**	**1**	**10**	**0**	**0**	**0**	**21:38**
2000-01	**Washington**	**NHL**	**54**	**2**	**4**	**6**	**60**	**0**	**0**	**0**	**58**	**3.4**	**–5**	**0**	**0.0**	**17:15**	**6**	**0**	**1**	**1**	**8**	**0**	**0**	**0**	**13:47**
2001-02	**Washington**	**NHL**	**68**	**8**	**8**	**16**	**38**	**2**	**0**	**3**	**85**	**9.4**	**4**	**2**	**0.0**	**19:24**	....	....	....	....	....	....	....	....	....
2002-03	**Washington**	**NHL**	**70**	**1**	**16**	**17**	**89**	**0**	**0**	**0**	**67**	**1.5**	**22**	**0**	**0.0**	**21:49**	**6**	**0**	**0**	**0**	**6**	**0**	**0**	**0**	**23:11**
2003-04	**Toronto**	**NHL**	**66**	**4**	**25**	**29**	**36**	**3**	**0**	**1**	**85**	**4.7**	**–1**	**1**	**100.0**	**22:08**	**11**	**0**	**0**	**0**	**6**	**0**	**0**	**0**	**18:45**
	NHL Totals		**636**	**47**	**93**	**140**	**644**	**5**	**1**	**12**	**786**	**6.0**		**3**	**33.3**	**20:07**	**45**	**1**	**2**	**3**	**44**	**0**	**0**	**0**	**19:09**

Signed as a free agent by **Toronto**, September 27, 2003.

KLEMM, Jon

(KLEHM, JAWN) **DAL.**

Defense. Shoots right. 6'2", 200 lbs. Born, Cranbrook, B.C., January 8, 1970.

Season	Club	League	GP	G	A	Pts	PIM	PP	SH	GW	S	%	+/-	TF	F%	Min	GP	G	A	Pts	PIM	PP	SH	GW	Min
1986-87	Cranbrook Colts	KIJHL	59	20	51	71	54	....	....	....	....	....	....	....	....	....	....	....	....	....	....	....	....	....	....
1987-88	Seattle	WHL	68	6	7	13	24	....	....	....	....	....	....	....	....	....	....	....	....	....	....	....	....	....	....
1988-89	Seattle	WHL	2	1	1	2	0	....	....	....	....	....	....	....	....	....	....	....	....	....	....	....	....	....	....
	Spokane Chiefs	WHL	66	6	34	40	42	....	....	....	....	....	....	....	....	....	....	....	....	....	....	....	....	....	....
1989-90	Spokane Chiefs	WHL	66	3	28	31	100	....	....	....	....	....	....	....	....	....	6	1	1	2	5	....	....	....	....
1990-91	Spokane Chiefs	WHL	72	7	58	65	65	....	....	....	....	....	....	....	....	....	15	3	6	9	8	....	....	....	....
1991-92	**Quebec**	**NHL**	**4**	**0**	**1**	**1**	**0**	**0**	**0**	**0**	**2**	**0.0**	**2**	....	....	....	....	....	....	....	....	....	....	....	....
	Halifax Citadels	AHL	70	6	13	19	40	....	....	....	....	....	....	....	....	....	....	....	....	....	....	....	....	....	....
1992-93	Halifax Citadels	AHL	80	3	20	23	32	....	....	....	....	....	....	....	....	....	....	....	....	....	....	....	....	....	....
1993-94	**Quebec**	**NHL**	**7**	**0**	**0**	**0**	**4**	**0**	**0**	**0**	**11**	**0.0**	**–1**	....	....	....	....	....	....	....	....	....	....	....	....
	Cornwall Aces	AHL	66	4	26	30	78	....	....	....	....	....	....	....	....	....	13	1	2	3	6	....	....	....	....
1994-95	Cornwall Aces	AHL	65	6	13	19	84	....	....	....	....	....	....	....	....	....	....	....	....	....	....	....	....	....	....
	Quebec	**NHL**	**4**	**1**	**0**	**1**	**2**	**0**	**0**	**0**	**5**	**20.0**	**3**	....	....	....	....	....	....	....	....	....	....	....	....
1995-96♦	**Colorado**	**NHL**	**56**	**3**	**12**	**15**	**20**	**0**	**1**	**1**	**61**	**4.9**	**12**	....	....	....	**15**	**2**	**1**	**3**	**0**	**1**	**0**	**0**	....
1996-97	**Colorado**	**NHL**	**80**	**9**	**15**	**24**	**37**	**1**	**2**	**1**	**103**	**8.7**	**12**	....	....	....	**17**	**1**	**1**	**2**	**6**	**0**	**0**	**0**	....
1997-98	**Colorado**	**NHL**	**67**	**6**	**8**	**14**	**30**	**0**	**0**	**0**	**60**	**10.0**	**–3**	....	....	....	**4**	**0**	**0**	**0**	**0**	**0**	**0**	**0**	....
1998-99	**Colorado**	**NHL**	**39**	**1**	**2**	**3**	**31**	**0**	**0**	**0**	**28**	**3.6**	**4**	**14**	**35.7**	**13:43**	**19**	**0**	**1**	**1**	**10**	**0**	**0**	**0**	**8:32**
99-2000	**Colorado**	**NHL**	**73**	**5**	**7**	**12**	**34**	**0**	**0**	**0**	**64**	**7.8**	**26**	**17**	**47.1**	**17:22**	**17**	**2**	**1**	**3**	**9**	**0**	**0**	**0**	**14:25**
2000-01♦	**Colorado**	**NHL**	**78**	**4**	**11**	**15**	**54**	**2**	**0**	**2**	**97**	**4.1**	**22**	**1**	**100.0**	**19:56**	**22**	**1**	**2**	**3**	**16**	**0**	**0**	**1**	**16:15**
2001-02	**Chicago**	**NHL**	**82**	**4**	**16**	**20**	**42**	**2**	**0**	**1**	**111**	**3.6**	**–3**	**1**	**0.0**	**23:50**	**5**	**0**	**1**	**1**	**4**	**0**	**0**	**0**	**21:58**
2002-03	**Chicago**	**NHL**	**70**	**2**	**14**	**16**	**44**	**1**	**0**	**1**	**74**	**2.7**	**–9**	**2**	**0.0**	**21:57**	....	....	....	....	....	....	....	....	....
2003-04	**Chicago**	**NHL**	**19**	**0**	**1**	**1**	**20**	**0**	**0**	**0**	**19**	**0.0**	**6**	**0**	**0.0**	**21:21**	....	....	....	....	....	....	....	....	....
	Dallas	**NHL**	**58**	**2**	**4**	**6**	**24**	**0**	**0**	**1**	**52**	**3.8**	**10**	**1**	**0.0**	**16:00**	....	....	....	....	....	....	....	....	....
	NHL Totals		**637**	**37**	**91**	**128**	**342**	**6**	**3**	**7**	**687**	**5.4**		**36**	**38.9**	**19:32**	**99**	**6**	**7**	**13**	**45**	**1**	**0**	**1**	**13:53**

WHL West Second All-Star Team (1991)

Signed as a free agent by **Quebec**, May 14, 1991. Transferred to **Colorado** after **Quebec** franchise relocated, June 21, 1995. • Missed majority of 1998-99 season recovering from knee injury suffered in game vs. Phoenix, November 10, 1998. Signed as a free agent by **Chicago**, July 1, 2001. Traded to **Dallas** by **Chicago** with NY Rangers' 4th round choice (previously acquired, Dallas selected Fredrik Naslund) in 2004 Entry Draft for Stephane Robidas and Dallas' 2nd round choice (Jakub Sindel) in 2004 Entry Draft, November 17, 2003.

KLESLA, Rostislav

(KLEHS-luh, RAHS-tih-slav) **CBJ**

Defense. Shoots left. 6'3", 206 lbs. Born, Novy Jicin, Czech., March 21, 1982. Columbus' 1st choice, 4th overall, in 2000 Entry Draft.

Season	Club	League	GP	G	A	Pts	PIM	PP	SH	GW	S	%	+/-	TF	F%	Min	GP	G	A	Pts	PIM	PP	SH	GW	Min
1997-98	HC Opava Jr.	Czech-Jr.	38	11	18	29	87	....	....	....	....	....	....	....	....	....	8	2	2	4	0	....	....	....	....
1998-99	Sioux City	USHL	54	4	12	16	100	....	....	....	....	....	....	....	....	....	5	2	0	2	2	....	....	....	....
99-2000	Brampton	OHL	67	16	29	45	174	....	....	....	....	....	....	....	....	....	6	1	1	2	21	....	....	....	....
2000-01	**Columbus**	**NHL**	**8**	**2**	**0**	**2**	**6**	**0**	**0**	**0**	**10**	**20.0**	**–1**	**0**	**0.0**	**18:25**	....	....	....	....	....	....	....	....	....
	Brampton	OHL	45	18	36	54	59	....	....	....	....	....	....	....	....	....	9	2	9	11	26	....	....	....	....
2001-02	**Columbus**	**NHL**	**75**	**8**	**8**	**16**	**74**	**1**	**0**	**0**	**102**	**7.8**	**–6**	**0**	**0.0**	**18:52**	....	....	....	....	....	....	....	....	....
2002-03	**Columbus**	**NHL**	**72**	**2**	**14**	**16**	**71**	**0**	**0**	**0**	**89**	**2.2**	**–22**	**0**	**0.0**	**18:45**	....	....	....	....	....	....	....	....	....
2003-04	**Columbus**	**NHL**	**47**	**2**	**11**	**13**	**27**	**0**	**0**	**1**	**74**	**2.7**	**–16**	**0**	**0.0**	**18:19**	....	....	....	....	....	....	....	....	....
	NHL Totals		**202**	**14**	**33**	**47**	**178**	**1**	**0**	**1**	**275**	**5.1**		**0**	**0.0**	**18:41**	....	....	....	....	....	....	....	....	....

OHL All-Rookie Team (2000) • Canadian Major Junior All-Rookie Team (2000) • OHL First All-Star Team (2001) • NHL All-Rookie Team (2002)

Returned to **Brampton** (OHL) by **Columbus**, October 28, 2000.

KLOUCEK, Tomas

(KLOH-chehk, TAW-mahsh) **ATL.**

Defense. Shoots left. 6'3", 225 lbs. Born, Prague, Czech., March 7, 1980. NY Rangers' 6th choice, 131st overall, in 1998 Entry Draft.

Season	Club	League	GP	G	A	Pts	PIM	PP	SH	GW	S	%	+/-	TF	F%	Min	GP	G	A	Pts	PIM	PP	SH	GW	Min
1995-96	Slavia Praha Jr.	Czech-Jr.	40	2	8	10	....	....	....	....	....	....	....	....	....	....	....	....	....	....	....	....	....	....	....
1996-97	Slavia Praha Jr.	Czech-Jr.	43	4	14	18	44	....	....	....	....	....	....	....	....	....	....	....	....	....	....	....	....	....	....
1997-98	Slavia Praha Jr.	Czech-Jr.	43	1	9	10	....	....	....	....	....	....	....	....	....	....	....	....	....	....	....	....	....	....	....
1998-99	Cape Breton	QMJHL	59	4	17	21	162	....	....	....	....	....	....	....	....	....	2	0	0	0	4	....	....	....	....
99-2000	Hartford	AHL	73	2	8	10	113	....	....	....	....	....	....	....	....	....	23	0	4	4	18	....	....	....	....
2000-01	**NY Rangers**	**NHL**	**43**	**1**	**4**	**5**	**74**	**0**	**0**	**0**	**22**	**4.5**	**–3**	**0**	**0.0**	**16:43**	....	....	....	....	....	....	....	....	....
	Hartford	AHL	21	0	2	2	44	....	....	....	....	....	....	....	....	....	....	....	....	....	....	....	....	....	....
2001-02	**NY Rangers**	**NHL**	**52**	**1**	**3**	**4**	**137**	**0**	**0**	**0**	**21**	**4.8**	**–2**	**1**	**0.0**	**11:58**	....	....	....	....	....	....	....	....	....
	Hartford	AHL	9	0	2	2	27	....	....	....	....	....	....	....	....	....	10	1	1	2	8	....	....	....	....
2002-03	Hartford	AHL	20	3	4	7	102	....	....	....	....	....	....	....	....	....	....	....	....	....	....	....	....	....	....
	Nashville	**NHL**	**3**	**0**	**0**	**0**	**2**	**0**	**0**	**0**	**1**	**0.0**	**1**	**0**	**0.0**	**9:45**	....	....	....	....	....	....	....	....	....
	Milwaukee	AHL	34	0	6	6	80	....	....	....	....	....	....	....	....	....	....	....	....	....	....	....	....	....	....
2003-04	**Nashville**	**NHL**	**5**	**0**	**1**	**1**	**10**	**0**	**0**	**0**	**0**	**0.0**	**3**	**0**	**0.0**	**11:34**	....	....	....	....	....	....	....	....	....
	Atlanta	**NHL**	**37**	**0**	**0**	**0**	**25**	**0**	**0**	**0**	**12**	**0.0**	**–8**	**0**	**0.0**	**8:00**	....	....	....	....	....	....	....	....	....
	NHL Totals		**140**	**2**	**8**	**10**	**248**	**0**	**0**	**0**	**56**	**3.6**		**1**	**0.0**	**12:19**	....	....	....	....	....	....	....	....	....

Traded to **Nashville** by **NY Rangers** with Rem Murray and Marek Zidlicky for Mike Dunham, December 12, 2002. Traded to **Atlanta** by **Nashville** with Ben Simon for Simon Gamache and Kirill Safronov, December 2, 2003.

KNUBLE, Mike

(kuh-NOO-buhl, MIGHK) **PHI.**

Right wing. Shoots right. 6'3", 228 lbs. Born, Toronto, Ont., July 4, 1972. Detroit's 4th choice, 76th overall, in 1991 Entry Draft.

Season	Club	League	GP	G	A	Pts	PIM	PP	SH	GW	S	%	+/-	TF	F%	Min	GP	G	A	Pts	PIM	PP	SH	GW	Min
1988-89	East Kentwood	Hi-School	28	52	37	89	60	....	....	....	....	....	....	....	....	....	....	....	....	....	....	....	....	....	....
1989-90	East Kentwood	Hi-School	29	63	40	103	40	....	....	....	....	....	....	....	....	....	....	....	....	....	....	....	....	....	....
1990-91	Kalamazoo	NAJHL	36	18	24	42	30	....	....	....	....	....	....	....	....	....	....	....	....	....	....	....	....	....	....
1991-92	U. of Michigan	CCHA	43	7	8	15	48	....	....	....	....	....	....	....	....	....	....	....	....	....	....	....	....	....	....
1992-93	U. of Michigan	CCHA	39	26	16	42	57	....	....	....	....	....	....	....	....	....	....	....	....	....	....	....	....	....	....
1993-94	U. of Michigan	CCHA	41	32	26	58	71	....	....	....	....	....	....	....	....	....	....	....	....	....	....	....	....	....	....
1994-95	U. of Michigan	CCHA	34	*38	22	60	62	....	....	....	....	....	....	....	....	....	....	....	....	....	....	....	....	....	....
	Adirondack	AHL	....	....	....	....	....	....	....	....	....	....	....	....	....	....	3	0	0	0	0	....	....	....	....
1995-96	Adirondack	AHL	80	22	23	45	59	....	....	....	....	....	....	....	....	....	3	1	0	1	0	....	....	....	....
1996-97	**Detroit**	**NHL**	**9**	**1**	**0**	**1**	**0**	**0**	**0**	**0**	**10**	**10.0**	**–1**	....	....	....	....	....	....	....	....	....	....	....	....
	Adirondack	AHL	68	28	35	63	54	....	....	....	....	....	....	....	....	....	....	....	....	....	....	....	....	....	....
1997-98♦	**Detroit**	**NHL**	**53**	**7**	**6**	**13**	**16**	**0**	**0**	**0**	**54**	**13.0**	**2**	....	....	....	**3**	**0**	**1**	**1**	**0**	**0**	**0**	**0**	....
1998-99	**NY Rangers**	**NHL**	**82**	**15**	**20**	**35**	**26**	**3**	**0**	**1**	**113**	**13.3**	**–7**	**1**	**100.0**	**14:52**	....	....	....	....	....	....	....	....	....
99-2000	**NY Rangers**	**NHL**	**59**	**9**	**5**	**14**	**18**	**1**	**0**	**1**	**50**	**18.0**	**–5**	**9**	**55.6**	**10:39**	....	....	....	....	....	....	....	....	....
	Boston	**NHL**	**14**	**3**	**3**	**6**	**8**	**1**	**0**	**1**	**28**	**10.7**	**–2**	**3**	**0.0**	**19:29**	....	....	....	....	....	....	....	....	....

Season	Club	League	GP	G	A	Pts	PIM	PP	SH	GW	S	%	+/-	TF	F%	Min	GP	G	A	Pts	PIM	PP	SH	GW	Min
2000-01	Boston	NHL	82	7	13	20	37	0	1		92	7.6	0	115	31.3	10:34									
2001-02	Boston	NHL	54	8	6	14	42	0	0	2	77	10.4	9	27	44.4	9:45	2	0	0	0	0	0	0	0	3:30
2002-03	Boston	NHL	75	30	29	59	45	9	0	4	185	16.2	18	34	44.1	17:24	5	0	2	2	2	0	0	0	17:35
2003-04	Boston	NHL	82	21	25	46	32	4	0	3	192	10.9	19	54	31.5	18:47	7	2	0	2	0	1	0	0	19:45
NHL Totals			510	101	107	208	224	18	1	13	801	12.6		243	35.4	14:12	17	2	3	5	2	1	0	0	16:39

CCHA Second All-Star Team (1994, 1995) • NCAA West Second All-American Team (1995)
Traded to **NY Rangers** by **Detroit** for NY Rangers' 2nd round choice (Tomas Kopecky) in 2000 Entry Draft, October 1, 1998. Traded to **Boston** by **NY Rangers** for Rob DiMaio, March 10, 2000. Signed as a free agent by **Philadelphia**, July 3, 2004.

KNUTSEN, Espen

(kuh-NOOT-suhn, EHS-pehn)

Center. Shoots left. 5'11", 188 lbs.   Born, Oslo, Norway, January 12, 1972. Hartford's 9th choice, 204th overall, in 1990 Entry Draft.

Season	Club	League	GP	G	A	Pts	PIM	PP	SH	GW	S	%	+/-	TF	F%	Min	GP	G	A	Pts	PIM
1988-89	Valerengen Jr.	Nor-Jr.	36	14	7	21	18														
1989-90	Valerengen IF	OsloNorway	40	25	28	53	44														
1990-91	Valerengen IF	OsloNorway	31	30	24	54	42										5	3	4	7	2
1991-92	Valerengen IF	OsloNorway	30	28	26	54	37										8	7	8	15	
1992-93	Valerengen IF	OsloNorway	13	11	13	24	4														
1993-94	Valerengen IF	OsloNorway	38	32	26	58	20														
	Norway	Olympics	7	1	3	4	2														
1994-95	Djurgarden	Sweden	30	6	14	20	18										3	0	1	1	0
1995-96	Djurgarden	Sweden	32	10	23	33	50										4	1	0	1	2
1996-97	Djurgarden	Sweden	39	16	33	49	20										4	2	4	6	6
1997-98	**Anaheim**	**NHL**	19	3	0	3	6	1	0	0	21	14.3	-10								
	Cincinnati	AHL	41	4	13	17	18														
1998-99	Djurgarden	Sweden	39	18	24	42	32										4	0	1	1	2
	Djurgarden	EuroHL	4	2	2	4	2														
99-2000	Djurgarden	Sweden	48	18	35	53	65										13	5	*16	*21	2
2000-01	**Columbus**	**NHL**	66	11	42	53	30	2	0	0	62	17.7	-3	125	52.8	15:59					
2001-02	**Columbus**	**NHL**	77	11	31	42	47	5	2	1	102	10.8	-28	500	46.4	20:15					
2002-03	**Columbus**	**NHL**	31	5	4	9	20	0	1	1	28	17.9	-15	325	39.4	16:44					
2003-04	**Columbus**	**NHL**	14	0	4	4	2	0	0	0	11	0.0	-5	41	51.2	15:28					
	Syracuse Crunch	AHL	2	1	1	2	0														
	Valerenga IF	Norway	1	0	0	0	0														
	Djurgarden	Sweden	6	2	3	5	4										3	0	0		6
NHL Totals			207	30	81	111	105	11	2	2	224	13.4		991	45.1	17:49					

Played in NHL All-Star Game (2002)
Rights traded to **Anaheim** by **Hartford** for Kevin Brown, October 1, 1996. Traded to **Columbus** by **Anaheim** for Columbus' 4th round choice (Vladmir Korsunov) in 2001 Entry Draft, May 25, 2000. • Missed majority of 2002-03 season recovering from groin (November 5, 2002 vs. Washington) and wrist (March 13, 2003 vs. Colorado) injuries. Signed as a free agent by **Valerenga** (Norway), December 17, 2003. Signed as a free agent by **Djurgarden** (Sweden), December 30, 2003.

KOBASEW, Chuck

(KOH-buh-soo, CHUK)   **CGY.**

Center. Shoots left. 5'11", 195 lbs.   Born, Osoyoos, B.C., April 17, 1982. Calgary's 1st choice, 14th overall, in 2001 Entry Draft.

Season	Club	League	GP	G	A	Pts	PIM	PP	SH	GW	S	%	+/-	TF	F%	Min	GP	G	A	Pts	PIM	PP	SH	GW	Min
1997-98	Osoyoos Heat	KIJHL	6	2	2	4	2																		
1998-99	Osoyoos Heat	KIJHL	23	25	24	49																			
	Penticton	BCHL	30	11	17	28	18																		
99-2000	Penticton	BCHL	58	*54	52	106	83																		
2000-01	Boston College	H-East	43	27	22	49	38																		
2001-02	Kelowna Rockets	WHL	55	41	21	62	114										15	10	5	15	22				
2002-03	**Calgary**	**NHL**	23	4	2	6	8	1	0	1	29	13.8	-3	5	0.0	11:48									
	Saint John Flames	AHL	48	21	12	33	61																		
2003-04	**Calgary**	**NHL**	70	6	11	17	51	3	0	1	78	7.7	-12	91	42.9	10:22	26	0	1	1	24	0	0	0	9:02
NHL Totals			93	10	13	23	59	4	0	1	107	9.3		96	40.6	10:44	26	0	1	1	24	0	0	0	9:02

Hockey East Second All-Star Team (2001) • Hockey East Rookie of the Year (2001) • NCAA Championship All-Tournament Team (2001) • NCAA Championship Tournament MVP (2001)
• Left **Boston College** (H-East) and signed with **Kelowna** (WHL), August 13, 2001.

KOIVISTO, Tom

(KOI-vihs-toh, TAWM)

Defense. Shoots right. 5'10", 194 lbs.   Born, Turku, Finland, June 4, 1974. St. Louis' 8th choice, 253rd overall, in 2002 Entry Draft.

Season	Club	League	GP	G	A	Pts	PIM	PP	SH	GW	S	%	+/-	TF	F%	Min	GP	G	A	Pts	PIM
1991-92	TPS Turku Jr.	Finn-Jr.	36	4	9	13	40										8	1	3	4	12
1992-93	TPS Turku Jr.	Finn-Jr.	21	10	8	18	30										5	1	1	2	6
	Kiekoo-67 Turku	Finland-2	16	0	4	4	4														
	TPS Turku	Fiinland	1	0	0	0	0										1	0	0	0	0
1993-94	TPS Turku Jr.	Finn-Jr.	10	4	5	9	16										7	0	5	5	4
	Kiekko-67 Turku	Finland-2	16	4	12	16	2														
	TPS Turku	Finland	18	2	5	7	4										1	0	1	1	2
1994-95	TPS Turku Jr.	Finn-Jr.	5	0	2	2	8														
	Kiekko-67 Turku	Finland-2	14	7	3	10	6														
	TPS Turku	Finland	4	0	0	0	0														
	HPK Hameenlina	Finland	25	3	3	6	16														
1995-96	HPK Hameenlina	Finland	50	8	11	19	52										9	1	2	3	6
1996-97	HPK Hameenlina	Finland	46	18	17	35	50										10	4	2	6	6
1997-98	HPK Hameenlina	Finland	23	6	6	12	28														
	HPK Hameenlina	EuroHL	3	1	0	1	0														
1998-99	HPK Hameenlina	Finland	52	13	26	39	91										8	5	1	6	14
99-2000	Jokerit Helsinki	Finland	43	8	20	28	58										11	2	1	3	2
2000-01	Jokerit Helsinki	Finland	47	8	15	23	36										5	0	0	0	2
2001-02	Jokerit Helsinki	Finland	43	8	14	22	30										12	3	*8	11	2
2002-03	**St. Louis**	**NHL**	22	2	4	6	10	0	0	1	26	7.7	1	0	0.0	16:44					
	Worcester IceCats	AHL	47	4	13	17	32										3	0	1	1	0
2003-04	Worcester IceCats	AHL	28	4	13	17	16														
	Springfield	AHL	17	0	8	8	14														
NHL Totals			22	2	4	6	10	0	0	1	26	7.7		0	0.0	16:44					

Finnish Elite League All-Star Team (2002) • Finnish Elite League Best Defenseman (2002)
Signed as a free agent by **SC Langnau** (Swiss), May 26, 2003. Traded to **Phoenix** by **St. Louis** for future considerations, March 9, 2004. Signed as a free agent by **Vastra Frolunda** (Sweden), April 15, 2004.

KOIVU, Saku

(KOI-voo, SA-koo)   **MTL.**

Center. Shoots left. 5'10", 181 lbs.   Born, Turku, Finland, November 23, 1974. Montreal's 1st choice, 21st overall, in 1993 Entry Draft.

Season	Club	League	GP	G	A	Pts	PIM	PP	SH	GW	S	%	+/-	TF	F%	Min	GP	G	A	Pts	PIM	PP	SH	GW	Min
1990-91	TPS Turku-B	Finn-Jr.	24	20	28	48	26																		
1991-92	TPS Turku-B	Finn-Jr.	12	3	7	10	6																		
	TPS Turku Jr.	Finn-Jr.	34	25	28	53	57										8	5	*9	*14	6				
1992-93	TPS Turku	Finland	46	3	7	10	28										11	3	2	5					
1993-94	TPS Turku	Finland	47	23	30	53	42										11	4	8	12	16				
	Finland	Olympics	8	4	3	7	12																		
1994-95	TPS Turku	Finland	45	27	*47	*74	73										13	*7	10	17	16				
1995-96	**Montreal**	**NHL**	82	20	25	45	40	8	3	2	136	14.7	-7				6	3	1	4	8	0	0	0	
1996-97	**Montreal**	**NHL**	50	17	39	56	38	5	0	3	135	12.6	7				5	1	3	4	10	0	0	0	
1997-98	**Montreal**	**NHL**	69	14	43	57	48	2	2	3	145	9.7	8				6	2	3	5	4				
	Finland	Olympics	6	2	*8	*10	4																		
1998-99	**Montreal**	**NHL**	65	14	30	44	38	4	0	2	145	9.7	-7	1427	52.6	20:02									
99-2000	**Montreal**	**NHL**	24	3	18	21	14	1	0	0	53	5.7	7	495	52.9	19:13									
2000-01	**Montreal**	**NHL**	54	17	30	47	40	7	0	3	113	15.0	2	1092	47.6	21:23									
2001-02	**Montreal**	**NHL**	3	0	2	2	0	0	0	0	2	0.0	2	13	61.5	13:57	12	4	6	10	4	1	0	1	15:54

			Regular Season														Playoffs								
Season	Club	League	GP	G	A	Pts	PIM	PP	SH	GW	S	%	+/-	TF	F%	Min	GP	G	A	Pts	PIM	PP	SH	GW	Min
2002-03	**Montreal**	**NHL**	82	21	50	71	72	5	1	5	147	14.3	5	1566	49.6	19:14	....	....	....	....	....	....	....	....	....
2003-04	**Montreal**	**NHL**	68	14	41	55	52	5	0	3	112	12.5	–5	1194	53.9	19:18	11	3	8	11	10	2	0	0	20:34
	NHL Totals		497	120	278	398	342	37	8	19	988	12.1		5787	51.2	19:46	40	13	21	34	34	4	0	1	18:08

Bill Masterton Memorial Trophy (2002)

Played in NHL All-Star Game (1998)

Missed majority of 1999-2000 season recovering from shoulder injury suffered in game vs. NY Rangers, October 30, 1999. • Missed majority of 2001-02 season recovering from non-Hodgkin's lymphoma, September 6, 2001.

KOLANOS, Krystofer

(koh-LA-nohs, KRIHS) **PHX.**

Center. Shoots right. 6'3", 206 lbs. Born, Calgary, Alta., July 27, 1981. Phoenix's 1st choice, 19th overall, in 2000 Entry Draft.

			Regular Season														Playoffs								
Season	Club	League	GP	G	A	Pts	PIM	PP	SH	GW	S	%	+/-	TF	F%	Min	GP	G	A	Pts	PIM	PP	SH	GW	Min
1996-97	Calgary Flames	AAHA	24	24	35	59	....	....	....	....	....	....	....	....	....	....	....	....	....	....	....	....	....	....	....
1997-98	Calgary Buffaloes	AMHL	34	34	43	77	29	....	....	....	....	....	....	....	....	....	....	....	....	....	....	....	....	....	....
1998-99	Calgary Royals	AJHL	58	43	67	110	98	....	....	....	....	....	....	....	....	....	....	....	....	....	....	....	....	....	....
99-2000	Boston College	H-East	42	16	16	32	48	....	....	....	....	....	....	....	....	....	....	....	....	....	....	....	....	....	....
2000-01	Boston College	H-East	41	25	25	50	54	....	....	....	....	....	....	....	....	....	....	....	....	....	....	....	....	....	....
2001-02	**Phoenix**	**NHL**	57	11	11	22	48	0	0	5	81	13.6	6	703	46.4	13:05	2	0	0	0	6	0	0	0	11:12
2002-03	**Phoenix**	**NHL**	2	0	0	0	0	0	0	0	8	0.0	0	16	31.3	14:06	....	....	....	....	....	....	....	....	....
2003-04	**Phoenix**	**NHL**	41	4	6	10	24	1	0	1	61	6.6	–9	283	43.8	13:31	....	....	....	....	....	....	....	....	....
	Springfield	AHL	32	10	11	21	38	....	....	....	....	....	....	....	....	....	....	....	....	....	....	....	....	....	....
	NHL Totals		100	15	17	32	72	1	0	6	150	10.0		1002	45.4	13:17	2	0	0	0	6	0	0	0	11:12

Hockey East All-Rookie Team (2000) • Hockey East Second All-Star Team (2001) • NCAA East Second All-American Team (2001) • NCAA Championship All-Tournament Team (2001) • Missed majority of 2002-03 season recovering from head injury suffered in game vs. Pittsburgh, March 20, 2002.

KOLNIK, Juraj

(KOHL-nihk, YEW-igh) **FLA.**

Right wing. Shoots right. 5'10", 190 lbs. Born, Nitra, Czech., November 13, 1980. NY Islanders' 7th choice, 101st overall, in 1999 Entry Draft.

			Regular Season														Playoffs								
Season	Club	League	GP	G	A	Pts	PIM	PP	SH	GW	S	%	+/-	TF	F%	Min	GP	G	A	Pts	PIM	PP	SH	GW	Min
1997-98	Nitra Jr.	Slovak-Jr.	26	28	16	44	50	....	....	....	....	....	....	....	....	....	....	....	....	....	....	....	....	....	....
	Nitra	Slovakia	28	1	3	4	6	....	....	....	....	....	....	....	....	....	....	....	....	....	....	....	....	....	....
1998-99	Quebec Remparts	QMJHL	12	6	5	11	6	....	....	....	....	....	....	....	....	....	....	....	....	....	....	....	....	....	....
	Rimouski Oceanic	QMJHL	50	36	37	73	34	....	....	....	....	....	....	....	....	....	11	9	6	15	6	....	....	....	....
99-2000	Rimouski Oceanic	QMJHL	47	53	53	106	53	....	....	....	....	....	....	....	....	....	14	10	17	27	16	....	....	....	....
2000-01	**NY Islanders**	**NHL**	29	4	3	7	12	0	0	0	38	10.5	–8	1	100.0	10:28	....	....	....	....	....	....	....	....	....
	Lowell	AHL	25	2	6	8	18	....	....	....	....	....	....	....	....	....	....	....	....	....	....	....	....	....	....
	Springfield	AHL	29	15	20	35	20	....	....	....	....	....	....	....	....	....	....	....	....	....	....	....	....	....	....
2001-02	**NY Islanders**	**NHL**	7	2	0	2	0	1	0	0	10	20.0	–2	1	0.0	7:57	....	....	....	....	....	....	....	....	....
	Bridgeport	AHL	67	18	30	48	40	....	....	....	....	....	....	....	....	....	20	7	14	21	17	....	....	....	....
2002-03	**Florida**	**NHL**	10	0	1	1	0	0	0	0	14	0.0	1	1	0.0	10:33	....	....	....	....	....	....	....	....	....
	San Antonio	AHL	65	25	15	40	36	....	....	....	....	....	....	....	....	....	3	0	1	1	4	....	....	....	....
2003-04	**Florida**	**NHL**	53	14	11	25	14	2	0	1	100	14.0	–7	25	64.0	16:05	....	....	....	....	....	....	....	....	....
	San Antonio	AHL	15	2	14	16	21	....	....	....	....	....	....	....	....	....	....	....	....	....	....	....	....	....	....
	NHL Totals		99	20	15	35	26	3	0	1	162	12.3		28	60.7	13:18	....	....	....	....	....	....	....	....	....

Memorial Cup All-Star Team (2000)

Traded to **Florida** by **NY Islanders** with NY Islanders' 9th round choice (later traded to San Jose – San Jose selected Carter Lee) in 2003 Entry Draft for Sven Butenschon, October 11, 2002.

KOLTSOV, Konstantin

(kohlt-SAHV, kawn-stuhn-TEEN) **PIT.**

Right wing. Shoots left. 6', 206 lbs. Born, Minsk, USSR, April 17, 1981. Pittsburgh's 1st choice, 18th overall, in 1999 Entry Draft.

			Regular Season														Playoffs								
Season	Club	League	GP	G	A	Pts	PIM	PP	SH	GW	S	%	+/-	TF	F%	Min	GP	G	A	Pts	PIM	PP	SH	GW	Min
1997-98	Cherepovets 2	Russia-3	44	11	12	23	16	....	....	....	....	....	....	....	....	....	....	....	....	....	....	....	....	....	....
	Cherepovets	Russia	2	0	0	0	2	....	....	....	....	....	....	....	....	....	....	....	....	....	....	....	....	....	....
1998-99	Cherepovets 3	Russia-4	2	0	1	1	2	....	....	....	....	....	....	....	....	....	....	....	....	....	....	....	....	....	....
	Cherepovets 2	Russia-3	11	1	4	5	18	....	....	....	....	....	....	....	....	....	....	....	....	....	....	....	....	....	....
	Cherepovets	Russia	33	3	0	3	8	....	....	....	....	....	....	....	....	....	1	0	0	0	2	....	....	....	....
99-2000	Magnitogorsk	Russia	30	3	4	7	12	....	....	....	....	....	....	....	....	....	11	1	1	2	6	....	....	....	....
2000-01	Ak Bars Kazan	Russia	24	7	8	15	10	....	....	....	....	....	....	....	....	....	2	0	0	0	4	....	....	....	....
2001-02	Ak Bars Kazan	Russia	10	1	2	3	2	....	....	....	....	....	....	....	....	....	....	....	....	....	....	....	....	....	....
	Spartak Mos. 2	Russia-3	2	0	1	1	0	....	....	....	....	....	....	....	....	....	....	....	....	....	....	....	....	....	....
	Spartak Moscow	Russia	23	1	0	1	12	....	....	....	....	....	....	....	....	....	....	....	....	....	....	....	....	....	....
	Belarus	Olympics	2	0	0	0	0	....	....	....	....	....	....	....	....	....	....	....	....	....	....	....	....	....	....
2002-03	**Pittsburgh**	**NHL**	2	0	0	0	0	0	0	0	4	0.0	–2	0	0.0	13:06	....	....	....	....	....	....	....	....	....
	Wilkes-Barre	AHL	65	9	21	30	41	....	....	....	....	....	....	....	....	....	6	2	4	6	4	....	....	....	....
2003-04	**Pittsburgh**	**NHL**	82	9	20	29	30	2	0	3	123	7.3	–30	12	33.3	15:21	....	....	....	....	....	....	....	....	....
	Wilkes-Barre	AHL	....	....	....	....	....	....	....	....	....	....	....	....	....	....	24	6	11	17	18	....	....	....	....
	NHL Totals		84	9	20	29	30	2	0	3	127	7.1		12	33.3	15:18	....	....	....	....	....	....	....	....	....

KOMARNISKI, Zenith

(KOH-mahr-NIHS-kee, ZEE-nihth) **CBJ**

Left wing. Shoots left. 6', 200 lbs. Born, Edmonton, Alta., August 13, 1978. Vancouver's 2nd choice, 75th overall, in 1996 Entry Draft.

			Regular Season														Playoffs								
Season	Club	League	GP	G	A	Pts	PIM	PP	SH	GW	S	%	+/-	TF	F%	Min	GP	G	A	Pts	PIM	PP	SH	GW	Min
1993-94	Ft. Saskatchewan	AMHL	32	14	32	46	42	....	....	....	....	....	....	....	....	....	....	....	....	....	....	....	....	....	....
1994-95	Tri-City	WHL	66	5	19	24	110	....	....	....	....	....	....	....	....	....	17	1	2	3	47	....	....	....	....
1995-96	Tri-City	WHL	42	5	21	26	85	....	....	....	....	....	....	....	....	....	....	....	....	....	....	....	....	....	....
1996-97	Tri-City	WHL	58	12	44	56	112	....	....	....	....	....	....	....	....	....	....	....	....	....	....	....	....	....	....
1997-98	Tri-City	WHL	3	0	4	4	18	....	....	....	....	....	....	....	....	....	....	....	....	....	....	....	....	....	....
	Spokane Chiefs	WHL	43	7	20	27	90	....	....	....	....	....	....	....	....	....	18	4	6	10	49	....	....	....	....
1998-99	Syracuse Crunch	AHL	58	9	19	28	89	....	....	....	....	....	....	....	....	....	....	....	....	....	....	....	....	....	....
99-2000	**Vancouver**	**NHL**	18	1	1	2	8	0	0	0	21	4.8	–1	0	0.0	16:11	....	....	....	....	....	....	....	....	....
	Syracuse Crunch	AHL	42	4	12	16	130	....	....	....	....	....	....	....	....	....	4	2	0	2	6	....	....	....	....
2000-01	Kansas City	IHL	70	7	22	29	191	....	....	....	....	....	....	....	....	....	....	....	....	....	....	....	....	....	....
2001-02	Manitoba Moose	AHL	77	5	20	25	153	....	....	....	....	....	....	....	....	....	7	0	2	2	13	....	....	....	....
2002-03	**Vancouver**	**NHL**	1	0	0	0	2	0	0	0	0	0.0	0	0	0.0	6:25	....	....	....	....	....	....	....	....	....
	Manitoba Moose	AHL	53	15	8	23	94	....	....	....	....	....	....	....	....	....	13	2	2	4	30	....	....	....	....
2003-04	Manitoba Moose	AHL	10	0	0	0	35	....	....	....	....	....	....	....	....	....	....	....	....	....	....	....	....	....	....
	Columbus	**NHL**	2	0	0	0	0	0	0	0	1	0.0	0	0	0.0	14:48	....	....	....	....	....	....	....	....	....
	Syracuse Crunch	AHL	54	2	22	24	84	....	....	....	....	....	....	....	....	....	7	0	1	1	4	....	....	....	....
	NHL Totals		21	1	1	2	10	0	0	0	22	4.5		0	0.0	15:35	....	....	....	....	....	....	....	....	....

WHL West First All-Star Team (1997)

Traded to **Columbus** by **Vancouver** for Sean Pronger, October 30, 2003.

KOMISAREK, Mike

(koh-mih-SAIR-ehk, MIGHK) **MTL.**

Defense. Shoots right. 6'4", 237 lbs. Born, Islip Terrace, NY, January 19, 1982. Montreal's 1st choice, 7th overall, in 2001 Entry Draft.

			Regular Season														Playoffs								
Season	Club	League	GP	G	A	Pts	PIM	PP	SH	GW	S	%	+/-	TF	F%	Min	GP	G	A	Pts	PIM	PP	SH	GW	Min
1998-99	New England	EJHL	53	17	24	51	....	....	....	....	....	....	....	....	....	....	....	....	....	....	....	....	....	....	....
99-2000	U.S. National U-18	USDP	51	5	8	13	124	....	....	....	....	....	....	....	....	....	....	....	....	....	....	....	....	....	....
2000-01	U. of Michigan	CCHA	41	4	12	16	77	....	....	....	....	....	....	....	....	....	....	....	....	....	....	....	....	....	....
2001-02	U. of Michigan	CCHA	40	11	19	30	70	....	....	....	....	....	....	....	....	....	....	....	....	....	....	....	....	....	....
2002-03	**Montreal**	**NHL**	21	0	1	1	28	0	0	0	26	0.0	–6	0	0.0	16:42	....	....	....	....	....	....	....	....	....
	Hamilton	AHL	56	5	25	30	79	....	....	....	....	....	....	....	....	....	23	1	5	6	60	....	....	....	....
2003-04	**Montreal**	**NHL**	46	0	4	4	34	0	0	0	40	0.0	4	0	0.0	12:00	7	0	0	0	8	0	0	0	14:09
	Hamilton	AHL	18	2	7	9	47	....	....	....	....	....	....	....	....	....	....	....	....	....	....	....	....	....	....
	NHL Totals		67	0	5	5	62	0	0	0	66	0.0		0	0.0	13:28	7	0	0	0	8	0	0	0	14:09

CCHA First All-Star Team (2002) • NCAA West First All-American Team (2002) • AHL All-Rookie Team (2003)

KONDRATIEV, Maxim

(kohn-DRAT-yehv, mahx-EEM) **NYR**

Defense. Shoots left. 6'1", 176 lbs. Born, Togliatti, USSR, January 20, 1983. Toronto's 7th choice, 168th overall, in 2001 Entry Draft.

			Regular Season														Playoffs								
Season	Club	League	GP	G	A	Pts	PIM	PP	SH	GW	S	%	+/-	TF	F%	Min	GP	G	A	Pts	PIM	PP	SH	GW	Min
99-2000	Lada Togliatti 2	Russia-3	16	0	2	2	6	....	....	....	....	....	....	....	....	....	....	....	....	....	....	....	....	....	....
	Lada Togliatti	Russia-2	20	1	1	2	....	....	....	....	....	....	....	....	....	....	....	....	....	....	....	....	....	....	....
2000-01	Lada Togliatti 2	Russia-3	STATISTICS NOT AVAILABLE																						
	CSK VVS Samara	Russia-2	18	2	1	3	24	....	....	....	....	....	....	....	....	....	....	....	....	....	....	....	....	....	....
2001-02	Lada Togliatti	Russia	43	3	3	6	32	....	....	....	....	....	....	....	....	....	4	0	0	0	0	....	....	....	....
2002-03	Lada Togliatti	Russia	47	2	3	5	56	....	....	....	....	....	....	....	....	....	10	0	0	0	6	....	....	....	....
2003-04	**Toronto**	**NHL**	**7**	**0**	**0**	**0**	**2**	**0**	**0**	**0**	**6**	**0.0**	**0**	**0**	**0.0**	**15:36**	....	....	....	....	....	....	....	....	....
	St. John's	AHL	18	3	5	8	10	....	....	....	....	....	....	....	....	....	....	....	....	....	....	....	....	....	....
	Lada Togliatti	Russia	29	2	3	5	85	....	....	....	....	....	....	....	....	....	6	0	0	0	16	....	....	....	....
	NHL Totals		**7**	**0**	**0**	**0**	**2**	**0**	**0**	**0**	**6**	**0.0**		**0**	**0.0**	**15:36**	....	....	....	....	....	....	....	....	....

Assigned to **Lada Togliatti** (Russia) by **Toronto**, December 16, 2003. Traded to **NY Rangers** by **Toronto** with Jarkko Immonen, Toronto's 1st round choice (later traded to Calgary - Calgary selected Kris Chucko) in 2004 Entry Draft and Toronto's 2nd round choice in 2005 Entry Draft for Brian Leetch and Edmonton's 4th round choice (previously acquired, Toronto selected Roman Kukumberg) in 2004 Entry Draft, March 3, 2004.

KONOWALCHUK, Steve

(kahn-uh-WAHL-chuhk, STEEV) **COL.**

Left wing. Shoots left. 6'2", 207 lbs. Born, Salt Lake City, UT, November 11, 1972. Washington's 5th choice, 58th overall, in 1991 Entry Draft.

			Regular Season														Playoffs								
Season	Club	League	GP	G	A	Pts	PIM	PP	SH	GW	S	%	+/-	TF	F%	Min	GP	G	A	Pts	PIM	PP	SH	GW	Min
1989-90	Prince Albert	SMHL	36	30	28	58	22	....	....	....	....	....	....	....	....	....	....	....	....	....	....	....	....	....	....
1990-91	Portland	WHL	72	43	49	92	78	....	....	....	....	....	....	....	....	....	....	....	....	....	....	....	....	....	....
1991-92	Portland	WHL	64	51	53	104	95	....	....	....	....	....	....	....	....	....	6	3	6	9	12	....	....	....	....
	Washington	**NHL**	**1**	**0**	**0**	**0**	**0**	**0**	**0**	**0**	**1**	**0.0**	**0**	....	....	....	....	....	....	....	....	....	....	....	....
	Baltimore	AHL	3	1	1	2	0	....	....	....	....	....	....	....	....	....	....	....	....	....	....	....	....	....	....
1992-93	**Washington**	**NHL**	**36**	**4**	**7**	**11**	**16**	**1**	**0**	**1**	**34**	**11.8**	**4**	....	....	....	**2**	**0**	**1**	**1**	**0**	**0**	**0**	**0**	....
	Baltimore	AHL	37	18	28	46	74	....	....	....	....	....	....	....	....	....	....	....	....	....	....	....	....	....	....
1993-94	**Washington**	**NHL**	**62**	**12**	**14**	**26**	**33**	**0**	**0**	**0**	**63**	**19.0**	**9**	....	....	....	**11**	**0**	**1**	**1**	**10**	**0**	**0**	**0**	....
	Portland Pirates	AHL	8	11	4	15	4	....	....	....	....	....	....	....	....	....	....	....	....	....	....	....	....	....	....
1994-95	**Washington**	**NHL**	**46**	**11**	**14**	**25**	**44**	**3**	**3**	**3**	**88**	**12.5**	**7**	....	....	....	**7**	**2**	**5**	**7**	**12**	**0**	**1**	**0**	....
1995-96	**Washington**	**NHL**	**70**	**23**	**22**	**45**	**92**	**7**	**1**	**3**	**197**	**11.7**	**13**	....	....	....	**2**	**0**	**2**	**2**	**0**	**0**	**0**	**0**	....
1996-97	**Washington**	**NHL**	**78**	**17**	**25**	**42**	**67**	**2**	**1**	**3**	**155**	**11.0**	**-3**	....	....	....	....	....	....	....	....	....	....	....	....
1997-98	**Washington**	**NHL**	**80**	**10**	**24**	**34**	**80**	**2**	**0**	**2**	**131**	**7.6**	**9**	....	....	....	....	....	....	....	....	....	....	....	....
1998-99	**Washington**	**NHL**	**45**	**12**	**12**	**24**	**26**	**4**	**1**	**2**	**98**	**12.2**	**0**	**124**	**51.6**	**17:50**	....	....	....	....	....	....	....	....	....
99-2000	**Washington**	**NHL**	**82**	**16**	**27**	**43**	**80**	**3**	**0**	**1**	**146**	**11.0**	**19**	**147**	**49.7**	**17:36**	**5**	**1**	**0**	**1**	**2**	**0**	**1**	**0**	**17:25**
2000-01	**Washington**	**NHL**	**82**	**24**	**23**	**47**	**87**	**6**	**0**	**5**	**163**	**14.7**	**8**	**91**	**55.0**	**17:04**	**6**	**2**	**3**	**5**	**14**	**2**	**0**	**0**	**19:39**
2001-02	**Washington**	**NHL**	**28**	**2**	**12**	**14**	**23**	**0**	**0**	**0**	**36**	**5.6**	**-2**	**64**	**56.3**	**16:29**	....	....	....	....	....	....	....	....	....
2002-03	**Washington**	**NHL**	**77**	**15**	**15**	**30**	**71**	**2**	**0**	**3**	**119**	**12.6**	**3**	**92**	**44.6**	**16:42**	**6**	**0**	**0**	**0**	**6**	**0**	**0**	**0**	**16:07**
2003-04	**Washington**	**NHL**	**6**	**0**	**1**	**1**	**0**	**0**	**0**	**0**	**7**	**0.0**	**-5**	**7**	**57.1**	**14:38**	....	....	....	....	....	....	....	....	....
	Colorado	**NHL**	**76**	**19**	**20**	**39**	**70**	**3**	**0**	**3**	**145**	**13.1**	**2**	**338**	**47.0**	**18:20**	**11**	**4**	**0**	**4**	**12**	**4**	**0**	**1**	**18:15**
	NHL Totals		**769**	**165**	**216**	**381**	**689**	**33**	**6**	**26**	**1383**	**11.9**		**863**	**49.5**	**17:22**	**50**	**9**	**12**	**21**	**56**	**6**	**2**	**1**	**17:57**

WHL West First All-Star Team (1992) • WHL MVP (1992)

• Missed majority of 2001-02 season recovering from shoulder injury suffered in game vs. Los Angeles, October 16, 2001. Traded to **Colorado** by **Washington** with Washington's 3rd round choice (later traded to Carolina – Carolina selected Casey Borer) in 2004 Entry Draft for Bates Battaglia and Jonas Johansson, October 22, 2003.

KOROLEV, Evgeny

(KOH-roh-lehv, ehv-GEHN-ee) **NYI**

Defense. Shoots left. 6'1", 214 lbs. Born, Moscow, USSR, July 24, 1978. NY Islanders' 6th choice, 182nd overall, in 1998 Entry Draft.

			Regular Season														Playoffs								
Season	Club	League	GP	G	A	Pts	PIM	PP	SH	GW	S	%	+/-	TF	F%	Min	GP	G	A	Pts	PIM	PP	SH	GW	Min
1995-96	Peterborough	OHL	60	2	12	14	60	....	....	....	....	....	....	....	....	....	6	0	0	0	2	....	....	....	....
1996-97	Peterborough	OHL	64	5	17	22	60	....	....	....	....	....	....	....	....	....	11	1	1	2	8	....	....	....	....
1997-98	Peterborough	OHL	37	5	21	26	39	....	....	....	....	....	....	....	....	....	....	....	....	....	....	....	....	....	....
	London Knights	OHL	27	4	10	14	36	....	....	....	....	....	....	....	....	....	15	2	7	9	29	....	....	....	....
1998-99	Roanoke Express	ECHL	2	0	1	1	0	....	....	....	....	....	....	....	....	....	....	....	....	....	....	....	....	....	....
	Lowell	AHL	54	2	6	8	48	....	....	....	....	....	....	....	....	....	2	0	1	1	0	....	....	....	....
99-2000	**NY Islanders**	**NHL**	**17**	**1**	**2**	**3**	**8**	**0**	**0**	**0**	**7**	**14.3**	**-10**	**0**	**0.0**	**16:12**	....	....	....	....	....	....	....	....	....
	Lowell	AHL	57	1	10	11	61	....	....	....	....	....	....	....	....	....	6	0	0	0	4	....	....	....	....
2000-01	**NY Islanders**	**NHL**	**8**	**0**	**0**	**0**	**6**	**0**	**0**	**0**	**11**	**0.0**	**0**	**0**	**0.0**	**16:40**	....	....	....	....	....	....	....	....	....
	Chicago Wolves	IHL	4	0	1	1	0	....	....	....	....	....	....	....	....	....	....	....	....	....	....	....	....	....	....
	Louisville Panthers	AHL	36	2	14	16	68	....	....	....	....	....	....	....	....	....	....	....	....	....	....	....	....	....	....
2001-02	**NY Islanders**	**NHL**	**17**	**0**	**2**	**2**	**6**	**0**	**0**	**0**	**9**	**0.0**	**0**	**0**	**0.0**	**10:22**	**2**	**0**	**0**	**0**	**0**	**0**	**0**	**0**	**5:35**
	Bridgeport	AHL	53	5	8	13	30	....	....	....	....	....	....	....	....	....	....	....	....	....	....	....	....	....	....
2002-03	Yaroslavl	Russia	16	1	2	3	22	....	....	....	....	....	....	....	....	....	8	0	0	0	6	....	....	....	....
2003-04	Yaroslav 2	Russia-3	3	0	1	1	0	....	....	....	....	....	....	....	....	....	....	....	....	....	....	....	....	....	....
	Yaroslavl	Russia	25	1	1	2	39	....	....	....	....	....	....	....	....	....	....	....	....	....	....	....	....	....	....
	Lada Togliatti	Russia	29	2	3	5	85	....	....	....	....	....	....	....	....	....	6	0	0	0	16	....	....	....	....
	NHL Totals		**42**	**1**	**4**	**5**	**20**	**0**	**0**	**0**	**27**	**3.7**		**0**	**0.0**	**13:56**	**2**	**0**	**0**	**0**	**0**	**0**	**0**	**0**	**5:35**

• Re-entered NHL Entry Draft. Originally NY Islanders' 9th choice, 192nd overall, in 1996 Entry Draft.
Signed as a free agent by **Yaroslavl** (Russia), October 14, 2002.

KOROLEV, Igor

(KOH-roh-lehv, EE-gohr)

Center. Shoots left. 6'1", 190 lbs. Born, Moscow, USSR, September 6, 1970. St. Louis' 1st choice, 38th overall, in 1992 Entry Draft.

			Regular Season														Playoffs								
Season	Club	League	GP	G	A	Pts	PIM	PP	SH	GW	S	%	+/-	TF	F%	Min	GP	G	A	Pts	PIM	PP	SH	GW	Min
1988-89	Dynamo Moscow	USSR	1	0	0	0	2	....	....	....	....	....	....	....	....	....	....	....	....	....	....	....	....	....	....
1989-90	Dynamo Moscow	USSR	17	3	2	5	2	....	....	....	....	....	....	....	....	....	....	....	....	....	....	....	....	....	....
1990-91	Dynamo Moscow	USSR	38	12	4	16	12	....	....	....	....	....	....	....	....	....	....	....	....	....	....	....	....	....	....
1991-92	Dynamo Moscow	CIS	39	15	12	27	16	....	....	....	....	....	....	....	....	....	....	....	....	....	....	....	....	....	....
1992-93	Dynamo Moscow	CIS	5	1	2	3	4	....	....	....	....	....	....	....	....	....	....	....	....	....	....	....	....	....	....
	St. Louis	**NHL**	**74**	**4**	**23**	**27**	**20**	**2**	**0**	**0**	**76**	**5.3**	**-1**	....	....	....	**3**	**0**	**0**	**0**	**0**	**0**	**0**	**0**	....
1993-94	**St. Louis**	**NHL**	**73**	**6**	**10**	**16**	**40**	**0**	**0**	**1**	**93**	**6.5**	**-12**	....	....	....	**2**	**0**	**0**	**0**	**0**	**0**	**0**	**0**	....
1994-95	Dynamo Moscow	CIS	13	4	6	10	18	....	....	....	....	....	....	....	....	....	....	....	....	....	....	....	....	....	....
	Winnipeg	**NHL**	**45**	**8**	**22**	**30**	**10**	**1**	**0**	**1**	**85**	**9.4**	**1**	....	....	....	....	....	....	....	....	....	....	....	....
1995-96	**Winnipeg**	**NHL**	**73**	**22**	**29**	**51**	**42**	**8**	**0**	**5**	**165**	**13.3**	**1**	....	....	....	**6**	**0**	**3**	**3**	**0**	**0**	**0**	**0**	....
1996-97	**Phoenix**	**NHL**	**41**	**3**	**7**	**10**	**28**	**2**	**0**	**0**	**41**	**7.3**	**-5**	....	....	....	**1**	**0**	**0**	**0**	**0**	**0**	**0**	**0**	....
	Michigan	IHL	4	2	2	4	0	....	....	....	....	....	....	....	....	....	....	....	....	....	....	....	....	....	....
	Phoenix	IHL	4	2	6	8	4	....	....	....	....	....	....	....	....	....	....	....	....	....	....	....	....	....	....
1997-98	**Toronto**	**NHL**	**78**	**17**	**22**	**39**	**22**	**6**	**3**	**5**	**97**	**17.5**	**-18**	....	....	....	....	....	....	....	....	....	....	....	....
1998-99	**Toronto**	**NHL**	**66**	**13**	**34**	**47**	**46**	**1**	**0**	**2**	**99**	**13.1**	**11**	**973**	**42.0**	**18:06**	**1**	**0**	**0**	**0**	**0**	**0**	**0**	**0**	**7:42**
99-2000	**Toronto**	**NHL**	**80**	**20**	**26**	**46**	**22**	**5**	**3**	**4**	**101**	**19.8**	**12**	**964**	**41.3**	**17:56**	**12**	**0**	**4**	**4**	**6**	**0**	**0**	**0**	**18:56**
2000-01	**Toronto**	**NHL**	**73**	**10**	**19**	**29**	**28**	**2**	**0**	**0**	**78**	**12.8**	**3**	**569**	**42.5**	**15:41**	**11**	**0**	**0**	**0**	**0**	**0**	**0**	**0**	**17:43**
2001-02	**Chicago**	**NHL**	**82**	**9**	**20**	**29**	**20**	**0**	**1**	**1**	**78**	**11.5**	**-5**	**1166**	**41.1**	**16:49**	**5**	**0**	**1**	**1**	**0**	**0**	**0**	**0**	**15:50**
2002-03	**Chicago**	**NHL**	**48**	**4**	**5**	**9**	**30**	**1**	**0**	**1**	**32**	**12.5**	**-1**	**375**	**42.4**	**13:39**	....	....	....	....	....	....	....	....	....
	Norfolk Admirals	AHL	14	4	3	7	0	....	....	....	....	....	....	....	....	....	9	2	4	6	4	....	....	....	....
2003-04	**Chicago**	**NHL**	**62**	**3**	**10**	**13**	**22**	**0**	**0**	**1**	**38**	**7.9**	**-15**	**462**	**47.2**	**11:11**	....	....	....	....	....	....	....	....	....
	Norfolk Admirals	AHL	10	1	4	5	4	....	....	....	....	....	....	....	....	....	....	....	....	....	....	....	....	....	....
	NHL Totals		**795**	**119**	**227**	**346**	**330**	**28**	**7**	**21**	**983**	**12.1**		**4509**	**42.2**	**15:49**	**41**	**0**	**8**	**8**	**6**	**0**	**0**	**0**	**17:33**

Claimed by **Winnipeg** from **St. Louis** in Waiver Draft, January 18, 1995. Transferred to **Phoenix** after **Winnipeg** franchise relocated, July 1, 1996. Signed as a free agent by **Toronto**, September 29, 1997. Traded to **Chicago** by **Toronto** for Philadelphia's 3rd round choice (previously acquired, Toronto selected Nicolas Corbeil) in 2001 Entry Draft, June 23, 2001.

KOROLYUK, Alexander

(koh-roh-LYUHK, al-ehx-AN-duhr) **S.J.**

Left wing. Shoots left. 5'9", 190 lbs. Born, Moscow, USSR, January 15, 1976. San Jose's 6th choice, 141st overall, in 1994 Entry Draft.

			Regular Season														Playoffs								
Season	Club	League	GP	G	A	Pts	PIM	PP	SH	GW	S	%	+/-	TF	F%	Min	GP	G	A	Pts	PIM	PP	SH	GW	Min
1993-94	Krylja Sovetov	CIS	22	4	4	8	20	....	....	....	....	....	....	....	....	....	3	1	0	1	4	....	....	....	....
1994-95	Krylja Sovetov	CIS	52	16	13	29	62	....	....	....	....	....	....	....	....	....	4	1	2	3	4	....	....	....	....
1995-96	Krylja Sovetov	CIS	50	30	19	49	77	....	....	....	....	....	....	....	....	....	....	....	....	....	....	....	....	....	....
1996-97	Krylja Sovetov	Russia	17	8	5	13	46	....	....	....	....	....	....	....	....	....	....	....	....	....	....	....	....	....	....
	Manitoba Moose	IHL	42	20	16	36	71	....	....	....	....	....	....	....	....	....	....	....	....	....	....	....	....	....	....
1997-98	**San Jose**	**NHL**	**19**	**2**	**3**	**5**	**6**	**1**	**0**	**0**	**23**	**8.7**	**-5**	....	....	....	....	....	....	....	....	....	....	....	....
	Kentucky	AHL	44	16	23	39	96	....	....	....	....	....	....	....	....	....	3	0	0	0	0	....	....	....	....
1998-99	**San Jose**	**NHL**	**55**	**12**	**18**	**30**	**26**	**2**	**0**	**0**	**96**	**12.5**	**3**	**4**	**50.0**	**13:53**	**6**	**1**	**3**	**4**	**2**	**0**	**0**	**1**	**11:01**
	Kentucky	AHL	23	9	13	22	16	....	....	....	....	....	....	....	....	....	....	....	....	....	....	....	....	....	....

			Regular Season														Playoffs								
Season	Club	League	GP	G	A	Pts	PIM	PP	SH	GW	S	%	+/-	TF	F%	Min	GP	G	A	Pts	PIM	PP	SH	GW	Min
99-2000	San Jose	NHL	57	14	21	35	35	3	0	1	124	11.3	4	1	100.0	13:36	9	0	3	3	6	0	0	0	11:37
2000-01	Ak Bars Kazan	Russia	6	0	5	5	4	....	....	....	....	....	....	....	....	....	....	....	....	....	....	....	....	....	....
	San Jose	NHL	70	12	13	25	41	3	0	1	140	8.6	2	30	33.3	11:56	2	0	0	0	0	0	0	0	8:11
2001-02	San Jose	NHL	32	3	7	10	14	0	0	1	49	6.1	2	10	30.0	12:16	....	....	....	....	....	....	....	....	....
2002-03	Ak Bars Kazan	Russia	45	14	17	31	46	....	....	....	....	....	....	....	....	....	4	0	0	0	0	....	....	....	....
2003-04	San Jose	NHL	63	19	18	37	18	4	0	2	108	17.6	20	14	50.0	14:55	17	5	2	7	10	2	0	1	16:40
	NHL Totals		296	62	80	142	140	13	0	5	540	11.5		59	39.0	13:23	34	6	8	14	18	2	0	2	13:50

• Spent majority of 2001-02 season on practice roster. Signed as a free agent by **Ak Bars Kazan** (Russia) with San Jose retaining NHL rights, July 9, 2002.

KOSTOPOULOS, Tom

(kaw-STAWP-oh-lihs, TAWM)

Right wing. Shoots right. 6', 200 lbs. Born, Mississauga, Ont., January 24, 1979. Pittsburgh's 9th choice, 204th overall, in 1999 Entry Draft.

1995-96	Brampton	OPJHL	24	9	9	18	28	....	....	....	....	....	....	....	....	....	....	....	....	....	....	....	....	....	....
1996-97	London Knights	OHL	64	13	12	25	67	....	....	....	....	....	....	....	....	....	....	....	....	....	....	....	....	....	....
1997-98	London Knights	OHL	66	24	26	50	108	....	....	....	....	....	....	....	....	....	16	6	4	10	26	....	....	....	....
1998-99	London Knights	OHL	66	27	60	87	114	....	....	....	....	....	....	....	....	....	25	19	16	35	32	....	....	....	....
99-2000	Wilkes-Barre	AHL	76	26	32	58	121	....	....	....	....	....	....	....	....	....	....	....	....	....	....	....	....	....	....
2000-01	Wilkes-Barre	AHL	80	16	36	52	120	....	....	....	....	....	....	....	....	....	21	3	9	12	6	....	....	....	....
2001-02	Pittsburgh	NHL	11	1	2	3	9	0	0	0	8	12.5	–1	0	0.0	12:03	....	....	....	....	....	....	....	....	....
	Wilkes-Barre	AHL	70	27	26	53	112	....	....	....	....	....	....	....	....	....	....	....	....	....	....	....	....	....	....
2002-03	Pittsburgh	NHL	8	0	1	1	0	0	0	0	6	0.0	–4	2	0.0	4:33	....	....	....	....	....	....	....	....	....
	Wilkes-Barre	AHL	71	21	42	63	131	....	....	....	....	....	....	....	....	....	6	1	2	3	7	....	....	....	....
2003-04	Pittsburgh	NHL	60	9	13	22	67	2	1	1	101	8.9	–14	10	30.0	14:26	....	....	....	....	....	....	....	....	....
	Wilkes-Barre	AHL	21	7	13	20	43	....	....	....	....	....	....	....	....	....	24	7	16	23	32	....	....	....	....
	NHL Totals		79	10	16	26	76	2	1	1	115	8.7		12	25.0	13:06	....	....	....	....	....	....	....	....	....

KOTALIK, Ales

(KOH-tahl-eek, ALehsh) **BUF.**

Right wing. Shoots right. 6'1", 217 lbs. Born, Jindrichuv Hradec, Czech., December 23, 1978. Buffalo's 7th choice, 164th overall, in 1998 Entry Draft.

1993-94	C. Budejovice Jr.	Czech-Jr.	28	12	12	24	....	....	....	....	....	....	....	....	....	....	....	....	....	....	....	....	....	....	....
1994-95	C. Budejovice Jr.	Czech-Jr.	36	26	17	43	....	....	....	....	....	....	....	....	....	....	....	....	....	....	....	....	....	....	....
1995-96	C. Budejovice Jr.	Czech-Jr.	28	6	7	13	....	....	....	....	....	....	....	....	....	....	....	....	....	....	....	....	....	....	....
1996-97	C. Budejovice Jr.	Czech-Jr.	36	15	16	31	24	....	....	....	....	....	....	....	....	....	....	....	....	....	....	....	....	....	....
1997-98	Ceske Budejovice	Czech	47	9	7	16	14	....	....	....	....	....	....	....	....	....	....	....	....	....	....	....	....	....	....
1998-99	Ceske Budejovice	Czech	41	8	13	21	16	....	....	....	....	....	....	....	....	....	3	0	0	0	....	....	....	....	....
99-2000	Ceske Budejovice	Czech	43	7	12	19	34	....	....	....	....	....	....	....	....	....	3	0	1	1	6	....	....	....	....
2000-01	Ceske Budejovice	Czech	52	19	29	48	54	....	....	....	....	....	....	....	....	....	....	....	....	....	....	....	....	....	....
2001-02	Rochester	AHL	68	18	25	43	55	....	....	....	....	....	....	....	....	....	1	0	0	0	0	....	....	....	....
	Buffalo	NHL	13	1	3	4	2	0	0	0	21	4.8	–1	11	27.3	12:35	....	....	....	....	....	....	....	....	....
2002-03	Buffalo	NHL	68	21	14	35	30	4	0	2	138	15.2	–2	37	51.4	15:15	....	....	....	....	....	....	....	....	....
	Rochester	AHL	8	0	2	2	4	....	....	....	....	....	....	....	....	....	....	....	....	....	....	....	....	....	....
2003-04	Buffalo	NHL	62	15	11	26	41	2	0	3	142	10.6	–1	14	50.0	15:11	....	....	....	....	....	....	....	....	....
	NHL Totals		143	37	28	65	73	6	0	5	301	12.3		62	46.8	14:59	....	....	....	....	....	....	....	....	....

KOVALCHUK, Ilya

(koh-vuhl-CHOOK, IHL-yah) **ATL.**

Left wing. Shoots right. 6'2", 220 lbs. Born, Tver, USSR, April 15, 1983. Atlanta's 1st choice, 1st overall, in 2001 Entry Draft.

99-2000	Spartak Moscow	Russia-2	49	12	5	17	75	....	....	....	....	....	....	....	....	....	....	....	....	....	....	....	....	....	....
	Spartak Mos. 2	Russia-3	2	2	1	3	14	....	....	....	....	....	....	....	....	....	....	....	....	....	....	....	....	....	....
2000-01	Spartak Moscow	Russia-2	51	42	22	64	112	....	....	....	....	....	....	....	....	....	....	....	....	....	....	....	....	....	....
2001-02	Atlanta	NHL	65	29	22	51	28	7	0	4	184	15.8	–19	6	16.7	18:32	....	....	....	....	....	....	....	....	....
	Russia	Olympics	6	1	2	3	14	....	....	....	....	....	....	....	....	....	....	....	....	....	....	....	....	....	....
2002-03	Atlanta	NHL	81	38	29	67	57	9	0	3	257	14.8	–24	15	40.0	19:27	....	....	....	....	....	....	....	....	....
2003-04	Atlanta	NHL	81	*41	46	87	63	16	1	6	341	12.0	–10	28	32.1	23:41	....	....	....	....	....	....	....	....	....
	NHL Totals		227	108	97	205	148	32	1	13	782	13.8		49	32.7	20:42	....	....	....	....	....	....	....	....	....

NHL All-Rookie Team (2002) • NHL Second All-Star Team (2004) • Maurice "Rocket" Richard Trophy (2004) (tied with Jarome Iginla and Rick Nash)
Played in NHL All-Star Game (2004)

KOVALEV, Alex

(koh-VAH-lehv, al-EHX)

Right wing. Shoots left. 6'1", 220 lbs. Born, Togliatti, USSR, February 24, 1973. NY Rangers' 1st choice, 15th overall, in 1991 Entry Draft.

1989-90	Dynamo Moscow	USSR	1	0	0	0	0	....	....	....	....	....	....	....	....	....	....	....	....	....	....	....	....	....	....
1990-91	Dynamo Moscow	USSR	18	1	2	3	4	....	....	....	....	....	....	....	....	....	....	....	....	....	....	....	....	....	....
1991-92	Dynamo Moscow	CIS	33	16	9	25	20	....	....	....	....	....	....	....	....	....	....	....	....	....	....	....	....	....	....
	Russia	Olympics	8	1	2	3	14	....	....	....	....	....	....	....	....	....	....	....	....	....	....	....	....	....	....
1992-93	NY Rangers	NHL	65	20	18	38	79	3	0	3	134	14.9	–10	....	....	....	....	....	....	....	....	....	....	....	....
	Binghamton	AHL	13	13	11	24	35	....	....	....	....	....	....	....	....	....	9	3	5	8	14	....	....	....	....
1993-94 ♦	NY Rangers	NHL	76	23	33	56	154	7	0	3	184	12.5	18	....	....	....	23	9	12	21	18	5	0	2	....
1994-95	Lada Togliatti	CIS	12	8	8	16	49	....	....	....	....	....	....	....	....	....	....	....	....	....	....	....	....	....	....
	NY Rangers	NHL	48	13	15	28	30	1	1	1	103	12.6	–6	....	....	....	10	4	7	11	10	0	0	0	....
1995-96	NY Rangers	NHL	81	24	34	58	98	8	1	7	206	11.7	5	....	....	....	11	3	4	7	14	0	0	1	....
1996-97	NY Rangers	NHL	45	13	22	35	42	1	0	0	110	11.8	11	....	....	....	....	....	....	....	....	....	....	....	....
1997-98	NY Rangers	NHL	73	23	30	53	44	8	0	3	173	13.3	–22	....	....	....	....	....	....	....	....	....	....	....	....
1998-99	NY Rangers	NHL	14	3	4	7	12	1	0	1	35	8.6	–6	18	44.4	19:53	....	....	....	....	....	....	....	....	....
	Pittsburgh	NHL	63	20	26	46	37	5	1	4	156	12.8	8	226	43.4	20:30	10	5	7	12	14	0	0	1	20:24
99-2000	Pittsburgh	NHL	82	26	40	66	94	9	2	4	254	10.2	–3	306	47.4	22:53	11	1	5	6	10	0	0	0	26:35
2000-01	Pittsburgh	NHL	79	44	51	95	96	12	2	9	307	14.3	12	255	40.0	23:35	18	5	5	10	16	1	0	0	20:57
2001-02	Pittsburgh	NHL	67	32	44	76	80	8	1	3	266	12.0	2	179	45.3	24:03	....	....	....	....	....	....	....	....	....
	Russia	Olympics	6	3	1	4	4	....	....	....	....	....	....	....	....	....	....	....	....	....	....	....	....	....	....
2002-03	Pittsburgh	NHL	54	27	37	64	50	8	0	1	212	12.7	–11	19	31.6	24:03	....	....	....	....	....	....	....	....	....
	NY Rangers	NHL	24	10	3	13	20	3	0	2	59	16.9	2	19	42.1	20:09	....	....	....	....	....	....	....	....	....
2003-04	NY Rangers	NHL	66	13	29	42	54	3	0	0	178	7.3	–5	29	48.3	19:37	....	....	....	....	....	....	....	....	....
	Montreal	NHL	12	1	2	3	12	0	0	1	29	3.4	–4	2	50.0	15:36	11	6	4	10	8	1	0	1	20:11
	NHL Totals		849	292	388	680	902	77	8	42	2406	12.1		1053	44.0	22:06	94	33	44	77	90	7	0	5	21:54

Played in NHL All-Star Game (2001, 2003)

Traded to **Pittsburgh** by **NY Rangers** with Harry York for Petr Nedved, Chris Tamer and Sean Pronger, November 25, 1998. Traded to **NY Rangers** by **Pittsburgh** with Mike Wilson, Janne Laukkanen and Dan LaCouture for Joel Bouchard, Richard Lintner, Rico Fata, Mikael Samuelsson and future considerations, February 10, 2003. Traded to **Montreal** by **NY Rangers** for Jozef Balej and Montreal's 2nd round choice (Bruce Graham) in 2004 Entry Draft, March 2, 2004.

KOZLOV, Viktor

(KAHS-lahf, VIHK-tohr) **N.J.**

Center. Shoots right. 6'5", 235 lbs. Born, Togliatti, USSR, February 14, 1975. San Jose's 1st choice, 6th overall, in 1993 Entry Draft.

1990-91	Lada Togliatti	USSR-2	2	2	0	2	0	....	....	....	....	....	....	....	....	....	....	....	....	....	....	....	....	....	....
1991-92	Lada Togliatti	CIS	3	0	0	0	0	....	....	....	....	....	....	....	....	....	....	....	....	....	....	....	....	....	....
1992-93	Dynamo Moscow	CIS	30	6	5	11	4	....	....	....	....	....	....	....	....	....	10	3	0	3	0	....	....	....	....
1993-94	Dynamo Moscow	CIS	42	16	9	25	14	....	....	....	....	....	....	....	....	....	7	3	2	5	0	....	....	....	....
1994-95	Dynamo Moscow	CIS	3	1	1	2	2	....	....	....	....	....	....	....	....	....	....	....	....	....	....	....	....	....	....
	San Jose	NHL	16	2	0	2	2	0	0	0	23	8.7	–5	....	....	....	....	....	....	....	....	....	....	....	....
	Kansas City	IHL	4	1	1	2	0	....	....	....	....	....	....	....	....	....	13	4	5	9	12	....	....	....	....
1995-96	San Jose	NHL	62	6	13	19	6	1	0	0	107	5.6	–15	....	....	....	....	....	....	....	....	....	....	....	....
	Kansas City	IHL	15	4	7	11	12	....	....	....	....	....	....	....	....	....	....	....	....	....	....	....	....	....	....
1996-97	San Jose	NHL	78	16	25	41	40	4	0	4	184	8.7	–16	....	....	....	....	....	....	....	....	....	....	....	....
1997-98	San Jose	NHL	18	5	2	7	2	2	0	0	51	9.8	–2	....	....	....	....	....	....	....	....	....	....	....	....
	Florida	NHL	46	12	11	23	14	3	2	0	114	10.5	–1	....	....	....	....	....	....	....	....	....	....	....	....
1998-99	Florida	NHL	65	16	35	51	24	5	1	1	209	7.7	13	985	41.2	19:03	....	....	....	....	....	....	....	....	....
99-2000	Florida	NHL	80	17	53	70	16	6	0	2	223	7.6	24	1616	42.9	19:27	4	0	1	1	0	0	0	0	16:05
2000-01	Florida	NHL	51	14	23	37	10	6	0	2	139	10.1	–4	817	41.6	18:23	....	....	....	....	....	....	....	....	....
2001-02	Florida	NHL	50	9	18	27	20	6	0	1	143	6.3	–16	840	43.1	19:54	....	....	....	....	....	....	....	....	....
2002-03	Florida	NHL	74	22	34	56	18	7	1	1	232	9.5	–8	404	42.8	22:35	....	....	....	....	....	....	....	....	....

Season	Club	League	GP	G	A	Pts	PIM	PP	SH	GW	S	%	+/-	TF	F%	Min	GP	G	A	Pts	PIM	PP	SH	GW	Min
			Regular Season														Playoffs								
2003-04	**Florida**	**NHL**	**48**	**11**	**16**	**27**	**16**	**3**	**1**	**1**	**117**	**9.4**	**–4**	**200**	**49.0**	**19:30**	....	....	....	....	....	....	....	....	....
	New Jersey	**NHL**	**11**	**2**	**4**	**6**	**2**	**0**	**0**	**0**	**26**	**7.7**	**0**	**112**	**56.3**	**13:26**	**2**	**0**	**0**	**0**	**0**	**0**	**0**	**0**	**8:55**
	NHL Totals		**599**	**132**	**234**	**366**	**170**	**43**	**5**	**12**	**1568**	**8.4**		**4974**	**42.9**	**19:45**	**6**	**0**	**1**	**1**	**0**	**0**	**0**	**0**	**13:42**

Played in NHL All-Star Game (2000)

Traded to **Florida** by **San Jose** with Florida's 5th round choice (previously acquired, Florida selected Jaroslav Spacek) in 1998 Entry Draft for Dave Lowry and Florida's 1st round choice (later traded to Tampa Bay – Tampa Bay selected Vincent Lecavalier) in 1998 Entry Draft, November 13, 1997. Traded to **New Jersey** by **Florida** for Christian Berglund and Victor Uchevatov, March 1, 2004.

KOZLOV, Vyacheslav
(KAHS-lahf, VYACH-ih-slav) **ATL.**

Right wing. Shoots left. 5'10", 185 lbs. Born, Voskresensk, USSR, May 3, 1972. Detroit's 2nd choice, 45th overall, in 1990 Entry Draft.

Season	Club	League	GP	G	A	Pts	PIM	PP	SH	GW	S	%	+/-	TF	F%	Min	GP	G	A	Pts	PIM	PP	SH	GW	Min
1987-88	Voskresensk	USSR	2	0	0	0	0	....	....	....	....	....	....	....	....	....	....	....	....	....	....	....	....	....	....
1988-89	Voskresensk	USSR	14	0	1	1	2	....	....	....	....	....	....	....	....	....	....	....	....	....	....	....	....	....	....
1989-90	Voskresensk	USSR	45	14	12	26	38	....	....	....	....	....	....	....	....	....	....	....	....	....	....	....	....	....	....
1990-91	Voskresensk	USSR	45	11	13	24	46	....	....	....	....	....	....	....	....	....	....	....	....	....	....	....	....	....	....
1991-92	CSKA Moscow	CIS	11	6	5	11	12	....	....	....	....	....	....	....	....	....	....	....	....	....	....	....	....	....	....
	Detroit	**NHL**	**7**	**0**	**2**	**2**	**2**	**0**	**0**	**0**	**9**	**0.0**	**–2**	....	....	....	....	....	....	....	....	....	....	....	....
1992-93	**Detroit**	**NHL**	**17**	**4**	**1**	**5**	**14**	**0**	**0**	**0**	**26**	**15.4**	**–1**	....	....	....	**4**	**0**	**2**	**2**	**2**	**0**	**0**	**0**	....
	Adirondack	AHL	45	23	36	59	54	....	....	....	....	....	....	....	....	....	4	1	1	2	4	....	....	....	....
1993-94	**Detroit**	**NHL**	**77**	**34**	**39**	**73**	**50**	**8**	**2**	**6**	**202**	**16.8**	**27**	....	....	....	**7**	**2**	**5**	**7**	**12**	**0**	**0**	**0**	....
	Adirondack	AHL	3	0	1	1	15	....	....	....	....	....	....	....	....	....	....	....	....	....	....	....	....	....	....
1994-95	CSKA Moscow	CIS	10	3	4	7	14	....	....	....	....	....	....	....	....	....	....	....	....	....	....	....	....	....	....
	Detroit	**NHL**	**46**	**13**	**20**	**33**	**45**	**5**	**0**	**3**	**97**	**13.4**	**12**	....	....	....	**18**	**9**	**7**	**16**	**10**	**1**	**0**	**4**	....
1995-96	**Detroit**	**NHL**	**82**	**36**	**37**	**73**	**70**	**9**	**0**	**7**	**237**	**15.2**	**33**	....	....	....	**19**	**5**	**7**	**12**	**10**	**2**	**0**	**1**	....
1996-97 ♦	**Detroit**	**NHL**	**75**	**23**	**22**	**45**	**46**	**3**	**0**	**6**	**211**	**10.9**	**21**	....	....	....	**20**	**8**	**5**	**13**	**14**	**4**	**0**	**2**	....
1997-98 ♦	**Detroit**	**NHL**	**80**	**25**	**27**	**52**	**46**	**6**	**0**	**1**	**221**	**11.3**	**14**	....	....	....	**22**	**6**	**8**	**14**	**10**	**1**	**0**	**4**	....
1998-99	**Detroit**	**NHL**	**79**	**29**	**29**	**58**	**45**	**6**	**1**	**4**	**209**	**13.9**	**10**	**38**	**36.8**	**16:02**	**10**	**6**	**1**	**7**	**4**	**3**	**0**	**0**	**14:44**
99-2000	**Detroit**	**NHL**	**72**	**18**	**18**	**36**	**28**	**4**	**0**	**3**	**165**	**10.9**	**11**	**28**	**35.7**	**15:30**	**8**	**2**	**1**	**3**	**12**	**1**	**0**	**1**	**12:20**
2000-01	**Detroit**	**NHL**	**72**	**20**	**18**	**38**	**30**	**4**	**0**	**5**	**187**	**10.7**	**9**	**51**	**47.1**	**14:43**	**6**	**4**	**1**	**5**	**2**	**2**	**0**	**0**	**16:27**
2001-02	**Buffalo**	**NHL**	**38**	**9**	**13**	**22**	**16**	**3**	**0**	**1**	**68**	**13.2**	**0**	**24**	**41.7**	**16:31**	....	....	....	....	....	....	....	....	....
2002-03	**Atlanta**	**NHL**	**79**	**21**	**49**	**70**	**66**	**9**	**1**	**2**	**185**	**11.4**	**–10**	**67**	**34.3**	**20:01**	....	....	....	....	....	....	....	....	....
2003-04	**Atlanta**	**NHL**	**76**	**20**	**32**	**52**	**74**	**6**	**0**	**1**	**191**	**10.5**	**–12**	**164**	**32.3**	**20:20**	....	....	....	....	....	....	....	....	....
	NHL Totals		**800**	**252**	**307**	**559**	**532**	**63**	**4**	**39**	**2008**	**12.5**		**372**	**36.0**	**17:18**	**114**	**42**	**37**	**79**	**76**	**14**	**0**	**12**	**14:22**

Traded to **Buffalo** by **Detroit** with Detroit's 1st round choice (later traded to Columbus – later traded to Atlanta – Atlanta selected Jim Slater) in 2002 Entry Draft and future considerations for Dominik Hasek, July 1, 2001. • Missed majority of 2001-02 season recovering from Achilles tendon injury suffered in game vs. Columbus, December 31, 2001. Traded to **Atlanta** by **Buffalo** with Buffalo's 2nd round choice (later traded to Nashville – Nashville selected Konstantin Glazachev) in 2003 Entry Draft for Atlanta's 2nd (later traded to Florida – Florida selected Kamil Kreps) and 3rd (later traded to Phoenix – Phoenix selected Tyler Redenbach) round choices in 2003 Entry Draft, June 22, 2002.

KRAFT, Milan
(KRAFT, MIH-lan) **PIT.**

Center. Shoots right. 6'4", 212 lbs. Born, Plzen, Czech., January 17, 1980. Pittsburgh's 1st choice, 23rd overall, in 1998 Entry Draft.

Season	Club	League	GP	G	A	Pts	PIM	PP	SH	GW	S	%	+/-	TF	F%	Min	GP	G	A	Pts	PIM	PP	SH	GW	Min
1995-96	HC ZKZ Plzen Jr.	Czech-Jr.	49	54	41	95	....	....	....	....	....	....	....	....	....	....	....	....	....	....	....	....	....	....	....
1996-97	HC ZKZ Plzen Jr.	Czech-Jr.	29	24	12	36	....	....	....	....	....	....	....	....	....	....	....	....	....	....	....	....	....	....	....
	HC ZKZ Plzen	Czech	9	0	1	1	2	....	....	....	....	....	....	....	....	....	....	....	....	....	....	....	....	....	....
1997-98	Plzen Jr.	Czech-Jr.	24	22	21	43	12	....	....	....	....	....	....	....	....	....	....	....	....	....	....	....	....	....	....
	Plzen	Czech	16	0	5	5	0	....	....	....	....	....	....	....	....	....	1	0	0	0	0	....	....	....	....
1998-99	Prince Albert	WHL	68	40	46	86	32	....	....	....	....	....	....	....	....	....	14	7	13	20	6	....	....	....	....
99-2000	Prince Albert	WHL	56	34	35	69	42	....	....	....	....	....	....	....	....	....	6	4	1	5	4	....	....	....	....
2000-01	**Pittsburgh**	**NHL**	**42**	**7**	**7**	**14**	**8**	**1**	**1**	**1**	**63**	**11.1**	**–6**	**427**	**37.9**	**11:41**	**8**	**0**	**0**	**0**	**2**	**0**	**0**	**0**	**12:13**
	Wilkes-Barre	AHL	40	21	23	44	27	....	....	....	....	....	....	....	....	....	14	12	7	19	6	....	....	....	....
2001-02	**Pittsburgh**	**NHL**	**68**	**8**	**8**	**16**	**16**	**1**	**0**	**2**	**103**	**7.8**	**–9**	**766**	**44.7**	**12:29**	....	....	....	....	....	....	....	....	....
	Wilkes-Barre	AHL	8	4	4	8	10	....	....	....	....	....	....	....	....	....	....	....	....	....	....	....	....	....	....
2002-03	**Pittsburgh**	**NHL**	**31**	**7**	**5**	**12**	**10**	**0**	**0**	**1**	**50**	**14.0**	**–8**	**392**	**43.1**	**13:56**	....	....	....	....	....	....	....	....	....
	Wilkes-Barre	AHL	40	13	24	37	28	....	....	....	....	....	....	....	....	....	6	2	4	6	4	....	....	....	....
2003-04	**Pittsburgh**	**NHL**	**66**	**19**	**21**	**40**	**18**	**6**	**0**	**1**	**134**	**14.2**	**–22**	**970**	**47.4**	**15:16**	....	....	....	....	....	....	....	....	....
	NHL Totals		**207**	**41**	**41**	**82**	**52**	**8**	**1**	**5**	**350**	**11.7**		**2555**	**44.3**	**13:26**	**8**	**0**	**0**	**0**	**2**	**0**	**0**	**0**	**12:13**

KRAFT, Ryan
(KRAFT, RIGH-uhn) **NYI**

Center. Shoots left. 5'9", 181 lbs. Born, Bottineau, ND, November 7, 1975. San Jose's 11th choice, 194th overall, in 1995 Entry Draft.

Season	Club	League	GP	G	A	Pts	PIM	PP	SH	GW	S	%	+/-	TF	F%	Min	GP	G	A	Pts	PIM	PP	SH	GW	Min
1993-94	Moorhead Spuds	Hi-School	25	40	45	85	....	....	....	....	....	....	....	....	....	....	....	....	....	....	....	....	....	....	....
1994-95	U. of Minnesota	WCHA	44	13	33	46	44	....	....	....	....	....	....	....	....	....	....	....	....	....	....	....	....	....	....
1995-96	U. of Minnesota	WCHA	41	13	24	37	24	....	....	....	....	....	....	....	....	....	....	....	....	....	....	....	....	....	....
1996-97	U. of Minnesota	WCHA	42	25	21	46	37	....	....	....	....	....	....	....	....	....	....	....	....	....	....	....	....	....	....
1997-98	U. of Minnesota	WCHA	32	11	26	37	16	....	....	....	....	....	....	....	....	....	....	....	....	....	....	....	....	....	....
1998-99	Richmond	ECHL	63	28	36	64	35	....	....	....	....	....	....	....	....	....	18	10	10	20	4	....	....	....	....
99-2000	Richmond	ECHL	44	32	35	67	32	....	....	....	....	....	....	....	....	....	....	....	....	....	....	....	....	....	....
	Cleveland	IHL	1	0	1	1	0	....	....	....	....	....	....	....	....	....	....	....	....	....	....	....	....	....	....
	Kentucky	AHL	15	7	6	13	2	....	....	....	....	....	....	....	....	....	5	3	1	4	0	....	....	....	....
2000-01	Kentucky	AHL	77	38	50	88	36	....	....	....	....	....	....	....	....	....	3	2	0	2	0	....	....	....	....
2001-02	Cleveland Barons	AHL	63	19	41	60	42	....	....	....	....	....	....	....	....	....	....	....	....	....	....	....	....	....	....
2002-03	**San Jose**	**NHL**	**7**	**0**	**1**	**1**	**0**	**0**	**0**	**0**	**1**	**0.0**	**2**	**41**	**34.2**	**8:33**	....	....	....	....	....	....	....	....	....
	Cleveland Barons	AHL	53	14	27	41	12	....	....	....	....	....	....	....	....	....	....	....	....	....	....	....	....	....	....
2003-04	Bridgeport	AHL	74	15	21	36	20	....	....	....	....	....	....	....	....	....	6	2	2	4	0	....	....	....	....
	NHL Totals		**7**	**0**	**1**	**1**	**0**	**0**	**0**	**0**	**1**	**0.0**		**41**	**34.1**	**8:33**									

WCHA All-Rookie Team (1995) • WCHA All-Academic Team (1996) • AHL Second All-Star Team (2001) • Dudley "Red" Garrett Memorial Trophy (Top Rookie – AHL) (2001)

Signed as a free agent by **NY Islanders**, July 8, 2003.

KRAJICEK, Lukas
(KRIGH-ee-chehk, LOO-kahsh) **FLA.**

Defense. Shoots left. 6'2", 185 lbs. Born, Prostejov, Czech., March 11, 1983. Florida's 2nd choice; 24th overall, in 2001 Entry Draft.

Season	Club	League	GP	G	A	Pts	PIM	PP	SH	GW	S	%	+/-	TF	F%	Min	GP	G	A	Pts	PIM	PP	SH	GW	Min
1998-99	Zlin Jr.	Czech-Jr.	48	8	18	26	40	....	....	....	....	....	....	....	....	....	....	....	....	....	....	....	....	....	....
99-2000	Det. Compuware	NAJHL	53	5	22	27	61	....	....	....	....	....	....	....	....	....	5	0	1	1	18	....	....	....	....
2000-01	Peterborough	OHL	61	8	27	35	53	....	....	....	....	....	....	....	....	....	7	0	5	5	0	....	....	....	....
2001-02	**Florida**	**NHL**	**5**	**0**	**0**	**0**	**0**	**0**	**0**	**0**	**3**	**0.0**	**0**	**0**	**0.0**	**13:23**	....	....	....	....	....	....	....	....	....
	Peterborough	OHL	55	10	32	42	56	....	....	....	....	....	....	....	....	....	6	0	5	5	6	....	....	....	....
2002-03	Peterborough	OHL	52	11	42	53	42	....	....	....	....	....	....	....	....	....	7	0	3	3	0	....	....	....	....
	San Antonio	AHL	3	0	1	1	0	....	....	....	....	....	....	....	....	....	3	0	0	0	0	....	....	....	....
2003-04	**Florida**	**NHL**	**18**	**1**	**6**	**7**	**12**	**1**	**0**	**0**	**16**	**6.3**	**–2**	**0**	**0.0**	**13:32**	....	....	....	....	....	....	....	....	....
	San Antonio	AHL	54	5	12	17	24	....	....	....	....	....	....	....	....	....	....	....	....	....	....	....	....	....	....
	NHL Totals		**23**	**1**	**6**	**7**	**12**	**1**	**0**	**0**	**19**	**5.3**		**0**	**0.0**	**13:30**	....	....	....	....	....	....	....	....	....

OHL All-Rookie Team (2001) • OHL First All-Star Team (2003)

• Returned to **Peterborough** (OHL) by **Florida**, October 28, 2001.

KRESTANOVICH, Jordan
(KREH-sta-noh-vihtch, JOHR-dan) **MIN.**

Left wing. Shoots left. 6'1", 180 lbs. Born, Langley, B.C., June 14, 1981. Colorado's 7th choice, 152nd overall, in 1999 Entry Draft.

Season	Club	League	GP	G	A	Pts	PIM	PP	SH	GW	S	%	+/-	TF	F%	Min	GP	G	A	Pts	PIM	PP	SH	GW	Min
1996-97	Surrey Chiefs	BCAHA	55	79	81	160	....	....	....	....	....	....	....	....	....	....	....	....	....	....	....	....	....	....	....
1997-98	Calgary Hitmen	WHL	22	1	0	1	0	....	....	....	....	....	....	....	....	....	13	0	0	0	0	....	....	....	....
1998-99	Calgary Hitmen	WHL	62	6	13	19	10	....	....	....	....	....	....	....	....	....	20	3	8	11	4	....	....	....	....
99-2000	Calgary Hitmen	WHL	72	19	24	43	22	....	....	....	....	....	....	....	....	....	13	7	7	14	4	....	....	....	....
	Hershey Bears	AHL	....	....	....	....	....	....	....	....	....	....	....	....	....	....	1	0	0	0	0	....	....	....	....
2000-01	Calgary Hitmen	WHL	70	40	60	100	32	....	....	....	....	....	....	....	....	....	12	8	4	12	8	....	....	....	....
	Hershey Bears	AHL	....	....	....	....	....	....	....	....	....	....	....	....	....	....	2	0	0	0	0	....	....	....	....
2001-02	**Colorado**	**NHL**	**8**	**0**	**2**	**2**	**0**	**0**	**0**	**0**	**6**	**0.0**	**1**	**0**	**0.0**	**8:34**	....	....	....	....	....	....	....	....	....
	Hershey Bears	AHL	68	12	22	34	18	....	....	....	....	....	....	....	....	....	8	1	0	1	0	....	....	....	....
2002-03	Hershey Bears	AHL	70	13	21	34	24	....	....	....	....	....	....	....	....	....	4	0	1	1	2	....	....	....	....

Season	Club	League	Regular Season GP	G	A	Pts	PIM	PP	SH	GW	S	%	+/-	TF	F%	Min	Playoffs GP	G	A	Pts	PIM	PP	SH	GW	Min
2003-04	**Colorado**	**NHL**	14	0	0	0	6	0	0	0	25	0.0	0	21	23.8	10:08	....	....	....	....	....	....	....	....	....
	Hershey Bears	AHL	38	4	15	19	11	....	....	....	....	....	....	....	....	....	....	....	....	....	....	....	....	....	....
	Houston Aeros	AHL	12	2	1	3	0	....	....	....	....	....	....	....	....	....	2	0	0	0	0	....	....	....	....
	NHL Totals		22	0	2	2	6	0	0	0	31	0.0		21	23.8	9:34	....	....	....	....	....	....	....	....	....

Traded to **Minnesota** by **Colorado** for Chris Bala, March 9, 2004.

KRISTEK, Jaroslav

(KRIHSH-tehk, YAH-roh-slahv) **BUF.**

Right wing. Shoots left. 6'1", 188 lbs. Born, Zlin, Czech., March 16, 1980. Buffalo's 4th choice, 50th overall, in 1998 Entry Draft.

Season	Club	League	GP	G	A	Pts	PIM	PP	SH	GW	S	%	+/-	TF	F%	Min	GP	G	A	Pts	PIM	PP	SH	GW	Min
1995-96	AC ZPS Zlin Jr.	Czech-Jr.	34	33	20	53	....	....	....	....	....	....	....	....	....	....	....	....	....	....	....	....	....	....	....
1996-97	AC ZPS Zlin Jr.	Czech-Jr.	44	28	27	55	....	....	....	....	....	....	....	....	....	....	....	....	....	....	....	....	....	....	....
1997-98	Zlin Jr.	Czech-Jr.	7	8	5	13	....	....	....	....	....	....	....	....	....	....	....	....	....	....	....	....	....	....	....
	HC Prostejov	Czech-2	4	0	0	0	....	....	....	....	....	....	....	....	....	....	....	....	....	....	....	....	....	....	....
	Zlin	Czech	37	2	8	10	20	....	....	....	....	....	....	....	....	....	....	....	....	....	....	....	....	....	....
1998-99	Tri-City	WHL	70	38	48	86	55	....	....	....	....	....	....	....	....	....	12	4	3	7	2	....	....	....	....
99-2000	Tri-City	WHL	45	26	25	51	16	....	....	....	....	....	....	....	....	....	2	0	0	0	0	....	....	....	....
2000-01	Rochester	AHL	35	5	3	8	20	....	....	....	....	....	....	....	....	....	....	....	....	....	....	....	....	....	....
2001-02	Rochester	AHL	43	3	6	9	20	....	....	....	....	....	....	....	....	....	1	0	0	0	0	....	....	....	....
2002-03	**Buffalo**	**NHL**	6	0	0	0	4	0	0	0	4	0.0	−2	0	0.0	11:37	....	....	....	....	....	....	....	....	....
	Rochester	AHL	47	15	17	32	24	....	....	....	....	....	....	....	....	....	....	....	....	....	....	....	....	....	....
2003-04	Ceske Budejovice	Czech	52	12	14	26	24	....	....	....	....	....	....	....	....	....	....	....	....	....	....	....	....	....	....
	NHL Totals		6	0	0	0	4	0	0	0	4	0.0		0	0.0	11:37	....	....	....	....	....	....	....	....	....

Signed as a free agent by **Ceske Budejovice** (Czech) with Buffalo retaining NHL rights, August 26, 2003.

KROG, Jason

(KROHG, JAY-suhn)

Center. Shoots right. 5'11", 191 lbs. Born, Fernie, B.C., October 9, 1975.

Season	Club	League	GP	G	A	Pts	PIM	PP	SH	GW	S	%	+/-	TF	F%	Min	GP	G	A	Pts	PIM	PP	SH	GW	Min
1992-93	Chilliwack Chiefs	BCJHL	52	30	27	57	52	....	....	....	....	....	....	....	....	....	....	....	....	....	....	....	....	....	....
1993-94	Chilliwack Chiefs	BCJHL	42	19	36	55	20	....	....	....	....	....	....	....	....	....	....	....	....	....	....	....	....	....	....
1994-95	Chilliwack Chiefs	BCJHL	60	47	81	128	36	....	....	....	....	....	....	....	....	....	....	....	....	....	....	....	....	....	....
1995-96	New Hampshire	H-East	34	4	16	20	20	....	....	....	....	....	....	....	....	....	....	....	....	....	....	....	....	....	....
1996-97	New Hampshire	H-East	39	23	*44	*67	28	....	....	....	....	....	....	....	....	....	....	....	....	....	....	....	....	....	....
1997-98	New Hampshire	H-East	38	*33	33	66	44	....	....	....	....	....	....	....	....	....	....	....	....	....	....	....	....	....	....
1998-99	New Hampshire	H-East	41	*34	*51	*85	38	....	....	....	....	....	....	....	....	....	....	....	....	....	....	....	....	....	....
99-2000	**NY Islanders**	**NHL**	17	2	4	6	6	1	0	0	22	9.1	−1	81	53.1	10:03	....	....	....	....	....	....	....	....	....
	Lowell	AHL	45	6	21	27	22	....	....	....	....	....	....	....	....	....	....	....	....	....	....	....	....	....	....
	Providence Bruins	AHL	11	9	8	17	4	....	....	....	....	....	....	....	....	....	6	2	2	4	0	....	....	....	....
2000-01	**NY Islanders**	**NHL**	9	0	3	3	0	0	0	0	7	0.0	4	60	48.3	10:32	....	....	....	....	....	....	....	....	....
	Lowell	AHL	26	11	16	27	6	....	....	....	....	....	....	....	....	....	....	....	....	....	....	....	....	....	....
	Springfield	AHL	24	7	23	30	4	....	....	....	....	....	....	....	....	....	....	....	....	....	....	....	....	....	....
2001-02	**NY Islanders**	**NHL**	2	0	0	0	0	0	0	0	0	0.0	0	13	46.2	6:40	....	....	....	....	....	....	....	....	....
	Bridgeport	AHL	64	26	36	62	13	....	....	....	....	....	....	....	....	....	20	10	13	23	8	....	....	....	....
2002-03	**Anaheim**	**NHL**	67	10	15	25	12	0	1	1	92	10.9	1	634	60.4	13:47	21	3	1	4	4	0	0	0	12:10
	Cincinnati	AHL	9	3	4	7	6	....	....	....	....	....	....	....	....	....	....	....	....	....	....	....	....	....	....
2003-04	**Anaheim**	**NHL**	80	6	12	18	16	1	0	1	111	5.4	−4	769	58.5	11:58	....	....	....	....	....	....	....	....	....
	NHL Totals		175	18	34	52	34	2	1	2	232	7.8		1557	58.5	12:21	21	3	1	4	4	0	0	0	12:10

Hockey East All-Star Team (1997) • NCAA East Second All-American Team (1997) • Hockey East First All-Star Team (1998, 1999) • Hockey East Player of the Year (1999) • NCAA East First All-American Team (1999) • NCAA Championship All-Tournament Team (1999) • Hobey Baker Memorial Award (Top U.S. Collegiate Player) (1999)

Signed as a free agent by **NY Islanders**, May 14, 1999. Loaned to **Providence** (AHL) by **NY Islanders**, March 1, 2000. Signed as a free agent by **Anaheim**, July 17, 2002.

KRONWALL, Niklas

(KRAHN-wuhl, NIHK-las) **DET.**

Defense. Shoots left. 5'11", 165 lbs. Born, Stockholm, Sweden, January 12, 1981. Detroit's 1st choice, 29th overall, in 2000 Entry Draft.

Season	Club	League	GP	G	A	Pts	PIM	PP	SH	GW	S	%	+/-	TF	F%	Min	GP	G	A	Pts	PIM	PP	SH	GW	Min
1996-97	Djurgarden Jr.	Swede-Jr.	1	0	0	0	0	....	....	....	....	....	....	....	....	....	....	....	....	....	....	....	....	....	....
1997-98	Djurgarden Jr.	Swede-Jr.	27	4	3	7	71	....	....	....	....	....	....	....	....	....	2	0	0	0	2	....	....	....	....
1998-99	Huddinge IK	Swede-2	14	0	1	1	10	....	....	....	....	....	....	....	....	....	....	....	....	....	....	....	....	....	....
	Huddinge IK	Swede-Q	10	1	0	1	14	....	....	....	....	....	....	....	....	....	....	....	....	....	....	....	....	....	....
	Huddinge IK Jr.	Swede-Jr.	2	0	0	0	6	....	....	....	....	....	....	....	....	....	....	....	....	....	....	....	....	....	....
99-2000	Djurgarden	Sweden	37	1	4	5	16	....	....	....	....	....	....	....	....	....	8	0	0	0	8	....	....	....	....
2000-01	Djurgarden	Sweden	31	1	9	10	32	....	....	....	....	....	....	....	....	....	15	0	1	1	8	....	....	....	....
2001-02	Djurgarden	Sweden	48	5	7	12	34	....	....	....	....	....	....	....	....	....	5	0	0	0	0	....	....	....	....
2002-03	Djurgarden	Sweden	50	5	13	18	46	....	....	....	....	....	....	....	....	....	12	3	2	5	18	....	....	....	....
2003-04	**Detroit**	**NHL**	20	1	4	5	16	0	0	1	18	5.6	5	0	0.0	13:51	....	....	....	....	....	....	....	....	....
	Grand Rapids	AHL	25	2	11	13	20	....	....	....	....	....	....	....	....	....	....	....	....	....	....	....	....	....	....
	NHL Totals		20	1	4	5	16	0	0	1	18	5.6		0	0.0	13:51	....	....	....	....	....	....	....	....	....

KUBA, Filip

(KOO-bah, FIHL-ihp) **MIN.**

Defense. Shoots left. 6'3", 205 lbs. Born, Ostrava, Czech., December 29, 1976. Florida's 8th choice, 192nd overall, in 1995 Entry Draft.

Season	Club	League	GP	G	A	Pts	PIM	PP	SH	GW	S	%	+/-	TF	F%	Min	GP	G	A	Pts	PIM	PP	SH	GW	Min
1994-95	HC Vitkovice Jr.	Czech-Jr.	35	10	15	25	....	....	....	....	....	....	....	....	....	....	....	....	....	....	....	....	....	....	....
	HC Vitkovice	Czech	....	....	....	....	....	....	....	....	....	....	....	....	....	....	4	0	0	0	2	....	....	....	....
1995-96	HC Vitkovice	Czech	19	0	1	1	....	....	....	....	....	....	....	....	....	....	....	....	....	....	....	....	....	....	....
1996-97	Carolina	AHL	51	0	12	12	38	....	....	....	....	....	....	....	....	....	....	....	....	....	....	....	....	....	....
1997-98	New Haven	AHL	77	4	13	17	58	....	....	....	....	....	....	....	....	....	3	1	1	2	0	....	....	....	....
1998-99	**Florida**	**NHL**	5	0	1	1	0	0	0	0	5	0.0	2	0	0.0	22:29	....	....	....	....	....	....	....	....	....
	Kentucky	AHL	45	2	8	10	33	....	....	....	....	....	....	....	....	....	10	0	1	1	4	....	....	....	....
99-2000	**Florida**	**NHL**	13	1	5	6	2	1	0	1	16	6.3	−3	0	0.0	13:52	....	....	....	....	....	....	....	....	....
	Houston Aeros	IHL	27	3	6	9	13	....	....	....	....	....	....	....	....	....	11	1	2	3	4	....	....	....	....
2000-01	**Minnesota**	**NHL**	75	9	21	30	28	4	0	4	141	6.4	−6	1	0.0	24:16	....	....	....	....	....	....	....	....	....
2001-02	**Minnesota**	**NHL**	62	5	19	24	32	3	0	1	101	5.0	−6	0	0.0	25:30	....	....	....	....	....	....	....	....	....
2002-03	**Minnesota**	**NHL**	78	8	21	29	29	4	2	1	129	6.2	0	1	0.0	23:56	18	3	5	8	24	3	0	0	26:46
2003-04	**Minnesota**	**NHL**	77	5	19	24	28	2	1	2	114	4.4	−7	2	0.0	24:06	....	....	....	....	....	....	....	....	....
	NHL Totals		310	28	86	114	119	14	3	9	506	5.5		4	0.0	23:55	18	3	5	8	24	3	0	0	26:46

Played in NHL All-Star Game (2004)

Traded to **Calgary** by **Florida** for Rocky Thompson, March 16, 2000. Selected by **Minnesota** from **Calgary** in Expansion Draft, June 23, 2000.

KUBINA, Pavel

(koo-BEE-nuh, PAH-vehl) **T.B.**

Defense. Shoots right. 6'4", 230 lbs. Born, Celadna, Czech., April 15, 1977. Tampa Bay's 6th choice, 179th overall, in 1996 Entry Draft.

Season	Club	League	GP	G	A	Pts	PIM	PP	SH	GW	S	%	+/-	TF	F%	Min	GP	G	A	Pts	PIM	PP	SH	GW	Min
1993-94	HC Vitkovice Jr.	Czech-Jr.	35	4	3	7	....	....	....	....	....	....	....	....	....	....	....	....	....	....	....	....	....	....	....
	HC Vitkovice	Czech	1	0	0	0	....	....	....	....	....	....	....	....	....	....	....	....	....	....	....	....	....	....	....
1994-95	HC Vitkovice Jr.	Czech-Jr.	20	6	10	16	....	....	....	....	....	....	....	....	....	....	....	....	....	....	....	....	....	....	....
	HC Vitkovice	Czech	8	2	0	2	10	....	....	....	....	....	....	....	....	....	4	0	0	0	0	....	....	....	....
1995-96	HC Vitkovice Jr.	Czech-Jr.	16	5	10	15	....	....	....	....	....	....	....	....	....	....	....	....	....	....	....	....	....	....	....
	HC Vitkovice	Czech	33	3	4	7	32	....	....	....	....	....	....	....	....	....	4	0	0	0	0	....	....	....	....
1996-97	HC Vitkovice	Czech	1	0	0	0	0	....	....	....	....	....	....	....	....	....	....	....	....	....	....	....	....	....	....
	Moose Jaw	WHL	61	12	32	44	116	....	....	....	....	....	....	....	....	....	11	2	5	7	27	....	....	....	....
1997-98	**Tampa Bay**	**NHL**	10	1	2	3	22	0	0	0	8	12.5	−1	....	....	....	....	....	....	....	....	....	....	....	....
	Adirondack	AHL	55	4	8	12	86	....	....	....	....	....	....	....	....	....	1	1	0	1	14	....	....	....	....
1998-99	**Tampa Bay**	**NHL**	68	9	12	21	80	3	1	1	119	7.6	−33	2	0.0	22:47	....	....	....	....	....	....	....	....	....
	Cleveland	IHL	6	2	2	4	16	....	....	....	....	....	....	....	....	....	....	....	....	....	....	....	....	....	....
99-2000	**Tampa Bay**	**NHL**	69	8	18	26	93	6	0	3	128	6.3	−19	0	0.0	22:32	....	....	....	....	....	....	....	....	....
2000-01	**Tampa Bay**	**NHL**	70	11	19	30	103	6	1	1	128	8.6	−14	2	0.0	24:06	....	....	....	....	....	....	....	....	....
2001-02	**Tampa Bay**	**NHL**	82	11	23	34	106	5	2	3	189	5.8	−22	1	100.0	23:39	....	....	....	....	....	....	....	....	....
	Czech Republic	Olympics	4	0	1	1	0	....	....	....	....	....	....	....	....	....	....	....	....	....	....	....	....	....	....
2002-03	**Tampa Bay**	**NHL**	75	3	19	22	78	0	0	0	139	2.2	−7	1	0.0	21:24	11	0	0	0	12	0	0	0	24:52
2003-04♦	**Tampa Bay**	**NHL**	81	17	18	35	85	8	1	4	153	11.1	9	1	0.0	21:09	22	0	4	4	50	0	0	0	22:54
	NHL Totals		455	60	111	171	567	28	5	12	864	6.9		7	14.3	22:35	33	0	4	4	62	0	0	0	23:33

Played in NHL All-Star Game (2004)

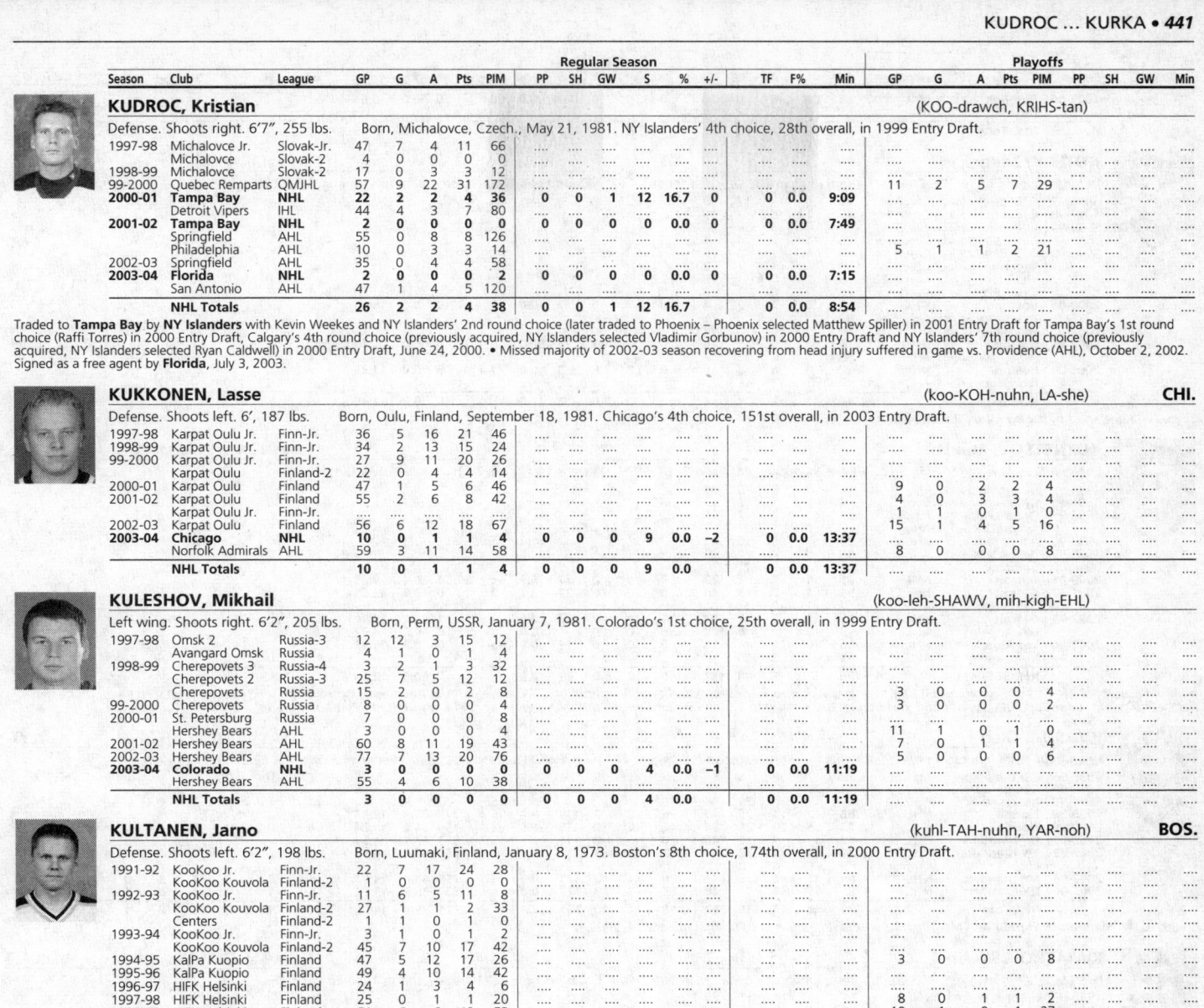

			Regular Season														Playoffs								
Season	Club	League	GP	G	A	Pts	PIM	PP	SH	GW	S	%	+/-	TF	F%	Min	GP	G	A	Pts	PIM	PP	SH	GW	Min

KUDROC, Kristian

(KOO-drawch, KRIHS-tan)

Defense. Shoots right. 6'7", 255 lbs. Born, Michalovce, Czech., May 21, 1981. NY Islanders' 4th choice, 28th overall, in 1999 Entry Draft.

1997-98	Michalovce Jr.	Slovak-Jr.	47	7	4	11	66	....	....	....	....	....	....	....	....	....	....	....	....	....	....	....	....	....	....
	Michalovce	Slovak-2	4	0	0	0	0	....	....	....	....	....	....	....	....	....	....	....	....	....	....	....	....	....	....
1998-99	Michalovce	Slovak-2	17	0	3	3	12	....	....	....	....	....	....	....	....	....	....	....	....	....	....	....	....	....	....
99-2000	Quebec Remparts	QMJHL	57	9	22	31	172	....	....	....	....	....	....	....	....	....	11	2	5	7	29	....	....	....	....
2000-01	**Tampa Bay**	**NHL**	**22**	**2**	**2**	**4**	**36**	**0**	**0**	**1**	**12**	**16.7**	**0**	**0**	**0.0**	**9:09**	....	....	....	....	....	....	....	....	....
	Detroit Vipers	IHL	44	4	3	7	80	....	....	....	....	....	....	....	....	....	....	....	....	....	....	....	....	....	....
2001-02	**Tampa Bay**	**NHL**	**2**	**0**	**0**	**0**	**0**	**0**	**0**	**0**	**0**	**0.0**	**0**	**0**	**0.0**	**7:49**	....	....	....	....	....	....	....	....	....
	Springfield	AHL	55	0	8	8	126	....	....	....	....	....	....	....	....	....	....	....	....	....	....	....	....	....	....
	Philadelphia	AHL	10	0	3	3	14	....	....	....	....	....	....	....	....	....	5	1	1	2	21	....	....	....	....
2002-03	Springfield	AHL	35	0	4	4	58	....	....	....	....	....	....	....	....	....	....	....	....	....	....	....	....	....	....
2003-04	**Florida**	**NHL**	**2**	**0**	**0**	**0**	**2**	**0**	**0**	**0**	**0**	**0.0**	**0**	**0**	**0.0**	**7:15**	....	....	....	....	....	....	....	....	....
	San Antonio	AHL	47	1	4	5	120	....	....	....	....	....	....	....	....	....	....	....	....	....	....	....	....	....	....
	NHL Totals		**26**	**2**	**2**	**4**	**38**	**0**	**0**	**1**	**12**	**16.7**		**0**	**0.0**	**8:54**	....	....	....	....	....	....	....	....	....

Traded to **Tampa Bay** by **NY Islanders** with Kevin Weekes and NY Islanders' 2nd round choice (later traded to Phoenix – Phoenix selected Matthew Spiller) in 2001 Entry Draft for Tampa Bay's 1st round choice (Raffi Torres) in 2000 Entry Draft, Calgary's 4th round choice (previously acquired, NY Islanders selected Vladimir Gorbunov) in 2000 Entry Draft and NY Islanders' 7th round choice (previously acquired, NY Islanders selected Ryan Caldwell) in 2000 Entry Draft, June 24, 2000. • Missed majority of 2002-03 season recovering from head injury suffered in game vs. Providence (AHL), October 2, 2002. Signed as a free agent by **Florida**, July 3, 2003.

KUKKONEN, Lasse

(koo-KOH-nuhn, LA-she) **CHI.**

Defense. Shoots left. 6', 187 lbs. Born, Oulu, Finland, September 18, 1981. Chicago's 4th choice, 151st overall, in 2003 Entry Draft.

1997-98	Karpat Oulu Jr.	Finn-Jr.	36	5	16	21	46	....	....	....	....	....	....	....	....	....	....	....	....	....	....	....	....	....	....
1998-99	Karpat Oulu Jr.	Finn-Jr.	34	2	13	15	24	....	....	....	....	....	....	....	....	....	....	....	....	....	....	....	....	....	....
99-2000	Karpat Oulu Jr.	Finn-Jr.	27	9	11	20	26	....	....	....	....	....	....	....	....	....	....	....	....	....	....	....	....	....	....
	Karpat Oulu	Finland-2	22	0	4	4	14	....	....	....	....	....	....	....	....	....	....	....	....	....	....	....	....	....	....
2000-01	Karpat Oulu	Finland	47	1	5	6	46	....	....	....	....	....	....	....	....	....	9	0	2	2	4	....	....	....	....
2001-02	Karpat Oulu	Finland	55	2	6	8	42	....	....	....	....	....	....	....	....	....	4	0	3	3	4	....	....	....	....
	Karpat Oulu Jr.	Finn-Jr.	....	....	....	....	....	....	....	....	....	....	....	....	....	....	1	1	0	1	0	....	....	....	....
2002-03	Karpat Oulu	Finland	56	6	12	18	67	....	....	....	....	....	....	....	....	....	15	1	4	5	16	....	....	....	....
2003-04	**Chicago**	**NHL**	**10**	**0**	**1**	**1**	**4**	**0**	**0**	**0**	**9**	**0.0**	**–2**	**0**	**0.0**	**13:37**	....	....	....	....	....	....	....	....	....
	Norfolk Admirals	AHL	59	3	11	14	58	....	....	....	....	....	....	....	....	....	8	0	0	0	8	....	....	....	....
	NHL Totals		**10**	**0**	**1**	**1**	**4**	**0**	**0**	**0**	**9**	**0.0**		**0**	**0.0**	**13:37**	....	....	....	....	....	....	....	....	....

KULESHOV, Mikhail

(koo-leh-SHAWV, mih-kigh-EHL)

Left wing. Shoots right. 6'2", 205 lbs. Born, Perm, USSR, January 7, 1981. Colorado's 1st choice, 25th overall, in 1999 Entry Draft.

1997-98	Omsk 2	Russia-3	12	12	3	15	12	....	....	....	....	....	....	....	....	....	....	....	....	....	....	....	....	....	....
	Avangard Omsk	Russia	4	1	0	1	4	....	....	....	....	....	....	....	....	....	....	....	....	....	....	....	....	....	....
1998-99	Cherepovets 3	Russia-4	3	2	1	3	32	....	....	....	....	....	....	....	....	....	....	....	....	....	....	....	....	....	....
	Cherepovets 2	Russia-3	25	7	5	12	12	....	....	....	....	....	....	....	....	....	....	....	....	....	....	....	....	....	....
	Cherepovets	Russia	15	2	0	2	8	....	....	....	....	....	....	....	....	....	3	0	0	0	4	....	....	....	....
99-2000	Cherepovets	Russia	8	0	0	0	4	....	....	....	....	....	....	....	....	....	3	0	0	0	2	....	....	....	....
2000-01	St. Petersburg	Russia	7	0	0	0	8	....	....	....	....	....	....	....	....	....	....	....	....	....	....	....	....	....	....
	Hershey Bears	AHL	3	0	0	0	4	....	....	....	....	....	....	....	....	....	11	1	0	1	0	....	....	....	....
2001-02	Hershey Bears	AHL	60	8	11	19	43	....	....	....	....	....	....	....	....	....	7	0	1	1	4	....	....	....	....
2002-03	Hershey Bears	AHL	77	7	13	20	76	....	....	....	....	....	....	....	....	....	5	0	0	0	6	....	....	....	....
2003-04	**Colorado**	**NHL**	**3**	**0**	**0**	**0**	**0**	**0**	**0**	**0**	**4**	**0.0**	**–1**	**0**	**0.0**	**11:19**	....	....	....	....	....	....	....	....	....
	Hershey Bears	AHL	55	4	6	10	38	....	....	....	....	....	....	....	....	....	....	....	....	....	....	....	....	....	....
	NHL Totals		**3**	**0**	**0**	**0**	**0**	**0**	**0**	**0**	**4**	**0.0**		**0**	**0.0**	**11:19**	....	....	....	....	....	....	....	....	....

KULTANEN, Jarno

(kuhl-TAH-nuhn, YAR-noh) **BOS.**

Defense. Shoots left. 6'2", 198 lbs. Born, Luumaki, Finland, January 8, 1973. Boston's 8th choice, 174th overall, in 2000 Entry Draft.

1991-92	KooKoo Jr.	Finn-Jr.	22	7	17	24	28	....	....	....	....	....	....	....	....	....	....	....	....	....	....	....	....	....	....
	KooKoo Kouvola	Finland-2	1	0	0	0	0	....	....	....	....	....	....	....	....	....	....	....	....	....	....	....	....	....	....
1992-93	KooKoo Jr.	Finn-Jr.	11	6	5	11	8	....	....	....	....	....	....	....	....	....	....	....	....	....	....	....	....	....	....
	KooKoo Kouvola	Finland-2	27	1	1	2	33	....	....	....	....	....	....	....	....	....	....	....	....	....	....	....	....	....	....
	Centers	Finland-2	1	1	0	1	0	....	....	....	....	....	....	....	....	....	....	....	....	....	....	....	....	....	....
1993-94	KooKoo Jr.	Finn-Jr.	3	1	0	1	2	....	....	....	....	....	....	....	....	....	....	....	....	....	....	....	....	....	....
	KooKoo Kouvola	Finland-2	45	7	10	17	42	....	....	....	....	....	....	....	....	....	....	....	....	....	....	....	....	....	....
1994-95	KalPa Kuopio	Finland	47	5	12	17	26	....	....	....	....	....	....	....	....	....	3	0	0	0	8	....	....	....	....
1995-96	KalPa Kuopio	Finland	49	4	10	14	42	....	....	....	....	....	....	....	....	....	....	....	....	....	....	....	....	....	....
1996-97	HIFK Helsinki	Finland	24	1	3	4	6	....	....	....	....	....	....	....	....	....	....	....	....	....	....	....	....	....	....
1997-98	HIFK Helsinki	Finland	25	0	1	1	20	....	....	....	....	....	....	....	....	....	8	0	1	1	2	....	....	....	....
1998-99	HIFK Helsinki	Finland	51	6	6	12	53	....	....	....	....	....	....	....	....	....	10	1	0	1	27	....	....	....	....
	HIFK Helsinki	EuroHL	5	1	0	1	4	....	....	....	....	....	....	....	....	....	4	0	1	1	2	....	....	....	....
99-2000	HIFK Helsinki	Finland	46	6	8	14	51	....	....	....	....	....	....	....	....	....	9	0	0	0	6	....	....	....	....
	HIFK Helsinki	EuroHL	5	2	2	4	31	....	....	....	....	....	....	....	....	....	2	0	0	0	2	....	....	....	....
2000-01	**Boston**	**NHL**	**62**	**2**	**8**	**10**	**26**	**0**	**0**	**1**	**76**	**2.6**	**–3**	**0**	**0.0**	**19:29**	....	....	....	....	....	....	....	....	....
2001-02	**Boston**	**NHL**	**38**	**0**	**3**	**3**	**33**	**0**	**0**	**0**	**31**	**0.0**	**–1**	**0**	**0.0**	**12:58**	....	....	....	....	....	....	....	....	....
2002-03	**Boston**	**NHL**	**2**	**0**	**0**	**0**	**0**	**0**	**0**	**0**	**3**	**0.0**	**1**	**0**	**0.0**	**10:16**	....	....	....	....	....	....	....	....	....
	Providence Bruins	AHL	59	9	25	34	35	....	....	....	....	....	....	....	....	....	4	0	0	0	6	....	....	....	....
2003-04	HIFK Helsinki	Finland	44	3	5	8	40	....	....	....	....	....	....	....	....	....	13	1	1	2	0	....	....	....	....
	NHL Totals		**102**	**2**	**11**	**13**	**59**	**0**	**0**	**1**	**110**	**1.8**		**0**	**0.0**	**16:52**	....	....	....	....	....	....	....	....	....

• Missed majority of 2001-02 season recovering from knee injury suffered in game vs. Minnesota, October 8, 2001. Signed as a free agent by **HIFK Helsinki** (Finland) with Boston retaining NHL rights, May 19, 2003.

KUNITZ, Chris

(KOO-hihtz, KRIHS) **ANA.**

Left wing. Shoots left. 6', 200 lbs. Born, Regina, Sask., September 26, 1979.

1996-97	Yorkton Mallers	SMHL	64	38	38	76	233	....	....	....	....	....	....	....	....	....	....	....	....	....	....	....	....	....	....
1997-98	Melville	SJHL	STATISTICS NOT AVAILABLE																						
1998-99	Melville	SJHL	63	57	32	89	222	....	....	....	....	....	....	....	....	....	....	....	....	....	....	....	....	....	....
99-2000	Ferris State	CCHA	38	20	9	29	70	....	....	....	....	....	....	....	....	....	....	....	....	....	....	....	....	....	....
2000-01	Ferris State	CCHA	37	16	13	29	81	....	....	....	....	....	....	....	....	....	....	....	....	....	....	....	....	....	....
2001-02	Ferris State	CCHA	35	*28	10	38	68	....	....	....	....	....	....	....	....	....	....	....	....	....	....	....	....	....	....
2002-03	Ferris State	CCHA	42	*35	*44	*79	56	....	....	....	....	....	....	....	....	....	....	....	....	....	....	....	....	....	....
2003-04	**Anaheim**	**NHL**	**21**	**0**	**6**	**6**	**12**	**0**	**0**	**0**	**31**	**0.0**	**1**	**7**	**14.3**	**9:07**	....	....	....	....	....	....	....	....	....
	Cincinnati	AHL	59	19	25	44	101	....	....	....	....	....	....	....	....	....	9	3	2	5	24	....	....	....	....
	NHL Totals		**21**	**0**	**6**	**6**	**12**	**0**	**0**	**0**	**31**	**0.0**		**7**	**14.3**	**9:07**	....	....	....	....	....	....	....	....	....

CCHA First All-Star Team (2002, 2003) • CCHA Player of the Year (2003) • NCAA West First All-American Team (2003)

Signed as a free agent by **Anaheim**, April 1, 2003.

KURKA, Tomas

(KUHR-kuh, TAW-mahsh) **CAR.**

Left wing. Shoots left. 5'11", 190 lbs. Born, Most, Czech., December 14, 1981. Carolina's 1st choice, 32nd overall, in 2000 Entry Draft.

1996-97	Litvinov Jr.	Czech-Jr.	38	25	20	45	20	....	....	....	....	....	....	....	....	....	....	....	....	....	....	....	....	....	....
1997-98	Litvinov Jr.	Czech-Jr.	44	38	23	61	90	....	....	....	....	....	....	....	....	....	....	....	....	....	....	....	....	....	....
1998-99	Litvinov Jr.	Czech-Jr.	42	23	16	39	47	....	....	....	....	....	....	....	....	....	....	....	....	....	....	....	....	....	....
	Litvinov	Czech	6	0	0	0	0	....	....	....	....	....	....	....	....	....	....	....	....	....	....	....	....	....	....
99-2000	Plymouth Whalers	OHL	64	36	28	64	37	....	....	....	....	....	....	....	....	....	17	7	6	13	6	....	....	....	....
2000-01	Plymouth Whalers	OHL	47	15	29	44	20	....	....	....	....	....	....	....	....	....	16	8	13	21	13	....	....	....	....
2001-02	Lowell	AHL	71	13	15	28	24	....	....	....	....	....	....	....	....	....	5	1	1	2	2	....	....	....	....
2002-03	**Carolina**	**NHL**	**14**	**3**	**2**	**5**	**2**	**0**	**0**	**0**	**22**	**13.6**	**1**	**4**	**50.0**	**14:59**	....	....	....	....	....	....	....	....	....
	Lowell	AHL	61	17	12	29	10	....	....	....	....	....	....	....	....	....	....	....	....	....	....	....	....	....	....

			Regular Season														Playoffs								
Season	Club	League	GP	G	A	Pts	PIM	PP	SH	GW	S	%	+/-	TF	F%	Min	GP	G	A	Pts	PIM	PP	SH	GW	Min
2003-04	Carolina	NHL	3	0	0	0	0	0	0	0	3	0.0	0	0	0.0	8:45	....	....	....	....	....	....	....	....	....
	Lowell	AHL	55	6	26	32	14	....	....	....	....	....	....	....	....	....	....	....	....	....	....	....	....	....	....
	NHL Totals		17	3	2	5	2	0	0	0	25	12.0		4	50.0	13:53	....	....	....	....	....	....	....	....	....

KUTLAK, Zdenek

(KUHT-lak, z'DEHN-ehk) **BOS.**

Defense. Shoots left. 6'3", 221 lbs. Born, Budejovice, Czech., February 13, 1980. Boston's 10th choice, 237th overall, in 2000 Entry Draft.

Season	Club	League	GP	G	A	Pts	PIM	PP	SH	GW	S	%	+/-	TF	F%	Min	GP	G	A	Pts	PIM	PP	SH	GW	Min
1996-97	C. Budejovice Jr.	Czech-Jr.	45	8	11	19	20	....	....	....	....	....	....	....	....	....	....	....	....	....	....	....	....	....	....
1997-98	C. Budejovice Jr.	Czech-Jr.	43	1	6	7	30	....	....	....	....	....	....	....	....	....	....	....	....	....	....	....	....	....	....
1998-99	C. Budejovice Jr.	Czech-Jr.	31	6	14	20	20	....	....	....	....	....	....	....	....	....	....	....	....	....	....	....	....	....	....
	Ceske Budejovice	Czech	22	1	3	4	4	....	....	....	....	....	....	....	....	....	3	0	0	0	0	....	....	....	....
99-2000	C. Budejovice Jr.	Czech-Jr.	8	4	2	6	26	....	....	....	....	....	....	....	....	....	....	....	....	....	....	....	....	....	....
	JindrichuvHradec	Czech-3	4	1	1	2	0	....	....	....	....	....	....	....	....	....	....	....	....	....	....	....	....	....	....
	IHC Pisek	Czech-2	3	1	0	1	0	....	....	....	....	....	....	....	....	....	2	0	0	0	2	....	....	....	....
	Ceske Budejovice	Czech	28	1	0	1	2	....	....	....	....	....	....	....	....	....	1	0	0	0	0	....	....	....	....
2000-01	Boston	NHL	10	0	2	2	4	0	0	0	7	0.0	–3	0	0.0	16:05	....	....	....	....	....	....	....	....	....
	Providence Bruins	AHL	62	4	5	9	16	....	....	....	....	....	....	....	....	....	....	....	....	....	....	....	....	....	....
2001-02	Providence Bruins	AHL	80	5	15	20	73	....	....	....	....	....	....	....	....	....	2	0	0	0	0	....	....	....	....
2002-03	Boston	NHL	4	1	0	1	0	0	0	0	1	100.0	0	0	0.0	5:16	....	....	....	....	....	....	....	....	....
	Providence Bruins	AHL	68	4	12	16	52	....	....	....	....	....	....	....	....	....	4	1	0	1	2	....	....	....	....
2003-04	Boston	NHL	2	0	0	0	0	0	0	0	0	0.0	–1	0	0.0	11:33	....	....	....	....	....	....	....	....	....
	Providence Bruins	AHL	47	7	12	19	22	....	....	....	....	....	....	....	....	....	2	0	0	0	2	....	....	....	....
	NHL Totals		16	1	2	3	4	0	0	0	8	12.5		0	0.0	12:49	....	....	....	....	....	....	....	....	....

Signed as a free agent by **Karlovy Vary** (Czech), May 16, 2004.

KUZNETSOV, Maxim

(kooz-NEHT-zahv, MAX-ihm)

Defense. Shoots left. 6'5", 230 lbs. Born, Pavlodar, USSR, March 24, 1977. Detroit's 1st choice, 26th overall, in 1995 Entry Draft.

Season	Club	League	GP	G	A	Pts	PIM	PP	SH	GW	S	%	+/-	TF	F%	Min	GP	G	A	Pts	PIM	PP	SH	GW	Min
1994-95	Dynamo Moscow	CIS	11	0	0	0	8	....	....	....	....	....	....	....	....	....	....	....	....	....	....	....	....	....	....
1995-96	Dynamo Moscow	CIS	9	1	1	2	22	....	....	....	....	....	....	....	....	....	4	0	0	0	0	....	....	....	....
1996-97	Dynamo Moscow	Russia	23	0	2	2	16	....	....	....	....	....	....	....	....	....	....	....	....	....	....	....	....	....	....
	Adirondack	AHL	2	0	1	1	6	....	....	....	....	....	....	....	....	....	2	0	0	0	0	....	....	....	....
1997-98	Adirondack	AHL	51	5	5	10	43	....	....	....	....	....	....	....	....	....	3	0	1	1	4	....	....	....	....
1998-99	Adirondack	AHL	60	0	4	4	30	....	....	....	....	....	....	....	....	....	3	0	0	0	0	....	....	....	....
99-2000	Cincinnati	AHL	47	2	9	11	36	....	....	....	....	....	....	....	....	....	....	....	....	....	....	....	....	....	....
2000-01	Detroit	NHL	25	1	2	3	23	0	0	0	17	5.9	–1	1	0.0	9:28	....	....	....	....	....	....	....	....	....
2001-02	Detroit	NHL	39	1	2	3	40	0	0	0	27	3.7	0	0	0.0	11:51	....	....	....	....	....	....	....	....	....
	Cincinnati	AHL	7	1	0	1	4	....	....	....	....	....	....	....	....	....	....	....	....	....	....	....	....	....	....
2002-03	Detroit	NHL	53	0	3	3	54	0	0	0	32	0.0	0	1	100.0	13:10	....	....	....	....	....	....	....	....	....
	Los Angeles	NHL	3	0	0	0	0	0	0	0	1	0.0	1	0	0.0	16:37	....	....	....	....	....	....	....	....	....
2003-04	Los Angeles	NHL	16	0	1	1	20	0	0	0	11	0.0	–5	0	0.0	15:11	....	....	....	....	....	....	....	....	....
	Manchester	AHL	39	2	8	10	57	....	....	....	....	....	....	....	....	....	2	0	0	0	4	....	....	....	....
	NHL Totals		136	2	8	10	137	0	0	0	88	2.3		2	50.0	12:25	....	....	....	....	....	....	....	....	....

• Missed majority of 2000-01 season recovering from knee injury suffered in game vs. Vancouver, November 24, 2000. Traded to **Los Angeles** by **Detroit** with Sean Avery, Detroit's 1st round choice (Jeff Tambellini) in 2003 Entry Draft and Detroit's 2nd round choice (later traded to Boston - Boston selected Martins Karsums) in 2004 Entry Draft for Mathieu Schneider, March 11, 2003.

KVASHA, Oleg

(kuh-VAH-shah, OH-lehg) **NYI**

Left wing/Center. Shoots right. 6'5", 230 lbs. Born, Moscow, USSR, July 26, 1978. Florida's 3rd choice, 65th overall, in 1996 Entry Draft.

Season	Club	League	GP	G	A	Pts	PIM	PP	SH	GW	S	%	+/-	TF	F%	Min	GP	G	A	Pts	PIM	PP	SH	GW	Min
1995-96	CSKA Moscow	CIS	38	2	3	5	14	....	....	....	....	....	....	....	....	....	2	0	0	0	0	....	....	....	....
1996-97	CSKA Moscow	Russia-2	44	20	22	42	115	....	....	....	....	....	....	....	....	....	....	....	....	....	....	....	....	....	....
1997-98	New Haven	AHL	57	13	16	29	46	....	....	....	....	....	....	....	....	....	3	2	1	3	0	....	....	....	....
1998-99	Florida	NHL	68	12	13	25	45	4	0	2	138	8.7	5	373	28.4	12:48	....	....	....	....	....	....	....	....	....
99-2000	Florida	NHL	78	5	20	25	34	2	0	0	110	4.5	3	553	34.9	11:24	4	0	0	0	0	0	0	0	10:18
2000-01	NY Islanders	NHL	62	11	9	20	46	0	0	0	118	9.3	–15	627	43.7	14:56	....	....	....	....	....	....	....	....	....
2001-02	NY Islanders	NHL	71	13	25	38	80	2	0	3	119	10.9	–4	456	47.4	14:12	7	0	1	1	6	0	0	0	15:17
	Russia	Olympics	5	0	0	0	0	....	....	....	....	....	....	....	....	....	....	....	....	....	....	....	....	....	....
2002-03	NY Islanders	NHL	69	12	14	26	44	0	1	2	121	9.9	4	256	43.0	13:03	5	0	1	1	2	0	0	0	16:26
2003-04	NY Islanders	NHL	81	15	36	51	48	5	3	3	147	10.2	4	656	38.3	17:52	5	1	0	1	0	1	0	0	16:05
	NHL Totals		429	68	117	185	297	13	4	10	753	9.0		2921	39.4	14:05	21	1	2	3	8	1	0	0	14:48

Traded to **NY Islanders** by **Florida** with Mark Parrish for Roberto Luongo and Olli Jokinen, June 24, 2000.

KWIATKOWSKI, Joel

(KWEE-at-KOW-skee, JOHL) **FLA.**

Defense. Shoots left. 6'2", 210 lbs. Born, Kindersley, Sask., March 22, 1977. Dallas' 7th choice, 194th overall, in 1996 Entry Draft.

Season	Club	League	GP	G	A	Pts	PIM	PP	SH	GW	S	%	+/-	TF	F%	Min	GP	G	A	Pts	PIM	PP	SH	GW	Min
1992-93	North Battleford	SJHL	51	3	14	17	89	....	....	....	....	....	....	....	....	....	....	....	....	....	....	....	....	....	....
1994-95	Tacoma Rockets	WHL	70	4	13	17	66	....	....	....	....	....	....	....	....	....	4	0	0	0	2	....	....	....	....
1995-96	Kelowna Rockets	WHL	40	6	17	23	85	....	....	....	....	....	....	....	....	....	....	....	....	....	....	....	....	....	....
	Prince George	WHL	32	6	11	17	48	....	....	....	....	....	....	....	....	....	....	....	....	....	....	....	....	....	....
1996-97	Prince George	WHL	72	15	37	52	94	....	....	....	....	....	....	....	....	....	15	4	2	6	24	....	....	....	....
1997-98	Prince George	WHL	62	21	43	64	65	....	....	....	....	....	....	....	....	....	11	3	6	9	6	....	....	....	....
1998-99	Cincinnati	AHL	80	12	21	33	48	....	....	....	....	....	....	....	....	....	3	2	0	2	0	....	....	....	....
99-2000	Cincinnati	AHL	70	4	22	26	28	....	....	....	....	....	....	....	....	....	....	....	....	....	....	....	....	....	....
2000-01	Ottawa	NHL	4	1	0	1	0	0	0	0	2	50.0	1	0	0.0	12:04	....	....	....	....	....	....	....	....	....
	Grand Rapids	IHL	77	4	17	21	58	....	....	....	....	....	....	....	....	....	10	1	0	1	4	....	....	....	....
2001-02	Ottawa	NHL	11	0	0	0	12	0	0	0	9	0.0	5	0	0.0	13:41	....	....	....	....	....	....	....	....	....
	Grand Rapids	AHL	65	8	21	29	94	....	....	....	....	....	....	....	....	....	5	1	2	3	12	....	....	....	....
2002-03	Ottawa	NHL	20	0	2	2	6	0	0	0	28	0.0	2	2	0.0	12:13	....	....	....	....	....	....	....	....	....
	Binghamton	AHL	1	0	0	0	2	....	....	....	....	....	....	....	....	....	....	....	....	....	....	....	....	....	....
	Washington	NHL	34	0	3	3	12	0	0	0	28	0.0	1	2	0.0	15:32	6	0	0	0	2	0	0	0	17:48
2003-04	Washington	NHL	80	6	6	12	89	2	0	0	90	6.7	–28	0	0.0	21:16	....	....	....	....	....	....	....	....	....
	NHL Totals		149	7	11	18	119	2	0	0	157	4.5		4	0.0	17:56	6	0	0	0	2	0	0	0	17:48

WHL West Second All-Star Team (1997) • WHL West First All-Star Team (1998)

Signed as a free agent by **Anaheim**, June 18, 1998. Traded to **Ottawa** by **Anaheim** for Patrick Traverse, June 12, 2000. Traded to **Washington** by **Ottawa** for Washington's 9th round choice (later traded back to Washington – Washington selected Mark Olafson) in 2003 Entry Draft, January 15, 2003. Signed as a free agent by **Florida**, July 16, 2004.

LAAKSONEN, Antti

(lah-AHK-soh-nehn, AHN-tee) **COL.**

Left wing. Shoots left. 6', 180 lbs. Born, Tammela, Finland, October 3, 1973. Boston's 10th choice, 191st overall, in 1997 Entry Draft.

Season	Club	League	GP	G	A	Pts	PIM	PP	SH	GW	S	%	+/-	TF	F%	Min	GP	G	A	Pts	PIM	PP	SH	GW	Min
1991-92	FoPS Forssa Jr.	Finn-Jr.	24	19	23	42	22	....	....	....	....	....	....	....	....	....	....	....	....	....	....	....	....	....	....
	FoPS Forssa	Finland-2	41	16	15	31	8	....	....	....	....	....	....	....	....	....	....	....	....	....	....	....	....	....	....
1992-93	FoPS Forssa Jr.	Finn-Jr.	9	5	3	8	10	....	....	....	....	....	....	....	....	....	....	....	....	....	....	....	....	....	....
	FoPS Forssa	Finland-2	34	11	19	30	36	....	....	....	....	....	....	....	....	....	....	....	....	....	....	....	....	....	....
	HPK Jr.	Finn-Jr.	1	1	1	2	0	....	....	....	....	....	....	....	....	....	....	....	....	....	....	....	....	....	....
	HPK Hameenlinna	Finland	2	0	0	0	0	....	....	....	....	....	....	....	....	....	....	....	....	....	....	....	....	....	....
1993-94	U. of Denver	WCHA	36	12	9	21	38	....	....	....	....	....	....	....	....	....	....	....	....	....	....	....	....	....	....
1994-95	U. of Denver	WCHA	40	17	18	35	42	....	....	....	....	....	....	....	....	....	....	....	....	....	....	....	....	....	....
1995-96	U. of Denver	WCHA	39	25	28	53	71	....	....	....	....	....	....	....	....	....	....	....	....	....	....	....	....	....	....
1996-97	U. of Denver	WCHA	39	21	17	38	63	....	....	....	....	....	....	....	....	....	....	....	....	....	....	....	....	....	....
1997-98	Providence Bruins	AHL	38	3	2	5	14	....	....	....	....	....	....	....	....	....	....	....	....	....	....	....	....	....	....
	Charlotte	ECHL	15	4	3	7	12	....	....	....	....	....	....	....	....	....	6	0	3	3	0	....	....	....	....
1998-99	Boston	NHL	11	1	2	3	2	0	0	0	8	12.5	–1	0	0.0	9:20	....	....	....	....	....	....	....	....	....
	Providence Bruins	AHL	66	25	33	58	52	....	....	....	....	....	....	....	....	....	19	7	2	9	28	....	....	....	....
99-2000	Boston	NHL	27	6	3	9	2	0	0	1	23	26.1	3	3	66.7	7:50	....	....	....	....	....	....	....	....	....
	Providence Bruins	AHL	40	10	12	22	57	....	....	....	....	....	....	....	....	....	14	5	4	9	4	....	....	....	....
2000-01	Minnesota	NHL	82	12	16	28	24	0	2	1	129	9.3	–7	15	26.7	16:27	....	....	....	....	....	....	....	....	....
2001-02	Minnesota	NHL	82	16	17	33	22	0	0	1	104	15.4	–5	19	42.1	16:20	....	....	....	....	....	....	....	....	....

			Regular Season														Playoffs								
Season	Club	League	GP	G	A	Pts	PIM	PP	SH	GW	S	%	+/-	TF	F%	Min	GP	G	A	Pts	PIM	PP	SH	GW	Min
2002-03	Minnesota	NHL	82	15	16	31	26	1	2	4	106	14.2	4	51	29.4	15:55	16	1	3	4	4	0	0	0	16:34
2003-04	Minnesota	NHL	77	12	14	26	20	0	1	1	100	12.0	0	144	36.1	16:03	....	....	....	....	....	....	....	....	....
	NHL Totals		361	62	68	130	96	1	5	8	470	13.2		232	34.9	15:21	16	1	3	4	4	0	0	0	16:34

WCHA Second All-Star Team (1996)

Signed as a free agent by **Minnesota**, July 14, 2000. Signed as a free agent by **Colorado**, July 2, 2004.

LACHANCE, Scott

(lah-CHANTS, SKAWT) **CBJ**

Defense. Shoots left. 6'1", 215 lbs. Born, Charlottesville, VA, October 22, 1972. NY Islanders' 1st choice, 4th overall, in 1991 Entry Draft.

1988-89	Springfield	NEJHL	36	8	28	36	20	....	....	....	....	....	....	....	....	....	....	....	....	....	....	....	....	....	....
1989-90	Springfield	NEJHL	34	25	41	66	62	....	....	....	....	....	....	....	....	....	....	....	....	....	....	....	....	....	....
1990-91	Boston University	H-East	31	5	19	24	48	....	....	....	....	....	....	....	....	....	....	....	....	....	....	....	....	....	....
1991-92	Team USA	Nat-Tm	36	1	10	11	34	....	....	....	....	....	....	....	....	....	....	....	....	....	....	....	....	....	....
	United States	Olympics	8	0	1	1	6	....	....	....	....	....	....	....	....	....	....	....	....	....	....	....	....	....	....
	NY Islanders	NHL	17	1	4	5	9	0	0	0	20	5.0	13	....	....	....	....	....	....	....	....	....	....	....	....
1992-93	NY Islanders	NHL	75	7	17	24	67	0	1	2	62	11.3	-1	....	....	....	....	....	....	....	....	....	....	....	....
1993-94	NY Islanders	NHL	74	3	11	14	70	0	0	1	59	5.1	-5	....	....	....	3	0	0	0	0	0	0	0	
1994-95	NY Islanders	NHL	26	6	7	13	26	3	0	0	56	10.7	2	....	....	....	....	....	....	....	....	....	....	....	....
1995-96	NY Islanders	NHL	55	3	10	13	54	1	0	0	81	3.7	-19	....	....	....	....	....	....	....	....	....	....	....	....
1996-97	NY Islanders	NHL	81	3	11	14	47	1	0	0	97	3.1	-7	....	....	....	....	....	....	....	....	....	....	....	....
1997-98	NY Islanders	NHL	63	2	11	13	45	1	0	0	62	3.2	-11	....	....	....	....	....	....	....	....	....	....	....	....
1998-99	NY Islanders	NHL	59	1	8	9	30	1	0	0	37	2.7	-19	0	0.0	21:34	....	....	....	....	....	....	....	....	....
	Montreal	NHL	17	1	1	2	11	0	0	0	22	4.5	-2	0	0.0	22:29	....	....	....	....	....	....	....	....	....
99-2000	Montreal	NHL	57	0	6	6	22	0	0	0	41	0.0	-4	0	0.0	17:47	....	....	....	....	....	....	....	....	....
2000-01	Vancouver	NHL	76	3	11	14	46	0	0	0	55	5.5	5	0	0.0	19:26	2	0	1	1	2	0	0	0	13:09
2001-02	Vancouver	NHL	81	1	10	11	50	0	0	0	48	2.1	15	2	100.0	20:02	6	1	1	2	4	0	0	1	20:33
2002-03	Columbus	NHL	61	0	1	1	46	0	0	0	35	0.0	-20	0	0.0	20:01	....	....	....	....	....	....	....	....	....
2003-04	Columbus	NHL	77	0	4	4	44	0	0	0	35	0.0	-23	1	0.0	18:59	....	....	....	....	....	....	....	....	....
	NHL Totals		819	31	112	143	567	7	1	3	710	4.4		3	66.7	19:45	11	1	2	3	6	0	0	1	18:41

Played in NHL All-Star Game (1997)

Traded to **Montreal** by **NY Islanders** for Montreal's 3rd round choice (Mattias Weinhandl) in 1999 Entry Draft, March 9, 1999. Signed as a free agent by **Vancouver**, August 13, 2000. Signed as a free agent by **Columbus**, July 4, 2002.

LaCOUTURE, Dan

(LA-koo-TUHR, DAN)

Left wing. Shoots left. 6'2", 208 lbs. Born, Hyannis, MA, April 18, 1977. NY Islanders' 2nd choice, 29th overall, in 1996 Entry Draft.

1992-93	Natick Redmen	Hi-School	20	38	34	72	46	....	....	....	....	....	....	....	....	....	....	....	....	....	....	....	....	....	....
1993-94	Natick Redmen	Hi-School	21	52	49	101	58	....	....	....	....	....	....	....	....	....	....	....	....	....	....	....	....	....	....
1994-95	Springfield Jr. Pics	NEJHL	52	44	56	100	98	....	....	....	....	....	....	....	....	....	....	....	....	....	....	....	....	....	....
1995-96	Springfield Jr. Pics	NEJHL	29	24	35	59	79	....	....	....	....	....	....	....	....	....	13	12	13	25	23	....	....	....	....
1996-97	Boston University	H-East	31	13	12	25	18	....	....	....	....	....	....	....	....	....	....	....	....	....	....	....	....	....	....
1997-98	Hamilton	AHL	77	15	10	25	31	....	....	....	....	....	....	....	....	....	5	1	0	1	0	....	....	....	....
1998-99	Edmonton	NHL	3	0	0	0	0	0	0	0	0	0.0	1	0	0.0	6:30	....	....	....	....	....	....	....	....	....
	Hamilton	AHL	72	17	14	31	73	....	....	....	....	....	....	....	....	....	9	2	1	3	2	....	....	....	....
99-2000	Edmonton	NHL	5	0	0	0	10	0	0	0	2	0.0	0	0	0.0	7:02	1	0	0	0	0	0	0	0	2:05
	Hamilton	AHL	70	23	17	40	85	....	....	....	....	....	....	....	....	....	6	2	1	3	0	....	....	....	....
2000-01	Edmonton	NHL	37	2	4	6	29	0	0	1	22	9.1	-2	5	20.0	7:06	....	....	....	....	....	....	....	....	....
	Pittsburgh	NHL	11	0	0	0	14	0	0	0	1	0.0	0	1	100.0	5:57	5	0	0	0	2	0	0	0	5:46
2001-02	Pittsburgh	NHL	82	6	11	17	71	0	1	0	77	7.8	-19	21	38.1	13:16	....	....	....	....	....	....	....	....	....
2002-03	Pittsburgh	NHL	44	2	2	4	72	0	0	0	30	6.7	-8	5	80.0	9:13	....	....	....	....	....	....	....	....	....
	NY Rangers	NHL	24	1	4	5	0	0	0	0	17	5.9	4	1	0.0	10:18	....	....	....	....	....	....	....	....	....
2003-04	NY Rangers	NHL	59	5	2	7	82	1	0	1	39	12.8	-13	8	50.0	9:29	....	....	....	....	....	....	....	....	....
	NHL Totals		265	16	23	39	278	1	1	2	188	8.5		41	43.9	10:08	6	0	0	0	2	0	0	0	5:09

Traded to **Edmonton** by **NY Islanders** for Mariusz Czerkawski, August 25, 1997. Traded to **Pittsburgh** by **Edmonton** for Sven Butenschon, March 13, 2001. Traded to **NY Rangers** by **Pittsburgh** with Mike Wilson, Alex Kovalev and Janne Laukkanen for Joel Bouchard, Richard Lintner, Rico Fata, Mikael Samuelsson and future considerations, February 10, 2003.

LAFLAMME, Christian

(lah-FLAM, KRIHS-tan)

Defense. Shoots right. 6'1", 206 lbs. Born, St-Charles, Que., November 24, 1976. Chicago's 2nd choice, 45th overall, in 1995 Entry Draft.

1991-92	Ste-Foy	QAAA	42	5	27	32	100	....	....	....	....	....	....	....	....	....	8	1	2	3	14	....	....	....	....
1992-93	Verdun	QMJHL	69	2	17	19	85	....	....	....	....	....	....	....	....	....	3	0	2	2	6	....	....	....	....
1993-94	Verdun	QMJHL	72	4	34	38	85	....	....	....	....	....	....	....	....	....	4	0	3	3	4	....	....	....	....
1994-95	Beauport	QMJHL	67	6	41	47	82	....	....	....	....	....	....	....	....	....	8	1	4	5	6	....	....	....	....
1995-96	Beauport	QMJHL	41	13	23	36	63	....	....	....	....	....	....	....	....	....	20	7	17	24	32	....	....	....	....
1996-97	Chicago	NHL	4	0	1	1	2	0	0	0	3	0.0	3	....	....	....	....	....	....	....	....	....	....	....	....
	Indianapolis Ice	IHL	62	5	15	20	60	....	....	....	....	....	....	....	....	....	4	1	1	2	16	....	....	....	....
1997-98	Chicago	NHL	72	0	11	11	59	0	0	0	75	0.0	14	....	....	....	....	....	....	....	....	....	....	....	....
1998-99	Chicago	NHL	62	2	11	13	70	0	0	0	53	3.8	0	0	0.0	18:51	....	....	....	....	....	....	....	....	....
	Portland Pirates	AHL	2	0	1	1	2	....	....	....	....	....	....	....	....	....	....	....	....	....	....	....	....	....	....
	Edmonton	NHL	11	0	1	1	0	0	0	0	15	0.0	-3	0	0.0	16:33	4	0	1	1	2	0	0	0	21:51
99-2000	Edmonton	NHL	50	0	5	5	32	0	0	0	18	0.0	-4	5	40.0	13:40	....	....	....	....	....	....	....	....	....
	Montreal	NHL	15	0	2	2	8	0	0	0	6	0.0	-5	0	0.0	14:32	....	....	....	....	....	....	....	....	....
2000-01	Montreal	NHL	39	0	3	3	42	0	0	0	16	0.0	-11	1	0.0	12:04	....	....	....	....	....	....	....	....	....
2001-02	St. Louis	NHL	8	0	1	1	4	0	0	0	6	0.0	3	0	0.0	13:54	....	....	....	....	....	....	....	....	....
	Worcester IceCats	AHL	62	2	17	19	52	....	....	....	....	....	....	....	....	....	....	....	....	....	....	....	....	....	....
2002-03	St. Louis	NHL	47	0	9	9	45	0	0	0	44	0.0	1	0	0.0	15:10	5	0	0	0	4	0	0	0	12:28
	Worcester IceCats	AHL	8	0	4	4	6	....	....	....	....	....	....	....	....	....	....	....	....	....	....	....	....	....	....
2003-04	St. Louis	NHL	16	0	1	1	20	0	0	0	9	0.0	-3	0	0.0	13:00	....	....	....	....	....	....	....	....	....
	Worcester IceCats	AHL	28	1	4	5	25	....	....	....	....	....	....	....	....	....	7	0	0	0	6	....	....	....	....
	NHL Totals		324	2	45	47	282	0	0	0	245	0.8		6	33.3	15:08	9	0	1	1	6	0	0	0	16:38

QMJHL All-Rookie Team (1993) • QMJHL Second All-Star Team (1995)

Traded to **Edmonton** by **Chicago** with Daniel Cleary, Ethan Moreau and Chad Kilger for Boris Mironov, Dean McAmmond and Jonas Elofsson, March 20, 1999. Traded to **Montreal** by **Edmonton** with Matthieu Descoteaux for Igor Ulanov and Alain Nasreddine, March 9, 2000. • Missed majority of 2000-01 season recovering from groin injury suffered in game vs. Calgary, December 13, 2000. Signed as a free agent by **St. Louis**, August 21, 2001. Signed as a free agent by **Kassel** (Germany), May 16, 2004.

LAICH, Brooks

(LAYCH, BROOKS) **WSH.**

Center. Shoots left. 6'2", 199 lbs. Born, Wawota, Alta., June 23, 1983. Ottawa's 7th choice, 193rd overall, in 2001 Entry Draft.

99-2000	Tisdale Trojans	SMHL	57	51	52	103	....	....	....	....	....	....	....	....	....	....	....	....	....	....	....	....	....	....	....
2000-01	Moose Jaw	WHL	71	9	21	30	28	....	....	....	....	....	....	....	....	....	4	0	0	0	5	....	....	....	....
2001-02	Moose Jaw	WHL	28	6	14	20	12	....	....	....	....	....	....	....	....	....	....	....	....	....	....	....	....	....	....
	Seattle	WHL	47	22	36	58	42	....	....	....	....	....	....	....	....	....	11	5	3	8	11	....	....	....	....
2002-03	Seattle	WHL	60	41	53	94	65	....	....	....	....	....	....	....	....	....	15	5	14	19	24	....	....	....	....
2003-04	Ottawa	NHL	1	0	0	0	2	0	0	0	1	0.0	0	7	42.9	9:34	....	....	....	....	....	....	....	....	....
	Binghamton	AHL	44	15	18	33	16	....	....	....	....	....	....	....	....	....	....	....	....	....	....	....	....	....	....
	Washington	NHL	4	0	1	1	0	0	0	0	2	0.0	-1	49	51.0	10:50	....	....	....	....	....	....	....	....	....
	Portland Pirates	AHL	22	1	3	4	12	....	....	....	....	....	....	....	....	....	6	0	0	0	0	....	....	....	....
	NHL Totals		5	0	1	1	2	0	0	0	3	0.0		56	50.0	10:35	....	....	....	....	....	....	....	....	....

WHL West First All-Star Team (2003)

Traded to **Washington** by **Ottawa** with Ottawa's 2nd round choice in 2005 Entry Draft and future considerations for Peter Bondra, February 18, 2004.

LAING, Quintin (LAY-ihng, QUIHN-tihn) CHI.

Left wing. Shoots left. 6'2", 175 lbs. Born, Rosetown, Sask., June 8, 1979. Detroit's 3rd choice, 102nd overall, in 1997 Entry Draft.

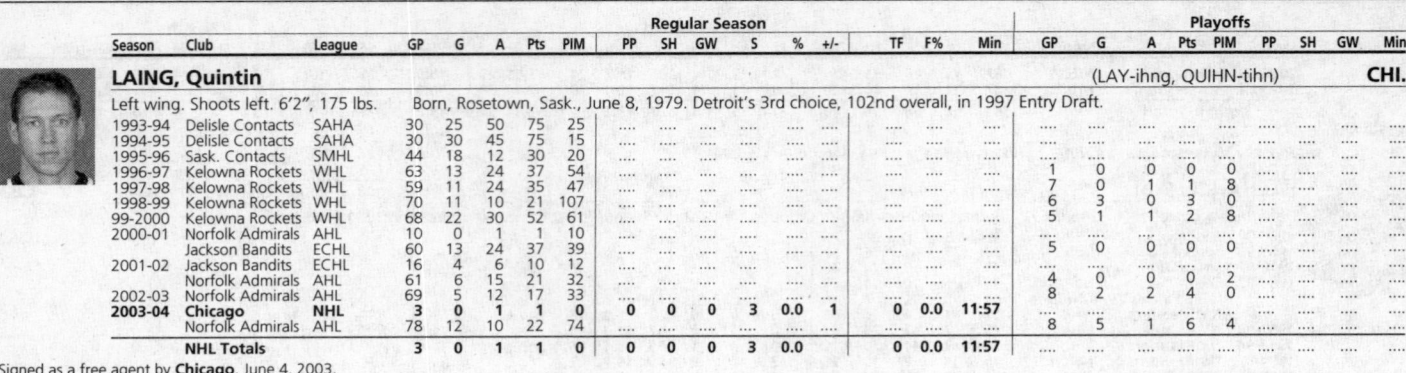

			Regular Season														Playoffs								
Season	Club	League	GP	G	A	Pts	PIM	PP	SH	GW	S	%	+/-	TF	F%	Min	GP	G	A	Pts	PIM	PP	SH	GW	Min
1993-94	Delisle Contacts	SAHA	30	25	50	75	25																		
1994-95	Delisle Contacts	SAHA	30	30	45	75	15																		
1995-96	Sask. Contacts	SMHL	44	18	12	30	20																		
1996-97	Kelowna Rockets	WHL	63	13	24	37	54										1	0	0	0	0				
1997-98	Kelowna Rockets	WHL	59	11	24	35	47										7	0	1	1	8				
1998-99	Kelowna Rockets	WHL	70	11	10	21	107										6	3	0	3	0				
99-2000	Kelowna Rockets	WHL	68	22	30	52	61										5	1	1	2	8				
2000-01	Norfolk Admirals	AHL	10	0	1	1	10																		
	Jackson Bandits	ECHL	60	13	24	37	39										5	0	0	0	0				
2001-02	Jackson Bandits	ECHL	16	4	6	10	12																		
	Norfolk Admirals	AHL	61	6	15	21	32										4	0	0	0	2				
2002-03	Norfolk Admirals	AHL	69	5	12	17	33										8	2	2	4	0				
2003-04	**Chicago**	**NHL**	**3**	**0**	**1**	**1**	**0**	**0**	**0**	**0**	**3**	**0.0**	**1**	**0**	**0.0**	**11:57**									
	Norfolk Admirals	AHL	78	12	10	22	74										8	5	1	6	4				
	NHL Totals		**3**	**0**	**1**	**1**	**0**	**0**	**0**	**0**	**3**	**0.0**		**0**	**0.0**	**11:57**									

Signed as a free agent by **Chicago**, June 4, 2003.

LAMPMAN, Bryce (LAMP-man, BRIGHS) NYR

Defense. Shoots left. 6'1", 193 lbs. Born, Rochester, MN, August 31, 1982. NY Rangers' 4th choice, 113th overall, in 2001 Entry Draft.

Season	Club	League	GP	G	A	Pts	PIM	PP	SH	GW	S	%	+/-	TF	F%	Min	GP	G	A	Pts	PIM	PP	SH	GW	Min
1998-99	Rochester	USHL	53	3	8	11	33																		
99-2000	Rochester	USHL	10	0	0	0	14																		
	Omaha Lancers	USHL	11	1	2	3	38										4	0	0	0	0				
2000-01	Omaha Lancers	USHL	55	10	11	21	77										12	1	4	5	12				
2001-02	Nebraska-Omaha	CCHA	26	0	4	4	28																		
2002-03	Kamloops Blazers	WHL	29	1	17	18	32																		
	Hartford	AHL	45	0	6	6	32										2	0	1	1	0				
2003-04	**NY Rangers**	**NHL**	**8**	**0**	**0**	**0**	**0**	**0**	**0**	**0**	**7**	**0.0**	**–4**	**0**	**0.0**	**19:34**									
	Hartford	AHL	68	4	11	15	50										16	1	3	4	14				
	NHL Totals		**8**	**0**	**0**	**0**	**0**	**0**	**0**	**0**	**7**	**0.0**		**0**	**0.0**	**19:34**									

• Left **Nebraska-Omaha** (CCHA) and signed as a free agent by **Kamloops** (WHL), August 1, 2002.

LANG, Robert (LANG, RAW-buhrt) DET.

Center. Shoots right. 6'2", 216 lbs. Born, Teplice, Czech., December 19, 1970. Los Angeles' 6th choice, 133rd overall, in 1990 Entry Draft.

Season	Club	League	GP	G	A	Pts	PIM	PP	SH	GW	S	%	+/-	TF	F%	Min	GP	G	A	Pts	PIM	PP	SH	GW	Min
1988-89	CHZ Litvinov	Czech	7	3	2	5	0																		
1989-90	CHZ Litvinov	Czech	32	8	7	15											8	3	3	6					
1990-91	CHZ Litvinov	Czech	56	26	26	52	38																		
1991-92	CHZ Litvinov	Czech	43	12	31	43	34																		
	Czechoslovakia	Olympics	8	5	8	13	8																		
1992-93	**Los Angeles**	**NHL**	**11**	**0**	**5**	**5**	**2**	**0**	**0**	**0**	**3**	**0.0**	**–3**												
	Phoenix	IHL	38	9	21	30	20																		
1993-94	**Los Angeles**	**NHL**	**32**	**9**	**10**	**19**	**10**	**0**	**0**	**0**	**41**	**22.0**	**7**												
	Phoenix	IHL	44	11	24	35	34																		
1994-95	Litvinov	Czech	16	4	19	23	28																		
	Los Angeles	**NHL**	**36**	**4**	**8**	**12**	**4**	**0**	**0**	**0**	**38**	**10.5**	**–7**												
1995-96	**Los Angeles**	**NHL**	**68**	**6**	**16**	**22**	**10**	**0**	**2**	**0**	**71**	**8.5**	**–15**												
1996-97	HC Sparta Praha	Czech	38	14	27	41	30										5	1	2	3	4				
	HC Sparta Praha	EuroHL	4	2	2	4	0										4	2	1	3	2				
1997-98	**Boston**	**NHL**	**3**	**0**	**0**	**0**	**2**	**0**	**0**	**0**	**2**	**0.0**	**1**												
	Pittsburgh	**NHL**	**51**	**9**	**13**	**22**	**14**	**1**	**1**	**2**	**64**	**14.1**	**6**				**6**	**0**	**3**	**3**	**2**	**0**	**0**	**0**	
	Czech Republic	Olympics	6	0	3	3	0																		
	Houston Aeros	IHL	9	1	7	8	4																		
1998-99	**Pittsburgh**	**NHL**	**72**	**21**	**23**	**44**	**24**	**7**	**0**	**3**	**137**	**15.3**	**–10**	**964**	**44.8**	**16:24**	**12**	**0**	**2**	**2**	**0**	**0**	**0**	**0**	**13:58**
99-2000	**Pittsburgh**	**NHL**	**78**	**23**	**42**	**65**	**14**	**13**	**0**	**5**	**142**	**16.2**	**–9**	**1433**	**50.7**	**19:22**	**11**	**3**	**3**	**6**	**0**	**2**	**0**	**0**	**21:42**
2000-01	**Pittsburgh**	**NHL**	**82**	**32**	**48**	**80**	**28**	**10**	**0**	**2**	**177**	**18.1**	**20**	**1348**	**43.9**	**20:24**	**16**	**4**	**4**	**8**	**4**	**0**	**0**	**0**	**19:21**
2001-02	**Pittsburgh**	**NHL**	**62**	**18**	**32**	**50**	**16**	**5**	**1**	**3**	**175**	**10.3**	**9**	**1172**	**46.3**	**22:56**									
	Czech Republic	Olympics	4	1	2	3	2																		
2002-03	**Washington**	**NHL**	**82**	**22**	**47**	**69**	**22**	**10**	**0**	**2**	**146**	**15.1**	**12**	**1069**	**45.9**	**18:47**	**6**	**2**	**1**	**3**	**2**	**0**	**0**	**1**	**21:55**
2003-04	**Washington**	**NHL**	**63**	**29**	**45**	**74**	**24**	**10**	**0**	**2**	**149**	**19.5**	**2**	**744**	**44.1**	**21:46**									
	Detroit	**NHL**	**6**	**1**	**4**	**5**	**0**	**0**	**0**	**1**	**14**	**7.1**	**2**	**96**	**57.3**	**16:20**	**12**	**4**	**5**	**9**	**6**	**0**	**0**	**0**	**18:10**
	NHL Totals		**646**	**174**	**293**	**467**	**170**	**56**	**4**	**20**	**1159**	**15.0**		**6826**	**46.4**	**19:46**	**63**	**13**	**18**	**31**	**14**	**2**	**0**	**1**	**18:42**

Played in NHL All-Star Game (2004)

Signed as a free agent by **Pittsburgh**, September 2, 1997. Claimed by **Boston** from **Pittsburgh** in Waiver Draft, September 28, 1997. Claimed on waivers by **Pittsburgh** from **Boston**, October 25, 1997. Signed as a free agent by **Washington**, July 1, 2002. Traded to **Detroit** by **Washington** for Tomas Fleischmann, Detroit's 1st round choice (Mike Green) in 2004 Entry Draft and Detroit's 4th round choice in 2006 Entry Draft, February 27, 2004.

LANGDON, Darren (LAING-duhn, DAIR-uhn) N.J.

Left wing. Shoots left. 6'1", 205 lbs. Born, Deer Lake, Nfld., January 8, 1971.

Season	Club	League	GP	G	A	Pts	PIM	PP	SH	GW	S	%	+/-	TF	F%	Min	GP	G	A	Pts	PIM	PP	SH	GW	Min
1991-92	Summerside	MJrHL	44	34	49	83	441																		
1992-93	Binghamton	AHL	18	3	4	7	115										8	0	1	1	14				
	Dayton Bombers	ECHL	54	23	22	45	429										3	0	1	1	40				
1993-94	Binghamton	AHL	54	2	7	9	327																		
1994-95	Binghamton	AHL	55	6	14	20	296										11	1	3	4	*84				
	NY Rangers	**NHL**	**18**	**1**	**1**	**2**	**62**	**0**	**0**	**0**	**6**	**16.7**	**0**												
1995-96	**NY Rangers**	**NHL**	**64**	**7**	**4**	**11**	**175**	**0**	**0**	**1**	**29**	**24.1**	**2**				**2**	**0**	**0**	**0**	**0**	**0**	**0**	**0**	
	Binghamton	AHL	1	0	0	0	12																		
1996-97	**NY Rangers**	**NHL**	**60**	**3**	**6**	**9**	**195**	**0**	**0**	**1**	**24**	**12.5**	**–1**				**10**	**0**	**0**	**0**	**2**	**0**	**0**	**0**	
1997-98	**NY Rangers**	**NHL**	**70**	**3**	**3**	**6**	**197**	**0**	**0**	**0**	**15**	**20.0**	**0**												
1998-99	**NY Rangers**	**NHL**	**44**	**0**	**0**	**0**	**80**	**0**	**0**	**0**	**8**	**0.0**	**–3**	**0**	**0.0**	**3:33**									
99-2000	**NY Rangers**	**NHL**	**21**	**0**	**1**	**1**	**26**	**0**	**0**	**0**	**13**	**0.0**	**–2**	**0**	**0.0**	**5:36**									
2000-01	**Carolina**	**NHL**	**54**	**0**	**2**	**2**	**94**	**0**	**0**	**0**	**6**	**0.0**	**–4**	**2**	**100.0**	**3:21**	**4**	**0**	**0**	**0**	**12**	**0**	**0**	**0**	**3:32**
2001-02	**Carolina**	**NHL**	**58**	**2**	**1**	**3**	**106**	**0**	**0**	**1**	**12**	**16.7**	**2**	**1**	**100.0**	**4:11**									
2002-03	**Carolina**	**NHL**	**9**	**0**	**0**	**0**	**16**	**0**	**0**	**0**	**4**	**0.0**	**0**	**0**	**0.0**	**2:45**									
	Vancouver	**NHL**	**45**	**0**	**1**	**1**	**143**	**0**	**0**	**0**	**15**	**0.0**	**–2**	**1**	**0.0**	**5:26**									
2003-04	**Montreal**	**NHL**	**64**	**0**	**3**	**3**	**135**	**0**	**0**	**0**	**22**	**0.0**	**–2**	**1**	**0.0**	**6:16**	**9**	**1**	**0**	**1**	**6**	**0**	**0**	**0**	**3:15**
	NHL Totals		**507**	**16**	**22**	**38**	**1229**	**0**	**0**	**3**	**154**	**10.4**		**5**	**60.0**	**4:38**	**25**	**1**	**0**	**1**	**20**	**0**	**0**	**0**	**3:20**

Signed as a free agent by **NY Rangers**, August 16, 1993. • Missed majority of 1999-2000 season recovering from hernia injury suffered in game vs. New Jersey, December 1, 1999. Traded to **Carolina** by **NY Rangers** with Rob DiMaio for Sandy McCarthy and Carolina's 4th round choice (Bryce Lampman) in 2001 Entry Draft, August 4, 2000. Traded to **Vancouver** by **Carolina** with Marek Malik for Jan Hlavac and Harold Druken, November 1, 2002. Claimed by **Montreal** from **Vancouver** in Waiver Draft, October 3, 2003. Signed as a free agent by **New Jersey**, July 3, 2004.

LANGENBRUNNER, Jamie (lan-gehn-BRUH-nuhr, JAY-mee) N.J.

Right wing. Shoots right. 6'1", 200 lbs. Born, Cloquet, MN, July 24, 1975. Dallas' 2nd choice, 35th overall, in 1993 Entry Draft.

Season	Club	League	GP	G	A	Pts	PIM	PP	SH	GW	S	%	+/-	TF	F%	Min	GP	G	A	Pts	PIM	PP	SH	GW	Min
1990-91	Cloquet High	Hi-School	20	6	16	22	8																		
1991-92	Cloquet High	Hi-School	23	16	23	39	24																		
1992-93	Cloquet High	Hi-School	27	27	62	89	18																		
1993-94	Peterborough	OHL	62	33	58	91	53										7	4	6	10	2				
1994-95	Peterborough	OHL	62	42	57	99	84										11	8	14	22	12				
	Dallas	**NHL**	**2**	**0**	**0**	**0**	**2**	**0**	**0**	**0**	**1**	**0.0**	**0**												
	Kalamazoo Wings	IHL															11	1	3	4	2				
1995-96	**Dallas**	**NHL**	**12**	**2**	**2**	**4**	**6**	**1**	**0**	**0**	**15**	**13.3**	**–2**												
	Michigan	IHL	59	25	40	65	129										10	3	10	13	8				
1996-97	**Dallas**	**NHL**	**76**	**13**	**26**	**39**	**51**	**3**	**0**	**3**	**112**	**11.6**	**–2**				**5**	**1**	**1**	**2**	**14**	**0**	**0**	**1**	
1997-98	**Dallas**	**NHL**	**81**	**23**	**29**	**52**	**61**	**8**	**0**	**6**	**159**	**14.5**	**9**				**16**	**1**	**4**	**5**	**14**	**0**	**0**	**1**	
	United States	Olympics	3	0	0	0	4																		

Season	Club	League	GP	G	A	Pts	PIM	PP	SH	GW	S	%	+/-	TF	F%	Min	GP	G	A	Pts	PIM	PP	SH	GW	Min
			Regular Season														Playoffs								
1998-99♦	**Dallas**	**NHL**	**75**	**12**	**33**	**45**	**62**	**4**	**0**	**1**	**145**	**8.3**	**10**	**217**	**46.1**	**15:51**	**23**	**10**	**7**	**17**	**16**	**4**	**0**	**3**	**17:43**
99-2000	**Dallas**	**NHL**	**65**	**18**	**21**	**39**	**68**	**4**	**2**	**6**	**153**	**11.8**	**16**	**40**	**50.0**	**17:33**	**15**	**1**	**7**	**8**	**18**	**1**	**0**	**0**	**15:28**
2000-01	**Dallas**	**NHL**	**53**	**12**	**18**	**30**	**57**	**3**	**2**	**4**	**104**	**11.5**	**4**	**316**	**45.3**	**16:30**	**10**	**2**	**2**	**4**	**6**	**0**	**0**	**1**	**19:26**
2001-02	**Dallas**	**NHL**	**68**	**10**	**16**	**26**	**54**	**0**	**1**	**2**	**132**	**7.6**	**-11**	**120**	**45.0**	**15:45**	....	....	....	....	....	....	....	....	....
	New Jersey	**NHL**	**14**	**3**	**3**	**6**	**23**	**0**	**0**	**2**	**31**	**9.7**	**2**	**2**	**50.0**	**15:27**	**5**	**0**	**1**	**1**	**8**	**0**	**0**	**0**	**14:57**
2002-03♦	**New Jersey**	**NHL**	**78**	**22**	**33**	**55**	**65**	**5**	**1**	**5**	**197**	**11.2**	**17**	**72**	**47.2**	**17:48**	**24**	***11**	**7**	***18**	**16**	**1**	**0**	**4**	**17:34**
2003-04	**New Jersey**	**NHL**	**53**	**10**	**16**	**26**	**43**	**1**	**2**	**2**	**130**	**7.7**	**9**	**31**	**51.6**	**16:01**	**5**	**0**	**2**	**2**	**2**	**0**	**0**	**0**	**15:04**
	NHL Totals		**577**	**125**	**197**	**322**	**492**	**29**	**8**	**31**	**1179**	**10.6**		**798**	**46.1**	**16:34**	**103**	**26**	**31**	**57**	**94**	**6**	**0**	**10**	**17:08**

Traded to **New Jersey** by **Dallas** with Joe Nieuwendyk for Jason Arnott, Randy McKay and New Jersey's 1st round choice (later traded to Columbus – later traded to Buffalo – Buffalo selected Dan Paille) in 2002 Entry Draft, March 19, 2002.

LANGFELD, Josh

(LANG-fehld, JAWSH) **OTT.**

Right wing. Shoots right. 6'3", 216 lbs. Born, Fridley, MN, July 17, 1977. Ottawa's 3rd choice, 66th overall, in 1997 Entry Draft.

Season	Club	League	GP	G	A	Pts	PIM	PP	SH	GW	S	%	+/-	TF	F%	Min	GP	G	A	Pts	PIM	PP	SH	GW	Min
1995-96	Great Falls	AFJHL	45	45	40	85	105	....	....	....	....	....	....	....	....	....	....	....	....	....	....	....	....	....	....
1996-97	Lincoln Stars	USHL	38	35	23	58	100	....	....	....	....	....	....	....	....	....	14	8	*13	*21	42	....	....	....	....
1997-98	U. of Michigan	CCHA	46	19	17	36	66	....	....	....	....	....	....	....	....	....	....	....	....	....	....	....	....	....	....
1998-99	U. of Michigan	CCHA	41	21	14	35	84	....	....	....	....	....	....	....	....	....	....	....	....	....	....	....	....	....	....
99-2000	U. of Michigan	CCHA	39	9	21	30	56	....	....	....	....	....	....	....	....	....	....	....	....	....	....	....	....	....	....
2000-01	U. of Michigan	CCHA	42	16	12	28	44	....	....	....	....	....	....	....	....	....	....	....	....	....	....	....	....	....	....
2001-02	**Ottawa**	**NHL**	**1**	**0**	**0**	**0**	**2**	**0**	**0**	**0**	**5**	**0.0**	**0**	**0**	**0.0**	**8:15**	....	....	....	....	....	....	....	....	....
	Grand Rapids	AHL	68	21	16	37	29	....	....	....	....	....	....	....	....	....	5	2	0	2	0	....	....	....	....
2002-03	**Ottawa**	**NHL**	**12**	**0**	**1**	**1**	**4**	**0**	**0**	**0**	**16**	**0.0**	**2**	**0**	**0.0**	**11:11**	....	....	....	....	....	....	....	....	....
	Binghamton	AHL	59	14	21	35	38	....	....	....	....	....	....	....	....	....	13	5	3	8	8	....	....	....	....
2003-04	**Ottawa**	**NHL**	**38**	**7**	**10**	**17**	**16**	**2**	**0**	**2**	**59**	**11.9**	**6**	**5**	**80.0**	**10:53**	....	....	....	....	....	....	....	....	....
	Binghamton	AHL	30	13	14	27	25	....	....	....	....	....	....	....	....	....	2	0	0	0	0	....	....	....	....
	NHL Totals		**51**	**7**	**11**	**18**	**22**	**2**	**0**	**2**	**80**	**8.8**		**5**	**80.0**	**10:54**	....	....	....	....	....	....	....	....	....

NCAA Championship All-Tournament Team (1998)

LANGKOW, Daymond

(LAING-kow, DAY-muhn) **PHX.**

Center. Shoots left. 5'11", 192 lbs. Born, Edmonton, Alta., September 27, 1976. Tampa Bay's 1st choice, 5th overall, in 1995 Entry Draft.

Season	Club	League	GP	G	A	Pts	PIM	PP	SH	GW	S	%	+/-	TF	F%	Min	GP	G	A	Pts	PIM	PP	SH	GW	Min
1991-92	Edmonton Pats	AMHL	35	36	45	81	100	....	....	....	....	....	....	....	....	....	....	....	....	....	....	....	....	....	....
	Tri-City	WHL	1	0	0	0	0	....	....	....	....	....	....	....	....	....	....	....	....	....	....	....	....	....	....
1992-93	Tri-City	WHL	64	22	42	64	100	....	....	....	....	....	....	....	....	....	4	1	0	1	4	....	....	....	....
1993-94	Tri-City	WHL	61	40	43	83	174	....	....	....	....	....	....	....	....	....	4	2	2	4	15	....	....	....	....
1994-95	Tri-City	WHL	72	*67	73	*140	142	....	....	....	....	....	....	....	....	....	17	12	15	27	52	....	....	....	....
1995-96	Tri-City	WHL	48	30	61	91	103	....	....	....	....	....	....	....	....	....	11	14	13	27	20	....	....	....	....
	Tampa Bay	**NHL**	**4**	**0**	**1**	**1**	**0**	**0**	**0**	**0**	**4**	**0.0**	**-1**	....	....	....	....	....	....	....	....	....	....	....	....
1996-97	**Tampa Bay**	**NHL**	**79**	**15**	**13**	**28**	**35**	**3**	**1**	**1**	**170**	**8.8**	**1**	....	....	....	....	....	....	....	....	....	....	....	....
	Adirondack	AHL	2	1	1	2	0	....	....	....	....	....	....	....	....	....	....	....	....	....	....	....	....	....	....
1997-98	**Tampa Bay**	**NHL**	**68**	**8**	**14**	**22**	**62**	**2**	**0**	**1**	**156**	**5.1**	**-9**	....	....	....	....	....	....	....	....	....	....	....	....
1998-99	**Tampa Bay**	**NHL**	**22**	**4**	**6**	**10**	**15**	**1**	**0**	**1**	**40**	**10.0**	**0**	**399**	**48.4**	**17:10**	....	....	....	....	....	....	....	....	....
	Cleveland	IHL	4	1	1	2	18	....	....	....	....	....	....	....	....	....	....	....	....	....	....	....	....	....	....
	Philadelphia	**NHL**	**56**	**10**	**13**	**23**	**24**	**3**	**1**	**1**	**109**	**9.2**	**-8**	**738**	**48.0**	**15:12**	**6**	**0**	**2**	**2**	**2**	**0**	**0**	**0**	**16:50**
99-2000	**Philadelphia**	**NHL**	**82**	**18**	**32**	**50**	**56**	**5**	**0**	**7**	**222**	**8.1**	**1**	**1263**	**45.1**	**16:57**	**16**	**5**	**5**	**10**	**23**	**1**	**1**	**2**	**20:03**
2000-01	**Philadelphia**	**NHL**	**71**	**13**	**41**	**54**	**50**	**3**	**0**	**2**	**190**	**6.8**	**12**	**1181**	**47.2**	**18:38**	**6**	**2**	**4**	**6**	**2**	**1**	**0**	**0**	**20:17**
2001-02	**Phoenix**	**NHL**	**80**	**27**	**35**	**62**	**36**	**6**	**3**	**2**	**171**	**15.8**	**18**	**1379**	**46.2**	**19:11**	**5**	**1**	**0**	**1**	**0**	**0**	**0**	**0**	**21:06**
2002-03	**Phoenix**	**NHL**	**82**	**20**	**32**	**52**	**56**	**4**	**2**	**2**	**196**	**10.2**	**20**	**1972**	**46.5**	**21:00**	....	....	....	....	....	....	....	....	....
2003-04	**Phoenix**	**NHL**	**81**	**21**	**31**	**52**	**40**	**4**	**1**	**2**	**174**	**12.1**	**4**	**1472**	**43.1**	**21:07**	....	....	....	....	....	....	....	....	....
	NHL Totals		**625**	**136**	**218**	**354**	**374**	**31**	**8**	**19**	**1432**	**9.5**		**8404**	**46.0**	**18:48**	**33**	**8**	**11**	**19**	**27**	**2**	**1**	**2**	**19:40**

WHL West First All-Star Team (1995) • Canadian Major Junior First All-Star Team (1995) • WHL West Second All-Star Team (1996)

Traded to **Philadelphia** by **Tampa Bay** with Mikael Renberg for Chris Gratton and Mike Sillinger, December 12, 1998. Traded to **Phoenix** by **Philadelphia** for Phoenix's 2nd round choice (later traded to Tampa Bay – later traded to San Jose – San Jose selected Dan Spang) in 2002 Entry Draft and Phoenix's 1st round choice (Jeff Carter) in 2003 Entry Draft, July 2, 2001.

LAPERRIERE, Ian

(luh-PAIR-ee-YAIR, EE-an) **COL.**

Right wing. Shoots right. 6'1", 201 lbs. Born, Montreal, Que., January 19, 1974. St. Louis' 6th choice, 158th overall, in 1992 Entry Draft.

Season	Club	League	GP	G	A	Pts	PIM	PP	SH	GW	S	%	+/-	TF	F%	Min	GP	G	A	Pts	PIM	PP	SH	GW	Min
1989-90	Mtl-Bourassa	QAAA	22	4	10	14	10	....	....	....	....	....	....	....	....	....	3	0	1	1	6	....	....	....	....
1990-91	Drummondville	QMJHL	65	19	29	48	117	....	....	....	....	....	....	....	....	....	14	2	9	11	48	....	....	....	....
1991-92	Drummondville	QMJHL	70	28	49	77	160	....	....	....	....	....	....	....	....	....	4	2	2	4	9	....	....	....	....
1992-93	Drummondville	QMJHL	60	44	*96	140	188	....	....	....	....	....	....	....	....	....	10	6	13	19	20	....	....	....	....
1993-94	Drummondville	QMJHL	62	41	72	113	150	....	....	....	....	....	....	....	....	....	9	4	6	10	35	....	....	....	....
	St. Louis	**NHL**	**1**	**0**	**0**	**0**	**0**	**0**	**0**	**0**	**1**	**0.0**	**0**	....	....	....	....	....	....	....	....	....	....	....	....
	Peoria Rivermen	IHL	....	....	....	....	....	....	....	....	....	....	....	....	....	....	5	1	3	4	2	....	....	....	....
1994-95	Peoria Rivermen	IHL	51	16	32	48	111	....	....	....	....	....	....	....	....	....	....	....	....	....	....	....	....	....	....
	St. Louis	**NHL**	**37**	**13**	**14**	**27**	**85**	**1**	**0**	**1**	**53**	**24.5**	**12**	....	....	....	**7**	**0**	**4**	**4**	**21**	**0**	**0**	**0**	....
1995-96	**St. Louis**	**NHL**	**33**	**3**	**6**	**9**	**87**	**1**	**0**	**1**	**31**	**9.7**	**-4**	....	....	....	....	....	....	....	....	....	....	....	....
	Worcester IceCats	AHL	3	2	1	3	22	....	....	....	....	....	....	....	....	....	....	....	....	....	....	....	....	....	....
	NY Rangers	**NHL**	**28**	**1**	**2**	**3**	**53**	**0**	**0**	**0**	**21**	**4.8**	**-5**	....	....	....	....	....	....	....	....	....	....	....	....
	Los Angeles	**NHL**	**10**	**2**	**3**	**5**	**15**	**0**	**0**	**0**	**18**	**11.1**	**-2**	....	....	....	....	....	....	....	....	....	....	....	....
1996-97	**Los Angeles**	**NHL**	**62**	**8**	**15**	**23**	**102**	**0**	**1**	**2**	**84**	**9.5**	**-25**	....	....	....	....	....	....	....	....	....	....	....	....
1997-98	**Los Angeles**	**NHL**	**77**	**6**	**15**	**21**	**131**	**0**	**1**	**1**	**74**	**8.1**	**0**	....	....	....	**4**	**1**	**0**	**1**	**6**	**0**	**0**	**0**	....
1998-99	**Los Angeles**	**NHL**	**72**	**3**	**10**	**13**	**138**	**0**	**0**	**1**	**62**	**4.8**	**-5**	**643**	**47.3**	**11:47**	....	....	....	....	....	....	....	....	....
99-2000	**Los Angeles**	**NHL**	**79**	**9**	**13**	**22**	**185**	**0**	**0**	**1**	**87**	**10.3**	**-14**	**1111**	**53.7**	**13:15**	**4**	**0**	**0**	**0**	**2**	**0**	**0**	**0**	**10:22**
2000-01	**Los Angeles**	**NHL**	**79**	**8**	**10**	**18**	**141**	**0**	**0**	**0**	**60**	**13.3**	**5**	**297**	**51.9**	**12:02**	**13**	**1**	**2**	**3**	**12**	**0**	**0**	**0**	**14:01**
2001-02	**Los Angeles**	**NHL**	**81**	**8**	**14**	**22**	**125**	**0**	**0**	**3**	**89**	**9.0**	**5**	**134**	**49.3**	**13:45**	**7**	**0**	**1**	**1**	**9**	**0**	**0**	**0**	**14:18**
2002-03	**Los Angeles**	**NHL**	**73**	**7**	**12**	**19**	**122**	**1**	**1**	**1**	**85**	**8.2**	**-9**	**317**	**49.2**	**15:46**	....	....	....	....	....	....	....	....	....
2003-04	**Los Angeles**	**NHL**	**62**	**10**	**12**	**22**	**58**	**1**	**0**	**3**	**59**	**16.9**	**-4**	**446**	**54.0**	**15:50**	....	....	....	....	....	....	....	....	....
	NHL Totals		**694**	**78**	**126**	**204**	**1242**	**4**	**3**	**14**	**724**	**10.8**		**2948**	**51.5**	**13:40**	**35**	**2**	**7**	**9**	**50**	**0**	**0**	**0**	**13:29**

QMJHL Second All-Star Team (1993)

Traded to **NY Rangers** by **St. Louis** for Stephane Matteau, December 28, 1995. Traded to **Los Angeles** by **NY Rangers** with Ray Ferraro, Mattias Norstrom, Nathan LaFayette and NY Rangers' 4th round choice (Sean Blanchard) in 1997 Entry Draft for Marty McSorley, Jari Kurri and Shane Churla, March 14, 1996. Signed as a free agent by **Colorado**, July 2, 2004.

LAPOINTE, Claude

(luh-POYNT, KLOHD) **PHI.**

Left wing/Center. Shoots left. 5'9", 188 lbs. Born, Lachine, Que., October 11, 1968. Quebec's 12th choice, 234th overall, in 1988 Entry Draft.

Season	Club	League	GP	G	A	Pts	PIM	PP	SH	GW	S	%	+/-	TF	F%	Min	GP	G	A	Pts	PIM	PP	SH	GW	Min
1983-84	Lac St-Louis Lions	QAAA	42	28	29	57	42	....	....	....	....	....	....	....	....	....	8	3	7	10	8	....	....	....	....
1984-85	Lac St-Louis Lions	QAAA	42	20	32	52	66	....	....	....	....	....	....	....	....	....	11	4	8	12	16	....	....	....	....
1985-86	Trois-Rivieres	QMJHL	63	14	32	46	70	....	....	....	....	....	....	....	....	....	9	5	6	11	4	....	....	....	....
1986-87	Trois-Rivieres	QMJHL	70	47	57	104	123	....	....	....	....	....	....	....	....	....	....	....	....	....	....	....	....	....	....
1987-88	Laval Titan	QMJHL	69	37	83	120	143	....	....	....	....	....	....	....	....	....	13	2	17	19	53	....	....	....	....
1988-89	Laval Titan	QMJHL	63	32	72	104	158	....	....	....	....	....	....	....	....	....	17	5	14	19	66	....	....	....	....
1989-90	Halifax Citadels	AHL	63	18	19	37	51	....	....	....	....	....	....	....	....	....	6	1	1	2	34	....	....	....	....
1990-91	**Quebec**	**NHL**	**13**	**2**	**2**	**4**	**4**	**0**	**0**	**0**	**7**	**28.6**	**3**	....	....	....	....	....	....	....	....	....	....	....	....
	Halifax Citadels	AHL	43	17	17	34	46	....	....	....	....	....	....	....	....	....	....	....	....	....	....	....	....	....	....
1991-92	**Quebec**	**NHL**	**78**	**13**	**20**	**33**	**86**	**0**	**2**	**2**	**95**	**13.7**	**-8**	....	....	....	....	....	....	....	....	....	....	....	....
1992-93	**Quebec**	**NHL**	**74**	**10**	**26**	**36**	**98**	**0**	**0**	**1**	**91**	**11.0**	**5**	....	....	....	**6**	**2**	**4**	**6**	**8**	**0**	**0**	**0**	....
1993-94	**Quebec**	**NHL**	**59**	**11**	**17**	**28**	**70**	**1**	**1**	**1**	**73**	**15.1**	**2**	....	....	....	....	....	....	....	....	....	....	....	....
1994-95	**Quebec**	**NHL**	**29**	**4**	**8**	**12**	**41**	**0**	**0**	**0**	**40**	**10.0**	**5**	....	....	....	**5**	**0**	**0**	**0**	**8**	**0**	**0**	**0**	....
1995-96	**Colorado**	**NHL**	**3**	**0**	**0**	**0**	**0**	**0**	**0**	**0**	**0**	**0.0**	**-1**	....	....	....	....	....	....	....	....	....	....	....	....
	Calgary	**NHL**	**32**	**4**	**5**	**9**	**20**	**0**	**2**	**1**	**44**	**9.1**	**2**	....	....	....	**2**	**0**	**0**	**0**	**0**	**0**	**0**	**0**	....
	Saint John Flames	AHL	12	5	3	8	10	....	....	....	....	....	....	....	....	....	....	....	....	....	....	....	....	....	....
1996-97	**NY Islanders**	**NHL**	**73**	**13**	**5**	**18**	**49**	**0**	**3**	**3**	**80**	**16.3**	**-12**	....	....	....	....	....	....	....	....	....	....	....	....
	Utah Grizzlies	IHL	9	7	6	13	14	....	....	....	....	....	....	....	....	....	....	....	....	....	....	....	....	....	....
1997-98	**NY Islanders**	**NHL**	**78**	**10**	**10**	**20**	**47**	**0**	**1**	**3**	**82**	**12.2**	**-9**	....	....	....	....	....	....	....	....	....	....	....	....
1998-99	**NY Islanders**	**NHL**	**82**	**14**	**23**	**37**	**62**	**2**	**2**	**1**	**134**	**10.4**	**-19**	**1218**	**56.6**	**19:21**	....	....	....	....	....	....	....	....	....
99-2000	**NY Islanders**	**NHL**	**76**	**15**	**16**	**31**	**60**	**2**	**1**	**3**	**129**	**11.6**	**-22**	**1284**	**54.0**	**19:39**	....	....	....	....	....	....	....	....	....
2000-01	**NY Islanders**	**NHL**	**80**	**9**	**23**	**32**	**56**	**1**	**1**	**1**	**94**	**9.6**	**-2**	**1074**	**50.4**	**18:40**	....	....	....	....	....	....	....	....	....
2001-02	**NY Islanders**	**NHL**	**80**	**9**	**12**	**21**	**60**	**0**	**3**	**0**	**74**	**12.2**	**-9**	**907**	**54.6**	**13:05**	**7**	**0**	**0**	**0**	**14**	**0**	**0**	**0**	**13:20**

			Regular Season														Playoffs								
Season	Club	League	GP	G	A	Pts	PIM	PP	SH	GW	S	%	+/-	TF	F%	Min	GP	G	A	Pts	PIM	PP	SH	GW	Min
2002-03	NY Islanders	NHL	66	6	6	12	20	0	0	1	67	9.0	–3	686	55.0	12:16	....	....	....	....	....	....	....	....	....
	Philadelphia	NHL	14	2	2	4	16	0	0	0	20	10.0	5	107	63.6	11:05	13	2	3	5	14	0	0	0	13:15
2003-04	Philadelphia	NHL	42	5	3	8	32	0	1	1	26	19.2	2	402	51.7	11:04	1	0	0	0	0	0	0	0	9:38
	Philadelphia	AHL	2	1	1	2	0	....	....	....	....	....	....	....	....	....	....	....	....	....	....	....	....	....	....
	NHL Totals		879	127	178	305	721	6	17	18	1056	12.0		5678	54.1	16:01	34	4	7	11	44	0	0	0	13:06

Transferred to **Colorado** after **Quebec** franchise relocated, June 21, 1995. Traded to **Calgary** by **Colorado** for Calgary's 7th round choice (Sami Pahlsson) in 1996 Entry Draft, November 1, 1995. Signed as a free agent by **NY Islanders**, August 14, 1996. Traded to **Philadelphia** by **NY Islanders** for Philadelphia's 5th round choice (later traded to Pittsburgh – Pittsburgh selected Evgeni Isakov) in 2003 Entry Draft, March 9, 2003.

LAPOINTE, Martin

(luh-POYNT, MAHR-tihn) **BOS.**

Right wing. Shoots right. 5'11", 215 lbs. Born, Ville St-Pierre, Que., September 12, 1973. Detroit's 1st choice, 10th overall, in 1991 Entry Draft.

Season	Club	League	GP	G	A	Pts	PIM	PP	SH	GW	S	%	+/-	TF	F%	Min	GP	G	A	Pts	PIM	PP	SH	GW	Min
1988-89	Lac St-Louis Lions	QAAA	42	39	45	84	46	....	....	....	....	....	....	....	....	....	3	6	2	8	4	....	....	....	....
1989-90	Laval Titan	QMJHL	65	42	54	96	77	....	....	....	....	....	....	....	....	....	14	8	17	25	54	....	....	....	....
1990-91	Laval Titan	QMJHL	64	44	54	98	66	....	....	....	....	....	....	....	....	....	13	7	14	21	26	....	....	....	....
1991-92	Laval Titan	QMJHL	31	25	30	55	84	....	....	....	....	....	....	....	....	....	10	4	10	14	32	....	....	....	....
	Detroit	NHL	4	0	1	1	5	0	0	0	2	0.0	2	....	....	....	3	0	1	1	4	0	0	0	....
	Adirondack	AHL	....	....	....	....	....	....	....	....	....	....	....	....	....	....	8	2	2	4	4	....	....	....	....
1992-93	Laval Titan	QMJHL	35	38	51	89	41	....	....	....	....	....	....	....	....	....	13	*13	*17	*30	22	....	....	....	....
	Detroit	NHL	3	0	0	0	0	0	0	0	2	0.0	–2	....	....	....	....	....	....	....	....	....	....	....	....
	Adirondack	AHL	8	1	2	3	9	....	....	....	....	....	....	....	....	....	....	....	....	....	....	....	....	....	....
1993-94	Detroit	NHL	50	8	8	16	55	2	0	0	45	17.8	7	....	....	....	4	0	0	0	6	0	0	0	....
	Adirondack	AHL	28	25	21	46	47	....	....	....	....	....	....	....	....	....	4	1	1	2	8	....	....	....	....
1994-95	Adirondack	AHL	39	29	16	45	80	....	....	....	....	....	....	....	....	....	....	....	....	....	....	....	....	....	....
	Detroit	NHL	39	4	6	10	73	0	0	1	46	8.7	1	....	....	....	2	0	1	1	8	0	0	0	....
1995-96	Detroit	NHL	58	6	3	9	93	1	0	0	76	7.9	0	....	....	....	11	1	2	3	12	0	0	0	....
1996-97♦	Detroit	NHL	78	16	17	33	167	5	1	1	149	10.7	–14	....	....	....	20	4	8	12	60	1	0	1	....
1997-98♦	Detroit	NHL	79	15	19	34	106	4	0	3	154	9.7	0	....	....	....	21	9	6	15	20	2	1	1	....
1998-99	Detroit	NHL	77	16	13	29	141	7	1	4	153	10.5	7	217	47.9	15:06	10	0	2	2	20	0	0	0	11:43
99-2000	Detroit	NHL	82	16	25	41	121	1	1	2	127	12.6	17	287	54.4	14:43	9	3	1	4	20	2	0	1	14:28
2000-01	Detroit	NHL	82	27	30	57	127	13	0	8	181	14.9	3	461	53.2	16:06	6	0	1	1	8	0	0	0	16:53
2001-02	Boston	NHL	68	17	23	40	101	4	0	2	141	12.1	12	222	53.6	17:22	6	1	2	3	12	1	0	1	16:58
2002-03	Boston	NHL	59	8	10	18	87	1	0	1	110	7.3	–19	52	48.1	15:22	5	1	0	1	14	0	0	0	14:39
2003-04	Boston	NHL	78	15	10	25	67	9	0	2	136	11.0	–5	101	51.5	14:26	7	0	0	0	14	0	0	0	15:21
	NHL Totals		757	148	165	313	1143	47	3	24	1322	11.2		1340	52.3	15:29	104	19	24	43	198	6	1	4	14:41

QMJHL First All-Star Team (1990, 1993) • QMJHL Offensive Rookie of the Year (1990) • QMJHL Second All-Star Team (1991) • Memorial Cup All-Star Team (1993)

Signed as a free agent by **Boston**, July 2, 2001.

LARAQUE, Georges

(luh-RAK, zhawrzh) **EDM.**

Right wing. Shoots right. 6'3", 243 lbs. Born, Montreal, Que., December 7, 1976. Edmonton's 2nd choice, 31st overall, in 1995 Entry Draft.

Season	Club	League	GP	G	A	Pts	PIM	PP	SH	GW	S	%	+/-	TF	F%	Min	GP	G	A	Pts	PIM	PP	SH	GW	Min
1991-92	Mtl-Bourassa	QAHA	28	20	20	40	30	....	....	....	....	....	....	....	....	....	....	....	....	....	....	....	....	....	....
1992-93	Mtl-Bourassa	QAAA	37	8	20	28	50	....	....	....	....	....	....	....	....	....	3	1	2	3	2	....	....	....	....
1993-94	St-Jean Lynx	QMJHL	70	11	11	22	142	....	....	....	....	....	....	....	....	....	4	0	0	0	7	....	....	....	....
1994-95	St-Jean Lynx	QMJHL	62	19	22	41	259	....	....	....	....	....	....	....	....	....	7	1	1	2	42	....	....	....	....
1995-96	Laval Titan	QMJHL	11	8	13	21	76	....	....	....	....	....	....	....	....	....	....	....	....	....	....	....	....	....	....
	St-Hyacinthe	QMJHL	8	3	4	7	59	....	....	....	....	....	....	....	....	....	....	....	....	....	....	....	....	....	....
	Granby	QMJHL	22	9	7	16	125	....	....	....	....	....	....	....	....	....	18	7	6	13	104	....	....	....	....
1996-97	Hamilton	AHL	73	14	20	34	179	....	....	....	....	....	....	....	....	....	15	1	3	4	12	....	....	....	....
1997-98	Edmonton	NHL	11	0	0	0	59	0	0	0	4	0.0	–4	....	....	....	....	....	....	....	....	....	....	....	....
	Hamilton	AHL	46	10	20	30	154	....	....	....	....	....	....	....	....	....	3	0	0	0	11	....	....	....	....
1998-99	Edmonton	NHL	39	3	2	5	57	0	0	0	17	17.6	–1	0	0.0	5:31	4	0	0	0	2	0	0	0	7:35
	Hamilton	AHL	25	6	8	14	93	....	....	....	....	....	....	....	....	....	....	....	....	....	....	....	....	....	....
99-2000	Edmonton	NHL	76	8	8	16	123	0	0	0	56	14.3	5	0	0.0	8:28	5	0	1	1	6	0	0	0	9:14
2000-01	Edmonton	NHL	82	13	16	29	148	1	0	1	73	17.8	5	0	0.0	9:03	6	1	1	2	8	0	0	0	9:54
2001-02	Edmonton	NHL	80	5	14	19	157	1	0	1	95	5.3	6	0	0.0	9:48	....	....	....	....	....	....	....	....	....
2002-03	Edmonton	NHL	64	6	7	13	110	0	0	2	46	13.0	–4	0	0.0	9:15	6	1	3	4	4	0	0	0	12:11
2003-04	Edmonton	NHL	66	6	11	17	99	1	0	1	54	11.1	7	0	0.0	9:22	....	....	....	....	....	....	....	....	....
	NHL Totals		418	41	58	99	753	3	0	5	345	11.9		0	0.0	8:50	21	2	5	7	20	0	0	0	9:57

LARIONOV, Igor

(LAIR-ee-AH-nohv, EE-gohr)

Center. Shoots left. 5'9", 170 lbs. Born, Voskresensk, USSR, December 3, 1960. Vancouver's 11th choice, 214th overall, in 1985 Entry Draft.

Season	Club	League	GP	G	A	Pts	PIM	PP	SH	GW	S	%	+/-	TF	F%	Min	GP	G	A	Pts	PIM	PP	SH	GW	Min
1977-78	Voskresensk	USSR	6	3	0	3	4	....	....	....	....	....	....	....	....	....	....	....	....	....	....	....	....	....	....
1978-79	Voskresensk	USSR	32	3	4	7	12	....	....	....	....	....	....	....	....	....	....	....	....	....	....	....	....	....	....
1979-80	Voskresensk	USSR	42	11	7	18	24	....	....	....	....	....	....	....	....	....	....	....	....	....	....	....	....	....	....
1980-81	Voskresensk	USSR	43	22	23	45	36	....	....	....	....	....	....	....	....	....	....	....	....	....	....	....	....	....	....
1981-82	CSKA Moscow	USSR	46	31	22	53	6	....	....	....	....	....	....	....	....	....	....	....	....	....	....	....	....	....	....
1982-83	CSKA Moscow	USSR	44	20	19	39	20	....	....	....	....	....	....	....	....	....	....	....	....	....	....	....	....	....	....
1983-84	CSKA Moscow	USSR	43	15	26	41	30	....	....	....	....	....	....	....	....	....	....	....	....	....	....	....	....	....	....
	Soviet Union	Olympics	6	1	4	5	6	....	....	....	....	....	....	....	....	....	....	....	....	....	....	....	....	....	....
1984-85	CSKA Moscow	USSR	40	18	28	46	20	....	....	....	....	....	....	....	....	....	....	....	....	....	....	....	....	....	....
1985-86	CSKA Moscow	USSR	40	21	31	52	33	....	....	....	....	....	....	....	....	....	....	....	....	....	....	....	....	....	....
1986-87	CSKA Moscow	USSR	39	20	26	46	34	....	....	....	....	....	....	....	....	....	....	....	....	....	....	....	....	....	....
1987-88	CSKA Moscow	USSR	51	25	32	57	54	....	....	....	....	....	....	....	....	....	....	....	....	....	....	....	....	....	....
	Soviet Union	Olympics	8	4	*9	13	4	....	....	....	....	....	....	....	....	....	....	....	....	....	....	....	....	....	....
1988-89	CSKA Moscow	USSR	31	15	12	27	22	....	....	....	....	....	....	....	....	....	....	....	....	....	....	....	....	....	....
1989-90	Vancouver	NHL	74	17	27	44	20	8	0	2	118	14.4	–5	....	....	....	....	....	....	....	....	....	....	....	....
1990-91	Vancouver	NHL	64	13	21	34	14	1	1	0	66	19.7	–3	....	....	....	6	1	0	1	6	0	0	0	....
1991-92	Vancouver	NHL	72	21	44	65	54	10	3	4	97	21.6	7	....	....	....	13	3	7	10	4	1	0	0	....
1992-93	HC Lugano	Swiss	24	10	19	29	44	....	....	....	....	....	....	....	....	....	8	3	15	18	0	....	....	....	....
1993-94	San Jose	NHL	60	18	38	56	40	3	2	2	72	25.0	20	....	....	....	14	5	13	18	10	0	0	0	....
1994-95	San Jose	NHL	33	4	20	24	14	0	0	1	69	5.8	–3	....	....	....	11	1	8	9	2	0	0	0	....
1995-96	San Jose	NHL	4	1	1	2	0	1	0	0	5	20.0	–6	....	....	....	....	....	....	....	....	....	....	....	....
	Detroit	NHL	69	21	50	71	34	9	1	5	108	19.4	37	....	....	....	19	6	7	13	6	3	0	2	....
1996-97♦	Detroit	NHL	64	12	42	54	26	2	1	4	95	12.6	31	....	....	....	20	4	8	12	8	3	0	1	....
1997-98♦	Detroit	NHL	69	8	39	47	40	3	0	2	93	8.6	14	....	....	....	22	3	10	13	12	0	0	0	....
1998-99	Detroit	NHL	75	14	49	63	48	4	2	2	83	16.9	13	867	49.8	17:20	7	0	2	2	0	0	0	0	13:51
99-2000	Detroit	NHL	79	9	38	47	28	3	0	4	69	13.0	13	729	43.6	16:05	9	1	2	3	6	1	0	0	14:10
2000-01	Florida	NHL	26	5	6	11	10	2	0	0	15	33.3	–11	299	48.8	16:33	....	....	....	....	....	....	....	....	....
	Detroit	NHL	39	4	25	29	28	2	0	1	31	12.9	6	311	44.4	16:36	6	1	3	4	2	1	0	0	17:06
2001-02♦	Detroit	NHL	70	11	32	43	50	4	0	1	50	22.0	–5	653	43.3	14:28	18	5	6	11	4	0	0	1	13:58
	Russia	Olympics	6	0	3	3	4	....	....	....	....	....	....	....	....	....	....	....	....	....	....	....	....	....	....
2002-03	Detroit	NHL	74	10	33	43	48	5	0	3	50	20.0	–7	454	43.0	13:55	4	0	1	1	0	0	0	0	15:11
2003-04	New Jersey	NHL	49	1	10	11	20	0	0	0	25	4.0	3	419	50.6	12:06	1	0	0	0	0	0	0	0	11:38
	NHL Totals		921	169	475	644	474	57	10	31	1046	16.2		3732	46.2	15:15	150	30	67	97	60	9	0	4	14:27

USSR First All-Star Team (1983, 1986, 1987, 1988) • USSR Player of the Year (1988)

Played in NHL All-Star Game (1998)

Claimed by **San Jose** from **Vancouver** in Waiver Draft, October 4, 1992. Traded to **Detroit** by **San Jose** for Ray Sheppard, October 24, 1995. Signed as a free agent by **Florida**, July 1, 2000. Traded to **Detroit** by **Florida** for Yan Golubovsky, December 28, 2000. Signed as a free agent by **New Jersey**, September 10, 2003. • Officially announced retirement, April 20, 2004.

LAROSE, Cory

(la-ROHZ, KOH-ree) **ATL.**

Center. Shoots left. 6', 190 lbs. Born, Campbellton, N.B., May 14, 1975.

Season	Club	League	GP	G	A	Pts	PIM	PP	SH	GW	S	%	+/-	TF	F%	Min	GP	G	A	Pts	PIM	PP	SH	GW	Min
1993-94	Kimball Union	Hi-School	21	18	11	29	14	....	....	....	....	....	....	....	....	....	....	....	....	....	....	....	....	....	....
1994-95	Langley Thunder	BCJHL	STATISTICS NOT AVAILABLE					....	....	....	....	....	....	....	....	....	....	....	....	....	....	....	....	....	....
1995-96	Langley Thunder	BCJHL	54	28	46	74	61	....	....	....	....	....	....	....	....	....	....	....	....	....	....	....	....	....	....
1996-97	U. of Maine	H-East	35	10	27	37	32	....	....	....	....	....	....	....	....	....	....	....	....	....	....	....	....	....	....
1997-98	U. of Maine	H-East	34	15	25	40	22	....	....	....	....	....	....	....	....	....	....	....	....	....	....	....	....	....	....
1998-99	U. of Maine	H-East	38	21	31	52	34	....	....	....	....	....	....	....	....	....	....	....	....	....	....	....	....	....	....

			Regular Season														Playoffs								
Season	**Club**	**League**	**GP**	**G**	**A**	**Pts**	**PIM**	**PP**	**SH**	**GW**	**S**	**%**	**+/-**	**TF**	**F%**	**Min**	**GP**	**G**	**A**	**Pts**	**PIM**	**PP**	**SH**	**GW**	**Min**
99-2000	U. of Maine	H-East	39	15	*36	51	45	....	....	....	....	....	....	....	....	....	....	....	....	....	....	....	....	....	....
2000-01	Cleveland	IHL	4	1	1	2	6	....	....	....	....	....	....	....	....	....	....	....	....	....	....	....	....	....	....
	Jackson Bandits	ECHL	63	21	32	53	73	....	....	....	....	....	....	....	....	....	5	2	2	4	12	....	....	....	....
2001-02	Houston Aeros	AHL	78	32	32	64	73	....	....	....	....	....	....	....	....	....	14	6	8	14	15	....	....	....	....
2002-03	Houston Aeros	AHL	58	18	38	56	57	....	....	....	....	....	....	....	....	....	....	....	....	....	....	....	....	....	....
	Hartford	AHL	24	9	10	19	20	....	....	....	....	....	....	....	....	....	2	0	1	1	0	....	....	....	....
2003-04	**NY Rangers**	**NHL**	**7**	**0**	**1**	**1**	**4**	**0**	**0**	**0**	**10**	**0.0**	**–2**	**40**	**47.5**	**11:27**	....	....	....	....	....	....	....	....	....
	Hartford	AHL	69	13	36	49	66	....	....	....	....	....	....	....	....	....	14	4	6	10	24	....	....	....	....
	NHL Totals		**7**	**0**	**1**	**1**	**4**	**0**	**0**	**0**	**10**	**0.0**		**40**	**47.5**	**11:27**	....	....	....	....	....	....	....	....	....

Hockey East First All-Star Team (2000) • NCAA East Second All-American Team (2000) • AHL All-Rookie Team (2002)

Signed as a free agent by **Minnesota**, May 10, 2000. Traded to **NY Rangers** by **Minnesota** for Jay Henderson, February 20, 2003. Signed as a free agent by **Atlanta**, July 14, 2004.

LARSEN, Brad

(LARH-sehn, BRAD) **ATL.**

Left wing. Shoots left. 6', 200 lbs. Born, Nakusp, B.C., June 28, 1977. Colorado's 5th choice, 87th overall, in 1997 Entry Draft.

Season	Club	League	GP	G	A	Pts	PIM	PP	SH	GW	S	%	+/-	TF	F%	Min	GP	G	A	Pts	PIM	PP	SH	GW	Min
1992-93	Nelson	RMJHL	42	31	37	68	164	....	....	....	....	....	....	....	....	....	....	....	....	....	....	....	....	....	....
1993-94	Swift Current	WHL	64	15	18	33	32	....	....	....	....	....	....	....	....	....	7	1	2	3	4	....	....	....	....
1994-95	Swift Current	WHL	62	24	33	57	73	....	....	....	....	....	....	....	....	....	6	0	1	1	2	....	....	....	....
1995-96	Swift Current	WHL	51	30	47	77	67	....	....	....	....	....	....	....	....	....	6	3	2	5	13	....	....	....	....
1996-97	Swift Current	WHL	61	36	46	82	61	....	....	....	....	....	....	....	....	....	....	....	....	....	....	....	....	....	....
1997-98	**Colorado**	**NHL**	**1**	**0**	**0**	**0**	**0**	**0**	**0**	**0**	**0**	**0.0**	**0**	....	....	....	....	....	....	....	....	....	....	....	....
	Hershey Bears	AHL	65	12	10	22	80	....	....	....	....	....	....	....	....	....	7	3	2	5	2	....	....	....	....
1998-99	Hershey Bears	AHL	18	3	4	7	11	....	....	....	....	....	....	....	....	....	5	0	1	1	6	....	....	....	....
99-2000	Hershey Bears	AHL	52	13	26	39	66	....	....	....	....	....	....	....	....	....	14	5	2	7	29	....	....	....	....
2000-01	**Colorado**	**NHL**	**9**	**0**	**0**	**0**	**0**	**0**	**0**	**0**	**3**	**0.0**	**1**	**14**	**57.1**	**9:17**	....	....	....	....	....	....	....	....	....
	Hershey Bears	AHL	67	21	25	46	93	....	....	....	....	....	....	....	....	....	10	1	3	4	6	....	....	....	....
2001-02	**Colorado**	**NHL**	**50**	**2**	**7**	**9**	**47**	**1**	**0**	**0**	**38**	**5.3**	**4**	**71**	**54.9**	**8:07**	**21**	**1**	**1**	**2**	**13**	**0**	**0**	**0**	**7:07**
2002-03	**Colorado**	**NHL**	**6**	**0**	**3**	**3**	**2**	**0**	**0**	**0**	**6**	**0.0**	**3**	**31**	**41.9**	**8:17**	....	....	....	....	....	....	....	....	....
	Hershey Bears	AHL	25	3	6	9	25	....	....	....	....	....	....	....	....	....	4	1	1	2	8	....	....	....	....
2003-04	**Colorado**	**NHL**	**26**	**2**	**2**	**4**	**11**	**0**	**0**	**0**	**17**	**11.8**	**2**	**9**	**44.4**	**7:41**	....	....	....	....	....	....	....	....	....
	Hershey Bears	AHL	21	4	13	17	40	....	....	....	....	....	....	....	....	....	....	....	....	....	....	....	....	....	....
	Atlanta	**NHL**	**6**	**0**	**0**	**0**	**2**	**0**	**0**	**0**	**6**	**0.0**	**–2**	**6**	**66.7**	**13:39**	....	....	....	....	....	....	....	....	....
	NHL Totals		**98**	**4**	**12**	**16**	**62**	**1**	**0**	**0**	**70**	**5.7**		**131**	**51.9**	**8:28**	**21**	**1**	**1**	**2**	**13**	**0**	**0**	**0**	**7:07**

• Re-entered NHL Entry Draft. Originally Ottawa's 3rd choice, 53rd overall, in 1995 Entry Draft.

WHL East Second All-Star Team (1997)

Rights traded to **Colorado** by **Ottawa** for Janne Laukkanen, January 26, 1996. • Missed majority of 1998-99 season recovering from abdominal injury suffered in game vs. Albany (AHL), November 20, 1998. • Missed majority of 2002-03 season recovering from groin (October 27, 2002 vs. Minnesota) and back (December 11, 2002 vs. Vancouver) injuries. Claimed on waivers by **Atlanta** from **Colorado**, February 25, 2004.

LAW, Kirby

(LAW, KUHR-bee) **MIN.**

Right wing. Shoots right. 6'1", 185 lbs. Born, McCreary, Man., March 11, 1977.

Season	Club	League	GP	G	A	Pts	PIM	PP	SH	GW	S	%	+/-	TF	F%	Min	GP	G	A	Pts	PIM	PP	SH	GW	Min
1991-92	McCreary	MAHA	60	89	103	192	60	....	....	....	....	....	....	....	....	....	....	....	....	....	....	....	....	....	....
1992-93	Dauphin Kings	MJHL	48	20	15	35	8	....	....	....	....	....	....	....	....	....	....	....	....	....	....	....	....	....	....
1993-94	Saskatoon Blades	WHL	66	9	11	20	39	....	....	....	....	....	....	....	....	....	16	0	0	0	6	....	....	....	....
1994-95	Saskatoon Blades	WHL	46	10	15	25	44	....	....	....	....	....	....	....	....	....	....	....	....	....	....	....	....	....	....
	Lethbridge	WHL	24	4	10	14	38	....	....	....	....	....	....	....	....	....	....	....	....	....	....	....	....	....	....
1995-96	Lethbridge	WHL	71	17	45	62	133	....	....	....	....	....	....	....	....	....	4	0	0	0	12	....	....	....	....
1996-97	Lethbridge	WHL	72	39	52	91	200	....	....	....	....	....	....	....	....	....	19	4	14	18	60	....	....	....	....
1997-98	Brandon	WHL	49	34	44	78	153	....	....	....	....	....	....	....	....	....	9	3	3	6	41	....	....	....	....
1998-99	Orlando	IHL	67	18	13	31	136	....	....	....	....	....	....	....	....	....	....	....	....	....	....	....	....	....	....
	Adirondack	AHL	11	2	3	5	40	....	....	....	....	....	....	....	....	....	3	1	0	1	2	....	....	....	....
99-2000	Louisville Panthers	AHL	66	31	21	52	173	....	....	....	....	....	....	....	....	....	....	....	....	....	....	....	....	....	....
	Orlando	IHL	1	1	0	1	0	....	....	....	....	....	....	....	....	....	....	....	....	....	....	....	....	....	....
	Philadelphia	AHL	12	1	4	5	6	....	....	....	....	....	....	....	....	....	5	2	0	2	2	....	....	....	....
2000-01	**Philadelphia**	**NHL**	**1**	**0**	**0**	**0**	**0**	**0**	**0**	**0**	**0**	**0.0**	**–1**	**0**	**0.0**	**3:23**	....	....	....	....	....	....	....	....	....
	Philadelphia	AHL	78	27	34	61	150	....	....	....	....	....	....	....	....	....	10	1	6	7	16	....	....	....	....
2001-02	Philadelphia	AHL	71	18	24	42	102	....	....	....	....	....	....	....	....	....	5	0	0	0	0	....	....	....	....
2002-03	**Philadelphia**	**NHL**	**2**	**0**	**0**	**0**	**2**	**0**	**0**	**0**	**0**	**0.0**	**0**	**0**	**0.0**	**1:41**	....	....	....	....	....	....	....	....	....
	Philadelphia	AHL	74	22	19	41	166	....	....	....	....	....	....	....	....	....	....	....	....	....	....	....	....	....	....
2003-04	**Philadelphia**	**NHL**	**6**	**0**	**1**	**1**	**2**	**0**	**0**	**0**	**1**	**0.0**	**0**	**0**	**0.0**	**8:09**	....	....	....	....	....	....	....	....	....
	Philadelphia	AHL	74	32	41	73	139	....	....	....	....	....	....	....	....	....	12	0	5	5	12	....	....	....	....
	NHL Totals		**9**	**0**	**1**	**1**	**4**	**0**	**0**	**0**	**1**	**0.0**		**0**	**0.0**	**6:11**	....	....	....	....	....	....	....	....	....

Signed as a free agent by **Atlanta**, July 27, 1999. Traded to **Philadelphia** by **Atlanta** for Vancouver's 6th round choice (previously acquired, Atlanta selected Jeff Dwyer) in 2000 Entry Draft and Philadelphia's 6th round choice (Pasi Nurminen) in 2001 Entry Draft, March 14, 2000. Signed as a free agent by **Minnesota**, July 6, 2004.

LEAHY, Patrick

(LEH-hey, PAT-rihk)

Right wing. Shoots right. 6'3", 190 lbs. Born, Brighton, MA, June 9, 1979. NY Rangers' 5th choice, 122nd overall, in 1998 Entry Draft.

Season	Club	League	GP	G	A	Pts	PIM	PP	SH	GW	S	%	+/-	TF	F%	Min	GP	G	A	Pts	PIM	PP	SH	GW	Min
1996-97	B.C. High Irish	Hi-School	25	24	24	48	....	....	....	....	....	....	....	....	....	....	....	....	....	....	....	....	....	....	....
1997-98	Miami University	CCHA	28	0	1	1	24	....	....	....	....	....	....	....	....	....	....	....	....	....	....	....	....	....	....
1998-99	Miami University	CCHA	34	10	20	30	40	....	....	....	....	....	....	....	....	....	....	....	....	....	....	....	....	....	....
99-2000	Miami University	CCHA	36	16	22	38	89	....	....	....	....	....	....	....	....	....	....	....	....	....	....	....	....	....	....
2000-01	Miami University	CCHA	37	13	19	32	14	....	....	....	....	....	....	....	....	....	....	....	....	....	....	....	....	....	....
2001-02	Trenton Titans	ECHL	41	20	21	41	64	....	....	....	....	....	....	....	....	....	....	....	....	....	....	....	....	....	....
	Hershey Bears	AHL	9	1	2	3	8	....	....	....	....	....	....	....	....	....	....	....	....	....	....	....	....	....	....
	Portland Pirates	AHL	9	1	1	2	8	....	....	....	....	....	....	....	....	....	....	....	....	....	....	....	....	....	....
	Bridgeport	AHL	14	2	2	4	2	....	....	....	....	....	....	....	....	....	20	3	4	7	4	....	....	....	....
2002-03	Providence Bruins	AHL	66	20	23	43	63	....	....	....	....	....	....	....	....	....	4	1	0	1	18	....	....	....	....
2003-04	**Boston**	**NHL**	**6**	**0**	**0**	**0**	**0**	**0**	**0**	**0**	**2**	**0.0**	**1**	**0**	**0.0**	**5:27**	....	....	....	....	....	....	....	....	....
	Providence Bruins	AHL	55	14	16	30	37	....	....	....	....	....	....	....	....	....	2	0	0	0	0	....	....	....	....
	NHL Totals		**6**	**0**	**0**	**0**	**0**	**0**	**0**	**0**	**2**	**0.0**		**0**	**0.0**	**5:27**	....	....	....	....	....	....	....	....	....

Signed as a free agent by **Boston**, July 28, 2003.

LECAVALIER, Vincent

(luh-KAV-uhl-YAY, VIHN-sihnt) **T.B.**

Center. Shoots left. 6'4", 205 lbs. Born, Ile Bizard, Que., April 21, 1980. Tampa Bay's 1st choice, 1st overall, in 1998 Entry Draft.

Season	Club	League	GP	G	A	Pts	PIM	PP	SH	GW	S	%	+/-	TF	F%	Min	GP	G	A	Pts	PIM	PP	SH	GW	Min
1995-96	Notre Dame	SMHL	22	52	52	104	....	....	....	....	....	....	....	....	....	....	....	....	....	....	....	....	....	....	....
1996-97	Rimouski Oceanic	QMJHL	64	42	61	103	38	....	....	....	....	....	....	....	....	....	4	4	3	7	2	....	....	....	....
1997-98	Rimouski Oceanic	QMJHL	58	44	71	115	117	....	....	....	....	....	....	....	....	....	18	*15	*26	*41	46	....	....	....	....
1998-99	**Tampa Bay**	**NHL**	**82**	**13**	**15**	**28**	**23**	**2**	**0**	**2**	**125**	**10.4**	**–19**	**953**	**40.3**	**13:40**	....	....	....	....	....	....	....	....	....
99-2000	**Tampa Bay**	**NHL**	**80**	**25**	**42**	**67**	**43**	**6**	**0**	**3**	**166**	**15.1**	**–25**	**1288**	**44.4**	**19:18**	....	....	....	....	....	....	....	....	....
2000-01	**Tampa Bay**	**NHL**	**68**	**23**	**28**	**51**	**66**	**7**	**0**	**3**	**165**	**13.9**	**–26**	**1278**	**44.9**	**19:57**	....	....	....	....	....	....	....	....	....
2001-02	**Tampa Bay**	**NHL**	**76**	**20**	**17**	**37**	**61**	**5**	**0**	**3**	**164**	**12.2**	**–18**	**931**	**41.5**	**17:09**	....	....	....	....	....	....	....	....	....
2002-03	**Tampa Bay**	**NHL**	**80**	**33**	**45**	**78**	**39**	**11**	**2**	**3**	**274**	**12.0**	**0**	**1200**	**43.9**	**19:33**	**11**	**3**	**3**	**6**	**22**	**1**	**0**	**1**	**22:36**
2003-04♦	**Tampa Bay**	**NHL**	**81**	**32**	**34**	**66**	**52**	**5**	**2**	**6**	**242**	**13.2**	**23**	**1119**	**41.4**	**18:04**	**23**	**9**	**7**	**16**	**25**	**2**	**0**	**0**	**19:39**
	NHL Totals		**467**	**146**	**181**	**327**	**284**	**36**	**4**	**20**	**1136**	**12.9**		**6769**	**42.9**	**17:53**	**34**	**12**	**10**	**22**	**47**	**3**	**0**	**1**	**20:36**

QMJHL All-Rookie Team (1997) • QMJHL Offensive Rookie of the Year (1997) • Canadian Major Junior Rookie of the Year (1997) • QMJHL First All-Star Team (1998) • Canadian Major Junior First All-Star Team (1998)

Played in NHL All-Star Game (2003)

			Regular Season														Playoffs								
Season	Club	League	GP	G	A	Pts	PIM	PP	SH	GW	S	%	+/-	TF	F%	Min	GP	G	A	Pts	PIM	PP	SH	GW	Min

LeCLAIR, John (luh-KLAIR, JAWN) PHI.

Left wing. Shoots left. 6'3", 226 lbs. Born, St. Albans, VT, July 5, 1969. Montreal's 2nd choice, 33rd overall, in 1987 Entry Draft.

Season	Club	League	GP	G	A	Pts	PIM	PP	SH	GW	S	%	+/-	TF	F%	Min	GP	G	A	Pts	PIM	PP	SH	GW	Min
1985-86	Bellows	Hi-School	22	41	28	69	14	....	....	....	....	....	....	....	....	....	....	....	....	....	....	....	....	....	....
1986-87	Bellows	Hi-School	23	44	40	84	14	....	....	....	....	....	....	....	....	....	....	....	....	....	....	....	....	....	....
1987-88	U. of Vermont	ECAC	31	12	22	34	62	....	....	....	....	....	....	....	....	....	....	....	....	....	....	....	....	....	....
1988-89	U. of Vermont	ECAC	18	9	12	21	40	....	....	....	....	....	....	....	....	....	....	....	....	....	....	....	....	....	....
1989-90	U. of Vermont	ECAC	10	10	6	16	38	....	....	....	....	....	....	....	....	....	....	....	....	....	....	....	....	....	....
1990-91	U. of Vermont	ECAC	33	25	20	45	58	....	....	....	....	....	....	....	....	....	....	....	....	....	....	....	....	....	....
	Montreal	**NHL**	**10**	**2**	**5**	**7**	**2**	**0**	**0**	**1**	**12**	**16.7**	**1**	....	....	....	**3**	**0**	**0**	**0**	**0**	**0**	**0**	**0**	....
1991-92	**Montreal**	**NHL**	**59**	**8**	**11**	**19**	**14**	**3**	**0**	**0**	**73**	**11.0**	**5**	....	....	....	**8**	**1**	**1**	**2**	**4**	**0**	**0**	**0**	....
	Fredericton	AHL	8	7	7	14	10	....	....	....	....	....	....	....	....	....	2	0	0	0	4	....	....	....	....
1992-93♦	**Montreal**	**NHL**	**72**	**19**	**25**	**44**	**33**	**2**	**0**	**2**	**139**	**13.7**	**11**	....	....	....	**20**	**4**	**6**	**10**	**14**	**0**	**0**	**3**	....
1993-94	**Montreal**	**NHL**	**74**	**19**	**24**	**43**	**32**	**1**	**0**	**1**	**153**	**12.4**	**17**	....	....	....	**7**	**2**	**1**	**3**	**8**	**1**	**0**	**0**	....
1994-95	**Montreal**	**NHL**	**9**	**1**	**4**	**5**	**10**	**1**	**0**	**0**	**18**	**5.6**	**–1**	....	....	....	....	....	....	....	....	....	....	....	....
	Philadelphia	**NHL**	**37**	**25**	**24**	**49**	**20**	**5**	**0**	**7**	**113**	**22.1**	**21**	....	....	....	**15**	**5**	**7**	**12**	**4**	**1**	**0**	**1**	....
1995-96	**Philadelphia**	**NHL**	**82**	**51**	**46**	**97**	**64**	**19**	**0**	**10**	**270**	**18.9**	**21**	....	....	....	**11**	**6**	**5**	**11**	**6**	**4**	**0**	**1**	....
1996-97	**Philadelphia**	**NHL**	**82**	**50**	**47**	**97**	**58**	**10**	**0**	**5**	**324**	**15.4**	**44**	....	....	....	**19**	**9**	**12**	**21**	**10**	**4**	**0**	**3**	....
1997-98	**Philadelphia**	**NHL**	**82**	**51**	**36**	**87**	**32**	**16**	**0**	**9**	**303**	**16.8**	**30**	....	....	....	**5**	**1**	**1**	**2**	**8**	**1**	**0**	**1**	....
	United States	Olympics	4	0	1	1	0	....	....	....	....	....	....	....	....	....	....	....	....	....	....	....	....	....	....
1998-99	**Philadelphia**	**NHL**	**76**	**43**	**47**	**90**	**30**	**16**	**0**	**7**	**246**	**17.5**	**36**	**7**	**14.3**	**21:03**	**6**	**3**	**0**	**3**	**12**	**2**	**0**	**0**	**20:14**
99-2000	**Philadelphia**	**NHL**	**82**	**40**	**37**	**77**	**36**	**13**	**0**	**7**	**249**	**16.1**	**8**	**7**	**28.6**	**20:18**	**18**	**6**	**7**	**13**	**6**	**4**	**0**	**2**	**21:16**
2000-01	**Philadelphia**	**NHL**	**16**	**7**	**5**	**12**	**0**	**3**	**0**	**2**	**48**	**14.6**	**2**	**0**	**0.0**	**19:06**	**6**	**1**	**2**	**3**	**2**	**0**	**0**	**0**	**19:34**
2001-02	**Philadelphia**	**NHL**	**82**	**25**	**26**	**51**	**30**	**4**	**0**	**6**	**220**	**11.4**	**5**	**4**	**75.0**	**17:30**	**5**	**0**	**0**	**0**	**2**	**0**	**0**	**0**	**17:18**
	United States	Olympics	6	*6	1	7	2	....	....	....	....	....	....	....	....	....	....	....	....	....	....	....	....	....	....
2002-03	**Philadelphia**	**NHL**	**35**	**18**	**10**	**28**	**16**	**8**	**0**	**4**	**99**	**18.2**	**10**	**3**	**66.7**	**16:09**	**13**	**2**	**3**	**5**	**10**	**1**	**0**	**0**	**17:09**
2003-04	**Philadelphia**	**NHL**	**75**	**23**	**32**	**55**	**51**	**8**	**0**	**4**	**182**	**12.6**	**20**	**9**	**33.3**	**16:06**	**18**	**2**	**2**	**4**	**8**	**0**	**0**	**0**	**15:57**
	NHL Totals		**873**	**382**	**379**	**761**	**428**	**109**	**0**	**65**	**2449**	**15.6**		**30**	**36.7**	**18:31**	**154**	**42**	**47**	**89**	**94**	**18**	**0**	**11**	**18:28**

ECAC Second All-Star Team (1991) • NHL First All-Star Team (1995, 1998) • NHL Second All-Star Team (1996, 1997, 1999) • Bud Ice Plus/Minus Award (1997) • Bud Light Plus/Minus Award (1999)
Played in NHL All-Star Game (1996, 1997, 1998, 1999, 2000)

• Missed majority of 1989-90 season recovering from knee surgery, January 20, 1990. Traded to **Philadelphia** by **Montreal** with Eric Desjardins and Gilbert Dionne for Mark Recchi and Philadelphia's 3rd round choice (Martin Hohenberger) in 1995 Entry Draft, February 9, 1995. • Missed majority of 2000-01 season recovering from back injury suffered in game vs. Boston, October 7, 2000. • Missed majority of 2002-03 season recovering from shoulder injury suffered in game vs. St. Louis, November 27, 2002.

LECLERC, Mike (luh-KLUHRK, MIGHK) ANA.

Left wing. Shoots left. 6'2", 208 lbs. Born, Winnipeg, Man., November 10, 1976. Anaheim's 3rd choice, 55th overall, in 1995 Entry Draft.

Season	Club	League	GP	G	A	Pts	PIM	PP	SH	GW	S	%	+/-	TF	F%	Min	GP	G	A	Pts	PIM	PP	SH	GW	Min
1991-92	St. Boniface	MJHL	43	16	12	28	25	....	....	....	....	....	....	....	....	....	....	....	....	....	....	....	....	....	....
	Victoria Cougars	WHL	2	0	0	0	0	....	....	....	....	....	....	....	....	....	....	....	....	....	....	....	....	....	....
1992-93	Victoria Cougars	WHL	70	4	11	15	118	....	....	....	....	....	....	....	....	....	....	....	....	....	....	....	....	....	....
1993-94	Victoria Cougars	WHL	68	29	11	40	112	....	....	....	....	....	....	....	....	....	....	....	....	....	....	....	....	....	....
1994-95	Prince George	WHL	43	20	36	56	78	....	....	....	....	....	....	....	....	....	....	....	....	....	....	....	....	....	....
	Brandon	WHL	23	5	8	13	50	....	....	....	....	....	....	....	....	....	18	10	6	16	33	....	....	....	....
1995-96	Brandon	WHL	71	58	53	111	161	....	....	....	....	....	....	....	....	....	19	6	19	25	25	....	....	....	....
1996-97	**Anaheim**	**NHL**	**5**	**1**	**1**	**2**	**0**	**0**	**0**	**1**	**3**	**33.3**	**2**	....	....	....	**1**	**0**	**0**	**0**	**0**	**0**	**0**	**0**	....
	Baltimore Bandits	AHL	71	29	27	56	134	....	....	....	....	....	....	....	....	....	....	....	....	....	....	....	....	....	....
1997-98	**Anaheim**	**NHL**	**7**	**0**	**0**	**0**	**6**	**0**	**0**	**0**	**11**	**0.0**	**–6**	....	....	....	....	....	....	....	....	....	....	....	....
	Cincinnati	AHL	48	18	22	40	83	....	....	....	....	....	....	....	....	....	....	....	....	....	....	....	....	....	....
1998-99	**Anaheim**	**NHL**	**7**	**0**	**0**	**0**	**4**	**0**	**0**	**0**	**1**	**0.0**	**–2**	**0**	**0.0**	**5:52**	**1**	**0**	**0**	**0**	**0**	**0**	**0**	**0**	**15:02**
	Cincinnati	AHL	65	25	28	53	153	....	....	....	....	....	....	....	....	....	3	0	1	1	19	....	....	....	....
99-2000	**Anaheim**	**NHL**	**69**	**8**	**11**	**19**	**70**	**0**	**0**	**2**	**105**	**7.6**	**–15**	**1**	**0.0**	**12:08**	....	....	....	....	....	....	....	....	....
2000-01	**Anaheim**	**NHL**	**54**	**15**	**20**	**35**	**26**	**3**	**0**	**3**	**130**	**11.5**	**–1**	**5**	**20.0**	**17:35**	....	....	....	....	....	....	....	....	....
2001-02	**Anaheim**	**NHL**	**82**	**20**	**24**	**44**	**107**	**8**	**0**	**4**	**178**	**11.2**	**–12**	**10**	**50.0**	**17:23**	....	....	....	....	....	....	....	....	....
2002-03	**Anaheim**	**NHL**	**57**	**9**	**19**	**28**	**34**	**1**	**0**	**4**	**122**	**7.4**	**–8**	**17**	**29.4**	**16:56**	**21**	**2**	**9**	**11**	**12**	**1**	**0**	**2**	**19:02**
2003-04	**Anaheim**	**NHL**	**10**	**1**	**3**	**4**	**4**	**0**	**0**	**0**	**19**	**5.3**	**–1**	**4**	**75.0**	**15:37**	....	....	....	....	....	....	....	....	....
	NHL Totals		**291**	**54**	**78**	**132**	**251**	**12**	**0**	**14**	**569**	**9.5**		**37**	**37.8**	**15:41**	**23**	**2**	**9**	**11**	**12**	**1**	**0**	**2**	**18:51**

WHL East Second All-Star Team (1996)

• Missed majority of 2003-04 season recovering from knee surgery, July 15, 2003.

LEEB, Brad (LEEB, BRAD) TOR.

Right wing. Shoots right. 5'11", 187 lbs. Born, Red Deer, Alta., August 27, 1979.

Season	Club	League	GP	G	A	Pts	PIM	PP	SH	GW	S	%	+/-	TF	F%	Min	GP	G	A	Pts	PIM	PP	SH	GW	Min
1994-95	Red Deer	AMHL	36	31	14	45	93	....	....	....	....	....	....	....	....	....	....	....	....	....	....	....	....	....	....
	Red Deer Rebels	WHL	3	0	0	0	4	....	....	....	....	....	....	....	....	....	....	....	....	....	....	....	....	....	....
1995-96	Red Deer Rebels	WHL	38	3	6	9	30	....	....	....	....	....	....	....	....	....	10	2	0	2	11	....	....	....	....
1996-97	Red Deer Rebels	WHL	70	15	20	35	76	....	....	....	....	....	....	....	....	....	16	3	3	6	6	....	....	....	....
1997-98	Red Deer Rebels	WHL	63	23	23	46	88	....	....	....	....	....	....	....	....	....	3	2	0	2	2	....	....	....	....
1998-99	Red Deer Rebels	WHL	64	32	47	79	84	....	....	....	....	....	....	....	....	....	9	5	9	14	10	....	....	....	....
99-2000	**Vancouver**	**NHL**	**2**	**0**	**0**	**0**	**2**	**0**	**0**	**0**	**3**	**0.0**	**–2**	**0**	**0.0**	**12:07**	....	....	....	....	....	....	....	....	....
	Syracuse Crunch	AHL	61	19	18	37	50	....	....	....	....	....	....	....	....	....	4	0	0	0	6	....	....	....	....
2000-01	Kansas City	IHL	53	18	16	34	53	....	....	....	....	....	....	....	....	....	....	....	....	....	....	....	....	....	....
2001-02	**Vancouver**	**NHL**	**2**	**0**	**0**	**0**	**0**	**0**	**0**	**0**	**1**	**0.0**	**1**	**0**	**0.0**	**9:35**	....	....	....	....	....	....	....	....	....
	Manitoba Moose	AHL	60	17	15	32	45	....	....	....	....	....	....	....	....	....	....	....	....	....	....	....	....	....	....
2002-03	St. John's	AHL	79	35	26	61	78	....	....	....	....	....	....	....	....	....	....	....	....	....	....	....	....	....	....
2003-04	**Toronto**	**NHL**	**1**	**0**	**0**	**0**	**0**	**0**	**0**	**0**	**1**	**0.0**	**–1**	**0**	**0.0**	**10:31**	....	....	....	....	....	....	....	....	....
	St. John's	AHL	77	24	25	49	116	....	....	....	....	....	....	....	....	....	....	....	....	....	....	....	....	....	....
	NHL Totals		**5**	**0**	**0**	**0**	**2**	**0**	**0**	**0**	**5**	**0.0**		**0**	**0.0**	**10:47**	....	....	....	....	....	....	....	....	....

WHL East Second All-Star Team (1999)

Signed as a free agent by **Vancouver**, October 8, 1999. Traded to **Toronto** by **Vancouver** for Tomas Mojzis, September 4, 2002.

LEETCH, Brian (LEECH, BRIGH-uhn) TOR.

Defense. Shoots left. 6'1", 190 lbs. Born, Corpus Christi, TX, March 3, 1968. NY Rangers' 1st choice, 9th overall, in 1986 Entry Draft.

Season	Club	League	GP	G	A	Pts	PIM	PP	SH	GW	S	%	+/-	TF	F%	Min	GP	G	A	Pts	PIM	PP	SH	GW	Min
1983-84	Cheshire High	Hi-School	28	52	49	101	24	....	....	....	....	....	....	....	....	....	....	....	....	....	....	....	....	....	....
1984-85	Avon Old Farms	Hi-School	26	30	46	76	15	....	....	....	....	....	....	....	....	....	....	....	....	....	....	....	....	....	....
1985-86	Avon Old Farms	Hi-School	28	40	44	84	18	....	....	....	....	....	....	....	....	....	....	....	....	....	....	....	....	....	....
1986-87	Boston College	H-East	37	9	38	47	10	....	....	....	....	....	....	....	....	....	....	....	....	....	....	....	....	....	....
1987-88	Team USA	Nat-Tm	50	13	61	74	38	....	....	....	....	....	....	....	....	....	....	....	....	....	....	....	....	....	....
	United States	Olympics	6	1	5	6	4	....	....	....	....	....	....	....	....	....	....	....	....	....	....	....	....	....	....
	NY Rangers	**NHL**	**17**	**2**	**12**	**14**	**0**	**1**	**0**	**1**	**40**	**5.0**	**5**	....	....	....	....	....	....	....	....	....	....	....	....
1988-89	**NY Rangers**	**NHL**	**68**	**23**	**48**	**71**	**50**	**8**	**3**	**1**	**268**	**8.6**	**8**	....	....	....	**4**	**3**	**2**	**5**	**2**	**2**	**0**	**0**	....
1989-90	**NY Rangers**	**NHL**	**72**	**11**	**45**	**56**	**26**	**5**	**0**	**2**	**222**	**5.0**	**–18**	....	....	....	....	....	....	....	....	....	....	....	....
1990-91	**NY Rangers**	**NHL**	**80**	**16**	**72**	**88**	**42**	**6**	**0**	**4**	**206**	**7.8**	**2**	....	....	....	**6**	**1**	**3**	**4**	**0**	**0**	**0**	**0**	....
1991-92	**NY Rangers**	**NHL**	**80**	**22**	**80**	**102**	**26**	**10**	**1**	**3**	**245**	**9.0**	**25**	....	....	....	**13**	**4**	**11**	**15**	**4**	**1**	**1**	**0**	....
1992-93	**NY Rangers**	**NHL**	**36**	**6**	**30**	**36**	**26**	**2**	**1**	**1**	**150**	**4.0**	**2**	....	....	....	....	....	....	....	....	....	....	....	....
1993-94♦	**NY Rangers**	**NHL**	**84**	**23**	**56**	**79**	**67**	**17**	**1**	**4**	**328**	**7.0**	**28**	....	....	....	**23**	**11**	***23**	***34**	**6**	**4**	**0**	**4**	....
1994-95	**NY Rangers**	**NHL**	**48**	**9**	**32**	**41**	**18**	**3**	**0**	**2**	**182**	**4.9**	**0**	....	....	....	**10**	**6**	**8**	**14**	**8**	**3**	**0**	**1**	....
1995-96	**NY Rangers**	**NHL**	**82**	**15**	**70**	**85**	**30**	**7**	**0**	**3**	**276**	**5.4**	**12**	....	....	....	**11**	**1**	**6**	**7**	**4**	**1**	**0**	**0**	....
1996-97	**NY Rangers**	**NHL**	**82**	**20**	**58**	**78**	**40**	**9**	**0**	**2**	**256**	**7.8**	**31**	....	....	....	**15**	**2**	**8**	**10**	**6**	**1**	**0**	**1**	....
1997-98	**NY Rangers**	**NHL**	**76**	**17**	**33**	**50**	**32**	**11**	**0**	**2**	**230**	**7.4**	**–36**	....	....	....	....	....	....	....	....	....	....	....	....
	United States	Olympics	4	1	1	2	0	....	....	....	....	....	....	....	....	....	....	....	....	....	....	....	....	....	....
1998-99	**NY Rangers**	**NHL**	**82**	**13**	**42**	**55**	**42**	**4**	**0**	**1**	**184**	**7.1**	**–7**	**0**	**0.0**	**29:52**	....	....	....	....	....	....	....	....	....
99-2000	**NY Rangers**	**NHL**	**50**	**7**	**19**	**26**	**20**	**3**	**0**	**2**	**124**	**5.6**	**–16**	**0**	**0.0**	**26:57**	....	....	....	....	....	....	....	....	....
2000-01	**NY Rangers**	**NHL**	**82**	**21**	**58**	**79**	**34**	**10**	**1**	**3**	**241**	**8.7**	**–18**	**0**	**0.0**	**29:21**	....	....	....	....	....	....	....	....	....
2001-02	**NY Rangers**	**NHL**	**82**	**10**	**45**	**55**	**28**	**1**	**0**	**3**	**202**	**5.0**	**14**	**0**	**0.0**	**25:52**	....	....	....	....	....	....	....	....	....
	United States	Olympics	6	0	5	5	0	....	....	....	....	....	....	....	....	....	....	....	....	....	....	....	....	....	....
2002-03	**NY Rangers**	**NHL**	**51**	**12**	**18**	**30**	**20**	**5**	**0**	**2**	**150**	**8.0**	**–3**	**0**	**0.0**	**26:06**	....	....	....	....	....	....	....	....	....

			Regular Season														Playoffs								
Season	**Club**	**League**	**GP**	**G**	**A**	**Pts**	**PIM**	**PP**	**SH**	**GW**	**S**	**%**	**+/-**	**TF**	**F%**	**Min**	**GP**	**G**	**A**	**Pts**	**PIM**	**PP**	**SH**	**GW**	**Min**
2003-04	**NY Rangers**	**NHL**	**57**	**13**	**23**	**36**	**24**	**4**	**1**	**1**	**165**	**7.9**	**–5**	**0**	**0.0**	**26:15**	....	....	....	....	....	....	....	....	....
	Toronto	**NHL**	**15**	**2**	**13**	**15**	**10**	**1**	**0**	**1**	**41**	**4.9**	**11**	**0**	**0.0**	**26:26**	**13**	**0**	**8**	**8**	**6**	**0**	**0**	**0**	**28:29**
	NHL Totals		**1144**	**242**	**754**	**996**	**535**	**107**	**8**	**38**	**3510**	**6.9**		**0**	**0.0**	**27:34**	**95**	**28**	**69**	**97**	**36**	**12**	**1**	**6**	**28:29**

Hockey East First All-Star Team (1987) • Hockey East Rookie of the Year (1987) • Hockey East Player of the Year (1987) • NCAA East First All-American Team (1987) • NHL All-Rookie Team (1989) • Calder Memorial Trophy (1989) • NHL Second All-Star Team (1991, 1994, 1996) • NHL First All-Star Team (1992, 1997) • James Norris Memorial Trophy (1992, 1997) • Conn Smythe Trophy (1994)

Played in NHL All-Star Game (1990, 1991, 1992, 1994, 1996, 1997, 1998, 2001, 2002)

Traded to **Edmonton** by **NY Rangers** for Jussi Markkanen and Edmonton's 4th round choice (later traded to Toronto – Toronto selected Roman Kukumberg), June 30, 2003. Signed as a free agent by **NY Rangers**, July 30, 2003. Traded to **Toronto** by **NY Rangers** with Edmonton's 4th round choice (previously acquired, Toronto selected Roman Kukumberg) in 2004 Entry Draft for Maxim Kondratiev, Jarkko Immonen, Toronto's 1st round choice (later traded to Calgary – Calgary selected Kris Chucko) in 2004 Entry Draft and Toronto's 2nd round choice in 2005 Entry Draft, March 3, 2004.

LEFEBVRE, Guillaume

(luh-FAYV, GEE-ohm) **PIT.**

Left wing. Shoots left. 6'1", 202 lbs. Born, Amos, Que., May 7, 1981. Philadelphia's 6th choice, 227th overall, in 2000 Entry Draft.

1996-97	Amos Forestiers	QAAA	40	7	12	19	14	....	....	....	....	....	....	....	....	....	....	....	....	....	....	....	....	....	....
1997-98	Amos Forestiers	QAAA	42	12	16	28	100	....	....	....	....	....	....	....	....	....	6	4	5	9	....	....	....	....	....
1998-99	Shawinigan	QMJHL	40	3	1	4	49	....	....	....	....	....	....	....	....	....	....	....	....	....	....	....	....	....	....
	Cape Breton	QMJHL	24	2	7	9	13	....	....	....	....	....	....	....	....	....	5	0	1	1	0	....	....	....	....
99-2000	Cape Breton	QMJHL	44	26	28	54	82	....	....	....	....	....	....	....	....	....	....	....	....	....	....	....	....	....	....
	Quebec Remparts	QMJHL	2	3	1	4	0	....	....	....	....	....	....	....	....	....	....	....	....	....	....	....	....	....	....
	Rouyn-Noranda	QMJHL	25	4	11	15	39	....	....	....	....	....	....	....	....	....	11	4	0	4	25	....	....	....	....
2000-01	Rouyn-Noranda	QMJHL	61	24	43	67	160	....	....	....	....	....	....	....	....	....	9	3	1	4	22	....	....	....	....
	Philadelphia	AHL	....	....	....	....	....	....	....	....	....	....	....	....	....	....	9	0	1	1	2	....	....	....	....
2001-02	**Philadelphia**	**NHL**	**3**	**0**	**0**	**0**	**0**	**0**	**0**	**0**	**3**	**0.0**	**–1**	**0**	**0.0**	**5:55**	....	....	....	....	....	....	....	....	....
	Philadelphia	AHL	78	19	15	34	111	....	....	....	....	....	....	....	....	....	5	0	0	0	4	....	....	....	....
2002-03	**Philadelphia**	**NHL**	**14**	**0**	**0**	**0**	**4**	**0**	**0**	**0**	**5**	**0.0**	**1**	**0**	**0.0**	**7:27**	....	....	....	....	....	....	....	....	....
	Philadelphia	AHL	47	7	6	13	113	....	....	....	....	....	....	....	....	....	....	....	....	....	....	....	....	....	....
	Pittsburgh	**NHL**	**12**	**2**	**4**	**6**	**0**	**0**	**0**	**0**	**14**	**14.3**	**1**	**1**	**100.0**	**17:30**	....	....	....	....	....	....	....	....	....
	Wilkes-Barre	AHL	1	1	0	1	0	....	....	....	....	....	....	....	....	....	5	0	0	0	6	....	....	....	....
2003-04	Wilkes-Barre	AHL	64	4	12	16	78	....	....	....	....	....	....	....	....	....	14	1	0	1	19	....	....	....	....
	NHL Totals		**29**	**2**	**4**	**6**	**4**	**0**	**0**	**0**	**22**	**9.1**		**1**	**100.0**	**11:27**	....	....	....	....	....	....	....	....	....

Traded to **Phoenix** by **Philadelphia** with Atlanta's 3rd round choice (previously acquired, Phoenix selected Tyler Redenbach) in 2003 Entry Draft and Philadelphia's 2nd round choice (later traded to NY Rangers – NY Rangers selected Brandon Dubinsky) in 2004 Entry Draft for Tony Amonte, March 10, 2003. Traded to **Pittsburgh** by **Phoenix** with Ramzi Abid and Dan Focht for Jan Hrdina and Francois Leroux, March 11, 2003.

LEGWAND, David

(LEHG-wuhnd, DAY-vihd) **NSH.**

Center. Shoots left. 6'2", 190 lbs. Born, Detroit, MI, August 17, 1980. Nashville's 1st choice, 2nd overall, in 1998 Entry Draft.

1996-97	Det. Compuware	MNHL	44	21	41	62	58	....	....	....	....	....	....	....	....	....	....	....	....	....	....	....	....	....	....
1997-98	Plymouth Whalers	OHL	59	54	51	105	56	....	....	....	....	....	....	....	....	....	15	8	12	20	24	....	....	....	....
1998-99	Plymouth Whalers	OHL	55	31	49	80	65	....	....	....	....	....	....	....	....	....	11	3	8	11	8	....	....	....	....
	Nashville	**NHL**	**1**	**0**	**0**	**0**	**0**	**0**	**0**	**0**	**2**	**0.0**	**0**	**9**	**55.6**	**12:50**	....	....	....	....	....	....	....	....	....
99-2000	**Nashville**	**NHL**	**71**	**13**	**15**	**28**	**30**	**4**	**0**	**2**	**111**	**11.7**	**–6**	**637**	**41.6**	**14:43**	....	....	....	....	....	....	....	....	....
2000-01	**Nashville**	**NHL**	**81**	**13**	**28**	**41**	**38**	**3**	**0**	**3**	**172**	**7.6**	**1**	**888**	**40.3**	**15:14**	....	....	....	....	....	....	....	....	....
2001-02	**Nashville**	**NHL**	**63**	**11**	**19**	**30**	**54**	**1**	**1**	**1**	**121**	**9.1**	**1**	**843**	**40.5**	**16:25**	....	....	....	....	....	....	....	....	....
2002-03	**Nashville**	**NHL**	**64**	**17**	**31**	**48**	**34**	**3**	**1**	**4**	**167**	**10.2**	**–2**	**1095**	**46.6**	**19:14**	....	....	....	....	....	....	....	....	....
2003-04	**Nashville**	**NHL**	**82**	**18**	**29**	**47**	**46**	**5**	**1**	**5**	**165**	**10.9**	**9**	**1109**	**45.1**	**17:16**	**6**	**1**	**0**	**1**	**8**	**0**	**1**	**0**	**15:41**
	NHL Totals		**362**	**72**	**122**	**194**	**202**	**16**	**3**	**15**	**738**	**9.8**		**4581**	**43.2**	**16:30**	**6**	**1**	**0**	**1**	**8**	**0**	**1**	**0**	**15:41**

OHL All-Rookie Team (1998) • OHL First All-Star Team (1998) • OHL Rookie of the Year (1998) • OHL MVP (1998) • Canadian Major Junior Rookie of the Year (1998)

LEHTINEN, Jere

(LEH-tih-nehn, YUH-ree) **DAL.**

Right wing. Shoots right. 6', 200 lbs. Born, Espoo, Finland, June 24, 1973. Minnesota's 3rd choice, 88th overall, in 1992 Entry Draft.

1989-90	Kiekko-67 Jr.	Finn-Jr.	32	23	23	46	6	....	....	....	....	....	....	....	....	....	5	0	3	3	0	....	....	....	....
1990-91	Kiekko Espoo Jr.	Finn-Jr.	3	3	1	4	0	....	....	....	....	....	....	....	....	....	....	....	....	....	....	....	....	....	....
	Kiekko Espoo	Finland-2	32	15	9	24	12	....	....	....	....	....	....	....	....	....	....	....	....	....	....	....	....	....	....
1991-92	Kiekko-67 Jr.	Finn-Jr.	8	5	4	9	2	....	....	....	....	....	....	....	....	....	....	....	....	....	....	....	....	....	....
	Kiekko Espoo	Finland-2	43	32	17	49	6	....	....	....	....	....	....	....	....	....	....	....	....	....	....	....	....	....	....
1992-93	Kiekko-67 Jr.	Finn-Jr.	4	5	3	8	8	....	....	....	....	....	....	....	....	....	....	....	....	....	....	....	....	....	....
	Kiekko Espoo	Finland	45	13	14	27	6	....	....	....	....	....	....	....	....	....	....	....	....	....	....	....	....	....	....
1993-94	TPS Turku	Finland	42	19	20	39	6	....	....	....	....	....	....	....	....	....	11	*11	2	13	*2	....	....	....	....
	Finland	Olympics	8	3	0	3	0	....	....	....	....	....	....	....	....	....	....	....	....	....	....	....	....	....	....
1994-95	TPS Turku	Finland	39	19	23	42	33	....	....	....	....	....	....	....	....	....	13	*8	6	14	4	....	....	....	....
1995-96	**Dallas**	**NHL**	**57**	**6**	**22**	**28**	**16**	**0**	**0**	**1**	**109**	**5.5**	**5**	....	....	....	....	....	....	....	....	....	....	....	....
	Michigan	IHL	1	1	0	1	0	....	....	....	....	....	....	....	....	....	....	....	....	....	....	....	....	....	....
1996-97	**Dallas**	**NHL**	**63**	**16**	**27**	**43**	**2**	**3**	**1**	**2**	**134**	**11.9**	**26**	....	....	....	**7**	**2**	**2**	**4**	**0**	**0**	**0**	**0**	....
1997-98	**Dallas**	**NHL**	**72**	**23**	**19**	**42**	**20**	**7**	**2**	**6**	**201**	**11.4**	**19**	....	....	....	**12**	**3**	**5**	**8**	**2**	**1**	**0**	**0**	....
	Finland	Olympics	6	4	2	6	2	....	....	....	....	....	....	....	....	....	....	....	....	....	....	....	....	....	....
1998-99♦	**Dallas**	**NHL**	**74**	**20**	**32**	**52**	**18**	**7**	**1**	**2**	**173**	**11.6**	**29**	**9**	**33.3**	**19:36**	**23**	**10**	**3**	**13**	**2**	**1**	**1**	**0**	**21:09**
99-2000	**Dallas**	**NHL**	**17**	**3**	**5**	**8**	**0**	**0**	**0**	**1**	**29**	**10.3**	**1**	**0**	**0.0**	**17:31**	**13**	**1**	**5**	**6**	**2**	**0**	**0**	**0**	**21:15**
2000-01	**Dallas**	**NHL**	**74**	**20**	**25**	**45**	**24**	**7**	**0**	**1**	**148**	**13.5**	**14**	**7**	**28.6**	**19:17**	**10**	**1**	**0**	**1**	**2**	**0**	**0**	**0**	**20:13**
2001-02	**Dallas**	**NHL**	**73**	**25**	**24**	**49**	**14**	**7**	**1**	**4**	**198**	**12.6**	**27**	**18**	**22.2**	**19:50**	....	....	....	....	....	....	....	....	....
	Finland	Olympics	4	1	2	3	2	....	....	....	....	....	....	....	....	....	....	....	....	....	....	....	....	....	....
2002-03	**Dallas**	**NHL**	**80**	**31**	**17**	**48**	**20**	**5**	**0**	**3**	**238**	**13.0**	**39**	**36**	**22.2**	**18:47**	**12**	**3**	**2**	**5**	**0**	**1**	**0**	**1**	**21:12**
2003-04	**Dallas**	**NHL**	**58**	**13**	**13**	**26**	**20**	**4**	**1**	**4**	**138**	**9.4**	**0**	**10**	**40.0**	**19:27**	**5**	**0**	**0**	**0**	**0**	**0**	**0**	**0**	**19:19**
	NHL Totals		**568**	**157**	**184**	**341**	**134**	**40**	**6**	**24**	**1368**	**11.5**		**80**	**26.3**	**19:18**	**82**	**20**	**17**	**37**	**8**	**3**	**1**	**1**	**20:53**

Frank J. Selke Trophy (1998, 1999, 2003)

Played in NHL All-Star Game (1998)

Rights transferred to **Dallas** after **Minnesota** franchise relocated, June 9, 1993. • Missed majority of 1999-2000 season recovering from leg injury suffered in game vs. Nashville, October 16, 1999.

LEMIEUX, Mario

(lehm-YOO, MAHR-ee-oh) **PIT.**

Center. Shoots right. 6'4", 230 lbs. Born, Montreal, Que., October 5, 1965. Pittsburgh's 1st choice, 1st overall, in 1984 Entry Draft.

1980-81	Mtl-Concordia	QAAA	47	62	62	124	127	....	....	....	....	....	....	....	....	....	3	2	5	7	8	....	....	....	....
1981-82	Laval Voisins	QMJHL	64	30	66	96	22	....	....	....	....	....	....	....	....	....	18	5	9	14	31	....	....	....	....
1982-83	Laval Voisins	QMJHL	66	84	100	184	76	....	....	....	....	....	....	....	....	....	12	14	18	32	18	....	....	....	....
1983-84	Laval Voisins	QMJHL	70	*133	*149	*282	92	....	....	....	....	....	....	....	....	....	14	*29	*23	*52	29	....	....	....	....
1984-85	**Pittsburgh**	**NHL**	**73**	**43**	**57**	**100**	**54**	**11**	**0**	**2**	**209**	**20.6**	**–35**	....	....	....	....	....	....	....	....	....	....	....	....
1985-86	**Pittsburgh**	**NHL**	**79**	**48**	**93**	**141**	**43**	**17**	**0**	**4**	**276**	**17.4**	**–6**	....	....	....	....	....	....	....	....	....	....	....	....
1986-87	**Pittsburgh**	**NHL**	**63**	**54**	**53**	**107**	**57**	**19**	**0**	**4**	**267**	**20.2**	**13**	....	....	....	....	....	....	....	....	....	....	....	....
1987-88	**Pittsburgh**	**NHL**	**77**	***70**	**98**	***168**	**92**	**22**	**10**	**7**	**382**	**18.3**	**23**	....	....	....	....	....	....	....	....	....	....	....	....
1988-89	**Pittsburgh**	**NHL**	**76**	***85**	***114**	***199**	**100**	**31**	**13**	**8**	**313**	**27.2**	**41**	....	....	....	**11**	**12**	**7**	**19**	**16**	**7**	**1**	**0**	....
1989-90	**Pittsburgh**	**NHL**	**59**	**45**	**78**	**123**	**78**	**14**	**3**	**4**	**226**	**19.9**	**–18**	....	....	....	....	....	....	....	....	....	....	....	....
1990-91♦	**Pittsburgh**	**NHL**	**26**	**19**	**26**	**45**	**30**	**6**	**1**	**2**	**89**	**21.3**	**8**	....	....	....	**23**	**16**	***28**	***44**	**16**	**6**	**2**	**0**	....
1991-92♦	**Pittsburgh**	**NHL**	**64**	**44**	**87**	***131**	**94**	**12**	**4**	**5**	**249**	**17.7**	**27**	....	....	....	**15**	***16**	**18**	***34**	**2**	**8**	**2**	**5**	....
1992-93	**Pittsburgh**	**NHL**	**60**	**69**	**91**	***160**	**38**	**16**	**6**	**10**	**286**	**24.1**	**55**	....	....	....	**11**	**8**	**10**	**18**	**10**	**3**	**1**	**1**	....
1993-94	**Pittsburgh**	**NHL**	**22**	**17**	**20**	**37**	**32**	**7**	**0**	**4**	**92**	**18.5**	**–2**	....	....	....	**6**	**4**	**3**	**7**	**2**	**1**	**0**	**0**	....
1994-95	**Pittsburgh**	**NHL**	DID NOT PLAY																						
1995-96	**Pittsburgh**	**NHL**	**70**	***69**	***92**	***161**	**54**	**31**	**8**	**8**	**338**	**20.4**	**10**	....	....	....	**18**	**11**	**16**	**27**	**33**	**3**	**1**	**2**	....
1996-97	**Pittsburgh**	**NHL**	**76**	**50**	***72**	***122**	**65**	**15**	**3**	**7**	**327**	**15.3**	**27**	....	....	....	**5**	**3**	**3**	**6**	**4**	**0**	**0**	**0**	....
1997-98			OUT OF HOCKEY – RETIRED																						
1998-99			OUT OF HOCKEY – RETIRED																						
99-2000			OUT OF HOCKEY – RETIRED																						
2000-01	**Pittsburgh**	**NHL**	**43**	**35**	**41**	**76**	**18**	**16**	**1**	**5**	**171**	**20.5**	**15**	**852**	**52.1**	**24:20**	**18**	**6**	**11**	**17**	**4**	**1**	**0**	**3**	**24:35**
2001-02	**Pittsburgh**	**NHL**	**24**	**6**	**25**	**31**	**14**	**2**	**0**	**0**	**75**	**8.0**	**0**	**354**	**44.6**	**22:16**	....	....	....	....	....	....	....	....	....
	Canada	Olympics	5	2	4	6	0	....	....	....	....	....	....	....	....	....	....	....	....	....	....	....	....	....	....

Season	Club	League	Regular Season GP	G	A	Pts	PIM	PP	SH	GW	S	%	+/-	TF	F%	Min	Playoffs GP	G	A	Pts	PIM	PP	SH	GW	Min
2002-03	Pittsburgh	NHL	67	28	63	91	43	14	0	4	235	11.9	–25	1029	46.1	23:05									
2003-04	Pittsburgh	NHL	10	1	8	9	6	0	0	0	21	4.8	–2	173	49.1	22:24									
	NHL Totals		889	683	1018	1701	818	233	49	74	3556	19.2		2408	48.2	23:16	107	76	96	172	87	29	7	11	24:35

QMJHL Second All-Star Team (1983) • QMJHL First All-Star Team (1984) • QMJHL MVP (1984) • Canadian Major Junior Player of the Year (1984) • NHL All-Rookie Team (1985) • Calder Memorial Trophy (1985) • NHL Second All-Star Team (1986, 1987, 1992, 2001) • Lester B. Pearson Award (1986, 1988, 1993, 1996) • Canada Cup All-Star Team (1987) • NHL First All-Star Team (1988, 1989, 1993, 1996, 1997) • Dodge Performance of the Year Award (1988) • Dodge Performer of the Year Award (1988, 1989) • Art Ross Trophy (1988, 1989, 1992, 1993, 1996, 1997) • Hart Trophy (1988, 1993, 1996) • Dodge Ram Tough Award (1989) • Conn Smythe Trophy (1991, 1992) • ProSet/NHL Player of the Year Award (1992) • Alka-Seltzer Plus Award (1993) • Bill Masterton Memorial Trophy (1993) • Lester Patrick Trophy (2000)

Played in NHL All-Star Game (1985, 1986, 1988, 1989, 1990, 1992, 1996, 1997, 2001, 2002)

• Missed remainder of 1989-90 and majority of 1990-91 seasons recovering from back injury suffered in game vs. NY Rangers, February 14, 1989. • Missed remainder of 1992-93 season after being diagnosed with Hodgkin's Disease, January 12, 1993. • Missed majority of 1993-94 season recovering from back injury suffered in game vs. Chicago, November 11, 1993. • Missed entire 1994-95 season recovering from effects of treatment for Hodgkin's Disease and back injury suffered in game vs. NY Rangers, March 12, 1994. • Became third player (Gordie Howe, Guy Lafleur) to appear in NHL game after being inducted into Hockey Hall of Fame, December 27, 2000. • Missed majority of 2001-02 season recovering from hip injury suffered in game vs. Anaheim, October 6, 2001. • Missed majority of 2003-04 season recovering from hip injury suffered in game vs. Boston, November 1, 2003.

LEOPOLD, Jordan

(LEE-oh-pohld, JOHR-dan) **CGY.**

Defense. Shoots left. 6', 193 lbs. Born, Golden Valley, MN, August 3, 1980. Anaheim's 1st choice, 44th overall, in 1999 Entry Draft.

Season	Club	League	GP	G	A	Pts	PIM	PP	SH	GW	S	%	+/-	TF	F%	Min	GP	G	A	Pts	PIM	PP	SH	GW	Min
1995-96	Armstrong	Hi-School	19	11	14	25	30																		
1996-97	Armstrong	Hi-School	30	24	36	60																			
1997-98	U.S. National U-18	USDP	60	11	12	23	16																		
1998-99	U. of Minnesota	WCHA	39	7	16	23	20																		
99-2000	U. of Minnesota	WCHA	39	6	18	24	20																		
2000-01	U. of Minnesota	WCHA	42	12	37	49	38																		
2001-02	U. of Minnesota	WCHA	44	20	28	48	28																		
2002-03	Calgary	NHL	58	4	10	14	12	3	0	0	78	5.1	–15	0	0.0	20:36									
	Saint John Flames	AHL	3	1	2	3	0																		
2003-04	Calgary	NHL	82	9	24	33	24	6	0	1	138	6.5	8	0	0.0	22:14	26	0	10	10	6	0	0	0	25:41
	NHL Totals		140	13	34	47	36	9	0	1	216	6.0		0	0.0	21:33	26	0	10	10	6	0	0	0	25:41

WCHA All-Rookie Team (1999) • WCHA Second All-Star Team (2000) • WCHA First All-Star Team (2001, 2002) • NCAA West First All-American Team (2001) • Hobey Baker Memorial Award (Top U.S. Collegiate Player) (2002)

Traded to **Calgary** by **Anaheim** for Andrei Nazarov and Calgary's 2nd round choice (later traded to Phoenix – later traded back to Calgary – Calgary selected Andrei Taratukhin) in 2001 Entry Draft, September 26, 2000.

LESCHYSHYN, Curtis

(luh-SIH-shuhn, KUHR-tihs)

Defense. Shoots left. 6'1", 207 lbs. Born, Thompson, Man., September 21, 1969. Quebec's 1st choice, 3rd overall, in 1988 Entry Draft.

Season	Club	League	GP	G	A	Pts	PIM	PP	SH	GW	S	%	+/-	TF	F%	Min	GP	G	A	Pts	PIM	PP	SH	GW	Min
1985-86	Saskatoon Blazers	SMHL	34	9	34	43	52																		
	Saskatoon Blades	WHL	1	0	0	0	0																		
1986-87	Saskatoon Blades	WHL	70	14	26	40	107										11	1	5	6	14				
1987-88	Saskatoon Blades	WHL	56	14	41	55	86										10	2	5	7	16				
1988-89	Quebec	NHL	71	4	9	13	71	1	1	0	58	6.9	–32												
1989-90	Quebec	NHL	68	2	6	8	44	1	0	0	42	4.8	–41												
1990-91	Quebec	NHL	55	3	7	10	49	2	0	1	57	5.3	–19												
1991-92	Quebec	NHL	42	5	12	17	42	3	0	1	61	8.2	–28												
	Halifax Citadels	AHL	6	0	2	2	4																		
1992-93	Quebec	NHL	82	9	23	32	61	4	0	2	73	12.3	25				6	1	1	2	6	1	0	0	
1993-94	Quebec	NHL	72	5	17	22	65	3	0	2	97	5.2	–2												
1994-95	Quebec	NHL	44	2	13	15	20	0	0	0	43	4.7	29				3	0	1	1	4	0	0	0	
1995-96♦	Colorado	NHL	77	4	15	19	73	0	0	1	76	5.3	32				17	1	2	3	8	0	0	0	
1996-97	Colorado	NHL	11	0	5	5	6	0	0	0	8	0.0	1												
	Washington	NHL	2	0	0	0	2	0	0	0	0	0.0	0												
	Hartford	NHL	64	4	13	17	30	1	1	1	94	4.3	–19												
1997-98	Carolina	NHL	73	2	10	12	45	1	0	1	53	3.8	–2												
1998-99	Carolina	NHL	65	2	7	9	50	0	0	0	35	5.7	–1	0	0.0	19:18	6	0	0	0	6	0	0	0	24:07
99-2000	Carolina	NHL	53	0	2	2	14	0	0	0	31	0.0	–19	0	0.0	17:47									
2000-01	Minnesota	NHL	54	2	3	5	19	1	0	1	43	4.7	–2	0	0.0	19:31									
	Ottawa	NHL	11	0	4	4	0	0	0	0	8	0.0	7	0	0.0	19:04	4	0	0	0	0	0	0	0	21:05
2001-02	Ottawa	NHL	79	1	9	10	44	0	0	0	59	1.7	–5	0	0.0	18:28	12	0	1	1	0	0	0	0	16:49
2002-03	Ottawa	NHL	54	1	6	7	18	0	0	0	30	3.3	11	0	0.0	15:13	18	0	1	1	10	0	0	0	14:11
2003-04	Ottawa	NHL	56	1	4	5	16	0	0	0	30	3.3	13	2	0.0	13:54	2	0	0	0	0	0	0	0	15:37
	NHL Totals		1033	47	165	212	669	17	2	10	898	5.2		2	0.0	17:32	68	2	6	8	34	1	0	0	17:05

WHL East First All-Star Team (1988)

Transferred to **Colorado** after **Quebec** franchise relcoated, June 21, 1995. Traded to **Washington** by **Colorado** with Chris Simon for Keith Jones, Washington's 1st (Scott Parker) and 4th (later traded back to Washington – Washington selected Krys Barch) round choices in 1998 Entry Draft, November 2, 1996. Traded to **Hartford** by **Washington** for Andrei Nikolishin, November 9, 1996. Transferred to **Carolina** after **Hartford** franchise relocated, June 25, 1997. Selected by **Minnesota** from **Carolina** in Expansion Draft, June 23, 2000. Traded to **Ottawa** by **Minnesota** for Ottawa's 3rd round choice (Stephane Veilleux) in 2001 Entry Draft and future considerations, March 13, 2001.

LESSARD, Francis

(leh-SAHR, FRAN-sihs) **ATL.**

Right wing. Shoots right. 6'2", 225 lbs. Born, Montreal, Que., May 30, 1979. Carolina's 3rd choice, 80th overall, in 1997 Entry Draft.

Season	Club	League	GP	G	A	Pts	PIM	PP	SH	GW	S	%	+/-	TF	F%	Min	GP	G	A	Pts	PIM	PP	SH	GW	Min
1994-95	Laval Laurentide	QAAA	1	0	0	0	0																		
1995-96	Laval Laurentide	QAAA	41	5	7	12	73										13	1	3	4					
1996-97	Val-d'Or Foreurs	QMJHL	66	1	9	10	287																		
1997-98	Val-d'Or Foreurs	QMJHL	63	3	20	23	338										19	1	6	7	*101				
1998-99	Drummondville	QMJHL	53	12	36	48	295																		
99-2000	Philadelphia	AHL	78	4	8	12	416										5	0	1	1	7				
2000-01	Philadelphia	AHL	64	3	7	10	330										10	0	0	0	33				
2001-02	Philadelphia	AHL	60	0	6	6	251																		
	Atlanta	NHL	5	0	0	0	26	0	0	0	2	0.0	0	0	0.0	12:45									
	Chicago Wolves	AHL	7	2	1	3	34										15	0	1	1	40				
2002-03	Atlanta	NHL	18	0	2	2	61	0	0	0	7	0.0	1	0	0.0	5:40									
	Chicago Wolves	AHL	50	2	5	7	194										1	0	0	0	0				
2003-04	Atlanta	NHL	62	1	1	2	181	0	0	0	19	5.3	–5	1	0.0	4:28									
	NHL Totals		85	1	3	4	268	0	0	0	28	3.6		1	0.0	5:12									

Memorial Cup All-Star Team (1998)

Traded to **Philadelphia** by **Carolina** for Philadelphia's 8th round choice (Antti Jokella) in 1999 Entry Draft, May 25, 1999. Traded to **Atlanta** by **Philadelphia** for David Harlock and Atlanta's 3rd (later traded to Phoenix – Phoenix selected Tyler Redenbach) and 7th (later traded to San Jose – San Jose selected Joe Pavelski) round choices in 2003 Entry Draft, March 15, 2002.

LETANG, Alan

(leh-TANG, A-luhn) **NYI**

Defense. Shoots left. 6'1", 201 lbs. Born, Renfrew, Ont., September 4, 1975. Montreal's 10th choice, 203rd overall, in 1993 Entry Draft.

Season	Club	League	GP	G	A	Pts	PIM	PP	SH	GW	S	%	+/-	TF	F%	Min	GP	G	A	Pts	PIM	PP	SH	GW	Min
1990-91	Ottawa Valley	ODMHA	32	3	26	29	16																		
1991-92	Cornwall Royals	OHL	47	1	4	5	16										6	0	0	0	2				
1992-93	Newmarket	OHL	66	1	25	26	14										6	0	3	3	2				
1993-94	Newmarket	OHL	58	3	21	24	30																		
1994-95	Sarnia Sting	OHL	62	5	36	41	35										4	2	2	4	6				
1995-96	Fredericton	AHL	71	0	26	26	40										10	0	3	3	4				
1996-97	Fredericton	AHL	60	2	9	11	8																		
1997-98	Kaufbeurer Adler	Germany	15	1	5	6	8																		
	SC Langnau	Swiss-2	11	4	3	7	6																		
	Augsburg	Germany	17	0	1	1	4																		
1998-99	Team Canada	Nat-Tm	41	3	9	12	20																		
	EV Zug	Swiss															9	0	4	4	4				
	Michigan	IHL	12	3	3	6	0										5	0	2	2	0				
99-2000	Dallas	NHL	8	0	0	0	2	0	0	0	1	0.0	–5	0	0.0	9:57									
	Michigan	IHL	51	1	12	13	30																		
2000-01	Utah Grizzlies	IHL	79	6	24	30	26																		

			Regular Season														Playoffs								
Season	Club	League	GP	G	A	Pts	PIM	PP	SH	GW	S	%	+/-	TF	F%	Min	GP	G	A	Pts	PIM	PP	SH	GW	Min
2001-02	Calgary	NHL	2	0	0	0	0	0	0	0	0	0.0	–2	0	0.0	11:06									
	Saint John Flames	AHL	61	4	24	28	33																		
2002-03	NY Islanders	NHL	4	0	0	0	0	0	0	0	2	0.0	–1	0	0.0	13:28									
	Bridgeport	AHL	70	3	21	24	21										8	1	0	1	0				
2003-04	Bridgeport	AHL	76	1	13	14	18										7	1	1	2	4				
	NHL Totals		14	0	0	0	2	0	0	0	3	0.0		0	0.0	11:07									

Signed as a free agent by **Dallas**, March 22, 1999. Signed as a free agent by **Calgary**, August 22, 2001. Signed as a free agent by **NY Islanders**, July 18, 2002.

LETOWSKI, Trevor

(leh-TOW-skee, TREH-vuhr) **CBJ**

Right wing. Shoots right. 5'10", 180 lbs. Born, Thunder Bay, Ont., April 5, 1977. Phoenix's 6th choice, 174th overall, in 1996 Entry Draft.

Season	Club	League	GP	G	A	Pts	PIM	PP	SH	GW	S	%	+/-	TF	F%	Min	GP	G	A	Pts	PIM	PP	SH	GW	Min
1993-94	T. Bay Kings	TBMHL	64	41	60	101	48																		
1994-95	Sarnia Sting	OHL	66	22	19	41	33										4	0	1	1	9				
1995-96	Sarnia Sting	OHL	66	36	63	99	66										10	9	5	14	10				
1996-97	Sarnia Sting	OHL	55	35	73	108	51										12	9	12	21	20				
1997-98	Springfield	AHL	75	11	20	31	26										4	1	0	1	2				
1998-99	Phoenix	NHL	14	2	2	4	2	0	0	0	8	25.0	1	49	55.1	6:01									
	Springfield	AHL	67	32	35	67	46										3	1	0	1	2				
99-2000	Phoenix	NHL	82	19	20	39	20	3	4	3	125	15.2	2	692	47.7	16:03	5	1	1	2	4	0	0	0	15:52
2000-01	Phoenix	NHL	77	7	15	22	32	0	1	3	110	6.4	–2	726	46.1	16:20									
2001-02	Phoenix	NHL	33	2	6	8	4	0	0	0	43	4.7	2	250	52.4	14:27									
	Vancouver	NHL	42	7	10	17	15	1	0	0	65	10.8	2	111	44.1	12:47	6	0	1	1	8	0	0	0	11:50
2002-03	Vancouver	NHL	78	11	14	25	36	1	1	2	136	8.1	8	70	41.4	12:26	6	0	1	1	0	0	0	0	9:40
2003-04	Columbus	NHL	73	15	17	32	16	4	0	1	126	11.9	–12	146	43.8	16:19									
	NHL Totals		399	63	84	147	125	9	6	9	613	10.3		2044	47.2	14:37	17	1	3	4	12	0	0	0	12:15

Traded to **Vancouver** by **Phoenix** with Todd Warriner, Tyler Bouck and Phoenix's 3rd round choice (later traded back to Phoenix – Phoenix selected Dimitri Pestunov) in 2003 Entry Draft for Drake Berehowsky and Denis Pederson, December 28, 2001. Signed as a free agent by **Columbus**, July 3, 2003.

LIDSTROM, Nicklas

(LID-struhm, NIHK-las) **DET.**

Defense. Shoots left. 6'2", 185 lbs. Born, Vasteras, Sweden, April 28, 1970. Detroit's 3rd choice, 53rd overall, in 1989 Entry Draft.

Season	Club	League	GP	G	A	Pts	PIM	PP	SH	GW	S	%	+/-	TF	F%	Min	GP	G	A	Pts	PIM	PP	SH	GW	Min
1987-88	Vasteras IK	Swede-2	3	0	0	0	0										5	0	0	0	6				
1988-89	Vasteras IK	Sweden	34	1	6	7	4										5	0	2	2	0				
1989-90	Vasteras IK	Sweden	39	8	8	16	14										2	0	1	1	2				
1990-91	Vasteras IK	Sweden	38	4	19	23	2										4	0	0	0	4				
1991-92	Detroit	NHL	80	11	49	60	22	5	0	1	168	6.5	36				11	1	2	3	0	1	0	0	
1992-93	Detroit	NHL	84	7	34	41	28	3	0	2	156	4.5	7				7	1	0	1	0	1	0	0	
1993-94	Detroit	NHL	84	10	46	56	26	4	0	3	200	5.0	43				7	3	2	5	0	1	1	0	
1994-95	Vasteras IK	Sweden	13	2	10	12	4																		
	Detroit	NHL	43	10	16	26	6	7	0	0	90	11.1	15				18	4	12	16	8	3	0	2	
1995-96	Detroit	NHL	81	17	50	67	20	8	1	1	211	8.1	29				19	5	9	14	10	1	0	0	
1996-97♦	Detroit	NHL	79	15	42	57	30	8	0	1	214	7.0	11				20	2	6	8	2	0	0	0	
1997-98♦	Detroit	NHL	80	17	42	59	18	7	1	1	205	8.3	22				22	6	13	19	8	2	0	2	
	Sweden	Olympics	4	1	1	2	2																		
1998-99	Detroit	NHL	81	14	43	57	14	6	2	3	205	6.8	14	0	0.0	26:31	10	2	9	11	4	2	0	0	30:21
99-2000	Detroit	NHL	81	20	53	73	18	9	4	3	218	9.2	19	0	0.0	28:45	9	2	4	6	4	1	0	0	30:28
2000-01	Detroit	NHL	82	15	56	71	18	8	0	0	272	5.5	9	0	0.0	28:27	6	1	7	8	0	0	0	0	29:17
2001-02♦	Detroit	NHL	78	9	50	59	20	6	0	0	215	4.2	13	0	0.0	28:49	23	5	11	16	2	2	1	2	31:10
	Sweden	Olympics	4	1	5	6	0																		
2002-03	Detroit	NHL	82	18	44	62	38	8	1	4	175	10.3	40	0	0.0	29:20	4	0	2	2	0	0	0	0	33:35
2003-04	Detroit	NHL	81	10	28	38	18	3	1	3	194	5.2	19	0	0.0	27:39	12	2	5	7	4	2	0	0	27:01
	NHL Totals		1016	173	553	726	276	82	10	22	2523	6.9		0	0.0	28:15	168	34	82	116	42	16	2	6	30:08

NHL All-Rookie Team (1992) • NHL First All-Star Team (1998, 1999, 2000, 2001, 2002, 2003) • James Norris Memorial Trophy (2001, 2002, 2003) • Conn Smythe Trophy (2002)
Played in NHL All-Star Game (1996, 1998, 1999, 2000, 2001, 2002, 2003, 2004)

LILES, John-Michael

(LIGH-uhls, JAWN-MIGHK-uhl) **COL.**

Defense. Shoots left. 5'10", 185 lbs. Born, Zionsville, IN, November 25, 1980. Colorado's 8th choice, 159th overall, in 2000 Entry Draft.

Season	Club	League	GP	G	A	Pts	PIM	PP	SH	GW	S	%	+/-	TF	F%	Min	GP	G	A	Pts	PIM	PP	SH	GW	Min
1997-98	U.S. National U-17	USDP	67	6	14	20	44																		
1998-99	U.S. National U-17	USDP	13	2	5	7	6																		
	U.S. National U-18	USDP	46	4	14	18	47																		
99-2000	Michigan State	CCHA	40	8	20	28	26																		
2000-01	Michigan State	CCHA	42	7	18	25	28																		
2001-02	Michigan State	CCHA	41	13	22	35	18																		
2002-03	Michigan State	CCHA	39	16	34	50	46																		
	Hershey Bears	AHL	5	0	1	1	4										5	0	0	0	2				
2003-04	Colorado	NHL	79	10	24	34	28	2	0	1	115	8.7	7	0	0.0	16:14	11	0	1	1	4	0	0	0	16:41
	NHL Totals		79	10	24	34	28	2	0	1	115	8.7		0	0.0	16:14	11	0	1	1	4	0	0	0	16:41

CCHA Second All-Star Team (2001) • CCHA First All-Star Team (2002, 2003) • NCAA West Second All-American Team (2002) • NCAA West First All-American Team (2003) • NHL All-Rookie Team (2004)

LILJA, Andreas

(LIHL-yuh, an-DRAY-uhs) **NSH.**

Defense. Shoots left. 6'3", 228 lbs. Born, Landskrona, Sweden, July 13, 1975. Los Angeles' 2nd choice, 54th overall, in 2000 Entry Draft.

Season	Club	League	GP	G	A	Pts	PIM	PP	SH	GW	S	%	+/-	TF	F%	Min	GP	G	A	Pts	PIM	PP	SH	GW	Min
1993-94	Malmo IF Jr.	Swede-Jr.	14	3	7	10	38																		
1994-95	Malmo IF Jr.	Swede-Jr.	30	7	13	20	82																		
	Malmo IF	Sweden	3	0	0	0	2																		
1995-96	Malmo IF Jr.	Swede-Jr.	3	0	1	1	6																		
	Malmo IF	Sweden	40	1	5	6	63										5	0	1	1	2				
1996-97	Malmo IF	Sweden	47	1	0	1	22										4	0	0	0	10				
1997-98	Malmo IF	Swede-2	11	6	5	11	24																		
	Malmo IF	Sweden	10	0	0	0	0																		
	Mora IK	Swede-2	13	1	4	5	30										4	1	0	1	14				
1998-99	Malmo IF	Sweden	41	0	3	3	44										1	0	0	0	4				
99-2000	Malmo IF	Sweden	49	8	11	19	88										6	0	0	0	8				
2000-01	Los Angeles	NHL	2	0	0	0	4	0	0	0	1	0.0	–2	0	0.0	12:22	1	0	0	0	0	0	0	0	6:56
	Lowell	AHL	61	7	29	36	149										4	0	6	6	6				
2001-02	Los Angeles	NHL	26	1	4	5	22	1	0	0	12	8.3	3	0	0.0	11:27	5	0	0	0	6	0	0	0	10:26
	Manchester	AHL	4	0	1	1	4																		
2002-03	Los Angeles	NHL	17	0	3	3	14	0	0	0	13	0.0	5	0	0.0	20:04									
	Florida	NHL	56	4	8	12	56	0	0	0	59	6.8	8	0	0.0	19:11									
2003-04	Florida	NHL	79	3	4	7	90	0	0	0	79	3.8	–8	1	0.0	19:34									
	NHL Totals		180	8	19	27	186	1	0	0	164	4.9		1	0.0	18:14	6	0	0	0	6	0	0	0	9:51

• Spent majority of 2001-02 season as a healthy reserve. Traded to **Florida** by **Los Angeles** with Jaroslav Bednar for Dmitry Yushkevich and Florida's 5th round choice (previously acquired, Los Angeles selected Brady Murray) in 2003 Entry Draft, Novermber 26, 2002. Signed as a free agent by **Nashville**, July 26, 2004.

LINDEN, Trevor

(LIHND-dehn, TREH-vuhr) **VAN.**

Right wing. Shoots right. 6'4", 215 lbs. Born, Medicine Hat, Alta., April 11, 1970. Vancouver's 1st choice, 2nd overall, in 1988 Entry Draft.

Season	Club	League	GP	G	A	Pts	PIM	PP	SH	GW	S	%	+/-	TF	F%	Min	GP	G	A	Pts	PIM	PP	SH	GW	Min
1985-86	Medicine Hat	AMHL	40	14	22	36	14																		
	Medicine Hat	WHL	5	2	0	2	0																		
1986-87	Medicine Hat	WHL	72	14	22	36	59										20	5	4	9	17				
1987-88	Medicine Hat	WHL	67	46	64	110	76										16	*13	12	25	19				
1988-89	Vancouver	NHL	80	30	29	59	41	10	1	2	186	16.1	–10				7	3	4	7	8	2	1	0	
1989-90	Vancouver	NHL	73	21	30	51	43	6	2	3	171	12.3	–17												
1990-91	Vancouver	NHL	80	33	37	70	65	16	2	4	229	14.4	–25				6	0	7	7	2	0	0	0	
1991-92	Vancouver	NHL	80	31	44	75	101	6	1	6	201	15.4	3				13	4	8	12	6	2	0	1	
1992-93	Vancouver	NHL	84	33	39	72	64	8	0	3	209	15.8	19				12	5	8	13	16	2	0	1	
1993-94	Vancouver	NHL	84	32	29	61	73	10	2	3	234	13.7	6				24	12	13	25	18	5	1	1	
1994-95	Vancouver	NHL	48	18	22	40	40	9	0	1	129	14.0	–5				11	2	6	8	12	1	0	0	

			Regular Season														Playoffs								
Season	Club	League	GP	G	A	Pts	PIM	PP	SH	GW	S	%	+/-	TF	F%	Min	GP	G	A	Pts	PIM	PP	SH	GW	Min
1995-96	Vancouver	NHL	82	33	47	80	42	12	1	2	202	16.3	6	....	....	....	6	4	4	8	6	2	0	0	....
1996-97	Vancouver	NHL	49	9	31	40	27	2	2	2	84	10.7	5	....	....	....	....	....	....	....	....	....	....	....	....
1997-98	Vancouver	NHL	42	7	14	21	49	2	0	1	74	9.5	–13	....	....	....	....	....	....	....	....	....	....	....	....
	NY Islanders	NHL	25	10	7	17	33	3	2	1	59	16.9	–1	....	....	....	....	....	....	....	....	....	....	....	....
	Canada	Olympics	6	1	0	1	10	....	....	....	....	....	....	....	....	....	....	....	....	....	....	....	....	....	....
1998-99	NY Islanders	NHL	82	18	29	47	32	8	1	1	167	10.8	–14	261	50.2	21:29	....	....	....	....	....	....	....	....	....
99-2000	Montreal	NHL	50	13	17	30	34	4	0	3	87	14.9	–3	860	56.3	17:51	....	....	....	....	....	....	....	....	....
2000-01	Montreal	NHL	57	12	21	33	52	6	0	3	96	12.5	–2	1142	52.7	20:47	....	....	....	....	....	....	....	....	....
	Washington	NHL	12	3	1	4	8	0	0	0	30	10.0	2	75	60.0	18:03	6	0	4	4	14	0	0	0	22:41
2001-02	Washington	NHL	16	1	2	3	6	1	0	0	19	5.3	–2	71	49.3	16:06	....	....	....	....	....	....	....	....	....
	Vancouver	NHL	64	12	22	34	65	2	0	2	122	9.8	–3	1190	53.4	19:23	6	1	4	5	0	0	0	0	19:36
2002-03	Vancouver	NHL	71	19	22	41	30	4	1	1	116	16.4	–1	568	54.4	15:52	14	1	2	3	10	0	1	0	17:38
2003-04	Vancouver	NHL	82	14	22	36	26	4	0	1	97	14.4	–6	1285	55.8	16:17	7	0	0	0	6	0	0	0	18:29
	NHL Totals		1161	349	465	814	831	113	15	39	2512	13.9		5452	54.3	18:28	112	32	60	92	98	14	3	3	19:05

WHL East Second All-Star Team (1988) • NHL All-Rookie Team (1989) • King Clancy Memorial Trophy (1997)

Played in NHL All-Star Game (1991, 1992)

Traded to **NY Islanders** by **Vancouver** for Todd Bertuzzi, Bryan McCabe and NY Islanders' 3rd round choice (Jarkko Ruutu) in 1998 Entry Draft, February 6, 1998. Traded to **Montreal** by **NY Islanders** for Montreal's 1st round choice (Branislav Mezei) in 1999 Entry Draft, May 29, 1999. Traded to **Washington** by **Montreal** with Dainius Zubrus and New Jersey's 2nd round choice (previously acquired, later traded to Tampa Bay – Tampa Bay selected Andreas Holmqvist) in 2001 Entry Draft for Richard Zednik, Jan Bulis and Washington's 1st round choice (Alexander Perezhogin) in 2001 Entry Draft, March 13, 2001. Traded to **Vancouver** by **Washington** with NY Islanders' 2nd round choice (previously acquired, Vancouver selected Denis Grot) in 2002 Entry Draft for Vancouver's 1st round choice (Boyd Gordon) in 2002 Entry Draft and Vancouver's 3rd round choice (later traded to Edmonton – Edmonton selected Zachery Stortini) in 2003 Entry Draft, November 10, 2001.

LINDGREN, Mats

(LIHND-gruhn, MAHTS)

Center/Left wing. Shoots left. 6'2", 202 lbs. Born, Skelleftea, Sweden, October 1, 1974. Winnipeg's 1st choice, 15th overall, in 1993 Entry Draft.

			Regular Season														Playoffs								
Season	Club	League	GP	G	A	Pts	PIM	PP	SH	GW	S	%	+/-	TF	F%	Min	GP	G	A	Pts	PIM	PP	SH	GW	Min
1990-91	Skelleftea AIK	Swede-2	10	0	1	1	0	....	....	....	....	....	....	....	....	....	....	....	....	....	....	....	....	....	....
1991-92	Skelleftea AIK	Swede-2	29	14	18	32	12	....	....	....	....	....	....	....	....	....	3	3	2	5	2	....	....	....	....
1992-93	Skelleftea AIK	Swede-2	32	20	18	38	18	....	....	....	....	....	....	....	....	....	3	0	0	0	2	....	....	....	....
1993-94	Farjestad	Sweden	22	11	6	17	26	....	....	....	....	....	....	....	....	....	....	....	....	....	....	....	....	....	....
1994-95	Farjestad	Sweden	37	17	15	32	20	....	....	....	....	....	....	....	....	....	3	0	0	0	4	....	....	....	....
1995-96	Cape Breton	AHL	13	7	5	12	6	....	....	....	....	....	....	....	....	....	....	....	....	....	....	....	....	....	....
1996-97	Edmonton	NHL	69	11	14	25	12	2	3	1	71	15.5	–7	....	....	....	12	0	4	4	0	0	0	0	....
	Hamilton	AHL	9	6	7	13	6	....	....	....	....	....	....	....	....	....	....	....	....	....	....	....	....	....	....
1997-98	Edmonton	NHL	82	13	13	26	42	1	3	3	131	9.9	0	....	....	....	12	1	1	2	10	0	0	0	....
	Sweden	Olympics	4	0	0	0	2	....	....	....	....	....	....	....	....	....	....	....	....	....	....	....	....	....	....
1998-99	Edmonton	NHL	48	5	12	17	22	0	1	0	53	9.4	4	363	47.9	11:31	....	....	....	....	....	....	....	....	....
	NY Islanders	NHL	12	5	3	8	2	3	0	1	30	16.7	2	180	48.9	20:08	....	....	....	....	....	....	....	....	....
99-2000	NY Islanders	NHL	43	9	7	16	24	1	0	1	68	13.2	0	551	49.2	19:17	....	....	....	....	....	....	....	....	....
2000-01	NY Islanders	NHL	20	3	4	7	10	0	2	0	34	8.8	4	176	48.3	15:14	....	....	....	....	....	....	....	....	....
2001-02	NY Islanders	NHL	59	3	12	15	16	0	0	1	35	8.6	0	237	59.1	8:21	....	....	....	....	....	....	....	....	....
2002-03	Vancouver	NHL	54	5	9	14	18	0	2	1	51	9.8	–2	763	54.5	13:54	....	....	....	....	....	....	....	....	....
	Manitoba Moose	AHL	4	0	1	1	6	....	....	....	....	....	....	....	....	....	....	....	....	....	....	....	....	....	....
2003-04	Vancouver	NHL	DID NOT PLAY – INJURED																						
	NHL Totals		387	54	74	128	146	7	11	8	473	11.4		2270	51.7	13:26	24	1	5	6	10	0	0	0	....

Traded to **Edmonton** by **Winnipeg** with Boris Mironov, Winnipeg's 1st round choice (Jason Bonsignore) in 1994 Entry Draft and Florida's 4th round choice (previously acquired, Edmonton selected Adam Copeland) in 1994 Entry Draft for Dave Manson and St. Louis' 6th round choice (previously acquired, Winnipeg selected Chris Kibermanis) in 1994 Entry Draft, March 15, 1994. Traded to **NY Islanders** by **Edmonton** with Edmonton's 8th round choice (Radek Martinek) in 1999 Entry Draft for Tommy Salo, March 20, 1999. • Missed majority of 2000-01 season recovering from shoulder injury suffered in game vs. Anaheim, November 25, 2000. Signed as a free agent by **Vancouver**, November 3, 2002. • Missed entire 2003-04 season recovering from back injury suffered in practice, October 10, 2003.

LINDROS, Eric

(LIHND-rahz, AIR-ihk)

Center. Shoots right. 6'4", 240 lbs. Born, London, Ont., February 28, 1973. Quebec's 1st choice, 1st overall, in 1991 Entry Draft.

			Regular Season														Playoffs								
Season	Club	League	GP	G	A	Pts	PIM	PP	SH	GW	S	%	+/-	TF	F%	Min	GP	G	A	Pts	PIM	PP	SH	GW	Min
1988-89	St. Michael's B	OJHL-B	37	24	43	67	193	....	....	....	....	....	....	....	....	....	27	23	25	48	155	....	....	....	....
1989-90	Det. Compuware	NAJHL	14	23	29	52	123	....	....	....	....	....	....	....	....	....	....	....	....	....	....	....	....	....	....
	Oshawa Generals	OHL	25	17	19	36	61	....	....	....	....	....	....	....	....	....	17	18	18	36	76	....	....	....	....
1990-91	Oshawa Generals	OHL	57	*71	78	*149	189	....	....	....	....	....	....	....	....	....	16	*18	20	*38	*93	....	....	....	....
1991-92	Oshawa Generals	OHL	13	9	22	31	54	....	....	....	....	....	....	....	....	....	....	....	....	....	....	....	....	....	....
	Team Canada	Nat-Tm	24	19	16	35	34	....	....	....	....	....	....	....	....	....	....	....	....	....	....	....	....	....	....
	Canada	Olympics	8	5	6	11	5	....	....	....	....	....	....	....	....	....	....	....	....	....	....	....	....	....	....
1992-93	Philadelphia	NHL	61	41	34	75	147	8	1	5	180	22.8	28	....	....	....	....	....	....	....	....	....	....	....	....
1993-94	Philadelphia	NHL	65	44	53	97	103	13	2	9	197	22.3	16	....	....	....	....	....	....	....	....	....	....	....	....
1994-95	Philadelphia	NHL	46	29	41	*70	60	7	0	4	144	20.1	27	....	....	....	12	4	11	15	18	0	0	1	....
1995-96	Philadelphia	NHL	73	47	68	115	163	15	0	4	294	16.0	26	....	....	....	12	6	6	12	43	3	0	2	....
1996-97	Philadelphia	NHL	52	32	47	79	136	9	0	7	198	16.2	31	....	....	....	19	12	14	*26	40	4	0	1	....
1997-98	Philadelphia	NHL	63	30	41	71	134	10	1	4	202	14.9	14	....	....	....	5	1	2	3	17	0	0	0	....
	Canada	Olympics	6	2	3	5	2	....	....	....	....	....	....	....	....	....	....	....	....	....	....	....	....	....	....
1998-99	Philadelphia	NHL	71	40	53	93	120	10	1	2	242	16.5	35	1529	60.0	22:56	....	....	....	....	....	....	....	....	....
99-2000	Philadelphia	NHL	55	27	32	59	83	10	1	2	187	14.4	11	1318	57.8	22:02	2	1	0	1	0	0	0	0	8:26
2000-01	Philadelphia	NHL	DID NOT PLAY – INJURED																						
2001-02	NY Rangers	NHL	72	37	36	73	138	12	1	4	196	18.9	19	1707	54.4	21:03	....	....	....	....	....	....	....	....	....
	Canada	Olympics	6	1	0	1	8	....	....	....	....	....	....	....	....	....	....	....	....	....	....	....	....	....	....
2002-03	NY Rangers	NHL	81	19	34	53	141	9	0	3	235	8.1	5	778	53.0	20:15	....	....	....	....	....	....	....	....	....
2003-04	NY Rangers	NHL	39	10	22	32	60	3	0	0	83	12.0	7	492	54.5	15:59	....	....	....	....	....	....	....	....	....
	NHL Totals		678	356	461	817	1285	106	7	44	2158	16.5		5824	56.5	20:49	50	24	33	57	118	7	0	4	8:26

Memorial Cup All-Star Team (1990) • OHL First All-Star Team (1991) • OHL MVP (1991) • Canadian Major Junior Player of the Year (1991) • NHL All-Rookie Team (1993) • NHL First All-Star Team (1995) • Lester B. Pearson Award (1995) • Hart Trophy (1995) • NHL Second All-Star Team (1996)

Played in NHL All-Star Game (1994, 1996, 1997, 1998, 1999, 2000)

Traded to **Philadelphia** by **Quebec** for Peter Forsberg, Steve Duchesne, Kerry Huffman, Mike Ricci, Ron Hextall, Philadelphia's 1st round choice (Jocelyn Thibault) in 1993 Entry Draft, $15,000,000 and future considerations (Chris Simon and Philadelphia's 1st round choice (later traded to Toronto – later traded to Washington – Washington selected Nolan Baumgartner) in 1994 Entry Draft, July 21, 1992), June 30, 1992. • Missed entire 2000-01 season recovering from head injury suffered in game vs. New Jersey, May 26, 2000 and contract dispute with Philadelphia Flyers management. Traded to **NY Rangers** by **Philadelphia** for Kim Johnsson, Jan Havac, Pavel Brendl and NY Rangers' 3rd round choice (Stefan Ruzicka) in 2003 Entry Draft, August 20, 2001. Missed majority of 2003-04 season recovering from shoulder (October 23, 2003 vs. Florida) and head (January 28, 2004 vs. Washington) injuries.

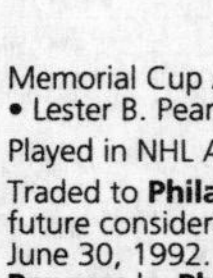

LINDSAY, Bill

(LIHND-see, BIHL)

Right wing. Shoots left. 6', 195 lbs. Born, Fernie, B.C., May 17, 1971. Quebec's 6th choice, 103rd overall, in 1991 Entry Draft.

			Regular Season														Playoffs								
Season	Club	League	GP	G	A	Pts	PIM	PP	SH	GW	S	%	+/-	TF	F%	Min	GP	G	A	Pts	PIM	PP	SH	GW	Min
1988-89	Vernon Lakers	BCJHL	56	24	29	53	166	....	....	....	....	....	....	....	....	....	....	....	....	....	....	....	....	....	....
1989-90	Tri-City	WHL	72	40	45	85	84	....	....	....	....	....	....	....	....	....	7	3	0	3	17	....	....	....	....
1990-91	Tri-City	WHL	63	46	47	93	151	....	....	....	....	....	....	....	....	....	5	3	6	9	10	....	....	....	....
1991-92	Tri-City	WHL	42	34	59	93	81	....	....	....	....	....	....	....	....	....	3	2	3	5	16	....	....	....	....
	Quebec	NHL	23	2	4	6	14	0	0	1	35	5.7	–6	....	....	....	....	....	....	....	....	....	....	....	....
1992-93	Quebec	NHL	44	4	9	13	16	0	0	0	58	6.9	0	....	....	....	....	....	....	....	....	....	....	....	....
	Halifax Citadels	AHL	20	11	13	24	18	....	....	....	....	....	....	....	....	....	....	....	....	....	....	....	....	....	....
1993-94	Florida	NHL	84	6	6	12	97	0	0	0	90	6.7	–2	....	....	....	....	....	....	....	....	....	....	....	....
1994-95	Florida	NHL	48	10	9	19	46	0	1	0	63	15.9	1	....	....	....	....	....	....	....	....	....	....	....	....
1995-96	Florida	NHL	73	12	22	34	57	0	3	2	118	10.2	13	....	....	....	22	5	5	10	18	0	1	1	....
1996-97	Florida	NHL	81	11	23	34	120	0	1	3	168	6.5	1	....	....	....	3	0	1	1	8	0	0	0	....
1997-98	Florida	NHL	82	12	16	28	80	0	2	5	150	8.0	–2	....	....	....	....	....	....	....	....	....	....	....	....
1998-99	Florida	NHL	75	12	15	27	92	0	1	2	135	8.9	–1	57	40.4	13:37	....	....	....	....	....	....	....	....	....
99-2000	Calgary	NHL	80	8	12	20	86	0	0	2	147	5.4	–7	28	39.3	12:55	....	....	....	....	....	....	....	....	....
2000-01	Calgary	NHL	52	1	9	10	97	0	0	0	57	1.8	–8	9	55.6	10:32	....	....	....	....	....	....	....	....	....
	San Jose	NHL	16	0	4	4	29	0	0	0	14	0.0	2	2	0.0	9:16	6	0	0	0	16	0	0	0	6:40
2001-02	Florida	NHL	63	4	7	11	117	0	0	1	63	6.3	–11	124	44.4	9:40	....	....	....	....	....	....	....	....	....
	Montreal	NHL	13	1	3	4	23	0	0	0	14	7.1	0	26	53.9	10:10	11	2	2	4	2	0	0	0	6:58
2002-03	Montreal	NHL	19	0	2	2	23	0	0	0	7	0.0	–1	21	42.9	5:20	....	....	....	....	....	....	....	....	....
	Hamilton	AHL	28	6	12	18	89	....	....	....	....	....	....	....	....	....	23	10	3	13	31	....	....	....	....

Season	Club	League	Regular Season GP	G	A	Pts	PIM	PP	SH	GW	S	%	+/-	TF	F%	Min	Playoffs GP	G	A	Pts	PIM	PP	SH	GW	Min
2003-04	**Atlanta**	**NHL**	**24**	**0**	**0**	**0**	**25**	**0**	**0**	**0**	**10**	**0.0**	**−6**	**8**	**50.0**	**5:55**	....	....	....	....	....	....	....	....	....
	Chicago Wolves	AHL	13	3	5	8	8	....	....	....	....	....	....	....	....	....	....	....	....	....	....	....	....	....	....
	NHL Totals		**777**	**83**	**141**	**224**	**922**	**0**	**8**	**16**	**1129**	**7.4**		**275**	**44.0**	**10:55**	**42**	**7**	**8**	**15**	**44**	**0**	**1**	**1**	**6:52**

WHL West Second All-Star Team (1992)

Claimed by **Florida** from **Quebec** in Expansion Draft, June 24, 1993. Traded to **Calgary** by **Florida** for Todd Simpson, September 30, 1999. Traded to **San Jose** by **Calgary** for Minnesota's 8th round choice (previously acquired, Calgary selected Joe Campbell) in 2001 Entry Draft, March 6, 2001. Signed as a free agent by **Florida**, August 23, 2001. Claimed on waivers by **Montreal** from **Florida**, March 19, 2002. Signed as a free agent by **Atlanta**, August 25, 2003. Claimed on waivers by **Washington** from **Atlanta**, March 9, 2004. • Missed majority of 2003-04 season recovering from throat injury suffered in game vs. Montreal, January 3, 2004.

LING, David

(LIHNG, DAY-vihd)

Right wing. Shoots right. 5'10", 204 lbs. Born, Halifax, N.S., January 9, 1975. Quebec's 9th choice, 179th overall, in 1993 Entry Draft.

Season	Club	League	GP	G	A	Pts	PIM	PP	SH	GW	S	%	+/-	TF	F%	Min	GP	G	A	Pts	PIM	PP	SH	GW	Min
1991-92	Charlottetown	MJrHL	30	33	42	75	270	....	....	....	....	....	....	....	....	....	....	....	....	....	....	....	....	....	....
	St. Michael's B	OJHL-B	8	5	14	19	25	....	....	....	....	....	....	....	....	....	....	....	....	....	....	....	....	....	....
1992-93	Kingston	OHL	64	17	46	63	275	....	....	....	....	....	....	....	....	....	16	3	12	15	*72	....	....	....	....
1993-94	Kingston	OHL	61	37	40	77	*254	....	....	....	....	....	....	....	....	....	6	4	2	6	16	....	....	....	....
1994-95	Kingston	OHL	62	*61	74	135	136	....	....	....	....	....	....	....	....	....	6	7	8	15	12	....	....	....	....
1995-96	Saint John Flames	AHL	75	24	32	56	179	....	....	....	....	....	....	....	....	....	9	0	5	5	12	....	....	....	....
1996-97	Saint John Flames	AHL	5	0	2	2	19	....	....	....	....	....	....	....	....	....	....	....	....	....	....	....	....	....	....
	Montreal	**NHL**	**2**	**0**	**0**	**0**	**0**	**0**	**0**	**0**	**0**	**0.0**	**0**	....	....	....	....	....	....	....	....	....	....	....	....
	Fredericton	AHL	48	22	36	58	229	....	....	....	....	....	....	....	....	....	....	....	....	....	....	....	....	....	....
1997-98	**Montreal**	**NHL**	**1**	**0**	**0**	**0**	**0**	**0**	**0**	**0**	**1**	**0.0**	**−1**	....	....	....	....	....	....	....	....	....	....	....	....
	Fredericton	AHL	67	25	41	66	148	....	....	....	....	....	....	....	....	....	....	....	....	....	....	....	....	....	....
	Indianapolis Ice	IHL	12	8	6	14	30	....	....	....	....	....	....	....	....	....	5	4	1	5	31	....	....	....	....
1998-99	Kansas City	IHL	82	30	42	72	112	....	....	....	....	....	....	....	....	....	3	1	0	1	20	....	....	....	....
99-2000	Kansas City	IHL	82	35	48	83	210	....	....	....	....	....	....	....	....	....	....	....	....	....	....	....	....	....	....
2000-01	Utah Grizzlies	IHL	79	15	28	43	202	....	....	....	....	....	....	....	....	....	....	....	....	....	....	....	....	....	....
2001-02	**Columbus**	**NHL**	**5**	**0**	**0**	**0**	**7**	**0**	**0**	**0**	**5**	**0.0**	**−1**	**1**	**0.0**	**9:47**	....	....	....	....	....	....	....	....	....
	Syracuse Crunch	AHL	71	19	41	60	240	....	....	....	....	....	....	....	....	....	10	5	5	10	16	....	....	....	....
2002-03	**Columbus**	**NHL**	**35**	**3**	**2**	**5**	**86**	**0**	**0**	**0**	**37**	**8.1**	**−6**	**15**	**40.0**	**7:56**	....	....	....	....	....	....	....	....	....
	Syracuse Crunch	AHL	46	7	34	41	129	....	....	....	....	....	....	....	....	....	....	....	....	....	....	....	....	....	....
2003-04	**Columbus**	**NHL**	**50**	**1**	**2**	**3**	**98**	**0**	**0**	**0**	**45**	**2.2**	**−3**	**8**	**37.5**	**7:45**	....	....	....	....	....	....	....	....	....
	Syracuse Crunch	AHL	14	7	10	17	25	....	....	....	....	....	....	....	....	....	7	0	1	1	36	....	....	....	....
	NHL Totals		**93**	**4**	**4**	**8**	**191**	**0**	**0**	**0**	**88**	**4.5**		**24**	**37.5**	**7:56**	....	....	....	....	....	....	....	....	....

OHL First All-Star Team (1995) • OHL MVP (1995) • Canadian Major Junior First All-Star Team (1995) • Canadian Major Junior Player of the Year (1995) • IHL First All-Star Team (2000)

Rights transferred to **Colorado** after **Quebec** franchise relocated, June 21, 1995. Traded to **Calgary** by **Colorado** with Colorado's 9th round choice (Steve Shirreffs) in 1995 Entry Draft for Calgary's 9th round choice (Chris George) in 1995 Entry Draft, July 7, 1995. Traded to **Montreal** by **Calgary** with Calgary's 6th round choice (Gordie Dwyer) in 1998 Entry Draft for Scott Fraser, October 24, 1996. Traded to **Chicago** by **Montreal** for Martin Gendron, March 14, 1998. Signed as a free agent by **Kansas City** (IHL) with Chicago retaining NHL rights, September 3, 1998. Traded to **Dallas** by **Chicago** for future considerations, August 11, 2000. Signed as a free agent by **Columbus**, July 7, 2001.

LOMBARDI, Matthew

(lawm-BAHR-dee, MA-thew) **CGY.**

Center. Shoots left. 5'11", 191 lbs. Born, Montreal, Que., March 18, 1982. Calgary's 3rd choice, 90th overall, in 2002 Entry Draft.

Season	Club	League	GP	G	A	Pts	PIM	PP	SH	GW	S	%	+/-	TF	F%	Min	GP	G	A	Pts	PIM	PP	SH	GW	Min
1997-98	Gatineau	QAAA	42	10	13	23	....	....	....	....	....	....	....	....	....	....	13	4	7	11	....	....	....	....	....
1998-99	Victoriaville Tigres	QMJHL	47	6	10	16	8	....	....	....	....	....	....	....	....	....	5	0	0	0	0	....	....	....	....
99-2000	Victoriaville Tigres	QMJHL	65	18	26	44	28	....	....	....	....	....	....	....	....	....	6	0	0	0	6	....	....	....	....
2000-01	Victoriaville Tigres	QMJHL	72	28	39	67	66	....	....	....	....	....	....	....	....	....	13	12	6	18	10	....	....	....	....
2001-02	Victoriaville Tigres	QMJHL	66	57	73	130	70	....	....	....	....	....	....	....	....	....	22	*17	18	35	18	....	....	....	....
2002-03	Saint John Flames	AHL	76	25	21	46	41	....	....	....	....	....	....	....	....	....	....	....	....	....	....	....	....	....	....
2003-04	**Calgary**	**NHL**	**79**	**16**	**13**	**29**	**32**	**3**	**2**	**4**	**130**	**12.3**	**4**	**992**	**47.9**	**14:26**	**13**	**1**	**5**	**6**	**4**	**0**	**0**	**1**	**14:46**
	NHL Totals		**79**	**16**	**13**	**29**	**32**	**3**	**2**	**4**	**130**	**12.3**		**992**	**47.9**	**14:26**	**13**	**1**	**5**	**6**	**4**	**0**	**0**	**1**	**14:46**

• Re-entered NHL Entry Draft. Originally Edmonton's 7th choice, 215th overall, in 2000 Entry Draft.

Memorial Cup All-Star Team (2002)

LOW, Reed

(LOH, REED) **ST.L.**

Right wing. Shoots right. 6'3", 222 lbs. Born, Moose Jaw, Sask., June 21, 1976. St. Louis' 7th choice, 177th overall, in 1996 Entry Draft.

Season	Club	League	GP	G	A	Pts	PIM	PP	SH	GW	S	%	+/-	TF	F%	Min	GP	G	A	Pts	PIM	PP	SH	GW	Min
1994-95	Minot Top Guns	SJHL	STATISTICS NOT AVAILABLE																						
	Regina Pats	WHL	2	0	0	0	5	....	....	....	....	....	....	....	....	....	....	....	....	....	....	....	....	....	....
1995-96	Moose Jaw	WHL	61	12	7	19	221	....	....	....	....	....	....	....	....	....	....	....	....	....	....	....	....	....	....
1996-97	Moose Jaw	WHL	62	16	11	27	228	....	....	....	....	....	....	....	....	....	12	2	1	3	50	....	....	....	....
1997-98	Worcester IceCats	AHL	17	1	1	2	75	....	....	....	....	....	....	....	....	....	3	0	0	0	0	....	....	....	....
	Baton Rouge	ECHL	39	4	2	6	145	....	....	....	....	....	....	....	....	....	....	....	....	....	....	....	....	....	....
1998-99	Worcester IceCats	AHL	77	5	6	11	239	....	....	....	....	....	....	....	....	....	4	0	0	0	2	....	....	....	....
99-2000	Worcester IceCats	AHL	80	12	16	28	203	....	....	....	....	....	....	....	....	....	9	1	3	4	16	....	....	....	....
2000-01	**St. Louis**	**NHL**	**56**	**1**	**5**	**6**	**159**	**0**	**0**	**0**	**31**	**3.2**	**4**	**2**	**50.0**	**6:17**	....	....	....	....	....	....	....	....	....
2001-02	**St. Louis**	**NHL**	**58**	**0**	**5**	**5**	**160**	**0**	**0**	**0**	**25**	**0.0**	**−3**	**0**	**0.0**	**5:22**	....	....	....	....	....	....	....	....	....
2002-03	**St. Louis**	**NHL**	**79**	**2**	**4**	**6**	**234**	**0**	**0**	**1**	**48**	**4.2**	**3**	**14**	**71.4**	**6:19**	....	....	....	....	....	....	....	....	....
2003-04	**St. Louis**	**NHL**	**57**	**0**	**2**	**2**	**141**	**0**	**0**	**0**	**28**	**0.0**	**−6**	**0**	**0.0**	**5:42**	....	....	....	....	....	....	....	....	....
	NHL Totals		**250**	**3**	**16**	**19**	**694**	**0**	**0**	**1**	**132**	**2.3**		**16**	**68.8**	**5:57**	....	....	....	....	....	....	....	....	....

LOWRY, Dave

(LOW-ree, DAYV)

Left wing. Shoots left. 6'1", 195 lbs. Born, Sudbury, Ont., February 14, 1965. Vancouver's 6th choice, 114th overall, in 1983 Entry Draft.

Season	Club	League	GP	G	A	Pts	PIM	PP	SH	GW	S	%	+/-	TF	F%	Min	GP	G	A	Pts	PIM	PP	SH	GW	Min
1981-82	Nepean	ODMHA	60	50	64	114	46	....	....	....	....	....	....	....	....	....	....	....	....	....	....	....	....	....	....
1982-83	London Knights	OHL	42	11	16	27	48	....	....	....	....	....	....	....	....	....	3	0	0	0	14	....	....	....	....
1983-84	London Knights	OHL	66	29	47	76	125	....	....	....	....	....	....	....	....	....	8	6	6	12	41	....	....	....	....
1984-85	London Knights	OHL	61	60	60	120	94	....	....	....	....	....	....	....	....	....	8	6	5	11	10	....	....	....	....
1985-86	**Vancouver**	**NHL**	**73**	**10**	**8**	**18**	**143**	**1**	**0**	**1**	**66**	**15.2**	**−21**	....	....	....	**3**	**0**	**0**	**0**	**0**	**0**	**0**	**0**	....
1986-87	**Vancouver**	**NHL**	**70**	**8**	**10**	**18**	**176**	**0**	**0**	**1**	**74**	**10.8**	**−23**	....	....	....	....	....	....	....	....	....	....	....	....
1987-88	**Vancouver**	**NHL**	**22**	**1**	**3**	**4**	**38**	**0**	**0**	**0**	**14**	**7.1**	**−2**	....	....	....	....	....	....	....	....	....	....	....	....
	Fredericton	AHL	46	18	27	45	59	....	....	....	....	....	....	....	....	....	14	7	3	10	72	....	....	....	....
1988-89	**St. Louis**	**NHL**	**21**	**3**	**3**	**6**	**11**	**0**	**1**	**0**	**22**	**13.6**	**1**	....	....	....	**10**	**0**	**5**	**5**	**4**	**0**	**0**	**0**	....
	Peoria Rivermen	IHL	58	31	35	66	45	....	....	....	....	....	....	....	....	....	....	....	....	....	....	....	....	....	....
1989-90	**St. Louis**	**NHL**	**78**	**19**	**6**	**25**	**75**	**0**	**2**	**1**	**98**	**19.4**	**1**	....	....	....	**12**	**2**	**1**	**3**	**39**	**0**	**0**	**0**	....
1990-91	**St. Louis**	**NHL**	**79**	**19**	**21**	**40**	**168**	**0**	**2**	**5**	**123**	**15.4**	**19**	....	....	....	**13**	**1**	**4**	**5**	**35**	**0**	**0**	**0**	....
1991-92	**St. Louis**	**NHL**	**75**	**7**	**13**	**20**	**77**	**0**	**0**	**1**	**85**	**8.2**	**−11**	....	....	....	**6**	**0**	**1**	**1**	**20**	**0**	**0**	**0**	....
1992-93	**St. Louis**	**NHL**	**58**	**5**	**8**	**13**	**101**	**0**	**0**	**0**	**59**	**8.5**	**−18**	....	....	....	**11**	**2**	**0**	**2**	**14**	**0**	**1**	**0**	....
1993-94	**Florida**	**NHL**	**80**	**15**	**22**	**37**	**64**	**3**	**0**	**3**	**122**	**12.3**	**−4**	....	....	....	....	....	....	....	....	....	....	....	....
1994-95	**Florida**	**NHL**	**45**	**10**	**10**	**20**	**25**	**2**	**0**	**3**	**70**	**14.3**	**−3**	....	....	....	....	....	....	....	....	....	....	....	....
1995-96	**Florida**	**NHL**	**63**	**10**	**14**	**24**	**36**	**0**	**0**	**1**	**83**	**12.0**	**−2**	....	....	....	**22**	**10**	**7**	**17**	**39**	**4**	**0**	**2**	....
1996-97	**Florida**	**NHL**	**77**	**15**	**14**	**29**	**51**	**2**	**0**	**2**	**96**	**15.6**	**2**	....	....	....	**5**	**0**	**0**	**0**	**0**	**0**	**0**	**0**	....
1997-98	**Florida**	**NHL**	**7**	**0**	**0**	**0**	**2**	**0**	**0**	**0**	**4**	**0.0**	**−1**	....	....	....	....	....	....	....	....	....	....	....	....
	San Jose	**NHL**	**50**	**4**	**4**	**8**	**51**	**0**	**0**	**1**	**47**	**8.5**	**0**	....	....	....	**6**	**0**	**0**	**0**	**18**	**0**	**0**	**0**	....
1998-99	**San Jose**	**NHL**	**61**	**6**	**9**	**15**	**24**	**2**	**0**	**0**	**58**	**10.3**	**−5**	**6**	**50.0**	**9:14**	**1**	**0**	**0**	**0**	**0**	**0**	**0**	**0**	**8:37**
99-2000	**San Jose**	**NHL**	**32**	**1**	**4**	**5**	**18**	**0**	**0**	**0**	**25**	**4.0**	**1**	**1**	**100.0**	**9:11**	**12**	**1**	**2**	**3**	**6**	**0**	**0**	**0**	**12:13**
2000-01	**Calgary**	**NHL**	**79**	**18**	**17**	**35**	**47**	**5**	**0**	**5**	**108**	**16.7**	**−2**	**20**	**20.0**	**15:57**	....	....	....	....	....	....	....	....	....
2001-02	**Calgary**	**NHL**	**62**	**7**	**6**	**13**	**51**	**2**	**1**	**1**	**74**	**9.5**	**−20**	**15**	**26.7**	**14:58**	....	....	....	....	....	....	....	....	....
2002-03	**Calgary**	**NHL**	**34**	**5**	**14**	**19**	**22**	**1**	**0**	**0**	**40**	**12.5**	**4**	**13**	**15.4**	**14:18**	....	....	....	....	....	....	....	....	....
	Saint John Flames	AHL	22	3	6	9	16	....	....	....	....	....	....	....	....	....	....	....	....	....	....	....	....	....	....
2003-04	**Calgary**	**NHL**	**18**	**1**	**1**	**2**	**11**	**0**	**0**	**0**	**9**	**11.1**	**−6**	**19**	**10.5**	**9:13**	**10**	**0**	**0**	**0**	**6**	**0**	**0**	**0**	**9:27**
	NHL Totals		**1084**	**164**	**187**	**351**	**1191**	**18**	**6**	**25**	**1277**	**12.8**		**74**	**21.6**	**12:55**	**111**	**16**	**20**	**36**	**181**	**4**	**1**	**2**	**10:51**

OHL First All-Star Team (1985)

Traded to **St. Louis** by **Vancouver** for Ernie Vargas, September 29, 1988. Claimed by **Florida** from **St. Louis** in Expansion Draft, June 24, 1993. Traded to **San Jose** by **Florida** with Florida's 1st round choice (later traded to Tampa Bay – Tampa Bay selected Vincent Lecavalier) in 1998 Entry Draft for Viktor Kozlov and Florida's 5th round choice (previously acquired, Florida selected Jaroslav Spacek) in 1998 Entry Draft, November 13, 1997. • Missed majority of 1999-2000 season recovering from shoulder injury suffered in game vs. Montreal, November 23, 1999. Signed as a free agent by **Calgary**, July 24, 2000. • Missed majority of 2003-04 season recovering from abdominal injury suffered in game vs. NY Islanders, January 6, 2004.

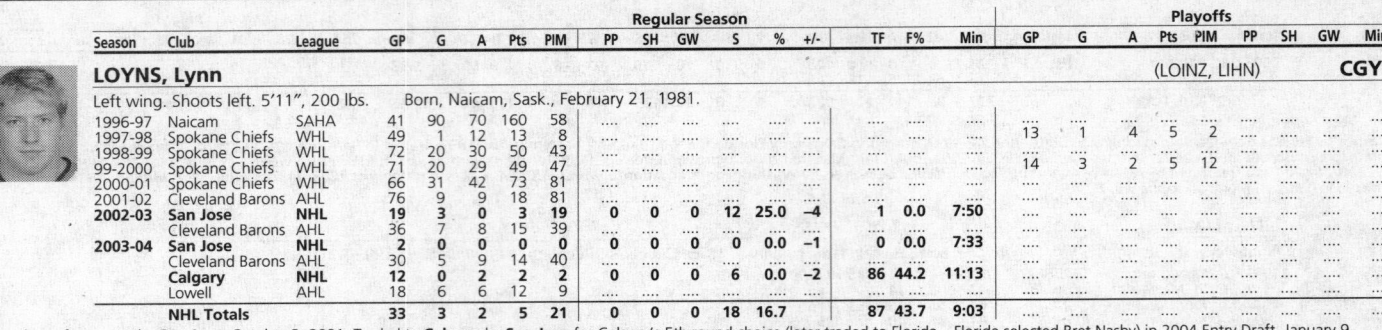

			Regular Season														Playoffs								
Season	Club	League	GP	G	A	Pts	PIM	PP	SH	GW	S	%	+/-	TF	F%	Min	GP	G	A	Pts	PIM	PP	SH	GW	Min

LOYNS, Lynn

(LOINZ, LIHN) **CGY.**

Left wing. Shoots left. 5'11", 200 lbs. Born, Naicam, Sask., February 21, 1981.

Season	Club	League	GP	G	A	Pts	PIM	PP	SH	GW	S	%	+/-	TF	F%	Min	GP	G	A	Pts	PIM	PP	SH	GW	Min
1996-97	Naicam	SAHA	41	90	70	160	58	....	....	....	....	....	....	....	....	....	....	....	....	....	....	....	....	....	....
1997-98	Spokane Chiefs	WHL	49	1	12	13	8	....	....	....	....	....	....	....	....	....	13	1	4	5	2	....	....	....	....
1998-99	Spokane Chiefs	WHL	72	20	30	50	43	....	....	....	....	....	....	....	....	....	....	....	....	....	....	....	....	....	....
99-2000	Spokane Chiefs	WHL	71	20	29	49	47	....	....	....	....	....	....	....	....	....	14	3	2	5	12	....	....	....	....
2000-01	Spokane Chiefs	WHL	66	31	42	73	81	....	....	....	....	....	....	....	....	....	....	....	....	....	....	....	....	....	....
2001-02	Cleveland Barons	AHL	76	9	9	18	81	....	....	....	....	....	....	....	....	....	....	....	....	....	....	....	....	....	....
2002-03	**San Jose**	**NHL**	**19**	**3**	**0**	**3**	**19**	**0**	**0**	**0**	**12**	**25.0**	**–4**	**1**	**0.0**	**7:50**	....	....	....	....	....	....	....	....	....
	Cleveland Barons	AHL	36	7	8	15	39	....	....	....	....	....	....	....	....	....	....	....	....	....	....	....	....	....	....
2003-04	**San Jose**	**NHL**	**2**	**0**	**0**	**0**	**0**	**0**	**0**	**0**	**0**	**0.0**	**–1**	**0**	**0.0**	**7:33**	....	....	....	....	....	....	....	....	....
	Cleveland Barons	AHL	30	5	9	14	40	....	....	....	....	....	....	....	....	....	....	....	....	....	....	....	....	....	....
	Calgary	**NHL**	**12**	**0**	**2**	**2**	**2**	**0**	**0**	**0**	**6**	**0.0**	**–2**	**86**	**44.2**	**11:13**	....	....	....	....	....	....	....	....	....
	Lowell	AHL	18	6	6	12	9	....	....	....	....	....	....	....	....	....	....	....	....	....	....	....	....	....	....
	NHL Totals		**33**	**3**	**2**	**5**	**21**	**0**	**0**	**0**	**18**	**16.7**		**87**	**43.7**	**9:03**	....	....	....	....	....	....	....	....	....

Signed as a free agent by **San Jose**, October 3, 2001. Traded to **Calgary** by **San Jose** for Calgary's 5th round choice (later traded to Florida – Florida selected Bret Nasby) in 2004 Entry Draft, January 9, 2004.

LUKOWICH, Brad

(loo-KUH-which, BRAD) **T.B.**

Defense. Shoots left. 6'1", 200 lbs. Born, Cranbrook, B.C., August 12, 1976. NY Islanders' 4th choice, 90th overall, in 1994 Entry Draft.

Season	Club	League	GP	G	A	Pts	PIM	PP	SH	GW	S	%	+/-	TF	F%	Min	GP	G	A	Pts	PIM	PP	SH	GW	Min
1992-93	Cranbrook Colts	RMJHL	54	21	41	62	162	....	....	....	....	....	....	....	....	....	....	....	....	....	....	....	....	....	....
	Kamloops Blazers	WHL	1	0	0	0	0	....	....	....	....	....	....	....	....	....	....	....	....	....	....	....	....	....	....
1993-94	Kamloops Blazers	WHL	42	5	11	16	166	....	....	....	....	....	....	....	....	....	16	0	1	1	35	....	....	....	....
1994-95	Kamloops Blazers	WHL	63	10	35	45	125	....	....	....	....	....	....	....	....	....	18	0	7	7	21	....	....	....	....
1995-96	Kamloops Blazers	WHL	65	14	55	69	114	....	....	....	....	....	....	....	....	....	13	2	10	12	29	....	....	....	....
1996-97	Michigan	IHL	69	2	6	8	77	....	....	....	....	....	....	....	....	....	4	0	1	1	2	....	....	....	....
1997-98	**Dallas**	**NHL**	**4**	**0**	**1**	**1**	**2**	**0**	**0**	**0**	**2**	**0.0**	**–2**	....	....	....	....	....	....	....	....	....	....	....	....
	Michigan	IHL	60	6	27	33	104	....	....	....	....	....	....	....	....	....	4	0	4	4	14	....	....	....	....
1998-99	**Dallas**	**NHL**	**14**	**1**	**2**	**3**	**19**	**0**	**0**	**0**	**8**	**12.5**	**3**	**0**	**0.0**	**16:18**	**8**	**0**	**1**	**1**	**4**	**0**	**0**	**0**	**10:00**
	Michigan	IHL	67	8	21	29	95	....	....	....	....	....	....	....	....	....	....	....	....	....	....	....	....	....	....
99-2000	**Dallas**	**NHL**	**60**	**3**	**1**	**4**	**50**	**0**	**0**	**1**	**33**	**9.1**	**–14**	**1**	**0.0**	**11:44**	....	....	....	....	....	....	....	....	....
2000-01	**Dallas**	**NHL**	**80**	**4**	**10**	**14**	**76**	**0**	**0**	**2**	**43**	**9.3**	**28**	**1**	**100.0**	**14:48**	**10**	**1**	**0**	**1**	**4**	**0**	**0**	**0**	**17:28**
2001-02	**Dallas**	**NHL**	**66**	**1**	**6**	**7**	**40**	**0**	**0**	**0**	**56**	**1.8**	**–1**	**0**	**0.0**	**13:14**	....	....	....	....	....	....	....	....	....
2002-03	**Tampa Bay**	**NHL**	**70**	**1**	**14**	**15**	**46**	**0**	**0**	**0**	**52**	**1.9**	**4**	**1**	**0.0**	**17:34**	**9**	**0**	**1**	**1**	**2**	**0**	**0**	**0**	**17:48**
2003-04♦	**Tampa Bay**	**NHL**	**79**	**5**	**14**	**19**	**24**	**0**	**0**	**1**	**86**	**5.8**	**29**	**3**	**0.0**	**18:45**	**18**	**0**	**2**	**2**	**6**	**0**	**0**	**0**	**15:51**
	NHL Totals		**373**	**15**	**48**	**63**	**257**	**0**	**0**	**4**	**280**	**5.4**		**6**	**16.7**	**15:27**	**45**	**1**	**4**	**5**	**16**	**0**	**0**	**0**	**15:34**

Traded to **Dallas** by **NY Islanders** for Dallas' 3rd round choice (Robert Schnabel) in 1997 Entry Draft, June 1, 1996. Traded to **Minnesota** by **Dallas** with Manny Fernandez for Minnesota's 3rd round choice (Joel Lundqvist) in 2000 Entry Draft and Minnesota's 4th round choice (later traded back to Minnesota – later traded to Los Angeles – Los Angeles selected Aaron Rome) in 2002 Entry Draft, June 12, 2000. Traded to **Dallas** by **Minnesota** with Minnesota's 3rd (Yared Hagos) and 9th (Dale Sullivan) round choices in 2001 Entry Draft for Aaron Gavey, Pavel Patera, Dallas' 8th round choice (Eric Johansson) in 2000 Entry Draft and Minnesota's 4th round choice (previously acquired, later traded to Los Angeles – Los Angeles selected Aaron Rome) in 2002 Entry Draft, June 25, 2000. Traded to **Tampa Bay** by **Dallas** with Dallas' 7th round choice (Jay Rosehill) in 2003 Entry Draft for Tampa Bay's 2nd round choice (previously acquired, later traded back to Tampa Bay – later traded to Dallas – Dallas selected Tobias Stephan) in 2002 Entry Draft, June 22, 2002.

LUNDMARK, Jamie

(LUHND-mahrk, JAY-mee) **NYR**

Center. Shoots right. 6', 174 lbs. Born, Edmonton, Alta., January 16, 1981. NY Rangers' 2nd choice, 9th overall, in 1999 Entry Draft.

Season	Club	League	GP	G	A	Pts	PIM	PP	SH	GW	S	%	+/-	TF	F%	Min	GP	G	A	Pts	PIM	PP	SH	GW	Min
1996-97	St. Albert Saints	AJHL	35	10	9	19	8	....	....	....	....	....	....	....	....	....	....	....	....	....	....	....	....	....	....
1997-98	St. Albert Saints	AJHL	57	33	58	91	171	....	....	....	....	....	....	....	....	....	19	13	18	31	5	....	....	....	....
1998-99	Moose Jaw	WHL	70	40	51	91	121	....	....	....	....	....	....	....	....	....	11	5	4	9	24	....	....	....	....
99-2000	Moose Jaw	WHL	37	21	27	48	33	....	....	....	....	....	....	....	....	....	....	....	....	....	....	....	....	....	....
2000-01	Seattle	WHL	52	35	42	77	49	....	....	....	....	....	....	....	....	....	9	4	4	8	16	....	....	....	....
2001-02	Hartford	AHL	79	27	32	59	56	....	....	....	....	....	....	....	....	....	10	3	4	7	16	....	....	....	....
2002-03	Hartford	AHL	22	9	9	18	18	....	....	....	....	....	....	....	....	....	2	0	0	0	0	....	....	....	....
	NY Rangers	**NHL**	**55**	**8**	**11**	**19**	**16**	**0**	**0**	**0**	**78**	**10.3**	**–3**	**62**	**43.6**	**12:04**	....	....	....	....	....	....	....	....	....
2003-04	**NY Rangers**	**NHL**	**56**	**2**	**8**	**10**	**33**	**0**	**0**	**1**	**68**	**2.9**	**–8**	**379**	**40.4**	**12:46**	....	....	....	....	....	....	....	....	....
	NHL Totals		**111**	**10**	**19**	**29**	**49**	**0**	**0**	**1**	**146**	**6.8**		**441**	**40.8**	**12:25**	....	....	....	....	....	....	....	....	....

WHL All-Rookie Team (1999) • WHL East Second All-Star Team (1999) • WHL West First All-Star Team (2001)

LUOMA, Mikko

(loo-OH-mah, MEE-koh) **EDM.**

Defense. Shoots left. 6'3", 207 lbs. Born, Jyvaskyla, Finland, June 22, 1976. Edmonton's 9th choice, 181st overall, in 2002 Entry Draft.

Season	Club	League	GP	G	A	Pts	PIM	PP	SH	GW	S	%	+/-	TF	F%	Min	GP	G	A	Pts	PIM	PP	SH	GW	Min
1993-94	JYP Jyvaskyla Jr.	Finn-Jr.	13	1	3	4	6	....	....	....	....	....	....	....	....	....	....	....	....	....	....	....	....	....	....
1994-95	JYP Jyvaskyla Jr.	Finn-Jr.	23	8	17	25	34	....	....	....	....	....	....	....	....	....	....	....	....	....	....	....	....	....	....
	JYP Jyvaskyla	Finn-2	....	....	....	....	....	....	....	....	....	....	....	....	....	....	7	1	2	3	2	....	....	....	....
1995-96	JYP Jyvaskyla Jr.	Finn-Jr.	27	4	10	14	56	....	....	....	....	....	....	....	....	....	....	....	....	....	....	....	....	....	....
	JYP Jyvaskyla	Finn-2	5	0	0	0	0	....	....	....	....	....	....	....	....	....	6	0	0	0	0	....	....	....	....
1996-97	JYP Jr.	Finn-Jr.	3	0	2	2	6	....	....	....	....	....	....	....	....	....	4	2	2	4	4	....	....	....	....
	JYP Jyvaskyla	Finn-2	34	15	52	67	34	....	....	....	....	....	....	....	....	....	....	....	....	....	....	....	....	....	....
1997-98	JYP Jyvaskyla	Finn-2	44	2	18	20	60	....	....	....	....	....	....	....	....	....	5	1	0	1	10	....	....	....	....
1998-99	JYP Jyvaskyla	Finland	53	2	8	10	60	....	....	....	....	....	....	....	....	....	3	0	0	0	4	....	....	....	....
99-2000	JYP Jyvaskyla	Finland	51	2	6	8	58	....	....	....	....	....	....	....	....	....	....	....	....	....	....	....	....	....	....
2000-01	Tappara Tampere	Finland	56	10	11	21	72	....	....	....	....	....	....	....	....	....	10	0	2	2	10	....	....	....	....
2001-02	Tappara Tampere	Finland	56	11	18	29	74	....	....	....	....	....	....	....	....	....	10	1	2	3	10	....	....	....	....
2002-03	Tappara Tampere	Finland	55	4	13	17	52	....	....	....	....	....	....	....	....	....	14	2	1	3	12	....	....	....	....
2003-04	**Edmonton**	**NHL**	**3**	**0**	**1**	**1**	**0**	**0**	**0**	**0**	**4**	**0.0**	**0**	**0**	**0.0**	**17:32**	....	....	....	....	....	....	....	....	....
	Toronto	AHL	65	4	22	26	54	....	....	....	....	....	....	....	....	....	3	1	0	1	8	....	....	....	....
	NHL Totals		**3**	**0**	**1**	**1**	**0**	**0**	**0**	**0**	**4**	**0.0**		**0**	**0.0**	**17:32**									

LUPASCHUK, Ross

(LOO-puhs-chuhk, RAWS) **PIT.**

Defense. Shoots right. 6'1", 210 lbs. Born, Edmonton, Alta., January 19, 1981. Washington's 4th choice, 34th overall, in 1999 Entry Draft.

Season	Club	League	GP	G	A	Pts	PIM	PP	SH	GW	S	%	+/-	TF	F%	Min	GP	G	A	Pts	PIM	PP	SH	GW	Min
1996-97	Edmonton Mets	AJHL	65	5	22	27	87	....	....	....	....	....	....	....	....	....	....	....	....	....	....	....	....	....	....
1997-98	Prince Albert	WHL	67	6	12	18	170	....	....	....	....	....	....	....	....	....	....	....	....	....	....	....	....	....	....
1998-99	Prince Albert	WHL	67	8	20	28	127	....	....	....	....	....	....	....	....	....	14	4	9	13	16	....	....	....	....
99-2000	Prince Albert	WHL	22	8	8	16	42	....	....	....	....	....	....	....	....	....	....	....	....	....	....	....	....	....	....
	Red Deer Rebels	WHL	46	13	27	40	116	....	....	....	....	....	....	....	....	....	4	0	1	1	10	....	....	....	....
2000-01	Red Deer Rebels	WHL	65	28	37	65	135	....	....	....	....	....	....	....	....	....	22	5	10	15	54	....	....	....	....
2001-02	Wilkes-Barre	AHL	72	9	20	29	91	....	....	....	....	....	....	....	....	....	....	....	....	....	....	....	....	....	....
2002-03	**Pittsburgh**	**NHL**	**3**	**0**	**0**	**0**	**4**	**0**	**0**	**0**	**3**	**0.0**	**–3**	**0**	**0.0**	**16:20**	....	....	....	....	....	....	....	....	....
	Wilkes-Barre	AHL	74	18	18	36	101	....	....	....	....	....	....	....	....	....	4	0	2	2	20	....	....	....	....
2003-04	Wilkes-Barre	AHL	58	4	17	21	96	....	....	....	....	....	....	....	....	....	8	0	2	2	37	....	....	....	....
	NHL Totals		**3**	**0**	**0**	**0**	**4**	**0**	**0**	**0**	**3**	**0.0**		**0**	**0.0**	**16:20**	....	....	....	....	....	....	....	....	....

WHL East Second All-Star Team (2001) • Memorial Cup All-Star Team (2001)

Traded to **Pittsburgh** by **Washington** with Kris Beech, Michal Sivek and future considerations for Jaromir Jagr and Frantisek Kucera, July 11, 2001.

LUPUL, Joffrey

(LOO-puhl, JAWF-ree) **ANA.**

Center. Shoots right. 6'1", 198 lbs. Born, Edmonton, Alta., September 23, 1983. Anaheim's 1st choice, 7th overall, in 2002 Entry Draft.

Season	Club	League	GP	G	A	Pts	PIM	PP	SH	GW	S	%	+/-	TF	F%	Min	GP	G	A	Pts	PIM	PP	SH	GW	Min
1998-99	Ft. Saskatchewan	ABHL	36	40	50	90	40	....	....	....	....	....	....	....	....	....	....	....	....	....	....	....	....	....	....
99-2000	Ft. Saskatchewan	AMHL	34	43	30	*73	47	....	....	....	....	....	....	....	....	....	4	0	1	1	2	....	....	....	....
2000-01	Medicine Hat	WHL	69	30	26	56	39	....	....	....	....	....	....	....	....	....	22	3	6	9	2	....	....	....	....
2001-02	Medicine Hat	WHL	72	*56	50	106	95	....	....	....	....	....	....	....	....	....	....	....	....	....	....	....	....	....	....
2002-03	Medicine Hat	WHL	50	41	37	78	82	....	....	....	....	....	....	....	....	....	11	4	11	15	20	....	....	....	....

			Regular Season														Playoffs								
Season	Club	League	GP	G	A	Pts	PIM	PP	SH	GW	S	%	+/-	TF	F%	Min	GP	G	A	Pts	PIM	PP	SH	GW	Min
2003-04	**Anaheim**	**NHL**	**75**	**13**	**21**	**34**	**28**	**4**	**0**	**2**	**137**	**9.5**	**–6**	**11**	**9.1**	**13:37**	....	....	....	....	....	....	....	....	....
	Cincinnati	AHL	3	3	2	5	2	....	....	....	....	....	....	....	....	....	....	....	....	....	....	....	....	....	....
	NHL Totals		**75**	**13**	**21**	**34**	**28**	**4**	**0**	**2**	**137**	**9.5**		**11**	**9.1**	**13:37**	....	....	....	....	....	....	....	....	....

WHL East First All-Star Team (2002) • Canadian Major Junior First All-Star Team (2002)

LYDMAN, Toni

(LEED-man, TOH-nee) **CGY.**

Defense. Shoots left. 6'1", 202 lbs. Born, Lahti, Finland, September 25, 1977. Calgary's 5th choice, 89th overall, in 1996 Entry Draft.

1992-93	Reipas Lahti C	Finn-Jr.	36	10	9	19	22	....	....	....	....	....	....	....	....	....	....	....	....	....	....	....	....	....	....
1993-94	Reipas Lahti B	Finn-Jr.	9	3	1	4	4	....	....	....	....	....	....	....	....	....	....	....	....	....	....	....	....	....	....
	Reipas Lahti Jr.	Finn-Jr.	1	0	0	0	0	....	....	....	....	....	....	....	....	....	....	....	....	....	....	....	....	....	....
1994-95	Reipas Lahti B	Finn-Jr.	9	7	4	11	12	....	....	....	....	....	....	....	....	....	....	....	....	....	....	....	....	....	....
	Reipas Lahti B	Finn-Jr.	26	6	4	10	10	....	....	....	....	....	....	....	....	....	....	....	....	....	....	....	....	....	....
1995-96	Reipas Lahti Jr.	Finn-Jr.	9	2	2	4	6	....	....	....	....	....	....	....	....	....	....	....	....	....	....	....	....	....	....
	Reipas Lahti	Finland	39	5	2	7	30	....	....	....	....	....	....	....	....	....	3	0	1	1	0	....	....	....	....
1996-97	Tappara Tampere	Finland	49	1	2	3	65	....	....	....	....	....	....	....	....	....	3	0	0	0	6	....	....	....	....
1997-98	Tappara Tampere	Finland	48	4	10	14	48	....	....	....	....	....	....	....	....	....	4	0	2	2	0	....	....	....	....
1998-99	HIFK Helsinki	Finland	42	4	7	11	36	....	....	....	....	....	....	....	....	....	11	0	3	3	2	....	....	....	....
	HIFK Helsinki	EuroHL	6	0	2	2	29	....	....	....	....	....	....	....	....	....	4	1	....	....	....	....	....	....	....
99-2000	HIFK Helsinki	Finland	46	4	18	22	36	....	....	....	....	....	....	....	....	....	9	0	4	4	6	....	....	....	....
2000-01	**Calgary**	**NHL**	**62**	**3**	**16**	**19**	**30**	**1**	**0**	**0**	**80**	**3.8**	**–7**	**0**	**0.0**	**20:36**	....	....	....	....	....	....	....	....	....
2001-02	**Calgary**	**NHL**	**79**	**6**	**22**	**28**	**52**	**1**	**0**	**0**	**126**	**4.8**	**–8**	**0**	**0.0**	**21:10**	....	....	....	....	....	....	....	....	....
2002-03	**Calgary**	**NHL**	**81**	**6**	**20**	**26**	**28**	**3**	**0**	**0**	**143**	**4.2**	**–7**	**0**	**0.0**	**25:47**	....	....	....	....	....	....	....	....	....
2003-04	**Calgary**	**NHL**	**67**	**4**	**16**	**20**	**30**	**2**	**0**	**1**	**93**	**4.3**	**6**	**0**	**0.0**	**21:13**	**6**	**0**	**1**	**1**	**2**	**0**	**0**	**0**	**14:30**
	NHL Totals		**289**	**19**	**74**	**93**	**140**	**7**	**0**	**1**	**442**	**4.3**		**0**	**0.0**	**22:21**	**6**	**0**	**1**	**1**	**2**	**0**	**0**	**0**	**14:30**

LYNCH, Doug

(LIHNCH, DUHG) **EDM.**

Defense. Shoots left. 6'3", 214 lbs. Born, North Vancouver, B.C., April 4, 1983. Edmonton's 2nd choice, 43rd overall, in 2001 Entry Draft.

1998-99	Port Coquitlam	BCAHA	45	47	48	95	120	....	....	....	....	....	....	....	....	....	....	....	....	....	....	....	....	....	....
	Red Deer Rebels	WHL	2	0	1	1	2	....	....	....	....	....	....	....	....	....	....	....	....	....	....	....	....	....	....
99-2000	Red Deer Rebels	WHL	65	9	5	14	57	....	....	....	....	....	....	....	....	....	4	0	0	0	5	....	....	....	....
2000-01	Red Deer Rebels	WHL	72	12	37	49	181	....	....	....	....	....	....	....	....	....	21	1	9	10	30	....	....	....	....
2001-02	Red Deer Rebels	WHL	71	21	27	48	202	....	....	....	....	....	....	....	....	....	22	5	4	9	12	....	....	....	....
2002-03	Red Deer Rebels	WHL	13	7	5	12	27	....	....	....	....	....	....	....	....	....	....	....	....	....	....	....	....	....	....
	Spokane Chiefs	WHL	42	6	12	18	129	....	....	....	....	....	....	....	....	....	4	1	0	1	16	....	....	....	....
2003-04	**Edmonton**	**NHL**	**2**	**0**	**0**	**0**	**0**	**0**	**0**	**0**	**2**	**0.0**	**0**	**0**	**0.0**	**10:16**	....	....	....	....	....	....	....	....	....
	Toronto	AHL	74	11	25	36	77	....	....	....	....	....	....	....	....	....	3	0	1	1	2	....	....	....	....
	NHL Totals		**2**	**0**	**0**	**0**	**0**	**0**	**0**	**0**	**2**	**0.0**		**0**	**0.0**	**10:16**	....	....	....	....	....	....	....	....	....

AHL All-Rookie Team (2004)

LYSAK, Brett

(LIGH-sak, BREHT) **CAR.**

Center. Shoots left. 6', 190 lbs. Born, Edmonton, Alta., December 30, 1980. Carolina's 2nd choice, 49th overall, in 1999 Entry Draft.

1994-95	St. Albert Sabres	AMBHL	STATISTICS NOT AVAILABLE																						
1995-96	St. Albert Raiders	AMHL	35	20	23	43	68	....	....	....	....	....	....	....	....	....	....	....	....	....	....	....	....	....	....
1996-97	Regina Pats	WHL	66	11	14	25	41	....	....	....	....	....	....	....	....	....	5	0	1	1	5	....	....	....	....
1997-98	Regina Pats	WHL	70	22	38	60	82	....	....	....	....	....	....	....	....	....	9	6	2	8	8	....	....	....	....
1998-99	Regina Pats	WHL	61	39	49	88	84	....	....	....	....	....	....	....	....	....	....	....	....	....	....	....	....	....	....
99-2000	Regina Pats	WHL	70	38	40	78	24	....	....	....	....	....	....	....	....	....	7	5	4	9	2	....	....	....	....
2000-01	Regina Pats	WHL	64	35	48	83	44	....	....	....	....	....	....	....	....	....	6	5	1	6	4	....	....	....	....
2001-02	Florida Everblades	ECHL	16	2	7	9	14	....	....	....	....	....	....	....	....	....	6	3	1	4	6	....	....	....	....
	Lowell	AHL	53	6	8	14	26	....	....	....	....	....	....	....	....	....	3	0	0	0	0	....	....	....	....
2002-03	Lowell	AHL	49	6	9	15	59	....	....	....	....	....	....	....	....	....	....	....	....	....	....	....	....	....	....
2003-04	**Carolina**	**NHL**	**2**	**0**	**0**	**0**	**2**	**0**	**0**	**0**	**0**	**0.0**	**0**	**1**	**0.0**	**3:24**	....	....	....	....	....	....	....	....	....
	Lowell	AHL	71	17	18	35	104	....	....	....	....	....	....	....	....	....	....	....	....	....	....	....	....	....	....
	NHL Totals		**2**	**0**	**0**	**0**	**2**	**0**	**0**	**0**	**0**	**0.0**		**1**	**0.0**	**3:24**	....	....	....	....	....	....	....	....	....

WHL East Second All-Star Team (1999) • Memorial Cup All-Star Team (2001)

MacDONALD, Craig

(MAK-DAWN-uhld, KRAYG)

Left wing. Shoots left. 6'1", 195 lbs. Born, Antigonish, N.S., April 7, 1977. Hartford's 3rd choice, 88th overall, in 1996 Entry Draft.

1994-95	Lawrence School	Hi-School	30	25	52	77	10	....	....	....	....	....	....	....	....	....	....	....	....	....	....	....	....	....	....
1995-96	Harvard Crimson	ECAC	34	7	10	17	10	....	....	....	....	....	....	....	....	....	....	....	....	....	....	....	....	....	....
1996-97	Harvard Crimson	ECAC	32	6	10	16	20	....	....	....	....	....	....	....	....	....	....	....	....	....	....	....	....	....	....
1997-98	Team Canada	Nat-Tm	58	18	29	47	38	....	....	....	....	....	....	....	....	....	....	....	....	....	....	....	....	....	....
1998-99	**Carolina**	**NHL**	**11**	**0**	**0**	**0**	**0**	**0**	**0**	**0**	**5**	**0.0**	**0**	**2**	**100.0**	**2:29**	**1**	**0**	**0**	**0**	**0**	**0**	**0**	**0**	**2:46**
	New Haven	AHL	62	17	31	48	77	....	....	....	....	....	....	....	....	....	....	....	....	....	....	....	....	....	....
99-2000	Cincinnati	IHL	78	12	24	36	76	....	....	....	....	....	....	....	....	....	11	4	1	5	8	....	....	....	....
2000-01	Cincinnati	IHL	82	20	28	48	104	....	....	....	....	....	....	....	....	....	5	0	1	1	6	....	....	....	....
2001-02	**Carolina**	**NHL**	**12**	**1**	**1**	**2**	**0**	**0**	**0**	**0**	**15**	**6.7**	**–1**	**19**	**47.4**	**10:11**	**4**	**0**	**0**	**0**	**2**	**0**	**0**	**0**	**4:42**
	Lowell	AHL	64	19	22	41	61	....	....	....	....	....	....	....	....	....	....	....	....	....	....	....	....	....	....
2002-03	**Carolina**	**NHL**	**35**	**1**	**3**	**4**	**20**	**0**	**0**	**0**	**43**	**2.3**	**–3**	**72**	**55.6**	**9:21**	....	....	....	....	....	....	....	....	....
	Lowell	AHL	27	7	20	27	38	....	....	....	....	....	....	....	....	....	....	....	....	....	....	....	....	....	....
2003-04	**Florida**	**NHL**	**34**	**0**	**3**	**3**	**25**	**0**	**0**	**0**	**42**	**0.0**	**–5**	**398**	**45.7**	**12:31**	....	....	....	....	....	....	....	....	....
	San Antonio	AHL	2	0	0	0	4	....	....	....	....	....	....	....	....	....	....	....	....	....	....	....	....	....	....
	Boston	**NHL**	**18**	**0**	**3**	**3**	**8**	**0**	**0**	**0**	**17**	**0.0**	**0**	**155**	**47.1**	**8:42**	**1**	**0**	**0**	**0**	**0**	**0**	**0**	**0**	**2:11**
	NHL Totals		**110**	**2**	**10**	**12**	**53**	**0**	**0**	**0**	**122**	**1.6**		**646**	**47.4**	**9:38**	**6**	**0**	**0**	**0**	**2**	**0**	**0**	**0**	**3:58**

Rights transferred to **Carolina** after **Hartford** franchise relocated, June 25, 1997. Signed as a free agent by **Florida**, August 14, 2003. Claimed on waivers by **Boston** from **Florida**, January 20, 2004.

MacDONALD, Jason

(MAK-DAWN-uhld, JAY-suhn)

Right wing. Shoots right. 5'11", 205 lbs. Born, Charlottetown, P.E.I., April 1, 1974. Detroit's 5th choice, 142nd overall, in 1992 Entry Draft.

1989-90	Charlottetown	MJrHL	29	11	29	40	206	....	....	....	....	....	....	....	....	....	....	....	....	....	....	....	....	....	....
1990-91	North Bay	OHL	57	12	15	27	126	....	....	....	....	....	....	....	....	....	10	3	3	6	15	....	....	....	....
1991-92	North Bay	OHL	17	5	8	13	50	....	....	....	....	....	....	....	....	....	....	....	....	....	....	....	....	....	....
	Owen Sound	OHL	42	17	19	36	129	....	....	....	....	....	....	....	....	....	5	0	3	3	16	....	....	....	....
1992-93	Owen Sound	OHL	56	46	43	89	197	....	....	....	....	....	....	....	....	....	8	6	5	11	28	....	....	....	....
1993-94	Owen Sound	OHL	66	55	61	116	177	....	....	....	....	....	....	....	....	....	9	7	11	18	36	....	....	....	....
	Adirondack	AHL	....	....	....	....	....	....	....	....	....	....	....	....	....	....	1	0	0	0	0	....	....	....	....
1994-95	Adirondack	AHL	68	14	21	35	238	....	....	....	....	....	....	....	....	....	4	0	0	0	2	....	....	....	....
1995-96	Adirondack	AHL	43	9	13	22	99	....	....	....	....	....	....	....	....	....	....	....	....	....	....	....	....	....	....
	Toledo Storm	ECHL	9	5	5	10	26	....	....	....	....	....	....	....	....	....	9	3	1	4	39	....	....	....	....
1996-97	Adirondack	AHL	1	0	0	0	2	....	....	....	....	....	....	....	....	....	....	....	....	....	....	....	....	....	....
	Fredericton	AHL	63	22	25	47	189	....	....	....	....	....	....	....	....	....	....	....	....	....	....	....	....	....	....
1997-98	Team Canada	Nat-Tm	51	15	20	35	133	....	....	....	....	....	....	....	....	....	....	....	....	....	....	....	....	....	....
	Saint John Flames	AHL	6	2	0	2	27	....	....	....	....	....	....	....	....	....	11	1	3	4	17	....	....	....	....
1998-99	Manitoba Moose	IHL	82	25	27	52	283	....	....	....	....	....	....	....	....	....	5	2	2	4	13	....	....	....	....
99-2000	Manitoba Moose	IHL	30	5	10	15	77	....	....	....	....	....	....	....	....	....	....	....	....	....	....	....	....	....	....
	Orlando	IHL	29	7	7	14	113	....	....	....	....	....	....	....	....	....	4	0	0	0	19	....	....	....	....
2000-01	Wilkes-Barre	AHL	74	17	16	33	290	....	....	....	....	....	....	....	....	....	17	1	3	4	*66	....	....	....	....
2001-02	Wilkes-Barre	AHL	57	8	13	21	330	....	....	....	....	....	....	....	....	....	....	....	....	....	....	....	....	....	....
2002-03	Wilkes-Barre	AHL	56	4	7	11	137	....	....	....	....	....	....	....	....	....	1	0	0	0	0	....	....	....	....
2003-04	Hartford	AHL	41	11	11	22	101	....	....	....	....	....	....	....	....	....	10	4	0	4	50	....	....	....	....
	NY Rangers	**NHL**	**4**	**0**	**0**	**0**	**19**	**0**	**0**	**0**	**3**	**0.0**	**–1**	**0**	**0.0**	**8:11**	....	....	....	....	....	....	....	....	....
	NHL Totals		**4**	**0**	**0**	**0**	**19**	**0**	**0**	**0**	**3**	**0.0**		**0**	**0.0**	**8:11**	....	....	....	....	....	....	....	....	....

OHL Second All-Star Team (1994)

Traded to **Montreal** by **Detroit** for cash, November 8, 1996. Signed as a free agent by **Pittsburgh**, July 18, 2001. Signed as a free agent by **Hartford** (AHL), September 9, 2003. Signed as a free agent by **NY Rangers**, December 11, 2003.

MacINNIS, Al

(MAK-IHN-his, AL) **ST.L.**

Defense. Shoots right. 6'2", 204 lbs. Born, Inverness, N.S., July 11, 1963. Calgary's 1st choice, 15th overall, in 1981 Entry Draft.

			Regular Season														Playoffs								
Season	Club	League	GP	G	A	Pts	PIM	PP	SH	GW	S	%	+/-	TF	F%	Min	GP	G	A	Pts	PIM	PP	SH	GW	Min
1979-80	Regina Blues	SJHL	59	20	28	48	110	....	....	....	....	....	....	....	....	....	....	....	....	....	....	....	....	....	....
1980-81	Kitchener Rangers	OMJHL	47	11	28	39	59	....	....	....	....	....	....	....	....	....	18	4	12	16	20	....	....	....	....
1981-82	Kitchener Rangers	OHL	59	25	50	75	145	....	....	....	....	....	....	....	....	....	15	5	10	15	44	....	....	....	....
	Calgary	**NHL**	**2**	**0**	**0**	**0**	**0**	**0**	**0**	**0**	**2**	**0.0**	**0**	....	....	....	....	....	....	....	....	....	....	....	....
1982-83	Kitchener Rangers	OHL	51	38	46	84	67	....	....	....	....	....	....	....	....	....	8	3	8	11	9	....	....	....	....
	Calgary	**NHL**	**14**	**1**	**3**	**4**	**9**	**0**	**0**	**0**	**7**	**14.3**	**0**	....	....	....	....	....	....	....	....	....	....	....	....
1983-84	**Calgary**	**NHL**	**51**	**11**	**34**	**45**	**42**	**7**	**0**	**2**	**160**	**6.9**	**0**	....	....	....	**11**	**2**	**12**	**14**	**13**	**2**	**0**	**1**	....
	Colorado Flames	CHL	19	5	14	19	22	....	....	....	....	....	....	....	....	....	....	....	....	....	....	....	....	....	....
1984-85	**Calgary**	**NHL**	**67**	**14**	**52**	**66**	**75**	**8**	**0**	**0**	**259**	**5.4**	**7**	....	....	....	**4**	**1**	**2**	**3**	**8**	**1**	**0**	**0**	....
1985-86	**Calgary**	**NHL**	**77**	**11**	**57**	**68**	**76**	**4**	**0**	**0**	**241**	**4.6**	**38**	....	....	....	**21**	**4**	***15**	**19**	**30**	**2**	**0**	**0**	....
1986-87	**Calgary**	**NHL**	**79**	**20**	**56**	**76**	**97**	**7**	**0**	**2**	**262**	**7.6**	**20**	....	....	....	**4**	**1**	**0**	**1**	**0**	**1**	**0**	**0**	....
1987-88	**Calgary**	**NHL**	**80**	**25**	**58**	**83**	**114**	**7**	**2**	**2**	**245**	**10.2**	**13**	....	....	....	**7**	**3**	**6**	**9**	**18**	**2**	**0**	**0**	....
1988-89 ♦	**Calgary**	**NHL**	**79**	**16**	**58**	**74**	**136**	**8**	**0**	**3**	**277**	**5.8**	**38**	....	....	....	**22**	**7**	***24**	***31**	**46**	**5**	**0**	**4**	....
1989-90	**Calgary**	**NHL**	**79**	**28**	**62**	**90**	**82**	**14**	**1**	**3**	**304**	**9.2**	**20**	....	....	....	**6**	**2**	**3**	**5**	**8**	**1**	**0**	**0**	....
1990-91	**Calgary**	**NHL**	**78**	**28**	**75**	**103**	**90**	**17**	**0**	**1**	**305**	**9.2**	**42**	....	....	....	**7**	**2**	**3**	**5**	**8**	**2**	**0**	**0**	....
1991-92	**Calgary**	**NHL**	**72**	**20**	**57**	**77**	**83**	**11**	**0**	**0**	**304**	**6.6**	**13**	....	....	....	....	....	....	....	....	....	....	....	....
1992-93	**Calgary**	**NHL**	**50**	**11**	**43**	**54**	**61**	**7**	**0**	**4**	**201**	**5.5**	**15**	....	....	....	**6**	**1**	**6**	**7**	**10**	**1**	**0**	**0**	....
1993-94	**Calgary**	**NHL**	**75**	**28**	**54**	**82**	**95**	**12**	**1**	**5**	**324**	**8.6**	**35**	....	....	....	**7**	**2**	**6**	**8**	**12**	**1**	**0**	**0**	....
1994-95	**St. Louis**	**NHL**	**32**	**8**	**20**	**28**	**43**	**2**	**0**	**0**	**110**	**7.3**	**19**	....	....	....	**7**	**1**	**5**	**6**	**10**	**0**	**0**	**0**	....
1995-96	**St. Louis**	**NHL**	**82**	**17**	**44**	**61**	**88**	**9**	**1**	**1**	**317**	**5.4**	**5**	....	....	....	**13**	**3**	**4**	**7**	**20**	**1**	**0**	**0**	....
1996-97	**St. Louis**	**NHL**	**72**	**13**	**30**	**43**	**65**	**6**	**1**	**1**	**296**	**4.4**	**2**	....	....	....	**6**	**1**	**2**	**3**	**4**	**1**	**0**	**0**	....
1997-98	**St. Louis**	**NHL**	**71**	**19**	**30**	**49**	**80**	**9**	**1**	**2**	**227**	**8.4**	**6**	....	....	....	**8**	**2**	**6**	**8**	**12**	**1**	**0**	**0**	....
	Canada	Olympics	6	2	0	2	2	....	....	....	....	....	....	....	....	....	....	....	....	....	....	....	....	....	....
1998-99	**St. Louis**	**NHL**	**82**	**20**	**42**	**62**	**70**	**11**	**1**	**2**	**314**	**6.4**	**33**	**0**	**0.0**	**29:07**	**13**	**4**	**8**	**12**	**20**	**2**	**0**	**0**	**35:14**
99-2000	**St. Louis**	**NHL**	**61**	**11**	**28**	**39**	**34**	**6**	**0**	**7**	**245**	**4.5**	**20**	**0**	**0.0**	**26:07**	**7**	**1**	**3**	**4**	**14**	**1**	**0**	**0**	**28:52**
2000-01	**St. Louis**	**NHL**	**59**	**12**	**42**	**54**	**52**	**6**	**1**	**3**	**218**	**5.5**	**23**	**0**	**0.0**	**26:32**	**15**	**2**	**8**	**10**	**18**	**2**	**0**	**0**	**30:46**
2001-02	**St. Louis**	**NHL**	**71**	**11**	**35**	**46**	**52**	**6**	**0**	**4**	**231**	**4.8**	**3**	**0**	**0.0**	**26:56**	**10**	**0**	**7**	**7**	**4**	**0**	**0**	**0**	**29:03**
	Canada	Olympics	6	0	0	0	8	....	....	....	....	....	....	....	....	....	....	....	....	....	....	....	....	....	....
2002-03	**St. Louis**	**NHL**	**80**	**16**	**52**	**68**	**61**	**9**	**1**	**2**	**299**	**5.4**	**22**	**2**	**100.0**	**26:55**	**3**	**0**	**1**	**1**	**0**	**0**	**0**	**0**	**12:41**
2003-04	**St. Louis**	**NHL**	**3**	**0**	**2**	**2**	**6**	**0**	**0**	**0**	**9**	**0.0**	**–1**	**0**	**0.0**	**24:59**	....	....	....	....	....	....	....	....	....
	NHL Totals		**1416**	**340**	**934**	**1274**	**1511**	**166**	**10**	**44**	**5157**	**6.6**		**2**	**100.0**	**27:13**	**177**	**39**	**121**	**160**	**255**	**26**	**0**	**5**	**30:13**

OHL First All-Star Team (1982, 1983) • NHL Second All-Star Team (1987, 1989, 1994) • Conn Smythe Trophy (1989) • NHL First All-Star Team (1990, 1991, 1999, 2003) • James Norris Memorial Trophy (1999)

Played in NHL All-Star Game (1985, 1988, 1990, 1991, 1992, 1994, 1996, 1997, 1998, 1999, 2000, 2003)

Traded to **St. Louis** by **Calgary** with Calgary's 4th round choice (Didier Tremblay) in 1997 Entry Draft for Phil Housley and St. Louis' 2nd round choices in 1996 (Steve Begin) and 1997 (John Tripp) Entry Drafts, July 4, 1994. • Missed majority of 2003-04 season recovering from eye injury suffered in game vs. Nashville, October 16, 2003.

MacKENZIE, Derek

(muh-KEHN-zee, DAIR-ihk) **ATL.**

Center. Shoots left. 5'11", 180 lbs. Born, Sudbury, Ont., June 11, 1981. Atlanta's 6th choice, 128th overall, in 1999 Entry Draft.

			Regular Season														Playoffs								
Season	Club	League	GP	G	A	Pts	PIM	PP	SH	GW	S	%	+/-	TF	F%	Min	GP	G	A	Pts	PIM	PP	SH	GW	Min
1996-97	Rayside-Balfour	NOJHA	40	23	32	55	40	....	....	....	....	....	....	....	....	....	....	....	....	....	....	....	....	....	....
1997-98	Sudbury Wolves	OHL	59	9	11	20	26	....	....	....	....	....	....	....	....	....	....	....	....	....	....	....	....	....	....
1998-99	Sudbury Wolves	OHL	68	22	65	87	74	....	....	....	....	....	....	....	....	....	4	2	4	6	2	....	....	....	....
99-2000	Sudbury Wolves	OHL	68	24	33	57	110	....	....	....	....	....	....	....	....	....	12	5	9	14	16	....	....	....	....
2000-01	Sudbury Wolves	OHL	62	40	49	89	89	....	....	....	....	....	....	....	....	....	12	6	8	14	16	....	....	....	....
2001-02	**Atlanta**	**NHL**	**1**	**0**	**0**	**0**	**2**	**0**	**0**	**0**	**1**	**0.0**	**–1**	**16**	**56.3**	**13:51**	....	....	....	....	....	....	....	....	....
	Chicago Wolves	AHL	68	13	12	25	80	....	....	....	....	....	....	....	....	....	25	4	2	6	20	....	....	....	....
2002-03	Chicago Wolves	AHL	80	14	18	32	97	....	....	....	....	....	....	....	....	....	9	0	0	0	4	....	....	....	....
2003-04	**Atlanta**	**NHL**	**12**	**0**	**1**	**1**	**10**	**0**	**0**	**0**	**7**	**0.0**	**0**	**63**	**46.0**	**6:38**	....	....	....	....	....	....	....	....	....
	Chicago Wolves	AHL	63	19	16	35	67	....	....	....	....	....	....	....	....	....	10	7	1	8	13	....	....	....	....
	NHL Totals		**13**	**0**	**1**	**1**	**12**	**0**	**0**	**0**	**8**	**0.0**		**79**	**48.1**	**7:12**	....	....	....	....	....	....	....	....	....

MacLEAN, Don

(mihk-LAYN, DAWN)

Center. Shoots left. 6'2", 199 lbs. Born, Sydney, N.S., January 14, 1977. Los Angeles' 2nd choice, 33rd overall, in 1995 Entry Draft.

			Regular Season														Playoffs								
Season	Club	League	GP	G	A	Pts	PIM	PP	SH	GW	S	%	+/-	TF	F%	Min	GP	G	A	Pts	PIM	PP	SH	GW	Min
1992-93	Halifax Hawks	NSMHL	27	15	25	40	34	....	....	....	....	....	....	....	....	....	....	....	....	....	....	....	....	....	....
1993-94	Halifax Hawks	NSMHL	25	35	35	70	151	....	....	....	....	....	....	....	....	....	....	....	....	....	....	....	....	....	....
1994-95	Beauport	QMJHL	64	15	27	42	37	....	....	....	....	....	....	....	....	....	17	4	4	8	6	....	....	....	....
1995-96	Beauport	QMJHL	1	0	1	1	0	....	....	....	....	....	....	....	....	....	....	....	....	....	....	....	....	....	....
	Laval Titan	QMJHL	21	17	11	28	29	....	....	....	....	....	....	....	....	....	....	....	....	....	....	....	....	....	....
	Hull Olympiques	QMJHL	39	26	34	60	44	....	....	....	....	....	....	....	....	....	17	6	7	13	14	....	....	....	....
1996-97	Hull Olympiques	QMJHL	69	34	47	81	67	....	....	....	....	....	....	....	....	....	14	11	10	21	39	....	....	....	....
1997-98	**Los Angeles**	**NHL**	**22**	**5**	**2**	**7**	**4**	**2**	**0**	**0**	**25**	**20.0**	**–1**	....	....	....	....	....	....	....	....	....	....	....	....
	Fredericton	AHL	39	9	5	14	32	....	....	....	....	....	....	....	....	....	4	1	3	4	2	....	....	....	....
1998-99	Springfield	AHL	41	5	14	19	31	....	....	....	....	....	....	....	....	....	....	....	....	....	....	....	....	....	....
	Grand Rapids	IHL	28	6	13	19	8	....	....	....	....	....	....	....	....	....	....	....	....	....	....	....	....	....	....
99-2000	Lowell	AHL	40	11	17	28	18	....	....	....	....	....	....	....	....	....	....	....	....	....	....	....	....	....	....
	St. John's	AHL	21	14	12	26	8	....	....	....	....	....	....	....	....	....	....	....	....	....	....	....	....	....	....
2000-01	**Toronto**	**NHL**	**3**	**0**	**1**	**1**	**2**	**0**	**0**	**0**	**2**	**0.0**	**–2**	**33**	**54.6**	**9:48**	....	....	....	....	....	....	....	....	....
	St. John's	AHL	61	26	34	60	48	....	....	....	....	....	....	....	....	....	4	2	1	3	2	....	....	....	....
2001-02	St. John's	AHL	75	33	*54	*87	49	....	....	....	....	....	....	....	....	....	9	5	5	10	6	....	....	....	....
	Toronto	**NHL**	....	....	....	....	....	....	....	....	....	....	....	....	....	....	**3**	**0**	**0**	**0**	**0**	**0**	**0**	**0**	**1:39**
2002-03	Syracuse Crunch	AHL	17	9	9	18	6	....	....	....	....	....	....	....	....	....	....	....	....	....	....	....	....	....	....
2003-04	**Columbus**	**NHL**	**4**	**1**	**0**	**1**	**0**	**0**	**0**	**0**	**10**	**10.0**	**–1**	**31**	**58.1**	**11:41**	....	....	....	....	....	....	....	....	....
	Syracuse Crunch	AHL	77	27	41	68	45	....	....	....	....	....	....	....	....	....	7	0	3	3	4	....	....	....	....
	NHL Totals		**29**	**6**	**3**	**9**	**6**	**2**	**0**	**0**	**37**	**16.2**		**64**	**56.3**	**10:52**	**3**	**0**	**0**	**0**	**0**	**0**	**0**	**0**	**1:39**

John P. Sollenberger Trophy (Top Scorer – AHL) (2002)

Traded to **Toronto** by **Los Angeles** for Craig Charron, February 23, 2000. Signed as a free agent by **Columbus**, July 17, 2002. • Missed majority of 2002-03 season recovering from neck surgery, September 16, 2002.

MacMILLAN, Jeff

(muhk-MIHL-uhn, JEHF) **NYR**

Defense. Shoots left. 6'3", 206 lbs. Born, Durham, Ont., March 30, 1979. Dallas' 8th choice, 215th overall, in 1999 Entry Draft.

			Regular Season														Playoffs								
Season	Club	League	GP	G	A	Pts	PIM	PP	SH	GW	S	%	+/-	TF	F%	Min	GP	G	A	Pts	PIM	PP	SH	GW	Min
1995-96	Hanover Barons	OJHL-C	29	7	13	20	26	....	....	....	....	....	....	....	....	....	....	....	....	....	....	....	....	....	....
1996-97	Oshawa Generals	OHL	39	0	4	4	15	....	....	....	....	....	....	....	....	....	15	0	0	0	4	....	....	....	....
1997-98	Oshawa Generals	OHL	64	3	12	15	72	....	....	....	....	....	....	....	....	....	7	0	3	3	11	....	....	....	....
1998-99	Oshawa Generals	OHL	65	3	18	21	109	....	....	....	....	....	....	....	....	....	15	3	6	9	28	....	....	....	....
99-2000	Michigan	IHL	53	0	3	3	54	....	....	....	....	....	....	....	....	....	....	....	....	....	....	....	....	....	....
	Fort Wayne	UHL	7	1	1	2	25	....	....	....	....	....	....	....	....	....	9	0	2	2	10	....	....	....	....
2000-01	Utah Grizzlies	IHL	81	5	15	20	105	....	....	....	....	....	....	....	....	....	....	....	....	....	....	....	....	....	....
2001-02	Utah Grizzlies	AHL	77	6	9	15	146	....	....	....	....	....	....	....	....	....	5	1	0	1	17	....	....	....	....
2002-03	Utah Grizzlies	AHL	78	8	7	15	132	....	....	....	....	....	....	....	....	....	2	0	0	0	6	....	....	....	....
2003-04	**Dallas**	**NHL**	**4**	**0**	**0**	**0**	**0**	**0**	**0**	**0**	**3**	**0.0**	**–2**	**0**	**0.0**	**8:19**	....	....	....	....	....	....	....	....	....
	Utah Grizzlies	AHL	73	4	6	10	108	....	....	....	....	....	....	....	....	....	....	....	....	....	....	....	....	....	....
	NHL Totals		**4**	**0**	**0**	**0**	**0**	**0**	**0**	**0**	**3**	**0.0**		**0**	**0.0**	**8:19**	....	....	....	....	....	....	....	....	....

Signed as a free agent by **NY Rangers**, July 22, 2004.

MacNEIL, Ian

(muhk-NEEL, EE-an)

Center. Shoots left. 6'2", 190 lbs. Born, Halifax, N.S., April 27, 1977. Hartford's 3rd choice, 85th overall, in 1995 Entry Draft.

			Regular Season														Playoffs								
Season	Club	League	GP	G	A	Pts	PIM	PP	SH	GW	S	%	+/-	TF	F%	Min	GP	G	A	Pts	PIM	PP	SH	GW	Min
1993-94	Whitby Lions	OMHA	50	30	22	52	102	....	....	....	....	....	....	....	....	....	....	....	....	....	....	....	....	....	....
1994-95	Oshawa Generals	OHL	60	7	21	28	62	....	....	....	....	....	....	....	....	....	7	0	2	2	0	....	....	....	....
1995-96	Oshawa Generals	OHL	49	15	17	32	54	....	....	....	....	....	....	....	....	....	5	1	2	3	8	....	....	....	....
1996-97	Oshawa Generals	OHL	64	23	20	43	96	....	....	....	....	....	....	....	....	....	18	2	3	5	37	....	....	....	....
1997-98	New Haven	AHL	68	12	21	33	67	....	....	....	....	....	....	....	....	....	3	1	0	1	10	....	....	....	....
1998-99	New Haven	AHL	47	6	4	10	62	....	....	....	....	....	....	....	....	....	....	....	....	....	....	....	....	....	....
99-2000	Cincinnati	IHL	81	19	18	37	100	....	....	....	....	....	....	....	....	....	11	3	2	5	25	....	....	....	....

			Regular Season														Playoffs								
Season	Club	League	GP	G	A	Pts	PIM	PP	SH	GW	S	%	+/-	TF	F%	Min	GP	G	A	Pts	PIM	PP	SH	GW	Min
2000-01	Cincinnati	IHL	82	17	22	39	139	....	....	....	....	....	....	....	....	....	5	0	1	1	4	....	....	....	....
2001-02	Lowell	AHL	79	14	20	34	128	....	....	....	....	....	....	....	....	....	2	0	1	1	4	....	....	....	....
2002-03	**Philadelphia**	**NHL**	**2**	**0**	**0**	**0**	**0**	**0**	**0**	**0**	**2**	**0.0**	**1**	**0**	**0.0**	**10:08**	....	....	....	....	....	....	....	....	....
	Philadelphia	AHL	71	10	13	23	132	....	....	....	....	....	....	....	....	....	....	....	....	....	....	....	....	....	....
2003-04	Philadelphia	AHL	71	13	15	28	151	....	....	....	....	....	....	....	....	....	12	2	6	8	34	....	....	....	....
	NHL Totals		**2**	**0**	**0**	**0**	**0**	**0**	**0**	**0**	**2**	**0.0**		**0**	**0.0**	**10:08**	....	....	....	....	....	....	....	....	....

Rights transferred to **Carolina** after **Hartford** franchise relocated, June 25, 1997. Signed as a free agent by **Philadelphia**, July 2, 2002.

MADDEN, John

(MA-dehn, JAWN) **N.J.**

Center. Shoots left. 5'11", 190 lbs. Born, Barrie, Ont., May 4, 1973.

Season	Club	League	GP	G	A	Pts	PIM	PP	SH	GW	S	%	+/-	TF	F%	Min	GP	G	A	Pts	PIM	PP	SH	GW	Min
1989-90	Alliston Hornets	OJHL-C	31	24	25	49	26	....	....	....	....	....	....	....	....	....	....	....	....	....	....	....	....	....	....
1990-91	Alliston Hornets	OJHL-C	14	15	21	36	10	....	....	....	....	....	....	....	....	....	....	....	....	....	....	....	....	....	....
	Barrie Colts	OJHL-B	1	0	0	0	0	....	....	....	....	....	....	....	....	....	....	....	....	....	....	....	....	....	....
1991-92	Barrie Colts	OJHL-B	42	50	54	104	46	....	....	....	....	....	....	....	....	....	13	10	9	19	14	....	....	....	....
1992-93	Barrie Colts	OJHL-B	43	49	75	124	62	....	....	....	....	....	....	....	....	....	....	....	....	....	....	....	....	....	....
1993-94	U. of Michigan	CCHA	36	6	11	17	14	....	....	....	....	....	....	....	....	....	....	....	....	....	....	....	....	....	....
1994-95	U. of Michigan	CCHA	39	21	22	43	8	....	....	....	....	....	....	....	....	....	....	....	....	....	....	....	....	....	....
1995-96	U. of Michigan	CCHA	43	27	30	57	45	....	....	....	....	....	....	....	....	....	....	....	....	....	....	....	....	....	....
1996-97	U. of Michigan	CCHA	42	26	37	63	56	....	....	....	....	....	....	....	....	....	....	....	....	....	....	....	....	....	....
1997-98	Albany River Rats	AHL	74	20	36	56	40	....	....	....	....	....	....	....	....	....	13	3	13	16	14	....	....	....	....
1998-99	**New Jersey**	**NHL**	**4**	**0**	**1**	**1**	**0**	**0**	**0**	**0**	**4**	**0.0**	**-2**	**0**	**0.0**	**9:13**	....	....	....	....	....	....	....	....	....
	Albany River Rats	AHL	75	38	60	98	44	....	....	....	....	....	....	....	....	....	5	2	2	4	6	....	....	....	....
99-2000♦	**New Jersey**	**NHL**	**74**	**16**	**9**	**25**	**6**	**0**	**6**	**3**	**115**	**13.9**	**7**	**770**	**47.5**	**11:40**	**20**	**3**	**4**	**7**	**0**	**0**	**1**	**2**	**15:30**
2000-01	**New Jersey**	**NHL**	**80**	**23**	**15**	**38**	**12**	**0**	**3**	**4**	**163**	**14.1**	**24**	**974**	**46.6**	**15:35**	**25**	**4**	**3**	**7**	**6**	**0**	**0**	**0**	**15:15**
2001-02	**New Jersey**	**NHL**	**82**	**15**	**8**	**23**	**25**	**0**	**0**	**2**	**170**	**8.8**	**6**	**1001**	**47.0**	**15:36**	**6**	**0**	**0**	**0**	**0**	**0**	**0**	**0**	**17:25**
2002-03♦	**New Jersey**	**NHL**	**80**	**19**	**22**	**41**	**26**	**2**	**2**	**3**	**207**	**9.2**	**13**	**1502**	**50.9**	**18:18**	**24**	**6**	**10**	**16**	**2**	**2**	**1**	**1**	**19:38**
2003-04	**New Jersey**	**NHL**	**80**	**12**	**23**	**35**	**22**	**1**	**1**	**1**	**210**	**5.7**	**7**	**1377**	**53.3**	**17:17**	**5**	**0**	**0**	**0**	**0**	**0**	**0**	**0**	**14:51**
	NHL Totals		**400**	**85**	**78**	**163**	**91**	**3**	**12**	**13**	**869**	**9.8**		**5624**	**49.6**	**15:41**	**80**	**13**	**17**	**30**	**8**	**2**	**2**	**3**	**16:46**

CCHA First All-Star Team (1997) • NCAA West First All-American Team (1997) • Frank J. Selke Trophy (2001)

Signed as a free agent by **New Jersey**, June 26, 1997.

MAIR, Adam

(MAIR, A-duhm) **BUF.**

Center. Shoots right. 6'2", 215 lbs. Born, Hamilton, Ont., February 15, 1979. Toronto's 2nd choice, 84th overall, in 1997 Entry Draft.

Season	Club	League	GP	G	A	Pts	PIM	PP	SH	GW	S	%	+/-	TF	F%	Min	GP	G	A	Pts	PIM	PP	SH	GW	Min
1994-95	Ohsweken	OJHL-B	39	21	23	44	91	....	....	....	....	....	....	....	....	....	....	....	....	....	....	....	....	....	....
1995-96	Owen Sound	OHL	62	12	15	27	63	....	....	....	....	....	....	....	....	....	6	0	0	0	2	....	....	....	....
1996-97	Owen Sound	OHL	65	16	35	51	113	....	....	....	....	....	....	....	....	....	4	1	0	1	2	....	....	....	....
1997-98	Owen Sound	OHL	56	25	27	52	179	....	....	....	....	....	....	....	....	....	11	6	3	9	31	....	....	....	....
1998-99	Owen Sound	OHL	43	23	41	64	109	....	....	....	....	....	....	....	....	....	16	10	10	20	*47	....	....	....	....
	St. John's	AHL	....	....	....	....	....	....	....	....	....	....	....	....	....	....	3	1	0	1	6	....	....	....	....
	Toronto	**NHL**	....	....	....	....	....	....	....	....	....	....	....	....	....	....	**5**	**1**	**0**	**1**	**14**	**0**	**0**	**0**	**5:37**
99-2000	**Toronto**	**NHL**	**8**	**1**	**0**	**1**	**6**	**0**	**0**	**0**	**7**	**14.3**	**-1**	**9**	**33.3**	**11:33**	**5**	**0**	**0**	**0**	**8**	**0**	**0**	**0**	**10:15**
	St. John's	AHL	66	22	27	49	124	....	....	....	....	....	....	....	....	....	....	....	....	....	....	....	....	....	....
2000-01	**Toronto**	**NHL**	**16**	**0**	**2**	**2**	**14**	**0**	**0**	**0**	**17**	**0.0**	**3**	**56**	**51.8**	**9:00**	....	....	....	....	....	....	....	....	....
	St. John's	AHL	47	18	27	45	69	....	....	....	....	....	....	....	....	....	....	....	....	....	....	....	....	....	....
	Los Angeles	**NHL**	**10**	**0**	**0**	**0**	**6**	**0**	**0**	**0**	**5**	**0.0**	**-3**	**21**	**61.9**	**6:14**	....	....	....	....	....	....	....	....	....
2001-02	**Los Angeles**	**NHL**	**18**	**1**	**1**	**2**	**57**	**0**	**0**	**0**	**10**	**10.0**	**1**	**31**	**58.1**	**7:11**	....	....	....	....	....	....	....	....	....
	Manchester	AHL	27	10	9	19	48	....	....	....	....	....	....	....	....	....	5	5	1	6	10	....	....	....	....
2002-03	**Buffalo**	**NHL**	**79**	**6**	**11**	**17**	**146**	**0**	**1**	**1**	**83**	**7.2**	**-4**	**572**	**51.2**	**10:37**	....	....	....	....	....	....	....	....	....
2003-04	**Buffalo**	**NHL**	**81**	**6**	**14**	**20**	**146**	**1**	**0**	**1**	**82**	**7.3**	**-3**	**340**	**45.9**	**9:38**	....	....	....	....	....	....	....	....	....
	NHL Totals		**212**	**14**	**28**	**42**	**375**	**1**	**1**	**2**	**204**	**6.9**		**1029**	**49.8**	**9:39**	**10**	**1**	**0**	**1**	**22**	**0**	**0**	**0**	**7:56**

Traded to **Los Angeles** by **Toronto** with Toronto's 2nd round choice (Mike Cammalleri) in 2001 Entry Draft for Aki Berg, March 13, 2001. Traded to **Buffalo** by **Los Angeles** with Los Angeles' 5th round choice (Thomas Morrow) in 2003 Entry Draft for Erik Rasmussen, July 24, 2002.

MAJESKY, Ivan

(migh-EHV-skee, ee-VAHN) **ATL.**

Defense. Shoots right. 6'5", 230 lbs. Born, Banska Bystrica, Czech., September 2, 1976. Florida's 12th choice, 267th overall, in 2001 Entry Draft.

Season	Club	League	GP	G	A	Pts	PIM	PP	SH	GW	S	%	+/-	TF	F%	Min	GP	G	A	Pts	PIM	PP	SH	GW	Min
1995-96	Banska Bystrica	Slovakia	17	0	0	0	18	....	....	....	....	....	....	....	....	....	....	....	....	....	....	....	....	....	....
1996-97	Banska Bystrica	Slovakia	49	2	4	6	....	....	....	....	....	....	....	....	....	....	....	....	....	....	....	....	....	....	....
1997-98	Banska Bystrica	Slovak-2	43	6	7	13	50	....	....	....	....	....	....	....	....	....	....	....	....	....	....	....	....	....	....
1998-99	Banska Bystrica	Slovak-2	48	7	7	14	68	....	....	....	....	....	....	....	....	....	....	....	....	....	....	....	....	....	....
	HKm Zvolen	Slovakia	....	....	....	....	....	....	....	....	....	....	....	....	....	....	6	0	2	2	2	....	....	....	....
99-2000	HKm Zvolen	Slovakia	51	7	9	16	68	....	....	....	....	....	....	....	....	....	10	0	4	4	2	....	....	....	....
2000-01	Ilves Tampere	Finland	54	2	14	16	99	....	....	....	....	....	....	....	....	....	9	0	1	1	6	....	....	....	....
2001-02	Ilves Tampere	Finland	44	6	6	12	84	....	....	....	....	....	....	....	....	....	....	....	....	....	....	....	....	....	....
	Slovakia	Olympics	4	0	1	1	4	....	....	....	....	....	....	....	....	....	....	....	....	....	....	....	....	....	....
2002-03	**Florida**	**NHL**	**82**	**4**	**8**	**12**	**92**	**0**	**0**	**2**	**52**	**7.7**	**-18**	**0**	**0.0**	**20:53**	....	....	....	....	....	....	....	....	....
2003-04	**Atlanta**	**NHL**	**63**	**3**	**7**	**10**	**76**	**0**	**0**	**0**	**35**	**8.6**	**-7**	**2**	**50.0**	**14:28**	....	....	....	....	....	....	....	....	....
	NHL Totals		**145**	**7**	**15**	**22**	**168**	**0**	**0**	**2**	**87**	**8.0**		**2**	**50.0**	**18:06**	....	....	....	....	....	....	....	....	....

Traded to **Atlanta** by **Florida** for Atlanta's 2nd round choice (Kamil Kreps) in 2003 Entry Draft, June 21, 2003.

MALAKHOV, Vladimir

(mah-LAH-kahf, vla-DIH-meer)

Defense. Shoots left. 6'4", 230 lbs. Born, Sverdlovsk, USSR, August 30, 1968. NY Islanders' 12th choice, 191st overall, in 1989 Entry Draft.

Season	Club	League	GP	G	A	Pts	PIM	PP	SH	GW	S	%	+/-	TF	F%	Min	GP	G	A	Pts	PIM	PP	SH	GW	Min
1986-87	Spartak Moscow	USSR	22	0	1	1	12	....	....	....	....	....	....	....	....	....	....	....	....	....	....	....	....	....	....
1987-88	Spartak Moscow	USSR	28	2	2	4	26	....	....	....	....	....	....	....	....	....	....	....	....	....	....	....	....	....	....
1988-89	CSKA Moscow	USSR	34	6	2	8	16	....	....	....	....	....	....	....	....	....	....	....	....	....	....	....	....	....	....
1989-90	CSKA Moscow	USSR	48	2	10	12	34	....	....	....	....	....	....	....	....	....	....	....	....	....	....	....	....	....	....
1990-91	CSKA Moscow	USSR	46	5	13	18	22	....	....	....	....	....	....	....	....	....	....	....	....	....	....	....	....	....	....
1991-92	CSKA Moscow	CIS	40	1	9	10	12	....	....	....	....	....	....	....	....	....	....	....	....	....	....	....	....	....	....
	Russia	Olympics	8	3	0	3	4	....	....	....	....	....	....	....	....	....	....	....	....	....	....	....	....	....	....
1992-93	**NY Islanders**	**NHL**	**64**	**14**	**38**	**52**	**59**	**7**	**0**	**0**	**178**	**7.9**	**14**	....	....	....	**17**	**3**	**6**	**9**	**12**	**0**	**0**	**0**	....
	Capital District	AHL	3	2	1	3	11	....	....	....	....	....	....	....	....	....	....	....	....	....	....	....	....	....	....
1993-94	**NY Islanders**	**NHL**	**76**	**10**	**47**	**57**	**80**	**4**	**0**	**2**	**235**	**4.3**	**29**	....	....	....	**4**	**0**	**0**	**0**	**6**	**0**	**0**	**0**	....
1994-95	**NY Islanders**	**NHL**	**26**	**3**	**13**	**16**	**32**	**1**	**0**	**0**	**61**	**4.9**	**-1**	....	....	....	....	....	....	....	....	....	....	....	....
	Montreal	**NHL**	**14**	**1**	**4**	**5**	**14**	**0**	**0**	**0**	**30**	**3.3**	**-2**	....	....	....	....	....	....	....	....	....	....	....	....
1995-96	**Montreal**	**NHL**	**61**	**5**	**23**	**28**	**79**	**2**	**0**	**0**	**122**	**4.1**	**7**	....	....	....	....	....	....	....	....	....	....	....	....
1996-97	**Montreal**	**NHL**	**65**	**10**	**20**	**30**	**43**	**5**	**0**	**1**	**177**	**5.6**	**3**	....	....	....	**5**	**0**	**0**	**0**	**6**	**0**	**0**	**0**	....
1997-98	**Montreal**	**NHL**	**74**	**13**	**31**	**44**	**70**	**8**	**0**	**2**	**166**	**7.8**	**16**	....	....	....	**9**	**3**	**4**	**7**	**10**	**2**	**0**	**0**	....
1998-99	**Montreal**	**NHL**	**62**	**13**	**21**	**34**	**77**	**8**	**0**	**3**	**143**	**9.1**	**-7**	**0**	**0.0**	**23:29**	....	....	....	....	....	....	....	....	....
99-2000	**Montreal**	**NHL**	**7**	**0**	**0**	**0**	**4**	**0**	**0**	**0**	**7**	**0.0**	**0**	**0**	**0.0**	**21:20**	....	....	....	....	....	....	....	....	....
	♦ New Jersey	**NHL**	**17**	**1**	**4**	**5**	**19**	**1**	**0**	**1**	**11**	**9.1**	**1**	**0**	**0.0**	**20:18**	**23**	**1**	**4**	**5**	**18**	**1**	**0**	**0**	**19:31**
2000-01	**NY Rangers**	**NHL**	**3**	**0**	**2**	**2**	**4**	**0**	**0**	**0**	**6**	**0.0**	**0**	**0**	**0.0**	**19:07**	....	....	....	....	....	....	....	....	....
2001-02	**NY Rangers**	**NHL**	**81**	**6**	**22**	**28**	**83**	**1**	**0**	**0**	**145**	**4.1**	**10**	**1**	**100.0**	**22:48**	....	....	....	....	....	....	....	....	....
	Russia	Olympics	6	1	3	4	4	....	....	....	....	....	....	....	....	....	....	....	....	....	....	....	....	....	....
2002-03	**NY Rangers**	**NHL**	**71**	**3**	**14**	**17**	**52**	**1**	**0**	**0**	**131**	**2.3**	**-7**	**0**	**0.0**	**21:24**	....	....	....	....	....	....	....	....	....
2003-04	**NY Rangers**	**NHL**	**56**	**3**	**15**	**18**	**53**	**1**	**0**	**0**	**83**	**3.6**	**-5**	**1**	**100.0**	**19:37**	....	....	....	....	....	....	....	....	....
	Philadelphia	**NHL**	**6**	**0**	**1**	**1**	**2**	**0**	**0**	**0**	**12**	**0.0**	**-1**	**0**	**0.0**	**22:57**	**17**	**1**	**5**	**6**	**12**	**0**	**0**	**0**	**24:56**
	NHL Totals		**683**	**82**	**255**	**337**	**671**	**39**	**0**	**9**	**1507**	**5.4**		**2**	**100.0**	**21:49**	**75**	**8**	**19**	**27**	**64**	**3**	**0**	**0**	**21:49**

NHL All-Rookie Team (1993)

Traded to **Montreal** by **NY Islanders** with Pierre Turgeon for Kirk Muller, Mathieu Schneider and Craig Darby, April 5, 1995. • Missed majority of 1999-2000 season recovering from knee injury suffered in exhibition game vs. Boston, September 27, 1999. Traded to **New Jersey** by **Montreal** for Sheldon Souray, Josh DeWolf and New Jersey's 2nd round choice (later traded to Washington – later traded to Tampa Bay – Tampa Bay selected Andreas Holmqvist) in 2001 Entry Draft, March 1, 2000. Signed as a free agent by **NY Rangers**, July 10, 2000. • Missed majority of 2000-01 season recovering from knee injury suffered in game vs. Montreal, November 11, 2000. Traded to **Philadelphia** by **NY Rangers** for Rick Kozak and Philadelphia's 2nd round choice in 2005 Entry Draft, March 8, 2004.

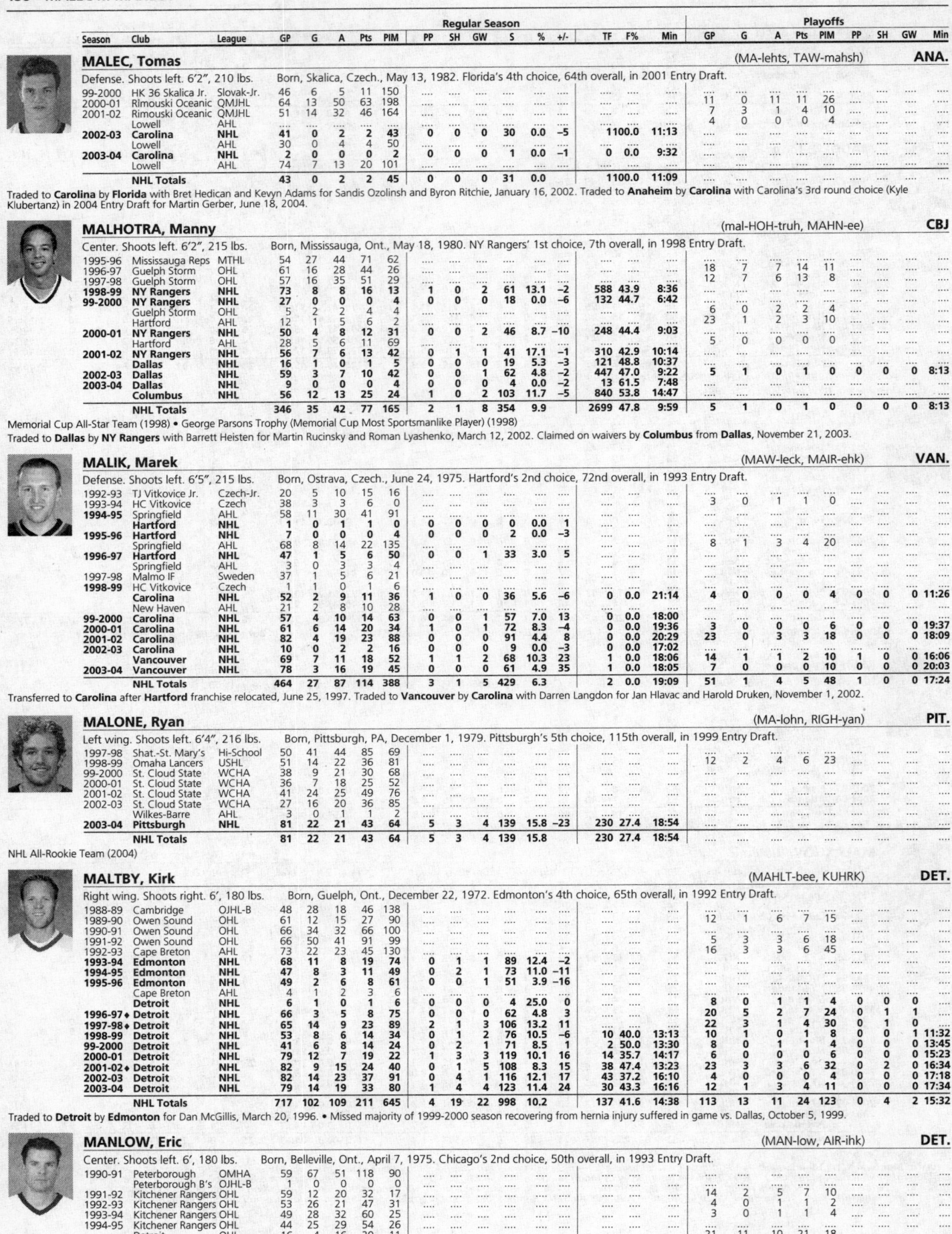

MALEC, Tomas
(MA-lehts, TAW-mahsh) **ANA.**

Defense. Shoots left. 6'2", 210 lbs. Born, Skalica, Czech., May 13, 1982. Florida's 4th choice, 64th overall, in 2001 Entry Draft.

			Regular Season														Playoffs								
Season	Club	League	GP	G	A	Pts	PIM	PP	SH	GW	S	%	+/-	TF	F%	Min	GP	G	A	Pts	PIM	PP	SH	GW	Min
99-2000	HK 36 Skalica Jr.	Slovak-Jr.	46	6	5	11	150	....	....	....	....	....	....	....	....	....	....	....	....	....	....	....	....	....	....
2000-01	Rimouski Oceanic	QMJHL	64	13	50	63	198	....	....	....	....	....	....	....	....	....	11	0	11	11	26	....	....	....	....
2001-02	Rimouski Oceanic	QMJHL	51	14	32	46	164	....	....	....	....	....	....	....	....	....	7	3	1	4	10	....	....	....	....
	Lowell	AHL	....	....	....	....	....	....	....	....	....	....	....	....	....	....	4	0	0	0	4	....	....	....	....
2002-03	**Carolina**	**NHL**	**41**	**0**	**2**	**2**	**43**	**0**	**0**	**0**	**30**	**0.0**	**–5**	**1**	**100.0**	**11:13**	....	....	....	....	....	....	....	....	....
	Lowell	AHL	30	0	4	4	50	....	....	....	....	....	....	....	....	....	....	....	....	....	....	....	....	....	....
2003-04	**Carolina**	**NHL**	**2**	**0**	**0**	**0**	**2**	**0**	**0**	**0**	**1**	**0.0**	**–1**	**0**	**0.0**	**9:32**	....	....	....	....	....	....	....	....	....
	Lowell	AHL	74	7	13	20	101	....	....	....	....	....	....	....	....	....	....	....	....	....	....	....	....	....	....
	NHL Totals		**43**	**0**	**2**	**2**	**45**	**0**	**0**	**0**	**31**	**0.0**		**1**	**100.0**	**11:09**	....	....	....	....	....	....	....	....	....

Traded to **Carolina** by **Florida** with Bret Hedican and Kevyn Adams for Sandis Ozolinsh and Byron Ritchie, January 16, 2002. Traded to **Anaheim** by **Carolina** with Carolina's 3rd round choice (Kyle Klubertanz) in 2004 Entry Draft for Martin Gerber, June 18, 2004.

MALHOTRA, Manny
(mal-HOH-truh, MAHN-ee) **CBJ**

Center. Shoots left. 6'2", 215 lbs. Born, Mississauga, Ont., May 18, 1980. NY Rangers' 1st choice, 7th overall, in 1998 Entry Draft.

Season	Club	League	GP	G	A	Pts	PIM	PP	SH	GW	S	%	+/-	TF	F%	Min	GP	G	A	Pts	PIM	PP	SH	GW	Min
1995-96	Mississauga Reps	MTHL	54	27	44	71	62	....	....	....	....	....	....	....	....	....	....	....	....	....	....	....	....	....	....
1996-97	Guelph Storm	OHL	61	16	28	44	26	....	....	....	....	....	....	....	....	....	18	7	7	14	11	....	....	....	....
1997-98	Guelph Storm	OHL	57	16	35	51	29	....	....	....	....	....	....	....	....	....	12	7	6	13	8	....	....	....	....
1998-99	**NY Rangers**	**NHL**	**73**	**8**	**8**	**16**	**13**	**1**	**0**	**2**	**61**	**13.1**	**–2**	**588**	**43.9**	**8:36**	....	....	....	....	....	....	....	....	....
99-2000	**NY Rangers**	**NHL**	**27**	**0**	**0**	**0**	**4**	**0**	**0**	**0**	**18**	**0.0**	**–6**	**132**	**44.7**	**6:42**	....	....	....	....	....	....	....	....	....
	Guelph Storm	OHL	5	2	2	4	4	....	....	....	....	....	....	....	....	....	6	0	2	2	4	....	....	....	....
	Hartford	AHL	12	1	5	6	2	....	....	....	....	....	....	....	....	....	23	1	2	3	10	....	....	....	....
2000-01	**NY Rangers**	**NHL**	**50**	**4**	**8**	**12**	**31**	**0**	**0**	**2**	**46**	**8.7**	**–10**	**248**	**44.4**	**9:03**	....	....	....	....	....	....	....	....	....
	Hartford	AHL	28	5	6	11	69	....	....	....	....	....	....	....	....	....	5	0	0	0	0	....	....	....	....
2001-02	**NY Rangers**	**NHL**	**56**	**7**	**6**	**13**	**42**	**0**	**1**	**1**	**41**	**17.1**	**–1**	**310**	**42.9**	**10:14**	....	....	....	....	....	....	....	....	....
	Dallas	**NHL**	**16**	**1**	**0**	**1**	**5**	**0**	**0**	**0**	**19**	**5.3**	**–3**	**121**	**48.8**	**10:37**	....	....	....	....	....	....	....	....	....
2002-03	**Dallas**	**NHL**	**59**	**3**	**7**	**10**	**42**	**0**	**0**	**1**	**62**	**4.8**	**–2**	**447**	**47.0**	**9:22**	**5**	**1**	**0**	**1**	**0**	**0**	**0**	**0**	**8:13**
2003-04	**Dallas**	**NHL**	**9**	**0**	**0**	**0**	**4**	**0**	**0**	**0**	**4**	**0.0**	**–2**	**13**	**61.5**	**7:48**	....	....	....	....	....	....	....	....	....
	Columbus	**NHL**	**56**	**12**	**13**	**25**	**24**	**1**	**0**	**2**	**103**	**11.7**	**–5**	**840**	**53.8**	**14:47**	....	....	....	....	....	....	....	....	....
	NHL Totals		**346**	**35**	**42**	**77**	**165**	**2**	**1**	**8**	**354**	**9.9**		**2699**	**47.8**	**9:59**	**5**	**1**	**0**	**1**	**0**	**0**	**0**	**0**	**8:13**

Memorial Cup All-Star Team (1998) • George Parsons Trophy (Memorial Cup Most Sportsmanlike Player) (1998)

Traded to **Dallas** by **NY Rangers** with Barrett Heisten for Martin Rucinsky and Roman Lyashenko, March 12, 2002. Claimed on waivers by **Columbus** from **Dallas**, November 21, 2003.

MALIK, Marek
(MAW-leck, MAIR-ehk) **VAN.**

Defense. Shoots left. 6'5", 215 lbs. Born, Ostrava, Czech., June 24, 1975. Hartford's 2nd choice, 72nd overall, in 1993 Entry Draft.

Season	Club	League	GP	G	A	Pts	PIM	PP	SH	GW	S	%	+/-	TF	F%	Min	GP	G	A	Pts	PIM	PP	SH	GW	Min
1992-93	TJ Vitkovice Jr.	Czech-Jr.	20	5	10	15	16	....	....	....	....	....	....	....	....	....	....	....	....	....	....	....	....	....	....
1993-94	HC Vitkovice	Czech	38	3	3	6	0	....	....	....	....	....	....	....	....	....	3	0	1	1	0	....	....	....	....
1994-95	Springfield	AHL	58	11	30	41	91	....	....	....	....	....	....	....	....	....	....	....	....	....	....	....	....	....	....
	Hartford	**NHL**	**1**	**0**	**1**	**1**	**0**	**0**	**0**	**0**	**0**	**0.0**	**1**	....	....	....	....	....	....	....	....	....	....	....	....
1995-96	**Hartford**	**NHL**	**7**	**0**	**0**	**0**	**4**	**0**	**0**	**0**	**2**	**0.0**	**–3**	....	....	....	....	....	....	....	....	....	....	....	....
	Springfield	AHL	68	8	14	22	135	....	....	....	....	....	....	....	....	....	8	1	3	4	20	....	....	....	....
1996-97	**Hartford**	**NHL**	**47**	**1**	**5**	**6**	**50**	**0**	**0**	**1**	**33**	**3.0**	**5**	....	....	....	....	....	....	....	....	....	....	....	....
	Springfield	AHL	3	0	3	3	4	....	....	....	....	....	....	....	....	....	....	....	....	....	....	....	....	....	....
1997-98	Malmo IF	Sweden	37	1	5	6	21	....	....	....	....	....	....	....	....	....	....	....	....	....	....	....	....	....	....
1998-99	HC Vitkovice	Czech	1	1	0	1	6	....	....	....	....	....	....	....	....	....	....	....	....	....	....	....	....	....	....
	Carolina	**NHL**	**52**	**2**	**9**	**11**	**36**	**1**	**0**	**0**	**36**	**5.6**	**–6**	**0**	**0.0**	**21:14**	**4**	**0**	**0**	**0**	**4**	**0**	**0**	**0**	**11:26**
	New Haven	AHL	21	2	8	10	28	....	....	....	....	....	....	....	....	....	....	....	....	....	....	....	....	....	....
99-2000	**Carolina**	**NHL**	**57**	**4**	**10**	**14**	**63**	**0**	**0**	**1**	**57**	**7.0**	**13**	**0**	**0.0**	**18:00**	....	....	....	....	....	....	....	....	....
2000-01	**Carolina**	**NHL**	**61**	**6**	**14**	**20**	**34**	**1**	**0**	**1**	**72**	**8.3**	**–4**	**0**	**0.0**	**19:36**	**3**	**0**	**0**	**0**	**6**	**0**	**0**	**0**	**19:37**
2001-02	**Carolina**	**NHL**	**82**	**4**	**19**	**23**	**88**	**0**	**0**	**0**	**91**	**4.4**	**8**	**0**	**0.0**	**20:29**	**23**	**0**	**3**	**3**	**18**	**0**	**0**	**0**	**18:09**
2002-03	**Carolina**	**NHL**	**10**	**0**	**2**	**2**	**16**	**0**	**0**	**0**	**9**	**0.0**	**–3**	**0**	**0.0**	**17:02**	....	....	....	....	....	....	....	....	....
	Vancouver	**NHL**	**69**	**7**	**11**	**18**	**52**	**1**	**1**	**2**	**68**	**10.3**	**23**	**1**	**0.0**	**18:06**	**14**	**1**	**1**	**2**	**10**	**1**	**0**	**0**	**16:06**
2003-04	**Vancouver**	**NHL**	**78**	**3**	**16**	**19**	**45**	**0**	**0**	**0**	**61**	**4.9**	**35**	**1**	**0.0**	**18:05**	**7**	**0**	**0**	**0**	**10**	**0**	**0**	**0**	**20:03**
	NHL Totals		**464**	**27**	**87**	**114**	**388**	**3**	**1**	**5**	**429**	**6.3**		**2**	**0.0**	**19:09**	**51**	**1**	**4**	**5**	**48**	**1**	**0**	**0**	**17:24**

Transferred to **Carolina** after **Hartford** franchise relocated, June 25, 1997. Traded to **Vancouver** by **Carolina** with Darren Langdon for Jan Hlavac and Harold Druken, November 1, 2002.

MALONE, Ryan
(MA-lohn, RIGH-yan) **PIT.**

Left wing. Shoots left. 6'4", 216 lbs. Born, Pittsburgh, PA, December 1, 1979. Pittsburgh's 5th choice, 115th overall, in 1999 Entry Draft.

Season	Club	League	GP	G	A	Pts	PIM	PP	SH	GW	S	%	+/-	TF	F%	Min	GP	G	A	Pts	PIM	PP	SH	GW	Min
1997-98	Shat.-St. Mary's	Hi-School	50	41	44	85	69	....	....	....	....	....	....	....	....	....	....	....	....	....	....	....	....	....	....
1998-99	Omaha Lancers	USHL	51	14	22	36	81	....	....	....	....	....	....	....	....	....	12	2	4	6	23	....	....	....	....
99-2000	St. Cloud State	WCHA	38	9	21	30	68	....	....	....	....	....	....	....	....	....	....	....	....	....	....	....	....	....	....
2000-01	St. Cloud State	WCHA	36	7	18	25	52	....	....	....	....	....	....	....	....	....	....	....	....	....	....	....	....	....	....
2001-02	St. Cloud State	WCHA	41	24	25	49	76	....	....	....	....	....	....	....	....	....	....	....	....	....	....	....	....	....	....
2002-03	St. Cloud State	WCHA	27	16	20	36	85	....	....	....	....	....	....	....	....	....	....	....	....	....	....	....	....	....	....
	Wilkes-Barre	AHL	3	0	1	1	2	....	....	....	....	....	....	....	....	....	....	....	....	....	....	....	....	....	....
2003-04	**Pittsburgh**	**NHL**	**81**	**22**	**21**	**43**	**64**	**5**	**3**	**4**	**139**	**15.8**	**–23**	**230**	**27.4**	**18:54**	....	....	....	....	....	....	....	....	....
	NHL Totals		**81**	**22**	**21**	**43**	**64**	**5**	**3**	**4**	**139**	**15.8**		**230**	**27.4**	**18:54**	....	....	....	....	....	....	....	....	....

NHL All-Rookie Team (2004)

MALTBY, Kirk
(MAHLT-bee, KUHRK) **DET.**

Right wing. Shoots right. 6', 180 lbs. Born, Guelph, Ont., December 22, 1972. Edmonton's 4th choice, 65th overall, in 1992 Entry Draft.

Season	Club	League	GP	G	A	Pts	PIM	PP	SH	GW	S	%	+/-	TF	F%	Min	GP	G	A	Pts	PIM	PP	SH	GW	Min
1988-89	Cambridge	OJHL-B	48	28	18	46	138	....	....	....	....	....	....	....	....	....	....	....	....	....	....	....	....	....	....
1989-90	Owen Sound	OHL	61	12	15	27	90	....	....	....	....	....	....	....	....	....	12	1	6	7	15	....	....	....	....
1990-91	Owen Sound	OHL	66	34	32	66	100	....	....	....	....	....	....	....	....	....	....	....	....	....	....	....	....	....	....
1991-92	Owen Sound	OHL	66	50	41	91	99	....	....	....	....	....	....	....	....	....	5	3	3	6	18	....	....	....	....
1992-93	Cape Breton	AHL	73	22	23	45	130	....	....	....	....	....	....	....	....	....	16	3	3	6	45	....	....	....	....
1993-94	**Edmonton**	**NHL**	**68**	**11**	**8**	**19**	**74**	**0**	**1**	**1**	**89**	**12.4**	**–2**	....	....	....	....	....	....	....	....	....	....	....	....
1994-95	**Edmonton**	**NHL**	**47**	**8**	**3**	**11**	**49**	**0**	**2**	**1**	**73**	**11.0**	**–11**	....	....	....	....	....	....	....	....	....	....	....	....
1995-96	**Edmonton**	**NHL**	**49**	**2**	**6**	**8**	**61**	**0**	**0**	**1**	**51**	**3.9**	**–16**	....	....	....	....	....	....	....	....	....	....	....	....
	Cape Breton	AHL	4	1	2	3	6	....	....	....	....	....	....	....	....	....	....	....	....	....	....	....	....	....	....
	Detroit	**NHL**	**6**	**1**	**0**	**1**	**6**	**0**	**0**	**0**	**4**	**25.0**	**0**	....	....	....	**8**	**0**	**1**	**1**	**4**	**0**	**0**	**0**	....
1996-97♦	**Detroit**	**NHL**	**66**	**3**	**5**	**8**	**75**	**0**	**0**	**0**	**62**	**4.8**	**3**	....	....	....	**20**	**5**	**2**	**7**	**24**	**0**	**1**	**1**	....
1997-98♦	**Detroit**	**NHL**	**65**	**14**	**9**	**23**	**89**	**2**	**1**	**3**	**106**	**13.2**	**11**	....	....	....	**22**	**3**	**1**	**4**	**30**	**0**	**1**	**0**	....
1998-99	**Detroit**	**NHL**	**53**	**8**	**6**	**14**	**34**	**0**	**1**	**2**	**76**	**10.5**	**–6**	**10**	**40.0**	**13:13**	**10**	**1**	**0**	**1**	**8**	**0**	**0**	**1**	**11:32**
99-2000	**Detroit**	**NHL**	**41**	**6**	**8**	**14**	**24**	**0**	**2**	**1**	**71**	**8.5**	**1**	**2**	**50.0**	**13:30**	**8**	**0**	**1**	**1**	**4**	**0**	**0**	**0**	**13:45**
2000-01	**Detroit**	**NHL**	**79**	**12**	**7**	**19**	**22**	**1**	**3**	**3**	**119**	**10.1**	**16**	**14**	**35.7**	**14:17**	**6**	**0**	**0**	**0**	**6**	**0**	**0**	**0**	**15:23**
2001-02♦	**Detroit**	**NHL**	**82**	**9**	**15**	**24**	**40**	**0**	**1**	**5**	**108**	**8.3**	**15**	**38**	**47.4**	**13:23**	**23**	**3**	**3**	**6**	**32**	**0**	**2**	**0**	**16:34**
2002-03	**Detroit**	**NHL**	**82**	**14**	**23**	**37**	**91**	**0**	**4**	**1**	**116**	**12.1**	**17**	**43**	**37.2**	**16:10**	**4**	**0**	**0**	**0**	**4**	**0**	**0**	**0**	**17:18**
2003-04	**Detroit**	**NHL**	**79**	**14**	**19**	**33**	**80**	**1**	**4**	**4**	**123**	**11.4**	**24**	**30**	**43.3**	**16:16**	**12**	**1**	**3**	**4**	**11**	**0**	**0**	**0**	**17:34**
	NHL Totals		**717**	**102**	**109**	**211**	**645**	**4**	**19**	**22**	**998**	**10.2**		**137**	**41.6**	**14:38**	**113**	**13**	**11**	**24**	**123**	**0**	**4**	**2**	**15:32**

Traded to **Detroit** by **Edmonton** for Dan McGillis, March 20, 1996. • Missed majority of 1999-2000 season recovering from hernia injury suffered in game vs. Dallas, October 5, 1999.

MANLOW, Eric
(MAN-low, AIR-ihk) **DET.**

Center. Shoots left. 6', 180 lbs. Born, Belleville, Ont., April 7, 1975. Chicago's 2nd choice, 50th overall, in 1993 Entry Draft.

Season	Club	League	GP	G	A	Pts	PIM	PP	SH	GW	S	%	+/-	TF	F%	Min	GP	G	A	Pts	PIM	PP	SH	GW	Min
1990-91	Peterborough	OMHA	59	67	51	118	90	....	....	....	....	....	....	....	....	....	....	....	....	....	....	....	....	....	....
	Peterborough B's	OJHL-B	1	0	0	0	0	....	....	....	....	....	....	....	....	....	....	....	....	....	....	....	....	....	....
1991-92	Kitchener Rangers	OHL	59	12	20	32	17	....	....	....	....	....	....	....	....	....	14	2	5	7	10	....	....	....	....
1992-93	Kitchener Rangers	OHL	53	26	21	47	31	....	....	....	....	....	....	....	....	....	4	0	1	1	2	....	....	....	....
1993-94	Kitchener Rangers	OHL	49	28	32	60	25	....	....	....	....	....	....	....	....	....	3	0	1	1	4	....	....	....	....
1994-95	Kitchener Rangers	OHL	44	25	29	54	26	....	....	....	....	....	....	....	....	....	....	....	....	....	....	....	....	....	....
	Detroit	OHL	16	4	16	20	11	....	....	....	....	....	....	....	....	....	21	11	10	21	18	....	....	....	....
1995-96	Indianapolis Ice	IHL	75	6	11	17	32	....	....	....	....	....	....	....	....	....	4	0	1	1	4	....	....	....	....

			Regular Season															Playoffs								
Season	Club	League	GP	G	A	Pts	PIM	PP	SH	GW	S	%	+/-	TF	F%	Min	GP	G	A	Pts	PIM	PP	SH	GW	Min
1996-97	Baltimore Bandits	AHL	36	6	6	12	13	....	....	....	....	....	....	....	....	....	3	0	0	0	0	....	....	....	....
	Columbus Chill	ECHL	32	18	18	36	20	....	....	....	....	....	....	....	....	....	....	....	....	....	....	....	....	....	....
1997-98	Indianapolis Ice	IHL	60	8	11	19	25	....	....	....	....	....	....	....	....	....	3	1	0	1	0	....	....	....	....
1998-99	Long Beach	IHL	51	9	19	28	30	....	....	....	....	....	....	....	....	....	8	0	0	0	8	....	....	....	....
	Florida Everblades	ECHL	18	8	15	23	11	....	....	....	....	....	....	....	....	....	....	....	....	....	....	....	....	....	....
99-2000	Florida Everblades	ECHL	26	14	24	38	24	....	....	....	....	....	....	....	....	....	....	....	....	....	....	....	....	....	....
	Providence Bruins	AHL	46	17	16	33	14	....	....	....	....	....	....	....	....	....	14	6	8	14	8	....	....	....	....
2000-01	**Boston**	**NHL**	**8**	**0**	**1**	**1**	**2**	**0**	**0**	**0**	**3**	**0.0**	**0**	**61**	**50.8**	**7:26**	....	....	....	....	....	....	....	....	....
	Providence Bruins	AHL	60	16	51	67	18	....	....	....	....	....	....	....	....	....	17	6	7	13	6	....	....	....	....
2001-02	**Boston**	**NHL**	**3**	**0**	**0**	**0**	**0**	**0**	**0**	**0**	**2**	**0.0**	**0**	**16**	**31.3**	**6:05**	....	....	....	....	....	....	....	....	....
	Providence Bruins	AHL	70	13	35	48	30	....	....	....	....	....	....	....	....	....	2	0	0	0	2	....	....	....	....
2002-03	**NY Islanders**	**NHL**	**8**	**2**	**1**	**3**	**4**	**1**	**0**	**0**	**7**	**28.6**	**2**	**84**	**54.8**	**12:27**	....	....	....	....	....	....	....	....	....
	Bridgeport	AHL	62	19	40	59	58	....	....	....	....	....	....	....	....	....	9	0	6	6	2	....	....	....	....
2003-04	**NY Islanders**	**NHL**	**18**	**0**	**2**	**2**	**2**	**0**	**0**	**0**	**10**	**0.0**	**–2**	**178**	**53.9**	**10:13**	....	....	....	....	....	....	....	....	....
	Bridgeport	AHL	40	8	27	35	16	....	....	....	....	....	....	....	....	....	1	0	0	0	2	....	....	....	....
	NHL Totals		**37**	**2**	**4**	**6**	**8**	**1**	**0**	**0**	**22**	**9.1**		**339**	**52.5**	**9:46**	....	....	....	....	....	....	....	....	....

Signed as a free agent by **Providence** (AHL), January 24, 2000. Signed as a free agent by **Boston**, July 11, 2000. Signed as a free agent by **NY Islanders**, July 21, 2002. Signed as a free agent by **Detroit**, July 21, 2004.

MANNING, Paul

(MAN-nihng, PAWL) **CBJ**

Defense. Shoots left. 6'4", 205 lbs. Born, Red Deer, Alta., April 15, 1979. Calgary's 3rd choice, 62nd overall, in 1998 Entry Draft.

Season	Club	League	GP	G	A	Pts	PIM	PP	SH	GW	S	%	+/-	TF	F%	Min	GP	G	A	Pts	PIM	PP	SH	GW	Min
1995-96	Red Deer	AMHL	32	8	32	40	....	....	....	....	....	....	....	....	....	....	....	....	....	....	....	....	....	....	....
1996-97	Red Deer Vipers	HJHL	36	9	33	42	....	....	....	....	....	....	....	....	....	....	....	....	....	....	....	....	....	....	....
1997-98	Colorado College	WCHA	30	1	5	6	16	....	....	....	....	....	....	....	....	....	....	....	....	....	....	....	....	....	....
1998-99	Colorado College	WCHA	41	3	10	13	75	....	....	....	....	....	....	....	....	....	....	....	....	....	....	....	....	....	....
99-2000	Colorado College	WCHA	39	6	17	23	26	....	....	....	....	....	....	....	....	....	....	....	....	....	....	....	....	....	....
2000-01	Colorado College	WCHA	34	2	28	30	48	....	....	....	....	....	....	....	....	....	....	....	....	....	....	....	....	....	....
2001-02	Syracuse Crunch	AHL	35	1	4	5	16	....	....	....	....	....	....	....	....	....	....	....	....	....	....	....	....	....	....
	Elmira Jackals	UHL	1	1	0	1	0	....	....	....	....	....	....	....	....	....	....	....	....	....	....	....	....	....	....
2002-03	**Columbus**	**NHL**	**8**	**0**	**0**	**0**	**2**	**0**	**0**	**0**	**4**	**0.0**	**0**	**0**	**0.0**	**13:02**	....	....	....	....	....	....	....	....	....
	Syracuse Crunch	AHL	52	2	5	7	37	....	....	....	....	....	....	....	....	....	....	....	....	....	....	....	....	....	....
2003-04	Hamburg Freezers	Germany	50	2	2	4	67	....	....	....	....	....	....	....	....	....	11	0	3	3	6	....	....	....	....
	NHL Totals		**8**	**0**	**0**	**0**	**2**	**0**	**0**	**0**	**4**	**0.0**		**0**	**0.0**	**13:02**	....	....	....	....	....	....	....	....	....

WCHA Second All-Star Team (2001)

Rights traded to **Columbus** by **Calgary** for Buffalo's 5th round choice (previously acquired, later traded to Detroit – Detroit selected Andreas Jamtin) in 2001 Entry Draft, June 24, 2001. Signed as a free agent by **Hamburg** (Germany), August 9, 2003.

MAPLETOFT, Justin

(MAPLE-tawft, JUHS-tihn) **NYI**

Center. Shoots left. 6'1", 180 lbs. Born, Lloydminster, Sask., January 11, 1981. NY Islanders' 9th choice, 130th overall, in 1999 Entry Draft.

Season	Club	League	GP	G	A	Pts	PIM	PP	SH	GW	S	%	+/-	TF	F%	Min	GP	G	A	Pts	PIM	PP	SH	GW	Min
1996-97	Calgary Royals	AMHL	36	25	36	51	....	....	....	....	....	....	....	....	....	....	....	....	....	....	....	....	....	....	....
	Red Deer Rebels	WHL	2	0	0	0	0	....	....	....	....	....	....	....	....	....	....	....	....	....	....	....	....	....	....
1997-98	Red Deer Rebels	WHL	65	9	4	13	41	....	....	....	....	....	....	....	....	....	....	....	....	....	....	....	....	....	....
1998-99	Red Deer Rebels	WHL	72	24	22	46	81	....	....	....	....	....	....	....	....	....	....	....	....	....	....	....	....	....	....
99-2000	Red Deer Rebels	WHL	72	39	57	96	135	....	....	....	....	....	....	....	....	....	4	2	1	3	28	....	....	....	....
2000-01	Red Deer Rebels	WHL	70	43	*77	*120	111	....	....	....	....	....	....	....	....	....	22	13	*21	34	59	....	....	....	....
2001-02	Bridgeport	AHL	80	13	20	33	60	....	....	....	....	....	....	....	....	....	20	7	10	17	23	....	....	....	....
2002-03	**NY Islanders**	**NHL**	**11**	**2**	**2**	**4**	**2**	**1**	**0**	**0**	**12**	**16.7**	**–1**	**138**	**41.3**	**12:17**	**2**	**0**	**0**	**0**	**0**	**0**	**0**	**0**	**7:23**
	Bridgeport	AHL	63	13	26	39	47	....	....	....	....	....	....	....	....	....	7	1	2	3	6	....	....	....	....
2003-04	**NY Islanders**	**NHL**	**27**	**1**	**4**	**5**	**6**	**0**	**0**	**0**	**15**	**6.7**	**–1**	**134**	**48.5**	**6:09**	....	....	....	....	....	....	....	....	....
	Bridgeport	AHL	36	10	13	23	59	....	....	....	....	....	....	....	....	....	....	....	....	....	....	....	....	....	....
	NHL Totals		**38**	**3**	**6**	**9**	**8**	**1**	**0**	**0**	**27**	**11.1**		**272**	**44.9**	**7:56**	**2**	**0**	**0**	**0**	**0**	**0**	**0**	**0**	**7:23**

WHL East First All-Star Team (2000, 2001) • Canadian Major Junior First All-Star Team (2001)

MARA, Paul

(MAIR-uh, PAWL) **PHX.**

Defense. Shoots left. 6'4", 219 lbs. Born, Ridgewood, NJ, September 7, 1979. Tampa Bay's 1st choice, 7th overall, in 1997 Entry Draft.

Season	Club	League	GP	G	A	Pts	PIM	PP	SH	GW	S	%	+/-	TF	F%	Min	GP	G	A	Pts	PIM	PP	SH	GW	Min
1994-95	Belmont Hill	Hi-School	28	5	17	22	28	....	....	....	....	....	....	....	....	....	....	....	....	....	....	....	....	....	....
1995-96	Belmont Hill	Hi-School	28	18	20	38	40	....	....	....	....	....	....	....	....	....	....	....	....	....	....	....	....	....	....
1996-97	Sudbury Wolves	OHL	44	9	34	43	61	....	....	....	....	....	....	....	....	....	....	....	....	....	....	....	....	....	....
1997-98	Sudbury Wolves	OHL	25	8	18	26	79	....	....	....	....	....	....	....	....	....	....	....	....	....	....	....	....	....	....
	Plymouth Whalers	OHL	25	8	15	23	30	....	....	....	....	....	....	....	....	....	15	3	14	17	30	....	....	....	....
1998-99	Plymouth Whalers	OHL	52	13	41	54	95	....	....	....	....	....	....	....	....	....	11	5	7	12	28	....	....	....	....
	Tampa Bay	**NHL**	**1**	**1**	**1**	**2**	**0**	**1**	**0**	**0**	**1**	**100.0**	**–3**	**0**	**0.0**	**19:34**	....	....	....	....	....	....	....	....	....
99-2000	**Tampa Bay**	**NHL**	**54**	**7**	**11**	**18**	**73**	**4**	**0**	**1**	**78**	**9.0**	**–27**	**0**	**0.0**	**22:13**	....	....	....	....	....	....	....	....	....
	Detroit Vipers	IHL	15	3	5	8	22	....	....	....	....	....	....	....	....	....	....	....	....	....	....	....	....	....	....
2000-01	**Tampa Bay**	**NHL**	**46**	**6**	**10**	**16**	**40**	**2**	**0**	**1**	**58**	**10.3**	**–17**	**0**	**0.0**	**23:06**	....	....	....	....	....	....	....	....	....
	Detroit Vipers	IHL	10	3	3	6	22	....	....	....	....	....	....	....	....	....	....	....	....	....	....	....	....	....	....
	Phoenix	**NHL**	**16**	**0**	**4**	**4**	**14**	**0**	**0**	**0**	**20**	**0.0**	**1**	**0**	**0.0**	**19:22**	....	....	....	....	....	....	....	....	....
2001-02	**Phoenix**	**NHL**	**75**	**7**	**17**	**24**	**58**	**2**	**0**	**0**	**112**	**6.3**	**–6**	**2**	**100.0**	**21:34**	**5**	**0**	**0**	**0**	**4**	**0**	**0**	**0**	**22:57**
2002-03	**Phoenix**	**NHL**	**73**	**10**	**15**	**25**	**78**	**1**	**0**	**0**	**95**	**10.5**	**–7**	**1**	**0.0**	**21:06**	....	....	....	....	....	....	....	....	....
2003-04	**Phoenix**	**NHL**	**81**	**6**	**36**	**42**	**48**	**1**	**0**	**0**	**140**	**4.3**	**–11**	**2**	**0.0**	**23:37**	....	....	....	....	....	....	....	....	....
	NHL Totals		**346**	**37**	**94**	**131**	**311**	**11**	**0**	**2**	**504**	**7.3**		**5**	**40.0**	**22:09**	**5**	**0**	**0**	**0**	**4**	**0**	**0**	**0**	**22:57**

Traded to **Phoenix** by **Tampa Bay** with Mike Johnson, Ruslan Zainullin and NY Islanders' 2nd round choice (previously acquired, Phoenix selected Matthew Spiller) in 2001 Entry Draft for Nikolai Khabibulin and Stan Neckar, March 5, 2001.

MARCHANT, Todd

(mahr-SHAHNT, TAWD) **CBJ**

Center. Shoots left. 5'10", 180 lbs. Born, Buffalo, NY, August 12, 1973. NY Rangers' 8th choice, 164th overall, in 1993 Entry Draft.

Season	Club	League	GP	G	A	Pts	PIM	PP	SH	GW	S	%	+/-	TF	F%	Min	GP	G	A	Pts	PIM	PP	SH	GW	Min
1990-91	Niagara Scenics	NAJHL	37	31	47	78	....	....	....	....	....	....	....	....	....	....	....	....	....	....	....	....	....	....	....
1991-92	Clarkson Knights	ECAC	32	20	12	32	32	....	....	....	....	....	....	....	....	....	....	....	....	....	....	....	....	....	....
1992-93	Clarkson Knights	ECAC	33	18	28	46	38	....	....	....	....	....	....	....	....	....	....	....	....	....	....	....	....	....	....
1993-94	Team USA	Nat-Tm	59	28	39	67	48	....	....	....	....	....	....	....	....	....	....	....	....	....	....	....	....	....	....
	United States	Olympics	8	1	1	2	6	....	....	....	....	....	....	....	....	....	....	....	....	....	....	....	....	....	....
	NY Rangers	**NHL**	**1**	**0**	**0**	**0**	**0**	**0**	**0**	**0**	**1**	**0.0**	**–1**	....	....	....	....	....	....	....	....	....	....	....	....
	Binghamton	AHL	8	2	7	9	6	....	....	....	....	....	....	....	....	....	....	....	....	....	....	....	....	....	....
	Edmonton	**NHL**	**3**	**0**	**1**	**1**	**2**	**0**	**0**	**0**	**5**	**0.0**	**–1**	....	....	....	....	....	....	....	....	....	....	....	....
	Cape Breton	AHL	3	1	4	5	2	....	....	....	....	....	....	....	....	....	5	1	1	2	0	....	....	....	....
1994-95	Cape Breton	AHL	38	22	25	47	25	....	....	....	....	....	....	....	....	....	....	....	....	....	....	....	....	....	....
	Edmonton	**NHL**	**45**	**13**	**14**	**27**	**32**	**3**	**2**	**2**	**95**	**13.7**	**–3**	....	....	....	....	....	....	....	....	....	....	....	....
1995-96	**Edmonton**	**NHL**	**81**	**19**	**19**	**38**	**66**	**2**	**3**	**2**	**221**	**8.6**	**–19**	....	....	....	....	....	....	....	....	....	....	....	....
1996-97	**Edmonton**	**NHL**	**79**	**14**	**19**	**33**	**44**	**0**	**4**	**3**	**202**	**6.9**	**11**	....	....	....	**12**	**4**	**2**	**6**	**12**	**0**	**3**	**1**	....
1997-98	**Edmonton**	**NHL**	**76**	**14**	**21**	**35**	**71**	**2**	**1**	**3**	**194**	**7.2**	**9**	....	....	....	**12**	**1**	**1**	**2**	**10**	**0**	**0**	**0**	....
1998-99	**Edmonton**	**NHL**	**82**	**14**	**22**	**36**	**65**	**3**	**1**	**2**	**183**	**7.7**	**3**	**1449**	**50.0**	**16:47**	**4**	**1**	**1**	**2**	**12**	**0**	**0**	**0**	**24:21**
99-2000	**Edmonton**	**NHL**	**82**	**17**	**23**	**40**	**70**	**0**	**1**	**0**	**170**	**10.0**	**7**	**1593**	**52.9**	**17:08**	**3**	**1**	**0**	**1**	**2**	**0**	**0**	**0**	**18:07**
2000-01	**Edmonton**	**NHL**	**71**	**13**	**26**	**39**	**51**	**0**	**4**	**2**	**113**	**11.5**	**1**	**1549**	**53.8**	**17:54**	**6**	**0**	**0**	**0**	**4**	**0**	**0**	**0**	**22:57**
2001-02	**Edmonton**	**NHL**	**82**	**12**	**22**	**34**	**41**	**0**	**3**	**1**	**124**	**9.7**	**7**	**1523**	**52.4**	**16:58**	....	....	....	....	....	....	....	....	....
2002-03	**Edmonton**	**NHL**	**77**	**20**	**40**	**60**	**48**	**7**	**1**	**3**	**146**	**13.7**	**13**	**1336**	**58.0**	**19:54**	**6**	**0**	**2**	**2**	**2**	**0**	**0**	**0**	**20:03**
2003-04	**Columbus**	**NHL**	**77**	**9**	**25**	**34**	**34**	**4**	**0**	**2**	**163**	**5.5**	**–17**	**1412**	**50.9**	**20:39**	....	....	....	....	....	....	....	....	....
	NHL Totals		**756**	**145**	**232**	**377**	**524**	**21**	**20**	**20**	**1617**	**9.0**		**8862**	**53.0**	**18:11**	**43**	**7**	**6**	**13**	**42**	**0**	**3**	**1**	**21:34**

ECAC Second All-Star Team (1993)

Traded to **Edmonton** by **NY Rangers** for Craig MacTavish, March 21, 1994. Signed as a free agent by **Columbus**, July 3, 2003.

MARCHMENT, Bryan

(MAHRCH-mehnt, BRIGH-uhn)

Defense. Shoots left. 6'1", 200 lbs. Born, Scarborough, Ont., May 1, 1969. Winnipeg's 1st choice, 16th overall, in 1987 Entry Draft.

			Regular Season														Playoffs								
Season	Club	League	GP	G	A	Pts	PIM	PP	SH	GW	S	%	+/-	TF	F%	Min	GP	G	A	Pts	PIM	PP	SH	GW	Min
1984-85	Tor. Young Nats	MTHL	69	14	35	49	229	....	....	....	....	....	....	....	....	....	....	....	....	....	....	....	....	....	....
1985-86	Belleville Bulls	OHL	57	5	15	20	225	....	....	....	....	....	....	....	....	....	21	0	7	7	83	....	....	....	....
1986-87	Belleville Bulls	OHL	52	6	38	44	238	....	....	....	....	....	....	....	....	....	6	0	4	4	17	....	....	....	....
1987-88	Belleville Bulls	OHL	56	7	51	58	200	....	....	....	....	....	....	....	....	....	6	1	3	4	19	....	....	....	....
1988-89	Belleville Bulls	OHL	43	14	36	50	118	....	....	....	....	....	....	....	....	....	5	0	1	1	12	....	....	....	....
	Winnipeg	NHL	2	0	0	0	2	0	0	0	1	0.0	0	....	....	....	....	....	....	....	....	....	....	....	....
1989-90	Winnipeg	NHL	7	0	2	2	28	0	0	0	5	0.0	0	....	....	....	....	....	....	....	....	....	....	....	....
	Moncton Hawks	AHL	56	4	19	23	217	....	....	....	....	....	....	....	....	....	....	....	....	....	....	....	....	....	....
1990-91	Winnipeg	NHL	28	2	2	4	91	0	0	0	24	8.3	-5	....	....	....	....	....	....	....	....	....	....	....	....
	Moncton Hawks	AHL	33	2	11	13	101	....	....	....	....	....	....	....	....	....	....	....	....	....	....	....	....	....	....
1991-92	Chicago	NHL	58	5	10	15	168	2	0	0	55	9.1	-4	....	....	....	16	1	0	1	36	0	0	0	....
1992-93	Chicago	NHL	78	5	15	20	313	1	0	1	75	6.7	15	....	....	....	4	0	0	0	12	0	0	0	....
1993-94	Chicago	NHL	13	1	4	5	42	0	0	0	18	5.6	-2	....	....	....	....	....	....	....	....	....	....	....	....
	Hartford	NHL	42	3	7	10	124	0	1	1	74	4.1	-12	....	....	....	....	....	....	....	....	....	....	....	....
1994-95	Edmonton	NHL	40	1	5	6	184	0	0	0	57	1.8	-11	....	....	....	....	....	....	....	....	....	....	....	....
1995-96	Edmonton	NHL	78	3	15	18	202	0	0	0	96	3.1	-7	....	....	....	....	....	....	....	....	....	....	....	....
1996-97	Edmonton	NHL	71	3	13	16	132	1	0	0	89	3.4	13	....	....	....	3	0	0	0	4	0	0	0	....
1997-98	Edmonton	NHL	27	0	4	4	58	0	0	0	23	0.0	-2	....	....	....	....	....	....	....	....	....	....	....	....
	Tampa Bay	NHL	22	2	4	6	43	0	0	0	20	10.0	-3	....	....	....	....	....	....	....	....	....	....	....	....
	San Jose	NHL	12	0	3	3	43	0	0	0	13	0.0	2	....	....	....	6	0	0	0	10	0	0	0	....
1998-99	San Jose	NHL	59	2	6	8	101	0	0	0	49	4.1	-7	0	0.0	17:43	6	0	0	0	4	0	0	0	16:41
99-2000	San Jose	NHL	49	0	4	4	72	0	0	0	51	0.0	3	0	0.0	18:55	11	2	1	3	12	0	0	0	18:40
2000-01	San Jose	NHL	75	7	11	18	204	0	1	3	73	9.6	15	1	100.0	18:12	5	0	1	1	2	0	0	0	17:00
2001-02	San Jose	NHL	72	2	20	22	178	0	0	0	68	2.9	22	0	0.0	18:47	12	1	1	2	10	0	0	0	15:29
2002-03	San Jose	NHL	67	2	9	11	108	0	0	0	66	3.0	-2	0	0.0	19:19	....	....	....	....	....	....	....	....	....
	Colorado	NHL	14	0	3	3	33	0	0	0	18	0.0	4	0	0.0	16:42	7	0	0	0	4	0	0	0	16:02
2003-04	Toronto	NHL	75	1	3	4	106	0	0	0	56	1.8	4	0	0.0	15:13	13	0	0	0	8	0	0	0	14:31
	NHL Totals		889	39	140	179	2232	4	2	5	931	4.2		1	100.0	17:54	83	4	3	7	102	0	0	0	16:15

OHL Second All-Star Team (1989)

Traded to **Chicago** by **Winnipeg** with Chris Norton for Troy Murray and Warren Rychel, July 22, 1991. Traded to **Hartford** by **Chicago** with Steve Larmer for Eric Weinrich and Patrick Poulin, November 2, 1993. Transferred to **Edmonton** from **Hartford** as compensation for Hartford's signing of free agent Steven Rice, August 30, 1994. Traded to **Tampa Bay** by **Edmonton** with Steve Kelly and Jason Bonsignore for Roman Hamrlik and Paul Comrie, December 30, 1997. Traded to **San Jose** by **Tampa Bay** with David Shaw and Tampa Bay's 1st round choice (later traded to Nashville – Nashville selected David Legwand) in 1998 Entry Draft for Andrei Nazarov and Florida's 1st round choice (previously acquired, Tampa Bay selected Vincent Lecavallier) in 1998 Entry Draft, March 24, 1998. Traded to **Colorado** by **San Jose** for Colorado's 3rd (later traded to Calgary – Calgary selected Ryan Donally) and 5th (later traded back to Colorado – Colorado selected Brad Richardson) round choices in 2003 Entry Draft, March 8, 2003. Signed as a free agent by **Toronto**, July 11, 2003.

MARKOV, Andrei

(MAHR-kahf, AHN-dray) **MTL.**

Defense. Shoots left. 6', 208 lbs. Born, Voskresensk, USSR, December 20, 1978. Montreal's 6th choice, 162nd overall, in 1998 Entry Draft.

Season	Club	League	GP	G	A	Pts	PIM	PP	SH	GW	S	%	+/-	TF	F%	Min	GP	G	A	Pts	PIM	PP	SH	GW	Min
1995-96	Voskresensk	CIS	38	0	0	0	14	....	....	....	....	....	....	....	....	....	....	....	....	....	....	....	....	....	....
1996-97	Voskresensk	Russia	43	8	4	12	32	....	....	....	....	....	....	....	....	....	2	1	1	2	0	....	....	....	....
1997-98	Voskresensk	Russia	43	10	5	15	83	....	....	....	....	....	....	....	....	....	....	....	....	....	....	....	....	....	....
1998-99	Dynamo Moscow	Russia	38	10	11	21	32	....	....	....	....	....	....	....	....	....	16	3	6	9	6	....	....	....	....
	Dynamo Moscow	EuroHL	12	7	5	12	12	....	....	....	....	....	....	....	....	....	6	2	2	4	4	....	....	....	....
99-2000	Dynamo Moscow	Russia	29	11	12	23	28	....	....	....	....	....	....	....	....	....	17	4	3	7	8	....	....	....	....
2000-01	Montreal	NHL	63	6	17	23	18	2	0	0	82	7.3	-6	2	50.0	16:53	....	....	....	....	....	....	....	....	....
	Quebec Citadelles	AHL	14	0	5	5	4	....	....	....	....	....	....	....	....	....	7	1	1	2	2	....	....	....	....
2001-02	Montreal	NHL	56	5	19	24	24	2	0	1	73	6.8	-1	0	0.0	17:15	12	1	3	4	8	0	0	1	15:53
	Quebec Citadelles	AHL	12	4	6	10	7	....	....	....	....	....	....	....	....	....	....	....	....	....	....	....	....	....	....
2002-03	Montreal	NHL	79	13	24	37	34	3	0	2	159	8.2	13	1	0.0	23:17	....	....	....	....	....	....	....	....	....
2003-04	Montreal	NHL	69	6	22	28	20	2	0	0	105	5.7	-2	2	50.0	21:29	11	1	4	5	8	0	0	1	22:52
	NHL Totals		267	30	82	112	96	9	0	3	419	7.2		5	40.0	20:03	23	2	7	9	16	0	0	2	19:14

MARKOV, Danny

(MAHR-kahf, DA-nee) **PHI.**

Defense. Shoots left. 6'1", 190 lbs. Born, Moscow, USSR, July 30, 1976. Toronto's 7th choice, 223rd overall, in 1995 Entry Draft.

Season	Club	League	GP	G	A	Pts	PIM	PP	SH	GW	S	%	+/-	TF	F%	Min	GP	G	A	Pts	PIM	PP	SH	GW	Min
1993-94	Spartak Moscow	CIS	13	1	0	1	6	....	....	....	....	....	....	....	....	....	1	0	0	0	0	....	....	....	....
1994-95	Spartak Moscow	CIS	39	0	1	1	36	....	....	....	....	....	....	....	....	....	....	....	....	....	....	....	....	....	....
1995-96	Spartak Moscow	CIS	38	2	0	2	12	....	....	....	....	....	....	....	....	....	2	0	0	0	2	....	....	....	....
1996-97	Spartak Moscow	Russia	39	3	6	9	41	....	....	....	....	....	....	....	....	....	....	....	....	....	....	....	....	....	....
	St. John's	AHL	10	2	4	6	18	....	....	....	....	....	....	....	....	....	11	2	6	8	14	....	....	....	....
1997-98	Toronto	NHL	25	2	5	7	28	1	0	0	15	13.3	0	....	....	....	....	....	....	....	....	....	....	....	....
	St. John's	AHL	52	3	23	26	124	....	....	....	....	....	....	....	....	....	2	0	1	1	0	....	....	....	....
1998-99	Toronto	NHL	57	4	8	12	47	0	0	0	34	11.8	5	0	0.0	18:41	17	0	6	6	18	0	0	0	22:24
99-2000	Toronto	NHL	59	0	10	10	28	0	0	0	38	0.0	13	1	0.0	20:08	12	0	3	3	10	0	0	0	21:05
2000-01	Toronto	NHL	59	3	13	16	34	1	0	2	49	6.1	6	0	0.0	19:02	11	1	1	2	12	0	0	0	21:30
2001-02	Phoenix	NHL	72	6	30	36	67	4	0	1	103	5.8	-7	0	0.0	22:55	....	....	....	....	....	....	....	....	....
	Russia	Olympics	5	0	1	1	0	....	....	....	....	....	....	....	....	....	....	....	....	....	....	....	....	....	....
2002-03	Phoenix	NHL	64	4	16	20	36	2	0	0	105	3.8	2	0	0.0	23:16	....	....	....	....	....	....	....	....	....
2003-04	Carolina	NHL	44	4	10	14	37	2	0	1	73	5.5	-6	0	0.0	23:39	....	....	....	....	....	....	....	....	....
	Philadelphia	NHL	34	2	3	5	58	1	0	1	27	7.4	0	0	0.0	21:16	18	1	2	3	25	0	0	1	23:03
	NHL Totals		414	25	95	120	335	11	0	5	444	5.6		1	0.0	21:17	58	2	12	14	65	0	0	1	22:09

Traded to **Phoenix** by **Toronto** for Robert Reichel, Travis Green and Craig Mills, June 12, 2001. Traded to **Carolina** by **Phoenix** with future considerations (Edmonton's 3rd round choice (previously acquired, later traded to NY Rangers - NY Rangers selected Billy Ryan) in 2004 Entry Draft, June 26, 2004) for David Tanabe and Igor Knyazev, June 21, 2003. Traded to **Philadelphia** by **Carolina** for Justin Williams, January 20, 2004.

MARLEAU, Patrick

(mahr-LOH, PAT-rihk) **S.J.**

Center. Shoots left. 6'2", 220 lbs. Born, Aneroid, Sask., September 15, 1979. San Jose's 1st choice, 2nd overall, in 1997 Entry Draft.

Season	Club	League	GP	G	A	Pts	PIM	PP	SH	GW	S	%	+/-	TF	F%	Min	GP	G	A	Pts	PIM	PP	SH	GW	Min
1993-94	Swift Current	SMHL	53	72	95	167	....	....	....	....	....	....	....	....	....	....	....	....	....	....	....	....	....	....	....
1994-95	Swift Current	SMHL	31	30	22	52	18	....	....	....	....	....	....	....	....	....	....	....	....	....	....	....	....	....	....
1995-96	Seattle	WHL	72	32	42	74	22	....	....	....	....	....	....	....	....	....	5	3	4	7	4	....	....	....	....
1996-97	Seattle	WHL	71	51	74	125	37	....	....	....	....	....	....	....	....	....	15	7	16	23	12	....	....	....	....
1997-98	San Jose	NHL	74	13	19	32	14	1	0	2	90	14.4	5	....	....	....	5	0	1	1	0	0	0	0	....
1998-99	San Jose	NHL	81	21	24	45	24	4	0	4	134	15.7	10	1121	43.4	15:11	6	2	1	3	4	2	0	0	11:08
99-2000	San Jose	NHL	81	17	23	40	36	3	0	3	161	10.6	-9	851	42.0	14:11	5	1	1	2	2	1	0	0	11:51
2000-01	San Jose	NHL	81	25	27	52	22	5	0	6	146	17.1	7	1088	44.8	16:17	6	2	0	2	4	0	0	0	14:50
2001-02	San Jose	NHL	79	21	23	44	40	3	0	5	121	17.4	9	897	47.3	14:04	12	6	5	11	6	1	0	3	15:50
2002-03	San Jose	NHL	82	28	29	57	33	8	1	3	172	16.3	-10	1403	47.3	18:31	....	....	....	....	....	....	....	....	....
2003-04	San Jose	NHL	80	28	29	57	24	9	0	5	220	12.7	-5	1014	41.6	18:12	17	8	4	12	6	4	1	2	19:16
	NHL Totals		558	153	174	327	193	33	1	28	1044	14.7		6374	44.6	16:05	51	19	12	31	22	8	1	5	15:56

WHL West First All-Star Team (1997)
Played in NHL All-Star Game (2004)

MARSHALL, Grant

(MAHR-shahl, GRANT) **N.J.**

Right wing. Shoots right. 6'1", 200 lbs. Born, Mississauga, Ont., June 9, 1973. Toronto's 2nd choice, 23rd overall, in 1992 Entry Draft.

Season	Club	League	GP	G	A	Pts	PIM	PP	SH	GW	S	%	+/-	TF	F%	Min	GP	G	A	Pts	PIM	PP	SH	GW	Min
1989-90	Tor. Young Nats	MTHL	39	15	28	43	56	....	....	....	....	....	....	....	....	....	....	....	....	....	....	....	....	....	....
1990-91	Ottawa 67's	OHL	26	6	11	17	25	....	....	....	....	....	....	....	....	....	1	0	0	0	0	....	....	....	....
1991-92	Ottawa 67's	OHL	61	32	51	83	132	....	....	....	....	....	....	....	....	....	11	6	11	17	11	....	....	....	....
1992-93	Ottawa 67's	OHL	30	14	29	43	83	....	....	....	....	....	....	....	....	....	....	....	....	....	....	....	....	....	....
	Newmarket	OHL	31	11	25	36	89	....	....	....	....	....	....	....	....	....	7	4	7	11	20	....	....	....	....
	St. John's	AHL	2	0	0	0	0	....	....	....	....	....	....	....	....	....	2	0	0	0	2	....	....	....	....
1993-94	St. John's	AHL	67	11	29	40	155	....	....	....	....	....	....	....	....	....	11	1	5	6	17	....	....	....	....
1994-95	Kalamazoo Wings	IHL	61	17	29	46	96	....	....	....	....	....	....	....	....	....	16	9	3	12	27	....	....	....	....
	Dallas	NHL	2	0	1	1	0	0	0	0	0	0.0	1	....	....	....	....	....	....	....	....	....	....	....	....
1995-96	Dallas	NHL	70	9	19	28	111	0	0	0	62	14.5	0	....	....	....	....	....	....	....	....	....	....	....	....

								Regular Season									Playoffs								
Season	Club	League	GP	G	A	Pts	PIM	PP	SH	GW	S	%	+/-	TF	F%	Min	GP	G	A	Pts	PIM	PP	SH	GW	Min
1996-97	Dallas	NHL	56	6	4	10	98	0	0	0	0	0.0	5	....	....	....	5	0	2	2	8	0	0	0	....
1997-98	Dallas	NHL	72	9	10	19	96	3	0	1	91	9.9	−2	....	....	....	17	0	2	2	*47	0	0	0	....
1998-99♦	Dallas	NHL	82	13	18	31	85	2	0	4	112	11.6	1	2	50.0	12:39	14	0	3	3	20	0	0	0	11:42
99-2000	Dallas	NHL	45	2	6	8	38	1	0	0	43	4.7	−5	3	0.0	11:19	14	0	1	1	4	0	0	0	10:08
2000-01	Dallas	NHL	75	13	24	37	64	4	0	1	93	14.0	1	16	56.3	11:05	9	0	0	0	0	0	0	0	11:15
2001-02	Columbus	NHL	81	15	18	33	86	6	0	4	152	9.9	−20	28	39.3	15:27	....	....	....	....	....	....	....	....	....
2002-03	Columbus	NHL	66	8	20	28	71	3	0	2	96	8.3	−8	26	46.2	13:56	....	....	....	....	....	....	....	....	....
	♦ New Jersey	NHL	10	1	3	4	7	0	0	0	17	5.9	−3	1	100.0	11:38	24	6	2	8	8	2	0	1	14:30
2003-04	New Jersey	NHL	65	8	7	15	67	5	0	2	76	10.5	−9	5	40.0	12:53	....	....	....	....	....	....	....	....	....
	NHL Totals		624	84	130	214	723	24	0	14	742	11.3		81	44.4	12:59	83	6	10	16	87	2	0	1	12:23

• Missed majority of 1990-91 season recovering from neck injury suffered in game vs. Sudbury (OHL), December 4, 1990. Transferred to **Dallas** from **Toronto** with Peter Zezel as compensation for Toronto's signing of free agent Mike Craig, August 10, 1994. Traded to **Columbus** by **Dallas** for Columbus' 2nd round choice (Loui Eriksson) in 2003 Entry Draft, August 29, 2001. Traded to **New Jersey** by **Columbus** for New Jersey's 4th round choice (later traded to Carolina – later traded to Calgary – Calgary selected Kristopher Hogg) in 2004 Entry Draft, March 10, 2003.

MARSHALL, Jason

(MAHR-shahl, JAY-suhn) **S.J.**

Defense. Shoots right. 6'2", 200 lbs. Born, Cranbrook, B.C., February 22, 1971. St. Louis' 1st choice, 9th overall, in 1989 Entry Draft.

Season	Club	League	GP	G	A	Pts	PIM	PP	SH	GW	S	%	+/-	TF	F%	Min	GP	G	A	Pts	PIM	PP	SH	GW	Min
1987-88	Columbia Valley	RMJHL	40	4	28	32	150	....	....	....	....	....	....	....	....	....	....	....	....	....	....	....	....	....	....
1988-89	Vernon Lakers	BCJHL	48	10	30	40	197	....	....	....	....	....	....	....	....	....	31	6	6	12	14	....	....	....	....
1989-90	Team Canada	Nat-Tm	73	1	11	12	57	....	....	....	....	....	....	....	....	....	....	....	....	....	....	....	....	....	....
1990-91	Tri-City	WHL	59	10	34	44	236	....	....	....	....	....	....	....	....	....	7	1	2	3	20	....	....	....	....
	Peoria Rivermen	IHL	....	....	....	....	....	....	....	....	....	....	....	....	....	....	18	0	1	1	48	....	....	....	....
1991-92	St. Louis	NHL	2	1	0	1	4	0	0	0	2	50.0	0	....	....	....	....	....	....	....	....	....	....	....	....
	Peoria Rivermen	IHL	78	4	18	22	178	....	....	....	....	....	....	....	....	....	10	0	1	1	16	....	....	....	....
1992-93	Peoria Rivermen	IHL	77	4	16	20	229	....	....	....	....	....	....	....	....	....	4	0	0	0	20	....	....	....	....
1993-94	Team Canada	Nat-Tm	41	3	10	13	60	....	....	....	....	....	....	....	....	....	....	....	....	....	....	....	....	....	....
	Peoria Rivermen	IHL	20	1	1	2	72	....	....	....	....	....	....	....	....	....	3	2	0	2	2	....	....	....	....
1994-95	San Diego Gulls	IHL	80	7	18	25	218	....	....	....	....	....	....	....	....	....	5	0	1	1	8	....	....	....	....
	Anaheim	NHL	1	0	0	0	0	0	0	0	1	0.0	−2	....	....	....	....	....	....	....	....	....	....	....	....
1995-96	Anaheim	NHL	24	0	1	1	42	0	0	0	9	0.0	3	....	....	....	....	....	....	....	....	....	....	....	....
	Baltimore Bandits	AHL	57	1	13	14	150	....	....	....	....	....	....	....	....	....	....	....	....	....	....	....	....	....	....
1996-97	Anaheim	NHL	73	1	9	10	140	0	0	0	34	2.9	6	....	....	....	7	0	1	1	4	0	0	0	....
1997-98	Anaheim	NHL	72	3	6	9	189	1	0	0	68	4.4	−8	....	....	....	....	....	....	....	....	....	....	....	....
1998-99	Anaheim	NHL	72	1	7	8	142	0	0	0	63	1.6	−5	0	0.0	19:06	4	1	0	1	10	1	0	0	21:29
99-2000	Anaheim	NHL	55	0	3	3	88	0	0	0	41	0.0	−10	2	50.0	16:33	....	....	....	....	....	....	....	....	....
2000-01	Anaheim	NHL	50	3	4	7	105	2	1	1	38	7.9	−12	1	0.0	14:36	....	....	....	....	....	....	....	....	....
	Washington	NHL	5	0	0	0	17	0	0	0	5	0.0	−1	0	0.0	11:48	....	....	....	....	....	....	....	....	....
2001-02	Minnesota	NHL	80	5	6	11	148	1	0	0	73	6.8	−8	0	0.0	16:18	....	....	....	....	....	....	....	....	....
2002-03	Minnesota	NHL	45	1	5	6	69	0	0	0	40	2.5	4	7	28.6	11:24	15	1	1	2	16	0	0	1	10:50
2003-04	Minnesota	NHL	12	1	4	5	18	1	0	0	16	6.3	−1	0	0.0	15:36	....	....	....	....	....	....	....	....	....
	Houston Aeros	AHL	49	7	12	19	87	....	....	....	....	....	....	....	....	....	....	....	....	....	....	....	....	....	....
	San Jose	NHL	12	0	2	2	8	0	0	0	14	0.0	−2	0	0.0	16:00	17	0	1	1	25	0	0	0	14:44
	NHL Totals		503	16	47	63	970	5	1	1	404	4.0		10	30.0	15:56	43	2	3	5	55	1	0	1	13:52

Traded to **Anaheim** by **St. Louis** for Bill Houlder, August 29, 1994. Traded to **Washington** by **Anaheim** for Alexei Tezikov and Edmonton's 4th round choice (previously acquired, Anaheim selected Brandon Rogers) in 2001 Entry Draft, March 13, 2001. Signed as a free agent by **Minnesota**, July 2, 2001. Traded to **San Jose** by **Minnesota** for San Jose's 5th round choice (Jean-Claude Sawyer) in 2004 Entry Draft, March 3, 2004.

MARTENSSON, Tony

(MOHR-tehn-suhn, TOH-nee) **ANA.**

Center. Shoots left. 6', 189 lbs. Born, Upplands Vasby, Sweden, June 23, 1980. Anaheim's 9th choice, 224th overall, in 2001 Entry Draft.

Season	Club	League	GP	G	A	Pts	PIM	PP	SH	GW	S	%	+/-	TF	F%	Min	GP	G	A	Pts	PIM	PP	SH	GW	Min
1997-98	Arlanda Mastra	Swede-2	12	2	4	6	0	....	....	....	....	....	....	....	....	....	2	0	0	0	0	....	....	....	....
1998-99	Arlanda Mastra	Swede-2	37	8	22	30	8	....	....	....	....	....	....	....	....	....	2	0	0	0	0	....	....	....	....
99-2000	Arlanda Mastra	Swede-2	44	21	28	49	14	....	....	....	....	....	....	....	....	....	....	....	....	....	....	....	....	....	....
2000-01	Brynas IF Gavle	Sweden	50	15	11	26	20	....	....	....	....	....	....	....	....	....	4	0	1	1	2	....	....	....	....
	Brynas IF Gavle Jr.	Swede-Jr.	1	1	0	1	0	....	....	....	....	....	....	....	....	....	....	....	....	....	....	....	....	....	....
2001-02	Brynas IF Gavle	Sweden	50	9	17	26	14	....	....	....	....	....	....	....	....	....	4	1	3	4	0	....	....	....	....
2002-03	Cincinnati	AHL	79	17	36	53	20	....	....	....	....	....	....	....	....	....	....	....	....	....	....	....	....	....	....
2003-04	Anaheim	NHL	6	1	1	2	0	0	0	0	4	25.0	−2	18	44.4	6:58	....	....	....	....	....	....	....	....	....
	Cincinnati	AHL	67	16	34	50	20	....	....	....	....	....	....	....	....	....	9	3	10	13	4	....	....	....	....
	NHL Totals		6	1	1	2	0	0	0	0	4	25.0		18	44.4	6:58	....	....	....	....	....	....	....	....	....

Signed as a free agent by **Linkopings HC** (Sweden), May 17, 2004.

MARTIN, Paul

(MAHR-tihn, PAWL) **N.J.**

Defense. Shoots left. 6'1", 190 lbs. Born, Minneapolis, MN, March 5, 1981. New Jersey's 5th choice, 62nd overall, in 2000 Entry Draft.

Season	Club	League	GP	G	A	Pts	PIM	PP	SH	GW	S	%	+/-	TF	F%	Min	GP	G	A	Pts	PIM	PP	SH	GW	Min
1998-99	Elk River Elks	Hi-School	24	9	11	20	....	....	....	....	....	....	....	....	....	....	....	....	....	....	....	....	....	....	....
99-2000	Elk River Elks	Hi-School	24	15	35	50	26	....	....	....	....	....	....	....	....	....	....	....	....	....	....	....	....	....	....
2000-01	U. of Minnesota	WCHA	38	3	17	20	8	....	....	....	....	....	....	....	....	....	....	....	....	....	....	....	....	....	....
2001-02	U. of Minnesota	WCHA	44	8	30	38	22	....	....	....	....	....	....	....	....	....	....	....	....	....	....	....	....	....	....
2002-03	U. of Minnesota	WCHA	45	9	30	39	32	....	....	....	....	....	....	....	....	....	....	....	....	....	....	....	....	....	....
2003-04	New Jersey	NHL	70	6	18	24	4	2	0	2	82	7.3	12	0	0.0	20:08	5	1	1	2	4	1	0	0	23:40
	NHL Totals		70	6	18	24	4	2	0	2	82	7.3		0	0.0	20:08	5	1	1	2	4	1	0	0	23:40

Minnesota High School Player of the Year (1999) • WCHA All-Rookie Team (2001) • WCHA Second All-Star Team (2002, 2003) • NCAA West Second All-American Team (2003) • NCAA Championship All-Tournament Team (2003)

MARTINEK, Radek

(MAHR-tih-nehk, RA-dehk) **NYI**

Defense. Shoots right. 6'1", 200 lbs. Born, Havlickuv Brod, Czech., August 31, 1976. NY Islanders' 12th choice, 228th overall, in 1999 Entry Draft.

Season	Club	League	GP	G	A	Pts	PIM	PP	SH	GW	S	%	+/-	TF	F%	Min	GP	G	A	Pts	PIM	PP	SH	GW	Min
1996-97	Ceske Budejovice	Czech	52	3	5	8	40	....	....	....	....	....	....	....	....	....	5	0	1	1	2	....	....	....	....
	Ceske Budejovice	EHL	6	0	0	0	0	....	....	....	....	....	....	....	....	....	2	0	0	0	0	....	....	....	....
1997-98	Ceske Budejovice	Czech	42	2	7	9	36	....	....	....	....	....	....	....	....	....	....	....	....	....	....	....	....	....	....
1998-99	Ceske Budejovice	Czech	52	12	13	25	50	....	....	....	....	....	....	....	....	....	3	0	2	2	....	....	....	....	....
99-2000	Ceske Budejovice	Czech	45	5	18	23	24	....	....	....	....	....	....	....	....	....	3	0	0	0	6	....	....	....	....
2000-01	Ceske Budejovice	Czech	44	8	10	18	45	....	....	....	....	....	....	....	....	....	....	....	....	....	....	....	....	....	....
2001-02	NY Islanders	NHL	23	1	4	5	16	0	0	1	25	4.0	5	0	0.0	21:07	....	....	....	....	....	....	....	....	....
2002-03	NY Islanders	NHL	66	2	11	13	26	0	0	1	67	3.0	15	0	0.0	17:15	4	0	0	0	4	0	0	0	10:16
	Bridgeport	AHL	3	0	3	3	2	....	....	....	....	....	....	....	....	....	....	....	....	....	....	....	....	....	....
2003-04	NY Islanders	NHL	47	4	3	7	43	0	0	1	48	8.3	−9	0	0.0	13:03	5	0	1	1	0	0	0	0	12:12
	NHL Totals		136	7	18	25	85	0	0	3	140	5.0		0	0.0	16:27	9	0	1	1	4	0	0	0	11:20

• Missed majority of 2001-02 season recovering from knee injury suffered in game vs. NY Rangers, November 11, 2001.

MARTINS, Steve

(MAHR-tihns, STEEV)

Center. Shoots left. 5'9", 185 lbs. Born, Gatineau, Que., April 13, 1972. Hartford's 1st choice, 5th overall, in 1994 Supplemental Draft.

Season	Club	League	GP	G	A	Pts	PIM	PP	SH	GW	S	%	+/-	TF	F%	Min	GP	G	A	Pts	PIM	PP	SH	GW	Min
1988-89	L'Outaouais	QAAA	38	18	33	51	70	....	....	....	....	....	....	....	....	....	....	....	....	....	....	....	....	....	....
1989-90	Choate-Rosemary	Hi-School	STATISTICS NOT AVAILABLE																						
1990-91	Choate-Rosemary	Hi-School	STATISTICS NOT AVAILABLE																						
1991-92	Harvard Crimson	ECAC	20	13	14	27	26	....	....	....	....	....	....	....	....	....	....	....	....	....	....	....	....	....	....
1992-93	Harvard Crimson	ECAC	18	6	8	14	40	....	....	....	....	....	....	....	....	....	....	....	....	....	....	....	....	....	....
1993-94	Harvard Crimson	ECAC	32	25	35	60	*93	....	....	....	....	....	....	....	....	....	....	....	....	....	....	....	....	....	....
1994-95	Harvard Crimson	ECAC	28	15	23	38	93	....	....	....	....	....	....	....	....	....	....	....	....	....	....	....	....	....	....
1995-96	Hartford	NHL	23	1	3	4	8	0	0	0	27	3.7	−3	....	....	....	....	....	....	....	....	....	....	....	....
	Springfield	AHL	30	9	20	29	10	....	....	....	....	....	....	....	....	....	....	....	....	....	....	....	....	....	....
1996-97	Hartford	NHL	2	0	1	1	0	0	0	0	2	0.0	0	....	....	....	....	....	....	....	....	....	....	....	....
	Springfield	AHL	63	12	31	43	78	....	....	....	....	....	....	....	....	....	17	1	3	4	26	....	....	....	....
1997-98	Carolina	NHL	3	0	0	0	0	0	0	0	0	0.0	0	....	....	....	....	....	....	....	....	....	....	....	....
	Chicago Wolves	IHL	78	20	41	61	122	....	....	....	....	....	....	....	....	....	21	6	14	20	28	....	....	....	....
1998-99	Ottawa	NHL	36	4	3	7	10	1	0	1	27	14.8	4	191	56.0	8:28	....	....	....	....	....	....	....	....	....
	Detroit Vipers	IHL	4	1	6	7	16	....	....	....	....	....	....	....	....	....	....	....	....	....	....	....	....	....	....

			Regular Season														Playoffs								
Season	Club	League	GP	G	A	Pts	PIM	PP	SH	GW	S	%	+/-	TF	F%	Min	GP	G	A	Pts	PIM	PP	SH	GW	Min
99-2000	Ottawa	NHL	2	1	0	1	0	0	0	0	3	33.3	–1	3	0.0	11:10	....	....	....	....	....	....	....	....	....
	Tampa Bay	NHL	57	5	7	12	37	0	1	1	62	8.1	–11	806	50.9	13:27	....	....	....	....	....	....	....	....	....
2000-01	Tampa Bay	NHL	20	1	1	2	13	0	0	0	18	5.6	–9	184	52.2	9:35	....	....	....	....	....	....	....	....	....
	Detroit Vipers	IHL	8	5	4	9	4	....	....	....	....	....	....	....	....	....	....	....	....	....	....	....	....	....	....
	NY Islanders	NHL	39	1	3	4	20	0	1	0	28	3.6	–7	302	58.0	9:41	....	....	....	....	....	....	....	....	....
	Chicago Wolves	IHL	5	1	2	3	0	....	....	....	....	....	....	....	....	....	16	1	6	7	22	....	....	....	....
2001-02	Ottawa	NHL	14	1	0	1	4	0	0	0	11	9.1	1	121	55.4	9:33	2	0	0	0	0	0	0	0	7:13
	Grand Rapids	AHL	51	10	21	31	66	....	....	....	....	....	....	....	....	....	3	0	0	0	0	....	....	....	....
2002-03	Ottawa	NHL	14	2	3	5	10	0	0	0	13	15.4	3	111	55.9	9:45	....	....	....	....	....	....	....	....	....
	Binghamton	AHL	26	5	11	16	31	....	....	....	....	....	....	....	....	....	....	....	....	....	....	....	....	....	....
	St. Louis	NHL	28	3	3	6	18	0	1	0	25	12.0	–8	369	54.7	13:38	2	0	1	1	0	0	0	0	9:23
2003-04	St. Louis	NHL	25	1	0	1	22	0	1	0	27	3.7	–7	172	61.1	10:29	1	0	0	0	0	0	0	0	5:29
	Worcester IceCats	AHL	22	4	9	13	16	....	....	....	....	....	....	....	....	....	....	....	....	....	....	....	....	....	....
	NHL Totals		263	20	24	44	142	1	4	2	243	8.2		2259	54.2	10:58	5	0	1	1	0	0	0	0	7:44

ECAC First All-Star Team (1994) • ECAC Player of the Year (1994) • NCAA East First All-American Team (1994) • NCAA Final Four All-Tournament Team (1994)

Transferred to **Carolina** after **Hartford** franchise relocated, June 25, 1997. Signed as a free agent by **Ottawa**, July 20, 1998. Claimed on waivers by **Tampa Bay** from **Ottawa**, October 29, 1999. Traded to **NY Islanders** by **Tampa Bay** for future considerations, January 3, 2001. Signed as a free agent by **Ottawa**, August 30, 2001. Claimed on waivers by **St. Louis** from **Ottawa**, January 15, 2003.

MATTEUCCI, Mike

(ma-TEW-chee, MIGHK)

Defense. Shoots left. 6'3", 210 lbs. Born, Trail, B.C., December 27, 1971.

Season	Club	League	GP	G	A	Pts	PIM	PP	SH	GW	S	%	+/-	TF	F%	Min	GP	G	A	Pts	PIM	PP	SH	GW	Min
1991-92	Estevan Bruins	SJHL	STATISTICS NOT AVAILABLE																						
1992-93	Lake Superior	CCHA	19	1	3	4	16	....	....	....	....	....	....	....	....	....	....	....	....	....	....	....	....	....	....
1993-94	Lake Superior	CCHA	45	6	11	17	64	....	....	....	....	....	....	....	....	....	....	....	....	....	....	....	....	....	....
1994-95	Lake Superior	CCHA	38	3	11	14	52	....	....	....	....	....	....	....	....	....	....	....	....	....	....	....	....	....	....
1995-96	Lake Superior	CCHA	40	3	13	16	82	....	....	....	....	....	....	....	....	....	....	....	....	....	....	....	....	....	....
	Los Angeles	IHL	4	0	0	0	7	....	....	....	....	....	....	....	....	....	....	....	....	....	....	....	....	....	....
1996-97	Long Beach	IHL	81	4	4	8	254	....	....	....	....	....	....	....	....	....	18	0	1	1	42	....	....	....	....
1997-98	Long Beach	IHL	79	1	7	8	258	....	....	....	....	....	....	....	....	....	17	0	2	2	57	....	....	....	....
1998-99	Long Beach	IHL	79	3	9	12	253	....	....	....	....	....	....	....	....	....	8	0	1	1	12	....	....	....	....
99-2000	Long Beach	IHL	64	0	4	4	170	....	....	....	....	....	....	....	....	....	6	0	0	0	16	....	....	....	....
2000-01	Minnesota	NHL	3	0	0	0	2	0	0	0	3	0.0	–2	1	100.0	11:29	....	....	....	....	....	....	....	....	....
	Cleveland	IHL	69	0	7	7	189	....	....	....	....	....	....	....	....	....	4	0	0	0	15	....	....	....	....
2001-02	Minnesota	NHL	3	0	0	0	2	0	0	0	0	0.0	1	0	0.0	10:06	....	....	....	....	....	....	....	....	....
	Houston Aeros	AHL	69	3	10	13	128	....	....	....	....	....	....	....	....	....	14	1	1	2	33	....	....	....	....
2002-03	Albany River Rats	AHL	68	1	3	4	133	....	....	....	....	....	....	....	....	....	....	....	....	....	....	....	....	....	....
2003-04	Albany River Rats	AHL	73	1	12	13	107	....	....	....	....	....	....	....	....	....	....	....	....	....	....	....	....	....	....
	NHL Totals		6	0	0	0	4	0	0	0	3	0.0		1	100.0	10:48	....	....	....	....	....	....	....	....	....

Signed as a free agent by **Edmonton**, September 10, 1998. Traded to **Boston** by **Edmonton** for Kay Whitmore, December 29, 1999. Signed as a free agent by **Minnesota**, July 20, 2000. Signed as a free agent by **New Jersey**, July 12, 2002.

MATVICHUK, Richard

(MAT-vih-chuhk, RIH-chuhrd) **N.J.**

Defense. Shoots left. 6'2", 215 lbs. Born, Edmonton, Alta., February 5, 1973. Minnesota's 1st choice, 8th overall, in 1991 Entry Draft.

Season	Club	League	GP	G	A	Pts	PIM	PP	SH	GW	S	%	+/-	TF	F%	Min	GP	G	A	Pts	PIM	PP	SH	GW	Min
1988-89	Ft. Saskatchewan	AJHL	58	7	36	43	147	....	....	....	....	....	....	....	....	....	....	....	....	....	....	....	....	....	....
1989-90	Saskatoon Blades	WHL	56	8	24	32	126	....	....	....	....	....	....	....	....	....	10	2	8	10	16	....	....	....	....
1990-91	Saskatoon Blades	WHL	68	13	36	49	117	....	....	....	....	....	....	....	....	....	....	....	....	....	....	....	....	....	....
1991-92	Saskatoon Blades	WHL	58	14	40	54	126	....	....	....	....	....	....	....	....	....	22	1	9	10	61	....	....	....	....
1992-93	Minnesota	NHL	53	2	3	5	26	1	0	0	51	3.9	–8	....	....	....	....	....	....	....	....	....	....	....	....
	Kalamazoo Wings	IHL	3	0	1	1	6	....	....	....	....	....	....	....	....	....	....	....	....	....	....	....	....	....	....
1993-94	Dallas	NHL	25	0	3	3	22	0	0	0	18	0.0	1	....	....	....	7	1	1	2	12	1	0	0	....
	Kalamazoo Wings	IHL	43	8	17	25	84	....	....	....	....	....	....	....	....	....	....	....	....	....	....	....	....	....	....
1994-95	Dallas	NHL	14	0	2	2	14	0	0	0	21	0.0	–7	....	....	....	5	0	2	2	4	0	0	0	....
	Kalamazoo Wings	IHL	17	0	6	6	16	....	....	....	....	....	....	....	....	....	....	....	....	....	....	....	....	....	....
1995-96	Dallas	NHL	73	6	16	22	71	0	0	1	81	7.4	4	....	....	....	....	....	....	....	....	....	....	....	....
1996-97	Dallas	NHL	57	5	7	12	87	0	2	0	83	6.0	1	....	....	....	7	0	1	1	20	0	0	0	....
1997-98	Dallas	NHL	74	3	15	18	63	0	0	0	71	4.2	7	....	....	....	16	1	1	2	14	0	0	0	....
1998-99♦	Dallas	NHL	64	3	9	12	51	1	0	0	54	5.6	23	0	0.0	21:19	22	1	5	6	20	0	0	0	22:40
99-2000	Dallas	NHL	70	4	21	25	42	0	0	1	73	5.5	7	0	0.0	24:27	23	2	5	7	14	0	0	0	25:51
2000-01	Dallas	NHL	78	4	16	20	62	2	0	1	85	4.7	5	1	100.0	22:53	10	0	0	0	14	0	0	0	22:43
2001-02	Dallas	NHL	82	9	12	21	52	4	0	2	109	8.3	11	1	0.0	23:47	....	....	....	....	....	....	....	....	....
2002-03	Dallas	NHL	68	1	5	6	58	0	0	1	59	1.7	1	3	0.0	19:23	12	0	3	3	8	0	0	0	19:55
2003-04	Dallas	NHL	75	1	20	21	36	0	0	1	85	1.2	0	2	50.0	21:50	5	0	1	1	8	0	0	0	22:15
	NHL Totals		733	38	129	167	584	8	2	7	790	4.8		7	28.6	22:21	107	5	19	24	114	1	0	0	23:12

WHL East First All-Star Team (1992)

Transferred to **Dallas** after **Minnesota** franchise relocated, June 9, 1993. Signed as a free agent by **New Jersey**, July 12, 2004.

MAULDIN, Greg

(MAWL-dihn, GREHG) **CBJ**

Center. Shoots right. 5'11", 180 lbs. Born, Boston, MA, June 10, 1982. Columbus' 10th choice, 199th overall, in 2002 Entry Draft.

Season	Club	League	GP	G	A	Pts	PIM	PP	SH	GW	S	%	+/-	TF	F%	Min	GP	G	A	Pts	PIM	PP	SH	GW	Min
99-2000	Boston Jr. Bruins	EJHL	58	45	42	87	14	....	....	....	....	....	....	....	....	....	....	....	....	....	....	....	....	....	....
2000-01	Boston Jr. Bruins	EJHL	53	48	58	106	73	....	....	....	....	....	....	....	....	....	....	....	....	....	....	....	....	....	....
2001-02	Massachusetts	H-East	33	12	12	24	10	....	....	....	....	....	....	....	....	....	....	....	....	....	....	....	....	....	....
2002-03	Massachusetts	H-East	36	21	20	41	26	....	....	....	....	....	....	....	....	....	....	....	....	....	....	....	....	....	....
2003-04	Massachusetts	H-East	29	15	14	29	15	....	....	....	....	....	....	....	....	....	....	....	....	....	....	....	....	....	....
	Columbus	NHL	6	0	0	0	4	0	0	0	6	0.0	–2	0	0.0	8:47	....	....	....	....	....	....	....	....	....
	Syracuse Crunch	AHL	2	0	0	0	0	....	....	....	....	....	....	....	....	....	1	0	0	0	0	....	....	....	....
	NHL Totals		6	0	0	0	4	0	0	0	6	0.0		0	0.0	8:47	....	....	....	....	....	....	....	....	....

EJHL First All-Star Team (2000, 2001) • EJHL MVP (2000)

MAY, Brad

(MAY, BRAD) **VAN.**

Left wing. Shoots left. 6'1", 217 lbs. Born, Toronto, Ont., November 29, 1971. Buffalo's 1st choice, 14th overall, in 1990 Entry Draft.

Season	Club	League	GP	G	A	Pts	PIM	PP	SH	GW	S	%	+/-	TF	F%	Min	GP	G	A	Pts	PIM	PP	SH	GW	Min
1987-88	Markham	OMHA	31	22	37	59	58	....	....	....	....	....	....	....	....	....	....	....	....	....	....	....	....	....	....
	Markham	MTJHL	6	1	1	2	21	....	....	....	....	....	....	....	....	....	....	....	....	....	....	....	....	....	....
1988-89	Niagara Falls	OHL	65	8	14	22	304	....	....	....	....	....	....	....	....	....	17	0	1	1	55	....	....	....	....
1989-90	Niagara Falls	OHL	61	32	58	90	223	....	....	....	....	....	....	....	....	....	16	9	13	22	64	....	....	....	....
1990-91	Niagara Falls	OHL	34	37	32	69	93	....	....	....	....	....	....	....	....	....	14	11	14	25	53	....	....	....	....
1991-92	Buffalo	NHL	69	11	6	17	309	1	0	3	82	13.4	–12	....	....	....	7	1	4	5	2	0	0	1	....
1992-93	Buffalo	NHL	82	13	13	26	242	0	0	1	114	11.4	3	....	....	....	8	1	1	2	14	0	0	1	....
1993-94	Buffalo	NHL	84	18	27	45	171	3	0	3	166	10.8	–6	....	....	....	7	0	2	2	9	0	0	0	....
1994-95	Buffalo	NHL	33	3	3	6	87	1	0	0	42	7.1	5	....	....	....	4	0	0	0	2	0	0	0	....
1995-96	Buffalo	NHL	79	15	29	44	295	3	0	4	168	8.9	6	....	....	....	....	....	....	....	....	....	....	....	....
1996-97	Buffalo	NHL	42	3	4	7	106	1	0	1	75	4.0	–8	....	....	....	10	1	1	2	32	0	0	0	....
1997-98	Buffalo	NHL	36	4	7	11	113	0	0	0	41	9.8	2	....	....	....	....	....	....	....	....	....	....	....	....
	Vancouver	NHL	27	9	3	12	41	4	0	2	56	16.1	0	....	....	....	....	....	....	....	....	....	....	....	....
1998-99	Vancouver	NHL	66	6	11	17	102	1	0	1	91	6.6	–14	8	12.5	13:04	....	....	....	....	....	....	....	....	....
99-2000	Vancouver	NHL	59	9	7	16	90	0	0	3	66	13.6	–2	3	0.0	10:24	....	....	....	....	....	....	....	....	....
2000-01	Phoenix	NHL	62	11	14	25	107	0	0	0	83	13.3	10	3	33.3	11:11	....	....	....	....	....	....	....	....	....
2001-02	Phoenix	NHL	72	10	12	22	95	1	0	3	105	9.5	11	3	0.0	12:04	5	0	0	0	0	0	0	0	10:19
2002-03	Phoenix	NHL	20	3	4	7	32	0	0	0	24	12.5	3	0	0.0	9:56	....	....	....	....	....	....	....	....	....
	Vancouver	NHL	3	0	0	0	10	0	0	0	1	0.0	1	0	0.0	7:48	14	0	0	0	15	0	0	0	7:25
2003-04	Vancouver	NHL	70	5	6	11	137	0	0	0	75	6.7	–2	8	50.0	8:56	6	1	0	1	6	0	0	0	7:07
	NHL Totals		804	120	146	266	1937	15	0	21	1189	10.1		25	24.0	11:02	61	4	8	12	80	0	0	2	7:55

OHL Second All-Star Team (1990, 1991)

• Missed majority of 1990-91 season recovering from knee injury suffered at Team Canada Juniors evaluation camp, August 21, 1990. Traded to **Vancouver** by **Buffalo** with Buffalo's 3rd round choice (later traded to Tampa Bay – Tampa Bay selected Jimmie Olvestad) in 1999 Entry Draft for Geoff Sanderson, February 4, 1998. Traded to **Phoenix** by **Vancouver** for future considerations, June 24, 2000. • Missed majority of 2002-03 season recovering from shoulder injury suffered in pre-season game vs. Detroit, October 6, 2002. Traded to **Vancouver** by **Phoenix** for Phoenix's 3rd round choice (previously acquired, Phoenix selected Dimitri Pestunov) in 2003 Entry Draft, March 11, 2003.

MAYERS, Jamal

(MAI-uhrz, JUH-MAHL) **ST.L.**

Right wing. Shoots right. 6'1", 217 lbs. Born, Toronto, Ont., October 24, 1974. St. Louis' 3rd choice, 89th overall, in 1993 Entry Draft.

Season	Club	League	GP	G	A	Pts	PIM	PP	SH	GW	S	%	+/-	TF	F%	Min	GP	G	A	Pts	PIM	PP	SH	GW	Min
			Regular Season														Playoffs								
1990-91	Thornhill Rattlers	MTJHL	44	12	24	36	78																		
1991-92	Thornhill Rattlers	MTJHL	56	38	69	107	36																		
1992-93	West. Michigan	CCHA	38	8	17	25	26																		
1993-94	West. Michigan	CCHA	40	17	32	49	40																		
1994-95	West. Michigan	CCHA	39	13	32	45	40																		
1995-96	West. Michigan	CCHA	38	17	22	39	75																		
1996-97	**St. Louis**	**NHL**	**6**	**0**	**1**	**1**	**2**	**0**	**0**	**0**	**7**	**0.0**	**-3**												
	Worcester IceCats	AHL	62	12	14	26	104										5	4	5	9	4				
1997-98	Worcester IceCats	AHL	61	19	24	43	117										11	3	4	7	10				
1998-99	**St. Louis**	**NHL**	**34**	**4**	**5**	**9**	**40**	**0**	**0**	**0**	**48**	**8.3**	**-3**	**2**	**50.0**	**8:08**	**11**	**0**	**1**	**1**	**8**	**0**	**0**	**0**	**8:34**
	Worcester IceCats	AHL	20	9	7	16	34																		
99-2000	**St. Louis**	**NHL**	**79**	**7**	**10**	**17**	**90**	**0**	**0**	**0**	**99**	**7.1**	**0**	**77**	**52.0**	**9:46**	**7**	**0**	**4**	**4**	**2**	**0**	**0**	**0**	**10:42**
2000-01	**St. Louis**	**NHL**	**77**	**8**	**13**	**21**	**117**	**0**	**0**	**0**	**132**	**6.1**	**-3**	**273**	**51.3**	**11:04**	**15**	**2**	**3**	**5**	**8**	**0**	**0**	**0**	**11:28**
2001-02	**St. Louis**	**NHL**	**77**	**9**	**8**	**17**	**99**	**0**	**1**	**0**	**105**	**8.6**	**9**	**761**	**52.6**	**11:36**	**10**	**3**	**0**	**3**	**2**	**0**	**0**	**2**	**11:14**
2002-03	**St. Louis**	**NHL**	**15**	**2**	**5**	**7**	**8**	**0**	**0**	**0**	**26**	**7.7**	**1**	**111**	**51.4**	**14:21**									
2003-04	**St. Louis**	**NHL**	**80**	**6**	**5**	**11**	**91**	**0**	**1**	**3**	**130**	**4.6**	**-19**	**681**	**48.6**	**13:01**	**5**	**0**	**0**	**0**	**0**	**0**	**0**	**0**	**12:55**
	NHL Totals		**368**	**36**	**47**	**83**	**447**	**0**	**2**	**3**	**547**	**6.6**		**1905**	**50.9**	**11:11**	**48**	**5**	**8**	**13**	**20**	**0**	**0**	**2**	**10:47**

• Missed majority of 2002-03 season recovering from knee injury suffered in game vs. Calgary, November 16, 2002.

McALLISTER, Chris

(mih-KAL-ihs-tuhr, KRIHS)

Defense. Shoots left. 6'8", 240 lbs. Born, Saskatoon, Sask., June 16, 1975. Vancouver's 1st choice, 40th overall, in 1995 Entry Draft.

Season	Club	League	GP	G	A	Pts	PIM	PP	SH	GW	S	%	+/-	TF	F%	Min	GP	G	A	Pts	PIM	PP	SH	GW	Min
1992-93	Saskatoon Royals	NSJHL	40	14	14	28	224																		
	Saskatoon Blades	WHL	4	0	0	0	2																		
1993-94	Humboldt	SJHL	50	3	5	8	150																		
	Saskatoon Blades	WHL	2	0	0	0	5																		
1994-95	Saskatoon Blades	WHL	65	2	8	10	134										10	0	0	0	28				
1995-96	Syracuse Crunch	AHL	68	0	2	2	142										16	0	0	0	34				
1996-97	Syracuse Crunch	AHL	43	3	1	4	108										3	0	0	0	6				
1997-98	**Vancouver**	**NHL**	**36**	**1**	**2**	**3**	**106**	**0**	**0**	**0**	**15**	**6.7**	**-12**												
	Syracuse Crunch	AHL	23	0	1	1	71										5	0	0	0	21				
1998-99	**Vancouver**	**NHL**	**28**	**1**	**1**	**2**	**63**	**0**	**0**	**0**	**6**	**16.7**	**-7**	**0**	**0.0**	**5:53**									
	Syracuse Crunch	AHL	5	0	0	0	24																		
	Toronto	**NHL**	**20**	**0**	**2**	**2**	**39**	**0**	**0**	**0**	**12**	**0.0**	**4**	**0**	**0.0**	**13:59**	**6**	**0**	**1**	**1**	**4**	**0**	**0**	**0**	**13:00**
99-2000	**Toronto**	**NHL**	**36**	**0**	**3**	**3**	**68**	**0**	**0**	**0**	**12**	**0.0**	**-4**	**0**	**0.0**	**12:02**									
2000-01	**Philadelphia**	**NHL**	**60**	**2**	**2**	**4**	**124**	**0**	**0**	**0**	**33**	**6.1**	**1**	**0**	**0.0**	**11:36**	**2**	**0**	**0**	**0**	**0**	**0**	**0**	**0**	**8:00**
2001-02	**Philadelphia**	**NHL**	**42**	**0**	**5**	**5**	**113**	**0**	**0**	**0**	**26**	**0.0**	**-7**	**0**	**0.0**	**9:12**									
2002-03	**Philadelphia**	**NHL**	**19**	**0**	**0**	**0**	**21**	**0**	**0**	**0**	**9**	**0.0**	**-2**	**0**	**0.0**	**9:32**									
	Philadelphia	AHL	4	0	0	0	12																		
	Colorado	**NHL**	**14**	**0**	**1**	**1**	**26**	**0**	**0**	**0**	**4**	**0.0**	**6**	**0**	**0.0**	**8:02**	**1**	**0**	**0**	**0**	**0**	**0**	**0**	**0**	**2:34**
2003-04	**Colorado**	**NHL**	**34**	**0**	**0**	**0**	**62**	**0**	**0**	**0**	**11**	**0.0**	**-2**	**0**	**0.0**	**5:34**									
	NY Rangers	**NHL**	**12**	**0**	**1**	**1**	**12**	**0**	**0**	**0**	**8**	**0.0**	**-4**	**4**	**50.0**	**12:49**									
	NHL Totals		**301**	**4**	**17**	**21**	**634**	**0**	**0**	**0**	**136**	**2.9**		**4**	**50.0**	**9:48**	**9**	**0**	**1**	**1**	**4**	**0**	**0**	**0**	**10:43**

Traded to **Toronto** by **Vancouver** for Darby Hendrickson, February 16, 1999. Traded to **Philadelphia** by **Toronto** for the rights to Regan Kelly, September 26, 2000. Traded to **Colorado** by **Philadelphia** for Colorado's 6th round choice (Ville Hostikka) in 2003 Entry Draft, February 5, 2003. Traded to **NY Rangers** by **Colorado** with David Liffiton and Florida's 2nd round choice (previously acquired, later traded back to Florida – Florida selected David Shantz) in 2004 Entry Draft for Matthew Barnaby and NY Rangers' 3rd round choice (Denis Parshin) in 2004 Entry Draft, March 8, 2004.

McAMMOND, Dean

(MIHK-AM-uhnd, DEEN)

Left wing. Shoots left. 5'11", 193 lbs. Born, Grand Cache, Alta., June 15, 1973. Chicago's 1st choice, 22nd overall, in 1991 Entry Draft.

Season	Club	League	GP	G	A	Pts	PIM	PP	SH	GW	S	%	+/-	TF	F%	Min	GP	G	A	Pts	PIM	PP	SH	GW	Min
1988-89	St. Albert Raiders	AMHL	36	33	44	77	132																		
1989-90	Prince Albert	WHL	53	11	11	22	49										14	2	3	5	18				
1990-91	Prince Albert	WHL	71	33	35	68	108										2	0	1	1	6				
1991-92	Prince Albert	WHL	63	37	54	91	189										10	12	11	23	26				
	Chicago	**NHL**	**5**	**0**	**2**	**2**	**0**	**0**	**0**	**0**	**4**	**0.0**	**-2**				**3**	**0**	**0**	**0**	**2**	**0**	**0**	**0**	
1992-93	Prince Albert	WHL	30	19	29	48	44																		
	Swift Current	WHL	18	10	13	23	24										17	*16	19	35	20				
1993-94	**Edmonton**	**NHL**	**45**	**6**	**21**	**27**	**16**	**2**	**0**	**0**	**52**	**11.5**	**12**												
	Cape Breton	AHL	28	9	12	21	38																		
1994-95	**Edmonton**	**NHL**	**6**	**0**	**0**	**0**	**0**	**0**	**0**	**0**	**3**	**0.0**	**-1**												
1995-96	**Edmonton**	**NHL**	**53**	**15**	**15**	**30**	**23**	**4**	**0**	**0**	**79**	**19.0**	**6**												
	Cape Breton	AHL	22	9	15	24	55																		
1996-97	**Edmonton**	**NHL**	**57**	**12**	**17**	**29**	**28**	**4**	**0**	**6**	**106**	**11.3**	**-15**												
1997-98	**Edmonton**	**NHL**	**77**	**19**	**31**	**50**	**46**	**8**	**0**	**3**	**128**	**14.8**	**9**				**12**	**1**	**4**	**5**	**12**	**0**	**0**	**0**	
1998-99	**Edmonton**	**NHL**	**65**	**9**	**16**	**25**	**36**	**1**	**0**	**0**	**122**	**7.4**	**5**	**26**	**38.5**	**14:15**									
	Chicago	**NHL**	**12**	**1**	**4**	**5**	**2**	**0**	**0**	**1**	**16**	**6.3**	**3**	**37**	**48.6**	**15:43**									
99-2000	**Chicago**	**NHL**	**76**	**14**	**18**	**32**	**72**	**1**	**0**	**1**	**118**	**11.9**	**11**	**257**	**39.7**	**16:25**									
2000-01	**Chicago**	**NHL**	**61**	**10**	**16**	**26**	**43**	**1**	**0**	**1**	**95**	**10.5**	**4**	**23**	**43.5**	**15:30**									
	Philadelphia	**NHL**	**10**	**1**	**1**	**2**	**0**	**1**	**0**	**0**	**17**	**5.9**	**-1**	**65**	**46.2**	**12:00**	**4**	**0**	**0**	**0**	**2**	**0**	**0**	**0**	**9:25**
2001-02	**Calgary**	**NHL**	**73**	**21**	**30**	**51**	**60**	**7**	**0**	**4**	**152**	**13.8**	**2**	**143**	**55.2**	**18:56**									
2002-03	**Colorado**	**NHL**	**41**	**10**	**8**	**18**	**10**	**2**	**0**	**2**	**72**	**13.9**	**1**	**9**	**55.6**	**14:24**									
2003-04	**Calgary**	**NHL**	**64**	**17**	**13**	**30**	**18**	**4**	**1**	**5**	**101**	**16.8**	**9**	**768**	**49.1**	**16:52**									
	NHL Totals		**645**	**135**	**192**	**327**	**354**	**35**	**1**	**23**	**1065**	**12.7**		**1328**	**47.5**	**16:07**	**19**	**1**	**4**	**5**	**16**	**0**	**0**	**0**	**9:25**

Traded to **Edmonton** by **Chicago** with Igor Kravchuk for Joe Murphy, February 24, 1993. Traded to **Chicago** by **Edmonton** with Boris Mironov and Jonas Elofsson for Chad Kilger, Daniel Cleary, Ethan Moreau and Christian Laflamme, March 20, 1999. Traded to **Philadelphia** by **Chicago** for Philadelphia's 3rd round choice (later traded to Toronto – Toronto selected Nicolas Corbeil) in 2001 Entry Draft, March 13, 2001. Traded to **Calgary** by **Philadelphia** for Calgary's 4th round choice (Rosario Ruggeri) in 2002 Entry Draft, June 24, 2001. Traded to **Colorado** by **Calgary** with Derek Morris and Jeff Shantz for Chris Drury and Stephane Yelle, October 1, 2002. Traded to **Calgary** by **Colorado** for Calgary's 5th round choice (Mark McCutcheon) in 2003 Entry Draft, March 11, 2003. • Ruled ineligible to play remainder of 2002-03 season by NHL due to transaction violation by Calgary, March 15, 2003.

McCABE, Bryan

(mih-KAYB, BRIGH-uhn) **TOR.**

Defense. Shoots left. 6'2", 220 lbs. Born, St. Catharines, Ont., June 8, 1975. NY Islanders' 2nd choice, 40th overall, in 1993 Entry Draft.

Season	Club	League	GP	G	A	Pts	PIM	PP	SH	GW	S	%	+/-	TF	F%	Min	GP	G	A	Pts	PIM	PP	SH	GW	Min
1990-91	Calgary Canucks	AMHL	33	14	34	48	55																		
1991-92	Medicine Hat	WHL	68	6	24	30	157										4	0	0	0	6				
1992-93	Medicine Hat	WHL	14	0	13	13	83																		
	Spokane Chiefs	WHL	46	3	44	47	134										6	1	5	6	28				
1993-94	Spokane Chiefs	WHL	64	22	62	84	218										3	0	4	4	4				
1994-95	Spokane Chiefs	WHL	42	14	39	53	115																		
	Brandon	WHL	20	6	10	16	38										18	4	13	17	59				
1995-96	**NY Islanders**	**NHL**	**82**	**7**	**16**	**23**	**156**	**3**	**0**	**1**	**130**	**5.4**	**-24**												
1996-97	**NY Islanders**	**NHL**	**82**	**8**	**20**	**28**	**165**	**2**	**1**	**2**	**117**	**6.8**	**-2**												
1997-98	**NY Islanders**	**NHL**	**56**	**3**	**9**	**12**	**145**	**1**	**0**	**0**	**81**	**3.7**	**9**												
	Vancouver	**NHL**	**26**	**1**	**11**	**12**	**64**	**0**	**1**	**0**	**42**	**2.4**	**10**												
1998-99	**Vancouver**	**NHL**	**69**	**7**	**14**	**21**	**120**	**1**	**2**	**0**	**98**	**7.1**	**-11**	**1**	**0.0**	**24:13**									
99-2000	**Chicago**	**NHL**	**79**	**6**	**19**	**25**	**139**	**2**	**0**	**2**	**119**	**5.0**	**-8**	**1**	**0.0**	**23:23**									
2000-01	**Toronto**	**NHL**	**82**	**5**	**24**	**29**	**123**	**3**	**0**	**2**	**159**	**3.1**	**16**	**0**	**0.0**	**23:49**	**11**	**2**	**3**	**5**	**16**	**1**	**0**	**0**	**23:56**
2001-02	**Toronto**	**NHL**	**82**	**17**	**26**	**43**	**129**	**8**	**0**	**1**	**157**	**10.8**	**16**	**1**	**0.0**	**24:34**	**20**	**5**	**5**	**10**	**30**	**3**	**0**	**1**	**29:33**
2002-03	**Toronto**	**NHL**	**75**	**6**	**18**	**24**	**135**	**3**	**0**	**1**	**149**	**4.0**	**9**	**1**	**0.0**	**23:39**	**7**	**0**	**3**	**3**	**10**	**0**	**0**	**0**	**27:28**
2003-04	**Toronto**	**NHL**	**75**	**16**	**37**	**53**	**86**	**8**	**0**	**2**	**168**	**9.5**	**22**	**2**	**50.0**	**25:44**	**13**	**3**	**5**	**8**	**14**	**2**	**0**	**0**	**28:47**
	NHL Totals		**708**	**76**	**194**	**270**	**1262**	**31**	**4**	**11**	**1220**	**6.2**		**6**	**16.7**	**24:13**	**51**	**10**	**16**	**26**	**70**	**6**	**0**	**1**	**27:51**

WHL West Second All-Star Team (1993) • WHL West First All-Star Team (1994) • WHL East First All-Star Team (1995) • Memorial Cup All-Star Team (1995) • NHL Second All-Star Team (2004)

Traded to **Vancouver** by **NY Islanders** with Todd Bertuzzi and NY Islanders' 3rd round choice (Jarkko Ruutu) in 1998 Entry Draft for Trevor Linden, February 6, 1998. Traded to **Chicago** by **Vancouver** with Vancouver's 1st round choice (Pavel Vorobiev) in 2000 Entry Draft for Chicago's 1st round choice (later traded to Tampa Bay – later traded to NY Rangers – NY Rangers selected Pavel Brendl) in 1999 Entry Draft, June 25, 1999. Traded to **Toronto** by **Chicago** for Alexander Karpovtsev and Toronto's 4th round choice (Vladimir Gusev) in 2001 Entry Draft, October 2, 2000.

			Regular Season														Playoffs								
Season	Club	League	GP	G	A	Pts	PIM	PP	SH	GW	S	%	+/-	TF	F%	Min	GP	G	A	Pts	PIM	PP	SH	GW	Min

McCARTHY, Sandy
(mih-KAHR-thee, SAN-dee)

Right wing. Shoots right. 6'3", 222 lbs. Born, Toronto, Ont., June 15, 1972. Calgary's 3rd choice, 52nd overall, in 1991 Entry Draft.

Season	Club	League	GP	G	A	Pts	PIM	PP	SH	GW	S	%	+/-	TF	F%	Min	GP	G	A	Pts	PIM	PP	SH	GW	Min
1987-88	Midland	OJHL-C	18	2	1	3	70	....	....	....	....	....	....				....	....	....	....	....	....	....	....	....
1988-89	Hawkesbury	OCJHL	42	4	11	15	139	....	....	....	....	....	....				14	3	3	6	60	....	....	....	....
1989-90	Laval Titan	QMJHL	65	10	11	21	269	....	....	....	....	....	....				13	6	5	11	67	....	....	....	....
1990-91	Laval Titan	QMJHL	68	21	19	40	297	....	....	....	....	....	....				8	4	5	9	81	....	....	....	....
1991-92	Laval Titan	QMJHL	62	39	51	90	326	....	....	....	....	....	....				....	....	....	....	....	....	....	....	....
1992-93	Salt Lake	IHL	77	18	20	38	220	....	....	....	....	....	....				7	0	0	0	34	0	0	0	
1993-94	Calgary	NHL	79	5	5	10	173	0	0	0	39	12.8	-3				6	0	1	1	17	0	0	0	
1994-95	Calgary	NHL	37	5	3	8	101	0	0	2	29	17.2	1				4	0	0	0	10	0	0	0	
1995-96	Calgary	NHL	75	9	7	16	173	3	0	1	98	9.2	-8				....	....	....	....	....	....	....	....	....
1996-97	Calgary	NHL	33	3	5	8	113	1	0	1	38	7.9	-8				....	....	....	....	....	....	....	....	....
1997-98	Calgary	NHL	52	8	5	13	170	1	0	1	68	11.8	-18				....	....	....	....	....	....	....	....	....
	Tampa Bay	NHL	14	0	5	5	71	0	0	0	26	0.0	-1				....	....	....	....	....	....	....	....	....
1998-99	Tampa Bay	NHL	67	5	7	12	135	1	0	0	89	5.6	-22	0	0.0	11:02	....	....	....	....	....	....	....	....	....
	Philadelphia	NHL	13	0	1	1	25	0	0	0	18	0.0	-2	2	50.0	11:09	6	0	1	1	0	0	0	0	6:33
99-2000	Philadelphia	NHL	58	6	5	11	111	1	0	0	68	8.8	-5	4	0.0	10:27	....	....	....	....	....	....	....	....	....
	Carolina	NHL	13	0	0	0	9	0	0	0	12	0.0	2	0	0.0	7:24	....	....	....	....	....	....	....	....	....
2000-01	NY Rangers	NHL	81	11	10	21	171	0	0	2	95	11.6	3	4	0.0	10:25	....	....	....	....	....	....	....	....	....
2001-02	NY Rangers	NHL	82	10	13	23	171	0	0	3	90	11.1	-8	6	50.0	8:29	....	....	....	....	....	....	....	....	....
2002-03	NY Rangers	NHL	82	6	9	15	81	0	0	1	81	7.4	-4	11	9.1	7:26	....	....	....	....	....	....	....	....	....
2003-04	Boston	NHL	37	3	1	4	28	0	0	1	27	11.1	0	1	0.0	6:22	....	....	....	....	....	....	....	....	....
	NY Rangers	NHL	13	1	0	1	2	1	0	0	11	9.1	-8	1	0.0	9:58	....	....	....	....	....	....	....	....	....
	NHL Totals		736	72	76	148	1534	9	0	12	789	9.1		29	17.2	9:12	23	0	2	2	61	0	0	0	6:33

Traded to **Tampa Bay** by **Calgary** with Calgary's 3rd (Brad Richards) and 5th (Curtis Rich) round choices in 1998 Entry Draft for Jason Wiemer, March 24, 1998. Traded to **Philadelphia** by **Tampa Bay** with Mikael Andersson for Colin Forbes and Philadelphia's 4th round choice (Michal Lanicek) in 1999 Entry Draft, March 20, 1999. Traded to **Carolina** by **Philadelphia** for Kent Manderville, March 14, 2000. Traded to **NY Rangers** by **Carolina** with Carolina's 4th round choice (Bryce Lampman) in 2001 Entry Draft for Darren Langdon and Rob DiMaio, August 4, 2000. Signed as a free agent by **Boston**, August 12, 2003. Claimed on waivers by **NY Rangers** from **Boston**, March 9, 2004.

McCARTHY, Steve
(mih-KAHR-thee, STEEV)   **CHI.**

Defense. Shoots left. 6'1", 198 lbs. Born, Trail, B.C., February 3, 1981. Chicago's 1st choice, 23rd overall, in 1999 Entry Draft.

Season	Club	League	GP	G	A	Pts	PIM	PP	SH	GW	S	%	+/-	TF	F%	Min	GP	G	A	Pts	PIM	PP	SH	GW	Min
1996-97	Trail Smokies	BCHL	57	25	52	77	81	....	....	....	....	....	....				....	....	....	....	....	....	....	....	....
	Edmonton Ice	WHL	2	0	0	0	0	....	....	....	....	....	....				....	....	....	....	....	....	....	....	....
1997-98	Edmonton Ice	WHL	58	11	29	40	59	....	....	....	....	....	....				....	....	....	....	....	....	....	....	....
1998-99	Kootenay Ice	WHL	57	19	33	52	79	....	....	....	....	....	....				6	0	5	5	8	....	....	....	....
99-2000	Chicago	NHL	5	1	1	2	4	1	0	0	4	25.0	0	0	0.0	15:09	....	....	....	....	....	....	....	....	....
	Kootenay Ice	WHL	37	13	23	36	36	....	....	....	....	....	....				....	....	....	....	....	....	....	....	....
2000-01	Chicago	NHL	44	0	5	5	8	0	0	0	32	0.0	-7	0	0.0	14:47	....	....	....	....	....	....	....	....	....
	Norfolk Admirals	AHL	7	0	4	4	2	....	....	....	....	....	....				....	....	....	....	....	....	....	....	....
2001-02	Chicago	NHL	3	0	0	0	2	0	0	0	2	0.0	-1	0	0.0	11:48	....	....	....	....	....	....	....	....	....
	Norfolk Admirals	AHL	77	7	21	28	37	....	....	....	....	....	....				9	0	3	3	2	....	....	....	....
2002-03	Chicago	NHL	• 57	1	4	5	23	0	0	0	55	1.8	-1	0	0.0	16:25	....	....	....	....	....	....	....	....	....
	Norfolk Admirals	AHL	19	1	6	7	14	....	....	....	....	....	....				9	0	4	4	0	....	....	....	....
2003-04	Chicago	NHL	25	1	3	4	8	0	0	0	29	3.4	-9	0	0.0	19:21	....	....	....	....	....	....	....	....	....
	NHL Totals		134	3	13	16	45	1	0	0	122	2.5		0	0.0	16:16	....	....	....	....	....	....	....	....	....

• Missed majority of 2003-04 season recovering from groin injury suffered in game vs. Calgary, November 22, 2003.

McCARTY, Darren
(mih-KAHR-tee, DAIR-ehn)   **DET.**

Right wing. Shoots right. 6'1", 210 lbs. Born, Burnaby, B.C., April 1, 1972. Detroit's 2nd choice, 46th overall, in 1992 Entry Draft.

Season	Club	League	GP	G	A	Pts	PIM	PP	SH	GW	S	%	+/-	TF	F%	Min	GP	G	A	Pts	PIM	PP	SH	GW	Min
1988-89	Peterboro B's	OJHL-B	34	18	17	35	135	....	....	....	....	....	....				11	1	1	2	21	....	....	....	....
1989-90	Belleville Bulls	OHL	63	12	15	27	142	....	....	....	....	....	....				6	2	2	4	13	....	....	....	....
1990-91	Belleville Bulls	OHL	60	30	37	67	151	....	....	....	....	....	....				5	1	4	5	13	....	....	....	....
1991-92	Belleville Bulls	OHL	65	*55	72	127	177	....	....	....	....	....	....				5	4	7	11	13	....	....	....	....
1992-93	Adirondack	AHL	73	17	19	36	278	....	....	....	....	....	....				11	0	1	1	33	....	....	....	....
1993-94	Detroit	NHL	67	9	17	26	181	0	0	2	81	11.1	12				7	2	2	4	8	0	0	0	
1994-95	Detroit	NHL	31	5	8	13	88	1	0	0	27	18.5	5				18	3	2	5	14	0	0	0	
1995-96	Detroit	NHL	63	15	14	29	158	8	0	1	102	14.7	14				19	3	2	5	20	0	0	1	
1996-97 ♦	Detroit	NHL	68	19	30	49	126	5	0	6	171	11.1	14				20	3	4	7	34	0	0	0	
1997-98 ♦	Detroit	NHL	71	15	22	37	157	5	1	2	166	9.0	0				22	3	8	11	34	0	0	1	
1998-99	Detroit	NHL	69	14	26	40	108	6	0	1	140	10.0	10	15	33.3	17:04	10	1	1	2	23	0	0	0	13:04
99-2000	Detroit	NHL	24	6	6	12	48	0	0	0	40	15.0	1	1	0.0	13:40	9	0	1	1	12	0	0	0	14:09
2000-01	Detroit	NHL	72	12	10	22	123	1	1	3	118	10.2	-5	26	53.9	13:26	6	1	0	1	2	0	0	0	13:11
2001-02 ♦	Detroit	NHL	62	5	7	12	98	0	0	0	74	6.8	2	26	38.5	11:47	23	4	4	8	34	0	0	1	13:33
2002-03	Detroit	NHL	73	13	9	22	112	1	0	2	129	10.1	10	320	57.8	13:18	4	0	0	0	6	0	0	0	15:45
2003-04	Detroit	NHL	43	6	5	11	50	1	0	0	61	9.8	2	141	50.4	12:20	12	0	1	1	7	0	0	0	11:30
	NHL Totals		643	119	154	273	1275	28	2	21	1109	10.7		529	53.9	13:43	150	20	25	45	194	0	0	5	13:17

OHL First All-Star Team (1992)
• Missed majority of 1999-2000 season recovering from hernia injury suffered in game vs. Dallas, November 10, 1999.

McCAULEY, Alyn
(mih-KAW-lee, AL-ihn)   **S.J.**

Center. Shoots left. 5'11", 200 lbs. Born, Brockville, Ont., May 29, 1977. New Jersey's 5th choice, 79th overall, in 1995 Entry Draft.

Season	Club	League	GP	G	A	Pts	PIM	PP	SH	GW	S	%	+/-	TF	F%	Min	GP	G	A	Pts	PIM	PP	SH	GW	Min
1991-92	Kingston	OCJHL	37	5	17	22	6	....	....	....	....	....	....				....	....	....	....	....	....	....	....	....
1992-93	Kingston	OCJHL	38	31	29	60	18	....	....	....	....	....	....				....	....	....	....	....	....	....	....	....
1993-94	Ottawa 67's	OHL	38	13	23	36	10	....	....	....	....	....	....				13	5	14	19	4	....	....	....	....
1994-95	Ottawa 67's	OHL	65	16	38	54	20	....	....	....	....	....	....				....	....	....	....	....	....	....	....	....
1995-96	Ottawa 67's	OHL	55	34	48	82	24	....	....	....	....	....	....				10	0	0	0	0	....	....	....	....
1996-97	Ottawa 67's	OHL	50	*56	56	112	16	....	....	....	....	....	....				22	14	22	36	14	....	....	....	....
	St. John's	AHL	....	....	....	....	....	....	....	....	....	....	....				3	0	1	1	0	....	....	....	....
1997-98	Toronto	NHL	60	6	10	16	6	0	0	1	77	7.8	-7				....	....	....	....	....	....	....	....	....
1998-99	Toronto	NHL	39	9	15	24	2	1	0	1	76	11.8	7	591	46.4	15:10	....	....	....	....	....	....	....	....	....
99-2000	Toronto	NHL	45	5	5	10	10	1	0	0	41	12.2	-6	450	47.8	10:46	5	0	0	0	6	0	0	0	7:51
	St. John's	AHL	5	1	1	2	0	....	....	....	....	....	....				....	....	....	....	....	....	....	....	....
2000-01	Toronto	NHL	14	1	0	1	0	0	0	0	13	7.7	0	139	46.8	10:28	10	0	0	0	0	0	0	0	9:34
	St. John's	AHL	47	16	28	44	12	....	....	....	....	....	....				....	....	....	....	....	....	....	....	....
2001-02	Toronto	NHL	82	6	10	16	18	0	1	0	95	6.3	10	951	48.1	11:24	20	5	10	15	14	1	0	2	19:12
2002-03	Toronto	NHL	64	6	9	15	16	0	0	0	79	7.6	3	515	44.5	12:54	....	....	....	....	....	....	....	....	....
	San Jose	NHL	16	3	7	10	4	3	0	0	29	10.3	-2	81	50.6	17:29	....	....	....	....	....	....	....	....	....
2003-04	San Jose	NHL	82	20	27	47	28	5	0	4	146	13.7	23	1216	47.7	16:51	11	2	1	3	2	0	0	0	14:17
	NHL Totals		402	56	83	139	84	10	1	7	556	10.1		3943	47.2	13:35	46	7	11	18	14	1	0	2	14:42

OHL First All-Star Team (1996, 1997) • OHL MVP (1996, 1997) • Canadian Major Junior First All-Star Team (1997) • Canadian Major Junior Player of the Year (1997)

Rights traded to **Toronto** by **New Jersey** with Jason Smith and Steve Sullivan for Doug Gilmour, Dave Ellett and New Jersey's 3rd round choice (previously acquired, New Jersey selected Andre Lakos) in 1999 Entry Draft, February 25, 1997. Traded to **San Jose** by **Toronto** with Brad Boyes and Toronto's 1st round choice (later traded to Boston – Boston selected Mark Stuart) in 2003 Entry Draft for Owen Nolan, March 5, 2003.

McCORMICK, Cody
(muh-KOHR-mihk, KOH-dee)   **COL.**

Center/Right wing. Shoots right. 6'2", 200 lbs. Born, London, Ont., April 18, 1983. Colorado's 5th choice, 144th overall, in 2001 Entry Draft.

Season	Club	League	GP	G	A	Pts	PIM	PP	SH	GW	S	%	+/-	TF	F%	Min	GP	G	A	Pts	PIM	PP	SH	GW	Min
1998-99	Elgin-Middlesex	MHAO	58	22	40	62	81	....	....	....	....	....	....				....	....	....	....	....	....	....	....	....
99-2000	Belleville Bulls	OHL	45	3	4	7	42	....	....	....	....	....	....				9	1	0	1	10	....	....	....	....
2000-01	Belleville Bulls	OHL	66	7	16	23	135	....	....	....	....	....	....				10	1	1	2	23	....	....	....	....
2001-02	Belleville Bulls	OHL	63	10	17	27	118	....	....	....	....	....	....				11	2	4	6	24	....	....	....	....
2002-03	Belleville Bulls	OHL	61	36	33	69	166	....	....	....	....	....	....				7	4	7	11	11	....	....	....	....

								Regular Season									Playoffs								
Season	Club	League	GP	G	A	Pts	PIM	PP	SH	GW	S	%	+/-	TF	F%	Min	GP	G	A	Pts	PIM	PP	SH	GW	Min
2003-04	**Colorado**	**NHL**	**44**	**2**	**3**	**5**	**73**	**0**	**0**	**1**	**33**	**6.1**	**–4**	**110**	**32.7**	**8:07**	....	....	....	....	....	....	....	....	....
	Hershey Bears	AHL	32	3	6	9	60	....	....	....	....	....	....	....	....	....	....	....	....	....	....	....	....	....	....
	NHL Totals		**44**	**2**	**3**	**5**	**73**	**0**	**0**	**1**	**33**	**6.1**		**110**	**32.7**	**8:07**	....	....	....	....	....	....	....	....	....

OHL First All-Star Team (2003)

McDONALD, Andy

(mihk-DAW-nuhld, AN-dee) **ANA.**

Center. Shoots left. 5'10", 186 lbs. Born, Strathroy, Ont., August 25, 1977.

1993-94	Strathroy Rockets	OJHL-B	7	2	2	4	0	....	....	....	....	....	....	....	....	....	....	....	....	....	....	....	....	....	....
1994-95	Strathroy Rockets	OJHL-B	50	32	41	73	24	....	....	....	....	....	....	....	....	....	....	....	....	....	....	....	....	....	....
1995-96	Strathroy Rockets	OJHL-B	52	31	56	87	103	....	....	....	....	....	....	....	....	....	....	....	....	....	....	....	....	....	....
1996-97	Colgate	ECAC	33	9	10	19	16	....	....	....	....	....	....	....	....	....	....	....	....	....	....	....	....	....	....
1997-98	Colgate	ECAC	35	13	19	32	26	....	....	....	....	....	....	....	....	....	....	....	....	....	....	....	....	....	....
1998-99	Colgate	ECAC	35	20	26	46	42	....	....	....	....	....	....	....	....	....	....	....	....	....	....	....	....	....	....
99-2000	Colgate	ECAC	34	25	*33	*58	49	....	....	....	....	....	....	....	....	....	....	....	....	....	....	....	....	....	....
2000-01	**Anaheim**	**NHL**	**16**	**1**	**0**	**1**	**6**	**0**	**0**	**0**	**21**	**4.8**	**0**	**139**	**48.9**	**11:11**	....	....	....	....	....	....	....	....	....
	Cincinnati	AHL	46	15	25	40	21	....	....	....	....	....	....	....	....	....	3	0	1	1	2	....	....	....	....
2001-02	**Anaheim**	**NHL**	**53**	**7**	**21**	**28**	**10**	**2**	**0**	**3**	**79**	**8.9**	**2**	**818**	**53.7**	**15:59**	....	....	....	....	....	....	....	....	....
	Cincinnati	AHL	21	7	25	32	6	....	....	....	....	....	....	....	....	....	....	....	....	....	....	....	....	....	....
2002-03	**Anaheim**	**NHL**	**46**	**10**	**11**	**21**	**14**	**3**	**0**	**1**	**92**	**10.9**	**–1**	**604**	**56.0**	**18:31**	....	....	....	....	....	....	....	....	....
2003-04	**Anaheim**	**NHL**	**79**	**9**	**21**	**30**	**24**	**2**	**1**	**1**	**162**	**5.6**	**–13**	**282**	**54.3**	**16:34**	....	....	....	....	....	....	....	....	....
	NHL Totals		**194**	**27**	**53**	**80**	**54**	**7**	**1**	**5**	**354**	**7.6**		**1843**	**54.2**	**16:25**	....	....	....	....	....	....	....	....	....

ECAC Second All-Star Team (1999) • ECAC First All-Star Team (2000) • NCAA East First All-American Team (2000)

Signed as a free agent by **Anaheim**, April 3, 2000.

McDONELL, Kent

(MAHK-dah-NEHL, KEHNT) **CBJ**

Right wing. Shoots right. 6'2", 205 lbs. Born, Williamstown, Ont., March 1, 1979. Detroit's 3rd choice, 181st overall, in 1999 Entry Draft.

1995-96	Cornwall Colts	OCJHL	33	21	14	35	64	....	....	....	....	....	....	....	....	....	....	....	....	....	....	....	....	....	....
1996-97	Guelph Storm	OHL	56	7	5	12	57	....	....	....	....	....	....	....	....	....	16	0	2	2	4	....	....	....	....
1997-98	Guelph Storm	OHL	64	28	23	51	76	....	....	....	....	....	....	....	....	....	12	7	4	11	18	....	....	....	....
1998-99	Guelph Storm	OHL	60	31	38	69	110	....	....	....	....	....	....	....	....	....	11	4	3	7	36	....	....	....	....
99-2000	Guelph Storm	OHL	56	35	35	70	100	....	....	....	....	....	....	....	....	....	6	1	4	5	6	....	....	....	....
2000-01	Dayton Bombers	ECHL	28	16	9	25	94	....	....	....	....	....	....	....	....	....	3	0	0	0	4	....	....	....	....
	Syracuse Crunch	AHL	32	3	3	6	36	....	....	....	....	....	....	....	....	....	3	1	0	1	0	....	....	....	....
2001-02	Syracuse Crunch	AHL	72	18	13	31	122	....	....	....	....	....	....	....	....	....	3	0	2	2	0	....	....	....	....
2002-03	**Columbus**	**NHL**	**3**	**0**	**0**	**0**	**0**	**0**	**0**	**0**	**4**	**0.0**	**–1**	**0**	**0.0**	**8:40**	....	....	....	....	....	....	....	....	....
	Syracuse Crunch	AHL	72	14	24	38	93	....	....	....	....	....	....	....	....	....	....	....	....	....	....	....	....	....	....
2003-04	**Columbus**	**NHL**	**29**	**1**	**2**	**3**	**36**	**0**	**0**	**0**	**23**	**4.3**	**–7**	**5**	**60.0**	**10:18**	....	....	....	....	....	....	....	....	....
	Syracuse Crunch	AHL	51	17	31	48	102	....	....	....	....	....	....	....	....	....	5	0	1	1	10	....	....	....	....
	NHL Totals		**32**	**1**	**2**	**3**	**36**	**0**	**0**	**0**	**27**	**3.7**		**5**	**60.0**	**10:09**	....	....	....	....	....	....	....	....	....

• Re-entered NHL Entry Draft. Originally Carolina's 9th choice, 225th overall, in 1997 Entry Draft.

Traded to **Columbus** by **Detroit** for Columbus's 6th round choice (Andreas Sundin) in 2003 Entry Draft, August 14, 2000.

McEACHERN, Shawn

(muh-GEH-kruhn, SHAWN) **ATL.**

Right wing. Shoots left. 5'11", 200 lbs. Born, Waltham, MA, February 28, 1969. Pittsburgh's 6th choice, 110th overall, in 1987 Entry Draft.

1985-86	Matignon	Hi-School	20	32	20	52	....	....	....	....	....	....	....	....	....	....	....	....	....	....	....	....	....	....	....
1986-87	Matignon	Hi-School	16	29	28	57	....	....	....	....	....	....	....	....	....	....	....	....	....	....	....	....	....	....	....
1987-88	Matignon	Hi-School	22	52	40	92	....	....	....	....	....	....	....	....	....	....	....	....	....	....	....	....	....	....	....
1988-89	Boston University	H-East	36	20	28	48	32	....	....	....	....	....	....	....	....	....	....	....	....	....	....	....	....	....	....
1989-90	Boston University	H-East	43	25	31	56	78	....	....	....	....	....	....	....	....	....	....	....	....	....	....	....	....	....	....
1990-91	Boston University	H-East	41	34	48	82	43	....	....	....	....	....	....	....	....	....	....	....	....	....	....	....	....	....	....
1991-92	Team USA	Nat-Tm	57	26	23	49	38	....	....	....	....	....	....	....	....	....	....	....	....	....	....	....	....	....	....
	United States	Olympics	8	1	0	1	10	....	....	....	....	....	....	....	....	....	....	....	....	....	....	....	....	....	....
	♦ **Pittsburgh**	**NHL**	**15**	**0**	**4**	**4**	**0**	**0**	**0**	**0**	**14**	**0.0**	**1**	....	....	....	**19**	**2**	**7**	**9**	**4**	**0**	**0**	**0**	....
1992-93	**Pittsburgh**	**NHL**	**84**	**28**	**33**	**61**	**46**	**7**	**0**	**6**	**196**	**14.3**	**21**	....	....	....	**12**	**3**	**2**	**5**	**10**	**0**	**0**	**1**	....
1993-94	**Los Angeles**	**NHL**	**49**	**8**	**13**	**21**	**24**	**0**	**3**	**0**	**81**	**9.9**	**1**	....	....	....	....	....	....	....	....	....	....	....	....
	Pittsburgh	**NHL**	**27**	**12**	**9**	**21**	**10**	**0**	**2**	**1**	**78**	**15.4**	**13**	....	....	....	**6**	**1**	**0**	**1**	**2**	**0**	**0**	**0**	....
1994-95	Kiekko Espoo	Finland	8	1	3	4	6	....	....	....	....	....	....	....	....	....	....	....	....	....	....	....	....	....	....
	Pittsburgh	**NHL**	**44**	**13**	**13**	**26**	**22**	**1**	**2**	**1**	**97**	**13.4**	**4**	....	....	....	**11**	**0**	**2**	**2**	**8**	**0**	**0**	**0**	....
1995-96	**Boston**	**NHL**	**82**	**24**	**29**	**53**	**34**	**3**	**2**	**3**	**238**	**10.1**	**–5**	....	....	....	**5**	**2**	**1**	**3**	**8**	**0**	**0**	**0**	....
1996-97	**Ottawa**	**NHL**	**65**	**11**	**20**	**31**	**18**	**0**	**1**	**2**	**150**	**7.3**	**–5**	....	....	....	**7**	**2**	**0**	**2**	**8**	**1**	**0**	**0**	....
1997-98	**Ottawa**	**NHL**	**81**	**24**	**24**	**48**	**42**	**8**	**2**	**4**	**229**	**10.5**	**1**	....	....	....	**11**	**0**	**4**	**4**	**8**	**0**	**0**	**0**	....
1998-99	**Ottawa**	**NHL**	**77**	**31**	**25**	**56**	**46**	**7**	**0**	**4**	**223**	**13.9**	**8**	**441**	**48.5**	**18:45**	**4**	**2**	**0**	**2**	**6**	**1**	**0**	**0**	**21:51**
99-2000	**Ottawa**	**NHL**	**69**	**29**	**22**	**51**	**24**	**10**	**0**	**4**	**219**	**13.2**	**2**	**54**	**50.0**	**17:50**	**6**	**0**	**3**	**3**	**4**	**0**	**0**	**0**	**18:08**
2000-01	**Ottawa**	**NHL**	**82**	**32**	**40**	**72**	**62**	**9**	**0**	**1**	**231**	**13.9**	**10**	**420**	**48.8**	**18:25**	**4**	**0**	**2**	**2**	**2**	**0**	**0**	**0**	**20:49**
2001-02	**Ottawa**	**NHL**	**80**	**15**	**31**	**46**	**52**	**5**	**0**	**3**	**196**	**7.7**	**9**	**210**	**52.4**	**17:40**	**12**	**0**	**4**	**4**	**2**	**0**	**0**	**0**	**16:59**
2002-03	**Atlanta**	**NHL**	**46**	**10**	**16**	**26**	**28**	**4**	**1**	**1**	**120**	**8.3**	**–27**	**154**	**43.5**	**19:18**	....	....	....	....	....	....	....	....	....
2003-04	**Atlanta**	**NHL**	**82**	**17**	**38**	**55**	**76**	**5**	**1**	**3**	**176**	**9.7**	**5**	**181**	**44.2**	**20:14**	....	....	....	....	....	....	....	....	....
	NHL Totals		**883**	**254**	**317**	**571**	**484**	**59**	**14**	**33**	**2248**	**11.3**		**1460**	**48.2**	**18:41**	**97**	**12**	**25**	**37**	**62**	**2**	**0**	**1**	**18:35**

Hockey East Second All-Star Team (1990) • Hockey East First All-Star Team (1991) • NCAA East First All-American Team (1991)

Traded to **Los Angeles** by **Pittsburgh** for Marty McSorley, August 27, 1993. Traded to **Pittsburgh** by **Los Angeles** with Tomas Sandstrom for Marty McSorley and Jim Paek, February 16, 1994. Traded to **Boston** by **Pittsburgh** with Kevin Stevens for Glen Murray, Bryan Smolinski and Boston's 3rd round choice (Boyd Kane) in 1996 Entry Draft, August 2, 1995. Traded to **Ottawa** by **Boston** for Trent McCleary and Ottawa's 3rd round choice (Eric Naud) in 1996 Entry Draft, June 22, 1996. Traded to **Atlanta** by **Ottawa** with Ottawa's 6th round choice (Dan Turple) in 2004 Entry Draft for Brian Pothier, June 29, 2002.

McGILLIS, Dan

(MIHK-gihl-his, DAN)

Defense. Shoots left. 6'2", 230 lbs. Born, Hawkesbury, Ont., July 1, 1972. Detroit's 10th choice, 238th overall, in 1992 Entry Draft.

1989-90	Hawkesbury	OCJHL	55	2	1	3	52	....	....	....	....	....	....	....	....	....	....	....	....	....	....	....	....	....	....
1990-91	Hawkesbury	OCJHL	56	8	22	30	92	....	....	....	....	....	....	....	....	....	....	....	....	....	....	....	....	....	....
1991-92	Hawkesbury	OCJHL	36	5	19	24	106	....	....	....	....	....	....	....	....	....	....	....	....	....	....	....	....	....	....
1992-93	Northeastern	H-East	35	5	12	17	42	....	....	....	....	....	....	....	....	....	....	....	....	....	....	....	....	....	....
1993-94	Northeastern	H-East	38	4	25	29	82	....	....	....	....	....	....	....	....	....	....	....	....	....	....	....	....	....	....
1994-95	Northeastern	H-East	34	9	22	31	70	....	....	....	....	....	....	....	....	....	....	....	....	....	....	....	....	....	....
1995-96	Northeastern	H-East	34	12	24	36	50	....	....	....	....	....	....	....	....	....	....	....	....	....	....	....	....	....	....
1996-97	**Edmonton**	**NHL**	**73**	**6**	**16**	**22**	**52**	**2**	**1**	**2**	**139**	**4.3**	**2**	....	....	....	**12**	**0**	**5**	**5**	**24**	**0**	**0**	**0**	....
1997-98	**Edmonton**	**NHL**	**67**	**10**	**15**	**25**	**74**	**5**	**0**	**3**	**119**	**8.4**	**–17**	....	....	....	....	....	....	....	....	....	....	....	....
	Philadelphia	**NHL**	**13**	**1**	**5**	**6**	**35**	**1**	**0**	**0**	**18**	**5.6**	**–4**	....	....	....	**5**	**1**	**2**	**3**	**10**	**1**	**0**	**0**	....
1998-99	**Philadelphia**	**NHL**	**78**	**8**	**37**	**45**	**61**	**6**	**0**	**4**	**164**	**4.9**	**16**	**0**	**0.0**	**21:41**	**6**	**0**	**1**	**1**	**12**	**0**	**0**	**0**	**19:36**
99-2000	**Philadelphia**	**NHL**	**68**	**4**	**14**	**18**	**55**	**3**	**0**	**1**	**128**	**3.1**	**16**	**0**	**0.0**	**20:04**	**18**	**2**	**6**	**8**	**12**	**0**	**0**	**0**	**24:42**
2000-01	**Philadelphia**	**NHL**	**82**	**14**	**35**	**49**	**86**	**4**	**0**	**4**	**207**	**6.8**	**13**	**1**	**0.0**	**23:23**	**6**	**1**	**0**	**1**	**6**	**0**	**1**	**0**	**24:12**
2001-02	**Philadelphia**	**NHL**	**75**	**5**	**14**	**19**	**46**	**2**	**0**	**1**	**147**	**3.4**	**17**	**0**	**0.0**	**21:04**	**5**	**1**	**0**	**1**	**8**	**1**	**0**	**0**	**20:27**
2002-03	**Philadelphia**	**NHL**	**24**	**0**	**3**	**3**	**20**	**0**	**0**	**0**	**41**	**0.0**	**7**	**0**	**0.0**	**18:13**	....	....	....	....	....	....	....	....	....
	San Jose	**NHL**	**37**	**3**	**13**	**16**	**30**	**2**	**0**	**0**	**71**	**4.2**	**–6**	**0**	**0.0**	**21:54**	....	....	....	....	....	....	....	....	....
	Boston	**NHL**	**10**	**0**	**1**	**1**	**10**	**0**	**0**	**0**	**18**	**0.0**	**2**	**0**	**0.0**	**21:15**	**5**	**3**	**0**	**3**	**2**	**2**	**0**	**1**	**18:54**
2003-04	**Boston**	**NHL**	**80**	**5**	**23**	**28**	**65**	**1**	**0**	**2**	**117**	**4.3**	**–1**	**1**	**0.0**	**19:43**	**7**	**0**	**0**	**0**	**2**	**0**	**0**	**0**	**18:38**
	NHL Totals		**607**	**56**	**176**	**232**	**534**	**26**	**1**	**17**	**1169**	**4.8**		**2**	**0.0**	**21:08**	**64**	**8**	**14**	**22**	**76**	**4**	**1**	**1**	**22:01**

Hockey East First All-Star Team (1995, 1996) • NCAA East First All-American Team (1996)

Traded to **Edmonton** by **Detroit** for Kirk Maltby, March 20, 1996. Traded to **Philadelphia** by **Edmonton** with Edmonton's 2nd round choice (Jason Beckett) in 1998 Entry Draft for Janne Niinimaa, March 24, 1998. Traded to **San Jose** by **Philadelphia** for Marcus Ragnarsson, December 6, 2002. Traded to **Boston** by **San Jose** for Boston's 2nd round choice (later traded to NY Rangers – NY Rangers selected Ivan Baranka) in 2003 Entry Draft, March 11, 2003.

McKEE, Jay

(mih-KEE, JAY) **BUF.**

Defense. Shoots left. 6'4", 212 lbs. Born, Kingston, Ont., September 8, 1977. Buffalo's 1st choice, 14th overall, in 1995 Entry Draft.

			Regular Season														Playoffs								
Season	Club	League	GP	G	A	Pts	PIM	PP	SH	GW	S	%	+/-	TF	F%	Min	GP	G	A	Pts	PIM	PP	SH	GW	Min
1992-93	Ernestown Jets	OJHL-C	36	0	17	17	37	....	....	....	....	....	....	....	....	....	....	....	....	....	....	....	....	....	....
	Kingston	MTJHL	2	0	0	0	0	....	....	....	....	....	....	....	....	....	....	....	....	....	....	....	....	....	....
1993-94	Sudbury Wolves	OHL	51	0	1	1	51	....	....	....	....	....	....	....	....	....	3	0	0	0	0	....	....	....	....
1994-95	Sudbury Wolves	OHL	39	6	6	12	91	....	....	....	....	....	....	....	....	....	....	....	....	....	....	....	....	....	....
	Niagara Falls	OHL	26	3	13	16	60	....	....	....	....	....	....	....	....	....	6	2	3	5	10	....	....	....	....
1995-96	Niagara Falls	OHL	64	5	41	46	129	....	....	....	....	....	....	....	....	....	10	1	5	6	16	....	....	....	....
	Buffalo	**NHL**	**1**	**0**	**1**	**1**	**2**	**0**	**0**	**0**	**2**	**0.0**	**1**	....	....	....	....	....	....	....	....	....	....	....	....
	Rochester	AHL	4	0	1	1	15	....	....	....	....	....	....	....	....	....	....	....	....	....	....	....	....	....	....
1996-97	**Buffalo**	**NHL**	**43**	**1**	**9**	**10**	**35**	**0**	**0**	**0**	**29**	**3.4**	**3**	....	....	....	**3**	**0**	**0**	**0**	**0**	**0**	**0**	**0**	....
	Rochester	AHL	7	2	5	7	4	....	....	....	....	....	....	....	....	....	....	....	....	....	....	....	....	....	....
1997-98	**Buffalo**	**NHL**	**56**	**1**	**13**	**14**	**42**	**0**	**0**	**0**	**55**	**1.8**	**–1**	....	....	....	**1**	**0**	**0**	**0**	**0**	**0**	**0**	**0**	....
	Rochester	AHL	13	1	7	8	11	....	....	....	....	....	....	....	....	....	....	....	....	....	....	....	....	....	....
1998-99	**Buffalo**	**NHL**	**72**	**0**	**6**	**6**	**75**	**0**	**0**	**0**	**57**	**0.0**	**20**	**0**	**0.0**	**20:28**	**21**	**0**	**3**	**3**	**24**	**0**	**0**	**0**	**22:31**
99-2000	**Buffalo**	**NHL**	**78**	**5**	**12**	**17**	**50**	**1**	**0**	**1**	**84**	**6.0**	**5**	**0**	**0.0**	**20:58**	**1**	**0**	**0**	**0**	**0**	**0**	**0**	**0**	**17:57**
2000-01	**Buffalo**	**NHL**	**74**	**1**	**10**	**11**	**76**	**0**	**0**	**0**	**62**	**1.6**	**9**	**2**	**0.0**	**19:24**	**8**	**1**	**0**	**1**	**6**	**0**	**0**	**1**	**19:23**
2001-02	**Buffalo**	**NHL**	**81**	**2**	**11**	**13**	**43**	**0**	**0**	**1**	**50**	**4.0**	**18**	**0**	**0.0**	**19:26**	....	....	....	....	....	....	....	....	....
2002-03	**Buffalo**	**NHL**	**59**	**0**	**5**	**5**	**49**	**0**	**0**	**0**	**44**	**0.0**	**–16**	**0**	**0.0**	**18:45**	....	....	....	....	....	....	....	....	....
2003-04	**Buffalo**	**NHL**	**43**	**2**	**3**	**5**	**41**	**0**	**0**	**1**	**29**	**6.9**	**6**	**0**	**0.0**	**17:44**	....	....	....	....	....	....	....	....	....
	NHL Totals		**507**	**12**	**70**	**82**	**413**	**1**	**0**	**3**	**412**	**2.9**		**2**	**0.0**	**19:37**	**34**	**1**	**3**	**4**	**30**	**0**	**0**	**1**	**21:32**

OHL Second All-Star Team (1996)

McKENNA, Steve

(mih-KEHN-ah, STEEV)

Left wing. Shoots left. 6'8", 252 lbs. Born, Toronto, Ont., August 21, 1973.

Season	Club	League	GP	G	A	Pts	PIM	PP	SH	GW	S	%	+/-	TF	F%	Min	GP	G	A	Pts	PIM	PP	SH	GW	Min
1991-92	Cambridge	OJHL-B	48	21	23	44	173	....	....	....	....	....	....	....	....	....	....	....	....	....	....	....	....	....	....
1992-93	Notre Dame	SJHL	STATISTICS NOT AVAILABLE																						
1993-94	Merrimack	H-East	37	1	2	3	74	....	....	....	....	....	....	....	....	....	....	....	....	....	....	....	....	....	....
1994-95	Merrimack	H-East	37	1	9	10	74	....	....	....	....	....	....	....	....	....	....	....	....	....	....	....	....	....	....
1995-96	Merrimack	H-East	33	3	11	14	67	....	....	....	....	....	....	....	....	....	....	....	....	....	....	....	....	....	....
1996-97	**Los Angeles**	**NHL**	**9**	**0**	**0**	**0**	**37**	**0**	**0**	**0**	**6**	**0.0**	**1**	....	....	....	....	....	....	....	....	....	....	....	....
	Phoenix	IHL	66	6	5	11	187	....	....	....	....	....	....	....	....	....	....	....	....	....	....	....	....	....	....
1997-98	**Los Angeles**	**NHL**	**62**	**4**	**4**	**8**	**150**	**1**	**0**	**0**	**42**	**9.5**	**–9**	....	....	....	**3**	**0**	**1**	**1**	**8**	**0**	**0**	**0**	....
	Fredericton	AHL	6	2	1	3	48	....	....	....	....	....	....	....	....	....	....	....	....	....	....	....	....	....	....
1998-99	**Los Angeles**	**NHL**	**20**	**1**	**0**	**1**	**36**	**0**	**0**	**0**	**12**	**8.3**	**–3**	**0**	**0.0**	**8:24**	....	....	....	....	....	....	....	....	....
99-2000	**Los Angeles**	**NHL**	**46**	**0**	**5**	**5**	**125**	**0**	**0**	**0**	**14**	**0.0**	**3**	**1**	**0.0**	**4:53**	....	....	....	....	....	....	....	....	....
2000-01	**Minnesota**	**NHL**	**20**	**1**	**1**	**2**	**19**	**0**	**0**	**0**	**12**	**8.3**	**0**	**0**	**0.0**	**7:59**	....	....	....	....	....	....	....	....	....
	Pittsburgh	**NHL**	**34**	**0**	**0**	**0**	**100**	**0**	**0**	**0**	**7**	**0.0**	**–4**	**0**	**0.0**	**3:16**	....	....	....	....	....	....	....	....	....
2001-02	**NY Rangers**	**NHL**	**54**	**2**	**1**	**3**	**144**	**1**	**0**	**1**	**17**	**11.8**	**0**	**2**	**0.0**	**3:59**	....	....	....	....	....	....	....	....	....
	Hartford	AHL	3	0	0	0	11	....	....	....	....	....	....	....	....	....	....	....	....	....	....	....	....	....	....
2002-03	**Pittsburgh**	**NHL**	**79**	**9**	**1**	**10**	**128**	**5**	**0**	**3**	**59**	**15.3**	**–18**	**1**	**0.0**	**7:45**	....	....	....	....	....	....	....	....	....
2003-04	**Pittsburgh**	**NHL**	**49**	**1**	**2**	**3**	**85**	**0**	**0**	**0**	**30**	**3.3**	**–10**	**3**	**0.0**	**6:19**	....	....	....	....	....	....	....	....	....
	NHL Totals		**373**	**18**	**14**	**32**	**824**	**7**	**0**	**4**	**199**	**9.0**		**7**	**0.0**	**5:58**	**3**	**0**	**1**	**1**	**8**	**0**	**0**	**0**	....

Signed as a free agent by **Los Angeles**, May 23, 1996. Selected by **Minnesota** from **Los Angeles** in Expansion Draft, June 23, 2000. Traded to **Pittsburgh** by **Minnesota** for Roman Simicek, January 13, 2001. Signed as a free agent by **NY Rangers**, August 28, 2001. Signed as a free agent by **Pittsburgh**, July 12, 2002.

McKENZIE, Jim

(MIHK-ehn-zee, JIHM) **NSH.**

Left wing. Shoots left. 6'4", 230 lbs. Born, Gull Lake, Sask., November 3, 1969. Hartford's 3rd choice, 73rd overall, in 1989 Entry Draft.

Season	Club	League	GP	G	A	Pts	PIM	PP	SH	GW	S	%	+/-	TF	F%	Min	GP	G	A	Pts	PIM	PP	SH	GW	Min
1985-86	Moose Jaw	SMHL	36	18	26	44	89	....	....	....	....	....	....	....	....	....	....	....	....	....	....	....	....	....	....
	Moose Jaw	WHL	3	0	2	2	0	....	....	....	....	....	....	....	....	....	....	....	....	....	....	....	....	....	....
1986-87	Moose Jaw	WHL	65	5	3	8	125	....	....	....	....	....	....	....	....	....	9	0	0	0	7	....	....	....	....
1987-88	Moose Jaw	WHL	62	1	17	18	134	....	....	....	....	....	....	....	....	....	....	....	....	....	....	....	....	....	....
1988-89	Victoria Cougars	WHL	67	15	27	42	176	....	....	....	....	....	....	....	....	....	8	1	4	5	30	....	....	....	....
1989-90	**Hartford**	**NHL**	**5**	**0**	**0**	**0**	**4**	**0**	**0**	**0**	**0**	**0.0**	**0**	....	....	....	....	....	....	....	....	....	....	....	....
	Binghamton	AHL	56	4	12	16	149	....	....	....	....	....	....	....	....	....	....	....	....	....	....	....	....	....	....
1990-91	**Hartford**	**NHL**	**41**	**4**	**3**	**7**	**108**	**0**	**0**	**0**	**16**	**25.0**	**–7**	....	....	....	**6**	**0**	**0**	**0**	**8**	**0**	**0**	**0**	....
	Springfield	AHL	24	3	4	7	102	....	....	....	....	....	....	....	....	....	....	....	....	....	....	....	....	....	....
1991-92	**Hartford**	**NHL**	**67**	**5**	**1**	**6**	**87**	**0**	**0**	**0**	**34**	**14.7**	**–6**	....	....	....	....	....	....	....	....	....	....	....	....
1992-93	**Hartford**	**NHL**	**64**	**3**	**6**	**9**	**202**	**0**	**0**	**0**	**36**	**8.3**	**–10**	....	....	....	....	....	....	....	....	....	....	....	....
1993-94	**Hartford**	**NHL**	**26**	**1**	**2**	**3**	**67**	**0**	**0**	**0**	**9**	**11.1**	**–6**	....	....	....	....	....	....	....	....	....	....	....	....
	Dallas	**NHL**	**34**	**2**	**3**	**5**	**63**	**0**	**0**	**1**	**18**	**11.1**	**4**	....	....	....	....	....	....	....	....	....	....	....	....
	Pittsburgh	**NHL**	**11**	**0**	**0**	**0**	**16**	**0**	**0**	**0**	**6**	**0.0**	**–5**	....	....	....	**3**	**0**	**0**	**0**	**0**	**0**	**0**	**0**	....
1994-95	**Pittsburgh**	**NHL**	**39**	**2**	**1**	**3**	**63**	**0**	**0**	**1**	**16**	**12.5**	**–7**	....	....	....	**5**	**0**	**0**	**0**	**4**	**0**	**0**	**0**	....
1995-96	**Winnipeg**	**NHL**	**73**	**4**	**2**	**6**	**202**	**0**	**0**	**0**	**28**	**14.3**	**–4**	....	....	....	**1**	**0**	**0**	**0**	**2**	**0**	**0**	**0**	....
1996-97	**Phoenix**	**NHL**	**65**	**5**	**3**	**8**	**200**	**0**	**0**	**1**	**38**	**13.2**	**–5**	....	....	....	**7**	**0**	**0**	**0**	**2**	**0**	**0**	**0**	....
1997-98	**Phoenix**	**NHL**	**64**	**3**	**4**	**7**	**146**	**0**	**0**	**0**	**35**	**8.6**	**–7**	....	....	....	**1**	**0**	**0**	**0**	**0**	**0**	**0**	**0**	....
1998-99	**Anaheim**	**NHL**	**73**	**5**	**4**	**9**	**99**	**1**	**0**	**1**	**59**	**8.5**	**–18**	**8**	**50.0**	**10:22**	**4**	**0**	**0**	**0**	**4**	**0**	**0**	**0**	**6:58**
99-2000	**Anaheim**	**NHL**	**31**	**3**	**3**	**6**	**48**	**0**	**0**	**0**	**22**	**13.6**	**–5**	**2**	**0.0**	**10:26**	....	....	....	....	....	....	....	....	....
	Washington	**NHL**	**30**	**1**	**2**	**3**	**16**	**0**	**0**	**0**	**10**	**10.0**	**0**	**0**	**0.0**	**6:22**	**1**	**0**	**0**	**0**	**0**	**0**	**0**	**0**	**0:17**
2000-01	**New Jersey**	**NHL**	**53**	**2**	**2**	**4**	**119**	**0**	**0**	**0**	**32**	**6.3**	**0**	**0**	**0.0**	**7:56**	**3**	**0**	**0**	**0**	**2**	**0**	**0**	**0**	**5:42**
2001-02	**New Jersey**	**NHL**	**67**	**3**	**5**	**8**	**123**	**1**	**0**	**0**	**33**	**9.1**	**0**	**3**	**0.0**	**7:19**	**6**	**0**	**0**	**0**	**2**	**0**	**0**	**0**	**9:47**
2002-03♦	**New Jersey**	**NHL**	**76**	**4**	**8**	**12**	**88**	**0**	**0**	**2**	**42**	**9.5**	**3**	**5**	**60.0**	**7:42**	**13**	**0**	**0**	**0**	**14**	**0**	**0**	**0**	**8:00**
2003-04	**Nashville**	**NHL**	**61**	**1**	**3**	**4**	**88**	**0**	**0**	**0**	**10**	**10.0**	**–13**	**3**	**66.7**	**6:14**	**1**	**0**	**0**	**0**	**0**	**0**	**0**	**0**	**3:32**
	NHL Totals		**880**	**48**	**52**	**100**	**1739**	**2**	**0**	**6**	**444**	**10.8**		**21**	**42.9**	**8:03**	**51**	**0**	**0**	**0**	**38**	**0**	**0**	**0**	**7:33**

Traded to **Florida** by **Hartford** for Alexander Godynyuk, December 16, 1993. Traded to **Dallas** by **Florida** for Dallas' 4th round choice (later traded to Ottawa – Ottawa selected Kevin Bolibruck) in 1995 Entry Draft, December 16, 1993. Traded to **Pittsburgh** by **Dallas** for Mike Needham, March 21, 1994. Signed as a free agent by **NY Islanders**, August 2, 1995. Claimed by **Winnipeg** from **NY Islanders** in Waiver Draft, October 2, 1995. Transferred to **Phoenix** after **Winnipeg** franchise relocated, July 1, 1996. Traded to **Anaheim** by **Phoenix** for Jean-Francois Jomphe, June 18, 1998. Claimed on waivers by **Washington** from **Anaheim**, January 20, 2000. Signed as a free agent by **New Jersey**, July 3, 2000. Signed as a free agent by **Nashville**, July 22, 2003.

McLAREN, Kyle

(mih-KLAIR-uhn, KIGHL) **S.J.**

Defense. Shoots left. 6'4", 225 lbs. Born, Humboldt, Sask., June 18, 1977. Boston's 1st choice, 9th overall, in 1995 Entry Draft.

Season	Club	League	GP	G	A	Pts	PIM	PP	SH	GW	S	%	+/-	TF	F%	Min	GP	G	A	Pts	PIM	PP	SH	GW	Min
1992-93	Lethbridge	AMHL	60	28	28	56	84	....	....	....	....	....	....	....	....	....	....	....	....	....	....	....	....	....	....
1993-94	Tacoma Rockets	WHL	62	1	9	10	53	....	....	....	....	....	....	....	....	....	6	1	4	5	6	....	....	....	....
1994-95	Tacoma Rockets	WHL	47	13	19	32	68	....	....	....	....	....	....	....	....	....	4	1	1	2	4	....	....	....	....
1995-96	**Boston**	**NHL**	**74**	**5**	**12**	**17**	**73**	**0**	**0**	**0**	**74**	**6.8**	**16**	....	....	....	**5**	**0**	**0**	**0**	**14**	**0**	**0**	**0**	....
1996-97	**Boston**	**NHL**	**58**	**5**	**9**	**14**	**54**	**0**	**0**	**1**	**68**	**7.4**	**–9**	....	....	....	....	....	....	....	....	....	....	....	....
1997-98	**Boston**	**NHL**	**66**	**5**	**20**	**25**	**56**	**2**	**0**	**0**	**101**	**5.0**	**13**	....	....	....	**6**	**1**	**0**	**1**	**4**	**1**	**0**	**0**	....
1998-99	**Boston**	**NHL**	**52**	**6**	**18**	**24**	**48**	**3**	**0**	**0**	**97**	**6.2**	**1**	**0**	**0.0**	**23:25**	**12**	**0**	**3**	**3**	**10**	**0**	**0**	**0**	**26:45**
99-2000	**Boston**	**NHL**	**71**	**8**	**11**	**19**	**67**	**2**	**0**	**3**	**142**	**5.6**	**–4**	**5**	**40.0**	**23:18**	....	....	....	....	....	....	....	....	....
2000-01	**Boston**	**NHL**	**58**	**5**	**12**	**17**	**53**	**2**	**0**	**0**	**91**	**5.5**	**–5**	**4**	**50.0**	**24:14**	....	....	....	....	....	....	....	....	....
2001-02	**Boston**	**NHL**	**38**	**0**	**8**	**8**	**19**	**0**	**0**	**0**	**57**	**0.0**	**–4**	**1**	**0.0**	**19:21**	**4**	**0**	**0**	**0**	**20**	**0**	**0**	**0**	**18:37**
2002-03	**San Jose**	**NHL**	**33**	**0**	**8**	**8**	**30**	**0**	**0**	**0**	**43**	**0.0**	**–10**	**0**	**0.0**	**22:40**	....	....	....	....	....	....	....	....	....
2003-04	**San Jose**	**NHL**	**64**	**2**	**22**	**24**	**60**	**0**	**1**	**0**	**67**	**3.0**	**10**	**1**	**0.0**	**21:01**	**16**	**0**	**3**	**3**	**10**	**0**	**0**	**0**	**24:09**
	NHL Totals		**514**	**36**	**120**	**156**	**460**	**9**	**1**	**4**	**740**	**4.9**		**11**	**36.4**	**22:29**	**43**	**1**	**6**	**7**	**58**	**1**	**0**	**0**	**24:26**

NHL All-Rookie Team (1996)

• Missed majority of 2001-02 season recovering from chest (October 10, 2001 vs. Minnesota) and wrist (December 26, 2001 vs. Ottawa) injuries. • Missed majority of 2002-03 season in contract dispute with Boston. Traded to **San Jose** by **Boston** with Boston's 4th round choice (Torrey Mitchell) in 2004 Entry Draft for Jeff Hackett and Jeff Jillson, January 23, 2003.

							Regular Season												Playoffs						
Season	Club	League	GP	G	A	Pts	PIM	PP	SH	GW	S	%	+/-	TF	F%	Min	GP	G	A	Pts	PIM	PP	SH	GW	Min

McLAREN, Steve (muh-KLAIR-uhn, STEEV) — T.B.

Defense. Shoots left. 6', 210 lbs. Born, Owen Sound, Ont., February 3, 1975. Chicago's 3rd choice, 85th overall, in 1994 Entry Draft.

Season	Club	League	GP	G	A	Pts	PIM	PP	SH	GW	S	%	+/-	TF	F%	Min	GP	G	A	Pts	PIM	PP	SH	GW	Min
1992-93	N. Bay Trappers	NOJHA	30	15	18	33	110																		
1993-94	North Bay	OHL	55	2	15	17	130											18	0	3	3	50				
1994-95	North Bay	OHL	27	3	10	13	119											6	2	1	3	23				
1995-96	Indianapolis Ice	IHL	54	1	2	3	170											3	0	0	0	2				
1996-97	Indianapolis Ice	IHL	63	2	5	7	309											4	0	0	0	10				
1997-98	Indianapolis Ice	IHL	61	3	5	8	208											5	0	0	0	24				
1998-99	Philadelphia	AHL	52	4	3	7	216											7	0	0	0	2				
99-2000	Philadelphia	AHL	64	1	2	3	247																			
2000-01	Philadelphia	AHL	48	3	1	4	177											8	0	0	0	38				
2001-02	Worcester IceCats	AHL	58	0	4	4	251											1	0	0	0	0				
2002-03	Worcester IceCats	AHL	40	0	0	0	80											3	0	0	0	4				
2003-04	**St. Louis**	**NHL**	6	0	0	0	25	0	0	0	2	0.0	0	0	0.0	2:47									
	Worcester IceCats	AHL	35	2	1	3	146											6	0	0	0	2				
	NHL Totals		6	0	0	0	25	0	0	0	2	0.0		0	0.0	2:47									

Signed as a free agent by **Philadelphia**, August 24, 1998. Signed as a free agent by **St. Louis**, July 16, 2001. • Missed majority of 2003-04 season recovering from head injury suffered in game vs. Columbus, December 29, 2003. Signed as a free agent by **Tampa Bay**, July 28, 2004.

McLEAN, Brett (mihk-LAYN, BREHT) — COL.

Center. Shoots left. 5'11", 194 lbs. Born, Comox, B.C., August 14, 1978. Dallas' 9th choice, 242nd overall, in 1997 Entry Draft.

Season	Club	League	GP	G	A	Pts	PIM	PP	SH	GW	S	%	+/-	TF	F%	Min	GP	G	A	Pts	PIM	PP	SH	GW	Min
1993-94	Notre Dame	SMBHL	71	109	124	233	70																			
1994-95	Tacoma Rockets	WHL	67	11	23	34	33											4	0	1	1	0				
1995-96	Kelowna Rockets	WHL	71	37	42	79	60											6	2	2	4	6				
1996-97	Kelowna Rockets	WHL	72	44	60	104	98											6	4	2	6	12				
1997-98	Kelowna Rockets	WHL	54	42	45	87	91											7	4	5	9	17				
1998-99	Kelowna Rockets	WHL	44	32	38	70	46																			
	Brandon	WHL	21	15	16	31	20											5	1	6	7	6				
	Cincinnati	AHL	7	0	3	3	6																			
99-2000	Johnstown Chiefs	ECHL	8	4	7	11	6																			
	Saint John Flames	AHL	72	15	23	38	115											3	0	1	1	2				
2000-01	Cleveland	IHL	74	20	24	44	54											4	0	0	0	18				
2001-02	Houston Aeros	AHL	78	24	21	45	71											14	1	6	7	12				
2002-03	**Chicago**	**NHL**	2	0	0	0	0	0	0	0	1	0.0	-1	19	26.3	10:47									
	Norfolk Admirals	AHL	77	23	38	61	60											9	2	6	8	9				
2003-04	**Chicago**	**NHL**	76	11	20	31	54	5	1	0	125	8.8	-11	1135	51.1	17:33									
	Norfolk Admirals	AHL	4	3	3	6	6																			
	NHL Totals		78	11	20	31	54	5	1	0	126	8.7		1154	50.7	17:23									

WHL West Second All-Star Team (1998)

Signed as a free agent by **Calgary**, September, 1999. Signed as a free agent by **Minnesota**, July 13, 2000. Signed as a free agent by **Chicago**, July 23, 2002. Signed as a free agent by **Colorado**, July 22, 2004.

McMORROW, Sean (muhk-MOHR-roh, SHAWN) — BUF.

Left wing. Shoots right. 6'4", 214 lbs. Born, Vancouver, B.C., January 19, 1982. Buffalo's 7th choice, 258th overall, in 2000 Entry Draft.

Season	Club	League	GP	G	A	Pts	PIM	PP	SH	GW	S	%	+/-	TF	F%	Min	GP	G	A	Pts	PIM	PP	SH	GW	Min
1998-99	Pickering Panthers	OPJHL	35	2	10	12	175																			
99-2000	Sarnia Sting	OHL	31	0	1	1	75																			
	Kitchener Rangers	OHL	31	0	1	1	67											4	0	0	0	12				
2000-01	Mississauga	OHL	13	0	0	0	34																			
	Kingston	OHL	7	0	1	1	22											5	0	0	0	0				
	London Knights	OHL	29	0	3	3	75																			
2001-02	London Knights	OHL	38	0	1	1	107											5	1	1	2	12				
	Oshawa Generals	OHL	27	6	1	7	63																			
2002-03	**Buffalo**	**NHL**	1	0	0	0	0	0	0	0	0	0.0	0	0	0.0	1:27									
	Rochester	AHL	64	0	1	1	315											3	0	0	0	17				
2003-04	Rochester	AHL	57	0	0	0	287											14	1	0	1	15				
	NHL Totals		1	0	0	0	0	0	0	0	0	0.0		0	0.0	1:27									

McNEILL, Grant (muhk-NEEL, GRANT) — FLA.

Defense. Shoots left. 6'2", 210 lbs. Born, Vermillion, Alta., June 8, 1983. Florida's 5th choice, 68th overall, in 2001 Entry Draft.

Season	Club	League	GP	G	A	Pts	PIM	PP	SH	GW	S	%	+/-	TF	F%	Min	GP	G	A	Pts	PIM	PP	SH	GW	Min
1998-99	Wainwright	AAHL	26	2	11	13	83											6	0	6	6	14				
99-2000	Prince Albert	WHL	58	1	1	2	43											6	0	1	1	0				
2000-01	Prince Albert	WHL	61	2	6	8	280																			
2001-02	Prince Albert	WHL	70	7	6	13	*326																			
2002-03	Prince Albert	WHL	71	1	8	9	280																			
2003-04	**Florida**	**NHL**	3	0	0	0	5	0	0	0	0	0.0	0	0	0.0	2:43									
	San Antonio	AHL	33	0	0	0	110																			
	NHL Totals		3	0	0	0	5	0	0	0	0	0.0		0	0.0	2:43									

• Missed majority of 2003-04 season recovering from jaw injury suffered in game vs. Cincinnati (AHL), January 21, 2004.

MELICHAR, Josef (mehl-ee-KHAHR, YOH-sehf) — PIT.

Defense. Shoots left. 6'2", 220 lbs. Born, Ceske Budejovice, Czech., January 20, 1979. Pittsburgh's 3rd choice, 71st overall, in 1997 Entry Draft.

Season	Club	League	GP	G	A	Pts	PIM	PP	SH	GW	S	%	+/-	TF	F%	Min	GP	G	A	Pts	PIM	PP	SH	GW	Min
1995-96	C. Budejovice Jr.	Czech-Jr.	38	3	4	7																				
1996-97	C. Budejovice Jr.	Czech-Jr.	41	2	3	5	10																			
1997-98	Tri-City	WHL	67	9	24	33	154																			
1998-99	Tri-City	WHL	65	8	28	36	125											11	1	0	1	15				
99-2000	Wilkes-Barre	AHL	80	3	9	12	126																			
2000-01	**Pittsburgh**	**NHL**	18	0	2	2	21	0	0	0	9	0.0	-5	0	0.0	14:54									
	Wilkes-Barre	AHL	46	2	5	7	69											21	0	5	5	6				
2001-02	**Pittsburgh**	**NHL**	60	0	3	3	68	0	0	0	46	0.0	-1	0	0.0	16:46									
2002-03	**Pittsburgh**	**NHL**	8	0	0	0	2	0	0	0	6	0.0	-2	0	0.0	15:19									
2003-04	**Pittsburgh**	**NHL**	82	3	5	8	62	0	0	0	78	3.8	-17	0	0.0	19:01									
	NHL Totals		168	3	10	13	153	0	0	0	139	2.2		0	0.0	17:36									

• Missed majority of 2002-03 season recovering from shoulder injury suffered in game vs. Boston, October 13, 2002.

MELLANBY, Scott (MEH-lihn-bee, SKAWT) — ATL.

Right wing. Shoots right. 6'1", 210 lbs. Born, Montreal, Que., June 11, 1966. Philadelphia's 2nd choice, 27th overall, in 1984 Entry Draft.

Season	Club	League	GP	G	A	Pts	PIM	PP	SH	GW	S	%	+/-	TF	F%	Min	GP	G	A	Pts	PIM	PP	SH	GW	Min
1982-83	Don Mills	MTHL	72	66	52	118	38																			
1983-84	Henry Carr	MTJHL	39	37	37	74	97																			
1984-85	U. of Wisconsin	WCHA	40	14	24	38	60																			
1985-86	U. of Wisconsin	WCHA	32	21	23	44	89																			
	Philadelphia	**NHL**	2	0	0	0	0	0	0	0	0	0.0	-1													
1986-87	**Philadelphia**	**NHL**	71	11	21	32	94	1	0	0	118	9.3	8					24	5	5	10	46	0	0	1	
1987-88	**Philadelphia**	**NHL**	75	25	26	51	185	7	0	2	190	13.2	-7					7	0	1	1	16	0	0	0	
1988-89	**Philadelphia**	**NHL**	76	21	29	50	183	11	0	3	202	10.4	-13					19	4	5	9	28	0	0	0	
1989-90	**Philadelphia**	**NHL**	57	6	17	23	77	0	0	1	104	5.8	-4													
1990-91	**Philadelphia**	**NHL**	74	20	21	41	155	5	0	6	165	12.1	6													
1991-92	**Edmonton**	**NHL**	80	23	27	50	197	7	0	5	159	14.5	5					16	2	1	3	29	1	0	1	
1992-93	**Edmonton**	**NHL**	69	15	17	32	147	6	0	3	114	13.2	-4													
1993-94	**Florida**	**NHL**	80	30	30	60	149	17	0	4	204	14.7	0													
1994-95	**Florida**	**NHL**	48	13	12	25	90	4	0	5	130	10.0	-16													
1995-96	**Florida**	**NHL**	79	32	38	70	160	19	0	5	225	14.2	4					22	3	6	9	44	2	0	0	
1996-97	**Florida**	**NHL**	82	27	29	56	170	9	1	4	221	12.2	7					5	0	2	2	4	0	0	0	
1997-98	**Florida**	**NHL**	79	15	24	39	127	6	0	1	188	8.0	-14													

			Regular Season														Playoffs								
Season	Club	League	GP	G	A	Pts	PIM	PP	SH	GW	S	%	+/-	TF	F%	Min	GP	G	A	Pts	PIM	PP	SH	GW	Min
1998-99	Florida	NHL	67	18	27	45	85	4	0	3	136	13.2	5	11	27.3	16:14	....	....	....	....	....	....	....	....	....
99-2000	Florida	NHL	77	18	28	46	126	6	0	2	134	13.4	14	20	60.0	14:51	4	0	1	1	2	0	0	0	13:09
2000-01	Florida	NHL	40	4	9	13	46	1	0	0	58	6.9	–13	4	50.0	14:59	....	....	....	....	....	....	....	....	....
	St. Louis	NHL	23	7	1	8	25	2	0	0	37	18.9	0	1	0.0	15:00	15	3	3	6	17	2	0	0	14:43
2001-02	St. Louis	NHL	64	15	26	41	93	8	0	2	137	10.9	–5	3	0.0	15:40	10	7	3	10	18	4	0	1	17:54
2002-03	St. Louis	NHL	80	26	31	57	176	13	0	4	132	19.7	1	11	45.5	16:39	6	0	1	1	10	0	0	0	16:18
2003-04	St. Louis	NHL	68	14	17	31	76	6	0	3	103	13.6	–7	4	50.0	15:29	4	0	1	1	2	0	0	0	14:16
	NHL Totals		1291	340	430	770	2361	132	1	51	2757	12.3		54	44.4	15:40	132	24	29	53	216	9	0	3	15:34

Played in NHL All-Star Game (1996)

Traded to **Edmonton** by **Philadelphia** with Craig Fisher and Craig Berube for Dave Brown, Corey Foster and Jari Kurri, May 30, 1991. Claimed by **Florida** from **Edmonton** in Expansion Draft, June 24, 1993. Traded to **St. Louis** by **Florida** for rights to Dave Morisset and St. Louis' 5th round choice (Vince Bellissimo) in 2002 Entry Draft, February 9, 2001. Signed as a free agent by **Atlanta**, July 26, 2004.

MELOCHE, Eric

(muh-LAWSH, AIR-ihk) **PHI.**

Right wing. Shoots right. 5'10", 197 lbs. Born, Montreal, Que., May 1, 1976. Pittsburgh's 7th choice, 186th overall, in 1996 Entry Draft.

Season	Club	League	GP	G	A	Pts	PIM	PP	SH	GW	S	%	+/-	TF	F%	Min	GP	G	A	Pts	PIM	PP	SH	GW	Min
1994-95	Cornwall Colts	OCJHL	40	7	15	22	51	....	....	....	....	....	....	....	....	....	....	....	....	....	....	....	....	....	....
1995-96	Cornwall Colts	OCJHL	64	68	53	121	162	....	....	....	....	....	....	....	....	....	....	....	....	....	....	....	....	....	....
1996-97	Ohio State	CCHA	39	12	11	23	78	....	....	....	....	....	....	....	....	....	....	....	....	....	....	....	....	....	....
1997-98	Ohio State	CCHA	42	26	22	48	86	....	....	....	....	....	....	....	....	....	....	....	....	....	....	....	....	....	....
1998-99	Ohio State	CCHA	35	11	16	27	87	....	....	....	....	....	....	....	....	....	....	....	....	....	....	....	....	....	....
99-2000	Ohio State	CCHA	36	20	11	31	*138	....	....	....	....	....	....	....	....	....	....	....	....	....	....	....	....	....	....
2000-01	Wilkes-Barre	AHL	79	20	20	40	72	....	....	....	....	....	....	....	....	....	21	6	10	16	17	....	....	....	....
2001-02	Pittsburgh	NHL	23	0	1	1	8	0	0	0	29	0.0	–7	4	0.0	10:10	....	....	....	....	....	....	....	....	....
	Wilkes-Barre	AHL	55	13	14	27	91	....	....	....	....	....	....	....	....	....	....	....	....	....	....	....	....	....	....
2002-03	Pittsburgh	NHL	13	5	1	6	4	2	0	1	34	14.7	–2	27	55.6	0:00	....	....	....	....	....	....	....	....	....
	Wilkes-Barre	AHL	59	12	17	29	95	....	....	....	....	....	....	....	....	....	6	1	0	1	20	....	....	....	....
2003-04	Pittsburgh	NHL	25	3	7	10	20	0	0	0	28	10.7	–6	92	39.1	14:47	....	....	....	....	....	....	....	....	....
	Wilkes-Barre	AHL	56	16	26	42	49	....	....	....	....	....	....	....	....	....	23	9	6	15	14	....	....	....	....
	NHL Totals		61	8	9	17	32	2	0	1	91	8.8		123	29.3	9:54	....	....	....	....	....	....	....	....	....

Signed as a free agent by **Philadelphia**, July 14, 2004.

MESSIER, Eric

(MEHS-see-ay, AIR-ihk)

Left wing. Shoots left. 6'2", 195 lbs. Born, Drummondville, Que., October 29, 1973.

Season	Club	League	GP	G	A	Pts	PIM	PP	SH	GW	S	%	+/-	TF	F%	Min	GP	G	A	Pts	PIM	PP	SH	GW	Min
1990-91	Swift Textile	QAHA	STATISTICS NOT AVAILABLE																						
	Mtl-Bourassa	QAAA	3	0	1	1	0	....	....	....	....	....	....	....	....	....	2	0	0	0	0	....	....	....	....
1991-92	Trois-Rivieres	QMJHL	58	2	10	12	28	....	....	....	....	....	....	....	....	....	15	2	2	4	13	....	....	....	....
1992-93	Sherbrooke	QMJHL	51	4	17	21	82	....	....	....	....	....	....	....	....	....	15	0	4	4	18	....	....	....	....
1993-94	Sherbrooke	QMJHL	67	4	24	28	69	....	....	....	....	....	....	....	....	....	12	1	7	8	14	....	....	....	....
1994-95	U. Quebec T-R	OUAA	13	8	5	13	20	....	....	....	....	....	....	....	....	....	4	0	3	3	8	....	....	....	....
1995-96	Cornwall Aces	AHL	72	5	9	14	111	....	....	....	....	....	....	....	....	....	8	1	1	2	20	....	....	....	....
1996-97	Colorado	NHL	21	0	0	0	4	0	0	0	11	0.0	7	....	....	....	6	0	0	0	4	0	0	0	....
	Hershey Bears	AHL	55	16	26	42	69	....	....	....	....	....	....	....	....	....	9	3	8	11	14	....	....	....	....
1997-98	Colorado	NHL	62	4	12	16	20	0	0	0	66	6.1	4	....	....	....	....	....	....	....	....	....	....	....	....
1998-99	Colorado	NHL	31	4	2	6	14	1	0	1	30	13.3	0	0	0.0	13:43	3	0	0	0	0	0	0	0	4:40
	Hershey Bears	AHL	6	1	3	4	4	....	....	....	....	....	....	....	....	....	....	....	....	....	....	....	....	....	....
99-2000	Colorado	NHL	61	3	6	9	24	1	0	0	28	10.7	0	4	25.0	10:27	14	0	1	1	4	0	0	0	4:55
2000-01 ♦	Colorado	NHL	64	5	7	12	26	0	0	1	60	8.3	–3	9	44.4	12:16	23	2	2	4	14	0	0	0	16:16
2001-02	Colorado	NHL	74	5	10	15	26	0	0	3	84	6.0	–5	8	25.0	15:15	21	1	2	3	0	0	0	0	16:34
2002-03	Colorado	NHL	72	4	10	14	16	0	1	1	52	7.7	–2	17	17.7	12:20	5	0	0	0	0	0	0	0	6:57
2003-04	Florida	NHL	21	0	3	3	16	0	0	0	13	0.0	–2	19	10.5	11:16	....	....	....	....	....	....	....	....	....
	NHL Totals		406	25	50	75	146	2	1	6	344	7.3		57	21.1	12:42	72	3	5	8	22	0	0	0	12:43

QMJHL Second All-Star Team (1994)

Signed as a free agent by **Colorado**, June 14, 1995. • Missed majority of 1998-99 season recovering from elbow injury suffered in game vs. Ottawa, October 10, 1998. Traded to **Florida** by **Colorado** with Vaclav Nedorost for Peter Worrell and Florida's 2nd round choice (later traded to NY Rangers – later traded back to Florida – Florida selected David Shantz) in 2004 Entry Draft, July 18, 2003. • Missed majority of 2003-04 season recovering from wrist injury suffered in game vs. Atlanta, November 21, 2003.

MESSIER, Mark

(MEHS-see-ay, MAHRK)

Center. Shoots left. 6'1", 210 lbs. Born, Edmonton, Alta., January 18, 1961. Edmonton's 2nd choice, 48th overall, in 1979 Entry Draft.

Season	Club	League	GP	G	A	Pts	PIM	PP	SH	GW	S	%	+/-	TF	F%	Min	GP	G	A	Pts	PIM	PP	SH	GW	Min
1976-77	Spruce Grove	AJHL	57	27	39	66	91	....	....	....	....	....	....	....	....	....	....	....	....	....	....	....	....	....	....
1977-78	St. Albert Saints	AJHL	54	25	49	74	194	....	....	....	....	....	....	....	....	....	....	....	....	....	....	....	....	....	....
	Portland	WHL	....	....	....	....	....	....	....	....	....	....	....	....	....	....	7	4	1	5	2	....	....	....	....
1978-79	St. Albert Saints	AJHL	17	15	18	33	64	....	....	....	....	....	....	....	....	....	....	....	....	....	....	....	....	....	....
	Indianapolis	WHA	5	0	0	0	0	....	....	....	....	....	....	....	....	....	....	....	....	....	....	....	....	....	....
	Cincinnati	WHA	47	1	10	11	58	....	....	....	....	....	....	....	....	....	....	....	....	....	....	....	....	....	....
1979-80	Edmonton	NHL	75	12	21	33	120	1	1	1	113	10.6	–10	....	....	....	3	1	2	3	2	0	1	0	....
	Houston Apollos	CHL	4	0	3	3	4	....	....	....	....	....	....	....	....	....	....	....	....	....	....	....	....	....	....
1980-81	Edmonton	NHL	72	23	40	63	102	4	0	1	179	12.8	–12	....	....	....	9	2	5	7	13	0	0	0	....
1981-82	Edmonton	NHL	78	50	38	88	119	10	0	3	235	21.3	21	....	....	....	5	1	2	3	8	0	0	0	....
1982-83	Edmonton	NHL	77	48	58	106	72	12	1	2	237	20.3	19	....	....	....	15	15	6	21	14	4	2	0	....
1983-84 ♦	Edmonton	NHL	73	37	64	101	165	7	4	7	219	16.9	40	....	....	....	19	8	18	26	19	1	1	2	....
1984-85 ♦	Edmonton	NHL	55	23	31	54	57	4	5	1	136	16.9	8	....	....	....	18	12	13	25	12	1	1	1	....
1985-86	Edmonton	NHL	63	35	49	84	68	10	5	7	201	17.4	36	....	....	....	10	4	6	10	18	0	2	0	....
1986-87 ♦	Edmonton	NHL	77	37	70	107	73	7	4	5	208	17.8	21	....	....	....	21	12	16	28	16	1	2	1	....
1987-88 ♦	Edmonton	NHL	77	37	74	111	103	12	3	7	182	20.3	21	....	....	....	19	11	23	34	29	7	1	0	....
1988-89	Edmonton	NHL	72	33	61	94	130	6	6	4	164	20.1	–5	....	....	....	7	1	11	12	8	0	0	0	....
1989-90 ♦	Edmonton	NHL	79	45	84	129	79	13	6	3	211	21.3	19	....	....	....	22	9	*22	*31	20	1	1	1	....
1990-91	Edmonton	NHL	53	12	52	64	34	3	1	2	109	11.0	15	....	....	....	18	4	11	15	16	1	0	0	....
1991-92	NY Rangers	NHL	79	35	72	107	76	12	4	6	212	16.5	31	....	....	....	11	7	7	14	6	2	2	0	....
1992-93	NY Rangers	NHL	75	25	66	91	72	7	2	2	215	11.6	–6	....	....	....	....	....	....	....	....	....	....	....	....
1993-94 ♦	NY Rangers	NHL	76	26	58	84	76	6	2	5	216	12.0	25	....	....	....	23	12	18	30	33	2	1	4	....
1994-95	NY Rangers	NHL	46	14	39	53	40	3	3	2	126	11.1	8	....	....	....	10	3	10	13	8	2	0	1	....
1995-96	NY Rangers	NHL	74	47	52	99	122	14	1	5	241	19.5	29	....	....	....	11	4	7	11	16	2	0	1	....
1996-97	NY Rangers	NHL	71	36	48	84	88	7	5	9	227	15.9	12	....	....	....	15	3	9	12	6	0	0	1	....
1997-98	Vancouver	NHL	82	22	38	60	58	8	2	2	139	15.8	–10	....	....	....	....	....	....	....	....	....	....	....	....
1998-99	Vancouver	NHL	59	13	35	48	33	4	2	2	97	13.4	–12	1536	53.9	22:36	....	....	....	....	....	....	....	....	....
99-2000	Vancouver	NHL	66	17	37	54	30	6	0	4	131	13.0	–15	1684	56.8	21:12	....	....	....	....	....	....	....	....	....
2000-01	NY Rangers	NHL	82	24	43	67	89	12	3	2	131	18.3	–25	1879	55.5	19:14	....	....	....	....	....	....	....	....	....
2001-02	NY Rangers	NHL	41	7	16	23	32	2	0	2	69	10.1	–1	787	53.6	18:31	....	....	....	....	....	....	....	....	....
2002-03	NY Rangers	NHL	78	18	22	40	30	8	1	5	117	15.4	–2	1280	52.9	18:38	....	....	....	....	....	....	....	....	....
2003-04	NY Rangers	NHL	76	18	25	43	42	1	2	3	104	17.3	3	1241	55.0	16:29	....	....	....	....	....	....	....	....	....
	NHL Totals		1756	694	1193	1887	1910	179	63	92	4219	16.4		8407	54.8	19:20	236	109	186	295	244	24	14	12	....

NHL First All-Star Team (1982, 1983, 1990, 1992) • NHL Second All-Star Team (1984) • Conn Smythe Trophy (1984) • Lester B. Pearson Award (1990, 1992) • Hart Trophy (1990, 1992)

Played in NHL All-Star Game (1982, 1983, 1984, 1986, 1988, 1989, 1990, 1991, 1992, 1994, 1996, 1997, 1998, 2000, 2004)

Signed as an underage free agent by **Indianapolis** (WHA) to a 10-game tryout contract, November 5, 1978. Signed as a free agent by **Cincinnati** (WHA) after **Indianapolis** (WHA) franchise folded, December, 1978. Traded to **NY Rangers** by **Edmonton** with future considerations (Jeff Beukeboom for David Shaw, November 12, 1991) for Bernie Nicholls, Steven Rice and Louie DeBrusk, October 4, 1991. Signed as a free agent by **Vancouver**, July 30, 1997. Signed as a free agent by **NY Rangers**, July 13, 2000. • Missed majority of 2001-02 season recovering from back injury suffered in game vs. Toronto, December 8, 2001. Traded to **San Jose** by **NY Rangers** for San Jose's 4th round choice (Ryan Callahan) in 2004 Entry Draft, June 30, 2003. Signed as a free agent by **NY Rangers**, September 5, 2003.

MEYER, Freddy
(MAY-uhr, FREHD) **PHI.**

Defense. Shoots left. 5'10", 192 lbs. Born, Sanbornville, NH, January 4, 1981.

			Regular Season														Playoffs								
Season	Club	League	GP	G	A	Pts	PIM	PP	SH	GW	S	%	+/-	TF	F%	Min	GP	G	A	Pts	PIM	PP	SH	GW	Min
1996-97	Cardigan Prep	Hi-School	Statistics Not Available																						
1997-98	U.S. National U-17	USDP	Statistics Not Available																						
1998-99	U.S. National U-17	USDP	3	0	2	2	0	....	....	....	....	....	....	....	....	....	....	....	....	....	....	....	....	....	....
	U.S. National U-18	USDP	54	10	23	33	151	....	....	....	....	....	....	....	....	....	....	....	....	....	....	....	....	....	....
99-2000	U.S. National U-18	USDP	28	3	8	11	60	....	....	....	....	....	....	....	....	....	....	....	....	....	....	....	....	....	....
	Boston University	H-East	25	1	11	12	52	....	....	....	....	....	....	....	....	....	....	....	....	....	....	....	....	....	....
2000-01	Boston University	H-East	28	6	13	19	82	....	....	....	....	....	....	....	....	....	....	....	....	....	....	....	....	....	....
2001-02	Boston University	H-East	37	5	15	20	78	....	....	....	....	....	....	....	....	....	....	....	....	....	....	....	....	....	....
2002-03	Boston University	H-East	36	5	16	21	76	....	....	....	....	....	....	....	....	....	....	....	....	....	....	....	....	....	....
2003-04	**Philadelphia**	**NHL**	**1**	**0**	**0**	**0**	**0**	**0**	**0**	**0**	**1**	**0.0**	**0**	**0**	**0.0**	**15:24**	....	....	....	....	....	....	....	....	....
	Philadelphia	AHL	59	14	14	28	50	....	....	....	....	....	....	....	....	....	12	0	3	3	8	....	....	....	....
	NHL Totals		**1**	**0**	**0**	**0**	**0**	**0**	**0**	**0**	**1**	**0.0**		**0**	**0.0**	**15:24**	....	....	....	....	....	....	....	....	....

Hockey East All-Rookie Team (2000) • Hockey East First All-Star Team (2003) • NCAA East First All-American Team (2003)

Signed as a free agent by **Philadelphia**, May 21, 2003.

MEZEI, Branislav
(MEH-tzay, BRAN-ih-slav) **FLA.**

Defense. Shoots left. 6'5", 236 lbs. Born, Nitra, Czech., October 8, 1980. NY Islanders' 3rd choice, 10th overall, in 1999 Entry Draft.

Season	Club	League	GP	G	A	Pts	PIM	PP	SH	GW	S	%	+/-	TF	F%	Min	GP	G	A	Pts	PIM	PP	SH	GW	Min
1996-97	HC Nitra Jr.	Slovak-Jr.	40	8	17	25	42	....	....	....	....	....	....	....	....	....	....	....	....	....	....	....	....	....	....
1997-98	Belleville Bulls	OHL	53	3	5	8	58	....	....	....	....	....	....	....	....	....	8	0	2	2	8	....	....	....	....
1998-99	Belleville Bulls	OHL	60	5	18	23	90	....	....	....	....	....	....	....	....	....	18	0	4	4	29	....	....	....	....
99-2000	Belleville Bulls	OHL	58	7	21	28	99	....	....	....	....	....	....	....	....	....	6	0	3	3	10	....	....	....	....
2000-01	**NY Islanders**	**NHL**	**42**	**1**	**4**	**5**	**53**	**0**	**0**	**0**	**29**	**3.4**	**–5**	**0**	**0.0**	**14:48**	....	....	....	....	....	....	....	....	....
	Lowell	AHL	20	0	3	3	28	....	....	....	....	....	....	....	....	....	....	....	....	....	....	....	....	....	....
2001-02	**NY Islanders**	**NHL**	**24**	**0**	**2**	**2**	**12**	**0**	**0**	**0**	**4**	**0.0**	**2**	**0**	**0.0**	**8:28**	....	....	....	....	....	....	....	....	....
	Bridgeport	AHL	59	1	9	10	137	....	....	....	....	....	....	....	....	....	20	0	1	1	48	....	....	....	....
2002-03	**Florida**	**NHL**	**11**	**2**	**0**	**2**	**10**	**0**	**0**	**1**	**10**	**20.0**	**–2**	**0**	**0.0**	**18:22**	....	....	....	....	....	....	....	....	....
	San Antonio	AHL	1	0	0	0	0	....	....	....	....	....	....	....	....	....	3	0	0	0	0	....	....	....	....
2003-04	**Florida**	**NHL**	**45**	**0**	**7**	**7**	**80**	**0**	**0**	**0**	**26**	**0.0**	**–4**	**0**	**0.0**	**17:43**	....	....	....	....	....	....	....	....	....
	NHL Totals		**122**	**3**	**13**	**16**	**155**	**0**	**0**	**1**	**69**	**4.3**		**0**	**0.0**	**14:57**	....	....	....	....	....	....	....	....	....

OHL First All-Star Team (2000)

Traded to **Florida** by **NY Islanders** for Jason Wiemer, July 3, 2002. • Missed majority of 2002-03 season recovering from ankle (October 12, 2002 vs. Atlanta) and foot (January 1, 2003 vs. New Jersey) injuries.

MICHALEK, Milan
(mih-KHAL-ihk, MEE-lahn) **S.J.**

Right wing. Shoots left. 6'2", 220 lbs. Born, Jindrichuv Hradec, Czech., December 7, 1984. San Jose's 1st choice, 6th overall, in 2003 Entry Draft.

Season	Club	League	GP	G	A	Pts	PIM	PP	SH	GW	S	%	+/-	TF	F%	Min	GP	G	A	Pts	PIM	PP	SH	GW	Min
99-2000	HC Hradek 16	Czech-Jr.	3	2	5	7	0	....	....	....	....	....	....	....	....	....	....	....	....	....	....	....	....	....	....
	C. Budejovice Jr.	Czech-Jr.	48	16	26	42	42	....	....	....	....	....	....	....	....	....	6	3	1	4	4	....	....	....	....
2000-01	C. Budejovice Jr.	Czech-Jr.	30	10	13	23	30	....	....	....	....	....	....	....	....	....	4	1	3	4	2	....	....	....	....
	Ceske Budejovice	Czech	5	0	0	0	0	....	....	....	....	....	....	....	....	....	....	....	....	....	....	....	....	....	....
2001-02	Ceske Budejovice	Czech	47	6	11	17	12	....	....	....	....	....	....	....	....	....	....	....	....	....	....	....	....	....	....
	C. Budejovice Jr.	Czech-Jr.	5	3	2	5	4	....	....	....	....	....	....	....	....	....	7	5	4	9	14	....	....	....	....
	HC Hradek	Czech-2	3	2	0	2	0	....	....	....	....	....	....	....	....	....	....	....	....	....	....	....	....	....	....
2002-03	Ceske Budejovice	Czech	46	3	5	8	14	....	....	....	....	....	....	....	....	....	4	1	0	1	2	....	....	....	....
	Kladno	Czech-2	....	....	....	....	....	....	....	....	....	....	....	....	....	....	6	2	2	4	16	....	....	....	....
2003-04	**San Jose**	**NHL**	**2**	**1**	**0**	**1**	**4**	**0**	**0**	**0**	**1**	**100.0**	**1**	**0**	**0.0**	**9:05**	....	....	....	....	....	....	....	....	....
	Cleveland Barons	AHL	7	2	2	4	4	....	....	....	....	....	....	....	....	....	....	....	....	....	....	....	....	....	....
	NHL Totals		**2**	**1**	**0**	**1**	**4**	**0**	**0**	**0**	**1**	**100.0**		**0**	**0.0**	**9:05**	....	....	....	....	....	....	....	....	....

• Missed majority of 2003-04 season recovering from knee injury suffered in game vs. Calgary, October 11, 2003.

MICHALEK, Zbynek
(mih-KHAL-ihk, ZBIGH-nehk) **MIN.**

Defense. Shoots right. 6'1", 199 lbs. Born, Jindrichuv Hradec, Czech., December 23, 1982.

Season	Club	League	GP	G	A	Pts	PIM	PP	SH	GW	S	%	+/-	TF	F%	Min	GP	G	A	Pts	PIM	PP	SH	GW	Min
99-2000	Karlovy Vary Jr.	Czech-Jr.	40	2	10	12	20	....	....	....	....	....	....	....	....	....	....	....	....	....	....	....	....	....	....
2000-01	Shawinigan	QMJHL	69	10	29	39	52	....	....	....	....	....	....	....	....	....	3	0	0	0	0	....	....	....	....
2001-02	Shawinigan	QMJHL	68	16	35	51	54	....	....	....	....	....	....	....	....	....	10	8	7	15	10	....	....	....	....
2002-03	Houston Aeros	AHL	62	4	10	14	26	....	....	....	....	....	....	....	....	....	23	1	1	2	6	....	....	....	....
2003-04	**Minnesota**	**NHL**	**22**	**1**	**1**	**2**	**4**	**0**	**0**	**0**	**17**	**5.9**	**–7**	**0**	**0.0**	**14:13**	....	....	....	....	....	....	....	....	....
	Houston Aeros	AHL	55	5	16	21	32	....	....	....	....	....	....	....	....	....	2	1	0	1	0	....	....	....	....
	NHL Totals		**22**	**1**	**1**	**2**	**4**	**0**	**0**	**0**	**17**	**5.9**		**0**	**0.0**	**14:13**	....	....	....	....	....	....	....	....	....

Signed as a free agent by **Minnesota**, September 29, 2001.

MIETTINEN, Antti
(mih-EHT-tih-nehn, AN-tee) **DAL.**

Center. Shoots right. 5'11", 180 lbs. Born, Hameenlinna, Finland, July 3, 1980. Dallas' 10th choice, 224th overall, in 2000 Entry Draft.

Season	Club	League	GP	G	A	Pts	PIM	PP	SH	GW	S	%	+/-	TF	F%	Min	GP	G	A	Pts	PIM	PP	SH	GW	Min
1996-97	HPK B	Finn-Jr.	36	24	29	53	34	....	....	....	....	....	....	....	....	....	....	....	....	....	....	....	....	....	....
1997-98	HPK B	Finn-Jr.	34	13	28	41	63	....	....	....	....	....	....	....	....	....	8	1	0	1	2	....	....	....	....
	HPK Jr.	Finn-Jr.	8	1	0	1	2	....	....	....	....	....	....	....	....	....	....	....	....	....	....	....	....	....	....
1998-99	HPK Jr.	Finn-Jr.	35	17	22	39	28	....	....	....	....	....	....	....	....	....	....	....	....	....	....	....	....	....	....
	FoPS Forssa	Finland-2	4	3	1	4	6	....	....	....	....	....	....	....	....	....	....	....	....	....	....	....	....	....	....
	HPK Hameenlinna	Finland	13	0	0	0	2	....	....	....	....	....	....	....	....	....	4	0	0	0	0	....	....	....	....
99-2000	HPK Jr.	Finn-Jr.	16	11	13	24	16	....	....	....	....	....	....	....	....	....	....	....	....	....	....	....	....	....	....
	HPK Hameenlinna	Finland	39	2	1	3	8	....	....	....	....	....	....	....	....	....	7	1	0	1	0	....	....	....	....
2000-01	HPK Jr.	Finn-Jr.	4	3	10	13	2	....	....	....	....	....	....	....	....	....	....	....	....	....	....	....	....	....	....
	HPK Hameenlinna	Finland	55	13	11	24	20	....	....	....	....	....	....	....	....	....	....	....	....	....	....	....	....	....	....
2001-02	HPK Hameenlinna	Finland	56	19	37	56	50	....	....	....	....	....	....	....	....	....	8	2	4	6	8	....	....	....	....
2002-03	HPK Hameenlinna	Finland	53	25	25	50	54	....	....	....	....	....	....	....	....	....	10	1	7	8	29	....	....	....	....
2003-04	**Dallas**	**NHL**	**16**	**1**	**0**	**1**	**0**	**0**	**0**	**1**	**17**	**5.9**	**–9**	**1**	**0.0**	**9:51**	....	....	....	....	....	....	....	....	....
	Utah Grizzlies	AHL	48	7	23	30	20	....	....	....	....	....	....	....	....	....	....	....	....	....	....	....	....	....	....
	NHL Totals		**16**	**1**	**0**	**1**	**0**	**0**	**0**	**1**	**17**	**5.9**		**1**	**0.0**	**9:51**	....	....	....	....	....	....	....	....	....

MILLER, Aaron
(MIHL-luhr, AIR-ruhn) **L.A.**

Defense. Shoots right. 6'4", 200 lbs. Born, Buffalo, NY, August 11, 1971. NY Rangers' 6th choice, 88th overall, in 1989 Entry Draft.

Season	Club	League	GP	G	A	Pts	PIM	PP	SH	GW	S	%	+/-	TF	F%	Min	GP	G	A	Pts	PIM	PP	SH	GW	Min
1987-88	Niagara Scenics	NAJHL	30	4	9	13	2	....	....	....	....	....	....	....	....	....	....	....	....	....	....	....	....	....	....
1988-89	Niagara Scenics	NAJHL	59	24	38	62	60	....	....	....	....	....	....	....	....	....	....	....	....	....	....	....	....	....	....
1989-90	U. of Vermont	ECAC	31	1	15	16	24	....	....	....	....	....	....	....	....	....	....	....	....	....	....	....	....	....	....
1990-91	U. of Vermont	ECAC	30	3	7	10	22	....	....	....	....	....	....	....	....	....	....	....	....	....	....	....	....	....	....
1991-92	U. of Vermont	ECAC	31	3	16	19	28	....	....	....	....	....	....	....	....	....	....	....	....	....	....	....	....	....	....
1992-93	U. of Vermont	ECAC	30	4	13	17	16	....	....	....	....	....	....	....	....	....	....	....	....	....	....	....	....	....	....
1993-94	**Quebec**	**NHL**	**1**	**0**	**0**	**0**	**0**	**0**	**0**	**0**	**0**	**0.0**	**–1**	....	....	....	....	....	....	....	....	....	....	....	....
	Cornwall Aces	AHL	64	4	10	14	49	....	....	....	....	....	....	....	....	....	13	0	2	2	10	....	....	....	....
1994-95	Cornwall Aces	AHL	76	4	18	22	69	....	....	....	....	....	....	....	....	....	....	....	....	....	....	....	....	....	....
	Quebec	**NHL**	**9**	**0**	**3**	**3**	**6**	**0**	**0**	**0**	**12**	**0.0**	**2**	....	....	....	....	....	....	....	....	....	....	....	....
1995-96	**Colorado**	**NHL**	**5**	**0**	**0**	**0**	**0**	**0**	**0**	**0**	**2**	**0.0**	**0**	....	....	....	....	....	....	....	....	....	....	....	....
	Cornwall Aces	AHL	62	4	23	27	77	....	....	....	....	....	....	....	....	....	8	0	1	1	6	....	....	....	....
1996-97	**Colorado**	**NHL**	**56**	**5**	**12**	**17**	**15**	**0**	**0**	**3**	**47**	**10.6**	**15**	....	....	....	**17**	**1**	**2**	**3**	**10**	**0**	**0**	**0**	....
1997-98	**Colorado**	**NHL**	**55**	**2**	**2**	**4**	**51**	**0**	**0**	**0**	**29**	**6.9**	**0**	....	....	....	**7**	**0**	**0**	**0**	**8**	**0**	**0**	**0**	....
1998-99	**Colorado**	**NHL**	**76**	**5**	**13**	**18**	**42**	**1**	**0**	**2**	**87**	**5.7**	**3**	**0**	**0.0**	**21:49**	**19**	**1**	**5**	**6**	**10**	**0**	**0**	**0**	**21:13**
99-2000	**Colorado**	**NHL**	**53**	**1**	**7**	**8**	**36**	**0**	**0**	**0**	**44**	**2.3**	**3**	**0**	**0.0**	**19:05**	**17**	**1**	**1**	**2**	**6**	**0**	**0**	**0**	**19:12**
2000-01	**Colorado**	**NHL**	**56**	**4**	**9**	**13**	**29**	**0**	**0**	**0**	**49**	**8.2**	**19**	**0**	**0.0**	**18:25**	....	....	....	....	....	....	....	....	....
	Los Angeles	**NHL**	**13**	**0**	**5**	**5**	**14**	**0**	**0**	**0**	**10**	**0.0**	**3**	**1**	**0.0**	**22:44**	**13**	**0**	**1**	**1**	**6**	**0**	**0**	**0**	**22:02**
2001-02	**Los Angeles**	**NHL**	**74**	**5**	**12**	**17**	**54**	**0**	**1**	**3**	**75**	**6.7**	**14**	**0**	**0.0**	**22:21**	**7**	**0**	**0**	**0**	**0**	**0**	**0**	**0**	**26:28**
	United States	Olympics	6	0	0	0	4	....	....	....	....	....	....	....	....	....	....	....	....	....	....	....	....	....	....

			Regular Season														Playoffs								
Season	Club	League	GP	G	A	Pts	PIM	PP	SH	GW	S	%	+/-	TF	F%	Min	GP	G	A	Pts	PIM	PP	SH	GW	Min
2002-03	**Los Angeles**	**NHL**	**49**	**1**	**5**	**6**	**24**	**0**	**0**	**0**	**34**	**2.9**	**–7**	**1**	**100.0**	**21:30**									
2003-04	**Los Angeles**	**NHL**	**35**	**1**	**2**	**3**	**32**	**0**	**0**	**0**	**26**	**3.8**	**–3**	**0**	**0.0**	**19:00**									
	NHL Totals		**482**	**24**	**70**	**94**	**303**	**1**	**1**	**8**	**415**	**5.8**		**2**	**50.0**	**20:42**	**80**	**3**	**9**	**12**	**40**	**0**	**0**	**0**	**21:27**

ECAC First All-Star Team (1993) • NCAA East Second All-American Team (1993)

Traded to **Quebec** by **NY Rangers** with NY Rangers' 5th round choice (Bill Lindsay) in 1991 Entry Draft for Joe Cirella, January 17, 1991. Transferred to **Colorado** after **Quebec** franchise relocated, June 21, 1995. Traded to **Los Angeles** by **Colorado** with Adam Deadmarsh, a player to be named later (Jared Aulin, March 22, 2001), Colorado's 1st round choice (Dave Steckel) in 2001 Entry Draft and Colorado's 1st round choice (Brian Boyle) in 2003 Entry Draft for Rob Blake and Steve Reinprecht, February 21, 2001. • Missed majority of 2003-04 season recovering from cervical injury suffered in game vs. Atlanta, December 10, 2003.

MILLER, Kevin

(MIHL-luhr, KEH-vihn) **DET.**

Center. Shoots right. 5'11", 190 lbs. Born, Lansing, MI, September 2, 1965. NY Rangers' 10th choice, 202nd overall, in 1984 Entry Draft.

Season	Club	League	GP	G	A	Pts	PIM	PP	SH	GW	S	%	+/-	TF	F%	Min	GP	G	A	Pts	PIM	PP	SH	GW	Min
1983-84	Redford Royals	GLJHL	44	28	57	85																			
1984-85	Michigan State	CCHA	44	11	29	40	84																		
1985-86	Michigan State	CCHA	45	19	52	71	112																		
1986-87	Michigan State	CCHA	42	25	56	81	63																		
1987-88	Michigan State	CCHA	9	6	3	9	18																		
	Team USA	Nat-Tm	48	31	32	63	33																		
	United States	Olympics	5	1	3	4	4																		
1988-89	**NY Rangers**	**NHL**	**24**	**3**	**5**	**8**	**2**	**0**	**0**	**1**	**40**	**7.5**	**–1**												
	Denver Rangers	IHL	55	29	47	76	19										4	2	1	3	2				
1989-90	**NY Rangers**	**NHL**	**16**	**0**	**5**	**5**	**2**	**0**	**0**	**0**	**9**	**0.0**	**–1**				**1**	**0**	**0**	**0**	**0**	**0**	**0**	**0**	
	Flint Spirits	IHL	48	19	23	42	41																		
1990-91	**NY Rangers**	**NHL**	**63**	**17**	**27**	**44**	**63**	**1**	**2**	**3**	**113**	**15.0**	**1**												
	Detroit	**NHL**	**11**	**5**	**2**	**7**	**4**	**0**	**1**	**0**	**23**	**21.7**	**–4**				**7**	**3**	**2**	**5**	**20**	**0**	**1**	**0**	
1991-92	**Detroit**	**NHL**	**80**	**20**	**26**	**46**	**53**	**3**	**1**	**4**	**130**	**15.4**	**6**				**9**	**0**	**2**	**2**	**4**	**0**	**0**	**0**	
1992-93	**Washington**	**NHL**	**10**	**0**	**3**	**3**	**35**	**0**	**0**	**0**	**10**	**0.0**	**–4**												
	St. Louis	**NHL**	**72**	**24**	**22**	**46**	**65**	**8**	**3**	**4**	**153**	**15.7**	**6**				**10**	**0**	**3**	**3**	**11**	**0**	**0**	**0**	
1993-94	**St. Louis**	**NHL**	**75**	**23**	**25**	**48**	**83**	**6**	**3**	**5**	**154**	**14.9**	**6**				**3**	**1**	**0**	**1**	**4**	**0**	**1**	**0**	
1994-95	**St. Louis**	**NHL**	**15**	**2**	**5**	**7**	**0**	**0**	**0**	**0**	**19**	**10.5**	**4**												
	San Jose	**NHL**	**21**	**6**	**7**	**13**	**13**	**1**	**1**	**2**	**41**	**14.6**	**0**				**6**	**0**	**0**	**0**	**2**	**0**	**0**	**0**	
1995-96	**San Jose**	**NHL**	**68**	**22**	**20**	**42**	**41**	**2**	**2**	**2**	**146**	**15.1**	**–8**												
	Pittsburgh	**NHL**	**13**	**6**	**5**	**11**	**4**	**1**	**0**	**0**	**33**	**18.2**	**4**				**18**	**3**	**2**	**5**	**8**	**0**	**0**	**0**	
1996-97	**Chicago**	**NHL**	**69**	**14**	**17**	**31**	**41**	**5**	**1**	**2**	**139**	**10.1**	**–10**				**6**	**0**	**1**	**1**	**0**	**0**	**0**	**0**	
1997-98	**Chicago**	**NHL**	**37**	**4**	**7**	**11**	**8**	**0**	**0**	**1**	**37**	**10.8**	**–4**												
	Indianapolis Ice	IHL	26	11	11	22	41										2	1	1	2	0				
1998-99	**NY Islanders**	**NHL**	**33**	**1**	**5**	**6**	**13**	**0**	**0**	**0**	**37**	**2.7**	**–5**	**114**	**49.1**	**10:19**									
	Chicago Wolves	IHL	30	11	20	31	8										10	2	7	9	22				
99-2000	**Ottawa**	**NHL**	**9**	**3**	**2**	**5**	**2**	**1**	**0**	**2**	**11**	**27.3**	**1**	**34**	**41.2**	**8:10**	**1**	**0**	**0**	**0**	**0**	**0**	**0**	**0**	**4:33**
	Grand Rapids	IHL	63	20	34	54	51										17	*11	7	*18	30				
2000-01	HC Davos	Swiss	36	*29	27	56	61										4	3	0	3	2				
2001-02	HC Davos	Swiss	43	23	18	41	78										16	4	10	14	12				
2002-03	HC Davos	Swiss	44	14	24	38	40										17	8	3	11	4				
2003-04	**Detroit**	**NHL**	**4**	**0**	**2**	**2**	**0**	**0**	**0**	**0**	**2**	**0.0**	**2**	**4**	**75.0**	**7:21**									
	Grand Rapids	AHL	74	27	21	48	22										4	3	0	3	5				
	NHL Totals		**620**	**150**	**185**	**335**	**429**	**28**	**14**	**26**	**1097**	**13.7**		**152**	**48.0**	**9:38**	**61**	**7**	**10**	**17**	**49**	**0**	**2**	**0**	**4:33**

Traded to **Detroit** by **NY Rangers** with Jim Cummins and Dennis Vial for Joe Kocur and Per Djoos, March 5, 1991. Traded to **Washington** by **Detroit** for Dino Ciccarelli, June 20, 1992. Traded to **St. Louis** by **Washington** for Paul Cavallini, November 2, 1992. Traded to **San Jose** by **St. Louis** for Todd Elik, March 23, 1995. Traded to **Pittsburgh** by **San Jose** for Pittsburgh's 5th round choice (later traded to Boston – Boston selected Elias Abrahamsson) in 1996 Entry Draft , March 20, 1996. Signed as a free agent by **Chicago**, July 18, 1996. Signed as a free agent by **NY Islanders**, October 9, 1998. Signed as a free agent by **Ottawa**, August 24, 1999. Signed as a free agent by **HC Davos** (Swiss), July 26, 2000. Signed as a free agent by **Detroit**, August 27, 2003.

MILLER, Kip

(MIHL-luhr, KIHP)

Center. Shoots left. 5'10", 190 lbs. Born, Lansing, MI, June 11, 1969. Quebec's 4th choice, 72nd overall, in 1987 Entry Draft.

Season	Club	League	GP	G	A	Pts	PIM	PP	SH	GW	S	%	+/-	TF	F%	Min	GP	G	A	Pts	PIM	PP	SH	GW	Min
1984-85	Det. Compuware	MNHL	65	69	63	132																			
1985-86	Det. Compuware	GLJHL	30	25	28	53																			
1986-87	Michigan State	CCHA	41	20	19	39	92																		
1987-88	Michigan State	CCHA	39	16	25	41	51																		
1988-89	Michigan State	CCHA	47	32	45	77	94																		
1989-90	Michigan State	CCHA	45	*48	53	*101	60																		
1990-91	**Quebec**	**NHL**	**13**	**4**	**3**	**7**	**7**	**0**	**0**	**0**	**16**	**25.0**	**–1**												
	Halifax Citadels	AHL	66	36	33	69	40																		
1991-92	**Quebec**	**NHL**	**36**	**5**	**10**	**15**	**12**	**1**	**0**	**2**	**46**	**10.9**	**–21**												
	Halifax Citadels	AHL	24	9	17	26	8																		
	Minnesota	**NHL**	**3**	**1**	**2**	**3**	**2**	**1**	**0**	**0**	**3**	**33.3**	**–1**												
	Kalamazoo Wings	IHL	6	1	8	9	4										12	3	9	12	12				
1992-93	Kalamazoo Wings	IHL	61	17	39	56	59																		
1993-94	**San Jose**	**NHL**	**11**	**2**	**2**	**4**	**6**	**0**	**0**	**0**	**21**	**9.5**	**–1**												
	Kansas City	IHL	71	38	54	92	51																		
1994-95	Denver Grizzlies	IHL	71	46	60	106	54										17	*15	14	29	8				
	NY Islanders	**NHL**	**8**	**0**	**1**	**1**	**0**	**0**	**0**	**0**	**11**	**0.0**	**1**												
1995-96	**Chicago**	**NHL**	**10**	**1**	**4**	**5**	**2**	**0**	**0**	**0**	**12**	**8.3**	**1**												
	Indianapolis Ice	IHL	73	32	59	91	46										5	2	6	8	2				
1996-97	Chicago Wolves	IHL	43	11	41	52	32																		
	Indianapolis Ice	IHL	37	17	24	41	18										4	2	2	4	2				
1997-98	Utah Grizzlies	IHL	72	38	59	97	30										4	3	2	5	10				
	NY Islanders	**NHL**	**9**	**1**	**3**	**4**	**2**	**0**	**0**	**0**	**11**	**9.1**	**–2**												
1998-99	**Pittsburgh**	**NHL**	**77**	**19**	**23**	**42**	**22**	**1**	**0**	**4**	**125**	**15.2**	**1**	**150**	**44.7**	**16:55**	**13**	**2**	**7**	**9**	**19**	**1**	**0**	**0**	**18:56**
99-2000	**Pittsburgh**	**NHL**	**44**	**4**	**15**	**19**	**10**	**0**	**0**	**1**	**50**	**8.0**	**–1**	**132**	**40.2**	**14:18**									
	Anaheim	**NHL**	**30**	**6**	**17**	**23**	**4**	**2**	**0**	**1**	**32**	**18.8**	**1**	**7**	**42.9**	**13:44**									
2000-01	**Pittsburgh**	**NHL**	**33**	**3**	**8**	**11**	**6**	**1**	**0**	**0**	**38**	**7.9**	**0**	**61**	**50.8**	**9:46**									
	Grand Rapids	IHL	34	16	19	35	12										10	5	8	13	2				
2001-02	Grand Rapids	AHL	41	21	35	56	27																		
	NY Islanders	**NHL**	**37**	**7**	**17**	**24**	**6**	**2**	**0**	**1**	**52**	**13.5**	**2**	**119**	**58.8**	**14:07**	**7**	**4**	**2**	**6**	**2**	**2**	**0**	**1**	**11:14**
2002-03	**Washington**	**NHL**	**72**	**12**	**38**	**50**	**18**	**3**	**0**	**4**	**89**	**13.5**	**–1**	**171**	**49.7**	**14:58**	**5**	**0**	**2**	**2**	**2**	**0**	**0**	**0**	**10:36**
2003-04	**Washington**	**NHL**	**66**	**9**	**22**	**31**	**8**	**6**	**0**	**2**	**74**	**12.2**	**–10**	**297**	**47.5**	**14:03**									
	NHL Totals		**449**	**74**	**165**	**239**	**105**	**17**	**0**	**15**	**580**	**12.8**		**937**	**48.0**	**14:28**	**25**	**6**	**11**	**17**	**23**	**3**	**0**	**1**	**15:07**

CCHA First All-Star Team (1989, 1990) • CCHA Player of the Year (1990) • NCAA West First All-American Team (1989, 1990) • Hobey Baker Memorial Award (Top U.S. Collegiate Player) (1990)

Traded to **Minnesota** by **Quebec** for Steve Maltais, March 8, 1992. Signed as a free agent by **San Jose**, August 10, 1993. Signed as a free agent by **NY Islanders**, July 7, 1994. Signed as a free agent by **Chicago**, July 21, 1995. Signed as a free agent by **NY Islanders**, November 26, 1997. Claimed by **Pittsburgh** from **NY Islanders** in Waiver Draft, October 5, 1998. Traded to **Anaheim** by **Pittsburgh** for Anaheim's 9th round choice (Roman Simicek) in 2000 Entry Draft, January 29, 2000. Signed as a free agent by **Pittsburgh**, September 24, 2000. Signed as a free agent by **Grand Rapids** (AHL), May 31, 2001. Signed as a free agent by **NY Islanders**, January 16, 2002. Signed as a free agent by **Washington**, July 9, 2002.

MILLEY, Norm

(MIHL-lee, NOHR-man) **BUF.**

Right wing. Shoots right. 6', 200 lbs. Born, Toronto, Ont., February 14, 1980. Buffalo's 3rd choice, 47th overall, in 1998 Entry Draft.

Season	Club	League	GP	G	A	Pts	PIM	PP	SH	GW	S	%	+/-	TF	F%	Min	GP	G	A	Pts	PIM	PP	SH	GW	Min
1995-96	Tor. Red Wings	MTHL	42	42	36	78																			
	St. Michael's B	OJHL-B	5	2	1	3	0																		
1996-97	Sudbury Wolves	OHL	61	30	32	62	15																		
1997-98	Sudbury Wolves	OHL	62	33	41	74	48										10	0	1	1	4				
1998-99	Sudbury Wolves	OHL	68	52	68	120	47										4	2	3	5	4				
99-2000	Sudbury Wolves	OHL	68	*52	60	112	47										12	8	11	19	6				
2000-01	Rochester	AHL	77	20	27	47	56										4	0	0	0	2				
2001-02	**Buffalo**	**NHL**	**5**	**0**	**1**	**1**	**0**	**0**	**0**	**0**	**10**	**0.0**	**0**	**1**	**0.0**	**13:12**									
	Rochester	AHL	74	20	18	38	20										2	0	3	3	6				
2002-03	**Buffalo**	**NHL**	**8**	**0**	**2**	**2**	**6**	**0**	**0**	**0**	**8**	**0.0**	**–2**	**2**	**50.0**	**10:41**									
	Rochester	AHL	67	16	32	48	39										3	2	0	2	2				
2003-04	**Buffalo**	**NHL**	**2**	**0**	**0**	**0**	**2**	**0**	**0**	**0**	**2**	**0.0**	**0**	**0**	**0.0**	**8:20**									
	Rochester	AHL	77	18	19	37	60										16	7	6	13	10				
	NHL Totals		**15**	**0**	**3**	**3**	**8**	**0**	**0**	**0**	**20**	**0.0**		**3**	**33.3**	**11:12**									

OHL All-Rookie Team (1997) • OHL Second All-Star Team (1999) • OHL First All-Star Team (2000) • Canadian Major Junior First All-Star Team (2000)

MINK, Graham

(MIHNK, GRAY-uhm) **WSH.**

Center. Shoots right. 6'3", 217 lbs. Born, Stowe, VT, May 21, 1979.

			Regular Season														Playoffs								
Season	Club	League	GP	G	A	Pts	PIM	PP	SH	GW	S	%	+/-	TF	F%	Min	GP	G	A	Pts	PIM	PP	SH	GW	Min
1997-98	Mount Hermon	Hi-School	25	17	25	42																			
1998-99	U. of Vermont	ECAC	27	4	2	6	34																		
99-2000	U. of Vermont	ECAC	17	7	4	11	14																		
2000-01	U. of Vermont	ECAC	32	17	12	29	52																		
2001-02	Richmond	ECHL	29	8	9	17	78																		
	Portland Pirates	AHL	56	17	17	34	50																		
2002-03	Portland Pirates	AHL	71	22	15	37	115																		
2003-04	**Washington**	**NHL**	**2**	**0**	**0**	**0**	**2**	**0**	**0**	**0**	**0**	**0.0**	**–1**	**1**	**0.0**	**5:32**									
	Portland Pirates	AHL	68	18	19	37	74										3	0	1	1	4				
	NHL Totals		**2**	**0**	**0**	**0**	**2**	**0**	**0**	**0**	**0**	**0.0**		**1**	**0.0**	**5:32**									

Signed as a free agent by **Portland** (AHL), September 30, 2001. Signed as a free agent by **Washington**, April 9, 2002.

MIRONOV, Boris

(mih-RAWN-ohv, BOHR-ihs)

Defense. Shoots right. 6'3", 223 lbs. Born, Moscow, USSR, March 21, 1972. Winnipeg's 2nd choice, 27th overall, in 1992 Entry Draft.

			Regular Season														Playoffs								
Season	Club	League	GP	G	A	Pts	PIM	PP	SH	GW	S	%	+/-	TF	F%	Min	GP	G	A	Pts	PIM	PP	SH	GW	Min
1988-89	CSKA Moscow	USSR	1	0	0	0	0																		
1989-90	CSKA Moscow	USSR	7	0	0	0	0																		
1990-91	CSKA Moscow	USSR	36	1	5	6	16																		
1991-92	CSKA Moscow	CIS	36	2	1	3	22																		
1992-93	CSKA Moscow	CIS	19	0	5	5	20																		
1993-94	**Winnipeg**	**NHL**	**65**	**7**	**22**	**29**	**96**	**5**	**0**	**0**	**122**	**5.7**	**–29**												
	Edmonton	**NHL**	**14**	**0**	**2**	**2**	**14**	**0**	**0**	**0**	**23**	**0.0**	**–4**												
1994-95	**Edmonton**	**NHL**	**29**	**1**	**7**	**8**	**40**	**0**	**0**	**0**	**48**	**2.1**	**–9**												
	Cape Breton	AHL	4	2	5	7	23																		
1995-96	**Edmonton**	**NHL**	**78**	**8**	**24**	**32**	**101**	**7**	**0**	**1**	**158**	**5.1**	**–23**												
1996-97	**Edmonton**	**NHL**	**55**	**6**	**26**	**32**	**85**	**2**	**0**	**1**	**147**	**4.1**	**2**				**12**	**2**	**8**	**10**	**16**	**2**	**0**	**0**	
1997-98	**Edmonton**	**NHL**	**81**	**16**	**30**	**46**	**100**	**10**	**1**	**1**	**203**	**7.9**	**–8**				**12**	**3**	**3**	**6**	**27**	**1**	**0**	**1**	
	Russia	Olympics	6	0	2	2	2																		
1998-99	**Edmonton**	**NHL**	**63**	**11**	**29**	**40**	**104**	**5**	**0**	**4**	**138**	**8.0**	**6**	**0**	**0.0**	**25:55**									
	Chicago	**NHL**	**12**	**0**	**9**	**9**	**27**	**0**	**0**	**0**	**35**	**0.0**	**7**	**0**	**0.0**	**24:17**									
99-2000	**Chicago**	**NHL**	**58**	**9**	**28**	**37**	**72**	**4**	**2**	**1**	**144**	**6.3**	**–3**	**1**	**100.0**	**24:53**									
2000-01	**Chicago**	**NHL**	**66**	**5**	**17**	**22**	**42**	**3**	**0**	**0**	**143**	**3.5**	**–14**	**0**	**0.0**	**22:05**									
2001-02	**Chicago**	**NHL**	**64**	**4**	**14**	**18**	**68**	**0**	**0**	**1**	**129**	**3.1**	**15**	**0**	**0.0**	**22:43**	**1**	**0**	**0**	**0**	**2**	**0**	**0**	**0**	**5:41**
	Russia	Olympics	6	1	0	1	2																		
2002-03	**Chicago**	**NHL**	**20**	**3**	**1**	**4**	**22**	**1**	**0**	**0**	**14**	**21.4**	**–1**	**0**	**0.0**	**19:12**									
	NY Rangers	**NHL**	**36**	**3**	**9**	**12**	**34**	**1**	**0**	**0**	**56**	**5.4**	**3**	**0**	**0.0**	**20:35**									
2003-04	**NY Rangers**	**NHL**	**75**	**3**	**13**	**16**	**86**	**1**	**0**	**1**	**129**	**2.3**	**1**	**1**	**0.0**	**20:37**									
	NHL Totals		**716**	**76**	**231**	**307**	**891**	**39**	**3**	**10**	**1489**	**5.1**		**2**	**50.0**	**22:43**	**25**	**5**	**11**	**16**	**45**	**3**	**0**	**1**	**5:41**

NHL All-Rookie Team (1994)

Traded to **Edmonton** by **Winnipeg** with Mats Lindgren, Winnipeg's 1st round choice (Jason Bonsignore) in 1994 Entry Draft and Florida's 4th round choice (previously acquired, Edmonton selected Adam Copeland) in 1994 Entry Draft for Dave Manson and St. Louis' 6th round choice (previously acquired, Winnipeg selected Chris Kibermanis) in 1994 Entry Draft, March 15, 1994. Traded to **Chicago** by **Edmonton** with Dean McAmmond and Jonas Elofsson for Chad Kilger, Daniel Cleary, Ethan Moreau and Christian Laflamme, March 20, 1999. Traded to **NY Rangers** by **Chicago** for NY Rangers' 4th round choice (later traded to Dallas – Dallas selected Fredrik Naslund) in 2004 Entry Draft, January 8, 2003.

MITCHELL, Willie

(MIH-chuhl, WIHL-lee) **MIN.**

Defense. Shoots left. 6'3", 205 lbs. Born, Port McNeill, B.C., April 23, 1977. New Jersey's 12th choice, 199th overall, in 1996 Entry Draft.

			Regular Season														Playoffs								
Season	Club	League	GP	G	A	Pts	PIM	PP	SH	GW	S	%	+/-	TF	F%	Min	GP	G	A	Pts	PIM	PP	SH	GW	Min
1993-94	Notre Dame	SMHL	31	4	11	15	81																		
1994-95	Kelowna Spartans	BCHL	42	3	8	11	71																		
1995-96	Melfort Mustangs	SJHL	19	2	6	8											14	0	2	2	12				
1996-97	Melfort Mustangs	SJHL	64	14	42	56	227										4	0	1	1	23				
1997-98	Clarkson Knights	ECAC	34	9	17	26	105																		
1998-99	Clarkson Knights	ECAC	34	10	19	29	40																		
	Albany River Rats	AHL	6	1	3	4	29																		
99-2000	**New Jersey**	**NHL**	**2**	**0**	**0**	**0**	**0**	**0**	**0**	**0**	**2**	**0.0**	**1**	**0**	**0.0**	**16:04**									
	Albany River Rats	AHL	63	5	14	19	71										5	1	2	3	4				
2000-01	**New Jersey**	**NHL**	**16**	**0**	**2**	**2**	**29**	**0**	**0**	**0**	**14**	**0.0**	**0**	**0**	**0.0**	**14:52**									
	Albany River Rats	AHL	41	3	13	16	94																		
	Minnesota	**NHL**	**17**	**1**	**7**	**8**	**11**	**0**	**0**	**0**	**16**	**6.3**	**4**	**0**	**0.0**	**20:49**									
2001-02	**Minnesota**	**NHL**	**68**	**3**	**10**	**13**	**68**	**0**	**0**	**1**	**67**	**4.5**	**–16**	**0**	**0.0**	**21:25**									
2002-03	**Minnesota**	**NHL**	**69**	**2**	**12**	**14**	**84**	**0**	**1**	**1**	**67**	**3.0**	**13**	**0**	**0.0**	**21:28**	**18**	**1**	**3**	**4**	**14**	**0**	**0**	**0**	**24:48**
2003-04	**Minnesota**	**NHL**	**70**	**1**	**13**	**14**	**83**	**0**	**0**	**0**	**58**	**1.7**	**12**	**2**	**50.0**	**22:36**									
	NHL Totals		**242**	**7**	**44**	**51**	**275**	**0**	**1**	**2**	**224**	**3.1**		**2**	**50.0**	**21:15**	**18**	**1**	**3**	**4**	**14**	**0**	**0**	**0**	**24:48**

SJHL First All-Star Team (1997) • SJHL Top Defenseman Award (1997) • ECAC Second All-Star Team (1998) • ECAC Rookie of the Year (1998) (co-winner - Erik Cole) • ECAC First All-Star Team (1999) • NCAA East Second All-American Team (1999)

Traded to **Minnesota** by **New Jersey** for Sean O'Donnell, March 4, 2001.

MODANO, Mike

(moh-DA-noh, MIGHK) **DAL.**

Center. Shoots left. 6'3", 205 lbs. Born, Livonia, MI, June 7, 1970. Minnesota's 1st choice, 1st overall, in 1988 Entry Draft.

			Regular Season														Playoffs								
Season	Club	League	GP	G	A	Pts	PIM	PP	SH	GW	S	%	+/-	TF	F%	Min	GP	G	A	Pts	PIM	PP	SH	GW	Min
1985-86	Det. Compuware	MNHL	69	66	65	131	32																		
1986-87	Prince Albert	WHL	70	32	30	62	96										8	1	4	5	4				
1987-88	Prince Albert	WHL	65	47	80	127	80										9	7	11	18	18				
1988-89	Prince Albert	WHL	41	39	66	105	74																		
	Minnesota	**NHL**															**2**	**0**	**0**	**0**	**0**	**0**	**0**	**0**	
1989-90	**Minnesota**	**NHL**	**80**	**29**	**46**	**75**	**63**	**12**	**0**	**2**	**172**	**16.9**	**–7**				**7**	**1**	**1**	**2**	**12**	**0**	**0**	**0**	
1990-91	**Minnesota**	**NHL**	**79**	**28**	**36**	**64**	**65**	**9**	**0**	**2**	**232**	**12.1**	**2**				**23**	**8**	**12**	**20**	**16**	**3**	**0**	**1**	
1991-92	**Minnesota**	**NHL**	**76**	**33**	**44**	**77**	**46**	**5**	**0**	**8**	**256**	**12.9**	**–9**				**7**	**3**	**2**	**5**	**4**	**1**	**0**	**0**	
1992-93	**Minnesota**	**NHL**	**82**	**33**	**60**	**93**	**83**	**9**	**0**	**7**	**307**	**10.7**	**–7**												
1993-94	**Dallas**	**NHL**	**76**	**50**	**43**	**93**	**54**	**18**	**0**	**4**	**281**	**17.8**	**–8**				**9**	**7**	**3**	**10**	**16**	**2**	**0**	**2**	
1994-95	**Dallas**	**NHL**	**30**	**12**	**17**	**29**	**8**	**4**	**1**	**0**	**100**	**12.0**	**7**												
1995-96	**Dallas**	**NHL**	**78**	**36**	**45**	**81**	**63**	**8**	**4**	**4**	**320**	**11.3**	**–12**												
1996-97	**Dallas**	**NHL**	**80**	**35**	**48**	**83**	**42**	**9**	**5**	**9**	**291**	**12.0**	**43**				**7**	**4**	**1**	**5**	**0**	**1**	**1**	**2**	
1997-98	**Dallas**	**NHL**	**52**	**21**	**38**	**59**	**32**	**7**	**5**	**2**	**191**	**11.0**	**25**				**17**	**4**	**10**	**14**	**12**	**1**	**0**	**1**	
	United States	Olympics	4	2	0	2	0																		
1998-99♦	**Dallas**	**NHL**	**77**	**34**	**47**	**81**	**44**	**6**	**4**	**7**	**224**	**15.2**	**29**	**1572**	**51.1**	**20:50**	**23**	**5**	***18**	**23**	**16**	**1**	**1**	**1**	**24:40**
99-2000	**Dallas**	**NHL**	**77**	**38**	**43**	**81**	**48**	**11**	**1**	**8**	**188**	**20.2**	**0**	**1763**	**51.4**	**22:55**	**23**	**10**	***13**	**23**	**10**	**4**	**0**	**2**	**25:26**
2000-01	**Dallas**	**NHL**	**81**	**33**	**51**	**84**	**52**	**8**	**3**	**7**	**208**	**15.9**	**26**	**1791**	**52.0**	**22:24**	**9**	**3**	**4**	**7**	**0**	**2**	**0**	**0**	**25:43**
2001-02	**Dallas**	**NHL**	**78**	**34**	**43**	**77**	**38**	**6**	**2**	**5**	**219**	**15.5**	**14**	**1710**	**53.7**	**22:27**									
	United States	Olympics	6	0	*6	6	4																		
2002-03	**Dallas**	**NHL**	**79**	**28**	**57**	**85**	**30**	**5**	**2**	**6**	**193**	**14.5**	**34**	**1808**	**51.4**	**20:53**	**12**	**5**	**10**	**15**	**4**	**1**	**0**	**2**	**23:53**
2003-04	**Dallas**	**NHL**	**76**	**14**	**30**	**44**	**46**	**6**	**0**	**0**	**152**	**9.2**	**–21**	**1523**	**52.6**	**20:27**	**5**	**1**	**2**	**3**	**8**	**1**	**0**	**0**	**23:17**
	NHL Totals		**1101**	**458**	**648**	**1106**	**714**	**123**	**27**	**71**	**3334**	**13.7**		**10167**	**52.0**	**21:40**	**144**	**51**	**76**	**127**	**98**	**17**	**2**	**11**	**24:49**

WHL East First All-Star Team (1989) • NHL All-Rookie Team (1990) • NHL Second All-Star Team (2000)

Played in NHL All-Star Game (1993, 1998, 1999, 2000, 2003, 2004)

Transferred to **Dallas** after **Minnesota** franchise relocated, June 9, 1993.

MODIN, Fredrik

(moh-DEEN, FREHD-rihk) **T.B.**

Left wing. Shoots left. 6'4", 225 lbs. Born, Sundsvall, Sweden, October 8, 1974. Toronto's 3rd choice, 64th overall, in 1994 Entry Draft.

			Regular Season														Playoffs								
Season	Club	League	GP	G	A	Pts	PIM	PP	SH	GW	S	%	+/-	TF	F%	Min	GP	G	A	Pts	PIM	PP	SH	GW	Min
1991-92	Timra IK	Swede-2	11	1	0	1	0																		
1992-93	Timra IK	Swede-2	30	5	7	12	12										5	1	0	1	0				
1993-94	Timra IK	Swede-2	30	16	15	31	36										2	0	1	1	6				
1994-95	Brynas IF Gavle	Sweden	38	9	10	19	33										14	4	4	8	6				
1995-96	Brynas IF Gavle	Sweden	22	4	8	12	22																		
1996-97	**Toronto**	**NHL**	**76**	**6**	**7**	**13**	**24**	**0**	**0**	**0**	**85**	**7.1**	**–14**												

			Regular Season														Playoffs								
Season	Club	League	GP	G	A	Pts	PIM	PP	SH	GW	S	%	+/-	TF	F%	Min	GP	G	A	Pts	PIM	PP	SH	GW	Min
1997-98	Toronto	NHL	74	16	16	32	32	1	0	4	137	11.7	-5												
1998-99	Toronto	NHL	67	16	15	31	35	1	0	3	108	14.8	14	2	50.0	13:34	8	0	0	0	6	0	0	0	9:50
99-2000	Tampa Bay	NHL	80	22	26	48	18	3	0	5	167	13.2	-26	6	50.0	15:32									
2000-01	Tampa Bay	NHL	76	32	24	56	48	8	0	4	217	14.7	-1	21	42.9	17:15									
2001-02	Tampa Bay	NHL	54	14	17	31	27	2	0	4	141	9.9	0	25	40.0	19:05									
2002-03	Tampa Bay	NHL	76	17	23	40	43	2	1	4	179	9.5	7	35	28.6	17:35	11	2	0	2	18	0	0	0	19:18
2003-04♦	Tampa Bay	NHL	82	29	28	57	32	5	1	2	206	14.1	31	138	38.4	18:12	23	8	11	19	10	3	0	2	20:47
	NHL Totals		585	152	156	308	259	22	2	26	1240	12.3		227	37.9	16:50	42	10	11	21	34	3	0	2	18:18

Played in NHL All-Star Game (2001)

Traded to **Tampa Bay** by **Toronto** for Cory Cross and Tampa Bay's 7th round choice (Ivan Kolozvary) in 2001 Entry Draft, October 1, 1999.

MODRY, Jaroslav

(MOH-dree, YAHRO-slahv) **ATL.**

Defense. Shoots left. 6'2", 220 lbs. Born, Ceske Budejovice, Czech., February 27, 1971. New Jersey's 11th choice, 179th overall, in 1990 Entry Draft.

Season	Club	League	GP	G	A	Pts	PIM	PP	SH	GW	S	%	+/-	TF	F%	Min	GP	G	A	Pts	PIM	PP	SH	GW	Min
1987-88	Ceske Budejovice	Czech	3	0	0	0	0																		
1988-89	Ceske Budejovice	Czech	28	0	1	1	8																		
1989-90	Ceske Budejovice	Czech	41	2	2	4																			
1990-91	Dukla Trencin	Czech	33	1	9	10	6																		
1991-92	Ceske Budejovice	Czech-2	14	4	10	14																			
	Dukla Trencin	Czech	18	0	4	4	6																		
1992-93	Utica Devils	AHL	80	7	35	42	62										5	0	2	2	2				
1993-94	New Jersey	NHL	41	2	15	17	18	2	0	0	35	5.7	10												
	Albany River Rats	AHL	19	1	5	6	25																		
1994-95	Ceske Budejovice	Czech	19	1	3	4	30																		
	New Jersey	NHL	11	0	0	0	0	0	0	0	10	0.0	-1												
	Albany River Rats	AHL	18	5	6	11	14										14	3	3	6	4				
1995-96	Ottawa	NHL	64	4	14	18	38	1	0	1	89	4.5	-17												
	Los Angeles	NHL	9	0	3	3	6	0	0	0	17	0.0	-4												
1996-97	Los Angeles	NHL	30	3	3	6	25	1	1	0	32	9.4	-13												
	Phoenix	IHL	23	3	12	15	17																		
	Utah Grizzlies	IHL	11	1	4	5	20										7	0	1	1	6				
1997-98	Utah Grizzlies	IHL	74	12	21	33	72										4	0	2	2	6				
1998-99	Los Angeles	NHL	5	0	1	1	0	0	0	0	11	0.0	1	0	0.0	26:00									
	Long Beach	IHL	64	6	29	35	44										8	4	2	6	4				
99-2000	Los Angeles	NHL	26	5	4	9	18	5	0	1	32	15.6	-2	0	0.0	19:13	2	0	0	0	2	0	0	0	16:48
	Long Beach	IHL	11	2	4	6	8																		
2000-01	Los Angeles	NHL	63	4	15	19	48	0	0	0	72	5.6	16	0	0.0	18:22	10	1	0	1	4	1	0	1	16:08
2001-02	Los Angeles	NHL	80	4	38	42	65	4	0	0	119	3.4	-4	0	0.0	19:31	7	0	2	2	0	0	0	0	21:26
2002-03	Los Angeles	NHL	82	13	25	38	68	8	0	1	205	6.3	-13	1	0.0	22:39									
2003-04	Los Angeles	NHL	79	5	27	32	44	1	0	1	196	2.6	11	1	0.0	24:24									
	NHL Totals		490	40	145	185	330	22	1	4	818	4.9		2	0.0	21:18	19	1	2	3	6	1	0	1	18:09

Played in NHL All-Star Game (2002)

Traded to **Ottawa** by **New Jersey** for Ottawa's 4th round choice (Alyn McCauley) in 1995 Entry Draft, July 8, 1995. Traded to **Los Angeles** by **Ottawa** with Ottawa's 8th round choice (Stephen Valiquette) in 1996 Entry Draft for Kevin Brown, March 20, 1996. Signed as a free agent by **Atlanta**, July 1, 2004.

MOEN, Travis

(MOH-ehn, TRA-vihs) **CHI.**

Left wing. Shoots left. 6'2", 210 lbs. Born, Stewart Valley, Sask., April 6, 1982. Calgary's 6th choice, 155th overall, in 2000 Entry Draft.

Season	Club	League	GP	G	A	Pts	PIM	PP	SH	GW	S	%	+/-	TF	F%	Min	GP	G	A	Pts	PIM	PP	SH	GW	Min
1998-99	Swift Current	SMHL	STATISTICS NOT AVAILABLE																						
	Kelowna Rockets	WHL	4	0	0	0	0																		
99-2000	Kelowna Rockets	WHL	66	9	6	15	96										5	1	1	2	2				
2000-01	Kelowna Rockets	WHL	40	8	8	16	106																		
2001-02	Kelowna Rockets	WHL	71	10	17	27	197										13	1	0	1	28				
2002-03	Norfolk Admirals	AHL	42	1	2	3	62										9	0	0	0	20				
2003-04	Chicago	NHL	82	4	2	6	142	0	0	2	51	7.8	-17	19	15.8	10:57									
	NHL Totals		82	4	2	6	142	0	0	2	51	7.8		19	15.8	10:57									

Signed as a free agent by **Chicago**, October 21, 2002.

MOGILNY, Alexander

(moh-GIHL-nee, al-ehx-AN-duhr) **TOR.**

Right wing. Shoots left. 6', 209 lbs. Born, Khabarovsk, USSR, February 18, 1969. Buffalo's 4th choice, 89th overall, in 1988 Entry Draft.

Season	Club	League	GP	G	A	Pts	PIM	PP	SH	GW	S	%	+/-	TF	F%	Min	GP	G	A	Pts	PIM	PP	SH	GW	Min
1986-87	CSKA Moscow	USSR	28	15	1	16	4																		
1987-88	CSKA Moscow	USSR	39	12	8	20	14																		
	Soviet Union	Olympics	6	3	2	5	2																		
1988-89	CSKA Moscow	USSR	31	11	11	22	24																		
1989-90	Buffalo	NHL	65	15	28	43	16	4	0	2	130	11.5	8				4	0	1	1	2	0	0	0	
1990-91	Buffalo	NHL	62	30	34	64	16	3	3	5	201	14.9	14				6	0	6	6	2	0	0	0	
1991-92	Buffalo	NHL	67	39	45	84	73	15	0	2	236	16.5	7				2	0	2	2	0	0	0	0	
1992-93	Buffalo	NHL	77	*76	51	127	40	27	0	11	360	21.1	7				7	7	3	10	6	2	0	0	
1993-94	Buffalo	NHL	66	32	47	79	22	17	0	7	258	12.4	8				7	4	2	6	6	1	0	0	
1994-95	Spartak Moscow	CIS	1	0	1	1	0																		
	Buffalo	NHL	44	19	28	47	36	12	0	2	148	12.8	0				5	3	2	5	2	0	0	0	
1995-96	Vancouver	NHL	79	55	52	107	16	10	5	6	292	18.8	14				6	1	8	9	8	0	0	0	
1996-97	Vancouver	NHL	76	31	42	73	18	7	1	4	174	17.8	9												
1997-98	Vancouver	NHL	51	18	27	45	36	5	4	1	118	15.3	-6												
1998-99	Vancouver	NHL	59	14	31	45	58	3	2	1	110	12.7	0	47	23.4	20:35									
99-2000	Vancouver	NHL	47	21	17	38	16	3	1	1	126	16.7	7	9	11.1	19:34									
♦	New Jersey	NHL	12	3	3	6	4	2	0	0	35	8.6	-4	0	0.0	17:04	23	4	3	7	4	2	0	1	16:06
2000-01	New Jersey	NHL	75	43	40	83	43	12	0	7	240	17.9	10	11	36.4	16:53	25	5	11	16	8	1	0	2	16:42
2001-02	Toronto	NHL	66	24	33	57	8	5	0	4	188	12.8	1	5	40.0	17:38	20	8	3	11	8	2	0	2	19:23
2002-03	Toronto	NHL	73	33	46	79	12	5	3	9	165	20.0	4	18	33.3	20:03	6	5	2	7	4	0	1	0	21:43
2003-04	Toronto	NHL	37	8	22	30	12	4	1	1	92	8.7	9	10	60.0	18:29	13	2	4	6	8	0	0	0	16:28
	NHL Totals		956	461	546	1007	426	134	20	63	2873	16.0		100	30.0	18:45	124	39	47	86	58	8	1	5	17:28

NHL Second All-Star Team (1993, 1996) • Lady Byng Trophy (2003)

Played in NHL All-Star Game (1992, 1993, 1994, 1996)

Traded to **Vancouver** by **Buffalo** with Buffalo's 5th round choice (Todd Norman) in 1995 Entry Draft for Michael Peca, Mike Wilson and Vancouver's 1st round choice (Jay McKee) in 1995 Entry Draft, July 8, 1995. Traded to **New Jersey** by **Vancouver** for Brendan Morrison and Denis Pederson, March 14, 2000. Signed as a free agent by **Toronto**, July 3, 2001. • Missed majority of 2003-04 season recovering from hip injury suffered in game vs. Edmonton, November 20, 2003.

MONTADOR, Steve

(MAWN-tuh-dohr, STEEV) **CGY.**

Defense. Shoots right. 6', 210 lbs. Born, Vancouver, B.C., December 21, 1979.

Season	Club	League	GP	G	A	Pts	PIM	PP	SH	GW	S	%	+/-	TF	F%	Min	GP	G	A	Pts	PIM	PP	SH	GW	Min
1995-96	St. Michael's B	OPJHL	46	3	16	19	145																		
1996-97	North Bay	OHL	63	7	28	35	129																		
1997-98	North Bay	OHL	37	5	16	21	54																		
	Erie Otters	OHL	26	3	17	20	35										7	1	1	2	9				
1998-99	Erie Otters	OHL	61	9	33	42	114										5	0	2	2	4				
99-2000	Peterborough	OHL	64	14	42	56	97										5	0	2	2	4				
	Saint John Flames	AHL															2	0	0	0	0				
2000-01	Saint John Flames	AHL	58	1	6	7	95										19	0	8	8	13				
2001-02	Calgary	NHL	11	1	2	3	26	0	0	0	10	10.0	-2	0	0.0	12:12									
	Saint John Flames	AHL	67	9	16	25	107																		
2002-03	Calgary	NHL	50	1	1	2	114	0	0	0	64	1.6	-9	0	0.0	15:11									
	Saint John Flames	AHL	11	1	7	8	20																		
2003-04	Calgary	NHL	26	1	2	3	50	0	0	1	31	3.2	-1	1	0.0	11:46	20	1	2	3	6	0	0	1	17:43
	NHL Totals		87	3	5	8	190	0	0	1	105	2.9		1	0.0	13:47	20	1	2	3	6	0	0	1	17:43

Signed as a free agent by **Calgary**, April 10, 2000. • Spent majority of 2003-04 season as a healthy reserve.

MOORE, Dominic

(MOOR, DOHM-ih-nihk) **NYR**

Center. Shoots left. 6', 180 lbs. Born, Thornhill, Ont., August 3, 1980. NY Rangers' 2nd choice, 95th overall, in 2000 Entry Draft.

			Regular Season														Playoffs								
Season	Club	League	GP	G	A	Pts	PIM	PP	SH	GW	S	%	+/-	TF	F%	Min	GP	G	A	Pts	PIM	PP	SH	GW	Min
1996-97	Thornhill Islanders	MTJHL	29	4	6	10	48	....	....	....	....	....	....	....	....	....	1	0	1	1	0	....	....	....	....
1997-98	Aurora Tigers	OPJHL	51	10	15	25	16	....	....	....	....	....	....	....	....	....	....	....	....	....	....	....	....	....	....
1998-99	Aurora Tigers	OPJHL	51	34	53	87	70	....	....	....	....	....	....	....	....	....	....	....	....	....	....	....	....	....	....
99-2000	Harvard Crimson	ECAC	30	12	24	28	16	....	....	....	....	....	....	....	....	....	....	....	....	....	....	....	....	....	....
2000-01	Harvard Crimson	ECAC	32	15	28	43	40	....	....	....	....	....	....	....	....	....	....	....	....	....	....	....	....	....	....
2001-02	Harvard Crimson	ECAC	32	13	16	29	37	....	....	....	....	....	....	....	....	....	....	....	....	....	....	....	....	....	....
2002-03	Harvard Crimson	ECAC	34	*24	27	*51	30	....	....	....	....	....	....	....	....	....	....	....	....	....	....	....	....	....	....
2003-04	**NY Rangers**	**NHL**	**5**	**0**	**3**	**3**	**0**	**0**	**0**	**0**	**3**	**0.0**	**0**	**36**	**30.6**	**9:18**	....	....	....	....	....	....	....	....	....
	Hartford	AHL	70	14	25	39	60	....	....	....	....	....	....	....	....	....	16	3	3	6	8	....	....	....	....
	NHL Totals		**5**	**0**	**3**	**3**	**0**	**0**	**0**	**0**	**3**	**0.0**		**36**	**30.6**	**9:18**	....	....	....	....	....	....	....	....	....

ECAC All-Rookie Team (2000) • ECAC Second All-Star Team (2001) • ECAC First All-Star Team (2003) • NCAA East First All-American Team (2003)

MOORE, Steve

(MOOR, STEEV)

Center. Shoots right. 6'2", 205 lbs. Born, Windsor, Ont., September 22, 1978. Colorado's 7th choice, 53rd overall, in 1998 Entry Draft.

Season	Club	League	GP	G	A	Pts	PIM	PP	SH	GW	S	%	+/-	TF	F%	Min	GP	G	A	Pts	PIM	PP	SH	GW	Min
1995-96	Thornhill Islanders	MTJHL	50	25	27	52	57	....	....	....	....	....	....	....	....	....	18	4	5	9		....	....	....	....
1996-97	Thornhill Islanders	MTJHL	50	34	52	86	52	....	....	....	....	....	....	....	....	....	13	10	11	21	2	....	....	....	....
1997-98	Harvard Crimson	ECAC	33	10	23	33	46	....	....	....	....	....	....	....	....	....	....	....	....	....	....	....	....	....	....
1998-99	Harvard Crimson	ECAC	30	18	13	31	34	....	....	....	....	....	....	....	....	....	....	....	....	....	....	....	....	....	....
99-2000	Harvard Crimson	ECAC	27	10	16	26	53	....	....	....	....	....	....	....	....	....	....	....	....	....	....	....	....	....	....
2000-01	Harvard Crimson	ECAC	32	7	26	33	43	....	....	....	....	....	....	....	....	....	....	....	....	....	....	....	....	....	....
2001-02	**Colorado**	**NHL**	**8**	**0**	**0**	**0**	**4**	**0**	**0**	**0**	**5**	**0.0**	**–4**	**33**	**51.5**	**7:05**	....	....	....	....	....	....	....	....	....
	Hershey Bears	AHL	68	10	17	27	31	....	....	....	....	....	....	....	....	....	8	0	1	1	6	....	....	....	....
2002-03	**Colorado**	**NHL**	**4**	**0**	**0**	**0**	**0**	**0**	**0**	**0**	**0**	**0.0**	**0**	**23**	**30.4**	**8:56**	....	....	....	....	....	....	....	....	....
	Hershey Bears	AHL	58	10	13	23	41	....	....	....	....	....	....	....	....	....	5	0	1	1	4	....	....	....	....
2003-04	**Colorado**	**NHL**	**57**	**5**	**7**	**12**	**37**	**0**	**0**	**1**	**52**	**9.6**	**–5**	**387**	**40.3**	**13:06**	....	....	....	....	....	....	....	....	....
	Hershey Bears	AHL	13	4	4	8	6	....	....	....	....	....	....	....	....	....	....	....	....	....	....	....	....	....	....
	NHL Totals		**69**	**5**	**7**	**12**	**41**	**0**	**0**	**1**	**57**	**8.8**		**443**	**40.6**	**12:10**	....	....	....	....	....	....	....	....	....

MORAN, Brad

(moh-RAN, BRAD) **CBJ**

Center. Shoots left. 5'11", 187 lbs. Born, Abbotsford, B.C., March 20, 1979. Buffalo's 8th choice, 191st overall, in 1998 Entry Draft.

Season	Club	League	GP	G	A	Pts	PIM	PP	SH	GW	S	%	+/-	TF	F%	Min	GP	G	A	Pts	PIM	PP	SH	GW	Min
1994-95	Abbotsford	BCAHA	56	66	93	159	40	....	....	....	....	....	....	....	....	....	....	....	....	....	....	....	....	....	....
1995-96	Calgary Hitmen	WHL	70	13	31	44	28	....	....	....	....	....	....	....	....	....	....	....	....	....	....	....	....	....	....
1996-97	Calgary Hitmen	WHL	72	30	36	66	61	....	....	....	....	....	....	....	....	....	....	....	....	....	....	....	....	....	....
1997-98	Calgary Hitmen	WHL	72	53	49	102	64	....	....	....	....	....	....	....	....	....	18	10	8	18	20	....	....	....	....
1998-99	Calgary Hitmen	WHL	71	60	58	118	96	....	....	....	....	....	....	....	....	....	21	17	*25	42	26	....	....	....	....
99-2000	Calgary Hitmen	WHL	72	48	*72	*120	84	....	....	....	....	....	....	....	....	....	13	7	15	22	18	....	....	....	....
2000-01	Syracuse Crunch	AHL	71	11	19	30	30	....	....	....	....	....	....	....	....	....	5	3	4	7	2	....	....	....	....
2001-02	**Columbus**	**NHL**	**3**	**0**	**0**	**0**	**0**	**0**	**0**	**0**	**2**	**0.0**	**0**	**22**	**40.9**	**7:39**	....	....	....	....	....	....	....	....	....
	Syracuse Crunch	AHL	64	25	24	49	51	....	....	....	....	....	....	....	....	....	10	5	8	13	2	....	....	....	....
2002-03	Syracuse Crunch	AHL	47	12	19	31	22	....	....	....	....	....	....	....	....	....	....	....	....	....	....	....	....	....	....
2003-04	**Columbus**	**NHL**	**2**	**1**	**1**	**2**	**2**	**0**	**0**	**0**	**4**	**25.0**	**–1**	**25**	**64.0**	**10:03**	....	....	....	....	....	....	....	....	....
	Syracuse Crunch	AHL	72	24	35	59	44	....	....	....	....	....	....	....	....	....	7	5	3	8	2	....	....	....	....
	NHL Totals		**5**	**1**	**1**	**2**	**2**	**0**	**0**	**0**	**6**	**16.7**		**47**	**53.2**	**8:36**	....	....	....	....	....	....	....	....	....

WHL East First All-Star Team (1999, 2000)

Signed as a free agent by **Columbus**, June 5, 2000. Signed as a free agent by **Lokomotiv Yaroslavl** (Russia), July 7, 2004.

MORAN, Ian

(moh-RAN, EE-an) **BOS.**

Defense. Shoots right. 6', 200 lbs. Born, Cleveland, OH, August 24, 1972. Pittsburgh's 5th choice, 107th overall, in 1990 Entry Draft.

Season	Club	League	GP	G	A	Pts	PIM	PP	SH	GW	S	%	+/-	TF	F%	Min	GP	G	A	Pts	PIM	PP	SH	GW	Min
1987-88	Belmont Hill	Hi-School	25	3	13	16	15	....	....	....	....	....	....	....	....	....	....	....	....	....	....	....	....	....	....
1988-89	Belmont Hill	Hi-School	23	7	25	32	8	....	....	....	....	....	....	....	....	....	....	....	....	....	....	....	....	....	....
1989-90	Belmont Hill	Hi-School	23	10	36	46	....	....	....	....	....	....	....	....	....	....	....	....	....	....	....	....	....	....	....
1990-91	Belmont Hill	Hi-School	23	7	44	51	12	....	....	....	....	....	....	....	....	....	....	....	....	....	....	....	....	....	....
1991-92	Boston College	H-East	30	2	16	18	44	....	....	....	....	....	....	....	....	....	....	....	....	....	....	....	....	....	....
1992-93	Boston College	H-East	31	8	12	20	32	....	....	....	....	....	....	....	....	....	....	....	....	....	....	....	....	....	....
1993-94	Team USA	Nat-Tm	50	8	15	23	69	....	....	....	....	....	....	....	....	....	....	....	....	....	....	....	....	....	....
	Cleveland	IHL	33	5	13	18	39	....	....	....	....	....	....	....	....	....	....	....	....	....	....	....	....	....	....
1994-95	Cleveland	IHL	64	7	31	38	94	....	....	....	....	....	....	....	....	....	4	0	1	1	2	....	....	....	....
	Pittsburgh	**NHL**	....	....	....	....	....	....	....	....	....	....	....	....	....	....	**8**	**0**	**0**	**0**	**0**	**0**	**0**	**0**	....
1995-96	**Pittsburgh**	**NHL**	**51**	**1**	**1**	**2**	**47**	**0**	**0**	**0**	**44**	**2.3**	**–1**	....	....	....	....	....	....	....	....	....	....	....	....
1996-97	**Pittsburgh**	**NHL**	**36**	**4**	**5**	**9**	**22**	**0**	**0**	**0**	**50**	**8.0**	**–11**	....	....	....	**5**	**1**	**2**	**3**	**4**	**0**	**0**	**0**	....
	Cleveland	IHL	36	6	23	29	26	....	....	....	....	....	....	....	....	....	....	....	....	....	....	....	....	....	....
1997-98	**Pittsburgh**	**NHL**	**37**	**1**	**6**	**7**	**19**	**0**	**0**	**1**	**33**	**3.0**	**0**	....	....	....	**6**	**0**	**0**	**0**	**2**	**0**	**0**	**0**	....
1998-99	**Pittsburgh**	**NHL**	**62**	**4**	**5**	**9**	**37**	**0**	**1**	**0**	**65**	**6.2**	**1**	**32**	**34.4**	**16:34**	**13**	**0**	**2**	**2**	**8**	**0**	**0**	**0**	**21:10**
99-2000	**Pittsburgh**	**NHL**	**73**	**4**	**8**	**12**	**28**	**0**	**0**	**0**	**58**	**6.9**	**–10**	**210**	**33.8**	**11:21**	**11**	**0**	**1**	**1**	**2**	**0**	**0**	**0**	**8:52**
2000-01	**Pittsburgh**	**NHL**	**40**	**3**	**4**	**7**	**28**	**0**	**0**	**1**	**73**	**4.1**	**5**	**4**	**25.0**	**17:42**	**18**	**0**	**1**	**1**	**4**	**0**	**0**	**0**	**15:54**
2001-02	**Pittsburgh**	**NHL**	**64**	**2**	**8**	**10**	**54**	**0**	**0**	**1**	**94**	**2.1**	**–11**	**2**	**100.0**	**20:00**	....	....	....	....	....	....	....	....	....
2002-03	**Pittsburgh**	**NHL**	**70**	**0**	**7**	**7**	**46**	**0**	**0**	**0**	**85**	**0.0**	**–17**	**4**	**75.0**	**18:37**	....	....	....	....	....	....	....	....	....
	Boston	**NHL**	**8**	**0**	**1**	**1**	**2**	**0**	**0**	**0**	**11**	**0.0**	**–1**	**1**	**100.0**	**16:22**	**5**	**0**	**1**	**1**	**4**	**0**	**0**	**0**	**18:24**
2003-04	**Boston**	**NHL**	**35**	**1**	**4**	**5**	**28**	**0**	**0**	**0**	**54**	**1.9**	**3**	**1**	**100.0**	**18:45**	....	....	....	....	....	....	....	....	....
	NHL Totals		**476**	**20**	**49**	**69**	**311**	**0**	**1**	**3**	**567**	**3.5**		**254**	**35.4**	**16:52**	**66**	**1**	**7**	**8**	**24**	**0**	**0**	**0**	**15:59**

Hockey East All-Rookie Team (1992) • Hockey East Rookie of the Year (1992) (co-winner - Craig Darby)

• Missed majority of 1997-98 season recovering from knee injury suffered in training camp, September 30, 1997. • Missed majority of 2000-01 season recovering from hand injury originally suffered in game vs. Edmonton, November 11, 2000. Traded to **Boston** by **Pittsburgh** for Boston's 4th round choice (Paul Bissonnette) in 2003 Entry Draft, March 11, 2003. • Missed majority of 2003-04 season recovering from ankle injury suffered in game vs. Tampa Bay, December 23, 2003.

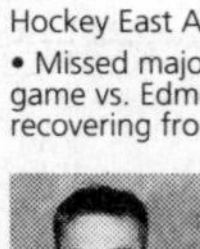

MOREAU, Ethan

(moh-ROH, EE-than) **EDM.**

Left wing. Shoots left. 6'2", 220 lbs. Born, Huntsville, Ont., September 22, 1975. Chicago's 1st choice, 14th overall, in 1994 Entry Draft.

Season	Club	League	GP	G	A	Pts	PIM	PP	SH	GW	S	%	+/-	TF	F%	Min	GP	G	A	Pts	PIM	PP	SH	GW	Min
1990-91	Orillia Terriers	OPJHL	42	17	22	39	26	....	....	....	....	....	....	....	....	....	12	6	6	12	18	....	....	....	....
1991-92	Niagara Falls	OHL	62	20	35	55	39	....	....	....	....	....	....	....	....	....	17	4	6	10	4	....	....	....	....
1992-93	Niagara Falls	OHL	65	32	41	73	69	....	....	....	....	....	....	....	....	....	4	0	3	3	4	....	....	....	....
1993-94	Niagara Falls	OHL	59	44	54	98	100	....	....	....	....	....	....	....	....	....	....	....	....	....	....	....	....	....	....
1994-95	Niagara Falls	OHL	39	25	41	66	69	....	....	....	....	....	....	....	....	....	....	....	....	....	....	....	....	....	....
	Sudbury Wolves	OHL	23	13	17	30	22	....	....	....	....	....	....	....	....	....	18	6	12	18	26	....	....	....	....
1995-96	**Chicago**	**NHL**	**8**	**0**	**1**	**1**	**4**	**0**	**0**	**0**	**1**	**0.0**	**1**	....	....	....	....	....	....	....	....	....	....	....	....
	Indianapolis Ice	IHL	71	21	20	41	126	....	....	....	....	....	....	....	....	....	5	4	0	4	8	....	....	....	....
1996-97	**Chicago**	**NHL**	**82**	**15**	**16**	**31**	**123**	**0**	**0**	**1**	**114**	**13.2**	**13**	....	....	....	**6**	**1**	**0**	**1**	**9**	**0**	**0**	**0**	....
1997-98	**Chicago**	**NHL**	**54**	**9**	**9**	**18**	**73**	**2**	**0**	**0**	**87**	**10.3**	**0**	....	....	....	....	....	....	....	....	....	....	....	....
1998-99	**Chicago**	**NHL**	**66**	**9**	**6**	**15**	**84**	**0**	**0**	**1**	**80**	**11.3**	**–5**	**3**	**33.3**	**12:30**	....	....	....	....	....	....	....	....	....
	Edmonton	**NHL**	**14**	**1**	**5**	**6**	**8**	**0**	**0**	**1**	**16**	**6.3**	**2**	**1**	**0.0**	**11:47**	**4**	**0**	**3**	**3**	**6**	**0**	**0**	**0**	**17:26**
99-2000	**Edmonton**	**NHL**	**73**	**17**	**10**	**27**	**62**	**1**	**0**	**3**	**106**	**16.0**	**8**	**8**	**62.5**	**15:07**	**5**	**0**	**1**	**1**	**0**	**0**	**0**	**0**	**15:46**
2000-01	**Edmonton**	**NHL**	**68**	**9**	**10**	**19**	**90**	**0**	**1**	**3**	**97**	**9.3**	**–6**	**2**	**0.0**	**14:11**	**4**	**0**	**0**	**0**	**2**	**0**	**0**	**0**	**10:35**
2001-02	**Edmonton**	**NHL**	**80**	**11**	**5**	**16**	**81**	**0**	**2**	**1**	**129**	**8.5**	**4**	**11**	**54.6**	**12:43**	....	....	....	....	....	....	....	....	....
2002-03	**Edmonton**	**NHL**	**78**	**14**	**17**	**31**	**112**	**2**	**3**	**2**	**137**	**10.2**	**–7**	**25**	**12.0**	**13:30**	**6**	**0**	**1**	**1**	**16**	**0**	**0**	**0**	**12:23**
2003-04	**Edmonton**	**NHL**	**81**	**20**	**12**	**32**	**96**	**0**	**3**	**5**	**180**	**11.1**	**7**	**59**	**44.1**	**15:04**	....	....	....	....	....	....	....	....	....
	NHL Totals		**604**	**105**	**91**	**196**	**733**	**5**	**9**	**17**	**947**	**11.1**		**109**	**37.6**	**13:48**	**25**	**1**	**5**	**6**	**33**	**0**	**0**	**0**	**13:57**

OHL All-Rookie Team (1992)

Traded to **Edmonton** by **Chicago** with Daniel Cleary, Chad Kilger and Christian Laflamme for Boris Mironov, Dean McAmmond and Jonas Elofsson, March 20, 1999.

MORGAN, Gavin

(MOHR-guhn, GA-vign) **MTL.**

Center. Shoots right. 5'11", 191 lbs. Born, Scarborough, Ont., July 9, 1976.

			Regular Season														Playoffs								
Season	Club	League	GP	G	A	Pts	PIM	PP	SH	GW	S	%	+/-	TF	F%	Min	GP	G	A	Pts	PIM	PP	SH	GW	Min
1992-93	Wexford Raiders	MTJHL	3	0	1	1	0	....	....	....	....	....	....	....	....	....	....	....	....	....	....	....	....	....	....
1993-94	Wexford Raiders	MTJHL	49	18	32	50	91	....	....	....	....	....	....	....	....	....	....	....	....	....	....	....	....	....	....
1994-95	Wexford Raiders	MTJHL	49	26	39	65	170	....	....	....	....	....	....	....	....	....	....	....	....	....	....	....	....	....	....
1995-96	U. of Denver	WCHA	28	2	9	11	47	....	....	....	....	....	....	....	....	....	....	....	....	....	....	....	....	....	....
1996-97	U. of Denver	WCHA	41	8	15	23	46	....	....	....	....	....	....	....	....	....	....	....	....	....	....	....	....	....	....
1997-98	U. of Denver	WCHA	37	9	8	17	42	....	....	....	....	....	....	....	....	....	....	....	....	....	....	....	....	....	....
1998-99	U. of Denver	WCHA	40	13	16	29	85	....	....	....	....	....	....	....	....	....	....	....	....	....	....	....	....	....	....
99-2000	Idaho Steelheads	WCHL	54	17	33	50	150	....	....	....	....	....	....	....	....	....	3	0	3	3	4	....	....	....	....
	Long Beach	IHL	7	0	1	1	10	....	....	....	....	....	....	....	....	....	....	....	....	....	....	....	....	....	....
	Utah Grizzlies	IHL	10	0	2	2	4	....	....	....	....	....	....	....	....	....	2	1	0	1	2	....	....	....	....
2000-01	Utah Grizzlies	IHL	79	7	14	21	187	....	....	....	....	....	....	....	....	....	....	....	....	....	....	....	....	....	....
2001-02	Utah Grizzlies	AHL	76	8	24	32	249	....	....	....	....	....	....	....	....	....	5	0	1	1	2	....	....	....	....
2002-03	Utah Grizzlies	AHL	73	15	24	39	244	....	....	....	....	....	....	....	....	....	2	0	1	1	17	....	....	....	....
2003-04	**Dallas**	**NHL**	**6**	**0**	**0**	**0**	**21**	**0**	**0**	**0**	**7**	**0.0**	**0**	**20**	**70.0**	**5:49**	....	....	....	....	....	....	....	....	....
	Hershey Bears	AHL	67	10	23	33	152	....	....	....	....	....	....	....	....	....	....	....	....	....	....	....	....	....	....
	NHL Totals		**6**	**0**	**0**	**0**	**21**	**0**	**0**	**0**	**7**	**0.0**		**20**	**70.0**	**5:49**	....	....	....	....	....	....	....	....	....

Signed as a free agent by **Idaho** (WCHL), August 25, 1999. Signed as a free agent by **Utah** (IHL), June 26, 2000. Signed as a free agent by **Dallas**, July 17, 2001. Signed as a free agent by **Montreal**, July 26, 2004.

MORGAN, Jason

(MOHR-gan, JAY-son) **CHI.**

Center. Shoots left. 6'1", 200 lbs. Born, St. John's, Nfld., October 9, 1976. Los Angeles' 5th choice, 118th overall, in 1995 Entry Draft.

			Regular Season														Playoffs								
Season	Club	League	GP	G	A	Pts	PIM	PP	SH	GW	S	%	+/-	TF	F%	Min	GP	G	A	Pts	PIM	PP	SH	GW	Min
1992-93	Kitchener AA	OMHA	69	44	40	84	85	....	....	....	....	....	....	....	....	....	....	....	....	....	....	....	....	....	....
1993-94	Kitchener Rangers	OHL	65	6	15	21	16	....	....	....	....	....	....	....	....	....	5	1	0	1	0	....	....	....	....
1994-95	Kitchener Rangers	OHL	35	3	15	18	25	....	....	....	....	....	....	....	....	....	....	....	....	....	....	....	....	....	....
	Kingston	OHL	20	0	3	3	14	....	....	....	....	....	....	....	....	....	6	0	2	2	0	....	....	....	....
1995-96	Kingston	OHL	66	16	38	54	50	....	....	....	....	....	....	....	....	....	6	1	2	3	0	....	....	....	....
1996-97	**Los Angeles**	**NHL**	**3**	**0**	**0**	**0**	**0**	**0**	**0**	**0**	**4**	**0.0**	**–3**	....	....	....	....	....	....	....	....	....	....	....	....
	Phoenix	IHL	57	3	6	9	29	....	....	....	....	....	....	....	....	....	....	....	....	....	....	....	....	....	....
	Mississippi	ECHL	6	3	0	3	0	....	....	....	....	....	....	....	....	....	3	1	1	2	6	....	....	....	....
1997-98	**Los Angeles**	**NHL**	**11**	**1**	**0**	**1**	**4**	**0**	**0**	**0**	**5**	**20.0**	**–7**	....	....	....	....	....	....	....	....	....	....	....	....
	Springfield	AHL	58	13	22	35	66	....	....	....	....	....	....	....	....	....	3	1	0	1	18	....	....	....	....
1998-99	Long Beach	IHL	13	4	6	10	18	....	....	....	....	....	....	....	....	....	....	....	....	....	....	....	....	....	....
	Springfield	AHL	46	6	16	22	51	....	....	....	....	....	....	....	....	....	3	0	0	0	6	....	....	....	....
99-2000	Cincinnati	IHL	15	1	3	4	14	....	....	....	....	....	....	....	....	....	....	....	....	....	....	....	....	....	....
	Florida Everblades	ECHL	48	14	25	39	79	....	....	....	....	....	....	....	....	....	5	2	2	4	16	....	....	....	....
2000-01	Florida Everblades	ECHL	37	15	22	37	41	....	....	....	....	....	....	....	....	....	5	2	3	5	17	....	....	....	....
	Hamilton	AHL	11	2	0	2	10	....	....	....	....	....	....	....	....	....	....	....	....	....	....	....	....	....	....
	Springfield	AHL	16	1	4	5	19	....	....	....	....	....	....	....	....	....	....	....	....	....	....	....	....	....	....
	Saint John Flames	AHL	....	....	....	....	....	....	....	....	....	....	....	....	....	....	6	0	1	1	2	....	....	....	....
2001-02	Saint John Flames	AHL	76	17	20	37	69	....	....	....	....	....	....	....	....	....	....	....	....	....	....	....	....	....	....
2002-03	Saint John Flames	AHL	80	13	40	53	63	....	....	....	....	....	....	....	....	....	....	....	....	....	....	....	....	....	....
2003-04	**Calgary**	**NHL**	**13**	**0**	**2**	**2**	**2**	**0**	**0**	**0**	**14**	**0.0**	**1**	**98**	**44.9**	**9:45**	....	....	....	....	....	....	....	....	....
	Lowell	AHL	21	6	13	19	16	....	....	....	....	....	....	....	....	....	....	....	....	....	....	....	....	....	....
	Nashville	**NHL**	**6**	**0**	**2**	**2**	**2**	**0**	**0**	**0**	**6**	**0.0**	**0**	**15**	**73.3**	**10:06**	....	....	....	....	....	....	....	....	....
	Norfolk Admirals	AHL	19	6	8	14	16	....	....	....	....	....	....	....	....	....	8	0	1	1	10	....	....	....	....
	NHL Totals		**33**	**1**	**4**	**5**	**8**	**0**	**0**	**0**	**29**	**3.4**		**113**	**48.7**	**9:51**	....	....	....	....	....	....	....	....	....

Signed to a PTO (tryout) contract by **Saint John** (AHL), April 22, 2001. Signed as a free agent by **Saint John** (AHL), August 28, 2001. Signed as a free agent by **Calgary**, July 11, 2002. Claimed on waivers by **Nashville** from **Calgary**, December 31, 2003. Claimed on waivers by **Calgary** from **Nashville**, February 19, 2004. Traded to **Chicago** by **Calgary** with future considerations for Ville Nieminen, February 24, 2004.

MORO, Marc

(MOH-roh, MAHRK) **TOR.**

Defense. Shoots left. 6'1", 218 lbs. Born, Toronto, Ont., July 17, 1977. Ottawa's 2nd choice, 27th overall, in 1995 Entry Draft.

			Regular Season														Playoffs								
Season	Club	League	GP	G	A	Pts	PIM	PP	SH	GW	S	%	+/-	TF	F%	Min	GP	G	A	Pts	PIM	PP	SH	GW	Min
1992-93	Miss. Senators	MTHL	42	9	18	27	56	....	....	....	....	....	....	....	....	....	....	....	....	....	....	....	....	....	....
	Miss. Senators	MTJHL	2	0	0	0	0	....	....	....	....	....	....	....	....	....	....	....	....	....	....	....	....	....	....
1993-94	Kingston	MTJHL	12	0	2	2	10	....	....	....	....	....	....	....	....	....	....	....	....	....	....	....	....	....	....
	Kingston	OHL	43	0	3	3	81	....	....	....	....	....	....	....	....	....	....	....	....	....	....	....	....	....	....
1994-95	Kingston	OHL	64	4	12	16	255	....	....	....	....	....	....	....	....	....	6	0	0	0	23	....	....	....	....
1995-96	Kingston	OHL	66	4	17	21	261	....	....	....	....	....	....	....	....	....	6	0	0	0	12	....	....	....	....
	P.E.I. Senators	AHL	2	0	0	0	7	....	....	....	....	....	....	....	....	....	2	0	0	0	4	....	....	....	....
1996-97	Kingston	OHL	37	4	8	12	97	....	....	....	....	....	....	....	....	....	....	....	....	....	....	....	....	....	....
	Sault Ste. Marie	OHL	26	0	5	5	74	....	....	....	....	....	....	....	....	....	11	1	6	7	38	....	....	....	....
1997-98	**Anaheim**	**NHL**	**1**	**0**	**0**	**0**	**0**	**0**	**0**	**0**	**0**	**0.0**	**0**	....	....	....	....	....	....	....	....	....	....	....	....
	Cincinnati	AHL	74	1	6	7	181	....	....	....	....	....	....	....	....	....	....	....	....	....	....	....	....	....	....
1998-99	Milwaukee	IHL	80	0	5	5	264	....	....	....	....	....	....	....	....	....	2	0	0	0	4	....	....	....	....
99-2000	**Nashville**	**NHL**	**8**	**0**	**0**	**0**	**40**	**0**	**0**	**0**	**3**	**0.0**	**–3**	**0**	**0.0**	**10:55**	....	....	....	....	....	....	....	....	....
	Milwaukee	IHL	64	5	5	10	203	....	....	....	....	....	....	....	....	....	....	....	....	....	....	....	....	....	....
2000-01	**Nashville**	**NHL**	**6**	**0**	**0**	**0**	**12**	**0**	**0**	**0**	**1**	**0.0**	**1**	**0**	**0.0**	**3:34**	....	....	....	....	....	....	....	....	....
	Milwaukee	IHL	68	2	9	11	190	....	....	....	....	....	....	....	....	....	5	1	0	1	10	....	....	....	....
2001-02	**Nashville**	**NHL**	**13**	**0**	**0**	**0**	**23**	**0**	**0**	**0**	**7**	**0.0**	**–3**	**0**	**0.0**	**12:02**	....	....	....	....	....	....	....	....	....
	Milwaukee	AHL	41	1	8	9	81	....	....	....	....	....	....	....	....	....	....	....	....	....	....	....	....	....	....
	Toronto	**NHL**	**2**	**0**	**0**	**0**	**2**	**0**	**0**	**0**	**0**	**0.0**	**0**	**0**	**0.0**	**11:23**	....	....	....	....	....	....	....	....	....
	St. John's	AHL	7	1	0	1	21	....	....	....	....	....	....	....	....	....	....	....	....	....	....	....	....	....	....
2002-03	St. John's	AHL	68	3	8	11	128	....	....	....	....	....	....	....	....	....	....	....	....	....	....	....	....	....	....
2003-04	St. John's	AHL	76	1	9	10	144	....	....	....	....	....	....	....	....	....	....	....	....	....	....	....	....	....	....
	NHL Totals		**30**	**0**	**0**	**0**	**77**	**0**	**0**	**0**	**11**	**0.0**		**0**	**0.0**	**9:56**	....	....	....	....	....	....	....	....	....

Rights traded to **Anaheim** by **Ottawa** with Ted Drury for Jason York and Shaun Van Allen, October 1, 1996. Traded to **Nashville** by **Anaheim** with Chris Mason for Dominic Roussel, October 5, 1998. Traded to **Toronto** by **Nashville** for D.J. Smith and Marty Wilford, March 1, 2002.

MOROZOV, Aleksey

(moh-ROH-zohv, ah-LEHK-see) **PIT.**

Right wing. Shoots left. 6'1", 204 lbs. Born, Moscow, USSR, February 16, 1977. Pittsburgh's 1st choice, 24th overall, in 1995 Entry Draft.

			Regular Season														Playoffs								
Season	Club	League	GP	G	A	Pts	PIM	PP	SH	GW	S	%	+/-	TF	F%	Min	GP	G	A	Pts	PIM	PP	SH	GW	Min
1993-94	Krylja Sovetov	CIS	7	0	0	0	0	....	....	....	....	....	....	....	....	....	3	0	0	0	2	....	....	....	....
1994-95	Krylja Sovetov	CIS	48	15	12	27	53	....	....	....	....	....	....	....	....	....	4	0	3	3	0	....	....	....	....
1995-96	Krylja Sovetov	CIS	47	13	9	22	26	....	....	....	....	....	....	....	....	....	....	....	....	....	....	....	....	....	....
1996-97	Krylja Sovetov	Russia	44	21	11	32	32	....	....	....	....	....	....	....	....	....	2	0	1	1	2	....	....	....	....
1997-98	Krylja Sovetov	Russia	6	2	1	3	4	....	....	....	....	....	....	....	....	....	....	....	....	....	....	....	....	....	....
	Pittsburgh	**NHL**	**76**	**13**	**13**	**26**	**8**	**2**	**0**	**3**	**80**	**16.3**	**–4**	....	....	....	**6**	**0**	**1**	**1**	**2**	**0**	**0**	**0**	....
	Russia	Olympics	6	2	2	4	0	....	....	....	....	....	....	....	....	....	....	....	....	....	....	....	....	....	....
1998-99	**Pittsburgh**	**NHL**	**67**	**9**	**10**	**19**	**14**	**0**	**0**	**0**	**75**	**12.0**	**5**	**7**	**42.9**	**11:50**	**10**	**1**	**1**	**2**	**0**	**0**	**0**	**0**	**12:01**
99-2000	**Pittsburgh**	**NHL**	**68**	**12**	**19**	**31**	**14**	**0**	**1**	**0**	**101**	**11.9**	**12**	**27**	**33.3**	**13:51**	**5**	**0**	**0**	**0**	**0**	**0**	**0**	**0**	**11:48**
2000-01	**Pittsburgh**	**NHL**	**66**	**5**	**14**	**19**	**6**	**0**	**0**	**1**	**72**	**6.9**	**–8**	**19**	**42.1**	**10:41**	**18**	**3**	**3**	**6**	**6**	**0**	**1**	**0**	**14:59**
2001-02	**Pittsburgh**	**NHL**	**72**	**20**	**29**	**49**	**16**	**7**	**0**	**3**	**162**	**12.3**	**–7**	**1**	**100.0**	**16:42**	....	....	....	....	....	....	....	....	....
2002-03	**Pittsburgh**	**NHL**	**27**	**9**	**16**	**25**	**16**	**6**	**0**	**2**	**46**	**19.6**	**–3**	**0**	**0.0**	**18:42**	....	....	....	....	....	....	....	....	....
2003-04	**Pittsburgh**	**NHL**	**75**	**16**	**34**	**50**	**24**	**8**	**0**	**5**	**132**	**12.1**	**–24**	**0**	**0.0**	**16:34**	....	....	....	....	....	....	....	....	....
	NHL Totals		**451**	**84**	**135**	**219**	**98**	**23**	**1**	**14**	**668**	**12.6**		**54**	**38.9**	**14:22**	**39**	**4**	**5**	**9**	**8**	**0**	**1**	**0**	**13:36**

• Missed majority of 2002-03 season recovering from wrist injury suffered in game vs. Toronto, December 10, 2002.

			Regular Season														Playoffs								
Season	Club	League	GP	G	A	Pts	PIM	PP	SH	GW	S	%	+/-	TF	F%	Min	GP	G	A	Pts	PIM	PP	SH	GW	Min

MORRIS, Derek

(MOH-rihs, DAIR-ihk) **PHX.**

Defense. Shoots right. 6', 220 lbs. Born, Edmonton, Alta., August 24, 1978. Calgary's 1st choice, 13th overall, in 1996 Entry Draft.

Season	Club	League	GP	G	A	Pts	PIM	PP	SH	GW	S	%	+/-	TF	F%	Min	GP	G	A	Pts	PIM	PP	SH	GW	Min
1994-95	Red Deer	AMHL	31	6	35	41	74																		
1995-96	Regina Pats	WHL	67	8	44	52	70										11	1	7	8	26				
1996-97	Regina Pats	WHL	67	18	57	75	180										5	0	3	3	9				
	Saint John Flames	AHL	7	0	3	3	7										5	0	3	3	7				
1997-98	**Calgary**	**NHL**	**82**	**9**	**20**	**29**	**88**	**5**	**1**	**1**	**120**	**7.5**	**1**												
1998-99	**Calgary**	**NHL**	**71**	**7**	**27**	**34**	**73**	**3**	**0**	**2**	**150**	**4.7**	**4**	**0**	**0.0**	**20:44**									
99-2000	**Calgary**	**NHL**	**78**	**9**	**29**	**38**	**80**	**3**	**0**	**2**	**193**	**4.7**	**2**	**0**	**0.0**	**24:51**									
2000-01	**Calgary**	**NHL**	**51**	**5**	**23**	**28**	**56**	**3**	**1**	**4**	**142**	**3.5**	**–15**	**0**	**0.0**	**25:51**									
	Saint John Flames	AHL	3	1	2	3	2																		
2001-02	**Calgary**	**NHL**	**61**	**4**	**30**	**34**	**88**	**2**	**0**	**1**	**166**	**2.4**	**–4**	**1**	**100.0**	**24:40**									
2002-03	**Colorado**	**NHL**	**75**	**11**	**37**	**48**	**68**	**9**	**0**	**7**	**191**	**5.8**	**16**	**0**	**0.0**	**23:49**	**7**	**0**	**3**	**3**	**6**	**0**	**0**	**0**	**22:44**
2003-04	**Colorado**	**NHL**	**69**	**6**	**22**	**28**	**47**	**2**	**0**	**1**	**139**	**4.3**	**4**	**0**	**0.0**	**20:53**									
	Phoenix	**NHL**	**14**	**0**	**4**	**4**	**2**	**0**	**0**	**0**	**28**	**0.0**	**–5**	**0**	**0.0**	**25:02**									
	NHL Totals		**501**	**51**	**192**	**243**	**502**	**27**	**2**	**18**	**1129**	**4.5**		**1**	**100.0**	**23:25**	**7**	**0**	**3**	**3**	**6**	**0**	**0**	**0**	**22:44**

WHL East First All-Star Team (1997) • NHL All-Rookie Team (1998)

Traded to **Colorado** by **Calgary** with Jeff Shantz and Dean McAmmond for Chris Drury and Stephane Yelle, October 1, 2002. Traded to **Phoenix** by **Colorado** with Keith Ballard for Ossi Vaananen, Chris Gratton and Phoenix's 2nd round choice in 2005 Entry Draft, March 8, 2004.

MORRISON, Brendan

(MOHR-ih-suhn, BREHN-duhn) **VAN.**

Center. Shoots left. 5'11", 190 lbs. Born, Pitt Meadows, B.C., August 15, 1975. New Jersey's 3rd choice, 39th overall, in 1993 Entry Draft.

Season	Club	League	GP	G	A	Pts	PIM	PP	SH	GW	S	%	+/-	TF	F%	Min	GP	G	A	Pts	PIM	PP	SH	GW	Min
1990-91	Ridge Meadows	BCAHA	77	126	127	253	88																		
1991-92	Ridge Meadows	BCAHA	55	56	111	167	56																		
1992-93	Penticton	BCJHL	56	35	59	94	45																		
1993-94	U. of Michigan	CCHA	38	20	28	48	24										5	2	7	9	2				
1994-95	U. of Michigan	CCHA	39	23	*53	*76	42										5	1	11	12	6				
1995-96	U. of Michigan	CCHA	35	28	44	*72	41										7	6	9	15	4				
1996-97	U. of Michigan	CCHA	43	31	*57	*88	52										6	6	8	14	8				
1997-98	**New Jersey**	**NHL**	**11**	**5**	**4**	**9**	**0**	**0**	**0**	**1**	**19**	**26.3**	**3**				**3**	**0**	**1**	**1**	**0**	**0**	**0**	**0**	
	Albany River Rats	AHL	72	35	49	84	44										8	3	4	7	19				
1998-99	**New Jersey**	**NHL**	**76**	**13**	**33**	**46**	**18**	**5**	**0**	**2**	**111**	**11.7**	**–4**	**920**	**51.1**	**13:55**	**7**	**0**	**2**	**2**	**0**	**0**	**0**	**0**	**13:04**
99-2000	Trebic	Czech-2	2	0	0	0	0																		
	Pardubice	Czech	6	5	2	7	2																		
	New Jersey	**NHL**	**44**	**5**	**21**	**26**	**8**	**2**	**0**	**1**	**79**	**6.3**	**8**	**572**	**51.1**	**16:09**									
	Vancouver	**NHL**	**12**	**2**	**7**	**9**	**10**	**0**	**0**	**0**	**17**	**11.8**	**4**	**48**	**54.2**	**14:41**									
2000-01	**Vancouver**	**NHL**	**82**	**16**	**38**	**54**	**42**	**3**	**2**	**3**	**179**	**8.9**	**2**	**1685**	**50.1**	**18:22**	**4**	**1**	**2**	**3**	**0**	**1**	**0**	**0**	**20:50**
2001-02	**Vancouver**	**NHL**	**82**	**23**	**44**	**67**	**26**	**6**	**0**	**4**	**183**	**12.6**	**18**	**1307**	**49.9**	**19:21**	**6**	**0**	**2**	**2**	**6**	**0**	**0**	**0**	**19:44**
2002-03	**Vancouver**	**NHL**	**82**	**25**	**46**	**71**	**36**	**6**	**2**	**8**	**167**	**15.0**	**18**	**1585**	**48.3**	**21:13**	**14**	**4**	**7**	**11**	**18**	**1**	**0**	**1**	**20:18**
2003-04	**Vancouver**	**NHL**	**82**	**22**	**38**	**60**	**50**	**5**	**1**	**4**	**161**	**13.7**	**16**	**1486**	**51.0**	**20:08**	**7**	**2**	**3**	**5**	**8**	**1**	**0**	**1**	**22:00**
	NHL Totals		**471**	**111**	**231**	**342**	**190**	**27**	**5**	**23**	**916**	**12.1**		**7603**	**50.1**	**18:19**	**41**	**7**	**17**	**24**	**32**	**3**	**0**	**2**	**19:15**

CCHA Rookie of the Year (1994) • CCHA First All-Star Team (1995, 1996, 1997) • NCAA West First All-American Team (1995, 1996, 1997) • CCHA Player of the Year (1996, 1997) • NCAA Championship All-Tournament Team (1996) • NCAA Championship Tournament MVP (1996) • Hobey Baker Memorial Award (Top U.S. Collegiate Player) (1997)

Traded to **Vancouver** by **New Jersey** with Denis Pederson for Alexander Mogilny, March 14, 2000.

MORRISONN, Shaone

(MOHR-ih-suhn, SHAWN) **WSH.**

Defense. Shoots left. 6'3", 205 lbs. Born, Vancouver, B.C., December 23, 1982. Boston's 1st choice, 19th overall, in 2001 Entry Draft.

Season	Club	League	GP	G	A	Pts	PIM	PP	SH	GW	S	%	+/-	TF	F%	Min	GP	G	A	Pts	PIM	PP	SH	GW	Min
1997-98	Vancouver T-Birds	BCAHA	45	16	44	60	75																		
1998-99	South Surrey	BCHL	19	0	2	2	13																		
99-2000	Kamloops Blazers	WHL	57	1	6	7	80										4	0	0	0	6				
2000-01	Kamloops Blazers	WHL	61	13	25	38	132										4	0	0	0	6				
2001-02	Kamloops Blazers	WHL	61	11	26	37	106										4	0	2	2	2				
2002-03	**Boston**	**NHL**	**11**	**0**	**0**	**0**	**8**	**0**	**0**	**0**	**4**	**0.0**	**0**	**0**	**0.0**	**8:57**									
	Providence Bruins	AHL	60	5	16	21	103										4	0	0	0	6				
2003-04	**Boston**	**NHL**	**30**	**1**	**7**	**8**	**10**	**0**	**0**	**0**	**13**	**7.7**	**10**	**0**	**0.0**	**18:11**									
	Providence Bruins	AHL	18	0	2	2	16																		
	Washington	**NHL**	**3**	**0**	**0**	**0**	**0**	**0**	**0**	**0**	**1**	**0.0**	**0**	**0**	**0.0**	**18:52**									
	Portland Pirates	AHL	13	1	4	5	10										7	0	1	1	4				
	NHL Totals		**44**	**1**	**7**	**8**	**18**	**0**	**0**	**0**	**18**	**5.6**		**0**	**0.0**	**15:55**									

Traded to **Washington** by **Boston** with Boston's 1st (Jeff Schultz) and 2nd (Michail Yunkov) round choices in 2004 Entry Draft for Sergei Gonchar, March 3, 2004.

MORROW, Brenden

(MOHR-roh, BREHN-duhn) **DAL.**

Left wing. Shoots left. 5'11", 210 lbs. Born, Carlyle, Sask., January 16, 1979. Dallas' 1st choice, 25th overall, in 1997 Entry Draft.

Season	Club	League	GP	G	A	Pts	PIM	PP	SH	GW	S	%	+/-	TF	F%	Min	GP	G	A	Pts	PIM	PP	SH	GW	Min
1994-95	Estevan	SMBHL	60	117	72	189	45																		
1995-96	Portland	WHL	65	13	12	25	61										7	0	0	0	8				
1996-97	Portland	WHL	71	39	49	88	178										6	2	1	3	4				
1997-98	Portland	WHL	68	34	52	86	184										16	10	8	18	65				
1998-99	Portland	WHL	61	41	44	85	248										4	0	4	4	18				
99-2000	**Dallas**	**NHL**	**64**	**14**	**19**	**33**	**81**	**3**	**0**	**3**	**113**	**12.4**	**8**	**25**	**48.0**	**15:51**	**21**	**2**	**4**	**6**	**22**	**1**	**0**	**0**	**15:04**
	Michigan	IHL	9	2	0	2	18																		
2000-01	**Dallas**	**NHL**	**82**	**20**	**24**	**44**	**128**	**7**	**0**	**6**	**121**	**16.5**	**18**	**22**	**45.5**	**15:29**	**10**	**0**	**3**	**3**	**12**	**0**	**0**	**0**	**17:00**
2001-02	**Dallas**	**NHL**	**72**	**17**	**18**	**35**	**109**	**4**	**0**	**3**	**102**	**16.7**	**12**	**39**	**41.0**	**16:52**									
2002-03	**Dallas**	**NHL**	**71**	**21**	**22**	**43**	**134**	**2**	**3**	**4**	**105**	**20.0**	**20**	**29**	**27.6**	**15:43**	**12**	**3**	**5**	**8**	**16**	**2**	**0**	**0**	**21:03**
2003-04	**Dallas**	**NHL**	**81**	**25**	**24**	**49**	**121**	**9**	**0**	**3**	**132**	**18.9**	**10**	**38**	**47.4**	**19:24**	**5**	**0**	**1**	**1**	**4**	**0**	**0**	**0**	**21:29**
	NHL Totals		**370**	**97**	**107**	**204**	**573**	**25**	**3**	**19**	**573**	**16.9**		**153**	**41.8**	**16:43**	**48**	**5**	**13**	**18**	**54**	**3**	**0**	**0**	**17:38**

WHL West First All-Star Team (1999)

MOTTAU, Mike

(MAW-tuh, MIGHK)

Defense. Shoots left. 6', 192 lbs. Born, Quincy, MA, March 19, 1978. NY Rangers' 10th choice, 182nd overall, in 1997 Entry Draft.

Season	Club	League	GP	G	A	Pts	PIM	PP	SH	GW	S	%	+/-	TF	F%	Min	GP	G	A	Pts	PIM	PP	SH	GW	Min
1994-95	Thayer Academy	Hi-School	29	7	19	26																			
1995-96	Thayer Academy	Hi-School	31	6	20	26	14																		
1996-97	Boston College	H-East	38	5	18	23	77																		
1997-98	Boston College	H-East	40	13	36	49	50																		
1998-99	Boston College	H-East	43	3	39	42	44																		
99-2000	Boston College	H-East	42	6	37	43	61																		
2000-01	**NY Rangers**	**NHL**	**18**	**0**	**3**	**3**	**13**	**0**	**0**	**0**	**17**	**0.0**	**–6**	**0**	**0.0**	**15:18**									
	Hartford	AHL	61	10	33	43	45										5	0	1	1	19				
2001-02	**NY Rangers**	**NHL**	**1**	**0**	**0**	**0**	**0**	**0**	**0**	**0**	**0**	**0.0**	**0**	**0**	**0.0**	**6:20**									
	Hartford	AHL	80	9	42	51	56										10	0	5	5	4				
2002-03	Hartford	AHL	29	1	18	19	24																		
	Calgary	**NHL**	**4**	**0**	**0**	**0**	**0**	**0**	**0**	**0**	**0**	**0.0**	**–1**	**0**	**0.0**	**9:50**									
	Saint John Flames	AHL	32	5	12	17	14																		
2003-04	Cincinnati	AHL	69	9	22	31	79										9	1	2	3	8				
	NHL Totals		**23**	**0**	**3**	**3**	**13**	**0**	**0**	**0**	**17**	**0.0**		**0**	**0.0**	**13:57**									

Hockey East First All-Star Team (1998, 2000) • NCAA East Second All-American Team (1998) • NCAA Championship All-Tournament Team (1998, 2000) • Hockey East Second All-Star Team (1999) • NCAA East First All-American Team (1999, 2000) • Hockey East Player of the Year (2000) (co-winner - Ty Conklin) • Hobey Baker Memorial Award (Top U.S. Collegiate Player) (2000)

Traded to **Calgary** by **NY Rangers** for Calgary's 6th round choice (Ivan Dornic) in 2003 Entry Draft and future considerations, January 22, 2003. Signed as a free agent by **Anaheim**, July 25, 2003.

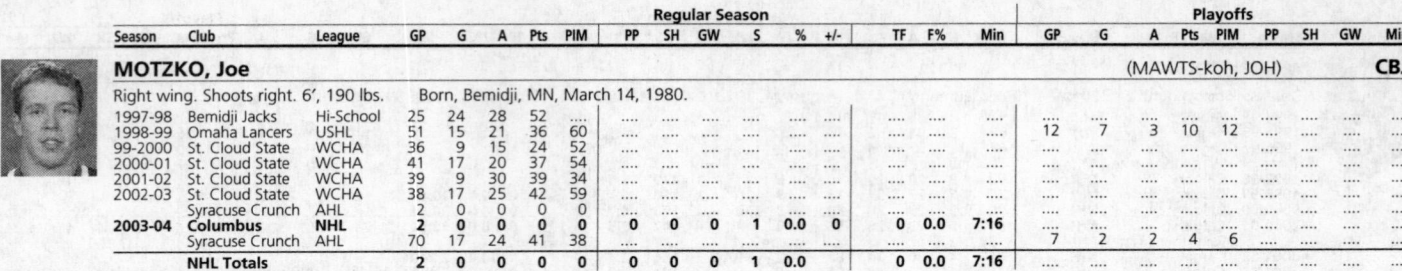

MOTZKO, Joe

(MAWTS-koh, JOH) **CBJ**

Right wing. Shoots right. 6', 190 lbs. Born, Bemidji, MN, March 14, 1980.

Season	Club	League	Regular Season GP	G	A	Pts	PIM	PP	SH	GW	S	%	+/-	TF	F%	Min	Playoffs GP	G	A	Pts	PIM	PP	SH	GW	Min
1997-98	Bemidji Jacks	Hi-School	25	24	28	52	....	....	....	....	....	....	....	....	....	....	....	....	....	....	....	....	....	....	....
1998-99	Omaha Lancers	USHL	51	15	21	36	60	....	....	....	....	....	....	....	....	....	12	7	3	10	12	....	....	....	....
99-2000	St. Cloud State	WCHA	36	9	15	24	52	....	....	....	....	....	....	....	....	....	....	....	....	....	....	....	....	....	....
2000-01	St. Cloud State	WCHA	41	17	20	37	54	....	....	....	....	....	....	....	....	....	....	....	....	....	....	....	....	....	....
2001-02	St. Cloud State	WCHA	39	9	30	39	34	....	....	....	....	....	....	....	....	....	....	....	....	....	....	....	....	....	....
2002-03	St. Cloud State	WCHA	38	17	25	42	59	....	....	....	....	....	....	....	....	....	....	....	....	....	....	....	....	....	....
	Syracuse Crunch	AHL	2	0	0	0	0	....	....	....	....	....	....	....	....	....	....	....	....	....	....	....	....	....	....
2003-04	**Columbus**	**NHL**	**2**	**0**	**0**	**0**	**0**	**0**	**0**	**0**	**1**	**0.0**	**0**	**0**	**0.0**	**7:16**	....	....	....	....	....	....	....	....	....
	Syracuse Crunch	AHL	70	17	24	41	38	....	....	....	....	....	....	....	....	....	7	2	2	4	6	....	....	....	....
	NHL Totals		**2**	**0**	**0**	**0**	**0**	**0**	**0**	**0**	**1**	**0.0**		**0**	**0.0**	**7:16**	....	....	....	....	....	....	....	....	....

Signed as a free agent by **Columbus**, May 15, 2003.

MOWERS, Mark

(MAHW-uhrs, MAHRK) **DET.**

Center. Shoots right. 5'11", 187 lbs. Born, Whitesboro, NY, February 16, 1974.

1992-93	Saginaw Gears	NAJHL	39	31	39	70	....	....	....	....	....	....	....	....	....	....	....	....	....	....	....	....	....	....	....
1993-94	Dubuque	USHL	47	51	31	82	80	....	....	....	....	....	....	....	....	....	....	....	....	....	....	....	....	....	....
1994-95	New Hampshire	H-East	36	13	23	36	16	....	....	....	....	....	....	....	....	....	....	....	....	....	....	....	....	....	....
1995-96	New Hampshire	H-East	34	21	26	47	18	....	....	....	....	....	....	....	....	....	....	....	....	....	....	....	....	....	....
1996-97	New Hampshire	H-East	39	26	32	58	52	....	....	....	....	....	....	....	....	....	....	....	....	....	....	....	....	....	....
1997-98	New Hampshire	H-East	35	25	31	56	32	....	....	....	....	....	....	....	....	....	....	....	....	....	....	....	....	....	....
1998-99	**Nashville**	**NHL**	**30**	**0**	**6**	**6**	**4**	**0**	**0**	**0**	**24**	**0.0**	**–4**	**241**	**49.0**	**9:22**	....	....	....	....	....	....	....	....	....
	Milwaukee	IHL	51	14	22	36	24	....	....	....	....	....	....	....	....	....	1	0	0	0	0	....	....	....	....
99-2000	**Nashville**	**NHL**	**41**	**4**	**5**	**9**	**10**	**0**	**0**	**0**	**50**	**8.0**	**0**	**312**	**45.2**	**10:58**	....	....	....	....	....	....	....	....	....
	Milwaukee	IHL	23	11	15	26	34	....	....	....	....	....	....	....	....	....	....	....	....	....	....	....	....	....	....
2000-01	Milwaukee	IHL	63	25	25	50	54	....	....	....	....	....	....	....	....	....	5	1	2	3	2	....	....	....	....
2001-02	**Nashville**	**NHL**	**14**	**1**	**2**	**3**	**2**	**0**	**0**	**0**	**5**	**20.0**	**–2**	**24**	**33.3**	**8:31**	....	....	....	....	....	....	....	....	....
	Milwaukee	AHL	45	19	20	39	34	....	....	....	....	....	....	....	....	....	....	....	....	....	....	....	....	....	....
2002-03	Grand Rapids	AHL	78	34	47	81	47	....	....	....	....	....	....	....	....	....	15	3	4	7	4	....	....	....	....
2003-04	**Detroit**	**NHL**	**52**	**3**	**8**	**11**	**4**	**1**	**0**	**1**	**48**	**6.3**	**3**	**400**	**47.8**	**10:27**	....	....	....	....	....	....	....	....	....
	Grand Rapids	AHL	16	8	6	14	4	....	....	....	....	....	....	....	....	....	....	....	....	....	....	....	....	....	....
	NHL Totals		**137**	**8**	**21**	**29**	**20**	**1**	**0**	**1**	**127**	**6.3**		**977**	**46.9**	**10:10**	....	....	....	....	....	....	....	....	....

Hockey East Rookie of the Year (1995) • Hockey East Second All-Star Team (1998) • NCAA East First All-American Team (1998) • Ken McKenzie Trophy (U.S. Born Rookie of the Year – IHL) (1999) • AHL Second All-Star Team (2003)

Signed as a free agent by **Nashville**, June 11, 1998. Signed as a free agent by **Detroit**, August 5, 2002.

MROZIK, Rick

(muh-ROH-zihk, RIHK)

Center. Shoots left. 6'2", 185 lbs. Born, Duluth, MN, January 2, 1975. Dallas' 4th choice, 136th overall, in 1993 Entry Draft.

1992-93	Cloquet High	Hi-School	28	9	38	47	12	....	....	....	....	....	....	....	....	....	....	....	....	....	....	....	....	....	....
1993-94	U. Minn-Duluth	WCHA	38	2	9	11	38	....	....	....	....	....	....	....	....	....	....	....	....	....	....	....	....	....	....
1994-95	U. Minn-Duluth	WCHA	3	0	0	0	2	....	....	....	....	....	....	....	....	....	....	....	....	....	....	....	....	....	....
1995-96	U. Minn-Duluth	WCHA	35	3	19	22	63	....	....	....	....	....	....	....	....	....	....	....	....	....	....	....	....	....	....
1996-97	U. Minn-Duluth	WCHA	38	11	23	34	56	....	....	....	....	....	....	....	....	....	....	....	....	....	....	....	....	....	....
1997-98	Portland Pirates	AHL	75	2	15	17	52	....	....	....	....	....	....	....	....	....	10	1	3	4	2	....	....	....	....
1998-99	Portland Pirates	AHL	70	4	8	12	63	....	....	....	....	....	....	....	....	....	....	....	....	....	....	....	....	....	....
99-2000	Worcester IceCats	AHL	3	0	0	0	0	....	....	....	....	....	....	....	....	....	....	....	....	....	....	....	....	....	....
	Pee Dee Pride	ECHL	60	9	19	28	44	....	....	....	....	....	....	....	....	....	5	2	0	2	6	....	....	....	....
	Syracuse Crunch	AHL	1	0	0	0	0	....	....	....	....	....	....	....	....	....	....	....	....	....	....	....	....	....	....
2000-01	Saint John Flames	AHL	76	5	11	16	26	....	....	....	....	....	....	....	....	....	19	1	1	2	6	....	....	....	....
2001-02	Saint John Flames	AHL	55	2	5	7	27	....	....	....	....	....	....	....	....	....	....	....	....	....	....	....	....	....	....
2002-03	**Calgary**	**NHL**	**2**	**0**	**0**	**0**	**0**	**0**	**0**	**0**	**2**	**0.0**	**0**	**0**	**0.0**	**10:02**	....	....	....	....	....	....	....	....	....
	Saint John Flames	AHL	68	2	10	12	46	....	....	....	....	....	....	....	....	....	....	....	....	....	....	....	....	....	....
2003-04	Rochester	AHL	72	4	10	14	47	....	....	....	....	....	....	....	....	....	15	1	4	5	4	....	....	....	....
	NHL Totals		**2**	**0**	**0**	**0**	**0**	**0**	**0**	**0**	**2**	**0.0**		**0**	**0.0**	**10:02**	....	....	....	....	....	....	....	....	....

WCHA Second All-Star Team (1997)

Traded to **Washington** by **Dallas** with Mark Tinordi for Kevin Hatcher, January 18, 1995. Signed as a free agent by **Calgary**, August 6, 2001. Signed as a free agent by **Buffalo**, August 21, 2003.

MUCKALT, Bill

(MUH-kawlt, BIHL)

Right wing. Shoots right. 6'1", 200 lbs. Born, Surrey, B.C., July 15, 1974. Vancouver's 9th choice, 221st overall, in 1994 Entry Draft.

1991-92	Merritt	BCJHL	55	14	11	25	75	....	....	....	....	....	....	....	....	....	....	....	....	....	....	....	....	....	....
1992-93	Merritt	BCJHL	59	31	43	74	80	....	....	....	....	....	....	....	....	....	....	....	....	....	....	....	....	....	....
1993-94	Merritt	BCJHL	43	58	51	109	99	....	....	....	....	....	....	....	....	....	....	....	....	....	....	....	....	....	....
	Kelowna Spartans	BCJHL	15	12	10	22	20	....	....	....	....	....	....	....	....	....	....	....	....	....	....	....	....	....	....
1994-95	U. of Michigan	CCHA	39	19	18	37	42	....	....	....	....	....	....	....	....	....	5	1	1	2	6	....	....	....	....
1995-96	U. of Michigan	CCHA	41	28	30	58	34	....	....	....	....	....	....	....	....	....	7	5	6	11	6	....	....	....	....
1996-97	U. of Michigan	CCHA	36	26	38	64	69	....	....	....	....	....	....	....	....	....	6	5	9	14	2	....	....	....	....
1997-98	U. of Michigan	CCHA	46	32	*35	*67	94	....	....	....	....	....	....	....	....	....	....	....	....	....	....	....	....	....	....
1998-99	**Vancouver**	**NHL**	**73**	**16**	**20**	**36**	**98**	**4**	**2**	**1**	**119**	**13.4**	**–9**	**68**	**55.9**	**15:24**	....	....	....	....	....	....	....	....	....
99-2000	**Vancouver**	**NHL**	**33**	**4**	**8**	**12**	**17**	**1**	**0**	**1**	**53**	**7.5**	**6**	**6**	**50.0**	**14:34**	....	....	....	....	....	....	....	....	....
	NY Islanders	**NHL**	**12**	**4**	**3**	**7**	**4**	**0**	**0**	**0**	**26**	**15.4**	**5**	**8**	**50.0**	**12:23**	....	....	....	....	....	....	....	....	....
2000-01	**NY Islanders**	**NHL**	**60**	**11**	**15**	**26**	**33**	**1**	**0**	**2**	**90**	**12.2**	**–4**	**7**	**14.3**	**13:43**	....	....	....	....	....	....	....	....	....
2001-02	**Ottawa**	**NHL**	**70**	**0**	**8**	**8**	**46**	**0**	**0**	**0**	**73**	**0.0**	**–3**	**13**	**69.2**	**9:46**	....	....	....	....	....	....	....	....	....
2002-03	**Minnesota**	**NHL**	**8**	**5**	**3**	**8**	**6**	**0**	**0**	**0**	**13**	**38.5**	**5**	**6**	**50.0**	**13:00**	**5**	**0**	**0**	**0**	**0**	**0**	**0**	**0**	**11:15**
2003-04	Houston Aeros	AHL	9	0	3	3	6	....	....	....	....	....	....	....	....	....	....	....	....	....	....	....	....	....	....
	NHL Totals		**256**	**40**	**57**	**97**	**204**	**6**	**2**	**4**	**374**	**10.7**		**108**	**53.7**	**13:08**	**5**	**0**	**0**	**0**	**0**	**0**	**0**	**0**	**11:15**

CCHA First All-Star Team (1998) • NCAA West First All-American Team (1998)

Traded to **NY Islanders** by **Vancouver** with Kevin Weekes and Dave Scatchard for Felix Potvin, NY Islanders' compensatory 2nd round choice (later traded to New Jersey – New Jersey selected Teemu Laine) in 2000 Entry Draft and NY Islanders' 3rd round choice (Thatcher Bell) in 2000 Entry Draft, December 19, 1999. • Missed majority of 1999-2000 season recovering from shoulder injury suffered in game vs. Tampa Bay, January 13, 2000. Traded to **Ottawa** by **NY Islanders** with Zdeno Chara and NY Islanders' 1st round choice (Jason Spezza) in 2001 Entry Draft for Alexei Yashin, June 23, 2001. Signed as a free agent by **Minnesota**, July 3, 2002. • Missed majority of 2002-03 and 2003-04 seasons recovering from shoulder injury suffered in game vs. Calgary, October 22, 2002.

MUIR, Bryan

(MEWR, BRIGH-uhn)

Defense. Shoots left. 6'4", 220 lbs. Born, Winnipeg, Man., June 8, 1973.

1991-92	Wexford Raiders	MTJHL	44	3	19	22	35	....	....	....	....	....	....	....	....	....	....	....	....	....	....	....	....	....	....
1992-93	New Hampshire	H-East	26	1	2	3	24	....	....	....	....	....	....	....	....	....	....	....	....	....	....	....	....	....	....
1993-94	New Hampshire	H-East	40	0	4	4	48	....	....	....	....	....	....	....	....	....	....	....	....	....	....	....	....	....	....
1994-95	New Hampshire	H-East	28	9	9	18	46	....	....	....	....	....	....	....	....	....	....	....	....	....	....	....	....	....	....
1995-96	Team Canada	Nat-Tm	42	6	12	18	38	....	....	....	....	....	....	....	....	....	....	....	....	....	....	....	....	....	....
	Edmonton	**NHL**	**5**	**0**	**0**	**0**	**6**	**0**	**0**	**0**	**4**	**0.0**	**–4**	....	....	....	....	....	....	....	....	....	....	....	....
1996-97	Hamilton	AHL	75	8	16	24	80	....	....	....	....	....	....	....	....	....	14	0	5	5	12	....	....	....	....
	Edmonton	**NHL**	....	....	....	....	....	....	....	....	....	....	....	....	....	....	**5**	**0**	**0**	**0**	**4**	**0**	**0**	**0**	....
1997-98	**Edmonton**	**NHL**	**7**	**0**	**0**	**0**	**17**	**0**	**0**	**0**	**6**	**0.0**	**0**	....	....	....	....	....	....	....	....	....	....	....	....
	Hamilton	AHL	28	3	10	13	62	....	....	....	....	....	....	....	....	....	....	....	....	....	....	....	....	....	....
	Albany River Rats	AHL	41	3	10	13	67	....	....	....	....	....	....	....	....	....	13	3	0	3	12	....	....	....	....
1998-99	**New Jersey**	**NHL**	**1**	**0**	**0**	**0**	**0**	**0**	**0**	**0**	**4**	**0.0**	**0**	**0**	**0.0**	**9:54**	....	....	....	....	....	....	....	....	....
	Albany River Rats	AHL	10	0	0	0	29	....	....	....	....	....	....	....	....	....	....	....	....	....	....	....	....	....	....
	Chicago	**NHL**	**53**	**1**	**4**	**5**	**50**	**0**	**0**	**0**	**78**	**1.3**	**1**	**0**	**0.0**	**18:49**	....	....	....	....	....	....	....	....	....
	Portland Pirates	AHL	2	1	1	2	2	....	....	....	....	....	....	....	....	....	....	....	....	....	....	....	....	....	....
99-2000	**Chicago**	**NHL**	**11**	**2**	**3**	**5**	**13**	**0**	**1**	**0**	**19**	**10.5**	**–1**	**0**	**0.0**	**17:54**	....	....	....	....	....	....	....	....	....
	Tampa Bay	**NHL**	**30**	**1**	**1**	**2**	**32**	**0**	**0**	**0**	**32**	**3.1**	**–8**	**1**	**100.0**	**19:29**	....	....	....	....	....	....	....	....	....

Season	Club	League	GP	G	A	Pts	PIM	PP	SH	GW	S	%	+/-	TF	F%	Min	GP	G	A	Pts	PIM	PP	SH	GW	Min
			Regular Season														Playoffs								
2000-01	**Tampa Bay**	**NHL**	**10**	**0**	**3**	**3**	**15**	**0**	**0**	**0**	**14**	**0.0**	**–7**	**1**	**0.0**	**18:34**	....	....	....	....	....	....	....	....	....
	Detroit Vipers	IHL	21	5	7	12	36	....	....	....	....	....	....	....	....	....	....	....	....	....	....	....	....	....	....
	Colorado	**NHL**	**8**	**0**	**0**	**0**	**4**	**0**	**0**	**0**	**3**	**0.0**	**0**	**0**	**0.0**	**8:14**	**3**	**0**	**0**	**0**	**0**	**0**	**0**	**0**	**3:15**
	Hershey Bears	AHL	26	5	8	13	50	....	....	....	....	....	....	....	....	....	....	....	....	....	....	....	....	....	....
2001-02	**Colorado**	**NHL**	**22**	**1**	**1**	**2**	**9**	**0**	**0**	**0**	**26**	**3.8**	**1**	**0**	**0.0**	**10:20**	**21**	**0**	**0**	**0**	**2**	**0**	**0**	**0**	**5:39**
	Hershey Bears	AHL	59	10	16	26	133	....	....	....	....	....	....	....	....	....	....	....	....	....	....	....	....	....	....
2002-03	**Colorado**	**NHL**	**32**	**0**	**2**	**2**	**19**	**0**	**0**	**0**	**9**	**0.0**	**3**	**0**	**0.0**	**6:33**	....	....	....	....	....	....	....	....	....
	Hershey Bears	AHL	36	9	12	21	75	....	....	....	....	....	....	....	....	....	5	2	6	8	6	....	....	....	....
2003-04	**Los Angeles**	**NHL**	**2**	**0**	**1**	**1**	**2**	**0**	**0**	**0**	**2**	**0.0**	**1**	**0**	**0.0**	**17:56**	....	....	....	....	....	....	....	....	....
	Manchester	AHL	73	13	37	50	141	....	....	....	....	....	....	....	....	....	6	2	3	5	12	....	....	....	....
	NHL Totals		**181**	**5**	**15**	**20**	**167**	**0**	**1**	**0**	**197**	**2.5**		**2**	**50.0**	**14:52**	**29**	**0**	**0**	**0**	**6**	**0**	**0**	**0**	**5:21**

AHL First All-Star Team (2004)

Signed to five-game amateur tryout contract by **Edmonton**, February 29, 1996. Signed as a free agent by **Edmonton**, April 30, 1996. Traded to **New Jersey** by **Edmonton** with Jason Arnott for Valeri Zelepukin and Bill Guerin, January 4, 1998. Traded to **Chicago** by **New Jersey** for Chicago's 3rd round choice (Mike Rupp) in 2000 Entry Draft. November 13, 1998. Traded to **Tampa Bay** by **Chicago** with Reid Simpson for Michael Nylander, November 12, 1999. • Missed majority of 1999-2000 season recovering from leg injury suffered in game vs. Atlanta, November 17, 1999. Traded to **Colorado** by **Tampa Bay** for Colorado's 8th round choice (Dmitri Bezrukov) in 2001 Entry Draft, January 23, 2001. Signed as a free agent by **Los Angeles**, July 31, 2003. Signed as a free agent by **MoDo** (Sweden), July 25, 2004.

MURLEY, Matt

(MUHR-lee, MAT) **PIT.**

Left wing. Shoots left. 6'1", 206 lbs. Born, Troy, NY, December 17, 1979. Pittsburgh's 2nd choice, 51st overall, in 1999 Entry Draft.

Season	Club	League	GP	G	A	Pts	PIM	PP	SH	GW	S	%	+/-	TF	F%	Min	GP	G	A	Pts	PIM	PP	SH	GW	Min
1996-97	Syracuse	MTJHL	48	52	58	110	111	....	....	....	....	....	....	....	....	....	....	....	....	....	....	....	....	....	....
1997-98	Syracuse	MTJHL	49	56	70	126	103	....	....	....	....	....	....	....	....	....	....	....	....	....	....	....	....	....	....
1998-99	RPI Engineers	ECAC	36	17	32	49	32	....	....	....	....	....	....	....	....	....	....	....	....	....	....	....	....	....	....
99-2000	RPI Engineers	ECAC	35	9	29	38	42	....	....	....	....	....	....	....	....	....	....	....	....	....	....	....	....	....	....
2000-01	RPI Engineers	ECAC	34	*24	18	42	34	....	....	....	....	....	....	....	....	....	....	....	....	....	....	....	....	....	....
2001-02	RPI Engineers	ECAC	32	*24	22	46	26	....	....	....	....	....	....	....	....	....	....	....	....	....	....	....	....	....	....
2002-03	Wilkes-Barre	AHL	73	21	37	58	45	....	....	....	....	....	....	....	....	....	6	0	2	2	15	....	....	....	....
2003-04	**Pittsburgh**	**NHL**	**18**	**1**	**1**	**2**	**14**	**0**	**0**	**0**	**20**	**5.0**	**–6**	**2**	**50.0**	**11:49**	....	....	....	....	....	....	....	....	....
	Wilkes-Barre	AHL	63	10	26	36	69	....	....	....	....	....	....	....	....	....	24	7	6	13	17	....	....	....	....
	NHL Totals		**18**	**1**	**1**	**2**	**14**	**0**	**0**	**0**	**20**	**5.0**		**2**	**50.0**	**11:49**	....	....	....	....	....	....	....	....	....

ECAC First All-Star Team (2002)

MURPHY, Curtis

(MUHR-fee, KUHR-this)

Defense. Shoots right. 5'8", 185 lbs. Born, Kerrobert, Sask., December 3, 1975.

Season	Club	League	GP	G	A	Pts	PIM	PP	SH	GW	S	%	+/-	TF	F%	Min	GP	G	A	Pts	PIM	PP	SH	GW	Min
1993-94	Nipawin Hawks	SJHL	60	21	33	54	....	....	....	....	....	....	....	....	....	....	....	....	....	....	....	....	....	....	....
1994-95	North Dakota	WCHA	33	6	10	16	28	....	....	....	....	....	....	....	....	....	....	....	....	....	....	....	....	....	....
1995-96	North Dakota	WCHA	38	6	12	18	58	....	....	....	....	....	....	....	....	....	....	....	....	....	....	....	....	....	....
1996-97	North Dakota	WCHA	43	12	30	42	36	....	....	....	....	....	....	....	....	....	....	....	....	....	....	....	....	....	....
1997-98	North Dakota	WCHA	39	8	34	42	78	....	....	....	....	....	....	....	....	....	....	....	....	....	....	....	....	....	....
1998-99	Orlando	IHL	80	22	35	57	60	....	....	....	....	....	....	....	....	....	17	4	5	9	16	....	....	....	....
99-2000	Orlando	IHL	81	8	43	51	59	....	....	....	....	....	....	....	....	....	6	0	2	2	6	....	....	....	....
2000-01	Orlando	IHL	51	19	30	49	55	....	....	....	....	....	....	....	....	....	10	2	9	11	12	....	....	....	....
2001-02	Houston Aeros	AHL	80	12	35	47	75	....	....	....	....	....	....	....	....	....	14	2	4	6	10	....	....	....	....
2002-03	**Minnesota**	**NHL**	**1**	**0**	**0**	**0**	**0**	**0**	**0**	**0**	**0**	**0.0**	**0**	**0**	**0.0**	**8:56**	....	....	....	....	....	....	....	....	....
	Houston Aeros	AHL	80	23	31	54	63	....	....	....	....	....	....	....	....	....	23	2	7	9	22	....	....	....	....
2003-04	Milwaukee	AHL	79	17	36	53	51	....	....	....	....	....	....	....	....	....	22	4	8	12	12	....	....	....	....
	NHL Totals		**1**	**0**	**0**	**0**	**0**	**0**	**0**	**0**	**0**	**0.0**		**0**	**0.0**	**8:56**	....	....	....	....	....	....	....	....	....

WCHA First All-Star Team (1997, 1998) • NCAA West Second All-American Team (1997) • WCHA Player of the Year (1998) • WCHA All-Tournament Team (1998) • NCAA West First All-American Team (1998) • IHL First All-Star Team (2001) • AHL First All-Star Team (2003, 2004) • Eddie Shore Award (Outstanding Defenseman – AHL) (2003, 2004)

Signed as a free agent by **Minnesota**, June 18, 2001. Traded to **Nashville** by **Minnesota** for Chris Bala, June 26, 2003.

MURRAY, Garth

(MUHR-ree, GARTH) **NYR**

Center. Shoots left. 6'1", 205 lbs. Born, Regina, Sask., September 17, 1982. NY Rangers' 3rd choice, 79th overall, in 2001 Entry Draft.

Season	Club	League	GP	G	A	Pts	PIM	PP	SH	GW	S	%	+/-	TF	F%	Min	GP	G	A	Pts	PIM	PP	SH	GW	Min
1997-98	Calgary Buffaloes	AMHL	56	26	34	60	110	....	....	....	....	....	....	....	....	....	....	....	....	....	....	....	....	....	....
	Regina Pats	WHL	4	0	0	0	2	....	....	....	....	....	....	....	....	....	2	0	0	0	0	....	....	....	....
1998-99	Regina Pats	WHL	60	3	5	8	101	....	....	....	....	....	....	....	....	....	....	....	....	....	....	....	....	....	....
99-2000	Regina Pats	WHL	68	14	26	40	155	....	....	....	....	....	....	....	....	....	7	1	1	2	7	....	....	....	....
2000-01	Regina Pats	WHL	72	28	16	44	183	....	....	....	....	....	....	....	....	....	6	1	1	2	10	....	....	....	....
2001-02	Regina Pats	WHL	62	33	30	63	154	....	....	....	....	....	....	....	....	....	6	2	3	5	9	....	....	....	....
	Hartford	AHL	4	0	0	0	0	....	....	....	....	....	....	....	....	....	9	1	3	4	6	....	....	....	....
2002-03	Hartford	AHL	64	10	14	24	121	....	....	....	....	....	....	....	....	....	2	0	0	0	6	....	....	....	....
2003-04	**NY Rangers**	**NHL**	**20**	**1**	**0**	**1**	**24**	**0**	**0**	**0**	**18**	**5.6**	**–5**	**5**	**20.0**	**9:16**	....	....	....	....	....	....	....	....	....
	Hartford	AHL	63	11	11	22	159	....	....	....	....	....	....	....	....	....	16	0	4	4	29	....	....	....	....
	NHL Totals		**20**	**1**	**0**	**1**	**24**	**0**	**0**	**0**	**18**	**5.6**		**5**	**20.0**	**9:16**	....	....	....	....	....	....	....	....	....

MURRAY, Glen

(MUHR-ree, GLEHN)

Right wing. Shoots right. 6'3", 225 lbs. Born, Halifax, N.S., November 1, 1972. Boston's 1st choice, 18th overall, in 1991 Entry Draft.

Season	Club	League	GP	G	A	Pts	PIM	PP	SH	GW	S	%	+/-	TF	F%	Min	GP	G	A	Pts	PIM	PP	SH	GW	Min
1988-89	Bridgewater	NSMHL	45	50	56	106	62	....	....	....	....	....	....	....	....	....	....	....	....	....	....	....	....	....	....
1989-90	Sudbury Wolves	OHL	62	8	28	36	17	....	....	....	....	....	....	....	....	....	7	0	0	0	4	....	....	....	....
1990-91	Sudbury Wolves	OHL	66	27	38	65	82	....	....	....	....	....	....	....	....	....	5	8	4	12	10	....	....	....	....
1991-92	Sudbury Wolves	OHL	54	37	47	84	93	....	....	....	....	....	....	....	....	....	11	7	4	11	18	....	....	....	....
	Boston	**NHL**	**5**	**3**	**1**	**4**	**0**	**1**	**0**	**0**	**20**	**15.0**	**2**	....	....	....	**15**	**4**	**2**	**6**	**10**	**1**	**0**	**0**	....
1992-93	**Boston**	**NHL**	**27**	**3**	**4**	**7**	**8**	**2**	**0**	**1**	**28**	**10.7**	**–6**	....	....	....	....	....	....	....	....	....	....	....	....
	Providence Bruins	AHL	48	30	26	56	42	....	....	....	....	....	....	....	....	....	6	1	4	5	4	....	....	....	....
1993-94	**Boston**	**NHL**	**81**	**18**	**13**	**31**	**48**	**0**	**0**	**4**	**114**	**15.8**	**–1**	....	....	....	**13**	**4**	**5**	**9**	**14**	**0**	**0**	**0**	....
1994-95	**Boston**	**NHL**	**35**	**5**	**2**	**7**	**46**	**0**	**0**	**2**	**64**	**7.8**	**–11**	....	....	....	**2**	**0**	**0**	**0**	**2**	**0**	**0**	**0**	....
1995-96	**Pittsburgh**	**NHL**	**69**	**14**	**15**	**29**	**57**	**0**	**0**	**2**	**100**	**14.0**	**4**	....	....	....	**18**	**2**	**6**	**8**	**10**	**0**	**0**	**1**	....
1996-97	**Pittsburgh**	**NHL**	**66**	**11**	**11**	**22**	**24**	**3**	**0**	**1**	**127**	**8.7**	**–19**	....	....	....	....	....	....	....	....	....	....	....	....
	Los Angeles	**NHL**	**11**	**5**	**3**	**8**	**8**	**0**	**0**	**0**	**26**	**19.2**	**–2**	....	....	....	....	....	....	....	....	....	....	....	....
1997-98	**Los Angeles**	**NHL**	**81**	**29**	**31**	**60**	**54**	**7**	**3**	**7**	**193**	**15.0**	**6**	....	....	....	**4**	**2**	**0**	**2**	**6**	**0**	**0**	**0**	....
1998-99	**Los Angeles**	**NHL**	**61**	**16**	**15**	**31**	**36**	**3**	**3**	**3**	**173**	**9.2**	**–14**	**12**	**25.0**	**20:33**	....	....	....	....	....	....	....	....	....
99-2000	**Los Angeles**	**NHL**	**78**	**29**	**33**	**62**	**60**	**10**	**1**	**2**	**202**	**14.4**	**13**	**15**	**80.0**	**18:30**	**4**	**0**	**0**	**0**	**2**	**0**	**0**	**0**	**19:04**
2000-01	**Los Angeles**	**NHL**	**64**	**18**	**21**	**39**	**32**	**3**	**1**	**1**	**138**	**13.0**	**9**	**7**	**42.9**	**18:12**	**13**	**4**	**3**	**7**	**4**	**1**	**0**	**1**	**19:51**
2001-02	**Los Angeles**	**NHL**	**9**	**6**	**5**	**11**	**0**	**4**	**0**	**2**	**34**	**17.6**	**5**	**1**	**100.0**	**19:08**	....	....	....	....	....	....	....	....	....
	Boston	**NHL**	**73**	**35**	**25**	**60**	**40**	**5**	**0**	**7**	**212**	**16.5**	**26**	**39**	**23.1**	**19:50**	**6**	**1**	**4**	**5**	**4**	**0**	**0**	**0**	**18:02**
2002-03	**Boston**	**NHL**	**82**	**44**	**48**	**92**	**64**	**12**	**0**	**5**	**331**	**13.3**	**9**	**32**	**37.5**	**22:36**	**5**	**1**	**1**	**2**	**4**	**0**	**0**	**0**	**19:36**
2003-04	**Boston**	**NHL**	**81**	**32**	**28**	**60**	**56**	**11**	**0**	**9**	**260**	**12.3**	**17**	**53**	**35.9**	**20:56**	**7**	**2**	**1**	**3**	**8**	**0**	**0**	**1**	**19:57**
	NHL Totals		**823**	**268**	**255**	**523**	**533**	**61**	**8**	**46**	**2022**	**13.3**		**159**	**37.1**	**20:10**	**87**	**20**	**22**	**42**	**64**	**2**	**0**	**3**	**19:26**

Played in NHL All-Star Game (2003, 2004)

Traded to **Pittsburgh** by **Boston** with Bryan Smolinski and Boston's 3rd round choice (Boyd Kane) in 1996 Entry Draft for Kevin Stevens and Shawn McEachern, August 2, 1995. Traded to **Los Angeles** by **Pittsburgh** for Ed Olczyk, March 18, 1997. Traded to **Boston** by **Los Angeles** with Jozef Stumpel for Jason Allison and Mikko Eloranta, October 24, 2001.

MURRAY, Marty

(MUHR-ree, MAHR-tee) **CAR.**

Center. Shoots left. 5'9", 180 lbs. Born, Lylton, Man., February 16, 1975. Calgary's 5th choice, 96th overall, in 1993 Entry Draft.

Season	Club	League	GP	G	A	Pts	PIM	PP	SH	GW	S	%	+/-	TF	F%	Min	GP	G	A	Pts	PIM	PP	SH	GW	Min
1990-91	S-W Cougars	MMHL	36	46	47	93	50	....	....	....	....	....	....	....	....	....	....	....	....	....	....	....	....	....	....
1991-92	Brandon	WHL	68	20	36	56	22	....	....	....	....	....	....	....	....	....	....	....	....	....	....	....	....	....	....
1992-93	Brandon	WHL	67	29	65	94	50	....	....	....	....	....	....	....	....	....	4	1	3	4	0	....	....	....	....
1993-94	Brandon	WHL	64	43	71	114	33	....	....	....	....	....	....	....	....	....	14	6	14	20	14	....	....	....	....
1994-95	Brandon	WHL	65	40	*88	128	53	....	....	....	....	....	....	....	....	....	18	9	*20	29	16	....	....	....	....
1995-96	**Calgary**	**NHL**	**15**	**3**	**3**	**6**	**0**	**2**	**0**	**0**	**22**	**13.6**	**–4**	....	....	....	....	....	....	....	....	....	....	....	....
	Saint John Flames	AHL	58	25	31	56	20	....	....	....	....	....	....	....	....	....	14	2	4	6	4	....	....	....	....
1996-97	**Calgary**	**NHL**	**2**	**0**	**0**	**0**	**4**	**0**	**0**	**0**	**2**	**0.0**	**0**	....	....	....	....	....	....	....	....	....	....	....	....
	Saint John Flames	AHL	67	19	39	58	40	....	....	....	....	....	....	....	....	....	5	2	3	5	4	....	....	....	....

			Regular Season														Playoffs								
Season	Club	League	GP	G	A	Pts	PIM	PP	SH	GW	S	%	+/-	TF	F%	Min	GP	G	A	Pts	PIM	PP	SH	GW	Min
1997-98	**Calgary**	**NHL**	**2**	**0**	**0**	**0**	**2**	**0**	**0**	**0**	**2**	**0.0**	**1**	....	....	....	....	....	....	....	....	....	....	....	....
	Saint John Flames	AHL	41	10	30	40	16	....	....	....	....	....	....	....	....	....	21	10	10	20	12	....	....	....	....
1998-99	EC Villacher SV	Alpenliga	33	26	41	67	12	....	....	....	....	....	....	....	....	....	....	....	....	....	....	....	....	....	....
	EC Villacher SV	Austria	17	13	17	30	6	....	....	....	....	....	....	....	....	....	6	1	4	5	0	....	....	....	....
99-2000	Kolner Haie	Germany	56	12	47	59	28	....	....	....	....	....	....	....	....	....	10	4	3	7	2	....	....	....	....
2000-01	**Calgary**	**NHL**	**7**	**0**	**0**	**0**	**0**	**0**	**0**	**0**	**6**	**0.0**	**–2**	**88**	**55.7**	**14:28**	....	....	....	....	....	....	....	....	....
	Saint John Flames	AHL	56	24	52	76	36	....	....	....	....	....	....	....	....	....	19	4	16	20	18	....	....	....	....
2001-02	**Philadelphia**	**NHL**	**74**	**12**	**15**	**27**	**10**	**1**	**1**	**2**	**109**	**11.0**	**10**	**913**	**50.7**	**13:56**	**5**	**0**	**1**	**1**	**0**	**0**	**0**	**0**	**13:14**
	Philadelphia	AHL	3	0	3	3	2	....	....	....	....	....	....	....	....	....	....	....	....	....	....	....	....	....	....
2002-03	**Philadelphia**	**NHL**	**76**	**11**	**15**	**26**	**13**	**1**	**1**	**0**	**105**	**10.5**	**–1**	**472**	**55.1**	**12:22**	**4**	**0**	**0**	**0**	**4**	**0**	**0**	**0**	**11:00**
2003-04	**Carolina**	**NHL**	**66**	**5**	**7**	**12**	**8**	**0**	**0**	**0**	**56**	**8.9**	**6**	**229**	**52.8**	**11:49**	....	....	....	....	....	....	....	....	....
	NHL Totals		**242**	**31**	**40**	**71**	**37**	**4**	**2**	**2**	**302**	**10.3**		**1702**	**52.5**	**12:47**	**9**	**0**	**1**	**1**	**4**	**0**	**0**	**0**	**12:15**

WHL East First All-Star Team (1994, 1995) • Canadian Major Junior Second All-Star Team (1994) • WHL MVP (1995)

Signed as a free agent by **Philadelphia**, July 9, 2001. Traded to **Carolina** by **Philadelphia** for Carolina's 6th round choice (Frederik Cabana) in 2004 Entry Draft, June 22, 2003.

MURRAY, Rem

(MUHR-ree, REHM)

Center/left wing. Shoots left. 6'2", 200 lbs. Born, Stratford, Ont., October 9, 1972. Los Angeles' 5th choice, 135th overall, in 1992 Entry Draft.

Season	Club	League	GP	G	A	Pts	PIM	PP	SH	GW	S	%	+/-	TF	F%	Min	GP	G	A	Pts	PIM	PP	SH	GW	Min
1989-90	Stratford Cullitons	OJHL-B	46	19	32	51	48	....	....	....	....	....	....	....	....	....	....	....	....	....	....	....	....	....	....
1990-91	Stratford Cullitons	OJHL-B	48	39	59	98	39	....	....	....	....	....	....	....	....	....	....	....	....	....	....	....	....	....	....
1991-92	Michigan State	CCHA	41	12	36	48	16	....	....	....	....	....	....	....	....	....	....	....	....	....	....	....	....	....	....
1992-93	Michigan State	CCHA	40	22	35	57	24	....	....	....	....	....	....	....	....	....	....	....	....	....	....	....	....	....	....
1993-94	Michigan State	CCHA	41	16	38	54	18	....	....	....	....	....	....	....	....	....	....	....	....	....	....	....	....	....	....
1994-95	Michigan State	CCHA	40	20	36	56	21	....	....	....	....	....	....	....	....	....	....	....	....	....	....	....	....	....	....
1995-96	Cape Breton	AHL	79	31	59	90	40	....	....	....	....	....	....	....	....	....	....	....	....	....	....	....	....	....	....
1996-97	**Edmonton**	**NHL**	**82**	**11**	**20**	**31**	**16**	**1**	**0**	**2**	**85**	**12.9**	**9**	....	....	....	**12**	**1**	**2**	**3**	**4**	**0**	**0**	**0**	....
1997-98	**Edmonton**	**NHL**	**61**	**9**	**9**	**18**	**39**	**2**	**2**	**0**	**59**	**15.3**	**–9**	....	....	....	**11**	**1**	**4**	**5**	**2**	**0**	**0**	**0**	....
1998-99	**Edmonton**	**NHL**	**78**	**21**	**18**	**39**	**20**	**4**	**1**	**4**	**116**	**18.1**	**4**	**1013**	**48.1**	**15:50**	**4**	**1**	**1**	**2**	**2**	**0**	**0**	**0**	**22:40**
99-2000	**Edmonton**	**NHL**	**44**	**9**	**5**	**14**	**8**	**2**	**0**	**3**	**65**	**13.8**	**–2**	**303**	**50.5**	**14:16**	**5**	**0**	**1**	**1**	**2**	**0**	**0**	**0**	**15:19**
2000-01	**Edmonton**	**NHL**	**82**	**15**	**21**	**36**	**24**	**1**	**3**	**3**	**122**	**12.3**	**5**	**694**	**49.3**	**15:21**	**6**	**2**	**0**	**2**	**6**	**1**	**0**	**0**	**18:10**
2001-02	**Edmonton**	**NHL**	**69**	**7**	**17**	**24**	**14**	**0**	**2**	**1**	**84**	**8.3**	**5**	**825**	**50.9**	**14:27**	....	....	....	....	....	....	....	....	....
	NY Rangers	**NHL**	**11**	**1**	**2**	**3**	**4**	**0**	**0**	**0**	**14**	**7.1**	**–9**	**151**	**51.7**	**15:51**	....	....	....	....	....	....	....	....	....
2002-03	**NY Rangers**	**NHL**	**32**	**6**	**6**	**12**	**4**	**1**	**1**	**1**	**62**	**9.7**	**–3**	**118**	**53.4**	**15:39**	....	....	....	....	....	....	....	....	....
	Nashville	**NHL**	**53**	**6**	**13**	**19**	**18**	**1**	**0**	**0**	**81**	**7.4**	**1**	**720**	**49.2**	**17:16**	....	....	....	....	....	....	....	....	....
2003-04	**Nashville**	**NHL**	**39**	**8**	**9**	**17**	**12**	**0**	**2**	**1**	**58**	**13.8**	**–1**	**169**	**46.2**	**16:37**	....	....	....	....	....	....	....	....	....
	NHL Totals		**551**	**93**	**120**	**213**	**159**	**12**	**11**	**15**	**746**	**12.5**		**3993**	**49.5**	**15:35**	**38**	**5**	**8**	**13**	**16**	**1**	**0**	**0**	**18:25**

CCHA Second All-Star Team (1995)

Signed as a free agent by **Edmonton**, September 19, 1995. Traded to **NY Rangers** by **Edmonton** with Tom Poti for Mike York and NY Rangers' 4th round choice (Ivan Koltsov) in 2002 Entry Draft, March 19, 2002. Traded to **Nashville** by **NY Rangers** with Tomas Kloucek and Marek Zidlicky for Mike Dunham, December 12, 2002. • Missed majority of 2003-04 season recovering from neck injury suffered in game vs. Detroit, January 5, 2004.

MYRVOLD, Anders

(MYOOR-vohld, AN-duhrs) **DET.**

Defense. Shoots left. 6'2", 200 lbs. Born, Lorenskog, Norway, August 12, 1975. Quebec's 6th choice, 127th overall, in 1993 Entry Draft.

Season	Club	League	GP	G	A	Pts	PIM	PP	SH	GW	S	%	+/-	TF	F%	Min	GP	G	A	Pts	PIM	PP	SH	GW	Min
1991-92	Storhamr IL	Norway	1	0	0	0	4	....	....	....	....	....	....	....	....	....	....	....	....	....	....	....	....	....	....
1992-93	Farjestad	Sweden	2	0	0	0	0	....	....	....	....	....	....	....	....	....	....	....	....	....	....	....	....	....	....
1993-94	Grums IK	Swede-2	24	1	0	1	59	....	....	....	....	....	....	....	....	....	2	1	0	1	5	....	....	....	....
1994-95	Laval Titan	QMJHL	64	14	50	64	173	....	....	....	....	....	....	....	....	....	20	4	10	14	68	....	....	....	....
	Cornwall Aces	AHL	....	....	....	....	....	....	....	....	....	....	....	....	....	....	3	0	1	1	2	....	....	....	....
1995-96	**Colorado**	**NHL**	**4**	**0**	**1**	**1**	**6**	**0**	**0**	**0**	**4**	**0.0**	**–2**	....	....	....	....	....	....	....	....	....	....	....	....
	Cornwall Aces	AHL	70	5	24	29	125	....	....	....	....	....	....	....	....	....	5	1	0	1	19	....	....	....	....
1996-97	Hershey Bears	AHL	20	0	3	3	16	....	....	....	....	....	....	....	....	....	....	....	....	....	....	....	....	....	....
	Boston	**NHL**	**9**	**0**	**2**	**2**	**4**	**0**	**0**	**0**	**8**	**0.0**	**–1**	....	....	....	....	....	....	....	....	....	....	....	....
	Providence Bruins	AHL	53	6	15	21	107	....	....	....	....	....	....	....	....	....	10	0	1	1	6	....	....	....	....
1997-98	Providence Bruins	AHL	75	4	21	25	91	....	....	....	....	....	....	....	....	....	....	....	....	....	....	....	....	....	....
1998-99	Djurgarden	Sweden	29	3	4	7	52	....	....	....	....	....	....	....	....	....	....	....	....	....	....	....	....	....	....
	Djurgarden	EuroHL	3	0	1	1	4	....	....	....	....	....	....	....	....	....	....	....	....	....	....	....	....	....	....
	AIK Solna	Sweden	19	1	3	4	24	....	....	....	....	....	....	....	....	....	....	....	....	....	....	....	....	....	....
99-2000	AIK Solna	Sweden	49	1	3	4	87	....	....	....	....	....	....	....	....	....	....	....	....	....	....	....	....	....	....
2000-01	**NY Islanders**	**NHL**	**12**	**0**	**1**	**1**	**0**	**0**	**0**	**0**	**8**	**0.0**	**–2**	**0**	**0.0**	**9:26**	....	....	....	....	....	....	....	....	....
	Springfield	AHL	69	5	25	30	129	....	....	....	....	....	....	....	....	....	....	....	....	....	....	....	....	....	....
2001-02	Hartford	AHL	19	3	3	6	28	....	....	....	....	....	....	....	....	....	....	....	....	....	....	....	....	....	....
	Fribourg	Swiss	6	0	0	0	16	....	....	....	....	....	....	....	....	....	4	0	1	1	6	....	....	....	....
2002-03	Adler Mannheim	Germany	45	0	3	3	82	....	....	....	....	....	....	....	....	....	7	0	0	0	4	....	....	....	....
2003-04	Grand Rapids	AHL	71	0	21	21	94	....	....	....	....	....	....	....	....	....	4	0	1	1	2	....	....	....	....
	Detroit	**NHL**	**8**	**0**	**1**	**1**	**2**	**0**	**0**	**0**	**6**	**0.0**	**–1**	**0**	**0.0**	**12:12**	....	....	....	....	....	....	....	....	....
	NHL Totals		**33**	**0**	**5**	**5**	**12**	**0**	**0**	**0**	**26**	**0.0**		**0**	**0.0**	**10:32**	....	....	....	....	....	....	....	....	....

QMJHL All-Rookie Team (1995)

Rights transferred to **Colorado** after **Quebec** franchise relocated, June 21, 1995. Traded to **Boston** by **Colorado** with Landon Wilson for Boston's 1st round choice (Robyn Regehr) in 1998 Entry Draft, November 22, 1996. Signed as a free agent by **NY Islanders**, August 28, 2000. Signed as a free agent by **Fribourg** (Swiss), January 10, 2002. Signed as a free agent by **Florida**, July 28, 2002. Signed as a free agent by **Detroit**, September 1, 2003.

NAGY, Ladislav

(NA-gee, LA-dih-slahv) **PHX.**

Left wing. Shoots left. 5'11", 192 lbs. Born, Saca, Czech., June 1, 1979. St. Louis' 6th choice, 177th overall, in 1997 Entry Draft.

Season	Club	League	GP	G	A	Pts	PIM	PP	SH	GW	S	%	+/-	TF	F%	Min	GP	G	A	Pts	PIM	PP	SH	GW	Min
1996-97	HC Kosice Jr.	Slovak-Jr.	45	29	30	59	105	....	....	....	....	....	....	....	....	....	....	....	....	....	....	....	....	....	....
	HK Dragon Presov	Slovak-2	11	6	5	11	....	....	....	....	....	....	....	....	....	....	....	....	....	....	....	....	....	....	....
1997-98	HC Kosice	Slovakia	29	19	15	34	41	....	....	....	....	....	....	....	....	....	11	2	4	6	6	....	....	....	....
1998-99	Halifax	QMJHL	63	71	55	126	148	....	....	....	....	....	....	....	....	....	5	3	3	6	18	....	....	....	....
	Worcester IceCats	AHL	....	....	....	....	....	....	....	....	....	....	....	....	....	....	3	2	2	4	0	....	....	....	....
99-2000	**St. Louis**	**NHL**	**11**	**2**	**4**	**6**	**2**	**1**	**0**	**0**	**15**	**13.3**	**2**	**6**	**33.3**	**12:19**	**6**	**1**	**1**	**2**	**0**	**0**	**0**	**0**	**13:29**
	Worcester IceCats	AHL	69	23	28	51	67	....	....	....	....	....	....	....	....	....	2	1	0	1	0	....	....	....	....
2000-01	**St. Louis**	**NHL**	**40**	**8**	**8**	**16**	**20**	**2**	**0**	**2**	**59**	**13.6**	**–2**	**28**	**50.0**	**13:03**	....	....	....	....	....	....	....	....	....
	Worcester IceCats	AHL	20	6	14	20	36	....	....	....	....	....	....	....	....	....	....	....	....	....	....	....	....	....	....
	Phoenix	**NHL**	**6**	**0**	**1**	**1**	**2**	**0**	**0**	**0**	**5**	**0.0**	**0**	**0**	**0.0**	**12:38**	....	....	....	....	....	....	....	....	....
2001-02	**Phoenix**	**NHL**	**74**	**23**	**19**	**42**	**50**	**5**	**0**	**5**	**187**	**12.3**	**6**	**17**	**47.1**	**15:04**	**5**	**0**	**0**	**0**	**21**	**0**	**0**	**0**	**15:45**
2002-03	HC Kosice	Slovakia	1	2	1	3	0	....	....	....	....	....	....	....	....	....	....	....	....	....	....	....	....	....	....
	Phoenix	**NHL**	**80**	**22**	**35**	**57**	**92**	**8**	**0**	**6**	**209**	**10.5**	**17**	**41**	**34.2**	**17:28**	....	....	....	....	....	....	....	....	....
2003-04	**Phoenix**	**NHL**	**55**	**24**	**28**	**52**	**46**	**11**	**0**	**6**	**160**	**15.0**	**11**	**33**	**42.4**	**18:10**	....	....	....	....	....	....	....	....	....
	NHL Totals		**266**	**79**	**95**	**174**	**212**	**27**	**0**	**19**	**635**	**12.4**		**125**	**41.6**	**15:57**	**11**	**1**	**1**	**2**	**21**	**0**	**0**	**0**	**14:30**

Traded to **Phoenix** by **St. Louis** with Michal Handzus, the rights to Jeff Taffe and St. Louis' 1st round choice (Ben Eager) in 2002 Entry Draft for Keith Tkachuk, March 13, 2001.

NASH, Rick

(NASH, RIHK) **CBJ**

Left wing. Shoots left. 6'4", 206 lbs. Born, Brampton, Ont., June 16, 1984. Columbus' 1st choice, 1st overall, in 2002 Entry Draft.

Season	Club	League	GP	G	A	Pts	PIM	PP	SH	GW	S	%	+/-	TF	F%	Min	GP	G	A	Pts	PIM	PP	SH	GW	Min
99-2000	Tor. Marlboros	GTHL	34	61	54	115	34	....	....	....	....	....	....	....	....	....	....	....	....	....	....	....	....	....	....
2000-01	London Knights	OHL	58	31	35	66	56	....	....	....	....	....	....	....	....	....	4	3	3	6	8	....	....	....	....
2001-02	London Knights	OHL	54	32	40	72	88	....	....	....	....	....	....	....	....	....	12	10	9	19	21	....	....	....	....
2002-03	**Columbus**	**NHL**	**74**	**17**	**22**	**39**	**78**	**6**	**0**	**2**	**154**	**11.0**	**–27**	**14**	**35.7**	**13:57**	....	....	....	....	....	....	....	....	....
2003-04	**Columbus**	**NHL**	**80**	***41**	**16**	**57**	**87**	**19**	**0**	**7**	**269**	**15.2**	**–35**	**21**	**28.6**	**17:38**	....	....	....	....	....	....	....	....	....
	NHL Totals		**154**	**58**	**38**	**96**	**165**	**25**	**0**	**9**	**423**	**13.7**		**35**	**31.4**	**15:52**	....	....	....	....	....	....	....	....	....

OHL All-Rookie Team (2001) • OHL Rookie of the Year (2001) • CHL All-Rookie Team (2001) • NHL All-Rookie Team (2003) • Maurice "Rocket" Richard Trophy (2004) (tied with Jarome Iginla and Ilya Kovalchuk)

Played in NHL All-Star Game (2004)

NASH, Tyson

(NASH, TIGH-sohn) **PHX.**

Left wing. Shoots left. 5'11", 191 lbs. Born, Edmonton, Alta., March 11, 1975. Vancouver's 10th choice, 247th overall, in 1994 Entry Draft.

			Regular Season														Playoffs								
Season	Club	League	GP	G	A	Pts	PIM	PP	SH	GW	S	%	+/-	TF	F%	Min	GP	G	A	Pts	PIM	PP	SH	GW	Min
1990-91	Sherwood Park	AMHL	40	17	28	43	63	....	....	....	....	....	....	....	....	....	....	....	....	....	....	....	....	....	....
1991-92	Kamloops Blazers	WHL	33	1	6	7	62	....	....	....	....	....	....	....	....	....	4	0	0	0	0	....	....	....	....
1992-93	Kamloops Blazers	WHL	61	10	16	26	78	....	....	....	....	....	....	....	....	....	13	3	2	5	32	....	....	....	....
1993-94	Kamloops Blazers	WHL	65	20	36	56	135	....	....	....	....	....	....	....	....	....	16	3	4	7	12	....	....	....	....
1994-95	Kamloops Blazers	WHL	63	34	41	75	70	....	....	....	....	....	....	....	....	....	21	10	7	17	30	....	....	....	....
1995-96	Syracuse Crunch	AHL	50	4	7	11	58	....	....	....	....	....	....	....	....	....	4	0	0	0	11	....	....	....	....
	Raleigh IceCaps	ECHL	6	1	1	2	8	....	....	....	....	....	....	....	....	....	....	....	....	....	....	....	....	....	....
1996-97	Syracuse Crunch	AHL	77	17	17	34	105	....	....	....	....	....	....	....	....	....	3	0	2	2	0	....	....	....	....
1997-98	Syracuse Crunch	AHL	74	20	20	40	184	....	....	....	....	....	....	....	....	....	5	0	2	2	28	....	....	....	....
1998-99	**St. Louis**	**NHL**	**2**	**0**	**0**	**0**	**5**	**0**	**0**	**0**	**1**	**0.0**	**–1**	**0**	**0.0**	**7:44**	**1**	**0**	**0**	**0**	**2**	**0**	**0**	**0**	**6:25**
	Worcester IceCats	AHL	55	14	22	36	143	....	....	....	....	....	....	....	....	....	4	4	1	5	27	....	....	....	....
99-2000	**St. Louis**	**NHL**	**66**	**4**	**9**	**13**	**150**	**0**	**1**	**1**	**68**	**5.9**	**6**	**0**	**0.0**	**8:35**	**6**	**1**	**0**	**1**	**24**	**0**	**0**	**0**	**8:36**
2000-01	**St. Louis**	**NHL**	**57**	**8**	**7**	**15**	**110**	**0**	**1**	**0**	**113**	**7.1**	**8**	**2**	**50.0**	**12:29**	....	....	....	....	....	....	....	....	....
2001-02	**St. Louis**	**NHL**	**64**	**6**	**7**	**13**	**100**	**0**	**0**	**1**	**66**	**9.1**	**2**	**14**	**35.7**	**10:02**	**9**	**0**	**1**	**1**	**20**	**0**	**0**	**0**	**8:03**
2002-03	**St. Louis**	**NHL**	**66**	**6**	**3**	**9**	**114**	**1**	**0**	**2**	**77**	**7.8**	**0**	**9**	**11.1**	**9:53**	**7**	**2**	**1**	**3**	**6**	**0**	**0**	**0**	**9:05**
2003-04	**Phoenix**	**NHL**	**69**	**3**	**5**	**8**	**110**	**0**	**0**	**0**	**83**	**3.6**	**–6**	**13**	**38.5**	**11:53**	....	....	....	....	....	....	....	....	....
	NHL Totals		**324**	**27**	**31**	**58**	**589**	**1**	**2**	**4**	**408**	**6.6**		**38**	**31.6**	**10:31**	**23**	**3**	**2**	**5**	**52**	**0**	**0**	**0**	**8:26**

Signed as a free agent by **St. Louis**, July 14, 1998. Traded to **Phoenix** by **St. Louis** for Phoenix's 5th round choice (Lee Stempniak) in 2003 Enrey Draft, June 21, 2003.

NASLUND, Markus

(NAZ-luhnd, MAHR-kuhs) **VAN.**

Left wing. Shoots left. 5'11", 195 lbs. Born, Ornskoldsvik, Sweden, July 30, 1973. Pittsburgh's 1st choice, 16th overall, in 1991 Entry Draft.

			Regular Season														Playoffs								
Season	Club	League	GP	G	A	Pts	PIM	PP	SH	GW	S	%	+/-	TF	F%	Min	GP	G	A	Pts	PIM	PP	SH	GW	Min
1988-89	Ornskoldsviks IF	Swede-3	14	7	6	13	....	....	....	....	....	....	....	....	....	....	....	....	....	....	....	....	....	....	....
1989-90	MoDo Jr.	Swede-Jr.	33	43	35	78	20	....	....	....	....	....	....	....	....	....	....	....	....	....	....	....	....	....	....
1990-91	MoDo	Sweden	32	10	9	19	14	....	....	....	....	....	....	....	....	....	....	....	....	....	....	....	....	....	....
1991-92	MoDo	Sweden	39	22	18	40	54	....	....	....	....	....	....	....	....	....	....	....	....	....	....	....	....	....	....
1992-93	MoDo Jr.	Swede-Jr.	2	4	1	5	2	....	....	....	....	....	....	....	....	....	....	....	....	....	....	....	....	....	....
	MoDo	Sweden	39	22	17	39	67	....	....	....	....	....	....	....	....	....	3	3	2	5	0	....	....	....	....
1993-94	**Pittsburgh**	**NHL**	**71**	**4**	**7**	**11**	**27**	**1**	**0**	**0**	**80**	**5.0**	**–3**	....	....	....	....	....	....	....	....	....	....	....	....
	Cleveland	IHL	5	1	6	7	4	....	....	....	....	....	....	....	....	....	....	....	....	....	....	....	....	....	....
1994-95	**Pittsburgh**	**NHL**	**14**	**2**	**2**	**4**	**2**	**0**	**0**	**0**	**13**	**15.4**	**0**	....	....	....	....	....	....	....	....	....	....	....	....
	Cleveland	IHL	7	3	4	7	6	....	....	....	....	....	....	....	....	....	4	1	3	4	8	....	....	....	....
1995-96	**Pittsburgh**	**NHL**	**66**	**19**	**33**	**52**	**36**	**3**	**0**	**4**	**125**	**15.2**	**17**	....	....	....	....	....	....	....	....	....	....	....	....
	Vancouver	**NHL**	**10**	**3**	**0**	**3**	**6**	**1**	**0**	**1**	**19**	**15.8**	**3**	....	....	....	**6**	**1**	**2**	**3**	**8**	**1**	**0**	**0**	....
1996-97	**Vancouver**	**NHL**	**78**	**21**	**20**	**41**	**30**	**4**	**0**	**4**	**120**	**17.5**	**–15**	....	....	....	....	....	....	....	....	....	....	....	....
1997-98	**Vancouver**	**NHL**	**76**	**14**	**20**	**34**	**56**	**2**	**1**	**0**	**106**	**13.2**	**5**	....	....	....	....	....	....	....	....	....	....	....	....
1998-99	**Vancouver**	**NHL**	**80**	**36**	**30**	**66**	**74**	**15**	**2**	**3**	**205**	**17.6**	**–13**	**14**	**57.1**	**19:57**	....	....	....	....	....	....	....	....	....
99-2000	**Vancouver**	**NHL**	**82**	**27**	**38**	**65**	**64**	**6**	**2**	**3**	**271**	**10.0**	**–5**	**13**	**46.2**	**20:13**	....	....	....	....	....	....	....	....	....
2000-01	**Vancouver**	**NHL**	**72**	**41**	**34**	**75**	**58**	**18**	**1**	**5**	**277**	**14.8**	**–2**	**6**	**50.0**	**19:03**	....	....	....	....	....	....	....	....	....
2001-02	**Vancouver**	**NHL**	**81**	**40**	**50**	**90**	**50**	**8**	**0**	**6**	**302**	**13.2**	**22**	**5**	**20.0**	**19:31**	**6**	**1**	**1**	**2**	**2**	**0**	**0**	**0**	**18:54**
	Sweden	Olympics	4	2	1	3	0	....	....	....	....	....	....	....	....	....	....	....	....	....	....	....	....	....	....
2002-03	**Vancouver**	**NHL**	**82**	**48**	**56**	**104**	**52**	**24**	**0**	**12**	**294**	**16.3**	**6**	**6**	**33.3**	**19:54**	**14**	**5**	**9**	**14**	**18**	**2**	**0**	**1**	**18:14**
2003-04	**Vancouver**	**NHL**	**78**	**35**	**49**	**84**	**58**	**5**	**0**	**6**	**296**	**11.8**	**24**	**14**	**35.7**	**19:23**	**7**	**2**	**7**	**9**	**2**	**2**	**0**	**0**	**19:21**
	NHL Totals		**790**	**290**	**339**	**629**	**513**	**87**	**6**	**44**	**2108**	**13.8**		**58**	**43.1**	**19:41**	**33**	**9**	**19**	**28**	**30**	**5**	**0**	**1**	**18:40**

NHL First All-Star Team (2002, 2003, 2004) • Lester B. Pearson Award (2003)
Played in NHL All-Star Game (1999, 2001, 2002, 2003, 2004)
Traded to **Vancouver** by **Pittsburgh** for Alek Stojanov, March 20, 1996.

NASREDDINE, Alain

(NAS-ruh-deen, AL-eh)

Defense. Shoots left. 6'1", 201 lbs. Born, Montreal, Que., July 10, 1975. Florida's 8th choice, 135th overall, in 1993 Entry Draft.

			Regular Season														Playoffs								
Season	Club	League	GP	G	A	Pts	PIM	PP	SH	GW	S	%	+/-	TF	F%	Min	GP	G	A	Pts	PIM	PP	SH	GW	Min
1990-91	Mtl-Bourassa	QAAA	35	10	25	35	50	....	....	....	....	....	....	....	....	....	....	....	....	....	....	....	....	....	....
1991-92	Drummondville	QMJHL	61	1	9	10	78	....	....	....	....	....	....	....	....	....	4	0	0	0	17	....	....	....	....
1992-93	Drummondville	QMJHL	64	0	14	14	137	....	....	....	....	....	....	....	....	....	10	0	1	1	36	....	....	....	....
1993-94	Chicoutimi	QMJHL	60	3	24	27	218	....	....	....	....	....	....	....	....	....	26	2	10	12	118	....	....	....	....
1994-95	Chicoutimi	QMJHL	67	8	31	39	342	....	....	....	....	....	....	....	....	....	13	3	5	8	40	....	....	....	....
1995-96	Carolina	AHL	63	0	5	5	245	....	....	....	....	....	....	....	....	....	....	....	....	....	....	....	....	....	....
1996-97	Carolina	AHL	26	0	4	4	109	....	....	....	....	....	....	....	....	....	....	....	....	....	....	....	....	....	....
	Indianapolis Ice	IHL	49	0	2	2	248	....	....	....	....	....	....	....	....	....	4	1	1	2	27	....	....	....	....
1997-98	Indianapolis Ice	IHL	75	1	12	13	258	....	....	....	....	....	....	....	....	....	5	0	2	2	12	....	....	....	....
1998-99	**Chicago**	**NHL**	**7**	**0**	**0**	**0**	**19**	**0**	**0**	**0**	**2**	**0.0**	**–2**	**0**	**0.0**	**12:11**	....	....	....	....	....	....	....	....	....
	Portland Pirates	AHL	7	0	1	1	36	....	....	....	....	....	....	....	....	....	....	....	....	....	....	....	....	....	....
	Montreal	**NHL**	**8**	**0**	**0**	**0**	**33**	**0**	**0**	**0**	**1**	**0.0**	**1**	**0**	**0.0**	**8:12**	....	....	....	....	....	....	....	....	....
	Fredericton	AHL	38	0	10	10	108	....	....	....	....	....	....	....	....	....	15	0	3	3	39	....	....	....	....
99-2000	Quebec Citadelles	AHL	59	1	6	7	178	....	....	....	....	....	....	....	....	....	....	....	....	....	....	....	....	....	....
	Hamilton	AHL	11	0	0	0	12	....	....	....	....	....	....	....	....	....	10	1	1	2	14	....	....	....	....
2000-01	Hamilton	AHL	74	4	14	18	164	....	....	....	....	....	....	....	....	....	....	....	....	....	....	....	....	....	....
2001-02	Hamilton	AHL	79	7	10	17	154	....	....	....	....	....	....	....	....	....	12	1	3	4	22	....	....	....	....
2002-03	**NY Islanders**	**NHL**	**3**	**0**	**0**	**0**	**2**	**0**	**0**	**0**	**0**	**0.0**	**0**	**0**	**0.0**	**12:11**	....	....	....	....	....	....	....	....	....
	Bridgeport	AHL	67	3	9	12	114	....	....	....	....	....	....	....	....	....	9	0	0	0	27	....	....	....	....
2003-04	Bridgeport	AHL	53	1	6	7	70	....	....	....	....	....	....	....	....	....	....	....	....	....	....	....	....	....	....
	Wilkes-Barre	AHL	17	1	1	2	16	....	....	....	....	....	....	....	....	....	24	1	0	1	48	....	....	....	....
	NHL Totals		**18**	**0**	**0**	**0**	**54**	**0**	**0**	**0**	**3**	**0.0**		**0**	**0.0**	**10:25**	....	....	....	....	....	....	....	....	....

QMJHL Second All-Star Team (1995)
Traded to **Chicago** by **Florida** for Ivan Droppa, December 18, 1996. Traded to **Montreal** by **Chicago** with Jeff Hackett, Eric Weinrich and Tampa Bay's 4th round choice (previously acquired, Montreal selected Chris Dyment) in 1999 Entry Draft for Jocelyn Thibault, Dave Manson and Brad Brown, November 16, 1998. Traded to **Edmonton** by **Montreal** with Igor Ulanov for Christian Laflamme and Matthieu Descoteaux, March 9, 2000. Signed as a free agent by **NY Islanders**, September 6, 2002. Traded to **Pittsburgh** by **NY Islanders** for Steve Webb, March 8, 2004.

NAZAROV, Andrei

(nah-ZAH-rohv, AWN-dray) **PHX.**

Left wing. Shoots right. 6'5", 242 lbs. Born, Chelyabinsk, USSR, May 22, 1974. San Jose's 2nd choice, 10th overall, in 1992 Entry Draft.

			Regular Season														Playoffs								
Season	Club	League	GP	G	A	Pts	PIM	PP	SH	GW	S	%	+/-	TF	F%	Min	GP	G	A	Pts	PIM	PP	SH	GW	Min
1991-92	Dynamo Moscow	CIS	2	1	0	1	2	....	....	....	....	....	....	....	....	....	....	....	....	....	....	....	....	....	....
1992-93	Dynamo Moscow	CIS	42	8	2	10	79	....	....	....	....	....	....	....	....	....	10	1	1	2	8	....	....	....	....
1993-94	Dynamo Moscow	CIS	6	2	2	4	0	....	....	....	....	....	....	....	....	....	....	....	....	....	....	....	....	....	....
	San Jose	**NHL**	**1**	**0**	**0**	**0**	**0**	**0**	**0**	**0**	**0**	**0.0**	**0**	....	....	....	....	....	....	....	....	....	....	....	....
	Kansas City	IHL	71	15	18	33	64	....	....	....	....	....	....	....	....	....	....	....	....	....	....	....	....	....	....
1994-95	Kansas City	IHL	43	15	10	25	55	....	....	....	....	....	....	....	....	....	....	....	....	....	....	....	....	....	....
	San Jose	**NHL**	**26**	**3**	**5**	**8**	**94**	**0**	**0**	**0**	**19**	**15.8**	**–1**	....	....	....	**6**	**0**	**0**	**0**	**9**	**0**	**0**	**0**	....
1995-96	**San Jose**	**NHL**	**42**	**7**	**7**	**14**	**62**	**2**	**0**	**1**	**55**	**12.7**	**–15**	....	....	....	....	....	....	....	....	....	....	....	....
	Kansas City	IHL	27	4	6	10	118	....	....	....	....	....	....	....	....	....	2	0	0	0	2	....	....	....	....
1996-97	**San Jose**	**NHL**	**60**	**12**	**15**	**27**	**222**	**1**	**0**	**1**	**116**	**10.3**	**–4**	....	....	....	....	....	....	....	....	....	....	....	....
	Kentucky	AHL	3	1	2	3	4	....	....	....	....	....	....	....	....	....	....	....	....	....	....	....	....	....	....
1997-98	**San Jose**	**NHL**	**40**	**1**	**1**	**2**	**112**	**0**	**0**	**0**	**31**	**3.2**	**–4**	....	....	....	....	....	....	....	....	....	....	....	....
	Tampa Bay	**NHL**	**14**	**1**	**1**	**2**	**58**	**0**	**0**	**0**	**19**	**5.3**	**–9**	....	....	....	....	....	....	....	....	....	....	....	....
1998-99	**Tampa Bay**	**NHL**	**26**	**2**	**0**	**2**	**43**	**0**	**0**	**0**	**18**	**11.1**	**–5**	**4**	**50.0**	**8:13**	....	....	....	....	....	....	....	....	....
	Calgary	**NHL**	**36**	**5**	**9**	**14**	**30**	**0**	**0**	**2**	**53**	**9.4**	**1**	**0**	**0.0**	**14:31**	....	....	....	....	....	....	....	....	....
99-2000	**Calgary**	**NHL**	**76**	**10**	**22**	**32**	**78**	**1**	**0**	**1**	**110**	**9.1**	**3**	**2**	**100.0**	**11:44**	....	....	....	....	....	....	....	....	....
2000-01	**Anaheim**	**NHL**	**16**	**1**	**0**	**1**	**29**	**0**	**0**	**0**	**13**	**7.7**	**–9**	**2**	**50.0**	**8:42**	....	....	....	....	....	....	....	....	....
	Boston	**NHL**	**63**	**1**	**4**	**5**	**200**	**0**	**0**	**0**	**50**	**2.0**	**–14**	**14**	**21.4**	**8:12**	....	....	....	....	....	....	....	....	....
2001-02	**Boston**	**NHL**	**47**	**0**	**2**	**2**	**164**	**0**	**0**	**0**	**18**	**0.0**	**–2**	**1**	**100.0**	**3:10**	....	....	....	....	....	....	....	....	....
	Phoenix	**NHL**	**30**	**6**	**3**	**9**	**51**	**0**	**0**	**0**	**38**	**15.8**	**7**	**1**	**100.0**	**7:35**	**3**	**0**	**0**	**0**	**2**	**0**	**0**	**0**	**9:34**

			Regular Season														Playoffs								
Season	Club	League	GP	G	A	Pts	PIM	PP	SH	GW	S	%	+/-	TF	F%	Min	GP	G	A	Pts	PIM	PP	SH	GW	Min
2002-03	Phoenix	NHL	59	3	0	3	135	2	0	0	35	8.6	–9	6	33.3	6:34	....	....	....	....	....	....	....	....	....
2003-04	Phoenix	NHL	33	1	2	3	125	0	0	0	17	5.9	–7	0	0.0	5:28	....	....	....	....	....	....	....	....	....
	NHL Totals		569	53	71	124	1403	6	0	5	592	9.0		30	40.0	8:22	9	0	0	0	11	0	0	0	9:34

Traded to **Tampa Bay** by **San Jose** with Florida's 1st round choice (previously acquired, Tampa Bay selected Vincent Lecavalier) in 1998 Entry Draft for Bryan Marchment, David Shaw and Tampa Bay's 1st round choice (later traded to Nashville – Nashville selected David Legwand) in 1998 Entry Draft, March 24, 1998. Traded to **Calgary** by **Tampa Bay** for Michael Nylander, January 19, 1999. Traded to **Anaheim** by **Calgary** with Calgary's 2nd round choice (later traded to Phoenix – later traded back to Calgary – Calgary selected Andrei Taratukhin) in 2001 Entry Draft for Jordan Leopold, September 26, 2000. Traded to **Boston** by **Anaheim** with Patrick Traverse for Samuel Pahlsson, November 18, 2000. Traded to **Phoenix** by **Boston** for Phoenix's 5th round choice (Peter Hamerlik) in 2002 Entry Draft, January 25, 2002. • Spent majority of 2003-04 season as a healthy reserve.

NECKAR, Stan

(NEHTS-kahzh, STAN)

Defense. Shoots left. 6'1", 214 lbs. Born, Ceske Budejovice, Czech., December 22, 1975. Ottawa's 2nd choice, 29th overall, in 1994 Entry Draft.

1991-92	C. Budejovice Jr.	Czech-Jr.	18	1	3	4	....	....	....	....	....	....	....	....	....	....	....	....	....	....	....	....	....	....	....
1992-93	Ceske Budejovice	Czech	42	2	9	11	12	....	....	....	....	....	....	....	....	....	....	....	....	....	....	....	....	....	....
1993-94	Ceske Budejovice	Czech	12	3	2	5	2	....	....	....	....	....	....	....	....	....	3	0	0	0	....	....	....	....	....
1994-95	Detroit Vipers	IHL	15	2	2	4	15	....	....	....	....	....	....	....	....	....	....	....	....	....	....	....	....	....	....
	Ottawa	NHL	48	1	3	4	37	0	0	0	34	2.9	–20	....	....	....	....	....	....	....	....	....	....	....	....
1995-96	Ottawa	NHL	82	3	9	12	54	1	0	0	57	5.3	–16	....	....	....	....	....	....	....	....	....	....	....	....
1996-97	Ottawa	NHL	5	0	0	0	2	0	0	0	3	0.0	2	....	....	....	....	....	....	....	....	....	....	....	....
1997-98	Ottawa	NHL	60	2	2	4	31	0	0	0	43	4.7	–14	....	....	....	9	0	0	0	2	0	0	0	....
1998-99	Ottawa	NHL	3	0	2	2	0	0	0	0	2	0.0	–1	0	0.0	15:53	....	....	....	....	....	....	....	....	....
	NY Rangers	NHL	18	0	0	0	8	0	0	0	8	0.0	–1	0	0.0	13:46	....	....	....	....	....	....	....	....	....
	Phoenix	NHL	11	0	1	1	10	0	0	0	6	0.0	3	0	0.0	15:08	6	0	1	1	4	0	0	0	10:20
99-2000	Phoenix	NHL	66	2	8	10	36	0	0	0	34	5.9	1	0	0.0	14:27	5	0	0	0	0	0	0	0	11:28
2000-01	Phoenix	NHL	53	2	2	4	63	0	0	1	16	12.5	–2	0	0.0	15:26	....	....	....	....	....	....	....	....	....
	Tampa Bay	NHL	16	0	2	2	8	0	0	0	10	0.0	–1	0	0.0	18:33	....	....	....	....	....	....	....	....	....
2001-02	Tampa Bay	NHL	77	1	7	8	24	0	1	0	38	2.6	–18	0	0.0	20:31	....	....	....	....	....	....	....	....	....
2002-03	Tampa Bay	NHL	70	1	4	5	43	0	0	1	38	2.6	–6	0	0.0	18:42	7	0	2	2	2	0	0	0	18:35
2003-04	Nashville	NHL	1	0	1	1	0	0	0	0	0	0.0	2	0	0.0	14:59	....	....	....	....	....	....	....	....	....
	Milwaukee	AHL	3	0	3	3	2	....	....	....	....	....	....	....	....	....	....	....	....	....	....	....	....	....	....
	Tampa Bay	NHL	....	....	....	....	....	....	....	....	....	....	....	....	....	....	2	0	0	0	0	0	0	0	13:48
	NHL Totals		510	12	41	53	316	1	1	2	289	4.2		0	0.0	17:15	29	0	3	3	8	0	0	0	13:51

Traded to **NY Rangers** by **Ottawa** for Bill Berg and NY Rangers' 2nd round choice (later traded to Anaheim – Anaheim selected Jordan Leopold) in 1999 Entry Draft, November 27, 1998. Traded to **Phoenix** by **NY Rangers** for Jason Doig and Phoenix's 6th round choice (Jay Dardis) in 1999 Entry Draft, March 23, 1999. Traded to **Tampa Bay** by **Phoenix** with Nikolai Khabibulin for Mike Johnson, Paul Mara, Ruslan Zainullin and NY Islanders' 2nd round choice (previously acquired, Phoenix selected Matthew Spiller) in 2001 Entry Draft, March 5, 2001. Signed as a free agent by **Nashville**, November 26, 2003. • Missed majority of 2003-04 season recovering from groin injury suffered in practice, November 29, 2003. Traded to **Tampa Bay** by **Nashville** for Tampa Bay's 6th round choice (Kevin Schaeffer) in 2004 Entry Draft, March 9, 2004.

NEDOROST, Andrej

(NEHD-ohr-ohst, AWN-dray) **CBJ**

Left wing. Shoots left. 6', 192 lbs. Born, Trencin, Czech., April 30, 1980. Columbus' 10th choice, 286th overall, in 2000 Entry Draft.

1996-96	Dukla Trencin Jr.	Slovak-Jr.	40	50	35	85	....	....	....	....	....	....	....	....	....	....	....	....	....	....	....	....	....	....	....
1996-97	Dukla Trencin Jr.	Slovak-Jr.	45	15	16	31	....	....	....	....	....	....	....	....	....	....	....	....	....	....	....	....	....	....	....
1997-98	Dukla Trencin Jr.	Slovak-Jr.	45	27	22	49	61	....	....	....	....	....	....	....	....	....	....	....	....	....	....	....	....	....	....
	Dukla Trencin	Slovakia	1	0	0	0	0	....	....	....	....	....	....	....	....	....	....	....	....	....	....	....	....	....	....
1998-99	Essen Jr.	German-Jr.	17	37	18	55	43	....	....	....	....	....	....	....	....	....	....	....	....	....	....	....	....	....	....
	Essen	German-2	30	3	5	8	22	....	....	....	....	....	....	....	....	....	....	....	....	....	....	....	....	....	....
99-2000	Essen	Germany	66	7	5	12	44	....	....	....	....	....	....	....	....	....	....	....	....	....	....	....	....	....	....
2000-01	Plzen	Czech	33	10	8	18	22	....	....	....	....	....	....	....	....	....	....	....	....	....	....	....	....	....	....
2001-02	Columbus	NHL	7	0	2	2	2	0	0	0	12	0.0	–3	1	100.0	12:56	....	....	....	....	....	....	....	....	....
	Syracuse Crunch	AHL	37	5	13	18	28	....	....	....	....	....	....	....	....	....	10	1	3	4	4	....	....	....	....
2002-03	Syracuse Crunch	AHL	63	14	19	33	85	....	....	....	....	....	....	....	....	....	....	....	....	....	....	....	....	....	....
	Columbus	NHL	12	0	1	1	4	0	0	0	10	0.0	–6	30	36.7	9:15	....	....	....	....	....	....	....	....	....
2003-04	Columbus	NHL	9	2	0	2	6	0	0	0	16	12.5	0	13	69.2	13:02	....	....	....	....	....	....	....	....	....
	Syracuse Crunch	AHL	8	0	2	2	6	....	....	....	....	....	....	....	....	....	....	....	....	....	....	....	....	....	....
	Magnitogorsk	Russia	16	3	4	7	12	....	....	....	....	....	....	....	....	....	7	0	3	3	4	....	....	....	....
	NHL Totals		28	2	3	5	12	0	0	0	38	5.3		44	47.7	11:23	....	....	....	....	....	....	....	....	....

Assigned to **Magnitogorsk** (Russia) by **Columbus**, December 17, 2003.

NEDOROST, Vaclav

(neh-DOHR-uhst, VAT-slav) **FLA.**

Center. Shoots left. 6'1", 190 lbs. Born, Budejovice, Czech., March 16, 1982. Colorado's 1st choice, 14th overall, in 2000 Entry Draft.

1997-98	C. Budejovice Jr.	Czech-Jr.	43	30	23	53	20	....	....	....	....	....	....	....	....	....	....	....	....	....	....	....	....	....	....
1998-99	C. Budejovice Jr.	Czech-Jr.	39	6	15	21	20	....	....	....	....	....	....	....	....	....	....	....	....	....	....	....	....	....	....
	Ceske Budejovice	Czech	7	0	2	2	0	....	....	....	....	....	....	....	....	....	....	....	....	....	....	....	....	....	....
99-2000	C. Budejovice Jr.	Czech-Jr.	14	4	7	11	4	....	....	....	....	....	....	....	....	....	....	....	....	....	....	....	....	....	....
	Ceske Budejovice	Czech	38	8	6	14	6	....	....	....	....	....	....	....	....	....	3	0	0	0	0	....	....	....	....
2000-01	Ceske Budejovice	Czech	36	3	12	15	14	....	....	....	....	....	....	....	....	....	....	....	....	....	....	....	....	....	....
2001-02	Colorado	NHL	25	2	2	4	2	1	0	0	22	9.1	–4	62	45.2	10:15	....	....	....	....	....	....	....	....	....
	Hershey Bears	AHL	49	12	22	34	16	....	....	....	....	....	....	....	....	....	7	2	3	5	2	....	....	....	....
2002-03	Colorado	NHL	42	4	5	9	20	1	0	0	35	11.4	8	151	44.4	10:29	....	....	....	....	....	....	....	....	....
	Hershey Bears	AHL	5	3	2	5	0	....	....	....	....	....	....	....	....	....	5	2	2	4	0	....	....	....	....
2003-04	Florida	NHL	32	4	3	7	12	2	0	0	38	10.5	–6	121	42.2	11:32	....	....	....	....	....	....	....	....	....
	San Antonio	AHL	21	9	6	15	2	....	....	....	....	....	....	....	....	....	....	....	....	....	....	....	....	....	....
	NHL Totals		99	10	10	20	34	4	0	0	95	10.5		334	43.7	10:46	....	....	....	....	....	....	....	....	....

Traded to **Florida** by **Colorado** with Eric Messier for Peter Worrell and Florida's 2nd round choice (later traded to NY Rangers – later traded back to Florida – Florida selected David Shantz) in 2004 Entry Draft, July 18, 2003.

NEDVED, Petr

(NEHD-VEHD, PEE-tuhr) **EDM.**

Center. Shoots left. 6'3", 195 lbs. Born, Liberec, Czech., December 9, 1971. Vancouver's 1st choice, 2nd overall, in 1990 Entry Draft.

1988-89	CHZ Litvinov Jr.	Czech-Jr.	20	32	19	51	12	....	....	....	....	....	....	....	....	....	....	....	....	....	....	....	....	....	....
1989-90	Seattle	WHL	71	65	80	145	80	....	....	....	....	....	....	....	....	....	11	4	9	13	2	....	....	....	....
1990-91	Vancouver	NHL	61	10	6	16	20	1	0	0	97	10.3	–21	....	....	....	6	0	1	1	0	0	0	0	....
1991-92	Vancouver	NHL	77	15	22	37	36	5	0	1	99	15.2	–3	....	....	....	10	1	4	5	16	0	0	0	....
1992-93	Vancouver	NHL	84	38	33	71	96	2	1	3	149	25.5	20	....	....	....	12	2	3	5	2	0	0	0	....
1993-94	Team Canada	Nat-Tm	17	19	12	31	16	....	....	....	....	....	....	....	....	....	....	....	....	....	....	....	....	....	....
	Canada	Olympics	8	5	1	6	6	....	....	....	....	....	....	....	....	....	....	....	....	....	....	....	....	....	....
	St. Louis	NHL	19	6	14	20	8	2	0	0	63	9.5	2	....	....	....	4	0	1	1	4	0	0	0	....
1994-95	NY Rangers	NHL	46	11	12	23	26	1	0	3	123	8.9	–1	....	....	....	10	3	2	5	6	2	0	0	....
1995-96	Pittsburgh	NHL	80	45	54	99	68	8	1	5	204	22.1	37	....	....	....	18	10	10	20	16	4	0	2	....
1996-97	Pittsburgh	NHL	74	33	38	71	66	12	3	4	189	17.5	–2	....	....	....	5	1	2	3	12	0	1	0	....
1997-98	Stadion Liberec	Czech-2	2	0	3	3	....	....	....	....	....	....	....	....	....	....	....	....	....	....	....	....	....	....	....
	TJ Novy Jicin	Czech-3	7	9	16	25	....	....	....	....	....	....	....	....	....	....	....	....	....	....	....	....	....	....	....
	HC Sparta Praha	Czech	5	2	3	5	8	....	....	....	....	....	....	....	....	....	6	0	2	2	52	....	....	....	....
	Las Vegas	IHL	3	3	3	6	4	....	....	....	....	....	....	....	....	....	....	....	....	....	....	....	....	....	....
1998-99	Las Vegas	IHL	13	8	10	18	32	....	....	....	....	....	....	....	....	....	....	....	....	....	....	....	....	....	....
	NY Rangers	NHL	56	20	27	47	50	9	1	3	153	13.1	–6	1069	52.5	20:31	....	....	....	....	....	....	....	....	....
99-2000	NY Rangers	NHL	76	24	44	68	40	6	2	4	201	11.9	2	1354	54.0	19:54	....	....	....	....	....	....	....	....	....
2000-01	NY Rangers	NHL	79	32	46	78	54	9	1	5	230	13.9	10	1349	49.7	20:16	....	....	....	....	....	....	....	....	....
2001-02	Liberec	Czech-2	1	3	0	3	2	....	....	....	....	....	....	....	....	....	....	....	....	....	....	....	....	....	....
	NY Rangers	NHL	78	21	25	46	36	6	1	3	175	12.0	–8	1402	52.1	19:22	....	....	....	....	....	....	....	....	....
2002-03	NY Rangers	NHL	78	27	31	58	64	8	3	4	205	13.2	–4	1142	53.0	20:21	....	....	....	....	....	....	....	....	....
2003-04	NY Rangers	NHL	65	14	17	31	42	5	0	3	153	9.2	–9	929	48.6	18:51	....	....	....	....	....	....	....	....	....
	Edmonton	NHL	16	5	10	15	4	2	0	0	37	13.5	1	226	46.9	18:11	....	....	....	....	....	....	....	....	....
	NHL Totals		889	301	379	680	610	76	13	38	2078	14.5		7471	51.6	19:49	65	17	23	40	56	6	1	2	....

WHL Rookie of the Year (1990) • Canadian Major Junior Rookie of the Year (1990)

Signed as a free agent by **St. Louis**, March 5, 1994. Traded to **NY Rangers** by **St. Louis** for Esa Tikkanen and Doug Lidster, July 24, 1994. Traded to **Pittsburgh** by **NY Rangers** with Sergei Zubov for Luc Robitaille and Ulf Samuelsson, August 31, 1995. Traded to **NY Rangers** by **Pittsburgh** with Chris Tamer and Sean Pronger for Alex Kovalev and Harry York, November 25, 1998. Traded to **Edmonton** by **NY Rangers** with Jussi Markkanen for Stephen Valiquette, Dwight Helminen, Edmonton's 2nd round compensatory choice (Dane Byers) in 2004 Entry Draft and future considerations, March 3, 2004.

Season	Club	League	Regular Season GP	G	A	Pts	PIM	PP	SH	GW	S	%	+/-	TF	F%	Min	Playoffs GP	G	A	Pts	PIM	PP	SH	GW	Min

NEIL, Chris

(NEEL, KRIHS) **OTT.**

Right wing. Shoots right. 6', 213 lbs. Born, Markdale, Ont., June 18, 1979. Ottawa's 7th choice, 161st overall, in 1998 Entry Draft.

Season	Club	League	GP	G	A	Pts	PIM	PP	SH	GW	S	%	+/-	TF	F%	Min	GP	G	A	Pts	PIM	PP	SH	GW	Min
1995-96	Orangeville	OJHL-B	43	15	15	30	50	....	....	....	....	....	....	....	....	....	....	....	....	....	....	....	....	....	....
1996-97	North Bay	OHL	65	13	16	29	150	....	....	....	....	....	....	....	....	....	....	....	....	....	....	....	....	....	....
1997-98	North Bay	OHL	59	26	29	55	231	....	....	....	....	....	....	....	....	....	....	....	....	....	....	....	....	....	....
1998-99	North Bay	OHL	66	26	46	72	215	....	....	....	....	....	....	....	....	....	4	1	0	1	15	....	....	....	....
99-2000	Mobile Mysticks	ECHL	4	0	2	2	39	....	....	....	....	....	....	....	....	....	....	....	....	....	....	....	....	....	....
	Grand Rapids	IHL	51	9	10	19	301	....	....	....	....	....	....	....	....	....	8	0	2	2	24	....	....	....	....
2000-01	Grand Rapids	IHL	78	15	21	36	354	....	....	....	....	....	....	....	....	....	10	2	2	4	22	....	....	....	....
2001-02	**Ottawa**	**NHL**	**72**	**10**	**7**	**17**	**231**	**1**	**0**	**0**	**56**	**17.9**	**5**	**0**	**0.0**	**8:22**	**12**	**0**	**0**	**0**	**12**	**0**	**0**	**0**	**7:12**
2002-03	**Ottawa**	**NHL**	**68**	**6**	**4**	**10**	**147**	**0**	**0**	**0**	**62**	**9.7**	**8**	**5**	**60.0**	**7:40**	**15**	**1**	**0**	**1**	**24**	**0**	**0**	**0**	**7:57**
2003-04	**Ottawa**	**NHL**	**82**	**8**	**8**	**16**	**194**	**0**	**0**	**1**	**76**	**10.5**	**13**	**14**	**42.9**	**8:51**	**7**	**0**	**1**	**1**	**19**	**0**	**0**	**0**	**6:45**
	NHL Totals		**222**	**24**	**19**	**43**	**572**	**1**	**0**	**1**	**194**	**12.4**		**19**	**47.4**	**8:20**	**34**	**1**	**1**	**2**	**55**	**0**	**0**	**0**	**7:27**

NELSON, Jeff

(NEHL-sohn, JEHF)

Center. Shoots left. 5'11", 190 lbs. Born, Prince Albert, Sask., December 18, 1972. Washington's 4th choice, 36th overall, in 1991 Entry Draft.

Season	Club	League	GP	G	A	Pts	PIM	PP	SH	GW	S	%	+/-	TF	F%	Min	GP	G	A	Pts	PIM	PP	SH	GW	Min
1987-88	Prince Albert	SMHL	31	24	32	56	32	....	....	....	....	....	....	....	....	....	....	....	....	....	....	....	....	....	....
1988-89	Prince Albert	WHL	71	30	57	87	74	....	....	....	....	....	....	....	....	....	4	0	3	3	4	....	....	....	....
1989-90	Prince Albert	WHL	72	28	69	97	79	....	....	....	....	....	....	....	....	....	14	2	11	13	10	....	....	....	....
1990-91	Prince Albert	WHL	72	46	74	120	58	....	....	....	....	....	....	....	....	....	3	1	1	2	4	....	....	....	....
1991-92	Prince Albert	WHL	64	48	65	113	84	....	....	....	....	....	....	....	....	....	9	7	14	21	18	....	....	....	....
1992-93	Baltimore	AHL	72	14	38	52	12	....	....	....	....	....	....	....	....	....	7	1	3	4	2	....	....	....	....
1993-94	Portland Pirates	AHL	80	34	73	107	92	....	....	....	....	....	....	....	....	....	17	10	5	15	20	....	....	....	....
1994-95	Portland Pirates	AHL	64	33	50	83	57	....	....	....	....	....	....	....	....	....	7	1	4	5	8	....	....	....	....
	Washington	**NHL**	**10**	**1**	**0**	**1**	**2**	**0**	**0**	**0**	**4**	**25.0**	**−2**	....	....	....	....	....	....	....	....	....	....	....	....
1995-96	**Washington**	**NHL**	**33**	**0**	**7**	**7**	**16**	**0**	**0**	**0**	**21**	**0.0**	**3**	....	....	....	**3**	**0**	**0**	**0**	**4**	**0**	**0**	**0**	....
	Portland Pirates	AHL	39	15	32	47	62	....	....	....	....	....	....	....	....	....	....	....	....	....	....	....	....	....	....
1996-97	Grand Rapids	IHL	82	34	55	89	85	....	....	....	....	....	....	....	....	....	5	0	4	4	4	....	....	....	....
1997-98	Milwaukee	IHL	52	20	34	54	30	....	....	....	....	....	....	....	....	....	10	2	7	9	15	....	....	....	....
1998-99	**Nashville**	**NHL**	**9**	**2**	**1**	**3**	**2**	**0**	**0**	**0**	**8**	**25.0**	**−1**	**138**	**55.1**	**16:09**	....	....	....	....	....	....	....	....	....
	Milwaukee	IHL	70	20	31	51	66	....	....	....	....	....	....	....	....	....	2	0	0	0	0	....	....	....	....
99-2000	Portland Pirates	AHL	73	24	30	54	38	....	....	....	....	....	....	....	....	....	1	0	0	0	0	....	....	....	....
2000-01	Portland Pirates	AHL	80	18	37	55	63	....	....	....	....	....	....	....	....	....	3	0	2	2	6	....	....	....	....
2001-02	Schwenningen	Germany	60	13	14	27	60	....	....	....	....	....	....	....	....	....	....	....	....	....	....	....	....	....	....
2002-03	Cleveland Barons	AHL	80	12	48	60	26	....	....	....	....	....	....	....	....	....	....	....	....	....	....	....	....	....	....
2003-04	Muskegon Fury	UHL	10	7	14	21	6	....	....	....	....	....	....	....	....	....	....	....	....	....	....	....	....	....	....
	Grand Rapids	AHL	64	14	30	44	43	....	....	....	....	....	....	....	....	....	4	1	0	1	4	....	....	....	....
	NHL Totals		**52**	**3**	**8**	**11**	**20**	**0**	**0**	**0**	**33**	**9.1**		**138**	**55.1**	**16:09**	**3**	**0**	**0**	**0**	**4**	**0**	**0**	**0**	....

Canadian Major Junior Scholastic Player of the Year (1989, 1990) • WHL East Second All-Star Team (1991, 1992)

Signed as a free agent by **Grand Rapids** (IHL), September 9, 1996. Signed as a free agent by **Nashville**, August 19, 1998. Traded to **Washington** by **Nashville** for cash, June 21, 1999. Signed as a free agent by **Schwenningen** (Germany), July 17, 2001. Signed as a free agent by **San Jose**, September 5, 2002. Signed as a free agent by **Muskegon** (UHL), August 21, 2003. Signed as a free agent by **Grand Rapids** (AHL), October 28, 2003.

NEMECEK, Jan

(NEHM-eh-chehk, YAHN) **L.A.**

Defense. Shoots Left. 6'1", 220 lbs. Born, Pisek, Czech., February 14, 1976. Los Angeles' 7th choice, 215th overall, in 1994 Entry Draft.

Season	Club	League	GP	G	A	Pts	PIM	PP	SH	GW	S	%	+/-	TF	F%	Min	GP	G	A	Pts	PIM	PP	SH	GW	Min
1992-93	Ceske Budejovice	Czech	15	0	0	0		....	....	....	....	....	....	....	....	....	....	....	....	....	....	....	....	....	....
1993-94	Ceske Budejovice	Czech	16	0	1	1	16	....	....	....	....	....	....	....	....	....	....	....	....	....	....	....	....	....	....
1994-95	Hull Olympiques	QMJHL	49	10	16	26	48	....	....	....	....	....	....	....	....	....	21	5	9	14	10	....	....	....	....
1995-96	Hull Olympiques	QMJHL	57	17	49	66	58	....	....	....	....	....	....	....	....	....	17	2	13	15	10	....	....	....	....
1996-97	Mississippi	ECHL	20	3	9	12	16	....	....	....	....	....	....	....	....	....	3	0	0	0	4	....	....	....	....
	Phoenix	IHL	24	1	1	2	2	....	....	....	....	....	....	....	....	....	....	....	....	....	....	....	....	....	....
1997-98	Fredericton	AHL	65	7	24	31	43	....	....	....	....	....	....	....	....	....	2	0	0	0	0	....	....	....	....
1998-99	**Los Angeles**	**NHL**	**6**	**1**	**0**	**1**	**4**	**0**	**0**	**1**	**8**	**12.5**	**−1**	**0**	**0.0**	**16:42**	....	....	....	....	....	....	....	....	....
	Long Beach	IHL	66	5	16	21	42	....	....	....	....	....	....	....	....	....	....	....	....	....	....	....	....	....	....
99-2000	**Los Angeles**	**NHL**	**1**	**0**	**0**	**0**	**0**	**0**	**0**	**0**	**0**	**0.0**	**0**	**0**	**0.0**	**9:36**	....	....	....	....	....	....	....	....	....
	Long Beach	IHL	71	9	15	24	22	....	....	....	....	....	....	....	....	....	6	1	0	1	4	....	....	....	....
2000-01	Nurnberg	Germany	60	5	16	21	18	....	....	....	....	....	....	....	....	....	4	1	0	1	0	....	....	....	....
2001-02	Nurnberg	Germany	60	6	18	24	18	....	....	....	....	....	....	....	....	....	4	0	3	3	2	....	....	....	....
2002-03	Karlovy Vary	Czech	30	1	9	10	16	....	....	....	....	....	....	....	....	....	....	....	....	....	....	....	....	....	....
	KLH Chumotov	Czech-2	2	0	0	0	0	....	....	....	....	....	....	....	....	....	....	....	....	....	....	....	....	....	....
2003-04	Timra IK	Sweden	50	4	8	12	18	....	....	....	....	....	....	....	....	....	9	0	1	1	2	....	....	....	....
	NHL Totals		**7**	**1**	**0**	**1**	**4**	**0**	**0**	**1**	**8**	**12.5**		**0**	**0.0**	**15:41**	....	....	....	....	....	....	....	....	....

QMJHL Second All-Star Team (1996)

NICHOL, Scott

(NIH-KOHL, SKAWT) **CHI.**

Center. Shoots right. 5'8", 173 lbs. Born, Edmonton, Alta., December 31, 1974. Buffalo's 9th choice, 272nd overall, in 1993 Entry Draft.

Season	Club	League	GP	G	A	Pts	PIM	PP	SH	GW	S	%	+/-	TF	F%	Min	GP	G	A	Pts	PIM	PP	SH	GW	Min
1991-92	Calgary Flames	AMHL	23	26	16	42	132	....	....	....	....	....	....	....	....	....	....	....	....	....	....	....	....	....	....
1992-93	Portland	WHL	67	31	33	64	146	....	....	....	....	....	....	....	....	....	16	8	8	16	41	....	....	....	....
1993-94	Portland	WHL	65	40	53	93	144	....	....	....	....	....	....	....	....	....	10	3	8	11	16	....	....	....	....
1994-95	Rochester	AHL	71	11	16	27	136	....	....	....	....	....	....	....	....	....	5	0	3	3	14	....	....	....	....
1995-96	**Buffalo**	**NHL**	**2**	**0**	**0**	**0**	**10**	**0**	**0**	**0**	**4**	**0.0**	**0**	....	....	....	....	....	....	....	....	....	....	....	....
	Rochester	AHL	62	14	18	32	170	....	....	....	....	....	....	....	....	....	19	7	6	13	36	....	....	....	....
1996-97	Rochester	AHL	68	22	21	43	133	....	....	....	....	....	....	....	....	....	10	2	1	3	26	....	....	....	....
1997-98	**Buffalo**	**NHL**	**3**	**0**	**0**	**0**	**4**	**0**	**0**	**0**	**5**	**0.0**	**0**	....	....	....	....	....	....	....	....	....	....	....	....
	Rochester	AHL	35	13	7	20	113	....	....	....	....	....	....	....	....	....	....	....	....	....	....	....	....	....	....
1998-99	Rochester	AHL	52	13	20	33	120	....	....	....	....	....	....	....	....	....	....	....	....	....	....	....	....	....	....
99-2000	Rochester	AHL	37	7	11	18	141	....	....	....	....	....	....	....	....	....	....	....	....	....	....	....	....	....	....
2000-01	Detroit Vipers	IHL	67	7	24	31	198	....	....	....	....	....	....	....	....	....	....	....	....	....	....	....	....	....	....
2001-02	**Calgary**	**NHL**	**60**	**8**	**9**	**17**	**107**	**2**	**1**	**0**	**49**	**16.3**	**−9**	**458**	**53.1**	**12:41**	....	....	....	....	....	....	....	....	....
2002-03	**Calgary**	**NHL**	**68**	**5**	**5**	**10**	**149**	**0**	**1**	**0**	**66**	**7.6**	**−7**	**357**	**58.3**	**10:47**	....	....	....	....	....	....	....	....	....
2003-04	**Chicago**	**NHL**	**75**	**7**	**11**	**18**	**145**	**0**	**0**	**1**	**112**	**6.3**	**−16**	**1178**	**57.4**	**15:46**	....	....	....	....	....	....	....	....	....
	NHL Totals		**208**	**20**	**25**	**45**	**415**	**2**	**2**	**1**	**236**	**8.5**		**1993**	**56.5**	**13:11**	....	....	....	....	....	....	....	....	....

• Missed majority of 1999-2000 season recovering from knee injury suffered in game vs. Saint John (AHL), February 16, 2000. Signed as a free agent by **Calgary**, July 1, 2001. Signed as a free agent by **Chicago**, July 1, 2003.

NICKULAS, Eric

(NICK-luhs, AIR-ihk) **CHI.**

Right wing. Shoots right. 5'11", 206 lbs. Born, Hyannis, MA, March 25, 1975. Boston's 3rd choice, 99th overall, in 1994 Entry Draft.

Season	Club	League	GP	G	A	Pts	PIM	PP	SH	GW	S	%	+/-	TF	F%	Min	GP	G	A	Pts	PIM	PP	SH	GW	Min
1991-92	Barnstable	Hi-School	24	30	25	55	....	....	....	....	....	....	....	....	....	....	....	....	....	....	....	....	....	....	....
1992-93	Tabor Academy	Hi-School	28	25	25	50	....	....	....	....	....	....	....	....	....	....	....	....	....	....	....	....	....	....	....
1993-94	Cushing Academy	Hi-School	25	46	36	82	....	....	....	....	....	....	....	....	....	....	....	....	....	....	....	....	....	....	....
1994-95	New Hampshire	H-East	33	15	9	24	32	....	....	....	....	....	....	....	....	....	....	....	....	....	....	....	....	....	....
1995-96	New Hampshire	H-East	34	26	12	38	66	....	....	....	....	....	....	....	....	....	....	....	....	....	....	....	....	....	....
1996-97	New Hampshire	H-East	39	29	22	51	80	....	....	....	....	....	....	....	....	....	....	....	....	....	....	....	....	....	....
1997-98	Orlando	IHL	76	22	9	31	77	....	....	....	....	....	....	....	....	....	6	0	0	0	10	....	....	....	....
1998-99	**Boston**	**NHL**	**2**	**0**	**0**	**0**	**0**	**0**	**0**	**0**	**0**	**0.0**	**0**	**0**	**0.0**	**3:27**	**1**	**0**	**0**	**0**	**2**	**0**	**0**	**0**	**4:35**
	Providence Bruins	AHL	75	31	27	58	83	....	....	....	....	....	....	....	....	....	18	8	12	20	33	....	....	....	....
99-2000	**Boston**	**NHL**	**20**	**5**	**6**	**11**	**12**	**1**	**0**	**0**	**28**	**17.9**	**−1**	**4**	**50.0**	**11:13**	....	....	....	....	....	....	....	....	....
	Providence Bruins	AHL	40	6	6	12	37	....	....	....	....	....	....	....	....	....	12	2	3	5	20	....	....	....	....
2000-01	**Boston**	**NHL**	**7**	**0**	**0**	**0**	**4**	**0**	**0**	**0**	**6**	**0.0**	**−2**	**1**	**100.0**	**7:07**	....	....	....	....	....	....	....	....	....
	Providence Bruins	AHL	62	20	23	43	100	....	....	....	....	....	....	....	....	....	12	4	4	8	24	....	....	....	....
2001-02	Worcester IceCats	AHL	54	11	25	36	48	....	....	....	....	....	....	....	....	....	3	0	1	1	2	....	....	....	....
2002-03	**St. Louis**	**NHL**	**8**	**0**	**1**	**1**	**6**	**0**	**0**	**0**	**3**	**0.0**	**−2**	**0**	**0.0**	**9:31**	....	....	....	....	....	....	....	....	....
	Worcester IceCats	AHL	39	17	16	33	40	....	....	....	....	....	....	....	....	....	3	0	0	0	2	....	....	....	....

			Regular Season														Playoffs								
Season	**Club**	**League**	**GP**	**G**	**A**	**Pts**	**PIM**	**PP**	**SH**	**GW**	**S**	**%**	**+/-**	**TF**	**F%**	**Min**	**GP**	**G**	**A**	**Pts**	**PIM**	**PP**	**SH**	**GW**	**Min**
2003-04	**St. Louis**	**NHL**	**44**	**7**	**11**	**18**	**44**	**1**	**0**	**1**	**80**	**8.8**	**–2**	**10**	**30.0**	**12:50**	....	....	....	....	....	....	....	....	....
	Chicago	**NHL**	**21**	**1**	**1**	**2**	**8**	**0**	**0**	**0**	**41**	**2.4**	**–6**	**11**	**45.5**	**13:46**	....	....	....	....	....	....	....	....	....
	NHL Totals		**102**	**13**	**19**	**32**	**74**	**2**	**0**	**1**	**158**	**8.2**		**26**	**42.3**	**11:52**	**1**	**0**	**0**	**0**	**2**	**0**	**0**	**0**	**4:35**

Ken McKenzie Trophy (U.S. Born Rookie of the Year – IHL) (1998)

Signed as a free agent by **Worcester** (AHL), November 10, 2001. Signed as a free agent by **St. Louis**, July 16, 2002. Claimed on waivers by **Chicago** from **St. Louis**, February 24, 2004.

NIEDERMAYER, Rob

(NEE-duhr-MIGH-uhr, RAWB) **ANA.**

Center. Shoots left. 6'2", 204 lbs. Born, Cassiar, B.C., December 28, 1974. Florida's 1st choice, 5th overall, in 1993 Entry Draft.

Season	Club	League	GP	G	A	Pts	PIM	PP	SH	GW	S	%	+/-	TF	F%	Min	GP	G	A	Pts	PIM	PP	SH	GW	Min
1989-90	Cranbrook Blazers	BCAHA	35	42	40	82	30	....	....	....	....	....	....	....	....	....	....	....	....	....	....	....	....	....	....
1990-91	Medicine Hat	WHL	71	24	26	50	8	....	....	....	....	....	....	....	....	....	12	3	7	10	2	....	....	....	....
1991-92	Medicine Hat	WHL	71	32	46	78	77	....	....	....	....	....	....	....	....	....	4	2	3	5	2	....	....	....	....
1992-93	Medicine Hat	WHL	52	43	34	77	67	....	....	....	....	....	....	....	....	....	....	....	....	....	....	....	....	....	....
1993-94	**Florida**	**NHL**	**65**	**9**	**17**	**26**	**51**	**3**	**0**	**2**	**67**	**13.4**	**–11**	....	....	....	....	....	....	....	....	....	....	....	....
1994-95	Medicine Hat	WHL	13	9	15	24	14	....	....	....	....	....	....	....	....	....	....	....	....	....	....	....	....	....	....
	Florida	**NHL**	**48**	**4**	**6**	**10**	**36**	**1**	**0**	**0**	**58**	**6.9**	**–13**	....	....	....	....	....	....	....	....	....	....	....	....
1995-96	**Florida**	**NHL**	**82**	**26**	**35**	**61**	**107**	**11**	**0**	**6**	**155**	**16.8**	**1**	....	....	....	**22**	**5**	**3**	**8**	**12**	**2**	**0**	**2**	....
1996-97	**Florida**	**NHL**	**60**	**14**	**24**	**38**	**54**	**3**	**0**	**2**	**136**	**10.3**	**4**	....	....	....	**5**	**2**	**1**	**3**	**6**	**1**	**0**	**0**	....
1997-98	**Florida**	**NHL**	**33**	**8**	**7**	**15**	**41**	**5**	**0**	**2**	**64**	**12.5**	**–9**	....	....	....	....	....	....	....	....	....	....	....	....
1998-99	**Florida**	**NHL**	**82**	**18**	**33**	**51**	**50**	**6**	**1**	**3**	**142**	**12.7**	**–13**	**1895**	**47.1**	**21:17**	....	....	....	....	....	....	....	....	....
99-2000	**Florida**	**NHL**	**81**	**10**	**23**	**33**	**46**	**1**	**0**	**4**	**135**	**7.4**	**–5**	**1632**	**47.9**	**19:04**	**4**	**1**	**0**	**1**	**6**	**0**	**0**	**0**	**15:55**
2000-01	**Florida**	**NHL**	**67**	**12**	**20**	**32**	**50**	**3**	**1**	**0**	**115**	**10.4**	**–12**	**997**	**45.0**	**20:30**	....	....	....	....	....	....	....	....	....
2001-02	**Calgary**	**NHL**	**57**	**6**	**14**	**20**	**49**	**1**	**2**	**1**	**87**	**6.9**	**–15**	**777**	**48.4**	**18:01**	....	....	....	....	....	....	....	....	....
2002-03	**Calgary**	**NHL**	**54**	**8**	**10**	**18**	**42**	**2**	**0**	**1**	**104**	**7.7**	**–13**	**139**	**48.9**	**17:29**	....	....	....	....	....	....	....	....	....
	Anaheim	**NHL**	**12**	**2**	**2**	**4**	**15**	**1**	**0**	**0**	**21**	**9.5**	**3**	**14**	**42.9**	**15:21**	**21**	**3**	**7**	**10**	**18**	**0**	**2**	**0**	**23:35**
2003-04	**Anaheim**	**NHL**	**55**	**12**	**16**	**28**	**34**	**6**	**0**	**2**	**111**	**10.8**	**–6**	**45**	**64.4**	**19:28**	....	....	....	....	....	....	....	....	....
	NHL Totals		**696**	**129**	**207**	**336**	**575**	**43**	**4**	**23**	**1195**	**10.8**		**5499**	**47.3**	**19:20**	**52**	**11**	**11**	**22**	**42**	**3**	**2**	**2**	**22:21**

WHL East First All-Star Team (1993)

• Missed majority of 1997-98 season recovering from thumb (November 26, 1997 vs. Boston) and head (March 19, 1998 vs. Buffalo) injuries. Traded to **Calgary** by **Florida** with Philadelphia's 2nd round choice (previously acquired, Calgary selected Andrei Medvedev) in 2001 Entry Draft for Valeri Bure and Jason Wiemer, June 23, 2001. Traded to **Anaheim** by **Calgary** for Mike Commodore and Jean-Francois Damphousse, March 11, 2003.

NIEDERMAYER, Scott

(NEE-duhr-MIGH-uhr, SKAWT) **N.J.**

Defense. Shoots left. 6'1", 200 lbs. Born, Edmonton, Alta., August 31, 1973. New Jersey's 1st choice, 3rd overall, in 1991 Entry Draft.

Season	Club	League	GP	G	A	Pts	PIM	PP	SH	GW	S	%	+/-	TF	F%	Min	GP	G	A	Pts	PIM	PP	SH	GW	Min
1988-89	Cranbrook Blazers	BCAHA	62	55	37	92	100	....	....	....	....	....	....	....	....	....	....	....	....	....	....	....	....	....	....
1989-90	Kamloops Blazers	WHL	64	14	55	69	64	....	....	....	....	....	....	....	....	....	17	2	14	16	35	....	....	....	....
1990-91	Kamloops Blazers	WHL	57	26	56	82	52	....	....	....	....	....	....	....	....	....	....	....	....	....	....	....	....	....	....
1991-92	Kamloops Blazers	WHL	35	7	32	39	61	....	....	....	....	....	....	....	....	....	17	9	14	23	28	....	....	....	....
	New Jersey	**NHL**	**4**	**0**	**1**	**1**	**2**	**0**	**0**	**0**	**4**	**0.0**	**1**	....	....	....	....	....	....	....	....	....	....	....	....
1992-93	**New Jersey**	**NHL**	**80**	**11**	**29**	**40**	**47**	**5**	**0**	**0**	**131**	**8.4**	**8**	....	....	....	**5**	**0**	**3**	**3**	**2**	**0**	**0**	**0**	....
1993-94	**New Jersey**	**NHL**	**81**	**10**	**36**	**46**	**42**	**5**	**0**	**2**	**135**	**7.4**	**34**	....	....	....	**20**	**2**	**2**	**4**	**8**	**1**	**0**	**0**	....
1994-95♦	**New Jersey**	**NHL**	**48**	**4**	**15**	**19**	**18**	**4**	**0**	**0**	**52**	**7.7**	**19**	....	....	....	**20**	**4**	**7**	**11**	**10**	**2**	**0**	**1**	....
1995-96	**New Jersey**	**NHL**	**79**	**8**	**25**	**33**	**46**	**6**	**0**	**0**	**179**	**4.5**	**5**	....	....	....	....	....	....	....	....	....	....	....	....
1996-97	**New Jersey**	**NHL**	**81**	**5**	**30**	**35**	**64**	**3**	**0**	**3**	**159**	**3.1**	**–4**	....	....	....	**10**	**2**	**4**	**6**	**6**	**2**	**0**	**1**	....
1997-98	**New Jersey**	**NHL**	**81**	**14**	**43**	**57**	**27**	**11**	**0**	**1**	**175**	**8.0**	**5**	....	....	....	**6**	**0**	**2**	**2**	**4**	**0**	**0**	**0**	....
1998-99	Utah Grizzlies	IHL	5	0	2	2	0	....	....	....	....	....	....	....	....	....	....	....	....	....	....	....	....	....	....
	New Jersey	**NHL**	**72**	**11**	**35**	**46**	**26**	**1**	**1**	**3**	**161**	**6.8**	**16**	**13**	**15.4**	**24:40**	**7**	**1**	**3**	**4**	**18**	**1**	**0**	**0**	**25:30**
99-2000♦	**New Jersey**	**NHL**	**71**	**7**	**31**	**38**	**48**	**1**	**0**	**0**	**109**	**6.4**	**19**	**8**	**37.5**	**24:21**	**22**	**5**	**2**	**7**	**10**	**0**	**2**	**1**	**25:28**
2000-01	**New Jersey**	**NHL**	**57**	**6**	**29**	**35**	**22**	**1**	**0**	**5**	**87**	**6.9**	**14**	**5**	**0.0**	**23:19**	**21**	**0**	**6**	**6**	**14**	**0**	**0**	**0**	**23:53**
2001-02	**New Jersey**	**NHL**	**76**	**11**	**22**	**33**	**30**	**2**	**0**	**6**	**129**	**8.5**	**12**	**1**	**100.0**	**24:17**	**6**	**0**	**2**	**2**	**6**	**0**	**0**	**0**	**26:37**
	Canada	Olympics	6	1	1	2	4	....	....	....	....	....	....	....	....	....	....	....	....	....	....	....	....	....	....
2002-03♦	**New Jersey**	**NHL**	**81**	**11**	**28**	**39**	**62**	**3**	**0**	**3**	**164**	**6.7**	**23**	**1**	**0.0**	**24:30**	**24**	**2**	***16**	***18**	**16**	**1**	**0**	**0**	**26:07**
2003-04	**New Jersey**	**NHL**	**81**	**14**	**40**	**54**	**44**	**9**	**0**	**3**	**165**	**8.5**	**20**	**1**	**0.0**	**25:56**	**5**	**1**	**0**	**1**	**6**	**0**	**0**	**0**	**27:21**
	NHL Totals		**892**	**112**	**364**	**476**	**478**	**51**	**1**	**26**	**1650**	**6.8**		**29**	**20.7**	**24:35**	**146**	**17**	**47**	**64**	**100**	**7**	**2**	**3**	**25:27**

WHL West First All-Star Team (1991, 1992) • Canadian Major Junior Scholastic Player of the Year (1991) • Memorial Cup All-Star Team (1992) • Stafford Smythe Memorial Trophy (Memorial Cup MVP) (1992) • NHL All-Rookie Team (1993) • NHL Second All-Star Team (1998) • NHL First All-Star Team (2004) • James Norris Trophy (2004)

Played in NHL All-Star Game (1998, 2001, 2004)

Signed to tryout (PTO) contract by **Utah** (IHL) with **New Jersey** retaining NHL rights, October 19, 1998.

NIELSEN, Chris

(NEEL-sehn, KRIHS)

Right wing. Shoots right. 6'2", 204 lbs. Born, Moshi, Tanzania, February 16, 1980. NY Islanders' 2nd choice, 36th overall, in 1998 Entry Draft.

Season	Club	League	GP	G	A	Pts	PIM	PP	SH	GW	S	%	+/-	TF	F%	Min	GP	G	A	Pts	PIM	PP	SH	GW	Min
1995-96	S-W Cougars	MMHL	39	37	35	72	59	....	....	....	....	....	....	....	....	....	....	....	....	....	....	....	....	....	....
	Calgary Hitmen	WHL	6	0	0	0	0	....	....	....	....	....	....	....	....	....	....	....	....	....	....	....	....	....	....
1996-97	Calgary Hitmen	WHL	62	11	19	30	39	....	....	....	....	....	....	....	....	....	....	....	....	....	....	....	....	....	....
1997-98	Calgary Hitmen	WHL	68	22	29	51	31	....	....	....	....	....	....	....	....	....	18	2	4	6	10	....	....	....	....
1998-99	Calgary Hitmen	WHL	70	22	24	46	45	....	....	....	....	....	....	....	....	....	21	11	5	16	28	....	....	....	....
99-2000	Calgary Hitmen	WHL	62	38	31	69	86	....	....	....	....	....	....	....	....	....	13	14	9	23	20	....	....	....	....
2000-01	**Columbus**	**NHL**	**29**	**4**	**5**	**9**	**4**	**0**	**0**	**1**	**36**	**11.1**	**4**	**18**	**55.6**	**10:30**	....	....	....	....	....	....	....	....	....
	Syracuse Crunch	AHL	47	10	11	21	24	....	....	....	....	....	....	....	....	....	5	2	2	4	4	....	....	....	....
2001-02	**Columbus**	**NHL**	**23**	**2**	**3**	**5**	**4**	**0**	**0**	**1**	**28**	**7.1**	**–3**	**6**	**33.3**	**10:47**	....	....	....	....	....	....	....	....	....
	Syracuse Crunch	AHL	47	12	12	24	18	....	....	....	....	....	....	....	....	....	10	2	2	4	2	....	....	....	....
2002-03	Syracuse Crunch	AHL	19	1	3	4	8	....	....	....	....	....	....	....	....	....	....	....	....	....	....	....	....	....	....
	Chicago Wolves	AHL	18	3	4	7	4	....	....	....	....	....	....	....	....	....	....	....	....	....	....	....	....	....	....
	Manitoba Moose	AHL	33	3	10	13	13	....	....	....	....	....	....	....	....	....	14	1	2	3	16	....	....	....	....
2003-04	Manitoba Moose	AHL	72	4	7	11	21	....	....	....	....	....	....	....	....	....	....	....	....	....	....	....	....	....	....
	NHL Totals		**52**	**6**	**8**	**14**	**8**	**0**	**0**	**2**	**64**	**9.4**		**24**	**50.0**	**10:38**									

Traded to **Columbus** by **NY Islanders** for Columbus' 4th (later traded to Anaheim – Anaheim selected Jonas Ronnqvist) and 9th (Dmitri Altarev) round choices in 2000 Entry Draft, May 11, 2000. Traded to **Atlanta** by **Columbus** with Petteri Nummelin for Tomi Kallio and Pauli Levokari, December 2, 2002. Traded to **Vancouver** by **Atlanta** with Chris Herperger for Jeff Farkas, January 20, 2003.

NIEMINEN, Ville

(nee-EHM-ih-nehn, VIHL-ee) **CGY.**

Left wing. Shoots left. 6', 200 lbs. Born, Tampere, Finland, April 6, 1977. Colorado's 4th choice, 78th overall, in 1997 Entry Draft.

Season	Club	League	GP	G	A	Pts	PIM	PP	SH	GW	S	%	+/-	TF	F%	Min	GP	G	A	Pts	PIM	PP	SH	GW	Min
1994-95	Tappara Jr.	Finn-Jr.	16	11	21	32	47	....	....	....	....	....	....	....	....	....	....	....	....	....	....	....	....	....	....
	Tappara Tampere	Finland	16	0	0	0	0	....	....	....	....	....	....	....	....	....	....	....	....	....	....	....	....	....	....
1995-96	Tappara Jr.	Finn-Jr.	20	20	23	43	63	....	....	....	....	....	....	....	....	....	....	....	....	....	....	....	....	....	....
	KooKoo Kouvola	Finland-2	7	2	1	3	4	....	....	....	....	....	....	....	....	....	....	....	....	....	....	....	....	....	....
	Tappara Tampere	Finland	4	0	1	1	8	....	....	....	....	....	....	....	....	....	....	....	....	....	....	....	....	....	....
1996-97	Tappara Tampere	Finland	49	10	13	23	120	....	....	....	....	....	....	....	....	....	3	1	0	1	8	....	....	....	....
1997-98	Hershey Bears	AHL	74	14	22	36	85	....	....	....	....	....	....	....	....	....	....	....	....	....	....	....	....	....	....
1998-99	Hershey Bears	AHL	67	24	19	43	127	....	....	....	....	....	....	....	....	....	3	0	1	1	0	....	....	....	....
99-2000	**Colorado**	**NHL**	**1**	**0**	**0**	**0**	**0**	**0**	**0**	**0**	**2**	**0.0**	**0**	**0**	**0.0**	**10:12**	....	....	....	....	....	....	....	....	....
	Hershey Bears	AHL	74	21	30	51	54	....	....	....	....	....	....	....	....	....	9	2	4	6	6	....	....	....	....
2000-01♦	**Colorado**	**NHL**	**50**	**14**	**8**	**22**	**38**	**2**	**0**	**3**	**68**	**20.6**	**8**	**3**	**33.3**	**12:26**	**23**	**4**	**6**	**10**	**20**	**3**	**0**	**1**	**14:10**
	Hershey Bears	AHL	28	10	11	21	48	....	....	....	....	....	....	....	....	....	....	....	....	....	....	....	....	....	....
2001-02	**Colorado**	**NHL**	**53**	**10**	**14**	**24**	**30**	**1**	**0**	**5**	**72**	**13.9**	**1**	**8**	**62.5**	**12:41**	....	....	....	....	....	....	....	....	....
	Finland	Olympics	4	0	1	1	2	....	....	....	....	....	....	....	....	....	....	....	....	....	....	....	....	....	....
	Pittsburgh	**NHL**	**13**	**1**	**2**	**3**	**8**	**0**	**0**	**0**	**11**	**9.1**	**–2**	**0**	**0.0**	**16:10**	....	....	....	....	....	....	....	....	....
2002-03	**Pittsburgh**	**NHL**	**75**	**9**	**12**	**21**	**93**	**0**	**2**	**1**	**86**	**10.5**	**–25**	**46**	**52.2**	**14:08**	....	....	....	....	....	....	....	....	....
2003-04	**Chicago**	**NHL**	**60**	**2**	**11**	**13**	**40**	**1**	**0**	**0**	**56**	**3.6**	**–15**	**4**	**25.0**	**11:46**	....	....	....	....	....	....	....	....	....
	Calgary	**NHL**	**19**	**3**	**5**	**8**	**18**	**0**	**0**	**1**	**27**	**11.1**	**6**	**5**	**0.0**	**14:36**	**24**	**4**	**4**	**8**	**55**	**1**	**0**	**0**	**16:17**
	NHL Totals		**271**	**39**	**52**	**91**	**227**	**4**	**2**	**10**	**322**	**12.1**		**66**	**47.0**	**13:08**	**47**	**8**	**10**	**18**	**75**	**4**	**0**	**1**	**15:15**

Traded to **Pittsburgh** by **Colorado** with Rick Berry for Darius Kasparaitis, March 19, 2002. Signed as a free agent by **Chicago**, July 29, 2003. Traded to **Calgary** by **Chicago** for Jason Morgan and future considerations, February 24, 2004.

NIEUWENDYK, Joe
(NOO-ihn-DIGHK, JOH) **TOR.**

Center. Shoots left. 6'2", 205 lbs. Born, Oshawa, Ont., September 10, 1966. Calgary's 2nd choice, 27th overall, in 1985 Entry Draft.

			Regular Season														Playoffs								
Season	Club	League	GP	G	A	Pts	PIM	PP	SH	GW	S	%	+/-	TF	F%	Min	GP	G	A	Pts	PIM	PP	SH	GW	Min
1983-84	Pickering Panthers	MTJHL	38	30	28	58	35	....	....	....	....	....	....	....	....	....	....	....	....	....	....	....	....	....	....
1984-85	Cornell Big Red	ECAC	29	21	24	45	30	....	....	....	....	....	....	....	....	....	....	....	....	....	....	....	....	....	....
1985-86	Cornell Big Red	ECAC	29	26	28	54	67	....	....	....	....	....	....	....	....	....	....	....	....	....	....	....	....	....	....
1986-87	Cornell Big Red	ECAC	23	26	26	52	26	....	....	....	....	....	....	....	....	....	....	....	....	....	....	....	....	....	....
	Calgary	NHL	9	5	1	6	0	2	0	1	16	31.3	0	....	....	....	6	2	2	4	0	0	0	0	....
1987-88	Calgary	NHL	75	51	41	92	23	31	3	8	212	24.1	20	....	....	....	8	3	4	7	2	1	0	0	....
1988-89♦	Calgary	NHL	77	51	31	82	40	19	3	11	215	23.7	26	....	....	....	22	10	4	14	10	6	0	1	....
1989-90	Calgary	NHL	79	45	50	95	40	18	0	3	226	19.9	32	....	....	....	6	4	6	10	4	1	0	0	....
1990-91	Calgary	NHL	79	45	40	85	36	22	4	1	222	20.3	19	....	....	....	7	4	1	5	10	2	0	0	....
1991-92	Calgary	NHL	69	22	34	56	55	7	0	2	137	16.1	–1	....	....	....	....	....	....	....	....	....	....	....	....
1992-93	Calgary	NHL	79	38	37	75	52	14	0	6	208	18.3	9	....	....	....	6	3	6	9	10	1	0	0	....
1993-94	Calgary	NHL	64	36	39	75	51	14	1	7	191	18.8	19	....	....	....	6	2	2	4	0	1	0	0	....
1994-95	Calgary	NHL	46	21	29	50	33	3	0	4	122	17.2	11	....	....	....	5	4	3	7	0	2	0	1	....
1995-96	Dallas	NHL	52	14	18	32	41	8	0	3	138	10.1	–17	....	....	....	....	....	....	....	....	....	....	....	....
1996-97	Dallas	NHL	66	30	21	51	32	8	0	2	173	17.3	–5	....	....	....	7	2	2	4	6	0	0	0	....
1997-98	Dallas	NHL	73	39	30	69	30	14	0	11	203	19.2	16	....	....	....	1	1	0	1	0	0	0	0	....
	Canada	Olympics	6	2	3	5	2	....	....	....	....	....	....	....	....	....	....	....	....	....	....	....	....	....	....
1998-99♦	Dallas	NHL	67	28	27	55	34	8	0	8	157	17.8	11	1170	63.2	15:33	23	*11	10	21	19	3	0	6	18:27
99-2000	Dallas	NHL	48	15	19	34	26	7	0	2	110	13.6	–1	924	59.1	16:15	23	7	3	10	18	3	0	2	16:41
2000-01	Dallas	NHL	69	29	23	52	30	12	0	4	166	17.5	5	1262	57.2	16:11	7	4	0	4	4	1	0	1	15:50
2001-02	Dallas	NHL	67	23	24	47	18	6	0	5	157	14.6	–2	1345	59.6	16:59	....	....	....	....	....	....	....	....	....
	Canada	Olympics	6	1	1	2	0	....	....	....	....	....	....	....	....	....	....	....	....	....	....	....	....	....	....
	New Jersey	NHL	14	2	9	11	4	0	0	1	32	6.3	2	275	55.3	16:22	5	0	1	1	0	0	0	0	19:22
2002-03♦	New Jersey	NHL	80	17	28	45	56	3	0	4	201	8.5	10	1383	58.5	16:45	17	3	6	9	4	1	0	0	15:03
2003-04	Toronto	NHL	64	22	28	50	26	10	1	5	131	16.8	7	970	60.4	15:38	9	6	0	6	4	1	0	2	15:24
	NHL Totals		1177	533	529	1062	627	206	12	88	3017	17.7		7329	59.4	16:15	158	66	50	116	91	23	0	13	16:47

ECAC Rookie of the Year (1985) • ECAC First All-Star Team (1986, 1987) • NCAA East First All-American Team (1986, 1987) • ECAC Player of the Year (1987) • Calder Memorial Trophy (1988) • NHL All-Rookie Team (1988) • Dodge Ram Tough Award (1988) • King Clancy Memorial Trophy (1995) • Conn Smythe Trophy (1999)

Played in NHL All-Star Game (1988, 1989, 1990, 1994)

Traded to **Dallas** by **Calgary** for Corey Millen and Jarome Iginla, December 19, 1995. Traded to **New Jersey** by **Dallas** with Jamie Langenbrunner for Jason Arnott, Randy McKay and New Jersey's 1st round choice (later traded to Columbus – later traded to Buffalo – Buffalo selected Dan Paille) in 2002 Entry Draft, March 19, 2002. Signed as a free agent by **Toronto**, September 9, 2003.

NIINIMAA, Janne
(nihn-EE-mah, YAH-nee) **NYI**

Defense. Shoots left. 6'1", 220 lbs. Born, Raahe, Finland, May 22, 1975. Philadelphia's 1st choice, 36th overall, in 1993 Entry Draft.

			Regular Season														Playoffs								
Season	Club	League	GP	G	A	Pts	PIM	PP	SH	GW	S	%	+/-	TF	F%	Min	GP	G	A	Pts	PIM	PP	SH	GW	Min
1990-91	Karpat Oulu Jr.	Finn-Jr.	3	1	0	1	2	....	....	....	....	....	....	....	....	....	....	....	....	....	....	....	....	....	....
1991-92	Karpat Oulu Jr.	Finn-Jr.	3	0	0	0	4	....	....	....	....	....	....	....	....	....	....	....	....	....	....	....	....	....	....
	Karpat Oulu	Finland-2	41	2	11	13	49	....	....	....	....	....	....	....	....	....	....	....	....	....	....	....	....	....	....
1992-93	Karpat Oulu Jr.	Finn-Jr.	10	3	9	12	16	....	....	....	....	....	....	....	....	....	....	....	....	....	....	....	....	....	....
	KKP Kiimimki	Finland-3	1	0	2	2	4	....	....	....	....	....	....	....	....	....	....	....	....	....	....	....	....	....	....
	Karpat Oulu	Finland-2	29	2	3	5	14	....	....	....	....	....	....	....	....	....	....	....	....	....	....	....	....	....	....
1993-94	Jokerit Helsinki Jr.	Finn-Jr.	10	2	6	8	41	....	....	....	....	....	....	....	....	....	....	....	....	....	....	....	....	....	....
	Jokerit Helsinki	Finland	45	3	8	11	24	....	....	....	....	....	....	....	....	....	12	1	1	2	4	....	....	....	....
1994-95	Jokerit Helsinki Jr.	Finn-Jr.	3	1	2	3	4	....	....	....	....	....	....	....	....	....	....	....	....	....	....	....	....	....	....
	Jokerit Helsinki	Finland	42	7	10	17	36	....	....	....	....	....	....	....	....	....	10	1	4	5	35	....	....	....	....
1995-96	Jokerit Helsinki	Finland	49	5	15	20	79	....	....	....	....	....	....	....	....	....	11	0	2	2	12	....	....	....	....
	Jokerit Helsinki Jr.	Finn-Jr.	....	....	....	....	....	....	....	....	....	....	....	....	....	....	2	3	4	7	6	....	....	....	....
1996-97	Philadelphia	NHL	77	4	40	44	58	1	0	2	141	2.8	12	....	....	....	19	1	12	13	16	1	0	1	....
1997-98	Philadelphia	NHL	66	3	31	34	56	2	0	1	115	2.6	6	....	....	....	....	....	....	....	....	....	....	....	....
	Edmonton	NHL	11	1	8	9	6	1	0	0	19	5.3	7	....	....	....	11	1	1	2	12	0	0	1	....
	Finland	Olympics	6	0	3	3	8	....	....	....	....	....	....	....	....	....	....	....	....	....	....	....	....	....	....
1998-99	Edmonton	NHL	81	4	24	28	88	2	0	1	142	2.8	7	1	0.0	23:54	4	0	0	0	2	0	0	0	28:16
99-2000	Edmonton	NHL	81	8	25	33	89	2	2	0	133	6.0	14	0	0.0	24:28	5	0	2	2	2	0	0	0	21:39
2000-01	Edmonton	NHL	82	12	34	46	90	8	0	1	122	9.8	6	0	0.0	25:20	6	0	2	2	6	0	0	0	28:33
2001-02	Edmonton	NHL	81	5	39	44	80	1	0	2	119	4.2	13	0	0.0	26:02	....	....	....	....	....	....	....	....	....
	Finland	Olympics	4	0	3	3	2	....	....	....	....	....	....	....	....	....	....	....	....	....	....	....	....	....	....
2002-03	Edmonton	NHL	63	4	24	28	66	2	0	0	90	4.4	–7	1	0.0	26:48	....	....	....	....	....	....	....	....	....
	NY Islanders	NHL	13	1	5	6	14	1	0	0	11	9.1	–2	0	0.0	23:02	5	0	1	1	12	0	0	0	23:32
2003-04	NY Islanders	NHL	82	9	19	28	64	4	0	2	97	9.3	12	0	0.0	23:15	5	1	2	3	2	1	0	1	24:31
	NHL Totals		637	51	249	300	611	24	2	9	989	5.2		2	0.0	24:50	55	3	20	23	52	2	0	3	25:19

NHL All-Rookie Team (1997)

Played in NHL All-Star Game (2001)

Traded to **Edmonton** by **Philadelphia** for Dan McGillis and Edmonton's 2nd round choice (Jason Beckett) in 1998 Entry Draft, March 24, 1998. Traded to **NY Islanders** by **Edmonton** with Washington's 2nd round choice (previously acquired, NY Islanders selected Evgeni Tunik) in 2003 Entry Draft for Brad Isbister and Raffi Torres, March 11, 2003.

NIKOLISHIN, Andrei
(nee-koh-LEE-shin, AWN-dray)

Center. Shoots left. 6', 213 lbs. Born, Vorkuta, USSR, March 25, 1973. Hartford's 2nd choice, 47th overall, in 1992 Entry Draft.

			Regular Season														Playoffs								
Season	Club	League	GP	G	A	Pts	PIM	PP	SH	GW	S	%	+/-	TF	F%	Min	GP	G	A	Pts	PIM	PP	SH	GW	Min
1990-91	Dynamo Moscow	USSR	2	0	0	0	0	....	....	....	....	....	....	....	....	....	....	....	....	....	....	....	....	....	....
1991-92	Dynamo Moscow	CIS	18	1	0	1	4	....	....	....	....	....	....	....	....	....	....	....	....	....	....	....	....	....	....
1992-93	Dynamo Moscow	CIS	42	5	7	12	30	....	....	....	....	....	....	....	....	....	10	2	1	3	8	....	....	....	....
1993-94	Dynamo Moscow	CIS	41	8	12	20	30	....	....	....	....	....	....	....	....	....	9	1	3	4	4	....	....	....	....
	Russia	Olympics	8	2	5	7	6	....	....	....	....	....	....	....	....	....	....	....	....	....	....	....	....	....	....
1994-95	Dynamo Moscow	CIS	12	7	2	9	6	....	....	....	....	....	....	....	....	....	....	....	....	....	....	....	....	....	....
	Hartford	NHL	39	8	10	18	10	1	1	0	57	14.0	7	....	....	....	....	....	....	....	....	....	....	....	....
1995-96	Hartford	NHL	61	14	37	51	34	4	1	3	83	16.9	–2	....	....	....	....	....	....	....	....	....	....	....	....
1996-97	Hartford	NHL	12	2	5	7	2	0	0	0	25	8.0	–2	....	....	....	....	....	....	....	....	....	....	....	....
	Washington	NHL	59	7	14	21	30	1	0	0	73	9.6	5	....	....	....	....	....	....	....	....	....	....	....	....
1997-98	Washington	NHL	38	6	10	16	14	1	0	1	40	15.0	1	....	....	....	21	1	13	14	12	1	0	0	....
	Portland Pirates	AHL	2	0	0	0	2	....	....	....	....	....	....	....	....	....	....	....	....	....	....	....	....	....	....
1998-99	Dynamo Moscow	Russia	4	0	0	0	0	....	....	....	....	....	....	....	....	....	....	....	....	....	....	....	....	....	....
	Washington	NHL	73	8	27	35	28	0	1	1	121	6.6	0	1354	52.5	17:34	....	....	....	....	....	....	....	....	....
99-2000	Washington	NHL	76	11	14	25	28	0	2	2	98	11.2	6	1190	54.7	15:44	5	0	2	2	4	0	0	0	17:27
2000-01	Washington	NHL	81	13	25	38	34	4	0	2	145	9.0	9	1214	55.4	15:32	6	0	0	0	2	0	0	0	16:50
2001-02	Washington	NHL	80	13	23	36	40	1	0	0	143	9.1	–1	1445	55.7	17:23	....	....	....	....	....	....	....	....	....
	Russia	Olympics	6	0	1	1	6	....	....	....	....	....	....	....	....	....	....	....	....	....	....	....	....	....	....
2002-03	Chicago	NHL	60	6	15	21	26	0	1	0	73	8.2	–3	947	56.6	17:01	....	....	....	....	....	....	....	....	....
2003-04	Colorado	NHL	49	5	7	12	24	0	0	0	71	7.0	3	1021	58.1	16:17	11	0	2	2	4	0	0	0	15:41
	NHL Totals		628	93	187	280	270	13	6	9	929	10.0		7171	55.3	16:35	43	1	17	18	22	1	0	0	16:24

Traded to **Washington** by **Hartford** for Curtis Leschyshyn, November 9, 1996. Traded to **Chicago** by **Washington** with Chris Simon for Michael Nylander, Chicago's 3rd round choice (Stephen Werner) in 2003 Entry Draft and future considerations, November 1, 2002. Traded to **Colorado** by **Chicago** for Colorado's 4th round choice (Mitch Maunu) in 2004 Entry Draft, June 21, 2003.

NILSON, Marcus
(NIHL-suhn, MAHR-kuhs) **CGY.**

Left wing. Shoots right. 6'2", 195 lbs. Born, Balsta, Sweden, March 1, 1978. Florida's 1st choice, 20th overall, in 1996 Entry Draft.

			Regular Season														Playoffs								
Season	Club	League	GP	G	A	Pts	PIM	PP	SH	GW	S	%	+/-	TF	F%	Min	GP	G	A	Pts	PIM	PP	SH	GW	Min
1994-95	Djurgarden Jr.	Swede-Jr.	24	7	8	15	22	....	....	....	....	....	....	....	....	....	....	....	....	....	....	....	....	....	....
1995-96	Djurgarden Jr.	Swede-Jr.	25	19	17	36	46	....	....	....	....	....	....	....	....	....	2	1	1	2	12	....	....	....	....
	Djurgarden	Sweden	12	0	0	0	0	....	....	....	....	....	....	....	....	....	1	0	0	0	0	....	....	....	....
1996-97	Djurgarden	Sweden	37	0	3	3	33	....	....	....	....	....	....	....	....	....	4	0	0	0	0	....	....	....	....
1997-98	Djurgarden	Sweden	41	4	7	11	18	....	....	....	....	....	....	....	....	....	15	2	1	3	16	....	....	....	....
1998-99	Florida	NHL	8	1	1	2	5	0	0	1	7	14.3	2	6	50.0	12:24	....	....	....	....	....	....	....	....	....
	New Haven	AHL	69	8	25	33	10	....	....	....	....	....	....	....	....	....	....	....	....	....	....	....	....	....	....
99-2000	Florida	NHL	9	0	2	2	2	0	0	0	6	0.0	2	14	64.3	7:56	....	....	....	....	....	....	....	....	....
	Louisville Panthers	AHL	64	9	23	32	52	....	....	....	....	....	....	....	....	....	4	0	0	0	2	....	....	....	....
2000-01	Florida	NHL	78	12	24	36	74	0	0	2	141	8.5	–3	169	40.8	15:46	....	....	....	....	....	....	....	....	....
2001-02	Florida	NHL	81	14	19	33	55	6	1	2	147	9.5	–14	539	43.8	16:31	....	....	....	....	....	....	....	....	....
2002-03	Florida	NHL	82	15	19	34	31	7	1	0	187	8.0	2	469	46.7	15:31	....	....	....	....	....	....	....	....	....

			Regular Season														Playoffs								
Season	Club	League	GP	G	A	Pts	PIM	PP	SH	GW	S	%	+/-	TF	F%	Min	GP	G	A	Pts	PIM	PP	SH	GW	Min
2003-04	**Florida**	**NHL**	**69**	**6**	**13**	**19**	**26**	**1**	**1**	**1**	**110**	**5.5**	**–9**	**151**	**44.4**	**15:30**	....	....	....	....	....	....	....	....	....
	Calgary	**NHL**	**14**	**5**	**0**	**5**	**14**	**1**	**0**	**2**	**23**	**21.7**	**3**	**173**	**45.1**	**16:43**	**26**	**4**	**7**	**11**	**12**	**0**	**0**	**1**	**19:25**
	NHL Totals		**341**	**53**	**78**	**131**	**207**	**15**	**3**	**8**	**621**	**8.5**		**1521**	**44.8**	**15:35**	**26**	**4**	**7**	**11**	**12**	**0**	**0**	**1**	**19:25**

Traded to **Calgary** by **Florida** for Calgary's 2nd round choice (David Booth) in 2004 Entry Draft, March 8, 2004.

NOLAN, Owen

(NOH-lan, OH-wehn) **TOR.**

Right wing. Shoots right. 6'1", 215 lbs. Born, Belfast, Ireland, February 12, 1972. Quebec's 1st choice, 1st overall, in 1990 Entry Draft.

Season	Club	League	GP	G	A	Pts	PIM	PP	SH	GW	S	%	+/-	TF	F%	Min	GP	G	A	Pts	PIM	PP	SH	GW	Min
1987-88	Thorold	OMHA	28	53	32	85	24	....	....	....	....	....	....	....	....	....	....	....	....	....	....	....	....	....	....
	Thorold	OJHL-B	3	1	0	1	2	....	....	....	....	....	....	....	....	....	....	....	....	....	....	....	....	....	....
1988-89	Cornwall Royals	OHL	62	34	25	59	213	....	....	....	....	....	....	....	....	....	18	5	11	16	41	....	....	....	....
1989-90	Cornwall Royals	OHL	58	51	59	110	240	....	....	....	....	....	....	....	....	....	6	7	5	12	26	....	....	....	....
1990-91	**Quebec**	**NHL**	**59**	**3**	**10**	**13**	**109**	**0**	**0**	**0**	**54**	**5.6**	**–19**	....	....	....	....	....	....	....	....	....	....	....	....
	Halifax Citadels	AHL	6	4	4	8	11	....	....	....	....	....	....	....	....	....	....	....	....	....	....	....	....	....	....
1991-92	**Quebec**	**NHL**	**75**	**42**	**31**	**73**	**183**	**17**	**0**	**0**	**190**	**22.1**	**–9**	....	....	....	....	....	....	....	....	....	....	....	....
1992-93	**Quebec**	**NHL**	**73**	**36**	**41**	**77**	**185**	**15**	**0**	**4**	**241**	**14.9**	**–1**	....	....	....	**5**	**1**	**0**	**1**	**2**	**0**	**0**	**0**	....
1993-94	**Quebec**	**NHL**	**6**	**2**	**2**	**4**	**8**	**0**	**0**	**0**	**15**	**13.3**	**2**	....	....	....	....	....	....	....	....	....	....	....	....
1994-95	**Quebec**	**NHL**	**46**	**30**	**19**	**49**	**46**	**13**	**2**	**8**	**137**	**21.9**	**21**	....	....	....	**6**	**2**	**3**	**5**	**6**	**0**	**0**	**0**	....
1995-96	**Colorado**	**NHL**	**9**	**4**	**4**	**8**	**9**	**4**	**0**	**0**	**23**	**17.4**	**–3**	....	....	....	....	....	....	....	....	....	....	....	....
	San Jose	**NHL**	**72**	**29**	**32**	**61**	**137**	**12**	**1**	**2**	**184**	**15.8**	**–30**	....	....	....	....	....	....	....	....	....	....	....	....
1996-97	**San Jose**	**NHL**	**72**	**31**	**32**	**63**	**155**	**10**	**0**	**3**	**225**	**13.8**	**–19**	....	....	....	....	....	....	....	....	....	....	....	....
1997-98	**San Jose**	**NHL**	**75**	**14**	**27**	**41**	**144**	**3**	**1**	**1**	**192**	**7.3**	**–2**	....	....	....	**6**	**2**	**2**	**4**	**26**	**2**	**0**	**1**	....
1998-99	**San Jose**	**NHL**	**78**	**19**	**26**	**45**	**129**	**6**	**2**	**3**	**207**	**9.2**	**16**	**657**	**49.3**	**19:09**	**6**	**1**	**1**	**2**	**6**	**0**	**0**	**0**	**20:15**
99-2000	**San Jose**	**NHL**	**78**	**44**	**40**	**84**	**110**	**18**	**4**	**6**	**261**	**16.9**	**–1**	**357**	**50.7**	**21:07**	**10**	**8**	**2**	**10**	**6**	**2**	**2**	**3**	**22:14**
2000-01	**San Jose**	**NHL**	**57**	**24**	**25**	**49**	**75**	**10**	**1**	**4**	**191**	**12.6**	**0**	**407**	**46.9**	**21:49**	**6**	**1**	**1**	**2**	**8**	**0**	**0**	**1**	**22:45**
2001-02	**San Jose**	**NHL**	**75**	**23**	**43**	**66**	**93**	**8**	**2**	**2**	**217**	**10.6**	**7**	**545**	**47.0**	**19:23**	**12**	**3**	**6**	**9**	**8**	**0**	**0**	**0**	**19:46**
	Canada	Olympics	6	0	3	3	2	....	....	....	....	....	....	....	....	....	....	....	....	....	....	....	....	....	....
2002-03	**San Jose**	**NHL**	**61**	**22**	**20**	**42**	**91**	**8**	**3**	**4**	**192**	**11.5**	**–5**	**226**	**50.4**	**18:08**	....	....	....	....	....	....	....	....	....
	Toronto	**NHL**	**14**	**7**	**5**	**12**	**16**	**5**	**0**	**1**	**29**	**24.1**	**2**	**56**	**48.2**	**17:00**	**7**	**0**	**2**	**2**	**2**	**0**	**0**	**0**	**23:19**
2003-04	**Toronto**	**NHL**	**65**	**19**	**29**	**48**	**110**	**7**	**2**	**3**	**154**	**12.3**	**4**	**242**	**53.3**	**17:57**	....	....	....	....	....	....	....	....	....
	NHL Totals		**915**	**349**	**386**	**735**	**1600**	**136**	**18**	**41**	**2512**	**13.9**		**2490**	**49.1**	**19:30**	**58**	**18**	**17**	**35**	**64**	**4**	**2**	**5**	**21:29**

OHL Rookie of the Year (1989) • OHL First All-Star Team (1990)

Played in NHL All-Star Game (1992, 1996, 1997, 2000, 2002)

• Missed majority of 1993-94 season recovering from shoulder injury suffered in game vs. Tampa Bay, November 13, 1993. Transferred to **Colorado** after **Quebec** franchise relocated, June 21, 1995. Traded to **San Jose** by **Colorado** for Sandis Ozolinsh, October 26, 1995. Traded to **Toronto** by **San Jose** for Alyn McCauley, Brad Boyes and Toronto's 1st round choice (later traded to Boston – Boston selected Mark Stuart) in 2003 Entry Draft, March 5, 2003.

NORSTROM, Mattias

(NOHR-struhm, MAT-tee-ahs) **L.A.**

Defense. Shoots left. 6'2", 210 lbs. Born, Stockholm, Sweden, January 2, 1972. NY Rangers' 2nd choice, 48th overall, in 1992 Entry Draft.

Season	Club	League	GP	G	A	Pts	PIM	PP	SH	GW	S	%	+/-	TF	F%	Min	GP	G	A	Pts	PIM	PP	SH	GW	Min
1990-91	Mora IK	Swede-2	9	1	1	2	6	....	....	....	....	....	....	....	....	....	1	0	0	0	2	....	....	....	....
1991-92	AIK Solna	Sweden	39	4	3	7	28	....	....	....	....	....	....	....	....	....	3	0	2	2	2	....	....	....	....
1992-93	AIK Solna	Sweden	22	0	1	1	16	....	....	....	....	....	....	....	....	....	....	....	....	....	....	....	....	....	....
1993-94	**NY Rangers**	**NHL**	**9**	**0**	**2**	**2**	**6**	**0**	**0**	**0**	**3**	**0.0**	**0**	....	....	....	....	....	....	....	....	....	....	....	....
	Binghamton	AHL	55	1	9	10	70	....	....	....	....	....	....	....	....	....	....	....	....	....	....	....	....	....	....
1994-95	Binghamton	AHL	63	9	10	19	91	....	....	....	....	....	....	....	....	....	....	....	....	....	....	....	....	....	....
	NY Rangers	**NHL**	**9**	**0**	**3**	**3**	**2**	**0**	**0**	**0**	**4**	**0.0**	**2**	....	....	....	**3**	**0**	**0**	**0**	**0**	**0**	**0**	**0**	....
1995-96	**NY Rangers**	**NHL**	**25**	**2**	**1**	**3**	**22**	**0**	**0**	**0**	**17**	**11.8**	**5**	....	....	....	....	....	....	....	....	....	....	....	....
	Los Angeles	**NHL**	**11**	**0**	**1**	**1**	**18**	**0**	**0**	**0**	**17**	**0.0**	**–8**	....	....	....	....	....	....	....	....	....	....	....	....
1996-97	**Los Angeles**	**NHL**	**80**	**1**	**21**	**22**	**84**	**0**	**0**	**0**	**106**	**0.9**	**–4**	....	....	....	....	....	....	....	....	....	....	....	....
1997-98	**Los Angeles**	**NHL**	**73**	**1**	**12**	**13**	**90**	**0**	**0**	**0**	**61**	**1.6**	**14**	....	....	....	**4**	**0**	**0**	**0**	**2**	**0**	**0**	**0**	....
	Sweden	Olympics	4	0	1	1	2	....	....	....	....	....	....	....	....	....	....	....	....	....	....	....	....	....	....
1998-99	**Los Angeles**	**NHL**	**78**	**2**	**5**	**7**	**36**	**0**	**1**	**0**	**61**	**3.3**	**–10**	**1**	**0.0**	**20:20**	....	....	....	....	....	....	....	....	....
99-2000	**Los Angeles**	**NHL**	**82**	**1**	**13**	**14**	**66**	**0**	**0**	**0**	**62**	**1.6**	**22**	**0**	**0.0**	**21:49**	**4**	**0**	**0**	**0**	**6**	**0**	**0**	**0**	**21:35**
2000-01	**Los Angeles**	**NHL**	**82**	**0**	**18**	**18**	**60**	**0**	**0**	**0**	**59**	**0.0**	**10**	**2**	**0.0**	**21:50**	**13**	**0**	**2**	**2**	**18**	**0**	**0**	**0**	**23:16**
2001-02	**Los Angeles**	**NHL**	**79**	**2**	**9**	**11**	**38**	**0**	**0**	**0**	**42**	**4.8**	**–2**	**0**	**0.0**	**23:01**	**7**	**0**	**0**	**0**	**4**	**0**	**0**	**0**	**23:24**
	Sweden	Olympics	4	0	0	0	0	....	....	....	....	....	....	....	....	....	....	....	....	....	....	....	....	....	....
2002-03	**Los Angeles**	**NHL**	**82**	**0**	**6**	**6**	**49**	**0**	**0**	**0**	**63**	**0.0**	**0**	**1**	**100.0**	**21:30**	....	....	....	....	....	....	....	....	....
2003-04	**Los Angeles**	**NHL**	**74**	**1**	**13**	**14**	**44**	**0**	**0**	**0**	**65**	**1.5**	**–3**	**1**	**100.0**	**22:26**	....	....	....	....	....	....	....	....	....
	NHL Totals		**684**	**10**	**104**	**114**	**515**	**0**	**1**	**0**	**560**	**1.8**		**5**	**40.0**	**21:49**	**31**	**0**	**2**	**2**	**30**	**0**	**0**	**0**	**23:02**

Played in NHL All-Star Game (1999, 2004)

Traded to **Los Angeles** by **NY Rangers** with Ray Ferraro, Ian Laperriere, Nathan Lafayette and NY Rangers' 4th round choice (Sean Blanchard) in 1997 Entry Draft for Marty McSorley, Jari Kurri and Shane Churla, March 14, 1996.

NORTON, Brad

(NOHR-tuhn, BRAD)

Defense. Shoots left. 6'4", 235 lbs. Born, Cambridge, MA, February 13, 1975. Edmonton's 9th choice, 215th overall, in 1993 Entry Draft.

Season	Club	League	GP	G	A	Pts	PIM	PP	SH	GW	S	%	+/-	TF	F%	Min	GP	G	A	Pts	PIM	PP	SH	GW	Min
1992-93	Cushing Academy	Hi-School	31	10	26	36	....	....	....	....	....	....	....	....	....	....	....	....	....	....	....	....	....	....	....
1993-94	Cushing Academy	Hi-School	STATISTICS NOT AVAILABLE																						
1994-95	U. Mass-Amherst	H-East	30	0	6	6	89	....	....	....	....	....	....	....	....	....	....	....	....	....	....	....	....	....	....
1995-96	U. Mass-Amherst	H-East	34	4	12	16	99	....	....	....	....	....	....	....	....	....	....	....	....	....	....	....	....	....	....
1996-97	U. Mass-Amherst	H-East	35	2	16	18	88	....	....	....	....	....	....	....	....	....	....	....	....	....	....	....	....	....	....
1997-98	U. Mass-Amherst	H-East	20	2	13	15	28	....	....	....	....	....	....	....	....	....	....	....	....	....	....	....	....	....	....
	Detroit Vipers	IHL	33	1	4	5	56	....	....	....	....	....	....	....	....	....	22	0	2	2	87	....	....	....	....
1998-99	Hamilton	AHL	58	1	8	9	134	....	....	....	....	....	....	....	....	....	11	0	1	1	6	....	....	....	....
99-2000	Hamilton	AHL	40	5	12	17	104	....	....	....	....	....	....	....	....	....	10	1	4	5	26	....	....	....	....
2000-01	Hamilton	AHL	46	3	15	18	114	....	....	....	....	....	....	....	....	....	....	....	....	....	....	....	....	....	....
2001-02	**Florida**	**NHL**	**22**	**0**	**2**	**2**	**45**	**0**	**0**	**0**	**6**	**0.0**	**–2**	**1**	**0.0**	**9:15**	....	....	....	....	....	....	....	....	....
	Hershey Bears	AHL	40	0	10	10	62	....	....	....	....	....	....	....	....	....	2	0	0	0	6	....	....	....	....
2002-03	**Los Angeles**	**NHL**	**53**	**3**	**3**	**6**	**97**	**0**	**0**	**0**	**19**	**15.8**	**1**	**2**	**0.0**	**6:04**	....	....	....	....	....	....	....	....	....
2003-04	**Los Angeles**	**NHL**	**20**	**0**	**1**	**1**	**77**	**0**	**0**	**0**	**10**	**0.0**	**–1**	**0**	**0.0**	**8:34**	....	....	....	....	....	....	....	....	....
	Washington	**NHL**	**16**	**0**	**1**	**1**	**17**	**0**	**0**	**0**	**6**	**0.0**	**–4**	**0**	**0.0**	**12:50**	....	....	....	....	....	....	....	....	....
	NHL Totals		**111**	**3**	**7**	**10**	**236**	**0**	**0**	**0**	**41**	**7.3**		**3**	**0.0**	**8:08**	....	....	....	....	....	....	....	....	....

Signed as a free agent by **Florida**, July 27, 2001. Signed as a free agent by **Los Angeles**, October, 8, 2002. Claimed on waivers by **Washington** from **Los Angeles**, March 4, 2004. • Missed majority of 2003-04 season recovering from arm injury suffered in pre-season game vs. Phoenix, September 20, 2003.

NOVOSELTSEV, Ivan

(noh-voh-SEHLT-sehv, ee-VAHN)

Right wing. Shoots left. 6'1", 210 lbs. Born, Golitsino, USSR, January 23, 1979. Florida's 5th choice, 95th overall, in 1997 Entry Draft.

Season	Club	League	GP	G	A	Pts	PIM	PP	SH	GW	S	%	+/-	TF	F%	Min	GP	G	A	Pts	PIM	PP	SH	GW	Min
1995-96	Krylja Sovetov	CIS	1	0	0	0	2	....	....	....	....	....	....	....	....	....	....	....	....	....	....	....	....	....	....
1996-97	Krylja Sovetov 2	Russia-3	19	5	3	8	39	....	....	....	....	....	....	....	....	....	....	....	....	....	....	....	....	....	....
	Krylja Sovetov	Russia	30	0	3	3	18	....	....	....	....	....	....	....	....	....	2	0	0	0	4	....	....	....	....
1997-98	Sarnia Sting	OHL	53	26	22	48	41	....	....	....	....	....	....	....	....	....	5	1	1	2	8	....	....	....	....
1998-99	Sarnia Sting	OHL	68	57	39	96	45	....	....	....	....	....	....	....	....	....	5	2	4	6	6	....	....	....	....
99-2000	**Florida**	**NHL**	**14**	**2**	**1**	**3**	**8**	**2**	**0**	**0**	**8**	**25.0**	**–3**	**1**	**100.0**	**10:29**	....	....	....	....	....	....	....	....	....
	Louisville Panthers	AHL	47	14	21	35	22	....	....	....	....	....	....	....	....	....	4	1	0	1	6	....	....	....	....
2000-01	**Florida**	**NHL**	**38**	**3**	**6**	**9**	**16**	**0**	**0**	**0**	**34**	**8.8**	**–5**	**1**	**0.0**	**10:44**	....	....	....	....	....	....	....	....	....
	Louisville Panthers	AHL	34	2	10	12	8	....	....	....	....	....	....	....	....	....	....	....	....	....	....	....	....	....	....
2001-02	**Florida**	**NHL**	**70**	**13**	**16**	**29**	**44**	**1**	**1**	**5**	**109**	**11.9**	**–10**	**27**	**44.4**	**14:53**	....	....	....	....	....	....	....	....	....
2002-03	**Florida**	**NHL**	**78**	**10**	**17**	**27**	**30**	**1**	**0**	**0**	**115**	**8.7**	**–16**	**39**	**30.8**	**15:02**	....	....	....	....	....	....	....	....	....
2003-04	**Florida**	**NHL**	**17**	**1**	**4**	**5**	**8**	**0**	**0**	**0**	**25**	**4.0**	**–6**	**8**	**75.0**	**11:55**	....	....	....	....	....	....	....	....	....
	Phoenix	**NHL**	**17**	**2**	**0**	**2**	**6**	**0**	**0**	**0**	**23**	**8.7**	**–7**	**1**	**0.0**	**10:11**	....	....	....	....	....	....	....	....	....
	Springfield	AHL	2	1	0	1	2	....	....	....	....	....	....	....	....	....	....	....	....	....	....	....	....	....	....
	NHL Totals		**234**	**31**	**44**	**75**	**112**	**4**	**1**	**5**	**314**	**9.9**		**77**	**40.3**	**13:26**	....	....	....	....	....	....	....	....	....

OHL First All-Star Team (1999)

Traded to **Phoenix** by **Florida** for future considerations, December 30, 2003. • Missed majority of 2003-04 season recovering from head injury suffered in game vs. Detroit, January 16, 2004.

			Regular Season														Playoffs								
Season	Club	League	GP	G	A	Pts	PIM	PP	SH	GW	S	%	+/-	TF	F%	Min	GP	G	A	Pts	PIM	PP	SH	GW	Min

NUMMINEN, Teppo

(NOO-mih-nehn, TEH-poh)

Defense. Shoots right. 6'2", 197 lbs. Born, Tampere, Finland, July 3, 1968. Winnipeg's 2nd choice, 29th overall, in 1986 Entry Draft.

Season	Club	League	GP	G	A	Pts	PIM	PP	SH	GW	S	%	+/-	TF	F%	Min	GP	G	A	Pts	PIM	PP	SH	GW	Min
1984-85	Tappara Jr.	Finn-Jr.	30	14	17	31	10																		
	Whitby Lawmen	OPJHL	16	3	9	12	0																		
1985-86	Tappara Jr.	Finn-Jr.	2	0	0	0	0										3	0	1	1	2				
	Tappara Tampere	Finland	31	2	4	6	6										8	0	0	0	0				
1986-87	Tappara Tampere	Finland	44	9	9	18	16										9	4	1	5	4				
1987-88	Tappara Tampere	Finland	40	10	10	20	29										10	6	6	12	6				
	Finland	Olympics	6	1	4	5	0																		
1988-89	**Winnipeg**	**NHL**	**69**	**1**	**14**	**15**	**36**	**0**	**1**	**0**	**85**	**1.2**	**-11**												
1989-90	**Winnipeg**	**NHL**	**79**	**11**	**32**	**43**	**20**	**1**	**0**	**1**	**105**	**10.5**	**-4**				**7**	**1**	**2**	**3**	**10**	**0**	**0**	**0**	
1990-91	**Winnipeg**	**NHL**	**80**	**8**	**25**	**33**	**28**	**3**	**0**	**0**	**151**	**5.3**	**-15**												
1991-92	**Winnipeg**	**NHL**	**80**	**5**	**34**	**39**	**32**	**4**	**0**	**1**	**143**	**3.5**	**15**				**7**	**0**	**0**	**0**	**0**	**0**	**0**	**0**	
1992-93	**Winnipeg**	**NHL**	**66**	**7**	**30**	**37**	**33**	**3**	**1**	**0**	**103**	**6.8**	**4**				**6**	**1**	**1**	**2**	**2**	**1**	**0**	**0**	
1993-94	**Winnipeg**	**NHL**	**57**	**5**	**18**	**23**	**28**	**4**	**0**	**1**	**89**	**5.6**	**-23**												
1994-95	TuTo Turku	Finland	12	3	8	11	4																		
	Winnipeg	**NHL**	**42**	**5**	**16**	**21**	**16**	**2**	**0**	**0**	**86**	**5.8**	**12**												
1995-96	**Winnipeg**	**NHL**	**74**	**11**	**43**	**54**	**22**	**6**	**0**	**3**	**165**	**6.7**	**-4**				**6**	**0**	**0**	**0**	**2**	**0**	**0**	**0**	
1996-97	**Phoenix**	**NHL**	**82**	**2**	**25**	**27**	**28**	**0**	**0**	**0**	**135**	**1.5**	**-3**				**7**	**3**	**3**	**6**	**0**	**1**	**0**	**1**	
1997-98	**Phoenix**	**NHL**	**82**	**11**	**40**	**51**	**30**	**6**	**0**	**2**	**126**	**8.7**	**25**				**1**	**0**	**0**	**0**	**0**	**0**	**0**	**0**	
	Finland	Olympics	6	1	1	2	2																		
1998-99	**Phoenix**	**NHL**	**82**	**10**	**30**	**40**	**30**	**1**	**0**	**0**	**156**	**6.4**	**3**	**2**	**0.0**	**24:26**	**7**	**2**	**1**	**3**	**4**	**2**	**0**	**0**	**26:09**
99-2000	**Phoenix**	**NHL**	**79**	**8**	**34**	**42**	**16**	**2**	**0**	**2**	**126**	**6.3**	**21**	**1**	**0.0**	**23:37**	**5**	**1**	**1**	**2**	**0**	**0**	**0**	**0**	**23:11**
2000-01	**Phoenix**	**NHL**	**72**	**5**	**26**	**31**	**36**	**1**	**0**	**2**	**109**	**4.6**	**9**	**0**	**0.0**	**24:28**									
2001-02	**Phoenix**	**NHL**	**76**	**13**	**35**	**48**	**20**	**4**	**0**	**6**	**117**	**11.1**	**13**	**0**	**0.0**	**23:51**	**4**	**0**	**0**	**0**	**2**	**0**	**0**	**0**	**25:33**
	Finland	Olympics	4	0	1	1	0																		
2002-03	**Phoenix**	**NHL**	**78**	**6**	**24**	**30**	**30**	**2**	**0**	**1**	**108**	**5.6**	**0**	**0**	**0.0**	**23:51**									
2003-04	**Dallas**	**NHL**	**62**	**3**	**14**	**17**	**18**	**0**	**0**	**0**	**83**	**3.6**	**-5**	**1**	**100.0**	**21:40**	**4**	**0**	**1**	**1**	**0**	**0**	**0**	**0**	**19:12**
	NHL Totals		**1160**	**111**	**440**	**551**	**423**	**39**	**2**	**19**	**1887**	**5.9**		**4**	**25.0**	**23:43**	**54**	**8**	**9**	**17**	**20**	**4**	**0**	**1**	**23:54**

Played in NHL All-Star Game (1999, 2000, 2001)

Transferred to **Phoenix** after **Winnipeg** franchise relocated, July 1, 1996. Traded to **Dallas** by **Phoenix** for Mike Sillinger, July 22, 2003.

NYCHOLAT, Lawrence

(NIH-coh-lat, LAW-rehnts) **NYR**

Defense. Shoots left. 6', 192 lbs. Born, Calgary, Alta., May 7, 1979.

Season	Club	League	GP	G	A	Pts	PIM	PP	SH	GW	S	%	+/-	TF	F%	Min	GP	G	A	Pts	PIM	PP	SH	GW	Min
1995-96	Notre Dame	SMHL	42	10	36	46	66																		
1996-97	Swift Current	WHL	67	8	13	21	82										10	0	0	0	24				
1997-98	Swift Current	WHL	71	13	35	48	108										1	0	0	0	0				
1998-99	Swift Current	WHL	72	16	44	60	125										6	2	2	4	12				
99-2000	Swift Current	WHL	70	22	58	80	92										2	0	0	0	0				
2000-01	Jackson Bandits	ECHL	5	1	2	3	5																		
	Cleveland	IHL	42	3	7	10	69										4	0	0	0	2				
2001-02	Houston Aeros	AHL	72	3	11	14	92										14	1	0	1	23				
2002-03	Houston Aeros	AHL	66	11	28	39	155																		
	Hartford	AHL	15	2	9	11	6										2	2	0	2	0				
2003-04	**NY Rangers**	**NHL**	**9**	**0**	**0**	**0**	**6**	**0**	**0**	**0**	**6**	**0.0**	**-2**	**0**	**0.0**	**17:09**									
	Hartford	AHL	72	6	26	32	130										16	0	5	5	28				
	NHL Totals		**9**	**0**	**0**	**0**	**6**	**0**	**0**	**0**	**6**	**0.0**		**0**	**0.0**	**17:09**									

Signed as a free agent by **Minnesota**, August 31, 2000. Traded to **NY Rangers** by **Minnesota** for Johan Holmqvist, March 11, 2003.

NYLANDER, Michael

(NEE-lan-duhr, MIGH-kuhl) **NYR**

Center. Shoots left. 6'1", 195 lbs. Born, Stockholm, Sweden, October 3, 1972. Hartford's 4th choice, 59th overall, in 1991 Entry Draft.

Season	Club	League	GP	G	A	Pts	PIM	PP	SH	GW	S	%	+/-	TF	F%	Min	GP	G	A	Pts	PIM	PP	SH	GW	Min
1989-90	Huddinge IK	Swede-2	31	7	15	22	4										5	3	0	3	0				
1990-91	Huddinge IK	Swede-2	33	14	20	34	10										2	0	0	0	0				
1991-92	AIK Solna	Sweden	40	11	17	28	30										3	1	4	5	4				
1992-93	**Hartford**	**NHL**	**59**	**11**	**22**	**33**	**36**	**3**	**0**	**1**	**85**	**12.9**	**-7**												
	Springfield	AHL															3	3	3	6	2				
1993-94	**Hartford**	**NHL**	**58**	**11**	**33**	**44**	**24**	**4**	**0**	**1**	**74**	**14.9**	**-2**												
	Springfield	AHL	4	0	9	9	0																		
	Calgary	**NHL**	**15**	**2**	**9**	**11**	**6**	**0**	**0**	**0**	**21**	**9.5**	**10**				**3**	**0**	**0**	**0**	**0**	**0**	**0**	**0**	
1994-95	JyP HT Jyvaskyla	Finland	16	11	19	30	63																		
	Calgary	**NHL**	**6**	**0**	**1**	**1**	**2**	**0**	**0**	**0**	**2**	**0.0**	**1**				**6**	**0**	**6**	**6**	**2**	**0**	**0**	**0**	
1995-96	**Calgary**	**NHL**	**73**	**17**	**38**	**55**	**20**	**0**	**0**	**6**	**163**	**10.4**	**0**				**4**	**0**	**0**	**0**	**0**	**0**	**0**	**0**	
1996-97	HC Lugano	Swiss	36	12	43	55	28										8	3	8	11	8				
1997-98	**Calgary**	**NHL**	**65**	**13**	**23**	**36**	**24**	**0**	**0**	**2**	**117**	**11.1**	**10**												
	Sweden	Olympics	4	0	0	0	6																		
1998-99	**Calgary**	**NHL**	**9**	**2**	**3**	**5**	**2**	**1**	**0**	**0**	**7**	**28.6**	**1**	**25**	**60.0**	**11:10**									
	Tampa Bay	**NHL**	**24**	**2**	**7**	**9**	**6**	**1**	**0**	**0**	**26**	**7.7**	**-10**	**75**	**44.0**	**13:29**									
99-2000	**Tampa Bay**	**NHL**	**11**	**1**	**2**	**3**	**4**	**1**	**0**	**0**	**10**	**10.0**	**-3**	**35**	**57.1**	**10:32**									
	Chicago	**NHL**	**66**	**23**	**28**	**51**	**26**	**4**	**0**	**2**	**112**	**20.5**	**9**	**561**	**46.9**	**16:39**									
2000-01	**Chicago**	**NHL**	**82**	**25**	**39**	**64**	**32**	**4**	**0**	**5**	**176**	**14.2**	**7**	**1036**	**48.3**	**18:52**									
2001-02	**Chicago**	**NHL**	**82**	**15**	**46**	**61**	**50**	**6**	**0**	**2**	**158**	**9.5**	**28**	**974**	**50.2**	**15:33**	**5**	**0**	**3**	**3**	**2**	**0**	**0**	**0**	**15:20**
	Sweden	Olympics	4	1	2	3	0																		
2002-03	**Chicago**	**NHL**	**9**	**0**	**4**	**4**	**4**	**0**	**0**	**0**	**20**	**0.0**	**0**	**86**	**48.8**	**15:19**									
	Washington	**NHL**	**71**	**17**	**39**	**56**	**36**	**7**	**0**	**2**	**141**	**12.1**	**3**	**1005**	**47.4**	**18:41**	**6**	**3**	**2**	**5**	**8**	**1**	**0**	**1**	**16:45**
2003-04	**Washington**	**NHL**	**3**	**0**	**2**	**2**	**8**	**0**	**0**	**0**	**1**	**0.0**	**1**	**22**	**54.6**	**14:57**									
	Boston	**NHL**	**15**	**1**	**11**	**12**	**14**	**0**	**0**	**1**	**29**	**3.4**	**3**	**128**	**46.1**	**15:43**	**6**	**3**	**3**	**6**	**0**	**0**	**0**	**0**	**18:57**
	NHL Totals		**648**	**140**	**307**	**447**	**294**	**34**	**0**	**22**	**1142**	**12.3**		**3947**	**48.4**	**16:41**	**30**	**6**	**14**	**20**	**12**	**1**	**0**	**1**	**17:06**

Traded to **Calgary** by **Hartford** with James Patrick and Zarley Zalapski for Gary Suter, Paul Ranheim and Ted Drury, March 10, 1994. • Missed majority of 1994-95 season recovering from wrist injury suffered in game vs. St. Louis, January 24, 1995. Traded to **Tampa Bay** by **Calgary** for Andrei Nazarov, January 19, 1999. Traded to **Chicago** by **Tampa Bay** for Bryan Muir and Reid Simpson, November 12, 1999. Traded to **Washington** by **Chicago** with Chicago's 3rd round choice (Stephen Werner) in 2003 Entry Draft and future considerations for Chris Simon and Andrei Nikolishin, November 1, 2002. • Missed majority of 2003-04 season recovering from leg injury suffered in practice, October 2, 2003. Traded to **Boston** by **Washington** for Boston's 2nd round choice in 2006 Entry Draft and future considerations, March 4, 2004. Signed as a free agent by **NY Rangers**, August 10, 2004.

OATES, Adam

(OHTS, A-duhm)

Center. Shoots right. 5'11", 190 lbs. Born, Weston, Ont., August 27, 1962.

Season	Club	League	GP	G	A	Pts	PIM	PP	SH	GW	S	%	+/-	TF	F%	Min	GP	G	A	Pts	PIM	PP	SH	GW	Min
1979-80	Port Credit Titans	OHA-B	34	30	36	66	41																		
	Markham Waxers	OHA-A	9	1	6	7	2																		
1980-81	Markham Waxers	OHA-A	43	36	53	89	89																		
1981-82	Markham Waxers	OJHL	40	59	110	169	....																		
1982-83	RPI Engineers	ECAC	22	9	33	42	8																		
1983-84	RPI Engineers	ECAC	38	26	57	83	15																		
1984-85	RPI Engineers	ECAC	38	31	60	91	29																		
1985-86	**Detroit**	**NHL**	**38**	**9**	**11**	**20**	**10**	**1**	**0**	**1**	**49**	**18.4**	**-24**												
	Adirondack	AHL	34	18	28	46	4										17	7	14	21	4				
1986-87	**Detroit**	**NHL**	**76**	**15**	**32**	**47**	**21**	**4**	**0**	**1**	**138**	**10.9**	**0**				**16**	**4**	**7**	**11**	**6**	**0**	**0**	**1**	
1987-88	**Detroit**	**NHL**	**63**	**14**	**40**	**54**	**20**	**3**	**0**	**3**	**111**	**12.6**	**16**				**16**	**8**	**12**	**20**	**6**	**4**	**0**	**1**	
1988-89	**Detroit**	**NHL**	**69**	**16**	**62**	**78**	**14**	**2**	**0**	**1**	**127**	**12.6**	**-1**				**6**	**0**	**8**	**8**	**2**	**0**	**0**	**0**	
1989-90	**St. Louis**	**NHL**	**80**	**23**	**79**	**102**	**30**	**6**	**2**	**3**	**168**	**13.7**	**9**				**12**	**2**	**12**	**14**	**4**	**1**	**0**	**0**	
1990-91	**St. Louis**	**NHL**	**61**	**25**	**90**	**115**	**29**	**3**	**1**	**3**	**139**	**18.0**	**15**				**13**	**7**	**13**	**20**	**10**	**2**	**0**	**1**	
1991-92	**St. Louis**	**NHL**	**54**	**10**	**59**	**69**	**12**	**3**	**1**	**3**	**118**	**8.5**	**-4**												
	Boston	**NHL**	**26**	**10**	**20**	**30**	**10**	**3**	**0**	**1**	**73**	**13.7**	**-5**				**15**	**5**	**14**	**19**	**4**	**3**	**0**	**2**	
1992-93	**Boston**	**NHL**	**84**	**45**	***97**	**142**	**32**	**24**	**1**	**11**	**254**	**17.7**	**15**				**4**	**0**	**9**	**9**	**4**	**0**	**0**	**0**	
1993-94	**Boston**	**NHL**	**77**	**32**	**80**	**112**	**45**	**16**	**2**	**3**	**197**	**16.2**	**10**				**13**	**3**	**9**	**12**	**8**	**2**	**0**	**0**	
1994-95	**Boston**	**NHL**	**48**	**12**	**41**	**53**	**8**	**4**	**1**	**2**	**109**	**11.0**	**-11**				**5**	**1**	**0**	**1**	**2**	**1**	**0**	**0**	
1995-96	**Boston**	**NHL**	**70**	**25**	**67**	**92**	**18**	**7**	**1**	**2**	**183**	**13.7**	**16**				**5**	**2**	**5**	**7**	**2**	**0**	**1**	**0**	
1996-97	**Boston**	**NHL**	**63**	**18**	**52**	**70**	**10**	**2**	**2**	**4**	**138**	**13.0**	**-3**												
	Washington	**NHL**	**17**	**4**	**8**	**12**	**4**	**1**	**0**	**1**	**22**	**18.2**	**-2**												

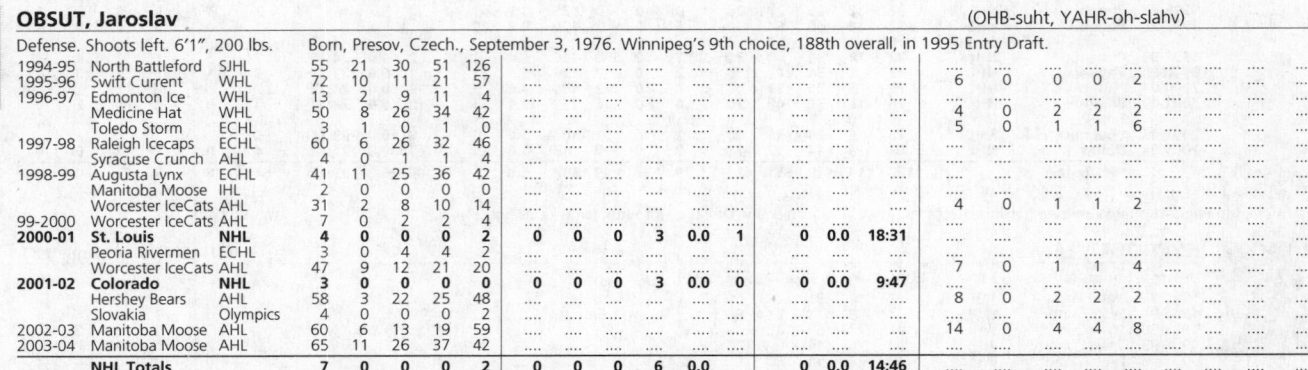

			Regular Season														Playoffs								
Season	Club	League	GP	G	A	Pts	PIM	PP	SH	GW	S	%	+/-	TF	F%	Min	GP	G	A	Pts	PIM	PP	SH	GW	Min
1997-98	Washington	NHL	82	18	58	76	36	3	2	3	121	14.9	6	....	....	....	21	6	11	17	8	1	1	1	....
1998-99	Washington	NHL	59	12	42	54	22	3	0	0	79	15.2	–1	1330	59.2	20:34	....	....	....	....	....	....	....	....	....
99-2000	Washington	NHL	82	15	56	71	14	5	0	6	93	16.1	13	2176	56.8	22:20	5	0	3	3	4	0	0	0	25:06
2000-01	Washington	NHL	81	13	*69	82	28	5	0	4	72	18.1	–9	1836	58.9	21:00	6	0	0	0	0	0	0	0	16:21
2001-02	Washington	NHL	66	11	*57	68	22	3	0	1	85	12.9	–2	1642	56.5	22:06	....	....	....	....	....	....	....	....	....
	Philadelphia	NHL	14	3	*7	10	6	0	0	0	17	17.6	–2	323	55.7	20:51	5	0	2	2	0	0	0	0	21:53
2002-03	Anaheim	NHL	67	9	36	45	16	4	0	2	67	13.4	–1	1064	57.8	18:38	21	4	9	13	6	3	0	1	19:15
2003-04	Edmonton	NHL	60	2	16	18	8	1	0	1	32	6.3	0	851	57.2	14:30	....	....	....	....	....	....	....	....	....
	NHL Totals		1337	341	1079	1420	415	103	12	56	2392	14.3		9222	57.6	20:05	163	42	114	156	66	17	2	7	19:56

ECAC Second All-Star Team (1984) • NCAA East First All-American Team (1984, 1985) • ECAC First All-Star Team (1985) • NCAA Championship All-Tournament Team (1985) • NHL Second All-Star Team (1991)

Played in NHL All-Star Game (1991, 1992, 1993, 1994, 1997)

Signed as a free agent by **Detroit**, June 28, 1985. Traded to **St. Louis** by **Detroit** with Paul MacLean for Bernie Federko and Tony McKegney, June 15, 1989. Traded to **Boston** by **St. Louis** for Craig Janney and Stephane Quintal, February 7, 1992. Traded to **Washington** by **Boston** with Bill Ranford and Rick Tocchet for Jim Carey, Anson Carter, Jason Allison and Washington's 3rd round choice (Lee Goren) in 1997 Entry Draft, March 1, 1997. Traded to **Philadelphia** by **Washington** for Maxime Ouellet and Philadelphia's 1st (later traded to Dallas – Dallas selected Martin Vagner), 2nd (Maxime Daigneault) and 3rd (Derek Krestanovich) round choices in 2002 Entry Draft, March 19, 2002. Signed as a free agent by **Anaheim**, July 1, 2002. Signed as a free agent by **Edmonton**, November 17, 2003. • Officially announced retirement, April 3, 2004.

OBSUT, Jaroslav

(OHB-suht, YAHR-oh-slahv)

Defense. Shoots left. 6'1", 200 lbs. Born, Presov, Czech., September 3, 1976. Winnipeg's 9th choice, 188th overall, in 1995 Entry Draft.

Season	Club	League	GP	G	A	Pts	PIM	PP	SH	GW	S	%	+/-	TF	F%	Min	GP	G	A	Pts	PIM	PP	SH	GW	Min
1994-95	North Battleford	SJHL	55	21	30	51	126	....	....	....	....	....	....	....	....	....	....	....	....	....	....	....	....	....	....
1995-96	Swift Current	WHL	72	10	11	21	57	....	....	....	....	....	....	....	....	....	6	0	0	0	2	....	....	....	....
1996-97	Edmonton Ice	WHL	13	2	9	11	4	....	....	....	....	....	....	....	....	....	....	....	....	....	....	....	....	....	....
	Medicine Hat	WHL	50	8	26	34	42	....	....	....	....	....	....	....	....	....	4	0	2	2	2	....	....	....	....
	Toledo Storm	ECHL	3	1	0	1	0	....	....	....	....	....	....	....	....	....	5	0	1	1	6	....	....	....	....
1997-98	Raleigh Icecaps	ECHL	60	6	26	32	46	....	....	....	....	....	....	....	....	....	....	....	....	....	....	....	....	....	....
	Syracuse Crunch	AHL	4	0	1	1	4	....	....	....	....	....	....	....	....	....	....	....	....	....	....	....	....	....	....
1998-99	Augusta Lynx	ECHL	41	11	25	36	42	....	....	....	....	....	....	....	....	....	....	....	....	....	....	....	....	....	....
	Manitoba Moose	IHL	2	0	0	0	0	....	....	....	....	....	....	....	....	....	....	....	....	....	....	....	....	....	....
	Worcester IceCats	AHL	31	2	8	10	14	....	....	....	....	....	....	....	....	....	4	0	1	1	2	....	....	....	....
99-2000	Worcester IceCats	AHL	7	0	2	2	4	....	....	....	....	....	....	....	....	....	....	....	....	....	....	....	....	....	....
2000-01	**St. Louis**	**NHL**	**4**	**0**	**0**	**0**	**2**	**0**	**0**	**0**	**3**	**0.0**	**1**	**0**	**0.0**	**18:31**	....	....	....	....	....	....	....	....	....
	Peoria Rivermen	ECHL	3	0	4	4	2	....	....	....	....	....	....	....	....	....	....	....	....	....	....	....	....	....	....
	Worcester IceCats	AHL	47	9	12	21	20	....	....	....	....	....	....	....	....	....	7	0	1	1	4	....	....	....	....
2001-02	**Colorado**	**NHL**	**3**	**0**	**0**	**0**	**0**	**0**	**0**	**0**	**3**	**0.0**	**0**	**0**	**0.0**	**9:47**	....	....	....	....	....	....	....	....	....
	Hershey Bears	AHL	58	3	22	25	48	....	....	....	....	....	....	....	....	....	8	0	2	2	2	....	....	....	....
	Slovakia	Olympics	4	0	0	0	2	....	....	....	....	....	....	....	....	....	....	....	....	....	....	....	....	....	....
2002-03	Manitoba Moose	AHL	60	6	13	19	59	....	....	....	....	....	....	....	....	....	14	0	4	4	8	....	....	....	....
2003-04	Manitoba Moose	AHL	65	11	26	37	42	....	....	....	....	....	....	....	....	....	....	....	....	....	....	....	....	....	....
	NHL Totals		**7**	**0**	**0**	**0**	**2**	**0**	**0**	**0**	**6**	**0.0**		**0**	**0.0**	**14:46**	....	....	....	....	....	....	....	....	....

Signed as a free agent by **St. Louis**, April 26, 1999. • Missed majority of 1999-2000 season recovering from knee injury suffered in practice, October, 1999. Signed as a free agent by **Colorado**, August 11, 2001. Signed as a free agent by **Vancouver**, July 10, 2002. Signed as a free agent by **Lulea HF** (Sweden), April 27, 2004.

ODELEIN, Lyle

(OH-duh-LIGHN, LIGHL)

Defense. Shoots right. 6', 210 lbs. Born, Quill Lake, Sask., July 21, 1968. Montreal's 8th choice, 141st overall, in 1986 Entry Draft.

Season	Club	League	GP	G	A	Pts	PIM	PP	SH	GW	S	%	+/-	TF	F%	Min	GP	G	A	Pts	PIM	PP	SH	GW	Min
1984-85	Regina Pat Cdns.	SMHL	26	12	13	25	30	....	....	....	....	....	....	....	....	....	....	....	....	....	....	....	....	....	....
1985-86	Moose Jaw	WHL	67	9	37	46	117	....	....	....	....	....	....	....	....	....	13	1	6	7	34	....	....	....	....
1986-87	Moose Jaw	WHL	59	9	50	59	70	....	....	....	....	....	....	....	....	....	9	2	5	7	26	....	....	....	....
1987-88	Moose Jaw	WHL	63	15	43	58	166	....	....	....	....	....	....	....	....	....	....	....	....	....	....	....	....	....	....
1988-89	Sherbrooke	AHL	33	3	4	7	120	....	....	....	....	....	....	....	....	....	3	0	2	2	5	....	....	....	....
	Peoria Rivermen	IHL	36	2	8	10	116	....	....	....	....	....	....	....	....	....	....	....	....	....	....	....	....	....	....
1989-90	**Montreal**	**NHL**	**8**	**0**	**2**	**2**	**33**	**0**	**0**	**0**	**1**	**0.0**	**–1**	....	....	....	....	....	....	....	....	....	....	....	....
	Sherbrooke	AHL	68	7	24	31	265	....	....	....	....	....	....	....	....	....	12	6	5	11	79	....	....	....	....
1990-91	**Montreal**	**NHL**	**52**	**0**	**2**	**2**	**259**	**0**	**0**	**0**	**25**	**0.0**	**7**	....	....	....	**12**	**0**	**0**	**0**	**54**	**0**	**0**	**0**	....
1991-92	**Montreal**	**NHL**	**71**	**1**	**7**	**8**	**212**	**0**	**0**	**0**	**43**	**2.3**	**15**	....	....	....	**7**	**0**	**0**	**0**	**11**	**0**	**0**	**0**	....
1992-93♦	**Montreal**	**NHL**	**83**	**2**	**14**	**16**	**205**	**0**	**0**	**0**	**79**	**2.5**	**35**	....	....	....	**20**	**1**	**5**	**6**	**30**	**0**	**0**	**0**	....
1993-94	**Montreal**	**NHL**	**79**	**11**	**29**	**40**	**276**	**6**	**0**	**2**	**116**	**9.5**	**8**	....	....	....	**7**	**0**	**0**	**0**	**17**	**0**	**0**	**0**	....
1994-95	**Montreal**	**NHL**	**48**	**3**	**7**	**10**	**152**	**0**	**0**	**0**	**74**	**4.1**	**–13**	....	....	....	....	....	....	....	....	....	....	....	....
1995-96	**Montreal**	**NHL**	**79**	**3**	**14**	**17**	**230**	**0**	**1**	**0**	**74**	**4.1**	**8**	....	....	....	**6**	**1**	**1**	**2**	**6**	**0**	**1**	**0**	....
1996-97	**New Jersey**	**NHL**	**79**	**3**	**13**	**16**	**110**	**1**	**0**	**2**	**93**	**3.2**	**16**	....	....	....	**10**	**2**	**2**	**4**	**19**	**1**	**0**	**0**	....
1997-98	**New Jersey**	**NHL**	**79**	**4**	**19**	**23**	**171**	**1**	**0**	**0**	**76**	**5.3**	**11**	....	....	....	**6**	**1**	**1**	**2**	**21**	**1**	**0**	**1**	....
1998-99	**New Jersey**	**NHL**	**70**	**5**	**26**	**31**	**114**	**1**	**0**	**0**	**101**	**5.0**	**6**	**0**	**0.0**	**19:53**	**7**	**0**	**3**	**3**	**10**	**0**	**0**	**0**	**18:28**
99-2000	**New Jersey**	**NHL**	**57**	**1**	**15**	**16**	**104**	**0**	**0**	**1**	**59**	**1.7**	**–10**	**0**	**0.0**	**16:42**	....	....	....	....	....	....	....	....	....
	Phoenix	**NHL**	**16**	**1**	**7**	**8**	**19**	**1**	**0**	**0**	**30**	**3.3**	**1**	**0**	**0.0**	**21:45**	**5**	**0**	**0**	**0**	**16**	**0**	**0**	**0**	**16:38**
2000-01	**Columbus**	**NHL**	**81**	**3**	**14**	**17**	**118**	**1**	**0**	**0**	**104**	**2.9**	**–16**	**0**	**0.0**	**21:31**	....	....	....	....	....	....	....	....	....
2001-02	**Columbus**	**NHL**	**65**	**2**	**14**	**16**	**89**	**0**	**0**	**0**	**76**	**2.6**	**–28**	**0**	**0.0**	**22:12**	....	....	....	....	....	....	....	....	....
	Chicago	**NHL**	**12**	**0**	**2**	**2**	**4**	**0**	**0**	**0**	**10**	**0.0**	**0**	**0**	**0.0**	**24:23**	**4**	**0**	**1**	**1**	**25**	**0**	**0**	**0**	**24:08**
2002-03	**Chicago**	**NHL**	**65**	**7**	**4**	**11**	**76**	**0**	**0**	**0**	**77**	**9.1**	**7**	**1**	**100.0**	**19:05**	....	....	....	....	....	....	....	....	....
	Dallas	**NHL**	**3**	**0**	**0**	**0**	**6**	**0**	**0**	**0**	**1**	**0.0**	**0**	**0**	**0.0**	**17:49**	**2**	**0**	**0**	**0**	**0**	**0**	**0**	**0**	**12:52**
2003-04	**Florida**	**NHL**	**82**	**4**	**12**	**16**	**88**	**2**	**0**	**0**	**67**	**6.0**	**–7**	**1**	**100.0**	**18:53**	....	....	....	....	....	....	....	....	....
	NHL Totals		**1029**	**50**	**201**	**251**	**2266**	**13**	**1**	**5**	**1106**	**4.5**		**2**	**100.0**	**19:59**	**86**	**5**	**13**	**18**	**209**	**2**	**1**	**1**	**18:36**

Traded to **New Jersey** by **Montreal** for Stephane Richer, August 22, 1996. Traded to **Phoenix** by **New Jersey** for Deron Quint and Phoenix's 3rd round choice (later traded back to Phoenix – Phoenix selected Beat Forster) in 2001 Entry Draft, March 7, 2000. Selected by **Columbus** from **Phoenix** in Expansion Draft, June 23, 2000. Traded to **Chicago** by **Columbus** for Jaroslav Spacek and Chicago's 2nd round choice (Dan Fritsche) in 2003 Entry Draft, March 19, 2002. Traded to **Dallas** by **Chicago** for Sami Helenius and Dallas's 7th round choice (Troy Brouwer) in 2004 Entry Draft, March 10, 2003. Signed as a free agent by **Florida**, September 9, 2003.

O'DONNELL, Sean

(oh-DOHN-ehl, SHAWN) **PHX.**

Defense. Shoots left. 6'3", 227 lbs. Born, Ottawa, Ont., October 13, 1971. Buffalo's 6th choice, 123rd overall, in 1991 Entry Draft.

Season	Club	League	GP	G	A	Pts	PIM	PP	SH	GW	S	%	+/-	TF	F%	Min	GP	G	A	Pts	PIM	PP	SH	GW	Min
1987-88	Kanata Valley	OCJHL	54	4	25	29	96	....	....	....	....	....	....	....	....	....	....	....	....	....	....	....	....	....	....
1988-89	Sudbury Wolves	OHL	56	1	9	10	49	....	....	....	....	....	....	....	....	....	....	....	....	....	....	....	....	....	....
1989-90	Sudbury Wolves	OHL	64	7	19	26	84	....	....	....	....	....	....	....	....	....	7	1	2	3	8	....	....	....	....
1990-91	Sudbury Wolves	OHL	66	8	23	31	114	....	....	....	....	....	....	....	....	....	5	1	4	5	10	....	....	....	....
1991-92	Rochester	AHL	73	4	9	13	193	....	....	....	....	....	....	....	....	....	16	1	2	3	21	....	....	....	....
1992-93	Rochester	AHL	74	3	18	21	203	....	....	....	....	....	....	....	....	....	17	1	6	7	38	....	....	....	....
1993-94	Rochester	AHL	64	2	10	12	242	....	....	....	....	....	....	....	....	....	4	0	1	1	21	....	....	....	....
1994-95	Phoenix	IHL	61	2	18	20	132	....	....	....	....	....	....	....	....	....	9	0	1	1	21	....	....	....	....
	Los Angeles	**NHL**	**15**	**0**	**2**	**2**	**49**	**0**	**0**	**0**	**12**	**0.0**	**–2**	....	....	....	....	....	....	....	....	....	....	....	....
1995-96	**Los Angeles**	**NHL**	**71**	**2**	**5**	**7**	**127**	**0**	**0**	**0**	**65**	**3.1**	**3**	....	....	....	....	....	....	....	....	....	....	....	....
1996-97	**Los Angeles**	**NHL**	**55**	**5**	**12**	**17**	**144**	**2**	**0**	**0**	**68**	**7.4**	**–13**	....	....	....	....	....	....	....	....	....	....	....	....
1997-98	**Los Angeles**	**NHL**	**80**	**2**	**15**	**17**	**179**	**0**	**0**	**1**	**71**	**2.8**	**7**	....	....	....	**4**	**1**	**0**	**1**	**36**	**0**	**0**	**0**	....
1998-99	**Los Angeles**	**NHL**	**80**	**1**	**13**	**14**	**186**	**0**	**0**	**0**	**64**	**1.6**	**1**	**0**	**0.0**	**19:10**	....	....	....	....	....	....	....	....	....
99-2000	**Los Angeles**	**NHL**	**80**	**2**	**12**	**14**	**114**	**0**	**0**	**1**	**51**	**3.9**	**4**	**0**	**0.0**	**17:41**	**4**	**1**	**0**	**1**	**4**	**0**	**0**	**0**	**16:26**
2000-01	**Minnesota**	**NHL**	**63**	**4**	**12**	**16**	**128**	**1**	**0**	**2**	**58**	**6.9**	**–2**	**12**	**50.0**	**23:00**	....	....	....	....	....	....	....	....	....
	New Jersey	**NHL**	**17**	**0**	**1**	**1**	**33**	**0**	**0**	**0**	**9**	**0.0**	**2**	**0**	**0.0**	**16:27**	**23**	**1**	**2**	**3**	**41**	**0**	**0**	**0**	**16:21**
2001-02	**Boston**	**NHL**	**80**	**3**	**22**	**25**	**89**	**1**	**0**	**2**	**112**	**2.7**	**27**	**0**	**0.0**	**24:50**	**6**	**0**	**2**	**2**	**4**	**0**	**0**	**0**	**24:57**
2002-03	**Boston**	**NHL**	**70**	**1**	**15**	**16**	**76**	**0**	**0**	**1**	**61**	**1.6**	**8**	**1**	**0.0**	**22:05**	....	....	....	....	....	....	....	....	....
2003-04	**Boston**	**NHL**	**82**	**1**	**10**	**11**	**110**	**0**	**0**	**0**	**72**	**1.4**	**10**	**3**	**33.3**	**20:36**	**7**	**0**	**0**	**0**	**0**	**0**	**0**	**0**	**19:53**
	NHL Totals		**693**	**21**	**119**	**140**	**1235**	**4**	**0**	**7**	**643**	**3.3**		**16**	**43.8**	**20:58**	**44**	**3**	**4**	**7**	**85**	**0**	**0**	**0**	**18:16**

Traded to **Los Angeles** by **Buffalo** for Doug Houda, July 26, 1994. Selected by **Minnesota** from **Los Angeles** in Expansion Draft, June 23, 2000. Traded to **New Jersey** by **Minnesota** for Willie Mitchell, March 4, 2001. Signed as a free agent by **Boston**, July 2, 2001. Signed as a free agent by **Phoenix**, July 6, 2004.

OHLUND, Mattias

(OH-luhnd, MAT-tee-ahs) **VAN.**

Defense. Shoots left. 6'2", 220 lbs. Born, Pitea, Sweden, September 9, 1976. Vancouver's 1st choice, 13th overall, in 1994 Entry Draft.

			Regular Season														Playoffs								
Season	Club	League	GP	G	A	Pts	PIM	PP	SH	GW	S	%	+/-	TF	F%	Min	GP	G	A	Pts	PIM	PP	SH	GW	Min
1992-93	Pitea HC	Swede-2	22	0	6	6	16	....	....	....	....	....	....	....	....	....	....	....	....	....	....	....	....	....	....
1993-94	Pitea HC	Swede-2	28	7	10	17	62	....	....	....	....	....	....	....	....	....	....	....	....	....	....	....	....	....	....
1994-95	Lulea HF	Sweden	34	6	10	16	34	....	....	....	....	....	....	....	....	....	9	4	0	4	16	....	....	....	....
1995-96	Lulea HF	Sweden	38	4	10	14	26	....	....	....	....	....	....	....	....	....	13	1	0	1	47	....	....	....	....
1996-97	Lulea HF	Sweden	47	7	9	16	38	....	....	....	....	....	....	....	....	....	10	1	2	3	8	....	....	....	....
	Lulea HF	EuroHL	6	0	3	3	0	....	....	....	....	....	....	....	....	....	....	....	....	....	....	....	....	....	....
1997-98	**Vancouver**	**NHL**	**77**	**7**	**23**	**30**	**76**	**1**	**0**	**0**	**172**	**4.1**	**3**	....	....	....	....	....	....	....	....	....	....	....	....
	Sweden	Olympics	4	0	1	1	4	....	....	....	....	....	....	....	....	....	....	....	....	....	....	....	....	....	....
1998-99	**Vancouver**	**NHL**	**74**	**9**	**26**	**35**	**83**	**2**	**1**	**1**	**129**	**7.0**	**–19**	**0**	**0.0**	**26:04**	....	....	....	....	....	....	....	....	....
99-2000	**Vancouver**	**NHL**	**42**	**4**	**16**	**20**	**24**	**2**	**1**	**1**	**63**	**6.3**	**6**	**0**	**0.0**	**27:41**	....	....	....	....	....	....	....	....	....
2000-01	**Vancouver**	**NHL**	**65**	**8**	**20**	**28**	**46**	**1**	**1**	**4**	**136**	**5.9**	**–16**	**0**	**0.0**	**25:00**	**4**	**1**	**3**	**4**	**6**	**1**	**0**	**0**	**26:32**
2001-02	**Vancouver**	**NHL**	**81**	**10**	**26**	**36**	**56**	**4**	**1**	**3**	**193**	**5.2**	**16**	**0**	**0.0**	**25:17**	**6**	**1**	**1**	**2**	**6**	**0**	**0**	**0**	**28:48**
	Sweden	Olympics	4	0	2	2	2	....	....	....	....	....	....	....	....	....	....	....	....	....	....	....	....	....	....
2002-03	**Vancouver**	**NHL**	**59**	**2**	**27**	**29**	**42**	**0**	**0**	**0**	**100**	**2.0**	**1**	**0**	**0.0**	**25:23**	**13**	**3**	**4**	**7**	**12**	**0**	**0**	**0**	**24:01**
2003-04	**Vancouver**	**NHL**	**82**	**14**	**20**	**34**	**73**	**5**	**0**	**3**	**129**	**10.9**	**14**	**0**	**0.0**	**25:47**	**7**	**1**	**4**	**5**	**13**	**0**	**0**	**1**	**27:25**
	NHL Totals		**480**	**54**	**158**	**212**	**400**	**15**	**4**	**12**	**922**	**5.9**		**0**	**0.0**	**25:45**	**30**	**6**	**12**	**18**	**37**	**1**	**0**	**1**	**26:06**

NHL All-Rookie Team (1998)
Played in NHL All-Star Game (1999)

OLIVER, David

(AWL-ih-vuhr, DAY-vihd)

Right wing. Shoots right. 6', 190 lbs. Born, Sechelt, B.C., April 17, 1971. Edmonton's 7th choice, 144th overall, in 1991 Entry Draft.

Season	Club	League	GP	G	A	Pts	PIM	PP	SH	GW	S	%	+/-	TF	F%	Min	GP	G	A	Pts	PIM	PP	SH	GW	Min
1988-89	Vernon Lakers	BCJHL	58	41	38	79	38	....	....	....	....	....	....	....	....	....	....	....	....	....	....	....	....	....	....
1989-90	Vernon Lakers	BCJHL	58	51	48	99	22	....	....	....	....	....	....	....	....	....	....	....	....	....	....	....	....	....	....
1990-91	U. of Michigan	CCHA	27	13	11	24	34	....	....	....	....	....	....	....	....	....	....	....	....	....	....	....	....	....	....
1991-92	U. of Michigan	CCHA	44	31	27	58	32	....	....	....	....	....	....	....	....	....	....	....	....	....	....	....	....	....	....
1992-93	U. of Michigan	CCHA	40	35	20	55	18	....	....	....	....	....	....	....	....	....	....	....	....	....	....	....	....	....	....
1993-94	U. of Michigan	CCHA	41	28	40	68	16	....	....	....	....	....	....	....	....	....	....	....	....	....	....	....	....	....	....
1994-95	Cape Breton	AHL	32	11	18	29	8	....	....	....	....	....	....	....	....	....	....	....	....	....	....	....	....	....	....
	Edmonton	**NHL**	**44**	**16**	**14**	**30**	**20**	**10**	**0**	**0**	**79**	**20.3**	**–11**	....	....	....	....	....	....	....	....	....	....	....	....
1995-96	**Edmonton**	**NHL**	**80**	**20**	**19**	**39**	**34**	**14**	**0**	**0**	**131**	**15.3**	**–22**	....	....	....	....	....	....	....	....	....	....	....	....
1996-97	**Edmonton**	**NHL**	**17**	**1**	**2**	**3**	**4**	**0**	**0**	**0**	**22**	**4.5**	**–8**	....	....	....	....	....	....	....	....	....	....	....	....
	NY Rangers	**NHL**	**14**	**2**	**1**	**3**	**4**	**0**	**0**	**0**	**13**	**15.4**	**3**	....	....	....	**3**	**0**	**0**	**0**	**0**	**0**	**0**	**0**	....
1997-98	Houston Aeros	IHL	78	38	27	65	60	....	....	....	....	....	....	....	....	....	4	3	0	3	4	....	....	....	....
1998-99	**Ottawa**	**NHL**	**17**	**2**	**5**	**7**	**4**	**0**	**0**	**0**	**18**	**11.1**	**1**	**3**	**33.3**	**10:34**	....	....	....	....	....	....	....	....	....
	Houston Aeros	IHL	37	18	17	35	30	....	....	....	....	....	....	....	....	....	19	10	6	16	22	....	....	....	....
99-2000	**Phoenix**	**NHL**	**9**	**1**	**0**	**1**	**2**	**1**	**0**	**0**	**6**	**16.7**	**0**	**0**	**0.0**	**7:38**	....	....	....	....	....	....	....	....	....
	Houston Aeros	IHL	45	16	11	27	40	....	....	....	....	....	....	....	....	....	11	3	4	7	8	....	....	....	....
2000-01	**Ottawa**	**NHL**	**7**	**0**	**0**	**0**	**2**	**0**	**0**	**0**	**2**	**0.0**	**0**	**0**	**0.0**	**5:37**	....	....	....	....	....	....	....	....	....
	Grand Rapids	IHL	51	14	17	31	35	....	....	....	....	....	....	....	....	....	10	6	2	8	8	....	....	....	....
2001-02	Munchen Barons	Germany	59	20	14	34	30	....	....	....	....	....	....	....	....	....	9	2	2	4	6	....	....	....	....
2002-03	**Dallas**	**NHL**	**6**	**0**	**3**	**3**	**2**	**0**	**0**	**0**	**5**	**0.0**	**1**	**0**	**0.0**	**9:13**	**6**	**0**	**0**	**0**	**2**	**0**	**0**	**0**	**6:33**
	Utah Grizzlies	AHL	37	11	14	25	14	....	....	....	....	....	....	....	....	....	....	....	....	....	....	....	....	....	....
2003-04	**Dallas**	**NHL**	**36**	**7**	**5**	**12**	**12**	**3**	**0**	**1**	**30**	**23.3**	**6**	**1**	**100.0**	**9:51**	**1**	**0**	**0**	**0**	**0**	**0**	**0**	**0**	**7:31**
	Utah Grizzlies	AHL	31	5	12	17	12	....	....	....	....	....	....	....	....	....	....	....	....	....	....	....	....	....	....
	NHL Totals		**230**	**49**	**49**	**98**	**84**	**28**	**0**	**1**	**306**	**16.0**		**4**	**50.0**	**9:18**	**10**	**0**	**0**	**0**	**2**	**0**	**0**	**0**	**6:41**

CCHA Second All-Star Team (1993) • CCHA First All-Star Team (1994) • CCHA Player of the Year (1994) • NCAA West First All-American Team (1994)

Claimed on waivers by **NY Rangers** from **Edmonton**, February 21, 1997. Signed as a free agent by **Ottawa**, July 2, 1998. Signed as a free agent by **Phoenix**, July 20, 1999. Signed as a free agent by **Ottawa**, August 2, 2000. Signed as a free agent by **Dallas**, July 30, 2002.

OLIWA, Krzysztof

(oh-LEE-vuh, KHRIH-stahf) **N.J.**

Left wing. Shoots left. 6'5", 245 lbs. Born, Tychy, Poland, April 12, 1973. New Jersey's 4th choice, 65th overall, in 1993 Entry Draft.

Season	Club	League	GP	G	A	Pts	PIM	PP	SH	GW	S	%	+/-	TF	F%	Min	GP	G	A	Pts	PIM	PP	SH	GW	Min
1990-91	GKS Katowski Jr.	Poland-Jr.	5	4	4	8	10	....	....	....	....	....	....	....	....	....	....	....	....	....	....	....	....	....	....
1991-92	GKS Tychy	Poland	10	3	7	10	6	....	....	....	....	....	....	....	....	....	....	....	....	....	....	....	....	....	....
1992-93	Welland Cougars	OJHL-B	30	13	21	34	127	....	....	....	....	....	....	....	....	....	....	....	....	....	....	....	....	....	....
1993-94	Albany River Rats	AHL	33	2	4	6	151	....	....	....	....	....	....	....	....	....	....	....	....	....	....	....	....	....	....
	Raleigh IceCaps	ECHL	15	0	2	2	65	....	....	....	....	....	....	....	....	....	9	0	0	0	35	....	....	....	....
1994-95	Albany River Rats	AHL	20	1	1	2	77	....	....	....	....	....	....	....	....	....	....	....	....	....	....	....	....	....	....
	Saint John Flames	AHL	14	1	4	5	79	....	....	....	....	....	....	....	....	....	....	....	....	....	....	....	....	....	....
	Raleigh IceCaps	ECHL	5	0	2	2	32	....	....	....	....	....	....	....	....	....	....	....	....	....	....	....	....	....	....
	Detroit Vipers	IHL	4	0	1	1	24	....	....	....	....	....	....	....	....	....	....	....	....	....	....	....	....	....	....
1995-96	Albany River Rats	AHL	51	5	11	16	217	....	....	....	....	....	....	....	....	....	....	....	....	....	....	....	....	....	....
	Raleigh IceCaps	ECHL	9	1	0	1	53	....	....	....	....	....	....	....	....	....	....	....	....	....	....	....	....	....	....
1996-97	**New Jersey**	**NHL**	**1**	**0**	**0**	**0**	**5**	**0**	**0**	**0**	**0**	**0.0**	**–1**	....	....	....	....	....	....	....	....	....	....	....	....
	Albany River Rats	AHL	60	13	14	27	322	....	....	....	....	....	....	....	....	....	15	7	1	8	49	....	....	....	....
1997-98	**New Jersey**	**NHL**	**73**	**2**	**3**	**5**	**295**	**0**	**0**	**2**	**53**	**3.8**	**3**	....	....	....	**6**	**0**	**0**	**0**	**23**	**0**	**0**	**0**	....
1998-99	**New Jersey**	**NHL**	**64**	**5**	**7**	**12**	**240**	**0**	**0**	**1**	**59**	**8.5**	**4**	**1**	**0.0**	**7:02**	**1**	**0**	**0**	**0**	**2**	**0**	**0**	**0**	**2:35**
99-2000♦	**New Jersey**	**NHL**	**69**	**6**	**10**	**16**	**184**	**1**	**0**	**2**	**61**	**9.8**	**–2**	**3**	**66.7**	**6:45**	....	....	....	....	....	....	....	....	....
2000-01	**Columbus**	**NHL**	**10**	**0**	**2**	**2**	**34**	**0**	**0**	**0**	**5**	**0.0**	**1**	**0**	**0.0**	**5:17**	....	....	....	....	....	....	....	....	....
	Pittsburgh	**NHL**	**26**	**1**	**2**	**3**	**131**	**0**	**0**	**0**	**17**	**5.9**	**–4**	**1**	**100.0**	**4:58**	**5**	**0**	**0**	**0**	**16**	**0**	**0**	**0**	**2:14**
2001-02	**Pittsburgh**	**NHL**	**57**	**0**	**2**	**2**	**150**	**0**	**0**	**0**	**31**	**0.0**	**–5**	**0**	**0.0**	**5:35**	....	....	....	....	....	....	....	....	....
2002-03	**NY Rangers**	**NHL**	**9**	**0**	**0**	**0**	**51**	**0**	**0**	**0**	**3**	**0.0**	**1**	**1**	**0.0**	**3:45**	....	....	....	....	....	....	....	....	....
	Hartford	AHL	15	0	1	1	30	....	....	....	....	....	....	....	....	....	....	....	....	....	....	....	....	....	....
	Boston	**NHL**	**33**	**0**	**0**	**0**	**110**	**0**	**0**	**0**	**11**	**0.0**	**–4**	**1**	**0.0**	**3:58**	....	....	....	....	....	....	....	....	....
2003-04	**Calgary**	**NHL**	**65**	**3**	**2**	**5**	**247**	**0**	**0**	**0**	**32**	**9.4**	**–8**	**5**	**20.0**	**4:56**	**20**	**2**	**0**	**2**	**6**	**0**	**0**	**0**	**3:44**
	NHL Totals		**407**	**17**	**28**	**45**	**1447**	**1**	**0**	**5**	**272**	**6.3**		**12**	**33.3**	**5:42**	**32**	**2**	**0**	**2**	**47**	**0**	**0**	**0**	**3:24**

Traded to **Columbus** by **New Jersey** with future considerations (Deron Quint, June 23, 2000) for Columbus' 3rd round choice (Brandon Nolan) in 2001 Entry Draft and future considerations (Turner Stevenson, June 23, 2000), June 12, 2000. • Missed majority of 2000-2001 season recovering from arm injury suffered in game vs. Detroit, October 28, 2000. Traded to **Pittsburgh** by **Columbus** for San Jose's 3rd round choice (previously acquired, Columbus selected Aaron Johnson) in 2001 Entry Draft, January 14, 2001. Traded to **NY Rangers** by **Pittsburgh** for NY Rangers' 9th round choice (later traded to Tampa Bay – Tampa Bay selected Albert Vishnyakov) in 2003 Entry Draft, June 23, 2002. Traded to **Boston** by **NY Rangers** for Boston's 9th round choice (later traded to San Jose - San Jose selected Brian Mahoney-Wilson) in 2004 Entry Draft, January 6, 2003. Signed as a free agent by **Calgary**, July 30, 2003. Signed as a free agent by **New Jersey**, July 15, 2004.

OLSON, Josh

(OHL-suhn, JAWSH) **FLA.**

Left wing. Shoots left. 6'5", 225 lbs. Born, Grand Forks, ND, July 13, 1981. Florida's 6th choice, 190th overall, in 2000 Entry Draft.

Season	Club	League	GP	G	A	Pts	PIM	PP	SH	GW	S	%	+/-	TF	F%	Min	GP	G	A	Pts	PIM	PP	SH	GW	Min
1998-99	Fargo-Moorhead	USHL	11	2	2	4	8	....	....	....	....	....	....	....	....	....	....	....	....	....	....	....	....	....	....
99-2000	Fargo-Moorhead	USHL	18	2	5	7	37	....	....	....	....	....	....	....	....	....	....	....	....	....	....	....	....	....	....
	Omaha Lancers	USHL	43	6	7	13	44	....	....	....	....	....	....	....	....	....	4	0	0	0	4	....	....	....	....
2000-01	Portland	WHL	72	22	38	60	86	....	....	....	....	....	....	....	....	....	16	5	4	9	17	....	....	....	....
2001-02	Portland	WHL	72	40	48	88	85	....	....	....	....	....	....	....	....	....	7	4	3	7	8	....	....	....	....
	Utah Grizzlies	AHL	1	0	0	0	0	....	....	....	....	....	....	....	....	....	1	0	0	0	0	....	....	....	....
2002-03	San Antonio	AHL	23	0	1	1	14	....	....	....	....	....	....	....	....	....	....	....	....	....	....	....	....	....	....
	Jackson Bandits	ECHL	39	10	17	27	13	....	....	....	....	....	....	....	....	....	1	0	1	1	0	....	....	....	....
2003-04	**Florida**	**NHL**	**5**	**1**	**0**	**1**	**0**	**0**	**0**	**0**	**6**	**16.7**	**1**	**0**	**0.0**	**8:17**	....	....	....	....	....	....	....	....	....
	San Antonio	AHL	73	22	16	38	33	....	....	....	....	....	....	....	....	....	....	....	....	....	....	....	....	....	....
	NHL Totals		**5**	**1**	**0**	**1**	**0**	**0**	**0**	**0**	**6**	**16.7**		**0**	**0.0**	**8:17**	....	....	....	....	....	....	....	....	....

OLVESTAD, Jimmie

(OHL-vuh-stahd, JIHM-mee)

Left wing. Shoots left. 6'1", 189 lbs. Born, Stockholm, Sweden, February 16, 1980. Tampa Bay's 4th choice, 88th overall, in 1999 Entry Draft.

Season	Club	League	GP	G	A	Pts	PIM	PP	SH	GW	S	%	+/-	TF	F%	Min	GP	G	A	Pts	PIM	PP	SH	GW	Min
1996-97	Huddinge IK Jr.	Swede-Jr.	40	15	16	31	....	....	....	....	....	....	....	....	....	....	....	....	....	....	....	....	....	....	....
1997-98	Djurgarden Jr.	Swede-Jr.	10	3	3	6	10	....	....	....	....	....	....	....	....	....	....	....	....	....	....	....	....	....	....
	Huddinge IK	Swede-2	11	0	0	0	6	....	....	....	....	....	....	....	....	....	....	....	....	....	....	....	....	....	....
1998-99	Djurgarden	Sweden	44	2	4	6	18	....	....	....	....	....	....	....	....	....	4	0	0	0	8	....	....	....	....
99-2000	Djurgarden	Sweden	50	6	3	9	34	....	....	....	....	....	....	....	....	....	13	1	2	3	12	....	....	....	....
2000-01	Djurgarden	Sweden	50	7	8	15	79	....	....	....	....	....	....	....	....	....	16	7	2	9	14	....	....	....	....

							Regular Season										Playoffs								
Season	Club	League	GP	G	A	Pts	PIM	PP	SH	GW	S	%	+/-	TF	F%	Min	GP	G	A	Pts	PIM	PP	SH	GW	Min
2001-02	**Tampa Bay**	**NHL**	**74**	**3**	**11**	**14**	**24**	**0**	**0**	**0**	**99**	**3.0**	**3**	**14**	**28.6**	**14:00**	....	....	....	....	....	....	....	....	....
2002-03	**Tampa Bay**	**NHL**	**37**	**0**	**3**	**3**	**16**	**0**	**0**	**0**	**30**	**0.0**	**–2**	**12**	**33.3**	**10:28**	....	....	....	....	....	....	....	....	....
	Springfield	AHL	6	0	1	1	13	....	....	....	....	....	....	....	....	....	....	....	....	....	....	....	....	....	....
2003-04	Hamilton	AHL	76	7	14	21	56	....	....	....	....	....	....	....	....	....	4	2	0	2	4	....	....	....	....
	NHL Totals		**111**	**3**	**14**	**17**	**40**	**0**	**0**	**0**	**129**	**2.3**		**26**	**30.8**	**12:49**	....	....	....	....	....	....	....	....	....

Signed as a free agent by **Djurgarden** (Sweden), April 27, 2004.

O'NEILL, Jeff

(oh-NEEL, JEHF) **CAR.**

Right wing. Shoots right. 6'1", 195 lbs. Born, Richmond Hill, Ont., February 23, 1976. Hartford's 1st choice, 5th overall, in 1994 Entry Draft.

1990-91	Richmond Hill	OMHA	78	56	134	190	....	....	....	....	....	....	....	....	....	....	....	....	....	....	....	....	....	....	....
1991-92	Thornhill	MTJHL	43	27	*53	80	48	....	....	....	....	....	....	....	....	....	....	....	....	....	....	....	....	....	....
1992-93	Guelph Storm	OHL	65	32	47	79	88	....	....	....	....	....	....	....	....	....	5	2	2	4	6	....	....	....	....
1993-94	Guelph Storm	OHL	66	45	81	126	95	....	....	....	....	....	....	....	....	....	9	2	11	13	31	....	....	....	....
1994-95	Guelph Storm	OHL	57	43	81	124	56	....	....	....	....	....	....	....	....	....	14	8	18	26	34	....	....	....	....
1995-96	**Hartford**	**NHL**	**65**	**8**	**19**	**27**	**40**	**1**	**0**	**1**	**65**	**12.3**	**–3**	....	....	....	....	....	....	....	....	....	....	....	....
1996-97	**Hartford**	**NHL**	**72**	**14**	**16**	**30**	**40**	**2**	**1**	**2**	**101**	**13.9**	**–24**	....	....	....	....	....	....	....	....	....	....	....	....
	Springfield	AHL	1	0	0	0	0	....	....	....	....	....	....	....	....	....	....	....	....	....	....	....	....	....	....
1997-98	**Carolina**	**NHL**	**74**	**19**	**20**	**39**	**67**	**7**	**1**	**4**	**114**	**16.7**	**–8**	....	....	....	....	....	....	....	....	....	....	....	....
1998-99	**Carolina**	**NHL**	**75**	**16**	**15**	**31**	**66**	**4**	**0**	**2**	**121**	**13.2**	**3**	**941**	**45.6**	**16:44**	**6**	**0**	**1**	**1**	**0**	**0**	**0**	**0**	**19:25**
99-2000	**Carolina**	**NHL**	**80**	**25**	**38**	**63**	**72**	**4**	**0**	**7**	**189**	**13.2**	**–9**	**1337**	**49.5**	**19:20**	....	....	....	....	....	....	....	....	....
2000-01	**Carolina**	**NHL**	**82**	**41**	**26**	**67**	**106**	**17**	**0**	**5**	**242**	**16.9**	**–18**	**726**	**50.0**	**18:20**	**6**	**1**	**2**	**3**	**10**	**0**	**0**	**1**	**17:33**
2001-02	**Carolina**	**NHL**	**76**	**31**	**33**	**64**	**63**	**11**	**0**	**6**	**272**	**11.4**	**–5**	**831**	**56.7**	**19:44**	**22**	**8**	**5**	**13**	**27**	**3**	**0**	**1**	**19:00**
2002-03	**Carolina**	**NHL**	**82**	**30**	**31**	**61**	**38**	**11**	**0**	**7**	**316**	**9.5**	**–21**	**986**	**54.1**	**19:09**	....	....	....	....	....	....	....	....	....
2003-04	**Carolina**	**NHL**	**67**	**14**	**20**	**34**	**60**	**7**	**0**	**4**	**207**	**6.8**	**–12**	**660**	**57.6**	**17:29**	....	....	....	....	....	....	....	....	....
	NHL Totals		**673**	**198**	**218**	**416**	**552**	**64**	**2**	**38**	**1627**	**12.2**		**5481**	**51.8**	**18:30**	**34**	**9**	**8**	**17**	**37**	**3**	**0**	**2**	**18:49**

OHL All-Rookie Team (1993) • OHL Rookie of the Year (1993) • OHL First All-Star Team (1995)
Played in NHL All-Star Game (2003)
Transferred to **Carolina** after **Hartford** franchise relocated, June 25, 1997.

ORPIK, Brooks

(OHR-pihk, BRUKS) **PIT.**

Defense. Shoots left. 6'2", 228 lbs. Born, San Francisco, CA, September 26, 1980. Pittsburgh's 1st choice, 18th overall, in 2000 Entry Draft.

1996-97	Thayer Academy	Hi-School	20	4	1	5	....	....	....	....	....	....	....	....	....	....	....	....	....	....	....	....	....	....	....
1997-98	Thayer Academy	Hi-School	22	0	7	7	....	....	....	....	....	....	....	....	....	....	....	....	....	....	....	....	....	....	....
1998-99	Boston College	H-East	41	1	10	11	*96	....	....	....	....	....	....	....	....	....	....	....	....	....	....	....	....	....	....
99-2000	Boston College	H-East	38	1	9	10	102	....	....	....	....	....	....	....	....	....	....	....	....	....	....	....	....	....	....
2000-01	Boston College	H-East	40	0	20	20	*124	....	....	....	....	....	....	....	....	....	....	....	....	....	....	....	....	....	....
2001-02	Wilkes-Barre	AHL	78	2	18	20	99	....	....	....	....	....	....	....	....	....	....	....	....	....	....	....	....	....	....
2002-03	**Pittsburgh**	**NHL**	**6**	**0**	**0**	**0**	**2**	**0**	**0**	**0**	**2**	**0.0**	**–5**	**0**	**0.0**	**18:19**	....	....	....	....	....	....	....	....	....
	Wilkes-Barre	AHL	71	4	14	18	105	....	....	....	....	....	....	....	....	....	6	0	0	0	14	....	....	....	....
2003-04	**Pittsburgh**	**NHL**	**79**	**1**	**9**	**10**	**127**	**0**	**0**	**0**	**56**	**1.8**	**–36**	**0**	**0.0**	**18:25**	....	....	....	....	....	....	....	....	....
	Wilkes-Barre	AHL	3	0	0	0	2	....	....	....	....	....	....	....	....	....	24	0	4	4	53	....	....	....	....
	NHL Totals		**85**	**1**	**9**	**10**	**129**	**0**	**0**	**0**	**58**	**1.7**		**0**	**0.0**	**18:25**	....	....	....	....	....	....	....	....	....

ORR, Colton

(OHR, KOHL-tuhn) **BOS.**

Right wing. Shoots right. 6'3", 210 lbs. Born, Winnipeg, Man., March 3, 1982.

1998-99	St. Boniface	MJHL	STATISTICS NOT AVAILABLE																						
	Swift Current	WHL	2	0	0	0	0	....	....	....	....	....	....	....	....	....	....	....	....	....	....	....	....	....	....
99-2000	Swift Current	WHL	61	3	2	5	130	....	....	....	....	....	....	....	....	....	12	1	0	1	25	....	....	....	....
2000-01	Swift Current	WHL	19	0	4	4	67	....	....	....	....	....	....	....	....	....	....	....	....	....	....	....	....	....	....
	Kamloops Blazers	WHL	41	8	1	9	179	....	....	....	....	....	....	....	....	....	3	0	0	0	20	....	....	....	....
2001-02	Kamloops Blazers	WHL	1	0	0	0	7	....	....	....	....	....	....	....	....	....	2	0	0	0	2	....	....	....	....
2002-03	Kamloops Blazers	WHL	3	2	0	2	17	....	....	....	....	....	....	....	....	....	....	....	....	....	....	....	....	....	....
	Regina Pats	WHL	37	6	2	8	170	....	....	....	....	....	....	....	....	....	3	0	0	0	19	....	....	....	....
	Providence Bruins	AHL	1	0	0	0	7	....	....	....	....	....	....	....	....	....	....	....	....	....	....	....	....	....	....
2003-04	**Boston**	**NHL**	**1**	**0**	**0**	**0**	**0**	**0**	**0**	**0**	**0**	**0.0**	**–1**	**0**	**0.0**	**2:13**	....	....	....	....	....	....	....	....	....
	Providence Bruins	AHL	64	1	4	5	257	....	....	....	....	....	....	....	....	....	2	0	0	0	9	....	....	....	....
	NHL Totals		**1**	**0**	**0**	**0**	**0**	**0**	**0**	**0**	**0**	**0.0**		**0**	**0.0**	**2:13**	....	....	....	....	....	....	....	....	....

Signed as a free agent by **Boston**, September 19, 2001. • Missed majority of 2001-02 season recovering from wrist injury suffered in game vs. Red Deer (WHL), October 20, 2001.

ORSZAGH, Vladimir

(OHR-sahg, vla-DIH-meer) **NSH.**

Right wing. Shoots left. 5'11", 195 lbs. Born, Banska Bystrica, Czech., May 24, 1977. NY Islanders' 4th choice, 106th overall, in 1995 Entry Draft.

1993-94	B. Bystrica Jr.	Slovak-Jr.	38	38	27	65	....	....	....	....	....	....	....	....	....	....	....	....	....	....	....	....	....	....	....
1994-95	Banska Bystrica	Slovak-2	38	18	12	30	....	....	....	....	....	....	....	....	....	....	....	....	....	....	....	....	....	....	....
1995-96	Banska Bystrica	Slovakia	31	9	5	14	22	....	....	....	....	....	....	....	....	....	....	....	....	....	....	....	....	....	....
1996-97	Utah Grizzlies	IHL	68	12	15	27	30	....	....	....	....	....	....	....	....	....	3	0	1	1	4	....	....	....	....
1997-98	**NY Islanders**	**NHL**	**11**	**0**	**1**	**1**	**2**	**0**	**0**	**0**	**9**	**0.0**	**–3**	....	....	....	....	....	....	....	....	....	....	....	....
	Utah Grizzlies	IHL	62	13	10	23	60	....	....	....	....	....	....	....	....	....	4	2	0	2	0	....	....	....	....
1998-99	**NY Islanders**	**NHL**	**12**	**1**	**0**	**1**	**6**	**0**	**0**	**0**	**4**	**20.0**	**2**	**0**	**0.0**	**6:36**	....	....	....	....	....	....	....	....	....
	Lowell	AHL	68	18	23	41	57	....	....	....	....	....	....	....	....	....	3	2	2	4	2	....	....	....	....
99-2000	**NY Islanders**	**NHL**	**11**	**2**	**1**	**3**	**4**	**0**	**0**	**0**	**16**	**12.5**	**1**	**0**	**0.0**	**11:55**	....	....	....	....	....	....	....	....	....
	Lowell	AHL	55	8	12	20	22	....	....	....	....	....	....	....	....	....	7	3	3	6	2	....	....	....	....
2000-01	Djurgarden	Sweden	50	23	13	36	62	....	....	....	....	....	....	....	....	....	16	*7	3	10	20	....	....	....	....
2001-02	**Nashville**	**NHL**	**79**	**15**	**21**	**36**	**56**	**5**	**0**	**3**	**113**	**13.3**	**–15**	**10**	**20.0**	**16:04**	....	....	....	....	....	....	....	....	....
2002-03	**Nashville**	**NHL**	**78**	**16**	**16**	**32**	**38**	**3**	**0**	**3**	**152**	**10.5**	**–1**	**17**	**29.4**	**17:34**	....	....	....	....	....	....	....	....	....
2003-04	**Nashville**	**NHL**	**82**	**16**	**21**	**37**	**74**	**2**	**2**	**3**	**124**	**12.9**	**–4**	**39**	**25.6**	**17:00**	**6**	**2**	**0**	**2**	**4**	**0**	**0**	**0**	**16:08**
	NHL Totals		**273**	**50**	**60**	**110**	**180**	**10**	**2**	**9**	**418**	**12.0**		**66**	**25.8**	**16:12**	**6**	**2**	**0**	**2**	**4**	**0**	**0**	**0**	**16:08**

Signed as a free agent by **Nashville**, May 30, 2001.

ORTMEYER, Jed

(OHRT-migh-uhr, JEHD) **NYR**

Center. Shoots right. 6'1", 186 lbs. Born, Omaha, NE, September 3, 1978.

1997-98	Omaha Lancers	USHL	54	23	25	48	52	....	....	....	....	....	....	....	....	....	14	3	4	7	31	....	....	....	....
1998-99	Omaha Lancers	USHL	52	23	36	59	81	....	....	....	....	....	....	....	....	....	12	5	6	11	16	....	....	....	....
99-2000	U. of Michigan	CCHA	41	8	16	24	40	....	....	....	....	....	....	....	....	....	....	....	....	....	....	....	....	....	....
2000-01	U. of Michigan	CCHA	27	10	11	21	52	....	....	....	....	....	....	....	....	....	....	....	....	....	....	....	....	....	....
2001-02	U. of Michigan	CCHA	41	15	23	38	40	....	....	....	....	....	....	....	....	....	....	....	....	....	....	....	....	....	....
2002-03	U. of Michigan	CCHA	36	18	16	34	48	....	....	....	....	....	....	....	....	....	....	....	....	....	....	....	....	....	....
2003-04	**NY Rangers**	**NHL**	**58**	**2**	**4**	**6**	**16**	**0**	**0**	**0**	**48**	**4.2**	**–10**	**16**	**31.3**	**9:52**	....	....	....	....	....	....	....	....	....
	Hartford	AHL	13	2	8	10	4	....	....	....	....	....	....	....	....	....	16	5	2	7	6	....	....	....	....
	NHL Totals		**58**	**2**	**4**	**6**	**16**	**0**	**0**	**0**	**48**	**4.2**		**16**	**31.3**	**9:52**	....	....	....	....	....	....	....	....	....

Signed as a free agent by **NY Rangers**, May 10, 2003.

OTT, Steve

(AWT, STEEV) **DAL.**

Center. Shoots left. 6', 185 lbs. Born, Summerside, P.E.I., August 19, 1982. Dallas' 1st choice, 25th overall, in 2000 Entry Draft.

1998-99	Leamington Flyers	OJHL-B	48	14	30	44	110	....	....	....	....	....	....	....	....	....	....	....	....	....	....	....	....	....	....
99-2000	Windsor Spitfires	OHL	66	23	39	62	131	....	....	....	....	....	....	....	....	....	12	3	5	8	21	....	....	....	....
2000-01	Windsor Spitfires	OHL	55	50	37	87	164	....	....	....	....	....	....	....	....	....	9	3	8	11	27	....	....	....	....
2001-02	Windsor Spitfires	OHL	53	43	45	88	178	....	....	....	....	....	....	....	....	....	14	6	10	16	49	....	....	....	....

			Regular Season														Playoffs								
Season	Club	League	GP	G	A	Pts	PIM	PP	SH	GW	S	%	+/-	TF	F%	Min	GP	G	A	Pts	PIM	PP	SH	GW	Min
2002-03	Dallas	NHL	26	3	4	7	31	0	0	0	25	12.0	6	4	50.0	8:46	1	0	0	0	0	0	0	0	6:57
	Utah Grizzlies	AHL	40	9	11	20	98																		
2003-04	Dallas	NHL	73	2	10	12	152	0	0	1	74	2.7	−2	59	49.2	10:14	4	1	0	1	0	0	0	1	6:55
	NHL Totals		99	5	14	19	183	0	0	1	99	5.1		63	49.2	9:51	5	1	0	1	0	0	0	1	6:55

OHL Second All-Star Team (2002)

OZOLINSH, Sandis

(OH-zoh-LIHNCH, SAN-dihz) **ANA.**

Defense. Shoots left. 6'3", 215 lbs. Born, Riga, Latvia, August 3, 1972. San Jose's 3rd choice, 30th overall, in 1991 Entry Draft.

Season	Club	League	GP	G	A	Pts	PIM	PP	SH	GW	S	%	+/-	TF	F%	Min	GP	G	A	Pts	PIM	PP	SH	GW	Min
1990-91	Dynamo Riga	USSR	44	0	3	3	51																		
1991-92	Riga Stars	CIS	30	6	0	6	42																		
	Kansas City	IHL	34	6	9	15	20										15	2	5	7	22				
1992-93	San Jose	NHL	37	7	16	23	40	2	0	0	83	8.4	−9												
1993-94	San Jose	NHL	81	26	38	64	24	4	0	3	157	16.6	16				14	0	10	10	8	0	0	0	
1994-95	San Jose	NHL	48	9	16	25	30	3	1	2	83	10.8	−6				11	3	2	5	6	1	0	0	
1995-96	San Francisco	IHL	2	1	0	1	0																		
	San Jose	NHL	7	1	3	4	4	1	0	0	21	4.8	2												
	♦ Colorado	NHL	66	13	37	50	50	7	1	1	145	9.0	0				22	5	14	19	16	2	0	1	
1996-97	Colorado	NHL	80	23	45	68	88	13	0	4	232	9.9	4				17	4	13	17	24	2	0	1	
1997-98	Colorado	NHL	66	13	38	51	65	9	0	2	135	9.6	−12				7	0	7	7	14	0	0	0	
1998-99	Colorado	NHL	39	7	25	32	22	4	0	3	81	8.6	10	0	0.0	22:06	19	4	8	12	22	3	0	1	22:24
99-2000	Colorado	NHL	82	16	36	52	46	6	0	1	210	7.6	17	0	0.0	22:41	17	5	5	10	20	3	0	1	18:35
2000-01	Carolina	NHL	72	12	32	44	71	4	2	2	145	8.3	−25	0	0.0	22:12	6	0	2	2	5	0	0	0	19:04
2001-02	Carolina	NHL	46	4	19	23	34	1	0	0	71	5.6	−4	0	0.0	19:30									
	Florida	NHL	37	10	19	29	24	2	0	1	101	9.9	−3	0	0.0	30:30									
	Latvia	Olympics	1	0	4	4	0																		
2002-03	Florida	NHL	51	7	19	26	40	5	0	2	83	8.4	−16	0	0.0	28:23									
	Anaheim	NHL	31	5	13	18	16	1	0	1	54	9.3	10	0	0.0	22:08	21	2	6	8	10	0	0	1	23:37
2003-04	Anaheim	NHL	36	5	11	16	24	1	0	2	58	8.6	−7	0	0.0	19:57									
	NHL Totals		779	158	367	525	578	63	4	24	1659	9.5		0	0.0	23:21	134	23	67	90	125	11	0	5	21:28

NHL First All-Star Team (1997)

Played in NHL All-Star Game (1994, 1997, 1998, 2000, 2001, 2002, 2003)

• Missed majority of 1992-93 season recovering from knee injury suffered in game vs. Philadelphia, December 30, 1992. Traded to **Colorado** by **San Jose** for Owen Nolan, October 26, 1995. Traded to **Carolina** by **Colorado** with Columbus' 2nd round choice (previously acquired, Carolina selected Tomas Kurka) in 2000 Entry Draft for Nolan Pratt, Carolina's 1st (Vaclav Nedorost) and 2nd (Jared Aulin) round choices in 2000 Entry Draft and Philadelphia's 2nd round choice (previously acquired, Colorado selected Agris Saviels) in 2000 Entry Draft, June 24, 2000. Traded to **Florida** by **Carolina** with Byron Ritchie for Bret Hedican, Kevyn Adams and Tomas Malec, January 16, 2002. Traded to **Anaheim** by **Florida** with Lance Ward for Pavel Trnka, Matt Cullen and Anaheim's 4th round choice (James Pemberton) in 2003 Entry Draft, January 30, 2003. • Missed majority of 2003-04 season recovering from shoulder injury suffered in game vs. Colorado, December 19, 2003.

PAHLSSON, Samuel

(PAWL-suhn, SAM-ew-l) **ANA.**

Center. Shoots left. 5'11", 212 lbs. Born, Ornskoldsvik, Sweden, December 17, 1977. Colorado's 10th choice, 176th overall, in 1996 Entry Draft.

Season	Club	League	GP	G	A	Pts	PIM	PP	SH	GW	S	%	+/-	TF	F%	Min	GP	G	A	Pts	PIM	PP	SH	GW	Min
1992-93	Ange IK	Swede-4	9	0	0	0	0																		
1993-94	Ange IK	Swede-4	STATISTICS NOT AVAILABLE																						
1994-95	MoDo Jr.	Swede-Jr.	30	10	11	21	26																		
	MoDo	Sweden	1	0	0	0	0																		
1995-96	MoDo Jr.	Swede-Jr.	5	2	6	8	2																		
	MoDo	Sweden	36	1	3	4	8										4	0	0	0	0				
1996-97	MoDo	Sweden	49	8	9	17	83																		
1997-98	MoDo	Sweden	23	6	11	17	24										9	3	0	3	6				
1998-99	MoDo	Sweden	50	17	17	34	44										13	3	3	6	10				
99-2000	MoDo	Sweden	47	16	11	27	67										13	3	3	6	8				
	MoDo	EuroHL	4	1	0	1	0										3	1	1	2	2				
2000-01	Boston	NHL	17	1	1	2	6	0	0	0	13	7.7	−5	239	40.2	14:19									
	Anaheim	NHL	59	3	4	7	14	1	1	1	46	6.5	−9	867	45.1	14:14									
2001-02	Anaheim	NHL	80	6	14	20	26	1	1	0	99	6.1	−16	1201	49.8	16:24									
2002-03	Anaheim	NHL	34	4	11	15	18	0	1	2	28	14.3	10	118	52.5	13:20	21	2	4	6	12	0	0	0	16:41
	Cincinnati	AHL	13	1	7	8	24																		
2003-04	Anaheim	NHL	82	8	14	22	52	1	0	2	134	6.0	−2	908	55.3	16:51									
	NHL Totals		272	22	44	66	116	3	3	5	320	6.9		3333	49.5	15:33	21	2	4	6	12	0	0	0	16:41

Traded to **Boston** by **Colorado** with Brian Rolston, Martin Grenier and New Jersey's 1st round choice (previously acquired, Boston selected Martin Samuelsson) in 2000 Entry Draft for Raymond Bourque and Dave Andreychuk, March 6, 2000. Traded to **Anaheim** by **Boston** for Patrick Traverse and Andrei Nazarov, November 18, 2000.

PALFFY, Ziggy

(PAHL-fee, ZIHG-gee)

Right wing. Shoots left. 5'10", 183 lbs. Born, Skalica, Czech., May 5, 1972. NY Islanders' 2nd choice, 26th overall, in 1991 Entry Draft.

Season	Club	League	GP	G	A	Pts	PIM	PP	SH	GW	S	%	+/-	TF	F%	Min	GP	G	A	Pts	PIM	PP	SH	GW	Min
1990-91	AC Nitra	Czech	50	34	16	50	18																		
1991-92	Dukla Trencin	Czech	45	41	33	74	36																		
1992-93	Dukla Trencin	Czech	43	38	41	79																			
1993-94	NY Islanders	NHL	5	0	0	0	0	0	0	0	5	0.0	−6												
	Salt Lake	IHL	57	25	32	57	83																		
	Slovakia	Olympics	8	3	*7	*10	8																		
1994-95	Denver Grizzlies	IHL	33	20	23	43	40																		
	NY Islanders	NHL	33	10	7	17	6	1	0	1	75	13.3	3												
1995-96	NY Islanders	NHL	81	43	44	87	56	17	1	6	257	16.7	−17												
1996-97	Dukla Trencin	Slovakia	1	0	0	0																			
	NY Islanders	NHL	80	48	42	90	43	6	4	6	292	16.4	21												
1997-98	NY Islanders	NHL	82	45	42	87	34	17	2	5	277	16.2	−2												
1998-99	HK 36 Skalica	Slovakia	9	11	8	19	6																		
	NY Islanders	NHL	50	22	28	50	34	5	2	1	168	13.1	−6	1	100.0	22:04									
99-2000	Los Angeles	NHL	64	27	39	66	32	4	0	3	186	14.5	18	7	42.9	19:39	4	2	0	2	0	0	0	0	21:21
2000-01	Los Angeles	NHL	73	38	51	89	20	12	4	8	217	17.5	22	5	80.0	19:46	13	3	5	8	8	0	0	0	22:27
2001-02	Los Angeles	NHL	63	32	27	59	26	15	1	6	161	19.9	5	3	66.7	20:18	7	4	5	9	0	0	0	0	22:23
	Slovakia	Olympics	1	0	0	0	0																		
2002-03	Los Angeles	NHL	76	37	48	85	47	10	2	5	277	13.4	22	10	30.0	22:27									
2003-04	Los Angeles	NHL	35	16	25	41	12	3	3	2	109	14.7	18	7	0.0	21:32									
	NHL Totals		642	318	353	671	310	90	19	43	2024	15.7		33	39.4	20:54	24	9	10	19	8	0	0	0	22:15

Played in NHL All-Star Game (1998, 2001, 2002)

Traded to **Los Angeles** by **NY Islanders** with Brian Smolinski, Marcel Cousineau and New Jersey's 4th round choice (previously acquired, Los Angeles selected Daniel Johansson) in 1999 Entry Draft for Olli Jokinen, Josh Green, Mathieu Biron and Los Angeles' 1st round choice (Taylor Pyatt) in 1999 Entry Draft, June 20, 1999. • Missed majority of 2003-04 season recovering from shoulder injury suffered in game vs. Anaheim, January 7, 2004.

PANDOLFO, Jay

(pan-DAHL-foh, JAY) **N.J.**

Left wing. Shoots left. 6'1", 190 lbs. Born, Winchester, MA, December 27, 1974. New Jersey's 2nd choice, 32nd overall, in 1993 Entry Draft.

Season	Club	League	GP	G	A	Pts	PIM	PP	SH	GW	S	%	+/-	TF	F%	Min	GP	G	A	Pts	PIM	PP	SH	GW	Min
1989-90	Burlington Prep	Hi-School	23	33	30	63	18																		
1990-91	Burlington Prep	Hi-School	20	19	27	46	10																		
1991-92	Burlington Prep	Hi-School	20	35	34	69	14																		
1992-93	Boston University	H-East	37	16	22	38	16																		
1993-94	Boston University	H-East	37	17	25	42	27																		
1994-95	Boston University	H-East	20	7	13	20	6																		
1995-96	Boston University	H-East	39	*38	29	67	6																		
	Albany River Rats	AHL	5	3	1	4	0										3	0	0	0	0				
1996-97	New Jersey	NHL	46	6	8	14	6	0	0	1	61	9.8	−1				6	0	1	1	0	0	0	0	
	Albany River Rats	AHL	12	3	9	12	0																		
1997-98	New Jersey	NHL	23	1	3	4	4	0	0	0	23	4.3	−4				3	0	2	2	0	0	0	0	
	Albany River Rats	AHL	51	18	19	37	24																		
1998-99	New Jersey	NHL	70	14	13	27	10	1	1	4	100	14.0	3	10	40.0	15:13	7	1	0	1	0	0	0	0	13:19
99-2000 ♦	New Jersey	NHL	71	7	8	15	4	0	0	0	86	8.1	0	19	47.4	13:25	23	0	5	5	0	0	0	0	15:35
2000-01	New Jersey	NHL	63	4	12	16	16	0	0	0	57	7.0	3	15	53.3	14:05	25	1	4	5	4	0	0	0	12:38
2001-02	New Jersey	NHL	65	4	10	14	15	0	1	0	72	5.6	12	12	41.7	13:59	6	0	0	0	0	0	0	0	16:11

Season	Club	League	GP	G	A	Pts	PIM	PP	SH	GW	S	%	+/-	TF	F%	Min	GP	G	A	Pts	PIM	PP	SH	GW	Min
			Regular Season														Playoffs								
2002-03♦	New Jersey	NHL	68	6	11	17	23	0	1	4	92	6.5	12	13	23.1	16:08	24	6	6	12	2	0	0	1	16:34
2003-04	New Jersey	NHL	82	13	13	26	14	1	2	4	140	9.3	5	25	44.0	16:00	5	0	0	0	0	0	0	0	13:41
	NHL Totals		488	55	78	133	92	2	5	13	631	8.7		94	42.6	14:51	99	8	18	26	6	0	0	1	14:47

Hockey East First All-Star Team (1996) • Hockey East Player of the Year (1996) • NCAA East First All-American Team (1996)

PANDOLFO, Mike

(pan-DAHL-foh, MIGHK) **CBJ**

Left wing. Shoots left. 6'3", 221 lbs. Born, Winchester, MA, September 15, 1979. Buffalo's 5th choice, 77th overall, in 1998 Entry Draft.

Season	Club	League	GP	G	A	Pts	PIM	PP	SH	GW	S	%	+/-	TF	F%	Min	GP	G	A	Pts	PIM	PP	SH	GW	Min
1996-97	St. Sebastian's	Hi-School	32	27	28	55	30																		
1997-98	St. Sebastian's	Hi-School	28	29	23	52	18																		
1998-99	Boston University	H-East	34	13	4	17	26																		
99-2000	Boston University	H-East	41	13	10	23	37																		
2000-01	Boston University	H-East	37	16	13	29	30																		
2001-02	Boston University	H-East	38	22	18	40	22																		
2002-03	Syracuse Crunch	AHL	74	9	9	18	31																		
2003-04	Columbus	NHL	3	0	0	0	0	0	0	0	3	0.0	−2	0	0.0	8:18									
	Syracuse Crunch	AHL	77	18	19	37	29										7	1	0	1	2				
	NHL Totals		3	0	0	0	0	0	0	0	3	0.0		0	0.0	8:18									

Rights traded to **Columbus** by **Buffalo** with Detroit's 1st round choice (previously acquired, later traded to Atlanta – Atlanta selected Jim Slater) in 2002 Entry Draft for New Jersey's 1st round choice (previously acquired, Buffalo selected Dan Paille) in 2002 Entry Draft, June 22, 2002.

PAPINEAU, Justin

(PA-pee-noh, JUHS-tihn) **NYI**

Center. Shoots left. 5'10", 178 lbs. Born, Ottawa, Ont., January 15, 1980. St. Louis' 3rd choice, 75th overall, in 2000 Entry Draft.

Season	Club	League	GP	G	A	Pts	PIM	PP	SH	GW	S	%	+/-	TF	F%	Min	GP	G	A	Pts	PIM	PP	SH	GW	Min
1995-96	Ottawa Jr. Sens	OCJHL	52	31	19	50	51																		
1996-97	Belleville Bulls	OHL	50	10	32	42	32																		
1997-98	Belleville Bulls	OHL	66	41	53	94	34										10	5	9	14	6				
1998-99	Belleville Bulls	OHL	68	52	47	99	28										21	*21	*30	*51	20				
99-2000	Belleville Bulls	OHL	60	40	36	76	52										16	4	12	16	16				
2000-01	Worcester IceCats	AHL	43	7	22	29	33										11	7	3	10	8				
2001-02	St. Louis	NHL	1	0	0	0	0	0	0	0	0	0.0	−2	7	42.9	8:40									
	Worcester IceCats	AHL	75	*38	38	76	86										3	1	2	3	4				
2002-03	St. Louis	NHL	11	2	1	3	0	0	0	1	15	13.3	−1	99	44.4	10:59									
	Worcester IceCats	AHL	44	21	17	38	42																		
	NY Islanders	NHL	5	1	2	3	4	0	0	1	8	12.5	1	15	53.3	14:50	1	0	0	0	0	0	0	0	5:12
	Bridgeport	AHL	5	7	1	8	4										7	1	3	4	7				
2003-04	NY Islanders	NHL	64	8	5	13	8	5	0	2	44	18.2	4	49	38.8	7:42									
	NHL Totals		81	11	8	19	12	5	0	4	67	16.4		170	43.5	8:36	1	0	0	0	0	0	0	0	5:12

• Re-entered NHL Entry Draft. Originally Los Angeles' 2nd choice, 46th overall, in 1998 Entry Draft.

Traded to **NY Islanders** by **St. Louis** with St. Louis' 2nd round choice (Jeremy Colliton) in 2003 Entry Draft for Chris Osgood and NY Islanders' 3rd round choice (Konstantin Barulin) in 2003 Entry Draft, March 11, 2003.

PARK, Richard

(PAHRK, RIH-chuhrd) **MIN.**

Right wing. Shoots right. 5'11", 190 lbs. Born, Seoul, South Korea, May 27, 1976. Pittsburgh's 2nd choice, 50th overall, in 1994 Entry Draft.

Season	Club	League	GP	G	A	Pts	PIM	PP	SH	GW	S	%	+/-	TF	F%	Min	GP	G	A	Pts	PIM	PP	SH	GW	Min
1991-92	Tor. Young Nats	MTHL	76	49	58	107	91																		
1992-93	Belleville Bulls	OHL	66	23	38	61	38										5	0	0	0	14				
1993-94	Belleville Bulls	OHL	59	27	49	76	70										12	3	5	8	18				
1994-95	Belleville Bulls	OHL	45	28	51	79	35										16	9	18	27	12				
	Pittsburgh	NHL	1	0	1	1	2	0	0	0	4	0.0	1				3	0	0	0	2	0	0	0	
1995-96	Belleville Bulls	OHL	6	7	6	13	2										14	18	12	30	10				
	Pittsburgh	NHL	56	4	6	10	36	0	1	1	62	6.5	3				1	0	0	0	0	0	0	0	
1996-97	Pittsburgh	NHL	1	0	0	0	0	0	0	0	1	0.0	−1												
	Cleveland	IHL	50	12	15	27	30																		
	Anaheim	NHL	11	1	1	2	10	0	0	0	9	11.1	0				11	0	1	1	2	0	0	0	
1997-98	Anaheim	NHL	15	0	2	2	8	0	0	0	14	0.0	−3												
	Cincinnati	AHL	56	17	26	43	36																		
1998-99	Philadelphia	NHL	7	0	0	0	0	0	0	0	5	0.0	−1	15	53.3	9:21									
	Philadelphia	AHL	75	41	42	83	33										16	9	6	15	4				
99-2000	Utah Grizzlies	IHL	82	28	32	60	36										5	1	0	1	0				
2000-01	Cleveland	IHL	75	27	21	48	29										4	0	2	2	4				
2001-02	Minnesota	NHL	63	10	15	25	10	2	1	2	115	8.7	−1	79	41.8	16:28									
	Houston Aeros	AHL	13	4	10	14	6																		
2002-03	Minnesota	NHL	81	14	10	24	16	2	2	3	149	9.4	−3	178	48.9	16:36	18	3	3	6	4	0	0	1	17:03
2003-04	Minnesota	NHL	73	13	12	25	28	4	0	1	142	9.2	0	379	40.1	16:30									
	NHL Totals		308	42	47	89	110	8	4	7	501	8.4		651	43.0	16:18	33	3	4	7	8	0	0	1	17:03

OHL All-Rookie Team (1993) • AHL Second All-Star Team (1999)

Traded to **Anaheim** by **Pittsburgh** for Roman Oksiuta, March 18, 1997. Signed as a free agent by **Philadelphia**, August 24, 1998. Signed as a free agent by **Utah** (IHL), September 22, 1999. Signed as a free agent by **Minnesota**, June 6, 2000.

PARKER, Scott

(PAR-kuhr, SKAWT) **S.J.**

Right wing. Shoots right. 6'5", 230 lbs. Born, Hanford, CA, January 29, 1978. Colorado's 4th choice, 20th overall, in 1998 Entry Draft.

Season	Club	League	GP	G	A	Pts	PIM	PP	SH	GW	S	%	+/-	TF	F%	Min	GP	G	A	Pts	PIM	PP	SH	GW	Min
1993-94	Alaska Arctic Ice	AAHL	34	8	12	20	86																		
1994-95	Spokane Braves	KIJHL	43	7	21	28	128																		
1995-96	Kelowna Rockets	WHL	64	3	4	7	159										6	0	0	0	12				
1996-97	Kelowna Rockets	WHL	68	18	8	26	*330										6	0	2	2	4				
1997-98	Kelowna Rockets	WHL	71	30	22	52	243										7	6	0	6	23				
1998-99	Colorado	NHL	27	0	0	0	71	0	0	0	3	0.0	−3	1	0.0	1:37									
	Hershey Bears	AHL	32	4	3	7	143										4	0	0	0	6				
99-2000	Hershey Bears	AHL	68	12	7	19	206										11	1	1	2	56				
2000-01♦	Colorado	NHL	69	2	3	5	155	0	0	1	35	5.7	−2	2	0.0	5:42	4	0	0	0	2	0	0	0	2:12
2001-02	Colorado	NHL	63	1	4	5	154	0	0	0	32	3.1	0	0	0.0	5:50									
2002-03	Colorado	NHL	43	1	3	4	82	0	0	0	20	5.0	6	0	0.0	6:15	1	0	0	0	2	0	0	0	1:44
2003-04	San Jose	NHL	50	1	3	4	101	0	0	0	20	5.0	0	5	40.0	6:37									
	NHL Totals		252	5	13	18	563	0	0	1	110	4.5		8	25.0	5:34	5	0	0	0	4	0	0	0	2:06

• Re-entered NHL Entry Draft. Originally New Jersey's 6th choice, 63rd overall, in 1996 Entry Draft.

Traded to **San Jose** by **Colorado** for Colorado's 5th round choice (previously acquired, Colorado selected Brad Richardson) in 2003 Entry Draft, June 21, 2003.

PARRISH, Mark

(PAIR-ihsh, MAHRK) **NYI**

Right wing. Shoots right. 5'11", 200 lbs. Born, Bloomington, MN, February 2, 1977. Colorado's 3rd choice, 79th overall, in 1996 Entry Draft.

Season	Club	League	GP	G	A	Pts	PIM	PP	SH	GW	S	%	+/-	TF	F%	Min	GP	G	A	Pts	PIM	PP	SH	GW	Min
1994-95	Jefferson Jaguars	Hi-School	27	40	20	60	42																		
1995-96	St. Cloud State	WCHA	39	15	13	28	30																		
1996-97	St. Cloud State	WCHA	35	*27	15	42	60																		
1997-98	Seattle	WHL	54	54	38	92	29										5	2	3	5	2				
	New Haven	AHL	1	1	0	1	2																		
1998-99	Florida	NHL	73	24	13	37	25	5	0	5	129	18.6	−6	1	0.0	13:59									
	New Haven	AHL	2	1	0	1	0																		
99-2000	Florida	NHL	81	26	18	44	39	6	0	3	152	17.1	1	8	75.0	14:04	4	0	1	1	0	0	0	0	12:37
2000-01	NY Islanders	NHL	70	17	13	30	28	6	0	3	123	13.8	−27	3	33.3	15:27									
2001-02	NY Islanders	NHL	78	30	30	60	32	9	1	6	162	18.5	10	10	40.0	16:48	7	2	1	3	6	2	0	0	17:27

Season	Club	League	GP	G	A	Pts	PIM	PP	SH	GW	S	%	+/-	TF	F%	Min	GP	G	A	Pts	PIM	PP	SH	GW	Min
								Regular Season									Playoffs								
2002-03	**NY Islanders**	**NHL**	**81**	**23**	**25**	**48**	**28**	**9**	**0**	**5**	**147**	**15.6**	**-11**	**9**	**44.4**	**16:12**	**5**	**1**	**0**	**1**	**4**	**1**	**0**	**0**	**16:02**
2003-04	**NY Islanders**	**NHL**	**59**	**24**	**11**	**35**	**18**	**6**	**0**	**6**	**105**	**22.9**	**8**	**5**	**20.0**	**17:20**	**5**	**1**	**2**	**3**	**0**	**0**	**0**	**0**	**20:35**
	NHL Totals		**442**	**144**	**110**	**254**	**170**	**41**	**1**	**28**	**818**	**17.6**		**36**	**44.4**	**15:35**	**21**	**4**	**4**	**8**	**10**	**3**	**0**	**0**	**16:56**

NCAA West Second All-American Team (1997) • WHL West First All-Star Team (1998)

Played in NHL All-Star Game (2002)

Rights traded to **Florida** by **Colorado** with Anaheim's 3rd round choice (previously acquired, Florida selected Lance Ward) in 1998 Entry Draft for Tom Fitzgerald, March 24, 1998. Traded to **NY Islanders** by **Florida** with Oleg Kvasha for Roberto Luongo and Olli Jokinen, June 24, 2000.

PATRICK, James
(PAT-rihk, JAYMS) **BUF.**

Defense. Shoots right. 6'2", 202 lbs. Born, Winnipeg, Man., June 14, 1963. NY Rangers' 1st choice, 9th overall, in 1981 Entry Draft.

Season	Club	League	GP	G	A	Pts	PIM	PP	SH	GW	S	%	+/-	TF	F%	Min	GP	G	A	Pts	PIM	PP	SH	GW	Min
1980-81	Prince Albert	SJHL	59	21	61	82	162																		
1981-82	North Dakota	WCHA	42	5	24	29	26																		
1982-83	North Dakota	WCHA	36	12	36	48	29																		
1983-84	Team Canada	Nat-Tm	63	7	24	31	52																		
	Canada	Olympics	7	0	3	3	4																		
	NY Rangers	**NHL**	**12**	**1**	**7**	**8**	**2**	**0**	**0**	**0**	**15**	**6.7**	**6**				**5**	**0**	**3**	**3**	**2**	**0**	**0**	**0**	
1984-85	**NY Rangers**	**NHL**	**75**	**8**	**28**	**36**	**71**	**4**	**1**	**1**	**101**	**7.9**	**-17**				**3**	**0**	**0**	**0**	**4**	**0**	**0**	**0**	
1985-86	**NY Rangers**	**NHL**	**75**	**14**	**29**	**43**	**88**	**2**	**1**	**1**	**131**	**10.7**	**14**				**16**	**1**	**5**	**6**	**34**	**0**	**0**	**0**	
1986-87	**NY Rangers**	**NHL**	**78**	**10**	**45**	**55**	**62**	**5**	**0**	**0**	**143**	**7.0**	**13**				**6**	**1**	**2**	**3**	**2**	**1**	**0**	**1**	
1987-88	**NY Rangers**	**NHL**	**70**	**17**	**45**	**62**	**52**	**9**	**0**	**1**	**187**	**9.1**	**16**												
1988-89	**NY Rangers**	**NHL**	**68**	**11**	**36**	**47**	**41**	**6**	**0**	**2**	**147**	**7.5**	**3**				**4**	**0**	**1**	**1**	**2**	**0**	**0**	**0**	
1989-90	**NY Rangers**	**NHL**	**73**	**14**	**43**	**57**	**50**	**9**	**0**	**0**	**136**	**10.3**	**4**				**10**	**3**	**8**	**11**	**0**	**2**	**0**	**1**	
1990-91	**NY Rangers**	**NHL**	**74**	**10**	**49**	**59**	**58**	**6**	**0**	**2**	**138**	**7.2**	**-5**				**6**	**0**	**0**	**0**	**6**	**0**	**0**	**0**	
1991-92	**NY Rangers**	**NHL**	**80**	**14**	**57**	**71**	**54**	**6**	**0**	**1**	**148**	**9.5**	**34**				**13**	**0**	**7**	**7**	**12**	**0**	**0**	**0**	
1992-93	**NY Rangers**	**NHL**	**60**	**5**	**21**	**26**	**61**	**3**	**0**	**0**	**99**	**5.1**	**1**												
1993-94	**NY Rangers**	**NHL**	**6**	**0**	**3**	**3**	**2**	**0**	**0**	**0**	**6**	**0.0**	**1**												
	Hartford	**NHL**	**47**	**8**	**20**	**28**	**32**	**4**	**1**	**2**	**65**	**12.3**	**-12**												
	Calgary	**NHL**	**15**	**2**	**2**	**4**	**6**	**1**	**0**	**0**	**20**	**10.0**	**6**				**7**	**0**	**1**	**1**	**6**	**0**	**0**	**0**	
1994-95	**Calgary**	**NHL**	**43**	**0**	**10**	**10**	**14**	**0**	**0**	**0**	**43**	**0.0**	**-3**				**5**	**0**	**1**	**1**	**0**	**0**	**0**	**0**	
1995-96	**Calgary**	**NHL**	**80**	**3**	**32**	**35**	**30**	**1**	**0**	**0**	**116**	**2.6**	**3**				**4**	**0**	**0**	**0**	**2**	**0**	**0**	**0**	
1996-97	**Calgary**	**NHL**	**19**	**3**	**1**	**4**	**6**	**1**	**0**	**0**	**22**	**13.6**	**2**												
1997-98	**Calgary**	**NHL**	**60**	**6**	**11**	**17**	**26**	**1**	**0**	**1**	**57**	**10.5**	**-2**												
1998-99	**Buffalo**	**NHL**	**45**	**1**	**7**	**8**	**16**	**0**	**0**	**0**	**31**	**3.2**	**12**	**0**	**0.0**	**14:45**	**20**	**0**	**1**	**1**	**12**	**0**	**0**	**0**	**13:57**
99-2000	**Buffalo**	**NHL**	**66**	**5**	**8**	**13**	**22**	**0**	**0**	**3**	**40**	**12.5**	**8**	**0**	**0.0**	**15:59**	**5**	**0**	**1**	**1**	**2**	**0**	**0**	**0**	**15:23**
2000-01	**Buffalo**	**NHL**	**54**	**4**	**9**	**13**	**12**	**1**	**0**	**0**	**48**	**8.3**	**9**	**0**	**0.0**	**17:16**	**13**	**1**	**2**	**3**	**2**	**0**	**0**	**0**	**20:10**
2001-02	**Buffalo**	**NHL**	**56**	**5**	**8**	**13**	**16**	**1**	**0**	**0**	**45**	**11.1**	**3**	**0**	**0.0**	**16:27**									
2002-03	**Buffalo**	**NHL**	**69**	**4**	**12**	**16**	**26**	**2**	**0**	**1**	**63**	**6.3**	**-3**	**2**	**100.0**	**18:55**									
2003-04	**Buffalo**	**NHL**	**55**	**4**	**7**	**11**	**12**	**0**	**0**	**1**	**44**	**9.1**	**11**	**0**	**0.0**	**18:59**									
	NHL Totals		**1280**	**149**	**490**	**639**	**759**	**62**	**3**	**16**	**1845**	**8.1**		**2**	**100.0**	**17:10**	**117**	**6**	**32**	**38**	**86**	**3**	**0**	**2**	**16:16**

WCHA Second All-Star Team (1982) • WCHA Freshman of the Year (1982) • NCAA Chamionship All-Tournament Team (1982) • WCHA First All-Star Team (1983) • NCAA West All American Team (1983)

Traded to **Hartford** by **NY Rangers** with Darren Turcotte for Steve Larmer, Nick Kypreos, Barry Richter and Hartford's 6th round choice (Yuri Litvinov) in 1994 Entry Draft, November 2, 1993. Traded to **Calgary** by **Hartford** with Zarley Zalapski and Michael Nylander for Gary Suter, Paul Ranheim and Ted Drury, March 10, 1994. • Missed majority of 1996-97 season recovering from knee injury suffered in game vs. Pittsburgh, October 24, 1996. Signed as a free agent by **Buffalo**, October 7, 1998.

PAUL, Jeff
(PAWL, JEHF) **WSH.**

Defense. Shoots right. 6'4", 225 lbs. Born, London, Ont., March 1, 1978. Chicago's 2nd choice, 42nd overall, in 1996 Entry Draft.

Season	Club	League	GP	G	A	Pts	PIM	PP	SH	GW	S	%	+/-	TF	F%	Min	GP	G	A	Pts	PIM	PP	SH	GW	Min
1993-94	Woodstock Vets	OJHL-C	36	1	6	7	73																		
1994-95	Niagara Falls	OHL	57	3	10	13	64										6	0	2	2	0				
1995-96	Niagara Falls	OHL	48	1	7	8	81										10	0	4	4	37				
1996-97	Erie Otters	OHL	60	4	23	27	152										5	2	0	2	12				
1997-98	Erie Otters	OHL	48	3	17	20	108										7	0	2	2	13				
1998-99	Portland Pirates	AHL	6	0	0	0	4																		
	Indianapolis Ice	IHL	55	0	7	7	120										7	0	2	2	12				
99-2000	Cleveland	IHL	69	6	6	12	210										9	1	0	1	12				
2000-01	Norfolk Admirals	AHL	59	5	6	11	171										9	0	2	2	12				
2001-02	Hershey Bears	AHL	58	1	13	14	201										7	0	1	1	6				
2002-03	**Colorado**	**NHL**	**2**	**0**	**0**	**0**	**7**	**0**	**0**	**0**	**0**	**0.0**	**0**	**0**	**0.0**	**3:32**									
	Hershey Bears	AHL	50	2	3	5	123																		
2003-04	San Antonio	AHL	57	2	6	8	174																		
	Hartford	AHL	17	0	5	5	38										15	1	2	3	31				
	NHL Totals		**2**	**0**	**0**	**0**	**7**	**0**	**0**	**0**	**0**	**0.0**		**0**	**0.0**	**3:32**									

Signed as a free agent by **Colorado**, August 8, 2001. Signed as a free agent by **Florida**, August 19, 2003. Traded to **NY Rangers** by **Florida** for Paul Healey, March 9, 2004. Signed as a free agent by **Washington**, August 2, 2004.

PAYER, Serge
(pie-YAY, SAIRZH) **FLA.**

Center. Shoots left. 6', 192 lbs. Born, Rockland, Ont., May 7, 1979.

Season	Club	League	GP	G	A	Pts	PIM	PP	SH	GW	S	%	+/-	TF	F%	Min	GP	G	A	Pts	PIM	PP	SH	GW	Min
1994-95	Cumberland Colts	ODMHA	42	37	46	83	55																		
1995-96	Kitchener Rangers	OHL	66	8	16	24	18										12	0	2	2	2				
1996-97	Kitchener Rangers	OHL	63	7	16	23	27										13	1	3	4	2				
1997-98	Kitchener Rangers	OHL	44	20	21	41	51										6	3	0	3	7				
1998-99	Kitchener Rangers	OHL	40	18	19	37	22																		
99-2000	Kitchener Rangers	OHL	44	10	26	36	53										5	0	3	3	6				
2000-01	**Florida**	**NHL**	**43**	**5**	**1**	**6**	**21**	**0**	**1**	**0**	**34**	**14.7**	**0**	**97**	**42.3**	**7:27**									
	Louisville Panthers	AHL	32	6	6	12	15																		
2001-02	Utah Grizzlies	AHL	20	6	2	8	9																		
2002-03	San Antonio	AHL	78	10	31	41	30										1	0	0	0	2				
2003-04	**Ottawa**	**NHL**	**5**	**0**	**1**	**1**	**2**	**0**	**0**	**0**	**2**	**0.0**	**1**	**43**	**46.5**	**10:30**									
	Binghamton	AHL	67	14	20	34	91										2	0	0	0	0				
	NHL Totals		**48**	**5**	**2**	**7**	**23**	**0**	**1**	**0**	**36**	**13.9**		**140**	**43.6**	**7:46**									

Signed as a free agent by **Florida**, September 30, 1997. • Missed majority of 2001-02 season recovering from back injury suffered in training camp, September, 2001. Traded to **Ottawa** by **Florida** for Ottawa's 9th round choice (Luke Beaverson) in 2004 Entry Draft, September 10, 2003. Signed as a free agent by **Florida**, July 23, 2004.

PEAT, Stephen
(PEET, STEE-vehn) **WSH.**

Right wing. Shoots right. 6'3", 230 lbs. Born, Princeton, B.C., March 10, 1980. Anaheim's 2nd choice, 32nd overall, in 1998 Entry Draft.

Season	Club	League	GP	G	A	Pts	PIM	PP	SH	GW	S	%	+/-	TF	F%	Min	GP	G	A	Pts	PIM	PP	SH	GW	Min
1995-96	Langley Thunder	BCJHL	59	5	15	20	112																		
	Red Deer Rebels	WHL	1	0	0	0	0																		
1996-97	Red Deer Rebels	WHL	68	3	14	17	161										16	0	2	2	22				
1997-98	Red Deer Rebels	WHL	63	6	12	18	189										5	0	0	0	8				
1998-99	Red Deer Rebels	WHL	31	2	6	8	98																		
	Tri-City	WHL	5	0	0	0	19																		
99-2000	Tri-City	WHL	12	0	2	2	48																		
	Calgary Hitmen	WHL	23	0	8	8	100										13	0	1	1	33				
2000-01	Portland Pirates	AHL	6	0	0	0	16																		
2001-02	**Washington**	**NHL**	**38**	**2**	**2**	**4**	**85**	**0**	**0**	**0**	**11**	**18.2**	**-1**	**0**	**0.0**	**5:04**									
	Portland Pirates	AHL	17	2	2	4	57																		
2002-03	**Washington**	**NHL**	**27**	**1**	**0**	**1**	**57**	**0**	**0**	**0**	**7**	**14.3**	**-3**	**0**	**0.0**	**4:09**									
	Portland Pirates	AHL	18	0	0	0	52																		
2003-04	**Washington**	**NHL**	**64**	**5**	**0**	**5**	**90**	**0**	**0**	**0**	**21**	**23.8**	**-10**	**4**	**0.0**	**6:38**									
	NHL Totals		**129**	**8**	**2**	**10**	**232**	**0**	**0**	**0**	**39**	**20.5**		**4**	**0.0**	**5:39**									

• Missed majority of 1999-2000 season recovering from injuries sustained off-ice, February 8, 2000. Rights traded to **Washington** by **Anaheim** for Washington's 4th round choice (later traded to Montreal – later traded to Pittsburgh – Pittsburgh selected Michel Ouellet) in 2000 Entry Draft, June 1, 2000. • Missed majority of 2000-01season recovering from groin injury suffered in training camp, September 29, 2000.

PECA, Michael

(PEH-kuh, MIGH-kuhl) **NYI**

Center. Shoots right. 5'11", 190 lbs. Born, Toronto, Ont., March 26, 1974. Vancouver's 2nd choice, 40th overall, in 1992 Entry Draft.

			Regular Season														Playoffs								
Season	Club	League	GP	G	A	Pts	PIM	PP	SH	GW	S	%	+/-	TF	F%	Min	GP	G	A	Pts	PIM	PP	SH	GW	Min
1989-90	Tor. Red Wings	MTHL	39	42	53	95	40	....	....	....	....	....	....	....	....	....	....	....	....	....	....	....	....	....	....
1990-91	Sudbury Wolves	OHL	62	14	27	41	24	....	....	....	....	....	....	....	....	....	5	1	0	1	7	....	....	....	....
1991-92	Sudbury Wolves	OHL	39	16	34	50	61	....	....	....	....	....	....	....	....	....	....	....	....	....	....	....	....	....	....
	Ottawa 67's	OHL	27	8	17	25	32	....	....	....	....	....	....	....	....	....	11	6	10	16	6	....	....	....	....
1992-93	Ottawa 67's	OHL	55	38	64	102	80	....	....	....	....	....	....	....	....	....	....	....	....	....	....	....	....	....	....
	Hamilton	AHL	9	6	3	9	11	....	....	....	....	....	....	....	....	....	....	....	....	....	....	....	....	....	....
1993-94	Ottawa 67's	OHL	55	50	63	113	101	....	....	....	....	....	....	....	....	....	17	7	22	29	30	....	....	....	....
	Vancouver	**NHL**	**4**	**0**	**0**	**0**	**2**	**0**	**0**	**0**	**5**	**0.0**	**–1**	....	....	....	....	....	....	....	....	....	....	....	....
1994-95	Syracuse Crunch	AHL	35	10	24	34	75	....	....	....	....	....	....	....	....	....	....	....	....	....	....	....	....	....	....
	Vancouver	**NHL**	**33**	**6**	**6**	**12**	**30**	**2**	**0**	**1**	**46**	**13.0**	**–6**	....	....	....	**5**	**0**	**1**	**1**	**8**	**0**	**0**	**0**	....
1995-96	**Buffalo**	**NHL**	**68**	**11**	**20**	**31**	**67**	**4**	**3**	**1**	**109**	**10.1**	**–1**	....	....	....	....	....	....	....	....	....	....	....	....
1996-97	**Buffalo**	**NHL**	**79**	**20**	**29**	**49**	**80**	**5**	**6**	**4**	**137**	**14.6**	**26**	....	....	....	**10**	**0**	**2**	**2**	**8**	**0**	**0**	**0**	....
1997-98	**Buffalo**	**NHL**	**61**	**18**	**22**	**40**	**57**	**6**	**5**	**1**	**132**	**13.6**	**12**	....	....	....	**13**	**3**	**2**	**5**	**8**	**0**	**0**	**1**	....
1998-99	**Buffalo**	**NHL**	**82**	**27**	**29**	**56**	**81**	**10**	**0**	**8**	**199**	**13.6**	**7**	**1855**	**49.4**	**20:44**	**21**	**5**	**8**	**13**	**18**	**2**	**1**	**0**	**22:28**
99-2000	**Buffalo**	**NHL**	**73**	**20**	**21**	**41**	**67**	**2**	**0**	**3**	**144**	**13.9**	**6**	**1604**	**48.6**	**19:57**	**5**	**0**	**1**	**1**	**4**	**0**	**0**	**0**	**18:42**
2000-01				DID NOT PLAY																					
2001-02	**NY Islanders**	**NHL**	**80**	**25**	**35**	**60**	**62**	**3**	**6**	**5**	**168**	**14.9**	**19**	**1804**	**52.4**	**20:14**	**5**	**1**	**0**	**1**	**2**	**0**	**0**	**0**	**16:15**
	Canada	Olympics	6	0	2	2	2	....	....	....	....	....	....	....	....	....	....	....	....	....	....	....	....	....	....
2002-03	**NY Islanders**	**NHL**	**66**	**13**	**29**	**42**	**43**	**4**	**2**	**2**	**117**	**11.1**	**–4**	**1315**	**53.0**	**18:57**	**5**	**0**	**0**	**0**	**4**	**0**	**0**	**0**	**20:10**
2003-04	**NY Islanders**	**NHL**	**76**	**11**	**29**	**40**	**71**	**0**	**1**	**0**	**117**	**9.4**	**17**	**1674**	**53.1**	**19:02**	**5**	**0**	**0**	**0**	**6**	**0**	**0**	**0**	**23:01**
	NHL Totals		**622**	**151**	**220**	**371**	**560**	**36**	**23**	**25**	**1174**	**12.9**		**8252**	**51.2**	**19:49**	**69**	**9**	**14**	**23**	**58**	**2**	**1**	**1**	**21:02**

Frank J. Selke Trophy (1997, 2002)

Traded to **Buffalo** by **Vancouver** with Mike Wilson and Vancouver's 1st round choice (Jay McKee) in 1995 Entry Draft for Alexander Mogilny and Buffalo's 5th round choice (Todd Norman) in 1995 Entry Draft, July 8, 1995. • Missed entire 2000-01 season after failing to come to contract terms with **Buffalo**. Rights traded to **NY Islanders** by **Buffalo** for Tim Connolly and Taylor Pyatt, June 24, 2001.

PEDERSON, Denis

(PEE-duhr-suhn, DEH-nihs)

Center/Right wing. Shoots right. 6'2", 205 lbs. Born, Prince Albert, Sask., September 10, 1975. New Jersey's 1st choice, 13th overall, in 1993 Entry Draft.

			Regular Season														Playoffs								
Season	Club	League	GP	G	A	Pts	PIM	PP	SH	GW	S	%	+/-	TF	F%	Min	GP	G	A	Pts	PIM	PP	SH	GW	Min
1990-91	Prince Albert	SMHL	30	25	17	42	84	....	....	....	....	....	....	....	....	....	....	....	....	....	....	....	....	....	....
1991-92	Prince Albert	SMHL	21	33	25	58	40	....	....	....	....	....	....	....	....	....	....	....	....	....	....	....	....	....	....
	Prince Albert	WHL	10	0	0	0	6	....	....	....	....	....	....	....	....	....	7	0	1	1	13	....	....	....	....
1992-93	Prince Albert	WHL	72	33	40	73	134	....	....	....	....	....	....	....	....	....	....	....	....	....	....	....	....	....	....
1993-94	Prince Albert	WHL	71	53	45	98	157	....	....	....	....	....	....	....	....	....	....	....	....	....	....	....	....	....	....
1994-95	Prince Albert	WHL	63	30	38	68	122	....	....	....	....	....	....	....	....	....	15	11	14	25	14	....	....	....	....
	Albany River Rats	AHL	....	....	....	....	....	....	....	....	....	....	....	....	....	....	3	0	0	0	2	....	....	....	....
1995-96	**New Jersey**	**NHL**	**10**	**3**	**1**	**4**	**0**	**1**	**0**	**2**	**6**	**50.0**	**–1**	....	....	....	....	....	....	....	....	....	....	....	....
	Albany River Rats	AHL	68	28	43	71	104	....	....	....	....	....	....	....	....	....	4	1	2	3	0	....	....	....	....
1996-97	**New Jersey**	**NHL**	**70**	**12**	**20**	**32**	**62**	**3**	**0**	**3**	**106**	**11.3**	**7**	....	....	....	**9**	**0**	**0**	**0**	**2**	**0**	**0**	**0**	....
	Albany River Rats	AHL	3	1	3	4	7	....	....	....	....	....	....	....	....	....	....	....	....	....	....	....	....	....	....
1997-98	**New Jersey**	**NHL**	**80**	**15**	**13**	**28**	**97**	**7**	**0**	**1**	**135**	**11.1**	**–6**	....	....	....	**6**	**1**	**1**	**2**	**2**	**0**	**1**	**0**	....
1998-99	**New Jersey**	**NHL**	**76**	**11**	**12**	**23**	**66**	**3**	**0**	**1**	**145**	**7.6**	**–10**	**540**	**42.8**	**15:19**	**3**	**0**	**1**	**1**	**0**	**0**	**0**	**0**	**9:36**
99-2000	**New Jersey**	**NHL**	**35**	**3**	**3**	**6**	**16**	**0**	**0**	**0**	**41**	**7.3**	**–7**	**125**	**48.8**	**10:42**	....	....	....	....	....	....	....	....	....
	Vancouver	**NHL**	**12**	**3**	**2**	**5**	**2**	**0**	**0**	**1**	**15**	**20.0**	**1**	**70**	**45.7**	**12:41**	....	....	....	....	....	....	....	....	....
2000-01	**Vancouver**	**NHL**	**61**	**4**	**8**	**12**	**65**	**0**	**1**	**3**	**70**	**5.7**	**0**	**351**	**42.7**	**11:42**	**4**	**0**	**1**	**1**	**4**	**0**	**0**	**0**	**15:53**
2001-02	**Vancouver**	**NHL**	**29**	**1**	**5**	**6**	**31**	**0**	**0**	**0**	**24**	**4.2**	**–2**	**142**	**47.2**	**8:18**	....	....	....	....	....	....	....	....	....
	Phoenix	**NHL**	**19**	**1**	**1**	**2**	**20**	**0**	**0**	**0**	**18**	**5.6**	**–2**	**202**	**49.0**	**10:32**	**5**	**0**	**2**	**2**	**0**	**0**	**0**	**0**	**10:36**
2002-03	**Nashville**	**NHL**	**43**	**4**	**6**	**10**	**39**	**0**	**0**	**0**	**64**	**6.3**	**2**	**440**	**50.2**	**12:48**	....	....	....	....	....	....	....	....	....
2003-04	Eisbaren Berlin	Germany	41	15	21	36	40	....	....	....	....	....	....	....	....	....	11	5	6	11	8	....	....	....	....
	NHL Totals		**435**	**57**	**71**	**128**	**398**	**14**	**1**	**11**	**624**	**9.1**		**1870**	**46.0**	**12:21**	**27**	**1**	**5**	**6**	**8**	**0**	**1**	**0**	**12:07**

WHL East Second All-Star Team (1994)

Traded to **Vancouver** by **New Jersey** with Brendan Morrison for Alexander Mogilny, March 14, 2000. Traded to **Phoenix** by **Vancouver** with Drake Berehowsky for Todd Warriner, Trevor Letowski, Tyler Bouck and Phoenix's 3rd round choice (later traded back to Phoenix – Phoenix selected Dimitri Pestunov) in 2003 Entry Draft, December 28, 2001. Signed as a free agent by **Nashville**, July 24, 2002. Signed as a free agent by **Eisbaren Berlin** (Germany), September 9, 2003.

PELLERIN, Scott

(PEHL-ih-rihn, SKAWT)

Left wing. Shoots left. 5'11", 190 lbs. Born, Shediac, N.B., January 9, 1970. New Jersey's 4th choice, 47th overall, in 1989 Entry Draft.

			Regular Season														Playoffs								
Season	Club	League	GP	G	A	Pts	PIM	PP	SH	GW	S	%	+/-	TF	F%	Min	GP	G	A	Pts	PIM	PP	SH	GW	Min
1985-86	Moncton Flyers	NBAHA	45	65	34	99	34	....	....	....	....	....	....	....	....	....	....	....	....	....	....	....	....	....	....
1986-87	Notre Dame	SMHL	72	62	68	130	98	....	....	....	....	....	....	....	....	....	....	....	....	....	....	....	....	....	....
1987-88	Notre Dame	SJHL	57	37	49	86	139	....	....	....	....	....	....	....	....	....	....	....	....	....	....	....	....	....	....
1988-89	U. of Maine	H-East	45	29	33	62	92	....	....	....	....	....	....	....	....	....	....	....	....	....	....	....	....	....	....
1989-90	U. of Maine	H-East	42	22	34	56	68	....	....	....	....	....	....	....	....	....	....	....	....	....	....	....	....	....	....
1990-91	U. of Maine	H-East	43	23	25	48	60	....	....	....	....	....	....	....	....	....	....	....	....	....	....	....	....	....	....
1991-92	U. of Maine	H-East	37	*32	25	57	54	....	....	....	....	....	....	....	....	....	....	....	....	....	....	....	....	....	....
	Utica Devils	AHL	....	....	....	....	....	....	....	....	....	....	....	....	....	....	3	1	0	1	0	....	....	....	....
1992-93	**New Jersey**	**NHL**	**45**	**10**	**11**	**21**	**41**	**1**	**2**	**0**	**60**	**16.7**	**–1**	....	....	....	....	....	....	....	....	....	....	....	....
	Utica Devils	AHL	27	15	18	33	33	....	....	....	....	....	....	....	....	....	2	0	1	1	0	....	....	....	....
1993-94	**New Jersey**	**NHL**	**1**	**0**	**0**	**0**	**2**	**0**	**0**	**0**	**0**	**0.0**	**0**	....	....	....	....	....	....	....	....	....	....	....	....
	Albany River Rats	AHL	73	28	46	74	84	....	....	....	....	....	....	....	....	....	5	2	1	3	11	....	....	....	....
1994-95	Albany River Rats	AHL	74	23	33	56	95	....	....	....	....	....	....	....	....	....	14	6	4	10	8	....	....	....	....
1995-96	**New Jersey**	**NHL**	**6**	**2**	**1**	**3**	**0**	**0**	**0**	**0**	**9**	**22.2**	**1**	....	....	....	....	....	....	....	....	....	....	....	....
	Albany River Rats	AHL	75	35	47	82	142	....	....	....	....	....	....	....	....	....	4	0	3	3	10	....	....	....	....
1996-97	**St. Louis**	**NHL**	**54**	**8**	**10**	**18**	**35**	**0**	**2**	**2**	**76**	**10.5**	**12**	....	....	....	**6**	**0**	**0**	**0**	**6**	**0**	**0**	**0**	....
	Worcester IceCats	AHL	24	10	16	26	37	....	....	....	....	....	....	....	....	....	....	....	....	....	....	....	....	....	....
1997-98	**St. Louis**	**NHL**	**80**	**8**	**21**	**29**	**62**	**1**	**1**	**0**	**96**	**8.3**	**14**	....	....	....	**10**	**0**	**2**	**2**	**10**	**0**	**0**	**0**	....
1998-99	**St. Louis**	**NHL**	**80**	**20**	**21**	**41**	**42**	**0**	**5**	**4**	**138**	**14.5**	**1**	**6**	**66.7**	**17:18**	**8**	**1**	**0**	**1**	**4**	**0**	**0**	**0**	**13:50**
99-2000	**St. Louis**	**NHL**	**80**	**8**	**15**	**23**	**48**	**0**	**2**	**2**	**120**	**6.7**	**9**	**6**	**16.7**	**14:47**	**7**	**0**	**0**	**0**	**2**	**0**	**0**	**0**	**14:55**
2000-01	**Minnesota**	**NHL**	**58**	**11**	**28**	**39**	**45**	**2**	**2**	**2**	**117**	**9.4**	**6**	**47**	**31.9**	**18:40**	....	....	....	....	....	....	....	....	....
	Carolina	**NHL**	**19**	**0**	**5**	**5**	**6**	**0**	**0**	**0**	**21**	**0.0**	**–4**	**52**	**44.2**	**14:14**	**6**	**0**	**0**	**0**	**4**	**0**	**0**	**0**	**11:10**
2001-02	**Boston**	**NHL**	**35**	**1**	**5**	**6**	**6**	**0**	**0**	**0**	**41**	**2.4**	**–6**	**24**	**37.5**	**11:38**	....	....	....	....	....	....	....	....	....
	Dallas	**NHL**	**33**	**3**	**5**	**8**	**15**	**0**	**0**	**0**	**22**	**13.6**	**–5**	**8**	**25.0**	**9:13**	....	....	....	....	....	....	....	....	....
2002-03	**Dallas**	**NHL**	**20**	**1**	**3**	**4**	**8**	**1**	**0**	**0**	**20**	**5.0**	**–3**	**5**	**20.0**	**10:43**	....	....	....	....	....	....	....	....	....
	Phoenix	**NHL**	**23**	**0**	**1**	**1**	**8**	**0**	**0**	**0**	**17**	**0.0**	**–5**	**12**	**58.3**	**9:32**	....	....	....	....	....	....	....	....	....
2003-04	Portland Pirates	AHL	6	0	3	3	0	....	....	....	....	....	....	....	....	....	....	....	....	....	....	....	....	....	....
	Worcester IceCats	AHL	49	9	21	30	38	....	....	....	....	....	....	....	....	....	10	3	1	4	19	....	....	....	....
	St. Louis	**NHL**	**2**	**0**	**0**	**0**	**2**	**0**	**0**	**0**	**1**	**0.0**	**–3**	**2**	**0.0**	**14:05**	....	....	....	....	....	....	....	....	....
	NHL Totals		**536**	**72**	**126**	**198**	**320**	**5**	**14**	**10**	**738**	**9.8**		**162**	**38.3**	**14:33**	**37**	**1**	**2**	**3**	**26**	**0**	**0**	**0**	**13:26**

Hockey East Rookie of the Year (1989) (co-winner - Rob Gaudreau) • Hockey East First All-Star Team (1992) • Hockey East Player of the Year (1992) • NCAA East First All-American Team (1992) • Hobey Baker Memorial Award (Top U.S. Collegiate Player) (1992)

Signed as a free agent by **St. Louis**, July 10, 1996. Selected by **Minnesota** from **St. Louis** in Expansion Draft, June 23, 2000. Traded to **Carolina** by **Minnesota** for Askhat Rakhmatullin, Carolina's 3rd round choice (later traded to NY Rangers – NY Rangers selected Garth Murray) in 2001 Entry Draft and Carolina's compensatory 5th round choice (Armands Berzins) in 2002 Entry Draft, March 1, 2001. Signed as a free agent by **Boston**, July 26, 2001. Claimed on waivers by **Dallas** from **Boston**, January 12, 2002. Traded to **Phoenix** by **Dallas** with Dallas' 4th round choice (Kevin Porter) in 2004 Entry Draft for Claude Lemieux, January 16, 2003. Signed as a free agent by **Portland** (AHL), September 12, 2003. Signed as a free agent by **Worcester** (AHL), November 5, 2003. Signed as a free agent by **St. Louis**, December 22, 2003.

PELUSO, Mike

(puh-LOO-soh, MIGHK)

Right wing. Shoots right. 6'1", 208 lbs. Born, Bismarck, ND, September 2, 1974. Calgary's 12th choice, 253rd overall, in 1994 Entry Draft.

			Regular Season														Playoffs								
Season	Club	League	GP	G	A	Pts	PIM	PP	SH	GW	S	%	+/-	TF	F%	Min	GP	G	A	Pts	PIM	PP	SH	GW	Min
1992-93	Omaha Lancers	USHL	45	21	12	33	31	....	....	....	....	....	....	....	....	....	....	....	....	....	....	....	....	....	....
1993-94	Omaha Lancers	USHL	48	36	29	65	77	....	....	....	....	....	....	....	....	....	....	....	....	....	....	....	....	....	....
1994-95	U. Minn-Duluth	WCHA	38	11	23	34	38	....	....	....	....	....	....	....	....	....	....	....	....	....	....	....	....	....	....
1995-96	U. Minn-Duluth	WCHA	38	25	19	44	64	....	....	....	....	....	....	....	....	....	....	....	....	....	....	....	....	....	....
1996-97	U. Minn-Duluth	WCHA	37	20	20	40	53	....	....	....	....	....	....	....	....	....	....	....	....	....	....	....	....	....	....
1997-98	U. Minn-Duluth	WCHA	40	24	21	45	100	....	....	....	....	....	....	....	....	....	....	....	....	....	....	....	....	....	....
1998-99	Portland Pirates	AHL	26	7	6	13	6	....	....	....	....	....	....	....	....	....	....	....	....	....	....	....	....	....	....
99-2000	Portland Pirates	AHL	71	25	29	54	86	....	....	....	....	....	....	....	....	....	4	2	0	2	0	....	....	....	....
2000-01	Portland Pirates	AHL	19	12	10	22	17	....	....	....	....	....	....	....	....	....	....	....	....	....	....	....	....	....	....
	Worcester IceCats	AHL	44	17	23	40	22	....	....	....	....	....	....	....	....	....	11	3	3	6	4	....	....	....	....

Season	Club	League	GP	G	A	Pts	PIM	PP	SH	GW	S	%	+/-	TF	F%	Min	GP	G	A	Pts	PIM	PP	SH	GW	Min
			Regular Season														Playoffs								
2001-02	**Chicago**	**NHL**	**37**	**4**	**2**	**6**	**19**	**0**	**0**	**1**	**45**	**8.9**	**–3**	**1**	**0.0**	**9:17**									
	Norfolk Admirals	AHL	29	18	9	27	4										4	1	0	1	0				
2002-03	Norfolk Admirals	AHL	74	24	31	55	35										9	1	2	3	4				
2003-04	**Philadelphia**	**NHL**	**1**	**0**	**0**	**0**	**0**	**0**	**0**	**0**	**2**	**0.0**	**0**	**0**	**0.0**	**9:34**									
	Philadelphia	AHL	72	13	18	31	87										5	0	1	1	4				
	NHL Totals		**38**	**4**	**2**	**6**	**19**	**0**	**0**	**1**	**47**	**8.5**		**1**	**0.0**	**9:17**									

WCHA Second All-Star Team (1997)

Signed as a free agent by **Washington**, October 9, 1998. Traded to **St. Louis** by **Washington** for Derek Bekar, November 29, 2000. Signed as a free agent by **Chicago**, August 1, 2001. Signed as a free agent by **Philadelphia**, July 24, 2003.

PERREAULT, Yanic

(puh-ROH, YAH-nihk)

Center. Shoots left. 5'11", 185 lbs. Born, Sherbrooke, Que., April 4, 1971. Toronto's 1st choice, 47th overall, in 1991 Entry Draft.

Season	Club	League	GP	G	A	Pts	PIM	PP	SH	GW	S	%	+/-	TF	F%	Min	GP	G	A	Pts	PIM	PP	SH	GW	Min
1987-88	L'est Cantonniers	QAAA	42	*70	57	*127	14										8	12	10	22	6				
1988-89	Trois-Rivieres	QMJHL	70	53	55	108	48																		
1989-90	Trois-Rivieres	QMJHL	63	51	63	114	75										7	6	5	11	19				
1990-91	Trois-Rivieres	QMJHL	67	*87	98	*185	103										6	4	7	11	6				
1991-92	St. John's	AHL	62	38	38	76	19										16	7	8	15	4				
1992-93	St. John's	AHL	79	49	46	95	56										9	4	5	9	2				
1993-94	**Toronto**	**NHL**	**13**	**3**	**3**	**6**	**0**	**2**	**0**	**0**	**24**	**12.5**	**1**												
	St. John's	AHL	62	45	60	105	38										11	*12	6	18	14				
1994-95	Phoenix	IHL	68	51	48	99	52																		
	Los Angeles	**NHL**	**26**	**2**	**5**	**7**	**20**	**0**	**0**	**1**	**43**	**4.7**	**3**												
1995-96	**Los Angeles**	**NHL**	**78**	**25**	**24**	**49**	**16**	**8**	**3**	**7**	**175**	**14.3**	**–11**												
1996-97	**Los Angeles**	**NHL**	**41**	**11**	**14**	**25**	**20**	**1**	**1**	**0**	**98**	**11.2**	**0**												
1997-98	**Los Angeles**	**NHL**	**79**	**28**	**20**	**48**	**32**	**3**	**2**	**3**	**206**	**13.6**	**6**				**4**	**1**	**2**	**3**	**6**	**1**	**0**	**0**	
1998-99	**Los Angeles**	**NHL**	**64**	**10**	**17**	**27**	**30**	**2**	**2**	**1**	**113**	**8.8**	**–3**	**1024**	**56.5**	**15:24**									
	Toronto	**NHL**	**12**	**7**	**8**	**15**	**12**	**2**	**1**	**2**	**28**	**25.0**	**10**	**164**	**62.8**	**13:20**	**17**	**3**	**6**	**9**	**6**	**0**	**0**	**2**	**15:55**
99-2000	**Toronto**	**NHL**	**58**	**18**	**27**	**45**	**22**	**5**	**0**	**4**	**114**	**15.8**	**3**	**987**	**61.8**	**15:18**	**1**	**0**	**1**	**1**	**0**	**0**	**0**	**0**	**12:56**
2000-01	**Toronto**	**NHL**	**76**	**24**	**28**	**52**	**52**	**5**	**0**	**2**	**134**	**17.9**	**0**	**1055**	**62.7**	**14:01**	**11**	**2**	**3**	**5**	**4**	**1**	**0**	**1**	**12:20**
2001-02	**Montreal**	**NHL**	**82**	**27**	**29**	**56**	**40**	**6**	**0**	**7**	**156**	**17.3**	**–3**	**1485**	**61.3**	**16:47**	**11**	**3**	**5**	**8**	**0**	**2**	**0**	**1**	**13:05**
2002-03	**Montreal**	**NHL**	**73**	**24**	**22**	**46**	**30**	**7**	**0**	**4**	**145**	**16.6**	**–11**	**1156**	**62.9**	**16:05**									
2003-04	**Montreal**	**NHL**	**69**	**16**	**15**	**31**	**40**	**5**	**0**	**3**	**114**	**14.0**	**–10**	**861**	**65.2**	**13:46**	**9**	**2**	**2**	**4**	**0**	**0**	**0**	**1**	**12:29**
	NHL Totals		**671**	**195**	**212**	**407**	**314**	**46**	**9**	**34**	**1350**	**14.4**		**6732**	**61.7**	**15:12**	**53**	**11**	**19**	**30**	**16**	**4**	**0**	**5**	**13:47**

QMJHL All-Rookie Team (1989) • QMJHL Offensive Rookie of the Year (1989) • Canadian Major Junior Rookie of the Year (1989) • QMJHL First All-Star Team (1991) • QMJHL MVP (1991)

Traded to **Los Angeles** by **Toronto** for Los Angeles' 4th round choice (later traded to Philadelphia – later traded back to Los Angeles – Los Angeles selected Mikael Simons) in 1996 Entry Draft, July 11, 1994. Traded to **Toronto** by **Los Angeles** for Jason Podollan and Toronto's 3rd round choice (Cory Campbell) in 1999 Entry Draft, March 23, 1999. Signed as a free agent by **Montreal**, July 4, 2001.

PERRIN, Eric

(peh-REHN, AIR-ihk) **T.B.**

Center. Shoots left. 5'9", 176 lbs. Born, Laval, Que., November 1, 1975.

Season	Club	League	GP	G	A	Pts	PIM	PP	SH	GW	S	%	+/-	TF	F%	Min	GP	G	A	Pts	PIM	PP	SH	GW	Min
1991-92	Laval-Laurentide	QAAA	42	41	50	91											12	7	16	23					
1992-93	Laval College	CEGEP	STATISTICS NOT AVAILABLE																						
1993-94	U. of Vermont	ECAC	32	24	21	45	34																		
1994-95	U. of Vermont	ECAC	35	28	39	67	38																		
1995-96	U. of Vermont	ECAC	38	29	56	85	38																		
1996-97	U. of Vermont	ECAC	36	26	33	59	40																		
1997-98	Cleveland	IHL	69	12	31	43	34																		
	Quebec Rafales	IHL	13	2	12	14	4																		
1998-99	Kansas City	IHL	82	24	37	61	71										3	0	0	0	0				
99-2000	Kansas City	IHL	21	3	15	18	16																		
2000-01	Jokerit Helsinki	Finland	6	1	1	2	4																		
	Assat Pori	Finland	43	15	23	38	70																		
2001-02	Assat Pori	Finland	45	13	13	26	16																		
	HPK Hameenlinna	Finland	12	5	10	15	4										8	2	4	6	6				
2002-03	JYP Jyvaskyla	Finland	56	18	28	46	36										7	4	6	10	8				
2003-04♦	**Tampa Bay**	**NHL**	**4**	**0**	**0**	**0**	**0**	**0**	**0**	**0**	**3**	**0.0**	**–1**	**30**	**60.0**	**8:32**	**12**	**0**	**1**	**1**	**6**	**0**	**0**	**0**	**5:20**
	Hershey Bears	AHL	71	21	54	75	49																		
	NHL Totals		**4**	**0**	**0**	**0**	**0**	**0**	**0**	**0**	**3**	**0.0**		**30**	**60.0**	**8:32**	**12**	**0**	**1**	**1**	**6**	**0**	**0**	**0**	**5:20**

ECAC All-Rookie Team (1994) • ECAC First All-Star Team (1995, 1996) • ECAC Player of the Year (1996) • NCAA East First All-American Team (1996) • AHL First All-Star Team (2004)

Signed as a free agent by **Tampa Bay**, June 19, 2003.

PERROTT, Nathan

(PEHR-roht, NAY-than) **TOR.**

Right wing. Shoots right. 6', 225 lbs. Born, Owen Sound, Ont., December 8, 1976. New Jersey's 2nd choice, 44th overall, in 1995 Entry Draft.

Season	Club	League	GP	G	A	Pts	PIM	PP	SH	GW	S	%	+/-	TF	F%	Min	GP	G	A	Pts	PIM	PP	SH	GW	Min
1992-93	Walkerton	OJHL-C	25	6	13	19	45																		
1993-94	St. Mary's Lincolns	OJHL-B	41	11	26	37	249																		
1994-95	Oshawa Generals	OHL	63	18	28	46	233										2	1	1	2	9				
1995-96	Oshawa Generals	OHL	59	30	32	62	158										5	2	3	5	8				
	Albany River Rats	AHL	4	0	0	0	12																		
1996-97	Oshawa Generals	OHL	5	1	0	1	17																		
	Sault Ste. Marie	OHL	37	18	23	41	120										11	5	5	10	60				
1997-98	Indianapolis Ice	IHL	31	4	3	7	76																		
	Jacksonville	ECHL	30	6	8	14	135																		
1998-99	Indianapolis Ice	IHL	72	14	11	25	307										7	3	1	4	45				
99-2000	Cleveland	IHL	65	12	9	21	248										9	2	1	3	19				
2000-01	Norfolk Admirals	AHL	73	11	17	28	268										9	2	0	2	18				
2001-02	Norfolk Admirals	AHL	2	0	0	0	5																		
	Nashville	**NHL**	**22**	**1**	**2**	**3**	**74**	**0**	**0**	**1**	**7**	**14.3**	**–1**	**1**	**0.0**	**4:55**									
	Milwaukee	AHL	56	6	10	16	190																		
2002-03	**Nashville**	**NHL**	**1**	**0**	**0**	**0**	**5**	**0**	**0**	**0**	**0**	**0.0**	**0**	**0**	**0.0**	**4:13**									
	Milwaukee	AHL	27	1	2	3	106																		
	St. John's	AHL	36	7	8	15	97																		
2003-04	**Toronto**	**NHL**	**40**	**1**	**2**	**3**	**116**	**0**	**0**	**0**	**47**	**2.1**	**–1**	**5**	**20.0**	**7:40**									
	NHL Totals		**63**	**2**	**4**	**6**	**195**	**0**	**0**	**1**	**54**	**3.7**		**6**	**16.7**	**6:39**									

Signed as a free agent by **Chicago**, August 27, 1997. Traded to **Nashville** by **Chicago** for future considerations, October 9, 2001. Traded to **Toronto** by **Nashville** for Bob Wren, Deceber 31, 2002.
• Spent majority of 2003-04 season as a healthy reserve.

PETERS, Andrew

(PEE-tuhrs, AN-droo) **BUF.**

Left wing. Shoots left. 6'4", 223 lbs. Born, St. Catharines, Ont., May 5, 1980. Buffalo's 2nd choice, 34th overall, in 1998 Entry Draft.

Season	Club	League	GP	G	A	Pts	PIM	PP	SH	GW	S	%	+/-	TF	F%	Min	GP	G	A	Pts	PIM	PP	SH	GW	Min
1996-97	Georgetown	OPJHL	46	11	16	27	65																		
1997-98	Oshawa Generals	OHL	60	11	7	18	220										7	2	0	2	19				
1998-99	Oshawa Generals	OHL	54	14	10	24	137										15	2	7	9	36				
99-2000	Kitchener Rangers	OHL	42	6	13	19	95										4	0	1	1	14				
2000-01	Rochester	AHL	49	0	4	4	118																		
2001-02	Rochester	AHL	67	4	1	5	*388																		
2002-03	Rochester	AHL	57	3	0	3	223										3	0	0	0	24				
2003-04	**Buffalo**	**NHL**	**42**	**2**	**0**	**2**	**151**	**0**	**0**	**0**	**19**	**10.5**	**–3**	**2**	**0.0**	**4:10**									
	NHL Totals		**42**	**2**	**0**	**2**	**151**	**0**	**0**	**0**	**19**	**10.5**		**2**	**0.0**	**4:10**									

PETERSEN, Toby
(PEE-tuhr-sohn, TOH-bee) **EDM.**

Center. Shoots left. 5'10", 197 lbs. Born, Minneapolis, MN, October 27, 1978. Pittsburgh's 9th choice, 244th overall, in 1998 Entry Draft.

			Regular Season														Playoffs								
Season	Club	League	GP	G	A	Pts	PIM	PP	SH	GW	S	%	+/-	TF	F%	Min	GP	G	A	Pts	PIM	PP	SH	GW	Min
1995-96	Jefferson Jaguars	Hi-School	25	29	30	59	....	....	....	....	....	....	....	....	....	....	....	....	....	....	....	....	....	....	....
1996-97	Colorado College	WCHA	40	17	21	38	18	....	....	....	....	....	....	....	....	....	....	....	....	....	....	....	....	....	....
1997-98	Colorado College	WCHA	40	16	17	33	34	....	....	....	....	....	....	....	....	....	....	....	....	....	....	....	....	....	....
1998-99	Colorado College	WCHA	21	12	12	24	2	....	....	....	....	....	....	....	....	....	....	....	....	....	....	....	....	....	....
99-2000	Colorado College	WCHA	37	14	19	33	8	....	....	....	....	....	....	....	....	....	....	....	....	....	....	....	....	....	....
2000-01	**Pittsburgh**	**NHL**	**12**	**2**	**6**	**8**	**4**	**0**	**0**	**1**	**25**	**8.0**	**3**	**39**	**35.9**	**13:22**	....	....	....	....	....	....	....	....	....
	Wilkes-Barre	AHL	73	26	41	67	22	....	....	....	....	....	....	....	....	....	21	7	6	13	4	....	....	....	....
2001-02	**Pittsburgh**	**NHL**	**79**	**8**	**10**	**18**	**4**	**1**	**1**	**0**	**116**	**6.9**	**–15**	**338**	**45.6**	**12:16**	....	....	....	....	....	....	....	....	....
2002-03	Wilkes-Barre	AHL	80	31	35	66	24	....	....	....	....	....	....	....	....	....	6	1	3	4	4	....	....	....	....
2003-04	Wilkes-Barre	AHL	62	15	29	44	4	....	....	....	....	....	....	....	....	....	21	2	10	12	12	....	....	....	....
	NHL Totals		**91**	**10**	**16**	**26**	**8**	**1**	**1**	**1**	**141**	**7.1**		**377**	**44.6**	**12:25**	....	....	....	....	....	....	....	....	....

WCHA All-Rookie Team (1997)

Signed as a free agent by **Edmonton**, July 30, 2004.

PETROVICKY, Ronald
(PEHT-roh-vih-kee, RAW-nohld) **ATL.**

Right wing. Shoots right. 5'11", 190 lbs. Born, Zilina, Czechoslovakia, February 15, 1977. Calgary's 9th choice, 228th overall, in 1996 Entry Draft.

Season	Club	League	GP	G	A	Pts	PIM	PP	SH	GW	S	%	+/-	TF	F%	Min	GP	G	A	Pts	PIM	PP	SH	GW	Min
1993-94	Dukla Trencin Jr.	Slovak-Jr.	36	28	27	55	42	....	....	....	....	....	....	....	....	....	....	....	....	....	....	....	....	....	....
	Dukla Trencin	Slovakia	1	0	0	0	0	....	....	....	....	....	....	....	....	....	....	....	....	....	....	....	....	....	....
1994-95	Tri-City	WHL	39	4	11	15	86	....	....	....	....	....	....	....	....	....	....	....	....	....	....	....	....	....	....
	Prince George	WHL	21	4	6	10	37	....	....	....	....	....	....	....	....	....	....	....	....	....	....	....	....	....	....
1995-96	Prince George	WHL	39	19	21	40	61	....	....	....	....	....	....	....	....	....	....	....	....	....	....	....	....	....	....
1996-97	Prince George	WHL	72	32	37	69	119	....	....	....	....	....	....	....	....	....	15	4	9	13	31	....	....	....	....
1997-98	Regina Pats	WHL	71	64	49	113	168	....	....	....	....	....	....	....	....	....	9	2	4	6	11	....	....	....	....
1998-99	Saint John Flames	AHL	78	12	21	33	114	....	....	....	....	....	....	....	....	....	7	1	2	3	19	....	....	....	....
99-2000	Saint John Flames	AHL	67	23	33	56	131	....	....	....	....	....	....	....	....	....	3	1	1	2	6	....	....	....	....
2000-01	**Calgary**	**NHL**	**30**	**4**	**5**	**9**	**54**	**1**	**0**	**1**	**30**	**13.3**	**0**	**7**	**42.9**	**11:33**	....	....	....	....	....	....	....	....	....
2001-02	**Calgary**	**NHL**	**77**	**5**	**7**	**12**	**85**	**1**	**0**	**1**	**78**	**6.4**	**0**	**28**	**46.4**	**11:42**	....	....	....	....	....	....	....	....	....
2002-03	**NY Rangers**	**NHL**	**66**	**5**	**9**	**14**	**77**	**2**	**1**	**1**	**65**	**7.7**	**–12**	**52**	**42.3**	**12:25**	....	....	....	....	....	....	....	....	....
2003-04	**Atlanta**	**NHL**	**78**	**16**	**15**	**31**	**123**	**0**	**0**	**1**	**102**	**15.7**	**–9**	**27**	**40.7**	**14:16**	....	....	....	....	....	....	....	....	....
	NHL Totals		**251**	**30**	**36**	**66**	**339**	**4**	**1**	**4**	**275**	**10.9**		**114**	**43.0**	**12:40**	....	....	....	....	....	....	....	....	....

WHL East Second All-Star Team (1998)

• Missed majority of 2000-01 season recovering from wrist injury suffered in game vs. Detroit, October 5, 2000. Claimed by **NY Rangers** from **Calgary** in Waiver Draft, October 4, 2002. Claimed by **Atlanta** from **NY Rangers** in Waiver Draft, October 3, 2003.

PETTINEN, Tomi
(peh-TIHN-ehn, TAW-mee) **NYI**

Defense. Shoots left. 6'3", 220 lbs. Born, Ylojarvi, Finland, June 17, 1977. NY Islanders' 9th choice, 267th overall, in 2000 Entry Draft.

Season	Club	League	GP	G	A	Pts	PIM	PP	SH	GW	S	%	+/-	TF	F%	Min	GP	G	A	Pts	PIM	PP	SH	GW	Min
1993-94	Ilves Tampere-C	Finn-Jr.	31	2	2	4	4	....	....	....	....	....	....	....	....	....	....	....	....	....	....	....	....	....	....
1994-95	Ilves Tampere-B	Finn-Jr.	31	1	6	7	46	....	....	....	....	....	....	....	....	....	4	0	0	0	2	....	....	....	....
	Ilves Tampere Jr.	Finn-Jr.	1	0	0	0	0	....	....	....	....	....	....	....	....	....	....	....	....	....	....	....	....	....	....
1995-96	KooVee Jr.	Finn-Jr.	21	0	0	0	64	....	....	....	....	....	....	....	....	....	....	....	....	....	....	....	....	....	....
	Ilves Tampere Jr.	Finn-Jr.	12	1	1	2	18	....	....	....	....	....	....	....	....	....	....	....	....	....	....	....	....	....	....
1996-97	Ilves Tampere Jr.	Finn-Jr.	26	3	8	11	44	....	....	....	....	....	....	....	....	....	....	....	....	....	....	....	....	....	....
	Ilves Tampere	Finland	16	1	0	1	12	....	....	....	....	....	....	....	....	....	....	....	....	....	....	....	....	....	....
1997-98	Ilves Tampere Jr.	Finn-Jr.	14	1	4	5	24	....	....	....	....	....	....	....	....	....	....	....	....	....	....	....	....	....	....
	Ilves Tampere	Finland	3	0	0	0	0	....	....	....	....	....	....	....	....	....	....	....	....	....	....	....	....	....	....
	Lukko Rauma Jr.	Finn-Jr.	11	2	6	8	14	....	....	....	....	....	....	....	....	....	....	....	....	....	....	....	....	....	....
	Lukko Rauma	Finland-2	4	0	0	0	2	....	....	....	....	....	....	....	....	....	....	....	....	....	....	....	....	....	....
	Lukko Rauma	Finland	27	0	2	2	16	....	....	....	....	....	....	....	....	....	....	....	....	....	....	....	....	....	....
1998-99	Hermes Kokkola	Finland-2	42	8	6	14	76	....	....	....	....	....	....	....	....	....	3	0	0	0	6	....	....	....	....
	HIFK Helsinki	Finland	4	0	0	0	2	....	....	....	....	....	....	....	....	....	....	....	....	....	....	....	....	....	....
99-2000	Ilves Tampere	Finland	51	1	6	7	78	....	....	....	....	....	....	....	....	....	3	1	2	3	2	....	....	....	....
2000-01	Ilves Tampere	Finland	56	2	2	4	86	....	....	....	....	....	....	....	....	....	9	0	0	0	4	....	....	....	....
2001-02	Ilves Tampere	Finland	48	5	4	9	51	....	....	....	....	....	....	....	....	....	3	0	0	0	4	....	....	....	....
	Bridgeport	AHL	....	....	....	....	....	....	....	....	....	....	....	....	....	....	9	0	1	1	0	....	....	....	....
2002-03	**NY Islanders**	**NHL**	**2**	**0**	**0**	**0**	**0**	**0**	**0**	**0**	**0**	**0.0**	**1**	**0**	**0.0**	**11:34**	....	....	....	....	....	....	....	....	....
	Bridgeport	AHL	75	1	8	9	56	....	....	....	....	....	....	....	....	....	9	0	0	0	17	....	....	....	....
2003-04	**NY Islanders**	**NHL**	**4**	**0**	**0**	**0**	**2**	**0**	**0**	**0**	**2**	**0.0**	**–2**	**0**	**0.0**	**10:24**	....	....	....	....	....	....	....	....	....
	Bridgeport	AHL	71	1	8	9	37	....	....	....	....	....	....	....	....	....	7	1	0	1	0	....	....	....	....
	NHL Totals		**6**	**0**	**0**	**0**	**2**	**0**	**0**	**0**	**2**	**0.0**		**0**	**0.0**	**10:47**	....	....	....	....	....	....	....	....	....

PETTINGER, Matt
(PEH-tihn-juhr, MAT) **WSH.**

Left wing. Shoots left. 6'1", 205 lbs. Born, Edmonton, Alta., October 22, 1980. Washington's 2nd choice, 43rd overall, in 2000 Entry Draft.

Season	Club	League	GP	G	A	Pts	PIM	PP	SH	GW	S	%	+/-	TF	F%	Min	GP	G	A	Pts	PIM	PP	SH	GW	Min
1994-95	Victoria Racquet	BCAHA	55	52	48	100	41	....	....	....	....	....	....	....	....	....	....	....	....	....	....	....	....	....	....
1995-96	Victoria Racquet	BCAHA	60	80	65	145	45	....	....	....	....	....	....	....	....	....	....	....	....	....	....	....	....	....	....
1996-97	Victoria Salsa	BCHL	49	22	14	36	31	....	....	....	....	....	....	....	....	....	....	....	....	....	....	....	....	....	....
1997-98	Victoria Salsa	BCHL	55	22	20	42	56	....	....	....	....	....	....	....	....	....	7	5	1	6	8	....	....	....	....
1998-99	U. of Denver	WCHA	33	6	14	20	44	....	....	....	....	....	....	....	....	....	....	....	....	....	....	....	....	....	....
99-2000	U. of Denver	WCHA	19	2	6	8	49	....	....	....	....	....	....	....	....	....	....	....	....	....	....	....	....	....	....
	Calgary Hitmen	WHL	27	14	6	20	41	....	....	....	....	....	....	....	....	....	11	2	6	8	30	....	....	....	....
2000-01	**Washington**	**NHL**	**10**	**0**	**0**	**0**	**2**	**0**	**0**	**0**	**6**	**0.0**	**–1**	**2**	**50.0**	**7:47**	....	....	....	....	....	....	....	....	....
	Portland Pirates	AHL	64	19	17	36	92	....	....	....	....	....	....	....	....	....	2	0	0	0	4	....	....	....	....
2001-02	**Washington**	**NHL**	**61**	**7**	**3**	**10**	**44**	**1**	**0**	**1**	**73**	**9.6**	**–8**	**5**	**20.0**	**9:39**	....	....	....	....	....	....	....	....	....
	Portland Pirates	AHL	9	3	3	6	24	....	....	....	....	....	....	....	....	....	....	....	....	....	....	....	....	....	....
2002-03	**Washington**	**NHL**	**1**	**0**	**0**	**0**	**0**	**0**	**0**	**0**	**0**	**0.0**	**0**	**1**	**0.0**	**3:30**	....	....	....	....	....	....	....	....	....
	Portland Pirates	AHL	69	14	13	27	72	....	....	....	....	....	....	....	....	....	3	0	2	2	2	....	....	....	....
2003-04	**Washington**	**NHL**	**71**	**7**	**5**	**12**	**37**	**1**	**0**	**1**	**92**	**7.6**	**–9**	**18**	**44.4**	**11:25**	....	....	....	....	....	....	....	....	....
	NHL Totals		**143**	**14**	**8**	**22**	**83**	**2**	**0**	**2**	**171**	**8.2**		**26**	**38.5**	**10:21**	....	....	....	....	....	....	....	....	....

Left **U. of Denver** (WCHA) and signed as a free agent with **Calgary** (WHL), January 10, 2000.

PHILLIPS, Chris
(FIHL-ihps, KRIHS) **OTT.**

Defense. Shoots left. 6'3", 215 lbs. Born, Calgary, Alta., March 9, 1978. Ottawa's 1st choice, 1st overall, in 1996 Entry Draft.

Season	Club	League	GP	G	A	Pts	PIM	PP	SH	GW	S	%	+/-	TF	F%	Min	GP	G	A	Pts	PIM	PP	SH	GW	Min
1993-94	Fort McMurray	AJHL	56	6	16	22	72	....	....	....	....	....	....	....	....	....	10	0	3	3	16	....	....	....	....
1994-95	Fort McMurray	AJHL	48	16	32	48	127	....	....	....	....	....	....	....	....	....	11	4	2	6	10	....	....	....	....
1995-96	Prince Albert	WHL	61	10	30	40	97	....	....	....	....	....	....	....	....	....	18	2	12	14	30	....	....	....	....
1996-97	Prince Albert	WHL	32	3	23	26	58	....	....	....	....	....	....	....	....	....	....	....	....	....	....	....	....	....	....
	Lethbridge	WHL	26	4	18	22	28	....	....	....	....	....	....	....	....	....	19	4	*21	25	20	....	....	....	....
1997-98	**Ottawa**	**NHL**	**72**	**5**	**11**	**16**	**38**	**2**	**0**	**2**	**107**	**4.7**	**2**	....	....	....	**11**	**0**	**2**	**2**	**2**	**0**	**0**	**0**	....
1998-99	**Ottawa**	**NHL**	**34**	**3**	**3**	**6**	**32**	**2**	**0**	**0**	**51**	**5.9**	**–5**	**0**	**0.0**	**18:06**	**3**	**0**	**0**	**0**	**0**	**0**	**0**	**0**	**13:50**
99-2000	**Ottawa**	**NHL**	**65**	**5**	**14**	**19**	**39**	**0**	**0**	**1**	**96**	**5.2**	**12**	**0**	**0.0**	**16:50**	**6**	**0**	**1**	**1**	**4**	**0**	**0**	**0**	**18:17**
2000-01	**Ottawa**	**NHL**	**73**	**2**	**12**	**14**	**31**	**2**	**0**	**0**	**77**	**2.6**	**8**	**1**	**0.0**	**21:28**	**1**	**1**	**0**	**1**	**0**	**0**	**0**	**0**	**20:52**
2001-02	**Ottawa**	**NHL**	**63**	**6**	**16**	**22**	**29**	**1**	**0**	**1**	**103**	**5.8**	**5**	**0**	**0.0**	**19:31**	**12**	**0**	**0**	**0**	**12**	**0**	**0**	**0**	**21:44**
2002-03	**Ottawa**	**NHL**	**78**	**3**	**16**	**19**	**71**	**2**	**0**	**1**	**97**	**3.1**	**7**	**0**	**0.0**	**20:13**	**18**	**2**	**4**	**6**	**12**	**0**	**0**	**1**	**21:36**
2003-04	**Ottawa**	**NHL**	**82**	**7**	**16**	**23**	**46**	**0**	**0**	**1**	**93**	**7.5**	**15**	**1**	**100.0**	**20:50**	**7**	**1**	**0**	**1**	**12**	**1**	**0**	**0**	**20:26**
	NHL Totals		**467**	**31**	**88**	**119**	**286**	**9**	**0**	**6**	**624**	**5.0**		**2**	**50.0**	**19:44**	**58**	**4**	**7**	**11**	**42**	**1**	**0**	**1**	**20:32**

WHL East First All-Star Team (1997) • Canadian Major Junior First All-Star Team (1997)

• Missed majority of 1998-99 season recovering from ankle injury suffered in game vs. Buffalo, December 30, 1998.

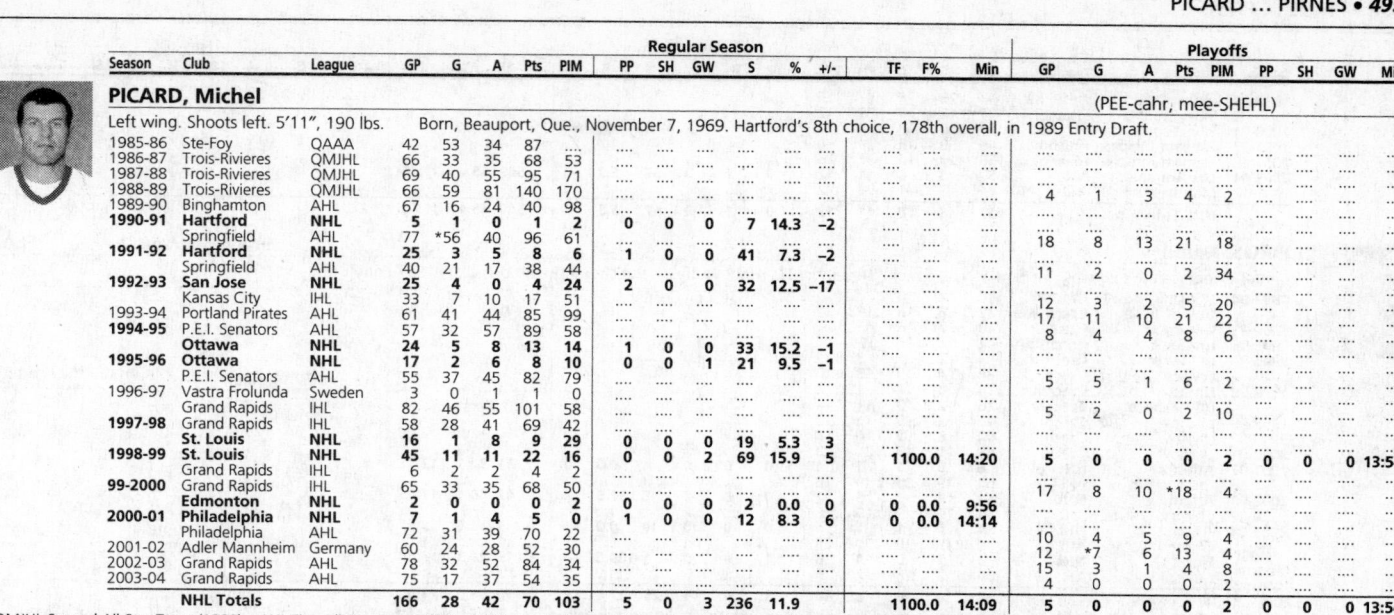

PICARD, Michel

(PEE-cahr, mee-SHEHL)

Left wing. Shoots left. 5'11", 190 lbs. Born, Beauport, Que., November 7, 1969. Hartford's 8th choice, 178th overall, in 1989 Entry Draft.

			Regular Season														Playoffs								
Season	Club	League	GP	G	A	Pts	PIM	PP	SH	GW	S	%	+/-	TF	F%	Min	GP	G	A	Pts	PIM	PP	SH	GW	Min
1985-86	Ste-Foy	QAAA	42	53	34	87	....																		
1986-87	Trois-Rivieres	QMJHL	66	33	35	68	53	....	....	....	....	....	....	....	....	....	....	....	....	....	....	....	....	....	....
1987-88	Trois-Rivieres	QMJHL	69	40	55	95	71	....	....	....	....	....	....	....	....	....	....	....	....	....	....	....	....	....	....
1988-89	Trois-Rivieres	QMJHL	66	59	81	140	170	....	....	....	....	....	....	....	....	....	4	1	3	4	2	....	....	....	....
1989-90	Binghamton	AHL	67	16	24	40	98	....	....	....	....	....	....	....	....	....	....	....	....	....	....	....	....	....	....
1990-91	**Hartford**	**NHL**	**5**	**1**	**0**	**1**	**2**	**0**	**0**	**0**	**7**	**14.3**	**–2**	....	....	....	....	....	....	....	....	....	....	....	....
	Springfield	AHL	77	*56	40	96	61	....	....	....	....	....	....	....	....	....	18	8	13	21	18	....	....	....	....
1991-92	**Hartford**	**NHL**	**25**	**3**	**5**	**8**	**6**	**1**	**0**	**0**	**41**	**7.3**	**–2**	....	....	....	....	....	....	....	....	....	....	....	....
	Springfield	AHL	40	21	17	38	44	....	....	....	....	....	....	....	....	....	11	2	0	2	34	....	....	....	....
1992-93	**San Jose**	**NHL**	**25**	**4**	**0**	**4**	**24**	**2**	**0**	**0**	**32**	**12.5**	**–17**	....	....	....	....	....	....	....	....	....	....	....	....
	Kansas City	IHL	33	7	10	17	51	....	....	....	....	....	....	....	....	....	12	3	2	5	20	....	....	....	....
1993-94	Portland Pirates	AHL	61	41	44	85	99	....	....	....	....	....	....	....	....	....	17	11	10	21	22	....	....	....	....
1994-95	P.E.I. Senators	AHL	57	32	57	89	58	....	....	....	....	....	....	....	....	....	8	4	4	8	6	....	....	....	....
	Ottawa	**NHL**	**24**	**5**	**8**	**13**	**14**	**1**	**0**	**0**	**33**	**15.2**	**–1**	....	....	....	....	....	....	....	....	....	....	....	....
1995-96	**Ottawa**	**NHL**	**17**	**2**	**6**	**8**	**10**	**0**	**0**	**1**	**21**	**9.5**	**–1**	....	....	....	....	....	....	....	....	....	....	....	....
	P.E.I. Senators	AHL	55	37	45	82	79	....	....	....	....	....	....	....	....	....	5	5	1	6	2	....	....	....	....
1996-97	Vastra Frolunda	Sweden	3	0	1	1	0	....	....	....	....	....	....	....	....	....	....	....	....	....	....	....	....	....	....
	Grand Rapids	IHL	82	46	55	101	58	....	....	....	....	....	....	....	....	....	5	2	0	2	10	....	....	....	....
1997-98	Grand Rapids	IHL	58	28	41	69	42	....	....	....	....	....	....	....	....	....	....	....	....	....	....	....	....	....	....
	St. Louis	**NHL**	**16**	**1**	**8**	**9**	**29**	**0**	**0**	**0**	**19**	**5.3**	**3**	....	....	....	....	....	....	....	....	....	....	....	....
1998-99	**St. Louis**	**NHL**	**45**	**11**	**11**	**22**	**16**	**0**	**0**	**2**	**69**	**15.9**	**5**	**1**	**100.0**	**14:20**	**5**	**0**	**0**	**0**	**2**	**0**	**0**	**0**	**13:54**
	Grand Rapids	IHL	6	2	2	4	2	....	....	....	....	....	....	....	....	....	....	....	....	....	....	....	....	....	....
99-2000	Grand Rapids	IHL	65	33	35	68	50	....	....	....	....	....	....	....	....	....	17	8	10	*18	4	....	....	....	....
	Edmonton	**NHL**	**2**	**0**	**0**	**0**	**2**	**0**	**0**	**0**	**2**	**0.0**	**0**	**0**	**0.0**	**9:56**	....	....	....	....	....	....	....	....	....
2000-01	**Philadelphia**	**NHL**	**7**	**1**	**4**	**5**	**0**	**1**	**0**	**0**	**12**	**8.3**	**6**	**0**	**0.0**	**14:14**	....	....	....	....	....	....	....	....	....
	Philadelphia	AHL	72	31	39	70	22	....	....	....	....	....	....	....	....	....	10	4	5	9	4	....	....	....	....
2001-02	Adler Mannheim	Germany	60	24	28	52	30	....	....	....	....	....	....	....	....	....	12	*7	6	13	4	....	....	....	....
2002-03	Grand Rapids	AHL	78	32	52	84	34	....	....	....	....	....	....	....	....	....	15	3	1	4	8	....	....	....	....
2003-04	Grand Rapids	AHL	75	17	37	54	35	....	....	....	....	....	....	....	....	....	4	0	0	0	2	....	....	....	....
	NHL Totals		**166**	**28**	**42**	**70**	**103**	**5**	**0**	**3**	**236**	**11.9**		**1**	**100.0**	**14:09**	**5**	**0**	**0**	**0**	**2**	**0**	**0**	**0**	**13:54**

QMJHL Second All-Star Team (1989) • AHL First All-Star Team (1991, 1995) • AHL Second All-Star Team (1994, 2003) • IHL First All-Star Team (1997)

Traded to **San Jose** by **Hartford** for future considerations (Yvon Corriveau, January 21, 1993), October 9, 1992. Signed as a free agent by **Portland** (AHL), September, 1993. Signed as a free agent by **Ottawa**, June 16, 1994. Traded to **Washington** by **Ottawa** for cash, May 21, 1996. Signed as a free agent by **St. Louis**, January 5, 1998. Signed as a free agent by **Edmonton**, December 2, 1999. Signed as a free agent by **Philadelphia**, August 14, 2000. Signed as a free agent by **Detroit**, July 15, 2002.

PIHLMAN, Tuomas

(PIHL-mahn, TAWH-muhs) **N.J.**

Left wing. Shoots left. 6'3", 210 lbs. Born, Espoo, Finland, November 13, 1982. New Jersey's 3rd choice, 48th overall, in 2001 Entry Draft.

Season	Club	League	GP	G	A	Pts	PIM	PP	SH	GW	S	%	+/-	TF	F%	Min	GP	G	A	Pts	PIM	PP	SH	GW	Min
1996-97	JYP Jyvaskyla C	Finn-Jr.	25	9	10	19	28	....	....	....	....	....	....	....	....	....	....	....	....	....	....	....	....	....	....
1997-98	JYP Jyvaskyla C	Finn-Jr.	1	0	1	1	0	....	....	....	....	....	....	....	....	....	....	....	....	....	....	....	....	....	....
	JYP Jyvaskyla B	Finn-Jr.	30	2	5	7	18	....	....	....	....	....	....	....	....	....	4	1	3	4	6	....	....	....	....
1998-99	JYP Jyvaskyla B	Finn-Jr.	35	21	20	41	64	....	....	....	....	....	....	....	....	....	6	1	1	2	12	....	....	....	....
99-2000	JYP Jyvaskyla Jr.	Finn-Jr.	20	4	4	8	54	....	....	....	....	....	....	....	....	....	4	0	0	0	8	....	....	....	....
	JYP Jyvaskyla	Finland	17	0	0	0	18	....	....	....	....	....	....	....	....	....	....	....	....	....	....	....	....	....	....
2000-01	JYP Jyvaskyla Jr.	Finn-Jr.	1	1	0	1	0	....	....	....	....	....	....	....	....	....	....	....	....	....	....	....	....	....	....
	JYP Jyvaskyla	Finland	47	3	6	9	59	....	....	....	....	....	....	....	....	....	....	....	....	....	....	....	....	....	....
2001-02	JYP Jyvaskyla Jr.	Finn-Jr.	3	1	1	2	4	....	....	....	....	....	....	....	....	....	....	....	....	....	....	....	....	....	....
	JYP Jyvaskyla	Finland	44	9	2	11	93	....	....	....	....	....	....	....	....	....	....	....	....	....	....	....	....	....	....
2002-03	JYP Jyvaskyla	Finland	53	19	15	34	58	....	....	....	....	....	....	....	....	....	1	0	0	0	0	....	....	....	....
2003-04	**New Jersey**	**NHL**	**2**	**0**	**0**	**0**	**2**	**0**	**0**	**0**	**1**	**0.0**	**0**	**0**	**0.0**	**6:56**	....	....	....	....	....	....	....	....	....
	Albany River Rats	AHL	73	10	19	29	59	....	....	....	....	....	....	....	....	....	....	....	....	....	....	....	....	....	....
	NHL Totals		**2**	**0**	**0**	**0**	**2**	**0**	**0**	**0**	**1**	**0.0**		**0**	**0.0**	**6:56**	....	....	....	....	....	....	....	....	....

PILAR, Karel

(PEE-lahr, KAH-rehl) **TOR.**

Defense. Shoots right. 6'3", 207 lbs. Born, Prague, Czech., December 23, 1977. Toronto's 2nd choice, 39th overall, in 2001 Entry Draft.

Season	Club	League	GP	G	A	Pts	PIM	PP	SH	GW	S	%	+/-	TF	F%	Min	GP	G	A	Pts	PIM	PP	SH	GW	Min
99-2000	Litvinov	Czech	49	2	12	14	61	....	....	....	....	....	....	....	....	....	7	0	0	0	4	....	....	....	....
2000-01	Litvinov	Czech	52	12	26	38	52	....	....	....	....	....	....	....	....	....	4	1	1	2	25	....	....	....	....
2001-02	**Toronto**	**NHL**	**23**	**1**	**3**	**4**	**8**	**0**	**0**	**0**	**32**	**3.1**	**3**	**0**	**0.0**	**16:03**	**11**	**0**	**4**	**4**	**12**	**0**	**0**	**0**	**17:47**
	St. John's	AHL	52	10	14	24	26	....	....	....	....	....	....	....	....	....	....	....	....	....	....	....	....	....	....
2002-03	**Toronto**	**NHL**	**17**	**3**	**4**	**7**	**12**	**1**	**0**	**1**	**22**	**13.6**	**–7**	**0**	**0.0**	**18:29**	....	....	....	....	....	....	....	....	....
	St. John's	AHL	7	2	5	7	28	....	....	....	....	....	....	....	....	....	....	....	....	....	....	....	....	....	....
2003-04	**Toronto**	**NHL**	**50**	**2**	**17**	**19**	**22**	**1**	**0**	**1**	**74**	**2.7**	**2**	**0**	**0.0**	**18:03**	**1**	**1**	**0**	**1**	**0**	**0**	**0**	**0**	**20:48**
	St. John's	AHL	6	3	4	7	6	....	....	....	....	....	....	....	....	....	....	....	....	....	....	....	....	....	....
	NHL Totals		**90**	**6**	**24**	**30**	**42**	**2**	**0**	**2**	**128**	**4.7**		**0**	**0.0**	**17:38**	**12**	**1**	**4**	**5**	**12**	**0**	**0**	**0**	**18:02**

• Spent majority of 2002-03 season as a healthy reserve.

PIRJETA, Lasse

(PEER-yeh-tuh, LAH-see) **PIT.**

Left wing. Shoots left. 6'4", 225 lbs. Born, Oulu, Finland, April 4, 1974. Columbus' 7th choice, 133rd overall, in 2002 Entry Draft.

Season	Club	League	GP	G	A	Pts	PIM	PP	SH	GW	S	%	+/-	TF	F%	Min	GP	G	A	Pts	PIM	PP	SH	GW	Min
1990-91	Karpat Oulu Jr.	Finn-Jr.	21	5	6	11	10	....	....	....	....	....	....	....	....	....	....	....	....	....	....	....	....	....	....
1991-92	Tacoma Rockets	WHL	16	5	2	7	4	....	....	....	....	....	....	....	....	....	....	....	....	....	....	....	....	....	....
	Karpat Oulu Jr.	Finn-Jr.	7	1	4	5	8	....	....	....	....	....	....	....	....	....	....	....	....	....	....	....	....	....	....
	Karpat Oulu	Finland-2	2	0	0	0	0	....	....	....	....	....	....	....	....	....	....	....	....	....	....	....	....	....	....
1992-93	Karpat Oulu Jr.	Finn-Jr.	24	13	19	32	34	....	....	....	....	....	....	....	....	....	....	....	....	....	....	....	....	....	....
	Karpat Oulu	Finland-2	20	4	3	7	6	....	....	....	....	....	....	....	....	....	....	....	....	....	....	....	....	....	....
1993-94	TPS Turku Jr.	Finn-Jr.	6	2	2	4	2	....	....	....	....	....	....	....	....	....	4	6	2	8	2	....	....	....	....
	Kiekko-67 Turku	Finland-2	2	2	1	3	0	....	....	....	....	....	....	....	....	....	....	....	....	....	....	....	....	....	....
	TPS Turku	Finland	43	9	9	18	14	....	....	....	....	....	....	....	....	....	11	4	0	4	2	....	....	....	....
1994-95	TPS Turku Jr.	Finn-Jr.	1	0	0	0	0	....	....	....	....	....	....	....	....	....	....	....	....	....	....	....	....	....	....
	TPS Turku	Finland	49	7	13	20	64	....	....	....	....	....	....	....	....	....	8	0	1	1	29	....	....	....	....
1995-96	TPS Turku	Finland	45	13	14	27	34	....	....	....	....	....	....	....	....	....	11	6	3	9	4	....	....	....	....
1996-97	Vastra Frolunda	Sweden	50	14	8	22	36	....	....	....	....	....	....	....	....	....	3	0	1	1	4	....	....	....	....
	Vastra Frolunda	EuroHL	5	2	6	8	4	....	....	....	....	....	....	....	....	....	....	....	....	....	....	....	....	....	....
1997-98	Tappara Tampere	Finland	48	24	22	46	20	....	....	....	....	....	....	....	....	....	4	1	1	2	2	....	....	....	....
1998-99	Tappara Tampere	Finland	54	22	19	41	32	....	....	....	....	....	....	....	....	....	....	....	....	....	....	....	....	....	....
99-2000	HIFK Helsinki	Finland	54	18	25	43	24	....	....	....	....	....	....	....	....	....	9	2	3	5	10	....	....	....	....
	HIFK Helsinki	EuroHL	6	1	3	4	6	....	....	....	....	....	....	....	....	....	2	1	1	2	0	....	....	....	....
2000-01	HIFK Helsinki	Finland	55	15	18	33	24	....	....	....	....	....	....	....	....	....	....	....	....	....	....	....	....	....	....
2001-02	Karpat Oulu	Finland	55	15	26	41	24	....	....	....	....	....	....	....	....	....	4	2	2	4	2	....	....	....	....
2002-03	**Columbus**	**NHL**	**51**	**11**	**10**	**21**	**12**	**2**	**0**	**2**	**80**	**13.8**	**–4**	**327**	**43.1**	**11:28**	....	....	....	....	....	....	....	....	....
2003-04	**Columbus**	**NHL**	**57**	**2**	**8**	**10**	**20**	**0**	**0**	**0**	**78**	**2.6**	**–6**	**465**	**49.5**	**10:46**	....	....	....	....	....	....	....	....	....
	Syracuse Crunch	AHL	5	1	2	3	2	....	....	....	....	....	....	....	....	....	....	....	....	....	....	....	....	....	....
	Pittsburgh	**NHL**	**13**	**6**	**6**	**12**	**0**	**1**	**0**	**1**	**33**	**18.2**	**3**	**187**	**51.9**	**14:22**	....	....	....	....	....	....	....	....	....
	NHL Totals		**121**	**19**	**24**	**43**	**32**	**3**	**0**	**3**	**191**	**9.9**		**979**	**47.8**	**11:27**	....	....	....	....	....	....	....	....	....

Traded to **Pittsburgh** by **Columbus** for Brian Holzinger, March 9, 2004.

PIRNES, Esa

(PEER-nehz, EH-sah) **L.A.**

Center. Shoots left. 6', 189 lbs. Born, Oulu, Finland, April 1, 1977. Los Angeles' 7th choice, 174th overall, in 2003 Entry Draft.

Season	Club	League	GP	G	A	Pts	PIM	PP	SH	GW	S	%	+/-	TF	F%	Min	GP	G	A	Pts	PIM	PP	SH	GW	Min
1994-95	Karpat Oulu Jr.	Finn-Jr.	18	3	3	6	10	....	....	....	....	....	....	....	....	....	14	5	6	11	6	....	....	....	....
1995-96	Karpat Oulu Jr.	Finn-Jr.	24	19	13	32	8	....	....	....	....	....	....	....	....	....	....	....	....	....	....	....	....	....	....
	Karpat Oulu	Finland-2	20	8	4	12	12	....	....	....	....	....	....	....	....	....	3	0	0	0	0	....	....	....	....
1996-97	Karpat Oulu Jr.	Finn-Jr.	9	5	5	10	6	....	....	....	....	....	....	....	....	....	....	....	....	....	....	....	....	....	....
	Karpat Oulu	Finland-2	36	17	16	33	20	....	....	....	....	....	....	....	....	....	3	0	0	0	12	....	....	....	....
1997-98	Karpat Oulu Jr.	Finn-Jr.	15	9	23	32	4	....	....	....	....	....	....	....	....	....	....	....	....	....	....	....	....	....	....
	Karpat Oulu	Finland-2	32	6	15	21	12	....	....	....	....	....	....	....	....	....	....	....	....	....	....	....	....	....	....

			Regular Season														Playoffs								
Season	Club	League	GP	G	A	Pts	PIM	PP	SH	GW	S	%	+/-	TF	F%	Min	GP	G	A	Pts	PIM	PP	SH	GW	Min
1998-99	Karpat Oulu	Finland-2	47	26	26	52	16										5	0	3	3	2				
99-2000	Blues Espoo	Finland	51	15	24	39	12										4	0	1	1	2				
2000-01	Blues Espoo	Finland	54	10	8	18	51																		
2001-02	Tappara Tampere	Finland	49	8	16	24	30										10	0	1	1	2				
2002-03	Tappara Tampere	Finland	56	23	14	37	6										15	5	*9	*14	2				
2003-04	**Los Angeles**	**NHL**	**57**	**3**	**8**	**11**	**12**	**0**	**1**	**0**	**57**	**5.3**	**–9**	**549**	**45.4**	**11:45**									
	Manchester	AHL	4	3	1	4	2																		
	NHL Totals		**57**	**3**	**8**	**11**	**12**	**0**	**1**	**0**	**57**	**5.3**		**549**	**45.4**	**11:45**									

PIROS, Kamil

(PIH-ruhsh, KA-mihl) **FLA.**

Center. Shoots left. 6', 200 lbs. Born, Most, Czech., November 20, 1978. Buffalo's 9th choice, 212th overall, in 1997 Entry Draft.

Season	Club	League	GP	G	A	Pts	PIM	PP	SH	GW	S	%	+/-	TF	F%	Min	GP	G	A	Pts	PIM	PP	SH	GW	Min
1993-94	HC Banik Most Jr.	Czech-Jr.	16	12	10	22																			
	Litvinov Jr.	Czech-Jr.	22	6	13	19																			
1994-95	Litvinov Jr.	Czech-Jr.	40	27	16	43																			
1995-96	Litvinov Jr.	Czech-Jr.	42	16	13	29																			
1996-97	Litvinov Jr.	Czech-Jr.	3	2	1	3																			
	Litvinov	Czech	38	4	9	13	10																		
1997-98	Litvinov	Czech	14	0	1	1	2																		
	HC Vitkovice	Czech	26	2	9	11	14																		
1998-99	Litvinov	Czech	41	7	9	16	10																		
99-2000	Litvinov	Czech	40	8	8	16	18										7	0	3	3	2				
2000-01	Litvinov	Czech	48	11	13	24	28										6	1	1	2	2				
2001-02	**Atlanta**	**NHL**	**8**	**0**	**1**	**1**	**4**	**0**	**0**	**0**	**4**	**0.0**	**–2**	**81**	**32.1**	**12:12**									
	Chicago Wolves	AHL	64	19	30	49	16										25	6	11	17	6				
2002-03	**Atlanta**	**NHL**	**3**	**3**	**2**	**5**	**2**	**0**	**0**	**1**	**8**	**37.5**	**4**	**47**	**40.4**	**17:05**									
	Chicago Wolves	AHL	51	10	9	19	16										9	1	0	1	4				
2003-04	**Atlanta**	**NHL**	**14**	**0**	**1**	**1**	**4**	**0**	**0**	**0**	**10**	**0.0**	**–3**	**3**	**33.3**	**9:57**									
	Chicago Wolves	AHL	50	10	20	30	20																		
	Florida	**NHL**	**3**	**1**	**0**	**1**	**0**	**1**	**0**	**0**	**1**	**100.0**	**–1**	**19**	**26.3**	**6:59**									
	San Antonio	AHL	14	2	5	7	6																		
	NHL Totals		**28**	**4**	**4**	**8**	**10**	**1**	**0**	**1**	**23**	**17.4**		**150**	**34.0**	**11:02**									

Rights traded to **Atlanta** by **Buffalo** with Buffalo's 4th round choice (later traded to St. Louis – St. Louis selected Igor Valeyev) in 2001 Entry Draft for Donald Audette, March 13, 2001. Signed as a free agent by **Yaroslavl** (Russia), September 8, 2003. Traded to **Florida** by **Atlanta** for Kyle Rossiter, March 8, 2004.

PISA, Ales

(PEE-sha, al-EHSH) **NYR**

Defense. Shoots left. 6', 195 lbs. Born, Pardibuce, Czech., January 2, 1977. Edmonton's 10th choice, 272nd overall, in 2001 Entry Draft.

Season	Club	League	GP	G	A	Pts	PIM	PP	SH	GW	S	%	+/-	TF	F%	Min	GP	G	A	Pts	PIM	PP	SH	GW	Min
1993-94	HC Pardubice	Czech	2	0	0	0	0																		
1994-95	HC Pardubice	Czech	22	0	0	0	18										2	0	0	0	0				
1995-96	Pardubice	Czech	33	0	4	4	82																		
1996-97	Pardubice	Czech	41	4	2	6	70										6	0	2	2	6				
1997-98	Pardubice	Czech	50	4	9	13	107										3	0	0	0	4				
1998-99	Pardubice	Czech	48	7	12	19	74										3	0	1	1					
99-2000	Pardubice	Czech	51	5	11	16	58										1	0	0	0	4				
2000-01	Pardubice	Czech	47	10	13	23	75										7	2	2	4	4				
2001-02	**Edmonton**	**NHL**	**2**	**0**	**0**	**0**	**2**	**0**	**0**	**0**	**3**	**0.0**	**0**	**0**	**0.0**	**15:02**									
	Hamilton	AHL	52	6	12	18	62										14	1	4	5	8				
2002-03	**Edmonton**	**NHL**	**48**	**1**	**3**	**4**	**24**	**1**	**0**	**0**	**34**	**2.9**	**11**	**0**	**0.0**	**12:56**									
	Hamilton	AHL	7	0	1	1	14																		
	NY Rangers	**NHL**	**3**	**0**	**0**	**0**	**0**	**0**	**0**	**0**	**3**	**0.0**	**1**	**0**	**0.0**	**13:55**									
2003-04	Cherepovets	Russia	31	1	11	12	46																		
	NHL Totals		**53**	**1**	**3**	**4**	**26**	**1**	**0**	**0**	**40**	**2.5**		**0**	**0.0**	**13:04**									

Traded to **NY Rangers** by **Edmonton** with Anson Carter for Radek Dvorak and Cory Cross, March 11, 2003.

PISANI, Fernando

(pih-ZAN-ee, FUHR-nan-DOH) **EDM.**

Right wing. Shoots left. 6'1", 205 lbs. Born, Edmonton, Alta., December 27, 1976. Edmonton's 9th choice, 195th overall, in 1996 Entry Draft.

Season	Club	League	GP	G	A	Pts	PIM	PP	SH	GW	S	%	+/-	TF	F%	Min	GP	G	A	Pts	PIM	PP	SH	GW	Min
1993-94	St. Albert Saints	AJHL	50	6	21	27	24																		
1994-95	Bonnyville	AJHL	16	4	34	37	97																		
	St. Albert Saints	AJHL	40	26	21	47	16																		
1995-96	St. Albert Saints	AJHL	58	40	63	103	134										18	7	22	29	28				
1996-97	Providence	H-East	35	12	18	30	36																		
1997-98	Providence	H-East	36	16	18	34	20																		
1998-99	Providence	H-East	38	14	37	51	42																		
99-2000	Providence	H-East	38	14	24	38	56																		
2000-01	Hamilton	AHL	52	12	13	25	28																		
2001-02	Hamilton	AHL	79	26	34	60	60										15	4	6	10	4				
2002-03	**Edmonton**	**NHL**	**35**	**8**	**5**	**13**	**10**	**0**	**1**	**0**	**32**	**25.0**	**9**	**1**	**100.0**	**10:43**	**6**	**1**	**0**	**1**	**2**	**0**	**0**	**0**	**13:48**
	Hamilton	AHL	41	17	15	32	24																		
2003-04	**Edmonton**	**NHL**	**76**	**16**	**14**	**30**	**46**	**4**	**1**	**1**	**99**	**16.2**	**14**	**10**	**20.0**	**12:46**									
	NHL Totals		**111**	**24**	**19**	**43**	**56**	**4**	**2**	**1**	**131**	**18.3**		**11**	**27.3**	**12:07**	**6**	**1**	**0**	**1**	**2**	**0**	**0**	**0**	**13:48**

PITKANEN, Joni

(PIHT-ka-nuhn, YOH-nee) **PHI.**

Defense. Shoots left. 6'3", 200 lbs. Born, Oulu, Finland, September 19, 1983. Philadelphia's 1st choice, 4th overall, in 2002 Entry Draft.

Season	Club	League	GP	G	A	Pts	PIM	PP	SH	GW	S	%	+/-	TF	F%	Min	GP	G	A	Pts	PIM	PP	SH	GW	Min
1998-99	Karpat Oulu Jr.	Finn-Jr.	30	1	5	6	12																		
99-2000	Karpat Oulu Jr.	Finn-Jr.	38	12	14	26	26										6	1	4	5	2				
2000-01	Karpat Oulu Jr.	Finn-Jr.	24	6	11	17	77																		
	Karpat Oulu	Finland	21	0	0	0	10										2	0	0	0	2				
2001-02	Karpat Oulu	Finland	49	4	15	19	65										4	0	0	0	12				
	Karpat Oulu Jr.	Finn-Jr.															1	0	0	0	0				
2002-03	Karpat Oulu	Finland	35	5	15	20	38																		
2003-04	**Philadelphia**	**NHL**	**71**	**8**	**19**	**27**	**44**	**5**	**0**	**2**	**133**	**6.0**	**15**	**0**	**0.0**	**16:35**	**15**	**0**	**3**	**3**	**6**	**0**	**0**	**0**	**12:13**
	NHL Totals		**71**	**8**	**19**	**27**	**44**	**5**	**0**	**2**	**133**	**6.0**		**0**	**0.0**	**16:35**	**15**	**0**	**3**	**3**	**6**	**0**	**0**	**0**	**12:13**

NHL All-Rookie Team (2004)

PITTIS, Domenic

(PIH-THIS, DOHM-ihn-ihk)

Center. Shoots left. 5'11", 190 lbs. Born, Calgary, Alta., October 1, 1974. Pittsburgh's 2nd choice, 52nd overall, in 1993 Entry Draft.

Season	Club	League	GP	G	A	Pts	PIM	PP	SH	GW	S	%	+/-	TF	F%	Min	GP	G	A	Pts	PIM	PP	SH	GW	Min
1990-91	Calgary Flames	AMHL	35	23	54	77	43																		
1991-92	Lethbridge	WHL	65	6	17	23	18										5	0	2	2	4				
1992-93	Lethbridge	WHL	66	46	73	119	69										4	3	3	6	8				
1993-94	Lethbridge	WHL	72	58	69	127	93										8	4	11	15	16				
1994-95	Cleveland	IHL	62	18	32	50	66										3	0	2	2	2				
1995-96	Cleveland	IHL	74	10	28	38	100										3	0	0	0	2				
1996-97	**Pittsburgh**	**NHL**	**1**	**0**	**0**	**0**	**0**	**0**	**0**	**0**	**0**	**0.0**	**–1**												
	Long Beach	IHL	65	23	43	66	91										18	5	9	14	26				
1997-98	Syracuse Crunch	AHL	75	23	41	64	90										5	1	3	4	4				
1998-99	**Buffalo**	**NHL**	**3**	**0**	**0**	**0**	**2**	**0**	**0**	**0**	**1**	**0.0**	**0**	**19**	**42.1**	**8:35**									
	Rochester	AHL	76	38	66	*104	108										20	7	*14	*21	40				
99-2000	**Buffalo**	**NHL**	**7**	**1**	**0**	**1**	**6**	**0**	**0**	**0**	**6**	**16.7**	**1**	**65**	**44.6**	**11:27**									
	Rochester	AHL	53	17	48	65	85										21	4	*26	*30	28				
2000-01	**Edmonton**	**NHL**	**47**	**4**	**5**	**9**	**49**	**0**	**0**	**2**	**42**	**9.5**	**–5**	**367**	**54.8**	**10:46**	**3**	**0**	**0**	**0**	**2**	**0**	**0**	**0**	**8:00**
2001-02	**Edmonton**	**NHL**	**22**	**0**	**6**	**6**	**8**	**0**	**0**	**0**	**18**	**0.0**	**–2**	**52**	**55.8**	**11:23**									
2002-03	**Nashville**	**NHL**	**2**	**0**	**0**	**0**	**2**	**0**	**0**	**0**	**1**	**0.0**	**0**	**6**	**16.7**	**5:00**									
	Milwaukee	AHL	30	11	21	32	65										6	2	4	6	8				

			Regular Season														Playoffs								
Season	Club	League	GP	G	A	Pts	PIM	PP	SH	GW	S	%	+/-	TF	F%	Min	GP	G	A	Pts	PIM	PP	SH	GW	Min
2003-04	Buffalo	NHL	4	0	0	0	4	0	0	0	3	0.0	–1	47	53.2	11:37									
	Rochester	AHL	75	20	*57	77	137										16	5	14	19	30				
	NHL Totals		86	5	11	16	71	0	0	2	71	7.0		556	52.7	10:49	3	0	0	0	2	0	0	0	8:00

WHL East Second All-Star Team (1994) • John P. Sollenberger Trophy (Top Scorer – AHL) (1999)

Signed as a free agent by **Buffalo**, August 10, 1998. Signed as a free agent by **Edmonton**, July 25, 2000. • Missed majority of 2001-02 season recovering from head injury suffered in game vs. Nashvile, February 28, 2002. Signed as a free agent by **Nashville**, July 24, 2002. • Missed majority of 2002-03 season recovering from head injury suffered in game vs. San Jose, November 7, 2002. Signed as a free agent by **Buffalo**, July 26, 2003. Signed as a free agent by **ERC Ingolstadt** (Germany), April 3, 2004.

PIVKO, Libor
(PIHV-koh, LEE-bohr) **NSH.**

Left wing. Shoots left. 6'2", 205 lbs. Born, Novy Vicin, Czech., March 29, 1980. Nashville's 4th choice, 89th overall, in 2000 Entry Draft.

Season	Club	League	GP	G	A	Pts	PIM	PP	SH	GW	S	%	+/-	TF	F%	Min	GP	G	A	Pts	PIM	PP	SH	GW	Min
1995-96	Slezan Opava Jr.	Czech-Jr.	37	19	14	33	30																		
1996-97	Slezan Opava Jr.	Czech-Jr.	16	12	9	21	22																		
1997-98	HC Opava Jr.	Czech-Jr.	37	15	11	26	36																		
1998-99	HC Opava Jr.	Czech-Jr.	38	21	14	35																			
	HC Opava	Czech	5	0	1	1	0																		
99-2000	Havirov Jr.	Czech-Jr.	5	1	3	4	4																		
	HC Femax Havirov	Czech	40	11	11	22	41																		
	HC Ytong Brno	Czech-3															4	3	4	7	0				
2000-01	HC Femax Havirov	Czech	45	7	12	19	58																		
2001-02	Zlin	Czech	46	8	20	28	36										9	5	3	8	8				
2002-03	HC Hame Zlin	Czech	52	13	12	25	60																		
2003-04	**Nashville**	**NHL**	**1**	**0**	**0**	**0**	**0**	**0**	**0**	**0**	**2**	**0.0**	**0**	**0**	**0.0**	**6:50**									
	Milwaukee	AHL	67	11	20	31	50										21	7	6	13	22				
	NHL Totals		**1**	**0**	**0**	**0**	**0**	**0**	**0**	**0**	**2**	**0.0**		**0**	**0.0**	**6:50**									

PLEKANEC, Tomas
(pleh-KA-nyehts, TAW-mahsh) **MTL.**

Left wing. Shoots left. 5'10", 200 lbs. Born, Kladno, Czech., October 31, 1982. Montreal's 4th choice, 71st overall, in 2001 Entry Draft.

Season	Club	League	GP	G	A	Pts	PIM	PP	SH	GW	S	%	+/-	TF	F%	Min	GP	G	A	Pts	PIM	PP	SH	GW	Min
1996-97	Kladno 18	Czech-Jr.	13	1	3	4																			
1997-98	Kladno 18	Czech-Jr.	45	38	26	64																			
1998-99	Kladno Jr.	Czech-Jr.	53	22	20	42																			
99-2000	Kladno Jr.	Czech-Jr.	43	14	16	30																			
	HK Kralupy	Czech-2	6	2	2	4	2																		
	HK Slany	Czech-2	3	0	1	1	6																		
2000-01	Kladno	Czech	47	9	9	18	24																		
	Kladno Jr.	Czech-Jr.	9	6	4	10	4																		
2001-02	Kladno	Czech	48	7	16	23	28																		
	HC Bolesav	Czech-2	6	6	3	9	14																		
	Kladno	Czech-Q	5	0	1	1	0																		
2002-03	Hamilton	AHL	77	19	27	46	74										13	3	2	5	8				
2003-04	**Montreal**	**NHL**	**2**	**0**	**0**	**0**	**0**	**0**	**0**	**0**	**0**	**0.0**	**0**	**11**	**45.5**	**9:02**									
	Hamilton	AHL	74	23	43	66	90										10	2	5	7	6				
	NHL Totals		**2**	**0**	**0**	**0**	**0**	**0**	**0**	**0**	**0**	**0.0**		**11**	**45.5**	**9:02**									

PLETKA, Vaclav
(PLEHT-kuh, VAT-slav) **PHI.**

Right wing. Shoots left. 5'11", 182 lbs. Born, Mlada Boleslav, Czech., June 8, 1979. Philadelphia's 5th choice, 208th overall, in 1999 Entry Draft.

Season	Club	League	GP	G	A	Pts	PIM	PP	SH	GW	S	%	+/-	TF	F%	Min	GP	G	A	Pts	PIM	PP	SH	GW	Min
1995-96	Mlada Boleslav Jr.	Czech-Jr.	35	22	17	39																			
1996-97	Mlada Boleslav Jr.	Czech-Jr.	37	28	13	41																			
1997-98	Mlada Boleslav Jr.	Czech-Jr.	36	23	25	48																			
1998-99	Trinec Jr.	Czech-Jr.	20	11	5	16																			
	Trinec	Czech	50	15	11	26	20										10	2	1	3					
99-2000	HC Ocelari Trinec	Czech	51	28	21	49	62										4	2	2	4	2				
2000-01	Philadelphia	AHL	71	20	21	41	51										10	1	3	4	4				
2001-02	**Philadelphia**	**NHL**	**1**	**0**	**0**	**0**	**0**	**0**	**0**	**0**	**2**	**0.0**	**0**	**0**	**0.0**	**11:34**									
	Philadelphia	AHL	61	20	19	39	43																		
2002-03	HC Ocelari Trinec	Czech	47	20	24	44	58										12	3	2	5	18				
2003-04	HC Ocelari Trinec	Czech	47	12	17	29	104										5	0	0	0	2				
	NHL Totals		**1**	**0**	**0**	**0**	**0**	**0**	**0**	**0**	**2**	**0.0**		**0**	**0.0**	**11:34**									

Signed as a free agent by **HC Ocelari Trinec** (Czech), July 27, 2002.

POAPST, Steve
(POHPST, STEEV) **CHI.**

Defense. Shoots left. 6', 199 lbs. Born, Cornwall, Ont., January 3, 1969.

Season	Club	League	GP	G	A	Pts	PIM	PP	SH	GW	S	%	+/-	TF	F%	Min	GP	G	A	Pts	PIM	PP	SH	GW	Min
1986-87	Smiths Falls Bears	OCJHL	54	10	27	37	94																		
1987-88	Colgate	ECAC	32	3	13	16	22																		
1988-89	Colgate	ECAC	30	0	5	5	38																		
1989-90	Colgate	ECAC	38	4	15	19	54																		
1990-91	Colgate	ECAC	32	6	15	21	43																		
1991-92	Hampton Roads	ECHL	55	8	20	28	29										14	1	4	5	12				
1992-93	Hampton Roads	ECHL	63	10	35	45	57										4	0	1	1	4				
	Baltimore	AHL	7	0	1	1	4										7	0	3	3	6				
1993-94	Portland Pirates	AHL	78	14	21	35	47										12	0	3	3	8				
1994-95	Portland Pirates	AHL	71	8	22	30	60										7	0	1	1	16				
1995-96	**Washington**	**NHL**	**3**	**1**	**0**	**1**	**0**	**0**	**0**	**1**	**2**	**50.0**	**–1**				**6**	**0**	**0**	**0**	**0**	**0**	**0**	**0**	
	Portland Pirates	AHL	70	10	24	34	79										20	2	6	8	16				
1996-97	Portland Pirates	AHL	47	1	20	21	34										5	0	1	1	6				
1997-98	Portland Pirates	AHL	76	8	29	37	46										10	2	3	5	8				
1998-99	**Washington**	**NHL**	**22**	**0**	**0**	**0**	**8**	**0**	**0**	**0**	**11**	**0.0**	**–8**	**0**	**0.0**	**12:26**									
	Portland Pirates	AHL	54	3	21	24	36																		
99-2000	Portland Pirates	AHL	58	0	14	14	20										3	1	0	1	2				
2000-01	**Chicago**	**NHL**	**36**	**2**	**3**	**5**	**12**	**0**	**0**	**0**	**27**	**7.4**	**3**	**0**	**0.0**	**17:03**									
	Norfolk Admirals	AHL	37	1	8	9	14																		
2001-02	**Chicago**	**NHL**	**56**	**1**	**7**	**8**	**30**	**0**	**0**	**0**	**48**	**2.1**	**6**	**0**	**0.0**	**14:52**	**5**	**0**	**0**	**0**	**0**	**0**	**0**	**0**	**23:14**
2002-03	**Chicago**	**NHL**	**75**	**2**	**11**	**13**	**50**	**0**	**0**	**0**	**49**	**4.1**	**14**	**0**	**0.0**	**22:51**									
2003-04	**Chicago**	**NHL**	**53**	**2**	**2**	**4**	**26**	**0**	**0**	**1**	**55**	**3.6**	**–16**	**1**	**0.0**	**22:15**									
	NHL Totals		**245**	**8**	**23**	**31**	**126**	**0**	**0**	**2**	**192**	**4.2**		**1**	**0.0**	**19:04**	**11**	**0**	**0**	**0**	**0**	**0**	**0**	**0**	**23:14**

ECHL First All-Star Team (1993)

Signed as a free agent by **Washington**, February 4, 1995. Signed as a free agent by **Chicago**, July 27, 2000.

POCK, Thomas
(PAWK, TAW-muhs) **NYR**

Defense. Shoots left. 6'1", 208 lbs. Born, Klagenfurt, Austria, December 2, 1981.

Season	Club	League	GP	G	A	Pts	PIM	PP	SH	GW	S	%	+/-	TF	F%	Min	GP	G	A	Pts	PIM	PP	SH	GW	Min
1998-99	Klagenfurt Jr.	Aust-Jr.	31	0	0	0	2																		
99-2000	Klagenfurt	Austria	15	3	8	11	14																		
	Klagenfurt	Alpen.	33	4	11	15	48																		
2000-01	Massachusetts	H-East	33	6	6	12	59																		
2001-02	Massachusetts	H-East	23	5	7	12	26																		
	Austria	Nat-Tm	10	1	2	3	4																		
	Austria	Olympics	4	0	0	0	2																		
2002-03	Massachusetts	H-East	37	17	20	37	46																		
2003-04	Massachusetts	H-East	37	16	25	41	48																		
	NY Rangers	**NHL**	**6**	**2**	**2**	**4**	**0**	**0**	**0**	**0**	**8**	**25.0**	**–4**	**0**	**0.0**	**18:38**									
	NHL Totals		**6**	**2**	**2**	**4**	**0**	**0**	**0**	**0**	**8**	**25.0**		**0**	**0.0**	**18:38**									

Hockey East Second All-Star Team (2003) • Hockey East First All-Star Team (2004) • NCAA East First All-American Team (2004)

Signed as a free agent by **NY Rangers**, March 23, 2004.

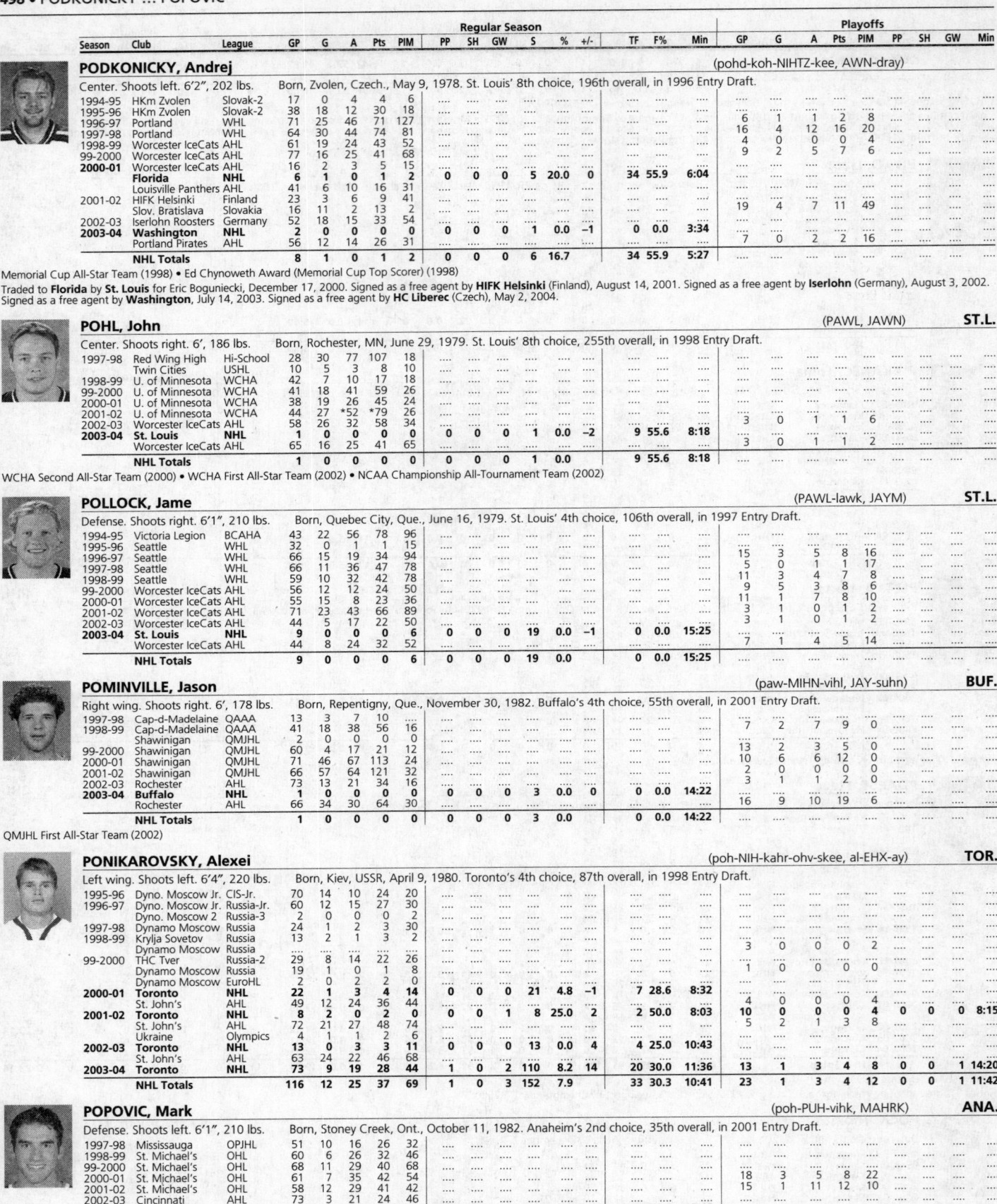

PODKONICKY, Andrej
(pohd-koh-NIHTZ-kee, AWN-dray)

Center. Shoots left. 6'2", 202 lbs. Born, Zvolen, Czech., May 9, 1978. St. Louis' 8th choice, 196th overall, in 1996 Entry Draft.

Season	Club	League	GP	G	A	Pts	PIM	PP	SH	GW	S	%	+/-	TF	F%	Min	Playoffs GP	G	A	Pts	PIM	PP	SH	GW	Min
1994-95	HKm Zvolen	Slovak-2	17	0	4	4	6	....	....	....	....	....	....	....	....	....	....	....	....	....	....	....	....	....	....
1995-96	HKm Zvolen	Slovak-2	38	18	12	30	18	....	....	....	....	....	....	....	....	....	....	....	....	....	....	....	....	....	....
1996-97	Portland	WHL	71	25	46	71	127	....	....	....	....	....	....	....	....	....	6	1	1	2	8	....	....	....	....
1997-98	Portland	WHL	64	30	44	74	81	....	....	....	....	....	....	....	....	....	16	4	12	16	20	....	....	....	....
1998-99	Worcester IceCats	AHL	61	19	24	43	52	....	....	....	....	....	....	....	....	....	4	0	0	0	4	....	....	....	....
99-2000	Worcester IceCats	AHL	77	16	25	41	68	....	....	....	....	....	....	....	....	....	9	2	5	7	6	....	....	....	....
2000-01	Worcester IceCats	AHL	16	2	3	5	15	....	....	....	....	....	....	....	....	....	....	....	....	....	....	....	....	....	....
	Florida	**NHL**	**6**	**1**	**0**	**1**	**2**	**0**	**0**	**0**	**5**	**20.0**	**0**	**34**	**55.9**	**6:04**	....	....	....	....	....	....	....	....	....
	Louisville Panthers	AHL	41	6	10	16	31	....	....	....	....	....	....	....	....	....	....	....	....	....	....	....	....	....	....
2001-02	HIFK Helsinki	Finland	23	3	6	9	41	....	....	....	....	....	....	....	....	....	....	....	....	....	....	....	....	....	....
	Slov. Bratislava	Slovakia	16	11	2	13	2	....	....	....	....	....	....	....	....	....	19	4	7	11	49	....	....	....	....
2002-03	Iserlohn Roosters	Germany	52	18	15	33	54	....	....	....	....	....	....	....	....	....	....	....	....	....	....	....	....	....	....
2003-04	**Washington**	**NHL**	**2**	**0**	**0**	**0**	**0**	**0**	**0**	**0**	**1**	**0.0**	**–1**	**0**	**0.0**	**3:34**	....	....	....	....	....	....	....	....	....
	Portland Pirates	AHL	56	12	14	26	31	....	....	....	....	....	....	....	....	....	7	0	2	2	16	....	....	....	....
	NHL Totals		**8**	**1**	**0**	**1**	**2**	**0**	**0**	**0**	**6**	**16.7**		**34**	**55.9**	**5:27**	....	....	....	....	....	....	....	....	....

Memorial Cup All-Star Team (1998) • Ed Chynoweth Award (Memorial Cup Top Scorer) (1998)

Traded to **Florida** by **St. Louis** for Eric Boguniecki, December 17, 2000. Signed as a free agent by **HIFK Helsinki** (Finland), August 14, 2001. Signed as a free agent by **Iserlohn** (Germany), August 3, 2002. Signed as a free agent by **Washington**, July 14, 2003. Signed as a free agent by **HC Liberec** (Czech), May 2, 2004.

POHL, John
(PAWL, JAWN) **ST.L.**

Center. Shoots right. 6', 186 lbs. Born, Rochester, MN, June 29, 1979. St. Louis' 8th choice, 255th overall, in 1998 Entry Draft.

Season	Club	League	GP	G	A	Pts	PIM	PP	SH	GW	S	%	+/-	TF	F%	Min	Playoffs GP	G	A	Pts	PIM	PP	SH	GW	Min
1997-98	Red Wing High	Hi-School	28	30	77	107	18	....	....	....	....	....	....	....	....	....	....	....	....	....	....	....	....	....	....
	Twin Cities	USHL	10	5	3	8	10	....	....	....	....	....	....	....	....	....	....	....	....	....	....	....	....	....	....
1998-99	U. of Minnesota	WCHA	42	7	10	17	18	....	....	....	....	....	....	....	....	....	....	....	....	....	....	....	....	....	....
99-2000	U. of Minnesota	WCHA	41	18	41	59	26	....	....	....	....	....	....	....	....	....	....	....	....	....	....	....	....	....	....
2000-01	U. of Minnesota	WCHA	38	19	26	45	24	....	....	....	....	....	....	....	....	....	....	....	....	....	....	....	....	....	....
2001-02	U. of Minnesota	WCHA	44	27	*52	*79	26	....	....	....	....	....	....	....	....	....	....	....	....	....	....	....	....	....	....
2002-03	Worcester IceCats	AHL	58	26	32	58	34	....	....	....	....	....	....	....	....	....	3	0	1	1	6	....	....	....	....
2003-04	**St. Louis**	**NHL**	**1**	**0**	**0**	**0**	**0**	**0**	**0**	**0**	**1**	**0.0**	**–2**	**9**	**55.6**	**8:18**	....	....	....	....	....	....	....	....	....
	Worcester IceCats	AHL	65	16	25	41	65	....	....	....	....	....	....	....	....	....	3	0	1	1	2	....	....	....	....
	NHL Totals		**1**	**0**	**0**	**0**	**0**	**0**	**0**	**0**	**1**	**0.0**		**9**	**55.6**	**8:18**	....	....	....	....	....	....	....	....	....

WCHA Second All-Star Team (2000) • WCHA First All-Star Team (2002) • NCAA Championship All-Tournament Team (2002)

POLLOCK, Jame
(PAWL-lawk, JAYM) **ST.L.**

Defense. Shoots right. 6'1", 210 lbs. Born, Quebec City, Que., June 16, 1979. St. Louis' 4th choice, 106th overall, in 1997 Entry Draft.

Season	Club	League	GP	G	A	Pts	PIM	PP	SH	GW	S	%	+/-	TF	F%	Min	Playoffs GP	G	A	Pts	PIM	PP	SH	GW	Min
1994-95	Victoria Legion	BCAHA	43	22	56	78	96	....	....	....	....	....	....	....	....	....	....	....	....	....	....	....	....	....	....
1995-96	Seattle	WHL	32	0	1	1	15	....	....	....	....	....	....	....	....	....	....	....	....	....	....	....	....	....	....
1996-97	Seattle	WHL	66	15	19	34	94	....	....	....	....	....	....	....	....	....	15	3	5	8	16	....	....	....	....
1997-98	Seattle	WHL	66	11	36	47	78	....	....	....	....	....	....	....	....	....	5	0	1	1	17	....	....	....	....
1998-99	Seattle	WHL	59	10	32	42	78	....	....	....	....	....	....	....	....	....	11	3	4	7	8	....	....	....	....
99-2000	Worcester IceCats	AHL	56	12	12	24	50	....	....	....	....	....	....	....	....	....	9	5	3	8	6	....	....	....	....
2000-01	Worcester IceCats	AHL	55	15	8	23	36	....	....	....	....	....	....	....	....	....	11	1	7	8	10	....	....	....	....
2001-02	Worcester IceCats	AHL	71	23	43	66	89	....	....	....	....	....	....	....	....	....	3	1	0	1	2	....	....	....	....
2002-03	Worcester IceCats	AHL	44	5	17	22	50	....	....	....	....	....	....	....	....	....	3	1	0	1	2	....	....	....	....
2003-04	**St. Louis**	**NHL**	**9**	**0**	**0**	**0**	**6**	**0**	**0**	**0**	**19**	**0.0**	**–1**	**0**	**0.0**	**15:25**	....	....	....	....	....	....	....	....	....
	Worcester IceCats	AHL	44	8	24	32	52	....	....	....	....	....	....	....	....	....	7	1	4	5	14	....	....	....	....
	NHL Totals		**9**	**0**	**0**	**0**	**6**	**0**	**0**	**0**	**19**	**0.0**		**0**	**0.0**	**15:25**	....	....	....	....	....	....	....	....	....

POMINVILLE, Jason
(paw-MIHN-vihl, JAY-suhn) **BUF.**

Right wing. Shoots right. 6', 178 lbs. Born, Repentigny, Que., November 30, 1982. Buffalo's 4th choice, 55th overall, in 2001 Entry Draft.

Season	Club	League	GP	G	A	Pts	PIM	PP	SH	GW	S	%	+/-	TF	F%	Min	Playoffs GP	G	A	Pts	PIM	PP	SH	GW	Min
1997-98	Cap-d-Madelaine	QAAA	13	3	7	10	....	....	....	....	....	....	....	....	....	....	....	....	....	....	....	....	....	....	....
1998-99	Cap-d-Madelaine	QAAA	41	18	38	56	16	....	....	....	....	....	....	....	....	....	7	2	7	9	0	....	....	....	....
	Shawinigan	QMJHL	2	0	0	0	0	....	....	....	....	....	....	....	....	....	....	....	....	....	....	....	....	....	....
99-2000	Shawinigan	QMJHL	60	4	17	21	12	....	....	....	....	....	....	....	....	....	13	2	3	5	0	....	....	....	....
2000-01	Shawinigan	QMJHL	71	46	67	113	24	....	....	....	....	....	....	....	....	....	10	6	6	12	0	....	....	....	....
2001-02	Shawinigan	QMJHL	66	57	64	121	32	....	....	....	....	....	....	....	....	....	2	0	0	0	0	....	....	....	....
2002-03	Rochester	AHL	73	13	21	34	16	....	....	....	....	....	....	....	....	....	3	1	1	2	0	....	....	....	....
2003-04	**Buffalo**	**NHL**	**1**	**0**	**0**	**0**	**0**	**0**	**0**	**0**	**3**	**0.0**	**0**	**0**	**0.0**	**14:22**	....	....	....	....	....	....	....	....	....
	Rochester	AHL	66	34	30	64	30	....	....	....	....	....	....	....	....	....	16	9	10	19	6	....	....	....	....
	NHL Totals		**1**	**0**	**0**	**0**	**0**	**0**	**0**	**0**	**3**	**0.0**		**0**	**0.0**	**14:22**	....	....	....	....	....	....	....	....	....

QMJHL First All-Star Team (2002)

PONIKAROVSKY, Alexei
(poh-NIH-kahr-ohv-skee, al-EHX-ay) **TOR.**

Left wing. Shoots left. 6'4", 220 lbs. Born, Kiev, USSR, April 9, 1980. Toronto's 4th choice, 87th overall, in 1998 Entry Draft.

Season	Club	League	GP	G	A	Pts	PIM	PP	SH	GW	S	%	+/-	TF	F%	Min	Playoffs GP	G	A	Pts	PIM	PP	SH	GW	Min
1995-96	Dyno. Moscow Jr.	CIS-Jr.	70	14	10	24	20	....	....	....	....	....	....	....	....	....	....	....	....	....	....	....	....	....	....
1996-97	Dyno. Moscow Jr.	Russia-Jr.	60	12	15	27	30	....	....	....	....	....	....	....	....	....	....	....	....	....	....	....	....	....	....
	Dyno. Moscow 2	Russia-3	2	0	0	0	2	....	....	....	....	....	....	....	....	....	....	....	....	....	....	....	....	....	....
1997-98	Dynamo Moscow	Russia	24	1	2	3	30	....	....	....	....	....	....	....	....	....	....	....	....	....	....	....	....	....	....
1998-99	Krylja Sovetov	Russia	13	2	1	3	2	....	....	....	....	....	....	....	....	....	....	....	....	....	....	....	....	....	....
	Dynamo Moscow	Russia	....	....	....	....	....	....	....	....	....	....	....	....	....	....	3	0	0	0	2	....	....	....	....
99-2000	THC Tver	Russia-2	29	8	14	22	26	....	....	....	....	....	....	....	....	....	....	....	....	....	....	....	....	....	....
	Dynamo Moscow	Russia	19	1	0	1	8	....	....	....	....	....	....	....	....	....	1	0	0	0	0	....	....	....	....
	Dynamo Moscow	EuroHL	2	0	2	2	0	....	....	....	....	....	....	....	....	....	....	....	....	....	....	....	....	....	....
2000-01	**Toronto**	**NHL**	**22**	**1**	**3**	**4**	**14**	**0**	**0**	**0**	**21**	**4.8**	**–1**	**7**	**28.6**	**8:32**	....	....	....	....	....	....	....	....	....
	St. John's	AHL	49	12	24	36	44	....	....	....	....	....	....	....	....	....	4	0	0	0	4	....	....	....	....
2001-02	**Toronto**	**NHL**	**8**	**2**	**0**	**2**	**0**	**0**	**0**	**1**	**8**	**25.0**	**2**	**2**	**50.0**	**8:03**	**10**	**0**	**0**	**0**	**4**	**0**	**0**	**0**	**8:15**
	St. John's	AHL	72	21	27	48	74	....	....	....	....	....	....	....	....	....	5	2	1	3	8	....	....	....	....
	Ukraine	Olympics	4	1	1	2	6	....	....	....	....	....	....	....	....	....	....	....	....	....	....	....	....	....	....
2002-03	**Toronto**	**NHL**	**13**	**0**	**3**	**3**	**11**	**0**	**0**	**0**	**13**	**0.0**	**4**	**4**	**25.0**	**10:43**	....	....	....	....	....	....	....	....	....
	St. John's	AHL	63	24	22	46	68	....	....	....	....	....	....	....	....	....	....	....	....	....	....	....	....	....	....
2003-04	**Toronto**	**NHL**	**73**	**9**	**19**	**28**	**44**	**1**	**0**	**2**	**110**	**8.2**	**14**	**20**	**30.0**	**11:36**	**13**	**1**	**3**	**4**	**8**	**0**	**0**	**1**	**14:20**
	NHL Totals		**116**	**12**	**25**	**37**	**69**	**1**	**0**	**3**	**152**	**7.9**		**33**	**30.3**	**10:41**	**23**	**1**	**3**	**4**	**12**	**0**	**0**	**1**	**11:42**

POPOVIC, Mark
(poh-PUH-vihk, MAHRK) **ANA.**

Defense. Shoots left. 6'1", 210 lbs. Born, Stoney Creek, Ont., October 11, 1982. Anaheim's 2nd choice, 35th overall, in 2001 Entry Draft.

Season	Club	League	GP	G	A	Pts	PIM	PP	SH	GW	S	%	+/-	TF	F%	Min	Playoffs GP	G	A	Pts	PIM	PP	SH	GW	Min
1997-98	Mississauga	OPJHL	51	10	16	26	32	....	....	....	....	....	....	....	....	....	....	....	....	....	....	....	....	....	....
1998-99	St. Michael's	OHL	60	6	26	32	46	....	....	....	....	....	....	....	....	....	....	....	....	....	....	....	....	....	....
99-2000	St. Michael's	OHL	68	11	29	40	68	....	....	....	....	....	....	....	....	....	....	....	....	....	....	....	....	....	....
2000-01	St. Michael's	OHL	61	7	35	42	54	....	....	....	....	....	....	....	....	....	18	3	5	8	22	....	....	....	....
2001-02	St. Michael's	OHL	58	12	29	41	42	....	....	....	....	....	....	....	....	....	15	1	11	12	10	....	....	....	....
2002-03	Cincinnati	AHL	73	3	21	24	46	....	....	....	....	....	....	....	....	....	....	....	....	....	....	....	....	....	....
2003-04	**Anaheim**	**NHL**	**1**	**0**	**0**	**0**	**0**	**0**	**0**	**0**	**1**	**0.0**	**0**	**0**	**0.0**	**13:48**	....	....	....	....	....	....	....	....	....
	Cincinnati	AHL	74	4	10	14	63	....	....	....	....	....	....	....	....	....	9	1	2	3	4	....	....	....	....
	NHL Totals		**1**	**0**	**0**	**0**	**0**	**0**	**0**	**0**	**1**	**0.0**		**0**	**0.0**	**13:48**	....	....	....	....	....	....	....	....	....

OHL First All-Star Team (2002)

POTHIER, Brian

(POH-thee-uhr, BRIGH-uhn) **OTT.**

Defense. Shoots right. 6', 195 lbs. Born, New Bedford, MA, April 15, 1977.

			Regular Season														Playoffs								
Season	Club	League	GP	G	A	Pts	PIM	PP	SH	GW	S	%	+/-	TF	F%	Min	GP	G	A	Pts	PIM	PP	SH	GW	Min
1995-96	Northfield High	Hi-School	27	11	22	33	36	....	....	....	....	....	....	....	....	....	....	....	....	....	....	....	....	....	....
1996-97	RPI Engineers	ECAC	34	1	11	12	42	....	....	....	....	....	....	....	....	....	....	....	....	....	....	....	....	....	....
1997-98	RPI Engineers	ECAC	35	2	9	11	28	....	....	....	....	....	....	....	....	....	....	....	....	....	....	....	....	....	....
1998-99	RPI Engineers	ECAC	37	5	13	18	36	....	....	....	....	....	....	....	....	....	....	....	....	....	....	....	....	....	....
99-2000	RPI Engineers	ECAC	36	9	24	33	44	....	....	....	....	....	....	....	....	....	....	....	....	....	....	....	....	....	....
2000-01	**Atlanta**	**NHL**	**3**	**0**	**0**	**0**	**2**	**0**	**0**	**0**	**0**	**0.0**	**4**	**0**	**0.0**	**20:38**	....	....	....	....	....	....	....	....	....
	Orlando	IHL	76	12	29	41	69	....	....	....	....	....	....	....	....	....	16	3	5	8	11	....	....	....	....
2001-02	**Atlanta**	**NHL**	**33**	**3**	**6**	**9**	**22**	**1**	**0**	**1**	**65**	**4.6**	**–19**	**0**	**0.0**	**21:41**	....	....	....	....	....	....	....	....	....
	Chicago Wolves	AHL	39	6	13	19	30	....	....	....	....	....	....	....	....	....	....	....	....	....	....	....	....	....	....
2002-03	**Ottawa**	**NHL**	**14**	**2**	**4**	**6**	**6**	**0**	**0**	**1**	**23**	**8.7**	**11**	**0**	**0.0**	**15:23**	**1**	**0**	**0**	**0**	**2**	**0**	**0**	**0**	**13:11**
	Binghamton	AHL	68	7	40	47	58	....	....	....	....	....	....	....	....	....	8	2	8	10	4	....	....	....	....
2003-04	**Ottawa**	**NHL**	**55**	**2**	**6**	**8**	**24**	**1**	**0**	**1**	**78**	**2.6**	**6**	**0**	**0.0**	**16:43**	**7**	**0**	**0**	**0**	**6**	**0**	**0**	**0**	**17:15**
	NHL Totals		**105**	**7**	**16**	**23**	**54**	**2**	**0**	**3**	**166**	**4.2**		**0**	**0.0**	**18:13**	**8**	**0**	**0**	**0**	**8**	**0**	**0**	**0**	**16:44**

ECAC Second All-Star Team (2000) • ECAC All-Tournament Team (2000) • NCAA East Second All-American Team (2000) • Garry F. Longman Memorial Trophy (Top Rookie – IHL) (2001) • AHL Second All-Star Team (2003)

Signed as a free agent by **Atlanta**, March 27, 2000. Traded to **Ottawa** by **Atlanta** for Shawn McEachern and Ottawa's 6th round choice (Dan Turple) in 2004 Entry Draft, June 29, 2002.

POTI, Tom

(POH-tee, TAWM) **NYR**

Defense. Shoots left. 6'3", 215 lbs. Born, Worcester, MA, March 22, 1977. Edmonton's 4th choice, 59th overall, in 1996 Entry Draft.

			Regular Season														Playoffs								
Season	Club	League	GP	G	A	Pts	PIM	PP	SH	GW	S	%	+/-	TF	F%	Min	GP	G	A	Pts	PIM	PP	SH	GW	Min
1992-93	St. Peter's High	Hi-School	55	25	46	71	....	....	....	....	....	....	....	....	....	....	....	....	....	....	....	....	....	....	....
1993-94	Cushing Academy	Hi-School	30	10	35	45	....	....	....	....	....	....	....	....	....	....	....	....	....	....	....	....	....	....	....
1994-95	Cushing Academy	Hi-School	36	17	54	71	35	....	....	....	....	....	....	....	....	....	....	....	....	....	....	....	....	....	....
	Central-Mass	MBAHL	8	8	10	18	....	....	....	....	....	....	....	....	....	....	....	....	....	....	....	....	....	....	....
1995-96	Cushing Academy	Hi-School	29	14	59	73	18	....	....	....	....	....	....	....	....	....	....	....	....	....	....	....	....	....	....
1996-97	Boston University	H-East	38	4	17	21	54	....	....	....	....	....	....	....	....	....	....	....	....	....	....	....	....	....	....
1997-98	Boston University	H-East	38	13	29	42	60	....	....	....	....	....	....	....	....	....	....	....	....	....	....	....	....	....	....
1998-99	**Edmonton**	**NHL**	**73**	**5**	**16**	**21**	**42**	**2**	**0**	**3**	**94**	**5.3**	**10**	**0**	**0.0**	**19:33**	**4**	**0**	**1**	**1**	**2**	**0**	**0**	**0**	**28:02**
99-2000	**Edmonton**	**NHL**	**76**	**9**	**26**	**35**	**65**	**2**	**1**	**1**	**125**	**7.2**	**8**	**0**	**0.0**	**24:10**	**5**	**0**	**1**	**1**	**0**	**0**	**0**	**0**	**23:53**
2000-01	**Edmonton**	**NHL**	**81**	**12**	**20**	**32**	**60**	**6**	**0**	**3**	**161**	**7.5**	**–4**	**0**	**0.0**	**22:44**	**6**	**0**	**2**	**2**	**2**	**0**	**0**	**0**	**20:25**
2001-02	**Edmonton**	**NHL**	**55**	**1**	**16**	**17**	**42**	**1**	**0**	**0**	**100**	**1.0**	**–6**	**0**	**0.0**	**24:32**	....	....	....	....	....	....	....	....	....
	United States	Olympics	6	0	1	1	4	....	....	....	....	....	....	....	....	....	....	....	....	....	....	....	....	....	....
	NY Rangers	**NHL**	**11**	**1**	**7**	**8**	**2**	**1**	**0**	**1**	**9**	**11.1**	**–4**	**0**	**0.0**	**21:45**	....	....	....	....	....	....	....	....	....
2002-03	**NY Rangers**	**NHL**	**80**	**11**	**37**	**48**	**58**	**3**	**0**	**2**	**148**	**7.4**	**–6**	**0**	**0.0**	**24:43**	....	....	....	....	....	....	....	....	....
2003-04	**NY Rangers**	**NHL**	**67**	**10**	**14**	**24**	**47**	**4**	**0**	**5**	**124**	**8.1**	**–1**	**0**	**0.0**	**22:28**	....	....	....	....	....	....	....	....	....
	NHL Totals		**443**	**49**	**136**	**185**	**316**	**19**	**1**	**15**	**761**	**6.4**		**0**	**0.0**	**22:58**	**15**	**0**	**4**	**4**	**4**	**0**	**0**	**0**	**23:36**

NCAA Championship All-Tournament Team (1997) • Hockey East First All-Star Team (1998) • NCAA East First All-American Team (1998) • NHL All-Rookie Team (1999)

Played in NHL All-Star Game (2003)

Traded to **NY Rangers** by **Edmonton** with Rem Murray for Mike York and NY Rangers' 4th round choice (Ivan Koltsov) in 2002 Entry Draft, March 19, 2002.

PRATT, Nolan

(PRAT, NOH-lan) **T.B.**

Defense. Shoots left. 6'3", 200 lbs. Born, Fort McMurray, Alta., August 14, 1975. Hartford's 4th choice, 115th overall, in 1993 Entry Draft.

			Regular Season														Playoffs								
Season	Club	League	GP	G	A	Pts	PIM	PP	SH	GW	S	%	+/-	TF	F%	Min	GP	G	A	Pts	PIM	PP	SH	GW	Min
1991-92	Bonnyville	AJHL	33	3	7	10	57	....	....	....	....	....	....	....	....	....	....	....	....	....	....	....	....	....	....
	Portland	WHL	22	2	9	11	13	....	....	....	....	....	....	....	....	....	6	1	3	4	12	....	....	....	....
1992-93	Portland	WHL	70	4	19	23	97	....	....	....	....	....	....	....	....	....	16	2	7	9	31	....	....	....	....
1993-94	Portland	WHL	72	4	32	36	105	....	....	....	....	....	....	....	....	....	10	1	2	3	14	....	....	....	....
1994-95	Portland	WHL	72	6	37	43	196	....	....	....	....	....	....	....	....	....	9	1	6	7	10	....	....	....	....
1995-96	Springfield	AHL	62	2	6	8	72	....	....	....	....	....	....	....	....	....	2	0	0	0	0	....	....	....	....
	Richmond	ECHL	4	1	0	1	2	....	....	....	....	....	....	....	....	....	....	....	....	....	....	....	....	....	....
1996-97	**Hartford**	**NHL**	**9**	**0**	**2**	**2**	**6**	**0**	**0**	**0**	**4**	**0.0**	**0**	....	....	....	....	....	....	....	....	....	....	....	....
	Springfield	AHL	66	1	18	19	127	....	....	....	....	....	....	....	....	....	17	0	3	3	18	....	....	....	....
1997-98	**Carolina**	**NHL**	**23**	**0**	**2**	**2**	**44**	**0**	**0**	**0**	**11**	**0.0**	**–2**	....	....	....	....	....	....	....	....	....	....	....	....
	New Haven	AHL	54	3	15	18	135	....	....	....	....	....	....	....	....	....	....	....	....	....	....	....	....	....	....
1998-99	**Carolina**	**NHL**	**61**	**1**	**14**	**15**	**95**	**0**	**0**	**1**	**46**	**2.2**	**15**	**0**	**0.0**	**16:45**	**3**	**0**	**0**	**0**	**2**	**0**	**0**	**0**	**19:58**
99-2000	**Carolina**	**NHL**	**64**	**3**	**1**	**4**	**90**	**0**	**0**	**1**	**47**	**6.4**	**–22**	**0**	**0.0**	**19:10**	....	....	....	....	....	....	....	....	....
2000-01	**Colorado**	**NHL**	**46**	**1**	**2**	**3**	**40**	**0**	**0**	**1**	**26**	**3.8**	**2**	**1**	**0.0**	**9:50**	....	....	....	....	....	....	....	....	....
2001-02	**Tampa Bay**	**NHL**	**46**	**0**	**3**	**3**	**51**	**0**	**0**	**0**	**38**	**0.0**	**–4**	**1**	**0.0**	**18:25**	....	....	....	....	....	....	....	....	....
2002-03	**Tampa Bay**	**NHL**	**67**	**1**	**7**	**8**	**35**	**0**	**0**	**0**	**38**	**2.6**	**–6**	**0**	**0.0**	**17:34**	**4**	**0**	**1**	**1**	**0**	**0**	**0**	**0**	**21:01**
2003-04♦	**Tampa Bay**	**NHL**	**58**	**1**	**3**	**4**	**42**	**0**	**0**	**0**	**35**	**2.9**	**11**	**0**	**0.0**	**16:25**	**20**	**0**	**0**	**0**	**8**	**0**	**0**	**0**	**18:06**
	NHL Totals		**374**	**7**	**34**	**41**	**403**	**0**	**0**	**3**	**245**	**2.9**		**2**	**0.0**	**16:36**	**27**	**0**	**1**	**1**	**10**	**0**	**0**	**0**	**18:44**

Transferred to **Carolina** after **Hartford** franchise relocated, June 25, 1997. Traded to **Colorado** by **Carolina** with Carolina's 1st (Vaclav Nedorost) and 2nd (Jared Aulin) round choices in 2000 Entry Draft and Philadelphia's 2nd round choice (previously acquired, Colorado selected Agris Saviels) in 2000 Entry Draft for Sandis Ozolinsh and Columbus' 2nd round choice (previously acquired, Carolina selected Tomas Kurka) in 2000 Entry Draft, June 24, 2000. Traded to **Tampa Bay** by **Colorado** for Los Angeles' 6th round choice (previously acquired, Colorado selected Scott Horvath) in 2001 Entry Draft, June 24, 2001.

PREISSING, Tom

(PREH-sihng, TAWM) **S.J.**

Defense. Shoots right. 6', 205 lbs. Born, Rosemount, MN, December 3, 1978.

			Regular Season														Playoffs								
Season	Club	League	GP	G	A	Pts	PIM	PP	SH	GW	S	%	+/-	TF	F%	Min	GP	G	A	Pts	PIM	PP	SH	GW	Min
1997-98	Green Bay	USHL	56	8	13	21	30	....	....	....	....	....	....	....	....	....	4	0	2	2	2	....	....	....	....
1998-99	Green Bay	USHL	53	18	37	55	40	....	....	....	....	....	....	....	....	....	6	3	6	9	2	....	....	....	....
99-2000	Colorado College	WCHA	36	4	14	18	20	....	....	....	....	....	....	....	....	....	....	....	....	....	....	....	....	....	....
2000-01	Colorado College	WCHA	33	6	18	24	26	....	....	....	....	....	....	....	....	....	....	....	....	....	....	....	....	....	....
2001-02	Colorado College	WCHA	43	6	26	32	42	....	....	....	....	....	....	....	....	....	....	....	....	....	....	....	....	....	....
2002-03	Colorado College	WCHA	42	23	29	52	16	....	....	....	....	....	....	....	....	....	....	....	....	....	....	....	....	....	....
2003-04	**San Jose**	**NHL**	**69**	**2**	**17**	**19**	**12**	**2**	**0**	**1**	**89**	**2.2**	**8**	**0**	**0.0**	**18:12**	**11**	**0**	**1**	**1**	**0**	**0**	**0**	**0**	**12:49**
	NHL Totals		**69**	**2**	**17**	**19**	**12**	**2**	**0**	**1**	**89**	**2.2**		**0**	**0.0**	**18:12**	**11**	**0**	**1**	**1**	**0**	**0**	**0**	**0**	**12:49**

WCHA First All-Star Team (2003) • NCAA West First All-American Team (2003)

Signed as a free agent by **San Jose**, April 4, 2003.

PRIMEAU, Keith

(PREE-moh, KEETH) **PHI.**

Center. Shoots left. 6'5", 220 lbs. Born, Toronto, Ont., November 24, 1971. Detroit's 1st choice, 3rd overall, in 1990 Entry Draft.

			Regular Season														Playoffs								
Season	Club	League	GP	G	A	Pts	PIM	PP	SH	GW	S	%	+/-	TF	F%	Min	GP	G	A	Pts	PIM	PP	SH	GW	Min
1986-87	Whitby Flyers	OMHA	65	69	80	149	116	....	....	....	....	....	....	....	....	....	....	....	....	....	....	....	....	....	....
1987-88	Hamilton Kilty B's	OJHL-B	19	19	17	36	16	....	....	....	....	....	....	....	....	....	....	....	....	....	....	....	....	....	....
	Hamilton	OHL	47	6	6	12	69	....	....	....	....	....	....	....	....	....	11	0	2	2	2	....	....	....	....
1988-89	Niagara Falls	OHL	48	20	35	55	56	....	....	....	....	....	....	....	....	....	17	9	16	25	12	....	....	....	....
1989-90	Niagara Falls	OHL	65	*57	70	*127	97	....	....	....	....	....	....	....	....	....	16	*16	17	*33	49	....	....	....	....
1990-91	**Detroit**	**NHL**	**58**	**3**	**12**	**15**	**106**	**0**	**0**	**1**	**33**	**9.1**	**–12**	....	....	....	**5**	**1**	**1**	**2**	**25**	**0**	**0**	**0**	....
	Adirondack	AHL	6	3	5	8	8	....	....	....	....	....	....	....	....	....	....	....	....	....	....	....	....	....	....
1991-92	**Detroit**	**NHL**	**35**	**6**	**10**	**16**	**83**	**0**	**0**	**0**	**27**	**22.2**	**9**	....	....	....	**11**	**0**	**0**	**0**	**14**	**0**	**0**	**0**	....
	Adirondack	AHL	42	21	24	45	89	....	....	....	....	....	....	....	....	....	9	1	7	8	27	....	....	....	....
1992-93	**Detroit**	**NHL**	**73**	**15**	**17**	**32**	**152**	**4**	**1**	**2**	**75**	**20.0**	**–6**	....	....	....	**7**	**0**	**2**	**2**	**26**	**0**	**0**	**0**	....
1993-94	**Detroit**	**NHL**	**78**	**31**	**42**	**73**	**173**	**7**	**3**	**4**	**155**	**20.0**	**34**	....	....	....	**7**	**0**	**2**	**2**	**6**	**0**	**0**	**0**	....
1994-95	**Detroit**	**NHL**	**45**	**15**	**27**	**42**	**99**	**1**	**0**	**3**	**96**	**15.6**	**17**	....	....	....	**17**	**4**	**5**	**9**	**45**	**2**	**0**	**0**	....
1995-96	**Detroit**	**NHL**	**74**	**27**	**25**	**52**	**168**	**6**	**2**	**7**	**150**	**18.0**	**19**	....	....	....	**17**	**1**	**4**	**5**	**28**	**0**	**0**	**0**	....
1996-97	**Hartford**	**NHL**	**75**	**26**	**25**	**51**	**161**	**6**	**3**	**2**	**169**	**15.4**	**–3**	....	....	....	....	....	....	....	....	....	....	....	....
1997-98	**Carolina**	**NHL**	**81**	**26**	**37**	**63**	**110**	**7**	**3**	**2**	**180**	**14.4**	**19**	....	....	....	....	....	....	....	....	....	....	....	....
	Canada	Olympics	6	2	1	3	4	....	....	....	....	....	....	....	....	....	....	....	....	....	....	....	....	....	....
1998-99	**Carolina**	**NHL**	**78**	**30**	**32**	**62**	**75**	**9**	**1**	**5**	**178**	**16.9**	**8**	**1823**	**53.5**	**21:21**	**6**	**0**	**3**	**3**	**6**	**0**	**0**	**0**	**24:35**
99-2000	**Philadelphia**	**NHL**	**23**	**7**	**10**	**17**	**31**	**1**	**0**	**1**	**51**	**13.7**	**10**	**478**	**54.2**	**17:38**	**18**	**2**	**11**	**13**	**13**	**0**	**0**	**1**	**20:25**
2000-01	**Philadelphia**	**NHL**	**71**	**34**	**39**	**73**	**76**	**11**	**0**	**4**	**165**	**20.6**	**17**	**1811**	**53.5**	**19:58**	**4**	**0**	**3**	**3**	**8**	**0**	**0**	**0**	**19:44**
2001-02	**Philadelphia**	**NHL**	**75**	**19**	**29**	**48**	**128**	**5**	**0**	**3**	**151**	**12.6**	**–3**	**1595**	**51.3**	**18:00**	**5**	**0**	**0**	**0**	**6**	**0**	**0**	**0**	**17:20**

			Regular Season														Playoffs								
Season	Club	League	GP	G	A	Pts	PIM	PP	SH	GW	S	%	+/-	TF	F%	Min	GP	G	A	Pts	PIM	PP	SH	GW	Min
2002-03	Philadelphia	NHL	80	19	27	46	93	6	0	4	171	11.1	4	1613	51.4	19:16	13	1	1	2	14	0	0	0	20:21
2003-04	Philadelphia	NHL	54	7	15	22	80	0	1	2	86	8.1	11	1010	53.3	16:36	18	9	7	16	22	0	2	3	18:58
	NHL Totals		900	265	347	612	1535	63	14	40	1687	15.7		8330	52.7	19:06	128	18	39	57	213	2	2	4	20:06

OHL Second All-Star Team (1990)

Played in NHL All-Star Game (1999, 2004)

Traded to **Hartford** by **Detroit** with Paul Coffey and Detroit's 1st round choice (Nikos Tselios) in 1997 Entry Draft for Brendan Shanahan and Brian Glynn, October 9, 1996. Transferred to **Carolina** after **Hartford** franchise relocated, June 25, 1997. • Missed majority of 1999-2000 season after failing to come to contract terms with **Carolina**. Traded to **Philadelphia** by **Carolina** with Carolina's 5th round choice (later traded to NY Islanders – NY Islanders selected Kristofer Ottosson) in 2000 Entry Draft for Rod Brind'Amour, Jean-Marc Pelletier and Philadelphia's 2nd round choice (later traded to Colorado – Colorado selected Agris Saviels) in 2000 Entry Draft, January 23, 2000.

PRIMEAU, Wayne

(PREE-moh, WAYN) **S.J.**

Center. Shoots left. 6'4", 230 lbs. Born, Scarborough, Ont., June 4, 1976. Buffalo's 1st choice, 17th overall, in 1994 Entry Draft.

1991-92	Whitby Flyers	OMHA	63	36	50	86	96	....	....	....	....	....	....	....	....	....	....	....	....	....	....	....	....	....	....
1992-93	Owen Sound	OHL	66	10	27	37	108	....	....	....	....	....	....	....	....	....	8	1	4	5	0	....	....	....	....
1993-94	Owen Sound	OHL	65	25	50	75	75	....	....	....	....	....	....	....	....	....	9	1	6	7	8	....	....	....	....
1994-95	Owen Sound	OHL	66	34	62	96	84	....	....	....	....	....	....	....	....	....	10	4	9	13	15	....	....	....	....
	Buffalo	NHL	1	1	0	1	0	0	0	1	2	50.0	–2	....	....	....	....	....	....	....	....	....	....	....	....
1995-96	Owen Sound	OHL	28	15	29	44	52	....	....	....	....	....	....	....	....	....	....	....	....	....	....	....	....	....	....
	Oshawa Generals	OHL	24	12	13	25	33	....	....	....	....	....	....	....	....	....	3	2	3	5	2	....	....	....	....
	Buffalo	NHL	2	0	0	0	0	0	0	0	0	0.0	0	....	....	....	....	....	....	....	....	....	....	....	....
	Rochester	AHL	8	2	3	5	6	....	....	....	....	....	....	....	....	....	17	3	1	4	11	....	....	....	....
1996-97	Buffalo	NHL	45	2	4	6	64	1	0	0	25	8.0	–2	....	....	....	9	0	0	0	6	0	0	0	....
	Rochester	AHL	24	9	5	14	27	....	....	....	....	....	....	....	....	....	1	0	0	0	0	....	....	....	....
1997-98	Buffalo	NHL	69	6	6	12	87	2	0	1	51	11.8	9	....	....	....	14	1	3	4	6	0	0	0	....
1998-99	Buffalo	NHL	67	5	8	13	38	0	0	0	55	9.1	–6	529	48.6	10:19	19	3	4	7	6	1	0	0	13:29
99-2000	Buffalo	NHL	41	5	7	12	38	2	0	1	40	12.5	–8	430	45.6	11:03	....	....	....	....	....	....	....	....	....
	Tampa Bay	NHL	17	2	3	5	25	0	0	0	35	5.7	–4	290	45.5	14:21	....	....	....	....	....	....	....	....	....
2000-01	Tampa Bay	NHL	47	2	13	15	77	0	0	0	47	4.3	–17	630	52.2	14:11	....	....	....	....	....	....	....	....	....
	Pittsburgh	NHL	28	1	6	7	54	0	0	0	30	3.3	0	318	51.3	12:45	18	1	3	4	2	0	0	0	15:06
2001-02	Pittsburgh	NHL	33	3	7	10	18	0	1	0	28	10.7	–1	519	53.2	12:38	....	....	....	....	....	....	....	....	....
2002-03	Pittsburgh	NHL	70	5	11	16	55	1	0	0	101	5.0	–30	1240	50.4	16:17	....	....	....	....	....	....	....	....	....
	San Jose	NHL	7	1	1	2	0	0	0	0	13	7.7	2	98	45.9	15:59	....	....	....	....	....	....	....	....	....
2003-04	San Jose	NHL	72	9	20	29	90	0	1	1	142	6.3	4	867	46.6	15:28	17	1	2	3	4	0	0	0	15:41
	NHL Totals		499	42	86	128	546	6	2	4	569	7.4		4921	49.3	13:36	77	6	12	18	24	1	0	0	14:43

Traded to **Tampa Bay** by **Buffalo** with Cory Sarich, Brian Holzinger and Buffalo's 3rd round choice (Alexander Kharitonov) in 2000 Entry Draft for Chris Gratton and Tampa Bay's 2nd round choice (Derek Roy) in 2001 Entry Draft, March 9, 2000. Traded to **Pittsburgh** by **Tampa Bay** for Matthew Barnaby, February 1, 2001. • Missed majority of 2001-02 season recovering from knee injury suffered in game vs. Buffalo, January 8, 2002. Traded to **San Jose** by **Pittsburgh** for Matt Bradley, March 11, 2003.

PRONGER, Chris

(PRAHN-guhr, KRIHS) **ST.L.**

Defense. Shoots left. 6'6", 220 lbs. Born, Dryden, Ont., October 10, 1974. Hartford's 1st choice, 2nd overall, in 1993 Entry Draft.

1990-91	Stratford Cullitons	OJHL-B	48	15	37	52	132	....	....	....	....	....	....	....	....	....	....	....	....	....	....	....	....	....	....
1991-92	Peterborough	OHL	63	17	45	62	90	....	....	....	....	....	....	....	....	....	10	1	8	9	28	....	....	....	....
1992-93	Peterborough	OHL	61	15	62	77	108	....	....	....	....	....	....	....	....	....	21	15	25	40	51	....	....	....	....
1993-94	Hartford	NHL	81	5	25	30	113	2	0	0	174	2.9	–3	....	....	....	....	....	....	....	....	....	....	....	....
1994-95	Hartford	NHL	43	5	9	14	54	3	0	1	94	5.3	–12	....	....	....	....	....	....	....	....	....	....	....	....
1995-96	St. Louis	NHL	78	7	18	25	110	3	1	1	138	5.1	–18	....	....	....	13	1	5	6	16	0	0	0	....
1996-97	St. Louis	NHL	79	11	24	35	143	4	0	0	147	7.5	15	....	....	....	6	1	1	2	22	0	0	0	....
1997-98	St. Louis	NHL	81	9	27	36	180	1	0	2	145	6.2	47	....	....	....	10	1	9	10	26	0	0	0	....
	Canada	Olympics	6	0	0	0	4	....	....	....	....	....	....	....	....	....	....	....	....	....	....	....	....	....	....
1998-99	St. Louis	NHL	67	13	33	46	113	8	0	0	172	7.6	3	0	0.0	30:36	13	1	4	5	28	1	0	0	35:53
99-2000	St. Louis	NHL	79	14	48	62	92	8	0	3	192	7.3	52	1	0.0	30:14	7	3	4	7	32	2	0	2	30:14
2000-01	St. Louis	NHL	51	8	39	47	75	4	0	0	121	6.6	21	0	0.0	27:45	15	1	7	8	32	0	0	0	33:50
2001-02	St. Louis	NHL	78	7	40	47	120	4	1	3	204	3.4	23	0	0.0	29:28	9	1	7	8	24	0	0	0	27:51
	Canada	Olympics	6	0	1	1	2	....	....	....	....	....	....	....	....	....	....	....	....	....	....	....	....	....	....
2002-03	St. Louis	NHL	5	1	3	4	10	0	0	0	11	9.1	–2	1	0.0	21:39	7	1	3	4	14	0	0	0	24:36
2003-04	St. Louis	NHL	80	14	40	54	88	7	0	3	203	6.9	–1	2	0.0	27:28	5	0	1	1	16	0	0	0	27:54
	NHL Totals		722	94	306	400	1098	44	2	13	1601	5.9		4	0.0	29:03	85	10	41	51	210	3	0	2	31:13

OHL All-Rookie Team (1992) • OHL First All-Star Team (1993) • Canadian Major Junior First All-Star Team (1993) • Canadian Major Junior Defenseman of the Year (1993) • NHL All-Rookie Team (1994) • NHL Second All-Star Team (1998, 2004) • Bud Ice Plus/Minus Award (1998) • NHL First All-Star Team (2000) • Bud Light Plus/Minus Award (2000) • James Norris Memorial Trophy (2000) • Hart Trophy (2000)

Played in NHL All-Star Game (1999, 2000, 2002, 2004)

Traded to **St. Louis** by **Hartford** for Brendan Shanahan, July 27, 1995. • Missed majority of 2002-03 season recovering from wrist and knee surgery, September 10, 2002.

PRONGER, Sean

(PRAHN-guhr, SHAWN)

Center. Shoots left. 6'3", 209 lbs. Born, Thunder Bay, Ont., November 30, 1972. Vancouver's 3rd choice, 51st overall, in 1991 Entry Draft.

1988-89	Kenora Boise	NOJHA	33	38	30	68	....	....	....	....	....	....	....	....	....	....	....	....	....	....	....	....	....	....	....
1989-90	Thunder Bay	USHL	48	18	34	52	61	....	....	....	....	....	....	....	....	....	....	....	....	....	....	....	....	....	....
1990-91	Bowling Green	CCHA	40	3	7	10	30	....	....	....	....	....	....	....	....	....	....	....	....	....	....	....	....	....	....
1991-92	Bowling Green	CCHA	34	9	7	16	28	....	....	....	....	....	....	....	....	....	....	....	....	....	....	....	....	....	....
1992-93	Bowling Green	CCHA	39	23	23	46	35	....	....	....	....	....	....	....	....	....	....	....	....	....	....	....	....	....	....
1993-94	Bowling Green	CCHA	38	17	17	34	38	....	....	....	....	....	....	....	....	....	....	....	....	....	....	....	....	....	....
1994-95	Knoxville	ECHL	34	18	23	41	55	....	....	....	....	....	....	....	....	....	....	....	....	....	....	....	....	....	....
	Greensboro	ECHL	2	0	2	2	0	....	....	....	....	....	....	....	....	....	....	....	....	....	....	....	....	....	....
	San Diego Gulls	IHL	8	0	0	0	2	....	....	....	....	....	....	....	....	....	....	....	....	....	....	....	....	....	....
1995-96	Anaheim	NHL	7	0	1	1	6	0	0	0	3	0.0	0	....	....	....	....	....	....	....	....	....	....	....	....
	Baltimore Bandits	AHL	72	16	17	33	61	....	....	....	....	....	....	....	....	....	12	3	7	10	16	....	....	....	....
1996-97	Anaheim	NHL	39	7	7	14	20	1	0	1	43	16.3	6	....	....	....	9	0	2	2	4	0	0	0	....
	Baltimore Bandits	AHL	41	26	17	43	17	....	....	....	....	....	....	....	....	....	....	....	....	....	....	....	....	....	....
1997-98	Anaheim	NHL	62	5	15	20	30	1	0	2	68	7.4	–9	....	....	....	....	....	....	....	....	....	....	....	....
	Pittsburgh	NHL	5	1	0	1	2	0	0	1	5	20.0	–1	....	....	....	5	0	0	0	4	0	0	0	....
1998-99	Pittsburgh	NHL	2	0	0	0	0	0	0	0	3	0.0	0	4	75.0	8:48	....	....	....	....	....	....	....	....	....
	Houston Aeros	IHL	16	11	7	18	32	....	....	....	....	....	....	....	....	....	....	....	....	....	....	....	....	....	....
	NY Rangers	NHL	14	0	3	3	4	0	0	0	3	0.0	–3	15	20.0	6:28	....	....	....	....	....	....	....	....	....
	Los Angeles	NHL	13	0	1	1	4	0	0	0	8	0.0	2	20	35.0	11:00	....	....	....	....	....	....	....	....	....
99-2000	Boston	NHL	11	0	1	1	13	0	0	0	7	0.0	–4	116	46.6	10:47	....	....	....	....	....	....	....	....	....
	Providence Bruins	AHL	51	11	18	29	26	....	....	....	....	....	....	....	....	....	....	....	....	....	....	....	....	....	....
	Manitoba Moose	IHL	14	3	5	8	21	....	....	....	....	....	....	....	....	....	2	0	1	1	2	....	....	....	....
2000-01	Manitoba Moose	IHL	82	18	21	39	85	....	....	....	....	....	....	....	....	....	13	3	6	9	2	....	....	....	....
2001-02	Columbus	NHL	26	3	1	4	4	0	0	0	25	12.0	–4	167	52.1	11:26	....	....	....	....	....	....	....	....	....
	Syracuse Crunch	AHL	54	23	26	49	53	....	....	....	....	....	....	....	....	....	8	4	1	5	10	....	....	....	....
2002-03	Columbus	NHL	78	7	6	13	72	1	0	0	67	10.4	–26	655	49.5	11:32	....	....	....	....	....	....	....	....	....
2003-04	Syracuse Crunch	AHL	7	2	0	2	7	....	....	....	....	....	....	....	....	....	....	....	....	....	....	....	....	....	....
	Vancouver	NHL	3	0	1	1	4	0	0	0	6	0.0	–1	35	42.9	10:17	....	....	....	....	....	....	....	....	....
	Manitoba Moose	AHL	68	17	15	32	68	....	....	....	....	....	....	....	....	....	....	....	....	....	....	....	....	....	....
	NHL Totals		260	23	36	59	159	3	0	4	238	9.7		1012	48.7	10:52	14	0	2	2	8	0	0	0	....

Signed as a free agent by **Anaheim**, February 14, 1995. Traded to **Pittsburgh** by **Anaheim** for the rights to Patrick Lalime, March 24, 1998. Traded to **NY Rangers** by **Pittsburgh** with Chris Tamer and Petr Nedved for Alex Kovalev and Harry York, November 25, 1998. Traded to **Los Angeles** by **NY Rangers** for Eric Lacroix, February 12, 1999. Signed as a free agent by **Boston**, August 25, 1999. Traded to **Manitoba** (IHL) by **Providence** (AHL) with Keith McCambridge for Terry Hollinger, March 16, 2000 with Boston retaining Pronger's NHL rights. Traded to **NY Islanders** by **Boston** for future considerations, December 5, 2000. Claimed on waivers by **Columbus** from **NY Islanders**, May 18, 2001. Traded to **Vancouver** by **Columbus** for Zenith Komarniski, October 30, 2003.

PROSPAL, Vaclav

(PRAWS-pahl, VAT-slav) **ANA.**

Center. Shoots left. 6'2", 195 lbs. Born, Ceske Budejovice, Czech., February 17, 1975. Philadelphia's 2nd choice, 71st overall, in 1993 Entry Draft.

			Regular Season														Playoffs								
Season	Club	League	GP	G	A	Pts	PIM	PP	SH	GW	S	%	+/-	TF	F%	Min	GP	G	A	Pts	PIM	PP	SH	GW	Min
1991-92	C. Budejovice Jr.	Czech-Jr.	36	16	16	32	12	....	....	....	....	....	....	....	....	....	....	....	....	....	....	....	....	....	....
1992-93	C. Budejovice Jr.	Czech-Jr.	32	26	31	57	24	....	....	....	....	....	....	....	....	....	....	....	....	....	....	....	....	....	....
1993-94	Hershey Bears	AHL	55	14	21	35	38	....	....	....	....	....	....	....	....	....	2	0	0	0	2	....	....	....	....
1994-95	Hershey Bears	AHL	69	13	32	45	36	....	....	....	....	....	....	....	....	....	2	1	0	1	4	....	....	....	....
1995-96	Hershey Bears	AHL	68	15	36	51	59	....	....	....	....	....	....	....	....	....	5	2	4	6	2	....	....	....	....
1996-97	**Philadelphia**	**NHL**	**18**	**5**	**10**	**15**	**4**	**0**	**0**	**0**	**35**	**14.3**	**3**	....	....	....	**5**	**1**	**3**	**4**	**4**	**0**	**0**	**0**	....
	Philadelphia	AHL	63	32	63	95	70	....	....	....	....	....	....	....	....	....	....	....	....	....	....	....	....	....	....
1997-98	**Philadelphia**	**NHL**	**41**	**5**	**13**	**18**	**17**	**4**	**0**	**0**	**60**	**8.3**	**-10**	....	....	....	....	....	....	....	....	....	....	....	....
	Ottawa	**NHL**	**15**	**1**	**6**	**7**	**4**	**0**	**0**	**0**	**28**	**3.6**	**-1**	....	....	....	**6**	**0**	**0**	**0**	**0**	**0**	**0**	**0**	....
1998-99	**Ottawa**	**NHL**	**79**	**10**	**26**	**36**	**58**	**2**	**0**	**3**	**114**	**8.8**	**8**	**997**	**56.2**	**13:03**	**4**	**0**	**0**	**0**	**0**	**0**	**0**	**0**	**12:37**
99-2000	**Ottawa**	**NHL**	**79**	**22**	**33**	**55**	**40**	**5**	**0**	**4**	**204**	**10.8**	**-2**	**1331**	**49.6**	**16:26**	**6**	**0**	**4**	**4**	**4**	**0**	**0**	**0**	**17:40**
2000-01	**Ottawa**	**NHL**	**40**	**1**	**12**	**13**	**12**	**0**	**0**	**0**	**68**	**1.5**	**1**	**501**	**50.1**	**12:57**	....	....	....	....	....	....	....	....	....
	Florida	**NHL**	**34**	**4**	**12**	**16**	**10**	**1**	**0**	**0**	**68**	**5.9**	**-2**	**487**	**54.6**	**16:36**	....	....	....	....	....	....	....	....	....
2001-02	**Tampa Bay**	**NHL**	**81**	**18**	**37**	**55**	**38**	**7**	**0**	**2**	**166**	**10.8**	**-11**	**555**	**52.8**	**17:31**	....	....	....	....	....	....	....	....	....
2002-03	**Tampa Bay**	**NHL**	**80**	**22**	**57**	**79**	**53**	**9**	**0**	**4**	**134**	**16.4**	**9**	**161**	**51.6**	**18:39**	**11**	**4**	**2**	**6**	**8**	**2**	**0**	**0**	**21:15**
2003-04	**Anaheim**	**NHL**	**82**	**19**	**35**	**54**	**54**	**7**	**0**	**4**	**185**	**10.3**	**-9**	**45**	**46.7**	**18:37**	....	....	....	....	....	....	....	....	....
	NHL Totals		**549**	**107**	**241**	**348**	**290**	**35**	**0**	**17**	**1062**	**10.1**		**4077**	**52.3**	**16:32**	**32**	**5**	**9**	**14**	**16**	**2**	**0**	**0**	**18:35**

AHL First All-Star Team (1997)

Traded to **Ottawa** by **Philadelphia** with Pat Falloon and Dallas' 2nd round choice (previously acquired, Ottawa selected Chris Bala) in 1998 Entry Draft for Alexandre Daigle, January 17, 1998. Traded to **Florida** by **Ottawa** for future considerations, January 20, 2001. Traded to **Tampa Bay** by **Florida** for Ryan Johnson and Tampa Bay's 6th round choice (later traded back to Tampa Bay – Tampa Bay selected Doug O'Brien) in 2003 Entry Draft, July 10, 2001. Signed as a free agent by **Anaheim**, July 17, 2003.

PURINTON, Dale

(PUHR-ihn-TOHN, DAYL) **NYR**

Defense. Shoots left. 6'3", 214 lbs. Born, Fort Wayne, IN, October 11, 1976. NY Rangers' 5th choice, 117th overall, in 1995 Entry Draft.

Season	Club	League	GP	G	A	Pts	PIM	PP	SH	GW	S	%	+/-	TF	F%	Min	GP	G	A	Pts	PIM	PP	SH	GW	Min
1992-93	Moose Jaw	SMHL	34	1	16	17	107	....	....	....	....	....	....	....	....	....	....	....	....	....	....	....	....	....	....
	Moose Jaw	WHL	2	0	0	0	2	....	....	....	....	....	....	....	....	....	....	....	....	....	....	....	....	....	....
1993-94	Vernon Vipers	BCJHL	42	1	6	7	194	....	....	....	....	....	....	....	....	....	....	....	....	....	....	....	....	....	....
1994-95	Tacoma Rockets	WHL	65	0	8	8	291	....	....	....	....	....	....	....	....	....	3	0	0	0	13	....	....	....	....
1995-96	Kelowna Rockets	WHL	22	1	4	5	88	....	....	....	....	....	....	....	....	....	....	....	....	....	....	....	....	....	....
	Lethbridge	WHL	37	3	6	9	144	....	....	....	....	....	....	....	....	....	4	1	1	2	25	....	....	....	....
1996-97	Lethbridge	WHL	51	6	26	32	254	....	....	....	....	....	....	....	....	....	18	3	5	8	*88	....	....	....	....
1997-98	Hartford	AHL	17	0	0	0	95	....	....	....	....	....	....	....	....	....	....	....	....	....	....	....	....	....	....
	Charlotte	ECHL	34	3	5	8	186	....	....	....	....	....	....	....	....	....	....	....	....	....	....	....	....	....	....
1998-99	Hartford	AHL	45	1	3	4	306	....	....	....	....	....	....	....	....	....	7	0	2	2	24	....	....	....	....
99-2000	**NY Rangers**	**NHL**	**1**	**0**	**0**	**0**	**7**	**0**	**0**	**0**	**1**	**0.0**	**-1**	**0**	**0.0**	**12:45**	....	....	....	....	....	....	....	....	....
	Hartford	AHL	62	4	4	8	415	....	....	....	....	....	....	....	....	....	23	0	3	3	*87	....	....	....	....
2000-01	**NY Rangers**	**NHL**	**42**	**0**	**2**	**2**	**180**	**0**	**0**	**0**	**13**	**0.0**	**5**	**0**	**0.0**	**9:33**	....	....	....	....	....	....	....	....	....
	Hartford	AHL	11	0	1	1	75	....	....	....	....	....	....	....	....	....	....	....	....	....	....	....	....	....	....
2001-02	**NY Rangers**	**NHL**	**40**	**0**	**4**	**4**	**113**	**0**	**0**	**0**	**11**	**0.0**	**4**	**0**	**0.0**	**7:37**	....	....	....	....	....	....	....	....	....
2002-03	**NY Rangers**	**NHL**	**58**	**3**	**9**	**12**	**161**	**0**	**0**	**0**	**50**	**6.0**	**-2**	**0**	**0.0**	**15:02**	....	....	....	....	....	....	....	....	....
2003-04	**NY Rangers**	**NHL**	**40**	**1**	**1**	**2**	**117**	**0**	**0**	**0**	**31**	**3.2**	**-9**	**0**	**0.0**	**12:47**	....	....	....	....	....	....	....	....	....
	NHL Totals		**181**	**4**	**16**	**20**	**578**	**0**	**0**	**0**	**106**	**3.8**		**0**	**0.0**	**11:37**	....	....	....	....	....	....	....	....	....

• Spent majority of 2003-04 season as a healthy reserve.

PUSHOR, Jamie

(PUH-shohr, JAY-mee)

Defense. Shoots right. 6'3", 218 lbs. Born, Lethbridge, Alta., February 11, 1973. Detroit's 2nd choice, 32nd overall, in 1991 Entry Draft.

Season	Club	League	GP	G	A	Pts	PIM	PP	SH	GW	S	%	+/-	TF	F%	Min	GP	G	A	Pts	PIM	PP	SH	GW	Min
1988-89	Lethbridge	AMHL	37	1	8	9	20	....	....	....	....	....	....	....	....	....	....	....	....	....	....	....	....	....	....
	Lethbridge	WHL	2	0	0	0	0	....	....	....	....	....	....	....	....	....	....	....	....	....	....	....	....	....	....
1989-90	Lethbridge	AMHL	35	6	27	33	92	....	....	....	....	....	....	....	....	....	....	....	....	....	....	....	....	....	....
	Lethbridge	WHL	10	0	2	2	2	....	....	....	....	....	....	....	....	....	16	0	0	0	63	....	....	....	....
1990-91	Lethbridge	WHL	71	1	13	14	202	....	....	....	....	....	....	....	....	....	....	....	....	....	....	....	....	....	....
1991-92	Lethbridge	WHL	49	2	15	17	232	....	....	....	....	....	....	....	....	....	5	0	0	0	33	....	....	....	....
1992-93	Lethbridge	WHL	72	6	22	28	200	....	....	....	....	....	....	....	....	....	4	0	1	1	9	....	....	....	....
1993-94	Adirondack	AHL	73	1	17	18	124	....	....	....	....	....	....	....	....	....	12	0	0	0	22	....	....	....	....
1994-95	Adirondack	AHL	58	2	11	13	129	....	....	....	....	....	....	....	....	....	4	0	1	1	0	....	....	....	....
1995-96	**Detroit**	**NHL**	**5**	**0**	**1**	**1**	**17**	**0**	**0**	**0**	**6**	**0.0**	**2**	....	....	....	....	....	....	....	....	....	....	....	....
	Adirondack	AHL	65	2	16	18	126	....	....	....	....	....	....	....	....	....	3	0	0	0	5	....	....	....	....
1996-97◆	**Detroit**	**NHL**	**75**	**4**	**7**	**11**	**129**	**0**	**0**	**0**	**63**	**6.3**	**1**	....	....	....	**5**	**0**	**1**	**1**	**5**	**0**	**0**	**0**	....
1997-98	**Detroit**	**NHL**	**54**	**2**	**5**	**7**	**71**	**0**	**0**	**0**	**43**	**4.7**	**2**	....	....	....	....	....	....	....	....	....	....	....	....
	Anaheim	**NHL**	**10**	**0**	**2**	**2**	**10**	**0**	**0**	**0**	**8**	**0.0**	**1**	....	....	....	....	....	....	....	....	....	....	....	....
1998-99	**Anaheim**	**NHL**	**70**	**1**	**2**	**3**	**112**	**0**	**0**	**0**	**75**	**1.3**	**-20**	**0**	**0.0**	**19:16**	**4**	**0**	**0**	**0**	**6**	**0**	**0**	**0**	**14:08**
99-2000	**Dallas**	**NHL**	**62**	**0**	**8**	**8**	**53**	**0**	**0**	**0**	**27**	**0.0**	**0**	**0**	**0.0**	**11:36**	**5**	**0**	**0**	**0**	**5**	**0**	**0**	**0**	**10:06**
2000-01	**Columbus**	**NHL**	**75**	**3**	**10**	**13**	**94**	**0**	**1**	**0**	**64**	**4.7**	**7**	**0**	**0.0**	**20:48**	....	....	....	....	....	....	....	....	....
2001-02	**Columbus**	**NHL**	**61**	**0**	**6**	**6**	**54**	**0**	**0**	**0**	**46**	**0.0**	**-10**	**0**	**0.0**	**17:06**	....	....	....	....	....	....	....	....	....
	Pittsburgh	**NHL**	**15**	**0**	**2**	**2**	**30**	**0**	**0**	**0**	**14**	**0.0**	**-3**	**0**	**0.0**	**19:03**	....	....	....	....	....	....	....	....	....
2002-03	**Pittsburgh**	**NHL**	**76**	**3**	**1**	**4**	**76**	**0**	**0**	**0**	**54**	**5.6**	**-28**	**0**	**0.0**	**16:58**	....	....	....	....	....	....	....	....	....
2003-04	Syracuse Crunch	AHL	17	1	4	5	24	....	....	....	....	....	....	....	....	....	....	....	....	....	....	....	....	....	....
	Columbus	**NHL**	**7**	**0**	**0**	**0**	**2**	**0**	**0**	**0**	**6**	**0.0**	**-2**	**0**	**0.0**	**13:12**	....	....	....	....	....	....	....	....	....
	NY Rangers	**NHL**	**7**	**0**	**0**	**0**	**0**	**0**	**0**	**0**	**4**	**0.0**	**-3**	**0**	**0.0**	**13:08**	....	....	....	....	....	....	....	....	....
	Hartford	AHL	14	0	2	2	21	....	....	....	....	....	....	....	....	....	16	1	1	2	18	....	....	....	....
	NHL Totals		**517**	**13**	**44**	**57**	**648**	**0**	**1**	**0**	**410**	**3.2**		**0**	**0.0**	**17:15**	**14**	**0**	**1**	**1**	**16**	**0**	**0**	**0**	**11:53**

Traded to **Anaheim** by **Detroit** with Detroit's 4th round choice (Viktor Wallin) in 1998 Entry Draft for Dmitri Mironov, March 24, 1998. Claimed by **Atlanta** from **Anaheim** in Expansion Draft, June 25, 1999. Traded to **Dallas** by **Atlanta** for Jason Botterill, July 15, 1999. Selected by **Columbus** from **Dallas** in Expansion Draft, June 23, 2000. Traded to **Pittsburgh** by **Columbus** for Pittsburgh's 4th round choice (Kevin Jarman) in 2003 Entry Draft, March 15, 2002. Signed as a free agent by **Syracuse** (AHL), November 18, 2003. Signed as a free agent by **Columbus**, December 10, 2003. Traded to **NY Rangers** by **Columbus** for NY Rangers' 8th round choice (Matt Greer) in 2004 Entry Draft, January 23, 2004.

PYATT, Taylor

(PIGH-at, TAY-luhr) **BUF.**

Left wing. Shoots left. 6'4", 222 lbs. Born, Thunder Bay, Ont., August 19, 1981. NY Islanders' 2nd choice, 8th overall, in 1999 Entry Draft.

Season	Club	League	GP	G	A	Pts	PIM	PP	SH	GW	S	%	+/-	TF	F%	Min	GP	G	A	Pts	PIM	PP	SH	GW	Min
1996-97	Thunder Bay	TBAHA	60	52	61	113	72	....	....	....	....	....	....	....	....	....	....	....	....	....	....	....	....	....	....
1997-98	Sudbury Wolves	OHL	58	14	17	31	104	....	....	....	....	....	....	....	....	....	10	3	1	4	8	....	....	....	....
1998-99	Sudbury Wolves	OHL	68	37	38	75	95	....	....	....	....	....	....	....	....	....	4	0	4	4	6	....	....	....	....
99-2000	Sudbury Wolves	OHL	68	40	49	89	98	....	....	....	....	....	....	....	....	....	12	8	7	15	25	....	....	....	....
2000-01	**NY Islanders**	**NHL**	**78**	**4**	**14**	**18**	**39**	**1**	**0**	**2**	**86**	**4.7**	**-17**	**1**	**0.0**	**12:14**	....	....	....	....	....	....	....	....	....
2001-02	**Buffalo**	**NHL**	**48**	**10**	**10**	**20**	**35**	**0**	**0**	**0**	**61**	**16.4**	**4**	**0**	**0.0**	**13:30**	....	....	....	....	....	....	....	....	....
	Rochester	AHL	27	6	4	10	36	....	....	....	....	....	....	....	....	....	....	....	....	....	....	....	....	....	....
2002-03	**Buffalo**	**NHL**	**78**	**14**	**14**	**28**	**38**	**2**	**0**	**0**	**110**	**12.7**	**-8**	**8**	**25.0**	**14:06**	....	....	....	....	....	....	....	....	....
2003-04	**Buffalo**	**NHL**	**63**	**8**	**12**	**20**	**25**	**1**	**2**	**4**	**98**	**8.2**	**-7**	**19**	**26.3**	**15:36**	....	....	....	....	....	....	....	....	....
	NHL Totals		**267**	**36**	**50**	**86**	**137**	**4**	**2**	**6**	**355**	**10.1**		**28**	**25.0**	**13:48**	....	....	....	....	....	....	....	....	....

OHL First All-Star Team (2000)

Traded to **Buffalo** by **NY Islanders** with Tim Connolly for Michael Peca, June 24, 2001.

QUINT, Deron

(KWIHNT, DAIR-ohn)

Defense. Shoots left. 6'2", 219 lbs. Born, Durham, NH, March 12, 1976. Winnipeg's 1st choice, 30th overall, in 1994 Entry Draft.

Season	Club	League	GP	G	A	Pts	PIM	PP	SH	GW	S	%	+/-	TF	F%	Min	GP	G	A	Pts	PIM	PP	SH	GW	Min
1990-91	Cardigan High	Hi-School	31	67	54	121	....	....	....	....	....	....	....	....	....	....	....	....	....	....	....	....	....	....	....
1991-92	Cardigan High	Hi-School	21	111	58	169	....	....	....	....	....	....	....	....	....	....	....	....	....	....	....	....	....	....	....
1992-93	Tabor Academy	Hi-School	28	15	26	41	30	....	....	....	....	....	....	....	....	....	1	0	2	2	0	....	....	....	....
1993-94	Seattle	WHL	63	15	29	44	47	....	....	....	....	....	....	....	....	....	9	4	12	16	8	....	....	....	....
1994-95	Seattle	WHL	65	29	60	89	82	....	....	....	....	....	....	....	....	....	3	1	2	3	6	....	....	....	....
1995-96	**Winnipeg**	**NHL**	**51**	**5**	**13**	**18**	**22**	**2**	**0**	**0**	**97**	**5.2**	**-2**	....	....	....	....	....	....	....	....	....	....	....	....
	Springfield	AHL	11	2	3	5	4	....	....	....	....	....	....	....	....	....	10	2	3	5	6	....	....	....	....
	Seattle	WHL	....	....	....	....	....	....	....	....	....	....	....	....	....	....	5	4	1	5	6	....	....	....	....
1996-97	**Phoenix**	**NHL**	**27**	**3**	**11**	**14**	**4**	**1**	**0**	**0**	**63**	**4.8**	**-4**	....	....	....	**7**	**0**	**2**	**2**	**0**	**0**	**0**	**0**	....
	Springfield	AHL	43	6	18	24	20	....	....	....	....	....	....	....	....	....	12	2	7	9	4	....	....	....	....

			Regular Season														Playoffs								
Season	Club	League	GP	G	A	Pts	PIM	PP	SH	GW	S	%	+/-	TF	F%	Min	GP	G	A	Pts	PIM	PP	SH	GW	Min
1997-98	**Phoenix**	**NHL**	**32**	**4**	**7**	**11**	**16**	**1**	**0**	**1**	**61**	**6.6**	**–6**	....	....	....	....	....	....	....	....	....	....	....	....
	Springfield	AHL	8	1	7	8	10	....	....	....	....	....	....	....	....	....	1	0	0	0	0	....	....	....	....
1998-99	**Phoenix**	**NHL**	**60**	**5**	**8**	**13**	**20**	**2**	**0**	**0**	**94**	**5.3**	**–10**	**0**	**0.0**	**16:12**	....	....	....	....	....	....	....	....	....
99-2000	**Phoenix**	**NHL**	**50**	**3**	**7**	**10**	**22**	**0**	**0**	**1**	**88**	**3.4**	**0**	**0**	**0.0**	**16:39**	....	....	....	....	....	....	....	....	....
	New Jersey	**NHL**	**4**	**1**	**0**	**1**	**2**	**0**	**0**	**0**	**6**	**16.7**	**–2**	**0**	**0.0**	**16:26**	....	....	....	....	....	....	....	....	....
2000-01	**Columbus**	**NHL**	**57**	**7**	**16**	**23**	**16**	**3**	**0**	**0**	**148**	**4.7**	**–19**	**1**	**100.0**	**24:06**	....	....	....	....	....	....	....	....	....
	Syracuse Crunch	AHL	21	5	15	20	30	....	....	....	....	....	....	....	....	....	....	....	....	....	....	....	....	....	....
2001-02	**Columbus**	**NHL**	**75**	**7**	**18**	**25**	**26**	**3**	**0**	**1**	**169**	**4.1**	**–34**	**0**	**0.0**	**22:01**	....	....	....	....	....	....	....	....	....
2002-03	Springfield	AHL	4	1	2	3	4	....	....	....	....	....	....	....	....	....	....	....	....	....	....	....	....	....	....
	Phoenix	**NHL**	**51**	**7**	**10**	**17**	**20**	**2**	**0**	**0**	**85**	**8.2**	**–5**	**0**	**0.0**	**15:51**	....	....	....	....	....	....	....	....	....
2003-04	**Chicago**	**NHL**	**51**	**4**	**7**	**11**	**18**	**2**	**0**	**0**	**72**	**5.6**	**–26**	**0**	**0.0**	**18:08**	....	....	....	....	....	....	....	....	....
	NHL Totals		**458**	**46**	**97**	**143**	**166**	**16**	**0**	**3**	**883**	**5.2**		**1**	**100.0**	**19:03**	**7**	**0**	**2**	**2**	**0**	**0**	**0**	**0**	....

WHL West First All-Star Team (1995)

Transferred to **Phoenix** after **Winnipeg** franchise relocated, July 1, 1996. Traded to **New Jersey** by **Phoenix** with Phoenix's 3rd round choice (later traded back to Phoenix – Phoenix selected Beat Forster) in 2001 Entry Draft for Lyle Odelein, March 7, 2000. Traded to **Columbus** by **New Jersey** to complete transaction that sent Krzysztof Oliwa to Columbus (June 12, 2000) and Turner Stevenson to New Jersey (June 23, 2000), June 23, 2000. Signed to a PTO (tryout) contract by **Springfield** (AHL), October 16, 2002. Signed as a free agent by **Phoenix**, October 26, 2002. Signed as a free agent by **Chicago**, August 5, 2003.

QUINTAL, Stephane

(KAYN-tahl, STEH-fan) **L.A.**

Defense. Shoots right. 6'3", 231 lbs. Born, Boucherville, Que., October 22, 1968. Boston's 2nd choice, 14th overall, in 1987 Entry Draft.

1984-85	Richelieu Riverains	QAAA	41	1	10	11	68	....	....	....	....	....	....	....	....	....	9	0	5	5	27	....	....	....	....
1985-86	Granby Bisons	QMJHL	67	2	17	19	144	....	....	....	....	....	....	....	....	....	....	....	....	....	....	....	....	....	....
1986-87	Granby Bisons	QMJHL	67	13	41	54	178	....	....	....	....	....	....	....	....	....	8	0	9	9	10	....	....	....	....
1987-88	Hull Olympiques	QMJHL	38	13	23	36	138	....	....	....	....	....	....	....	....	....	19	7	12	19	30	....	....	....	....
1988-89	**Boston**	**NHL**	**26**	**0**	**1**	**1**	**29**	**0**	**0**	**0**	**23**	**0.0**	**–5**	....	....	....	....	....	....	....	....	....	....	....	....
	Maine Mariners	AHL	16	4	10	14	28	....	....	....	....	....	....	....	....	....	....	....	....	....	....	....	....	....	....
1989-90	**Boston**	**NHL**	**38**	**2**	**2**	**4**	**22**	**0**	**0**	**0**	**43**	**4.7**	**–11**	....	....	....	....	....	....	....	....	....	....	....	....
	Maine Mariners	AHL	37	4	16	20	27	....	....	....	....	....	....	....	....	....	....	....	....	....	....	....	....	....	....
1990-91	**Boston**	**NHL**	**45**	**2**	**6**	**8**	**89**	**1**	**0**	**0**	**54**	**3.7**	**2**	....	....	....	**3**	**0**	**1**	**1**	**7**	**0**	**0**	**0**	....
	Maine Mariners	AHL	23	1	5	6	30	....	....	....	....	....	....	....	....	....	....	....	....	....	....	....	....	....	....
1991-92	**Boston**	**NHL**	**49**	**4**	**10**	**14**	**77**	**0**	**0**	**0**	**52**	**7.7**	**–8**	....	....	....	....	....	....	....	....	....	....	....	....
	St. Louis	**NHL**	**26**	**0**	**6**	**6**	**32**	**0**	**0**	**0**	**19**	**0.0**	**–3**	....	....	....	**4**	**1**	**2**	**3**	**6**	**1**	**0**	**0**	....
1992-93	**St. Louis**	**NHL**	**75**	**1**	**10**	**11**	**100**	**0**	**1**	**0**	**81**	**1.2**	**–6**	....	....	....	**9**	**0**	**0**	**0**	**8**	**0**	**0**	**0**	....
1993-94	**Winnipeg**	**NHL**	**81**	**8**	**18**	**26**	**119**	**1**	**1**	**1**	**154**	**5.2**	**–25**	....	....	....	....	....	....	....	....	....	....	....	....
1994-95	**Winnipeg**	**NHL**	**43**	**6**	**17**	**23**	**78**	**3**	**0**	**2**	**107**	**5.6**	**0**	....	....	....	....	....	....	....	....	....	....	....	....
1995-96	**Montreal**	**NHL**	**68**	**2**	**14**	**16**	**117**	**0**	**1**	**1**	**104**	**1.9**	**–4**	....	....	....	**6**	**0**	**1**	**1**	**6**	**0**	**0**	**0**	....
1996-97	**Montreal**	**NHL**	**71**	**7**	**15**	**22**	**100**	**1**	**0**	**0**	**139**	**5.0**	**1**	....	....	....	**5**	**0**	**1**	**1**	**6**	**0**	**0**	**0**	....
1997-98	**Montreal**	**NHL**	**71**	**6**	**10**	**16**	**97**	**0**	**0**	**0**	**88**	**6.8**	**13**	....	....	....	**9**	**0**	**2**	**2**	**4**	**0**	**0**	**0**	....
1998-99	**Montreal**	**NHL**	**82**	**8**	**19**	**27**	**84**	**1**	**1**	**4**	**159**	**5.0**	**–23**	**0**	**0.0**	**22:06**	....	....	....	....	....	....	....	....	....
99-2000	**NY Rangers**	**NHL**	**75**	**2**	**14**	**16**	**77**	**0**	**0**	**1**	**102**	**2.0**	**–10**	**0**	**0.0**	**19:04**	....	....	....	....	....	....	....	....	....
2000-01	**Chicago**	**NHL**	**72**	**1**	**18**	**19**	**60**	**0**	**0**	**0**	**109**	**0.9**	**–9**	**0**	**0.0**	**22:30**	....	....	....	....	....	....	....	....	....
2001-02	**Montreal**	**NHL**	**75**	**6**	**10**	**16**	**87**	**1**	**0**	**1**	**85**	**7.1**	**–7**	**0**	**0.0**	**18:52**	**12**	**1**	**3**	**4**	**12**	**0**	**0**	**0**	**22:41**
2002-03	**Montreal**	**NHL**	**67**	**5**	**5**	**10**	**70**	**0**	**0**	**0**	**73**	**6.8**	**–4**	**0**	**0.0**	**18:38**	....	....	....	....	....	....	....	....	....
2003-04	**Montreal**	**NHL**	**73**	**3**	**5**	**8**	**82**	**0**	**0**	**0**	**86**	**3.5**	**10**	**0**	**0.0**	**20:38**	**4**	**0**	**0**	**0**	**2**	**0**	**0**	**0**	**13:03**
	NHL Totals		**1037**	**63**	**180**	**243**	**1320**	**8**	**4**	**10**	**1478**	**4.3**		**0**	**0.0**	**20:21**	**52**	**2**	**10**	**12**	**51**	**1**	**0**	**0**	**20:17**

QMJHL First All-Star Team (1987)

Traded to **St. Louis** by **Boston** with Craig Janney for Adam Oates, February 7, 1992. Traded to **Winnipeg** by **St. Louis** with Nelson Emerson for Phil Housley, September 24, 1993. Traded to **Montreal** by **Winnipeg** for Montreal's 2nd round choice (Jason Doig) in 1995 Entry Draft, July 8, 1995. Signed as a free agent by **NY Rangers**, July 13, 1999. Claimed on waivers by **Chicago** from **NY Rangers**, October 5, 2000. Traded to **Montreal** by **Chicago** for Montreal's 4th round choice (Brent MacLellan) in 2001 Entry Draft, June 23, 2001. Traded to **Los Angeles** by **Montreal** for future considerations, June 27, 2004.

RACHUNEK, Karel

(ra-KHOO-nehk, KAH-rehl) **NYR**

Defense. Shoots right. 6'2", 211 lbs. Born, Zlin, Czech., August 27, 1979. Ottawa's 8th choice, 229th overall, in 1997 Entry Draft.

1995-96	AC ZPS Zlin Jr.	Czech-Jr.	38	8	11	19	....	....	....	....	....	....	....	....	....	....	....	....	....	....	....	....	....	....	....
1996-97	AC ZPS Zlin Jr.	Czech-Jr.	27	2	11	13	....	....	....	....	....	....	....	....	....	....	....	....	....	....	....	....	....	....	....
1997-98	Zlin	Czech	27	1	2	3	16	....	....	....	....	....	....	....	....	....	....	....	....	....	....	....	....	....	....
1998-99	Zlin	Czech	39	3	9	12	88	....	....	....	....	....	....	....	....	....	6	0	0	0	....	....	....	....	....
99-2000	**Ottawa**	**NHL**	**6**	**0**	**0**	**0**	**2**	**0**	**0**	**0**	**3**	**0.0**	**0**	**0**	**0.0**	**8:03**	....	....	....	....	....	....	....	....	....
	Grand Rapids	IHL	62	6	20	26	64	....	....	....	....	....	....	....	....	....	9	0	5	5	6	....	....	....	....
2000-01	**Ottawa**	**NHL**	**71**	**3**	**30**	**33**	**60**	**3**	**0**	**0**	**77**	**3.9**	**17**	**0**	**0.0**	**20:54**	**3**	**0**	**0**	**0**	**0**	**0**	**0**	**0**	**22:38**
2001-02	**Ottawa**	**NHL**	**51**	**3**	**15**	**18**	**24**	**1**	**0**	**2**	**55**	**5.5**	**7**	**2**	**0.0**	**19:19**	....	....	....	....	....	....	....	....	....
2002-03	Yaroslavl	Russia	9	3	0	3	8	....	....	....	....	....	....	....	....	....	....	....	....	....	....	....	....	....	....
	Ottawa	**NHL**	**58**	**4**	**25**	**29**	**30**	**3**	**0**	**1**	**110**	**3.6**	**23**	**3**	**33.3**	**21:46**	**17**	**1**	**3**	**4**	**14**	**0**	**0**	**0**	**23:14**
	Binghamton	AHL	6	0	2	2	10	....	....	....	....	....	....	....	....	....	....	....	....	....	....	....	....	....	....
2003-04	**Ottawa**	**NHL**	**60**	**1**	**16**	**17**	**29**	**0**	**0**	**0**	**99**	**1.0**	**17**	**0**	**0.0**	**19:43**	....	....	....	....	....	....	....	....	....
	NY Rangers	**NHL**	**12**	**1**	**3**	**4**	**4**	**1**	**0**	**0**	**21**	**4.8**	**–9**	**0**	**0.0**	**19:04**	....	....	....	....	....	....	....	....	....
	NHL Totals		**258**	**12**	**89**	**101**	**149**	**8**	**0**	**3**	**365**	**3.3**		**5**	**20.0**	**20:07**	**20**	**1**	**3**	**4**	**14**	**0**	**0**	**0**	**23:09**

Traded to **NY Rangers** by **Ottawa** with Alexandre Giroux for Greg De Vries, March 9, 2004.

RADIVOJEVIC, Branko

(ra-dih-VOI-uh-vihch, BRAN-koh) **PHI.**

Right wing. Shoots right. 6'1", 209 lbs. Born, Piestany, Czech., November 24, 1980. Colorado's 3rd choice, 93rd overall, in 1999 Entry Draft.

1997-98	Dukla Trencin Jr.	Slovak-Jr.	52	30	31	61	50	....	....	....	....	....	....	....	....	....	....	....	....	....	....	....	....	....	....
	Dukla Trencin	Slovakia	1	0	0	0	2	....	....	....	....	....	....	....	....	....	....	....	....	....	....	....	....	....	....
1998-99	Belleville Bulls	OHL	68	20	38	58	61	....	....	....	....	....	....	....	....	....	21	7	17	24	18	....	....	....	....
99-2000	Belleville Bulls	OHL	59	23	49	72	86	....	....	....	....	....	....	....	....	....	16	5	8	13	32	....	....	....	....
2000-01	Belleville Bulls	OHL	61	34	70	104	77	....	....	....	....	....	....	....	....	....	10	6	10	16	18	....	....	....	....
2001-02	**Phoenix**	**NHL**	**18**	**4**	**2**	**6**	**4**	**0**	**0**	**1**	**19**	**21.1**	**1**	**0**	**0.0**	**9:22**	**1**	**0**	**0**	**0**	**2**	**0**	**0**	**0**	**8:07**
	Springfield	AHL	62	18	21	39	64	....	....	....	....	....	....	....	....	....	....	....	....	....	....	....	....	....	....
2002-03	**Phoenix**	**NHL**	**79**	**12**	**15**	**27**	**63**	**1**	**0**	**3**	**109**	**11.0**	**–2**	**20**	**40.0**	**13:18**	....	....	....	....	....	....	....	....	....
2003-04	**Phoenix**	**NHL**	**53**	**9**	**14**	**23**	**36**	**2**	**1**	**2**	**83**	**10.8**	**–5**	**30**	**30.0**	**16:27**	....	....	....	....	....	....	....	....	....
	Philadelphia	**NHL**	**24**	**1**	**8**	**9**	**36**	**0**	**0**	**0**	**24**	**4.2**	**0**	**11**	**54.6**	**10:28**	**18**	**1**	**1**	**2**	**32**	**0**	**0**	**0**	**9:56**
	NHL Totals		**174**	**26**	**39**	**65**	**139**	**3**	**1**	**6**	**235**	**11.1**		**61**	**37.7**	**13:28**	**19**	**1**	**1**	**2**	**34**	**0**	**0**	**0**	**9:51**

OHL First All-Star Team (2001)

Signed as a free agent by **Phoenix**, June 19, 2001. Traded to **Philadelphia** by **Phoenix** with Sean Burke and Ben Eager for Mike Comrie, February 9, 2004.

RADULOV, Igor

(rah-DOO-lahf, EE-gohr) **CHI.**

Left wing. Shoots left. 6'1", 186 lbs. Born, Nizhny Tagil, USSR, August 23, 1982. Chicago's 4th choice, 74th overall, in 2000 Entry Draft.

1997-98	Yaroslavl	Russia	5	0	2	2	4	....	....	....	....	....	....	....	....	....	....	....	....	....	....	....	....	....	....
1998-99	Yaroslavl 2	Russia-3	21	2	3	5	4	....	....	....	....	....	....	....	....	....	....	....	....	....	....	....	....	....	....
99-2000	Yaroslavl 2	Russia-3	31	17	16	33	....	....	....	....	....	....	....	....	....	....	....	....	....	....	....	....	....	....	....
2000-01	Kristall Saratov	Russia-2	4	0	2	2	2	....	....	....	....	....	....	....	....	....	....	....	....	....	....	....	....	....	....
	St. Petersburg	Russia	8	1	0	1	6	....	....	....	....	....	....	....	....	....	....	....	....	....	....	....	....	....	....
2001-02	Mississauga	OHL	62	33	30	63	30	....	....	....	....	....	....	....	....	....	....	....	....	....	....	....	....	....	....
2002-03	**Chicago**	**NHL**	**7**	**5**	**0**	**5**	**4**	**3**	**0**	**0**	**14**	**35.7**	**–3**	**0**	**0.0**	**15:06**	....	....	....	....	....	....	....	....	....
	Norfolk Admirals	AHL	62	18	9	27	26	....	....	....	....	....	....	....	....	....	9	2	2	4	8	....	....	....	....
2003-04	**Chicago**	**NHL**	**36**	**4**	**7**	**11**	**18**	**0**	**0**	**0**	**47**	**8.5**	**–2**	**0**	**0.0**	**12:15**	....	....	....	....	....	....	....	....	....
	Norfolk Admirals	AHL	38	9	14	23	26	....	....	....	....	....	....	....	....	....	8	0	1	1	4	....	....	....	....
	NHL Totals		**43**	**9**	**7**	**16**	**22**	**3**	**0**	**0**	**61**	**14.8**		**0**	**0.0**	**12:43**	....	....	....	....	....	....	....	....	....

			Regular Season															Playoffs							
Season	Club	League	GP	G	A	Pts	PIM	PP	SH	GW	S	%	+/-	TF	F%	Min	GP	G	A	Pts	PIM	PP	SH	GW	Min

RAFALSKI, Brian
(ra-FAWL-skee, BRIGH-uhn)   N.J.

Defense. Shoots right. 5'10", 190 lbs.   Born, Dearborn, MI, September 28, 1973.

Season	Club	League	GP	G	A	Pts	PIM	PP	SH	GW	S	%	+/-	TF	F%	Min	GP	G	A	Pts	PIM	PP	SH	GW	Min
1990-91	Madison Capitols	USHL	47	12	11	23	28	....	....	....	....	....	....				....	....	....	....	....	....	....	....	....
1991-92	U. of Wisconsin	WCHA	34	3	14	17	34	....	....	....	....	....	....				....	....	....	....	....	....	....	....	....
1992-93	U. of Wisconsin	WCHA	32	0	13	13	10	....	....	....	....	....	....				....	....	....	....	....	....	....	....	....
1993-94	U. of Wisconsin	WCHA	37	6	17	23	26	....	....	....	....	....	....				....	....	....	....	....	....	....	....	....
1994-95	U. of Wisconsin	WCHA	43	11	34	45	48	....	....	....	....	....	....				....	....	....	....	....	....	....	....	....
1995-96	Brynas IF Gavle	Sweden	40	4	14	18	26	....	....	....	....	....	....				9	0	1	1	2	....	....	....	....
1996-97	HPK Hameenlinna	Finland	49	11	24	35	26	....	....	....	....	....	....				10	6	5	11	4	....	....	....	....
1997-98	HIFK Helsinki	Finland	40	13	10	23	20	....	....	....	....	....	....				9	5	6	11	0	....	....	....	....
1998-99	HIFK Helsinki	Finland	53	19	34	53	18	....	....	....	....	....	....				11	5	*9	*14	4	....	....	....	....
	HIFK Helsinki	EuroHL	6	4	6	10	10	....	....	....	....	....	....				4	1	0	1	2	....	....	....	....
99-2000♦	New Jersey	NHL	75	5	27	32	28	1	0	1	128	3.9	21	1	0.0	18:51	23	2	6	8	8	0	0	1	21:25
2000-01	New Jersey	NHL	78	9	43	52	26	6	0	1	142	6.3	36	2100.0		21:41	25	7	11	18	7	1	0	3	22:08
2001-02	New Jersey	NHL	76	7	40	47	18	2	0	4	125	5.6	15	0	0.0	22:08	6	3	2	5	4	3	0	0	21:45
	United States	Olympics	6	1	4	5	2										....	....	....	....	....	....	....	....	....
2002-03♦	New Jersey	NHL	79	3	37	40	14	2	0	0	178	1.7	18	1	0.0	23:09	23	2	9	11	8	0	0	0	25:46
2003-04	New Jersey	NHL	69	6	30	36	24	2	0	1	130	4.6	6	0	0.0	22:48	5	0	1	1	0	0	0	0	22:22
	NHL Totals		**377**	**30**	**177**	**207**	**110**	**13**	**0**	**7**	**703**	**4.3**		**4**	**50.0**	**21:43**	**82**	**14**	**29**	**43**	**27**	**6**	**0**	**4**	**22:56**

WCHA First All-Star Team (1995) • NCAA West First All-American Team (1995) • NHL All-Rookie Team (2000)
Played in NHL All-Star Game (2004)
Signed as a free agent by **New Jersey**, June 18, 1999.

RAGNARSSON, Marcus
(RAG-nahr-suhn, MAHR-kuhs)   PHI.

Defense. Shoots left. 6'1", 215 lbs.   Born, Ostervala, Sweden, August 13, 1971. San Jose's 5th choice, 99th overall, in 1992 Entry Draft.

Season	Club	League	GP	G	A	Pts	PIM	PP	SH	GW	S	%	+/-	TF	F%	Min	GP	G	A	Pts	PIM	PP	SH	GW	Min
1986-87	Ostervala IF	Swede-3	28	1	6	7	....	....	....	....	....	....	....				....	....	....	....	....	....	....	....	....
1987-88	Ostervala IF	Swede-3	25	3	12	15	....	....	....	....	....	....	....				....	....	....	....	....	....	....	....	....
1988-89	Ostervala IF	Swede-3	30	15	14	29	....	....	....	....	....	....	....				....	....	....	....	....	....	....	....	....
1989-90	Nacka HK	Swede-2	9	2	3	5	4	....	....	....	....	....	....				....	....	....	....	....	....	....	....	....
	Djurgarden	Sweden	13	0	2	2	0	....	....	....	....	....	....				1	0	0	0	0	....	....	....	....
1990-91	Djurgarden	Sweden	35	4	1	5	12	....	....	....	....	....	....				7	0	0	0	6	....	....	....	....
1991-92	Djurgarden	Sweden	40	8	5	13	14	....	....	....	....	....	....				10	0	1	1	4	....	....	....	....
1992-93	Djurgarden	Sweden	35	3	3	6	53	....	....	....	....	....	....				6	0	3	3	8	....	....	....	....
1993-94	Djurgarden	Sweden	19	0	4	4	24	....	....	....	....	....	....				....	....	....	....	....	....	....	....	....
1994-95	Djurgarden	Sweden	38	3	9	16	20	....	....	....	....	....	....				3	0	0	0	4	....	....	....	....
1995-96	San Jose	NHL	71	8	31	39	42	4	0	0	94	8.5	-24				....	....	....	....	....	....	....	....	....
1996-97	San Jose	NHL	69	3	14	17	63	2	0	0	57	5.3	-18				....	....	....	....	....	....	....	....	....
1997-98	San Jose	NHL	79	5	20	25	65	3	0	1	91	5.5	-11				6	0	0	0	4	....	....	....	....
	Sweden	Olympics	3	0	1	1	0										....	....	....	....	....	....	....	....	....
1998-99	San Jose	NHL	74	0	13	13	66	0	0	0	87	0.0	7	3	66.7	21:55	6	0	1	1	6	0	0	0	22:16
99-2000	San Jose	NHL	63	3	13	16	38	0	0	0	60	5.0	13	0	0.0	22:52	12	0	3	3	10	0	0	0	22:22
2000-01	San Jose	NHL	68	3	12	15	44	1	0	0	74	4.1	2	0	0.0	23:36	5	0	1	1	8	0	0	0	20:24
2001-02	San Jose	NHL	70	5	15	20	44	2	0	3	68	7.4	4	4	25.0	22:37	12	1	3	4	12	0	0	1	21:35
	Sweden	Olympics	4	0	2	2	2										....	....	....	....	....	....	....	....	....
2002-03	San Jose	NHL	25	1	7	8	30	0	0	0	27	3.7	2	2100.0		24:56	....	....	....	....	....	....	....	....	....
	Philadelphia	NHL	43	2	6	8	32	1	0	0	52	3.8	5	1100.0		21:10	13	0	4	4	6	0	0	0	25:23
2003-04	Philadelphia	NHL	70	7	9	16	58	2	0	2	82	8.5	12	0	0.0	20:55	14	1	4	5	14	0	0	1	21:58
	NHL Totals		**632**	**37**	**140**	**177**	**482**	**15**	**0**	**7**	**692**	**5.3**		**10**	**60.0**	**22:24**	**68**	**2**	**13**	**15**	**60**	**0**	**0**	**1**	**22:35**

Played in NHL All-Star Game (2001)
Traded to **Philadelphia** by **San Jose** for Dan McGillis, December 6, 2002.

RASMUSSEN, Erik
(RAS-moo-suhn, AIR-ihk)   N.J.

Left wing/Center. Shoots left. 6'1", 210 lbs.   Born, Minneapolis, MN, March 28, 1977. Buffalo's 1st choice, 7th overall, in 1996 Entry Draft.

Season	Club	League	GP	G	A	Pts	PIM	PP	SH	GW	S	%	+/-	TF	F%	Min	GP	G	A	Pts	PIM	PP	SH	GW	Min
1992-93	St. Louis Park	Hi-School	23	16	24	40	50	....	....	....	....	....	....				....	....	....	....	....	....	....	....	....
1993-94	St. Louis Park	Hi-School	18	25	18	43	80	....	....	....	....	....	....				....	....	....	....	....	....	....	....	....
1994-95	St. Louis Park	Hi-School	23	19	33	52	80	....	....	....	....	....	....				....	....	....	....	....	....	....	....	....
1995-96	U. of Minnesota	WCHA	40	16	32	48	55	....	....	....	....	....	....				....	....	....	....	....	....	....	....	....
1996-97	U. of Minnesota	WCHA	34	15	12	27	*123	....	....	....	....	....	....				....	....	....	....	....	....	....	....	....
1997-98	**Buffalo**	NHL	21	2	3	5	14	0	0	0	28	7.1	2				....	....	....	....	....	....	....	....	....
	Rochester	AHL	53	9	14	23	83	....	....	....	....	....	....				1	0	0	0	5	....	....	....	....
1998-99	**Buffalo**	NHL	42	3	7	10	37	0	0	0	40	7.5	6	67	40.3	12:22	21	2	4	6	18	0	0	1	12:51
	Rochester	AHL	37	12	14	26	47	....	....	....	....	....	....				....	....	....	....	....	....	....	....	....
99-2000	**Buffalo**	NHL	67	8	6	14	43	0	0	2	76	10.5	1	130	44.6	11:27	3	0	0	0	4	0	0	0	8:59
2000-01	**Buffalo**	NHL	82	12	19	31	51	1	0	3	95	12.6	0	565	43.7	13:47	3	0	1	1	0	0	0	0	16:26
2001-02	**Buffalo**	NHL	69	8	11	19	34	0	0	2	89	9.0	-1	236	43.2	13:03	....	....	....	....	....	....	....	....	....
2002-03	**Los Angeles**	NHL	57	4	12	16	28	0	0	1	75	5.3	-1	278	44.6	13:39	....	....	....	....	....	....	....	....	....
2003-04	**New Jersey**	NHL	69	7	6	13	41	0	0	0	68	10.3	5	423	44.4	11:34	5	0	2	2	2	0	0	0	14:44
	NHL Totals		**407**	**44**	**64**	**108**	**248**	**1**	**0**	**8**	**471**	**9.3**		**1699**	**43.4**	**12:41**	**32**	**2**	**7**	**9**	**24**	**0**	**0**	**1**	**13:07**

Minnesota High School Player of the Year (1995)
Traded to **Los Angeles** by **Buffalo** for Adam Mair and Los Angeles' 5th round choice (Thomas Morrow) in 2003 Entry Draft, July 24, 2002. Signed as a free agent by **New Jersey**, July 25, 2003.

RATHJE, Mike
(RATH-jee, MIGHK)   S.J.

Defense. Shoots left. 6'5", 235 lbs.   Born, Mannville, Alta., May 11, 1974. San Jose's 1st choice, 3rd overall, in 1992 Entry Draft.

Season	Club	League	GP	G	A	Pts	PIM	PP	SH	GW	S	%	+/-	TF	F%	Min	GP	G	A	Pts	PIM	PP	SH	GW	Min
1989-90	Sherwood Park	AMHL	33	6	11	17	30	....	....	....	....	....	....				6	1	1	2	2	....	....	....	....
1990-91	Medicine Hat	WHL	64	1	16	17	28	....	....	....	....	....	....				12	0	4	4	2	....	....	....	....
1991-92	Medicine Hat	WHL	67	11	23	34	99	....	....	....	....	....	....				4	0	1	1	2	....	....	....	....
1992-93	Medicine Hat	WHL	57	12	37	49	103	....	....	....	....	....	....				10	3	3	6	12	....	....	....	....
	Kansas City	IHL	....	....	....	....	....	....	....	....	....	....	....				5	0	0	0	12	....	....	....	....
1993-94	San Jose	NHL	47	1	9	10	59	1	0	0	30	3.3	-9				1	0	0	0	0	0	0	0	0
	Kansas City	IHL	6	0	2	2	0	....	....	....	....	....	....				....	....	....	....	....	....	....	....	....
1994-95	Kansas City	IHL	6	0	1	1	7	....	....	....	....	....	....				....	....	....	....	....	....	....	....	....
	San Jose	NHL	42	2	7	9	29	0	0	0	38	5.3	-1				11	0	3	3	4	0	0	0	....
1995-96	San Jose	NHL	27	0	7	7	14	0	0	0	26	0.0	-16				....	....	....	....	....	....	....	....	....
	Kansas City	IHL	36	6	11	17	34	....	....	....	....	....	....				....	....	....	....	....	....	....	....	....
1996-97	San Jose	NHL	31	0	8	8	21	0	0	0	22	0.0	-1				....	....	....	....	....	....	....	....	....
1997-98	San Jose	NHL	81	3	12	15	59	1	0	0	61	4.9	-4				6	1	0	1	6	1	0	0	....
1998-99	San Jose	NHL	82	5	9	14	36	0	0	1	67	7.5	15	0	0.0	20:07	6	0	0	0	4	0	0	0	22:08
99-2000	San Jose	NHL	66	2	14	16	31	0	0	0	46	4.3	-2	0	0.0	22:11	12	1	3	4	8	0	0	0	21:32
2000-01	San Jose	NHL	81	0	11	11	48	0	0	0	89	0.0	7	0	0.0	22:20	6	0	1	1	4	0	0	0	24:20
2001-02	San Jose	NHL	52	5	12	17	48	4	0	0	56	8.9	23	0	0.0	21:31	12	1	3	4	6	1	0	0	23:29
2002-03	San Jose	NHL	82	7	22	29	48	3	0	1	147	4.8	-19	1	0.0	24:07	....	....	....	....	....	....	....	....	....
2003-04	San Jose	NHL	80	2	17	19	46	0	1	0	105	1.9	18	0	0.0	23:27	17	1	5	6	13	0	0	0	23:26
	NHL Totals		**671**	**27**	**128**	**155**	**439**	**11**	**1**	**2**	**687**	**3.9**		**1**	**0.0**	**22:20**	**71**	**9**	**14**	**23**	**45**	**7**	**0**	**0**	**22:58**

WHL East Second All-Star Team (1992, 1993)
• Missed majority of 1996-97 season recovering from groin injury suffered in game vs. Dallas, November 8, 1996.

RAY, Rob

(RAY, RAWB)

Right wing. Shoots left. 6', 217 lbs. Born, Stirling, Ont., June 8, 1968. Buffalo's 5th choice, 97th overall, in 1988 Entry Draft.

Season	Club	League	GP	G	A	Pts	PIM	PP	SH	GW	S	%	+/-	TF	F%	Min	GP	G	A	Pts	PIM	PP	SH	GW	Min
			Regular Season														Playoffs								
1983-84	Trenton Bobcats	OJHL-B	40	11	10	21	57	....	....	....	....	....	....	....	....	....	....	....	....	....	....	....	....	....	....
1984-85	Whitby Lawmen	OPJHL	35	5	10	15	318	....	....	....	....	....	....	....	....	....	....	....	....	....	....	....	....	....	....
1985-86	Cornwall Royals	OHL	53	6	13	19	253	....	....	....	....	....	....	....	....	....	6	0	0	0	26	....	....	....	....
1986-87	Cornwall Royals	OHL	46	17	20	37	158	....	....	....	....	....	....	....	....	....	5	1	1	2	16	....	....	....	....
1987-88	Cornwall Royals	OHL	61	11	41	52	179	....	....	....	....	....	....	....	....	....	11	2	3	5	33	....	....	....	....
1988-89	Rochester	AHL	74	11	18	29	*446	....	....	....	....	....	....	....	....	....	....	....	....	....	....	....	....	....	....
1989-90	**Buffalo**	**NHL**	**27**	**2**	**1**	**3**	**99**	**0**	**0**	**0**	**20**	**10.0**	**-2**	....	....	....	....	....	....	....	....	....	....	....	....
	Rochester	AHL	43	2	13	15	335	....	....	....	....	....	....	....	....	....	17	1	3	4	115	....	....	....	....
1990-91	**Buffalo**	**NHL**	**66**	**8**	**8**	**16**	***350**	**0**	**0**	**1**	**54**	**14.8**	**-11**	....	....	....	**6**	**1**	**1**	**2**	**56**	**0**	**0**	**1**	....
	Rochester	AHL	8	1	1	2	15	....	....	....	....	....	....	....	....	....	....	....	....	....	....	....	....	....	....
1991-92	**Buffalo**	**NHL**	**63**	**5**	**3**	**8**	**354**	**0**	**0**	**0**	**29**	**17.2**	**-9**	....	....	....	**7**	**0**	**0**	**0**	**2**	**0**	**0**	**0**	....
1992-93	**Buffalo**	**NHL**	**68**	**3**	**2**	**5**	**211**	**1**	**0**	**0**	**28**	**10.7**	**-3**	....	....	....	....	....	....	....	....	....	....	....	....
1993-94	**Buffalo**	**NHL**	**82**	**3**	**4**	**7**	**274**	**0**	**0**	**0**	**34**	**8.8**	**2**	....	....	....	**7**	**1**	**0**	**1**	**43**	**0**	**0**	**0**	....
1994-95	**Buffalo**	**NHL**	**47**	**0**	**3**	**3**	**173**	**0**	**0**	**0**	**7**	**0.0**	**-4**	....	....	....	**5**	**0**	**0**	**0**	**14**	**0**	**0**	**0**	....
1995-96	**Buffalo**	**NHL**	**71**	**3**	**6**	**9**	**287**	**0**	**0**	**0**	**21**	**14.3**	**-8**	....	....	....	....	....	....	....	....	....	....	....	....
1996-97	**Buffalo**	**NHL**	**82**	**7**	**3**	**10**	**286**	**0**	**0**	**1**	**45**	**15.6**	**3**	....	....	....	**12**	**0**	**1**	**1**	**28**	**0**	**0**	**0**	....
1997-98	**Buffalo**	**NHL**	**63**	**2**	**4**	**6**	**234**	**1**	**0**	**1**	**19**	**10.5**	**2**	....	....	....	**10**	**0**	**0**	**0**	**24**	**0**	**0**	**0**	....
1998-99	**Buffalo**	**NHL**	**76**	**0**	**4**	**4**	***261**	**0**	**0**	**0**	**23**	**0.0**	**-2**	**0**	**0.0**	**5:11**	**5**	**1**	**0**	**1**	**0**	**0**	**0**	**1**	**3:11**
99-2000	**Buffalo**	**NHL**	**69**	**1**	**3**	**4**	**158**	**0**	**0**	**0**	**17**	**5.9**	**0**	**0**	**0.0**	**4:13**	....	....	....	....	....	....	....	....	....
2000-01	**Buffalo**	**NHL**	**63**	**4**	**6**	**10**	**210**	**0**	**0**	**1**	**33**	**12.1**	**2**	**1**	**100.0**	**5:38**	**3**	**0**	**0**	**0**	**2**	**0**	**0**	**0**	**1:05**
2001-02	**Buffalo**	**NHL**	**71**	**2**	**3**	**5**	**200**	**0**	**0**	**0**	**23**	**8.7**	**-3**	**0**	**0.0**	**5:08**	....	....	....	....	....	....	....	....	....
2002-03	**Buffalo**	**NHL**	**41**	**0**	**0**	**0**	**92**	**0**	**0**	**0**	**14**	**0.0**	**-5**	**3**	**33.3**	**4:24**	....	....	....	....	....	....	....	....	....
	Ottawa	**NHL**	**5**	**0**	**0**	**0**	**4**	**0**	**0**	**0**	**0**	**0.0**	**0**	**0**	**0.0**	**4:53**	....	....	....	....	....	....	....	....	....
2003-04	**Ottawa**	**NHL**	**6**	**1**	**0**	**1**	**14**	**0**	**0**	**0**	**3**	**33.3**	**0**	**0**	**0.0**	**4:40**	....	....	....	....	....	....	....	....	....
	Binghamton	AHL	5	2	0	2	11	....	....	....	....	....	....	....	....	....	....	....	....	....	....	....	....	....	....
	NHL Totals		**900**	**41**	**50**	**91**	**3207**	**2**	**0**	**4**	**370**	**11.1**		**4**	**50.0**	**4:57**	**55**	**3**	**2**	**5**	**169**	**0**	**0**	**2**	**2:24**

King Clancy Memorial Trophy (1999)

Traded to **Ottawa** by **Buffalo** for future considerations, March 10, 2003. Re-signed as a free agent by **Ottawa**, February 13, 2004.

REASONER, Marty

(REE-sohn-uhr, MAHR-tee) **EDM.**

Center. Shoots left. 6'1", 200 lbs. Born, Honeoye Falls, NY, February 26, 1977. St. Louis' 1st choice, 14th overall, in 1996 Entry Draft.

Season	Club	League	GP	G	A	Pts	PIM	PP	SH	GW	S	%	+/-	TF	F%	Min	GP	G	A	Pts	PIM	PP	SH	GW	Min
1993-94	Deerfield	Hi-School	22	27	25	52	....	....	....	....	....	....	....	....	....	....	....	....	....	....	....	....	....	....	....
1994-95	Deerfield	Hi-School	26	25	32	57	14	....	....	....	....	....	....	....	....	....	....	....	....	....	....	....	....	....	....
1995-96	Boston College	H-East	34	16	29	45	32	....	....	....	....	....	....	....	....	....	....	....	....	....	....	....	....	....	....
1996-97	Boston College	H-East	35	20	24	44	31	....	....	....	....	....	....	....	....	....	....	....	....	....	....	....	....	....	....
1997-98	Boston College	H-East	42	*33	40	*73	56	....	....	....	....	....	....	....	....	....	....	....	....	....	....	....	....	....	....
1998-99	**St. Louis**	**NHL**	**22**	**3**	**7**	**10**	**8**	**1**	**0**	**0**	**33**	**9.1**	**2**	**224**	**53.6**	**13:55**	....	....	....	....	....	....	....	....	....
	Worcester IceCats	AHL	44	17	22	39	24	....	....	....	....	....	....	....	....	....	4	2	1	3	6	....	....	....	....
99-2000	**St. Louis**	**NHL**	**32**	**10**	**14**	**24**	**20**	**3**	**0**	**0**	**51**	**19.6**	**9**	**379**	**49.6**	**15:20**	**7**	**2**	**1**	**3**	**4**	**1**	**0**	**0**	**13:12**
	Worcester IceCats	AHL	44	23	28	51	39	....	....	....	....	....	....	....	....	....	....	....	....	....	....	....	....	....	....
2000-01	**St. Louis**	**NHL**	**41**	**4**	**9**	**13**	**14**	**0**	**0**	**0**	**65**	**6.2**	**-5**	**454**	**53.1**	**14:00**	**10**	**3**	**1**	**4**	**0**	**0**	**0**	**1**	**12:21**
	Worcester IceCats	AHL	34	17	18	35	25	....	....	....	....	....	....	....	....	....	....	....	....	....	....	....	....	....	....
2001-02	**Edmonton**	**NHL**	**52**	**6**	**5**	**11**	**41**	**3**	**0**	**2**	**66**	**9.1**	**0**	**470**	**55.5**	**11:44**	....	....	....	....	....	....	....	....	....
2002-03	**Edmonton**	**NHL**	**70**	**11**	**20**	**31**	**28**	**2**	**2**	**0**	**102**	**10.8**	**19**	**968**	**53.5**	**14:50**	**6**	**1**	**0**	**1**	**2**	**1**	**0**	**0**	**14:22**
	Hamilton	AHL	2	0	2	2	2	....	....	....	....	....	....	....	....	....	....	....	....	....	....	....	....	....	....
2003-04	**Edmonton**	**NHL**	**17**	**2**	**6**	**8**	**10**	**0**	**1**	**0**	**28**	**7.1**	**5**	**321**	**52.7**	**16:30**	....	....	....	....	....	....	....	....	....
	NHL Totals		**234**	**36**	**61**	**97**	**121**	**9**	**3**	**2**	**345**	**10.4**		**2816**	**53.2**	**14:06**	**23**	**6**	**2**	**8**	**6**	**2**	**0**	**1**	**13:08**

Hockey East Rookie of the Year (1996) • Hockey East First All-Star Team (1997, 1998) • NCAA East First All-American Team (1998) • NCAA Championship All-Tournament Team (1998)

Traded to **Edmonton** by **St. Louis** with Jochen Hecht and Jan Horacek for Doug Weight and Michel Riesen, July 1, 2001. • Missed majority of 2003-04 season recovering from ankle (November 8, 2003 vs. Toronto) and knee (January 13, 2004 vs. Florida) injuries.

RECCHI, Mark

(REH-kee, MAHRK) **PIT.**

Right wing. Shoots left. 5'10", 190 lbs. Born, Kamloops, B.C., February 1, 1968. Pittsburgh's 4th choice, 67th overall, in 1988 Entry Draft.

Season	Club	League	GP	G	A	Pts	PIM	PP	SH	GW	S	%	+/-	TF	F%	Min	GP	G	A	Pts	PIM	PP	SH	GW	Min
1984-85	Langley Eagles	BCJHL	51	26	39	65	39	....	....	....	....	....	....	....	....	....	....	....	....	....	....	....	....	....	....
	New Westminster	WHL	4	1	0	1	0	....	....	....	....	....	....	....	....	....	....	....	....	....	....	....	....	....	....
1985-86	New Westminster	WHL	72	21	40	61	55	....	....	....	....	....	....	....	....	....	....	....	....	....	....	....	....	....	....
1986-87	Kamloops Blazers	WHL	40	26	50	76	63	....	....	....	....	....	....	....	....	....	13	3	16	19	17	....	....	....	....
1987-88	Kamloops Blazers	WHL	62	61	*93	154	75	....	....	....	....	....	....	....	....	....	17	10	*21	*31	18	....	....	....	....
1988-89	**Pittsburgh**	**NHL**	**15**	**1**	**1**	**2**	**0**	**0**	**0**	**0**	**11**	**9.1**	**-2**	....	....	....	....	....	....	....	....	....	....	....	....
	Muskegon	IHL	63	50	49	99	86	....	....	....	....	....	....	....	....	....	14	7	*14	*21	28	....	....	....	....
1989-90	**Pittsburgh**	**NHL**	**74**	**30**	**37**	**67**	**44**	**6**	**2**	**4**	**143**	**21.0**	**6**	....	....	....	....	....	....	....	....	....	....	....	....
	Muskegon	IHL	4	7	4	11	2	....	....	....	....	....	....	....	....	....	....	....	....	....	....	....	....	....	....
1990-91♦	**Pittsburgh**	**NHL**	**78**	**40**	**73**	**113**	**48**	**12**	**0**	**9**	**184**	**21.7**	**0**	....	....	....	**24**	**10**	**24**	**34**	**33**	**5**	**0**	**2**	....
1991-92	**Pittsburgh**	**NHL**	**58**	**33**	**37**	**70**	**78**	**16**	**1**	**4**	**156**	**21.2**	**-16**	....	....	....	....	....	....	....	....	....	....	....	....
	Philadelphia	**NHL**	**22**	**10**	**17**	**27**	**18**	**4**	**0**	**1**	**54**	**18.5**	**-5**	....	....	....	....	....	....	....	....	....	....	....	....
1992-93	**Philadelphia**	**NHL**	**84**	**53**	**70**	**123**	**95**	**15**	**4**	**6**	**274**	**19.3**	**1**	....	....	....	....	....	....	....	....	....	....	....	....
1993-94	**Philadelphia**	**NHL**	**84**	**40**	**67**	**107**	**46**	**11**	**0**	**5**	**217**	**18.4**	**-2**	....	....	....	....	....	....	....	....	....	....	....	....
1994-95	**Philadelphia**	**NHL**	**10**	**2**	**3**	**5**	**12**	**1**	**0**	**2**	**17**	**11.8**	**-6**	....	....	....	....	....	....	....	....	....	....	....	....
	Montreal	**NHL**	**39**	**14**	**29**	**43**	**16**	**8**	**0**	**1**	**104**	**13.5**	**-3**	....	....	....	....	....	....	....	....	....	....	....	....
1995-96	**Montreal**	**NHL**	**82**	**28**	**50**	**78**	**69**	**11**	**2**	**6**	**191**	**14.7**	**20**	....	....	....	**6**	**3**	**3**	**6**	**0**	**3**	**0**	**0**	....
1996-97	**Montreal**	**NHL**	**82**	**34**	**46**	**80**	**58**	**7**	**2**	**3**	**202**	**16.8**	**-1**	....	....	....	**5**	**4**	**2**	**6**	**2**	**0**	**0**	**0**	....
1997-98	**Montreal**	**NHL**	**82**	**32**	**42**	**74**	**51**	**9**	**1**	**6**	**216**	**14.8**	**11**	....	....	....	**10**	**4**	**8**	**12**	**6**	**0**	**0**	**2**	....
	Canada	Olympics	5	0	2	2	0	....	....	....	....	....	....	....	....	....	....	....	....	....	....	....	....	....	....
1998-99	**Montreal**	**NHL**	**61**	**12**	**35**	**47**	**28**	**3**	**0**	**2**	**152**	**7.9**	**-4**	**239**	**44.8**	**20:37**	....	....	....	....	....	....	....	....	....
	Philadelphia	**NHL**	**10**	**4**	**2**	**6**	**6**	**0**	**0**	**0**	**19**	**21.1**	**-3**	**4**	**25.0**	**19:30**	**6**	**0**	**1**	**1**	**2**	**0**	**0**	**0**	**19:35**
99-2000	**Philadelphia**	**NHL**	**82**	**28**	***63**	**91**	**50**	**7**	**1**	**5**	**223**	**12.6**	**20**	**353**	**49.6**	**21:43**	**18**	**6**	**12**	**18**	**6**	**2**	**0**	**1**	**23:10**
2000-01	**Philadelphia**	**NHL**	**69**	**27**	**50**	**77**	**33**	**7**	**1**	**8**	**191**	**14.1**	**15**	**138**	**42.8**	**21:40**	**6**	**2**	**2**	**4**	**2**	**1**	**0**	**1**	**23:00**
2001-02	**Philadelphia**	**NHL**	**80**	**22**	**42**	**64**	**46**	**7**	**2**	**4**	**205**	**10.7**	**5**	**82**	**53.7**	**20:40**	**4**	**0**	**0**	**0**	**2**	**0**	**0**	**0**	**21:10**
2002-03	**Philadelphia**	**NHL**	**79**	**20**	**32**	**52**	**35**	**8**	**1**	**3**	**171**	**11.7**	**0**	**168**	**52.4**	**18:50**	**13**	**7**	**3**	**10**	**2**	**1**	**0**	**1**	**18:00**
2003-04	**Philadelphia**	**NHL**	**82**	**26**	**49**	**75**	**47**	**14**	**1**	**5**	**167**	**15.6**	**18**	**298**	**52.4**	**17:12**	**18**	**4**	**2**	**6**	**4**	**2**	**0**	**0**	**16:46**
	NHL Totals		**1173**	**456**	**745**	**1201**	**780**	**146**	**18**	**74**	**2897**	**15.7**		**1282**	**49.1**	**20:03**	**110**	**40**	**57**	**97**	**59**	**14**	**0**	**7**	**19:53**

WHL West First All-Star Team (1988) • IHL Second All-Star Team (1989) • NHL Second All-Star Team (1992)

Played in NHL All-Star Game (1991, 1993, 1994, 1997, 1998, 1999, 2000)

Traded to **Philadelphia** by **Pittsburgh** with Brian Benning and Los Angeles' 1st round choice (previously acquired, Philadelphia selected Jason Bowen) in 1992 Entry Draft for Rick Tocchet, Kjell Samuelsson, Ken Wregget and Philadelphia's 3rd round choice (Dave Roche) in 1993 Entry Draft, February 19, 1992. Traded to **Montreal** by **Philadelphia** with Philadelphia's 3rd round choice (Martin Hohenberger) in 1995 Entry Draft for Eric Desjardins, Gilbert Dionne and John LeClair, February 9, 1995. Traded to **Philadelphia** by **Montreal** for Danius Zubrus, Philadelphia's 2nd round choice (Matt Carkner) in 1999 Entry Draft and NY Islanders' 6th round choice (previously acquired, Montreal selected Scott Selig) in 2000 Entry Draft, March 10, 1999. Signed as a free agent by **Pittsburgh**, July 9, 2004.

REDDEN, Wade

(REH-duhn, WAYD) **OTT.**

Defense. Shoots left. 6'2", 205 lbs. Born, Lloydminster, Sask., June 12, 1977. NY Islanders' 1st choice, 2nd overall, in 1995 Entry Draft.

Season	Club	League	GP	G	A	Pts	PIM	PP	SH	GW	S	%	+/-	TF	F%	Min	GP	G	A	Pts	PIM	PP	SH	GW	Min
1992-93	Lloydminster	AJHL	34	4	11	15	64	....	....	....	....	....	....	....	....	....	....	....	....	....	....	....	....	....	....
1993-94	Brandon	WHL	63	4	35	39	98	....	....	....	....	....	....	....	....	....	14	2	4	6	10	....	....	....	....
1994-95	Brandon	WHL	64	14	46	60	83	....	....	....	....	....	....	....	....	....	18	5	10	15	8	....	....	....	....
1995-96	Brandon	WHL	51	9	45	54	55	....	....	....	....	....	....	....	....	....	19	5	10	15	19	....	....	....	....
1996-97	**Ottawa**	**NHL**	**82**	**6**	**24**	**30**	**41**	**2**	**0**	**1**	**102**	**5.9**	**1**	....	....	....	**7**	**1**	**3**	**4**	**2**	**0**	**0**	**0**	....
1997-98	**Ottawa**	**NHL**	**80**	**8**	**14**	**22**	**27**	**3**	**0**	**2**	**103**	**7.8**	**17**	....	....	....	**9**	**0**	**2**	**2**	**2**	**0**	**0**	**0**	....
1998-99	**Ottawa**	**NHL**	**72**	**8**	**21**	**29**	**54**	**3**	**0**	**1**	**127**	**6.3**	**7**	**0**	**0.0**	**23:27**	**4**	**1**	**2**	**3**	**2**	**1**	**0**	**0**	**26:39**
99-2000	**Ottawa**	**NHL**	**81**	**10**	**26**	**36**	**49**	**3**	**0**	**2**	**163**	**6.1**	**-1**	**0**	**0.0**	**23:43**	....	....	....	....	....	....	....	....	....
2000-01	**Ottawa**	**NHL**	**78**	**10**	**37**	**47**	**49**	**4**	**0**	**0**	**159**	**6.3**	**22**	**0**	**0.0**	**25:17**	**4**	**0**	**0**	**0**	**0**	**0**	**0**	**0**	**27:29**
2001-02	**Ottawa**	**NHL**	**79**	**9**	**25**	**34**	**48**	**4**	**1**	**1**	**156**	**5.8**	**22**	**1**	**0.0**	**25:06**	**12**	**3**	**2**	**5**	**6**	**1**	**0**	**1**	**27:56**

			Regular Season														Playoffs								
Season	Club	League	GP	G	A	Pts	PIM	PP	SH	GW	S	%	+/-	TF	F%	Min	GP	G	A	Pts	PIM	PP	SH	GW	Min
2002-03	Ottawa	NHL	76	10	35	45	70	4	0	3	154	6.5	23	0	0.0	25:24	18	1	8	9	10	0	0	1	25:28
2003-04	Ottawa	NHL	81	17	26	43	65	12	0	3	175	9.7	21	0	0.0	24:54	7	1	0	1	2	1	0	0	26:47
	NHL Totals		629	78	208	286	403	35	1	13	1139	6.8		1	0.0	24:39	61	7	17	24	24	3	0	2	26:37

WHL Rookie of the Year (1994) • WHL East Second All-Star Team (1995) • WHL East First All-Star Team (1996) • Memorial Cup All-Star Team (1996)
Played in NHL All-Star Game (2002)
Traded to **Ottawa** by **NY Islanders** with Damian Rhodes for Don Beaupre, Martin Straka and Bryan Berard, January 23, 1996.

REGEHR, Robyn (reh-GEER, RAW-bihn) CGY.

Defense. Shoots left. 6'2", 226 lbs. Born, Recife, Brazil, April 19, 1980. Colorado's 3rd choice, 19th overall, in 1998 Entry Draft.

Season	Club	League	GP	G	A	Pts	PIM	PP	SH	GW	S	%	+/-	TF	F%	Min	GP	G	A	Pts	PIM	PP	SH	GW	Min
1995-96	Prince Albert	SMHL	59	8	24	32	157	....	....	....	....	....	....	....	....	....	....	....	....	....	....	....	....	....	....
1996-97	Kamloops Blazers	WHL	64	4	19	23	96	....	....	....	....	....	....	....	....	....	5	0	1	1	18	....	....	....	....
1997-98	Kamloops Blazers	WHL	65	4	10	14	120	....	....	....	....	....	....	....	....	....	5	0	3	3	8	....	....	....	....
1998-99	Kamloops Blazers	WHL	54	12	20	32	130	....	....	....	....	....	....	....	....	....	12	1	4	5	21	....	....	....	....
99-2000	Calgary	NHL	57	5	7	12	46	2	0	0	64	7.8	–2	0	0.0	18:24	....	....	....	....	....	....	....	....	....
	Saint John Flames	AHL	5	0	0	0	0	....	....	....	....	....	....	....	....	....	....	....	....	....	....	....	....	....	....
2000-01	Calgary	NHL	71	1	3	4	70	0	0	0	62	1.6	–7	1	0.0	19:43	....	....	....	....	....	....	....	....	....
2001-02	Calgary	NHL	77	2	6	8	93	0	0	0	82	2.4	–24	0	0.0	20:54	....	....	....	....	....	....	....	....	....
2002-03	Calgary	NHL	76	0	12	12	87	0	0	0	109	0.0	–9	1	100.0	22:45	....	....	....	....	....	....	....	....	....
2003-04	Calgary	NHL	82	4	14	18	74	2	0	1	106	3.8	14	2	50.0	22:21	26	2	7	9	20	0	0	0	26:27
	NHL Totals		363	12	42	54	370	4	0	1	423	2.8		4	50.0	20:59	26	2	7	9	20	0	0	0	26:27

WHL West First All-Star Team (1999)
Traded to **Calgary** by **Colorado** with Rene Corbet, Wade Belak and Colorado's 2nd round compensatory choice (Jarret Stoll) in 2000 Entry Draft for Theoren Fleury and Chris Dingman, February 28, 1999.

REICH, Jeremy (REECH, JAIR-eh-MEE) CBJ

Left wing. Shoots left. 6'1", 204 lbs. Born, Craik, Sask., February 11, 1979. Chicago's 3rd choice, 39th overall, in 1997 Entry Draft.

Season	Club	League	GP	G	A	Pts	PIM	PP	SH	GW	S	%	+/-	TF	F%	Min	GP	G	A	Pts	PIM	PP	SH	GW	Min
1993-94	Pilote Butte	SAHA	80	70	65	135	120	....	....	....	....	....	....	....	....	....	....	....	....	....	....	....	....	....	....
1994-95	Sask. Contacts	SMHL	35	13	20	33	81	....	....	....	....	....	....	....	....	....	....	....	....	....	....	....	....	....	....
1995-96	Seattle	WHL	65	11	11	22	88	....	....	....	....	....	....	....	....	....	5	0	1	1	10	....	....	....	....
1996-97	Seattle	WHL	62	19	31	50	134	....	....	....	....	....	....	....	....	....	15	2	5	7	36	....	....	....	....
1997-98	Seattle	WHL	43	24	23	47	121	....	....	....	....	....	....	....	....	....	....	....	....	....	....	....	....	....	....
	Swift Current	WHL	22	8	8	16	47	....	....	....	....	....	....	....	....	....	12	5	6	11	37	....	....	....	....
1998-99	Swift Current	WHL	67	21	28	49	220	....	....	....	....	....	....	....	....	....	6	0	3	3	26	....	....	....	....
99-2000	Swift Current	WHL	72	33	58	91	167	....	....	....	....	....	....	....	....	....	12	2	10	12	19	....	....	....	....
2000-01	Syracuse Crunch	AHL	56	6	9	15	108	....	....	....	....	....	....	....	....	....	5	0	0	0	6	....	....	....	....
2001-02	Syracuse Crunch	AHL	59	9	7	16	178	....	....	....	....	....	....	....	....	....	10	4	0	4	16	....	....	....	....
2002-03	Syracuse Crunch	AHL	78	14	13	27	195	....	....	....	....	....	....	....	....	....	....	....	....	....	....	....	....	....	....
2003-04	Columbus	NHL	9	0	1	1	20	0	0	0	3	0.0	–3	0	0.0	7:38	....	....	....	....	....	....	....	....	....
	Syracuse Crunch	AHL	72	14	37	51	150	....	....	....	....	....	....	....	....	....	6	1	1	2	13	....	....	....	....
	NHL Totals		9	0	1	1	20	0	0	0	3	0.0		0	0.0	7:38	....	....	....	....	....	....	....	....	....

Signed as a free agent by **Columbus**, May 17, 2000.

REICHEL, Robert (RIGH-khul, RAW-buhrt)

Center. Shoots left. 5'10", 180 lbs. Born, Litvinov, Czech., June 25, 1971. Calgary's 5th choice, 70th overall, in 1989 Entry Draft.

Season	Club	League	GP	G	A	Pts	PIM	PP	SH	GW	S	%	+/-	TF	F%	Min	GP	G	A	Pts	PIM	PP	SH	GW	Min
1987-88	CHZ Litvinov	Czech	36	17	10	27	8	....	....	....	....	....	....	....	....	....	....	....	....	....	....	....	....	....	....
1988-89	CHZ Litvinov	Czech	44	23	25	48	32	....	....	....	....	....	....	....	....	....	....	....	....	....	....	....	....	....	....
1989-90	CHZ Litvinov	Czech	44	*43	28	*71	....	....	....	....	....	....	....	....	....	....	8	6	6	12	....	....	....	....	....
1990-91	Calgary	NHL	66	19	22	41	22	3	0	3	131	14.5	17	....	....	....	6	1	1	2	0	1	0	0	....
1991-92	Calgary	NHL	77	20	34	54	32	8	0	3	181	11.0	1	....	....	....	....	....	....	....	....	....	....	....	....
1992-93	Calgary	NHL	80	40	48	88	54	12	0	5	238	16.8	25	....	....	....	6	2	4	6	2	2	0	0	....
1993-94	Calgary	NHL	84	40	53	93	58	14	0	6	249	16.1	20	....	....	....	7	0	5	5	0	0	0	0	....
1994-95	Frankfurt Lions	Germany	21	19	24	43	41	....	....	....	....	....	....	....	....	....	....	....	....	....	....	....	....	....	....
	Calgary	NHL	48	18	17	35	28	5	0	2	160	11.3	–2	....	....	....	7	2	4	6	4	0	0	1	....
1995-96	Frankfurt Lions	Germany	46	47	54	101	84	....	....	....	....	....	....	....	....	....	3	1	3	4	0	....	....	....	....
1996-97	Calgary	NHL	70	16	27	43	22	6	0	3	181	8.8	–2	....	....	....	....	....	....	....	....	....	....	....	....
	NY Islanders	NHL	12	5	14	19	4	0	1	0	33	15.2	7	....	....	....	....	....	....	....	....	....	....	....	....
1997-98	NY Islanders	NHL	82	25	40	65	32	8	0	2	201	12.4	–11	....	....	....	....	....	....	....	....	....	....	....	....
	Czech Republic	Olympics	6	3	0	3	0	....	....	....	....	....	....	....	....	....	....	....	....	....	....	....	....	....	....
1998-99	NY Islanders	NHL	70	19	37	56	50	5	1	1	186	10.2	–15	1241	51.7	19:36	....	....	....	....	....	....	....	....	....
	Phoenix	NHL	13	7	6	13	4	3	0	3	50	14.0	2	241	48.5	20:03	7	1	3	4	2	0	0	0	18:56
99-2000	Litvinov	Czech	45	25	32	57	24	....	....	....	....	....	....	....	....	....	7	3	4	7	2	....	....	....	....
2000-01	Litvinov	Czech	49	23	33	56	72	....	....	....	....	....	....	....	....	....	5	1	2	3	4	....	....	....	....
2001-02	Toronto	NHL	78	20	31	51	26	1	0	3	152	13.2	7	1045	49.6	15:11	18	0	3	3	4	0	0	0	12:40
	Czech Republic	Olympics	4	1	0	1	2	....	....	....	....	....	....	....	....	....	....	....	....	....	....	....	....	....	....
2002-03	Toronto	NHL	81	12	30	42	26	1	1	1	111	10.8	7	1123	52.2	14:33	7	2	1	3	0	0	0	0	20:54
2003-04	Toronto	NHL	69	11	19	30	30	2	0	2	100	11.0	2	1002	53.1	15:30	12	0	2	2	8	0	0	0	17:10
	NHL Totals		830	252	378	630	388	68	3	34	1973	12.8		4652	51.5	16:17	70	8	23	31	20	3	0	1	16:12

Traded to **NY Islanders** by **Calgary** for Marty McInnis, Tyrone Garner and Calgary's 6th round choice (previously acquired, Calgary selected Ilja Demidov) in 1997 Entry Draft, March 18, 1997. Traded to **Phoenix** by **NY Islanders** with NY Islanders' 3rd round choice (Jason Jaspers) in 1999 Entry Draft and Ottawa's 4th round choice (previously acquired, Phoenix selected Preston Mizzi) in 1999 Entry Draft for Brad Isbister and Phoenix's 3rd round choice (Brian Collins) in 1999 Entry Draft, March 20, 1999. Traded to **Toronto** by **Phoenix** with Travis Green and Craig Mills for Danny Markov, June 12, 2001.

REID, Brandon (REED, BRAN-duhn)

Center. Shoots right. 5'8", 165 lbs. Born, Kirkland, Que., March 9, 1981. Vancouver's 5th choice, 208th overall, in 2000 Entry Draft.

Season	Club	League	GP	G	A	Pts	PIM	PP	SH	GW	S	%	+/-	TF	F%	Min	GP	G	A	Pts	PIM	PP	SH	GW	Min
1996-97	Lac St-Louis Lions	QAAA	44	17	34	51	....	....	....	....	....	....	....	....	....	....	7	2	3	5	....	....	....	....	....
1997-98	Halifax	QMJHL	67	13	21	36	6	....	....	....	....	....	....	....	....	....	5	1	0	1	15	....	....	....	....
1998-99	Halifax	QMJHL	70	32	25	57	33	....	....	....	....	....	....	....	....	....	5	2	2	4	0	....	....	....	....
99-2000	Halifax	QMJHL	62	44	80	124	10	....	....	....	....	....	....	....	....	....	10	7	11	18	4	....	....	....	....
2000-01	Val-d'Or Foreurs	QMJHL	57	45	81	126	18	....	....	....	....	....	....	....	....	....	21	13	29	42	14	....	....	....	....
2001-02	Manitoba Moose	AHL	60	18	19	37	6	....	....	....	....	....	....	....	....	....	7	0	3	3	0	....	....	....	....
2002-03	Vancouver	NHL	7	2	3	5	0	0	0	0	15	13.3	4	69	55.1	9:47	9	0	1	1	0	0	0	0	9:36
	Manitoba Moose	AHL	73	18	36	54	18	....	....	....	....	....	....	....	....	....	1	1	1	2	0	....	....	....	....
2003-04	Vancouver	NHL	3	0	1	1	0	0	0	0	2	0.0	1	38	47.4	9:21	....	....	....	....	....	....	....	....	....
	Manitoba Moose	AHL	73	19	39	58	20	....	....	....	....	....	....	....	....	....	....	....	....	....	....	....	....	....	....
	NHL Totals		10	2	4	6	0	0	0	0	17	11.8		107	52.3	9:40	9	0	1	1	0	0	0	0	9:36

QMJHL Second All-Star Team (2000) • George Parsons Trophy (Memorial Cup Most Sportsmanlike Player) (2000, 2001) • QMJHL First All-Star Team (2001)
Signed as a free agent by **Hamburg** (Germany), July 7, 2004.

REINPRECHT, Steve (REIGHN-prehkt, STEEV) CGY.

Center. Shoots left. 6', 190 lbs. Born, Edmonton, Alta., May 7, 1976.

Season	Club	League	GP	G	A	Pts	PIM	PP	SH	GW	S	%	+/-	TF	F%	Min	GP	G	A	Pts	PIM	PP	SH	GW	Min
1993-94	Edmonton SSAC	AMHL	71	48	77	125	....	....	....	....	....	....	....	....	....	....	....	....	....	....	....	....	....	....	....
1994-95	St. Albert Saints	AJHL	56	35	44	79	14	....	....	....	....	....	....	....	....	....	....	....	....	....	....	....	....	....	....
1995-96	St. Albert Saints	AJHL	32	24	36	60	....	....	....	....	....	....	....	....	....	....	....	....	....	....	....	....	....	....	....
1996-97	U. of Wisconsin	WCHA	38	11	9	20	12	....	....	....	....	....	....	....	....	....	....	....	....	....	....	....	....	....	....
1997-98	U. of Wisconsin	WCHA	41	19	24	43	18	....	....	....	....	....	....	....	....	....	....	....	....	....	....	....	....	....	....
1998-99	U. of Wisconsin	WCHA	38	16	17	33	14	....	....	....	....	....	....	....	....	....	....	....	....	....	....	....	....	....	....
99-2000	U. of Wisconsin	WCHA	37	26	40	*66	14	....	....	....	....	....	....	....	....	....	....	....	....	....	....	....	....	....	....
	Los Angeles	NHL	1	0	0	0	2	0	0	0	0	0.0	0	6	50.0	6:01	....	....	....	....	....	....	....	....	....
2000-01	Los Angeles	NHL	59	12	17	29	12	3	2	3	72	16.7	11	676	41.4	12:39	....	....	....	....	....	....	....	....	....
	♦ Colorado	NHL	21	3	4	7	2	0	0	0	28	10.7	–1	209	51.2	15:38	22	2	3	5	2	0	0	0	12:09
2001-02	Colorado	NHL	67	19	27	46	18	4	0	3	111	17.1	14	413	52.1	16:32	21	7	5	12	8	0	0	2	16:23

			Regular Season														Playoffs								
Season	Club	League	GP	G	A	Pts	PIM	PP	SH	GW	S	%	+/-	TF	F%	Min	GP	G	A	Pts	PIM	PP	SH	GW	Min
2002-03	**Colorado**	**NHL**	**77**	**18**	**33**	**51**	**18**	**2**	**1**	**1**	**146**	**12.3**	**–6**	**928**	**46.4**	**17:22**	**7**	**1**	**2**	**3**	**0**	**0**	**0**	**0**	**15:32**
2003-04	**Calgary**	**NHL**	**44**	**7**	**22**	**29**	**4**	**3**	**0**	**1**	**68**	**10.3**	**1**	**120**	**40.0**	**17:05**	....	....	....	....	....	....	....	....	....
	NHL Totals		**269**	**59**	**103**	**162**	**56**	**12**	**3**	**8**	**425**	**13.9**		**2352**	**46.1**	**15:54**	**50**	**10**	**10**	**20**	**10**	**0**	**0**	**2**	**14:24**

WCHA Second All-Star Team (1998) • WCHA First All-Star Team (2000) • WCHA Player of the Year (2000) • NCAA West First All-American Team (2000)

Signed as a free agent by **Los Angeles**, March 31, 2000. Traded to **Colorado** by **Los Angeles** with Rob Blake for Adam Deadmarsh, Aaron Miller, a player to be named later (Jared Aulin, March 22, 2001), and Colorado's 1st round choices in 2001 (Dave Steckel) and 2003 (Brian Boyle) Entry Drafts, February 21, 2001. Traded to **Buffalo** by **Colorado** for Keith Ballard, July 3, 2003. Traded to **Calgary** by **Buffalo** with Rhett Warrener for Chris Drury and Steve Begin, July 3, 2003.

REIRDEN, Todd

(REER-dehn, TAWD)

Defense. Shoots left. 6'5", 225 lbs. Born, Deerfield, IL, June 25, 1971. New Jersey's 14th choice, 242nd overall, in 1990 Entry Draft.

Season	Club	League	GP	G	A	Pts	PIM	PP	SH	GW	S	%	+/-	TF	F%	Min	GP	G	A	Pts	PIM	PP	SH	GW	Min
1987-88	Deerfield	Hi-School	22	19	32	51	....	....	....	....	....	....	....	....	....	....	....	....	....	....	....	....	....	....	....
1988-89	Tabor Academy	Hi-School	22	6	16	22	....	....	....	....	....	....	....	....	....	....	....	....	....	....	....	....	....	....	....
1989-90	Tabor Academy	Hi-School	22	10	28	38	....	....	....	....	....	....	....	....	....	....	....	....	....	....	....	....	....	....	....
1990-91	Bowling Green	CCHA	28	1	5	6	22	....	....	....	....	....	....	....	....	....	....	....	....	....	....	....	....	....	....
1991-92	Bowling Green	CCHA	33	8	7	15	34	....	....	....	....	....	....	....	....	....	....	....	....	....	....	....	....	....	....
1992-93	Bowling Green	CCHA	41	8	17	25	48	....	....	....	....	....	....	....	....	....	....	....	....	....	....	....	....	....	....
1993-94	Bowling Green	CCHA	38	7	23	30	56	....	....	....	....	....	....	....	....	....	....	....	....	....	....	....	....	....	....
1994-95	Albany River Rats	AHL	2	0	1	1	2	....	....	....	....	....	....	....	....	....	....	....	....	....	....	....	....	....	....
	Raleigh Icecaps	ECHL	26	2	13	15	33	....	....	....	....	....	....	....	....	....	....	....	....	....	....	....	....	....	....
	Tallahassee	ECHL	43	5	25	30	61	....	....	....	....	....	....	....	....	....	13	2	5	7	40	....	....	....	....
1995-96	Tallahassee	ECHL	7	1	3	4	10	....	....	....	....	....	....	....	....	....	....	....	....	....	....	....	....	....	....
	Jacksonville	ECHL	15	1	10	11	41	....	....	....	....	....	....	....	....	....	1	0	2	2	4	....	....	....	....
	Chicago Wolves	IHL	31	0	2	2	39	....	....	....	....	....	....	....	....	....	9	0	2	2	16	....	....	....	....
1996-97	Chicago Wolves	IHL	57	3	10	13	108	....	....	....	....	....	....	....	....	....	....	....	....	....	....	....	....	....	....
	San Antonio	IHL	23	2	5	7	51	....	....	....	....	....	....	....	....	....	9	0	1	1	17	....	....	....	....
1997-98	San Antonio	IHL	70	5	14	19	132	....	....	....	....	....	....	....	....	....	....	....	....	....	....	....	....	....	....
	Fort Wayne	IHL	11	2	2	4	16	....	....	....	....	....	....	....	....	....	4	0	2	2	4	....	....	....	....
1998-99	**Edmonton**	**NHL**	**17**	**2**	**3**	**5**	**20**	**0**	**0**	**0**	**26**	**7.7**	**–1**	**0**	**0.0**	**17:17**	....	....	....	....	....	....	....	....	....
	Hamilton	AHL	58	9	25	34	84	....	....	....	....	....	....	....	....	....	11	0	5	5	6	....	....	....	....
99-2000	**St. Louis**	**NHL**	**56**	**4**	**21**	**25**	**32**	**0**	**0**	**1**	**77**	**5.2**	**18**	**1**	**0.0**	**18:18**	**4**	**0**	**1**	**1**	**0**	**0**	**0**	**0**	**13:43**
2000-01	**St. Louis**	**NHL**	**38**	**2**	**4**	**6**	**43**	**1**	**0**	**0**	**58**	**3.4**	**–2**	**2**	**50.0**	**16:50**	**1**	**0**	**0**	**0**	**0**	**0**	**0**	**0**	**2:52**
	Worcester IceCats	AHL	7	2	6	8	20	....	....	....	....	....	....	....	....	....	....	....	....	....	....	....	....	....	....
2001-02	**Atlanta**	**NHL**	**65**	**3**	**5**	**8**	**82**	**1**	**0**	**0**	**85**	**3.5**	**–25**	**1**	**0.0**	**18:02**	....	....	....	....	....	....	....	....	....
2002-03	Cincinnati	AHL	58	7	13	20	97	....	....	....	....	....	....	....	....	....	....	....	....	....	....	....	....	....	....
2003-04	**Phoenix**	**NHL**	**7**	**0**	**2**	**2**	**4**	**0**	**0**	**0**	**9**	**0.0**	**–4**	**0**	**0.0**	**15:22**	....	....	....	....	....	....	....	....	....
	Cincinnati	AHL	39	3	8	11	42	....	....	....	....	....	....	....	....	....	....	....	....	....	....	....	....	....	....
	Springfield	AHL	34	6	7	13	42	....	....	....	....	....	....	....	....	....	....	....	....	....	....	....	....	....	....
	NHL Totals		**183**	**11**	**35**	**46**	**181**	**2**	**0**	**1**	**255**	**4.3**		**4**	**25.0**	**17:42**	**5**	**0**	**1**	**1**	**0**	**0**	**0**	**0**	**11:33**

Signed as a free agent by **Edmonton**, September 17, 1998. Claimed on waivers by **St. Louis** from **Edmonton**, September 30, 1999. Signed as a free agent by **Atlanta**, July 16, 2001. Signed as a free agent by **Anaheim**, July 17, 2002. Traded to **Phoenix** by **Anaheim** for future considerations, January 17, 2004.

RENBERG, Mikael

(REHN-buhrg, MIGH-kuhl)

Right wing. Shoots left. 6'2", 235 lbs. Born, Pitea, Sweden, May 5, 1972. Philadelphia's 3rd choice, 40th overall, in 1990 Entry Draft.

Season	Club	League	GP	G	A	Pts	PIM	PP	SH	GW	S	%	+/-	TF	F%	Min	GP	G	A	Pts	PIM	PP	SH	GW	Min
1988-89	Pitea HC	Swede-2	12	6	3	9	....	....	....	....	....	....	....	....	....	....	....	....	....	....	....	....	....	....	....
1989-90	Pitea HC	Swede-2	29	15	19	34	....	....	....	....	....	....	....	....	....	....	....	....	....	....	....	....	....	....	....
1990-91	Lulea HF	Sweden	29	11	6	17	12	....	....	....	....	....	....	....	....	....	5	1	1	2	4	....	....	....	....
1991-92	Lulea HF	Sweden	38	8	15	23	20	....	....	....	....	....	....	....	....	....	2	0	0	0	0	....	....	....	....
1992-93	Lulea HF	Sweden	39	19	13	32	61	....	....	....	....	....	....	....	....	....	11	4	4	8	4	....	....	....	....
1993-94	**Philadelphia**	**NHL**	**83**	**38**	**44**	**82**	**36**	**9**	**0**	**1**	**195**	**19.5**	**8**	....	....	....	....	....	....	....	....	....	....	....	....
1994-95	Lulea HF	Sweden	10	9	4	13	16	....	....	....	....	....	....	....	....	....	....	....	....	....	....	....	....	....	....
	Philadelphia	**NHL**	**47**	**26**	**31**	**57**	**20**	**8**	**0**	**4**	**143**	**18.2**	**20**	....	....	....	**15**	**6**	**7**	**13**	**6**	**2**	**0**	**0**	....
1995-96	**Philadelphia**	**NHL**	**51**	**23**	**20**	**43**	**45**	**9**	**0**	**4**	**198**	**11.6**	**8**	....	....	....	**11**	**3**	**6**	**9**	**14**	**1**	**0**	**0**	....
1996-97	**Philadelphia**	**NHL**	**77**	**22**	**37**	**59**	**65**	**1**	**0**	**4**	**249**	**8.8**	**36**	....	....	....	**18**	**5**	**6**	**11**	**4**	**2**	**0**	**0**	....
1997-98	**Tampa Bay**	**NHL**	**68**	**16**	**22**	**38**	**34**	**6**	**3**	**0**	**175**	**9.1**	**–37**	....	....	....	....	....	....	....	....	....	....	....	....
	Sweden	Olympics	4	1	2	3	4	....	....	....	....	....	....	....	....	....	....	....	....	....	....	....	....	....	....
1998-99	**Tampa Bay**	**NHL**	**20**	**4**	**8**	**12**	**4**	**2**	**0**	**0**	**42**	**9.5**	**–2**	**2**	**100.0**	**15:32**	....	....	....	....	....	....	....	....	....
	Philadelphia	**NHL**	**46**	**11**	**15**	**26**	**14**	**4**	**0**	**2**	**112**	**9.8**	**7**	**1**	**0.0**	**16:00**	**6**	**0**	**1**	**1**	**0**	**0**	**0**	**0**	**13:26**
99-2000	**Philadelphia**	**NHL**	**62**	**8**	**21**	**29**	**30**	**3**	**0**	**1**	**106**	**7.5**	**–1**	**3**	**33.3**	**13:27**	....	....	....	....	....	....	....	....	....
	Phoenix	**NHL**	**10**	**2**	**4**	**6**	**2**	**0**	**0**	**0**	**16**	**12.5**	**0**	**0**	**0.0**	**15:31**	**5**	**1**	**2**	**3**	**4**	**0**	**0**	**1**	**15:02**
2000-01	Lulea HF	Sweden	48	22	32	54	36	....	....	....	....	....	....	....	....	....	11	6	5	11	35	....	....	....	....
2001-02	**Toronto**	**NHL**	**71**	**14**	**38**	**52**	**36**	**4**	**0**	**3**	**130**	**10.8**	**11**	**6**	**33.3**	**14:35**	**3**	**0**	**0**	**0**	**2**	**0**	**0**	**0**	**12:16**
	Sweden	Olympics	4	1	0	1	4	....	....	....	....	....	....	....	....	....	....	....	....	....	....	....	....	....	....
2002-03	**Toronto**	**NHL**	**67**	**14**	**21**	**35**	**36**	**7**	**0**	**1**	**137**	**10.2**	**5**	**9**	**33.3**	**13:32**	**7**	**1**	**0**	**1**	**8**	**1**	**0**	**1**	**14:39**
2003-04	**Toronto**	**NHL**	**59**	**12**	**13**	**25**	**50**	**2**	**0**	**1**	**88**	**13.6**	**–1**	**4**	**25.0**	**13:16**	**2**	**0**	**0**	**0**	**4**	**0**	**0**	**0**	**10:31**
	NHL Totals		**661**	**190**	**274**	**464**	**372**	**55**	**3**	**21**	**1591**	**11.9**		**25**	**36.0**	**14:13**	**67**	**16**	**22**	**38**	**42**	**6**	**0**	**2**	**13:45**

NHL All-Rookie Team (1994)

Traded to **Tampa Bay** by **Philadelphia** with Karl Dykhuis for Philadelphia's 1st round choices (previously acquired) in 1998 (Philadelphia selected Simon Gagne), 1999 (Philadelphia selected Maxime Ouellet), 2000 (Philadelphia selected Justin Williams) and 2001 (later traded to Ottawa – Ottawa selected Tim Gleason) Entry Drafts, August 20, 1997. Traded to **Philadelphia** by **Tampa Bay** with Daymond Langkow for Chris Gratton and Mike Sillinger, December 12, 1998. Traded to **Phoenix** by **Philadelphia** for Rick Tocchet, March 8, 2000. Traded to **Toronto** by **Phoenix** for Sergei Berezin, June 23, 2001.

RHEAUME, Pascal

(RAY-awm, pas-KAL) **N.J.**

Center. Shoots left. 6'1", 220 lbs. Born, Quebec City, Que., June 21, 1973.

Season	Club	League	GP	G	A	Pts	PIM	PP	SH	GW	S	%	+/-	TF	F%	Min	GP	G	A	Pts	PIM	PP	SH	GW	Min
1990-91	Ste-Foy	QAAA	37	20	38	58	25	....	....	....	....	....	....	....	....	....	7	7	1	8	6	....	....	....	....
1991-92	Trois-Rivieres	QMJHL	65	17	20	37	84	....	....	....	....	....	....	....	....	....	14	5	4	9	23	....	....	....	....
1992-93	Sherbrooke	QMJHL	65	28	34	62	88	....	....	....	....	....	....	....	....	....	14	6	5	11	31	....	....	....	....
1993-94	Albany River Rats	AHL	55	17	18	35	43	....	....	....	....	....	....	....	....	....	5	0	1	1	0	....	....	....	....
1994-95	Albany River Rats	AHL	78	19	25	44	46	....	....	....	....	....	....	....	....	....	14	3	6	9	19	....	....	....	....
1995-96	Albany River Rats	AHL	68	26	42	68	50	....	....	....	....	....	....	....	....	....	4	1	2	3	2	....	....	....	....
1996-97	**New Jersey**	**NHL**	**2**	**1**	**0**	**1**	**0**	**0**	**0**	**0**	**5**	**20.0**	**1**	....	....	....	....	....	....	....	....	....	....	....	....
	Albany River Rats	AHL	51	22	23	45	40	....	....	....	....	....	....	....	....	....	16	2	8	10	16	....	....	....	....
1997-98	**St. Louis**	**NHL**	**48**	**6**	**9**	**15**	**35**	**1**	**0**	**0**	**45**	**13.3**	**4**	....	....	....	**10**	**1**	**3**	**4**	**8**	**1**	**0**	**0**	....
1998-99	**St. Louis**	**NHL**	**60**	**9**	**18**	**27**	**24**	**2**	**0**	**0**	**85**	**10.6**	**10**	**21**	**71.4**	**13:19**	**5**	**1**	**0**	**1**	**4**	**0**	**0**	**0**	**11:36**
99-2000	**St. Louis**	**NHL**	**7**	**1**	**1**	**2**	**6**	**0**	**0**	**0**	**5**	**20.0**	**–2**	**2**	**0.0**	**10:08**	....	....	....	....	....	....	....	....	....
	Worcester IceCats	AHL	7	1	1	2	4	....	....	....	....	....	....	....	....	....	....	....	....	....	....	....	....	....	....
2000-01	**St. Louis**	**NHL**	**8**	**2**	**0**	**2**	**5**	**2**	**0**	**0**	**16**	**12.5**	**–1**	**7**	**42.9**	**11:56**	**3**	**0**	**1**	**1**	**0**	**0**	**0**	**0**	**11:30**
	Worcester IceCats	AHL	56	23	35	58	63	....	....	....	....	....	....	....	....	....	11	2	4	6	2	....	....	....	....
2001-02	**Chicago**	**NHL**	**19**	**0**	**2**	**2**	**4**	**0**	**0**	**0**	**19**	**0.0**	**–1**	**165**	**51.5**	**9:22**	....	....	....	....	....	....	....	....	....
	Atlanta	**NHL**	**42**	**11**	**9**	**20**	**25**	**6**	**0**	**2**	**61**	**18.0**	**–3**	**510**	**45.9**	**14:27**	....	....	....	....	....	....	....	....	....
2002-03	**Atlanta**	**NHL**	**56**	**4**	**9**	**13**	**24**	**0**	**2**	**1**	**70**	**5.7**	**–8**	**602**	**46.8**	**12:17**	....	....	....	....	....	....	....	....	....
	♦ New Jersey	**NHL**	**21**	**4**	**1**	**5**	**8**	**0**	**1**	**1**	**23**	**17.4**	**3**	**248**	**51.6**	**11:50**	**24**	**1**	**2**	**3**	**13**	**0**	**0**	**0**	**13:32**
2003-04	**NY Rangers**	**NHL**	**17**	**0**	**0**	**0**	**5**	**0**	**0**	**0**	**15**	**0.0**	**–3**	**46**	**56.5**	**10:02**	....	....	....	....	....	....	....	....	....
	Hartford	AHL	3	1	0	1	0	....	....	....	....	....	....	....	....	....	....	....	....	....	....	....	....	....	....
	St. Louis	**NHL**	**25**	**1**	**3**	**4**	**4**	**0**	**0**	**0**	**23**	**4.3**	**–3**	**26**	**38.5**	**10:19**	**3**	**0**	**0**	**0**	**2**	**0**	**0**	**0**	**6:55**
	NHL Totals		**305**	**39**	**52**	**91**	**140**	**11**	**3**	**4**	**367**	**10.6**		**1627**	**48.1**	**12:13**	**45**	**3**	**6**	**9**	**27**	**1**	**0**	**0**	**12:31**

Signed as a free agent by **New Jersey**, October 1, 1993. Claimed by **St. Louis** from **New Jersey** in Waiver Draft, September 28, 1997. • Missed majority of 1999-2000 season recovering from shoulder surgery, August, 1999. Signed as a free agent by **Chicago**, July 31, 2001. Claimed on waivers by **Atlanta** from **Chicago**, November 14, 2001. Traded to **New Jersey** by **Atlanta** for future considerations, February 24, 2003. Signed as a free agent by **NY Rangers**, October 22, 2003. Claimed on waivers by **St. Louis** from **NY Rangers**, January 29, 2004. Signed as a free agent by **New Jersey**, August, 2004.

RIBEIRO, Mike

(rih-bee-AIR-roh, MIGHK) **MTL.**

Center. Shoots left. 6', 177 lbs. Born, Montreal, Que., February 10, 1980. Montreal's 2nd choice, 45th overall, in 1998 Entry Draft.

Season	Club	League	GP	G	A	Pts	PIM	PP	SH	GW	S	%	+/-	TF	F%	Min	GP	G	A	Pts	PIM	PP	SH	GW	Min
1996-97	Mtl-Bourassa	QAAA	43	32	57	89	48	....	....	....	....	....	....	....	....	....	16	15	23	38	14	....	....	....	....
1997-98	Rouyn-Noranda	QMJHL	67	40	*85	125	55	....	....	....	....	....	....	....	....	....	6	3	1	4	0	....	....	....	....
1998-99	Rouyn-Noranda	QMJHL	69	*67	*100	*167	137	....	....	....	....	....	....	....	....	....	11	5	11	16	12	....	....	....	....
	Fredericton	AHL	....	....	....	....	....	....	....	....	....	....	....	....	....	....	5	0	1	1	2	....	....	....	....

			Regular Season														Playoffs								
Season	Club	League	GP	G	A	Pts	PIM	PP	SH	GW	S	%	+/-	TF	F%	Min	GP	G	A	Pts	PIM	PP	SH	GW	Min
99-2000	Montreal	NHL	19	1	1	2	2	1	0	0	18	5.6	–6	95	34.7	10:40	....	....	....	....	....	....	....	....	....
	Quebec Citadelles	AHL	3	0	0	0	2	....	....	....	....	....	....	....	....	....	....	....	....	....	....	....	....	....	....
	Rouyn-Noranda	QMJHL	2	1	3	4	0	....	....	....	....	....	....	....	....	....	....	....	....	....	....	....	....	....	....
	Quebec Remparts	QMJHL	21	17	28	45	30	....	....	....	....	....	....	....	....	....	11	3	20	23	38	....	....	....	....
2000-01	Montreal	NHL	2	0	0	0	2	0	0	0	3	0.0	0	11	18.2	10:38	....	....	....	....	....	....	....	....	....
	Quebec Citadelles	AHL	74	26	40	66	44	....	....	....	....	....	....	....	....	....	9	1	5	6	23	....	....	....	....
2001-02	Montreal	NHL	43	8	10	18	12	3	0	0	48	16.7	–11	141	44.0	13:55	....	....	....	....	....	....	....	....	....
	Quebec Citadelles	AHL	23	9	14	23	36	....	....	....	....	....	....	....	....	....	3	0	3	3	0	....	....	....	....
2002-03	Montreal	NHL	52	5	12	17	6	2	0	0	57	8.8	–3	358	50.3	11:07	....	....	....	....	....	....	....	....	....
	Hamilton	AHL	3	0	1	1	0	....	....	....	....	....	....	....	....	....	....	....	....	....	....	....	....	....	....
2003-04	Montreal	NHL	81	20	45	65	34	7	0	5	103	19.4	15	913	44.8	17:05	11	2	1	3	18	0	0	0	16:31
	NHL Totals		197	34	68	102	56	13	0	5	229	14.8		1518	45.2	14:08	11	2	1	3	18	0	0	0	16:31

QMJHL Second All-Star Team (1998) • QMJHL First All-Star Team (1999) • Canadian Major Junior First All-Star Team (1999)

RICCI, Mike
(REE-CHEE, MIGHK) **PHX.**

Center. Shoots left. 6', 200 lbs. Born, Scarborough, Ont., October 27, 1971. Philadelphia's 1st choice, 4th overall, in 1990 Entry Draft.

Season	Club	League	GP	G	A	Pts	PIM	PP	SH	GW	S	%	+/-	TF	F%	Min	GP	G	A	Pts	PIM	PP	SH	GW	Min
1986-87	Toronto Marlies	MTHL	38	39	42	81	27	....	....	....	....	....	....	....	....	....	....	....	....	....	....	....	....	....	....
1987-88	Peterborough	OHL	41	24	37	61	20	....	....	....	....	....	....	....	....	....	8	5	5	10	4	....	....	....	....
1988-89	Peterborough	OHL	60	54	52	106	43	....	....	....	....	....	....	....	....	....	17	19	16	35	18	....	....	....	....
1989-90	Peterborough	OHL	60	52	64	116	39	....	....	....	....	....	....	....	....	....	12	5	7	12	26	....	....	....	....
1990-91	Philadelphia	NHL	68	21	20	41	64	9	0	4	121	17.4	–8	....	....	....	....	....	....	....	....	....	....	....	....
1991-92	Philadelphia	NHL	78	20	36	56	93	11	2	0	149	13.4	–10	....	....	....	....	....	....	....	....	....	....	....	....
1992-93	Quebec	NHL	77	27	51	78	123	12	1	10	142	19.0	8	....	....	....	6	0	6	6	8	0	0	0	....
1993-94	Quebec	NHL	83	30	21	51	113	13	3	6	138	21.7	–9	....	....	....	....	....	....	....	....	....	....	....	....
1994-95	Quebec	NHL	48	15	21	36	40	9	0	1	73	20.5	5	....	....	....	6	1	3	4	8	0	0	0	....
1995-96♦	Colorado	NHL	62	6	21	27	52	3	0	1	73	8.2	1	....	....	....	22	6	11	17	18	3	0	1	....
1996-97	Colorado	NHL	63	13	19	32	59	5	0	3	74	17.6	–3	....	....	....	17	2	4	6	17	0	0	1	....
1997-98	Colorado	NHL	6	0	4	4	2	0	0	0	5	0.0	0	....	....	....	....	....	....	....	....	....	....	....	....
	San Jose	NHL	59	9	14	23	30	5	0	2	86	10.5	–4	....	....	....	6	1	3	4	6	0	0	0	....
1998-99	San Jose	NHL	82	13	26	39	68	2	1	2	98	13.3	1	1465	49.6	15:23	6	2	3	5	10	1	0	0	16:53
99-2000	San Jose	NHL	82	20	24	44	60	10	0	5	134	14.9	14	1522	50.7	16:52	12	5	1	6	2	3	0	1	17:37
2000-01	San Jose	NHL	81	22	22	44	60	9	2	4	141	15.6	3	1631	51.4	18:00	6	0	3	3	0	0	0	0	19:44
2001-02	San Jose	NHL	79	19	34	53	44	5	2	0	115	16.5	9	1501	49.0	17:04	12	4	6	10	4	0	0	1	19:51
2002-03	San Jose	NHL	75	11	23	34	53	5	1	2	101	10.9	–12	1152	51.6	16:31	....	....	....	....	....	....	....	....	....
2003-04	San Jose	NHL	71	7	19	26	40	2	0	0	48	14.6	8	1116	54.8	14:21	17	2	3	5	4	0	0	0	15:31
	NHL Totals		1014	233	355	588	901	100	12	40	1498	15.6		8387	51.0	16:24	110	23	43	66	77	7	0	4	17:36

OHL Second All-Star Team (1989) • OHL First All-Star Team (1990) • OHL MVP (1990) • Canadian Major Junior Player of the Year (1990) • OHL First All-Star Team (1990)

Traded to **Quebec** by **Philadelphia** with Steve Duchesne, Peter Forsberg, Kerry Huffman, Ron Hextall, Philadelphia's 1st round choice (Jocelyn Thibault) in 1993 Entry Draft, $15,000,000 and future considerations (Chris Simon and Philadelphia's 1st round choice (later traded to Toronto – later traded to Washington – Washington selected Nolan Baumgartner) in 1994 Entry Draft, July 21, 1992) for Eric Lindros, June 30, 1992. Transferred to **Colorado** after **Quebec** franchise relocated, June 21, 1995. Traded to **San Jose** by **Colorado** with Colorado's 2nd round choice (later traded to Buffalo – Buffalo selected Jaroslav Kristek) in 1998 Entry Draft for Shean Donovan and San Jose's 1st round choice (Alex Tanguay) in 1998 Entry Draft, November 21, 1997. Signed as a free agent by **Phoenix**, July 9, 2004.

RICHARDS, Brad
(RIH-chahrds, BRAD) **T.B.**

Center. Shoots left. 6'1", 198 lbs. Born, Murray Harbour, P.E.I., May 2, 1980. Tampa Bay's 2nd choice, 64th overall, in 1998 Entry Draft.

Season	Club	League	GP	G	A	Pts	PIM	PP	SH	GW	S	%	+/-	TF	F%	Min	GP	G	A	Pts	PIM	PP	SH	GW	Min
1996-97	Notre Dame	SJHL	63	39	48	87	73	....	....	....	....	....	....	....	....	....	....	....	....	....	....	....	....	....	....
1997-98	Rimouski Oceanic	QMJHL	68	33	82	115	44	....	....	....	....	....	....	....	....	....	19	8	24	32	2	....	....	....	....
1998-99	Rimouski Oceanic	QMJHL	59	39	92	131	55	....	....	....	....	....	....	....	....	....	11	9	12	21	6	....	....	....	....
99-2000	Rimouski Oceanic	QMJHL	63	*71	*115	*186	69	....	....	....	....	....	....	....	....	....	12	13	*24	*37	16	....	....	....	....
2000-01	Tampa Bay	NHL	82	21	41	62	14	7	0	3	179	11.7	–10	955	41.4	16:54	....	....	....	....	....	....	....	....	....
2001-02	Tampa Bay	NHL	82	20	42	62	13	5	0	0	251	8.0	–18	911	41.2	19:48	....	....	....	....	....	....	....	....	....
2002-03	Tampa Bay	NHL	80	17	57	74	24	4	0	2	277	6.1	3	1007	47.5	19:56	11	0	5	5	12	0	0	0	22:21
2003-04♦	Tampa Bay	NHL	82	26	53	79	12	5	1	6	244	10.7	14	1167	46.7	20:26	23	12	14	*26	4	7	0	7	23:28
	NHL Totals		326	84	193	277	63	21	1	11	951	8.8		4040	44.4	19:16	34	12	19	31	16	7	0	7	23:07

QMJHL First All-Star Team (2000) • Canadian Major Junior First All-Star Team (2000) • Canadian Major Junior Player of the Year (2000) • Memorial Cup All-Star Team (2000) • Stafford Smythe Memorial Trophy (Memorial Cup MVP) (2000) • NHL All-Rookie Team (2001) • Lady Byng Trophy (2004) • Conn Smythe Trophy (2004)

RICHARDSON, Luke
(RIH-chahrd-sohn, LEWK) **CBJ**

Defense. Shoots left. 6'4", 215 lbs. Born, Ottawa, Ont., March 26, 1969. Toronto's 1st choice, 7th overall, in 1987 Entry Draft.

Season	Club	League	GP	G	A	Pts	PIM	PP	SH	GW	S	%	+/-	TF	F%	Min	GP	G	A	Pts	PIM	PP	SH	GW	Min
1984-85	Ottawa Knights	OMHA	35	5	26	31	72	....	....	....	....	....	....	....	....	....	....	....	....	....	....	....	....	....	....
1985-86	Peterborough	OHL	63	6	18	24	57	....	....	....	....	....	....	....	....	....	16	2	1	3	50	....	....	....	....
1986-87	Peterborough	OHL	59	13	32	45	70	....	....	....	....	....	....	....	....	....	12	0	5	5	24	....	....	....	....
1987-88	Toronto	NHL	78	4	6	10	90	0	0	0	49	8.2	–25	....	....	....	2	0	0	0	0	0	0	0	....
1988-89	Toronto	NHL	55	2	7	9	106	0	0	0	59	3.4	–15	....	....	....	....	....	....	....	....	....	....	....	....
1989-90	Toronto	NHL	67	4	14	18	122	0	0	0	80	5.0	–1	....	....	....	5	0	0	0	22	0	0	0	....
1990-91	Toronto	NHL	78	1	9	10	238	0	0	0	68	1.5	–28	....	....	....	....	....	....	....	....	....	....	....	....
1991-92	Edmonton	NHL	75	2	19	21	118	0	0	0	85	2.4	–9	....	....	....	16	0	5	5	45	0	0	0	....
1992-93	Edmonton	NHL	82	3	10	13	142	0	2	0	78	3.8	–18	....	....	....	....	....	....	....	....	....	....	....	....
1993-94	Edmonton	NHL	69	2	6	8	131	0	0	0	92	2.2	–13	....	....	....	....	....	....	....	....	....	....	....	....
1994-95	Edmonton	NHL	46	3	10	13	40	1	1	1	51	5.9	–6	....	....	....	....	....	....	....	....	....	....	....	....
1995-96	Edmonton	NHL	82	2	9	11	108	0	0	0	61	3.3	–27	....	....	....	....	....	....	....	....	....	....	....	....
1996-97	Edmonton	NHL	82	1	11	12	91	0	0	0	67	1.5	9	....	....	....	12	0	2	2	14	0	0	0	....
1997-98	Philadelphia	NHL	81	2	3	5	139	2	0	0	57	3.5	7	....	....	....	5	0	0	0	0	0	0	0	....
1998-99	Philadelphia	NHL	78	0	6	6	106	0	0	0	49	0.0	–3	0	0.0	16:33	....	....	....	....	....	....	....	....	....
99-2000	Philadelphia	NHL	74	2	5	7	140	0	0	1	50	4.0	14	0	0.0	16:11	18	0	1	1	41	0	0	0	21:58
2000-01	Philadelphia	NHL	82	2	6	8	131	0	1	0	75	2.7	23	1	0.0	20:42	6	0	0	0	4	0	0	0	24:39
2001-02	Philadelphia	NHL	72	1	8	9	102	0	0	0	65	1.5	18	0	0.0	18:17	5	0	0	0	4	0	0	0	19:18
2002-03	Columbus	NHL	82	0	13	13	73	0	0	0	56	0.0	–16	2	50.0	23:31	....	....	....	....	....	....	....	....	....
2003-04	Columbus	NHL	64	1	5	6	48	0	0	1	34	2.9	–11	0	0.0	20:07	....	....	....	....	....	....	....	....	....
	NHL Totals		1247	32	147	179	1925	3	4	3	1076	3.0		3	33.3	19:17	69	0	8	8	130	0	0	0	22:04

Traded to **Edmonton** by **Toronto** with Vincent Damphousse, Peter Ing and Scott Thornton for Grant Fuhr, Glenn Anderson and Craig Berube, September 19, 1991. Signed as a free agent by **Philadelphia**, July 23, 1997. Signed as a free agent by **Columbus**, July 4, 2002.

RISSMILLER, Pat
(RIGHZ-mih-luhr, PAT) **S.J.**

Left wing. Shoots left. 6'4", 210 lbs. Born, Belmont, MA, October 26, 1978.

Season	Club	League	GP	G	A	Pts	PIM	PP	SH	GW	S	%	+/-	TF	F%	Min	GP	G	A	Pts	PIM	PP	SH	GW	Min
1997-98	The Hill School	Hi-School	STATISTICS NOT AVAILABLE																						
1998-99	Holy Cross	MAAC	34	13	28	41	23	....	....	....	....	....	....	....	....	....	....	....	....	....	....	....	....	....	....
99-2000	Holy Cross	MAAC	35	10	17	27	22	....	....	....	....	....	....	....	....	....	....	....	....	....	....	....	....	....	....
2000-01	Holy Cross	MAAC	29	14	15	29	40	....	....	....	....	....	....	....	....	....	....	....	....	....	....	....	....	....	....
2001-02	Holy Cross	MAAC	33	16	*30	*46	31	....	....	....	....	....	....	....	....	....	....	....	....	....	....	....	....	....	....
2002-03	Cleveland Barons	AHL	72	14	26	40	24	....	....	....	....	....	....	....	....	....	....	....	....	....	....	....	....	....	....
	Cincinnati	ECHL	2	2	2	4	0	....	....	....	....	....	....	....	....	....	....	....	....	....	....	....	....	....	....
2003-04	San Jose	NHL	4	0	0	0	0	0	0	0	2	0.0	0	26	53.9	7:07	....	....	....	....	....	....	....	....	....
	Cleveland Barons	AHL	75	14	31	45	66	....	....	....	....	....	....	....	....	....	9	0	1	1	8	....	....	....	....
	NHL Totals		4	0	0	0	0	0	0	0	2	0.0		26	53.8	7:07	....	....	....	....	....	....	....	....	....

MAAC All-Rookie Team (1999 • MAAC First All-Star Team (2002) • MAAC Offensive Player of the Year (2002)

Signed as a free agent by **Cleveland** (AHL), September 23, 2002. Signed as a free agent by **San Jose**, June 30, 2003.

RITA, Jani

(REETA, YA-nee) **EDM.**

Left wing. Shoots left. 6'1", 206 lbs. Born, Helsinki, Finland, July 25, 1981. Edmonton's 1st choice, 13th overall, in 1999 Entry Draft.

			Regular Season														Playoffs								
Season	Club	League	GP	G	A	Pts	PIM	PP	SH	GW	S	%	+/-	TF	F%	Min	GP	G	A	Pts	PIM	PP	SH	GW	Min
1994-95	Jokerit Helsinki C	Finn-Jr.	7	3	0	3	0	....	....	....	....	....	....	....	....	....	6	1	0	1	0	....	....	....	....
1995-96	Jokerit Helsinki C	Finn-Jr.	12	10	3	13	2	....	....	....	....	....	....	....	....	....	....	....	....	....	....	....	....	....	....
	Jokerit Helsinki B	Finn-Jr.	5	0	0	0	0	....	....	....	....	....	....	....	....	....	....	....	....	....	....	....	....	....	....
1996-97	Jokerit Helsinki B	Finn-Jr.	27	22	7	29	4	....	....	....	....	....	....	....	....	....	....	....	....	....	....	....	....	....	....
1997-98	Jokerit Helsinki B	Finn-Jr.	7	7	4	11	2	....	....	....	....	....	....	....	....	....	....	....	....	....	....	....	....	....	....
	Jokerit Helsinki Jr.	Finn-Jr.	36	15	9	24	2	....	....	....	....	....	....	....	....	....	8	4	1	5	0	....	....	....	....
	Jokerit Helsinki	Finland	....	....	....	....	....	....	....	....	....	....	....	....	....	....	1	0	0	0	0	....	....	....	....
1998-99	Jokerit Helsinki Jr.	Finn-Jr.	20	9	13	22	8	....	....	....	....	....	....	....	....	....	....	....	....	....	....	....	....	....	....
	Jokerit Helsinki	Finland	41	3	2	5	39	....	....	....	....	....	....	....	....	....	....	....	....	....	....	....	....	....	....
	Jokerit Helsinki	EuroHL	3	0	0	0	0	....	....	....	....	....	....	....	....	....	....	....	....	....	....	....	....	....	....
99-2000	Jokerit Helsinki Jr.	Finn-Jr.	1	1	0	1	0	....	....	....	....	....	....	....	....	....	....	....	....	....	....	....	....	....	....
	Jokerit Helsinki	Finland	49	6	3	9	10	....	....	....	....	....	....	....	....	....	11	1	0	1	0	....	....	....	....
2000-01	Jokerit Helsinki Jr.	Finn-Jr.	3	3	2	5	0	....	....	....	....	....	....	....	....	....	....	....	....	....	....	....	....	....	....
	Jokerit Helsinki	Finland	50	5	10	15	18	....	....	....	....	....	....	....	....	....	5	0	0	0	2	....	....	....	....
2001-02	**Edmonton**	**NHL**	**1**	**0**	**0**	**0**	**0**	**0**	**0**	**0**	**0**	**0.0**	**0**	**0**	**0.0**	**6:09**	....	....	....	....	....	....	....	....	....
	Hamilton	AHL	76	25	17	42	32	....	....	....	....	....	....	....	....	....	15	8	4	12	0	....	....	....	....
2002-03	**Edmonton**	**NHL**	**12**	**3**	**1**	**4**	**0**	**0**	**0**	**0**	**18**	**16.7**	**2**	**1**	**0.0**	**9:32**	....	....	....	....	....	....	....	....	....
	Hamilton	AHL	64	21	27	48	18	....	....	....	....	....	....	....	....	....	23	3	4	7	2	....	....	....	....
2003-04	**Edmonton**	**NHL**	**2**	**0**	**0**	**0**	**0**	**0**	**0**	**0**	**1**	**0.0**	**0**	**0**	**0.0**	**4:34**	....	....	....	....	....	....	....	....	....
	Toronto	AHL	64	17	24	41	18	....	....	....	....	....	....	....	....	....	1	1	0	1	0	....	....	....	....
	NHL Totals		**15**	**3**	**1**	**4**	**0**	**0**	**0**	**0**	**19**	**15.8**		**1**	**0.0**	**8:39**	....	....	....	....	....	....	....	....	....

RITCHIE, Byron

(RIHT-chee, BIGH-rohn) **CGY.**

Center. Shoots left. 5'10", 195 lbs. Born, Burnaby, B.C., April 24, 1977. Hartford's 6th choice, 165th overall, in 1995 Entry Draft.

			Regular Season														Playoffs								
Season	Club	League	GP	G	A	Pts	PIM	PP	SH	GW	S	%	+/-	TF	F%	Min	GP	G	A	Pts	PIM	PP	SH	GW	Min
1992-93	North Delta	BCAHA	60	102	151	253	147	....	....	....	....	....	....	....	....	....	....	....	....	....	....	....	....	....	....
1993-94	Lethbridge	WHL	44	4	11	15	44	....	....	....	....	....	....	....	....	....	6	0	0	0	14	....	....	....	....
1994-95	Lethbridge	WHL	58	22	28	50	132	....	....	....	....	....	....	....	....	....	....	....	....	....	....	....	....	....	....
1995-96	Lethbridge	WHL	66	55	51	106	163	....	....	....	....	....	....	....	....	....	4	0	2	2	4	....	....	....	....
	Springfield	AHL	6	2	1	3	4	....	....	....	....	....	....	....	....	....	8	0	3	3	0	....	....	....	....
1996-97	Lethbridge	WHL	63	50	76	126	115	....	....	....	....	....	....	....	....	....	18	*16	12	*28	28	....	....	....	....
1997-98	New Haven	AHL	65	13	18	31	97	....	....	....	....	....	....	....	....	....	....	....	....	....	....	....	....	....	....
1998-99	**Carolina**	**NHL**	**3**	**0**	**0**	**0**	**0**	**0**	**0**	**0**	**0**	**0.0**	**0**	**5**	**20.0**	**3:25**	....	....	....	....	....	....	....	....	....
	New Haven	AHL	66	24	33	57	139	....	....	....	....	....	....	....	....	....	....	....	....	....	....	....	....	....	....
99-2000	**Carolina**	**NHL**	**26**	**0**	**2**	**2**	**17**	**0**	**0**	**0**	**13**	**0.0**	**-10**	**155**	**49.7**	**7:24**	....	....	....	....	....	....	....	....	....
	Cincinnati	IHL	34	8	13	21	81	....	....	....	....	....	....	....	....	....	10	1	6	7	32	....	....	....	....
2000-01	Cincinnati	IHL	77	31	35	66	166	....	....	....	....	....	....	....	....	....	5	3	2	5	10	....	....	....	....
2001-02	**Carolina**	**NHL**	**4**	**0**	**0**	**0**	**2**	**0**	**0**	**0**	**5**	**0.0**	**0**	**9**	**44.4**	**11:30**	....	....	....	....	....	....	....	....	....
	Lowell	AHL	43	25	30	55	38	....	....	....	....	....	....	....	....	....	....	....	....	....	....	....	....	....	....
	Florida	**NHL**	**31**	**5**	**6**	**11**	**34**	**2**	**0**	**0**	**55**	**9.1**	**-2**	**324**	**50.9**	**12:26**	....	....	....	....	....	....	....	....	....
2002-03	**Florida**	**NHL**	**30**	**0**	**3**	**3**	**19**	**0**	**0**	**0**	**29**	**0.0**	**-4**	**251**	**48.2**	**9:18**	....	....	....	....	....	....	....	....	....
	San Antonio	AHL	26	3	14	17	68	....	....	....	....	....	....	....	....	....	3	1	0	1	0	....	....	....	....
2003-04	**Florida**	**NHL**	**50**	**5**	**6**	**11**	**84**	**0**	**0**	**2**	**65**	**7.7**	**-10**	**168**	**48.8**	**13:54**	....	....	....	....	....	....	....	....	....
	NHL Totals		**144**	**10**	**17**	**27**	**156**	**2**	**0**	**2**	**167**	**6.0**		**912**	**49.3**	**11:10**	....	....	....	....	....	....	....	....	....

WHL East Second All-Star Team (1996, 1997)

Rights transferred to **Carolina** after **Hartford** franchise relocated, June 25, 1997. Traded to **Florida** by **Carolina** with Sandis Ozolinsh for Bret Hedican, Kevyn Adams and Tomas Malec, January 16, 2002. Signed as a free agent by **Calgary**, July 2, 2004.

RIVERS, Jamie

(RIH-vuhrs, JAY-mee) **DET.**

Defense. Shoots left. 6', 195 lbs. Born, Ottawa, Ont., March 16, 1975. St. Louis' 2nd choice, 63rd overall, in 1993 Entry Draft.

			Regular Season														Playoffs								
Season	Club	League	GP	G	A	Pts	PIM	PP	SH	GW	S	%	+/-	TF	F%	Min	GP	G	A	Pts	PIM	PP	SH	GW	Min
1989-90	Ottawa South	ODMHA	50	26	46	72	46	....	....	....	....	....	....	....	....	....	....	....	....	....	....	....	....	....	....
1990-91	Ottawa Jr. Sens	OCJHL	55	4	30	34	74	....	....	....	....	....	....	....	....	....	....	....	....	....	....	....	....	....	....
1991-92	Sudbury Wolves	OHL	55	3	13	16	20	....	....	....	....	....	....	....	....	....	8	0	0	0	0	....	....	....	....
1992-93	Sudbury Wolves	OHL	62	12	43	55	20	....	....	....	....	....	....	....	....	....	14	7	19	26	4	....	....	....	....
1993-94	Sudbury Wolves	OHL	65	32	*89	121	58	....	....	....	....	....	....	....	....	....	10	1	9	10	14	....	....	....	....
1994-95	Sudbury Wolves	OHL	46	9	56	65	30	....	....	....	....	....	....	....	....	....	18	7	26	33	22	....	....	....	....
1995-96	**St. Louis**	**NHL**	**3**	**0**	**0**	**0**	**2**	**0**	**0**	**0**	**5**	**0.0**	**-1**	....	....	....	....	....	....	....	....	....	....	....	....
	Worcester IceCats	AHL	75	7	45	52	130	....	....	....	....	....	....	....	....	....	4	0	1	1	4	....	....	....	....
1996-97	**St. Louis**	**NHL**	**15**	**2**	**5**	**7**	**6**	**1**	**0**	**0**	**9**	**22.2**	**-4**	....	....	....	....	....	....	....	....	....	....	....	....
	Worcester IceCats	AHL	63	8	35	43	83	....	....	....	....	....	....	....	....	....	5	1	2	3	14	....	....	....	....
1997-98	**St. Louis**	**NHL**	**59**	**2**	**4**	**6**	**36**	**1**	**0**	**1**	**53**	**3.8**	**5**	....	....	....	....	....	....	....	....	....	....	....	....
1998-99	**St. Louis**	**NHL**	**76**	**2**	**5**	**7**	**47**	**1**	**0**	**0**	**78**	**2.6**	**-3**	**0**	**0.0**	**14:10**	**9**	**1**	**1**	**2**	**2**	**1**	**0**	**1**	**6:29**
99-2000	**NY Islanders**	**NHL**	**75**	**1**	**16**	**17**	**84**	**1**	**0**	**0**	**95**	**1.1**	**-4**	**0**	**0.0**	**19:39**	....	....	....	....	....	....	....	....	....
2000-01	**Ottawa**	**NHL**	**45**	**2**	**4**	**6**	**44**	**0**	**0**	**0**	**41**	**4.9**	**6**	**0**	**0.0**	**14:01**	**1**	**0**	**0**	**0**	**4**	**0**	**0**	**0**	**12:45**
	Grand Rapids	IHL	2	0	0	0	2	....	....	....	....	....	....	....	....	....	....	....	....	....	....	....	....	....	....
2001-02	**Ottawa**	**NHL**	**2**	**0**	**0**	**0**	**4**	**0**	**0**	**0**	**3**	**0.0**	**-3**	**0**	**0.0**	**11:37**	....	....	....	....	....	....	....	....	....
	Boston	**NHL**	**64**	**4**	**2**	**6**	**45**	**1**	**0**	**1**	**48**	**8.3**	**6**	**39**	**33.3**	**8:27**	**3**	**0**	**0**	**0**	**0**	**0**	**0**	**0**	**4:57**
2002-03	**Florida**	**NHL**	**1**	**0**	**0**	**0**	**2**	**0**	**0**	**0**	**2**	**0.0**	**-2**	**0**	**0.0**	**18:27**	....	....	....	....	....	....	....	....	....
	San Antonio	AHL	50	6	19	25	68	....	....	....	....	....	....	....	....	....	3	0	1	1	10	....	....	....	....
2003-04	**Detroit**	**NHL**	**50**	**3**	**4**	**7**	**41**	**0**	**0**	**0**	**31**	**9.7**	**9**	**1**	**0.0**	**10:14**	**2**	**0**	**0**	**0**	**2**	**0**	**0**	**0**	**5:40**
	Grand Rapids	AHL	2	0	0	0	4	....	....	....	....	....	....	....	....	....	....	....	....	....	....	....	....	....	....
	NHL Totals		**390**	**16**	**40**	**56**	**311**	**5**	**0**	**2**	**365**	**4.4**		**40**	**32.5**	**13:40**	**15**	**1**	**1**	**2**	**8**	**1**	**0**	**1**	**6:29**

OHL First All-Star Team (1994) • Canadian Major Junior Second All-Star Team (1994) • OHL Second All-Star Team (1995) • AHL Second All-Star Team (1997)

Claimed by **NY Islanders** from **St. Louis** in Waiver Draft, September 27, 1999. Signed as a free agent by **Ottawa**, November 30, 2000. Claimed on waivers by **Boston** from **Ottawa**, October 13, 2001. Signed as a free agent by **San Antonio** (AHL), November 2, 2002. Signed as a free agent by **Florida**, December 16, 2002. Signed as a free agent by **Detroit**, July 29, 2003.

RIVET, Craig

(rih-VAY, KRAYG) **MTL.**

Defense. Shoots right. 6'2", 207 lbs. Born, North Bay, Ont., September 13, 1974. Montreal's 4th choice, 68th overall, in 1992 Entry Draft.

			Regular Season														Playoffs								
Season	Club	League	GP	G	A	Pts	PIM	PP	SH	GW	S	%	+/-	TF	F%	Min	GP	G	A	Pts	PIM	PP	SH	GW	Min
1990-91	Barrie Colts	OJHL-B	42	9	17	26	55	....	....	....	....	....	....	....	....	....	....	....	....	....	....	....	....	....	....
1991-92	Kingston	OHL	66	5	21	26	97	....	....	....	....	....	....	....	....	....	....	....	....	....	....	....	....	....	....
1992-93	Kingston	OHL	64	19	55	74	117	....	....	....	....	....	....	....	....	....	16	5	7	12	39	....	....	....	....
1993-94	Kingston	OHL	61	12	52	64	100	....	....	....	....	....	....	....	....	....	6	0	3	3	6	....	....	....	....
	Fredericton	AHL	4	0	2	2	2	....	....	....	....	....	....	....	....	....	....	....	....	....	....	....	....	....	....
1994-95	Fredericton	AHL	78	5	27	32	126	....	....	....	....	....	....	....	....	....	12	0	4	4	17	....	....	....	....
	Montreal	**NHL**	**5**	**0**	**1**	**1**	**5**	**0**	**0**	**0**	**2**	**0.0**	**2**	....	....	....	....	....	....	....	....	....	....	....	....
1995-96	**Montreal**	**NHL**	**19**	**1**	**4**	**5**	**54**	**0**	**0**	**0**	**9**	**11.1**	**4**	....	....	....	....	....	....	....	....	....	....	....	....
	Fredericton	AHL	49	5	18	23	189	....	....	....	....	....	....	....	....	....	6	0	0	0	12	....	....	....	....
1996-97	**Montreal**	**NHL**	**35**	**0**	**4**	**4**	**54**	**0**	**0**	**0**	**24**	**0.0**	**7**	....	....	....	**5**	**0**	**1**	**1**	**14**	**0**	**0**	**0**	....
	Fredericton	AHL	23	3	12	15	99	....	....	....	....	....	....	....	....	....	....	....	....	....	....	....	....	....	....
1997-98	**Montreal**	**NHL**	**61**	**0**	**2**	**2**	**93**	**0**	**0**	**0**	**26**	**0.0**	**-3**	....	....	....	**5**	**0**	**0**	**0**	**2**	**0**	**0**	**0**	....
1998-99	**Montreal**	**NHL**	**66**	**2**	**8**	**10**	**66**	**0**	**0**	**0**	**39**	**5.1**	**-3**	**0**	**0.0**	**14:20**	....	....	....	....	....	....	....	....	....
99-2000	**Montreal**	**NHL**	**61**	**3**	**14**	**17**	**76**	**0**	**0**	**1**	**71**	**4.2**	**11**	**0**	**0.0**	**19:03**	....	....	....	....	....	....	....	....	....
2000-01	**Montreal**	**NHL**	**26**	**1**	**2**	**3**	**36**	**0**	**0**	**0**	**22**	**4.5**	**-8**	**0**	**0.0**	**19:04**	....	....	....	....	....	....	....	....	....
2001-02	**Montreal**	**NHL**	**82**	**8**	**17**	**25**	**76**	**0**	**0**	**0**	**90**	**8.9**	**1**	**1**	**0.0**	**19:00**	**12**	**0**	**3**	**3**	**4**	**0**	**0**	**0**	**21:26**
2002-03	**Montreal**	**NHL**	**82**	**7**	**15**	**22**	**71**	**3**	**0**	**2**	**118**	**5.9**	**1**	**0**	**0.0**	**22:00**	....	....	....	....	....	....	....	....	....
2003-04	**Montreal**	**NHL**	**80**	**4**	**8**	**12**	**98**	**2**	**0**	**1**	**96**	**4.2**	**-1**	**0**	**0.0**	**19:28**	**11**	**1**	**4**	**5**	**2**	**1**	**0**	**0**	**24:07**
	NHL Totals		**517**	**26**	**75**	**101**	**629**	**5**	**0**	**4**	**497**	**5.2**		**1**	**0.0**	**18:57**	**33**	**1**	**8**	**9**	**22**	**1**	**0**	**0**	**22:43**

• Missed majority of 2000-01 season recovering from shoulder injury suffered in game vs. Vancouver, October 30, 2000.

ROBERTS, Gary

(RAW-buhrts, GAIR-ree) **TOR.**

Left wing. Shoots left. 6'2", 215 lbs. Born, North York, Ont., May 23, 1966. Calgary's 1st choice, 12th overall, in 1984 Entry Draft.

Season	Club	League	Regular Season GP	G	A	Pts	PIM	PP	SH	GW	S	%	+/-	TF	F%	Min	Playoffs GP	G	A	Pts	PIM	PP	SH	GW	Min
1980-81	Hamilton Kilty B's	OHA-B	3	0	1	1	0	....	....	....	....	....	....	....	....	....	....	....	....	....	....	....	....	....	....
1981-82	Whitby	OMHA	44	55	31	86	133	....	....	....	....	....	....	....	....	....	....	....	....	....	....	....	....	....	....
1982-83	Ottawa 67's	OHL	53	12	8	20	83	....	....	....	....	....	....	....	....	....	5	1	0	1	19	....	....	....	....
1983-84	Ottawa 67's	OHL	48	27	30	57	144	....	....	....	....	....	....	....	....	....	13	10	7	17	62	....	....	....	....
1984-85	Ottawa 67's	OHL	59	44	62	106	186	....	....	....	....	....	....	....	....	....	5	2	8	10	10	....	....	....	....
	Moncton	AHL	7	4	2	6	7	....	....	....	....	....	....	....	....	....	....	....	....	....	....	....	....	....	....
1985-86	Ottawa 67's	OHL	24	26	25	51	83	....	....	....	....	....	....	....	....	....	....	....	....	....	....	....	....	....	....
	Guelph Platers	OHL	23	18	15	33	65	....	....	....	....	....	....	....	....	....	20	18	13	31	43	....	....	....	....
1986-87	**Calgary**	**NHL**	**32**	**5**	**10**	**15**	**85**	**0**	**0**	**0**	**38**	**13.2**	**6**	....	....	....	**2**	**0**	**0**	**0**	**4**	**0**	**0**	**0**	....
	Moncton	AHL	38	20	18	38	72	....	....	....	....	....	....	....	....	....	....	....	....	....	....	....	....	....	....
1987-88	**Calgary**	**NHL**	**74**	**13**	**15**	**28**	**282**	**0**	**0**	**1**	**118**	**11.0**	**24**	....	....	....	**9**	**2**	**3**	**5**	**29**	**0**	**0**	**0**	....
1988-89♦	**Calgary**	**NHL**	**71**	**22**	**16**	**38**	**250**	**0**	**1**	**2**	**123**	**17.9**	**32**	....	....	....	**22**	**5**	**7**	**12**	**57**	**0**	**0**	**0**	....
1989-90	**Calgary**	**NHL**	**78**	**39**	**33**	**72**	**222**	**5**	**0**	**5**	**175**	**22.3**	**31**	....	....	....	**6**	**2**	**5**	**7**	**41**	**0**	**0**	**0**	....
1990-91	**Calgary**	**NHL**	**80**	**22**	**31**	**53**	**252**	**0**	**0**	**3**	**132**	**16.7**	**15**	....	....	....	**7**	**1**	**3**	**4**	**18**	**0**	**0**	**0**	....
1991-92	**Calgary**	**NHL**	**76**	**53**	**37**	**90**	**207**	**15**	**0**	**2**	**196**	**27.0**	**32**	....	....	....	....	....	....	....	....	....	....	....	....
1992-93	**Calgary**	**NHL**	**58**	**38**	**41**	**79**	**172**	**8**	**3**	**4**	**166**	**22.9**	**32**	....	....	....	**5**	**1**	**6**	**7**	**43**	**1**	**0**	**0**	....
1993-94	**Calgary**	**NHL**	**73**	**41**	**43**	**84**	**145**	**12**	**3**	**5**	**202**	**20.3**	**37**	....	....	....	**7**	**2**	**6**	**8**	**24**	**1**	**0**	**1**	....
1994-95	**Calgary**	**NHL**	**8**	**2**	**2**	**4**	**43**	**2**	**0**	**0**	**20**	**10.0**	**1**	....	....	....	....	....	....	....	....	....	....	....	....
1995-96	**Calgary**	**NHL**	**35**	**22**	**20**	**42**	**78**	**9**	**0**	**5**	**84**	**26.2**	**15**	....	....	....	....	....	....	....	....	....	....	....	....
1996-97	**Calgary**	**NHL**	DID NOT PLAY – INJURED																						
1997-98	**Carolina**	**NHL**	**61**	**20**	**29**	**49**	**103**	**4**	**0**	**2**	**106**	**18.9**	**3**	....	....	....	....	....	....	....	....	....	....	....	....
1998-99	**Carolina**	**NHL**	**77**	**14**	**28**	**42**	**178**	**1**	**1**	**4**	**138**	**10.1**	**2**	**15**	**46.7**	**19:36**	**6**	**1**	**1**	**2**	**8**	**0**	**0**	**0**	**21:01**
99-2000	**Carolina**	**NHL**	**69**	**23**	**30**	**53**	**62**	**12**	**0**	**1**	**150**	**15.3**	**–10**	**7**	**28.6**	**18:31**	....	....	....	....	....	....	....	....	....
2000-01	**Toronto**	**NHL**	**82**	**29**	**24**	**53**	**109**	**8**	**2**	**3**	**138**	**21.0**	**16**	**13**	**46.2**	**17:08**	**11**	**2**	**9**	**11**	**0**	**0**	**0**	**0**	**19:49**
2001-02	**Toronto**	**NHL**	**69**	**21**	**27**	**48**	**63**	**6**	**2**	**2**	**122**	**17.2**	**–4**	**6**	**33.3**	**17:23**	**19**	**7**	**12**	**19**	**56**	**3**	**0**	**1**	**19:28**
2002-03	**Toronto**	**NHL**	**14**	**5**	**3**	**8**	**10**	**3**	**0**	**0**	**22**	**22.7**	**–2**	**4**	**50.0**	**15:35**	**7**	**1**	**1**	**2**	**8**	**0**	**0**	**0**	**21:04**
2003-04	**Toronto**	**NHL**	**72**	**28**	**20**	**48**	**84**	**11**	**1**	**7**	**124**	**22.6**	**9**	**12**	**33.3**	**17:33**	**13**	**4**	**4**	**8**	**10**	**2**	**0**	**1**	**17:45**
	NHL Totals		**1029**	**397**	**409**	**806**	**2345**	**96**	**13**	**46**	**2054**	**19.3**		**57**	**40.4**	**17:57**	**114**	**28**	**57**	**85**	**298**	**7**	**0**	**3**	**19:30**

OHL Second All-Star Team (1985, 1986) • Bill Masterton Memorial Trophy (1996)

Played in NHL All-Star Game (1992, 1993, 2004)

• Missed remainder of 1994-95 and majority of 1995-96 seasons recovering from neck injury suffered in game vs. Toronto, February 4, 1995. • Missed remainder of 1995-96 and entire 1996-97 seasons recovering from neck injury suffered in game vs. Vancouver, April 3, 1996. Traded to **Carolina** by **Calgary** with Trevor Kidd for Andrew Cassels and Jean-Sebastien Giguere, August 25, 1997. Signed as a free agent by **Toronto**, July 4, 2000. • Missed majority of 2002-03 season recovering from off-season shoulder surgery, August 13, 2002.

ROBIDAS, Stephane

(ROH-bih-dah, STEH-fan) **CHI.**

Defense. Shoots right. 5'11", 188 lbs. Born, Sherbrooke, Que., March 3, 1977. Montreal's 7th choice, 164th overall, in 1995 Entry Draft.

Season	Club	League	Regular Season GP	G	A	Pts	PIM	PP	SH	GW	S	%	+/-	TF	F%	Min	Playoffs GP	G	A	Pts	PIM	PP	SH	GW	Min
1992-93	Magog	QAAA	41	3	12	15	16	....	....	....	....	....	....	....	....	....	5	1	1	2	2	....	....	....	....
1993-94	Shawinigan	QMJHL	67	3	18	21	33	....	....	....	....	....	....	....	....	....	1	0	0	0	0	....	....	....	....
1994-95	Shawinigan	QMJHL	71	13	56	69	44	....	....	....	....	....	....	....	....	....	15	7	12	19	4	....	....	....	....
1995-96	Shawinigan	QMJHL	67	23	56	79	53	....	....	....	....	....	....	....	....	....	6	1	5	6	10	....	....	....	....
1996-97	Shawinigan	QMJHL	67	24	51	75	59	....	....	....	....	....	....	....	....	....	7	4	6	10	14	....	....	....	....
1997-98	Fredericton	AHL	79	10	21	31	50	....	....	....	....	....	....	....	....	....	4	0	2	2	0	....	....	....	....
1998-99	Fredericton	AHL	79	8	33	41	59	....	....	....	....	....	....	....	....	....	15	1	5	6	10	....	....	....	....
99-2000	**Montreal**	**NHL**	**1**	**0**	**0**	**0**	**0**	**0**	**0**	**0**	**0**	**0.0**	**0**	**0**	**0.0**	**15:54**	....	....	....	....	....	....	....	....	....
	Quebec Citadelles	AHL	76	14	31	45	36	....	....	....	....	....	....	....	....	....	3	0	1	1	0	....	....	....	....
2000-01	**Montreal**	**NHL**	**65**	**6**	**6**	**12**	**14**	**1**	**0**	**0**	**77**	**7.8**	**0**	**1**	**100.0**	**20:44**	....	....	....	....	....	....	....	....	....
2001-02	**Montreal**	**NHL**	**56**	**1**	**10**	**11**	**14**	**1**	**0**	**0**	**68**	**1.5**	**–25**	**3**	**33.3**	**18:58**	**2**	**0**	**0**	**0**	**4**	**0**	**0**	**0**	**13:07**
2002-03	**Dallas**	**NHL**	**76**	**3**	**7**	**10**	**35**	**0**	**0**	**1**	**47**	**6.4**	**15**	**1**	**100.0**	**12:54**	**12**	**0**	**1**	**1**	**20**	**0**	**0**	**0**	**13:54**
2003-04	**Dallas**	**NHL**	**14**	**1**	**0**	**1**	**8**	**1**	**0**	**0**	**8**	**12.5**	**–2**	**1**	**100.0**	**12:57**	....	....	....	....	....	....	....	....	....
	Chicago	**NHL**	**45**	**2**	**10**	**12**	**33**	**0**	**1**	**1**	**55**	**3.6**	**6**	**0**	**0.0**	**20:56**	....	....	....	....	....	....	....	....	....
	NHL Totals		**257**	**13**	**33**	**46**	**104**	**3**	**1**	**2**	**255**	**5.1**		**6**	**66.7**	**17:37**	**14**	**0**	**1**	**1**	**24**	**0**	**0**	**0**	**13:47**

QMJHL First All-Star Team (1996, 1997)

Claimed by **Atlanta** from **Montreal** in Waiver Draft, October 4, 2002. Traded to **Dallas** by **Atlanta** for future considerations, October 4, 2002. Traded to **Chicago** by **Dallas** with Dallas' 2nd round choice (Jakub Sindel) in 2004 Entry Draft for Jon Klemm and NY Rangers' 4th round choice (previously acquired, Dallas selected Fredrik Naslund) in 2004 Entry Draft, November 17, 2004.

ROBINSON, Nathan

DET.

Center. Shoots left. 5'9", 180 lbs. Born, Kingston, Ont., December 31, 1981.

Season	Club	League	Regular Season GP	G	A	Pts	PIM	PP	SH	GW	S	%	+/-	TF	F%	Min	Playoffs GP	G	A	Pts	PIM	PP	SH	GW	Min
1998-99	Belleville Bulls	OHL	50	11	8	19	23	....	....	....	....	....	....	....	....	....	21	4	4	8	14	....	....	....	....
99-2000	Belleville Bulls	OHL	61	19	18	37	45	....	....	....	....	....	....	....	....	....	15	3	4	7	10	....	....	....	....
2000-01	Belleville Bulls	OHL	66	32	37	69	57	....	....	....	....	....	....	....	....	....	10	6	10	16	7	....	....	....	....
2001-02	Belleville Bulls	OHL	67	47	63	*110	74	....	....	....	....	....	....	....	....	....	11	8	6	14	10	....	....	....	....
2002-03	Toledo Storm	ECHL	9	5	9	14	29	....	....	....	....	....	....	....	....	....	....	....	....	....	....	....	....	....	....
	Grand Rapids	AHL	53	3	14	17	24	....	....	....	....	....	....	....	....	....	8	0	3	3	0	....	....	....	....
2003-04	**Detroit**	**NHL**	**5**	**0**	**0**	**0**	**2**	**0**	**0**	**0**	**5**	**0.0**	**–1**	**0**	**0.0**	**6:01**	....	....	....	....	....	....	....	....	....
	Grand Rapids	AHL	69	24	26	50	41	....	....	....	....	....	....	....	....	....	3	0	0	0	2	....	....	....	....
	NHL Totals		**5**	**0**	**0**	**0**	**2**	**0**	**0**	**0**	**5**	**0.0**		**0**	**0.0**	**6:01**	....	....	....	....	....	....	....	....	....

Signed as a free agent by **Detroit**, October 12, 2002.

ROBITAILLE, Luc

(ROH-buh-tigh, LEWK) **L.A.**

Left wing. Shoots left. 6'1", 215 lbs. Born, Montreal, Que., February 17, 1966. Los Angeles' 9th choice, 171st overall, in 1984 Entry Draft.

Season	Club	League	Regular Season GP	G	A	Pts	PIM	PP	SH	GW	S	%	+/-	TF	F%	Min	Playoffs GP	G	A	Pts	PIM	PP	SH	GW	Min
1982-83	Mtl-Bourassa	QAAA	48	36	57	93	28	....	....	....	....	....	....	....	....	....	7	9	6	15	14	....	....	....	....
1983-84	Hull Olympiques	QMJHL	70	32	53	85	48	....	....	....	....	....	....	....	....	....	....	....	....	....	....	....	....	....	....
1984-85	Hull Olympiques	QMJHL	64	55	94	149	115	....	....	....	....	....	....	....	....	....	5	4	2	6	27	....	....	....	....
1985-86	Hull Olympiques	QMJHL	63	68	123	191	91	....	....	....	....	....	....	....	....	....	15	17	27	44	28	....	....	....	....
1986-87	**Los Angeles**	**NHL**	**79**	**45**	**39**	**84**	**28**	**18**	**0**	**3**	**199**	**22.6**	**–18**	....	....	....	**5**	**1**	**4**	**5**	**2**	**0**	**0**	**0**	....
1987-88	**Los Angeles**	**NHL**	**80**	**53**	**58**	**111**	**82**	**17**	**0**	**6**	**220**	**24.1**	**–9**	....	....	....	**5**	**2**	**5**	**7**	**18**	**2**	**0**	**1**	....
1988-89	**Los Angeles**	**NHL**	**78**	**46**	**52**	**98**	**65**	**10**	**0**	**4**	**237**	**19.4**	**5**	....	....	....	**11**	**2**	**6**	**8**	**10**	**0**	**0**	**1**	....
1989-90	**Los Angeles**	**NHL**	**80**	**52**	**49**	**101**	**38**	**20**	**0**	**7**	**210**	**24.8**	**8**	....	....	....	**10**	**5**	**5**	**10**	**12**	**1**	**0**	**1**	....
1990-91	**Los Angeles**	**NHL**	**76**	**45**	**46**	**91**	**68**	**11**	**0**	**5**	**229**	**19.7**	**28**	....	....	....	**12**	**12**	**4**	**16**	**22**	**5**	**0**	**2**	....
1991-92	**Los Angeles**	**NHL**	**80**	**44**	**63**	**107**	**95**	**26**	**0**	**6**	**240**	**18.3**	**–4**	....	....	....	**6**	**3**	**4**	**7**	**12**	**1**	**0**	**1**	....
1992-93	**Los Angeles**	**NHL**	**84**	**63**	**62**	**125**	**100**	**24**	**2**	**8**	**265**	**23.8**	**18**	....	....	....	**24**	**9**	**13**	**22**	**28**	**4**	**0**	**2**	....
1993-94	**Los Angeles**	**NHL**	**83**	**44**	**42**	**86**	**86**	**24**	**0**	**3**	**267**	**16.5**	**–20**	....	....	....	....	....	....	....	....	....	....	....	....
1994-95	**Pittsburgh**	**NHL**	**46**	**23**	**19**	**42**	**37**	**5**	**0**	**3**	**109**	**21.1**	**10**	....	....	....	**12**	**7**	**4**	**11**	**26**	**0**	**0**	**2**	....
1995-96	**NY Rangers**	**NHL**	**77**	**23**	**46**	**69**	**80**	**11**	**0**	**4**	**223**	**10.3**	**13**	....	....	....	**11**	**1**	**5**	**6**	**8**	**0**	**0**	**0**	....
1996-97	**NY Rangers**	**NHL**	**69**	**24**	**24**	**48**	**48**	**5**	**0**	**4**	**200**	**12.0**	**16**	....	....	....	**15**	**4**	**7**	**11**	**4**	**0**	**0**	**0**	....
1997-98	**Los Angeles**	**NHL**	**57**	**16**	**24**	**40**	**66**	**5**	**0**	**7**	**130**	**12.3**	**5**	....	....	....	**4**	**1**	**2**	**3**	**6**	**0**	**0**	**0**	....
1998-99	**Los Angeles**	**NHL**	**82**	**39**	**35**	**74**	**54**	**11**	**0**	**7**	**292**	**13.4**	**–1**	**7**	**57.1**	**19:11**	....	....	....	....	....	....	....	....	....
99-2000	**Los Angeles**	**NHL**	**71**	**36**	**38**	**74**	**68**	**13**	**0**	**7**	**221**	**16.3**	**11**	**10**	**30.0**	**18:34**	**4**	**2**	**2**	**4**	**6**	**0**	**0**	**0**	**20:25**
2000-01	**Los Angeles**	**NHL**	**82**	**37**	**51**	**88**	**66**	**16**	**1**	**4**	**235**	**15.7**	**10**	**12**	**33.3**	**18:42**	**13**	**4**	**3**	**7**	**10**	**1**	**0**	**1**	**18:19**
2001-02♦	**Detroit**	**NHL**	**81**	**30**	**20**	**50**	**38**	**13**	**0**	**5**	**190**	**15.8**	**–2**	**12**	**41.7**	**14:51**	**23**	**4**	**5**	**9**	**10**	**1**	**0**	**1**	**13:16**
2002-03	**Detroit**	**NHL**	**81**	**11**	**20**	**31**	**50**	**3**	**0**	**0**	**148**	**7.4**	**4**	**18**	**50.0**	**12:49**	**4**	**1**	**0**	**1**	**0**	**0**	**0**	**0**	**11:30**
2003-04	**Los Angeles**	**NHL**	**80**	**22**	**29**	**51**	**56**	**12**	**0**	**4**	**221**	**10.0**	**4**	**2**	**0.0**	**16:41**	....	....	....	....	....	....	....	....	....
	NHL Totals		**1366**	**653**	**717**	**1370**	**1125**	**244**	**3**	**87**	**3836**	**17.0**		**61**	**41.0**	**16:46**	**159**	**58**	**69**	**127**	**174**	**15**	**0**	**12**	**15:15**

QMJHL Second All-Star Team (1985) • QMJHL First All-Star Team (1986) • Canadian Major Junior Player of the Year (1986) • NHL All-Rookie Team (1987) • NHL Second All-Star Team (1987, 1992, 2001) • Calder Memorial Trophy (1987) • NHL First All-Star Team (1988, 1989, 1990, 1991, 1993)

Played in NHL All-Star Game (1988, 1989, 1990, 1991, 1992, 1993, 1999, 2001)

Traded to **Pittsburgh** by **Los Angeles** for Rick Tocchet and Pittsburgh's 2nd round choice (Pavel Rosa) in 1995 Entry Draft, July 29, 1994. Traded to **NY Rangers** by **Pittsburgh** with Ulf Samuelsson for Petr Nedved and Sergei Zubov, August 31, 1995. Traded to **Los Angeles** by **NY Rangers** for Kevin Stevens, August 28, 1997. Signed as a free agent by **Detroit**, July 5, 2001. Signed as a free agent by **Los Angeles**, July 24, 2003.

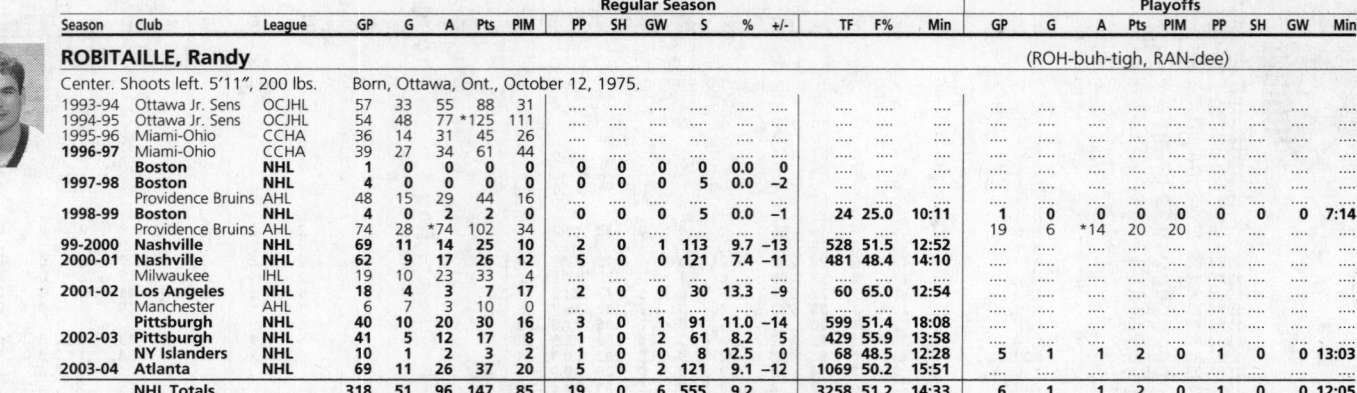

ROBITAILLE, Randy
(ROH-buh-tigh, RAN-dee)

Center. Shoots left. 5'11", 200 lbs. Born, Ottawa, Ont., October 12, 1975.

			Regular Season														Playoffs								
Season	Club	League	GP	G	A	Pts	PIM	PP	SH	GW	S	%	+/-	TF	F%	Min	GP	G	A	Pts	PIM	PP	SH	GW	Min
1993-94	Ottawa Jr. Sens	OCJHL	57	33	55	88	31																		
1994-95	Ottawa Jr. Sens	OCJHL	54	48	77	*125	111																		
1995-96	Miami-Ohio	CCHA	36	14	31	45	26																		
1996-97	Miami-Ohio	CCHA	39	27	34	61	44																		
	Boston	**NHL**	1	0	0	0	0	0	0	0	0	0.0	0												
1997-98	**Boston**	**NHL**	4	0	0	0	0	0	0	0	5	0.0	−2												
	Providence Bruins	AHL	48	15	29	44	16																		
1998-99	**Boston**	**NHL**	4	0	2	2	0	0	0	0	5	0.0	−1	24	25.0	10:11	1	0	0	0	0	0	0	0	7:14
	Providence Bruins	AHL	74	28	*74	102	34										19	6	*14	20	20				
99-2000	**Nashville**	**NHL**	69	11	14	25	10	2	0	1	113	9.7	−13	528	51.5	12:52									
2000-01	**Nashville**	**NHL**	62	9	17	26	12	5	0	0	121	7.4	−11	481	48.4	14:10									
	Milwaukee	IHL	19	10	23	33	4																		
2001-02	**Los Angeles**	**NHL**	18	4	3	7	17	2	0	0	30	13.3	−9	60	65.0	12:54									
	Manchester	AHL	6	7	3	10	0																		
	Pittsburgh	**NHL**	40	10	20	30	16	3	0	1	91	11.0	−14	599	51.4	18:08									
2002-03	**Pittsburgh**	**NHL**	41	5	12	17	8	1	0	2	61	8.2	5	429	55.9	13:58									
	NY Islanders	**NHL**	10	1	2	3	2	1	0	0	8	12.5	0	68	48.5	12:28	5	1	1	2	0	1	0	0	13:03
2003-04	**Atlanta**	**NHL**	69	11	26	37	20	5	0	2	121	9.1	−12	1069	50.2	15:51									
	NHL Totals		**318**	**51**	**96**	**147**	**85**	**19**	**0**	**6**	**555**	**9.2**		**3258**	**51.2**	**14:33**	**6**	**1**	**1**	**2**	**0**	**1**	**0**	**0**	**12:05**

CCHA First All-Star Team (1997) • NCAA West First All-American Team (1997) • AHL First All-Star Team (1999) • Les Cunningham Award (MVP – AHL) (1999)

Signed as a free agent by **Boston**, March 27, 1997. Traded to **Atlanta** by **Boston** for Peter Ferraro, June 25, 1999. Traded to **Nashville** by **Atlanta** for Denny Lambert, August 16, 1999. Signed as a free agent by **Los Angeles**, July 6, 2001. Claimed on waivers by **Pittsburgh** from **Los Angeles**, January 4, 2002. Traded to **NY Islanders** by **Pittsburgh** for Philadelphia's 5th round choice (previously acquired, Pittsburgh selected Evgeni Isakov) in 2003 Entry Draft, March 9, 2003. Signed as a free agent by **Atlanta**, August 12, 2003. Signed as a free agent by **Zurich** (Swiss), April 26, 2004.

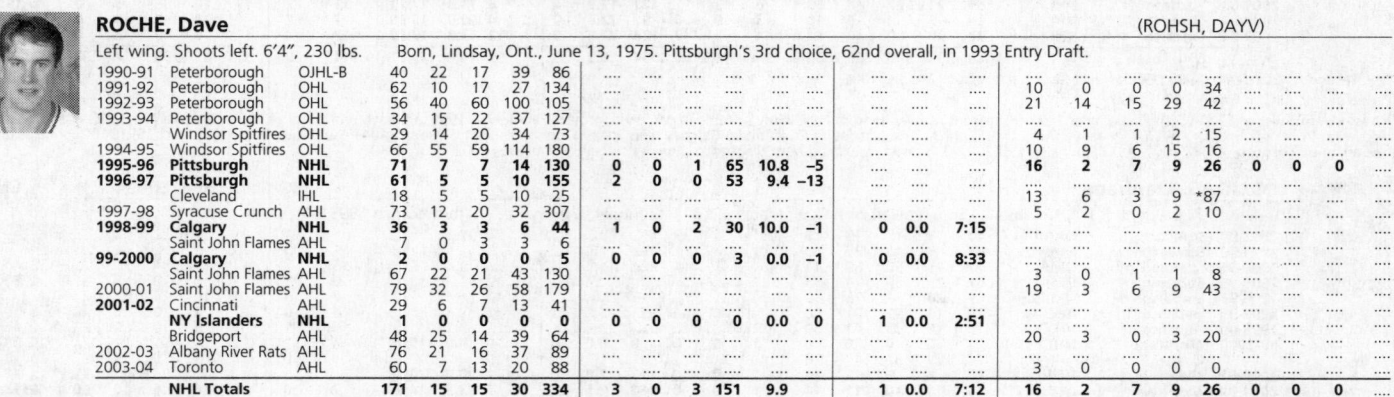

ROCHE, Dave
(ROHSH, DAYV)

Left wing. Shoots left. 6'4", 230 lbs. Born, Lindsay, Ont., June 13, 1975. Pittsburgh's 3rd choice, 62nd overall, in 1993 Entry Draft.

Season	Club	League	GP	G	A	Pts	PIM	PP	SH	GW	S	%	+/-	TF	F%	Min	GP	G	A	Pts	PIM	PP	SH	GW	Min
1990-91	Peterborough	OJHL-B	40	22	17	39	86																		
1991-92	Peterborough	OHL	62	10	17	27	134										10	0	0	0	34				
1992-93	Peterborough	OHL	56	40	60	100	105										21	14	15	29	42				
1993-94	Peterborough	OHL	34	15	22	37	127																		
	Windsor Spitfires	OHL	29	14	20	34	73										4	1	1	2	15				
1994-95	Windsor Spitfires	OHL	66	55	59	114	180										10	9	6	15	16				
1995-96	**Pittsburgh**	**NHL**	71	7	7	14	130	0	0	1	65	10.8	−5				16	2	7	9	26	0	0	0	
1996-97	**Pittsburgh**	**NHL**	61	5	5	10	155	2	0	0	53	9.4	−13												
	Cleveland	IHL	18	5	5	10	25										13	6	3	9	*87				
1997-98	Syracuse Crunch	AHL	73	12	20	32	307										5	2	0	2	10				
1998-99	**Calgary**	**NHL**	36	3	3	6	44	1	0	2	30	10.0	−1	0	0.0	7:15									
	Saint John Flames	AHL	7	0	3	3	6																		
99-2000	**Calgary**	**NHL**	2	0	0	0	5	0	0	0	3	0.0	−1	0	0.0	8:33									
	Saint John Flames	AHL	67	22	21	43	130										3	0	1	1	8				
2000-01	Saint John Flames	AHL	79	32	26	58	179										19	3	6	9	43				
2001-02	Cincinnati	AHL	29	6	7	13	41																		
	NY Islanders	**NHL**	1	0	0	0	0	0	0	0	0	0.0	0	1	0.0	2:51									
	Bridgeport	AHL	48	25	14	39	64										20	3	0	3	20				
2002-03	Albany River Rats	AHL	76	21	16	37	89																		
2003-04	Toronto	AHL	60	7	13	20	88										3	0	0	0	0				
	NHL Totals		**171**	**15**	**15**	**30**	**334**	**3**	**0**	**3**	**151**	**9.9**		**1**	**0.0**	**7:12**	**16**	**2**	**7**	**9**	**26**	**0**	**0**	**0**	

OHL First All-Star Team (1995)

Traded to **Calgary** by **Pittsburgh** with Ken Wregget for German Titov and Todd Hlushko, June 17, 1998. Signed as a free agent by **NY Islanders**, August 17, 2001. Traded to **Anaheim** by **NY Islanders** for Jim Cummins, January 14, 2002. Traded to **NY Islanders** by **Anaheim** for Ben Guite and the rights to Bjorn Mellin, March 19, 2002. Signed as a free agent by **New Jersey**, August 27, 2002. Signed as a free agent by **Toronto** (AHL), October 3, 2003.

ROCHE, Travis
(ROHSH, TRA-vihs) **ATL.**

Defense. Shoots right. 6'1", 190 lbs. Born, Grand Cache, Alta., June 17, 1978.

Season	Club	League	GP	G	A	Pts	PIM	PP	SH	GW	S	%	+/-	TF	F%	Min	GP	G	A	Pts	PIM	PP	SH	GW	Min
1996-97	Trail	BCHL	49	17	40	57	159																		
1997-98	Trail	BCHL	38	11	31	42	104										11	0	8	8	21				
1998-99	North Dakota	WCHA	DID NOT PLAY – FRESHMAN																						
99-2000	North Dakota	WCHA	42	6	22	28	60																		
2000-01	North Dakota	WCHA	42	11	38	49	42																		
	Minnesota	**NHL**	1	0	0	0	0	0	0	0	0	0.0	0	0	0.0	15:22									
2001-02	**Minnesota**	**NHL**	4	0	0	0	2	0	0	0	1	0.0	−1	0	0.0	12:30									
	Houston Aeros	AHL	60	13	21	34	107										12	2	3	5	6				
2002-03	Houston Aeros	AHL	65	14	34	48	42										23	3	5	8	26				
2003-04	**Minnesota**	**NHL**	5	0	1	1	0	0	0	0	5	0.0	−3	0	0.0	16:07									
	Houston Aeros	AHL	60	8	30	38	18										2	0	0	0	2				
	NHL Totals		**10**	**0**	**1**	**1**	**2**	**0**	**0**	**0**	**6**	**0.0**		**0**	**0.0**	**14:36**									

BCHL Second All-Star Team (1997) • BCHL Rookie of the Year Award (1997) • BCHL Playoff MVP Award (1997) • BCHL First All-Star Team (1998) • BCHL Best Defenseman Award (1998) • WCHA All-Rookie Team (2000) • WCHA First All-Star Team (2001) • NCAA West First All-American Team (2001) • NCAA Championship All-Tournament Team (2001)

Signed as a free agent by **Minnesota**, April 8, 2001. Signed as a free agent by **Atlanta**, July 14, 2004.

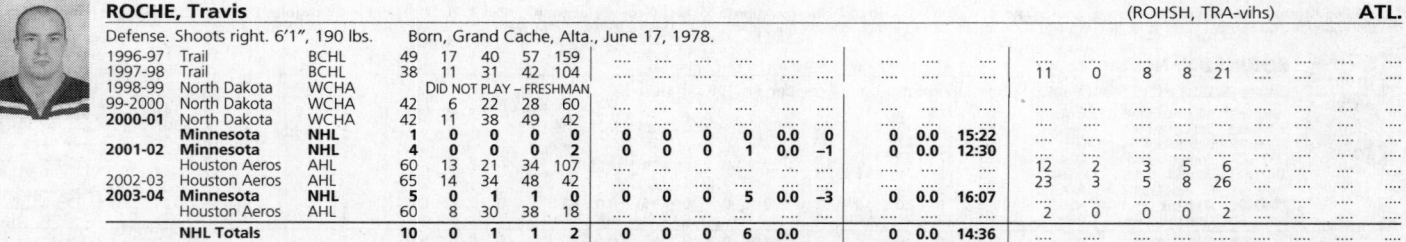

ROENICK, Jeremy
(ROH-nihk, JAIR-eh-mee) **PHI.**

Center. Shoots right. 6'1", 196 lbs. Born, Boston, MA, January 17, 1970. Chicago's 1st choice, 8th overall, in 1988 Entry Draft.

Season	Club	League	GP	G	A	Pts	PIM	PP	SH	GW	S	%	+/-	TF	F%	Min	GP	G	A	Pts	PIM	PP	SH	GW	Min
1986-87	Thayer Academy	Hi-School	24	31	34	65																			
1987-88	Thayer Academy	Hi-School	24	34	50	84																			
1988-89	Hull Olympiques	QMJHL	28	34	36	70	14																		
	Chicago	**NHL**	20	9	9	18	4	2	0	0	52	17.3	4				10	1	3	4	7	1	0	1	
1989-90	**Chicago**	**NHL**	78	26	40	66	54	6	0	4	173	15.0	2				20	11	7	18	8	4	0	1	
1990-91	**Chicago**	**NHL**	79	41	53	94	80	15	4	10	194	21.1	38				6	3	5	8	4	1	0	1	
1991-92	**Chicago**	**NHL**	80	53	50	103	98	22	3	13	234	22.6	23				18	12	10	22	12	4	0	3	
1992-93	**Chicago**	**NHL**	84	50	57	107	86	22	3	3	255	19.6	15				4	1	2	3	2	0	0	0	
1993-94	**Chicago**	**NHL**	84	46	61	107	125	24	5	5	281	16.4	21				6	1	6	7	2	0	0	1	
1994-95	Kolner Haie	Germany	3	3	1	4	2																		
	Chicago	**NHL**	33	10	24	34	14	5	0	1	93	10.8	5				8	1	2	3	16	0	0	0	
1995-96	**Chicago**	**NHL**	66	32	35	67	109	12	4	2	171	18.7	9				10	5	7	12	2	1	0	1	
1996-97	**Phoenix**	**NHL**	72	29	40	69	115	10	3	7	228	12.7	−7				6	2	4	6	4	0	0	0	
1997-98	**Phoenix**	**NHL**	79	24	32	56	103	6	1	3	182	13.2	5				6	5	3	8	4	2	2	2	
	United States	Olympics	4	0	1	1	6																		
1998-99	**Phoenix**	**NHL**	78	24	48	72	130	4	0	3	203	11.8	7	956	47.6	20:10	1	0	0	0	0	0	0	0	26:55
99-2000	**Phoenix**	**NHL**	75	34	44	78	102	6	3	12	192	17.7	11	925	50.1	20:51	5	2	2	4	10	1	0	0	19:46
2000-01	**Phoenix**	**NHL**	80	30	46	76	114	13	0	7	192	15.6	−1	888	49.1	21:00									
2001-02	**Philadelphia**	**NHL**	75	21	46	67	74	5	0	3	167	12.6	32	1329	49.1	18:14	5	0	0	0	14	0	0	0	18:41
	United States	Olympics	6	1	4	5	2																		
2002-03	**Philadelphia**	**NHL**	79	27	32	59	75	8	1	6	197	13.7	20	1088	53.0	18:48	13	3	5	8	8	0	0	1	21:07
2003-04	**Philadelphia**	**NHL**	62	19	28	47	62	10	1	1	128	14.8	1	846	51.5	17:37	18	4	9	13	8	2	0	1	18:05
	NHL Totals		**1124**	**475**	**645**	**1120**	**1345**	**170**	**28**	**80**	**2942**	**16.1**		**6032**	**50.1**	**19:31**	**136**	**51**	**65**	**116**	**101**	**16**	**2**	**12**	**19:30**

QMJHL Second All-Star Team (1989)

Played in NHL All-Star Game (1991, 1992, 1993, 1994, 1999, 2000, 2002, 2003, 2004)

Traded to **Phoenix** by **Chicago** for Alex Zhamnov, Craig Mills and Phoenix's 1st round choice (Ty Jones) in 1997 Entry Draft, August 16, 1996. Signed as a free agent by **Philadelphia**, July 2, 2001.

Season	Club	League	Regular Season GP	G	A	Pts	PIM	PP	SH	GW	S	%	+/-	TF	F%	Min	Playoffs GP	G	A	Pts	PIM	PP	SH	GW	Min

ROHLOFF, Todd

(ROH-lawf, TAWD)

Defense. Shoots left. 6'3", 213 lbs. Born, Grand Rapids, IL, January 16, 1974.

Season	Club	League	GP	G	A	Pts	PIM	PP	SH	GW	S	%	+/-	TF	F%	Min	GP	G	A	Pts	PIM	PP	SH	GW	Min
1992-93	St. Paul Vulcans	USHL	33	2	9	11	52	....	....	....	....	....	....	....	....	....	....	....	....	....	....	....	....	....	....
1993-94	St. Paul Vulcans	USHL	47	4	22	26	....	....	....	....	....	....	....	....	....	....	....	....	....	....	....	....	....	....	....
1994-95	Miami University	CCHA	38	1	6	7	22	....	....	....	....	....	....	....	....	....	....	....	....	....	....	....	....	....	....
1995-96	Miami University	CCHA	23	2	4	6	24	....	....	....	....	....	....	....	....	....	....	....	....	....	....	....	....	....	....
1996-97	Miami University	CCHA	38	2	12	14	48	....	....	....	....	....	....	....	....	....	....	....	....	....	....	....	....	....	....
1997-98	Miami University	CCHA	17	2	5	7	38	....	....	....	....	....	....	....	....	....	....	....	....	....	....	....	....	....	....
	Indianapolis Ice	IHL	5	0	1	1	6	....	....	....	....	....	....	....	....	....	1	0	0	0	0	....	....	....	....
1998-99	Portland Pirates	AHL	58	1	6	7	58	....	....	....	....	....	....	....	....	....	....	....	....	....	....	....	....	....	....
	Indianapolis Ice	IHL	12	2	0	2	8	....	....	....	....	....	....	....	....	....	5	1	1	2	6	....	....	....	....
99-2000	Cleveland	IHL	77	1	13	14	88	....	....	....	....	....	....	....	....	....	9	0	0	0	6	....	....	....	....
2000-01	Portland Pirates	AHL	58	3	8	11	59	....	....	....	....	....	....	....	....	....	3	0	0	0	2	....	....	....	....
2001-02	**Washington**	**NHL**	**16**	**0**	**1**	**1**	**14**	**0**	**0**	**0**	**6**	**0.0**	**–2**	**0**	**0.0**	**14:11**	....	....	....	....	....	....	....	....	....
	Portland Pirates	AHL	17	1	3	4	22	....	....	....	....	....	....	....	....	....	....	....	....	....	....	....	....	....	....
2002-03	Portland Pirates	AHL	64	2	10	12	65	....	....	....	....	....	....	....	....	....	3	0	0	0	2	....	....	....	....
2003-04	**Columbus**	**NHL**	**24**	**0**	**2**	**2**	**8**	**0**	**0**	**0**	**16**	**0.0**	**–12**	**2**	**50.0**	**19:15**	....	....	....	....	....	....	....	....	....
	Syracuse Crunch	AHL	14	1	5	6	16	....	....	....	....	....	....	....	....	....	....	....	....	....	....	....	....	....	....
	Washington	**NHL**	**35**	**0**	**3**	**3**	**18**	**0**	**0**	**0**	**19**	**0.0**	**–5**	**0**	**0.0**	**14:07**	....	....	....	....	....	....	....	....	....
	NHL Totals		**75**	**0**	**6**	**6**	**40**	**0**	**0**	**0**	**41**	**0.0**		**2**	**50.0**	**15:46**	....	....	....	....	....	....	....	....	....

Signed as a free agent by **Chicago**, March 24, 1998. Signed as a free agent by **Washington**, July 21, 2000. • Missed majority of 2001-02 season recovering from ankle injury suffered in off-season, September, 2001. Signed as a free agent by **Columbus**, September 5, 2003. Claimed on waivers by **Washington** from **Columbus**, January 9, 2004.

ROLSTON, Brian

(ROHL-stuhn, BRIGH-uhn) **MIN.**

Center/Right wing. Shoots left. 6'2", 210 lbs. Born, Flint, MI, February 21, 1973. New Jersey's 2nd choice, 11th overall, in 1991 Entry Draft.

Season	Club	League	GP	G	A	Pts	PIM	PP	SH	GW	S	%	+/-	TF	F%	Min	GP	G	A	Pts	PIM	PP	SH	GW	Min
1989-90	Det. Compuware	NAJHL	40	36	37	73	57	....	....	....	....	....	....	....	....	....	....	....	....	....	....	....	....	....	....
1990-91	Det. Compuware	NAJHL	36	49	46	95	14	....	....	....	....	....	....	....	....	....	....	....	....	....	....	....	....	....	....
1991-92	Lake Superior	CCHA	37	14	23	37	14	....	....	....	....	....	....	....	....	....	....	....	....	....	....	....	....	....	....
1992-93	Lake Superior	CCHA	39	33	31	64	20	....	....	....	....	....	....	....	....	....	....	....	....	....	....	....	....	....	....
1993-94	Team USA	Nat-Tm	41	20	28	48	36	....	....	....	....	....	....	....	....	....	....	....	....	....	....	....	....	....	....
	United States	Olympics	8	7	0	7	8	....	....	....	....	....	....	....	....	....	....	....	....	....	....	....	....	....	....
	Albany River Rats	AHL	17	5	5	10	8	....	....	....	....	....	....	....	....	....	5	1	2	3	0	....	....	....	....
1994-95	Albany River Rats	AHL	18	9	11	20	10	....	....	....	....	....	....	....	....	....	....	....	....	....	....	....	....	....	....
	♦ New Jersey	**NHL**	**40**	**7**	**11**	**18**	**17**	**2**	**0**	**3**	**92**	**7.6**	**5**	....	....	....	**6**	**2**	**1**	**3**	**4**	**1**	**0**	**0**	....
1995-96	**New Jersey**	**NHL**	**58**	**13**	**11**	**24**	**8**	**3**	**1**	**4**	**139**	**9.4**	**9**	....	....	....	....	....	....	....	....	....	....	....	....
1996-97	**New Jersey**	**NHL**	**81**	**18**	**27**	**45**	**20**	**2**	**2**	**3**	**237**	**7.6**	**6**	....	....	....	**10**	**4**	**1**	**5**	**6**	**1**	**2**	**0**	....
1997-98	**New Jersey**	**NHL**	**76**	**16**	**14**	**30**	**16**	**0**	**2**	**1**	**185**	**8.6**	**7**	....	....	....	**6**	**1**	**0**	**1**	**2**	**0**	**1**	**0**	....
1998-99	**New Jersey**	**NHL**	**82**	**24**	**33**	**57**	**14**	**5**	**5**	**3**	**210**	**11.4**	**11**	**51**	**45.1**	**18:49**	**7**	**1**	**0**	**1**	**2**	**0**	**1**	**0**	**17:36**
99-2000	**New Jersey**	**NHL**	**11**	**3**	**1**	**4**	**0**	**1**	**0**	**2**	**33**	**9.1**	**–2**	**37**	**37.8**	**19:09**	....	....	....	....	....	....	....	....	....
	Colorado	**NHL**	**50**	**8**	**10**	**18**	**12**	**1**	**0**	**3**	**107**	**7.5**	**–6**	**65**	**41.5**	**16:18**	....	....	....	....	....	....	....	....	....
	Boston	**NHL**	**16**	**5**	**4**	**9**	**6**	**3**	**0**	**1**	**66**	**7.6**	**–4**	**265**	**41.1**	**22:13**	....	....	....	....	....	....	....	....	....
2000-01	**Boston**	**NHL**	**77**	**19**	**39**	**58**	**28**	**5**	**0**	**4**	**286**	**6.6**	**6**	**666**	**45.7**	**19:19**	....	....	....	....	....	....	....	....	....
2001-02	**Boston**	**NHL**	**82**	**31**	**31**	**62**	**30**	**6**	**9**	**7**	**331**	**9.4**	**11**	**1289**	**46.6**	**20:24**	**6**	**4**	**1**	**5**	**0**	**1**	**1**	**0**	**20:37**
	United States	Olympics	6	0	3	3	0	....	....	....	....	....	....	....	....	....	....	....	....	....	....	....	....	....	....
2002-03	**Boston**	**NHL**	**81**	**27**	**32**	**59**	**32**	**6**	**5**	**5**	**281**	**9.6**	**1**	**1148**	**47.6**	**20:28**	**5**	**0**	**2**	**2**	**0**	**0**	**0**	**0**	**18:39**
2003-04	**Boston**	**NHL**	**82**	**19**	**29**	**48**	**40**	**3**	**2**	**3**	**257**	**7.4**	**9**	**1205**	**50.7**	**19:38**	**7**	**1**	**0**	**1**	**8**	**0**	**0**	**0**	**16:33**
	NHL Totals		**736**	**190**	**242**	**432**	**223**	**37**	**26**	**39**	**2224**	**8.5**		**4726**	**47.3**	**19:26**	**47**	**13**	**5**	**18**	**22**	**3**	**5**	**0**	**18:15**

NCAA Championship All-Tournament Team (1992, 1993) • CCHA First All-Star Team (1993) • NCAA West Second All-American Team (1993)

Traded to **Colorado** by **New Jersey** with New Jersey's 1st round choice (later traded to Boston – Boston selected Martin Samuelsson) in 2000 Entry Draft for Claude Lemieux and Colorado's 1st (David Hale) and 2nd (Matt DeMarchi) round choices in 2000 Entry Draft, November 3, 1999. Traded to **Boston** by **Colorado** with Martin Grenier, Samuel Pahlsson and New Jersey's 1st round choice (previously acquired, Boston selected Martin Samuelsson) in 2000 Entry Draft for Raymond Bourque and Dave Andreychuk, March 6, 2000. Signed as a free agent by **Minnesota**, July 8, 2004.

RONNING, Cliff

(RAWN-ihng, KLIHF)

Center. Shoots left. 5'8", 165 lbs. Born, Burnaby, B.C., October 1, 1965. St. Louis' 9th choice, 134th overall, in 1984 Entry Draft.

Season	Club	League	GP	G	A	Pts	PIM	PP	SH	GW	S	%	+/-	TF	F%	Min	GP	G	A	Pts	PIM	PP	SH	GW	Min
1982-83	New Westminster	BCJHL	52	83	68	151	22	....	....	....	....	....	....	....	....	....	....	....	....	....	....	....	....	....	....
1983-84	New Westminster	WHL	71	69	67	136	10	....	....	....	....	....	....	....	....	....	9	8	13	21	10	....	....	....	....
1984-85	New Westminster	WHL	70	*89	108	*197	20	....	....	....	....	....	....	....	....	....	11	10	14	24	4	....	....	....	....
1985-86	Team Canada	Nat-Tm	71	*55	*63	*118	53	....	....	....	....	....	....	....	....	....	....	....	....	....	....	....	....	....	....
	St. Louis	**NHL**	....	....	....	....	....	....	....	....	....	....	....	....	....	....	**5**	**1**	**1**	**2**	**2**	**1**	**0**	**0**	....
1986-87	Team Canada	Nat-Tm	26	17	16	33	12	....	....	....	....	....	....	....	....	....	....	....	....	....	....	....	....	....	....
	St. Louis	**NHL**	**42**	**11**	**14**	**25**	**6**	**2**	**0**	**2**	**68**	**16.2**	**–1**	....	....	....	**4**	**0**	**1**	**1**	**0**	**0**	**0**	**0**	....
1987-88	**St. Louis**	**NHL**	**26**	**5**	**8**	**13**	**12**	**1**	**0**	**1**	**38**	**13.2**	**6**	....	....	....	....	....	....	....	....	....	....	....	....
1988-89	**St. Louis**	**NHL**	**64**	**24**	**31**	**55**	**18**	**16**	**0**	**1**	**150**	**16.0**	**3**	....	....	....	**7**	**1**	**3**	**4**	**0**	**1**	**0**	**0**	....
	Peoria Rivermen	IHL	12	11	20	31	8	....	....	....	....	....	....	....	....	....	....	....	....	....	....	....	....	....	....
1989-90	HC Asiago	Italy	36	67	49	116	25	....	....	....	....	....	....	....	....	....	6	7	12	19	4	....	....	....	....
1990-91	**St. Louis**	**NHL**	**48**	**14**	**18**	**32**	**10**	**5**	**0**	**2**	**81**	**17.3**	**2**	....	....	....	....	....	....	....	....	....	....	....	....
	Vancouver	**NHL**	**11**	**6**	**6**	**12**	**0**	**2**	**0**	**0**	**32**	**18.8**	**–2**	....	....	....	**6**	**6**	**3**	**9**	**12**	**2**	**0**	**2**	....
1991-92	**Vancouver**	**NHL**	**80**	**24**	**47**	**71**	**42**	**6**	**0**	**2**	**216**	**11.1**	**18**	....	....	....	**13**	**8**	**5**	**13**	**6**	**1**	**0**	**1**	....
1992-93	**Vancouver**	**NHL**	**79**	**29**	**56**	**85**	**30**	**10**	**0**	**2**	**209**	**13.9**	**19**	....	....	....	**12**	**2**	**9**	**11**	**6**	**0**	**0**	**0**	....
1993-94	**Vancouver**	**NHL**	**76**	**25**	**43**	**68**	**42**	**10**	**0**	**4**	**197**	**12.7**	**7**	....	....	....	**24**	**5**	**10**	**15**	**16**	**2**	**0**	**2**	....
1994-95	**Vancouver**	**NHL**	**41**	**6**	**19**	**25**	**27**	**3**	**0**	**2**	**93**	**6.5**	**–4**	....	....	....	**11**	**3**	**5**	**8**	**2**	**1**	**0**	**2**	....
1995-96	**Vancouver**	**NHL**	**79**	**22**	**45**	**67**	**42**	**5**	**0**	**1**	**187**	**11.8**	**16**	....	....	....	**6**	**0**	**2**	**2**	**6**	**0**	**0**	**0**	....
1996-97	**Phoenix**	**NHL**	**69**	**19**	**32**	**51**	**26**	**8**	**0**	**2**	**171**	**11.1**	**–9**	....	....	....	**7**	**0**	**7**	**7**	**12**	**0**	**0**	**0**	....
1997-98	**Phoenix**	**NHL**	**80**	**11**	**44**	**55**	**36**	**3**	**0**	**0**	**197**	**5.6**	**5**	....	....	....	**6**	**1**	**3**	**4**	**4**	**0**	**0**	**0**	....
1998-99	**Phoenix**	**NHL**	**7**	**2**	**5**	**7**	**2**	**2**	**0**	**1**	**18**	**11.1**	**3**	**81**	**51.9**	**15:22**	....	....	....	....	....	....	....	....	....
	Nashville	**NHL**	**72**	**18**	**35**	**53**	**40**	**8**	**0**	**3**	**239**	**7.5**	**–6**	**1129**	**47.7**	**19:42**	....	....	....	....	....	....	....	....	....
99-2000	**Nashville**	**NHL**	**82**	**26**	**36**	**62**	**34**	**7**	**0**	**2**	**248**	**10.5**	**–13**	**611**	**45.7**	**18:11**	....	....	....	....	....	....	....	....	....
2000-01	**Nashville**	**NHL**	**80**	**19**	**43**	**62**	**28**	**6**	**0**	**4**	**237**	**8.0**	**4**	**331**	**45.0**	**17:23**	....	....	....	....	....	....	....	....	....
2001-02	**Nashville**	**NHL**	**67**	**18**	**31**	**49**	**24**	**4**	**0**	**0**	**164**	**11.0**	**0**	**98**	**51.0**	**16:44**	....	....	....	....	....	....	....	....	....
	Los Angeles	**NHL**	**14**	**1**	**4**	**5**	**8**	**1**	**0**	**0**	**35**	**2.9**	**0**	**14**	**50.0**	**16:53**	**4**	**0**	**1**	**1**	**2**	**0**	**0**	**0**	**11:09**
2002-03	**Minnesota**	**NHL**	**80**	**17**	**31**	**48**	**24**	**8**	**0**	**5**	**171**	**9.9**	**–6**	**566**	**47.0**	**17:25**	**17**	**2**	**7**	**9**	**4**	**1**	**0**	**0**	**16:39**
2003-04	**NY Islanders**	**NHL**	**40**	**9**	**15**	**24**	**2**	**2**	**0**	**0**	**55**	**16.4**	**3**	**174**	**45.4**	**11:56**	**4**	**0**	**0**	**0**	**0**	**0**	**0**	**0**	**5:44**
	NHL Totals		**1137**	**306**	**563**	**869**	**453**	**109**	**0**	**34**	**2806**	**10.9**		**3004**	**47.0**	**17:16**	**126**	**29**	**57**	**86**	**72**	**9**	**0**	**7**	**14:01**

WHL Rookie of the Year (1984) • WHL West First All-Star Team (1985) • WHL MVP (1985)

Traded to **Vancouver** by **St. Louis** with Geoff Courtnall, Robert Dirk, Sergio Momesso and St. Louis' 5th round choice (Brian Loney) in 1992 Entry Draft for Dan Quinn and Garth Butcher, March 5, 1991. Signed as a free agent by **Phoenix**, July 1, 1996. Traded to **Nashville** by **Phoenix** with Richard Lintner for future considerations, October 31, 1998. Traded to **Los Angeles** by **Nashville** for Jere Karalahti and Los Angeles' 4th round choice (Teemu Lassila) in 2003 Entry Draft, March 16, 2002. Traded to **Minnesota** by **Los Angeles** for Minnesota's 4th round choice (Aaron Rome) in 2002 Entry Draft, June 22, 2002. Signed as a free agent by **NY Islanders**, January 9, 2004.

ROSA, Pavel

(ROHZA, PAH-vehl)

Right wing. Shoots right. 5'11", 188 lbs. Born, Most, Czech., June 7, 1977. Los Angeles' 3rd choice, 50th overall, in 1995 Entry Draft.

Season	Club	League	GP	G	A	Pts	PIM	PP	SH	GW	S	%	+/-	TF	F%	Min	GP	G	A	Pts	PIM	PP	SH	GW	Min
1994-95	Litvinov Jr.	Czech-Jr.	40	56	42	98	....	....	....	....	....	....	....	....	....	....	....	....	....	....	....	....	....	....	....
	Litvinov	Czech	2	0	0	0	0	....	....	....	....	....	....	....	....	....	1	0	0	0	0	....	....	....	....
1995-96	Hull Olympiques	QMJHL	61	46	70	116	39	....	....	....	....	....	....	....	....	....	18	14	22	36	25	....	....	....	....
1996-97	Hull Olympiques	QMJHL	68	*63	*90	*153	66	....	....	....	....	....	....	....	....	....	14	18	13	31	16	....	....	....	....
1997-98	Fredericton	AHL	1	0	0	0	0	....	....	....	....	....	....	....	....	....	....	....	....	....	....	....	....	....	....
	Long Beach	IHL	2	0	1	1	0	....	....	....	....	....	....	....	....	....	1	1	1	2	0	....	....	....	....
1998-99	**Los Angeles**	**NHL**	**29**	**4**	**12**	**16**	**6**	**0**	**0**	**0**	**61**	**6.6**	**0**	**0**	**0.0**	**13:34**	....	....	....	....	....	....	....	....	....
	Long Beach	IHL	31	17	13	30	28	....	....	....	....	....	....	....	....	....	6	1	2	3	0	....	....	....	....
99-2000	**Los Angeles**	**NHL**	**3**	**0**	**0**	**0**	**0**	**0**	**0**	**0**	**1**	**0.0**	**–1**	**0**	**0.0**	**11:21**	....	....	....	....	....	....	....	....	....
	Long Beach	IHL	74	22	31	53	76	....	....	....	....	....	....	....	....	....	6	2	2	4	4	....	....	....	....
2000-01	HPK Hameenlinna	Finland	54	25	25	50	53	....	....	....	....	....	....	....	....	....	....	....	....	....	....	....	....	....	....
2001-02	Jokerit Helsinki	Finland	46	21	22	43	37	....	....	....	....	....	....	....	....	....	12	3	5	8	18	....	....	....	....
2002-03	**Los Angeles**	**NHL**	**2**	**0**	**0**	**0**	**0**	**0**	**0**	**0**	**4**	**0.0**	**–1**	**0**	**0.0**	**13:57**	....	....	....	....	....	....	....	....	....
	Manchester	AHL	61	28	35	63	20	....	....	....	....	....	....	....	....	....	3	3	1	4	4	....	....	....	....

			Regular Season														Playoffs								
Season	Club	League	GP	G	A	Pts	PIM	PP	SH	GW	S	%	+/-	TF	F%	Min	GP	G	A	Pts	PIM	PP	SH	GW	Min
2003-04	**Los Angeles**	**NHL**	**2**	**1**	**1**	**2**	**0**	**0**	**0**	**0**	**4**	**25.0**	**1**	**0**	**0.0**	**12:41**	....	....	....	....	....	....	....	....	....
	Manchester	AHL	77	39	49	*88	32	....	....	....	....	....	....	....	....	....	6	3	6	9	6	....	....	....	....
	NHL Totals		**36**	**5**	**13**	**18**	**6**	**0**	**0**	**0**	**70**	**7.1**		**0**	**0.0**	**13:21**	....	....	....	....	....	....	....	....	....

QMJHL All-Rookie Team (1996) • QMJHL Offensive Rookie of the Year (1996) • QMJHL First All-Star Team (1997) • Canadian Major Junior First All-Star Team (1997) • AHL Second All-Star Team (2004) • Won John P. Sollenger Trophy (Top Scorer - AHL) (2004)

• Missed majority of 1997-98 season recovering from head injury suffered in training camp, September, 1997. Signed as a free agent by **Dynamo Moscow** (Russia), May 4, 2004.

ROSSITER, Kyle

(RAWS-ih-tuhr, KIGHL) **ATL.**

Defense. Shoots left. 6'3", 220 lbs. Born, Edmonton, Alta., June 9, 1980. Florida's 1st choice, 30th overall, in 1998 Entry Draft.

1995-96	Edmonton SSAC	AMHL	34	5	19	24	116	....	....	....	....	....	....	....	....	....	....	....	....	....	....	....	....	....	....
1996-97	Spokane Chiefs	WHL	50	0	2	2	65	....	....	....	....	....	....	....	....	....	9	0	0	0	6	....	....	....	....
1997-98	Spokane Chiefs	WHL	61	6	16	22	190	....	....	....	....	....	....	....	....	....	15	0	3	3	28	....	....	....	....
1998-99	Spokane Chiefs	WHL	71	4	17	21	206	....	....	....	....	....	....	....	....	....	....	....	....	....	....	....	....	....	....
99-2000	Spokane Chiefs	WHL	63	11	22	33	155	....	....	....	....	....	....	....	....	....	15	1	4	5	25	....	....	....	....
2000-01	Louisville Panthers	AHL	78	2	5	7	110	....	....	....	....	....	....	....	....	....	....	....	....	....	....	....	....	....	....
2001-02	**Florida**	**NHL**	**2**	**0**	**0**	**0**	**2**	**0**	**0**	**0**	**0**	**0.0**	**–1**	**0**	**0.0**	**15:27**	....	....	....	....	....	....	....	....	....
	Utah Grizzlies	AHL	74	3	7	10	88	....	....	....	....	....	....	....	....	....	5	0	1	1	0	....	....	....	....
2002-03	**Florida**	**NHL**	**3**	**0**	**0**	**0**	**0**	**0**	**0**	**0**	**0**	**0.0**	**–2**	**0**	**0.0**	**10:09**	....	....	....	....	....	....	....	....	....
	San Antonio	AHL	67	0	7	7	107	....	....	....	....	....	....	....	....	....	3	0	0	0	0	....	....	....	....
2003-04	**Florida**	**NHL**	**4**	**0**	**0**	**0**	**7**	**0**	**0**	**0**	**1**	**0.0**	**–1**	**0**	**0.0**	**11:55**	....	....	....	....	....	....	....	....	....
	San Antonio	AHL	51	5	7	12	70	....	....	....	....	....	....	....	....	....	....	....	....	....	....	....	....	....	....
	Atlanta	**NHL**	**2**	**0**	**1**	**1**	**0**	**0**	**0**	**0**	**0**	**0.0**	**1**	**0**	**0.0**	**10:14**	....	....	....	....	....	....	....	....	....
	Chicago Wolves	AHL	12	0	1	1	25	....	....	....	....	....	....	....	....	....	6	0	0	0	19	....	....	....	....
	NHL Totals		**11**	**0**	**1**	**1**	**9**	**0**	**0**	**0**	**1**	**0.0**		**0**	**0.0**	**11:46**	....	....	....	....	....	....	....	....	....

Canadian Major Junior Scholastic Player of the Year (1998)

Traded to **Atlanta** by **Florida** for Kamil Piros, March 8, 2004.

ROURKE, Allan

(RAWRK, AL-lan) **CAR.**

Defense. Shoots left. 6'1", 214 lbs. Born, Mississauga, Ont., March 6, 1980. Toronto's 6th choice, 154th overall, in 1998 Entry Draft.

1995-96	Mississauga Reps	MTHL	38	15	25	40	173	....	....	....	....	....	....	....	....	....	....	....	....	....	....	....	....	....	....
1996-97	Kitchener Rangers	OHL	25	1	1	2	12	....	....	....	....	....	....	....	....	....	6	0	0	0	0	....	....	....	....
1997-98	Kitchener Rangers	OHL	48	5	17	22	59	....	....	....	....	....	....	....	....	....	6	1	1	2	6	....	....	....	....
1998-99	Kitchener Rangers	OHL	66	11	28	39	79	....	....	....	....	....	....	....	....	....	1	0	0	0	2	....	....	....	....
99-2000	Kitchener Rangers	OHL	67	31	43	74	57	....	....	....	....	....	....	....	....	....	5	0	6	6	13	....	....	....	....
2000-01	St. John's	AHL	64	9	19	28	36	....	....	....	....	....	....	....	....	....	....	....	....	....	....	....	....	....	....
2001-02	St. John's	AHL	62	2	9	11	48	....	....	....	....	....	....	....	....	....	10	0	2	2	6	....	....	....	....
2002-03	St. John's	AHL	65	12	19	31	49	....	....	....	....	....	....	....	....	....	....	....	....	....	....	....	....	....	....
2003-04	**Carolina**	**NHL**	**25**	**1**	**2**	**3**	**22**	**0**	**0**	**0**	**24**	**4.2**	**4**	**0**	**0.0**	**12:28**	....	....	....	....	....	....	....	....	....
	Lowell	AHL	45	5	9	14	45	....	....	....	....	....	....	....	....	....	....	....	....	....	....	....	....	....	....
	NHL Totals		**25**	**1**	**2**	**3**	**22**	**0**	**0**	**0**	**24**	**4.2**		**0**	**0.0**	**12:28**	....	....	....	....	....	....	....	....	....

OHL Second All-Star Team (2000)

Traded to **Carolina** by **Toronto** for Harold Druken, May 29, 2003.

ROY, Andre

(WAH, AHN-dray) **T.B.**

Right wing. Shoots left. 6'4", 221 lbs. Born, Port Chester, NY, February 8, 1975. Boston's 5th choice, 151st overall, in 1994 Entry Draft.

1992-93	Nord Selects	QAHA	STATISTICS NOT AVAILABLE																						
1993-94	Goulbourn Royals	OJHL-C	9	9	13	22	98	....	....	....	....	....	....	....	....	....	....	....	....	....	....	....	....	....	....
	Beauport	QMJHL	33	6	7	13	125	....	....	....	....	....	....	....	....	....	....	....	....	....	....	....	....	....	....
	Chicoutimi	QMJHL	32	4	14	18	152	....	....	....	....	....	....	....	....	....	25	3	6	9	94	....	....	....	....
1994-95	Chicoutimi	QMJHL	20	15	8	23	90	....	....	....	....	....	....	....	....	....	....	....	....	....	....	....	....	....	....
	Drummondville	QMJHL	34	18	13	31	233	....	....	....	....	....	....	....	....	....	4	2	0	2	34	....	....	....	....
1995-96	**Boston**	**NHL**	**3**	**0**	**0**	**0**	**0**	**0**	**0**	**0**	**0**	**0.0**	**0**	....	....	....	....	....	....	....	....	....	....	....	....
	Providence Bruins	AHL	58	7	8	15	167	....	....	....	....	....	....	....	....	....	1	0	0	0	10	....	....	....	....
1996-97	**Boston**	**NHL**	**10**	**0**	**2**	**2**	**12**	**0**	**0**	**0**	**12**	**0.0**	**–5**	....	....	....	....	....	....	....	....	....	....	....	....
	Providence Bruins	AHL	50	17	11	28	234	....	....	....	....	....	....	....	....	....	....	....	....	....	....	....	....	....	....
1997-98	Providence Bruins	AHL	36	3	11	14	154	....	....	....	....	....	....	....	....	....	....	....	....	....	....	....	....	....	....
	Charlotte	ECHL	27	10	8	18	132	....	....	....	....	....	....	....	....	....	7	2	3	5	34	....	....	....	....
1998-99	Fort Wayne	IHL	65	15	6	21	*395	....	....	....	....	....	....	....	....	....	2	0	0	0	11	....	....	....	....
99-2000	**Ottawa**	**NHL**	**73**	**4**	**3**	**7**	**145**	**0**	**0**	**1**	**39**	**10.3**	**3**	**3**	**33.3**	**6:29**	**5**	**0**	**0**	**0**	**2**	**0**	**0**	**0**	**5:54**
2000-01	**Ottawa**	**NHL**	**64**	**3**	**5**	**8**	**169**	**0**	**0**	**0**	**33**	**9.1**	**1**	**2**	**50.0**	**4:36**	**2**	**0**	**0**	**0**	**16**	**0**	**0**	**0**	**4:16**
2001-02	**Ottawa**	**NHL**	**56**	**6**	**8**	**14**	**148**	**0**	**0**	**0**	**60**	**10.0**	**3**	**1**	**100.0**	**8:23**	....	....	....	....	....	....	....	....	....
	Tampa Bay	**NHL**	**9**	**1**	**1**	**2**	**63**	**0**	**0**	**0**	**6**	**16.7**	**–5**	**0**	**0.0**	**8:58**	....	....	....	....	....	....	....	....	....
2002-03	**Tampa Bay**	**NHL**	**62**	**10**	**7**	**17**	**119**	**0**	**0**	**2**	**85**	**11.8**	**0**	**7**	**57.1**	**10:46**	**5**	**0**	**1**	**1**	**2**	**0**	**0**	**0**	**12:31**
2003-04♦	**Tampa Bay**	**NHL**	**33**	**1**	**1**	**2**	**78**	**0**	**0**	**0**	**24**	**4.2**	**–5**	**2**	**50.0**	**7:52**	**21**	**1**	**2**	**3**	**61**	**0**	**0**	**1**	**6:11**
	NHL Totals		**310**	**25**	**27**	**52**	**734**	**0**	**0**	**3**	**259**	**9.7**		**15**	**53.3**	**7:33**	**33**	**1**	**3**	**4**	**81**	**0**	**0**	**1**	**6:59**

Signed as a free agent by **Ottawa**, April 28, 1999. Traded to **Tampa Bay** by **Ottawa** with Ottawa's 6th round choice (Paul Ranger) in 2002 Entry Draft for Juha Ylonen, March 15, 2002. • Spent majority of 2003-04 season as a healthy reserve.

ROY, Derek

(ROI, DAIR-ihk) **BUF.**

Center. Shoots left. 5'9", 186 lbs. Born, Ottawa, Ont., May 4, 1983. Buffalo's 2nd choice, 32nd overall, in 2001 Entry Draft.

1998-99	Ontario East	OMHA	34	61	31	92	42	....	....	....	....	....	....	....	....	....	....	....	....	....	....	....	....	....	....
99-2000	Kitchener Rangers	OHL	66	34	53	87	44	....	....	....	....	....	....	....	....	....	5	4	1	5	6	....	....	....	....
2000-01	Kitchener Rangers	OHL	65	42	39	81	114	....	....	....	....	....	....	....	....	....	....	....	....	....	....	....	....	....	....
2001-02	Kitchener Rangers	OHL	62	43	46	89	92	....	....	....	....	....	....	....	....	....	4	1	2	3	2	....	....	....	....
2002-03	Kitchener Rangers	OHL	49	28	50	78	73	....	....	....	....	....	....	....	....	....	21	9	*23	32	14	....	....	....	....
2003-04	**Buffalo**	**NHL**	**49**	**9**	**10**	**19**	**12**	**1**	**0**	**4**	**71**	**12.7**	**–8**	**715**	**47.4**	**15:19**	....	....	....	....	....	....	....	....	....
	Rochester	AHL	26	10	16	26	20	....	....	....	....	....	....	....	....	....	16	6	8	14	18	....	....	....	....
	NHL Totals		**49**	**9**	**10**	**19**	**12**	**1**	**0**	**4**	**71**	**12.7**		**715**	**47.4**	**15:19**	....	....	....	....	....	....	....	....	....

OHL All-Rookie Team (2000) • OHL Rookie of the Year (2000) • CHL All-Rookie Team (2000) • CHL Plus/Minus Award (2000) • CHL Most Sportsmanlike Playerr (2000) • Memorial Cup All-Star Team (2003) • Stafford Smythe Memorial Trophy (Memorial Cup MVP) (2003)

ROZSIVAL, Michal

(roh-ZIH-vahl, MEE-khahl) **PIT.**

Defense. Shoots right. 6'1", 212 lbs. Born, Vlasim, Czech., September 3, 1978. Pittsburgh's 5th choice, 105th overall, in 1996 Entry Draft.

1994-95	Dukla Jihlava Jr.	Czech-Jr.	31	8	13	21	....	....	....	....	....	....	....	....	....	....	....	....	....	....	....	....	....	....	....
1995-96	HC Dukla Jihlava	Czech	36	3	4	7	....	....	....	....	....	....	....	....	....	....	....	....	....	....	....	....	....	....	....
1996-97	Swift Current	WHL	63	8	31	39	80	....	....	....	....	....	....	....	....	....	10	0	6	6	15	....	....	....	....
1997-98	Swift Current	WHL	71	14	55	69	122	....	....	....	....	....	....	....	....	....	12	0	5	5	33	....	....	....	....
1998-99	Syracuse Crunch	AHL	49	3	22	25	72	....	....	....	....	....	....	....	....	....	....	....	....	....	....	....	....	....	....
99-2000	**Pittsburgh**	**NHL**	**75**	**4**	**17**	**21**	**48**	**1**	**0**	**1**	**73**	**5.5**	**11**	**1**	**0.0**	**19:01**	**2**	**0**	**0**	**0**	**4**	**0**	**0**	**0**	**30:56**
2000-01	**Pittsburgh**	**NHL**	**30**	**1**	**4**	**5**	**26**	**0**	**0**	**0**	**17**	**5.9**	**3**	**1**	**100.0**	**17:06**	....	....	....	....	....	....	....	....	....
	Wilkes-Barre	AHL	29	8	8	16	32	....	....	....	....	....	....	....	....	....	21	3	*19	22	23	....	....	....	....
2001-02	**Pittsburgh**	**NHL**	**79**	**9**	**20**	**29**	**47**	**4**	**0**	**4**	**89**	**10.1**	**–6**	**0**	**0.0**	**20:01**	....	....	....	....	....	....	....	....	....
2002-03	**Pittsburgh**	**NHL**	**53**	**4**	**6**	**10**	**40**	**1**	**0**	**0**	**61**	**6.6**	**–5**	**0**	**0.0**	**20:25**	....	....	....	....	....	....	....	....	....
2003-04	Wilkes-Barre	AHL	1	0	0	0	2	....	....	....	....	....	....	....	....	....	....	....	....	....	....	....	....	....	....
	NHL Totals		**237**	**18**	**47**	**65**	**161**	**6**	**0**	**5**	**240**	**7.5**		**2**	**50.0**	**19:25**	**2**	**0**	**0**	**0**	**4**	**0**	**0**	**0**	**30:56**

WHL East First All-Star Team (1998)

• Missed majority of 2003-04 season recovering from knee injury suffered in training camp, September 18, 2003.

RUCCHIN, Steve

(ROO-chihn, STEEV) **ANA.**

Center. Shoots left. 6'2", 211 lbs. Born, Thunder Bay, Ont., July 4, 1971. Anaheim's 1st choice, 2nd overall, in 1994 Supplemental Draft.

Season	Club	League	Regular Season GP	G	A	Pts	PIM	PP	SH	GW	S	%	+/-	TF	F%	Min	Playoffs GP	G	A	Pts	PIM	PP	SH	GW	Min
1989-90	Banting High	Hi-School	STATISTICS NOT AVAILABLE																						
	Thamesford	OJHL-D	2	1	2	3	0																		
1990-91	Western Ontario	OUAA	34	13	16	29	14																		
1991-92	Western Ontario	OUAA	37	28	34	62	36																		
1992-93	Western Ontario	OUAA	34	22	26	48	16																		
1993-94	Western Ontario	OUAA	35	30	23	53	30																		
1994-95	San Diego Gulls	IHL	41	11	15	26	14																		
	Anaheim	**NHL**	**43**	**6**	**11**	**17**	**23**	**0**	**0**	**1**	**59**	**10.2**	**7**												
1995-96	**Anaheim**	**NHL**	**64**	**19**	**25**	**44**	**12**	**8**	**1**	**4**	**113**	**16.8**	**3**												
1996-97	**Anaheim**	**NHL**	**79**	**19**	**48**	**67**	**24**	**6**	**1**	**2**	**153**	**12.4**	**26**				**8**	**1**	**2**	**3**	**10**	**0**	**0**	**0**	
1997-98	**Anaheim**	**NHL**	**72**	**17**	**36**	**53**	**13**	**8**	**1**	**3**	**131**	**13.0**	**8**												
1998-99	**Anaheim**	**NHL**	**69**	**23**	**39**	**62**	**22**	**5**	**1**	**5**	**145**	**15.9**	**11**	**1845**	**52.3**	**22:33**	**4**	**0**	**3**	**3**	**0**	**0**	**0**	**0**	**21:55**
99-2000	**Anaheim**	**NHL**	**71**	**19**	**38**	**57**	**16**	**10**	**0**	**2**	**131**	**14.5**	**9**	**1996**	**53.4**	**22:12**									
2000-01	**Anaheim**	**NHL**	**16**	**3**	**5**	**8**	**0**	**2**	**0**	**0**	**19**	**15.8**	**–5**	**289**	**51.6**	**18:47**									
2001-02	**Anaheim**	**NHL**	**38**	**7**	**16**	**23**	**6**	**4**	**0**	**1**	**57**	**12.3**	**–3**	**808**	**52.2**	**19:17**									
2002-03	**Anaheim**	**NHL**	**82**	**20**	**38**	**58**	**12**	**6**	**1**	**4**	**194**	**10.3**	**–14**	**1613**	**54.2**	**21:05**	**21**	**7**	**3**	**10**	**2**	**1**	**0**	**2**	**23:35**
2003-04	**Anaheim**	**NHL**	**82**	**20**	**23**	**43**	**12**	**9**	**1**	**1**	**148**	**13.5**	**–14**	**1446**	**53.6**	**19:46**									
	NHL Totals		**616**	**153**	**279**	**432**	**140**	**58**	**6**	**23**	**1150**	**13.3**		**7997**	**53.2**	**21:00**	**33**	**8**	**8**	**16**	**12**	**1**	**0**	**2**	**23:19**

• Missed majority of 2000-01 season recovering from jaw injury suffered in game vs. Colorado, November 15, 2000. • Missed majority of 2001-02 season recovering from leg injury suffered in game vs. San Jose, November 16, 2001.

RUCINSKY, Martin

(roo-CHIHN-skee, MAHR-tihn)

Left wing. Shoots left. 6'1", 205 lbs. Born, Most, Czech., March 11, 1971. Edmonton's 2nd choice, 20th overall, in 1991 Entry Draft.

Season	Club	League	Regular Season GP	G	A	Pts	PIM	PP	SH	GW	S	%	+/-	TF	F%	Min	Playoffs GP	G	A	Pts	PIM	PP	SH	GW	Min
1988-89	CHZ Litvinov	Czech	3	1	0	1	2																		
1989-90	CHZ Litvinov	Czech	39	12	6	18											8	5	3	8					
1990-91	CHZ Litvinov	Czech	56	24	20	44	69																		
1991-92	**Edmonton**	**NHL**	**2**	**0**	**0**	**0**	**0**	**0**	**0**	**0**	**1**	**0.0**	**–3**												
	Cape Breton	AHL	35	11	12	23	34																		
	Quebec	**NHL**	**4**	**1**	**1**	**2**	**2**	**0**	**0**	**0**	**4**	**25.0**	**1**												
	Halifax Citadels	AHL	7	1	1	2	6																		
1992-93	**Quebec**	**NHL**	**77**	**18**	**30**	**48**	**51**	**4**	**0**	**1**	**133**	**13.5**	**16**				**6**	**1**	**1**	**2**	**4**	**1**	**0**	**0**	
1993-94	**Quebec**	**NHL**	**60**	**9**	**23**	**32**	**58**	**4**	**0**	**1**	**96**	**9.4**	**4**												
1994-95	Litvinov	Czech	13	12	10	22	54																		
	Quebec	**NHL**	**20**	**3**	**6**	**9**	**14**	**0**	**0**	**0**	**32**	**9.4**	**5**												
1995-96	HC Petra Vsetin	Czech	1	1	1	2	0																		
	Colorado	**NHL**	**22**	**4**	**11**	**15**	**14**	**0**	**0**	**1**	**39**	**10.3**	**10**												
	Montreal	**NHL**	**56**	**25**	**35**	**60**	**54**	**9**	**2**	**3**	**142**	**17.6**	**8**												
1996-97	**Montreal**	**NHL**	**70**	**28**	**27**	**55**	**62**	**6**	**3**	**3**	**172**	**16.3**	**1**				**5**	**0**	**0**	**0**	**4**	**0**	**0**	**0**	
1997-98	**Montreal**	**NHL**	**78**	**21**	**32**	**53**	**84**	**5**	**3**	**3**	**192**	**10.9**	**13**				**10**	**3**	**0**	**3**	**4**	**1**	**0**	**0**	
	Czech Republic	Olympics	6	3	1	4	4																		
1998-99	Litvinov	Czech	3	2	2	4	0																		
	Montreal	**NHL**	**73**	**17**	**17**	**34**	**50**	**5**	**0**	**1**	**180**	**9.4**	**–25**	**12**	**50.0**	**18:12**									
99-2000	**Montreal**	**NHL**	**80**	**25**	**24**	**49**	**70**	**7**	**1**	**4**	**242**	**10.3**	**1**	**31**	**54.8**	**18:54**									
2000-01	**Montreal**	**NHL**	**57**	**16**	**22**	**38**	**66**	**5**	**1**	**4**	**141**	**11.3**	**–5**	**5**	**40.0**	**19:11**									
2001-02	**Montreal**	**NHL**	**18**	**2**	**6**	**8**	**12**	**1**	**0**	**0**	**41**	**4.9**	**–1**	**5**	**80.0**	**16:15**									
	Dallas	**NHL**	**42**	**6**	**11**	**17**	**24**	**2**	**0**	**1**	**63**	**9.5**	**3**	**7**	**57.1**	**14:33**									
	Czech Republic	Olympics	4	0	3	3	2																		
	NY Rangers	**NHL**	**15**	**3**	**10**	**13**	**6**	**0**	**0**	**1**	**24**	**12.5**	**6**	**3**	**33.3**	**16:39**									
2002-03	Litvinov	Czech	2	1	0	1	2																		
	St. Louis	**NHL**	**61**	**16**	**14**	**30**	**38**	**4**	**4**	**3**	**135**	**11.9**	**–1**	**19**	**57.9**	**16:55**	**7**	**4**	**2**	**6**	**4**	**0**	**0**	**0**	**16:52**
2003-04	**NY Rangers**	**NHL**	**69**	**13**	**29**	**42**	**62**	**0**	**1**	**2**	**161**	**8.1**	**13**	**14**	**14.3**	**18:51**									
	Vancouver	**NHL**	**13**	**1**	**2**	**3**	**10**	**0**	**0**	**0**	**45**	**2.2**	**2**	**2**	**0.0**	**19:03**	**7**	**1**	**1**	**2**	**6**	**1**	**0**	**0**	**17:02**
	NHL Totals		**817**	**208**	**300**	**508**	**677**	**52**	**15**	**28**	**1843**	**11.3**		**98**	**48.0**	**17:55**	**35**	**9**	**4**	**13**	**22**	**3**	**0**	**0**	**16:57**

Played in NHL All-Star Game (2000)

Traded to **Quebec** by **Edmonton** for Ron Tugnutt and Brad Zavisha, March 10, 1992. Transferred to **Colorado** after **Quebec** franchise relocated, June 21, 1995. Traded to **Montreal** by **Colorado** with Andrei Kovalenko and Jocelyn Thibault for Patrick Roy and Mike Keane, December 6, 1995. Traded to **Dallas** by **Montreal** with Benoit Brunet for Donald Audette and Shaun Van Allen, November 21, 2001. Traded to **NY Rangers** by **Dallas** with Roman Lyashenko for Manny Malhotra and Barrett Heisten, March 12, 2002. Signed as a free agent by **St. Louis**, October 30, 2002. Signed as a free agent by **NY Rangers**, August 28, 2003. Traded to **Vancouver** by **NY Rangers** for R.J. Umberger and Martin Grenier, March 9, 2004.

RUMBLE, Darren

(RUHM-buhl, DAIR-rehn)

Defense. Shoots left. 6'1", 200 lbs. Born, Barrie, Ont., January 23, 1969. Philadelphia's 1st choice, 20th overall, in 1987 Entry Draft.

Season	Club	League	Regular Season GP	G	A	Pts	PIM	PP	SH	GW	S	%	+/-	TF	F%	Min	Playoffs GP	G	A	Pts	PIM	PP	SH	GW	Min
1985-86	Barrie Colts	OJHL-B	46	14	32	46	91																		
1986-87	Kitchener Rangers	OHL	64	11	32	43	44										4	0	1	1	9				
1987-88	Kitchener Rangers	OHL	55	15	50	65	64																		
1988-89	Kitchener Rangers	OHL	46	11	28	39	25										5	1	0	1	2				
1989-90	Hershey Bears	AHL	57	2	13	15	31																		
1990-91	**Philadelphia**	**NHL**	**3**	**1**	**0**	**1**	**0**	**0**	**0**	**0**	**2**	**50.0**	**1**												
	Hershey Bears	AHL	73	6	35	41	48										3	0	5	5	2				
1991-92	Hershey Bears	AHL	79	12	54	66	118										6	0	3	3	2				
1992-93	**Ottawa**	**NHL**	**69**	**3**	**13**	**16**	**61**	**0**	**0**	**0**	**92**	**3.3**	**–24**												
	New Haven	AHL	2	1	0	1	0																		
1993-94	**Ottawa**	**NHL**	**70**	**6**	**9**	**15**	**116**	**0**	**0**	**0**	**95**	**6.3**	**–50**												
	P.E.I. Senators	AHL	3	2	0	2	0																		
1994-95	P.E.I. Senators	AHL	70	7	46	53	77										11	0	6	6	4				
1995-96	**Philadelphia**	**NHL**	**5**	**0**	**0**	**0**	**4**	**0**	**0**	**0**	**7**	**0.0**	**0**												
	Hershey Bears	AHL	58	13	37	50	83										5	0	0	0	6				
1996-97	**Philadelphia**	**NHL**	**10**	**0**	**0**	**0**	**0**	**0**	**0**	**0**	**9**	**0.0**	**–2**												
	Philadelphia	AHL	72	18	44	62	83										7	0	3	3	19				
1997-98	Adler Mannheim	Germany	21	2	7	9	18																		
	Adler Mannheim	EuroHL	4	0	1	1	4																		
	San Antonio	IHL	46	7	22	29	47																		
1998-99	Utah Grizzlies	IHL	10	1	4	5	10																		
	Grand Rapids	IHL	53	6	22	28	44																		
99-2000	Grand Rapids	IHL	29	3	10	13	20																		
	Worcester IceCats	AHL	39	0	17	17	31										9	0	2	2	6				
2000-01	**St. Louis**	**NHL**	**12**	**0**	**4**	**4**	**27**	**0**	**0**	**0**	**11**	**0.0**	**7**	**0**	**0.0**	**18:12**									
	Worcester IceCats	AHL	53	6	24	30	65										8	0	1	1	10				
2001-02	Worcester IceCats	AHL	60	3	29	32	48										3	0	4	4	2				
2002-03	**Tampa Bay**	**NHL**	**19**	**0**	**0**	**0**	**6**	**0**	**0**	**0**	**10**	**0.0**	**–2**	**0**	**0.0**	**11:07**									
	Springfield	AHL	33	5	17	22	18																		
2003-04	**Tampa Bay**	**NHL**	**5**	**0**	**0**	**0**	**2**	**0**	**0**	**0**	**5**	**0.0**	**–2**	**0**	**0.0**	**11:34**									
	Hershey Bears	AHL	5	2	0	2	6																		
	NHL Totals		**193**	**10**	**26**	**36**	**216**	**0**	**0**	**0**	**231**	**4.3**		**0**	**0.0**	**13:33**									

AHL Second All-Star Team (1995) • AHL First All-Star Team (1997) • Eddie Shore Award (Top Defenseman – AHL) (1997)

Claimed by **Ottawa** from **Philadelphia** in Expansion Draft, June 18, 1992. Signed as a free agent by **Philadelphia**, July 31, 1995. Signed as a free agent by **St. Louis**, February 1, 2000. Signed as a free agent by **Tampa Bay**, September 11, 2002. • Spent majority of 2003-04 seaon as a healthy reserve.

RUPP, Mike

(RUHP, MIGHK) **PHX.**

Right wing. Shoots left. 6'5", 230 lbs. Born, Cleveland, OH, January 13, 1980. New Jersey's 7th choice, 76th overall, in 2000 Entry Draft.

Season	Club	League	Regular Season GP	G	A	Pts	PIM	PP	SH	GW	S	%	+/-	TF	F%	Min	Playoffs GP	G	A	Pts	PIM	PP	SH	GW	Min
1996-97	St. Edward's	Hi-School	20	26	24	50																			
1997-98	Windsor Spitfires	OHL	38	9	8	17	60																		
	Erie Otters	OHL	26	7	3	10	57										7	3	1	4	6				
1998-99	Erie Otters	OHL	63	22	25	47	102										5	0	2	2	25				
99-2000	Erie Otters	OHL	58	32	21	53	134										13	5	5	10	22				
2000-01	Albany River Rats	AHL	71	10	10	20	63																		

			Regular Season														Playoffs								
Season	Club	League	GP	G	A	Pts	PIM	PP	SH	GW	S	%	+/-	TF	F%	Min	GP	G	A	Pts	PIM	PP	SH	GW	Min
2001-02	Albany River Rats	AHL	78	13	17	30	90	....	....	....	....	....	....	....	....	....	....	....	....	....	....	....	....	....	....
2002-03♦	**New Jersey**	**NHL**	**26**	**5**	**3**	**8**	**21**	**2**	**0**	**3**	**34**	**14.7**	**0**	**150**	**44.7**	**11:39**	**4**	**1**	**3**	**4**	**0**	**0**	**0**	**1**	**11:28**
	Albany River Rats	AHL	47	8	11	19	74	....	....	....	....	....	....	....	....	....	....	....	....	....	....	....	....	....	....
2003-04	**New Jersey**	**NHL**	**51**	**6**	**5**	**11**	**41**	**1**	**0**	**1**	**64**	**9.4**	**–1**	**386**	**47.9**	**10:38**	....	....	....	....	....	....	....	....	....
	Phoenix	**NHL**	**6**	**0**	**1**	**1**	**6**	**0**	**0**	**0**	**12**	**0.0**	**–3**	**94**	**57.5**	**16:59**	....	....	....	....	....	....	....	....	....
	NHL Totals		**83**	**11**	**9**	**20**	**68**	**3**	**0**	**4**	**110**	**10.0**		**630**	**48.6**	**11:25**	**4**	**1**	**3**	**4**	**0**	**0**	**0**	**1**	**11:28**

• Re-entered NHL Entry Draft. Originally NY Islanders' 1st choice, 9th overall, in 1998 Entry Draft.
Traded to **Phoenix** by **New Jersey** with New Jersey's 2nd round choice (later traded to Edmonton – Edmonton selected Geoff Paukovich) in 2004 Entry Draft for Jan Hrdina, March 5, 2004.

RUUTU, Jarkko

(ROO-too, YAHR-koh) **VAN.**

Right wing. Shoots left. 6'2", 194 lbs. Born, Vantaa, Finland, August 23, 1975. Vancouver's 3rd choice, 68th overall, in 1998 Entry Draft.

Season	Club	League	GP	G	A	Pts	PIM	PP	SH	GW	S	%	+/-	TF	F%	Min	GP	G	A	Pts	PIM	PP	SH	GW	Min
1991-92	HIFK Helsinki Jr.	Finn-Jr.	1	0	0	0	0	....	....	....	....	....	....	....	....	....	....	....	....	....	....	....	....	....	....
1992-93	HIFK Helsinki B	Finn-Jr.	33	26	21	47	53	....	....	....	....	....	....	....	....	....	....	....	....	....	....	....	....	....	....
	HIFK Helsinki Jr.	Finn-Jr.	1	0	0	0	0	....	....	....	....	....	....	....	....	....	....	....	....	....	....	....	....	....	....
1993-94	HIFK Helsinki Jr.	Finn-Jr.	19	9	12	21	44	....	....	....	....	....	....	....	....	....	....	....	....	....	....	....	....	....	....
1994-95	HIFK Helsinki Jr.	Finn-Jr.	35	26	22	48	117	....	....	....	....	....	....	....	....	....	....	....	....	....	....	....	....	....	....
1995-96	Michigan Tech	WCHA	39	12	10	22	96	....	....	....	....	....	....	....	....	....	....	....	....	....	....	....	....	....	....
1996-97	HIFK Helsinki	Finland	48	11	10	21	*155	....	....	....	....	....	....	....	....	....	....	....	....	....	....	....	....	....	....
1997-98	HIFK Helsinki	Finland	37	10	10	20	87	....	....	....	....	....	....	....	....	....	8	*7	4	11	10	....	....	....	....
1998-99	HIFK Helsinki	Finland	25	10	4	14	136	....	....	....	....	....	....	....	....	....	9	0	2	2	43	....	....	....	....
	HIFK Helsinki	EuroHL	5	1	2	3	8	....	....	....	....	....	....	....	....	....	....	....	....	....	....	....	....	....	....
99-2000	**Vancouver**	**NHL**	**8**	**0**	**1**	**1**	**6**	**0**	**0**	**0**	**4**	**0.0**	**–1**	**0**	**0.0**	**8:47**	....	....	....	....	....	....	....	....	....
	Syracuse Crunch	AHL	65	26	32	58	164	....	....	....	....	....	....	....	....	....	4	3	1	4	8	....	....	....	....
2000-01	**Vancouver**	**NHL**	**21**	**3**	**3**	**6**	**32**	**0**	**1**	**0**	**23**	**13.0**	**1**	**0**	**0.0**	**10:39**	**4**	**0**	**1**	**1**	**8**	**0**	**0**	**0**	**10:18**
	Kansas City	IHL	46	11	18	29	111	....	....	....	....	....	....	....	....	....	....	....	....	....	....	....	....	....	....
2001-02	**Vancouver**	**NHL**	**49**	**2**	**7**	**9**	**74**	**0**	**0**	**0**	**37**	**5.4**	**–1**	**5**	**0.0**	**10:11**	**1**	**0**	**0**	**0**	**0**	**0**	**0**	**0**	**8:53**
	Finland	Olympics	4	0	0	0	4	....	....	....	....	....	....	....	....	....	....	....	....	....	....	....	....	....	....
2002-03	**Vancouver**	**NHL**	**36**	**2**	**2**	**4**	**66**	**0**	**0**	**1**	**36**	**5.6**	**–7**	**6**	**16.7**	**8:58**	**13**	**0**	**2**	**2**	**14**	**0**	**0**	**0**	**11:59**
2003-04	**Vancouver**	**NHL**	**71**	**6**	**8**	**14**	**133**	**1**	**0**	**0**	**70**	**8.6**	**–13**	**20**	**30.0**	**11:29**	**6**	**1**	**0**	**1**	**10**	**0**	**0**	**0**	**9:13**
	NHL Totals		**185**	**13**	**21**	**34**	**311**	**1**	**1**	**1**	**170**	**7.6**		**31**	**22.6**	**10:26**	**24**	**1**	**3**	**4**	**32**	**0**	**0**	**0**	**10:53**

• Spent majority of 2002-03 season as a healthy reserve.

RUUTU, Tuomo

(ROO-too, TOO-oh-moh) **CHI.**

Center/Left wing. Shoots left. 6'2", 208 lbs. Born, Vantaa, Finland, February 16, 1983. Chicago's 1st choice, 9th overall, in 2001 Entry Draft.

Season	Club	League	GP	G	A	Pts	PIM	PP	SH	GW	S	%	+/-	TF	F%	Min	GP	G	A	Pts	PIM	PP	SH	GW	Min
1997-98	HIFK Helsinki C	Finn-Jr.	22	4	11	15	10	....	....	....	....	....	....	....	....	....	3	0	1	1	4	....	....	....	....
1998-99	HIFK Helsinki C	Finn-Jr.	3	6	3	9	25	....	....	....	....	....	....	....	....	....	5	*4	2	6	8	....	....	....	....
	HIFK Helsinki B	Finn-Jr.	25	9	11	20	88	....	....	....	....	....	....	....	....	....	2	1	1	2	2	....	....	....	....
99-2000	HIFK Helsinki Jr.	Finn-Jr.	35	11	16	27	32	....	....	....	....	....	....	....	....	....	3	0	1	1	4	....	....	....	....
	HIFK Helsinki	Finland	1	0	0	0	2	....	....	....	....	....	....	....	....	....	....	....	....	....	....	....	....	....	....
2000-01	HIFK Helsinki Jr.	Finn-Jr.	2	1	0	1	0	....	....	....	....	....	....	....	....	....	....	....	....	....	....	....	....	....	....
	Jokerit Helsinki	Finland	47	11	11	22	86	....	....	....	....	....	....	....	....	....	5	0	0	0	4	....	....	....	....
2001-02	Jokerit Helsinki	Finland	51	7	16	23	69	....	....	....	....	....	....	....	....	....	10	0	6	6	29	....	....	....	....
2002-03	HIFK Helsinki	Finland	30	12	15	27	24	....	....	....	....	....	....	....	....	....	....	....	....	....	....	....	....	....	....
2003-04	**Chicago**	**NHL**	**82**	**23**	**21**	**44**	**58**	**10**	**0**	**3**	**174**	**13.2**	**–31**	**317**	**46.4**	**16:24**	....	....	....	....	....	....	....	....	....
	NHL Totals		**82**	**23**	**21**	**44**	**58**	**10**	**0**	**3**	**174**	**13.2**		**317**	**46.4**	**16:24**	....	....	....	....	....	....	....	....	....

RYCROFT, Mark

(RIGH-krawft, MAHRK) **ST.L.**

Right wing. Shoots right. 5'11", 192 lbs. Born, Penticton, B.C., July 12, 1978.

Season	Club	League	GP	G	A	Pts	PIM	PP	SH	GW	S	%	+/-	TF	F%	Min	GP	G	A	Pts	PIM	PP	SH	GW	Min
1993-94	Penticton Ice	BCAHA	60	47	65	112	100	....	....	....	....	....	....	....	....	....	....	....	....	....	....	....	....	....	....
1994-95	Penticton Ice	BCAHA	43	33	43	76	90	....	....	....	....	....	....	....	....	....	....	....	....	....	....	....	....	....	....
1995-96	Nanaimo Clippers	BCHL	60	17	28	45	28	....	....	....	....	....	....	....	....	....	....	....	....	....	....	....	....	....	....
1996-97	Nanaimo Clippers	BCHL	58	32	35	67	79	....	....	....	....	....	....	....	....	....	....	....	....	....	....	....	....	....	....
1997-98	U. of Denver	WCHA	35	15	17	32	28	....	....	....	....	....	....	....	....	....	....	....	....	....	....	....	....	....	....
1998-99	U. of Denver	WCHA	41	19	18	37	36	....	....	....	....	....	....	....	....	....	....	....	....	....	....	....	....	....	....
99-2000	U. of Denver	WCHA	41	17	17	34	87	....	....	....	....	....	....	....	....	....	....	....	....	....	....	....	....	....	....
2000-01	Worcester IceCats	AHL	71	24	26	50	68	....	....	....	....	....	....	....	....	....	11	2	5	7	4	....	....	....	....
2001-02	**St. Louis**	**NHL**	**9**	**0**	**3**	**3**	**4**	**0**	**0**	**0**	**14**	**0.0**	**0**	**1**	**0.0**	**9:50**	....	....	....	....	....	....	....	....	....
	Worcester IceCats	AHL	66	12	19	31	68	....	....	....	....	....	....	....	....	....	3	0	1	1	0	....	....	....	....
2002-03	Worcester IceCats	AHL	45	8	18	26	35	....	....	....	....	....	....	....	....	....	1	0	0	0	0	....	....	....	....
2003-04	**St. Louis**	**NHL**	**71**	**9**	**12**	**21**	**32**	**0**	**0**	**0**	**110**	**8.2**	**2**	**11**	**63.6**	**14:23**	**3**	**0**	**0**	**0**	**2**	**0**	**0**	**0**	**9:41**
	NHL Totals		**80**	**9**	**15**	**24**	**36**	**0**	**0**	**0**	**124**	**7.3**		**12**	**58.3**	**13:52**	**3**	**0**	**0**	**0**	**2**	**0**	**0**	**0**	**9:41**

WCHA All-Rookie Team (1998)
Signed as a free agent by **St. Louis**, May 15, 2000.

RYDER, Michael

(RIGH-duhr, MIGH-kuhl) **MTL.**

Right wing. Shoots right. 6'1", 196 lbs. Born, St. John's, Nfld., March 31, 1980. Montreal's 9th choice, 216th overall, in 1998 Entry Draft.

Season	Club	League	GP	G	A	Pts	PIM	PP	SH	GW	S	%	+/-	TF	F%	Min	GP	G	A	Pts	PIM	PP	SH	GW	Min
1996-97	Bonavista Saints	NFAHA	23	31	17	48	....	....	....	....	....	....	....	....	....	....	....	....	....	....	....	....	....	....	....
1997-98	Hull Olympiques	QMJHL	69	34	28	62	41	....	....	....	....	....	....	....	....	....	10	4	2	6	4	....	....	....	....
1998-99	Hull Olympiques	QMJHL	69	44	43	87	65	....	....	....	....	....	....	....	....	....	23	*20	16	36	39	....	....	....	....
99-2000	Hull Olympiques	QMJHL	63	50	58	108	50	....	....	....	....	....	....	....	....	....	15	11	17	28	28	....	....	....	....
2000-01	Tallahassee	ECHL	5	4	5	9	6	....	....	....	....	....	....	....	....	....	....	....	....	....	....	....	....	....	....
	Quebec Citadelles	AHL	61	6	9	15	14	....	....	....	....	....	....	....	....	....	....	....	....	....	....	....	....	....	....
2001-02	Mississippi	ECHL	20	14	13	27	2	....	....	....	....	....	....	....	....	....	....	....	....	....	....	....	....	....	....
	Quebec Citadelles	AHL	50	11	17	28	9	....	....	....	....	....	....	....	....	....	3	0	1	1	2	....	....	....	....
2002-03	Hamilton	AHL	69	34	33	67	43	....	....	....	....	....	....	....	....	....	23	11	6	17	8	....	....	....	....
2003-04	**Montreal**	**NHL**	**81**	**25**	**38**	**63**	**26**	**10**	**0**	**4**	**215**	**11.6**	**10**	**25**	**24.0**	**16:00**	**11**	**1**	**2**	**3**	**4**	**0**	**0**	**0**	**16:52**
	NHL Totals		**81**	**25**	**38**	**63**	**26**	**10**	**0**	**4**	**215**	**11.6**		**25**	**24.0**	**16:00**	**11**	**1**	**2**	**3**	**4**	**0**	**0**	**0**	**16:52**

NHL All-Rookie Team (2004)

SAFRONOV, Kirill

(sah-FRAW-nawf, kih-RIHL) **NSH.**

Defense. Shoots left. 6'2", 215 lbs. Born, Leningrad, USSR, February 26, 1981. Phoenix's 2nd choice, 19th overall, in 1999 Entry Draft.

Season	Club	League	GP	G	A	Pts	PIM	PP	SH	GW	S	%	+/-	TF	F%	Min	GP	G	A	Pts	PIM	PP	SH	GW	Min
1996-97	St. Petersburg 2	Russia-3	9	0	0	0	6	....	....	....	....	....	....	....	....	....	....	....	....	....	....	....	....	....	....
	St. Petersburg	Russia	1	0	0	0	0	....	....	....	....	....	....	....	....	....	....	....	....	....	....	....	....	....	....
1997-98	St. Petersburg 2	Russia-3	34	4	3	7	36	....	....	....	....	....	....	....	....	....	....	....	....	....	....	....	....	....	....
	St. Petersburg	Russia	9	0	1	1	4	....	....	....	....	....	....	....	....	....	1	0	0	0	0	....	....	....	....
1998-99	St. Petersburg 2	Russia-4	4	2	1	3	2	....	....	....	....	....	....	....	....	....	....	....	....	....	....	....	....	....	....
	St. Petersburg	Russia	45	1	3	4	32	....	....	....	....	....	....	....	....	....	....	....	....	....	....	....	....	....	....
99-2000	Quebec Remparts	QMJHL	55	11	32	43	95	....	....	....	....	....	....	....	....	....	11	2	4	6	14	....	....	....	....
2000-01	Springfield	AHL	65	5	13	18	77	....	....	....	....	....	....	....	....	....	....	....	....	....	....	....	....	....	....
2001-02	**Phoenix**	**NHL**	**1**	**0**	**0**	**0**	**0**	**0**	**0**	**0**	**0**	**0.0**	**–2**	**0**	**0.0**	**6:08**	....	....	....	....	....	....	....	....	....
	Springfield	AHL	68	3	19	22	26	....	....	....	....	....	....	....	....	....	....	....	....	....	....	....	....	....	....
	Atlanta	**NHL**	**2**	**0**	**0**	**0**	**2**	**0**	**0**	**0**	**2**	**0.0**	**–3**	**0**	**0.0**	**21:11**	....	....	....	....	....	....	....	....	....
	Chicago Wolves	AHL	8	0	2	2	2	....	....	....	....	....	....	....	....	....	25	2	6	8	8	....	....	....	....
2002-03	**Atlanta**	**NHL**	**32**	**2**	**2**	**4**	**14**	**0**	**0**	**0**	**21**	**9.5**	**–10**	**1**	**0.0**	**15:02**	....	....	....	....	....	....	....	....	....
	Chicago Wolves	AHL	44	4	15	19	29	....	....	....	....	....	....	....	....	....	9	1	2	3	4	....	....	....	....
2003-04	Chicago Wolves	AHL	21	1	4	5	8	....	....	....	....	....	....	....	....	....	....	....	....	....	....	....	....	....	....
	Milwaukee	AHL	59	4	16	20	41	....	....	....	....	....	....	....	....	....	21	0	6	6	20	....	....	....	....
	NHL Totals		**35**	**2**	**2**	**4**	**16**	**0**	**0**	**0**	**23**	**8.7**		**1**	**0.0**	**15:08**	....	....	....	....	....	....	....	....	....

Traded to **Atlanta** by **Phoenix** with the rights to Ruslan Zainullin and Phoenix's 5th round choice (Patrick Dwyer) in 2002 Entry Draft for Darcy Hordichuk and Atlanta's 4th (Lance Monych) and 5th (John Zeiler) round choices in 2002 Entry Draft, March 19, 2002. Traded to **Nashville** by **Atlanta** with Simon Gamache for Ben Simon and Tomas Kloucek, December 2, 2003.

ST. JACQUES, Bruno

(SAINT ZHAWK, BROO-noh) **CAR.**

Defense. Shoots left. 6'2", 204 lbs. Born, Montreal, Que., August 22, 1980. Philadelphia's 12th choice, 253rd overall, in 1998 Entry Draft.

			Regular Season														Playoffs								
Season	Club	League	GP	G	A	Pts	PIM	PP	SH	GW	S	%	+/-	TF	F%	Min	GP	G	A	Pts	PIM	PP	SH	GW	Min
1996-97	Mtl-Bourassa	QAAA	40	5	8	13	....	....	....	....	....	....	....	....	....	....	16	0	7	7	....	....	....	....	....
1997-98	Baie-Comeau	QMJHL	63	1	11	12	140	....	....	....	....	....	....	....	....	....	....	....	....	....	....	....	....	....	....
1998-99	Baie-Comeau	QMJHL	49	8	13	21	85	....	....	....	....	....	....	....	....	....	....	....	....	....	....	....	....	....	....
99-2000	Baie-Comeau	QMJHL	60	8	28	36	120	....	....	....	....	....	....	....	....	....	6	0	2	2	10	....	....	....	....
	Philadelphia	AHL	3	0	1	1	0	....	....	....	....	....	....	....	....	....	1	0	0	0	0	....	....	....	....
2000-01	Philadelphia	AHL	45	1	16	17	83	....	....	....	....	....	....	....	....	....	10	1	0	1	16	....	....	....	....
2001-02	**Philadelphia**	**NHL**	**7**	**0**	**0**	**0**	**2**	**0**	**0**	**0**	**4**	**0.0**	**4**	**0**	**0.0**	**13:51**	....	....	....	....	....	....	....	....	....
	Philadelphia	AHL	55	3	11	14	59	....	....	....	....	....	....	....	....	....	4	0	0	0	0	....	....	....	....
2002-03	**Philadelphia**	**NHL**	**6**	**0**	**0**	**0**	**2**	**0**	**0**	**0**	**5**	**0.0**	**–1**	**0**	**0.0**	**14:35**	....	....	....	....	....	....	....	....	....
	Philadelphia	AHL	30	0	7	7	46	....	....	....	....	....	....	....	....	....	....	....	....	....	....	....	....	....	....
	Carolina	**NHL**	**18**	**2**	**5**	**7**	**12**	**0**	**0**	**0**	**14**	**14.3**	**–3**	**0**	**0.0**	**18:15**	....	....	....	....	....	....	....	....	....
	Lowell	AHL	8	1	1	2	8	....	....	....	....	....	....	....	....	....	....	....	....	....	....	....	....	....	....
2003-04	**Carolina**	**NHL**	**35**	**0**	**2**	**2**	**31**	**0**	**0**	**0**	**16**	**0.0**	**–7**	**0**	**0.0**	**11:50**	....	....	....	....	....	....	....	....	....
	Lowell	AHL	6	0	0	0	8	....	....	....	....	....	....	....	....	....	....	....	....	....	....	....	....	....	....
	NHL Totals		**66**	**2**	**7**	**9**	**47**	**0**	**0**	**0**	**39**	**5.1**		**0**	**0.0**	**14:03**	....	....	....	....	....	....	....	....	....

Traded to **Carolina** by **Philadelphia** with Pavel Brendl for Sami Kapanen and Ryan Bast, February 7, 2003. • Missed majority of 2003-04 season recovering from abdominal injury suffered in game vs. Philadelphia, November 28, 2003.

ST. LOUIS, Martin

(sehn-loo-EE, mahr-TEHN) **T.B.**

Right wing. Shoots left. 5'9", 185 lbs. Born, Laval, Que., June 18, 1975.

Season	Club	League	GP	G	A	Pts	PIM	PP	SH	GW	S	%	+/-	TF	F%	Min	GP	G	A	Pts	PIM	PP	SH	GW	Min
1991-92	Laval Laurentide	QAAA	42	29	*74	*103	38	....	....	....	....	....	....	....	....	....	12	7	15	22	16	....	....	....	....
1992-93	Hawkesbury	OCJHL	31	37	50	87	70	....	....	....	....	....	....	....	....	....	....	....	....	....	....	....	....	....	....
1993-94	U. of Vermont	ECAC	33	15	36	51	24	....	....	....	....	....	....	....	....	....	....	....	....	....	....	....	....	....	....
1994-95	U. of Vermont	ECAC	35	23	48	71	36	....	....	....	....	....	....	....	....	....	....	....	....	....	....	....	....	....	....
1995-96	U. of Vermont	ECAC	35	29	56	85	38	....	....	....	....	....	....	....	....	....	....	....	....	....	....	....	....	....	....
1996-97	U. of Vermont	ECAC	36	24	*36	60	65	....	....	....	....	....	....	....	....	....	....	....	....	....	....	....	....	....	....
1997-98	Cleveland	IHL	56	16	34	50	24	....	....	....	....	....	....	....	....	....	....	....	....	....	....	....	....	....	....
	Saint John Flames	AHL	25	15	11	26	20	....	....	....	....	....	....	....	....	....	20	5	15	20	16	....	....	....	....
1998-99	**Calgary**	**NHL**	**13**	**1**	**1**	**2**	**10**	**0**	**0**	**0**	**14**	**7.1**	**–2**	**0**	**0.0**	**8:15**	....	....	....	....	....	....	....	....	....
	Saint John Flames	AHL	53	28	34	62	30	....	....	....	....	....	....	....	....	....	7	4	4	8	2	....	....	....	....
99-2000	**Calgary**	**NHL**	**56**	**3**	**15**	**18**	**22**	**0**	**0**	**1**	**73**	**4.1**	**–5**	**3**	**0.0**	**14:41**	....	....	....	....	....	....	....	....	....
	Saint John Flames	AHL	17	15	11	26	14	....	....	....	....	....	....	....	....	....	....	....	....	....	....	....	....	....	....
2000-01	**Tampa Bay**	**NHL**	**78**	**18**	**22**	**40**	**12**	**3**	**3**	**4**	**141**	**12.8**	**–4**	**48**	**41.7**	**15:14**	....	....	....	....	....	....	....	....	....
2001-02	**Tampa Bay**	**NHL**	**53**	**16**	**19**	**35**	**20**	**6**	**1**	**2**	**105**	**15.2**	**4**	**33**	**39.4**	**18:41**	....	....	....	....	....	....	....	....	....
2002-03	**Tampa Bay**	**NHL**	**82**	**33**	**37**	**70**	**32**	**12**	**3**	**5**	**201**	**16.4**	**10**	**37**	**37.8**	**19:43**	**11**	**7**	**5**	**12**	**0**	**1**	**2**	**3**	**22:21**
2003-04♦	**Tampa Bay**	**NHL**	**82**	**38**	***56**	***94**	**24**	**8**	**8**	**7**	**212**	**17.9**	**35**	**24**	**33.3**	**20:35**	**23**	**9**	***15**	**24**	**14**	**3**	**1**	**3**	**22:52**
	NHL Totals		**364**	**109**	**150**	**259**	**120**	**29**	**15**	**19**	**746**	**14.6**		**145**	**37.9**	**17:37**	**34**	**16**	**20**	**36**	**14**	**4**	**3**	**6**	**22:42**

ECAC First All-Star Team (1995, 1996, 1997) • ECAC Player of the Year (1995) • NCAA East First All-American Team (1995, 1996, 1997) • NCAA Championship All-Tournament Team (1996) • NHL First All-Star Team (2004) • Art Ross Trophy (2004) • Lester B. Pearson Award (2004) • Hart Trophy (2004)

Played in NHL All-Star Game (2003, 2004)

Signed as a free agent by **Calgary**, February 19, 1998. Signed as a free agent by **Tampa Bay**, July 31, 2000.

SAKIC, Joe

(SAK-ihk, JOH) **COL.**

Center. Shoots left. 5'11", 195 lbs. Born, Burnaby, B.C., July 7, 1969. Quebec's 2nd choice, 15th overall, in 1987 Entry Draft.

Season	Club	League	GP	G	A	Pts	PIM	PP	SH	GW	S	%	+/-	TF	F%	Min	GP	G	A	Pts	PIM	PP	SH	GW	Min
1985-86	Burnaby	BCAHA	80	83	73	156	96	....	....	....	....	....	....	....	....	....	....	....	....	....	....	....	....	....	....
	Lethbridge	WHL	3	0	0	0	0	....	....	....	....	....	....	....	....	....	....	....	....	....	....	....	....	....	....
1986-87	Swift Current	WHL	72	60	73	133	31	....	....	....	....	....	....	....	....	....	4	0	1	1	0	....	....	....	....
1987-88	Swift Current	WHL	64	*78	82	*160	64	....	....	....	....	....	....	....	....	....	10	11	13	24	12	....	....	....	....
1988-89	**Quebec**	**NHL**	**70**	**23**	**39**	**62**	**24**	**10**	**0**	**2**	**148**	**15.5**	**–36**	....	....	....	....	....	....	....	....	....	....	....	....
1989-90	**Quebec**	**NHL**	**80**	**39**	**63**	**102**	**27**	**8**	**1**	**2**	**234**	**16.7**	**–40**	....	....	....	....	....	....	....	....	....	....	....	....
1990-91	**Quebec**	**NHL**	**80**	**48**	**61**	**109**	**24**	**12**	**3**	**7**	**245**	**19.6**	**–26**	....	....	....	....	....	....	....	....	....	....	....	....
1991-92	**Quebec**	**NHL**	**69**	**29**	**65**	**94**	**20**	**6**	**3**	**1**	**217**	**13.4**	**5**	....	....	....	....	....	....	....	....	....	....	....	....
1992-93	**Quebec**	**NHL**	**78**	**48**	**57**	**105**	**40**	**20**	**2**	**4**	**264**	**18.2**	**–3**	....	....	....	**6**	**3**	**3**	**6**	**2**	**1**	**0**	**0**	....
1993-94	**Quebec**	**NHL**	**84**	**28**	**64**	**92**	**18**	**10**	**1**	**9**	**279**	**10.0**	**–8**	....	....	....	....	....	....	....	....	....	....	....	....
1994-95	**Quebec**	**NHL**	**47**	**19**	**43**	**62**	**30**	**3**	**2**	**5**	**157**	**12.1**	**7**	....	....	....	**6**	**4**	**1**	**5**	**0**	**1**	**1**	**1**	....
1995-96♦	**Colorado**	**NHL**	**82**	**51**	**69**	**120**	**44**	**17**	**6**	**7**	**339**	**15.0**	**14**	....	....	....	**22**	***18**	**16**	***34**	**14**	**6**	**0**	**6**	....
1996-97	**Colorado**	**NHL**	**65**	**22**	**52**	**74**	**34**	**10**	**2**	**5**	**261**	**8.4**	**–10**	....	....	....	**17**	**8**	***17**	**25**	**14**	**3**	**0**	**0**	....
1997-98	**Colorado**	**NHL**	**64**	**27**	**36**	**63**	**50**	**12**	**1**	**2**	**254**	**10.6**	**0**	....	....	....	**6**	**2**	**3**	**5**	**6**	**0**	**1**	**2**	....
	Canada	Olympics	4	1	2	3	4	....	....	....	....	....	....	....	....	....	....	....	....	....	....	....	....	....	....
1998-99	**Colorado**	**NHL**	**73**	**41**	**55**	**96**	**29**	**12**	**5**	**6**	**255**	**16.1**	**23**	**1723**	**51.4**	**25:35**	**19**	**6**	**13**	**19**	**8**	**1**	**1**	**1**	**25:01**
99-2000	**Colorado**	**NHL**	**60**	**28**	**53**	**81**	**28**	**5**	**1**	**5**	**242**	**11.6**	**30**	**1392**	**53.8**	**23:16**	**17**	**2**	**7**	**9**	**8**	**2**	**0**	**0**	**23:50**
2000-01♦	**Colorado**	**NHL**	**82**	**54**	**64**	**118**	**30**	**19**	**3**	**12**	**332**	**16.3**	**45**	**2292**	**53.0**	**23:01**	**21**	***13**	**13**	***26**	**6**	**5**	**0**	**3**	**21:33**
2001-02	**Colorado**	**NHL**	**82**	**26**	**53**	**79**	**18**	**9**	**1**	**4**	**260**	**10.0**	**12**	**2148**	**52.2**	**22:00**	**21**	**9**	**10**	**19**	**4**	**4**	**0**	**1**	**22:44**
	Canada	Olympics	6	4	3	7	0	....	....	....	....	....	....	....	....	....	....	....	....	....	....	....	....	....	....
2002-03	**Colorado**	**NHL**	**58**	**26**	**32**	**58**	**24**	**8**	**0**	**1**	**190**	**13.7**	**4**	**1359**	**50.8**	**21:12**	**7**	**6**	**3**	**9**	**2**	**2**	**0**	**1**	**22:29**
2003-04	**Colorado**	**NHL**	**81**	**33**	**54**	**87**	**42**	**13**	**1**	**3**	**253**	**13.0**	**11**	**1705**	**52.6**	**20:16**	**11**	**7**	**5**	**12**	**8**	**1**	**1**	**2**	**21:15**
	NHL Totals		**1155**	**542**	**860**	**1402**	**482**	**174**	**32**	**75**	**3930**	**13.8**		**10619**	**52.3**	**22:32**	**153**	**78**	**91**	**169**	**72**	**26**	**4**	**17**	**22:56**

WHL East Second All-Star Team (1987) • WHL East Rookie of the Year (1987) • WHL East MVP (1987) • WHL East First All-Star Team (1988) • WHL MVP (1988) • Canadian Major Junior Player of the Year (1988) • Conn Smythe Trophy (1996) • NHL First All-Star Team (2001, 2002, 2004) • Bud Light Plus/Minus Award (2001) (tied with Patrik Elias) • Lady Byng Trophy (2001) • Lester B. Pearson Award (2001) • Hart Trophy (2001)

Played in NHL All-Star Game (1990, 1991, 1992, 1993, 1994, 1996, 1998, 2000, 2001, 2002, 2004)

Transferred to **Colorado** after **Quebec** franchise relocated, June 21, 1995.

SALEI, Ruslan

(sah-LAY, roos-LAHN) **ANA.**

Defense. Shoots left. 6'1", 205 lbs. Born, Minsk, USSR, November 2, 1974. Anaheim's 1st choice, 9th overall, in 1996 Entry Draft.

Season	Club	League	GP	G	A	Pts	PIM	PP	SH	GW	S	%	+/-	TF	F%	Min	GP	G	A	Pts	PIM	PP	SH	GW	Min
1992-93	Dynamo Minsk	CIS	9	1	0	1	10	....	....	....	....	....	....	....	....	....	....	....	....	....	....	....	....	....	....
1993-94	Tivali Minsk	CIS	39	2	3	5	50	....	....	....	....	....	....	....	....	....	....	....	....	....	....	....	....	....	....
1994-95	Tivali Minsk	CIS	51	4	2	6	44	....	....	....	....	....	....	....	....	....	....	....	....	....	....	....	....	....	....
1995-96	Las Vegas	IHL	76	7	23	30	123	....	....	....	....	....	....	....	....	....	15	3	7	10	18	....	....	....	....
1996-97	**Anaheim**	**NHL**	**30**	**0**	**1**	**1**	**37**	**0**	**0**	**0**	**14**	**0.0**	**–8**	....	....	....	....	....	....	....	....	....	....	....	....
	Baltimore Bandits	AHL	12	1	4	5	12	....	....	....	....	....	....	....	....	....	....	....	....	....	....	....	....	....	....
	Las Vegas	IHL	8	0	2	2	24	....	....	....	....	....	....	....	....	....	3	2	1	3	6	....	....	....	....
1997-98	**Anaheim**	**NHL**	**66**	**5**	**10**	**15**	**70**	**1**	**0**	**0**	**104**	**4.8**	**7**	....	....	....	....	....	....	....	....	....	....	....	....
	Cincinnati	AHL	6	3	6	9	14	....	....	....	....	....	....	....	....	....	....	....	....	....	....	....	....	....	....
	Belarus	Olympics	7	1	0	1	4	....	....	....	....	....	....	....	....	....	....	....	....	....	....	....	....	....	....
1998-99	**Anaheim**	**NHL**	**74**	**2**	**14**	**16**	**65**	**1**	**0**	**0**	**123**	**1.6**	**1**	**0**	**0.0**	**22:03**	**3**	**0**	**0**	**0**	**4**	**0**	**0**	**0**	**15:40**
99-2000	**Anaheim**	**NHL**	**71**	**5**	**5**	**10**	**94**	**1**	**0**	**0**	**116**	**4.3**	**3**	**0**	**0.0**	**20:21**	....	....	....	....	....	....	....	....	....
2000-01	**Anaheim**	**NHL**	**50**	**1**	**5**	**6**	**70**	**0**	**0**	**0**	**73**	**1.4**	**–14**	**0**	**0.0**	**20:40**	....	....	....	....	....	....	....	....	....
2001-02	**Anaheim**	**NHL**	**82**	**4**	**7**	**11**	**97**	**0**	**0**	**1**	**96**	**4.2**	**–10**	**0**	**0.0**	**21:25**	....	....	....	....	....	....	....	....	....
	Belarus	Olympics	6	2	1	3	4	....	....	....	....	....	....	....	....	....	....	....	....	....	....	....	....	....	....
2002-03	**Anaheim**	**NHL**	**61**	**4**	**8**	**12**	**78**	**0**	**0**	**0**	**93**	**4.3**	**2**	**0**	**0.0**	**21:53**	**21**	**2**	**3**	**5**	**26**	**0**	**0**	**1**	**26:05**
2003-04	**Anaheim**	**NHL**	**82**	**4**	**11**	**15**	**110**	**0**	**1**	**2**	**145**	**2.8**	**–1**	**0**	**0.0**	**23:42**	....	....	....	....	....	....	....	....	....
	NHL Totals		**516**	**25**	**61**	**86**	**621**	**3**	**1**	**3**	**764**	**3.3**		**0**	**0.0**	**21:46**	**24**	**2**	**3**	**5**	**30**	**0**	**0**	**1**	**24:47**

SALMELAINEN, Tony

(sal-meh-LIGH-nehn, TOH-nee) **EDM.**

Left wing. Shoots right. 5'9", 185 lbs. Born, Espoo, Finland, August 8, 1981. Edmonton's 3rd choice, 41st overall, in 1999 Entry Draft.

Season	Club	League	GP	G	A	Pts	PIM	PP	SH	GW	S	%	+/-	TF	F%	Min	GP	G	A	Pts	PIM	PP	SH	GW	Min
1996-97	Kiekko Espoo Jr.	Finn-Jr.	30	8	5	13	38	....	....	....	....	....	....	....	....	....	....	....	....	....	....	....	....	....	....
1997-98	Kiekko Espoo B	Finn-Jr.	5	2	2	4	10	....	....	....	....	....	....	....	....	....	....	....	....	....	....	....	....	....	....
	HIFK Helsinki B	Finn-Jr.	28	23	16	39	30	....	....	....	....	....	....	....	....	....	....	....	....	....	....	....	....	....	....
	HIFK Helsinki Jr.	Finn-Jr.	5	0	0	0	0	....	....	....	....	....	....	....	....	....	....	....	....	....	....	....	....	....	....
1998-99	HIFK Helsinki B	Finn-Jr.	21	13	10	23	45	....	....	....	....	....	....	....	....	....	....	....	....	....	....	....	....	....	....
	HIFK Helsinki Jr.	Finn-Jr.	....	....	....	....	....	....	....	....	....	....	....	....	....	....	10	10	8	18	10	....	....	....	....

Season	Club	League	GP	G	A	Pts	PIM	PP	SH	GW	S	%	+/-	TF	F%	Min	GP	G	A	Pts	PIM	PP	SH	GW	Min
					Regular Season															Playoffs					
99-2000	HIFK Helsinki Jr.	Finn-Jr.	1	0	1	1	0	....	....	....	....	....	....	....	....	....	....	....	....	....	....	....	....	....	....
	HIFK Helsinki	Finland	1	1	0	1	0	....	....	....	....	....	....	....	....	....	....	....	....	....	....	....	....	....	....
	HIFK Helsinki	EuroHL	1	0	0	0	0	....	....	....	....	....	....	....	....	....	....	....	....	....	....	....	....	....	....
2000-01	HIFK Helsinki Jr.	Finn-Jr.	3	3	3	6	0	....	....	....	....	....	....	....	....	....	....	....	....	....	....	....	....	....	....
	HIFK Helsinki	Finland	19	1	0	1	6	....	....	....	....	....	....	....	....	....	....	....	....	....	....	....	....	....	....
	Ilves Tampere Jr.	Finn-Jr.	3	1	2	3	2	....	....	....	....	....	....	....	....	....	....	....	....	....	....	....	....	....	....
	Ilves Tampere	Finland	26	3	10	13	4	....	....	....	....	....	....	....	....	....	3	0	0	0	0	....	....	....	....
2001-02	Ilves Tampere Jr.	Finn-Jr.	6	2	2	4	27	....	....	....	....	....	....	....	....	....	....	....	....	....	....	....	....	....	....
	Ilves Tampere	Finland	49	10	9	19	30	....	....	....	....	....	....	....	....	....	3	0	0	0	2	....	....	....	....
2002-03	Hamilton	AHL	67	14	19	33	14	....	....	....	....	....	....	....	....	....	17	6	8	14	0	....	....	....	....
2003-04	**Edmonton**	**NHL**	**13**	**0**	**1**	**1**	**4**	**0**	**0**	**0**	**17**	**0.0**	**–1**	**0**	**0.0**	**9:39**	....	....	....	....	....	....	....	....	....
	Toronto	AHL	58	19	25	44	27	....	....	....	....	....	....	....	....	....	3	0	1	1	0	....	....	....	....
	NHL Totals		**13**	**0**	**1**	**1**	**4**	**0**	**0**	**0**	**17**	**0.0**		**0**	**0.0**	**9:39**	....	....	....	....	....	....	....	....	....

SALO, Sami
(SA-loh, SA-mee) **VAN.**

Defense. Shoots right. 6'3", 215 lbs. Born, Turku, Finland, September 2, 1974. Ottawa's 7th choice, 239th overall, in 1996 Entry Draft.

Season	Club	League	GP	G	A	Pts	PIM	PP	SH	GW	S	%	+/-	TF	F%	Min	GP	G	A	Pts	PIM	PP	SH	GW	Min
1991-92	Kiekko 67 Jr.	Finn-Jr.	23	4	5	9	26	....	....	....	....	....	....	....	....	....	....	....	....	....	....	....	....	....	....
1992-93	Kiekko 67 Turku B	Finn-Jr.	21	9	4	13	4	....	....	....	....	....	....	....	....	....	....	....	....	....	....	....	....	....	....
	Kiekko 67 Jr.	Finn-Jr.	13	6	2	8	2	....	....	....	....	....	....	....	....	....	....	....	....	....	....	....	....	....	....
1993-94	TPS Turku Jr.	Finn-Jr.	36	7	13	20	16	....	....	....	....	....	....	....	....	....	7	0	1	1	10	....	....	....	....
1994-95	TPS Turku Jr.	Finn-Jr.	14	1	3	4	6	....	....	....	....	....	....	....	....	....	....	....	....	....	....	....	....	....	....
	Kiekko 67 Turku	Finland-2	19	4	2	6	4	....	....	....	....	....	....	....	....	....	....	....	....	....	....	....	....	....	....
	TPS Turku	Finland	7	1	2	3	8	....	....	....	....	....	....	....	....	....	1	0	0	0	0	....	....	....	....
1995-96	TPS Turku	Finland	47	7	14	21	32	....	....	....	....	....	....	....	....	....	11	1	3	4	8	....	....	....	....
1996-97	TPS Turku	Finland	48	9	6	15	10	....	....	....	....	....	....	....	....	....	10	2	3	5	4	....	....	....	....
	TPS Turku	EuroHL	6	0	2	2	6	....	....	....	....	....	....	....	....	....	2	0	0	0	2	....	....	....	....
1997-98	Jokerit Helsinki	Finland	35	3	5	8	10	....	....	....	....	....	....	....	....	....	8	0	1	1	2	....	....	....	....
	Jokerit Helsinki	EuroHL	6	1	1	2	2	....	....	....	....	....	....	....	....	....	....	....	....	....	....	....	....	....	....
1998-99	**Ottawa**	**NHL**	**61**	**7**	**12**	**19**	**24**	**2**	**0**	**1**	**106**	**6.6**	**20**	**0**	**0.0**	**19:42**	**4**	**0**	**0**	**0**	**0**	**0**	**0**	**0**	**21:32**
	Detroit Vipers	IHL	5	0	2	2	0	....	....	....	....	....	....	....	....	....	....	....	....	....	....	....	....	....	....
99-2000	**Ottawa**	**NHL**	**37**	**6**	**8**	**14**	**2**	**3**	**0**	**1**	**85**	**7.1**	**6**	**0**	**0.0**	**20:18**	**6**	**1**	**1**	**2**	**0**	**1**	**0**	**0**	**24:11**
2000-01	**Ottawa**	**NHL**	**31**	**2**	**16**	**18**	**10**	**1**	**0**	**0**	**61**	**3.3**	**9**	**0**	**0.0**	**19:44**	**4**	**0**	**0**	**0**	**0**	**0**	**0**	**0**	**22:30**
2001-02	**Ottawa**	**NHL**	**66**	**4**	**14**	**18**	**14**	**1**	**1**	**2**	**122**	**3.3**	**1**	**0**	**0.0**	**19:52**	**12**	**2**	**1**	**3**	**4**	**0**	**0**	**0**	**20:23**
	Finland	Olympics	4	0	0	0	0	....	....	....	....	....	....	....	....	....	....	....	....	....	....	....	....	....	....
2002-03	**Vancouver**	**NHL**	**79**	**9**	**21**	**30**	**10**	**4**	**0**	**1**	**126**	**7.1**	**9**	**0**	**0.0**	**20:08**	**12**	**1**	**3**	**4**	**0**	**0**	**0**	**0**	**20:52**
2003-04	**Vancouver**	**NHL**	**74**	**7**	**19**	**26**	**22**	**5**	**0**	**2**	**143**	**4.9**	**8**	**1**	**100.0**	**22:14**	**7**	**1**	**2**	**3**	**2**	**1**	**0**	**0**	**22:59**
	NHL Totals		**348**	**35**	**90**	**125**	**82**	**16**	**1**	**7**	**643**	**5.4**		**1**	**100.0**	**20:26**	**45**	**5**	**7**	**12**	**6**	**2**	**0**	**0**	**21:43**

NHL All-Rookie Team (1999)

• Missed majority of 1999-2000 season recovering from wrist injury suffered in game vs. Philadelphia, November 28, 1999. • Missed majority of 2000-01 season recovering from shoulder injury suffered in game vs. Atlanta, December 14, 2000. Traded to **Vancouver** by **Ottawa** for Peter Schaefer, September 21, 2002.

SALOMONSSON, Andreas
(sal-oh-MAWN-suhn, an-DRAY-uhs) **WSH.**

Right wing. Shoots left. 6'1", 200 lbs. Born, Ornskoldsvik, Sweden, December 19, 1973. New Jersey's 8th choice, 163rd overall, in 2001 Entry Draft.

Season	Club	League	GP	G	A	Pts	PIM	PP	SH	GW	S	%	+/-	TF	F%	Min	GP	G	A	Pts	PIM	PP	SH	GW	Min
1990-91	MoDo	Sweden	2	0	0	0	0	....	....	....	....	....	....	....	....	....	....	....	....	....	....	....	....	....	....
1991-92	MoDo	Sweden	20	1	1	2	26	....	....	....	....	....	....	....	....	....	....	....	....	....	....	....	....	....	....
1992-93	MoDo Jr.	Swede-Jr.	10	4	16	20	8	....	....	....	....	....	....	....	....	....	....	....	....	....	....	....	....	....	....
	MoDo	Sweden	33	1	1	2	0	....	....	....	....	....	....	....	....	....	....	....	....	....	....	....	....	....	....
1993-94	MoDo	Sweden	38	15	8	23	33	....	....	....	....	....	....	....	....	....	11	1	2	3	4	....	....	....	....
1994-95	MoDo	Sweden	40	5	9	14	34	....	....	....	....	....	....	....	....	....	....	....	....	....	....	....	....	....	....
1995-96	MoDo	Sweden	38	13	6	19	22	....	....	....	....	....	....	....	....	....	7	0	4	4	8	....	....	....	....
1996-97	MoDo	Sweden	23	6	6	12	22	....	....	....	....	....	....	....	....	....	....	....	....	....	....	....	....	....	....
	Ratingen	Germany	21	5	1	6	49	....	....	....	....	....	....	....	....	....	....	....	....	....	....	....	....	....	....
1997-98	MoDo	Sweden	45	6	15	21	69	....	....	....	....	....	....	....	....	....	8	4	3	7	4	....	....	....	....
1998-99	MoDo	Sweden	46	13	13	26	60	....	....	....	....	....	....	....	....	....	13	4	5	9	12	....	....	....	....
99-2000	MoDo	Sweden	48	9	15	24	38	....	....	....	....	....	....	....	....	....	12	0	4	4	12	....	....	....	....
	MoDo	EuroHL	5	2	2	4	4	....	....	....	....	....	....	....	....	....	3	1	1	2	4	....	....	....	....
2000-01	Djurgarden	Sweden	48	10	12	22	46	....	....	....	....	....	....	....	....	....	13	3	4	7	31	....	....	....	....
2001-02	**New Jersey**	**NHL**	**39**	**4**	**5**	**9**	**22**	**1**	**0**	**1**	**58**	**6.9**	**–12**	**6**	**33.3**	**13:30**	**4**	**0**	**1**	**1**	**0**	**0**	**0**	**0**	**12:16**
	Albany River Rats	AHL	19	3	10	13	6	....	....	....	....	....	....	....	....	....	....	....	....	....	....	....	....	....	....
2002-03	**Washington**	**NHL**	**32**	**1**	**4**	**5**	**14**	**0**	**0**	**0**	**20**	**5.0**	**–1**	**29**	**37.9**	**8:50**	....	....	....	....	....	....	....	....	....
	Portland Pirates	AHL	31	7	17	24	23	....	....	....	....	....	....	....	....	....	3	4	0	4	0	....	....	....	....
2003-04	MoDo	Sweden	47	13	26	39	48	....	....	....	....	....	....	....	....	....	6	1	5	6	6	....	....	....	....
	NHL Totals		**71**	**5**	**9**	**14**	**36**	**1**	**0**	**1**	**78**	**6.4**		**35**	**37.1**	**11:24**	**4**	**0**	**1**	**1**	**0**	**0**	**0**	**0**	**12:15**

Claimed on waivers by **Washington** from **New Jersey**, October 15, 2002. Signed as a free agent by **MoDo** (Sweden), with Washington retaining NHL rights, August 7, 2003.

SALVADOR, Bryce
(SAL-vuh-dohr, BRIGHS) **ST.L.**

Defense. Shoots left. 6'2", 215 lbs. Born, Brandon, Man., February 11, 1976. Tampa Bay's 6th choice, 138th overall, in 1994 Entry Draft.

Season	Club	League	GP	G	A	Pts	PIM	PP	SH	GW	S	%	+/-	TF	F%	Min	GP	G	A	Pts	PIM	PP	SH	GW	Min
1991-92	Brandon	MAHA	52	6	23	29	38	....	....	....	....	....	....	....	....	....	....	....	....	....	....	....	....	....	....
1992-93	Lethbridge	WHL	64	1	4	5	29	....	....	....	....	....	....	....	....	....	4	0	0	0	0	....	....	....	....
1993-94	Lethbridge	WHL	61	4	14	18	36	....	....	....	....	....	....	....	....	....	9	0	1	1	2	....	....	....	....
1994-95	Lethbridge	WHL	67	1	9	10	88	....	....	....	....	....	....	....	....	....	....	....	....	....	....	....	....	....	....
1995-96	Lethbridge	WHL	56	4	12	16	75	....	....	....	....	....	....	....	....	....	3	0	1	1	2	....	....	....	....
1996-97	Lethbridge	WHL	63	8	32	40	81	....	....	....	....	....	....	....	....	....	19	0	7	7	14	....	....	....	....
1997-98	Worcester IceCats	AHL	46	2	8	10	74	....	....	....	....	....	....	....	....	....	11	0	1	1	45	....	....	....	....
1998-99	Worcester IceCats	AHL	69	5	13	18	129	....	....	....	....	....	....	....	....	....	4	0	1	1	2	....	....	....	....
99-2000	Worcester IceCats	AHL	55	0	13	13	53	....	....	....	....	....	....	....	....	....	9	0	1	1	2	....	....	....	....
2000-01	**St. Louis**	**NHL**	**75**	**2**	**8**	**10**	**69**	**0**	**0**	**1**	**60**	**3.3**	**–4**	**1**	**0.0**	**16:38**	**14**	**2**	**0**	**2**	**18**	**0**	**0**	**1**	**14:41**
2001-02	**St. Louis**	**NHL**	**66**	**5**	**7**	**12**	**78**	**1**	**0**	**2**	**37**	**13.5**	**3**	**0**	**0.0**	**16:55**	**10**	**0**	**1**	**1**	**4**	**0**	**0**	**0**	**12:34**
2002-03	**St. Louis**	**NHL**	**71**	**2**	**8**	**10**	**95**	**1**	**0**	**0**	**73**	**2.7**	**7**	**0**	**0.0**	**18:57**	**7**	**0**	**0**	**0**	**2**	**0**	**0**	**0**	**17:17**
2003-04	**St. Louis**	**NHL**	**69**	**3**	**5**	**8**	**47**	**0**	**0**	**1**	**60**	**5.0**	**–4**	**0**	**0.0**	**17:29**	**5**	**0**	**0**	**0**	**2**	**0**	**0**	**0**	**14:31**
	Worcester IceCats	AHL	2	0	1	1	0	....	....	....	....	....	....	....	....	....	....	....	....	....	....	....	....	....	....
	NHL Totals		**281**	**12**	**28**	**40**	**289**	**2**	**0**	**4**	**230**	**5.2**		**1**	**0.0**	**17:30**	**36**	**2**	**1**	**3**	**26**	**0**	**0**	**1**	**14:35**

Signed as a free agent by **St. Louis**, December 16, 1996.

SAMSONOV, Sergei
(sam-SAWN-nahf, SAIR-gay) **BOS.**

Left wing. Shoots right. 5'8", 194 lbs. Born, Moscow, USSR, October 27, 1978. Boston's 2nd choice, 8th overall, in 1997 Entry Draft.

Season	Club	League	GP	G	A	Pts	PIM	PP	SH	GW	S	%	+/-	TF	F%	Min	GP	G	A	Pts	PIM	PP	SH	GW	Min
1994-95	CSKA Moscow Jr.	CIS-Jr.	50	110	72	182	....	....	....	....	....	....	....	....	....	....	....	....	....	....	....	....	....	....	....
	CSKA Moscow	CIS	13	2	2	4	14	....	....	....	....	....	....	....	....	....	2	0	0	0	0	....	....	....	....
1995-96	CSKA Moscow	CIS	51	21	17	38	12	....	....	....	....	....	....	....	....	....	3	1	1	2	4	....	....	....	....
1996-97	Detroit Vipers	IHL	73	29	35	64	18	....	....	....	....	....	....	....	....	....	19	8	4	12	12	....	....	....	....
1997-98	**Boston**	**NHL**	**81**	**22**	**25**	**47**	**8**	**7**	**0**	**3**	**159**	**13.8**	**9**	....	....	....	**6**	**2**	**5**	**7**	**0**	**0**	**0**	**1**	....
1998-99	**Boston**	**NHL**	**79**	**25**	**26**	**51**	**18**	**6**	**0**	**8**	**160**	**15.6**	**–6**	**0**	**0.0**	**16:23**	**11**	**3**	**1**	**4**	**0**	**0**	**0**	**0**	**16:11**
99-2000	**Boston**	**NHL**	**77**	**19**	**26**	**45**	**4**	**6**	**0**	**3**	**145**	**13.1**	**–6**	**3**	**0.0**	**16:32**	....	....	....	....	....	....	....	....	....
2000-01	**Boston**	**NHL**	**82**	**29**	**46**	**75**	**18**	**3**	**0**	**3**	**215**	**13.5**	**6**	**14**	**42.9**	**19:23**	....	....	....	....	....	....	....	....	....
2001-02	**Boston**	**NHL**	**74**	**29**	**41**	**70**	**27**	**3**	**0**	**4**	**192**	**15.1**	**21**	**1**	**0.0**	**18:47**	**6**	**2**	**2**	**4**	**0**	**0**	**0**	**0**	**17:41**
	Russia	Olympics	6	1	2	3	4	....	....	....	....	....	....	....	....	....	....	....	....	....	....	....	....	....	....
2002-03	**Boston**	**NHL**	**8**	**5**	**6**	**11**	**2**	**1**	**0**	**3**	**23**	**21.7**	**8**	**0**	**0.0**	**20:20**	**5**	**0**	**2**	**2**	**0**	**0**	**0**	**0**	**17:07**
2003-04	**Boston**	**NHL**	**58**	**17**	**23**	**40**	**4**	**3**	**0**	**5**	**132**	**12.9**	**12**	**4**	**25.0**	**17:27**	**7**	**2**	**5**	**7**	**0**	**0**	**0**	**0**	**17:18**
	NHL Totals		**459**	**146**	**193**	**339**	**81**	**29**	**0**	**29**	**1026**	**14.2**		**22**	**31.8**	**17:47**	**35**	**9**	**15**	**24**	**0**	**0**	**0**	**1**	**16:55**

Garry F. Longman Memorial Trophy (Top Rookie – IHL) (1997) • NHL All-Rookie Team (1998) • Calder Memorial Trophy (1998)

Played in NHL All-Star Game (2001)

• Missed majority of 2002-03 season recovering from wrist injury suffered in game vs. Columbus, October 18, 2002.

			Regular Season														Playoffs								
Season	Club	League	GP	G	A	Pts	PIM	PP	SH	GW	S	%	+/-	TF	F%	Min	GP	G	A	Pts	PIM	PP	SH	GW	Min

SAMUELSSON, Martin

(SAM-yuhl-suhn, MAHR-tihn) **BOS.**

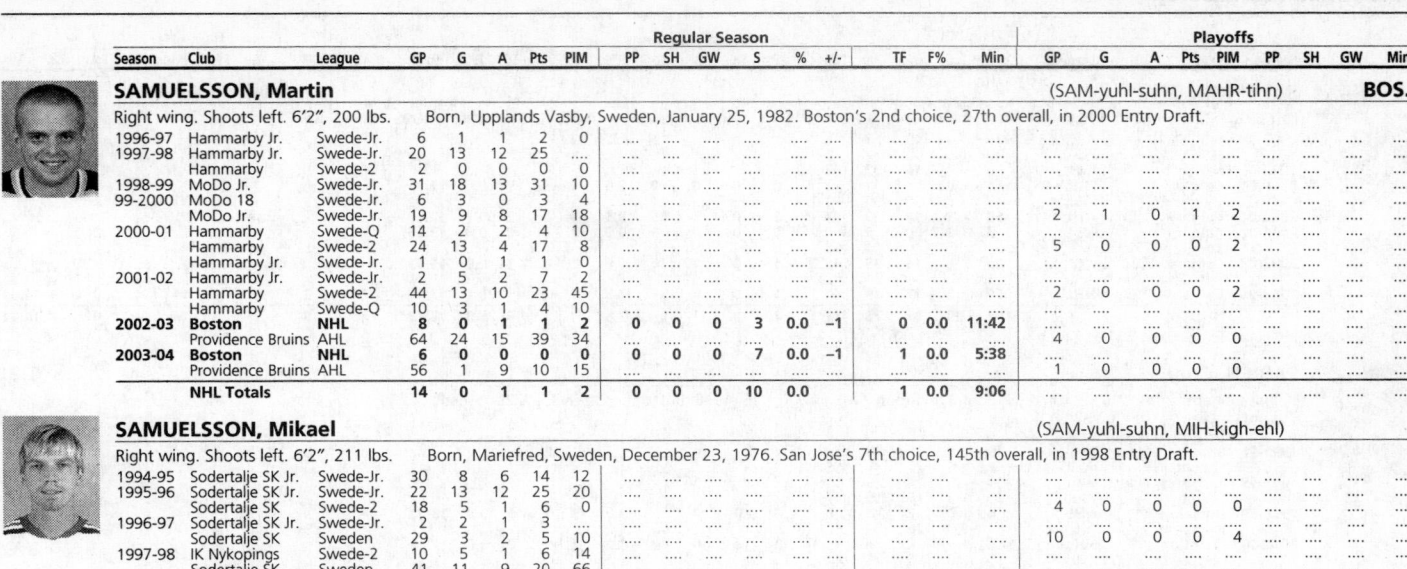

Right wing. Shoots left. 6'2", 200 lbs. Born, Upplands Vasby, Sweden, January 25, 1982. Boston's 2nd choice, 27th overall, in 2000 Entry Draft.

Season	Club	League	GP	G	A	Pts	PIM	PP	SH	GW	S	%	+/-	TF	F%	Min	GP	G	A	Pts	PIM	PP	SH	GW	Min
1996-97	Hammarby Jr.	Swede-Jr.	6	1	1	2	0	....	....	....	....	....	....	....	....	....	....	....	....	....	....	....	....	....	....
1997-98	Hammarby Jr.	Swede-Jr.	20	13	12	25	....	....	....	....	....	....	....	....	....	....	....	....	....	....	....	....	....	....	....
	Hammarby	Swede-2	2	0	0	0	0	....	....	....	....	....	....	....	....	....	....	....	....	....	....	....	....	....	....
1998-99	MoDo Jr.	Swede-Jr.	31	18	13	31	10	....	....	....	....	....	....	....	....	....	....	....	....	....	....	....	....	....	....
99-2000	MoDo 18	Swede-Jr.	6	3	0	3	4	....	....	....	....	....	....	....	....	....	....	....	....	....	....	....	....	....	....
	MoDo Jr.	Swede-Jr.	19	9	8	17	18	....	....	....	....	....	....	....	....	....	2	1	0	1	2	....	....	....	....
2000-01	Hammarby	Swede-Q	14	2	2	4	10	....	....	....	....	....	....	....	....	....	....	....	....	....	....	....	....	....	....
	Hammarby	Swede-2	24	13	4	17	8	....	....	....	....	....	....	....	....	....	5	0	0	0	2	....	....	....	....
	Hammarby Jr.	Swede-Jr.	1	0	1	1	0	....	....	....	....	....	....	....	....	....	....	....	....	....	....	....	....	....	....
2001-02	Hammarby Jr.	Swede-Jr.	2	5	2	7	2	....	....	....	....	....	....	....	....	....	....	....	....	....	....	....	....	....	....
	Hammarby	Swede-2	44	13	10	23	45	....	....	....	....	....	....	....	....	....	2	0	0	0	2	....	....	....	....
	Hammarby	Swede-Q	10	3	1	4	10	....	....	....	....	....	....	....	....	....	....	....	....	....	....	....	....	....	....
2002-03	**Boston**	**NHL**	**8**	**0**	**1**	**1**	**2**	**0**	**0**	**0**	**3**	**0.0**	**–1**	**0**	**0.0**	**11:42**	....	....	....	....	....	....	....	....	....
	Providence Bruins	AHL	64	24	15	39	34	....	....	....	....	....	....	....	....	....	4	0	0	0	0	....	....	....	....
2003-04	**Boston**	**NHL**	**6**	**0**	**0**	**0**	**0**	**0**	**0**	**0**	**7**	**0.0**	**–1**	**1**	**0.0**	**5:38**	....	....	....	....	....	....	....	....	....
	Providence Bruins	AHL	56	1	9	10	15	....	....	....	....	....	....	....	....	....	1	0	0	0	0	....	....	....	....
	NHL Totals		**14**	**0**	**1**	**1**	**2**	**0**	**0**	**0**	**10**	**0.0**		**1**	**0.0**	**9:06**	....	....	....	....	....	....	....	....	....

SAMUELSSON, Mikael

(SAM-yuhl-suhn, MIH-kigh-ehl)

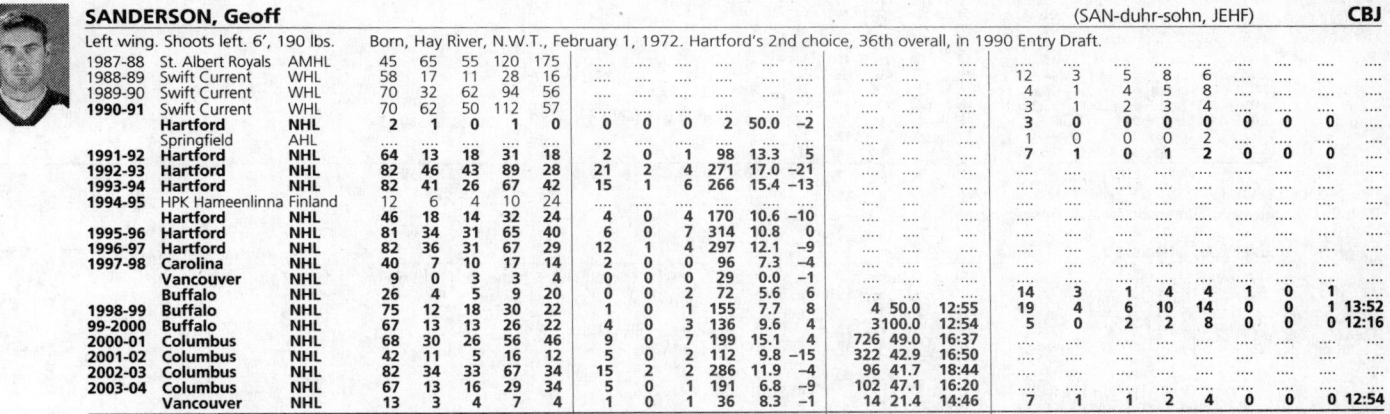

Right wing. Shoots left. 6'2", 211 lbs. Born, Mariefred, Sweden, December 23, 1976. San Jose's 7th choice, 145th overall, in 1998 Entry Draft.

Season	Club	League	GP	G	A	Pts	PIM	PP	SH	GW	S	%	+/-	TF	F%	Min	GP	G	A	Pts	PIM	PP	SH	GW	Min
1994-95	Sodertalje SK Jr.	Swede-Jr.	30	8	6	14	12	....	....	....	....	....	....	....	....	....	....	....	....	....	....	....	....	....	....
1995-96	Sodertalje SK Jr.	Swede-Jr.	22	13	12	25	20	....	....	....	....	....	....	....	....	....	....	....	....	....	....	....	....	....	....
	Sodertalje SK	Swede-2	18	5	1	6	0	....	....	....	....	....	....	....	....	....	4	0	0	0	0	....	....	....	....
1996-97	Sodertalje SK Jr.	Swede-Jr.	2	2	1	3	....	....	....	....	....	....	....	....	....	....	....	....	....	....	....	....	....	....	....
	Sodertalje SK	Sweden	29	3	2	5	10	....	....	....	....	....	....	....	....	....	10	0	0	0	4	....	....	....	....
1997-98	IK Nykopings	Swede-2	10	5	1	6	14	....	....	....	....	....	....	....	....	....	....	....	....	....	....	....	....	....	....
	Sodertalje SK	Sweden	41	11	9	20	66	....	....	....	....	....	....	....	....	....	....	....	....	....	....	....	....	....	....
1998-99	Sodertalje SK	Swede-2	18	13	10	23	26	....	....	....	....	....	....	....	....	....	10	2	2	4	12	....	....	....	....
	Vastra Frolunda	Sweden	27	0	5	5	10	....	....	....	....	....	....	....	....	....	....	....	....	....	....	....	....	....	....
99-2000	Brynas IF Gavle	Sweden	40	4	3	7	76	....	....	....	....	....	....	....	....	....	11	7	2	9	6	....	....	....	....
	Brynas IF Gavle	EuroHL	4	0	2	2	4	....	....	....	....	....	....	....	....	....	....	....	....	....	....	....	....	....	....
2000-01	**San Jose**	**NHL**	**4**	**0**	**0**	**0**	**0**	**0**	**0**	**0**	**3**	**0.0**	**0**	**0**	**0.0**	**4:41**	....	....	....	....	....	....	....	....	....
	Kentucky	AHL	66	32	46	78	58	....	....	....	....	....	....	....	....	....	3	1	0	1	0	....	....	....	....
2001-02	**NY Rangers**	**NHL**	**67**	**6**	**10**	**16**	**23**	**1**	**2**	**1**	**94**	**6.4**	**10**	**5**	**40.0**	**11:52**	....	....	....	....	....	....	....	....	....
	Hartford	AHL	8	3	6	9	12	....	....	....	....	....	....	....	....	....	....	....	....	....	....	....	....	....	....
2002-03	**NY Rangers**	**NHL**	**58**	**8**	**14**	**22**	**32**	**1**	**1**	**2**	**118**	**6.8**	**0**	**35**	**42.9**	**15:32**	....	....	....	....	....	....	....	....	....
	Pittsburgh	**NHL**	**22**	**2**	**0**	**2**	**8**	**1**	**0**	**0**	**36**	**5.6**	**–21**	**8**	**75.0**	**14:04**	....	....	....	....	....	....	....	....	....
2003-04	**Florida**	**NHL**	**37**	**3**	**6**	**9**	**35**	**0**	**0**	**1**	**50**	**6.0**	**0**	**28**	**28.6**	**12:15**	....	....	....	....	....	....	....	....	....
	NHL Totals		**188**	**19**	**30**	**49**	**98**	**3**	**3**	**4**	**301**	**6.3**		**76**	**40.8**	**13:11**	....	....	....	....	....	....	....	....	....

Traded to **NY Rangers** by **San Jose** with Christian Gosselin for Adam Graves and future considerations, June 24, 2001. Traded to **Pittsburgh** by **NY Rangers** with Joel Bouchard, Richard Lintner and Rico Fata for Mike Wilson, Alex Kovalev, Janne Laukkanen and Dan LaCouture, February 10, 2003. Traded to **Florida** by **Pittsburgh** with Pittsburgh's 1st round choice (Nathan Horton) and 2nd round compensatory choice (Stefan Meyer) in 2003 Entry Draft for Florida's 1st (Marc-Andre Fleury) and 3rd (Daniel Carcillo) round choices in 2003 Entry Draft, June 21, 2003. • Missed majority of 2003-04 season recovering from jaw (November 21, 2003 vs. Washington) and hand (January 21, 2004 vs. Columbus) injuries.

SANDERSON, Geoff

(SAN-duhr-sohn, JEHF) **CBJ**

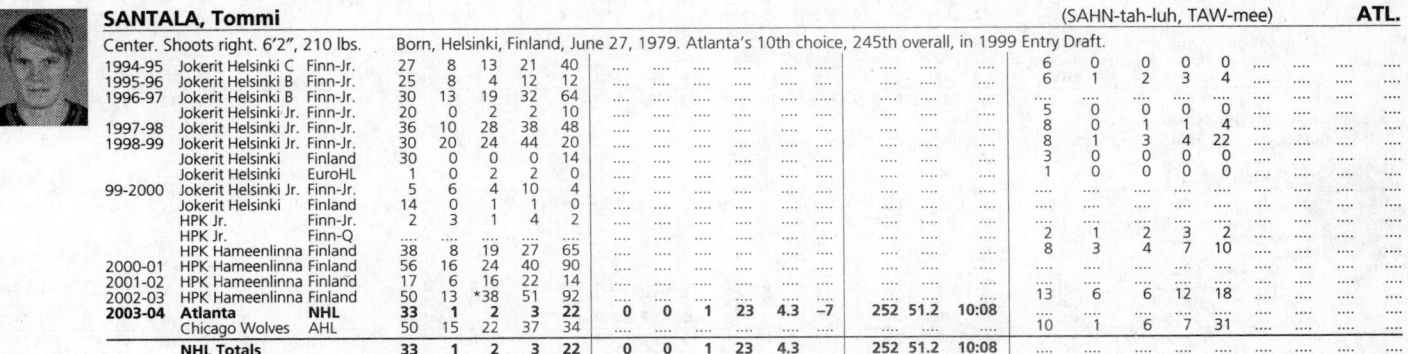

Left wing. Shoots left. 6', 190 lbs. Born, Hay River, N.W.T., February 1, 1972. Hartford's 2nd choice, 36th overall, in 1990 Entry Draft.

Season	Club	League	GP	G	A	Pts	PIM	PP	SH	GW	S	%	+/-	TF	F%	Min	GP	G	A	Pts	PIM	PP	SH	GW	Min
1987-88	St. Albert Royals	AMHL	45	65	55	120	175	....	....	....	....	....	....	....	....	....	....	....	....	....	....	....	....	....	....
1988-89	Swift Current	WHL	58	17	11	28	16	....	....	....	....	....	....	....	....	....	12	3	5	8	6	....	....	....	....
1989-90	Swift Current	WHL	70	32	62	94	56	....	....	....	....	....	....	....	....	....	4	1	4	5	8	....	....	....	....
1990-91	Swift Current	WHL	70	62	50	112	57	....	....	....	....	....	....	....	....	....	3	1	2	3	4	....	....	....	....
	Hartford	**NHL**	**2**	**1**	**0**	**1**	**0**	**0**	**0**	**0**	**2**	**50.0**	**–2**	....	....	....	**3**	**0**	**0**	**0**	**0**	**0**	**0**	**0**	....
	Springfield	AHL	....	....	....	....	....	....	....	....	....	....	....	....	....	....	1	0	0	0	2	....	....	....	....
1991-92	**Hartford**	**NHL**	**64**	**13**	**18**	**31**	**18**	**2**	**0**	**1**	**98**	**13.3**	**5**	....	....	....	**7**	**1**	**0**	**1**	**2**	**0**	**0**	**0**	....
1992-93	**Hartford**	**NHL**	**82**	**46**	**43**	**89**	**28**	**21**	**2**	**4**	**271**	**17.0**	**–21**	....	....	....	....	....	....	....	....	....	....	....	....
1993-94	**Hartford**	**NHL**	**82**	**41**	**26**	**67**	**42**	**15**	**1**	**6**	**266**	**15.4**	**–13**	....	....	....	....	....	....	....	....	....	....	....	....
1994-95	HPK Hameenlinna	Finland	12	6	4	10	24	....	....	....	....	....	....	....	....	....	....	....	....	....	....	....	....	....	....
	Hartford	**NHL**	**46**	**18**	**14**	**32**	**24**	**4**	**0**	**4**	**170**	**10.6**	**–10**	....	....	....	....	....	....	....	....	....	....	....	....
1995-96	**Hartford**	**NHL**	**81**	**34**	**31**	**65**	**40**	**6**	**0**	**7**	**314**	**10.8**	**0**	....	....	....	....	....	....	....	....	....	....	....	....
1996-97	**Hartford**	**NHL**	**82**	**36**	**31**	**67**	**29**	**12**	**1**	**4**	**297**	**12.1**	**–9**	....	....	....	....	....	....	....	....	....	....	....	....
1997-98	**Carolina**	**NHL**	**40**	**7**	**10**	**17**	**14**	**2**	**0**	**0**	**96**	**7.3**	**–4**	....	....	....	....	....	....	....	....	....	....	....	....
	Vancouver	**NHL**	**9**	**0**	**3**	**3**	**4**	**0**	**0**	**0**	**29**	**0.0**	**–1**	....	....	....	....	....	....	....	....	....	....	....	....
	Buffalo	**NHL**	**26**	**4**	**5**	**9**	**20**	**0**	**0**	**2**	**72**	**5.6**	**6**	....	....	....	**14**	**3**	**1**	**4**	**4**	**1**	**0**	**1**	....
1998-99	**Buffalo**	**NHL**	**75**	**12**	**18**	**30**	**22**	**1**	**0**	**1**	**155**	**7.7**	**8**	**4**	**50.0**	**12:55**	**19**	**4**	**6**	**10**	**14**	**0**	**0**	**1**	**13:52**
99-2000	**Buffalo**	**NHL**	**67**	**13**	**13**	**26**	**22**	**4**	**0**	**3**	**136**	**9.6**	**4**	**3**	**100.0**	**12:54**	**5**	**0**	**2**	**2**	**8**	**0**	**0**	**0**	**12:16**
2000-01	**Columbus**	**NHL**	**68**	**30**	**26**	**56**	**46**	**9**	**0**	**7**	**199**	**15.1**	**4**	**726**	**49.0**	**16:37**	....	....	....	....	....	....	....	....	....
2001-02	**Columbus**	**NHL**	**42**	**11**	**5**	**16**	**12**	**5**	**0**	**2**	**112**	**9.8**	**–15**	**322**	**42.9**	**16:50**	....	....	....	....	....	....	....	....	....
2002-03	**Columbus**	**NHL**	**82**	**34**	**33**	**67**	**34**	**15**	**2**	**2**	**286**	**11.9**	**–4**	**96**	**41.7**	**18:44**	....	....	....	....	....	....	....	....	....
2003-04	**Columbus**	**NHL**	**67**	**13**	**16**	**29**	**34**	**5**	**0**	**1**	**191**	**6.8**	**–9**	**102**	**47.1**	**16:20**	....	....	....	....	....	....	....	....	....
	Vancouver	**NHL**	**13**	**3**	**4**	**7**	**4**	**1**	**0**	**1**	**36**	**8.3**	**–1**	**14**	**21.4**	**14:46**	**7**	**1**	**1**	**2**	**4**	**0**	**0**	**0**	**12:54**
	NHL Totals		**928**	**316**	**296**	**612**	**393**	**102**	**6**	**45**	**2730**	**11.6**		**1267**	**46.6**	**15:41**	**55**	**9**	**10**	**19**	**32**	**1**	**0**	**2**	**13:23**

Played in NHL All-Star Game (1994, 1997)

Transferred to **Carolina** after **Hartford** franchise relocated, June 25, 1997. Traded to **Vancouver** by **Carolina** with Sean Burke and Enrico Ciccone for Kirk McLean and Martin Gelinas, January 3, 1998. Traded to **Buffalo** by **Vancouver** for Brad May and Buffalo's 3rd round choice (later traded to Tampa Bay – Tampa Bay selected Jimmie Olvestad) in 1999 Entry Draft, February 4, 1998. Selected by **Columbus** from **Buffalo** in Expansion Draft, June 23, 2000. Traded to **Vancouver** by **Columbus** for Vancouver's 3rd round choice (Daniel Lacosta) in 2004 Entry Draft, March 9, 2004. Claimed on waivers by **Columbus** from **Vancouver**, June 28, 2004.

SANTALA, Tommi

(SAHN-tah-luh, TAW-mee) **ATL.**

Center. Shoots right. 6'2", 210 lbs. Born, Helsinki, Finland, June 27, 1979. Atlanta's 10th choice, 245th overall, in 1999 Entry Draft.

Season	Club	League	GP	G	A	Pts	PIM	PP	SH	GW	S	%	+/-	TF	F%	Min	GP	G	A	Pts	PIM	PP	SH	GW	Min
1994-95	Jokerit Helsinki C	Finn-Jr.	27	8	13	21	40	....	....	....	....	....	....	....	....	....	6	0	0	0	0	....	....	....	....
1995-96	Jokerit Helsinki B	Finn-Jr.	25	8	4	12	12	....	....	....	....	....	....	....	....	....	6	1	2	3	4	....	....	....	....
1996-97	Jokerit Helsinki B	Finn-Jr.	30	13	19	32	64	....	....	....	....	....	....	....	....	....	....	....	....	....	....	....	....	....	....
	Jokerit Helsinki Jr.	Finn-Jr.	20	0	2	2	10	....	....	....	....	....	....	....	....	....	5	0	0	0	0	....	....	....	....
1997-98	Jokerit Helsinki Jr.	Finn-Jr.	36	10	28	38	48	....	....	....	....	....	....	....	....	....	8	0	1	1	4	....	....	....	....
1998-99	Jokerit Helsinki Jr.	Finn-Jr.	30	20	24	44	20	....	....	....	....	....	....	....	....	....	8	1	3	4	22	....	....	....	....
	Jokerit Helsinki	Finland	30	0	0	0	14	....	....	....	....	....	....	....	....	....	3	0	0	0	0	....	....	....	....
	Jokerit Helsinki	EuroHL	1	0	2	2	0	....	....	....	....	....	....	....	....	....	1	0	0	0	0	....	....	....	....
99-2000	Jokerit Helsinki Jr.	Finn-Jr.	5	6	4	10	4	....	....	....	....	....	....	....	....	....	....	....	....	....	....	....	....	....	....
	Jokerit Helsinki	Finland	14	0	1	1	0	....	....	....	....	....	....	....	....	....	....	....	....	....	....	....	....	....	....
	HPK Jr.	Finn-Jr.	2	3	1	4	2	....	....	....	....	....	....	....	....	....	....	....	....	....	....	....	....	....	....
	HPK Jr.	Finn-Q	....	....	....	....	....	....	....	....	....	....	....	....	....	....	2	1	2	3	2	....	....	....	....
	HPK Hameenlinna	Finland	38	8	19	27	65	....	....	....	....	....	....	....	....	....	8	3	4	7	10	....	....	....	....
2000-01	HPK Hameenlinna	Finland	56	16	24	40	90	....	....	....	....	....	....	....	....	....	....	....	....	....	....	....	....	....	....
2001-02	HPK Hameenlinna	Finland	17	6	16	22	14	....	....	....	....	....	....	....	....	....	....	....	....	....	....	....	....	....	....
2002-03	HPK Hameenlinna	Finland	50	13	*38	51	92	....	....	....	....	....	....	....	....	....	13	6	6	12	18	....	....	....	....
2003-04	**Atlanta**	**NHL**	**33**	**1**	**2**	**3**	**22**	**0**	**0**	**1**	**23**	**4.3**	**–7**	**252**	**51.2**	**10:08**	....	....	....	....	....	....	....	....	....
	Chicago Wolves	AHL	50	15	22	37	34	....	....	....	....	....	....	....	....	....	10	1	6	7	31	....	....	....	....
	NHL Totals		**33**	**1**	**2**	**3**	**22**	**0**	**0**	**1**	**23**	**4.3**		**252**	**51.2**	**10:08**	....	....	....	....	....	....	....	....	....

			Regular Season														Playoffs								
Season	Club	League	GP	G	A	Pts	PIM	PP	SH	GW	S	%	+/-	TF	F%	Min	GP	G	A	Pts	PIM	PP	SH	GW	Min

SAPRYKIN, Oleg
(sah-PRIH-kihn, OH-lehg) **CGY.**

Left wing. Shoots left. 6', 195 lbs. Born, Moscow, USSR, February 12, 1981. Calgary's 1st choice, 11th overall, in 1999 Entry Draft.

1997-98	HC CSKA 2	Russia-3	15	0	3	3	6	....	....	....	....	....	....	....	....	....	....	....	....	....	....	....	....	....	....
	HC CSKA	Russia	20	0	2	2	8	....	....	....	....	....	....	....	....	....	....	....	....	....	....	....	....	....	....
1998-99	Seattle	WHL	66	47	46	93	107	....	....	....	....	....	....	....	....	....	11	5	11	16	36	....	....	....	....
99-2000	**Calgary**	**NHL**	**4**	**0**	**1**	**1**	**2**	**0**	**0**	**0**	**2**	**0.0**	**–4**	**0**	**0.0**	**12:35**	....	....	....	....	....	....	....	....	....
	Seattle	WHL	48	30	36	66	91	....	....	....	....	....	....	....	....	....	6	3	3	6	37	....	....	....	....
2000-01	**Calgary**	**NHL**	**59**	**9**	**14**	**23**	**43**	**2**	**0**	**0**	**95**	**9.5**	**4**	**2**	**50.0**	**12:10**	....	....	....	....	....	....	....	....	....
2001-02	**Calgary**	**NHL**	**3**	**0**	**0**	**0**	**0**	**0**	**0**	**0**	**9**	**0.0**	**–2**	**0**	**0.0**	**13:25**	....	....	....	....	....	....	....	....	....
	Saint John Flames	AHL	52	5	19	24	53	....	....	....	....	....	....	....	....	....	....	....	....	....	....	....	....	....	....
2002-03	**Calgary**	**NHL**	**52**	**8**	**15**	**23**	**46**	**1**	**0**	**1**	**116**	**6.9**	**5**	**1**	**0.0**	**11:53**	....	....	....	....	....	....	....	....	....
	Saint John Flames	AHL	21	12	9	21	22	....	....	....	....	....	....	....	....	....	....	....	....	....	....	....	....	....	....
2003-04	**Calgary**	**NHL**	**69**	**12**	**17**	**29**	**41**	**4**	**0**	**0**	**151**	**7.9**	**1**	**13**	**23.1**	**13:48**	**26**	**3**	**3**	**6**	**14**	**1**	**0**	**1**	**14:01**
	NHL Totals		**187**	**29**	**47**	**76**	**132**	**7**	**0**	**1**	**373**	**7.8**		**16**	**25.0**	**12:43**	**26**	**3**	**3**	**6**	**14**	**1**	**0**	**1**	**14:01**

WHL West Second All-Star Team (1999, 2000)

SARICH, Cory
(SAHR-ihch, KOH-ree) **T.B.**

Defense. Shoots right. 6'5", 204 lbs. Born, Saskatoon, Sask., August 16, 1978. Buffalo's 2nd choice, 27th overall, in 1996 Entry Draft.

1994-95	Sask. Contacts	SMHL	31	5	22	27	99	....	....	....	....	....	....	....	....	....	....	....	....	....	....	....	....	....	....
	Saskatoon Blades	WHL	6	0	0	0	4	....	....	....	....	....	....	....	....	....	3	0	1	1	0	....	....	....	....
1995-96	Saskatoon Blades	WHL	59	5	18	23	54	....	....	....	....	....	....	....	....	....	3	0	0	0	4	....	....	....	....
1996-97	Saskatoon Blades	WHL	58	6	27	33	158	....	....	....	....	....	....	....	....	....	....	....	....	....	....	....	....	....	....
1997-98	Saskatoon Blades	WHL	33	5	24	29	90	....	....	....	....	....	....	....	....	....	....	....	....	....	....	....	....	....	....
	Seattle	WHL	13	3	16	19	47	....	....	....	....	....	....	....	....	....	....	....	....	....	....	....	....	....	....
1998-99	**Buffalo**	**NHL**	**4**	**0**	**0**	**0**	**0**	**0**	**0**	**0**	**2**	**0.0**	**3**	**0**	**0.0**	**13:11**	....	....	....	....	....	....	....	....	....
	Rochester	AHL	77	3	26	29	82	....	....	....	....	....	....	....	....	....	20	2	4	6	14	....	....	....	....
99-2000	**Buffalo**	**NHL**	**42**	**0**	**4**	**4**	**35**	**0**	**0**	**0**	**49**	**0.0**	**2**	**0**	**0.0**	**17:42**	....	....	....	....	....	....	....	....	....
	Rochester	AHL	15	0	6	6	44	....	....	....	....	....	....	....	....	....	....	....	....	....	....	....	....	....	....
	Tampa Bay	**NHL**	**17**	**0**	**2**	**2**	**42**	**0**	**0**	**0**	**20**	**0.0**	**–8**	**0**	**0.0**	**20:42**	....	....	....	....	....	....	....	....	....
2000-01	**Tampa Bay**	**NHL**	**73**	**1**	**8**	**9**	**106**	**0**	**0**	**1**	**66**	**1.5**	**–25**	**3**	**0.0**	**18:44**	....	....	....	....	....	....	....	....	....
	Detroit Vipers	IHL	3	0	2	2	2	....	....	....	....	....	....	....	....	....	....	....	....	....	....	....	....	....	....
2001-02	Springfield	AHL	2	0	0	0	0	....	....	....	....	....	....	....	....	....	....	....	....	....	....	....	....	....	....
	Tampa Bay	**NHL**	**72**	**0**	**11**	**11**	**105**	**0**	**0**	**0**	**55**	**0.0**	**–4**	**2**	**50.0**	**16:06**	....	....	....	....	....	....	....	....	....
2002-03	**Tampa Bay**	**NHL**	**82**	**5**	**9**	**14**	**63**	**0**	**0**	**2**	**79**	**6.3**	**–3**	**3**	**0.0**	**19:36**	**11**	**0**	**2**	**2**	**6**	**0**	**0**	**0**	**21:18**
2003-04♦	**Tampa Bay**	**NHL**	**82**	**3**	**16**	**19**	**89**	**0**	**1**	**1**	**93**	**3.2**	**5**	**1**	**0.0**	**18:31**	**23**	**0**	**2**	**2**	**25**	**0**	**0**	**0**	**19:11**
	NHL Totals		**372**	**9**	**50**	**59**	**440**	**0**	**1**	**4**	**364**	**2.5**		**9**	**11.1**	**18:17**	**34**	**0**	**4**	**4**	**31**	**0**	**0**	**0**	**19:52**

WHL West Second All-Star Team (1998)

Traded to **Tampa Bay** by **Buffalo** with Wayne Primeau, Brian Holzinger and Buffalo's 3rd round choice (Alexander Kharitonov) in 2000 Entry Draft for Chris Gratton and Tampa Bay's 2nd round choice (Derek Roy) in 2001 Entry Draft, March 9, 2000.

SARNO, Peter
(SAHR-noh, PEE-tuhr) **VAN.**

Center. Shoots left. 5'11", 185 lbs. Born, Toronto, Ont., July 26, 1979. Edmonton's 6th choice, 141st overall, in 1997 Entry Draft.

1995-96	North York	MTJHL	52	39	57	96	27	....	....	....	....	....	....	....	....	....	....	....	....	....	....	....	....	....	....
1996-97	Windsor Spitfires	OHL	66	20	63	83	59	....	....	....	....	....	....	....	....	....	5	0	3	3	6	....	....	....	....
1997-98	Windsor Spitfires	OHL	64	33	*88	*121	18	....	....	....	....	....	....	....	....	....	....	....	....	....	....	....	....	....	....
	Hamilton	AHL	8	1	1	2	2	....	....	....	....	....	....	....	....	....	....	....	....	....	....	....	....	....	....
1998-99	Sarnia Sting	OHL	68	37	*93	*130	49	....	....	....	....	....	....	....	....	....	6	1	7	8	2	....	....	....	....
99-2000	Hamilton	AHL	67	10	36	46	31	....	....	....	....	....	....	....	....	....	....	....	....	....	....	....	....	....	....
2000-01	Hamilton	AHL	79	19	46	65	64	....	....	....	....	....	....	....	....	....	....	....	....	....	....	....	....	....	....
2001-02	Hamilton	AHL	76	12	40	52	38	....	....	....	....	....	....	....	....	....	15	6	7	13	4	....	....	....	....
2002-03	Blues Espoo	Finland	45	17	23	40	34	....	....	....	....	....	....	....	....	....	7	2	1	3	2	....	....	....	....
2003-04	**Edmonton**	**NHL**	**6**	**1**	**0**	**1**	**2**	**0**	**0**	**0**	**5**	**20.0**	**2**	**59**	**52.5**	**10:15**	....	....	....	....	....	....	....	....	....
	Toronto	AHL	31	6	12	18	29	....	....	....	....	....	....	....	....	....	....	....	....	....	....	....	....	....	....
	Manitoba Moose	AHL	23	5	9	14	6	....	....	....	....	....	....	....	....	....	....	....	....	....	....	....	....	....	....
	NHL Totals		**6**	**1**	**0**	**1**	**2**	**0**	**0**	**0**	**5**	**20.0**		**59**	**52.5**	**10:15**	....	....	....	....	....	....	....	....	....

OHL All-Rookie Team (1997) • OHL Rookie of the Year (1997)

Traded to **Vancouver** by **Edmonton** for Tyler Moss, February 16, 2004.

SATAN, Miroslav
(SHA-tuhn, MEER-oh-slav) **BUF.**

Left wing. Shoots left. 6'3", 190 lbs. Born, Topolcany, Czech., October 22, 1974. Edmonton's 6th choice, 111th overall, in 1993 Entry Draft.

1991-92	VTJ Topolcany Jr.	Czech-Jr.	31	30	22	52	....	....	....	....	....	....	....	....	....	....	....	....	....	....	....	....	....	....	....
	VTJ Topolcany	Czech-2	9	2	1	3	6	....	....	....	....	....	....	....	....	....	....	....	....	....	....	....	....	....	....
1992-93	Dukla Trencin	Czech	38	11	6	17	....	....	....	....	....	....	....	....	....	....	....	....	....	....	....	....	....	....	....
1993-94	Dukla Trencin	Slovakia	30	32	16	48	16	....	....	....	....	....	....	....	....	....	....	....	....	....	....	....	....	....	....
	Slovakia	Olympics	8	*9	0	9	0	....	....	....	....	....	....	....	....	....	....	....	....	....	....	....	....	....	....
1994-95	Cape Breton	AHL	25	24	16	40	15	....	....	....	....	....	....	....	....	....	....	....	....	....	....	....	....	....	....
	Detroit Vipers	IHL	8	1	3	4	4	....	....	....	....	....	....	....	....	....	....	....	....	....	....	....	....	....	....
	San Diego Gulls	IHL	6	0	2	2	6	....	....	....	....	....	....	....	....	....	....	....	....	....	....	....	....	....	....
1995-96	**Edmonton**	**NHL**	**62**	**18**	**17**	**35**	**22**	**6**	**0**	**4**	**113**	**15.9**	**0**	....	....	....	....	....	....	....	....	....	....	....	....
1996-97	**Edmonton**	**NHL**	**64**	**17**	**11**	**28**	**22**	**5**	**0**	**2**	**90**	**18.9**	**–4**	....	....	....	....	....	....	....	....	....	....	....	....
	Buffalo	**NHL**	**12**	**8**	**2**	**10**	**4**	**2**	**0**	**1**	**29**	**27.6**	**1**	....	....	....	**7**	**0**	**0**	**0**	**0**	**0**	**0**	**0**	....
1997-98	**Buffalo**	**NHL**	**79**	**22**	**24**	**46**	**34**	**9**	**0**	**4**	**139**	**15.8**	**2**	....	....	....	**14**	**5**	**4**	**9**	**4**	**4**	**0**	**1**	....
1998-99	**Buffalo**	**NHL**	**81**	**40**	**26**	**66**	**44**	**13**	**3**	**6**	**208**	**19.2**	**24**	**9**	**55.6**	**20:49**	**12**	**3**	**5**	**8**	**2**	**1**	**0**	**1**	**21:18**
99-2000	Dukla Trencin	Slovakia	3	2	8	10	2	....	....	....	....	....	....	....	....	....	....	....	....	....	....	....	....	....	....
	Buffalo	**NHL**	**81**	**33**	**34**	**67**	**32**	**5**	**3**	**5**	**265**	**12.5**	**16**	**7**	**14.3**	**20:35**	**5**	**3**	**2**	**5**	**0**	**0**	**0**	**0**	**19:52**
2000-01	**Buffalo**	**NHL**	**82**	**29**	**33**	**62**	**36**	**8**	**2**	**4**	**206**	**14.1**	**5**	**11**	**36.4**	**19:56**	**13**	**3**	**10**	**13**	**8**	**1**	**0**	**0**	**21:18**
2001-02	**Buffalo**	**NHL**	**82**	**37**	**36**	**73**	**33**	**15**	**5**	**5**	**267**	**13.9**	**14**	**4**	**50.0**	**21:10**	....	....	....	....	....	....	....	....	....
	Slovakia	Olympics	2	0	1	1	0	....	....	....	....	....	....	....	....	....	....	....	....	....	....	....	....	....	....
2002-03	**Buffalo**	**NHL**	**79**	**26**	**49**	**75**	**20**	**11**	**1**	**3**	**240**	**10.8**	**–3**	**10**	**20.0**	**21:23**	....	....	....	....	....	....	....	....	....
2003-04	Slovan Bratislava	Slovakia	7	6	4	10	41	....	....	....	....	....	....	....	....	....	....	....	....	....	....	....	....	....	....
	Buffalo	**NHL**	**82**	**29**	**28**	**57**	**30**	**11**	**1**	**5**	**206**	**14.1**	**–15**	**9**	**22.2**	**20:02**	....	....	....	....	....	....	....	....	....
	NHL Totals		**704**	**259**	**260**	**519**	**277**	**85**	**15**	**39**	**1763**	**14.7**		**50**	**32.0**	**20:39**	**51**	**14**	**21**	**35**	**14**	**6**	**0**	**2**	**21:04**

Played in NHL All-Star Game (2000, 2003)

Traded to **Buffalo** by **Edmonton** for Barrie Moore and Craig Millar, March 18, 1997.

SAUER, Kurt
(SAW-uhr, KUHRT) **COL.**

Defense. Shoots left. 6'4", 225 lbs. Born, St. Cloud, MN, January 16, 1981. Colorado's 5th choice, 88th overall, in 2000 Entry Draft.

1998-99	North Iowa	USHL	52	1	4	5	67	....	....	....	....	....	....	....	....	....	....	....	....	....	....	....	....	....	....
99-2000	Spokane Chiefs	WHL	71	3	12	15	48	....	....	....	....	....	....	....	....	....	15	2	1	3	8	....	....	....	....
2000-01	Spokane Chiefs	WHL	48	5	10	15	85	....	....	....	....	....	....	....	....	....	3	1	0	1	2	....	....	....	....
2001-02	Spokane Chiefs	WHL	61	4	20	24	73	....	....	....	....	....	....	....	....	....	11	0	3	3	12	....	....	....	....
2002-03	**Anaheim**	**NHL**	**80**	**1**	**2**	**3**	**74**	**0**	**0**	**0**	**50**	**2.0**	**–23**	**0**	**0.0**	**18:33**	**21**	**1**	**1**	**2**	**6**	**0**	**1**	**1**	**20:45**
2003-04	**Anaheim**	**NHL**	**55**	**1**	**4**	**5**	**32**	**0**	**0**	**0**	**32**	**3.1**	**–8**	**0**	**0.0**	**16:54**	....	....	....	....	....	....	....	....	....
	Colorado	**NHL**	**14**	**0**	**1**	**1**	**19**	**0**	**0**	**0**	**12**	**0.0**	**–3**	**0**	**0.0**	**15:04**	**3**	**0**	**0**	**0**	**0**	**0**	**0**	**0**	**11:56**
	NHL Totals		**149**	**2**	**7**	**9**	**125**	**0**	**0**	**0**	**94**	**2.1**		**0**	**0.0**	**17:37**	**24**	**1**	**1**	**2**	**6**	**0**	**1**	**1**	**19:39**

WHL West First All-Star Team (2002)

Signed as a free agent by **Anaheim**, July 6, 2002. Traded to **Colorado** by **Anaheim** with Anaheim's 4th round choice in 2005 Entry Draft for Martin Skoula, February 21, 2004.

SAVAGE, Andre

(SA-vahj, AWN-dray) **COL.**

Center. Shoots right. 6', 195 lbs. Born, Ottawa, Ont., May 27, 1975.

			Regular Season														Playoffs								
Season	Club	League	GP	G	A	Pts	PIM	PP	SH	GW	S	%	+/-	TF	F%	Min	GP	G	A	Pts	PIM	PP	SH	GW	Min
1992-93	Gloucester	OCJHL	54	34	34	68	38	....	....	....	....	....	....	....	....	....	....	....	....	....	....	....	....	....	....
1993-94	Gloucester	OCJHL	57	43	74	117	44	....	....	....	....	....	....	....	....	....	....	....	....	....	....	....	....	....	....
1994-95	Michigan Tech	WCHA	39	7	17	24	56	....	....	....	....	....	....	....	....	....	....	....	....	....	....	....	....	....	....
1995-96	Michigan Tech	WCHA	38	13	27	40	42	....	....	....	....	....	....	....	....	....	....	....	....	....	....	....	....	....	....
1996-97	Michigan Tech	WCHA	37	18	20	38	34	....	....	....	....	....	....	....	....	....	....	....	....	....	....	....	....	....	....
1997-98	Michigan Tech	WCHA	33	14	27	41	34	....	....	....	....	....	....	....	....	....	....	....	....	....	....	....	....	....	....
1998-99	**Boston**	**NHL**	**6**	**1**	**0**	**1**	**0**	**0**	**0**	**0**	**8**	**12.5**	**2**	**32**	**65.6**	**9:31**	....	....	....	....	....	....	....	....	....
	Providence Bruins	AHL	63	27	42	69	54	....	....	....	....	....	....	....	....	....	5	0	1	1	0	....	....	....	....
99-2000	**Boston**	**NHL**	**43**	**7**	**13**	**20**	**10**	**2**	**0**	**1**	**70**	**10.0**	**–8**	**619**	**55.1**	**14:40**	....	....	....	....	....	....	....	....	....
	Providence Bruins	AHL	30	15	17	32	22	....	....	....	....	....	....	....	....	....	14	6	7	13	22	....	....	....	....
2000-01	**Boston**	**NHL**	**1**	**0**	**0**	**0**	**0**	**0**	**0**	**0**	**1**	**0.0**	**0**	**3**	**100.0**	**4:38**	....	....	....	....	....	....	....	....	....
	Providence Bruins	AHL	35	13	15	28	47	....	....	....	....	....	....	....	....	....	17	3	4	7	18	....	....	....	....
2001-02	Manitoba Moose	AHL	76	35	26	61	115	....	....	....	....	....	....	....	....	....	6	2	3	5	16	....	....	....	....
2002-03	Philadelphia	AHL	64	11	31	42	66	....	....	....	....	....	....	....	....	....	....	....	....	....	....	....	....	....	....
	Philadelphia	**NHL**	**16**	**2**	**1**	**3**	**4**	**0**	**0**	**1**	**13**	**15.4**	**2**	**74**	**55.4**	**7:49**	....	....	....	....	....	....	....	....	....
2003-04	Philadelphia	AHL	8	1	0	1	12	....	....	....	....	....	....	....	....	....	....	....	....	....	....	....	....	....	....
	Providence Bruins	AHL	63	16	30	46	94	....	....	....	....	....	....	....	....	....	1	0	0	0	2	....	....	....	....
	NHL Totals		**66**	**10**	**14**	**24**	**14**	**2**	**0**	**2**	**92**	**10.9**		**728**	**55.8**	**12:23**	....	....	....	....	....	....	....	....	....

WCHA First All-Star Team (1998)

Signed as a free agent by **Boston**, June 18, 1998. Signed as a free agent by **Vancouver**, August 2, 2001. Signed as a free agent by **Philadelphia**, August 20, 2002. Loaned to **Providence** (AHL) by **Philadelphia** (AHL) for the loan of P.J. Stock, October 29, 2003. Signed as a free agent by **Colorado**, July 22, 2004.

SAVAGE, Brian

(SA-vuhj, BRIGH-uhn) **PHX.**

Left wing. Shoots left. 6'1", 200 lbs. Born, Sudbury, Ont., February 24, 1971. Montreal's 11th choice, 171st overall, in 1991 Entry Draft.

Season	Club	League	GP	G	A	Pts	PIM	PP	SH	GW	S	%	+/-	TF	F%	Min	GP	G	A	Pts	PIM	PP	SH	GW	Min
1989-90	Sud. Cub Wolves	NOJHA	32	45	40	85	61	....	....	....	....	....	....	....	....	....	....	....	....	....	....	....	....	....	....
1990-91	Miami University	CCHA	28	5	6	11	26	....	....	....	....	....	....	....	....	....	....	....	....	....	....	....	....	....	....
1991-92	Miami University	CCHA	40	24	16	40	43	....	....	....	....	....	....	....	....	....	....	....	....	....	....	....	....	....	....
1992-93	Miami University	CCHA	38	*37	21	58	44	....	....	....	....	....	....	....	....	....	....	....	....	....	....	....	....	....	....
1993-94	Team Canada	Nat-Tm	51	20	26	46	38	....	....	....	....	....	....	....	....	....	....	....	....	....	....	....	....	....	....
	Canada	Olympics	8	2	2	4	6	....	....	....	....	....	....	....	....	....	....	....	....	....	....	....	....	....	....
	Montreal	**NHL**	**3**	**1**	**0**	**1**	**0**	**0**	**0**	**0**	**3**	**33.3**	**0**	....	....	....	**3**	**0**	**2**	**2**	**0**	**0**	**0**	**0**	....
	Fredericton	AHL	17	12	15	27	4	....	....	....	....	....	....	....	....	....	....	....	....	....	....	....	....	....	....
1994-95	**Montreal**	**NHL**	**37**	**12**	**7**	**19**	**27**	**0**	**0**	**0**	**64**	**18.8**	**5**	....	....	....	....	....	....	....	....	....	....	....	....
1995-96	**Montreal**	**NHL**	**75**	**25**	**8**	**33**	**28**	**4**	**0**	**4**	**150**	**16.7**	**–8**	....	....	....	**6**	**0**	**2**	**2**	**2**	**0**	**0**	**0**	....
1996-97	**Montreal**	**NHL**	**81**	**23**	**37**	**60**	**39**	**5**	**0**	**2**	**219**	**10.5**	**–14**	....	....	....	**5**	**1**	**1**	**2**	**0**	**0**	**0**	**0**	....
1997-98	**Montreal**	**NHL**	**64**	**26**	**17**	**43**	**36**	**8**	**0**	**7**	**152**	**17.1**	**11**	....	....	....	**9**	**0**	**2**	**2**	**6**	**0**	**0**	**0**	....
1998-99	**Montreal**	**NHL**	**54**	**16**	**10**	**26**	**20**	**5**	**0**	**4**	**124**	**12.9**	**–14**	**70**	**44.3**	**16:30**	....	....	....	....	....	....	....	....	....
99-2000	**Montreal**	**NHL**	**38**	**17**	**12**	**29**	**19**	**6**	**1**	**5**	**107**	**15.9**	**–4**	**67**	**47.8**	**17:56**	....	....	....	....	....	....	....	....	....
2000-01	**Montreal**	**NHL**	**62**	**21**	**24**	**45**	**26**	**12**	**0**	**1**	**172**	**12.2**	**–13**	**30**	**56.7**	**18:50**	....	....	....	....	....	....	....	....	....
2001-02	**Montreal**	**NHL**	**47**	**14**	**15**	**29**	**30**	**7**	**0**	**2**	**117**	**12.0**	**–14**	**3**	**0.0**	**18:12**	....	....	....	....	....	....	....	....	....
	Phoenix	**NHL**	**30**	**6**	**6**	**12**	**8**	**2**	**0**	**2**	**47**	**12.8**	**1**	**4**	**50.0**	**15:02**	**5**	**0**	**0**	**0**	**0**	**0**	**0**	**0**	**11:13**
2002-03	**Phoenix**	**NHL**	**43**	**6**	**10**	**16**	**22**	**1**	**0**	**1**	**68**	**8.8**	**–4**	**14**	**35.7**	**13:22**	....	....	....	....	....	....	....	....	....
2003-04	**Phoenix**	**NHL**	**61**	**12**	**13**	**25**	**36**	**3**	**0**	**1**	**101**	**11.9**	**–5**	**13**	**38.5**	**14:19**	....	....	....	....	....	....	....	....	....
	St. Louis	**NHL**	**13**	**4**	**3**	**7**	**2**	**1**	**0**	**1**	**23**	**17.4**	**–3**	**0**	**0.0**	**16:15**	**5**	**1**	**1**	**2**	**0**	**0**	**0**	**0**	**15:10**
	NHL Totals		**608**	**183**	**162**	**345**	**293**	**54**	**1**	**30**	**1347**	**13.6**		**201**	**45.8**	**16:24**	**33**	**2**	**8**	**10**	**8**	**0**	**0**	**0**	**13:11**

CCHA First All-Star Team (1993) • CCHA Player of the Year (1993) • NCAA West Second All-American Team (1993)

• Missed majority of 1999-2000 season recovering from neck injury suffered in game vs. Los Angeles, November 20, 1999. Traded to **Phoenix** by **Montreal** with Montreal's 3rd round choice (Matt Jones) in 2002 Entry Draft and future considerations for Sergei Berezin, January 25, 2002. Traded to **St. Louis** by **Phoenix** for future considerations, March 9, 2004. Claimed on waivers by **Phoenix** from **St. Louis**, June 29, 2004.

SAVARD, Marc

(sa-VAHR, MAHRK) **ATL.**

Center. Shoots left. 5'10", 195 lbs. Born, Ottawa, Ont., July 17, 1977. NY Rangers' 3rd choice, 91st overall, in 1995 Entry Draft.

Season	Club	League	GP	G	A	Pts	PIM	PP	SH	GW	S	%	+/-	TF	F%	Min	GP	G	A	Pts	PIM	PP	SH	GW	Min
1992-93	Metcalfe Jets	OJHL-B	36	*44	55	*99	38	....	....	....	....	....	....	....	....	....	....	....	....	....	....	....	....	....	....
1993-94	Oshawa Generals	OHL	61	18	39	57	20	....	....	....	....	....	....	....	....	....	5	4	3	7	8	....	....	....	....
1994-95	Oshawa Generals	OHL	66	43	96	*139	78	....	....	....	....	....	....	....	....	....	7	5	6	11	8	....	....	....	....
1995-96	Oshawa Generals	OHL	48	28	59	87	77	....	....	....	....	....	....	....	....	....	5	4	5	9	6	....	....	....	....
1996-97	Oshawa Generals	OHL	64	43	*87	*130	94	....	....	....	....	....	....	....	....	....	18	13	*24	*37	20	....	....	....	....
1997-98	**NY Rangers**	**NHL**	**28**	**1**	**5**	**6**	**4**	**0**	**0**	**0**	**32**	**3.1**	**–4**	....	....	....	....	....	....	....	....	....	....	....	....
	Hartford	AHL	58	21	53	74	66	....	....	....	....	....	....	....	....	....	15	8	19	27	24	....	....	....	....
1998-99	**NY Rangers**	**NHL**	**70**	**9**	**36**	**45**	**38**	**4**	**0**	**1**	**116**	**7.8**	**–7**	**956**	**48.4**	**14:35**	....	....	....	....	....	....	....	....	....
	Hartford	AHL	9	3	10	13	16	....	....	....	....	....	....	....	....	....	7	1	12	13	16	....	....	....	....
99-2000	**Calgary**	**NHL**	**78**	**22**	**31**	**53**	**56**	**4**	**0**	**3**	**184**	**12.0**	**–2**	**1021**	**49.6**	**16:36**	....	....	....	....	....	....	....	....	....
2000-01	**Calgary**	**NHL**	**77**	**23**	**42**	**65**	**46**	**10**	**1**	**5**	**197**	**11.7**	**–12**	**1050**	**53.1**	**19:13**	....	....	....	....	....	....	....	....	....
2001-02	**Calgary**	**NHL**	**56**	**14**	**19**	**33**	**48**	**7**	**0**	**3**	**140**	**10.0**	**–18**	**577**	**54.8**	**17:20**	....	....	....	....	....	....	....	....	....
2002-03	**Calgary**	**NHL**	**10**	**1**	**2**	**3**	**8**	**0**	**0**	**0**	**21**	**4.8**	**–3**	**89**	**52.8**	**14:41**	....	....	....	....	....	....	....	....	....
	Atlanta	**NHL**	**57**	**16**	**31**	**47**	**77**	**6**	**0**	**4**	**127**	**12.6**	**–11**	**1247**	**50.9**	**19:50**	....	....	....	....	....	....	....	....	....
2003-04	**Atlanta**	**NHL**	**45**	**19**	**33**	**52**	**85**	**6**	**1**	**3**	**133**	**14.3**	**–8**	**1083**	**49.9**	**22:19**	....	....	....	....	....	....	....	....	....
	NHL Totals		**421**	**105**	**199**	**304**	**362**	**37**	**2**	**19**	**950**	**11.1**		**6023**	**50.9**	**17:56**	....	....	....	....	....	....	....	....	....

OHL Second All-Star Team (1995)

Traded to **Calgary** by **NY Rangers** with NY Rangers 1st round choice (Oleg Saprykin) in 1999 Entry Draft for the rights to Jan Hlavac and Calgary's 1st (Jamie Lundmark) and 3rd (later traded back to Calgary – Calgary selected Craig Andersson) round choices in 1999 Entry Draft, June 26, 1999. Traded to **Atlanta** by **Calgary** for Ruslan Zainullin, November 15, 2002.

SCATCHARD, Dave

(SKAT-chuhrd, DAYV) **NYI**

Center. Shoots right. 6'2", 224 lbs. Born, Hinton, Alta., February 20, 1976. Vancouver's 3rd choice, 42nd overall, in 1994 Entry Draft.

Season	Club	League	GP	G	A	Pts	PIM	PP	SH	GW	S	%	+/-	TF	F%	Min	GP	G	A	Pts	PIM	PP	SH	GW	Min
1991-92	Salmon Arm	BCAHA	65	98	100	198	167	....	....	....	....	....	....	....	....	....	....	....	....	....	....	....	....	....	....
1992-93	Kimberley	RMJHL	51	20	23	43	61	....	....	....	....	....	....	....	....	....	....	....	....	....	....	....	....	....	....
1993-94	Portland	WHL	47	9	11	20	46	....	....	....	....	....	....	....	....	....	10	2	1	3	4	....	....	....	....
1994-95	Portland	WHL	71	20	30	50	148	....	....	....	....	....	....	....	....	....	8	0	3	3	21	....	....	....	....
1995-96	Portland	WHL	59	19	28	47	146	....	....	....	....	....	....	....	....	....	7	1	8	9	14	....	....	....	....
	Syracuse Crunch	AHL	1	0	0	0	0	....	....	....	....	....	....	....	....	....	15	2	5	7	29	....	....	....	....
1996-97	Syracuse Crunch	AHL	26	8	7	15	65	....	....	....	....	....	....	....	....	....	....	....	....	....	....	....	....	....	....
1997-98	**Vancouver**	**NHL**	**76**	**13**	**11**	**24**	**165**	**0**	**0**	**1**	**85**	**15.3**	**–4**	....	....	....	....	....	....	....	....	....	....	....	....
1998-99	**Vancouver**	**NHL**	**82**	**13**	**13**	**26**	**140**	**0**	**2**	**2**	**130**	**10.0**	**–12**	**1007**	**56.3**	**13:46**	....	....	....	....	....	....	....	....	....
99-2000	**Vancouver**	**NHL**	**21**	**0**	**4**	**4**	**24**	**0**	**0**	**0**	**25**	**0.0**	**–3**	**190**	**59.5**	**10:12**	....	....	....	....	....	....	....	....	....
	NY Islanders	**NHL**	**44**	**12**	**14**	**26**	**93**	**0**	**1**	**1**	**103**	**11.7**	**0**	**710**	**55.8**	**13:42**	....	....	....	....	....	....	....	....	....
2000-01	**NY Islanders**	**NHL**	**81**	**21**	**24**	**45**	**114**	**4**	**0**	**5**	**176**	**11.9**	**–9**	**1322**	**55.1**	**16:50**	....	....	....	....	....	....	....	....	....
2001-02	**NY Islanders**	**NHL**	**80**	**12**	**15**	**27**	**111**	**3**	**1**	**4**	**117**	**10.3**	**–4**	**788**	**53.8**	**12:31**	**7**	**1**	**1**	**2**	**22**	**0**	**0**	**0**	**12:38**
2002-03	**NY Islanders**	**NHL**	**81**	**27**	**18**	**45**	**108**	**5**	**0**	**2**	**165**	**16.4**	**9**	**1147**	**52.7**	**14:30**	**5**	**1**	**0**	**1**	**6**	**0**	**0**	**1**	**15:58**
2003-04	**NY Islanders**	**NHL**	**61**	**9**	**16**	**25**	**78**	**1**	**1**	**1**	**111**	**8.1**	**12**	**1052**	**52.7**	**16:13**	**5**	**0**	**1**	**1**	**6**	**0**	**0**	**0**	**16:18**
	NHL Totals		**526**	**107**	**115**	**222**	**833**	**13**	**5**	**16**	**912**	**11.7**		**6216**	**54.5**	**14:23**	**17**	**2**	**2**	**4**	**34**	**0**	**0**	**1**	**14:41**

Traded to **NY Islanders** by **Vancouver** with Kevin Weekes and Bill Muckalt for Felix Potvin, NY Islanders' compensatory 2nd round choice (later traded to New Jersey – New Jersey selected Teemu Laine) in 2000 Entry Draft and NY Islanders' 3rd round choice (Thatcher Bell) in 2000 Entry Draft, December 19, 1999.

SCHAEFER, Peter

(SHAY-fuhr, PEE-tuhr) **OTT.**

Left wing. Shoots left. 5'11", 195 lbs. Born, Yellow Grass, Sask., July 12, 1977. Vancouver's 3rd choice, 66th overall, in 1995 Entry Draft.

Season	Club	League	GP	G	A	Pts	PIM	PP	SH	GW	S	%	+/-	TF	F%	Min	GP	G	A	Pts	PIM	PP	SH	GW	Min
1993-94	Yorkton Mallers	SMHL	32	27	14	41	133	....	....	....	....	....	....	....	....	....	....	....	....	....	....	....	....	....	....
	Brandon	WHL	2	1	0	1	0	....	....	....	....	....	....	....	....	....	....	....	....	....	....	....	....	....	....
1994-95	Brandon	WHL	68	27	32	59	34	....	....	....	....	....	....	....	....	....	18	5	3	8	18	....	....	....	....
1995-96	Brandon	WHL	69	47	61	108	53	....	....	....	....	....	....	....	....	....	19	10	13	23	5	....	....	....	....
1996-97	Brandon	WHL	61	49	74	123	85	....	....	....	....	....	....	....	....	....	6	1	4	5	4	....	....	....	....
	Syracuse Crunch	AHL	5	0	3	3	0	....	....	....	....	....	....	....	....	....	3	1	3	4	14	....	....	....	....
1997-98	Syracuse Crunch	AHL	73	19	44	63	41	....	....	....	....	....	....	....	....	....	5	2	1	3	2	....	....	....	....

			Regular Season														Playoffs								
Season	Club	League	GP	G	A	Pts	PIM	PP	SH	GW	S	%	+/-	TF	F%	Min	GP	G	A	Pts	PIM	PP	SH	GW	Min
1998-99	Vancouver	NHL	25	4	4	8	8	1	0	1	24	16.7	−1	6	0.0	13:21	....	....	....	....	....	....	....	....	....
	Syracuse Crunch	AHL	41	10	19	29	66	....	....	....	....	....	....	....	....	....	....	....	....	....	....	....	....	....	....
99-2000	Vancouver	NHL	71	16	15	31	20	2	2	4	101	15.8	0	21	19.1	15:28	....	....	....	....	....	....	....	....	....
	Syracuse Crunch	AHL	2	0	0	0	2	....	....	....	....	....	....	....	....	....	....	....	....	....	....	....	....	....	....
2000-01	Vancouver	NHL	82	16	20	36	22	3	4	2	163	9.8	4	25	32.0	16:18	3	0	0	0	0	0	0	0	13:08
2001-02	TPS Turku	Finland	33	16	15	31	93	....	....	....	....	....	....	....	....	....	8	1	2	3	2	....	....	....	....
2002-03	Ottawa	NHL	75	6	17	23	32	0	0	1	93	6.5	11	44	20.5	14:59	16	2	3	5	6	0	1	0	11:51
2003-04	Ottawa	NHL	81	15	24	39	26	2	2	3	112	13.4	22	39	23.1	15:36	7	0	2	2	4	0	0	0	14:25
	NHL Totals		334	57	80	137	108	8	8	11	493	11.6		135	22.2	15:26	26	2	5	7	10	0	1	0	12:42

WHL East First All-Star Team (1996, 1997) • Canadian Major Junior First All-Star Team (1997)

Signed as a free agent by **TPS Turku** (Finland) with Vancouver retaining NHL rights, October 18, 2001. Traded to **Ottawa** by **Vancouver** for Sami Salo, September 21, 2002.

SCHASTLIVY, Petr
(schust-LEE-vee, PEH-tuhr)

Left wing. Shoots left. 6'1", 204 lbs. Born, Angarsk, USSR, April 18, 1979. Ottawa's 5th choice, 101st overall, in 1998 Entry Draft.

Season	Club	League	GP	G	A	Pts	PIM	PP	SH	GW	S	%	+/-	TF	F%	Min	GP	G	A	Pts	PIM	PP	SH	GW	Min
1997-98	Yaroslavl	Russia	47	15	9	24	34	....	....	....	....	....	....	....	....	....	....	....	....	....	....	....	....	....	....
	Yaroslavl	Russia	4	0	0	0	0	....	....	....	....	....	....	....	....	....	....	....	....	....	....	....	....	....	....
1998-99	Yaroslavl	Russia	40	6	1	7	28	....	....	....	....	....	....	....	....	....	6	0	0	0	2	....	....	....	....
99-2000	Ottawa	NHL	13	2	5	7	2	1	0	1	22	9.1	4	0	0.0	12:18	1	0	0	0	0	0	0	0	13:09
	Grand Rapids	IHL	46	16	12	28	10	....	....	....	....	....	....	....	....	....	17	8	7	15	6	....	....	....	....
2000-01	Ottawa	NHL	17	3	2	5	6	0	0	0	32	9.4	−1	0	0.0	11:20	....	....	....	....	....	....	....	....	....
	Grand Rapids	IHL	43	10	14	24	10	....	....	....	....	....	....	....	....	....	7	4	4	8	0	....	....	....	....
2001-02	Ottawa	NHL	1	0	1	1	0	0	0	0	0	0.0	1	0	0.0	3:21	....	....	....	....	....	....	....	....	....
	Grand Rapids	AHL	31	22	13	35	10	....	....	....	....	....	....	....	....	....	....	....	....	....	....	....	....	....	....
2002-03	Ottawa	NHL	33	9	10	19	4	5	0	2	68	13.2	3	2	0.0	13:21	....	....	....	....	....	....	....	....	....
2003-04	Ottawa	NHL	43	2	4	6	14	1	0	1	37	5.4	−1	11	45.5	9:32	....	....	....	....	....	....	....	....	....
	Anaheim	NHL	22	2	0	2	4	0	0	1	48	4.2	−3	2	50.0	11:21	....	....	....	....	....	....	....	....	....
	NHL Totals		129	18	22	40	30	7	0	5	207	8.7		15	40.0	11:17	1	0	0	0	0	0	0	0	13:09

• Missed majority of 2001-02 season recovering from knee injury suffered in game vs. Chicago, December 31, 2001. • Missed majority of 2002-03 season recovering from groin injury suffered in practice, October 5, 2002. Traded to **Anaheim** by **Ottawa** for Todd Simpson, February 4, 2004.

SCHMIDT, Chris
(SHMIHT, KRIHS) **L.A.**

Center. Shoots left. 6'3", 212 lbs. Born, Beaver Lodge, Alta., March 1, 1976. Los Angeles' 4th choice, 111th overall, in 1994 Entry Draft.

Season	Club	League	GP	G	A	Pts	PIM	PP	SH	GW	S	%	+/-	TF	F%	Min	GP	G	A	Pts	PIM	PP	SH	GW	Min
1992-93	Seattle	WHL	61	6	7	13	17	....	....	....	....	....	....	....	....	....	5	0	1	1	0	....	....	....	....
1993-94	Seattle	WHL	68	7	17	24	26	....	....	....	....	....	....	....	....	....	9	3	1	4	2	....	....	....	....
1994-95	Seattle	WHL	61	21	11	32	31	....	....	....	....	....	....	....	....	....	3	0	0	0	0	....	....	....	....
1995-96	Seattle	WHL	61	39	23	62	135	....	....	....	....	....	....	....	....	....	5	1	5	6	9	....	....	....	....
1996-97	Mississippi	ECHL	18	7	7	14	35	....	....	....	....	....	....	....	....	....	....	....	....	....	....	....	....	....	....
	Phoenix	IHL	37	3	6	9	60	....	....	....	....	....	....	....	....	....	....	....	....	....	....	....	....	....	....
1997-98	Fredericton	AHL	69	8	5	13	67	....	....	....	....	....	....	....	....	....	4	0	0	0	2	....	....	....	....
1998-99	Springfield	AHL	17	3	2	5	19	....	....	....	....	....	....	....	....	....	1	0	0	0	0	....	....	....	....
	Mississippi	ECHL	6	1	0	1	2	....	....	....	....	....	....	....	....	....	18	6	8	14	10	....	....	....	....
99-2000	Team Canada	Nat-Tm	33	1	9	10	28	....	....	....	....	....	....	....	....	....	....	....	....	....	....	....	....	....	....
	Lowell	AHL	38	8	10	18	38	....	....	....	....	....	....	....	....	....	7	2	1	3	8	....	....	....	....
2000-01	Lowell	AHL	79	21	32	53	84	....	....	....	....	....	....	....	....	....	4	2	2	4	2	....	....	....	....
2001-02	Manchester	AHL	62	9	12	21	43	....	....	....	....	....	....	....	....	....	5	0	2	2	0	....	....	....	....
2002-03	Los Angeles	NHL	10	0	2	2	5	0	0	0	10	0.0	−1	2	100.0	10:01	....	....	....	....	....	....	....	....	....
	Manchester	AHL	53	12	13	25	58	....	....	....	....	....	....	....	....	....	2	0	1	1	4	....	....	....	....
2003-04	Manchester	AHL	54	6	13	19	39	....	....	....	....	....	....	....	....	....	6	0	1	1	4	....	....	....	....
	NHL Totals		10	0	2	2	5	0	0	0	10	0.0		2	100.0	10:01	....	....	....	....	....	....	....	....	....

SCHNABEL, Robert
(SHNAH-buhl, RAW-buhrt)

Defense. Shoots left. 6'5", 230 lbs. Born, Prague, Czech., November 10, 1978. Phoenix's 7th choice, 129th overall, in 1998 Entry Draft.

Season	Club	League	GP	G	A	Pts	PIM	PP	SH	GW	S	%	+/-	TF	F%	Min	GP	G	A	Pts	PIM	PP	SH	GW	Min
1994-95	Slavia Praha Jr.	Czech-Jr.	35	11	6	17	14	....	....	....	....	....	....	....	....	....	....	....	....	....	....	....	....	....	....
1995-96	Slavia Praha Jr.	Czech-Jr.	38	3	5	8	....	....	....	....	....	....	....	....	....	....	....	....	....	....	....	....	....	....	....
1996-97	Slavia Praha Jr.	Czech-Jr.	36	5	2	7	....	....	....	....	....	....	....	....	....	....	....	....	....	....	....	....	....	....	....
	HC Slavia Praha	Czech	4	0	0	0	4	....	....	....	....	....	....	....	....	....	1	0	0	0	0	....	....	....	....
1997-98	Red Deer Rebels	WHL	61	1	22	23	143	....	....	....	....	....	....	....	....	....	5	0	0	0	16	....	....	....	....
1998-99	Red Deer Rebels	WHL	1	0	0	0	2	....	....	....	....	....	....	....	....	....	....	....	....	....	....	....	....	....	....
	Springfield	AHL	77	1	7	8	155	....	....	....	....	....	....	....	....	....	3	1	0	1	4	....	....	....	....
99-2000	Springfield	AHL	40	2	8	10	133	....	....	....	....	....	....	....	....	....	5	0	0	0	4	....	....	....	....
2000-01	Springfield	AHL	22	1	2	3	38	....	....	....	....	....	....	....	....	....	....	....	....	....	....	....	....	....	....
	Timra IK	Sweden	16	0	2	2	72	....	....	....	....	....	....	....	....	....	....	....	....	....	....	....	....	....	....
2001-02	Nashville	NHL	1	0	0	0	0	0	0	0	0	0.0	0	0	0.0	7:16	....	....	....	....	....	....	....	....	....
	Milwaukee	AHL	67	2	7	9	130	....	....	....	....	....	....	....	....	....	....	....	....	....	....	....	....	....	....
2002-03	Milwaukee	AHL	62	3	6	9	178	....	....	....	....	....	....	....	....	....	6	0	0	0	34	....	....	....	....
	Nashville	NHL	1	0	0	0	0	0	0	0	0	0.0	0	0	0.0	4:28	....	....	....	....	....	....	....	....	....
2003-04	Nashville	NHL	20	0	3	3	34	0	0	0	10	0.0	6	0	0.0	14:36	....	....	....	....	....	....	....	....	....
	Milwaukee	AHL	11	1	0	1	27	....	....	....	....	....	....	....	....	....	0	0	0	0	0	....	....	....	....
	NHL Totals		22	0	3	3	34	0	0	0	10	0.0		0	0.0	13:48	....	....	....	....	....	....	....	....	....

• Re-entered NHL Entry Draft. Originally NY Islanders' 5th choice, 79th overall, in 1997 Entry Draft.

Claimed on waivers by **Nashville** from **Phoenix**, January 2, 2001. • Missed majority of 2003-04 season recovering from wrist injury suffered in game vs. Columbus, October 18, 2003. Signed as a free agent by **HC Sparta Praha** (Czech), May 19, 2004.

SCHNEIDER, Mathieu
(SHNIGH-duhr, MA-thew) **DET.**

Defense. Shoots left. 5'10", 192 lbs. Born, New York, NY, June 12, 1969. Montreal's 4th choice, 44th overall, in 1987 Entry Draft.

Season	Club	League	GP	G	A	Pts	PIM	PP	SH	GW	S	%	+/-	TF	F%	Min	GP	G	A	Pts	PIM	PP	SH	GW	Min
1985-86	Mount St. Charles	Hi-School	19	3	27	30	....	....	....	....	....	....	....	....	....	....	....	....	....	....	....	....	....	....	....
1986-87	Cornwall Royals	OHL	63	7	29	36	75	....	....	....	....	....	....	....	....	....	5	0	0	0	22	....	....	....	....
1987-88	Cornwall Royals	OHL	48	21	40	61	83	....	....	....	....	....	....	....	....	....	11	2	6	8	14	....	....	....	....
	Montreal	NHL	4	0	0	0	2	0	0	0	2	0.0	−1	....	....	....	....	....	....	....	....	....	....	....	....
	Sherbrooke	AHL	....	....	....	....	....	....	....	....	....	....	....	....	....	....	3	0	3	3	12	....	....	....	....
1988-89	Cornwall Royals	OHL	59	16	57	73	96	....	....	....	....	....	....	....	....	....	18	7	20	27	30	....	....	....	....
1989-90	Montreal	NHL	44	7	14	21	25	5	0	1	84	8.3	2	....	....	....	9	1	3	4	31	1	0	0	....
	Sherbrooke	AHL	28	6	13	19	20	....	....	....	....	....	....	....	....	....	....	....	....	....	....	....	....	....	....
1990-91	Montreal	NHL	69	10	20	30	63	5	0	3	164	6.1	7	....	....	....	13	2	7	9	18	1	0	0	....
1991-92	Montreal	NHL	78	8	24	32	72	2	0	1	194	4.1	10	....	....	....	10	1	4	5	6	1	0	0	....
1992-93♦	Montreal	NHL	60	13	31	44	91	3	0	2	169	7.7	8	....	....	....	11	1	2	3	16	0	0	0	....
1993-94	Montreal	NHL	75	20	32	52	62	11	0	4	193	10.4	15	....	....	....	1	0	0	0	0	0	0	0	....
1994-95	Montreal	NHL	30	5	15	20	49	2	0	0	82	6.1	−3	....	....	....	....	....	....	....	....	....	....	....	....
	NY Islanders	NHL	13	3	6	9	30	1	0	2	36	8.3	−5	....	....	....	....	....	....	....	....	....	....	....	....
1995-96	NY Islanders	NHL	65	11	36	47	93	7	0	1	155	7.1	−18	....	....	....	....	....	....	....	....	....	....	....	....
	Toronto	NHL	13	2	5	7	10	0	0	0	36	5.6	−2	....	....	....	6	0	4	4	8	0	0	0	....
1996-97	Toronto	NHL	26	5	7	12	20	1	0	1	63	7.9	3	....	....	....	....	....	....	....	....	....	....	....	....
1997-98	Toronto	NHL	76	11	26	37	44	4	1	1	181	6.1	−12	....	....	....	....	....	....	....	....	....	....	....	....
	United States	Olympics	4	0	0	0	6	....	....	....	....	....	....	....	....	....	....	....	....	....	....	....	....	....	....
1998-99	NY Rangers	NHL	75	10	24	34	71	5	0	2	159	6.3	−19	0	0.0	24:35	....	....	....	....	....	....	....	....	....
99-2000	NY Rangers	NHL	80	10	20	30	78	3	0	1	228	4.4	−6	0	0.0	22:31	....	....	....	....	....	....	....	....	....
2000-01	Los Angeles	NHL	73	16	35	51	56	7	1	2	183	8.7	0	0	0.0	23:04	13	0	9	9	10	0	0	0	25:51
2001-02	Los Angeles	NHL	55	7	23	30	68	4	0	0	123	5.7	3	0	0.0	22:25	7	0	1	1	18	0	0	0	22:52

			Regular Season														Playoffs								
Season	Club	League	GP	G	A	Pts	PIM	PP	SH	GW	S	%	+/-	TF	F%	Min	GP	G	A	Pts	PIM	PP	SH	GW	Min
2002-03	**Los Angeles**	**NHL**	**65**	**14**	**29**	**43**	**57**	**10**	**0**	**1**	**162**	**8.6**	**0**	**0**	**0.0**	**22:20**	....	....	....	....	....	....	....	....	....
	Detroit	**NHL**	**13**	**2**	**5**	**7**	**16**	**1**	**0**	**0**	**37**	**5.4**	**2**	**0**	**0.0**	**22:42**	**4**	**0**	**0**	**0**	**6**	**0**	**0**	**0**	**28:16**
2003-04	**Detroit**	**NHL**	**78**	**14**	**32**	**46**	**56**	**4**	**1**	**4**	**165**	**8.5**	**22**	**4**	**0.0**	**24:29**	**12**	**1**	**2**	**3**	**8**	**1**	**0**	**1**	**26:30**
	NHL Totals		**992**	**168**	**384**	**552**	**963**	**75**	**3**	**26**	**2416**	**7.0**		**4**	**0.0**	**23:17**	**86**	**6**	**32**	**38**	**121**	**4**	**0**	**1**	**25:45**

OHL First All-Star Team (1988, 1989)

Played in NHL All-Star Game (1996, 2003)

Traded to **NY Islanders** by **Montreal** with Kirk Muller and Craig Darby for Pierre Turgeon and Vladimir Malakhov, April 5, 1995. Traded to **Toronto** by **NY Islanders** with Wendel Clark and D.J. Smith for Darby Hendrickson, Sean Haggerty, Kenny Jonsson and Toronto's 1st round choice (Roberto Luongo) in 1997 Entry Draft, March 13, 1996. • Missed majority of 1996-97 season recovering from groin injury suffered in game vs. St. Louis, December 27, 1996. Rights traded to **NY Rangers** by **Toronto** for Alexander Karpovtsev and NY Rangers' 4th round choice (Mirko Murovic) in 1999 Entry Draft, October 14, 1998. Selected by **Columbus** from **NY Rangers** in Expansion Draft, June 23, 2000. Signed as a free agent by **Los Angeles**, August 14, 2000. Traded to **Detroit** by **Los Angeles** for Sean Avery, Maxim Kuznetsov, Detroit's 1st round choice (Jeff Tambellini) in 2003 Entry Draft and Detroit's 2nd round choice (later traded to Boston – Boston selected Martins Karsums) in 2004 Entry Draft, March 11, 2003.

SCHULTZ, Nick

(SHUHLTZ, NIHK) **MIN.**

Defense. Shoots left. 6'1", 207 lbs. Born, Strasbourg, Sask., August 25, 1982. Minnesota's 2nd choice, 33rd overall, in 2000 Entry Draft.

Season	Club	League	GP	G	A	Pts	PIM	PP	SH	GW	S	%	+/-	TF	F%	Min	GP	G	A	Pts	PIM	PP	SH	GW	Min
1997-98	Yorkton Mallers	SMHL	59	10	30	40	74	....	....	....	....	....	....	....	....	....	....	....	....	....	....	....	....	....	....
1998-99	Prince Albert	WHL	58	5	18	23	37	....	....	....	....	....	....	....	....	....	14	0	7	7	0	....	....	....	....
99-2000	Prince Albert	WHL	72	11	33	44	38	....	....	....	....	....	....	....	....	....	6	0	3	3	2	....	....	....	....
2000-01	Prince Albert	WHL	59	17	30	47	120	....	....	....	....	....	....	....	....	....	....	....	....	....	....	....	....	....	....
	Cleveland	IHL	4	1	1	2	2	....	....	....	....	....	....	....	....	....	3	0	1	1	0	....	....	....	....
2001-02	**Minnesota**	**NHL**	**52**	**4**	**6**	**10**	**14**	**1**	**0**	**1**	**47**	**8.5**	**0**	**0**	**0.0**	**16:08**	....	....	....	....	....	....	....	....	....
	Houston Aeros	AHL	....	....	....	....	....	....	....	....	....	....	....	....	....	....	14	1	5	6	2	....	....	....	....
2002-03	**Minnesota**	**NHL**	**75**	**3**	**7**	**10**	**23**	**0**	**0**	**1**	**70**	**4.3**	**11**	**0**	**0.0**	**18:28**	**18**	**0**	**1**	**1**	**10**	**0**	**0**	**0**	**19:39**
2003-04	**Minnesota**	**NHL**	**79**	**6**	**10**	**16**	**16**	**1**	**0**	**0**	**72**	**8.3**	**12**	**0**	**0.0**	**20:19**	....	....	....	....	....	....	....	....	....
	NHL Totals		**206**	**13**	**23**	**36**	**53**	**2**	**0**	**2**	**189**	**6.9**		**0**	**0.0**	**18:35**	**18**	**0**	**1**	**1**	**10**	**0**	**0**	**0**	**19:39**

SCHULTZ, Ray

(SHUHLTZ, RAY) **N.J.**

Defense. Shoots left. 6'2", 215 lbs. Born, Red Deer, Alta., November 14, 1976. Ottawa's 8th choice, 184th overall, in 1995 Entry Draft.

Season	Club	League	GP	G	A	Pts	PIM	PP	SH	GW	S	%	+/-	TF	F%	Min	GP	G	A	Pts	PIM	PP	SH	GW	Min
1993-94	Edmonton SSAC	AMHL	31	3	24	27	94	....	....	....	....	....	....	....	....	....	....	....	....	....	....	....	....	....	....
	Tri-City	WHL	3	0	0	0	11	....	....	....	....	....	....	....	....	....	....	....	....	....	....	....	....	....	....
1994-95	Tri-City	WHL	63	1	8	9	209	....	....	....	....	....	....	....	....	....	11	0	0	0	16	....	....	....	....
1995-96	Calgary Hitmen	WHL	66	3	17	20	282	....	....	....	....	....	....	....	....	....	....	....	....	....	....	....	....	....	....
1996-97	Calgary Hitmen	WHL	32	3	17	20	141	....	....	....	....	....	....	....	....	....	....	....	....	....	....	....	....	....	....
	Kelowna Rockets	WHL	23	3	11	14	63	....	....	....	....	....	....	....	....	....	6	0	2	2	12	....	....	....	....
1997-98	**NY Islanders**	**NHL**	**13**	**0**	**1**	**1**	**45**	**0**	**0**	**0**	**4**	**0.0**	**3**	....	....	....	....	....	....	....	....	....	....	....	....
	Kentucky	AHL	51	2	4	6	179	....	....	....	....	....	....	....	....	....	1	0	0	0	25	....	....	....	....
1998-99	**NY Islanders**	**NHL**	**4**	**0**	**0**	**0**	**7**	**0**	**0**	**0**	**2**	**0.0**	**–2**	**1**	**0.0**	**15:21**	....	....	....	....	....	....	....	....	....
	Lowell	AHL	54	0	3	3	184	....	....	....	....	....	....	....	....	....	1	0	0	0	4	....	....	....	....
99-2000	**NY Islanders**	**NHL**	**9**	**0**	**1**	**1**	**30**	**0**	**0**	**0**	**2**	**0.0**	**1**	**0**	**0.0**	**14:18**	....	....	....	....	....	....	....	....	....
	Kansas City	IHL	65	5	5	10	208	....	....	....	....	....	....	....	....	....	....	....	....	....	....	....	....	....	....
2000-01	**NY Islanders**	**NHL**	**13**	**0**	**2**	**2**	**40**	**0**	**0**	**0**	**3**	**0.0**	**–1**	**0**	**0.0**	**10:50**	....	....	....	....	....	....	....	....	....
	Lowell	AHL	13	0	1	1	33	....	....	....	....	....	....	....	....	....	....	....	....	....	....	....	....	....	....
	Cleveland	IHL	44	3	5	8	127	....	....	....	....	....	....	....	....	....	3	1	0	1	16	....	....	....	....
2001-02	**NY Islanders**	**NHL**	**2**	**0**	**0**	**0**	**5**	**0**	**0**	**0**	**0**	**0.0**	**–1**	**0**	**0.0**	**3:22**	**2**	**0**	**0**	**0**	**2**	**0**	**0**	**0**	**9:11**
	Bridgeport	AHL	69	0	15	15	205	....	....	....	....	....	....	....	....	....	19	1	3	4	18	....	....	....	....
2002-03	**NY Islanders**	**NHL**	**4**	**0**	**0**	**0**	**28**	**0**	**0**	**0**	**1**	**0.0**	**–1**	**0**	**0.0**	**5:23**	....	....	....	....	....	....	....	....	....
	Bridgeport	AHL	51	2	8	10	105	....	....	....	....	....	....	....	....	....	9	1	0	1	14	....	....	....	....
2003-04	Milwaukee	AHL	73	2	10	12	153	....	....	....	....	....	....	....	....	....	22	1	2	3	31	....	....	....	....
	NHL Totals		**45**	**0**	**4**	**4**	**155**	**0**	**0**	**0**	**12**	**0.0**		**1**	**0.0**	**11:13**	**2**	**0**	**0**	**0**	**2**	**0**	**0**	**0**	**9:11**

Signed as a free agent by **NY Islanders**, June 9, 1997. Signed as a free agent by **Nashville**, July 17, 2003. Signed as a free agent by **New Jersey**, July 6, 2004.

SCOTT, Richard

(SKAWT, RIH-chuhrd) **NYR**

Left wing. Shoots left. 6'2", 195 lbs. Born, Orillia, Ont., August 1, 1978.

Season	Club	League	GP	G	A	Pts	PIM	PP	SH	GW	S	%	+/-	TF	F%	Min	GP	G	A	Pts	PIM	PP	SH	GW	Min
1996-97	Orillia Terriers	OPJHL	10	0	0	0	23	....	....	....	....	....	....	....	....	....	....	....	....	....	....	....	....	....	....
1997-98	Couchiching	OPJHL	45	13	19	32	166	....	....	....	....	....	....	....	....	....	....	....	....	....	....	....	....	....	....
1998-99	Oshawa Generals	OHL	54	12	12	24	193	....	....	....	....	....	....	....	....	....	....	....	....	....	....	....	....	....	....
99-2000	Charlotte	ECHL	55	1	5	6	317	....	....	....	....	....	....	....	....	....	....	....	....	....	....	....	....	....	....
2000-01	Charlotte	ECHL	4	1	1	2	22	....	....	....	....	....	....	....	....	....	....	....	....	....	....	....	....	....	....
	Hartford	AHL	64	2	5	7	320	....	....	....	....	....	....	....	....	....	1	0	0	0	0	....	....	....	....
2001-02	**NY Rangers**	**NHL**	**5**	**0**	**0**	**0**	**5**	**0**	**0**	**0**	**1**	**0.0**	**0**	**0**	**0.0**	**2:25**	....	....	....	....	....	....	....	....	....
	Hartford	AHL	39	2	3	5	211	....	....	....	....	....	....	....	....	....	....	....	....	....	....	....	....	....	....
2002-03	Charlotte	ECHL	3	0	1	1	4	....	....	....	....	....	....	....	....	....	....	....	....	....	....	....	....	....	....
	Hartford	AHL	32	0	5	5	150	....	....	....	....	....	....	....	....	....	2	0	0	0	16	....	....	....	....
2003-04	**NY Rangers**	**NHL**	**5**	**0**	**0**	**0**	**23**	**0**	**0**	**0**	**1**	**0.0**	**0**	**1**	**100.0**	**6:01**	....	....	....	....	....	....	....	....	....
	Hartford	AHL	15	2	2	4	79	....	....	....	....	....	....	....	....	....	....	....	....	....	....	....	....	....	....
	NHL Totals		**10**	**0**	**0**	**0**	**28**	**0**	**0**	**0**	**2**	**0.0**		**1**	**100.0**	**4:13**	....	....	....	....	....	....	....	....	....

Signed as a free agent by **NY Rangers**, May 8, 2001. • Missed majority of 2003-04 season recovering from head injury suffered in game vs. NY Islanders, December 4, 2003.

SCOVILLE, Darrel

(SKO-vihl, DAIR-uhl) **CBJ**

Defense. Shoots left. 6'3", 208 lbs. Born, Swift Current, Sask., October 13, 1975.

Season	Club	League	GP	G	A	Pts	PIM	PP	SH	GW	S	%	+/-	TF	F%	Min	GP	G	A	Pts	PIM	PP	SH	GW	Min
1994-95	Lebret Eagles	SJHL	61	15	50	65	....	....	....	....	....	....	....	....	....	....	....	....	....	....	....	....	....	....	....
1995-96	Merrimack	H-East	34	6	20	26	54	....	....	....	....	....	....	....	....	....	....	....	....	....	....	....	....	....	....
1996-97	Merrimack	H-East	35	7	16	23	71	....	....	....	....	....	....	....	....	....	....	....	....	....	....	....	....	....	....
1997-98	Merrimack	H-East	38	4	26	30	84	....	....	....	....	....	....	....	....	....	....	....	....	....	....	....	....	....	....
1998-99	Saint John Flames	AHL	61	1	7	8	66	....	....	....	....	....	....	....	....	....	7	1	2	3	13	....	....	....	....
99-2000	**Calgary**	**NHL**	**6**	**0**	**0**	**0**	**2**	**0**	**0**	**0**	**1**	**0.0**	**1**	**0**	**0.0**	**9:18**	....	....	....	....	....	....	....	....	....
	Saint John Flames	AHL	64	11	25	36	99	....	....	....	....	....	....	....	....	....	3	1	2	3	0	....	....	....	....
2000-01	Saint John Flames	AHL	76	11	32	47	125	....	....	....	....	....	....	....	....	....	11	2	6	8	8	....	....	....	....
2001-02	Syracuse Crunch	AHL	51	5	16	21	60	....	....	....	....	....	....	....	....	....	10	0	0	0	6	....	....	....	....
2002-03	**Columbus**	**NHL**	**2**	**0**	**0**	**0**	**4**	**0**	**0**	**0**	**1**	**0.0**	**0**	**0**	**0.0**	**14:31**	....	....	....	....	....	....	....	....	....
	Syracuse Crunch	AHL	24	4	9	13	26	....	....	....	....	....	....	....	....	....	....	....	....	....	....	....	....	....	....
2003-04	**Columbus**	**NHL**	**8**	**0**	**1**	**1**	**6**	**0**	**0**	**0**	**5**	**0.0**	**–4**	**0**	**0.0**	**19:14**	....	....	....	....	....	....	....	....	....
	Syracuse Crunch	AHL	70	10	32	42	73	....	....	....	....	....	....	....	....	....	6	0	2	2	4	....	....	....	....
	NHL Totals		**16**	**0**	**1**	**1**	**12**	**0**	**0**	**0**	**7**	**0.0**		**0**	**0.0**	**14:55**	....	....	....	....	....	....	....	....	....

Hockey East All-Rookie Team (1996)

Signed as a free agent by **Calgary**, June 12, 1998. Signed as a free agent by **Columbus**, July 10, 2001. • Missed majority of 2002-03 season recovering from abdominal (October 26, 2002 vs. Grand Rapids - AHL) and foot (January 6, 2003. vs. Philadelphia - AHL) injuries.

SCUDERI, Rob

(SKUD-uhree, RAWB) **PIT.**

Defense. Shoots left. 6', 214 lbs. Born, Syosset, NY, December 30, 1978. Pittsburgh's 5th choice, 134th overall, in 1998 Entry Draft.

Season	Club	League	GP	G	A	Pts	PIM	PP	SH	GW	S	%	+/-	TF	F%	Min	GP	G	A	Pts	PIM	PP	SH	GW	Min
1995-96	NY Apple Core	MJBHL	76	18	60	78	....	....	....	....	....	....	....	....	....	....	....	....	....	....	....	....	....	....	....
1996-97	NY Apple Core	MJBHL	82	42	70	112	64	....	....	....	....	....	....	....	....	....	....	....	....	....	....	....	....	....	....
1997-98	Boston College	H-East	42	0	24	24	12	....	....	....	....	....	....	....	....	....	....	....	....	....	....	....	....	....	....
1998-99	Boston College	H-East	41	2	8	10	20	....	....	....	....	....	....	....	....	....	....	....	....	....	....	....	....	....	....
99-2000	Boston College	H-East	42	1	12	13	22	....	....	....	....	....	....	....	....	....	....	....	....	....	....	....	....	....	....
2000-01	Boston College	H-East	43	4	19	23	42	....	....	....	....	....	....	....	....	....	....	....	....	....	....	....	....	....	....
2001-02	Wilkes-Barre	AHL	75	1	22	23	66	....	....	....	....	....	....	....	....	....	....	....	....	....	....	....	....	....	....
2002-03	Wilkes-Barre	AHL	74	4	17	21	44	....	....	....	....	....	....	....	....	....	6	0	1	1	4	....	....	....	....
2003-04	**Pittsburgh**	**NHL**	**13**	**1**	**2**	**3**	**4**	**0**	**0**	**0**	**4**	**25.0**	**2**	**0**	**0.0**	**20:06**	....	....	....	....	....	....	....	....	....
	Wilkes-Barre	AHL	64	1	15	16	54	....	....	....	....	....	....	....	....	....	24	0	3	3	14	....	....	....	....
	NHL Totals		**13**	**1**	**2**	**3**	**4**	**0**	**0**	**0**	**4**	**25.0**		**0**	**0.0**	**20:06**	....	....	....	....	....	....	....	....	....

NCAA Championship All-Tournament Team (2001)

SEDIN, Daniel
(suh-DEEN, DAN-yehl) **VAN.**

Left wing. Shoots left. 6'1", 200 lbs. Born, Ornskoldsvik, Sweden, September 26, 1980. Vancouver's 1st choice, 2nd overall, in 1999 Entry Draft.

			Regular Season														Playoffs								
Season	Club	League	GP	G	A	Pts	PIM	PP	SH	GW	S	%	+/-	TF	F%	Min	GP	G	A	Pts	PIM	PP	SH	GW	Min
1996-97	MoDo Jr.	Swede-Jr.	26	26	14	40																			
1997-98	MoDo Jr.	Swede-Jr.	4	3	3	6	4																		
	MoDo	Sweden	45	4	8	12	26										9	0	0	0	2				
1998-99	MoDo	Sweden	50	21	21	42	20										13	4	8	12	14				
99-2000	MoDo	Sweden	50	19	26	45	28										13	*8	6	14	18				
	MoDo	EuroHL	4	3	3	6	0										2	0	0	0	0				
2000-01	**Vancouver**	**NHL**	**75**	**20**	**14**	**34**	**24**	**10**	**0**	**3**	**127**	**15.7**	**-3**	**10**	**60.0**	**13:00**	**4**	**1**	**2**	**3**	**0**	**0**	**0**	**0**	**16:15**
2001-02	**Vancouver**	**NHL**	**79**	**9**	**23**	**32**	**32**	**4**	**0**	**2**	**117**	**7.7**	**1**	**18**	**33.3**	**12:22**	**6**	**0**	**1**	**1**	**0**	**0**	**0**	**0**	**10:44**
2002-03	**Vancouver**	**NHL**	**79**	**14**	**17**	**31**	**34**	**4**	**0**	**2**	**134**	**10.4**	**8**	**24**	**45.8**	**12:26**	**14**	**1**	**5**	**6**	**8**	**1**	**0**	**1**	**12:23**
2003-04	**Vancouver**	**NHL**	**82**	**18**	**36**	**54**	**18**	**1**	**0**	**3**	**153**	**11.8**	**18**	**71**	**47.9**	**13:33**	**7**	**1**	**2**	**3**	**0**	**1**	**0**	**0**	**16:03**
	NHL Totals		**315**	**61**	**90**	**151**	**108**	**19**	**0**	**10**	**531**	**11.5**		**123**	**46.3**	**12:50**	**31**	**3**	**10**	**13**	**8**	**2**	**0**	**1**	**13:24**

SEDIN, Henrik
(suh-DEEN, HEHN-rihk) **VAN.**

Center. Shoots left. 6'2", 200 lbs. Born, Ornskoldsvik, Sweden, September 26, 1980. Vancouver's 2nd choice, 3rd overall, in 1999 Entry Draft.

Season	Club	League	GP	G	A	Pts	PIM	PP	SH	GW	S	%	+/-	TF	F%	Min	GP	G	A	Pts	PIM	PP	SH	GW	Min
1996-97	MoDo Jr.	Swede-Jr.	26	14	22	36																			
1997-98	MoDo Jr.	Swede-Jr.	8	4	7	11	6																		
	MoDo	Sweden	39	1	4	5	8										7	0	0	0	0				
1998-99	MoDo	Sweden	49	12	22	34	32										13	2	8	10	6				
99-2000	MoDo	Sweden	50	9	38	47	22										13	5	9	14	2				
2000-01	**Vancouver**	**NHL**	**82**	**9**	**20**	**29**	**38**	**2**	**0**	**1**	**98**	**9.2**	**-2**	**1020**	**44.1**	**13:31**	**4**	**0**	**4**	**4**	**0**	**0**	**0**	**0**	**16:31**
2001-02	**Vancouver**	**NHL**	**82**	**16**	**20**	**36**	**36**	**3**	**0**	**1**	**78**	**20.5**	**9**	**785**	**47.4**	**12:48**	**6**	**3**	**0**	**3**	**0**	**0**	**0**	**1**	**11:55**
2002-03	**Vancouver**	**NHL**	**78**	**8**	**31**	**39**	**38**	**4**	**1**	**1**	**81**	**9.9**	**9**	**995**	**48.2**	**13:58**	**14**	**3**	**2**	**5**	**8**	**1**	**0**	**0**	**13:01**
2003-04	**Vancouver**	**NHL**	**76**	**11**	**31**	**42**	**32**	**2**	**0**	**2**	**99**	**11.1**	**23**	**961**	**50.0**	**14:02**	**7**	**2**	**2**	**4**	**2**	**2**	**0**	**0**	**16:02**
	NHL Totals		**318**	**44**	**102**	**146**	**144**	**11**	**1**	**5**	**356**	**12.4**		**3761**	**47.4**	**13:34**	**31**	**8**	**8**	**16**	**10**	**3**	**0**	**1**	**13:56**

SEIDENBERG, Dennis
(ZIGH-dehn-buhrg, DEH-nihs) **PHI.**

Defense. Shoots left. 6', 200 lbs. Born, Schwenningen, West Germany, July 18, 1981. Philadelphia's 6th choice, 172nd overall, in 2001 Entry Draft.

Season	Club	League	GP	G	A	Pts	PIM	PP	SH	GW	S	%	+/-	TF	F%	Min	GP	G	A	Pts	PIM	PP	SH	GW	Min
99-2000	Mannheim Jr.	German-Jr.	52	12	28	40	28																		
	Adler Mannheim	Germany	3	0	0	0	0																		
2000-01	Mannheim Jr.	German-Jr.	9	3	8	11	20																		
	Adler Mannheim	Germany	55	2	5	7	6										12	0	1	1	10				
2001-02	Adler Mannheim	Germany	55	7	13	20	56										8	0	0	0	2				
2002-03	**Philadelphia**	**NHL**	**58**	**4**	**9**	**13**	**20**	**1**	**0**	**0**	**123**	**3.3**	**8**	**1**	**0.0**	**16:50**									
	Philadelphia	AHL	19	5	6	11	17																		
2003-04	**Philadelphia**	**NHL**	**5**	**0**	**0**	**0**	**2**	**0**	**0**	**0**	**14**	**0.0**	**-4**	**0**	**0.0**	**17:20**	**3**	**0**	**0**	**0**	**0**	**0**	**0**	**0**	**7:36**
	Philadelphia	AHL	33	7	12	19	31										9	2	2	4	4				
	NHL Totals		**63**	**4**	**9**	**13**	**22**	**1**	**0**	**0**	**137**	**2.9**		**1**	**0.0**	**16:52**	**3**	**0**	**0**	**0**	**0**	**0**	**0**	**0**	**7:36**

• Missed majority of 2003-04 season recovering from leg injury suffered in game vs. Edmonton, January 10, 2004.

SEJNA, Peter
(SHAY-nah, PEE-tuhr) **ST.L.**

Left wing. Shoots left. 5'11", 198 lbs. Born, Liptovsky Mikulas, Czech., October 5, 1979.

Season	Club	League	GP	G	A	Pts	PIM	PP	SH	GW	S	%	+/-	TF	F%	Min	GP	G	A	Pts	PIM	PP	SH	GW	Min
1995-96	HK Liptovsky 18	Slovak-Jr.	44	40	23	63	20																		
1996-97	HK Liptovsky 18	Slovak-Jr.	40	32	19	51	6																		
	HK Liptovsky	Slovakia	29	3	5	8	2																		
	HK Liptovsky Jr.	Slovak-Jr.	17	14	10	24	8																		
1997-98	HK Liptovsky	Slovakia	34	5	6	11	6																		
1998-99	Des Moines	USHL	52	40	23	63	26										14	11	6	17	8				
99-2000	Des Moines	USHL	58	41	53	94	36										9	4	5	9	4				
2000-01	Colorado College	WCHA	41	29	29	58	10																		
2001-02	Colorado College	WCHA	43	26	24	50	16																		
2002-03	Colorado College	WCHA	42	*36	46	*82	12																		
	St. Louis	**NHL**	**1**	**1**	**0**	**1**	**0**	**1**	**0**	**0**	**3**	**33.3**	**0**	**0**	**0.0**	**15:22**									
2003-04	**St. Louis**	**NHL**	**20**	**2**	**2**	**4**	**4**	**2**	**0**	**0**	**36**	**5.6**	**-9**	**7**	**42.9**	**14:58**									
	Worcester IceCats	AHL	59	12	29	41	13										10	3	3	6	10				
	NHL Totals		**21**	**3**	**2**	**5**	**4**	**3**	**0**	**0**	**39**	**7.7**		**7**	**42.9**	**14:59**									

WCHA First All-Star Team (2003) • WCHA Player of the Year (2003) • NCAA West First All-American Team (2003) • Hobey Baker Memorial Award (Top U.S. Collegiate Player) (2003)

Signed as a free agent by **St. Louis**, April 6, 2003.

SEKERAS, Lubomir
(SEH-kuhr-ahsh, LOO-boh-mihr)

Defense. Shoots left. 6', 183 lbs. Born, Trencin, Czech., November 18, 1968. Minnesota's 8th choice, 232nd overall, in 2000 Entry Draft.

Season	Club	League	GP	G	A	Pts	PIM	PP	SH	GW	S	%	+/-	TF	F%	Min	GP	G	A	Pts	PIM	PP	SH	GW	Min
1987-88	Dukla Trencin Jr.	Czech-Jr.	STATISTICS NOT AVAILABLE																						
	Dukla Trencin	Czech															9	0	0	0	0				
1988-89	Dukla Trencin	Czech	16	2	5	7	22										11	0	4	4	0				
1989-90	Dukla Trencin	Czech	44	6	8	14											9	0	2	2					
1990-91	Dukla Trencin	Czech	52	6	16	22											6	0	1	1					
1991-92	Dukla Trencin	Czech	30	2	6	8	32										13	1	1	2	0				
1992-93	Dukla Trencin	Czech	40	5	19	24	48										11	4	9	13	0				
1993-94	Dukla Trencin	Slovakia	36	9	12	21	46										9	2	4	6	10				
1994-95	Dukla Trencin	Slovakia	36	11	11	22	24										9	2	7	9	8				
1995-96	Trinec	Czech	40	11	13	24	44										3	0	0	0	0				
1996-97	Trinec	Czech	52	14	21	35	56										4	1	0	1	2				
1997-98	Trinec	Czech	50	11	33	44	42										13	2	10	12	4				
1998-99	Trinec	Czech	50	8	15	23	38										10	2	6	8					
99-2000	HC Ocelari Trinec	Czech	52	7	24	31	36										4	0	2	2	2				
2000-01	**Minnesota**	**NHL**	**80**	**11**	**23**	**34**	**52**	**4**	**0**	**2**	**102**	**10.8**	**-8**	**0**	**0.0**	**21:13**									
2001-02	**Minnesota**	**NHL**	**69**	**4**	**20**	**24**	**38**	**4**	**0**	**1**	**82**	**4.9**	**-7**	**0**	**0.0**	**22:37**									
2002-03	**Minnesota**	**NHL**	**60**	**2**	**9**	**11**	**30**	**1**	**0**	**1**	**50**	**4.0**	**-12**	**3**	**100.0**	**18:52**	**15**	**1**	**1**	**2**	**6**	**1**	**0**	**1**	**16:51**
2003-04	Yaroslavl	Russia	15	0	3	3	6																		
	Sodertalje SK	Sweden	33	4	13	17	30																		
	Dallas	**NHL**	**4**	**1**	**1**	**2**	**2**	**0**	**0**	**0**	**2**	**50.0**	**0**	**0**	**0.0**	**16:30**									
	NHL Totals		**213**	**18**	**53**	**71**	**122**	**9**	**0**	**4**	**236**	**7.6**		**3**	**100.0**	**20:55**	**15**	**1**	**1**	**2**	**6**	**1**	**0**	**1**	**16:51**

Signed as a free agent by **Yaroslavl** (Russia), September 16, 2003. Signed as a free agent by **Dallas**, March 9, 2004. Signed as a free agent by **Nurnberg** (Germany), July 8, 2004.

SELANNE, Teemu
(SEH-lahn-nay, TEE-moo)

Right wing. Shoots right. 6', 204 lbs. Born, Helsinki, Finland, July 3, 1970. Winnipeg's 1st choice, 10th overall, in 1988 Entry Draft.

Season	Club	League	GP	G	A	Pts	PIM	PP	SH	GW	S	%	+/-	TF	F%	Min	GP	G	A	Pts	PIM	PP	SH	GW	Min
1986-87	Jokerit Helsinki Jr.	Finn-Jr.	33	10	12	22	8																		
1987-88	Jokerit Helsinki Jr.	Finn-Jr.	33	*43	23	*66	18										5	4	3	7	2				
	Jokerit Helsinki	Finland-2	5	1	1	2	0																		
1988-89	Army Jr.	Finn-Jr.	3	3	1	4	2																		
	Jokerit Helsinki Jr.	Finn-Jr.	3	8	8	16	4																		
	Jokerit Helsinki	Finland-2	34	35	33	68	12										5	7	3	10	4				
1989-90	Jokerit Helsinki	Finland	11	4	8	12	0																		
1990-91	Jokerit Helsinki Jr.	Finn-Jr.	1	0	0	0	0																		
	Jokerit Helsinki	Finland	42	33	25	58	12																		
1991-92	Jokerit Helsinki	Finland	44	*39	23	62	20										10	*10	7	*17	18				
	Finland	Olympics	8	7	4	11	6																		
1992-93	**Winnipeg**	**NHL**	**84**	***76**	**56**	**132**	**45**	**24**	**0**	**7**	**387**	**19.6**	**8**				**6**	**4**	**2**	**6**	**2**	**2**	**0**	**2**	
1993-94	**Winnipeg**	**NHL**	**51**	**25**	**29**	**54**	**22**	**11**	**0**	**2**	**191**	**13.1**	**-23**												
1994-95	Jokerit Helsinki	Finland	20	7	12	19	6																		
	Winnipeg	**NHL**	**45**	**22**	**26**	**48**	**2**	**8**	**2**	**1**	**167**	**13.2**	**1**												

			Regular Season														Playoffs								
Season	Club	League	GP	G	A	Pts	PIM	PP	SH	GW	S	%	+/-	TF	F%	Min	GP	G	A	Pts	PIM	PP	SH	GW	Min
1995-96	**Winnipeg**	**NHL**	**51**	**24**	**48**	**72**	**18**	**6**	**1**	**4**	**163**	**14.7**	**3**	....	....	....	....	....	....	....	....	....	....	....	....
	Anaheim	**NHL**	**28**	**16**	**20**	**36**	**4**	**3**	**0**	**1**	**104**	**15.4**	**2**	....	....	....	....	....	....	....	....	....	....	....	....
1996-97	**Anaheim**	**NHL**	**78**	**51**	**58**	**109**	**34**	**11**	**1**	**8**	**273**	**18.7**	**28**	....	....	....	**11**	**7**	**3**	**10**	**4**	**3**	**0**	**1**	....
1997-98	**Anaheim**	**NHL**	**73**	***52**	**34**	**86**	**30**	**10**	**1**	**10**	**268**	**19.4**	**12**	....	....	....	....	....	....	....	....	....	....	....	....
	Finland	Olympics	5	4	6	*10	8	....	....	....	....	....	....	....	....	....	....	....	....	....	....	....	....	....	....
1998-99	**Anaheim**	**NHL**	**75**	***47**	**60**	**107**	**30**	**25**	**0**	**7**	**281**	**16.7**	**18**	**5**	**20.0**	**22:47**	**4**	**2**	**2**	**4**	**2**	**1**	**0**	**0**	**22:23**
99-2000	**Anaheim**	**NHL**	**79**	**33**	**52**	**85**	**12**	**8**	**0**	**6**	**236**	**14.0**	**6**	**13**	**23.1**	**22:44**	....	....	....	....	....	....	....	....	....
2000-01	**Anaheim**	**NHL**	**61**	**26**	**33**	**59**	**36**	**10**	**0**	**5**	**202**	**12.9**	**–8**	**4**	**50.0**	**21:51**	....	....	....	....	....	....	....	....	....
	San Jose	**NHL**	**12**	**7**	**6**	**13**	**0**	**2**	**0**	**2**	**31**	**22.6**	**1**	**4**	**75.0**	**18:14**	**6**	**0**	**2**	**2**	**2**	**0**	**0**	**0**	**17:13**
2001-02	**San Jose**	**NHL**	**82**	**29**	**25**	**54**	**40**	**9**	**1**	**8**	**202**	**14.4**	**–11**	**12**	**25.0**	**16:58**	**12**	**5**	**3**	**8**	**2**	**2**	**0**	**1**	**16:51**
	Finland	Olympics	4	3	0	3	2	....	....	....	....	....	....	....	....	....	....	....	....	....	....	....	....	....	....
2002-03	**San Jose**	**NHL**	**82**	**28**	**36**	**64**	**30**	**7**	**0**	**5**	**253**	**11.1**	**–6**	**107**	**42.1**	**19:14**	....	....	....	....	....	....	....	....	....
2003-04	**Colorado**	**NHL**	**78**	**16**	**16**	**32**	**32**	**6**	**1**	**4**	**182**	**8.8**	**2**	**80**	**43.8**	**16:10**	**10**	**0**	**3**	**3**	**2**	**0**	**0**	**0**	**12:53**
	NHL Totals		**879**	**452**	**499**	**951**	**335**	**140**	**7**	**70**	**2940**	**15.4**		**225**	**40.9**	**19:48**	**49**	**18**	**15**	**33**	**14**	**8**	**0**	**4**	**16:22**

NHL All-Rookie Team (1993) • NHL First All-Star Team (1993, 1997) • Calder Memorial Trophy (1993) • NHL Second All-Star Team (1998, 1999) • Maurice "Rocket" Richard Trophy (1999)

Played in NHL All-Star Game (1993, 1994, 1996, 1997, 1998, 1999, 2000, 2002, 2003)

• Missed majority of 1989-90 season recovering from leg injury suffered in game vs. HIFK Helsinki (Finland), October 19, 1989. Traded to **Anaheim** by **Winnipeg** with Marc Chouinard and Winnipeg's 4th round choice (later traded to Toronto – later traded to Montreal – Montreal selected Kim Staal) in 1996 Entry Draft for Chad Kilger, Oleg Tverdovsky and Anaheim's 3rd round choice (Per-Anton Lundstrom) in 1996 Entry Draft, February 7, 1996. Traded to **San Jose** by **Anaheim** for Jeff Friesen, Steve Shields and San Jose's 2nd round choice (later traded to Dallas – Dallas selected Vojtech Polak) in 2003 Entry Draft, March 5, 2001. Signed as a free agent by **Colorado**, July 3, 2003.

SELLARS, Luke

(SEHL-lahrs, LEWK) **ATL.**

Defense. Shoots left. 6'1", 210 lbs. Born, Toronto, Ont., May 21, 1981. Atlanta's 2nd choice, 30th overall, in 1999 Entry Draft.

Season	Club	League	GP	G	A	Pts	PIM	PP	SH	GW	S	%	+/-	TF	F%	Min	GP	G	A	Pts	PIM	PP	SH	GW	Min
1997-98	Wexford Raiders	MTJHL	46	2	18	20	155	....	....	....	....	....	....	....	....	....	....	....	....	....	....	....	....	....	....
1998-99	Ottawa 67's	OHL	56	4	19	23	87	....	....	....	....	....	....	....	....	....	9	1	2	3	7	....	....	....	....
99-2000	Ottawa 67's	OHL	56	8	34	42	147	....	....	....	....	....	....	....	....	....	11	4	6	10	28	....	....	....	....
2000-01	Ottawa 67's	OHL	59	9	21	30	136	....	....	....	....	....	....	....	....	....	18	4	10	14	47	....	....	....	....
2001-02	**Atlanta**	**NHL**	**1**	**0**	**0**	**0**	**2**	**0**	**0**	**0**	**0**	**0.0**	**0**	**0**	**0.0**	**3:27**	....	....	....	....	....	....	....	....	....
	Chicago Wolves	AHL	31	2	4	6	87	....	....	....	....	....	....	....	....	....	....	....	....	....	....	....	....	....	....
	Greenville	ECHL	21	2	6	8	61	....	....	....	....	....	....	....	....	....	17	7	6	13	44	....	....	....	....
2002-03	Chicago Wolves	AHL	42	4	11	15	117	....	....	....	....	....	....	....	....	....	....	....	....	....	....	....	....	....	....
	Greenville	ECHL	4	2	2	4	6	....	....	....	....	....	....	....	....	....	....	....	....	....	....	....	....	....	....
2003-04	Chicago Wolves	AHL	32	2	6	8	72	....	....	....	....	....	....	....	....	....	....	....	....	....	....	....	....	....	....
	NHL Totals		**1**	**0**	**0**	**0**	**2**	**0**	**0**	**0**	**0**	**0.0**		**0**	**0.0**	**3:27**	....	....	....	....	....	....	....	....	....

OHL All-Rookie Team (1999)

• Missed majority of 2003-04 season recovering from knee injury suffered in game vs. San Antonio (AHL), February 2, 2004.

SEMENOV, Alexei

(seh-MEH-nahv, al-EHX-ay) **EDM.**

Defense. Shoots left. 6'6", 235 lbs. Born, Murmansk, USSR, April 10, 1981. Edmonton's 2nd choice, 36th overall, in 1999 Entry Draft.

Season	Club	League	GP	G	A	Pts	PIM	PP	SH	GW	S	%	+/-	TF	F%	Min	GP	G	A	Pts	PIM	PP	SH	GW	Min
1997-98	Krylja Sovetov 2	Russia-3	52	1	2	3	48	....	....	....	....	....	....	....	....	....	....	....	....	....	....	....	....	....	....
1998-99	St. Petersburg 2	Russia-4	19	0	1	1	20	....	....	....	....	....	....	....	....	....	....	....	....	....	....	....	....	....	....
	Sudbury Wolves	OHL	28	0	3	3	28	....	....	....	....	....	....	....	....	....	2	0	0	0	4	....	....	....	....
99-2000	Sudbury Wolves	OHL	65	9	35	44	135	....	....	....	....	....	....	....	....	....	12	1	3	4	23	....	....	....	....
	Hamilton	AHL	....	....	....	....	....	....	....	....	....	....	....	....	....	....	3	0	0	0	0	....	....	....	....
2000-01	Sudbury Wolves	OHL	65	21	42	63	106	....	....	....	....	....	....	....	....	....	12	4	13	17	17	....	....	....	....
2001-02	Hamilton	AHL	78	5	11	16	67	....	....	....	....	....	....	....	....	....	....	....	....	....	....	....	....	....	....
2002-03	**Edmonton**	**NHL**	**46**	**1**	**6**	**7**	**58**	**0**	**0**	**0**	**33**	**3.0**	**–7**	**0**	**0.0**	**19:41**	**6**	**0**	**0**	**0**	**0**	**0**	**0**	**0**	**13:05**
	Hamilton	AHL	37	4	3	7	45	....	....	....	....	....	....	....	....	....	....	....	....	....	....	....	....	....	....
2003-04	**Edmonton**	**NHL**	**46**	**2**	**3**	**5**	**32**	**1**	**0**	**0**	**36**	**5.6**	**8**	**0**	**0.0**	**17:16**	....	....	....	....	....	....	....	....	....
	NHL Totals		**92**	**3**	**9**	**12**	**90**	**1**	**0**	**0**	**69**	**4.3**		**0**	**0.0**	**18:28**	**6**	**0**	**0**	**0**	**0**	**0**	**0**	**0**	**13:05**

OHL First All-Star Team (2001)

SEMIN, Alexander

(SEH-min, al-ehx-AN-duhr) **WSH.**

Left wing. Shoots left. 6', 181 lbs. Born, Krasnoyarsk, USSR, March 3, 1984. Washington's 2nd choice, 13th overall, in 2002 Entry Draft.

Season	Club	League	GP	G	A	Pts	PIM	PP	SH	GW	S	%	+/-	TF	F%	Min	GP	G	A	Pts	PIM	PP	SH	GW	Min
2001-02	Chelyabinsk	Russia-2	46	13	8	21	52	....	....	....	....	....	....	....	....	....	2	2	0	2	0	....	....	....	....
2002-03	Lada Togliatti	Russia	47	10	7	17	36	....	....	....	....	....	....	....	....	....	10	*5	3	8	10	....	....	....	....
2003-04	**Washington**	**NHL**	**52**	**10**	**12**	**22**	**36**	**4**	**0**	**2**	**92**	**10.9**	**–2**	**6**	**50.0**	**12:37**	....	....	....	....	....	....	....	....	....
	Portland Pirates	AHL	4	3	1	4	6	....	....	....	....	....	....	....	....	....	7	4	7	11	19	....	....	....	....
	NHL Totals		**52**	**10**	**12**	**22**	**36**	**4**	**0**	**2**	**92**	**10.9**		**6**	**50.0**	**12:37**	....	....	....	....	....	....	....	....	....

SEVERSON, Cam

(SEH-vuhr-SOHN, KAM) **NSH.**

Left wing. Shoots left. 6'1", 215 lbs. Born, Canora, Sask., January 15, 1978. San Jose's 6th choice, 192nd overall, in 1997 Entry Draft.

Season	Club	League	GP	G	A	Pts	PIM	PP	SH	GW	S	%	+/-	TF	F%	Min	GP	G	A	Pts	PIM	PP	SH	GW	Min
1996-97	Lethbridge	WHL	45	12	13	25	169	....	....	....	....	....	....	....	....	....	....	....	....	....	....	....	....	....	....
	Prince Albert	WHL	16	5	13	18	54	....	....	....	....	....	....	....	....	....	4	4	0	4	8	....	....	....	....
1997-98	Prince Albert	WHL	41	23	25	48	129	....	....	....	....	....	....	....	....	....	....	....	....	....	....	....	....	....	....
	Spokane Chiefs	WHL	23	9	11	20	88	....	....	....	....	....	....	....	....	....	18	11	4	15	51	....	....	....	....
1998-99	Spokane Chiefs	WHL	46	16	17	33	190	....	....	....	....	....	....	....	....	....	....	....	....	....	....	....	....	....	....
	Oklahoma City	CHL	5	6	3	9	4	....	....	....	....	....	....	....	....	....	10	4	0	4	26	....	....	....	....
99-2000	Louisiana	ECHL	7	0	2	2	22	....	....	....	....	....	....	....	....	....	....	....	....	....	....	....	....	....	....
	Peoria Rivermen	ECHL	56	19	8	27	138	....	....	....	....	....	....	....	....	....	18	3	4	7	41	....	....	....	....
2000-01	Portland Pirates	AHL	8	0	0	0	11	....	....	....	....	....	....	....	....	....	....	....	....	....	....	....	....	....	....
	Quad City	UHL	46	22	26	48	129	....	....	....	....	....	....	....	....	....	....	....	....	....	....	....	....	....	....
	Cincinnati	AHL	20	4	7	11	60	....	....	....	....	....	....	....	....	....	3	1	1	2	0	....	....	....	....
2001-02	Hartford	AHL	65	11	10	21	116	....	....	....	....	....	....	....	....	....	5	0	0	0	7	....	....	....	....
2002-03	**Anaheim**	**NHL**	**2**	**0**	**0**	**0**	**8**	**0**	**0**	**0**	**1**	**0.0**	**0**	**0**	**0.0**	**6:44**	**1**	**0**	**0**	**0**	**0**	**0**	**0**	**0**	**2:24**
	Cincinnati	AHL	71	12	9	21	156	....	....	....	....	....	....	....	....	....	....	....	....	....	....	....	....	....	....
2003-04	**Anaheim**	**NHL**	**31**	**3**	**0**	**3**	**50**	**1**	**0**	**0**	**24**	**12.5**	**–3**	**3**	**66.7**	**7:21**	....	....	....	....	....	....	....	....	....
	Cincinnati	AHL	38	7	7	14	145	....	....	....	....	....	....	....	....	....	....	....	....	....	....	....	....	....	....
	NHL Totals		**33**	**3**	**0**	**3**	**58**	**1**	**0**	**0**	**25**	**12.0**		**3**	**66.7**	**7:19**	**1**	**0**	**0**	**0**	**0**	**0**	**0**	**0**	**2:24**

Signed as a free agent by **Hartford** (AHL), September 24, 2001. Signed as a free agent by **Anaheim**, August 22, 2002. Signed as a free agent by **Nashville**, July 21, 2004.

SHANAHAN, Brendan

(SHAN-na-HAN, BREHN-duhn) **DET.**

Left wing. Shoots right. 6'3", 218 lbs. Born, Mimico, Ont., January 23, 1969. New Jersey's 1st choice, 2nd overall, in 1987 Entry Draft.

Season	Club	League	GP	G	A	Pts	PIM	PP	SH	GW	S	%	+/-	TF	F%	Min	GP	G	A	Pts	PIM	PP	SH	GW	Min
1984-85	Mississauga Reps	MTHL	36	20	21	41	26	....	....	....	....	....	....	....	....	....	....	....	....	....	....	....	....	....	....
	Dixie Beehives	MTJHL	1	0	0	0	0	....	....	....	....	....	....	....	....	....	....	....	....	....	....	....	....	....	....
1985-86	London Knights	OHL	59	28	34	62	70	....	....	....	....	....	....	....	....	....	5	5	5	10	5	....	....	....	....
1986-87	London Knights	OHL	56	39	53	92	92	....	....	....	....	....	....	....	....	....	....	....	....	....	....	....	....	....	....
1987-88	**New Jersey**	**NHL**	**65**	**7**	**19**	**26**	**131**	**2**	**0**	**2**	**72**	**9.7**	**–20**	....	....	....	**12**	**2**	**1**	**3**	**44**	**1**	**0**	**0**	....
1988-89	**New Jersey**	**NHL**	**68**	**22**	**28**	**50**	**115**	**9**	**0**	**0**	**152**	**14.5**	**2**	....	....	....	....	....	....	....	....	....	....	....	....
1989-90	**New Jersey**	**NHL**	**73**	**30**	**42**	**72**	**137**	**8**	**0**	**5**	**196**	**15.3**	**15**	....	....	....	**6**	**3**	**3**	**6**	**20**	**1**	**0**	**1**	....
1990-91	**New Jersey**	**NHL**	**75**	**29**	**37**	**66**	**141**	**7**	**0**	**2**	**195**	**14.9**	**4**	....	....	....	**7**	**3**	**5**	**8**	**12**	**2**	**0**	**0**	....
1991-92	**St. Louis**	**NHL**	**80**	**33**	**36**	**69**	**171**	**13**	**0**	**2**	**215**	**15.3**	**–3**	....	....	....	**6**	**2**	**3**	**5**	**14**	**1**	**0**	**0**	....
1992-93	**St. Louis**	**NHL**	**71**	**51**	**43**	**94**	**174**	**18**	**0**	**8**	**232**	**22.0**	**10**	....	....	....	**11**	**4**	**3**	**7**	**18**	**2**	**0**	**0**	....
1993-94	**St. Louis**	**NHL**	**81**	**52**	**50**	**102**	**211**	**15**	**7**	**8**	**397**	**13.1**	**–9**	....	....	....	**4**	**2**	**5**	**7**	**4**	**0**	**0**	**0**	....
1994-95	Dusseldorfer EG	Germany	3	5	3	8	4	....	....	....	....	....	....	....	....	....	....	....	....	....	....	....	....	....	....
	St. Louis	**NHL**	**45**	**20**	**21**	**41**	**136**	**6**	**2**	**6**	**153**	**13.1**	**7**	....	....	....	**5**	**4**	**5**	**9**	**14**	**1**	**0**	**1**	....
1995-96	**Hartford**	**NHL**	**74**	**44**	**34**	**78**	**125**	**17**	**2**	**6**	**280**	**15.7**	**2**	....	....	....	....	....	....	....	....	....	....	....	....
1996-97	**Hartford**	**NHL**	**2**	**1**	**0**	**1**	**0**	**0**	**1**	**0**	**13**	**7.7**	**1**	....	....	....	....	....	....	....	....	....	....	....	....
	♦ **Detroit**	**NHL**	**79**	**46**	**41**	**87**	**131**	**20**	**2**	**7**	**323**	**14.2**	**31**	....	....	....	**20**	**9**	**8**	**17**	**43**	**2**	**0**	**2**	....
1997-98	♦ **Detroit**	**NHL**	**75**	**28**	**29**	**57**	**154**	**15**	**1**	**9**	**266**	**10.5**	**6**	....	....	....	**20**	**5**	**4**	**9**	**22**	**3**	**0**	**2**	....
	Canada	Olympics	6	2	0	2	0	....	....	....	....	....	....	....	....	....	....	....	....	....	....	....	....	....	....
1998-99	**Detroit**	**NHL**	**81**	**31**	**27**	**58**	**123**	**5**	**0**	**5**	**288**	**10.8**	**2**	**18**	**44.4**	**17:31**	**10**	**3**	**7**	**10**	**6**	**1**	**0**	**1**	**18:31**
99-2000	**Detroit**	**NHL**	**78**	**41**	**37**	**78**	**105**	**13**	**1**	**9**	**283**	**14.5**	**24**	**24**	**50.0**	**18:35**	**9**	**3**	**2**	**5**	**10**	**0**	**0**	**0**	**17:36**
2000-01	**Detroit**	**NHL**	**81**	**31**	**45**	**76**	**81**	**15**	**1**	**7**	**278**	**11.2**	**9**	**115**	**43.5**	**18:22**	**2**	**2**	**2**	**4**	**0**	**0**	**0**	**1**	**21:01**

			Regular Season														Playoffs								
Season	Club	League	GP	G	A	Pts	PIM	PP	SH	GW	S	%	+/-	TF	F%	Min	GP	G	A	Pts	PIM	PP	SH	GW	Min
2001-02 ♦	**Detroit**	**NHL**	**80**	**37**	**38**	**75**	**118**	**12**	**3**	**7**	**277**	**13.4**	**23**	**70**	**47.1**	**18:55**	**23**	**8**	**11**	**19**	**20**	**1**	**0**	**2**	**19:06**
	Canada	Olympics	6	0	1	1	0																		
2002-03	**Detroit**	**NHL**	**78**	**30**	**38**	**68**	**103**	**13**	**0**	**6**	**260**	**11.5**	**5**	**28**	**60.7**	**18:38**	**4**	**1**	**1**	**2**	**4**	**1**	**0**	**0**	**22:03**
2003-04	**Detroit**	**NHL**	**82**	**25**	**28**	**53**	**117**	**8**	**0**	**7**	**280**	**8.9**	**15**	**32**	**46.9**	**18:05**	**12**	**1**	**5**	**6**	**20**	**0**	**1**	**0**	**16:49**
	NHL Totals		**1268**	**558**	**593**	**1151**	**2273**	**196**	**20**	**96**	**4160**	**13.4**		**287**	**47.0**	**18:21**	**151**	**52**	**65**	**117**	**251**	**16**	**1**	**10**	**18:35**

NHL First All-Star Team (1994, 2000) • NHL Second All-Star Team (2002) • King Clancy Memorial Trophy (2003)

Played in NHL All-Star Game (1994, 1996, 1997, 1998, 1999, 2000, 2002)

Signed as a free agent by **St. Louis**, July 25, 1991. Traded to **Hartford** by **St. Louis** for Chris Pronger, July 27, 1995. Traded to **Detroit** by **Hartford** with Brian Glynn for Paul Coffey, Keith Primeau and Detroit's 1st round choice (Nikos Tselios) in 1997 Entry Draft, October 9, 1996.

SHANTZ, Jeff

(SHAWNTS, JEHF)

Center. Shoots right. 6', 195 lbs. Born, Duchess, Alta., October 10, 1973. Chicago's 2nd choice, 36th overall, in 1992 Entry Draft.

1989-90	Medicine Hat	AMHL	36	18	31	49	30																		
	Regina Pats	WHL	1	0	0	0	0																		
1990-91	Regina Pats	WHL	69	16	21	37	22										8	2	2	4	2				
1991-92	Regina Pats	WHL	72	39	50	89	35																		
1992-93	Regina Pats	WHL	64	29	54	83	75										13	2	12	14	14				
1993-94	**Chicago**	**NHL**	**52**	**3**	**13**	**16**	**30**	**0**	**0**	**0**	**56**	**5.4**	**–14**				**6**	**0**	**0**	**0**	**6**	**0**	**0**	**0**	
	Indianapolis Ice	IHL	19	5	9	14	20																		
1994-95	Indianapolis Ice	IHL	32	9	15	24	20																		
	Chicago	**NHL**	**45**	**6**	**12**	**18**	**33**	**0**	**2**	**0**	**58**	**10.3**	**11**				**16**	**3**	**1**	**4**	**2**	**0**	**0**	**0**	
1995-96	**Chicago**	**NHL**	**78**	**6**	**14**	**20**	**24**	**1**	**2**	**0**	**72**	**8.3**	**12**				**10**	**2**	**3**	**5**	**6**	**0**	**0**	**0**	
1996-97	**Chicago**	**NHL**	**69**	**9**	**21**	**30**	**28**	**0**	**1**	**1**	**86**	**10.5**	**11**				**6**	**0**	**4**	**4**	**6**	**0**	**0**	**0**	
1997-98	**Chicago**	**NHL**	**61**	**11**	**20**	**31**	**36**	**1**	**2**	**2**	**69**	**15.9**	**0**												
1998-99	**Chicago**	**NHL**	**7**	**1**	**0**	**1**	**4**	**0**	**0**	**0**	**5**	**20.0**	**–1**	**72**	**38.9**	**15:14**									
	Calgary	**NHL**	**69**	**12**	**17**	**29**	**40**	**1**	**1**	**3**	**77**	**15.6**	**15**	**1112**	**48.4**	**16:47**									
99-2000	**Calgary**	**NHL**	**74**	**13**	**18**	**31**	**30**	**6**	**0**	**1**	**112**	**11.6**	**–13**	**1576**	**51.1**	**18:15**									
2000-01	**Calgary**	**NHL**	**73**	**5**	**15**	**20**	**58**	**0**	**0**	**0**	**88**	**5.7**	**–7**	**876**	**53.5**	**14:51**									
2001-02	**Calgary**	**NHL**	**40**	**3**	**3**	**6**	**23**	**2**	**0**	**0**	**37**	**8.1**	**–3**	**298**	**53.0**	**11:26**									
	Saint John Flames	AHL	2	0	1	1	0																		
2002-03	**Colorado**	**NHL**	**74**	**3**	**6**	**9**	**35**	**0**	**0**	**2**	**68**	**4.4**	**–12**	**874**	**52.1**	**11:28**	**6**	**0**	**0**	**0**	**4**	**0**	**0**	**0**	**9:42**
2003-04	Langnau	Swiss	48	18	27	45	40																		
	NHL Totals		**642**	**72**	**139**	**211**	**341**	**11**	**8**	**9**	**728**	**9.9**		**4808**	**51.0**	**14:51**	**44**	**5**	**8**	**13**	**24**	**0**	**0**	**0**	**9:42**

WHL East First All-Star Team (1993)

Traded to **Calgary** by **Chicago** with Steve Dubinsky for Marty McInnis, Jamie Allison and Eric Andersson, October 27, 1998. Traded to **Colorado** by **Calgary** with Derek Morris and Dean McAmmond for Chris Drury and Stephane Yelle, October 1, 2002. Signed as a free agent by **Langnau** (Swiss), August 19, 2003.

SHARP, Patrick

(SHAHRP, PAT-rihk) **PHI.**

Center. Shoots right. 6', 197 lbs. Born, Thunder Bay, Ont., December 27, 1981. Philadelphia's 2nd choice, 95th overall, in 2001 Entry Draft.

1998-99	Thunder Bay	USHL	55	19	24	43	48										3	1	1	2	0				
99-2000	Thunder Bay	USHL	56	20	35	55	41																		
2000-01	U. of Vermont	ECAC	34	12	15	27	36																		
2001-02	U. of Vermont	ECAC	31	13	13	26	50																		
2002-03	**Philadelphia**	**NHL**	**3**	**0**	**0**	**0**	**2**	**0**	**0**	**0**	**3**	**0.0**	**0**	**7**	**42.9**	**5:59**									
	Philadelphia	AHL	53	14	19	33	39																		
2003-04	**Philadelphia**	**NHL**	**41**	**5**	**2**	**7**	**55**	**0**	**0**	**1**	**44**	**11.4**	**–3**	**272**	**46.7**	**9:56**	**12**	**1**	**0**	**1**	**2**	**0**	**0**	**0**	**6:12**
	Philadelphia	AHL	35	15	14	29	45										1	2	0	2	0				
	NHL Totals		**44**	**5**	**2**	**7**	**57**	**0**	**0**	**1**	**47**	**10.6**		**279**	**46.6**	**9:40**	**12**	**1**	**0**	**1**	**2**	**0**	**0**	**0**	**6:12**

SHELLEY, Jody

(SHEH-lee, JOH-dee) **CBJ**

Left wing. Shoots left. 6'4", 225 lbs. Born, Thompson, Man., February 7, 1976.

1994-95	Halifax	QMJHL	72	10	12	22	194										7	0	1	1	12				
1995-96	Halifax	QMJHL	50	13	19	32	319										6	0	2	2	36				
1996-97	Halifax	QMJHL	58	25	19	44	*448										17	6	6	12	*123				
1997-98	Dalhousie	AUAA	19	6	11	17	145																		
	Saint John Flames	AHL	18	1	1	2	50																		
1998-99	Saint John Flames	AHL	8	0	0	0	46																		
	Johnstown Chiefs	ECHL	52	12	17	29	325																		
99-2000	Johnstown Chiefs	ECHL	36	9	17	26	256																		
	Saint John Flames	AHL	22	1	4	5	93										3	0	0	0	2				
2000-01	Syracuse Crunch	AHL	69	1	7	8	*357										5	0	0	0	21				
	Columbus	**NHL**	**1**	**0**	**0**	**0**	**10**	**0**	**0**	**0**	**0**	**0.0**	**0**	**0**	**0.0**	**1:33**									
2001-02	**Columbus**	**NHL**	**52**	**3**	**3**	**6**	**206**	**0**	**0**	**0**	**35**	**8.6**	**1**	**0**	**0.0**	**6:32**									
	Syracuse Crunch	AHL	22	3	5	8	165																		
2002-03	**Columbus**	**NHL**	**68**	**1**	**4**	**5**	***249**	**0**	**0**	**0**	**39**	**2.6**	**–5**	**1**	**0.0**	**6:08**									
2003-04	**Columbus**	**NHL**	**76**	**3**	**3**	**6**	**228**	**1**	**0**	**0**	**62**	**4.8**	**–10**	**3**	**0.0**	**7:14**									
	NHL Totals		**197**	**7**	**10**	**17**	**693**	**1**	**0**	**0**	**136**	**5.1**		**4**	**0.0**	**6:38**									

Signed as a free agent by **Calgary**, September 1, 1998. Signed as a free agent by **Syracuse** (AHL), September 15, 2000. Signed as a free agent by **Columbus**, January 31, 2001.

SHISHKANOV, Timofei

(SHIHSH-kuh-nahv, tee-moh-FAY) **NSH.**

Left wing. Shoots right. 6'1", 213 lbs. Born, Moscow, USSR, June 10, 1983. Nashville's 2nd choice, 33rd overall, in 2001 Entry Draft.

99-2000	Spartak Mos. 2	Russia-3	14	6	5	11	10																		
	Spartak Moscow	Russia-2	14	1	0	1	2																		
2000-01	Spartak Mos. 2	Russia-3	STATISTICS NOT AVAILABLE																						
	Spartak Moscow	Russia-2	12	0	0	0	2																		
2001-02	HC CSKA Moscow	Russia-2	23	7	6	13	8																		
	HC CSKA 2	Russia-3	13	7	9	16	14																		
2002-03	Quebec Remparts	QMJHL	51	36	46	82	60										11	5	12	17	14				
2003-04	**Nashville**	**NHL**	**2**	**0**	**0**	**0**	**0**	**0**	**0**	**0**	**0**	**0.0**	**–1**	**0**	**0.0**	**6:32**									
	Milwaukee	AHL	63	23	20	43	46										22	2	6	8	17				
	NHL Totals		**2**	**0**	**0**	**0**	**0**	**0**	**0**	**0**	**0**	**0.0**		**0**	**0.0**	**6:32**									

QMJHL First All-Star Team (2003) • AHL All-Rookie Team (2004)

SHVIDKI, Denis

(SHVIHD-kee, DEH-nihs)

Right wing. Shoots left. 6', 195 lbs. Born, Kharkov, USSR, November 21, 1980. Florida's 1st choice, 12th overall, in 1999 Entry Draft.

1996-97	Yaroslavl 2	Russia-3	35	21	12	33	32																		
	Yaroslavl	Russia	17	3	2	5	6																		
1997-98	Yaroslavl 2	Russia-2	32	20	13	33	20																		
	Yaroslavl	Russia	15	1	1	2	2																		
1998-99	Barrie Colts	OHL	61	35	59	94	8										12	7	9	16	2				
99-2000	Barrie Colts	OHL	61	41	65	106	55										9	3	1	4	2				
2000-01	**Florida**	**NHL**	**43**	**6**	**10**	**16**	**16**	**0**	**0**	**1**	**28**	**21.4**	**6**	**4**	**50.0**	**10:21**									
	Louisville Panthers	AHL	34	15	11	26	20																		
2001-02	**Florida**	**NHL**	**8**	**1**	**2**	**3**	**2**	**0**	**0**	**0**	**11**	**9.1**	**–4**	**1**	**0.0**	**11:57**									
	Utah Grizzlies	AHL	8	2	4	6	2																		
2002-03	**Florida**	**NHL**	**23**	**4**	**2**	**6**	**12**	**2**	**0**	**1**	**29**	**13.8**	**–7**	**5**	**60.0**	**14:14**									
	San Antonio	AHL	54	8	18	26	28																		
2003-04	**Florida**	**NHL**	**2**	**0**	**0**	**0**	**0**	**0**	**0**	**0**	**4**	**0.0**	**0**	**0**	**0.0**	**14:05**									
	San Antonio	AHL	77	15	39	54	30																		
	NHL Totals		**76**	**11**	**14**	**25**	**30**	**2**	**0**	**2**	**72**	**15.3**		**10**	**50.0**	**11:47**									

OHL All-Rookie Team (1999) • OHL Second All-Star Team (1999)

• Missed majority of 2001-02 season recovering from head injury suffered in game vs. Philadelphia, October 4, 2001. Signed as a free agent by **Yaroslavl** (Russia), July 7, 2004.

			Regular Season														Playoffs								
Season	Club	League	GP	G	A	Pts	PIM	PP	SH	GW	S	%	+/-	TF	F%	Min	GP	G	A	Pts	PIM	PP	SH	GW	Min

SIKLENKA, Mike
(sih-KLEHN-kuh, MIGHK) **DAL.**

Right wing. Shoots right. 6'5", 224 lbs. Born, Meadow Lake, Sask., December 18, 1979. Washington's 5th choice, 118th overall, in 1998 Entry Draft.

Season	Club	League	GP	G	A	Pts	PIM	PP	SH	GW	S	%	+/-	TF	F%	Min	GP	G	A	Pts	PIM	PP	SH	GW	Min
1997-98	Lloydminster	AJHL	54	10	17	27	120	....	....	....	....	....	....	....	....	....	....	....	....	....	....	....	....	....	....
1998-99	Seattle	WHL	68	19	13	32	115	....	....	....	....	....	....	....	....	....	11	6	6	12	24	....	....	....	....
99-2000	Portland Pirates	AHL	9	0	0	0	14	....	....	....	....	....	....	....	....	....	....	....	....	....	....	....	....	....	....
	Hampton Roads	ECHL	58	7	4	11	62	....	....	....	....	....	....	....	....	....	8	1	0	1	15	....	....	....	....
2000-01	Richmond	ECHL	65	19	18	37	117	....	....	....	....	....	....	....	....	....	4	0	0	0	34	....	....	....	....
	Portland Pirates	AHL	3	0	0	0	0	....	....	....	....	....	....	....	....	....	....	....	....	....	....	....	....	....	....
2001-02	Richmond	ECHL	55	13	21	34	111	....	....	....	....	....	....	....	....	....	....	....	....	....	....	....	....	....	....
	Portland Pirates	AHL	8	1	0	1	2	....	....	....	....	....	....	....	....	....	....	....	....	....	....	....	....	....	....
2002-03	**Philadelphia**	**NHL**	**1**	**0**	**0**	**0**	**0**	**0**	**0**	**0**	**1**	**0.0**	**0**	**0**	**0.0**	**4:26**	....	....	....	....	....	....	....	....	....
	Philadelphia	AHL	64	6	6	12	169	....	....	....	....	....	....	....	....	....	....	....	....	....	....	....	....	....	....
2003-04	**NY Rangers**	**NHL**	**1**	**0**	**0**	**0**	**0**	**0**	**0**	**0**	**0**	**0.0**	**0**	**0**	**0.0**	**2:22**	....	....	....	....	....	....	....	....	....
	Trenton Titans	ECHL	1	1	0	1	0	....	....	....	....	....	....	....	....	....	....	....	....	....	....	....	....	....	....
	Philadelphia	AHL	18	1	5	6	29	....	....	....	....	....	....	....	....	....	....	....	....	....	....	....	....	....	....
	Utah Grizzlies	AHL	26	3	6	9	74	....	....	....	....	....	....	....	....	....	....	....	....	....	....	....	....	....	....
	NHL Totals		**2**	**0**	**0**	**0**	**0**	**0**	**0**	**0**	**1**	**0.0**		**0**	**0.0**	**3:24**	....	....	....	....	....	....	....	....	....

Signed as a free agent by **Philadelphia**, January 27, 2002. Claimed by **NY Rangers** from **Philadelphia** in Waiver Draft, October 3, 2003. Claimed on waivers by **Philadelphia** from **NY Rangers**, November 5, 2003. Traded to **Dallas** by **Philadelphia** for Steve Gainey, February 16, 2004.

SILLINGER, Mike
(sih-LIHN-juhr, MIGHK) **ST.L.**

Center. Shoots right. 5'11", 196 lbs. Born, Regina, Sask., June 29, 1971. Detroit's 1st choice, 11th overall, in 1989 Entry Draft.

Season	Club	League	GP	G	A	Pts	PIM	PP	SH	GW	S	%	+/-	TF	F%	Min	GP	G	A	Pts	PIM	PP	SH	GW	Min
1986-87	Regina Kings	SMHL	31	83	51	134	....	....	....	....	....	....	....	....	....	....	....	....	....	....	....	....	....	....	....
1987-88	Regina Pats	WHL	67	18	25	43	17	....	....	....	....	....	....	....	....	....	4	2	2	4	0	....	....	....	....
1988-89	Regina Pats	WHL	72	53	78	131	52	....	....	....	....	....	....	....	....	....	....	....	....	....	....	....	....	....	....
1989-90	Regina Pats	WHL	70	57	72	129	41	....	....	....	....	....	....	....	....	....	11	12	10	22	2	....	....	....	....
	Adirondack	AHL	....	....	....	....	....	....	....	....	....	....	....	....	....	....	1	0	0	0	0	....	....	....	....
1990-91	Regina Pats	WHL	57	50	66	116	42	....	....	....	....	....	....	....	....	....	8	6	9	15	4	....	....	....	....
	Detroit	**NHL**	**3**	**0**	**1**	**1**	**0**	**0**	**0**	**0**	**6**	**0.0**	**–2**	....	....	....	**3**	**0**	**1**	**1**	**0**	**0**	**0**	**0**	....
1991-92	Adirondack	AHL	64	25	41	66	26	....	....	....	....	....	....	....	....	....	15	9	*19	*28	12	....	....	....	....
	Detroit	**NHL**	....	....	....	....	....	....	....	....	....	....	....	....	....	....	**8**	**2**	**2**	**4**	**2**	**0**	**0**	**0**	....
1992-93	**Detroit**	**NHL**	**51**	**4**	**17**	**21**	**16**	**0**	**0**	**0**	**47**	**8.5**	**0**	....	....	....	....	....	....	....	....	....	....	....	....
	Adirondack	AHL	15	10	20	30	31	....	....	....	....	....	....	....	....	....	11	5	13	18	10	....	....	....	....
1993-94	**Detroit**	**NHL**	**62**	**8**	**21**	**29**	**10**	**0**	**1**	**1**	**91**	**8.8**	**2**	....	....	....	....	....	....	....	....	....	....	....	....
1994-95	CE Wien	Austria	13	13	14	27	10	....	....	....	....	....	....	....	....	....	....	....	....	....	....	....	....	....	....
	Anaheim	**NHL**	**15**	**2**	**5**	**7**	**6**	**2**	**0**	**0**	**28**	**7.1**	**1**	....	....	....	....	....	....	....	....	....	....	....	....
	Detroit	**NHL**	**13**	**2**	**6**	**8**	**2**	**0**	**0**	**0**	**11**	**18.2**	**3**	....	....	....	....	....	....	....	....	....	....	....	....
1995-96	**Anaheim**	**NHL**	**62**	**13**	**21**	**34**	**32**	**7**	**0**	**2**	**143**	**9.1**	**–20**	....	....	....	....	....	....	....	....	....	....	....	....
	Vancouver	**NHL**	**12**	**1**	**3**	**4**	**6**	**0**	**1**	**0**	**16**	**6.3**	**2**	....	....	....	**6**	**0**	**0**	**0**	**2**	**0**	**0**	**0**	....
1996-97	**Vancouver**	**NHL**	**78**	**17**	**20**	**37**	**25**	**3**	**3**	**2**	**112**	**15.2**	**–3**	....	....	....	....	....	....	....	....	....	....	....	....
1997-98	**Vancouver**	**NHL**	**48**	**10**	**9**	**19**	**34**	**1**	**2**	**1**	**56**	**17.9**	**–14**	....	....	....	....	....	....	....	....	....	....	....	....
	Philadelphia	**NHL**	**27**	**11**	**11**	**22**	**16**	**1**	**2**	**0**	**40**	**27.5**	**3**	....	....	....	**3**	**1**	**0**	**1**	**0**	**0**	**0**	**0**	....
1998-99	**Philadelphia**	**NHL**	**25**	**0**	**3**	**3**	**8**	**0**	**0**	**0**	**23**	**0.0**	**–9**	**229**	**62.9**	**10:42**	....	....	....	....	....	....	....	....	....
	Tampa Bay	**NHL**	**54**	**8**	**2**	**10**	**28**	**0**	**2**	**0**	**69**	**11.6**	**–20**	**320**	**57.8**	**13:57**	....	....	....	....	....	....	....	....	....
99-2000	**Tampa Bay**	**NHL**	**67**	**19**	**25**	**44**	**86**	**6**	**3**	**1**	**126**	**15.1**	**–29**	**493**	**56.0**	**19:42**	....	....	....	....	....	....	....	....	....
	Florida	**NHL**	**13**	**4**	**4**	**8**	**16**	**2**	**0**	**1**	**20**	**20.0**	**–1**	**248**	**61.3**	**19:33**	**4**	**2**	**1**	**3**	**2**	**0**	**0**	**0**	**20:24**
2000-01	**Florida**	**NHL**	**55**	**13**	**21**	**34**	**44**	**1**	**0**	**2**	**100**	**13.0**	**–12**	**1028**	**59.7**	**18:52**	....	....	....	....	....	....	....	....	....
	Ottawa	**NHL**	**13**	**3**	**4**	**7**	**4**	**0**	**0**	**0**	**19**	**15.8**	**1**	**215**	**63.3**	**14:31**	**4**	**0**	**0**	**0**	**2**	**0**	**0**	**0**	**13:40**
2001-02	**Columbus**	**NHL**	**80**	**20**	**23**	**43**	**54**	**8**	**0**	**5**	**150**	**13.3**	**–35**	**2024**	**57.0**	**20:51**	....	....	....	....	....	....	....	....	....
2002-03	**Columbus**	**NHL**	**75**	**18**	**25**	**43**	**52**	**9**	**3**	**3**	**128**	**14.1**	**–21**	**1490**	**56.5**	**19:08**	....	....	....	....	....	....	....	....	....
2003-04	**Phoenix**	**NHL**	**60**	**8**	**6**	**14**	**54**	**0**	**1**	**0**	**66**	**12.1**	**–14**	**771**	**56.3**	**15:22**	....	....	....	....	....	....	....	....	....
	St. Louis	**NHL**	**16**	**5**	**5**	**10**	**14**	**0**	**1**	**0**	**40**	**12.5**	**4**	**351**	**57.8**	**20:08**	**5**	**3**	**1**	**4**	**6**	**0**	**1**	**0**	**22:17**
	NHL Totals		**829**	**166**	**232**	**398**	**507**	**40**	**19**	**18**	**1291**	**12.9**		**7169**	**57.7**	**17:50**	**33**	**8**	**5**	**13**	**14**	**0**	**1**	**0**	**19:03**

WHL East Second All-Star Team (1990) • WHL East First All-Star Team (1991)

Traded to **Anaheim** by **Detroit** with Jason York for Stu Grimson, Mark Ferner and Anaheim's 6th round choice (Magnus Nilsson) in 1996 Entry Draft, April 4, 1995. Traded to **Vancouver** by **Anaheim** for Roman Oksiuta, March 15, 1996. Traded to **Philadelphia** by **Vancouver** for Philadelphia's 5th round choice (later traded back to Philadelphia – Philadelphia selected Garrett Prosofsky) in 1998 Entry Draft, February 5, 1998. Traded to **Tampa Bay** by **Philadelphia** with Chris Gratton for Mikael Renberg and Daymond Langkow, December 12, 1998. Traded to **Florida** by **Tampa Bay** for Ryan Johnson and Dwayne Hay, March 14, 2000. Traded to **Ottawa** by **Florida** for future considerations, March 13, 2001. Signed as a free agent by **Columbus**, July 7, 2001. Traded to **Dallas** by **Columbus** with Columbus' 2nd round choice (Johan Fransson) in 2004 Entry Draft for Darryl Sydor, July 22, 2003. Traded to **Phoenix** by **Dallas** with future considerations for Teppo Numminen, July 22, 2003. Traded to **St. Louis** by **Phoenix** for Brent Johnson, March 4, 2004.

SIM, Jon
(SIHM, JAWN)

Left wing. Shoots left. 5'10", 190 lbs. Born, New Glasgow, N.S., September 29, 1977. Dallas' 2nd choice, 70th overall, in 1996 Entry Draft.

Season	Club	League	GP	G	A	Pts	PIM	PP	SH	GW	S	%	+/-	TF	F%	Min	GP	G	A	Pts	PIM	PP	SH	GW	Min
1994-95	Laval Titan	QMJHL	9	0	1	1	6	....	....	....	....	....	....	....	....	....	....	....	....	....	....	....	....	....	....
	Sarnia Sting	OHL	25	9	12	21	19	....	....	....	....	....	....	....	....	....	4	3	2	5	2	....	....	....	....
1995-96	Sarnia Sting	OHL	63	56	46	102	130	....	....	....	....	....	....	....	....	....	10	8	7	15	26	....	....	....	....
1996-97	Sarnia Sting	OHL	64	*56	39	95	109	....	....	....	....	....	....	....	....	....	12	9	5	14	32	....	....	....	....
1997-98	Sarnia Sting	OHL	59	44	50	94	95	....	....	....	....	....	....	....	....	....	5	1	4	5	14	....	....	....	....
1998-99 ♦	**Dallas**	**NHL**	**7**	**1**	**0**	**1**	**12**	**0**	**0**	**0**	**8**	**12.5**	**1**	**6**	**50.0**	**11:26**	**4**	**0**	**0**	**0**	**0**	**0**	**0**	**0**	**6:27**
	Michigan	IHL	68	24	27	51	91	....	....	....	....	....	....	....	....	....	5	3	1	4	18	....	....	....	....
99-2000	**Dallas**	**NHL**	**25**	**5**	**3**	**8**	**10**	**2**	**0**	**1**	**44**	**11.4**	**4**	**4**	**75.0**	**10:51**	**7**	**1**	**0**	**1**	**6**	**0**	**0**	**0**	**11:11**
	Michigan	IHL	35	14	16	30	65	....	....	....	....	....	....	....	....	....	....	....	....	....	....	....	....	....	....
2000-01	**Dallas**	**NHL**	**15**	**0**	**3**	**3**	**6**	**0**	**0**	**0**	**18**	**0.0**	**–2**	**1**	**100.0**	**8:47**	....	....	....	....	....	....	....	....	....
	Utah Grizzlies	IHL	39	16	13	29	44	....	....	....	....	....	....	....	....	....	....	....	....	....	....	....	....	....	....
2001-02	**Dallas**	**NHL**	**26**	**3**	**0**	**3**	**10**	**1**	**0**	**0**	**43**	**7.0**	**–3**	**3**	**0.0**	**9:30**	....	....	....	....	....	....	....	....	....
	Utah Grizzlies	AHL	31	21	6	27	63	....	....	....	....	....	....	....	....	....	....	....	....	....	....	....	....	....	....
2002-03	**Dallas**	**NHL**	**4**	**0**	**0**	**0**	**0**	**0**	**0**	**0**	**7**	**0.0**	**–1**	**2**	**50.0**	**9:10**	....	....	....	....	....	....	....	....	....
	Utah Grizzlies	AHL	42	16	31	47	85	....	....	....	....	....	....	....	....	....	....	....	....	....	....	....	....	....	....
	Nashville	**NHL**	**4**	**1**	**0**	**1**	**0**	**0**	**0**	**0**	**3**	**33.3**	**0**	**14**	**35.7**	**9:18**	....	....	....	....	....	....	....	....	....
	Los Angeles	**NHL**	**14**	**0**	**2**	**2**	**19**	**0**	**0**	**0**	**29**	**0.0**	**–3**	**3**	**33.3**	**12:05**	....	....	....	....	....	....	....	....	....
2003-04	**Los Angeles**	**NHL**	**48**	**6**	**7**	**13**	**27**	**0**	**0**	**1**	**73**	**8.2**	**0**	**19**	**31.6**	**10:01**	....	....	....	....	....	....	....	....	....
	Pittsburgh	**NHL**	**15**	**2**	**3**	**5**	**6**	**0**	**0**	**1**	**27**	**7.4**	**–4**	**0**	**0.0**	**13:39**	....	....	....	....	....	....	....	....	....
	NHL Totals		**158**	**18**	**18**	**36**	**90**	**3**	**0**	**3**	**252**	**7.1**		**52**	**38.5**	**10:30**	**11**	**1**	**0**	**1**	**6**	**0**	**0**	**0**	**9:27**

OHL Second All-Star Team (1998)

Traded to **Nashville** by **Dallas** for Bubba Berenzweig and future considerations, February 17, 2003. Claimed on waivers by **Los Angeles** from **Nashville**, March 8, 2003. Claimed on waivers by **Pittsburgh** from **Los Angeles**, March 4, 2004.

SIMON, Ben
(SIGH-mohn, BEN) **ATL.**

Left wing. Shoots left. 6', 200 lbs. Born, Shaker Heights, OH, June 14, 1978. Chicago's 5th choice, 110th overall, in 1997 Entry Draft.

Season	Club	League	GP	G	A	Pts	PIM	PP	SH	GW	S	%	+/-	TF	F%	Min	GP	G	A	Pts	PIM	PP	SH	GW	Min
1992-93	Shaker Heights	Hi-School	25	15	21	36	....	....	....	....	....	....	....	....	....	....	....	....	....	....	....	....	....	....	....
1993-94	Shaker Heights	Hi-School	24	45	41	86	....	....	....	....	....	....	....	....	....	....	....	....	....	....	....	....	....	....	....
1994-95	Shaker Heights	Hi-School	25	61	68	129	....	....	....	....	....	....	....	....	....	....	....	....	....	....	....	....	....	....	....
1995-96	Cleveland Barons	NAJHL	45	38	33	71	....	....	....	....	....	....	....	....	....	....	5	7	13	20	....	....	....	....	....
1996-97	U. of Notre Dame	CCHA	30	4	15	19	79	....	....	....	....	....	....	....	....	....	....	....	....	....	....	....	....	....	....
1997-98	U. of Notre Dame	CCHA	37	9	28	37	91	....	....	....	....	....	....	....	....	....	....	....	....	....	....	....	....	....	....
1998-99	U. of Notre Dame	CCHA	37	18	24	42	65	....	....	....	....	....	....	....	....	....	....	....	....	....	....	....	....	....	....
99-2000	U. of Notre Dame	CCHA	40	13	19	32	53	....	....	....	....	....	....	....	....	....	....	....	....	....	....	....	....	....	....
2000-01	Orlando	IHL	77	8	12	20	47	....	....	....	....	....	....	....	....	....	16	6	5	11	20	....	....	....	....
2001-02	**Atlanta**	**NHL**	**6**	**0**	**0**	**0**	**6**	**0**	**0**	**0**	**7**	**0.0**	**1**	**32**	**40.6**	**9:20**	....	....	....	....	....	....	....	....	....
	Chicago Wolves	AHL	74	11	23	34	56	....	....	....	....	....	....	....	....	....	25	2	3	5	24	....	....	....	....
2002-03	**Atlanta**	**NHL**	**10**	**0**	**1**	**1**	**9**	**0**	**0**	**0**	**7**	**0.0**	**0**	**54**	**31.5**	**9:25**	....	....	....	....	....	....	....	....	....
	Chicago Wolves	AHL	69	15	17	32	78	....	....	....	....	....	....	....	....	....	9	0	0	0	6	....	....	....	....

			Regular Season														Playoffs								
Season	Club	League	GP	G	A	Pts	PIM	PP	SH	GW	S	%	+/-	TF	F%	Min	GP	G	A	Pts	PIM	PP	SH	GW	Min
2003-04	Milwaukee	AHL	18	1	3	4	6	....	....	....	....	....	....	....	....	....	....	....	....	....	....	....	....	....	....
	Atlanta	**NHL**	**52**	**3**	**0**	**3**	**28**	0	0	0	30	10.0	–10	203	33.0	6:05	....	....	....	....	....	....	....	....	....
	NHL Totals		**68**	**3**	**1**	**4**	**43**	0	0	0	44	6.8		289	33.6	6:51	....	....	....	....	....	....	....	....	....

CCHA Second All-Star Team (1999)

Rights traded to **Atlanta** by **Chicago** for Atlanta's 9th round choice (Peter Flache) in 2000 Entry Draft, June 25, 2000. Signed as a free agent by **Nashville**, July 14, 2003. Traded to **Atlanta** by **Nashville** with Tomas Kloucek for Simon Gamache and Kirill Safronov, December 2, 2003.

SIMON, Chris

(SIGH-mohn, KRIHS) **CGY.**

Left wing. Shoots left. 6'4", 235 lbs. Born, Wawa, Ont., January 30, 1972. Philadelphia's 2nd choice, 25th overall, in 1990 Entry Draft.

1986-87	Wawa Flyers	NOHA	36	12	20	32	108	....	....	....	....	....	....	....	....	....	....	....	....	....	....	....	....	....	....
1987-88	Soo Thunderbirds	NOJHA	55	42	36	78	172	....	....	....	....	....	....	....	....	....	....	....	....	....	....	....	....	....	....
1988-89	Ottawa 67's	OHL	36	4	2	6	31	....	....	....	....	....	....	....	....	....	....	....	....	....	....	....	....	....	....
1989-90	Ottawa 67's	OHL	57	36	38	74	146	....	....	....	....	....	....	....	....	....	3	2	1	3	4	....	....	....	....
1990-91	Ottawa 67's	OHL	20	16	6	22	69	....	....	....	....	....	....	....	....	....	17	5	9	14	59	....	....	....	....
1991-92	Ottawa 67's	OHL	2	1	1	2	24	....	....	....	....	....	....	....	....	....	....	....	....	....	....	....	....	....	....
	Sault Ste. Marie	OHL	31	19	25	44	143	....	....	....	....	....	....	....	....	....	11	5	8	13	49	....	....	....	....
1992-93	**Quebec**	**NHL**	**16**	**1**	**1**	**2**	**67**	0	0	1	15	6.7	–2	....	....	....	**5**	**0**	**0**	**0**	**26**	0	0	0	....
	Halifax Citadels	AHL	36	12	6	18	131	....	....	....	....	....	....	....	....	....	....	....	....	....	....	....	....	....	....
1993-94	**Quebec**	**NHL**	**37**	**4**	**4**	**8**	**132**	0	0	1	39	10.3	–2	....	....	....	....	....	....	....	....	....	....	....	....
1994-95	**Quebec**	**NHL**	**29**	**3**	**9**	**12**	**106**	0	0	0	33	9.1	14	....	....	....	**6**	**1**	**1**	**2**	**19**	0	0	1	....
1995-96♦	**Colorado**	**NHL**	**64**	**16**	**18**	**34**	**250**	4	0	1	105	15.2	10	....	....	....	**12**	**1**	**2**	**3**	**11**	0	0	0	....
1996-97	**Washington**	**NHL**	**42**	**9**	**13**	**22**	**165**	3	0	1	89	10.1	–1	....	....	....	....	....	....	....	....	....	....	....	....
1997-98	**Washington**	**NHL**	**28**	**7**	**10**	**17**	**38**	4	0	1	71	9.9	–1	....	....	....	**18**	**1**	**0**	**1**	**26**	0	0	0	....
1998-99	**Washington**	**NHL**	**23**	**3**	**7**	**10**	**48**	0	0	0	29	10.3	–4	2	50.0	12:08	....	....	....	....	....	....	....	....	....
99-2000	**Washington**	**NHL**	**75**	**29**	**20**	**49**	**146**	7	0	5	201	14.4	11	7	28.6	15:32	**4**	**2**	**0**	**2**	**24**	0	0	0	18:07
2000-01	**Washington**	**NHL**	**60**	**10**	**10**	**20**	**109**	4	0	2	123	8.1	–12	3	33.3	14:34	**6**	**0**	**1**	**1**	**4**	0	0	0	9:55
2001-02	**Washington**	**NHL**	**82**	**14**	**17**	**31**	**137**	1	0	1	121	11.6	–8	7	28.6	12:11	....	....	....	....	....	....	....	....	....
2002-03	**Washington**	**NHL**	**10**	**0**	**2**	**2**	**23**	0	0	0	16	0.0	–3	0	0.0	8:53	....	....	....	....	....	....	....	....	....
	Chicago	**NHL**	**61**	**12**	**6**	**18**	**125**	2	0	2	72	16.7	–4	5	20.0	11:06	....	....	....	....	....	....	....	....	....
2003-04	**NY Rangers**	**NHL**	**65**	**14**	**9**	**23**	**225**	3	0	0	116	12.1	14	3	0.0	11:56	....	....	....	....	....	....	....	....	....
	Calgary	**NHL**	**13**	**3**	**2**	**5**	**25**	1	0	0	31	9.7	1	2	100.0	16:38	**16**	**5**	**2**	**7**	***74**	4	0	1	15:06
	NHL Totals		**605**	**125**	**128**	**253**	**1596**	29	0	15	1061	11.8		29	31.0	13:03	**67**	**10**	**6**	**16**	**184**	4	0	2	14:22

• Missed majority of 1990-91 season recovering from shoulder surgery, October, 1990. Traded to **Quebec** by **Philadelphia** with Philadelphia's 1st round choice (later traded to Toronto – later traded to Washington – Washington selected Nolan Baumgartner) in 1994 Entry Draft to complete transaction that sent Eric Lindros to Philadelphia (June 30, 1992), July 21, 1992. Transferred to **Colorado** after **Quebec** franchise relocated, June 21, 1995. Traded to **Washington** by **Colorado** with Curtis Leschyshyn for Keith Jones and Washington's 1st (Scott Parker) and 4th (later traded back to Washington – Washington selected Krys Barch) round choices in 1998 Entry Drarft, November 2, 1996. Traded to **Chicago** by **Washington** with Andrei Nikolishin for Michael Nylander, Chicago's 3rd round choice (Stephen Werner) in 2003 Entry Draft and future considerations, November 1, 2002. Signed as a free agent by **NY Rangers**, July 25, 2003. Traded to **Calgary** by **NY Rangers** with NY Rangers' 7th round choice (Matt Schneider) in 2004 Entry Draft for Jamie McLennan, Blair Betts and Greg Moore, March 6, 2004

SIMPSON, Reid

(SIHMP-sohn, REED)

Left wing. Shoots left. 6'2", 216 lbs. Born, Flin Flon, Man., May 21, 1969. Philadelphia's 3rd choice, 72nd overall, in 1989 Entry Draft.

1984-85	Flin Flon Bombers	MMHL	50	60	70	130	100	....	....	....	....	....	....	....	....	....	....	....	....	....	....	....	....	....	....
1985-86	Flin Flon Bombers	MJHL	40	20	21	41	200	....	....	....	....	....	....	....	....	....	....	....	....	....	....	....	....	....	....
	New Westminster	WHL	2	0	0	0	0	....	....	....	....	....	....	....	....	....	....	....	....	....	....	....	....	....	....
1986-87	Prince Albert	WHL	47	3	8	11	105	....	....	....	....	....	....	....	....	....	8	2	3	5	13	....	....	....	....
1987-88	Prince Albert	WHL	72	13	14	27	164	....	....	....	....	....	....	....	....	....	10	1	0	1	43	....	....	....	....
1988-89	Prince Albert	WHL	59	26	29	55	264	....	....	....	....	....	....	....	....	....	4	2	1	3	30	....	....	....	....
1989-90	Prince Albert	WHL	29	15	17	32	121	....	....	....	....	....	....	....	....	....	14	4	7	11	34	....	....	....	....
	Hershey Bears	AHL	28	2	2	4	175	....	....	....	....	....	....	....	....	....	....	....	....	....	....	....	....	....	....
1990-91	Hershey Bears	AHL	54	9	15	24	183	....	....	....	....	....	....	....	....	....	1	0	0	0	0	....	....	....	....
1991-92	**Philadelphia**	**NHL**	**1**	**0**	**0**	**0**	**0**	0	0	0	0	0.0	0	....	....	....	....	....	....	....	....	....	....	....	....
	Hershey Bears	AHL	60	11	7	18	145	....	....	....	....	....	....	....	....	....	....	....	....	....	....	....	....	....	....
1992-93	**Minnesota**	**NHL**	**1**	**0**	**0**	**0**	**5**	0	0	0	0	0.0	0	....	....	....	....	....	....	....	....	....	....	....	....
	Kalamazoo Wings	IHL	45	5	5	10	193	....	....	....	....	....	....	....	....	....	....	....	....	....	....	....	....	....	....
1993-94	Kalamazoo Wings	IHL	5	0	0	0	16	....	....	....	....	....	....	....	....	....	....	....	....	....	....	....	....	....	....
	Albany River Rats	AHL	37	9	5	14	135	....	....	....	....	....	....	....	....	....	5	1	1	2	18	....	....	....	....
1994-95	Albany River Rats	AHL	70	18	25	43	268	....	....	....	....	....	....	....	....	....	14	1	8	9	13	....	....	....	....
	New Jersey	**NHL**	**9**	**0**	**0**	**0**	**27**	0	0	0	5	0.0	–1	....	....	....	....	....	....	....	....	....	....	....	....
1995-96	**New Jersey**	**NHL**	**23**	**1**	**5**	**6**	**79**	0	0	0	8	12.5	2	....	....	....	....	....	....	....	....	....	....	....	....
	Albany River Rats	AHL	6	1	3	4	17	....	....	....	....	....	....	....	....	....	....	....	....	....	....	....	....	....	....
1996-97	**New Jersey**	**NHL**	**27**	**0**	**4**	**4**	**60**	0	0	0	17	0.0	0	....	....	....	**5**	**0**	**0**	**0**	**29**	0	0	0	....
	Albany River Rats	AHL	3	0	0	0	10	....	....	....	....	....	....	....	....	....	....	....	....	....	....	....	....	....	....
1997-98	**New Jersey**	**NHL**	**6**	**0**	**0**	**0**	**16**	0	0	0	5	0.0	–2	....	....	....	....	....	....	....	....	....	....	....	....
	Chicago	**NHL**	**38**	**3**	**2**	**5**	**102**	1	0	0	19	15.8	–1	....	....	....	....	....	....	....	....	....	....	....	....
1998-99	**Chicago**	**NHL**	**53**	**5**	**4**	**9**	**145**	1	0	0	23	21.7	2	5	40.0	5:56	....	....	....	....	....	....	....	....	....
99-2000	Cleveland	IHL	12	2	2	4	56	....	....	....	....	....	....	....	....	....	....	....	....	....	....	....	....	....	....
	Tampa Bay	**NHL**	**26**	**1**	**0**	**1**	**103**	0	0	0	13	7.7	–3	1	100.0	4:33	....	....	....	....	....	....	....	....	....
2000-01	**St. Louis**	**NHL**	**38**	**2**	**1**	**3**	**96**	0	0	1	23	8.7	–3	1	0.0	6:57	**5**	**0**	**0**	**0**	**2**	0	0	0	6:13
2001-02	**Montreal**	**NHL**	**25**	**1**	**1**	**2**	**63**	0	0	1	9	11.1	0	0	0.0	4:22	....	....	....	....	....	....	....	....	....
	Nashville	**NHL**	**26**	**5**	**0**	**5**	**69**	0	0	0	13	38.5	–1	5	60.0	5:45	....	....	....	....	....	....	....	....	....
	Milwaukee	AHL	2	1	0	1	37	....	....	....	....	....	....	....	....	....	....	....	....	....	....	....	....	....	....
2002-03	**Nashville**	**NHL**	**26**	**0**	**1**	**1**	**56**	0	0	0	11	0.0	–4	1	0.0	5:04	....	....	....	....	....	....	....	....	....
	Milwaukee	AHL	17	6	6	12	40	....	....	....	....	....	....	....	....	....	....	....	....	....	....	....	....	....	....
2003-04	**Pittsburgh**	**NHL**	**2**	**0**	**0**	**0**	**17**	0	0	0	2	0.0	0	0	0.0	4:46	....	....	....	....	....	....	....	....	....
	Wilkes-Barre	AHL	51	6	11	17	168	....	....	....	....	....	....	....	....	....	2	0	0	0	0	....	....	....	....
	NHL Totals		**301**	**18**	**18**	**36**	**838**	2	0	2	148	12.2		13	46.2	5:36	**10**	**0**	**0**	**0**	**31**	0	0	0	6:13

Signed as a free agent by **Minnesota**, December 14, 1992. Transferred to **Dallas** after **Minnesota** franchise relocated, June 9, 1993. Traded to **New Jersey** by **Dallas** with Roy Mitchell for future considerations, March 21, 1994. Traded to **Chicago** by **New Jersey** for Chicago's 4th round choice (Mikko Jokela) in 1998 Entry Draft and future considerations, January 8, 1998. Traded to **Tampa Bay** by **Chicago** with Bryan Muir for Michael Nylander, November 12, 1999. • Missed majority of 1999-2000 season recovering from jaw injury suffered in game vs. NY Islanders, January 13, 2000. Signed as a free agent by **St. Louis**, August 24, 2000. • Missed majority of 2000-01 season recovering from groin injury suffered in game vs. Nashville, November 24, 2000. Signed as a free agent by **Montreal**, September 10, 2001. Claimed on waivers by **Nashville** from **Montreal**, January 28, 2002. Signed as a free agent by **Pittsburgh**, August 29, 2003.

SIMPSON, Todd

(SIHMP-sohn, TAWD)

Defense. Shoots left. 6'3", 218 lbs. Born, North Vancouver, B.C., May 28, 1973.

1991-92	Brown University	ECAC	18	1	4	5	38	....	....	....	....	....	....	....	....	....	....	....	....	....	....	....	....	....	....
1992-93	Tri-City	WHL	69	5	18	23	196	....	....	....	....	....	....	....	....	....	4	0	0	0	13	....	....	....	....
1993-94	Tri-City	WHL	12	2	3	5	32	....	....	....	....	....	....	....	....	....	....	....	....	....	....	....	....	....	....
	Saskatoon Blades	WHL	51	7	19	26	175	....	....	....	....	....	....	....	....	....	16	1	5	6	42	....	....	....	....
1994-95	Saint John Flames	AHL	80	3	10	13	321	....	....	....	....	....	....	....	....	....	5	0	0	0	4	....	....	....	....
1995-96	**Calgary**	**NHL**	**6**	**0**	**0**	**0**	**32**	0	0	0	3	0.0	0	....	....	....	....	....	....	....	....	....	....	....	....
	Saint John Flames	AHL	66	4	13	17	277	....	....	....	....	....	....	....	....	....	16	2	3	5	32	....	....	....	....
1996-97	**Calgary**	**NHL**	**82**	**1**	**13**	**14**	**208**	0	0	0	85	1.2	–14	....	....	....	....	....	....	....	....	....	....	....	....
1997-98	**Calgary**	**NHL**	**53**	**1**	**5**	**6**	**109**	0	0	1	51	2.0	–10	....	....	....	....	....	....	....	....	....	....	....	....
1998-99	**Calgary**	**NHL**	**73**	**2**	**8**	**10**	**151**	0	0	0	52	3.8	18	1	100.0	17:19	....	....	....	....	....	....	....	....	....
99-2000	**Florida**	**NHL**	**82**	**1**	**6**	**7**	**202**	0	0	0	50	2.0	5	0	0.0	16:35	**4**	**0**	**0**	**0**	**4**	0	0	0	15:24
2000-01	**Florida**	**NHL**	**25**	**1**	**3**	**4**	**74**	0	0	1	26	3.8	0	0	0.0	16:29	....	....	....	....	....	....	....	....	....
	Phoenix	**NHL**	**13**	**0**	**1**	**1**	**12**	0	0	0	9	0.0	–4	0	0.0	13:56	....	....	....	....	....	....	....	....	....
2001-02	**Phoenix**	**NHL**	**67**	**2**	**13**	**15**	**152**	0	0	0	51	3.9	20	0	0.0	17:20	**5**	**0**	**2**	**2**	**6**	0	0	0	18:30
2002-03	**Phoenix**	**NHL**	**66**	**2**	**7**	**9**	**135**	0	0	0	67	3.0	7	0	0.0	16:59	....	....	....	....	....	....	....	....	....
2003-04	**Anaheim**	**NHL**	**46**	**4**	**3**	**7**	**105**	0	0	0	42	9.5	–6	0	0.0	14:18	....	....	....	....	....	....	....	....	....
	Ottawa	**NHL**	**16**	**0**	**1**	**1**	**47**	0	0	0	10	0.0	–1	1	0.0	14:21	....	....	....	....	....	....	....	....	....
	NHL Totals		**529**	**14**	**60**	**74**	**1227**	0	0	2	446	3.1		2	50.0	16:28	**9**	**0**	**2**	**2**	**10**	0	0	0	17:07

Signed as free agent by **Calgary**, July 6, 1994. Traded to **Florida** by **Calgary** for Bill Lindsay, September 30, 1999. • Missed majority of 2000-01 season recovering from head injury suffered in game vs. NY Islanders, December 6, 2000. Traded to **Phoenix** by **Florida** for Phoenix's 2nd round choice (later traded to New Jersey – New Jersey selected Tuomas Pihlman) in 2001 Entry Draft, March 13, 2001. Claimed by **Anaheim** from **Phoenix** in Waiver Draft, October 3, 2003. Traded to **Ottawa** by **Anaheim** for Petr Schastlivy, February 4, 2004.

SIVEK, Michal

(sih-VIHK, MEE-khahl) **PIT.**

Center. Shoots left. 6'3", 214 lbs. Born, Nachod, Czech., January 21, 1981. Washington's 2nd choice, 29th overall, in 1999 Entry Draft.

			Regular Season														Playoffs								
Season	Club	League	GP	G	A	Pts	PIM	PP	SH	GW	S	%	+/-	TF	F%	Min	GP	G	A	Pts	PIM	PP	SH	GW	Min
1997-98	Sparta Praha Jr.	Czech-Jr.	31	13	8	21	....	....	....	....	....	....	....	....	....	....	....	....	....	....	....	....	....	....	....
	HC Sparta Praha	Czech	25	1	1	2	10	....	....	....	....	....	....	....	....	....	5	1	0	1	0	....	....	....	....
1998-99	HC Sparta Praha	Czech	1	1	0	1	....	....	....	....	....	....	....	....	....	....	....	....	....	....	....	....	....	....	....
	Kladno	Czech	34	3	8	11	24	....	....	....	....	....	....	....	....	....	....	....	....	....	....	....	....	....	....
99-2000	Prince Albert	WHL	53	23	37	60	65	....	....	....	....	....	....	....	....	....	6	1	4	5	10	....	....	....	....
2000-01	HC Sparta Praha	Czech	32	6	7	13	28	....	....	....	....	....	....	....	....	....	13	4	2	6	8	....	....	....	....
2001-02	Wilkes-Barre	AHL	25	4	8	12	30	....	....	....	....	....	....	....	....	....	....	....	....	....	....	....	....	....	....
	HC Sparta Praha	Czech	17	5	3	8	20	....	....	....	....	....	....	....	....	....	12	0	1	1	10	....	....	....	....
2002-03	**Pittsburgh**	**NHL**	**38**	**3**	**3**	**6**	**14**	**1**	**0**	**0**	**45**	**6.7**	**–5**	**32**	**43.8**	**13:05**	....	....	....	....	....	....	....	....	....
	Wilkes-Barre	AHL	40	10	17	27	33	....	....	....	....	....	....	....	....	....	6	3	2	5	20	....	....	....	....
2003-04	Wilkes-Barre	AHL	22	4	7	11	6	....	....	....	....	....	....	....	....	....	....	....	....	....	....	....	....	....	....
	NHL Totals		**38**	**3**	**3**	**6**	**14**	**1**	**0**	**0**	**45**	**6.7**		**32**	**43.8**	**13:05**	....	....	....	....	....	....	....	....	....

Traded to **Pittsburgh** by **Washington** with Kris Beech, Ross Lupaschuk and future considerations for Jaromir Jagr and Frantisek Kucera, July 11, 2001. • Missed majority of 2003-04 season recovering from finger injury suffered in game vs. Syracuse (AHL), October 17, 2003. Signed as a free agent by **HC Sparta Praha** (Czech), May 19, 2004.

SJOSTROM, Fredrik

(SHAW-strahm, FREHD-rihk) **PHX.**

Right wing. Shoots left. 6'1", 217 lbs. Born, Fargelanda, Sweden, May 6, 1983. Phoenix's 1st choice, 11th overall, in 2001 Entry Draft.

			Regular Season														Playoffs								
Season	Club	League	GP	G	A	Pts	PIM	PP	SH	GW	S	%	+/-	TF	F%	Min	GP	G	A	Pts	PIM	PP	SH	GW	Min
99-2000	MoDo 18	Swede-Jr.	4	0	2	2	6	....	....	....	....	....	....	....	....	....	....	....	....	....	....	....	....	....	....
	MoDo Jr.	Swede-Jr.	18	4	6	10	8	....	....	....	....	....	....	....	....	....	....	....	....	....	....	....	....	....	....
2000-01	V. Frolunda Jr.	Swede-Jr.	11	3	7	10	12	....	....	....	....	....	....	....	....	....	4	1	2	3	6	....	....	....	....
	Vastra Frolunda	Sweden	31	3	2	5	6	....	....	....	....	....	....	....	....	....	5	0	0	0	2	....	....	....	....
2001-02	Calgary Hitmen	WHL	58	19	31	50	51	....	....	....	....	....	....	....	....	....	4	1	1	2	8	....	....	....	....
2002-03	Calgary Hitmen	WHL	63	34	43	77	95	....	....	....	....	....	....	....	....	....	5	1	3	4	4	....	....	....	....
	Springfield	AHL	2	1	0	1	0	....	....	....	....	....	....	....	....	....	6	2	0	2	12	....	....	....	....
2003-04	**Phoenix**	**NHL**	**57**	**7**	**6**	**13**	**22**	**0**	**0**	**1**	**73**	**9.6**	**–7**	**7**	**28.6**	**11:35**	....	....	....	....	....	....	....	....	....
	Springfield	AHL	17	0	7	7	8	....	....	....	....	....	....	....	....	....	....	....	....	....	....	....	....	....	....
	NHL Totals		**57**	**7**	**6**	**13**	**22**	**0**	**0**	**1**	**73**	**9.6**		**7**	**28.6**	**11:35**	....	....	....	....	....	....	....	....	....

SKALDE, Jarrod

(SKAHL-dee, JAIR-ruhd) **T.B.**

Center. Shoots left. 6', 185 lbs. Born, Niagara Falls, Ont., February 26, 1971. New Jersey's 3rd choice, 26th overall, in 1989 Entry Draft.

			Regular Season														Playoffs								
Season	Club	League	GP	G	A	Pts	PIM	PP	SH	GW	S	%	+/-	TF	F%	Min	GP	G	A	Pts	PIM	PP	SH	GW	Min
1986-87	Fort Erie Meteors	OJHL-B	41	27	34	61	36	....	....	....	....	....	....	....	....	....	....	....	....	....	....	....	....	....	....
1987-88	Oshawa Generals	OHL	60	12	16	28	24	....	....	....	....	....	....	....	....	....	7	2	1	3	2	....	....	....	....
1988-89	Oshawa Generals	OHL	65	38	38	76	36	....	....	....	....	....	....	....	....	....	6	1	5	6	2	....	....	....	....
1989-90	Oshawa Generals	OHL	62	40	52	92	66	....	....	....	....	....	....	....	....	....	17	10	7	17	6	....	....	....	....
1990-91	Oshawa Generals	OHL	15	8	14	22	14	....	....	....	....	....	....	....	....	....	....	....	....	....	....	....	....	....	....
	Belleville Bulls	OHL	40	30	52	82	21	....	....	....	....	....	....	....	....	....	6	9	6	15	10	....	....	....	....
	New Jersey	**NHL**	**1**	**0**	**1**	**1**	**0**	**0**	**0**	**0**	**2**	**0.0**	**0**	....	....	....	....	....	....	....	....	....	....	....	....
	Utica Devils	AHL	3	3	2	5	0	....	....	....	....	....	....	....	....	....	....	....	....	....	....	....	....	....	....
1991-92	**New Jersey**	**NHL**	**15**	**2**	**4**	**6**	**4**	**0**	**0**	**2**	**25**	**8.0**	**–1**	....	....	....	....	....	....	....	....	....	....	....	....
	Utica Devils	AHL	62	20	20	40	56	....	....	....	....	....	....	....	....	....	4	3	1	4	8	....	....	....	....
1992-93	**New Jersey**	**NHL**	**11**	**0**	**2**	**2**	**4**	**0**	**0**	**0**	**11**	**0.0**	**–3**	....	....	....	....	....	....	....	....	....	....	....	....
	Utica Devils	AHL	59	21	39	60	76	....	....	....	....	....	....	....	....	....	5	0	2	2	19	....	....	....	....
	Cincinnati	IHL	4	1	2	3	4	....	....	....	....	....	....	....	....	....	....	....	....	....	....	....	....	....	....
1993-94	**Anaheim**	**NHL**	**20**	**5**	**4**	**9**	**10**	**2**	**0**	**2**	**25**	**20.0**	**–3**	....	....	....	....	....	....	....	....	....	....	....	....
	San Diego Gulls	IHL	57	25	38	63	79	....	....	....	....	....	....	....	....	....	9	3	12	15	10	....	....	....	....
1994-95	Las Vegas	IHL	74	34	41	75	103	....	....	....	....	....	....	....	....	....	9	2	4	6	8	....	....	....	....
1995-96	Baltimore Bandits	AHL	11	2	6	8	55	....	....	....	....	....	....	....	....	....	....	....	....	....	....	....	....	....	....
	Calgary	**NHL**	**1**	**0**	**0**	**0**	**0**	**0**	**0**	**0**	**0**	**0.0**	**0**	....	....	....	....	....	....	....	....	....	....	....	....
	Saint John Flames	AHL	68	27	40	67	98	....	....	....	....	....	....	....	....	....	16	4	9	13	6	....	....	....	....
1996-97	Saint John Flames	AHL	65	32	36	68	94	....	....	....	....	....	....	....	....	....	3	0	0	0	14	....	....	....	....
1997-98	**San Jose**	**NHL**	**22**	**4**	**6**	**10**	**14**	**0**	**0**	**0**	**30**	**13.3**	**–2**	....	....	....	....	....	....	....	....	....	....	....	....
	Kentucky	AHL	6	2	6	8	10	....	....	....	....	....	....	....	....	....	....	....	....	....	....	....	....	....	....
	Chicago	**NHL**	**4**	**0**	**1**	**1**	**2**	**0**	**0**	**0**	**4**	**0.0**	**0**	....	....	....	....	....	....	....	....	....	....	....	....
	Indianapolis Ice	IHL	2	0	2	2	0	....	....	....	....	....	....	....	....	....	....	....	....	....	....	....	....	....	....
	Dallas	**NHL**	**1**	**0**	**0**	**0**	**0**	**0**	**0**	**0**	**0**	**0.0**	**0**	....	....	....	....	....	....	....	....	....	....	....	....
	Chicago	**NHL**	**3**	**0**	**0**	**0**	**2**	**0**	**0**	**0**	**0**	**0.0**	**0**	....	....	....	....	....	....	....	....	....	....	....	....
	Kentucky	AHL	17	3	9	12	38	....	....	....	....	....	....	....	....	....	3	3	0	3	6	....	....	....	....
1998-99	**San Jose**	**NHL**	**17**	**1**	**1**	**2**	**4**	**0**	**0**	**0**	**17**	**5.9**	**–6**	**191**	**52.4**	**10:07**	....	....	....	....	....	....	....	....	....
	Kentucky	AHL	54	17	40	57	75	....	....	....	....	....	....	....	....	....	12	4	5	9	16	....	....	....	....
99-2000	Utah Grizzlies	IHL	77	25	54	79	98	....	....	....	....	....	....	....	....	....	5	0	1	1	10	....	....	....	....
2000-01	**Atlanta**	**NHL**	**19**	**1**	**2**	**3**	**20**	**0**	**0**	**0**	**24**	**4.2**	**–8**	**291**	**47.1**	**13:57**	....	....	....	....	....	....	....	....	....
	Orlando	IHL	60	14	40	54	56	....	....	....	....	....	....	....	....	....	15	3	6	9	20	....	....	....	....
2001-02	Chicago Wolves	AHL	64	15	37	52	71	....	....	....	....	....	....	....	....	....	....	....	....	....	....	....	....	....	....
	Philadelphia	**NHL**	**1**	**0**	**0**	**0**	**2**	**0**	**0**	**0**	**5**	**0.0**	**0**	**15**	**60.0**	**12:25**	....	....	....	....	....	....	....	....	....
	Philadelphia	AHL	16	4	4	8	23	....	....	....	....	....	....	....	....	....	4	0	2	2	4	....	....	....	....
2002-03	Lausanne HC	Swiss	23	7	8	15	30	....	....	....	....	....	....	....	....	....	....	....	....	....	....	....	....	....	....
2003-04	Utah Grizzlies	AHL	77	23	35	58	55	....	....	....	....	....	....	....	....	....	....	....	....	....	....	....	....	....	....
	NHL Totals		**115**	**13**	**21**	**34**	**62**	**2**	**0**	**4**	**143**	**9.1**		**497**	**49.5**	**12:09**	....	....	....	....	....	....	....	....	....

OHL Second All-Star Team (1991) • IHL First All-Star Team (2000)

Claimed by **Anaheim** from **New Jersey** in Expansion Draft, June 24, 1993. Traded to **Calgary** by **Anaheim** for Bobby Marshall, October 30, 1995. Signed as a free agent by **San Jose**, August 14, 1997. Claimed on waivers by **Chicago** from **San Jose**, January 8, 1998. Claimed on waivers by **San Jose** from **Chicago**, January 23, 1998. Claimed on waivers by **Dallas** from **San Jose**, January 27, 1998. Claimed on waivers by **Chicago** from **Dallas**, February 10, 1998. Claimed on waivers by **San Jose** from **Chicago**, March 6, 1998. Signed as a free agent by **Atlanta**, July 21, 2000. Traded to **Philadelphia** by **Atlanta** for Joe DiPenta, March 5, 2002. Signed as a free agent by **Lausanne HC** (Swiss), March 21, 2002. Signed as a free agent by **Dallas**, July 17, 2003. Signed as a free agent by **Tampa Bay**, July 28, 2004.

SKOULA, Martin

(SHKOH-la, MAHR-tihn) **ANA.**

Defense. Shoots left. 6'2", 195 lbs. Born, Litomerice, Czech., October 28, 1979. Colorado's 2nd choice, 17th overall, in 1998 Entry Draft.

			Regular Season														Playoffs								
Season	Club	League	GP	G	A	Pts	PIM	PP	SH	GW	S	%	+/-	TF	F%	Min	GP	G	A	Pts	PIM	PP	SH	GW	Min
1995-96	Litvinov Jr.	Czech-Jr.	38	0	4	4	....	....	....	....	....	....	....	....	....	....	....	....	....	....	....	....	....	....	....
	Litvinov	Czech	....	....	....	....	....	....	....	....	....	....	....	....	....	....	1	0	0	0	0	....	....	....	....
1996-97	Litvinov Jr.	Czech-Jr.	38	2	9	11	....	....	....	....	....	....	....	....	....	....	....	....	....	....	....	....	....	....	....
	Litvinov	Czech	1	0	0	0	0	....	....	....	....	....	....	....	....	....	....	....	....	....	....	....	....	....	....
1997-98	Barrie Colts	OHL	66	8	36	44	36	....	....	....	....	....	....	....	....	....	6	1	3	4	4	....	....	....	....
1998-99	Barrie Colts	OHL	67	13	46	59	46	....	....	....	....	....	....	....	....	....	12	3	10	13	13	....	....	....	....
	Hershey Bears	AHL	....	....	....	....	....	....	....	....	....	....	....	....	....	....	1	0	0	0	0	....	....	....	....
99-2000	**Colorado**	**NHL**	**80**	**3**	**13**	**16**	**20**	**2**	**0**	**0**	**66**	**4.5**	**5**	**0**	**0.0**	**18:15**	**17**	**0**	**2**	**2**	**4**	**0**	**0**	**0**	**18:45**
2000-01♦	**Colorado**	**NHL**	**82**	**8**	**17**	**25**	**38**	**3**	**0**	**2**	**108**	**7.4**	**8**	**1**	**100.0**	**20:41**	**23**	**1**	**4**	**5**	**8**	**0**	**0**	**0**	**11:59**
2001-02	**Colorado**	**NHL**	**82**	**10**	**21**	**31**	**42**	**5**	**0**	**1**	**100**	**10.0**	**–3**	**0**	**0.0**	**22:18**	**21**	**0**	**6**	**6**	**2**	**0**	**0**	**0**	**14:37**
	Czech Republic	Olympics	4	0	0	0	0	....	....	....	....	....	....	....	....	....	....	....	....	....	....	....	....	....	....
2002-03	**Colorado**	**NHL**	**81**	**4**	**21**	**25**	**68**	**2**	**0**	**0**	**93**	**4.3**	**11**	**1**	**100.0**	**18:27**	**7**	**0**	**1**	**1**	**4**	**0**	**0**	**0**	**11:05**
2003-04	**Colorado**	**NHL**	**58**	**2**	**14**	**16**	**30**	**0**	**0**	**0**	**54**	**3.7**	**2**	**0**	**0.0**	**17:21**	....	....	....	....	....	....	....	....	....
	Anaheim	**NHL**	**21**	**2**	**7**	**9**	**2**	**1**	**0**	**0**	**30**	**6.7**	**3**	**1**	**0.0**	**21:14**	....	....	....	....	....	....	....	....	....
	NHL Totals		**404**	**29**	**93**	**122**	**200**	**13**	**0**	**3**	**451**	**6.4**		**3**	**66.7**	**19:38**	**68**	**1**	**13**	**14**	**18**	**0**	**0**	**0**	**14:24**

OHL All-Rookie Team (1998) • OHL Second All-Star Team (1999)

Traded to **Anaheim** by **Colorado** for Kurt Sauer and Anaheim's 4th round choice in 2005 Entry Draft, February 21, 2004.

SKRASTINS, Karlis

(SKRAS-tinsh, KAR-lihs) **COL.**

Defense. Shoots left. 6'1", 212 lbs. Born, Riga, USSR, July 9, 1974. Nashville's 8th choice, 230th overall, in 1998 Entry Draft.

			Regular Season														Playoffs								
Season	Club	League	GP	G	A	Pts	PIM	PP	SH	GW	S	%	+/-	TF	F%	Min	GP	G	A	Pts	PIM	PP	SH	GW	Min
1992-93	Pardaugava Riga	CIS	40	3	5	8	16	....	....	....	....	....	....	....	....	....	2	0	0	0	0	....	....	....	....
1993-94	Pardaugava Riga	CIS	42	7	5	12	18	....	....	....	....	....	....	....	....	....	2	1	0	1	4	....	....	....	....
1994-95	Pardaugava Riga	CIS	52	4	14	18	69	....	....	....	....	....	....	....	....	....	....	....	....	....	....	....	....	....	....
1995-96	TPS Turku	Finland	50	4	11	15	32	....	....	....	....	....	....	....	....	....	11	2	2	4	10	....	....	....	....
1996-97	TPS Turku	Finland	50	2	8	10	20	....	....	....	....	....	....	....	....	....	12	0	4	4	2	....	....	....	....
	TPS Turku	EuroHL	6	0	1	1	4	....	....	....	....	....	....	....	....	....	4	0	0	0	14	....	....	....	....

			Regular Season														Playoffs								
Season	Club	League	GP	G	A	Pts	PIM	PP	SH	GW	S	%	+/-	TF	F%	Min	GP	G	A	Pts	PIM	PP	SH	GW	Min
1997-98	TPS Turku	Finland	48	4	15	19	67	....	....	....	....	....	....	....	....	....	4	0	0	0	0	....	....	....	....
	TPS Turku	EuroHL	6	0	1	1	6	....	....	....	....	....	....	....	....	....	....	....	....	....	....	....	....	....	....
1998-99	**Nashville**	**NHL**	**2**	**0**	**1**	**1**	**0**	**0**	**0**	**0**	**0**	**0.0**	**0**	**0**	**0.0**	**11:47**	....	....	....	....	....	....	....	....	....
	Milwaukee	IHL	75	8	36	44	47	....	....	....	....	....	....	....	....	....	2	0	1	1	2	....	....	....	....
99-2000	**Nashville**	**NHL**	**59**	**5**	**6**	**11**	**20**	**1**	**0**	**2**	**51**	**9.8**	**–7**	**0**	**0.0**	**20:51**	....	....	....	....	....	....	....	....	....
	Milwaukee	IHL	19	3	8	11	10	....	....	....	....	....	....	....	....	....	....	....	....	....	....	....	....	....	....
2000-01	**Nashville**	**NHL**	**82**	**1**	**11**	**12**	**30**	**0**	**0**	**1**	**66**	**1.5**	**–12**	**0**	**0.0**	**19:12**	....	....	....	....	....	....	....	....	....
2001-02	**Nashville**	**NHL**	**82**	**4**	**13**	**17**	**36**	**0**	**0**	**1**	**84**	**4.8**	**–12**	**0**	**0.0**	**20:29**	....	....	....	....	....	....	....	....	....
	Latvia	Olympics	1	0	0	0	0	....	....	....	....	....	....	....	....	....	....	....	....	....	....	....	....	....	....
2002-03	**Nashville**	**NHL**	**82**	**3**	**10**	**13**	**44**	**0**	**1**	**0**	**86**	**3.5**	**–18**	**0**	**0.0**	**20:17**	....	....	....	....	....	....	....	....	....
2003-04	**Colorado**	**NHL**	**82**	**5**	**8**	**13**	**26**	**0**	**1**	**1**	**102**	**4.9**	**18**	**0**	**0.0**	**21:49**	**11**	**0**	**2**	**2**	**2**	**0**	**0**	**0**	**23:07**
	NHL Totals		**389**	**18**	**49**	**67**	**156**	**1**	**2**	**5**	**389**	**4.6**		**0**	**0.0**	**20:28**	**11**	**0**	**2**	**2**	**2**	**0**	**0**	**0**	**23:07**

Traded to **Colorado** by **Nashville** for Colorado's 3rd round choice (later traded to Ottawa – Ottawa selected Peter Regin Jensen) in 2004 Entry Draft, June 30, 2003.

SKRBEK, Pavel

(SKUHR-behk, PAH-vehl) **NSH.**

Defense. Shoots left. 6'3", 217 lbs. Born, Kladno, Czech., August 9, 1978. Pittsburgh's 2nd choice, 28th overall, in 1996 Entry Draft.

			Regular Season														Playoffs								
Season	Club	League	GP	G	A	Pts	PIM	PP	SH	GW	S	%	+/-	TF	F%	Min	GP	G	A	Pts	PIM	PP	SH	GW	Min
1994-95	HC Kladno Jr.	Czech-Jr.	29	7	6	13	....	....	....	....	....	....	....	....	....	....	....	....	....	....	....	....	....	....	....
1995-96	Kladno Jr.	Czech-Jr.	29	10	12	22	....	....	....	....	....	....	....	....	....	....	....	....	....	....	....	....	....	....	....
	HC Poldi Kladno	Czech	13	0	1	1		....	....	....	....	....	....	....	....	....	5	0	0	0	....	....	....	....	....
1996-97	HC Poldi Kladno	Czech	35	1	5	6	26	....	....	....	....	....	....	....	....	....	3	0	0	0	4	....	....	....	....
1997-98	Kladno	Czech	47	4	10	14	126	....	....	....	....	....	....	....	....	....	....	....	....	....	....	....	....	....	....
1998-99	**Pittsburgh**	**NHL**	**4**	**0**	**0**	**0**	**2**	**0**	**0**	**0**	**1**	**0.0**	**2**	**0**	**0.0**	**14:21**	....	....	....	....	....	....	....	....	....
	Syracuse Crunch	AHL	64	6	16	22	38	....	....	....	....	....	....	....	....	....	....	....	....	....	....	....	....	....	....
99-2000	Wilkes-Barre	AHL	51	7	16	23	50	....	....	....	....	....	....	....	....	....	....	....	....	....	....	....	....	....	....
	Milwaukee	IHL	6	0	0	0	0	....	....	....	....	....	....	....	....	....	....	....	....	....	....	....	....	....	....
2000-01	**Nashville**	**NHL**	**5**	**0**	**0**	**0**	**4**	**0**	**0**	**0**	**2**	**0.0**	**1**	**0**	**0.0**	**11:44**	....	....	....	....	....	....	....	....	....
	Milwaukee	IHL	54	2	22	24	55	....	....	....	....	....	....	....	....	....	5	0	0	0	2	....	....	....	....
2001-02	**Nashville**	**NHL**	**3**	**0**	**0**	**0**	**2**	**0**	**0**	**0**	**0**	**0.0**	**–2**	**0**	**0.0**	**10:18**	....	....	....	....	....	....	....	....	....
	Kladno	Czech	24	2	3	5	30	....	....	....	....	....	....	....	....	....	....	....	....	....	....	....	....	....	....
2002-03	Lulea HF	Sweden	39	2	2	4	61	....	....	....	....	....	....	....	....	....	4	0	0	0	10	....	....	....	....
2003-04	Lulea HF	Sweden	34	4	4	8	84	....	....	....	....	....	....	....	....	....	5	0	4	4	6	....	....	....	....
	NHL Totals		**12**	**0**	**0**	**0**	**8**	**0**	**0**	**0**	**3**	**0.0**		**0**	**0.0**	**12:15**	....	....	....	....	....	....	....	....	....

Traded to **Nashville** by **Pittsburgh** for Bob Boughner, March 13, 2000. Assigned to **Kladno** (Czech) by **Nashville**, October 31, 2001. Signed as a free agent by **Lulea HF** (Sweden), June 20, 2002.

SKRLAC, Rob

(SKUHR-lak, RAWB) **N.J.**

Left wing. Shoots left. 6'5", 245 lbs. Born, Port McNeill, B.C., June 10, 1976. Buffalo's 11th choice, 224th overall, in 1995 Entry Draft.

			Regular Season														Playoffs								
Season	Club	League	GP	G	A	Pts	PIM	PP	SH	GW	S	%	+/-	TF	F%	Min	GP	G	A	Pts	PIM	PP	SH	GW	Min
1993-94	Richmond	BCAHA	49	44	55	99	56	....	....	....	....	....	....	....	....	....	....	....	....	....	....	....	....	....	....
1994-95	Kamloops Blazers	WHL	23	0	1	1	177	....	....	....	....	....	....	....	....	....	....	....	....	....	....	....	....	....	....
1995-96	Kamloops Blazers	WHL	63	1	4	5	216	....	....	....	....	....	....	....	....	....	13	0	0	0	52	....	....	....	....
1996-97	Kamloops Blazers	WHL	61	8	10	18	278	....	....	....	....	....	....	....	....	....	5	0	0	0	35	....	....	....	....
1997-98	Albany River Rats	AHL	53	0	2	2	256	....	....	....	....	....	....	....	....	....	....	....	....	....	....	....	....	....	....
1998-99	Albany River Rats	AHL	61	1	1	2	213	....	....	....	....	....	....	....	....	....	1	0	0	0	0	....	....	....	....
99-2000	Albany River Rats	AHL	37	0	0	0	115	....	....	....	....	....	....	....	....	....	....	....	....	....	....	....	....	....	....
2000-01	Albany River Rats	AHL	38	0	0	0	105	....	....	....	....	....	....	....	....	....	....	....	....	....	....	....	....	....	....
2001-02	Albany River Rats	AHL	2	0	0	0	22	....	....	....	....	....	....	....	....	....	....	....	....	....	....	....	....	....	....
	Mississippi	ECHL	29	1	3	4	161	....	....	....	....	....	....	....	....	....	....	....	....	....	....	....	....	....	....
	Portland Pirates	AHL	33	0	3	3	87	....	....	....	....	....	....	....	....	....	....	....	....	....	....	....	....	....	....
2002-03	Albany River Rats	AHL	42	2	3	5	165	....	....	....	....	....	....	....	....	....	....	....	....	....	....	....	....	....	....
2003-04	**New Jersey**	**NHL**	**8**	**1**	**0**	**1**	**22**	**0**	**0**	**1**	**3**	**33.3**	**1**	**0**	**0.0**	**2:15**	....	....	....	....	....	....	....	....	....
	Albany River Rats	AHL	36	1	0	1	137	....	....	....	....	....	....	....	....	....	....	....	....	....	....	....	....	....	....
	NHL Totals		**8**	**1**	**0**	**1**	**22**	**0**	**0**	**1**	**3**	**33.3**		**0**	**0.0**	**2:15**	....	....	....	....	....	....	....	....	....

Signed as a free agent by **New Jersey**, June 17, 1997.

SLANEY, John

(SLAY-nee, JAWN) **PHI.**

Defense. Shoots left. 6', 189 lbs. Born, St. John's, Nfld., February 7, 1972. Washington's 1st choice, 9th overall, in 1990 Entry Draft.

			Regular Season														Playoffs								
Season	Club	League	GP	G	A	Pts	PIM	PP	SH	GW	S	%	+/-	TF	F%	Min	GP	G	A	Pts	PIM	PP	SH	GW	Min
1987-88	St. John's	NFAHA	65	41	69	110	70	....	....	....	....	....	....	....	....	....	....	....	....	....	....	....	....	....	....
1988-89	Cornwall Royals	OHL	66	16	43	59	23	....	....	....	....	....	....	....	....	....	18	8	16	24	10	....	....	....	....
1989-90	Cornwall Royals	OHL	64	38	59	97	68	....	....	....	....	....	....	....	....	....	6	0	8	8	11	....	....	....	....
1990-91	Cornwall Royals	OHL	34	21	25	46	28	....	....	....	....	....	....	....	....	....	....	....	....	....	....	....	....	....	....
1991-92	Cornwall Royals	OHL	34	19	41	60	43	....	....	....	....	....	....	....	....	....	6	3	8	11	0	....	....	....	....
	Baltimore	AHL	6	2	4	6	0	....	....	....	....	....	....	....	....	....	....	....	....	....	....	....	....	....	....
1992-93	Baltimore	AHL	79	20	46	66	60	....	....	....	....	....	....	....	....	....	7	0	7	7	8	....	....	....	....
1993-94	**Washington**	**NHL**	**47**	**7**	**9**	**16**	**27**	**3**	**0**	**1**	**70**	**10.0**	**3**	....	....	....	**11**	**1**	**1**	**2**	**2**	**1**	**0**	**0**	....
	Portland Pirates	AHL	29	14	13	27	17	....	....	....	....	....	....	....	....	....	....	....	....	....	....	....	....	....	....
1994-95	**Washington**	**NHL**	**16**	**0**	**3**	**3**	**6**	**0**	**0**	**0**	**21**	**0.0**	**–3**	....	....	....	....	....	....	....	....	....	....	....	....
	Portland Pirates	AHL	8	3	10	13	4	....	....	....	....	....	....	....	....	....	7	1	3	4	4	....	....	....	....
1995-96	**Colorado**	**NHL**	**7**	**0**	**3**	**3**	**4**	**0**	**0**	**0**	**12**	**0.0**	**2**	....	....	....	....	....	....	....	....	....	....	....	....
	Cornwall Aces	AHL	5	0	4	4	2	....	....	....	....	....	....	....	....	....	....	....	....	....	....	....	....	....	....
	Los Angeles	**NHL**	**31**	**6**	**11**	**17**	**10**	**3**	**1**	**0**	**63**	**9.5**	**5**	....	....	....	....	....	....	....	....	....	....	....	....
1996-97	**Los Angeles**	**NHL**	**32**	**3**	**11**	**14**	**4**	**1**	**0**	**1**	**60**	**5.0**	**–10**	....	....	....	....	....	....	....	....	....	....	....	....
	Phoenix	IHL	35	9	25	34	8	....	....	....	....	....	....	....	....	....	....	....	....	....	....	....	....	....	....
1997-98	**Phoenix**	**NHL**	**55**	**3**	**14**	**17**	**24**	**1**	**0**	**1**	**74**	**4.1**	**–3**	....	....	....	....	....	....	....	....	....	....	....	....
	Las Vegas	IHL	5	2	2	4	10	....	....	....	....	....	....	....	....	....	....	....	....	....	....	....	....	....	....
1998-99	**Nashville**	**NHL**	**46**	**2**	**12**	**14**	**14**	**0**	**0**	**1**	**84**	**2.4**	**–12**	**0**	**0.0**	**20:39**	....	....	....	....	....	....	....	....	....
	Milwaukee	IHL	7	0	1	1	0	....	....	....	....	....	....	....	....	....	....	....	....	....	....	....	....	....	....
99-2000	**Pittsburgh**	**NHL**	**29**	**1**	**4**	**5**	**10**	**1**	**0**	**0**	**27**	**3.7**	**–10**	**35**	**40.0**	**12:13**	**2**	**1**	**0**	**1**	**2**	**1**	**0**	**0**	**5:43**
	Wilkes-Barre	AHL	49	30	30	60	25	....	....	....	....	....	....	....	....	....	....	....	....	....	....	....	....	....	....
2000-01	Wilkes-Barre	AHL	40	12	38	50	4	....	....	....	....	....	....	....	....	....	....	....	....	....	....	....	....	....	....
	Philadelphia	AHL	25	6	11	17	10	....	....	....	....	....	....	....	....	....	10	2	6	8	6	....	....	....	....
2001-02	**Philadelphia**	**NHL**	**1**	**0**	**0**	**0**	**0**	**0**	**0**	**0**	**1**	**0.0**	**2**	**0**	**0.0**	**23:33**	**1**	**0**	**0**	**0**	**0**	**0**	**0**	**0**	**11:20**
	Philadelphia	AHL	64	20	39	59	26	....	....	....	....	....	....	....	....	....	5	2	1	3	0	....	....	....	....
2002-03	Philadelphia	AHL	55	9	33	42	36	....	....	....	....	....	....	....	....	....	....	....	....	....	....	....	....	....	....
2003-04	**Philadelphia**	**NHL**	**4**	**0**	**2**	**2**	**0**	**0**	**0**	**0**	**0**	**0.0**	**0**	**0**	**0.0**	**13:38**	....	....	....	....	....	....	....	....	....
	Philadelphia	AHL	59	19	29	48	31	....	....	....	....	....	....	....	....	....	12	3	4	7	6	....	....	....	....
	NHL Totals		**268**	**22**	**69**	**91**	**99**	**9**	**1**	**4**	**412**	**5.3**		**35**	**40.0**	**17:17**	**14**	**2**	**1**	**3**	**4**	**2**	**0**	**0**	**7:35**

OHL First All-Star Team (1990) • Canadian Major Junior Defenseman of the Year (1990) • OHL Second All-Star Team (1991) • AHL First All-Star Team (2001, 2002) • Eddie Shore Award (Top Defenseman – AHL) (2001, 2002) • AHL Second All-Star Team (2004)

Traded to **Colorado** by **Washington** for Philadelphia's 3rd round choice (previously acquired, Washington selected Shawn McNeil) in 1996 Entry Draft, July 12, 1995. Traded to **Los Angeles** by **Colorado** for Winnipeg's 6th round choice (previously acquired, Colorado selected Brian Willsie) in 1996 Entry Draft, December 28, 1995. Signed as a free agent by **Phoenix**, August 19, 1997. Claimed by **Nashville** from **Phoenix** in Expansion Draft, June 26, 1998. Signed as a free agent by **Pittsburgh**, September 30, 1999. Traded to **Philadelphia** by **Pittsburgh** for Kevin Stevens, January 14, 2001.

SLEGR, Jiri

(SLAY-guhr, YEE-ree)

Defense. Shoots left. 6', 216 lbs. Born, Jihlava, Czech., May 30, 1971. Vancouver's 3rd choice, 23rd overall, in 1990 Entry Draft.

			Regular Season														Playoffs								
Season	Club	League	GP	G	A	Pts	PIM	PP	SH	GW	S	%	+/-	TF	F%	Min	GP	G	A	Pts	PIM	PP	SH	GW	Min
1987-88	CHZ Litvinov	Czech	4	1	1	2	0	....	....	....	....	....	....	....	....	....	....	....	....	....	....	....	....	....	....
1988-89	CHZ Litvinov	Czech	8	0	0	0	4	....	....	....	....	....	....	....	....	....	....	....	....	....	....	....	....	....	....
1989-90	CHZ Litvinov	Czech	51	4	15	19		....	....	....	....	....	....	....	....	....	....	....	....	....	....	....	....	....	....
1990-91	HC CHZ Litvinov	Czech	47	11	36	47	26	....	....	....	....	....	....	....	....	....	....	....	....	....	....	....	....	....	....
1991-92	Litvinov	Czech	42	9	23	32	38	....	....	....	....	....	....	....	....	....	....	....	....	....	....	....	....	....	....
	Czechoslovakia	Olympics	8	1	1	2	14	....	....	....	....	....	....	....	....	....	....	....	....	....	....	....	....	....	....
1992-93	**Vancouver**	**NHL**	**41**	**4**	**22**	**26**	**109**	**2**	**0**	**0**	**89**	**4.5**	**16**	....	....	....	**5**	**0**	**3**	**3**	**4**	**0**	**0**	**0**	....
	Hamilton	AHL	21	4	14	18	42	....	....	....	....	....	....	....	....	....	....	....	....	....	....	....	....	....	....
1993-94	**Vancouver**	**NHL**	**78**	**5**	**33**	**38**	**86**	**1**	**0**	**0**	**160**	**3.1**	**0**	....	....	....	....	....	....	....	....	....	....	....	....
1994-95	Litvinov	Czech	11	3	10	13	80	....	....	....	....	....	....	....	....	....	....	....	....	....	....	....	....	....	....
	Vancouver	**NHL**	**19**	**1**	**5**	**6**	**32**	**0**	**0**	**1**	**42**	**2.4**	**0**	....	....	....	....	....	....	....	....	....	....	....	....
	Edmonton	**NHL**	**12**	**1**	**5**	**6**	**14**	**1**	**0**	**0**	**27**	**3.7**	**–5**	....	....	....	....	....	....	....	....	....	....	....	....
1995-96	**Edmonton**	**NHL**	**57**	**4**	**13**	**17**	**74**	**0**	**1**	**1**	**91**	**4.4**	**–1**	....	....	....	....	....	....	....	....	....	....	....	....
	Cape Breton	AHL	4	1	2	3	4	....	....	....	....	....	....	....	....	....	....	....	....	....	....	....	....	....	....

Season	Club	League	Regular Season GP	G	A	Pts	PIM	PP	SH	GW	S	%	+/-	TF	F%	Min	Playoffs GP	G	A	Pts	PIM	PP	SH	GW	Min
1996-97	Litvinov	Czech	1	0	0	0	0	....	....	....	....	....	....	....	....	....	....	....	....	....	....	....	....	....	....
	Sodertalje SK	Sweden	30	4	14	18	62	....	....	....	....	....	....	....	....	....	10	4	2	6	32	....	....	....	....
1997-98	**Pittsburgh**	**NHL**	**73**	**5**	**12**	**17**	**109**	**1**	**1**	**0**	**131**	**3.8**	**10**	....	....	....	**6**	**0**	**4**	**4**	**2**	**0**	**0**	**0**	....
	Czech Republic	Olympics	6	1	0	1	8	....	....	....	....	....	....	....	....	....	....	....	....	....	....	....	....	....	....
1998-99	**Pittsburgh**	**NHL**	**63**	**3**	**20**	**23**	**86**	**1**	**0**	**0**	**91**	**3.3**	**13**	**2**	**0.0**	**18:42**	**13**	**1**	**3**	**4**	**12**	**0**	**0**	**1**	**19:50**
99-2000	**Pittsburgh**	**NHL**	**74**	**11**	**20**	**31**	**82**	**0**	**0**	**2**	**144**	**7.6**	**20**	**3**	**66.7**	**21:22**	**10**	**2**	**3**	**5**	**19**	**0**	**0**	**1**	**20:02**
2000-01	**Pittsburgh**	**NHL**	**42**	**5**	**10**	**15**	**60**	**0**	**1**	**1**	**67**	**7.5**	**–9**	**0**	**0.0**	**17:37**	....	....	....	....	....	....	....	....	....
	Atlanta	**NHL**	**33**	**3**	**16**	**19**	**36**	**2**	**0**	**0**	**78**	**3.8**	**–1**	**1**	**0.0**	**21:34**	....	....	....	....	....	....	....	....	....
2001-02	**Atlanta**	**NHL**	**38**	**3**	**5**	**8**	**51**	**1**	**0**	**0**	**56**	**5.4**	**–21**	**0**	**0.0**	**21:21**	....	....	....	....	....	....	....	....	....
	♦ Detroit	**NHL**	**8**	**0**	**1**	**1**	**8**	**0**	**0**	**0**	**11**	**0.0**	**1**	**0**	**0.0**	**19:16**	**1**	**0**	**0**	**0**	**2**	**0**	**0**	**0**	**17:11**
2002-03	Litvinov	Czech	10	2	3	5	14	....	....	....	....	....	....	....	....	....	....	....	....	....	....	....	....	....	....
	Avangard Omsk	Russia	6	1	2	3	8	....	....	....	....	....	....	....	....	....	9	0	3	3	*45	....	....	....	....
2003-04	**Vancouver**	**NHL**	**16**	**2**	**5**	**7**	**8**	**1**	**1**	**1**	**15**	**13.3**	**6**	**0**	**0.0**	**12:16**	....	....	....	....	....	....	....	....	....
	Boston	**NHL**	**36**	**4**	**15**	**19**	**27**	**0**	**0**	**1**	**83**	**4.8**	**5**	**0**	**0.0**	**20:03**	**7**	**1**	**1**	**2**	**0**	**0**	**0**	**0**	**18:08**
	NHL Totals		**590**	**51**	**182**	**233**	**782**	**10**	**4**	**7**	**1085**	**4.7**		**6**	**33.3**	**19:39**	**42**	**4**	**14**	**18**	**39**	**0**	**0**	**2**	**19:26**

Czechoslovakian First All-Star Team (1991)

Traded to **Edmonton** by **Vancouver** for Roman Oksiuta, April 7, 1995. Traded to **Pittsburgh** by **Edmonton** for Pittsburgh's 3rd round choice (later traded to New Jersey – New Jersey selected Brian Gionta) in 1998 Entry Draft, August 12, 1997. Traded to **Atlanta** by **Pittsburgh** for San Jose's 3rd round choice (previously acquired, later traded to Columbus – Columbus selected Aaron Johnson) in 2001 Entry Draft, January 14, 2001. Traded to **Detroit** by **Atlanta** for Yuri Butsayev and Detroit's 3rd round choice (later traded to Columbus – Columbus selected Jeff Genovy) in 2002 Entry Draft, March 19, 2002. Signed as a free agent by **Vancouver**, September 4, 2003. Traded to **Boston** by **Vancouver** for future considerations, January 17, 2004.

SLOAN, Blake

(SLOHN, BLAYK)

Right wing. Shoots right. 5'10", 196 lbs. Born, Park Ridge, IL, July 27, 1975.

Season	Club	League	GP	G	A	Pts	PIM	PP	SH	GW	S	%	+/-	TF	F%	Min	GP	G	A	Pts	PIM	PP	SH	GW	Min
1992-93	Tabor Academy	Hi-School	33	7	15	22	....	....	....	....	....	....	....	....	....	....	....	....	....	....	....	....	....	....	....
1993-94	U. of Michigan	CCHA	38	2	4	6	48	....	....	....	....	....	....	....	....	....	....	....	....	....	....	....	....	....	....
1994-95	U. of Michigan	CCHA	39	2	15	17	60	....	....	....	....	....	....	....	....	....	....	....	....	....	....	....	....	....	....
1995-96	U. of Michigan	CCHA	41	6	24	30	55	....	....	....	....	....	....	....	....	....	....	....	....	....	....	....	....	....	....
1996-97	U. of Michigan	CCHA	41	2	15	17	52	....	....	....	....	....	....	....	....	....	....	....	....	....	....	....	....	....	....
1997-98	Houston Aeros	IHL	70	2	13	15	86	....	....	....	....	....	....	....	....	....	2	0	0	0	0	....	....	....	....
1998-99♦	**Dallas**	**NHL**	**14**	**0**	**0**	**0**	**10**	**0**	**0**	**0**	**7**	**0.0**	**–1**	**0**	**0.0**	**9:01**	**19**	**0**	**2**	**2**	**8**	**0**	**0**	**0**	**9:58**
	Houston Aeros	IHL	62	8	10	18	76	....	....	....	....	....	....	....	....	....	....	....	....	....	....	....	....	....	....
99-2000	**Dallas**	**NHL**	**67**	**4**	**13**	**17**	**50**	**0**	**0**	**1**	**78**	**5.1**	**11**	**2**	**50.0**	**13:30**	**16**	**0**	**0**	**0**	**12**	**0**	**0**	**0**	**8:55**
2000-01	**Dallas**	**NHL**	**33**	**2**	**2**	**4**	**4**	**0**	**0**	**1**	**29**	**6.9**	**–2**	**4**	**25.0**	**9:56**	....	....	....	....	....	....	....	....	....
	Houston Aeros	IHL	20	7	4	11	18	....	....	....	....	....	....	....	....	....	....	....	....	....	....	....	....	....	....
	Columbus	**NHL**	**14**	**1**	**0**	**1**	**13**	**0**	**0**	**0**	**16**	**6.3**	**–2**	**7**	**28.6**	**13:19**	....	....	....	....	....	....	....	....	....
2001-02	**Columbus**	**NHL**	**60**	**2**	**7**	**9**	**46**	**0**	**0**	**0**	**49**	**4.1**	**–18**	**3**	**66.7**	**10:56**	....	....	....	....	....	....	....	....	....
	Calgary	**NHL**	**7**	**0**	**2**	**2**	**4**	**0**	**0**	**0**	**7**	**0.0**	**1**	**2**	**0.0**	**12:16**	....	....	....	....	....	....	....	....	....
2002-03	**Calgary**	**NHL**	**67**	**2**	**8**	**10**	**28**	**0**	**0**	**0**	**56**	**3.6**	**–5**	**31**	**12.9**	**12:23**	....	....	....	....	....	....	....	....	....
2003-04	**Dallas**	**NHL**	**28**	**0**	**0**	**0**	**7**	**0**	**0**	**0**	**23**	**0.0**	**–1**	**4**	**0.0**	**7:11**	....	....	....	....	....	....	....	....	....
	Grand Rapids	AHL	7	4	2	6	4	....	....	....	....	....	....	....	....	....	....	....	....	....	....	....	....	....	....
	NHL Totals		**290**	**11**	**32**	**43**	**162**	**0**	**0**	**2**	**265**	**4.2**		**53**	**18.9**	**11:26**	**35**	**0**	**2**	**2**	**20**	**0**	**0**	**0**	**9:29**

Signed as a free agent by **Dallas**, March 10, 1998. Claimed on waivers by **Columbus** from **Dallas**, March 13, 2001. Traded to **Calgary** by **Columbus** for Jamie Allison, March 19, 2002. Signed as a free agent by **Grand Rapids** (AHL), November 18, 2003. Signed as a free agent by **Detroit**, December 1, 2003. Claimed on waivers by **Dallas** from **Detroit**, December 3, 2003. • Spent majority of 2003-04 season as a healthy reserve.

SMIRNOV, Alexei

(smihr-NAHV, al-EHX-ay) **ANA.**

Left wing. Shoots left. 6'3", 211 lbs. Born, Tver, USSR, January 28, 1982. Anaheim's 1st choice, 12th overall, in 2000 Entry Draft.

Season	Club	League	GP	G	A	Pts	PIM	PP	SH	GW	S	%	+/-	TF	F%	Min	GP	G	A	Pts	PIM	PP	SH	GW	Min
1997-98	Dyno. Moscow 2	Russia-2	11	1	1	2	4	....	....	....	....	....	....	....	....	....	....	....	....	....	....	....	....	....	....
1998-99	Dyno. Moscow 2	Russia-3	27	9	3	12	24	....	....	....	....	....	....	....	....	....	....	....	....	....	....	....	....	....	....
99-2000	Dyno. Moscow 2	Russia-3	12	5	3	8	34	....	....	....	....	....	....	....	....	....	....	....	....	....	....	....	....	....	....
	THC Tver	Russia-2	35	3	5	8	24	....	....	....	....	....	....	....	....	....	....	....	....	....	....	....	....	....	....
	Dynamo Moscow	Russia	1	0	0	0	0	....	....	....	....	....	....	....	....	....	....	....	....	....	....	....	....	....	....
2000-01	Dynamo Moscow	Russia	29	2	0	2	16	....	....	....	....	....	....	....	....	....	....	....	....	....	....	....	....	....	....
2001-02	CSKA Moscow 2	Russia-3	2	1	0	1	0	....	....	....	....	....	....	....	....	....	....	....	....	....	....	....	....	....	....
	CSKA Moscow	Russia	51	5	11	16	42	....	....	....	....	....	....	....	....	....	....	....	....	....	....	....	....	....	....
2002-03	**Anaheim**	**NHL**	**44**	**3**	**2**	**5**	**18**	**0**	**0**	**1**	**46**	**6.5**	**–1**	**6**	**16.7**	**8:50**	**4**	**0**	**0**	**0**	**2**	**0**	**0**	**0**	**4:22**
	Cincinnati	AHL	19	7	3	10	12	....	....	....	....	....	....	....	....	....	....	....	....	....	....	....	....	....	....
2003-04	**Anaheim**	**NHL**	**8**	**0**	**1**	**1**	**2**	**0**	**0**	**0**	**8**	**0.0**	**0**	**3**	**0.0**	**7:17**	....	....	....	....	....	....	....	....	....
	Cincinnati	AHL	51	9	10	19	34	....	....	....	....	....	....	....	....	....	2	0	0	0	2	....	....	....	....
	NHL Totals		**52**	**3**	**3**	**6**	**20**	**0**	**0**	**1**	**54**	**5.6**		**9**	**11.1**	**8:36**	**4**	**0**	**0**	**0**	**2**	**0**	**0**	**0**	**4:22**

SMITH, Brandon

(SMIHTH, BRAN-duhn) **NYI**

Defense. Shoots left. 6'1", 209 lbs. Born, Hazelton, B.C., February 25, 1973.

Season	Club	League	GP	G	A	Pts	PIM	PP	SH	GW	S	%	+/-	TF	F%	Min	GP	G	A	Pts	PIM	PP	SH	GW	Min
1989-90	Portland	WHL	59	2	17	19	16	....	....	....	....	....	....	....	....	....	....	....	....	....	....	....	....	....	....
1990-91	Portland	WHL	17	8	5	13	8	....	....	....	....	....	....	....	....	....	....	....	....	....	....	....	....	....	....
1991-92	Portland	WHL	70	12	32	44	63	....	....	....	....	....	....	....	....	....	....	....	....	....	....	....	....	....	....
1992-93	Portland	WHL	72	20	54	74	38	....	....	....	....	....	....	....	....	....	16	4	9	13	6	....	....	....	....
1993-94	Portland	WHL	72	19	63	82	47	....	....	....	....	....	....	....	....	....	10	2	10	12	8	....	....	....	....
1994-95	Dayton Bombers	ECHL	60	16	49	65	57	....	....	....	....	....	....	....	....	....	4	2	3	5	0	....	....	....	....
	Minnesota Moose	IHL	1	0	0	0	0	....	....	....	....	....	....	....	....	....	....	....	....	....	....	....	....	....	....
	Adirondack	AHL	14	1	2	3	7	....	....	....	....	....	....	....	....	....	3	0	0	0	2	....	....	....	....
1995-96	Adirondack	AHL	48	4	13	17	22	....	....	....	....	....	....	....	....	....	3	0	1	1	2	....	....	....	....
1996-97	Adirondack	AHL	80	8	26	34	30	....	....	....	....	....	....	....	....	....	4	0	0	0	0	....	....	....	....
1997-98	Adirondack	AHL	64	9	27	36	26	....	....	....	....	....	....	....	....	....	1	0	1	1	0	....	....	....	....
1998-99	**Boston**	**NHL**	**5**	**0**	**0**	**0**	**0**	**0**	**0**	**0**	**2**	**0.0**	**2**	**0**	**0.0**	**9:38**	....	....	....	....	....	....	....	....	....
	Providence Bruins	AHL	72	16	46	62	32	....	....	....	....	....	....	....	....	....	19	1	9	10	12	....	....	....	....
99-2000	**Boston**	**NHL**	**22**	**2**	**4**	**6**	**10**	**0**	**0**	**0**	**24**	**8.3**	**–4**	**0**	**0.0**	**19:29**	....	....	....	....	....	....	....	....	....
	Providence Bruins	AHL	55	8	30	38	20	....	....	....	....	....	....	....	....	....	14	1	11	12	2	....	....	....	....
2000-01	**Boston**	**NHL**	**3**	**1**	**0**	**1**	**0**	**1**	**0**	**0**	**2**	**50.0**	**–1**	**0**	**0.0**	**6:46**	....	....	....	....	....	....	....	....	....
	Providence Bruins	AHL	63	11	28	39	30	....	....	....	....	....	....	....	....	....	17	0	5	5	6	....	....	....	....
2001-02	Cleveland Barons	AHL	59	6	29	35	26	....	....	....	....	....	....	....	....	....	....	....	....	....	....	....	....	....	....
2002-03	**NY Islanders**	**NHL**	**3**	**0**	**0**	**0**	**0**	**0**	**0**	**0**	**1**	**0.0**	**–2**	**0**	**0.0**	**9:59**	....	....	....	....	....	....	....	....	....
	Bridgeport	AHL	63	9	32	41	37	....	....	....	....	....	....	....	....	....	9	1	3	4	5	....	....	....	....
2003-04	Bridgeport	AHL	74	5	23	28	39	....	....	....	....	....	....	....	....	....	7	1	3	4	9	....	....	....	....
	NHL Totals		**33**	**3**	**4**	**7**	**10**	**1**	**0**	**0**	**29**	**10.3**		**0**	**0.0**	**15:58**	....	....	....	....	....	....	....	....	....

WHL West Second All-Star Team (1993, 1994) • ECHL First All-Star Team (1995) • ECHL Top Defenseman Award (1995) • AHL First All-Star Team (1999)

Signed as a free agent by **Detroit**, July 22, 1997. Signed as a free agent by **Boston**, August 5, 1998. Signed as a free agent by **San Jose**, July 23, 2001. Signed as a free agent by **NY Islanders**, August 3, 2002.

SMITH, D.J.

(SMIHTH, DEE-JAY) **COL.**

Defense. Shoots left. 6'1", 205 lbs. Born, Windsor, Ont., May 13, 1977. NY Islanders' 3rd choice, 41st overall, in 1995 Entry Draft.

Season	Club	League	GP	G	A	Pts	PIM	PP	SH	GW	S	%	+/-	TF	F%	Min	GP	G	A	Pts	PIM	PP	SH	GW	Min
1992-93	Belle River	OJHL-C	40	5	18	23	39	....	....	....	....	....	....	....	....	....	....	....	....	....	....	....	....	....	....
	Windsor Bulldogs	OJHL-B	1	0	0	0	0	....	....	....	....	....	....	....	....	....	....	....	....	....	....	....	....	....	....
1993-94	Windsor Bulldogs	OJHL-B	51	8	34	42	267	....	....	....	....	....	....	....	....	....	....	....	....	....	....	....	....	....	....
1994-95	Windsor Spitfires	OHL	61	4	13	17	201	....	....	....	....	....	....	....	....	....	10	1	3	4	41	....	....	....	....
1995-96	Windsor Spitfires	OHL	64	14	45	59	260	....	....	....	....	....	....	....	....	....	7	1	7	8	23	....	....	....	....
	St. John's	AHL	1	0	0	0	0	....	....	....	....	....	....	....	....	....	....	....	....	....	....	....	....	....	....
1996-97	Windsor Spitfires	OHL	63	15	52	67	190	....	....	....	....	....	....	....	....	....	5	1	7	8	11	....	....	....	....
	Toronto	**NHL**	**8**	**0**	**1**	**1**	**7**	**0**	**0**	**0**	**4**	**0.0**	**–5**	....	....	....	....	....	....	....	....	....	....	....	....
	St. John's	AHL	....	....	....	....	....	....	....	....	....	....	....	....	....	....	1	0	0	0	0	....	....	....	....
1997-98	St. John's	AHL	65	4	11	15	237	....	....	....	....	....	....	....	....	....	4	0	0	0	4	....	....	....	....
1998-99	St. John's	AHL	79	7	28	35	216	....	....	....	....	....	....	....	....	....	5	0	1	1	0	....	....	....	....
99-2000	**Toronto**	**NHL**	**3**	**0**	**0**	**0**	**5**	**0**	**0**	**0**	**2**	**0.0**	**–1**	**0**	**0.0**	**12:37**	....	....	....	....	....	....	....	....	....
	St. John's	AHL	74	6	22	28	197	....	....	....	....	....	....	....	....	....	....	....	....	....	....	....	....	....	....
2000-01	St. John's	AHL	59	7	12	19	106	....	....	....	....	....	....	....	....	....	4	0	0	0	11	....	....	....	....

			Regular Season														Playoffs								
Season	Club	League	GP	G	A	Pts	PIM	PP	SH	GW	S	%	+/-	TF	F%	Min	GP	G	A	Pts	PIM	PP	SH	GW	Min
2001-02	St. John's	AHL	59	6	10	16	152	....	....	....	....	....	....	....	....	....	....	....	....	....	....	....	....	....	....
	Hershey Bears	AHL	14	0	3	3	33	....	....	....	....	....	....	....	....	....	8	1	0	1	33	....	....	....	....
2002-03	**Colorado**	**NHL**	**34**	**1**	**0**	**1**	**55**	**0**	**0**	**0**	**7**	**14.3**	**2**	**0**	**0.0**	**3:49**	....	....	....	....	....	....	....	....	....
	Hershey Bears	AHL	2	0	0	0	4	....	....	....	....	....	....	....	....	....	....	....	....	....	....	....	....	....	....
2003-04	Hershey Bears	AHL	35	7	7	14	71	....	....	....	....	....	....	....	....	....	....	....	....	....	....	....	....	....	....
	NHL Totals		**45**	**1**	**1**	**2**	**67**	**0**	**0**	**0**	**13**	**7.7**		**0**	**0.0**	**4:32**	....	....	....	....	....	....	....	....	....

OHL Second All-Star Team (1997)

Traded to **Toronto** by **NY Islanders** with Wendel Clark and Mathieu Schneider for Darby Hendrickson, Sean Haggerty, Kenny Jonsson and Toronto's 1st round choice (Roberto Luongo) in 1997 Entry Draft, March 13, 1996. Traded to **Nashville** by **Toronto** with Marty Wilford for Marc Moro, March 1, 2002. Traded to **Colorado** by **Nashville** for Tampa Bay's 9th round choice (previously acquired, Nashville selected Matt Davis) in 2002 Entry Draft, March 1, 2002. • Missed majority of 2002-03 season recovering from head injury suffered in game vs. San Jose, November 5, 2002. • Missed majority of 2003-04 season recovering from knee injury suffered in game vs. Norfolk (AHL), January 14, 2004.

SMITH, Dan

(SMIHTH, DAN) **EDM.**

Defense. Shoots left. 6'2", 200 lbs. Born, Fernie, B.C., October 19, 1976. Colorado's 7th choice, 181st overall, in 1995 Entry Draft.

Season	Club	League	GP	G	A	Pts	PIM	PP	SH	GW	S	%	+/-	TF	F%	Min	GP	G	A	Pts	PIM	PP	SH	GW	Min
1994-95	U.B.C.	CWUAA	28	1	3	4	26	....	....	....	....	....	....	....	....	....	....	....	....	....	....	....	....	....	....
1995-96	Tri-City	WHL	58	1	21	22	70	....	....	....	....	....	....	....	....	....	11	1	3	4	14	....	....	....	....
1996-97	Tri-City	WHL	72	5	19	24	174	....	....	....	....	....	....	....	....	....	....	....	....	....	....	....	....	....	....
	Hershey Bears	AHL	8	0	1	1	6	....	....	....	....	....	....	....	....	....	15	0	1	1	25	....	....	....	....
1997-98	Hershey Bears	AHL	50	1	2	3	71	....	....	....	....	....	....	....	....	....	6	0	0	0	4	....	....	....	....
1998-99	**Colorado**	**NHL**	**12**	**0**	**0**	**0**	**9**	**0**	**0**	**0**	**6**	**0.0**	**5**	**0**	**0.0**	**12:14**	....	....	....	....	....	....	....	....	....
	Hershey Bears	AHL	54	5	7	12	72	....	....	....	....	....	....	....	....	....	5	0	1	1	0	....	....	....	....
99-2000	**Colorado**	**NHL**	**3**	**0**	**0**	**0**	**0**	**0**	**0**	**0**	**0**	**0.0**	**2**	**0**	**0.0**	**11:03**	....	....	....	....	....	....	....	....	....
	Hershey Bears	AHL	49	7	15	22	56	....	....	....	....	....	....	....	....	....	....	....	....	....	....	....	....	....	....
2000-01	Hershey Bears	AHL	58	2	12	14	34	....	....	....	....	....	....	....	....	....	12	0	1	1	4	....	....	....	....
2001-02	Colorado	WCHL	12	0	2	2	16	....	....	....	....	....	....	....	....	....	....	....	....	....	....	....	....	....	....
	Lukko Rauma	Finland	32	1	2	3	18	....	....	....	....	....	....	....	....	....	....	....	....	....	....	....	....	....	....
2002-03	Springfield	AHL	69	1	14	15	53	....	....	....	....	....	....	....	....	....	6	0	2	2	0	....	....	....	....
2003-04	Toronto	AHL	66	4	9	13	41	....	....	....	....	....	....	....	....	....	....	....	....	....	....	....	....	....	....
	NHL Totals		**15**	**0**	**0**	**0**	**9**	**0**	**0**	**0**	**6**	**0.0**		**0**	**0.0**	**12:00**	....	....	....	....	....	....	....	....	....

Signed as a free agent by **Colorado** (WCHL), October 26, 2001. Signed as a free agent by **Lukko** (Finland) after receiving release from Colorado (WCHL), November 21, 2001. Signed as a free agent by **Edmonton**, August 21, 2003.

SMITH, Jason

(SMIHTH, JAY-suhn) **EDM.**

Defense. Shoots right. 6'3", 215 lbs. Born, Calgary, Alta., November 2, 1973. New Jersey's 1st choice, 18th overall, in 1992 Entry Draft.

Season	Club	League	GP	G	A	Pts	PIM	PP	SH	GW	S	%	+/-	TF	F%	Min	GP	G	A	Pts	PIM	PP	SH	GW	Min
1990-91	Calgary Canucks	AJHL	45	3	15	18	69	....	....	....	....	....	....	....	....	....	....	....	....	....	....	....	....	....	....
	Regina Pats	WHL	2	0	0	0	7	....	....	....	....	....	....	....	....	....	4	0	0	0	2	....	....	....	....
1991-92	Regina Pats	WHL	62	9	29	38	138	....	....	....	....	....	....	....	....	....	....	....	....	....	....	....	....	....	....
1992-93	Regina Pats	WHL	64	14	52	66	175	....	....	....	....	....	....	....	....	....	13	4	8	12	39	....	....	....	....
	Utica Devils	AHL	....	....	....	....	....	....	....	....	....	....	....	....	....	....	1	0	0	0	2	....	....	....	....
1993-94	**New Jersey**	**NHL**	**41**	**0**	**5**	**5**	**43**	**0**	**0**	**0**	**47**	**0.0**	**7**	....	....	....	**6**	**0**	**0**	**0**	**7**	**0**	**0**	**0**	....
	Albany River Rats	AHL	20	6	3	9	31	....	....	....	....	....	....	....	....	....	....	....	....	....	....	....	....	....	....
1994-95	Albany River Rats	AHL	7	0	2	2	15	....	....	....	....	....	....	....	....	....	11	2	2	4	19	....	....	....	....
	New Jersey	**NHL**	**2**	**0**	**0**	**0**	**0**	**0**	**0**	**0**	**5**	**0.0**	**–3**	....	....	....	....	....	....	....	....	....	....	....	....
1995-96	**New Jersey**	**NHL**	**64**	**2**	**1**	**3**	**86**	**0**	**0**	**0**	**52**	**3.8**	**5**	....	....	....	....	....	....	....	....	....	....	....	....
1996-97	**New Jersey**	**NHL**	**57**	**1**	**2**	**3**	**38**	**0**	**0**	**0**	**48**	**2.1**	**–8**	....	....	....	....	....	....	....	....	....	....	....	....
	Toronto	**NHL**	**21**	**0**	**5**	**5**	**16**	**0**	**0**	**0**	**26**	**0.0**	**–4**	....	....	....	....	....	....	....	....	....	....	....	....
1997-98	**Toronto**	**NHL**	**81**	**3**	**13**	**16**	**100**	**0**	**0**	**0**	**97**	**3.1**	**–5**	....	....	....	....	....	....	....	....	....	....	....	....
1998-99	**Toronto**	**NHL**	**60**	**2**	**11**	**13**	**40**	**0**	**0**	**0**	**53**	**3.8**	**–9**	**0**	**0.0**	**17:31**	....	....	....	....	....	....	....	....	....
	Edmonton	**NHL**	**12**	**1**	**1**	**2**	**11**	**0**	**0**	**0**	**15**	**6.7**	**0**	**0**	**0.0**	**20:26**	**4**	**0**	**1**	**1**	**4**	**0**	**0**	**0**	**26:29**
99-2000	**Edmonton**	**NHL**	**80**	**3**	**11**	**14**	**60**	**0**	**0**	**1**	**96**	**3.1**	**16**	**1**	**100.0**	**21:15**	**5**	**0**	**1**	**1**	**4**	**0**	**0**	**0**	**21:56**
2000-01	**Edmonton**	**NHL**	**82**	**5**	**15**	**20**	**120**	**1**	**1**	**0**	**140**	**3.6**	**14**	**1**	**0.0**	**21:40**	**6**	**0**	**2**	**2**	**6**	**0**	**0**	**0**	**25:27**
2001-02	**Edmonton**	**NHL**	**74**	**5**	**13**	**18**	**103**	**0**	**1**	**1**	**85**	**5.9**	**14**	**0**	**0.0**	**21:00**	....	....	....	....	....	....	....	....	....
2002-03	**Edmonton**	**NHL**	**68**	**4**	**8**	**12**	**64**	**0**	**0**	**1**	**93**	**4.3**	**5**	**0**	**0.0**	**21:46**	**6**	**0**	**0**	**0**	**19**	**0**	**0**	**0**	**21:16**
2003-04	**Edmonton**	**NHL**	**68**	**7**	**12**	**19**	**98**	**0**	**1**	**1**	**84**	**8.3**	**13**	**2**	**50.0**	**21:21**	....	....	....	....	....	....	....	....	....
	NHL Totals		**710**	**33**	**97**	**130**	**779**	**1**	**3**	**4**	**841**	**3.9**		**4**	**25.0**	**20:46**	**27**	**0**	**4**	**4**	**40**	**0**	**0**	**0**	**23:37**

WHL East First All-Star Team (1993) • Canadian Major Junior First All-Star Team (1993)

• Missed majority of 1994-95 season recovering from knee injury suffered in practice, November 5, 1994. Traded to **Toronto** by **New Jersey** with Steve Sullivan and the rights to Alyn McCauley for Doug Gilmour, Dave Ellett and New Jersey's 4th round choice (previously acquired, New Jersey selected Andre Lakos) in 1999 Entry Draft, February 25, 1997. Traded to **Edmonton** by **Toronto** for Edmonton's 4th round choice (Jonathon Zion) in 1999 Entry Draft and Edmonton's 2nd round choice (Kris Vernarsky) in 2000 Entry Draft, March 23, 1999.

SMITH, Mark

(SMIHTH, MAHRK) **S.J.**

Center. Shoots left. 5'10", 215 lbs. Born, Edmonton, Alta., October 24, 1977. San Jose's 7th choice, 219th overall, in 1997 Entry Draft.

Season	Club	League	GP	G	A	Pts	PIM	PP	SH	GW	S	%	+/-	TF	F%	Min	GP	G	A	Pts	PIM	PP	SH	GW	Min
1993-94	Nipawin Hawks	SJHL	62	14	12	26	44	....	....	....	....	....	....	....	....	....	....	....	....	....	....	....	....	....	....
1994-95	Lethbridge	WHL	49	3	4	7	25	....	....	....	....	....	....	....	....	....	....	....	....	....	....	....	....	....	....
1995-96	Lethbridge	WHL	71	11	24	35	59	....	....	....	....	....	....	....	....	....	4	2	0	2	2	....	....	....	....
1996-97	Lethbridge	WHL	62	19	38	57	125	....	....	....	....	....	....	....	....	....	19	7	13	20	51	....	....	....	....
1997-98	Lethbridge	WHL	70	42	67	109	206	....	....	....	....	....	....	....	....	....	3	0	2	2	18	....	....	....	....
	Kentucky	AHL	2	0	0	0	0	....	....	....	....	....	....	....	....	....	....	....	....	....	....	....	....	....	....
1998-99	Kentucky	AHL	78	18	21	39	101	....	....	....	....	....	....	....	....	....	12	2	7	9	16	....	....	....	....
99-2000	Kentucky	AHL	79	21	45	66	153	....	....	....	....	....	....	....	....	....	9	0	5	5	22	....	....	....	....
2000-01	**San Jose**	**NHL**	**42**	**2**	**2**	**4**	**51**	**0**	**0**	**0**	**39**	**5.1**	**2**	**308**	**52.9**	**8:48**	....	....	....	....	....	....	....	....	....
	Kentucky	AHL	6	2	6	8	23	....	....	....	....	....	....	....	....	....	....	....	....	....	....	....	....	....	....
2001-02	**San Jose**	**NHL**	**49**	**3**	**3**	**6**	**72**	**0**	**0**	**1**	**40**	**7.5**	**–1**	**368**	**54.1**	**8:03**	....	....	....	....	....	....	....	....	....
2002-03	**San Jose**	**NHL**	**75**	**4**	**11**	**15**	**64**	**0**	**0**	**0**	**68**	**5.9**	**1**	**632**	**57.0**	**9:21**	....	....	....	....	....	....	....	....	....
2003-04	**San Jose**	**NHL**	**36**	**1**	**3**	**4**	**72**	**0**	**0**	**0**	**31**	**3.2**	**–5**	**207**	**50.2**	**8:22**	**10**	**1**	**0**	**1**	**11**	**0**	**0**	**1**	**7:44**
	NHL Totals		**202**	**10**	**19**	**29**	**259**	**0**	**0**	**1**	**178**	**5.6**		**1515**	**54.5**	**8:45**	**10**	**1**	**0**	**1**	**11**	**0**	**0**	**1**	**7:44**

WHL East Second All-Star Team (1998)

• Spent majority of 2003-04 season as a healthy reserve.

SMITH, Nathan

(SMIHTH, NAY-thun) **VAN.**

Center. Shoots left. 6'2", 192 lbs. Born, Edmonton, Alta., February 9, 1982. Vancouver's 1st choice, 23rd overall, in 2000 Entry Draft.

Season	Club	League	GP	G	A	Pts	PIM	PP	SH	GW	S	%	+/-	TF	F%	Min	GP	G	A	Pts	PIM	PP	SH	GW	Min
1997-98	Sherwood Park	AMHL	35	15	13	28	24	....	....	....	....	....	....	....	....	....	....	....	....	....	....	....	....	....	....
1998-99	Swift Current	WHL	47	5	8	13	26	....	....	....	....	....	....	....	....	....	....	....	....	....	....	....	....	....	....
99-2000	Swift Current	WHL	70	21	28	49	72	....	....	....	....	....	....	....	....	....	12	1	6	7	4	....	....	....	....
2000-01	Swift Current	WHL	67	28	62	90	78	....	....	....	....	....	....	....	....	....	19	4	3	7	20	....	....	....	....
2001-02	Swift Current	WHL	47	22	38	60	52	....	....	....	....	....	....	....	....	....	12	3	6	9	18	....	....	....	....
2002-03	Manitoba Moose	AHL	53	9	8	17	30	....	....	....	....	....	....	....	....	....	14	1	3	4	25	....	....	....	....
2003-04	**Vancouver**	**NHL**	**2**	**0**	**0**	**0**	**0**	**0**	**0**	**0**	**1**	**0.0**	**–1**	**12**	**33.3**	**5:16**	....	....	....	....	....	....	....	....	....
	Manitoba Moose	AHL	76	4	16	20	71	....	....	....	....	....	....	....	....	....	....	....	....	....	....	....	....	....	....
	NHL Totals		**2**	**0**	**0**	**0**	**0**	**0**	**0**	**0**	**1**	**0.0**		**12**	**33.3**	**5:16**	....	....	....	....	....	....	....	....	....

SMITH, Nick

(SMIHTH, NIHK)

Center. Shoots left. 6'2", 196 lbs. Born, Hamilton, Ont., March 23, 1979. Florida's 4th choice, 74th overall, in 1997 Entry Draft.

Season	Club	League	GP	G	A	Pts	PIM	PP	SH	GW	S	%	+/-	TF	F%	Min	GP	G	A	Pts	PIM	PP	SH	GW	Min
1995-96	Shelburne Wolves	MTJHL	42	13	18	31	12	....	....	....	....	....	....	....	....	....	....	....	....	....	....	....	....	....	....
1996-97	Barrie Colts	OHL	63	10	18	28	15	....	....	....	....	....	....	....	....	....	9	3	8	11	13	....	....	....	....
1997-98	Barrie Colts	OHL	63	13	21	34	21	....	....	....	....	....	....	....	....	....	6	1	2	3	4	....	....	....	....
1998-99	Barrie Colts	OHL	68	19	34	53	18	....	....	....	....	....	....	....	....	....	12	3	8	11	8	....	....	....	....
99-2000	Louisville Panthers	AHL	53	8	4	12	8	....	....	....	....	....	....	....	....	....	4	0	0	0	0	....	....	....	....
	Port Huron	UHL	2	1	1	2	0	....	....	....	....	....	....	....	....	....	....	....	....	....	....	....	....	....	....
2000-01	Louisville Panthers	AHL	23	1	2	3	25	....	....	....	....	....	....	....	....	....	....	....	....	....	....	....	....	....	....
2001-02	**Florida**	**NHL**	**15**	**0**	**0**	**0**	**0**	**0**	**0**	**0**	**2**	**0.0**	**–1**	**53**	**47.2**	**4:09**	....	....	....	....	....	....	....	....	....
	Bridgeport	AHL	22	3	6	9	4	....	....	....	....	....	....	....	....	....	....	....	....	....	....	....	....	....	....
	Saint John Flames	AHL	41	8	9	17	10	....	....	....	....	....	....	....	....	....	....	....	....	....	....	....	....	....	....

			Regular Season														Playoffs								
Season	Club	League	GP	G	A	Pts	PIM	PP	SH	GW	S	%	+/-	TF	F%	Min	GP	G	A	Pts	PIM	PP	SH	GW	Min
2002-03	Cincinnati	AHL	79	12	26	38	28	....	....	....	....	....	....	....	....	....	....	....	....	....	....	....	....	....	....
2003-04	Cincinnati	AHL	67	4	11	15	66	....	....	....	....	....	....	....	....	....	3	0	1	1	0	....	....	....	....
	NHL Totals		**15**	**0**	**0**	**0**	**0**	**0**	**0**	**0**	**2**	**0.0**		**53**	**47.2**	**4:09**	....	....	....	....	....	....	....	....	....

• Missed majority of 2000-01 season recovering from knee injury suffered in training camp, September 25, 2000. Signed as a free agent by **Anaheim**, August 22, 2002.

SMITH, Wyatt

(SMIHTH, WIGH-uht) **NSH.**

Center. Shoots left. 5'11", 200 lbs. Born, Thief River Falls, MN, February 13, 1977. Phoenix's 6th choice, 233rd overall, in 1997 Entry Draft.

1994-95	Warroad Warriors	Hi-School	28	29	31	60	28	....	....	....	....	....	....	....	....	....	....	....	....	....	....	....	....	....	....
1995-96	U. of Minnesota	WCHA	32	4	5	9	32	....	....	....	....	....	....	....	....	....	....	....	....	....	....	....	....	....	....
1996-97	U. of Minnesota	WCHA	38	16	14	30	44	....	....	....	....	....	....	....	....	....	....	....	....	....	....	....	....	....	....
1997-98	U. of Minnesota	WCHA	39	24	23	47	62	....	....	....	....	....	....	....	....	....	....	....	....	....	....	....	....	....	....
1998-99	U. of Minnesota	WCHA	43	23	20	43	37	....	....	....	....	....	....	....	....	....	....	....	....	....	....	....	....	....	....
99-2000	**Phoenix**	**NHL**	**2**	**0**	**0**	**0**	**0**	**0**	**0**	**0**	**0**	**0.0**	**–2**	**20**	**30.0**	**11:39**	....	....	....	....	....	....	....	....	....
	Springfield	AHL	60	14	26	40	26	....	....	....	....	....	....	....	....	....	5	2	3	5	13	....	....	....	....
2000-01	**Phoenix**	**NHL**	**42**	**3**	**7**	**10**	**13**	**0**	**1**	**0**	**40**	**7.5**	**7**	**335**	**40.9**	**12:20**	....	....	....	....	....	....	....	....	....
	Springfield	AHL	18	5	7	12	11	....	....	....	....	....	....	....	....	....	....	....	....	....	....	....	....	....	....
2001-02	**Phoenix**	**NHL**	**10**	**0**	**0**	**0**	**0**	**0**	**0**	**0**	**4**	**0.0**	**–5**	**81**	**48.2**	**10:36**	....	....	....	....	....	....	....	....	....
	Springfield	AHL	69	23	32	55	69	....	....	....	....	....	....	....	....	....	....	....	....	....	....	....	....	....	....
2002-03	**Nashville**	**NHL**	**11**	**1**	**0**	**1**	**0**	**0**	**0**	**0**	**8**	**12.5**	**–1**	**123**	**49.6**	**11:56**	....	....	....	....	....	....	....	....	....
	Milwaukee	AHL	56	24	27	51	89	....	....	....	....	....	....	....	....	....	4	1	0	1	2	....	....	....	....
2003-04	**Nashville**	**NHL**	**18**	**3**	**1**	**4**	**2**	**0**	**1**	**0**	**21**	**14.3**	**2**	**193**	**57.0**	**10:22**	....	....	....	....	....	....	....	....	....
	Milwaukee	AHL	40	9	7	16	40	....	....	....	....	....	....	....	....	....	22	5	7	12	25	....	....	....	....
	NHL Totals		**83**	**7**	**8**	**15**	**15**	**0**	**2**	**0**	**73**	**9.6**		**752**	**46.9**	**11:38**	....	....	....	....	....	....	....	....	....

Signed as a free agent by **Nashville**, July 15, 2002.

SMITHSON, Jerred

(SMIHTH-suhn, JEHR-rehd) **NSH.**

Center. Shoots right. 6'2", 197 lbs. Born, Vernon, B.C., February 4, 1979.

1994-95	Vernon	BCAHA	64	39	46	85	120	....	....	....	....	....	....	....	....	....	....	....	....	....	....	....	....	....	....
1995-96	Calgary Hitmen	WHL	60	4	2	6	16	....	....	....	....	....	....	....	....	....	....	....	....	....	....	....	....	....	....
1996-97	Calgary Hitmen	WHL	65	3	6	9	49	....	....	....	....	....	....	....	....	....	....	....	....	....	....	....	....	....	....
1997-98	Calgary Hitmen	WHL	65	12	9	21	65	....	....	....	....	....	....	....	....	....	18	0	2	2	25	....	....	....	....
1998-99	Calgary Hitmen	WHL	63	14	22	36	108	....	....	....	....	....	....	....	....	....	21	3	7	10	17	....	....	....	....
99-2000	Calgary Hitmen	WHL	66	14	25	39	111	....	....	....	....	....	....	....	....	....	10	1	1	2	16	....	....	....	....
2000-01	Lowell	AHL	24	1	1	2	10	....	....	....	....	....	....	....	....	....	4	0	0	0	2	....	....	....	....
2001-02	Manchester	AHL	78	5	13	18	45	....	....	....	....	....	....	....	....	....	5	0	1	1	4	....	....	....	....
2002-03	**Los Angeles**	**NHL**	**22**	**0**	**2**	**2**	**21**	**0**	**0**	**0**	**9**	**0.0**	**–5**	**175**	**48.0**	**8:50**	....	....	....	....	....	....	....	....	....
	Manchester	AHL	38	4	21	25	60	....	....	....	....	....	....	....	....	....	3	0	0	0	4	....	....	....	....
2003-04	**Los Angeles**	**NHL**	**8**	**0**	**1**	**1**	**4**	**0**	**0**	**0**	**2**	**0.0**	**0**	**86**	**64.0**	**10:39**	....	....	....	....	....	....	....	....	....
	Manchester	AHL	66	7	13	20	51	....	....	....	....	....	....	....	....	....	6	0	1	1	10	....	....	....	....
	NHL Totals		**30**	**0**	**3**	**3**	**25**	**0**	**0**	**0**	**11**	**0.0**		**261**	**53.3**	**9:19**	....	....	....	....	....	....	....	....	....

Signed as a free agent by **Los Angeles**, February 18, 2000. Signed as a free agent by **Nashville**, July 21, 2004.

SMOLINSKI, Bryan

(smoh-LIHN-skee, BRIGH-uhn) **OTT.**

Center. Shoots right. 6'1", 208 lbs. Born, Toledo, OH, December 27, 1971. Boston's 1st choice, 21st overall, in 1990 Entry Draft.

1987-88	Det. Caesars	MNHL	80	43	77	120	....	....	....	....	....	....	....	....	....	....	....	....	....	....	....	....	....	....	....
1988-89	Stratford Cullitons	OJHL-B	46	32	62	94	132	....	....	....	....	....	....	....	....	....	....	....	....	....	....	....	....	....	....
1989-90	Michigan State	CCHA	35	9	13	22	34	....	....	....	....	....	....	....	....	....	....	....	....	....	....	....	....	....	....
1990-91	Michigan State	CCHA	35	9	12	21	24	....	....	....	....	....	....	....	....	....	....	....	....	....	....	....	....	....	....
1991-92	Michigan State	CCHA	41	28	33	61	55	....	....	....	....	....	....	....	....	....	....	....	....	....	....	....	....	....	....
1992-93	Michigan State	CCHA	40	31	37	*68	93	....	....	....	....	....	....	....	....	....	....	....	....	....	....	....	....	....	....
	Boston	**NHL**	**9**	**1**	**3**	**4**	**0**	**0**	**0**	**0**	**10**	**10.0**	**3**	....	....	....	**4**	**1**	**0**	**1**	**2**	**0**	**0**	**0**	....
1993-94	**Boston**	**NHL**	**83**	**31**	**20**	**51**	**82**	**4**	**3**	**5**	**179**	**17.3**	**4**	....	....	....	**13**	**5**	**4**	**9**	**4**	**2**	**0**	**0**	....
1994-95	**Boston**	**NHL**	**44**	**18**	**13**	**31**	**31**	**6**	**0**	**5**	**121**	**14.9**	**–3**	....	....	....	**5**	**0**	**1**	**1**	**4**	**0**	**0**	**0**	....
1995-96	**Pittsburgh**	**NHL**	**81**	**24**	**40**	**64**	**69**	**8**	**2**	**1**	**229**	**10.5**	**6**	....	....	....	**18**	**5**	**4**	**9**	**10**	**0**	**0**	**1**	....
1996-97	Detroit Vipers	IHL	6	5	7	12	10	....	....	....	....	....	....	....	....	....	....	....	....	....	....	....	....	....	....
	NY Islanders	**NHL**	**64**	**28**	**28**	**56**	**25**	**9**	**0**	**1**	**183**	**15.3**	**9**	....	....	....	....	....	....	....	....	....	....	....	....
1997-98	**NY Islanders**	**NHL**	**81**	**13**	**30**	**43**	**34**	**3**	**0**	**4**	**203**	**6.4**	**–16**	....	....	....	....	....	....	....	....	....	....	....	....
1998-99	**NY Islanders**	**NHL**	**82**	**16**	**24**	**40**	**49**	**7**	**0**	**3**	**223**	**7.2**	**–7**	**1011**	**48.3**	**19:19**	....	....	....	....	....	....	....	....	....
99-2000	**Los Angeles**	**NHL**	**79**	**20**	**36**	**56**	**48**	**2**	**0**	**0**	**160**	**12.5**	**2**	**1545**	**50.9**	**18:35**	**4**	**0**	**0**	**0**	**2**	**0**	**0**	**0**	**18:22**
2000-01	**Los Angeles**	**NHL**	**78**	**27**	**32**	**59**	**40**	**5**	**3**	**5**	**183**	**14.8**	**10**	**952**	**48.7**	**18:32**	**13**	**1**	**5**	**6**	**14**	**0**	**0**	**0**	**20:35**
2001-02	**Los Angeles**	**NHL**	**80**	**13**	**25**	**38**	**56**	**4**	**1**	**0**	**187**	**7.0**	**7**	**1316**	**45.7**	**19:23**	**7**	**2**	**0**	**2**	**2**	**1**	**0**	**0**	**18:15**
2002-03	**Los Angeles**	**NHL**	**58**	**18**	**20**	**38**	**18**	**6**	**1**	**8**	**150**	**12.0**	**–1**	**831**	**46.3**	**19:02**	....	....	....	....	....	....	....	....	....
	Ottawa	**NHL**	**10**	**3**	**5**	**8**	**2**	**0**	**0**	**0**	**26**	**11.5**	**1**	**127**	**46.5**	**15:42**	**18**	**2**	**7**	**9**	**6**	**0**	**0**	**0**	**15:21**
2003-04	**Ottawa**	**NHL**	**80**	**19**	**27**	**46**	**49**	**4**	**0**	**3**	**182**	**10.4**	**22**	**880**	**44.7**	**16:39**	**7**	**1**	**1**	**2**	**4**	**0**	**0**	**0**	**16:04**
	NHL Totals		**829**	**231**	**303**	**534**	**503**	**58**	**10**	**35**	**2036**	**11.3**		**6662**	**47.7**	**18:30**	**89**	**17**	**22**	**39**	**48**	**3**	**0**	**1**	**17:30**

CCHA First All-Star Team (1993) • NCAA West First All-American Team (1993)

Traded to **Pittsburgh** by **Boston** with Glen Murray and Boston's 3rd round choice (Boyd Kane) in 1996 Entry Draft for Kevin Stevens and Shawn McEachern, August 2, 1995. Traded to **NY Islanders** by **Pittsburgh** for Darius Kasparaitis and Andreas Johansson, November 17, 1996. Traded to **Los Angeles** by **NY Islanders** with Ziggy Palffy, Marcel Cousineau and New Jersey's 4th round choice (previously acquired, Los Angeles selected Daniel Johansson) in 1999 Entry Draft for Olli Jokinen, Josh Green, Mathieu Biron and Los Angeles' 1st round choice (Taylor Pyatt) in 1999 Entry Draft, June 20, 1999. Traded to **Ottawa** by **Los Angeles** for the rights to Tim Gleason and future considerations, March 11, 2003.

SMREK, Peter

(SMUHR-ehk, PEE-tuhr)

Defense. Shoots left. 6'1", 215 lbs. Born, Martin, Czech., February 16, 1979. St. Louis' 2nd choice, 85th overall, in 1999 Entry Draft.

1996-97	Martin	Slovakia	12	1	0	1	....	....	....	....	....	....	....	....	....	....	3	0	0	0	....	....	....	....	....
1997-98	Martin Jr.	Slovak-Jr.	19	7	6	13	32	....	....	....	....	....	....	....	....	....	....	....	....	....	....	....	....	....	....
	Martin	Slovakia	23	0	5	5	24	....	....	....	....	....	....	....	....	....	1	0	0	0	0	....	....	....	....
1998-99	Des Moines	USHL	52	6	26	32	59	....	....	....	....	....	....	....	....	....	14	2	7	9	8	....	....	....	....
99-2000	Peoria Rivermen	ECHL	4	1	1	2	2	....	....	....	....	....	....	....	....	....	....	....	....	....	....	....	....	....	....
	Worcester IceCats	AHL	64	5	19	24	26	....	....	....	....	....	....	....	....	....	2	0	0	0	4	....	....	....	....
2000-01	**St. Louis**	**NHL**	**6**	**2**	**0**	**2**	**2**	**0**	**0**	**1**	**5**	**40.0**	**1**	**0**	**0.0**	**13:01**	....	....	....	....	....	....	....	....	....
	Worcester IceCats	AHL	50	2	7	9	71	....	....	....	....	....	....	....	....	....	....	....	....	....	....	....	....	....	....
	NY Rangers	**NHL**	**14**	**0**	**3**	**3**	**12**	**0**	**0**	**0**	**9**	**0.0**	**1**	**0**	**0.0**	**16:47**	....	....	....	....	....	....	....	....	....
	Hartford	AHL	....	....	....	....	....	....	....	....	....	....	....	....	....	....	5	0	2	2	2	....	....	....	....
2001-02	**NY Rangers**	**NHL**	**8**	**0**	**1**	**1**	**4**	**0**	**0**	**0**	**2**	**0.0**	**–7**	**0**	**0.0**	**14:28**	....	....	....	....	....	....	....	....	....
	Hartford	AHL	50	2	5	7	36	....	....	....	....	....	....	....	....	....	....	....	....	....	....	....	....	....	....
	Slovakia	Olympics	4	0	0	0	0	....	....	....	....	....	....	....	....	....	....	....	....	....	....	....	....	....	....
	Milwaukee	AHL	8	0	2	2	4	....	....	....	....	....	....	....	....	....	....	....	....	....	....	....	....	....	....
2002-03	Milwaukee	AHL	68	3	20	23	70	....	....	....	....	....	....	....	....	....	5	0	0	0	0	....	....	....	....
2003-04	Binghamton	AHL	80	5	18	23	91	....	....	....	....	....	....	....	....	....	2	0	0	0	4	....	....	....	....
	NHL Totals		**28**	**2**	**4**	**6**	**18**	**0**	**0**	**1**	**16**	**12.5**		**0**	**0.0**	**15:19**	....	....	....	....	....	....	....	....	....

Traded to **NY Rangers** by **St. Louis** for Alexei Gusarov, March 5, 2001. Traded to **Nashville** by **NY Rangers** for Richard Lintner, March 19, 2002. Traded to **Ottawa** by **Nashville** for Chris Bala, June 26, 2003. Signed as a free agent by **EHC Wolfsburg** (Germany), May 7, 2004.

SMYTH, Brad

(SMIHTH, BRAD) **L.A.**

Right wing. Shoots right. 6', 195 lbs. Born, Ottawa, Ont., March 13, 1973.

1989-90	Nepean	OMHA	55	53	36	89	105	....	....	....	....	....	....	....	....	....	....	....	....	....	....	....	....	....	....
1990-91	London Knights	OHL	29	2	6	8	22	....	....	....	....	....	....	....	....	....	....	....	....	....	....	....	....	....	....
1991-92	London Knights	OHL	58	17	18	35	93	....	....	....	....	....	....	....	....	....	10	2	0	2	8	....	....	....	....
1992-93	London Knights	OHL	66	54	55	109	118	....	....	....	....	....	....	....	....	....	12	7	8	15	25	....	....	....	....
1993-94	Cincinnati	IHL	30	7	3	10	54	....	....	....	....	....	....	....	....	....	....	....	....	....	....	....	....	....	....
	Birmingham Bulls	ECHL	29	26	30	56	38	....	....	....	....	....	....	....	....	....	10	8	8	16	19	....	....	....	....
1994-95	Springfield	AHL	3	0	0	0	7	....	....	....	....	....	....	....	....	....	....	....	....	....	....	....	....	....	....
	Birmingham Bulls	ECHL	36	33	35	68	52	....	....	....	....	....	....	....	....	....	3	5	2	7	0	....	....	....	....
	Cincinnati	IHL	26	2	11	13	34	....	....	....	....	....	....	....	....	....	1	0	0	0	2	....	....	....	....

			Regular Season														Playoffs								
Season	Club	League	GP	G	A	Pts	PIM	PP	SH	GW	S	%	+/-	TF	F%	Min	GP	G	A	Pts	PIM	PP	SH	GW	Min
1995-96	**Florida**	**NHL**	7	1	1	2	4	1	0	0	12	8.3	–3	....	....	....	....	....	....	....	....	....	....	....	....
	Carolina	AHL	68	*68	58	*126	80	....	....	....	....	....	....	....	....	....	....	....	....	....	....	....	....	....	....
1996-97	**Florida**	**NHL**	8	1	0	1	2	0	0	0	10	10.0	–3	....	....	....	....	....	....	....	....	....	....	....	....
	Los Angeles	**NHL**	44	8	8	16	74	0	0	1	74	10.8	–7	....	....	....	....	....	....	....	....	....	....	....	....
	Phoenix	IHL	3	5	2	7	0	....	....	....	....	....	....	....	....	....	....	....	....	....	....	....	....	....	....
1997-98	**Los Angeles**	**NHL**	9	1	3	4	4	0	0	0	12	8.3	–1	....	....	....	....	....	....	....	....	....	....	....	....
	NY Rangers	**NHL**	1	0	0	0	0	0	0	0	1	0.0	0	....	....	....	....	....	....	....	....	....	....	....	....
	Hartford	AHL	57	29	33	62	79	....	....	....	....	....	....	....	....	....	15	12	8	20	11	....	....	....	....
1998-99	**Nashville**	**NHL**	3	0	0	0	6	0	0	0	5	0.0	–1	0	0.0	9:54	....	....	....	....	....	....	....	....	....
	Milwaukee	IHL	34	11	16	27	21	....	....	....	....	....	....	....	....	....	....	....	....	....	....	....	....	....	....
	Hartford	AHL	36	25	19	44	48	....	....	....	....	....	....	....	....	....	7	6	0	6	14	....	....	....	....
99-2000	Hartford	AHL	80	39	37	76	62	....	....	....	....	....	....	....	....	....	23	*13	10	23	8	....	....	....	....
2000-01	**NY Rangers**	**NHL**	4	1	0	1	4	0	0	0	10	10.0	0	0	0.0	13:57	....	....	....	....	....	....	....	....	....
	Hartford	AHL	77	*50	29	79	110	....	....	....	....	....	....	....	....	....	5	2	3	5	8	....	....	....	....
2001-02	Hartford	AHL	79	34	48	82	90	....	....	....	....	....	....	....	....	....	10	3	8	11	14	....	....	....	....
2002-03	**Ottawa**	**NHL**	12	3	1	4	15	2	0	0	16	18.8	–2	2	0.0	9:30	....	....	....	....	....	....	....	....	....
	Binghamton	AHL	69	24	32	56	77	....	....	....	....	....	....	....	....	....	14	7	6	13	12	....	....	....	....
2003-04	Karpat Oulu	Finland	48	20	18	38	85	....	....	....	....	....	....	....	....	....	15	3	5	8	4	....	....	....	....
	NHL Totals		**88**	**15**	**13**	**28**	**109**	**3**	**0**	**1**	**140**	**10.7**		**2**	**0.0**	**10:30**	....	....	....	....	....	....	....	....	....

AHL First All-Star Team (1996, 2001, 2002) • John B. Sollenberger Trophy (Top Scorer – AHL) (1996) • Les Cunningham Award (MVP – AHL) (1996)

Signed as a free agent by **Florida**, October 4, 1993. Traded to **Los Angeles** by **Florida** for Los Angeles' 3rd round choice (Vratislav Cech) in 1997 Entry Draft, November 28, 1996. Traded to **NY Rangers** by **Los Angeles** for future considerations, November 14, 1997. Signed as a free agent by **Nashville**, July 16, 1998. Traded to **NY Rangers** by **Nashville** for future considerations, May 3, 1999. Signed as a free agent by **Ottawa**, August 1, 2002. Signed as a free agent by **Karpat Oulu** (Finland), October 1, 2003. Signed as a free agent by **Los Angeles**, July 16, 2004.

SMYTH, Ryan (SMIHTH, RIGH-uhn) EDM.

Left wing. Shoots left. 6'1", 190 lbs. Born, Banff, Alta., February 21, 1976. Edmonton's 2nd choice, 6th overall, in 1994 Entry Draft.

Season	Club	League	GP	G	A	Pts	PIM	PP	SH	GW	S	%	+/-	TF	F%	Min	GP	G	A	Pts	PIM	PP	SH	GW	Min
1990-91	Banff Blazers	ABHL	25	100	50	150	....	....	....	....	....	....	....	....	....	....	....	....	....	....	....	....	....	....	....
	Lethbridge	AMHL	34	8	21	29	....	....	....	....	....	....	....	....	....	....	....	....	....	....	....	....	....	....	....
1991-92	Caronport	SMHL	35	55	61	116	98	....	....	....	....	....	....	....	....	....	....	....	....	....	....	....	....	....	....
	Moose Jaw	WHL	2	0	0	0	0	....	....	....	....	....	....	....	....	....	....	....	....	....	....	....	....	....	....
1992-93	Moose Jaw	WHL	64	19	14	33	59	....	....	....	....	....	....	....	....	....	....	....	....	....	....	....	....	....	....
1993-94	Moose Jaw	WHL	72	50	55	105	88	....	....	....	....	....	....	....	....	....	....	....	....	....	....	....	....	....	....
1994-95	Moose Jaw	WHL	50	41	45	86	66	....	....	....	....	....	....	....	....	....	10	6	9	15	22	....	....	....	....
	Edmonton	**NHL**	3	0	0	0	0	0	0	0	2	0.0	–1	....	....	....	....	....	....	....	....	....	....	....	....
1995-96	**Edmonton**	**NHL**	48	2	9	11	28	1	0	0	65	3.1	–10	....	....	....	....	....	....	....	....	....	....	....	....
	Cape Breton	AHL	9	6	5	11	4	....	....	....	....	....	....	....	....	....	....	....	....	....	....	....	....	....	....
1996-97	**Edmonton**	**NHL**	82	39	22	61	76	20	0	4	265	14.7	–7	....	....	....	12	5	5	10	12	1	0	2	....
1997-98	**Edmonton**	**NHL**	65	20	13	33	44	10	0	2	205	9.8	–24	....	....	....	12	1	3	4	16	1	0	0	....
1998-99	**Edmonton**	**NHL**	71	13	18	31	62	6	0	2	161	8.1	0	5	20.0	14:26	3	3	0	3	0	2	0	0	24:35
99-2000	**Edmonton**	**NHL**	82	28	26	54	58	11	0	4	238	11.8	–2	24	54.2	19:12	5	1	0	1	6	0	1	0	19:18
2000-01	**Edmonton**	**NHL**	82	31	39	70	58	11	0	6	245	12.7	10	17	35.3	19:58	6	3	4	7	4	0	0	0	24:46
2001-02	**Edmonton**	**NHL**	61	15	35	50	48	7	1	5	150	10.0	7	12	41.7	19:27	....	....	....	....	....	....	....	....	....
	Canada	Olympics	6	0	1	1	0	....	....	....	....	....	....	....	....	....	....	....	....	....	....	....	....	....	....
2002-03	**Edmonton**	**NHL**	66	27	34	61	67	10	0	3	199	13.6	5	42	42.9	19:21	6	2	0	2	16	0	1	0	17:39
2003-04	**Edmonton**	**NHL**	82	23	36	59	70	8	2	6	245	9.4	11	484	47.1	19:39	....	....	....	....	....	....	....	....	....
	NHL Totals		**642**	**198**	**232**	**430**	**511**	**84**	**3**	**32**	**1775**	**11.2**		**584**	**46.4**	**18:43**	**44**	**15**	**12**	**27**	**54**	**4**	**2**	**2**	**21:15**

WHL East Second All-Star Team (1995)

SOMIK, Radovan (SAW-mihk, RAH-doh-vahn) PHI.

Right wing. Shoots right. 6'2", 194 lbs. Born, Martin, Czech., May 5, 1977. Philadelphia's 3rd choice, 100th overall, in 1995 Entry Draft.

Season	Club	League	GP	G	A	Pts	PIM	PP	SH	GW	S	%	+/-	TF	F%	Min	GP	G	A	Pts	PIM	PP	SH	GW	Min
1993-94	Martin	Slovakia	1	0	0	0	0	....	....	....	....	....	....	....	....	....	....	....	....	....	....	....	....	....	....
1994-95	Martin	Slovakia	25	3	0	3	39	....	....	....	....	....	....	....	....	....	3	1	0	1	2	....	....	....	....
1995-96	Martin	Slovakia	25	3	6	9	8	....	....	....	....	....	....	....	....	....	9	1	0	1		....	....	....	....
1996-97	Martin	Slovakia	35	3	5	8	....	....	....	....	....	....	....	....	....	....	3	0	0	0		....	....	....	....
1997-98	Martin	Slovakia	26	6	9	15	10	....	....	....	....	....	....	....	....	....	3	0	0	0	0	....	....	....	....
1998-99	Dukla Trencin	Slovakia	26	1	4	5	6	....	....	....	....	....	....	....	....	....	....	....	....	....	....	....	....	....	....
99-2000	Martin	Slovak-2	40	38	28	66	32	....	....	....	....	....	....	....	....	....	....	....	....	....	....	....	....	....	....
2000-01	Zlin	Czech	46	15	10	25	22	....	....	....	....	....	....	....	....	....	6	1	0	1	0	....	....	....	....
2001-02	Zlin	Czech	37	14	14	28	22	....	....	....	....	....	....	....	....	....	11	4	3	7	37	....	....	....	....
2002-03	**Philadelphia**	**NHL**	60	8	10	18	10	0	1	2	95	8.4	9	20	35.0	15:49	5	1	1	2	6	0	0	0	11:39
2003-04	**Philadelphia**	**NHL**	53	4	10	14	17	0	0	0	41	9.8	–2	32	59.4	11:01	10	1	1	2	4	0	0	0	8:08
	Philadelphia	AHL	1	0	0	0	2	....	....	....	....	....	....	....	....	....	....	....	....	....	....	....	....	....	....
	NHL Totals		**113**	**12**	**20**	**32**	**27**	**0**	**1**	**2**	**136**	**8.8**		**52**	**50.0**	**13:34**	**15**	**2**	**2**	**4**	**10**	**0**	**0**	**0**	**9:18**

SONNENBERG, Martin (SOHN-nehn-BUHRG, MAHR-tihn)

Left wing. Shoots left. 6', 197 lbs. Born, Wetaskiwin, Alta., January 23, 1978.

Season	Club	League	GP	G	A	Pts	PIM	PP	SH	GW	S	%	+/-	TF	F%	Min	GP	G	A	Pts	PIM	PP	SH	GW	Min
1994-95	Leduc Oil Barons	AMHL	35	28	40	68	34	....	....	....	....	....	....	....	....	....	....	....	....	....	....	....	....	....	....
1995-96	Saskatoon Blades	WHL	58	8	7	15	24	....	....	....	....	....	....	....	....	....	3	0	0	0	2	....	....	....	....
1996-97	Saskatoon Blades	WHL	72	38	26	64	79	....	....	....	....	....	....	....	....	....	....	....	....	....	....	....	....	....	....
1997-98	Saskatoon Blades	WHL	72	40	52	92	87	....	....	....	....	....	....	....	....	....	6	1	3	4	9	....	....	....	....
1998-99	**Pittsburgh**	**NHL**	44	1	1	2	19	0	0	0	12	8.3	–2	2	0.0	4:00	7	0	0	0	0	0	0	0	3:03
	Syracuse Crunch	AHL	36	15	9	24	31	....	....	....	....	....	....	....	....	....	....	....	....	....	....	....	....	....	....
99-2000	**Pittsburgh**	**NHL**	14	1	2	3	0	1	0	0	19	5.3	0	7	28.6	7:26	....	....	....	....	....	....	....	....	....
	Wilkes-Barre	AHL	62	20	33	53	109	....	....	....	....	....	....	....	....	....	....	....	....	....	....	....	....	....	....
2000-01	Wilkes-Barre	AHL	73	14	18	32	89	....	....	....	....	....	....	....	....	....	21	4	3	7	6	....	....	....	....
2001-02	Wilkes-Barre	AHL	78	20	30	50	127	....	....	....	....	....	....	....	....	....	....	....	....	....	....	....	....	....	....
2002-03	Saint John Flames	AHL	54	11	10	21	63	....	....	....	....	....	....	....	....	....	....	....	....	....	....	....	....	....	....
2003-04	**Calgary**	**NHL**	5	0	0	0	2	0	0	0	7	0.0	–2	5	80.0	8:51	....	....	....	....	....	....	....	....	....
	Lowell	AHL	48	20	22	42	46	....	....	....	....	....	....	....	....	....	....	....	....	....	....	....	....	....	....
	NHL Totals		**63**	**2**	**3**	**5**	**21**	**1**	**0**	**0**	**38**	**5.3**		**14**	**42.9**	**5:09**	**7**	**0**	**0**	**0**	**0**	**0**	**0**	**0**	**3:03**

Signed as a free agent by **Pittsburgh**, October 9, 1998. Signed as a free agent by **Calgary**, July 9, 2002.

SOPEL, Brent (SOH-puhl, BREHNT) VAN.

Defense. Shoots right. 6'1", 205 lbs. Born, Calgary, Alta., January 7, 1977. Vancouver's 6th choice, 144th overall, in 1995 Entry Draft.

Season	Club	League	GP	G	A	Pts	PIM	PP	SH	GW	S	%	+/-	TF	F%	Min	GP	G	A	Pts	PIM	PP	SH	GW	Min
1992-93	Sask. Legion	SMHL	36	7	17	24	95	....	....	....	....	....	....	....	....	....	....	....	....	....	....	....	....	....	....
1993-94	Saskatoon Blazers	SMHL	34	9	30	39	180	....	....	....	....	....	....	....	....	....	....	....	....	....	....	....	....	....	....
	Saskatoon Blades	WHL	11	2	2	4	2	....	....	....	....	....	....	....	....	....	....	....	....	....	....	....	....	....	....
1994-95	Saskatoon Blades	WHL	22	1	10	11	31	....	....	....	....	....	....	....	....	....	....	....	....	....	....	....	....	....	....
	Swift Current	WHL	41	4	19	23	50	....	....	....	....	....	....	....	....	....	3	0	3	3	0	....	....	....	....
1995-96	Swift Current	WHL	71	13	48	61	87	....	....	....	....	....	....	....	....	....	6	1	2	3	4	....	....	....	....
	Syracuse Crunch	AHL	1	0	0	0	0	....	....	....	....	....	....	....	....	....	....	....	....	....	....	....	....	....	....
1996-97	Swift Current	WHL	62	15	41	56	109	....	....	....	....	....	....	....	....	....	10	5	11	16	32	....	....	....	....
	Syracuse Crunch	AHL	2	0	0	0	0	....	....	....	....	....	....	....	....	....	3	0	0	0	0	....	....	....	....
1997-98	Syracuse Crunch	AHL	76	10	33	43	70	....	....	....	....	....	....	....	....	....	5	0	7	7	12	....	....	....	....
1998-99	**Vancouver**	**NHL**	5	1	0	1	4	1	0	0	5	20.0	–1	0	0.0	11:58	....	....	....	....	....	....	....	....	....
	Syracuse Crunch	AHL	53	10	21	31	59	....	....	....	....	....	....	....	....	....	....	....	....	....	....	....	....	....	....
99-2000	**Vancouver**	**NHL**	18	2	4	6	12	0	0	1	11	18.2	9	0	0.0	10:31	....	....	....	....	....	....	....	....	....
	Syracuse Crunch	AHL	50	6	25	31	67	....	....	....	....	....	....	....	....	....	4	0	2	2	8	....	....	....	....
2000-01	**Vancouver**	**NHL**	52	4	10	14	10	0	0	1	57	7.0	4	0	0.0	16:01	4	0	0	0	2	0	0	0	19:05
	Kansas City	IHL	4	0	1	1	0	....	....	....	....	....	....	....	....	....	....	....	....	....	....	....	....	....	....
2001-02	**Vancouver**	**NHL**	66	8	17	25	44	1	0	3	116	6.9	21	0	0.0	19:01	6	0	2	2	2	0	0	0	24:45
2002-03	**Vancouver**	**NHL**	81	7	30	37	23	6	0	1	167	4.2	–15	0	0.0	21:42	14	2	6	8	4	1	0	1	22:33
2003-04	**Vancouver**	**NHL**	80	10	32	42	36	6	0	2	173	5.8	11	0	0.0	21:56	7	0	1	1	0	0	0	0	23:55
	NHL Totals		**302**	**32**	**93**	**125**	**129**	**14**	**0**	**8**	**529**	**6.0**		**0**	**0.0**	**19:22**	**31**	**2**	**9**	**11**	**8**	**1**	**0**	**1**	**22:50**

SOURAY, Sheldon
(SUHR-ee, SHEHL-dohn) **MTL.**

Defense. Shoots left. 6'4", 227 lbs. Born, Elk Point, Alta., July 13, 1976. New Jersey's 3rd choice, 71st overall, in 1994 Entry Draft.

			Regular Season														Playoffs								
Season	Club	League	GP	G	A	Pts	PIM	PP	SH	GW	S	%	+/-	TF	F%	Min	GP	G	A	Pts	PIM	PP	SH	GW	Min
1990-91	Bonnyville Sabres	AAHA	30	15	20	35	100																		
1991-92	Quesnel	BCAHA	20	5	15	20	200																		
	Alberta Cycle	AMHL	11	0	5	5	67																		
1992-93	Ft. Saskatchewan	AJHL	35	0	12	12	125																		
	Tri-City	WHL	2	0	0	0	0																		
1993-94	Tri-City	WHL	42	3	6	9	122																		
1994-95	Tri-City	WHL	40	2	24	26	140																		
	Prince George	WHL	11	2	3	5	23																		
	Albany River Rats	AHL	7	0	2	2	8																		
1995-96	Prince George	WHL	32	9	18	27	91																		
	Kelowna Rockets	WHL	27	7	20	27	94										6	0	5	5	2				
	Albany River Rats	AHL	6	0	2	2	12										4	0	1	1	4				
1996-97	Albany River Rats	AHL	70	2	11	13	160										16	2	3	5	47				
1997-98	**New Jersey**	**NHL**	**60**	**3**	**7**	**10**	**85**	**0**	**0**	**1**	**74**	**4.1**	**18**				**3**	**0**	**1**	**1**	**2**	**0**	**0**	**0**	
	Albany River Rats	AHL	6	0	0	0	8																		
1998-99	**New Jersey**	**NHL**	**70**	**1**	**7**	**8**	**110**	**0**	**0**	**0**	**101**	**1.0**	**5**	**0**	**0.0**	**14:56**	**2**	**0**	**1**	**1**	**0**	**0**	**0**	**0**	**12:57**
99-2000	**New Jersey**	**NHL**	**52**	**0**	**8**	**8**	**70**	**0**	**0**	**0**	**74**	**0.0**	**–6**	**0**	**0.0**	**17:12**									
	Montreal	**NHL**	**19**	**3**	**0**	**3**	**44**	**0**	**0**	**0**	**39**	**7.7**	**7**	**0**	**0.0**	**19:18**									
2000-01	**Montreal**	**NHL**	**52**	**3**	**8**	**11**	**95**	**0**	**0**	**2**	**103**	**2.9**	**–11**	**0**	**0.0**	**20:36**									
2001-02	**Montreal**	**NHL**	**34**	**3**	**5**	**8**	**62**	**1**	**0**	**0**	**56**	**5.4**	**–5**	**1**	**100.0**	**18:11**	**12**	**0**	**1**	**1**	**16**	**0**	**0**	**0**	**19:01**
2002-03	**Montreal**	**NHL**	DID NOT PLAY – INJURED																						
2003-04	**Montreal**	**NHL**	**63**	**15**	**20**	**35**	**104**	**6**	**1**	**3**	**186**	**8.1**	**4**	**0**	**0.0**	**23:26**	**11**	**0**	**2**	**2**	**39**	**0**	**0**	**0**	**23:55**
	NHL Totals		**350**	**28**	**55**	**83**	**570**	**7**	**1**	**6**	**633**	**4.4**		**1**	**100.0**	**18:52**	**28**	**0**	**5**	**5**	**57**	**0**	**0**	**0**	**20:41**

WHL West Second All-Star Team (1996)

Traded to **Montreal** by **New Jersey** with Josh DeWolf and New Jersey's 2nd round choice (later traded to Washington – later traded to Tampa Bay – Tampa Bay selected Andreas Holmqvist) in 2001 Entry Draft for Vladimir Malakhov, March 1, 2000. • Missed remainder of 2001-02 season and entire 2002-03 season recovering from wrist injury suffered in game vs. Tampa Bay, November 17, 2001.

Played in NHL All-Star Game (2004)

SPACEK, Jaroslav
(SPAH-chehk, YA-roh-slahv) **CBJ**

Defense. Shoots left. 5'11", 206 lbs. Born, Rokycany, Czech., February 11, 1974. Florida's 5th choice, 117th overall, in 1998 Entry Draft.

			Regular Season														Playoffs								
Season	Club	League	GP	G	A	Pts	PIM	PP	SH	GW	S	%	+/-	TF	F%	Min	GP	G	A	Pts	PIM	PP	SH	GW	Min
1992-93	HC Skoda Plzen	Czech	16	1	3	4																			
1993-94	HC Skoda Plzen	Czech	34	2	6	8																			
1994-95	Plzen	Czech	38	4	8	12	14										3	1	0	1	2				
1995-96	HC ZKZ Plzen	Czech	40	3	10	13	42										3	0	1	1	4				
1996-97	HC ZKZ Plzen	Czech	52	9	29	38	44																		
1997-98	Farjestad	Sweden	45	10	16	26	63										12	2	5	7	14				
	Farjestad	EuroHL	6	2	3	5	2																		
1998-99	**Florida**	**NHL**	**63**	**3**	**12**	**15**	**28**	**2**	**1**	**0**	**92**	**3.3**	**15**	**1**	**100.0**	**19:27**									
	New Haven	AHL	14	4	8	12	15																		
99-2000	**Florida**	**NHL**	**82**	**10**	**26**	**36**	**53**	**4**	**0**	**1**	**111**	**9.0**	**7**	**1**	**0.0**	**22:40**	**4**	**0**	**0**	**0**	**0**	**0**	**0**	**0**	**20:29**
2000-01	**Florida**	**NHL**	**12**	**2**	**1**	**3**	**8**	**1**	**0**	**0**	**21**	**9.5**	**–4**	**0**	**0.0**	**19:12**									
	Chicago	**NHL**	**50**	**5**	**18**	**23**	**20**	**2**	**0**	**1**	**85**	**5.9**	**7**	**0**	**0.0**	**21:31**									
2001-02	**Chicago**	**NHL**	**60**	**3**	**10**	**13**	**29**	**0**	**0**	**1**	**64**	**4.7**	**5**	**0**	**0.0**	**16:25**									
	Czech Republic	Olympics	4	0	0	0	0																		
	Columbus	**NHL**	**14**	**2**	**3**	**5**	**24**	**1**	**1**	**1**	**29**	**6.9**	**–9**	**0**	**0.0**	**23:35**									
2002-03	**Columbus**	**NHL**	**81**	**9**	**36**	**45**	**70**	**5**	**0**	**1**	**166**	**5.4**	**–23**	**0**	**0.0**	**24:47**									
2003-04	**Columbus**	**NHL**	**58**	**5**	**17**	**22**	**45**	**2**	**1**	**2**	**108**	**4.6**	**–13**	**0**	**0.0**	**23:26**									
	NHL Totals		**420**	**39**	**123**	**162**	**277**	**17**	**3**	**7**	**676**	**5.8**		**2**	**50.0**	**21:36**	**4**	**0**	**0**	**0**	**0**	**0**	**0**	**0**	**20:29**

Traded to **Chicago** by **Florida** for Anders Eriksson, November 6, 2000. Traded to **Columbus** by **Chicago** with Chicago's 2nd round choice (Dan Fritsche) in 2003 Entry Draft for Lyle Odelein, March 19, 2002.

SPANHEL, Martin
(SPAN-hehl, MAHR-tihn) **CBJ**

Left wing. Shoots left. 6'2", 206 lbs. Born, Zlin, Czech., July 1, 1977. Philadelphia's 6th choice, 152nd overall, in 1995 Entry Draft.

			Regular Season														Playoffs								
Season	Club	League	GP	G	A	Pts	PIM	PP	SH	GW	S	%	+/-	TF	F%	Min	GP	G	A	Pts	PIM	PP	SH	GW	Min
1994-95	AC ZPS Zlin Jr.	Czech-Jr.	33	25	16	41	0																		
	AC ZPS Zlin	Czech	1	0	0	0	0																		
1995-96	Lethbridge	WHL	6	1	0	1	0																		
	Moose Jaw	WHL	61	4	12	16	33																		
1996-97	AC ZPS Zlin	Czech	22	3	6	9	20																		
1997-98	Zlin	Czech	40	7	9	16	70																		
1998-99	Plzen	Czech	49	12	12	24	60										5	2	1	3	27				
99-2000	Plzen	Czech	52	21	27	48	86										7	1	4	5	12				
2000-01	**Columbus**	**NHL**	**6**	**1**	**0**	**1**	**2**	**0**	**0**	**0**	**8**	**12.5**	**–1**	**1**	**0.0**	**12:29**									
	Syracuse Crunch	AHL	67	11	13	24	75										2	0	0	0	8				
2001-02	**Columbus**	**NHL**	**4**	**1**	**0**	**1**	**2**	**0**	**0**	**0**	**6**	**16.7**	**–2**	**0**	**0.0**	**11:12**									
	Syracuse Crunch	AHL	50	7	12	19	43																		
2002-03	HC Sparta Praha	Czech	40	5	5	10	46										8	1	0	1	6				
2003-04	HIFK Helsinki	Finland	36	2	11	13	22													0					
	Plzen	Czech	14	1	2	3	20										12	2	2	4	10				
	NHL Totals		**10**	**2**	**0**	**2**	**4**	**0**	**0**	**0**	**14**	**14.3**		**1**	**0.0**	**11:58**									

Traded to **San Jose** by **Philadelphia** with Philadelphia's 1st round choice (later traded to Buffalo – later traded to Phoenix – Phoenix selected Daniel Briere) in 1996 Entry Draft and Philadelphia's 4th round choice (later traded to Buffalo – Buffalo selected Mike Martone) in 1996 Entry Draft for Pat Falloon, November 16, 1995. Traded to **Buffalo** by **San Jose** with Vaclav Varada and Philadelphia's 1st (previously acquired, later traded to Phoenix – Phoenix selected Daniel Briere) and 4th (previously acquired, Buffalo selected Mike Martone) round choices in 1996 Entry Draft for Doug Bodger, November 16, 1995. Signed as a free agent by **Columbus**, May 30, 2000. Signed as a free agent by **HC Sparta Praha** (Czech) with Columbus retaining NHL rights, July 26, 2002.

SPEZZA, Jason
(SPEHT-zah, JAY-suhn) **OTT.**

Center. Shoots right. 6'2", 206 lbs. Born, Mississauga, Ont., June 13, 1983. Ottawa's 1st choice, 2nd overall, in 2001 Entry Draft.

			Regular Season														Playoffs								
Season	Club	League	GP	G	A	Pts	PIM	PP	SH	GW	S	%	+/-	TF	F%	Min	GP	G	A	Pts	PIM	PP	SH	GW	Min
1997-98	Tor. Marlboros	MTHL	54	53	61	114	42																		
1998-99	Brampton	OHL	67	22	49	71	18																		
99-2000	Mississauga	OHL	52	24	37	61	33																		
2000-01	Mississauga	OHL	15	7	23	30	11																		
	Windsor Spitfires	OHL	41	36	50	86	32										9	4	5	9	10				
2001-02	Windsor Spitfires	OHL	27	19	26	45	16																		
	Belleville Bulls	OHL	26	23	37	60	26										11	5	6	11	18				
	Grand Rapids	AHL															3	1	0	1	2				
2002-03	**Ottawa**	**NHL**	**33**	**7**	**14**	**21**	**8**	**3**	**0**	**0**	**65**	**10.8**	**–3**	**330**	**45.8**	**12:40**	**3**	**1**	**1**	**2**	**0**	**1**	**0**	**0**	**11:34**
	Binghamton	AHL	43	22	32	54	71										2	1	2	3	4				
2003-04	**Ottawa**	**NHL**	**78**	**22**	**33**	**55**	**71**	**5**	**0**	**3**	**142**	**15.5**	**22**	**956**	**47.7**	**14:38**	**3**	**0**	**0**	**0**	**2**	**0**	**0**	**0**	**9:44**
	NHL Totals		**111**	**29**	**47**	**76**	**79**	**8**	**0**	**3**	**207**	**14.0**		**1286**	**47.2**	**14:03**	**6**	**1**	**1**	**2**	**2**	**1**	**0**	**0**	**10:39**

OHL All-Rookie Team (1999) • AHL All-Rookie Team (2003)

SPILLER, Matthew
(SPIHL-uhr, MA-thew) **PHX.**

Defense. Shoots left. 6'5", 233 lbs. Born, Daysland, Alta., February 7, 1983. Phoenix's 2nd choice, 31st overall, in 2001 Entry Draft.

			Regular Season														Playoffs								
Season	Club	League	GP	G	A	Pts	PIM	PP	SH	GW	S	%	+/-	TF	F%	Min	GP	G	A	Pts	PIM	PP	SH	GW	Min
1998-99	East Central Chill	AMBHL	36	8	19	27	140																		
99-2000	Seattle	WHL	60	1	10	11	108										7	0	0	0	25				
2000-01	Seattle	WHL	71	4	7	11	174																		
2001-02	Seattle	WHL	72	8	23	31	168										1	0	0	0	4				
2002-03	Seattle	WHL	68	11	24	35	198										15	2	7	9	36				
2003-04	**Phoenix**	**NHL**	**51**	**0**	**0**	**0**	**54**	**0**	**0**	**0**	**22**	**0.0**	**–11**	**0**	**0.0**	**10:42**									
	Springfield	AHL	21	1	2	3	32																		
	NHL Totals		**51**	**0**	**0**	**0**	**54**	**0**	**0**	**0**	**22**	**0.0**		**0**	**0.0**	**10:42**									

Season	Club	League	GP	G	A	Pts	PIM	PP	SH	GW	S	%	+/-	TF	F%	Min	Playoffs GP	G	A	Pts	PIM	PP	SH	GW	Min

STAAL, Eric (STAHL, AIR-ihk) **CAR.**

Center. Shoots left. 6'3", 182 lbs. Born, Thunder Bay, Ont., October 29, 1984. Carolina's 1st choice, 2nd overall, in 2003 Entry Draft.

Season	Club	League	GP	G	A	Pts	PIM	PP	SH	GW	S	%	+/-	TF	F%	Min	GP	G	A	Pts	PIM	PP	SH	GW	Min
99-2000	Thunder Bay	Exhib.	7	4	8	12	0	....	....	....	....	....	....	....	....	....	....	....	....	....	....	....	....	....	....
2000-01	Peterborough	OHL	63	19	30	49	23	....	....	....	....	....	....	....	....	....	7	2	5	7	4	....	....	....	....
2001-02	Peterborough	OHL	56	23	39	62	40	....	....	....	....	....	....	....	....	....	6	3	6	9	10	....	....	....	....
2002-03	Peterborough	OHL	66	39	59	98	36	....	....	....	....	....	....	....	....	....	7	9	5	14	6	....	....	....	....
2003-04	**Carolina**	**NHL**	**81**	**11**	**20**	**31**	**40**	**2**	**1**	**3**	**164**	**6.7**	**–6**	**669**	**43.1**	**16:40**	....	....	....	....	....	....	....	....	....
	NHL Totals		**81**	**11**	**20**	**31**	**40**	**2**	**1**	**3**	**164**	**6.7**		**669**	**43.0**	**16:40**	....	....	....	....	....	....	....	....	....

OHL Second All-Star Team (2003) • Canadian Major Junior First All-Star Team (2003)

STAIOS, Steve (STAY-uhs, STEEV) **EDM.**

Defense. Shoots right. 6'1", 200 lbs. Born, Hamilton, Ont., July 28, 1973. St. Louis' 1st choice, 27th overall, in 1991 Entry Draft.

Season	Club	League	GP	G	A	Pts	PIM	PP	SH	GW	S	%	+/-	TF	F%	Min	GP	G	A	Pts	PIM	PP	SH	GW	Min
1988-89	Hamilton Huskies	OMHA	58	13	39	52	78	....	....	....	....	....	....	....	....	....	....	....	....	....	....	....	....	....	....
1989-90	Hamilton Kilty B's	OJHL-B	40	9	27	36	66	....	....	....	....	....	....	....	....	....	....	....	....	....	....	....	....	....	....
1990-91	Niagara Falls	OHL	66	17	29	46	115	....	....	....	....	....	....	....	....	....	12	2	3	5	10	....	....	....	....
1991-92	Niagara Falls	OHL	65	11	42	53	122	....	....	....	....	....	....	....	....	....	17	7	8	15	27	....	....	....	....
1992-93	Niagara Falls	OHL	12	4	14	18	30	....	....	....	....	....	....	....	....	....	....	....	....	....	....	....	....	....	....
	Sudbury Wolves	OHL	53	13	44	57	67	....	....	....	....	....	....	....	....	....	11	5	6	11	22	....	....	....	....
1993-94	Peoria Rivermen	IHL	38	3	9	12	42	....	....	....	....	....	....	....	....	....	....	....	....	....	....	....	....	....	....
1994-95	Peoria Rivermen	IHL	60	3	13	16	64	....	....	....	....	....	....	....	....	....	6	0	0	0	10	....	....	....	....
1995-96	Peoria Rivermen	IHL	6	0	1	1	14	....	....	....	....	....	....	....	....	....	....	....	....	....	....	....	....	....	....
	Worcester IceCats	AHL	57	1	11	12	114	....	....	....	....	....	....	....	....	....	....	....	....	....	....	....	....	....	....
	Boston	**NHL**	**12**	**0**	**0**	**0**	**4**	**0**	**0**	**0**	**4**	**0.0**	**–5**	....	....	....	**3**	**0**	**0**	**0**	**0**	**0**	**0**	**0**	....
	Providence Bruins	AHL	7	1	4	5	8	....	....	....	....	....	....	....	....	....	....	....	....	....	....	....	....	....	....
1996-97	**Boston**	**NHL**	**54**	**3**	**8**	**11**	**71**	**0**	**0**	**0**	**56**	**5.4**	**–26**	....	....	....	....	....	....	....	....	....	....	....	....
	Vancouver	**NHL**	**9**	**0**	**6**	**6**	**20**	**0**	**0**	**0**	**10**	**0.0**	**2**	....	....	....	....	....	....	....	....	....	....	....	....
1997-98	**Vancouver**	**NHL**	**77**	**3**	**4**	**7**	**134**	**0**	**0**	**1**	**45**	**6.7**	**–3**	....	....	....	....	....	....	....	....	....	....	....	....
1998-99	**Vancouver**	**NHL**	**57**	**0**	**2**	**2**	**54**	**0**	**0**	**0**	**33**	**0.0**	**–12**	**4**	**25.0**	**6:53**	....	....	....	....	....	....	....	....	....
99-2000	**Atlanta**	**NHL**	**27**	**2**	**3**	**5**	**66**	**0**	**0**	**0**	**38**	**5.3**	**–5**	**2**	**50.0**	**13:01**	....	....	....	....	....	....	....	....	....
2000-01	**Atlanta**	**NHL**	**70**	**9**	**13**	**22**	**137**	**4**	**0**	**0**	**156**	**5.8**	**–23**	**1**	**0.0**	**21:45**	....	....	....	....	....	....	....	....	....
2001-02	**Edmonton**	**NHL**	**73**	**5**	**5**	**10**	**108**	**0**	**0**	**1**	**101**	**5.0**	**10**	**0**	**0.0**	**18:05**	....	....	....	....	....	....	....	....	....
2002-03	**Edmonton**	**NHL**	**76**	**5**	**21**	**26**	**96**	**1**	**3**	**0**	**126**	**4.0**	**13**	**1**	**0.0**	**22:17**	**6**	**0**	**0**	**0**	**4**	**0**	**0**	**0**	**23:27**
2003-04	**Edmonton**	**NHL**	**82**	**6**	**22**	**28**	**86**	**1**	**0**	**1**	**153**	**3.9**	**17**	**0**	**0.0**	**23:03**	....	....	....	....	....	....	....	....	....
	NHL Totals		**537**	**33**	**84**	**117**	**776**	**6**	**3**	**3**	**722**	**4.6**		**8**	**25.0**	**18:37**	**9**	**0**	**0**	**0**	**4**	**0**	**0**	**0**	**23:27**

Traded to **Boston** by **St. Louis** with Kevin Sawyer for Steve Leach, March 8, 1996. Claimed on waivers by **Vancouver** from **Boston**, March 18, 1997. Claimed by **Atlanta** from **Vancouver** in Expansion Draft, June 25, 1999. • Missed majority of 1999-2000 season recovering from knee injury suffered in game vs. Colorado, October 23, 1999. Traded to **New Jersey** by **Atlanta** for New Jersey's 9th round choice (Simon Gamache) in 2000 Entry Draft, June 12, 2000. Traded to **Atlanta** by **New Jersey** for future considerations, July 10, 2000. Signed as a free agent by **Edmonton**, July 12, 2001.

STAJAN, Matt (STAY-juhn, MAHT) **TOR.**

Center. Shoots left. 6'1", 180 lbs. Born, Mississauga, Ont., December 19, 1983. Toronto's 2nd choice, 57th overall, in 2002 Entry Draft.

Season	Club	League	GP	G	A	Pts	PIM	PP	SH	GW	S	%	+/-	TF	F%	Min	GP	G	A	Pts	PIM	PP	SH	GW	Min
99-2000	Miss. Senators	GTHL	STATISTICS NOT AVAILABLE																						
2000-01	Belleville Bulls	OHL	57	9	18	27	27	....	....	....	....	....	....	....	....	....	7	1	6	7	5	....	....	....	....
2001-02	Belleville Bulls	OHL	68	33	52	85	50	....	....	....	....	....	....	....	....	....	11	3	8	11	14	....	....	....	....
2002-03	Belleville Bulls	OHL	57	34	60	94	75	....	....	....	....	....	....	....	....	....	7	5	8	13	16	....	....	....	....
	St. John's	AHL	1	0	1	1	0	....	....	....	....	....	....	....	....	....	....	....	....	....	....	....	....	....	....
	Toronto	**NHL**	**1**	**1**	**0**	**1**	**0**	**0**	**0**	**0**	**1**	**100.0**	**1**	**12**	**33.3**	**11:00**	....	....	....	....	....	....	....	....	....
2003-04	**Toronto**	**NHL**	**69**	**14**	**13**	**27**	**22**	**0**	**0**	**0**	**63**	**22.2**	**7**	**450**	**38.9**	**11:00**	**3**	**0**	**0**	**0**	**2**	**0**	**0**	**0**	**11:13**
	NHL Totals		**70**	**15**	**13**	**28**	**22**	**0**	**0**	**0**	**64**	**23.4**		**462**	**38.7**	**11:00**	**3**	**0**	**0**	**0**	**2**	**0**	**0**	**0**	**11:13**

• Scored a goal in his first NHL game (April 5, 2003, at home vs. Ottawa).

STEFAN, Patrik (SHTEH-fan, PAT-rihk) **ATL.**

Center. Shoots left. 6'2", 210 lbs. Born, Pribram, Czech., September 16, 1980. Atlanta's 1st choice, 1st overall, in 1999 Entry Draft.

Season	Club	League	GP	G	A	Pts	PIM	PP	SH	GW	S	%	+/-	TF	F%	Min	GP	G	A	Pts	PIM	PP	SH	GW	Min
1996-97	HC Sparta Praha	Czech	5	0	1	1	2	....	....	....	....	....	....	....	....	....	7	1	0	1	0	....	....	....	....
1997-98	HC Sparta Praha	Czech	27	2	6	8	16	....	....	....	....	....	....	....	....	....	....	....	....	....	....	....	....	....	....
	Long Beach	IHL	25	5	10	15	10	....	....	....	....	....	....	....	....	....	10	1	1	2	2	....	....	....	....
1998-99	Long Beach	IHL	33	11	24	35	26	....	....	....	....	....	....	....	....	....	....	....	....	....	....	....	....	....	....
99-2000	**Atlanta**	**NHL**	**72**	**5**	**20**	**25**	**30**	**1**	**0**	**0**	**117**	**4.3**	**–20**	**988**	**41.4**	**14:49**	....	....	....	....	....	....	....	....	....
2000-01	**Atlanta**	**NHL**	**66**	**10**	**21**	**31**	**22**	**0**	**0**	**1**	**93**	**10.8**	**–3**	**834**	**42.9**	**14:07**	....	....	....	....	....	....	....	....	....
2001-02	**Atlanta**	**NHL**	**59**	**7**	**16**	**23**	**22**	**0**	**1**	**0**	**67**	**10.4**	**–4**	**628**	**41.9**	**15:58**	....	....	....	....	....	....	....	....	....
	Chicago Wolves	AHL	5	3	0	3	0	....	....	....	....	....	....	....	....	....	....	....	....	....	....	....	....	....	....
2002-03	**Atlanta**	**NHL**	**71**	**13**	**21**	**34**	**12**	**3**	**0**	**2**	**96**	**13.5**	**–10**	**1125**	**45.7**	**16:50**	....	....	....	....	....	....	....	....	....
2003-04	**Atlanta**	**NHL**	**82**	**14**	**26**	**40**	**26**	**3**	**2**	**2**	**110**	**12.7**	**–7**	**1446**	**45.6**	**16:29**	....	....	....	....	....	....	....	....	....
	NHL Totals		**350**	**49**	**104**	**153**	**112**	**7**	**3**	**5**	**483**	**10.1**		**5021**	**43.9**	**15:41**	....	....	....	....	....	....	....	....	....

STEPHENS, Charlie (STEE-vuhns, CHAHR-lee) **OTT.**

Center/Right wing. Shoots right. 6'3", 220 lbs. Born, London, Ont., April 5, 1981. Colorado's 9th choice, 196th overall, in 2001 Entry Draft.

Season	Club	League	GP	G	A	Pts	PIM	PP	SH	GW	S	%	+/-	TF	F%	Min	GP	G	A	Pts	PIM	PP	SH	GW	Min
1995-96	Elgin-Middlesex	MHAO	60	25	29	54	60	....	....	....	....	....	....	....	....	....	....	....	....	....	....	....	....	....	....
1996-97	Leamington Flyers	OJHL-B	50	26	36	62	103	....	....	....	....	....	....	....	....	....	....	....	....	....	....	....	....	....	....
1997-98	St. Michael's	OHL	58	9	21	30	38	....	....	....	....	....	....	....	....	....	....	....	....	....	....	....	....	....	....
1998-99	St. Michael's	OHL	7	2	4	6	8	....	....	....	....	....	....	....	....	....	....	....	....	....	....	....	....	....	....
	Guelph Storm	OHL	61	24	28	52	72	....	....	....	....	....	....	....	....	....	11	3	5	8	19	....	....	....	....
99-2000	Guelph Storm	OHL	56	16	34	50	87	....	....	....	....	....	....	....	....	....	6	1	3	4	15	....	....	....	....
2000-01	Guelph Storm	OHL	67	38	38	76	53	....	....	....	....	....	....	....	....	....	4	0	2	2	2	....	....	....	....
2001-02	Guelph Storm	OHL	4	1	2	3	2	....	....	....	....	....	....	....	....	....	....	....	....	....	....	....	....	....	....
	London Knights	OHL	56	23	33	56	55	....	....	....	....	....	....	....	....	....	12	6	10	16	18	....	....	....	....
	Hershey Bears	AHL	....	....	....	....	....	....	....	....	....	....	....	....	....	....	1	0	0	0	0	....	....	....	....
2002-03	**Colorado**	**NHL**	**2**	**0**	**0**	**0**	**0**	**0**	**0**	**0**	**1**	**0.0**	**0**	**0**	**0.0**	**5:20**	....	....	....	....	....	....	....	....	....
	Hershey Bears	AHL	74	17	33	50	38	....	....	....	....	....	....	....	....	....	5	1	1	2	2	....	....	....	....
2003-04	**Colorado**	**NHL**	**6**	**0**	**2**	**2**	**4**	**0**	**0**	**0**	**1**	**0.0**	**–1**	**22**	**45.5**	**6:12**	....	....	....	....	....	....	....	....	....
	Hershey Bears	AHL	32	5	9	14	21	....	....	....	....	....	....	....	....	....	....	....	....	....	....	....	....	....	....
	Quad City	UHL	7	0	1	1	0	....	....	....	....	....	....	....	....	....	....	....	....	....	....	....	....	....	....
	Binghamton	AHL	37	15	17	32	43	....	....	....	....	....	....	....	....	....	2	0	0	0	0	....	....	....	....
	NHL Totals		**8**	**0**	**2**	**2**	**4**	**0**	**0**	**0**	**2**	**0.0**		**22**	**45.5**	**5:59**	....	....	....	....	....	....	....	....	....

• Re-entered NHL Entry Draft. Originally Washington's 3rd choice, 31st overall, in 1999 Entry Draft.
Traded to **Ottawa** by **Colorado** for Dennis Bonvie, January 23, 2004.

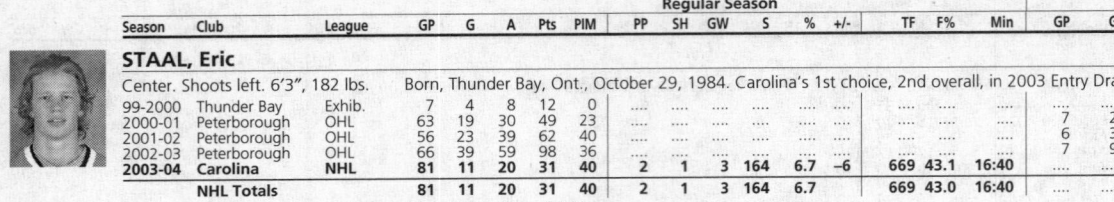

STEVENS, Scott (STEE-vehns, SKAWT) **N.J.**

Defense. Shoots left. 6'2", 215 lbs. Born, Kitchener, Ont., April 1, 1964. Washington's 1st choice, 5th overall, in 1982 Entry Draft.

Season	Club	League	GP	G	A	Pts	PIM	PP	SH	GW	S	%	+/-	TF	F%	Min	GP	G	A	Pts	PIM	PP	SH	GW	Min
1980-81	Kitchener	OHA-B	39	7	33	40	82	....	....	....	....	....	....				....	....	....	....	....	....	....	....	....
	Kitchener Rangers	OMJHL	1	0	0	0	0	....	....	....	....	....	....				....	....	....	....	....	....	....	....	....
1981-82	Kitchener Rangers	OHL	68	6	36	42	158	....	....	....	....	....	....				15	1	10	11	71	....	....	....	....
1982-83	**Washington**	**NHL**	**77**	**9**	**16**	**25**	**195**	**0**	**0**	**0**	**121**	**7.4**	**14**				**4**	**1**	**0**	**1**	**26**	**0**	**0**	**0**	
1983-84	**Washington**	**NHL**	**78**	**13**	**32**	**45**	**201**	**7**	**0**	**2**	**155**	**8.4**	**26**				**8**	**1**	**8**	**9**	**21**	**1**	**0**	**0**	
1984-85	**Washington**	**NHL**	**80**	**21**	**44**	**65**	**221**	**16**	**0**	**5**	**170**	**12.4**	**19**				**5**	**0**	**1**	**1**	**20**	**0**	**0**	**0**	
1985-86	**Washington**	**NHL**	**73**	**15**	**38**	**53**	**165**	**3**	**0**	**2**	**121**	**12.4**	**0**				**9**	**3**	**8**	**11**	**12**	**2**	**0**	**2**	
1986-87	**Washington**	**NHL**	**77**	**10**	**51**	**61**	**283**	**2**	**0**	**0**	**165**	**6.1**	**13**				**7**	**0**	**5**	**5**	**19**	**0**	**0**	**0**	
1987-88	**Washington**	**NHL**	**80**	**12**	**60**	**72**	**184**	**5**	**1**	**2**	**231**	**5.2**	**14**				**13**	**1**	**11**	**12**	**46**	**0**	**0**	**0**	
1988-89	**Washington**	**NHL**	**80**	**7**	**61**	**68**	**225**	**6**	**0**	**3**	**195**	**3.6**	**1**				**6**	**1**	**4**	**5**	**11**	**0**	**0**	**0**	
1989-90	**Washington**	**NHL**	**56**	**11**	**29**	**40**	**154**	**7**	**0**	**0**	**143**	**7.7**	**1**				**15**	**2**	**7**	**9**	**25**	**1**	**0**	**0**	
1990-91	**St. Louis**	**NHL**	**78**	**5**	**44**	**49**	**150**	**1**	**0**	**1**	**160**	**3.1**	**23**				**13**	**0**	**3**	**3**	**36**	**0**	**0**	**0**	
1991-92	**New Jersey**	**NHL**	**68**	**17**	**42**	**59**	**124**	**7**	**1**	**2**	**156**	**10.9**	**24**				**7**	**2**	**1**	**3**	**29**	**2**	**0**	**1**	
1992-93	**New Jersey**	**NHL**	**81**	**12**	**45**	**57**	**120**	**8**	**0**	**1**	**146**	**8.2**	**14**				**5**	**2**	**2**	**4**	**10**	**1**	**0**	**0**	
1993-94	**New Jersey**	**NHL**	**83**	**18**	**60**	**78**	**112**	**5**	**1**	**4**	**215**	**8.4**	**53**				**20**	**2**	**9**	**11**	**42**	**2**	**0**	**1**	

							Regular Season										Playoffs								
Season	Club	League	GP	G	A	Pts	PIM	PP	SH	GW	S	%	+/-	TF	F%	Min	GP	G	A	Pts	PIM	PP	SH	GW	Min
1994-95♦	New Jersey	NHL	48	2	20	22	56	1	0	1	111	1.8	4	....	....	....	20	1	7	8	24	0	0	1	....
1995-96	New Jersey	NHL	82	5	23	28	100	2	1	1	174	2.9	7	....	....	....	....	....	....	....	....	....	....	....	....
1996-97	New Jersey	NHL	79	5	19	24	70	0	0	1	166	3.0	26	....	....	....	10	0	4	4	2	0	0	0	....
1997-98	New Jersey	NHL	80	4	22	26	80	1	0	1	94	4.3	19	....	....	....	6	1	0	1	8	0	0	0	....
	Canada	Olympics	6	0	0	0	2	....	....	....	....	....	....	....	....	....	....	....	....	....	....	....	....	....	....
1998-99	New Jersey	NHL	75	5	22	27	64	0	0	1	111	4.5	29	1	0.0	24:11	7	2	1	3	10	2	0	0	24:28
99-2000♦	New Jersey	NHL	78	8	21	29	103	0	1	1	133	6.0	30	0	0.0	23:23	23	3	8	11	6	0	0	2	25:25
2000-01	New Jersey	NHL	81	9	22	31	71	3	0	2	171	5.3	40	0	0.0	24:37	25	1	7	8	37	0	0	0	22:37
2001-02	New Jersey	NHL	82	1	16	17	44	0	0	1	121	0.8	15	0	0.0	23:19	6	0	0	0	4	0	0	0	22:14
2002-03♦	New Jersey	NHL	81	4	16	20	41	0	0	2	113	3.5	18	0	0.0	23:05	24	3	6	9	14	1	0	1	24:44
2003-04	New Jersey	NHL	38	3	9	12	22	1	0	1	68	4.4	3	0	0.0	24:01	....	....	....	....	....	....	....	....	....
	NHL Totals		1635	196	712	908	2785	75	5	34	3240	6.0		1	0.0	23:44	233	26	92	118	402	12	0	8	24:06

NHL All-Rookie Team (1983) • NHL First All-Star Team (1988, 1994) • NHL Second All-Star Team (1992, 1997, 2001) • Alka-Seltzer Plus Award (1994) • Conn Smythe Trophy (2000)

Played in NHL All-Star Game (1985, 1989, 1991, 1992, 1993, 1994, 1996, 1997, 1998, 1999, 2000, 2001, 2003)

Signed as a free agent by **St. Louis**, July 16, 1990. Transferred to **New Jersey** from **St. Louis** as compensation for St. Louis' signing of free agent Brendan Shanahan, September 3, 1991. • Missed majority of 2003-04 season recovering from head injury suffered in game vs. Pittsburgh, January 7, 2004.

STEVENSON, Jeremy

(STEE-vehn-suhn, JAIR-eh-mee) **NSH.**

Left wing. Shoots left. 6'1", 215 lbs. Born, San Bernardino, CA, July 28, 1974. Anaheim's 10th choice, 262nd overall, in 1994 Entry Draft.

Season	Club	League	GP	G	A	Pts	PIM	PP	SH	GW	S	%	+/-	TF	F%	Min	GP	G	A	Pts	PIM	PP	SH	GW	Min
1989-90	Elliot Lake Vikings	NOHA	61	39	26	65	203	....	....	....	....	....	....	....	....	....	....	....	....	....	....	....	....	....	....
1990-91	Cornwall Royals	OHL	58	13	20	33	124	....	....	....	....	....	....	....	....	....	....	....	....	....	....	....	....	....	....
1991-92	Cornwall Royals	OHL	63	15	23	38	176	....	....	....	....	....	....	....	....	....	6	3	1	4	4	....	....	....	....
1992-93	Newmarket	OHL	54	28	28	56	144	....	....	....	....	....	....	....	....	....	5	5	1	6	28	....	....	....	....
1993-94	Newmarket	OHL	9	2	4	6	27	....	....	....	....	....	....	....	....	....	....	....	....	....	....	....	....	....	....
	Sault Ste. Marie	OHL	48	18	19	37	183	....	....	....	....	....	....	....	....	....	14	1	1	2	23	....	....	....	....
1994-95	Greensboro	ECHL	43	14	13	27	231	....	....	....	....	....	....	....	....	....	17	6	11	17	64	....	....	....	....
1995-96	Anaheim	NHL	3	0	1	1	12	0	0	0	1	0.0	1	....	....	....	....	....	....	....	....	....	....	....	....
	Baltimore Bandits	AHL	60	11	10	21	295	....	....	....	....	....	....	....	....	....	12	4	2	6	23	....	....	....	....
1996-97	Anaheim	NHL	5	0	0	0	14	0	0	0	1	0.0	–1	....	....	....	....	....	....	....	....	....	....	....	....
	Baltimore Bandits	AHL	25	8	8	16	125	....	....	....	....	....	....	....	....	....	3	0	0	0	8	....	....	....	....
1997-98	Anaheim	NHL	45	3	5	8	101	0	0	1	43	7.0	–4	....	....	....	....	....	....	....	....	....	....	....	....
	Cincinnati	AHL	10	5	0	5	34	....	....	....	....	....	....	....	....	....	....	....	....	....	....	....	....	....	....
1998-99	Cincinnati	AHL	22	4	4	8	83	....	....	....	....	....	....	....	....	....	3	1	0	1	2	....	....	....	....
99-2000	Anaheim	NHL	3	0	0	0	7	0	0	0	2	0.0	–1	0	0.0	6:50	....	....	....	....	....	....	....	....	....
	Cincinnati	AHL	41	11	14	25	100	....	....	....	....	....	....	....	....	....	....	....	....	....	....	....	....	....	....
2000-01	Milwaukee	IHL	60	16	13	29	262	....	....	....	....	....	....	....	....	....	5	2	0	2	12	....	....	....	....
	Nashville	NHL	8	1	0	1	39	0	0	0	6	16.7	–1	0	0.0	6:24	....	....	....	....	....	....	....	....	....
2001-02	Nashville	NHL	4	0	0	0	9	0	0	0	0	0.0	0	0	0.0	5:53	....	....	....	....	....	....	....	....	....
	Milwaukee	AHL	53	12	7	19	192	....	....	....	....	....	....	....	....	....	....	....	....	....	....	....	....	....	....
2002-03	Minnesota	NHL	32	5	6	11	69	1	0	1	29	17.2	6	0	0.0	10:48	14	0	5	5	12	0	0	0	12:32
	Houston Aeros	AHL	18	6	7	13	77	....	....	....	....	....	....	....	....	....	....	....	....	....	....	....	....	....	....
2003-04	Minnesota	NHL	3	0	0	0	2	0	0	0	5	0.0	–1	0	0.0	11:24	....	....	....	....	....	....	....	....	....
	Nashville	NHL	53	5	4	9	103	3	0	0	62	8.1	–2	4	50.0	10:03	6	0	0	0	8	0	0	0	6:43
	NHL Totals		156	14	16	30	356	4	0	2	149	9.4		4	50.0	9:47	20	0	5	5	20	0	0	0	10:48

• Re-entered NHL Entry Draft. Originally Winnipeg's 3rd choice, 60th overall, in 1992 Entry Draft.

Signed as a free agent by **Nashville**, September 25, 2000. Signed as a free agent by **Minnesota**, November 26, 2002. Claimed on waivers by **Nashville** from **Minnesota**, October 22, 2003.

STEVENSON, Turner

(STEE-vehn-suhn, TUHR-nuhr) **PHI.**

Right wing. Shoots right. 6'3", 220 lbs. Born, Prince George, B.C., May 18, 1972. Montreal's 1st choice, 12th overall, in 1990 Entry Draft.

Season	Club	League	GP	G	A	Pts	PIM	PP	SH	GW	S	%	+/-	TF	F%	Min	GP	G	A	Pts	PIM	PP	SH	GW	Min
1987-88	Prince George	BCAHA	53	45	46	91	127	....	....	....	....	....	....	....	....	....	....	....	....	....	....	....	....	....	....
1988-89	Seattle	WHL	69	15	12	27	84	....	....	....	....	....	....	....	....	....	....	....	....	....	....	....	....	....	....
1989-90	Seattle	WHL	62	29	32	61	276	....	....	....	....	....	....	....	....	....	13	3	2	5	35	....	....	....	....
1990-91	Seattle	WHL	57	36	27	63	222	....	....	....	....	....	....	....	....	....	6	1	5	6	15	....	....	....	....
	Fredericton	AHL	....	....	....	....	....	....	....	....	....	....	....	....	....	....	4	0	0	0	5	....	....	....	....
1991-92	Seattle	WHL	58	20	32	52	264	....	....	....	....	....	....	....	....	....	15	9	3	12	55	....	....	....	....
1992-93	Montreal	NHL	1	0	0	0	0	0	0	0	1	0.0	–1	....	....	....	....	....	....	....	....	....	....	....	....
	Fredericton	AHL	79	25	34	59	102	....	....	....	....	....	....	....	....	....	5	2	3	5	11	....	....	....	....
1993-94	Montreal	NHL	2	0	0	0	2	0	0	0	0	0.0	–2	....	....	....	3	0	2	2	0	0	0	0	....
	Fredericton	AHL	66	19	28	47	155	....	....	....	....	....	....	....	....	....	....	....	....	....	....	....	....	....	....
1994-95	Fredericton	AHL	37	12	12	24	109	....	....	....	....	....	....	....	....	....	....	....	....	....	....	....	....	....	....
	Montreal	NHL	41	6	1	7	86	0	0	1	35	17.1	0	....	....	....	....	....	....	....	....	....	....	....	....
1995-96	Montreal	NHL	80	9	16	25	167	0	0	2	101	8.9	–2	....	....	....	6	0	1	1	2	0	0	0	....
1996-97	Montreal	NHL	65	8	13	21	97	1	0	0	76	10.5	–14	....	....	....	5	1	1	2	2	0	0	0	....
1997-98	Montreal	NHL	63	4	6	10	110	1	0	0	43	9.3	–8	....	....	....	10	3	4	7	12	0	0	0	....
1998-99	Montreal	NHL	69	10	17	27	88	0	0	2	102	9.8	6	29	37.9	12:57	....	....	....	....	....	....	....	....	....
99-2000	Montreal	NHL	64	8	13	21	61	0	0	2	94	8.5	–1	5	20.0	13:10	....	....	....	....	....	....	....	....	....
2000-01	New Jersey	NHL	69	8	18	26	97	2	0	1	92	8.7	11	0	0.0	11:00	23	1	3	4	20	0	0	1	9:27
2001-02	New Jersey	NHL	21	0	2	2	25	0	0	0	33	0.0	–3	0	0.0	11:38	1	0	0	0	4	0	0	0	10:13
2002-03♦	New Jersey	NHL	77	7	13	20	115	0	0	0	85	8.2	7	12	41.7	11:53	14	1	1	2	26	0	0	0	13:01
2003-04	New Jersey	NHL	61	14	13	27	76	4	0	2	76	18.4	0	5	60.0	12:42	5	0	0	0	0	0	0	0	13:29
	NHL Totals		613	74	112	186	924	8	0	10	738	10.0		51	39.2	12:16	67	6	12	18	66	0	0	1	11:06

WHL West First All-Star Team (1992) • Memorial Cup All-Star Team (1992).

Selected by **Columbus** from **Montreal** in Expansion Draft, June 23, 2000. Traded to **New Jersey** by **Columbus** to complete transaction that sent Krzysztof Oliwa (June 12, 2000) and Deron Quint (June 23, 2000) to **Columbus**, June 23, 2000. • Missed majority of 2001-02 season recovering from knee injury suffered in game vs. Vancouver, December 29, 2001. Signed as a free agent by **Philadelphia**, July 3, 2004.

STEWART, Karl

(STEW-ahrt, KARL) **ATL.**

Center. Shoots left. 5'10", 175 lbs. Born, Aurora, Ont., June 30, 1983.

Season	Club	League	GP	G	A	Pts	PIM	PP	SH	GW	S	%	+/-	TF	F%	Min	GP	G	A	Pts	PIM	PP	SH	GW	Min
99-2000	Thornhill	OJHL	49	15	19	34	61	....	....	....	....	....	....	....	....	....	....	....	....	....	....	....	....	....	....
2000-01	Plymoth Whalers	OHL	68	9	14	23	87	....	....	....	....	....	....	....	....	....	19	3	4	7	14	....	....	....	....
2001-02	Plymouth Whalers	OHL	65	20	23	43	104	....	....	....	....	....	....	....	....	....	6	0	2	2	21	....	....	....	....
2002-03	Plymouth Whalers	OHL	68	35	50	85	120	....	....	....	....	....	....	....	....	....	17	7	10	17	31	....	....	....	....
2003-04	Atlanta	NHL	5	0	1	1	4	0	0	0	2	0.0	0	10	10.0	4:27	....	....	....	....	....	....	....	....	....
	Chicago Wolves	AHL	72	10	32	42	186	....	....	....	....	....	....	....	....	....	10	2	3	5	29	....	....	....	....
	NHL Totals		5	0	1	1	4	0	0	0	2	0.0		10	10.0	4:27	....	....	....	....	....	....	....	....	....

Signed as a free agent by **Atlanta**, September 28, 2001.

STILLMAN, Cory

(STIHL-mahn, KOHR-ee) **T.B.**

Left wing. Shoots left. 6', 194 lbs. Born, Peterborough, Ont., December 20, 1973. Calgary's 1st choice, 6th overall, in 1992 Entry Draft.

Season	Club	League	GP	G	A	Pts	PIM	PP	SH	GW	S	%	+/-	TF	F%	Min	GP	G	A	Pts	PIM	PP	SH	GW	Min
1989-90	Peterboro B's	OJHL-B	41	30	*54	84	76	....	....	....	....	....	....	....	....	....	....	....	....	....	....	....	....	....	....
1990-91	Windsor Spitfires	OHL	64	31	70	101	31	....	....	....	....	....	....	....	....	....	11	3	6	9	8	....	....	....	....
1991-92	Windsor Spitfires	OHL	53	29	61	90	59	....	....	....	....	....	....	....	....	....	7	2	4	6	8	....	....	....	....
1992-93	Peterborough	OHL	61	25	55	80	55	....	....	....	....	....	....	....	....	....	18	3	8	11	18	....	....	....	....
1993-94	Saint John Flames	AHL	79	35	48	83	52	....	....	....	....	....	....	....	....	....	7	2	4	6	16	....	....	....	....
1994-95	Saint John Flames	AHL	63	28	53	81	70	....	....	....	....	....	....	....	....	....	5	0	2	2	2	....	....	....	....
	Calgary	NHL	10	0	2	2	2	0	0	0	7	0.0	1	....	....	....	....	....	....	....	....	....	....	....	....
1995-96	Calgary	NHL	74	16	19	35	41	4	1	3	132	12.1	–5	....	....	....	2	1	1	2	0	0	0	0	....
1996-97	Calgary	NHL	58	6	20	26	14	2	0	0	112	5.4	–6	....	....	....	....	....	....	....	....	....	....	....	....
1997-98	Calgary	NHL	72	27	22	49	40	9	4	1	178	15.2	–9	....	....	....	....	....	....	....	....	....	....	....	....
1998-99	Calgary	NHL	76	27	30	57	38	9	3	5	175	15.4	7	535	46.5	16:19	....	....	....	....	....	....	....	....	....
99-2000	Calgary	NHL	37	12	9	21	12	6	0	3	59	20.3	–9	283	54.4	17:45	....	....	....	....	....	....	....	....	....
2000-01	Calgary	NHL	66	21	24	45	45	7	0	4	148	14.2	–6	346	43.9	18:50	....	....	....	....	....	....	....	....	....
	St. Louis	NHL	12	3	4	7	6	3	0	0	26	11.5	–2	36	61.1	18:37	15	3	5	8	8	1	0	1	14:58
2001-02	St. Louis	NHL	80	23	22	45	36	6	0	4	140	16.4	8	196	46.4	0:00	9	0	2	2	2	0	0	0	....

			Regular Season														Playoffs								
Season	Club	League	GP	G	A	Pts	PIM	PP	SH	GW	S	%	+/-	TF	F%	Min	GP	G	A	Pts	PIM	PP	SH	GW	Min
2002-03	**St. Louis**	**NHL**	**79**	**24**	**43**	**67**	**56**	**6**	**0**	**4**	**157**	**15.3**	**12**	**266**	**41.7**	**0:00**	**6**	**2**	**2**	**4**	**2**	**2**	**0**	**1**	....
2003-04♦	**Tampa Bay**	**NHL**	**81**	**25**	**55**	**80**	**36**	**11**	**1**	**6**	**178**	**14.0**	**18**	**38**	**31.6**	**19:31**	**21**	**2**	**5**	**7**	**15**	**0**	**1**	**0**	**0:00**
	NHL Totals		**645**	**184**	**250**	**434**	**326**	**63**	**9**	**30**	**1312**	**14.0**		**1700**	**33.9**	**9:37**	**53**	**8**	**15**	**23**	**27**	**3**	**1**	**2**	**6:14**

OHL Rookie of the Year (1991)

• Missed majority of 1999-2000 season recovering from shoulder injury suffered in game vs. Philadelphia, December 27, 1999. Traded to **St. Louis by Calgary** for Craig Conroy and St. Louis' 7th round choice (David Moss) in 2001 Entry Draft, March 13, 2001. Traded to **Tampa Bay** by **St. Louis** for Tampa Bay's 2nd round choice (David Backes) in 2003 Entry Draft, June 21, 2003.

STOCK, P.J. (STAWK, PEE-JAY) BOS.

Center. Shoots left. 5'10", 197 lbs. Born, Montreal, Que., May 26, 1975.

Season	Club	League	GP	G	A	Pts	PIM	PP	SH	GW	S	%	+/-	TF	F%	Min	GP	G	A	Pts	PIM	PP	SH	GW	Min
1992-93	Pembroke	OCJHL	55	10	38	48	189																		
1993-94	Pembroke	OCJHL	52	25	48	73	262																		
1994-95	Victoriaville Tigres	QMJHL	70	9	46	55	386										4	0	0	0	60				
1995-96	Victoriaville Tigres	QMJHL	67	19	43	62	432										12	5	4	9	79				
1996-97	St. FX University	AUAA	27	11	20	31	110										3	0	4	4	14				
1997-98	Hartford	AHL	41	8	8	16	202										11	1	3	4	79				
	NY Rangers	**NHL**	**38**	**2**	**3**	**5**	**114**	**0**	**0**	**1**	**9**	**22.2**	**4**												
1998-99	**NY Rangers**	**NHL**	**5**	**0**	**0**	**0**	**6**	**0**	**0**	**0**	**0**	**0.0**	**–1**	**8**	**50.0**	**2:42**									
	Hartford	AHL	55	4	14	18	250										6	0	1	1	35				
99-2000	**NY Rangers**	**NHL**	**11**	**0**	**1**	**1**	**11**	**0**	**0**	**0**	**2**	**0.0**	**1**	**63**	**31.8**	**6:13**									
	Hartford	AHL	64	13	23	36	290										23	1	11	12	69				
2000-01	**Montreal**	**NHL**	**20**	**1**	**2**	**3**	**32**	**0**	**0**	**0**	**9**	**11.1**	**–1**	**83**	**53.0**	**5:31**									
	Philadelphia	**NHL**	**31**	**1**	**3**	**4**	**78**	**0**	**0**	**0**	**18**	**5.6**	**–2**	**12**	**50.0**	**7:48**	**2**	**0**	**0**	**0**	**0**	**0**	**0**	**0**	**5:00**
	Philadelphia	AHL	9	1	2	3	37																		
2001-02	**Boston**	**NHL**	**58**	**0**	**3**	**3**	**122**	**0**	**0**	**0**	**12**	**0.0**	**–2**	**120**	**45.8**	**5:09**	**6**	**1**	**0**	**1**	**19**	**0**	**0**	**0**	**3:15**
2002-03	**Boston**	**NHL**	**71**	**1**	**9**	**10**	**160**	**1**	**0**	**0**	**38**	**2.6**	**–5**	**185**	**44.9**	**6:14**									
2003-04	**Boston**	**NHL**	**1**	**0**	**0**	**0**	**0**	**0**	**0**	**0**	**1**	**0.0**	**0**	**2**	**50.0**	**6:04**									
	Providence Bruins	AHL	4	1	0	1	2																		
	Philadelphia	AHL	66	5	18	23	207										12	0	2	2	34				
	NHL Totals		**235**	**5**	**21**	**26**	**523**	**1**	**0**	**1**	**89**	**5.6**		**473**	**45.0**	**6:00**	**8**	**1**	**0**	**1**	**19**	**0**	**0**	**0**	**3:41**

Signed as a free agent by **NY Rangers**, November 18, 1997. Signed as a free agent by **Montreal**, July 7, 2000. Traded to **Philadelphia** by **Montreal** with Montreal's 6th round choice (Dennis Seidenberg) in 2001 Entry Draft for Gino Odjick, December 7, 2000. Signed as a free agent by **NY Rangers**, August 23, 2001. Claimed by **Boston** from **NY Rangers** in Waiver Draft, September 28, 2001. Loaned to **Philadelphia** (AHL) by **Providence** (AHL) for the loan of Andre Savage, October 29, 2003.

STOLL, Jarret (STOHL, JEHR-eht) EDM.

Center. Shoots right. 6'1", 200 lbs. Born, Melville, Sask., June 25, 1982. Edmonton's 3rd choice, 36th overall, in 2002 Entry Draft.

Season	Club	League	GP	G	A	Pts	PIM	PP	SH	GW	S	%	+/-	TF	F%	Min	GP	G	A	Pts	PIM	PP	SH	GW	Min
1997-98	Saskatoon Blazers	SMHL	44	45	44	*89	78																		
	Edmonton Ice	WHL	8	2	3	5	4																		
1998-99	Kootenay Ice	WHL	57	13	21	34	38										4	0	0	0	2				
99-2000	Kootenay Ice	WHL	71	37	38	75	64										20	7	9	16	24				
2000-01	Kootenay Ice	WHL	62	40	66	106	105										11	5	9	14	22				
2001-02	Kootenay Ice	WHL	47	32	34	66	64										22	6	14	20	35				
2002-03	**Edmonton**	**NHL**	**4**	**0**	**1**	**1**	**0**	**0**	**0**	**0**	**5**	**0.0**	**–3**	**30**	**63.3**	**7:44**									
	Hamilton	AHL	76	21	33	54	86										23	5	8	13	25				
2003-04	**Edmonton**	**NHL**	**68**	**10**	**11**	**21**	**42**	**1**	**1**	**2**	**107**	**9.3**	**8**	**1019**	**54.1**	**13:54**									
	NHL Totals		**72**	**10**	**12**	**22**	**42**	**1**	**1**	**2**	**112**	**8.9**		**1049**	**54.3**	**13:34**									

• Re-entered NHL Entry Draft. Originally Calgary's 3rd choice, 46th overall, in 2000 Entry Draft.

WHL East First All-Star Team (2001) • Canadian Major Junior First All-Star Team (2001) • WHL West First All-Star Team (2002)

STRAKA, Martin (STRAH-kuh, MAHR-tihn) L.A.

Center. Shoots left. 5'9", 178 lbs. Born, Plzen, Czech., September 3, 1972. Pittsburgh's 1st choice, 19th overall, in 1992 Entry Draft.

Season	Club	League	GP	G	A	Pts	PIM	PP	SH	GW	S	%	+/-	TF	F%	Min	GP	G	A	Pts	PIM	PP	SH	GW	Min
1989-90	TJ Skoda Plzen	Czech	1	0	3	3																			
1990-91	HC Skoda Plzen	Czech	47	7	24	31	6																		
1991-92	HC Skoda Plzen	Czech	50	27	28	55	20																		
1992-93	**Pittsburgh**	**NHL**	**42**	**3**	**13**	**16**	**29**	**0**	**0**	**1**	**28**	**10.7**	**2**				**11**	**2**	**1**	**3**	**2**	**0**	**0**	**0**	
	Cleveland	IHL	4	4	3	7	0																		
1993-94	**Pittsburgh**	**NHL**	**84**	**30**	**34**	**64**	**24**	**2**	**0**	**6**	**130**	**23.1**	**24**				**6**	**1**	**0**	**1**	**2**	**0**	**0**	**0**	
1994-95	Plzen	Czech	19	10	11	21	18																		
	Pittsburgh	**NHL**	**31**	**4**	**12**	**16**	**16**	**0**	**0**	**0**	**36**	**11.1**	**0**												
	Ottawa	**NHL**	**6**	**1**	**1**	**2**	**0**	**0**	**0**	**0**	**13**	**7.7**	**–1**												
1995-96	**Ottawa**	**NHL**	**43**	**9**	**16**	**25**	**29**	**5**	**0**	**1**	**63**	**14.3**	**–14**												
	NY Islanders	**NHL**	**22**	**2**	**10**	**12**	**6**	**0**	**0**	**0**	**18**	**11.1**	**–6**												
	Florida	**NHL**	**12**	**2**	**4**	**6**	**6**	**1**	**0**	**0**	**17**	**11.8**	**1**				**13**	**2**	**2**	**4**	**2**	**0**	**0**	**0**	
1996-97	**Florida**	**NHL**	**55**	**7**	**22**	**29**	**12**	**2**	**0**	**1**	**94**	**7.4**	**9**				**4**	**0**	**0**	**0**	**0**	**0**	**0**	**0**	
1997-98	**Pittsburgh**	**NHL**	**75**	**19**	**23**	**42**	**28**	**4**	**3**	**4**	**117**	**16.2**	**–1**				**6**	**2**	**0**	**2**	**2**	**0**	**1**	**0**	
	Czech Republic	Olympics	6	1	2	3	0																		
1998-99	**Pittsburgh**	**NHL**	**80**	**35**	**48**	**83**	**26**	**5**	**4**	**4**	**177**	**19.8**	**12**	**845**	**43.6**	**23:35**	**13**	**6**	**9**	**15**	**6**	**1**	**0**	**0**	**25:00**
99-2000	**Pittsburgh**	**NHL**	**71**	**20**	**39**	**59**	**26**	**3**	**1**	**2**	**146**	**13.7**	**24**	**651**	**42.9**	**23:58**	**11**	**3**	**9**	**12**	**10**	**1**	**0**	**0**	**24:27**
2000-01	**Pittsburgh**	**NHL**	**82**	**27**	**68**	**95**	**38**	**7**	**1**	**4**	**185**	**14.6**	**19**	**331**	**43.2**	**23:01**	**18**	**5**	**8**	**13**	**8**	**3**	**0**	**2**	**21:24**
2001-02	**Pittsburgh**	**NHL**	**13**	**5**	**4**	**9**	**0**	**1**	**0**	**1**	**33**	**15.2**	**3**	**5**	**60.0**	**18:00**									
2002-03	**Pittsburgh**	**NHL**	**60**	**18**	**28**	**46**	**12**	**7**	**0**	**4**	**136**	**13.2**	**–18**	**115**	**45.2**	**20:37**									
2003-04	**Pittsburgh**	**NHL**	**22**	**4**	**8**	**12**	**16**	**1**	**0**	**0**	**34**	**11.8**	**–16**	**121**	**38.8**	**21:32**									
	Los Angeles	**NHL**	**32**	**6**	**8**	**14**	**4**	**1**	**1**	**0**	**34**	**17.6**	**–9**	**66**	**48.5**	**16:47**									
	NHL Totals		**730**	**192**	**338**	**530**	**272**	**39**	**10**	**28**	**1261**	**15.2**		**2134**	**43.3**	**22:06**	**82**	**21**	**29**	**50**	**32**	**5**	**1**	**2**	**23:19**

Czechoslovakian First All-Star Team (1992)

Played in NHL All-Star Game (1999)

Traded to **Ottawa** by **Pittsburgh** for Troy Murray and Norm Maciver, April 7, 1995. Traded to **NY Islanders** by **Ottawa** with Don Beaupre and Bryan Berard for Damian Rhodes and Wade Redden, January 23, 1996. Claimed on waivers by **Florida** from **NY Islanders**, March 15, 1996. Signed as a free agent by **Pittsburgh**, August 6, 1997. • Missed majority of 2001-02 season recovering from leg injury suffered in game vs. Florida, October 28, 2001. Traded to **Los Angeles** by **Pittsburgh** for Martin Strbak and Sergei Anshakov, November 30, 2003.

STRBAK, Martin (SHTUHR-bak, MAHR-tehn) PIT.

Defense. Shoots left. 6'3", 210 lbs. Born, Presov, Czech., January 15, 1975. Los Angeles' 10th choice, 224th overall, in 1993 Entry Draft.

Season	Club	League	GP	G	A	Pts	PIM	PP	SH	GW	S	%	+/-	TF	F%	Min	GP	G	A	Pts	PIM	PP	SH	GW	Min
1994-95	Slovan Bratislava	Slovakia	26	3	4	7	10																		
1995-96	Slovan Bratislava	Slovakia	44	4	4	8	22																		
1996-97	Slovan Bratislava	Slovakia	38	3	2	5	24																		
	Slovan Bratislava	EuroHL	5	0	0	0	4																		
1997-98	Spisska Nova Vis	Slovakia	33	1	1	2	18																		
1998-99	Slovan Bratislava	Slovakia	18	0	0	0	4										2	0	0	0	4				
	HC Trnava	Slovak-2	15	3	6	9	12																		
99-2000	Litvinov	Czech	50	3	6	9	28																		
2000-01	Vsetin	Czech	49	2	6	8	46										14	2	1	3	35				
2001-02	Vsetin	Czech	33	8	9	17	46																		
	Yaroslavl	Russia	19	1	1	2	10										9	1	2	3	8				
2002-03	Yaroslavl	Russia	27	0	6	6	28																		
	HPK Hameenlinna	Finland	20	4	9	13	68										13	2	3	5	8				
2003-04	**Los Angeles**	**NHL**	**5**	**2**	**0**	**2**	**8**	**0**	**0**	**1**	**7**	**28.6**	**1**	**0**	**0.0**	**19:14**									
	Manchester	AHL	12	0	1	1	25																		
	Pittsburgh	**NHL**	**44**	**3**	**11**	**14**	**38**	**0**	**0**	**0**	**47**	**6.4**	**–11**	**2**	**50.0**	**19:31**									
	NHL Totals		**49**	**5**	**11**	**16**	**46**	**0**	**0**	**1**	**54**	**9.3**		**2**	**50.0**	**19:29**									

Traded to **Pittsburgh** by **Los Angeles** with Sergei Anshakov for Martin Straka, November 30, 2003.

STROSHEIN, Garret
(STROH-shighn, GAIR-reht) **WSH.**

Right wing. Shoots right. 6'7", 245 lbs. Born, Edmonton, Alta., April 4, 1980.

			Regular Season														Playoffs								
Season	Club	League	GP	G	A	Pts	PIM	PP	SH	GW	S	%	+/-	TF	F%	Min	GP	G	A	Pts	PIM	PP	SH	GW	Min
1998-99	Seattle	WHL	11	0	0	0	32	....	....	....	....	....	....	....	....	....	4	0	0	0	7	....	....	....	....
99-2000	Chilliwack Chiefs	BCHL	58	3	1	4	176	....	....	....	....	....	....	....	....	....	....	....	....	....	....	....	....	....	....
2000-01	Chilliwack Chiefs	BCHL	55	7	8	15	187	....	....	....	....	....	....	....	....	....	....	....	....	....	....	....	....	....	....
	San Diego Gulls	WCHL	3	0	0	0	5	....	....	....	....	....	....	....	....	....	....	....	....	....	....	....	....	....	....
2001-02	Mobile Mysticks	ECHL	3	0	0	0	13	....	....	....	....	....	....	....	....	....	....	....	....	....	....	....	....	....	....
	San Diego Gulls	WCHL	24	0	0	0	90	....	....	....	....	....	....	....	....	....	....	....	....	....	....	....	....	....	....
	Fresno Falcons	WCHL	20	1	0	1	67	....	....	....	....	....	....	....	....	....	....	....	....	....	....	....	....	....	....
	Bakersfield	WCHL	....	....	....	....	....	....	....	....	....	....	....	....	....	....	4	0	0	0	2	....	....	....	....
2002-03	Richmond	ECHL	2	0	0	0	7	....	....	....	....	....	....	....	....	....	....	....	....	....	....	....	....	....	....
	Portland Pirates	WHL	28	0	1	1	86	....	....	....	....	....	....	....	....	....	2	0	0	0	6	....	....	....	....
2003-04	**Washington**	**NHL**	**3**	**0**	**0**	**0**	**14**	**0**	**0**	**0**	**2**	**0.0**	**–1**	**0**	**0.0**	**7:16**	....	....	....	....	....	....	....	....	....
	Portland Pirates	AHL	35	1	1	2	73	....	....	....	....	....	....	....	....	....	....	....	....	....	....	....	....	....	....
	NHL Totals		**3**	**0**	**0**	**0**	**14**	**0**	**0**	**0**	**2**	**0.0**		**0**	**0.0**	**7:16**	....	....	....	....	....	....	....	....	....

Signed as a free agent by **Washington**, July 14, 2003.

STRUDWICK, Jason
(STRUHD-wihk, JAY-suhn) **NYR**

Wing/Defense. Shoots left. 6'3", 210 lbs. Born, Edmonton, Alta., July 17, 1975. NY Islanders' 3rd choice, 63rd overall, in 1994 Entry Draft.

Season	Club	League	GP	G	A	Pts	PIM	PP	SH	GW	S	%	+/-	TF	F%	Min	GP	G	A	Pts	PIM	PP	SH	GW	Min
1991-92	Edmonton Legion	AMHL	35	3	8	11	67	....	....	....	....	....	....	....	....	....	....	....	....	....	....	....	....	....	....
1992-93	Edmonton Pats	AMHL	33	8	20	28	135	....	....	....	....	....	....	....	....	....	....	....	....	....	....	....	....	....	....
1993-94	Kamloops Blazers	WHL	61	6	8	14	118	....	....	....	....	....	....	....	....	....	19	0	4	4	24	....	....	....	....
1994-95	Kamloops Blazers	WHL	72	3	11	14	183	....	....	....	....	....	....	....	....	....	21	1	1	2	39	....	....	....	....
1995-96	**NY Islanders**	**NHL**	**1**	**0**	**0**	**0**	**7**	**0**	**0**	**0**	**0**	**0.0**	**0**	....	....	....	....	....	....	....	....	....	....	....	....
	Worcester IceCats	AHL	60	2	7	9	119	....	....	....	....	....	....	....	....	....	4	0	1	1	0	....	....	....	....
1996-97	Kentucky	AHL	80	1	9	10	198	....	....	....	....	....	....	....	....	....	4	0	0	0	0	....	....	....	....
1997-98	**NY Islanders**	**NHL**	**17**	**0**	**1**	**1**	**36**	**0**	**0**	**0**	**3**	**0.0**	**1**	....	....	....	....	....	....	....	....	....	....	....	....
	Kentucky	AHL	39	3	1	4	87	....	....	....	....	....	....	....	....	....	....	....	....	....	....	....	....	....	....
	Vancouver	**NHL**	**11**	**0**	**1**	**1**	**29**	**0**	**0**	**0**	**5**	**0.0**	**–3**	....	....	....	....	....	....	....	....	....	....	....	....
	Syracuse Crunch	AHL	....	....	....	....	....	....	....	....	....	....	....	....	....	....	3	0	0	0	6	....	....	....	....
1998-99	**Vancouver**	**NHL**	**65**	**0**	**3**	**3**	**114**	**0**	**0**	**0**	**25**	**0.0**	**–19**	**0**	**0.0**	**12:49**	....	....	....	....	....	....	....	....	....
99-2000	**Vancouver**	**NHL**	**63**	**1**	**3**	**4**	**64**	**0**	**0**	**0**	**18**	**5.6**	**–13**	**0**	**0.0**	**15:12**	....	....	....	....	....	....	....	....	....
2000-01	**Vancouver**	**NHL**	**60**	**1**	**4**	**5**	**64**	**0**	**0**	**1**	**21**	**4.8**	**16**	**0**	**0.0**	**9:59**	**2**	**0**	**0**	**0**	**0**	**0**	**0**	**0**	**2:15**
2001-02	**Vancouver**	**NHL**	**44**	**2**	**4**	**6**	**96**	**0**	**0**	**0**	**13**	**15.4**	**4**	**0**	**0.0**	**9:45**	....	....	....	....	....	....	....	....	....
2002-03	**Chicago**	**NHL**	**48**	**2**	**3**	**5**	**87**	**0**	**0**	**0**	**19**	**10.5**	**–4**	**3**	**0.0**	**8:32**	....	....	....	....	....	....	....	....	....
2003-04	**Chicago**	**NHL**	**54**	**1**	**3**	**4**	**73**	**0**	**0**	**0**	**32**	**3.1**	**–16**	**1**	**0.0**	**14:55**	....	....	....	....	....	....	....	....	....
	NHL Totals		**363**	**7**	**22**	**29**	**570**	**0**	**0**	**1**	**136**	**5.1**		**4**	**0.0**	**12:05**	**2**	**0**	**0**	**0**	**0**	**0**	**0**	**0**	**2:15**

Traded to **Vancouver** by **NY Islanders** for Gino Odjick, March 23, 1998. Signed as a free agent by **Chicago**, July 15, 2002. Signed as a free agent by **NY Rangers**, July 20, 2004.

STUART, Brad
(STEW-ahrt, BRAD) **S.J.**

Defense. Shoots left. 6'2", 220 lbs. Born, Rocky Mountain House, Alta., November 6, 1979. San Jose's 1st choice, 3rd overall, in 1998 Entry Draft.

Season	Club	League	GP	G	A	Pts	PIM	PP	SH	GW	S	%	+/-	TF	F%	Min	GP	G	A	Pts	PIM	PP	SH	GW	Min
1995-96	Red Deer	AMHL	35	12	25	37	83	....	....	....	....	....	....	....	....	....	....	....	....	....	....	....	....	....	....
	Regina Pats	WHL	3	0	0	0	0	....	....	....	....	....	....	....	....	....	....	....	....	....	....	....	....	....	....
1996-97	Regina Pats	WHL	57	7	36	43	58	....	....	....	....	....	....	....	....	....	5	0	4	4	14	....	....	....	....
1997-98	Regina Pats	WHL	72	20	45	65	82	....	....	....	....	....	....	....	....	....	9	3	4	7	10	....	....	....	....
1998-99	Regina Pats	WHL	29	10	19	29	43	....	....	....	....	....	....	....	....	....	....	....	....	....	....	....	....	....	....
	Calgary Hitmen	WHL	30	11	22	33	26	....	....	....	....	....	....	....	....	....	21	8	15	23	59	....	....	....	....
99-2000	**San Jose**	**NHL**	**82**	**10**	**26**	**36**	**32**	**5**	**1**	**3**	**133**	**7.5**	**3**	**0**	**0.0**	**20:24**	**12**	**1**	**0**	**1**	**6**	**1**	**0**	**0**	**16:30**
2000-01	**San Jose**	**NHL**	**77**	**5**	**18**	**23**	**56**	**1**	**0**	**2**	**119**	**4.2**	**10**	**0**	**0.0**	**20:06**	**5**	**1**	**0**	**1**	**0**	**0**	**0**	**0**	**20:19**
2001-02	**San Jose**	**NHL**	**82**	**6**	**23**	**29**	**39**	**2**	**0**	**2**	**96**	**6.3**	**13**	**0**	**0.0**	**21:41**	**12**	**0**	**3**	**3**	**8**	**0**	**0**	**0**	**19:42**
2002-03	**San Jose**	**NHL**	**36**	**4**	**10**	**14**	**46**	**2**	**0**	**1**	**63**	**6.3**	**–6**	**0**	**0.0**	**20:53**	....	....	....	....	....	....	....	....	....
2003-04	**San Jose**	**NHL**	**77**	**9**	**30**	**39**	**34**	**5**	**0**	**0**	**129**	**7.0**	**9**	**0**	**0.0**	**22:09**	**17**	**1**	**5**	**6**	**13**	**0**	**0**	**0**	**23:23**
	NHL Totals		**354**	**34**	**107**	**141**	**207**	**15**	**1**	**8**	**540**	**6.3**		**0**	**0.0**	**21:04**	**46**	**3**	**8**	**11**	**27**	**1**	**0**	**0**	**20:18**

WHL East Second All-Star Team (1998) • WHL East First All-Star Team (1999) • Canadian Major Junior First All-Star Team (1999) • Canadian Major Junior Defenseman of the Year (1999) • NHL All-Rookie Team (2000)

• Missed majority of 2002-03 season recovering from ankle (January 4, 2003 vs. Los Angeles) and head (February 21, 2003 vs. Columbus) injuries.

STUART, Mike
(STEW-ahrt, MIGHK) **ST.L.**

Defense. Shoots right. 6', 200 lbs. Born, Rochester, MN, August 31, 1980. Nashville's 6th choice, 137th overall, in 2000 Entry Draft.

Season	Club	League	GP	G	A	Pts	PIM	PP	SH	GW	S	%	+/-	TF	F%	Min	GP	G	A	Pts	PIM	PP	SH	GW	Min
1996-97	Rochester	USHL	46	4	9	13	22	....	....	....	....	....	....	....	....	....	....	....	....	....	....	....	....	....	....
1997-98	Rochester	USHL	50	4	15	19	40	....	....	....	....	....	....	....	....	....	....	....	....	....	....	....	....	....	....
1998-99	Colorado College	WCHA	40	2	12	14	44	....	....	....	....	....	....	....	....	....	....	....	....	....	....	....	....	....	....
99-2000	Colorado College	WCHA	32	2	5	7	26	....	....	....	....	....	....	....	....	....	....	....	....	....	....	....	....	....	....
2000-01	Colorado College	WCHA	33	1	13	14	36	....	....	....	....	....	....	....	....	....	....	....	....	....	....	....	....	....	....
2001-02	Colorado College	WCHA	35	3	9	12	46	....	....	....	....	....	....	....	....	....	....	....	....	....	....	....	....	....	....
2002-03	Worcester IceCats	AHL	41	1	5	6	19	....	....	....	....	....	....	....	....	....	3	0	0	0	2	....	....	....	....
	Peoria Rivermen	ECHL	19	2	7	9	12	....	....	....	....	....	....	....	....	....	....	....	....	....	....	....	....	....	....
2003-04	**St. Louis**	**NHL**	**2**	**0**	**0**	**0**	**0**	**0**	**0**	**0**	**0**	**0.0**	**0**	**0**	**0.0**	**9:31**	....	....	....	....	....	....	....	....	....
	Worcester IceCats	AHL	30	0	4	4	20	....	....	....	....	....	....	....	....	....	....	....	....	....	....	....	....	....	....
	NHL Totals		**2**	**0**	**0**	**0**	**0**	**0**	**0**	**0**	**0**	**0.0**		**0**	**0.0**	**9:31**	....	....	....	....	....	....	....	....	....

USHL All-Rookie Team (1997)

Signed as a free agent by **St. Louis**, October 7, 2002. • Missed majority of 2003-04 season recovering from groin injury suffered in game vs. Hartford (AHL), January 28, 2004.

STUMPEL, Jozef
(STUM-puhl, JOH-zehf)

Center. Shoots right. 6'3", 225 lbs. Born, Nitra, Czech., July 20, 1972. Boston's 2nd choice, 40th overall, in 1991 Entry Draft.

Season	Club	League	GP	G	A	Pts	PIM	PP	SH	GW	S	%	+/-	TF	F%	Min	GP	G	A	Pts	PIM	PP	SH	GW	Min
1989-90	Plastika Nitra	Czech-2	38	12	11	23	....	....	....	....	....	....	....	....	....	....	....	....	....	....	....	....	....	....	....
1990-91	AC Nitra	Czech	49	23	22	45	14	....	....	....	....	....	....	....	....	....	....	....	....	....	....	....	....	....	....
1991-92	Kolner EC	Germany	33	19	18	37	35	....	....	....	....	....	....	....	....	....	4	1	1	2	0	....	....	....	....
	Boston	**NHL**	**4**	**1**	**0**	**1**	**0**	**0**	**0**	**0**	**3**	**33.3**	**1**	....	....	....	....	....	....	....	....	....	....	....	....
1992-93	**Boston**	**NHL**	**13**	**1**	**3**	**4**	**4**	**0**	**0**	**0**	**8**	**12.5**	**–3**	....	....	....	....	....	....	....	....	....	....	....	....
	Providence Bruins	AHL	56	31	61	92	26	....	....	....	....	....	....	....	....	....	6	4	4	8	0	....	....	....	....
1993-94	**Boston**	**NHL**	**59**	**8**	**15**	**23**	**14**	**0**	**0**	**1**	**62**	**12.9**	**4**	....	....	....	**13**	**1**	**7**	**8**	**4**	**0**	**0**	**0**	....
	Providence Bruins	AHL	17	5	12	17	4	....	....	....	....	....	....	....	....	....	....	....	....	....	....	....	....	....	....
1994-95	Kolner Haie	Germany	25	16	23	39	18	....	....	....	....	....	....	....	....	....	....	....	....	....	....	....	....	....	....
	Boston	**NHL**	**44**	**5**	**13**	**18**	**8**	**1**	**0**	**2**	**46**	**10.9**	**4**	....	....	....	**5**	**0**	**0**	**0**	**0**	**0**	**0**	**0**	....
1995-96	**Boston**	**NHL**	**76**	**18**	**36**	**54**	**14**	**5**	**0**	**2**	**158**	**11.4**	**–8**	....	....	....	**5**	**1**	**2**	**3**	**0**	**0**	**0**	**0**	....
1996-97	**Boston**	**NHL**	**78**	**21**	**55**	**76**	**14**	**6**	**0**	**1**	**168**	**12.5**	**–22**	....	....	....	....	....	....	....	....	....	....	....	....
1997-98	**Los Angeles**	**NHL**	**77**	**21**	**58**	**79**	**53**	**4**	**0**	**2**	**162**	**13.0**	**17**	....	....	....	**4**	**1**	**2**	**3**	**2**	**0**	**0**	**0**	....
1998-99	**Los Angeles**	**NHL**	**64**	**13**	**21**	**34**	**10**	**1**	**0**	**1**	**131**	**9.9**	**–18**	**1484**	**54.0**	**19:44**	....	....	....	....	....	....	....	....	....
99-2000	**Los Angeles**	**NHL**	**57**	**17**	**41**	**58**	**10**	**3**	**0**	**7**	**126**	**13.5**	**23**	**1088**	**50.6**	**19:16**	**4**	**0**	**4**	**4**	**8**	**0**	**0**	**0**	**21:05**
2000-01	Slov. Bratislava	Slovakia	9	2	4	6	16	....	....	....	....	....	....	....	....	....	....	....	....	....	....	....	....	....	....
	Los Angeles	**NHL**	**63**	**16**	**39**	**55**	**14**	**9**	**0**	**6**	**95**	**16.8**	**20**	**1278**	**52.7**	**19:35**	**13**	**3**	**5**	**8**	**10**	**2**	**0**	**1**	**21:56**
2001-02	**Los Angeles**	**NHL**	**9**	**1**	**3**	**4**	**4**	**0**	**0**	**0**	**7**	**14.3**	**1**	**164**	**48.2**	**20:06**	....	....	....	....	....	....	....	....	....
	Boston	**NHL**	**72**	**7**	**47**	**54**	**14**	**1**	**0**	**3**	**93**	**7.5**	**21**	**1346**	**49.7**	**18:36**	**6**	**0**	**2**	**2**	**0**	**0**	**0**	**0**	**16:43**
	Slovakia	Olympics	2	2	1	3	0	....	....	....	....	....	....	....	....	....	....	....	....	....	....	....	....	....	....
2002-03	**Boston**	**NHL**	**78**	**14**	**37**	**51**	**12**	**4**	**0**	**2**	**110**	**12.7**	**0**	**1601**	**54.7**	**18:27**	**5**	**0**	**2**	**2**	**0**	**0**	**0**	**0**	**17:31**
2003-04	**Los Angeles**	**NHL**	**64**	**8**	**29**	**37**	**16**	**4**	**0**	**0**	**78**	**10.3**	**5**	**1105**	**49.3**	**18:46**	....	....	....	....	....	....	....	....	....
	NHL Totals		**758**	**151**	**397**	**548**	**187**	**38**	**0**	**27**	**1247**	**12.1**		**8066**	**52.0**	**19:03**	**55**	**6**	**24**	**30**	**24**	**2**	**0**	**1**	**19:55**

Traded to **Los Angeles** by **Boston** with Sandy Moger and Boston's 4th round choice (later traded to New Jersey – New Jersey selected Pierre Dagenais) in 1998 Entry Draft for Dmitri Kristich and Byron Dafoe, August 29, 1997. Traded to **Boston** by **Los Angeles** with Glen Murray for Jason Allison and Mikko Eloranta, October 24, 2001. Traded to **Los Angeles** by **Boston** with Boston's 7th round choice (later traded to Nashville – Nashville selected Miroslav Hanuljak) in 2003 Entry Draft for Philadelphia's 4th round choice (previously acquired, Boston selected Patrick Valcak) in 2003 Entry Draft and Detroit's 2nd round choice (previously acquired, Boston selected Martins Karsums) in 2004 Entry Draft, June 22, 2003.

			Regular Season														Playoffs								
Season	Club	League	GP	G	A	Pts	PIM	PP	SH	GW	S	%	+/-	TF	F%	Min	GP	G	A	Pts	PIM	PP	SH	GW	Min

STURM, Marco
(STURHM, MAHR-koh) **S.J.**

Left wing. Shoots left. 6', 195 lbs. Born, Dingolfing, West Germany, September 8, 1978. San Jose's 2nd choice, 21st overall, in 1996 Entry Draft.

Season	Club	League	GP	G	A	Pts	PIM	PP	SH	GW	S	%	+/-	TF	F%	Min	GP	G	A	Pts	PIM	PP	SH	GW	Min
1995-96	EV Landshut	Germany	47	12	20	32	50	....	....	....	....	....	....	....	....	....	11	1	3	4	18	....	....	....	....
1996-97	EV Landshut	Germany	46	16	27	43	40	....	....	....	....	....	....	....	....	....	7	1	4	5	6	....	....	....	....
1997-98	**San Jose**	**NHL**	**74**	**10**	**20**	**30**	**40**	**2**	**0**	**3**	**118**	**8.5**	**–2**	....	....	....	**2**	**0**	**0**	**0**	**0**	**0**	**0**	**0**	....
	Germany	Olympics	2	0	0	0	0	....	....	....	....	....	....	....	....	....	....	....	....	....	....	....	....	....	....
1998-99	**San Jose**	**NHL**	**78**	**16**	**22**	**38**	**52**	**3**	**2**	**3**	**140**	**11.4**	**7**	**576**	**45.0**	**15:23**	**6**	**2**	**2**	**4**	**4**	**0**	**0**	**1**	**14:16**
99-2000	**San Jose**	**NHL**	**74**	**12**	**15**	**27**	**22**	**2**	**4**	**3**	**120**	**10.0**	**4**	**183**	**45.4**	**14:07**	**12**	**1**	**3**	**4**	**6**	**0**	**0**	**0**	**13:00**
2000-01	**San Jose**	**NHL**	**81**	**14**	**18**	**32**	**28**	**2**	**3**	**5**	**153**	**9.2**	**9**	**517**	**40.2**	**16:06**	**6**	**0**	**2**	**2**	**0**	**0**	**0**	**0**	**18:18**
2001-02	**San Jose**	**NHL**	**77**	**21**	**20**	**41**	**32**	**4**	**3**	**5**	**174**	**12.1**	**23**	**105**	**47.6**	**15:39**	**12**	**3**	**2**	**5**	**2**	**0**	**0**	**0**	**15:33**
	Germany	Olympics	5	0	1	1	0	....	....	....	....	....	....	....	....	....	....	....	....	....	....	....	....	....	....
2002-03	**San Jose**	**NHL**	**82**	**28**	**20**	**48**	**16**	**6**	**0**	**2**	**208**	**13.5**	**9**	**83**	**48.2**	**16:31**	....	....	....	....	....	....	....	....	....
2003-04	**San Jose**	**NHL**	**64**	**21**	**20**	**41**	**36**	**10**	**2**	**6**	**158**	**13.3**	**0**	**7**	**42.9**	**16:25**	....	....	....	....	....	....	....	....	....
	NHL Totals		**530**	**122**	**135**	**257**	**226**	**29**	**14**	**27**	**1071**	**11.4**		**1471**	**43.7**	**15:42**	**38**	**6**	**9**	**15**	**12**	**0**	**0**	**1**	**14:56**

Played in NHL All-Star Game (1999)

STUTZEL, Mike
(STUHT-zuhl, MIGHK) **PHX.**

Left wing. Shoots left. 6'2", 216 lbs. Born, Victoria, B.C., February 28, 1979.

Season	Club	League	GP	G	A	Pts	PIM	PP	SH	GW	S	%	+/-	TF	F%	Min	GP	G	A	Pts	PIM	PP	SH	GW	Min
1997-98	Powell River Kings	BCHL	24	7	5	12	38	....	....	....	....	....	....	....	....	....	....	....	....	....	....	....	....	....	....
	Prince George	BCHL	28	13	22	35	20	....	....	....	....	....	....	....	....	....	9	4	1	5	18	....	....	....	....
1998-99	Prince George	BCHL	58	41	51	92	102	....	....	....	....	....	....	....	....	....	....	....	....	....	....	....	....	....	....
99-2000	North. Michigan	CCHA	29	3	6	9	44	....	....	....	....	....	....	....	....	....	....	....	....	....	....	....	....	....	....
2000-01	North. Michigan	CCHA	16	3	5	8	6	....	....	....	....	....	....	....	....	....	....	....	....	....	....	....	....	....	....
2001-02	North. Michigan	CCHA	40	16	17	33	20	....	....	....	....	....	....	....	....	....	....	....	....	....	....	....	....	....	....
2002-03	North. Michigan	CCHA	41	27	15	42	50	....	....	....	....	....	....	....	....	....	....	....	....	....	....	....	....	....	....
2003-04	**Phoenix**	**NHL**	**9**	**0**	**0**	**0**	**0**	**0**	**0**	**0**	**3**	**0.0**	**–4**	**1**	**0.0**	**5:47**	....	....	....	....	....	....	....	....	....
	Springfield	AHL	62	12	12	24	39	....	....	....	....	....	....	....	....	....	....	....	....	....	....	....	....	....	....
	NHL Totals		**9**	**0**	**0**	**0**	**0**	**0**	**0**	**0**	**3**	**0.0**		**1**	**0.0**	**5:47**	....	....	....	....	....	....	....	....	....

Signed as a free agent by **Phoenix**, April 10, 2003.

SUCHY, Radoslav
(soo-KHEE, RAD-oh-slav) **CBJ**

Defense. Shoots left. 6'2", 204 lbs. Born, Kezmarok, Czech., April 7, 1976.

Season	Club	League	GP	G	A	Pts	PIM	PP	SH	GW	S	%	+/-	TF	F%	Min	GP	G	A	Pts	PIM	PP	SH	GW	Min
1993-94	SKP PS Poprad Jr.	Slovak-Jr.	30	11	12	23	16	....	....	....	....	....	....	....	....	....	....	....	....	....	....	....	....	....	....
	SKP PS Poprad	Slovakia	3	0	0	0	0	....	....	....	....	....	....	....	....	....	....	....	....	....	....	....	....	....	....
1994-95	Sherbrooke	QMJHL	69	12	32	44	30	....	....	....	....	....	....	....	....	....	7	0	3	3	2	....	....	....	....
1995-96	Sherbrooke	QMJHL	68	15	53	68	68	....	....	....	....	....	....	....	....	....	7	0	3	3	2	....	....	....	....
1996-97	Sherbrooke	QMJHL	32	6	34	40	14	....	....	....	....	....	....	....	....	....	....	....	....	....	....	....	....	....	....
	Chicoutimi	QMJHL	28	5	24	29	26	....	....	....	....	....	....	....	....	....	19	6	15	21	12	....	....	....	....
1997-98	Las Vegas	IHL	26	1	4	5	10	....	....	....	....	....	....	....	....	....	....	....	....	....	....	....	....	....	....
	Springfield	AHL	41	6	15	21	16	....	....	....	....	....	....	....	....	....	4	0	1	1	2	....	....	....	....
1998-99	Springfield	AHL	69	4	32	36	10	....	....	....	....	....	....	....	....	....	3	0	1	1	0	....	....	....	....
99-2000	**Phoenix**	**NHL**	**60**	**0**	**6**	**6**	**16**	**0**	**0**	**0**	**36**	**0.0**	**2**	**0**	**0.0**	**15:09**	**5**	**0**	**1**	**1**	**0**	**0**	**0**	**0**	**16:18**
	Springfield	AHL	2	0	1	1	0	....	....	....	....	....	....	....	....	....	....	....	....	....	....	....	....	....	....
2000-01	**Phoenix**	**NHL**	**72**	**0**	**10**	**10**	**22**	**0**	**0**	**0**	**33**	**0.0**	**1**	**0**	**0.0**	**17:09**	....	....	....	....	....	....	....	....	....
2001-02	**Phoenix**	**NHL**	**81**	**4**	**13**	**17**	**10**	**1**	**0**	**0**	**49**	**8.2**	**25**	**1**	**100.0**	**18:05**	**5**	**1**	**0**	**1**	**0**	**0**	**0**	**0**	**20:35**
2002-03	**Phoenix**	**NHL**	**77**	**1**	**8**	**9**	**18**	**1**	**0**	**0**	**48**	**2.1**	**2**	**1**	**0.0**	**16:26**	....	....	....	....	....	....	....	....	....
2003-04	**Phoenix**	**NHL**	**82**	**7**	**14**	**21**	**8**	**2**	**0**	**2**	**82**	**8.5**	**1**	**1**	**100.0**	**19:40**	....	....	....	....	....	....	....	....	....
	NHL Totals		**372**	**12**	**51**	**63**	**74**	**4**	**0**	**2**	**248**	**4.8**		**3**	**66.7**	**17:26**	**10**	**1**	**1**	**2**	**0**	**0**	**0**	**0**	**18:27**

QMJHL All-Rookie Team (1995) • QMJHL Second All-Star Team (1997) • George Parsons Trophy (Memorial Cup Most Sportsmanlike Player) (1997)

Signed as a free agent by **Phoenix**, September 26, 1997. Traded to **Columbus** by **Phoenix** with Phoenix's 6th round choice in 2005 Entry Draft for Columbus' 4th round choice in 2005 Entry Draft, July 6, 2004.

SUGLOBOV, Aleksander
(suh-GLOH-bahf, al-ehx-AN-duhr) **N.J.**

Right wing. Shoots left. 6', 200 lbs. Born, Elektrostal, USSR, January 15, 1982. New Jersey's 3rd choice, 56th overall, in 2000 Entry Draft.

Season	Club	League	GP	G	A	Pts	PIM	PP	SH	GW	S	%	+/-	TF	F%	Min	GP	G	A	Pts	PIM	PP	SH	GW	Min
1998-99	Spartak Mos. 2	Russia-4	1	0	0	0	0	....	....	....	....	....	....	....	....	....	....	....	....	....	....	....	....	....	....
	Spartak Moscow	Russia	1	0	0	0	0	....	....	....	....	....	....	....	....	....	....	....	....	....	....	....	....	....	....
99-2000	Yaroslavl 2	Russia-3	38	23	10	33	....	....	....	....	....	....	....	....	....	....	....	....	....	....	....	....	....	....	....
2000-01	St. Petersburg	Russia	8	1	0	1	6	....	....	....	....	....	....	....	....	....	....	....	....	....	....	....	....	....	....
	Ufa Salavat	Russia	6	0	0	0	4	....	....	....	....	....	....	....	....	....	....	....	....	....	....	....	....	....	....
	Yaroslavl	Russia	4	0	0	0	2	....	....	....	....	....	....	....	....	....	11	1	2	3	6	....	....	....	....
2001-02	Yaroslavl 2	Russia-3	6	5	2	7	20	....	....	....	....	....	....	....	....	....	....	....	....	....	....	....	....	....	....
	Yaroslavl	Russia	25	4	2	6	26	....	....	....	....	....	....	....	....	....	5	1	1	2	18	....	....	....	....
2002-03	Nizhnekamsk	Russia	6	0	0	0	4	....	....	....	....	....	....	....	....	....	....	....	....	....	....	....	....	....	....
	Yaroslavl	Russia	17	4	2	6	12	....	....	....	....	....	....	....	....	....	5	1	0	1	2	....	....	....	....
2003-04	**New Jersey**	**NHL**	**1**	**0**	**0**	**0**	**0**	**0**	**0**	**0**	**2**	**0.0**	**0**	**0**	**0.0**	**8:18**	....	....	....	....	....	....	....	....	....
	Albany River Rats	AHL	35	11	11	22	54	....	....	....	....	....	....	....	....	....	....	....	....	....	....	....	....	....	....
	NHL Totals		**1**	**0**	**0**	**0**	**0**	**0**	**0**	**0**	**2**	**0.0**		**0**	**0.0**	**8:18**	....	....	....	....	....	....	....	....	....

• Missed majority of 2003-04 season recovering from wrist injury suffered in game vs. Edmonton, January 5, 2004.

SULLIVAN, Steve
(SUHL-ih-vuhn, STEEV) **NSH.**

Right wing. Shoots right. 5'9", 155 lbs. Born, Timmins, Ont., July 6, 1974. New Jersey's 10th choice, 233rd overall, in 1994 Entry Draft.

Season	Club	League	GP	G	A	Pts	PIM	PP	SH	GW	S	%	+/-	TF	F%	Min	GP	G	A	Pts	PIM	PP	SH	GW	Min
1991-92	Timmins	NOJHA	47	66	55	121	141	....	....	....	....	....	....	....	....	....	....	....	....	....	....	....	....	....	....
1992-93	Sault Ste. Marie	OHL	62	36	27	63	44	....	....	....	....	....	....	....	....	....	16	3	8	11	18	....	....	....	....
1993-94	Sault Ste. Marie	OHL	63	51	62	113	82	....	....	....	....	....	....	....	....	....	14	9	16	25	22	....	....	....	....
1994-95	Albany River Rats	AHL	75	31	50	81	124	....	....	....	....	....	....	....	....	....	14	4	7	11	10	....	....	....	....
1995-96	**New Jersey**	**NHL**	**16**	**5**	**4**	**9**	**8**	**2**	**0**	**1**	**23**	**21.7**	**3**	....	....	....	....	....	....	....	....	....	....	....	....
	Albany River Rats	AHL	53	33	42	75	127	....	....	....	....	....	....	....	....	....	4	3	0	3	6	....	....	....	....
1996-97	**New Jersey**	**NHL**	**33**	**8**	**14**	**22**	**14**	**2**	**0**	**2**	**63**	**12.7**	**9**	....	....	....	....	....	....	....	....	....	....	....	....
	Albany River Rats	AHL	15	8	7	15	16	....	....	....	....	....	....	....	....	....	....	....	....	....	....	....	....	....	....
	Toronto	**NHL**	**21**	**5**	**11**	**16**	**23**	**1**	**0**	**1**	**45**	**11.1**	**5**	....	....	....	....	....	....	....	....	....	....	....	....
1997-98	**Toronto**	**NHL**	**63**	**10**	**18**	**28**	**40**	**1**	**0**	**1**	**112**	**8.9**	**–8**	....	....	....	....	....	....	....	....	....	....	....	....
1998-99	**Toronto**	**NHL**	**63**	**20**	**20**	**40**	**28**	**4**	**0**	**5**	**110**	**18.2**	**12**	**685**	**44.4**	**14:12**	**13**	**3**	**3**	**6**	**14**	**2**	**0**	**0**	**16:20**
99-2000	**Toronto**	**NHL**	**7**	**0**	**1**	**1**	**4**	**0**	**0**	**0**	**11**	**0.0**	**–1**	**47**	**48.9**	**11:52**	....	....	....	....	....	....	....	....	....
	Chicago	**NHL**	**73**	**22**	**42**	**64**	**52**	**2**	**1**	**6**	**169**	**13.0**	**20**	**692**	**48.0**	**18:05**	....	....	....	....	....	....	....	....	....
2000-01	**Chicago**	**NHL**	**81**	**34**	**41**	**75**	**54**	**6**	**8**	**3**	**204**	**16.7**	**3**	**649**	**42.4**	**20:32**	....	....	....	....	....	....	....	....	....
2001-02	**Chicago**	**NHL**	**78**	**21**	**39**	**60**	**67**	**3**	**0**	**8**	**155**	**13.5**	**23**	**758**	**48.9**	**19:10**	**5**	**1**	**0**	**1**	**2**	**0**	**0**	**0**	**18:04**
2002-03	**Chicago**	**NHL**	**82**	**26**	**35**	**61**	**42**	**4**	**2**	**3**	**190**	**13.7**	**15**	**382**	**46.1**	**19:15**	....	....	....	....	....	....	....	....	....
2003-04	**Chicago**	**NHL**	**56**	**15**	**28**	**43**	**36**	**4**	**2**	**4**	**140**	**10.7**	**–7**	**103**	**44.7**	**21:19**	....	....	....	....	....	....	....	....	....
	Nashville	**NHL**	**24**	**9**	**21**	**30**	**12**	**7**	**0**	**0**	**78**	**11.5**	**8**	**124**	**43.6**	**20:02**	**6**	**1**	**1**	**2**	**6**	**0**	**0**	**1**	**18:58**
	NHL Totals		**597**	**175**	**274**	**449**	**380**	**36**	**13**	**34**	**1300**	**13.5**		**3440**	**46.0**	**18:46**	**24**	**5**	**4**	**9**	**22**	**2**	**0**	**1**	**17:21**

AHL First All-Star Team (1996)

Traded to **Toronto** by **New Jersey** with Jason Smith and the rights to Alyn McCauley for Doug Gilmour, Dave Ellett and New Jersey's 3rd round choice (previously acquired, New Jersey selected Andre Lakos) in 1999 Entry Draft, February 25, 1997. Claimed on waivers by **Chicago** from **Toronto**, October 23, 1999. Traded to **Nashville** by **Chicago** for Nashville's 2nd round choices in 2004 (Ryan Garlock) and 2005 Entry Drafts, February 16, 2004.

SUNDIN, Mats
(suhn-DEEN, MATS) **TOR.**

Center. Shoots right. 6'5", 231 lbs. Born, Bromma, Sweden, February 13, 1971. Quebec's 1st choice, 1st overall, in 1989 Entry Draft.

Season	Club	League	GP	G	A	Pts	PIM	PP	SH	GW	S	%	+/-	TF	F%	Min	GP	G	A	Pts	PIM	PP	SH	GW	Min
1988-89	Nacka HK	Swede-2	25	10	8	18	18	....	....	....	....	....	....	....	....	....	....	....	....	....	....	....	....	....	....
1989-90	Djurgarden	Sweden	34	10	8	18	16	....	....	....	....	....	....	....	....	....	8	7	0	7	4	....	....	....	....
1990-91	**Quebec**	**NHL**	**80**	**23**	**36**	**59**	**58**	**4**	**0**	**0**	**155**	**14.8**	**–24**	....	....	....	....	....	....	....	....	....	....	....	....
1991-92	**Quebec**	**NHL**	**80**	**33**	**43**	**76**	**103**	**8**	**2**	**2**	**231**	**14.3**	**–19**	....	....	....	....	....	....	....	....	....	....	....	....
1992-93	**Quebec**	**NHL**	**80**	**47**	**67**	**114**	**96**	**13**	**4**	**9**	**215**	**21.9**	**21**	....	....	....	**6**	**3**	**1**	**4**	**6**	**1**	**0**	**0**	....
1993-94	**Quebec**	**NHL**	**84**	**32**	**53**	**85**	**60**	**6**	**2**	**4**	**226**	**14.2**	**1**	....	....	....	....	....	....	....	....	....	....	....	....

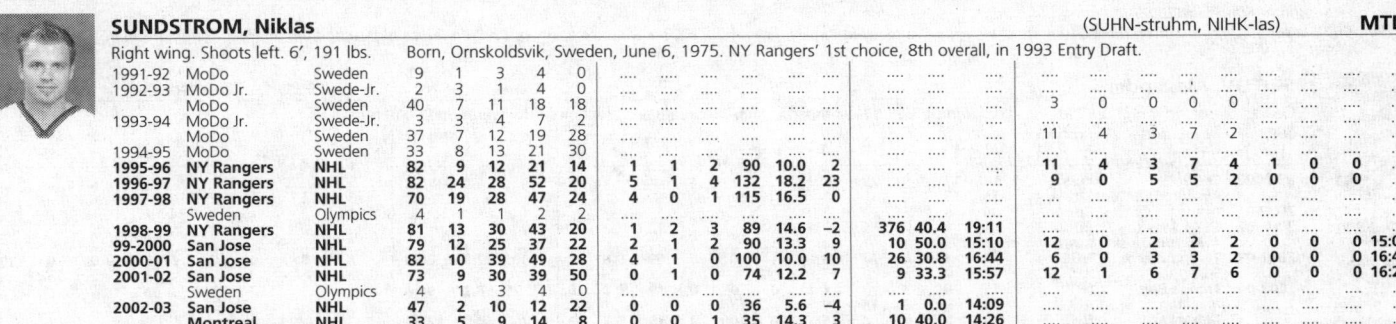

			Regular Season														Playoffs								
Season	Club	League	GP	G	A	Pts	PIM	PP	SH	GW	S	%	+/-	TF	F%	Min	GP	G	A	Pts	PIM	PP	SH	GW	Min
1994-95	Djurgarden	Sweden	12	7	2	9	14	....	....	....	....	....	....	....	....	....	....	....	....	....	....	....	....	....	....
	Toronto	NHL	47	23	24	47	14	9	0	4	173	13.3	–5	....	....	....	7	5	4	9	4	2	0	1	....
1995-96	Toronto	NHL	76	33	50	83	46	7	6	7	301	11.0	8	....	....	....	6	3	1	4	4	2	0	1	....
1996-97	Toronto	NHL	82	41	53	94	59	7	4	8	281	14.6	6	....	....	....	....	....	....	....	....	....	....	....	....
1997-98	Toronto	NHL	82	33	41	74	49	9	1	5	219	15.1	–3	....	....	....	....	....	....	....	....	....	....	....	....
	Sweden	Olympics	4	3	0	3	4	....	....	....	....	....	....	....	....	....	....	....	....	....	....	....	....	....	....
1998-99	Toronto	NHL	82	31	52	83	58	4	0	6	209	14.8	22	1993	57.3	20:41	17	8	8	16	16	3	0	2	22:46
99-2000	Toronto	NHL	73	32	41	73	46	10	2	7	184	17.4	16	1619	50.8	20:11	12	3	5	8	10	0	0	1	21:27
2000-01	Toronto	NHL	82	28	46	74	76	9	0	6	226	12.4	15	1870	56.6	19:21	11	6	7	13	14	2	1	1	20:12
2001-02	Toronto	NHL	82	41	39	80	94	10	2	9	262	15.6	6	1812	57.5	19:20	8	2	5	7	4	0	0	0	20:07
	Sweden	Olympics	4	5	4	*9	10	....	....	....	....	....	....	....	....	....	....	....	....	....	....	....	....	....	....
2002-03	Toronto	NHL	75	37	35	72	58	16	3	8	223	16.6	1	1774	56.1	20:15	7	1	3	4	6	1	0	0	24:17
2003-04	Toronto	NHL	81	31	44	75	52	11	1	10	226	13.7	11	1705	53.0	19:52	9	4	5	9	8	0	0	1	18:24
	NHL Totals		1086	465	624	1089	869	123	27	85	3131	14.9		10773	55.4	19:56	83	35	39	74	72	11	1	7	21:18

NHL Second All-Star Team (2002, 2004)

Played in NHL All-Star Game (1996, 1997, 1998, 1999, 2000, 2001, 2002, 2004)

Traded to **Toronto** by **Quebec** with Garth Butcher, Todd Warriner and Philadelphia's 1st round choice (previously acquired, later traded to Washington – Washington selected Nolan Baumgartner) in 1994 Entry Draft for Wendel Clark, Sylvain Lefebvre, Landon Wilson and Toronto's 1st round choice (Jeffrey Kealty) in 1994 Entry Draft, June 28, 1994.

SUNDSTROM, Niklas

(SUHN-struhm, NIHK-las) **MTL.**

Right wing. Shoots left. 6', 191 lbs. Born, Ornskoldsvik, Sweden, June 6, 1975. NY Rangers' 1st choice, 8th overall, in 1993 Entry Draft.

1991-92	MoDo	Sweden	9	1	3	4	0	....	....	....	....	....	....	....	....	....	....	....	....	....	....	....	....	....	....
1992-93	MoDo Jr.	Swede-Jr.	2	3	1	4	0	....	....	....	....	....	....	....	....	....	....	....	....	....	....	....	....	....	....
	MoDo	Sweden	40	7	11	18	18	....	....	....	....	....	....	....	....	....	3	0	0	0	0	....	....	....	....
1993-94	MoDo Jr.	Swede-Jr.	3	3	4	7	2	....	....	....	....	....	....	....	....	....	....	....	....	....	....	....	....	....	....
	MoDo	Sweden	37	7	12	19	28	....	....	....	....	....	....	....	....	....	11	4	3	7	2	....	....	....	....
1994-95	MoDo	Sweden	33	8	13	21	30	....	....	....	....	....	....	....	....	....	....	....	....	....	....	....	....	....	....
1995-96	NY Rangers	NHL	82	9	12	21	14	1	1	2	90	10.0	2	....	....	....	11	4	3	7	4	1	0	0	....
1996-97	NY Rangers	NHL	82	24	28	52	20	5	1	4	132	18.2	23	....	....	....	9	0	5	5	2	0	0	0	....
1997-98	NY Rangers	NHL	70	19	28	47	24	4	0	1	115	16.5	0	....	....	....	....	....	....	....	....	....	....	....	....
	Sweden	Olympics	4	1	1	2	2	....	....	....	....	....	....	....	....	....	....	....	....	....	....	....	....	....	....
1998-99	NY Rangers	NHL	81	13	30	43	20	1	2	3	89	14.6	–2	376	40.4	19:11	....	....	....	....	....	....	....	....	....
99-2000	San Jose	NHL	79	12	25	37	22	2	1	2	90	13.3	9	10	50.0	15:10	12	0	2	2	2	0	0	0	15:09
2000-01	San Jose	NHL	82	10	39	49	28	4	1	0	100	10.0	10	26	30.8	16:44	6	0	3	3	2	0	0	0	16:40
2001-02	San Jose	NHL	73	9	30	39	50	0	1	0	74	12.2	7	9	33.3	15:57	12	1	6	7	6	0	0	0	16:25
	Sweden	Olympics	4	1	3	4	0	....	....	....	....	....	....	....	....	....	....	....	....	....	....	....	....	....	....
2002-03	San Jose	NHL	47	2	10	12	22	0	0	0	36	5.6	–4	1	0.0	14:09	....	....	....	....	....	....	....	....	....
	Montreal	NHL	33	5	9	14	8	0	0	1	35	14.3	3	10	40.0	14:26	....	....	....	....	....	....	....	....	....
2003-04	Montreal	NHL	66	8	12	20	18	0	0	2	67	11.9	3	20	15.0	14:17	4	1	0	1	2	0	0	0	13:10
	NHL Totals		695	111	223	334	226	17	7	15	828	13.4		452	38.7	16:00	54	6	19	25	18	1	0	0	15:38

Traded to **Tampa Bay** by **NY Rangers** with Dan Cloutier and NY Rangers' 1st (Nikita Alexeev) and 3rd (later traded to San Jose – later traded to Chicago – Chicago selected Igor Radulov) round choices in 2000 Entry Draft for Chicago's 1st round choice (previously acquired, NY Rangers selected Pavel Brendl) in 1999 Entry Draft, June 26, 1999. Traded to **San Jose** by **Tampa Bay** with NY Rangers' 3rd round choice (previously acquired, later traded to Chicago – Chicago selected Igor Radulov) in 2000 Entry Draft for Bill Houlder, Andrei Zyuzin, Shawn Burr and Steve Guolla, August 4, 1999. Traded to **Montreal** by **San Jose** with San Jose's 3rd round choice (later traded to Los Angeles – Los Angeles selected Paul Baier) in 2004 Entry Draft for Jeff Hackett, January 23, 2003.

SURMA, Damian

(SUHR-ma, DAY-mee-an) **CAR.**

Center. Shoots left. 5'10", 200 lbs. Born, Lincoln Park, MI, January 22, 1981. Carolina's 5th choice, 174th overall, in 1999 Entry Draft.

1997-98	Det. Compuware	NAJHL	54	12	18	30	54	....	....	....	....	....	....	....	....	....	7	1	4	5	10	....	....	....	....
1998-99	Plymouth Whalers	OHL	65	17	15	32	62	....	....	....	....	....	....	....	....	....	11	3	6	9	15	....	....	....	....
99-2000	Plymouth Whalers	OHL	66	34	44	78	114	....	....	....	....	....	....	....	....	....	20	9	8	17	10	....	....	....	....
2000-01	Plymouth Whalers	OHL	55	26	34	60	62	....	....	....	....	....	....	....	....	....	19	8	9	17	25	....	....	....	....
2001-02	Plymouth Whalers	OHL	55	28	27	55	68	....	....	....	....	....	....	....	....	....	6	3	0	3	10	....	....	....	....
	Lowell	AHL	1	0	0	0	0	....	....	....	....	....	....	....	....	....	4	0	0	0	0	....	....	....	....
2002-03	Carolina	NHL	1	1	0	1	0	0	0	0	1	100.0	0	0	0.0	7:15	....	....	....	....	....	....	....	....	....
	Lowell	AHL	68	11	11	22	46	....	....	....	....	....	....	....	....	....	....	....	....	....	....	....	....	....	....
2003-04	Carolina	NHL	1	0	1	1	0	0	0	0	0	0.0	1	0	0.0	9:26	....	....	....	....	....	....	....	....	....
	Lowell	AHL	48	3	5	8	21	....	....	....	....	....	....	....	....	....	....	....	....	....	....	....	....	....	....
	Florida Everblades	ECHL	18	6	9	15	20	....	....	....	....	....	....	....	....	....	16	5	4	9	20	....	....	....	....
	NHL Totals		2	1	1	2	0	0	0	0	1	100.0		0	0.0	8:21	....	....	....	....	....	....	....	....	....

SUROVY, Tomas

(suh-ROH-vee, TAW-mahsh) **PIT.**

Center. Shoots left. 6'1", 205 lbs. Born, Banska Bystrica, Czech., September 24, 1981. Pittsburgh's 5th choice, 120th overall, in 2001 Entry Draft.

99-2000	Banska Bystrica	Slovak-2	39	25	29	54	4	....	....	....	....	....	....	....	....	....	....	....	....	....	....	....	....	....	....
2000-01	HC SKP Poprad	Slovakia	53	22	28	50	30	....	....	....	....	....	....	....	....	....	6	2	1	3	14	....	....	....	....
2001-02	Wilkes-Barre	AHL	65	23	10	33	37	....	....	....	....	....	....	....	....	....	....	....	....	....	....	....	....	....	....
2002-03	Pittsburgh	NHL	26	4	7	11	10	1	0	2	47	8.5	0	2	50.0	14:19	....	....	....	....	....	....	....	....	....
	Wilkes-Barre	AHL	39	19	20	39	18	....	....	....	....	....	....	....	....	....	6	2	3	5	2	....	....	....	....
2003-04	Pittsburgh	NHL	47	11	12	23	16	3	0	1	112	9.8	–8	4	25.0	12:28	....	....	....	....	....	....	....	....	....
	Wilkes-Barre	AHL	30	14	15	29	14	....	....	....	....	....	....	....	....	....	24	6	10	16	8	....	....	....	....
	NHL Totals		73	15	19	34	26	4	0	3	159	9.4		6	33.3	13:08	....	....	....	....	....	....	....	....	....

SUTHERBY, Brian

(SUH-thur-bee, BRIGH-uhn) **WSH.**

Center. Shoots left. 6'3", 205 lbs. Born, Edmonton, Alta., March 1, 1982. Washington's 1st choice, 26th overall, in 2000 Entry Draft.

1997-98	CAC Cement	AMHL	36	36	23	59	60	....	....	....	....	....	....	....	....	....	....	....	....	....	....	....	....	....	....
1998-99	Moose Jaw	WHL	66	9	12	21	47	....	....	....	....	....	....	....	....	....	11	0	1	1	0	....	....	....	....
99-2000	Moose Jaw	WHL	47	18	17	35	102	....	....	....	....	....	....	....	....	....	4	1	1	2	12	....	....	....	....
2000-01	Moose Jaw	WHL	59	34	43	77	138	....	....	....	....	....	....	....	....	....	4	2	1	3	10	....	....	....	....
2001-02	Washington	NHL	7	0	0	0	2	0	0	0	3	0.0	–3	39	35.9	7:17	....	....	....	....	....	....	....	....	....
	Moose Jaw	WHL	36	18	27	45	75	....	....	....	....	....	....	....	....	....	12	7	5	12	33	....	....	....	....
2002-03	Washington	NHL	72	2	9	11	93	0	0	0	38	5.3	7	288	43.8	9:44	5	0	0	0	10	0	0	0	4:10
	Portland Pirates	AHL	5	0	5	5	11	....	....	....	....	....	....	....	....	....	....	....	....	....	....	....	....	....	....
2003-04	Washington	NHL	30	2	0	2	28	0	0	0	24	8.3	–5	116	41.4	10:15	....	....	....	....	....	....	....	....	....
	Portland Pirates	AHL	6	2	4	6	16	....	....	....	....	....	....	....	....	....	....	....	....	....	....	....	....	....	....
	NHL Totals		109	4	9	13	123	0	0	0	65	6.2		443	42.4	9:43	5	0	0	0	10	0	0	0	4:10

• Missed majority of 2003-04 season recovering from groin injury suffered in game vs. St. Louis, October 18, 2003.

SUTTON, Andy

(SUH-tohn, AN-dee) **ATL.**

Defense. Shoots left. 6'6", 245 lbs. Born, Kingston, Ont., March 10, 1975.

1991-92	Gananoque	OJHL-B	36	11	9	20	....	....	....	....	....	....	....	....	....	....	14	9	21	30	....	....	....	....	....
1992-93	Gananoque	OJHL-B	38	14	9	23	....	....	....	....	....	....	....	....	....	....	12	16	13	29	....	....	....	....	....
1993-94	St. Michael's B	MTJHL	48	17	23	40	161	....	....	....	....	....	....	....	....	....	3	0	0	0	20	....	....	....	....
1994-95	Michigan Tech	WCHA	19	2	1	3	42	....	....	....	....	....	....	....	....	....	....	....	....	....	....	....	....	....	....
1995-96	Michigan Tech	WCHA	33	2	2	4	58	....	....	....	....	....	....	....	....	....	....	....	....	....	....	....	....	....	....
1996-97	Michigan Tech	WCHA	32	2	7	9	73	....	....	....	....	....	....	....	....	....	....	....	....	....	....	....	....	....	....
1997-98	Michigan Tech	WCHA	38	16	24	40	97	....	....	....	....	....	....	....	....	....	....	....	....	....	....	....	....	....	....
	Kentucky	AHL	7	0	0	0	33	....	....	....	....	....	....	....	....	....	....	....	....	....	....	....	....	....	....
1998-99	San Jose	NHL	31	0	3	3	65	0	0	0	24	0.0	–4	0	0.0	12:58	....	....	....	....	....	....	....	....	....
	Kentucky	AHL	21	5	10	15	53	....	....	....	....	....	....	....	....	....	5	0	0	0	23	....	....	....	....
99-2000	San Jose	NHL	40	1	1	2	80	0	0	0	29	3.4	–5	0	0.0	12:57	....	....	....	....	....	....	....	....	....
	Kentucky	AHL	3	0	1	1	0	....	....	....	....	....	....	....	....	....	....	....	....	....	....	....	....	....	....
2000-01	Minnesota	NHL	69	3	4	7	131	2	0	0	64	4.7	–11	3	33.3	12:55	....	....	....	....	....	....	....	....	....
2001-02	Minnesota	NHL	19	2	4	6	35	1	0	0	21	9.5	–4	2	0.0	10:57	....	....	....	....	....	....	....	....	....
	Atlanta	NHL	24	0	4	4	46	0	0	0	20	0.0	0	0	0.0	15:25	....	....	....	....	....	....	....	....	....

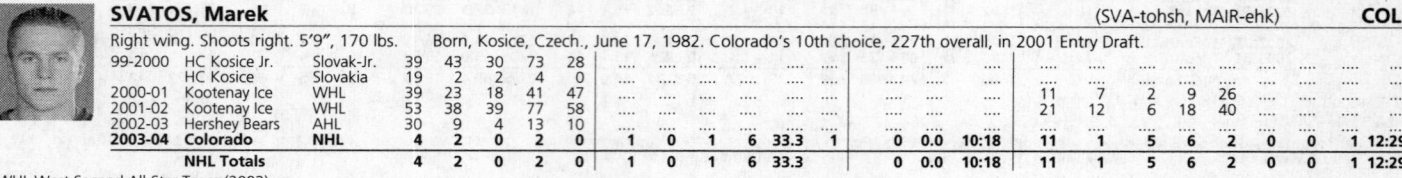

Season	Club	League	GP	G	A	Pts	PIM	PP	SH	GW	S	%	+/-	TF	F%	Min	GP	G	A	Pts	PIM	PP	SH	GW	Min
												Regular Season								**Playoffs**				
2002-03	Atlanta	NHL	53	3	18	21	114	1	1	0	65	4.6	–8	3	33.3	18:00	....	....	....	....	....	....	....	....	....
2003-04	Atlanta	NHL	65	8	13	21	94	7	1	1	102	7.8	0	1	0.0	23:21	....	....	....	....	....	....	....	....	....
	NHL Totals		301	17	47	64	565	11	2	1	325	5.2		9	22.2	16:09	....	....	....	....	....	....	....	....	....

WCHA Second All-Star Team (1998)

Signed as a free agent by **San Jose**, March 20, 1998. Traded to **Minnesota** by **San Jose** with San Jose's 7th round choice (Peter Bartos) in 2000 Entry Draft and 3rd round choice (later traded to Atlanta – later traded to Pittsburgh – later traded to Columbus – Columbus selected Aaron Johnson) in 2001 Entry Draft for Minnesota's 8th round choice (later traded to Calgary – Calgary selected Joe Campbell) in 2001 Entry Draft and future considerations, June 12, 2000. Traded to **Atlanta** by **Minnesota** for Hnat Domenichelli, January 22, 2002.

SVATOS, Marek

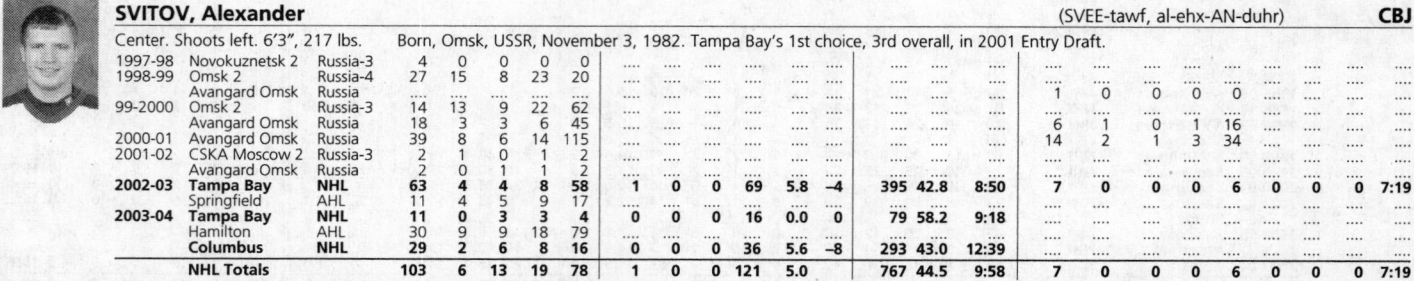

(SVA-tohsh, MAIR-ehk)   **COL.**

Right wing. Shoots right. 5'9", 170 lbs.   Born, Kosice, Czech., June 17, 1982. Colorado's 10th choice, 227th overall, in 2001 Entry Draft.

Season	Club	League	GP	G	A	Pts	PIM	PP	SH	GW	S	%	+/-	TF	F%	Min	GP	G	A	Pts	PIM	PP	SH	GW	Min
99-2000	HC Kosice Jr.	Slovak-Jr.	39	43	30	73	28	....	....	....	....	....	....				....	....	....	....	....				
	HC Kosice	Slovakia	19	2	2	4	0	....	....	....	....	....	....				....	....	....	....	....				
2000-01	Kootenay Ice	WHL	39	23	18	41	47	....	....	....	....	....	....				11	7	2	9	26				
2001-02	Kootenay Ice	WHL	53	38	39	77	58	....	....	....	....	....	....				21	12	6	18	40				
2002-03	Hershey Bears	AHL	30	9	4	13	10	....	....	....	....	....	....				....	....	....	....	....				
2003-04	**Colorado**	**NHL**	4	2	0	2	0	1	0	1	6	33.3	1	0	0.0	10:18	11	1	5	6	2	0	0	1	12:29
	NHL Totals		4	2	0	2	0	1	0	1	6	33.3		0	0.0	10:18	11	1	5	6	2	0	0	1	12:29

WHL West Second All-Star Team (2002)

• Missed majority of 2002-03 season recovering from shoulder injury that required surgery, January 28, 2003. • Missed majority of 2003-04 season recovering from shoulder injury suffered in game vs. St. Louis, October 12, 2003.

SVITOV, Alexander

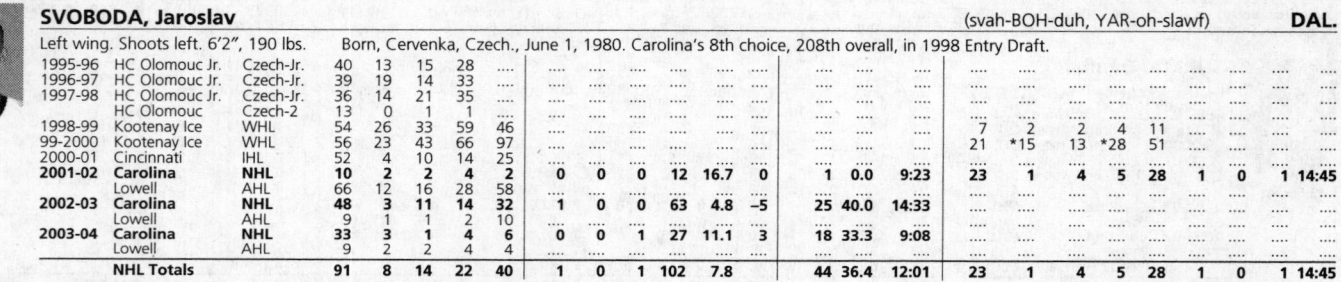

(SVEE-tawf, al-ehx-AN-duhr)   **CBJ**

Center. Shoots left. 6'3", 217 lbs.   Born, Omsk, USSR, November 3, 1982. Tampa Bay's 1st choice, 3rd overall, in 2001 Entry Draft.

Season	Club	League	GP	G	A	Pts	PIM	PP	SH	GW	S	%	+/-	TF	F%	Min	GP	G	A	Pts	PIM	PP	SH	GW	Min
1997-98	Novokuznetsk 2	Russia-3	4	0	0	0	0	....	....	....	....	....	....				....	....	....	....	....				
1998-99	Omsk 2	Russia-4	27	15	8	23	20	....	....	....	....	....	....				....	....	....	....	....				
	Avangard Omsk	Russia						....	....	....	....	....	....				1	0	0	0	0				
99-2000	Omsk 2	Russia-3	14	13	9	22	62	....	....	....	....	....	....				....	....	....	....	....				
	Avangard Omsk	Russia	18	3	3	6	45	....	....	....	....	....	....				6	1	0	1	16				
2000-01	Avangard Omsk	Russia	39	8	6	14	115	....	....	....	....	....	....				14	2	1	3	34				
2001-02	CSKA Moscow 2	Russia-3	2	1	0	1	2	....	....	....	....	....	....				....	....	....	....	....				
	Avangard Omsk	Russia	2	0	1	1	2	....	....	....	....	....	....				....	....	....	....	....				
2002-03	**Tampa Bay**	**NHL**	63	4	4	8	58	1	0	0	69	5.8	–4	395	42.8	8:50	7	0	0	0	6	0	0	0	7:19
	Springfield	AHL	11	4	5	9	17	....	....	....	....	....	....				....	....	....	....	....				
2003-04	**Tampa Bay**	**NHL**	11	0	3	3	4	0	0	0	16	0.0	0	79	58.2	9:18	....	....	....	....	....				
	Hamilton	AHL	30	9	9	18	79	....	....	....	....	....	....				....	....	....	....	....				
	Columbus	NHL	29	2	6	8	16	0	0	0	36	5.6	–8	293	43.0	12:39	....	....	....	....	....				
	NHL Totals		103	6	13	19	78	1	0	0	121	5.0		767	44.5	9:58	7	0	0	0	6	0	0	0	7:19

Traded to **Columbus** by **Tampa Bay** with Tampa Bay's 3rd round choice (later traded to Calgary – Calgary selected Dustin Boyd) in 2004 Entry Draft for Darryl Sydor and Columbus' 4th round choice (Mike Lundin) in 2004 Entry Draft, January 27, 2004.

SVOBODA, Jaroslav

(svah-BOH-duh, YAR-oh-slawf)   **DAL.**

Left wing. Shoots left. 6'2", 190 lbs.   Born, Cervenka, Czech., June 1, 1980. Carolina's 8th choice, 208th overall, in 1998 Entry Draft.

Season	Club	League	GP	G	A	Pts	PIM	PP	SH	GW	S	%	+/-	TF	F%	Min	GP	G	A	Pts	PIM	PP	SH	GW	Min
1995-96	HC Olomouc Jr.	Czech-Jr.	40	13	15	28	....	....	....	....	....	....	....				....	....	....	....	....				
1996-97	HC Olomouc Jr.	Czech-Jr.	39	19	14	33	....	....	....	....	....	....	....				....	....	....	....	....				
1997-98	HC Olomouc Jr.	Czech-Jr.	36	14	21	35	....	....	....	....	....	....	....				....	....	....	....	....				
	HC Olomouc	Czech-2	13	0	1	1	....	....	....	....	....	....	....				....	....	....	....	....				
1998-99	Kootenay Ice	WHL	54	26	33	59	46	....	....	....	....	....	....				7	2	2	4	11				
99-2000	Kootenay Ice	WHL	56	23	43	66	97	....	....	....	....	....	....				21	*15	13	*28	51				
2000-01	Cincinnati	IHL	52	4	10	14	25	....	....	....	....	....	....				....	....	....	....	....				
2001-02	**Carolina**	**NHL**	10	2	2	4	2	0	0	0	12	16.7	0	1	0.0	9:23	23	1	4	5	28	1	0	1	14:45
	Lowell	AHL	66	12	16	28	58	....	....	....	....	....	....				....	....	....	....	....				
2002-03	**Carolina**	**NHL**	48	3	11	14	32	1	0	0	63	4.8	–5	25	40.0	14:33	....	....	....	....	....				
	Lowell	AHL	9	1	1	2	10	....	....	....	....	....	....				....	....	....	....	....				
2003-04	**Carolina**	**NHL**	33	3	1	4	6	0	0	1	27	11.1	3	18	33.3	9:08	....	....	....	....	....				
	Lowell	AHL	9	2	2	4	4	....	....	....	....	....	....				....	....	....	....	....				
	NHL Totals		91	8	14	22	40	1	0	1	102	7.8		44	36.4	12:01	23	1	4	5	28	1	0	1	14:45

Traded to **Dallas** by **Carolina** for Dallas' 4th round choice in 2005 Entry Draft, June 29, 2004.

SWANSON, Brian

(SWAHN-suhn, BRIGH-uhn)

Center. Shoots left. 5'10", 185 lbs.   Born, Eagle River, AK, March 24, 1976. San Jose's 5th choice, 115th overall, in 1994 Entry Draft.

Season	Club	League	GP	G	A	Pts	PIM	PP	SH	GW	S	%	+/-	TF	F%	Min	GP	G	A	Pts	PIM	PP	SH	GW	Min
1991-92	Anchorage	AAHL	50	35	40	75	10	....	....	....	....	....	....				....	....	....	....	....				
1992-93	Anchorage	AAHL	45	40	50	90	12	....	....	....	....	....	....				....	....	....	....	....				
1993-94	Omaha Lancers	USHL	47	38	42	80	40	....	....	....	....	....	....				....	....	....	....	....				
1994-95	Omaha Lancers	USHL	33	14	35	49	12	....	....	....	....	....	....				....	....	....	....	....				
1995-96	Colorado College	WCHA	40	26	33	59	24	....	....	....	....	....	....				....	....	....	....	....				
1996-97	Colorado College	WCHA	43	19	32	51	47	....	....	....	....	....	....				....	....	....	....	....				
1997-98	Colorado College	WCHA	42	18	*38	*56	26	....	....	....	....	....	....				....	....	....	....	....				
1998-99	Colorado College	WCHA	42	25	*41	66	28	....	....	....	....	....	....				....	....	....	....	....				
	Hartford	AHL	4	0	0	0	4	....	....	....	....	....	....				....	....	....	....	....				
99-2000	Hamilton	AHL	69	19	40	59	18	....	....	....	....	....	....				10	2	5	7	6				
2000-01	**Edmonton**	**NHL**	16	1	1	2	6	0	0	0	8	12.5	–1	150	44.0	10:55	....	....	....	....	....				
	Hamilton	AHL	49	18	29	47	20	....	....	....	....	....	....				....	....	....	....	....				
2001-02	**Edmonton**	**NHL**	8	1	1	2	0	0	0	0	7	14.3	–1	59	54.2	10:10	....	....	....	....	....				
	Hamilton	AHL	65	34	39	73	26	....	....	....	....	....	....				15	7	6	13	8				
2002-03	**Edmonton**	**NHL**	44	2	10	12	10	1	0	1	67	3.0	–7	405	52.4	11:55	....	....	....	....	....				
2003-04	**Atlanta**	**NHL**	2	0	1	1	0	0	0	0	0	0.0	0	17	29.4	6:35	....	....	....	....	....				
	Chicago Wolves	AHL	70	13	34	47	30	....	....	....	....	....	....				10	4	4	8	6				
	NHL Totals		70	4	13	17	16	1	0	1	82	4.9		631	49.9	11:20	....	....	....	....	....				

USHL First All-Star Team (1994) • USHL Second Team All-Star (1995) • WCHA Second All-Star Team (1996) • WCHA Rookie of the Year (1996) • WCHA First All-Star Team (1997, 1998, 1999) • NCAA West Second All-American Team (1998) • NCAA West First All-American Team (1999) • AHL Second All-Star Team (2002)

Traded to **NY Rangers** by **San Jose** with Jayson More and San Jose's 4th round choice (later traded back to San Jose – San Jose selected Adam Colagiacomo) in 1997 Entry Draft for Marty McSorley, August 20, 1996. Signed as a free agent by **Edmonton**, August 19, 1999. Signed as a free agent by **Atlanta**, July 24, 2003. Signed as a free agent by **Kassel** (Germany), May 10, 2004.

SWEENEY, Don

(SWEE-nee, DAWN)   **DAL.**

Defense. Shoots left. 5'10", 185 lbs.   Born, St. Stephen, N.B., August 17, 1966. Boston's 8th choice, 166th overall, in 1984 Entry Draft.

Season	Club	League	GP	G	A	Pts	PIM	PP	SH	GW	S	%	+/-	TF	F%	Min	GP	G	A	Pts	PIM	PP	SH	GW	Min
1983-84	South St. Paul	Hi-School	22	33	26	59		....	....	....	....	....	....				....	....	....	....	....				
1984-85	Harvard Crimson	ECAC	29	3	7	10	30	....	....	....	....	....	....				....	....	....	....	....				
1985-86	Harvard Crimson	ECAC	31	4	5	9	12	....	....	....	....	....	....				....	....	....	....	....				
1986-87	Harvard Crimson	ECAC	34	7	4	11	22	....	....	....	....	....	....				....	....	....	....	....				
1987-88	Harvard Crimson	ECAC	30	6	23	29	37	....	....	....	....	....	....				....	....	....	....	....				
	Maine Mariners	AHL						....	....	....	....	....	....				6	1	3	4	0				
1988-89	**Boston**	**NHL**	36	3	5	8	20	0	0	0	35	8.6	–6				....	....	....	....	....				
	Maine Mariners	AHL	42	8	17	25	24	....	....	....	....	....	....				....	....	....	....	....				
1989-90	**Boston**	**NHL**	58	3	5	8	58	0	0	0	49	6.1	11				21	1	5	6	18	1	0	0	
	Maine Mariners	AHL	11	0	8	8	8	....	....	....	....	....	....				....	....	....	....	....				
1990-91	**Boston**	**NHL**	77	8	13	21	67	0	1	3	102	7.8	2				19	3	0	3	25	0	0	0	
1991-92	**Boston**	**NHL**	75	3	11	14	74	0	0	1	92	3.3	–5				15	0	0	0	10	0	0	0	
1992-93	**Boston**	**NHL**	84	7	27	34	68	0	1	0	107	6.5	34				4	0	0	0	0	0	0	0	
1993-94	**Boston**	**NHL**	75	6	15	21	50	1	2	2	136	4.4	29				12	2	1	3	4	0	0	1	
1994-95	**Boston**	**NHL**	47	3	19	22	24	1	0	0	102	2.9	6				5	0	2	2	6	0	0	0	
1995-96	**Boston**	**NHL**	77	4	24	28	42	2	0	3	142	2.8	–4				5	0	2	2	6	0	0	0	
1996-97	**Boston**	**NHL**	82	3	23	26	39	0	0	0	113	2.7	–5				....	....	....	....	....				
1997-98	**Boston**	**NHL**	59	1	15	16	24	0	0	0	55	1.8	12				....	....	....	....	....				
1998-99	**Boston**	**NHL**	81	2	10	12	64	0	0	0	79	2.5	14	0	0.0	19:31	11	0	3	6	1	0	0	0	21:48

			Regular Season														Playoffs								
Season	Club	League	GP	G	A	Pts	PIM	PP	SH	GW	S	%	+/-	TF	F%	Min	GP	G	A	Pts	PIM	PP	SH	GW	Min
99-2000	**Boston**	**NHL**	**81**	**1**	**13**	**14**	**48**	**0**	**0**	**0**	**82**	**1.2**	**–14**	**1**	**0.0**	**21:08**	....	....	....	....	....	....	....	....	....
2000-01	**Boston**	**NHL**	**72**	**2**	**10**	**12**	**26**	**1**	**0**	**1**	**60**	**3.3**	**–1**	**0**	**0.0**	**19:16**	....	....	....	....	....	....	....	....	....
2001-02	**Boston**	**NHL**	**81**	**3**	**15**	**18**	**35**	**1**	**0**	**0**	**70**	**4.3**	**22**	**0**	**0.0**	**20:09**	**6**	**0**	**1**	**1**	**2**	**0**	**0**	**0**	**17:44**
2002-03	**Boston**	**NHL**	**67**	**3**	**5**	**8**	**24**	**0**	**0**	**0**	**55**	**5.5**	**–1**	**0**	**0.0**	**13:13**	**5**	**0**	**1**	**1**	**0**	**0**	**0**	**0**	**14:40**
2003-04	**Dallas**	**NHL**	**63**	**0**	**11**	**11**	**18**	**0**	**0**	**0**	**39**	**0.0**	**22**	**0**	**0.0**	**15:53**	**5**	**0**	**0**	**0**	**2**	**0**	**0**	**0**	**16:59**
	NHL Totals		**1115**	**52**	**221**	**273**	**681**	**6**	**4**	**12**	**1318**	**3.9**		**1**	**0.0**	**18:25**	**108**	**9**	**10**	**19**	**81**	**2**	**0**	**1**	**18:41**

ECAC First All-Star Team (1988) • NCAA East All-American Team (1988)

Signed as a free agent by **Dallas**, July 14, 2003.

SYDOR, Darryl

(sih-DOHR, DAIR-ihl) **T.B.**

Defense. Shoots left. 6'1", 205 lbs. Born, Edmonton, Alta., May 13, 1972. Los Angeles' 1st choice, 7th overall, in 1990 Entry Draft.

Season	Club	League	GP	G	A	Pts	PIM	PP	SH	GW	S	%	+/-	TF	F%	Min	GP	G	A	Pts	PIM	PP	SH	GW	Min
1985-86	Genstar Cement	AAHA	34	20	17	37	60	....	....	....	....	....	....	....	....	....	....	....	....	....	....	....	....	....	....
1986-87	Genstar Cement	AAHA	36	15	20	35	60	....	....	....	....	....	....	....	....	....	....	....	....	....	....	....	....	....	....
1987-88	Edmonton Mets	AJHL	38	10	11	21	54	....	....	....	....	....	....	....	....	....	....	....	....	....	....	....	....	....	....
1988-89	Kamloops Blazers	WHL	65	12	14	26	86	....	....	....	....	....	....	....	....	....	15	1	4	5	19	....	....	....	....
1989-90	Kamloops Blazers	WHL	67	29	66	95	129	....	....	....	....	....	....	....	....	....	17	2	9	11	28	....	....	....	....
1990-91	Kamloops Blazers	WHL	66	27	78	105	88	....	....	....	....	....	....	....	....	....	12	3	*22	25	10	....	....	....	....
1991-92	Kamloops Blazers	WHL	29	9	39	48	33	....	....	....	....	....	....	....	....	....	17	3	15	18	18	....	....	....	....
	Los Angeles	**NHL**	**18**	**1**	**5**	**6**	**22**	**0**	**0**	**0**	**18**	**5.6**	**–3**	....	....	....	....	....	....	....	....	....	....	....	....
1992-93	**Los Angeles**	**NHL**	**80**	**6**	**23**	**29**	**63**	**0**	**0**	**1**	**112**	**5.4**	**–2**	....	....	....	**24**	**3**	**8**	**11**	**16**	**2**	**0**	**0**	....
1993-94	**Los Angeles**	**NHL**	**84**	**8**	**27**	**35**	**94**	**1**	**0**	**0**	**146**	**5.5**	**–9**	....	....	....	....	....	....	....	....	....	....	....	....
1994-95	**Los Angeles**	**NHL**	**48**	**4**	**19**	**23**	**36**	**3**	**0**	**0**	**96**	**4.2**	**–2**	....	....	....	....	....	....	....	....	....	....	....	....
1995-96	**Los Angeles**	**NHL**	**58**	**1**	**11**	**12**	**34**	**1**	**0**	**0**	**84**	**1.2**	**–11**	....	....	....	....	....	....	....	....	....	....	....	....
	Dallas	**NHL**	**26**	**2**	**6**	**8**	**41**	**1**	**0**	**0**	**33**	**6.1**	**–1**	....	....	....	....	....	....	....	....	....	....	....	....
1996-97	**Dallas**	**NHL**	**82**	**8**	**40**	**48**	**51**	**2**	**0**	**2**	**142**	**5.6**	**37**	....	....	....	**7**	**0**	**2**	**2**	**0**	**0**	**0**	**0**	....
1997-98	**Dallas**	**NHL**	**79**	**11**	**35**	**46**	**51**	**4**	**1**	**1**	**166**	**6.6**	**17**	....	....	....	**17**	**0**	**5**	**5**	**14**	**0**	**0**	**0**	....
1998-99♦	**Dallas**	**NHL**	**74**	**14**	**34**	**48**	**50**	**9**	**0**	**2**	**163**	**8.6**	**–1**	**1**	**100.0**	**21:16**	**23**	**3**	**9**	**12**	**16**	**1**	**0**	**1**	**22:20**
99-2000	**Dallas**	**NHL**	**74**	**8**	**26**	**34**	**32**	**5**	**0**	**1**	**132**	**6.1**	**6**	**1**	**0.0**	**23:09**	**23**	**1**	**6**	**7**	**6**	**0**	**0**	**0**	**20:48**
2000-01	**Dallas**	**NHL**	**81**	**10**	**37**	**47**	**34**	**8**	**0**	**1**	**140**	**7.1**	**5**	**1**	**0.0**	**21:25**	**10**	**1**	**3**	**4**	**0**	**1**	**0**	**0**	**22:42**
2001-02	**Dallas**	**NHL**	**78**	**4**	**29**	**33**	**50**	**2**	**0**	**0**	**183**	**2.2**	**3**	**0**	**0.0**	**21:07**	....	....	....	....	....	....	....	....	....
2002-03	**Dallas**	**NHL**	**81**	**5**	**31**	**36**	**40**	**2**	**0**	**1**	**132**	**3.8**	**22**	**0**	**0.0**	**18:19**	**12**	**0**	**6**	**6**	**6**	**0**	**0**	**0**	**19:14**
2003-04	**Columbus**	**NHL**	**49**	**2**	**13**	**15**	**26**	**1**	**0**	**0**	**80**	**2.5**	**–19**	**1**	**0.0**	**21:54**	....	....	....	....	....	....	....	....	....
	♦ Tampa Bay	**NHL**	**31**	**1**	**6**	**7**	**6**	**0**	**0**	**0**	**42**	**2.4**	**3**	**0**	**0.0**	**19:06**	**23**	**0**	**6**	**6**	**9**	**0**	**0**	**0**	**21:50**
	NHL Totals		**943**	**85**	**342**	**427**	**630**	**39**	**1**	**9**	**1669**	**5.1**		**4**	**25.0**	**20:59**	**139**	**8**	**45**	**53**	**67**	**4**	**0**	**1**	**21:27**

WHL West First All-Star Team (1990, 1991, 1992)

Played in NHL All-Star Game (1998, 1999)

Traded to **Dallas** by **Los Angeles** with Los Angeles' 5th round choice (Ryan Christie) in 1996 Entry Draft for Shane Churla and Doug Zmolek, February 17, 1996. Traded to **Columbus** by **Dallas** for Mike Sillinger and Columbus' 2nd round choice (Johan Fransson) in 2004 Entry Draft, July 22, 2003. Traded to **Tampa Bay** by **Columbus** with Columbus' 4th round choice (Mike Lundin) in 2004 Entry Draft for Alexander Svitov and Tampa Bay's 3rd round choice (later traded to Calgary – Calgary selected Dustin Boyd) in 2004 Entry Draft, January 27, 2004.

SYKORA, Petr

(SEE-koh-ra, PEE-tuhr) **ANA.**

Right wing. Shoots left. 6', 190 lbs. Born, Plzen, Czech., November 19, 1976. New Jersey's 1st choice, 18th overall, in 1995 Entry Draft.

Season	Club	League	GP	G	A	Pts	PIM	PP	SH	GW	S	%	+/-	TF	F%	Min	GP	G	A	Pts	PIM	PP	SH	GW	Min
1991-92	Plzen Jr.	Czech-Jr.	30	50	50	100	....	....	....	....	....	....	....	....	....	....	....	....	....	....	....	....	....	....	....
1992-93	HC Skoda Plzen	Czech	19	12	5	17	....	....	....	....	....	....	....	....	....	....	....	....	....	....	....	....	....	....	....
1993-94	HC Skoda Plzen	Czech	37	10	16	26	....	....	....	....	....	....	....	....	....	....	4	0	1	1	....	....	....	....	....
	Cleveland	IHL	13	4	5	9	8	....	....	....	....	....	....	....	....	....	....	....	....	....	....	....	....	....	....
1994-95	Detroit Vipers	IHL	29	12	17	29	16	....	....	....	....	....	....	....	....	....	....	....	....	....	....	....	....	....	....
1995-96	**New Jersey**	**NHL**	**63**	**18**	**24**	**42**	**32**	**8**	**0**	**3**	**128**	**14.1**	**7**	....	....	....	....	....	....	....	....	....	....	....	....
	Albany River Rats	AHL	5	4	1	5	0	....	....	....	....	....	....	....	....	....	....	....	....	....	....	....	....	....	....
1996-97	**New Jersey**	**NHL**	**19**	**1**	**2**	**3**	**4**	**0**	**0**	**0**	**26**	**3.8**	**–8**	....	....	....	**2**	**0**	**0**	**0**	**2**	**0**	**0**	**0**	....
	Albany River Rats	AHL	43	20	25	45	48	....	....	....	....	....	....	....	....	....	4	1	4	5	2	....	....	....	....
1997-98	**New Jersey**	**NHL**	**58**	**16**	**20**	**36**	**22**	**3**	**1**	**4**	**130**	**12.3**	**0**	....	....	....	**2**	**0**	**0**	**0**	**0**	**0**	**0**	**0**	....
	Albany River Rats	AHL	2	4	1	5	0	....	....	....	....	....	....	....	....	....	....	....	....	....	....	....	....	....	....
1998-99	**New Jersey**	**NHL**	**80**	**29**	**43**	**72**	**22**	**15**	**0**	**7**	**222**	**13.1**	**16**	**33**	**33.3**	**16:14**	**7**	**3**	**3**	**6**	**4**	**0**	**0**	**1**	**18:11**
99-2000♦	**New Jersey**	**NHL**	**79**	**25**	**43**	**68**	**26**	**5**	**1**	**4**	**222**	**11.3**	**24**	**47**	**61.7**	**17:06**	**23**	**9**	**8**	**17**	**10**	**1**	**0**	**3**	**15:20**
2000-01	**New Jersey**	**NHL**	**73**	**35**	**46**	**81**	**32**	**9**	**2**	**3**	**249**	**14.1**	**36**	**15**	**33.3**	**17:44**	**25**	**10**	**12**	**22**	**12**	**2**	**2**	**2**	**18:40**
2001-02	**New Jersey**	**NHL**	**73**	**21**	**27**	**48**	**44**	**4**	**0**	**4**	**194**	**10.8**	**12**	**1**	**0.0**	**17:51**	**4**	**0**	**1**	**1**	**0**	**0**	**0**	**0**	**17:57**
	Czech Republic	Olympics	4	1	0	1	0	....	....	....	....	....	....	....	....	....	....	....	....	....	....	....	....	....	....
2002-03	**Anaheim**	**NHL**	**82**	**34**	**25**	**59**	**24**	**15**	**1**	**5**	**299**	**11.4**	**–7**	**23**	**39.1**	**0:00**	**21**	**4**	**9**	**13**	**12**	**1**	**0**	**2**	....
2003-04	**Anaheim**	**NHL**	**81**	**23**	**29**	**52**	**34**	**6**	**0**	**2**	**277**	**8.3**	**–9**	**9**	**22.2**	**17:57**	....	....	....	....	....	....	....	....	....
	NHL Totals		**608**	**202**	**259**	**461**	**240**	**65**	**5**	**32**	**1747**	**11.6**		**128**	**35.2**	**13:34**	**84**	**26**	**33**	**59**	**40**	**4**	**2**	**8**	**17:16**

NHL All-Rookie Team (1996)

Traded to **Anaheim** by **New Jersey** with Mike Commodore, Jean-Francois Damphousse and Igor Pohanka for Jeff Friesen, Oleg Tverdovsky and Maxim Balmochnykh, July 6, 2002.

SYKORA, Petr

(SEE-koh-ra, PEE-tuhr) **WSH.**

Center. Shoots right. 6'3", 206 lbs. Born, Pardubice, Czech., December 21, 1978. Detroit's 2nd choice, 76th overall, in 1997 Entry Draft.

Season	Club	League	GP	G	A	Pts	PIM	PP	SH	GW	S	%	+/-	TF	F%	Min	GP	G	A	Pts	PIM	PP	SH	GW	Min
1994-95	HC Pardubice Jr.	Czech-Jr.	38	35	33	68	....	....	....	....	....	....	....	....	....	....	....	....	....	....	....	....	....	....	....
1995-96	HC Pardubice Jr.	Czech-Jr.	16	26	17	43	....	....	....	....	....	....	....	....	....	....	....	....	....	....	....	....	....	....	....
1996-97	HC Pardubice Jr.	Czech-Jr.	12	14	4	18	....	....	....	....	....	....	....	....	....	....	....	....	....	....	....	....	....	....	....
	Pardubice	Czech	29	1	3	4	4	....	....	....	....	....	....	....	....	....	....	....	....	....	....	....	....	....	....
1997-98	Pardubice	Czech	39	4	5	9	8	....	....	....	....	....	....	....	....	....	3	0	0	0	....	....	....	....	....
1998-99	**Nashville**	**NHL**	**2**	**0**	**0**	**0**	**0**	**0**	**0**	**0**	**2**	**0.0**	**–1**	**11**	**45.5**	**8:19**	....	....	....	....	....	....	....	....	....
	Milwaukee	IHL	73	14	15	29	50	....	....	....	....	....	....	....	....	....	2	1	1	2	0	....	....	....	....
99-2000	Milwaukee	IHL	3	0	1	1	2	....	....	....	....	....	....	....	....	....	....	....	....	....	....	....	....	....	....
	Pardubice	Czech	36	7	13	20	49	....	....	....	....	....	....	....	....	....	3	0	0	0	2	....	....	....	....
2000-01	Pardubice	Czech	47	26	18	44	42	....	....	....	....	....	....	....	....	....	7	5	3	8	6	....	....	....	....
2001-02	Pardubice	Czech	32	18	8	26	72	....	....	....	....	....	....	....	....	....	6	1	2	3	26	....	....	....	....
2002-03	Pardubice	Czech	45	18	18	36	86	....	....	....	....	....	....	....	....	....	19	7	7	14	39	....	....	....	....
2003-04	Pardubice	Czech	48	23	23	46	20	....	....	....	....	....	....	....	....	....	7	1	0	1	6	....	....	....	....
	NHL Totals		**2**	**0**	**0**	**0**	**0**	**0**	**0**	**0**	**2**	**0.0**		**11**	**45.5**	**8:19**	....	....	....	....	....	....	....	....	....

Traded to **Nashville** by **Detroit** with Detroit's 3rd round choice (later traded to Edmonton – Edmonton selected Mike Comrie) and 4th round compensatory choice (Alexander Krevsun) in 1999 Entry Draft for Doug Brown, July 14, 1998. Traded to **Washington** by **Nashville** for Washington's 3rd round choice (Paul Brown) in 2003 Entry Draft, June 22, 2002.

TAFFE, Jeff

(TAYF, JEHF) **PHX.**

Center. Shoots left. 6'3", 201 lbs. Born, Hastings, MN, February 19, 1981. St. Louis' 1st choice, 30th overall, in 2000 Entry Draft.

Season	Club	League	GP	G	A	Pts	PIM	PP	SH	GW	S	%	+/-	TF	F%	Min	GP	G	A	Pts	PIM	PP	SH	GW	Min
1996-97	Hastings Huskies	Hi-School	25	21	37	58	....	....	....	....	....	....	....	....	....	....	....	....	....	....	....	....	....	....	....
1997-98	Hastings Huskies	Hi-School	28	37	29	66	....	....	....	....	....	....	....	....	....	....	....	....	....	....	....	....	....	....	....
1998-99	Hastings Huskies	Hi-School	28	39	51	90	....	....	....	....	....	....	....	....	....	....	....	....	....	....	....	....	....	....	....
	Rochester	USHL	17	12	9	21	26	....	....	....	....	....	....	....	....	....	....	....	....	....	....	....	....	....	....
99-2000	U. of Minnesota	WCHA	39	10	10	20	22	....	....	....	....	....	....	....	....	....	....	....	....	....	....	....	....	....	....
2000-01	U. of Minnesota	WCHA	38	12	23	35	56	....	....	....	....	....	....	....	....	....	....	....	....	....	....	....	....	....	....
2001-02	U. of Minnesota	WCHA	43	34	24	58	86	....	....	....	....	....	....	....	....	....	....	....	....	....	....	....	....	....	....
2002-03	**Phoenix**	**NHL**	**20**	**3**	**1**	**4**	**4**	**1**	**0**	**1**	**18**	**16.7**	**–4**	**113**	**29.2**	**11:34**	....	....	....	....	....	....	....	....	....
	Springfield	AHL	57	23	26	49	44	....	....	....	....	....	....	....	....	....	5	0	3	3	8	....	....	....	....
2003-04	**Phoenix**	**NHL**	**59**	**8**	**10**	**18**	**20**	**5**	**0**	**0**	**67**	**11.9**	**–8**	**219**	**43.4**	**11:02**	....	....	....	....	....	....	....	....	....
	Springfield	AHL	15	10	6	16	19	....	....	....	....	....	....	....	....	....	....	....	....	....	....	....	....	....	....
	NHL Totals		**79**	**11**	**11**	**22**	**24**	**6**	**0**	**1**	**85**	**12.9**		**332**	**38.6**	**11:10**	....	....	....	....	....	....	....	....	....

Rights traded to **Phoenix** by **St. Louis** with Michal Handzus, Ladislav Nagy and St. Louis' 1st round choice (Ben Eager) in 2002 Entry Draft for Keith Tkachuk, March 13, 2001.

TALLINDER, Henrik

(tah-LIHN-duhr, HEHN-rihk) **BUF.**

Defense. Shoots left. 6'3", 210 lbs. Born, Stockholm, Sweden, January 10, 1979. Buffalo's 2nd choice, 48th overall, in 1997 Entry Draft.

			Regular Season														Playoffs								
Season	Club	League	GP	G	A	Pts	PIM	PP	SH	GW	S	%	+/-	TF	F%	Min	GP	G	A	Pts	PIM	PP	SH	GW	Min
1996-97	AIK Solna Jr.	Swede-Jr.	40	4	13	17	55	....	....	....	....	....	....	....	....	....	....	....	....	....	....	....	....	....	....
	AIK Solna	Sweden	1	0	0	0	0	....	....	....	....	....	....	....	....	....	....	....	....	....	....	....	....	....	....
1997-98	AIK Solna	Sweden	34	0	0	0	26	....	....	....	....	....	....	....	....	....	....	....	....	....	....	....	....	....	....
1998-99	AIK Solna	Sweden	36	0	0	0	30	....	....	....	....	....	....	....	....	....	....	....	....	....	....	....	....	....	....
99-2000	AIK Solna	Sweden	50	0	2	2	59	....	....	....	....	....	....	....	....	....	....	....	....	....	....	....	....	....	....
2000-01	TPS Turku	Finland	56	5	9	14	62	....	....	....	....	....	....	....	....	....	10	2	1	3	8	....	....	....	....
2001-02	**Buffalo**	**NHL**	**2**	**0**	**0**	**0**	**0**	**0**	**0**	**0**	**4**	**0.0**	**−1**	**0**	**0.0**	**18:10**	....	....	....	....	....	....	....	....	....
	Rochester	AHL	73	6	14	20	26	....	....	....	....	....	....	....	....	....	2	0	0	0	0	....	....	....	....
2002-03	**Buffalo**	**NHL**	**46**	**3**	**10**	**13**	**28**	**1**	**0**	**0**	**37**	**8.1**	**−3**	**0**	**0.0**	**19:53**	....	....	....	....	....	....	....	....	....
2003-04	**Buffalo**	**NHL**	**72**	**1**	**9**	**10**	**26**	**0**	**0**	**0**	**63**	**1.6**	**5**	**1**	**0.0**	**18:23**	....	....	....	....	....	....	....	....	....
	NHL Totals		**120**	**4**	**19**	**23**	**54**	**1**	**0**	**0**	**104**	**3.8**		**1**	**0.0**	**18:57**	....	....	....	....	....	....	....	....	....

TAMER, Chris

(TAY-muhr, KRIHS)

Defense. Shoots left. 6'2", 205 lbs. Born, Dearborn, MI, November 17, 1970. Pittsburgh's 3rd choice, 68th overall, in 1990 Entry Draft.

Season	Club	League	GP	G	A	Pts	PIM	PP	SH	GW	S	%	+/-	TF	F%	Min	GP	G	A	Pts	PIM	PP	SH	GW	Min
1987-88	Redford Royals	NAJHL	40	10	20	30	217	....	....	....	....	....	....	....	....	....	....	....	....	....	....	....	....	....	....
1988-89	Redford Royals	NAJHL	31	6	13	19	79	....	....	....	....	....	....	....	....	....	....	....	....	....	....	....	....	....	....
1989-90	U. of Michigan	CCHA	42	2	7	9	147	....	....	....	....	....	....	....	....	....	....	....	....	....	....	....	....	....	....
1990-91	U. of Michigan	CCHA	45	8	19	27	130	....	....	....	....	....	....	....	....	....	....	....	....	....	....	....	....	....	....
1991-92	U. of Michigan	CCHA	43	4	15	19	125	....	....	....	....	....	....	....	....	....	....	....	....	....	....	....	....	....	....
1992-93	U. of Michigan	CCHA	39	5	18	23	113	....	....	....	....	....	....	....	....	....	....	....	....	....	....	....	....	....	....
1993-94	**Pittsburgh**	**NHL**	**12**	**0**	**0**	**0**	**9**	**0**	**0**	**0**	**10**	**0.0**	**3**	....	....	....	**5**	**0**	**0**	**0**	**2**	**0**	**0**	**0**	....
	Cleveland	IHL	53	1	2	3	160	....	....	....	....	....	....	....	....	....	....	....	....	....	....	....	....	....	....
1994-95	Cleveland	IHL	48	4	10	14	204	....	....	....	....	....	....	....	....	....	....	....	....	....	....	....	....	....	....
	Pittsburgh	**NHL**	**36**	**2**	**0**	**2**	**82**	**0**	**0**	**0**	**26**	**7.7**	**0**	....	....	....	**4**	**0**	**0**	**0**	**18**	**0**	**0**	**0**	....
1995-96	**Pittsburgh**	**NHL**	**70**	**4**	**10**	**14**	**153**	**0**	**0**	**1**	**75**	**5.3**	**20**	....	....	....	**18**	**0**	**7**	**7**	**24**	**0**	**0**	**0**	....
1996-97	**Pittsburgh**	**NHL**	**45**	**2**	**4**	**6**	**131**	**0**	**1**	**0**	**56**	**3.6**	**−25**	....	....	....	**4**	**0**	**0**	**0**	**4**	**0**	**0**	**0**	....
1997-98	**Pittsburgh**	**NHL**	**79**	**0**	**7**	**7**	**181**	**0**	**0**	**0**	**55**	**0.0**	**4**	....	....	....	**6**	**0**	**1**	**1**	**4**	**0**	**0**	**0**	....
1998-99	**Pittsburgh**	**NHL**	**11**	**0**	**0**	**0**	**32**	**0**	**0**	**0**	**2**	**0.0**	**−2**	**0**	**0.0**	**5:59**	....	....	....	....	....	....	....	....	....
	NY Rangers	**NHL**	**52**	**1**	**5**	**6**	**92**	**0**	**0**	**1**	**46**	**2.2**	**−12**	**0**	**0.0**	**15:25**	....	....	....	....	....	....	....	....	....
99-2000	**Atlanta**	**NHL**	**69**	**2**	**8**	**10**	**91**	**0**	**0**	**0**	**61**	**3.3**	**−32**	**5**	**40.0**	**18:29**	....	....	....	....	....	....	....	....	....
2000-01	**Atlanta**	**NHL**	**82**	**4**	**13**	**17**	**128**	**0**	**1**	**1**	**90**	**4.4**	**−1**	**1**	**0.0**	**19:42**	....	....	....	....	....	....	....	....	....
2001-02	**Atlanta**	**NHL**	**78**	**3**	**3**	**6**	**111**	**0**	**1**	**0**	**66**	**4.5**	**−11**	**0**	**0.0**	**18:30**	....	....	....	....	....	....	....	....	....
2002-03	**Atlanta**	**NHL**	**72**	**1**	**9**	**10**	**118**	**0**	**0**	**0**	**53**	**1.9**	**−10**	**0**	**0.0**	**15:41**	....	....	....	....	....	....	....	....	....
2003-04	**Atlanta**	**NHL**	**38**	**2**	**5**	**7**	**55**	**0**	**0**	**1**	**40**	**5.0**	**−9**	**0**	**0.0**	**17:58**	....	....	....	....	....	....	....	....	....
	NHL Totals		**644**	**21**	**64**	**85**	**1183**	**0**	**3**	**4**	**580**	**3.6**		**6**	**33.3**	**17:27**	**37**	**0**	**8**	**8**	**52**	**0**	**0**	**0**	....

Traded to **NY Rangers** by **Pittsburgh** with Petr Nedved and Sean Pronger for Alex Kovalev and Harry York, November 25, 1998. Claimed by **Atlanta** from **NY Rangers** in Expansion Draft, June 25, 1999. • Missed majority of 2003-04 season recovering from back injury suffered in game vs. Phoenix, January 11, 2004.

TANABE, David

(tuh-NA-bee, DAY-vihd) **PHX.**

Defense. Shoots right. 6'1", 212 lbs. Born, White Bear Lake, MN, July 19, 1980. Carolina's 1st choice, 16th overall, in 1999 Entry Draft.

Season	Club	League	GP	G	A	Pts	PIM	PP	SH	GW	S	%	+/-	TF	F%	Min	GP	G	A	Pts	PIM	PP	SH	GW	Min
1996-97	Hill-Murray	Hi-School	28	12	14	26	....	....	....	....	....	....	....	....	....	....	....	....	....	....	....	....	....	....	....
1997-98	U.S. National U-18	USDP	73	8	21	29	96	....	....	....	....	....	....	....	....	....	....	....	....	....	....	....	....	....	....
1998-99	U. of Wisconsin	WCHA	35	10	12	22	44	....	....	....	....	....	....	....	....	....	....	....	....	....	....	....	....	....	....
99-2000	**Carolina**	**NHL**	**31**	**4**	**0**	**4**	**14**	**3**	**0**	**0**	**28**	**14.3**	**−4**	**0**	**0.0**	**12:53**	....	....	....	....	....	....	....	....	....
	Cincinnati	IHL	32	0	13	13	14	....	....	....	....	....	....	....	....	....	11	1	4	5	6	....	....	....	....
2000-01	**Carolina**	**NHL**	**74**	**7**	**22**	**29**	**42**	**5**	**0**	**1**	**130**	**5.4**	**−9**	**0**	**0.0**	**17:55**	**6**	**2**	**0**	**2**	**12**	**2**	**0**	**0**	**20:47**
2001-02	**Carolina**	**NHL**	**78**	**1**	**15**	**16**	**35**	**0**	**0**	**0**	**113**	**0.9**	**−13**	**0**	**0.0**	**18:27**	**1**	**0**	**1**	**1**	**0**	**0**	**0**	**0**	**7:31**
2002-03	**Carolina**	**NHL**	**68**	**3**	**10**	**13**	**24**	**2**	**0**	**0**	**104**	**2.9**	**−27**	**0**	**0.0**	**18:12**	....	....	....	....	....	....	....	....	....
2003-04	**Phoenix**	**NHL**	**45**	**5**	**7**	**12**	**22**	**2**	**0**	**2**	**88**	**5.7**	**4**	**0**	**0.0**	**23:02**	....	....	....	....	....	....	....	....	....
	NHL Totals		**296**	**20**	**54**	**74**	**137**	**12**	**0**	**3**	**463**	**4.3**		**0**	**0.0**	**18:23**	**7**	**2**	**1**	**3**	**12**	**2**	**0**	**0**	**18:53**

WCHA All-Rookie Team (1999)

Traded to **Phoenix** by **Carolina** with Igor Knyazev for Danny Markov and future considerations (Edmonton's 3rd round choice (previously acquired, later traded to NY Rangers - NY Rangers selected Billy Ryan) in 2004 Entry Draft, June 26, 2004), June 21, 2003.

TANGUAY, Alex

(TAN-guay, AL-ehx) **COL.**

Left wing. Shoots left. 6', 190 lbs. Born, Ste-Justine, Que., November 21, 1979. Colorado's 1st choice, 12th overall, in 1998 Entry Draft.

Season	Club	League	GP	G	A	Pts	PIM	PP	SH	GW	S	%	+/-	TF	F%	Min	GP	G	A	Pts	PIM	PP	SH	GW	Min
1994-95	Cap-d-Madeleine	QAAA	1	0	1	1	0	....	....	....	....	....	....	....	....	....	....	....	....	....	....	....	....	....	....
1995-96	Cap-d-Madeleine	QAAA	44	29	34	63	64	....	....	....	....	....	....	....	....	....	5	2	4	6	14	....	....	....	....
1996-97	Halifax	QMJHL	70	27	41	68	60	....	....	....	....	....	....	....	....	....	12	5	8	13	8	....	....	....	....
1997-98	Halifax	QMJHL	51	47	38	85	32	....	....	....	....	....	....	....	....	....	5	7	6	13	4	....	....	....	....
1998-99	Halifax	QMJHL	31	27	34	61	30	....	....	....	....	....	....	....	....	....	5	1	2	3	2	....	....	....	....
	Hershey Bears	AHL	5	1	2	3	2	....	....	....	....	....	....	....	....	....	5	0	2	2	0	....	....	....	....
99-2000	**Colorado**	**NHL**	**76**	**17**	**34**	**51**	**22**	**5**	**0**	**3**	**74**	**23.0**	**6**	**11**	**45.5**	**15:38**	**17**	**2**	**1**	**3**	**2**	**1**	**0**	**1**	**10:49**
2000-01 ◆	**Colorado**	**NHL**	**82**	**27**	**50**	**77**	**37**	**7**	**1**	**3**	**135**	**20.0**	**35**	**30**	**43.3**	**17:51**	**23**	**6**	**15**	**21**	**8**	**1**	**0**	**2**	**19:18**
2001-02	**Colorado**	**NHL**	**70**	**13**	**35**	**48**	**36**	**7**	**0**	**2**	**90**	**14.4**	**8**	**37**	**40.5**	**18:20**	**19**	**5**	**8**	**13**	**0**	**3**	**0**	**0**	**17:25**
2002-03	**Colorado**	**NHL**	**82**	**26**	**41**	**67**	**36**	**3**	**0**	**5**	**142**	**18.3**	**34**	**123**	**39.0**	**17:48**	**7**	**1**	**2**	**3**	**4**	**0**	**0**	**1**	**19:06**
2003-04	**Colorado**	**NHL**	**69**	**25**	**54**	**79**	**42**	**7**	**0**	**5**	**117**	**21.4**	**30**	**71**	**40.9**	**18:21**	**8**	**2**	**2**	**4**	**2**	**1**	**0**	**1**	**15:46**
	NHL Totals		**379**	**108**	**214**	**322**	**173**	**29**	**1**	**18**	**558**	**19.4**		**272**	**40.4**	**17:35**	**74**	**16**	**28**	**44**	**16**	**6**	**0**	**5**	**16:28**

QMJHL All-Rookie Team (1997)

Played in NHL All-Star Game (2004)

TAPPER, Brad

(TA-puhr, BRAD)

Right wing. Shoots right. 6', 185 lbs. Born, Scarborough, Ont., April 28, 1978.

Season	Club	League	GP	G	A	Pts	PIM	PP	SH	GW	S	%	+/-	TF	F%	Min	GP	G	A	Pts	PIM	PP	SH	GW	Min
1996-97	Wexford Raiders	MTJHL	50	42	70	112	169	....	....	....	....	....	....	....	....	....	....	....	....	....	....	....	....	....	....
1997-98	RPI Engineers	ECAC	34	14	11	25	62	....	....	....	....	....	....	....	....	....	....	....	....	....	....	....	....	....	....
1998-99	RPI Engineers	ECAC	35	20	20	40	60	....	....	....	....	....	....	....	....	....	....	....	....	....	....	....	....	....	....
99-2000	RPI Engineers	ECAC	37	*31	20	51	81	....	....	....	....	....	....	....	....	....	....	....	....	....	....	....	....	....	....
2000-01	**Atlanta**	**NHL**	**16**	**2**	**3**	**5**	**6**	**0**	**0**	**0**	**21**	**9.5**	**1**	**0**	**0.0**	**12:44**	....	....	....	....	....	....	....	....	....
	Orlando	IHL	45	7	9	16	39	....	....	....	....	....	....	....	....	....	2	0	0	0	2	....	....	....	....
2001-02	**Atlanta**	**NHL**	**20**	**2**	**4**	**6**	**43**	**0**	**0**	**0**	**34**	**5.9**	**−3**	**3**	**66.7**	**13:21**	....	....	....	....	....	....	....	....	....
	Chicago Wolves	AHL	50	14	12	26	62	....	....	....	....	....	....	....	....	....	19	3	4	7	42	....	....	....	....
2002-03	**Atlanta**	**NHL**	**35**	**10**	**4**	**14**	**23**	**1**	**0**	**3**	**68**	**14.7**	**2**	**4**	**25.0**	**13:03**	....	....	....	....	....	....	....	....	....
	Chicago Wolves	AHL	28	9	14	23	42	....	....	....	....	....	....	....	....	....	9	1	3	4	10	....	....	....	....
2003-04	Chicago Wolves	AHL	20	1	8	9	26	....	....	....	....	....	....	....	....	....	....	....	....	....	....	....	....	....	....
	Binghamton	AHL	29	9	12	21	26	....	....	....	....	....	....	....	....	....	....	....	....	....	....	....	....	....	....
	NHL Totals		**71**	**14**	**11**	**25**	**72**	**1**	**0**	**3**	**123**	**11.4**		**7**	**42.9**	**13:04**	....	....	....	....	....	....	....	....	....

ECAC First All-Star Team (2000) • NCAA East Second All-American Team (2000)

Signed as a free agent by **Atlanta**, April 11, 2000. Traded to **Ottawa** by **Atlanta** for Daniel Corso, January 6, 2004.

TARNSTROM, Dick

(TAHRN-struhm, DIHK) **PIT.**

Defense. Shoots left. 6'1", 205 lbs. Born, Sundbyberg, Sweden, January 20, 1975. NY Islanders' 12th choice, 272nd overall, in 1994 Entry Draft.

Season	Club	League	GP	G	A	Pts	PIM	PP	SH	GW	S	%	+/-	TF	F%	Min	GP	G	A	Pts	PIM	PP	SH	GW	Min
1992-93	AIK Solna	Sweden	3	0	0	0	0	....	....	....	....	....	....	....	....	....	....	....	....	....	....	....	....	....	....
1993-94	AIK Solna	Sweden	33	1	4	5	....	....	....	....	....	....	....	....	....	....	....	....	....	....	....	....	....	....	....
1994-95	AIK Solna	Swede-2	37	8	4	12	26	....	....	....	....	....	....	....	....	....	....	....	....	....	....	....	....	....	....
1995-96	AIK Solna	Sweden	40	0	5	5	32	....	....	....	....	....	....	....	....	....	....	....	....	....	....	....	....	....	....
1996-97	AIK Solna	Sweden	49	5	3	8	38	....	....	....	....	....	....	....	....	....	7	0	1	1	6	....	....	....	....
1997-98	AIK Solna	Sweden	45	2	12	14	30	....	....	....	....	....	....	....	....	....	....	....	....	....	....	....	....	....	....
1998-99	AIK Solna	Sweden	47	9	14	23	36	....	....	....	....	....	....	....	....	....	....	....	....	....	....	....	....	....	....
99-2000	AIK Solna	Sweden	42	7	15	22	20	....	....	....	....	....	....	....	....	....	....	....	....	....	....	....	....	....	....
2000-01	AIK Solna	Sweden	50	10	18	28	28	....	....	....	....	....	....	....	....	....	5	0	0	0	8	....	....	....	....

			Regular Season														Playoffs								
Season	Club	League	GP	G	A	Pts	PIM	PP	SH	GW	S	%	+/-	TF	F%	Min	GP	G	A	Pts	PIM	PP	SH	GW	Min
2001-02	**NY Islanders**	**NHL**	62	3	16	19	38	0	0	0	59	5.1	−12	0	0.0	17:39	5	0	0	0	2	0	0	0	7:13
	Bridgeport	AHL	9	0	2	2	2																		
2002-03	**Pittsburgh**	**NHL**	61	7	34	41	50	3	0	0	115	6.1	−11	0	0.0	23:54									
2003-04	**Pittsburgh**	**NHL**	80	16	36	52	38	12	0	0	158	10.1	−37	0	0.0	24:03									
	NHL Totals		203	26	86	112	126	15	0	0	332	7.8		0	0.0	22:03	5	0	0	0	2	0	0	0	7:13

Claimed on waivers by **Pittsburgh** from **NY Islanders**, August 6, 2002.

TAYLOR, Chris

(TAY-luhr, KRIHS) **BUF.**

Center. Shoots left. 6'2", 192 lbs. Born, Stratford, Ont., March 6, 1972. NY Islanders' 2nd choice, 27th overall, in 1990 Entry Draft.

Season	Club	League	GP	G	A	Pts	PIM	PP	SH	GW	S	%	+/-	TF	F%	Min	GP	G	A	Pts	PIM	PP	SH	GW	Min
1987-88	Stratford Cullitons	OJHL-B	52	28	37	65	112																		
1988-89	London Knights	OHL	62	7	16	23	52										15	0	2	2	15				
1989-90	London Knights	OHL	66	45	60	105	60										6	3	2	5	6				
1990-91	London Knights	OHL	65	50	78	128	50										7	4	8	12	6				
1991-92	London Knights	OHL	66	48	74	122	57										10	8	16	24	9				
1992-93	Capital District	AHL	77	19	43	62	32										4	0	1	1	2				
1993-94	Salt Lake	IHL	79	21	20	41	38																		
1994-95	Denver Grizzlies	IHL	78	38	48	86	47										14	7	6	13	10				
	NY Islanders	**NHL**	10	0	3	3	2	0	0	0	13	0.0	1												
1995-96	**NY Islanders**	**NHL**	11	0	1	1	2	0	0	0	4	0.0	1												
	Utah Grizzlies	IHL	50	18	23	41	60										22	5	11	16	26				
1996-97	**NY Islanders**	**NHL**	1	0	0	0	0	0	0	0	1	0.0	0												
	Utah Grizzlies	IHL	71	27	40	67	24										7	1	2	3	0				
1997-98	Utah Grizzlies	IHL	79	28	56	84	66										4	0	2	2	6				
1998-99	**Boston**	**NHL**	37	3	5	8	12	0	1	0	60	5.0	−3	512	53.7	14:24									
	Providence Bruins	AHL	21	6	11	17	6																		
	Las Vegas	IHL	14	3	12	15	2																		
99-2000	**Buffalo**	**NHL**	11	1	1	2	2	0	0	0	15	6.7	−2	125	45.6	10:54	2	0	0	0	2	0	0	0	10:32
	Rochester	AHL	49	21	28	49	21																		
2000-01	**Buffalo**	**NHL**	14	0	2	2	6	0	0	0	21	0.0	1	138	50.7	11:08									
	Rochester	AHL	45	20	24	44	25																		
2001-02	Rochester	AHL	77	21	45	66	66										2	0	1	1	0				
2002-03	**Buffalo**	**NHL**	11	1	3	4	2	0	0	0	10	10.0	−1	152	47.4	13:55									
	Rochester	AHL	61	12	55	67	44										3	3	1	4	2				
2003-04	**Buffalo**	**NHL**	54	6	6	12	22	0	0	0	50	12.0	−2	531	51.0	10:10									
	Rochester	AHL	24	9	18	27	20										16	5	12	17	0				
	NHL Totals		149	11	21	32	48	0	1	0	174	6.3		1458	51.1	11:54	2	0	0	0	2	0	0	0	10:32

Signed as a free agent by **Los Angeles**, July 25, 1997. Signed as a free agent by **Boston**, August 5, 1998. Signed as a free agent by **Buffalo**, August 13, 1999.

TAYLOR, Tim

(TAY-luhr, TIHM) **T.B.**

Center. Shoots left. 6'1", 189 lbs. Born, Stratford, Ont., February 6, 1969. Washington's 2nd choice, 36th overall, in 1988 Entry Draft.

Season	Club	League	GP	G	A	Pts	PIM	PP	SH	GW	S	%	+/-	TF	F%	Min	GP	G	A	Pts	PIM	PP	SH	GW	Min
1985-86	Stratford Cullitons	OJHL-B	1	0	0	0	0																		
1986-87	Stratford Cullitons	OJHL-B	31	25	26	51	51																		
	London Knights	OHL	34	7	9	16	11																		
1987-88	London Knights	OHL	64	46	50	96	66										12	9	9	18	26				
1988-89	London Knights	OHL	61	34	80	114	93										21	*21	25	*46	58				
1989-90	Baltimore	AHL	79	31	36	67	124										9	2	2	4	13				
1990-91	Baltimore	AHL	79	25	42	67	75										5	0	1	1	4				
1991-92	Baltimore	AHL	65	9	18	27	131																		
1992-93	Baltimore	AHL	41	15	16	31	49																		
	Hamilton	AHL	36	15	22	37	37																		
1993-94	**Detroit**	**NHL**	1	1	0	1	0	0	0	0	4	25.0	−1												
	Adirondack	AHL	79	36	*81	*117	86										12	2	10	12	12				
1994-95	**Detroit**	**NHL**	22	0	4	4	16	0	0	0	21	0.0	3				6	0	1	1	12	0	0	0	
1995-96	**Detroit**	**NHL**	72	11	14	25	39	1	1	4	81	13.6	11				18	0	4	4	4	0	0	0	
1996-97♦	**Detroit**	**NHL**	44	3	4	7	52	0	1	0	44	6.8	−6				2	0	0	0	0	0	0	0	
1997-98	**Boston**	**NHL**	79	20	11	31	57	1	3	0	127	15.7	−16				6	0	0	0	10	0	0	0	
1998-99	**Boston**	**NHL**	49	4	7	11	55	0	0	1	76	5.3	−10	834	58.3	15:56	12	0	3	3	8	0	0	0	15:09
99-2000	**NY Rangers**	**NHL**	76	9	11	20	72	0	0	2	79	11.4	−4	1276	58.9	14:09									
2000-01	**NY Rangers**	**NHL**	38	2	5	7	16	0	0	1	34	5.9	−6	292	59.3	8:57									
2001-02	**Tampa Bay**	**NHL**	48	4	4	8	25	0	1	0	50	8.0	−2	559	54.6	13:29									
2002-03	**Tampa Bay**	**NHL**	82	4	8	12	38	0	0	1	95	4.2	−13	961	57.9	13:43	11	0	1	1	6	0	0	0	13:54
2003-04♦	**Tampa Bay**	**NHL**	82	7	15	22	25	0	0	1	95	7.4	−5	666	59.6	12:54	23	2	3	5	31	0	0	0	14:17
	NHL Totals		593	65	83	148	395	2	6	10	706	9.2		4588	58.2	13:24	78	2	12	14	71	0	0	0	14:25

AHL First All-Star Team (1994) • John B. Sollenberger Trophy (Top Scorer – AHL) (1994)

Traded to **Vancouver** by **Washington** for Eric Murano, January 29, 1993. Signed as a free agent by **Detroit**, July 28, 1993. Claimed by **Boston** from **Detroit** in Waiver Draft, September 28, 1997. Signed as a free agent by **NY Rangers**, July 30, 1999. • Missed majority of 2000-01 season recovering from abdominal injury suffered in game vs. Phoenix, January 4, 2001. Traded to **Tampa Bay** by **NY Rangers** for Kyle Freadrich and Nils Ekman, June 30, 2001.

TENKRAT, Petr

(TEHN-krat, PEE-tuhr) **TOR.**

Right wing. Shoots right. 5'11", 200 lbs. Born, Kladno, Czech., May 31, 1977. Anaheim's 6th choice, 230th overall, in 1999 Entry Draft.

Season	Club	League	GP	G	A	Pts	PIM	PP	SH	GW	S	%	+/-	TF	F%	Min	GP	G	A	Pts	PIM	PP	SH	GW	Min
1994-95	HC Kladno	Czech	1	0	0	0	0																		
1995-96	HC Poldi Kladno	Czech	20	0	4	4	4										3	0	1	1	0				
1996-97	HC Poldi Kladno	Czech	43	5	9	14	6										3	0	1	1	0				
1997-98	Kladno	Czech	52	9	10	19	24																		
1998-99	Kladno	Czech	50	21	14	35	32																		
99-2000	HPK Hameenlinna	Finland	32	20	9	29	31																		
	Ilves Tampere	Finland	22	15	5	20	44										3	1	1	2	14				
2000-01	**Anaheim**	**NHL**	46	5	9	14	16	0	0	2	79	6.3	−11	0	0.0	12:48									
	Cincinnati	AHL	25	9	9	18	24										4	3	2	5	0				
2001-02	**Anaheim**	**NHL**	9	0	0	0	6	0	0	0	13	0.0	−6	1	0.0	11:47									
	Cincinnati	AHL	3	2	3	5	2																		
	Nashville	**NHL**	58	8	16	24	28	0	1	2	82	9.8	−4	7	28.6	12:00									
	Milwaukee	AHL	4	0	0	0	2																		
2002-03	Karpat Oulu	Finland	51	21	19	40	60										14	4	2	6	6				
2003-04	Karpat Oulu	Finland	35	22	15	37	30										15	3	7	10	*45				
	Voskresensk	Russia	19	0	2	2	18																		
	NHL Totals		113	13	25	38	50	0	1	4	174	7.5		8	25.0	12:18									

Traded to **Nashville** by **Anaheim** for Patrick Kjellberg, November 1, 2001. Claimed by **Florida** from **Nashville** in Waiver Draft, October 4, 2002. Traded to **Columbus** by **Florida** for Mathieu Biron, October 4, 2002. Signed as a free agent by **Karpat** (Finland), May 15, 2002. Claimed by **Toronto** from **Columbus** in Waiver Draft, October 3, 2003.

TETARENKO, Joey

(teh-tar-EHN-koh, JOH-ee) **CAR.**

Right wing. Shoots right. 6'2", 215 lbs. Born, Prince Albert, Sask., March 3, 1978. Florida's 4th choice, 82nd overall, in 1996 Entry Draft.

Season	Club	League	GP	G	A	Pts	PIM	PP	SH	GW	S	%	+/-	TF	F%	Min	GP	G	A	Pts	PIM	PP	SH	GW	Min
1993-94	North Battleford	SMHL	36	6	13	19	75																		
1994-95	Portland	WHL	59	0	1	1	134										9	0	0	0	8				
1995-96	Portland	WHL	71	4	11	15	190										7	0	1	1	17				
1996-97	Portland	WHL	68	8	18	26	182										2	0	0	0	2				
1997-98	Portland	WHL	49	2	12	14	148										16	0	2	2	30				
1998-99	New Haven	AHL	65	4	10	14	154																		
99-2000	Louisville Panthers	AHL	57	3	11	14	136										4	0	0	0	2				
2000-01	**Florida**	**NHL**	29	3	1	4	44	0	0	0	21	14.3	−1	0	0.0	6:12									
	Louisville Panthers	AHL	29	1	4	5	74																		
2001-02	**Florida**	**NHL**	38	1	0	1	123	0	0	0	10	10.0	−5	0	0.0	5:08									
2002-03	San Antonio	AHL	50	4	12	16	123																		
	Florida	**NHL**	2	0	0	0	4	0	0	0	2	0.0	−1	0	0.0	6:19									
	Binghamton	AHL	14	2	2	4	33										14	0	0	0	36				
	Ottawa	**NHL**	2	0	0	0	5	0	0	0	1	0.0	0	0	0.0	6:29									

			Regular Season														Playoffs								
Season	Club	League	GP	G	A	Pts	PIM	PP	SH	GW	S	%	+/-	TF	F%	Min	GP	G	A	Pts	PIM	PP	SH	GW	Min
2003-04	**Carolina**	**NHL**	**2**	**0**	**0**	**0**	**0**	**0**	**0**	**0**	**0**	**0.0**	**0**	**1**	**0.0**	**3:31**	....	....	....	....	....	....	....	....	....
	Lowell	AHL	57	1	6	7	167	....	....	....	....	....	....	....	....	....	....	....	....	....	....	....	....	....	....
	NHL Totals		**73**	**4**	**1**	**5**	**176**	**0**	**0**	**0**	**34**	**11.8**		**1**	**0.0**	**5:35**	....	....	....	....	....	....	....	....	....

• Missed majority of 2001-02 season recovering from jaw injury suffered in game vs. NY Rangers, November 3, 2001. Traded to **Ottawa** by **Florida** for Simon Lajeunesse, March 4, 2003. Signed as a free agent by **Carolina**, July 2, 2003.

THERIEN, Chris

(TEH-ree-ehn, KRIHS)

Defense. Shoots left. 6'5", 235 lbs. Born, Ottawa, Ont., December 14, 1971. Philadelphia's 7th choice, 47th overall, in 1990 Entry Draft.

Season	Club	League	GP	G	A	Pts	PIM	PP	SH	GW	S	%	+/-	TF	F%	Min	GP	G	A	Pts	PIM	PP	SH	GW	Min
1988-89	Ottawa Jr. Sens	OCJHL	8	3	1	4	22	....	....	....	....	....	....	....	....	....	....	....	....	....	....	....	....	....	....
1989-90	Ottawa Jr. Sens	OCJHL	3	0	2	2	2	....	....	....	....	....	....	....	....	....	....	....	....	....	....	....	....	....	....
	Northfield Prep	Hi-School	31	35	37	72	54	....	....	....	....	....	....	....	....	....	....	....	....	....	....	....	....	....	....
1990-91	Providence	H-East	36	4	18	22	36	....	....	....	....	....	....	....	....	....	....	....	....	....	....	....	....	....	....
1991-92	Providence	H-East	36	16	25	41	38	....	....	....	....	....	....	....	....	....	....	....	....	....	....	....	....	....	....
1992-93	Providence	H-East	33	8	11	19	52	....	....	....	....	....	....	....	....	....	....	....	....	....	....	....	....	....	....
	Team Canada	Nat-Tm	8	1	4	5	8	....	....	....	....	....	....	....	....	....	....	....	....	....	....	....	....	....	....
1993-94	Team Canada	Nat-Tm	59	7	15	22	46	....	....	....	....	....	....	....	....	....	....	....	....	....	....	....	....	....	....
	Canada	Olympics	4	0	0	0	4	....	....	....	....	....	....	....	....	....	....	....	....	....	....	....	....	....	....
	Hershey Bears	AHL	6	0	0	0	2	....	....	....	....	....	....	....	....	....	....	....	....	....	....	....	....	....	....
1994-95	Hershey Bears	AHL	34	3	13	16	27	....	....	....	....	....	....	....	....	....	....	....	....	....	....	....	....	....	....
	Philadelphia	**NHL**	**48**	**3**	**10**	**13**	**38**	**1**	**0**	**0**	**53**	**5.7**	**8**	....	....	....	**15**	**0**	**0**	**0**	**10**	**0**	**0**	**0**	....
1995-96	**Philadelphia**	**NHL**	**82**	**6**	**17**	**23**	**89**	**3**	**0**	**1**	**123**	**4.9**	**16**	....	....	....	**12**	**0**	**0**	**0**	**18**	**0**	**0**	**0**	....
1996-97	**Philadelphia**	**NHL**	**71**	**2**	**22**	**24**	**64**	**0**	**0**	**1**	**107**	**1.9**	**27**	....	....	....	**19**	**1**	**6**	**7**	**6**	**0**	**0**	**1**	....
1997-98	**Philadelphia**	**NHL**	**78**	**3**	**16**	**19**	**80**	**1**	**0**	**1**	**102**	**2.9**	**5**	....	....	....	**5**	**0**	**1**	**1**	**4**	**0**	**0**	**0**	....
1998-99	**Philadelphia**	**NHL**	**74**	**3**	**15**	**18**	**48**	**1**	**0**	**0**	**115**	**2.6**	**16**	**0**	**0.0**	**20:45**	**6**	**0**	**0**	**0**	**6**	**0**	**0**	**0**	**20:23**
99-2000	**Philadelphia**	**NHL**	**80**	**4**	**9**	**13**	**66**	**1**	**0**	**1**	**126**	**3.2**	**11**	**0**	**0.0**	**20:12**	**18**	**0**	**1**	**1**	**12**	**0**	**0**	**0**	**21:40**
2000-01	**Philadelphia**	**NHL**	**73**	**2**	**12**	**14**	**48**	**1**	**0**	**0**	**103**	**1.9**	**22**	**0**	**0.0**	**20:38**	**6**	**1**	**0**	**1**	**8**	**0**	**0**	**0**	**20:55**
2001-02	**Philadelphia**	**NHL**	**77**	**4**	**10**	**14**	**30**	**0**	**2**	**3**	**105**	**3.8**	**16**	**0**	**0.0**	**18:42**	**5**	**0**	**0**	**0**	**2**	**0**	**0**	**0**	**19:50**
2002-03	**Philadelphia**	**NHL**	**67**	**1**	**6**	**7**	**36**	**0**	**0**	**0**	**93**	**1.1**	**10**	**0**	**0.0**	**17:24**	**13**	**0**	**2**	**2**	**2**	**0**	**0**	**0**	**17:51**
2003-04	**Philadelphia**	**NHL**	**56**	**1**	**9**	**10**	**50**	**0**	**0**	**0**	**59**	**1.7**	**2**	**0**	**0.0**	**18:31**	....	....	....	....	....	....	....	....	....
	Philadelphia	AHL	2	0	0	0	0	....	....	....	....	....	....	....	....	....	....	....	....	....	....	....	....	....	....
	Dallas	**NHL**	**11**	**0**	**0**	**0**	**2**	**0**	**0**	**0**	**9**	**0.0**	**4**	**1**	**0.0**	**18:13**	**5**	**2**	**0**	**2**	**0**	**0**	**0**	**0**	**17:04**
	NHL Totals		**717**	**29**	**126**	**155**	**551**	**8**	**2**	**6**	**995**	**2.9**		**1**	**0.0**	**19:25**	**104**	**4**	**10**	**14**	**68**	**0**	**0**	**1**	**19:54**

Hockey East Second All-Star Team (1993) • NHL All-Rookie Team (1995)

Traded to **Dallas** by **Philadelphia** for Phoenix's 8th round choice (previously acquired, Philadelphia selected Martin Houle) in 2004 Entry Draft and Dallas' 3rd round choice in 2005 Entry Draft, March 8, 2004.

THOMAS, Steve

(TAW-mas, STEEV)

Left wing. Shoots left. 5'10", 185 lbs. Born, Stockport, England, July 15, 1963.

Season	Club	League	GP	G	A	Pts	PIM	PP	SH	GW	S	%	+/-	TF	F%	Min	GP	G	A	Pts	PIM	PP	SH	GW	Min
1980-81	Markham Waxers	OHA-A	42	22	25	47	76	....	....	....	....	....	....	....	....	....	....	....	....	....	....	....	....	....	....
	Toronto	OMJHL	1	0	0	0	0	....	....	....	....	....	....	....	....	....	....	....	....	....	....	....	....	....	....
1981-82	Markham Waxers	OJHL	48	68	57	125	113	....	....	....	....	....	....	....	....	....	....	....	....	....	....	....	....	....	....
	Toronto	OHL	1	0	0	0	0	....	....	....	....	....	....	....	....	....	....	....	....	....	....	....	....	....	....
1982-83	Toronto	OHL	61	18	20	38	42	....	....	....	....	....	....	....	....	....	....	....	....	....	....	....	....	....	....
1983-84	Toronto	OHL	70	51	54	105	77	....	....	....	....	....	....	....	....	....	....	....	....	....	....	....	....	....	....
1984-85	**Toronto**	**NHL**	**18**	**1**	**1**	**2**	**2**	**0**	**0**	**0**	**26**	**3.8**	**–13**	....	....	....	....	....	....	....	....	....	....	....	....
	St. Catharines	AHL	64	42	48	90	56	....	....	....	....	....	....	....	....	....	....	....	....	....	....	....	....	....	....
1985-86	**Toronto**	**NHL**	**65**	**20**	**37**	**57**	**36**	**5**	**0**	**5**	**197**	**10.2**	**–15**	....	....	....	**10**	**6**	**8**	**14**	**9**	**3**	**0**	**0**	....
	St. Catharines	AHL	19	18	14	32	35	....	....	....	....	....	....	....	....	....	....	....	....	....	....	....	....	....	....
1986-87	**Toronto**	**NHL**	**78**	**35**	**27**	**62**	**114**	**3**	**0**	**7**	**245**	**14.3**	**–3**	....	....	....	**13**	**2**	**3**	**5**	**13**	**0**	**0**	**0**	....
1987-88	**Chicago**	**NHL**	**30**	**13**	**13**	**26**	**40**	**5**	**0**	**3**	**69**	**18.8**	**1**	....	....	....	**3**	**1**	**2**	**3**	**6**	**0**	**0**	**0**	....
1988-89	**Chicago**	**NHL**	**45**	**21**	**19**	**40**	**69**	**8**	**0**	**0**	**124**	**16.9**	**–2**	....	....	....	**12**	**3**	**5**	**8**	**10**	**1**	**0**	**2**	....
1989-90	**Chicago**	**NHL**	**76**	**40**	**30**	**70**	**91**	**13**	**0**	**7**	**235**	**17.0**	**–3**	....	....	....	**20**	**7**	**6**	**13**	**33**	**1**	**0**	**3**	....
1990-91	**Chicago**	**NHL**	**69**	**19**	**35**	**54**	**129**	**2**	**0**	**3**	**192**	**9.9**	**8**	....	....	....	**6**	**1**	**2**	**3**	**15**	**0**	**0**	**0**	....
1991-92	**Chicago**	**NHL**	**11**	**2**	**6**	**8**	**26**	**0**	**0**	**1**	**35**	**5.7**	**–3**	....	....	....	....	....	....	....	....	....	....	....	....
	NY Islanders	**NHL**	**71**	**28**	**42**	**70**	**71**	**3**	**0**	**2**	**210**	**13.3**	**11**	....	....	....	....	....	....	....	....	....	....	....	....
1992-93	**NY Islanders**	**NHL**	**79**	**37**	**50**	**87**	**111**	**12**	**0**	**7**	**264**	**14.0**	**3**	....	....	....	**18**	**9**	**8**	**17**	**37**	**0**	**0**	**0**	....
1993-94	**NY Islanders**	**NHL**	**78**	**42**	**33**	**75**	**139**	**17**	**0**	**5**	**249**	**16.9**	**–9**	....	....	....	**4**	**1**	**0**	**1**	**8**	**1**	**0**	**0**	....
1994-95	**NY Islanders**	**NHL**	**47**	**11**	**15**	**26**	**60**	**3**	**0**	**2**	**133**	**8.3**	**–14**	....	....	....	....	....	....	....	....	....	....	....	....
1995-96	**New Jersey**	**NHL**	**81**	**26**	**35**	**61**	**98**	**6**	**0**	**6**	**192**	**13.5**	**–2**	....	....	....	....	....	....	....	....	....	....	....	....
1996-97	**New Jersey**	**NHL**	**57**	**15**	**19**	**34**	**46**	**1**	**0**	**2**	**124**	**12.1**	**9**	....	....	....	**10**	**1**	**1**	**2**	**18**	**0**	**0**	**0**	....
1997-98	**New Jersey**	**NHL**	**55**	**14**	**10**	**24**	**32**	**3**	**0**	**4**	**111**	**12.6**	**4**	....	....	....	**6**	**0**	**3**	**3**	**2**	**0**	**0**	**0**	....
1998-99	**Toronto**	**NHL**	**78**	**28**	**45**	**73**	**33**	**11**	**0**	**7**	**209**	**13.4**	**26**	**4**	**25.0**	**18:23**	**17**	**6**	**3**	**9**	**12**	**2**	**0**	**1**	**20:37**
99-2000	**Toronto**	**NHL**	**81**	**26**	**37**	**63**	**68**	**9**	**0**	**9**	**151**	**17.2**	**1**	**8**	**50.0**	**16:19**	**12**	**6**	**3**	**9**	**10**	**0**	**0**	**1**	**18:21**
2000-01	**Toronto**	**NHL**	**57**	**8**	**26**	**34**	**46**	**1**	**0**	**1**	**140**	**5.7**	**0**	**3**	**33.3**	**16:02**	**11**	**6**	**3**	**9**	**4**	**4**	**0**	**0**	**16:22**
2001-02	**Chicago**	**NHL**	**34**	**11**	**4**	**15**	**17**	**3**	**0**	**0**	**66**	**16.7**	**0**	**0**	**0.0**	**17:21**	**5**	**1**	**1**	**2**	**0**	**0**	**0**	**0**	**15:45**
2002-03	**Chicago**	**NHL**	**69**	**4**	**13**	**17**	**51**	**0**	**0**	**1**	**91**	**4.4**	**0**	**19**	**36.8**	**12:45**	....	....	....	....	....	....	....	....	....
	Anaheim	**NHL**	**12**	**10**	**3**	**13**	**2**	**1**	**0**	**3**	**27**	**37.0**	**10**	**5**	**20.0**	**13:42**	**21**	**4**	**4**	**8**	**8**	**2**	**0**	**3**	**15:13**
2003-04	**Detroit**	**NHL**	**44**	**10**	**12**	**22**	**25**	**0**	**0**	**3**	**80**	**12.5**	**8**	**7**	**28.6**	**12:45**	**6**	**0**	**1**	**1**	**2**	**0**	**0**	**0**	**8:18**
	NHL Totals		**1235**	**421**	**512**	**933**	**1306**	**106**	**0**	**78**	**3170**	**13.3**		**46**	**34.8**	**15:38**	**174**	**54**	**53**	**107**	**187**	**14**	**0**	**10**	**16:39**

AHL First All-Star Team (1985) • Dudley "Red" Garrett Memorial Trophy (Top Rookie – AHL) (1985)

Signed as a free agent by **Toronto**, May 12, 1984. Traded to **Chicago** by **Toronto** with Rick Vaive and Bob McGill for Al Secord and Ed Olczyk, September 3, 1987. Traded to **NY Islanders** by **Chicago** with Adam Creighton for Brent Sutter and Brad Lauer, October 25, 1991. Traded to **New Jersey** by **NY Islanders** for Claude Lemieux, October 3, 1995. Signed as a free agent by **Toronto**, July 30, 1998. Signed as a free agent by **Chicago**, July 17, 2001. • Missed majority of 2001-02 season recovering from ankle injury suffered in game vs. Calgary, November 15, 2001. Traded to **Anaheim** by **Chicago** for Anaheim's 5th round choice (Alexei Ivanov) in 2003 Entry Draft, March 11, 2003. Signed as a free agent by **Detroit**, November 5, 2003.

THOMPSON, Rocky

(TAWM-suhn, RAW-kee) **EDM.**

Defense. Shoots right. 6'2", 205 lbs. Born, Calgary, Alta., August 8, 1977. Calgary's 3rd choice, 72nd overall, in 1995 Entry Draft.

Season	Club	League	GP	G	A	Pts	PIM	PP	SH	GW	S	%	+/-	TF	F%	Min	GP	G	A	Pts	PIM	PP	SH	GW	Min
1992-93	Spruce Grove	AMHL	65	13	50	63	295	....	....	....	....	....	....	....	....	....	....	....	....	....	....	....	....	....	....
1993-94	Medicine Hat	WHL	68	1	4	5	166	....	....	....	....	....	....	....	....	....	3	0	0	0	2	....	....	....	....
1994-95	Medicine Hat	WHL	63	1	6	7	220	....	....	....	....	....	....	....	....	....	5	0	0	0	17	....	....	....	....
1995-96	Medicine Hat	WHL	71	9	20	29	260	....	....	....	....	....	....	....	....	....	5	2	3	5	26	....	....	....	....
	Saint John Flames	AHL	4	0	0	0	33	....	....	....	....	....	....	....	....	....	....	....	....	....	....	....	....	....	....
1996-97	Medicine Hat	WHL	47	6	9	15	170	....	....	....	....	....	....	....	....	....	....	....	....	....	....	....	....	....	....
	Swift Current	WHL	22	3	5	8	90	....	....	....	....	....	....	....	....	....	10	1	2	3	22	....	....	....	....
1997-98	**Calgary**	**NHL**	**12**	**0**	**0**	**0**	**61**	**0**	**0**	**0**	**3**	**0.0**	**0**	....	....	....	....	....	....	....	....	....	....	....	....
	Saint John Flames	AHL	51	3	0	3	187	....	....	....	....	....	....	....	....	....	18	1	1	2	47	....	....	....	....
1998-99	**Calgary**	**NHL**	**3**	**0**	**0**	**0**	**25**	**0**	**0**	**0**	**0**	**0.0**	**0**	**0**	**0.0**	**2:01**	....	....	....	....	....	....	....	....	....
	Saint John Flames	AHL	27	2	2	4	108	....	....	....	....	....	....	....	....	....	....	....	....	....	....	....	....	....	....
99-2000	Saint John Flames	AHL	53	2	8	10	125	....	....	....	....	....	....	....	....	....	....	....	....	....	....	....	....	....	....
	Louisville Panthers	AHL	3	0	1	1	54	....	....	....	....	....	....	....	....	....	4	0	0	0	4	....	....	....	....
2000-01	**Florida**	**NHL**	**4**	**0**	**0**	**0**	**19**	**0**	**0**	**0**	**0**	**0.0**	**0**	**0**	**0.0**	**1:28**	....	....	....	....	....	....	....	....	....
	Louisville Panthers	AHL	55	3	5	8	193	....	....	....	....	....	....	....	....	....	....	....	....	....	....	....	....	....	....
2001-02	**Florida**	**NHL**	**6**	**0**	**0**	**0**	**12**	**0**	**0**	**0**	**1**	**0.0**	**0**	**1**	**0.0**	**4:03**	....	....	....	....	....	....	....	....	....
	Hershey Bears	AHL	42	0	3	3	143	....	....	....	....	....	....	....	....	....	8	1	0	1	19	....	....	....	....
2002-03	San Antonio	AHL	79	1	11	12	275	....	....	....	....	....	....	....	....	....	3	0	0	0	4	....	....	....	....
2003-04	Toronto	AHL	69	1	8	9	196	....	....	....	....	....	....	....	....	....	3	1	1	2	0	....	....	....	....
	NHL Totals		**25**	**0**	**0**	**0**	**117**	**0**	**0**	**0**	**4**	**0.0**		**1**	**0.0**	**2:47**	....	....	....	....	....	....	....	....	....

Traded to **Florida** by **Calgary** for Filip Kuba, March 16, 2000. Signed as a free agent by **Edmonton**, July 20, 2003.

Season	Club	League	Regular Season GP	G	A	Pts	PIM	PP	SH	GW	S	%	+/-	TF	F%	Min	Playoffs GP	G	A	Pts	PIM	PP	SH	GW	Min

THORNTON, Joe

(THOHRN-tuhn, JOH) **BOS.**

Center. Shoots left. 6'4", 223 lbs. Born, London, Ont., July 2, 1979. Boston's 1st choice, 1st overall, in 1997 Entry Draft.

Season	Club	League	GP	G	A	Pts	PIM	PP	SH	GW	S	%	+/-	TF	F%	Min	GP	G	A	Pts	PIM	PP	SH	GW	Min
1993-94	Elgin-Middlesex	OMHA	67	*83	*85	*168	45	....	....	....	....	....	....	....	....	....	....	....	....	....	....	....	....	....	....
	St. Thomas Stars	OJHL-B	6	2	6	8	2	....	....	....	....	....	....	....	....	....	....	....	....	....	....	....	....	....	....
1994-95	St. Thomas Stars	OJHL-B	50	40	64	104	53	....	....	....	....	....	....	....	....	....	....	....	....	....	....	....	....	....	....
1995-96	Sault Ste. Marie	OHL	66	30	46	76	53	....	....	....	....	....	....	....	....	....	4	1	1	2	11	....	....	....	....
1996-97	Sault Ste. Marie	OHL	59	41	81	122	123	....	....	....	....	....	....	....	....	....	11	11	8	19	24	....	....	....	....
1997-98	**Boston**	**NHL**	**55**	**3**	**4**	**7**	**19**	**0**	**0**	**1**	**33**	**9.1**	**-6**	....	....	....	**6**	**0**	**0**	**0**	**9**	**0**	**0**	**0**	....
1998-99	**Boston**	**NHL**	**81**	**16**	**25**	**41**	**69**	**7**	**0**	**1**	**128**	**12.5**	**3**	**1073**	**48.7**	**15:21**	**11**	**3**	**6**	**9**	**4**	**2**	**0**	**2**	**19:52**
99-2000	**Boston**	**NHL**	**81**	**23**	**37**	**60**	**82**	**5**	**0**	**3**	**171**	**13.5**	**-5**	**1861**	**49.5**	**21:18**	....	....	....	....	....	....	....	....	....
2000-01	**Boston**	**NHL**	**72**	**37**	**34**	**71**	**107**	**19**	**1**	**5**	**181**	**20.4**	**-4**	**1651**	**52.1**	**21:45**	....	....	....	....	....	....	....	....	....
2001-02	**Boston**	**NHL**	**66**	**22**	**46**	**68**	**127**	**6**	**0**	**5**	**152**	**14.5**	**7**	**1341**	**49.1**	**19:59**	**6**	**2**	**4**	**6**	**10**	**0**	**0**	**0**	**21:09**
2002-03	**Boston**	**NHL**	**77**	**36**	**65**	**101**	**109**	**12**	**2**	**4**	**196**	**18.4**	**12**	**1766**	**49.5**	**22:33**	**5**	**1**	**2**	**3**	**4**	**1**	**0**	**0**	**20:13**
2003-04	**Boston**	**NHL**	**77**	**23**	**50**	**73**	**98**	**4**	**0**	**6**	**187**	**12.3**	**18**	**1671**	**56.3**	**21:38**	**7**	**0**	**0**	**0**	**14**	**0**	**0**	**0**	**21:30**
	NHL Totals		**509**	**160**	**261**	**421**	**611**	**53**	**3**	**25**	**1048**	**15.3**		**9363**	**51.0**	**20:23**	**35**	**6**	**12**	**18**	**41**	**3**	**0**	**2**	**20:35**

OHL All-Rookie Team (1996) • OHL Rookie of the Year (1996) • Canadian Major Junior Rookie of the Year (1996) • OHL Second All-Star Team (1997) • NHL Second All-Star Team (2003)
Played in NHL All-Star Game (2002, 2003, 2004)

THORNTON, Scott

(THOHRN-tuhn, SKAWT) **S.J.**

Left wing. Shoots left. 6'3", 225 lbs. Born, London, Ont., January 9, 1971. Toronto's 1st choice, 3rd overall, in 1989 Entry Draft.

Season	Club	League	GP	G	A	Pts	PIM	PP	SH	GW	S	%	+/-	TF	F%	Min	GP	G	A	Pts	PIM	PP	SH	GW	Min
1986-87	London	OJHL-B	31	10	7	17	10	....	....	....	....	....	....	....	....	....	....	....	....	....	....	....	....	....	....
1987-88	Belleville Bulls	OHL	62	11	19	30	54	....	....	....	....	....	....	....	....	....	6	0	1	1	2	....	....	....	....
1988-89	Belleville Bulls	OHL	59	28	34	62	103	....	....	....	....	....	....	....	....	....	5	1	1	2	6	....	....	....	....
1989-90	Belleville Bulls	OHL	47	21	28	49	91	....	....	....	....	....	....	....	....	....	11	2	10	12	15	....	....	....	....
1990-91	Belleville Bulls	OHL	3	2	1	3	2	....	....	....	....	....	....	....	....	....	6	0	7	7	14	....	....	....	....
	Toronto	**NHL**	**33**	**1**	**3**	**4**	**30**	**0**	**0**	**0**	**31**	**3.2**	**-15**	....	....	....	....	....	....	....	....	....	....	....	....
	Newmarket Saints	AHL	5	1	0	1	4	....	....	....	....	....	....	....	....	....	....	....	....	....	....	....	....	....	....
1991-92	**Edmonton**	**NHL**	**15**	**0**	**1**	**1**	**43**	**0**	**0**	**0**	**11**	**0.0**	**-6**	....	....	....	**1**	**0**	**0**	**0**	**0**	**0**	**0**	**0**	....
	Cape Breton	AHL	49	9	14	23	40	....	....	....	....	....	....	....	....	....	5	1	0	1	8	....	....	....	....
1992-93	**Edmonton**	**NHL**	**9**	**0**	**1**	**1**	**0**	**0**	**0**	**0**	**7**	**0.0**	**-4**	....	....	....	....	....	....	....	....	....	....	....	....
	Cape Breton	AHL	58	23	27	50	102	....	....	....	....	....	....	....	....	....	16	1	2	3	35	....	....	....	....
1993-94	**Edmonton**	**NHL**	**61**	**4**	**7**	**11**	**104**	**0**	**0**	**0**	**65**	**6.2**	**-15**	....	....	....	....	....	....	....	....	....	....	....	....
	Cape Breton	AHL	2	1	1	2	31	....	....	....	....	....	....	....	....	....	....	....	....	....	....	....	....	....	....
1994-95	**Edmonton**	**NHL**	**47**	**10**	**12**	**22**	**89**	**0**	**1**	**1**	**69**	**14.5**	**-4**	....	....	....	....	....	....	....	....	....	....	....	....
1995-96	**Edmonton**	**NHL**	**77**	**9**	**9**	**18**	**149**	**0**	**2**	**3**	**95**	**9.5**	**-25**	....	....	....	....	....	....	....	....	....	....	....	....
1996-97	**Montreal**	**NHL**	**73**	**10**	**10**	**20**	**128**	**1**	**1**	**1**	**110**	**9.1**	**-19**	....	....	....	**5**	**1**	**0**	**1**	**2**	**0**	**0**	**0**	....
1997-98	**Montreal**	**NHL**	**67**	**6**	**9**	**15**	**158**	**1**	**0**	**1**	**51**	**11.8**	**0**	....	....	....	**9**	**0**	**2**	**2**	**10**	**0**	**0**	**0**	....
1998-99	**Montreal**	**NHL**	**47**	**7**	**4**	**11**	**87**	**1**	**0**	**1**	**56**	**12.5**	**-2**	**466**	**52.8**	**12:24**	....	....	....	....	....	....	....	....	....
99-2000	**Montreal**	**NHL**	**35**	**2**	**3**	**5**	**70**	**0**	**0**	**1**	**36**	**5.6**	**-7**	**253**	**51.8**	**12:40**	....	....	....	....	....	....	....	....	....
	Dallas	**NHL**	**30**	**6**	**3**	**9**	**38**	**1**	**0**	**0**	**47**	**12.8**	**-5**	**14**	**14.3**	**13:03**	**23**	**2**	**7**	**9**	**28**	**0**	**0**	**1**	**14:11**
2000-01	**San Jose**	**NHL**	**73**	**19**	**17**	**36**	**114**	**4**	**0**	**1**	**159**	**11.9**	**4**	**29**	**41.4**	**13:54**	**6**	**3**	**0**	**3**	**8**	**0**	**0**	**1**	**15:50**
2001-02	**San Jose**	**NHL**	**77**	**26**	**16**	**42**	**116**	**6**	**0**	**5**	**144**	**18.1**	**11**	**18**	**61.1**	**13:31**	**12**	**3**	**3**	**6**	**6**	**0**	**0**	**0**	**15:52**
2002-03	**San Jose**	**NHL**	**41**	**9**	**12**	**21**	**41**	**4**	**0**	**1**	**64**	**14.1**	**-7**	**6**	**50.0**	**13:53**	....	....	....	....	....	....	....	....	....
2003-04	**San Jose**	**NHL**	**80**	**13**	**14**	**27**	**84**	**1**	**0**	**1**	**127**	**10.2**	**-6**	**27**	**40.7**	**13:57**	**12**	**2**	**2**	**4**	**22**	**0**	**0**	**0**	**12:31**
	NHL Totals		**765**	**122**	**121**	**243**	**1251**	**19**	**4**	**16**	**1072**	**11.4**		**813**	**51.2**	**13:28**	**68**	**11**	**14**	**25**	**76**	**0**	**0**	**2**	**14:22**

Traded to **Edmonton** by **Toronto** with Vincent Damphousse, Peter Ing and Luke Richardson for Grant Fuhr, Glenn Anderson and Craig Berube, September 19, 1991. Traded to **Montreal** by **Edmonton** for Andrei Kovalenko, September 6, 1996. Traded to **Dallas** by **Montreal** for Juha Lind, January 22, 2000. Signed as a free agent by **San Jose**, July 1, 2000. • Missed majority of 2002-03 season recovering from shoulder (October 7, 2002 in training camp) and head (February 21, 2003 vs. Columbus) injuries.

THORNTON, Shawn

(THOHRN-tohn, SHAWN) **CHI.**

Right wing. Shoots right. 6'1", 209 lbs. Born, Oshawa, Ont., July 23, 1977. Toronto's 6th choice, 190th overall, in 1997 Entry Draft.

Season	Club	League	GP	G	A	Pts	PIM	PP	SH	GW	S	%	+/-	TF	F%	Min	GP	G	A	Pts	PIM	PP	SH	GW	Min
1995-96	Peterborough	OHL	63	4	10	14	192	....	....	....	....	....	....	....	....	....	24	3	0	3	25	....	....	....	....
1996-97	Peterborough	OHL	61	19	10	29	204	....	....	....	....	....	....	....	....	....	11	2	4	6	20	....	....	....	....
1997-98	St. John's	AHL	59	0	3	3	225	....	....	....	....	....	....	....	....	....	....	....	....	....	....	....	....	....	....
1998-99	St. John's	AHL	78	8	11	19	354	....	....	....	....	....	....	....	....	....	5	0	0	0	9	....	....	....	....
99-2000	St. John's	AHL	60	4	12	16	316	....	....	....	....	....	....	....	....	....	....	....	....	....	....	....	....	....	....
2000-01	St. John's	AHL	79	5	12	17	320	....	....	....	....	....	....	....	....	....	3	1	2	3	2	....	....	....	....
2001-02	Norfolk Admirals	AHL	70	8	14	22	281	....	....	....	....	....	....	....	....	....	4	0	0	0	4	....	....	....	....
2002-03	**Chicago**	**NHL**	**13**	**1**	**1**	**2**	**31**	**0**	**0**	**0**	**15**	**6.7**	**-4**	**3**	**66.7**	**8:30**	....	....	....	....	....	....	....	....	....
	Norfolk Admirals	AHL	50	11	2	13	213	....	....	....	....	....	....	....	....	....	9	0	2	2	28	....	....	....	....
2003-04	**Chicago**	**NHL**	**8**	**1**	**0**	**1**	**23**	**0**	**0**	**0**	**14**	**7.1**	**2**	**19**	**42.1**	**11:14**	....	....	....	....	....	....	....	....	....
	Norfolk Admirals	AHL	64	6	11	17	259	....	....	....	....	....	....	....	....	....	8	1	1	2	6	....	....	....	....
	NHL Totals		**21**	**2**	**1**	**3**	**54**	**0**	**0**	**0**	**29**	**6.9**		**22**	**45.5**	**9:32**	....	....	....	....	....	....	....	....	....

Traded to **Chicago** by **Toronto** for Marty Wilford, September 30, 2001.

TIBBETTS, Billy

(TIH-buhts, BIHL-ee)

Right wing. Shoots right. 6'2", 215 lbs. Born, Boston, MA, October 14, 1974.

Season	Club	League	GP	G	A	Pts	PIM	PP	SH	GW	S	%	+/-	TF	F%	Min	GP	G	A	Pts	PIM	PP	SH	GW	Min
1992-93	Boston Jr. Bruins	NEJHL	73	60	80	140	150	....	....	....	....	....	....	....	....	....	....	....	....	....	....	....	....	....	....
1993-94	Sioux City	USHL	7	1	4	5	27	....	....	....	....	....	....	....	....	....	....	....	....	....	....	....	....	....	....
	London Knights	OHL	14	6	6	12	49	....	....	....	....	....	....	....	....	....	....	....	....	....	....	....	....	....	....
	Tri-City	WHL	9	0	2	2	39	....	....	....	....	....	....	....	....	....	....	....	....	....	....	....	....	....	....
1994-95	Antigonish	MJrHL	30	13	12	25	....	....	....	....	....	....	....	....	....	....	....	....	....	....	....	....	....	....	....
	Birmingham Bulls	ECHL	2	0	1	1	18	....	....	....	....	....	....	....	....	....	....	....	....	....	....	....	....	....	....
1995-96	Johnstown Chiefs	ECHL	58	37	31	68	300	....	....	....	....	....	....	....	....	....	....	....	....	....	....	....	....	....	....
1996/00			DID NOT PLAY																						
2000-01	**Pittsburgh**	**NHL**	**29**	**1**	**2**	**3**	**79**	**0**	**0**	**0**	**16**	**6.3**	**-2**	**115**	**28.7**	**7:14**	....	....	....	....	....	....	....	....	....
	Wilkes-Barre	AHL	38	14	24	38	185	....	....	....	....	....	....	....	....	....	12	4	6	10	55	....	....	....	....
2001-02	**Pittsburgh**	**NHL**	**33**	**1**	**5**	**6**	**109**	**0**	**0**	**1**	**42**	**2.4**	**-13**	**87**	**36.8**	**12:05**	....	....	....	....	....	....	....	....	....
	Wilkes-Barre	AHL	24	13	17	30	193	....	....	....	....	....	....	....	....	....	....	....	....	....	....	....	....	....	....
	Philadelphia	**NHL**	**9**	**0**	**1**	**1**	**69**	**0**	**0**	**0**	**6**	**0.0**	**-3**	**25**	**32.0**	**6:41**	....	....	....	....	....	....	....	....	....
2002-03	**NY Rangers**	**NHL**	**11**	**0**	**0**	**0**	**12**	**0**	**0**	**0**	**6**	**0.0**	**-2**	**75**	**41.3**	**9:58**	....	....	....	....	....	....	....	....	....
	Hartford	AHL	35	7	10	17	172	....	....	....	....	....	....	....	....	....	....	....	....	....	....	....	....	....	....
2003-04	San Diego Gulls	ECHL	• 40	18	35	53	266	....	....	....	....	....	....	....	....	....	....	....	....	....	....	....	....	....	....
	Springfield	AHL	6	0	2	2	25	....	....	....	....	....	....	....	....	....	....	....	....	....	....	....	....	....	....
	Houston Aeros	AHL	8	0	8	8	22	....	....	....	....	....	....	....	....	....	1	0	0	0	0	....	....	....	....
	NHL Totals		**82**	**2**	**8**	**10**	**269**	**0**	**0**	**1**	**70**	**2.9**		**302**	**34.4**	**9:29**	....	....	....	....	....	....	....	....	....

• Missed 1996-97 through 1999-2000 seasons serving prison sentence that commenced July 12, 1996. Signed as a free agent by **Pittsburgh**, April 10, 2000. Traded to **Philadelphia** by **Pittsburgh** for Kent Manderville, March 17, 2002. Signed as a free agent by **NY Rangers**, December 16, 2002. Signed as a free agent by **San Diego** (ECHL), October 17, 2003. Signed to a PTO (tryout) contract by **Springfield** (AHL), January 8, 2004. Signed to a PTO (tryout) contract by **Houston** (AHL), March 21, 2004.

TILEY, Brad

(TIHL-ee, BRAD)

Defense. Shoots left. 6'1", 199 lbs. Born, Markdale, Ont., July 5, 1971. Boston's 4th choice, 84th overall, in 1991 Entry Draft.

Season	Club	League	GP	G	A	Pts	PIM	PP	SH	GW	S	%	+/-	TF	F%	Min	GP	G	A	Pts	PIM	PP	SH	GW	Min
1987-88	Owen Sound	OJHL-B	45	18	25	43	69	....	....	....	....	....	....	....	....	....	....	....	....	....	....	....	....	....	....
1988-89	Sault Ste. Marie	OHL	50	4	11	15	31	....	....	....	....	....	....	....	....	....	....	....	....	....	....	....	....	....	....
1989-90	Sault Ste. Marie	OHL	66	9	32	41	47	....	....	....	....	....	....	....	....	....	....	....	....	....	....	....	....	....	....
1990-91	Sault Ste. Marie	OHL	66	11	55	66	29	....	....	....	....	....	....	....	....	....	14	4	15	19	12	....	....	....	....
1991-92	Maine Mariners	AHL	62	7	22	29	36	....	....	....	....	....	....	....	....	....	....	....	....	....	....	....	....	....	....
1992-93	Phoenix	IHL	46	11	27	38	35	....	....	....	....	....	....	....	....	....	....	....	....	....	....	....	....	....	....
	Binghamton	AHL	26	6	10	16	19	....	....	....	....	....	....	....	....	....	8	0	1	1	2	....	....	....	....
1993-94	Binghamton	AHL	29	6	10	16	6	....	....	....	....	....	....	....	....	....	....	....	....	....	....	....	....	....	....
	Phoenix	IHL	35	8	15	23	21	....	....	....	....	....	....	....	....	....	....	....	....	....	....	....	....	....	....
1994-95	Detroit Vipers	IHL	56	7	19	26	32	....	....	....	....	....	....	....	....	....	....	....	....	....	....	....	....	....	....
	Fort Wayne	IHL	14	1	6	7	2	....	....	....	....	....	....	....	....	....	3	1	2	3	0	....	....	....	....
1995-96	Orlando	IHL	69	11	23	34	82	....	....	....	....	....	....	....	....	....	23	2	4	6	16	....	....	....	....

Season	Club	League	Regular Season														Playoffs								
			GP	G	A	Pts	PIM	PP	SH	GW	S	%	+/-	TF	F%	Min	GP	G	A	Pts	PIM	PP	SH	GW	Min
1996-97	Phoenix	IHL	66	8	28	36	34																		
	Long Beach	IHL	3	1	0	1	2																		
1997-98	**Phoenix**	**NHL**	**1**	**0**	**0**	**0**	**0**																		
	Springfield	AHL	60	10	31	41	36										4	0	4	4	2				
1998-99	**Phoenix**	**NHL**	**8**	**0**	**0**	**0**	**0**	**0**	**0**	**0**	**1**	**0.0**	**−1**	**0**	**0.0**	**11:29**	**1**	**0**	**0**	**0**	**0**	**0**	**0**	**0**	**13:11**
	Springfield	AHL	69	9	35	44	14										1	0	0	0	0				
99-2000	Springfield	AHL	80	14	54	68	51										5	0	4	4	2				
2000-01	**Philadelphia**	**NHL**	**2**	**0**	**0**	**0**	**0**	**0**	**0**	**0**	**1**	**0.0**	**−1**	**0**	**0.0**	**15:46**									
	Philadelphia	AHL	56	11	19	30	10										10	1	2	3	2				
2001-02	Philadelphia	AHL	56	6	15	21	14																		
2002-03	Philadelphia	AHL	79	8	28	36	28																		
2003-04	Milwaukee	AHL	75	13	34	47	14										22	1	6	7	6				
	NHL Totals		**11**	**0**	**0**	**0**	**0**	**0**	**0**	**0**	**2**	**0.0**		**0**	**0.0**	**12:20**	**1**	**0**	**0**	**0**	**0**	**0**	**0**	**0**	**13:11**

Memorial Cup All-Star Team (1991) • AHL First All-Star Team (2000) • Eddie Shore Award (Top Defenseman – AHL) (2000)

Signed as a free agent by **NY Rangers**, September 4, 1992. Traded to **Los Angeles** by **NY Rangers** for Los Angeles' 11th round choice (Jamie Butt) in 1994 Entry Draft, January 28, 1994. Signed as a free agent by **Phoenix**, September 4, 1997. Signed as a free agent by **Philadelphia**, July 14, 2000. Signed as a free agent by **Milwaukee** (AHL), October 22, 2003.

TIMANDER, Mattias

(tih-MAHN-duhr, MA-tee-uhs)

Defense. Shoots left. 6'2", 230 lbs. Born, Solleftea, Sweden, April 16, 1974. Boston's 7th choice, 208th overall, in 1992 Entry Draft.

Season	Club	League	GP	G	A	Pts	PIM	PP	SH	GW	S	%	+/-	TF	F%	Min	GP	G	A	Pts	PIM	PP	SH	GW	Min
1992-93	MoDo Jr.	Swede-Jr.	4	0	0	0	0																		
	Husums IF	Swede-2	27	4	9	13	22																		
	MoDo	Sweden	1	0	0	0	0																		
1993-94	MoDo Jr.	Swede-Jr.	3	2	2	4	10																		
	MoDo	Sweden	23	2	2	4	6										11	2	0	2	10				
1994-95	MoDo	Sweden	39	8	9	17	24																		
1995-96	MoDo	Sweden	37	4	10	14	34										7	1	1	2	8				
1996-97	**Boston**	**NHL**	**41**	**1**	**8**	**9**	**14**	**0**	**0**	**0**	**62**	**1.6**	**−9**												
	Providence Bruins	AHL	32	3	11	14	20										10	1	1	2	12				
1997-98	**Boston**	**NHL**	**23**	**1**	**1**	**2**	**6**	**0**	**0**	**0**	**17**	**5.9**	**−9**												
	Providence Bruins	AHL	31	3	7	10	25																		
1998-99	**Boston**	**NHL**	**22**	**0**	**6**	**6**	**10**	**0**	**0**	**0**	**22**	**0.0**	**4**	**0**	**0.0**	**12:54**	**4**	**1**	**1**	**2**	**2**	**0**	**0**	**0**	**13:03**
	Providence Bruins	AHL	43	2	22	24	24																		
99-2000	**Boston**	**NHL**	**60**	**0**	**8**	**8**	**22**	**0**	**0**	**0**	**39**	**0.0**	**−11**	**0**	**0.0**	**12:29**									
	Hershey Bears	AHL	1	0	0	0	2																		
2000-01	**Columbus**	**NHL**	**76**	**2**	**9**	**11**	**24**	**0**	**0**	**1**	**68**	**2.9**	**−8**	**2**	**100.0**	**21:02**									
2001-02	**Columbus**	**NHL**	**78**	**4**	**7**	**11**	**44**	**1**	**0**	**0**	**68**	**5.9**	**−34**	**1**	**0.0**	**19:52**									
2002-03	**NY Islanders**	**NHL**	**80**	**3**	**13**	**16**	**24**	**0**	**0**	**1**	**83**	**3.6**	**−2**	**0**	**0.0**	**17:29**	**1**	**0**	**0**	**0**	**0**	**0**	**0**	**0**	**4:08**
2003-04	**NY Islanders**	**NHL**	**5**	**1**	**1**	**2**	**2**	**0**	**0**	**1**	**3**	**33.3**	**2**	**0**	**0.0**	**14:35**									
	Bridgeport	AHL	35	2	6	8	12																		
	Philadelphia	**NHL**	**34**	**1**	**4**	**5**	**19**	**0**	**1**	**0**	**43**	**2.3**	**13**	**0**	**0.0**	**18:25**	**18**	**2**	**4**	**6**	**6**	**0**	**0**	**1**	**17:28**
	NHL Totals		**419**	**13**	**57**	**70**	**165**	**1**	**1**	**3**	**405**	**3.2**		**3**	**66.7**	**17:41**	**23**	**3**	**5**	**8**	**8**	**0**	**0**	**1**	**16:07**

Selected by **Columbus** from **Boston** in Expansion Draft, June 23, 2000. Traded to **NY Islanders** by **Columbus** for NY Islanders' 4th round choice (Jekabs Redlihs) in 2002 Entry Draft, June 22, 2002. Traded to **Philadelphia** by **NY Islanders** for Tampa Bay's 7th round choice (previously acquired, NY Islanders selected Chris Campoli) in 2004 Entry Draft, January 22, 2004.

TIMONEN, Kimmo

(TEEM-oh-nehn, KEE-moh) **NSH.**

Defense. Shoots left. 5'10", 196 lbs. Born, Kuopio, Finland, March 18, 1975. Los Angeles' 11th choice, 250th overall, in 1993 Entry Draft.

Season	Club	League	GP	G	A	Pts	PIM	PP	SH	GW	S	%	+/-	TF	F%	Min	GP	G	A	Pts	PIM	PP	SH	GW	Min
1990-91	KalPa Kuopio Jr.	Finn-Jr.	4	0	1	1	2																		
1991-92	KalPa Kuopio Jr.	Finn-Jr.	32	7	10	17	4																		
	KalPa Kuopio	Finland	5	0	0	0	0																		
1992-93	KalPa Kuopio Jr.	Finn-Jr.	16	9	15	24	10																		
	KalPa Kuopio	Finland	33	0	2	2	4																		
1993-94	KalPa Kuopio Jr.	Finn-Jr.	5	4	7	11	0																		
	KalPa Kuopio	Finland	46	6	7	13	55																		
1994-95	TPS Turku Jr.	Finn-Jr.	1	0	0	0	0																		
	TPS Turku	Finland	45	3	4	7	10										13	0	1	1	6				
1995-96	TPS Turku	Finland	48	3	21	24	22										9	1	2	3	12				
1996-97	TPS Turku	Finland	50	10	14	24	18										12	2	7	9	8				
	TPS Turku	EuroHL	6	1	0	1	27										4	0	1	1	0				
1997-98	HIFK Helsinki	Finland	45	10	15	25	59										9	3	4	7	8				
	Finland	Olympics	6	0	1	1	2																		
1998-99	**Nashville**	**NHL**	**50**	**4**	**8**	**12**	**30**	**1**	**0**	**0**	**75**	**5.3**	**−4**	**0**	**0.0**	**19:04**									
	Milwaukee	IHL	29	2	13	15	22																		
99-2000	**Nashville**	**NHL**	**51**	**8**	**25**	**33**	**26**	**2**	**1**	**2**	**97**	**8.2**	**−5**	**0**	**0.0**	**21:06**									
2000-01	**Nashville**	**NHL**	**82**	**12**	**13**	**25**	**50**	**6**	**0**	**3**	**151**	**7.9**	**−6**	**2**	**50.0**	**23:11**									
2001-02	**Nashville**	**NHL**	**82**	**13**	**29**	**42**	**28**	**9**	**0**	**1**	**154**	**8.4**	**2**	**0**	**0.0**	**24:12**									
	Finland	Olympics	4	0	1	1	2																		
2002-03	**Nashville**	**NHL**	**72**	**6**	**34**	**40**	**46**	**4**	**0**	**0**	**144**	**4.2**	**−3**	**0**	**0.0**	**22:25**									
2003-04	**Nashville**	**NHL**	**77**	**12**	**32**	**44**	**52**	**8**	**0**	**1**	**180**	**6.7**	**−7**	**1**	**0.0**	**23:52**	**6**	**0**	**0**	**0**	**10**	**0**	**0**	**0**	**24:16**
	NHL Totals		**414**	**55**	**141**	**196**	**232**	**30**	**1**	**7**	**801**	**6.9**		**3**	**33.3**	**22:37**	**6**	**0**	**0**	**0**	**10**	**0**	**0**	**0**	**24:15**

Played in NHL All-Star Game (2004)

Traded to **Nashville** by **Los Angeles** with Jan Vopat for future considerations, June 26, 1998.

TJARNQVIST, Daniel

(TUH-yahrn-kvihst, DAN-yehl) **ATL.**

Defense. Shoots left. 6'2", 200 lbs. Born, Umea, Sweden, October 14, 1976. Florida's 5th choice, 88th overall, in 1995 Entry Draft.

Season	Club	League	GP	G	A	Pts	PIM	PP	SH	GW	S	%	+/-	TF	F%	Min	GP	G	A	Pts	PIM	PP	SH	GW	Min
1992-93	Rogle Jr.	Swede-Jr.	7	1	0	1	0																		
1993-94	Rogle 18	Swede-Jr.	STATISTICS NOT AVAILABLE																						
1994-95	Rogle	Sweden	18	0	1	1	2																		
	Rogle	Swede-Q	15	2	3	5	0																		
1995-96	Rogle	Sweden	22	1	7	8	6																		
1996-97	Jokerit Helsinki	Finland	44	3	8	11	4										9	0	3	3	4				
	Jokerit Helsinki	EuroHL	6	1	1	2	2																		
	Rogle	Sweden-Q	18	5	16	21	7										11	1	4	5	4				
1997-98	Djurgarden	Sweden	40	5	9	14	12										15	1	1	2	2				
1998-99	Djurgarden	Sweden	40	4	3	7	16										4	0	0	0	2				
99-2000	Djurgarden	Sweden	42	3	16	19	8										5	0	0	0	2				
2000-01	Djurgarden	Sweden	45	9	17	26	26										16	6	5	11	2				
2001-02	**Atlanta**	**NHL**	**75**	**2**	**16**	**18**	**14**	**1**	**0**	**0**	**68**	**2.9**	**−22**	**4**	**25.0**	**21:32**									
2002-03	**Atlanta**	**NHL**	**75**	**3**	**12**	**15**	**26**	**1**	**0**	**0**	**65**	**4.6**	**−20**	**3**	**66.7**	**21:53**									
2003-04	**Atlanta**	**NHL**	**68**	**5**	**15**	**20**	**20**	**0**	**2**	**1**	**65**	**7.7**	**−4**	**4**	**25.0**	**22:17**									
	NHL Totals		**218**	**10**	**43**	**53**	**60**	**2**	**2**	**1**	**198**	**5.1**		**11**	**36.4**	**21:53**									

Traded to **Atlanta** by **Florida** with Gord Murphy, Herbert Vasiljevs and Ottawa's 6th round choice (previously acquired, later traded to Dallas – Dallas selected Justin Cox) in 1999 Entry Draft for Trevor Kidd, June 25, 1999.

TJARNQVIST, Mathias

(TUH-yahrn-kvihst, MAT-ee-uhs) **DAL.**

Right wing. Shoots left. 6'1", 183 lbs. Born, Umea, Sweden, April 15, 1979. Dallas' 3rd choice, 96th overall, in 1999 Entry Draft.

Season	Club	League	GP	G	A	Pts	PIM	PP	SH	GW	S	%	+/-	TF	F%	Min	GP	G	A	Pts	PIM	PP	SH	GW	Min
1995-96	Rogle Jr.	Swede-Jr.	4	2	0	2	0																		
1996-97	Rogle Jr.	Swede-Jr.	18	5	8	13	....																		
	Rogle	Swede-2	15	1	4	5	4																		
1997-98	Rogle	Swede-2	31	12	11	23	30										4	2	0	2	6				
1998-99	Rogle	Swede-2	34	18	16	34	44										5	4	1	5	4				
99-2000	Djurgarden	Sweden	50	12	12	24	20										13	3	2	5	16				
2000-01	Djurgarden	Sweden	47	11	8	19	53										16	1	2	3	6				
2001-02	Djurgarden	Sweden	6	0	1	1	4										2	0	0	0	2				
2002-03	Djurgarden	Sweden	38	11	13	24	30										9	4	1	5	12				

			Regular Season														Playoffs								
Season	Club	League	GP	G	A	Pts	PIM	PP	SH	GW	S	%	+/-	TF	F%	Min	GP	G	A	Pts	PIM	PP	SH	GW	Min
2003-04	Dallas	NHL	18	1	1	2	2	0	0	1	11	9.1	−6	4	25.0	9:43									
	Utah Grizzlies	AHL	60	15	13	28	51																		
	NHL Totals		18	1	1	2	2	0	0	1	11	9.1		4	25.0	9:43									

TJUTIN, Fedor

(TYOO-tihn, feh-DUHR) **NYR**

Defense. Shoots left. 6'2", 196 lbs. Born, Izhevsk, USSR, July 19, 1983. NY Rangers' 2nd choice, 40th overall, in 2001 Entry Draft.

Season	Club	League	GP	G	A	Pts	PIM	PP	SH	GW	S	%	+/-	TF	F%	Min	GP	G	A	Pts	PIM	PP	SH	GW	Min
1998-99	Magnitogorsk 2	Russia-4	7	0	1	1	2																		
99-2000	Izhstal Izhevsk 2	Russia-3	38	11	8	19	68																		
	Izhstal Izhevsk	Russia-2	10	0	1	1	12																		
2000-01	St. Petersburg	Russia	34	2	4	6	20																		
2001-02	Guelph Storm	OHL	53	19	40	59	54										9	2	8	10	8				
2002-03	St. Petersburg	Russia	10	1	1	2	16																		
	Ak Bars Kazan	Russia	10	0	0	0	8										5	0	0	0	4				
2003-04	NY Rangers	NHL	25	2	5	7	14	0	1	0	33	6.1	−4	1	0.0	20:08									
	Hartford	AHL	43	5	9	14	50										16	0	5	5	18				
	NHL Totals		25	2	5	7	14	0	1	0	33	6.1		1	0.0	20:08									

TKACHUK, Keith

(kuh-CHUK, KEETH) **ST.L.**

Left wing. Shoots left. 6'2", 225 lbs. Born, Melrose, MA, March 28, 1972. Winnipeg's 1st choice, 19th overall, in 1990 Entry Draft.

Season	Club	League	GP	G	A	Pts	PIM	PP	SH	GW	S	%	+/-	TF	F%	Min	GP	G	A	Pts	PIM	PP	SH	GW	Min
1988-89	Malden	Hi-School	21	30	16	46																			
1989-90	Malden	Hi-School	6	12	14	26																			
1990-91	Boston University	H-East	36	17	23	40	70																		
1991-92	Team USA	Nat-Tm	45	10	10	20	141																		
	United States	Olympics	8	1	1	2	12																		
	Winnipeg	NHL	17	3	5	8	28	2	0	0	22	13.6	0				7	3	0	3	30	0	0	0	
1992-93	Winnipeg	NHL	83	28	23	51	201	12	0	2	199	14.1	−13				6	4	0	4	14	1	0	0	
1993-94	Winnipeg	NHL	84	41	40	81	255	22	3	3	218	18.8	−12												
1994-95	Winnipeg	NHL	48	22	29	51	152	7	2	2	129	17.1	−4												
1995-96	Winnipeg	NHL	76	50	48	98	156	20	2	6	249	20.1	11				6	1	2	3	22	0	0	0	
1996-97	Phoenix	NHL	81	*52	34	86	228	9	2	7	296	17.6	−1				7	6	0	6	7	2	0	0	
1997-98	Phoenix	NHL	69	40	26	66	147	11	0	8	232	17.2	9				6	3	3	6	10	0	0	0	
	United States	Olympics	4	0	2	2	6																		
1998-99	Phoenix	NHL	68	36	32	68	151	11	2	7	258	14.0	22	770	47.7	20:59	7	1	3	4	13	1	0	0	25:09
99-2000	Phoenix	NHL	50	22	21	43	82	5	1	1	183	12.0	7	500	50.4	19:21	5	1	1	2	4	1	0	0	18:46
2000-01	Phoenix	NHL	64	29	42	71	108	15	0	4	230	12.6	6	646	51.9	20:11									
	St. Louis	NHL	12	6	2	8	14	2	0	1	41	14.6	−3	87	54.0	19:39	15	2	7	9	20	2	0	1	19:17
2001-02	St. Louis	NHL	73	38	37	75	117	13	0	7	244	15.6	21	88	43.2	19:38	10	5	5	10	18	1	0	0	19:24
	United States	Olympics	5	2	0	2	2																		
2002-03	St. Louis	NHL	56	31	24	55	139	14	0	5	185	16.8	1	346	55.8	19:16	7	1	3	4	14	0	0	0	19:22
2003-04	St. Louis	NHL	75	33	38	71	83	18	0	8	233	14.2	8	410	49.5	19:39	5	0	2	2	10	0	0	0	19:18
	NHL Totals		856	431	401	832	1861	161	12	61	2719	15.9		2847	50.4	19:52	81	27	26	53	162	8	0	1	20:06

NHL Second All-Star Team (1995, 1998)

Played in NHL All-Star Game (1997, 1998, 1999, 2004)

Transferred to **Phoenix** after **Winnipeg** franchise relocated, July 1, 1996. Traded to **St. Louis** by **Phoenix** for Michal Handzus, Ladislav Nagy, the rights to Jeff Taffe and St. Louis' 1st round choice (Ben Eager) in 2002 Entry Draft, March 13, 2001.

TOBLER, Ryan

(TOH-bluhr, RIGH-uhn)

Left wing. Shoots left. 6'3", 227 lbs. Born, Calgary, Alta., May 13, 1976.

Season	Club	League	GP	G	A	Pts	PIM	PP	SH	GW	S	%	+/-	TF	F%	Min	GP	G	A	Pts	PIM	PP	SH	GW	Min
1993-94	Calgary Royals	AJHL	56	32	17	49	195																		
1994-95	Saskatoon Blades	WHL	61	11	19	30	81										10	1	2	3	8				
1995-96	Calgary Hitmen	WHL	16	10	3	13	8																		
	Swift Current	WHL	25	17	11	28	31										6	1	1	2	2				
1996-97	Swift Current	WHL	39	10	17	27	40																		
	Moose Jaw	WHL	24	6	15	21	16										12	1	6	7	16				
1997-98	Lake Charles	WPHL	66	22	34	56	204										4	2	3	5	18				
	Utah Grizzlies	IHL	3	1	0	1	2																		
1998-99	Adirondack	AHL	64	9	18	27	157										3	0	0	0	2				
99-2000	Milwaukee	IHL	78	19	28	47	293										2	0	0	0	0				
2000-01	Milwaukee	IHL	49	7	9	16	196																		
	Hartford	AHL	13	1	5	6	71										5	0	0	0	2				
2001-02	Tampa Bay	NHL	4	0	0	0	5	0	0	0	1	0.0	−2	0	0.0	4:08									
	Springfield	AHL	73	17	24	41	215																		
2002-03	Springfield	AHL	11	0	2	2	44																		
	Chicago Wolves	AHL	58	13	18	31	143										2	0	0	0	0				
2003-04	Colorado Eagles	CHL	51	30	49	79	93																		
	Wilkes-Barre	AHL	12	0	1	1	34										9	0	1	1	20				
	NHL Totals		4	0	0	0	5	0	0	0	1	0.0		0	0.0	4:08									

Signed as a free agent by **Nashville**, May 1, 2000. Traded to **NY Rangers** by **Nashville** for Bert Robertsson, March 7, 2001. Signed as a free agent by **Tampa Bay**, August 21, 2001. Signed as a free agent by **Colorado** (CHL), September 1, 2003. Signed as a free agent by **Wilkes-Barre** (AHL), February 18, 2004.

TOMS, Jeff

(TAWMS, JEHF)

Center. Shoots left. 6'5", 200 lbs. Born, Swift Current, Sask., June 4, 1974. New Jersey's 10th choice, 210th overall, in 1992 Entry Draft.

Season	Club	League	GP	G	A	Pts	PIM	PP	SH	GW	S	%	+/-	TF	F%	Min	GP	G	A	Pts	PIM	PP	SH	GW	Min
1990-91	Oakville	OMHA	58	34	47	81	72																		
1991-92	Sault Ste. Marie	OHL	36	9	5	14	0										16	0	1	1	2				
1992-93	Sault Ste. Marie	OHL	59	16	23	39	20										16	4	4	8	7				
1993-94	Sault Ste. Marie	OHL	64	52	45	97	19										14	11	4	15	2				
1994-95	Atlanta Knights	IHL	40	7	8	15	10										4	0	0	0	4				
1995-96	Tampa Bay	NHL	1	0	0	0	0	0	0	0	1	0.0	0												
	Atlanta Knights	IHL	68	16	18	34	18										1	0	0	0	0				
1996-97	Tampa Bay	NHL	34	2	8	10	10	0	0	1	53	3.8	2												
	Adirondack	AHL	37	11	16	27	8										4	1	2	3	0				
1997-98	Tampa Bay	NHL	13	1	2	3	7	0	0	0	14	7.1	−6												
	Washington	NHL	33	3	4	7	8	0	0	1	55	5.5	−11				1	0	0	0	0	0	0	0	
1998-99	Washington	NHL	21	1	5	6	2	0	0	0	30	3.3	0	92	54.3	13:35									
	Portland Pirates	AHL	20	3	7	10	8																		
99-2000	Washington	NHL	20	1	2	3	4	0	0	1	18	5.6	−1	17	52.9	8:26									
	Portland Pirates	AHL	33	16	21	37	16										4	1	1	2	2				
2000-01	NY Islanders	NHL	39	2	4	6	10	0	0	0	37	5.4	−7	172	42.4	9:44									
	Springfield	AHL	5	6	5	11	0																		
	NY Rangers	NHL	15	1	1	2	0	0	0	0	12	8.3	−3	21	33.3	6:34									
	Hartford	AHL	12	4	9	13	2										5	6	0	6	2				
2001-02	NY Rangers	NHL	38	7	4	11	10	2	0	0	62	11.3	−4	243	45.3	10:31									
	Hartford	AHL	9	6	6	12	4																		
	Pittsburgh	NHL	14	2	1	3	4	0	0	0	22	9.1	−5	71	40.9	12:19									
2002-03	Florida	NHL	8	2	2	4	4	0	0	1	12	16.7	2	83	53.0	11:36									
	San Antonio	AHL	64	30	33	63	28										1	0	0	0	0				
2003-04	Cherepovets	Russia	14	0	2	2	8																		
	EHC Basel	Swiss	25	14	11	25	14																		
	EHC Basel	Swiss-Q	8	3	2	5	0																		
	NHL Totals		236	22	33	55	59	2	0	4	316	7.0		699	46.1	10:18	1	0	0	0	0	0	0	0	

Traded to **Tampa Bay** by **New Jersey** for Vancouver's 4th round choice (previously acquired, later traded to New Jersey – later traded to Calgary – Calgary selected Ryan Duthie) in 1994 Entry Draft, May 31, 1994. Claimed by on waivers by **Washington** from **Tampa Bay**, November 19, 1997. Signed as a free agent by **NY Islanders**, July 27, 2000. Claimed on waivers by **NY Rangers** from **NY Islanders**, January 13, 2001. Claimed on waivers by **Pittsburgh** from **NY Rangers**, March 16, 2002. Signed as a free agent by **Florida**, July 11, 2002. Assigned to **Cherepovets** (Russia) by **Florida**, July 1, 2003. Signed as a free agent by **EHC Basel** (Swiss), November 11, 2003.

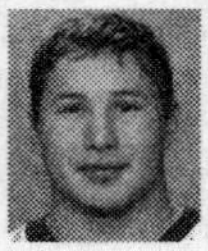

TOOTOO, Jordin
(TOO-TOO, JOHR-dihn) **NSH.**

Right wing. Shoots right. 5'9", 195 lbs. Born, Churchill, Man., February 2, 1983. Nashville's 6th choice, 98th overall, in 2001 Entry Draft.

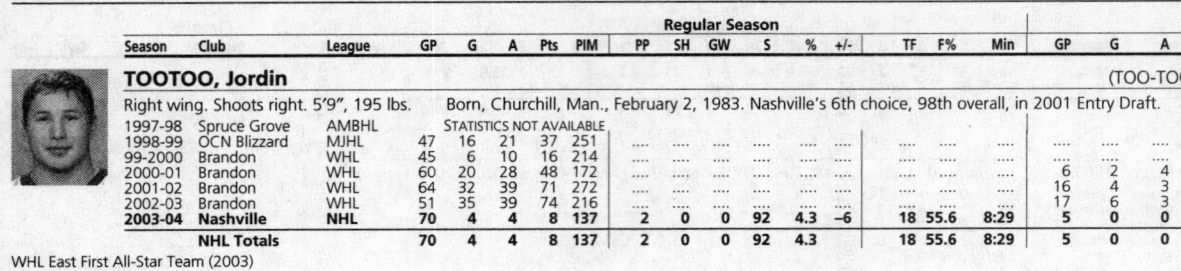

			Regular Season															Playoffs								
Season	Club	League	GP	G	A	Pts	PIM	PP	SH	GW	S	%	+/-	TF	F%	Min	GP	G	A	Pts	PIM	PP	SH	GW	Min
1997-98	Spruce Grove	AMBHL	STATISTICS NOT AVAILABLE																						
1998-99	OCN Blizzard	MJHL	47	16	21	37	251																		
99-2000	Brandon	WHL	45	6	10	16	214																		
2000-01	Brandon	WHL	60	20	28	48	172										6	2	4	6	18				
2001-02	Brandon	WHL	64	32	39	71	272										16	4	3	7	*58				
2002-03	Brandon	WHL	51	35	39	74	216										17	6	3	9	49				
2003-04	**Nashville**	**NHL**	**70**	**4**	**4**	**8**	**137**	**2**	**0**	**0**	**92**	**4.3**	**–6**	**18**	**55.6**	**8:29**	**5**	**0**	**0**	**0**	**4**	**0**	**0**	**0**	**5:09**
	NHL Totals		**70**	**4**	**4**	**8**	**137**	**2**	**0**	**0**	**92**	**4.3**		**18**	**55.6**	**8:29**	**5**	**0**	**0**	**0**	**4**	**0**	**0**	**0**	**5:09**

WHL East First All-Star Team (2003)

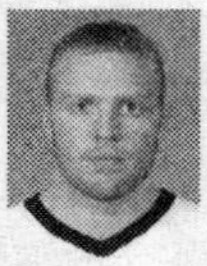

TORRES, Raffi
(TAW-rehs, RA-fee) **EDM.**

Left wing. Shoots left. 6', 216 lbs. Born, Toronto, Ont., October 8, 1981. NY Islanders' 2nd choice, 5th overall, in 2000 Entry Draft.

Season	Club	League	GP	G	A	Pts	PIM	PP	SH	GW	S	%	+/-	TF	F%	Min	GP	G	A	Pts	PIM	PP	SH	GW	Min
1997-98	Thornhill Rattlers	MTJHL	46	17	16	33	90																		
1998-99	Brampton	OHL	62	35	27	62	32																		
99-2000	Brampton	OHL	68	43	48	91	40										6	5	2	7	23				
2000-01	Brampton	OHL	55	33	37	70	76										8	7	4	11	19				
2001-02	**NY Islanders**	**NHL**	**14**	**0**	**1**	**1**	**6**	**0**	**0**	**0**	**9**	**0.0**	**2**	**0**	**0.0**	**7:35**									
	Bridgeport	AHL	59	20	10	30	45										20	8	9	17	26				
2002-03	**NY Islanders**	**NHL**	**17**	**0**	**5**	**5**	**10**	**0**	**0**	**0**	**12**	**0.0**	**0**	**4**	**25.0**	**7:40**									
	Bridgeport	AHL	49	17	15	32	54																		
	Hamilton	AHL	11	1	7	8	14										23	6	1	7	29				
2003-04	**Edmonton**	**NHL**	**80**	**20**	**14**	**34**	**65**	**5**	**0**	**3**	**136**	**14.7**	**12**	**21**	**28.6**	**12:38**									
	NHL Totals		**111**	**20**	**20**	**40**	**81**	**5**	**0**	**3**	**157**	**12.7**		**25**	**28.0**	**11:14**									

OHL All-Rookie Team (1999) • OHL Second All-Star Team (2000, 2001)

Traded to **Edmonton** by **NY Islanders** with Brad Isbister for Janne Niinimaa and Washington's 2nd round choice (previously acquired, NY Islanders selected Evgeni Tunik) in 2003 Entry Draft, March 11, 2003.

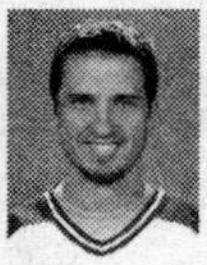

TRAVERSE, Patrick
(tra-VAIRZ, PAT-rihk)

Defense. Shoots left. 6'4", 207 lbs. Born, Montreal, Que., March 14, 1974. Ottawa's 3rd choice, 50th overall, in 1992 Entry Draft.

Season	Club	League	GP	G	A	Pts	PIM	PP	SH	GW	S	%	+/-	TF	F%	Min	GP	G	A	Pts	PIM	PP	SH	GW	Min
1990-91	Mtl-Bourassa	QAAA	42	4	19	23	10										5	0	3	3	2				
1991-92	Shawinigan	QMJHL	59	3	11	14	12										10	0	0	0	4				
1992-93	Shawinigan	QMJHL	53	5	24	29	24																		
	St-Jean Lynx	QMJHL	15	1	6	7	0										4	0	1	1	2				
	New Haven	AHL	2	0	0	0	2																		
1993-94	St-Jean Lynx	QMJHL	66	15	37	52	30										5	0	4	4	4				
	P.E.I. Senators	AHL	3	0	1	1	2																		
1994-95	P.E.I. Senators	AHL	70	5	13	18	19										7	0	2	2	0				
1995-96	**Ottawa**	**NHL**	**5**	**0**	**0**	**0**	**2**	**0**	**0**	**0**	**2**	**0.0**	**–1**												
	P.E.I. Senators	AHL	55	4	21	25	32										5	1	2	3	2				
1996-97	Worcester IceCats	AHL	24	0	4	4	23																		
	Grand Rapids	IHL	10	2	1	3	10										2	0	1	1	2				
1997-98	Hershey Bears	AHL	71	14	15	29	67										7	1	3	4	4				
1998-99	**Ottawa**	**NHL**	**46**	**1**	**9**	**10**	**22**	**0**	**0**	**0**	**35**	**2.9**	**12**	**0**	**0.0**	**14:56**									
99-2000	**Ottawa**	**NHL**	**66**	**6**	**17**	**23**	**21**	**1**	**0**	**0**	**73**	**8.2**	**17**	**0**	**0.0**	**18:43**	**6**	**0**	**0**	**0**	**2**	**0**	**0**	**0**	**17:50**
2000-01	**Anaheim**	**NHL**	**15**	**1**	**0**	**1**	**6**	**0**	**0**	**0**	**7**	**14.3**	**–6**	**0**	**0.0**	**17:19**									
	Boston	**NHL**	**37**	**2**	**6**	**8**	**14**	**1**	**0**	**1**	**39**	**5.1**	**4**	**0**	**0.0**	**16:38**									
	Montreal	**NHL**	**19**	**2**	**3**	**5**	**10**	**0**	**0**	**0**	**16**	**12.5**	**–8**	**0**	**0.0**	**21:36**									
2001-02	**Montreal**	**NHL**	**25**	**2**	**3**	**5**	**14**	**2**	**0**	**0**	**24**	**8.3**	**–7**	**0**	**0.0**	**18:14**									
	Quebec Citadelles	AHL	4	0	2	2	4																		
2002-03	**Montreal**	**NHL**	**65**	**0**	**13**	**13**	**24**	**0**	**0**	**0**	**63**	**0.0**	**–9**	**0**	**0.0**	**20:12**									
2003-04	Hamilton	AHL	80	5	21	26	31										10	1	2	3	0				
	NHL Totals		**278**	**14**	**51**	**65**	**113**	**4**	**0**	**1**	**259**	**5.4**		**0**	**0.0**	**18:14**	**6**	**0**	**0**	**0**	**2**	**0**	**0**	**0**	**17:49**

Traded to **Anaheim** by **Ottawa** for Joel Kwiatkowski, June 12, 2000. Traded to **Boston** by **Anaheim** with Andrei Nazarov for Samuel Pahlsson, November 18, 2000. Traded to **Montreal** by **Boston** for Eric Weinrich, February 21, 2001. • Missed majority of 2001-02 season recovering from knee (November 3, 2001 vs. Calgary) and head (January 10, 2002 vs. NY Islanders) injuries.

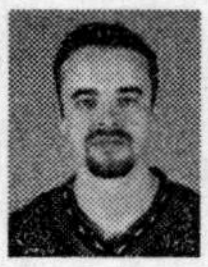

TREMBLAY, Yannick
(TRAHM-blay, YA-nihk)

Defense. Shoots right. 6'2", 200 lbs. Born, Pointe-aux-Trembles, Que., November 15, 1975. Toronto's 4th choice, 145th overall, in 1995 Entry Draft.

Season	Club	League	GP	G	A	Pts	PIM	PP	SH	GW	S	%	+/-	TF	F%	Min	GP	G	A	Pts	PIM	PP	SH	GW	Min
1991-92	Mtl-Bourassa	QAAA	35	2	5	7	55										8	0	4	4	2				
1992-93	Mtl-Bourassa	CEGEP	21	2	5	7	10										3	0	0	0	2				
1993-94	St. Thomas	AUAA	25	2	3	5	10																		
1994-95	Beauport	QMJHL	70	10	32	42	22										17	6	8	14	6				
1995-96	Beauport	QMJHL	61	12	33	45	42										20	3	16	19	18				
	St. John's	AHL	3	0	1	1	0																		
1996-97	**Toronto**	**NHL**	**5**	**0**	**0**	**0**	**0**	**0**	**0**	**0**	**2**	**0.0**	**–4**												
	St. John's	AHL	67	7	25	32	34										11	2	9	11	0				
1997-98	**Toronto**	**NHL**	**38**	**2**	**4**	**6**	**6**	**1**	**0**	**0**	**45**	**4.4**	**–6**												
	St. John's	AHL	17	3	7	10	4										4	0	1	1	5				
1998-99	**Toronto**	**NHL**	**35**	**2**	**7**	**9**	**16**	**0**	**0**	**0**	**37**	**5.4**	**0**	**0**	**0.0**	**17:39**									
99-2000	**Atlanta**	**NHL**	**75**	**10**	**21**	**31**	**22**	**4**	**1**	**2**	**139**	**7.2**	**–42**	**3**	**0.0**	**19:27**									
2000-01	**Atlanta**	**NHL**	**46**	**4**	**8**	**12**	**30**	**1**	**0**	**1**	**102**	**3.9**	**–6**	**1**	**100.0**	**20:27**									
2001-02	**Atlanta**	**NHL**	**66**	**9**	**15**	**24**	**47**	**1**	**0**	**1**	**115**	**7.8**	**–15**	**0**	**0.0**	**21:50**									
2002-03	**Atlanta**	**NHL**	**75**	**8**	**22**	**30**	**32**	**5**	**0**	**1**	**151**	**5.3**	**–27**	**1**	**0.0**	**21:45**									
2003-04	**Atlanta**	**NHL**	**38**	**2**	**8**	**10**	**13**	**1**	**0**	**1**	**47**	**4.3**	**–13**	**2**	**50.0**	**21:36**									
	NHL Totals		**378**	**37**	**85**	**122**	**166**	**13**	**1**	**6**	**638**	**5.8**		**7**	**28.6**	**20:38**									

Claimed by **Atlanta** from **Toronto** in Expansion Draft, June 25, 1999. • Missed majority of 2003-04 season recovering from foot (November 15, 2003 vs. Philadelphia) and hip (January 30, 2004 vs. Toronto) injuries.

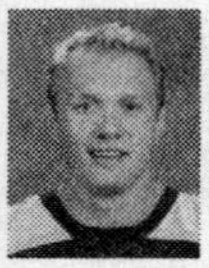

TREPANIER, Pascal
(TREHP-uhn-yay, pas-KAL)

Defense. Shoots right. 6', 210 lbs. Born, Gaspe, Que., September 4, 1973.

Season	Club	League	GP	G	A	Pts	PIM	PP	SH	GW	S	%	+/-	TF	F%	Min	GP	G	A	Pts	PIM	PP	SH	GW	Min
1989-90	Jonquiere Elites	QAAA	40	2	8	10	46																		
1990-91	Hull Olympiques	QMJHL	46	3	3	6	56										4	0	2	2	7				
1991-92	Trois-Rivieres	QMJHL	53	4	18	22	125										15	3	5	8	21				
1992-93	Sherbrooke	QMJHL	59	15	33	48	130										15	5	7	12	36				
1993-94	Sherbrooke	QMJHL	48	16	41	57	67										12	1	8	9	14				
1994-95	Dayton Bombers	ECHL	36	16	28	44	113										9	2	4	6	20				
	Kalamazoo Wings	IHL	14	1	2	3	47																		
	Cornwall Aces	AHL	4	0	0	0	9										14	2	7	9	32				
1995-96	Cornwall Aces	AHL	70	13	20	33	142										8	1	2	3	24				
1996-97	Hershey Bears	AHL	73	14	39	53	151										23	6	13	19	59				
1997-98	**Colorado**	**NHL**	**15**	**0**	**1**	**1**	**18**	**0**	**0**	**0**	**9**	**0.0**	**–2**												
	Hershey Bears	AHL	43	13	18	31	105										7	4	2	6	8				
1998-99	**Anaheim**	**NHL**	**45**	**2**	**4**	**6**	**48**	**0**	**0**	**1**	**49**	**4.1**	**0**	**1**	**0.0**	**12:42**									
99-2000	**Anaheim**	**NHL**	**37**	**0**	**4**	**4**	**54**	**0**	**0**	**0**	**33**	**0.0**	**2**	**1**	**0.0**	**11:18**									
2000-01	**Anaheim**	**NHL**	**57**	**6**	**4**	**10**	**73**	**3**	**0**	**0**	**86**	**7.0**	**–12**	**1**	**100.0**	**16:47**									
2001-02	**Colorado**	**NHL**	**74**	**4**	**9**	**13**	**59**	**2**	**0**	**0**	**87**	**4.6**	**4**	**0**	**0.0**	**14:37**	**2**	**0**	**0**	**0**	**0**	**0**	**0**	**0**	**5:43**

			Regular Season														Playoffs								
Season	**Club**	**League**	**GP**	**G**	**A**	**Pts**	**PIM**	**PP**	**SH**	**GW**	**S**	**%**	**+/-**	**TF**	**F%**	**Min**	**GP**	**G**	**A**	**Pts**	**PIM**	**PP**	**SH**	**GW**	**Min**
2002-03	**Nashville**	**NHL**	**1**	**0**	**0**	**0**	**0**	**0**	**0**	**0**	**1**	**0.0**	**0**	**0**	**0.0**	**9:55**	....	....	....	....	....	....	....	....	....
	Milwaukee	AHL	52	9	15	24	33	....	....	....	....	....	....	....	....	....	....	....	....	....	....	....	....	....	....
	San Antonio	AHL	12	4	6	10	10	....	....	....	....	....	....	....	....	....	2	0	0	0	2	....	....	....	....
2003-04	Hershey Bears	AHL	75	11	33	44	53	....	....	....	....	....	....	....	....	....	....	....	....	....	....	....	....	....	....
	NHL Totals		**229**	**12**	**22**	**34**	**252**	**5**	**0**	**1**	**265**	**4.5**		**3**	**33.3**	**14:12**	**2**	**0**	**0**	**0**	**0**	**0**	**0**	**0**	**5:43**

AHL Second All-Star Team (1997)

Signed as a free agent by **Colorado**, August 30, 1995. Claimed by **Anaheim** from **Colorado** in Waiver Draft, October 5, 1998. Signed as a free agent by **Colorado**, September, 2001. Signed as a free agent by **Nashville**, July 16, 2002. Traded to **Florida** by **Nashville** for Wade Flaherty, March 9, 2003. Signed as a free agent by **Tampa Bay**, July 23, 2003.

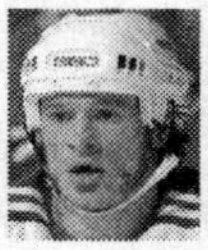

TRIPP, John

(TRIHP, JAWN)

Right wing. Shoots right. 6'2", 215 lbs. Born, Kingston, Ont., May 4, 1977. Calgary's 3rd choice, 42nd overall, in 1997 Entry Draft.

1993-94	St. Mary's Lincolns	OJHL-B	42	15	29	44	116	....	....	....	....	....	....	....	....	....	....	....	....	....	....	....	....	....	....
1994-95	Oshawa Generals	OHL	58	6	11	17	53	....	....	....	....	....	....	....	....	....	7	0	1	1	4	....	....	....	....
1995-96	Oshawa Generals	OHL	56	13	14	27	95	....	....	....	....	....	....	....	....	....	5	1	1	2	13	....	....	....	....
1996-97	Oshawa Generals	OHL	59	28	20	48	126	....	....	....	....	....	....	....	....	....	18	*16	10	26	42	....	....	....	....
1997-98	Roanoke Express	ECHL	9	0	2	2	22	....	....	....	....	....	....	....	....	....	....	....	....	....	....	....	....	....	....
	Saint John Flames	AHL	61	1	11	12	66	....	....	....	....	....	....	....	....	....	2	0	1	1	0	....	....	....	....
1998-99	Saint John Flames	AHL	2	0	0	0	10	....	....	....	....	....	....	....	....	....	....	....	....	....	....	....	....	....	....
	Johnstown Chiefs	ECHL	7	2	0	2	12	....	....	....	....	....	....	....	....	....	....	....	....	....	....	....	....	....	....
99-2000	Johnstown Chiefs	ECHL	38	13	11	24	64	....	....	....	....	....	....	....	....	....	....	....	....	....	....	....	....	....	....
	Saint John Flames	AHL	29	8	7	15	38	....	....	....	....	....	....	....	....	....	3	0	0	0	2	....	....	....	....
2000-01	Pensacola	ECHL	36	19	14	33	110	....	....	....	....	....	....	....	....	....	....	....	....	....	....	....	....	....	....
	Houston Aeros	IHL	15	0	6	6	14	....	....	....	....	....	....	....	....	....	....	....	....	....	....	....	....	....	....
	Hershey Bears	AHL	5	0	1	1	0	....	....	....	....	....	....	....	....	....	....	....	....	....	....	....	....	....	....
	Milwaukee	IHL	12	0	1	1	31	....	....	....	....	....	....	....	....	....	....	....	....	....	....	....	....	....	....
2001-02	Pensacola	ECHL	49	25	27	52	114	....	....	....	....	....	....	....	....	....	....	....	....	....	....	....	....	....	....
	Hartford	AHL	23	4	9	13	22	....	....	....	....	....	....	....	....	....	10	4	2	6	17	....	....	....	....
2002-03	**NY Rangers**	**NHL**	**9**	**1**	**2**	**3**	**2**	**0**	**0**	**0**	**16**	**6.3**	**1**	**0**	**0.0**	**8:43**	....	....	....	....	....	....	....	....	....
	Hartford	AHL	57	29	21	50	68	....	....	....	....	....	....	....	....	....	2	0	0	0	2	....	....	....	....
2003-04	**Los Angeles**	**NHL**	**34**	**1**	**5**	**6**	**33**	**0**	**0**	**0**	**45**	**2.2**	**–4**	**2**	**100.0**	**8:05**	....	....	....	....	....	....	....	....	....
	Manchester	AHL	24	8	7	15	33	....	....	....	....	....	....	....	....	....	....	....	....	....	....	....	....	....	....
	NHL Totals		**43**	**2**	**7**	**9**	**35**	**0**	**0**	**0**	**61**	**3.3**		**2**	**100.0**	**8:13**	....	....	....	....	....	....	....	....	....

• Re-entered NHL Entry Draft. Originally Colorado's 3rd choice, 77th overall, in 1995 Entry Draft.

Signed to tryout contract by **Hartford** (AHL), January 29, 2002. Signed as a free agent by **Hartford** (AHL), September 3, 2002. Signed as a free agent by **Los Angeles**, August 6, 2003. Signed as a free agent by **Alder Mannheim** (Germany), April 20, 2004.

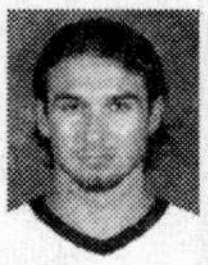

TRNKA, Pavel

(truhn-KAH, PAH-vehl)

Defense. Shoots left. 6'2", 206 lbs. Born, Plzen, Czech., July 27, 1976. Anaheim's 5th choice, 106th overall, in 1994 Entry Draft.

1993-94	HC Skoda Plzen	Czech	12	0	1	1	....	....	....	....	....	....	....	....	....	....	....	....	....	....	....	....	....	....	....
1994-95	HC Kladno	Czech	28	0	5	5	24	....	....	....	....	....	....	....	....	....	....	....	....	....	....	....	....	....	....
	Plzen	Czech	6	0	0	0	0	....	....	....	....	....	....	....	....	....	....	....	....	....	....	....	....	....	....
1995-96	Baltimore Bandits	AHL	69	2	6	8	44	....	....	....	....	....	....	....	....	....	6	0	0	0	2	....	....	....	....
1996-97	Baltimore Bandits	AHL	69	6	14	20	86	....	....	....	....	....	....	....	....	....	3	0	0	0	2	....	....	....	....
1997-98	**Anaheim**	**NHL**	**48**	**3**	**4**	**7**	**40**	**1**	**0**	**0**	**46**	**6.5**	**–4**	....	....	....	....	....	....	....	....	....	....	....	....
	Cincinnati	AHL	23	3	5	8	28	....	....	....	....	....	....	....	....	....	....	....	....	....	....	....	....	....	....
1998-99	**Anaheim**	**NHL**	**63**	**0**	**4**	**4**	**60**	**0**	**0**	**0**	**50**	**0.0**	**–6**	**0**	**0.0**	**16:06**	**4**	**0**	**1**	**1**	**2**	**0**	**0**	**0**	**21:26**
99-2000	**Anaheim**	**NHL**	**57**	**2**	**15**	**17**	**34**	**0**	**0**	**0**	**54**	**3.7**	**12**	**0**	**0.0**	**19:21**	....	....	....	....	....	....	....	....	....
2000-01	**Anaheim**	**NHL**	**59**	**1**	**7**	**8**	**42**	**0**	**0**	**0**	**59**	**1.7**	**–12**	**0**	**0.0**	**20:07**	....	....	....	....	....	....	....	....	....
2001-02	**Anaheim**	**NHL**	**71**	**2**	**11**	**13**	**66**	**1**	**0**	**0**	**78**	**2.6**	**–5**	**0**	**0.0**	**17:03**	....	....	....	....	....	....	....	....	....
2002-03	**Anaheim**	**NHL**	**24**	**3**	**6**	**9**	**6**	**1**	**0**	**0**	**33**	**9.1**	**2**	**0**	**0.0**	**16:00**	....	....	....	....	....	....	....	....	....
	Florida	**NHL**	**22**	**0**	**3**	**3**	**24**	**0**	**0**	**0**	**25**	**0.0**	**–1**	**0**	**0.0**	**17:24**	....	....	....	....	....	....	....	....	....
2003-04	**Florida**	**NHL**	**67**	**3**	**13**	**16**	**51**	**1**	**0**	**0**	**66**	**4.5**	**2**	**0**	**0.0**	**17:07**	....	....	....	....	....	....	....	....	....
	NHL Totals		**411**	**14**	**63**	**77**	**323**	**4**	**0**	**0**	**411**	**3.4**		**0**	**0.0**	**17:43**	**4**	**0**	**1**	**1**	**2**	**0**	**0**	**0**	**21:26**

Traded to **Florida** by **Anaheim** with Matt Cullen and Anaheim's 4th round choice (James Pemberton) in 2003 Entry Draft for Sandis Ozolinsh and Lance Ward, January 30, 2003.

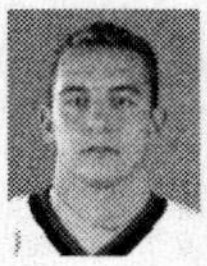

TSELIOS, Nikos

(TSEHL-ee-ohs, NEE-kohs) **PHX.**

Defense. Shoots left. 6'5", 226 lbs. Born, Oak Park, IL, January 20, 1979. Carolina's 1st choice, 22nd overall, in 1997 Entry Draft.

1995-96	Chicago	MEHL	27	5	8	13	40	....	....	....	....	....	....	....	....	....	....	....	....	....	....	....	....	....	....
1996-97	Belleville Bulls	OHL	64	9	37	46	61	....	....	....	....	....	....	....	....	....	6	1	1	2	2	....	....	....	....
1997-98	Belleville Bulls	OHL	20	2	10	12	16	....	....	....	....	....	....	....	....	....	....	....	....	....	....	....	....	....	....
	Plymouth Whalers	OHL	41	8	20	28	27	....	....	....	....	....	....	....	....	....	15	1	8	9	27	....	....	....	....
1998-99	Plymouth Whalers	OHL	60	21	39	60	60	....	....	....	....	....	....	....	....	....	11	4	10	14	8	....	....	....	....
99-2000	Cincinnati	IHL	80	3	19	22	75	....	....	....	....	....	....	....	....	....	10	0	2	2	4	....	....	....	....
2000-01	Cincinnati	IHL	79	7	18	25	98	....	....	....	....	....	....	....	....	....	5	0	3	3	0	....	....	....	....
2001-02	**Carolina**	**NHL**	**2**	**0**	**0**	**0**	**6**	**0**	**0**	**0**	**3**	**0.0**	**–2**	**0**	**0.0**	**13:13**	....	....	....	....	....	....	....	....	....
	Lowell	AHL	70	3	16	19	64	....	....	....	....	....	....	....	....	....	....	....	....	....	....	....	....	....	....
2002-03	Lowell	AHL	61	4	8	12	65	....	....	....	....	....	....	....	....	....	....	....	....	....	....	....	....	....	....
	Springfield	AHL	13	0	2	2	12	....	....	....	....	....	....	....	....	....	6	0	0	0	4	....	....	....	....
2003-04	Springfield	AHL	75	5	8	13	105	....	....	....	....	....	....	....	....	....	....	....	....	....	....	....	....	....	....
	NHL Totals		**2**	**0**	**0**	**0**	**6**	**0**	**0**	**0**	**3**	**0.0**		**0**	**0.0**	**13:13**	....	....	....	....	....	....	....	....	....

OHL All-Rookie Team (1997)

Signed as a free agent by **Phoenix**, July 21, 2003.

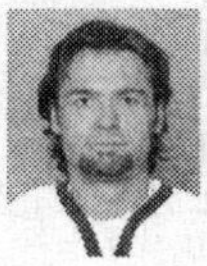

TUCKER, Darcy

(TUH-kuhr, DAHR-see) **TOR.**

Right wing. Shoots left. 5'10", 178 lbs. Born, Castor, Alta., March 15, 1975. Montreal's 8th choice, 151st overall, in 1993 Entry Draft.

1990-91	Red Deer	AMHL	47	70	90	160	48	....	....	....	....	....	....	....	....	....	....	....	....	....	....	....	....	....	....
1991-92	Kamloops Blazers	WHL	26	3	10	13	32	....	....	....	....	....	....	....	....	....	9	0	1	1	16	....	....	....	....
1992-93	Kamloops Blazers	WHL	67	31	58	89	155	....	....	....	....	....	....	....	....	....	13	7	6	13	34	....	....	....	....
1993-94	Kamloops Blazers	WHL	66	52	88	140	143	....	....	....	....	....	....	....	....	....	19	9	*18	*27	43	....	....	....	....
1994-95	Kamloops Blazers	WHL	64	64	73	137	94	....	....	....	....	....	....	....	....	....	21	*16	15	*31	19	....	....	....	....
1995-96	**Montreal**	**NHL**	**3**	**0**	**0**	**0**	**0**	**0**	**0**	**0**	**1**	**0.0**	**–1**	....	....	....	....	....	....	....	....	....	....	....	....
	Fredericton	AHL	74	29	64	93	174	....	....	....	....	....	....	....	....	....	7	7	3	10	14	....	....	....	....
1996-97	**Montreal**	**NHL**	**73**	**7**	**13**	**20**	**110**	**1**	**0**	**3**	**62**	**11.3**	**–5**	....	....	....	**4**	**0**	**0**	**0**	**0**	**0**	**0**	**0**	....
1997-98	**Montreal**	**NHL**	**39**	**1**	**5**	**6**	**57**	**0**	**0**	**0**	**19**	**5.3**	**–6**	....	....	....	....	....	....	....	....	....	....	....	....
	Tampa Bay	**NHL**	**35**	**6**	**8**	**14**	**89**	**1**	**1**	**0**	**44**	**13.6**	**–8**	....	....	....	....	....	....	....	....	....	....	....	....
1998-99	**Tampa Bay**	**NHL**	**82**	**21**	**22**	**43**	**176**	**8**	**2**	**3**	**178**	**11.8**	**–34**	**1470**	**45.6**	**19:24**	....	....	....	....	....	....	....	....	....
99-2000	**Tampa Bay**	**NHL**	**50**	**14**	**20**	**34**	**108**	**1**	**0**	**2**	**98**	**14.3**	**–15**	**152**	**48.7**	**19:58**	....	....	....	....	....	....	....	....	....
	Toronto	**NHL**	**27**	**7**	**10**	**17**	**55**	**0**	**2**	**3**	**40**	**17.5**	**3**	**11**	**54.6**	**16:41**	**12**	**4**	**2**	**6**	**15**	**1**	**0**	**2**	**17:23**
2000-01	**Toronto**	**NHL**	**82**	**16**	**21**	**37**	**141**	**2**	**0**	**4**	**122**	**13.1**	**6**	**413**	**47.0**	**16:09**	**11**	**0**	**2**	**2**	**6**	**0**	**0**	**0**	**13:59**
2001-02	**Toronto**	**NHL**	**77**	**24**	**35**	**59**	**92**	**7**	**0**	**5**	**124**	**19.4**	**24**	**138**	**43.5**	**16:59**	**17**	**4**	**4**	**8**	**38**	**1**	**0**	**1**	**16:50**
2002-03	**Toronto**	**NHL**	**77**	**10**	**26**	**36**	**119**	**4**	**1**	**2**	**108**	**9.3**	**–7**	**68**	**45.6**	**15:21**	**6**	**0**	**3**	**3**	**6**	**0**	**0**	**0**	**21:07**
2003-04	**Toronto**	**NHL**	**64**	**21**	**11**	**32**	**68**	**8**	**1**	**2**	**146**	**14.4**	**4**	**136**	**50.7**	**17:50**	**12**	**2**	**0**	**2**	**14**	**1**	**0**	**0**	**13:54**
	NHL Totals		**609**	**127**	**171**	**298**	**1015**	**32**	**7**	**24**	**942**	**13.5**		**2388**	**46.2**	**17:25**	**62**	**10**	**11**	**21**	**79**	**3**	**0**	**3**	**16:15**

WHL West First All-Star Team (1994, 1995) • Canadian Major Junior First All-Star Team (1994) • Memorial Cup All-Star Team (1994, 1995) • Stafford Smythe Memorial Trophy (Memorial Cup MVP) (1994) • Dudley "Red" Garrett Memorial Trophy (Top Rookie – AHL) (1996)

Traded to **Tampa Bay** by **Montreal** with Stephane Richer and David Wilkie for Patrick Poulin, Mick Vukota and Igor Ulanov, January 15, 1998. Traded to **Toronto** by **Tampa Bay** with Tampa Bay's 4th round choice (Miguel Delisle) in 2000 Entry Draft and future considerations for Mike Johnson, Marek Posmyk, Toronto's 5th (Pavel Sedov) and 6th (Aaron Gionet) round choices in 2000 Entry Draft and future considerations, February 9, 2000.

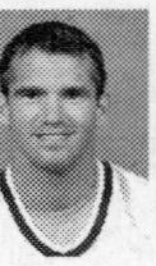

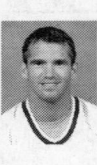

TURGEON, Pierre

(TUHR-zhaw, PEE-air) **DAL.**

Center. Shoots left. 6'1", 199 lbs. Born, Rouyn, Que., August 28, 1969. Buffalo's 1st choice, 1st overall, in 1987 Entry Draft.

Season	Club	League	GP	G	A	Pts	PIM	PP	SH	GW	S	%	+/-	TF	F%	Min	GP	G	A	Pts	PIM	PP	SH	GW	Min
			Regular Season														Playoffs								
1984-85	Mtl-Bourassa	QAAA	41	49	52	101	26	....	....	....	....	....	....	....	....	....	5	3	8	11	2	....	....	....	....
1985-86	Granby Bisons	QMJHL	69	47	67	114	31	....	....	....	....	....	....	....	....	....	....	....	....	....	....	....	....	....	....
1986-87	Granby Bisons	QMJHL	58	69	85	154	8	....	....	....	....	....	....	....	....	....	7	9	6	15	15	....	....	....	....
1987-88	**Buffalo**	**NHL**	76	14	28	42	34	8	0	3	101	13.9	–8	....	....	....	6	4	3	7	4	3	0	0	....
1988-89	**Buffalo**	**NHL**	80	34	54	88	26	19	0	5	182	18.7	–2	....	....	....	5	3	5	8	2	1	0	0	....
1989-90	**Buffalo**	**NHL**	80	40	66	106	29	17	1	10	193	20.7	10	....	....	....	6	2	4	6	2	0	0	1	....
1990-91	**Buffalo**	**NHL**	78	32	47	79	26	13	2	3	174	18.4	14	....	....	....	6	3	1	4	6	1	0	0	....
1991-92	**Buffalo**	**NHL**	8	2	6	8	4	0	0	0	14	14.3	–1	....	....	....	....	....	....	....	....	....	....	....	....
	NY Islanders	**NHL**	69	38	49	87	16	13	0	6	193	19.7	8	....	....	....	....	....	....	....	....	....	....	....	....
1992-93	**NY Islanders**	**NHL**	83	58	74	132	26	24	0	10	301	19.3	–1	....	....	....	11	6	7	13	0	0	0	0	....
1993-94	**NY Islanders**	**NHL**	69	38	56	94	18	10	4	6	254	15.0	14	....	....	....	4	0	1	1	0	0	0	0	....
1994-95	**NY Islanders**	**NHL**	34	13	14	27	10	3	2	2	93	14.0	–12	....	....	....	....	....	....	....	....	....	....	....	....
	Montreal	**NHL**	15	11	9	20	4	2	0	2	67	16.4	12	....	....	....	....	....	....	....	....	....	....	....	....
1995-96	**Montreal**	**NHL**	80	38	58	96	44	17	1	6	297	12.8	19	....	....	....	6	2	4	6	2	0	0	0	....
1996-97	**Montreal**	**NHL**	9	1	10	11	2	0	0	0	22	4.5	4	....	....	....	....	....	....	....	....	....	....	....	....
	St. Louis	**NHL**	69	25	49	74	12	5	0	7	194	12.9	4	....	....	....	5	1	1	2	2	1	0	0	....
1997-98	**St. Louis**	**NHL**	60	22	46	68	24	6	0	4	140	15.7	13	....	....	....	10	4	4	8	2	2	0	0	....
1998-99	**St. Louis**	**NHL**	67	31	34	65	36	10	0	5	193	16.1	4	1285	50.0	19:07	13	4	9	13	6	0	0	2	19:35
99-2000	**St. Louis**	**NHL**	52	26	40	66	8	8	0	3	139	18.7	30	1016	53.2	19:13	7	0	7	7	0	0	0	0	19:45
2000-01	**St. Louis**	**NHL**	79	30	52	82	37	11	0	6	171	17.5	14	1569	49.7	18:50	15	5	10	15	2	1	0	0	19:07
2001-02	**Dallas**	**NHL**	66	15	32	47	16	7	0	1	121	12.4	–4	822	48.4	16:31	....	....	....	....	....	....	....	....	....
2002-03	**Dallas**	**NHL**	65	12	30	42	18	3	0	5	76	15.8	4	290	53.8	14:38	5	0	1	1	0	0	0	0	12:21
2003-04	**Dallas**	**NHL**	76	15	25	40	20	6	0	1	104	14.4	17	578	49.3	14:13	5	1	3	4	2	0	0	0	15:53
	NHL Totals		1215	495	779	1274	410	182	10	85	3029	16.3		5560	50.4	17:01	104	35	60	95	30	9	0	3	18:14

QMJHL Offensive Rookie of the Year) (1986) • Lady Byng Memorial Trophy (1993)

Played in NHL All-Star Game (1990, 1993, 1994, 1996)

Traded to **NY Islanders** by **Buffalo** with Uwe Krupp, Benoit Hogue and Dave McLlwain for Pat LaFontaine, Randy Hillier, Randy Wood and NY Islanders' 4th round choice (Dean Melanson) in 1992 Entry Draft, October 25, 1991. Traded to **Montreal** by **NY Islanders** with Vladimir Malakhov for Kirk Muller, Mathieu Schneider and Craig Darby, April 5, 1995. Traded to **St. Louis** by **Montreal** with Rory Fitzpatrick and Craig Conroy for Murray Baron, Shayne Corson and St. Louis' 5th round choice (Gennady Razin) in 1997 Entry Draft, October 29, 1996. Signed as a free agent by **Dallas**, July 1, 2001.

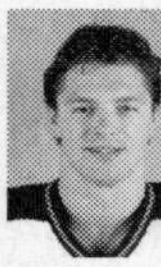

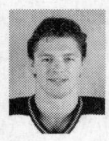

TVERDOVSKY, Oleg

(tvehr-DOHV-skee, OH-lehg)

Defense. Shoots left. 6'1", 205 lbs. Born, Donetsk, USSR, May 18, 1976. Anaheim's 1st choice, 2nd overall, in 1994 Entry Draft.

Season	Club	League	GP	G	A	Pts	PIM	PP	SH	GW	S	%	+/-	TF	F%	Min	GP	G	A	Pts	PIM	PP	SH	GW	Min
1992-93	Krylja Sovetov	CIS	21	0	1	1	6	....	....	....	....	....	....	....	....	....	6	0	0	0	0	....	....	....	....
1993-94	Krylja Sovetov	CIS	46	4	10	14	22	....	....	....	....	....	....	....	....	....	3	1	0	1	2	....	....	....	....
1994-95	Brandon	WHL	7	1	4	5	4	....	....	....	....	....	....	....	....	....	....	....	....	....	....	....	....	....	....
	Anaheim	**NHL**	36	3	9	12	14	1	1	0	26	11.5	–6	....	....	....	....	....	....	....	....	....	....	....	....
1995-96	**Anaheim**	**NHL**	51	7	15	22	35	2	0	0	84	8.3	0	....	....	....	....	....	....	....	....	....	....	....	....
	Winnipeg	**NHL**	31	0	8	8	6	0	0	0	35	0.0	–7	....	....	....	6	0	1	1	0	0	0	0	....
1996-97	**Phoenix**	**NHL**	82	10	45	55	30	3	1	2	144	6.9	–5	....	....	....	7	0	1	1	0	0	0	0	....
1997-98	Hamilton	AHL	9	8	6	14	2	....	....	....	....	....	....	....	....	....	....	....	....	....	....	....	....	....	....
	Phoenix	**NHL**	46	7	12	19	12	4	0	1	83	8.4	1	....	....	....	6	0	7	7	0	0	0	0	....
1998-99	**Phoenix**	**NHL**	82	7	18	25	32	2	0	2	117	6.0	11	1	0.0	20:48	6	0	2	2	6	0	0	0	17:43
99-2000	**Anaheim**	**NHL**	82	15	36	51	30	5	0	5	153	9.8	5	1	0.0	22:46	....	....	....	....	....	....	....	....	....
2000-01	**Anaheim**	**NHL**	82	14	39	53	32	8	0	3	188	7.4	–11	0	0.0	24:25	....	....	....	....	....	....	....	....	....
2001-02	**Anaheim**	**NHL**	73	6	26	32	31	2	0	1	147	4.1	0	0	0.0	22:50	....	....	....	....	....	....	....	....	....
	Russia	Olympics	6	1	1	2	0	....	....	....	....	....	....	....	....	....	....	....	....	....	....	....	....	....	....
2002-03♦	**New Jersey**	**NHL**	50	5	8	13	22	2	0	1	76	6.6	2	0	0.0	16:48	15	0	3	3	0	0	0	0	15:06
2003-04	Avangard Omsk	Russia	57	16	17	33	58	....	....	....	....	....	....	....	....	....	11	0	2	2	2	....	....	....	....
	NHL Totals		615	74	216	290	244	29	2	15	1053	7.0		2	0.0	21:54	40	0	14	14	6	0	0	0	15:51

Played in NHL All-Star Game (1997)

Traded to **Winnipeg** by **Anaheim** with Chad Kilger and Anaheim's 3rd round choice (Per-Anton Lundstrom) in 1996 Entry Draft for Teemu Selanne, Marc Chouinard and Winnipeg's 4th round choice (later traded to Toronto – later traded to Montreal – Montreal selected Kim Staal) in 1996 Entry Draft, February 7, 1996. Transferred to **Phoenix** after **Winnipeg** franchise relocated, July 1, 1996. Traded to **Anaheim** by **Phoenix** for Travis Green and Anaheim's 1st round choice (Scott Kelman) in 1999 Entry Draft, June 26, 1999. Traded to **New Jersey** by **Anaheim** with Jeff Friesen and Maxim Balmochnykh for Petr Sykora, Mike Commodore, Jean-Francois Damphousse and Igor Pohanka, July 6, 2002. Signed as a free agent by **Avangard Omsk** (Russia), August 29, 2003.

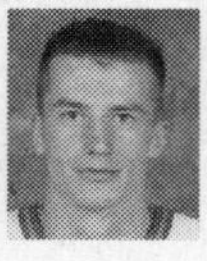

TVRDON, Roman

(t-vahr-DAWN, ROH-muhn)

Center. Shoots left. 6'1", 189 lbs. Born, Trencin, Czech., January 29, 1981. Washington's 6th choice, 132nd overall, in 1999 Entry Draft.

Season	Club	League	GP	G	A	Pts	PIM	PP	SH	GW	S	%	+/-	TF	F%	Min	GP	G	A	Pts	PIM	PP	SH	GW	Min
1995-96	Dukla Trencin 18	Slovak-Jr.	46	25	15	40	32	....	....	....	....	....	....	....	....	....	....	....	....	....	....	....	....	....	....
1996-97	Dukla Trencin 18	Slovak-Jr.	42	25	13	38	10	....	....	....	....	....	....	....	....	....	....	....	....	....	....	....	....	....	....
1997-98	Dukla Trencin Jr.	Slovak-Jr.	48	4	12	16	39	....	....	....	....	....	....	....	....	....	....	....	....	....	....	....	....	....	....
1998-99	Dukla Trencin Jr.	Slovak-Jr.	49	23	23	46	20	....	....	....	....	....	....	....	....	....	6	4	4	8	4	....	....	....	....
99-2000	Spokane Chiefs	WHL	69	26	44	70	40	....	....	....	....	....	....	....	....	....	15	4	7	11	16	....	....	....	....
2000-01	Spokane Chiefs	WHL	62	28	34	62	55	....	....	....	....	....	....	....	....	....	12	5	11	16	0	....	....	....	....
2001-02	Portland Pirates	AHL	49	5	9	14	22	....	....	....	....	....	....	....	....	....	....	....	....	....	....	....	....	....	....
2002-03	Portland Pirates	AHL	35	5	4	9	17	....	....	....	....	....	....	....	....	....	....	....	....	....	....	....	....	....	....
2003-04	**Washington**	**NHL**	9	0	1	1	2	0	0	0	7	0.0	–3	45	35.6	10:41	....	....	....	....	....	....	....	....	....
	Portland Pirates	AHL	51	2	4	6	20	....	....	....	....	....	....	....	....	....	7	0	0	0	2	....	....	....	....
	NHL Totals		9	0	1	1	2	0	0	0	7	0.0		45	35.6	10:41	....	....	....	....	....	....	....	....	....

• Missed majority of 2002-03 season recovering from shoulder injury suffered in game vs. Saint John (AHL), December 28, 2002.

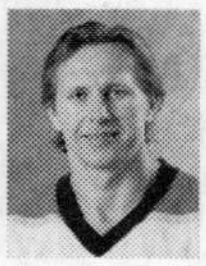

ULANOV, Igor

(yoo-LAH-nahf, EE-gohr) **EDM.**

Defense. Shoots left. 6'3", 220 lbs. Born, Krasnokamsk, USSR, October 1, 1969. Winnipeg's 8th choice, 203rd overall, in 1991 Entry Draft.

Season	Club	League	GP	G	A	Pts	PIM	PP	SH	GW	S	%	+/-	TF	F%	Min	GP	G	A	Pts	PIM	PP	SH	GW	Min
1990-91	Voskresensk	USSR	41	2	2	4	52	....	....	....	....	....	....	....	....	....	....	....	....	....	....	....	....	....	....
1991-92	Voskresensk	CIS	27	1	4	5	24	....	....	....	....	....	....	....	....	....	....	....	....	....	....	....	....	....	....
	Winnipeg	**NHL**	27	2	9	11	67	0	0	0	23	8.7	5	....	....	....	7	0	0	0	39	0	0	0	....
	Moncton Hawks	AHL	3	0	1	1	16	....	....	....	....	....	....	....	....	....	....	....	....	....	....	....	....	....	....
1992-93	**Winnipeg**	**NHL**	56	2	14	16	124	0	0	0	26	7.7	6	....	....	....	4	0	0	0	4	0	0	0	....
	Moncton Hawks	AHL	9	1	3	4	26	....	....	....	....	....	....	....	....	....	....	....	....	....	....	....	....	....	....
	Fort Wayne	IHL	3	0	1	1	29	....	....	....	....	....	....	....	....	....	....	....	....	....	....	....	....	....	....
1993-94	**Winnipeg**	**NHL**	74	0	17	17	165	0	0	0	46	0.0	–11	....	....	....	....	....	....	....	....	....	....	....	....
1994-95	**Winnipeg**	**NHL**	19	1	3	4	27	0	0	0	13	7.7	–2	....	....	....	....	....	....	....	....	....	....	....	....
	Washington	**NHL**	3	0	1	1	2	0	0	0	0	0.0	3	....	....	....	2	0	0	0	4	0	0	0	....
1995-96	**Chicago**	**NHL**	53	1	8	9	92	0	0	0	24	4.2	12	....	....	....	....	....	....	....	....	....	....	....	....
	Indianapolis Ice	IHL	1	0	0	0	0	....	....	....	....	....	....	....	....	....	....	....	....	....	....	....	....	....	....
	Tampa Bay	**NHL**	11	2	1	3	24	0	0	1	13	15.4	–1	....	....	....	5	0	0	0	15	0	0	0	....
1996-97	**Tampa Bay**	**NHL**	59	1	7	8	108	0	0	0	56	1.8	2	....	....	....	....	....	....	....	....	....	....	....	....
1997-98	**Tampa Bay**	**NHL**	45	2	7	9	85	1	0	0	32	6.3	–5	....	....	....	....	....	....	....	....	....	....	....	....
	Montreal	**NHL**	4	0	1	1	12	0	0	0	4	0.0	–2	....	....	....	10	1	4	5	12	0	0	0	....
1998-99	**Montreal**	**NHL**	76	3	9	12	109	0	0	0	55	5.5	–3	0	0.0	17:35	....	....	....	....	....	....	....	....	....
99-2000	**Montreal**	**NHL**	43	1	5	6	76	0	0	0	33	3.0	–11	0	0.0	16:33	....	....	....	....	....	....	....	....	....
	Edmonton	**NHL**	14	0	3	3	10	0	0	0	6	0.0	–3	0	0.0	16:23	5	0	0	0	6	0	0	0	16:59
2000-01	**Edmonton**	**NHL**	67	3	20	23	90	1	0	0	74	4.1	15	0	0.0	23:01	6	0	0	0	4	0	0	0	24:25
2001-02	**NY Rangers**	**NHL**	39	0	6	6	53	0	0	0	17	0.0	–4	0	0.0	16:19	....	....	....	....	....	....	....	....	....
	Hartford	AHL	6	1	1	2	2	....	....	....	....	....	....	....	....	....	....	....	....	....	....	....	....	....	....
	Florida	**NHL**	14	0	4	4	11	0	0	0	9	0.0	–3	0	0.0	20:50	....	....	....	....	....	....	....	....	....
2002-03	**Florida**	**NHL**	56	1	1	2	39	0	0	0	20	5.0	7	0	0.0	16:42	....	....	....	....	....	....	....	....	....
	San Antonio	AHL	5	1	0	1	4	....	....	....	....	....	....	....	....	....	....	....	....	....	....	....	....	....	....

			Regular Season														Playoffs								
Season	Club	League	GP	G	A	Pts	PIM	PP	SH	GW	S	%	+/-	TF	F%	Min	GP	G	A	Pts	PIM	PP	SH	GW	Min
2003-04	Edmonton	NHL	42	5	13	18	28	1	0	3	49	10.2	19	0	0.0	19:51									
	Toronto	AHL	10	0	5	5	8																		
	NHL Totals		702	24	129	153	1122	3	0	4	500	4.8		0	0.0	18:34	39	1	4	5	84	0	0	0	21:02

Traded to **Washington** by **Winnipeg** with Mike Eagles for Washington's 3rd (later traded to Dallas – Dallas selected Sergey Gusev) and 5th (Brian Elder) round choices in 1995 Entry Draft, April 7, 1995. Traded to **Chicago** by **Washington** for Chicago's 3rd round choice (Dave Weninger) in 1996 Entry Draft, October 17, 1995. Traded to **Tampa Bay** by **Chicago** with Patrick Poulin and Chicago's 2nd round choice (later traded to New Jersey – New Jersey selected Pierre Dagenais) in 1996 Entry Draft for Enrico Ciccone and Tampa Bay's 2nd round choice (Jeff Paul) in 1996 Entry Draft, March 20, 1996. Traded to **Montreal** by **Tampa Bay** with Patrick Poulin and Mick Vukota for Stephane Richer, Darcy Tucker and David Wilkie, January 15, 1998. Traded to **Edmonton** by **Montreal** with Alain Nasreddine for Christian Laflamme and Matthieu Descoteaux, March 9, 2000. Signed as a free agent by **NY Rangers**, July 20, 2001. Traded to **Florida** by **NY Rangers** with Filip Novak, NY Rangers' 1st (later traded to Calgary – Calgary selected Eric Nystrom) and 2nd (Rob Globke) round choices in 2002 Entry Draft and NY Rangers' 4th round choice (later traded to Atlanta – Atlanta selected Guillaume Desbiens) in 2003 Entry Draft for Pavel Bure and Florida's 2nd round choice (Lee Falardeau) in 2002 Entry Draft, March 18, 2002. Signed to a PTO (tryout) contract by **Toronto** (AHL), December 13, 2003. Signed as a free agent by **Edmonton**, January 5, 2004.

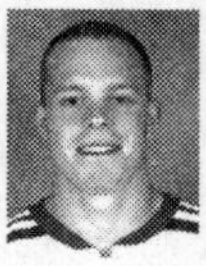

ULMER, Jeff

(UHL-muhr, JEHF) **COL.**

Right wing. Shoots right. 5'11", 195 lbs. Born, Wilcox, Sask., April 27, 1977.

Season	Club	League	GP	G	A	Pts	PIM	PP	SH	GW	S	%	+/-	TF	F%	Min	GP	G	A	Pts	PIM	PP	SH	GW	Min
1994-95	Notre Dame	AJHL	63	25	35	60																			
1995-96	North Dakota	WCHA	29	5	3	8	26																		
1996-97	North Dakota	WCHA	26	6	11	17	16																		
1997-98	North Dakota	WCHA	32	12	12	24	44																		
1998-99	North Dakota	WCHA	38	16	20	36	46																		
99-2000	Team Canada	Nat-Tm	48	14	25	39	20																		
	Houston Aeros	IHL	5	1	0	1	0										11	2	4	6	6				
2000-01	NY Rangers	NHL	21	3	0	3	8	0	0	0	22	13.6	-6	16	31.3	10:23									
	Hartford	AHL	48	11	14	25	34																		
2001-02	Grand Rapids	AHL	73	9	17	26	65										5	0	1	1	11				
2002-03	Binghamton	AHL	57	8	12	20	40										13	0	1	1	30				
2003-04	Cardiff Devils	Britain	9	9	9	18	6																		
	Lukko Rauma	Finland	34	13	8	21	67										4	0	0	0	2				
	NHL Totals		21	3	0	3	8	0	0	0	22	13.6		16	31.3	10:23									

Signed as a free agent by **Houston** (IHL), March 30, 2000. Signed as a free agent by **NY Rangers**, July 27, 2000. Traded to **Ottawa** by **NY Rangers** with Jason Doig for Sean Gagnon, June 29, 2001. Signed as a free agent by **Cardiff** (Britain), October 10, 2003. Signed as a free agent by **Lukko Rauma** (Finland), November 11, 2003. Signed as a free agent by **Colorado**, June 10, 2004.

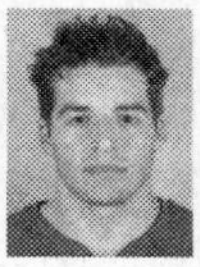

ULMER, Layne

(UHL-muhr, LAYN) **NYR**

Center. Shoots left. 6'1", 205 lbs. Born, North Battleford, Sask., September 14, 1980. Ottawa's 8th choice, 209th overall, in 1999 Entry Draft.

Season	Club	League	GP	G	A	Pts	PIM	PP	SH	GW	S	%	+/-	TF	F%	Min	GP	G	A	Pts	PIM	PP	SH	GW	Min
1996-97	Swift Current	SMHL	43	35	49	84	71																		
1997-98	Swift Current	WHL	50	8	9	17	23										12	3	1	4	0				
1998-99	Swift Current	WHL	72	40	35	75	34										6	2	1	3	4				
99-2000	Swift Current	WHL	71	50	54	104	66										12	12	6	18	16				
2000-01	Swift Current	WHL	68	*63	56	119	75										19	7	3	10	20				
2001-02	Hartford	AHL	22	0	5	5	17																		
	Charlotte	ECHL	38	18	17	35	12										5	2	2	4	4				
2002-03	Hartford	AHL	68	12	20	32	16										2	0	0	0	0				
2003-04	NY Rangers	NHL	1	0	0	0	0	0	0	0	1	0.0	-1	8	75.0	9:27									
	Hartford	AHL	76	22	16	38	26										7	2	5	7	0				
	NHL Totals		1	0	0	0	0	0	0	0	1	0.0		8	75.0	9:27									

WHL East First All-Star Team (2000, 2001)

Signed as a free agent by **NY Rangers**, June 13, 2001.

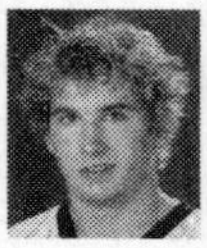

UPSHALL, Scottie

(UHP-shuhl, SKAW-tee) **NSH.**

Right wing. Shoots left. 6', 187 lbs. Born, Fort McMurray, Alta., October 7, 1983. Nashville's 1st choice, 6th overall, in 2002 Entry Draft.

Season	Club	League	GP	G	A	Pts	PIM	PP	SH	GW	S	%	+/-	TF	F%	Min	GP	G	A	Pts	PIM	PP	SH	GW	Min
1998-99	Fort McMurray	AMHL	28	62	40	102	100																		
99-2000	Fort McMurray	AJHL	52	26	26	52	65																		
2000-01	Kamloops Blazers	WHL	70	42	45	87	111										4	0	2	2	10				
2001-02	Kamloops Blazers	WHL	61	32	51	83	139										4	1	2	3	21				
2002-03	Nashville	NHL	8	1	0	1	0	0	0	0	6	16.7	2	2	0.0	8:42									
	Kamloops Blazers	WHL	42	25	31	56	111										6	0	2	2	34				
	Milwaukee	AHL	2	1	0	1	2										6	0	0	0	2				
2003-04	Nashville	NHL	7	0	1	1	0	0	0	0	6	0.0	-2	8	37.5	9:11									
	Milwaukee	AHL	31	13	11	24	42										8	3	0	3	4				
	NHL Totals		15	1	1	2	0	0	0	0	12	8.3		10	30.0	8:56									

WHL All-Rookie Team (2001) • WHL Rookie of the Year (2001) • CHL All-Rookie Team (2001) • Canadian Major Junior Rookie of the Year (2001) • WHL West Second All-Star Team (2002) • Missed majority of 2003-04 season recovering from knee injury suffered in game vs. Phoenix, December 22, 2003.

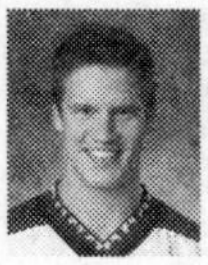

VAANANEN, Ossi

(VAN-ih-nehn, AW-see) **COL.**

Defense. Shoots left. 6'4", 215 lbs. Born, Vantaa, Finland, August 18, 1980. Phoenix's 2nd choice, 43rd overall, in 1998 Entry Draft.

Season	Club	League	GP	G	A	Pts	PIM	PP	SH	GW	S	%	+/-	TF	F%	Min	GP	G	A	Pts	PIM	PP	SH	GW	Min
1994-95	Jokerit Helsinki C	Finn-Jr.	23	0	1	1	10										6	0	0	0	8				
1995-96	Jokerit Helsinki C	Finn-Jr.	12	0	0	0	10																		
	Jokerit Helsinki B	Finn-Jr.	1	0	0	0	0										1	0	0	0	0				
1996-97	Jokerit Helsinki Jr.	Finn-Jr.	17	1	2	3	43																		
1997-98	Jokerit Helsinki Jr.	Finn-Jr.	31	0	6	6	24																		
1998-99	Jokerit Helsinki Jr.	Finn-Jr.	12	1	6	7	16																		
	Jokerit Helsinki	EuroHL	5	0	0	0	2										1	0	1	1	2				
	Jokerit Helsinki	Finland	48	0	1	1	42										3	0	1	1	2				
99-2000	Jokerit Helsinki	Finland	49	1	6	7	46										11	1	1	2	2				
2000-01	Phoenix	NHL	81	4	12	16	90	0	0	2	69	5.8	9	0	0.0	19:09									
2001-02	Phoenix	NHL	76	2	12	14	74	0	1	0	41	4.9	6	0	0.0	20:13	5	0	0	0	6	0	0	0	20:33
	Finland	Olympics	2	0	1	1	0																		
2002-03	Phoenix	NHL	67	2	7	9	82	0	0	0	49	4.1	1	0	0.0	19:15									
2003-04	Phoenix	NHL	67	2	4	6	87	0	0	1	39	5.1	-10	0	0.0	19:21									
	Colorado	NHL	12	0	0	0	2	0	0	0	6	0.0	-4	0	0.0	18:36	11	0	1	1	18	0	0	0	22:06
	NHL Totals		303	10	35	45	335	0	1	3	204	4.9		0	0.0	19:28	16	0	1	1	24	0	0	0	21:37

Traded to **Colorado** by **Phoenix** with Chris Gratton and Phoenix's 2nd round choice in 2005 Entry Draft for Derek Morris and Keith Ballard, March 8, 2004.

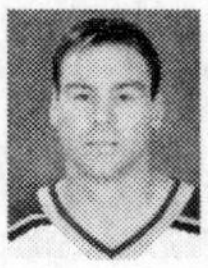

VALICEVIC, Rob

(val-IH-seh-VIK, RAWB)

Right wing. Shoots right. 6'1", 198 lbs. Born, Detroit, MI, January 6, 1971. NY Islanders' 6th choice, 114th overall, in 1991 Entry Draft.

Season	Club	League	GP	G	A	Pts	PIM	PP	SH	GW	S	%	+/-	TF	F%	Min	GP	G	A	Pts	PIM	PP	SH	GW	Min
1990-91	Det. Compuware	NAJHL	39	31	44	75	54																		
1991-92	Lake Superior	CCHA	32	8	4	12	12																		
1992-93	Lake Superior	CCHA	43	21	20	41	28																		
1993-94	Lake Superior	CCHA	45	18	20	38	46																		
1994-95	Lake Superior	CCHA	37	10	21	31	40																		
1995-96	Louisiana	ECHL	60	42	20	62	85										5	2	3	5	8				
	Springfield	AHL	2	0	0	0	2																		
1996-97	Louisiana	ECHL	8	7	2	9	21																		
	Houston Aeros	IHL	58	11	12	23	42										12	1	3	4	11				
1997-98	Houston Aeros	IHL	72	29	28	57	47										4	2	0	2	2				
1998-99	Nashville	NHL	19	4	2	6	2	0	0	2	23	17.4	4	17	29.4	11:01									
	Houston Aeros	IHL	57	16	33	49	62										19	7	10	17	8				
99-2000	Nashville	NHL	80	14	11	25	21	2	1	3	113	12.4	-11	50	44.0	14:31									
2000-01	Nashville	NHL	60	8	6	14	26	1	0	4	62	12.9	-2	35	40.0	14:06									
2001-02	Los Angeles	NHL	17	1	1	2	8	0	0	0	9	11.1	-4	166	41.6	9:34									
	Manchester	AHL	59	11	23	34	25										5	1	0	1	4				
2002-03	Anaheim	NHL	10	1	0	1	2	0	0	1	7	14.3	1	0	0.0	8:35									
	Cincinnati	AHL	69	17	26	43	38																		

			Regular Season														Playoffs								
Season	Club	League	GP	G	A	Pts	PIM	PP	SH	GW	S	%	+/-	TF	F%	Min	GP	G	A	Pts	PIM	PP	SH	GW	Min
2003-04	**Dallas**	**NHL**	**7**	**0**	**0**	**0**	**2**	**0**	**0**	**0**	**4**	**0.0**	**-1**	**27**	**48.2**	**7:50**	....	....	....	....	....	....	....	....	....
	Utah Grizzlies	AHL	67	11	26	37	44	....	....	....	....	....	....	....	....	....	....	....	....	....	....	....	....	....	....
	NHL Totals		**193**	**28**	**20**	**48**	**61**	**3**	**1**	**10**	**218**	**12.8**		**295**	**41.7**	**13:03**	....	....	....	....	....	....	....	....	....

Signed as a free agent by **Nashville**, May 28, 1998. Signed as a free agent by **Los Angeles**, August 16, 2001. Signed as a free agent by **Anaheim**, July 24, 2002. Signed as a free agent by **Dallas**, August 28, 2003.

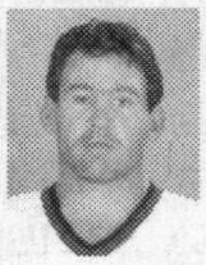

VAN ALLEN, Shaun

(VAN-AL-ehn, SHAWN)

Center. Shoots left. 6'1", 205 lbs. Born, Calgary, Alta., August 29, 1967. Edmonton's 5th choice, 105th overall, in 1987 Entry Draft.

Season	Club	League	GP	G	A	Pts	PIM	PP	SH	GW	S	%	+/-	TF	F%	Min	GP	G	A	Pts	PIM	PP	SH	GW	Min
1984-85	Swift Current	SJHL	61	12	20	32	136	....	....	....	....	....	....	....	....	....	....	....	....	....	....	....	....	....	....
1985-86	Saskatoon Blades	WHL	55	12	11	23	43	....	....	....	....	....	....	....	....	....	13	4	8	12	28	....	....	....	....
1986-87	Saskatoon Blades	WHL	72	38	59	97	116	....	....	....	....	....	....	....	....	....	11	4	6	10	24	....	....	....	....
1987-88	Milwaukee	IHL	40	14	28	42	34	....	....	....	....	....	....	....	....	....	....	....	....	....	....	....	....	....	....
	Nova Scotia Oilers	AHL	19	4	10	14	17	....	....	....	....	....	....	....	....	....	4	1	1	2	4	....	....	....	....
1988-89	Cape Breton	AHL	76	32	42	74	81	....	....	....	....	....	....	....	....	....	....	....	....	....	....	....	....	....	....
1989-90	Cape Breton	AHL	61	25	44	69	83	....	....	....	....	....	....	....	....	....	4	0	2	2	8	....	....	....	....
1990-91	**Edmonton**	**NHL**	**2**	**0**	**0**	**0**	**0**	**0**	**0**	**0**	**0**	**0.0**	**0**	....	....	....	....	....	....	....	....	....	....	....	....
	Cape Breton	AHL	76	25	75	100	182	....	....	....	....	....	....	....	....	....	4	0	1	1	8	....	....	....	....
1991-92	Cape Breton	AHL	77	29	*84	*113	80	....	....	....	....	....	....	....	....	....	5	3	7	10	14	....	....	....	....
1992-93	**Edmonton**	**NHL**	**21**	**1**	**4**	**5**	**6**	**0**	**0**	**0**	**19**	**5.3**	**-2**	....	....	....	....	....	....	....	....	....	....	....	....
	Cape Breton	AHL	43	14	62	76	68	....	....	....	....	....	....	....	....	....	15	8	9	17	18	....	....	....	....
1993-94	**Anaheim**	**NHL**	**80**	**8**	**25**	**33**	**64**	**2**	**2**	**1**	**104**	**7.7**	**0**	....	....	....	....	....	....	....	....	....	....	....	....
1994-95	**Anaheim**	**NHL**	**45**	**8**	**21**	**29**	**32**	**1**	**1**	**1**	**68**	**11.8**	**-4**	....	....	....	....	....	....	....	....	....	....	....	....
1995-96	**Anaheim**	**NHL**	**49**	**8**	**17**	**25**	**41**	**0**	**0**	**2**	**78**	**10.3**	**13**	....	....	....	....	....	....	....	....	....	....	....	....
1996-97	**Ottawa**	**NHL**	**80**	**11**	**14**	**25**	**35**	**1**	**1**	**2**	**123**	**8.9**	**-8**	....	....	....	**7**	**0**	**1**	**1**	**4**	**0**	**0**	**0**	....
1997-98	**Ottawa**	**NHL**	**80**	**4**	**15**	**19**	**48**	**0**	**0**	**0**	**104**	**3.8**	**4**	....	....	....	**11**	**0**	**1**	**1**	**10**	**0**	**0**	**0**	....
1998-99	**Ottawa**	**NHL**	**79**	**6**	**11**	**17**	**30**	**0**	**1**	**0**	**47**	**12.8**	**3**	**656**	**47.4**	**11:07**	**4**	**0**	**0**	**0**	**0**	**0**	**0**	**0**	**8:42**
99-2000	**Ottawa**	**NHL**	**75**	**9**	**19**	**28**	**37**	**0**	**2**	**4**	**75**	**12.0**	**20**	**911**	**48.6**	**11:49**	**6**	**0**	**1**	**1**	**9**	**0**	**0**	**0**	**12:09**
2000-01	**Dallas**	**NHL**	**59**	**7**	**16**	**23**	**16**	**0**	**2**	**3**	**51**	**13.7**	**5**	**559**	**47.1**	**12:05**	**8**	**0**	**2**	**2**	**8**	**0**	**0**	**0**	**13:56**
2001-02	**Dallas**	**NHL**	**19**	**2**	**4**	**6**	**6**	**0**	**0**	**0**	**20**	**10.0**	**-5**	**177**	**53.1**	**12:57**	....	....	....	....	....	....	....	....	....
	Montreal	**NHL**	**54**	**6**	**9**	**15**	**20**	**0**	**1**	**1**	**28**	**21.4**	**5**	**381**	**47.8**	**10:08**	**7**	**0**	**1**	**1**	**2**	**0**	**0**	**0**	**9:25**
2002-03	**Ottawa**	**NHL**	**78**	**12**	**20**	**32**	**66**	**2**	**2**	**3**	**53**	**22.6**	**17**	**838**	**45.0**	**12:29**	**18**	**1**	**1**	**2**	**12**	**0**	**0**	**1**	**11:54**
2003-04	**Ottawa**	**NHL**	**73**	**2**	**10**	**12**	**80**	**0**	**1**	**0**	**41**	**4.9**	**6**	**792**	**52.3**	**11:29**	....	....	....	....	....	....	....	....	....
	NHL Totals		**794**	**84**	**185**	**269**	**481**	**6**	**13**	**17**	**811**	**10.4**		**4314**	**48.3**	**11:38**	**61**	**1**	**7**	**8**	**45**	**0**	**0**	**1**	**11:37**

AHL Second All-Star Team (1991) • AHL First All-Star Team (1992) • John B. Sollenberger Trophy (Top Scorer – AHL) (1992)

Signed as a free agent by **Anaheim**, July 22, 1993. Traded to **Ottawa** by **Anaheim** with Jason York for Ted Drury and the rights to Marc Moro, October 1, 1996. Signed as a free agent by **Dallas**, July 12, 2000. Traded to **Montreal** by **Dallas** with Donald Audette for Martin Rucinsky and Benoit Brunet, November 21, 2001. Signed as a free agent by **Ottawa**, July 24, 2002.

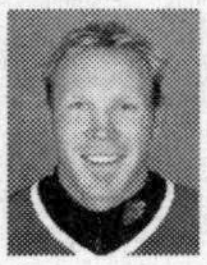

VANDENBUSSCHE, Ryan

(van-dehn-BUHSH, RIGH-yuhn) **PIT.**

Right wing. Shoots right. 6', 200 lbs. Born, Simcoe, Ont., February 28, 1973. Toronto's 9th choice, 173rd overall, in 1992 Entry Draft.

Season	Club	League	GP	G	A	Pts	PIM	PP	SH	GW	S	%	+/-	TF	F%	Min	GP	G	A	Pts	PIM	PP	SH	GW	Min
1988-89	Delhi Flames	OJHL-D	3	1	1	2	2	....	....	....	....	....	....	....	....	....	....	....	....	....	....	....	....	....	....
1989-90	Norwich	OJHL-C	21	12	10	22	146	....	....	....	....	....	....	....	....	....	....	....	....	....	....	....	....	....	....
	Tillsonburg Titans	OJHL-B	24	0	5	5	113	....	....	....	....	....	....	....	....	....	....	....	....	....	....	....	....	....	....
1990-91	Massena	OCJHL	10	2	3	5	46	....	....	....	....	....	....	....	....	....	....	....	....	....	....	....	....	....	....
	Cornwall Royals	OHL	49	3	8	11	139	....	....	....	....	....	....	....	....	....	....	....	....	....	....	....	....	....	....
1991-92	Cornwall Royals	OHL	61	13	15	28	232	....	....	....	....	....	....	....	....	....	6	0	2	2	9	....	....	....	....
1992-93	Newmarket	OHL	30	15	12	27	161	....	....	....	....	....	....	....	....	....	....	....	....	....	....	....	....	....	....
	Guelph Storm	OHL	29	3	14	17	99	....	....	....	....	....	....	....	....	....	5	1	3	4	13	....	....	....	....
	St. John's	AHL	1	0	0	0	0	....	....	....	....	....	....	....	....	....	....	....	....	....	....	....	....	....	....
1993-94	St. John's	AHL	44	4	10	14	124	....	....	....	....	....	....	....	....	....	....	....	....	....	....	....	....	....	....
	Springfield	AHL	9	1	2	3	29	....	....	....	....	....	....	....	....	....	5	0	0	0	16	....	....	....	....
1994-95	St. John's	AHL	53	2	13	15	239	....	....	....	....	....	....	....	....	....	3	0	0	0	17	....	....	....	....
1995-96	Binghamton	AHL	68	3	17	20	240	....	....	....	....	....	....	....	....	....	4	0	0	0	9	....	....	....	....
1996-97	**NY Rangers**	**NHL**	**11**	**1**	**0**	**1**	**30**	**0**	**0**	**0**	**4**	**25.0**	**-2**	....	....	....	....	....	....	....	....	....	....	....	....
	Binghamton	AHL	38	8	11	19	133	....	....	....	....	....	....	....	....	....	....	....	....	....	....	....	....	....	....
1997-98	**NY Rangers**	**NHL**	**16**	**1**	**0**	**1**	**38**	**0**	**0**	**0**	**2**	**50.0**	**-2**	....	....	....	....	....	....	....	....	....	....	....	....
	Hartford	AHL	15	2	0	2	45	....	....	....	....	....	....	....	....	....	....	....	....	....	....	....	....	....	....
	Chicago	**NHL**	**4**	**0**	**1**	**1**	**5**	**0**	**0**	**0**	**0**	**0.0**	**0**	....	....	....	....	....	....	....	....	....	....	....	....
	Indianapolis Ice	IHL	3	1	1	2	4	....	....	....	....	....	....	....	....	....	....	....	....	....	....	....	....	....	....
1998-99	**Chicago**	**NHL**	**6**	**0**	**0**	**0**	**17**	**0**	**0**	**0**	**3**	**0.0**	**0**	**0**	**0.0**	**9:29**	....	....	....	....	....	....	....	....	....
	Indianapolis Ice	IHL	34	3	10	13	130	....	....	....	....	....	....	....	....	....	....	....	....	....	....	....	....	....	....
	Portland Pirates	AHL	37	4	1	5	119	....	....	....	....	....	....	....	....	....	....	....	....	....	....	....	....	....	....
99-2000	**Chicago**	**NHL**	**52**	**0**	**1**	**1**	**143**	**0**	**0**	**0**	**19**	**0.0**	**-3**	**3**	**0.0**	**5:37**	....	....	....	....	....	....	....	....	....
2000-01	**Chicago**	**NHL**	**64**	**2**	**5**	**7**	**146**	**0**	**0**	**0**	**24**	**8.3**	**-8**	**2**	**0.0**	**7:46**	....	....	....	....	....	....	....	....	....
2001-02	**Chicago**	**NHL**	**50**	**1**	**2**	**3**	**103**	**0**	**0**	**0**	**22**	**4.5**	**-10**	**2**	**50.0**	**6:19**	**1**	**0**	**0**	**0**	**0**	**0**	**0**	**0**	**7:20**
2002-03	**Chicago**	**NHL**	**22**	**0**	**0**	**0**	**58**	**0**	**0**	**0**	**7**	**0.0**	**0**	**1**	**100.0**	**6:30**	....	....	....	....	....	....	....	....	....
	Norfolk Admirals	AHL	4	0	1	1	5	....	....	....	....	....	....	....	....	....	....	....	....	....	....	....	....	....	....
2003-04	**Chicago**	**NHL**	**65**	**4**	**1**	**5**	**120**	**2**	**0**	**0**	**25**	**16.0**	**-10**	**0**	**0.0**	**6:16**	....	....	....	....	....	....	....	....	....
	NHL Totals		**290**	**9**	**10**	**19**	**660**	**2**	**0**	**0**	**106**	**8.5**		**8**	**25.0**	**6:37**	**1**	**0**	**0**	**0**	**0**	**0**	**0**	**0**	**7:20**

Signed as a free agent by **NY Rangers**, August 22, 1995. Traded to **Chicago** by **NY Rangers** for Ryan Risidore, March 24, 1998. • Missed majority of 2002-03 season recovering from hand injury suffered in game vs. Detroit, January 5, 2003. Signed as a free agent by **Pittsburgh**, July 12, 2004.

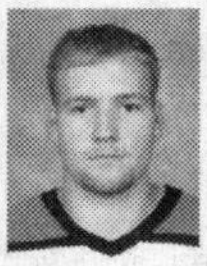

VANDERMEER, Jim

(VAN-duhr-meer, JIHM) **CHI.**

Defense. Shoots left. 6'1", 218 lbs. Born, Caroline, Alta., February 21, 1980.

Season	Club	League	GP	G	A	Pts	PIM	PP	SH	GW	S	%	+/-	TF	F%	Min	GP	G	A	Pts	PIM	PP	SH	GW	Min
1997-98	Red Deer	AMHL	26	4	8	12	51	....	....	....	....	....	....	....	....	....	....	....	....	....	....	....	....	....	....
	Red Deer Rebels	WHL	35	0	3	3	55	....	....	....	....	....	....	....	....	....	2	0	0	0	0	....	....	....	....
1998-99	Red Deer Rebels	WHL	70	5	23	28	258	....	....	....	....	....	....	....	....	....	9	0	1	1	24	....	....	....	....
99-2000	Red Deer Rebels	WHL	71	8	30	38	221	....	....	....	....	....	....	....	....	....	4	0	1	1	16	....	....	....	....
2000-01	Red Deer Rebels	WHL	72	21	44	65	180	....	....	....	....	....	....	....	....	....	22	3	13	16	43	....	....	....	....
2001-02	Philadelphia	AHL	74	1	13	14	88	....	....	....	....	....	....	....	....	....	5	0	2	2	14	....	....	....	....
2002-03	**Philadelphia**	**NHL**	**24**	**2**	**1**	**3**	**27**	**0**	**0**	**0**	**22**	**9.1**	**9**	**0**	**0.0**	**13:42**	**8**	**0**	**1**	**1**	**9**	**0**	**0**	**0**	**12:42**
	Philadelphia	AHL	48	4	8	12	122	....	....	....	....	....	....	....	....	....	....	....	....	....	....	....	....	....	....
2003-04	**Philadelphia**	**NHL**	**23**	**3**	**2**	**5**	**25**	**0**	**0**	**1**	**24**	**12.5**	**-5**	**0**	**0.0**	**15:47**	....	....	....	....	....	....	....	....	....
	Philadelphia	AHL	26	1	6	7	120	....	....	....	....	....	....	....	....	....	....	....	....	....	....	....	....	....	....
	Chicago	**NHL**	**23**	**2**	**10**	**12**	**58**	**1**	**1**	**0**	**37**	**5.4**	**-6**	**1**	**100.0**	**22:03**	....	....	....	....	....	....	....	....	....
	NHL Totals		**70**	**7**	**13**	**20**	**110**	**1**	**1**	**1**	**83**	**8.4**		**1**	**100.0**	**17:08**	**8**	**0**	**1**	**1**	**9**	**0**	**0**	**0**	**12:42**

WHL East First All-Star Team (2001) • Canadian Major Junior Humanitarian Player of the Year (2001)

Signed as a free agent by **Philadelphia**, December 21, 2000. Traded to **Chicago** by **Philadelphia** with the rights to Colin Fraser and Los Angeles' 2nd round choice (previously acquired, Chicago selected Bryan Bickell) in 2004 Entry Draft for Alex Zhamnov and Washington's 4th round choice (previously acquired, Philadelphia selected R.J. Anderson) in 2004 Entry Draft, February 19, 2004.

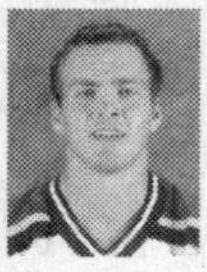

VAN RYN, Mike

(VAN RIHN, MIGHK) **FLA.**

Defense. Shoots right. 6'1", 202 lbs. Born, London, Ont., May 14, 1979. New Jersey's 1st choice, 26th overall, in 1998 Entry Draft.

Season	Club	League	GP	G	A	Pts	PIM	PP	SH	GW	S	%	+/-	TF	F%	Min	GP	G	A	Pts	PIM	PP	SH	GW	Min
1995-96	London Nationals	OJHL-B	44	9	14	23	24	....	....	....	....	....	....	....	....	....	....	....	....	....	....	....	....	....	....
1996-97	London Nationals	OJHL-B	46	14	31	45	32	....	....	....	....	....	....	....	....	....	....	....	....	....	....	....	....	....	....
1997-98	U. of Michigan	CCHA	38	4	14	18	44	....	....	....	....	....	....	....	....	....	....	....	....	....	....	....	....	....	....
1998-99	U. of Michigan	CCHA	37	10	13	23	52	....	....	....	....	....	....	....	....	....	....	....	....	....	....	....	....	....	....
99-2000	Sarnia Sting	OHL	61	6	35	41	34	....	....	....	....	....	....	....	....	....	7	0	5	5	4	....	....	....	....
2000-01	**St. Louis**	**NHL**	**1**	**0**	**0**	**0**	**0**	**0**	**0**	**0**	**1**	**0.0**	**-2**	**0**	**0.0**	**13:43**	....	....	....	....	....	....	....	....	....
	Worcester IceCats	AHL	37	3	10	13	12	....	....	....	....	....	....	....	....	....	7	1	1	2	2	....	....	....	....
2001-02	**St. Louis**	**NHL**	**48**	**2**	**8**	**10**	**18**	**0**	**0**	**1**	**52**	**3.8**	**10**	**0**	**0.0**	**16:23**	**9**	**0**	**0**	**0**	**0**	**0**	**0**	**0**	**16:04**
	Worcester IceCats	AHL	24	2	7	9	17	....	....	....	....	....	....	....	....	....	....	....	....	....	....	....	....	....	....

			Regular Season														Playoffs								
Season	Club	League	GP	G	A	Pts	PIM	PP	SH	GW	S	%	+/-	TF	F%	Min	GP	G	A	Pts	PIM	PP	SH	GW	Min
2002-03	St. Louis	NHL	20	0	3	3	8	0	0	0	21	0.0	3	0	0.0	15:04									
	Worcester IceCats	AHL	33	2	8	10	16																		
	San Antonio	AHL	11	0	3	3	20										3	0	0	0	0				
2003-04	Florida	NHL	79	13	24	37	52	6	1	0	136	9.6	−16	3	33.3	24:26									
	NHL Totals		148	15	35	50	78	6	1	1	210	7.1		3	33.3	20:29	9	0	0	0	0	0	0	0	16:04

OJHL-B First All-Star Team (1997)

Signed as a free agent by **St. Louis**, June 30, 2000. • Missed majority of 2000-01 season recovering from shoulder injury suffered in game vs. Phoenix, October 5, 2000. Traded to **Florida** by **St. Louis** for Valeri Bure and Florida's 5th round choice (Nikita Nikitin) in 2004 Entry Draft, March 11, 2003.

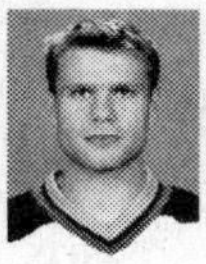

VARADA, Vaclav
(vuh-RA-da, VAT-slav) **OTT.**

Right wing. Shoots left. 6', 208 lbs. Born, Vsetin, Czech., April 26, 1976. San Jose's 4th choice, 89th overall, in 1994 Entry Draft.

1993-94	HC Vitkovice	Czech	24	6	7	13	....										5	1	1	2					
1994-95	Tacoma Rockets	WHL	68	50	38	88	108										4	4	3	7	11				
1995-96	Kelowna Rockets	WHL	59	39	46	85	100										6	3	3	6	16				
	Buffalo	NHL	1	0	0	0	0	0	0	0	2	0.0	0												
	Rochester	AHL	5	3	0	3	4																		
1996-97	Buffalo	NHL	5	0	0	0	2	0	0	0	2	0.0	0												
	Rochester	AHL	53	23	25	48	81										10	1	6	7	27				
1997-98	Buffalo	NHL	27	5	6	11	15	0	0	1	27	18.5	0				15	3	4	7	18	0	0	0	
	Rochester	AHL	45	30	26	56	74																		
1998-99	Buffalo	NHL	72	7	24	31	61	1	0	1	123	5.7	11	1	0.0	14:30	21	5	4	9	14	1	0	0	16:31
99-2000	HC Vitkovice	Czech	5	2	3	5	12																		
	Buffalo	NHL	76	10	27	37	62	0	0	0	140	7.1	12	1	0.0	14:58	5	0	0	0	8	0	0	0	14:19
2000-01	Buffalo	NHL	75	10	21	31	81	2	0	2	112	8.9	−2	2	0.0	15:57	13	0	4	4	8	0	0	0	18:08
2001-02	Buffalo	NHL	76	7	16	23	82	1	0	1	138	5.1	−7	3	0.0	16:33									
2002-03	Buffalo	NHL	44	7	4	11	23	1	0	0	64	10.9	−2	13	53.9	16:07									
	Ottawa	NHL	11	2	6	8	8	1	0	0	17	11.8	3	8	0.0	14:57	18	2	4	6	18	0	0	0	13:57
2003-04	Ottawa	NHL	30	5	5	10	26	0	0	1	47	10.6	2	14	35.7	14:21	7	1	1	2	4	0	0	0	12:03
	NHL Totals		417	53	109	162	360	6	0	6	672	7.9		42	28.6	15:28	79	11	17	28	70	1	0	0	15:28

Traded to **Buffalo** by **San Jose** with Martin Spahnel and Philadelphia's 1st (previously acquired, later traded to Phoenix – Phoenix selected Daniel Briere) and 4th (previously acquired, Buffalo selected Mike Martone) round choices in 1996 Entry Draft for Doug Bodger, November 16, 1995. Traded to **Ottawa** by **Buffalo** with Buffalo's 5th round choice (Tim Cook) in 2003 Entry Draft for Jakub Klepis, February 25, 2003. • Missed majority of 2003-04 season recovering from knee injury suffered in game vs. Boston, December 13, 2003.

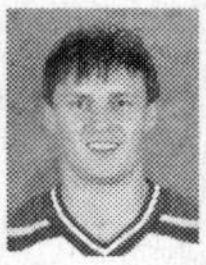

VARLAMOV, Sergei
(vahr-LAHM-uhf, SAIR-gay)

Left wing. Shoots left. 5'11", 203 lbs. Born, Kiev, USSR, July 21, 1978.

1994-95	Nelson	RMJHL	26	11	15	26	56																		
1995-96	Swift Current	WHL	55	23	21	44	65																		
1996-97	Swift Current	WHL	72	46	39	85	94										10	3	8	11	10				
	Saint John Flames	AHL	1	0	0	0	0																		
1997-98	Swift Current	WHL	72	*66	53	*119	132										12	10	5	15	28				
	Calgary	NHL	1	0	0	0	0	0	0	0	0	0.0	0												
	Saint John Flames	AHL	....	....	....	....	....										3	0	0	0	0				
1998-99	Saint John Flames	AHL	76	24	33	57	66										7	0	4	4	8				
99-2000	Calgary	NHL	7	3	0	3	0	0	0	1	11	27.3	0	1	0.0	10:22									
	Saint John Flames	AHL	68	20	21	41	88										3	0	0	0	24				
2000-01	Saint John Flames	AHL	55	21	30	51	56										19	*15	8	23	10				
2001-02	St. Louis	NHL	52	5	7	12	26	0	0	0	83	6.0	4	1	0.0	11:10	1	0	0	0	2	0	0	0	8:45
	Ukraine	Olympics	2	0	1	1	14																		
2002-03	St. Louis	NHL	3	0	0	0	0	0	0	0	5	0.0	1	0	0.0	11:26									
	Worcester IceCats	AHL	72	23	38	61	79										3	2	0	2	0				
2003-04	Worcester IceCats	AHL	43	7	16	23	18																		
	Manitoba Moose	AHL	12	4	2	6	10																		
	NHL Totals		63	8	7	15	26	0	0	1	99	8.1		2	0.0	11:06	1	0	0	0	2	0	0	0	8:45

WHL East First All-Star Team (1998) • Canadian Major Junior First All-Star Team (1998) • Canadian Major Junior Player of the Year (1998)

Signed as a free agent by **Calgary**, September 18, 1996. Traded to **St. Louis** by **Calgary** with Fred Brathwaite, Daniel Tkaczuk and Calgary's 9th round choice (Grant Jacobsen) in 2001 Entry Draft for Roman Turek and St. Louis' 4th round choice (Yegor Shastin) in 2001 Entry Draft, June 23, 2001. Traded to **Vancouver** by **St. Louis** for Ryan Ready, March 9, 2004.

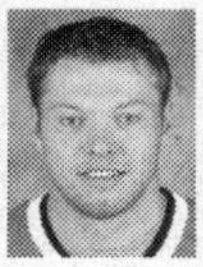

VASICEK, Josef
(VAHSH-ih-chehk, YOH-zehf) **CAR.**

Center. Shoots left. 6'4", 200 lbs. Born, Havlickuv Brod, Czech., September 12, 1980. Carolina's 4th choice, 91st overall, in 1998 Entry Draft.

1995-96	Jiskra Havlickuv 18	Czech-Jr.	36	25	25	50	....																		
1996-97	Slavia Praha 18	Czech-Jr.	37	20	40	60	....																		
1997-98	Slavia Praha Jr.	Czech-Jr.	34	13	20	33	....																		
1998-99	Sault Ste. Marie	OHL	66	21	35	56	30										5	3	0	3	10				
99-2000	Sault Ste. Marie	OHL	54	26	46	72	49										17	5	15	20	8				
2000-01	Carolina	NHL	76	8	13	21	53	1	0	0	103	7.8	−8	786	46.6	11:49	6	2	0	2	0	0	0	0	13:56
	Cincinnati	IHL	....	....	....	....	....										3	0	0	0	0				
2001-02	Carolina	NHL	78	14	17	31	53	3	0	3	117	12.0	−7	878	48.3	14:11	23	3	2	5	12	0	0	1	14:50
2002-03	Carolina	NHL	57	10	10	20	33	4	0	1	87	11.5	−19	652	49.5	15:57									
2003-04	Carolina	NHL	82	19	26	45	60	6	0	5	161	11.8	−3	262	48.9	17:06									
	NHL Totals		293	51	66	117	199	14	0	9	468	10.9		2578	48.1	14:44	29	5	2	7	12	0	0	1	14:39

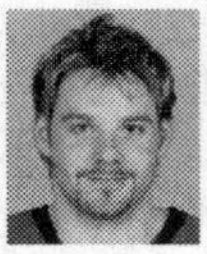

VAUCLAIR, Julien
(voh-KLAIR, JEW-lee-ehn)

Defense. Shoots left. 6', 205 lbs. Born, Delemont, Switz., October 2, 1979. Ottawa's 4th choice, 74th overall, in 1998 Entry Draft.

1995-96	HC Ajoie	Swiss-3	20	4	10	14	....																		
1996-97	HC Ajoie	Swiss-2	40	0	6	6	24										9	0	2	2	8				
1997-98	HC Lugano Jr.	Swiss-Jr.	10	7	4	11	10																		
	HC Lugano	Swiss	36	1	2	3	12										7	0	0	0	25				
1998-99	HC Lugano	Swiss	38	0	3	3	8																		
	HC Lugano Jr.	Swiss-Jr.	19	10	14	24	14										1	0	0	0	0				
99-2000	HC Lugano	Swiss	45	3	3	6	16										14	0	0	0	0				
	HC Lugano Jr.	EuroHL	6	1	0	1	0										4	1	0	1	2				
2000-01	HC Lugano	Swiss	42	3	4	7	57										18	0	1	1	4				
2001-02	Grand Rapids	AHL	71	5	14	19	18										4	0	1	1	4				
	Switzerland	Olympics	4	1	0	1	2																		
2002-03	Binghamton	AHL	67	6	16	22	30										14	0	1	1	8				
2003-04	Ottawa	NHL	1	0	0	0	2	0	0	0	0	0.0	1	0	0.0	12:48									
	Binghamton	AHL	78	9	30	39	39										2	0	0	0	0				
	NHL Totals		1	0	0	0	2	0	0	0	0	0.0		0	0.0	12:48									

Signed as a free agent by **HC Lugano** (Swiss), May 12, 2004.

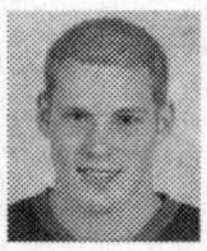

VEILLEUX, Stephane
(VAY-oo, STEH-fan) **MIN.**

Left wing. Shoots left. 6'1", 187 lbs. Born, Beauceville, Que., November 16, 1981. Minnesota's 4th choice, 93rd overall, in 2001 Entry Draft.

1997-98	Beauce-Amiante	QAAA	21	20	17	37	....																		
	Levis-Lauzon	QAAA	14	3	5	8	....										1	0	0	0	0				
1998-99	Victoriaville Tigres	QMJHL	65	6	13	19	35										6	1	3	4	2				
99-2000	Victoriaville Tigres	QMJHL	22	1	4	5	17																		
	Val-d'Or Foreurs	QMJHL	50	14	28	42	100																		
2000-01	Val-d'Or Foreurs	QMJHL	68	48	67	115	90										21	15	18	33	42				
2001-02	Houston Aeros	AHL	77	13	22	35	113										14	2	4	6	20				
2002-03	Minnesota	NHL	38	3	2	5	23	1	0	0	52	5.8	−6	13	7.7	12:08									
	Houston Aeros	AHL	29	8	4	12	43										23	7	11	18	12				
2003-04	Minnesota	NHL	19	2	8	10	20	1	1	1	37	5.4	0	10	40.0	14:20									
	Houston Aeros	AHL	64	13	25	38	66										2	1	1	2	2				
	NHL Totals		57	5	10	15	43	2	1	1	89	5.6		23	21.7	12:52									

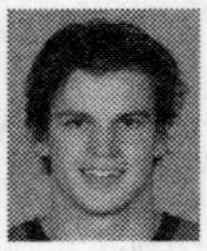

VERMETTE, Antoine

(vuhr-MEHT, AN-twuhn) **OTT.**

Center. Shoots left. 6'1", 184 lbs. Born, St-Agapit, Que., July 20, 1982. Ottawa's 3rd choice, 55th overall, in 2000 Entry Draft.

			Regular Season														Playoffs								
Season	**Club**	**League**	**GP**	**G**	**A**	**Pts**	**PIM**	**PP**	**SH**	**GW**	**S**	**%**	**+/-**	**TF**	**F%**	**Min**	**GP**	**G**	**A**	**Pts**	**PIM**	**PP**	**SH**	**GW**	**Min**
1997-98	Quebec Select	QAHA	19	11	20	31	36	....	....	....	....	....	....	....	....	....	....	....	....	....	....	....	....	....	....
	Levis-Lauzon	QAAA	8	1	1	2	4	....	....	....	....	....	....	....	....	....	1	0	0	0	0	....	....	....	....
1998-99	Quebec Remparts	QMJHL	57	9	17	26	32	....	....	....	....	....	....	....	....	....	13	0	0	0	2	....	....	....	....
99-2000	Victoriaville Tigres	QMJHL	71	30	41	71	87	....	....	....	....	....	....	....	....	....	6	0	1	1	6	....	....	....	....
2000-01	Victoriaville Tigres	QMJHL	71	57	62	119	102	....	....	....	....	....	....	....	....	....	9	4	6	10	14	....	....	....	....
2001-02	Victoriaville Tigres	QMJHL	4	0	2	2	6	....	....	....	....	....	....	....	....	....	22	10	16	26	10	....	....	....	....
2002-03	Binghamton	AHL	80	34	28	62	57	....	....	....	....	....	....	....	....	....	14	2	9	11	10	....	....	....	....
2003-04	**Ottawa**	**NHL**	**57**	**7**	**7**	**14**	**16**	**0**	**1**	**0**	**63**	**11.1**	**5**	**100**	**44.0**	**11:59**	**4**	**0**	**1**	**1**	**4**	**0**	**0**	**0**	**11:35**
	Binghamton	AHL	3	0	0	0	6	....	....	....	....	....	....	....	....	....	....	....	....	....	....	....	....	....	....
	NHL Totals		**57**	**7**	**7**	**14**	**16**	**0**	**1**	**0**	**63**	**11.1**		**100**	**44.0**	**11:59**	**4**	**0**	**1**	**1**	**4**	**0**	**0**	**0**	**11:35**

AHL All-Rookie Team (2003)

• Missed majority of 2001-02 season recovering from neck injury suffered at Team Canada Jr. Selection Camp, June 3, 2001.

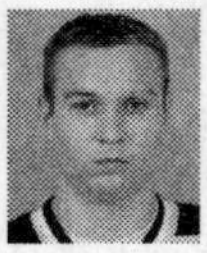

VERNARSKY, Kris

(veh-NAHR-skee, KRIHS) **BOS.**

Center. Shoots left. 6'3", 201 lbs. Born, Detroit, MI, April 5, 1982. Toronto's 2nd choice, 51st overall, in 2000 Entry Draft.

			Regular Season														Playoffs								
Season	**Club**	**League**	**GP**	**G**	**A**	**Pts**	**PIM**	**PP**	**SH**	**GW**	**S**	**%**	**+/-**	**TF**	**F%**	**Min**	**GP**	**G**	**A**	**Pts**	**PIM**	**PP**	**SH**	**GW**	**Min**
1997-98	U.S. National U-18	USDP	69	11	18	29	97	....	....	....	....	....	....	....	....	....	....	....	....	....	....	....	....	....	....
1998-99	Plymouth Whalers	OHL	45	3	14	17	30	....	....	....	....	....	....	....	....	....	11	0	0	0	2	....	....	....	....
99-2000	Plymouth Whalers	OHL	64	16	22	38	63	....	....	....	....	....	....	....	....	....	19	3	6	9	24	....	....	....	....
2000-01	Plymouth Whalers	OHL	60	14	21	35	35	....	....	....	....	....	....	....	....	....	19	7	10	17	19	....	....	....	....
2001-02	Plymouth Whalers	OHL	59	19	36	55	98	....	....	....	....	....	....	....	....	....	6	1	2	3	15	....	....	....	....
2002-03	**Boston**	**NHL**	**14**	**1**	**0**	**1**	**2**	**0**	**0**	**0**	**18**	**5.6**	**–2**	**22**	**54.6**	**10:15**	....	....	....	....	....	....	....	....	....
	Providence Bruins	AHL	65	12	15	27	49	....	....	....	....	....	....	....	....	....	4	0	0	0	20	....	....	....	....
2003-04	**Boston**	**NHL**	**3**	**0**	**0**	**0**	**0**	**0**	**0**	**0**	**0**	**0.0**	**–1**	**12**	**33.3**	**6:33**	....	....	....	....	....	....	....	....	....
	Providence Bruins	AHL	55	8	9	17	61	....	....	....	....	....	....	....	....	....	2	0	0	0	4	....	....	....	....
	NHL Totals		**17**	**1**	**0**	**1**	**2**	**0**	**0**	**0**	**18**	**5.6**		**34**	**47.1**	**9:36**	....	....	....	....	....	....	....	....	....

Rights traded to **Boston** by **Toronto** for Ric Jackman, May 13, 2002.

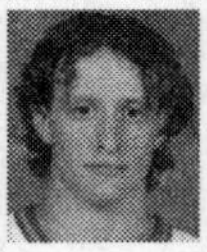

VEROT, Darcy

(vuhr-AWT, DAHR-see) **WSH.**

Left wing. Shoots left. 6', 199 lbs. Born, Radville, Sask., July 13, 1976.

			Regular Season														Playoffs								
Season	**Club**	**League**	**GP**	**G**	**A**	**Pts**	**PIM**	**PP**	**SH**	**GW**	**S**	**%**	**+/-**	**TF**	**F%**	**Min**	**GP**	**G**	**A**	**Pts**	**PIM**	**PP**	**SH**	**GW**	**Min**
1994-95	Weyburn	SJHL	57	8	18	26	240	....	....	....	....	....	....	....	....	....	16	5	2	7	50	....	....	....	....
1995-96	Weyburn	SJHL	64	15	30	45	191	....	....	....	....	....	....	....	....	....	3	1	0	1	20	....	....	....	....
1996-97	Weyburn	SJHL	61	26	51	77	218	....	....	....	....	....	....	....	....	....	13	3	8	11	24	....	....	....	....
1997-98	Lake Charles	WPHL	68	11	26	37	269	....	....	....	....	....	....	....	....	....	4	0	1	1	25	....	....	....	....
1998-99	Lake Charles	WPHL	68	17	23	40	236	....	....	....	....	....	....	....	....	....	9	2	4	6	53	....	....	....	....
99-2000	Wheeling Nailers	ECHL	44	7	12	19	240	....	....	....	....	....	....	....	....	....	....	....	....	....	....	....	....	....	....
	Wilkes-Barre	AHL	23	5	5	10	96	....	....	....	....	....	....	....	....	....	....	....	....	....	....	....	....	....	....
2000-01	Wilkes-Barre	AHL	78	10	15	25	347	....	....	....	....	....	....	....	....	....	21	2	3	5	40	....	....	....	....
2001-02	Wilkes-Barre	AHL	71	6	10	16	387	....	....	....	....	....	....	....	....	....	....	....	....	....	....	....	....	....	....
2002-03	Saint John Flames	AHL	73	5	11	16	299	....	....	....	....	....	....	....	....	....	....	....	....	....	....	....	....	....	....
2003-04	**Washington**	**NHL**	**37**	**0**	**2**	**2**	**135**	**0**	**0**	**0**	**11**	**0.0**	**–6**	**183**	**48.6**	**8:48**	....	....	....	....	....	....	....	....	....
	Portland Pirates	AHL	28	3	5	8	89	....	....	....	....	....	....	....	....	....	....	....	....	....	....	....	....	....	....
	NHL Totals		**37**	**0**	**2**	**2**	**135**	**0**	**0**	**0**	**11**	**0.0**		**183**	**48.6**	**8:48**	....	....	....	....	....	....	....	....	....

Signed as a free agent by **Wilkes-Barre** (AHL), February 25, 2000. Signed as a free agent by **Pittsburgh**, July 28, 2000. Signed as a free agent by **Calgary**, July 9, 2002. Signed as a free agent by **Washingon**, September 5, 2003.

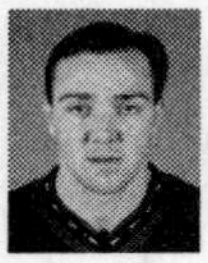

VIGIER, J.P.

(vih-ZHAY, JAY-pee) **ATL.**

Right wing. Shoots right. 6', 200 lbs. Born, Notre Dame de Lourdes, Man., September 11, 1976.

			Regular Season														Playoffs								
Season	**Club**	**League**	**GP**	**G**	**A**	**Pts**	**PIM**	**PP**	**SH**	**GW**	**S**	**%**	**+/-**	**TF**	**F%**	**Min**	**GP**	**G**	**A**	**Pts**	**PIM**	**PP**	**SH**	**GW**	**Min**
1995-96	Portage Terriers	MJHL	56	32	49	81	....	....	....	....	....	....	....	....	....	....	....	....	....	....	....	....	....	....	....
1996-97	North. Michigan	WCHA	36	10	14	24	54	....	....	....	....	....	....	....	....	....	....	....	....	....	....	....	....	....	....
1997-98	North. Michigan	CCHA	36	12	15	27	60	....	....	....	....	....	....	....	....	....	....	....	....	....	....	....	....	....	....
1998-99	North. Michigan	CCHA	42	21	18	39	80	....	....	....	....	....	....	....	....	....	....	....	....	....	....	....	....	....	....
99-2000	North. Michigan	CCHA	39	18	17	35	72	....	....	....	....	....	....	....	....	....	....	....	....	....	....	....	....	....	....
	Orlando	IHL	3	1	0	1	0	....	....	....	....	....	....	....	....	....	....	....	....	....	....	....	....	....	....
2000-01	**Atlanta**	**NHL**	**2**	**0**	**0**	**0**	**0**	**0**	**0**	**0**	**1**	**0.0**	**–2**	**1**	**100.0**	**9:56**	....	....	....	....	....	....	....	....	....
	Orlando	IHL	78	23	17	40	66	....	....	....	....	....	....	....	....	....	16	6	6	12	14	....	....	....	....
2001-02	**Atlanta**	**NHL**	**15**	**4**	**1**	**5**	**4**	**0**	**0**	**0**	**18**	**22.2**	**–5**	**3**	**66.7**	**13:13**	....	....	....	....	....	....	....	....	....
	Chicago Wolves	AHL	62	25	16	41	26	....	....	....	....	....	....	....	....	....	21	7	7	14	20	....	....	....	....
2002-03	**Atlanta**	**NHL**	**13**	**0**	**0**	**0**	**4**	**0**	**0**	**0**	**21**	**0.0**	**–13**	**1**	**0.0**	**14:07**	....	....	....	....	....	....	....	....	....
	Chicago Wolves	AHL	63	29	27	56	54	....	....	....	....	....	....	....	....	....	9	3	1	4	4	....	....	....	....
2003-04	**Atlanta**	**NHL**	**70**	**10**	**8**	**18**	**22**	**2**	**2**	**3**	**110**	**9.1**	**–18**	**53**	**47.2**	**14:36**	....	....	....	....	....	....	....	....	....
	NHL Totals		**100**	**14**	**9**	**23**	**30**	**2**	**2**	**3**	**150**	**9.3**		**58**	**48.3**	**14:14**	....	....	....	....	....	....	....	....	....

CCHA Second All-Star Team (1999) • CCHA All-Tournament Team (1999)

Signed as a free agent by **Atlanta**, April 20, 2000.

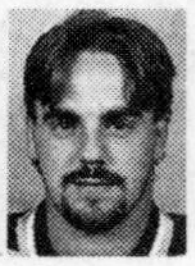

VIRTUE, Terry

(VIR-too, TAIR-ee) **T.B.**

Defense. Shoots right. 6', 198 lbs. Born, Scarborough, Ont., August 12, 1970.

			Regular Season														Playoffs								
Season	**Club**	**League**	**GP**	**G**	**A**	**Pts**	**PIM**	**PP**	**SH**	**GW**	**S**	**%**	**+/-**	**TF**	**F%**	**Min**	**GP**	**G**	**A**	**Pts**	**PIM**	**PP**	**SH**	**GW**	**Min**
1988-89	Hobbema Hawks	AJHL	56	6	31	37	339	....	....	....	....	....	....	....	....	....	....	....	....	....	....	....	....	....	....
	Victoria Cougars	WHL	8	1	1	2	13	....	....	....	....	....	....	....	....	....	....	....	....	....	....	....	....	....	....
1989-90	Victoria Cougars	WHL	24	1	9	10	85	....	....	....	....	....	....	....	....	....	....	....	....	....	....	....	....	....	....
	Tri-City	WHL	34	1	10	11	82	....	....	....	....	....	....	....	....	....	6	0	0	0	30	....	....	....	....
1990-91	Tri-City	WHL	11	1	8	9	24	....	....	....	....	....	....	....	....	....	....	....	....	....	....	....	....	....	....
	Portland	WHL	59	9	44	53	127	....	....	....	....	....	....	....	....	....	....	....	....	....	....	....	....	....	....
1991-92	Roanoke Valley	ECHL	38	4	22	26	165	....	....	....	....	....	....	....	....	....	....	....	....	....	....	....	....	....	....
	Louisville	ECHL	23	1	15	16	58	....	....	....	....	....	....	....	....	....	13	0	8	8	49	....	....	....	....
1992-93	Louisville	ECHL	28	0	17	17	84	....	....	....	....	....	....	....	....	....	....	....	....	....	....	....	....	....	....
	Wheeling	ECHL	31	3	15	18	86	....	....	....	....	....	....	....	....	....	16	3	5	8	18	....	....	....	....
1993-94	Wheeling	ECHL	34	5	28	33	61	....	....	....	....	....	....	....	....	....	6	2	2	4	4	....	....	....	....
	Cape Breton	AHL	26	4	6	10	10	....	....	....	....	....	....	....	....	....	5	0	0	0	17	....	....	....	....
1994-95	Worcester IceCats	AHL	73	14	25	39	183	....	....	....	....	....	....	....	....	....	....	....	....	....	....	....	....	....	....
	Atlanta Knights	IHL	1	0	0	0	2	....	....	....	....	....	....	....	....	....	....	....	....	....	....	....	....	....	....
1995-96	Worcester IceCats	AHL	76	7	31	38	234	....	....	....	....	....	....	....	....	....	4	0	0	0	4	....	....	....	....
1996-97	Worcester IceCats	AHL	80	16	26	42	220	....	....	....	....	....	....	....	....	....	5	0	4	4	8	....	....	....	....
1997-98	Worcester IceCats	AHL	74	8	26	34	233	....	....	....	....	....	....	....	....	....	11	1	4	5	41	....	....	....	....
1998-99	**Boston**	**NHL**	**4**	**0**	**0**	**0**	**0**	**0**	**0**	**0**	**2**	**0.0**	**2**	**0**	**0.0**	**9:41**	....	....	....	....	....	....	....	....	....
	Providence Bruins	AHL	76	8	48	56	117	....	....	....	....	....	....	....	....	....	17	2	12	14	29	....	....	....	....
99-2000	**NY Rangers**	**NHL**	**1**	**0**	**0**	**0**	**0**	**0**	**0**	**0**	**2**	**0.0**	**–2**	**0**	**0.0**	**12:32**	....	....	....	....	....	....	....	....	....
	Hartford	AHL	67	5	22	27	166	....	....	....	....	....	....	....	....	....	23	3	7	10	51	....	....	....	....
2000-01	Hartford	AHL	71	5	24	29	166	....	....	....	....	....	....	....	....	....	5	1	0	1	2	....	....	....	....
2001-02	Hartford	AHL	76	4	20	24	117	....	....	....	....	....	....	....	....	....	10	0	1	1	19	....	....	....	....
2002-03	Worcester IceCats	AHL	78	5	30	35	144	....	....	....	....	....	....	....	....	....	....	....	....	....	....	....	....	....	....
2003-04	Worcester IceCats	AHL	74	6	16	22	66	....	....	....	....	....	....	....	....	....	10	1	4	5	36	....	....	....	....
	NHL Totals		**5**	**0**	**0**	**0**	**0**	**0**	**0**	**0**	**4**	**0.0**		**0**	**0.0**	**10:15**	....	....	....	....	....	....	....	....	....

AHL Second All-Star Team (1999)

Signed as a free agent by **St. Louis**, January 29, 1996. Signed as a free agent by **Boston**, August 28, 1998. Signed as a free agent by **NY Rangers**, July 29, 1999. Signed as a free agent by **St. Louis**, July 14, 2002. Signed as a free agent by **Springfield** (AHL), July 30, 2004.

Regular Season / Playoffs

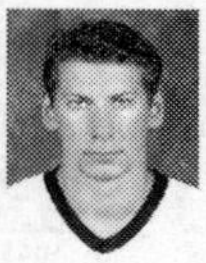

VISHNEVSKI, Vitaly (vihsh-NEHV-skee, vih-TAL-ee) **ANA.**

Defense. Shoots left. 6'2", 206 lbs. Born, Kharkov, USSR, March 18, 1980. Anaheim's 1st choice, 5th overall, in 1998 Entry Draft.

Season	Club	League	GP	G	A	Pts	PIM	PP	SH	GW	S	%	+/-	TF	F%	Min	Playoffs GP	G	A	Pts	PIM	PP	SH	GW	Min
1995-96	Yaroslavl 2	CIS-2	40	4	4	8	20																		
1996-97	Yaroslavl 2	Russia-3	45	0	2	2	30																		
1997-98	Yaroslavl 2	Russia-2	47	8	9	17	164																		
1998-99	Yaroslavl	Russia	34	3	4	7	38										10	0	0	0	4				
99-2000	Anaheim	NHL	31	1	1	2	26	1	0	0	17	5.9	0	0	0.0	16:38									
	Cincinnati	AHL	35	1	3	4	45																		
2000-01	Anaheim	NHL	76	1	10	11	99	0	0	0	49	2.0	−1	0	0.0	19:14									
2001-02	Anaheim	NHL	74	0	3	3	60	0	0	0	54	0.0	−10	0	0.0	17:36									
2002-03	Anaheim	NHL	80	2	6	8	76	0	1	0	65	3.1	−8	0	0.0	14:10	21	0	1	1	6	0	0	0	10:02
2003-04	Anaheim	NHL	73	6	10	16	51	0	0	0	86	7.0	0	0	0.0	17:10									
	NHL Totals		334	10	30	40	312	1	1	0	271	3.7		0	0.0	16:58	21	0	1	1	6	0	0	0	10:02

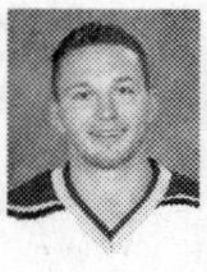

VISNOVSKY, Lubomir (vihsh-NAWV-skee, LOO-boh-mihr) **L.A.**

Defense. Shoots left. 5'10", 188 lbs. Born, Topolcany, Czech., August 11, 1976. Los Angeles' 4th choice, 118th overall, in 2000 Entry Draft.

Season	Club	League	GP	G	A	Pts	PIM	PP	SH	GW	S	%	+/-	TF	F%	Min	Playoffs GP	G	A	Pts	PIM	PP	SH	GW	Min
1994-95	Slov. Bratislava	Slovakia	36	11	12	23	10										9	1	3	4	2				
1995-96	Slov. Bratislava	Slovakia	35	8	6	14	22										13	1	5	6	2				
1996-97	Slov. Bratislava	Slovakia	44	11	12	23											2	0	1	1					
	Slov. Bratislava	EuroHL	6	3	1	4	2										2	0	0	0	6				
1997-98	Slov. Bratislava	Slovakia	36	7	9	16	16										11	2	4	6	8				
	Slov. Bratislava	EuroHL	6	1	0	1	4																		
1998-99	Slov. Bratislava	Slovakia	40	9	10	19	31										10	5	5	10	0				
	Slov. Bratislava	EuroHL	6	0	3	3	4																		
99-2000	Slov. Bratislava	Slovakia	52	21	24	45	38										8	5	3	8	16				
2000-01	Los Angeles	NHL	81	7	32	39	36	3	0	3	105	6.7	16	0	0.0	16:58	8	0	0	0	0	0	0	0	13:57
2001-02	Los Angeles	NHL	72	4	17	21	14	1	0	2	95	4.2	−5	0	0.0	16:15	4	0	1	1	0	0	0	0	8:22
	Slovakia	Olympics	3	1	2	3	0																		
2002-03	Los Angeles	NHL	57	8	16	24	28	1	0	1	85	9.4	2	0	0.0	19:20									
2003-04	Los Angeles	NHL	58	8	21	29	26	5	0	0	114	7.0	8	0	0.0	24:02									
	NHL Totals		268	27	86	113	104	10	0	6	399	6.8		0	0.0	18:49	12	0	1	1	0	0	0	0	12:05

NHL All-Rookie Team (2001)

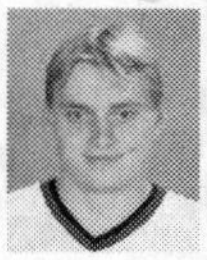

VOLCHENKOV, Anton (vohl-chen-KAHF, AN-tawn) **OTT.**

Defense. Shoots left. 6'1", 227 lbs. Born, Moscow, USSR, February 25, 1982. Ottawa's 1st choice, 21st overall, in 2000 Entry Draft.

Season	Club	League	GP	G	A	Pts	PIM	PP	SH	GW	S	%	+/-	TF	F%	Min	Playoffs GP	G	A	Pts	PIM	PP	SH	GW	Min
99-2000	HC CSKA 2	Russia-3	6	0	1	1	10																		
	HC CSKA	Russia-2	30	2	9	11	36																		
2000-01	Krylja Sovetov	Russia-2	34	3	4	7	56																		
2001-02	Krylja Sovetov 2	Russia-3	1	0	0	0	0																		
	Krylja Sovetov	Russia	47	4	16	20	50										3	0	0	0	29				
2002-03	Ottawa	NHL	57	3	13	16	40	0	0	0	75	4.0	−4	0	0.0	15:30	17	1	1	2	4	0	0	1	13:31
2003-04	Ottawa	NHL	19	1	2	3	8	0	0	0	15	6.7	1	0	0.0	13:04	5	0	0	0	6	0	0	0	11:52
	NHL Totals		76	4	15	19	48	0	0	0	90	4.4		0	0.0	14:54	22	1	1	2	10	0	0	1	13:09

• Missed majority of 2003-04 season recovering from shoulder injury suffered in game vs. Boston, December 8, 2003.

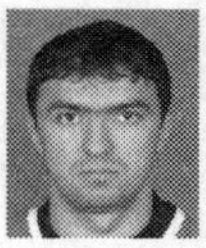

VOROBIEV, Pavel (voh-roh-BEE-ehf, PAH-vehl) **CHI.**

Right wing. Shoots left. 6', 194 lbs. Born, Karaganda, USSR, May 5, 1982. Chicago's 2nd choice, 11th overall, in 2000 Entry Draft.

Season	Club	League	GP	G	A	Pts	PIM	PP	SH	GW	S	%	+/-	TF	F%	Min	Playoffs GP	G	A	Pts	PIM	PP	SH	GW	Min
1996-97	Molot Perm 2	Russia-3	2	0	0	0	0																		
1997-98	Yaroslavl 2	Russia-2	16	2	0	2	6																		
1998-99	Yaroslavl 2	Russia-3	17	0	1	1	0																		
99-2000	Yaroslavl 2	Russia-3	40	19	15	34	20																		
	Yaroslavl	Russia	8	2	0	2	4										10	2	2	4	0				
2000-01	Yaroslavl	Russia	36	8	8	16	28										10	4	1	5	8				
2001-02	Yaroslavl	Russia	9	3	2	5	6										7	0	0	0	4				
2002-03	Yaroslavl	Russia	44	10	18	28	10										7	0	1	1	2				
2003-04	Chicago	NHL	18	1	3	4	4	1	0	1	20	5.0	1	0	0.0	12:48									
	Norfolk Admirals	AHL	57	13	16	29	8										4	0	0	0	0				
	NHL Totals		18	1	3	4	4	1	0	1	20	5.0		0	0.0	12:48									

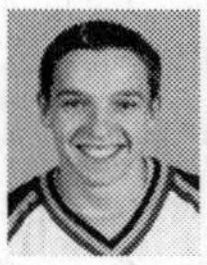

VRBATA, Radim (vuhr-BA-tuh, ra-DEEM) **CAR.**

Right wing. Shoots right. 6'1", 190 lbs. Born, Mlada Boleslav, Czech., June 13, 1981. Colorado's 10th choice, 212th overall, in 1999 Entry Draft.

Season	Club	League	GP	G	A	Pts	PIM	PP	SH	GW	S	%	+/-	TF	F%	Min	Playoffs GP	G	A	Pts	PIM	PP	SH	GW	Min
1997-98	Mlada Boleslav Jr.	Czech-Jr.	35	42	31	73	4																		
1998-99	Hull Olympiques	QMJHL	54	22	38	60	16										23	6	13	19	6				
99-2000	Hull Olympiques	QMJHL	58	29	45	74	26										15	3	9	12	8				
2000-01	Shawinigan	QMJHL	55	56	64	120	67										10	4	7	11	4				
	Hershey Bears	AHL															1	0	1	1	2				
2001-02	Colorado	NHL	52	18	12	30	14	6	0	3	112	16.1	7	8	37.5	14:32	9	0	0	0	0	0	0	0	13:05
	Hershey Bears	AHL	20	8	14	22	8																		
2002-03	Colorado	NHL	66	11	19	30	16	3	0	4	171	6.4	0	14	50.0	13:55									
	Carolina	NHL	10	5	0	5	2	3	0	0	44	11.4	−7	15	46.7	19:00									
2003-04	Carolina	NHL	80	12	13	25	24	4	0	2	195	6.2	−10	21	38.1	13:42									
	NHL Totals		208	46	44	90	56	16	0	9	522	8.8		58	43.1	14:14	9	0	0	0	0	0	0	0	13:05

QMJHL First All-Star Team (2001)
Traded to **Carolina** by **Colorado** for Bates Battaglia, March 11, 2003.

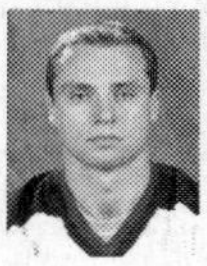

VYBORNY, David (vih-BOHR-nee, DAY-vihd) **CBJ**

Right wing. Shoots left. 5'10", 189 lbs. Born, Jihlava, Czech., June 2, 1975. Edmonton's 3rd choice, 33rd overall, in 1993 Entry Draft.

Season	Club	League	GP	G	A	Pts	PIM	PP	SH	GW	S	%	+/-	TF	F%	Min	Playoffs GP	G	A	Pts	PIM	PP	SH	GW	Min
1991-92	HC Sparta Praha	Czech	32	6	9	15	2																		
1992-93	HC Sparta Praha	Czech	52	20	24	44																			
1993-94	HC Sparta Praha	Czech	44	15	20	35	0										6	4	7	11	0				
1994-95	Cape Breton	AHL	76	23	38	61	30																		
1995-96	HC Sparta Praha	Czech	40	12	18	30											12	6	5	11					
1996-97	HC Sparta Praha	Czech	47	20	29	49	14										10	7	7	14	6				
1997-98	MoDo	Sweden	45	16	21	37	34										9	0	2	2	2				
1998-99	HC Sparta Praha	Czech	52	24	*46	*70	22										8	1	3	4					
99-2000	HC Sparta Praha	Czech	50	25	38	63	30										9	3	*8	*11	4				
2000-01	Columbus	NHL	79	13	19	32	22	5	0	1	125	10.4	−9	36	44.4	15:25									
2001-02	Columbus	NHL	75	13	18	31	6	6	0	2	103	12.6	−14	25	44.0	15:27									
2002-03	Columbus	NHL	79	20	26	46	16	4	1	4	125	16.0	12	46	32.6	16:20									
2003-04	Columbus	NHL	82	22	31	53	40	8	4	2	158	13.9	−26	97	21.7	20:23									
	NHL Totals		315	68	94	162	84	23	5	9	511	13.3		204	30.9	16:57									

Signed as a free agent by **Columbus**, June 8, 2000.

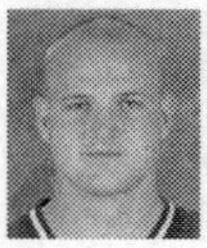

WALKER, Matt (WAH-kuhr, MAT) **ST.L.**

Defense. Shoots right. 6'2", 236 lbs. Born, Beaverlodge, Alta., April 7, 1980. St. Louis' 3rd choice, 83rd overall, in 1998 Entry Draft.

Season	Club	League	GP	G	A	Pts	PIM	PP	SH	GW	S	%	+/-	TF	F%	Min	Playoffs GP	G	A	Pts	PIM	PP	SH	GW	Min
1996-97	Grand Prairie	AAHA	68	22	62	74	186																		
1997-98	Portland	WHL	64	2	13	15	124										16	0	0	0	21				
1998-99	Portland	WHL	64	1	10	11	151										4	0	1	1	6				
99-2000	Portland	WHL	38	2	7	9	97																		
	Kootenay Ice	WHL	31	4	19	23	53										21	5	13	18	24				

Season	Club	League	Regular Season GP	G	A	Pts	PIM	PP	SH	GW	S	%	+/-	TF	F%	Min	Playoffs GP	G	A	Pts	PIM	PP	SH	GW	Min
2000-01	Peoria Rivermen	ECHL	8	1	0	1	70																		
	Worcester IceCats	AHL	61	4	8	12	131										11	0	0	0	6				
2001-02	Worcester IceCats	AHL	49	2	11	13	164										3	0	0	0	8				
2002-03	St. Louis	NHL	16	0	1	1	38	0	0	0	13	0.0	0	1	100.0	11:09									
	Worcester IceCats	AHL	40	1	8	9	58																		
2003-04	St. Louis	NHL	14	0	1	1	25	0	0	0	8	0.0	0	0	0.0	11:23	4	0	0	0	0	0	0	0	9:43
	Worcester IceCats	AHL	4	0	1	1	7																		
	NHL Totals		30	0	2	2	63	0	0	0	21	0.0		1	100.0	11:15	4	0	0	0	0	0	0	0	9:43

• Missed majority of 2003-04 season recovering from groin injury suffered in training camp, September 23, 2003.

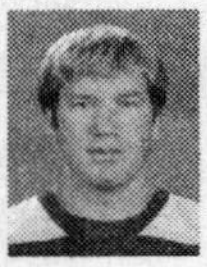

WALKER, Scott (WAH-kuhr, SKAWT) NSH.

Right wing. Shoots right. 5'10", 196 lbs. Born, Cambridge, Ont., July 19, 1973. Vancouver's 4th choice, 124th overall, in 1993 Entry Draft.

1989-90	Kitchener	OJHL-B	6	0	5	5	4																		
	Cambridge	OJHL-B	27	7	22	29	87																		
1990-91	Cambridge	OJHL-B	45	10	27	37	241																		
1991-92	Owen Sound	OHL	53	7	31	38	128										5	0	7	7	8				
1992-93	Owen Sound	OHL	57	23	68	91	110										8	1	5	6	16				
1993-94	Hamilton	AHL	77	10	29	39	272										4	0	1	1	25				
1994-95	Syracuse Crunch	AHL	74	14	38	52	334																		
	Vancouver	NHL	11	0	1	1	33	0	0	0	8	0.0	0												
1995-96	Vancouver	NHL	63	4	8	12	137	0	1	1	45	8.9	−7												
	Syracuse Crunch	AHL	15	3	12	15	52										16	9	8	17	39				
1996-97	Vancouver	NHL	64	3	15	18	132	0	0	0	55	5.5	2												
1997-98	Vancouver	NHL	59	3	10	13	164	0	1	1	40	7.5	−8												
1998-99	Nashville	NHL	71	15	25	40	103	0	1	2	96	15.6	0	265	48.3	16:21									
99-2000	Nashville	NHL	69	7	21	28	90	0	1	0	98	7.1	−16	30	36.7	15:49									
2000-01	Nashville	NHL	74	25	29	54	66	9	3	1	159	15.7	−2	541	51.4	19:17									
2001-02	Nashville	NHL	28	4	5	9	18	1	0	0	46	8.7	−13	149	38.9	18:38									
2002-03	Nashville	NHL	60	15	18	33	58	7	0	5	124	12.1	2	336	49.1	19:50									
2003-04	Nashville	NHL	75	25	42	67	94	9	3	3	157	15.9	4	367	41.4	20:03	6	0	1	1	6	0	0	0	20:10
	NHL Totals		574	101	174	275	895	26	10	13	828	12.2		1688	46.9	18:17	6	0	1	1	6	0	0	0	20:10

OHL Second All-Star Team (1993)

Claimed by **Nashville** from **Vancouver** in Expansion Draft, June 26, 1998.

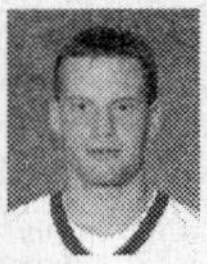

WALLIN, Jesse (WAHL-ihn, JEH-see)

Defense. Shoots left. 6'2", 190 lbs. Born, Saskatoon, Sask., March 10, 1978. Detroit's 1st choice, 26th overall, in 1996 Entry Draft.

1993-94	North Battleford	SMHL	32	1	7	8	41																		
1994-95	Red Deer Rebels	WHL	72	4	20	24	72																		
1995-96	Red Deer Rebels	WHL	70	5	19	24	61										9	0	3	3	4				
1996-97	Red Deer Rebels	WHL	59	6	33	39	70										16	1	4	5	10				
1997-98	Red Deer Rebels	WHL	14	1	6	7	17										5	0	1	1	2				
1998-99	Adirondack	AHL	76	4	12	16	34										3	0	2	2	2				
99-2000	Detroit	NHL	1	0	0	0	0	0	0	0	0	0.0	−2	0	0.0	19:22									
	Cincinnati	AHL	75	3	14	17	61																		
2000-01	Detroit	NHL	1	0	0	0	2	0	0	0	1	0.0	0	0	0.0	3:50									
	Cincinnati	AHL	76	2	15	17	50										4	0	1	1	4				
2001-02	Detroit	NHL	15	0	1	1	13	0	0	0	8	0.0	−1	0	0.0	10:42									
	Cincinnati	AHL	5	1	1	2	2																		
2002-03	Detroit	NHL	32	0	1	1	19	0	0	0	23	0.0	−2	0	0.0	13:16									
2003-04	Lowell	AHL	1	0	0	0	0																		
	NHL Totals		49	0	2	2	34	0	0	0	32	0.0		0	0.0	12:25									

Canadian Major Junior Humanitarian Player of the Year (1997)

• Missed majority of 1997-98 season recovering from arm injury suffered in automobile accident (September 10, 1997) and foot injury suffered in World Junior Championship game vs. Germany, December 30, 1997 • Missed majority of 2001-02 season recovering from groin injury suffered in training camp, October 1, 2001. • Missed majority of 2002-03 season recovering from elbow (December 17, 2002 vs. NY Islanders), wrist (January 5, 2003 vs. Chicago) and knee (March 16, 2003 vs. Colorado) injuries. Signed as a free agent by **Calgary**, July 31, 2003. • Missed majority of 2003-04 season recovering from head injury suffered in game vs. Hartford (AHL), October 18, 2003.

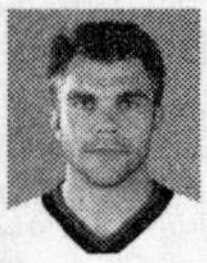

WALLIN, Niclas (VAH-lihn, NIH-kluhs) CAR.

Defense. Shoots left. 6'3", 220 lbs. Born, Boden, Sweden, February 20, 1975. Carolina's 3rd choice, 97th overall, in 2000 Entry Draft.

1994-95	Bodens IK Jr.	Swede-Jr.	30	2	13	15	125																		
	Bodens IK	Swede-2	13	0	0	0	0										2	0	0	0	0				
1995-96	Bodens IK Jr.	Swede-Jr.	2	2	2	4	0																		
	Bodens IK	Swede-2	30	2	7	9	26										2	0	1	1	2				
1996-97	Brynas IF Gavle	Sweden	47	1	1	2	14																		
1997-98	Brynas IF Gavle	Sweden	44	2	3	5	57										3	0	1	1	4				
1998-99	Brynas IF Gavle	Sweden	46	2	4	6	52										14	0	1	1	8				
99-2000	Brynas IF Gavle	Sweden	48	7	9	16	73										11	2	1	3	14				
	Brynas IF Gavle	EuroHL	5	1	1	2	10																		
2000-01	Carolina	NHL	37	2	3	5	21	0	0	0	19	10.5	−11	0	0.0	14:57	3	0	0	0	2	0	0	0	19:10
	Cincinnati	IHL	8	1	2	3	4										3	0	0	0	2				
2001-02	Carolina	NHL	52	1	2	3	36	0	0	0	33	3.0	1	0	0.0	12:12	23	2	1	3	12	0	0	2	15:26
2002-03	Carolina	NHL	77	2	8	10	71	0	0	2	69	2.9	−19	0	0.0	16:12									
2003-04	Carolina	NHL	57	3	7	10	51	0	0	0	74	4.1	−8	0	0.0	18:40									
	NHL Totals		223	8	20	28	179	0	0	2	195	4.1		0	0.0	15:41	26	2	1	3	14	0	0	2	15:52

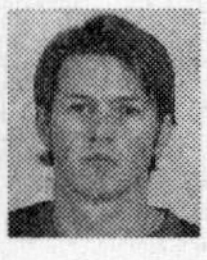

WALLIN, Rickard (WAHL-in, RIH-kahrd) MIN.

Center. Shoots left. 6'2", 185 lbs. Born, Stockholm, Sweden, April 19, 1980. Phoenix's 8th choice, 160th overall, in 1998 Entry Draft.

1996-97	Vasteras IK Jr.	Swede-Jr.	26	3	3	6																			
1997-98	Farjestad Jr.	Swede-Jr.	29	20	30	50	32										2	1	1	2	2				
1998-99	Farjestad Jr.	Swede-Jr.	21	11	15	26	30																		
	Farjestad	Sweden	5	0	0	0	0																		
99-2000	IF Troja-Ljungby	Swede-2	46	15	22	37	54																		
2000-01	Farjestad	Sweden	47	9	22	31	24										16	11	3	14	4				
2001-02	Farjestad	Sweden	50	12	31	43	56										10	4	9	13	8				
2002-03	Minnesota	NHL	4	1	0	1	0	0	0	1	1	100.0	1	28	53.6	7:44									
	Houston Aeros	AHL	52	13	22	35	70										23	4	11	15	22				
2003-04	Minnesota	NHL	15	5	4	9	14	3	0	1	16	31.3	1	189	45.5	14:20									
	Houston Aeros	AHL	47	14	18	32	36										2	0	0	0	2				
	NHL Totals		19	6	4	10	14	3	0	2	17	35.3		217	46.5	12:56									

Rights traded to **Minnesota** by **Phoenix** for Joe Juneau, June 23, 2000.

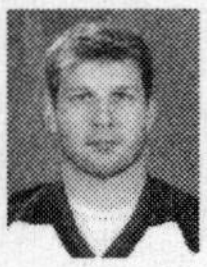

WALSER, Derrick (WAHL-zuhr, DEHR-rihk) CBJ

Defense. Shoots left. 5'10", 196 lbs. Born, New Glasgow, N.S., May 12, 1978.

1994-95	Beauport	QMJHL	48	4	18	22	34										12	2	5	7	2				
1995-96	Beauport	QMJHL	69	9	31	40	56										20	2	11	13	16				
1996-97	Beauport	QMJHL	37	13	25	38	26																		
	Rimouski Oceanic	QMJHL	31	15	30	45	44										4	2	2	4	6				
1997-98	Rimouski Oceanic	QMJHL	70	41	69	110	135										18	10	*26	36	49				
1998-99	Saint John Flames	AHL	40	3	7	10	24																		
	Johnstown Chiefs	ECHL	24	8	12	20	29																		
99-2000	Saint John Flames	AHL	14	2	3	5	10																		
	Johnstown Chiefs	ECHL	54	17	26	43	104										7	3	3	6	8				
2000-01	Saint John Flames	AHL	76	19	36	55	36										19	7	9	16	14				

Season	Club	League	Regular Season GP	G	A	Pts	PIM	PP	SH	GW	S	%	+/-	TF	F%	Min	Playoffs GP	G	A	Pts	PIM	PP	SH	GW	Min
2001-02	Columbus	NHL	2	1	0	1	0	0	0	0	2	50.0	-2	0	0.0	16:18	....	....	....	....	....	....	....	....	....
	Syracuse Crunch	AHL	73	23	38	61	70	....	....	....	....	....	....	....	....	....	10	1	5	6	12	....	....	....	....
2002-03	Columbus	NHL	53	4	13	17	34	3	0	2	86	4.7	-9	1	100.0	14:52	....	....	....	....	....	....	....	....	....
	Syracuse Crunch	AHL	28	7	14	21	30	....	....	....	....	....	....	....	....	....	....	....	....	....	....	....	....	....	....
2003-04	Columbus	NHL	27	1	8	9	22	1	0	0	35	2.9	-6	0	0.0	18:23	....	....	....	....	....	....	....	....	....
	Syracuse Crunch	AHL	48	10	26	36	82	....	....	....	....	....	....	....	....	....	3	1	1	2	4	....	....	....	....
	NHL Totals		82	6	21	27	56	4	0	2	123	4.9		1	100.0	16:03	....	....	....	....	....	....	....	....	....

QMJHL First All-Star Team (1997) • Emile Bouchard Trophy (Top Defenseman – QMJHL) (1998) • QMJHL First All-Star Team (1998) • Canadian Major Junior First All-Star Team (1998) • Canadian Major Junior Defenseman of the Year (1998)

Signed as a free agent by **Calgary**, October 16, 1998. Signed as a free agent by **Columbus**, September 17, 2001. Signed as a free agent by **Eisbaren Berlin** (Germany), May 13, 2004.

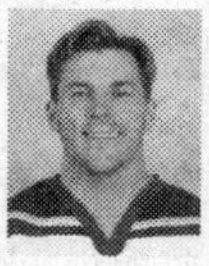

WALZ, Wes

(WAHLZ, WEHS) **MIN.**

Center. Shoots right. 5'10", 180 lbs. Born, Calgary, Alta., May 15, 1970. Boston's 3rd choice, 57th overall, in 1989 Entry Draft.

Season	Club	League	GP	G	A	Pts	PIM	PP	SH	GW	S	%	+/-	TF	F%	Min	GP	G	A	Pts	PIM	PP	SH	GW	Min
1987-88	Cgy. North Stars	AMHL	35	47	52	99	72	....	....	....	....	....	....	....	....	....	....	....	....	....	....	....	....	....	....
	Prince Albert	WHL	1	1	1	2	0	....	....	....	....	....	....	....	....	....	....	....	....	....	....	....	....	....	....
1988-89	Lethbridge	WHL	63	29	75	104	32	....	....	....	....	....	....	....	....	....	8	1	5	6	6	....	....	....	....
1989-90	Lethbridge	WHL	56	54	86	140	69	....	....	....	....	....	....	....	....	....	19	13	*24	*37	33	....	....	....	....
	Boston	NHL	2	1	1	2	0	1	0	0	1	100.0	-1	....	....	....	....	....	....	....	....	....	....	....	....
1990-91	Boston	NHL	56	8	8	16	32	1	0	1	57	14.0	-14	....	....	....	2	0	0	0	0	0	0	0	....
	Maine Mariners	AHL	20	8	12	20	19	....	....	....	....	....	....	....	....	....	2	0	0	0	21	....	....	....	....
1991-92	Boston	NHL	15	0	3	3	12	0	0	0	17	0.0	-3	....	....	....	....	....	....	....	....	....	....	....	....
	Maine Mariners	AHL	21	13	11	24	38	....	....	....	....	....	....	....	....	....	....	....	....	....	....	....	....	....	....
	Philadelphia	NHL	2	1	0	1	0	0	0	1	2	50.0	1	....	....	....	....	....	....	....	....	....	....	....	....
	Hershey Bears	AHL	41	13	28	41	37	....	....	....	....	....	....	....	....	....	6	1	2	3	0	....	....	....	....
1992-93	Hershey Bears	AHL	78	35	45	80	106	....	....	....	....	....	....	....	....	....	....	....	....	....	....	....	....	....	....
1993-94	Calgary	NHL	53	11	27	38	16	1	0	0	79	13.9	20	....	....	....	6	3	0	3	2	0	0	0	....
	Saint John Flames	AHL	15	6	6	12	14	....	....	....	....	....	....	....	....	....	....	....	....	....	....	....	....	....	....
1994-95	Calgary	NHL	39	6	12	18	11	4	0	1	73	8.2	7	....	....	....	1	0	0	0	0	0	0	0	....
1995-96	Detroit	NHL	2	0	0	0	0	0	0	0	2	0.0	0	....	....	....	....	....	....	....	....	....	....	....	....
	Adirondack	AHL	38	20	35	55	58	....	....	....	....	....	....	....	....	....	....	....	....	....	....	....	....	....	....
1996-97	EV Zug	Swiss	41	24	22	46	67	....	....	....	....	....	....	....	....	....	9	5	1	6	39	....	....	....	....
1997-98	EV Zug	Swiss	38	18	34	52	32	....	....	....	....	....	....	....	....	....	20	*16	*12	*28	18	....	....	....	....
	EV Zug	EuroHL	5	1	3	4	10	....	....	....	....	....	....	....	....	....	....	....	....	....	....	....	....	....	....
1998-99	EV Zug	Swiss	42	22	27	49	75	....	....	....	....	....	....	....	....	....	10	3	9	12	2	....	....	....	....
	EV Zug	EuroHL	6	7	5	12	4	....	....	....	....	....	....	....	....	....	2	0	0	0	12	....	....	....	....
99-2000	Long Beach	IHL	6	4	3	7	8	....	....	....	....	....	....	....	....	....	....	....	....	....	....	....	....	....	....
	HC Lugano	Swiss	13	7	11	18	14	....	....	....	....	....	....	....	....	....	5	3	4	7	4	....	....	....	....
2000-01	Minnesota	NHL	82	18	12	30	37	0	7	3	152	11.8	-8	1533	47.2	16:45	....	....	....	....	....	....	....	....	....
2001-02	Minnesota	NHL	64	10	20	30	43	0	2	5	97	10.3	0	1231	44.8	16:42	....	....	....	....	....	....	....	....	....
2002-03	Minnesota	NHL	80	13	19	32	63	0	0	4	115	11.3	11	1505	50.4	15:56	18	7	6	13	14	0	2	2	17:24
2003-04	Minnesota	NHL	57	12	13	25	32	0	3	2	70	17.1	5	909	46.3	16:18	....	....	....	....	....	....	....	....	....
	NHL Totals		452	80	115	195	246	7	12	17	665	12.0		5178	47.4	16:25	27	10	6	16	16	0	2	2	17:24

WHL Rookie of the Year (1989) • WHL East First All-Star Team (1990)

Traded to **Philadelphia** by **Boston** with Garry Galley and Boston's 3rd round choice (Milos Holan) in 1993 Entry Draft for Gord Murphy, Brian Dobbin, Philadelphia's 3rd round choice (Sergei Zholtok) in 1992 Entry Draft and Philadelphia's 4th round choice (Charles Paquette) in 1993 Entry Draft, January 2, 1992. Signed as a free agent by **Calgary**, August 26, 1993. Signed as a free agent by **Detroit**, September 6, 1995. Signed as a free agent by **Long Beach** (IHL), October 12, 1999. Signed as a free agent by **Minnesota**, June 28, 2000.

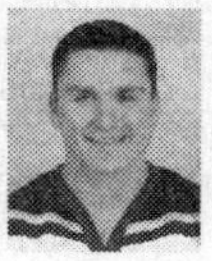

WANVIG, Kyle

(WEHN-vihg, KIGHL) **MIN.**

Right wing. Shoots right. 6'2", 219 lbs. Born, Calgary, Alta., January 29, 1981. Minnesota's 2nd choice, 36th overall, in 2001 Entry Draft.

Season	Club	League	GP	G	A	Pts	PIM	PP	SH	GW	S	%	+/-	TF	F%	Min	GP	G	A	Pts	PIM	PP	SH	GW	Min
1996-97	Calgary Blazers	AMHL	26	31	48	79	85	....	....	....	....	....	....	....	....	....	....	....	....	....	....	....	....	....	....
1997-98	Edmonton Ice	WHL	62	17	12	29	69	....	....	....	....	....	....	....	....	....	....	....	....	....	....	....	....	....	....
1998-99	Kootenay Ice	WHL	71	12	20	32	119	....	....	....	....	....	....	....	....	....	7	1	3	4	18	....	....	....	....
99-2000	Kootenay Ice	WHL	6	2	2	4	12	....	....	....	....	....	....	....	....	....	....	....	....	....	....	....	....	....	....
	Red Deer Rebels	WHL	58	21	18	39	123	....	....	....	....	....	....	....	....	....	4	1	0	1	4	....	....	....	....
2000-01	Red Deer Rebels	WHL	69	55	46	101	202	....	....	....	....	....	....	....	....	....	22	10	12	22	47	....	....	....	....
2001-02	Houston Aeros	AHL	34	6	7	13	43	....	....	....	....	....	....	....	....	....	9	0	1	1	23	....	....	....	....
2002-03	Minnesota	NHL	7	1	0	1	13	0	0	0	5	20.0	0	1	100.0	9:14	....	....	....	....	....	....	....	....	....
	Houston Aeros	AHL	57	13	16	29	137	....	....	....	....	....	....	....	....	....	21	6	4	10	27	....	....	....	....
2003-04	Minnesota	NHL	6	0	1	1	10	0	0	0	16	0.0	-2	4	75.0	13:48	....	....	....	....	....	....	....	....	....
	Houston Aeros	AHL	72	25	16	41	147	....	....	....	....	....	....	....	....	....	2	0	1	1	0	....	....	....	....
	NHL Totals		13	1	1	2	23	0	0	0	21	4.8		5	80.0	11:21	....	....	....	....	....	....	....	....	....

• Re-entered NHL Entry Draft. Originally Boston's 3rd choice, 89th overall, in 1999 Entry Draft.

WHL East Second All-Star Team (2001) • Memorial Cup All-Star Team (2001) • Stafford Smythe Memorial Trophy (Memorial Cup MVP) (2001)

• Missed majority of 2001-02 season recovering from ankle injury suffered in game vs. Grand Rapids (AHL), December 30, 2001.

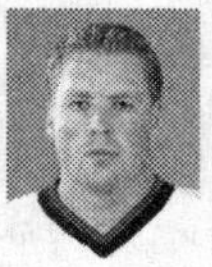

WARD, Aaron

(WOHRD, AIR-ruhn) **CAR.**

Defense. Shoots right. 6'2", 225 lbs. Born, Windsor, Ont., January 17, 1973. Winnipeg's 1st choice, 5th overall, in 1991 Entry Draft.

Season	Club	League	GP	G	A	Pts	PIM	PP	SH	GW	S	%	+/-	TF	F%	Min	GP	G	A	Pts	PIM	PP	SH	GW	Min
1988-89	Nepean Raiders	OCJHL	54	1	14	15	40	....	....	....	....	....	....	....	....	....	....	....	....	....	....	....	....	....	....
1989-90	Nepean Raiders	OCJHL	52	6	33	39	85	....	....	....	....	....	....	....	....	....	....	....	....	....	....	....	....	....	....
1990-91	U. of Michigan	CCHA	46	8	11	19	126	....	....	....	....	....	....	....	....	....	....	....	....	....	....	....	....	....	....
1991-92	U. of Michigan	CCHA	42	7	12	19	64	....	....	....	....	....	....	....	....	....	....	....	....	....	....	....	....	....	....
1992-93	U. of Michigan	CCHA	30	5	8	13	73	....	....	....	....	....	....	....	....	....	....	....	....	....	....	....	....	....	....
1993-94	Detroit	NHL	5	1	0	1	4	0	0	0	3	33.3	2	....	....	....	....	....	....	....	....	....	....	....	....
	Adirondack	AHL	58	4	12	16	87	....	....	....	....	....	....	....	....	....	9	2	6	8	6	....	....	....	....
1994-95	Adirondack	AHL	76	11	24	35	87	....	....	....	....	....	....	....	....	....	4	0	1	1	0	....	....	....	....
	Detroit	NHL	1	0	1	1	2	0	0	0	0	0.0	1	....	....	....	....	....	....	....	....	....	....	....	....
1995-96	Adirondack	AHL	74	5	10	15	133	....	....	....	....	....	....	....	....	....	3	0	0	0	6	....	....	....	....
1996-97♦	Detroit	NHL	49	2	5	7	52	0	0	0	40	5.0	-9	....	....	....	19	0	0	0	17	0	0	0	....
1997-98♦	Detroit	NHL	52	5	5	10	47	0	0	1	47	10.6	-1	....	....	....	....	....	....	....	....	....	....	....	....
1998-99	Detroit	NHL	60	3	8	11	52	0	0	0	46	6.5	-5	0	0.0	13:55	8	0	1	1	8	0	0	0	10:15
99-2000	Detroit	NHL	36	1	3	4	24	0	0	0	25	4.0	-4	0	0.0	12:36	3	0	0	0	0	0	0	0	7:36
2000-01	Detroit	NHL	73	4	5	9	57	0	0	1	48	8.3	-4	0	0.0	17:00	....	....	....	....	....	....	....	....	....
2001-02	Carolina	NHL	79	3	11	14	74	0	0	2	69	4.3	0	1	100.0	19:40	23	1	1	2	22	0	0	0	21:12
2002-03	Carolina	NHL	77	3	6	9	90	0	0	1	66	4.5	-23	0	0.0	18:43	....	....	....	....	....	....	....	....	....
2003-04	Carolina	NHL	49	3	5	8	37	2	0	0	51	5.9	1	0	0.0	17:52	....	....	....	....	....	....	....	....	....
	NHL Totals		481	25	49	74	439	2	0	5	395	6.3		1	100.0	17:07	53	1	2	3	47	0	0	0	17:26

Traded to **Detroit** by **Winnipeg** with Toronto's 4th round choice (previously acquired, Detroit selected John Jakopin) in 1993 Entry Draft for Paul Ysebaert and future considerations (Alan Kerr, June 18, 1993), June 11, 1993. • Missed majority of 1999-2000 season recovering from shoulder injury suffered in game vs. Vancouver, January 19, 2000. Traded to **Carolina** by **Detroit** for Carolina's 2nd round choice (Jiri Hudler) in 2002 Entry Draft, July 9, 2001.

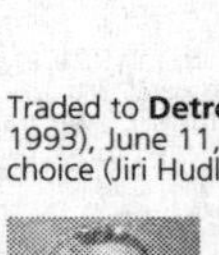

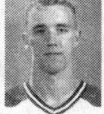

WARD, Jason

(WOHRD, JAY-suhn) **MTL.**

Right wing. Shoots right. 6'3", 203 lbs. Born, Chapleau, Ont., January 16, 1979. Montreal's 1st choice, 11th overall, in 1997 Entry Draft.

Season	Club	League	GP	G	A	Pts	PIM	PP	SH	GW	S	%	+/-	TF	F%	Min	GP	G	A	Pts	PIM	PP	SH	GW	Min
1994-95	Oshawa	OJHL-B	47	30	31	61	75	....	....	....	....	....	....	....	....	....	....	....	....	....	....	....	....	....	....
1995-96	Niagara Falls	OHL	64	15	35	50	139	....	....	....	....	....	....	....	....	....	10	6	4	10	23	....	....	....	....
1996-97	Erie Otters	OHL	58	25	39	64	137	....	....	....	....	....	....	....	....	....	5	1	2	3	2	....	....	....	....
1997-98	Erie Otters	OHL	21	7	9	16	42	....	....	....	....	....	....	....	....	....	....	....	....	....	....	....	....	....	....
	Windsor Spitfires	OHL	26	19	27	46	34	....	....	....	....	....	....	....	....	....	....	....	....	....	....	....	....	....	....
	Fredericton	AHL	7	1	0	1	2	....	....	....	....	....	....	....	....	....	1	0	0	0	2	....	....	....	....
1998-99	Windsor Spitfires	OHL	12	8	11	19	25	....	....	....	....	....	....	....	....	....	....	....	....	....	....	....	....	....	....
	Plymouth Whalers	OHL	23	14	13	27	28	....	....	....	....	....	....	....	....	....	11	6	8	14	12	....	....	....	....
	Fredericton	AHL	....	....	....	....	....	....	....	....	....	....	....	....	....	....	10	4	2	6	22	....	....	....	....
99-2000	Montreal	NHL	32	2	1	3	10	1	0	0	24	8.3	-1	86	44.2	9:10	....	....	....	....	....	....	....	....	....
	Quebec Citadelles	AHL	40	14	12	26	30	....	....	....	....	....	....	....	....	....	3	2	1	3	4	....	....	....	....
2000-01	Montreal	NHL	12	0	0	0	12	0	0	0	4	0.0	3	2	50.0	8:16	....	....	....	....	....	....	....	....	....
	Quebec Citadelles	AHL	23	7	12	19	69	....	....	....	....	....	....	....	....	....	....	....	....	....	....	....	....	....	....

			Regular Season														Playoffs								
Season	Club	League	GP	G	A	Pts	PIM	PP	SH	GW	S	%	+/-	TF	F%	Min	GP	G	A	Pts	PIM	PP	SH	GW	Min
2001-02	Quebec Citadelles	AHL	78	24	33	57	128	....	....	....	....	....	....	....	....	....	3	0	0	0	2	....	....	....	....
2002-03	**Montreal**	**NHL**	**8**	**3**	**2**	**5**	**0**	**0**	**0**	**0**	**10**	**30.0**	**3**	**6**	**50.0**	**11:17**	....	....	....	....	....	....	....	....	....
	Hamilton	AHL	69	31	41	72	78	....	....	....	....	....	....	....	....	....	23	*12	9	*21	20	....	....	....	....
2003-04	**Montreal**	**NHL**	**53**	**5**	**7**	**12**	**21**	**2**	**0**	**1**	**56**	**8.9**	**3**	**98**	**41.8**	**12:39**	**5**	**0**	**2**	**2**	**2**	**0**	**0**	**0**	**15:39**
	Hamilton	AHL	2	0	3	3	17	....	....	....	....	....	....	....	....	....	....	....	....	....	....	....	....	....	....
	NHL Totals		**105**	**10**	**10**	**20**	**43**	**3**	**0**	**1**	**94**	**10.6**		**192**	**43.2**	**10:59**	**5**	**0**	**2**	**2**	**2**	**0**	**0**	**0**	**15:39**

AHL First All-Star Team (2003)

• Missed majority of 2000-01 season recovering from knee injury suffered in game vs. Carolina, January 16, 2001.

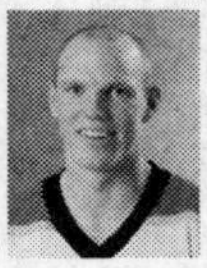

WARD, Lance

(WAWRD, LANTS) **ANA.**

Defense. Shoots left. 6'3", 220 lbs. Born, Lloydminster, Alta., June 2, 1978. Florida's 3rd choice, 63rd overall, in 1998 Entry Draft.

Season	Club	League	GP	G	A	Pts	PIM	PP	SH	GW	S	%	+/-	TF	F%	Min	GP	G	A	Pts	PIM	PP	SH	GW	Min
1993-94	Lloydminister	AAHA	20	8	12	20	68	....	....	....	....	....	....	....	....	....	....	....	....	....	....	....	....	....	....
1994-95	Red Deer Rebels	WHL	28	0	0	0	57	....	....	....	....	....	....	....	....	....	....	....	....	....	....	....	....	....	....
1995-96	Red Deer Rebels	WHL	72	4	13	17	127	....	....	....	....	....	....	....	....	....	10	0	4	4	10	....	....	....	....
1996-97	Red Deer Rebels	WHL	70	5	34	39	229	....	....	....	....	....	....	....	....	....	16	0	3	3	36	....	....	....	....
1997-98	Red Deer Rebels	WHL	71	8	25	33	233	....	....	....	....	....	....	....	....	....	5	0	0	0	16	....	....	....	....
1998-99	Miami Matadors	ECHL	6	1	0	1	12	....	....	....	....	....	....	....	....	....	....	....	....	....	....	....	....	....	....
	Fort Wayne	IHL	13	0	2	2	28	....	....	....	....	....	....	....	....	....	....	....	....	....	....	....	....	....	....
	New Haven	AHL	43	2	5	7	51	....	....	....	....	....	....	....	....	....	....	....	....	....	....	....	....	....	....
99-2000	Louisville Panthers	AHL	80	4	16	20	190	....	....	....	....	....	....	....	....	....	4	0	0	0	6	....	....	....	....
2000-01	**Florida**	**NHL**	**30**	**0**	**2**	**2**	**45**	**0**	**0**	**0**	**17**	**0.0**	**–3**	**0**	**0.0**	**15:50**	....	....	....	....	....	....	....	....	....
	Louisville Panthers	AHL	35	3	2	5	78	....	....	....	....	....	....	....	....	....	....	....	....	....	....	....	....	....	....
2001-02	**Florida**	**NHL**	**68**	**1**	**4**	**5**	**131**	**0**	**0**	**0**	**39**	**2.6**	**–20**	**1**	**0.0**	**14:31**	....	....	....	....	....	....	....	....	....
2002-03	**Florida**	**NHL**	**36**	**3**	**1**	**4**	**78**	**0**	**0**	**1**	**34**	**8.8**	**–4**	**0**	**0.0**	**9:07**	....	....	....	....	....	....	....	....	....
	Anaheim	**NHL**	**29**	**0**	**1**	**1**	**43**	**0**	**0**	**0**	**18**	**0.0**	**–2**	**0**	**0.0**	**7:08**	....	....	....	....	....	....	....	....	....
2003-04	**Anaheim**	**NHL**	**46**	**0**	**4**	**4**	**94**	**0**	**0**	**0**	**26**	**0.0**	**–1**	**0**	**0.0**	**8:41**	....	....	....	....	....	....	....	....	....
	Cincinnati	AHL	5	0	1	1	6	....	....	....	....	....	....	....	....	....	....	....	....	....	....	....	....	....	....
	NHL Totals		**209**	**4**	**12**	**16**	**391**	**0**	**0**	**1**	**134**	**3.0**		**1**	**0.0**	**11:28**	....	....	....	....	....	....	....	....	....

• Re-entered NHL Entry Draft. Originally New Jersey's 1st choice, 10th overall, in 1996 Entry Draft.

Traded to **Anaheim** by **Florida** with Sandis Ozolinsh for Pavel Trnka, Matt Cullen and Anaheim's 4th round choice (James Pemberton) in 2003 Entry Draft, January 30, 2003.

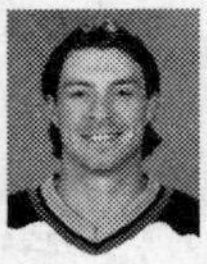

WARRENER, Rhett

(WAHR-ihn-uhr, REHT) **CGY.**

Defense. Shoots right. 6'2", 217 lbs. Born, Shaunavon, Sask., January 27, 1976. Florida's 2nd choice, 27th overall, in 1994 Entry Draft.

Season	Club	League	GP	G	A	Pts	PIM	PP	SH	GW	S	%	+/-	TF	F%	Min	GP	G	A	Pts	PIM	PP	SH	GW	Min
1991-92	Saskatoon Blazers	SMHL	33	6	5	11	71	....	....	....	....	....	....	....	....	....	....	....	....	....	....	....	....	....	....
	Saskatoon Blades	WHL	2	0	0	0	0	....	....	....	....	....	....	....	....	....	....	....	....	....	....	....	....	....	....
1992-93	Saskatoon Blades	WHL	68	2	17	19	100	....	....	....	....	....	....	....	....	....	9	0	0	0	14	....	....	....	....
1993-94	Saskatoon Blades	WHL	61	7	19	26	131	....	....	....	....	....	....	....	....	....	16	0	5	5	33	....	....	....	....
1994-95	Saskatoon Blades	WHL	66	13	26	39	137	....	....	....	....	....	....	....	....	....	10	0	3	3	6	....	....	....	....
1995-96	**Florida**	**NHL**	**28**	**0**	**3**	**3**	**46**	**0**	**0**	**0**	**19**	**0.0**	**4**	....	....	....	**21**	**0**	**1**	**1**	**0**	**0**	**0**	**0**	....
	Carolina	AHL	9	0	0	0	4	....	....	....	....	....	....	....	....	....	....	....	....	....	....	....	....	....	....
1996-97	**Florida**	**NHL**	**62**	**4**	**9**	**13**	**88**	**1**	**0**	**1**	**58**	**6.9**	**20**	....	....	....	**5**	**0**	**0**	**0**	**0**	**0**	**0**	**0**	....
1997-98	**Florida**	**NHL**	**79**	**0**	**4**	**4**	**99**	**0**	**0**	**0**	**66**	**0.0**	**–16**	....	....	....	....	....	....	....	....	....	....	....	....
1998-99	**Florida**	**NHL**	**48**	**0**	**7**	**7**	**64**	**0**	**0**	**0**	**33**	**0.0**	**–1**	**0**	**0.0**	**19:01**	....	....	....	....	....	....	....	....	....
	Buffalo	**NHL**	**13**	**1**	**0**	**1**	**20**	**0**	**0**	**0**	**11**	**9.1**	**3**	**0**	**0.0**	**18:13**	**20**	**1**	**3**	**4**	**32**	**0**	**0**	**0**	**22:08**
99-2000	**Buffalo**	**NHL**	**61**	**0**	**3**	**3**	**89**	**0**	**0**	**0**	**68**	**0.0**	**18**	**0**	**0.0**	**19:51**	**5**	**0**	**0**	**0**	**2**	**0**	**0**	**0**	**21:42**
2000-01	**Buffalo**	**NHL**	**77**	**3**	**16**	**19**	**78**	**0**	**0**	**2**	**103**	**2.9**	**10**	**0**	**0.0**	**20:24**	**13**	**0**	**2**	**2**	**4**	**0**	**0**	**0**	**22:37**
2001-02	**Buffalo**	**NHL**	**65**	**5**	**5**	**10**	**113**	**0**	**0**	**1**	**66**	**7.6**	**15**	**0**	**0.0**	**19:39**	....	....	....	....	....	....	....	....	....
2002-03	**Buffalo**	**NHL**	**50**	**0**	**9**	**9**	**63**	**0**	**0**	**0**	**47**	**0.0**	**1**	**0**	**0.0**	**18:14**	....	....	....	....	....	....	....	....	....
2003-04	**Calgary**	**NHL**	**77**	**3**	**14**	**17**	**97**	**0**	**1**	**1**	**82**	**3.7**	**8**	**1**	**0.0**	**19:52**	**24**	**0**	**1**	**1**	**6**	**0**	**0**	**0**	**24:06**
	NHL Totals		**560**	**16**	**70**	**86**	**757**	**1**	**1**	**5**	**553**	**2.9**		**1**	**0.0**	**19:34**	**88**	**1**	**7**	**8**	**44**	**0**	**0**	**0**	**22:57**

Traded to **Buffalo** by **Florida** with Florida's 5th round choice (Ryan Miller) in 1999 Entry Draft for Mike Wilson, March 23, 1999. Traded to **Calgary** by **Buffalo** with Steve Reinprecht for Chris Drury and Steve Begin, July 3, 2003.

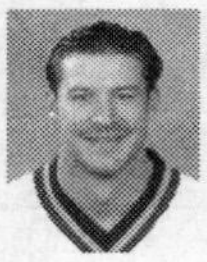

WARRINER, Todd

(WAHR-ihn-uhr, TAWD)

Left wing. Shoots left. 6'1", 200 lbs. Born, Blenheim, Ont., January 3, 1974. Quebec's 1st choice, 4th overall, in 1992 Entry Draft.

Season	Club	League	GP	G	A	Pts	PIM	PP	SH	GW	S	%	+/-	TF	F%	Min	GP	G	A	Pts	PIM	PP	SH	GW	Min
1988-89	Blenheim Blades	OJHL-C	10	1	4	5	0	....	....	....	....	....	....	....	....	....	....	....	....	....	....	....	....	....	....
1989-90	Chatham	OJHL-B	40	24	21	45	12	....	....	....	....	....	....	....	....	....	....	....	....	....	....	....	....	....	....
1990-91	Windsor Spitfires	OHL	57	36	28	64	26	....	....	....	....	....	....	....	....	....	11	5	6	11	12	....	....	....	....
1991-92	Windsor Spitfires	OHL	50	41	41	82	64	....	....	....	....	....	....	....	....	....	7	5	4	9	6	....	....	....	....
1992-93	Windsor Spitfires	OHL	23	13	21	34	29	....	....	....	....	....	....	....	....	....	....	....	....	....	....	....	....	....	....
	Kitchener Rangers	OHL	32	19	24	43	35	....	....	....	....	....	....	....	....	....	7	5	14	19	14	....	....	....	....
1993-94	Team Canada	Nat-Tm	50	11	20	31	33	....	....	....	....	....	....	....	....	....	....	....	....	....	....	....	....	....	....
	Canada	Olympics	4	1	1	2	0	....	....	....	....	....	....	....	....	....	....	....	....	....	....	....	....	....	....
	Kitchener Rangers	OHL	....	....	....	....	....	....	....	....	....	....	....	....	....	....	1	0	1	1	0	....	....	....	....
	Cornwall Aces	AHL	....	....	....	....	....	....	....	....	....	....	....	....	....	....	10	1	4	5	4	....	....	....	....
1994-95	St. John's	AHL	46	8	10	18	22	....	....	....	....	....	....	....	....	....	4	1	0	1	2	....	....	....	....
	Toronto	**NHL**	**5**	**0**	**0**	**0**	**0**	**0**	**0**	**0**	**1**	**0.0**	**–3**	....	....	....	....	....	....	....	....	....	....	....	....
1995-96	**Toronto**	**NHL**	**57**	**7**	**8**	**15**	**26**	**1**	**0**	**0**	**79**	**8.9**	**–11**	....	....	....	**6**	**1**	**1**	**2**	**2**	**0**	**0**	**0**	....
	St. John's	AHL	11	5	6	11	16	....	....	....	....	....	....	....	....	....	....	....	....	....	....	....	....	....	....
1996-97	**Toronto**	**NHL**	**75**	**12**	**21**	**33**	**41**	**2**	**2**	**0**	**146**	**8.2**	**–3**	....	....	....	....	....	....	....	....	....	....	....	....
1997-98	**Toronto**	**NHL**	**45**	**5**	**8**	**13**	**20**	**0**	**0**	**1**	**73**	**6.8**	**5**	....	....	....	....	....	....	....	....	....	....	....	....
1998-99	**Toronto**	**NHL**	**53**	**9**	**10**	**19**	**28**	**1**	**0**	**1**	**96**	**9.4**	**–6**	**579**	**47.8**	**14:06**	**9**	**0**	**0**	**0**	**2**	**0**	**0**	**0**	**13:56**
99-2000	**Toronto**	**NHL**	**18**	**3**	**1**	**4**	**2**	**0**	**0**	**0**	**33**	**9.1**	**6**	**33**	**45.5**	**12:33**	....	....	....	....	....	....	....	....	....
	Tampa Bay	**NHL**	**55**	**11**	**13**	**24**	**34**	**3**	**1**	**0**	**100**	**11.0**	**–14**	**175**	**52.0**	**16:28**	....	....	....	....	....	....	....	....	....
2000-01	**Tampa Bay**	**NHL**	**64**	**10**	**11**	**21**	**46**	**3**	**2**	**1**	**99**	**10.1**	**–13**	**400**	**50.5**	**14:43**	....	....	....	....	....	....	....	....	....
2001-02	**Phoenix**	**NHL**	**18**	**0**	**3**	**3**	**8**	**0**	**0**	**0**	**10**	**0.0**	**–3**	**16**	**62.5**	**10:53**	....	....	....	....	....	....	....	....	....
	Springfield	AHL	2	0	0	0	0	....	....	....	....	....	....	....	....	....	....	....	....	....	....	....	....	....	....
	Vancouver	**NHL**	**14**	**2**	**4**	**6**	**12**	**0**	**0**	**0**	**18**	**11.1**	**4**	**4**	**100.0**	**9:01**	**6**	**1**	**0**	**1**	**2**	**0**	**0**	**0**	**11:28**
	Manitoba Moose	AHL	30	7	13	20	32	....	....	....	....	....	....	....	....	....	....	....	....	....	....	....	....	....	....
2002-03	**Vancouver**	**NHL**	**30**	**4**	**6**	**10**	**22**	**0**	**0**	**0**	**53**	**7.5**	**0**	**29**	**41.4**	**11:41**	....	....	....	....	....	....	....	....	....
	Philadelphia	**NHL**	**13**	**2**	**3**	**5**	**6**	**0**	**0**	**1**	**13**	**15.4**	**2**	**0**	**0.0**	**8:30**	....	....	....	....	....	....	....	....	....
	Nashville	**NHL**	**6**	**0**	**1**	**1**	**4**	**0**	**0**	**0**	**6**	**0.0**	**–1**	**5**	**60.0**	**11:16**	....	....	....	....	....	....	....	....	....
2003-04	Jokerit Helsinki	Finland	13	5	1	6	8	....	....	....	....	....	....	....	....	....	8	0	2	2	29	....	....	....	....
	NHL Totals		**453**	**65**	**89**	**154**	**249**	**10**	**5**	**4**	**727**	**8.9**		**1241**	**49.5**	**13:33**	**21**	**2**	**1**	**3**	**6**	**0**	**0**	**0**	**12:57**

OHL First All-Star Team (1992)

Traded to **Toronto** by **Quebec** with Mats Sundin, Garth Butcher and Philadelphia's 1st round choice (previously acquired, later traded to Washington – Washington selected Nolan Baumgartner) in 1994 Entry Draft for Wendel Clark, Sylvain Lefebvre, Landon Wilson and Toronto's 1st round choice (Jeffrey Kealty) in 1994 Entry Draft, June 28, 1994. Traded to **Tampa Bay** by **Toronto** for Tampa Bay's 3rd round choice (Mikael Tellqvist) in 2000 Entry Draft, November 29, 1999. Traded to **Phoenix** by **Tampa Bay** for Juha Ylonen, June 18, 2001. Traded to **Vancouver** by **Phoenix** with Trevor Letowski, Tyler Bouck and Phoenix's 3rd round choice (later traded back to Phoenix – Phoenix selected Dimitri Pestunov) in 2003 Entry Draft for Drake Berehowsky and Denis Pederson, December 28, 2001. Traded to **Philadelphia** by **Vancouver** for future considerations, February 5, 2003. Claimed on waivers by **Nashville** from **Philadelphia**, March 11, 2003. Signed as a free agent by **Jokerit Helsinki** (Finland), October 19, 2003.

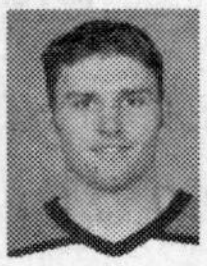

WATT, Mike

(WAHT, MIGHK)

Left wing. Shoots left. 6'2", 212 lbs. Born, Seaforth, Ont., March 31, 1976. Edmonton's 3rd choice, 32nd overall, in 1994 Entry Draft.

Season	Club	League	GP	G	A	Pts	PIM	PP	SH	GW	S	%	+/-	TF	F%	Min	GP	G	A	Pts	PIM	PP	SH	GW	Min
1990-91	Seaforth	OJHL-D	39	15	23	38	43	....	....	....	....	....	....	....	....	....	....	....	....	....	....	....	....	....	....
1991-92	Stratford Cullitons	OJHL-B	40	5	21	26	103	....	....	....	....	....	....	....	....	....	....	....	....	....	....	....	....	....	....
1992-93	Stratford Cullitons	OJHL-B	45	20	35	55	100	....	....	....	....	....	....	....	....	....	....	....	....	....	....	....	....	....	....
1993-94	Stratford Cullitons	OJHL-B	48	34	34	68	165	....	....	....	....	....	....	....	....	....	....	....	....	....	....	....	....	....	....
1994-95	Michigan State	CCHA	39	12	6	18	64	....	....	....	....	....	....	....	....	....	....	....	....	....	....	....	....	....	....
1995-96	Michigan State	CCHA	37	17	22	39	60	....	....	....	....	....	....	....	....	....	....	....	....	....	....	....	....	....	....
1996-97	Michigan State	CCHA	39	24	17	41	109	....	....	....	....	....	....	....	....	....	....	....	....	....	....	....	....	....	....
1997-98	**Edmonton**	**NHL**	**14**	**1**	**2**	**3**	**4**	**0**	**0**	**1**	**14**	**7.1**	**–4**	....	....	....	....	....	....	....	....	....	....	....	....
	Hamilton	AHL	63	24	25	49	65	....	....	....	....	....	....	....	....	....	9	2	2	4	8	....	....	....	....
1998-99	**NY Islanders**	**NHL**	**75**	**8**	**17**	**25**	**12**	**0**	**0**	**4**	**75**	**10.7**	**–2**	**180**	**50.6**	**11:15**	....	....	....	....	....	....	....	....	....
99-2000	**NY Islanders**	**NHL**	**45**	**5**	**6**	**11**	**17**	**0**	**1**	**0**	**49**	**10.2**	**–8**	**81**	**48.2**	**12:02**	....	....	....	....	....	....	....	....	....
	Lowell	AHL	16	6	11	17	6	....	....	....	....	....	....	....	....	....	7	1	1	2	4	....	....	....	....

			Regular Season													Playoffs								
Season	Club	League	GP	G	A	Pts	PIM	PP	SH	GW	S	%	+/-	TF	F%	Min	GP	G	A	Pts	PIM	PP	SH	GW	Min
2000-01	**Nashville**	**NHL**	**18**	**1**	**1**	**2**	**8**	**0**	**0**	**1**	**18**	**5.6**	**–2**	**2**	**50.0**	**11:02**	....	....	....	....	....	....	....	....	....
	Milwaukee	IHL	60	20	20	40	48	....	....	....	....	....	....	....	....	....	5	1	2	3	6	....	....	....	....
2001-02	Philadelphia	AHL	53	11	13	24	38	....	....	....	....	....	....	....	....	....	5	2	1	3	6	....	....	....	....
2002-03	**Carolina**	**NHL**	**5**	**0**	**0**	**0**	**0**	**0**	**0**	**0**	**2**	**0.0**	**–1**	**19**	**47.4**	**7:30**	....	....	....	....	....	....	....	....	....
	Lowell	AHL	61	9	14	23	35	....	....	....	....	....	....	....	....	....	....	....	....	....	....	....	....	....	....
2003-04	St. Petersburg	Russia	57	11	13	24	77	....	....	....	....	....	....	....	....	....	....	....	....	....	....	....	....	....	....
	NHL Totals		**157**	**15**	**26**	**41**	**41**	**0**	**1**	**6**	**158**	**9.5**		**282**	**49.6**	**11:20**	....	....	....	....	....	....	....	....	....

Traded to **NY Islanders** by **Edmonton** for Eric Fichaud, June 18, 1998. Claimed on waivers by **Nashville** from **NY Islanders**, May 23, 2000. Traded to **Philadelphia** by **Nashville** for Mikhail Chernov, May 24, 2001. Signed as a free agent by **Carolina**, August 7, 2002. Signed as a free agent by **St. Petersburg** (Russia), June 27, 2003.

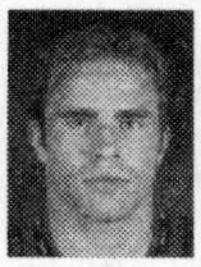

WEAVER, Mike

(WEE-vuhr, MIGHK) **L.A.**

Defense. Shoots right. 5'9", 180 lbs. Born, Bramalea, Ont., May 2, 1978.

Season	Club	League	GP	G	A	Pts	PIM	PP	SH	GW	S	%	+/-	TF	F%	Min	GP	G	A	Pts	PIM	PP	SH	GW	Min
1995-96	Bramalea Blues	OPJHL	48	10	39	49	103	....	....	....	....	....	....	....	....	....	....	....	....	....	....	....	....	....	....
1996-97	Michigan State	CCHA	39	0	7	7	46	....	....	....	....	....	....	....	....	....	....	....	....	....	....	....	....	....	....
1997-98	Michigan State	CCHA	44	4	22	26	68	....	....	....	....	....	....	....	....	....	....	....	....	....	....	....	....	....	....
1998-99	Michigan State	CCHA	42	1	6	7	54	....	....	....	....	....	....	....	....	....	....	....	....	....	....	....	....	....	....
99-2000	Michigan State	CCHA	26	0	7	7	20	....	....	....	....	....	....	....	....	....	....	....	....	....	....	....	....	....	....
2000-01	Orlando	IHL	68	0	8	8	34	....	....	....	....	....	....	....	....	....	16	0	2	2	8	....	....	....	....
2001-02	**Atlanta**	**NHL**	**16**	**0**	**1**	**1**	**10**	**0**	**0**	**0**	**9**	**0.0**	**0**	**0**	**0.0**	**13:54**	....	....	....	....	....	....	....	....	....
	Chicago Wolves	AHL	58	2	8	10	67	....	....	....	....	....	....	....	....	....	25	1	3	4	21	....	....	....	....
2002-03	**Atlanta**	**NHL**	**40**	**0**	**5**	**5**	**20**	**0**	**0**	**0**	**21**	**0.0**	**–5**	**0**	**0.0**	**18:38**	....	....	....	....	....	....	....	....	....
	Chicago Wolves	AHL	33	2	2	4	32	....	....	....	....	....	....	....	....	....	9	0	3	3	4	....	....	....	....
2003-04	**Atlanta**	**NHL**	**1**	**0**	**0**	**0**	**0**	**0**	**0**	**0**	**0**	**0.0**	**–1**	**0**	**0.0**	**8:28**	....	....	....	....	....	....	....	....	....
	Chicago Wolves	AHL	78	3	14	17	89	....	....	....	....	....	....	....	....	....	9	2	2	4	20	....	....	....	....
	NHL Totals		**57**	**0**	**6**	**6**	**30**	**0**	**0**	**0**	**30**	**0.0**		**0**	**0.0**	**17:08**	....	....	....	....	....	....	....	....	....

OPJHL Defenseman of the Year (1996) • CCHA All-Tournament Team (1997) • CCHA First All-Star Team (1999, 2000) • CCHA Best Defensive Defenseman Award (1999, 2000) • NCAA West Second All-American Team (1999, 2000)

Signed as a free agent by **Atlanta**, June 15, 2000. Signed as a free agent by **Los Angeles**, July 16, 2004.

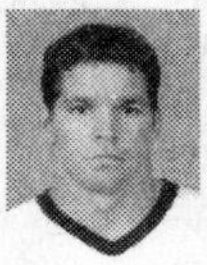

WEBB, Steve

(WEHB, STEEV)

Right wing. Shoots right. 6', 211 lbs. Born, Peterborough, Ont., April 30, 1975. Buffalo's 8th choice, 176th overall, in 1994 Entry Draft.

Season	Club	League	GP	G	A	Pts	PIM	PP	SH	GW	S	%	+/-	TF	F%	Min	GP	G	A	Pts	PIM	PP	SH	GW	Min
1991-92	Peterborough	OJHL-B	37	9	9	18	195	....	....	....	....	....	....	....	....	....	....	....	....	....	....	....	....	....	....
1992-93	Windsor Spitfires	OHL	63	14	25	39	184	....	....	....	....	....	....	....	....	....	....	....	....	....	....	....	....	....	....
1993-94	Windsor Spitfires	OHL	2	0	1	1	9	....	....	....	....	....	....	....	....	....	....	....	....	....	....	....	....	....	....
	Peterborough	OHL	33	6	15	21	117	....	....	....	....	....	....	....	....	....	6	1	1	2	20	....	....	....	....
1994-95	Peterborough	OHL	42	8	16	24	109	....	....	....	....	....	....	....	....	....	11	3	3	6	22	....	....	....	....
1995-96	Muskegon Fury	ColHL	58	18	24	42	263	....	....	....	....	....	....	....	....	....	5	1	2	3	22	....	....	....	....
	Detroit Vipers	IHL	4	0	0	0	24	....	....	....	....	....	....	....	....	....	....	....	....	....	....	....	....	....	....
1996-97	**NY Islanders**	**NHL**	**41**	**1**	**4**	**5**	**144**	**1**	**0**	**0**	**21**	**4.8**	**–10**	....	....	....	....	....	....	....	....	....	....	....	....
	Kentucky	AHL	25	6	6	12	103	....	....	....	....	....	....	....	....	....	2	0	0	0	19	....	....	....	....
1997-98	**NY Islanders**	**NHL**	**20**	**0**	**0**	**0**	**35**	**0**	**0**	**0**	**6**	**0.0**	**–2**	....	....	....	....	....	....	....	....	....	....	....	....
	Kentucky	AHL	37	5	13	18	139	....	....	....	....	....	....	....	....	....	3	0	1	1	10	....	....	....	....
1998-99	**NY Islanders**	**NHL**	**45**	**0**	**0**	**0**	**32**	**0**	**0**	**0**	**18**	**0.0**	**–10**	**0**	**0.0**	**4:13**	....	....	....	....	....	....	....	....	....
	Lowell	AHL	23	2	4	6	80	....	....	....	....	....	....	....	....	....	....	....	....	....	....	....	....	....	....
99-2000	**NY Islanders**	**NHL**	**65**	**1**	**3**	**4**	**103**	**0**	**0**	**0**	**27**	**3.7**	**–4**	**1**	**0.0**	**7:00**	....	....	....	....	....	....	....	....	....
2000-01	**NY Islanders**	**NHL**	**31**	**0**	**2**	**2**	**35**	**0**	**0**	**0**	**8**	**0.0**	**1**	**0**	**0.0**	**6:26**	....	....	....	....	....	....	....	....	....
2001-02	**NY Islanders**	**NHL**	**60**	**2**	**4**	**6**	**104**	**0**	**0**	**0**	**31**	**6.5**	**0**	**1**	**100.0**	**6:29**	**7**	**0**	**0**	**0**	**12**	**0**	**0**	**0**	**6:52**
2002-03	**NY Islanders**	**NHL**	**49**	**1**	**0**	**1**	**75**	**0**	**0**	**0**	**27**	**3.7**	**–5**	**0**	**0.0**	**6:02**	**5**	**0**	**0**	**0**	**10**	**0**	**0**	**0**	**6:46**
2003-04	**Pittsburgh**	**NHL**	**5**	**0**	**0**	**0**	**2**	**0**	**0**	**0**	**3**	**0.0**	**–3**	**0**	**0.0**	**5:20**	....	....	....	....	....	....	....	....	....
	Wilkes-Barre	AHL	30	4	7	11	48	....	....	....	....	....	....	....	....	....	....	....	....	....	....	....	....	....	....
	NY Islanders	**NHL**	**5**	**0**	**0**	**0**	**2**	**0**	**0**	**0**	**0**	**0.0**	**–1**	**1**	**0.0**	**4:57**	**2**	**0**	**0**	**0**	**6**	**0**	**0**	**0**	**4:01**
	Bridgeport	AHL	7	0	1	1	29	....	....	....	....	....	....	....	....	....	5	0	0	0	4	....	....	....	....
	NHL Totals		**321**	**5**	**13**	**18**	**532**	**1**	**0**	**0**	**141**	**3.5**		**3**	**33.3**	**6:05**	**14**	**0**	**0**	**0**	**28**	**0**	**0**	**0**	**6:25**

Signed as a free agent by **NY Islanders**, October 10, 1996. • Missed majority of 2000-01 season recovering from knee injury suffered in game vs. Anaheim, November 19, 2000. Signed as a free agent by **Philadelphia**, October 21, 2003. Claimed on waivers by **Pittsburgh** from **Philadelphia**, October 22, 2003. Traded to **NY Islanders** by **Pittsburgh** for Alain Nasreddine, March 8, 2004.

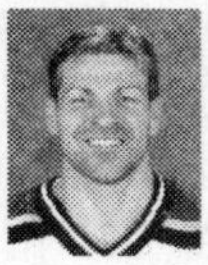

WEIGHT, Doug

(WAYT, DUHG) **ST.L.**

Center. Shoots left. 5'11", 200 lbs. Born, Warren, MI, January 21, 1971. NY Rangers' 2nd choice, 34th overall, in 1990 Entry Draft.

Season	Club	League	GP	G	A	Pts	PIM	PP	SH	GW	S	%	+/-	TF	F%	Min	GP	G	A	Pts	PIM	PP	SH	GW	Min
1988-89	Bloomfield Jets	NAJHL	34	26	53	79	105	....	....	....	....	....	....	....	....	....	....	....	....	....	....	....	....	....	....
1989-90	Lake Superior	CCHA	46	21	48	69	44	....	....	....	....	....	....	....	....	....	....	....	....	....	....	....	....	....	....
1990-91	Lake Superior	CCHA	42	29	46	75	86	....	....	....	....	....	....	....	....	....	....	....	....	....	....	....	....	....	....
	NY Rangers	**NHL**	....	....	....	....	....	....	....	....	....	....	....	....	....	....	**1**	**0**	**0**	**0**	**0**	**0**	**0**	**0**	....
1991-92	**NY Rangers**	**NHL**	**53**	**8**	**22**	**30**	**23**	**0**	**0**	**2**	**72**	**11.1**	**–3**	....	....	....	**7**	**2**	**2**	**4**	**0**	**1**	**0**	**0**	....
	Binghamton	AHL	9	3	14	17	2	....	....	....	....	....	....	....	....	....	4	1	4	5	6	....	....	....	....
1992-93	**NY Rangers**	**NHL**	**65**	**15**	**25**	**40**	**55**	**3**	**0**	**1**	**90**	**16.7**	**4**	....	....	....	....	....	....	....	....	....	....	....	....
	Edmonton	**NHL**	**13**	**2**	**6**	**8**	**10**	**0**	**0**	**0**	**35**	**5.7**	**–2**	....	....	....	....	....	....	....	....	....	....	....	....
1993-94	**Edmonton**	**NHL**	**84**	**24**	**50**	**74**	**47**	**4**	**1**	**1**	**188**	**12.8**	**–22**	....	....	....	....	....	....	....	....	....	....	....	....
1994-95	Rosenheim	Germany	8	2	3	5	18	....	....	....	....	....	....	....	....	....	....	....	....	....	....	....	....	....	....
	Edmonton	**NHL**	**48**	**7**	**33**	**40**	**69**	**1**	**0**	**1**	**104**	**6.7**	**–17**	....	....	....	....	....	....	....	....	....	....	....	....
1995-96	**Edmonton**	**NHL**	**82**	**25**	**79**	**104**	**95**	**9**	**0**	**2**	**204**	**12.3**	**–19**	....	....	....	....	....	....	....	....	....	....	....	....
1996-97	**Edmonton**	**NHL**	**80**	**21**	**61**	**82**	**80**	**4**	**0**	**2**	**235**	**8.9**	**1**	....	....	....	**12**	**3**	**8**	**11**	**8**	**0**	**0**	**0**	....
1997-98	**Edmonton**	**NHL**	**79**	**26**	**44**	**70**	**69**	**9**	**0**	**4**	**205**	**12.7**	**1**	....	....	....	**12**	**2**	**7**	**9**	**14**	**2**	**0**	**1**	....
	United States	Olympics	4	0	2	2	2	....	....	....	....	....	....	....	....	....	....	....	....	....	....	....	....	....	....
1998-99	**Edmonton**	**NHL**	**43**	**6**	**31**	**37**	**12**	**1**	**0**	**0**	**79**	**7.6**	**–8**	**853**	**49.5**	**19:51**	**4**	**1**	**1**	**2**	**15**	**0**	**0**	**0**	**14:43**
99-2000	**Edmonton**	**NHL**	**77**	**21**	**51**	**72**	**54**	**3**	**1**	**4**	**167**	**12.6**	**6**	**1588**	**50.4**	**20:35**	**5**	**3**	**2**	**5**	**4**	**2**	**0**	**1**	**21:05**
2000-01	**Edmonton**	**NHL**	**82**	**25**	**65**	**90**	**91**	**8**	**0**	**3**	**188**	**13.3**	**12**	**1514**	**51.3**	**22:08**	**6**	**1**	**5**	**6**	**17**	**0**	**0**	**0**	**22:45**
2001-02	**St. Louis**	**NHL**	**61**	**15**	**34**	**49**	**40**	**3**	**0**	**1**	**131**	**11.5**	**20**	**1123**	**49.2**	**19:48**	**10**	**1**	**1**	**2**	**4**	**1**	**0**	**1**	**16:26**
	United States	Olympics	6	0	3	3	4	....	....	....	....	....	....	....	....	....	....	....	....	....	....	....	....	....	....
2002-03	**St. Louis**	**NHL**	**70**	**15**	**52**	**67**	**52**	**7**	**0**	**3**	**182**	**8.2**	**–6**	**1048**	**50.4**	**20:23**	**7**	**5**	**8**	**13**	**2**	**5**	**0**	**1**	**22:26**
2003-04	**St. Louis**	**NHL**	**75**	**14**	**51**	**65**	**37**	**6**	**0**	**5**	**198**	**7.1**	**–3**	**1115**	**50.4**	**20:25**	**5**	**2**	**1**	**3**	**6**	**1**	**1**	**0**	**19:24**
	NHL Totals		**912**	**224**	**604**	**828**	**734**	**58**	**2**	**29**	**2078**	**10.8**		**7241**	**50.3**	**20:38**	**69**	**20**	**35**	**55**	**70**	**12**	**1**	**4**	**19:26**

CCHA First All-Star Team (1991) • NCAA West Second All-American Team (1991)

Played in NHL All-Star Game (1996, 1998, 2001, 2003)

Traded to **Edmonton** by **NY Rangers** for Esa Tikkanen, March 17, 1993. Traded to **St. Louis** by **Edmonton** with Michel Riesen for Marty Reasoner, Jochen Hecht and Jan Horacek, July 1, 2001.

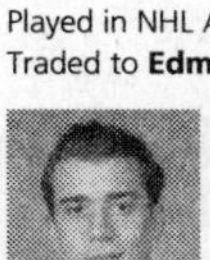

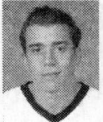

WEINHANDL, Mattias

(vayn-hanh-duhl, mah-TEE-uhs) **NYI**

Right wing. Shoots right. 6', 183 lbs. Born, Ljungby, Sweden, June 1, 1980. NY Islanders' 5th choice, 78th overall, in 1999 Entry Draft.

Season	Club	League	GP	G	A	Pts	PIM	PP	SH	GW	S	%	+/-	TF	F%	Min	GP	G	A	Pts	PIM	PP	SH	GW	Min
1995-96	Troja-Ljungby Jr.	Swede-Jr.	28	38	40	78	....	....	....	....	....	....	....	....	....	....	....	....	....	....	....	....	....	....	....
1996-97	Troja-Ljungby Jr.	Swede-Jr.	48	61	69	130	46	....	....	....	....	....	....	....	....	....	....	....	....	....	....	....	....	....	....
1997-98	IF Troja-Ljungby	Swede-2	28	3	2	5	2	....	....	....	....	....	....	....	....	....	5	0	0	0	2	....	....	....	....
1998-99	IF Troja-Ljungby	Swede-2	38	20	20	40	30	....	....	....	....	....	....	....	....	....	5	4	3	7	4	....	....	....	....
99-2000	MoDo Jr.	Swede-Jr.	1	2	2	4	2	....	....	....	....	....	....	....	....	....	....	....	....	....	....	....	....	....	....
	MoDo	Sweden	32	15	9	24	6	....	....	....	....	....	....	....	....	....	13	5	3	8	8	....	....	....	....
2000-01	MoDo	Sweden	48	16	16	32	14	....	....	....	....	....	....	....	....	....	6	1	3	4	6	....	....	....	....
2001-02	MoDo	Sweden	50	18	16	34	10	....	....	....	....	....	....	....	....	....	14	4	*11	*15	4	....	....	....	....
2002-03	**NY Islanders**	**NHL**	**47**	**6**	**17**	**23**	**10**	**1**	**0**	**0**	**66**	**9.1**	**–2**	**5**	**60.0**	**13:52**	....	....	....	....	....	....	....	....	....
	Bridgeport	AHL	23	9	12	21	14	....	....	....	....	....	....	....	....	....	....	....	....	....	....	....	....	....	....
2003-04	**NY Islanders**	**NHL**	**55**	**8**	**12**	**20**	**26**	**4**	**0**	**2**	**49**	**16.3**	**9**	**6**	**33.3**	**12:20**	**5**	**0**	**0**	**0**	**2**	**0**	**0**	**0**	**13:07**
	Bridgeport	AHL	10	3	6	9	10	....	....	....	....	....	....	....	....	....	....	....	....	....	....	....	....	....	....
	NHL Totals		**102**	**14**	**29**	**43**	**36**	**5**	**0**	**2**	**115**	**12.2**		**11**	**45.5**	**13:02**	**5**	**0**	**0**	**0**	**2**	**0**	**0**	**0**	**13:07**

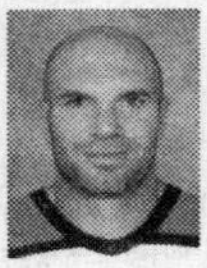

WEINRICH, Eric (WIGHN-rihch, AIR-ihk) ST.L.

Defense. Shoots left. 6'1", 207 lbs. Born, Roanoke, VA, December 19, 1966. New Jersey's 3rd choice, 32nd overall, in 1985 Entry Draft.

			Regular Season														Playoffs								
Season	Club	League	GP	G	A	Pts	PIM	PP	SH	GW	S	%	+/-	TF	F%	Min	GP	G	A	Pts	PIM	PP	SH	GW	Min
1983-84	N. Yarmouth	Hi-School	17	23	33	56																			
1984-85	N. Yarmouth	Hi-School	20	6	21	27																			
1985-86	U. of Maine	H-East	34	0	14	14	26																		
1986-87	U. of Maine	H-East	41	12	32	44	59																		
1987-88	U. of Maine	H-East	8	4	7	11	22																		
	Team USA	Nat-Tm	38	3	9	12	24																		
	United States	Olympics	3	0	0	0	0																		
1988-89	**New Jersey**	**NHL**	**2**	**0**	**0**	**0**	**0**	**0**	**0**	**0**	**3**	**0.0**	**–1**												
	Utica Devils	AHL	80	17	27	44	70										5	0	1	1	4				
1989-90	**New Jersey**	**NHL**	**19**	**2**	**7**	**9**	**11**	**1**	**0**	**1**	**16**	**12.5**	**1**				**6**	**1**	**3**	**4**	**17**	**0**	**0**	**0**	
	Utica Devils	AHL	57	12	48	60	38																		
1990-91	**New Jersey**	**NHL**	**76**	**4**	**34**	**38**	**48**	**1**	**0**	**0**	**96**	**4.2**	**10**				**7**	**1**	**2**	**3**	**6**	**1**	**0**	**0**	
1991-92	**New Jersey**	**NHL**	**76**	**7**	**25**	**32**	**55**	**5**	**0**	**0**	**97**	**7.2**	**10**				**7**	**0**	**2**	**2**	**4**	**0**	**0**	**0**	
1992-93	**Hartford**	**NHL**	**79**	**7**	**29**	**36**	**76**	**0**	**2**	**2**	**104**	**6.7**	**–11**												
1993-94	**Hartford**	**NHL**	**8**	**1**	**1**	**2**	**2**	**1**	**0**	**0**	**10**	**10.0**	**–5**												
	Chicago	**NHL**	**54**	**3**	**23**	**26**	**31**	**1**	**0**	**2**	**105**	**2.9**	**6**				**6**	**0**	**2**	**2**	**6**	**0**	**0**	**0**	
1994-95	**Chicago**	**NHL**	**48**	**3**	**10**	**13**	**33**	**1**	**0**	**2**	**50**	**6.0**	**1**				**16**	**1**	**5**	**6**	**4**	**0**	**0**	**0**	
1995-96	**Chicago**	**NHL**	**77**	**5**	**10**	**15**	**65**	**0**	**0**	**0**	**76**	**6.6**	**14**				**10**	**1**	**4**	**5**	**10**	**1**	**0**	**0**	
1996-97	**Chicago**	**NHL**	**81**	**7**	**25**	**32**	**62**	**1**	**0**	**0**	**115**	**6.1**	**19**				**6**	**0**	**1**	**1**	**4**	**0**	**0**	**0**	
1997-98	**Chicago**	**NHL**	**82**	**2**	**21**	**23**	**106**	**0**	**0**	**0**	**85**	**2.4**	**10**												
1998-99	**Chicago**	**NHL**	**14**	**1**	**3**	**4**	**12**	**0**	**0**	**0**	**24**	**4.2**	**–13**	**0**	**0.0**	**20:12**									
	Montreal	**NHL**	**66**	**6**	**12**	**18**	**77**	**4**	**0**	**1**	**95**	**6.3**	**–12**	**0**	**0.0**	**24:44**									
99-2000	**Montreal**	**NHL**	**77**	**4**	**25**	**29**	**39**	**2**	**0**	**0**	**120**	**3.3**	**4**	**0**	**0.0**	**25:21**									
2000-01	**Montreal**	**NHL**	**60**	**6**	**19**	**25**	**34**	**2**	**0**	**1**	**81**	**7.4**	**–1**	**1**	**100.0**	**24:27**									
	Boston	**NHL**	**22**	**1**	**5**	**6**	**10**	**1**	**0**	**1**	**28**	**3.6**	**–8**	**0**	**0.0**	**25:52**									
2001-02	**Philadelphia**	**NHL**	**80**	**4**	**20**	**24**	**26**	**0**	**0**	**2**	**102**	**3.9**	**27**	**0**	**0.0**	**21:53**	**5**	**0**	**0**	**0**	**4**	**0**	**0**	**0**	**18:42**
2002-03	**Philadelphia**	**NHL**	**81**	**2**	**18**	**20**	**40**	**1**	**1**	**0**	**103**	**1.9**	**16**	**1**	**0.0**	**21:24**	**13**	**2**	**3**	**5**	**12**	**1**	**0**	**0**	**24:59**
2003-04	**Philadelphia**	**NHL**	**54**	**2**	**7**	**9**	**32**	**1**	**0**	**1**	**56**	**3.6**	**11**	**0**	**0.0**	**20:48**									
	St. Louis	**NHL**	**26**	**2**	**8**	**10**	**14**	**1**	**0**	**0**	**27**	**7.4**	**1**	**0**	**0.0**	**23:05**	**5**	**0**	**1**	**1**	**0**	**0**	**0**	**0**	**23:36**
	NHL Totals		**1082**	**69**	**302**	**371**	**773**	**23**	**3**	**13**	**1393**	**5.0**		**2**	**50.0**	**23:09**	**81**	**6**	**23**	**29**	**67**	**3**	**0**	**0**	**23:19**

Hockey East First All-Star Team (1987) • NCAA East Second All-American Team (1987) • AHL First All-Star Team (1990) • Eddie Shore Award (Top Defenseman – AHL) (1990) • NHL All-Rookie Team (1991)

Traded to **Hartford** by **New Jersey** with Sean Burke for Bobby Holik and Hartford's 2nd round choice (Jay Pandolfo) in 1993 Entry Draft, August 28, 1992. Traded to **Chicago** by **Hartford** with Patrick Poulin for Steve Larmer and Bryan Marchment, November 2, 1993. Traded to **Montreal** by **Chicago** with Jeff Hackett, Alain Nasreddine and Tampa Bay's 4th round choice (previously acquired, Montreal selected Chris Dyment) in 1999 Entry Draft for Jocelyn Thibault, Dave Manson and Brad Brown, November 16, 1998. Traded to **Boston** by **Montreal** for Patrick Traverse, February 21, 2001. Signed as a free agent by **Philadelphia**, July 5, 2001. Traded to **St. Louis** by **Philadelphia** for St. Louis' 5th round choice (Gino Pisellini) in 2004 Entry Draft, February 9, 2004.

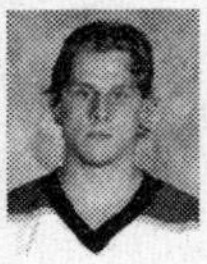

WEISS, Stephen (WIGHS, STEEV-ehn) FLA.

Center. Shoots left. 5'11", 185 lbs. Born, Toronto, Ont., April 3, 1983. Florida's 1st choice, 4th overall, in 2001 Entry Draft.

Season	Club	League	GP	G	A	Pts	PIM	PP	SH	GW	S	%	+/-	TF	F%	Min	GP	G	A	Pts	PIM	PP	SH	GW	Min
1997-98	Tor. Young Nats	MTHL	48	51	58	109																			
1998-99	North York	OPJHL	35	15	22	37	10																		
99-2000	Plymouth Whalers	OHL	64	24	42	66	35										23	8	18	26	18				
2000-01	Plymouth Whalers	OHL	62	40	47	87	45										18	7	16	23	10				
2001-02	**Florida**	**NHL**	**7**	**1**	**1**	**2**	**0**	**1**	**0**	**0**	**15**	**6.7**	**0**	**107**	**52.3**	**16:14**									
	Plymouth Whalers	OHL	46	25	45	70	69										6	2	7	9	13				
2002-03	**Florida**	**NHL**	**77**	**6**	**15**	**21**	**17**	**0**	**0**	**2**	**87**	**6.9**	**–13**	**1065**	**46.3**	**14:17**									
2003-04	**Florida**	**NHL**	**50**	**12**	**17**	**29**	**10**	**3**	**0**	**2**	**82**	**14.6**	**–10**	**799**	**44.9**	**17:42**									
	San Antonio	AHL	10	6	3	9	14																		
	NHL Totals		**134**	**19**	**33**	**52**	**27**	**4**	**0**	**4**	**184**	**10.3**		**1971**	**46.1**	**15:40**									

OHL All-Rookie Team (2000)

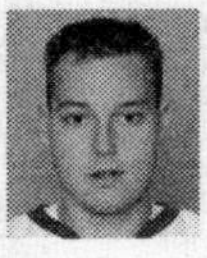

WELLWOOD, Kyle (WEHL-wud, KIGHL) TOR.

Center. Shoots right. 5'10", 190 lbs. Born, Windsor, Ont., May 16, 1983. Toronto's 6th choice, 134th overall, in 2001 Entry Draft.

Season	Club	League	GP	G	A	Pts	PIM	PP	SH	GW	S	%	+/-	TF	F%	Min	GP	G	A	Pts	PIM	PP	SH	GW	Min
1998-99	Tecumseh	OJHL-B	51	22	41	63	12																		
99-2000	Belleville Bulls	OHL	65	14	37	51	14										16	3	7	10	6				
2000-01	Belleville Bulls	OHL	68	35	*83	*118	24										10	3	16	19	4				
2001-02	Belleville Bulls	OHL	28	16	24	40	4																		
	Windsor Spitfires	OHL	26	14	21	35	0										16	12	12	24	0				
2002-03	Windsor Spitfires	OHL	57	41	59	100	0										7	5	9	14	0				
2003-04	**Toronto**	**NHL**	**1**	**0**	**0**	**0**	**0**	**0**	**0**	**0**	**1**	**0.0**	**–1**	**13**	**30.8**	**7:56**									
	St. John's	AHL	76	20	35	55	6																		
	NHL Totals		**1**	**0**	**0**	**0**	**0**	**0**	**0**	**0**	**1**	**0.0**		**13**	**30.8**	**7:56**									

OHL First All-Star Team (2001)

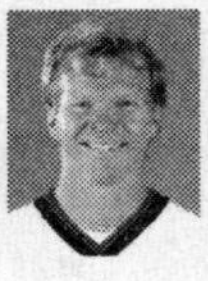

WESLEY, Glen (WEH-slee, GLEHN) CAR.

Defense. Shoots left. 6'1", 205 lbs. Born, Red Deer, Alta., October 2, 1968. Boston's 1st choice, 3rd overall, in 1987 Entry Draft.

Season	Club	League	GP	G	A	Pts	PIM	PP	SH	GW	S	%	+/-	TF	F%	Min	GP	G	A	Pts	PIM	PP	SH	GW	Min
1983-84	Red Deer Rustlers	AJHL	57	9	20	29	40																		
	Portland	WHL	3	1	2	3	0																		
1984-85	Portland	WHL	67	16	52	68	76										6	1	6	7	8				
1985-86	Portland	WHL	69	16	75	91	96										15	3	11	14	29				
1986-87	Portland	WHL	63	16	46	62	72										20	8	18	26	27				
1987-88	**Boston**	**NHL**	**79**	**7**	**30**	**37**	**69**	**1**	**2**	**0**	**158**	**4.4**	**21**				**23**	**6**	**8**	**14**	**22**	**4**	**1**	**0**	
1988-89	**Boston**	**NHL**	**77**	**19**	**35**	**54**	**61**	**8**	**1**	**1**	**181**	**10.5**	**23**				**10**	**0**	**2**	**2**	**4**	**0**	**0**	**0**	
1989-90	**Boston**	**NHL**	**78**	**9**	**27**	**36**	**48**	**5**	**0**	**4**	**166**	**5.4**	**6**				**21**	**2**	**6**	**8**	**36**	**0**	**0**	**1**	
1990-91	**Boston**	**NHL**	**80**	**11**	**32**	**43**	**78**	**5**	**1**	**1**	**199**	**5.5**	**0**				**19**	**2**	**9**	**11**	**19**	**2**	**0**	**0**	
1991-92	**Boston**	**NHL**	**78**	**9**	**37**	**46**	**54**	**4**	**0**	**1**	**211**	**4.3**	**–9**				**15**	**2**	**4**	**6**	**16**	**0**	**0**	**0**	
1992-93	**Boston**	**NHL**	**64**	**8**	**25**	**33**	**47**	**4**	**1**	**0**	**183**	**4.4**	**–2**				**4**	**0**	**0**	**0**	**0**	**0**	**0**	**0**	
1993-94	**Boston**	**NHL**	**81**	**14**	**44**	**58**	**64**	**6**	**1**	**1**	**265**	**5.3**	**1**				**13**	**3**	**3**	**6**	**12**	**1**	**0**	**0**	
1994-95	**Hartford**	**NHL**	**48**	**2**	**14**	**16**	**50**	**1**	**0**	**1**	**125**	**1.6**	**–6**												
1995-96	**Hartford**	**NHL**	**68**	**8**	**16**	**24**	**88**	**6**	**0**	**1**	**129**	**6.2**	**–9**												
1996-97	**Hartford**	**NHL**	**68**	**6**	**26**	**32**	**40**	**3**	**1**	**0**	**126**	**4.8**	**0**												
1997-98	**Carolina**	**NHL**	**82**	**6**	**19**	**25**	**36**	**1**	**0**	**1**	**121**	**5.0**	**7**												
1998-99	**Carolina**	**NHL**	**74**	**7**	**17**	**24**	**44**	**0**	**0**	**2**	**112**	**6.3**	**14**	**1**	**0.0**	**22:31**	**6**	**0**	**0**	**0**	**2**	**0**	**0**	**0**	**28:21**
99-2000	**Carolina**	**NHL**	**78**	**7**	**15**	**22**	**38**	**1**	**0**	**0**	**99**	**7.1**	**–4**	**0**	**0.0**	**21:32**									
2000-01	**Carolina**	**NHL**	**71**	**5**	**16**	**21**	**42**	**3**	**0**	**0**	**92**	**5.4**	**–2**	**0**	**0.0**	**22:21**	**6**	**0**	**0**	**0**	**0**	**0**	**0**	**0**	**22:07**
2001-02	**Carolina**	**NHL**	**77**	**5**	**13**	**18**	**56**	**1**	**0**	**0**	**88**	**5.7**	**–8**	**0**	**0.0**	**20:13**	**22**	**0**	**2**	**2**	**12**	**0**	**0**	**0**	**21:04**
2002-03	**Carolina**	**NHL**	**63**	**1**	**7**	**8**	**40**	**1**	**0**	**0**	**72**	**1.4**	**–5**	**0**	**0.0**	**21:24**									
	Toronto	**NHL**	**7**	**0**	**3**	**3**	**4**	**0**	**0**	**0**	**5**	**0.0**	**3**	**0**	**0.0**	**20:41**	**5**	**0**	**1**	**1**	**2**	**0**	**0**	**0**	**27:39**
2003-04	**Carolina**	**NHL**	**74**	**0**	**6**	**6**	**32**	**0**	**0**	**0**	**82**	**0.0**	**18**	**0**	**0.0**	**21:22**									
	NHL Totals		**1247**	**124**	**382**	**506**	**891**	**50**	**7**	**13**	**2414**	**5.1**		**1**	**0.0**	**21:33**	**144**	**15**	**35**	**50**	**125**	**7**	**1**	**1**	**23:11**

WHL West First All-Star Team (1986, 1987) • NHL All-Rookie Team (1988)

Played in NHL All-Star Game (1989)

Traded to **Hartford** by **Boston** for Hartford's 1st round choices in 1995 (Kyle McLaren), 1996 (Johnathan Aitken) and 1997 (Sergei Samsonov) Entry Drafts, August 26, 1994. Transferred to **Carolina** after **Hartford** franchise relocated, June 25, 1997. Traded to **Toronto** by **Carolina** for Toronto's 2nd round choice (later traded to Columbus – Columbus selected Kyle Wharton) in 2004 Entry Draft, March 9, 2003. Signed as a free agent by **Carolina**, July 8, 2003.

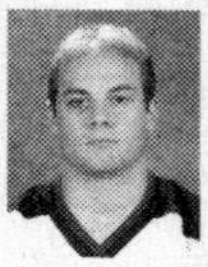

WESTCOTT, Duvie

(WEST-coht, DOO-vee) **CBJ**

Defense. Shoots right. 5'11", 192 lbs. Born, Winnipeg, Man., October 30, 1977.

			Regular Season														Playoffs								
Season	Club	League	GP	G	A	Pts	PIM	PP	SH	GW	S	%	+/-	TF	F%	Min	GP	G	A	Pts	PIM	PP	SH	GW	Min
1996-97	Winnipeg South	MJHL	52	12	47	59																			
1997-98	Alaska-Anchorage	WCHA	25	3	5	8	43																		
	Omaha Lancers	USHL	12	3	3	6	31										14	0	8	8	84				
1998-99	St. Cloud State	WCHA	DID NOT PLAY – TRANSFERRED COLLEGES																						
99-2000	St. Cloud State	WCHA	36	1	18	19	67																		
2000-01	St. Cloud State	WCHA	38	10	24	34	116																		
2001-02	**Columbus**	**NHL**	**4**	**0**	**0**	**0**	**2**	**0**	**0**	**0**	**3**	**0.0**	**–2**	**0**	**0.0**	**15:08**									
	Syracuse Crunch	AHL	68	4	29	33	99										10	0	1	1	12				
2002-03	**Columbus**	**NHL**	**39**	**0**	**7**	**7**	**77**	**0**	**0**	**0**	**27**	**0.0**	**–3**	**0**	**0.0**	**18:41**									
	Syracuse Crunch	AHL	22	1	10	11	54																		
2003-04	**Columbus**	**NHL**	**34**	**0**	**7**	**7**	**39**	**0**	**0**	**0**	**43**	**0.0**	**–15**	**0**	**0.0**	**21:11**									
	NHL Totals		**77**	**0**	**14**	**14**	**118**	**0**	**0**	**0**	**73**	**0.0**		**0**	**0.0**	**19:36**									

WCHA Second All-Star Team (2001)

Signed as a free agent by **Columbus**, May 10, 2001. • Missed majority of 2003-04 season recovering from ankle (October 13, 2003 vs. Vancouver) and hand (January 31, 2004 vs. Minnesota) injuries.

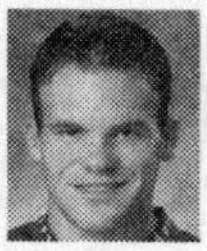

WESTRUM, Erik

(WEHST-ruhm, AIR-ihk) **PHX.**

Center. Shoots left. 6', 204 lbs. Born, Minneapolis, MN, July 26, 1979. Phoenix's 9th choice, 187th overall, in 1998 Entry Draft.

			Regular Season														Playoffs								
Season	Club	League	GP	G	A	Pts	PIM	PP	SH	GW	S	%	+/-	TF	F%	Min	GP	G	A	Pts	PIM	PP	SH	GW	Min
1995/97	Apple Valley	Hi-School	78	56	84	140																			
1997-98	U. of Minnesota	WCHA	39	6	12	18	43																		
1998-99	U. of Minnesota	WCHA	41	10	26	36	81																		
99-2000	U. of Minnesota	WCHA	39	27	26	53	99																		
2000-01	U. of Minnesota	WCHA	42	26	35	61	84																		
2001-02	Springfield	AHL	73	13	29	42	116																		
2002-03	Springfield	AHL	70	10	22	32	65										6	0	4	4	6				
2003-04	**Phoenix**	**NHL**	**15**	**1**	**1**	**2**	**20**	**0**	**0**	**0**	**29**	**3.4**	**–3**	**106**	**39.6**	**16:00**									
	Springfield	AHL	56	14	18	32	91																		
	NHL Totals		**15**	**1**	**1**	**2**	**20**	**0**	**0**	**0**	**29**	**3.4**		**106**	**39.6**	**16:00**									

• Statistics for **Apple Valley** (Hi-School) are career totals for 1995-1997 seasons. • WCHA Second All-Star Team (2001)

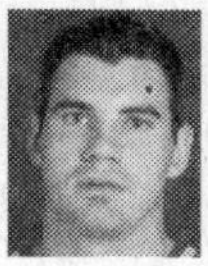

WHITE, Brian

(WIGHT, BRIGH-uhn)

Defense. Shoots right. 6'1", 195 lbs. Born, Winchester, MA, February 7, 1976. Tampa Bay's 11th choice, 268th overall, in 1994 Entry Draft.

			Regular Season														Playoffs								
Season	Club	League	GP	G	A	Pts	PIM	PP	SH	GW	S	%	+/-	TF	F%	Min	GP	G	A	Pts	PIM	PP	SH	GW	Min
1993-94	Arlington	Hi-School	40	14	18	32	81																		
1994-95	U. of Maine	H-East	28	1	1	2	16																		
1995-96	U. of Maine	H-East	39	0	4	4	18																		
1996-97	U. of Maine	H-East	35	4	12	16	36																		
1997-98	U. of Maine	H-East	33	0	12	12	45																		
	Long Beach	IHL	1	0	0	0	0																		
1998-99	**Colorado**	**NHL**	**2**	**0**	**0**	**0**	**0**	**0**	**0**	**0**	**0**	**0.0**	**0**	**0**	**0.0**	**0:40**									
	Hershey Bears	AHL	71	4	8	12	41										4	0	1	1	2				
99-2000	Hershey Bears	AHL	79	3	19	22	78										14	0	3	3	21				
2000-01	Hershey Bears	AHL	75	2	9	11	44										9	0	1	1	12				
2001-02	Cincinnati	AHL	73	0	8	8	32										3	0	0	0	2				
2002-03	Providence Bruins	AHL	51	2	5	7	34										4	0	1	1	8				
2003-04	Providence Bruins	AHL	71	2	7	9	40										2	0	0	0	0				
	NHL Totals		**2**	**0**	**0**	**0**	**0**	**0**	**0**	**0**	**0**	**0.0**		**0**	**0.0**	**0:40**									

Signed as a free agent by **Colorado**, July 7, 1998. Signed as a free agent by **Anaheim**, August 14, 2001. Signed as a free agent by **Providence** (AHL), September 23, 2002.

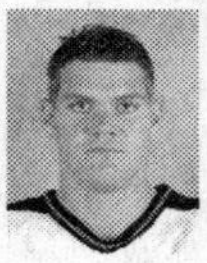

WHITE, Colin

(WIGHT, CAWl-ihn) **N.J.**

Defense. Shoots left. 6'4", 215 lbs. Born, New Glasgow, N.S., December 12, 1977. New Jersey's 5th choice, 49th overall, in 1996 Entry Draft.

			Regular Season														Playoffs								
Season	Club	League	GP	G	A	Pts	PIM	PP	SH	GW	S	%	+/-	TF	F%	Min	GP	G	A	Pts	PIM	PP	SH	GW	Min
1994-95	Laval Titan	QMJHL	7	0	1	1	32																		
	Hull Olympiques	QMJHL	5	0	1	1	4										12	0	0	0	23				
1995-96	Hull Olympiques	QMJHL	62	2	8	10	303										18	0	4	4	42				
1996-97	Hull Olympiques	QMJHL	63	3	12	15	297										14	3	12	15	65				
1997-98	Albany River Rats	AHL	76	3	13	16	235										13	0	0	0	55				
1998-99	Albany River Rats	AHL	77	2	12	14	265										5	0	1	1	8				
99-2000♦	**New Jersey**	**NHL**	**21**	**2**	**1**	**3**	**40**	**0**	**0**	**1**	**29**	**6.9**	**3**	**0**	**0.0**	**14:45**	**23**	**1**	**5**	**6**	**18**	**0**	**0**	**1**	**14:25**
	Albany River Rats	AHL	52	5	21	26	176																		
2000-01	**New Jersey**	**NHL**	**82**	**1**	**19**	**20**	**155**	**0**	**0**	**1**	**114**	**0.9**	**32**	**0**	**0.0**	**19:06**	**25**	**0**	**3**	**3**	**42**	**0**	**0**	**0**	**16:45**
2001-02	**New Jersey**	**NHL**	**73**	**2**	**3**	**5**	**133**	**0**	**0**	**0**	**81**	**2.5**	**6**	**0**	**0.0**	**20:06**	**6**	**0**	**0**	**0**	**2**	**0**	**0**	**0**	**21:50**
2002-03♦	**New Jersey**	**NHL**	**72**	**5**	**8**	**13**	**98**	**0**	**0**	**1**	**81**	**6.2**	**19**	**0**	**0.0**	**19:41**	**24**	**0**	**5**	**5**	**29**	**0**	**0**	**0**	**22:02**
2003-04	**New Jersey**	**NHL**	**75**	**2**	**11**	**13**	**96**	**0**	**0**	**0**	**61**	**3.3**	**10**	**0**	**0.0**	**21:02**	**5**	**0**	**0**	**0**	**4**	**0**	**0**	**0**	**19:40**
	NHL Totals		**323**	**12**	**42**	**54**	**522**	**0**	**0**	**3**	**366**	**3.3**		**0**	**0.0**	**19:37**	**83**	**1**	**13**	**14**	**95**	**0**	**0**	**1**	**18:10**

QMJHL All-Rookie Team (1996) • NHL All-Rookie Team (2001)

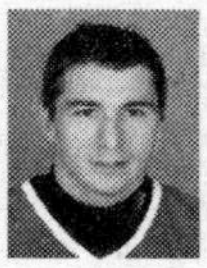

WHITE, Peter

(WIGHT, PEE-tuhr) **PHI.**

Center. Shoots left. 5'11", 200 lbs. Born, Montreal, Que., March 15, 1969. Edmonton's 4th choice, 92nd overall, in 1989 Entry Draft.

			Regular Season														Playoffs								
Season	Club	League	GP	G	A	Pts	PIM	PP	SH	GW	S	%	+/-	TF	F%	Min	GP	G	A	Pts	PIM	PP	SH	GW	Min
1984-85	Lac St-Louis Lions	QAAA	42	16	32	48	18										11	4	3	7	4				
1985-86	Lac St-Louis Lions	QAAA	42	38	62	100	28										2	3	1	4	2				
1986-87	Pembroke	OCJHL	55	20	34	54	20																		
1987-88	Pembroke	OCJHL	56	*90	*136	*226	32																		
1988-89	Michigan State	CCHA	46	20	33	53	17																		
1989-90	Michigan State	CCHA	45	22	40	62	6																		
1990-91	Michigan State	CCHA	37	7	31	38	28																		
1991-92	Michigan State	CCHA	41	26	49	75	32																		
1992-93	Cape Breton	AHL	64	12	28	40	10										16	3	3	6	12				
1993-94	**Edmonton**	**NHL**	**26**	**3**	**5**	**8**	**2**	**0**	**0**	**0**	**17**	**17.6**	**1**												
	Cape Breton	AHL	45	21	49	70	12										5	2	3	5	2				
1994-95	Cape Breton	AHL	65	36	*69	*105	30																		
	Edmonton	**NHL**	**9**	**2**	**4**	**6**	**0**	**2**	**0**	**0**	**13**	**15.4**	**1**												
1995-96	**Edmonton**	**NHL**	**26**	**5**	**3**	**8**	**0**	**1**	**0**	**0**	**34**	**14.7**	**–14**												
	Toronto	**NHL**	**1**	**0**	**0**	**0**	**0**	**0**	**0**	**0**	**0**	**0.0**	**0**												
	St. John's	AHL	17	6	7	13	6																		
	Atlanta Knights	IHL	36	21	20	41	4										3	0	3	3	2				
1996-97	Philadelphia	AHL	80	*44	61	*105	28										10	6	8	14	6				
1997-98	Philadelphia	AHL	80	27	*78	*105	28										20	9	9	18	6				
1998-99	**Philadelphia**	**NHL**	**3**	**0**	**0**	**0**	**0**	**0**	**0**	**0**	**0**	**0.0**	**0**	**8**	**37.5**	**2:02**									
	Philadelphia	AHL	77	31	59	90	20										16	4	13	17	12				
99-2000	**Philadelphia**	**NHL**	**21**	**1**	**5**	**6**	**6**	**0**	**0**	**0**	**24**	**4.2**	**1**	**277**	**54.5**	**13:04**	**16**	**0**	**2**	**2**	**0**	**0**	**0**	**0**	**11:54**
	Philadelphia	AHL	62	20	41	61	38																		
2000-01	**Philadelphia**	**NHL**	**77**	**9**	**16**	**25**	**16**	**1**	**0**	**1**	**68**	**13.2**	**1**	**1038**	**54.3**	**12:56**	**3**	**0**	**0**	**0**	**0**	**0**	**0**	**0**	**11:47**
2001-02	**Chicago**	**NHL**	**48**	**3**	**3**	**6**	**10**	**1**	**0**	**1**	**21**	**14.3**	**–8**	**513**	**53.0**	**10:31**									
	Norfolk Admirals	AHL	24	4	19	23	18										4	0	1	1	0				
2002-03	**Chicago**	**NHL**	**6**	**0**	**1**	**1**	**0**	**0**	**0**	**0**	**2**	**0.0**	**0**	**58**	**39.7**	**9:01**									
	Norfolk Admirals	AHL	31	6	17	23	21										9	2	4	6	5				
	Philadelphia	AHL	47	17	26	43	16																		
2003-04	**Philadelphia**	**NHL**	**3**	**0**	**0**	**0**	**2**	**0**	**0**	**0**	**2**	**0.0**	**–1**	**10**	**30.0**	**6:25**									
	Philadelphia	AHL	75	12	48	60	39										12	2	1	3	10				
	NHL Totals		**220**	**23**	**37**	**60**	**36**	**5**	**0**	**2**	**181**	**12.7**		**1904**	**53.4**	**11:44**	**19**	**0**	**2**	**2**	**0**	**0**	**0**	**0**	**11:53**

AHL Second All-Star Team (1995, 1997) • John B. Sollenberger Trophy (Top Scorer – AHL) (1995, 1997, 1998)

Traded to **Toronto** by **Edmonton** with Edmonton's 4th round choice (Jason Sessa) in 1996 Entry Draft for Kent Manderville, December 4, 1995. Signed as a free agent by **Philadelphia**, August 19, 1996. Signed as a free agent by **Chicago**, September 10, 2001. Traded to **Philadelphia** by **Chicago** for future considerations, March 11, 2003.

Season	Club	League	GP	G	A	Pts	PIM	PP	SH	GW	S	%	+/-	TF	F%	Min	GP	G	A	Pts	PIM	PP	SH	GW	Min
			Regular Season														Playoffs								

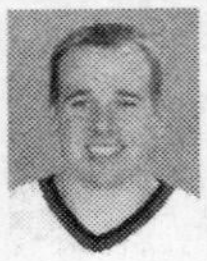

WHITE, Todd

(WIGHT, TAWD) **OTT.**

Center. Shoots left. 5'10", 194 lbs. Born, Kanata, Ont., May 21, 1975.

Season	Club	League	GP	G	A	Pts	PIM	PP	SH	GW	S	%	+/-	TF	F%	Min	GP	G	A	Pts	PIM	PP	SH	GW	Min
1990-91	Powassan Hawks	NOJHA	38	34	38	72	118	....	....	....	....	....	....	....	....	....	....	....	....	....	....	....	....	....	....
1991-92	Kanata Valley	OCJHL	55	39	49	88	30	....	....	....	....	....	....	....	....	....	....	....	....	....	....	....	....	....	....
1992-93	Kanata Valley	OCJHL	49	51	87	138	46	....	....	....	....	....	....	....	....	....	....	....	....	....	....	....	....	....	....
1993-94	Clarkson Knights	ECAC	33	10	12	22	28	....	....	....	....	....	....	....	....	....	....	....	....	....	....	....	....	....	....
1994-95	Clarkson Knights	ECAC	34	13	16	29	44	....	....	....	....	....	....	....	....	....	....	....	....	....	....	....	....	....	....
1995-96	Clarkson Knights	ECAC	38	29	43	72	36	....	....	....	....	....	....	....	....	....	....	....	....	....	....	....	....	....	....
1996-97	Clarkson Knights	ECAC	37	*38	*36	*74	22	....	....	....	....	....	....	....	....	....	....	....	....	....	....	....	....	....	....
1997-98	**Chicago**	**NHL**	**7**	**1**	**0**	**1**	**2**	**0**	**0**	**0**	**3**	**33.3**	**0**	....	....	....	....	....	....	....	....	....	....	....	....
	Indianapolis Ice	IHL	65	46	36	82	28	....	....	....	....	....	....	....	....	....	5	2	3	5	4	....	....	....	....
1998-99	**Chicago**	**NHL**	**35**	**5**	**8**	**13**	**20**	**2**	**0**	**0**	**43**	**11.6**	**–1**	**452**	**46.0**	**13:39**	....	....	....	....	....	....	....	....	....
	Chicago Wolves	IHL	25	11	13	24	8	....	....	....	....	....	....	....	....	....	10	1	4	5	8	....	....	....	....
99-2000	**Chicago**	**NHL**	**1**	**0**	**0**	**0**	**0**	**0**	**0**	**0**	**0**	**0.0**	**0**	**9**	**55.6**	**13:02**	....	....	....	....	....	....	....	....	....
	Cleveland	IHL	42	21	30	51	32	....	....	....	....	....	....	....	....	....	....	....	....	....	....	....	....	....	....
	Philadelphia	**NHL**	**3**	**1**	**0**	**1**	**0**	**0**	**0**	**0**	**4**	**25.0**	**–1**	**25**	**40.0**	**10:29**	....	....	....	....	....	....	....	....	....
	Philadelphia	AHL	32	19	24	43	12	....	....	....	....	....	....	....	....	....	5	2	1	3	8	....	....	....	....
2000-01	**Ottawa**	**NHL**	**16**	**4**	**1**	**5**	**4**	**0**	**0**	**0**	**12**	**33.3**	**5**	**133**	**57.1**	**8:33**	**2**	**0**	**0**	**0**	**0**	**0**	**0**	**0**	**7:29**
	Grand Rapids	IHL	64	22	32	54	20	....	....	....	....	....	....	....	....	....	10	4	4	8	10	....	....	....	....
2001-02	**Ottawa**	**NHL**	**81**	**20**	**30**	**50**	**24**	**4**	**0**	**1**	**147**	**13.6**	**12**	**1508**	**50.5**	**18:22**	**12**	**2**	**2**	**4**	**6**	**0**	**0**	**0**	**18:57**
2002-03	**Ottawa**	**NHL**	**80**	**25**	**35**	**60**	**28**	**8**	**1**	**5**	**144**	**17.4**	**19**	**1396**	**50.5**	**17:58**	**18**	**5**	**1**	**6**	**6**	**1**	**1**	**2**	**16:59**
2003-04	**Ottawa**	**NHL**	**53**	**9**	**20**	**29**	**22**	**1**	**1**	**2**	**98**	**9.2**	**12**	**879**	**52.0**	**17:32**	**7**	**1**	**0**	**1**	**4**	**0**	**0**	**0**	**18:04**
	NHL Totals		**276**	**65**	**94**	**159**	**100**	**15**	**2**	**8**	**451**	**14.4**		**4402**	**50.5**	**16:46**	**39**	**8**	**3**	**11**	**16**	**1**	**1**	**2**	**17:18**

ECAC Second All-Star Team (1996) • NCAA East Second All-American Team (1996) • ECAC First All-Star Team (1997) • NCAA East First All-American Team (1997) • Garry F. Longman Memorial Trophy (Top Rookie – IHL) (1998)

Signed as a free agent by **Chicago**, August 27, 1997. Traded to **Philadelphia** by **Chicago** for future considerations, January 26, 2000. Signed as a free agent by **Ottawa**, July 12, 2000.

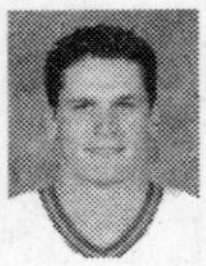

WHITFIELD, Trent

(WHIHT-feeld, TREHNT) **WSH.**

Center. Shoots left. 5'11", 204 lbs. Born, Estevan, Sask., June 17, 1977. Boston's 5th choice, 100th overall, in 1996 Entry Draft.

Season	Club	League	GP	G	A	Pts	PIM	PP	SH	GW	S	%	+/-	TF	F%	Min	GP	G	A	Pts	PIM	PP	SH	GW	Min
1993-94	Saskatoon Blazers	SMHL	36	26	22	48	42	....	....	....	....	....	....	....	....	....	....	....	....	....	....	....	....	....	....
	Spokane Chiefs	WHL	5	1	1	2	0	....	....	....	....	....	....	....	....	....	....	....	....	....	....	....	....	....	....
1994-95	Spokane Chiefs	WHL	48	8	17	25	26	....	....	....	....	....	....	....	....	....	11	7	6	13	5	....	....	....	....
1995-96	Spokane Chiefs	WHL	72	33	51	84	75	....	....	....	....	....	....	....	....	....	18	8	10	18	10	....	....	....	....
1996-97	Spokane Chiefs	WHL	58	34	42	76	74	....	....	....	....	....	....	....	....	....	9	5	7	12	10	....	....	....	....
1997-98	Spokane Chiefs	WHL	65	38	44	82	97	....	....	....	....	....	....	....	....	....	18	9	10	19	15	....	....	....	....
1998-99	Portland Pirates	AHL	50	10	8	18	20	....	....	....	....	....	....	....	....	....	....	....	....	....	....	....	....	....	....
	Hampton Roads	ECHL	19	13	12	25	12	....	....	....	....	....	....	....	....	....	4	2	0	2	14	....	....	....	....
99-2000	Portland Pirates	AHL	79	18	35	53	52	....	....	....	....	....	....	....	....	....	3	1	1	2	2	....	....	....	....
	Washington	**NHL**	....	....	....	....	....	....	....	....	....	....	....	....	....	....	**3**	**0**	**0**	**0**	**0**	**0**	**0**	**0**	**5:47**
2000-01	**Washington**	**NHL**	**61**	**2**	**4**	**6**	**35**	**0**	**0**	**0**	**47**	**4.3**	**3**	**520**	**51.9**	**9:39**	**5**	**0**	**0**	**0**	**2**	**0**	**0**	**0**	**7:07**
	Portland Pirates	AHL	19	9	11	20	27	....	....	....	....	....	....	....	....	....	....	....	....	....	....	....	....	....	....
2001-02	**Washington**	**NHL**	**24**	**0**	**1**	**1**	**28**	**0**	**0**	**0**	**15**	**0.0**	**–3**	**189**	**54.0**	**7:06**	....	....	....	....	....	....	....	....	....
	Portland Pirates	AHL	10	4	4	8	8	....	....	....	....	....	....	....	....	....	....	....	....	....	....	....	....	....	....
	NY Rangers	**NHL**	**1**	**0**	**0**	**0**	**0**	**0**	**0**	**0**	**0**	**0.0**	**1**	**18**	**50.0**	**12:44**	....	....	....	....	....	....	....	....	....
	Portland Pirates	AHL	24	10	16	26	16	....	....	....	....	....	....	....	....	....	....	....	....	....	....	....	....	....	....
2002-03	**Washington**	**NHL**	**14**	**1**	**1**	**2**	**6**	**0**	**0**	**1**	**4**	**25.0**	**1**	**124**	**57.3**	**8:30**	**6**	**0**	**0**	**0**	**10**	**0**	**0**	**0**	**11:01**
	Portland Pirates	AHL	64	27	34	61	42	....	....	....	....	....	....	....	....	....	....	....	....	....	....	....	....	....	....
2003-04	**Washington**	**NHL**	**44**	**6**	**5**	**11**	**14**	**0**	**1**	**2**	**38**	**15.8**	**–2**	**598**	**55.4**	**12:48**	....	....	....	....	....	....	....	....	....
	Portland Pirates	AHL	24	8	7	15	22	....	....	....	....	....	....	....	....	....	....	....	....	....	....	....	....	....	....
	NHL Totals		**144**	**9**	**11**	**20**	**83**	**0**	**1**	**3**	**104**	**8.7**		**1449**	**54.0**	**10:06**	**14**	**0**	**0**	**0**	**12**	**0**	**0**	**0**	**8:30**

WHL West First All-Star Team (1997) • WHL West Second All-Star Team (1998)

Signed as a free agent by **Washington**, September 1, 1998. Claimed on waivers by **NY Rangers** from **Washington**, January 16, 2002. Claimed on waivers by **Washington** from **NY Rangers**, February 1, 2002.

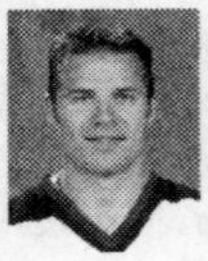

WHITNEY, Ray

(WHIHT-nee, RAY) **DET.**

Left wing. Shoots right. 5'10", 175 lbs. Born, Fort Saskatchewan, Alta., May 8, 1972. San Jose's 2nd choice, 23rd overall, in 1991 Entry Draft.

Season	Club	League	GP	G	A	Pts	PIM	PP	SH	GW	S	%	+/-	TF	F%	Min	GP	G	A	Pts	PIM	PP	SH	GW	Min
1987-88	Ft. Saskatchewan	AMHL	71	80	155	235	119	....	....	....	....	....	....	....	....	....	....	....	....	....	....	....	....	....	....
1988-89	Spokane Chiefs	WHL	71	17	33	50	16	....	....	....	....	....	....	....	....	....	....	....	....	....	....	....	....	....	....
1989-90	Spokane Chiefs	WHL	71	57	56	113	50	....	....	....	....	....	....	....	....	....	6	3	4	7	6	....	....	....	....
1990-91	Spokane Chiefs	WHL	72	67	118	*185	36	....	....	....	....	....	....	....	....	....	15	13	18	*31	12	....	....	....	....
1991-92	Kolner EC	Germany	10	3	6	9	4	....	....	....	....	....	....	....	....	....	....	....	....	....	....	....	....	....	....
	Team Canada	Nat-Tm	5	1	0	1	6	....	....	....	....	....	....	....	....	....	....	....	....	....	....	....	....	....	....
	San Jose	**NHL**	**2**	**0**	**3**	**3**	**0**	**0**	**0**	**0**	**4**	**0.0**	**–1**	....	....	....	....	....	....	....	....	....	....	....	....
	San Diego Gulls	IHL	63	36	54	90	12	....	....	....	....	....	....	....	....	....	4	0	0	0	0	....	....	....	....
1992-93	**San Jose**	**NHL**	**26**	**4**	**6**	**10**	**4**	**1**	**0**	**0**	**24**	**16.7**	**–14**	....	....	....	....	....	....	....	....	....	....	....	....
	Kansas City	IHL	46	20	33	53	14	....	....	....	....	....	....	....	....	....	12	5	7	12	2	....	....	....	....
1993-94	**San Jose**	**NHL**	**61**	**14**	**26**	**40**	**14**	**1**	**0**	**0**	**82**	**17.1**	**2**	....	....	....	**14**	**0**	**4**	**4**	**8**	**0**	**0**	**0**	....
1994-95	**San Jose**	**NHL**	**39**	**13**	**12**	**25**	**14**	**4**	**0**	**1**	**67**	**19.4**	**–7**	....	....	....	**11**	**4**	**4**	**8**	**2**	**0**	**0**	**1**	....
1995-96	**San Jose**	**NHL**	**60**	**17**	**24**	**41**	**16**	**4**	**2**	**2**	**106**	**16.0**	**–23**	....	....	....	....	....	....	....	....	....	....	....	....
1996-97	**San Jose**	**NHL**	**12**	**0**	**2**	**2**	**4**	**0**	**0**	**0**	**24**	**0.0**	**–6**	....	....	....	....	....	....	....	....	....	....	....	....
	Kentucky	AHL	9	1	7	8	2	....	....	....	....	....	....	....	....	....	....	....	....	....	....	....	....	....	....
	Utah Grizzlies	IHL	43	13	35	48	34	....	....	....	....	....	....	....	....	....	7	3	1	4	6	....	....	....	....
1997-98	**Edmonton**	**NHL**	**9**	**1**	**3**	**4**	**0**	**0**	**0**	**0**	**19**	**5.3**	**–1**	....	....	....	....	....	....	....	....	....	....	....	....
	Florida	**NHL**	**68**	**32**	**29**	**61**	**28**	**12**	**0**	**2**	**156**	**20.5**	**10**	....	....	....	....	....	....	....	....	....	....	....	....
1998-99	**Florida**	**NHL**	**81**	**26**	**38**	**64**	**18**	**7**	**0**	**6**	**193**	**13.5**	**–3**	**144**	**43.8**	**18:20**	....	....	....	....	....	....	....	....	....
99-2000	**Florida**	**NHL**	**81**	**29**	**42**	**71**	**35**	**5**	**0**	**3**	**198**	**14.6**	**16**	**198**	**49.0**	**18:41**	**4**	**1**	**0**	**1**	**4**	**0**	**0**	**0**	**18:13**
2000-01	**Florida**	**NHL**	**43**	**10**	**21**	**31**	**28**	**5**	**0**	**0**	**117**	**8.5**	**–16**	**38**	**39.5**	**17:41**	....	....	....	....	....	....	....	....	....
	Columbus	**NHL**	**3**	**0**	**3**	**3**	**2**	**0**	**0**	**0**	**3**	**0.0**	**–1**	**19**	**36.8**	**20:17**	....	....	....	....	....	....	....	....	....
2001-02	**Columbus**	**NHL**	**67**	**21**	**40**	**61**	**12**	**6**	**0**	**3**	**210**	**10.0**	**–22**	**21**	**47.6**	**20:13**	....	....	....	....	....	....	....	....	....
2002-03	**Columbus**	**NHL**	**81**	**24**	**52**	**76**	**22**	**8**	**2**	**2**	**235**	**10.2**	**–26**	**29**	**44.8**	**21:00**	....	....	....	....	....	....	....	....	....
2003-04	**Detroit**	**NHL**	**67**	**14**	**29**	**43**	**22**	**3**	**1**	**4**	**119**	**11.8**	**7**	**18**	**38.9**	**16:24**	**12**	**1**	**3**	**4**	**4**	**0**	**0**	**1**	**11:56**
	NHL Totals		**700**	**205**	**330**	**535**	**219**	**56**	**5**	**23**	**1557**	**13.2**		**467**	**45.4**	**18:51**	**41**	**6**	**11**	**17**	**18**	**0**	**0**	**2**	**13:30**

WHL West First All-Star Team (1991) • WHL MVP (1991) • Memorial Cup All-Star Team (1991) • George Parsons Trophy (Memorial Cup Most Sportsmanlike Player) (1991)

Played in NHL All-Star Game (2000, 2003)

Signed as a free agent by **Edmonton**, October 1, 1997. Claimed on waivers by **Florida** from **Edmonton**, November 6, 1997. Traded to **Columbus** by **Florida** with future considerations for Kevyn Adams and Columbus's 4th round choice (Michael Woodford) in 2001 Entry Draft, March 13, 2001. Signed as a free agent by **Detroit**, July 30, 2003.

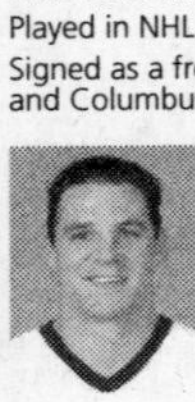

WIEMER, Jason

(WEE-muhr, JAY-suhn) **CGY.**

Center. Shoots left. 6'1", 225 lbs. Born, Kimberley, B.C., April 14, 1976. Tampa Bay's 1st choice, 8th overall, in 1994 Entry Draft.

Season	Club	League	GP	G	A	Pts	PIM	PP	SH	GW	S	%	+/-	TF	F%	Min	GP	G	A	Pts	PIM	PP	SH	GW	Min
1991-92	Kimberley	RMJHL	45	33	33	66	211	....	....	....	....	....	....	....	....	....	....	....	....	....	....	....	....	....	....
	Portland	WHL	2	0	1	1	0	....	....	....	....	....	....	....	....	....	....	....	....	....	....	....	....	....	....
1992-93	Portland	WHL	68	18	34	52	159	....	....	....	....	....	....	....	....	....	16	7	3	10	27	....	....	....	....
1993-94	Portland	WHL	72	45	51	96	236	....	....	....	....	....	....	....	....	....	10	4	4	8	32	....	....	....	....
1994-95	Portland	WHL	16	10	14	24	63	....	....	....	....	....	....	....	....	....	....	....	....	....	....	....	....	....	....
	Tampa Bay	**NHL**	**36**	**1**	**4**	**5**	**44**	**0**	**0**	**0**	**10**	**10.0**	**–2**	....	....	....	....	....	....	....	....	....	....	....	....
1995-96	**Tampa Bay**	**NHL**	**66**	**9**	**9**	**18**	**81**	**4**	**0**	**1**	**89**	**10.1**	**–9**	....	....	....	**6**	**1**	**0**	**1**	**28**	**1**	**0**	**0**	....
1996-97	**Tampa Bay**	**NHL**	**63**	**9**	**5**	**14**	**134**	**2**	**0**	**0**	**103**	**8.7**	**–13**	....	....	....	....	....	....	....	....	....	....	....	....
	Adirondack	AHL	4	1	0	1	7	....	....	....	....	....	....	....	....	....	....	....	....	....	....	....	....	....	....
1997-98	**Tampa Bay**	**NHL**	**67**	**8**	**9**	**17**	**132**	**2**	**0**	**0**	**106**	**7.5**	**–9**	....	....	....	....	....	....	....	....	....	....	....	....
	Calgary	**NHL**	**12**	**4**	**1**	**5**	**28**	**1**	**0**	**2**	**16**	**25.0**	**–1**	....	....	....	....	....	....	....	....	....	....	....	....
1998-99	**Calgary**	**NHL**	**78**	**8**	**13**	**21**	**177**	**1**	**0**	**1**	**128**	**6.3**	**–12**	**867**	**40.9**	**13:17**	....	....	....	....	....	....	....	....	....
99-2000	**Calgary**	**NHL**	**64**	**11**	**11**	**22**	**120**	**2**	**0**	**3**	**104**	**10.6**	**–10**	**955**	**47.6**	**14:41**	....	....	....	....	....	....	....	....	....
2000-01	**Calgary**	**NHL**	**65**	**10**	**5**	**15**	**177**	**3**	**0**	**1**	**76**	**13.2**	**–15**	**599**	**51.1**	**13:56**	....	....	....	....	....	....	....	....	....
2001-02	**Florida**	**NHL**	**70**	**11**	**20**	**31**	**178**	**5**	**1**	**1**	**115**	**9.6**	**–4**	**1241**	**44.1**	**17:09**	....	....	....	....	....	....	....	....	....
2002-03	**NY Islanders**	**NHL**	**81**	**9**	**19**	**28**	**116**	**0**	**1**	**2**	**139**	**6.5**	**5**	**347**	**49.0**	**12:26**	**5**	**0**	**0**	**0**	**23**	**0**	**0**	**0**	**13:37**

								Regular Season									Playoffs								
Season	Club	League	GP	G	A	Pts	PIM	PP	SH	GW	S	%	+/-	TF	F%	Min	GP	G	A	Pts	PIM	PP	SH	GW	Min
2003-04	NY Islanders	NHL	13	1	3	4	24	0	0	0	14	7.1	–1	72	47.2	11:36	....	....	....	....	....	....	....	....	....
	Minnesota	NHL	62	7	11	18	106	1	0	0	89	7.9	–6	726	44.4	13:57	....	....	....	....	....	....	....	....	....
	NHL Totals		677	88	110	198	1317	21	2	11	989	8.9		4807	45.5	14:06	11	1	0	1	51	1	0	0	13:37

Traded to **Calgary** by **Tampa Bay** for Sandy McCarthy and Calgary's 3rd (Brad Richards) and 5th (Curtis Rich) round choices in 1998 Entry Draft, March 24, 1998. Traded to **Florida** by **Calgary** with Valeri Bure for Rob Neidermayer and Philadelphia's 2nd round choice (previously acquired, Calgary selected Andrei Medvedev) in 2001 Entry Draft, June 24, 2001. Traded to **NY Islanders** by **Florida** for Branislav Mezei, July 3, 2002. Claimed on waivers by **Minnesota** from **NY Islanders**, November 13, 2003. Signed as a free agent by **Calgary**, August 5, 2004.

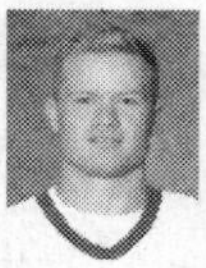

WILLIAMS, Jason
(WIHL-yuhms, JAY-suhn) **DET.**

Center. Shoots right. 5'11", 185 lbs. Born, London, Ont., August 11, 1980.

Season	Club	League	GP	G	A	Pts	PIM	PP	SH	GW	S	%	+/-	TF	F%	Min	GP	G	A	Pts	PIM	PP	SH	GW	Min
1995-96	Mount Brydges	OJHL-D	36	31	28	59	18	....	....	....	....	....	....	....	....	....	....	....	....	....	....	....	....	....	....
1996-97	Peterborough	OHL	60	4	8	12	8	....	....	....	....	....	....	....	....	....	10	1	0	1	2	....	....	....	....
1997-98	Peterborough	OHL	55	8	27	35	31	....	....	....	....	....	....	....	....	....	4	0	1	1	2	....	....	....	....
1998-99	Peterborough	OHL	68	26	48	74	42	....	....	....	....	....	....	....	....	....	5	1	2	3	2	....	....	....	....
99-2000	Peterborough	OHL	66	36	37	75	64	....	....	....	....	....	....	....	....	....	5	2	1	3	2	....	....	....	....
2000-01	**Detroit**	**NHL**	**5**	**0**	**3**	**3**	**2**	**0**	**0**	**0**	**7**	**0.0**	**1**	**56**	**39.3**	**12:24**	**2**	**0**	**0**	**0**	**0**	**0**	**0**	**0**	**11:45**
	Cincinnati	AHL	76	24	45	69	48	....	....	....	....	....	....	....	....	....	1	0	0	0	2	....	....	....	....
2001-02♦	**Detroit**	**NHL**	**25**	**8**	**2**	**10**	**4**	**4**	**0**	**0**	**32**	**25.0**	**2**	**208**	**47.6**	**10:50**	**9**	**0**	**0**	**0**	**2**	**0**	**0**	**0**	**6:12**
	Cincinnati	AHL	52	23	27	50	27	....	....	....	....	....	....	....	....	....	3	0	1	1	6	....	....	....	....
2002-03	**Detroit**	**NHL**	**16**	**3**	**3**	**6**	**2**	**1**	**0**	**0**	**20**	**15.0**	**3**	**78**	**51.3**	**10:43**	....	....	....	....	....	....	....	....	....
	Grand Rapids	AHL	45	23	22	45	18	....	....	....	....	....	....	....	....	....	15	1	7	8	16	....	....	....	....
2003-04	**Detroit**	**NHL**	**49**	**6**	**7**	**13**	**15**	**0**	**0**	**0**	**44**	**13.6**	**1**	**315**	**49.2**	**9:27**	**3**	**0**	**0**	**0**	**2**	**0**	**0**	**0**	**6:11**
	NHL Totals		**95**	**17**	**15**	**32**	**23**	**5**	**0**	**0**	**103**	**16.5**		**657**	**48.1**	**10:11**	**14**	**0**	**0**	**0**	**4**	**0**	**0**	**0**	**6:59**

Signed as a free agent by **Detroit**, September 18, 2000.

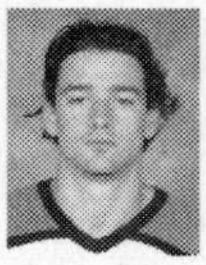

WILLIAMS, Justin
(WIHL-yuhms, JUHS-tihn) **CAR.**

Right wing. Shoots right. 6'1", 190 lbs. Born, Cobourg, Ont., October 4, 1981. Philadelphia's 1st choice, 28th overall, in 2000 Entry Draft.

Season	Club	League	GP	G	A	Pts	PIM	PP	SH	GW	S	%	+/-	TF	F%	Min	GP	G	A	Pts	PIM	PP	SH	GW	Min
1997-98	Colborne Colts	OJHL-C	36	32	35	67	26	....	....	....	....	....	....	....	....	....	....	....	....	....	....	....	....	....	....
	Cobourg Cougars	OPJHL	17	0	3	3	5	....	....	....	....	....	....	....	....	....	....	....	....	....	....	....	....	....	....
1998-99	Plymouth Whalers	OHL	47	4	8	12	28	....	....	....	....	....	....	....	....	....	7	1	2	3	0	....	....	....	....
99-2000	Plymouth Whalers	OHL	68	37	46	83	46	....	....	....	....	....	....	....	....	....	23	*14	16	*30	10	....	....	....	....
2000-01	**Philadelphia**	**NHL**	**63**	**12**	**13**	**25**	**22**	**0**	**0**	**0**	**99**	**12.1**	**6**	**13**	**53.9**	**12:31**	....	....	....	....	....	....	....	....	....
2001-02	**Philadelphia**	**NHL**	**75**	**17**	**23**	**40**	**32**	**0**	**0**	**1**	**162**	**10.5**	**11**	**16**	**25.0**	**14:27**	**5**	**0**	**0**	**0**	**4**	**0**	**0**	**0**	**16:42**
2002-03	**Philadelphia**	**NHL**	**41**	**8**	**16**	**24**	**22**	**0**	**0**	**2**	**105**	**7.6**	**15**	**16**	**50.0**	**15:57**	**12**	**1**	**5**	**6**	**8**	**0**	**0**	**1**	**14:11**
2003-04	**Philadelphia**	**NHL**	**47**	**6**	**20**	**26**	**32**	**3**	**0**	**1**	**107**	**5.6**	**10**	**38**	**31.6**	**15:30**	....	....	....	....	....	....	....	....	....
	Carolina	**NHL**	**32**	**5**	**13**	**18**	**32**	**1**	**0**	**0**	**96**	**5.2**	**2**	**25**	**36.0**	**18:52**	....	....	....	....	....	....	....	....	....
	NHL Totals		**258**	**48**	**85**	**133**	**140**	**4**	**0**	**4**	**569**	**8.4**		**108**	**37.0**	**14:58**	**17**	**1**	**5**	**6**	**12**	**0**	**0**	**1**	**14:56**

• Missed majority of 2002-03 season recovering from shoulder (November 15, 2002 vs. Carolina) and knee (January 18, 2003 vs. Tampa Bay) injuries. Traded to **Carolina** by **Philadelphia** for Danny Markov, January 20, 2004.

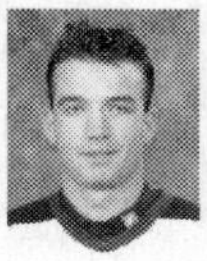

WILLIS, Shane
(WIH-lihs, SHAYN) **T.B.**

Right wing. Shoots right. 6'1", 190 lbs. Born, Edmonton, Alta., June 13, 1977. Carolina's 4th choice, 88th overall, in 1997 Entry Draft.

Season	Club	League	GP	G	A	Pts	PIM	PP	SH	GW	S	%	+/-	TF	F%	Min	GP	G	A	Pts	PIM	PP	SH	GW	Min
1992-93	Red Deer	ABHL	36	32	18	50	88	....	....	....	....	....	....	....	....	....	....	....	....	....	....	....	....	....	....
1993-94	Red Deer	AMHL	34	40	26	66	103	....	....	....	....	....	....	....	....	....	....	....	....	....	....	....	....	....	....
1994-95	Prince Albert	WHL	65	24	19	43	38	....	....	....	....	....	....	....	....	....	13	3	4	7	6	....	....	....	....
1995-96	Prince Albert	WHL	69	41	40	81	47	....	....	....	....	....	....	....	....	....	18	11	10	21	18	....	....	....	....
1996-97	Prince Albert	WHL	41	34	22	56	63	....	....	....	....	....	....	....	....	....	....	....	....	....	....	....	....	....	....
	Lethbridge	WHL	26	22	17	39	24	....	....	....	....	....	....	....	....	....	19	13	11	24	20	....	....	....	....
1997-98	Lethbridge	WHL	64	58	54	112	73	....	....	....	....	....	....	....	....	....	4	2	3	5	6	....	....	....	....
	New Haven	AHL	1	0	1	1	2	....	....	....	....	....	....	....	....	....	....	....	....	....	....	....	....	....	....
1998-99	**Carolina**	**NHL**	**7**	**0**	**0**	**0**	**0**	**0**	**0**	**0**	**1**	**0.0**	**–2**	**0**	**0.0**	**2:14**	....	....	....	....	....	....	....	....	....
	New Haven	AHL	73	31	50	81	49	....	....	....	....	....	....	....	....	....	....	....	....	....	....	....	....	....	....
99-2000	**Carolina**	**NHL**	**2**	**0**	**0**	**0**	**0**	**0**	**0**	**0**	**1**	**0.0**	**–1**	**0**	**0.0**	**5:50**	....	....	....	....	....	....	....	....	....
	Cincinnati	IHL	80	35	25	60	64	....	....	....	....	....	....	....	....	....	11	5	3	8	8	....	....	....	....
2000-01	**Carolina**	**NHL**	**73**	**20**	**24**	**44**	**45**	**9**	**0**	**6**	**172**	**11.6**	**–6**	**10**	**20.0**	**15:58**	**2**	**0**	**0**	**0**	**0**	**0**	**0**	**0**	**12:56**
2001-02	**Carolina**	**NHL**	**59**	**7**	**10**	**17**	**24**	**2**	**0**	**0**	**126**	**5.6**	**–8**	**10**	**50.0**	**13:00**	....	....	....	....	....	....	....	....	....
	Tampa Bay	**NHL**	**21**	**4**	**3**	**7**	**6**	**0**	**0**	**0**	**29**	**13.8**	**0**	**12**	**8.3**	**11:18**	....	....	....	....	....	....	....	....	....
2002-03	Springfield	AHL	56	16	16	32	26	....	....	....	....	....	....	....	....	....	6	4	2	6	4	....	....	....	....
2003-04	**Tampa Bay**	**NHL**	**12**	**0**	**6**	**6**	**2**	**0**	**0**	**0**	**27**	**0.0**	**1**	**2**	**0.0**	**13:50**	....	....	....	....	....	....	....	....	....
	Hershey Bears	AHL	55	27	21	48	71	....	....	....	....	....	....	....	....	....	....	....	....	....	....	....	....	....	....
	NHL Totals		**174**	**31**	**43**	**74**	**77**	**11**	**0**	**6**	**356**	**8.7**		**34**	**23.5**	**13:35**	**2**	**0**	**0**	**0**	**0**	**0**	**0**	**0**	**12:56**

• Re-entered NHL Entry Draft. Originally Tampa Bay's 3rd choice, 56th overall, in 1995 Entry Draft.
WHL East First All-Star Team (1997, 1998) • AHL First All-Star Team (1999) • Dudley "Red" Garrett Memorial Trophy (Top Rookie – AHL) (1999) • NHL All-Rookie Team (2001)
Traded to **Tampa Bay** by **Carolina** with Chris Dingman for Kevin Weekes, March 5, 2002.

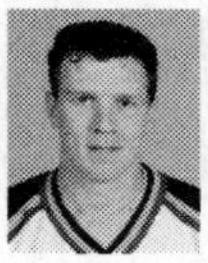

WILLSIE, Brian
(WIHL-see, BRIGH-uhn) **WSH.**

Right wing. Shoots right. 6'1", 195 lbs. Born, London, Ont., March 16, 1978. Colorado's 7th choice, 146th overall, in 1996 Entry Draft.

Season	Club	League	GP	G	A	Pts	PIM	PP	SH	GW	S	%	+/-	TF	F%	Min	GP	G	A	Pts	PIM	PP	SH	GW	Min
1993-94	Belmont Bombers	OJHL-D	13	9	5	14	14	....	....	....	....	....	....	....	....	....	....	....	....	....	....	....	....	....	....
1994-95	St. Thomas Stars	OJHL-B	45	35	47	82	47	....	....	....	....	....	....	....	....	....	....	....	....	....	....	....	....	....	....
1995-96	Guelph Storm	OHL	65	13	21	34	18	....	....	....	....	....	....	....	....	....	16	4	2	6	6	....	....	....	....
1996-97	Guelph Storm	OHL	64	37	31	68	37	....	....	....	....	....	....	....	....	....	18	15	4	19	10	....	....	....	....
1997-98	Guelph Storm	OHL	57	45	31	76	41	....	....	....	....	....	....	....	....	....	12	9	5	14	18	....	....	....	....
1998-99	Hershey Bears	AHL	72	19	10	29	28	....	....	....	....	....	....	....	....	....	3	1	0	1	0	....	....	....	....
99-2000	**Colorado**	**NHL**	**1**	**0**	**0**	**0**	**0**	**0**	**0**	**0**	**1**	**0.0**	**0**	**0**	**0.0**	**8:16**	....	....	....	....	....	....	....	....	....
	Hershey Bears	AHL	78	20	39	59	44	....	....	....	....	....	....	....	....	....	12	2	6	8	8	....	....	....	....
2000-01	Hershey Bears	AHL	48	18	23	41	20	....	....	....	....	....	....	....	....	....	12	7	2	9	14	....	....	....	....
2001-02	**Colorado**	**NHL**	**56**	**7**	**7**	**14**	**14**	**2**	**0**	**1**	**66**	**10.6**	**4**	**8**	**12.5**	**11:24**	**4**	**0**	**1**	**1**	**2**	**0**	**0**	**0**	**11:54**
2002-03	**Colorado**	**NHL**	**12**	**0**	**1**	**1**	**15**	**0**	**0**	**0**	**12**	**0.0**	**0**	**7**	**14.3**	**9:36**	**6**	**1**	**0**	**1**	**2**	**0**	**0**	**1**	**10:48**
	Hershey Bears	AHL	59	29	28	57	49	....	....	....	....	....	....	....	....	....	....	....	....	....	....	....	....	....	....
2003-04	**Washington**	**NHL**	**49**	**10**	**5**	**15**	**18**	**1**	**1**	**1**	**85**	**11.8**	**–7**	**46**	**34.8**	**12:42**	....	....	....	....	....	....	....	....	....
	NHL Totals		**118**	**17**	**13**	**30**	**47**	**3**	**1**	**2**	**164**	**10.4**		**61**	**29.5**	**11:44**	**10**	**1**	**1**	**2**	**4**	**0**	**0**	**1**	**11:14**

OHL First All-Star Team (1998)
Claimed by **Washington** from **Colorado** in Waiver Draft, October 3, 2003.

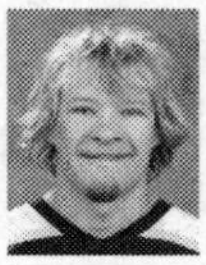

WILM, Clarke
(WIHLM, KLAHRK) **TOR.**

Center. Shoots left. 6', 202 lbs. Born, Central Butte, Sask., October 24, 1976. Calgary's 5th choice, 150th overall, in 1995 Entry Draft.

Season	Club	League	GP	G	A	Pts	PIM	PP	SH	GW	S	%	+/-	TF	F%	Min	GP	G	A	Pts	PIM	PP	SH	GW	Min
1991-92	Saskatoon Blazers	SMHL	36	18	28	46	16	....	....	....	....	....	....	....	....	....	....	....	....	....	....	....	....	....	....
	Saskatoon Blades	WHL	....	....	....	....	....	....	....	....	....	....	....	....	....	....	1	0	0	0	0	....	....	....	....
1992-93	Saskatoon Blades	WHL	69	14	19	33	71	....	....	....	....	....	....	....	....	....	9	4	2	6	13	....	....	....	....
1993-94	Saskatoon Blades	WHL	70	18	32	50	181	....	....	....	....	....	....	....	....	....	16	0	9	9	19	....	....	....	....
1994-95	Saskatoon Blades	WHL	71	20	39	59	179	....	....	....	....	....	....	....	....	....	10	6	1	7	21	....	....	....	....
1995-96	Saskatoon Blades	WHL	72	49	61	110	83	....	....	....	....	....	....	....	....	....	4	1	1	2	4	....	....	....	....
1996-97	Saint John Flames	AHL	62	9	19	28	107	....	....	....	....	....	....	....	....	....	5	2	0	2	15	....	....	....	....
1997-98	Saint John Flames	AHL	68	13	26	39	112	....	....	....	....	....	....	....	....	....	21	5	9	14	8	....	....	....	....
1998-99	**Calgary**	**NHL**	**78**	**10**	**8**	**18**	**53**	**2**	**2**	**0**	**94**	**10.6**	**11**	**609**	**40.9**	**11:32**	....	....	....	....	....	....	....	....	....
99-2000	**Calgary**	**NHL**	**78**	**10**	**12**	**22**	**67**	**1**	**3**	**0**	**81**	**12.3**	**–6**	**872**	**44.4**	**12:38**	....	....	....	....	....	....	....	....	....
2000-01	**Calgary**	**NHL**	**81**	**7**	**8**	**15**	**69**	**2**	**0**	**0**	**85**	**8.2**	**–11**	**992**	**51.9**	**14:11**	....	....	....	....	....	....	....	....	....
2001-02	**Calgary**	**NHL**	**66**	**4**	**14**	**18**	**61**	**0**	**1**	**0**	**83**	**4.8**	**–1**	**995**	**51.1**	**15:00**	....	....	....	....	....	....	....	....	....
2002-03	**Nashville**	**NHL**	**82**	**5**	**11**	**16**	**36**	**0**	**0**	**0**	**108**	**4.6**	**–11**	**339**	**50.4**	**11:58**	....	....	....	....	....	....	....	....	....
2003-04	**Toronto**	**NHL**	**10**	**0**	**0**	**0**	**7**	**0**	**0**	**0**	**10**	**0.0**	**0**	**43**	**46.5**	**11:45**	**5**	**0**	**1**	**1**	**2**	**0**	**0**	**0**	**12:45**
	St. John's	AHL	47	16	17	33	97	....	....	....	....	....	....	....	....	....	....	....	....	....	....	....	....	....	....
	NHL Totals		**395**	**36**	**53**	**89**	**293**	**5**	**6**	**0**	**461**	**7.8**		**3850**	**48.1**	**12:58**	**5**	**0**	**1**	**1**	**2**	**0**	**0**	**0**	**12:45**

Signed as a free agent by **Nashville**, July 11, 2002. Signed as a free agent by **Toronto**, October 28, 2003.

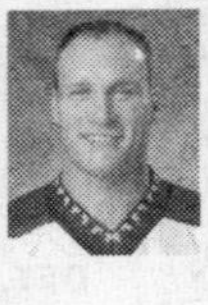

WILSON, Landon
(WIHL-suhn, LAN-duhn)

Right wing. Shoots right. 6'3", 226 lbs. Born, St. Louis, MO, March 13, 1975. Toronto's 2nd choice, 19th overall, in 1993 Entry Draft.

Season	Club	League	GP	G	A	Pts	PIM	PP	SH	GW	S	%	+/-	TF	F%	Min	Playoffs GP	G	A	Pts	PIM	PP	SH	GW	Min
1991-92	California	WSJHL	38	50	42	92	135																			
1992-93	Dubuque	USHL	43	29	36	65	284																			
1993-94	North Dakota	WCHA	35	18	15	33	*147																			
1994-95	North Dakota	WCHA	31	7	16	23	141																			
	Cornwall Aces	AHL	8	4	4	8	25										13	3	4	7	68				
1995-96	**Colorado**	**NHL**	**7**	**1**	**0**	**1**	**6**	**0**	**0**	**0**	**6**	**16.7**	**3**												
	Cornwall Aces	AHL	53	21	13	34	154										8	1	3	4	22				
1996-97	**Colorado**	**NHL**	**9**	**1**	**2**	**3**	**23**	**0**	**0**	**0**	**7**	**14.3**	**1**												
	Boston	**NHL**	**40**	**7**	**10**	**17**	**49**	**0**	**0**	**0**	**76**	**9.2**	**-6**												
	Providence Bruins	AHL	2	2	1	3	2										10	3	4	7	16				
1997-98	**Boston**	**NHL**	**28**	**1**	**5**	**6**	**7**	**0**	**0**	**0**	**26**	**3.8**	**3**				**1**	**0**	**0**	**0**	**0**	**0**	**0**	**0**	
	Providence Bruins	AHL	42	18	10	28	146																		
1998-99	**Boston**	**NHL**	**22**	**3**	**3**	**6**	**17**	**0**	**0**	**0**	**32**	**9.4**	**0**	**3**	**0.0**	**10:04**	**8**	**1**	**1**	**2**	**8**	**1**	**0**	**1**	**13:41**
	Providence Bruins	AHL	48	31	22	53	89										11	7	1	8	19				
99-2000	**Boston**	**NHL**	**40**	**1**	**3**	**4**	**18**	**0**	**0**	**0**	**67**	**1.5**	**-6**	**14**	**42.9**	**10:09**									
	Providence Bruins	AHL	17	5	5	10	45										9	2	3	5	38				
2000-01	**Phoenix**	**NHL**	**70**	**18**	**13**	**31**	**92**	**2**	**0**	**3**	**123**	**14.6**	**3**	**13**	**46.2**	**11:26**									
2001-02	**Phoenix**	**NHL**	**47**	**7**	**12**	**19**	**46**	**1**	**0**	**0**	**100**	**7.0**	**4**	**15**	**53.3**	**12:51**	**4**	**0**	**0**	**0**	**12**	**0**	**0**	**0**	**12:03**
	Springfield	AHL	2	2	1	3	2																		
2002-03	**Phoenix**	**NHL**	**31**	**6**	**8**	**14**	**26**	**0**	**0**	**3**	**92**	**6.5**	**1**	**35**	**54.3**	**12:11**									
2003-04	**Phoenix**	**NHL**	**35**	**1**	**3**	**4**	**16**	**0**	**0**	**0**	**41**	**2.4**	**-3**	**44**	**31.8**	**9:51**									
	Pittsburgh	**NHL**	**19**	**5**	**1**	**6**	**31**	**2**	**0**	**0**	**35**	**14.3**	**0**	**2**	**0.0**	**11:21**									
	NHL Totals		**348**	**51**	**60**	**111**	**331**	**5**	**0**	**6**	**605**	**8.4**		**126**	**42.1**	**11:15**	**13**	**1**	**1**	**2**	**20**	**1**	**0**	**1**	**13:08**

WCHA Rookie of the Year (1994) • AHL First All-Star Team (1999)

Traded to **Quebec** by **Toronto** with Wendel Clark, Sylvain Lefebvre and Toronto's 1st round choice (Jeffrey Kealty) in 1994 Entry Draft for Mats Sundin, Garth Butcher, Todd Warriner and Philadelphia's 1st round choice (previously acquired, later traded to Washington – Washington selected Nolan Baumgartner) in 1994 Entry Draft, June 28, 1994. Transferred to **Colorado** after **Quebec** franchise relocated, June 21, 1995. Traded to **Boston** by **Colorado** with Anders Myrvold for Boston's 1st round choice (Robyn Regehr) in 1998 Entry Draft, November 22, 1996. Signed as a free agent by **Phoenix**, July 7, 2000. • Missed majority of 2002-03 season recovering from eye injury suffered in game vs. Washington, December 13, 2002. Traded to **Pittsburgh** by **Phoenix** for future considerations, February 22, 2004.

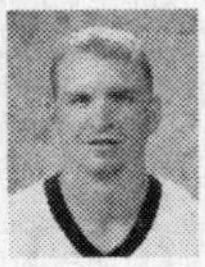

WILSON, Mike
(WIHL-suhn, MIGHK)

Defense. Shoots left. 6'6", 229 lbs. Born, Brampton, Ont., February 26, 1975. Vancouver's 1st choice, 20th overall, in 1993 Entry Draft.

Season	Club	League	GP	G	A	Pts	PIM	PP	SH	GW	S	%	+/-	TF	F%	Min	Playoffs GP	G	A	Pts	PIM	PP	SH	GW	Min
1991-92	Georgetown	OJHL-B	41	9	13	22	65																		
1992-93	Sudbury Wolves	OHL	53	6	7	13	58										14	1	1	2	2				
1993-94	Sudbury Wolves	OHL	60	4	22	26	62										9	1	3	4	8				
1994-95	Sudbury Wolves	OHL	64	13	34	47	46										18	1	8	9	10				
1995-96	**Buffalo**	**NHL**	**58**	**4**	**8**	**12**	**41**	**1**	**0**	**1**	**52**	**7.7**	**13**												
	Rochester	AHL	15	0	5	5	38																		
1996-97	**Buffalo**	**NHL**	**77**	**2**	**9**	**11**	**51**	**0**	**0**	**1**	**57**	**3.5**	**13**				**10**	**0**	**1**	**1**	**2**	**0**	**0**	**0**	
1997-98	**Buffalo**	**NHL**	**66**	**4**	**4**	**8**	**48**	**0**	**0**	**1**	**52**	**7.7**	**13**				**15**	**0**	**1**	**1**	**13**	**0**	**0**	**0**	
1998-99	Las Vegas	IHL	6	3	1	4	6																		
	Buffalo	**NHL**	**30**	**1**	**2**	**3**	**47**	**0**	**0**	**1**	**40**	**2.5**	**10**	**0**	**0.0**	**16:40**									
	Florida	**NHL**	**4**	**0**	**0**	**0**	**0**	**0**	**0**	**0**	**8**	**0.0**	**2**	**0**	**0.0**	**19:23**									
99-2000	**Florida**	**NHL**	**60**	**4**	**16**	**20**	**35**	**0**	**0**	**2**	**65**	**6.2**	**10**	**0**	**0.0**	**18:07**	**4**	**0**	**0**	**0**	**0**	**0**	**0**	**0**	**18:52**
2000-01	**Florida**	**NHL**	**19**	**0**	**1**	**1**	**25**	**0**	**0**	**0**	**26**	**0.0**	**-7**	**0**	**0.0**	**13:20**									
	Louisville Panthers	AHL	4	0	2	2	5																		
2001-02	Wilkes-Barre	AHL	46	3	9	12	59																		
	Pittsburgh	**NHL**	**21**	**1**	**1**	**2**	**17**	**0**	**0**	**0**	**14**	**7.1**	**-12**	**0**	**0.0**	**14:51**									
2002-03	Wilkes-Barre	AHL	45	4	5	9	89																		
	NY Rangers	**NHL**	**1**	**0**	**0**	**0**	**0**	**0**	**0**	**0**	**0**	**0.0**	**1**	**0**	**0.0**	**12:41**									
	Hartford	AHL	5	1	2	3	5																		
2003-04	Springfield	AHL	45	3	8	11	28																		
	NHL Totals		**336**	**16**	**41**	**57**	**264**	**1**	**0**	**6**	**314**	**5.1**		**0**	**0.0**	**16:37**	**29**	**0**	**2**	**2**	**15**	**0**	**0**	**0**	**18:52**

OHL All-Rookie Team (1993)

Traded to **Buffalo** by **Vancouver** with Michael Peca and Vancouver's 1st round choice (Jay McKee) in 1995 Entry Draft for Alexander Mogilny and Buffalo's 5th round choice (Todd Norman) in 1995 Entry Draft, July 8, 1995. Traded to **Florida** by **Buffalo** for Rhett Warrener and Florida's 5th round choice (Ryan Miller) in 1999 Entry Draft, March 23, 1999. • Missed majority of 2000-01 season recovering from shoulder injury suffered in game vs. New Jersey, October 25, 2000. Signed as a free agent by **Pittsburgh**, July 5, 2001. Traded to **NY Rangers** by **Pittsburgh** with Alex Kovalev, Janne Laukkanen and Dan LaCouture for Joel Bouchard, Richard Lintner, Rico Fata, Mikael Samuelsson and future considerations, February 10, 2003. Signed as a free agent by **Phoenix**, September 23, 2003.

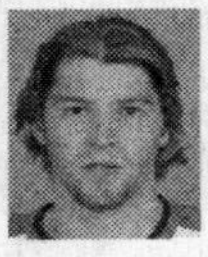

WISEMAN, Chad
(WIGHZ-man, CHAD) **NYR**

Left wing. Shoots left. 6', 190 lbs. Born, Burlington, Ont., March 25, 1981. San Jose's 8th choice, 246th overall, in 2000 Entry Draft.

Season	Club	League	GP	G	A	Pts	PIM	PP	SH	GW	S	%	+/-	TF	F%	Min	Playoffs GP	G	A	Pts	PIM	PP	SH	GW	Min
1997-98	Burlington	OPJHL	50	28	36	64	31																		
1998-99	Mississauga	OHL	64	11	25	36	29																		
99-2000	Mississauga	OHL	68	23	45	68	53																		
2000-01	Mississauga	OHL	30	15	29	44	22																		
	Plymouth Whalers	OHL	32	11	16	27	12										19	12	8	20	22				
2001-02	Cleveland Barons	AHL	76	21	29	50	61																		
2002-03	**San Jose**	**NHL**	**4**	**0**	**0**	**0**	**4**	**0**	**0**	**0**	**1**	**0.0**	**-2**	**0**	**0.0**	**9:19**									
	Cleveland Barons	AHL	77	17	35	52	44																		
2003-04	**NY Rangers**	**NHL**	**4**	**1**	**0**	**1**	**0**	**0**	**0**	**0**	**3**	**33.3**	**-1**	**0**	**0.0**	**8:49**									
	Hartford	AHL	62	25	27	52	45										15	5	6	11	12				
	NHL Totals		**8**	**1**	**0**	**1**	**4**	**0**	**0**	**0**	**4**	**25.0**		**0**	**0.0**	**9:04**									

Traded to **NY Rangers** by **San Jose** for Nils Ekman, August 12, 2003.

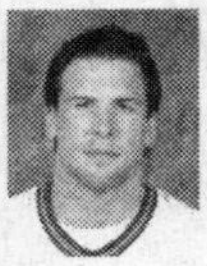

WITT, Brendan
(WIHT, BREHN-duhn) **WSH.**

Defense. Shoots left. 6'2", 219 lbs. Born, Humboldt, Sask., February 20, 1975. Washington's 1st choice, 11th overall, in 1993 Entry Draft.

Season	Club	League	GP	G	A	Pts	PIM	PP	SH	GW	S	%	+/-	TF	F%	Min	Playoffs GP	G	A	Pts	PIM	PP	SH	GW	Min
1990-91	Saskatoon Blazers	SMHL	31	5	13	18	42																		
	Seattle	WHL															1	0	0	0	0				
1991-92	Seattle	WHL	67	3	9	12	212										15	1	1	2	84				
1992-93	Seattle	WHL	70	2	26	28	239										5	1	2	3	30				
1993-94	Seattle	WHL	56	8	31	39	235										9	3	8	11	23				
1994-95			DID NOT PLAY																						
1995-96	**Washington**	**NHL**	**48**	**2**	**3**	**5**	**85**	**0**	**0**	**1**	**44**	**4.5**	**-4**												
1996-97	**Washington**	**NHL**	**44**	**3**	**2**	**5**	**88**	**0**	**0**	**0**	**41**	**7.3**	**-20**												
	Portland Pirates	AHL	30	2	4	6	56										5	1	0	1	30				
1997-98	**Washington**	**NHL**	**64**	**1**	**7**	**8**	**112**	**0**	**0**	**0**	**68**	**1.5**	**-11**				**16**	**1**	**0**	**1**	**14**	**0**	**0**	**0**	
1998-99	**Washington**	**NHL**	**54**	**2**	**5**	**7**	**87**	**0**	**0**	**0**	**51**	**3.9**	**-6**	**0**	**0.0**	**15:50**									
99-2000	**Washington**	**NHL**	**77**	**1**	**7**	**8**	**114**	**0**	**0**	**0**	**64**	**1.6**	**5**	**2**	**50.0**	**20:56**	**3**	**0**	**0**	**0**	**0**	**0**	**0**	**0**	**20:52**
2000-01	**Washington**	**NHL**	**72**	**3**	**3**	**6**	**101**	**0**	**0**	**0**	**87**	**3.4**	**2**	**1**	**100.0**	**20:41**	**6**	**2**	**0**	**2**	**12**	**1**	**0**	**0**	**20:50**
2001-02	**Washington**	**NHL**	**68**	**3**	**7**	**10**	**78**	**0**	**0**	**0**	**81**	**3.7**	**-1**	**1**	**100.0**	**20:03**									
2002-03	**Washington**	**NHL**	**69**	**2**	**9**	**11**	**106**	**0**	**0**	**0**	**80**	**2.5**	**12**	**0**	**0.0**	**20:55**	**6**	**1**	**0**	**1**	**0**	**0**	**0**	**0**	**23:33**
2003-04	**Washington**	**NHL**	**72**	**2**	**10**	**12**	**123**	**0**	**0**	**0**	**91**	**2.2**	**-22**	**3**	**66.7**	**22:48**									
	NHL Totals		**568**	**19**	**53**	**72**	**894**	**0**	**0**	**1**	**607**	**3.1**		**7**	**71.4**	**20:24**	**31**	**4**	**0**	**4**	**26**	**1**	**0**	**0**	**21:55**

WHL West First All-Star Team (1993, 1994) • Canadian Major Junior First All-Star Team (1994)

• Missed entire 1994-95 season after failing to come to contract terms with **Washington**.

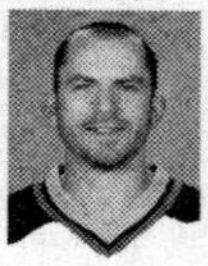

WOOLLEY, Jason

(WU-lee, JAY-suhn) **DET.**

Defense. Shoots left. 6', 203 lbs. Born, Toronto, Ont., July 27, 1969. Washington's 4th choice, 61st overall, in 1989 Entry Draft.

			Regular Season														Playoffs								
Season	Club	League	GP	G	A	Pts	PIM	PP	SH	GW	S	%	+/-	TF	F%	Min	GP	G	A	Pts	PIM	PP	SH	GW	Min
1986-87	St. Michael's B	OJHL-B	35	13	22	35	40																		
1987-88	St. Michael's B	OJHL-B	31	19	37	56	22																		
1988-89	Michigan State	CCHA	47	12	25	37	26																		
1989-90	Michigan State	CCHA	45	10	38	48	26																		
1990-91	Michigan State	CCHA	40	15	44	59	24																		
1991-92	Team Canada	Nat-Tm	60	14	30	44	36																		
	Canada	Olympics	8	0	5	5	4																		
	Washington	**NHL**	**1**	**0**	**0**	**0**	**0**	**0**	**0**	**0**	**2**	**0.0**	**1**												
	Baltimore	AHL	15	1	10	11	6																		
1992-93	**Washington**	**NHL**	**26**	**0**	**2**	**2**	**10**	**0**	**0**	**0**	**11**	**0.0**	**3**												
	Baltimore	AHL	29	14	27	41	22										1	0	2	2	0				
1993-94	**Washington**	**NHL**	**10**	**1**	**2**	**3**	**4**	**0**	**0**	**0**	**15**	**6.7**	**2**				**4**	**1**	**0**	**1**	**4**	**0**	**0**	**1**	
	Portland Pirates	AHL	41	12	29	41	14										9	2	2	4	4				
1994-95	Detroit Vipers	IHL	48	8	28	36	38																		
	Florida	**NHL**	**34**	**4**	**9**	**13**	**18**	**1**	**0**	**0**	**76**	**5.3**	**–1**												
1995-96	**Florida**	**NHL**	**52**	**6**	**28**	**34**	**32**	**3**	**0**	**0**	**98**	**6.1**	**–9**				**13**	**2**	**6**	**8**	**14**	**1**	**0**	**1**	
1996-97	**Florida**	**NHL**	**3**	**0**	**0**	**0**	**2**	**0**	**0**	**0**	**7**	**0.0**	**1**												
	Pittsburgh	**NHL**	**57**	**6**	**30**	**36**	**28**	**2**	**0**	**1**	**79**	**7.6**	**3**				**5**	**0**	**3**	**3**	**0**	**0**	**0**	**0**	
1997-98	**Buffalo**	**NHL**	**71**	**9**	**26**	**35**	**35**	**3**	**0**	**2**	**129**	**7.0**	**8**				**15**	**2**	**9**	**11**	**12**	**1**	**0**	**1**	
1998-99	**Buffalo**	**NHL**	**80**	**10**	**33**	**43**	**62**	**4**	**0**	**2**	**154**	**6.5**	**16**	**0**	**0.0**	**18:43**	**21**	**4**	**11**	**15**	**10**	**2**	**0**	**1**	**17:54**
99-2000	**Buffalo**	**NHL**	**74**	**8**	**25**	**33**	**52**	**2**	**0**	**2**	**113**	**7.1**	**14**	**0**	**0.0**	**17:51**	**5**	**0**	**2**	**2**	**2**	**0**	**0**	**0**	**18:06**
2000-01	**Buffalo**	**NHL**	**67**	**5**	**18**	**23**	**46**	**4**	**0**	**3**	**92**	**5.4**	**0**	**0**	**0.0**	**17:22**	**8**	**1**	**5**	**6**	**2**	**0**	**0**	**1**	**18:30**
2001-02	**Buffalo**	**NHL**	**59**	**8**	**20**	**28**	**34**	**6**	**0**	**2**	**90**	**8.9**	**–6**	**0**	**0.0**	**17:11**									
2002-03	**Buffalo**	**NHL**	**14**	**0**	**3**	**3**	**29**	**0**	**0**	**0**	**29**	**0.0**	**–1**	**0**	**0.0**	**15:59**									
	Detroit	**NHL**	**62**	**6**	**17**	**23**	**22**	**1**	**0**	**2**	**52**	**11.5**	**12**	**0**	**0.0**	**16:59**	**4**	**1**	**0**	**1**	**0**	**0**	**0**	**0**	**15:25**
2003-04	**Detroit**	**NHL**	**55**	**4**	**15**	**19**	**28**	**0**	**0**	**1**	**60**	**6.7**	**19**	**2**	**50.0**	**15:42**	**4**	**0**	**0**	**0**	**0**	**0**	**0**	**0**	**17:00**
	NHL Totals		**665**	**67**	**228**	**295**	**402**	**26**	**0**	**15**	**1007**	**6.7**		**2**	**50.0**	**17:22**	**79**	**11**	**36**	**47**	**44**	**4**	**0**	**5**	**17:43**

CCHA First All-Star Team (1991) • NCAA West First All-American Team (1991)

Signed as a free agent by **Florida**, February 15, 1995. Traded to **Pittsburgh** by **Florida** with Stu Barnes for Chris Wells, November 19, 1996. Traded to **Buffalo** by **Pittsburgh** for Buffalo's 5th round choice (Robert Scuderi) in 1998 Entry Draft, September 24, 1997. Traded to **Detroit** by **Buffalo** for future considerations, November 16, 2002.

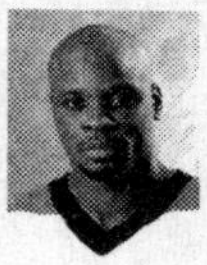

WORRELL, Peter

(woh-REHL, PEE-tuhr) **COL.**

Left wing. Shoots left. 6'6", 235 lbs. Born, Pierrefonds, Que., August 18, 1977. Florida's 7th choice, 166th overall, in 1995 Entry Draft.

1993-94	Lac St-Louis Lions	QAAA	1	0	0	0	0										1	0	0	0	0				
1994-95	Hull Olympiques	QMJHL	56	1	8	9	243										21	0	1	1	91				
1995-96	Hull Olympiques	QMJHL	63	23	36	59	464										18	11	8	19	81				
1996-97	Hull Olympiques	QMJHL	62	17	46	63	437										14	3	13	16	83				
1997-98	**Florida**	**NHL**	**19**	**0**	**0**	**0**	**153**	**0**	**0**	**0**	**15**	**0.0**	**–4**												
	New Haven	AHL	50	15	12	27	309										1	0	1	1	6				
1998-99	**Florida**	**NHL**	**62**	**4**	**5**	**9**	**258**	**0**	**0**	**2**	**50**	**8.0**	**0**	**0**	**0.0**	**6:15**									
	New Haven	AHL	10	3	1	4	65																		
99-2000	**Florida**	**NHL**	**48**	**3**	**6**	**9**	**169**	**2**	**0**	**1**	**45**	**6.7**	**–7**	**1**	**100.0**	**8:25**	**4**	**1**	**0**	**1**	**8**	**0**	**0**	**0**	**11:17**
2000-01	**Florida**	**NHL**	**71**	**3**	**7**	**10**	**248**	**0**	**0**	**0**	**86**	**3.5**	**–10**	**3**	**33.3**	**9:28**									
2001-02	**Florida**	**NHL**	**79**	**4**	**5**	**9**	***354**	**0**	**0**	**1**	**65**	**6.2**	**–15**	**9**	**0.0**	**8:45**									
2002-03	**Florida**	**NHL**	**63**	**2**	**3**	**5**	**193**	**0**	**0**	**0**	**52**	**3.8**	**–14**	**13**	**15.4**	**9:16**									
2003-04	**Colorado**	**NHL**	**49**	**3**	**1**	**4**	**179**	**0**	**0**	**0**	**32**	**9.4**	**2**	**5**	**0.0**	**5:55**									
	NHL Totals		**391**	**19**	**27**	**46**	**1554**	**2**	**0**	**4**	**345**	**5.5**		**31**	**12.9**	**8:08**	**4**	**1**	**0**	**1**	**8**	**0**	**0**	**0**	**11:17**

Traded to **Colorado** by **Florida** with Florida's 2nd round choice (later traded to NY Rangers – later traded back to Florida – Florida selected David Shantz) in 2004 Entry Draft for Eric Messier and Vaclav Nedorost, July 18, 2003.

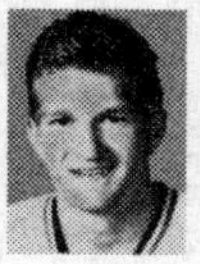

WOTTON, Mark

(WAH-tuhn, MAHRK)

Defense. Shoots left. 6'1", 195 lbs. Born, Foxwarren, Man., November 16, 1973. Vancouver's 11th choice, 237th overall, in 1992 Entry Draft.

1988-89	Foxwarren Blades	MAHA	60	10	30	40	70																		
1989-90	Saskatoon Blades	WHL	51	2	3	5	31										7	1	1	2	15				
1990-91	Saskatoon Blades	WHL	45	4	11	15	37																		
1991-92	Saskatoon Blades	WHL	64	11	25	36	62										21	2	6	8	22				
1992-93	Saskatoon Blades	WHL	71	15	51	66	90										9	6	5	11	18				
1993-94	Saskatoon Blades	WHL	65	12	34	46	108										16	3	12	15	32				
1994-95	Syracuse Crunch	AHL	75	12	29	41	50																		
	Vancouver	**NHL**	**1**	**0**	**0**	**0**	**0**	**0**	**0**	**0**	**2**	**0.0**	**1**				**5**	**0**	**0**	**0**	**4**	**0**	**0**	**0**	
1995-96	Syracuse Crunch	AHL	80	10	35	45	96										15	1	12	13	20				
1996-97	**Vancouver**	**NHL**	**36**	**3**	**6**	**9**	**19**	**0**	**1**	**0**	**41**	**7.3**	**8**												
	Syracuse Crunch	AHL	27	2	8	10	25										2	0	0	0	4				
1997-98	**Vancouver**	**NHL**	**5**	**0**	**0**	**0**	**6**	**0**	**0**	**0**	**3**	**0.0**	**–2**												
	Syracuse Crunch	AHL	56	12	21	33	80										5	0	0	0	12				
1998-99	Syracuse Crunch	AHL	72	4	31	35	74																		
99-2000	Michigan	IHL	70	3	7	10	72																		
2000-01	**Dallas**	**NHL**	**1**	**0**	**0**	**0**	**0**	**0**	**0**	**0**	**0**	**0.0**	**0**	**0**	**0.0**	**13:45**									
	Utah Grizzlies	IHL	63	2	2	4	64																		
2001-02	Utah Grizzlies	AHL	57	9	18	27	68										4	0	1	1	6				
2002-03	Utah Grizzlies	AHL	69	8	26	34	68										2	0	0	0	2				
2003-04	Utah Grizzlies	AHL	23	1	3	4	25																		
	NHL Totals		**43**	**3**	**6**	**9**	**25**	**0**	**1**	**0**	**46**	**6.5**		**0**	**0.0**	**13:45**	**5**	**0**	**0**	**0**	**4**	**0**	**0**	**0**	

WHL East Second All-Star Team (1994)

Signed as a free agent by **Dallas**, July 9, 1999. • Missed majority of 2003-04 season recovering from knee injury suffered in game vs. Cincinnati (AHL), December 6, 2003.

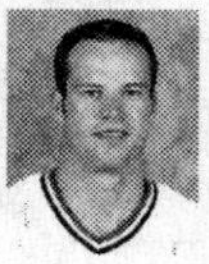

WRIGHT, Jamie

(RIGHT, JAY-mee) **EDM.**

Left wing. Shoots left. 6', 195 lbs. Born, Kitchener, Ont., May 13, 1976. Dallas' 3rd choice, 98th overall, in 1994 Entry Draft.

1991-92	Elmira	OJHL-B	44	17	11	28	46																		
1992-93	Elmira	OJHL-B	47	22	32	54	52																		
1993-94	Guelph Storm	OHL	65	17	15	32	34										8	2	1	3	10				
1994-95	Guelph Storm	OHL	65	43	39	82	36										14	6	8	14	6				
1995-96	Guelph Storm	OHL	55	30	36	66	45										16	10	12	22	35				
1996-97	Michigan	IHL	60	6	8	14	34										1	0	0	0	0				
1997-98	**Dallas**	**NHL**	**21**	**4**	**2**	**6**	**2**	**0**	**0**	**2**	**15**	**26.7**	**8**				**5**	**0**	**0**	**0**	**0**	**0**	**0**	**0**	
	Michigan	IHL	53	15	11	26	31																		
1998-99	**Dallas**	**NHL**	**11**	**0**	**0**	**0**	**0**	**0**	**0**	**0**	**10**	**0.0**	**–3**	**0**	**0.0**	**7:37**									
	Michigan	IHL	64	16	15	31	92										2	0	0	0	2				
99-2000	**Dallas**	**NHL**	**23**	**1**	**4**	**5**	**16**	**0**	**0**	**0**	**15**	**6.7**	**4**	**2**	**50.0**	**9:50**									
	Michigan	IHL	49	12	4	16	64																		
2000-01	**Dallas**	**NHL**	**2**	**1**	**0**	**1**	**0**	**0**	**0**	**0**	**4**	**25.0**	**–3**	**1**	**0.0**	**10:45**									
	Utah Grizzlies	IHL	74	25	27	52	126																		
2001-02	**Calgary**	**NHL**	**44**	**4**	**12**	**16**	**20**	**0**	**0**	**0**	**64**	**6.3**	**6**	**10**	**60.0**	**13:44**									
	Saint John Flames	AHL	34	11	13	24	34																		
2002-03	**Calgary**	**NHL**	**19**	**2**	**2**	**4**	**12**	**0**	**0**	**0**	**16**	**12.5**	**1**	**14**	**42.9**	**11:43**									
	Saint John Flames	AHL	3	2	1	3	0																		
	Philadelphia	**NHL**	**4**	**0**	**0**	**0**	**4**	**0**	**0**	**0**	**2**	**0.0**	**–1**	**0**	**0.0**	**9:27**									
	Philadelphia	AHL	33	10	14	24	31																		
2003-04	Toronto	AHL	78	25	30	55	101																		
	NHL Totals		**124**	**12**	**20**	**32**	**54**	**0**	**0**	**2**	**126**	**9.5**		**27**	**48.1**	**11:37**	**5**	**0**	**0**	**0**	**0**	**0**	**0**	**0**	

Signed as a free agent by **Calgary**, August 2, 2001. Traded to **Philadelphia** by **Calgary** for future considerations, January 22, 2003. Signed as a free agent by **Edmonton**, August 8, 2003.

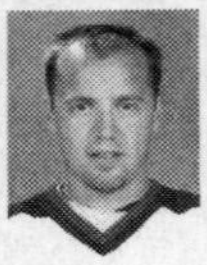

WRIGHT, Tyler

(RIGHT, TIGH-luhr) **CBJ**

Center. Shoots right. 6', 190 lbs. Born, Kamsack, Sask., April 6, 1973. Edmonton's 1st choice, 12th overall, in 1991 Entry Draft.

			Regular Season														Playoffs								
Season	Club	League	GP	G	A	Pts	PIM	PP	SH	GW	S	%	+/-	TF	F%	Min	GP	G	A	Pts	PIM	PP	SH	GW	Min
1988-89	Swift Current	SMHL	36	20	13	33	102	....	....	....	....	....	....	....	....	....	....	....	....	....	....	....	....	....	....
1989-90	Swift Current	WHL	67	14	18	32	119	....	....	....	....	....	....	....	....	....	4	0	0	0	12	....	....	....	....
1990-91	Swift Current	WHL	66	41	51	92	157	....	....	....	....	....	....	....	....	....	3	0	0	0	6	....	....	....	....
1991-92	Swift Current	WHL	63	36	46	82	185	....	....	....	....	....	....	....	....	....	8	2	5	7	16	....	....	....	....
1992-93	Swift Current	WHL	37	24	41	65	76	....	....	....	....	....	....	....	....	....	17	9	17	26	*49	....	....	....	....
	Edmonton	NHL	7	1	1	2	19	0	0	0	7	14.3	–4	....	....	....	....	....	....	....	....	....	....	....	....
1993-94	Edmonton	NHL	5	0	0	0	4	0	0	0	2	0.0	–3	....	....	....	....	....	....	....	....	....	....	....	....
	Cape Breton	AHL	65	14	27	41	160	....	....	....	....	....	....	....	....	....	5	2	0	2	11	....	....	....	....
1994-95	Cape Breton	AHL	70	16	15	31	184	....	....	....	....	....	....	....	....	....	....	....	....	....	....	....	....	....	....
	Edmonton	NHL	6	1	0	1	14	0	0	0	6	16.7	1	....	....	....	....	....	....	....	....	....	....	....	....
1995-96	Edmonton	NHL	23	1	0	1	33	0	0	0	18	5.6	–7	....	....	....	....	....	....	....	....	....	....	....	....
	Cape Breton	AHL	31	6	12	18	158	....	....	....	....	....	....	....	....	....	....	....	....	....	....	....	....	....	....
1996-97	Pittsburgh	NHL	45	2	2	4	70	0	0	2	30	6.7	–7	....	....	....	....	....	....	....	....	....	....	....	....
	Cleveland	IHL	10	4	3	7	34	....	....	....	....	....	....	....	....	....	14	4	2	6	44	....	....	....	....
1997-98	Pittsburgh	NHL	82	3	4	7	112	1	0	0	46	6.5	–3	....	....	....	6	0	1	1	4	0	0	0	....
1998-99	Pittsburgh	NHL	61	0	0	0	90	0	0	0	16	0.0	–2	122	46.7	3:46	13	0	0	0	19	0	0	0	3:22
99-2000	Pittsburgh	NHL	50	12	10	22	45	0	0	1	68	17.6	4	698	47.1	13:24	11	3	1	4	17	0	0	0	16:12
	Wilkes-Barre	AHL	25	5	15	20	86	....	....	....	....	....	....	....	....	....	....	....	....	....	....	....	....	....	....
2000-01	Columbus	NHL	76	16	16	32	140	4	1	2	141	11.3	–9	999	45.1	17:41	....	....	....	....	....	....	....	....	....
2001-02	Columbus	NHL	77	13	11	24	100	4	0	1	120	10.8	–40	1036	43.9	17:12	....	....	....	....	....	....	....	....	....
2002-03	Columbus	NHL	70	19	11	30	113	3	2	3	108	17.6	–25	760	41.3	16:07	....	....	....	....	....	....	....	....	....
2003-04	Columbus	NHL	68	9	9	18	63	2	0	3	109	8.3	–19	316	43.7	14:34	....	....	....	....	....	....	....	....	....
	NHL Totals		570	77	64	141	803	14	3	12	671	11.5		3931	44.3	14:09	30	3	2	5	40	0	0	0	9:15

Traded to **Pittsburgh** by **Edmonton** for Pittsburgh's 7th round choice (Brandon Lafrance) in 1996 Entry Draft, June 22, 1996. Selected by **Columbus** from **Pittsburgh** in Expansion Draft, June 23, 2000.

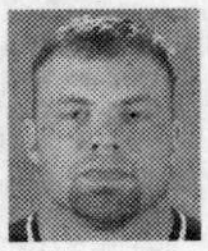

YABLONSKI, Jeremy

(ya-BLAWN-skee, JAIR-eh-mee) **NSH.**

Left wing. Shoots right. 6', 232 lbs. Born, Meadow Lake, Sask., March 21, 1980.

Season	Club	League	GP	G	A	Pts	PIM	PP	SH	GW	S	%	+/-	TF	F%	Min	GP	G	A	Pts	PIM	PP	SH	GW	Min
1996-97	Beardy's Blackhawks		SMHL	38	7	3	10	284	....	....	....	....	....	....	....	....	....	....	....	....	....	....	....	....	....
....																									
1997-98	Edmonton Ice	WHL	47	3	0	3	143	....	....	....	....	....	....	....	....	....	....	....	....	....	....	....	....	....	....
1998-99	Kootenay Ice	WHL	27	1	1	2	77	....	....	....	....	....	....	....	....	....	....	....	....	....	....	....	....	....	....
99-2000	Kootenay Ice	WHL	DID NOT PLAY – INJURED																						
2000-01	Phoenix	WCHL	44	2	1	3	169	....	....	....	....	....	....	....	....	....	....	....	....	....	....	....	....	....	....
2001-02	Idaho Steelheads	WCHL	69	2	1	3	303	....	....	....	....	....	....	....	....	....	....	....	....	....	....	....	....	....	....
2002-03	Peoria Riverman	ECHL	24	1	2	3	154	....	....	....	....	....	....	....	....	....	....	....	....	....	....	....	....	....	....
	Cincinnati	AHL	9	0	0	0	42	....	....	....	....	....	....	....	....	....	....	....	....	....	....	....	....	....	....
	Worcester IceCats	AHL	20	1	0	1	50	....	....	....	....	....	....	....	....	....	....	....	....	....	....	....	....	....	....
2003-04	Worcester IceCats	AHL	6	0	0	0	19	....	....	....	....	....	....	....	....	....	....	....	....	....	....	....	....	....	....
	St. Louis	NHL	1	0	0	0	5	0	0	0	1	0.0	–1	0	0.0	7:53	....	....	....	....	....	....	....	....	....
	Peoria Rivermen	ECHL	13	0	2	2	62	....	....	....	....	....	....	....	....	....	....	....	....	....	....	....	....	....	....
	Milwaukee	AHL	2	0	0	0	11	....	....	....	....	....	....	....	....	....	....	....	....	....	....	....	....	....	....
	NHL Totals		1	0	0	0	5	0	0	0	1	0.0		0	0.0	7:53	....	....	....	....	....	....	....	....	....

• Missed majority of 1998-99 season and entire 1999-2000 season recovering from head injury suffered in practice, January 3, 1999. Signed as a free agent by **Worcester** (AHL), July 17, 2003. Signed as a free agent by **St. Louis**, December 30, 2003. Claimed on waivers by **Nashville** from **St. Louis**, January 30, 2004.

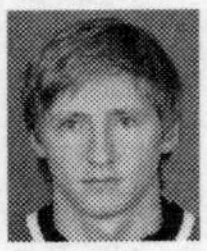

YAKUBOV, Mikhail

(yuh-KOO-bahf, mih-kigh-EHL) **CHI.**

Center. Shoots left. 6'3", 202 lbs. Born, Barnaul, USSR, February 16, 1982. Chicago's 1st choice, 10th overall, in 2000 Entry Draft.

Season	Club	League	GP	G	A	Pts	PIM	PP	SH	GW	S	%	+/-	TF	F%	Min	GP	G	A	Pts	PIM	PP	SH	GW	Min
1997-98	Lada Togliatti 2	Russia-3	7	0	0	0	0	....	....	....	....	....	....	....	....	....	....	....	....	....	....	....	....	....	....
1998-99	Lada Togliatti 2	Russia-4	38	11	4	15	32	....	....	....	....	....	....	....	....	....	....	....	....	....	....	....	....	....	....
99-2000	Lada Togliatti 2	Russia-3	26	12	19	31	14	....	....	....	....	....	....	....	....	....	....	....	....	....	....	....	....	....	....
2000-01	Lada Togliatti	Russia	25	0	0	0	4	....	....	....	....	....	....	....	....	....	4	0	0	0	0	....	....	....	....
2001-02	Red Deer Rebels	WHL	71	32	57	89	54	....	....	....	....	....	....	....	....	....	23	14	9	23	28	....	....	....	....
2002-03	Norfolk Admirals	AHL	62	6	5	11	36	....	....	....	....	....	....	....	....	....	9	0	0	0	8	....	....	....	....
2003-04	Chicago	NHL	30	1	7	8	8	0	0	0	32	3.1	–12	337	45.7	13:44	....	....	....	....	....	....	....	....	....
	Norfolk Admirals	AHL	51	9	18	27	22	....	....	....	....	....	....	....	....	....	8	0	3	3	2	....	....	....	....
	NHL Totals		30	1	7	8	8	0	0	0	32	3.1		337	45.7	13:44	....	....	....	....	....	....	....	....	....

WHL East Second All-Star Team (2002)

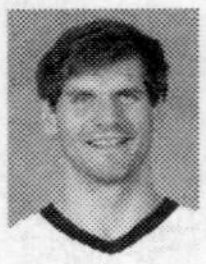

YASHIN, Alexei

(YAH-shin, al-EHX-ay) **NYI**

Center. Shoots right. 6'3", 225 lbs. Born, Sverdlovsk, USSR, November 5, 1973. Ottawa's 1st choice, 2nd overall, in 1992 Entry Draft.

Season	Club	League	GP	G	A	Pts	PIM	PP	SH	GW	S	%	+/-	TF	F%	Min	GP	G	A	Pts	PIM	PP	SH	GW	Min
1990-91	Sverdlovsk	USSR	26	2	1	3	10	....	....	....	....	....	....	....	....	....	....	....	....	....	....	....	....	....	....
1991-92	Dynamo Moscow	CIS	35	7	5	12	19	....	....	....	....	....	....	....	....	....	....	....	....	....	....	....	....	....	....
1992-93	Dynamo Moscow	CIS	27	10	12	22	18	....	....	....	....	....	....	....	....	....	10	7	3	10	18	....	....	....	....
1993-94	Ottawa	NHL	83	30	49	79	22	11	2	3	232	12.9	–49	....	....	....	....	....	....	....	....	....	....	....	....
1994-95	Las Vegas	IHL	24	15	20	35	32	....	....	....	....	....	....	....	....	....	....	....	....	....	....	....	....	....	....
	Ottawa	NHL	47	21	23	44	20	11	0	1	154	13.6	–20	....	....	....	....	....	....	....	....	....	....	....	....
1995-96	CSKA Moscow	CIS	4	2	2	4	4	....	....	....	....	....	....	....	....	....	....	....	....	....	....	....	....	....	....
	Ottawa	NHL	46	15	24	39	28	8	0	1	143	10.5	–15	....	....	....	....	....	....	....	....	....	....	....	....
1996-97	Ottawa	NHL	82	35	40	75	44	10	0	5	291	12.0	–7	....	....	....	7	1	5	6	2	1	0	0	....
1997-98	Ottawa	NHL	82	33	39	72	24	5	0	6	291	11.3	6	....	....	....	11	5	3	8	8	3	0	2	....
	Russia	Olympics	6	3	3	6	0	....	....	....	....	....	....	....	....	....	....	....	....	....	....	....	....	....	....
1998-99	Ottawa	NHL	82	44	50	94	54	19	0	5	337	13.1	16	1428	41.9	22:05	4	0	0	0	10	0	0	0	26:06
99-2000	Ottawa	NHL	DID NOT PLAY – SUSPENDED																						
2000-01	Ottawa	NHL	82	40	48	88	30	13	2	10	263	15.2	10	1414	43.1	20:24	4	0	1	1	0	0	0	0	24:53
2001-02	NY Islanders	NHL	78	32	43	75	25	15	0	5	239	13.4	–3	828	46.7	20:37	7	3	4	7	2	1	0	0	21:54
	Russia	Olympics	6	1	1	2	0	....	....	....	....	....	....	....	....	....	....	....	....	....	....	....	....	....	....
2002-03	NY Islanders	NHL	81	26	39	65	32	14	0	7	274	9.5	–12	1074	47.2	18:32	5	2	2	4	2	0	0	0	21:06
2003-04	NY Islanders	NHL	47	15	19	34	10	3	0	1	148	10.1	–1	603	42.8	17:19	5	0	1	1	0	0	0	0	15:33
	NHL Totals		710	291	374	665	289	109	4	44	2372	12.3		5347	44.1	20:01	43	11	16	27	24	5	0	2	21:37

NHL Second All-Star Team (1999)

Played in NHL All-Star Game (1994, 1999, 2002)

• Suspended for entire 1999-2000 season by **Ottawa** for refusing to report to team, November 9, 1999. Traded to **NY Islanders** by **Ottawa** for Bill Muckalt, Zdeno Chara and NY Islanders' 1st round choice (Jason Spezza) in 2001 Entry Draft, June 23, 2001.

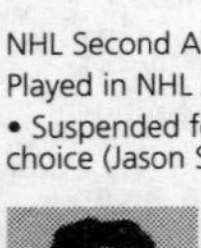

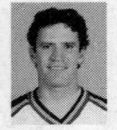

YELLE, Stephane

(YEHL, STEH-fan) **CGY.**

Center. Shoots left. 6'1", 190 lbs. Born, Ottawa, Ont., May 9, 1974. New Jersey's 9th choice, 186th overall, in 1992 Entry Draft.

Season	Club	League	GP	G	A	Pts	PIM	PP	SH	GW	S	%	+/-	TF	F%	Min	GP	G	A	Pts	PIM	PP	SH	GW	Min
1990-91	Cumberland	OJHL-B	33	20	30	50	16	....	....	....	....	....	....	....	....	....	....	....	....	....	....	....	....	....	....
1991-92	Oshawa Generals	OHL	55	12	14	26	20	....	....	....	....	....	....	....	....	....	7	2	0	2	2	....	....	....	....
1992-93	Oshawa Generals	OHL	66	24	50	74	20	....	....	....	....	....	....	....	....	....	10	2	4	6	4	....	....	....	....
1993-94	Oshawa Generals	OHL	66	35	69	104	22	....	....	....	....	....	....	....	....	....	5	1	7	8	2	....	....	....	....
1994-95	Cornwall Aces	AHL	40	18	15	33	22	....	....	....	....	....	....	....	....	....	13	7	7	14	8	....	....	....	....
1995-96♦	Colorado	NHL	71	13	14	27	30	0	2	1	93	14.0	15	....	....	....	22	1	4	5	8	0	1	0	....
1996-97	Colorado	NHL	79	9	17	26	38	0	1	1	89	10.1	1	....	....	....	12	1	6	7	2	0	0	0	....
1997-98	Colorado	NHL	81	7	15	22	48	0	1	0	93	7.5	–10	....	....	....	7	1	0	1	12	0	0	0	....
1998-99	Colorado	NHL	72	8	7	15	40	1	0	0	99	8.1	–8	1201	51.2	15:15	10	0	1	1	6	0	0	0	15:13
99-2000	Colorado	NHL	79	8	14	22	28	0	1	1	90	8.9	9	1294	52.2	15:51	17	1	2	3	4	0	0	0	15:38
2000-01♦	Colorado	NHL	50	4	10	14	20	0	1	0	54	7.4	–3	736	56.4	14:28	23	1	2	3	8	0	0	1	13:52
2001-02	Colorado	NHL	73	5	12	17	48	0	1	1	71	7.0	1	1036	51.8	14:02	20	0	2	2	14	0	0	0	13:26

Season	Club	League	GP	G	A	Pts	PIM	PP	SH	GW	S	%	+/-	TF	F%	Min	GP	G	A	Pts	PIM	PP	SH	GW	Min
			Regular Season														Playoffs								
2002-03	**Calgary**	**NHL**	**82**	**10**	**15**	**25**	**50**	**3**	**0**	**3**	**121**	**8.3**	**–10**	**1494**	**53.4**	**18:06**									
2003-04	**Calgary**	**NHL**	**53**	**4**	**13**	**17**	**24**	**1**	**0**	**0**	**76**	**5.3**	**1**	**996**	**56.6**	**15:48**	**23**	**3**	**3**	**6**	**16**	**0**	**1**	**1**	**17:04**
	NHL Totals		**640**	**68**	**117**	**185**	**326**	**5**	**7**	**7**	**786**	**8.7**		**6757**	**53.4**	**15:42**	**134**	**8**	**20**	**28**	**70**	**0**	**2**	**2**	**15:02**

Traded to **Quebec** by **New Jersey** with New Jersey's 11th round choice (Steven Low) in 1994 Entry Draft for Quebec's 11th round choice (Mike Hanson) in 1994 Entry Draft, June 1, 1994. Transferred to **Colorado** after **Quebec** franchise relocated, June 21, 1995. Traded to **Calgary** by **Colorado** with Chris Drury for Derek Morris, Jeff Shantz and Dean McAmmond, October 1, 2002.

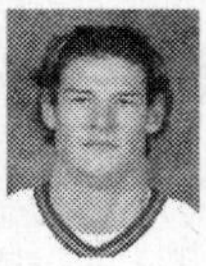

YONKMAN, Nolan

(YAWK-man, NOH-lan) **WSH.**

Defense. Shoots right. 6'6", 245 lbs. Born, Punnichy, Sask., April 1, 1981. Washington's 5th choice, 37th overall, in 1999 Entry Draft.

Season	Club	League	GP	G	A	Pts	PIM	PP	SH	GW	S	%	+/-	TF	F%	Min	GP	G	A	Pts	PIM	PP	SH	GW	Min
1996-97	Naicam Vikings	SAHA	64	15	23	38	36																		
	Kelowna Rockets	WHL	4	0	0	0	0																		
1997-98	Kelowna Rockets	WHL	65	0	2	2	36										7	0	0	0	2				
1998-99	Kelowna Rockets	WHL	61	1	6	7	129										6	0	0	0	6				
99-2000	Kelowna Rockets	WHL	71	5	7	12	153										5	0	0	0	8				
2000-01	Kelowna Rockets	WHL	7	0	1	1	19																		
	Brandon	WHL	51	6	10	16	94										6	0	1	1	12				
2001-02	**Washington**	**NHL**	**11**	**1**	**0**	**1**	**4**	**0**	**0**	**0**	**7**	**14.3**	**3**	**0**	**0.0**	**12:44**									
	Portland Pirates	AHL	59	4	3	7	116																		
2002-03	Portland Pirates	AHL	24	1	4	5	40										3	0	1	1	2				
2003-04	**Washington**	**NHL**	**1**	**0**	**0**	**0**	**0**	**0**	**0**	**0**	**0**	**0.0**	**0**	**0**	**0.0**	**5:00**									
	Portland Pirates	AHL	4	0	0	0	11																		
	NHL Totals		**12**	**1**	**0**	**1**	**4**	**0**	**0**	**0**	**7**	**14.3**		**0**	**0.0**	**12:05**									

• Missed majority of 2002-03 season recovering from abdominal injury suffered in training camp, September 25, 2002. • Missed majority of 2003-04 season recovering from knee injury suffered in game vs. Worcester (AHL), October 23, 2003.

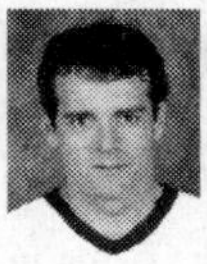

YORK, Jason

(YOHRK, JAY-suhn)

Defense. Shoots right. 6'1", 208 lbs. Born, Nepean, Ont., May 20, 1970. Detroit's 6th choice, 129th overall, in 1990 Entry Draft.

Season	Club	League	GP	G	A	Pts	PIM	PP	SH	GW	S	%	+/-	TF	F%	Min	GP	G	A	Pts	PIM	PP	SH	GW	Min
1986-87	Smiths Falls Bears	OCJHL	46	6	13	19	86																		
1987-88	Hamilton	OHL	58	4	9	13	110																		
1988-89	Windsor Spitfires	OHL	65	19	44	63	105																		
1989-90	Windsor Spitfires	OHL	39	9	30	39	38																		
	Kitchener Rangers	OHL	25	11	25	36	17										17	3	19	22	10				
1990-91	Windsor Spitfires	OHL	66	13	80	93	40										11	3	10	13	12				
1991-92	Adirondack	AHL	49	4	20	24	32										5	0	1	1	0				
1992-93	**Detroit**	**NHL**	**2**	**0**	**0**	**0**	**0**	**0**	**0**	**0**	**1**	**0.0**	**0**												
	Adirondack	AHL	77	15	40	55	86										11	0	3	3	18				
1993-94	**Detroit**	**NHL**	**7**	**1**	**2**	**3**	**2**	**0**	**0**	**0**	**9**	**11.1**	**0**												
	Adirondack	AHL	74	10	56	66	98										12	3	11	14	22				
1994-95	**Detroit**	**NHL**	**10**	**1**	**2**	**3**	**2**	**0**	**0**	**0**	**6**	**16.7**	**0**												
	Adirondack	AHL	5	1	3	4	4																		
	Anaheim	**NHL**	**15**	**0**	**8**	**8**	**12**	**0**	**0**	**0**	**22**	**0.0**	**4**												
1995-96	**Anaheim**	**NHL**	**79**	**3**	**21**	**24**	**88**	**0**	**0**	**0**	**106**	**2.8**	**–7**												
1996-97	**Ottawa**	**NHL**	**75**	**4**	**17**	**21**	**67**	**1**	**0**	**0**	**121**	**3.3**	**–8**				**7**	**0**	**0**	**0**	**4**	**0**	**0**	**0**	
1997-98	**Ottawa**	**NHL**	**73**	**3**	**13**	**16**	**62**	**0**	**0**	**0**	**109**	**2.8**	**8**				**7**	**1**	**1**	**2**	**7**	**1**	**0**	**0**	
1998-99	**Ottawa**	**NHL**	**79**	**4**	**31**	**35**	**48**	**2**	**0**	**0**	**177**	**2.3**	**17**	**2**	**0.0**	**23:49**	**4**	**1**	**1**	**2**	**4**	**0**	**0**	**0**	**24:59**
99-2000	**Ottawa**	**NHL**	**79**	**8**	**22**	**30**	**60**	**1**	**0**	**1**	**159**	**5.0**	**–3**	**0**	**0.0**	**23:20**	**6**	**0**	**2**	**2**	**2**	**0**	**0**	**0**	**25:30**
2000-01	**Ottawa**	**NHL**	**74**	**6**	**16**	**22**	**72**	**3**	**0**	**2**	**133**	**4.5**	**7**	**0**	**0.0**	**23:49**	**4**	**0**	**0**	**0**	**4**	**0**	**0**	**0**	**20:58**
2001-02	**Anaheim**	**NHL**	**74**	**5**	**20**	**25**	**60**	**3**	**0**	**2**	**104**	**4.8**	**–11**	**0**	**0.0**	**19:19**									
2002-03	**Nashville**	**NHL**	**74**	**4**	**15**	**19**	**52**	**2**	**0**	**0**	**107**	**3.7**	**13**	**0**	**0.0**	**19:57**									
	Cincinnati	AHL	4	3	2	5	8																		
2003-04	**Nashville**	**NHL**	**67**	**2**	**13**	**15**	**64**	**0**	**0**	**1**	**80**	**2.5**	**–4**	**1**	**0.0**	**21:17**	**6**	**0**	**3**	**3**	**4**	**0**	**0**	**0**	**21:27**
	NHL Totals		**708**	**41**	**180**	**221**	**589**	**12**	**0**	**6**	**1134**	**3.6**		**3**	**0.0**	**21:58**	**34**	**2**	**7**	**9**	**25**	**1**	**0**	**0**	**23:16**

AHL First All-Star Team (1994)

Traded to **Anaheim** by **Detroit** with Mike Sillinger for Stu Grimson, Mark Ferner and Anaheim's 6th round choice (Magnus Nilsson) in 1996 Entry Draft, April 4, 1995. Traded to **Ottawa** by **Anaheim** with Shaun Van Allen for Ted Drury and the rights to Marc Moro, October 1, 1996. Signed as a free agent by **Anaheim**, July 3, 2001. Traded to **Nashville** by **Anaheim** for future considerations, October 23, 2002.

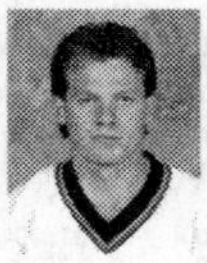

YORK, Mike

(YOHRK, MIGHK) **EDM.**

Left wing. Shoots right. 5'10", 185 lbs. Born, Waterford, MI, January 3, 1978. NY Rangers' 7th choice, 136th overall, in 1997 Entry Draft.

Season	Club	League	GP	G	A	Pts	PIM	PP	SH	GW	S	%	+/-	TF	F%	Min	GP	G	A	Pts	PIM	PP	SH	GW	Min
1992-93	Michigan	MNHL	50	45	50	95																			
1993-94	Det. Compuware	MNHL	85	136	140	276																			
1994-95	Thornhill Islanders	MTJHL	49	39	54	*93	44										11	7	6	13	0				
1995-96	Michigan State	CCHA	39	12	27	39	20																		
1996-97	Michigan State	CCHA	37	18	29	47	42																		
1997-98	Michigan State	CCHA	40	27	34	61	38																		
1998-99	Michigan State	CCHA	42	22	32	*54	41																		
	Hartford	AHL	3	2	2	4	0										6	3	1	4	0				
99-2000	**NY Rangers**	**NHL**	**82**	**26**	**24**	**50**	**18**	**8**	**0**	**4**	**177**	**14.7**	**–17**	**1131**	**48.1**	**1:35**									
2000-01	**NY Rangers**	**NHL**	**79**	**14**	**17**	**31**	**20**	**3**	**2**	**4**	**171**	**8.2**	**1**	**1098**	**46.9**	**17:45**									
2001-02	**NY Rangers**	**NHL**	**69**	**18**	**39**	**57**	**16**	**2**	**0**	**5**	**188**	**9.6**	**8**	**267**	**43.1**	**20:24**									
	United States	Olympics	6	0	1	1	0																		
	Edmonton	**NHL**	**12**	**2**	**2**	**4**	**0**	**1**	**0**	**1**	**30**	**6.7**	**–1**	**100**	**56.0**	**16:35**									
2002-03	**Edmonton**	**NHL**	**71**	**22**	**29**	**51**	**10**	**7**	**2**	**4**	**177**	**12.4**	**–8**	**390**	**43.9**	**19:04**	**6**	**0**	**2**	**2**	**2**	**0**	**0**	**0**	**14:20**
2003-04	**Edmonton**	**NHL**	**61**	**16**	**26**	**42**	**15**	**1**	**2**	**0**	**144**	**11.1**	**18**	**656**	**45.9**	**19:17**									
	NHL Totals		**374**	**98**	**137**	**235**	**79**	**22**	**6**	**18**	**887**	**11.0**		**3642**	**46.7**	**15:10**	**6**	**0**	**2**	**2**	**2**	**0**	**0**	**0**	**14:20**

CCHA Second All-Star Team (1998) • NCAA West First All-American Team (1998, 1999) • CCHA First All-Star Team (1999) • CCHA Player of the Year (1999) • NHL All-Rookie Team (2000)

Played in NHL All-Star Game (2002)

Traded to **Edmonton** by **NY Rangers** with NY Rangers' 4th round choice (Ivan Koltsov) in 2002 Entry Draft for Tom Poti and Rem Murray, March 19, 2002.

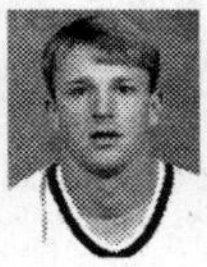

YOUNG, Scott

(YUHNG, SKAWT)

Right wing. Shoots right. 6'1", 200 lbs. Born, Clinton, MA, October 1, 1967. Hartford's 1st choice, 11th overall, in 1986 Entry Draft.

Season	Club	League	GP	G	A	Pts	PIM	PP	SH	GW	S	%	+/-	TF	F%	Min	GP	G	A	Pts	PIM	PP	SH	GW	Min
1984-85	St. Mark's	Hi-School	23	28	41	69																			
1985-86	Boston University	H-East	38	16	13	29	31																		
1986-87	Boston University	H-East	33	15	21	36	24																		
1987-88	Team USA	Nat-Tm	56	11	47	58	31																		
	United States	Olympics	6	2	6	8	4																		
	Hartford	**NHL**	**7**	**0**	**0**	**0**	**2**	**0**	**0**	**0**	**6**	**0.0**	**–6**				**4**	**1**	**0**	**1**	**0**	**0**	**0**	**0**	
1988-89	**Hartford**	**NHL**	**76**	**19**	**40**	**59**	**27**	**6**	**0**	**2**	**203**	**9.4**	**–21**				**4**	**2**	**0**	**2**	**4**	**0**	**0**	**0**	
1989-90	**Hartford**	**NHL**	**80**	**24**	**40**	**64**	**47**	**10**	**2**	**5**	**239**	**10.0**	**–24**				**7**	**2**	**0**	**2**	**2**	**0**	**0**	**0**	
1990-91	**Hartford**	**NHL**	**34**	**6**	**9**	**15**	**8**	**3**	**1**	**2**	**94**	**6.4**	**–9**												
	♦ **Pittsburgh**	**NHL**	**43**	**11**	**16**	**27**	**33**	**3**	**1**	**3**	**116**	**9.5**	**3**				**17**	**1**	**6**	**7**	**2**	**1**	**0**	**0**	
1991-92	HC Bolzano	Alpenliga	15	19	11	30	14																		
	HC Bolzano	Italy	18	22	17	39	6										5	4	3	7	7				
	Team USA	Nat-Tm	10	2	4	6	21																		
	United States	Olympics	8	2	1	3	2																		
1992-93	**Quebec**	**NHL**	**82**	**30**	**30**	**60**	**20**	**9**	**6**	**5**	**225**	**13.3**	**5**				**6**	**4**	**1**	**5**	**0**	**0**	**0**	**2**	
1993-94	**Quebec**	**NHL**	**76**	**26**	**25**	**51**	**14**	**6**	**1**	**1**	**236**	**11.0**	**–4**												
1994-95	EV Landshut	Germany	4	6	1	7	6																		
	Frankfurt Lions	Germany	1	1	0	1	0																		
	Quebec	**NHL**	**48**	**18**	**21**	**39**	**14**	**3**	**3**	**0**	**167**	**10.8**	**9**				**6**	**3**	**3**	**6**	**2**	**0**	**1**	**0**	
1995-96 ♦	**Colorado**	**NHL**	**81**	**21**	**39**	**60**	**50**	**7**	**0**	**5**	**229**	**9.2**	**2**				**22**	**3**	**12**	**15**	**10**	**0**	**0**	**0**	
1996-97	**Colorado**	**NHL**	**72**	**18**	**19**	**37**	**14**	**7**	**0**	**0**	**164**	**11.0**	**–5**				**17**	**4**	**2**	**6**	**14**	**2**	**0**	**0**	
1997-98	**Anaheim**	**NHL**	**73**	**13**	**20**	**33**	**22**	**4**	**2**	**1**	**187**	**7.0**	**–13**												
1998-99	**St. Louis**	**NHL**	**75**	**24**	**28**	**52**	**27**	**8**	**0**	**4**	**205**	**11.7**	**8**	**4**	**25.0**	**15:14**	**13**	**4**	**7**	**11**	**10**	**1**	**0**	**1**	**17:56**
99-2000	**St. Louis**	**NHL**	**75**	**24**	**15**	**39**	**18**	**6**	**1**	**7**	**244**	**9.8**	**12**	**2**	**50.0**	**16:06**	**6**	**6**	**2**	**8**	**8**	**3**	**0**	**0**	**17:18**
2000-01	**St. Louis**	**NHL**	**81**	**40**	**33**	**73**	**30**	**14**	**3**	**7**	**321**	**12.5**	**15**	**4**	**25.0**	**19:18**	**15**	**6**	**7**	**13**	**2**	**0**	**2**	**3**	**20:34**

			Regular Season														Playoffs								
Season	Club	League	GP	G	A	Pts	PIM	PP	SH	GW	S	%	+/-	TF	F%	Min	GP	G	A	Pts	PIM	PP	SH	GW	Min
2001-02	**St. Louis**	**NHL**	**67**	**19**	**22**	**41**	**26**	**5**	**0**	**1**	**210**	**9.0**	**11**	**4**	**0.0**	**18:31**	**10**	**3**	**0**	**3**	**2**	**1**	**1**	**0**	**17:40**
	United States	Olympics	6	4	0	4	2	....	....	....	....	....	....	....	....	....	....	....	....	....	....	....	....	....	....
2002-03	**Dallas**	**NHL**	**79**	**23**	**19**	**42**	**30**	**5**	**1**	**4**	**237**	**9.7**	**24**	**8**	**37.5**	**16:08**	**10**	**4**	**3**	**7**	**6**	**2**	**0**	**1**	**19:12**
2003-04	**Dallas**	**NHL**	**53**	**8**	**8**	**16**	**14**	**2**	**0**	**2**	**134**	**6.0**	**–15**	**5**	**20.0**	**14:45**	**4**	**1**	**0**	**1**	**2**	**1**	**0**	**0**	**15:05**
	NHL Totals		**1102**	**324**	**384**	**708**	**396**	**98**	**21**	**49**	**3217**	**10.1**		**27**	**25.9**	**16:46**	**141**	**44**	**43**	**87**	**64**	**11**	**4**	**7**	**18:32**

Hockey East Rookie of the Year (1986) (co-winner - Al Loring)

Traded to **Pittsburgh** by **Hartford** for Rob Brown, December 21, 1990. Traded to **Quebec** by **Pittsburgh** for Bryan Fogarty, March 10, 1992. Transferred to **Colorado** after **Quebec** franchise relocated, June 21, 1995. Traded to **Anaheim** by **Colorado** for Anaheim's 3rd round choice (later traded to Florida – Florida selected Lance Ward) in 1998 Entry Draft, September 17, 1997. Signed as a free agent by **St. Louis**, July 28, 1998. Signed as a free agent by **Dallas**, July 5, 2002.

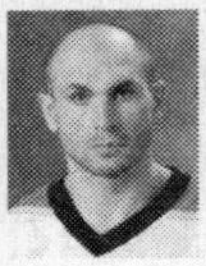

YUSHKEVICH, Dmitry

(yoosh-KAY-vihch, dih-MEE-tree)

Defense. Shoots right. 5'11", 208 lbs. Born, Cherepovets, USSR, November 19, 1971. Philadelphia's 6th choice, 122nd overall, in 1991 Entry Draft.

Season	Club	League	GP	G	A	Pts	PIM	PP	SH	GW	S	%	+/-	TF	F%	Min	GP	G	A	Pts	PIM	PP	SH	GW	Min
1988-89	Yaroslavl	USSR	23	2	1	3	8	....	....	....	....	....	....	....	....	....	....	....	....	....	....	....	....	....	....
1989-90	Yaroslavl	USSR	41	2	3	5	39	....	....	....	....	....	....	....	....	....	....	....	....	....	....	....	....	....	....
1990-91	Yaroslavl	USSR	41	10	4	14	22	....	....	....	....	....	....	....	....	....	....	....	....	....	....	....	....	....	....
1991-92	Dynamo Moscow	CIS	35	5	7	12	14	....	....	....	....	....	....	....	....	....	....	....	....	....	....	....	....	....	....
	Russia	Olympics	8	1	2	3	4	....	....	....	....	....	....	....	....	....	....	....	....	....	....	....	....	....	....
1992-93	**Philadelphia**	**NHL**	**82**	**5**	**27**	**32**	**71**	**1**	**0**	**1**	**155**	**3.2**	**12**	....	....	....	....	....	....	....	....	....	....	....	....
1993-94	**Philadelphia**	**NHL**	**75**	**5**	**25**	**30**	**86**	**1**	**0**	**2**	**136**	**3.7**	**–8**	....	....	....	....	....	....	....	....	....	....	....	....
1994-95	Yaroslavl	CIS	10	3	4	7	8	....	....	....	....	....	....	....	....	....	....	....	....	....	....	....	....	....	....
	Philadelphia	**NHL**	**40**	**5**	**9**	**14**	**47**	**3**	**1**	**1**	**80**	**6.3**	**–4**	....	....	....	**15**	**1**	**5**	**6**	**12**	**0**	**0**	**0**	....
1995-96	**Toronto**	**NHL**	**69**	**1**	**10**	**11**	**54**	**1**	**0**	**0**	**96**	**1.0**	**–14**	....	....	....	**4**	**0**	**0**	**0**	**0**	**0**	**0**	**0**	....
1996-97	**Toronto**	**NHL**	**74**	**4**	**10**	**14**	**56**	**1**	**1**	**1**	**99**	**4.0**	**–24**	....	....	....	....	....	....	....	....	....	....	....	....
1997-98	**Toronto**	**NHL**	**72**	**0**	**12**	**12**	**78**	**0**	**0**	**0**	**92**	**0.0**	**–13**	....	....	....	....	....	....	....	....	....	....	....	....
	Russia	Olympics	6	0	0	0	2	....	....	....	....	....	....	....	....	....	....	....	....	....	....	....	....	....	....
1998-99	**Toronto**	**NHL**	**78**	**6**	**22**	**28**	**88**	**2**	**1**	**0**	**95**	**6.3**	**25**	**0**	**0.0**	**22:20**	**17**	**1**	**5**	**6**	**22**	**1**	**0**	**0**	**23:13**
99-2000	Yaroslavl	Russia	7	2	3	5	2	....	....	....	....	....	....	....	....	....	....	....	....	....	....	....	....	....	....
	Toronto	**NHL**	**77**	**3**	**24**	**27**	**55**	**2**	**1**	**1**	**103**	**2.9**	**2**	**0**	**0.0**	**23:18**	**12**	**1**	**1**	**2**	**4**	**0**	**0**	**0**	**24:45**
2000-01	**Toronto**	**NHL**	**81**	**5**	**19**	**24**	**52**	**1**	**0**	**0**	**110**	**4.5**	**–2**	**0**	**0.0**	**24:14**	**11**	**0**	**4**	**4**	**12**	**0**	**0**	**0**	**25:18**
2001-02	**Toronto**	**NHL**	**55**	**6**	**13**	**19**	**26**	**3**	**0**	**0**	**79**	**7.6**	**14**	**1**	**100.0**	**23:25**	....	....	....	....	....	....	....	....	....
2002-03	**Florida**	**NHL**	**23**	**1**	**6**	**7**	**14**	**0**	**0**	**0**	**23**	**4.3**	**–12**	**3**	**33.3**	**23:40**	....	....	....	....	....	....	....	....	....
	Los Angeles	**NHL**	**42**	**0**	**3**	**3**	**24**	**0**	**0**	**0**	**36**	**0.0**	**–4**	**2**	**0.0**	**19:57**	....	....	....	....	....	....	....	....	....
	Philadelphia	**NHL**	**18**	**2**	**2**	**4**	**8**	**0**	**0**	**0**	**16**	**12.5**	**7**	**0**	**0.0**	**18:05**	**13**	**1**	**4**	**5**	**2**	**0**	**0**	**1**	**24:20**
2003-04	Yaroslavl	Russia	35	7	11	18	38	....	....	....	....	....	....	....	....	....	3	0	2	2	2	....	....	....	....
	NHL Totals		**786**	**43**	**182**	**225**	**659**	**15**	**4**	**6**	**1120**	**3.8**		**6**	**33.3**	**22:43**	**72**	**4**	**19**	**23**	**52**	**1**	**0**	**1**	**24:16**

Played in NHL All-Star Game (2000)

Traded to **Toronto** by **Philadelphia** with Philadelphia's 2nd round choice (Francis Larivee) in 1996 Entry Draft for Toronto's 1st round choice (Dainius Zubrus) in 1996 Entry Draft, Toronto's 2nd round choice (Jean-Marc Pelletier) in 1997 Entry Draft and Los Angeles' 4th round choice (previously acquired, later traded back to Los Angeles – Los Angeles selected Mikael Simons) in 1996 Entry Draft, August 30, 1995. Traded to **Florida** by **Toronto** for Robert Svehla, July 18, 2002. Traded to **Los Angeles** by **Florida** with NY Islanders' 5th round choice (previously acquired, Los Angeles selected Brady Murray) in 2003 Entry Draft for Jaroslav Bednar and Andreas Lilja, November 26, 2002. Traded to **Philadelphia** by **Los Angeles** for Philadelphia's 4th round choice (later traded to Boston – Boston selected Patrick Valcak) in 2003 Entry Draft and Philadelphia's 7th round choice (Daniel Taylor) in 2004 Entry Draft, March 1, 2003. Signed as a free agent by **Yaroslavl** (Russia), November 11, 2003.

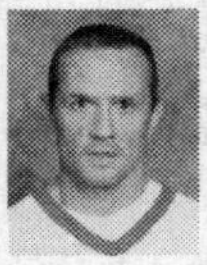

YZERMAN, Steve

(IGH-zuhr-muhn, STEEV) **DET.**

Center. Shoots right. 5'11", 185 lbs. Born, Cranbrook, B.C., May 9, 1965. Detroit's 1st choice, 4th overall, in 1983 Entry Draft.

Season	Club	League	GP	G	A	Pts	PIM	PP	SH	GW	S	%	+/-	TF	F%	Min	GP	G	A	Pts	PIM	PP	SH	GW	Min
1980-81	Nepean Raiders	OCJHL	50	38	*54	92	44	....	....	....	....	....	....	....	....	....	....	....	....	....	....	....	....	....	....
1981-82	Peterborough	OHL	58	21	43	64	65	....	....	....	....	....	....	....	....	....	6	0	1	1	16	....	....	....	....
1982-83	Peterborough	OHL	56	42	49	91	33	....	....	....	....	....	....	....	....	....	4	1	4	5	0	....	....	....	....
1983-84	**Detroit**	**NHL**	**80**	**39**	**48**	**87**	**33**	**13**	**0**	**2**	**177**	**22.0**	**–17**	....	....	....	**4**	**3**	**3**	**6**	**0**	**1**	**0**	**1**	....
1984-85	**Detroit**	**NHL**	**80**	**30**	**59**	**89**	**58**	**9**	**0**	**3**	**231**	**13.0**	**–17**	....	....	....	**3**	**2**	**1**	**3**	**2**	**0**	**0**	**0**	....
1985-86	**Detroit**	**NHL**	**51**	**14**	**28**	**42**	**16**	**3**	**0**	**3**	**132**	**10.6**	**–24**	....	....	....	....	....	....	....	....	....	....	....	....
1986-87	**Detroit**	**NHL**	**80**	**31**	**59**	**90**	**43**	**9**	**1**	**2**	**217**	**14.3**	**–1**	....	....	....	**16**	**5**	**13**	**18**	**8**	**1**	**0**	**0**	....
1987-88	**Detroit**	**NHL**	**64**	**50**	**52**	**102**	**44**	**10**	**6**	**6**	**242**	**20.7**	**30**	....	....	....	**3**	**1**	**3**	**4**	**6**	**0**	**0**	**0**	....
1988-89	**Detroit**	**NHL**	**80**	**65**	**90**	**155**	**61**	**17**	**3**	**7**	**388**	**16.8**	**17**	....	....	....	**6**	**5**	**5**	**10**	**2**	**2**	**0**	**0**	....
1989-90	**Detroit**	**NHL**	**79**	**62**	**65**	**127**	**79**	**16**	**7**	**8**	**332**	**18.7**	**–6**	....	....	....	....	....	....	....	....	....	....	....	....
1990-91	**Detroit**	**NHL**	**80**	**51**	**57**	**108**	**34**	**12**	**6**	**4**	**326**	**15.6**	**–2**	....	....	....	**7**	**3**	**3**	**6**	**4**	**1**	**0**	**0**	....
1991-92	**Detroit**	**NHL**	**79**	**45**	**58**	**103**	**64**	**9**	**8**	**9**	**295**	**15.3**	**26**	....	....	....	**11**	**3**	**5**	**8**	**12**	**0**	**1**	**1**	....
1992-93	**Detroit**	**NHL**	**84**	**58**	**79**	**137**	**44**	**13**	**7**	**6**	**307**	**18.9**	**33**	....	....	....	**7**	**4**	**3**	**7**	**4**	**1**	**1**	**1**	....
1993-94	**Detroit**	**NHL**	**58**	**24**	**58**	**82**	**36**	**7**	**3**	**3**	**217**	**11.1**	**11**	....	....	....	**3**	**1**	**3**	**4**	**0**	**0**	**0**	**0**	....
1994-95	**Detroit**	**NHL**	**47**	**12**	**26**	**38**	**40**	**4**	**0**	**1**	**134**	**9.0**	**6**	....	....	....	**15**	**4**	**8**	**12**	**0**	**2**	**0**	**1**	....
1995-96	**Detroit**	**NHL**	**80**	**36**	**59**	**95**	**64**	**16**	**2**	**8**	**220**	**16.4**	**29**	....	....	....	**18**	**8**	**12**	**20**	**4**	**4**	**0**	**1**	....
1996-97♦	**Detroit**	**NHL**	**81**	**22**	**63**	**85**	**78**	**8**	**0**	**3**	**232**	**9.5**	**22**	....	....	....	**20**	**7**	**6**	**13**	**4**	**3**	**0**	**2**	....
1997-98♦	**Detroit**	**NHL**	**75**	**24**	**45**	**69**	**46**	**6**	**2**	**0**	**188**	**12.8**	**3**	....	....	....	**22**	**6**	***18**	***24**	**22**	**3**	**1**	**0**	....
	Canada	Olympics	6	1	1	2	10	....	....	....	....	....	....	....	....	....	....	....	....	....	....	....	....	....	....
1998-99	**Detroit**	**NHL**	**80**	**29**	**45**	**74**	**42**	**13**	**2**	**4**	**231**	**12.6**	**8**	**1600**	**56.9**	**21:35**	**10**	**9**	**4**	**13**	**0**	**4**	**0**	**2**	**21:49**
99-2000	**Detroit**	**NHL**	**78**	**35**	**44**	**79**	**34**	**15**	**2**	**6**	**234**	**15.0**	**28**	**1868**	**56.8**	**21:07**	**8**	**0**	**4**	**4**	**0**	**0**	**0**	**0**	**22:39**
2000-01	**Detroit**	**NHL**	**54**	**18**	**34**	**52**	**18**	**5**	**0**	**7**	**155**	**11.6**	**4**	**1197**	**59.6**	**22:14**	**1**	**0**	**0**	**0**	**0**	**0**	**0**	**0**	**5:58**
2001-02♦	**Detroit**	**NHL**	**52**	**13**	**35**	**48**	**18**	**5**	**1**	**5**	**104**	**12.5**	**11**	**1182**	**58.4**	**20:35**	**23**	**6**	**17**	**23**	**10**	**4**	**0**	**2**	**21:22**
	Canada	Olympics	6	2	4	6	2	....	....	....	....	....	....	....	....	....	....	....	....	....	....	....	....	....	....
2002-03	**Detroit**	**NHL**	**16**	**2**	**6**	**8**	**8**	**1**	**0**	**1**	**13**	**15.4**	**6**	**134**	**56.0**	**15:35**	**4**	**0**	**1**	**1**	**2**	**0**	**0**	**0**	**20:33**
2003-04	**Detroit**	**NHL**	**75**	**18**	**33**	**51**	**46**	**7**	**0**	**3**	**141**	**12.8**	**10**	**1134**	**55.3**	**17:32**	**11**	**3**	**2**	**5**	**0**	**0**	**0**	**1**	**17:02**
	NHL Totals		**1453**	**678**	**1043**	**1721**	**906**	**198**	**50**	**91**	**4516**	**15.0**		**7115**	**57.3**	**20:18**	**192**	**70**	**111**	**181**	**80**	**26**	**3**	**12**	**20:28**

NHL All-Rookie Team (1984) • Lester B. Pearson Award (1989) • Conn Smythe Trophy (1998) • NHL First All-Star Team (2000) • Frank J. Selke Trophy (2000) • Bill Masterton Memorial Trophy (2003)

Played in NHL All-Star Game (1984, 1988, 1989, 1990, 1991, 1992, 1993, 1997, 2000)

• Missed majority of 2002-03 season recovering from off-season knee surgery, August 2, 2002.

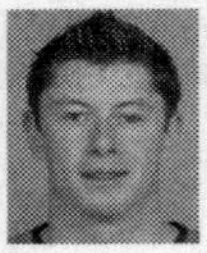

ZALESAK, Miroslav

(zah-LIH-sahk, MEER-oh-slav) **S.J.**

Right wing. Shoots left. 6', 200 lbs. Born, Skalica, Czech., January 2, 1980. San Jose's 5th choice, 104th overall, in 1998 Entry Draft.

Season	Club	League	GP	G	A	Pts	PIM	PP	SH	GW	S	%	+/-	TF	F%	Min	GP	G	A	Pts	PIM	PP	SH	GW	Min
1995-96	HC Nitra Jr.	Slovak-Jr.	49	53	29	82	....	....	....	....	....	....	....	....	....	....	....	....	....	....	....	....	....	....	....
1996-97	HC Nitra Jr.	Slovak-Jr.	58	51	31	82	....	....	....	....	....	....	....	....	....	....	....	....	....	....	....	....	....	....	....
1997-98	Nitra Jr.	Slovak-Jr.	27	32	29	61	30	....	....	....	....	....	....	....	....	....	....	....	....	....	....	....	....	....	....
	Nitra	Slovakia	30	8	6	14	0	....	....	....	....	....	....	....	....	....	....	....	....	....	....	....	....	....	....
1998-99	Nitra	Slovakia	15	4	3	7	10	....	....	....	....	....	....	....	....	....	....	....	....	....	....	....	....	....	....
	Drummondville	QMJHL	45	24	27	51	18	....	....	....	....	....	....	....	....	....	....	....	....	....	....	....	....	....	....
99-2000	Drummondville	QMJHL	60	50	61	111	40	....	....	....	....	....	....	....	....	....	16	7	11	18	4	....	....	....	....
2000-01	Kentucky	AHL	60	14	11	25	26	....	....	....	....	....	....	....	....	....	3	0	1	1	4	....	....	....	....
2001-02	Cleveland Barons	AHL	74	22	20	42	44	....	....	....	....	....	....	....	....	....	....	....	....	....	....	....	....	....	....
2002-03	**San Jose**	**NHL**	**10**	**1**	**2**	**3**	**0**	**0**	**0**	**0**	**8**	**12.5**	**–2**	**1**	**0.0**	**9:28**	....	....	....	....	....	....	....	....	....
	Cleveland Barons	AHL	50	27	22	49	35	....	....	....	....	....	....	....	....	....	....	....	....	....	....	....	....	....	....
2003-04	**San Jose**	**NHL**	**2**	**0**	**0**	**0**	**0**	**0**	**0**	**0**	**3**	**0.0**	**–1**	**0**	**0.0**	**12:02**	....	....	....	....	....	....	....	....	....
	Cleveland Barons	AHL	72	35	40	75	80	....	....	....	....	....	....	....	....	....	9	1	4	5	14	....	....	....	....
	NHL Totals		**12**	**1**	**2**	**3**	**0**	**0**	**0**	**0**	**11**	**9.1**		**1**	**0.0**	**9:54**	....	....	....	....	....	....	....	....	....

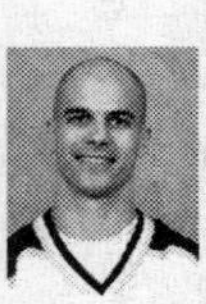

ZAMUNER, Rob

(ZAM-nuhr, RAWB)

Left wing. Shoots left. 6'3", 203 lbs. Born, Oakville, Ont., September 17, 1969. NY Rangers' 3rd choice, 45th overall, in 1989 Entry Draft.

Season	Club	League	GP	G	A	Pts	PIM	PP	SH	GW	S	%	+/-	TF	F%	Min	GP	G	A	Pts	PIM	PP	SH	GW	Min
1985-86	Oakville Oaks	OMHA	48	43	50	93	66	....	....	....	....	....	....	....	....	....	....	....	....	....	....	....	....	....	....
1986-87	Guelph Jr. B's	OJHL-B	3	6	7	13	15	....	....	....	....	....	....	....	....	....	....	....	....	....	....	....	....	....	....
	Guelph Platers	OHL	62	6	15	21	8	....	....	....	....	....	....	....	....	....	....	....	....	....	....	....	....	....	....
1987-88	Guelph Platers	OHL	58	20	41	61	18	....	....	....	....	....	....	....	....	....	....	....	....	....	....	....	....	....	....
1988-89	Guelph Platers	OHL	66	46	65	111	38	....	....	....	....	....	....	....	....	....	7	5	5	10	9	....	....	....	....
1989-90	Flint Spirits	IHL	77	44	35	79	32	....	....	....	....	....	....	....	....	....	4	1	0	1	6	....	....	....	....
1990-91	Binghamton	AHL	80	25	58	83	50	....	....	....	....	....	....	....	....	....	9	7	6	13	35	....	....	....	....
1991-92	**NY Rangers**	**NHL**	**9**	**1**	**2**	**3**	**2**	**0**	**0**	**0**	**11**	**9.1**	**0**	....	....	....	....	....	....	....	....	....	....	....	....
	Binghamton	AHL	61	19	53	72	42	....	....	....	....	....	....	....	....	....	11	8	9	17	8	....	....	....	....
1992-93	**Tampa Bay**	**NHL**	**84**	**15**	**28**	**43**	**74**	**1**	**0**	**0**	**183**	**8.2**	**–25**	....	....	....	....	....	....	....	....	....	....	....	....
1993-94	**Tampa Bay**	**NHL**	**59**	**6**	**6**	**12**	**42**	**0**	**0**	**1**	**109**	**5.5**	**–9**	....	....	....	....	....	....	....	....	....	....	....	....
1994-95	**Tampa Bay**	**NHL**	**43**	**9**	**6**	**15**	**24**	**0**	**3**	**1**	**74**	**12.2**	**–3**	....	....	....	....	....	....	....	....	....	....	....	....

			Regular Season														Playoffs								
Season	Club	League	GP	G	A	Pts	PIM	PP	SH	GW	S	%	+/-	TF	F%	Min	GP	G	A	Pts	PIM	PP	SH	GW	Min
1995-96	Tampa Bay	NHL	72	15	20	35	62	0	3	4	152	9.9	11	....	....	....	6	2	3	5	10	0	1	0	....
1996-97	Tampa Bay	NHL	82	17	33	50	56	0	4	3	216	7.9	3	....	....	....	....	....	....	....	....	....	....	....	....
1997-98	Tampa Bay	NHL	77	14	12	26	41	0	3	4	126	11.1	–31	....	....	....	....	....	....	....	....	....	....	....	....
	Canada	Olympics	6	1	0	1	8	....	....	....	....	....	....	....	....	....	....	....	....	....	....	....	....	....	....
1998-99	Tampa Bay	NHL	58	8	11	19	24	1	1	2	89	9.0	–15	34	47.1	16:26	....	....	....	....	....	....	....	....	....
99-2000	Ottawa	NHL	57	9	12	21	32	0	1	0	103	8.7	–6	29	37.9	14:56	6	2	0	2	2	0	0	1	12:59
2000-01	Ottawa	NHL	79	19	18	37	52	1	2	4	123	15.4	7	162	35.8	14:46	4	0	0	0	6	0	0	0	13:51
2001-02	Boston	NHL	66	12	13	25	24	1	2	0	98	12.2	6	192	41.7	13:13	6	0	2	2	4	0	0	0	12:35
2002-03	Boston	NHL	55	10	6	16	18	3	0	1	94	10.6	2	97	45.4	12:08	5	0	0	0	4	0	0	0	9:23
2003-04	Boston	NHL	57	4	5	9	16	0	0	0	49	8.2	3	58	50.0	9:43	7	0	0	0	0	0	0	0	5:35
	Providence Bruins	AHL	4	0	1	1	2	....	....	....	....	....	....	....	....	....	....	....	....	....	....	....	....	....	....
	NHL Totals		798	139	172	311	467	7	19	20	1427	9.7		572	41.6	13:37	34	4	5	9	26	0	1	1	10:32

Signed as a free agent by **Tampa Bay**, July 13, 1992. Traded to **Ottawa** by **Tampa Bay** with Tampa Bay's 2nd round choice (later traded to Philadelphia – later traded back to Tampa Bay – later traded to Dallas – Dallas selected Tobias Stephan) in 2002 Entry Draft for Andreas Johansson, June 29, 1999. Signed as a free agent by **Boston**, July 6, 2001.

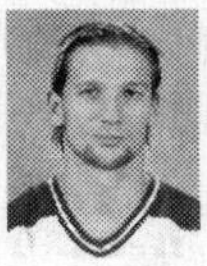

ZEDNIK, Richard (ZEHD-nihk, RIH-chuhrd) MTL.

Right wing. Shoots left. 6'1", 196 lbs. Born, Bystrica, Czech., January 6, 1976. Washington's 10th choice, 249th overall, in 1994 Entry Draft.

Season	Club	League	GP	G	A	Pts	PIM	PP	SH	GW	S	%	+/-	TF	F%	Min	GP	G	A	Pts	PIM	PP	SH	GW	Min
1993-94	Banska Bystrica	Slovak-2	25	3	6	9	....	....	....	....	....	....	....	....	....	....	....	....	....	....	....	....	....	....	....
1994-95	Portland	WHL	65	35	51	86	89	....	....	....	....	....	....	....	....	....	9	5	5	10	20	....	....	....	....
1995-96	Portland	WHL	61	44	37	81	154	....	....	....	....	....	....	....	....	....	7	8	4	12	23	....	....	....	....
	Washington	NHL	1	0	0	0	0	0	0	0	0	0.0	0	....	....	....	....	....	....	....	....	....	....	....	....
	Portland Pirates	AHL	1	1	1	2	0	....	....	....	....	....	....	....	....	....	21	4	5	9	26	....	....	....	....
1996-97	Washington	NHL	11	2	1	3	4	1	0	0	21	9.5	–5	....	....	....	....	....	....	....	....	....	....	....	....
	Portland Pirates	AHL	56	15	20	35	70	....	....	....	....	....	....	....	....	....	5	1	0	1	6	....	....	....	....
1997-98	Washington	NHL	65	17	9	26	28	2	0	2	148	11.5	–2	....	....	....	17	7	3	10	16	2	0	0	....
1998-99	Washington	NHL	49	9	8	17	50	1	0	2	115	7.8	–6	2	0.0	15:08	....	....	....	....	....	....	....	....	....
99-2000	Washington	NHL	69	19	16	35	54	1	0	2	179	10.6	6	1	100.0	15:34	5	0	0	0	5	0	0	0	16:57
2000-01	Washington	NHL	62	16	19	35	61	4	0	3	155	10.3	–2	1	0.0	15:32	....	....	....	....	....	....	....	....	....
	Montreal	NHL	12	3	6	9	10	1	0	0	23	13.0	–2	0	0.0	18:29	....	....	....	....	....	....	....	....	....
2001-02	Montreal	NHL	82	22	22	44	59	4	0	3	249	8.8	–3	10	30.0	17:39	4	4	4	8	6	2	0	0	21:19
2002-03	Montreal	NHL	80	31	19	50	79	9	0	2	250	12.4	4	10	30.0	18:25	....	....	....	....	....	....	....	....	....
2003-04	Montreal	NHL	81	26	24	50	63	7	0	9	218	11.9	5	6	50.0	17:30	11	3	3	6	2	0	0	1	18:52
	NHL Totals		512	145	124	269	408	30	0	23	1358	10.7		30	33.3	16:52	37	14	10	24	29	4	0	1	18:53

WHL West Second All-Star Team (1996)

Traded to **Montreal** by **Washington** with Jan Bulis and Washington's 1st round choice (Alexander Perezhogin) in 2001 Entry Draft for Trevor Linden, Dainius Zubrus and New Jersey's 2nd round choice (previously acquired, later traded to Tampa Bay – Tampa Bay selected Andreas Holmqvist) in 2001 Entry Draft, March 13, 2001.

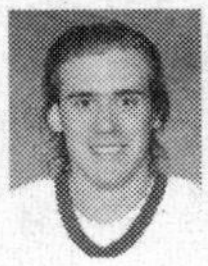

ZETTERBERG, Henrik (ZEH-tuhr-buhrg, HEHN-rihk) DET.

Left wing. Shoots left. 5'11", 176 lbs. Born, Njurunda, Sweden, October 9, 1980. Detroit's 4th choice, 210th overall, in 1999 Entry Draft.

Season	Club	League	GP	G	A	Pts	PIM	PP	SH	GW	S	%	+/-	TF	F%	Min	GP	G	A	Pts	PIM	PP	SH	GW	Min
1997-98	Timra IK Jr.	Swede-Jr.	18	9	5	14	4	....	....	....	....	....	....	....	....	....	....	....	....	....	....	....	....	....	....
	Timra IK	Swede-2	16	1	2	3	4	....	....	....	....	....	....	....	....	....	4	0	1	1	0	....	....	....	....
1998-99	Timra IK	Swede-2	37	15	13	28	2	....	....	....	....	....	....	....	....	....	4	2	1	3	2	....	....	....	....
99-2000	Timra IK	Swede-2	32	20	14	34	20	....	....	....	....	....	....	....	....	....	10	10	4	14	4	....	....	....	....
2000-01	Timra IK	Sweden	47	15	31	46	24	....	....	....	....	....	....	....	....	....	....	....	....	....	....	....	....	....	....
2001-02	Timra IK	Sweden	48	10	22	32	20	....	....	....	....	....	....	....	....	....	....	....	....	....	....	....	....	....	....
	Sweden	Olympics	4	0	1	1	0	....	....	....	....	....	....	....	....	....	....	....	....	....	....	....	....	....	....
2002-03	Detroit	NHL	79	22	22	44	8	5	1	4	135	16.3	6	401	46.1	16:19	4	1	0	1	0	0	0	0	18:19
2003-04	Detroit	NHL	61	15	28	43	14	7	1	2	137	10.9	15	627	45.6	18:15	12	2	2	4	4	0	0	0	17:17
	NHL Totals		140	37	50	87	22	12	2	6	272	13.6		1028	45.8	17:09	16	3	2	5	4	0	0	0	17:32

Swedish Elite League Rookie of the Year (2001) • NHL All-Rookie Team (2003)

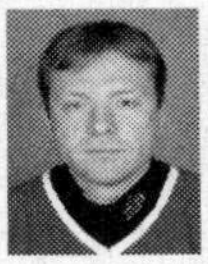

ZHAMNOV, Alex (ZHAHM-nahf, al-EHX)

Center. Shoots left. 6'1", 204 lbs. Born, Moscow, USSR, October 1, 1970. Winnipeg's 5th choice, 77th overall, in 1990 Entry Draft.

Season	Club	League	GP	G	A	Pts	PIM	PP	SH	GW	S	%	+/-	TF	F%	Min	GP	G	A	Pts	PIM	PP	SH	GW	Min
1988-89	Dynamo Moscow	USSR	4	0	0	0	0	....	....	....	....	....	....	....	....	....	....	....	....	....	....	....	....	....	....
1989-90	Dynamo Moscow	USSR	43	11	6	17	21	....	....	....	....	....	....	....	....	....	....	....	....	....	....	....	....	....	....
1990-91	Dynamo Moscow	USSR	46	16	12	28	24	....	....	....	....	....	....	....	....	....	....	....	....	....	....	....	....	....	....
1991-92	Dynamo Moscow	CIS	39	15	21	36	28	....	....	....	....	....	....	....	....	....	....	....	....	....	....	....	....	....	....
	Russia	Olympics	8	0	3	3	8	....	....	....	....	....	....	....	....	....	....	....	....	....	....	....	....	....	....
1992-93	Winnipeg	NHL	68	25	47	72	58	6	1	4	163	15.3	7	....	....	....	6	0	2	2	2	0	0	0	....
1993-94	Winnipeg	NHL	61	26	45	71	62	7	0	1	196	13.3	–20	....	....	....	....	....	....	....	....	....	....	....	....
1994-95	Winnipeg	NHL	48	30	35	65	20	9	0	4	155	19.4	5	....	....	....	....	....	....	....	....	....	....	....	....
1995-96	Winnipeg	NHL	58	22	37	59	65	5	0	2	199	11.1	–4	....	....	....	6	2	1	3	8	0	0	0	....
1996-97	Chicago	NHL	74	20	42	62	56	6	1	2	208	9.6	18	....	....	....	....	....	....	....	....	....	....	....	....
1997-98	Chicago	NHL	70	21	28	49	61	6	2	3	193	10.9	16	....	....	....	....	....	....	....	....	....	....	....	....
	Russia	Olympics	6	2	1	3	2	....	....	....	....	....	....	....	....	....	....	....	....	....	....	....	....	....	....
1998-99	Chicago	NHL	76	20	41	61	50	8	1	2	200	10.0	–10	1299	48.9	21:30	....	....	....	....	....	....	....	....	....
99-2000	Chicago	NHL	71	23	37	60	61	5	0	7	175	13.1	7	1171	45.8	22:08	....	....	....	....	....	....	....	....	....
2000-01	Chicago	NHL	63	13	36	49	40	3	1	3	117	11.1	–12	1486	48.1	21:15	....	....	....	....	....	....	....	....	....
2001-02	Chicago	NHL	77	22	45	67	67	6	0	3	173	12.7	8	1634	50.0	22:19	5	0	0	0	0	0	0	0	21:16
	Russia	Olympics	6	1	0	1	4	....	....	....	....	....	....	....	....	....	....	....	....	....	....	....	....	....	....
2002-03	Chicago	NHL	74	15	43	58	70	2	3	1	166	9.0	0	1345	51.3	21:06	....	....	....	....	....	....	....	....	....
2003-04	Chicago	NHL	23	6	12	18	14	1	0	1	63	9.5	–8	514	49.2	19:34	....	....	....	....	....	....	....	....	....
	Philadelphia	NHL	20	5	13	18	14	0	0	0	33	15.2	7	355	46.2	18:32	18	4	10	14	8	1	0	1	18:39
	NHL Totals		783	248	461	709	638	64	9	33	2041	12.2		7804	48.8	21:24	35	6	13	19	18	1	0	1	19:13

NHL Second All-Star Team (1995)

Played in NHL All-Star Game (2002)

Traded to **Chicago** by **Phoenix** with Craig Mills and Phoenix's 1st round choice (Ty Jones) in 1997 Entry Draft for Jeremy Roenick, August 16, 1996. Traded to **Philadelphia** by **Chicago** with Washington's 4th round choice (previously acquired, Philadelphia selected R.J. Anderson) in 2004 Entry Draft for Jim Vandermeer, the rights to Colin Fraser and Los Angeles' 2nd round choice (previously acquired, Chicago selected Bryan Bickell) in 2004 Entry Draft, February 19, 2004.

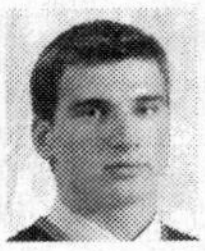

ZHERDEV, Nikolai (ZHAIR-dehv, NIH-koh-ligh) CBJ

Wing. Shoots right. 6', 186 lbs. Born, Kiev, USSR, November 5, 1984. Columbus' 1st choice, 4th overall, in 2003 Entry Draft.

Season	Club	League	GP	G	A	Pts	PIM	PP	SH	GW	S	%	+/-	TF	F%	Min	GP	G	A	Pts	PIM	PP	SH	GW	Min
99-2000	Elektrostal 2	Russia-3	21	10	7	17	26	....	....	....	....	....	....	....	....	....	7	0	0	0	0	....	....	....	....
	Kristal Jr.	Russia-Jr.	6	0	4	4	2	....	....	....	....	....	....	....	....	....	....	....	....	....	....	....	....	....	....
2000-01	Elektrostal	Russia-2	18	5	8	13	12	....	....	....	....	....	....	....	....	....	....	....	....	....	....	....	....	....	....
	Russia	Exhib.	17	10	11	21	17	....	....	....	....	....	....	....	....	....	....	....	....	....	....	....	....	....	....
2001-02	Elektrostal	Russia-2	53	13	15	28	62	....	....	....	....	....	....	....	....	....	....	....	....	....	....	....	....	....	....
	Elektrostal 2	Russia-3	1	1	0	1	4	....	....	....	....	....	....	....	....	....	....	....	....	....	....	....	....	....	....
2002-03	CSKA Moscow	Russia	44	12	12	24	34	....	....	....	....	....	....	....	....	....	....	....	....	....	....	....	....	....	....
2003-04	CSKA Moscow	Russia	20	2	2	4	14	....	....	....	....	....	....	....	....	....	....	....	....	....	....	....	....	....	....
	Columbus	NHL	57	13	21	34	54	5	0	1	137	9.5	–11	9	11.1	16:11	....	....	....	....	....	....	....	....	....
	NHL Totals		57	13	21	34	54	5	0	1	137	9.5		9	11.1	16:11	....	....	....	....	....	....	....	....	....

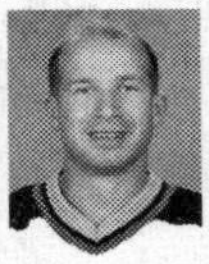

ZHITNIK, Alexei (ZHIHT-nihk, al-EHX-ay)

Defense. Shoots left. 5'11", 215 lbs. Born, Kiev, USSR, October 10, 1972. Los Angeles' 3rd choice, 81st overall, in 1991 Entry Draft.

Season	Club	League	GP	G	A	Pts	PIM	PP	SH	GW	S	%	+/-	TF	F%	Min	GP	G	A	Pts	PIM	PP	SH	GW	Min
1989-90	Sokol Kiev	USSR	31	3	4	7	16	....	....	....	....	....	....	....	....	....	....	....	....	....	....	....	....	....	....
1990-91	Sokol Kiev	USSR	46	1	4	5	46	....	....	....	....	....	....	....	....	....	....	....	....	....	....	....	....	....	....
1991-92	CSKA Moscow	CIS	44	2	7	9	52	....	....	....	....	....	....	....	....	....	....	....	....	....	....	....	....	....	....
	Russia	Olympics	8	1	0	1	0	....	....	....	....	....	....	....	....	....	....	....	....	....	....	....	....	....	....
1992-93	Los Angeles	NHL	78	12	36	48	80	5	0	2	136	8.8	–3	....	....	....	24	3	9	12	26	2	0	1	....
1993-94	Los Angeles	NHL	81	12	40	52	101	11	0	1	227	5.3	–11	....	....	....	....	....	....	....	....	....	....	....	....
1994-95	Los Angeles	NHL	11	2	5	7	27	2	0	0	33	6.1	–3	....	....	....	....	....	....	....	....	....	....	....	....
	Buffalo	NHL	21	2	5	7	34	1	0	0	33	6.1	–3	....	....	....	5	0	1	1	14	0	0	0	....
1995-96	Buffalo	NHL	80	6	30	36	58	5	0	0	193	3.1	–25	....	....	....	....	....	....	....	....	....	....	....	....

			Regular Season														Playoffs								
Season	Club	League	GP	G	A	Pts	PIM	PP	SH	GW	S	%	+/-	TF	F%	Min	GP	G	A	Pts	PIM	PP	SH	GW	Min
1996-97	**Buffalo**	**NHL**	**80**	**7**	**28**	**35**	**95**	**3**	**1**	**0**	**170**	**4.1**	**10**	....	....	....	**12**	**1**	**0**	**1**	**16**	**0**	**0**	**0**	....
1997-98	**Buffalo**	**NHL**	**78**	**15**	**30**	**45**	**102**	**2**	**3**	**3**	**191**	**7.9**	**19**	....	....	....	**15**	**0**	**3**	**3**	**36**	**0**	**0**	**0**	....
	Russia	Olympics	6	0	2	2	2	....	....	....	....	....	....	....	....	....	....	....	....	....	....	....	....	....	....
1998-99	**Buffalo**	**NHL**	**81**	**7**	**26**	**33**	**96**	**3**	**1**	**2**	**185**	**3.8**	**-6**	**0**	**0.0**	**25:39**	**21**	**4**	**11**	**15**	***52**	**4**	**0**	**2**	**27:07**
99-2000	**Buffalo**	**NHL**	**74**	**2**	**11**	**13**	**95**	**1**	**0**	**0**	**139**	**1.4**	**-6**	**0**	**0.0**	**24:48**	**4**	**0**	**0**	**0**	**8**	**0**	**0**	**0**	**25:50**
2000-01	**Buffalo**	**NHL**	**78**	**8**	**29**	**37**	**75**	**5**	**0**	**1**	**149**	**5.4**	**-3**	**0**	**0.0**	**24:15**	**13**	**1**	**6**	**7**	**12**	**0**	**0**	**0**	**25:38**
2001-02	**Buffalo**	**NHL**	**82**	**1**	**33**	**34**	**80**	**1**	**0**	**0**	**150**	**0.7**	**-1**	**0**	**0.0**	**25:36**	....	....	....	....	....	....	....	....	....
2002-03	**Buffalo**	**NHL**	**70**	**3**	**18**	**21**	**85**	**0**	**0**	**1**	**138**	**2.2**	**-5**	**1**	**0.0**	**26:33**	....	....	....	....	....	....	....	....	....
2003-04	**Buffalo**	**NHL**	**68**	**4**	**24**	**28**	**102**	**2**	**0**	**0**	**134**	**3.0**	**-13**	**0**	**0.0**	**25:01**	....	....	....	....	....	....	....	....	....
	NHL Totals		**882**	**81**	**315**	**396**	**1030**	**41**	**5**	**10**	**1878**	**4.3**		**1**	**0.0**	**25:18**	**94**	**9**	**30**	**39**	**164**	**6**	**0**	**3**	**26:29**

Played in NHL All-Star Game (1999, 2002)

Traded to **Buffalo** by **Los Angeles** with Robb Stauber, Charlie Huddy and Los Angeles' 5th round choice (Marian Menhart) in 1995 Entry Draft for Philippe Boucher, Denis Tsygurov and Grant Fuhr, February 14, 1995.

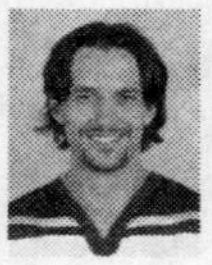

ZHOLTOK, Sergei

(ZHOL-tok, SAIR-gay)

Center. Shoots right. 6'2", 197 lbs. Born, Riga, Latvia, December 2, 1972. Boston's 2nd choice, 55th overall, in 1992 Entry Draft.

Season	Club	League	GP	G	A	Pts	PIM	PP	SH	GW	S	%	+/-	TF	F%	Min	GP	G	A	Pts	PIM	PP	SH	GW	Min
1990-91	Dynamo Riga	USSR	39	4	0	4	16	....	....	....	....	....	....	....	....	....	....	....	....	....	....	....	....	....	....
1991-92	Riga Stars	CIS	27	6	3	9	6	....	....	....	....	....	....	....	....	....	....	....	....	....	....	....	....	....	....
1992-93	**Boston**	**NHL**	**1**	**0**	**1**	**1**	**0**	**0**	**0**	**0**	**2**	**0.0**	**1**	....	....	....	....	....	....	....	....	....	....	....	....
	Providence Bruins	AHL	64	31	35	66	57	....	....	....	....	....	....	....	....	....	6	3	5	8	4	....	....	....	....
1993-94	**Boston**	**NHL**	**24**	**2**	**1**	**3**	**2**	**1**	**0**	**0**	**25**	**8.0**	**-7**	....	....	....	....	....	....	....	....	....	....	....	....
	Providence Bruins	AHL	54	29	33	62	16	....	....	....	....	....	....	....	....	....	....	....	....	....	....	....	....	....	....
1994-95	Providence Bruins	AHL	78	23	35	58	42	....	....	....	....	....	....	....	....	....	13	8	5	13	6	....	....	....	....
1995-96	Las Vegas	IHL	82	51	50	101	30	....	....	....	....	....	....	....	....	....	15	7	13	20	6	....	....	....	....
1996-97	**Ottawa**	**NHL**	**57**	**12**	**16**	**28**	**19**	**5**	**0**	**0**	**96**	**12.5**	**2**	....	....	....	**7**	**1**	**1**	**2**	**0**	**1**	**0**	**0**	....
	Las Vegas	IHL	19	13	14	27	20	....	....	....	....	....	....	....	....	....	....	....	....	....	....	....	....	....	....
1997-98	**Ottawa**	**NHL**	**78**	**10**	**13**	**23**	**16**	**7**	**0**	**1**	**127**	**7.9**	**-7**	....	....	....	**11**	**0**	**2**	**2**	**0**	**0**	**0**	**0**	....
1998-99	**Montreal**	**NHL**	**70**	**7**	**15**	**22**	**6**	**2**	**0**	**3**	**102**	**6.9**	**-12**	**522**	**49.0**	**11:11**	....	....	....	....	....	....	....	....	....
	Fredericton	AHL	7	3	4	7	0	....	....	....	....	....	....	....	....	....	....	....	....	....	....	....	....	....	....
99-2000	**Montreal**	**NHL**	**68**	**26**	**12**	**38**	**28**	**9**	**0**	**7**	**163**	**16.0**	**2**	**914**	**48.9**	**17:17**	....	....	....	....	....	....	....	....	....
	Quebec Citadelles	AHL	1	0	1	1	2	....	....	....	....	....	....	....	....	....	....	....	....	....	....	....	....	....	....
2000-01	**Montreal**	**NHL**	**32**	**1**	**10**	**11**	**8**	**0**	**0**	**0**	**78**	**1.3**	**-15**	**318**	**52.2**	**15:38**	....	....	....	....	....	....	....	....	....
	Edmonton	**NHL**	**37**	**4**	**16**	**20**	**22**	**1**	**0**	**0**	**61**	**6.6**	**8**	**109**	**60.6**	**12:55**	**3**	**0**	**0**	**0**	**0**	**0**	**0**	**0**	**9:23**
2001-02	**Minnesota**	**NHL**	**73**	**19**	**20**	**39**	**28**	**10**	**0**	**2**	**146**	**13.0**	**-10**	**823**	**45.6**	**16:04**	....	....	....	....	....	....	....	....	....
2002-03	**Minnesota**	**NHL**	**78**	**16**	**26**	**42**	**18**	**3**	**0**	**2**	**153**	**10.5**	**1**	**998**	**45.2**	**16:36**	**18**	**2**	**11**	**13**	**0**	**1**	**0**	**0**	**15:43**
2003-04	**Minnesota**	**NHL**	**59**	**13**	**16**	**29**	**19**	**3**	**0**	**3**	**115**	**11.3**	**4**	**676**	**46.0**	**16:13**	....	....	....	....	....	....	....	....	....
	Nashville	**NHL**	**11**	**1**	**1**	**2**	**0**	**0**	**0**	**0**	**17**	**5.9**	**-2**	**122**	**54.1**	**11:41**	**6**	**1**	**0**	**1**	**0**	**1**	**0**	**0**	**10:34**
	NHL Totals		**588**	**111**	**147**	**258**	**166**	**41**	**0**	**18**	**1085**	**10.2**		**4482**	**47.7**	**15:10**	**45**	**4**	**14**	**18**	**0**	**3**	**0**	**0**	**13:52**

Signed as a free agent by **Las Vegas** (IHL), August 5, 1995. Signed as a free agent by **Ottawa**, July 10, 1996. Signed as a free agent by **Montreal**, September 9, 1998. Traded to **Edmonton** by **Montreal** for Chad Kilger, December 18, 2000. Traded to **Minnesota** by **Edmonton** for Minnesota's 7th round choice (J.F. Dufort) in 2002 Entry Draft, June 29, 2001. Traded to **Nashville** by **Minnesota** with Brad Bombardir for Buffalo's 3rd round choice (previously acquired, Minnesota selected Clayton Stoner) in 2004 Entry Draft and Nashville's 4th round choice (Patrick Bordeleau) in 2004 Entry Draft, March 5, 2004.

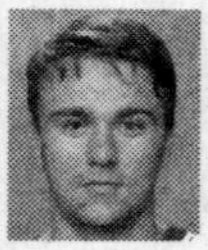

ZIDLICKY, Marek

(zhihd-LIHTS-kee, MAIR-ehk) **NSH.**

Defense. Shoots right. 5'11", 187 lbs. Born, Most, Czech., February 3, 1977. NY Rangers' 6th choice, 176th overall, in 2001 Entry Draft.

Season	Club	League	GP	G	A	Pts	PIM	PP	SH	GW	S	%	+/-	TF	F%	Min	GP	G	A	Pts	PIM	PP	SH	GW	Min
1994-95	HC Kladno	Czech	30	2	2	4	38	....	....	....	....	....	....	....	....	....	11	1	1	2	10	....	....	....	....
1995-96	HC Poldi Kladno	Czech	37	4	5	9	74	....	....	....	....	....	....	....	....	....	7	1	1	2	8	....	....	....	....
1996-97	HC Poldi Kladno	Czech	49	5	16	21	60	....	....	....	....	....	....	....	....	....	2	0	0	0	0	....	....	....	....
1997-98	Kladno	Czech	51	2	13	15	121	....	....	....	....	....	....	....	....	....	....	....	....	....	....	....	....	....	....
1998-99	Kladno	Czech	50	10	12	22	94	....	....	....	....	....	....	....	....	....	....	....	....	....	....	....	....	....	....
99-2000	HIFK Helsinki	Finland	47	4	16	20	66	....	....	....	....	....	....	....	....	....	9	3	2	5	24	....	....	....	....
	HIFK Helsinki	EuroHL	4	2	2	4	10	....	....	....	....	....	....	....	....	....	1	0	0	0	0	....	....	....	....
2000-01	HIFK Helsinki	Finland	51	12	25	37	146	....	....	....	....	....	....	....	....	....	5	0	1	1	6	....	....	....	....
2001-02	HIFK Helsinki	Finland	56	11	29	40	107	....	....	....	....	....	....	....	....	....	....	....	....	....	....	....	....	....	....
2002-03	HIFK Helsinki	Finland	54	10	37	47	79	....	....	....	....	....	....	....	....	....	4	0	0	0	4	....	....	....	....
2003-04	**Nashville**	**NHL**	**82**	**14**	**39**	**53**	**82**	**9**	**0**	**4**	**143**	**9.8**	**-16**	**0**	**0.0**	**20:02**	**1**	**0**	**0**	**0**	**0**	**0**	**0**	**0**	**2:16**
	NHL Totals		**82**	**14**	**39**	**53**	**82**	**9**	**0**	**4**	**143**	**9.8**		**0**	**0.0**	**20:02**	**1**	**0**	**0**	**0**	**0**	**0**	**0**	**0**	**2:16**

Traded to **Nashville** by NY Rangers with Rem Murray and Tomas Kloucek for Mike Dunham, December 12, 2002.

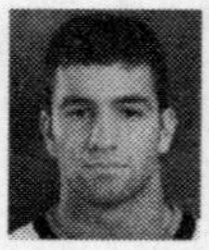

ZIGOMANIS, Mike

(zih-goh-MAN-his, MIGHK) **CAR.**

Center. Shoots right. 6'1", 189 lbs. Born, North York, Ont., January 17, 1981. Carolina's 2nd choice, 46th overall, in 2001 Entry Draft.

Season	Club	League	GP	G	A	Pts	PIM	PP	SH	GW	S	%	+/-	TF	F%	Min	GP	G	A	Pts	PIM	PP	SH	GW	Min
1996-97	Wexford Raiders	MTHL	40	37	48	85	23	....	....	....	....	....	....	....	....	....	....	....	....	....	....	....	....	....	....
	Wexford Raiders	MTJHL	8	2	5	7	2	....	....	....	....	....	....	....	....	....	....	....	....	....	....	....	....	....	....
1997-98	Kingston	OHL	62	23	51	74	30	....	....	....	....	....	....	....	....	....	12	1	6	7	2	....	....	....	....
1998-99	Kingston	OHL	67	29	56	85	36	....	....	....	....	....	....	....	....	....	5	1	7	8	2	....	....	....	....
99-2000	Kingston	OHL	59	40	54	94	49	....	....	....	....	....	....	....	....	....	5	0	4	4	0	....	....	....	....
2000-01	Kingston	OHL	52	40	37	77	44	....	....	....	....	....	....	....	....	....	....	....	....	....	....	....	....	....	....
2001-02	Lowell	AHL	79	18	30	48	24	....	....	....	....	....	....	....	....	....	5	1	1	2	2	....	....	....	....
2002-03	**Carolina**	**NHL**	**19**	**2**	**1**	**3**	**0**	**1**	**1**	**0**	**19**	**10.5**	**-4**	**147**	**59.2**	**9:43**	....	....	....	....	....	....	....	....	....
	Lowell	AHL	38	13	18	31	19	....	....	....	....	....	....	....	....	....	....	....	....	....	....	....	....	....	....
2003-04	**Carolina**	**NHL**	**17**	**0**	**3**	**3**	**2**	**0**	**0**	**0**	**13**	**0.0**	**-1**	**108**	**53.7**	**8:37**	....	....	....	....	....	....	....	....	....
	Lowell	AHL	61	17	35	52	56	....	....	....	....	....	....	....	....	....	....	....	....	....	....	....	....	....	....
	NHL Totals		**36**	**2**	**4**	**6**	**2**	**1**	**1**	**0**	**32**	**6.3**		**255**	**56.9**	**9:12**	....	....	....	....	....	....	....	....	....

• Re-entered NHL Entry Draft. Originally Buffalo's 4th choice, 64th overall, in 1999 Entry Draft.

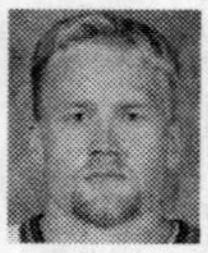

ZINGER, Dwayne

(ZIHN-guhr, DWAYN) **WSH.**

Defense. Shoots left. 6'4", 216 lbs. Born, Coronation, Alta., July 5, 1976.

Season	Club	League	GP	G	A	Pts	PIM	PP	SH	GW	S	%	+/-	TF	F%	Min	GP	G	A	Pts	PIM	PP	SH	GW	Min
1995-96	Melville	SJHL	64	7	17	24	....	....	....	....	....	....	....	....	....	....	....	....	....	....	....	....	....	....	....
1996-97	Alaska-Fairbanks	CCHA	32	1	5	6	45	....	....	....	....	....	....	....	....	....	....	....	....	....	....	....	....	....	....
1997-98	Alaska-Fairbanks	CCHA	32	1	3	4	91	....	....	....	....	....	....	....	....	....	....	....	....	....	....	....	....	....	....
1998-99	Alaska-Fairbanks	CCHA	33	4	14	18	42	....	....	....	....	....	....	....	....	....	....	....	....	....	....	....	....	....	....
99-2000	Alaska-Fairbanks	CCHA	34	10	4	14	34	....	....	....	....	....	....	....	....	....	....	....	....	....	....	....	....	....	....
	Cincinnati	AHL	13	0	2	2	33	....	....	....	....	....	....	....	....	....	....	....	....	....	....	....	....	....	....
2000-01	Cincinnati	AHL	68	6	9	15	120	....	....	....	....	....	....	....	....	....	4	1	1	2	2	....	....	....	....
2001-02	Cincinnati	AHL	67	6	13	19	156	....	....	....	....	....	....	....	....	....	3	0	1	1	2	....	....	....	....
2002-03	Portland Pirates	AHL	65	1	7	8	67	....	....	....	....	....	....	....	....	....	3	0	0	0	2	....	....	....	....
2003-04	**Washington**	**NHL**	**7**	**0**	**1**	**1**	**9**	**0**	**0**	**0**	**0**	**0.0**	**2**	**0**	**0.0**	**5:24**	....	....	....	....	....	....	....	....	....
	Portland Pirates	AHL	68	6	10	16	49	....	....	....	....	....	....	....	....	....	7	0	0	0	16	....	....	....	....
	NHL Totals		**7**	**0**	**1**	**1**	**9**	**0**	**0**	**0**	**0**	**0.0**		**0**	**0.0**	**5:24**	....	....	....	....	....	....	....	....	....

SJHL First All-Star Team (1996)

Signed as a free agent by **Detroit**, March 13, 2000. Signed as a free agent by **Washington**, July 9, 2002.

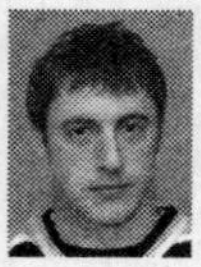

ZINOVJEV, Sergei

(zih-NOH-vee-ehv, SAIR-gay) **BOS.**

Center/Left wing. Shoots left. 5'10", 178 lbs. Born, Novokuznetsk, USSR, March 4, 1980. Boston's 6th choice, 73rd overall, in 2000 Entry Draft.

Season	Club	League	GP	G	A	Pts	PIM	PP	SH	GW	S	%	+/-	TF	F%	Min	GP	G	A	Pts	PIM	PP	SH	GW	Min
1995-96	Novokuznetsk 2	Russia-3	10	1	0	1	2	....	....	....	....	....	....	....	....	....	....	....	....	....	....	....	....	....	....
1996-97	Novokuznetsk 2	Russia-3	29	2	1	3	8	....	....	....	....	....	....	....	....	....	....	....	....	....	....	....	....	....	....
1997-98	Novokuznetsk 2	Russia-3	40	7	7	14	36	....	....	....	....	....	....	....	....	....	....	....	....	....	....	....	....	....	....
	Novokuznetsk	Russia-2	2	1	0	1	0	....	....	....	....	....	....	....	....	....	....	....	....	....	....	....	....	....	....
1998-99	Novokuznetsk 2	Russia-4	4	0	1	1	8	....	....	....	....	....	....	....	....	....	....	....	....	....	....	....	....	....	....
	Magnitogorsk	Russia	31	2	4	6	14	....	....	....	....	....	....	....	....	....	3	0	0	0	0	....	....	....	....
99-2000	Magnitogorsk	Russia	28	0	2	2	16	....	....	....	....	....	....	....	....	....	....	....	....	....	....	....	....	....	....
2000-01	Yaroslavl	Russia	27	2	10	12	36	....	....	....	....	....	....	....	....	....	....	....	....	....	....	....	....	....	....
	Ufa Salavat	Russia	8	4	5	9	6	....	....	....	....	....	....	....	....	....	....	....	....	....	....	....	....	....	....
2001-02	Spartak Moscow	Russia	51	12	18	30	43																		

			Regular Season														Playoffs								
Season	Club	League	GP	G	A	Pts	PIM	PP	SH	GW	S	%	+/-	TF	F%	Min	GP	G	A	Pts	PIM	PP	SH	GW	Min
2002-03	Ak Bars Kazan	Russia	47	14	17	31	50										5	1	1	2	6				
2003-04	**Boston**	**NHL**	**10**	**0**	**1**	**1**	**2**	**0**	**0**	**0**	**8**	**0.0**	**1**	**72**	**41.7**	**9:48**									
	Providence Bruins	AHL	4	1	2	3	0																		
	Ak Bars Kazan	Russia	27	5	9	14	75										8	0	1	1	12				
	NHL Totals		**10**	**0**	**1**	**1**	**2**	**0**	**0**	**0**	**8**	**0.0**		**72**	**41.7**	**9:48**									

Signed as a free agent by **Ak Bars Kazan** (Russia), December 9, 2003, with **Boston** retaining NHL rights.

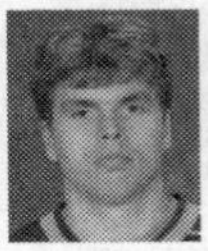

ZIZKA, Tomas

(ZHIHZH-kuh, TAW-mahsh) **L.A.**

Defense. Shoots left. 6'1", 198 lbs. Born, Sternberk, Czech., October 10, 1979. Los Angeles' 6th choice, 163rd overall, in 1998 Entry Draft.

Season	Club	League	GP	G	A	Pts	PIM	PP	SH	GW	S	%	+/-	TF	F%	Min	GP	G	A	Pts	PIM	PP	SH	GW	Min
1994-95	AC ZPS Zlin Jr.	Czech-Jr.	39	1	10	11																			
1995-96	AC ZPS Zlin Jr.	Czech-Jr.	47	2	8	10																			
1996-97	AC ZPS Zlin Jr.	Czech-Jr.	14	1	0	1																			
1997-98	Zlin Jr.	Czech-Jr.	11	3	4	7																			
	Zlin	Czech	33	0	3	3	2																		
1998-99	Zlin	Czech	44	3	7	10	14										11	1	2	3					
99-2000	Zlin	Czech	46	4	6	10	30										4	1	0	1	4				
2000-01	Zlin	Czech	43	2	11	13	16										6	0	0	0	6				
2001-02	Manchester	AHL	58	4	17	21	22										4	1	0	1	14				
2002-03	**Los Angeles**	**NHL**	**10**	**0**	**3**	**3**	**4**	**0**	**0**	**0**	**12**	**0.0**	**–4**	**0**	**0.0**	**15:24**									
	Manchester	AHL	61	13	30	43	50										3	0	2	2	2				
2003-04	**Los Angeles**	**NHL**	**15**	**2**	**3**	**5**	**12**	**1**	**0**	**0**	**24**	**8.3**	**–4**	**0**	**0.0**	**16:54**									
	Manchester	AHL	58	4	24	28	31										5	0	3	3	10				
	NHL Totals		**25**	**2**	**6**	**8**	**16**	**1**	**0**	**0**	**36**	**5.6**		**0**	**0.0**	**16:18**									

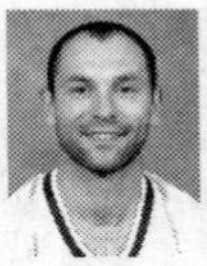

ZUBOV, Sergei

(ZOO-bahf, SAIR-gay) **DAL.**

Defense. Shoots right. 6'1", 200 lbs. Born, Moscow, USSR, July 22, 1970. NY Rangers' 6th choice, 85th overall, in 1990 Entry Draft.

Season	Club	League	GP	G	A	Pts	PIM	PP	SH	GW	S	%	+/-	TF	F%	Min	GP	G	A	Pts	PIM	PP	SH	GW	Min
1988-89	CSKA Moscow	USSR	29	1	4	5	10																		
1989-90	CSKA Moscow	USSR	48	6	2	8	16																		
1990-91	CSKA Moscow	USSR	41	6	5	11	12																		
1991-92	CSKA Moscow	CIS	44	4	7	11	8																		
	Russia	Olympics	8	0	1	1	0																		
1992-93	CSKA Moscow	CIS	1	0	1	1	0																		
	NY Rangers	**NHL**	**49**	**8**	**23**	**31**	**4**	**3**	**0**	**0**	**93**	**8.6**	**–1**												
	Binghamton	AHL	30	7	29	36	14										11	5	5	10	2				
1993-94♦	**NY Rangers**	**NHL**	**78**	**12**	**77**	**89**	**39**	**9**	**0**	**1**	**222**	**5.4**	**20**				**22**	**5**	**14**	**19**	**0**	**2**	**0**	**0**	
	Binghamton	AHL	2	1	2	3	0																		
1994-95	**NY Rangers**	**NHL**	**38**	**10**	**26**	**36**	**18**	**6**	**0**	**0**	**116**	**8.6**	**–2**				**10**	**3**	**8**	**11**	**2**	**1**	**0**	**0**	
1995-96	**Pittsburgh**	**NHL**	**64**	**11**	**55**	**66**	**22**	**3**	**2**	**1**	**141**	**7.8**	**28**				**18**	**1**	**14**	**15**	**26**	**1**	**0**	**0**	
1996-97	**Dallas**	**NHL**	**78**	**13**	**30**	**43**	**24**	**1**	**0**	**3**	**133**	**9.8**	**19**				**7**	**0**	**3**	**3**	**2**	**0**	**0**	**0**	
1997-98	**Dallas**	**NHL**	**73**	**10**	**47**	**57**	**16**	**5**	**1**	**2**	**148**	**6.8**	**16**				**17**	**4**	**5**	**9**	**2**	**3**	**0**	**1**	
1998-99♦	**Dallas**	**NHL**	**81**	**10**	**41**	**51**	**20**	**5**	**0**	**3**	**155**	**6.5**	**9**	**0**	**0.0**	**24:14**	**23**	**1**	**12**	**13**	**4**	**0**	**0**	**0**	**30:16**
99-2000	**Dallas**	**NHL**	**77**	**9**	**33**	**42**	**18**	**3**	**1**	**3**	**179**	**5.0**	**–2**	**0**	**0.0**	**28:50**	**18**	**2**	**7**	**9**	**6**	**1**	**1**	**0**	**26:28**
2000-01	**Dallas**	**NHL**	**79**	**10**	**41**	**51**	**24**	**6**	**0**	**1**	**173**	**5.8**	**22**	**0**	**0.0**	**26:37**	**10**	**1**	**5**	**6**	**4**	**0**	**0**	**0**	**30:37**
2001-02	**Dallas**	**NHL**	**80**	**12**	**32**	**44**	**22**	**8**	**0**	**2**	**198**	**6.1**	**–4**	**0**	**0.0**	**26:46**									
2002-03	**Dallas**	**NHL**	**82**	**11**	**44**	**55**	**26**	**8**	**0**	**2**	**158**	**7.0**	**21**	**0**	**0.0**	**25:50**	**12**	**4**	**10**	**14**	**4**	**2**	**0**	**0**	**30:45**
2003-04	**Dallas**	**NHL**	**77**	**7**	**35**	**42**	**20**	**4**	**1**	**1**	**154**	**4.5**	**0**	**0**	**0.0**	**25:50**	**5**	**1**	**1**	**2**	**0**	**1**	**0**	**0**	**28:01**
	NHL Totals		**856**	**123**	**484**	**607**	**253**	**61**	**5**	**19**	**1870**	**6.6**		**0**	**0.0**	**26:20**	**142**	**22**	**79**	**101**	**50**	**11**	**1**	**1**	**29:14**

Played in NHL All-Star Game (1998, 1999, 2000)

Traded to **Pittsburgh** by **NY Rangers** with Petr Nedved for Luc Robitaille and Ulf Samuelsson, August 31, 1995. Traded to **Dallas** by **Pittsburgh** for Kevin Hatcher, June 22, 1996.

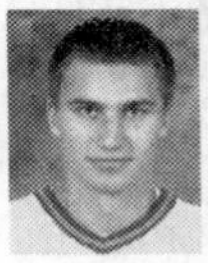

ZUBRUS, Dainius

(ZOO-bruhs, DAYN-ihs) **WSH.**

Right wing. Shoots left. 6'4", 226 lbs. Born, Elektrenai, USSR, June 16, 1978. Philadelphia's 1st choice, 15th overall, in 1996 Entry Draft.

Season	Club	League	GP	G	A	Pts	PIM	PP	SH	GW	S	%	+/-	TF	F%	Min	GP	G	A	Pts	PIM	PP	SH	GW	Min
1995-96	Pembroke	OCJHL	28	19	13	32	73																		
	Caledon	MTJHL	7	3	7	10	2										17	11	12	23	4				
1996-97	**Philadelphia**	**NHL**	**68**	**8**	**13**	**21**	**22**	**1**	**0**	**2**	**71**	**11.3**	**3**				**19**	**5**	**4**	**9**	**12**	**1**	**0**	**1**	
1997-98	**Philadelphia**	**NHL**	**69**	**8**	**25**	**33**	**42**	**1**	**0**	**5**	**101**	**7.9**	**29**				**5**	**0**	**1**	**1**	**2**	**0**	**0**	**0**	
1998-99	**Philadelphia**	**NHL**	**63**	**3**	**5**	**8**	**25**	**0**	**1**	**0**	**49**	**6.1**	**–5**	**29**	**51.7**	**11:00**									
	Montreal	**NHL**	**17**	**3**	**5**	**8**	**4**	**0**	**0**	**1**	**31**	**9.7**	**–3**	**2**	**50.0**	**16:53**									
99-2000	**Montreal**	**NHL**	**73**	**14**	**28**	**42**	**54**	**3**	**0**	**1**	**139**	**10.1**	**–1**	**212**	**39.2**	**17:37**									
2000-01	**Montreal**	**NHL**	**49**	**12**	**12**	**24**	**30**	**3**	**0**	**0**	**70**	**17.1**	**–7**	**190**	**41.1**	**18:30**									
	Washington	**NHL**	**12**	**1**	**1**	**2**	**7**	**1**	**0**	**0**	**13**	**7.7**	**–4**	**0**	**0.0**	**13:05**	**6**	**0**	**0**	**0**	**2**	**0**	**0**	**0**	**17:23**
2001-02	**Washington**	**NHL**	**71**	**17**	**26**	**43**	**38**	**4**	**0**	**3**	**138**	**12.3**	**5**	**131**	**37.4**	**18:52**									
2002-03	**Washington**	**NHL**	**63**	**13**	**22**	**35**	**43**	**2**	**0**	**0**	**104**	**12.5**	**15**	**565**	**50.3**	**16:26**	**6**	**2**	**2**	**4**	**4**	**1**	**0**	**0**	**21:30**
2003-04	**Washington**	**NHL**	**54**	**12**	**15**	**27**	**38**	**6**	**1**	**2**	**115**	**10.4**	**–16**	**916**	**48.0**	**19:31**									
	NHL Totals		**539**	**91**	**152**	**243**	**303**	**21**	**2**	**14**	**831**	**11.0**		**2045**	**46.5**	**16:49**	**36**	**7**	**7**	**14**	**20**	**2**	**0**	**1**	**19:27**

Traded to **Montreal** by **Philadelphia** with Philadelphia's 2nd round choice (Matt Carkner) in 1999 Entry Draft and NY Islanders' 6th round choice (previously acquired, Montreal selected Scott Selig) in 2000 Entry Draft for Mark Recchi, March 10, 1999. Traded to **Washington** by **Montreal** with Trevor Linden and New Jersey's 2nd round choice (previously acquired, later traded to Tampa Bay – Tampa Bay selected Andreas Holmqvist) in 2001 Entry Draft for Richard Zednik, Jan Bulis and Washington's 1st round choice (Alexander Perezhogin) in 2001 Entry Draft, March 13, 2001.

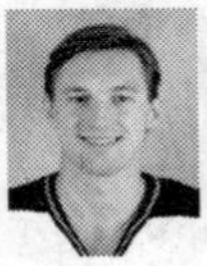

ZYUZIN, Andrei

(ZYOO-zin, AWN-dray) **MIN.**

Defense. Shoots left. 6'1", 215 lbs. Born, Ufa, USSR, January 21, 1978. San Jose's 1st choice, 2nd overall, in 1996 Entry Draft.

Season	Club	League	GP	G	A	Pts	PIM	PP	SH	GW	S	%	+/-	TF	F%	Min	GP	G	A	Pts	PIM	PP	SH	GW	Min
1994-95	Ufa Salavat	CIS	30	3	0	3	16																		
1995-96	Ufa Salavat	CIS	41	6	3	9	24																		
1996-97	Ufa Salavat	Russia	32	7	10	17	28										7	1	1	2	4				
1997-98	**San Jose**	**NHL**	**56**	**6**	**7**	**13**	**66**	**2**	**0**	**2**	**72**	**8.3**	**8**				**6**	**1**	**0**	**1**	**14**	**0**	**0**	**1**	
	Kentucky	AHL	17	4	5	9	28																		
1998-99	**San Jose**	**NHL**	**25**	**3**	**1**	**4**	**38**	**2**	**0**	**0**	**44**	**6.8**	**5**	**0**	**0.0**	**15:56**									
	Kentucky	AHL	23	2	12	14	42																		
99-2000	**Tampa Bay**	**NHL**	**34**	**2**	**9**	**11**	**33**	**0**	**0**	**0**	**47**	**4.3**	**–11**	**0**	**0.0**	**20:28**									
2000-01	**Tampa Bay**	**NHL**	**64**	**4**	**16**	**20**	**76**	**2**	**1**	**1**	**92**	**4.3**	**–8**	**0**	**0.0**	**18:39**									
	Detroit Vipers	IHL	2	0	1	1	0																		
2001-02	**Tampa Bay**	**NHL**	**9**	**0**	**2**	**2**	**6**	**0**	**0**	**0**	**14**	**0.0**	**–6**	**0**	**0.0**	**19:41**									
	New Jersey	**NHL**	**38**	**1**	**2**	**3**	**25**	**1**	**0**	**0**	**47**	**2.1**	**1**	**0**	**0.0**	**15:04**									
	Albany River Rats	AHL	3	0	1	1	2																		
2002-03	**New Jersey**	**NHL**	**1**	**0**	**1**	**1**	**2**	**0**	**0**	**0**	**0**	**0.0**	**–1**	**0**	**0.0**	**20:03**									
	Minnesota	**NHL**	**66**	**4**	**12**	**16**	**34**	**2**	**0**	**0**	**113**	**3.5**	**–7**	**4**	**25.0**	**21:38**	**18**	**0**	**1**	**1**	**14**	**0**	**0**	**0**	**23:07**
2003-04	**Minnesota**	**NHL**	**65**	**8**	**13**	**21**	**48**	**4**	**0**	**1**	**104**	**7.7**	**4**	**0**	**0.0**	**20:22**									
	NHL Totals		**358**	**28**	**63**	**91**	**328**	**13**	**1**	**4**	**533**	**5.3**		**4**	**25.0**	**19:14**	**24**	**1**	**1**	**2**	**28**	**0**	**0**	**1**	**23:07**

• Suspended for remainder of 1998-99 season by **San Jose** for leaving team without permission, April 1, 1999. Traded to **Tampa Bay** by **San Jose** with Bill Houlder, Shawn Burr and Steve Guolla for Niklas Sundstrom and NY Rangers' 3rd round choice (previously acquired, later traded to Chicago – Chicago selected Igor Radulov) in 2000 Entry Draft, August 4, 1999. • Missed majority of 1999-2000 season recovering from shoulder injury suffered in game vs. NY Islanders, January 13, 2000. Traded to **New Jersey** by **Tampa Bay** for Josef Boumedienne, Sascha Goc and the rights to Anton But, November 9, 2001. Claimed on waivers by **Minnesota** from **New Jersey**, November 2, 2002.

NHL Goaltenders

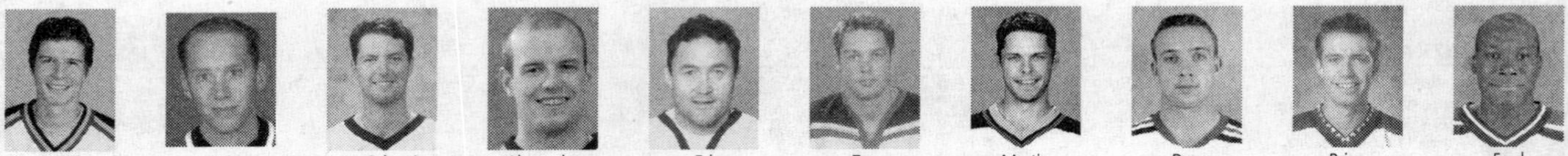

David Aebischer | Craig Anderson | Jean-Sebastien Aubin | Alexander Auld | Ed Belfour | Zac Bierk | Martin Biron | Dan Blackburn | Brian Boucher | Fred Brathwaite

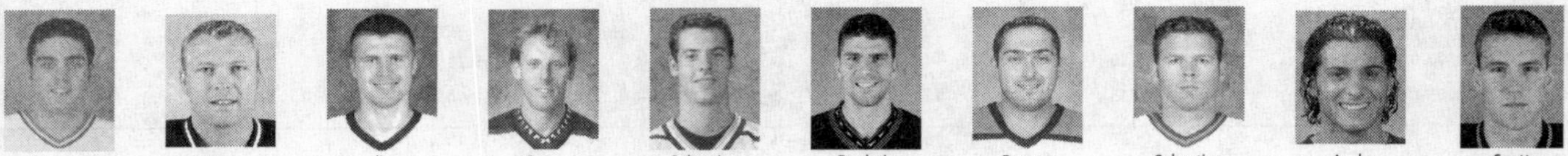

Martin Brochu | Martin Brodeur | Ilja Bryzgalov | Sean Burke | Sebastian Caron | Frederic Cassivi | Roman Cechmanek | Sebastien Charpentier | Andy Chiodo | Scott Clemmensen

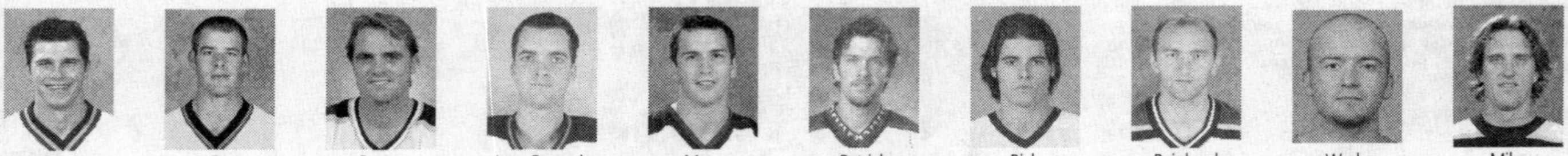

Dan Cloutier | Ty Conklin | Byron Dafoe | Jean-Francois Damphousse | Marc Denis | Patrick DesRochers | Rick DiPietro | Reinhard Divis | Wade Dubielewicz | Mike Dunham

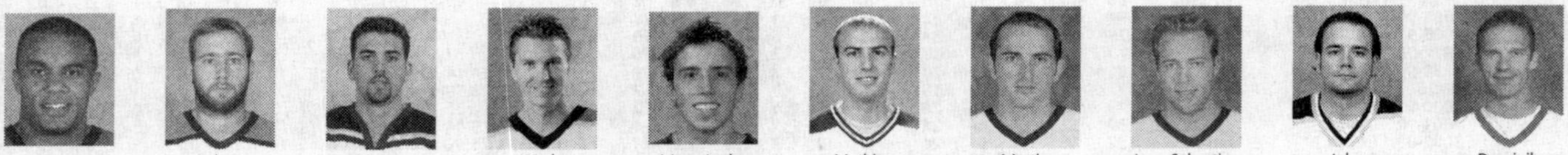

Ray Emery | Robert Esche | Manny Fernandez | Wade Flaherty | Marc-Andre Fleury | Mathieu Garon | Martin Gerber | Jean-Sebastien Giguere | John Grahame | Dominik Hasek

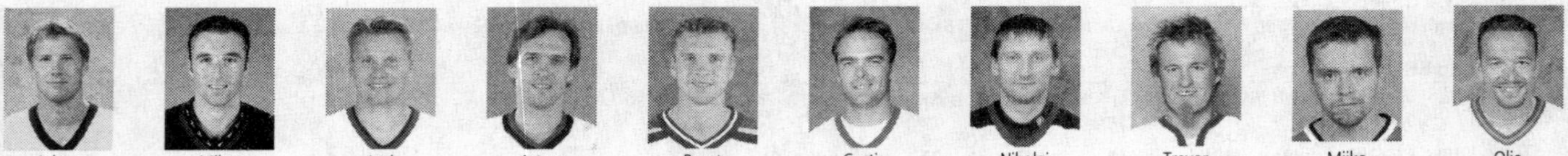

Johan Hedberg | Milan Hnilicka | Jani Hurme | Arturs Irbe | Brent Johnson | Curtis Joseph | Nikolai Khabibulin | Trevor Kidd | Miika Kiprusoff | Olie Kolzig

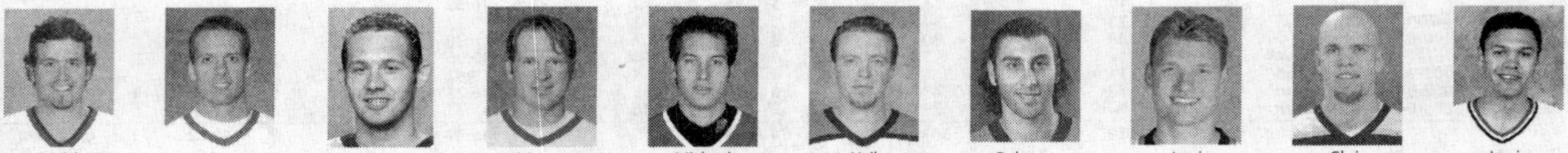

Patrick Lalime | Marc Lamothe | Jan Lasak | Manny Legace | Michael Leighton | Neil Little | Roberto Luongo | Jussi Markkanen | Chris Mason | Jamie McLennan

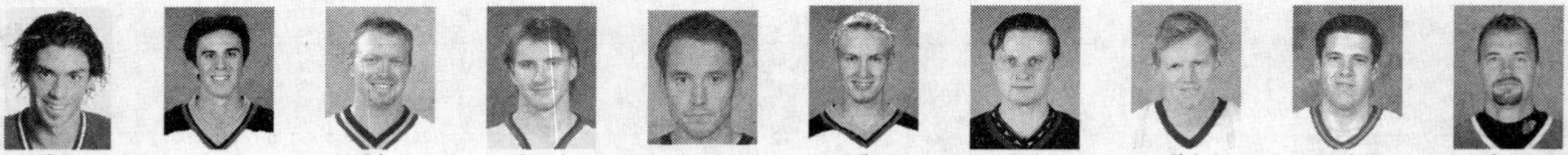

Olivier Michaud | Ryan Miller | Tyler Moss | Evgeni Nabokov | Antero Niittymaki | Mika Noronen | Pasi Nurminen | Chris Osgood | Maxime Ouellet | Steve Passmore

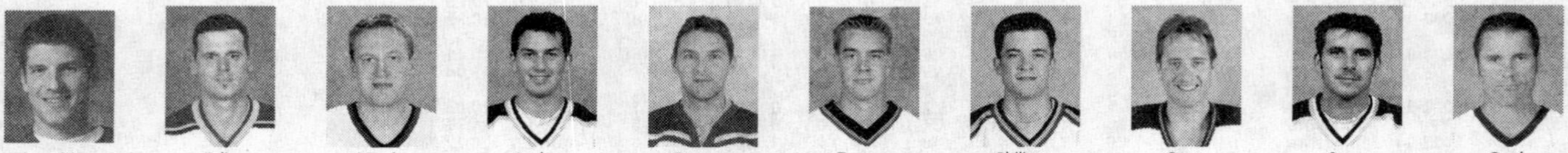

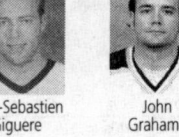

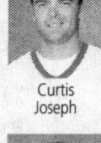

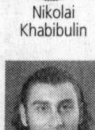

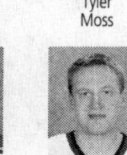

Jean-Marc Pelletier | Felix Potvin | Martin Prusek | Andrew Raycroft | Dwayne Roloson | Tommy Salo | Philippe Sauve | Corey Schwab | Steve Shields | Garth Snow

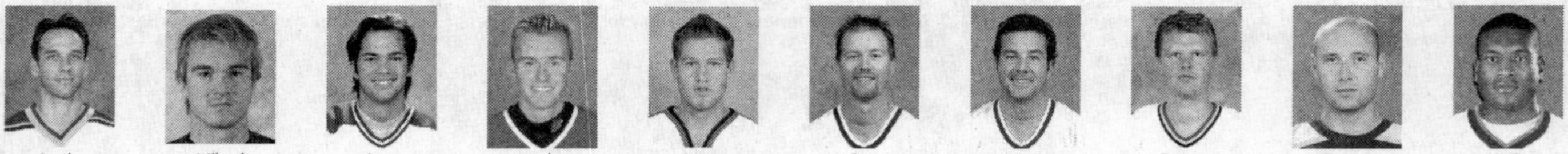

Jamie Storr | Mikael Tellqvist | Jose Theodore | Jocelyn Thibault | Vesa Toskala | Ron Tugnutt | Marty Turco | Roman Turek | Tomas Vokoun | Kevin Weekes

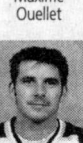

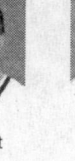

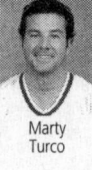

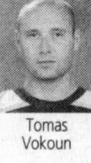

2004-05 Goaltender Register

Note: The 2004-05 Goaltender Register lists every goaltender who appeared in an NHL game in the 2003-04 season, every goaltender drafted in the first five rounds of the 2004 Entry Draft, goaltenders on NHL Reserve Lists and other goaltenders.

Trades and roster changes are current as of August 11, 2004.

To calculate a goaltender's goals-against per game average **(Avg)**, divide goals against **(GA)** by minutes played **(Mins)** and multiply this result by **60**.

Abbreviations: GP – games played; **W** – wins; **L** – losses; **T** – ties; **GA** – goals against; **SO** – shutouts; **Avg** – goals-against per game average.
♦ – member of Stanley Cup-winning team.

NHL Player Register begins on page 339.
Prospect Register begins on page 267.
League Abbreviations are listed on page 337.

AEBISCHER, David (A-bih-shuhr, DAY-vihd) COL.

Goaltender. Catches left. 6'1", 190 lbs. Born, Fribourg, Switz., February 7, 1978.
(Colorado's 7th choice, 161st overall, in 1997 Entry Draft).

			Regular Season								Playoffs						
Season	**Club**	**League**	**GP**	**W**	**L**	**T**	**Mins**	**GA**	**SO**	**Avg**	**GP**	**W**	**L**	**Mins**	**GA**	**SO**	**Avg**
1996-97	Fribourg	Swiss	10	....	....	....	577	34	0	3.54	3	1	2	184	13	0	4.24
1997-98	Chesapeake	ECHL	17	5	7	2	930	52	0	3.35	....	....	....	....	....	....	....
	Wheeling Nailers	ECHL	10	5	3	1	564	30	1	3.19	....	....	....	....	....	....	....
	Hershey Bears	AHL	2	0	0	1	79	5	0	3.76	....	....	....	....	....	....	....
	Fribourg	Swiss	1	1	0	0	60	1	0	1.00	4	....	....	240	17	....	4.25
1998-99	Hershey Bears	AHL	38	17	10	5	1932	79	2	2.45	3	1	2	152	6	0	2.37
99-2000	Hershey Bears	AHL	58	29	23	2	3259	180	1	3.31	14	7	6	788	40	2	3.05
2000-01♦	**Colorado**	**NHL**	**26**	**12**	**7**	**3**	**1393**	**52**	**3**	**2.24**	**1**	**0**	**0**	**1**	**0**	**0**	**0.00**
2001-02	**Colorado**	**NHL**	**21**	**13**	**6**	**0**	**1184**	**37**	**2**	**1.88**	**1**	**0**	**0**	**34**	**1**	**0**	**1.76**
	Switzerland	Olympics	2	1	0	0	81	6	0	4.43	....	....	....	....	....	....	....
2002-03	**Colorado**	**NHL**	**22**	**7**	**12**	**0**	**1235**	**50**	**1**	**2.43**	....	....	....	....	....	....	....
2003-04	**Colorado**	**NHL**	**62**	**32**	**19**	**9**	**3703**	**129**	**4**	**2.09**	**11**	**6**	**5**	**662**	**23**	**1**	**2.08**
	NHL Totals		**131**	**64**	**44**	**12**	**7515**	**268**	**10**	**2.14**	**13**	**6**	**5**	**697**	**24**	**1**	**2.07**

AHONEN, Ari (ah-HOH-nuhn, AH-ree) N.J.

Goaltender. Catches left. 6'2", 195 lbs. Born, Jyvaskyla, Finland, February 6, 1981.
(New Jersey's 1st choice, 27th overall, in 1999 Entry Draft).

			Regular Season								Playoffs						
Season	**Club**	**League**	**GP**	**W**	**L**	**T**	**Mins**	**GA**	**SO**	**Avg**	**GP**	**W**	**L**	**Mins**	**GA**	**SO**	**Avg**
1997-98	JYP Jyvaskyla Jr.	Finn-Jr.	31	....	....	....	1853	64	....	2.09	....	....	....	....	....	....	....
1998-99	JYP Jyvaskyla Jr.	Finn-Jr.	24	....	....	....	1447	70	....	2.90	....	....	....	....	....	....	....
99-2000	HIFK Helsinki	Finland	24	11	7	1	1347	70	1	3.12	2	0	2	119	7	0	3.53
	HIFK Helsinki	EuroHL	5	4	1	0	285	15	1	3.16	....	....	....	....	....	....	....
2000-01	HIFK Helsinki	Finland	37	18	13	4	2101	97	2	2.77	5	2	3	395	9	1	1.37
2001-02	Albany River Rats	AHL	36	6	22	6	2106	106	0	3.02	....	....	....	....	....	....	....
2002-03	Albany River Rats	AHL	38	13	20	3	2171	110	1	3.04	....	....	....	....	....	....	....
2003-04	Albany River Rats	AHL	50	13	30	6	3012	150	2	2.99	....	....	....	....	....	....	....

AKERLUND, Magnus (AK-uhr-luhnd, MAG-nuhs) CAR.

Goaltender. Catches right. 6'1", 183 lbs. Born, Osby, Sweden, April 25, 1986.
(Carolina's 5th choice, 137th overall, in 2004 Entry Draft).

			Regular Season								Playoffs						
Season	**Club**	**League**	**GP**	**W**	**L**	**T**	**Mins**	**GA**	**SO**	**Avg**	**GP**	**W**	**L**	**Mins**	**GA**	**SO**	**Avg**
2002-03	HV 71 Jr.	Swede-Jr.	18	....	....	....	861	44	1	3.07	2	....	....	80	6	0	4.50
2003-04	HV 71 Jr.	Swede-Jr.	26	....	....	....	1556	85	1	3.28	2	....	....	119	10	0	5.04

ANDERSON, Craig (AN-duhr-suhn, KRAYG) CHI.

Goaltender. Catches left. 6'2", 174 lbs. Born, Park Ridge, IL, May 21, 1981.
(Chicago's 4th choice, 73rd overall, in 2001 Entry Draft).

			Regular Season								Playoffs						
Season	**Club**	**League**	**GP**	**W**	**L**	**T**	**Mins**	**GA**	**SO**	**Avg**	**GP**	**W**	**L**	**Mins**	**GA**	**SO**	**Avg**
1997-98	Chicago Jets	MEHL	50	....	....	....	2991	143	2	2.86	....	....	....	....	....	....	....
1998-99	Chicago Freeze	NAJHL	14	11	3	0	840	40	0	2.56	....	....	....	....	....	....	....
	Guelph Storm	OHL	21	12	5	1	1006	52	1	3.10	3	0	2	114	9	0	4.74
99-2000	Guelph Storm	OHL	38	12	17	2	1955	117	0	3.59	3	0	1	110	5	0	2.73
2000-01	Guelph Storm	OHL	59	30	19	9	3555	156	3	2.63	4	0	4	240	17	0	4.25
2001-02	Norfolk Admirals	AHL	28	9	13	4	1568	77	2	2.95	1	0	1	21	1	0	2.83
2002-03	**Chicago**	**NHL**	**6**	**0**	**3**	**2**	**270**	**18**	**0**	**4.00**	....	....	....	....	....	....	....
	Norfolk Admirals	AHL	32	15	11	5	1795	58	4	1.94	5	2	3	345	15	0	2.61
2003-04	**Chicago**	**NHL**	**21**	**6**	**14**	**0**	**1205**	**57**	**1**	**2.84**	....	....	....	....	....	....	....
	Norfolk Admirals	AHL	37	17	20	0	2108	74	3	2.11	5	2	3	327	10	0	1.84
	NHL Totals		**27**	**6**	**17**	**2**	**1475**	**75**	**1**	**3.05**	....	....	....	....	....	....	....

• Re-entered NHL Entry Draft. Originally Calgary's 3rd choice, 77th overall, in 1999 Entry Draft.

OHL First All-Star Team (2001)

ANDERSSON, Andreas (AN-duhr-suhn, an-DRAY-uhs) ANA.

Goaltender. Catches left. 6', 180 lbs. Born, Jonkoping, Sweden, April 9, 1979.
(Anaheim's 8th choice, 245th overall, in 1998 Entry Draft).

			Regular Season								Playoffs						
Season	**Club**	**League**	**GP**	**W**	**L**	**T**	**Mins**	**GA**	**SO**	**Avg**	**GP**	**W**	**L**	**Mins**	**GA**	**SO**	**Avg**
1997-98	HV 71 Jr.	Swede-Jr.	10	....	....	....	600	31	....	3.10	....	....	....	....	....	....	....
	HV 71 Jonkoping	Sweden	7	....	....	....	420	20	....	2.86	....	....	....	....	....	....	....
1998-99	Mora IK Jr.	Swede-Jr.	12	....	....	....	720	28	0	1.92	....	....	....	....	....	....	....
	HV 71 Jonkoping	Sweden	12	....	....	....	633	35	0	3.32	....	....	....	....	....	....	....
99-2000	Tranas AIF	Swede-2	5	....	....	....	297	17	0	3.44	....	....	....	....	....	....	....
	HV 71 Jonkoping	Sweden	1	....	....	....	51	5	0	5.88	....	....	....	....	....	....	....
2000-01	IF Troja-Ljungby	Swede-2	19	....	....	....	1076	66	0	3.68	2	1	1	120	5	0	2.50
2001-02	IF Troja-Ljungby	Swede-2	6	....	....	....	360	27	0	4.50	....	....	....	....	....	....	....
2002-03	IF Troja-Ljungby	Swede-2	9	....	....	....	419	20	0	2.86	2	....	....	116	3	0	1.55
2003-04	IF Troja-Ljungby	Swede-2	32	....	....	....	1735	76	4	2.63	....	....	....	....	....	....	....

ANTILA, Kristian (AN-tih-luh, KRIHS-tan) EDM.

Goaltender. Catches left. 6'3", 207 lbs. Born, Vammala, Finland, January 10, 1980.
(Edmonton's 4th choice, 113th overall, in 1998 Entry Draft).

			Regular Season								Playoffs						
Season	**Club**	**League**	**GP**	**W**	**L**	**T**	**Mins**	**GA**	**SO**	**Avg**	**GP**	**W**	**L**	**Mins**	**GA**	**SO**	**Avg**
1997-98	Ilves Tampere Jr.	Finn-Jr.	11	....	....	....	564	28	0	2.97	....	....	....	....	....	....	....
1998-99	Ilves Tampere Jr.	Finn-Jr.	18	8	8	1	1080	48	0	2.63	5	....	....	300	11	....	2.22
	Ilves Tampere	Finland	5	1	2	0	207	12	0	3.48	....	....	....	....	....	....	....
99-2000	Ilves Tampere Jr.	Finn-Jr.	6	4	2	0	360	21	0	3.56	....	....	....	....	....	....	....
	Diskos Jyvaskyla	Finland-2	5	1	4	0	300	23	0	4.67	....	....	....	....	....	....	....
	Ilves Tampere	Finland	25	4	11	4	1239	74	1	3.58	1	0	1	20	4	0	12.00
2000-01	Assat Pori	Finland	42	9	27	7	2417	146	1	3.62	....	....	....	....	....	....	....
2001-02	Assat Pori	Finland	35	7	22	3	1951	112	3	3.44	....	....	....	....	....	....	....
2002-03	Hamilton Bulldogs	AHL	2	1	1	0	97	6	0	3.71	....	....	....	....	....	....	....
	Wichita Thunder	CHL	21	10	7	2	1147	70	0	3.66	....	....	....	....	....	....	....
2003-04	Columbus	ECHL	9	1	5	0	334	17	1	3.06	....	....	....	....	....	....	....
	AIK Solna	Swede-2	4	....	....	....	241	7	2	1.74	5	....	....	308	6	1	1.17

Loaned to **AIK Solna** (Sweden-2) by **Edmonton**, January 28, 2004.

ASKEY, Tom (AS-kee, TAWM) BUF.

Goaltender. Catches left. 6'1", 195 lbs. Born, Kenmore, NY, October 4, 1974.
(Anaheim's 8th choice, 186th overall, in 1993 Entry Draft).

			Regular Season								Playoffs						
Season	**Club**	**League**	**GP**	**W**	**L**	**T**	**Mins**	**GA**	**SO**	**Avg**	**GP**	**W**	**L**	**Mins**	**GA**	**SO**	**Avg**
1992-93	Ohio State	CCHA	25	2	19	0	1235	125	0	6.07	....	....	....	....	....	....	....
1993-94	Ohio State	CCHA	27	3	19	4	1488	103	0	4.15	....	....	....	....	....	....	....
1994-95	Ohio State	CCHA	26	4	19	2	1387	121	0	5.23	....	....	....	....	....	....	....
1995-96	Ohio State	CCHA	26	8	11	4	1340	68	0	3.05	....	....	....	....	....	....	....
1996-97	Baltimore Bandits	AHL	40	17	18	2	2238	140	1	3.75	3	0	3	137	11	0	4.79
1997-98	**Anaheim**	**NHL**	**7**	**0**	**1**	**2**	**273**	**12**	**0**	**2.64**	....	....	....	....	....	....	....
	Cincinnati	AHL	32	10	16	4	1753	104	3	3.56	....	....	....	....	....	....	....
1998-99	Cincinnati	AHL	53	21	22	3	2893	131	3	2.72	3	0	3	178	13	0	4.38
	Anaheim	**NHL**	....	....	....	....	....	....	....	....	**1**	**0**	**1**	**30**	**2**	**0**	**4.00**
99-2000	Kansas City Blades	IHL	13	3	5	3	658	43	0	3.92	....	....	....	....	....	....	....
	Houston Aeros	IHL	13	4	7	1	727	33	0	2.72	....	....	....	....	....	....	....
2000-01	Rochester	AHL	29	15	8	4	1671	71	1	2.55	....	....	....	....	....	....	....
2001-02	Rochester	AHL	34	16	15	3	2048	86	3	2.52	1	0	1	58	4	0	4.11
2002-03	Rochester	AHL	16	3	8	4	895	49	0	3.28	....	....	....	....	....	....	....
2003-04	Rochester	AHL	21	10	8	3	1273	48	1	2.26	2	2	0	120	5	1	2.50
	NHL Totals		**7**	**0**	**1**	**2**	**273**	**12**	**0**	**2.64**	**1**	**0**	**1**	**30**	**2**	**0**	**4.00**

CCHA Second All-Star Team (1996) • Shared Harry "Hap" Holmes Memorial Trophy (fewest goals against – AHL) (2001) with Mika Noronen

Signed as a free agent by **Rochester** (AHL), September 29, 2000. Signed as a free agent by **Buffalo**, August 10, 2001.

ASPLUND, Johan (AS-pluhnd, YOH-hahn) NYR

Goaltender. Catches left. 6'1", 180 lbs. Born, Slutskar, Sweden, December 15, 1980.
(NY Rangers' 4th choice, 79th overall, in 1999 Entry Draft).

			Regular Season								Playoffs						
Season	**Club**	**League**	**GP**	**W**	**L**	**T**	**Mins**	**GA**	**SO**	**Avg**	**GP**	**W**	**L**	**Mins**	**GA**	**SO**	**Avg**
1998-99	Brynas IF Gavle	Sweden	12	....	....	....	646	32	0	2.97	....	....	....	....	....	....	....
99-2000	Mora IK	Swede-2	3	3	0	0	180	6	0	2.00	....	....	....	....	....	....	....
	Brynas IF Gavle	Sweden	10	....	....	....	622	30	0	2.89	....	....	....	....	....	....	....
2000-01	Brynas IF Gavle	Sweden	29	....	....	....	1761	79	2	2.69	3	0	3	177	11	0	3.73
2001-02	Brynas IF Gavle	Sweden	34	....	....	....	2069	102	1	2.96	3	0	3	188	16	0	5.11
2002-03	Brynas IF Gavle	Sweden	13	....	....	....	680	43	0	3.79	....	....	....	....	....	....	....
2003-04	Nykopings 90	Swede-2	20	....	....	....	1092	48	2	2.64	2	....	....	100	4	0	2.40

Signed as a free agent by **Nykopings 90** (Swede-2) with NY Rangers retaining NHL rights, May 11, 2003.

AUBIN, Jean-Sebastien (OH-behn, ZHAWN-suh-BAS-tee-yeh)

Goaltender. Catches right. 5'11", 180 lbs. Born, Montreal, Que., July 19, 1977.
(Pittsburgh's 2nd choice, 76th overall, in 1995 Entry Draft).

			Regular Season								Playoffs						
Season	**Club**	**League**	**GP**	**W**	**L**	**T**	**Mins**	**GA**	**SO**	**Avg**	**GP**	**W**	**L**	**Mins**	**GA**	**SO**	**Avg**
1993-94	Montreal-Bourassa	QAAA	27	14	13	0	1524	96	1	3.74	4	1	3	222	19	0	5.14
1994-95	Sherbrooke	QMJHL	27	13	10	1	1287	73	1	3.40	3	1	2	185	11	0	3.57
1995-96	Sherbrooke	QMJHL	40	18	14	2	2140	127	0	3.57	4	1	3	238	23	0	5.55

Season	Club	League	GP	W	L	T	Mins	GA	SO	Avg	GP	W	L	Mins	GA	SO	Avg
1996-97	Sherbrooke	QMJHL	4	3	1	0	249	8	0	1.93	1	0	1	60	4	0	4.00
	Moncton Wildcats	QMJHL	22	9	12	0	1252	67	1	3.21	....	....	....	....	....	....	....
	Laval Titan	QMJHL	11	2	6	1	532	41	0	4.62	....	....	....	....	....	....	....
1997-98	Syracuse Crunch	AHL	8	2	4	1	380	26	0	4.10	....	....	....	....	....	....	....
	Dayton Bombers	ECHL	21	15	2	2	1177	59	1	3.01	3	1	1	142	4	0	1.69
1998-99	**Pittsburgh**	**NHL**	**17**	**4**	**3**	**6**	**756**	**28**	**2**	**2.22**	....	....	....	....	....	....	....
	Kansas City Blades	IHL	13	5	7	1	751	41	0	3.28	....	....	....	....	....	....	....
99-2000	**Pittsburgh**	**NHL**	**51**	**23**	**21**	**3**	**2789**	**120**	**2**	**2.58**	....	....	....	....	....	....	....
	Wilkes-Barre	AHL	11	2	8	0	538	39	0	4.35	....	....	....	....	....	....	....
2000-01	**Pittsburgh**	**NHL**	**36**	**20**	**14**	**1**	**2050**	**107**	**0**	**3.13**	**1**	**0**	**0**	**1**	**0**	**0**	**0.00**
2001-02	**Pittsburgh**	**NHL**	**21**	**3**	**12**	**1**	**1094**	**65**	**0**	**3.56**	....	....	....	....	....	....	....
2002-03	**Pittsburgh**	**NHL**	**21**	**6**	**13**	**0**	**1132**	**59**	**1**	**3.13**	....	....	....	....	....	....	....
	Wilkes-Barre	AHL	16	8	6	1	919	29	3	1.89	6	3	3	356	12	0	2.02
2003-04	**Pittsburgh**	**NHL**	**22**	**7**	**9**	**0**	**1067**	**53**	**1**	**2.98**	....	....	....	....	....	....	....
	Wilkes-Barre	AHL	13	4	5	2	670	31	0	2.78	....	....	....	....	....	....	....
	NHL Totals		**168**	**63**	**72**	**11**	**8888**	**432**	**6**	**2.92**	**1**	**0**	**0**	**1**	**0**	**0**	**0.00**

AULD, Alexander (AWLD, al-ehx-AN-duhr) VAN.

Goaltender. Catches left. 6'4", 197 lbs. Born, Cold Lake, Alta., January 7, 1981.
(Florida's 2nd choice, 40th overall, in 1999 Entry Draft).

			Regular Season								Playoffs						
Season	Club	League	GP	W	L	T	Mins	GA	SO	Avg	GP	W	L	Mins	GA	SO	Avg
1996-97	Thunder Bay Kings	TBMHL	35	....	....	....	2100	46	10	1.35	....	....	....	....	....	....	....
1997-98	Sturgeon Falls Lynx	NOJHA	11	4	6	0	611	46	0	4.52	....	....	....	....	....	....	....
	North Bay	OHL	6	0	4	0	206	17	0	4.95	....	....	....	....	....	....	....
1998-99	North Bay	OHL	37	9	20	1	1894	106	1	3.36	3	0	3	170	10	0	3.53
99-2000	North Bay	OHL	55	21	26	6	3047	167	2	3.29	6	2	4	374	12	0	*1.93
2000-01	North Bay	OHL	40	22	11	5	2319	98	1	2.54	4	0	4	240	15	0	3.75
2001-02	**Vancouver**	**NHL**	**1**	**1**	**0**	**0**	**60**	**2**	**0**	**2.00**	....	....	....	....	....	....	....
	Columbia Inferno	ECHL	6	3	1	2	375	12	0	1.92	....	....	....	....	....	....	....
	Manitoba Moose	AHL	21	11	9	0	1104	65	1	3.53	1	0	0	20	0	0	0.00
2002-03	**Vancouver**	**NHL**	**7**	**3**	**3**	**0**	**382**	**10**	**1**	**1.57**	**1**	**0**	**0**	**20**	**1**	**0**	**3.00**
	Manitoba Moose	AHL	37	15	19	3	2209	97	3	2.64	....	....	....	....	....	....	....
2003-04	**Vancouver**	**NHL**	**6**	**2**	**2**	**2**	**349**	**12**	**0**	**2.06**	**3**	**1**	**2**	**222**	**9**	**0**	**2.43**
	Manitoba Moose	AHL	40	18	16	4	2329	99	4	2.55	....	....	....	....	....	....	....
	NHL Totals		**14**	**6**	**5**	**2**	**791**	**24**	**1**	**1.82**	**4**	**1**	**2**	**242**	**10**	**0**	**2.48**

Rights traded to **Vancouver** by **Florida** for Vancouver's compensatory 2nd round choice (later traded to New Jersey – New Jersey selected Tuomas Pihlman) in 2001 Entry Draft and Vancouver's 3rd round choice (later traded to Atlanta – later traded to Buffalo – Buffalo selected John Adams) in 2002 Entry Draft, May 31, 2001.

BACASHIHUA, Jason (bak-ah-SHIH-hu-ah, JAY-suhn) ST.L.

Goaltender. Catches left. 5'11", 175 lbs. Born, Garden City, MI, September 20, 1982.
(Dallas' 1st choice, 26th overall, in 2001 Entry Draft).

			Regular Season								Playoffs						
Season	Club	League	GP	W	L	T	Mins	GA	SO	Avg	GP	W	L	Mins	GA	SO	Avg
99-2000	Chicago Freeze	NAJHL	41	20	19	2	2432	118	2	2.91	2	0	2	103	12	0	6.97
2000-01	Chicago Freeze	NAJHL	39	24	14	0	2246	121	1	3.23	3	1	2	190	12	0	3.79
2001-02	Plymouth Whalers	OHL	46	26	12	7	2688	105	*5	2.34	6	2	4	360	15	0	2.50
	Utah Grizzlies	AHL	1	0	1	0	61	3	0	2.97	....	....	....	....	....	....	....
2002-03	Utah Grizzlies	AHL	39	18	18	2	2245	118	3	3.15	1	0	1	59	2	0	2.05
2003-04	Utah Grizzlies	AHL	39	13	19	5	2234	99	3	2.66	....	....	....	....	....	....	....

Traded to **St. Louis** by **Dallas** for the rights to Shawn Belle, June 25, 2004.

BARULIN, Konstantin (bah-ROO-lihn, kawn-stuhn-TIHN) ST.L.

Goaltender. Catches left. 6', 180 lbs. Born, Karaganda, USSR, September 4, 1984.
(St. Louis' 3rd choice, 84th overall, in 2003 Entry Draft).

			Regular Season								Playoffs						
Season	Club	League	GP	W	L	T	Mins	GA	SO	Avg	GP	W	L	Mins	GA	SO	Avg
2001-02	Gazovik Tyumen	Russia-2	4	....	....	....	188	15	0	4.79	....	....	....	....	....	....	....
2002-03	Gazovik Tyumen	Russia-2	28	....	....	....	1672	47	5	1.69	....	....	....	....	....	....	....
2003-04	Gazovik Tyumen	Russia-2	11	....	....	....	663	24	....	2.17	....	....	....	....	....	....	....
	SKA St. Petersburg	Russia	1	....	....	....	1	0	0	0.00	....	....	....	....	....	....	....
	St. Petersburg 2	Russia-3	11	6	4	1	668	24	1	2.15	....	....	....	....	....	....	....

BEAUCHEMIN, Rejean (boh-sheh-MEH, ray-JAWN) PHI.

Goaltender. Catches left. 6'1", 193 lbs. Born, Winnipeg, Man., May 3, 1985.
(Philadelphia's 10th choice, 191st overall, in 2003 Entry Draft).

			Regular Season								Playoffs						
Season	Club	League	GP	W	L	T	Mins	GA	SO	Avg	GP	W	L	Mins	GA	SO	Avg
2001-02	Winnipeg Warriors	MMHL	29	6	8	4	1026	54	0	3.15	4	3	1	240	12	0	3.00
2002-03	Prince Albert	WHL	34	12	15	1	1618	86	1	3.19	....	....	....	....	....	....	....
2003-04	Prince Albert	WHL	62	30	21	6	3540	137	6	2.32	6	2	4	360	14	0	2.33

WHL East Second All-Star Team (2004)

BECKFORD-TSEU, Chris (BEHK-fuhrd-TSEW, KRIHS) ST.L.

Goaltender. Catches left. 6'3", 196 lbs. Born, Toronto, Ont., June 22, 1984.
(St. Louis' 8th choice, 159th overall, in 2003 Entry Draft).

			Regular Season								Playoffs						
Season	Club	League	GP	W	L	T	Mins	GA	SO	Avg	GP	W	L	Mins	GA	SO	Avg
2000-01	St. Michael's	OJHL-B	26	....	....	....	1506	121	0	4.83	....	....	....	....	....	....	....
2001-02	Oshawa	OPJHL	STATISTICS NOT AVAILABLE														
	Guelph Storm	OHL	5	2	0	0	207	16	0	4.64	....	....	....	....	....	....	....
	Oshawa Generals	OHL	7	2	3	0	341	19	0	3.34	5	1	4	310	16	0	3.10
2002-03	Oshawa Generals	OHL	54	25	26	2	2978	157	4	3.16	13	6	7	727	48	1	3.96
2003-04	Oshawa Generals	OHL	9	1	5	2	495	28	0	3.39	....	....	....	....	....	....	....
	Kingston	OHL	40	16	19	2	2226	121	3	3.26	5	1	4	303	18	0	3.56

BELFOUR, Ed (BEHL-fohr, EHD) TOR.

Goaltender. Catches left. 5'11", 202 lbs. Born, Carman, Man., April 21, 1965.

			Regular Season								Playoffs						
Season	Club	League	GP	W	L	T	Mins	GA	SO	Avg	GP	W	L	Mins	GA	SO	Avg
1983-84	Winkler Flyers	MJHL	14	....	....	....	818	68	0	4.99	....	....	....	....	....	....	....
1984-85	Winkler Flyers	MJHL	34	....	....	....	1973	145	1	4.41	7	3	4	528	41	0	4.66
1985-86	Winkler Flyers	MJHL	33	....	....	....	1943	124	1	3.83	....	....	....	....	....	....	....
1986-87	North Dakota	WCHA	34	29	4	0	2049	81	3	2.37	....	....	....	....	....	....	....
1987-88	Saginaw Hawks	IHL	61	32	25	0	*3446	183	3	3.19	9	4	5	561	33	0	3.53
1988-89	**Chicago**	**NHL**	**23**	**4**	**12**	**3**	**1148**	**74**	**0**	**3.87**	....	....	....	....	....	....	....
	Saginaw Hawks	IHL	29	12	10	0	1760	92	0	3.14	5	2	3	298	14	0	2.82
1989-90	Canada	Nat-Tm	33	13	12	6	1808	93	0	3.09	....	....	....	....	....	....	....
	Chicago	**NHL**	....	....	....	....	....	....	....	....	**9**	**4**	**2**	**409**	**17**	**0**	**2.49**
1990-91	**Chicago**	**NHL**	***74**	***43**	**19**	**7**	***4127**	**170**	**4**	***2.47**	**6**	**2**	**4**	**295**	**20**	**0**	**4.07**
1991-92	**Chicago**	**NHL**	**52**	**21**	**18**	**10**	**2928**	**132**	***5**	**2.70**	**18**	**12**	**4**	**949**	**39**	**1**	***2.47**
1992-93	**Chicago**	**NHL**	***71**	**41**	**18**	**11**	***4106**	**177**	***7**	**2.59**	**4**	**0**	**4**	**249**	**13**	**0**	**3.13**
1993-94	**Chicago**	**NHL**	**70**	**37**	**24**	**6**	**3998**	**178**	***7**	**2.67**	**6**	**2**	**4**	**360**	**15**	**0**	**2.50**
1994-95	**Chicago**	**NHL**	**42**	**22**	**15**	**3**	**2450**	**93**	***5**	**2.28**	**16**	**9**	**7**	**1014**	**37**	**1**	**2.19**
1995-96	**Chicago**	**NHL**	**50**	**22**	**17**	**10**	**2956**	**135**	**1**	**2.74**	**9**	**6**	**3**	**666**	**23**	**1**	***2.07**
1996-97	**Chicago**	**NHL**	**33**	**11**	**15**	**6**	**1966**	**88**	**1**	**2.69**	....	....	....	....	....	....	....
	San Jose	**NHL**	**13**	**3**	**9**	**0**	**757**	**43**	**1**	**3.41**	....	....	....	....	....	....	....
1997-98	**Dallas**	**NHL**	**61**	**37**	**12**	**10**	**3581**	**112**	**9**	***1.88**	**17**	**10**	**7**	**1039**	**31**	**1**	***1.79**
1998-99◆	**Dallas**	**NHL**	**61**	**35**	**15**	**9**	**3536**	**117**	**5**	**1.99**	***23**	***16**	**7**	***1544**	**43**	***3**	***1.67**
99-2000	**Dallas**	**NHL**	**62**	**32**	**21**	**7**	**3620**	**127**	**4**	**2.10**	***23**	**14**	**9**	**1443**	**45**	***4**	**1.87**
2000-01	**Dallas**	**NHL**	**63**	**35**	**20**	**7**	**3687**	**144**	**8**	**2.34**	**10**	**4**	**6**	**671**	**25**	**0**	**2.24**
2001-02	**Dallas**	**NHL**	**60**	**21**	**27**	**11**	**3467**	**153**	**1**	**2.65**	....	....	....	....	....	....	....
	Canada	Olympics	DID NOT PLAY – SPARE GOALTENDER														
2002-03	**Toronto**	**NHL**	**62**	**37**	**20**	**5**	**3738**	**141**	**7**	**2.26**	**7**	**3**	**4**	**532**	**24**	**0**	**2.71**
2003-04	**Toronto**	**NHL**	**59**	**34**	**19**	**6**	**3444**	**122**	**10**	**2.13**	**13**	**6**	**7**	**774**	**27**	**3**	**2.09**
	NHL Totals		**856**	**435**	**281**	**111**	**49509**	**2006**	**75**	**2.43**	**161**	**88**	**68**	**9945**	**359**	**14**	**2.17**

WCHA First All-Star Team (1987) • NCAA Championship All-Tournament Team (1987) • IHL First All-Star Team (1988) • Garry F. Longman Memorial Trophy (Top Rookie – IHL) (1988) (co-winner - John Cullen) • NHL All-Rookie Team (1991) • NHL First All-Star Team (1991, 1993) • Trico Goaltender Award (1991) • Calder Memorial Trophy (1991) • William M. Jennings Trophy (1991, 1993, 1995) • Vezina Trophy (1991, 1993) • NHL Second All-Star Team (1995) • Shared William M. Jennings Trophy (1999) with Roman Turek • MBNA Roger Crozier Saving Grace Award (2000)

Played in NHL All-Star Game (1992, 1993, 1996, 1998, 1999)

Signed as a free agent by **Chicago**, September 25, 1987. Traded to **San Jose** by **Chicago** for Chris Terreri, Ulf Dahlen and Michal Sykora, January 25, 1997. Signed as a free agent by **Dallas**, July 2, 1997. Traded to **Nashville** by **Dallas** with Cameron Mann for David Gosselin and Nashville's 5th round choice (Eero Kilpelainen) in 2003 Entry Draft, June 29, 2002. Signed as a free agent by **Toronto**, July 2, 2002.

BENDERA, Shane (behn-DEHR-ah, SHAYN) CBJ

Goaltender. Catches left. 5'11", 170 lbs. Born, St. Albert, Alta., July 13, 1982.
(Columbus' 6th choice, 169th overall, in 2000 Entry Draft).

			Regular Season								Playoffs						
Season	Club	League	GP	W	L	T	Mins	GA	SO	Avg	GP	W	L	Mins	GA	SO	Avg
1997-98	Edmonton KC Pats	AMHL	22	8	10	2	1284	82	0	3.84	....	....	....	....	....	....	....
	Red Deer Rebels	WHL	1	0	0	0	8	0	0	0.00	....	....	....	....	....	....	....
1998-99	Bonnyville Pontiacs	AJHL	20	....	....	....	956	70	0	4.38	....	....	....	....	....	....	....
	Red Deer Rebels	WHL	2	0	1	0	72	7	0	5.83	....	....	....	....	....	....	....
99-2000	Red Deer Rebels	WHL	*69	31	27	9	*4003	202	0	3.03	3	0	2	76	15	0	11.84
2000-01	Red Deer Rebels	WHL	45	32	8	2	2603	108	*5	*2.49	*22	*16	6	*1404	43	*4	1.84
2001-02	Red Deer Rebels	WHL	20	11	6	3	1211	46	1	2.28	....	....	....	....	....	....	....
	Kelowna Rockets	WHL	30	13	9	8	1816	79	0	2.61	15	9	6	918	29	*2	*1.90
2002-03	Dayton Bombers	ECHL	39	13	19	5	2243	106	1	2.84	....	....	....	....	....	....	....
2003-04	Bakersfield	ECHL	30	12	15	3	1731	95	2	3.29	....	....	....	....	....	....	....
	Elmira Jackals	UHL	1	0	1	0	40	4	0	6.00	....	....	....	....	....	....	....

WHL East Second All-Star Team (2001) • WHL West Second All-Star Team (2002)

BERKHOEL, Adam (BUHRK-uhl, A-duhm) ATL.

Goaltender. Catches left. 5'11", 190 lbs. Born, St. Paul, MN, May 16, 1981.
(Chicago's 12th choice, 240th overall, in 2000 Entry Draft).

			Regular Season								Playoffs						
Season	Club	League	GP	W	L	T	Mins	GA	SO	Avg	GP	W	L	Mins	GA	SO	Avg
99-2000	Twin Cities	USHL	49	25	15	7	2848	129	0	2.72	13	7	6	797	43	0	3.24
2000-01	U. of Denver	WCHA	15	7	6	1	745	38	1	3.06	....	....	....	....	....	....	....
2001-02	U. of Denver	WCHA	18	12	4	1	1026	40	1	2.34	....	....	....	....	....	....	....
2002-03	U. of Denver	WCHA	26	12	6	4	1436	55	3	*2.30	....	....	....	....	....	....	....
2003-04	U. of Denver	WCHA	39	24	11	4	2225	91	*7	2.45	....	....	....	....	....	....	....

USHL All-Rookie Team (2000) • USHL Second All-Star Team (2000) • NCAA Championship All-Tournament Team (2004) • NCAA Championship Tournament MVP (2004)

Traded to **Atlanta** by **Chicago** for future considerations, June 27, 2004.

BIERK, Zac (BUHRK, ZAK)

Goaltender. Catches left. 6'5", 205 lbs. Born, Peterborough, Ont., September 17, 1976.
(Tampa Bay's 8th choice, 212th overall, in 1995 Entry Draft).

			Regular Season								Playoffs						
Season	Club	League	GP	W	L	T	Mins	GA	SO	Avg	GP	W	L	Mins	GA	SO	Avg
1993-94	Peterborough	OPJHL	4	....	....	....	205	17	0	4.98	....	....	....	....	....	....	....
	Peterborough	OHL	9	0	4	2	423	37	0	5.22	1	0	0	33	7	0	12.70
1994-95	Peterborough	OHL	35	11	15	5	1779	117	0	3.95	6	2	3	301	24	0	4.78
1995-96	Peterborough	OHL	58	31	16	6	3292	174	2	3.17	*22	*14	7	*1383	83	0	3.60
1996-97	Peterborough	OHL	49	*28	16	0	2744	151	2	3.30	11	6	5	666	35	0	3.15
1997-98	**Tampa Bay**	**NHL**	**13**	**1**	**4**	**1**	**433**	**30**	**0**	**4.16**	....	....	....	....	....	....	....
	Adirondack	AHL	12	1	6	1	557	36	0	3.87	....	....	....	....	....	....	....
1998-99	**Tampa Bay**	**NHL**	**1**	**0**	**1**	**0**	**59**	**2**	**0**	**2.03**	....	....	....	....	....	....	....
	Cleveland	IHL	27	11	12	4	1556	79	0	3.05	....	....	....	....	....	....	....
99-2000	**Tampa Bay**	**NHL**	**12**	**4**	**4**	**1**	**509**	**31**	**0**	**3.65**	....	....	....	....	....	....	....
	Detroit Vipers	IHL	15	4	8	2	846	46	1	3.26	....	....	....	....	....	....	....
2000-01	**Minnesota**	**NHL**	**1**	**0**	**1**	**0**	**60**	**6**	**0**	**6.00**	....	....	....	....	....	....	....
	Cleveland	IHL	49	24	18	5	2785	134	6	2.89	4	0	3	182	10	0	3.29
2001-02	Augusta Lynx	ECHL	30	16	9	3	1748	68	1	2.33	....	....	....	....	....	....	....
	Springfield Falcons	AHL	1	0	1	0	20	4	0	12.00	....	....	....	....	....	....	....
2002-03	**Phoenix**	**NHL**	**16**	**4**	**9**	**1**	**884**	**32**	**1**	**2.17**	....	....	....	....	....	....	....
	Springfield Falcons	AHL	13	6	4	1	685	33	0	2.89	....	....	....	....	....	....	....
2003-04	**Phoenix**	**NHL**	**4**	**0**	**1**	**2**	**190**	**12**	**0**	**3.79**	....	....	....	....	....	....	....
	Springfield Falcons	AHL	2	0	1	1	106	6	0	3.38	....	....	....	....	....	....	....
	NHL Totals		**47**	**9**	**20**	**5**	**2135**	**113**	**1**	**3.18**	....	....	....	....	....	....	....

OHL First All-Star Team (1997) • Canadian Major Junior Second All-Star Team (1997)

• Missed remainder of 1998-99 season and majority of 1999-2000 season recovering from Meniere's Disease which was diagnosed on March 25, 1999. Claimed by **Minnesota** from **Tampa Bay** in Expansion Draft, June 23, 2000. Signed as a free agent by **Phoenix**, August 30, 2001.
• Missed majority of 2003-04 season recovering from hip injury suffered in game vs. Anaheim, November 9, 2003.

BIRON, Martin (BIH-rohn, MAHR-tihn) BUF.

Goaltender. Catches left. 6'2", 168 lbs. Born, Lac-St-Charles, Que., August 15, 1977.
(Buffalo's 2nd choice, 16th overall, in 1995 Entry Draft).

			Regular Season								Playoffs						
Season	Club	League	GP	W	L	T	Mins	GA	SO	Avg	GP	W	L	Mins	GA	SO	Avg
1993-94	Trois-Rivieres	QAAA	23	14	8	1	1412	80	1	3.40	2	1	1	112	7	0	3.73
1994-95	Beauport Harfangs	QMJHL	56	29	16	9	3193	132	3	*2.48	16	8	7	900	37	*4	2.47
1995-96	Beauport Harfangs	QMJHL	55	29	17	7	3201	152	1	2.85	*19	*12	7	1134	64	0	3.39
	Buffalo	**NHL**	**3**	**0**	**2**	**0**	**119**	**10**	**0**	**5.04**	....	....	....	....	....	....	....
1996-97	Beauport Harfangs	QMJHL	18	6	9	1	928	61	1	3.94	....	....	....	....	....	....	....
	Hull Olympiques	QMJHL	16	11	4	1	974	43	2	2.65	6	3	1	325	19	0	3.51
1997-98	South Carolina	ECHL	2	0	1	1	86	3	0	2.09	....	....	....	....	....	....	....
	Rochester	AHL	41	14	18	6	2312	113	*5	2.93	4	1	3	239	16	0	4.01
1998-99	**Buffalo**	**NHL**	**6**	**1**	**2**	**1**	**281**	**10**	**0**	**2.14**	....	....	....	....	....	....	....
	Rochester	AHL	52	36	13	3	3129	108	*6	*2.07	*20	12	8	1167	42	1	*2.16
99-2000	**Buffalo**	**NHL**	**41**	**19**	**18**	**2**	**2229**	**90**	**5**	**2.42**	....	....	....	....	....	....	....
	Rochester	AHL	6	6	0	0	344	12	1	2.09	....	....	....	....	....	....	....
2000-01	**Buffalo**	**NHL**	**18**	**7**	**7**	**1**	**918**	**39**	**2**	**2.55**	....	....	....	....	....	....	....
	Rochester	AHL	4	3	1	0	239	4	1	1.00	....	....	....	....	....	....	....
2001-02	**Buffalo**	**NHL**	**72**	**31**	**28**	**10**	**4085**	**151**	**4**	**2.22**	....	....	....	....	....	....	....
2002-03	**Buffalo**	**NHL**	**54**	**17**	**28**	**6**	**3170**	**135**	**4**	**2.56**	....	....	....	....	....	....	....
2003-04	**Buffalo**	**NHL**	**52**	**26**	**18**	**5**	**2972**	**125**	**2**	**2.52**	....	....	....	....	....	....	....
	NHL Totals		**246**	**101**	**103**	**25**	**13774**	**560**	**17**	**2.44**	....	....	....	....	....	....	....

QMJHL All-Rookie Team (1995) • Canadian Major Junior First All-Star Team (1995) • Canadian Major Junior Goaltender of the Year (1995) • AHL First All-Star Team (1999) • Shared Harry "Hap" Holmes Memorial Trophy (fewest goals against – AHL) (1999) with Tom Draper • Baz Bastien Memorial Trophy (Top Goaltender – AHL) (1999)

BLACKBURN, Dan (BLAK-buhrn, DAN) NYR

Goaltender. Catches left. 6', 180 lbs. Born, Montreal, Que., May 20, 1983.
(NY Rangers' 1st choice, 10th overall, in 2001 Entry Draft).

			Regular Season								Playoffs						
Season	Club	League	GP	W	L	T	Mins	GA	SO	Avg	GP	W	L	Mins	GA	SO	Avg
1997-98	Bow Valley Eagles	AJHL	20	9	6	1	1039	58	1	3.35	3	0	0	97	8	0	4.95
1998-99	Bow Valley Eagles	AJHL	38	7	19	6	1941	146	0	4.51	2	0	2	118	8	0	4.07
99-2000	Kootenay Ice	WHL	51	34	8	7	3004	126	3	2.52	*21	*16	5	*1272	43	2	*2.03
2000-01	Kootenay Ice	WHL	50	*33	14	2	2922	135	1	2.77	11	7	4	706	23	1	1.95
2001-02	**NY Rangers**	**NHL**	**31**	**12**	**16**	**0**	**1737**	**95**	**0**	**3.28**	....	....	....	....	....	....	....
	Hartford Wolf Pack	AHL	4	2	1	1	244	11	0	2.71	....	....	....	....	....	....	....
2002-03	**NY Rangers**	**NHL**	**32**	**8**	**16**	**4**	**1762**	**93**	**1**	**3.17**	....	....	....	....	....	....	....
2003-04			DID NOT PLAY – INJURED														
	NHL Totals		**63**	**20**	**32**	**4**	**3499**	**188**	**1**	**3.22**	....	....	....	....	....	....	....

WHL East First All-Star Team (2001) • Canadian Major Junior First All-Star Team (2001) • Canadian Major Junior Goaltender of the Year (2001) • NHL All-Rookie Team (2002)

• Missed entire 2003-04 season recovering from shoulder injury suffered in training camp, September 2, 2003.

BOISCLAIR, Daniel (BWUH-klair, DAN-yehl) CAR.

Goaltender. Catches left. 6'2", 180 lbs. Born, St. Aug. de Desmaures, Que., November 2, 1982.
(Carolina's 5th choice, 181st overall, in 2001 Entry Draft).

			Regular Season								Playoffs						
Season	Club	League	GP	W	L	T	Mins	GA	SO	Avg	GP	W	L	Mins	GA	SO	Avg
1998-99	Charles-Lemoyne	QAAA	25	14	7	2	1360	69	0	3.04	....	....	....	....	....	....	....
99-2000	Cape Breton	QMJHL	29	7	14	1	1421	95	0	4.01	3	0	1	86	6	0	4.21
2000-01	Cape Breton	QMJHL	47	16	23	2	2426	161	0	3.98	12	5	6	685	36	0	3.16
2001-02	Cape Breton	QMJHL	25	9	10	2	1151	73	1	3.81	....	....	....	....	....	....	....
	Victoriaville Tigres	QMJHL	15	5	5	3	780	42	0	3.23	*19	*13	6	*1107	53	0	2.87
2002-03	Florida Everblades	ECHL	4	0	2	1	224	15	0	4.03	....	....	....	....	....	....	....
2003-04	Florida Everblades	ECHL	2	1	1	0	119	9	0	4.55	....	....	....	....	....	....	....
	Peoria Rivermen	ECHL	5	2	2	1	304	9	1	1.78	....	....	....	....	....	....	....
	Greenville Grrrowl	ECHL	25	4	20	0	1355	88	0	3.90	....	....	....	....	....	....	....

• Missed majority of 2002-03 season after being diagnosed with anemia, November 19, 2002.

BOUCHER, Brian (BOO-shay, BRIGH-uhn) PHX.

Goaltender. Catches left. 6'2", 198 lbs. Born, Woonsocket, RI, January 2, 1977.
(Philadelphia's 1st choice, 22nd overall, in 1995 Entry Draft).

			Regular Season								Playoffs						
Season	Club	League	GP	W	L	T	Mins	GA	SO	Avg	GP	W	L	Mins	GA	SO	Avg
1993-94	Mount St. Charles	Hi-School	15	*14	0	1	*504	*8	*9	*0.57	4	*4	0	*180	*6	*1	*1.20
1994-95	Wexford Raiders	MTJHL	8	....	....	....	425	23	0	3.25	....	....	....	....	....	....	....
	Tri-City Americans	WHL	35	17	11	2	1969	108	1	3.29	13	6	5	795	50	0	3.77
1995-96	Tri-City Americans	WHL	55	33	19	2	3183	181	1	3.41	11	6	5	653	37	*2	3.40
1996-97	Tri-City Americans	WHL	41	10	24	6	2458	149	1	3.64	....	....	....	....	....	....	....
1997-98	Philadelphia	AHL	34	16	12	3	1901	101	0	3.19	2	0	0	30	1	0	1.95
1998-99	Philadelphia	AHL	36	20	8	5	2061	89	2	2.59	16	9	7	947	45	0	2.85
99-2000	**Philadelphia**	**NHL**	**35**	**20**	**10**	**3**	**2038**	**65**	**4**	***1.91**	**18**	**11**	**7**	**1183**	**40**	**1**	**2.03**
	Philadelphia	AHL	1	0	0	1	65	3	0	2.77	....	....	....	....	....	....	....
2000-01	**Philadelphia**	**NHL**	**27**	**8**	**12**	**5**	**1470**	**80**	**1**	**3.27**	**1**	**0**	**0**	**37**	**3**	**0**	**4.86**
2001-02	**Philadelphia**	**NHL**	**41**	**18**	**16**	**4**	**2295**	**92**	**2**	**2.41**	**2**	**0**	**1**	**88**	**2**	**0**	**1.36**
2002-03	**Phoenix**	**NHL**	**45**	**15**	**20**	**8**	**2544**	**128**	**0**	**3.02**	....	....	....	....	....	....	....
2003-04	**Phoenix**	**NHL**	**40**	**10**	**19**	**10**	**2364**	**108**	**5**	**2.74**	....	....	....	....	....	....	....
	NHL Totals		**188**	**71**	**77**	**30**	**10711**	**473**	**12**	**2.65**	**21**	**11**	**8**	**1308**	**45**	**1**	**2.06**

WHL West Second All-Star Team (1996) • WHL West First All-Star Team (1997) • NHL All-Rookie Team (2000)

Traded to **Phoenix** by **Philadelphia** with Nashville's 3rd round choice (previously acquired, Phoenix selected Joe Callahan) in 2002 Entry Draft for Michal Handzus and Robert Esche, June 12, 2002.

BOUTIN, Jonathan (boo-TEHN, JAWN-ah-thuhn) T.B.

Goaltender. Catches left. 6'1", 200 lbs. Born, Granby, Que., March 28, 1985.
(Tampa Bay's 3rd choice, 96th overall, in 2003 Entry Draft).

			Regular Season								Playoffs						
Season	Club	League	GP	W	L	T	Mins	GA	SO	Avg	GP	W	L	Mins	GA	SO	Avg
2000-01	Yamaska-Missiquoi	QBAA	STATISTICS NOT AVAILABLE														
2001-02	Halifax	QMJHL	11	4	1	1	459	18	0	2.35	2	0	0	15	0	0	0.00
2002-03	Halifax	QMJHL	47	22	11	2	2190	106	4	2.90	1	0	0	27	0	0	0.00
2003-04	PEI Rocket	QMJHL	30	13	12	2	1612	80	1	2.98	11	6	5	672	23	0	2.06

BRATHWAITE, Fred (BRAYTH-wayt, FREHD)

Goaltender. Catches left. 5'7", 175 lbs. Born, Ottawa, Ont., November 24, 1972.

			Regular Season								Playoffs						
Season	Club	League	GP	W	L	T	Mins	GA	SO	Avg	GP	W	L	Mins	GA	SO	Avg
1988-89	Smiths Falls Bears	COJHL	38	16	18	1	2130	187	0	5.27	....	....	....	....	....	....	....
1989-90	Orillia Terriers	OJHL-B	15	....	....	....	782	47	0	3.61	....	....	....	....	....	....	....
	Oshawa Generals	OHL	20	11	2	1	886	43	1	2.91	10	4	2	451	22	0	*2.93
1990-91	Oshawa Generals	OHL	39	25	6	3	1986	112	1	3.38	13	*9	2	677	43	0	3.81
1991-92	Oshawa Generals	OHL	24	12	7	2	1248	81	0	3.89	....	....	....	....	....	....	....
	London Knights	OHL	23	15	6	2	1325	61	*4	2.76	10	5	5	615	36	0	3.51
1992-93	Detroit	OHL	37	23	10	4	2192	134	0	3.67	15	9	6	858	48	1	3.36
1993-94	**Edmonton**	**NHL**	**19**	**3**	**10**	**3**	**982**	**58**	**0**	**3.54**	....	....	....	....	....	....	....
	Cape Breton Oilers	AHL	2	1	1	0	119	6	0	3.04	....	....	....	....	....	....	....
1994-95	**Edmonton**	**NHL**	**14**	**2**	**5**	**1**	**601**	**40**	**0**	**3.99**	....	....	....	....	....	....	....
1995-96	**Edmonton**	**NHL**	**7**	**0**	**2**	**0**	**293**	**12**	**0**	**2.46**	....	....	....	....	....	....	....
	Cape Breton Oilers	AHL	31	12	16	0	1699	110	1	3.88	....	....	....	....	....	....	....
1996-97	Manitoba Moose	IHL	58	22	22	5	2945	167	1	3.40	....	....	....	....	....	....	....
1997-98	Manitoba Moose	IHL	51	23	18	4	2736	138	1	3.03	2	0	1	72	4	0	3.30
1998-99	Canada	Nat-Tm	24	6	8	3	989	47	2	2.85	....	....	....	....	....	....	....
	Calgary	**NHL**	**28**	**11**	**9**	**7**	**1663**	**68**	**1**	**2.45**	....	....	....	....	....	....	....
99-2000	**Calgary**	**NHL**	**61**	**25**	**25**	**7**	**3448**	**158**	**5**	**2.75**	....	....	....	....	....	....	....
	Saint John Flames	AHL	2	2	0	0	120	4	0	2.00	....	....	....	....	....	....	....
2000-01	**Calgary**	**NHL**	**49**	**15**	**17**	**10**	**2742**	**106**	**5**	**2.32**	....	....	....	....	....	....	....
2001-02	**St. Louis**	**NHL**	**25**	**9**	**11**	**4**	**1446**	**54**	**2**	**2.24**	**1**	**0**	**0**	**1**	**0**	**0**	**0.00**
2002-03	**St. Louis**	**NHL**	**30**	**12**	**9**	**4**	**1615**	**74**	**2**	**2.75**	....	....	....	....	....	....	....
2003-04	**Columbus**	**NHL**	**21**	**4**	**11**	**1**	**1050**	**59**	**0**	**3.37**	....	....	....	....	....	....	....
	Syracuse Crunch	AHL	3	0	2	1	188	7	1	2.23	....	....	....	....	....	....	....
	NHL Totals		**254**	**81**	**99**	**37**	**13840**	**629**	**15**	**2.73**	**1**	**0**	**0**	**1**	**0**	**0**	**0.00**

• Scored a goal while with Detroit (OHL), April 20, 1993. Signed as a free agent by **Edmonton**, October 6, 1993. • Scored a goal while with Manitoba (IHL), November 9, 1996. Signed as a free agent by **Calgary**, January 6, 1999. Traded to **St. Louis** by **Calgary** with Daniel Tkaczuk, Sergei Varlamov and Calgary's 9th round choice (Grant Jacobsen) in 2001 Entry Draft for Roman Turek and St. Louis' 4th round choice (Yegor Shastin) in 2001 Entry Draft, June 23, 2001. • Played 6 seconds of playoff game vs. Detroit, May 4, 2002. Signed as a free agent by **Columbus**, June 2, 2003.

BROCHU, Martin (broh-SHOO, MAHR-tihn)

Goaltender. Catches left. 6', 199 lbs. Born, Anjou, Que., March 10, 1973.

			Regular Season								Playoffs						
Season	Club	League	GP	W	L	T	Mins	GA	SO	Avg	GP	W	L	Mins	GA	SO	Avg
1989-90	Montreal-Bourassa	QAAA	27	11	14	1	1471	103	3.	4.20	3	1	2	193	10	1	3.10
1990-91	Granby Bisons	QMJHL	16	6	5	0	622	39	1	3.76	....	....	....	....	....	....	....
1991-92	Granby Bisons	QMJHL	52	15	29	2	2772	278	0	4.72	....	....	....	....	....	....	....
1992-93	Hull Olympiques	QMJHL	29	9	15	1	1453	137	0	5.66	2	0	1	69	7	0	6.07
1993-94	Fredericton	AHL	32	10	11	3	1505	76	2	3.03	....	....	....	....	....	....	....
1994-95	Fredericton	AHL	44	18	18	4	2475	145	0	3.51	....	....	....	....	....	....	....
1995-96	Fredericton	AHL	17	6	8	2	986	70	0	4.26	....	....	....	....	....	....	....
	Wheeling	ECHL	19	10	6	2	1060	51	1	2.89	....	....	....	....	....	....	....
	Portland Pirates	AHL	5	2	2	1	287	15	0	3.14	12	7	4	700	28	*2	*2.40
1996-97	Portland Pirates	AHL	55	23	17	7	2962	150	2	3.04	5	2	3	324	13	0	2.41
1997-98	Portland Pirates	AHL	37	16	14	1	1926	96	2	2.99	6	3	2	296	16	0	3.24
1998-99	**Washington**	**NHL**	**2**	**0**	**2**	**0**	**120**	**6**	**0**	**3.00**	....	....	....	....	....	....	....
	Portland Pirates	AHL	20	6	10	3	1164	57	2	2.94	....	....	....	....	....	....	....
	Utah Grizzlies	IHL	5	1	3	1	298	13	0	2.62	....	....	....	....	....	....	....
99-2000	Portland Pirates	AHL	54	32	15	6	3192	116	4	2.18	2	0	2	80	7	0	5.27
2000-01	Saint John Flames	AHL	55	27	19	5	3049	132	2	2.60	19	*14	4	1148	39	*4	2.04
2001-02	**Vancouver**	**NHL**	**6**	**0**	**3**	**0**	**216**	**15**	**0**	**4.17**	....	....	....	....	....	....	....
	Manitoba Moose	AHL	29	10	14	3	1625	91	1	3.36	....	....	....	....	....	....	....
2002-03	Verdun Dragons	QSPHL	1	1	0	0	60	2	0	2.00	....	....	....	....	....	....	....
	Cherepovets	Russia	8	....	....	....	480	15	2	1.88	....	....	....	....	....	....	....
2003-04	**Pittsburgh**	**NHL**	**1**	**0**	**0**	**0**	**33**	**1**	**0**	**1.82**	....	....	....	....	....	....	....
	Wilkes-Barre	AHL	15	4	9	1	731	31	1	2.55	....	....	....	....	....	....	....
	Wheeling Nailers	ECHL	9	6	2	1	521	23	1	2.65	....	....	....	....	....	....	....
	NHL Totals		**9**	**0**	**5**	**0**	**369**	**22**	**0**	**3.58**	....	....	....	....	....	....	....

AHL First All-Star Team (2000) • Baz Bastien Memorial Trophy (Top Goaltender – AHL) (2000) • Les Cunningham Award (MVP – AHL) (2000)

Signed as a free agent by **Montreal**, September 22, 1992. Traded to **Washington** by **Montreal** for future considerations, March 15, 1996. Signed as a free agent by **Calgary**, August 25, 2000. Signed as a free agent by **Minnesota**, July 17, 2001. Claimed by **Vancouver** from **Minnesota** in Waiver Draft, September 28, 2001. Signed as a free agent by **Verdun** (QSPHL), October 22, 2002. Signed as a free agent by **Pittsburgh**, August 22, 2003.

BRODEUR, Martin (broh-DUHR, MAHR-tihn) N.J.

Goaltender. Catches left. 6'2", 210 lbs. Born, Montreal, Que., May 6, 1972.
(New Jersey's 1st choice, 20th overall, in 1990 Entry Draft).

			Regular Season								Playoffs						
Season	Club	League	GP	W	L	T	Mins	GA	SO	Avg	GP	W	L	Mins	GA	SO	Avg
1988-89	Montreal-Bourassa	QAAA	27	13	12	1	1580	98	0	3.72	3	0	3	210	14	0	3.99
1989-90	St-Hyacinthe Laser	QMJHL	42	23	13	2	2333	156	0	4.01	12	5	7	678	46	0	4.07
1990-91	St-Hyacinthe Laser	QMJHL	52	22	24	4	2946	162	2	3.30	4	0	4	232	16	0	4.14
1991-92	St-Hyacinthe Laser	QMJHL	48	27	16	4	2846	161	2	3.39	5	2	3	317	14	0	2.65
	New Jersey	**NHL**	**4**	**2**	**1**	**0**	**179**	**10**	**0**	**3.35**	**1**	**0**	**1**	**32**	**3**	**0**	**5.63**
1992-93	Utica Devils	AHL	32	14	13	5	1952	131	0	4.03	4	1	3	258	18	0	4.19
1993-94	**New Jersey**	**NHL**	**47**	**27**	**11**	**8**	**2625**	**105**	**3**	**2.40**	**17**	**8**	**9**	**1171**	**38**	**1**	**1.95**
1994-95♦	**New Jersey**	**NHL**	**40**	**19**	**11**	**6**	**2184**	**89**	**3**	**2.45**	***20**	***16**	**4**	***1222**	**34**	***3**	***1.67**
1995-96	**New Jersey**	**NHL**	**77**	**34**	**30**	**12**	***4433**	**173**	**6**	**2.34**	....	....	....	....	....	....	....
1996-97	**New Jersey**	**NHL**	**67**	**37**	**14**	**13**	**3838**	**120**	***10**	***1.88**	**10**	**5**	**5**	**659**	**19**	**2**	***1.73**
1997-98	**New Jersey**	**NHL**	**70**	***43**	**17**	**8**	**4128**	**130**	**10**	**1.89**	**6**	**2**	**4**	**366**	**12**	**0**	**1.97**
1998-99	**New Jersey**	**NHL**	***70**	***39**	**21**	**10**	***4239**	**162**	**4**	**2.29**	**7**	**3**	**4**	**425**	**20**	**0**	**2.82**
99-2000♦	**New Jersey**	**NHL**	**72**	***43**	**20**	**8**	**4312**	**161**	**6**	**2.24**	***23**	***16**	**7**	***1450**	**39**	**2**	***1.61**
2000-01	**New Jersey**	**NHL**	**72**	***42**	**17**	**11**	**4297**	**166**	**9**	**2.32**	***25**	**15**	**10**	***1505**	**52**	***4**	**2.07**
2001-02	**New Jersey**	**NHL**	***73**	**38**	**26**	**9**	***4347**	**156**	**4**	**2.15**	**6**	**2**	**4**	**381**	**9**	**1**	**1.42**
	Canada	Olympics	5	*4	0	1	300	9	0	*1.80	....	....	....	....	....	....	....
2002-03♦	**New Jersey**	**NHL**	**73**	***41**	**23**	**9**	**4374**	**147**	***9**	**2.02**	***24**	***16**	**8**	***1491**	**41**	***7**	**1.65**
2003-04	**New Jersey**	**NHL**	***75**	***38**	**26**	**11**	***4555**	**154**	***11**	**2.03**	**5**	**1**	**4**	**298**	**13**	**0**	**2.62**
	NHL Totals		**740**	**403**	**217**	**105**	**43511**	**1573**	**75**	**2.17**	**144**	**84**	**60**	**9000**	**280**	**20**	**1.87**

QMJHL All-Rookie Team (1990) • QMJHL Second All-Star Team (1992) • NHL All-Rookie Team (1994) • Calder Memorial Trophy (1994) • NHL Second All-Star Team (1997, 1998) • Shared William M. Jennings Trophy (1997) with Mike Dunham • William M. Jennings Trophy (1998, 2004) • NHL First All-Star Team (2003, 2004) • William M. Jennings Trophy (2003) (tied with Roman Cechmanek/Robert Esche) • Vezina Trophy (2003, 2004)

Played in NHL All-Star Game (1996, 1997, 1998, 1999, 2000, 2001, 2003, 2004)

• Scored a goal in playoffs vs. Montreal, April 17, 1997.

BRODEUR, Mike (broh-DUHR, MIGHK) CHI.

Goaltender. Catches left. 6'2", 170 lbs. Born, Calgary, Alta., March 30, 1983.
(Chicago's 7th choice, 211th overall, in 2003 Entry Draft).

			Regular Season								Playoffs						
Season	Club	League	GP	W	L	T	Mins	GA	SO	Avg	GP	W	L	Mins	GA	SO	Avg
2000-01	Calgary	AMHL	21	11	8	3	1231	54	1	2.63	10	6	4	620	31	0	3.00
2001-02	Camrose Kodiacs	AJHL	24	13	9	1	1299	65	1	2.91	....	....	....	....	....	....	....
2002-03	Camrose Kodiacs	AJHL	48	28	16	2	2570	113	2	2.64	21	16	5	1378	48	4	2.09
2003-04	Moose Jaw	WHL	41	23	12	5	2385	84	5	2.11	10	6	4	624	18	1	*1.73

BROWN, Mike (BROWN, MIGHK) BOS.

Goaltender. Catches left. 6', 177 lbs. Born, Syracuse, NY, March 4, 1985.
(Boston's 7th choice, 153rd overall, in 2003 Entry Draft).

			Regular Season								Playoffs						
Season	Club	League	GP	W	L	T	Mins	GA	SO	Avg	GP	W	L	Mins	GA	SO	Avg
2001-02	Baldwinsville Bees	Hi-School	7	....	....	....	420	8	4	0.86	5	3	2	300	6	1	1.20
2002-03	Saginaw Spirit	OHL	39	8	23	3	2186	134	0	3.68	....	....	....	....	....	....	....
2003-04	Saginaw Spirit	OHL	51	14	32	3	2886	156	4	3.24	....	....	....	....	....	....	....

BRUCKLER, Bernd (BRUK-luhr, BUHRND) PHI.

Goaltender. Catches left. 6'1", 180 lbs. Born, Graz, Austria, September 26, 1981.
(Philadelphia's 4th choice, 150th overall, in 2001 Entry Draft).

			Regular Season								Playoffs						
Season	Club	League	GP	W	L	T	Mins	GA	SO	Avg	GP	W	L	Mins	GA	SO	Avg
2000-01	Tri-City Storm	USHL	28	15	8	3	1624	67	2	2.48	7	3	4	459	21	1	2.75
2001-02	U. of Wisconsin	WCHA	18	6	8	2	973	50	1	3.08	....	....	....	....	....	....	....
2002-03	U. of Wisconsin	WCHA	24	9	11	3	1358	64	0	2.83	....	....	....	....	....	....	....
2003-04	U. of Wisconsin	WCHA	38	19	10	8	2300	80	4	2.09	....	....	....	....	....	....	....

USHL Second All-Star Team (2001) • WCHA All-Rookie Team (2002) • WCHA First All-Star Team (2004) • NCAA West First All-American Team (2004)

BRUST, Barry (BRUHST, BAIR-ree) L.A.

Goaltender. Catches left. 6'2", 210 lbs. Born, Swan River, Man., August 8, 1983.
(Minnesota's 4th choice, 73rd overall, in 2002 Entry Draft).

			Regular Season								Playoffs						
Season	Club	League	GP	W	L	T	Mins	GA	SO	Avg	GP	W	L	Mins	GA	SO	Avg
99-2000	Swan Valley	MJHL	19	10	9	0	1140	67	0	3.50	....	....	....	....	....	....	....
2000-01	Spokane Chiefs	WHL	16	4	6	1	777	42	0	3.24	....	....	....	....	....	....	....
2001-02	Spokane Chiefs	WHL	60	28	21	10	3540	152	1	2.58	11	6	5	677	23	0	2.04
2002-03	Spokane Chiefs	WHL	*59	22	31	4	*3385	194	0	3.44	11	4	7	722	37	0	3.07
2003-04	Spokane Chiefs	WHL	27	10	13	2	1505	75	0	2.99	....	....	....	....	....	....	....
	Calgary Hitmen	WHL	25	12	8	3	1448	54	2	2.24	7	3	4	457	15	2	1.97

WHL West First All-Star Team (2002)

Signed as a free agent by **Los Angeles**, June 10, 2004.

BRYZGALOV, Ilya (breez-GAH-lahf, ihl-YUH) ANA.

Goaltender. Catches left. 6'3", 198 lbs. Born, Togliatti, USSR, June 22, 1980.
(Anaheim's 2nd choice, 44th overall, in 2000 Entry Draft).

			Regular Season								Playoffs						
Season	Club	League	GP	W	L	T	Mins	GA	SO	Avg	GP	W	L	Mins	GA	SO	Avg
1997-98	Lada Togliatti 2	Russia-3	8	....	....	....	480	28	....	3.50	....	....	....	....	....	....	....
1998-99	Lada Togliatti 2	Russia-4	20	....	....	....	1200	43	....	2.15	....	....	....	....	....	....	....
99-2000	Spartak Moscow	Russia-2	9	....	....	....	500	21	....	2.52	....	....	....	....	....	....	....
	Lada Togliatti	Russia	14	....	....	....	796	18	3	1.36	7	....	....	407	10	1	1.47
2000-01	Lada Togliatti	Russia	34	....	....	....	1992	61	*8	1.84	5	....	....	249	8	0	1.93
2001-02	**Anaheim**	**NHL**	**1**	**0**	**0**	**0**	**32**	**1**	**0**	**1.88**	....	....	....	....	....	....	....
	Russia	Olympics	DID NOT PLAY – SPARE GOALTENDER														
	Cincinnati	AHL	45	20	16	4	2399	99	4	2.48	....	....	....	....	....	....	....
2002-03	Cincinnati	AHL	54	12	26	9	3020	142	1	2.82	....	....	....	....	....	....	....
2003-04	**Anaheim**	**NHL**	**1**	**1**	**0**	**0**	**60**	**2**	**0**	**2.00**	....	....	....	....	....	....	....
	Cincinnati	AHL	*64	27	25	10	*3748	145	6	2.32	9	5	4	536	27	1	3.02
	NHL Totals		**2**	**1**	**0**	**0**	**92**	**3**	**0**	**1.96**	....	....	....	....	....	....	....

BUDAJ, Peter (BOO-digh, PEE-tuhr) COL.

Goaltender. Catches left. 6'1", 200 lbs. Born, Bystrica, Czech., September 18, 1982.
(Colorado's 1st choice, 63rd overall, in 2001 Entry Draft).

			Regular Season								Playoffs						
Season	Club	League	GP	W	L	T	Mins	GA	SO	Avg	GP	W	L	Mins	GA	SO	Avg
99-2000	St. Michael's	OHL	34	6	18	1	1676	112	1	4.01	....	....	....	....	....	....	....
2000-01	St. Michael's	OHL	37	17	12	3	1996	95	3	2.86	11	6	4	621	26	1	2.51
2001-02	St. Michael's	OHL	42	26	9	5	2329	89	2	*2.29	12	5	6	620	34	*1	3.29
2002-03	Hershey Bears	AHL	28	10	10	2	1467	65	2	2.66	1	0	0	6	2	0	20.81
2003-04	Hershey Bears	AHL	46	17	20	6	2574	120	3	2.80	....	....	....	....	....	....	....

OHL Second All-Star Team (2002)

BURKE, Sean (BUHRK, SHAWN) PHI.

Goaltender. Catches left. 6'4", 211 lbs. Born, Windsor, Ont., January 29, 1967.
(New Jersey's 2nd choice, 24th overall, in 1985 Entry Draft).

			Regular Season								Playoffs						
Season	Club	League	GP	W	L	T	Mins	GA	SO	Avg	GP	W	L	Mins	GA	SO	Avg
1983-84	St. Michael's B	MTJHL	25	....	....	....	1482	120	0	4.86	....	....	....	....	....	....	....
1984-85	Toronto Marlboros	OHL	49	25	21	3	2987	211	0	4.24	5	1	3	266	25	0	5.64
1985-86	Toronto Marlboros	OHL	47	16	27	3	2840	233	0	4.92	4	0	4	238	24	0	6.05
1986-87	Canada	Nat-Tm	42	27	13	2	2550	130	0	3.05	....	....	....	....	....	....	....
1987-88	Canada	Nat-Tm	37	19	9	2	1962	92	1	2.81	....	....	....	....	....	....	....
	Canada	Olympics	4	1	2	1	238	12	0	3.02	....	....	....	....	....	....	....
	New Jersey	**NHL**	**13**	**10**	**1**	**0**	**689**	**35**	**1**	**3.05**	**17**	**9**	**8**	**1001**	**57**	***1**	**3.42**
1988-89	**New Jersey**	**NHL**	**62**	**22**	**31**	**9**	**3590**	**230**	**3**	**3.84**	....	....	....	....	....	....	....
1989-90	**New Jersey**	**NHL**	**52**	**22**	**22**	**6**	**2914**	**175**	**0**	**3.60**	**2**	**0**	**2**	**125**	**8**	**0**	**3.84**
1990-91	**New Jersey**	**NHL**	**35**	**8**	**12**	**8**	**1870**	**112**	**0**	**3.59**	....	....	....	....	....	....	....
1991-92	Canada	Nat-Tm	31	18	6	4	1721	75	1	2.61	....	....	....	....	....	....	....
	Canada	Olympics	7	5	2	0	429	17	0	2.37	....	....	....	....	....	....	....
	San Diego Gulls	IHL	7	4	2	1	424	17	0	2.41	3	0	3	160	13	0	4.88
1992-93	**Hartford**	**NHL**	**50**	**16**	**27**	**3**	**2656**	**184**	**0**	**4.16**	....	....	....	....	....	....	....
1993-94	**Hartford**	**NHL**	**47**	**17**	**24**	**5**	**2750**	**137**	**2**	**2.99**	....	....	....	....	....	....	....
1994-95	**Hartford**	**NHL**	**42**	**17**	**19**	**4**	**2418**	**108**	**0**	**2.68**	....	....	....	....	....	....	....
1995-96	**Hartford**	**NHL**	**66**	**28**	**28**	**6**	**3669**	**190**	**4**	**3.11**	....	....	....	....	....	....	....
1996-97	**Hartford**	**NHL**	**51**	**22**	**22**	**6**	**2985**	**134**	**4**	**2.69**	....	....	....	....	....	....	....
1997-98	**Carolina**	**NHL**	**25**	**7**	**11**	**5**	**1415**	**66**	**1**	**2.80**	....	....	....	....	....	....	....
	Vancouver	**NHL**	**16**	**2**	**9**	**4**	**838**	**49**	**0**	**3.51**	....	....	....	....	....	....	....
	Philadelphia	**NHL**	**11**	**7**	**3**	**0**	**632**	**27**	**1**	**2.56**	**5**	**1**	**4**	**283**	**17**	**0**	**3.60**
1998-99	**Florida**	**NHL**	**59**	**21**	**24**	**14**	**3402**	**151**	**3**	**2.66**	....	....	....	....	....	....	....
99-2000	**Florida**	**NHL**	**7**	**2**	**5**	**0**	**418**	**18**	**0**	**2.58**	....	....	....	....	....	....	....
	Phoenix	**NHL**	**35**	**17**	**14**	**3**	**2074**	**88**	**3**	**2.55**	**5**	**1**	**4**	**296**	**16**	**0**	**3.24**
2000-01	**Phoenix**	**NHL**	**62**	**25**	**22**	**13**	**3644**	**138**	**4**	**2.27**	....	....	....	....	....	....	....
2001-02	**Phoenix**	**NHL**	**60**	**33**	**21**	**6**	**3587**	**137**	**5**	**2.29**	**5**	**1**	**4**	**297**	**13**	**0**	**2.63**
2002-03	**Phoenix**	**NHL**	**22**	**12**	**6**	**2**	**1248**	**44**	**2**	**2.12**	....	....	....	....	....	....	....
2003-04	**Phoenix**	**NHL**	**32**	**10**	**15**	**5**	**1795**	**84**	**1**	**2.81**	....	....	....	....	....	....	....
	Philadelphia	**NHL**	**15**	**6**	**5**	**2**	**825**	**35**	**1**	**2.55**	**1**	**0**	**0**	**40**	**1**	**0**	**1.50**
	NHL Totals		**762**	**304**	**321**	**101**	**43419**	**2142**	**35**	**2.96**	**35**	**12**	**22**	**2042**	**112**	**1**	**3.29**

Played in NHL All-Star Game (1989, 2001, 2002)

Traded to **Hartford** by **New Jersey** with Eric Weinrich for Bobby Holik and Hartford's 2nd round choice (Jay Pandolfo) in 1993 Entry Draft, August 28, 1992. Transferred to **Carolina** after **Hartford** franchise relocated, June 25, 1997. Traded to **Vancouver** by **Carolina** with Geoff Sanderson and Enrico Ciccone for Kirk McLean and Martin Gelinas, January 3, 1998. Traded to **Philadelphia** by **Vancouver** for Garth Snow, March 4, 1998. Signed as a free agent by **Florida**, September 12, 1998. Traded to **Phoenix** by **Florida** with Florida's 5th round choice (Nate Kiser) in 2000 Entry Draft for Mikhail Shtalenkov and Phoenix's 4th round choice (Chris Eade) in 2000 Entry Draft, November 18, 1999. Traded to **Philadelphia** by **Phoenix** with Branko Radivojevic and Ben Eager for Mike Comrie, February 9, 2004.

CARON, Sebastian (KAIR-aw, suh-BAS-tee-yeh) PIT.

Goaltender. Catches left. 6'1", 170 lbs. Born, Amqui, Que., June 25, 1980.
(Pittsburgh's 4th choice, 86th overall, in 1999 Entry Draft).

			Regular Season								Playoffs						
Season	Club	League	GP	W	L	T	Mins	GA	SO	Avg	GP	W	L	Mins	GA	SO	Avg
1997-98	TGV Pentagone	QAHA	17	....	....	....	762	48	1	2.84	....	....	....	....	....	....	....
1998-99	Rimouski Oceanic	QMJHL	30	13	10	3	1570	85	0	3.25	2	1	0	68	0	0	0.00
99-2000	Rimouski Oceanic	QMJHL	54	*38	11	3	3040	179	1	3.53	14	*12	2	828	50	0	3.62
2000-01	Wilkes-Barre	AHL	30	12	14	3	1746	103	4	3.54	....	....	....	....	....	....	....
2001-02	Wilkes-Barre	AHL	46	14	22	8	2671	139	1	3.12	....	....	....	....	....	....	....
2002-03	**Pittsburgh**	**NHL**	**24**	**7**	**14**	**2**	**1408**	**62**	**2**	**2.64**	....	....	....	....	....	....	....
	Wilkes-Barre	AHL	27	12	14	1	1561	81	1	3.11	....	....	....	....	....	....	....
2003-04	**Pittsburgh**	**NHL**	**40**	**9**	**24**	**5**	**2213**	**138**	**1**	**3.74**	....	....	....	....	....	....	....
	NHL Totals		**64**	**16**	**38**	**7**	**3621**	**200**	**3**	**3.31**	....	....	....	....	....	....	....

Memorial Cup All-Star Team (2000) • Hap Emms Memorial Trophy (Memorial Cup Top Goaltender) (2000) • NHL All-Rookie Team (2003)

CASSIVI, Frederic (KASS-ih-vee, FREHD-uhr-ihk)

Goaltender. Catches left. 6'4", 215 lbs. Born, Sorel, Que., June 12, 1975.
(Ottawa's 7th choice, 210th overall, in 1994 Entry Draft).

			Regular Season								Playoffs						
Season	Club	League	GP	W	L	T	Mins	GA	SO	Avg	GP	W	L	Mins	GA	SO	Avg
1991-92	Abitibi Forestiers	QAAA	22	5	17	0	1320	106	0	4.84	3	1	2	180	15	0	5.06
1992-93			STATISTICS NOT AVAILABLE														
1993-94	St-Hyacinthe Laser	QMJHL	35	15	13	3	1751	127	1	4.35	....	....	....	....	....	....	....
1994-95	Halifax	QMJHL	24	9	12	1	1362	105	0	4.63	....	....	....	....	....	....	....
	St-Jean Lynx	QMJHL	19	12	6	0	1021	55	1	3.23	5	2	3	258	18	0	4.19
1995-96	Thunder Bay	ColHL	12	6	4	2	715	51	0	4.28	....	....	....	....	....	....	....
	P.E.I. Senators	AHL	41	20	14	3	2347	128	1	3.27	5	2	3	317	24	0	4.54
1996-97	Syracuse Crunch	AHL	55	23	22	8	3069	164	2	3.21	1	0	1	60	3	0	3.01
1997-98	Worcester IceCats	AHL	45	20	22	2	2593	140	1	3.24	6	3	3	326	18	0	3.31
1998-99	Cincinnati	IHL	44	21	17	2	2418	123	1	3.05	3	1	2	139	6	0	2.59
99-2000	Hershey Bears	AHL	31	14	9	3	1554	78	1	3.01	2	0	1	63	5	0	4.75
2000-01	Hershey Bears	AHL	49	17	24	3	2620	124	2	2.84	9	7	2	564	14	1	*1.49
2001-02	Hershey Bears	AHL	21	6	10	4	1201	50	0	2.50	....	....	....	....	....	....	....
	Atlanta	**NHL**	**6**	**2**	**3**	**0**	**307**	**17**	**0**	**3.32**	....	....	....	....	....	....	....
	Chicago Wolves	AHL	12	6	2	1	625	26	0	2.50	5	2	2	264	11	0	2.50
2002-03	**Atlanta**	**NHL**	**2**	**1**	**1**	**0**	**123**	**11**	**0**	**5.37**	....	....	....	....	....	....	....
	Chicago Wolves	AHL	21	10	8	1	1171	62	0	3.18	2	0	2	90	3	0	2.00
2003-04	Chicago Wolves	AHL	34	15	12	5	1911	82	1	2.57	....	....	....	....	....	....	....
	NHL Totals		**8**	**3**	**4**	**0**	**430**	**28**	**0**	**3.91**	....	....	....	....	....	....	....

Signed as a free agent by **Colorado**, August 17, 1999. Traded to **Atlanta** by **Colorado** for Brett Clark, January 24, 2002.

CECHMANEK, Roman (chehkh-MAN-ehk, ROH-muhn) L.A.

Goaltender. Catches left. 6'3", 187 lbs. Born, Gottwaldov, Czech., March 2, 1971.
(Philadelphia's 3rd choice, 171st overall, in 2000 Entry Draft).

			Regular Season								Playoffs						
Season	Club	League	GP	W	L	T	Mins	GA	SO	Avg	GP	W	L	Mins	GA	SO	Avg
1988-89	TJ Gottwaldov	Czech	1	0	0	0	13	0	0	0.00	....	....	....	....	....	....	....
1989-90	TJ Zlin	Czech	2	0	0	0	89	5	0	3.37	....	....	....	....	....	....	....
1990-91	Dukla Jihlava	Czech	9	....	....	....	447	18	2	2.42	....	....	....	....	....	....	....
1991-92	DS Olomouc	Czech	13	....	....	....	731	54	0	4.43	....	....	....	....	....	....	....
	AC ZPS Zlin	Czech	2	0	1	0	67	8	0	7.73	....	....	....	....	....	....	....
1992-93	Banik Hodonin	Czech-2	STATISTICS NOT AVAILABLE														
1993-94	HC Zbojovka Vsetin	Czech-2	STATISTICS NOT AVAILABLE														
1994-95	HC Dadak Vsetin	Czech	41	....	....	....	2413	98	5	2.44	11	....	....	619	23	1	2.23
1995-96	HC Petra Vsetin	Czech	36	....	....	....	2142	77	4	2.16	13	....	....	783	17	2	1.30
1996-97	HC Petra Vsetin	Czech	48	....	....	....	2762	98	3	2.13	10	....	....	602	11	2	1.10
1997-98	HC Petra Vsetin	Czech	41	....	....	....	2306	76	....	*1.98	10	....	....	600	16	1	*1.60
1998-99	HC Slovnaft Vsetin	Czech	45	....	....	....	2696	77	5	*1.71	12	8	4	*747	23	1	1.85
99-2000	HC Slovnaft Vsetin	Czech	37	....	....	....	2141	88	0	2.47	9	5	4	545	15	3	1.65
2000-01	**Philadelphia**	**NHL**	**59**	**35**	**15**	**6**	**3431**	**115**	**10**	**2.01**	**6**	**2**	**4**	**347**	**18**	**0**	**3.11**
	Philadelphia	AHL	3	1	1	0	160	3	0	1.12	....	....	....	....	....	....	....
2001-02	**Philadelphia**	**NHL**	**46**	**24**	**13**	**6**	**2603**	**89**	**4**	**2.05**	**4**	**1**	**3**	**227**	**7**	**1**	**1.85**
	Czech Republic	Olympics	DID NOT PLAY – SPARE GOALTENDER														
2002-03	**Philadelphia**	**NHL**	**58**	**33**	**15**	**10**	**3350**	**102**	**6**	**1.83**	**13**	**6**	**7**	**867**	**31**	**2**	**2.15**
2003-04	**Los Angeles**	**NHL**	**49**	**18**	**21**	**6**	**2701**	**113**	**5**	**2.51**	....	....	....	....	....	....	....
	NHL Totals		**212**	**110**	**64**	**28**	**12085**	**419**	**25**	**2.08**	**23**	**9**	**14**	**1441**	**56**	**3**	**2.33**

NHL Second All-Star Team (2001) • Shared William M. Jennings Trophy (2003) with Robert Esche (tied with Martin Brodeur)

Played in NHL All-Star Game (2001)

Traded to **Los Angeles** by **Philadelphia** for Los Angeles' 2nd round choice (later traded to Chicago – Chicago selected Bryan Bickell) in 2004 Entry Draft, May 28, 2003.

CENTOMO, Sebastien (sehn-TOH-moh, suh-BAS-tee-yeh)

Goaltender. Catches right. 6'1", 200 lbs. Born, Montreal, Que., March 26, 1981.

			Regular Season								Playoffs						
Season	Club	League	GP	W	L	T	Mins	GA	SO	Avg	GP	W	L	Mins	GA	SO	Avg
1996-97	Laval-Laurentides	QAAA	27	10	10	2	1298	102	0	4.71	5	2	3	348	18	0	3.10
1997-98	Laval-Laurentides	QAAA	30	16	11	2	1696	87	0	2.86	....	....	....	....	....	....	....
1998-99	Rouyn-Noranda	QMJHL	32	14	9	4	1658	104	1	3.76	2	0	1	28	5	0	10.71
99-2000	Rouyn-Noranda	QMJHL	50	24	17	3	2758	160	1	3.48	11	6	5	695	41	0	3.54
2000-01	Rouyn-Noranda	QMJHL	46	25	14	4	2599	158	3	3.65	1	0	1	60	4	0	4.00
2001-02	**Toronto**	**NHL**	**1**	**0**	**0**	**0**	**40**	**3**	**0**	**4.50**	....	....	....	....	....	....	....
	Memphis	CHL	19	16	1	0	1035	36	1	2.09	....	....	....	....	....	....	....
	St. John's	AHL	25	12	7	4	1429	60	2	2.52	11	4	6	691	29	2	2.52
2002-03	St. John's	AHL	19	7	10	1	1045	68	0	3.90	....	....	....	....	....	....	....
	Greensboro	ECHL	10	3	3	3	565	24	1	2.55	....	....	....	....	....	....	....
2003-04	St. John's	AHL	39	13	17	4	2097	110	2	3.15	....	....	....	....	....	....	....
	NHL Totals		**1**	**0**	**0**	**0**	**40**	**3**	**0**	**4.50**	....	....	....	....	....	....	....

CHL Rookie of the Year (2002)

Signed as a free agent by **Toronto**, September 10, 1999.

CHARPENTIER, Sebastien (shahr-PUHNT-yay, suh-BAS-tee-yeh)

Goaltender. Catches left. 5'9", 177 lbs. Born, Drummondville, Que., April 18, 1977.
(Washington's 4th choice, 93rd overall, in 1995 Entry Draft).

			Regular Season								Playoffs						
Season	Club	League	GP	W	L	T	Mins	GA	SO	Avg	GP	W	L	Mins	GA	SO	Avg
1991-92	Drummondville	QAHA	14	....	....	....	840	34	2	2.42	....	....	....	....	....	....	....
1992-93	Drummondville	QAHA	20	....	....	....	1215	37	*7	*1.80	....	....	....	....	....	....	....
1993-94	Magog	QAAA	24	14	5	1	1443	75	1	3.16	....	....	....	....	....	....	....
1994-95	Laval Titan	QMJHL	41	25	12	1	2152	99	2	2.76	16	9	4	886	45	0	3.05
1995-96	Laval Titan	QMJHL	18	4	10	0	938	97	0	6.20	....	....	....	....	....	....	....
	Val-d'Or Foreurs	QMJHL	33	21	9	1	1906	87	1	2.74	13	7	5	740	45	0	3.64
1996-97	Shawinigan	QMJHL	*62	*37	17	4	*3480	177	1	3.05	4	2	1	196	13	0	3.98
1997-98	Portland Pirates	AHL	4	1	3	0	229	10	0	2.61	....	....	....	....	....	....	....
	Hampton Roads	ECHL	43	20	16	6	2388	114	0	2.86	18	*14	4	*1183	38	1	*1.93
1998-99	Quad City Mallards	UHL	6	0	0	0	4	0	0	0.00	....	....	....	....	....	....	....
	Portland Pirates	AHL	3	0	3	0	180	10	0	3.34	....	....	....	....	....	....	....
99-2000	Portland Pirates	AHL	18	10	4	3	1041	48	0	2.77	3	1	1	183	9	0	2.96
2000-01	Portland Pirates	AHL	34	16	16	1	1978	113	1	3.43	1	0	1	102	3	0	1.76
2001-02	**Washington**	**NHL**	**2**	**1**	**1**	**0**	**122**	**5**	**0**	**2.46**	....	....	....	....	....	....	....
	Portland Pirates	AHL	49	20	18	10	2941	131	3	2.67	....	....	....	....	....	....	....
2002-03	**Washington**	**NHL**	**17**	**5**	**7**	**1**	**859**	**40**	**0**	**2.79**	....	....	....	....	....	....	....
	Porland Pirates	AHL	12	3	7	2	727	28	2	2.31	....	....	....	....	....	....	....
2003-04	**Washington**	**NHL**	**7**	**0**	**6**	**0**	**369**	**21**	**0**	**3.41**	....	....	....	....	....	....	....
	NHL Totals		**26**	**6**	**14**	**1**	**1350**	**66**	**0**	**2.93**	....	....	....	....	....	....	....

ECHL Playoff MVP (1998)

• Missed majority of 2003-04 season recovering from leg injury suffered in practice, November 3, 2003.

CHIODO, Andy (KEE-aw-doh, AN-dee) PIT.

Goaltender. Catches left. 5'11", 192 lbs. Born, Toronto, Ont., April 25, 1983.
(Pittsburgh's 8th choice, 199th overall, in 2003 Entry Draft).

			Regular Season								Playoffs						
Season	Club	League	GP	W	L	T	Mins	GA	SO	Avg	GP	W	L	Mins	GA	SO	Avg
1998-99	Wexford Raiders	OPJHL	26	....	....	....	1519	105	0	4.05	....	....	....	....	....	....	....
99-2000	Wexford Raiders	OPJHL	24	....	....	....	1389	89	0	3.84	....	....	....	....	....	....	....
2000-01	St. Michael's	OHL	38	18	12	5	2069	86	*4	2.49	9	2	6	479	30	0	3.76
2001-02	St. Michael's	OHL	33	14	10	3	1743	79	2	2.72	7	3	1	288	17	*1	3.54
2002-03	St. Michael's	OHL	57	26	18	6	3065	154	3	3.01	18	10	8	1021	56	1	3.29
2003-04	**Pittsburgh**	**NHL**	**8**	**3**	**4**	**1**	**486**	**28**	**0**	**3.46**	....	....	....	....	....	....	....
	Wilkes-Barre	AHL	44	18	19	2	2448	98	4	2.40	18	9	7	1048	38	*3	2.18
	Wheeling Nailers	ECHL	2	0	2	0	86	9	0	6.26	....	....	....	....	....	....	....
	NHL Totals		**8**	**3**	**4**	**1**	**486**	**28**	**0**	**3.46**	....	....	....	....	....	....	....

• Re-entered NHL Entry Draft. Originally NY Islanders' 3rd choice, 166th overall, in 2001 Entry Draft.

OHL First All-Star Team (2003)

CHOUINARD, Mathieu (SHWEE-nuhr, MA-tyew)

Goaltender. Catches left. 6'1", 211 lbs. Born, Laval, Que., April 11, 1980.
(Ottawa's 2nd choice, 45th overall, in 2000 Entry Draft).

			Regular Season								Playoffs						
Season	Club	League	GP	W	L	T	Mins	GA	SO	Avg	GP	W	L	Mins	GA	SO	Avg
1995-96	Amos Forestiers	QAAA	31	14	14	1	1613	114	1	4.24	1	1	2	190	11	0	3.48
1996-97	Shawinigan	QMJHL	17	4	7	1	795	51	0	3.85	4	1	3	264	15	0	3.41
1997-98	Shawinigan	QMJHL	55	*32	18	3	3055	142	2	2.79	6	2	4	348	24	0	4.14
1998-99	Shawinigan	QMJHL	56	36	16	4	3288	150	*5	2.74	6	2	4	392	27	0	4.13
99-2000	Shawinigan	QMJHL	*59	32	20	5	*3339	186	4	3.34	13	7	6	769	41	0	3.20
2000-01	Grand Rapids	IHL	28	17	7	1	1567	69	1	2.64	3	1	1	135	4	0	1.78
2001-02	Grand Rapids	AHL	25	11	12	1	1404	58	2	2.48	....	....	....	....	....	....	....
2002-03	Peoria Rivermen	ECHL	15	12	2	0	820	29	3	2.12	....	....	....	....	....	....	....
	Binghamton	AHL	4	2	0	0	152	5	0	1.98	1	0	0	2	0	0	0.00
2003-04	**Los Angeles**	**NHL**	**1**	**0**	**0**	**0**	**3**	**0**	**0**	**0.00**	....	....	....	....	....	....	....
	Manchester	AHL	22	10	6	0	1093	41	4	2.25	....	....	....	....	....	....	....
	Reading Royals	ECHL	3	1	1	1	185	7	0	2.27	....	....	....	....	....	....	....
	NHL Totals		**1**	**0**	**0**	**0**	**3**	**0**	**0**	**0.00**	....	....	....	....	....	....	....

• Re-entered NHL Entry Draft. Originally Ottawa's 1st choice, 15th overall, in 1998 Entry Draft.

QMJHL First All-Star Team (1999) • Shared Harry "Hap" Holmes Memorial Trophy (fewest goals against – AHL) (2002) with Martin Prusek and Simon Lajeunesse

Signed as a free agent by **Los Angeles**, July 7, 2003.

CHURCHILL, Jason (CHUHR-chihl, JAY-suhn) S.J.

Goaltender. Catches left. 6'3", 184 lbs. Born, St. John's, Nfld., November 5, 1985.
(San Jose's 4th choice, 129th overall, in 2004 Entry Draft).

			Regular Season								Playoffs						
Season	Club	League	GP	W	L	T	Mins	GA	SO	Avg	GP	W	L	Mins	GA	SO	Avg
2002-03	Antigonish	MJrHL	36	16	18	1	2050	137	1	4.01	....	....	....	....	....	....	....
	Halifax	QMJHL	4	1	0	1	160	9	0	3.39	....	....	....	....	....	....	....
2003-04	Halifax	QMJHL	53	15	28	4	2894	180	2	3.73	....	....	....	....	....	....	....

CLEMMENSEN, Scott (KLEH-mehn-sehn, SKAWT) N.J.

Goaltender. Catches left. 6'3", 205 lbs. Born, Des Moines, IA, July 23, 1977.
(New Jersey's 7th choice, 215th overall, in 1997 Entry Draft).

			Regular Season								Playoffs						
Season	Club	League	GP	W	L	T	Mins	GA	SO	Avg	GP	W	L	Mins	GA	SO	Avg
1995-96	Des Moines	USHL	20	10	7	1	1082	62	0	3.44	....	....	....	....	....	....	....
1996-97	Des Moines	USHL	36	22	9	2	2042	111	1	3.26	4	1	2	200	9	1	2.70
1997-98	Boston College	H-East	37	24	9	4	2205	102	*4	2.78	....	....	....	....	....	....	....
1998-99	Boston College	H-East	*42	26	12	4	*2507	120	1	2.87	....	....	....	....	....	....	....
99-2000	Boston College	H-East	29	19	7	0	1610	59	*5	2.20	....	....	....	....	....	....	....
2000-01	Boston College	H-East	*39	*30	7	2	*2312	82	3	2.13	....	....	....	....	....	....	....
2001-02	**New Jersey**	**NHL**	**2**	**0**	**0**	**0**	**20**	**1**	**0**	**3.00**	....	....	....	....	....	....	....
	Albany River Rats	AHL	29	5	19	4	1677	92	0	3.29	....	....	....	....	....	....	....
2002-03	Albany River Rats	AHL	47	12	24	8	2694	119	1	2.65	....	....	....	....	....	....	....
2003-04	**New Jersey**	**NHL**	**4**	**3**	**1**	**0**	**238**	**4**	**2**	**1.01**	....	....	....	....	....	....	....
	Albany River Rats	AHL	22	5	12	4	1309	67	0	3.07	....	....	....	....	....	....	....
	NHL Totals		**6**	**3**	**1**	**0**	**258**	**5**	**2**	**1.16**	....	....	....	....	....	....	....

NCAA Championship All-Tournament Team (2001)

CLOUTIER, Dan (KLOO-tyay, DAN) VAN.

Goaltender. Catches left. 6'1", 182 lbs. Born, Mont-Laurier, Que., April 22, 1976.
(NY Rangers' 1st choice, 26th overall, in 1994 Entry Draft).

			Regular Season								Playoffs						
Season	Club	League	GP	W	L	T	Mins	GA	SO	Avg	GP	W	L	Mins	GA	SO	Avg
1991-92	St. Thomas Stars	OJHL-B	14	....	....	....	823	80	0	5.83	....	....	....	....	....	....	....
1992-93	Timmins	NOJHA	5	4	0	0	255	10	0	2.35	....	....	....	....	....	....	....
	Sault Ste. Marie	OHL	12	4	6	0	572	44	0	4.62	4	1	2	231	12	0	3.12
1993-94	Sault Ste. Marie	OHL	55	28	14	6	2934	174	*2	3.56	14	*10	4	833	52	0	3.75
1994-95	Sault Ste. Marie	OHL	45	15	26	2	2518	185	1	4.41	....	....	....	....	....	....	....
1995-96	Sault Ste. Marie	OHL	13	9	3	0	641	43	0	4.02	....	....	....	....	....	....	....
	Guelph Storm	OHL	17	12	2	2	1004	35	2	2.09	16	11	5	993	52	*2	3.14
1996-97	Binghamton	AHL	60	23	28	8	3367	199	3	3.55	4	1	3	236	13	0	3.31
1997-98	**NY Rangers**	**NHL**	**12**	**4**	**5**	**1**	**551**	**23**	**0**	**2.50**	....	....	....	....	....	....	....
	Hartford Wolf Pack	AHL	24	12	8	3	1417	62	0	2.63	8	5	3	478	24	0	3.01
1998-99	**NY Rangers**	**NHL**	**22**	**6**	**8**	**3**	**1097**	**49**	**0**	**2.68**	....	....	....	....	....	....	....
99-2000	**Tampa Bay**	**NHL**	**52**	**9**	**30**	**3**	**2492**	**145**	**0**	**3.49**	....	....	....	....	....	....	....
2000-01	**Tampa Bay**	**NHL**	**24**	**3**	**13**	**3**	**1005**	**59**	**1**	**3.52**	....	....	....	....	....	....	....
	Detroit Vipers	IHL	1	0	1	0	59	3	0	3.05	....	....	....	....	....	....	....
	Vancouver	**NHL**	**16**	**4**	**6**	**5**	**914**	**37**	**0**	**2.43**	**2**	**0**	**2**	**117**	**9**	**0**	**4.62**
2001-02	**Vancouver**	**NHL**	**62**	**31**	**22**	**5**	**3502**	**142**	**7**	**2.43**	**6**	**2**	**3**	**273**	**16**	**0**	**3.52**
2002-03	**Vancouver**	**NHL**	**57**	**33**	**16**	**7**	**3376**	**136**	**2**	**2.42**	**14**	**7**	**7**	**833**	**45**	**0**	**3.24**
2003-04	**Vancouver**	**NHL**	**60**	**33**	**21**	**6**	**3539**	**134**	**5**	**2.27**	**3**	**1**	**1**	**138**	**5**	**0**	**2.17**
	NHL Totals		**305**	**123**	**121**	**33**	**16476**	**725**	**15**	**2.64**	**25**	**10**	**13**	**1361**	**75**	**0**	**3.31**

OHL Second All-Star Team (1996)

Traded to **Tampa Bay** by **NY Rangers** with Niklas Sundstrom and NY Rangers' 1st (Nikita Alexeev) and 3rd (later traded to San Jose – later traded to Chicago – Chicago selected Igor Radulov) round choices in 2000 Entry Draft for Chicago's 1st round choice (previously acquired, NY Rangers selected Pavel Brendl) in 1999 Entry Draft, June 26, 1999. Traded to **Vancouver** by **Tampa Bay** for Adrian Aucoin and Vancouver's 2nd round choice (Alexander Polushin) in 2001 Entry Draft, February 7, 2001.

COLEMAN, Gerald (KOHL-man, JAIR-uhld) T.B.

Goaltender. Catches left. 6'4", 189 lbs. Born, Chicago, IL, April 3, 1985.
(Tampa Bay's 5th choice, 224th overall, in 2003 Entry Draft).

			Regular Season								Playoffs						
Season	Club	League	GP	W	L	T	Mins	GA	SO	Avg	GP	W	L	Mins	GA	SO	Avg
99-2000	Chicago	MEHL	26	....	....	....	1560	65	0	2.50	....	....	....	....	....	....	....
2000-01	U.S. National U-17	USDP	45	11	23	5	2386	158	0	3.97	....	....	....	....	....	....	....
2001-02	U.S. National U-17	USDP	26	9	13	4	1436	86	0	3.59	....	....	....	....	....	....	....
	U.S. National U-18	USDP	11	5	3	1	570	31	1	3.28	....	....	....	....	....	....	....
2002-03	London Knights	OHL	26	6	9	3	1074	59	1	3.30	....	....	....	....	....	....	....
2003-04	London Knights	OHL	33	24	8	0	1852	68	*5	2.20	8	5	2	442	19	1	2.58

CONKLIN, Ty (KAWN-klihn, TIGH) EDM.

Goaltender. Catches left. 6', 184 lbs. Born, Anchorage, AK, March 30, 1976.

			Regular Season								Playoffs						
Season	Club	League	GP	W	L	T	Mins	GA	SO	Avg	GP	W	L	Mins	GA	SO	Avg
1995-96	Green Bay	USHL	30	....	....	....	1727	82	1	2.85	....	....	....	....	....	....	....
1996-97	Alaska-Anchorage	WCHA	DID NOT PLAY – FRESHMAN														
	Green Bay	USHL	30	19	7	1	1609	86	1	3.21	17	8	9	980	56	1	3.43
1997-98	New Hampshire	H-East	DID NOT PLAY – TRANSFERRED COLLEGES														
1998-99	New Hampshire	H-East	22	18	3	1	1338	41	0	*1.84	....	....	....	....	....	....	....
99-2000	New Hampshire	H-East	*37	*22	8	6	*2194	91	2	2.49	....	....	....	....	....	....	....
2000-01	New Hampshire	H-East	34	17	12	5	2048	70	*5	*2.05	....	....	....	....	....	....	....
2001-02	**Edmonton**	**NHL**	**4**	**2**	**0**	**0**	**148**	**4**	**0**	**1.62**	....	....	....	....	....	....	....
	Hamilton Bulldogs	AHL	37	13	12	8	2043	89	1	2.61	7	4	2	416	18	0	2.60
2002-03	Hamilton Bulldogs	AHL	38	19	13	3	2140	91	4	2.55	17	9	6	1024	38	1	2.23
2003-04	**Edmonton**	**NHL**	**38**	**17**	**14**	**4**	**2086**	**84**	**1**	**2.42**	....	....	....	....	....	....	....
	NHL Totals		**42**	**19**	**14**	**4**	**2234**	**88**	**1**	**2.36**	....	....	....	....	....	....	....

USHL Second All-Star Team (1996) • Hockey East All-Rookie Team (1999) • Hockey East Second All-Star Team (1999) • Hockey East First All-Star Team (2000, 2001) • Hockey East Player of the Year (2000) (co-winner - Mike Mottau) • NCAA East Second All-American Team (2000) • NCAA East First All-American Team (2001) • Walter Brown Award (New England's Outstanding American-born College player) (2001) (co-winner - Brian Gionta)

• Left **Alaska-Anchorage** (WCHA) and returned to **Green Bay** (USHL), November 14, 1996. Signed as a free agent by **Edmonton**, April 18, 2001.

CRAWFORD, Corey (KRAW-fohrd, KOHR-ee) CHI.

Goaltender. Catches left. 6'2", 183 lbs. Born, Montreal, Que., December 31, 1984.
(Chicago's 2nd choice, 52nd overall, in 2003 Entry Draft).

			Regular Season								Playoffs						
Season	Club	League	GP	W	L	T	Mins	GA	SO	Avg	GP	W	L	Mins	GA	SO	Avg
2000-01	Gatineau Intrepide	QAAA	21	17	3	1	1260	40	2	1.92	....	....	....	....	....	....	....
2001-02	Moncton Wildcats	QMJHL	38	9	20	3	1863	116	1	3.74	....	....	....	....	....	....	....
2002-03	Moncton Wildcats	QMJHL	50	24	17	6	2855	130	2	2.73	6	2	3	303	20	0	3.97
2003-04	Moncton Wildcats	QMJHL	54	*35	15	3	3019	132	2	2.62	*20	*13	6	*1170	42	0	2.15

QMJHL Second All-Star Team (2004)

CRAWFORD-WEST, Brandon (KRAW-fohrd-WEHST, BRAN-duhn) PIT.

Goaltender. Catches right. 6', 180 lbs. Born, San Diego, CA, July 1, 1982.
(Pittsburgh's 9th choice, 250th overall, in 2001 Entry Draft).

			Regular Season								Playoffs						
Season	Club	League	GP	W	L	T	Mins	GA	SO	Avg	GP	W	L	Mins	GA	SO	Avg
2000-01	Texas Tornado	NAJHL	43	30	9	3	2534	110	4	2.60	7	6	1	452	6	3	0.80
2001-02	Texas Tornado	NAJHL	50	35	11	2	2825	109	4	2.32	6	3	3	389	13	0	2.01
2002-03	Tri-City Storm	USHL	22	7	12	1	1207	61	0	3.03	....	....	....	....	....	....	....
	Bozeman Icedogs	AWHL	15	7	7	1	825	47	0	3.42	5	2	3	309	14	0	2.71
2003-04	Miami University	CCHA	33	21	8	3	1947	81	3	2.50	....	....	....	....	....	....	....

DAFOE, Byron (duh-FOH, BIGH-ruhn)

Goaltender. Catches left. 5'11", 200 lbs. Born, Sussex, England, February 25, 1971.
(Washington's 2nd choice, 35th overall, in 1989 Entry Draft).

			Regular Season								Playoffs						
Season	Club	League	GP	W	L	T	Mins	GA	SO	Avg	GP	W	L	Mins	GA	SO	Avg
1987-88	Juan de Fuca	BCJHL	32	....	....	....	1716	129	0	4.51	....	....	....	....	....	....	....
1988-89	Portland	WHL	59	29	24	3	3279	291	1	5.32	*18	10	8	*1091	81	*1	4.45
1989-90	Portland	WHL	40	14	21	3	2265	193	0	5.11	....	....	....	....	....	....	....
1990-91	Portland	WHL	8	1	5	1	414	41	0	5.94	....	....	....	....	....	....	....
	Prince Albert	WHL	32	13	12	4	1839	124	0	4.05	....	....	....	....	....	....	....
1991-92	Baltimore Skipjacks	AHL	33	12	16	4	1847	119	0	3.87	....	....	....	....	....	....	....
	New Haven	AHL	7	3	2	1	364	22	0	3.63	....	....	....	....	....	....	....
	Hampton Roads	ECHL	10	6	4	0	562	26	0	2.78	....	....	....	....	....	....	....
1992-93	**Washington**	**NHL**	**1**	**0**	**0**	**0**	**1**	**0**	**0**	**0.00**	....	....	....	....	....	....	....
	Baltimore Skipjacks	AHL	48	16	20	7	2617	191	1	4.38	5	2	3	241	22	0	5.48
1993-94	**Washington**	**NHL**	**5**	**2**	**2**	**0**	**230**	**13**	**0**	**3.39**	**2**	**0**	**2**	**118**	**5**	**0**	**2.54**
	Portland Pirates	AHL	47	24	16	4	2661	148	1	3.34	1	0	0	9	1	0	6.79
1994-95	**Washington**	**NHL**	**4**	**1**	**1**	**1**	**187**	**11**	**0**	**3.53**	**1**	**0**	**0**	**20**	**1**	**0**	**3.00**
	Phoenix	IHL	49	25	16	6	2743	169	2	3.70	....	....	....	....	....	....	....
	Portland Pirates	AHL	6	5	0	0	330	16	0	2.91	7	3	4	416	29	0	4.18
1995-96	**Los Angeles**	**NHL**	**47**	**14**	**24**	**8**	**2666**	**172**	**1**	**3.87**	....	....	....	....	....	....	....
1996-97	**Los Angeles**	**NHL**	**40**	**13**	**17**	**5**	**2162**	**112**	**0**	**3.11**	....	....	....	....	....	....	....
1997-98	**Boston**	**NHL**	**65**	**30**	**25**	**9**	**3693**	**138**	**6**	**2.24**	**6**	**2**	**4**	**422**	**14**	**1**	**1.99**
1998-99	**Boston**	**NHL**	**68**	**32**	**23**	**11**	**4001**	**133**	***10**	**1.99**	**12**	**6**	**6**	**768**	**26**	**2**	**2.03**
99-2000	**Boston**	**NHL**	**41**	**13**	**16**	**10**	**2307**	**114**	**3**	**2.96**	....	....	....	....	....	....	....
2000-01	**Boston**	**NHL**	**45**	**22**	**14**	**7**	**2536**	**101**	**2**	**2.39**	....	....	....	....	....	....	....
2001-02	**Boston**	**NHL**	**64**	**35**	**26**	**3**	**3827**	**141**	**4**	**2.21**	**6**	**2**	**4**	**358**	**19**	**0**	**3.18**
2002-03	**Atlanta**	**NHL**	**17**	**5**	**11**	**1**	**895**	**65**	**0**	**4.36**	....	....	....	....	....	....	....
2003-04	**Atlanta**	**NHL**	**18**	**4**	**11**	**1**	**973**	**51**	**0**	**3.14**	....	....	....	....	....	....	....
	NHL Totals		**415**	**171**	**170**	**56**	**23478**	**1051**	**26**	**2.69**	**27**	**10**	**16**	**1686**	**65**	**3**	**2.31**

AHL First All-Star Team (1994) • Shared Harry ''Hap'' Holmes Memorial Trophy (fewest goals against – AHL) (1994) with Olaf Kolzig • NHL Second All-Star Team (1999)

Traded to **Los Angeles** by **Washington** with Dmitri Khristich for Los Angeles' 1st round choice (Alexandre Volchkov) in 1996 Entry Draft and Dallas' 4th round choice (previously acquired, Washington selected Justin Davis) in 1996 Entry Draft, July 8, 1995. Traded to **Boston** by **Los Angeles** with Dimitri Khristich for Jozef Stumpel, Sandy Moger and Boston's 4th round choice (later traded to New Jersey – New Jersey selected Pierre Dagenais) in 1998 Entry Draft, August 29, 1997. Signed as a free agent by **Atlanta**, November 19, 2002.

DAIGNEAULT, Maxime (DAYN-yoh, mahx-EEM) WSH.

Goaltender. Catches left. 6'3", 202 lbs. Born, St-Jacques-le-Mineur, Que., January 23, 1984.
(Washington's 4th choice, 59th overall, in 2002 Entry Draft).

			Regular Season								Playoffs						
Season	Club	League	GP	W	L	T	Mins	GA	SO	Avg	GP	W	L	Mins	GA	SO	Avg
99-2000	Magog	QAAA	19	12	3	3	1108	53	3	2.87	18	12	5	945	42	1	2.67
2000-01	Val-d'Or Foreurs	QMJHL	28	14	8	1	1386	82	0	3.55	10	8	1	504	21	0	2.50
2001-02	Val-d'Or Foreurs	QMJHL	61	25	27	5	3270	184	3	3.38	7	3	4	431	23	0	3.20
2002-03	Val-d'Or Foreurs	QMJHL	48	23	18	3	2694	138	2	3.07	8	4	3	487	23	1	2.83
2003-04	Val-d'Or Foreurs	QMJHL	57	23	22	9	3250	158	2	2.92	7	3	4	416	16	0	2.31

Memorial Cup All-Star Team (2002) • Hap Emms Memorial Trophy (Memorial Cup Top Goaltender) (2002)

DAMPHOUSSE, Jean-Francois (DAHM-fooz, ZHAWN-fran-SWUH)

Goaltender. Catches left. 6', 180 lbs. Born, St-Alexis-des-Monts, Que., July 21, 1979.
(New Jersey's 1st choice, 24th overall, in 1997 Entry Draft).

			Regular Season								Playoffs						
Season	Club	League	GP	W	L	T	Mins	GA	SO	Avg	GP	W	L	Mins	GA	SO	Avg
1993-94	Ste-Foy	QAHA	18	10	1	0	1078	53	0	2.95	14	10	4	842	50	0	3.52
1994-95	Ste-Foy	QAHA	16	....	....	....	958	48	0	3.01	....	....	....	....	....	....	....
	Ste-Foy	QAAA	2	1	0	1	120	8	0	3.84	....	....	....	....	....	....	....
1995-96	Ste-Foy	QAAA	32	18	10	1	1629	83	2	3.06	....	....	....	....	....	....	....
1996-97	Moncton Wildcats	QMJHL	39	6	25	2	2063	190	0	5.53	....	....	....	....	....	....	....
1997-98	Moncton Wildcats	QMJHL	59	24	26	6	3400	174	1	3.07	10	5	5	595	28	0	2.82
1998-99	Moncton Wildcats	QMJHL	40	19	17	2	2163	121	1	3.36	4	0	4	200	12	0	3.60
	Albany River Rats	AHL	1	0	1	0	59	3	0	3.06	....	....	....	....	....	....	....
99-2000	Augusta Lynx	ECHL	14	4	7	0	676	49	0	4.35	....	....	....	....	....	....	....
	Albany River Rats	AHL	26	9	11	2	1326	62	0	2.81	2	0	1	62	4	0	3.86
2000-01	Albany River Rats	AHL	55	24	23	3	2963	141	1	2.86	....	....	....	....	....	....	....
2001-02	**New Jersey**	**NHL**	**6**	**1**	**3**	**0**	**294**	**12**	**0**	**2.45**	....	....	....	....	....	....	....
	Albany River Rats	AHL	18	3	11	2	1001	57	0	3.42	....	....	....	....	....	....	....
2002-03	Cincinnati	AHL	31	12	14	4	1669	87	0	3.13	....	....	....	....	....	....	....
	Saint John Flames	AHL	10	5	5	0	591	23	0	2.33	....	....	....	....	....	....	....
2003-04	Hamilton Bulldogs	AHL	35	19	11	4	2010	77	2	2.30	10	4	6	592	25	1	2.54
	NHL Totals		**6**	**1**	**3**	**0**	**294**	**12**	**0**	**2.45**	....	....	....	....	....	....	....

Traded to **Anaheim** by **New Jersey** with Petr Sykora, Mike Commodore and Igor Pohanka for Jeff Friesen, Oleg Tverdovsky and Maxim Balmochnykh, July 6, 2002. Traded to **Calgary** by **Anaheim** with Mike Commodore for Rob Niedermayer, March 11, 2003. Signed as a free agent by **Montreal**, July 4, 2003.

DANIS, Yann (DA-nihs, YAN) MTL.

Goaltender. Catches left. 6', 185 lbs. Born, Lafontaine, Que., June 21, 1981.

			Regular Season								Playoffs						
Season	Club	League	GP	W	L	T	Mins	GA	SO	Avg	GP	W	L	Mins	GA	SO	Avg
99-2000	St-Jerome	QJHL	STATISTICS NOT AVAILABLE														
	Cornwall Colts	COJHL	26	....	....	....	1367	71	0	3.12	....	....	....	....	....	....	....
2000-01	Brown University	ECAC	12	2	8	1	667	40	0	3.60	....	....	....	....	....	....	....
2001-02	Brown University	ECAC	24	11	10	2	1451	45	3	1.86	....	....	....	....	....	....	....
2002-03	Brown University	ECAC	*34	15	14	5	*2074	80	5	2.31	....	....	....	....	....	....	....
2003-04	Brown University	ECAC	30	15	11	4	1821	55	*5	*1.81	....	....	....	....	....	....	....
	Hamilton Bulldogs	AHL	2	2	0	0	120	3	1	1.50	1	0	0	12	0	0	0.00

ECAC Second All-Star Team (2002, 2003) • ECAC First All-Star Team (2004) • ECAC Goaltender of the Year (2004) • ECAC Player of the Year (2004) • NCAA East First All-American Team (2004)

Signed as a free agent by **Montreal**, March 19, 2004.

DENIS, Marc (deh-NEE, MAHRK) CBJ

Goaltender. Catches left. 6'1", 190 lbs. Born, Montreal, Que., August 1, 1977.
(Colorado's 1st choice, 25th overall, in 1995 Entry Draft).

			Regular Season								Playoffs						
Season	Club	League	GP	W	L	T	Mins	GA	SO	Avg	GP	W	L	Mins	GA	SO	Avg
1992-93	Montreal-Bourassa	QAAA	26	....	....	....	1559	74	5	2.87	....	....	....	....	....	....	....
1993-94	Trois-Rivieres	QAAA	36	10	22	3	2093	158	0	4.53	4	1	3	249	20	0	4.83
1994-95	Chicoutimi	QMJHL	32	17	9	1	1688	98	0	3.48	6	4	2	372	19	1	3.06
1995-96	Chicoutimi	QMJHL	51	23	21	4	2951	157	2	3.19	16	8	8	957	69	0	4.33
1996-97	Chicoutimi	QMJHL	41	22	15	2	2323	104	4	*2.69	*21	*11	10	*1229	70	*1	3.42
	Colorado	**NHL**	**1**	**0**	**1**	**0**	**60**	**3**	**0**	**3.00**	....	....	....	....	....	....	....
	Hershey Bears	AHL	....	....	....	....	....	....	....	....	4	1	0	56	1	0	1.08
1997-98	Hershey Bears	AHL	47	17	23	4	2588	125	1	2.90	6	3	3	346	15	0	2.59
1998-99	**Colorado**	**NHL**	**4**	**1**	**1**	**1**	**217**	**9**	**0**	**2.49**	....	....	....	....	....	....	....
	Hershey Bears	AHL	52	20	23	5	2908	137	4	2.83	3	1	1	143	7	0	2.93
99-2000	**Colorado**	**NHL**	**23**	**9**	**8**	**3**	**1203**	**51**	**3**	**2.54**	....	....	....	....	....	....	....
2000-01	**Columbus**	**NHL**	**32**	**6**	**20**	**4**	**1830**	**99**	**0**	**3.25**	....	....	....	....	....	....	....
2001-02	**Columbus**	**NHL**	**42**	**9**	**24**	**5**	**2335**	**121**	**1**	**3.11**	....	....	....	....	....	....	....
2002-03	**Columbus**	**NHL**	***77**	**27**	**41**	**8**	***4511**	**232**	**5**	**3.09**	....	....	....	....	....	....	....
2003-04	**Columbus**	**NHL**	**66**	**21**	**36**	**7**	**3796**	**162**	**5**	**2.56**	....	....	....	....	....	....	....
	NHL Totals		**245**	**73**	**131**	**28**	**13952**	**677**	**14**	**2.91**	....	....	....	....	....	....	....

QMJHL First All-Star Team (1997) • Canadian Major Junior First All-Star Team (1997) • Canadian Major Junior Goaltender of the Year (1997)

Traded to **Columbus** by **Colorado** for Columbus' 2nd round choice (later traded to Carolina – Carolina selected Tomas Kurka) in 2000 Entry Draft, June 7, 2000.

DESLAURIERS, Jeff (duh-LAW-ree-yay, JEHF) EDM.

Goaltender. Catches right. 6'3", 175 lbs. Born, St-Jean-Richelieu, Que., May 15, 1984.
(Edmonton's 2nd choice, 31st overall, in 2002 Entry Draft).

			Regular Season								Playoffs						
Season	Club	League	GP	W	L	T	Mins	GA	SO	Avg	GP	W	L	Mins	GA	SO	Avg
2000-01	Gatineau Intrepide	QAAA	22	10	9	2	1194	61	2	3.07	2	1	0	125	6	0	2.89
2001-02	Chicoutimi	QMJHL	51	28	20	1	2909	170	1	3.51	4	0	3	197	20	0	6.11
2002-03	Chicoutimi	QMJHL	54	18	24	1	2582	164	0	3.81	4	0	4	240	15	0	9.00
2003-04	Chicoutimi	QMJHL	50	21	20	6	2701	129	1	2.87	18	10	8	956	50	1	3.14

DesROCHERS, Patrick (duh-RAWSH-ay, PAT-rihk) CAR.

Goaltender. Catches left. 6'3", 209 lbs. Born, Penetanguishene, Ont., October 27, 1979.
(Phoenix's 1st choice, 14th overall, in 1998 Entry Draft).

			Regular Season								Playoffs						
Season	Club	League	GP	W	L	T	Mins	GA	SO	Avg	GP	W	L	Mins	GA	SO	Avg
1994-95	Barrie Colts	OPJHL	26	....	....	....	3205	179	3	3.08	....	....	....	....	....	....	....
1995-96	Sarnia Sting	OHL	29	12	6	2	1265	96	0	4.55	3	0	1	71	5	0	4.23
1996-97	Sarnia Sting	OHL	50	22	17	4	2667	154	*4	3.46	11	6	5	576	42	0	4.38
1997-98	Sarnia Sting	OHL	56	26	17	11	3205	179	1	3.35	4	1	2	160	12	0	4.50
1998-99	Sarnia Sting	OHL	8	3	5	0	425	26	0	3.67	....	....	....	....	....	....	....
	Kingston	OHL	44	14	22	3	2389	177	1	4.45	5	1	4	323	21	0	3.90
99-2000	Springfield Falcons	AHL	52	21	17	7	2710	137	1	3.03	2	1	1	120	7	1	3.50
2000-01	Springfield Falcons	AHL	50	17	24	5	2807	156	0	3.33	....	....	....	....	....	....	....
2001-02	Springfield Falcons	AHL	34	12	18	1	1864	94	2	3.03	....	....	....	....	....	....	....
	Phoenix	**NHL**	**5**	**1**	**2**	**1**	**243**	**15**	**0**	**3.70**	....	....	....	....	....	....	....
2002-03	**Phoenix**	**NHL**	**4**	**0**	**3**	**0**	**175**	**11**	**0**	**3.77**	....	....	....	....	....	....	....
	Springfield Falcons	AHL	8	2	4	1	454	20	0	2.64	....	....	....	....	....	....	....
	Carolina	**NHL**	**2**	**1**	**1**	**0**	**122**	**7**	**0**	**3.44**	....	....	....	....	....	....	....
	Lowell	AHL	17	4	12	1	1030	48	0	2.80	....	....	....	....	....	....	....
2003-04	Lowell	AHL	50	23	25	1	2838	138	0	2.92	....	....	....	....	....	....	....
	NHL Totals		**11**	**2**	**6**	**1**	**540**	**33**	**0**	**3.67**	....	....	....	....	....	....	....

Traded to **Carolina** by **Phoenix** for Jean-Marc Pelletier and future considerations, December 31, 2002.

DiPIETRO, Rick (dee-pee-EHT-roh, RIHK) NYI

Goaltender. Catches right. 5'11", 185 lbs. Born, Winthrop, MA, September 19, 1981.
(NY Islanders' 1st choice, 1st overall, in 2000 Entry Draft).

			Regular Season								Playoffs						
Season	Club	League	GP	W	L	T	Mins	GA	SO	Avg	GP	W	L	Mins	GA	SO	Avg
1997-98	U.S. National U-18	USDP	46	21	19	0	2526	131	2	3.11	....	....	....	....	....	....	....
1998-99	U.S. National U-18	USDP	46	31	11	2	2760	113	2	2.46	....	....	....	....	....	....	....
99-2000	Boston University	H-East	29	18	5	5	1790	73	2	2.45	....	....	....	....	....	....	....
2000-01	**NY Islanders**	**NHL**	**20**	**3**	**15**	**1**	**1083**	**63**	**0**	**3.49**	....	....	....	....	....	....	....
	Chicago Wolves	IHL	14	4	5	2	778	44	0	3.39	....	....	....	....	....	....	....
2001-02	Bridgeport	AHL	59	*30	22	7	3472	134	4	2.32	20	12	8	*1270	45	*3	2.13
2002-03	**NY Islanders**	**NHL**	**10**	**2**	**5**	**2**	**585**	**29**	**0**	**2.97**	**1**	**0**	**0**	**15**	**0**	**0**	**0.00**
	Bridgeport	AHL	34	16	10	8	2044	73	3	2.14	5	2	3	299	10	1	2.01
2003-04	**NY Islanders**	**NHL**	**50**	**23**	**18**	**5**	**2844**	**112**	**5**	**2.36**	**5**	**1**	**4**	**303**	**11**	**1**	**2.18**
	Bridgeport	AHL	2	0	2	0	119	3	0	1.51	....	....	....	....	....	....	....
	NHL Totals		**80**	**28**	**38**	**8**	**4512**	**204**	**5**	**2.71**	**6**	**1**	**4**	**318**	**11**	**1**	**2.08**

Hockey East Second All-Star Team (2000) • Hockey East Rookie of the Year (2000)

DISHER, Josh (DIH-shur, JAWSH) N.J.

Goaltender. Catches left. 6'1", 165 lbs. Born, Chatham, Ont., June 24, 1985.
(New Jersey's 3rd choice, 185th overall, in 2004 Entry Draft).

			Regular Season								Playoffs						
Season	Club	League	GP	W	L	T	Mins	GA	SO	Avg	GP	W	L	Mins	GA	SO	Avg
2003-04	Erie Otters	OHL	*63	26	27	5	*3524	168	*5	2.86	9	4	5	506	29	0	3.44

DIVIS, Reinhard (DIH-vihs, RIGHN-hard) ST.L.

Goaltender. Catches left. 5'11", 200 lbs. Born, Vienna, Austria, July 4, 1975.
(St. Louis' 8th choice, 261st overall, in 2000 Entry Draft).

			Regular Season								Playoffs						
Season	Club	League	GP	W	L	T	Mins	GA	SO	Avg	GP	W	L	Mins	GA	SO	Avg
1995-96	VEU Feldkirch	Austria	37	....	....	....	2200	85	0	2.32	....	....	....	....	....	....	....
1996-97	VEU Feldkirch	Alpenliga	45	....	....	....	2738	105	0	2.30	....	....	....	....	....	....	....
	VEU Feldkirch	Austria	....	....	....	....	....	....	....	....	11	....	....	620	27	0	2.61
1997-98	VEU Feldkirch	Alpenliga	13	....	....	....	779	22	0	1.69	....	....	....	....	....	....	....
	VEU Feldkirch	Austria	27	....	....	....	1620	55	0	2.07	....	....	....	....	....	....	....
1998-99	VEU Feldkirch	Austria	15	....	....	....	900	58	0	3.86	....	....	....	....	....	....	....
99-2000	Leksands IF	Sweden	48	....	....	....	2839	160	3	3.38	....	....	....	....	....	....	....
2000-01	Leksands IF	Sweden	41	....	....	....	2451	141	3	3.45	....	....	....	....	....	....	....
2001-02	**St. Louis**	**NHL**	**1**	**0**	**0**	**0**	**25**	**0**	**0**	**0.00**	....	....	....	....	....	....	....
	Worcester IceCats	AHL	55	28	20	5	3173	137	3	2.59	3	1	2	205	8	0	2.34
	Austria	Olympics	4	1	1	2	238	12	0	3.02	....	....	....	....	....	....	....
2002-03	**St. Louis**	**NHL**	**2**	**2**	**0**	**0**	**83**	**1**	**0**	**0.72**	....	....	....	....	....	....	....
	Worcester IceCats	AHL	9	6	1	0	453	17	0	2.25	....	....	....	....	....	....	....
2003-04	**St. Louis**	**NHL**	**13**	**4**	**4**	**2**	**629**	**29**	**0**	**2.77**	**1**	**0**	**0**	**18**	**0**	**0**	**0.00**
	Worcester IceCats	AHL	31	12	10	8	1709	63	3	2.21	....	....	....	....	....	....	....
	NHL Totals		**16**	**6**	**4**	**2**	**737**	**30**	**0**	**2.44**	**1**	**0**	**0**	**18**	**0**	**0**	**0.00**

DUBA, Tomas (DOO-bah, TAW-mash) PIT.

Goaltender. Catches left. 6', 176 lbs. Born, Prague, Czech., July 2, 1981.
(Pittsburgh's 8th choice, 217th overall, in 2001 Entry Draft).

			Regular Season								Playoffs						
Season	Club	League	GP	W	L	T	Mins	GA	SO	Avg	GP	W	L	Mins	GA	SO	Avg
1998-99	Sparta Praha Jr.	Czech-Jr.	34	....	....	....	1850	95	....	3.08	....	....	....	....	....	....	....
99-2000	Sparta Praha Jr.	Czech-Jr.	30	....	....	....	1670	73	....	2.62	....	....	....	....	....	....	....
	HC CKD Slany	Czech-3	1	0	1	0	60	5	0	5.00	....	....	....	....	....	....	....
2000-01	Sparta Praha Jr.	Czech-Jr.	14	....	....	....	774	41	0	3.18	2	....	....	60	6	0	6.00
	Beroun	Czech-2	8	....	....	....	426	18	....	2.54	....	....	....	....	....	....	....
2001-02	SaiPa	Finland	47	10	31	4	2755	152	3	3.31	....	....	....	....	....	....	....
2002-03	SaiPa	Finland	34	9	17	5	1888	86	3	2.73	....	....	....	....	....	....	....
2003-04	Znojmo	Czech	47	....	....	....	2568	103	4	2.41	7	3	4	412	20	0	2.91

DUBIELEWICZ, Wade (DOO-bih-wihtz, WAYD) NYI

Goaltender. Catches left. 5'10", 178 lbs. Born, Invermere, B.C., January 30, 1978.

			Regular Season								Playoffs						
Season	Club	League	GP	W	L	T	Mins	GA	SO	Avg	GP	W	L	Mins	GA	SO	Avg
1997-98	Trail Smoke Eaters	BCHL	41	....	....	....	2225	118	0	3.18	....	....	....	....	....	....	....
1998-99	Trail Smoke Eaters	BCHL	STATISTICS NOT AVAILABLE														
	Chilliwack Chiefs	BCHL	14	10	4	0	834	....	0	....	....	....	....	....	....	....	....
99-2000	U. of Denver	WCHA	13	3	5	1	596	27	1	2.72	....	....	....	....	....	....	....
2000-01	U. of Denver	WCHA	29	12	9	3	1542	59	2	2.30	....	....	....	....	....	....	....
2001-02	U. of Denver	WCHA	24	20	4	0	1431	41	2	*1.72	....	....	....	....	....	....	....
2002-03	U. of Denver	WCHA	19	9	8	2	1060	43	3	2.43	....	....	....	....	....	....	....
2003-04	**NY Islanders**	**NHL**	**2**	**1**	**0**	**1**	**105**	**3**	**0**	**1.71**	....	....	....	....	....	....	....
	Bridgeport	AHL	33	20	8	5	1959	45	9	*1.38	3	2	1	181	11	0	3.64
	NHL Totals		**2**	**1**	**0**	**1**	**105**	**3**	**0**	**1.71**	....	....	....	....	....	....	....

WCHA Second All-Star Team (2003) • AHL All-Rookie Team (2004) • AHL Second All-Star Team (2004) • Dudley "Red" Garrett Memorial Trophy (Top Rookie - AHL) (2004) • Shared Harry "Hap" Holmes Memorial Trophy (fewest goals against - AHL) with Dieter Kochan (2004)

Signed as a free agent by **NY Islanders**, May 25, 2003.

DUBNYK, Devan (DUHN-nihk, DEH-vuhn) EDM.

Goaltender. Catches left. 6'5", 194 lbs. Born, Regina, Sask., May 4, 1986.
(Edmonton's 1st choice, 14th overall, in 2004 Entry Draft).

			Regular Season								Playoffs						
Season	Club	League	GP	W	L	T	Mins	GA	SO	Avg	GP	W	L	Mins	GA	SO	Avg
2000-01	Calgary Bruins	CBHL	14	....	....	....	815	39	2	3.10	....	....	....	....	....	....	....
2001-02	Calgary Bruins	CBHL	18	7	9	2	1105	68	1	3.69	....	....	....	....	....	....	....
	Kamloops Blazers	WHL	3	1	1	0	143	13	0	5.45	....	....	....	....	....	....	....
2002-03	Kamloops Blazers	WHL	26	12	8	1	1279	68	2	3.19	....	....	....	....	....	....	....
2003-04	Kamloops Blazers	WHL	44	20	18	5	2533	106	6	2.51	4	1	3	245	12	0	2.94

Canadian Major Junior Scholastic Player of the Year (2004)

DUNHAM, Mike (DUHN-uhm, MIGHK) NYR

Goaltender. Catches left. 6'3", 200 lbs. Born, Johnson City, NY, June 1, 1972.
(New Jersey's 4th choice, 53rd overall, in 1990 Entry Draft).

			Regular Season								Playoffs						
Season	Club	League	GP	W	L	T	Mins	GA	SO	Avg	GP	W	L	Mins	GA	SO	Avg
1987-88	Canterbury School	Hi-School	29	....	....	....	1740	69	4	2.38	....	....	....	....	....	....	....
1988-89	Canterbury School	Hi-School	25	....	....	....	1500	63	2	2.52	....	....	....	....	....	....	....
1989-90	Canterbury School	Hi-School	32	....	....	....	1558	68	3	1.96	....	....	....	....	....	....	....
1990-91	University of Maine	H-East	23	14	5	2	1275	63	0	*2.96	....	....	....	....	....	....	....
1991-92	University of Maine	H-East	7	6	0	0	382	14	1	2.20	....	....	....	....	....	....	....
	United States	Nat-Tm	3	0	1	1	157	10	0	3.82	....	....	....	....	....	....	....
1992-93	University of Maine	H-East	25	*21	1	1	1429	63	0	2.65	....	....	....	....	....	....	....
1993-94	United States	Nat-Tm	33	22	9	2	1983	125	2	3.78	....	....	....	....	....	....	....
	United States	Olympics	3	0	1	2	180	15	0	5.00	....	....	....	....	....	....	....
	Albany River Rats	AHL	5	2	2	1	304	26	0	5.12	....	....	....	....	....	....	....
1994-95	Albany River Rats	AHL	35	20	7	8	2120	99	1	2.80	7	6	1	419	20	1	2.86
1995-96	Albany River Rats	AHL	44	30	10	2	2592	109	1	2.52	3	1	2	182	5	1	1.65
1996-97	**New Jersey**	**NHL**	**26**	**8**	**7**	**1**	**1013**	**43**	**2**	**2.55**	....	....	....	....	....	....	....
	Albany River Rats	AHL	3	1	1	1	184	12	0	3.91	....	....	....	....	....	....	....
1997-98	**New Jersey**	**NHL**	**15**	**5**	**5**	**3**	**773**	**29**	**1**	**2.25**	....	....	....	....	....	....	....
1998-99	**Nashville**	**NHL**	**44**	**16**	**23**	**3**	**2472**	**127**	**1**	**3.08**	....	....	....	....	....	....	....
99-2000	**Nashville**	**NHL**	**52**	**19**	**27**	**6**	**3077**	**146**	**0**	**2.85**	....	....	....	....	....	....	....
	Milwaukee	IHL	1	1	0	0	60	1	0	1.00	....	....	....	....	....	....	....
2000-01	**Nashville**	**NHL**	**48**	**21**	**21**	**4**	**2810**	**107**	**4**	**2.28**	....	....	....	....	....	....	....
2001-02	**Nashville**	**NHL**	**58**	**23**	**24**	**9**	**3316**	**144**	**3**	**2.61**	....	....	....	....	....	....	....
	United States	Olympics	1	1	0	0	60	0	*1	0.00	....	....	....	....	....	....	....
2002-03	**Nashville**	**NHL**	**15**	**2**	**9**	**2**	**819**	**43**	**0**	**3.15**	....	....	....	....	....	....	....
	NY Rangers	**NHL**	**43**	**19**	**17**	**5**	**2467**	**94**	**5**	**2.29**	....	....	....	....	....	....	....
2003-04	**NY Rangers**	**NHL**	**57**	**16**	**30**	**7**	**3148**	**159**	**2**	**3.03**	....	....	....	....	....	....	....
	NHL Totals		**358**	**129**	**163**	**39**	**19895**	**892**	**18**	**2.69**	....	....	....	....	....	....	....

Hockey East First All-Star Team (1993) • NCAA East First All-American Team (1993) • Shared Harry "Hap" Holmes Memorial Trophy (fewest goals against – AHL) (1995) with Corey Schwab • Jack A. Butterfield Trophy (Playoff MVP – AHL) (1995) (co-winner - Corey Schwab) • AHL Second All-Star Team (1996) • Shared William M. Jennings Trophy (1997) with Martin Brodeur

Claimed by **Nashville** from **New Jersey** in Expansion Draft, June 26, 1998. Traded to **NY Rangers** by **Nashville** for Rem Murray, Tomas Kloucek and Marek Zidlicky, December 12, 2002.

EDDY, Justin (EH-dee, JUHS-tihn) WSH.

Goaltender. Catches left. 6'3", 200 lbs. Born, New Haven, CT, September 2, 1980.

			Regular Season								Playoffs						
Season	Club	League	GP	W	L	T	Mins	GA	SO	Avg	GP	W	L	Mins	GA	SO	Avg
99-2000	Lincoln Stars	USHL	12	9	2	0	662	26	1	2.35	2	0	0	27	3	0	6.55
2000-01	Quinnipiac	MAAC	27	14	9	3	1580	73	0	2.80	....	....	....	....	....	....	....
2001-02	Quinnipiac	MAAC	17	5	6	2	887	44	1	2.98	....	....	....	....	....	....	....
2002-03	Quinnipiac	MAAC	17	9	5	5	900	44	2	2.93	....	....	....	....	....	....	....
2003-04	Quinnipiac	AH	14	4	6	3	835	35	0	2.52	....	....	....	....	....	....	....

MAAC All-Rookie Team (2001)

Signed as a free agent by **Washington**, April 26, 2004.

EHELECHNER, Patrick (eh-heh-LEHCH-nuhr, PAT-rihk) **S.J.**

Goaltender. Catches left. 6'2", 169 lbs. Born, Rosenheim, West Germany, September 23, 1984.
(San Jose's 5th choice, 139th overall, in 2003 Entry Draft).

			Regular Season								Playoffs						
Season	Club	League	GP	W	L	T	Mins	GA	SO	Avg	GP	W	L	Mins	GA	SO	Avg
2000-01	Mannheim	German-4	40	....	....	....	2423	171	2	4.23	....	....	....	....	....	....	....
2001-02	EV Landshut	German-3	2	....	....	....	130	6	0	2.77	....	....	....	....	....	....	....
	Hannover	Germany	8	....	....	....	475	24	0	3.03	....	....	....	....	....	....	....
2002-03	ESC Wedemark	German-4	STATISTICS NOT AVAILABLE														
	Hannover	Germany	4	....	....	....	162	16	0	5.90	....	....	....	....	....	....	....
2003-04	Sudbury Wolves	OHL	56	22	26	6	3089	148	3	2.87	7	2	4	390	14	2	2.15

OHL Second All-Star Team (2004)

EKLUND, Brian (EHK-luhnd, BRIGH-uhn) **T.B.**

Goaltender. Catches left. 6'5", 205 lbs. Born, Braintree, MA, May 24, 1980.
(Tampa Bay's 8th choice, 226th overall, in 2000 Entry Draft).

			Regular Season								Playoffs						
Season	Club	League	GP	W	L	T	Mins	GA	SO	Avg	GP	W	L	Mins	GA	SO	Avg
1997-98	Archbishop Prep	Hi-School	22	....	....	....	1320	40	*6	*1.84	....	....	....	....	....	....	....
1998-99	Brown University	ECAC	8	1	3	0	299	17	0	3.41	....	....	....	....	....	....	....
99-2000	Brown University	ECAC	12	1	6	2	569	28	1	2.95	....	....	....	....	....	....	....
2000-01	Brown University	ECAC	19	2	13	3	1084	62	0	3.43	....	....	....	....	....	....	....
2001-02	Brown University	ECAC	9	3	5	0	454	30	0	3.97	....	....	....	....	....	....	....
2002-03	Springfield Falcons	AHL	1	1	0	0	60	1	0	1.00	....	....	....	....	....	....	....
	Pensacola Ice Pilots	ECHL	19	10	6	0	999	61	0	3.66	....	....	....	....	....	....	....
2003-04	Pensacola Ice Pilots	ECHL	*62	*38	17	7	*3725	187	1	3.01	5	2	3	333	16	0	2.88

ELLIOTT, Brian (EHL-lee-awt, BRIGH-uhn) **OTT.**

Goaltender. Catches left. 6'3", 186 lbs. Born, Newmarket, Ont., April 9, 1985.
(Ottawa's 9th choice, 291st overall, in 2003 Entry Draft).

			Regular Season								Playoffs						
Season	Club	League	GP	W	L	T	Mins	GA	SO	Avg	GP	W	L	Mins	GA	SO	Avg
2002-03	Ajax Axemen	OPJHL	39	....	....	....	2097	135	0	3.86	....	....	....	....	....	....	....
2003-04	U. of Wisconsin	WCHA	6	3	3	0	336	12	0	2.14	....	....	....	....	....	....	....

ELLIS, Dan (EHL-ihs, DAN) **DAL.**

Goaltender. Catches left. 6', 185 lbs. Born, Saskatoon, Sask., June 19, 1980.
(Dallas' 2nd choice, 60th overall, in 2000 Entry Draft).

			Regular Season								Playoffs						
Season	Club	League	GP	W	L	T	Mins	GA	SO	Avg	GP	W	L	Mins	GA	SO	Avg
1998-99	Newmarket	OPJHL	28	24	3	1	1670	63	3	2.25	....	....	....	....	....	....	....
99-2000	Omaha Lancers	USHL	55	*34	16	4	*3274	123	*11	*2.25	4	1	3	238	10	0	2.52
2000-01	Nebraska-Omaha	CCHA	40	21	14	3	2285	95	2	2.49	....	....	....	....	....	....	....
2001-02	Nebraska-Omaha	CCHA	40	20	15	4	2405	97	3	2.42	....	....	....	....	....	....	....
2002-03	Nebraska-Omaha	CCHA	39	11	21	5	2211	117	3	3.18	....	....	....	....	....	....	....
2003-04	**Dallas**	**NHL**	**1**	**1**	**0**	**0**	**60**	**3**	**0**	**3.00**	....	....	....	....	....	....	....
	Utah Grizzlies	AHL	20	5	14	0	1130	55	2	2.92	....	....	....	....	....	....	....
	Idaho Steelheads	ECHL	23	13	8	1	1334	57	2	2.56	*16	*13	3	*966	30	*3	*1.86
	NHL Totals		**1**	**1**	**0**	**0**	**60**	**3**	**0**	**3.00**	....	....	....	....	....	....	....

USHL First All-Star Team (2000) • USHL Goaltender of the Year (2000) • USHL Player of the Year (2000) • CCHA Second All-Star Team (2002) • ECHL Playoff MVP (2004)

EMERY, Ray (EH-muhr-ee, RAY) **OTT.**

Goaltender. Catches left. 6'3", 198 lbs. Born, Cayuga, Ont., September 28, 1982.
(Ottawa's 4th choice, 99th overall, in 2001 Entry Draft).

			Regular Season								Playoffs						
Season	Club	League	GP	W	L	T	Mins	GA	SO	Avg	GP	W	L	Mins	GA	SO	Avg
1998-99	Dunnville Terriers	OJHL-C	22	3	19	0	1320	140	0	6.37	....	....	....	....	....	....	....
99-2000	Welland Cougars	OJHL-B	23	13	10	1	1323	62	1	2.68	....	....	....	....	....	....	....
	Sault Ste. Marie	OHL	16	9	3	0	716	36	1	3.02	15	8	7	883	33	*3	2.24
2000-01	Sault Ste. Marie	OHL	52	18	29	2	2938	174	1	3.55	....	....	....	....	....	....	....
2001-02	Sault Ste. Marie	OHL	*59	*33	17	9	*3477	158	4	2.73	6	2	4	360	19	*1	3.17
2002-03	**Ottawa**	**NHL**	**3**	**1**	**0**	**0**	**85**	**2**	**0**	**1.41**	....	....	....	....	....	....	....
	Binghamton	AHL	50	27	17	6	2924	118	*7	2.42	14	8	6	848	40	*2	2.83
2003-04	**Ottawa**	**NHL**	**3**	**2**	**0**	**0**	**126**	**5**	**0**	**2.38**	....	....	....	....	....	....	....
	Binghamton	AHL	53	21	23	7	3109	128	3	2.47	2	0	2	120	6	0	3.01
	NHL Totals		**6**	**3**	**0**	**0**	**211**	**7**	**0**	**1.99**	....	....	....	....	....	....	....

OHL First All-Star Team (2002) • Canadian Major Junior First All-Star Team (2002) • Canadian Major Junior Goaltender of the Year (2002) • AHL All-Rookie Team (2003)

ESCHE, Robert (EHSH, RAW-buhrt) **PHI.**

Goaltender. Catches left. 6'1", 210 lbs. Born, Whitesboro, NY, January 22, 1978.
(Phoenix's 5th choice, 139th overall, in 1996 Entry Draft).

			Regular Season								Playoffs						
Season	Club	League	GP	W	L	T	Mins	GA	SO	Avg	GP	W	L	Mins	GA	SO	Avg
1994-95	Gloucester	COJHL	20	10	6	0	1034	70	0	4.06	....	....	....	....	....	....	....
1995-96	Detroit Jr. Whalers	OHL	23	13	6	0	1219	76	1	3.74	3	0	2	105	4	0	2.29
1996-97	Detroit Jr. Whalers	OHL	58	24	28	2	3241	206	2	3.81	5	1	4	317	19	0	3.60
1997-98	Plymouth Whalers	OHL	48	29	13	4	2810	135	3	2.88	15	8	7	869	45	0	3.11
1998-99	**Phoenix**	**NHL**	**3**	**0**	**1**	**0**	**130**	**7**	**0**	**3.23**	....	....	....	....	....	....	....
	Springfield Falcons	AHL	55	24	20	6	2957	138	1	2.80	1	0	1	60	4	0	4.02
99-2000	**Phoenix**	**NHL**	**8**	**2**	**5**	**0**	**408**	**23**	**0**	**3.38**	....	....	....	....	....	....	....
	Houston Aeros	IHL	7	4	2	1	419	16	2	2.29	....	....	....	....	....	....	....
	Springfield Falcons	AHL	21	9	9	2	1207	61	2	3.03	3	1	2	180	12	0	4.01
2000-01	**Phoenix**	**NHL**	**25**	**10**	**8**	**4**	**1350**	**68**	**2**	**3.02**	....	....	....	....	....	....	....
2001-02	**Phoenix**	**NHL**	**22**	**6**	**10**	**2**	**1145**	**52**	**1**	**2.72**	....	....	....	....	....	....	....
	Springfield Falcons	AHL	1	1	0	0	60	0	1	0.00	....	....	....	....	....	....	....
2002-03	**Philadelphia**	**NHL**	**30**	**12**	**9**	**3**	**1638**	**60**	**2**	**2.20**	**1**	**0**	**0**	**30**	**1**	**0**	**2.00**
2003-04	**Philadelphia**	**NHL**	**40**	**21**	**11**	**7**	**2322**	**79**	**3**	**2.04**	**18**	**11**	**7**	**1061**	**41**	**1**	**2.32**
	NHL Totals		**128**	**51**	**44**	**16**	**6993**	**289**	**8**	**2.48**	**19**	**11**	**7**	**1091**	**42**	**1**	**2.31**

OHL Second All-Star Team (1998) • Shared William M. Jennings Trophy (2003) with Roman Cechmanek (tied with Martin Brodeur)

Traded to **Philadelphia** by **Phoenix** with Michal Handzus for Brian Boucher and Nashville's 3rd round choice (previously acquired, Phoenix selected Joe Callahan) in 2002 Entry Draft, June 12, 2002.

FERHI, Eddy (feh-REE, EH-dee) **ANA.**

Goaltender. Catches left. 6'3", 181 lbs. Born, Charenton, France, November 26, 1979.

			Regular Season								Playoffs						
Season	Club	League	GP	W	L	T	Mins	GA	SO	Avg	GP	W	L	Mins	GA	SO	Avg
1998-99	Levis Faucons	CEGEP	STATISTICS NOT AVAILABLE														
99-2000	Sacred Heart	MAAC	7	2	4	0	367	19	0	3.11	....	....	....	....	....	....	....
2000-01	Sacred Heart	MAAC	21	9	7	4	1248	50	2	*2.40	....	....	....	....	....	....	....
2001-02	Sacred Heart	MAAC	31	13	12	4	1775	90	2	3.04	....	....	....	....	....	....	....
2002-03	Sacred Heart	MAAC	29	12	12	5	1770	67	3	*2.27	....	....	....	....	....	....	....
	Cincinnati	AHL	1	1	0	0	60	2	0	2.00	....	....	....	....	....	....	....
2003-04	Cincinnati	AHL	19	2	12	3	1061	55	0	3.11	1	0	0	24	2	0	5.07

MAAC Second All-Star Team (2002) • MAAC First All-Star Team (2003)

Signed to PTO (tryout) contract by **Cincinnati** (AHL), April 3, 2003. Signed as a free agent by **Anaheim**, July 23, 2003.

FERNANDEZ, Manny (fuhr-NAN-dehz, MAN-ee) **MIN.**

Goaltender. Catches left. 6', 180 lbs. Born, Etobicoke, Ont., August 27, 1974.
(Quebec's 4th choice, 52nd overall, in 1992 Entry Draft).

			Regular Season								Playoffs						
Season	Club	League	GP	W	L	T	Mins	GA	SO	Avg	GP	W	L	Mins	GA	SO	Avg
1990-91	Lac St-Louis Lions	QAAA	20	13	5	0	1176	69	*3	3.52	3	2	1	181	12	0	3.98
1991-92	Laval Titan	QMJHL	31	14	13	2	1593	99	1	3.73	9	3	5	468	39	0	5.00
1992-93	Laval Titan	QMJHL	43	26	14	2	2347	141	1	3.60	13	*12	1	818	42	0	3.08
1993-94	Laval Titan	QMJHL	51	29	14	1	2776	143	*5	3.09	19	14	5	1116	49	*1	*2.63
1994-95	Kalamazoo Wings	IHL	46	21	10	9	2470	115	2	2.79	14	10	2	753	34	1	2.71
	Dallas	**NHL**	**1**	**0**	**1**	**0**	**59**	**3**	**0**	**3.05**	....	....	....	....	....	....	....
1995-96	**Dallas**	**NHL**	**5**	**0**	**1**	**1**	**249**	**19**	**0**	**4.58**	....	....	....	....	....	....	....
	Michigan K-Wings	IHL	47	22	15	9	2664	133	*4	3.00	6	5	1	372	14	0	*2.26
1996-97	Michigan K-Wings	IHL	48	20	24	2	2720	142	2	3.13	4	1	3	277	15	0	3.25
1997-98	**Dallas**	**NHL**	**2**	**1**	**0**	**0**	**69**	**2**	**0**	**1.74**	**1**	**0**	**0**	**2**	**0**	**0**	**0.00**
	Michigan K-Wings	IHL	55	27	17	5	3022	139	5	2.76	2	0	2	88	7	0	4.73
1998-99	**Dallas**	**NHL**	**1**	**0**	**1**	**0**	**60**	**2**	**0**	**2.00**	....	....	....	....	....	....	....
	Houston Aeros	IHL	50	34	6	9	2949	116	2	2.36	*19	*11	8	*1126	49	1	2.61
99-2000	**Dallas**	**NHL**	**24**	**11**	**8**	**3**	**1353**	**48**	**1**	**2.13**	**1**	**0**	**0**	**17**	**1**	**0**	**3.53**
2000-01	**Minnesota**	**NHL**	**42**	**19**	**17**	**4**	**2461**	**92**	**4**	**2.24**	....	....	....	....	....	....	....
2001-02	**Minnesota**	**NHL**	**44**	**12**	**24**	**5**	**2463**	**125**	**1**	**3.05**	....	....	....	....	....	....	....
2002-03	**Minnesota**	**NHL**	**35**	**19**	**13**	**2**	**1979**	**74**	**2**	**2.24**	**9**	**3**	**4**	**552**	**18**	**0**	**1.96**
2003-04	**Minnesota**	**NHL**	**37**	**11**	**14**	**9**	**2166**	**90**	**2**	**2.49**	....	....	....	....	....	....	....
	NHL Totals		**191**	**73**	**79**	**24**	**10859**	**455**	**10**	**2.51**	**11**	**3**	**4**	**571**	**19**	**0**	**2.00**

QMJHL First All-Star Team (1994) • QMJHL MVP (1994) • IHL Second All-Star Team (1995)

Rights traded to **Dallas** by **Quebec** for Tommy Sjodin and Dallas' 3rd round choice (Chris Drury) in 1994 Entry Draft, February 13, 1994. Traded to **Minnesota** by **Dallas** with Brad Lukowich for Minnesota's 3rd round choice (Joel Lundqvist) in 2000 Entry Draft and Minnesota's 4th round choice (later traded back to Minnesota – later traded to Los Angeles – Los Angeles selected Aaron Rome) in 2002 Entry Draft, June 12, 2000.

FICHAUD, Eric (FEE-shoh, AIR-ihk)

Goaltender. Catches left. 5'11", 179 lbs. Born, Anjou, Que., November 4, 1975.
(Toronto's 1st choice, 16th overall, in 1994 Entry Draft).

			Regular Season								Playoffs						
Season	Club	League	GP	W	L	T	Mins	GA	SO	Avg	GP	W	L	Mins	GA	SO	Avg
1991-92	Montreal-Bourassa	QAAA	28	12	15	1	1678	110	0	3.95	9	5	4	567	32	0	3.39
1992-93	Chicoutimi	QMJHL	43	18	13	1	2039	149	0	4.38	....	....	....	....	....	....	....
1993-94	Chicoutimi	QMJHL	*63	*37	21	3	*3493	192	4	3.30	*26	*16	10	*1560	86	*1	3.31
1994-95	Chicoutimi	QMJHL	46	21	19	4	2637	151	4	3.44	7	2	5	428	20	0	2.80
1995-96	**NY Islanders**	**NHL**	**24**	**7**	**12**	**2**	**1234**	**68**	**1**	**3.31**	....	....	....	....	....	....	....
	Worcester IceCats	AHL	34	13	15	6	1989	97	1	2.93	2	1	1	127	7	0	3.30
1996-97	**NY Islanders**	**NHL**	**34**	**9**	**14**	**4**	**1759**	**91**	**0**	**3.10**	....	....	....	....	....	....	....
1997-98	**NY Islanders**	**NHL**	**17**	**3**	**8**	**3**	**807**	**40**	**0**	**2.97**	....	....	....	....	....	....	....
	Utah Grizzlies	IHL	1	0	0	0	40	3	0	4.45	....	....	....	....	....	....	....
1998-99	**Nashville**	**NHL**	**9**	**0**	**6**	**0**	**447**	**24**	**0**	**3.22**	....	....	....	....	....	....	....
	Milwaukee	IHL	8	5	2	1	480	25	0	3.13	....	....	....	....	....	....	....
99-2000	**Carolina**	**NHL**	**9**	**3**	**5**	**1**	**490**	**24**	**1**	**2.94**	....	....	....	....	....	....	....
	Quebec Citadelles	AHL	6	4	1	1	368	17	0	2.77	3	0	3	177	10	0	3.39
2000-01	**Montreal**	**NHL**	**2**	**0**	**2**	**0**	**62**	**4**	**0**	**3.87**	....	....	....	....	....	....	....
	Quebec Citadelles	AHL	42	19	19	2	2441	127	1	3.12	2	0	1	98	3	0	1.84
2001-02	Manitoba Moose	AHL	5	2	3	0	279	13	1	2.80	....	....	....	....	....	....	....
	Krefeld Pinguine	Germany	9	....	....	....	401	11	0	1.65	3	....	....	197	8	0	2.44
2002-03	Hamilton Bulldogs	AHL	27	14	7	3	1447	55	4	2.28	8	5	3	472	17	0	2.16
2003-04	Hamilton Bulldogs	AHL	31	16	11	3	1836	70	1	2.29	....	....	....	....	....	....	....
	NHL Totals		**95**	**22**	**47**	**10**	**4799**	**251**	**2**	**3.14**	....	....	....	....	....	....	....

Canadian Major Junior Second All-Star Team (1994) • Memorial Cup All-Star Team (1994) • Hap Emms Memorial Trophy (Memorial Cup Top Goaltender) (1994) • QMJHL First All-Star Team (1995)

Traded to **NY Islanders** by **Toronto** for Benoit Hogue, NY Islanders' 3rd round choice (Ryan Pepperall) in 1995 Entry Draft and NY Islanders' 5th round choice (Brandon Sugden) in 1996 Entry Draft, April 6, 1995. Traded to **Edmonton** by **NY Islanders** for Mike Watt, June 18, 1998. Traded to **Nashville** by **Edmonton** with Drake Berehowsky and Greg de Vries for Mikhail Shtalenkov and Jim Dowd, October 1, 1998. Traded to **Carolina** by **Nashville** for Toronto's 4th round choice (previously acquired, Nashville selected Yevgeny Pavlov) in 1999 Entry Draft and future considerations, June 26, 1999. Claimed on waivers by **Montreal** from **Carolina**, February 11, 2000. Signed as a free agent by **Krefeld** (Germany) following release by **Manitoba** (AHL), January 11, 2002. Signed as a free agent by **Montreal**, September 10, 2002.

FINLEY, Brian (FIHN-lee, BRIGH-uhn) **NSH.**

Goaltender. Catches right. 6'3", 205 lbs. Born, Sault Ste. Marie, Ont., July 13, 1981.
(Nashville's 1st choice, 6th overall, in 1999 Entry Draft).

			Regular Season								Playoffs						
Season	Club	League	GP	W	L	T	Mins	GA	SO	Avg	GP	W	L	Mins	GA	SO	Avg
1996-97	Soo Carlucci's	NOBHL	45	....	....	....	1943	109	3	2.38	....	....	....	....	....	....	....
1997-98	Barrie Colts	OHL	41	23	14	1	2154	105	3	2.92	5	1	3	260	13	0	3.00
1998-99	Barrie Colts	OHL	52	*36	10	4	3063	136	3	2.66	5	4	1	323	15	0	2.79
99-2000	Barrie Colts	OHL	47	24	12	6	2540	130	2	3.07	*23	14	8	1353	58	1	2.57
2000-01	Barrie Colts	OHL	16	5	8	0	818	42	0	3.08	....	....	....	....	....	....	....
	Brampton Battalion	OHL	11	7	3	1	631	31	0	2.95	9	5	4	503	26	1	3.10
2001-02			DID NOT PLAY – INJURED														
2002-03	**Nashville**	**NHL**	**1**	**0**	**0**	**0**	**47**	**3**	**0**	**3.83**	....	....	....	....	....	....	....
	Milwaukee	AHL	22	7	11	2	1207	59	2	2.93	....	....	....	....	....	....	....
	Toledo Storm	ECHL	7	4	2	0	305	12	0	2.36	1	0	1	60	4	0	4.00
2003-04	Milwaukee	AHL	43	23	15	4	2561	100	2	2.34	1	0	1	59	2	0	2.05
	NHL Totals		**1**	**0**	**0**	**0**	**47**	**3**	**0**	**3.83**	....	....	....	....	....	....	....

OHL All-Rookie Team (1998) • OHL First All-Star Team (1999) • OHL Playoff MVP (2000)

• Missed entire 2001-02 season recovering from groin injury suffered during 2000-01 season and re-injured in training camp, October 3, 2001.

FISHER, Glenn (FIH-shuhr, GLEHN) **EDM.**

Goaltender. Catches left. 6'1", 160 lbs. Born, Edmonton, Alta., April 25, 1983.
(Edmonton's 9th choice, 148th overall, in 2002 Entry Draft).

			Regular Season								Playoffs						
Season	Club	League	GP	W	L	T	Mins	GA	SO	Avg	GP	W	L	Mins	GA	SO	Avg
99-2000	Edm. Leafs	AMBHL	16	9	5	2	944	62	0	3.94	....	....	....	....	....	....	....
2000-01	Edm. Leafs	AMHL	19	6	9	3	1116	77	0	4.14	....	....	....	....	....	....	....
2001-02	Ft. Saskatchewan	AJHL	47	....	....	....	2649	196	2	4.44	....	....	....	....	....	....	....
2002-03	Ft. Saskatchewan	AJHL	41	15	21	5	2401	159	0	3.97	....	....	....	....	....	....	....
2003-04	U. of Denver	WCHA	9	3	1	1	436	26	0	3.58	....	....	....	....	....	....	....

FLAHERTY, Wade (FLAY-uhr-tee, WAYD) **VAN.**

Goaltender. Catches left. 6', 185 lbs. Born, Terrace, B.C., January 11, 1968.
(Buffalo's 10th choice, 181st overall, in 1988 Entry Draft).

			Regular Season								Playoffs						
Season	Club	League	GP	W	L	T	Mins	GA	SO	Avg	GP	W	L	Mins	GA	SO	Avg
1984-85	Kelowna Wings	WHL	1	0	0	0	55	5	0	5.45	....	....	....	....	....	....	....
1985-86	Seattle	WHL	9	1	3	0	271	36	0	7.97	....	....	....	....	....	....	....
	Spokane Chiefs	WHL	5	0	3	0	161	21	0	7.83	....	....	....	....	....	....	....
1986-87	Nanaimo Clippers	BCJHL	15	....	....	....	830	53	0	3.83	....	....	....	....	....	....	....
	Victoria Cougars	WHL	3	0	2	0	127	16	0	7.56	....	....	....	....	....	....	....
1987-88	Victoria Cougars	WHL	36	20	15	0	2052	135	0	3.95	5	2	3	300	18	0	3.60
1988-89	Victoria Cougars	WHL	42	21	19	0	2408	180	4	4.49	....	....	....	....	....	....	....

1989-90	Greensboro	ECHL	27	12	10	0	1308	96	0	4.40	....	....	....	....	....	....	....
1990-91	Kansas City Blades	IHL	*56	16	31	4	2990	224	0	4.49	....	....	....	....	....	....	....
1991-92	San Jose	NHL	3	0	3	0	178	13	0	4.38	....	....	....	....	....	....	....
	Kansas City Blades	IHL	43	26	14	3	2603	140	1	3.23	1	0	0	1	0	0	0.00
1992-93	San Jose	NHL	1	0	1	0	60	5	0	5.00	....	....	....	....	....	....	....
	Kansas City Blades	IHL	*61	*34	19	7	*3642	195	2	3.21	*12	6	6	733	34	*1	2.78
1993-94	Kansas City Blades	IHL	*60	32	19	9	*3564	202	0	3.40	....	....	....	....	....	....	....
1994-95	San Jose	NHL	18	5	6	1	852	44	1	3.10	7	2	3	377	31	0	4.93
1995-96	San Jose	NHL	24	3	12	1	1137	92	0	4.85	....	....	....	....	....	....	....
1996-97	San Jose	NHL	7	2	4	0	359	31	0	5.18	....	....	....	....	....	....	....
	Kentucky	AHL	19	8	6	2	1032	54	1	3.14	3	1	2	200	11	0	3.30
1997-98	NY Islanders	NHL	16	4	4	3	694	23	3	1.99	....	....	....	....	....	....	....
	Utah Grizzlies	IHL	24	16	5	3	1341	40	3	1.79	....	....	....	....	....	....	....
1998-99	NY Islanders	NHL	20	5	11	2	1048	53	0	3.03	....	....	....	....	....	....	....
	Lowell	AHL	5	1	3	1	305	16	0	3.15	....	....	....	....	....	....	....
99-2000	NY Islanders	NHL	4	0	1	1	182	7	0	2.31	....	....	....	....	....	....	....
2000-01	NY Islanders	NHL	20	6	10	0	1017	56	1	3.30	....	....	....	....	....	....	....
	Tampa Bay	NHL	2	0	2	0	118	8	0	4.07	....	....	....	....	....	....	....
2001-02	Florida	NHL	4	2	1	1	245	12	0	2.94	....	....	....	....	....	....	....
	Utah Grizzlies	AHL	45	22	13	5	2351	92	2	2.35	5	2	3	312	11	0	2.12
2002-03	Nashville	NHL	1	0	1	0	51	4	0	4.71	....	....	....	....	....	....	....
	San Antonio	AHL	30	11	13	5	1791	86	1	2.88	....	....	....	....	....	....	....
2003-04	Milwaukee	AHL	36	21	12	3	2146	78	3	2.18	*21	*16	5	*1371	44	1	1.93
	NHL Totals		120	27	56	9	5941	348	5	3.51	7	2	3	377	31	0	4.93

WHL West Second All-Star Team (1988) • ECHL Playoff MVP (1990) • Shared James Norris Memorial Trophy (fewest goals against – IHL) (1992) with Arturs Irbe • IHL Second All-Star Team (1993, 1994) • Won Jack A. Butterfield Trophy (Playoff MVP - AHL) (2004)

Signed as a free agent by **San Jose**, September 3, 1991. Signed as a free agent by **NY Islanders**, July 22, 1997. Traded to **Tampa Bay** by **NY Islanders** for future considerations, February 16, 2001. Signed as a free agent by **Florida**, August 2, 2001. Traded to **Nashville** by **Florida** for Pascal Trepanier, March 9, 2003. Signed as a free agent by **Vancouver**, July 7, 2004.

FLEURY, Marc-Andre (fluh-REE, MAHRK-AWN-dray) PIT.

Goaltender. Catches left. 6'1", 175 lbs. Born, Sorel, Que., November 28, 1984.
(Pittsburgh's 1st choice, 1st overall, in 2003 Entry Draft).

					Regular Season								Playoffs				
Season	Club	League	GP	W	L	T	Mins	GA	SO	Avg	GP	W	L	Mins	GA	SO	Avg
99-2000	Charles-Lemoyne	QAAA	15	4	9	0	780	36	1	2.77	....	....	....	....	....	....	....
2000-01	Cape Breton	QMJHL	35	12	13	2	1705	115	0	4.05	2	0	1	32	4	0	7.50
2001-02	Cape Breton	QMJHL	55	26	14	8	3043	141	2	2.78	16	9	7	1003	55	0	3.29
2002-03	Cape Breton	QMJHL	51	17	24	6	2889	162	2	3.36	4	0	4	228	17	0	4.47
2003-04	Pittsburgh	NHL	21	4	14	2	1154	70	1	3.64	....	....	....	....	....	....	....
	Cape Breton	QMJHL	10	8	1	1	606	20	0	1.98	4	1	3	251	13	0	3.10
	Wilkes-Barre	AHL	....	....	....	....	....	....	....	....	2	0	1	92	6	0	3.90
	NHL Totals		21	4	14	2	1154	70	1	3.64	....	....	....	....	....	....	....

QMJHL Second All-Star Team (2003)

Returned to **Cape Breton** (QMJHL) by **Pittsburgh**, January 29, 2004.

FORD, Todd (FOHRD, TAWD) TOR.

Goaltender. Catches left. 6'4", 176 lbs. Born, Calgary, Alta., May 1, 1984.
(Toronto's 3rd choice, 74th overall, in 2002 Entry Draft).

					Regular Season								Playoffs				
Season	Club	League	GP	W	L	T	Mins	GA	SO	Avg	GP	W	L	Mins	GA	SO	Avg
99-2000	Calgary Stamps	CBHL					STATISTICS NOT AVAILABLE										
2000-01	Swift Current	WHL	20	12	4	2	1066	53	0	2.98	1	0	0	26	2	0	4.62
2001-02	Swift Current	WHL	37	18	12	3	2003	99	2	2.97	10	5	5	603	28	0	2.79
2002-03	Swift Current	WHL	28	12	9	5	1588	71	2	2.68	....	....	....	....	....	....	....
	Prince George	WHL	17	4	9	2	936	70	0	4.49	1	0	1	60	7	0	7.00
2003-04	Prince George	WHL	28	8	14	4	1480	82	0	3.32	....	....	....	....	....	....	....
	Vancouver Giants	WHL	10	1	7	1	570	33	0	3.47	1	0	0	32	0	0	0.00

FRANEK, Petr (FRAH-nehk, PEE-tuhr) COL.

Goaltender. Catches left. 5'11", 185 lbs. Born, Most, Czech., April 6, 1975.
(Quebec's 10th choice, 205th overall, in 1993 Entry Draft).

					Regular Season								Playoffs				
Season	Club	League	GP	W	L	T	Mins	GA	SO	Avg	GP	W	L	Mins	GA	SO	Avg
1992-93	Litvinov	Czech	5	....	....	....	273	15	0	3.29	....	....	....	....	....	....	....
1993-94	Litvinov	Czech	11	....	....	....	535	34	0	3.81	2	0	1	61	10	0	9.83
1994-95	Litvinov	Czech	12	....	....	....	657	47	0	4.29	1	0	0	16	0	0	0.00
1995-96	Litvinov	Czech	36	....	....	....	2096	85	3	2.43	16	....	....	948	47	1	2.97
1996-97	Hershey Bears	AHL	15	4	1	0	457	23	3	3.02	....	....	....	....	....	....	....
	Brantford Smoke	ColHL	6	4	1	0	321	14	0	2.61	....	....	....	....	....	....	....
	Quebec Rafales	IHL	6	3	3	0	357	18	0	3.02	1	0	1	40	4	0	6.00
1997-98	Hershey Bears	AHL	43	19	14	2	2169	98	2	2.71	1	0	1	60	4	0	4.00
1998-99	Utah Grizzlies	IHL	8	1	6	1	446	26	0	3.50	....	....	....	....	....	....	....
	Las Vegas Thunder	IHL	37	17	13	2	1879	107	0	3.42	....	....	....	....	....	....	....
99-2000	Nurnberg	Germany	30	....	....	....	1603	73	2	2.73	....	....	....	....	....	....	....
2000-01	HC Karlovy Vary	Czech	44	....	....	....	2507	121	....	2.90	....	....	....	....	....	....	....
2001-02	HC Karlovy Vary	Czech	40	....	....	....	2189	109	....	2.99	....	....	....	....	....	....	....
2002-03	HC Karlovy Vary	Czech	45	....	....	....	2570	107	5	2.50	....	....	....	....	....	....	....
2003-04	HC Karlovy Vary	Czech	25	....	....	....	1471	58	2	2.37	....	....	....	....	....	....	....
	HC Slavia Praha	Czech	4	....	....	....	245	8	0	1.96	*19	9	10	*1186	39	*3	1.97

Rights transferred to **Colorado** after **Quebec** franchise relocated, June 21, 1995.

GARNETT, Michael (gahr-NEHT, MIGH-kuhl) ATL.

Goaltender. Catches left. 6'1", 200 lbs. Born, Saskatoon, Sask., November 25, 1982.
(Atlanta's 2nd choice, 80th overall, in 2001 Entry Draft).

					Regular Season								Playoffs				
Season	Club	League	GP	W	L	T	Mins	GA	SO	Avg	GP	W	L	Mins	GA	SO	Avg
1997-98	Sask. Contacts	SMHL	3	1	1	0	82	8	0	5.85	....	....	....	....	....	....	....
1998-99	Sask. Contacts	SMHL					STATISTICS NOT AVAILABLE										
99-2000	Kindersley Klippers	SJHL	36	....	....	....	2067	140	1	3.57	....	....	....	....	....	....	....
	Red Deer Rebels	WHL	1	0	0	0	14	0	0	0.00	1	0	1	65	2	0	1.85
2000-01	Red Deer Rebels	WHL	21	14	5	1	1133	39	3	2.07	....	....	....	....	....	....	....
	Saskatoon Blades	WHL	28	7	17	2	1501	83	1	3.32	....	....	....	....	....	....	....
2001-02	Saskatoon Blades	WHL	*67	27	34	4	*3738	205	2	3.29	7	3	4	450	15	0	2.00
2002-03	Chicago Wolves	AHL	2	0	1	0	33	2	0	3.64	....	....	....	....	....	....	....
	Greenville Grrrowl	ECHL	38	16	15	3	2092	119	0	3.41	3	1	2	178	13	0	4.38
2003-04	Gwinnett	ECHL	33	21	10	2	1936	69	4	2.14	12	7	5	770	34	0	2.65
	Chicago Wolves	AHL	13	7	3	2	731	32	0	2.63	....	....	....	....	....	....	....

GARON, Mathieu (gah-ROHN, MA-tyew) L.A.

Goaltender. Catches right. 6'2", 192 lbs. Born, Chandler, Que., January 9, 1978.
(Montreal's 2nd choice, 44th overall, in 1996 Entry Draft).

					Regular Season								Playoffs				
Season	Club	League	GP	W	L	T	Mins	GA	SO	Avg	GP	W	L	Mins	GA	SO	Avg
1993-94	Jonquiere Elites	QAAA	17	0	13	0	834	88	0	6.33	....	....	....	....	....	....	....
1994-95	Jonquiere Elites	QAAA	27	13	13	1	1554	94	0	3.63	9	6	2	467	26	0	3.34
1995-96	Victoriaville Tigres	QMJHL	51	18	27	0	2709	189	1	4.19	12	7	4	676	38	1	3.39
1996-97	Victoriaville Tigres	QMJHL	53	29	18	3	3032	150	*6	2.97	6	2	4	330	23	0	4.18
1997-98	Victoriaville Tigres	QMJHL	47	27	18	2	2802	125	5	2.68	6	2	4	345	22	0	3.82
1998-99	Fredericton	AHL	40	14	22	2	2222	114	3	3.08	6	1	1	208	12	0	3.47
99-2000	Quebec Citadelles	AHL	53	17	28	3	2884	149	2	3.10	1	0	0	20	3	0	8.82
2000-01	Montreal	NHL	11	4	5	1	589	24	2	2.44	....	....	....	....	....	....	....
	Quebec Citadelles	AHL	31	16	13	1	1768	86	1	2.92	8	4	4	459	22	1	2.88
2001-02	Montreal	NHL	5	1	4	0	261	19	0	4.37	....	....	....	....	....	....	....
	Quebec Citadelles	AHL	50	21	15	12	2988	136	2	2.73	3	0	3	198	12	0	3.63
2002-03	Montreal	NHL	8	3	5	0	482	16	2	1.99	....	....	....	....	....	....	....
	Hamilton Bulldogs	AHL	20	15	2	2	1150	34	4	1.77	....	....	....	....	....	....	....
2003-04	Montreal	NHL	19	8	6	2	1003	38	0	2.27	1	0	0	12	0	0	0.00
	NHL Totals		43	16	20	3	2335	97	4	2.49	1	0	0	12	0	0	0.00

QMJHL All-Rookie Team (1996) • QMJHL Defensive Rookie of the Year (1996) • QMJHL First All-Star Team (1998) • Canadian Major Junior First All-Star Team (1998) • Canadian Major Junior Goaltender of the Year (1998)

Traded to **Los Angeles** by **Montreal** with San Jose's 3rd round choice (previously acquired, Los Angeles selected Paul Baier) in 2004 Entry Draft for Radek Bonk and Cristobal Huet, June 26, 2004.

GERBER, Martin (GUHR-buhr, MAHR-tihn) CAR.

Goaltender. Catches left. 6', 185 lbs. Born, Burgdorf, Switz., September 3, 1974.
(Anaheim's 10th choice, 232nd overall, in 2001 Entry Draft).

					Regular Season								Playoffs				
Season	Club	League	GP	W	L	T	Mins	GA	SO	Avg	GP	W	L	Mins	GA	SO	Avg
1996-97	SC Langnau Tigers	Swiss-2	38	....	....	....	2286	121	0	3.18	8	....	....	488	29	0	3.57
1997-98	SC Langnau Tigers	Swiss-2	40	....	....	....	2430	141	2	3.48	16	....	....	961	42	0	2.62
1998-99	SC Langnau Tigers	Swiss	42	....	....	....	2521	203	1	4.83	11	....	....	664	50	0	4.52
99-2000	SC Langnau Tigers	Swiss	44	....	....	....	2652	161	3	3.64	6	....	....	360	13	*2	*2.17
2000-01	SC Langnau Tigers	Swiss	*44	....	....	....	2671	114	3	2.56	5	....	....	319	7	1	1.32
2001-02	Farjestad	Sweden	44	....	....	....	2664	87	*4	*1.96	*10	....	....	*657	18	*2	*1.64
	Switzerland	Olympics	3	1	1	1	158	4	0	1.52	....	....	....	....	....	....	....
2002-03	Anaheim	NHL	22	6	11	3	1203	39	1	1.95	2	0	0	20	1	0	3.00
	Cincinnati	AHL	1	1	0	0	60	2	0	2.00	....	....	....	....	....	....	....
2003-04	Anaheim	NHL	32	11	12	4	1698	64	2	2.26	....	....	....	....	....	....	....
	NHL Totals		54	17	23	7	2901	103	3	2.13	2	0	0	20	1	0	3.00

• Scored a goal in playoffs vs. Martigny (Swiss-2), February 27, 1997. Traded to **Carolina** by **Anaheim** for Tomas Malec and Carolina's 3rd round choice (Kyle Klubertanz) in 2004 Entry Draft, June 18, 2004.

GIGUERE, Jean-Sebastien (ZHEE-gair, ZHAWN-suh-BAS-tee-yeh) ANA.

Goaltender. Catches left. 6'1", 199 lbs. Born, Montreal, Que., May 16, 1977.
(Hartford's 1st choice, 13th overall, in 1995 Entry Draft).

					Regular Season								Playoffs				
Season	Club	League	GP	W	L	T	Mins	GA	SO	Avg	GP	W	L	Mins	GA	SO	Avg
1992-93	Laval-Laurentides	QAAA	25	12	11	2	1498	76	0	3.02	11	6	5	654	38	0	3.49
1993-94	Verdun	QMJHL	25	13	5	2	1234	66	1	3.21	....	....	....	....	....	....	....
1994-95	Halifax	QMJHL	47	14	27	5	2755	181	2	3.94	7	3	4	417	17	1	*2.45
1995-96	Halifax	QMJHL	55	26	23	2	3230	185	1	3.44	6	1	5	354	24	0	4.07
1996-97	Hartford	NHL	8	1	4	0	394	24	0	3.65	....	....	....	....	....	....	....
	Halifax	QMJHL	50	28	19	3	3014	170	2	3.38	16	9	7	954	58	0	3.65
1997-98	Saint John Flames	AHL	31	16	10	3	1758	72	2	2.46	10	5	3	536	27	0	3.02
1998-99	Calgary	NHL	15	6	7	1	860	46	0	3.21	....	....	....	....	....	....	....
	Saint John Flames	AHL	39	18	16	3	2145	123	3	3.44	7	3	2	304	21	0	4.14
99-2000	Calgary	NHL	7	1	3	1	330	15	0	2.73	....	....	....	....	....	....	....
	Saint John Flames	AHL	41	17	17	3	2243	114	0	3.05	3	0	3	178	9	0	3.03
2000-01	Anaheim	NHL	34	11	17	5	2031	87	4	2.57	....	....	....	....	....	....	....
	Cincinnati	AHL	23	12	7	2	1306	53	0	2.43	....	....	....	....	....	....	....
2001-02	Anaheim	NHL	53	20	25	6	3127	111	4	2.13	....	....	....	....	....	....	....
2002-03	Anaheim	NHL	65	34	22	6	3775	145	8	2.30	21	15	6	1407	38	5	*1.62
2003-04	Anaheim	NHL	55	17	31	6	3210	140	3	2.62	....	....	....	....	....	....	....
	NHL Totals		237	90	109	25	13727	568	19	2.48	21	15	6	1407	38	5	1.62

QMJHL Second All-Star Team (1997) • Shared Harry "Hap" Holmes Memorial Trophy (fewest goals against – AHL) (1998) with Tyler Moss • Conn Smythe Trophy (2003)

Transferred to **Carolina** after **Hartford** franchise relocated, June 25, 1997. Traded to **Calgary** by **Carolina** with Andrew Cassels for Gary Roberts and Trevor Kidd, August 25, 1997. Traded to **Anaheim** by **Calgary** for Anaheim's 2nd round choice (later traded to Washington – Washington selected Matt Pettinger) in 2000 Entry Draft, June 10, 2000.

GLASS, Jeff (GLAS, JEHF) OTT.

Goaltender. Catches left. 6'2", 182 lbs. Born, Calgary, Alta., November 19, 1985.
(Ottawa's 5th choice, 89th overall, in 2004 Entry Draft).

					Regular Season								Playoffs				
Season	Club	League	GP	W	L	T	Mins	GA	SO	Avg	GP	W	L	Mins	GA	SO	Avg
2002-03	Kootenay Ice	WHL	35	15	16	3	1884	77	4	2.45	9	4	5	643	23	0	2.15
2003-04	Kootenay Ice	WHL	57	26	20	6	3263	128	5	2.35	4	0	4	239	14	0	3.51

GOEHRING, Karl (GAIR-ihng, KAHRL) CBJ

Goaltender. Catches left. 5'8", 160 lbs. Born, Apple Valley, MN, August 23, 1978.

					Regular Season								Playoffs				
Season	Club	League	GP	W	L	T	Mins	GA	SO	Avg	GP	W	L	Mins	GA	SO	Avg
1996-97	Fargo-Moorhead	USHL	32	13	18	1	1909	79	*4	*2.48	5	2	3	251	15	1	3.58
1997-98	North Dakota	WCHA	27	23	3	1	1504	57	1	*2.27	....	....	....	....	....	....	....
1998-99	North Dakota	WCHA	31	22	5	2	1774	71	3	2.40	....	....	....	....	....	....	....
99-2000	North Dakota	WCHA	30	19	6	4	1747	55	*8	*1.89	....	....	....	....	....	....	....
2000-01	North Dakota	WCHA	30	16	6	6	1662	66	*3	2.38	....	....	....	....	....	....	....
2001-02	Syracuse Crunch	AHL	15	5	6	3	891	37	1	2.49	....	....	....	....	....	....	....
	Dayton Bombers	ECHL	23	11	9	3	1393	52	2	2.24	*14	9	5	*866	35	1	2.43
2002-03	Syracuse Crunch	AHL	49	18	21	4	2608	116	4	2.67	....	....	....	....	....	....	....
2003-04	Syracuse Crunch	AHL	38	17	14	6	2234	97	1	2.60	5	2	2	295	16	0	3.26

WCHA First All-Star Team (1998, 2000) • WCHA Rookie of the Year (1998) • NCAA West First All-American Team (1998, 2000) • WCHA Second All-Star Team (1999)

Signed as a free agent by **Columbus**, May 7, 2001.

GOEPFERT, Robert (GEHP-fuhrt, RAW-buhrt) PIT.

Goaltender. Catches left. 5'10", 170 lbs. Born, Ozone Park, NY, May 9, 1983.
(Pittsburgh's 7th choice, 171st overall, in 2002 Entry Draft).

					Regular Season								Playoffs				
Season	Club	League	GP	W	L	T	Mins	GA	SO	Avg	GP	W	L	Mins	GA	SO	Avg
99-2000	Suffolk PAL	Metro-Jr.	38	....	....	....	2280	87	....	2.36	....	....	....	....	....	....	....
2000-01	Cedar Rapids	USHL	41	25	12	4	2565	125	1	2.92	4	1	3	188	18	0	5.73
2001-02	Cedar Rapids	USHL	51	27	16	5	2918	99	8	2.04	8	4	4	581	19	0	1.97
2002-03	Providence College	H-East	13	6	6	1	754	30	1	2.39	....	....	....	....	....	....	....
2003-04	Providence College	H-East	28	15	9	3	1641	68	2	2.49	....	....	....	....	....	....	....

USHL All-Rookie Team (2001) • USHL Goaltender of the Year (2001, 2002) • USHL First All-Star Team (2002• USHL Player of the Year (2002)

GRAHAME, John (GRAY-uhm, JAWN) T.B.

Goaltender. Catches left. 6'2", 220 lbs. Born, Denver, CO, August 31, 1975.
(Boston's 7th choice, 229th overall, in 1994 Entry Draft).

					Regular Season								Playoffs				
Season	Club	League	GP	W	L	T	Mins	GA	SO	Avg	GP	W	L	Mins	GA	SO	Avg
1993-94	Sioux City	USHL	20	....	....	....	1200	73	0	3.70	....	....	....	....	....	....	....
1994-95	Lake Superior State	CCHA	28	16	7	3	1616	75	2	2.79	....	....	....	....	....	....	....
1995-96	Lake Superior State	CCHA	29	21	4	2	1558	66	2	2.54	....	....	....	....	....	....	....
1996-97	Lake Superior State	CCHA	37	19	13	4	2197	134	3	3.66	....	....	....	....	....	....	....

1997-98	Providence Bruins	AHL	55	15	31	4	3053	164	3	3.22							
1998-99	Providence Bruins	AHL	48	*37	9	1	2771	134	3	2.90	19	*15	4	*1209	48	1	2.38
99-2000	**Boston**	**NHL**	**24**	**7**	**10**	**5**	**1344**	**55**	**2**	**2.46**							
	Providence Bruins	AHL	27	11	13	2	1528	86	1	3.38	13	10	3	839	35	0	2.50
2000-01	**Boston**	**NHL**	**10**	**3**	**4**	**0**	**471**	**28**	**0**	**3.57**							
	Providence Bruins	AHL	16	4	7	3	893	47	0	3.16	17	8	9	1043	46	2	2.65
2001-02	**Boston**	**NHL**	**19**	**8**	**7**	**2**	**1079**	**52**	**1**	**2.89**							
2002-03	**Boston**	**NHL**	**23**	**11**	**9**	**2**	**1352**	**61**	**1**	**2.71**							
	Tampa Bay	**NHL**	**17**	**6**	**5**	**4**	**914**	**34**	**2**	**2.23**	**1**	**0**	**1**	**111**	**2**	**0**	**1.08**
2003-04♦	**Tampa Bay**	**NHL**	**29**	**18**	**9**	**1**	**1688**	**58**	**1**	**2.06**	**1**	**0**	**0**	**34**	**2**	**0**	**3.53**
	NHL Totals		**122**	**53**	**44**	**14**	**6848**	**288**	**7**	**2.52**	**2**	**0**	**1**	**145**	**4**	**0**	**1.66**

Traded to **Tampa Bay** by **Boston** for Tampa Bay's 4th round choice (later traded to San Jose – San Jose selected Jason Churchill) in 2004 Entry Draft, January 13, 2003.

GRAHN, Carl (GRAHN, KARL) L.A.

Goaltender. Catches left. 6', 175 lbs. Born, Koupolo, Finland, January 8, 1981.
(Los Angeles' 11th choice, 282nd overall, in 2000 Entry Draft).

			Regular Season								Playoffs						
Season	**Club**	**League**	**GP**	**W**	**L**	**T**	**Mins**	**GA**	**SO**	**Avg**	**GP**	**W**	**L**	**Mins**	**GA**	**SO**	**Avg**
1998-99	KalPa Kuopio Jr.	Finn-Jr.	20	7	10	1	1153	63	1	3.28							
	KalPa Kuopio	Finland	3	0	2	0	126	16	0	7.63							
99-2000	KooKoo Jr.	Finn-Jr.	38				2165	124	1	3.44							
2000-01	KooKoo Kouvola	Finland-2	14	2	8	1	631	41	0	3.90							
2001-02	KooKoo Kouvola	Finland-2	36	19	10	6	2059	88	4	2.56	10	4	5	562	29	0	3.11
2002-03	KooKoo Kouvola	Finland-2	21	11	5	5	1276	49	2	2.30	8	4	3	466	21	1	2.71
2003-04	Pelicans Lahti	Finland	21	1	11	3	1121	72	0	3.85							
	Kiekko-Vantaa	Finland-2	8	4	3	1	475	22	0	2.78							

GREISS, Thomas (GRIGHS, TAW-muhs) S.J.

Goaltender. Catches left. 6'1", 192 lbs. Born, Straubing, West Germany, January 29, 1986.
(San Jose's 2nd choice, 94th overall, in 2004 Entry Draft).

			Regular Season								Playoffs						
Season	**Club**	**League**	**GP**	**W**	**L**	**T**	**Mins**	**GA**	**SO**	**Avg**	**GP**	**W**	**L**	**Mins**	**GA**	**SO**	**Avg**
2001-02	EV Fussen Jr.	Ger-Jr.					STATISTICS NOT AVAILABLE										
2002-03	Kolner Haie Jr.	Ger-Jr.	25				1613	58	0	2.16	3	1	2	180	8	1	2.67
2003-04	Kolner Haie Jr.	Ger-Jr.	24				1286	56		2.61							
	Kolner Haie	Germany	1				20	4	0	12.00							

GRUMET-MORRIS, Dov (groo-MAY-MAW-rihs, DAWV) PHI.

Goaltender. Catches left. 6'2", 190 lbs. Born, Evanston, IL, February 28, 1982.
(Philadelphia's 4th choice, 161st overall, in 2002 Entry Draft).

			Regular Season								Playoffs						
Season	**Club**	**League**	**GP**	**W**	**L**	**T**	**Mins**	**GA**	**SO**	**Avg**	**GP**	**W**	**L**	**Mins**	**GA**	**SO**	**Avg**
2000-01	Danville Wings	NAJHL	27	19	5	2	1547	57	3	2.21	5	2	2	300	17	0	3.40
2001-02	Harvard Crimson	ECAC	21	10	8	1	1226	58	1	2.84							
2002-03	Harvard Crimson	ECAC	29	18	9	2	1741	69	1	2.38							
2003-04	Harvard Crimson	ECAC	33	16	14	3	1933	76	3	2.36							

GUARD, Kelly (G'YEW-uhrd, KEHL-lee) OTT.

Goaltender. Catches left. 6'1", 203 lbs. Born, Prince Albert, Sask., June 10, 1983.

			Regular Season								Playoffs						
Season	**Club**	**League**	**GP**	**W**	**L**	**T**	**Mins**	**GA**	**SO**	**Avg**	**GP**	**W**	**L**	**Mins**	**GA**	**SO**	**Avg**
99-2000	Prince Albert	SMHL					STATISTICS NOT AVAILABLE										
2000-01	Prince Albert	SMHL	25				1488	81	0	3.27							
	La Ronge	SJHL					STATISTICS NOT AVAILABLE										
2001-02	Kindersley Klippers	SJHL	45	29	11	4	2628	130	1	2.97	19	12	6	1145	60	1	3.14
2002-03	Kelowna Rockets	WHL	53	39	10	3	3018	97	*6	*1.93	19	*16	3	1233	36	*4	*1.75
2003-04	Kelowna Rockets	WHL	62	*44	14	4	3652	95	*13	*1.56	17	11	6	1042	31	1	1.79

WHL West First All-Star Team (2003, 2004) • Memorial Cup All-Star Team (2004) • Won Hap Emms Memorial Trophy (Memorial Cup Tournament Top Goaltender) (2004) • Won Stafford Smythe Memorial Trophy (Memorial Cup Tournament MVP) (2004)

Signed as a free agent by **Ottawa**, May 11, 2004.

GUSTAFSON, Derek (GUHST-ahf-suhn, DAIR-ihk)

Goaltender. Catches left. 5'11", 210 lbs. Born, Gresham, OR, June 21, 1979.

			Regular Season								Playoffs						
Season	**Club**	**League**	**GP**	**W**	**L**	**T**	**Mins**	**GA**	**SO**	**Avg**	**GP**	**W**	**L**	**Mins**	**GA**	**SO**	**Avg**
1995-96	Seattle Ironmen	BCAHA	16				913	46	0	3.02							
1996-97	Vernon Vipers	BCHL	23				1241	70	0	3.38							
1997-98	Vernon Vipers	BCHL	42	27	13	2	2270	144	1	3.81	6	2	1	257	13	0	3.04
1998-99	Vernon Vipers	BCHL	42	39	3	0	2505	94	3	2.25							
99-2000	St. Lawrence	ECAC	24	17	4	2	1475	51	2	2.07							
2000-01	**Minnesota**	**NHL**	**4**	**1**	**3**	**0**	**239**	**10**	**0**	**2.51**							
	Jackson Bandits	ECHL	7	4	3	0	404	15	1	2.23							
	Cleveland	IHL	24	14	7	1	1293	59	2	2.74	2	0	1	53	5	0	5.64
2001-02	**Minnesota**	**NHL**	**1**	**0**	**0**	**0**	**26**	**0**	**0**	**0.00**							
	Houston Aeros	AHL	38	14	13	6	2016	92	4	2.74	2	0	0	25	1	0	2.37
2002-03	Houston Aeros	AHL	41	23	14	2	2301	108	2	2.82							
	Louisiana	ECHL	2	1	1	0	118	8	0	4.07							
2003-04	Louisiana	ECHL	43	28	14	0	2499	87	*5	2.09	8	4	4	560	19	1	2.03
	NHL Totals		**5**	**1**	**3**	**0**	**265**	**10**	**0**	**2.26**							

ECAC Second All-Star Team (2000) • ECAC Rookie of the Year (2000) • ECHL Second All-Star Team (2004)

Signed as a free agent by **Minnesota**, June 9, 2000. Signed as a free agent by **Louisiana** (ECHL), October 1, 2003.

HACKETT, Jeff (HA-keht, JEHF)

Goaltender. Catches left. 6'1", 198 lbs. Born, London, Ont., June 1, 1968.
(NY Islanders' 2nd choice, 34th overall, in 1987 Entry Draft).

			Regular Season								Playoffs						
Season	**Club**	**League**	**GP**	**W**	**L**	**T**	**Mins**	**GA**	**SO**	**Avg**	**GP**	**W**	**L**	**Mins**	**GA**	**SO**	**Avg**
1984-85	London Diamonds	OJHL-B	18				1078	73	1	4.06							
1985-86	London Diamonds	OJHL-B	19				1150	66	0	3.43							
1986-87	Oshawa Generals	OHL	31	18	9	2	1672	85	2	3.05	15	8	7	895	40	0	2.68
1987-88	Oshawa Generals	OHL	53	30	21	2	3165	205	0	3.89	7	3	4	438	31	0	4.25
1988-89	**NY Islanders**	**NHL**	**13**	**4**	**7**	**0**	**662**	**39**	**0**	**3.53**							
	Springfield Indians	AHL	29	12	14	2	1677	116	0	4.15							
1989-90	Springfield Indians	AHL	54	24	25	3	3045	187	1	3.68	*17	*10	5	934	60	0	3.85
1990-91	**NY Islanders**	**NHL**	**30**	**5**	**18**	**1**	**1508**	**91**	**0**	**3.62**							
1991-92	**San Jose**	**NHL**	**42**	**11**	**27**	**1**	**2314**	**148**	**0**	**3.84**							
1992-93	**San Jose**	**NHL**	**36**	**2**	**30**	**1**	**2000**	**176**	**0**	**5.28**							
1993-94	**Chicago**	**NHL**	**22**	**2**	**12**	**3**	**1084**	**62**	**0**	**3.43**							
1994-95	**Chicago**	**NHL**	**7**	**1**	**3**	**2**	**328**	**13**	**0**	**2.38**	**2**	**0**	**0**	**26**	**1**	**0**	**2.31**
1995-96	**Chicago**	**NHL**	**35**	**18**	**11**	**4**	**2000**	**80**	**4**	**2.40**	**1**	**0**	**1**	**60**	**5**	**0**	**5.00**
1996-97	**Chicago**	**NHL**	**41**	**19**	**18**	**4**	**2473**	**89**	**2**	**2.16**	**6**	**2**	**4**	**345**	**25**	**0**	**4.35**
1997-98	**Chicago**	**NHL**	**58**	**21**	**25**	**11**	**3441**	**126**	**8**	**2.20**							
1998-99	**Chicago**	**NHL**	**10**	**2**	**6**	**1**	**524**	**33**	**0**	**3.78**							
	Montreal	**NHL**	**53**	**24**	**20**	**9**	**3091**	**117**	**5**	**2.27**							
99-2000	**Montreal**	**NHL**	**56**	**23**	**25**	**7**	**3301**	**132**	**3**	**2.40**							
2000-01	**Montreal**	**NHL**	**19**	**4**	**10**	**2**	**998**	**54**	**0**	**3.25**							
2001-02	**Montreal**	**NHL**	**15**	**5**	**5**	**2**	**717**	**38**	**0**	**3.18**							
2002-03	**Montreal**	**NHL**	**18**	**7**	**8**	**2**	**1063**	**45**	**0**	**2.54**							
	Boston	**NHL**	**18**	**8**	**9**	**0**	**991**	**53**	**1**	**3.21**	**3**	**1**	**2**	**179**	**5**	**0**	**1.68**
2003-04	**Philadelphia**	**NHL**	**27**	**10**	**10**	**6**	**1630**	**65**	**3**	**2.39**							
	Philadelphia	AHL	1	1	0	0	60	2	0	2.00							
	NHL Totals		**500**	**166**	**244**	**56**	**28125**	**1361**	**26**	**2.90**	**12**	**3**	**7**	**610**	**36**	**0**	**3.54**

Jack A. Butterfield Trophy (Playoff MVP – AHL) (1990)

Claimed by **San Jose** from **NY Islanders** in Expansion Draft, May 30, 1991. Traded to **Chicago** by **San Jose** for Chicago's 3rd round choice (Alexei Yegorov) in 1994 Entry Draft, July 13, 1993. Traded to **Montreal** by **Chicago** with Eric Weinrich, Alain Nasreddine and Tampa Bay's 4th round choice (previously acquired, Montreal selected Chris Dyment) in 1999 Entry Draft for Jocelyn Thibault, Dave Manson and Brad Brown, November 16, 1998. • Missed majority of 2000-01 season recovering from hand injury suffered in game vs. Minnesota, October 24, 2000. • Missed majority of 2001-02 season recovering from shoulder injury suffered in game vs. Buffalo, October 20, 2001. Traded to **San Jose** by **Montreal** for Niklas Sundstrom and San Jose's 3rd round choice (later traded to Los Angeles – Los Angeles selected Paul Baier) in 2004 Entry Draft, January 23, 2003. Traded to **Boston** by **San Jose** with Jeff Jillson for Kyle McLaren and Boston's 4th round choice (Torrey Mitchell) in 2004 Entry Draft, January 23, 2003. Signed as a free agent by **Philadelphia**, July 1, 2003. • Missed majority of 2003-04 season recovering from the effects of vertigo, January 19, 2004. • Officially announced retirement, February 9, 2004.

HALAK, Jaroslav (HAH-lak, YAHR-roh-slav) MTL.

Goaltender. Catches left. 5'11", 171 lbs. Born, Bratislava, Slovakia, May 13, 1985.
(Montreal's 11th choice, 271st overall, in 2003 Entry Draft).

			Regular Season								Playoffs						
Season	**Club**	**League**	**GP**	**W**	**L**	**T**	**Mins**	**GA**	**SO**	**Avg**	**GP**	**W**	**L**	**Mins**	**GA**	**SO**	**Avg**
2001-02	Bratislava Jr.	Slovak-Jr.	22				1257	41	0	1.96	6	6	0	353	7	2	1.19
2002-03	Bratislava Jr.	Czech-Jr.	20	13	3	3	1200	41	1	2.02							
2003-04	Slov. Bratislava Jr.	Slovak-Jr.	29				1694	51		1.81							
	HC Dukla Senica	Slovak-2	21				1240	54		2.61							
	Slovan Bratislava	Slovakia	12				650	18	0	1.66	1			45	6	0	8.00

HAMERLIK, Peter (HAHM-ehr-lik, PEE-tuhr) BOS.

Goaltender. Catches left. 6'1", 194 lbs. Born, Myjava, Czech., January 2, 1982.
(Boston's 4th choice, 153rd overall, in 2002 Entry Draft).

			Regular Season								Playoffs						
Season	**Club**	**League**	**GP**	**W**	**L**	**T**	**Mins**	**GA**	**SO**	**Avg**	**GP**	**W**	**L**	**Mins**	**GA**	**SO**	**Avg**
1997-98	HK 36 Skalica Jr.	Slovak-Jr.	49				2969	168		3.40							
1998-99	HK 36 Skalica	Slovakia	1	0	1	0	24	3	0	7.50							
99-2000	HK 36 Skalica Jr.	Slovak-Jr.	37				1850	121		3.92							
	HK 36 Skalica	Slovakia	7				286	16		3.36							
2000-01	Kingston	OHL	56	21	21	8	3026	153	*4	3.03	3	0	2	131	13	0	5.95
2001-02	Kingston	OHL	43	12	21	6	2371	144	1	3.64	1	0	1	60	6	0	6.00
2002-03	Kingston	OHL	47	19	22	2	2566	153	3	3.58							
	Providence Bruins	AHL	1	0	0	1	65	4	0	3.69							
	Cincinnati	ECHL	5	2	1	1	250	14	0	3.35	6	3	1	308	12	0	2.34
2003-04	Providence Bruins	AHL	3	1	1	1	157	5	0	1.91	1	0	0	34	2	0	3.54
	Augusta Lynx	ECHL	8	1	5	1	424	27	0	3.82							
	Reading Royals	ECHL	16	8	3	3	880	30	0	2.05							
	Trenton Titans	ECHL	7	4	3	0	408	19	1	2.79							

• Re-entered NHL Entry Draft. Originally Pittsburgh's 3rd choice, 84th overall, in 2000 Entry Draft.

HANULJAK, Miroslav (HA-nuhl-yak, MEER-oh-slav) NSH.

Goaltender. Catches left. 5'11", 165 lbs. Born, Litvinov, Czech., September 12, 1984.
(Nashville's 12th choice, 213th overall, in 2003 Entry Draft).

			Regular Season								Playoffs						
Season	**Club**	**League**	**GP**	**W**	**L**	**T**	**Mins**	**GA**	**SO**	**Avg**	**GP**	**W**	**L**	**Mins**	**GA**	**SO**	**Avg**
99-2000	Litvinov Jr.	Czech-Jr.	42				2274	130	3	3.43							
2000-01	Litvinov Jr.	Czech-Jr.	48				2647	97	11	2.20	6			361	19	0	3.16
2001-02	Litvinov Jr.	Czech-Jr.	5				274	9	0	1.97							
2002-03	Litvinov Jr.	Czech-Jr.	30				1515	67	1	2.65							
2003-04	Litvinov Jr.	Czech-Jr.	6				287	10	2	2.09							
	Havirov Jr.	Czech-Jr.	26				1494	66	3	2.65							

HARDING, Josh (HAHR-dihng, JAWSH) MIN.

Goaltender. Catches right. 6'1", 180 lbs. Born, Regina, Sask., June 18, 1984.
(Minnesota's 2nd choice, 38th overall, in 2002 Entry Draft).

			Regular Season								Playoffs						
Season	**Club**	**League**	**GP**	**W**	**L**	**T**	**Mins**	**GA**	**SO**	**Avg**	**GP**	**W**	**L**	**Mins**	**GA**	**SO**	**Avg**
2000-01	Regina Pat Cdns.	SMHL	36	17	13	0	2106	96	2	2.75	3	1	2	170	11	0	3.88
2001-02	Regina Pats	WHL	42	27	13	1	2389	95	*4	2.39	6	2	4	325	16	0	2.95
2002-03	Regina Pats	WHL	57	18	24	13	*3385	155	3	2.75	5	1	4	321	13	0	2.43
2003-04	Regina Pats	WHL	28	12	14	2	1665	67	2	2.41							
	Brandon	WHL	27	13	11	3	1612	65	5	2.42	11	5	6	660	36	0	3.27

WHL East Second All-Star Team (2002) • WHL East First All-Star Team (2003)

HASEK, Dominik (HAH-shihk, DOHM-ihn-ihk) OTT.

Goaltender. Catches left. 5'11", 180 lbs. Born, Pardubice, Czech., January 29, 1965.
(Chicago's 11th choice, 207th overall, in 1983 Entry Draft).

			Regular Season								Playoffs						
Season	**Club**	**League**	**GP**	**W**	**L**	**T**	**Mins**	**GA**	**SO**	**Avg**	**GP**	**W**	**L**	**Mins**	**GA**	**SO**	**Avg**
1981-82	HC Pardubice	Czech	12				661	34		3.09							
1982-83	HC Pardubice	Czech	42				2358	105		2.67							
1983-84	HC Pardubice	Czech	40				2304	108		2.81							
1984-85	HC Pardubice	Czech	42				2419	131		3.25							
1985-86	HC Pardubice	Czech	45				2689	138		3.08							
1986-87	HC Pardubice	Czech	43				2515	103		2.46							
1987-88	HC Pardubice	Czech	31				1862	93		3.00							
	Czechoslovakia	Olympics	5	3	2	0	217	18	1	4.98							
1988-89	HC Pardubice	Czech	42				2507	114		2.73							
1989-90	Dukla Jihlava	Czech	40				2251	80		2.13							
1990-91	**Chicago**	**NHL**	**5**	**3**	**0**	**1**	**195**	**8**	**0**	**2.46**	**3**	**0**	**0**	**69**	**3**	**0**	**2.61**
	Indianapolis Ice	IHL	33	20	11	1	1903	80	*5	*2.52	1	1	0	60	3	0	3.00
1991-92	**Chicago**	**NHL**	**20**	**10**	**4**	**1**	**1014**	**44**	**1**	**2.60**	**3**	**0**	**2**	**158**	**8**	**0**	**3.04**
	Indianapolis Ice	IHL	20	7	10	3	1162	69	1	3.56							
1992-93	**Buffalo**	**NHL**	**28**	**11**	**10**	**4**	**1429**	**75**	**0**	**3.15**	**1**	**1**	**0**	**45**	**1**	**0**	**1.33**
1993-94	**Buffalo**	**NHL**	**58**	**30**	**20**	**6**	**3358**	**109**	***7**	***1.95**	**7**	**3**	**4**	**484**	**13**	**2**	***1.61**
1994-95	HC Pardubice	Czech	2	1	0	1	124	6	0	2.90							
	Buffalo	**NHL**	**41**	**19**	**14**	**7**	**2416**	**85**	***5**	***2.11**	**5**	**1**	**4**	**309**	**18**	**0**	**3.50**
1995-96	**Buffalo**	**NHL**	**59**	**22**	**30**	**6**	**3417**	**161**	**2**	**2.83**							
1996-97	**Buffalo**	**NHL**	**67**	**37**	**20**	**10**	**4037**	**153**	**5**	**2.27**	**3**	**1**	**1**	**153**	**5**	**0**	**1.96**
1997-98	**Buffalo**	**NHL**	***72**	**33**	**23**	**13**	***4220**	**147**	***13**	**2.09**	**15**	**10**	**5**	**948**	**32**	**1**	**2.03**
	Czech Republic	Olympics	6	*5	1	0	*369	6	*2	*0.97							
1998-99	**Buffalo**	**NHL**	**64**	**30**	**18**	**14**	**3817**	**119**	**9**	**1.87**	**19**	**13**	**6**	**1217**	**36**	**2**	**1.77**
99-2000	**Buffalo**	**NHL**	**35**	**15**	**11**	**6**	**2066**	**76**	**3**	**2.21**	**5**	**1**	**4**	**301**	**12**	**0**	**2.39**
2000-01	**Buffalo**	**NHL**	**67**	**37**	**24**	**4**	**3904**	**137**	***11**	**2.11**	**13**	**7**	**6**	**833**	**29**	**1**	**2.09**
2001-02♦	**Detroit**	**NHL**	**65**	***41**	**15**	**8**	**3872**	**140**	**5**	**2.17**	***23**	***16**	**7**	***1455**	**45**	***6**	**1.86**
	Czech Republic	Olympics	4	1	2	1	239	8	0	2.01							

2002-03			Out of Hockey – Retired														
2003-04	**Detroit**	**NHL**	**14**	**8**	**3**	**2**	**817**	**30**	**2**	**2.20**	....	....	....	....	....	....	....
	NHL Totals		**595**	**296**	**192**	**82**	**34562**	**1284**	**63**	**2.23**	**97**	**53**	**39**	**5972**	**202**	**12**	**2.03**

Czechoslovakian Goaltender of the Year (1986, 1987, 1988, 1989, 1990) • Czechoslovakian Player of the Year (1987, 1989, 1990) • Czechoslovakian First All-Star Team (1988, 1989, 1990) • IHL First All-Star Team (1991) • NHL All-Rookie Team (1992) • NHL First All-Star Team (1994, 1995, 1997, 1998, 1999, 2001) • Shared William M. Jennings Trophy (1994) with Grant Fuhr • Vezina Trophy (1994, 1995, 1997, 1998, 1999, 2001) • Lester B. Pearson Award (1997, 1998) • Hart Trophy (1997, 1998) • William M. Jennings Trophy (2001)

Played in NHL All-Star Game (1996, 1997, 1998, 1999, 2001, 2002)

Traded to **Buffalo** by **Chicago** for Stephane Beauregard and Buffalo's 4th round choice (Eric Daze) in 1993 Entry Draft, August 7, 1992. Traded to **Detroit** by **Buffalo** for Vyacheslav Kozlov, Detroit's 1st round choice (later traded to Columbus – later traded to Atlanta – Atlanta selected Jim Slater) in 2002 Entry Draft and future considerations, July 1, 2001. • Officially announced retirement, June 25, 2002. • **Detroit** picked up the option on his contract, July 1, 2003. • Missed majority of 2003-04 season recovering from groin injury suffered in game vs. St. Louis, October 29, 2003. Signed as a free agent by **Ottawa**, July 6, 2004.

HAUSER, Adam (HOW-suhr, A-duhm) L.A.

Goaltender. Catches left. 6'2", 195 lbs. Born, Bovey, MN, May 27, 1980.
(Edmonton's 4th choice, 81st overall, in 1999 Entry Draft).

			Regular Season								Playoffs						
Season	Club	League	GP	W	L	T	Mins	GA	SO	Avg	GP	W	L	Mins	GA	SO	Avg
1996-97	Greenway High	Hi-School	25	....	....	....	1496	63	0	2.54	....	....	....	....	....	....	....
1997-98	U.S. National U-18	USDP	38	19	10	7	2110	94	4	2.67	....	....	....	....	....	....	....
1998-99	U. of Minnesota	WCHA	*40	14	18	8	*2350	136	3	3.47	....	....	....	....	....	....	....
99-2000	U. of Minnesota	WCHA	36	20	14	2	2114	104	1	2.95	....	....	....	....	....	....	....
2000-01	U. of Minnesota	WCHA	40	*26	12	2	2366	101	*3	2.56	....	....	....	....	....	....	....
2001-02	U. of Minnesota	WCHA	35	*23	6	4	2003	80	1	2.40	....	....	....	....	....	....	....
2002-03	Jackson Bandits	ECHL	34	20	9	4	2021	83	*5	2.46	....	....	....	....	....	....	....
	Providence Bruins	AHL	1	0	0	1	64	3	0	2.80	....	....	....	....	....	....	....
2003-04	Manchester	AHL	43	20	15	7	2536	82	7	1.94	4	2	2	286	9	2	1.89
	Reading Royals	ECHL	4	3	0	1	245	7	1	1.71	....	....	....	....	....	....	....

NCAA Championship All-Tournament Team (2002) • ECHL All-Rookie Team (2003)

Signed as a free agent by **Manchester** (AHL), August 19, 2003. Signed as a free agent by **Los Angeles**, July 8, 2004.

HEDBERG, Johan (HEHD-buhrg, YO-han)

Goaltender. Catches left. 6', 184 lbs. Born, Leksand, Sweden, May 5, 1973.
(Philadelphia's 8th choice, 218th overall, in 1994 Entry Draft).

			Regular Season								Playoffs						
Season	Club	League	GP	W	L	T	Mins	GA	SO	Avg	GP	W	L	Mins	GA	SO	Avg
1992-93	Leksands IF	Sweden	10	....	....	....	600	24	....	2.40	....	....	....	....	....	....	....
1993-94	Leksands IF	Sweden	17	....	....	....	1020	48	....	2.82	....	....	....	....	....	....	....
1994-95	Leksands IF	Sweden	17	....	....	....	986	58	....	3.53	....	....	....	....	....	....	....
1995-96	Leksands IF	Sweden	34	....	....	....	2013	95	....	2.83	4	....	....	240	13	....	3.25
1996-97	Leksands IF	Sweden	38	....	....	....	2260	95	3	2.52	8	....	....	581	18	1	1.86
1997-98	Baton Rouge	ECHL	2	1	1	0	100	7	0	4.20	....	....	....	....	....	....	....
	Detroit Vipers	IHL	16	7	2	2	726	32	1	2.64	....	....	....	....	....	....	....
	Manitoba Moose	IHL	14	8	4	1	745	32	1	2.58	2	0	2	105	6	0	3.40
1998-99	Leksands IF	Sweden	*48	....	....	....	*2940	140	0	2.86	4	....	....	255	15	0	3.53
99-2000	Kentucky	AHL	33	18	9	5	1973	88	3	2.68	5	3	2	311	10	1	1.93
2000-01	Manitoba Moose	IHL	46	23	13	7	2697	115	1	2.56	....	....	....	....	....	....	....
	Pittsburgh	**NHL**	**9**	**7**	**1**	**1**	**545**	**24**	**0**	**2.64**	**18**	**9**	**9**	**1123**	**43**	**2**	**2.30**
2001-02	**Pittsburgh**	**NHL**	**66**	**25**	**34**	**7**	**3877**	**178**	**6**	**2.75**	....	....	....	....	....	....	....
	Sweden	Olympics	1	1	0	0	60	1	0	1.00	....	....	....	....	....	....	....
2002-03	**Pittsburgh**	**NHL**	**41**	**14**	**22**	**4**	**2410**	**126**	**1**	**3.14**	....	....	....	....	....	....	....
2003-04	**Vancouver**	**NHL**	**21**	**8**	**6**	**2**	**1098**	**46**	**3**	**2.51**	**2**	**1**	**1**	**98**	**4**	**0**	**2.45**
	Manitoba Moose	AHL	2	0	2	0	125	9	0	4.32	....	....	....	....	....	....	....
	NHL Totals		**137**	**54**	**63**	**14**	**7930**	**374**	**10**	**2.83**	**20**	**10**	**10**	**1221**	**47**	**2**	**2.31**

Rights traded to **San Jose** by **Philadelphia** for San Jose's 7th round choice (Pavel Kasparik) in 1999 Entry Draft, August 6, 1998. Traded to **Pittsburgh** by **San Jose** with Bobby Dollas for Jeff Norton, March 12, 2001. Traded to **Vancouver** by **Pittsburgh** for Vancouver's 2nd round choice (Alex Goligoski) in 2004 Entry Draft, August 25, 2003.

HEINO-LINDBERG, Christopher (HAY-noh-LIHND-buhrg) MTL.

Goaltender. Catches right. 6', 163 lbs. Born, Helsingborg, Sweden, January 29, 1985.
(Montreal's 7th choice, 177th overall, in 2003 Entry Draft).

			Regular Season								Playoffs						
Season	Club	League	GP	W	L	T	Mins	GA	SO	Avg	GP	W	L	Mins	GA	SO	Avg
2001-02	Hammarby Jr.	Swede-Jr.	17	....	....	....	987	59	0	3.59	....	....	....	....	....	....	....
2002-03	Hammarby 18	Swede-Jr.	3	....	....	....	180	9	0	3.00	....	....	....	....	....	....	....
	Hammarby Jr.	Swede-Jr.	23	....	....	....	1383	80	0	3.47	2	....	....	128	6	0	2.81
	Hammarby	Swede-2	1	....	....	....	60	2	0	2.00	....	....	....	....	....	....	....
2003-04	IF Vallentuna BK	Swede-2	23	....	....	....	1157	92	0	4.77	....	....	....	....	....	....	....
	Hammarby	Swede-2	3	....	....	....	105	8	0	4.57	....	....	....	....	....	....	....
	Hammarby Jr.	Swede-Jr.	8	....	....	....	483	20	0	2.48	2	....	....	122	10	0	4.92

HNILICKA, Milan (huh-LEETCH-kuh, MEE-lan)

Goaltender. Catches left. 6'1", 190 lbs. Born, Pardubice, Czech., June 25, 1973.
(NY Islanders' 4th choice, 70th overall, in 1991 Entry Draft).

			Regular Season								Playoffs						
Season	Club	League	GP	W	L	T	Mins	GA	SO	Avg	GP	W	L	Mins	GA	SO	Avg
1989-90	Poldi Kladno	Czech	24	....	....	....	1113	70	....	3.77	....	....	....	....	....	....	....
1990-91	Poldi Kladno	Czech	40	....	....	....	2122	98	0	2.80	....	....	....	....	....	....	....
1991-92	Poldi Kladno	Czech	38	....	....	....	2066	128	0	3.73	....	....	....	....	....	....	....
1992-93	Swift Current	WHL	*65	*46	12	2	3679	206	2	3.36	*17	*12	5	*1017	54	*2	3.19
1993-94	Richmond	ECHL	43	18	16	5	2299	155	4	4.05	....	....	....	....	....	....	....
	Salt Lake	IHL	8	5	1	0	378	25	0	3.97	....	....	....	....	....	....	....
1994-95	Denver Grizzlies	IHL	15	9	4	1	798	47	1	3.53	....	....	....	....	....	....	....
1995-96	HC Poldi Kladno	Czech	33	....	....	....	1959	93	1	2.84	8	....	....	493	24	....	2.92
1996-97	HC Poldi Kladno	Czech	48	....	....	....	2736	120	*4	2.63	3	....	....	151	14	0	5.56
1997-98	HC Sparta Praha	Czech	49	....	....	....	2847	99	....	2.09	11	....	....	632	31	....	3.00
1998-99	HC Sparta Praha	Czech	*50	....	....	....	*2877	109	....	2.27	8	....	....	507	13	....	*1.54
99-2000	**NY Rangers**	**NHL**	**2**	**0**	**1**	**0**	**86**	**5**	**0**	**3.49**	....	....	....	....	....	....	....
	Hartford Wolf Pack	AHL	36	22	11	0	1979	71	5	*2.15	3	0	1	99	6	0	3.64
2000-01	**Atlanta**	**NHL**	**36**	**12**	**19**	**2**	**1879**	**105**	**2**	**3.35**	....	....	....	....	....	....	....
2001-02	**Atlanta**	**NHL**	**60**	**13**	**33**	**10**	**3367**	**179**	**3**	**3.19**	....	....	....	....	....	....	....
2002-03	**Atlanta**	**NHL**	**21**	**4**	**13**	**1**	**1097**	**65**	**0**	**3.56**	....	....	....	....	....	....	....
	Chicago Wolves	AHL	15	11	2	1	838	33	1	2.36	....	....	....	....	....	....	....
2003-04	**Los Angeles**	**NHL**	**2**	**0**	**1**	**0**	**80**	**5**	**0**	**3.75**	....	....	....	....	....	....	....
	Manchester	AHL	20	8	10	0	1022	44	1	2.58	2	0	2	127	5	0	2.37
	NHL Totals		**121**	**29**	**67**	**13**	**6509**	**359**	**5**	**3.31**	....	....	....	....	....	....	....

Shared Harry "Hap" Holmes Memorial Trophy (fewest goals against – AHL) (2000) with Jean-Francois Labbe

Signed as a free agent by **NY Rangers**, July 15, 1999. Signed as a free agent by **Atlanta**, July 28, 2000. Traded to **Los Angeles** by **Atlanta** for future considerations, September 15, 2003. • Missed majority of 2003-04 season recovering from finger injury suffered in game vs. Phoenix, December 31, 2003. Signed as a free agent by **Liberec** (Czech), May 18, 2004.

HODSON, Jamie (HAWD-suhn, JAY-mee)

Goaltender. Catches left. 6'2", 205 lbs. Born, Brandon, Man., April 8, 1980.
(Toronto's 3rd choice, 69th overall, in 1998 Entry Draft).

			Regular Season								Playoffs						
Season	Club	League	GP	W	L	T	Mins	GA	SO	Avg	GP	W	L	Mins	GA	SO	Avg
1996-97	Yellowhead Chiefs	MMHL	12	....	....	....	720	58	1	4.83	....	....	....	....	....	....	....
1997-98	Brandon	WHL	20	12	2	2	964	52	2	3.24	6	5	0	337	16	0	2.85
1998-99	Brandon	WHL	43	23	12	3	2295	123	4	3.22	5	1	4	275	26	0	5.67
99-2000	Brandon	WHL	39	13	22	3	2321	130	2	3.36	....	....	....	....	....	....	....
2000-01	St. John's	AHL	4	0	2	0	137	13	0	5.71	....	....	....	....	....	....	....
	Brandon	WHL	29	9	17	1	1587	92	0	3.48	1	0	1	59	3	0	3.05
2001-02	South Carolina	ECHL	36	20	9	3	1996	100	1	3.01	1	0	1	60	3	0	3.01
2002-03	St. John's	AHL	22	8	7	2	1136	64	1	3.38	....	....	....	....	....	....	....
	Greensboro	ECHL	14	9	4	1	816	33	0	2.43	....	....	....	....	....	....	....
2003-04	Greensboro	ECHL	30	17	11	1	1799	81	2	2.70	....	....	....	....	....	....	....
	St. John's	AHL	12	3	6	1	572	40	0	4.20	....	....	....	....	....	....	....

HOLMQVIST, Johan (HOHLM-kvihst, YOH-han)

Goaltender. Catches left. 6'3", 195 lbs. Born, Tolfta, Sweden, May 24, 1978.
(NY Rangers' 9th choice, 175th overall, in 1997 Entry Draft).

			Regular Season								Playoffs						
Season	Club	League	GP	W	L	T	Mins	GA	SO	Avg	GP	W	L	Mins	GA	SO	Avg
1996-97	Brynas IF Gavle	Sweden	2	0	0	0	80	4	0	3.00	....	....	....	....	....	....	....
1997-98	Brynas IF Gavle	Sweden	33	....	....	....	1897	82	....	2.59	3	0	3	180	14	....	4.67
1998-99	Brynas IF Gavle	Sweden	41	....	....	....	2383	111	4	2.79	*14	9	5	*855	34	0	2.39
99-2000	Brynas IF Gavle	Sweden	41	....	....	....	2402	104	4	2.60	11	....	....	671	30	1	2.68
2000-01	**NY Rangers**	**NHL**	**2**	**0**	**2**	**0**	**119**	**10**	**0**	**5.04**	....	....	....	....	....	....	....
	Hartford Wolf Pack	AHL	43	19	14	4	2305	111	2	2.89	5	2	3	314	13	0	2.48
2001-02	**NY Rangers**	**NHL**	**1**	**0**	**0**	**0**	**9**	**0**	**0**	**0.00**	....	....	....	....	....	....	....
	Hartford Wolf Pack	AHL	48	26	12	6	2734	140	1	3.07	4	1	2	163	12	0	4.41
2002-03	**NY Rangers**	**NHL**	**1**	**0**	**1**	**0**	**39**	**2**	**0**	**3.08**	....	....	....	....	....	....	....
	Hartford Wolf Pack	AHL	35	14	13	5	1904	84	2	2.65	....	....	....	....	....	....	....
	Charlotte Checkers	ECHL	1	1	0	0	60	2	0	2.00	....	....	....	....	....	....	....
	Houston Aeros	AHL	8	5	3	0	479	23	1	2.88	*23	*15	8	*1499	50	1	2.00
2003-04	Houston Aeros	AHL	59	23	27	7	3467	148	4	2.56	....	....	....	....	....	....	....
	NHL Totals		**4**	**0**	**3**	**0**	**167**	**12**	**0**	**4.31**	....	....	....	....	....	....	....

Jack A. Butterfield Trophy (Playoff MVP – AHL) (2003)

Traded to **Minnesota** by **NY Rangers** for Lawrence Nycholat, March 11, 2003.

HOLT, Chris (HOHLT, KRIHS) NYR

Goaltender. Catches left. 6'2", 218 lbs. Born, Vancouver, B.C., June 5, 1985.
(NY Rangers' 8th choice, 180th overall, in 2003 Entry Draft).

			Regular Season								Playoffs						
Season	Club	League	GP	W	L	T	Mins	GA	SO	Avg	GP	W	L	Mins	GA	SO	Avg
2001-02	Billings Bulls	AWHL	24	13	7	1	1184	59	2	2.99	....	....	....	....	....	....	....
2002-03	U.S. National U-18	USDP	32	9	15	2	1774	95	1	3.21	....	....	....	....	....	....	....
2003-04	Nebraska-Omaha	CCHA	27	5	17	2	1499	81	0	3.24	....	....	....	....	....	....	....

HOSTIKKA, Ville (HAWS-tih-kuh, VIHL-ee) PHI.

Goaltender. Catches left. 6'3", 209 lbs. Born, Lappeenranta, Finland, March 21, 1985.
(Philadelphia's 11th choice, 193rd overall, in 2003 Entry Draft).

			Regular Season								Playoffs						
Season	Club	League	GP	W	L	T	Mins	GA	SO	Avg	GP	W	L	Mins	GA	SO	Avg
2001-02	SaiPa Jr.	Finn-Jr.	4	4	0	0	240	9	1	2.25	2	0	0	68	5	0	4.41
	SaiPa B	Finn-Jr.	24	11	8	4	1392	82	2	3.53	....	....	....	....	....	....	....
2002-03	SaiPa Jr.	Finn-Jr.	30	14	8	4	1750	79	2	2.71	1	0	1	58	5	0	5.17
2003-04	SaiPa Jr.	Finn-Jr.	12	1	6	3	645	41	0	3.81	....	....	....	....	....	....	....

HOWARD, James (HOW-uhrd, JAYMZ) DET.

Goaltender. Catches left. 6', 218 lbs. Born, Syracuse, NY, March 26, 1984.
(Detroit's 1st choice, 64th overall, in 2003 Entry Draft).

			Regular Season								Playoffs						
Season	Club	League	GP	W	L	T	Mins	GA	SO	Avg	GP	W	L	Mins	GA	SO	Avg
2001-02	U.S. National U-17	USDP	9	6	3	0	484	29	1	3.67	....	....	....	....	....	....	....
	U.S. National U-18	USDP	26	16	8	1	1492	47	3	1.89	....	....	....	....	....	....	....
2002-03	University of Maine	H-East	21	14	6	0	1151	47	3	2.45	....	....	....	....	....	....	....
2003-04	University of Maine	H-East	23	14	4	3	1364	27	6	1.19	....	....	....	....	....	....	....

Hockey East All-Rookie Team (2003) • Hockey East Rookie of the Year (2003) • Hockey East First All-Star Team (2004) • NCAA East Second All-American Team (2004)

HUET, Cristobal (oo-AY, KRIHS-toh-bahl) MTL.

Goaltender. Catches left. 6', 194 lbs. Born, St. Martin D'Heres, France, September 3, 1975.
(Los Angeles' 9th choice, 214th overall, in 2001 Entry Draft).

			Regular Season								Playoffs						
Season	Club	League	GP	W	L	T	Mins	GA	SO	Avg	GP	W	L	Mins	GA	SO	Avg
1997-98	CSG Grenoble	France	Statistics not available														
	France	Olympics	2	1	1	0	120	5	0	2.50	....	....	....	....	....	....	....
1998-99	HC Lugano	Swiss	21	....	....	....	1275	58	1	2.73	10	....	....	628	18	1	*1.72
99-2000	HC Lugano	Swiss	31	....	....	....	1886	50	*8	*1.59	13	....	....	783	29	0	2.22
2000-01	HC Lugano	Swiss	39	....	....	....	2365	77	*6	*1.95	*18	....	....	*1141	39	2	2.05
2001-02	HC Lugano	Swiss	39	....	....	....	2313	107	*4	2.78	1	0	1	60	3	0	3.00
	France	Olympics	3	0	2	1	179	10	0	3.36	....	....	....	....	....	....	....
2002-03	**Los Angeles**	**NHL**	**12**	**4**	**4**	**1**	**541**	**21**	**1**	**2.33**	....	....	....	....	....	....	....
	Manchester	AHL	30	16	8	5	1784	68	1	2.29	1	0	1	30	4	0	8.08
2003-04	**Los Angeles**	**NHL**	**41**	**10**	**16**	**10**	**2199**	**89**	**3**	**2.43**	....	....	....	....	....	....	....
	NHL Totals		**53**	**14**	**20**	**11**	**2740**	**110**	**4**	**2.41**	....	....	....	....	....	....	....

Traded to **Montreal** by **Los Angeles** with Radek Bonk for Mathieu Garon and San Jose's 3rd round choice (previously acquired, Los Angeles selected Paul Baier) in 2004 Entry Draft, June 26, 2004.

HURME, Jani (HOOR-meh, YAN-ee) ATL.

Goaltender. Catches left. 6', 190 lbs. Born, Turku, Finland, January 7, 1975.
(Ottawa's 2nd choice, 58th overall, in 1997 Entry Draft).

			Regular Season								Playoffs						
Season	Club	League	GP	W	L	T	Mins	GA	SO	Avg	GP	W	L	Mins	GA	SO	Avg
1992-93	TPS Turku Jr.	Finn-Jr.	12	....	....	....	669	47	0	4.22	1	....	....	60	0	1	0.00
1993-94	Kiekko 67 Jr.	Finn-Jr.	18	....	....	....	1082	57	0	3.16	....	....	....	....	....	....	....
	Kiekko 67 Turku	Finland-2	3	....	....	....	190	7	0	2.21	....	....	....	....	....	....	....
	TPS Turku	Finland	1	....	....	....	2	0	0	0.00	....	....	....	....	....	....	....
1994-95	TPS Turku Jr.	Finn-Jr.	2	....	....	....	125	5	0	2.40	....	....	....	....	....	....	....
	Kiekko 67 Jr.	Finn-Jr.	9	....	....	....	540	47	....	5.22	....	....	....	....	....	....	....
	Kiekko 67 Turku	Finland-2	19	....	....	....	1049	53	....	3.03	3	....	....	180	6	....	2.00
1995-96	TPS Turku Jr.	Finn-Jr.	13	....	....	....	777	34	1	2.63	....	....	....	....	....	....	....
	Kiekko 67 Turku	Finland-2	16	....	....	....	968	39	1	2.42	....	....	....	....	....	....	....
	TPS Turku	Finland	16	....	....	....	946	34	2	2.16	10	....	....	545	22	2	2.42
1996-97	TPS Turku	Finland	48	*31	11	6	*2917	101	*6	*2.08	*12	6	6	*722	39	0	3.24
1997-98	Detroit Vipers	IHL	6	2	2	2	290	20	0	4.13	....	....	....	....	....	....	....
	Indianapolis Ice	IHL	29	11	11	3	1506	83	1	3.30	3	1	0	129	10	0	4.62
1998-99	Detroit Vipers	IHL	12	7	3	1	643	26	1	2.43	....	....	....	....	....	....	....
	Cincinnati	IHL	26	14	9	2	1428	81	0	3.40	....	....	....	....	....	....	....
99-2000	**Ottawa**	**NHL**	**1**	**1**	**0**	**0**	**60**	**2**	**0**	**2.00**	....	....	....	....	....	....	....
	Grand Rapids	IHL	52	29	15	4	2948	107	4	2.18	*17	*10	7	*1028	37	1	2.16

2000-01	Ottawa	NHL	22	12	5	4	1296	54	2	2.50	....	....	....	....	....	....	....
2001-02	Ottawa	NHL	25	12	9	1	1309	54	3	2.48	....	....	....	....	....	....	....
	Finland	Olympics	3	1	2	0	179	9	0	3.01	....	....	....	....	....	....	....
2002-03	Florida	NHL	28	4	11	6	1376	66	1	2.88	....	....	....	....	....	....	....
2003-04							DID NOT PLAY – INJURED										
	NHL Totals		76	29	25	11	4041	176	6	2.61	....	....	....	....	....	....	....

Finnish Elite League Rookie of the Year (1996) • Finnish Elite League Player of the Year (1997) • IHL Second All-Star Team (2000)

Traded to **Florida** by **Ottawa** for Billy Thompson and Greg Watson, October 1, 2002. Claimed by **Carolina** from **Florida** in Waiver Draft, October 3, 2003. Traded to **Atlanta** by **Carolina** for Atlanta's 4th round choice (Brett Carson) in 2004 Entry Draft, October 3, 2003. • Missed entire 2003-04 season recovering from back injury suffered in training camp, October 3, 2003.

IRBE, Arturs (UHR-bay, AHR-tuhrs) CBJ

Goaltender. Catches left. 5'8", 190 lbs. Born, Riga, Latvia, February 2, 1967.
(Minnesota's 11th choice, 196th overall, in 1989 Entry Draft).

							Regular Season							Playoffs			
Season	Club	League	GP	W	L	T	Mins	GA	SO	Avg	GP	W	L	Mins	GA	SO	Avg
1986-87	Dynamo Riga	USSR	2	....	....	....	27	1	0	2.22	....	....	....	....	....	....	....
1987-88	Dynamo Riga	USSR	34	....	....	....	1870	86	4	2.76	....	....	....	....	....	....	....
1988-89	Dynamo Riga	USSR	40	....	....	....	2460	116	4	2.83	....	....	....	....	....	....	....
1989-90	Dynamo Riga	USSR	48	....	....	....	2880	115	2	2.40	....	....	....	....	....	....	....
1990-91	Dynamo Riga	USSR	46	....	....	....	2713	133	5	2.94	....	....	....	....	....	....	....
1991-92	San Jose	NHL	13	2	6	3	645	48	0	4.47	....	....	....	....	....	....	....
	Kansas City Blades	IHL	32	24	7	1	1955	80	0	*2.46	*15	*12	3	914	44	0	*2.89
1992-93	San Jose	NHL	36	7	26	0	2074	142	1	4.11	....	....	....	....	....	....	....
	Kansas City Blades	IHL	6	3	3	0	364	20	0	3.30	....	....	....	....	....	....	....
1993-94	San Jose	NHL	*74	30	28	16	*4412	209	3	2.84	14	7	7	806	50	0	3.72
1994-95	San Jose	NHL	38	14	19	3	2043	111	4	3.26	6	2	4	316	27	0	5.13
1995-96	San Jose	NHL	22	4	12	4	1112	85	0	4.59	....	....	....	....	....	....	....
	Kansas City Blades	IHL	4	1	2	1	226	16	0	4.24	....	....	....	....	....	....	....
1996-97	Dallas	NHL	35	17	12	3	1965	88	3	2.69	1	0	0	13	0	0	0.00
1997-98	Vancouver	NHL	41	14	11	6	1999	91	2	2.73	....	....	....	....	....	....	....
1998-99	Carolina	NHL	62	27	20	12	3643	135	6	2.22	6	2	4	408	15	0	2.21
99-2000	Carolina	NHL	*75	34	28	9	4345	175	5	2.42	....	....	....	....	....	....	....
2000-01	Carolina	NHL	*77	37	29	9	*4406	180	6	2.45	6	2	4	360	20	0	3.33
2001-02	Carolina	NHL	51	20	19	11	2974	126	3	2.54	18	10	8	1078	30	1	1.67
	Latvia	Olympics	1	0	1	0	60	4	0	4.00	....	....	....	....	....	....	....
2002-03	Carolina	NHL	34	7	24	2	1884	100	0	3.18	....	....	....	....	....	....	....
	Lowell	AHL	7	3	3	1	427	21	0	2.95	....	....	....	....	....	....	....
2003-04	Carolina	NHL	10	5	2	1	564	23	0	2.45	....	....	....	....	....	....	....
	Johnstown Chiefs	ECHL	14	10	3	1	847	30	1	2.13	....	....	....	....	....	....	....
	NHL Totals		568	218	236	79	32066	1513	33	2.83	51	23	27	2981	142	1	2.86

IHL First All-Star Team (1992) • Shared James Norris Memorial Trophy (fewest goals against – IHL) (1992) with Wade Flaherty

Played in NHL All-Star Game (1994, 1999)

Claimed by **San Jose** from **Minnesota** in Dispersal Draft, May 30, 1991. Signed as a free agent by **Dallas**, August 19, 1996. Signed as a free agent by **Vancouver**, August 25, 1997. Signed as a free agent by **Carolina**, September 14, 1998. Traded to **Columbus** by **Carolina** for future considerations, June 16, 2004.

JOHNSON, Brent (JAWN-suhn, BREHNT) PHX.

Goaltender. Catches left. 6'3", 196 lbs. Born, Farmington, MI, March 12, 1977.
(Colorado's 5th choice, 129th overall, in 1995 Entry Draft).

							Regular Season							Playoffs			
Season	Club	League	GP	W	L	T	Mins	GA	SO	Avg	GP	W	L	Mins	GA	SO	Avg
1993-94	Det. Compuware	NAJHL	18	....	....	....	1024	49	1	3.52	....	....	....	....	....	....	....
1994-95	Owen Sound	OHL	18	3	9	1	904	75	0	4.98	....	....	....	....	....	....	....
1995-96	Owen Sound	OHL	58	24	28	1	3211	243	1	4.54	6	2	4	371	29	0	4.69
1996-97	Owen Sound	OHL	50	20	28	1	2798	201	1	4.31	4	0	4	253	24	0	5.69
1997-98	Worcester IceCats	AHL	42	14	15	7	2240	119	0	3.19	6	3	2	332	19	0	3.43
1998-99	St. Louis	NHL	6	3	2	0	286	10	0	2.10	....	....	....	....	....	....	....
	Worcester IceCats	AHL	49	22	22	4	2925	146	2	2.99	4	1	3	238	12	0	3.02
99-2000	Worcester IceCats	AHL	58	24	27	5	3319	161	3	2.91	9	4	5	561	23	1	2.46
2000-01	St. Louis	NHL	31	19	9	2	1744	63	4	2.17	2	0	1	62	2	0	1.94
2001-02	St. Louis	NHL	58	34	20	4	3491	127	5	2.18	10	5	5	590	18	3	1.83
2002-03	St. Louis	NHL	38	16	13	5	2042	84	2	2.47	....	....	....	....	....	....	....
	Worcester IceCats	AHL	2	0	1	1	125	8	0	3.84	....	....	....	....	....	....	....
2003-04	St. Louis	NHL	10	4	3	1	493	20	1	2.43	....	....	....	....	....	....	....
	Worcester IceCats	AHL	8	2	2	2	365	14	0	2.30	....	....	....	....	....	....	....
	Phoenix	NHL	8	1	6	1	486	21	0	2.59	....	....	....	....	....	....	....
	NHL Totals		151	77	53	13	8542	325	12	2.28	12	5	6	652	20	3	1.84

Traded to **St. Louis** by **Colorado** for San Jose's 3rd round choice (previously acquired, Colorado selected Rick Berry) in 1997 Entry Draft, May 30, 1997. Traded to **Phoenix** by **St. Louis** for Mike Sillinger, March 4, 2004.

JOKELA, Antti (YOH-keh-luh, AHN-tee) CAR.

Goaltender. Catches left. 5'11", 175 lbs. Born, Rauma, Finland, May 7, 1981.
(Carolina's 8th choice, 237th overall, in 1999 Entry Draft).

							Regular Season							Playoffs			
Season	Club	League	GP	W	L	T	Mins	GA	SO	Avg	GP	W	L	Mins	GA	SO	Avg
1998-99	Lukko Rauma B	Finn-Jr.	8	....	....	....	480	26	0	3.25	....	....	....	....	....	....	....
	Lukko Rauma Jr.	Finn-Jr.	18	....	....	....	1038	66	1	3.81	....	....	....	....	....	....	....
99-2000	Lukko Rauma Jr.	Finn-Jr.	21	....	....	....	1196	71	0	3.56	....	....	....	....	....	....	....
2000-01	Jaa Kotkat	Finn-Jr.	42	20	20	2	2520	100	4	2.38	....	....	....	....	....	....	....
	Lukko Rauma	Finland	1	0	0	0	19	2	0	6.32	....	....	....	....	....	....	....
2001-02	Jaa Kotkat	Finland-2	28	....	....	....	1680	100	0	3.51	....	....	....	....	....	....	....
	Jaa Kotkat Jr.	Finn-Jr.	....	....	....	....	....	....	....	....	4	1	3	240	14	0	3.46
2002-03	Assat Pori	Finland	10	3	1	3	510	28	0	3.29	....	....	....	....	....	....	....
	Ahmat	Finland-2	1	0	1	0	59	5	0	5.02	....	....	....	....	....	....	....
2003-04	Lukko Rauma	Finland	11	2	5	4	672	27	0	2.41	1	0	1	59	3	0	3.05
	HC Salamat	Finland-2	1	0	1	0	60	4	0	4.00	....	....	....	....	....	....	....

JOSEPH, Curtis (JOH-sehf, KUR-tihs) DET.

Goaltender. Catches left. 5'11", 190 lbs. Born, Keswick, Ont., April 29, 1967.

							Regular Season							Playoffs			
Season	Club	League	GP	W	L	T	Mins	GA	SO	Avg	GP	W	L	Mins	GA	SO	Avg
1984-85	King City Dukes	OJHL-B	18	....	....	....	947	76	0	4.82	....	....	....	....	....	....	....
	Newmarket Flyers	OPJHL	2	1	1	0	120	16	0	8.00	....	....	....	....	....	....	....
1985-86	Richmond Hill	OPJHL	33	12	18	0	1716	156	1	5.45	....	....	....	....	....	....	....
1986-87	Richmond Hill	OPJHL	30	14	7	6	1764	128	1	4.35	....	....	....	....	....	....	....
1987-88	Notre Dame	SJHL	36	25	4	7	2174	94	1	2.59	....	....	....	....	....	....	....
1988-89	U. of Wisconsin	WCHA	38	21	11	5	2267	94	1	2.49	....	....	....	....	....	....	....
1989-90	Peoria Rivermen	IHL	23	10	8	2	1241	80	0	3.87	....	....	....	....	....	....	....
	St. Louis	NHL	15	9	5	1	852	48	0	3.38	6	4	1	327	18	0	3.30
1990-91	St. Louis	NHL	30	16	10	2	1710	89	0	3.12	....	....	....	....	....	....	....
1991-92	St. Louis	NHL	60	27	20	10	3494	175	2	3.01	6	2	4	379	23	0	3.64
1992-93	St. Louis	NHL	68	29	28	9	3890	196	1	3.02	11	7	4	715	27	*2	2.27
1993-94	St. Louis	NHL	71	36	23	11	4127	213	1	3.10	4	0	4	246	15	0	3.66
1994-95	St. Louis	NHL	36	20	10	1	1914	89	1	2.79	7	3	3	392	24	0	3.67
1995-96	Las Vegas Thunder	IHL	15	12	2	1	874	29	1	1.99	....	....	....	....	....	....	....
	Edmonton	NHL	34	15	16	2	1936	111	0	3.44	....	....	....	....	....	....	....
1996-97	Edmonton	NHL	72	32	29	9	4100	200	6	2.93	12	5	7	767	36	2	2.82
1997-98	Edmonton	NHL	71	29	31	9	4132	181	8	2.63	12	5	7	716	23	3	1.93
1998-99	Toronto	NHL	67	35	24	7	4001	171	3	2.56	17	9	8	1011	41	1	2.43
99-2000	Toronto	NHL	63	36	20	7	3801	158	4	2.49	12	6	6	729	25	1	2.06
2000-01	Toronto	NHL	68	33	27	8	4100	163	6	2.39	11	7	4	685	24	3	2.10
2001-02	Toronto	NHL	51	29	17	5	3065	114	4	2.23	20	10	10	1253	48	3	2.30
	Canada	Olympics	1	0	1	0	60	5	0	5.00	....	....	....	....	....	....	....
2002-03	Detroit	NHL	61	34	19	6	3566	148	5	2.49	4	0	4	289	10	0	2.08
2003-04	Detroit	NHL	31	16	10	3	1708	68	2	2.39	9	4	4	518	12	1	*1.39
	Grand Rapids	AHL	1	1	0	0	60	1	0	1.00	....	....	....	....	....	....	....
	NHL Totals		798	396	289	90	46396	2124	43	2.75	131	62	66	8027	326	16	2.44

WCHA First All-Star Team (1989) • WCHA Freshman of the Year (1989) • WCHA Player of the Year (1989) • NCAA West Second All-American Team (1989) • King Clancy Memorial Trophy (2000)

Played in NHL All-Star Game (1994, 2000)

Signed as a free agent by **St. Louis**, June 16, 1989. Traded to **Edmonton** by **St. Louis** with the rights to Mike Grier for St. Louis' 1st round choices (previously acquired) in 1996 (Marty Reasoner) and 1997 (later traded to Los Angeles – Los Angeles selected Matt Zultek) Entry Drafts, August 4, 1995. Signed as a free agent by **Toronto**, July 15, 1998. Traded to **Calgary** by **Toronto** for Calgary's 3rd round choice (later traded to Minnesota – Minnesota selected Danny Irmen) in 2003 Entry Draft and future considerations, June 30, 2002. Signed as a free agent by **Detroit**, July 2, 2002.

KALTIAINEN, Matti (kal-tee-AY-nehn, MAT-tee) BOS.

Goaltender. Catches left. 6'2", 216 lbs. Born, Espoo, Finland, April 30, 1982.
(Boston's 3rd choice, 111th overall, in 2001 Entry Draft).

							Regular Season							Playoffs			
Season	Club	League	GP	W	L	T	Mins	GA	SO	Avg	GP	W	L	Mins	GA	SO	Avg
1998-99	Blues Espoo Jr.	Finn-Jr.	4	....	....	....	258	10	0	2.33	....	....	....	....	....	....	....
99-2000	Blues Espoo Jr.	Finn-Jr.	23	....	....	....	1337	56	0	2.51	4	2	2	244	15	0	3.93
2000-01	Blues Espoo Jr.	Finn-Jr.	25	....	....	....	1500	65	0	2.60	....	....	....	....	....	....	....
2001-02	Boston College	H-East	18	8	10	0	1080	48	1	2.67	....	....	....	....	....	....	....
2002-03	Boston College	H-East	30	18	9	3	1843	68	1	2.21	....	....	....	....	....	....	....
2003-04	Boston College	H-East	*38	*27	7	4	*2284	67	4	1.76	....	....	....	....	....	....	....

Hockey East Second All-Star Team (2004)

KETTLES, Kyle (KEH-tuhls, KIGHL) MIN.

Goaltender. Catches left. 6'3", 180 lbs. Born, Lac du Bonnet, Man., February 19, 1981.
(Nashville's 13th choice, 205th overall, in 1999 Entry Draft).

							Regular Season							Playoffs			
Season	Club	League	GP	W	L	T	Mins	GA	SO	Avg	GP	W	L	Mins	GA	SO	Avg
1997-98	Selkirk Steelers	MJHL	32	9	19	1	1613	119	0	4.43	....	....	....	....	....	....	....
	Brandon	WHL	....	....	....	....	....	....	....	....	1	0	0	10	2	0	12.00
1998-99	Selkirk Steelers	MJHL	17	7	8	0	939	65	0	4.15	....	....	....	....	....	....	....
	Neepawa Natives	MJHL	6	2	4	0	361	27	0	4.49	....	....	....	....	....	....	....
99-2000	Medicine Hat	WHL	57	16	33	5	3260	215	1	3.96	....	....	....	....	....	....	....
2000-01	Medicine Hat	WHL	47	15	24	2	2586	183	0	4.25	....	....	....	....	....	....	....
2001-02	Medicine Hat	WHL	5	1	4	0	274	23	0	5.04	....	....	....	....	....	....	....
	Moose Jaw	WHL	54	24	25	4	3089	160	*4	3.11	12	6	6	735	29	1	2.37
2002-03	Louisiana	ECHL	41	21	12	7	2439	106	*5	2.61	6	3	3	359	13	1	2.17
2003-04	Houston Aeros	AHL	22	4	9	5	1094	51	1	2.80	....	....	....	....	....	....	....

Signed as a free agent by **Minnesota**, April 23, 2002.

KHABIBULIN, Nikolai (khah-bee-BOO-lihn, NIH-koh-ligh) T.B.

Goaltender. Catches left. 6'1", 203 lbs. Born, Sverdlovsk, USSR, January 13, 1973.
(Winnipeg's 8th choice, 204th overall, in 1992 Entry Draft).

							Regular Season							Playoffs			
Season	Club	League	GP	W	L	T	Mins	GA	SO	Avg	GP	W	L	Mins	GA	SO	Avg
1991-92	CSKA Moscow	CIS	2	0	0	0	34	2	0	3.53	....	....	....	....	....	....	....
1992-93	CSKA Moscow	CIS	13	....	....	....	491	27	....	3.29	....	....	....	....	....	....	....
1993-94	CSKA Moscow	CIS	46	....	....	....	2625	116	....	2.65	3	....	....	193	11	....	3.42
	Russian Penguins	IHL	12	2	7	2	639	47	0	4.41	....	....	....	....	....	....	....
1994-95	Springfield Falcons	AHL	23	9	9	3	1240	80	0	3.87	....	....	....	....	....	....	....
	Winnipeg	NHL	26	8	9	4	1339	76	0	3.41	....	....	....	....	....	....	....
1995-96	Winnipeg	NHL	53	26	20	3	2914	152	2	3.13	6	2	4	359	19	0	3.18
1996-97	Phoenix	NHL	72	30	33	6	4091	193	7	2.83	7	3	4	426	15	1	2.11
1997-98	Phoenix	NHL	70	30	28	10	4026	184	4	2.74	4	2	1	185	13	0	4.22
1998-99	Phoenix	NHL	63	32	23	7	3657	130	8	2.13	7	3	4	449	18	0	2.41
99-2000	Long Beach	IHL	33	21	11	1	1936	59	5	*1.83	5	2	3	321	15	0	2.81
2000-01	Tampa Bay	NHL	2	1	1	0	123	6	0	2.93	....	....	....	....	....	....	....
2001-02	Tampa Bay	NHL	70	24	32	10	3896	153	7	2.36	....	....	....	....	....	....	....
	Russia	Olympics	6	3	2	1	*359	14	*1	2.34	....	....	....	....	....	....	....
2002-03	Tampa Bay	NHL	65	30	22	11	3787	156	4	2.47	10	5	5	644	26	0	2.42
2003-04◆	Tampa Bay	NHL	55	28	19	7	3274	127	3	2.33	23	*16	7	1401	40	*5	1.71
	NHL Totals		476	209	187	58	27107	1177	35	2.61	57	31	25	3464	131	6	2.27

James Gatschene Memorial Trophy (MVP – IHL) (2000) (co-winner - Frederic Chabot)

Played in NHL All-Star Game (1998, 1999, 2002, 2003)

Transferred to **Phoenix** after **Winnipeg** franchise relocated, July 1, 1996. • Missed entire 1999-2000 NHL season and majority of 2000-01 season after failing to come to contract terms with **Phoenix**. Signed as a free agent by **Long Beach** (IHL) with **Phoenix** retaining NHL rights, January 14, 2000. Traded to **Tampa Bay** by **Phoenix** with Stan Neckar for Mike Johnson, Paul Mara, Ruslan Zainullin and NY Islanders' 2nd round choice (previously acquired, Phoenix selected Matthew Spiller) in 2001 Entry Draft, March 5, 2001.

KHLOPTONOV, Denis (khloh-POHT-nahv, DEH-nihs) FLA.

Goaltender. Catches left. 6'4", 198 lbs. Born, Moscow, USSR, January 27, 1978.
(Florida's 8th choice, 209th overall, in 1996 Entry Draft).

							Regular Season							Playoffs			
Season	Club	League	GP	W	L	T	Mins	GA	SO	Avg	GP	W	L	Mins	GA	SO	Avg
1996-97	HC CSKA	Russia	21	....	....	....	1260	42	0	2.00	....	....	....	....	....	....	....
1997-98	HC CSKA	Russia	20	....	....	....	987	58	....	3.53	....	....	....	....	....	....	....
1998-99	Muskegon Fury	UHL	37	21	8	2	1950	98	1	3.02	4	1	1	166	9	0	3.25
99-2000	CSKA Moscow	Russia	10	....	....	....	540	22	1	2.44	2	....	....	119	7	0	3.53
2000-01	CSKA Moscow	Russia	14	....	....	....	753	26	1	2.07	....	....	....	....	....	....	....
2001-02	Magnitogorsk	Russia	14	....	....	....	572	36	0	3.78	....	....	....	....	....	....	....
2002-03	CSKA Moscow	Russia					DID NOT PLAY – INJURED										
2003-04	Kristall Elektrostal	Russia-2	16	....	....	....	851	33	....	2.33	....	....	....	....	....	....	....
	Voskresensk	Russia-2	5	3	2	0	262	13	0	2.98	....	....	....	....	....	....	....

KIDD, Trevor (KIHD, TREH-vuhr)

Goaltender. Catches left. 6'2", 213 lbs. Born, Dugald, Man., March 26, 1972.
(Calgary's 1st choice, 11th overall, in 1990 Entry Draft).

							Regular Season							Playoffs			
Season	Club	League	GP	W	L	T	Mins	GA	SO	Avg	GP	W	L	Mins	GA	SO	Avg
1987-88	Eastman Selects	MAHA	14	....	....	....	840	66	0	4.72	....	....	....	....	....	....	....
1988-89	Brandon	WHL	32	11	13	1	1509	102	0	4.06	....	....	....	....	....	....	....
1989-90	Brandon	WHL	*63	24	32	2	*3676	254	2	4.15	....	....	....	....	....	....	....
1990-91	Brandon	WHL	30	10	19	1	1730	117	0	4.06	....	....	....	....	....	....	....
	Spokane Chiefs	WHL	14	8	3	0	749	44	0	3.52	15	*14	1	926	32	2	*2.07
1991-92	Canada	Nat-Tm	28	18	4	4	1349	79	2	3.51	....	....	....	....	....	....	....
	Canada	Olympics	1	1	0	0	60	0	1	0.00	....	....	....	....	....	....	....
	Calgary	NHL	2	1	1	0	120	8	0	4.00	....	....	....	....	....	....	....
1992-93	Salt Lake	IHL	29	10	16	1	1696	111	1	3.93	....	....	....	....	....	....	....
1993-94	Calgary	NHL	31	13	7	6	1614	85	0	3.16	....	....	....	....	....	....	....

1994-95	Calgary	NHL	*43	22	14	6	*2463	107	3	2.61	7	3	4	434	26	1	3.59
1995-96	Calgary	NHL	47	15	21	8	2570	119	3	2.78	2	0	1	83	9	0	6.51
1996-97	Calgary	NHL	55	21	23	6	2979	141	4	2.84	....	....	....	....	....	....	....
1997-98	Carolina	NHL	47	21	21	3	2685	97	3	2.17	....	....	....	....	....	....	....
1998-99	Carolina	NHL	25	7	10	6	1358	61	2	2.70	....	....	....	....	....	....	....
99-2000	Florida	NHL	28	14	11	2	1574	69	1	2.63	....	....	....	....	....	....	....
	Louisville Panthers	AHL	1	0	1	0	60	5	0	5.04	....	....	....	....	....	....	....
2000-01	Florida	NHL	42	10	23	6	2354	130	1	3.31	....	....	....	....	....	....	....
2001-02	Florida	NHL	33	4	16	5	1683	90	1	3.21	....	....	....	....	....	....	....
2002-03	Toronto	NHL	19	6	10	2	1143	59	0	3.10	....	....	....	....	....	....	....
2003-04	Toronto	NHL	15	6	5	2	883	48	1	3.26	1	0	0	33	1	0	1.82
	St. John's	AHL	1	1	0	0	60	1	0	1.00	....	....	....	....	....	....	....
	NHL Totals		**387**	**140**	**162**	**52**	**21426**	**1014**	**19**	**2.84**	**10**	**3**	**5**	**550**	**36**	**1**	**3.93**

WHL East First All-Star Team (1990) • Canadian Major Junior Goaltender of the Year (1990)

Traded to **Carolina** by **Calgary** with Gary Roberts for Andrew Cassels and Jean-Sebastien Giguere, August 25, 1997. Claimed by **Atlanta** from **Carolina** in Expansion Draft, June 25, 1999. Traded to **Florida** by **Atlanta** for Gord Murphy, Herbert Vasiljevs, Daniel Tjarnqvist and Ottawa's 6th round choice (previously acquired, later traded to Dallas – Dallas selected Justin Cox) in 1999 Entry Draft, June 25, 1999. Signed as a free agent by **Toronto**, August 26, 2002.

KILPELAINEN, Eero (kih-pehl-AI-nehn, EE-roh) DAL.

Goaltender. Catches left. 5'11", 152 lbs. Born, Juva, Finland, May 7, 1985.
(Dallas' 6th choice, 144th overall, in 2003 Entry Draft).

			Regular Season								Playoffs						
Season	**Club**	**League**	**GP**	**W**	**L**	**T**	**Mins**	**GA**	**SO**	**Avg**	**GP**	**W**	**L**	**Mins**	**GA**	**SO**	**Avg**
2002-03	KalPa Kuopio Jr.	Finn-Jr.	20	8	6	1	991	57	0	3.45	....	....	....	....	....	....	....
	KalPa Kuopio	Finland-2	1	0	0	0	17	4	0	14.12	....	....	....	....	....	....	....
2003-04	KalPa Kuopio Jr.	Finn-Jr.	43	17	19	6	2528	118	2	2.80	2	0	2	116	4	0	2.07

KIPRUSOFF, Miikka (KIHP-ruh-sohf, MEE-kah) CGY.

Goaltender. Catches left. 6'2", 190 lbs. Born, Turku, Finland, October 26, 1976.
(San Jose's 5th choice, 116th overall, in 1995 Entry Draft).

			Regular Season								Playoffs						
Season	**Club**	**League**	**GP**	**W**	**L**	**T**	**Mins**	**GA**	**SO**	**Avg**	**GP**	**W**	**L**	**Mins**	**GA**	**SO**	**Avg**
1994-95	TPS Turku Jr.	Finn-Jr.	31	....	....	....	1896	92	....	2.91	....	....	....	....	....	....	....
	TPS Turku	Finland	4	....	....	....	240	12	0	3.00	2	....	....	120	7	....	3.50
1995-96	TPS Turku Jr.	Finn-Jr.	3	....	....	....	180	9	....	3.00	....	....	....	....	....	....	....
	Kiekko 67 Turku	Finland-2	5	....	....	....	300	7	....	1.40	....	....	....	....	....	....	....
	TPS Turku	Finland	12	....	....	....	550	38	0	4.14	3	....	....	114	4	....	2.11
1996-97	AIK Solna	Sweden	42	....	....	....	2466	104	3	2.53	7	....	....	420	23	0	3.28
1997-98	AIK Solna	Sweden	42	....	....	....	2457	110	....	2.69	....	....	....	....	....	....	....
1998-99	TPS Turku	Finland	39	*26	6	6	2259	70	4	1.86	10	*9	1	580	15	*3	*1.55
99-2000	Kentucky	AHL	47	23	19	4	2759	114	3	2.48	5	1	3	239	13	0	3.27
2000-01	San Jose	NHL	5	2	1	0	154	5	0	1.95	3	1	1	149	5	0	2.01
	Kentucky	AHL	36	19	9	6	2038	76	2	2.24	....	....	....	....	....	....	....
2001-02	San Jose	NHL	20	7	6	3	1037	43	2	2.49	1	0	0	8	0	0	0.00
	Cleveland Barons	AHL	4	4	0	0	242	7	0	1.73	....	....	....	....	....	....	....
2002-03	San Jose	NHL	22	5	14	0	1199	65	1	3.25	....	....	....	....	....	....	....
2003-04	Calgary	NHL	38	24	10	4	2301	65	4	*1.69	*26	15	11	*1655	51	*5	1.85
	NHL Totals		**85**	**38**	**31**	**7**	**4691**	**178**	**7**	**2.28**	**30**	**16**	**12**	**1812**	**56**	**5**	**1.85**

Traded to **Calgary** by **San Jose** for future considerations, November 16, 2003.

KOCHAN, Dieter (KAH-kuhn, DEE-tuhr) NYI

Goaltender. Catches left. 6'1", 180 lbs. Born, Saskatoon, Sask., May 11, 1974.
(Vancouver's 3rd choice, 98th overall, in 1993 Entry Draft).

			Regular Season								Playoffs						
Season	**Club**	**League**	**GP**	**W**	**L**	**T**	**Mins**	**GA**	**SO**	**Avg**	**GP**	**W**	**L**	**Mins**	**GA**	**SO**	**Avg**
1991-92	Sioux City	USHL	23	7	10	0	1131	100	0	5.31	....	....	....	....	....	....	....
1992-93	Kelowna Spartans	BCJHL	44	34	8	0	2582	137	1	3.18	15	12	3	927	48	1	3.10
1993-94	Northern Michigan	WCHA	20	9	7	0	985	57	2	3.47	....	....	....	....	....	....	....
1994-95	Northern Michigan	WCHA	29	8	17	3	1512	107	0	4.25	....	....	....	....	....	....	....
1995-96	Northern Michigan	WCHA	31	7	21	2	1627	123	0	4.54	....	....	....	....	....	....	....
1996-97	Northern Michigan	WCHA	26	8	15	2	1528	99	0	3.89	....	....	....	....	....	....	....
1997-98	Louisville	ECHL	18	7	9	2	980	61	1	3.73	....	....	....	....	....	....	....
1998-99	Binghamton	UHL	40	18	16	5	2322	115	2	2.97	4	1	2	208	9	0	2.60
99-2000	Binghamton	UHL	43	29	11	3	2544	110	4	2.59	....	....	....	....	....	....	....
	Orlando	IHL	4	4	0	0	240	4	1	1.00	....	....	....	....	....	....	....
	Springfield Falcons	AHL	2	1	1	0	120	5	1	2.50	....	....	....	....	....	....	....
	Tampa Bay	NHL	5	1	4	0	238	17	0	4.29	....	....	....	....	....	....	....
	Grand Rapids	IHL	2	1	0	1	93	1	0	0.64	....	....	....	....	....	....	....
2000-01	Tampa Bay	NHL	10	0	3	0	314	18	0	3.44	....	....	....	....	....	....	....
	Detroit Vipers	IHL	49	13	28	3	2606	154	0	3.55	....	....	....	....	....	....	....
2001-02	Tampa Bay	NHL	5	0	3	1	237	16	0	4.05	....	....	....	....	....	....	....
	Springfield Falcons	AHL	45	21	20	1	2518	112	2	2.67	....	....	....	....	....	....	....
2002-03	Minnesota	NHL	1	0	1	0	60	5	0	5.00	....	....	....	....	....	....	....
	Houston Aeros	AHL	25	15	6	3	1447	61	1	2.53	2	0	0	20	0	0	0.00
2003-04	Bridgeport	AHL	45	20	17	7	2728	85	6	1.87	4	1	3	281	12	0	2.57
	NHL Totals		**21**	**1**	**11**	**1**	**849**	**56**	**0**	**3.96**	....	....	....	....	....	....	....

UHL Second All-Star Team (2000) • Shared Harry "Hap" Holmes Memorial Trophy (fewest goals against - AHL) with Wade Dubielewicz (2004)

• Scored a goal vs. Winston-Salem (UHL), January 5, 1999. Signed as a free agent by **Tampa Bay**, March 27, 2000. Signed as a free agent by **Minnesota**, August 5, 2002. Signed as a free agent by **NY Islanders**, August 7, 2003.

KOLZIG, Olie (KOHL-zihg, OH-lee) WSH.

Goaltender. Catches left. 6'3", 225 lbs. Born, Johannesburg, South Africa, April 6, 1970.
(Washington's 1st choice, 19th overall, in 1989 Entry Draft).

			Regular Season								Playoffs						
Season	**Club**	**League**	**GP**	**W**	**L**	**T**	**Mins**	**GA**	**SO**	**Avg**	**GP**	**W**	**L**	**Mins**	**GA**	**SO**	**Avg**
1986-87	Abbotsford Pilots	BCAHA	17	5	9	0	857	81	0	5.67	....	....	....	....	....	....	....
1987-88	New Westminster	WHL	15	6	5	0	650	48	1	4.43	3	0	3	149	11	0	4.43
1988-89	Tri-City Americans	WHL	30	16	10	2	1671	97	1	*3.48	....	....	....	....	....	....	....
1989-90	Washington	NHL	2	0	2	0	120	12	0	6.00	....	....	....	....	....	....	....
	Tri-City Americans	WHL	48	27	27	3	2504	187	1	4.48	6	4	0	318	27	0	5.09
1990-91	Baltimore Skipjacks	AHL	26	10	12	1	1367	72	0	3.16	....	....	....	....	....	....	....
	Hampton Roads	ECHL	21	11	9	1	1248	71	2	3.41	3	1	2	180	14	0	4.66
1991-92	Baltimore Skipjacks	AHL	28	5	17	2	1503	105	1	4.19	....	....	....	....	....	....	....
	Hampton Roads	ECHL	14	11	3	0	847	41	0	2.90	....	....	....	....	....	....	....
1992-93	Washington	NHL	1	0	0	0	20	2	0	6.00	....	....	....	....	....	....	....
	Rochester	AHL	49	25	16	4	2737	168	0	3.68	*17	9	8	*1040	61	0	3.52
1993-94	Washington	NHL	7	0	3	0	224	20	0	5.36	....	....	....	....	....	....	....
	Portland Pirates	AHL	29	16	8	5	1725	88	3	3.06	17	*12	5	1035	44	0	*2.55
1994-95	Washington	NHL	14	2	8	2	724	30	0	2.49	2	1	0	44	1	0	1.36
	Portland Pirates	AHL	2	1	0	1	125	3	0	1.44	....	....	....	....	....	....	....
1995-96	Washington	NHL	18	4	8	2	897	46	0	3.08	5	2	3	341	11	0	*1.94
	Portland Pirates	AHL	5	5	0	0	300	7	1	1.40	....	....	....	....	....	....	....
1996-97	Washington	NHL	29	8	15	4	1645	71	2	2.59	....	....	....	....	....	....	....
1997-98	Washington	NHL	64	33	18	10	3788	139	5	2.20	21	12	9	1351	44	*4	1.95
	Germany	Olympics	2	2	0	0	120	2	1	1.00	....	....	....	....	....	....	....
1998-99	Washington	NHL	64	26	31	3	3586	154	4	2.58	....	....	....	....	....	....	....
99-2000	Washington	NHL	73	41	20	11	*4371	163	5	2.24	5	1	4	284	16	0	3.38
2000-01	Washington	NHL	72	37	26	8	4279	177	5	2.48	6	2	4	375	14	1	2.24
2001-02	Washington	NHL	71	31	29	8	4131	192	6	2.79	....	....	....	....	....	....	....
2002-03	Washington	NHL	66	33	25	6	3894	156	4	2.40	6	2	4	404	14	1	2.08
2003-04	Washington	NHL	63	19	35	9	3738	180	2	2.89	....	....	....	....	....	....	....
	NHL Totals		**544**	**234**	**220**	**63**	**31417**	**1342**	**33**	**2.56**	**45**	**20**	**24**	**2799**	**100**	**6**	**2.14**

WHL West Second All-Star Team (1989) • Shared Harry ''Hap'' Holmes Memorial Trophy (fewest goals against – AHL) (1994) with Byron Dafoe • Jack A. Butterfield Trophy (Playoff MVP – AHL) (1994) • NHL First All-Star Team (2000) • Vezina Trophy (2000)

Played in NHL All-Star Game (1998, 2000)

• Scored a goal while with Tri-City (WHL), November 29, 1989.

KONSTANTINOV, Evgeny (kohn-stahn-TEE-nahf, ehv-GEH-nee)

Goaltender. Catches left. 6', 176 lbs. Born, Kazan, USSR, March 29, 1981.
(Tampa Bay's 2nd choice, 67th overall, in 1999 Entry Draft).

			Regular Season								Playoffs						
Season	**Club**	**League**	**GP**	**W**	**L**	**T**	**Mins**	**GA**	**SO**	**Avg**	**GP**	**W**	**L**	**Mins**	**GA**	**SO**	**Avg**
1997-98	Ak Bars Kazan 2	Russia-3	34	....	....	....	2040	129	....	3.79	....	....	....	....	....	....	....
1998-99	Ak Bars Kazan 2	Russia-4	17	....	....	....	1020	38	....	2.24	....	....	....	....	....	....	....
99-2000	Leninogorsk	Russia-2					STATISTICS NOT AVAILABLE										
	Ak Bars Kazan	Russia	2	....	....	....	59	5	0	5.08	....	....	....	....	....	....	....
2000-01	Detroit Vipers	IHL	27	4	15	2	1197	85	0	4.26	....	....	....	....	....	....	....
	Tampa Bay	NHL	1	0	0	0	1	0	0	0.00	....	....	....	....	....	....	....
	Louisiana	ECHL	8	4	4	0	458	21	0	2.75	12	5	6	637	32	0	3.01
2001-02	Pensacola Ice Pilots	ECHL	24	10	10	0	1229	71	0	3.47	....	....	....	....	....	....	....
	Springfield Falcons	AHL	3	1	2	0	178	5	0	1.69	....	....	....	....	....	....	....
2002-03	Tampa Bay	NHL	1	0	0	0	20	1	0	3.00	....	....	....	....	....	....	....
	Springfield Falcons	AHL	39	13	23	1	2188	118	1	3.24	....	....	....	....	....	....	....
2003-04	Pensacola Ice Pilots	ECHL	12	2	6	2	651	40	0	3.68	....	....	....	....	....	....	....
	Severstal 2	Russia-3	1	1	0	0	60	2	0	2.00	....	....	....	....	....	....	....
	NHL Totals		**2**	**0**	**0**	**0**	**21**	**1**	**0**	**2.86**	....	....	....	....	....	....	....

• Played 24 seconds of game vs. Colorado, December 8, 2000.

KOOPMANS, Logan (KOOP-manz, LOH-guhn) DET.

Goaltender. Catches left. 6'2", 182 lbs. Born, Cranbrook, B.C., May 18, 1984.
(Detroit's 5th choice, 166th overall, in 2002 Entry Draft).

			Regular Season								Playoffs						
Season	**Club**	**League**	**GP**	**W**	**L**	**T**	**Mins**	**GA**	**SO**	**Avg**	**GP**	**W**	**L**	**Mins**	**GA**	**SO**	**Avg**
99-2000	Lethbridge	WHL	5	1	3	0	282	19	0	4.04	....	....	....	....	....	....	....
2000-01	Columbia Valley	KIJHL	37	....	....	....	2140	144	1	3.90	....	....	....	....	....	....	....
2001-02	Lethbridge	WHL	37	20	12	2	2057	97	3	2.83	4	0	4	237	14	0	3.54
2002-03	Lethbridge	WHL	34	9	17	0	1628	131	1	4.83	....	....	....	....	....	....	....
2003-04	Lethbridge	WHL	62	27	25	8	3565	155	5	2.61	....	....	....	....	....	....	....

KOPRIVA, Miroslav (koh-PREE-vuh, MEER-oh-slav) MIN.

Goaltender. Catches left. 6'2", 176 lbs. Born, Kladno, Czech., December 5, 1983.
(Minnesota's 5th choice, 187th overall, in 2003 Entry Draft).

			Regular Season								Playoffs						
Season	**Club**	**League**	**GP**	**W**	**L**	**T**	**Mins**	**GA**	**SO**	**Avg**	**GP**	**W**	**L**	**Mins**	**GA**	**SO**	**Avg**
99-2000	Kladno Jr.	Czech-Jr.	46	....	....	....	2510	121	4	2.89	4	....	....	249	13	0	3.13
2000-01	Kladno Jr.	Czech-Jr.	26	....	....	....	1478	65	2	2.64	....	....	....	....	....	....	....
2001-02	Kladno Jr.	Czech-Jr.	41	....	....	....	2367	124	6	3.14	....	....	....	....	....	....	....
2002-03	Kladno Jr.	Czech-Jr.	42	....	....	....	2464	80	5	1.95	11	....	....	661	16	2	1.45
2003-04	Kladno Jr.	Czech-Jr.	4	....	....	....	240	10	1	2.50	....	....	....	....	....	....	....
	Beroun	Czech-2	31	....	....	....	1837	58	3	1.89	....	....	....	....	....	....	....
	HC Rabat Kladno	Czech	13	....	....	....	687	46	2	4.02	....	....	....	....	....	....	....

KOSTUR, Matus (KAW-stuhr, ma-TOOSH) N.J.

Goaltender. Catches left. 6'1", 195 lbs. Born, Banska Bystrica, Czech., March 28, 1980.
(New Jersey's 10th choice, 164th overall, in 2000 Entry Draft).

			Regular Season								Playoffs						
Season	**Club**	**League**	**GP**	**W**	**L**	**T**	**Mins**	**GA**	**SO**	**Avg**	**GP**	**W**	**L**	**Mins**	**GA**	**SO**	**Avg**
1997-98	B. Bystrica Jr.	Slovak-Jr.	36	....	....	....	2152	120	0	3.35	....	....	....	....	....	....	....
1998-99	Banska Bystrica	Slovak-2	3	....	....	....	133	9	0	4.06	....	....	....	....	....	....	....
99-2000	HKm Zvolen	Slovak-2	10	....	....	....	538	32	0	3.57	....	....	....	....	....	....	....
	HKm Zvolen	Slovakia	20	....	....	....	768	36	0	2.81	2	0	0	41	3	0	4.39
2000-01	HC Nitra	Slovak-2	20	18	1	1	1132	24	4	1.53	....	....	....	....	....	....	....
	HKm Zvolen	Slovakia	3	....	....	....	110	11	0	6.00	....	....	....	....	....	....	....
2001-02	HKm Zvolen	Slovakia	39	....	....	....	2163	78	5	2.16	2	....	....	99	5	0	3.03
2002-03	Columbus	ECHL	44	16	21	2	2422	150	1	3.72	....	....	....	....	....	....	....
2003-04	Columbus	ECHL	13	9	2	1	702	23	2	1.97	....	....	....	....	....	....	....
	Albany River Rats	AHL	10	3	6	1	544	32	1	3.53	....	....	....	....	....	....	....

KOTYK, Seamus (koh-TIHK, SHAY-muhs)

Goaltender. Catches left. 5'11", 180 lbs. Born, London, Ont., October 7, 1980.
(Boston's 5th choice, 147th overall, in 1999 Entry Draft).

			Regular Season								Playoffs						
Season	**Club**	**League**	**GP**	**W**	**L**	**T**	**Mins**	**GA**	**SO**	**Avg**	**GP**	**W**	**L**	**Mins**	**GA**	**SO**	**Avg**
1996-97	Stratford Cullitons	OJHL-B	28	....	....	....	1615	105	0	3.82	....	....	....	....	....	....	....
1997-98	Ottawa 67's	OHL	31	13	5	5	1422	63	4	2.66	7	3	2	332	11	0	1.99
1998-99	Ottawa 67's	OHL	41	26	7	4	2314	92	5	2.39	5	3	2	338	13	0	*2.31
99-2000	Ottawa 67's	OHL	26	12	6	2	1241	65	1	3.14	....	....	....	....	....	....	....
2000-01	Ottawa 67's	OHL	55	24	20	7	3087	141	2	2.74	*20	*16	4	*1157	46	*3	2.39
2001-02	Cleveland Barons	AHL	24	6	11	0	981	61	1	3.73	....	....	....	....	....	....	....
2002-03	Cleveland Barons	AHL	34	7	22	2	1838	118	2	3.85	....	....	....	....	....	....	....
2003-04	Cleveland Barons	AHL	30	13	10	5	1768	73	1	2.48	....	....	....	....	....	....	....

• Missed majority of 1999-2000 season recovering from surgery for cardiac arrhythmia, October 18, 1999. Signed as a free agent by **San Jose**, July 23, 2001.

KOWALSKI, Craig (koh-WAHL-skee, KRAYG) CAR.

Goaltender. Catches left. 5'10", 190 lbs. Born, Warren, MI, January 15, 1981.
(Carolina's 6th choice, 235th overall, in 2000 Entry Draft).

			Regular Season								Playoffs						
Season	**Club**	**League**	**GP**	**W**	**L**	**T**	**Mins**	**GA**	**SO**	**Avg**	**GP**	**W**	**L**	**Mins**	**GA**	**SO**	**Avg**
1998-99	Det. Compuware	NAJHL	42	*34	7	6	2733	96	3	*2.10	7	*7	0	420	13	1	*1.86
99-2000	Det. Compuware	NAJHL	49	33	12	3	2850	113	4	2.38	5	2	3	334	13	0	2.34
2000-01	Northern Michigan	CCHA	19	7	8	4	1078	49	1	2.73	....	....	....	....	....	....	....
2001-02	Northern Michigan	CCHA	38	24	11	2	2271	89	4	2.35	....	....	....	....	....	....	....
2002-03	Northern Michigan	CCHA	38	20	16	2	2213	104	3	2.82	....	....	....	....	....	....	....
2003-04	Northern Michigan	CCHA	37	17	14	4	2058	93	4	2.71	....	....	....	....	....	....	....

KRAHN, Brent (KRAWN, BREHNT) CGY.

Goaltender. Catches left. 6'4", 200 lbs. Born, Winnipeg, Man., April 2, 1982.
(Calgary's 1st choice, 9th overall, in 2000 Entry Draft).

			Regular Season								Playoffs						
Season	**Club**	**League**	**GP**	**W**	**L**	**T**	**Mins**	**GA**	**SO**	**Avg**	**GP**	**W**	**L**	**Mins**	**GA**	**SO**	**Avg**
1997-98	Pembina Valley	MMHL	22	20	0	1	1265	40	3	1.90	2	2	0	120	2	1	1.00
1998-99	Pembina Valley	MMHL	13	10	3	0	770	30	2	2.34	....	....	....	....	....	....	....
99-2000	Calgary Hitmen	WHL	39	33	6	0	2315	92	4	2.38	5	2	2	266	13	0	2.93
2000-01	Calgary Hitmen	WHL	37	22	10	3	2087	104	1	2.99	....	....	....	....	....	....	....
2001-02	Calgary Hitmen	WHL	18	8	6	2	1033	61	0	3.54	2	1	1	119	6	0	3.03
2002-03	Calgary Hitmen	WHL	23	11	10	2	1343	72	2	3.22	....	....	....	....	....	....	....
	Seattle	WHL	5	5	0	0	302	9	2	1.79	15	9	6	960	38	2	2.38
2003-04	Lowell	AHL	7	2	3	0	344	15	0	2.62	....	....	....	....	....	....	....

Season	Club	League	GP	W	L	T	Mins	GA	SO	Avg	GP	W	L	Mins	GA	SO	Avg
	Las Vegas	ECHL	14	7	5	2	828	36	0	2.61	....	....	....	....	....	....	....
	San Antonio	AHL	14	3	7	1	715	41	0	3.44	....	....	....	....	....	....	....

• Missed majority of 2001-02 season recovering from off-season knee surgery, June, 2001.

LABARBERA, Jason (lah-BAR-buhr-uh, JAY-suhn) NYR

Goaltender. Catches left. 6'2", 205 lbs. Born, Prince George, B.C., January 18, 1980.
(NY Rangers' 3rd choice, 66th overall, in 1998 Entry Draft).

			Regular Season								Playoffs						
Season	Club	League	GP	W	L	T	Mins	GA	SO	Avg	GP	W	L	Mins	GA	SO	Avg
1995-96	Prince George	BCAHA	31	....	....	....	1860	83	0	2.68	....	....	....	....	....	....	....
1996-97	Tri-City Americans	WHL	2	1	0	0	63	4	0	3.81	....	....	....	....	....	....	....
	Portland	WHL	9	5	1	1	443	18	0	2.44	....	....	....	....	....	....	....
1997-98	Portland	WHL	23	18	4	0	1305	72	1	3.31	....	....	....	....	....	....	....
1998-99	Portland	WHL	51	18	23	9	2991	170	4	3.41	4	0	4	252	19	0	4.52
99-2000	Portland	WHL	34	8	24	2	2005	123	1	3.68	....	....	....	....	....	....	....
	Spokane Chiefs	WHL	21	12	6	2	1146	50	0	2.62	9	6	1	435	18	1	2.48
2000-01	**NY Rangers**	**NHL**	**1**	**0**	**0**	**0**	**10**	**0**	**0**	**0.00**	....	....	....	....	....	....	....
	Hartford Wolf Pack	AHL	4	1	1	0	156	12	0	4.61	....	....	....	....	....	....	....
	Charlotte Checkers	ECHL	35	18	10	7	2100	112	1	3.20	2	1	1	143	5	0	2.09
2001-02	Charlotte Checkers	ECHL	13	9	3	1	744	29	0	2.34	4	2	2	212	12	0	3.39
	Hartford Wolf Pack	AHL	20	7	11	1	1058	55	0	3.12	....	....	....	....	....	....	....
2002-03	Hartford Wolf Pack	AHL	46	18	17	6	2452	105	2	2.57	2	0	2	117	6	0	3.07
2003-04	**NY Rangers**	**NHL**	**4**	**1**	**2**	**0**	**198**	**16**	**0**	**4.85**	....	....	....	....	....	....	....
	Hartford Wolf Pack	AHL	59	34	9	9	3393	90	*13	1.59	16	11	5	1043	30	*3	*1.73
	NHL Totals		**5**	**1**	**2**	**0**	**208**	**16**	**0**	**4.62**	....	....	....	....	....	....	....

AHL First All-Star Team (2004) • Baz Bastien Memorial Trophy (Top Goaltender - AHL) (2004) • Les Cunningham Plaque (MVP - AHL) (2004)

LABBE, Jean-Francois (lah-BAY, ZHAWN-fran-SWUH)

Goaltender. Catches left. 5'10", 175 lbs. Born, Sherbrooke, Que., June 15, 1972.

			Regular Season								Playoffs						
Season	Club	League	GP	W	L	T	Mins	GA	SO	Avg	GP	W	L	Mins	GA	SO	Avg
1988-89	L'est Cantonniers	QAAA	29	*22	7	0	1764	94	1	3.20	5	1	4	333	19	0	3.42
1989-90	Trois-Rivieres	QMJHL	28	13	10	0	1499	106	1	4.24	3	1	1	132	8	0	3.64
1990-91	Trois-Rivieres	QMJHL	54	*35	14	0	2870	158	5	3.30	5	1	4	230	19	0	4.96
1991-92	Trois-Rivieres	QMJHL	48	*31	13	3	2749	142	1	3.10	*15	*10	3	791	33	*1	*2.50
1992-93	Hull Olympiques	QMJHL	46	26	18	2	2701	156	2	3.46	10	6	3	518	24	*1	*2.78
1993-94	Thunder Bay	ColHL	52	*35	11	4	*2900	150	*2	*3.10	8	7	1	493	18	*2	*2.19
	P.E.I. Senators	AHL	7	4	3	0	389	22	0	3.39	....	....	....	....	....	....	....
1994-95	P.E.I. Senators	AHL	32	13	14	3	1817	94	2	3.10	....	....	....	....	....	....	....
1995-96	Cornwall Aces	AHL	55	25	21	5	2972	144	3	2.91	8	3	5	471	21	1	2.68
1996-97	Hershey Bears	AHL	66	*34	22	9	3811	160	*6	*2.52	*23	*14	8	*1364	59	1	2.60
1997-98	Hamilton Bulldogs	AHL	52	24	17	11	3138	149	2	2.85	7	3	4	413	20	0	2.90
1998-99	Hartford Wolf Pack	AHL	*59	28	26	3	*3392	182	2	3.22	7	3	4	447	22	0	2.95
99-2000	**NY Rangers**	**NHL**	**1**	**0**	**1**	**0**	**60**	**3**	**0**	**3.00**	....	....	....	....	....	....	....
	Hartford Wolf Pack	AHL	49	27	13	7	2853	120	1	2.52	*22	*15	7	*1320	48	3	2.18
2000-01	Hartford Wolf Pack	AHL	8	4	2	1	394	20	0	3.04	....	....	....	....	....	....	....
	Syracuse Crunch	AHL	37	15	15	5	2201	105	2	2.86	5	2	3	323	18	0	3.34
2001-02	**Columbus**	**NHL**	**3**	**1**	**1**	**0**	**117**	**6**	**0**	**3.08**	....	....	....	....	....	....	....
	Syracuse Crunch	AHL	51	27	16	7	2993	109	*9	2.18	10	6	4	596	19	2	*1.91
2002-03	**Columbus**	**NHL**	**11**	**2**	**4**	**0**	**451**	**27**	**0**	**3.59**	....	....	....	....	....	....	....
	Syracuse Crunch	AHL	4	1	2	1	247	11	0	2.68	....	....	....	....	....	....	....
2003-04	Lada Togliatti	Russia	30	....	....	....	1725	43	8	1.50	....	....	....	....	....	....	....
	NHL Totals		**15**	**3**	**6**	**0**	**628**	**36**	**0**	**3.44**	....	....	....	....	....	....	....

QMJHL First All-Star Team (1992) • ColHL First All-Star Team (1994) • ColHL Rookie of the Year (1994) • ColHL Outstanding Goaltender (1994) • ColHL Playoff MVP (1994) • AHL First All-Star Team (1997) • Harry "Hap" Holmes Memorial Trophy (fewest goals against – AHL) (1997) • Baz Bastien Memorial Trophy (Top Goaltender – AHL) (1997) • Les Cunningham Award (MVP – AHL) (1997) • Shared Harry "Hap" Holmes Memorial Trophy (fewest goals against – AHL) (2000) with Milan Hnilicka • AHL Second All-Star Team (2002)

Signed as a free agent by **Ottawa**, May 12, 1994. Traded to **Colorado** by **Ottawa** for future considerations, September 20, 1995. Signed as a free agent by **Edmonton**, September 2, 1997. Signed as a free agent by **NY Rangers**, July 30, 1998. • Scored a goal vs. Quebec (AHL), February 5, 2000. Traded to **Columbus** by **NY Rangers** for Bert Robertsson, November 9, 2000. Signed as a free agent by **Lada Togliatti** (Russia), July 1, 2003.

LACOSTA, Dan (luh-KAWS-tah, DAN) CBJ

Goaltender. Catches left. 6'1", 186 lbs. Born, Labrador City, Nfld., March 28, 1986.
(Columbus' 4th choice, 93rd overall, in 2004 Entry Draft).

			Regular Season								Playoffs						
Season	Club	League	GP	W	L	T	Mins	GA	SO	Avg	GP	W	L	Mins	GA	SO	Avg
2002-03	Owen Sound	OHL	28	8	10	3	1321	82	0	3.72	....	....	....	....	....	....	....
2003-04	Owen Sound	OHL	37	17	10	1	1810	82	4	2.72	....	....	....	....	....	....	....

LAJEUNESSE, Simon (lah-ZHUH-nehs, SIGH-mohn)

Goaltender. Catches left. 6'1", 178 lbs. Born, Quebec City, Que., January 22, 1981.
(Ottawa's 2nd choice, 48th overall, in 1999 Entry Draft).

			Regular Season								Playoffs						
Season	Club	League	GP	W	L	T	Mins	GA	SO	Avg	GP	W	L	Mins	GA	SO	Avg
1996-97	Cap-d-Madeleine	QAAA	23	15	5	1	1300	89	0	4.11	4	1	3	240	26	0	4.72
1997-98	Moncton Wildcats	QMJHL	19	5	6	3	925	51	1	3.31	2	0	0	1	0	0	0.00
1998-99	Moncton Wildcats	QMJHL	36	18	9	3	1993	98	1	2.95	1	0	0	43	2	0	2.79
99-2000	Moncton Wildcats	QMJHL	55	31	15	1	2922	127	6	2.61	16	9	6	910	56	1	3.69
2000-01	Acadie-Bathurst	QMJHL	36	10	19	2	1879	121	1	3.86	....	....	....	....	....	....	....
	Val-d'Or Foreurs	QMJHL	21	16	3	1	1159	54	1	2.80	14	8	4	760	52	0	4.10
2001-02	**Ottawa**	**NHL**	**1**	**0**	**0**	**0**	**24**	**0**	**0**	**0.00**	....	....	....	....	....	....	....
	Mobile Mysticks	ECHL	13	7	2	3	755	36	2	2.86	....	....	....	....	....	....	....
	Grand Rapids	AHL	26	13	7	5	1534	54	3	2.11	2	0	0	21	1	0	2.82
2002-03	Binghamton	AHL	19	7	7	1	966	47	1	2.92	....	....	....	....	....	....	....
	San Antonio	AHL	2	0	1	0	78	6	0	4.60	....	....	....	....	....	....	....
	Peoria Rivermen	ECHL	4	2	2	0	239	8	0	2.01	....	....	....	....	....	....	....
2003-04	San Antonio	AHL	8	1	4	1	351	23	0	3.93	....	....	....	....	....	....	....
	Augusta Lynx	ECHL	2	1	1	0	125	8	0	3.84	....	....	....	....	....	....	....
	Columbus	ECHL	1	0	0	0	26	1	0	2.31	....	....	....	....	....	....	....
	NHL Totals		**1**	**0**	**0**	**0**	**24**	**0**	**0**	**0.00**	....	....	....	....	....	....	....

QMJHL First All-Star Team (2000) • Shared Harry "Hap" Holmes Memorial Trophy (fewest goals against – AHL) (2002) with Martin Prusek and Mathieu Chouinard

Traded to **Florida** by **Ottawa** for Joey Tetarenko, March 4, 2003. • Missed majority of 2003-04 season recovering from groin injury suffered in game vs. Grand Rapids (AHL), January 13, 2004.

LALIME, Patrick (lah-LEEM, PAT-rihk) ST.L.

Goaltender. Catches left. 6'3", 185 lbs. Born, St-Bonaventure, Que., July 7, 1974.
(Pittsburgh's 6th choice, 156th overall, in 1993 Entry Draft).

			Regular Season								Playoffs						
Season	Club	League	GP	W	L	T	Mins	GA	SO	Avg	GP	W	L	Mins	GA	SO	Avg
1990-91	Abitibi Forestiers	QAAA	26	9	17	0	1595	151	0	5.81	....	....	....	....	....	....	....
1991-92	Shawinigan	QMJHL	6	....	....	....	272	25	0	5.50	....	....	....	....	....	....	....
1992-93	Shawinigan	QMJHL	44	10	24	4	2467	192	0	4.67	....	....	....	....	....	....	....
1993-94	Shawinigan	QMJHL	48	22	20	0	2733	192	1	4.22	5	1	3	223	25	0	6.73
1994-95	Hampton Roads	ECHL	26	15	7	3	1470	82	2	3.35	....	....	....	....	....	....	....
	Cleveland	IHL	23	7	10	4	1230	91	0	4.44	....	....	....	....	....	....	....
1995-96	Cleveland	IHL	41	20	12	7	2314	149	0	3.86	....	....	....	....	....	....	....
1996-97	**Pittsburgh**	**NHL**	**39**	**21**	**12**	**2**	**2058**	**101**	**3**	**2.94**	....	....	....	....	....	....	....
	Cleveland	IHL	14	6	6	2	834	45	1	3.24	....	....	....	....	....	....	....
1997-98	Grand Rapids	IHL	31	10	10	9	1749	76	2	2.61	1	0	1	77	4	0	3.11
1998-99	Kansas City Blades	IHL	*66	*39	20	4	*3789	190	2	3.01	3	1	2	179	6	1	2.01
99-2000	**Ottawa**	**NHL**	**38**	**19**	**14**	**3**	**2038**	**79**	**3**	**2.33**	....	....	....	....	....	....	....
2000-01	**Ottawa**	**NHL**	**60**	**36**	**19**	**5**	**3607**	**141**	**7**	**2.35**	**4**	**0**	**4**	**251**	**10**	**0**	**2.39**
2001-02	**Ottawa**	**NHL**	**61**	**27**	**24**	**8**	**3583**	**148**	**7**	**2.48**	**12**	**7**	**5**	**778**	**18**	**4**	***1.39**
2002-03	**Ottawa**	**NHL**	**67**	**39**	**20**	**7**	**3943**	**142**	**8**	**2.16**	**18**	**11**	**7**	**1122**	**34**	**1**	**1.82**
2003-04	**Ottawa**	**NHL**	**57**	**25**	**23**	**7**	**3324**	**127**	**5**	**2.29**	**7**	**3**	**4**	**398**	**13**	**0**	**1.96**
	NHL Totals		**322**	**167**	**112**	**32**	**18553**	**738**	**33**	**2.39**	**41**	**21**	**20**	**2549**	**75**	**5**	**1.77**

NHL All-Rookie Team (1997) • IHL First All-Star Team (1999)

Played in NHL All-Star Game (2003)

Rights traded to **Anaheim** by **Pittsburgh** for Sean Pronger, March 24, 1998. Traded to **Ottawa** by **Anaheim** for Ted Donato and the rights to Antti-Jussi Niemi, June 18, 1999. Traded to **St. Louis** by **Ottawa** for future considerations, June 27, 2004.

LAMOTHE, Marc (luh-MAWTH, MAHRK)

Goaltender. Catches left. 6'2", 210 lbs. Born, New Liskeard, Ont., February 27, 1974.
(Montreal's 6th choice, 92nd overall, in 1992 Entry Draft).

			Regular Season								Playoffs						
Season	Club	League	GP	W	L	T	Mins	GA	SO	Avg	GP	W	L	Mins	GA	SO	Avg
1990-91	Ottawa Jr. Sens	OCJHL	25	13	7	0	1220	82	1	4.03	....	....	....	....	....	....	....
1991-92	Kingston	OHL	42	10	25	2	2378	189	1	4.77	....	....	....	....	....	....	....
1992-93	Kingston	OHL	45	23	12	6	2489	162	1	3.91	15	8	5	753	48	1	3.82
1993-94	Kingston	OHL	48	23	20	5	2828	177	*2	3.76	6	2	2	224	12	0	3.21
1994-95	Wheeling	ECHL	13	9	2	1	737	38	0	3.10	....	....	....	....	....	....	....
	Fredericton	AHL	9	2	5	0	428	32	0	4.48	....	....	....	....	....	....	....
1995-96	Fredericton	AHL	23	5	9	3	1166	73	1	3.76	3	1	2	161	9	0	3.36
1996-97	Indianapolis Ice	IHL	38	20	14	4	2271	100	1	2.64	1	0	0	20	1	0	3.00
1997-98	Indianapolis Ice	IHL	31	18	10	2	1772	72	3	2.44	4	1	3	177	10	0	3.38
1998-99	Indianapolis Ice	IHL	32	9	16	6	1823	115	1	3.78	6	3	3	338	10	*2	1.78
99-2000	**Chicago**	**NHL**	**2**	**1**	**1**	**0**	**116**	**10**	**0**	**5.17**	....	....	....	....	....	....	....
	Cleveland	IHL	44	19	18	4	2455	112	2	2.74	4	2	2	325	12	0	2.21
2000-01	Syracuse Crunch	AHL	42	17	15	7	2323	112	2	2.89	....	....	....	....	....	....	....
2001-02	Hamilton Bulldogs	AHL	45	22	19	2	2569	102	3	2.38	9	6	3	551	18	0	1.96
2002-03	Grand Rapids	AHL	*60	*33	18	8	*3438	122	6	2.13	15	10	5	945	29	1	1.84
2003-04	**Detroit**	**NHL**	**2**	**1**	**0**	**1**	**125**	**3**	**0**	**1.44**	....	....	....	....	....	....	....
	Grand Rapids	AHL	43	21	16	5	2535	87	4	2.06	4	0	3	200	12	0	3.60
	NHL Totals		**4**	**2**	**1**	**1**	**241**	**13**	**0**	**3.24**	....	....	....	....	....	....	....

AHL First All-Star Team (2003) • Baz Bastien Memorial Trophy (Top Goaltender – AHL) (2003)

Signed as a free agent by **Chicago**, September 26, 1996. Signed as a free agent by **Edmonton**, August 16, 2001. Signed as a free agent by **Detroit**, August 5, 2002.

LASSILA, Teemu (la-SIHL-uh, TEE-moo) NSH.

Goaltender. Catches left. 5'11", 180 lbs. Born, Helsinki, Finland, March 26, 1983.
(Nashville's 9th choice, 117th overall, in 2003 Entry Draft).

			Regular Season								Playoffs						
Season	Club	League	GP	W	L	T	Mins	GA	SO	Avg	GP	W	L	Mins	GA	SO	Avg
2001-02	TPS Turku Jr.	Finn-Jr.	43	26	12	5	2577	77	5	1.79	9	4	2	571	21	1	2.21
2002-03	Hermes Kokkola	Finland-2	21	9	5	6	1268	45	2	2.13	....	....	....	....	....	....	....
	TPS Turku	Finland	21	12	6	1	1190	38	*6	1.92	7	3	4	416	21	1	3.03
2003-04	Assat Pori	Finland	5	3	2	0	300	16	0	3.20	....	....	....	....	....	....	....
	TPS Turku	Finland	19	7	5	6	1079	31	3	*1.72	12	8	4	680	17	*4	1.50

LAWSON, Tom (LAW-suhn, TAWM) COL.

Goaltender. Catches left. 6'5", 200 lbs. Born, Whitby, Ont., August 15, 1979.

			Regular Season								Playoffs						
Season	Club	League	GP	W	L	T	Mins	GA	SO	Avg	GP	W	L	Mins	GA	SO	Avg
1998-99	Markham Waxers	OPJHL	32	19	10	2	1793	101	....	3.38	....	....	....	....	....	....	....
99-2000	Bowling Green	CCHA	3	0	3	0	173	14	0	4.86	....	....	....	....	....	....	....
2000-01	Knoxville Speed	UHL	35	16	16	2	2002	116	0	3.48	....	....	....	....	....	....	....
	Cincinnati	AHL	1	0	0	0	23	1	0	2.58	....	....	....	....	....	....	....
2001-02	Anchorage Aces	WCHL	1	1	0	0	54	2	0	2.22	....	....	....	....	....	....	....
2002-03	Fort Wayne	UHL	56	29	15	10	3178	106	*7	*2.00	12	*11	1	750	21	*2	*1.68
2003-04	Hershey Bears	AHL	32	13	12	2	1693	65	4	2.30	....	....	....	....	....	....	....
	Reading Royals	ECHL	2	0	2	0	120	10	0	5.02	....	....	....	....	....	....	....

UHL First All-Star Team (2003)

Signed as a free agent by **Knoxville** (UHL) after leaving Bowling Green (CCHA), September 30, 2000. • Missed majority of 2001-02 season recovering from leg injury suffered in game vs. Colorado (WCHL), October 13, 2001. Signed as a free agent by **Fort Wayne** (UHL), October 13, 2002. Signed as a free agent by **Colorado**, June 3, 2003.

LECLAIRE, Pascal (lah-CLAIR, pas-KAL) CBJ

Goaltender. Catches left. 6'2", 190 lbs. Born, Repentigny, Que., November 7, 1982.
(Columbus' 1st choice, 8th overall, in 2001 Entry Draft).

			Regular Season								Playoffs						
Season	Club	League	GP	W	L	T	Mins	GA	SO	Avg	GP	W	L	Mins	GA	SO	Avg
1997-98	Cap-d-Madeleine	QAAA	26	6	17	3	1580	127	0	4.90	....	....	....	....	....	....	....
1998-99	Halifax	QMJHL	33	19	11	1	1828	96	2	3.15	1	0	0	17	2	0	7.06
99-2000	Halifax	QMJHL	31	16	8	4	1729	103	1	3.57	5	1	2	198	12	0	3.65
2000-01	Halifax	QMJHL	35	14	16	5	2111	126	1	3.58	2	0	2	109	10	0	5.49
2001-02	Montreal Rocket	QMJHL	45	15	23	4	2513	138	1	3.29	7	3	4	441	15	0	*2.04
2002-03	Syracuse Crunch	AHL	36	8	21	3	1886	112	0	3.56	....	....	....	....	....	....	....
2003-04	**Columbus**	**NHL**	**2**	**0**	**2**	**0**	**119**	**7**	**0**	**3.53**	....	....	....	....	....	....	....
	Syracuse Crunch	AHL	44	21	16	3	2447	125	2	3.06	3	1	2	142	12	0	5.07
	NHL Totals		**2**	**0**	**2**	**0**	**119**	**7**	**0**	**3.53**	....	....	....	....	....	....	....

LEGACE, Manny (LEH-gah-see, MAN-nee) DET.

Goaltender. Catches left. 5'9", 162 lbs. Born, Toronto, Ont., February 4, 1973.
(Hartford's 5th choice, 188th overall, in 1993 Entry Draft).

			Regular Season								Playoffs						
Season	Club	League	GP	W	L	T	Mins	GA	SO	Avg	GP	W	L	Mins	GA	SO	Avg
1987-88	Alliston Hornets	OJHL-C	16	7	9	0	960	83	0	5.17	....	....	....	....	....	....	....
1988-89	Vaughan Raiders	MTJHL	23	....	....	....	1303	92	1	4.24	....	....	....	....	....	....	....
1989-90	Vaughan Raiders	MTJHL	21	8	11	1	1180	89	1	4.53	....	....	....	....	....	....	....
	Thornhill	MTJHL	8	3	3	2	480	30	0	3.75	....	....	....	....	....	....	....
1990-91	Niagara Falls	OHL	30	13	11	2	1515	107	0	4.24	4	1	1	119	10	0	5.04
1991-92	Niagara Falls	OHL	43	21	16	3	2384	143	0	3.60	14	8	5	791	56	0	4.25
1992-93	Niagara Falls	OHL	48	22	19	3	2630	171	0	3.90	4	0	4	240	18	0	4.50
1993-94	Canada	Nat-Tm	16	8	6	0	859	36	2	2.51	....	....	....	....	....	....	....
1994-95	Springfield Falcons	AHL	39	12	17	6	2169	128	2	3.54	....	....	....	....	....	....	....
1995-96	Springfield Falcons	AHL	37	20	12	4	2196	83	*5	*2.27	4	1	3	220	18	0	4.91
1996-97	Springfield Falcons	AHL	36	17	14	5	2119	107	1	3.03	12	9	3	745	25	*2	2.01
	Richmond	ECHL	3	2	1	0	157	8	0	3.05	....	....	....	....	....	....	....
1997-98	Springfield Falcons	AHL	6	4	2	0	345	16	0	2.78	....	....	....	....	....	....	....
	Las Vegas Thunder	IHL	41	18	16	4	2106	111	1	3.16	4	1	3	237	16	0	4.05
1998-99	**Los Angeles**	**NHL**	**17**	**2**	**9**	**2**	**899**	**39**	**0**	**2.60**	....	....	....	....	....	....	....
	Long Beach	IHL	33	22	8	1	1796	67	2	2.24	6	4	2	338	9	0	*1.60
99-2000	**Detroit**	**NHL**	**4**	**4**	**0**	**0**	**240**	**11**	**0**	**2.75**	....	....	....	....	....	....	....
	Manitoba Moose	IHL	42	17	18	5	2409	104	2	2.59	2	0	2	141	7	0	2.97
2000-01	**Detroit**	**NHL**	**39**	**24**	**5**	**5**	**2136**	**73**	**2**	**2.05**	....	....	....	....	....	....	....

2001-02 ◆	Detroit	NHL	20	10	6	2	1117	45	1	2.42	1	0	0	11	1	0	5.45
2002-03	Detroit	NHL	25	14	5	4	1406	51	0	2.18	....	....	....	....	....	....	....
2003-04	Detroit	NHL	41	23	10	5	2325	82	3	2.12	4	2	2	220	8	0	2.18
	NHL Totals		146	77	35	18	8123	301	6	2.22	5	2	2	231	9	0	2.34

OHL First All-Star Team (1993) • AHL First All-Star Team (1996) • Shared Harry "Hap" Holmes Memorial Trophy (fewest goals against – AHL) (1996) with Scott Langkow • Baz Bastien Memorial Trophy (Top Goaltender – AHL) (1996)

Rights transferred to **Carolina** after **Hartford** franchise relocated, June 25, 1997. Traded to **Los Angeles** by **Carolina** for future considerations, July 31, 1998. Signed as a free agent by **Detroit**, August 9, 1999. Claimed on waivers by **Vancouver** from **Detroit**, September 30, 1999. Claimed on waivers by **Detroit** from **Vancouver**, October 13, 1999.

LEHTO, Mika (leh-TOH, MEE-kuh) PIT.

Goaltender. Catches left. 5'11", 175 lbs. Born, Vammala, Finland, April 12, 1979.
(Pittsburgh's 8th choice, 224th overall, in 1998 Entry Draft).

			Regular Season								Playoffs						
Season	Club	League	GP	W	L	T	Mins	GA	SO	Avg	GP	W	L	Mins	GA	SO	Avg
1996-97	Assat Pori Jr.	Finn-Jr.	6	....	....	....	304	17	0	3.35	....	....	....	....	....	....	....
1997-98	Assat Pori Jr.	Finn-Jr.	36	16	14	6	2160	103	2	2.86	....	....	....	....	....	....	....
	Assat Pori	Finland	1	0	0	0	35	1	0	1.71	1	0	0	17	0	0	0.00
1998-99	Assat Pori Jr.	Finn-Jr.	20	7	10	3	1202	68	....	3.39	....	....	....	....	....	....	....
	Assat Pori	Finland	15	4	6	1	773	38	1	2.95	....	....	....	....	....	....	....
99-2000	Assat Pori	Finland	23	4	11	3	1099	87	0	4.75	....	....	....	....	....	....	....
	Hermes Kokkola	Finland-2	6	3	2	1	339	19	1	3.36	....	....	....	....	....	....	....
	Assat Pori Jr.	Finn-Jr.	2	0	0	2	118	8	0	4.05	....	....	....	....	....	....	....
2000-01	JYP Jyvaskyla	Finland	41	12	20	8	2384	126	1	3.17	....	....	....	....	....	....	....
2001-02	JYP Jyvaskyla	Finland	37	10	17	10	2167	107	6	2.96	....	....	....	....	....	....	....
2002-03	Tappara Tampere	Finland	27	12	11	4	1512	45	3	*1.79	14	*10	3	928	23	*2	*1.49
2003-04	Tappara Tampere	Finland	*46	17	19	8	2639	111	3	2.52	3	1	2	190	5	0	1.58

LEHTONEN, Kari (LEH-tuh-nehn, KAH-ree) ATL.

Goaltender. Catches left. 6'3", 205 lbs. Born, Helsinki, Finland, November 16, 1983.
(Atlanta's 1st choice, 2nd overall, in 2002 Entry Draft).

			Regular Season								Playoffs						
Season	Club	League	GP	W	L	T	Mins	GA	SO	Avg	GP	W	L	Mins	GA	SO	Avg
1998-99	Jokerit Helsinki C	Finn-Jr.	17	....	....	....	1020	61	0	3.61	....	....	....	....	....	....	....
	Jokerit Helsinki B	Finn-Jr.	....	....	....	....	....	....	....	....	4	2	2	240	7	0	1.75
99-2000	Jokerit Helsinki Jr.	Finn-Jr.	33	21	9	3	1974	86	2	2.61	12	9	3	758	14	4	1.11
2000-01	Jokerit Helsinki	Finn-Jr.	31	20	9	1	1799	71	3	2.37	1	0	1	54	4	0	4.44
	Jokerit Helsinki	Finland	4	3	0	0	189	6	0	1.90	....	....	....	....	....	....	....
2001-02	Jokerit Helsinki Jr.	Finn-Jr.	6	5	1	0	360	11	1	1.83	....	....	....	....	....	....	....
	Jokerit Helsinki	Finland	23	13	5	3	1242	37	4	1.79	*11	*8	3	*623	18	*3	1.73
2002-03	Jokerit Helsinki	Finland	45	*23	14	6	2635	87	5	1.98	10	6	4	626	17	*2	1.63
2003-04	Atlanta	NHL	4	4	0	0	240	5	1	1.25	....	....	....	....	....	....	....
	Chicago Wolves	AHL	39	20	14	2	2192	88	3	2.41	10	6	4	663	23	1	2.08
	NHL Totals		4	4	0	0	240	5	1	1.25	....	....	....	....	....	....	....

LEIGHTON, Michael (LAY-tohn, MIGH-kuhl) CHI.

Goaltender. Catches left. 6'3", 186 lbs. Born, Petrolia, Ont., May 19, 1981.
(Chicago's 5th choice, 165th overall, in 1999 Entry Draft).

			Regular Season								Playoffs						
Season	Club	League	GP	W	L	T	Mins	GA	SO	Avg	GP	W	L	Mins	GA	SO	Avg
1997-98	Petrolia Jets	OJHL-B	30	....	....	....	1583	87	2	3.30	....	....	....	....	....	....	....
1998-99	Windsor Spitfires	OHL	28	4	17	2	1389	112	0	4.84	3	0	1	80	10	0	7.50
99-2000	Windsor Spitfires	OHL	42	17	17	2	2272	118	1	3.12	12	5	6	616	32	0	3.12
2000-01	Windsor Spitfires	OHL	54	32	13	5	3035	138	2	2.73	9	4	5	519	27	1	3.12
2001-02	Norfolk Admirals	AHL	52	27	16	8	3114	111	6	2.14	4	1	2	238	8	0	2.02
2002-03	Chicago	NHL	8	2	3	2	447	21	1	2.82	....	....	....	....	....	....	....
	Norfolk Admirals	AHL	36	18	13	5	2184	91	4	2.50	4	3	1	240	7	1	1.75
2003-04	Chicago	NHL	34	6	18	8	1988	99	2	2.99	....	....	....	....	....	....	....
	Norfolk Admirals	AHL	18	10	7	1	1081	33	1	1.83	4	2	1	212	2	2	0.57
	NHL Totals		42	8	21	10	2435	120	3	2.96	....	....	....	....	....	....	....

AHL All-Rookie Team (2002)

LENEVEU, David (LEH-neh-voo, DAY-vihd) PHX.

Goaltender. Catches left. 6'1", 187 lbs. Born, Fernie, B.C., May 23, 1983.
(Phoenix's 3rd choice, 46th overall, in 2002 Entry Draft).

			Regular Season								Playoffs						
Season	Club	League	GP	W	L	T	Mins	GA	SO	Avg	GP	W	L	Mins	GA	SO	Avg
99-2000	Fernie Ghostriders	AWJHL	22	15	2	0	1140	48	0	2.49	....	....	....	....	....	....	....
2000-01	Nanaimo Clippers	BCHL	41	....	....	....	2330	127	6	3.29	....	....	....	....	....	....	....
2001-02	Cornell Big Red	ECAC	14	11	2	1	842	21	2	*1.50	....	....	....	....	....	....	....
2002-03	Cornell Big Red	ECAC	32	*28	3	1	1946	39	*9	*1.20	....	....	....	....	....	....	....
2003-04	Springfield Falcons	AHL	38	16	19	3	2217	102	1	2.76	....	....	....	....	....	....	....

ECAC All-Rookie Team (2002) • ECAC First All-Star Team (2003) • ECAC Player of the Year (2003) (co-winner - Christopher Higgins) • NCAA East First All-American Team (2003)

LITTLE, Neil (LIH-tuhl, NEEL) PHI.

Goaltender. Catches left. 6'1", 193 lbs. Born, Medicine Hat, Alta., December 18, 1971.
(Philadelphia's 10th choice, 226th overall, in 1991 Entry Draft).

			Regular Season								Playoffs						
Season	Club	League	GP	W	L	T	Mins	GA	SO	Avg	GP	W	L	Mins	GA	SO	Avg
1989-90	Estevan Bruins	SJHL	46	21	19	4	2707	150	1	3.32	....	....	....	....	....	....	....
1990-91	RPI Engineers	ECAC	18	9	8	0	1032	71	0	4.13	....	....	....	....	....	....	....
1991-92	RPI Engineers	ECAC	28	11	11	3	1532	96	0	3.76	....	....	....	....	....	....	....
1992-93	RPI Engineers	ECAC	*31	*19	9	3	*1801	88	0	2.93	....	....	....	....	....	....	....
1993-94	RPI Engineers	ECAC	27	16	7	4	1570	88	0	3.36	....	....	....	....	....	....	....
	Hershey Bears	AHL	1	0	0	0	18	1	0	3.33	....	....	....	....	....	....	....
1994-95	Hershey Bears	AHL	19	5	7	3	919	60	0	3.91	....	....	....	....	....	....	....
	Johnstown Chiefs	ECHL	16	7	6	1	897	55	0	3.68	3	0	2	145	11	0	4.55
1995-96	Hershey Bears	AHL	48	21	18	6	2680	149	0	3.34	1	0	1	60	4	0	4.02
1996-97	Philadelphia	AHL	54	31	12	7	3007	145	0	2.89	10	6	4	620	20	1	*1.94
1997-98	Philadelphia	AHL	51	*31	11	7	2960	145	0	2.94	*20	*15	5	*1193	48	*3	2.41
1998-99	Grand Rapids	IHL	50	18	21	5	2740	144	3	3.15	....	....	....	....	....	....	....
99-2000	Philadelphia	AHL	51	26	18	2	2830	143	1	3.03	5	2	3	298	15	0	3.02
2000-01	Philadelphia	AHL	*58	22	27	4	3117	148	2	2.85	10	5	5	631	23	1	2.19
2001-02	Philadelphia	NHL	1	0	1	0	60	4	0	4.00	....	....	....	....	....	....	....
	Philadelphia	AHL	35	13	15	7	2079	70	2	2.02	5	2	3	298	13	0	2.62
2002-03	Philadelphia	AHL	42	18	19	4	2478	103	4	2.49	....	....	....	....	....	....	....
2003-04	Philadelphia	NHL	1	0	1	0	33	2	0	3.64	....	....	....	....	....	....	....
	Philadelphia	AHL	34	21	12	1	1900	62	6	1.96	....	....	....	....	....	....	....
	NHL Totals		2	0	2	0	93	6	0	3.87	....	....	....	....	....	....	....

ECAC First All-Star Team (1993) • NCAA East Second All-American Team (1993)

LIV, Stefan (LIHV, STEH-fuhn) DET.

Goaltender. Catches left. 6', 172 lbs. Born, Jonkoping, Sweden, December 21, 1980.
(Detroit's 3rd choice, 102nd overall, in 2000 Entry Draft).

			Regular Season								Playoffs						
Season	Club	League	GP	W	L	T	Mins	GA	SO	Avg	GP	W	L	Mins	GA	SO	Avg
1997-98	HV 71 Jr.	Swede-Jr.	17	....	....	....	1020	47	....	2.76	....	....	....	....	....	....	....
1998-99	HV 71 Jonkoping	Sweden	DID NOT PLAY – SPARE GOALTENDER														
99-2000	HV 71 Jr.	Swede-Jr.	10	....	....	....	600	17	2	1.70	....	....	....	....	....	....	....
	Tranas AIF	Swede-2	9	....	....	....	541	20	0	2.17	....	....	....	....	....	....	....
	HV 71 Jonkoping	Sweden	12	....	....	....	716	24	1	2.01	3	....	....	178	12	0	4.04
2000-01	HV 71 Jonkoping	Sweden	*46	....	....	....	*2752	127	4	2.77	....	....	....	....	....	....	....
2001-02	HV 71 Jonkoping	Sweden	38	....	....	....	2184	95	*4	2.61	8	....	....	517	27	0	3.13
2002-03	HV 71 Jonkoping	Sweden	46	....	....	....	2723	124	3	2.73	7	....	....	391	17	1	2.61
2003-04	HV 71 Jonkoping	Sweden	41	....	....	....	2450	91	6	2.23	*18	....	....	*1091	35	*5	1.92

LUNDQVIST, Henrik (LUHND-kvihst, HEHN-rihk) NYR

Goaltender. Catches left. 5'11", 167 lbs. Born, Are, Sweden, March 2, 1982.
(NY Rangers' 7th choice, 205th overall, in 2000 Entry Draft).

			Regular Season								Playoffs						
Season	Club	League	GP	W	L	T	Mins	GA	SO	Avg	GP	W	L	Mins	GA	SO	Avg
1998-99	V. Frolunda Jr.	Swede-Jr.	35	....	....	....	2100	95	0	2.73	....	....	....	....	....	....	....
99-2000	V. Frolunda Jr.	Swede-Jr.	30	....	....	....	1726	73	0	2.54	5	4	1	300	7	2	1.40
2000-01	V. Frolunda 18	Swede-Jr.	2	....	....	....	120	5	0	2.50	3	2	1	182	5	0	1.62
	V. Frolunda Jr.	Swede-Jr.	19	....	....	....	1140	50	2	2.64	....	....	....	....	....	....	....
	Molndals IF	Swede-2	7	....	....	....	420	29	0	4.22	....	....	....	....	....	....	....
	Vastra Frolunda	Sweden	4	....	....	....	190	11	0	3.47	....	....	....	....	....	....	....
2001-02	Vastra Frolunda	Sweden	20	....	....	....	1152	52	2	2.71	8	8	0	489	18	*2	2.21
	Vastra Frolunda Jr.	Swede-Jr.	1	1	0	0	60	4	0	4.00	....	....	....	....	....	....	....
2002-03	Vastra Frolunda	Sweden	28	....	....	....	1650	40	*6	*1.45	12	....	....	739	26	*2	2.11
	V. Frolunda Jr.	Swede-Jr.	1	1	0	0	60	4	0	4.00	....	....	....	....	....	....	....
2003-04	Vastra Frolunda	Sweden	*48	....	....	....	*2897	105	7	2.17	10	....	....	610	20	0	1.97

LUONGO, Roberto (loo-WAHN-goh, roh-BUHR-toh) FLA.

Goaltender. Catches left. 6'3", 205 lbs. Born, Montreal, Que., April 4, 1979.
(NY Islanders' 1st choice, 4th overall, in 1997 Entry Draft).

			Regular Season								Playoffs						
Season	Club	League	GP	W	L	T	Mins	GA	SO	Avg	GP	W	L	Mins	GA	SO	Avg
1994-95	Montreal-Bourassa	QAAA	25	10	14	0	94	1465	0	3.85	....	....	....	....	....	....	....
1995-96	Val-d'Or Foreurs	QMJHL	23	6	11	4	1201	74	0	3.70	3	0	1	68	5	0	4.41
1996-97	Val-d'Or Foreurs	QMJHL	60	32	22	2	3305	171	2	3.10	13	8	5	777	44	0	3.40
1997-98	Val-d'Or Foreurs	QMJHL	54	27	20	5	3046	157	*7	3.09	*17	*14	3	*1019	37	*2	*2.18
1998-99	Val-d'Or Foreurs	QMJHL	21	6	10	2	1176	77	1	3.93	....	....	....	....	....	....	....
	Acadie-Bathurst	QMJHL	22	14	7	1	1340	74	0	3.31	*23	*16	6	*1400	64	0	2.74
99-2000	NY Islanders	NHL	24	7	14	1	1292	70	1	3.25	....	....	....	....	....	....	....
	Lowell	AHL	26	10	12	4	1517	74	1	2.93	6	3	3	359	18	0	3.01
2000-01	Florida	NHL	47	12	24	7	2628	107	5	2.44	....	....	....	....	....	....	....
	Louisville Panthers	AHL	3	1	2	0	178	10	0	3.38	....	....	....	....	....	....	....
2001-02	Florida	NHL	58	16	33	4	3030	140	4	2.77	....	....	....	....	....	....	....
2002-03	Florida	NHL	65	20	34	7	3627	164	6	2.71	....	....	....	....	....	....	....
2003-04	Florida	NHL	72	25	33	14	4252	172	7	2.43	....	....	....	....	....	....	....
	NHL Totals		266	80	138	33	14829	653	23	2.64	....	....	....	....	....	....	....

NHL Second All-Star Team (2004)

Played in NHL All-Star Game (2004)

Traded to **Florida** by **NY Islanders** with Olli Jokinen for Mark Parrish and Oleg Kvasha, June 24, 2000.

MacINTYRE, Drew (MAK-ihn-tighr, DROO) DET.

Goaltender. Catches left. 6', 173 lbs. Born, Charlottetown, P.E.I., June 24, 1983.
(Detroit's 2nd choice, 121st overall, in 2001 Entry Draft).

			Regular Season								Playoffs						
Season	Club	League	GP	W	L	T	Mins	GA	SO	Avg	GP	W	L	Mins	GA	SO	Avg
1998-99	Trenton Sting	OPJHL	20	....	....	....	1173	71	2	3.63	....	....	....	....	....	....	....
99-2000	Sherbrooke	QMJHL	24	10	7	2	1253	67	0	3.21	....	....	....	....	....	....	....
2000-01	Sherbrooke	QMJHL	48	17	22	3	2552	139	4	3.27	4	0	4	238	19	0	4.78
2001-02	Sherbrooke	QMJHL	55	15	34	3	3028	201	1	3.98	....	....	....	....	....	....	....
2002-03	Sherbrooke	QMJHL	*61	31	24	5	*3515	161	2	2.75	12	5	7	767	52	0	4.07
2003-04	Toledo Storm	ECHL	11	6	4	0	574	25	0	2.61	....	....	....	....	....	....	....

• Missed majority of 2003-04 season recovering from thigh injury suffered in practice, December 27, 2003.

MALEK, Roman (MAHL-ehk, ROH-muhn) PHI.

Goaltender. Catches left. 5'11", 161 lbs. Born, Prague, Czech., September 25, 1977.
(Philadelphia's 5th choice, 158th overall, in 2001 Entry Draft).

			Regular Season								Playoffs						
Season	Club	League	GP	W	L	T	Mins	GA	SO	Avg	GP	W	L	Mins	GA	SO	Avg
1996-97	Slavia Praha Jr.	Czech-Jr.	31	....	....	....	1820	55	....	1.81	....	....	....	....	....	....	....
	HC Beroun	Czech-2	9	....	....	....	469	28	....	3.50	....	....	....	....	....	....	....
	HC Slavia Praha	Czech-2	2	....	....	....	61	8	0	7.86	....	....	....	....	....	....	....
1997-98	HC Beroun	Czech-2	36	....	....	....	2150	98	....	2.73	....	....	....	....	....	....	....
1998-99	HC Slavia Praha	Czech	18	....	....	....	830	51	....	3.69	....	....	....	....	....	....	....
99-2000	HC Slavia Praha	Czech	25	....	....	....	1342	59	....	2.64	....	....	....	....	....	....	....
	HC Beroun	Czech-2	3	....	....	....	150	7	0	2.80	....	....	....	....	....	....	....
2000-01	HC Slavia Praha	Czech	46	....	....	....	2550	100	....	2.35	11	....	....	665	28	....	2.53
2001-02	HC Slavia Praha	Czech	33	....	....	....	1967	80	....	2.44	9	....	....	485	22	....	2.72
2002-03	HC Slavia Praha	Czech	50	....	....	....	2844	77	*11	*1.62	17	....	....	1064	28	*5	1.58
2003-04	HC Slavia Praha	Czech	23	....	....	....	1273	49	2	2.31	....	....	....	....	....	....	....
	Plzen	Czech	17	....	....	....	1033	37	3	2.15	12	....	....	715	40	0	3.36

MANZATO, Daniel (man-ZA-toh, DAN-yehl) CAR.

Goaltender. Catches left. 6', 178 lbs. Born, Fribourg, Switz., January 17, 1984.
(Carolina's 3rd choice, 160th overall, in 2002 Entry Draft).

			Regular Season								Playoffs						
Season	Club	League	GP	W	L	T	Mins	GA	SO	Avg	GP	W	L	Mins	GA	SO	Avg
2000-01	Fribourg Jr.	Swiss-Jr.	36	....	....	....	2160	32	6	0.91	....	....	....	....	....	....	....
2001-02	Victoriaville Tigres	QMJHL	36	20	8	2	1894	102	0	3.23	6	3	0	249	17	0	4.09
2002-03	Victoriaville Tigres	QMJHL	48	23	18	5	2756	155	3	3.37	3	0	3	125	11	0	5.27
2003-04	Victoriaville Tigres	QMJHL	23	7	13	0	1170	78	0	4.00	....	....	....	....	....	....	....
	Kloten Flyers	Swiss	15	....	....	....	912	39	1	2.57	....	....	....	....	....	....	....
	Kloten Flyers	Swiss-Q	5	....	....	....	240	13	1	3.25	....	....	....	....	....	....	....

Signed as a free agent by **HC Kloten** (Swiss), January 5, 2004, following release by **Victoriaville** (QMJHL), January 4, 2004.

MARACLE, Norm (MAHR-ah-kuhl, NOHRM)

Goaltender. Catches left. 5'9", 195 lbs. Born, Belleville, Ont., October 2, 1974.
(Detroit's 6th choice, 126th overall, in 1993 Entry Draft).

			Regular Season								Playoffs						
Season	Club	League	GP	W	L	T	Mins	GA	SO	Avg	GP	W	L	Mins	GA	SO	Avg
1990-91	Cgy. North Stars	AMHL	29	....	....	....	1740	99	0	3.43	....	....	....	....	....	....	....
1991-92	Saskatoon Blades	WHL	29	13	6	3	1529	87	1	3.41	15	9	5	860	37	0	3.38
1992-93	Saskatoon Blades	WHL	53	27	18	3	1939	160	1	3.27	9	4	5	569	33	0	3.48
1993-94	Saskatoon Blades	WHL	56	*41	13	1	3219	148	2	2.76	16	*11	5	940	48	*1	3.06
1994-95	Adirondack	AHL	39	12	15	2	1997	119	0	3.57	....	....	....	....	....	....	....
1995-96	Adirondack	AHL	54	24	18	6	2949	135	2	2.75	1	0	1	30	4	0	8.11
1996-97	Adirondack	AHL	*68	*34	22	9	*3843	173	5	2.70	4	1	3	192	10	1	3.13
1997-98	Detroit	NHL	4	2	0	1	178	6	0	2.02	....	....	....	....	....	....	....
	Adirondack	AHL	*66	27	29	8	*3709	190	1	3.07	3	0	3	180	10	0	3.33
1998-99	Detroit	NHL	16	6	5	2	821	31	0	2.27	2	0	0	58	3	0	3.10
	Adirondack	AHL	6	3	3	0	359	18	0	3.01	....	....	....	....	....	....	....
99-2000	Atlanta	NHL	32	4	19	2	1618	94	1	3.49	....	....	....	....	....	....	....

Season	Club	League	GP	W	L	T	Mins	GA	SO	Avg	GP	W	L	Mins	GA	SO	Avg
2000-01	**Atlanta**	**NHL**	**13**	**2**	**8**	**3**	**753**	**43**	**0**	**3.43**							
	Orlando	IHL	51	33	13	3	2963	100	*8	*2.02	*16	*12	4	*1003	37	1	2.21
2001-02	**Atlanta**	**NHL**	**1**	**0**	**1**	**0**	**60**	**3**	**0**	**3.00**							
	Chicago Wolves	AHL	51	21	25	4	2919	141	3	2.90	2	0	1	55	4	0	4.36
2002-03	Chicago Wolves	AHL	49	22	18	6	2795	134	2	2.88	8	3	4	462	17	1	2.21
2003-04	Magnitogorsk	Russia	46				2463	84	8	2.05	*14			*857	22	2	1.54
	NHL Totals		**66**	**14**	**33**	**8**	**3430**	**177**	**1**	**3.10**	**2**	**0**	**0**	**58**	**3**	**0**	**3.10**

WHL East Second All-Star Team (1993) • WHL East First All-Star Team (1994) • Canadian Major Junior First All-Star Team (1994) • Canadian Major Junior Goaltender of the Year (1994) • AHL Second All-Star Team (1997, 1998) • IHL First All-Star Team (2001) • Shared James Norris Memorial Trophy (fewest goals against – IHL) (2001) with Scott Fankhouser • James Gatschene Memorial Trophy (MVP – IHL) (2001) • "Bud" Poile Trophy (Playoff MVP – IHL) (2001)

Claimed by **Atlanta** from **Detroit** in Expansion Draft, June 25, 1999. Signed as a free agent by **Magnitogorsk** (Russia), June 8, 2003.

MARKKANEN, Jussi (MAHR-kah-nehn, YOO-see) EDM.

Goaltender. Catches left. 6', 182 lbs. Born, Imatra, Finland, May 8, 1975.
(Edmonton's 5th choice, 133rd overall, in 2001 Entry Draft).

			Regular Season								Playoffs						
Season	Club	League	GP	W	L	T	Mins	GA	SO	Avg	GP	W	L	Mins	GA	SO	Avg
1991-92	SaiPa Jr.	Finn-Jr.	2				120	11	0	5.50							
1992-93	SaiPa Jr.	Finn-Jr.	7				367	28		4.58							
	SaiPa	Finland-2	16				798	60		4.51							
1993-94	SaiPa	Finland-2	30				1726	97		3.37							
1994-95	SaiPa	Finland-2	43				2493	122		2.94	3			179	5		1.68
1995-96	Tappara Jr.	Finn-Jr.	5				298	21		4.23							
	Tappara Tampere	Finland	23	11	8	2	1238	59	1	2.86							
1996-97	SaiPa	Finland	41	9	24	7	2340	132	0	3.38							
1997-98	SaiPa	Finland	*48	21	20	5	*2870	138	4	2.89	3	0	3	164	11	0	4.02
1998-99	SaiPa	Finland	48	21	19	4	2633	105	4	2.39	7	3	3	366	21	0	3.44
99-2000	SaiPa	Finland	48	4	23	9	2794	150	2	3.22							
2000-01	Tappara Tampere	Finland	52	*30	17	5	3076	107	*9	2.09	*10	7	3	*608	18	1	1.78
2001-02	**Edmonton**	**NHL**	**14**	**6**	**4**	**2**	**784**	**24**	**2**	**1.84**							
	Hamilton Bulldogs	AHL	4	2	2	0	239	9	0	2.26							
	Finland	Olympics	DID NOT PLAY – SPARE GOALTENDER														
2002-03	**Edmonton**	**NHL**	**22**	**7**	**8**	**3**	**1180**	**51**	**3**	**2.59**	**1**	**0**	**0**	**14**	**1**	**0**	**4.29**
2003-04	**NY Rangers**	**NHL**	**26**	**8**	**12**	**3**	**1244**	**53**	**2**	**2.56**							
	Edmonton	**NHL**	**7**	**2**	**2**	**2**	**394**	**12**	**0**	**1.83**							
	NHL Totals		**69**	**23**	**26**	**8**	**3602**	**140**	**7**	**2.33**	**1**	**0**	**0**	**14**	**1**	**0**	**4.29**

Traded to **NY Rangers** by **Edmonton** with Edmonton's 4th round choice (later traded to Toronto – Toronto selected Roman Kukumberg) for Brian Leetch, June 30, 2003. Traded to **Edmonton** by **NY Rangers** with Petr Nedved for Stephen Valiquette, Dwight Helminen, Edmonton's 2nd round compensatory choice (Dane Byers) in 2004 Entry Draft and future consideratons, March 3, 2004.

MARSTERS, Nathan (MAHR-stuhrs, NAY-thuhn) L.A.

Goaltender. Catches left. 6'4", 190 lbs. Born, Burlington, Ont., January 28, 1980.
(Los Angeles' 5th choice, 165th overall, in 2000 Entry Draft).

			Regular Season								Playoffs						
Season	Club	League	GP	W	L	T	Mins	GA	SO	Avg	GP	W	L	Mins	GA	SO	Avg
1997-98	Bramalea Blues	OPJHL	12				539	25	2	2.78							
1998-99	Bramalea Blues	OPJHL	29				1711	91	3	3.19							
99-2000	Bramalea Blues	OPJHL	28				1668	98	2	3.53							
	Chilliwack Chiefs	BCHL	15	9	6	0	825	63	0	4.58	20	15	5	1187	62	0	3.13
2000-01	RPI Engineers	ECAC	28	14	13	1	1631	64	*4	2.35							
2001-02	RPI Engineers	ECAC	28	15	9	3	1627	70	1	2.58							
2002-03	RPI Engineers	ECAC	24	7	15	1	1286	73	0	3.41							
2003-04	RPI Engineers	ECAC	35	*21	13	1	2094	75	*5	2.15							

ECAC Second All-Star Team (2004)

MASON, Chris (MAY-sohn, KRIHS) NSH.

Goaltender. Catches left. 6', 195 lbs. Born, Red Deer, Alta., April 20, 1976.
(New Jersey's 7th choice, 122nd overall, in 1995 Entry Draft).

			Regular Season								Playoffs						
Season	Club	League	GP	W	L	T	Mins	GA	SO	Avg	GP	W	L	Mins	GA	SO	Avg
1992-93	Red Deer Chiefs	AMHL	20				1280	76	0	3.35							
1993-94	Victoria Cougars	WHL	5	1	4	0	237	27	0	6.84							
1994-95	Prince George	WHL	44	8	30	1	2288	192	1	5.03							
1995-96	Prince George	WHL	59	16	37	1	3289	236	1	4.31							
1996-97	Prince George	WHL	50	19	24	4	2851	172	2	3.62	15	9	6	938	44	*1	2.81
1997-98	Cincinnati	AHL	47	13	19	7	2368	136	0	3.45							
1998-99	**Nashville**	**NHL**	**3**	**0**	**0**	**0**	**69**	**6**	**0**	**5.22**							
	Milwaukee	IHL	34	15	12	6	1901	92	1	2.90							
99-2000	Milwaukee	IHL	53	20	21	8	2952	137	2	2.78	3	1	2	252	11	0	2.62
2000-01	**Nashville**	**NHL**	**1**	**0**	**1**	**0**	**59**	**2**	**0**	**2.03**							
	Milwaukee	IHL	37	17	14	5	2226	87	5	2.35	4	1	3	239	12	0	3.02
2001-02	Milwaukee	AHL	48	17	21	7	2755	116	2	2.53							
2002-03	San Antonio	AHL	50	25	18	6	2914	122	1	2.51	3	0	3	195	9	0	2.77
2003-04	**Nashville**	**NHL**	**17**	**4**	**4**	**1**	**744**	**27**	**1**	**2.18**							
	Milwaukee	AHL	1	1	0	0	60	2	0	2.00							
	NHL Totals		**21**	**4**	**5**	**1**	**872**	**35**	**1**	**2.41**							

Signed as a free agent by **Anaheim**, June 27, 1997. Traded to **Nashville** by **Anaheim** with Marc Moro for Dominic Roussel, October 5, 1998. Signed as a free agent by **Florida**, August 20, 2002. Claimed by **Nashville** from **Florida** in Waiver Draft, October 3, 2003.

McELHINNEY, Curtis (MAK-IHL-ehn-ee, KUHR-this) CGY.

Goaltender. Catches left. 6'2", 185 lbs. Born, London, Ont., May 23, 1983.
(Calgary's 9th choice, 176th overall, in 2002 Entry Draft).

			Regular Season								Playoffs						
Season	Club	League	GP	W	L	T	Mins	GA	SO	Avg	GP	W	L	Mins	GA	SO	Avg
2000-01	Notre Dame	SJHL	STATISTICS NOT AVAILABLE														
2001-02	Colorado College	WCHA	9	6	0	1	441	15	1	2.04							
2002-03	Colorado College	WCHA	*37	*25	6	5	*2147	85	*4	2.37							
2003-04	Colorado College	WCHA	19	10	6	1	1015	41	2	2.42							

WCHA First All-Star Team (2003) • NCAA West Second All-American Team (2003)

McKENNA, Mike (mih-KEHN-ah, MIGHK) NSH.

Goaltender. Catches right. 6'3", 195 lbs. Born, St. Louis, MO, April 11, 1983.
(Nashville's 4th choice, 172nd overall, in 2002 Entry Draft).

			Regular Season								Playoffs						
Season	Club	League	GP	W	L	T	Mins	GA	SO	Avg	GP	W	L	Mins	GA	SO	Avg
99-2000	Springfield	NAJHL	16	6	8	0	879	48	0	3.28							
2000-01	Springfield	NAJHL	48	18	28	0	2743	209	0	4.57	2	0	2	120	11	0	5.50
2001-02	St. Lawrence	ECAC	20	7	10	1	1121	59	0	3.16							
2002-03	St. Lawrence	ECAC	15	1	7	2	618	38	0	3.69							
2003-04	St. Lawrence	ECAC	27	9	10	3	1475	60	3	2.44							

McLENNAN, Jamie (muh-KLEH-nuhn, JAY-mee) FLA.

Goaltender. Catches left. 6', 190 lbs. Born, Edmonton, Alta., June 30, 1971.
(NY Islanders' 3rd choice, 48th overall, in 1991 Entry Draft).

			Regular Season								Playoffs						
Season	Club	League	GP	W	L	T	Mins	GA	SO	Avg	GP	W	L	Mins	GA	SO	Avg
1987-88	St. Albert Royals	AMHL	21				1224	80	0	3.92							
1988-89	Spokane Chiefs	WHL	11				578	63	0	6.54							
	Lethbridge	WHL	7				368	22	0	3.59							
1989-90	Lethbridge	WHL	34	20	4	2	1690	110	1	3.91	13	6	5	677	44	0	3.90
1990-91	Lethbridge	WHL	56	32	18	4	3230	205	0	3.81	*16	8	8	*970	56	0	3.46
1991-92	Capital District	AHL	18	4	10	2	952	60	1	3.78							
	Richmond	ECHL	32	16	12	2	1837	114	0	3.72							
1992-93	Capital District	AHL	38	17	14	6	2171	117	1	3.23	1	0	1	20	5	0	15.00
1993-94	**NY Islanders**	**NHL**	**22**	**8**	**7**	**6**	**1287**	**61**	**0**	**2.84**	**2**	**0**	**1**	**82**	**6**	**0**	**4.39**
	Salt Lake	IHL	24	8	12	2	1320	80	0	3.64							
1994-95	**NY Islanders**	**NHL**	**21**	**6**	**11**	**2**	**1185**	**67**	**0**	**3.39**							
	Denver Grizzlies	IHL	4	3	0	1	239	12	0	3.00	11	8	2	640	23	1	*2.15
1995-96	**NY Islanders**	**NHL**	**13**	**3**	**9**	**1**	**636**	**39**	**0**	**3.68**							
	Utah Grizzlies	IHL	14	9	2	2	728	29	0	2.39							
	Worcester IceCats	AHL	22	14	7	1	1216	57	0	2.81	2	0	2	119	8	0	4.04
1996-97	Worcester IceCats	AHL	39	18	13	4	2152	100	2	2.79	4	2	2	262	16	0	3.67
1997-98	**St. Louis**	**NHL**	**30**	**16**	**8**	**2**	**1658**	**60**	**2**	**2.17**	**1**	**0**	**0**	**14**	**1**	**0**	**4.29**
1998-99	**St. Louis**	**NHL**	**33**	**13**	**14**	**4**	**1763**	**70**	**3**	**2.38**	**1**	**0**	**1**	**37**	**0**	**0**	**0.00**
99-2000	**St. Louis**	**NHL**	**19**	**9**	**5**	**2**	**1009**	**33**	**2**	**1.96**							
2000-01	**Minnesota**	**NHL**	**38**	**5**	**23**	**9**	**2230**	**98**	**2**	**2.64**							
2001-02	Houston Aeros	AHL	51	25	18	4	2852	130	3	2.74	14	8	6	880	31	2	2.11
2002-03	**Calgary**	**NHL**	**22**	**2**	**11**	**4**	**1165**	**58**	**0**	**2.99**							
2003-04	**Calgary**	**NHL**	**26**	**12**	**9**	**3**	**1446**	**53**	**4**	**2.20**							
	NY Rangers	**NHL**	**4**	**1**	**3**	**0**	**244**	**12**	**0**	**2.95**							
	NHL Totals		**228**	**75**	**100**	**33**	**12623**	**551**	**13**	**2.62**	**4**	**0**	**2**	**133**	**7**	**0**	**3.16**

WHL East First All-Star Team (1991) • Bill Masterton Memorial Trophy (1998)

Signed as a free agent by **St. Louis**, July 15, 1996. Claimed by **Minnesota** from **St. Louis** in Expansion Draft, June 23, 2000. Traded to **Calgary** by **Minnesota** for Calgary's 9th round choice (Mika Hannula) in 2002 Entry Draft, June 22, 2002. Traded to **NY Rangers** by **Calgary** with Blair Betts and Greg Moore for Chris Simon and NY Rangers' 7th round choice (Matt Schneider) in 2004 Entry Draft, March 6, 2004. Signed as a free agent by **Florida**, July 2, 2004.

McVICAR, Rob (mihk-VIH-kuhr, RAWB) VAN.

Goaltender. Catches left. 6'4", 195 lbs. Born, Hay River, NWT, January 15, 1982.
(Vancouver's 6th choice, 151st overall, in 2002 Entry Draft).

			Regular Season								Playoffs						
Season	Club	League	GP	W	L	T	Mins	GA	SO	Avg	GP	W	L	Mins	GA	SO	Avg
1998-99	Brandon Kings	MMMHL	21				1217	69	0	3.40							
99-2000	Brandon	WHL	14	5	6	0	687	43	0	3.76							
2000-01	Brandon	WHL	27	12	10	2	1537	76	0	2.97	5	2	3	324	13	1	2.41
2001-02	Brandon	WHL	55	*33	18	2	3276	151	1	2.77	19	11	8	1255	44	1	2.10
2002-03	Brandon	WHL	51	31	14	5	3027	136	2	2.70	13	6	7	737	32	0	2.61
2003-04	Manitoba Moose	AHL	10	4	3	2	514	25	0	2.92							
	Columbia Inferno	ECHL	19	11	5	2	1088	47	0	2.59							

MEDVEDEV, Andrei (mehd-VEH-dehv, AN-dray) CGY.

Goaltender. Catches left. 6', 211 lbs. Born, Moscow, USSR, April 1, 1983.
(Calgary's 3rd choice, 56th overall, in 2001 Entry Draft).

			Regular Season								Playoffs						
Season	Club	League	GP	W	L	T	Mins	GA	SO	Avg	GP	W	L	Mins	GA	SO	Avg
1998-99	Spartak Moscow	Russia	2				80	2	1	1.50							
99-2000	Spartak Moscow	Russia-2	STATISTICS NOT AVAILABLE														
2000-01	Spartak Moscow	Russia-2	11				208	8	0	2.31							
2001-02	Spartak Moscow 2	Russia-3	STATISTICS NOT AVAILABLE														
	Spartak Moscow	Russia	2				61	4	0	3.93							
2002-03	Spartak Moscow	Russia	17				810	28	1	2.07							
2003-04	Spartak Moscow	Russia-2	29				1640	48		1.76	3			107	3	1	1.68

MENSATOR, Lukas (MEHN-suh-tohr, loo-KAHSH) VAN.

Goaltender. Catches left. 5'8", 167 lbs. Born, Sokolov, Czech., August 18, 1984.
(Vancouver's 4th choice, 83rd overall, in 2002 Entry Draft).

			Regular Season								Playoffs						
Season	Club	League	GP	W	L	T	Mins	GA	SO	Avg	GP	W	L	Mins	GA	SO	Avg
99-2000	HC Karlovy Vary 18	Czech-Jr.	42				2406	160	0	3.99							
	Karlovy Vary Jr.	Czech-Jr.	1	1	0	0	60	3	0	3.00							
2000-01	HC Karlovy Vary 18	Czech-Jr.	6				360	15	0	2.50							
	Karlovy Vary Jr.	Czech-Jr.	19				1085	60	0	3.32							
2001-02	Karlovy Vary Jr.	Czech-Jr.	31				1809	93	0	3.08	9			459	17	0	2.22
	Banik CHZ Sokolov	Czech-3	3				180	12	0	4.00							
2002-03	Ottawa 67's	OHL	42	26	8	5	2395	122	0	3.06	*23	13	8	*1381	63	*2	2.74
2003-04	Ottawa 67's	OHL	50	18	22	7	2924	162	0	3.32	7	3	4	447	23	0	3.09

Signed as a free agent by **HC Karlovy Vary** (Czech) with Vancouver retaining NHL rights, May 17, 2004.

MICHAUD, Olivier (MEE-shoh, OH-lihv-ee-ay) MTL.

Goaltender. Catches left. 5'11", 179 lbs. Born, Beloeil, Que., September 14, 1983.

			Regular Season								Playoffs						
Season	Club	League	GP	W	L	T	Mins	GA	SO	Avg	GP	W	L	Mins	GA	SO	Avg
1998-99	Eclaireur Bantams	QAHA	23	14	4	5	1380	58		2.50							
99-2000	Antoine-Girouard	QAAA	7	6	1	0	420	15	1	2.14							
	Charles Lemonthe	QAAA	16	8	4	2	886	57	0	3.86	16	8	8	1015	29	2	1.71
	Shawinigan	QMJHL	1	0	1	0	49	2	0	2.44							
2000-01	Shawinigan	QMJHL	21	12	4	4	1096	54	1	2.96	3	1	2	150	6	0	2.41
2001-02	**Montreal**	**NHL**	**1**	**0**	**0**	**0**	**18**	**0**	**0**	**0.00**							
	Shawinigan	QMJHL	46	29	11	3	2650	108	3	*2.45	12	7	5	744	36	0	2.91
2002-03	Shawinigan	QMJHL	27	8	13	3	1497	82	1	3.29							
	Baie-Comeau	QMJHL	31	23	5	2	1775	90	3	3.04	12	7	5	748	38	0	3.05
2003-04	Columbus	ECHL	22	8	10	2	1234	62	1	3.01							
	Hamilton Bulldogs	AHL	16	4	7	3	900	38	2	2.53							
	NHL Totals		**1**	**0**	**0**	**0**	**18**	**0**	**0**	**0.00**							

Signed as a free agent by **Montreal**, September 18, 2001. • Promoted to **Montreal** from **Shawinigan** (QMJHL) and replaced injured Jose Theodore, October 26, 2001. • Returned to **Shawinigan** (QMJHL) by **Montreal**, November 5, 2001.

MILLER, Ryan (MIHL-luhr, RIGH-uhn) BUF.

Goaltender. Catches left. 6'2", 150 lbs. Born, East Lansing, MI, July 17, 1980.
(Buffalo's 7th choice, 138th overall, in 1999 Entry Draft).

			Regular Season								Playoffs						
Season	Club	League	GP	W	L	T	Mins	GA	SO	Avg	GP	W	L	Mins	GA	SO	Avg
1997-98	Sault Ste. Marie	NAJHL	37	21	14	0	2113	82	3	2.33	2	0	2	158	7	0	2.66
1998-99	Sault Ste. Marie	NAJHL	47	31	14	1	2711	104	8	2.30	4	2	2	218	10	1	2.76
99-2000	Michigan State	CCHA	26	16	5	3	1525	39	*8	*1.53							
2000-01	Michigan State	CCHA	40	*31	5	4	2447	54	*10	*1.32							
2001-02	Michigan State	CCHA	40	26	9	5	2411	71	*8	*1.77							
2002-03	**Buffalo**	**NHL**	**15**	**6**	**8**	**1**	**912**	**40**	**1**	**2.63**							
	Rochester	AHL	47	23	18	5	2817	110	2	2.34	3	1	2	190	13	0	4.11

2003-04	**Buffalo**	**NHL**	**3**	**0**	**3**	**0**	**178**	**15**	**0**	**5.06**	....	....	....	....	....	....	....
	Rochester	AHL	60	27	25	7	3579	132	5	2.21	14	7	7	857	26	2	1.82
	NHL Totals		**18**	**6**	**11**	**1**	**1090**	**55**	**1**	**3.03**	....	....	....	....	....	....	....

CCHA Second All-Star Team (2000) • CCHA First All-Star Team (2001, 2002) • NCAA West First All-American Team (2001, 2002) • Hobey Baker Memorial Award (Top U.S. Collegiate Player) (2001) • CCHA Player of the Year (2002)

MOIR, Kyle (MOI-uhr, KIGHL) NSH.

Goaltender. Catches left. 6'2", 190 lbs. Born, Calgary, Alta., May 25, 1986.
(Nashville's 4th choice, 139th overall, in 2004 Entry Draft).

			Regular Season								Playoffs						
Season	Club	League	GP	W	L	T	Mins	GA	SO	Avg	GP	W	L	Mins	GA	SO	Avg
2002-03	Calgary Flames	AMHL	15	8	2	4	922	44	0	2.86	....	....	....	....	....	....	....
	Swift Current	WHL	7	4	1	0	283	14	1	2.97	1	0	1	60	7	0	7.00
2003-04	Swift Current	WHL	46	22	15	4	2460	119	3	2.90	1	0	0	20	2	0	6.00

MONTOYA, Al (mawn-TOI-uh, AL) NYR

Goaltender. Catches left. 6'1", 190 lbs. Born, Chicago, IL, February 13, 1985.
(NY Rangers' 1st choice, 6th overall, in 2004 Entry Draft).

			Regular Season								Playoffs						
Season	Club	League	GP	W	L	T	Mins	GA	SO	Avg	GP	W	L	Mins	GA	SO	Avg
99-2000	Loyola Academy	Hi-School	28	12	13	3	1685	56	1	2.01	....	....	....	....	....	....	....
2000-01	Texas Tornados	NAJHL	15	10	3	0	780	38	0	2.92	1	1	0	60	2	0	2.00
	U.S. National	Nat-Tm	2	2	0	0	120	4	0	2.00	....	....	....	....	....	....	....
2001-02	U.S. National U-17	USDP	34	11	16	2	1914	103	0	3.23	....	....	....	....	....	....	....
2002-03	U. of Michigan	CCHA	*43	*30	10	3	*2547	99	4	2.33	....	....	....	....	....	....	....
2003-04	U. of Michigan	CCHA	*40	*26	12	2	*2340	87	6	2.23	....	....	....	....	....	....	....

CCHA All-Rookie Team (2003) • NCAA West Second All-American Team (2004)

MORRISON, Mike (MOHR-ih-suhn, MIGHK) EDM.

Goaltender. Catches right. 6'3", 194 lbs. Born, Medford, MA, July 11, 1979.
(Edmonton's 8th choice, 186th overall, in 1998 Entry Draft).

			Regular Season								Playoffs						
Season	Club	League	GP	W	L	T	Mins	GA	SO	Avg	GP	W	L	Mins	GA	SO	Avg
1997-98	Exeter Academy	Hi-School	27	15	11	2	1632	64	1	2.35	....	....	....	....	....	....	....
1998-99	University of Maine	H-East	11	3	0	1	347	10	1	1.73	....	....	....	....	....	....	....
99-2000	University of Maine	H-East	12	7	2	1	608	27	1	2.67	....	....	....	....	....	....	....
2000-01	University of Maine	H-East	10	2	3	3	490	16	1	1.96	....	....	....	....	....	....	....
2001-02	University of Maine	H-East	30	20	3	4	1645	60	2	2.19	....	....	....	....	....	....	....
2002-03	Columbus	ECHL	38	9	18	6	1948	113	1	3.48	....	....	....	....	....	....	....
2003-04	Toronto	AHL	27	12	8	2	1309	55	3	2.52	....	....	....	....	....	....	....

Hockey East First All-Star Team (2002)

MOSS, Tyler (MAWS, TIGH-luhr)

Goaltender. Catches right. 6', 185 lbs. Born, Ottawa, Ont., June 29, 1975.
(Tampa Bay's 2nd choice, 29th overall, in 1993 Entry Draft).

			Regular Season								Playoffs						
Season	Club	League	GP	W	L	T	Mins	GA	SO	Avg	GP	W	L	Mins	GA	SO	Avg
1991-92	Nepean Raiders	OCJHL	26	7	12	1	1335	109	0	4.90	....	....	....	....	....	....	....
1992-93	Kingston	OHL	31	13	7	5	1537	97	0	3.79	6	1	2	228	19	0	5.00
1993-94	Kingston	OHL	13	6	4	3	795	42	1	3.17	3	0	2	136	8	0	3.53
1994-95	Kingston	OHL	*57	33	17	5	*3249	164	1	3.03	6	2	4	333	27	0	4.86
1995-96	Atlanta Knights	IHL	40	11	19	4	2030	138	1	4.08	3	0	3	213	11	0	3.10
1996-97	Adirondack	AHL	11	1	5	2	507	42	1	4.97	....	....	....	....	....	....	....
	Grand Rapids	IHL	15	5	6	1	715	35	0	2.94	....	....	....	....	....	....	....
	Muskegon Fury	ColHL	2	1	1	0	119	5	0	2.51	....	....	....	....	....	....	....
	Saint John Flames	AHL	9	6	1	1	534	17	0	1.91	5	2	3	242	15	0	3.72
1997-98	**Calgary**	**NHL**	**6**	**2**	**3**	**1**	**367**	**20**	**0**	**3.27**	....	....	....	....	....	....	....
	Saint John Flames	AHL	39	19	10	7	2194	91	0	2.49	15	8	5	761	37	0	2.91
1998-99	**Calgary**	**NHL**	**11**	**3**	**7**	**0**	**550**	**23**	**0**	**2.51**	....	....	....	....	....	....	....
	Saint John Flames	AHL	9	2	5	1	475	25	0	3.16	....	....	....	....	....	....	....
	Orlando	IHL	9	6	2	1	515	21	1	2.45	17	10	7	1017	53	0	3.13
99-2000	Wilkes-Barre	AHL	4	1	1	1	188	11	0	3.52	....	....	....	....	....	....	....
	Kansas City Blades	IHL	36	18	12	5	2116	105	3	2.98	....	....	....	....	....	....	....
2000-01	**Carolina**	**NHL**	**12**	**1**	**6**	**0**	**557**	**37**	**0**	**3.99**	....	....	....	....	....	....	....
	Cincinnati	IHL	9	5	3	1	506	24	2	2.85	....	....	....	....	....	....	....
2001-02	Lowell	AHL	43	20	16	7	2572	106	1	2.47	....	....	....	....	....	....	....
2002-03	**Vancouver**	**NHL**	**1**	**0**	**0**	**0**	**22**	**1**	**0**	**2.73**	....	....	....	....	....	....	....
	Manitoba Moose	AHL	42	21	15	5	2502	117	3	2.81	10	6	4	618	23	0	2.23
2003-04	Manitoba Moose	AHL	32	10	16	5	1883	91	3	2.90	....	....	....	....	....	....	....
	Toronto	AHL	16	7	9	0	932	41	3	2.64	3	1	2	211	8	0	2.28
	NHL Totals		**30**	**6**	**16**	**1**	**1496**	**81**	**0**	**3.25**	....	....	....	....	....	....	....

OHL All-Rookie Team (1993) • OHL First All-Star Team (1995) • Shared Harry "Hap" Holmes Memorial Trophy (fewest goals against – AHL) (1998) with Jean-Sebastien Giguere

Traded to **Calgary** by **Tampa Bay** for Jamie Huscroft, March 18, 1997. Traded to **Pittsburgh** by **Calgary** with Rene Corbet for Brad Werenka, March 14, 2000. Signed as a free agent by **Carolina**, August 9, 2000. Signed as a free agent by **Vancouver**, July 5, 2002. Traded to **Edmonton** by **Vancouver** for Peter Sarno, February 16, 2004.

MULLER, Robert (MEW-luhr, RAW-buhrt) WSH.

Goaltender. Catches left. 5'8", 165 lbs. Born, Rosenheim, West Germany, June 25, 1980.
(Washington's 9th choice, 275th overall, in 2001 Entry Draft).

			Regular Season								Playoffs						
Season	Club	League	GP	W	L	T	Mins	GA	SO	Avg	GP	W	L	Mins	GA	SO	Avg
1997-98	EHC Klostersee	German-3					STATISTICS NOT AVAILABLE										
1998-99	Rosenheim	Germany	33	....	....	....	1863	105	1	3.38	....	....	....	....	....	....	....
99-2000	Rosenheim	Germany	39	....	....	....	2228	131	1	3.53	....	....	....	....	....	....	....
2000-01	Adler Mannheim	Germany	23	....	....	....	1195	49	1	2.46	2	....	....	103	2	0	1.17
	Germany	Olympic-Q	1	1	0	0	60	4	0	4.00	....	....	....	....	....	....	....
2001-02	Adler Mannheim	Germany	15	....	....	....	637	26	1	2.45	....	....	....	....	....	....	....
	Germany	Olympics	2	0	1	0	78	4	0	3.07	....	....	....	....	....	....	....
2002-03	Krefeld Pinguine	Germany	47	....	....	....	2762	107	5	2.32	14	....	....	843	28	*1	*1.99
2003-04	Krefeld Pinguine	Germany	49	....	....	....	2893	131	6	2.72	....	....	....	....	....	....	....

MUNCE, Ryan (MUNTS, RIGH-uhn) L.A.

Goaltender. Catches left. 6'2", 180 lbs. Born, Mississauga, Ont., April 16, 1985.
(Los Angeles' 5th choice, 82nd overall, in 2003 Entry Draft).

			Regular Season								Playoffs						
Season	Club	League	GP	W	L	T	Mins	GA	SO	Avg	GP	W	L	Mins	GA	SO	Avg
2002-03	Sarnia Sting	OHL	27	15	7	0	1410	62	3	2.64	4	1	1	149	8	1	3.22
2003-04	Sarnia Sting	OHL	54	28	21	4	3160	158	2	3.00	5	1	4	298	17	0	3.42

MUNRO, Adam (MUHN-roh, A-duhm) CHI.

Goaltender. Catches left. 6'2", 219 lbs. Born, St. George, Ont., November 12, 1982.
(Chicago's 1st choice, 29th overall, in 2001 Entry Draft).

			Regular Season								Playoffs						
Season	Club	League	GP	W	L	T	Mins	GA	SO	Avg	GP	W	L	Mins	GA	SO	Avg
1997-98	Brantford Classics	OMHA	15	13	2	0	660	20	*4	*1.36	....	....	....	....	....	....	....
1998-99	Brant County	OJHL-B	10	....	....	....	348	30	0	5.17	....	....	....	....	....	....	....
	Bowmanville	OPJHL	14	....	....	....	816	50	0	3.68	....	....	....	....	....	....	....
	Erie Otters	OHL	1	0	0	0	1	0	0	0.00	....	....	....	....	....	....	....
99-2000	Bowmanville	OPJHL	2	2	0	0	125	5	0	2.40	....	....	....	....	....	....	....
	Erie Otters	OHL	22	8	7	1	948	48	1	3.04	1	0	0	5	1	0	12.00
2000-01	Erie Otters	OHL	41	26	6	6	2283	88	*4	2.31	10	6	2	509	27	1	3.18
2001-02	Erie Otters	OHL	43	24	13	1	2277	128	3	3.37	6	4	2	361	17	0	2.83
2002-03	Erie Otters	OHL	8	2	6	0	426	24	1	3.38	....	....	....	....	....	....	....
	Sault Ste. Marie	OHL	42	20	20	2	2494	160	1	3.85	4	0	4	240	12	0	3.00
2003-04	**Chicago**	**NHL**	**7**	**1**	**5**	**1**	**426**	**26**	**0**	**3.66**	....	....	....	....	....	....	....
	Norfolk Admirals	AHL	12	5	4	1	695	26	0	2.24	....	....	....	....	....	....	....
	Gwinnett	ECHL	6	4	1	1	370	17	0	2.76	1	0	1	60	2	0	2.01
	NHL Totals		**7**	**1**	**5**	**1**	**426**	**26**	**0**	**3.66**	....	....	....	....	....	....	....

NABOKOV, Evgeni (na-BAW-kahv, ehv-GEH-nee) S.J.

Goaltender. Catches left. 6', 200 lbs. Born, Ust-Kamenogorsk, USSR, July 25, 1975.
(San Jose's 9th choice, 219th overall, in 1994 Entry Draft).

			Regular Season								Playoffs						
Season	Club	League	GP	W	L	T	Mins	GA	SO	Avg	GP	W	L	Mins	GA	SO	Avg
1992-93	Ust Kamenogorsk	CIS	4	1	0	0	109	5	0	2.75	....	....	....	....	....	....	....
1993-94	Ust Kamenogorsk	CIS	11	....	....	....	539	29	0	3.23	....	....	....	....	....	....	....
1994-95	Dynamo Moscow	CIS	24	....	....	....	1265	40	....	1.90	13	....	....	810	30	....	2.22
1995-96	Dynamo Moscow	CIS	39	....	....	....	2008	67	5	2.00	6	....	....	298	7	....	1.41
1996-97	Dynamo Moscow	Russia	27	....	....	....	1588	56	2	2.12	4	....	....	255	12	0	2.82
1997-98	Kentucky	AHL	33	10	21	2	1866	122	0	3.92	1	0	0	23	1	0	2.59
1998-99	Kentucky	AHL	43	26	14	1	2429	106	5	2.62	11	6	5	599	30	*2	3.00
99-2000	**San Jose**	**NHL**	**11**	**2**	**2**	**1**	**414**	**15**	**1**	**2.17**	**1**	**0**	**0**	**20**	**0**	**0**	**0.00**
	Cleveland	IHL	20	12	4	3	1164	52	0	2.68	....	....	....	....	....	....	....
	Kentucky	AHL	2	1	1	0	120	3	1	1.50	....	....	....	....	....	....	....
2000-01	**San Jose**	**NHL**	**66**	**32**	**21**	**7**	**3700**	**135**	**6**	**2.19**	**4**	**1**	**3**	**218**	**10**	**1**	**2.75**
2001-02	**San Jose**	**NHL**	**67**	**37**	**24**	**5**	**3901**	**149**	**7**	**2.29**	**12**	**7**	**5**	**712**	**31**	**0**	**2.61**
2002-03	**San Jose**	**NHL**	**55**	**19**	**28**	**8**	**3227**	**146**	**3**	**2.71**	....	....	....	....	....	....	....
2003-04	**San Jose**	**NHL**	**59**	**31**	**19**	**8**	**3456**	**127**	**9**	**2.20**	**17**	**10**	**7**	**1052**	**30**	**3**	**1.71**
	NHL Totals		**258**	**121**	**94**	**29**	**14698**	**572**	**26**	**2.34**	**34**	**18**	**15**	**2002**	**71**	**4**	**2.13**

NHL All-Rookie Team (2001) • Calder Memorial Trophy (2001)

Played in NHL All-Star Game (2001)

• Scored a goal vs. Vancouver, March 10, 2002.

NASTIUK, Kevin (NAZ-tee-uhk, KEH-vihn) CAR.

Goaltender. Catches left. 6'2", 176 lbs. Born, Edmonton, Alta., July 20, 1985.
(Carolina's 4th choice, 126th overall, in 2003 Entry Draft).

			Regular Season								Playoffs						
Season	Club	League	GP	W	L	T	Mins	GA	SO	Avg	GP	W	L	Mins	GA	SO	Avg
99-2000	Inland Real Estate	EMHA	20	9	6	5	998	59	0	3.25	....	....	....	....	....	....	....
	Inland Cement	AMBHL	1	0	1	0	50	8	0	9.60	....	....	....	....	....	....	....
2000-01	Inland Cement	AMBHL	20	12	7	1	1233	64	0	3.11	1	1	0	60	2	0	2.00
2001-02	Medicine Hat	WHL	19	4	10	0	877	66	0	4.52	....	....	....	....	....	....	....
2002-03	Medicine Hat	WHL	42	15	20	2	2344	172	0	4.40	11	7	4	693	33	0	2.86
2003-04	Medicine Hat	WHL	*68	40	19	8	*4056	187	4	2.77	*20	*16	4	*1182	38	*4	1.93

WHL Playoff MVP (2004)

NIITTYMAKI, Antero (NEE-too-mah-kee, AN-tehr-oh) PHI.

Goaltender. Catches left. 6', 195 lbs. Born, Turku, Finland, June 18, 1980.
(Philadelphia's 7th choice, 168th overall, in 1998 Entry Draft).

			Regular Season								Playoffs						
Season	Club	League	GP	W	L	T	Mins	GA	SO	Avg	GP	W	L	Mins	GA	SO	Avg
1998-99	TPS Turku Jr.	Finn-Jr.	35	....	....	....	2095	60	0	1.72	....	....	....	....	....	....	....
99-2000	TPS Turku Jr.	Finn-Jr.	1	1	0	0	60	1	0	1.00	....	....	....	....	....	....	....
	TPS Turku	Finland	32	23	6	2	1899	68	3	2.15	8	6	1	453	13	0	1.72
2000-01	TPS Turku	Finland	21	10	6	1	1112	46	2	2.48	....	....	....	....	....	....	....
2001-02	TPS Turku	Finland	27	16	8	1	1498	46	3	1.84	4	2	2	295	11	0	2.24
2002-03	Philadelphia	AHL	40	14	21	2	2283	98	0	2.58	....	....	....	....	....	....	....
2003-04	**Philadelphia**	**NHL**	**3**	**3**	**0**	**0**	**180**	**3**	**0**	**1.00**	....	....	....	....	....	....	....
	Philadelphia	AHL	49	24	13	6	2728	92	7	2.02	12	6	6	796	24	0	1.81
	NHL Totals		**3**	**3**	**0**	**0**	**180**	**3**	**0**	**1.00**	....	....	....	....	....	....	....

NISSINEN, Tuomas (NIHS-ih-nehn, too-OH-muhs) ST.L.

Goaltender. Catches left. 6'1", 176 lbs. Born, Kuopio, Finland, July 17, 1983.
(St. Louis' 2nd choice, 89th overall, in 2001 Entry Draft).

			Regular Season								Playoffs						
Season	Club	League	GP	W	L	T	Mins	GA	SO	Avg	GP	W	L	Mins	GA	SO	Avg
2000-01	KalPa Kuopio Jr.	Finn-Jr.	40	15	14	5	2327	125	2	3.22	1	0	1	60	4	0	4.00
2001-02	KalPa Kuopio Jr.	Finn-Jr.	33	20	11	2	1988	81	3	2.44	1	0	1	59	4	0	4.04
	Kalpa Kuopio	Finland-2	4	2	2	0	208	10	1	2.88	....	....	....	....	....	....	....
2002-03	Ilves Tampere	Finland	32	4	23	3	1750	108	1	3.70	....	....	....	....	....	....	....
2003-04	Hermes Kokkola	Finland-2	2	1	1	0	118	4	0	2.03	....	....	....	....	....	....	....
	Ilves Tampere Jr.	Finn-Jr.	1	1	0	0	60	4	0	4.00	....	....	....	....	....	....	....
	Ilves Tampere	Finland	23	7	7	5	1267	56	2	2.65	1	0	0	40	0	0	0.00

NORONEN, Mika (NOH-rah-nehn, MEE-kah) BUF.

Goaltender. Catches left. 6'2", 196 lbs. Born, Tampere, Finland, June 17, 1979.
(Buffalo's 1st choice, 21st overall, in 1997 Entry Draft).

			Regular Season								Playoffs						
Season	Club	League	GP	W	L	T	Mins	GA	SO	Avg	GP	W	L	Mins	GA	SO	Avg
1995-96	Tappara Jr.	Finn-Jr.	16	....	....	....	962	37	2	2.31	....	....	....	....	....	....	....
1996-97	Tappara Tampere	Finland	5	1	3	0	215	17	0	4.73	....	....	....	....	....	....	....
1997-98	Tappara Tampere	Finland	37	14	12	3	1704	83	1	2.92	4	1	2	196	12	0	3.67
1998-99	Tappara Tampere	Finland	43	18	20	5	2494	135	2	3.25	....	....	....	....	....	....	....
99-2000	Rochester	AHL	54	*33	13	4	3089	112	*6	2.18	21	13	8	1235	37	*6	*1.80
2000-01	**Buffalo**	**NHL**	**2**	**2**	**0**	**0**	**108**	**5**	**0**	**2.78**	....	....	....	....	....	....	....
	Rochester	AHL	47	26	15	5	2753	100	4	2.18	4	1	3	250	11	0	2.64
2001-02	**Buffalo**	**NHL**	**10**	**4**	**3**	**1**	**518**	**23**	**0**	**2.66**	....	....	....	....	....	....	....
	Rochester	AHL	45	16	17	12	2764	115	3	2.50	1	0	1	59	3	0	3.06
2002-03	**Buffalo**	**NHL**	**16**	**4**	**9**	**3**	**891**	**36**	**1**	**2.42**	....	....	....	....	....	....	....
	Rochester	AHL	19	5	9	5	1169	55	2	2.82	....	....	....	....	....	....	....
2003-04	**Buffalo**	**NHL**	**35**	**11**	**17**	**2**	**1796**	**77**	**2**	**2.57**	....	....	....	....	....	....	....
	NHL Totals		**63**	**21**	**29**	**6**	**3313**	**141**	**3**	**2.55**	....	....	....	....	....	....	....

AHL Second All-Star Team (2000, 2001) • Dudley "Red" Garrett Memorial Trophy (Top Rookie – AHL) (2000) • Shared Harry "Hap" Holmes Memorial Trophy (fewest goals against – AHL) (2001) with Tom Askey

NORRENA, Fredrik (noh-REH-nah, FREHD-rihk) T.B.

Goaltender. Catches left. 6', 189 lbs. Born, Pietarsaari, Finland, November 29, 1973.
(Tampa Bay's 8th choice, 213th overall, in 2002 Entry Draft).

			Regular Season								Playoffs						
Season	Club	League	GP	W	L	T	Mins	GA	SO	Avg	GP	W	L	Mins	GA	SO	Avg
1992-93	TPS Turku	Finland-2	2	0	0	0	29	1	0	2.01	....	....	....	....	....	....	....
	TPS Turku Jr.	Finn-Jr.	25	....	....	....	1449	74	1	3.06	5	....	....	307	11	0	2.14
1993-94	TPS Turku Jr.	Finn-Jr.	2	0	1	0	80	5	0	3.75	1	0	1	58	4	0	4.10
	TPS Turku	Finland	10	3	3	0	387	19	0	2.95	....	....	....	....	....	....	....
	Kiekko 67	Finland-2	15	7	7	1	875	42	2	2.88	....	....	....	....	....	....	....
1994-95	TPS Turku	Finland-2	22	....	....	....	1328	60	....	2.71	....	....	....	....	....	....	....
	Kiekko 67	Finland-2	15	....	....	....	828	34	0	2.46	....	....	....	....	....	....	....
1995-96	TPS Turku	Finland	26	....	....	....	1540	68	0	2.65	....	....	....	....	....	....	....

1996-97	Kiekko 67	Finland-2	12	....	....	....	725	35	0	2.98	....	....	....	....	....	....	....
	AIK Solna	Sweden	5	....	....	....	274	15	1	3.28	....	....	....	....	....	....	....
1997-98	Lukko Rauma	Finland	48	12	19	4	2174	105	0	2.90	....	....	....	....	....	....	....
1998-99	TPS Turku	Finland	20	11	4	1	1010	35	2	2.08	1	0	0	20	2	0	6.00
99-2000	TPS Turku	Finland	21	15	4	0	1175	35	2	*1.79	4	3	1	234	10	0	2.56
	TuTu Turku	Finland-2	2	1	1	0	118	7	0	3.54	....	....	....	....	....	....	....
2000-01	TPS Turku	Finland	39	26	10	3	2266	66	6	*1.75	*10	*9	1	603	13	*2	*1.29
2001-02	TPS Turku	Finland	32	14	11	5	1877	62	2	1.98	4	1	3	256	7	1	*1.64
2002-03	Vastra Frolunda	Sweden	23	....	....	....	1386	56	1	2.42	4	....	....	287	6	1	*1.25
2003-04	Linkopings HC	Sweden	40	....	....	....	2414	68	*9	*1.69	3	....	....	176	6	0	2.05

NURMINEN, Pasi (NUR-mih-nehn, PA-see) ATL.

Goaltender. Catches left. 5'10", 215 lbs. Born, Lahti, Finland, December 17, 1975.
(Atlanta's 6th choice, 189th overall, in 2001 Entry Draft).

			Regular Season								Playoffs						
Season	Club	League	GP	W	L	T	Mins	GA	SO	Avg	GP	W	L	Mins	GA	SO	Avg
1993-94	Reipas Lahti Jr.	Finn-Jr.	14	....	....	....	847	58	0	4.11	....	....	....	....	....	....	....
	Reipas Lahti	Finland	1	....	....	....	30	2	0	4.00	....	....	....	....	....	....	....
1994-95	Reipas Lahti Jr.	Finn-Jr.	9	....	....	....	542	22	....	2.44	....	....	....	....	....	....	....
	Reipas Lahti	Finland-2	9	....	....	....	423	44	0	6.24	....	....	....	....	....	....	....
1995-96	Kettera Imatra	Finland-2	38	....	....	....	2204	146	0	3.97	....	....	....	....	....	....	....
1996-97	Pelicans Lahti	Finland-2	30	....	....	....	1726	69	0	2.40	3	....	....	204	8	....	2.35
1997-98	Pelicans Lahti	Finland-2	35	....	....	....	3044	59	....	1.73	3	....	....	180	4	....	1.33
1998-99	HPK Hameenlinna	Finland	*48	24	17	6	*2810	127	2	2.71	7	3	4	425	24	1	3.39
99-2000	Jokerit Helsinki	Finland	48	24	15	8	2770	104	*6	2.25	*11	*7	4	*719	22	*2	1.84
2000-01	Jokerit Helsinki	Finland	52	*30	13	7	2971	107	5	2.16	5	2	3	308	11	1	2.14
2001-02	**Atlanta**	**NHL**	**9**	**2**	**5**	**0**	**465**	**28**	**0**	**3.61**	....	....	....	....	....	....	....
	Chicago Wolves	AHL	20	9	9	1	1165	57	2	2.93	*21	*15	5	1267	41	2	1.94
	Finland	Olympics	1	1	0	0	60	1	0	1.00	....	....	....	....	....	....	....
2002-03	**Atlanta**	**NHL**	**52**	**21**	**19**	**5**	**2856**	**137**	**2**	**2.88**	....	....	....	....	....	....	....
2003-04	**Atlanta**	**NHL**	**64**	**25**	**30**	**7**	**3738**	**173**	**3**	**2.78**	....	....	....	....	....	....	....
	NHL Totals		**125**	**48**	**54**	**12**	**7059**	**338**	**5**	**2.87**	....	....	....	....	....	....	....

Jack A. Butterfield Trophy (Playoff MVP – AHL) (2002)

OSAER, Phil (OH-shar, FIHL)

Goaltender. Catches left. 6'1", 186 lbs. Born, Dearborn, MI, February 10, 1980.
(St. Louis' 6th choice, 203rd overall, in 1999 Entry Draft).

			Regular Season								Playoffs						
Season	Club	League	GP	W	L	T	Mins	GA	SO	Avg	GP	W	L	Mins	GA	SO	Avg
1997-98	Waterloo	USHL	36	12	20	2	2094	107	2	3.07	5	1	4	295	17	0	3.46
1998-99	Ferris State	CCHA	9	2	2	1	399	10	0	1.51	....	....	....	....	....	....	....
99-2000	Ferris State	CCHA	25	13	8	2	1350	49	3	2.18	....	....	....	....	....	....	....
2000-01	Ferris State	CCHA	25	9	12	3	1449	57	3	2.36	....	....	....	....	....	....	....
2001-02	Peoria Rivermen	ECHL	29	16	11	2	1705	69	2	2.43	4	2	2	222	9	1	2.43
2002-03	Worcester IceCats	AHL	24	9	9	3	1328	64	1	2.89	....	....	....	....	....	....	....
	Trenton Titans	ECHL	2	0	2	0	118	7	0	3.57	....	....	....	....	....	....	....
	Louisiana	ECHL	4	2	1	1	244	9	0	2.21	....	....	....	....	....	....	....
2003-04	Hartford Wolf Pack	AHL	21	8	10	2	1055	39	3	2.22	....	....	....	....	....	....	....

CCHA Second All-Star Team (2001)

Signed as a free agent by **Hartford** (AHL), October 10, 2003. Signed as a free agent by **NY Rangers**, November 23, 2003.

OSGOOD, Chris (AWS-gud, KRIHS)

Goaltender. Catches left. 5'10", 175 lbs. Born, Peace River, Alta., November 26, 1972.
(Detroit's 3rd choice, 54th overall, in 1991 Entry Draft).

			Regular Season								Playoffs						
Season	Club	League	GP	W	L	T	Mins	GA	SO	Avg	GP	W	L	Mins	GA	SO	Avg
1988-89	Medicine Hat	AMHL	26	....	....	....	1441	88	0	3.66	....	....	....	....	....	....	....
1989-90	Medicine Hat	WHL	57	24	28	2	3094	228	0	4.42	3	0	3	173	17	0	5.91
1990-91	Medicine Hat	WHL	46	23	18	3	2630	173	2	3.95	12	7	5	712	42	0	3.54
1991-92	Medicine Hat	WHL	15	10	3	0	819	44	0	3.22	....	....	....	....	....	....	....
	Brandon	WHL	16	3	10	1	890	60	1	4.04	....	....	....	....	....	....	....
	Seattle	WHL	21	12	7	1	1217	65	1	3.20	15	9	6	904	51	0	3.38
1992-93	Adirondack	AHL	45	19	19	4	2438	159	0	3.91	1	0	1	59	2	0	2.03
1993-94	**Detroit**	**NHL**	**41**	**23**	**8**	**5**	**2206**	**105**	**2**	**2.86**	**6**	**3**	**2**	**307**	**12**	**1**	**2.35**
	Adirondack	AHL	4	3	1	0	239	13	0	3.26	....	....	....	....	....	....	....
1994-95	**Detroit**	**NHL**	**19**	**14**	**5**	**0**	**1087**	**41**	**1**	**2.26**	**2**	**0**	**0**	**68**	**2**	**0**	**1.76**
	Adirondack	AHL	2	1	1	0	120	6	0	3.00	....	....	....	....	....	....	....
1995-96	**Detroit**	**NHL**	**50**	***39**	**6**	**5**	**2933**	**106**	**5**	**2.17**	**15**	**8**	**7**	**936**	**33**	**2**	**2.12**
1996-97♦	**Detroit**	**NHL**	**47**	**23**	**13**	**9**	**2769**	**106**	**6**	**2.30**	**2**	**0**	**0**	**47**	**2**	**0**	**2.55**
1997-98♦	**Detroit**	**NHL**	**64**	**33**	**20**	**11**	**3807**	**140**	**6**	**2.21**	***22**	***16**	**6**	***1361**	**48**	**2**	**2.12**
1998-99	**Detroit**	**NHL**	**63**	**34**	**25**	**4**	**3691**	**149**	**3**	**2.42**	**6**	**4**	**2**	**358**	**14**	**1**	**2.35**
99-2000	**Detroit**	**NHL**	**53**	**30**	**14**	**8**	**3148**	**126**	**6**	**2.40**	**9**	**5**	**4**	**547**	**18**	**2**	**1.97**
2000-01	**Detroit**	**NHL**	**52**	**25**	**19**	**4**	**2834**	**127**	**1**	**2.69**	**6**	**2**	**4**	**365**	**15**	**1**	**2.47**
2001-02	**NY Islanders**	**NHL**	**66**	**32**	**25**	**6**	**3743**	**156**	**4**	**2.50**	**7**	**3**	**4**	**392**	**17**	**0**	**2.60**
2002-03	**NY Islanders**	**NHL**	**37**	**17**	**14**	**4**	**1993**	**97**	**2**	**2.92**	....	....	....	....	....	....	....
	St. Louis	**NHL**	**9**	**4**	**3**	**2**	**532**	**27**	**2**	**3.05**	**7**	**3**	**4**	**417**	**17**	**1**	**2.45**
2003-04	**St. Louis**	**NHL**	**67**	**31**	**25**	**8**	**3861**	**144**	**3**	**2.24**	**5**	**1**	**4**	**287**	**12**	**0**	**2.51**
	NHL Totals		**568**	**305**	**177**	**66**	**32604**	**1324**	**41**	**2.44**	**87**	**45**	**37**	**5085**	**190**	**10**	**2.24**

WHL East Second All-Star Team (1991) • NHL Second All-Star Team (1996) • Shared William M. Jennings Trophy (1996) with Mike Vernon

Played in NHL All-Star Game (1996, 1997, 1998)

• Scored a goal while with Medicine Hat (WHL), January 3, 1991. • Scored a goal vs. Hartford, March 6, 1996. Claimed by **NY Islanders** from **Detroit** in Waiver Draft, September 28, 2001. Traded to **St. Louis** by **NY Islanders** with NY Islanders' 3rd round choice (Konstantin Barulin) in 2003 Entry Draft for Justin Papineau and St. Louis' 2nd round choice (Jeremy Colliton) in 2003 Entry Draft, March 11, 2003.

OUELLET, Maxime (OO-leht, MAX-eem) WSH.

Goaltender. Catches left. 6'2", 195 lbs. Born, Beauport, Que., June 17, 1981.
(Philadelphia's 1st choice, 22nd overall, in 1999 Entry Draft).

			Regular Season								Playoffs						
Season	Club	League	GP	W	L	T	Mins	GA	SO	Avg	GP	W	L	Mins	GA	SO	Avg
1996-97	Ste-Foy	QAAA	29	16	8	0	1470	81	0	2.75	9	4	5	555	31	0	3.37
1997-98	Quebec Remparts	QMJHL	24	12	7	1	1188	66	0	3.33	7	3	1	305	16	0	3.15
1998-99	Quebec Remparts	QMJHL	*59	*40	12	6	*3447	155	3	*2.70	13	6	7	803	41	*1	3.06
99-2000	Quebec Remparts	QMJHL	53	31	16	4	2984	133	2	2.67	11	7	4	638	28	*2	*2.63
2000-01	**Philadelphia**	**NHL**	**2**	**0**	**1**	**0**	**76**	**3**	**0**	**2.37**	....	....	....	....	....	....	....
	Philadelphia	AHL	2	1	0	0	86	4	0	2.78	....	....	....	....	....	....	....
	Rouyn-Noranda	QMJHL	25	18	6	1	1471	65	3	2.65	8	4	4	490	25	0	3.06
2001-02	Philadelphia	AHL	41	16	13	8	2294	104	1	2.72	....	....	....	....	....	....	....
	Portland Pirates	AHL	6	3	3	0	358	17	0	2.85	....	....	....	....	....	....	....
2002-03	Portland Pirates	AHL	48	22	16	7	2773	111	*7	2.40	2	1	1	120	8	0	4.00
2003-04	**Washington**	**NHL**	**6**	**2**	**3**	**1**	**365**	**19**	**1**	**3.12**	....	....	....	....	....	....	....
	Portland Pirates	AHL	52	15	29	8	3050	101	10	1.99	5	2	2	303	8	0	1.59
	NHL Totals		**8**	**2**	**4**	**1**	**441**	**22**	**1**	**2.99**	....	....	....	....	....	....	....

QMJHL Second All-Star Team (1999, 2000, 2001) • Jacques Plante Trophy (fewest goals against – QMJHL) (1999) • AHL Second All-Star Team (2003)

• Returned to **Rouyn-Noranda** (QMJHL) by **Philadelphia**, October 27, 2000. Traded to **Washington** by **Philadelphia** with Philadelphia's 1st (later traded to Dallas – Dallas selected Martin Vagner), 2nd (Maxime Daigneault) and 3rd (Derek Krestanovich) round choices in 2002 Entry Draft for Adam Oates, March 19, 2002.

PARLEY, Davis (PAHR-lee, DAY-vihs) CGY.

Goaltender. Catches left. 6'2", 183 lbs. Born, Surrey, B.C., September 4, 1982.
(Florida's 5th choice, 120th overall, in 2000 Entry Draft).

			Regular Season								Playoffs						
Season	Club	League	GP	W	L	T	Mins	GA	SO	Avg	GP	W	L	Mins	GA	SO	Avg
1998-99	Campbell River	VIJHL	23	....	....	....	1380	43	4	1.87	....	....	....	....	....	....	....
99-2000	Kamloops Blazers	WHL	26	8	15	2	1497	80	2	3.21	1	0	0	37	3	0	4.86
2000-01	Kamloops Blazers	WHL	52	27	16	3	2948	170	1	3.46	3	0	3	154	13	0	5.06
2001-02	Kamloops Blazers	WHL	36	20	11	1	1994	92	1	2.77	3	0	3	169	11	0	3.91
2002-03	Kamloops Blazers	WHL	50	25	18	4	2856	132	3	2.77	6	2	4	495	16	1	1.94
2003-04	Texas Wildcatters	ECHL	52	18	29	3	2786	185	1	3.98	....	....	....	....	....	....	....

Signed as a free agent by **Calgary**, July, 2004.

PASSMORE, Steve (PAS-mohr, STEEV)

Goaltender. Catches left. 5'9", 165 lbs. Born, Thunder Bay, Ont., January 29, 1973.
(Quebec's 10th choice, 196th overall, in 1992 Entry Draft).

			Regular Season								Playoffs						
Season	Club	League	GP	W	L	T	Mins	GA	SO	Avg	GP	W	L	Mins	GA	SO	Avg
1988-89	Tri-City Americans	WHL	1	0	1	0	60	6	0	6.00	....	....	....	....	....	....	....
1989-90	West Island Deltas	BCAHA					STATISTICS NOT AVAILABLE										
	Tri-City Americans	WHL	4	....	....	....	215	17	0	4.74	....	....	....	....	....	....	....
1990-91	Victoria Cougars	WHL	35	3	25	1	1838	190	0	6.20	....	....	....	....	....	....	....
1991-92	Victoria Cougars	WHL	*71	15	50	5	*4228	347	0	4.92	....	....	....	....	....	....	....
1992-93	Victoria Cougars	WHL	43	14	24	2	2402	150	1	3.75	....	....	....	....	....	....	....
	Kamloops Blazers	WHL	25	19	6	0	1479	69	1	2.80	7	4	2	401	22	1	3.29
1993-94	Kamloops Blazers	WHL	36	22	9	2	1927	88	1	*2.74	*18	*11	7	*1099	60	0	3.28
1994-95	Cape Breton Oilers	AHL	25	8	13	3	1455	93	0	3.83	....	....	....	....	....	....	....
1995-96	Cape Breton Oilers	AHL	2	1	0	0	90	2	0	1.33	....	....	....	....	....	....	....
1996-97	Hamilton Bulldogs	AHL	27	12	12	3	1568	70	1	2.68	22	12	10	1325	61	*2	2.76
	Raleigh IceCaps	ECHL	2	1	1	0	118	13	0	6.56	....	....	....	....	....	....	....
1997-98	San Antonio	IHL	14	3	8	2	736	56	0	4.56	....	....	....	....	....	....	....
	Hamilton Bulldogs	AHL	27	11	10	6	1655	87	2	3.15	3	0	2	132	14	0	6.33
1998-99	**Edmonton**	**NHL**	**6**	**1**	**4**	**1**	**362**	**17**	**0**	**2.82**	....	....	....	....	....	....	....
	Hamilton Bulldogs	AHL	54	24	21	7	3148	117	4	2.23	11	5	6	680	31	0	2.74
99-2000	**Chicago**	**NHL**	**24**	**7**	**12**	**3**	**1388**	**63**	**1**	**2.72**	....	....	....	....	....	....	....
	Cleveland	IHL	2	1	0	1	120	3	1	1.50	....	....	....	....	....	....	....
2000-01	**Los Angeles**	**NHL**	**14**	**3**	**8**	**1**	**718**	**37**	**1**	**3.09**	....	....	....	....	....	....	....
	Lowell	AHL	6	2	4	0	334	24	0	4.32	....	....	....	....	....	....	....
	Chicago	**NHL**	**6**	**0**	**4**	**1**	**340**	**14**	**0**	**2.47**	....	....	....	....	....	....	....
	Chicago Wolves	IHL	6	2	2	2	340	22	0	3.88	....	....	....	....	....	....	....
2001-02	**Chicago**	**NHL**	**23**	**8**	**5**	**4**	**1142**	**43**	**0**	**2.26**	**3**	**0**	**2**	**138**	**6**	**0**	**2.61**
	Norfolk Admirals	AHL	2	2	0	0	120	6	0	3.00	....	....	....	....	....	....	....
2002-03	**Chicago**	**NHL**	**11**	**2**	**5**	**2**	**617**	**38**	**0**	**3.70**	....	....	....	....	....	....	....
	Norfolk Admirals	AHL	14	4	7	2	832	33	2	2.38	....	....	....	....	....	....	....
2003-04	**Chicago**	**NHL**	**9**	**2**	**6**	**0**	**478**	**23**	**0**	**2.89**	....	....	....	....	....	....	....
	Norfolk Admirals	AHL	15	3	10	2	889	39	2	2.63	....	....	....	....	....	....	....
	NHL Totals		**93**	**23**	**44**	**12**	**5045**	**235**	**2**	**2.79**	**3**	**0**	**2**	**138**	**6**	**0**	**2.61**

WHL West First All-Star Team (1993, 1994) • Fred Hunt Memorial Trophy (Sportsmanship – AHL) (1997) • AHL Second All-Star Team (1999)

Traded to **Edmonton** by **Quebec** for Brad Werenka, March 21, 1994. • Missed majority of the 1995-96 season recovering from blood disorder, October, 1995. Signed as a free agent by **Chicago**, July 8, 1999. Traded to **Los Angeles** by **Chicago** for Los Angeles' 4th round choice (Olli Malmivaara) in 2000 Entry Draft, May 1, 2000. Traded to **Chicago** by **Los Angeles** for Chicago's 8th round choice (Mike Gabinet) in 2001 Entry Draft, February 28, 2001.

PATZOLD, Dimitri (PATZ-ohld, dih-MEE-tree) S.J.

Goaltender. Catches left. 6', 200 lbs. Born, Ust-Kamenogorsk, USSR, February 3, 1983.
(San Jose's 3rd choice, 107th overall, in 2001 Entry Draft).

			Regular Season								Playoffs						
Season	Club	League	GP	W	L	T	Mins	GA	SO	Avg	GP	W	L	Mins	GA	SO	Avg
99-2000	Kolner Haie Jr.	Ger-Jr.	38	....	....	....	2131	73	0	2.06	....	....	....	....	....	....	....
	Kolner Haie 2	German-5	16	....	....	....	896	58	0	3.88	....	....	....	....	....	....	....
2000-01	EV Duisburg	German-2	6	....	....	....	360	17	0	2.83	....	....	....	....	....	....	....
	TSV Erding Jets	German-2	24	....	....	....	1378	89	0	3.88	....	....	....	....	....	....	....
2001-02	Kolner Haie	Germany	7	....	....	....	260	16	0	3.69	....	....	....	....	....	....	....
	EV Duisburg	German-2	6	....	....	....	360	17	0	2.83	....	....	....	....	....	....	....
2002-03	Adler Mannheim	Germany	15	....	....	....	817	35	0	2.57	2	....	....	34	2	0	3.53
2003-04	Cleveland Barons	AHL	27	10	15	0	1457	70	3	2.88	....	....	....	....	....	....	....
	Johnstown Chiefs	ECHL	8	7	0	0	443	20	0	2.71	1	0	1	59	2	0	2.02

PEARCE, Joseph (PEERS-JOH-sehf) T.B.

Goaltender. Catches left. 6'5", 215 lbs. Born, Brick, NJ, June 24, 1982.
(Tampa Bay's 3rd choice, 135th overall, in 2002 Entry Draft).

			Regular Season								Playoffs						
Season	Club	League	GP	W	L	T	Mins	GA	SO	Avg	GP	W	L	Mins	GA	SO	Avg
2000-01	Bismark Bobcats	AWJHL	17	....	....	....	1020	40	1	2.31	....	....	....	....	....	....	....
2001-02	N.H. Jr. Monarchs	EJHL	32	....	....	....	1885	57	1	1.82	....	....	....	....	....	....	....
2002-03	Chicago Steel	USHL	37	18	12	3	1980	96	1	2.91	....	....	....	....	....	....	....
2003-04	Boston College	H-East	5	2	2	0	270	14	0	3.11	....	....	....	....	....	....	....

PELLETIER, Jean-Marc (PEHL-tyay, ZHAWN-MAHRK) PHX.

Goaltender. Catches left. 6'3", 209 lbs. Born, Atlanta, GA, March 4, 1978.
(Philadelphia's 1st choice, 30th overall, in 1997 Entry Draft).

			Regular Season								Playoffs						
Season	Club	League	GP	W	L	T	Mins	GA	SO	Avg	GP	W	L	Mins	GA	SO	Avg
1993-94	Richelieu Riverains	QAAA	24	14	8	2	1440	91	0	3.79	2	1	0	104	11	0	6.32
1994-95	Richelieu Riverains	QAAA	21	15	6	0	1260	71	0	3.36	2	1	1	153	11	0	4.32
1995-96	Cornell Big Red	ECAC	5	1	2	0	179	15	0	5.03	....	....	....	....	....	....	....
1996-97	Cornell Big Red	ECAC	11	5	2	3	679	28	1	2.47	....	....	....	....	....	....	....
1997-98	Rimouski Oceanic	QMJHL	34	17	11	3	1913	118	0	3.70	16	11	3	895	51	1	3.42
1998-99	**Philadelphia**	**NHL**	**1**	**0**	**1**	**0**	**60**	**5**	**0**	**5.00**	....	....	....	....	....	....	....
	Philadelphia	AHL	47	25	16	4	2636	122	2	2.78	1	0	0	27	0	0	0.00
99-2000	Philadelphia	AHL	24	14	10	0	1405	58	3	2.48	....	....	....	....	....	....	....
	Cincinnati	IHL	22	14	4	2	1278	52	2	2.44	3	1	1	160	8	1	3.00
2000-01	Cincinnati	IHL	39	18	14	5	2261	119	2	3.16	5	1	4	318	15	0	2.83
2001-02	Lowell	AHL	40	21	12	4	2284	98	2	2.57	5	2	3	298	13	0	2.62
2002-03	Lowell	AHL	17	6	10	0	861	51	1	3.55	....	....	....	....	....	....	....
	Phoenix	**NHL**	**2**	**0**	**2**	**0**	**119**	**6**	**0**	**3.03**	....	....	....	....	....	....	....
	Springfield Falcons	AHL	24	12	7	4	1391	55	2	2.37	6	3	3	368	16	1	2.61
2003-04	**Phoenix**	**NHL**	**4**	**1**	**1**	**0**	**175**	**12**	**0**	**4.11**	....	....	....	....	....	....	....
	Springfield Falcons	AHL	43	10	24	5	2433	109	2	2.69	....	....	....	....	....	....	....
	NHL Totals		**7**	**1**	**4**	**0**	**354**	**23**	**0**	**3.90**	....	....	....	....	....	....	....

Traded to **Carolina** by **Philadelphia** with Rod Brind'Amour and Philadelphia's 2nd round choice (later traded to Colorado – Colorado selected Argis Saviels) in 2000 Entry Draft for Keith Primeau and Carolina's 5th round choice (later traded to NY Islanders – NY Islanders selected Kristofer Ottosson) in 2000 Entry Draft, January 23, 2000. Traded to **Phoenix** by **Carolina** with future considerations for Patrick DesRochers, December 31, 2002.

PENNER, Andrew (PEH-nuhr, AN-droo) CBJ

Goaltender. Catches left. 6'2", 205 lbs. Born, Scarborough, Ont., December 21, 1982.

			Regular Season								Playoffs						
Season	Club	League	GP	W	L	T	Mins	GA	SO	Avg	GP	W	L	Mins	GA	SO	Avg
1998-99	North York	OPJHL	26	....	....	....	1497	107	0	4.29	....	....	....	....	....	....	....
99-2000	North Bay	OHL	22	3	12	0	1070	79	0	4.43	....	....	....	....	....	....	....
2000-01	North Bay	OHL	32	10	19	1	1787	117	1	3.93	....	....	....	....	....	....	....
2001-02	North Bay	OHL	18	4	8	4	917	52	1	3.40	....	....	....	....	....	....	....
	Guelph Storm	OHL	36	18	12	5	2066	107	0	3.11	9	5	4	546	29	0	3.19
2002-03	Guelph Storm	OHL	51	21	21	7	2975	137	0	2.76	11	5	5	665	34	0	3.07
2003-04	Dayton Bombers	ECHL	50	15	27	2	2764	175	0	3.80	....	....	....	....	....	....	....

Signed as a free agent by **Columbus**, September 17, 2001.

PETERS, Justin (PEE-tuhrs, JUHS-tihn) CAR.

Goaltender. Catches left. 6', 209 lbs. Born, Blyth, Ont., August 30, 1986.
(Carolina's 2nd choice, 38th overall, in 2004 Entry Draft).

			Regular Season								Playoffs						
Season	Club	League	GP	W	L	T	Mins	GA	SO	Avg	GP	W	L	Mins	GA	SO	Avg
2002-03	St. Michael's	OHL	23	6	10	1	1052	54	0	3.08	7	1	0	126	4	0	1.90
2003-04	St. Michael's	OHL	53	30	16	6	3149	139	4	2.65	18	10	8	1109	37	4	2.00

PIETRASIAK, Jeff (peh-TRAZ-ee-ak, JEHF) PHX.

Goaltender. Catches left. 6'1", 180 lbs. Born, Marlboro, MA, April 5, 1983.
(Phoenix's 8th choice, 186th overall, in 2002 Entry Draft).

			Regular Season								Playoffs						
Season	Club	League	GP	W	L	T	Mins	GA	SO	Avg	GP	W	L	Mins	GA	SO	Avg
2000-01	Berkshire High	Hi-School	25	....	....	....	1150	26	8	1.37	....	....	....	....	....	....	....
2001-02	Berkshire High	Hi-School	32	....	....	....	1471	51	5	2.05	....	....	....	....	....	....	....
2002-03	New Hampshire	H-East	2	1	0	0	67	2	0	1.78	....	....	....	....	....	....	....
2003-04	New Hampshire	H-East	11	3	1	1	387	12	0	1.86	....	....	....	....	....	....	....

POGGE, Justin (POHG, JUHS-tihn) TOR.

Goaltender. Catches left. 6'3", 183 lbs. Born, Ft. McMurray, Alta., April 22, 1986.
(Toronto's 1st choice, 90th overall, in 2004 Entry Draft).

			Regular Season								Playoffs						
Season	Club	League	GP	W	L	T	Mins	GA	SO	Avg	GP	W	L	Mins	GA	SO	Avg
2002-03	Summerland	KIJHL	30	....	....	....	1761	91	0	3.13	....	....	....	....	....	....	....
2003-04	Prince George	WHL	44	17	18	2	2271	107	3	2.83	....	....	....	....	....	....	....

POTVIN, Felix (PAHT-vihn, FEEL-ihx)

Goaltender. Catches left. 6'1", 190 lbs. Born, Anjou, Que., June 23, 1971.
(Toronto's 2nd choice, 31st overall, in 1990 Entry Draft).

			Regular Season								Playoffs						
Season	Club	League	GP	W	L	T	Mins	GA	SO	Avg	GP	W	L	Mins	GA	SO	Avg
1987-88	Montreal-Bourassa	QAAA	27	15	7	3	1585	103	3	3.90	6	2	4	341	20	0	3.51
1988-89	Chicoutimi	QMJHL	*65	25	31	1	*3489	271	*2	4.66	....	....	....	....	....	....	....
1989-90	Chicoutimi	QMJHL	*62	*31	26	2	*3478	231	*2	3.99	....	....	....	....	....	....	....
1990-91	Chicoutimi	QMJHL	54	33	15	4	3216	145	*6	*2.70	*16	*11	5	*992	46	0	*2.78
1991-92	**Toronto**	**NHL**	**4**	**0**	**2**	**1**	**210**	**8**	**0**	**2.29**	....	....	....	....	....	....	....
	St. John's	AHL	35	18	10	6	2070	101	2	2.93	11	7	4	642	41	0	3.83
1992-93	**Toronto**	**NHL**	**48**	**25**	**15**	**7**	**2781**	**116**	**2**	***2.50**	***21**	**11**	**10**	***1308**	**62**	**1**	**2.84**
	St. John's	AHL	5	3	0	2	309	18	0	3.50	....	....	....	....	....	....	....
1993-94	**Toronto**	**NHL**	**66**	**34**	**22**	**9**	**3883**	**187**	**3**	**2.89**	**18**	**9**	**9**	**1124**	**46**	**3**	**2.46**
1994-95	**Toronto**	**NHL**	**36**	**15**	**13**	**7**	**2144**	**104**	**0**	**2.91**	**7**	**3**	**4**	**424**	**20**	**1**	**2.83**
1995-96	**Toronto**	**NHL**	**69**	**30**	**26**	**11**	**4009**	**192**	**2**	**2.87**	**6**	**2**	**4**	**350**	**19**	**0**	**3.26**
1996-97	**Toronto**	**NHL**	***74**	**27**	**36**	**7**	***4271**	**224**	**0**	**3.15**	....	....	....	....	....	....	....
1997-98	**Toronto**	**NHL**	**67**	**26**	**33**	**7**	**3864**	**176**	**5**	**2.73**	....	....	....	....	....	....	....
1998-99	**Toronto**	**NHL**	**5**	**3**	**2**	**0**	**299**	**19**	**0**	**3.81**	....	....	....	....	....	....	....
	NY Islanders	**NHL**	**11**	**2**	**7**	**1**	**606**	**37**	**0**	**3.66**	....	....	....	....	....	....	....
99-2000	**NY Islanders**	**NHL**	**22**	**5**	**14**	**3**	**1273**	**68**	**1**	**3.21**	....	....	....	....	....	....	....
	Vancouver	**NHL**	**34**	**12**	**13**	**7**	**1966**	**85**	**0**	**2.59**	....	....	....	....	....	....	....
2000-01	**Vancouver**	**NHL**	**35**	**14**	**17**	**3**	**2006**	**103**	**1**	**3.08**	....	....	....	....	....	....	....
	Los Angeles	**NHL**	**23**	**13**	**5**	**5**	**1410**	**46**	**5**	**1.96**	**13**	**7**	**6**	**812**	**33**	**2**	**2.44**
2001-02	**Los Angeles**	**NHL**	**71**	**31**	**27**	**8**	**4071**	**157**	**6**	**2.31**	**7**	**3**	**4**	**417**	**15**	**1**	**2.16**
2002-03	**Los Angeles**	**NHL**	**42**	**17**	**20**	**3**	**2367**	**105**	**3**	**2.66**	....	....	....	....	....	....	....
2003-04	**Boston**	**NHL**	**28**	**12**	**8**	**6**	**1605**	**67**	**4**	**2.50**	....	....	....	....	....	....	....
	NHL Totals		**635**	**266**	**260**	**85**	**36765**	**1694**	**32**	**2.76**	**72**	**35**	**37**	**4435**	**195**	**8**	**2.64**

QMJHL All-Rookie Team (1989) • QMJHL Second All-Star Team (1990) • QMJHL First All-Star Team (1991) • Canadian Major Junior Goaltender of the Year (1991) • Memorial Cup All-Star Team (1991) • Hap Emms Memorial Trophy (Memorial Cup Top Goaltender) (1991) • AHL First All-Star Team (1992) • Dudley "Red" Garrett Memorial Trophy (Top Rookie – AHL) (1992) • Baz Bastien Memorial Trophy (Top Goaltender – AHL) (1992) • NHL All-Rookie Team (1993)

Played in NHL All-Star Game (1994, 1996)

Traded to **NY Islanders** by **Toronto** with Toronto's 6th round choice (later traded to Tampa Bay – Tampa Bay selected Fedor Fedorov) in 1999 Entry Draft for Bryan Berard and NY Islanders' 6th round choice (Jan Sochor) in 1999 Entry Draft, January 9, 1999. Traded to **Vancouver** by **NY Islanders** with NY Islanders' compensatory 2nd round choice (later traded to New Jersey – New Jersey selected Teemu Laine) in 2000 Entry Draft and NY Islanders' 3rd round choice (Thatcher Bell) in 2000 Entry Draft for Kevin Weekes, Dave Scatchard and Bill Muckalt, December 19, 1999. Traded to **Los Angeles** by **Vancouver** for future considerations, February 15, 2001. Signed as a free agent by **Boston**, September 3, 2003.

PRUSEK, Martin (PREW-sehk, MAHR-tihn) OTT.

Goaltender. Catches left. 6'1", 176 lbs. Born, Ostrava, Czech., December 11, 1975.
(Ottawa's 6th choice, 164th overall, in 1999 Entry Draft).

			Regular Season								Playoffs						
Season	Club	League	GP	W	L	T	Mins	GA	SO	Avg	GP	W	L	Mins	GA	SO	Avg
1994-95	HC Vitkovice	Czech	5	....	....	....	232	18	....	4.65	....	....	....	....	....	....	....
1995-96	HC Vitkovice	Czech	40	....	....	....	2336	113	1	2.90	4	....	....	250	10	1	2.40
1996-97	HC Vitkovice	Czech	49	....	....	....	2841	109	8	2.30	9	....	....	546	19	1	2.08
1997-98	HC Vitkovice	Czech	50	....	....	....	2901	129	....	2.67	9	....	....	529	26	....	3.00
1998-99	HC Vitkovice	Czech	37	....	....	....	1905	85	....	2.68	4	....	....	250	12	....	2.88
99-2000	HC Vitkovice	Czech	50	....	....	....	2647	132	....	2.99	....	....	....	....	....	....	....
2000-01	HC Vitkovice	Czech	30	....	....	....	1679	64	....	2.29	9	....	....	460	25	....	3.26
2001-02	**Ottawa**	**NHL**	**1**	**0**	**1**	**0**	**62**	**3**	**0**	**2.90**	....	....	....	....	....	....	....
	Grand Rapids	AHL	33	18	8	5	1903	58	4	*1.83	5	2	3	278	10	0	2.16
2002-03	**Ottawa**	**NHL**	**18**	**12**	**2**	**1**	**935**	**37**	**0**	**2.37**	....	....	....	....	....	....	....
	Binghamton	AHL	4	1	2	1	243	7	1	1.73	....	....	....	....	....	....	....
2003-04	**Ottawa**	**NHL**	**29**	**16**	**6**	**3**	**1528**	**54**	**3**	**2.12**	**1**	**0**	**0**	**40**	**1**	**0**	**1.50**
	NHL Totals		**48**	**28**	**9**	**4**	**2525**	**94**	**3**	**2.23**	**1**	**0**	**0**	**40**	**1**	**0**	**1.50**

AHL First All-Star Team (2002) • Shared Harry "Hap" Holmes Memorial Trophy (fewest goals against – AHL) (2002) with Simon Lajeunesse and Mathieu Chouinard • Baz Bastien Memorial Trophy (Top Goaltender – AHL) (2002)

PUURULA, Joni (pu-u-ROO-luh, YOHN-ee) MTL.

Goaltender. Catches left. 5'11", 180 lbs. Born, Kokkola, Finland, August 4, 1982.
(Montreal's 10th choice, 243rd overall, in 2000 Entry Draft).

			Regular Season								Playoffs						
Season	Club	League	GP	W	L	T	Mins	GA	SO	Avg	GP	W	L	Mins	GA	SO	Avg
1998-99	Junkkarit	Finland-2	12	....	....	....	782	37	0	2.84	....	....	....	....	....	....	....
99-2000	Hermes Kokkola	Finland-2	23	8	12	2	1251	81	1	3.88	....	....	....	....	....	....	....
2000-01	FoPS Forssa	Finland-2	39	13	22	2	2264	142	1	3.76	....	....	....	....	....	....	....
	FoPS Forssa Jr.	Finn-Jr.	....	....	....	....	....	....	....	....	4	1	3	240	8	0	2.00
2001-02	HPK Jr.	Finn-Jr.	2	0	0	2	119	11	0	5.51	....	....	....	....	....	....	....
	FPS Fossa	Finland-2	5	2	2	1	305	18	0	3.54	....	....	....	....	....	....	....
	HPK Hameenlinna	Finland	9	8	0	1	515	18	0	2.10	8	4	3	453	13	0	1.72
2002-03	HPK Hameenlinna	Finland	34	19	6	9	1972	71	4	2.16	11	6	5	676	19	1	1.69
2003-04	Ahmat Hyvinkaa	Finland-2	3	2	0	1	182	9	0	2.97	....	....	....	....	....	....	....
	HPK Hameenlinna	Finland	33	16	9	7	1890	69	4	2.19	8	4	4	482	14	2	1.74

RACINE, Jean-Francois (RAY-seen, ZHAWN-fran-SWUH) TOR.

Goaltender. Catches left. 6'3", 194 lbs. Born, St-Hyacinthe, Que., April 27, 1982.
(Toronto's 4th choice, 90th overall, in 2000 Entry Draft).

			Regular Season								Playoffs						
Season	Club	League	GP	W	L	T	Mins	GA	SO	Avg	GP	W	L	Mins	GA	SO	Avg
1998-99	Magog	QAAA	36	19	12	1	2160	107	3	2.98	11	5	6	656	37	0	3.39
99-2000	Moncton Wildcats	QMJHL	10	3	3	1	410	28	0	4.10	....	....	....	....	....	....	....
	Drummondville	QMJHL	20	14	6	0	1152	63	1	3.28	3	0	0	65	5	0	4.60
2000-01	Drummondville	QMJHL	61	27	26	3	3362	189	4	3.37	5	2	3	303	20	0	3.97
2001-02	Drummondville	QMJHL	65	29	30	3	3640	208	2	3.43	12	5	7	720	42	1	3.50
2002-03	Memphis	CHL	35	22	9	3	2050	94	0	2.75	1	0	1	58	5	0	5.14
2003-04	Memphis	CHL	30	15	10	2	1645	74	2	2.70	....	....	....	....	....	....	....
	St. John's	AHL	9	4	5	0	496	24	1	2.90	....	....	....	....	....	....	....

RAYCROFT, Andrew (RAY-krawft, AN-droo) BOS.

Goaltender. Catches left. 6', 171 lbs. Born, Belleville, Ont., May 4, 1980.
(Boston's 4th choice, 135th overall, in 1998 Entry Draft).

			Regular Season								Playoffs						
Season	Club	League	GP	W	L	T	Mins	GA	SO	Avg	GP	W	L	Mins	GA	SO	Avg
1996-97	Wellington Dukes	MTJHL	27	....	....	....	1402	92	0	3.94	....	....	....	....	....	....	....
1997-98	Sudbury Wolves	OHL	33	8	16	5	1802	125	0	4.16	2	0	1	89	8	0	5.39
1998-99	Sudbury Wolves	OHL	45	17	22	5	2528	173	1	4.11	3	0	2	96	13	0	8.13
99-2000	Kingston	OHL	*61	33	20	5	3340	191	0	3.43	5	1	4	300	21	0	4.20
2000-01	**Boston**	**NHL**	**15**	**4**	**6**	**0**	**649**	**32**	**0**	**2.96**	....	....	....	....	....	....	....
	Providence Bruins	AHL	26	8	14	4	1459	82	1	3.37	....	....	....	....	....	....	....
2001-02	**Boston**	**NHL**	**1**	**0**	**0**	**1**	**65**	**3**	**0**	**2.77**	....	....	....	....	....	....	....
	Providence Bruins	AHL	56	25	24	6	3317	142	4	2.57	2	0	2	119	5	0	2.52
2002-03	**Boston**	**NHL**	**5**	**2**	**3**	**0**	**300**	**12**	**0**	**2.40**	....	....	....	....	....	....	....
	Providence Bruins	AHL	39	23	10	3	2255	94	1	2.50	4	1	3	264	6	1	*1.36
2003-04	**Boston**	**NHL**	**57**	**29**	**18**	**9**	**3420**	**117**	**3**	**2.05**	**7**	**3**	**4**	**447**	**16**	**1**	**2.15**
	NHL Totals		**78**	**35**	**27**	**10**	**4434**	**164**	**3**	**2.22**	**7**	**3**	**4**	**447**	**16**	**1**	**2.15**

OHL First All-Star Team (2000) • Canadian Major Junior First All-Star Team (2000) • Canadian Major Junior Goaltender of the Year (2000) • NHL All-Rookie Team (2004) • Calder Memorial Trophy (2004)

REGAN, Kevin (REE-guhn, KEH-vihn) BOS.

Goaltender. Catches left. 6', 195 lbs. Born, Boston, MA, July 25, 1984.
(Boston's 10th choice, 277th overall, in 2003 Entry Draft).

			Regular Season								Playoffs						
Season	Club	League	GP	W	L	T	Mins	GA	SO	Avg	GP	W	L	Mins	GA	SO	Avg
2001-02	St. Sebastian's	Hi-School	31	27	4	0	1860	56	0	1.91	....	....	....	....	....	....	....
	U.S. National U-18	USDP	1	0	0	0	12	0	0	0.00	....	....	....	....	....	....	....
	South Boston	USHA	3	3	0	0	158	8	0	2.58	....	....	....	....	....	....	....
2002-03	St. Sebastian's	Hi-School	28	....	....	....	1215	47	4	1.81	....	....	....	....	....	....	....
2003-04	Waterloo	USHL	50	*28	19	1	0	111	*6	2.37	*12	*9	3	*735	19	*1	*1.55

RHODES, Damian (ROHDZ, DAY-mee-uhn)

Goaltender. Catches left. 5'11", 195 lbs. Born, St. Paul, MN, May 28, 1969.
(Toronto's 6th choice, 112th overall, in 1987 Entry Draft).

			Regular Season								Playoffs						
Season	Club	League	GP	W	L	T	Mins	GA	SO	Avg	GP	W	L	Mins	GA	SO	Avg
1985-86	Richfield Spartans	Hi-School	16	....	....	....	720	56	0	3.50	....	....	....	....	....	....	....
1986-87	Richfield Spartans	Hi-School	19	....	....	....	673	51	1	4.55	....	....	....	....	....	....	....
1987-88	Michigan Tech	WCHA	29	16	10	1	1625	114	0	4.20	....	....	....	....	....	....	....
1988-89	Michigan Tech	WCHA	37	15	22	0	2216	163	0	4.41	....	....	....	....	....	....	....
1989-90	Michigan Tech	WCHA	25	6	17	0	1358	119	0	6.26	....	....	....	....	....	....	....
1990-91	**Toronto**	**NHL**	**1**	**1**	**0**	**0**	**60**	**1**	**0**	**1.00**	....	....	....	....	....	....	....
	Newmarket Saints	AHL	38	8	24	3	2154	144	1	4.01	....	....	....	....	....	....	....
1991-92	St. John's	AHL	43	20	16	5	2454	148	0	3.62	6	4	1	331	16	0	2.90
1992-93	St. John's	AHL	*52	27	16	8	*3074	184	1	3.59	9	4	5	538	37	0	4.13
1993-94	**Toronto**	**NHL**	**22**	**9**	**7**	**3**	**1213**	**53**	**0**	**2.62**	**1**	**0**	**0**	**1**	**0**	**0**	**0.00**
1994-95	**Toronto**	**NHL**	**13**	**6**	**6**	**1**	**760**	**34**	**0**	**2.68**	....	....	....	....	....	....	....
1995-96	**Toronto**	**NHL**	**11**	**4**	**5**	**1**	**624**	**29**	**0**	**2.79**	....	....	....	....	....	....	....
	Ottawa	**NHL**	**36**	**10**	**22**	**4**	**2123**	**98**	**2**	**2.77**	....	....	....	....	....	....	....
1996-97	**Ottawa**	**NHL**	**50**	**14**	**20**	**14**	**2934**	**133**	**1**	**2.72**	....	....	....	....	....	....	....
1997-98	**Ottawa**	**NHL**	**50**	**19**	**19**	**7**	**2743**	**107**	**5**	**2.34**	**10**	**5**	**5**	**590**	**21**	**0**	**2.14**
1998-99	**Ottawa**	**NHL**	**45**	**22**	**13**	**7**	**2480**	**101**	**3**	**2.44**	**2**	**0**	**2**	**150**	**6**	**0**	**2.40**
99-2000	**Atlanta**	**NHL**	**28**	**5**	**19**	**3**	**1561**	**101**	**1**	**3.88**	....	....	....	....	....	....	....
2000-01	**Atlanta**	**NHL**	**38**	**7**	**19**	**7**	**2072**	**116**	**0**	**3.36**	....	....	....	....	....	....	....
2001-02	**Atlanta**	**NHL**	**15**	**2**	**10**	**1**	**769**	**47**	**0**	**3.67**	....	....	....	....	....	....	....
2002-03	Lowell	AHL	7	1	4	0	379	26	0	4.12	....	....	....	....	....	....	....
	Greenville Grrrowl	ECHL	12	2	8	2	687	43	1	3.76	1	0	1	60	6	0	6.00
2003-04	Lowell	AHL	7	1	4	0	379	26	0	4.12	....	....	....	....	....	....	....
	NHL Totals		**309**	**99**	**140**	**48**	**17339**	**820**	**12**	**2.84**	**13**	**5**	**7**	**741**	**27**	**0**	**2.19**

• Credited with scoring a goal while with Michigan Tech (WCHA), January 21, 1989. • Played 10 seconds of playoff game vs. San Jose, May 6, 1994. Traded to **NY Islanders** by **Toronto** with Ken Belanger for future considerations (Kirk Muller and Don Beaupre, January 23, 1996), January 23, 1996. Traded to **Ottawa** by **NY Islanders** with Wade Redden for Don Beaupre, Martin Straka and Bryan Berard, January 23, 1996. • Credited with scoring a goal vs. New Jersey, January 2, 1999. Traded to **Atlanta** by **Ottawa** for future considerations, June 18, 1999. • Missed majority of 2002-03 and 2003-04 seasons recovering from hernia surgery, March 26, 2002.

ROLOSON, Dwayne (ROH-loh-suhn, DWAYN) MIN.

Goaltender. Catches left. 6'1", 178 lbs. Born, Simcoe, Ont., October 12, 1969.

			Regular Season								Playoffs						
Season	Club	League	GP	W	L	T	Mins	GA	SO	Avg	GP	W	L	Mins	GA	SO	Avg
1984-85	Simcoe Penguins	OJHL-C	3	....	....	....	100	21	0	12.60	....	....	....	....	....	....	....
1985-86	Simcoe Rams	OJHL-C	1	....	....	....	60	6	0	6.00	....	....	....	....	....	....	....
1986-87	Norwich	OJHL-C	19	....	....	....	1091	55	0	*3.03	....	....	....	....	....	....	....
1987-88	Belleville Bobcats	OJHL-B	21	9	6	1	1070	60	*2	3.36	....	....	....	....	....	....	....
1988-89	Thorold	OJHL-B	27	15	6	4	1490	82	0	3.30	....	....	....	....	....	....	....
1989-90	Thorold	OJHL-B	30	18	8	1	1683	108	0	3.85	....	....	....	....	....	....	....
1990-91	U. Mass-Lowell	H-East	15	5	9	0	823	63	0	4.59	....	....	....	....	....	....	....
1991-92	U. Mass-Lowell	H-East	12	3	8	0	660	52	0	4.73	....	....	....	....	....	....	....
1992-93	U. Mass-Lowell	H-East	*39	20	17	2	*2342	150	0	3.84	....	....	....	....	....	....	....
1993-94	U. Mass-Lowell	H-East	*40	*23	10	7	*2305	106	0	2.76	....	....	....	....	....	....	....
1994-95	Saint John Flames	AHL	46	16	21	8	2734	156	1	3.42	5	1	4	298	13	0	2.61
1995-96	Saint John Flames	AHL	67	*33	22	11	4026	190	1	2.83	16	10	6	1027	49	1	2.86
1996-97	**Calgary**	**NHL**	**31**	**9**	**14**	**3**	**1618**	**78**	**1**	**2.89**	....	....	....	....	....	....	....
	Saint John Flames	AHL	8	6	2	0	481	22	1	2.75	....	....	....	....	....	....	....
1997-98	**Calgary**	**NHL**	**39**	**11**	**16**	**8**	**2205**	**110**	**0**	**2.99**	....	....	....	....	....	....	....
	Saint John Flames	AHL	4	3	0	1	245	8	0	1.96	....	....	....	....	....	....	....
1998-99	**Buffalo**	**NHL**	**18**	**6**	**8**	**2**	**911**	**42**	**1**	**2.77**	**4**	**1**	**1**	**139**	**10**	**0**	**4.32**
	Rochester	AHL	2	2	0	0	120	4	0	2.00	....	....	....	....	....	....	....
99-2000	**Buffalo**	**NHL**	**14**	**1**	**7**	**3**	**677**	**32**	**0**	**2.84**	....	....	....	....	....	....	....

2000-01	Worcester IceCats	AHL	52	*32	15	5	*3127	113	*6	*2.17	11	6	5	697	23	1	1.98
2001-02	**Minnesota**	**NHL**	**45**	**14**	**20**	**7**	**2506**	**112**	**5**	**2.68**	....	....	....	....	....	....	....
2002-03	**Minnesota**	**NHL**	**50**	**23**	**16**	**8**	**2945**	**98**	**4**	**2.00**	**11**	**5**	**6**	**579**	**25**	**0**	**2.59**
2003-04	**Minnesota**	**NHL**	**48**	**19**	**18**	**11**	**2847**	**89**	**5**	**1.88**	....	....	....	....	....	....	....
	NHL Totals		**245**	**83**	**99**	**42**	**13709**	**561**	**16**	**2.46**	**15**	**6**	**7**	**718**	**35**	**0**	**2.92**

Hockey East First All-Star Team (1994) • Hockey East Player of the Year (1994) • NCAA East First All-American Team (1994) • AHL First All-Star Team (2001) • Baz Bastien Memorial Trophy (Top Goaltender – AHL) (2001) • MBNA/Mastercard Roger Crozier Saving Grace Award (2004)

Played in NHL All-Star Game (2004)

Signed as a free agent by **Calgary**, July 4, 1994. Signed as a free agent by **Buffalo**, July 15, 1998. Claimed by **Columbus** from **Buffalo** in Expansion Draft, June 23, 2000. Signed as a free agent by **St. Louis**, July 14, 2000. Signed as a free agent by **Minnesota**, July 2, 2001.

RUDKOWSKY, Cody (RUHD-kow-skee, KOH-dee)

Goaltender. Catches left. 6'1", 206 lbs. Born, Willingdon, Alta., July 21, 1978.

			Regular Season								Playoffs						
Season	**Club**	**League**	**GP**	**W**	**L**	**T**	**Mins**	**GA**	**SO**	**Avg**	**GP**	**W**	**L**	**Mins**	**GA**	**SO**	**Avg**
1995-96	Langley Thunder	BCJHL	23	....	....	....	1172	73	1	3.73	....	....	....	....	....	....	....
	Seattle	WHL	2	0	0	0	21	3	0	8.57	....	....	....	....	....	....	....
1996-97	Seattle	WHL	40	19	16	1	2162	124	0	3.44	1	1	0	30	0	0	0.00
1997-98	Seattle	WHL	53	20	22	3	2805	176	1	3.74	5	1	4	278	18	0	3.88
1998-99	Seattle	WHL	64	34	17	10	3665	177	*7	2.90	11	5	6	637	31	1	2.92
99-2000	Worcester IceCats	AHL	28	9	7	6	1405	75	0	3.20	....	....	....	....	....	....	....
	Peoria Rivermen	ECHL	10	6	4	0	599	32	0	3.20	2	1	1	119	6	0	3.02
2000-01	Worcester IceCats	AHL	25	13	8	3	1477	66	3	2.68	....	....	....	....	....	....	....
2001-02	Worcester IceCats	AHL	21	6	10	2	1108	50	1	2.71	....	....	....	....	....	....	....
	Peoria Rivermen	ECHL	12	5	2	4	709	24	3	2.03	2	0	1	78	4	0	3.08
2002-03	**St. Louis**	**NHL**	**1**	**1**	**0**	**0**	**30**	**0**	**0**	**0.00**	....	....	....	....	....	....	....
	Worcester IceCats	AHL	10	1	5	3	577	28	0	2.91	....	....	....	....	....	....	....
	Trenton Titans	ECHL	31	17	9	5	1867	85	2	2.73	3	0	3	178	14	0	4.72
2003-04	Reading Royals	ECHL	46	24	18	4	2728	108	1	2.38	14	8	6	834	28	1	2.02
	Worcester IceCats	AHL	1	0	0	0	49	3	0	3.67	1	0	1	58	2	0	2.07
	NHL Totals		**1**	**1**	**0**	**0**	**30**	**0**	**0**	**0.00**	....	....	....	....	....	....	....

WHL West First All-Star Team (1999) • Canadian Major Junior First All-Star Team (1999) • Canadian Major Junior Goaltender of the Year (1999)

Signed as a free agent by **St. Louis**, March 25, 1999.

SABOURIN, Dany (SA-boo-rihn, DAN-ee)

Goaltender. Catches left. 6'2", 182 lbs. Born, Val-d'Or, Que., September 2, 1980.
(Calgary's 5th choice, 108th overall, in 1998 Entry Draft).

			Regular Season								Playoffs						
Season	**Club**	**League**	**GP**	**W**	**L**	**T**	**Mins**	**GA**	**SO**	**Avg**	**GP**	**W**	**L**	**Mins**	**GA**	**SO**	**Avg**
1996-97	Amos Forestiers	QAAA	24	6	16	0	1440	107	0	4.48	....	....	....	....	....	....	....
1997-98	Sherbrooke	QMJHL	37	15	15	2	1906	128	1	4.03	....	....	....	....	....	....	....
1998-99	Sherbrooke	QMJHL	30	8	13	2	1477	102	1	4.14	1	0	1	49	2	0	2.45
	Saint John Flames	AHL	....	....	....	....	....	....	....	....	1	0	1	57	4	0	4.19
99-2000	Sherbrooke	QMJHL	55	25	22	5	3067	181	1	3.54	5	1	4	324	18	0	3.33
2000-01	Saint John Flames	AHL	1	1	0	0	40	0	0	0.00	....	....	....	....	....	....	....
	Johnstown Chiefs	ECHL	19	4	9	1	903	56	0	3.72	1	0	0	40	2	0	3.00
2001-02	Johnstown Chiefs	ECHL	27	14	10	1	1539	84	0	3.28	3	0	2	137	5	0	2.18
2002-03	Saint John Flames	AHL	41	15	17	4	2220	100	4	2.70	....	....	....	....	....	....	....
2003-04	**Calgary**	**NHL**	**4**	**0**	**3**	**0**	**169**	**10**	**0**	**3.55**	....	....	....	....	....	....	....
	Lowell	AHL	14	5	7	2	821	39	0	2.85	....	....	....	....	....	....	....
	Las Vegas	ECHL	10	6	3	1	613	24	0	2.35	1	0	1	58	2	0	2.07
	NHL Totals		**4**	**0**	**3**	**0**	**169**	**10**	**0**	**3.55**	....	....	....	....	....	....	....

SALFICKY, Dusan (sal-FITZ-kee, DOO-shahn) NYI

Goaltender. Catches left. 6'1", 185 lbs. Born, Chrudim, Czech., March 28, 1972.
(NY Islanders' 2nd choice, 132nd overall, in 2001 Entry Draft).

			Regular Season								Playoffs						
Season	**Club**	**League**	**GP**	**W**	**L**	**T**	**Mins**	**GA**	**SO**	**Avg**	**GP**	**W**	**L**	**Mins**	**GA**	**SO**	**Avg**
1990-91	Tri-City Americans	WHL	2	1	1	0	119	11	0	5.55	....	....	....	....	....	....	....
	Tesla Pardubice	Czech	18	....	....	....	1000	60	....	3.60	....	....	....	....	....	....	....
1991-92	Tesla Pardubice	Czech-Jr.					STATISTICS NOT AVAILABLE										
1992-93	VTJ Tabor	Czech-2					STATISTICS NOT AVAILABLE										
1993-94	HC Pardubice	Czech	1	0	0	1	59	0	1	0.00	....	....	....	....	....	....	....
1994-95	HC Pardubice	Czech	10	....	....	....	548	23	1	2.52	3	....	....	185	12	0	3.89
1995-96	Pardubice	Czech	8	....	....	....	315	22	0	4.19	....	....	....	....	....	....	....
1996-97	Pardubice	Czech	21	....	....	....	1180	48	0	2.44	3	....	....	134	12	0	5.37
1997-98	HC Keramika Plzen	Czech	50	....	....	....	2939	134	0	2.75	5	2	3	310	14	0	2.71
1998-99	HC Keramika Plzen	Czech	44	....	....	....	2506	100	0	2.39	5	2	3	233	14	0	3.32
99-2000	HC Keramika Plzen	Czech	*52	....	....	....	*3061	108	3	2.12	7	....	....	415	15	....	2.17
2000-01	HC Keramika Plzen	Czech	*52	....	....	....	*3014	132	0	2.63	....	....	....	....	....	....	....
2001-02	Bridgeport	AHL	4	3	1	0	239	4	1	1.00	....	....	....	....	....	....	....
	Pardubice	Czech	13	....	....	....	779	35	....	2.70	6	....	....	367	14	....	2.29
2002-03	CSKA Moscow	Russia	41	....	....	....	2300	77	7	2.01	....	....	....	....	....	....	....
2003-04	CSKA Moscow	Russia	45	....	....	....	2656	101	6	2.28	....	....	....	....	....	....	....

SALO, Tommy (SA-loh,TAW-mee)

Goaltender. Catches left. 5'11", 182 lbs. Born, Surahammar, Sweden, February 1, 1971.
(NY Islanders' 5th choice, 118th overall, in 1993 Entry Draft).

			Regular Season								Playoffs						
Season	**Club**	**League**	**GP**	**W**	**L**	**T**	**Mins**	**GA**	**SO**	**Avg**	**GP**	**W**	**L**	**Mins**	**GA**	**SO**	**Avg**
1992-93	Vasteras IK	Sweden	24	....	....	....	1431	59	2	2.47	2	....	....	120	6	0	3.00
1993-94	Vasteras IK	Sweden	32	....	....	....	1896	106	0	3.35	....	....	....	....	....	....	....
	Sweden	Olympics	6	5	1	0	370	13	1	2.11	....	....	....	....	....	....	....
1994-95	Denver Grizzlies	IHL	*65	*45	14	4	*3810	165	*3	*2.60	8	7	0	390	20	0	3.07
	NY Islanders	**NHL**	**6**	**1**	**5**	**0**	**358**	**18**	**0**	**3.02**	....	....	....	....	....	....	....
1995-96	**NY Islanders**	**NHL**	**10**	**1**	**7**	**1**	**523**	**35**	**0**	**4.02**	....	....	....	....	....	....	....
	Utah Grizzlies	IHL	45	28	15	2	2695	119	*4	2.65	22	*15	7	1342	51	*3	2.28
1996-97	**NY Islanders**	**NHL**	**58**	**20**	**27**	**8**	**3208**	**151**	**5**	**2.82**	....	....	....	....	....	....	....
1997-98	**NY Islanders**	**NHL**	**62**	**23**	**29**	**5**	**3461**	**152**	**4**	**2.64**	....	....	....	....	....	....	....
	Sweden	Olympics	4	2	2	0	238	9	0	2.27	....	....	....	....	....	....	....
1998-99	**NY Islanders**	**NHL**	**51**	**17**	**26**	**7**	**3018**	**132**	**5**	**2.62**	....	....	....	....	....	....	....
	Edmonton	**NHL**	**13**	**8**	**2**	**2**	**700**	**27**	**0**	**2.31**	**4**	**0**	**4**	**296**	**11**	**0**	**2.23**
99-2000	**Edmonton**	**NHL**	**70**	**27**	**28**	**13**	**4164**	**162**	**2**	**2.33**	**5**	**1**	**4**	**297**	**14**	**0**	**2.83**
2000-01	**Edmonton**	**NHL**	**73**	**36**	**25**	**12**	**4364**	**179**	**8**	**2.46**	**6**	**2**	**4**	**406**	**15**	**0**	**2.22**
2001-02	**Edmonton**	**NHL**	**69**	**30**	**28**	**10**	**4035**	**149**	**6**	**2.22**	....	....	....	....	....	....	....
	Sweden	Olympics	3	2	1	0	179	7	0	2.35	....	....	....	....	....	....	....
2002-03	**Edmonton**	**NHL**	**65**	**29**	**27**	**8**	**3814**	**172**	**4**	**2.71**	**6**	**2**	**4**	**343**	**18**	**0**	**3.15**
2003-04	**Edmonton**	**NHL**	**44**	**17**	**18**	**6**	**2487**	**107**	**3**	**2.58**	....	....	....	....	....	....	....
	Colorado	**NHL**	**5**	**1**	**3**	**1**	**304**	**12**	**0**	**2.37**	**1**	**0**	**0**	**27**	**0**	**0**	**0.00**
	NHL Totals		**526**	**210**	**225**	**73**	**30436**	**1296**	**37**	**2.55**	**22**	**5**	**16**	**1369**	**58**	**0**	**2.54**

IHL First All-Star Team (1995) • Garry F. Longman Memorial Trophy (Top Rookie – IHL) (1995) • James Norris Memorial Trophy (fewest goals against – IHL) (1995) • James Gatschene Memorial Trophy (MVP – IHL) (1995) • Shared James Norris Memorial Trophy (fewest goals against – IHL) (1996) with Mark McArthur • ''Bud'' Poile Trophy (Playoff MVP – IHL) (1996)

Played in NHL All-Star Game (2000, 2002)

Traded to **Edmonton** by **NY Islanders** for Mats Lindgren and Edmonton's 8th round choice (Radek Martinek) in 1999 Entry Draft, March 20, 1999. Traded to **Colorado** by **Edmonton** with Edmonton's 6th round choice in 2005 Entry Draft for Tom Gilbert, March 8, 2004.

SANFORD, Curtis (SAN-fohrd, KUHR-this) ST.L.

Goaltender. Catches right. 5'10", 187 lbs. Born, Owen Sound, Ont., October 5, 1979.

			Regular Season								Playoffs						
Season	**Club**	**League**	**GP**	**W**	**L**	**T**	**Mins**	**GA**	**SO**	**Avg**	**GP**	**W**	**L**	**Mins**	**GA**	**SO**	**Avg**
1994-95	Wiarton	OJHL-C	18	....	....	....	949	98	0	6.20	....	....	....	....	....	....	....
1995-96	Collingwood	OJHL	21	....	....	....	2128	74	0	3.54	....	....	....	....	....	....	....
1996-97	Owen Sound	OHL	19	4	8	1	847	77	0	5.45	....	....	....	....	....	....	....
	Owen Sound	OJHL-B	6	....	....	....	360	28	0	4.68	....	....	....	....	....	....	....
1997-98	Owen Sound	OHL	30	13	10	2	1542	114	1	4.44	9	4	4	456	30	1	3.95
1998-99	Owen Sound	OHL	56	30	16	5	2998	191	2	3.82	16	9	7	960	58	0	3.63
99-2000	Owen Sound	OHL	53	18	26	6	3124	198	1	3.80	....	....	....	....	....	....	....
	Missouri	UHL	6	3	1	0	237	6	0	1.52	....	....	....	....	....	....	....
2000-01	Peoria Rivermen	ECHL	27	15	7	4	1511	48	3	*1.91	14	9	4	813	28	*2	2.07
	Worcester IceCats	AHL	5	3	0	1	237	16	0	4.06	....	....	....	....	....	....	....
2001-02	Peoria Rivermen	ECHL	24	13	8	2	1418	58	1	2.45	....	....	....	....	....	....	....
	Worcester IceCats	AHL	9	5	4	0	537	22	0	2.46	....	....	....	....	....	....	....
2002-03	**St. Louis**	**NHL**	**8**	**5**	**1**	**0**	**397**	**13**	**1**	**1.96**	....	....	....	....	....	....	....
	Worcester IceCats	AHL	41	18	14	8	2317	93	3	2.41	3	0	3	179	8	0	2.68
2003-04	Worcester IceCats	AHL	43	20	16	3	2367	84	5	2.13	9	4	5	569	24	0	2.53
	NHL Totals		**8**	**5**	**1**	**0**	**397**	**13**	**1**	**1.96**	....	....	....	....	....	....	....

ECHL Second All-Star Team (2001)

Signed as a free agent by **St. Louis**, October 1, 2000.

SAUVE, Philippe (SOH-vay, FIHL-ihp) COL.

Goaltender. Catches left. 6', 180 lbs. Born, Buffalo, NY, February 27, 1980.
(Colorado's 6th choice, 38th overall, in 1998 Entry Draft).

			Regular Season								Playoffs						
Season	**Club**	**League**	**GP**	**W**	**L**	**T**	**Mins**	**GA**	**SO**	**Avg**	**GP**	**W**	**L**	**Mins**	**GA**	**SO**	**Avg**
1995-96	Laval-Laurentides	QAAA	25	9	10	0	1184	87	1	4.11	15	7	8	900	54	0	3.58
1996-97	Rimouski Oceanic	QMJHL	26	11	9	2	1334	84	0	3.78	1	0	0	14	3	0	12.90
1997-98	Rimouski Oceanic	QMJHL	40	23	16	0	2326	131	1	3.38	7	0	5	262	33	0	7.55
1998-99	Rimouski Oceanic	QMJHL	44	16	19	4	2401	155	0	3.87	11	6	4	595	30	*1	3.03
99-2000	Drummondville	QMJHL	28	12	12	2	1526	106	0	4.17	....	....	....	....	....	....	....
	Hull Olympiques	QMJHL	17	9	7	1	992	57	0	3.45	12	6	6	735	47	0	3.84
2000-01	Hershey Bears	AHL	42	17	18	1	2182	100	3	2.75	3	0	3	218	10	0	2.75
2001-02	Hershey Bears	AHL	55	25	20	6	3130	111	6	2.13	8	3	5	486	21	0	2.59
2002-03	Hershey Bears	AHL	*60	26	20	12	3394	134	5	2.37	5	2	3	295	14	0	2.85
2003-04	**Colorado**	**NHL**	**17**	**7**	**7**	**3**	**986**	**50**	**0**	**3.04**	....	....	....	....	....	....	....
	Hershey Bears	AHL	10	3	7	0	578	25	2	2.59	....	....	....	....	....	....	....
	NHL Totals		**17**	**7**	**7**	**3**	**986**	**50**	**0**	**3.04**	....	....	....	....	....	....	....

Canadian Major Junior Humanitarian Player of the Year (1999)

SCHAEFER, Nolan (SHAY-fuhr, NOH-luhn) S.J.

Goaltender. Catches right. 6'2", 200 lbs. Born, Yellow Grass, Sask., January 15, 1980.
(San Jose's 4th choice, 166th overall, in 2000 Entry Draft).

			Regular Season								Playoffs						
Season	**Club**	**League**	**GP**	**W**	**L**	**T**	**Mins**	**GA**	**SO**	**Avg**	**GP**	**W**	**L**	**Mins**	**GA**	**SO**	**Avg**
1996-97	Yorkton Mallers	SMHL	36	....	....	....	1854	132	0	4.27	....	....	....	....	....	....	....
1997-98	Yorkton Mallers	SMHL	5	....	....	....	239	17	0	4.25	....	....	....	....	....	....	....
	Nipawin Hawks	SJHL	21	12	4	3	1080	42	*3	*2.33	....	....	....	....	....	....	....
1998-99	Niapawin Hawks	SJHL	46	....	....	....	2478	165	0	3.60	....	....	....	....	....	....	....
99-2000	Providence College	H-East	14	6	5	1	778	42	0	3.24	....	....	....	....	....	....	....
2000-01	Providence College	H-East	25	15	8	2	1529	63	3	2.47	....	....	....	....	....	....	....
2001-02	Providence College	H-East	*35	11	18	5	*2062	113	0	3.29	....	....	....	....	....	....	....
2002-03	Providence College	H-East	25	13	8	2	1440	71	0	2.96	....	....	....	....	....	....	....
2003-04	Cleveland Barons	AHL	27	14	9	3	1592	62	2	2.34	9	4	5	573	24	0	2.51
	Fresno Falcons	ECHL	12	5	5	0	654	34	1	3.12	....	....	....	....	....	....	....

Hockey East Second All-Star Team (2001) • NCAA East Second All-American Team (2001)

SCHNEIDER, Cory (SHNIGH-duhr), KOHR-ee) VAN.

Goaltender. Catches left. 6'2", 195 lbs. Born, Salem, MA, March 18, 1986.
(Vancouver's 1st choice, 26th overall, in 2004 Entry Draft).

			Regular Season								Playoffs						
Season	**Club**	**League**	**GP**	**W**	**L**	**T**	**Mins**	**GA**	**SO**	**Avg**	**GP**	**W**	**L**	**Mins**	**GA**	**SO**	**Avg**
2002-03	Phillips-Andover	Hi-School	23	13	7	2	1385	39	3	1.69	....	....	....	....	....	....	....
2003-04	Phillips-Andover	Hi-School	24	17	5	2	1336	32	6	1.42	....	....	....	....	....	....	....
	U.S. National U-18	USDP	12	11	1	0	679	21	1	1.86	....	....	....	....	....	....	....

SCHWAB, Corey (SHWAHB, KOHR-ree)

Goaltender. Catches left. 6', 180 lbs. Born, North Battleford, Sask., November 4, 1970.
(New Jersey's 12th choice, 200th overall, in 1990 Entry Draft).

			Regular Season								Playoffs						
Season	**Club**	**League**	**GP**	**W**	**L**	**T**	**Mins**	**GA**	**SO**	**Avg**	**GP**	**W**	**L**	**Mins**	**GA**	**SO**	**Avg**
1988-89	Seattle	WHL	10	2	2	0	386	31	0	4.82	....	....	....	....	....	....	....
1989-90	Seattle	WHL	27	15	2	1	1150	69	1	3.60	3	0	0	49	2	0	2.45
1990-91	Seattle	WHL	*58	32	18	3	*3289	224	0	4.09	6	1	5	382	25	0	3.93
1991-92	Utica Devils	AHL	24	9	12	1	1322	95	0	4.31	....	....	....	....	....	....	....
	Cincinnati	ECHL	8	6	0	1	450	31	0	4.13	9	6	3	540	29	0	3.22
1992-93	Utica Devils	AHL	40	18	16	5	2387	169	*2	4.25	1	0	1	59	6	0	6.10
	Cincinnati	IHL	3	1	2	0	185	17	0	5.51	....	....	....	....	....	....	....
1993-94	Albany River Rats	AHL	51	27	21	3	3058	184	0	3.61	5	1	4	298	20	0	4.02
1994-95	Albany River Rats	AHL	45	25	10	9	2711	117	3	*2.59	7	6	1	425	19	0	2.68
1995-96	**New Jersey**	**NHL**	**10**	**0**	**3**	**0**	**331**	**12**	**0**	**2.18**	....	....	....	....	....	....	....
	Albany River Rats	AHL	5	3	2	0	299	13	0	2.61	....	....	....	....	....	....	....
1996-97	**Tampa Bay**	**NHL**	**31**	**11**	**12**	**1**	**1462**	**74**	**2**	**3.04**	....	....	....	....	....	....	....
1997-98	**Tampa Bay**	**NHL**	**16**	**2**	**9**	**1**	**821**	**40**	**1**	**2.92**	....	....	....	....	....	....	....
1998-99	**Tampa Bay**	**NHL**	**40**	**8**	**25**	**3**	**2146**	**126**	**0**	**3.52**	....	....	....	....	....	....	....
	Cleveland	IHL	8	1	6	1	477	31	0	3.90	....	....	....	....	....	....	....
99-2000	Orlando	IHL	16	9	4	2	868	31	1	2.14	....	....	....	....	....	....	....
	Vancouver	**NHL**	**6**	**2**	**1**	**1**	**269**	**16**	**0**	**3.57**	....	....	....	....	....	....	....
	Syracuse Crunch	AHL	12	7	5	0	720	42	0	3.50	4	1	3	246	11	1	2.69
2000-01	Kansas City Blades	IHL	50	22	24	1	2866	150	2	3.14	....	....	....	....	....	....	....
2001-02	**Toronto**	**NHL**	**30**	**12**	**10**	**5**	**1646**	**75**	**1**	**2.73**	**1**	**0**	**0**	**12**	**0**	**0**	**0.00**
2002-03♦	**New Jersey**	**NHL**	**11**	**5**	**3**	**1**	**614**	**15**	**1**	**1.47**	**2**	**0**	**0**	**28**	**0**	**0**	**0.00**
2003-04	**New Jersey**	**NHL**	**3**	**2**	**0**	**1**	**187**	**2**	**1**	**0.64**	....	....	....	....	....	....	....
	NHL Totals		**147**	**42**	**63**	**13**	**7476**	**360**	**6**	**2.89**	**3**	**0**	**0**	**40**	**0**	**0**	**0.00**

AHL Second All-Star Team (1995) • Shared Harry ''Hap'' Holmes Memorial Trophy (fewest goals against – AHL) (1995) with Mike Dunham • Jack A. Butterfield Trophy (Playoff MVP – AHL) (1995) (co-winner - Mike Dunham)

Traded to **Tampa Bay** by **New Jersey** for Jeff Reese, Chicago's 2nd round choice (previously acquired, New Jersey selected Pierre Dagenais) in 1996 Entry Draft and Tampa Bay's 8th round choice (Jay Bertsch) in 1996 Entry Draft, June 22, 1996. Claimed by **Atlanta** from **Tampa Bay** in Expansion Draft, June 25, 1999. Traded to **Vancouver** by **Atlanta** for Vancouver's 4th round choice (Carl Mallette) in 2000 Entry Draft, October 29, 1999. Signed as a free agent by **Toronto**, October 1, 2001. Signed as a free agent by **New Jersey**, July 8, 2002. • Missed majority of the 2003-04 season recovering from groin injury suffered in game vs. NY Rangers, November 15, 2003.

SCHWARZ, Marek (SHWAHRTS, MAIR-ehk) ST.L.

Goaltender. Catches right. 5'11", 176 lbs. Born, Mlada Boleslav, Czech., April 1, 1986.
(St. Louis' 1st choice, 17th overall, in 2004 Entry Draft).

			Regular Season								Playoffs						
Season	Club	League	GP	W	L	T	Mins	GA	SO	Avg	GP	W	L	Mins	GA	SO	Avg
2000-01	Mlada Boleslav Jr.	Czech-Jr.	45	....	....	....	1969	154	0	4.69	....	....	....	....	....	....	....
2001-02	Sparta Praha Jr.	Czech-Jr.	46	....	....	....	2692	86	9	1.92	6	....	....	368	16	0	2.61
2002-03	Sparta Praha Jr.	Czech-Jr.	34	....	....	....	1778	57	3	1.92	2	....	....	120	5	0	2.50
	HC Sparta Praha	Czech	1	....	....	....	1	0	0	0.00	....	....	....	....	....	....	....
2003-04	Sparta Praha Jr.	Czech-Jr.	7	....	....	....	352	14	2	2.39	....	....	....	....	....	....	....
	Plzen	Czech	10	....	....	....	603	33	0	3.28	....	....	....	....	....	....	....
	HC Sparta Praha	Czech	8	....	....	....	335	20	0	3.58	....	....	....	....	....	....	....
	HC Ocelari Trinec	Czech	5	....	....	....	280	12	0	2.57	....	....	....	....	....	....	....
	HC Mlada Boleslav	Czech-2	1	....	....	....	63	6	0	5.71	....	....	....	....	....	....	....

SCOTT, Travis (SKAWT, TRA-vihs) FLA.

Goaltender. Catches left. 6'2", 185 lbs. Born, Kanata, Ont., September 14, 1975.

			Regular Season								Playoffs						
Season	Club	League	GP	W	L	T	Mins	GA	SO	Avg	GP	W	L	Mins	GA	SO	Avg
1991-92	Nepean Raiders	COJHL	19	14	5	0	1065	71	1	4.00	....	....	....	....	....	....	....
1992-93	Nepean Raiders	COJHL	36	19	10	2	1968	133	0	4.05	....	....	....	....	....	....	....
1993-94	Windsor Spitfires	OHL	45	20	18	0	2312	158	1	4.10	4	0	4	240	16	0	4.00
1994-95	Windsor Spitfires	OHL	48	26	14	3	2644	147	3	3.34	3	0	1	94	6	1	3.83
1995-96	Oshawa Generals	OHL	31	15	9	4	1763	78	3	2.65	5	1	4	315	23	0	4.38
1996-97	Baton Rouge	ECHL	10	5	2	1	501	22	0	2.63	....	....	....	....	....	....	....
	Worcester IceCats	AHL	29	14	10	1	1482	75	1	3.04	....	....	....	....	....	....	....
1997-98	Baton Rouge	ECHL	36	14	11	6	1949	96	1	2.96	....	....	....	....	....	....	....
1998-99	Mississippi	ECHL	44	22	12	5	2337	112	1	2.88	*18	*14	4	*1252	42	3	2.01
99-2000	Lowell	AHL	46	15	23	3	2595	126	3	2.91	1	0	1	60	2	0	2.01
2000-01	**Los Angeles**	**NHL**	**1**	**0**	**0**	**0**	**25**	**3**	**0**	**7.20**	....	....	....	....	....	....	....
	Lowell	AHL	34	16	15	1	1977	83	2	2.52	4	1	2	209	7	1	2.01
2001-02	Manchester	AHL	39	21	12	3	2170	83	6	2.30	5	2	3	327	15	0	2.75
2002-03	Manchester	AHL	50	23	19	5	2829	116	4	2.46	3	0	2	148	9	0	3.65
2003-04	San Antonio	AHL	*64	26	31	6	3747	156	4	2.50	....	....	....	....	....	....	....
	NHL Totals		**1**	**0**	**0**	**0**	**25**	**3**	**0**	**7.20**	....	....	....	....	....	....	....

ECHL Playoff MVP (1999)

Signed as a free agent by **St. Louis**, December 30, 1996. Signed as a free agent by **Los Angeles**, February 18, 2000. Signed as a free agent by **Florida**, August 12, 2003.

SHANTZ, David (SHANTS, DAY-vihd) FLA.

Goaltender. Catches left. 6'1", 202 lbs. Born, Burlington, Ont., May 5, 1986.
(Florida's 2nd choice, 37th overall, in 2004 Entry Draft).

			Regular Season								Playoffs						
Season	Club	League	GP	W	L	T	Mins	GA	SO	Avg	GP	W	L	Mins	GA	SO	Avg
2002-03	Thorold	OJHL-B	36	30	3	3	2107	63	8	1.79	....	....	....	....	....	....	....
2003-04	Mississauga	OHL	43	21	18	3	2483	120	1	2.90	*24	12	12	*1449	49	*5	2.03

OHL All-Rookie Team (2004) • Canadian Major Junior All-Rookie Team (2004)

SHIELDS, Steve (SHEELDS, STEEV)

Goaltender. Catches left. 6'3", 215 lbs. Born, Toronto, Ont., July 19, 1972.
(Buffalo's 5th choice, 101st overall, in 1991 Entry Draft).

			Regular Season								Playoffs						
Season	Club	League	GP	W	L	T	Mins	GA	SO	Avg	GP	W	L	Mins	GA	SO	Avg
1989-90	St. Marys Lincolns	OJHL-B	26	....	....	....	1512	121	0	4.80	....	....	....	....	....	....	....
1990-91	U. of Michigan	CCHA	37	26	6	3	1963	106	0	3.24	....	....	....	....	....	....	....
1991-92	U. of Michigan	CCHA	*37	*27	7	2	*2090	99	1	2.84	....	....	....	....	....	....	....
1992-93	U. of Michigan	CCHA	*39	*30	6	2	2027	75	2	*2.22	....	....	....	....	....	....	....
1993-94	U. of Michigan	CCHA	36	*28	6	1	1961	87	0	2.66	....	....	....	....	....	....	....
1994-95	Rochester	AHL	13	3	8	0	673	53	0	4.72	1	0	0	20	3	0	9.00
	South Carolina	ECHL	21	11	5	2	1158	52	2	2.69	3	0	2	144	11	0	4.58
1995-96	**Buffalo**	**NHL**	**2**	**1**	**0**	**0**	**75**	**4**	**0**	**3.20**	....	....	....	....	....	....	....
	Rochester	AHL	43	20	17	2	2357	140	1	3.56	*19	*15	3	*1127	47	1	2.50
1996-97	**Buffalo**	**NHL**	**13**	**3**	**8**	**2**	**789**	**39**	**0**	**2.97**	**10**	**4**	**6**	**570**	**26**	**1**	**2.74**
	Rochester	AHL	23	14	6	2	1331	60	1	2.70	....	....	....	....	....	....	....
1997-98	**Buffalo**	**NHL**	**16**	**3**	**6**	**4**	**785**	**37**	**0**	**2.83**	....	....	....	....	....	....	....
	Rochester	AHL	1	0	1	0	59	3	0	3.04	....	....	....	....	....	....	....
1998-99	**San Jose**	**NHL**	**37**	**15**	**11**	**8**	**2162**	**80**	**4**	**2.22**	**1**	**0**	**1**	**60**	**6**	**0**	**6.00**
99-2000	**San Jose**	**NHL**	**67**	**27**	**30**	**8**	**3797**	**162**	**4**	**2.56**	**12**	**5**	**7**	**696**	**36**	**0**	**3.10**
2000-01	**San Jose**	**NHL**	**21**	**6**	**8**	**5**	**1135**	**47**	**2**	**2.48**	....	....	....	....	....	....	....
2001-02	**Anaheim**	**NHL**	**33**	**9**	**20**	**2**	**1777**	**79**	**0**	**2.67**	....	....	....	....	....	....	....
2002-03	**Boston**	**NHL**	**36**	**12**	**13**	**9**	**2112**	**97**	**0**	**2.76**	**2**	**0**	**2**	**119**	**6**	**0**	**3.03**
2003-04	**Florida**	**NHL**	**16**	**3**	**6**	**1**	**732**	**42**	**0**	**3.44**	....	....	....	....	....	....	....
	NHL Totals		**241**	**79**	**102**	**39**	**13364**	**587**	**10**	**2.64**	**25**	**9**	**16**	**1445**	**74**	**1**	**3.07**

CCHA First All-Star Team (1993, 1994) • NCAA West Second All-American Team (1993, 1994)

Traded to **San Jose** by **Buffalo** with Buffalo's 4th round choice (Miroslav Zalesak) in 1998 Entry Draft for Kay Whitmore, Colorado's 2nd round choice (previously acquired, Buffalo selected Jaroslav Kristek) in 1998 Entry Draft and San Jose's 5th round choice (later traded to Columbus – Columbus selected Tyler Kolarik) in 2000 Entry Draft, June 18, 1998. Traded to **Anaheim** by **San Jose** with Jeff Friesen and San Jose's 2nd round choice (later traded to Dallas – Dallas selected Vojtech Polak) in 2003 Entry Draft for Teemu Selanne, March 5, 2001. Traded to **Boston** by **Anaheim** for Boston's 3rd round choice (Shane Hynes) in 2003 Entry Draft, June 25, 2002. Traded to **Florida** by **Boston** for future considerations, October 5, 2003.

SIDIKOV, Rustam (SIH-dih-kawf, ROOS-tuhm) NSH.

Goaltender. Catches left. 6', 165 lbs. Born, Moscow, USSR, July 5, 1985.
(Nashville's 10th choice, 133rd overall, in 2003 Entry Draft).

			Regular Season								Playoffs						
Season	Club	League	GP	W	L	T	Mins	GA	SO	Avg	GP	W	L	Mins	GA	SO	Avg
2000-01	CSKA Moscow Jr.	Russia-Jr.	23	....	....	....	1204	50	....	2.50	....	....	....	103	4	0	2.33
2001-02	CSKA Moscow 2	Russia-3	1	....	....	....	60	5	0	5.00	....	....	....	....	....	....	....
2002-03	CSKA Moscow 18	Russia-Jr.	15	....	....	....	764	33		0255.00	7	....	....	409	14	0	2.05
	CSKA Moscow 2	Russia-3	2	....	....	....	120	2	0	1.00	....	....	....	....	....	....	....
2003-04	CSKA Moscow 2	Russia-3					STATISTICS NOT AVAILABLE										

SIGALET, Jordan (SIH-ga-leht, JOHR-duhn) BOS.

Goaltender. Catches left. 6'1", 180 lbs. Born, New Westminster, B.C., February 19, 1981.
(Boston's 6th choice, 209th overall, in 2001 Entry Draft).

			Regular Season								Playoffs						
Season	Club	League	GP	W	L	T	Mins	GA	SO	Avg	GP	W	L	Mins	GA	SO	Avg
99-2000	Victoria Salsa	BCHL	33	....	....	....	1980	108	0	3.28	....	....	....	....	....	....	....
2000-01	Victoria Salsa	BCHL	48	23	22	0	2820	142	0	3.03	18	12	5	1060	143	0	2.62
2001-02	Bowling Green	CCHA	13	2	6	2	657	38	0	3.47	....	....	....	....	....	....	....
2002-03	Bowling Green	CCHA	20	6	11	2	1208	66	1	3.28	....	....	....	....	....	....	....
2003-04	Bowling Green	CCHA	37	10	17	9	2210	101	2	2.74	....	....	....	....	....	....	....

CCHA First All-Star Team (2004)

SKUDRA, Peter (SKOO-druh, PEE-tuhr)

Goaltender. Catches left. 6'1", 189 lbs. Born, Riga, Latvia, April 24, 1973.

			Regular Season								Playoffs						
Season	Club	League	GP	W	L	T	Mins	GA	SO	Avg	GP	W	L	Mins	GA	SO	Avg
1992-93	Pardaugava Riga	CIS	27	....	....	....	1498	74	....	2.96	1	....	....	60	5	0	5.00
1993-94	Pardaugava Riga	CIS	14	....	....	....	783	42	....	3.22	1	....	....	55	4	0	4.36
1994-95	Greensboro	ECHL	33	13	9	5	1612	113	0	4.20	6	2	2	341	28	0	4.92
	Memphis	CHL	2	0	1	0	80	8	0	6.00	....	....	....	....	....	....	....
1995-96	Erie Panthers	ECHL	12	3	8	1	681	47	0	4.14	....	....	....	....	....	....	....
	Johnstown Chiefs	ECHL	30	12	11	4	1657	98	0	3.55	....	....	....	....	....	....	....
1996-97	Hamilton Bulldogs	AHL	32	8	16	2	1615	101	0	3.75	....	....	....	....	....	....	....
	Johnstown Chiefs	ECHL	4	2	1	1	200	11	0	3.30	....	....	....	....	....	....	....
1997-98	**Pittsburgh**	**NHL**	**17**	**6**	**4**	**3**	**851**	**26**	**0**	**1.83**	....	....	....	....	....	....	....
	Houston Aeros	IHL	9	5	3	1	499	23	0	2.77	....	....	....	....	....	....	....
	Kansas City Blades	IHL	13	10	3	0	775	37	0	2.86	8	4	4	512	20	1	*2.34
1998-99	**Pittsburgh**	**NHL**	**37**	**15**	**11**	**5**	**1914**	**89**	**3**	**2.79**	....	....	....	....	....	....	....
99-2000	**Pittsburgh**	**NHL**	**20**	**5**	**7**	**3**	**922**	**48**	**1**	**3.12**	**1**	**0**	**0**	**20**	**1**	**0**	**3.00**
2000-01	**Buffalo**	**NHL**	**1**	**0**	**0**	**0**	**1**	**0**	**0**	**0.00**	....	....	....	....	....	....	....
	Rochester	AHL	2	2	0	0	120	5	0	2.50	....	....	....	....	....	....	....
	Boston	**NHL**	**25**	**6**	**12**	**1**	**1116**	**62**	**0**	**3.33**	....	....	....	....	....	....	....
	Providence Bruins	AHL	3	3	0	0	180	5	0	1.67	....	....	....	....	....	....	....
2001-02	**Vancouver**	**NHL**	**23**	**10**	**8**	**2**	**1166**	**47**	**1**	**2.42**	**2**	**0**	**1**	**96**	**5**	**0**	**3.13**
	Hartford Wolf Pack	AHL	3	2	1	0	179	8	0	2.69	....	....	....	....	....	....	....
2002-03	**Vancouver**	**NHL**	**23**	**9**	**5**	**6**	**1192**	**54**	**1**	**2.72**	....	....	....	....	....	....	....
	Manitoba Moose	AHL	1	1	0	0	60	3	0	3.00	....	....	....	....	....	....	....
2003-04	Ak Bars Kazan	Russia	9	....	....	....	545	20	0	2.20	....	....	....	....	....	....	....
	Khimik Voskresensk	Russia	34	....	....	....	2045	59	6	1.73	....	....	....	....	....	....	....
	NHL Totals		**146**	**51**	**47**	**20**	**7162**	**326**	**6**	**2.73**	**3**	**0**	**1**	**116**	**6**	**0**	**3.10**

Signed as a free agent by **Pittsburgh**, September 25, 1997. Signed as a free agent by **Boston**, October 3, 2000. Claimed on waivers by **Buffalo** from **Boston**, October 6, 2000. • Played 27 seconds of game vs. Anaheim, October 20, 2000. Claimed on waivers by **Boston** from **Buffalo**, November 14, 2000. Signed as a free agent by **Vancouver**, November 7, 2001.

SMID, Zdenek (SHMIHD, z'DEHN-ehk) ATL.

Goaltender. Catches left. 5'10", 180 lbs. Born, Plzen, Czech., February 3, 1980.
(Atlanta's 7th choice, 168th overall, in 2000 Entry Draft).

			Regular Season								Playoffs						
Season	Club	League	GP	W	L	T	Mins	GA	SO	Avg	GP	W	L	Mins	GA	SO	Avg
1996-97	HC ZKZ Plzen Jr.	Czech-Jr.	23	....	....	....	1304	48	....	2.21	....	....	....	....	....	....	....
1997-98	Plzen Jr.	Czech-Jr.	30	....	....	....	1601	91	....	3.41	....	....	....	....	....	....	....
1998-99	Karlovy Vary Jr.	Czech-Jr.					STATISTICS NOT AVAILABLE										
	HC Karlovy Vary	Czech	3	....	....	....	160	11	....	4.13	....	....	....	....	....	....	....
99-2000	Karlovy Vary Jr.	Czech-Jr.	24	....	....	....	1409	54	2	2.30	2	1	1	86	9	0	6.28
	HC Karlovy Vary	Czech	14	....	....	....	650	41	1	3.78	3	....	....	150	8	....	3.20
2000-01	HC Karlovy Vary	Czech	12	....	....	....	630	34	1	3.24	....	....	....	....	....	....	....
	Sport Kadan	Czech-2	7	....	....	....	372	22	0	3.55	....	....	....	....	....	....	....
	Karlovy Vary Jr.	Czech-Jr.	19	....	....	....	1140	51	1	2.68	....	....	....	....	....	....	....
2001-02	HPK Hameenlinna	Finland	18	10	4	4	1055	44	2	2.50	....	....	....	....	....	....	....
	Lulea HF	Sweden	1	0	1	0	58	3	0	3.10	1	0	1	40	5	0	7.50
2002-03	Liberec	Czech	2	....	....	....	111	8	0	4.32	....	....	....	....	....	....	....
	HC Keramika Plzen	Czech	15	....	....	....	828	39	0	2.83	....	....	....	....	....	....	....
2003-04	Plzen	Czech	5	....	....	....	253	15	0	3.56	....	....	....	....	....	....	....
	HC Slavia Praha	Czech	5	....	....	....	203	8	0	2.36	....	....	....	....	....	....	....
	IHC Pisek	Czech-2	10	....	....	....	547	21	0	2.30	....	....	....	....	....	....	....

SMITH, Jason (SMIHTH, JAY-suhn) N.J.

Goaltender. Catches left. 6'1", 170 lbs. Born, St-Lambert, Que., July 17, 1985.
(New Jersey's 5th choice, 197th overall, in 2003 Entry Draft).

			Regular Season								Playoffs						
Season	Club	League	GP	W	L	T	Mins	GA	SO	Avg	GP	W	L	Mins	GA	SO	Avg
2002-03	Lennoxville	QJHL	29	22	4	1	1622	62	3	2.29	14	11	3	816	34	1	2.52
2003-04	Sacred Heart	AH	5	1	4	0	302	19	0	3.78	....	....	....	....	....	....	....

SMITH, Mike (SMIHTH, MIGHK) DAL.

Goaltender. Catches left. 6'3", 189 lbs. Born, Kingston, Ont., March 22, 1982.
(Dallas' 5th choice, 161st overall, in 2001 Entry Draft).

			Regular Season								Playoffs						
Season	Club	League	GP	W	L	T	Mins	GA	SO	Avg	GP	W	L	Mins	GA	SO	Avg
1998-99	Kingston	OPJHL	16	....	....	....	906	53	0	3.51	....	....	....	....	....	....	....
99-2000	Kingston	OHL	15	4	5	0	666	42	0	3.78	....	....	....	....	....	....	....
2000-01	Kingston	OHL	3	0	0	2	136	8	0	3.53	....	....	....	....	....	....	....
	Sudbury Wolves	OHL	43	22	13	7	2571	108	3	2.52	12	7	5	735	26	2	*2.12
2001-02	Sudbury Wolves	OHL	53	19	28	5	3082	157	3	3.06	5	1	4	302	15	0	2.98
2002-03	Lexington	ECHL	27	11	10	4	1553	66	1	2.55	2	0	1	93	8	0	5.14
	Utah Grizzlies	AHL	11	5	5	0	614	33	0	3.23	....	....	....	....	....	....	....
2003-04	Utah Grizzlies	AHL	21	8	11	0	1186	56	2	2.83	....	....	....	....	....	....	....

SNOW, Garth (SNOH, GAHRTH)

Goaltender. Catches left. 6'3", 200 lbs. Born, Wrentham, MA, July 28, 1969.
(Quebec's 6th choice, 114th overall, in 1987 Entry Draft).

			Regular Season								Playoffs						
Season	Club	League	GP	W	L	T	Mins	GA	SO	Avg	GP	W	L	Mins	GA	SO	Avg
1986-87	Mount St. Charles	Hi-School	30	....	....	....	1795	53	10	1.77	....	....	....	....	....	....	....
1987-88	Stratford Cullitons	OJHL-B	30	20	6	0	1642	93	2	3.40	....	....	....	....	....	....	....
1988-89	University of Maine	H-East	5	2	2	0	241	14	1	3.49	....	....	....	....	....	....	....
1989-90	University of Maine	H-East					DID NOT PLAY – ACADEMICALLY INELIGIBLE										
1990-91	University of Maine	H-East	25	*18	4	0	1290	64	2	2.98	....	....	....	....	....	....	....
1991-92	University of Maine	H-East	31	*25	4	2	1792	73	*2	*2.44	....	....	....	....	....	....	....
1992-93	University of Maine	H-East	23	*21	0	1	1210	42	1	*2.08	....	....	....	....	....	....	....
1993-94	United States	Nat-Tm	23	13	5	3	1324	71	1	3.22	....	....	....	....	....	....	....
	United States	Olympics	5	1	3	1	299	17	0	3.41	....	....	....	....	....	....	....
	Quebec	**NHL**	**5**	**3**	**2**	**0**	**279**	**16**	**0**	**3.44**	....	....	....	....	....	....	....
	Cornwall Aces	AHL	16	6	5	3	927	51	0	3.30	13	8	5	790	42	0	3.19
1994-95	Cornwall Aces	AHL	*62	*32	20	7	*3558	162	3	2.73	8	4	3	402	14	*2	*2.09
	Quebec	**NHL**	**2**	**1**	**1**	**0**	**119**	**11**	**0**	**5.55**	**1**	**0**	**0**	**9**	**1**	**0**	**6.67**
1995-96	**Philadelphia**	**NHL**	**26**	**12**	**8**	**4**	**1437**	**69**	**0**	**2.88**	**1**	**0**	**0**	**1**	**0**	**0**	**0.00**
1996-97	**Philadelphia**	**NHL**	**35**	**14**	**8**	**8**	**1884**	**79**	**2**	**2.52**	**12**	**8**	**4**	**699**	**33**	**0**	**2.83**
1997-98	**Philadelphia**	**NHL**	**29**	**14**	**9**	**4**	**1651**	**67**	**1**	**2.43**	....	....	....	....	....	....	....
	Vancouver	**NHL**	**12**	**3**	**6**	**0**	**504**	**26**	**0**	**3.10**	....	....	....	....	....	....	....
1998-99	**Vancouver**	**NHL**	**65**	**20**	**31**	**8**	**3501**	**171**	**6**	**2.93**	....	....	....	....	....	....	....
99-2000	**Vancouver**	**NHL**	**32**	**10**	**15**	**3**	**1712**	**76**	**0**	**2.66**	....	....	....	....	....	....	....
2000-01	**Pittsburgh**	**NHL**	**35**	**14**	**15**	**4**	**2032**	**101**	**3**	**2.98**	....	....	....	....	....	....	....
	Wilkes-Barre	AHL	3	2	1	0	178	7	0	2.36	....	....	....	....	....	....	....
2001-02	**NY Islanders**	**NHL**	**25**	**10**	**7**	**2**	**1217**	**55**	**2**	**2.71**	**1**	**0**	**0**	**26**	**2**	**0**	**4.62**
2002-03	**NY Islanders**	**NHL**	**43**	**16**	**17**	**5**	**2390**	**92**	**1**	**2.31**	**5**	**1**	**4**	**305**	**12**	**1**	**2.36**
2003-04	**NY Islanders**	**NHL**	**39**	**14**	**15**	**5**	**2015**	**94**	**1**	**2.80**	....	....	....	....	....	....	....
	NHL Totals		**348**	**131**	**134**	**43**	**18741**	**857**	**16**	**2.74**	**20**	**9**	**8**	**1040**	**48**	**1**	**2.77**

Hockey East Second All-Star Team (1992, 1993) • NCAA Championship All-Tournament Team (1993)

Transferred to **Colorado** after **Quebec** franchise relocated, June 21, 1995. Traded to **Philadelphia** by **Colorado** for Philadelphia's 3rd (later traded to Washington – Washington selected Shawn McNeil) and 6th (Kai Fischer) round choices in 1996 Entry Draft, July 12, 1995. Traded to **Vancouver** by **Philadelphia** for Sean Burke, March 4, 1998. Signed as a free agent by **Pittsburgh**, October 10, 2000. Signed as a free agent by **NY Islanders**, July 14, 2001.

STANA, Rastislav (STAN-ah, RAH-tih-slahv) WSH.

Goaltender. Catches left. 6'2", 184 lbs. Born, Kosice, Czech., January 10, 1980.
(Washington's 8th choice, 193rd overall, in 1998 Entry Draft).

			Regular Season								Playoffs						
Season	Club	League	GP	W	L	T	Mins	GA	SO	Avg	GP	W	L	Mins	GA	SO	Avg
1997-98	HC Kosice Jr.	Slovak-Jr.	32				1920	56	2	1.75							
1998-99	Moose Jaw	WHL	36	21	14	1	2131	123	2	3.46	9	4	5	544	30	0	3.31
99-2000	Moose Jaw	WHL	14	4	9	0	730	48	0	3.95							
	Calgary Hitmen	WHL	16	13	2	1	971	37	1	2.29	9	7	2	526	21	1	2.40
2000-01	Richmond	ECHL	38	15	16	2	2111	90	1	2.56	3	1	2	178	7	1	2.34
2001-02	Richmond	ECHL	36	20	12	3	2098	95	1	2.72							
	Portland Pirates	AHL	3	1	2	0	180	11	0	3.66							
	Slovakia	Olympics	1	1	0	0	60	1	0	1.00							
2002-03	Portland Pirates	AHL	24	8	11	4	1355	49	2	2.17	1	0	1	59	3	0	3.08
2003-04	**Washington**	**NHL**	**6**	**1**	**2**	**0**	**211**	**11**	**0**	**3.13**							
	Portland Pirates	AHL	24	14	5	4	1429	40	5	1.68	3	1	2	139	7	0	3.02
	NHL Totals		**6**	**1**	**2**	**0**	**211**	**11**	**0**	**3.13**							

STEPHAN, Tobias (STEH-fan, toh-BEE-uhs) DAL.

Goaltender. Catches left. 6'3", 178 lbs. Born, Zurich, Switz., January 21, 1984.
(Dallas' 3rd choice, 34th overall, in 2002 Entry Draft).

			Regular Season								Playoffs						
Season	Club	League	GP	W	L	T	Mins	GA	SO	Avg	GP	W	L	Mins	GA	SO	Avg
2000-01	Kloten Flyers Jr.	Swiss-Jr.					STATISTICS NOT AVAILABLE										
2001-02	EHC Chur	Swiss	23				1396	80	0	3.44	10			604	39	0	3.87
2002-03	Kloten Flyers	Swiss	*44				2670	125	2	2.81	5			292	20	0	4.11
2003-04	Kloten Flyers	Swiss	26				1547	61	5	2.37							

STORR, Jamie (STOHR, JAY-mee)

Goaltender. Catches left. 6'2", 195 lbs. Born, Brampton, Ont., December 28, 1975.
(Los Angeles' 1st choice, 7th overall, in 1994 Entry Draft).

			Regular Season								Playoffs						
Season	Club	League	GP	W	L	T	Mins	GA	SO	Avg	GP	W	L	Mins	GA	SO	Avg
1990-91	Brampton Capitals	MTJHL	24				1145	91	0	4.77	15			885	60	0	4.07
1991-92	Owen Sound	OHL	34	11	16	1	1732	128	0	4.43	5	1	4	299	28	0	5.62
1992-93	Owen Sound	OHL	41	20	17	3	2362	180	0	4.57	8	4	4	454	35	0	4.63
1993-94	Owen Sound	OHL	35	21	11	1	2004	120	1	3.59	9	4	5	547	44	0	4.83
1994-95	Owen Sound	OHL	17	5	9	2	977	64	0	3.93							
	Los Angeles	**NHL**	**5**	**1**	**3**	**1**	**263**	**17**	**0**	**3.88**							
	Windsor Spitfires	OHL	4	3	1	0	241	8	1	1.99	10	6	3	520	34	1	3.92
1995-96	**Los Angeles**	**NHL**	**5**	**3**	**1**	**0**	**262**	**12**	**0**	**2.75**							
	Phoenix	IHL	48	22	20	4	2711	139	2	3.08	2	1	1	118	4	1	2.03
1996-97	**Los Angeles**	**NHL**	**5**	**2**	**1**	**1**	**265**	**11**	**0**	**2.49**							
	Phoenix	IHL	44	16	22	4	2441	147	0	3.61							
1997-98	**Los Angeles**	**NHL**	**17**	**9**	**5**	**1**	**920**	**34**	**2**	**2.22**	**3**	**0**	**2**	**145**	**9**	**0**	**3.72**
	Long Beach	IHL	11	7	2	1	629	31	0	2.96							
1998-99	**Los Angeles**	**NHL**	**28**	**12**	**12**	**2**	**1525**	**61**	**4**	**2.40**							
99-2000	**Los Angeles**	**NHL**	**42**	**18**	**15**	**5**	**2206**	**93**	**1**	**2.53**	**1**	**0**	**1**	**36**	**2**	**0**	**3.33**
2000-01	**Los Angeles**	**NHL**	**45**	**19**	**18**	**6**	**2498**	**114**	**4**	**2.74**							
2001-02	**Los Angeles**	**NHL**	**19**	**9**	**4**	**3**	**886**	**28**	**2**	**1.90**	**1**	**0**	**0**	**1**	**0**	**0**	**0.00**
2002-03	**Los Angeles**	**NHL**	**39**	**12**	**19**	**2**	**2027**	**86**	**3**	**2.55**							
2003-04	**Carolina**	**NHL**	**14**	**0**	**8**	**2**	**660**	**32**	**0**	**2.91**							
	Lowell	AHL	13	2	6	2	712	38	0	3.20							
	NHL Totals		**219**	**85**	**86**	**23**	**11512**	**488**	**16**	**2.54**	**5**	**0**	**3**	**182**	**11**	**0**	**3.63**

OHL All-Rookie Team (1992) • OHL First All-Star Team (1994) • NHL All-Rookie Team (1998, 1999)

• Played 8 seconds of playoff game vs. Colorado, April 29, 2002. Signed as a free agent by **Carolina**, October 3, 2003. Signed as a free agent by **Mannheim** (Germany), May 5, 2004.

SZUPER, Levente (SHOO-puhr, leh-VEHN-teh)

Goaltender. Catches left. 5'11", 180 lbs. Born, Budapest, Hungary, June 11, 1980.
(Calgary's 4th choice, 116th overall, in 2000 Entry Draft).

			Regular Season								Playoffs						
Season	Club	League	GP	W	L	T	Mins	GA	SO	Avg	GP	W	L	Mins	GA	SO	Avg
1996-97	Ferencvaros Jr.	Hungary	10				600	9		0.90							
	Ferencvaros	Hungary	30				1660	74	3	2.67							
1997-98	Krefeld Jr.	Ger.-Jr.	40				2300	103	3	2.69							
1998-99	Ottawa 67's	OHL	32	22	6	3	1800	70	4	2.33	4	2	2	241	11	*1	2.74
99-2000	Ottawa 67's	OHL	53	31	15	2	2862	122	*5	2.56	11	6	5	680	35	1	3.09
2000-01	Saint John Flames	AHL	34	16	10	2	1750	73	2	2.50	1	1	0	36	0	0	0.00
2001-02	Saint John Flames	AHL	43	15	18	5	2429	98	5	2.42							
2002-03	Saint John Flames	AHL	35	12	18	2	1904	82	1	2.58							
2003-04	Peoria Rivermen	ECHL	32	23	8	1	1897	73	4	2.31	3	1	1	162	6	0	2.22
	Worcester IceCats	AHL	3	0	0	0	93	7	0	4.53							

Signed as a free agent by **St. Louis**, September 10, 2003.

TARASOV, Vadim (ta-RA-sahf, va-DEEM) MTL.

Goaltender. Catches left. 5'11", 187 lbs. Born, Ust-Kamenogorsk, USSR, December 31, 1976.
(Montreal's 9th choice, 196th overall, in 1999 Entry Draft).

			Regular Season								Playoffs						
Season	Club	League	GP	W	L	T	Mins	GA	SO	Avg	GP	W	L	Mins	GA	SO	Avg
1995-96	Novokuznetsk	CIS	26				1355	60	1	2.66							
1996-97	Novokuznetsk	Russia	34				1971	87	0	2.65							
1997-98	Novokuznetsk	Russia	23				1364	61	2	2.68							
1998-99	Novokuznetsk	Russia	*41				*2346	56	*8	1.43	6			349	16	0	2.75
99-2000	Novokuznetsk	Russia	28				1583	66	1	2.50	14			791	26	1	1.97
2000-01	Novokuznetsk	Russia	33				1960	69	4	2.11							
2001-02	Quebec Citadelles	AHL	14	7	4	2	801	42	0	3.15							
2002-03	Novokuznetsk	Russia	29				1450	64	0	2.65							
2003-04	Novokuznetsk	Russia	39				2165	63	4	1.75	3			169	9	0	3.20

Russian League Best Goaltender (1999, 2000, 2001)

Signed as a free agent by **Novokuznetsk** (Russia) with Montreal retaining NHL rights, July 18, 2002.

TELLQVIST, Mikael (TEHL-kvihst, MIGH-kuhl) TOR.

Goaltender. Catches left. 5'11", 194 lbs. Born, Sundbyberg, Sweden, September 19, 1979.
(Toronto's 3rd choice, 70th overall, in 2000 Entry Draft).

			Regular Season								Playoffs						
Season	Club	League	GP	W	L	T	Mins	GA	SO	Avg	GP	W	L	Mins	GA	SO	Avg
1997-98	Djurgarden Jr.	Swede-Jr.	23				1380	55		2.39	2	0	2	120	8	0	4.00
1998-99	Djurgarden	Sweden	3	1	2	0	124	8	0	3.87	4			240	11	0	2.75
	Djurgarden	EuroHL	3	2	1	0	180	8		2.33							
99-2000	Huddinge IK	Swede-2	11	4	7	0	660	33		3.30							
	Djurgarden	Sweden	30				1909	66	2	*2.07	*13			*814	21	*3	*1.55
2000-01	Djurgarden	Sweden	43				2622	91	*5	*2.08	*16			*1006	45	*1	2.68
2001-02	St. John's	AHL	28	8	11	6	1521	79	0	3.12	1	1	0	15	0	0	0.00
	Sweden	Olympics					DID NOT PLAY – SPARE GOALTENDER										
2002-03	**Toronto**	**NHL**	**3**	**1**	**1**	**0**	**86**	**4**	**0**	**2.79**							
	St. John's	AHL	47	17	25	3	2651	148	1	3.35							
2003-04	**Toronto**	**NHL**	**11**	**5**	**3**	**2**	**647**	**31**	**0**	**2.87**							
	St. John's	AHL	23	10	11	1	1343	59	1	2.64							
	NHL Totals		**14**	**6**	**4**	**2**	**733**	**35**	**0**	**2.86**							

THEODORE, Jose (TEE-uh-dohr, joh-SAY) MTL.

Goaltender. Catches right. 5'11", 182 lbs. Born, Laval, Que., September 13, 1976.
(Montreal's 2nd choice, 44th overall, in 1994 Entry Draft).

			Regular Season								Playoffs						
Season	Club	League	GP	W	L	T	Mins	GA	SO	Avg	GP	W	L	Mins	GA	SO	Avg
1990-91	Richelieu	QAHA	42				2520	80	0	1.90							
1991-92	Richelieu Riverains	QAAA	24	9	13	2	1440	96	0	3.99	5	2	3	295	26	0	5.28
1992-93	St-Jean Lynx	QMJHL	34	12	16	2	1776	112	0	3.78	3	0	2	175	11	0	3.77
1993-94	St-Jean Lynx	QMJHL	57	20	29	6	3225	194	0	3.61	5	1	4	296	18	0	3.65
1994-95	Hull Olympiques	QMJHL	*58	*32	22	2	*3348	193	5	3.46	*21	*15	6	*1263	59	*1	2.80
	Fredericton	AHL									1	0	1	60	3	0	3.00
1995-96	**Montreal**	**NHL**	**1**	**0**	**0**	**0**	**9**	**1**	**0**	**6.67**							
	Hull Olympiques	QMJHL	48	33	11	2	2807	158	0	3.38	5	2	3	299	20	0	4.01
1996-97	**Montreal**	**NHL**	**16**	**5**	**6**	**2**	**821**	**53**	**0**	**3.87**	**2**	**1**	**1**	**168**	**7**	**0**	**2.50**
	Fredericton	AHL	26	12	12	0	1469	87	0	3.55							
1997-98	Fredericton	AHL	53	20	23	8	3053	145	2	2.85	4	1	3	237	13	0	3.28
	Montreal	**NHL**									**3**	**0**	**1**	**120**	**1**	**0**	**0.50**
1998-99	**Montreal**	**NHL**	**18**	**4**	**12**	**0**	**913**	**50**	**1**	**3.29**							
	Fredericton	AHL	27	12	13	2	1609	77	2	2.87	13	8	5	694	35	1	3.03
99-2000	**Montreal**	**NHL**	**30**	**12**	**13**	**2**	**1655**	**58**	**5**	**2.10**							
2000-01	**Montreal**	**NHL**	**59**	**20**	**29**	**5**	**3298**	**141**	**2**	**2.57**							
	Quebec Citadelles	AHL	3	3	0	0	180	9	0	3.00							
2001-02	**Montreal**	**NHL**	**67**	**30**	**24**	**10**	**3864**	**136**	**7**	**2.11**	**12**	**6**	**6**	**686**	**35**	**0**	**3.06**
2002-03	**Montreal**	**NHL**	**57**	**20**	**31**	**6**	**3419**	**165**	**2**	**2.90**							
2003-04	**Montreal**	**NHL**	**67**	**33**	**28**	**5**	**3961**	**150**	**6**	**2.27**	**11**	**4**	**7**	**678**	**27**	**1**	**2.39**
	NHL Totals		**315**	**124**	**143**	**30**	**17940**	**754**	**23**	**2.52**	**28**	**11**	**15**	**1652**	**70**	**1**	**2.54**

QMJHL Second All-Star Team (1995, 1996) • NHL Second All-Star Team (2002) • MBNA Roger Crozier Saving Grace Award (2002) • Vezina Trophy (2002) • Hart Trophy (2002)

Played in NHL All-Star Game (2002, 2004)

• Scored a goal vs. NY Islanders, January 2, 2001.

THIBAULT, Jocelyn (TEE-boh, JAW-seh-lihn) CHI.

Goaltender. Catches left. 5'11", 169 lbs. Born, Montreal, Que., January 12, 1975.
(Quebec's 1st choice, 10th overall, in 1993 Entry Draft).

			Regular Season								Playoffs						
Season	Club	League	GP	W	L	T	Mins	GA	SO	Avg	GP	W	L	Mins	GA	SO	Avg
1990-91	Laval-Laurentides	QAAA	20	14	5	0	1178	78	1	3.94	5	2	3	300	20	0	4.00
1991-92	Trois-Rivieres	QMJHL	30	14	7	1	1496	77	0	3.09	3	1	1	110	4	0	2.19
1992-93	Sherbrooke	QMJHL	56	34	14	5	3190	159	3	2.99	15	9	6	882	57	0	3.87
1993-94	**Quebec**	**NHL**	**29**	**8**	**13**	**3**	**1504**	**83**	**0**	**3.31**							
	Cornwall Aces	AHL	4	4	0	0	240	9	1	2.25							
1994-95	Sherbrooke	QMJHL	13	6	6	1	776	38	1	2.94							
	Quebec	**NHL**	**18**	**12**	**2**	**2**	**898**	**35**	**1**	**2.34**	**3**	**1**	**2**	**148**	**8**	**0**	**3.24**
1995-96	**Colorado**	**NHL**	**10**	**3**	**4**	**2**	**558**	**28**	**0**	**3.01**							
	Montreal	**NHL**	**40**	**23**	**13**	**3**	**2334**	**110**	**3**	**2.83**	**6**	**2**	**4**	**311**	**18**	**0**	**3.47**
1996-97	**Montreal**	**NHL**	**61**	**22**	**24**	**11**	**3397**	**164**	**1**	**2.90**	**3**	**0**	**3**	**179**	**13**	**0**	**4.36**
1997-98	**Montreal**	**NHL**	**47**	**19**	**15**	**8**	**2652**	**109**	**2**	**2.47**	**2**	**0**	**0**	**43**	**4**	**0**	**5.58**
1998-99	**Montreal**	**NHL**	**10**	**3**	**4**	**2**	**529**	**23**	**1**	**2.61**							
	Chicago	**NHL**	**52**	**21**	**26**	**5**	**3014**	**136**	**4**	**2.71**							
99-2000	**Chicago**	**NHL**	**60**	**25**	**26**	**7**	**3438**	**158**	**3**	**2.76**							
2000-01	**Chicago**	**NHL**	**66**	**27**	**32**	**7**	**3844**	**180**	**6**	**2.81**							
2001-02	**Chicago**	**NHL**	**67**	**33**	**23**	**9**	**3838**	**159**	**6**	**2.49**	**3**	**1**	**2**	**159**	**7**	**0**	**2.64**
2002-03	**Chicago**	**NHL**	**62**	**26**	**28**	**7**	**3650**	**144**	**8**	**2.37**							
2003-04	**Chicago**	**NHL**	**14**	**5**	**7**	**2**	**821**	**39**	**1**	**2.85**							
	NHL Totals		**536**	**227**	**217**	**68**	**30477**	**1368**	**36**	**2.69**	**17**	**4**	**11**	**840**	**50**	**0**	**3.57**

QMJHL All-Rookie Team (1992) • QMJHL First All-Star Team (1993) • QMJHL MVP (1993) • Canadian Major Junior First All-Star Team (1993) • Canadian Major Junior Goaltender of the Year (1993)

Played in NHL All-Star Game (2003)

Transferred to **Colorado** after **Quebec** franchise relocated, June 21, 1995. Traded to **Montreal** by **Colorado** with Andrei Kovalenko and Martin Rucinsky for Patrick Roy and Mike Keane, December 6, 1995. Traded to **Chicago** by **Montreal** with Dave Manson and Brad Brown for Jeff Hackett, Eric Weinrich, Alain Nasreddine and Tampa Bay's 4th round choice (previously acquired, Montreal selected Chris Dyment) in 1999 Entry Draft, November 16, 1998. • Missed majority of 2003-04 season recovering from hip injury suffered in practice, November 9, 2003.

THOMAS, Tim (TAW-mas, TIHM)

Goaltender. Catches left. 5'11", 181 lbs. Born, Flint, MI, April 15, 1974.
(Quebec's 11th choice, 217th overall, in 1994 Entry Draft).

			Regular Season								Playoffs						
Season	Club	League	GP	W	L	T	Mins	GA	SO	Avg	GP	W	L	Mins	GA	SO	Avg
1992-93	Davison Academy	Hi-School	27				1580	87		3.30							
1993-94	U. of Vermont	ECAC	*33	15	12	6	1864	94	0	3.03							
1994-95	U. of Vermont	ECAC	34	18	13	2	2010	90	*4	*2.69							
1995-96	U. of Vermont	ECAC	37	*26	7	4	*2254	88	*3	*2.34							
1996-97	U. of Vermont	ECAC	36	22	11	3	2158	101	2	2.81							
1997-98	HIFK Helsinki	Finland	18	13	4	1	1035	28	2	*1.62	*9	*9	0	*551	14	*3	*1.52
	Birmingham Bulls	ECHL	6	4	1	1	360	13	1	2.17							
	Houston Aeros	IHL	1	0	1	0	59	4	0	4.01							
1998-99	HIFK Helsinki	Finland	14	8	3	3	833	31	2	2.23	*11	7	4	*658	25	0	2.28
	Hamilton Bulldogs	AHL	15	6	8	0	837	45	0	3.23							
99-2000	Detroit Vipers	IHL	36	10	21	3	2020	120	1	3.56							
2000-01	AIK Solna	Sweden	43				2542	105	3	2.48	5			299	20	0	4.01
2001-02	Karpat Oulu	Finland	32	15	12	5	1937	79	4	2.45	3	1	2	180	12	0	4.00
2002-03	**Boston**	**NHL**	**4**	**3**	**1**	**0**	**220**	**11**	**0**	**3.00**							
	Providence Bruins	AHL	35	18	12	5	2049	98	1	2.87							
2003-04	Providence Bruins	AHL	43	20	16	6	2544	78	9	1.84	2	0	2	84	10	0	7.13
	NHL Totals		**4**	**3**	**1**	**0**	**220**	**11**	**0**	**3.00**							

ECAC First All-Star Team (1995, 1996) • NCAA East Second All-American Team (1995) • NCAA East First All-American Team (1996)

Signed as a free agent by **Edmonton**, June 4, 1998. Signed as a free agent by **Boston**, August 8, 2002. Signed as a free agent by **Jokerit Helsinki** (Finland), May 17, 2004.

THOMPSON, Billy (TAWM-suhn, BIHL-lee) OTT.

Goaltender. Catches left. 6'2", 200 lbs. Born, Saskatoon, Sask., September 24, 1982.
(Florida's 7th choice, 136th overall, in 2001 Entry Draft).

			Regular Season								Playoffs						
Season	Club	League	GP	W	L	T	Mins	GA	SO	Avg	GP	W	L	Mins	GA	SO	Avg
1997-98	Sask. Contacts	SMHL	23	14	5	3	1336	65	2	2.92							
1998-99	Lebret Eagles	SJHL					STATISTICS NOT AVAILABLE										
99-2000	Estevan Bruins	SJHL	31				1763	132	1	4.49	5	1	3	328	17	0	3.11
	Prince George	WHL	1	0	1	0	60	5	0	5.00							
2000-01	Prince George	WHL	57	24	24	3	3185	178	1	3.35	6	2	4	324	22	0	4.07
2001-02	Prince George	WHL	42	20	17	2	2375	108	2	2.73	7	3	4	402	21	0	3.13
2002-03	Prince George	WHL	50	20	26	0	2776	186	0	4.02	5	1	3	239	12	0	3.01
	Binghamton	AHL	1	1	0	0	60	5	0	5.00							
2003-04	Binghamton	AHL	34	13	14	2	1725	83	2	2.89							

WHL West Second All-Star Team (2003)

Traded to **Ottawa** by **Florida** with Greg Watson for Jani Hurme, October 1, 2002.

TOIVONEN, Hannu (TOI-voh-nuhn, HA-noo) BOS.

Goaltender. Catches left. 6'2", 191 lbs. Born, Kalvola, Finland, May 18, 1984.
(Boston's 1st choice, 29th overall, in 2002 Entry Draft).

			Regular Season								Playoffs						
Season	Club	League	GP	W	L	T	Mins	GA	SO	Avg	GP	W	L	Mins	GA	SO	Avg
2001-02	HPK Jr.	Finn-Jr.	31	15	12	4	1877	103	2	3.29	7	3	4	440	31	0	4.23
	HPK 18	Finn-Jr.	5	4	0	1	300	11	0	2.23	....	....	....	....	....	....	....
2002-03	HPK Hameenlinna	Finland	24	16	2	4	1432	54	2	2.26	2	1	1	118	3	1	1.53
2003-04	Providence Bruins	AHL	36	15	16	4	2162	83	2	2.30	0	0	0	0	0	0	0.00

TOSKALA, Vesa (TAWS-kah-lah, VEH-sa) S.J.

Goaltender. Catches left. 5'10", 190 lbs. Born, Tampere, Finland, May 20, 1977.
(San Jose's 4th choice, 90th overall, in 1995 Entry Draft).

			Regular Season								Playoffs						
Season	Club	League	GP	W	L	T	Mins	GA	SO	Avg	GP	W	L	Mins	GA	SO	Avg
1994-95	Ilves Tampere	Finn-Jr.	17	....	....	....	956	36	....	2.26	....	....	....	....	....	....	....
1995-96	Ilves Tampere	Finn-Jr.	3	....	....	....	180	3	....	1.00	....	....	....	....	....	....	....
	KooVee Tampere	Finland-2	2	....	....	....	119	5	....	2.51	....	....	....	....	....	....	....
	Ilves Tampere	Finland	37	....	....	....	2073	109	1	3.16	2	....	....	78	11	....	8.49
1996-97	Ilves Tampere	Finland	40	22	12	5	2270	108	0	2.85	8	3	5	479	29	0	3.63
1997-98	Ilves Tampere	Finland	43	*26	13	3	2555	118	1	2.77	*9	6	3	519	18	1	2.08
1998-99	Ilves Tampere	Finland	33	21	12	0	1966	70	*5	2.14	4	1	3	248	14	0	3.39
99-2000	Farjestad	Sweden	44	....	....	....	2652	118	3	2.67	7	....	....	439	19	0	2.60
2000-01	Kentucky	AHL	44	22	13	5	2466	114	2	2.77	3	0	3	197	8	0	2.43
2001-02	San Jose	NHL	1	0	0	0	10	0	0	0.00	....	....	....	....	....	....	....
	Cleveland Barons	AHL	*62	19	33	7	*3574	178	3	2.99	....	....	....	....	....	....	....
2002-03	San Jose	NHL	11	4	3	1	537	21	1	2.35	....	....	....	....	....	....	....
	Cleveland Barons	AHL	49	15	30	2	2824	151	1	3.21	....	....	....	....	....	....	....
2003-04	San Jose	NHL	28	12	8	4	1541	53	1	2.06	....	....	....	....	....	....	....
	NHL Totals		40	16	11	5	2088	74	2	2.13	....	....	....	....	....	....	....

TREMBLAY, David (TRAHM-blay, DAY-vihd) PHI.

Goaltender. Catches left. 6'2", 180 lbs. Born, Hull, Que., August 16, 1985.
(Philadelphia's 9th choice, 140th overall, in 2003 Entry Draft).

			Regular Season								Playoffs						
Season	Club	League	GP	W	L	T	Mins	GA	SO	Avg	GP	W	L	Mins	GA	SO	Avg
2002-03	Hull Olympiques	QMJHL	30	14	9	2	1513	71	0	2.82	1	0	0	8	0	0	0.00
2003-04	Gatineau	QMJHL	47	33	10	3	2671	117	3	2.63	15	12	2	859	28	*2	*1.96

QMJHL All-Rookie Team (2003)

TUGNUTT, Ron (TUHG-nuht, RAWN)

Goaltender. Catches left. 5'11", 160 lbs. Born, Scarborough, Ont., October 22, 1967.
(Quebec's 4th choice, 81st overall, in 1986 Entry Draft).

			Regular Season								Playoffs						
Season	Club	League	GP	W	L	T	Mins	GA	SO	Avg	GP	W	L	Mins	GA	SO	Avg
1983-84	Tor. Red Wings	MTHL	34	....	....	....	1690	91	3	2.67	....	....	....	....	....	....	....
	Weston Dukes	MTJHL	1	0	0	0	20	2	0	6.00	....	....	....	....	....	....	....
1984-85	Peterborough	OHL	18	7	4	2	938	59	0	3.77	....	....	....	....	....	....	....
1985-86	Peterborough	OHL	26	18	7	0	1543	74	1	2.88	3	2	0	133	6	0	2.71
1986-87	Peterborough	OHL	31	21	7	2	1891	88	2	*2.79	6	3	3	374	21	1	3.37
1987-88	Quebec	NHL	6	2	3	0	284	16	0	3.38	....	....	....	....	....	....	....
	Fredericton Express	AHL	34	20	9	4	1964	118	1	3.60	4	1	2	204	11	0	3.24
1988-89	Quebec	NHL	26	10	10	3	1367	82	0	3.60	....	....	....	....	....	....	....
	Halifax Citadels	AHL	24	14	7	2	1368	79	1	3.46	....	....	....	....	....	....	....
1989-90	Quebec	NHL	35	5	24	3	1978	152	0	4.61	....	....	....	....	....	....	....
	Halifax Citadels	AHL	6	1	5	0	366	23	0	3.77	....	....	....	....	....	....	....
1990-91	Quebec	NHL	56	12	29	10	3144	212	0	4.05	....	....	....	....	....	....	....
	Halifax Citadels	AHL	2	0	1	0	100	8	0	4.80	....	....	....	....	....	....	....
1991-92	Quebec	NHL	30	6	17	3	1583	106	1	4.02	....	....	....	....	....	....	....
	Halifax Citadels	AHL	8	3	3	1	447	30	0	4.03	....	....	....	....	....	....	....
	Edmonton	NHL	3	1	1	0	124	10	0	4.84	2	0	0	60	3	0	3.00
1992-93	Edmonton	NHL	26	9	12	2	1338	93	0	4.17	....	....	....	....	....	....	....
1993-94	Anaheim	NHL	28	10	15	1	1520	76	1	3.00	....	....	....	....	....	....	....
	Montreal	NHL	8	2	3	1	378	24	0	3.81	1	0	1	59	5	0	5.08
1994-95	Montreal	NHL	7	1	3	1	346	18	0	3.12	....	....	....	....	....	....	....
1995-96	Portland Pirates	AHL	58	21	23	6	3068	171	2	3.34	13	7	6	782	36	1	2.76
1996-97	Ottawa	NHL	37	17	15	1	1991	93	3	2.80	7	3	4	425	14	1	1.98
1997-98	Ottawa	NHL	42	15	14	8	2236	84	3	2.25	2	0	1	74	6	0	4.86
1998-99	Ottawa	NHL	43	22	10	8	2508	75	3	*1.79	2	0	2	118	6	0	3.05
99-2000	Ottawa	NHL	44	18	12	8	2435	103	4	2.54	....	....	....	....	....	....	....
	Pittsburgh	NHL	7	4	2	0	374	15	0	2.41	11	6	5	746	22	2	1.77
2000-01	Columbus	NHL	53	22	25	5	3129	127	4	2.44	....	....	....	....	....	....	....
2001-02	Columbus	NHL	44	12	27	3	2502	119	2	2.85	....	....	....	....	....	....	....
2002-03	Dallas	NHL	31	15	10	5	1701	70	4	2.47	....	....	....	....	....	....	....
	Utah Grizzlies	AHL	5	1	3	1	281	14	0	2.99	....	....	....	....	....	....	....
2003-04	Dallas	NHL	11	3	7	0	548	22	1	2.41	....	....	....	....	....	....	....
	Utah Grizzlies	AHL	5	1	3	1	281	14	0	2.99	....	....	....	....	....	....	....
	NHL Totals		537	186	239	62	29486	1497	26	3.05	25	9	13	1482	56	3	2.27

OHL First All-Star Team (1987)

Played in NHL All-Star Game (1999)

Traded to **Edmonton** by **Quebec** with Brad Zavisha for Martin Rucinsky, March 10, 1992. Claimed by **Anaheim** from **Edmonton** in Expansion Draft, June 24, 1993. Traded to **Montreal** by **Anaheim** for Stephan Lebeau, February 20, 1994. Signed as a free agent by **Washington**, September 25, 1995. Signed as a free agent by **Ottawa**, August 14, 1996. Traded to **Pittsburgh** by **Ottawa** with Janne Laukkanen for Tom Barrasso, March 14, 2000. Signed as a free agent by **Columbus**, July 4, 2000. Traded to **Dallas** by **Columbus** with Columbus' 2nd round choice (Janos Vas) in 2002 Entry Draft for New Jersey's 1st round choice (previously acquired, later traded to Buffalo – Buffalo selected Dan Paille) in 2002 Entry Draft, June 18, 2002. • Missed majority of 2003-04 season recovering from knee (December 2, 2003 in practice) and groin (January 2, 2004 vs. Phoenix) injuries.

TURCO, Marty (TUHR-koh, MAHR-tee) DAL.

Goaltender. Catches left. 5'11", 183 lbs. Born, Sault Ste. Marie, Ont., August 13, 1975.
(Dallas' 4th choice, 124th overall, in 1994 Entry Draft).

			Regular Season								Playoffs						
Season	Club	League	GP	W	L	T	Mins	GA	SO	Avg	GP	W	L	Mins	GA	SO	Avg
1993-94	Cambridge	OJHL-B	34	19	10	3	1973	114	0	3.47	....	....	....	....	....	....	....
1994-95	U. of Michigan	CCHA	37	*27	7	1	2063	95	1	2.76	....	....	....	....	....	....	....
1995-96	U. of Michigan	CCHA	*42	*34	7	1	*2335	84	*5	*2.16	....	....	....	....	....	....	....
1996-97	U. of Michigan	CCHA	*41	*33	4	4	*2296	87	*4	*2.27	....	....	....	....	....	....	....
1997-98	U. of Michigan	CCHA	*45	*33	10	1	*2640	95	4	2.16	....	....	....	....	....	....	....
1998-99	Michigan K-Wings	IHL	54	24	17	10	3127	136	1	2.61	5	2	3	300	14	0	2.80
99-2000	Michigan K-Wings	IHL	60	23	27	*7	3399	139	*7	2.45	....	....	....	....	....	....	....
2000-01	Dallas	NHL	26	13	6	1	1266	40	3	*1.90	....	....	....	....	....	....	....
2001-02	Dallas	NHL	31	15	6	2	1519	53	2	2.09	....	....	....	....	....	....	....
2002-03	Dallas	NHL	55	31	10	10	3203	92	7	*1.72	12	6	6	798	25	0	1.88
2003-04	Dallas	NHL	73	37	21	13	4359	144	9	1.98	5	1	4	325	18	0	3.32
	NHL Totals		185	96	43	26	10347	329	21	1.91	17	7	10	1123	43	0	2.30

CCHA Rookie of the Year (1995) • NCAA Championship All-Tournament Team (1996, 1998) • CCHA First All-Star Team (1997) • NCAA West First All-American Team (1997) • CCHA Second All-Star Team (1998) • NCAA Championship Tournament MVP (1998) • Garry F. Longman Memorial Trophy (Top Rookie – IHL) (1999) • MBNA Roger Crozier Saving Grace Award (2001, 2003) • NHL Second All-Star Team (2003)

Played in NHL All-Star Game (2003, 2004)

TUREK, Roman (TOOR-ehk, ROH-muhn) CGY.

Goaltender. Catches right. 6'3", 220 lbs. Born, Strakonice, Czech., May 21, 1970.
(Minnesota's 6th choice, 113th overall, in 1990 Entry Draft).

			Regular Season								Playoffs						
Season	Club	League	GP	W	L	T	Mins	GA	SO	Avg	GP	W	L	Mins	GA	SO	Avg
1990-91	Ceske Budejovice	Czech	26	....	....	....	1244	98	0	4.73	....	....	....	....	....	....	....
1991-92	Ceske Budejovice	Czech-2					STATISTICS NOT AVAILABLE										
1992-93	Ceske Budejovice	Czech	43	....	....	....	2555	121	....	2.84	....	....	....	....	....	....	....
1993-94	Ceske Budejovice	Czech	44	....	....	....	2584	111	....	2.58	3	....	....	180	12	0	4.00
	Czech Republic	Olympics	2	2	0	0	120	3	0	1.50	....	....	....	....	....	....	....
1994-95	Ceske Budejovice	Czech	44	....	....	....	2587	119	....	2.76	9	....	....	498	25	....	3.01
1995-96	Nurnberg	Germany	48	....	....	....	2787	154	....	3.32	5	....	....	338	14	....	2.48
1996-97	Dallas	NHL	6	3	1	0	263	9	0	2.05	....	....	....	....	....	....	....
	Michigan K-Wings	IHL	29	8	13	4	1555	77	0	2.97	....	....	....	....	....	....	....
1997-98	Dallas	NHL	23	11	10	1	1324	49	1	2.22	....	....	....	....	....	....	....
	Michigan K-Wings	IHL	2	1	1	0	119	5	0	2.52	....	....	....	....	....	....	....
1998-99◆	Dallas	NHL	26	16	3	3	1382	48	1	2.08	....	....	....	....	....	....	....
99-2000	St. Louis	NHL	67	42	15	9	3960	129	*7	1.95	7	3	4	415	19	0	2.75
2000-01	St. Louis	NHL	54	24	18	10	3232	123	6	2.28	14	9	5	908	31	0	2.05
2001-02	Calgary	NHL	69	30	28	11	4081	172	5	2.53	....	....	....	....	....	....	....
2002-03	Calgary	NHL	65	27	29	9	3822	164	4	2.57	....	....	....	....	....	....	....
2003-04	Calgary	NHL	18	6	11	0	1031	40	3	2.33	1	0	0	19	0	0	0.00
	NHL Totals		328	159	115	43	19095	734	27	2.31	22	12	9	1342	50	0	2.24

Shared William M. Jennings Trophy (1999) with Ed Belfour • NHL Second All-Star Team (2000) • William M. Jennings Trophy (2000)

Played in NHL All-Star Game (2000)

Rights transferred to **Dallas** after **Minnesota** franchise relocated, June 9, 1993. Traded to **St. Louis** by **Dallas** for St. Louis' compensatory 2nd round choice (Dan Jancevski) in 1999 Entry Draft, June 20, 1999. Traded to **Calgary** by **St. Louis** with St. Louis' 4th round choice (Yegor Shastin) in 2001 Entry Draft for Fred Brathwaite, Daniel Tkaczuk, Sergei Varlamov and Calgary's 9th round choice (Grant Jacobsen) in 2001 Entry Draft, June 23, 2001. • Missed majority of 2003-04 season recovering from knee injury suffered in game vs. Buffalo, October 14, 2003.

UNDERHILL, Matt (UHN-duhr-hihl, MAT) CHI.

Goaltender. Catches left. 6'2", 195 lbs. Born, Merritt, B.C., September 16, 1979.
(Calgary's 8th choice, 170th overall, in 1999 Entry Draft).

			Regular Season								Playoffs						
Season	Club	League	GP	W	L	T	Mins	GA	SO	Avg	GP	W	L	Mins	GA	SO	Avg
1997-98	Notre Dame	SJHL	43	18	22	3	2573	132	2	3.07	....	....	....	....	....	....	....
1998-99	Cornell Big Red	ECAC	25	7	10	4	1320	65	1	2.95	....	....	....	....	....	....	....
99-2000	Cornell Big Red	ECAC	18	8	7	1	912	44	1	2.89	....	....	....	....	....	....	....
2000-01	Cornell Big Red	ECAC	25	13	8	3	1504	47	1	1.88	....	....	....	....	....	....	....
2001-02	Cornell Big Red	ECAC	21	14	6	1	1334	40	3	1.80	....	....	....	....	....	....	....
2002-03	Pee Dee Pride	ECHL	33	16	13	2	1878	88	0	2.81	....	....	....	....	....	....	....
	Providence Bruins	AHL	7	3	3	1	429	22	0	3.08	....	....	....	....	....	....	....
2003-04	Florence Pride	ECHL	29	10	14	4	1686	97	1	3.45	....	....	....	....	....	....	....
	Manchester	AHL	4	2	2	0	186	9	0	2.90	....	....	....	....	....	....	....
	Chicago	NHL	1	0	1	0	61	4	0	3.93	....	....	....	....	....	....	....
	Norfolk Admirals	AHL	1	0	0	0	20	0	0	0.00	....	....	....	....	....	....	....
	NHL Totals		1	0	1	0	61	4	0	3.93	....	....	....	....	....	....	....

ECAC First All-Star Team (2002)

Signed as a free agent by **Pee Dee** (ECHL), August 13, 2002. Signed as a free agent by **Chicago**, March 4, 2004.

VALENT, Michal (VAH-lehnt, MEE-khahl) BUF.

Goaltender. Catches left. 6'2", 176 lbs. Born, Martin, Czechoslovakia, March 5, 1986.
(Buffalo's 4th choice, 145th overall, in 2004 Entry Draft).

			Regular Season								Playoffs						
Season	Club	League	GP	W	L	T	Mins	GA	SO	Avg	GP	W	L	Mins	GA	SO	Avg
2002-03	MHC Martin 18	Slovak-Jr.	24	....	....	....	1343	48	3	2.14	....	....	....	....	....	....	....
2003-04	MHC Martin Jr.	Slovak-Jr.	38	....	....	....	2188	118	1	3.24	....	....	....	....	....	....	....

VALIQUETTE, Stephen (val-ih-KEHT, STEE-vehn) NYR

Goaltender. Catches left. 6'5", 205 lbs. Born, Etobicoke, Ont., August 20, 1977.
(Los Angeles' 8th choice, 190th overall, in 1996 Entry Draft).

			Regular Season								Playoffs						
Season	Club	League	GP	W	L	T	Mins	GA	SO	Avg	GP	W	L	Mins	GA	SO	Avg
1993-94	Burlington	OPJHL	30	....	....	....	1663	112	1	4.04	....	....	....	....	....	....	....
1994-95	Rayside-Balfour	NOJHA	2	0	2	0	89	12	0	8.09	....	....	....	....	....	....	....
	Smiths Falls Bears	OCJHL	21	10	8	3	1275	75	0	3.53	....	....	....	....	....	....	....
	Sudbury Wolves	OHL	4	2	0	0	138	6	0	2.61	....	....	....	....	....	....	....
1995-96	Sudbury Wolves	OHL	39	13	16	2	1887	123	0	3.91	....	....	....	....	....	....	....
1996-97	Sudbury Wolves	OHL	*61	21	29	7	3311	232	1	4.20	....	....	....	....	....	....	....
	Dayton Bombers	ECHL	3	1	0	0	89	6	0	4.03	2	1	1	118	5	0	2.54
1997-98	Sudbury Wolves	OHL	14	5	7	1	807	50	0	3.72	....	....	....	....	....	....	....
	Erie Otters	OHL	28	16	7	3	1525	65	3	2.56	7	3	4	467	15	1	1.93
1998-99	Hampton Roads	ECHL	31	18	7	3	1713	84	1	2.94	2	0	1	60	7	0	7.00
	Lowell	AHL	1	0	1	0	59	3	0	3.05	....	....	....	....	....	....	....
99-2000	NY Islanders	NHL	6	2	0	0	193	6	0	1.87	....	....	....	....	....	....	....
	Lowell	AHL	14	8	5	0	727	36	0	2.97	....	....	....	....	....	....	....
	Providence Bruins	AHL	1	1	0	0	60	3	0	3.00	....	....	....	....	....	....	....
	Trenton Titans	ECHL	12	5	6	1	692	36	1	3.12	....	....	....	....	....	....	....
2000-01	Springfield Falcons	AHL	20	7	10	1	1066	54	0	3.04	....	....	....	....	....	....	....
2001-02	Bridgeport	AHL	20	10	5	1	1071	45	2	2.52	1	0	0	18	1	0	3.30
2002-03	Bridgeport	AHL	34	15	14	3	1962	86	2	2.63	4	3	1	253	9	0	2.13
2003-04	Edmonton	NHL	1	0	0	0	14	2	0	8.57	....	....	....	....	....	....	....
	Toronto	AHL	35	14	14	5	2064	89	2	2.59	....	....	....	....	....	....	....
	NY Rangers	NHL	2	1	1	0	120	6	0	3.00	....	....	....	....	....	....	....
	Hartford Wolf Pack	AHL	7	2	4	1	400	15	1	2.25	1	0	0	11	0	0	0.00
	NHL Totals		9	3	1	0	327	14	0	2.57	....	....	....	....	....	....	....

Signed as a free agent by **NY Islanders**, August 18, 1998. Signed as a free agent by **Edmonton**, July 20, 2003. Claimed by **Florida** from **Edmonton** in Waiver Draft, October 3, 2003. Claimed on waivers by **Edmonton** from **Florida**, October 9, 2003. Traded to **NY Rangers** by **Edmonton** with Dwight Helminen, Edmonton's compensatory 2nd round choice (Dane Byers) in 2004 Entry Draft and future considerations for Petr Nedved and Jussi Markkanen, March 3, 2004.

VIOLIN, Matt (vigh-oh-LIHN, MAT) VAN.

Goaltender. Catches left. 6'1", 180 lbs. Born, Etobicoke, Ont., February 8, 1982.
(Vancouver's 9th choice, 247th overall, in 2002 Entry Draft).

			Regular Season								Playoffs						
Season	Club	League	GP	W	L	T	Mins	GA	SO	Avg	GP	W	L	Mins	GA	SO	Avg
2000-01	Oakville Blades	OPJHL	28	....	....	....	1643	110	0	4.02	....	....	....	....	....	....	....

2001-02	Lake Superior State	CCHA	21	4	11	2	1060	54	0	3.06	....	....	....	....	....	....	....
2002-03	Lake Superior State	CCHA	31	4	23	3	1572	96	1	3.66	....	....	....	....	....	....	....
2003-04	Lake Superior State	CCHA	19	4	10	3	983	55	0	3.36	....	....	....	....	....	....	....

VOKOUN, Tomas (voh-KOON, TAW-mas) NSH.

Goaltender. Catches right. 6', 195 lbs. Born, Karlovy Vary, Czech., July 2, 1976.
(Montreal's 11th choice, 226th overall, in 1994 Entry Draft).

			Regular Season								Playoffs						
Season	Club	League	GP	W	L	T	Mins	GA	SO	Avg	GP	W	L	Mins	GA	SO	Avg
1993-94	HC Kladno	Czech	1	0	0	0	20	2	0	6.01	....	....	....	....	....	....	....
1994-95	HC Kladno	Czech	26	....	....	....	1368	70	....	3.07	5	....	....	240	19	....	4.75
1995-96	Wheeling	ECHL	35	20	10	2	1912	117	0	3.67	7	4	3	436	19	0	2.61
	Fredericton	AHL	....	....	....	....	....	....	....	....	1	0	1	59	4	0	4.09
1996-97	**Montreal**	**NHL**	**1**	**0**	**0**	**0**	**20**	**4**	**0**	**12.00**	....	....	....	....	....	....	....
	Fredericton	AHL	47	12	26	7	2645	154	2	3.49	....	....	....	....	....	....	....
1997-98	Fredericton	AHL	31	13	13	2	1735	90	0	3.11	....	....	....	....	....	....	....
1998-99	**Nashville**	**NHL**	**37**	**12**	**18**	**4**	**1954**	**96**	**1**	**2.95**	....	....	....	....	....	....	....
	Milwaukee	IHL	9	3	2	4	539	22	1	2.45	2	0	2	149	8	0	3.22
99-2000	**Nashville**	**NHL**	**33**	**9**	**20**	**1**	**1879**	**87**	**1**	**2.78**	....	....	....	....	....	....	....
	Milwaukee	IHL	7	5	2	0	364	17	0	2.80	....	....	....	....	....	....	....
2000-01	**Nashville**	**NHL**	**37**	**13**	**17**	**5**	**2088**	**85**	**2**	**2.44**	....	....	....	....	....	....	....
2001-02	**Nashville**	**NHL**	**29**	**5**	**14**	**4**	**1471**	**66**	**2**	**2.69**	....	....	....	....	....	....	....
2002-03	**Nashville**	**NHL**	**69**	**25**	**31**	**11**	**3974**	**146**	**3**	**2.20**	....	....	....	....	....	....	....
2003-04	**Nashville**	**NHL**	**73**	**34**	**29**	**10**	**4221**	**178**	**3**	**2.53**	**6**	**2**	**4**	**356**	**12**	**1**	**2.02**
	NHL Totals		**279**	**98**	**129**	**35**	**15607**	**662**	**12**	**2.55**	**6**	**2**	**4**	**356**	**12**	**1**	**2.02**

Played in NHL All-Star Game (2004)

Claimed by **Nashville** from **Montreal** in Expansion Draft, June 26, 1998.

WARD, Cam (WOHRD, KAM) CAR.

Goaltender. Catches left. 6', 176 lbs. Born, Sherwood Park, Alta., February 29, 1984.
(Carolina's 1st choice, 25th overall, in 2002 Entry Draft).

			Regular Season								Playoffs						
Season	Club	League	GP	W	L	T	Mins	GA	SO	Avg	GP	W	L	Mins	GA	SO	Avg
1998-99	Sherwood Park	ABHL	24	13	7	4	1403	85	0	3.64	....	....	....	....	....	....	....
99-2000	Sherwood Park	AMHL	20	9	5	1	1194	71	0	3.57	7	4	3	262	22	0	3.57
2000-01	Sherwood Park	AMHL	25	14	6	3	1449	70	0	2.90	....	....	....	....	....	....	....
	Red Deer Rebels	WHL	1	1	0	0	60	0	1	0.00	....	....	....	....	....	....	....
2001-02	Red Deer Rebels	WHL	46	30	11	4	2694	102	1	*2.27	*23	14	9	*1502	53	*2	2.12
2002-03	Red Deer Rebels	WHL	57	*40	13	3	3368	118	5	2.10	*23	14	9	*1407	49	3	2.09
2003-04	Red Deer Rebels	WHL	56	31	16	8	3338	114	4	2.05	19	10	9	1200	37	3	1.85

WHL East First All-Star Team (2002, 2004) • WHL East Second All-Star Team (2003) • WHL Goaltender of the Year (2004) • WHL Player of the Year (2004) • Canadian Major Junior First All-Star Team (2004) • Canadian Major Junior Goaltender of the Year (2004)

WEBER, Jeff (WEH-buhr, JEHF) BUF.

Goaltender. Catches left. 6'2", 183 lbs. Born, Burlington, Ont., September 24, 1984.
(Buffalo's 9th choice, 235th overall, in 2003 Entry Draft).

			Regular Season								Playoffs						
Season	Club	League	GP	W	L	T	Mins	GA	SO	Avg	GP	W	L	Mins	GA	SO	Avg
99-2000	Ottawa Valley	OMHA					STATISTICS NOT AVAILABLE										
2000-01	Metcalfe Jets	OJHL	42	....	....	....	2520	129	0	3.07	....	....	....	....	....	....	....
2001-02	Sault Ste. Marie	OHL	4	2	1	0	228	16	0	4.21	....	....	....	....	....	....	....
2002-03	Sault Ste. Marie	OHL	4	0	2	1	187	12	0	3.85	....	....	....	....	....	....	....
	Plymouth Whalers	OHL	19	13	2	2	1086	42	1	2.32	3	0	1	70	2	0	1.71
2003-04	Plymouth Whalers	OHL	13	2	4	4	670	34	2	3.04	....	....	....	....	....	....	....
	Barrie Colts	OHL	13	6	3	0	663	30	0	2.71	2	0	1	49	3	0	3.67

WEEKES, Kevin (WEEKS, KEH-vihn)

Goaltender. Catches left. 6', 195 lbs. Born, Toronto, Ont., April 4, 1975.
(Florida's 2nd choice, 41st overall, in 1993 Entry Draft).

			Regular Season								Playoffs						
Season	Club	League	GP	W	L	T	Mins	GA	SO	Avg	GP	W	L	Mins	GA	SO	Avg
1990-91	Tor. Red Wings	MTHL					STATISTICS NOT AVAILABLE										
	St. Michael's B	MTJHL	1	0	0	0	41	1	0	1.46	....	....	....	....	....	....	....
1991-92	Tor. Red Wings	MTHL	35	....	....	....	1575	68	4	1.94	....	....	....	....	....	....	....
	St. Michael's B	MTJHL	2	0	1	1	127	11	0	5.20	4	1	2	214	15	1	4.21
1992-93	Owen Sound	OHL	29	9	12	5	1645	143	0	5.22	1	0	0	26	5	0	11.50
1993-94	Owen Sound	OHL	34	13	19	1	1974	158	0	4.80	....	....	....	....	....	....	....
1994-95	Ottawa 67's	OHL	41	13	23	4	2266	153	1	4.05	....	....	....	....	....	....	....
1995-96	Carolina Monarchs	AHL	60	24	25	8	3404	229	2	4.04	....	....	....	....	....	....	....
1996-97	Carolina Monarchs	AHL	51	17	28	4	2899	172	1	3.56	....	....	....	....	....	....	....
1997-98	**Florida**	**NHL**	**11**	**0**	**5**	**1**	**485**	**32**	**0**	**3.96**	....	....	....	....	....	....	....
	Fort Wayne	IHL	12	9	2	1	719	34	1	2.84	....	....	....	....	....	....	....
1998-99	Detroit Vipers	IHL	33	19	5	7	1857	64	*4	*2.07	....	....	....	....	....	....	....
	Vancouver	**NHL**	**11**	**0**	**8**	**1**	**532**	**34**	**0**	**3.83**	....	....	....	....	....	....	....
99-2000	**Vancouver**	**NHL**	**20**	**6**	**7**	**4**	**987**	**47**	**1**	**2.86**	....	....	....	....	....	....	....
	NY Islanders	**NHL**	**36**	**10**	**20**	**4**	**2026**	**115**	**1**	**3.41**	....	....	....	....	....	....	....
2000-01	**Tampa Bay**	**NHL**	**61**	**20**	**33**	**3**	**3378**	**177**	**4**	**3.14**	....	....	....	....	....	....	....
2001-02	**Tampa Bay**	**NHL**	**19**	**3**	**9**	**0**	**830**	**40**	**2**	**2.89**	....	....	....	....	....	....	....
	Carolina	**NHL**	**2**	**2**	**0**	**0**	**120**	**3**	**0**	**1.50**	**8**	**3**	**2**	**408**	**11**	**2**	**1.62**
2002-03	**Carolina**	**NHL**	**51**	**14**	**24**	**9**	**2965**	**126**	**5**	**2.55**	....	....	....	....	....	....	....
2003-04	**Carolina**	**NHL**	**66**	**23**	**30**	**11**	**3765**	**146**	**6**	**2.33**	....	....	....	....	....	....	....
	NHL Totals		**277**	**78**	**136**	**33**	**15088**	**720**	**19**	**2.86**	**8**	**3**	**2**	**408**	**11**	**2**	**1.62**

Shared James Norris Memorial Trophy (fewest goals against – IHL) (1999) with Andrei Trefilov

Traded to **Vancouver** by **Florida** with Ed Jovanovski, Dave Gagner, Mike Brown and Florida's 1st round choice (Nathan Smith) in 2000 Entry Draft for Pavel Bure, Bret Hedican, Brad Ference and Vancouver's 3rd round choice (Robert Fried) in 2000 Entry Draft, January 17, 1999. Traded to **NY Islanders** by **Vancouver** with Dave Scatchard and Bill Muckalt for Felix Potvin, NY Islanders' compensatory 2nd round choice (later traded to New Jersey – New Jersey selected Teemu Laine) in 2000 Entry Draft and NY Islanders' 3rd round choice (Thatcher Bell) in 2000 Entry Draft, December 19, 1999. Traded to **Tampa Bay** by **NY Islanders** with the rights to Kristian Kudroc and NY Islanders' 2nd round choice (later traded to Phoenix – Phoenix selected Matthew Spiller) in 2001 Entry Draft for Tampa Bay's 1st round choice (Raffi Torres) in 2000 Entry Draft, Calgary's 4th round choice (previously acquired, NY Islanders selected Vladimir Gorbunov) in 2000 Entry Draft and NY Islanders' 7th round choice (previously acquired, NY Islanders selected Ryan Caldwell) in 2000 Entry Draft, June 24, 2000. Traded to **Carolina** by **Tampa Bay** for Shane Willis and Chris Dingman, March 5, 2002.

WEIMAN, Tyler (WIGH-muhn, TIGH-luhr) COL.

Goaltender. Catches left. 5'11", 160 lbs. Born, Saskatoon, Sask., June 5, 1984.
(Colorado's 6th choice, 164th overall, in 2002 Entry Draft).

			Regular Season								Playoffs						
Season	Club	League	GP	W	L	T	Mins	GA	SO	Avg	GP	W	L	Mins	GA	SO	Avg
99-2000	Ft. Saskatchewan	AMBHL	21	15	4	2	1239	60	0	2.91	....	....	....	....	....	....	....
2000-01	Tri-City Americans	WHL	44	10	25	4	2464	155	0	3.77	....	....	....	....	....	....	....
2001-02	Tri-City Americans	WHL	47	18	17	5	2492	149	2	3.59	5	1	4	300	14	0	2.80
2002-03	Tri-City Americans	WHL	55	16	34	2	3129	207	1	3.97	....	....	....	....	....	....	....
2003-04	Tri-City Americans	WHL	54	23	21	7	3023	134	1	2.66	5	1	2	234	11	0	2.82

YEATS, Matthew (YAYTS, MA-thew)

Goaltender. Catches left. 5'11", 165 lbs. Born, Montreal, Que., April 6, 1979.
(Los Angeles' 9th choice, 248th overall, in 1998 Entry Draft).

			Regular Season								Playoffs						
Season	Club	League	GP	W	L	T	Mins	GA	SO	Avg	GP	W	L	Mins	GA	SO	Avg
1995-96	Lethbridge	WHL	1	0	0	0	20	3	0	9.00	....	....	....	....	....	....	....
1996-97	Olds Grizzlies	AJHL	32	....	....	....	1678	95	1	3.41	....	....	....	....	....	....	....
1997-98	Olds Grizzlies	AJHL	26	12	12	1	1498	96	0	3.85	....	....	....	....	....	....	....
1998-99	University of Maine	H-East						DID NOT PLAY									
99-2000	University of Maine	H-East	32	20	6	4	1821	79	0	2.60	....	....	....	....	....	....	....
2000-01	University of Maine	H-East	33	18	9	4	1897	76	2	2.40	....	....	....	....	....	....	....
2001-02	University of Maine	H-East	20	6	8	3	1048	54	0	3.09	....	....	....	....	....	....	....
2002-03	Philadelphia	AHL	2	1	1	0	90	4	0	2.67	....	....	....	....	....	....	....
	Atlantic City	ECHL	48	23	16	8	2811	141	4	3.01	8	4	1	397	16	1	2.42
2003-04	Portland Pirates	AHL	7	2	1	1	332	12	1	2.17	....	....	....	....	....	....	....
	Washington	**NHL**	**5**	**1**	**3**	**0**	**258**	**13**	**0**	**3.02**	....	....	....	....	....	....	....
	NHL Totals		**5**	**1**	**3**	**0**	**258**	**13**	**0**	**3.02**	....	....	....	....	....	....	....

• Ruled ineligible to play 1998-99 season by NCAA due to appearance with **Lethbridge** (WHL) in 1995-96. Signed as a free agent by **Portland** (AHL), November 6, 2003. Signed as a free agent by **Washington**, March 20, 2004.

ZABA, Matt (ZA-buh, MAT) L.A.

Goaltender. Catches left. 6'1", 168 lbs. Born, Yorkton, Sask., July 14, 1983.
(Los Angeles' 8th choice, 231st overall, in 2003 Entry Draft).

			Regular Season								Playoffs						
Season	Club	League	GP	W	L	T	Mins	GA	SO	Avg	GP	W	L	Mins	GA	SO	Avg
2000-01	Yorkton Mallers	SMHL	26	13	10	3	1480	79	0	3.20	....	....	....	....	....	....	....
2001-02	Penticton Panthers	BCHL	33	....	....	....	1980	128	0	3.69	....	....	....	....	....	....	....
2002-03	Vernon Vipers	BCHL	44	34	9	0	2012	96	2	2.21	17	14	3	1006	25	3	1.49
2003-04	Colorado College	WCHA	23	10	10	2	1323	50	1	2.27	....	....	....	....	....	....	....

WCHA All-Rookie Team (2004)

ZEPP, Rob (ZEHP, RAWB) CAR.

Goaltender. Catches left. 6'1", 181 lbs. Born, Scarborough, Ont., September 7, 1981.
(Carolina's 4th choice, 110th overall, in 2001 Entry Draft).

			Regular Season								Playoffs						
Season	Club	League	GP	W	L	T	Mins	GA	SO	Avg	GP	W	L	Mins	GA	SO	Avg
1997-98	Newmarket	OPJHL	3	....	....	....	181	13	0	4.31	....	....	....	....	....	....	....
1998-99	Plymouth Whalers	OHL	31	19	3	4	1662	76	3	2.74	3	1	0	100	10	0	6.00
99-2000	Plymouth Whalers	OHL	53	*36	11	3	3005	119	3	*2.38	*23	*15	8	*1374	52	2	2.27
2000-01	Plymouth Whalers	OHL	55	*34	18	3	3246	122	*4	*2.26	19	14	5	1139	51	2	2.69
2001-02	Florida Everblades	ECHL	13	6	5	2	739	41	0	3.33	....	....	....	....	....	....	....
2002-03	Florida Everblades	ECHL	41	20	13	7	2372	112	3	2.83	....	....	....	....	....	....	....
	Lowell	AHL	5	1	3	1	303	16	1	3.16	....	....	....	....	....	....	....
2003-04	Lowell	AHL	2	0	1	1	124	7	0	3.40	....	....	....	....	....	....	....
	Florida Everblades	ECHL	35	14	13	7	2052	101	0	2.95	12	8	3	683	31	1	2.72

• Re-entered NHL Entry Draft. Originally Atlanta's 5th choice, 99th overall, in 1999 Entry Draft.

Canadian Major Junior Scholastic Player of the Year (1999) • OHL Second All-Star Team (2000, 2001)

• Missed majority of 2001-02 season recovering from groin injury suffered in practice, January 3, 2002.

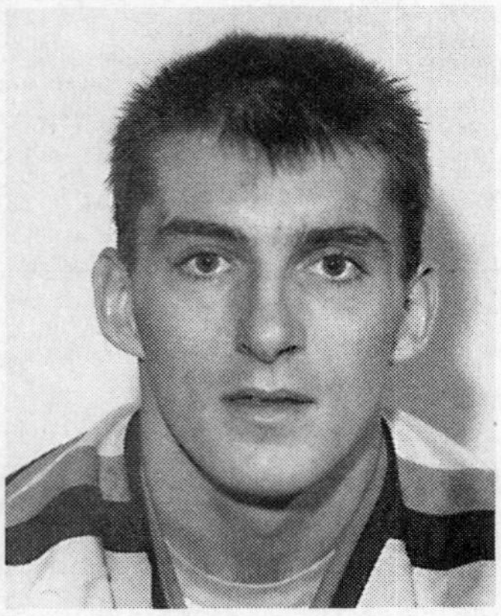
Jim Agnew

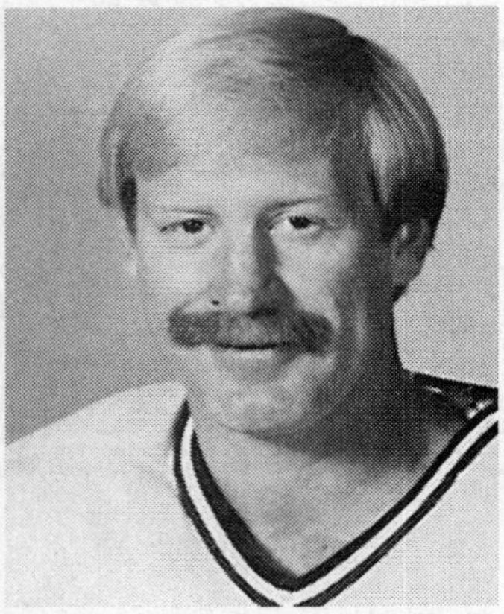
John Anderson

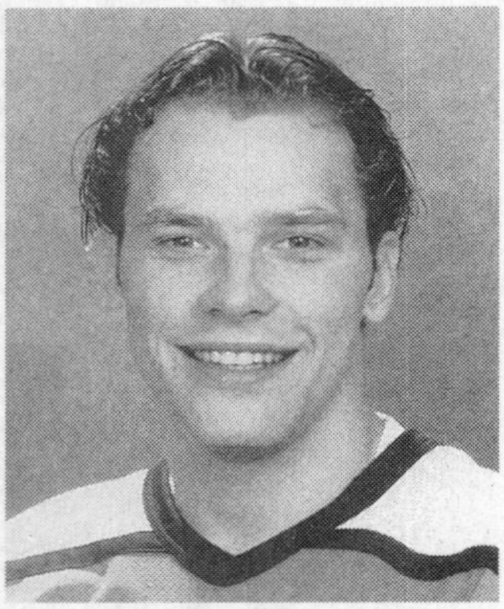
Shawn Antoski

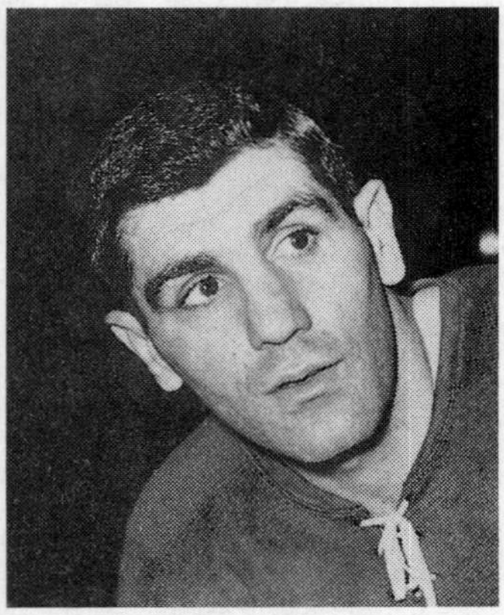
Lou Angotti

Retired NHL Player Index

Abbreviations: Teams/Cities: – **Ana.** – Anaheim; **Atl.** – Atlanta; **Bos.** – Boston; **Bro.** – Brooklyn; **Buf.** – Buffalo; **Cal.** – California; **Cgy.** – Calgary; **Cle.** – Cleveland; **Col.** – Colorado; **CBJ** – Columbus; **Dal.** – Dallas; **Det.** – Detroit; **Edm.** – Edmonton; **Fla.** – Florida; **Ham.** – Hamilton; **Hfd.** – Hartford;
K.C. – Kansas City; **L.A.** – Los Angeles; **Min.** – Minnesota; **Mtl.** – Montreal; **Mtl.M.** – Montreal Maroons; **Mtl.W.** – Montreal Wanderers; **N.J.** – New Jersey; **NYA** – NY Americans; **NYI** – NY Islanders; **NYR** – New York Rangers; – **Oak.** – Oakland; **Ott.** – Ottawa; – **Phi.** – Philadelphia; **Phx.** – Phoenix; **Pit.** – Pittsburgh; **Que.** – Quebec; **St.L.** – St. Louis; **S.J.** – San Jose; **T.B.** – Tampa Bay; **Tor.** – Toronto; **Van.** – Vancouver; **Wpg.** – Winnipeg; **Wsh.** – Washington

Total seasons are rounded off to the nearest full season. **A** – assists; **G** – goals; **GP** – games played; **PIM** – penalties in minutes; **TP** – total points.
● – deceased. Assists not recorded during 1917-18 season ‡ – Remains active in other leagues.

			Regular Schedule					Playoffs							
Name	NHL Teams	NHL Seasons	GP	G	A	TP	PIM	GP	G	A	TP	PIM	NHL Cup Wins	First NHL Season	Last NHL Season
A															
‡ Aalto, Antti	Ana.	4	151	11	17	28	52	4	0	0	0	2	....	1997-98	2000-01
Abbott, Reg	Mtl.	1	3	0	0	0	0	....	....	....	....	....	....	1952-53	1952-53
● Abel, Clarence	NYR, Chi.	8	333	19	18	37	359	38	1	1	2	58	2	1926-27	1933-34
Abel, Gerry	Det.	1	1	0	0	0	0	....	....	....	....	....	....	1966-67	1966-67
● Abel, Sid	Det., Chi.	14	612	189	283	472	376	97	28	30	58	79	3	1938-39	1953-54
Abgrall, Dennis	L.A.	1	13	0	2	2	4	....	....	....	....	....	....	1975-76	1975-76
Abrahamsson, Thommy	Hfd.	1	32	6	11	17	16	....	....	....	....	....	....	1980-81	1980-81
Achtymichuk, Gene	Mtl., Det.	4	32	3	5	8	2	....	....	....	....	....	....	1951-52	1958-59
Acomb, Doug	Tor.	1	2	0	1	1	0	....	....	....	....	....	....	1969-70	1969-70
Acton, Keith	Mtl., Min., Edm., Phi., Wsh., NYI	15	1023	226	358	584	1172	66	12	21	33	88	1	1979-80	1993-94
Adam, Douglas	NYR	1	4	0	1	1	0	....	....	....	....	....	....	1949-50	1949-50
Adam, Russ	Tor.	1	8	1	2	3	11	....	....	....	....	....	....	1982-83	1982-83
‡ Adams, Bryan	Atl.	2	11	0	1	1	2	....	....	....	....	....	....	1999-00	2000-01
Adams, Greg	Phi., Hfd., Wsh., Edm., Van., Que., Det.	10	545	84	143	227	1173	43	2	11	13	153	....	1980-81	1989-90
Adams, Greg	N.J., Van., Dal., Phx., Fla.	17	1056	355	388	743	326	81	20	22	42	16	....	1984-85	2000-01
● Adams, Jack	Tor., Ott.	7	173	83	32	115	366	10	2	0	2	13	2	1917-18	1926-27
Adams, John	Mtl.	1	42	6	12	18	11	3	0	0	0	0	....	1940-41	1940-41
● Adams, Stew	Chi., Tor.	4	95	9	26	35	60	11	3	3	6	14	....	1929-30	1932-33
Adduono, Rick	Bos., Atl.	2	4	0	0	0	2	....	....	....	....	....	....	1975-76	1979-80
Affleck, Bruce	St.L., Van., NYI	7	280	14	66	80	86	8	0	0	0	0	....	1974-75	1983-84
Agnew, Jim	Van., Hfd.	6	81	0	1	1	257	4	0	0	0	6	....	1986-87	1992-93
Ahern, Fred	Cal., Cle., Col.	4	146	31	30	61	130	2	0	1	1	2	....	1974-75	1977-78
Ahlin, Tony	Chi.	1	1	0	0	0	0	....	....	....	....	....	....	1937-38	1937-38
Ahola, Peter	L.A., Pit., S.J., Cgy.	3	123	10	17	27	137	6	0	0	0	2	....	1991-92	1993-94
Ahrens, Chris	Min.	6	52	0	3	3	84	1	0	0	0	0	....	1972-73	1977-78
Ailsby, Lloyd	NYR	1	3	0	0	0	2	....	....	....	....	....	....	1951-52	1951-52
Aitken, Brad	Pit., Edm.	2	14	1	3	4	25	....	....	....	....	....	....	1987-88	1990-91
Aivazoff, Micah	Det., Edm., NYI	3	92	4	6	10	46	....	....	....	....	....	....	1993-94	1995-96
‡ Alatalo, Mika	Phx.	2	152	17	29	46	58	5	0	0	0	2	....	1999-00	2000-01
● Albright, Clint	NYR	1	59	14	5	19	19	....	....	....	....	....	....	1948-49	1948-49
Aldcorn, Gary	Tor., Det., Bos.	5	226	41	56	97	78	6	1	2	3	4	....	1956-57	1960-61
‡ Aldridge, Keith	Dal.	1	4	0	0	0	0	....	....	....	....	....	....	1999-00	1999-00
Alexander, Claire	Tor., Van.	4	155	18	47	65	36	16	2	4	6	4	....	1974-75	1977-78
● Alexandre, Art	Mtl.	2	11	0	2	2	8	4	0	0	0	0	....	1931-32	1932-33
Allan, Jeff	Cle.	1	4	0	0	0	2	....	....	....	....	....	....	1977-78	1977-78
‡ Allen, Chris	Fla.	2	2	0	0	0	2	....	....	....	....	....	....	1997-98	1998-99
Allen, George	NYR, Chi., Mtl.	8	339	82	115	197	179	41	9	10	19	32	....	1938-39	1946-47
Allen, Keith	Det.	2	28	0	4	4	8	5	0	0	0	0	1	1953-54	1954-55
Allen, Peter	Pit.	1	8	0	0	0	8	....	....	....	....	....	....	1995-96	1995-96
● Allen, Viv	NYA	1	6	0	1	1	0	....	....	....	....	....	....	1940-41	1940-41
Alley, Steve	Hfd.	2	15	3	3	6	11	3	0	1	1	0	....	1979-80	1980-81
Allison, Dave	Mtl.	1	3	0	0	0	12	....	....	....	....	....	....	1983-84	1983-84
Allison, Mike	NYR, Tor., L.A.	10	499	102	166	268	630	82	9	17	26	135	....	1980-81	1989-90
Allison, Ray	Hfd., Phi.	7	238	64	93	157	223	12	2	3	5	20	....	1979-80	1986-87
● Allum, Bill	NYR	1	1	0	1	1	0	....	....	....	....	....	....	1940-41	1940-41
● Amadio, Dave	Det., L.A.	3	125	5	11	16	163	16	1	2	3	18	....	1957-58	1968-69
‡ Ambroziak, Peter	Buf.	1	12	0	1	1	0	....	....	....	....	....	....	1994-95	1994-95
Amodeo, Mike	Wpg.	1	19	0	0	0	2	....	....	....	....	....	....	1979-80	1979-80
● Anderson, Bill	Bos.	1	....	....	....	....	....	1	0	0	0	0	....	1942-43	1942-43
Anderson, Dale	Det.	1	13	0	0	0	6	2	0	0	0	0	....	1956-57	1956-57
Anderson, Doug	Mtl.	1	....	....	....	....	....	2	0	0	0	0	1	1952-53	1952-53
Anderson, Earl	Det., Bos.	3	109	19	19	38	22	5	0	1	1	0	....	1974-75	1976-77
Anderson, Glenn	Edm., Tor., NYR, St.L.	16	1129	498	601	1099	1120	225	93	121	214	442	6	1980-81	1995-96
Anderson, Jim	L.A.	1	7	1	2	3	2	....	....	....	....	....	....	1967-68	1967-68
Anderson, John	Tor., Que., Hfd.	12	814	282	349	631	263	37	9	18	27	2	....	1977-78	1988-89
Anderson, Murray	Wsh.	1	40	0	1	1	68	....	....	....	....	....	....	1974-75	1974-75
Anderson, Perry	St.L., N.J., S.J.	10	400	50	59	109	1051	36	2	1	3	161	....	1981-82	1991-92
Anderson, Ron	Det., L.A., St.L., Buf.	5	251	28	30	58	146	5	0	0	0	4	....	1967-68	1971-72
Anderson, Ron	Wsh.	1	28	9	7	16	8	....	....	....	....	....	....	1974-75	1974-75
Anderson, Russ	Pit., Hfd., L.A.	9	519	22	99	121	1086	10	0	3	3	28	....	1976-77	1984-85
‡ Anderson, Shawn	Buf., Que., Wsh., Phi.	8	255	11	51	62	117	19	1	1	2	16	....	1986-87	1994-95
● Anderson, Tom	Det., NYA, Bro.	8	319	62	127	189	180	16	2	7	9	8	....	1934-35	1941-42
Andersson, Erik	Cgy.	1	12	2	1	3	8	....	....	....	....	....	....	1997-98	1997-98
‡ Andersson, Jonas	Nsh.	1	5	0	0	0	2	....	....	....	....	....	....	2001-02	2001-02
Andersson, Kent-Erik	Min., NYR	7	456	72	103	175	78	50	4	11	15	4	....	1977-78	1983-84
Andersson, Mikael	Buf., Hfd., T.B., Phi., NYI	15	761	95	169	264	134	25	2	7	9	10	....	1985-86	1999-00
‡ Andersson, Niklas	Que., NYI, S.J., Nsh., Cgy.	6	164	29	53	82	85	....	....	....	....	....	....	1992-93	2000-01
Andersson, Peter	Wsh., Que.	3	172	10	41	51	81	7	0	2	2	2	....	1983-84	1985-86
‡ Andersson, Peter	NYR, Fla.	2	47	6	13	19	20	....	....	....	....	....	....	1992-93	1993-94
Andrascik, Steve	NYR	1	....	....	....	....	....	1	0	0	0	0	....	1971-72	1971-72
Andrea, Paul	NYR, Pit., Cal., Buf.	4	150	31	49	80	10	....	....	....	....	....	....	1965-66	1970-71
● Andrews, Lloyd	Tor.	4	53	8	5	13	10	2	0	0	0	0	1	1921-22	1924-25
Andrievski, Alexander	Chi.	1	1	0	0	0	0	....	....	....	....	....	....	1992-93	1992-93
Andruff, Ron	Mtl., Col.	5	153	19	36	55	54	2	0	0	0	0	....	1974-75	1978-79
Andrusak, Greg	Pit., Tor.	5	28	0	6	6	16	15	1	0	1	8	....	1993-94	1999-00
Angotti, Lou	NYR, Chi., Phi., Pit., St.L.	10	653	103	186	289	228	65	8	8	16	17	....	1964-65	1973-74
Anholt, Darrel	Chi.	1	1	0	0	0	0	....	....	....	....	....	....	1983-84	1983-84
Anslow, Hub	NYR	1	2	0	0	0	0	....	....	....	....	....	....	1947-48	1947-48
Antonovich, Mike	Min., Hfd., N.J.	5	87	10	15	25	37	....	....	....	....	....	....	1975-76	1983-84
Antoski, Shawn	Van., Phi., Pit., Ana.	8	183	3	5	8	599	36	1	3	4	74	....	1990-91	1997-98
● Apps, Syl	Tor.	10	423	201	231	432	56	69	25	29	54	8	3	1936-37	1947-48
Apps, Syl	NYR, Pit., L.A.	10	727	183	423	606	311	23	5	5	10	23	....	1970-71	1979-80
Arbour, Al	Det., Chi., Tor., St.L.	16	626	12	58	70	617	86	1	8	9	92	4	1953-54	1970-71
● Arbour, Amos	Mtl., Ham., Tor.	6	113	52	20	72	77	....	....	....	....	....	....	1918-19	1923-24
● Arbour, Jack	Det., Tor.	2	47	5	1	6	56	....	....	....	....	....	....	1926-27	1928-29
Arbour, John	Bos., Pit., Van., St.L.	5	106	1	9	10	149	5	0	0	0	0	....	1965-66	1971-72
● Arbour, Ty	Pit., Chi.	5	207	28	28	56	112	11	2	0	2	6	....	1926-27	1930-31
Archambault, Michel	Chi.	1	3	0	0	0	0	....	....	....	....	....	....	1976-77	1976-77
Archibald, Dave	Min., NYR, Ott., NYI	8	323	57	67	124	139	5	0	1	1	0	....	1987-88	1996-97
Archibald, Jim	Min.	3	16	1	2	3	45	....	....	....	....	....	....	1984-85	1986-87
Areshenkoff, Ron	Edm.	1	4	0	0	0	0	....	....	....	....	....	....	1979-80	1979-80
Armstrong, Bill	Phi.	1	1	0	1	1	0	....	....	....	....	....	....	1990-91	1990-91
● Armstrong, Bob	Bos.	12	542	13	86	99	671	42	1	7	8	28	....	1950-51	1961-62
Armstrong, George	Tor.	21	1187	296	417	713	721	110	26	34	60	52	4	1949-50	1970-71
Armstrong, Murray	Tor., NYA, Bro., Det.	8	270	67	121	188	72	30	4	6	10	2	....	1937-38	1945-46
● Armstrong, Norm	Tor.	1	7	1	1	2	2	....	....	....	....	....	....	1962-63	1962-63
Armstrong, Tim	Tor.	1	11	1	0	1	6	....	....	....	....	....	....	1988-89	1988-89
Arnason, Chuck	Mtl., Atl., Pit., K.C., Col., Cle., Min., Wsh.	8	401	109	90	199	122	9	2	4	6	4	....	1971-72	1978-79
Arniel, Scott	Wpg., Buf., Bos.	12	730	149	189	338	599	34	3	3	6	39	....	1981-82	1991-92
Arthur, Fred	Hfd., Phi.	3	80	1	8	9	49	4	0	0	0	2	....	1980-81	1982-83
Arundel, John	Tor.	1	3	0	0	0	9	....	....	....	....	....	....	1949-50	1949-50
● Ashbee, Barry	Bos., Phi.	5	284	15	70	85	291	17	0	4	4	22	1	1965-66	1973-74

Name	NHL Teams	NHL Seasons	Regular Schedule GP	G	A	TP	PIM	Playoffs GP	G	A	TP	PIM	NHL Cup Wins	First NHL Season	Last NHL Season
• Ashby, Don	Tor., Col., Edm.	6	188	40	56	96	40	12	1	0	1	4	....	1975-76	1980-81
Ashton, Brent	Van., Col., N.J., Min., Que., Det., Wpg., Bos., Cgy.	14	998	284	345	629	635	85	24	25	49	70	....	1979-80	1992-93
Ashworth, Frank	Chi.	1	18	5	4	9	2	....	....	....	....	....	....	1946-47	1946-47
Asmundson, Oscar	NYR, Det., St.L., NYA, Mtl.	5	111	11	23	34	30	9	0	2	2	4	1	1932-33	1937-38
‡ Astashenko, Kaspars	T.B.	2	23	1	2	3	8	....	....	....	....	....	....	1999-00	2000-01
‡ Astley, Mark	Buf.	3	75	4	19	23	92	2	0	0	0	0	....	1993-94	1995-96
• Atanas, Walt	NYR	1	49	13	8	21	40	....	....	....	....	....	....	1944-45	1944-45
Atcheynum, Blair	Ott., St.L., Nsh., Chi.	5	196	27	33	60	36	23	1	3	4	8	....	1992-93	2000-01
• Atkinson, Steve	Bos., Buf., Wsh.	6	302	60	51	111	104	1	0	0	0	0	....	1968-69	1974-75
Attwell, Bob	Col.	2	22	1	5	6	0	....	....	....	....	....	....	1979-80	1980-81
Attwell, Ron	St.L., NYR	1	22	1	7	8	8	....	....	....	....	....	....	1967-68	1967-68
Aubin, Norm	Tor.	2	69	18	13	31	30	1	0	0	0	0	....	1981-82	1982-83
Aubry, Pierre	Que., Det.	5	202	24	26	50	133	20	1	1	2	32	....	1980-81	1984-85
Aubuchon, Ossie	Bos., NYR	2	50	20	12	32	4	6	1	0	1	0	....	1942-43	1943-44
‡ Audet, Philippe	Det.	1	4	0	0	0	0	....	....	....	....	....	....	1998-99	1998-99
Auge, Les	Col.	1	6	0	3	3	4	....	....	....	....	....	....	1980-81	1980-81
‡ Augusta, Patrik	Tor., Wsh.	2	4	0	0	0	0	....	....	....	....	....	....	1993-94	1998-99
• Aurie, Larry	Det.	12	489	147	129	276	279	24	6	9	15	10	2	1927-28	1938-39
Awrey, Don	Bos., St.L., Mtl., Pit., NYR, Col.	16	979	31	158	189	1065	71	0	18	18	150	2	1963-64	1978-79
• Ayres, Vern	NYA, Mtl.M., St.L., NYR	6	211	6	11	17	350	....	....	....	....	....	....	1930-31	1935-36

B

Name	NHL Teams	NHL Seasons	Regular Schedule GP	G	A	TP	PIM	Playoffs GP	G	A	TP	PIM	NHL Cup Wins	First NHL Season	Last NHL Season
Babando, Pete	Bos., Det., Chi., NYR	6	351	86	73	159	194	17	3	3	6	6	1	1947-48	1952-53
Babcock, Bobby	Wsh.	2	2	0	0	0	2	....	....	....	....	....	....	1990-91	1992-93
Babe, Warren	Min.	3	21	2	5	7	23	2	0	0	0	0	....	1987-88	1990-91
‡ Babenko, Yuri	Col.	1	3	0	0	0	0	....	....	....	....	....	....	2000-01	2000-01
Babin, Mitch	St.L.	1	8	0	0	0	0	....	....	....	....	....	....	1975-76	1975-76
Baby, John	Cle., Min.	2	26	2	8	10	26	....	....	....	....	....	....	1977-78	1978-79
Babych, Dave	Wpg., Hfd., Van., Phi., L.A.	19	1195	142	581	723	970	114	21	41	62	113	....	1980-81	1998-99
Babych, Wayne	St.L., Pit., Que., Hfd.	9	519	192	246	438	498	41	7	9	16	24	....	1978-79	1986-87
‡ Baca, Jergus	Hfd.	2	10	0	2	2	14	....	....	....	....	....	....	1990-91	1991-92
Backman, Mike	NYR	3	18	1	6	7	18	10	2	2	4	2	....	1981-82	1983-84
• Backor, Pete	Tor.	1	36	4	5	9	6	....	....	....	....	....	1	1944-45	1944-45
Backstrom, Ralph	Mtl., L.A., Chi.	17	1032	278	361	639	386	116	27	32	59	68	6	1956-57	1972-73
• Bailey, Ace	Tor.	8	313	111	82	193	472	21	3	4	7	12	1	1926-27	1933-34
• Bailey, Bob	Tor., Det., Chi.	5	150	15	21	36	207	15	0	4	4	22	....	1953-54	1957-58
• Bailey, Garnet	Bos., Det., St.L., Wsh.	10	568	107	171	278	633	15	2	4	6	28	1	1968-69	1977-78
Bailey, Reid	Phi., Tor., Hfd.	4	40	1	3	4	105	16	0	2	2	25	....	1980-81	1983-84
Baillargeon, Joel	Wpg., Que.	3	20	0	2	2	31	....	....	....	....	....	....	1986-87	1988-89
Baird, Ken	Cal.	1	10	0	2	2	15	....	....	....	....	....	....	1971-72	1971-72
Baker, Bill	Mtl., Col., St.L., NYR	3	143	7	25	32	175	6	0	0	0	0	....	1980-81	1982-83
Baker, Jamie	Que., Ott., S.J., Tor.	10	404	71	79	150	271	25	5	4	9	42	....	1989-90	1998-99
Bakovic, Peter	Van.	1	10	2	0	2	48	....	....	....	....	....	....	1987-88	1987-88
Balderis, Helmut	Min.	1	26	3	6	9	2	....	....	....	....	....	....	1989-90	1989-90
Baldwin, Doug	Tor., Det., Chi.	3	24	0	1	1	8	....	....	....	....	....	....	1945-46	1947-48
Balfour, Earl	Tor., Chi.	7	288	30	22	52	78	26	0	3	3	4	1	1951-52	1960-61
• Balfour, Murray	Mtl., Chi., Bos.	8	306	67	90	157	393	40	9	10	19	45	1	1956-57	1964-65
Ball, Terry	Phi., Buf.	4	74	7	19	26	26	....	....	....	....	....	....	1967-68	1971-72
Balon, Dave	NYR, Mtl., Min., Van.	14	776	192	222	414	607	78	14	21	35	109	2	1959-60	1972-73
Baltimore, Bryon	Edm.	1	2	0	0	0	4	....	....	....	....	....	....	1979-80	1979-80
Baluik, Stan	Bos.	1	7	0	0	0	2	....	....	....	....	....	....	1959-60	1959-60
Bandura, Jeff	NYR	1	2	0	1	1	0	....	....	....	....	....	....	1980-81	1980-81
Banks, Darren	Bos.	2	20	2	2	4	73	....	....	....	....	....	....	1992-93	1993-94
‡ Bannister, Drew	T.B., Edm., Ana., NYR	6	164	5	25	30	161	12	0	0	0	30	....	1995-96	2001-02
Barahona, Ralph	Bos.	2	6	2	2	4	0	....	....	....	....	....	....	1990-91	1991-92
• Barbe, Andy	Tor.	1	1	0	0	0	2	....	....	....	....	....	....	1950-51	1950-51
Barber, Bill	Phi.	14	903	420	463	883	623	129	53	55	108	109	2	1972-73	1983-84
Barber, Don	Min., Wpg., Que., S.J.	4	115	25	32	57	64	11	4	4	8	10	....	1988-89	1991-92
• Barilko, Bill	Tor.	5	252	26	36	62	456	47	5	7	12	104	4	1946-47	1950-51
Barkley, Doug	Chi., Det.	6	253	24	80	104	382	30	0	9	9	63	....	1957-58	1965-66
Barlow, Bob	Min.	2	77	16	17	33	10	6	2	2	4	6	....	1969-70	1970-71
Barnes, Blair	L.A.	1	1	0	0	0	0	....	....	....	....	....	....	1982-83	1982-83
Barnes, Norm	Phi., Hfd.	5	156	6	38	44	178	12	0	0	0	8	....	1976-77	1981-82
Baron, Normand	Mtl., St.L.	2	27	2	0	2	51	3	0	0	0	22	....	1983-84	1985-86
Barr, Dave	Bos., NYR, St.L., Hfd., Det., N.J., Dal.	13	614	128	204	332	520	71	12	10	22	70	....	1981-82	1993-94
Barrault, Doug	Min., Fla.	2	4	0	0	0	2	....	....	....	....	....	....	1992-93	1993-94
Barrett, Fred	Min., L.A.	13	745	25	123	148	671	44	0	2	2	60	....	1970-71	1983-84
Barrett, John	Det., Wsh., Min.	8	488	20	77	97	604	16	2	2	4	50	....	1980-81	1987-88
Barrie, Doug	Pit., Buf., L.A.	3	158	10	42	52	268	....	....	....	....	....	....	1968-69	1971-72
Barrie, Len	Phi., Fla., Pit., L.A.	7	184	19	45	64	290	8	1	0	1	8	....	1989-90	2000-01
Barry, Ed	Bos.	1	19	1	3	4	2	....	....	....	....	....	....	1946-47	1946-47
• Barry, Marty	NYA, Bos., Det., Mtl.	12	509	195	192	387	231	43	15	18	33	34	2	1927-28	1939-40
Barry, Ray	Bos.	1	18	1	2	3	6	....	....	....	....	....	....	1951-52	1951-52
Bartel, Robin	Cgy., Van.	2	41	0	1	1	14	6	0	0	0	16	....	1985-86	1986-87
Bartlett, Jim	Mtl., NYR, Bos.	5	191	34	23	57	273	2	0	0	0	0	....	1954-55	1960-61
• Barton, Cliff	Pit., Phi., NYR	3	85	10	9	19	22	....	....	....	....	....	....	1929-30	1939-40
‡ Bartos, Peter	Min.	1	13	4	2	6	6	....	....	....	....	....	....	2000-01	2000-01
‡ Bashkirov, Andrei	Mtl.	3	30	0	3	3	0	....	....	....	....	....	....	1998-99	2000-01
Bassen, Bob	NYI, Chi., St.L., Que., Dal., Cgy.	15	765	88	144	232	1004	93	9	15	24	134	....	1985-86	1999-00
‡ Bast, Ryan	Phi.	1	2	0	1	1	0	....	....	....	....	....	....	1998-99	1998-99
Bathe, Frank	Det., Phi.	9	224	3	28	31	542	27	1	3	4	42	....	1974-75	1983-84
Bathgate, Andy	NYR, Tor., Det., Pit.	17	1069	349	624	973	624	54	21	14	35	76	1	1952-53	1970-71
Bathgate, Frank	NYR	1	2	0	0	0	2	....	....	....	....	....	....	1952-53	1952-53
• Batters, Jeff	St.L.	2	16	0	0	0	28	....	....	....	....	....	....	1993-94	1994-95
‡ Batyrshin, Ruslan	L.A.	1	2	0	0	0	6	....	....	....	....	....	....	1995-96	1995-96
• Bauer, Bobby	Bos.	9	327	123	137	260	36	48	11	8	19	6	2	1936-37	1951-52
Baumgartner, Ken	L.A., NYI, Tor., Ana., Bos.	12	696	13	41	54	2244	51	1	2	3	106	....	1987-88	1998-99
Baumgartner, Mike	K.C.	1	17	0	0	0	0	....	....	....	....	....	....	1974-75	1974-75
Baun, Bob	Tor., Oak., Det.	17	964	37	187	224	1493	96	3	12	15	171	4	1956-57	1972-73
Bautin, Sergei	Wpg., Det., S.J.	3	132	5	25	30	176	6	0	0	0	2	....	1992-93	1995-96
Bawa, Robin	Wsh., Van., S.J., Ana.	4	61	6	1	7	60	1	0	0	0	0	....	1989-90	1993-94
Baxter, Paul	Que., Pit., Cgy.	8	472	48	121	169	1564	40	0	5	5	162	....	1979-80	1986-87
Beadle, Sandy	Wpg.	1	6	1	0	1	2	....	....	....	....	....	....	1980-81	1980-81
Beaton, Frank	NYR	2	25	1	1	2	43	....	....	....	....	....	....	1978-79	1979-80
• Beattie, Red	Bos., Det., NYA	9	334	62	85	147	137	24	4	2	6	8	....	1930-31	1938-39
Beaudin, Norm	St.L., Min.	2	25	1	2	3	4	....	....	....	....	....	....	1967-68	1970-71
Beaudoin, Serge	Atl.	1	3	0	0	0	0	....	....	....	....	....	....	1979-80	1979-80
Beaudoin, Yves	Wsh.	3	11	0	0	0	5	....	....	....	....	....	....	1985-86	1987-88
‡ Beaufait, Mark	S.J.	1	5	1	0	1	0	....	....	....	....	....	....	1992-93	1992-93
Beck, Barry	Col., NYR, L.A.	10	615	104	251	355	1016	51	10	23	33	77	....	1977-78	1989-90
Beckett, Bob	Bos.	4	68	7	6	13	18	....	....	....	....	....	....	1956-57	1963-64
Bedard, James	Chi.	2	22	1	1	2	8	....	....	....	....	....	....	1949-50	1950-51
Beddoes, Clayton	Bos.	2	60	2	8	10	57	....	....	....	....	....	....	1995-96	1996-97
Bednarski, John	NYR, Edm.	4	100	2	18	20	114	1	0	0	0	17	....	1974-75	1979-80
Beers, Bob	Bos., T.B., Edm., NYI	8	258	28	79	107	225	21	1	1	2	22	....	1989-90	1996-97
Beers, Eddy	Cgy., St.L.	5	250	94	116	210	256	41	7	10	17	47	....	1981-82	1985-86
• Behling, Dick	Det.	2	5	1	0	1	2	....	....	....	....	....	....	1940-41	1942-43
Beisler, Frank	NYA	2	2	0	0	0	0	....	....	....	....	....	....	1936-37	1939-40
Belanger, Alain	Tor.	1	9	0	1	1	6	....	....	....	....	....	....	1977-78	1977-78
‡ Belanger, Francis	Mtl.	1	10	0	0	0	29	....	....	....	....	....	....	2000-01	2000-01
‡ Belanger, Jesse	Mtl., Fla., Van., Edm., NYI	8	246	59	76	135	56	12	0	3	3	2	....	1991-92	2000-01
Belanger, Roger	Pit.	1	44	3	5	8	32	....	....	....	....	....	....	1984-85	1984-85
Belisle, Danny	NYR	1	4	2	0	2	0	....	....	....	....	....	....	1960-61	1960-61
Beliveau, Jean	Mtl.	20	1125	507	712	1219	1029	162	79	97	176	211	10	1950-51	1970-71
• Bell, Billy	Mtl.W., Mtl., Ott.	6	72	4	2	6	14	5	0	0	0	0	1	1917-18	1923-24
Bell, Bruce	Que., St.L., NYR, Edm.	5	209	12	64	76	113	34	3	5	8	41	....	1984-85	1989-90
Bell, Harry	NYR	1	1	0	1	1	0	....	....	....	....	....	....	1946-47	1946-47
Bell, Joe	NYR	2	62	8	9	17	18	....	....	....	....	....	....	1942-43	1946-47
Belland, Neil	Van., Pit.	6	109	13	32	45	54	21	2	9	11	23	....	1981-82	1986-87
• Bellefeuille, Pete	Tor., Det.	4	92	26	4	30	58	....	....	....	....	....	....	1925-26	1929-30
• Bellemer, Andy	Mtl.M.	1	15	0	0	0	0	....	....	....	....	....	....	1932-33	1932-33
Bellows, Brian	Min., Mtl., T.B., Ana., Wsh.	17	1188	485	537	1022	718	143	51	71	122	143	1	1982-83	1998-99
• Bend, Lin	NYR	1	8	3	1	4	2	....	....	....	....	....	....	1942-43	1942-43
‡ Benda, Jan	Wsh.	1	9	0	3	3	6	....	....	....	....	....	....	1997-98	1997-98

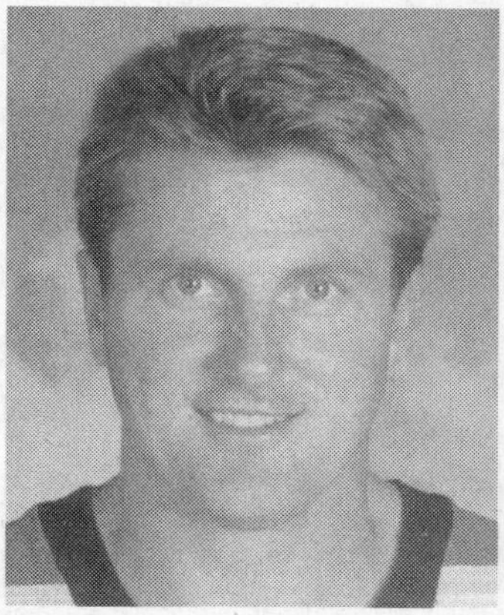

Len Barrie

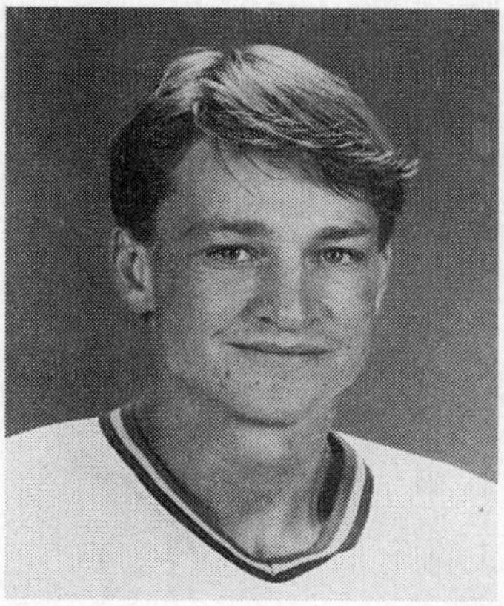

Bob Bassen

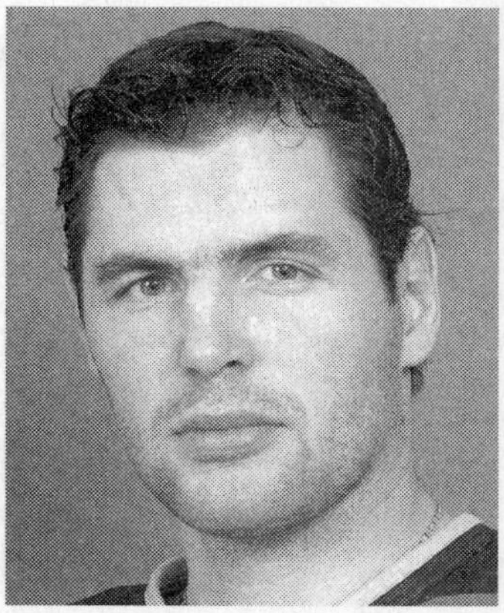

Jan Benda

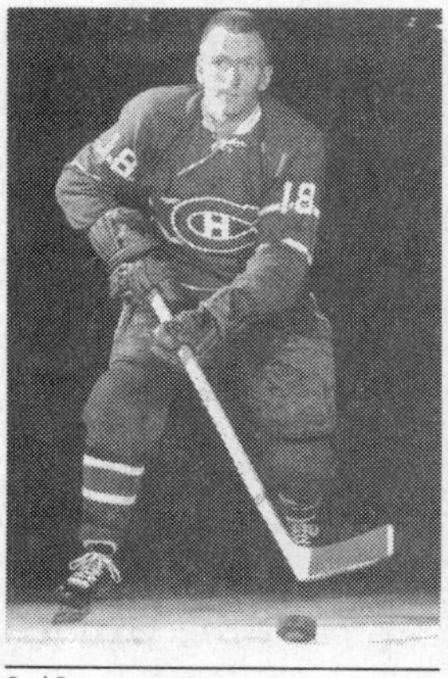

Red Berenson

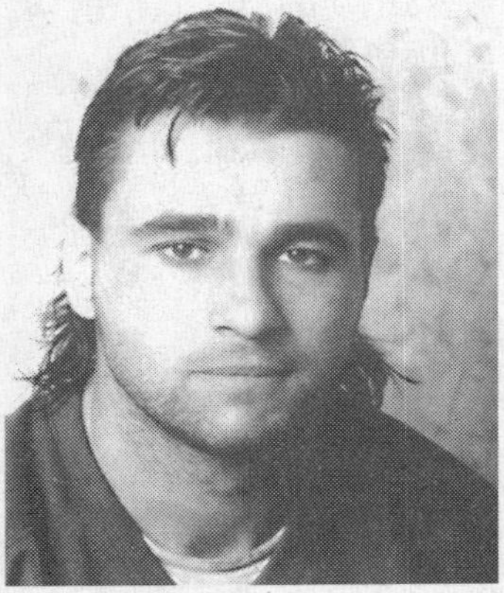

Frank Bialowas

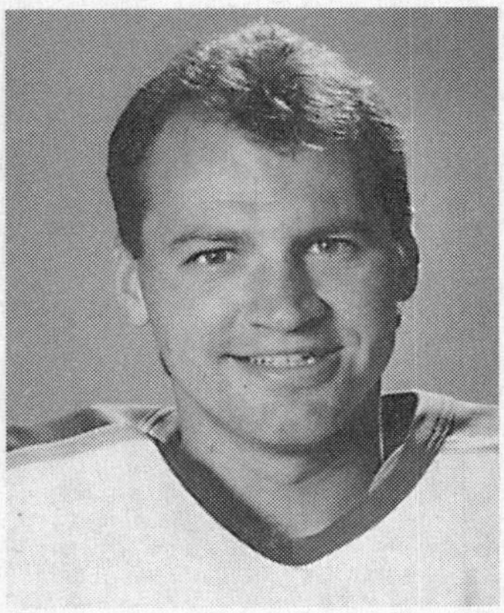

Doug Bodger

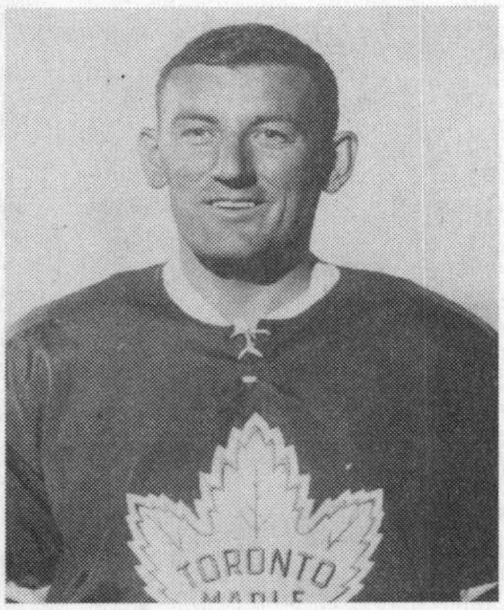

Don Blackburn

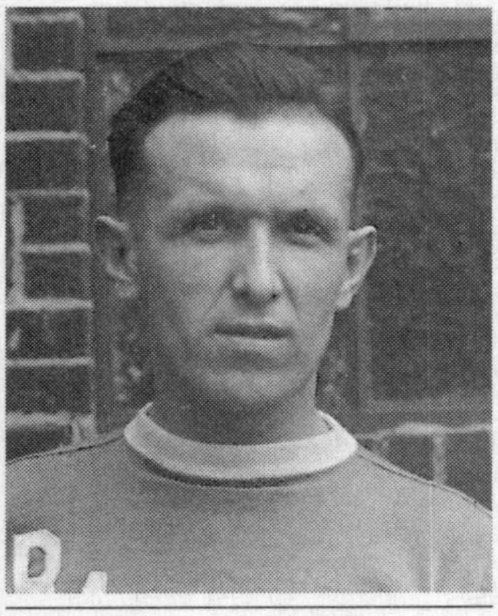

Frank Boucher

Name	NHL Teams	NHL Seasons	Regular Schedule GP	G	A	TP	PIM	Playoffs GP	G	A	TP	PIM	NHL Cup Wins	First NHL Season	Last NHL Season
Bennett, Adam	Chi., Edm.	3	69	3	8	11	69	....	....	....	....	....	....	1991-92	1993-94
Bennett, Bill	Bos., Hfd.	2	31	4	7	11	65	....	....	....	....	....	....	1978-79	1979-80
Bennett, Curt	St.L., NYR, Atl.	10	580	152	182	334	347	21	1	1	2	57	....	1970-71	1979-80
Bennett, Frank	Det.	1	7	0	1	1	2	....	....	....	....	....	....	1943-44	1943-44
Bennett, Harvey	Pit., Wsh., Phi., Min., St.L.	5	268	44	46	90	347	4	0	0	0	2	....	1974-75	1978-79
• Bennett, Max	Mtl.	1	1	0	0	0	0	....	....	....	....	....	....	1935-36	1935-36
Bennett, Rick	NYR	3	15	1	1	2	13	....	....	....	....	....	....	1989-90	1991-92
Benning, Brian	St.L., L.A., Phi., Edm., Fla.	11	568	63	233	296	963	48	3	20	23	74	....	1984-85	1994-95
Benning, Jim	Tor., Van.	9	605	52	191	243	461	7	1	1	2	2	....	1981-82	1989-90
• Benoit, Joe	Mtl.	5	185	75	69	144	94	11	6	3	9	11	1	1940-41	1946-47
Benson, Bill	NYA, Bro.	2	67	11	25	36	35	....	....	....	....	....	....	1940-41	1941-42
• Benson, Bobby	Bos.	1	8	0	1	1	4	....	....	....	....	....	....	1924-25	1924-25
• Bentley, Doug	Chi., NYR	13	566	219	324	543	217	23	9	8	17	12	....	1939-40	1953-54
• Bentley, Max	Chi., Tor., NYR	12	646	245	299	544	179	51	18	27	45	14	3	1940-41	1953-54
Bentley, Reg	Chi.	1	11	1	2	3	2	....	....	....	....	....	....	1942-43	1942-43
‡ Benysek, Ladislav	Edm., Min.	4	161	3	12	15	74	....	....	....	....	....	....	1997-98	2002-03
Beraldo, Paul	Bos.	2	10	0	0	0	4	....	....	....	....	....	....	1987-88	1988-89
‡ Beranek, Josef	Edm., Phi., Van., Pit.	9	531	118	144	262	398	57	5	8	13	24	....	1991-92	2000-01
Berenson, Red	Mtl., NYR, St.L., Det.	17	987	261	397	658	305	85	23	14	37	49	1	1961-62	1977-78
Berezan, Perry	Cgy., Min., S.J.	9	378	61	75	136	279	31	4	7	11	34	....	1984-85	1992-93
‡ Berezin, Sergei	Tor., Phx., Mtl., Chi., Wsh.	7	502	160	126	286	54	52	13	17	30	6	....	1996-97	2002-03
Berg, Bill	NYI, Tor., NYR, Ott.	10	546	55	67	122	488	61	3	4	7	34	....	1988-89	1998-99
• Bergdinon, Fred	Bos.	1	2	0	0	0	0	....	....	....	....	....	....	1925-26	1925-26
Bergen, Todd	Phi.	1	14	11	5	16	4	17	4	9	13	8	....	1984-85	1984-85
Berger, Mike	Min.	2	30	3	1	4	67	....	....	....	....	....	....	1987-88	1988-89
Bergeron, Michel	Det., NYI, Wsh.	5	229	80	58	138	165	....	....	....	....	....	....	1974-75	1978-79
Bergeron, Yves	Pit.	2	3	0	0	0	0	....	....	....	....	....	....	1974-75	1976-77
Bergkvist, Stefan	Pit.	2	7	0	0	0	9	4	0	0	0	2	....	1995-96	1996-97
Bergland, Tim	Wsh., T.B.	5	182	17	26	43	75	26	2	2	4	22	....	1989-90	1993-94
Bergloff, Bob	Min.	1	2	0	0	0	5	....	....	....	....	....	....	1982-83	1982-83
Berglund, Bo	Que., Min., Phi.	3	130	28	39	67	40	9	2	0	2	6	....	1983-84	1985-86
• Bergman, Gary	Det., Min., K.C.	12	838	68	299	367	1249	21	0	5	5	20	....	1964-65	1975-76
Bergman, Thommie	Det.	6	246	21	44	65	243	7	0	2	2	2	....	1972-73	1979-80
Bergqvist, Jonas	Cgy.	1	22	2	5	7	10	....	....	....	....	....	....	1989-90	1989-90
• Berlinquette, Louis	Mtl., Mtl.M., Pit.	8	193	45	33	78	129	11	0	5	5	9	....	1917-18	1925-26
Bernier, Serge	Phi., L.A., Que.	7	302	78	119	197	234	5	1	1	2	0	....	1968-69	1980-81
Berry, Bob	Mtl., L.A.	8	541	159	191	350	344	26	2	6	8	6	....	1968-69	1976-77
Berry, Brad	Wpg., Min., Dal.	8	241	4	28	32	323	13	0	1	1	16	....	1985-86	1993-94
Berry, Doug	Col.	2	121	10	33	43	25	....	....	....	....	....	....	1979-80	1980-81
Berry, Fred	Det.	1	3	0	0	0	0	....	....	....	....	....	....	1976-77	1976-77
Berry, Ken	Edm., Van.	4	55	8	10	18	30	....	....	....	....	....	....	1981-82	1988-89
‡ Bertrand, Eric	N.J., Atl., Mtl.	2	15	0	0	0	4	....	....	....	....	....	....	1999-00	2000-01
Berube, Craig	Phi., Tor., Cgy., Wsh., NYI	17	1054	61	98	159	3149	89	3	1	4	211	....	1986-87	2002-03
• Besler, Phil	Bos., Chi., Det.	2	30	1	4	5	18	....	....	....	....	....	....	1935-36	1938-39
• Bessone, Pete	Det.	1	6	0	1	1	6	....	....	....	....	....	....	1937-38	1937-38
Bethel, John	Wpg.	1	17	0	2	2	4	....	....	....	....	....	....	1979-80	1979-80
‡ Betik, Karel	T.B.	1	3	0	2	2	2	....	....	....	....	....	....	1998-99	1998-99
Bets, Maxim	Ana.	1	3	0	0	0	0	....	....	....	....	....	....	1993-94	1993-94
Bettio, Sam	Bos.	1	44	9	12	21	32	....	....	....	....	....	....	1949-50	1949-50
Beukeboom, Jeff	Edm., NYR	14	804	30	129	159	1890	99	3	16	19	197	4	1985-86	1998-99
Beverley, Nick	Bos., Pit., NYR, Min., L.A., Col.	11	502	18	94	112	156	7	0	1	1	0	....	1966-67	1979-80
Bialowas, Dwight	Atl., Min.	4	164	11	46	57	46	....	....	....	....	....	....	1973-74	1976-77
Bialowas, Frank	Tor.	1	3	0	0	0	12	....	....	....	....	....	....	1993-94	1993-94
Bianchin, Wayne	Pit., Edm.	7	276	68	41	109	137	3	0	1	1	6	....	1973-74	1979-80
‡ Bicanek, Radim	Ott., Chi., CBJ	7	122	1	11	12	62	7	0	0	0	8	....	1994-95	2001-02
Bidner, Todd	Wsh.	1	12	2	1	3	7	....	....	....	....	....	....	1981-82	1981-82
Biggs, Don	Min., Phi.	2	12	2	0	2	8	....	....	....	....	....	....	1984-85	1989-90
Bignell, Larry	Pit.	2	20	0	3	3	2	3	0	0	0	2	....	1973-74	1974-75
Bilodeau, Gilles	Que.	1	9	0	1	1	25	....	....	....	....	....	....	1979-80	1979-80
• Bionda, Jack	Tor., Bos.	4	93	3	9	12	113	11	0	1	1	14	....	1955-56	1958-59
Bissett, Tom	Det.	1	5	0	0	0	0	....	....	....	....	....	....	1990-91	1990-91
Bjugstad, Scott	Min., Pit., L.A.	9	317	76	68	144	144	9	0	1	1	2	....	1983-84	1991-92
‡ Black, James	Hfd., Min., Dal., Buf., Chi., Wsh.	11	352	58	57	115	84	13	2	1	3	4	....	1989-90	2000-01
Black, Steve	Det., Chi.	2	113	11	20	31	77	13	0	0	0	13	1	1949-50	1950-51
Blackburn, Bob	NYR, Pit.	3	135	8	12	20	105	6	0	0	0	4	....	1968-69	1970-71
Blackburn, Don	Bos., Phi., NYR, NYI, Min.	6	185	23	44	67	87	12	3	0	3	10	....	1962-63	1972-73
Blade, Hank	Chi.	2	24	2	3	5	2	....	....	....	....	....	....	1946-47	1947-48
Bladon, Tom	Phi., Pit., Edm., Wpg., Det.	9	610	73	197	270	392	86	8	29	37	70	2	1972-73	1980-81
• Blaine, Garry	Mtl.	1	1	0	0	0	0	....	....	....	....	....	....	1954-55	1954-55
• Blair, Andy	Tor., Chi.	9	402	74	86	160	323	38	6	6	12	32	1	1928-29	1936-37
Blair, Chuck	Tor.	1	1	0	0	0	0	....	....	....	....	....	....	1948-49	1948-49
Blair, Dusty	Tor.	1	2	0	0	0	0	....	....	....	....	....	....	1950-51	1950-51
Blaisdell, Mike	Det., NYR, Pit., Tor.	9	343	70	84	154	166	6	1	2	3	10	....	1980-81	1988-89
Blake, Bob	Bos.	1	12	0	0	0	0	....	....	....	....	....	....	1935-36	1935-36
• Blake, Mickey	Mtl.M., St.L., Tor.	3	10	1	1	2	4	....	....	....	....	....	....	1932-33	1935-36
• Blake, Toe	Mtl.M., Mtl.	14	577	235	292	527	272	58	25	37	62	23	3	1934-35	1947-48
Blight, Rick	Van., L.A.	7	326	96	125	221	170	5	0	5	5	2	....	1975-76	1982-83
• Blinco, Russ	Mtl.M., Chi.	6	268	59	66	125	24	19	3	3	6	4	1	1933-34	1938-39
Block, Ken	Van.	1	1	0	0	0	0	....	....	....	....	....	....	1970-71	1970-71
Bloemberg, Jeff	NYR	4	43	3	6	9	25	7	0	3	3	5	....	1988-89	1991-92
Blomqvist, Timo	Wsh., N.J.	5	243	4	53	57	293	13	0	0	0	24	....	1981-82	1986-87
Blomsten, Arto	Wpg., L.A.	3	25	0	4	4	8	....	....	....	....	....	....	1993-94	1995-96
Bloom, Mike	Wsh., Det.	3	201	30	47	77	215	....	....	....	....	....	....	1974-75	1976-77
Blum, John	Edm., Bos., Wsh., Det.	8	250	7	34	41	610	20	0	2	2	27	....	1982-83	1989-90
Bodak, Bob	Cgy., Hfd.	2	4	0	0	0	29	....	....	....	....	....	....	1987-88	1989-90
Boddy, Gregg	Van.	5	273	23	44	67	263	3	0	0	0	0	....	1971-72	1975-76
Bodger, Doug	Pit., Buf., S.J., N.J., L.A., Van.	16	1071	106	422	528	1007	47	6	18	24	25	....	1984-85	1999-00
Bodnar, Gus	Tor., Chi., Bos.	12	667	142	254	396	207	32	4	3	7	10	2	1943-44	1954-55
Boehm, Ron	Oak.	1	16	2	1	3	10	....	....	....	....	....	....	1967-68	1967-68
• Boesch, Garth	Tor.	4	197	9	28	37	205	34	2	5	7	18	3	1946-47	1949-50
Boh, Rick	Min.	1	8	2	1	3	4	....	....	....	....	....	....	1987-88	1987-88
‡ Bohonos, Lonny	Van., Tor.	4	83	19	16	35	22	9	3	6	9	2	....	1995-96	1998-99
‡ Boikov, Alexandre	Nsh.	2	10	0	0	0	15	....	....	....	....	....	....	1999-00	2000-01
Boileau, Marc	Det.	1	54	5	6	11	8	....	....	....	....	....	....	1961-62	1961-62
Boileau, Rene	NYA	1	7	0	0	0	0	....	....	....	....	....	....	1925-26	1925-26
Boimistruck, Fred	Tor.	2	83	4	14	18	45	....	....	....	....	....	....	1981-82	1982-83
Boisvert, Serge	Tor., Mtl.	5	46	5	7	12	8	23	3	7	10	4	1	1982-83	1987-88
Boivin, Claude	Phi., Ott.	4	132	12	19	31	364	....	....	....	....	....	....	1991-92	1994-95
Boivin, Leo	Tor., Bos., Det., Pit., Min.	19	1150	72	250	322	1192	54	3	10	13	59	....	1951-52	1969-70
Boland, Mike	K.C., Buf.	2	23	1	2	3	29	3	1	0	1	2	....	1974-75	1978-79
Boland, Mike	Phi.	1	2	0	0	0	0	....	....	....	....	....	....	1974-75	1974-75
Boldirev, Ivan	Bos., Cal., Chi., Atl., Van., Det.	15	1052	361	505	866	507	48	13	20	33	14	....	1970-71	1984-85
Bolduc, Danny	Det., Cgy.	3	102	22	19	41	33	1	0	0	0	0	....	1978-79	1983-84
Bolduc, Michel	Que.	2	10	0	0	0	6	....	....	....	....	....	....	1981-82	1982-83
• Boll, Buzz	Tor., NYA, Bro., Bos.	12	437	133	130	263	148	31	7	3	10	13	....	1932-33	1943-44
Bolonchuk, Larry	Van., Wsh.	4	74	3	9	12	97	....	....	....	....	....	....	1972-73	1977-78
• Bolton, Hugh	Tor.	8	235	10	51	61	221	17	0	5	5	14	1	1949-50	1956-57
Bonar, Dan	L.A.	3	170	25	39	64	208	14	3	4	7	22	....	1980-81	1982-83
‡ Bonin, Brian	Pit., Min.	2	12	0	0	0	0	3	0	0	0	0	....	1998-99	2000-01
Bonin, Marcel	Det., Bos., Mtl.	9	454	97	175	272	336	50	11	14	25	51	4	1952-53	1961-62
‡ Bonsignore, Jason	Edm., T.B.	4	79	3	13	16	34	....	....	....	....	....	....	1994-95	1998-99
Boo, Jim	Min.	1	6	0	0	0	22	....	....	....	....	....	....	1977-78	1977-78
• Boone, Buddy	Bos.	2	34	5	3	8	28	22	2	1	3	25	....	1956-57	1957-58
Boothman, George	Tor.	2	58	17	19	36	18	5	2	1	3	2	....	1942-43	1943-44
Bordeleau, Christian	Mtl., St.L., Chi.	4	205	38	65	103	82	19	4	7	11	17	1	1968-69	1971-72
Bordeleau, J.P.	Chi.	10	519	97	126	223	143	48	3	6	9	12	....	1969-70	1979-80
Bordeleau, Paulin	Van.	3	183	33	56	89	47	5	2	1	3	0	....	1973-74	1975-76
‡ Bordeleau, Sebastien	Mtl., Nsh., Min., Phx.	7	251	37	61	98	118	5	0	0	0	2	....	1995-96	2001-02
Borotsik, Jack	St.L.	1	1	0	0	0	0	....	....	....	....	....	....	1974-75	1974-75
Borsato, Luciano	Wpg.	5	203	35	55	90	113	7	1	0	1	4	....	1990-91	1994-95
Borschevsky, Nikolai	Tor., Cgy., Dal.	4	162	49	73	122	44	31	4	9	13	4	....	1992-93	1995-96
Boschman, Laurie	Tor., Edm., Wpg., N.J., Ott.	14	1009	229	348	577	2265	57	8	13	21	140	....	1979-80	1992-93
Bossy, Mike	NYI	10	752	573	553	1126	210	129	85	75	160	38	4	1977-78	1986-87
• Bostrom, Helge	Chi.	4	96	3	3	6	58	13	0	0	0	16	....	1929-30	1932-33
Botell, Mark	Phi.	1	32	4	10	14	31	....	....	....	....	....	....	1981-82	1981-82
Bothwell, Tim	NYR, St.L., Hfd.	12	502	28	93	121	382	49	0	3	3	56	....	1978-79	1988-89

			Regular Schedule					Playoffs							
Name	NHL Teams	NHL Seasons	GP	G	A	TP	PIM	GP	G	A	TP	PIM	NHL Cup Wins	First NHL Season	Last NHL Season
Botting, Cam	Atl.	1	2	0	1	1	0	....	....	....	....	....	....	1975-76	1975-76
Boucha, Henry	Det., Min., K.C., Col.	6	247	53	49	102	157	....	....	....	....	....	....	1971-72	1976-77
Bouchard, Butch	Mtl.	15	785	49	144	193	863	113	11	21	32	121	4	1941-42	1955-56
Bouchard, Dick	NYR	1	1	0	0	0	0	....	....	....	....	....	....	1954-55	1954-55
• Bouchard, Edmond	Mtl., Ham., NYA, Pit.	8	211	19	21	40	117	....	....	....	....	....	....	1921-22	1928-29
Bouchard, Pierre	Mtl., Wsh.	12	595	24	82	106	433	76	3	10	13	56	5	1970-71	1981-82
• Boucher, Billy	Mtl., Bos., NYA	7	213	93	38	131	409	14	3	0	3	17	1	1921-22	1927-28
• Boucher, Bobby	Mtl.	1	11	1	0	1	0	2	0	0	0	0	1	1923-24	1923-24
• Boucher, Clarence	NYA	2	47	2	2	4	133	....	....	....	....	....	....	1926-27	1927-28
• Boucher, Frank	Ott., NYR	14	557	160	263	423	119	55	16	20	36	12	2	1921-22	1943-44
• Boucher, Georges	Ott., Mtl.M., Chi.	15	449	117	87	204	838	28	5	3	8	88	4	1917-18	1931-32
Boudreau, Bruce	Tor., Chi.	8	141	28	42	70	46	9	2	0	2	0	....	1976-77	1985-86
Boudrias, Andre	Mtl., Min., Chi., St.L., Van.	12	662	151	340	491	216	34	6	10	16	12	....	1963-64	1975-76
Boughner, Barry	Oak., Cal.	2	20	0	0	0	11	....	....	....	....	....	....	1969-70	1970-71
Bourbonnais, Dan	Hfd.	2	59	3	25	28	11	....	....	....	....	....	....	1981-82	1983-84
Bourbonnais, Rick	St.L.	3	71	9	15	24	29	4	0	1	1	0	....	1975-76	1977-78
• Bourcier, Conrad	Mtl.	1	6	0	0	0	0	....	....	....	....	....	....	1935-36	1935-36
Bourcier, Jean	Mtl.	1	9	0	1	1	0	....	....	....	....	....	....	1935-36	1935-36
• Bourgeault, Leo	Tor., NYR, Ott., Mtl.	8	307	24	20	44	269	24	1	1	2	18	1	1926-27	1934-35
Bourgeois, Charlie	Cgy., St.L., Hfd.	7	290	16	54	70	788	40	2	3	5	194	....	1981-82	1987-88
Bourne, Bob	NYI, L.A.	14	964	258	324	582	605	139	40	56	96	108	4	1974-75	1987-88
Bourque, Phil	Pit., NYR, Ott.	12	477	88	111	199	516	56	13	12	25	107	2	1983-84	1995-96
Bourque, Raymond	Bos., Col.	22	1612	410	1169	1579	1141	214	41	139	180	171	1	1979-80	2000-01
Boutette, Pat	Tor., Hfd., Pit.	10	756	171	282	453	1354	46	10	14	24	109	....	1975-76	1984-85
Boutilier, Paul	NYI, Bos., Min., NYR, Wpg.	8	288	27	83	110	358	41	1	9	10	45	1	1981-82	1988-89
Bowen, Jason	Phi., Edm.	6	77	2	6	8	109	....	....	....	....	....	....	1992-93	1997-98
Bowler, Bill	CBJ	1	9	0	2	2	8	....	....	....	....	....	....	2000-01	2000-01
Bowman, Kirk	Chi.	3	88	11	17	28	19	7	1	0	1	0	....	1976-77	1978-79
• Bowman, Ralph	Ott., St.L., Det.	7	274	8	17	25	260	22	2	2	4	6	2	1933-34	1939-40
Bownass, Jack	Mtl., NYR	4	80	3	8	11	58	....	....	....	....	....	....	1957-58	1961-62
Bowness, Rick	Atl., Det., St.L., Wpg.	7	173	18	37	55	191	5	0	0	0	2	....	1975-76	1981-82
• Boyd, Bill	NYR, NYA	4	138	15	7	22	72	10	0	0	0	4	1	1926-27	1929-30
Boyd, Irvin	Bos., Det.	4	96	10	10	20	30	5	0	1	1	4	....	1931-32	1943-44
Boyd, Randy	Pit., Chi., NYI, Van.	8	257	20	67	87	328	13	0	2	2	26	....	1981-82	1988-89
Boyer, Wally	Tor., Chi., Oak., Pit.	7	365	54	105	159	163	15	1	3	4	0	....	1965-66	1971-72
Boyer, Zac	Dal.	2	3	0	0	0	0	2	0	0	0	0	....	1994-95	1995-96
Boyko, Darren	Wpg.	1	1	0	0	0	0	....	....	....	....	....	....	1988-89	1988-89
Bozek, Steve	L.A., Cgy., St.L., Van., S.J.	11	641	164	167	331	309	58	12	11	23	69	....	1981-82	1991-92
‡ Bozon, Philippe	St.L.	4	144	16	25	41	101	19	2	0	2	31	....	1991-92	1994-95
• Brackenborough, John	Bos.	1	7	0	0	0	0	....	....	....	....	....	....	1925-26	1925-26
Brackenbury, Curt	Que., Edm., St.L.	4	141	9	17	26	226	2	0	0	0	0	....	1979-80	1982-83
Bradley, Bart	Bos.	1	1	0	0	0	0	....	....	....	....	....	....	1949-50	1949-50
Bradley, Brian	Cgy., Van., Tor., T.B.	13	651	182	321	503	528	13	3	7	10	16	....	1985-86	1997-98
Bradley, Lyle	Cal., Cle.	2	6	1	0	1	2	....	....	....	....	....	....	1973-74	1976-77
Brady, Neil	N.J., Ott., Dal.	5	89	9	22	31	95	....	....	....	....	....	....	1989-90	1993-94
Bragnalo, Rick	Wsh.	4	145	15	35	50	46	....	....	....	....	....	....	1975-76	1978-79
• Branigan, Andy	NYA, Bro.	2	27	1	2	3	31	....	....	....	....	....	....	1940-41	1941-42
Brasar, Per-Olov	Min., Van.	5	348	64	142	206	33	13	1	2	3	0	....	1977-78	1981-82
• Brayshaw, Russ	Chi.	1	43	5	9	14	24	....	....	....	....	....	....	1944-45	1944-45
Breault, Francois	L.A.	3	27	2	4	6	42	....	....	....	....	....	....	1990-91	1992-93
Breitenbach, Ken	Buf.	3	68	1	13	14	49	8	0	1	1	4	....	1975-76	1978-79
Brennan, Dan	L.A.	2	8	0	1	1	9	....	....	....	....	....	....	1983-84	1985-86
Brennan, Doug	NYR	3	123	9	7	16	152	16	1	0	1	21	1	1931-32	1933-34
• Brennan, Tom	Bos.	2	12	2	2	4	2	....	....	....	....	....	....	1943-44	1944-45
Brenneman, John	Chi., NYR, Tor., Det., Oak.	5	152	21	19	40	46	....	....	....	....	....	1	1964-65	1968-69
Bretto, Joe	Chi.	1	3	0	0	0	4	....	....	....	....	....	....	1944-45	1944-45
• Brewer, Carl	Tor., Det., St.L.	12	604	25	198	223	1037	72	3	17	20	146	3	1957-58	1979-80
Brickley, Andy	Phi., Pit., N.J., Bos., Wpg.	11	385	82	140	222	81	17	1	4	5	4	....	1982-83	1993-94
• Briden, Archie	Bos., Det., Pit.	2	71	9	5	14	56	....	....	....	....	....	....	1926-27	1929-30
Bridgman, Mel	Phi., Cgy., N.J., Det., Van.	14	977	252	449	701	1625	125	28	39	67	298	....	1975-76	1988-89
• Briere, Michel	Pit.	1	76	12	32	44	20	10	5	3	8	17	....	1969-70	1969-70
Brindley, Doug	Tor.	1	3	0	0	0	0	....	....	....	....	....	....	1970-71	1970-71
• Brink, Milt	Chi.	1	5	0	0	0	0	....	....	....	....	....	....	1936-37	1936-37
Brisson, Gerry	Mtl.	1	4	0	2	2	4	....	....	....	....	....	....	1962-63	1962-63
Britz, Greg	Tor., Hfd.	3	8	0	0	0	4	....	....	....	....	....	....	1983-84	1986-87
• Broadbent, Punch	Ott., Mtl.M., NYA	11	303	121	51	172	564	23	4	6	10	60	4	1918-19	1928-29
Brochu, Stephane	NYR	1	1	0	0	0	0	....	....	....	....	....	....	1988-89	1988-89
Broden, Connie	Mtl.	3	6	2	1	3	2	7	0	1	1	0	2	1955-56	1957-58
Brooke, Bob	NYR, Min., N.J.	7	447	69	97	166	520	34	9	9	18	59	....	1983-84	1989-90
Brooks, Gord	St.L., Wsh.	3	70	7	18	25	37	....	....	....	....	....	....	1971-72	1974-75
• Brophy, Bernie	Mtl.M., Det.	3	62	4	4	8	25	2	0	0	0	2	1	1925-26	1929-30
Brossart, Willie	Phi., Tor., Wsh.	6	129	1	14	15	88	1	0	0	0	0	....	1970-71	1975-76
Broten, Aaron	Col., N.J., Min., Que., Tor., Wpg.	12	748	186	329	515	441	34	7	18	25	40	....	1980-81	1991-92
Broten, Neal	Min., Dal., N.J., L.A.	17	1099	289	634	923	569	135	35	63	98	77	1	1980-81	1996-97
Broten, Paul	NYR, Dal., St.L.	7	322	46	55	101	264	38	4	6	10	18	....	1989-90	1995-96
‡ Brousseau, Paul	Col., T.B., Fla.	4	26	1	3	4	29	....	....	....	....	....	....	1995-96	2000-01
• Brown, Adam	Det., Chi., Bos.	10	391	104	113	217	378	26	2	4	6	14	1	1941-42	1951-52
Brown, Arnie	Tor., NYR, Det., NYI, Atl.	12	681	44	141	185	738	22	0	6	6	23	....	1961-62	1973-74
‡ Brown, Cam	Van.	1	1	0	0	0	7	....	....	....	....	....	....	1990-91	1990-91
• Brown, Connie	Det.	5	73	15	24	39	12	14	2	3	5	0	1	1938-39	1942-43
Brown, Dave	Phi., Edm., S.J.	14	729	45	52	97	1789	80	2	3	5	209	1	1982-83	1995-96
Brown, Doug	N.J., Pit., Det.	15	854	160	214	374	210	109	23	23	46	26	2	1986-87	2000-01
• Brown, Fred	Mtl.M.	1	19	1	0	1	0	9	0	0	0	0	....	1927-28	1927-28
Brown, George	Mtl.	3	79	6	22	28	34	7	0	0	0	2	....	1936-37	1938-39
• Brown, Gerry	Det.	2	23	4	5	9	2	12	2	1	3	4	....	1941-42	1945-46
Brown, Greg	Buf., Pit., Wpg.	4	94	4	14	18	86	6	0	1	1	4	....	1990-91	1994-95
Brown, Harold	NYR	1	13	2	1	3	2	....	....	....	....	....	....	1945-46	1945-46
Brown, Jeff	Que., St.L., Van., Hfd., Car., Tor., Wsh.	13	747	154	430	584	498	87	20	45	65	59	....	1985-86	1997-98
Brown, Jim	L.A.	1	3	0	1	1	5	....	....	....	....	....	....	1982-83	1982-83
Brown, Keith	Chi., Fla.	16	876	68	274	342	916	103	4	32	36	184	....	1979-80	1994-95
Brown, Kevin	L.A., Hfd., Car., Edm.	6	64	7	9	16	28	1	0	0	0	0	....	1994-95	1999-00
Brown, Larry	NYR, Det., Phi., L.A.	9	455	7	53	60	180	35	0	4	4	10	....	1969-70	1977-78
Brown, Rob	Pit., Hfd., Chi., Dal., L.A.	11	543	190	248	438	599	54	12	14	26	45	....	1987-88	1999-00
• Brown, Stan	NYR, Det.	2	48	8	2	10	18	2	0	0	0	0	....	1926-27	1927-28
Brown, Wayne	Bos.	1	....	....	....	....	....	4	0	0	0	2	....	1953-54	1953-54
• Browne, Cecil	Chi.	1	13	2	0	2	4	....	....	....	....	....	....	1927-28	1927-28
Brownschidle, Jack	St.L., Hfd.	9	494	39	162	201	151	26	0	5	5	18	....	1977-78	1985-86
Brownschidle, Jeff	Hfd.	2	7	0	1	1	2	....	....	....	....	....	....	1981-82	1982-83
Brubaker, Jeff	Hfd., Mtl., Cgy., Tor., Edm., NYR, Det.	8	178	16	9	25	512	2	0	0	0	27	....	1979-80	1988-89
Bruce, David	Van., St.L., S.J.	8	234	48	39	87	338	3	0	0	0	2	....	1985-86	1993-94
• Bruce, Gordie	Bos.	3	28	4	9	13	13	7	2	3	5	4	....	1940-41	1945-46
• Bruce, Morley	Ott.	4	71	8	3	11	27	3	0	0	0	2	2	1917-18	1921-22
Brumwell, Murray	Min., N.J.	7	128	12	31	43	70	2	0	0	0	2	....	1980-81	1987-88
Brunet, Benoit	Mtl., Dal., Ott.	13	539	101	161	262	229	54	5	20	25	32	1	1988-89	2001-02
• Bruneteau, Eddie	Det.	7	180	40	42	82	35	31	7	6	13	0	....	1940-41	1948-49
• Bruneteau, Mud	Det.	11	411	139	138	277	80	77	23	14	37	22	3	1935-36	1945-46
• Brydge, Bill	Tor., Det., NYA	9	368	26	52	78	506	2	0	0	0	4	....	1926-27	1935-36
Brydges, Paul	Buf.	1	15	2	2	4	6	....	....	....	....	....	....	1986-87	1986-87
• Brydson, Glenn	Mtl.M., St.L., NYR, Chi.	8	299	56	79	135	203	11	0	0	0	8	....	1930-31	1937-38
• Brydson, Gord	Tor.	1	8	2	0	2	8	....	....	....	....	....	....	1929-30	1929-30
Bubla, Jiri	Van.	5	256	17	101	118	202	6	0	0	0	7	....	1981-82	1985-86
• Buchanan, Al	Tor.	2	4	0	1	1	2	....	....	....	....	....	....	1948-49	1949-50
Buchanan, Bucky	NYR	1	2	0	0	0	0	....	....	....	....	....	....	1948-49	1948-49
Buchanan, Jeff	Col.	1	6	0	0	0	6	....	....	....	....	....	....	1998-99	1998-99
Buchanan, Mike	Chi.	1	1	0	0	0	0	....	....	....	....	....	....	1951-52	1951-52
Buchanan, Ron	Bos., St.L.	2	5	0	0	0	0	....	....	....	....	....	....	1966-67	1969-70
Bucyk, John	Det., Bos.	23	1540	556	813	1369	497	124	41	62	103	42	2	1955-56	1977-78
Bucyk, Randy	Mtl., Cgy.	2	19	4	2	6	8	2	0	0	0	0	....	1985-86	1987-88
Buhr, Doug	K.C.	1	6	0	2	2	4	....	....	....	....	....	....	1974-75	1974-75
Bukovich, Tony	Det.	2	17	7	3	10	6	6	0	1	1	0	....	1943-44	1944-45
Bullard, Mike	Pit., Cgy., St.L., Phi., Tor.	11	727	329	345	674	703	40	11	18	29	44	....	1980-81	1991-92
• Buller, Hy	Det., NYR	5	188	22	58	80	215	....	....	....	....	....	....	1943-44	1953-54
Bulley, Ted	Chi., Wsh., Pit.	8	414	101	113	214	704	29	5	5	10	24	....	1976-77	1983-84
Burakovsky, Robert	Ott.	1	23	2	3	5	6	....	....	....	....	....	....	1993-94	1993-94
• Burch, Billy	Ham., NYA, Bos., Chi.	11	390	137	61	198	255	2	0	0	0	0	....	1922-23	1932-33
• Burchell, Fred	Mtl.	2	4	0	0	0	2	....	....	....	....	....	....	1950-51	1953-54

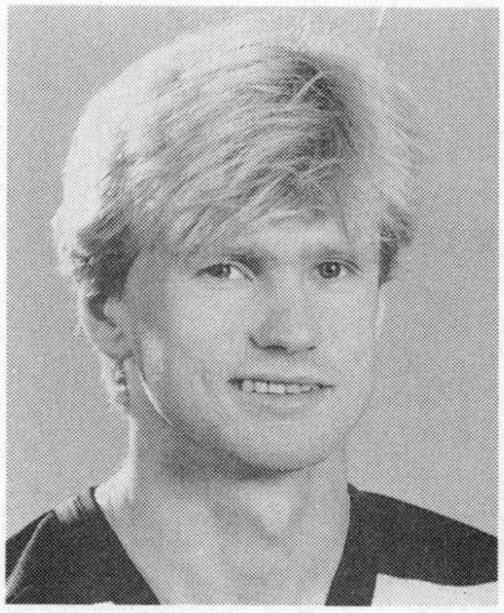

Nikolai Borschevsky

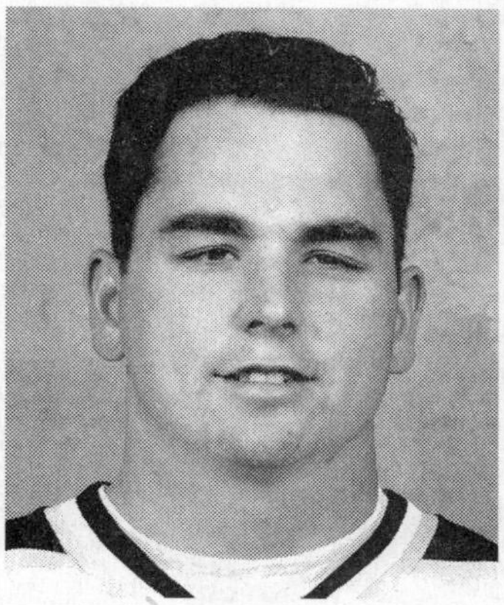

Bill Bowler

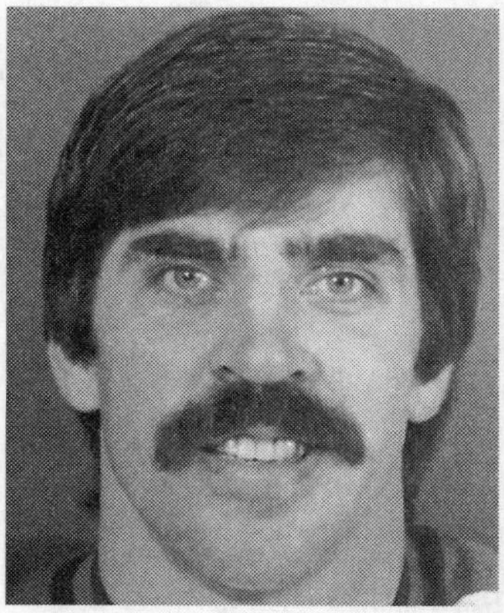

Mel Bridgman

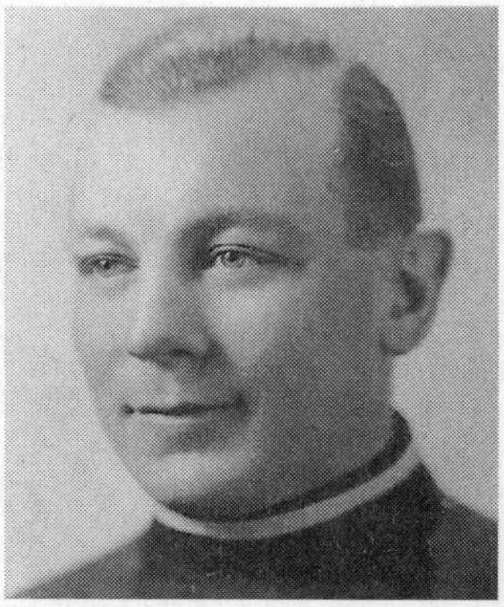

Punch Broadbent

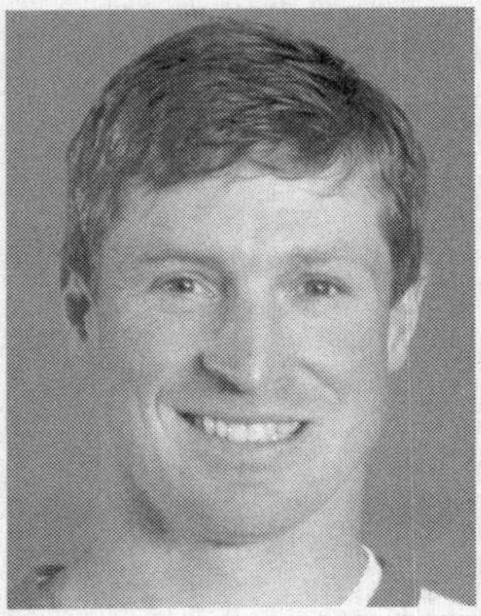

Doug Brown

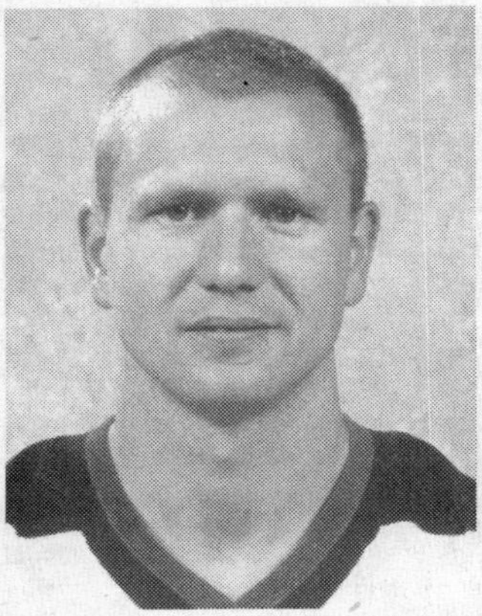

Jan Caloun

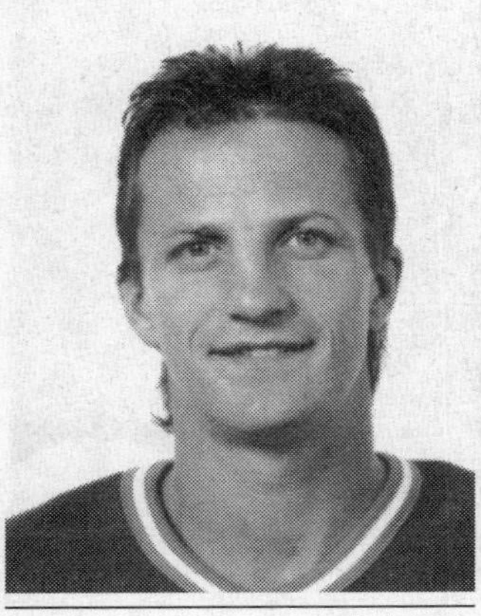

Guy Carbonneau

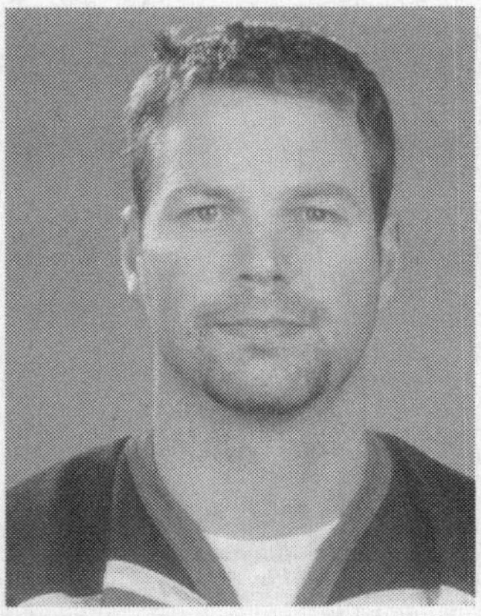

Eric Charron

			Regular Schedule					Playoffs					NHL	First	Last
Name	NHL Teams	NHL Seasons	GP	G	A	TP	PIM	GP	G	A	TP	PIM	Cup Wins	NHL Season	NHL Season
Burdon, Glen	K.C.	1	11	0	2	2	0	....	....	....	....	....	....	1974-75	1974-75
Bure, Pavel	Van., Fla., NYR	12	702	437	342	779	484	64	35	35	70	74	....	1991-92	2002-03
Bureau, Marc	Cgy., Min., T.B., Mtl., Phi.	11	567	55	83	138	327	50	5	7	12	46	....	1989-90	1999-00
Burega, Bill	Tor.	1	4	0	1	1	4	....	....	....	....	....	....	1955-56	1955-56
• Burke, Eddie	Bos., NYA	4	106	29	20	49	55	....	....	....	....	....	....	1931-32	1934-35
• Burke, Marty	Mtl., Pit., Ott., Chi.	11	494	19	47	66	560	31	2	4	6	44	2	1927-28	1937-38
• Burmister, Roy	NYA	3	67	4	3	7	2	....	....	....	....	....	....	1929-30	1931-32
Burnett, Kelly	NYR	1	3	1	0	1	0	....	....	....	....	....	....	1952-53	1952-53
• Burns, Bobby	Chi.	3	20	1	0	1	8	....	....	....	....	....	....	1927-28	1929-30
Burns, Charlie	Det., Bos., Oak., Pit., Min.	11	749	106	198	304	252	31	5	4	9	6	....	1958-59	1972-73
Burns, Gary	NYR	2	11	2	2	4	18	5	0	0	0	2	....	1980-81	1981-82
• Burns, Norm	NYR	1	11	0	4	4	2	....	....	....	....	....	....	1941-42	1941-42
Burns, Robin	Pit., K.C.	5	190	31	38	69	139	....	....	....	....	....	....	1970-71	1975-76
Burr, Shawn	Det., T.B., S.J.	16	878	181	259	440	1069	91	16	19	35	95	....	1984-85	1999-00
Burridge, Randy	Bos., Wsh., L.A., Buf.	13	706	199	251	450	458	107	18	34	52	103	....	1985-86	1997-98
Burrows, Dave	Pit., Tor.	10	724	29	135	164	373	29	1	5	6	25	....	1971-72	1980-81
• Burry, Bert	Ott.	1	4	0	0	0	0	....	....	....	....	....	....	1932-33	1932-33
Burt, Adam	Hfd., Car., Phi., Atl.	13	737	37	115	152	961	21	0	1	1	8	....	1988-89	2000-01
Burton, Cummy	Det.	3	43	0	2	2	21	3	0	0	0	0	....	1955-56	1958-59
Burton, Nelson	Wsh.	2	8	1	0	1	21	....	....	....	....	....	....	1977-78	1978-79
• Bush, Eddie	Det.	2	26	4	6	10	40	11	1	6	7	23	....	1938-39	1941-42
Buskas, Rod	Pit., Van., L.A., Chi.	11	556	19	63	82	1294	18	0	3	3	45	....	1982-83	1992-93
Busniuk, Mike	Phi.	2	143	3	23	26	297	25	2	5	7	34	....	1979-80	1980-81
Busniuk, Ron	Buf.	2	6	0	3	3	13	....	....	....	....	....	....	1972-73	1973-74
• Buswell, Walt	Det., Mtl.	8	368	10	40	50	164	24	2	1	3	10	....	1932-33	1939-40
Butcher, Garth	Van., St.L., Que., Tor.	14	897	48	158	206	2302	50	6	5	11	122	....	1981-82	1994-95
Butler, Dick	Chi.	1	7	2	0	2	0	....	....	....	....	....	....	1947-48	1947-48
Butler, Jerry	NYR, St.L., Tor., Van., Wpg.	11	641	99	120	219	515	48	3	3	6	79	....	1972-73	1982-83
‡ Butsayev, Viacheslav	Phi., S.J., Ana., Fla., Ott., T.B.	6	132	17	26	43	133	....	....	....	....	....	....	1992-93	1999-00
‡ Butsayev, Yuri	Det., Atl.	4	99	10	4	14	28	....	....	....	....	....	....	1999-00	2002-03
Butters, Bill	Min.	2	72	1	4	5	77	....	....	....	....	....	....	1977-78	1978-79
Buttrey, Gord	Chi.	1	10	0	0	0	0	....	....	....	....	....	....	1943-44	1943-44
Buynak, Gord	St.L.	1	4	0	0	0	2	....	....	....	....	....	....	1974-75	1974-75
Byakin, Ilja	Edm., S.J.	2	57	8	25	33	44	....	....	....	....	....	....	1993-94	1994-95
Byce, John	Bos.	3	21	2	3	5	6	8	2	0	2	2	....	1989-90	1991-92
Byers, Gord	Bos.	1	1	0	1	1	0	....	....	....	....	....	....	1949-50	1949-50
Byers, Jerry	Min., Atl., NYR	4	43	3	4	7	15	....	....	....	....	....	....	1972-73	1977-78
Byers, Lyndon	Bos., S.J.	10	279	28	43	71	1081	37	2	2	4	96	....	1983-84	1992-93
Byers, Mike	Tor., Phi., L.A., Buf.	4	166	42	34	76	39	4	0	1	1	0	....	1967-68	1971-72
Byram, Shawn	NYI, Chi.	2	5	0	0	0	14	....	....	....	....	....	....	1990-91	1991-92

C

• Caffery, Jack	Tor., Bos.	3	57	3	2	5	22	10	1	0	1	4	....	1954-55	1957-58
Caffery, Terry	Chi., Min.	2	14	0	0	0	0	1	0	0	0	0	....	1969-70	1970-71
• Cahan, Larry	Tor., NYR, Oak., L.A.	13	666	38	92	130	700	29	1	1	2	38	....	1954-55	1970-71
• Cahill, Charles	Bos.	2	32	0	1	1	4	....	....	....	....	....	....	1925-26	1926-27
• Cain, Francis	Mtl.M., Tor.	2	61	4	0	4	35	....	....	....	....	....	....	1924-25	1925-26
• Cain, Herb	Mtl.M., Mtl., Bos.	13	570	206	194	400	178	67	16	13	29	13	2	1933-34	1945-46
Cairns, Don	K.C., Col.	2	9	0	1	1	2	....	....	....	....	....	....	1975-76	1976-77
Calder, Eric	Wsh.	2	2	0	0	0	0	....	....	....	....	....	....	1981-82	1982-83
• Calladine, Norm	Bos.	3	63	19	29	48	8	....	....	....	....	....	....	1942-43	1944-45
Callander, Drew	Phi., Van.	4	39	6	2	8	7	....	....	....	....	....	....	1976-77	1979-80
Callander, Jock	Pit., T.B.	5	109	22	29	51	116	22	3	8	11	12	1	1987-88	1992-93
Callighen, Brett	Edm.	3	160	56	89	145	132	14	4	6	10	8	....	1979-80	1981-82
Callighen, Patsy	NYR	1	36	0	0	0	32	9	0	0	0	0	1	1927-28	1927-28
‡ Caloun, Jan	S.J., CBJ	3	24	8	6	14	2	....	....	....	....	....	....	1995-96	2000-01
Camazzola, James	Chi.	2	3	0	0	0	0	....	....	....	....	....	....	1983-84	1986-87
Camazzola, Tony	Wsh.	1	3	0	0	0	4	....	....	....	....	....	....	1981-82	1981-82
Cameron, Al	Det., Wpg.	6	282	11	44	55	356	7	0	1	1	2	....	1975-76	1980-81
• Cameron, Billy	Mtl., NYA	2	39	0	0	0	2	2	0	0	0	0	1	1923-24	1925-26
Cameron, Craig	Det., St.L., Min., NYI	9	552	87	65	152	196	27	3	1	4	17	....	1966-67	1975-76
Cameron, Dave	Col., N.J.	3	168	25	28	53	238	....	....	....	....	....	....	1981-82	1983-84
• Cameron, Harry	Tor., Ott., Mtl.	6	128	88	51	139	189	11	5	4	9	16	2	1917-18	1922-23
• Cameron, Scotty	NYR	1	35	8	11	19	0	....	....	....	....	....	....	1942-43	1942-43
Campbell, Bryan	L.A., Chi.	5	260	35	71	106	74	22	3	4	7	2	....	1967-68	1971-72
Campbell, Colin	Pit., Col., Edm., Van., Det.	11	636	25	103	128	1292	45	4	10	14	181	....	1974-75	1984-85
• Campbell, Dave	Mtl.	1	2	0	0	0	0	....	....	....	....	....	....	1920-21	1920-21
Campbell, Don	Chi.	1	17	1	3	4	8	....	....	....	....	....	....	1943-44	1943-44
• Campbell, Earl	Ott., NYA	3	76	6	3	9	14	1	0	0	0	6	....	1923-24	1925-26
Campbell, Scott	Wpg., St.L.	3	80	4	21	25	243	....	....	....	....	....	....	1979-80	1981-82
Campbell, Wade	Wpg., Bos.	6	213	9	27	36	305	10	0	0	0	20	....	1982-83	1987-88
Campeau, Tod	Mtl.	3	42	5	9	14	16	1	0	0	0	0	....	1943-44	1948-49
Campedelli, Dom	Mtl.	1	2	0	0	0	0	....	....	....	....	....	....	1985-86	1985-86
Capuano, Dave	Pit., Van., T.B., S.J.	4	104	17	38	55	56	6	1	1	2	5	....	1989-90	1993-94
Capuano, Jack	Tor., Van., Bos.	3	6	0	0	0	0	....	....	....	....	....	....	1989-90	1991-92
Carbol, Leo	Chi.	1	6	0	1	1	4	....	....	....	....	....	....	1942-43	1942-43
Carbonneau, Guy	Mtl., St.L., Dal.	19	1318	260	403	663	820	231	38	55	93	161	3	1980-81	1999-00
Cardin, Claude	St.L.	1	1	0	0	0	0	....	....	....	....	....	....	1967-68	1967-68
Cardwell, Steve	Pit.	3	53	9	11	20	35	4	0	0	0	2	....	1970-71	1972-73
• Carey, George	Que., Ham., Tor.	5	72	21	12	33	20	....	....	....	....	....	....	1919-20	1923-24
Carkner, Terry	NYR, Que., Phi., Det., Fla.	13	858	42	188	230	1588	54	1	9	10	48	....	1986-87	1998-99
Carleton, Wayne	Tor., Bos., Cal.	7	278	55	73	128	172	18	2	4	6	14	1	1965-66	1971-72
Carlin, Brian	L.A.	1	5	1	0	1	0	....	....	....	....	....	....	1971-72	1971-72
Carlson, Jack	Min., St.L.	6	236	30	15	45	417	25	1	2	3	72	....	1978-79	1986-87
Carlson, Kent	Mtl., St.L., Wsh.	5	113	7	11	18	148	8	0	0	0	13	....	1983-84	1988-89
Carlson, Steve	L.A.	1	52	9	12	21	23	4	1	1	2	7	....	1979-80	1979-80
Carlsson, Anders	N.J.	3	104	7	26	33	34	3	1	0	1	2	....	1986-87	1988-89
Carlyle, Randy	Tor., Pit., Wpg.	18	1055	148	499	647	1400	69	9	24	33	120	....	1976-77	1992-93
Carnback, Patrik	Mtl., Ana.	4	154	24	38	62	122	....	....	....	....	....	....	1992-93	1995-96
• Caron, Alain	Oak., Mtl.	2	60	9	13	22	18	....	....	....	....	....	....	1967-68	1968-69
Carpenter, Bob	Wsh., NYR, L.A., Bos., N.J.	19	1178	320	408	728	919	140	21	38	59	136	1	1981-82	1998-99
• Carpenter, Ed	Que., Ham.	2	45	10	5	15	41	....	....	....	....	....	....	1919-20	1920-21
Carr, Gene	St.L., NYR, L.A., Pit., Atl.	8	465	79	136	215	365	35	5	8	13	66	....	1971-72	1978-79
Carr, Lorne	NYR, NYA, Tor.	13	580	204	222	426	132	53	10	9	19	13	2	1933-34	1945-46
Carr, Red	Tor.	1	5	0	1	1	2	....	....	....	....	....	....	1943-44	1943-44
Carriere, Larry	Buf., Atl., Van., L.A., Tor.	7	367	16	74	90	462	27	0	3	3	42	....	1972-73	1979-80
• Carrigan, Gene	NYR, Det., St.L.	3	37	2	1	3	13	4	0	0	0	0	....	1930-31	1934-35
Carroll, Billy	NYI, Edm., Det.	7	322	30	54	84	113	71	6	12	18	18	4	1980-81	1986-87
• Carroll, George	Mtl.M., Bos.	1	16	0	0	0	11	....	....	....	....	....	....	1924-25	1924-25
Carroll, Greg	Wsh., Det., Hfd.	2	131	20	34	54	44	....	....	....	....	....	....	1978-79	1979-80
Carruthers, Dwight	Det., Phi.	2	2	0	0	0	0	....	....	....	....	....	....	1965-66	1967-68
• Carse, Bill	NYR, Chi.	4	124	28	43	71	38	13	3	2	5	0	....	1938-39	1941-42
• Carse, Bob	Chi., Mtl.	5	167	32	55	87	52	10	0	2	2	2	....	1939-40	1947-48
• Carson, Bill	Tor., Bos.	4	159	54	24	78	156	11	3	0	3	14	1	1926-27	1929-30
• Carson, Frank	Mtl.M., NYA, Det.	7	248	42	48	90	166	27	0	2	2	9	1	1925-26	1933-34
• Carson, Gerry	Mtl., NYR, Mtl.M.	6	261	12	11	23	205	22	0	0	0	12	1	1928-29	1936-37
Carson, Jimmy	L.A., Edm., Det., Van., Hfd.	10	626	275	286	561	254	55	17	15	32	22	....	1986-87	1995-96
Carson, Lindsay	Phi., Hfd.	7	373	66	80	146	524	49	4	10	14	56	....	1981-82	1987-88
Carter, Billy	Mtl., Bos.	3	16	0	0	0	6	....	....	....	....	....	....	1957-58	1961-62
Carter, John	Bos., S.J.	8	244	40	50	90	201	31	7	5	12	51	....	1985-86	1992-93
Carter, Ron	Edm.	1	2	0	0	0	0	....	....	....	....	....	....	1979-80	1979-80
• Carveth, Joe	Det., Bos., Mtl.	11	504	150	189	339	81	69	21	16	37	28	2	1940-41	1950-51
Cashman, Wayne	Bos.	17	1027	277	516	793	1041	145	31	57	88	250	2	1964-65	1982-83
‡ Casselman, Mike	Fla.	1	3	0	0	0	0	....	....	....	....	....	....	1995-96	1995-96
Cassidy, Bruce	Chi.	7	36	4	13	17	10	1	0	0	0	0	....	1983-84	1989-90
Cassidy, Tom	Pit.	1	26	3	4	7	15	....	....	....	....	....	....	1977-78	1977-78
Cassolato, Tony	Wsh.	3	23	1	6	7	4	....	....	....	....	....	....	1979-80	1981-82
Caufield, Jay	NYR, Min., Pit.	7	208	5	8	13	759	17	0	0	0	42	2	1986-87	1992-93
Cavallini, Gino	Cgy., St.L., Que.	9	593	114	159	273	507	74	14	19	33	66	....	1984-85	1992-93
Cavallini, Paul	Wsh., St.L., Dal.	10	564	56	177	233	750	69	8	27	35	114	....	1986-87	1995-96
Ceresino, Ray	Tor.	1	12	1	1	2	2	....	....	....	....	....	....	1948-49	1948-49
Cernik, Frantisek	Det.	1	49	5	4	9	13	....	....	....	....	....	....	1984-85	1984-85
Chabot, John	Mtl., Pit., Det.	8	508	84	228	312	85	33	6	20	26	2	....	1983-84	1990-91
• Chad, John	Chi.	3	80	15	22	37	29	10	0	1	1	2	....	1939-40	1945-46
• Chalmers, Chick	NYR	1	1	0	0	0	0	....	....	....	....	....	....	1953-54	1953-54

Name	NHL Teams	NHL Seasons	Regular Schedule GP	G	A	TP	PIM	Playoffs GP	G	A	TP	PIM	NHL Cup Wins	First NHL Season	Last NHL Season
Chalupa, Milan	Det.	1	14	0	5	5	6	....	....	....	....	....	....	1984-85	1984-85
● Chamberlain, Murph	Tor., Mtl., Bro., Bos.	12	510	100	175	275	769	66	14	17	31	96	2	1937-38	1948-49
Chambers, Shawn	Min., Wsh., T.B., N.J., Dal.	13	625	50	185	235	364	94	7	26	33	72	2	1987-88	1999-00
Champagne, Andre	Tor.	1	2	0	0	0	0	....	....	....	....	....	....	1962-63	1962-63
Chapdelaine, Rene	L.A.	3	32	0	2	2	32	....	....	....	....	....	....	1990-91	1992-93
● Chapman, Art	Bos., NYA	10	438	62	176	238	140	26	1	5	6	9	....	1930-31	1939-40
Chapman, Blair	Pit., St.L.	7	402	106	125	231	158	25	4	6	10	15	....	1976-77	1982-83
‡ Chapman, Brian	Hfd.	1	3	0	0	0	29	....	....	....	....	....	....	1990-91	1990-91
Charbonneau, Jose	Mtl., Van.	4	71	9	13	22	67	11	1	0	1	8	....	1987-88	1994-95
Charbonneau, Stephane	Que.	1	2	0	0	0	0	....	....	....	....	....	....	1991-92	1991-92
Charlebois, Bob	Min.	1	7	1	0	1	0	....	....	....	....	....	....	1967-68	1967-68
Charlesworth, Todd	Pit., NYR	6	93	3	9	12	47	....	....	....	....	....	....	1983-84	1989-90
‡ Charron, Eric	Mtl., T.B., Wsh., Cgy.	8	130	2	7	9	127	6	0	0	0	8	....	1992-93	1999-00
Charron, Guy	Mtl., Det., K.C., Wsh.	12	734	221	309	530	146	....	....	....	....	....	....	1969-70	1980-81
Chartier, Dave	Wpg.	1	1	0	0	0	0	....	....	....	....	....	....	1980-81	1980-81
Chartraw, Rick	Mtl., L.A., NYR, Edm.	10	420	28	64	92	399	75	7	9	16	80	4	1974-75	1983-84
Chase, Kelly	St.L., Hfd., Tor.	11	458	17	36	53	2017	27	1	1	2	100	....	1989-90	1999-00
Chasse, Denis	St.L., Wsh., Wpg., Ott.	4	132	11	14	25	292	7	1	7	8	23	....	1993-94	1996-97
‡ Chebaturkin, Vladimir	NYI, St.L., Chi.	5	62	2	7	9	52	3	0	0	0	2	....	1997-98	2001-02
Check, Lude	Det., Chi.	2	27	6	2	8	4	....	....	....	....	....	....	1943-44	1944-45
Chernoff, Mike	Min.	1	1	0	0	0	0	....	....	....	....	....	....	1968-69	1968-69
Chernomaz, Rich	Col., N.J., Cgy.	7	51	9	7	16	18	....	....	....	....	....	....	1981-82	1991-92
Cherry, Dick	Bos., Phi.	3	145	12	10	22	45	4	1	0	1	4	....	1956-57	1969-70
Cherry, Don	Bos.	1	....	....	....	....	....	1	0	0	0	0	....	1954-55	1954-55
Chervyakov, Denis	Bos.	1	2	0	0	0	2	....	....	....	....	....	....	1992-93	1992-93
● Chevrefils, Real	Bos., Det.	8	387	104	97	201	185	30	5	4	9	20	....	1951-52	1958-59
● Chiasson, Steve	Det., Cgy., Hfd., Car.	13	751	93	305	398	1107	63	16	19	35	119	....	1986-87	1998-99
Chibirev, Igor	Hfd.	2	45	7	12	19	2	....	....	....	....	....	....	1993-94	1994-95
Chicoine, Dan	Cle., Min.	3	31	1	2	3	12	1	0	0	0	0	....	1977-78	1979-80
Chinnick, Rick	Min.	2	4	0	2	2	0	....	....	....	....	....	....	1973-74	1974-75
Chipperfield, Ron	Edm., Que.	2	83	22	24	46	34	....	....	....	....	....	....	1979-80	1980-81
Chisholm, Art	Bos.	1	3	0	0	0	0	....	....	....	....	....	....	1960-61	1960-61
Chisholm, Colin	Min.	1	1	0	0	0	0	....	....	....	....	....	....	1986-87	1986-87
● Chisholm, Lex	Tor.	2	54	10	8	18	19	3	1	0	1	0	....	1939-40	1940-41
Chorney, Marc	Pit., L.A.	4	210	8	27	35	209	7	0	1	1	2	....	1980-81	1983-84
Chorske, Tom	Mtl., N.J., Ott., NYI, Wsh., Cgy., Pit.	11	596	115	122	237	225	50	5	12	17	10	1	1989-90	1999-00
● Chouinard, Gene	Ott.	1	8	0	0	0	0	....	....	....	....	....	....	1927-28	1927-28
Chouinard, Guy	Atl., Cgy., St.L.	10	578	205	370	575	120	46	9	28	37	12	....	1974-75	1983-84
Christian, Dave	Wpg., Wsh., Bos., St.L., Chi.	15	1009	340	433	773	284	102	32	25	57	27	....	1979-80	1993-94
‡ Christian, Jeff	N.J., Pit., Phx.	5	18	2	2	4	17	....	....	....	....	....	....	1991-92	1997-98
Christie, Mike	Cal., Cle., Col., Van.	7	412	15	101	116	550	2	0	0	0	0	....	1974-75	1980-81
Christoff, Steve	Min., Cgy., L.A.	5	248	77	64	141	108	35	16	12	28	25	....	1979-80	1983-84
Chrystal, Bob	NYR	2	132	11	14	25	112	....	....	....	....	....	....	1953-54	1954-55
‡ Church, Brad	Wsh.	1	2	0	0	0	0	....	....	....	....	....	....	1997-98	1997-98
● Church, Jack	Tor., Bro., Bos.	5	130	4	19	23	154	25	1	1	2	18	....	1938-39	1945-46
Churla, Shane	Hfd., Cgy., Min., Dal., L.A., NYR	11	488	26	45	71	2301	78	5	7	12	282	....	1986-87	1996-97
Chychrun, Jeff	Phi., L.A., Pit., Edm.	8	262	3	22	25	744	19	0	2	2	65	1	1986-87	1993-94
Chynoweth, Dean	NYI, Bos.	9	241	4	18	22	667	6	0	0	0	26	....	1988-89	1997-98
Chyzowski, Dave	NYI, Chi.	6	126	15	16	31	144	2	0	0	0	0	....	1989-90	1996-97
Ciavaglia, Peter	Buf.	2	5	0	0	0	0	....	....	....	....	....	....	1991-92	1992-93
Ciccarelli, Dino	Min., Wsh., Det., T.B., Fla.	19	1232	608	592	1200	1425	141	73	45	118	211	....	1980-81	1998-99
Ciccone, Enrico	Min., Wsh., T.B., Chi., Car., Van., Mtl.	9	374	10	18	28	1469	13	1	0	1	48	....	1991-92	2000-01
Cichocki, Chris	Det., N.J.	4	68	11	12	23	27	....	....	....	....	....	....	1985-86	1988-89
Cierny, Jozef	Edm.	1	1	0	0	0	0	....	....	....	....	....	....	1993-94	1993-94
● Ciesla, Hank	Chi., NYR	4	269	26	51	77	87	6	0	2	2	0	....	1955-56	1958-59
‡ Ciger, Zdeno	N.J., Edm., NYR, T.B.	7	352	94	134	228	101	13	2	6	8	4	....	1990-91	2001-02
Cimellaro, Tony	Ott.	1	2	0	0	0	0	....	....	....	....	....	....	1992-93	1992-93
Cimetta, Rob	Bos., Tor.	4	103	16	16	32	66	1	0	0	0	15	....	1988-89	1991-92
Cirella, Joe	Col., N.J., Que., NYR, Fla., Ott.	15	828	64	211	275	1446	38	0	13	13	98	....	1981-82	1995-96
‡ Cirone, Jason	Wpg.	1	3	0	0	0	2	....	....	....	....	....	....	1991-92	1991-92
‡ Cisar, Marian	Nsh.	3	73	13	17	30	57	....	....	....	....	....	....	1999-00	2001-02
Clackson, Kim	Pit., Que.	2	106	0	8	8	370	8	0	0	0	70	....	1979-80	1980-81
● Clancy, King	Ott., Tor.	16	592	136	147	283	914	55	8	8	16	88	3	1921-22	1936-37
Clancy, Terry	Oak., Tor.	4	93	6	6	12	39	....	....	....	....	....	....	1967-68	1972-73
● Clapper, Dit	Bos.	20	833	228	246	474	462	82	13	17	30	50	3	1927-28	1946-47
Clark, Dan	NYR	1	4	0	1	1	6	....	....	....	....	....	....	1978-79	1978-79
Clark, Dean	Edm.	1	1	0	0	0	0	....	....	....	....	....	....	1983-84	1983-84
Clark, Gordie	Bos.	2	8	0	1	1	0	1	0	0	0	0	....	1974-75	1975-76
● Clark, Nobby	Bos.	1	5	0	0	0	0	....	....	....	....	....	....	1927-28	1927-28
Clark, Wendel	Tor., Que., NYI, T.B., Det., Chi.	15	793	330	234	564	1690	95	37	32	69	201	....	1985-86	1999-00
Clarke, Bobby	Phi.	15	1144	358	852	1210	1453	136	42	77	119	152	2	1969-70	1983-84
‡ Clarke, Dale	St.L.	1	3	0	0	0	0	....	....	....	....	....	....	2000-01	2000-01
● Cleghorn, Odie	Mtl., Pit.	10	181	95	34	129	142	12	7	2	9	5	1	1918-19	1927-28
● Cleghorn, Sprague	Ott., Tor., Mtl., Bos.	10	259	83	55	138	538	21	4	3	7	26	2	1918-19	1927-28
Clement, Bill	Phi., Wsh., Atl., Cgy.	11	719	148	208	356	383	50	5	3	8	26	2	1971-72	1981-82
Cline, Bruce	NYR	1	30	2	3	5	10	....	....	....	....	....	....	1956-57	1956-57
Clippingdale, Steve	L.A., Wsh.	2	19	1	2	3	9	1	0	0	0	0	....	1976-77	1979-80
Cloutier, Real	Que., Buf.	6	317	146	198	344	119	25	7	5	12	20	....	1979-80	1984-85
Cloutier, Rejean	Det.	2	5	0	2	2	2	....	....	....	....	....	....	1979-80	1981-82
Cloutier, Roland	Det., Que.	3	34	8	9	17	2	....	....	....	....	....	....	1977-78	1979-80
‡ Cloutier, Sylvain	Chi.	1	7	0	0	0	0	....	....	....	....	....	....	1998-99	1998-99
● Clune, Wally	Mtl.	1	5	0	0	0	6	....	....	....	....	....	....	1955-56	1955-56
Coalter, Gary	Cal., K.C.	2	34	2	4	6	2	....	....	....	....	....	....	1973-74	1974-75
Coates, Steve	Det.	1	5	1	0	1	24	....	....	....	....	....	....	1976-77	1976-77
Cochrane, Glen	Phi., Van., Chi., Edm.	10	411	17	72	89	1556	18	1	1	2	31	....	1978-79	1988-89
Coffey, Paul	Edm., Pit., L.A., Det., Hfd., Phi., Chi., Car., Bos.	21	1409	396	1135	1531	1802	194	59	137	196	264	4	1980-81	2000-01
Coflin, Hugh	Chi.	1	31	0	3	3	33	....	....	....	....	....	....	1950-51	1950-51
Cole, Danton	Wpg., T.B., N.J., NYI, Chi.	7	318	58	60	118	125	1	0	0	0	0	1	1989-90	1995-96
Colley, Tom	Min.	1	1	0	0	0	2	....	....	....	....	....	....	1974-75	1974-75
Collings, Norm	Mtl.	1	1	0	1	1	0	....	....	....	....	....	....	1934-35	1934-35
Collins, Bill	Min., Mtl., Det., St.L., NYR, Phi., Wsh.	11	768	157	154	311	415	18	3	5	8	12	....	1967-68	1977-78
Collins, Gary	Tor.	1	....	....	....	....	....	2	0	0	0	0	....	1958-59	1958-59
Collyard, Bob	St.L.	1	10	1	3	4	4	....	....	....	....	....	....	1973-74	1973-74
● Colman, Michael	S.J.	1	15	0	1	1	32	....	....	....	....	....	....	1991-92	1991-92
● Colville, Mac	NYR	9	353	71	104	175	130	40	9	10	19	14	1	1935-36	1946-47
● Colville, Neil	NYR	12	464	99	166	265	213	46	7	19	26	32	1	1935-36	1948-49
Colwill, Les	NYR	1	69	7	6	13	16	....	....	....	....	....	....	1958-59	1958-59
Comeau, Rey	Mtl., Atl., Col.	9	564	98	141	239	175	9	2	1	3	8	....	1971-72	1979-80
Comrie, Paul	Edm.	1	15	1	2	3	4	....	....	....	....	....	....	1999-00	1999-00
Conacher, Brian	Tor., Det.	5	155	28	28	56	84	12	3	2	5	21	1	1961-62	1971-72
● Conacher, Charlie	Tor., Det., NYA	12	459	225	173	398	523	49	17	18	35	49	1	1929-30	1940-41
Conacher, Jim	Det., Chi., NYR	8	328	85	117	202	91	19	5	2	7	4	....	1945-46	1952-53
● Conacher, Lionel	Pit., NYA, Mtl.M., Chi.	12	498	80	105	185	882	35	2	2	4	34	2	1925-26	1936-37
Conacher, Pat	NYR, Edm., N.J., L.A., Cgy., NYI	13	521	63	76	139	235	66	11	10	21	40	1	1979-80	1995-96
Conacher, Pete	Chi., NYR, Tor.	6	229	47	39	86	57	7	0	0	0	0	....	1951-52	1957-58
● Conacher, Roy	Bos., Det., Chi.	11	490	226	200	426	90	42	15	15	30	14	2	1938-39	1951-52
● Conn, Red	NYA	2	96	9	28	37	22	....	....	....	....	....	....	1933-34	1934-35
Conn, Rob	Chi., Buf.	2	30	2	5	7	20	....	....	....	....	....	....	1991-92	1995-96
● Connelly, Bert	NYR, Chi.	3	87	13	15	28	37	14	1	0	1	0	1	1934-35	1937-38
Connelly, Wayne	Mtl., Bos., Min., Det., St.L., Van.	10	543	133	174	307	156	24	11	7	18	4	....	1960-61	1971-72
Connor, Cam	Mtl., Edm., NYR	5	89	9	22	31	256	20	5	0	5	6	1	1978-79	1982-83
● Connor, Harry	Bos., NYA, Ott.	4	134	16	5	21	149	10	0	0	0	2	....	1927-28	1930-31
● Connors, Bob	NYA, Det.	3	78	17	10	27	110	2	0	0	0	10	....	1926-27	1929-30
Conroy, Al	Phi.	3	114	9	14	23	156	....	....	....	....	....	....	1991-92	1993-94
Contini, Joe	Col., Min.	3	68	17	21	38	34	2	0	0	0	0	....	1977-78	1980-81
‡ Convery, Brandon	Tor., Van., L.A.	4	72	9	19	28	36	5	0	0	0	2	....	1995-96	1998-99
● Convey, Eddie	NYA	3	36	1	1	2	33	....	....	....	....	....	....	1930-31	1932-33
● Cook, Bill	NYR	11	474	229	138	367	386	46	13	11	24	68	2	1926-27	1936-37
● Cook, Bob	Van., Det., NYI, Min.	4	72	13	9	22	22	....	....	....	....	....	....	1970-71	1974-75
● Cook, Bud	Bos., Ott., St.L.	3	50	5	4	9	22	....	....	....	....	....	....	1931-32	1934-35
● Cook, Bun	NYR, Bos.	11	473	158	144	302	444	46	15	3	18	50	2	1926-27	1936-37
● Cook, Lloyd	Bos.	1	4	1	0	1	0	....	....	....	....	....	....	1924-25	1924-25
● Cook, Tom	Chi., Mtl.M.	9	349	77	98	175	184	24	2	4	6	19	1	1929-30	1937-38
● Cooper, Carson	Bos., Mtl., Det.	8	294	110	57	167	111	7	0	0	0	2	....	1924-25	1931-32
‡ Cooper, David	Tor.	3	30	3	7	10	24	....	....	....	....	....	....	1996-97	2000-01

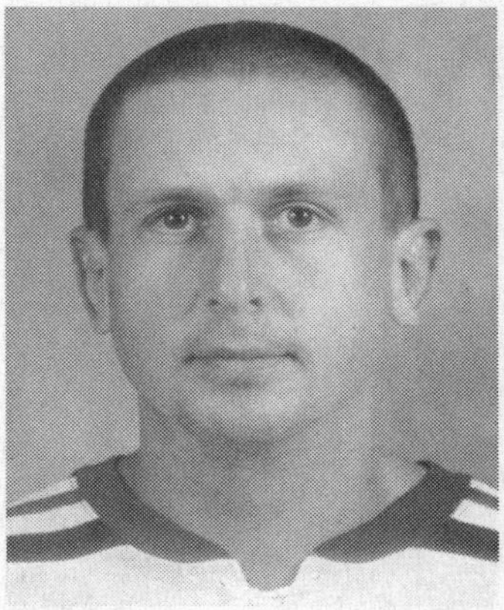
Zdeno Ciger

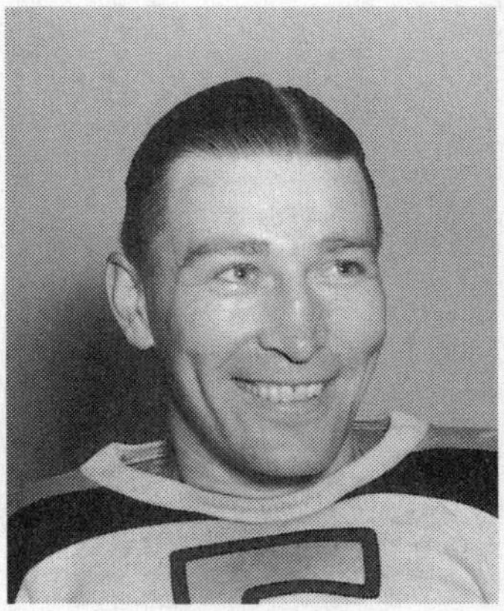
Dit Clapper

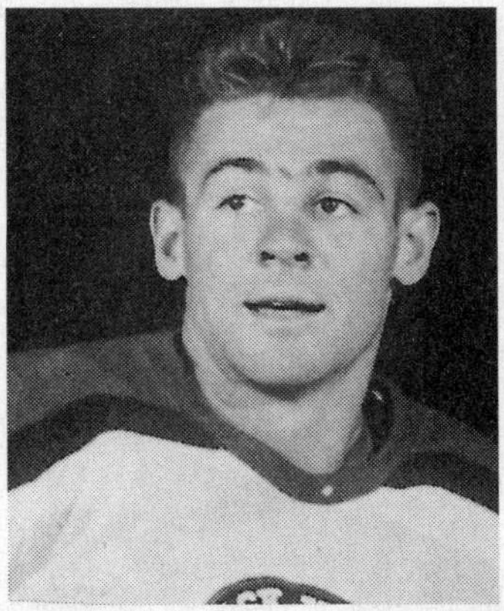
Pete Conacher

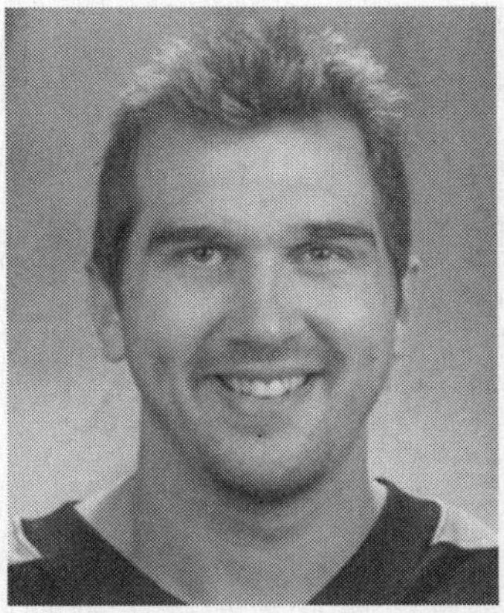
Rene Corbet

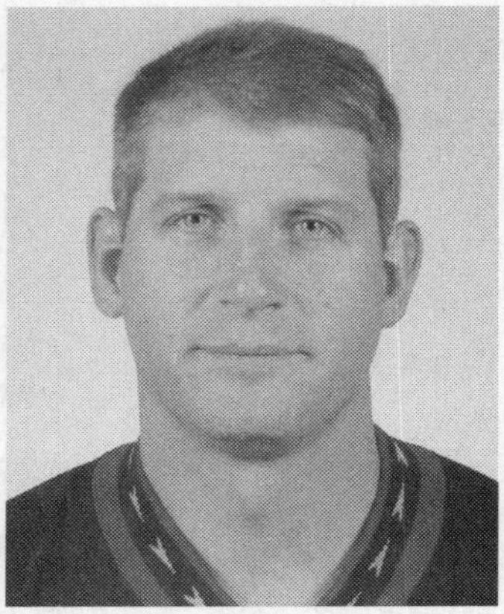

Bob Corkum

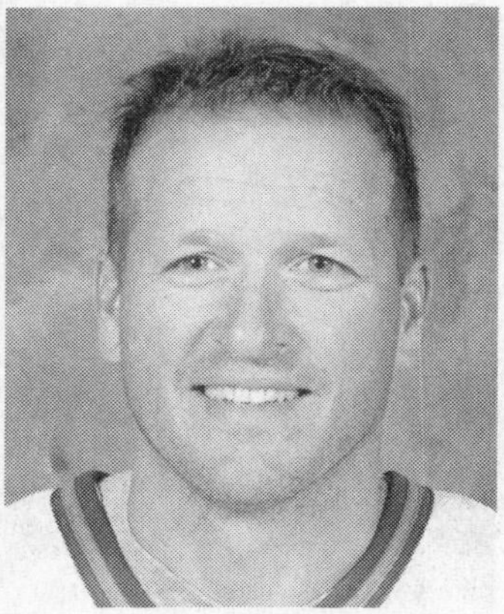

Sylvain Cote

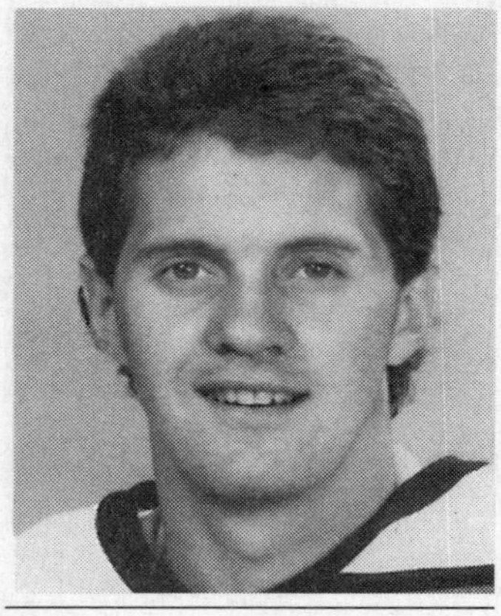

Murray Craven

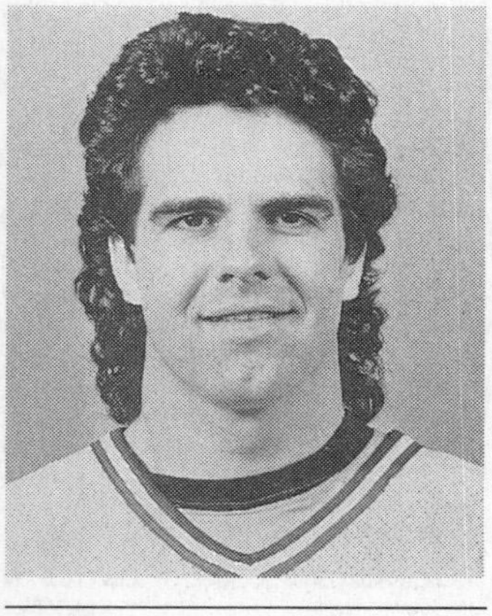

John Cullen

			Regular Schedule					Playoffs							
Name	NHL Teams	NHL Seasons	GP	G	A	TP	PIM	GP	G	A	TP	PIM	NHL Cup Wins	First NHL Season	Last NHL Season
Cooper, Ed	Col.	2	49	8	7	15	46	....	....	....	....	....	....	1980-81	1981-82
• Cooper, Hal	NYR	1	8	0	0	0	2	....	....	....	....	....	....	1944-45	1944-45
• Cooper, Joe	NYR, Chi.	11	420	30	66	96	442	35	3	5	8	58	....	1935-36	1946-47
Copp, Bob	Tor.	2	40	3	9	12	26	....	....	....	....	....	....	1942-43	1950-51
• Corbeau, Bert	Mtl., Ham., Tor.	10	258	63	49	112	629	9	2	2	4	38	....	1917-18	1926-27
Corbet, Rene	Que., Col., Cgy., Pit.	8	362	58	74	132	420	53	7	6	13	52	1	1993-94	2000-01
• Corbett, Mike	L.A.	1	....	....	....	....	....	2	0	1	1	2	....	1967-68	1967-68
Corcoran, Norm	Bos., Det., Chi.	4	29	1	3	4	21	4	0	0	0	6	....	1949-50	1955-56
Corkum, Bob	Buf., Ana., Phi., Phx., L.A., N.J., Atl.	12	720	97	103	200	281	62	7	7	14	24	....	1989-90	2001-02
• Cormier, Roger	Mtl.	1	1	0	0	0	0	....	....	....	....	....	....	1925-26	1925-26
Cornforth, Mark	Bos.	1	6	0	0	0	4	....	....	....	....	....	....	1995-96	1995-96
Corrigan, Chuck	Tor., NYA	2	19	2	2	4	2	....	....	....	....	....	....	1937-38	1940-41
Corrigan, Mike	L.A., Van., Pit.	10	594	152	195	347	698	17	2	3	5	20	....	1967-68	1977-78
‡ Corrinet, Chris	Wsh.	1	8	0	1	1	6	....	....	....	....	....	....	2001-02	2001-02
• Corriveau, Andre	Mtl.	1	3	0	1	1	0	....	....	....	....	....	....	1953-54	1953-54
‡ Corriveau, Yvon	Wsh., Hfd., S.J.	9	280	48	40	88	310	29	5	7	12	50	....	1985-86	1993-94
Cory, Ross	Wpg.	2	51	2	10	12	41	....	....	....	....	....	....	1979-80	1980-81
Cossette, Jacques	Pit.	3	64	8	6	14	29	3	0	1	1	4	....	1975-76	1978-79
• Costello, Les	Tor.	3	15	2	3	5	11	6	2	2	4	2	1	1947-48	1949-50
Costello, Murray	Chi., Bos., Det.	4	162	13	19	32	54	5	0	0	0	2	....	1953-54	1956-57
Costello, Rich	Tor.	2	12	2	2	4	2	....	....	....	....	....	....	1983-84	1985-86
• Cotch, Charlie	Ham., Tor.	1	12	1	0	1	0	....	....	....	....	....	....	1924-25	1924-25
Cote, Alain	Que.	10	696	103	190	293	383	67	9	15	24	44	....	1979-80	1988-89
Cote, Alain	Bos., Wsh., Mtl., T.B., Que.	9	119	2	18	20	124	11	0	2	2	26	....	1985-86	1993-94
Cote, Patrick	Dal., Nsh., Edm.	6	105	1	2	3	377	....	....	....	....	....	....	1995-96	2000-01
Cote, Ray	Edm.	3	15	0	0	0	4	14	3	2	5	0	....	1982-83	1984-85
Cote, Sylvain	Hfd., Wsh., Tor., Chi., Dal.	19	1171	122	313	435	545	102	11	22	33	62	....	1984-85	2002-03
• Cotton, Baldy	Pit., Tor., NYA	12	503	101	103	204	419	43	4	9	13	46	1	1925-26	1936-37
• Coughlin, Jack	Tor., Que., Mtl., Ham.	3	19	2	0	2	3	....	....	....	....	....	1	1917-18	1920-21
Coulis, Tim	Wsh., Min.	4	47	4	5	9	138	3	1	0	1	2	....	1979-80	1985-86
Coulson, D'arcy	Phi.	1	28	0	0	0	103	....	....	....	....	....	....	1930-31	1930-31
• Coulter, Art	Chi., NYR	11	465	30	82	112	543	49	4	5	9	61	2	1931-32	1941-42
Coulter, Neal	NYI	3	26	5	5	10	11	....	....	....	....	....	....	1985-86	1987-88
Cournoyer, Yvan	Mtl.	16	968	428	435	863	255	147	64	63	127	47	10	1963-64	1978-79
Courteau, Yves	Cgy., Hfd.	3	22	2	5	7	4	1	0	0	0	0	....	1984-85	1986-87
‡ Courtenay, Ed	S.J.	2	44	7	13	20	10	....	....	....	....	....	....	1991-92	1992-93
Courtnall, Geoff	Bos., Edm., Wsh., St.L., Van.	17	1048	367	432	799	1465	156	39	70	109	262	1	1983-84	1999-00
Courtnall, Russ	Tor., Mtl., Min., Dal., Van., NYR, L.A.	16	1029	297	447	744	557	129	39	44	83	83	....	1983-84	1998-99
‡ Courville, Larry	Van.	3	33	1	2	3	16	....	....	....	....	....	....	1995-96	1997-98
• Coutu, Billy	Mtl., Ham., Bos.	10	244	33	21	54	478	19	1	1	2	39	1	1917-18	1926-27
• Couture, Gerry	Det., Mtl., Chi.	10	385	86	70	156	89	45	9	7	16	4	1	1944-45	1953-54
• Couture, Rosie	Chi., Mtl.	8	309	48	56	104	184	23	1	5	6	15	1	1928-29	1935-36
Couturier, Sylvain	L.A.	3	33	4	5	9	4	....	....	....	....	....	....	1988-89	1991-92
Cowick, Bruce	Phi., Wsh., St.L.	3	70	5	6	11	43	8	0	0	0	9	1	1973-74	1975-76
Cowie, Rob	L.A.	2	78	7	12	19	52	....	....	....	....	....	....	1994-95	1995-96
• Cowley, Bill	St.L., Bos.	13	549	195	353	548	143	64	12	34	46	22	2	1934-35	1946-47
• Cox, Danny	Tor., Ott., Det., NYR	8	319	47	49	96	128	10	0	1	1	6	....	1926-27	1933-34
Coxe, Craig	Van., Cgy., St.L., S.J.	8	235	14	31	45	713	5	1	0	1	18	....	1984-85	1991-92
‡ Craig, Mike	Min., Dal., Tor., S.J.	9	423	71	97	168	550	26	2	2	4	49	....	1990-91	2001-02
‡ Craighead, John	Tor.	1	5	0	0	0	10	....	....	....	....	....	....	1996-97	1996-97
Craigwell, Dale	S.J.	3	98	11	18	29	28	....	....	....	....	....	....	1991-92	1993-94
Crashley, Bart	Det., K.C., L.A.	6	140	7	36	43	50	....	....	....	....	....	....	1965-66	1975-76
Craven, Murray	Det., Phi., Hfd., Van., Chi., S.J.	18	1071	266	493	759	524	118	27	43	70	64	....	1982-83	1999-00
Crawford, Bob	St.L., Hfd., NYR, Wsh.	7	246	71	71	142	72	11	0	1	1	8	....	1979-80	1986-87
Crawford, Bobby	Col., Det.	2	16	1	3	4	6	....	....	....	....	....	....	1980-81	1982-83
• Crawford, Jack	Bos.	13	548	38	140	178	202	66	3	13	16	36	2	1937-38	1949-50
Crawford, Lou	Bos.	2	26	2	1	3	29	1	0	0	0	0	....	1989-90	1991-92
Crawford, Marc	Van.	6	176	19	31	50	229	20	1	2	3	44	....	1981-82	1986-87
• Crawford, Rusty	Ott., Tor.	2	38	10	8	18	117	2	2	1	3	9	1	1917-18	1918-19
Creighton, Adam	Buf., Chi., NYI, T.B., St.L.	14	708	187	216	403	1077	61	11	14	25	137	....	1983-84	1996-97
Creighton, Dave	Bos., Tor., Chi., NYR	12	616	140	174	314	223	51	11	13	24	20	....	1948-49	1959-60
• Creighton, Jimmy	Det.	1	11	1	0	1	2	....	....	....	....	....	....	1930-31	1930-31
Cressman, Dave	Min.	2	85	6	8	14	37	....	....	....	....	....	....	1974-75	1975-76
Cressman, Glen	Mtl.	1	4	0	0	0	2	....	....	....	....	....	....	1956-57	1956-57
Crisp, Terry	Bos., St.L., NYI, Phi.	11	536	67	134	201	135	110	15	28	43	40	2	1965-66	1976-77
Cristofoli, Ed	Mtl.	1	9	0	1	1	4	....	....	....	....	....	....	1989-90	1989-90
• Croghan, Maurice	Mtl.M.	1	16	0	0	0	4	....	....	....	....	....	....	1937-38	1937-38
Crombeen, Mike	Cle., St.L., Hfd.	8	475	55	68	123	218	27	6	2	8	32	....	1977-78	1984-85
Cronin, Shawn	Wsh., Wpg., Phi., S.J.	7	292	3	18	21	877	32	1	0	1	38	....	1988-89	1994-95
• Crossett, Stan	Phi.	1	21	0	0	0	10	....	....	....	....	....	....	1930-31	1930-31
Crossman, Doug	Chi., Phi., L.A., NYI, Hfd., Det., T.B., St.L.	14	914	105	359	464	534	97	12	39	51	105	....	1980-81	1993-94
Croteau, Gary	L.A., Det., Cal., K.C., Col.	12	684	144	175	319	143	11	3	2	5	8	....	1968-69	1979-80
Crowder, Bruce	Bos., Pit.	4	243	47	51	98	156	31	8	4	12	41	....	1981-82	1984-85
Crowder, Keith	Bos., L.A.	10	662	223	271	494	1354	85	14	22	36	218	....	1980-81	1989-90
Crowder, Troy	N.J., Det., L.A., Van.	7	150	9	7	16	433	4	0	0	0	22	....	1987-88	1996-97
‡ Crowe, Phil	L.A., Phi., Ott., Nsh.	6	94	4	5	9	173	3	0	0	0	16	....	1993-94	1999-00
Crowley, Mike	Ana.	3	67	5	15	20	44	....	....	....	....	....	....	1997-98	2000-01
‡ Crowley, Ted	Hfd., Col., NYI	2	34	2	4	6	12	....	....	....	....	....	....	1993-94	1998-99
‡ Crozier, Greg	Pit.	1	1	0	0	0	0	....	....	....	....	....	....	2000-01	2000-01
Crozier, Joe	Tor.	1	5	0	3	3	2	....	....	....	....	....	....	1959-60	1959-60
• Crutchfield, Nels	Mtl.	1	41	5	5	10	20	2	0	1	1	22	....	1934-35	1934-35
Culhane, Jim	Hfd.	1	6	0	1	1	4	....	....	....	....	....	....	1989-90	1989-90
Cullen, Barry	Tor., Det.	5	219	32	52	84	111	6	0	0	0	2	....	1955-56	1959-60
Cullen, Brian	Tor., NYR	7	326	56	100	156	92	19	3	0	3	2	....	1954-55	1960-61
Cullen, John	Pit., Hfd., Tor., T.B.	11	621	187	363	550	898	53	12	22	34	58	....	1988-89	1998-99
Cullen, Ray	NYR, Det., Min., Van.	6	313	92	123	215	120	20	3	10	13	2	....	1965-66	1970-71
Cummins, Barry	Cal.	1	36	1	2	3	39	....	....	....	....	....	....	1973-74	1973-74
Cunneyworth, Randy	Buf., Pit., Wpg., Hfd., Chi., Ott.	16	866	189	225	414	1280	45	7	7	14	61	....	1980-81	1998-99
Cunningham, Bob	NYR	2	4	0	1	1	0	....	....	....	....	....	....	1960-61	1961-62
Cunningham, Jim	Phi.	1	1	0	0	0	4	....	....	....	....	....	....	1977-78	1977-78
• Cunningham, Les	NYA, Chi.	2	60	7	19	26	21	1	0	0	0	0	....	1936-37	1939-40
Cupolo, Bill	Bos.	1	47	11	13	24	10	7	1	2	3	0	....	1944-45	1944-45
Curran, Brian	Bos., NYI, Tor., Buf., Wsh.	10	381	7	33	40	1461	24	0	1	1	122	....	1983-84	1993-94
Currie, Dan	Edm., L.A.	4	22	2	1	3	4	....	....	....	....	....	....	1990-91	1993-94
Currie, Glen	Wsh., L.A.	8	326	39	79	118	100	12	1	3	4	4	....	1979-80	1987-88
Currie, Hugh	Mtl.	1	1	0	0	0	0	....	....	....	....	....	....	1950-51	1950-51
Currie, Tony	St.L., Van., Hfd.	8	290	92	119	211	83	16	4	12	16	14	....	1977-78	1984-85
Curry, Floyd	Mtl.	11	601	105	99	204	147	91	23	17	40	38	4	1947-48	1957-58
Curtale, Tony	Cgy.	1	2	0	0	0	0	....	....	....	....	....	....	1980-81	1980-81
Curtis, Paul	Mtl., L.A., St.L.	4	185	3	34	37	161	5	0	0	0	2	....	1969-70	1972-73
Cushenan, Ian	Chi., Mtl., NYR, Det.	5	129	3	11	14	134	....	....	....	....	....	1	1956-57	1963-64
Cusson, Jean	Oak.	1	2	0	0	0	0	....	....	....	....	....	....	1967-68	1967-68
Cyr, Denis	Cgy., Chi., St.L.	6	193	41	43	84	36	4	0	0	0	0	....	1980-81	1985-86
Cyr, Paul	Buf., NYR, Hfd.	9	470	101	140	241	623	24	4	6	10	31	....	1982-83	1991-92

D

Name	NHL Teams	NHL Seasons	GP	G	A	TP	PIM	GP	G	A	TP	PIM	NHL Cup Wins	First NHL Season	Last NHL Season
‡ Dahl, Kevin	Cgy., Phx., Tor., CBJ	8	188	7	22	29	153	16	0	2	2	12	....	1992-93	2000-01
Dahlen, Ulf	NYR, Min., Dal., S.J., Chi., Wsh.	14	966	301	354	655	230	85	15	25	40	12	....	1987-88	2002-03
Dahlin, Kjell	Mtl.	3	166	57	59	116	10	35	6	11	17	6	1	1985-86	1987-88
‡ Dahlman, Toni	Ott.	2	22	1	1	2	0	....	....	....	....	....	....	2001-02	2002-03
Dahlquist, Chris	Pit., Min., Cgy., Ott.	11	532	19	71	90	488	39	4	7	11	30	....	1985-86	1995-96
• Dahlstrom, Cully	Chi.	8	342	88	118	206	58	29	6	8	14	4	1	1937-38	1944-45
Daigle, Alain	Chi.	6	389	56	50	106	122	17	0	1	1	0	....	1974-75	1979-80
Daigneault, J.J.	Van., Phi., Mtl., St.L., Pit., Ana., NYI, Nsh., Phx., Min.	16	899	53	197	250	687	99	5	26	31	100	1	1984-85	2000-01
Dailey, Bob	Van., Phi.	9	561	94	231	325	814	63	12	34	46	105	....	1973-74	1981-82
• Daley, Frank	Det.	1	5	0	0	0	0	2	0	0	0	0	....	1928-29	1928-29
Daley, Pat	Wpg.	2	12	1	0	1	13	....	....	....	....	....	....	1979-80	1980-81
Dalgarno, Brad	NYI	10	321	49	71	120	332	27	2	4	6	37	....	1985-86	1995-96
Dallman, Marty	Tor.	2	6	0	1	1	0	....	....	....	....	....	....	1987-88	1988-89
Dallman, Rod	NYI, Phi.	4	6	1	0	1	26	1	0	1	1	0	....	1987-88	1991-92
Dame, Bunny	Mtl.	1	34	2	5	7	4	....	....	....	....	....	....	1941-42	1941-42
Damore, Hank	NYR	1	4	1	0	1	2	....	....	....	....	....	....	1943-44	1943-44
Daneyko, Ken	N.J.	20	1283	36	142	178	2519	175	5	17	22	296	3	1983-84	2002-03

Name	NHL Teams	NHL Seasons	Regular Schedule GP	G	A	TP	PIM	Playoffs GP	G	A	TP	PIM	NHL Cup Wins	First NHL Season	Last NHL Season
Daniels, Jeff	Pit., Fla., Hfd., Car., Nsh.	12	425	17	26	43	83	41	3	5	8	2	1	1990-91	2002-03
‡ Daniels, Kimbi	Phi.	2	27	1	2	3	4	....	....	....	....	....	....	1990-91	1991-92
Daniels, Scott	Hfd., Phi., N.J.	6	149	8	12	20	667	1	0	0	0	0	....	1992-93	1998-99
Daoust, Dan	Mtl., Tor.	8	522	87	167	254	544	32	7	5	12	83	....	1982-83	1989-90
Dark, Michael	St.L.	2	43	5	6	11	14	....	....	....	....	....	....	1986-87	1987-88
• Darragh, Harold	Pit., Phi., Bos., Tor.	8	308	68	49	117	50	16	1	3	4	4	1	1925-26	1932-33
• Darragh, Jack	Ott.	6	121	66	46	112	113	11	3	0	3	9	3	1917-18	1923-24
David, Richard	Que.	3	31	4	4	8	10	1	0	0	0	0	....	1979-80	1982-83
• Davidson, Bob	Tor.	12	491	94	160	254	398	79	5	17	22	76	2	1934-35	1945-46
• Davidson, Gord	NYR	2	51	3	6	9	8	....	....	....	....	....	....	1942-43	1943-44
‡ Davidsson, Johan	Ana., NYI	2	83	6	9	15	16	1	0	0	0	0	....	1998-99	1999-00
• Davie, Bob	Bos.	3	41	0	1	1	25	....	....	....	....	....	....	1933-34	1935-36
Davies, Buck	NYR	1	....	....	....	....	....	1	0	0	0	0	....	1947-48	1947-48
• Davis, Bob	Det.	1	3	0	0	0	0	....	....	....	....	....	....	1932-33	1932-33
Davis, Kim	Pit., Tor.	4	36	5	7	12	51	4	0	0	0	0	....	1977-78	1980-81
Davis, Lorne	Mtl., Chi., Det., Bos.	6	95	8	12	20	20	18	3	1	4	10	1	1951-52	1959-60
Davis, Mal	Det., Buf.	6	100	31	22	53	34	7	1	0	1	0	....	1978-79	1985-86
• Davison, Murray	Bos.	1	1	0	0	0	0	....	....	....	....	....	....	1965-66	1965-66
Davydov, Evgeny	Wpg., Fla., Ott.	4	155	40	39	79	120	11	2	2	4	2	....	1991-92	1994-95
‡ Dawe, Jason	Buf., NYI, Mtl., NYR	8	366	86	90	176	162	22	4	3	7	18	....	1993-94	2001-02
Dawes, Bob	Tor., Mtl.	4	32	2	7	9	6	10	0	0	0	2	1	1946-47	1950-51
• Day, Hap	Tor., NYA	14	581	86	116	202	601	53	4	7	11	56	1	1924-25	1937-38
Day, Joe	Hfd., NYI	3	72	1	10	11	87	....	....	....	....	....	....	1991-92	1993-94
Dea, Billy	NYR, Det., Chi., Pit.	8	397	67	54	121	44	11	2	1	3	6	....	1953-54	1970-71
• Deacon, Don	Det.	3	30	6	4	10	6	2	2	1	3	0	....	1936-37	1939-40
Deadmarsh, Butch	Buf., Atl., K.C.	5	137	12	5	17	155	4	0	0	0	17	....	1970-71	1974-75
Dean, Barry	Col., Phi.	3	165	25	56	81	146	....	....	....	....	....	....	1976-77	1978-79
Dean, Kevin	N.J., Atl., Dal., Chi.	7	331	7	48	55	138	16	2	2	4	2	1	1994-95	2000-01
Debenedet, Nelson	Det., Pit.	2	46	10	4	14	13	....	....	....	....	....	....	1973-74	1974-75
DeBlois, Lucien	NYR, Col., Wpg., Mtl., Que., Tor.	15	993	249	276	525	814	52	7	6	13	38	1	1977-78	1991-92
Debol, Dave	Hfd.	2	92	26	26	52	4	3	0	0	0	0	....	1979-80	1980-81
DeBrusk, Louie	Edm., T.B., Phx., Chi.	11	401	24	17	41	1161	15	2	0	2	10	....	1991-92	2002-03
Defazio, Dean	Pit.	1	22	0	2	2	28	....	....	....	....	....	....	1983-84	1983-84
DeGray, Dale	Cgy., Tor., L.A., Buf.	5	153	18	47	65	195	13	1	3	4	28	....	1985-86	1989-90
‡ Delisle, Jonathan	Mtl.	1	1	0	0	0	0	....	....	....	....	....	....	1998-99	1998-99
‡ Delisle, Xavier	T.B., Mtl.	2	16	3	2	5	6	....	....	....	....	....	....	1998-99	2000-01
• Delmonte, Armand	Bos.	1	1	0	0	0	0	....	....	....	....	....	....	1945-46	1945-46
Delorme, Gilbert	Mtl., St.L., Que., Det., Pit.	9	541	31	92	123	520	56	1	9	10	56	....	1981-82	1989-90
Delorme, Ron	Col., Van.	9	524	83	83	166	667	25	1	2	3	59	....	1976-77	1984-85
Delory, Val	NYR	1	1	0	0	0	0	....	....	....	....	....	....	1948-49	1948-49
Delparte, Guy	Col.	1	48	1	8	9	18	....	....	....	....	....	....	1976-77	1976-77
Delvecchio, Alex	Det.	24	1549	456	825	1281	383	121	35	69	104	29	3	1950-51	1973-74
• DeMarco, Ab	Chi., Tor., Bos., NYR	7	209	72	93	165	53	11	3	0	3	2	....	1938-39	1946-47
DeMarco, Ab	NYR, St.L., Pit., Van., L.A., Bos.	9	344	44	80	124	75	25	1	2	3	17	....	1969-70	1978-79
• Demers, Tony	Mtl., NYR	6	83	20	22	42	23	2	0	0	0	0	....	1937-38	1943-44
Denis, Jean-Paul	NYR	2	10	0	2	2	2	....	....	....	....	....	....	1946-47	1949-50
Denis, Lulu	Mtl.	2	3	0	1	1	0	....	....	....	....	....	....	1949-50	1950-51
• Denneny, Corb	Tor., Ham., Chi.	9	176	103	42	145	148	6	1	0	1	7	2	1917-18	1927-28
• Denneny, Cy	Ott., Bos.	12	328	248	85	333	301	25	16	2	18	23	5	1917-18	1928-29
Dennis, Norm	St.L.	4	12	3	0	3	11	5	0	0	0	2	....	1968-69	1971-72
• Denoird, Gerry	Tor.	1	17	0	1	1	0	....	....	....	....	....	....	1922-23	1922-23
DePalma, Larry	Min., S.J., Pit.	7	148	21	20	41	408	3	0	0	0	6	....	1985-86	1993-94
Derlago, Bill	Van., Tor., Bos., Wpg., Que.	9	555	189	227	416	247	13	5	0	5	8	....	1978-79	1986-87
• Desaulniers, Gerard	Mtl.	3	8	0	2	2	4	....	....	....	....	....	....	1950-51	1953-54
‡ Descoteaux, Matthieu	Mtl.	1	5	1	1	2	4	....	....	....	....	....	....	2000-01	2000-01
• Desilets, Joffre	Mtl., Chi.	5	192	37	45	82	57	7	1	0	1	7	....	1935-36	1939-40
Desjardins, Martin	Mtl.	1	8	0	2	2	2	....	....	....	....	....	....	1989-90	1989-90
• Desjardins, Vic	Chi., NYR	2	87	6	15	21	27	16	0	0	0	0	....	1930-31	1931-32
Deslauriers, Jacques	Mtl.	1	2	0	0	0	0	....	....	....	....	....	....	1955-56	1955-56
Deuling, Jarrett	NYI	2	15	0	1	1	11	....	....	....	....	....	....	1995-96	1996-97
Devine, Kevin	NYI	1	2	0	1	1	8	....	....	....	....	....	....	1982-83	1982-83
• Dewar, Tom	NYR	1	9	0	2	2	4	....	....	....	....	....	....	1943-44	1943-44
Dewsbury, Al	Det., Chi.	9	347	30	78	108	365	14	1	5	6	16	1	1946-47	1955-56
Deziel, Michel	Buf.	1	....	....	....	....	....	1	0	0	0	0	....	1974-75	1974-75
Dheere, Marcel	Mtl.	1	11	1	2	3	2	5	0	0	0	6	....	1942-43	1942-43
Diachuk, Edward	Det.	1	12	0	0	0	19	....	....	....	....	....	....	1960-61	1960-61
Dick, Harry	Chi.	1	12	0	1	1	12	....	....	....	....	....	....	1946-47	1946-47
Dickens, Ernie	Tor., Chi.	6	278	12	44	56	98	13	0	0	0	4	1	1941-42	1950-51
Dickenson, Herb	NYR	2	48	18	17	35	10	....	....	....	....	....	....	1951-52	1952-53
Diduck, Gerald	NYI, Mtl., Van., Chi., Hfd., Phx., Tor., Dal.	17	932	56	156	212	1612	114	8	16	24	212	....	1984-85	2000-01
Dietrich, Don	Chi., N.J.	2	28	0	7	7	10	....	....	....	....	....	....	1983-84	1985-86
• Dill, Bob	NYR	2	76	15	15	30	135	....	....	....	....	....	....	1943-44	1944-45
• Dillabough, Bob	Det., Bos., Pit., Oak.	9	283	32	54	86	76	17	3	0	3	0	....	1961-62	1969-70
• Dillon, Cecil	NYR, Det.	10	453	167	131	298	105	43	14	9	23	14	1	1930-31	1939-40
Dillon, Gary	Col.	1	13	1	1	2	29	....	....	....	....	....	....	1980-81	1980-81
Dillon, Wayne	NYR, Wpg.	4	229	43	66	109	60	3	0	1	1	0	....	1975-76	1979-80
Dineen, Bill	Det., Chi.	5	323	51	44	95	122	37	1	1	2	18	2	1953-54	1957-58
Dineen, Gary	Min.	1	4	0	1	1	0	....	....	....	....	....	....	1968-69	1968-69
Dineen, Gord	NYI, Min., Pit., Ott.	13	528	16	90	106	695	40	1	7	8	68	....	1982-83	1994-95
Dineen, Kevin	Hfd., Phi., Car., Ott., CBJ	19	1188	355	405	760	2229	59	23	18	41	127	....	1984-85	2002-03
Dineen, Peter	L.A., Det.	2	13	0	2	2	13	....	....	....	....	....	....	1986-87	1989-90
• Dinsmore, Chuck	Mtl.M.	4	100	6	2	8	50	8	1	0	1	2	1	1924-25	1929-30
Dionne, Gilbert	Mtl., Phi., Fla.	6	223	61	79	140	108	39	10	12	22	34	1	1990-91	1995-96
Dionne, Marcel	Det., L.A., NYR	18	1348	731	1040	1771	600	49	21	24	45	17	....	1971-72	1988-89
‡ DiPietro, Paul	Mtl., Tor., L.A.	6	192	31	49	80	96	31	11	10	21	10	1	1991-92	1996-97
Dirk, Robert	St.L., Van., Chi., Ana., Mtl.	9	402	13	29	42	786	39	0	1	1	56	....	1987-88	1995-96
‡ Divisek, Tomas	Phi.	2	5	1	0	1	0	....	....	....	....	....	....	2000-01	2001-02
Djoos, Per	Det., NYR	3	82	2	31	33	58	....	....	....	....	....	....	1990-91	1992-93
Doak, Gary	Det., Bos., Van., NYR	16	789	23	107	130	908	78	2	4	6	121	1	1965-66	1980-81
Dobbin, Brian	Phi., Bos.	5	63	7	8	15	61	2	0	0	0	17	....	1986-87	1991-92
Dobson, Jim	Min., Col., Que.	4	12	0	0	0	6	....	....	....	....	....	....	1979-80	1983-84
• Doherty, Fred	Mtl.	1	1	0	0	0	0	....	....	....	....	....	....	1918-19	1918-19
Dollas, Bobby	Wpg., Que., Det., Ana., Edm., Pit., Ott., Cgy., S.J.	16	646	42	96	138	467	47	2	1	3	41	....	1983-84	2000-01
‡ Domenichelli, Hnat	Hfd., Cgy., Atl., Min.	7	267	52	61	113	104	....	....	....	....	....	....	1996-97	2002-03
Donaldson, Gary	Chi.	1	1	0	0	0	0	....	....	....	....	....	....	1973-74	1973-74
Donatelli, Clark	Min., Bos.	2	35	3	4	7	39	2	0	0	0	0	....	1989-90	1991-92
• Donnelly, Babe	Mtl.M.	1	34	0	1	1	14	2	0	0	0	0	....	1926-27	1926-27
Donnelly, Dave	Bos., Chi., Edm.	5	137	15	24	39	150	5	0	0	0	0	....	1983-84	1987-88
Donnelly, Gord	Que., Wpg., Buf., Dal.	12	554	28	41	69	2069	26	0	2	2	61	....	1983-84	1994-95
Donnelly, Mike	NYR, Buf., L.A., Dal., NYI	11	465	114	121	235	255	47	12	12	24	30	....	1986-87	1996-97
‡ Dopita, Jiri	Phi., Edm.	2	73	12	21	33	19	....	....	....	....	....	....	2001-02	2002-03
• Doran, John	NYA, Det., Mtl.	5	98	5	10	15	110	3	0	0	0	0	....	1933-34	1939-40
Doran, Lloyd	Det.	1	24	3	2	5	10	....	....	....	....	....	....	1946-47	1946-47
• Doraty, Ken	Chi., Tor., Det.	5	103	15	26	41	24	15	7	2	9	2	....	1926-27	1937-38
Dore, Andre	NYR, St.L., Que.	7	257	14	81	95	261	23	1	2	3	32	....	1978-79	1984-85
Dore, Daniel	Que.	2	17	2	3	5	59	....	....	....	....	....	....	1989-90	1990-91
Dorey, Jim	Tor., NYR	4	232	25	74	99	553	11	0	2	2	40	....	1968-69	1971-72
Dorion, Dan	N.J.	2	4	1	1	2	2	....	....	....	....	....	....	1985-86	1987-88
Dornhoefer, Gary	Bos., Phi.	14	787	214	328	542	1291	80	17	19	36	203	2	1963-64	1977-78
Dorohoy, Eddie	Mtl.	1	16	0	0	0	6	....	....	....	....	....	....	1948-49	1948-49
Douglas, Jordy	Hfd., Min., Wpg.	6	268	76	62	138	160	6	0	0	0	4	....	1979-80	1984-85
Douglas, Kent	Tor., Oak., Det.	7	428	33	115	148	631	19	1	3	4	33	3	1962-63	1968-69
• Douglas, Les	Det.	4	52	6	12	18	8	10	3	2	5	2	1	1940-41	1946-47
Douris, Peter	Wpg., Bos., Ana., Dal.	11	321	54	67	121	80	27	3	5	8	14	....	1985-86	1997-98
• Downie, Dave	Tor.	1	11	0	1	1	2	....	....	....	....	....	....	1932-33	1932-33
‡ Doyon, Mario	Chi., Que.	3	28	3	4	7	16	....	....	....	....	....	....	1988-89	1990-91
• Draper, Bruce	Tor.	1	1	0	0	0	0	....	....	....	....	....	....	1962-63	1962-63
• Drillon, Gordie	Tor., Mtl.	7	311	155	139	294	56	50	26	15	41	10	1	1936-37	1942-43
Driscoll, Peter	Edm.	2	60	3	8	11	97	3	0	0	0	0	....	1979-80	1980-81
Driver, Bruce	N.J., NYR	15	922	96	390	486	670	108	10	40	50	64	1	1983-84	1997-98
Drolet, Rene	Phi., Det.	2	2	0	0	0	0	....	....	....	....	....	....	1971-72	1974-75
‡ Droppa, Ivan	Chi.	2	19	0	1	1	14	....	....	....	....	....	....	1993-94	1995-96
• Drouillard, Clarence	Det.	1	10	0	1	1	0	....	....	....	....	....	....	1937-38	1937-38
Drouin, Jude	Mtl., Min., NYI, Wpg.	12	666	151	305	456	346	72	27	41	68	33	....	1968-69	1980-81

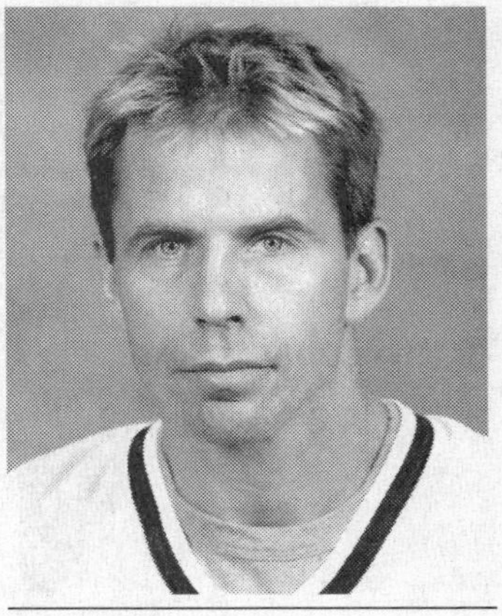

Ulf Dahlen

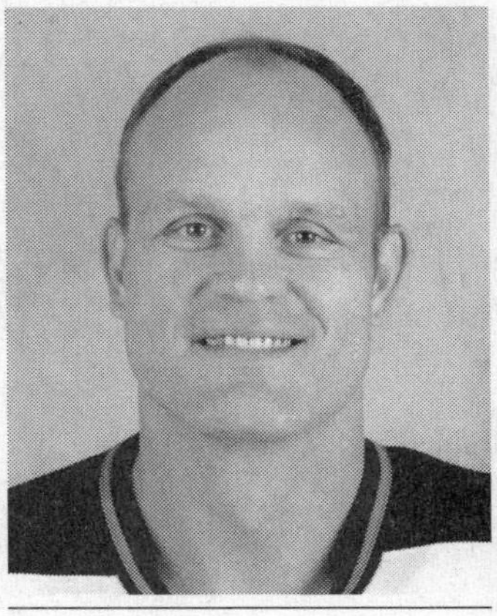

Ken Daneyko

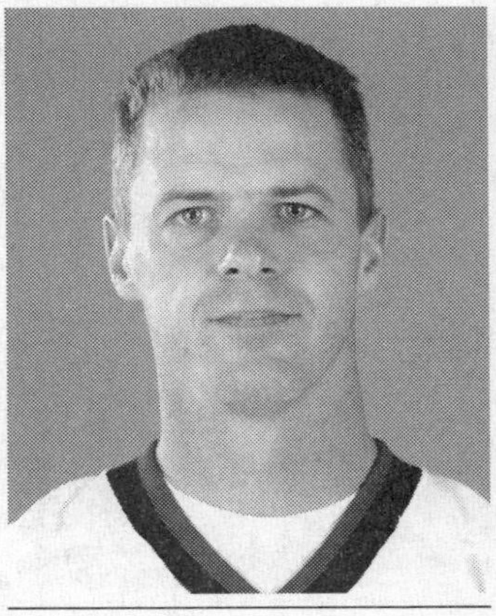

Jeff Daniels

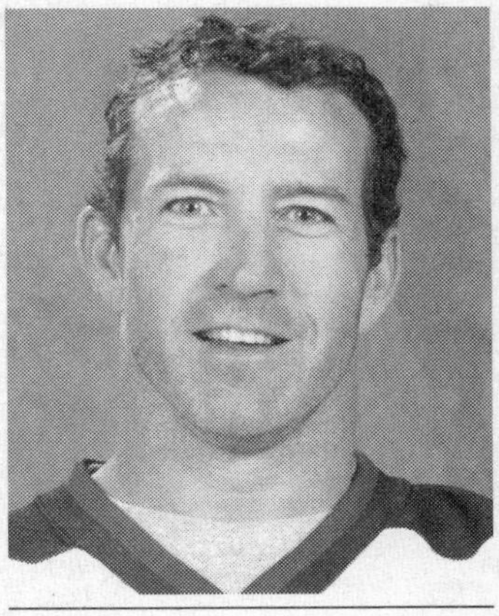

Kevin Dineen

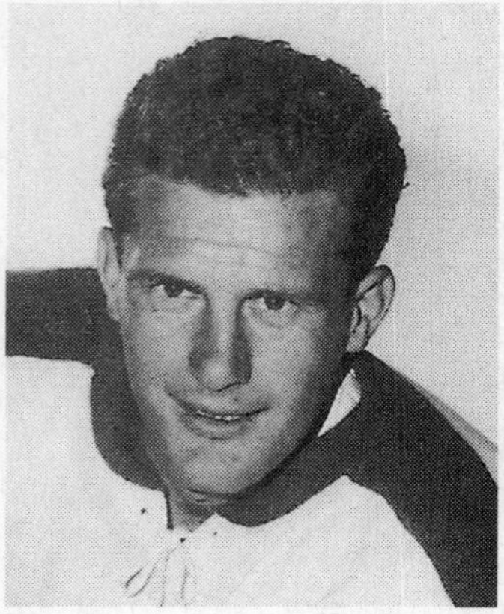

Kent Douglas

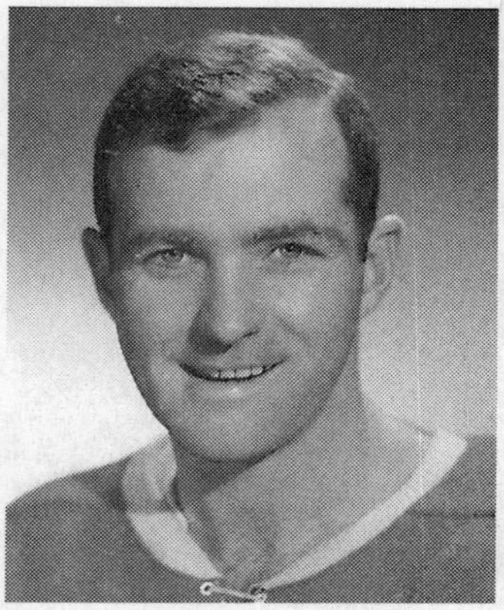

Dick Duff

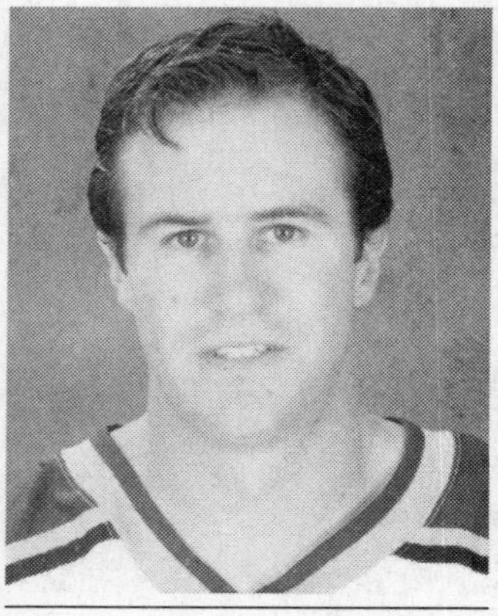

Nelson Emerson

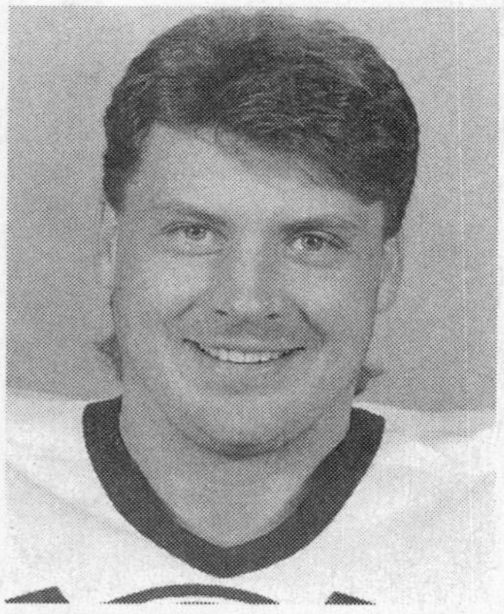

Todd Ewen

			Regular Schedule					Playoffs					NHL	First	Last
Name	NHL Teams	NHL Seasons	GP	G	A	TP	PIM	GP	G	A	TP	PIM	Cup Wins	NHL Season	NHL Season
Drouin, P.C.	Bos.	1	3	0	0	0	0	....	....	....	....	....	....	1996-97	1996-97
• Drouin, Polly	Mtl.	7	160	23	50	73	80	5	0	1	1	5	....	1934-35	1940-41
Druce, John	Wsh., Wpg., L.A., Phi.	10	531	113	126	239	347	53	17	6	23	38	....	1988-89	1997-98
Drulia, Stan	T.B.	3	126	15	27	42	52	....	....	....	....	....	....	1992-93	2000-01
• Drummond, Jim	NYR	1	2	0	0	0	0	....	....	....	....	....	....	1944-45	1944-45
• Drury, Herb	Pit., Phi.	6	213	24	13	37	203	4	1	1	2	0	....	1925-26	1930-31
‡ Drury, Ted	Cgy., Hfd., Ott., Ana., NYI, CBJ	8	414	41	52	93	367	14	1	0	1	4	....	1993-94	2000-01
‡ Dube, Christian	NYR	2	33	1	1	2	4	3	0	0	0	0	....	1996-97	1998-99
Dube, Gilles	Mtl., Det.	2	12	1	2	3	2	2	0	0	0	0	1	1949-50	1953-54
Dube, Norm	K.C.	2	57	8	10	18	54	....	....	....	....	....	....	1974-75	1975-76
Duberman, Justin	Pit.	1	4	0	0	0	0	....	....	....	....	....	....	1993-94	1993-94
Dubinsky, Steve	Chi., Cgy., Nsh., St.L.	10	375	25	45	70	164	10	1	0	1	14	....	1993-94	2002-03
Duchesne, Gaetan	Wsh., Que., Min., S.J., Fla.	14	1028	179	254	433	617	84	14	13	27	97	....	1981-82	1994-95
Duchesne, Steve	L.A., Phi., Que., St.L., Ott., Det.	16	1113	227	525	752	824	121	16	61	77	96	1	1986-87	2001-02
Dudley, Rick	Buf., Wpg.	6	309	75	99	174	292	25	7	2	9	69	....	1972-73	1980-81
Duerden, Dave	Fla.	1	2	0	0	0	0	....	....	....	....	....	....	1999-00	1999-00
Duff, Dick	Tor., NYR, Mtl., L.A., Buf.	18	1030	283	289	572	743	114	30	49	79	78	6	1954-55	1971-72
Dufour, Luc	Bos., Que., St.L.	3	167	23	21	44	199	18	1	0	1	32	....	1982-83	1984-85
Dufour, Marc	NYR, L.A.	3	14	1	0	1	2	....	....	....	....	....	....	1963-64	1968-69
Dufresne, Donald	Mtl., T.B., L.A., St.L., Edm.	9	268	6	36	42	258	34	1	3	4	47	1	1988-89	1996-97
• Duggan, John	Ott.	1	27	0	0	0	0	2	0	0	0	0	....	1925-26	1925-26
Duggan, Ken	Min.	1	1	0	0	0	0	....	....	....	....	....	....	1987-88	1987-88
Duguay, Ron	NYR, Det., Pit., L.A.	12	864	274	346	620	582	89	31	22	53	118	....	1977-78	1988-89
• Duguid, Lorne	Mtl.M., Det., Bos.	6	135	9	15	24	57	4	1	0	1	6	....	1931-32	1936-37
• Dukowski, Duke	Chi., NYA, NYR	5	200	16	30	46	172	6	0	0	0	6	....	1926-27	1933-34
• Dumart, Woody	Bos.	16	772	211	218	429	99	88	12	15	27	23	2	1935-36	1953-54
Dunbar, Dale	Van., Bos.	2	2	0	0	0	2	....	....	....	....	....	....	1985-86	1988-89
• Duncan, Art	Det., Tor.	5	156	18	16	34	225	5	0	0	0	4	....	1926-27	1930-31
Duncan, Iain	Wpg.	4	127	34	55	89	149	11	0	3	3	6	....	1986-87	1990-91
Duncanson, Craig	L.A., Wpg., NYR	7	38	5	4	9	61	....	....	....	....	....	....	1985-86	1992-93
Dundas, Rocky	Tor.	1	5	0	0	0	14	....	....	....	....	....	....	1989-90	1989-90
• Dunlap, Frank	Tor.	1	15	0	1	1	2	....	....	....	....	....	....	1943-44	1943-44
Dunlop, Blake	Min., Phi., St.L., Det.	11	550	130	274	404	172	40	4	10	14	18	....	1973-74	1983-84
Dunn, Dave	Van., Tor.	3	184	14	41	55	313	10	1	1	2	41	....	1973-74	1975-76
Dunn, Richie	Buf., Cgy., Hfd.	12	483	36	140	176	314	36	3	15	18	24	....	1977-78	1988-89
Dupere, Denis	Tor., Wsh., St.L., K.C., Col.	8	421	80	99	179	66	16	1	0	1	0	....	1970-71	1977-78
Dupont, Andre	NYR, St.L., Phi., Que.	13	800	59	185	244	1986	140	14	18	32	352	2	1970-71	1982-83
Dupont, Jerome	Chi., Tor.	6	214	7	29	36	468	20	0	2	2	56	....	1981-82	1986-87
‡ DuPont, Micki	Cgy.	2	18	1	2	3	6	....	....	....	....	....	....	2001-02	2002-03
Dupont, Norm	Mtl., Wpg., Hfd.	5	256	55	85	140	52	13	4	2	6	0	....	1979-80	1983-84
• Dupre, Yanick	Phi.	3	35	2	0	2	16	....	....	....	....	....	....	1991-92	1995-96
• Durbano, Steve	St.L., Pit., K.C., Col.	6	220	13	60	73	1127	5	0	2	2	8	....	1972-73	1978-79
Duris, Vitezslav	Tor.	2	89	3	20	23	62	3	0	1	1	2	....	1980-81	1982-83
Dussault, Norm	Mtl.	4	206	31	62	93	47	7	3	1	4	0	....	1947-48	1950-51
• Dutton, Red	Mtl.M., NYA	10	449	29	67	96	871	18	1	0	1	33	....	1926-27	1935-36
Dvorak, Miroslav	Phi.	3	193	11	74	85	51	18	0	2	2	6	....	1982-83	1984-85
Dwyer, Mike	Col., Cgy.	4	31	2	6	8	25	1	1	0	1	0	....	1978-79	1981-82
• Dyck, Henry	NYR	1	1	0	0	0	0	....	....	....	....	....	....	1943-44	1943-44
• Dye, Babe	Tor., Ham., Chi., NYA	11	271	201	47	248	221	10	2	0	2	11	1	1919-20	1930-31
Dykstra, Steve	Buf., Edm., Pit., Hfd.	5	217	8	32	40	545	1	0	0	0	2	....	1985-86	1989-90
Dyte, Jack	Chi.	1	27	1	0	1	31	....	....	....	....	....	....	1943-44	1943-44
Dziedzic, Joe	Pit., Phx.	3	130	14	14	28	131	21	1	3	4	23	....	1995-96	1998-99
E															
Eagles, Mike	Que., Chi., Wpg., Wsh.	16	853	74	122	196	928	44	2	6	8	34	....	1982-83	1999-00
Eakin, Bruce	Cgy., Det.	4	13	2	2	4	4	....	....	....	....	....	....	1981-82	1985-86
Eatough, Jeff	Buf.	1	1	0	0	0	0	....	....	....	....	....	....	1981-82	1981-82
Eaves, Mike	Min., Cgy.	8	324	83	143	226	80	43	7	10	17	14	....	1978-79	1985-86
Eaves, Murray	Wpg., Det.	8	57	4	13	17	9	4	0	1	1	2	....	1980-81	1989-90
Ecclestone, Tim	St.L., Det., Tor., Atl.	11	692	126	233	359	344	48	6	11	17	76	....	1967-68	1977-78
Edberg, Rolf	Wsh.	3	184	45	58	103	24	....	....	....	....	....	....	1978-79	1980-81
• Eddolls, Frank	Mtl., NYR	8	317	23	43	66	114	31	0	2	2	10	1	1944-45	1951-52
Edestrand, Darryl	St.L., Phi., Pit., Bos., L.A.	10	455	34	90	124	404	42	3	9	12	57	....	1967-68	1978-79
Edmundson, Garry	Mtl., Tor.	3	43	4	6	10	49	11	0	1	1	8	....	1951-52	1960-61
Edur, Tom	Col., Pit.	2	158	17	70	87	67	....	....	....	....	....	....	1976-77	1977-78
Egan, Pat	NYA, Bro., Det., Bos., NYR	11	554	77	153	230	776	46	9	4	13	48	....	1939-40	1950-51
‡ Egeland, Allan	T.B.	3	17	0	0	0	16	....	....	....	....	....	....	1995-96	1997-98
Egers, Jack	NYR, St.L., Wsh.	7	284	64	69	133	154	32	5	6	11	32	....	1969-70	1975-76
Ehman, Gerry	Bos., Det., Tor., Oak., Cal.	9	429	96	118	214	100	41	10	10	20	12	1	1957-58	1970-71
Eisenhut, Neil	Van., Cgy.	2	16	1	3	4	21	....	....	....	....	....	....	1993-94	1994-95
Eklund, Pelle	Phi., Dal.	9	594	120	335	455	109	66	10	36	46	8	....	1985-86	1993-94
Eldebrink, Anders	Van., Que.	2	55	3	11	14	29	14	0	0	0	10	....	1981-82	1982-83
‡ Elich, Matt	T.B.	2	16	1	1	2	0	....	....	....	....	....	....	1999-00	2000-01
Elik, Bo	Det.	1	3	0	0	0	0	....	....	....	....	....	....	1962-63	1962-63
‡ Elik, Todd	L.A., Min., Edm., S.J., St.L., Bos.	8	448	110	219	329	453	52	15	27	42	48	....	1989-90	1996-97
Ellett, Dave	Wpg., Tor., N.J., Bos., St.L.	16	1129	153	415	568	985	116	11	46	57	87	....	1984-85	1999-00
• Elliott, Fred	Ott.	1	43	2	0	2	6	....	....	....	....	....	....	1928-29	1928-29
Ellis, Ron	Tor.	16	1034	332	308	640	207	70	18	8	26	20	1	1963-64	1980-81
‡ Elomo, Miika	Wsh.	1	2	0	1	1	2	....	....	....	....	....	....	1999-00	1999-00
Eloranta, Kari	Cgy., St.L.	5	267	13	103	116	155	26	1	7	8	19	....	1981-82	1986-87
Elynuik, Pat	Wpg., Wsh., T.B., Ott.	9	506	154	188	342	459	20	6	9	15	25	....	1987-88	1995-96
Emberg, Eddie	Mtl.	1	....	....	....	....	....	2	1	0	1	0	....	1944-45	1944-45
Emerson, Nelson	St.L., Wpg., Hfd., Car., Chi., Ott., Atl., L.A.	12	771	195	293	488	575	40	7	15	22	33	....	1990-91	2001-02
Emma, David	N.J., Bos., Fla.	5	34	5	6	11	2	....	....	....	....	....	....	1992-93	2000-01
Emmons, Gary	S.J.	1	3	1	0	1	0	....	....	....	....	....	....	1993-94	1993-94
Emmons, John	Ott., T.B., Bos.	3	85	2	4	6	64	....	....	....	....	....	....	1999-00	2001-02
• Emms, Hap	Mtl.M., NYA, Det., Bos.	10	320	36	53	89	311	14	0	0	0	12	....	1926-27	1937-38
Endean, Craig	Wpg.	1	2	0	1	1	0	....	....	....	....	....	....	1986-87	1986-87
Engblom, Brian	Mtl., Wsh., L.A., Buf., Cgy.	11	659	29	177	206	599	48	3	9	12	43	3	1976-77	1986-87
Engele, Jerry	Min.	3	100	2	13	15	162	2	0	1	1	0	....	1975-76	1977-78
English, John	L.A.	1	3	1	3	4	4	1	0	0	0	0	....	1987-88	1987-88
Ennis, Jim	Edm.	1	5	1	0	1	10	....	....	....	....	....	....	1987-88	1987-88
Erickson, Aut	Bos., Chi., Tor., Oak.	7	226	7	24	31	182	7	0	0	0	2	1	1959-60	1969-70
Erickson, Bryan	Wsh., L.A., Pit., Wpg.	9	351	80	125	205	141	14	3	4	7	7	....	1983-84	1993-94
Erickson, Grant	Bos., Min.	2	6	1	0	1	0	....	....	....	....	....	....	1968-69	1969-70
Eriksson, Peter	Edm.	1	20	3	3	6	24	....	....	....	....	....	....	1989-90	1989-90
Eriksson, Roland	Min., Van.	3	193	48	95	143	26	2	1	0	1	0	....	1976-77	1978-79
Eriksson, Thomas	Phi.	5	208	22	76	98	107	19	0	3	3	12	....	1980-81	1985-86
Erixon, Jan	NYR	10	556	57	159	216	167	58	7	7	14	16	....	1983-84	1992-93
Errey, Bob	Pit., Buf., S.J., Det., Dal., NYR	15	895	170	212	382	1005	99	13	16	29	109	2	1983-84	1997-98
Esau, Len	Tor., Que., Cgy., Edm.	4	27	0	10	10	24	....	....	....	....	....	....	1991-92	1994-95
Esposito, Phil	Chi., Bos., NYR	18	1282	717	873	1590	910	130	61	76	137	138	2	1963-64	1980-81
• Evans, Chris	Tor., Buf., St.L., Det., K.C.	5	241	19	42	61	143	12	1	1	2	8	....	1969-70	1974-75
Evans, Daryl	L.A., Wsh., Tor.	6	113	22	30	52	25	11	5	8	13	12	....	1981-82	1986-87
Evans, Doug	St.L., Wpg., Phi.	8	355	48	87	135	502	22	3	4	7	38	....	1985-86	1992-93
• Evans, Jack	NYR, Chi.	14	752	19	80	99	989	56	2	2	4	97	1	1948-49	1962-63
Evans, John Paul	Phi.	3	103	14	25	39	34	1	0	0	0	0	....	1978-79	1982-83
Evans, Kevin	Min., S.J.	2	9	0	1	1	44	....	....	....	....	....	....	1990-91	1991-92
Evans, Paul	Tor.	2	11	1	1	2	21	2	0	0	0	0	....	1976-77	1977-78
Evans, Shawn	St.L., NYI	2	9	1	0	1	2	....	....	....	....	....	....	1985-86	1989-90
• Evans, Stewart	Det., Mtl.M., Mtl.	8	367	28	49	77	425	26	0	0	0	20	1	1930-31	1938-39
Evason, Dean	Wsh., Hfd., S.J., Dal., Cgy.	13	803	139	233	372	1002	55	9	20	29	132	....	1983-84	1995-96
Ewen, Todd	St.L., Mtl., Ana., S.J.	11	518	36	40	76	1911	26	0	0	0	87	1	1986-87	1996-97
Ezinicki, Bill	Tor., Bos., NYR	9	368	79	105	184	713	40	5	8	13	87	3	1944-45	1954-55
F															
Fahey, Trevor	NYR	1	1	0	0	0	0	....	....	....	....	....	....	1964-65	1964-65
Fairbairn, Bill	NYR, Min., St.L.	11	658	162	261	423	173	54	13	22	35	42	....	1968-69	1978-79
‡ Fairchild, Kelly	Tor., Dal., Col.	4	34	2	3	5	6	....	....	....	....	....	....	1995-96	2001-02
Falkenberg, Bob	Det.	5	54	1	5	6	26	....	....	....	....	....	....	1966-67	1971-72
‡ Falloon, Pat	S.J., Phi., Ott., Edm., Pit.	9	575	143	179	322	141	66	11	7	18	16	....	1991-92	1999-00
Farkas, Jeff	Tor., Atl.	4	11	0	2	2	6	5	1	0	1	0	....	1999-00	2002-03
Farrant, Walt	Chi.	1	1	0	0	0	0	....	....	....	....	....	....	1943-44	1943-44

			Regular Schedule					Playoffs							
Name	**NHL Teams**	**NHL Seasons**	**GP**	**G**	**A**	**TP**	**PIM**	**GP**	**G**	**A**	**TP**	**PIM**	**NHL Cup Wins**	**First NHL Season**	**Last NHL Season**
Farrish, Dave	NYR, Que., Tor.	7	430	17	110	127	440	14	0	2	2	24	....	1976-77	1983-84
Fashoway, Gordie	Chi.	1	13	3	2	5	14	....	....	....	....	....	....	1950-51	1950-51
Faubert, Mario	Pit.	7	231	21	90	111	292	10	2	2	4	6	....	1974-75	1981-82
Faulkner, Alex	Tor., Det.	3	101	15	17	32	15	12	5	0	5	2	....	1961-62	1963-64
Fauss, Ted	Tor.	2	28	0	2	2	15	....	....	....	....	....	....	1986-87	1987-88
Faust, Andre	Phi.	2	47	10	7	17	14	....	....	....	....	....	....	1992-93	1993-94
Feamster, Dave	Chi.	4	169	13	24	37	154	33	3	5	8	61	....	1981-82	1984-85
Featherstone, Glen	St.L., Bos., NYR, Hfd., Cgy.	9	384	19	61	80	939	28	0	2	2	103	....	1988-89	1996-97
Featherstone, Tony	Oak., Cal., Min.	3	130	17	21	38	65	2	0	0	0	0	....	1969-70	1973-74
Federko, Bernie	St.L., Det.	14	1000	369	761	1130	487	91	35	66	101	83	....	1976-77	1989-90
Fedotov, Anatoli	Wpg., Ana.	2	4	0	2	2	0	....	....	....	....	....	....	1992-93	1993-94
Fedyk, Brent	Det., Phi., Dal., NYR	10	470	97	112	209	308	16	3	2	5	12	....	1987-88	1998-99
Felix, Chris	Wsh.	4	35	1	12	13	10	2	0	1	1	0	....	1987-88	1990-91
‡ Felsner, Brian	Chi.	1	12	1	3	4	12	....	....	....	....	....	....	1997-98	1997-98
Felsner, Denny	St.L.	4	18	1	4	5	6	10	2	3	5	2	....	1991-92	1994-95
Feltrin, Tony	Pit., NYR	4	48	3	3	6	65	....	....	....	....	....	....	1980-81	1985-86
Fenton, Paul	Hfd., NYR, L.A., Wpg., Tor., Cgy., S.J.	8	411	100	83	183	198	17	4	1	5	27	....	1984-85	1991-92
Fenyves, David	Buf., Phi.	9	206	3	32	35	119	11	0	0	0	9	....	1982-83	1990-91
Fergus, Tom	Bos., Tor., Van.	12	726	235	346	581	499	65	21	17	38	48	....	1981-82	1992-93
‡ Ferguson, Craig	Mtl., Cgy., Fla.	5	27	1	1	2	6	....	....	....	....	....	....	1993-94	1999-00
Ferguson, George	Tor., Pit., Min.	12	797	160	238	398	431	86	14	23	37	44	....	1972-73	1983-84
Ferguson, John	Mtl.	8	500	145	158	303	1214	85	20	18	38	260	5	1963-64	1970-71
Ferguson, Lorne	Bos., Det., Chi.	8	422	82	80	162	193	31	6	3	9	24	....	1949-50	1958-59
Ferguson, Norm	Oak., Cal.	4	279	73	66	139	72	10	1	4	5	7	....	1968-69	1971-72
Ferner, Mark	Buf., Wsh., Ana., Det.	6	91	3	10	13	51	....	....	....	....	....	....	1986-87	1994-95
Ferraro, Ray	Hfd., NYI, NYR, L.A., Atl., St.L.	18	1258	408	490	898	1288	68	21	22	43	54	....	1984-85	2001-02
Fetisov, Viacheslav	N.J., Det.	9	546	36	192	228	656	116	2	26	28	147	2	1989-90	1997-98
Fidler, Mike	Cle., Min., Hfd., Chi.	7	271	84	97	181	124	....	....	....	....	....	....	1976-77	1982-83
• Field, Wilf	NYA, Bro., Mtl., Chi.	6	219	17	25	42	151	2	0	0	0	2	....	1936-37	1944-45
Fielder, Guyle	Chi., Det., Bos.	4	9	0	0	0	2	6	0	0	0	2	....	1950-51	1957-58
‡ Filimonov, Dmitri	Ott.	1	30	1	4	5	18	....	....	....	....	....	....	1993-94	1993-94
Fillion, Bob	Mtl.	7	327	42	61	103	84	33	7	4	11	10	2	1943-44	1949-50
• Fillion, Marcel	Bos.	1	1	0	0	0	0	....	....	....	....	....	....	1944-45	1944-45
• Filmore, Tommy	Det., NYA, Bos.	4	117	15	12	27	33	....	....	....	....	....	....	1930-31	1933-34
• Finkbeiner, Lloyd	NYA	1	2	0	0	0	0	....	....	....	....	....	....	1940-41	1940-41
Finn, Steven	Que., T.B., L.A.	12	725	34	78	112	1724	23	0	4	4	39	....	1985-86	1996-97
Finney, Sid	Chi.	3	59	10	7	17	4	7	0	2	2	0	....	1951-52	1953-54
• Finnigan, Ed	St.L., Bos.	2	15	1	1	2	2	....	....	....	....	....	....	1934-35	1935-36
• Finnigan, Frank	Ott., Tor., St.L.	14	553	115	88	203	407	38	6	9	15	22	2	1923-24	1936-37
Fiorentino, Peter	NYR	1	1	0	0	0	0	....	....	....	....	....	....	1991-92	1991-92
Fischer, Ron	Buf.	2	18	0	7	7	6	....	....	....	....	....	....	1981-82	1982-83
• Fisher, Alvin	Tor.	1	9	1	0	1	4	....	....	....	....	....	....	1924-25	1924-25
Fisher, Craig	Phi., Wpg., Fla.	4	12	0	0	0	2	....	....	....	....	....	....	1989-90	1996-97
Fisher, Dunc	NYR, Bos., Det.	7	275	45	70	115	104	21	4	4	8	14	....	1947-48	1958-59
• Fisher, Joe	Det.	4	65	8	12	20	13	12	2	1	3	6	1	1939-40	1942-43
Fitchner, Bob	Que.	2	78	12	20	32	59	3	0	0	0	10	....	1979-80	1980-81
Fitzgerald, Rusty	Pit.	2	25	2	2	4	12	5	0	0	0	4	....	1994-95	1995-96
Fitzpatrick, Ross	Phi.	4	20	5	2	7	0	....	....	....	....	....	....	1982-83	1985-86
Fitzpatrick, Sandy	NYR, Min.	2	22	3	6	9	8	12	0	0	0	0	....	1964-65	1967-68
Flaman, Fern	Bos., Tor.	17	910	34	174	208	1370	63	4	8	12	93	1	1944-45	1960-61
Flatley, Pat	NYI, NYR	14	780	170	340	510	686	70	18	15	33	75	....	1983-84	1996-97
Fleming, Gerry	Mtl.	2	11	0	0	0	42	....	....	....	....	....	....	1993-94	1994-95
Fleming, Reggie	Mtl., Chi., Bos., NYR, Phi., Buf.	12	749	108	132	240	1468	50	3	6	9	106	1	1959-60	1970-71
Flesch, John	Min., Pit., Col.	4	124	18	23	41	117	....	....	....	....	....	....	1974-75	1979-80
Fletcher, Steven	Mtl., Wpg.	2	3	0	0	0	5	1	0	0	0	5	....	1987-88	1988-89
• Flett, Bill	L.A., Phi., Tor., Atl., Edm.	11	689	202	215	417	501	52	7	16	23	42	1	1967-68	1979-80
Fleury, Theoren	Cgy., Col., NYR, Chi.	15	1084	455	633	1088	1840	77	34	45	79	116	1	1988-89	2002-03
Flichel, Todd	Wpg.	3	6	0	1	1	4	....	....	....	....	....	....	1987-88	1989-90
Flockhart, Rob	Van., Min.	5	55	2	5	7	14	1	1	0	1	2	....	1976-77	1980-81
Flockhart, Ron	Phi., Pit., Mtl., St.L., Bos.	9	453	145	183	328	208	19	4	6	10	14	....	1980-81	1988-89
Floyd, Larry	N.J.	2	12	2	3	5	9	....	....	....	....	....	....	1982-83	1983-84
• Fogarty, Bryan	Que., Pit., Mtl.	6	156	22	52	74	119	....	....	....	....	....	....	1989-90	1994-95
• Fogolin, Lee	Det., Chi.	9	427	10	48	58	575	28	0	2	2	30	1	1947-48	1955-56
Fogolin Jr., Lee	Buf., Edm.	13	924	44	195	239	1318	108	5	19	24	173	2	1974-75	1986-87
Folco, Peter	Van.	1	2	0	0	0	0	....	....	....	....	....	....	1973-74	1973-74
Foley, Gerry	Tor., NYR, L.A.	4	142	9	14	23	99	9	0	1	1	2	....	1954-55	1968-69
Foley, Rick	Chi., Phi., Det.	3	67	11	26	37	180	4	0	1	1	4	....	1970-71	1973-74
Foligno, Mike	Det., Buf., Tor., Fla.	15	1018	355	372	727	2049	57	15	17	32	185	....	1979-80	1993-94
Folk, Bill	Det.	2	12	0	0	0	4	....	....	....	....	....	....	1951-52	1952-53
Fontaine, Len	Det.	2	46	8	11	19	10	....	....	....	....	....	....	1972-73	1973-74
Fontas, Jon	Min.	2	2	0	0	0	0	....	....	....	....	....	....	1979-80	1980-81
Fonteyne, Val	Det., NYR, Pit.	13	820	75	154	229	26	59	3	10	13	8	....	1959-60	1971-72
Fontinato, Lou	NYR, Mtl.	9	535	26	78	104	1247	21	0	2	2	42	....	1954-55	1962-63
Forbes, Dave	Bos., Wsh.	6	363	64	64	128	341	45	1	4	5	13	....	1973-74	1978-79
Forbes, Mike	Bos., Edm.	3	50	1	11	12	41	....	....	....	....	....	....	1977-78	1981-82
Forey, Connie	St.L.	1	4	0	0	0	2	....	....	....	....	....	....	1973-74	1973-74
• Forsey, Jack	Tor.	1	19	7	9	16	10	3	0	1	1	0	....	1942-43	1942-43
• Forslund, Gus	Ott.	1	48	4	9	13	2	....	....	....	....	....	....	1932-33	1932-33
Forslund, Tomas	Cgy.	2	44	5	11	16	12	....	....	....	....	....	....	1991-92	1992-93
Forsyth, Alex	Wsh.	1	1	0	0	0	0	....	....	....	....	....	....	1976-77	1976-77
Fortier, Dave	Tor., NYI, Van.	4	205	8	21	29	335	20	0	2	2	33	....	1972-73	1976-77
Fortier, Marc	Que., Ott., L.A.	6	212	42	60	102	135	....	....	....	....	....	....	1987-88	1992-93
Fortin, Ray	St.L.	3	92	2	6	8	33	6	0	0	0	8	....	1967-68	1969-70
Foster, Corey	N.J., Phi., Pit., NYI	4	45	5	6	11	24	3	0	0	0	4	....	1988-89	1996-97
Foster, Dwight	Bos., Col., N.J., Det.	10	541	111	163	274	420	35	5	12	17	4	....	1977-78	1986-87
Foster, Herb	NYR	2	6	1	0	1	5	....	....	....	....	....	....	1940-41	1947-48
• Foster, Yip	NYR, Bos., Det.	4	83	3	2	5	32	....	....	....	....	....	....	1929-30	1934-35
Fotiu, Nick	NYR, Hfd., Cgy., Phi., Edm.	13	646	60	77	137	1362	38	0	4	4	67	....	1976-77	1988-89
• Fowler, Jimmy	Tor.	3	135	18	29	47	39	18	0	3	3	2	....	1936-37	1938-39
Fowler, Tom	Chi.	1	24	0	1	1	18	....	....	....	....	....	....	1946-47	1946-47
Fox, Greg	Atl., Chi., Pit.	8	494	14	92	106	637	44	1	9	10	67	....	1977-78	1984-85
Fox, Jim	L.A.	9	578	186	293	479	143	22	4	8	12	0	....	1980-81	1989-90
• Foyston, Frank	Det.	2	64	17	7	24	32	....	....	....	....	....	....	1926-27	1927-28
Frampton, Bob	Mtl.	1	2	0	0	0	0	3	0	0	0	0	....	1949-50	1949-50
Franceschetti, Lou	Wsh., Tor., Buf.	10	459	59	81	140	747	44	3	2	5	111	....	1981-82	1991-92
Francis, Bobby	Det.	1	14	2	0	2	0	....	....	....	....	....	....	1982-83	1982-83
• Fraser, Archie	NYR	1	3	0	1	1	0	....	....	....	....	....	....	1943-44	1943-44
• Fraser, Charles	Ham.	1	1	0	0	0	0	....	....	....	....	....	....	1923-24	1923-24
Fraser, Curt	Van., Chi., Min.	12	704	193	240	433	1306	65	15	18	33	198	....	1978-79	1989-90
• Fraser, Gord	Chi., Det., Mtl., Pit., Phi.	5	144	24	12	36	224	2	1	0	1	6	....	1926-27	1930-31
Fraser, Harvey	Chi.	1	21	5	4	9	0	....	....	....	....	....	....	1944-45	1944-45
Fraser, Iain	NYI, Que., Dal., Edm., Wpg., S.J.	5	94	23	23	46	31	4	0	0	0	0	....	1992-93	1996-97
Fraser, Scott	Mtl., Edm., NYR	3	72	16	15	31	24	11	1	1	2	0	....	1995-96	1998-99
Frawley, Dan	Chi., Pit.	6	273	37	40	77	674	1	0	0	0	0	....	1983-84	1988-89
Freadrich, Kyle	T.B.	2	23	0	1	1	75	....	....	....	....	....	....	1999-00	2000-01
• Fredrickson, Frank	Det., Bos., Pit.	5	161	39	34	73	206	10	2	3	5	24	....	1926-27	1930-31
Freer, Mark	Phi., Ott., Cgy.	7	124	16	23	39	61	....	....	....	....	....	....	1986-87	1993-94
• Frew, Irv	Mtl.M., St.L., Mtl.	3	96	2	5	7	146	4	0	0	0	6	....	1933-34	1935-36
Friday, Tim	Det.	1	23	0	3	3	6	....	....	....	....	....	....	1985-86	1985-86
Fridgen, Dan	Hfd.	2	13	2	3	5	2	....	....	....	....	....	....	1981-82	1982-83
Friedman, Doug	Edm., Nsh.	2	18	0	1	1	34	....	....	....	....	....	....	1997-98	1998-99
Friest, Ron	Min.	3	64	7	7	14	191	6	1	0	1	7	....	1980-81	1982-83
Frig, Len	Chi., Cal., Cle., St.L.	7	311	13	51	64	479	14	2	1	3	0	....	1972-73	1979-80
Frost, Harry	Bos.	1	4	0	0	0	0	1	0	0	0	0	1	1938-39	1938-39
Frycer, Miroslav	Que., Tor., Det., Edm.	8	415	147	183	330	486	17	3	8	11	16	....	1981-82	1988-89
Fryday, Bob	Mtl.	2	5	1	0	1	0	....	....	....	....	....	....	1949-50	1951-52
Ftorek, Robbie	Det., Que., NYR	8	334	77	150	227	262	19	9	6	15	28	....	1972-73	1984-85
Fullan, Larry	Wsh.	1	4	1	0	1	0	....	....	....	....	....	....	1974-75	1974-75
Fusco, Mark	Hfd.	2	80	3	12	15	42	....	....	....	....	....	....	1983-84	1984-85

G

Gadsby, Bill	Chi., NYR, Det.	20	1248	130	438	568	1539	67	4	23	27	92	....	1946-47	1965-66
Gaetz, Link	Min., S.J.	3	65	6	8	14	412	....	....	....	....	....	....	1988-89	1991-92
Gage, Jody	Det., Buf.	6	68	14	15	29	26	....	....	....	....	....	....	1980-81	1991-92
• Gagne, Art	Mtl., Bos., Ott., Det.	6	228	67	33	100	257	11	2	1	3	20	....	1926-27	1931-32

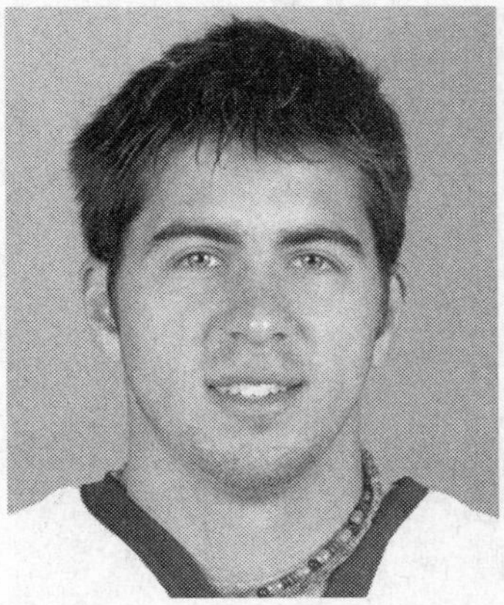
Jeff Farkas

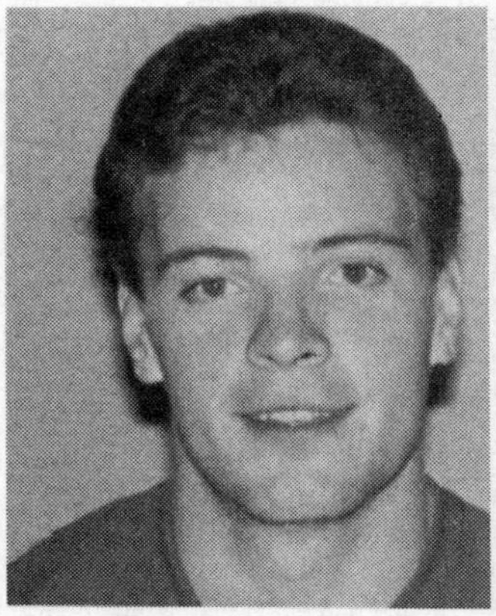
Tom Fergus

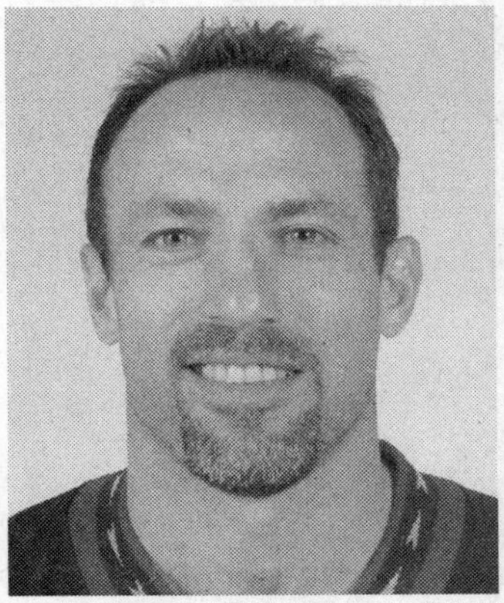
Ray Ferraro

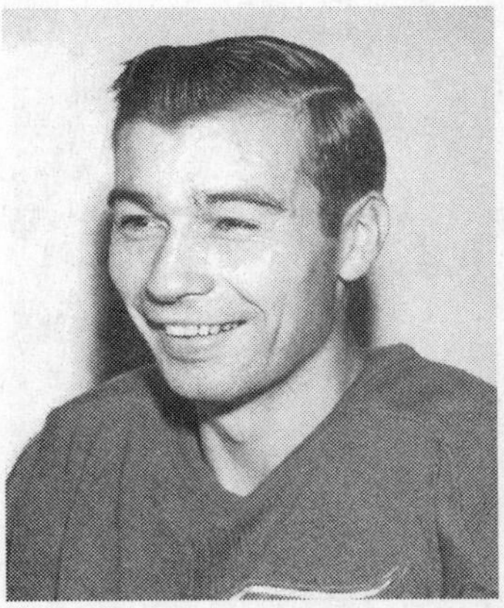
Guyle Fielder

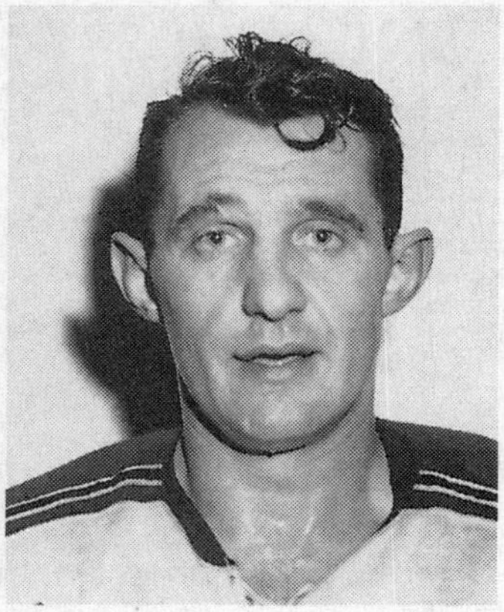

Bill Gadsby

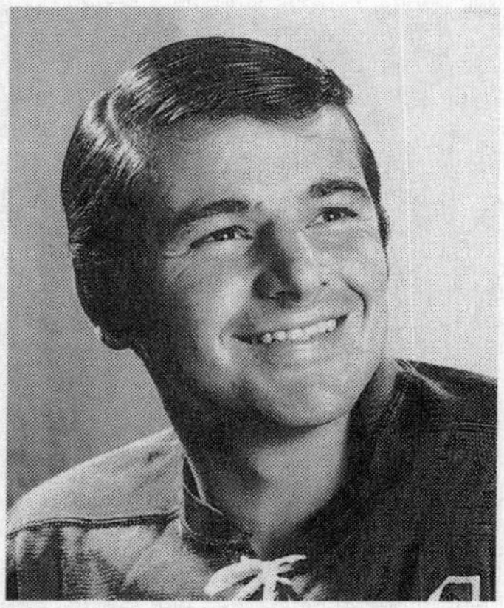

Rod Gilbert

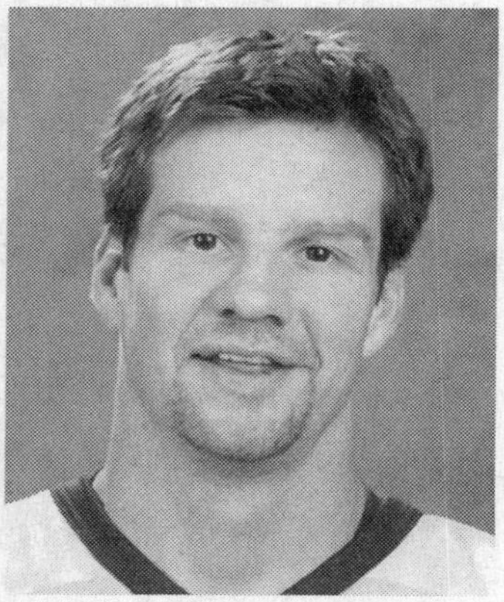

Brent Gilchrist

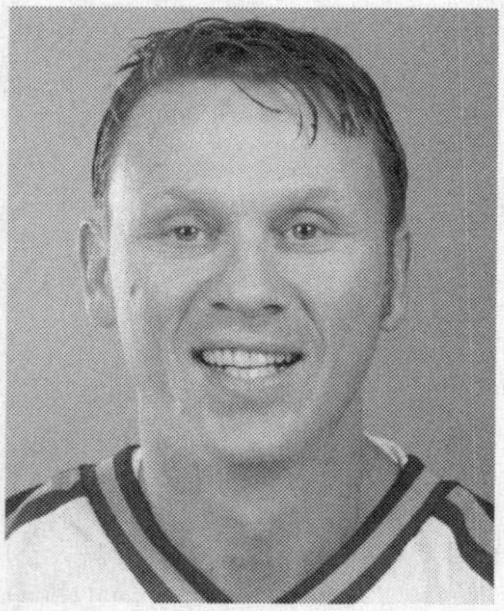

Todd Gill

			Regular Schedule					Playoffs					NHL	First	Last
Name	NHL Teams	NHL Seasons	GP	G	A	TP	PIM	GP	G	A	TP	PIM	Cup Wins	NHL Season	NHL Season
Gagne, Paul	Col., N.J., Tor., NYI	8	390	110	101	211	127	....	....	....	....	....	....	1980-81	1989-90
Gagne, Pierre	Bos.	1	2	0	0	0	0	....	....	....	....	....	....	1959-60	1959-60
Gagner, Dave	NYR, Min., Dal., Tor., Cgy., Fla., Van.	15	946	318	401	719	1018	57	22	26	48	64	....	1984-85	1998-99
Gagnon, Germain	Mtl., NYI, Chi., K.C.	5	259	40	101	141	72	19	2	3	5	2	....	1971-72	1975-76
• Gagnon, Johnny	Mtl., Bos., NYA	10	454	120	141	261	295	32	12	12	24	37	1	1930-31	1939-40
‡ Gagnon, Sean	Phx., Ott.	3	12	0	1	1	34	....	....	....	....	....	....	1997-98	2000-01
Gainey, Bob	Mtl.	16	1160	239	262	501	585	182	25	48	73	151	5	1973-74	1988-89
• Gainor, Dutch	Bos., NYR, Ott., Mtl.M.	7	246	51	56	107	129	22	2	1	3	14	2	1927-28	1934-35
‡ Galanov, Maxim	NYR, Pit., Atl., T.B.	4	122	8	12	20	44	1	0	0	0	0	....	1997-98	2000-01
Galarneau, Michel	Hfd.	3	78	7	10	17	34	....	....	....	....	....	....	1980-81	1982-83
• Galbraith, Percy	Bos., Ott.	8	347	29	31	60	224	31	4	7	11	24	1	1926-27	1933-34
• Gallagher, John	Mtl.M., Det., NYA	7	205	14	19	33	153	24	2	3	5	27	1	1930-31	1938-39
Gallant, Gerard	Det., T.B.	11	615	211	269	480	1674	58	18	21	39	178	....	1984-85	1994-95
Galley, Garry	L.A., Wsh., Bos., Phi., Buf., NYI	17	1149	125	475	600	1218	89	7	23	30	119	....	1984-85	2000-01
Gallimore, Jamie	Min.	1	2	0	0	0	0	....	....	....	....	....	....	1977-78	1977-78
• Gallinger, Don	Bos.	5	222	65	88	153	89	23	5	5	10	19	....	1942-43	1947-48
Gamble, Dick	Mtl., Chi., Tor.	8	195	41	41	82	66	14	1	2	3	4	1	1950-51	1966-67
Gambucci, Gary	Min.	2	51	2	7	9	9	....	....	....	....	....	....	1971-72	1973-74
Ganchar, Perry	St.L., Mtl., Pit.	4	42	3	7	10	36	7	3	1	4	0	....	1983-84	1988-89
Gans, Dave	L.A.	2	6	0	0	0	2	....	....	....	....	....	....	1982-83	1985-86
‡ Gardiner, Bruce	Ott., T.B., CBJ, N.J.	6	312	34	54	88	263	21	1	4	5	8	....	1996-97	2001-02
• Gardiner, Herb	Mtl., Chi.	3	108	10	9	19	52	9	0	1	1	16	....	1926-27	1928-29
Gardner, Bill	Chi., Hfd.	9	380	73	115	188	68	45	3	8	11	17	....	1980-81	1988-89
• Gardner, Cal	NYR, Tor., Chi., Bos.	12	696	154	238	392	517	61	7	10	17	20	2	1945-46	1956-57
Gardner, Dave	Mtl., St.L., Cal., Cle., Phi.	7	350	75	115	190	41	....	....	....	....	....	....	1972-73	1979-80
Gardner, Paul	Col., Tor., Pit., Wsh., Buf.	10	447	201	201	402	207	16	2	6	8	14	....	1976-77	1985-86
Gare, Danny	Buf., Det., Edm.	13	827	354	331	685	1285	64	25	21	46	195	....	1974-75	1986-87
Gariepy, Ray	Bos., Tor.	2	36	1	6	7	43	....	....	....	....	....	....	1953-54	1955-56
• Garland, Scott	Tor., L.A.	3	91	13	24	37	115	7	1	2	3	35	....	1975-76	1978-79
Garner, Rob	Pit.	1	1	0	0	0	0	....	....	....	....	....	....	1982-83	1982-83
Garpenlov, Johan	Det., S.J., Fla., Atl.	10	609	114	197	311	276	44	10	9	19	22	....	1990-91	1999-00
• Garrett, Red	NYR	1	23	1	1	2	18	....	....	....	....	....	....	1942-43	1942-43
Gartner, Mike	Wsh., Min., NYR, Tor., Phx.	19	1432	708	627	1335	1159	122	43	50	93	125	....	1979-80	1997-98
• Gassoff, Bob	St.L.	4	245	11	47	58	866	9	0	1	1	16	....	1973-74	1976-77
Gassoff, Brad	Van.	4	122	19	17	36	163	3	0	0	0	0	....	1975-76	1978-79
Gatzos, Steve	Pit.	4	89	15	20	35	83	1	0	0	0	0	....	1981-82	1984-85
Gaudreau, Rob	S.J., Ott.	4	231	51	54	105	69	14	2	0	2	0	....	1992-93	1995-96
Gaudreault, Armand	Bos.	1	44	15	9	24	27	7	0	2	2	8	....	1944-45	1944-45
• Gaudreault, Leo	Mtl.	3	67	8	4	12	30	....	....	....	....	....	....	1927-28	1932-33
‡ Gaul, Mike	Col., CBJ	2	3	0	0	0	4	....	....	....	....	....	....	1998-99	2000-01
Gaulin, Jean-Marc	Que.	4	26	4	3	7	8	1	0	0	0	0	....	1982-83	1985-86
Gaume, Dallas	Hfd.	1	4	1	1	2	0	....	....	....	....	....	....	1988-89	1988-89
• Gauthier, Art	Mtl.	1	13	0	0	0	0	1	0	0	0	0	....	1926-27	1926-27
Gauthier, Daniel	Chi.	1	5	0	0	0	0	....	....	....	....	....	....	1994-95	1994-95
• Gauthier, Fern	NYR, Mtl., Det.	6	229	46	50	96	35	22	5	1	6	7	....	1943-44	1948-49
Gauthier, Jean	Mtl., Phi., Bos.	10	166	6	29	35	150	14	1	3	4	22	1	1960-61	1969-70
Gauthier, Luc	Mtl.	1	3	0	0	0	2	....	....	....	....	....	....	1990-91	1990-91
Gauvreau, Jocelyn	Mtl.	1	2	0	0	0	0	....	....	....	....	....	....	1983-84	1983-84
Gavin, Stew	Tor., Hfd., Min.	13	768	130	155	285	584	66	14	20	34	75	....	1980-81	1992-93
Geale, Bob	Pit.	1	1	0	0	0	2	....	....	....	....	....	....	1984-85	1984-85
• Gee, George	Chi., Det.	9	551	135	183	318	345	41	6	13	19	32	1	1945-46	1953-54
Geldart, Gary	Min.	1	4	0	0	0	5	....	....	....	....	....	....	1970-71	1970-71
Gendron, Jean-Guy	NYR, Bos., Mtl., Phi.	14	863	182	201	383	701	42	7	4	11	47	....	1955-56	1971-72
Gendron, Martin	Wsh., Chi.	3	30	4	2	6	10	....	....	....	....	....	....	1994-95	1997-98
Geoffrion, Bernie	Mtl., NYR	16	883	393	429	822	689	132	58	60	118	88	6	1950-51	1967-68
Geoffrion, Danny	Mtl., Wpg.	3	111	20	32	52	99	2	0	0	0	7	....	1979-80	1981-82
• Geran, Gerry	Mtl.W., Bos.	2	37	5	1	6	6	....	....	....	....	....	....	1917-18	1925-26
• Gerard, Eddie	Ott.	6	128	50	48	98	108	11	4	0	4	17	3	1917-18	1922-23
Germain, Eric	L.A.	1	4	0	1	1	13	1	0	0	0	4	....	1987-88	1987-88
Getliffe, Ray	Bos., Mtl.	10	393	136	137	273	250	45	9	10	19	30	2	1935-36	1944-45
Giallonardo, Mario	Col.	2	23	0	3	3	6	....	....	....	....	....	....	1979-80	1980-81
Gibbs, Barry	Bos., Min., Atl., St.L., L.A.	13	797	58	224	282	945	36	4	2	6	67	....	1967-68	1979-80
Gibson, Don	Van.	1	14	0	3	3	20	....	....	....	....	....	....	1990-91	1990-91
Gibson, Doug	Bos., Wsh.	3	63	9	19	28	0	1	0	0	0	0	....	1973-74	1977-78
Gibson, John	L.A., Tor., Wpg.	3	48	0	2	2	120	....	....	....	....	....	....	1980-81	1983-84
Giesebrecht, Gus	Det.	4	135	27	51	78	13	17	2	3	5	0	....	1938-39	1941-42
Giffin, Lee	Pit.	2	27	1	3	4	9	....	....	....	....	....	....	1986-87	1987-88
Gilbert, Ed	K.C., Pit.	3	166	21	31	52	22	....	....	....	....	....	....	1974-75	1976-77
Gilbert, Greg	NYI, Chi., NYR, St.L.	15	837	150	228	378	576	133	17	33	50	162	3	1981-82	1995-96
Gilbert, Jeannot	Bos.	2	9	0	1	1	4	....	....	....	....	....	....	1962-63	1964-65
Gilbert, Rod	NYR	18	1065	406	615	1021	508	79	34	33	67	43	....	1960-61	1977-78
Gilbertson, Stan	Cal., St.L., Wsh., Pit.	6	428	85	89	174	148	3	1	1	2	2	....	1971-72	1976-77
Gilchrist, Brent	Mtl., Edm., Min., Dal., Det., Nsh.	15	792	135	170	305	400	90	17	14	31	48	1	1988-89	2002-03
Giles, Curt	Min., NYR, St.L.	14	895	43	199	242	733	103	6	16	22	118	....	1979-80	1992-93
Gilhen, Randy	Hfd., Wpg., Pit., L.A., NYR, T.B., Fla.	11	457	55	60	115	314	33	3	2	5	26	1	1982-83	1995-96
Gill, Todd	Tor., S.J., St.L., Det., Phx., Col., Chi.	19	1007	82	272	354	1214	103	7	30	37	193	....	1984-85	2002-03
Gillen, Don	Phi., Hfd.	2	35	2	4	6	22	....	....	....	....	....	....	1979-80	1981-82
• Gillie, Farrand	Det.	1	1	0	0	0	0	....	....	....	....	....	....	1928-29	1928-29
Gillies, Clark	NYI, Buf.	14	958	319	378	697	1023	164	47	47	94	287	4	1974-75	1987-88
Gillis, Jere	Van., NYR, Que., Buf., Phi.	9	386	78	95	173	230	19	4	7	11	9	....	1977-78	1986-87
Gillis, Mike	Col., Bos.	6	246	33	43	76	186	27	2	5	7	10	....	1978-79	1983-84
Gillis, Paul	Que., Chi., Hfd.	11	624	88	154	242	1498	42	3	14	17	156	....	1982-83	1992-93
Gilmour, Doug	St.L., Cgy., Tor., N.J., Chi., Buf., Mtl.	20	1474	450	964	1414	1301	182	60	128	188	235	1	1983-84	2002-03
Gingras, Gaston	Mtl., Tor., St.L.	10	476	61	174	235	161	52	6	18	24	20	1	1979-80	1988-89
Girard, Bob	Cal., Cle., Wsh.	5	305	45	69	114	140	....	....	....	....	....	....	1975-76	1979-80
Girard, Kenny	Tor.	3	7	0	1	1	2	....	....	....	....	....	....	1956-57	1959-60
• Giroux, Art	Mtl., Bos., Det.	3	54	6	4	10	14	2	0	0	0	0	....	1932-33	1935-36
Giroux, Larry	St.L., K.C., Det., Hfd.	7	274	15	74	89	333	5	0	0	0	4	....	1973-74	1979-80
Giroux, Pierre	L.A.	1	6	1	0	1	17	....	....	....	....	....	....	1982-83	1982-83
Gladney, Bob	L.A., Pit.	2	14	1	5	6	4	....	....	....	....	....	....	1982-83	1983-84
Gladu, Jean-Paul	Bos.	1	40	6	14	20	2	7	2	2	4	0	....	1944-45	1944-45
Glennie, Brian	Tor., L.A.	10	572	14	100	114	621	32	0	1	1	66	....	1969-70	1978-79
Glennon, Matt	Bos.	1	3	0	0	0	2	....	....	....	....	....	....	1991-92	1991-92
Gloeckner, Lorry	Det.	1	13	0	2	2	6	....	....	....	....	....	....	1978-79	1978-79
Gloor, Dan	Van.	1	2	0	0	0	0	....	....	....	....	....	....	1973-74	1973-74
• Glover, Fred	Det., Chi.	5	92	13	11	24	62	8	0	0	0	0	1	1948-49	1952-53
Glover, Howie	Chi., Det., NYR, Mtl.	5	144	29	17	46	101	11	1	2	3	2	....	1958-59	1968-69
Glynn, Brian	Cgy., Min., Edm., Ott., Van., Hfd.	10	431	25	79	104	410	57	6	10	16	40	....	1987-88	1996-97
Godden, Ernie	Tor.	1	5	1	1	2	6	....	....	....	....	....	....	1981-82	1981-82
• Godfrey, Warren	Bos., Det.	16	786	32	125	157	752	52	1	4	5	42	....	1952-53	1967-68
Godin, Eddy	Wsh.	2	27	3	6	9	12	....	....	....	....	....	....	1977-78	1978-79
• Godin, Sam	Ott., Mtl.	3	83	4	3	7	36	....	....	....	....	....	....	1927-28	1933-34
Godynyuk, Alexander	Tor., Cgy., Fla., Hfd.	7	223	10	39	49	224	....	....	....	....	....	....	1990-91	1996-97
Goegan, Pete	Det., NYR, Min.	11	383	19	67	86	365	33	1	3	4	61	....	1957-58	1967-68
Goertz, Dave	Pit.	1	2	0	0	0	2	....	....	....	....	....	....	1987-88	1987-88
• Goldham, Bob	Tor., Chi., Det.	12	650	28	143	171	400	66	3	14	17	53	5	1941-42	1955-56
‡ Goldmann, Erich	Ott.	1	1	0	0	0	0	....	....	....	....	....	....	1999-00	1999-00
• Goldsworthy, Bill	Bos., Min., NYR	14	771	283	258	541	793	40	18	19	37	30	....	1964-65	1977-78
• Goldsworthy, Leroy	NYR, Det., Chi., Mtl., Bos., NYA	10	336	66	57	123	79	24	1	0	1	4	1	1928-29	1938-39
Goldup, Glenn	Mtl., L.A.	9	291	52	67	119	303	16	4	3	7	22	....	1973-74	1981-82
Goldup, Hank	Tor., NYR	6	202	63	80	143	97	26	5	1	6	6	1	1939-40	1945-46
‡ Golubovsky, Yan	Det., Fla.	4	56	1	7	8	32	....	....	....	....	....	....	1997-98	2000-01
Goneau, Daniel	NYR	3	53	12	3	15	14	....	....	....	....	....	....	1996-97	1999-00
• Gooden, Bill	NYR	2	53	9	11	20	15	....	....	....	....	....	....	1942-43	1943-44
Goodenough, Larry	Phi., Van.	6	242	22	77	99	179	22	3	15	18	10	1	1974-75	1979-80
• Goodfellow, Ebbie	Det.	14	557	134	190	324	511	45	8	8	16	65	3	1929-30	1942-43
Gordiouk, Viktor	Buf.	2	26	3	8	11	0	....	....	....	....	....	....	1992-93	1994-95
Gordon, Fred	Det., Bos.	2	81	8	7	15	68	2	0	0	0	0	....	1926-27	1927-28
Gordon, Jack	NYR	3	36	3	10	13	0	9	1	1	2	7	....	1948-49	1950-51
Gordon, Robb	Van.	1	4	0	0	0	2	....	....	....	....	....	....	1998-99	1998-99
Gorence, Tom	Phi., Edm.	6	303	58	53	111	89	37	9	6	15	47	....	1978-79	1983-84
Goring, Butch	L.A., NYI, Bos.	16	1107	375	513	888	102	134	38	50	88	32	4	1969-70	1984-85
Gorman, Dave	Atl.	1	3	0	0	0	0	....	....	....	....	....	....	1979-80	1979-80
• Gorman, Ed	Ott., Tor.	4	111	14	6	20	108	8	0	0	0	2	1	1924-25	1927-28
Gosselin, Benoit	NYR	1	7	0	0	0	33	....	....	....	....	....	....	1977-78	1977-78
‡ Gosselin, David	Nsh.	2	13	2	1	3	11	....	....	....	....	....	....	1999-00	2001-02

Name	NHL Teams	NHL Seasons	Regular Schedule GP	G	A	TP	PIM	Playoffs GP	G	A	TP	PIM	NHL Cup Wins	First NHL Season	Last NHL Season
Gosselin, Guy	Wpg.	1	5	0	0	0	6	....	....	....	....	....	....	1987-88	1987-88
Gotaas, Steve	Pit., Min.	3	49	6	9	15	53	3	0	1	1	5	....	1987-88	1990-91
• Gottselig, Johnny	Chi.	16	589	176	195	371	203	43	13	13	26	18	2	1928-29	1944-45
Gould, Bobby	Atl., Cgy., Wsh., Bos.	11	697	145	159	304	572	78	15	13	28	58	....	1979-80	1989-90
Gould, John	Buf., Van., Atl.	9	504	131	138	269	113	14	3	2	5	4	....	1971-72	1979-80
Gould, Larry	Van.	1	2	0	0	0	0	....	....	....	....	....	....	1973-74	1973-74
Goulet, Michel	Que., Chi.	15	1089	548	604	1152	825	92	39	39	78	110	....	1979-80	1993-94
Goupille, Red	Mtl.	8	222	12	28	40	256	8	2	0	2	6	....	1935-36	1942-43
Govedaris, Chris	Hfd., Tor.	4	45	4	6	10	24	4	0	0	0	2	....	1989-90	1993-94
Goyer, Gerry	Chi.	1	40	1	2	3	4	3	0	0	0	2	....	1967-68	1967-68
Goyette, Phil	Mtl., NYR, St.L., Buf.	16	941	207	467	674	131	94	17	29	46	26	4	1956-57	1971-72
Graboski, Tony	Mtl.	3	66	6	10	16	24	3	0	0	0	6	....	1940-41	1942-43
• Gracie, Bob	Tor., Bos., NYA, Mtl.M., Mtl., Chi.	9	379	82	109	191	205	33	4	7	11	4	2	1930-31	1938-39
Gradin, Thomas	Van., Bos.	9	677	209	384	593	298	42	17	25	42	20	....	1978-79	1986-87
Graham, Dirk	Min., Chi.	12	772	219	270	489	917	90	17	27	44	92	....	1983-84	1994-95
• Graham, Leth	Ott., Ham.	6	27	3	0	3	0	1	0	0	0	0	1	1920-21	1925-26
Graham, Pat	Pit., Tor.	3	103	11	17	28	136	4	0	0	0	2	....	1981-82	1983-84
Graham, Rod	Bos.	1	14	2	1	3	7	....	....	....	....	....	....	1974-75	1974-75
• Graham, Ted	Chi., Mtl.M., Det., St.L., Bos., NYA	9	346	14	25	39	300	24	3	1	4	30	....	1927-28	1936-37
Granato, Tony	NYR, L.A., S.J.	14	773	248	244	492	1425	79	16	27	43	141	....	1988-89	2000-01
Grant, Danny	Mtl., Min., Det., L.A.	13	736	263	273	536	239	43	10	14	24	19	1	1965-66	1978-79
Gratton, Dan	L.A.	1	7	1	0	1	5	....	....	....	....	....	....	1987-88	1987-88
Gratton, Norm	NYR, Atl., Buf., Min.	5	201	39	44	83	64	6	0	1	1	2	....	1971-72	1975-76
Gravelle, Leo	Mtl., Det.	5	223	44	34	78	42	17	4	1	5	2	....	1946-47	1950-51
Graves, Adam	Det., Edm., NYR, S.J.	16	1152	329	287	616	1224	125	38	27	65	119	2	1987-88	2002-03
Graves, Hilliard	Cal., Atl., Van., Wpg.	9	556	118	163	281	209	2	0	0	0	0	....	1970-71	1979-80
Graves, Steve	Edm.	3	35	5	4	9	10	....	....	....	....	....	....	1983-84	1987-88
• Gray, Alex	NYR, Tor.	2	50	7	0	7	32	13	1	0	1	0	1	1927-28	1928-29
Gray, Terry	Bos., Mtl., L.A., St.L.	6	147	26	28	54	64	35	5	5	10	22	....	1961-62	1970-71
• Green, Red	Ham., NYA, Bos., Det.	6	195	59	26	85	290	1	0	0	0	0	1	1923-24	1928-29
Green, Rick	Wsh., Mtl., Det., NYI	15	845	43	220	263	588	100	3	16	19	73	1	1976-77	1991-92
• Green, Shorty	Ham., NYA	4	103	33	20	53	151	....	....	....	....	....	....	1923-24	1926-27
Green, Ted	Bos.	11	620	48	206	254	1029	31	4	8	12	54	1	1960-61	1971-72
Greenlaw, Jeff	Wsh., Fla.	6	57	3	6	9	108	2	0	0	0	21	....	1986-87	1993-94
Gregg, Randy	Edm., Van.	10	474	41	152	193	333	137	13	38	51	127	5	1981-82	1991-92
Greig, Bruce	Cal.	2	9	0	1	1	46	....	....	....	....	....	....	1973-74	1974-75
‡ Greig, Mark	Hfd., Tor., Cgy., Phi.	9	125	13	27	40	90	5	0	1	1	0	....	1990-91	2002-03
Grenier, Lucien	Mtl., L.A.	4	151	14	14	28	18	2	0	0	0	0	1	1968-69	1971-72
Grenier, Richard	NYI	1	10	1	1	2	2	....	....	....	....	....	....	1972-73	1972-73
Greschner, Ron	NYR	16	982	179	431	610	1226	84	17	32	49	106	....	1974-75	1989-90
‡ Gretzky, Brent	T.B.	2	13	1	3	4	2	....	....	....	....	....	....	1993-94	1994-95
Gretzky, Wayne	Edm., L.A., St.L., NYR	20	1487	894	1963	2857	577	208	122	260	382	66	4	1979-80	1998-99
Grieve, Brent	NYI, Edm., Chi., L.A.	4	97	20	16	36	87	....	....	....	....	....	....	1993-94	1996-97
Grigor, George	Chi.	1	2	1	0	1	0	1	0	0	0	0	....	1943-44	1943-44
Grimson, Stu	Cgy., Chi., Ana., Det., Hfd., Car., L.A., Nsh.	14	729	17	22	39	2113	42	1	1	2	120	....	1988-89	2001-02
Grisdale, John	Tor., Van.	6	250	4	39	43	346	10	0	1	1	15	....	1972-73	1978-79
‡ Groleau, Francois	Mtl.	3	8	0	1	1	6	....	....	....	....	....	....	1995-96	1997-98
‡ Gron, Stanislav	N.J.	1	1	0	0	0	0	....	....	....	....	....	....	2000-01	2000-01
‡ Gronman, Tuomas	Chi., Pit.	2	38	1	3	4	38	1	0	0	0	0	....	1996-97	1997-98
Gronsdahl, Lloyd	Bos.	1	10	1	2	3	0	....	....	....	....	....	....	1941-42	1941-42
Gronstrand, Jari	Min., NYR, Que., NYI	5	185	8	26	34	135	3	0	0	0	4	....	1986-87	1990-91
Gross, Lloyd	Tor., NYA, Bos., Det.	3	62	11	5	16	20	1	0	0	0	0	....	1926-27	1934-35
• Grosso, Don	Det., Chi., Bos.	9	336	87	117	204	90	48	15	14	29	63	1	1938-39	1946-47
Grosvenor, Len	Ott., NYA, Mtl.	6	149	9	11	20	78	4	0	0	0	2	....	1927-28	1932-33
Groulx, Wayne	Que.	1	1	0	0	0	0	....	....	....	....	....	....	1984-85	1984-85
Gruen, Danny	Det., Col.	3	49	9	13	22	19	....	....	....	....	....	....	1972-73	1976-77
Gruhl, Scott	L.A., Pit.	3	20	3	3	6	6	....	....	....	....	....	....	1981-82	1987-88
Gryp, Bob	Bos., Wsh.	3	74	11	13	24	33	....	....	....	....	....	....	1973-74	1975-76
Guay, Francois	Buf.	1	1	0	0	0	0	....	....	....	....	....	....	1989-90	1989-90
Guay, Paul	Phi., L.A., Bos., NYI	7	117	11	23	34	92	9	0	1	1	12	....	1983-84	1990-91
Guerard, Daniel	Ott.	1	2	0	0	0	0	....	....	....	....	....	....	1994-95	1994-95
Guerard, Stephane	Que.	2	34	0	0	0	40	....	....	....	....	....	....	1987-88	1989-90
Guevremont, Jocelyn	Van., Buf., NYR	9	571	84	223	307	319	40	4	17	21	18	....	1971-72	1979-80
Guidolin, Aldo	NYR	4	182	9	15	24	117	....	....	....	....	....	....	1952-53	1955-56
Guidolin, Bep	Bos., Det., Chi.	9	519	107	171	278	606	24	5	7	12	35	....	1942-43	1951-52
Guindon, Bobby	Wpg.	1	6	0	1	1	0	....	....	....	....	....	....	1979-80	1979-80
‡ Guren, Miloslav	Mtl.	2	36	1	3	4	16	....	....	....	....	....	....	1998-99	1999-00
Gusarov, Alexei	Que., Col., NYR, St.L.	11	607	39	128	167	313	68	0	14	14	38	1	1990-91	2000-01
‡ Gusev, Sergey	Dal., T.B.	4	89	4	10	14	34	....	....	....	....	....	....	1997-98	2000-01
‡ Gusmanov, Ravil	Wpg.	1	4	0	0	0	0	....	....	....	....	....	....	1995-96	1995-96
Gustafsson, Bengt-Ake	Wsh.	9	629	196	359	555	196	32	9	19	28	16	....	1979-80	1988-89
‡ Gustafsson, Per	Fla., Tor., Ott.	2	89	8	27	35	38	1	0	0	0	0	....	1996-97	1997-98
Gustavsson, Peter	Col.	1	2	0	0	0	0	....	....	....	....	....	....	1981-82	1981-82
Guy, Kevan	Cgy., Van.	6	156	5	20	25	138	5	0	1	1	23	....	1986-87	1991-92

H

Name	NHL Teams	NHL Seasons	Regular Schedule GP	G	A	TP	PIM	Playoffs GP	G	A	TP	PIM	NHL Cup Wins	First NHL Season	Last NHL Season
Haanpaa, Ari	NYI	3	60	6	11	17	37	6	0	0	0	10	....	1985-86	1987-88
‡ Haas, David	Edm., Cgy.	2	7	2	1	3	7	....	....	....	....	....	....	1990-91	1993-94
Habscheid, Marc	Edm., Min., Det., Cgy.	11	345	72	91	163	171	12	1	3	4	13	....	1981-82	1991-92
Hachborn, Len	Phi., L.A.	3	102	20	39	59	29	7	0	3	3	7	....	1983-84	1985-86
Haddon, Lloyd	Det.	1	8	0	0	0	2	1	0	0	0	0	....	1959-60	1959-60
Hadfield, Vic	NYR, Pit.	16	1002	323	389	712	1154	73	27	21	48	117	....	1961-62	1976-77
• Haggarty, Jim	Mtl.	1	5	1	1	2	0	3	2	1	3	0	....	1941-42	1941-42
Haggerty, Sean	Tor., NYI, Nsh.	4	14	1	2	3	4	....	....	....	....	....	....	1995-96	2000-01
• Hagglund, Roger	Que.	1	3	0	0	0	0	....	....	....	....	....	....	1984-85	1984-85
Hagman, Matti	Bos., Edm.	4	237	56	89	145	36	20	5	2	7	6	....	1976-77	1981-82
Haidy, Gord	Det.	1	....	....	....	....	....	1	0	0	0	0	1	1949-50	1949-50
Hajdu, Richard	Buf.	2	5	0	0	0	4	....	....	....	....	....	....	1985-86	1986-87
Hajt, Bill	Buf.	14	854	42	202	244	433	80	2	16	18	70	....	1973-74	1986-87
Hakansson, Anders	Min., Pit., L.A.	5	330	52	46	98	141	6	0	0	0	2	....	1981-82	1985-86
• Halderson, Harold	Det., Tor.	1	44	3	2	5	65	....	....	....	....	....	....	1926-27	1926-27
Hale, Larry	Phi.	4	196	5	37	42	90	8	0	0	0	12	....	1968-69	1971-72
Haley, Len	Det.	2	30	2	2	4	14	6	1	3	4	6	....	1959-60	1960-61
Halkidis, Bob	Buf., L.A., Tor., Det., T.B., NYI	11	256	8	32	40	825	20	0	1	1	51	....	1984-85	1995-96
‡ Halko, Steven	Car.	6	155	0	15	15	71	4	0	0	0	2	....	1997-98	2002-03
• Hall, Bob	NYA	1	8	0	0	0	0	....	....	....	....	....	....	1925-26	1925-26
Hall, Del	Cal.	3	9	2	0	2	2	....	....	....	....	....	....	1971-72	1973-74
• Hall, Joe	Mtl.	2	38	15	8	23	189	7	0	1	1	38	....	1917-18	1918-19
Hall, Murray	Chi., Det., Min., Van.	9	164	35	48	83	46	6	0	0	0	0	....	1961-62	1971-72
Hall, Taylor	Van., Bos.	5	41	7	9	16	29	....	....	....	....	....	....	1983-84	1987-88
Hall, Wayne	NYR	1	4	0	0	0	0	....	....	....	....	....	....	1960-61	1960-61
Haller, Kevin	Buf., Mtl., Phi., Hfd., Car., Ana., NYI	13	642	41	97	138	907	64	7	16	23	71	1	1989-90	2001-02
• Halliday, Milt	Ott.	3	67	1	0	1	4	6	0	0	0	0	1	1926-27	1928-29
Hallin, Mats	NYI, Min.	5	152	17	14	31	193	15	1	0	1	13	1	1982-83	1986-87
Halverson, Trevor	Wsh.	1	17	0	4	4	28	....	....	....	....	....	....	1998-99	1998-99
Halward, Doug	Bos., L.A., Van., Det., Edm.	14	653	69	224	293	774	47	7	10	17	113	....	1975-76	1988-89
Hamel, Gilles	Buf., Wpg., L.A.	9	519	127	147	274	276	27	4	5	9	10	....	1980-81	1988-89
• Hamel, Herb	Tor.	1	2	0	0	0	4	....	....	....	....	....	....	1930-31	1930-31
Hamel, Jean	St.L., Det., Que., Mtl.	12	699	26	95	121	766	33	0	2	2	44	....	1972-73	1983-84
• Hamill, Red	Bos., Chi.	12	419	128	94	222	160	24	1	2	3	20	1	1937-38	1950-51
Hamilton, Al	NYR, Buf., Edm.	7	257	10	78	88	258	7	0	0	0	2	....	1965-66	1979-80
Hamilton, Chuck	Mtl., St.L.	2	4	0	2	2	2	....	....	....	....	....	....	1961-62	1972-73
• Hamilton, Jack	Tor.	3	102	28	32	60	20	11	2	1	3	0	....	1942-43	1945-46
Hamilton, Jim	Pit.	8	95	14	18	32	28	6	3	0	3	0	....	1977-78	1984-85
• Hamilton, Reg	Tor., Chi.	12	424	21	87	108	412	64	3	8	11	46	2	1935-36	1946-47
Hammarstrom, Inge	Tor., St.L.	6	427	116	123	239	86	13	2	3	5	4	....	1973-74	1978-79
Hammond, Ken	L.A., Edm., NYR, Tor., Bos., S.J., Van., Ott.	8	193	18	29	47	290	15	0	0	0	24	....	1984-85	1992-93
Hampson, Gord	Cgy.	1	4	0	0	0	5	....	....	....	....	....	....	1982-83	1982-83
Hampson, Ted	Tor., NYR, Det., Oak., Cal., Min.	14	676	108	245	353	94	35	7	10	17	2	....	1959-60	1971-72
Hampton, Rick	Cal., Cle., L.A.	6	337	59	113	172	147	2	0	0	0	0	....	1974-75	1979-80
‡ Hamr, Radek	Ott.	2	11	0	0	0	0	....	....	....	....	....	....	1992-93	1993-94
Hamway, Mark	NYI	3	53	5	13	18	9	1	0	0	0	0	....	1984-85	1986-87
Handy, Ron	NYI, St.L.	2	14	0	3	3	0	....	....	....	....	....	....	1984-85	1987-88

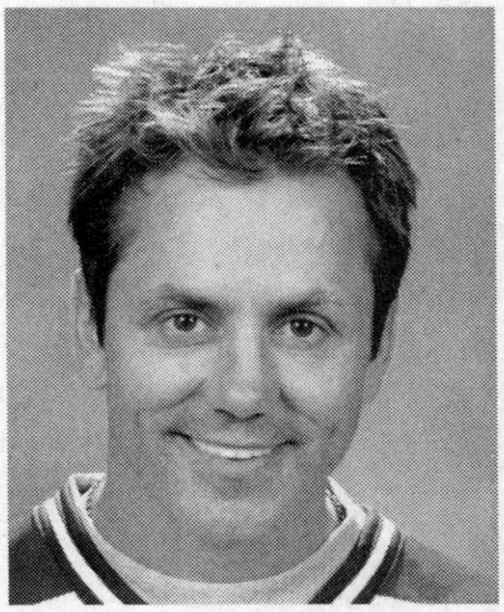

Doug Gilmour

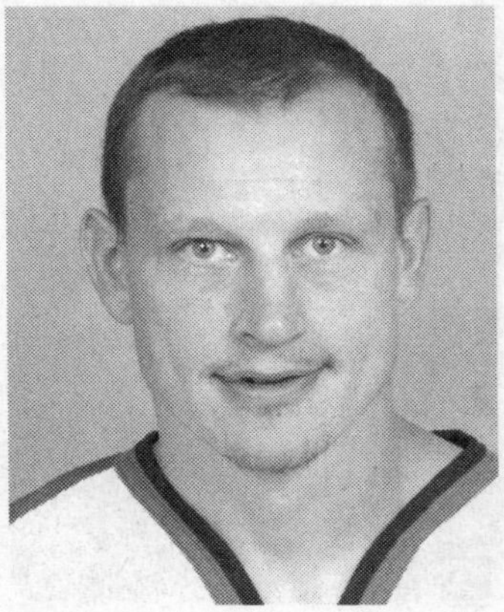

Adam Graves

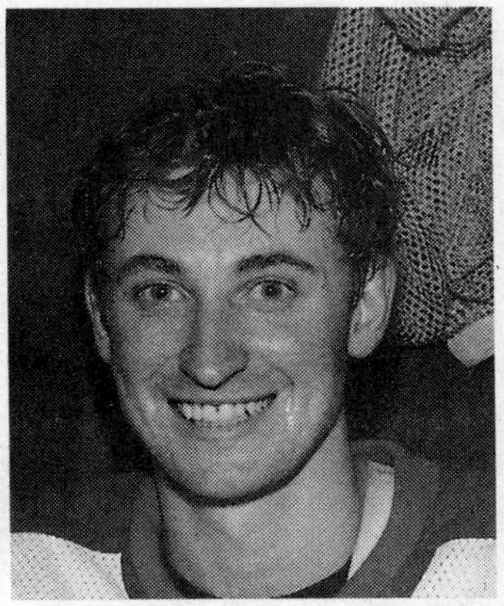

Wayne Gretzky

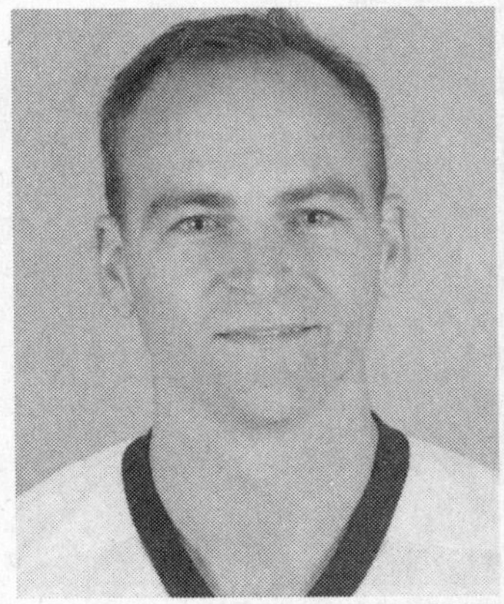

Kevin Haller

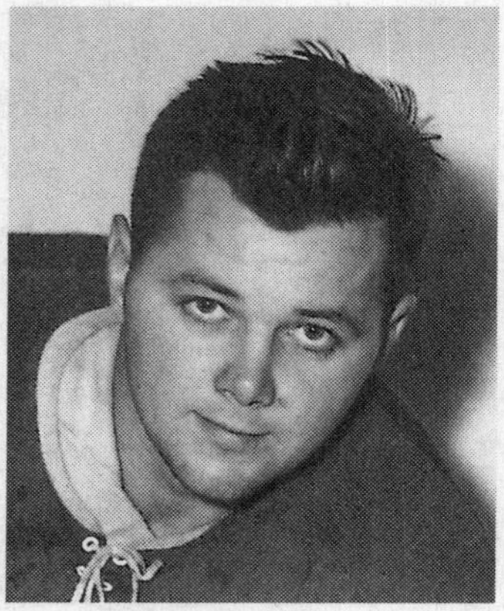

Doug Harvey

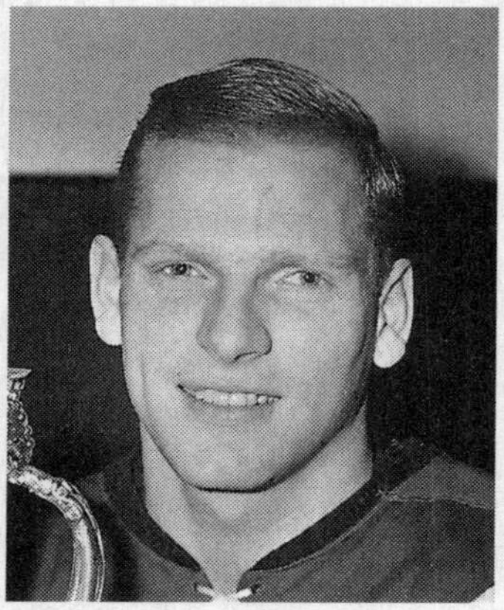

Bill Hay

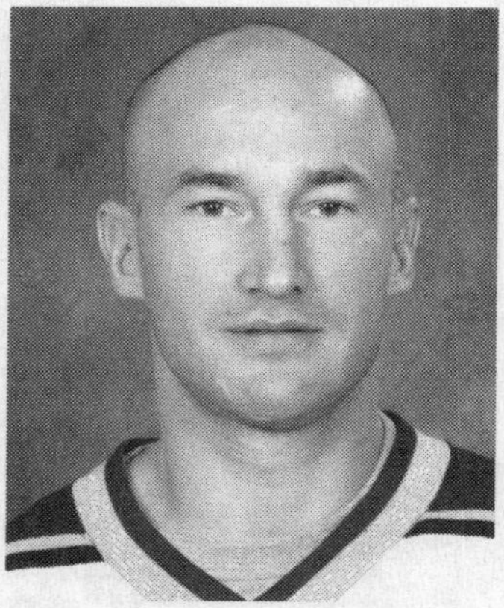

Steve Heinze

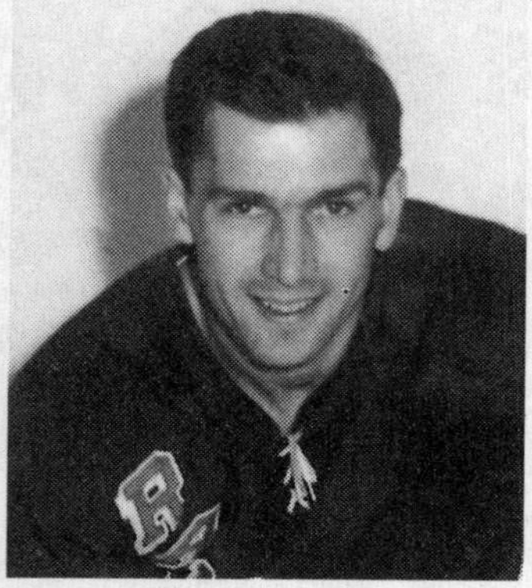

Wally Hergesheimer

Name	NHL Teams	NHL Seasons	Regular Schedule GP	G	A	TP	PIM	Playoffs GP	G	A	TP	PIM	NHL Cup Wins	First NHL Season	Last NHL Season
Hangsleben, Al	Hfd., Wsh., L.A.	3	185	21	48	69	396	....	....	....	....	....	....	1979-80	1981-82
Hankinson, Ben	N.J., T.B.	3	43	3	3	6	45	2	1	0	1	4	....	1992-93	1994-95
Hanna, John	NYR, Mtl., Phi.	5	198	6	26	32	206	....	....	....	....	....	....	1958-59	1967-68
Hannan, Dave	Pit., Edm., Tor., Buf., Col., Ott.	16	841	114	191	305	942	63	6	7	13	46	2	1981-82	1996-97
• Hannigan, Gord	Tor.	4	161	29	31	60	117	9	2	0	2	8	....	1952-53	1955-56
Hannigan, Pat	Tor., NYR, Phi.	5	182	30	39	69	116	11	1	2	3	11	....	1959-60	1968-69
Hannigan, Ray	Tor.	1	3	0	0	0	2	....	....	....	....	....	....	1948-49	1948-49
Hansen, Richie	NYI, St.L.	4	20	2	8	10	4	....	....	....	....	....	....	1976-77	1981-82
Hanson, Dave	Det., Min.	2	33	1	1	2	65	....	....	....	....	....	....	1978-79	1979-80
• Hanson, Emil	Det.	1	7	0	0	0	6	....	....	....	....	....	....	1932-33	1932-33
Hanson, Keith	Cgy.	1	25	0	2	2	77	....	....	....	....	....	....	1983-84	1983-84
• Hanson, Oscar	Chi.	1	8	0	0	0	0	....	....	....	....	....	....	1937-38	1937-38
Harbaruk, Nick	Pit., St.L.	5	364	45	75	120	273	14	3	1	4	20	....	1969-70	1973-74
Harding, Jeff	Phi.	2	15	0	0	0	47	....	....	....	....	....	....	1988-89	1989-90
Hardy, Joe	Oak., Cal.	2	63	9	14	23	51	4	0	0	0	0	....	1969-70	1970-71
Hardy, Mark	L.A., NYR, Min.	15	915	62	306	368	1293	67	5	16	21	158	....	1979-80	1993-94
Hargreaves, Jim	Van.	2	66	1	7	8	105	....	....	....	....	....	....	1970-71	1972-73
‡ Harkins, Brett	Bos., Fla., CBJ	4	78	6	30	36	22	....	....	....	....	....	....	1994-95	2001-02
Harkins, Todd	Cgy., Hfd.	3	48	3	3	6	78	....	....	....	....	....	....	1991-92	1993-94
Harlock, David	Tor., Wsh., NYI, Atl.	8	212	2	14	16	188	....	....	....	....	....	....	1993-94	2001-02
Harlow, Scott	St.L.	1	1	0	1	1	0	....	....	....	....	....	....	1987-88	1987-88
Harmon, Glen	Mtl.	9	452	50	96	146	334	53	5	10	15	37	2	1942-43	1950-51
Harms, John	Chi.	2	44	5	5	10	21	4	3	0	3	2	....	1943-44	1944-45
• Harnott, Walter	Bos.	1	6	0	0	0	2	....	....	....	....	....	....	1933-34	1933-34
Harper, Terry	Mtl., L.A., Det., St.L., Col.	19	1066	35	221	256	1362	112	4	13	17	140	5	1962-63	1980-81
Harrer, Tim	Cgy.	1	3	0	0	0	2	....	....	....	....	....	....	1982-83	1982-83
• Harrington, Hago	Bos., Mtl.	3	72	9	3	12	15	4	1	0	1	2	....	1925-26	1932-33
• Harris, Billy	Tor., Det., Oak., Pit.	13	769	126	219	345	205	62	8	10	18	30	3	1955-56	1968-69
Harris, Billy	NYI, L.A., Tor.	12	897	231	327	558	394	71	19	19	38	48	....	1972-73	1983-84
Harris, Duke	Min., Tor.	1	26	1	4	5	4	....	....	....	....	....	....	1967-68	1967-68
• Harris, Henry	Bos.	1	32	2	4	6	20	....	....	....	....	....	....	1930-31	1930-31
Harris, Hugh	Buf.	1	60	12	26	38	17	3	0	0	0	0	....	1972-73	1972-73
Harris, Ron	Det., Oak., Atl., NYR	11	476	20	91	111	474	28	4	3	7	33	....	1962-63	1975-76
• Harris, Smokey	Bos.	1	6	3	1	4	8	....	....	....	....	....	....	1924-25	1924-25
Harris, Ted	Mtl., Min., Det., St.L., Phi.	12	788	30	168	198	1000	100	1	22	23	230	5	1963-64	1974-75
Harrison, Ed	Bos., NYR	4	194	27	24	51	53	9	1	0	1	2	....	1947-48	1950-51
Harrison, Jim	Bos., Tor., Chi., Edm.	8	324	67	86	153	435	13	1	1	2	43	....	1968-69	1979-80
Hart, Gerry	Det., NYI, Que., St.L.	15	730	29	150	179	1240	78	3	12	15	175	....	1968-69	1982-83
• Hart, Gizzy	Det., Mtl.	3	104	6	8	14	12	8	0	1	1	0	....	1926-27	1932-33
Hartman, Mike	Buf., Wpg., T.B., NYR	9	397	43	35	78	1388	21	0	0	0	106	1	1986-87	1994-95
Hartsburg, Craig	Min.	10	570	98	315	413	818	61	15	27	42	70	....	1979-80	1988-89
Harvey, Buster	Min., Atl., K.C., Det.	7	407	90	118	208	131	14	0	2	2	8	....	1970-71	1976-77
• Harvey, Doug	Mtl., NYR, Det., St.L.	20	1113	88	452	540	1216	137	8	64	72	152	6	1947-48	1968-69
Harvey, Hugh	K.C.	2	18	1	1	2	4	....	....	....	....	....	....	1974-75	1975-76
Hassard, Bob	Tor., Chi.	5	126	9	28	37	22	....	....	....	....	....	1	1949-50	1954-55
Hatcher, Kevin	Wsh., Dal., Pit., NYR, Car.	17	1157	227	450	677	1392	118	22	37	59	252	....	1984-85	2000-01
Hatoum, Ed	Det., Van.	3	47	3	6	9	25	....	....	....	....	....	....	1968-69	1970-71
‡ Hauer, Brett	Edm., Nsh.	3	37	4	4	8	38	....	....	....	....	....	....	1995-96	2001-02
Hawerchuk, Dale	Wpg., Buf., St.L., Phi.	16	1188	518	891	1409	730	97	30	69	99	67	....	1981-82	1996-97
‡ Hawgood, Greg	Bos., Edm., Phi., Fla., Pit., S.J., Van., Dal.	12	474	60	164	224	426	42	2	8	10	37	....	1987-88	2001-02
Hawkins, Todd	Van., Tor.	3	10	0	0	0	15	....	....	....	....	....	....	1988-89	1991-92
Haworth, Alan	Buf., Wsh., Que.	8	524	189	211	400	425	42	12	16	28	28	....	1980-81	1987-88
Haworth, Gord	NYR	1	2	0	1	1	0	....	....	....	....	....	....	1952-53	1952-53
Hawryliw, Neil	NYI	1	1	0	0	0	0	....	....	....	....	....	....	1981-82	1981-82
Hay, Bill	Chi.	8	506	113	273	386	244	67	15	21	36	62	1	1959-60	1966-67
• Hay, George	Chi., Det.	7	239	74	60	134	84	8	2	3	5	2	....	1926-27	1933-34
Hay, Jim	Det.	3	75	1	5	6	22	9	1	0	1	2	1	1952-53	1954-55
Hayek, Peter	Min.	1	1	0	0	0	0	....	....	....	....	....	....	1981-82	1981-82
Hayes, Chris	Bos.	1	....	....	....	....	....	1	0	0	0	0	1	1971-72	1971-72
• Haynes, Paul	Mtl.M., Bos., Mtl.	11	391	61	134	195	164	24	2	8	10	13	....	1930-31	1940-41
Hayward, Rick	L.A.	1	4	0	0	0	5	....	....	....	....	....	....	1990-91	1990-91
Hazlett, Steve	Van.	1	1	0	0	0	0	....	....	....	....	....	....	1979-80	1979-80
Head, Galen	Det.	1	1	0	0	0	0	....	....	....	....	....	....	1967-68	1967-68
• Headley, Fern	Bos., Mtl.	1	30	1	3	4	10	1	0	0	0	0	....	1924-25	1924-25
Healey, Rich	Det.	1	1	0	0	0	2	....	....	....	....	....	....	1960-61	1960-61
Heaphy, Shawn	Cgy.	1	1	0	0	0	0	....	....	....	....	....	....	1992-93	1992-93
Heaslip, Mark	NYR, L.A.	3	117	10	19	29	110	5	0	0	0	2	....	1976-77	1978-79
Heath, Randy	NYR	2	13	2	4	6	15	....	....	....	....	....	....	1984-85	1985-86
Hebenton, Andy	NYR, Bos.	9	630	189	202	391	83	22	6	5	11	8	....	1955-56	1963-64
‡ Hecl, Radoslav	Buf.	1	14	0	0	0	2	....	....	....	....	....	....	2002-03	2002-03
Hedberg, Anders	NYR	7	465	172	225	397	144	58	22	24	46	31	....	1978-79	1984-85
• Heffernan, Frank	Tor.	1	19	0	1	1	10	....	....	....	....	....	....	1919-20	1919-20
Heffernan, Gerry	Mtl.	3	83	33	35	68	27	11	3	3	6	8	1	1941-42	1943-44
Heidt, Mike	L.A.	1	6	0	1	1	7	....	....	....	....	....	....	1983-84	1983-84
• Heindl, Bill	Min., NYR	3	18	2	1	3	0	....	....	....	....	....	....	1970-71	1972-73
Heinrich, Lionel	Bos.	1	35	1	1	2	33	....	....	....	....	....	....	1955-56	1955-56
Heinze, Steve	Bos., CBJ, Buf., L.A.	12	694	178	158	336	379	69	11	15	26	48	....	1991-92	2002-03
Heiskala, Earl	Phi.	3	127	13	11	24	294	....	....	....	....	....	....	1968-69	1970-71
Helander, Peter	L.A.	1	7	0	1	1	0	....	....	....	....	....	....	1982-83	1982-83
‡ Helenius, Sami	Cgy., T.B., Col., Dal., Chi.	6	155	2	4	6	260	1	0	0	0	0	....	1996-97	2002-03
• Heller, Ott	NYR	15	647	55	176	231	465	61	6	8	14	61	2	1931-32	1945-46
Helman, Harry	Ott.	3	44	1	0	1	7	2	0	0	0	0	1	1922-23	1924-25
‡ Helminen, Raimo	NYR, Min., NYI	3	117	13	46	59	16	2	0	0	0	0	....	1985-86	1988-89
• Hemmerling, Tony	NYA	2	22	3	3	6	4	....	....	....	....	....	....	1935-36	1936-37
Henderson, Archie	Wsh., Min., Hfd.	3	23	3	1	4	92	....	....	....	....	....	....	1980-81	1982-83
‡ Henderson, Matt	Nsh., Chi.	2	6	0	1	1	2	....	....	....	....	....	....	1998-99	2001-02
Henderson, Murray	Bos.	8	405	24	62	86	305	41	2	3	5	23	....	1944-45	1951-52
Henderson, Paul	Det., Tor., Atl.	13	707	236	241	477	304	56	11	14	25	28	....	1962-63	1979-80
Hendrickson, John	Det.	3	5	0	0	0	4	....	....	....	....	....	....	1957-58	1961-62
Henning, Lorne	NYI	9	544	73	111	184	102	81	7	7	14	8	2	1972-73	1980-81
• Henry, Camille	NYR, Chi., St.L.	14	727	279	249	528	88	47	6	12	18	7	....	1953-54	1969-70
Henry, Dale	NYI	6	132	13	26	39	263	14	1	0	1	19	....	1984-85	1989-90
‡ Hentunen, Jukka	Cgy., Nsh.	1	38	4	5	9	4	....	....	....	....	....	....	2001-02	2001-02
Hepple, Alan	N.J.	3	3	0	0	0	7	....	....	....	....	....	....	1983-84	1985-86
Herbers, Ian	Edm., T.B., NYI	2	65	0	5	5	79	....	....	....	....	....	....	1993-94	1999-00
• Herberts, Jimmy	Bos., Tor., Det.	6	206	83	31	114	253	9	3	0	3	10	....	1924-25	1929-30
Herchenratter, Art	Det.	1	10	1	2	3	2	....	....	....	....	....	....	1940-41	1940-41
Hergerts, Fred	NYA	2	20	2	4	6	2	....	....	....	....	....	....	1934-35	1935-36
Hergesheimer, Phil	Chi., Bos.	4	125	21	41	62	19	6	0	0	0	2	....	1939-40	1942-43
Hergesheimer, Wally	NYR, Chi.	7	351	114	85	199	106	5	1	0	1	0	....	1951-52	1958-59
• Heron, Red	Tor., Bro., Mtl.	4	106	21	19	40	38	21	2	2	4	6	....	1938-39	1941-42
Heroux, Yves	Que.	1	1	0	0	0	0	....	....	....	....	....	....	1986-87	1986-87
Herter, Jason	NYI	1	1	0	1	1	0	....	....	....	....	....	....	1995-96	1995-96
Hervey, Matt	Wpg., Bos., T.B.	3	35	0	5	5	97	5	0	0	0	6	....	1988-89	1992-93
Hess, Bob	St.L., Buf., Hfd.	8	329	27	95	122	178	4	1	1	2	2	....	1974-75	1983-84
‡ Heward, Jamie	Tor., Nsh., NYI, CBJ	6	239	25	45	70	116	....	....	....	....	....	....	1995-96	2001-02
• Heximer, Obs	NYR, Bos., NYA	3	84	13	7	20	16	5	0	0	0	2	....	1929-30	1934-35
• Hextall, Bryan	NYR	11	449	187	175	362	227	37	8	9	17	19	1	1936-37	1947-48
Hextall, Bryan	NYR, Pit., Atl., Det., Min.	8	549	99	161	260	738	18	0	4	4	59	....	1962-63	1975-76
Hextall, Dennis	NYR, L.A., Cal., Min., Det., Wsh.	13	681	153	350	503	1398	22	3	3	6	45	....	1967-68	1979-80
Heyliger, Vic	Chi.	2	33	2	3	5	2	....	....	....	....	....	....	1937-38	1943-44
Hicke, Bill	Mtl., NYR, Oak., Cal., Pit.	14	729	168	234	402	395	42	3	10	13	41	2	1958-59	1971-72
Hicke, Ernie	Cal., Atl., NYI, Min., L.A.	8	520	132	140	272	407	2	1	0	1	0	....	1970-71	1977-78
Hickey, Greg	NYR	1	1	0	0	0	0	....	....	....	....	....	....	1977-78	1977-78
Hickey, Pat	NYR, Col., Tor., Que., St.L.	10	646	192	212	404	351	55	5	11	16	37	....	1975-76	1984-85
Hicks, Alex	Ana., Pit., S.J., Fla.	5	258	25	54	79	247	15	0	2	2	8	....	1995-96	1999-00
Hicks, Doug	Min., Chi., Edm., Wsh.	9	561	37	131	168	442	18	2	1	3	15	....	1974-75	1982-83
Hicks, Glenn	Det.	2	108	6	12	18	127	....	....	....	....	....	....	1979-80	1980-81
• Hicks, Henry	Mtl.M., Det.	3	96	7	2	9	72	....	....	....	....	....	....	1928-29	1930-31
Hicks, Wayne	Chi., Bos., Mtl., Phi., Pit.	5	115	13	23	36	22	2	0	1	1	2	1	1959-60	1967-68
Hidi, Andre	Wsh.	2	7	2	1	3	9	2	0	0	0	0	....	1983-84	1984-85
Hiemer, Uli	N.J.	3	143	19	54	73	176	....	....	....	....	....	....	1984-85	1986-87
‡ Higgins, Matt	Mtl.	4	57	1	2	3	6	....	....	....	....	....	....	1997-98	2000-01
Higgins, Paul	Tor.	2	25	0	0	0	152	1	0	0	0	0	....	1981-82	1982-83
Higgins, Tim	Chi., N.J., Det.	11	706	154	198	352	719	65	5	8	13	77	....	1978-79	1988-89

Name	NHL Teams	NHL Seasons	Regular Schedule GP	G	A	TP	PIM	Playoffs GP	G	A	TP	PIM	NHL Cup Wins	First NHL Season	Last NHL Season
Hildebrand, Ike	NYR, Chi.	2	41	7	11	18	16	....	....	....	....	....	....	1953-54	1954-55
Hill, Al	Phi.	8	221	40	55	95	227	51	8	11	19	43	....	1976-77	1987-88
Hill, Brian	Hfd.	1	19	1	1	2	4	....	....	....	....	....	....	1979-80	1979-80
• Hill, Mel	Bos., Bro., Tor.	9	324	89	109	198	128	43	12	7	19	18	3	1937-38	1945-46
Hiller, Dutch	NYR, Det., Bos., Mtl.	9	383	91	113	204	163	48	9	8	17	21	2	1937-38	1945-46
Hiller, Jim	L.A., Det., NYR	2	63	8	12	20	116	2	0	0	0	4	....	1992-93	1993-94
Hillier, Randy	Bos., Pit., NYI, Buf.	11	543	16	110	126	906	28	0	2	2	93	1	1981-82	1991-92
Hillman, Floyd	Bos.	1	6	0	0	0	10	....	....	....	....	....	....	1956-57	1956-57
Hillman, Larry	Det., Bos., Tor., Min., Mtl., Phi., L.A., Buf.	19	790	36	196	232	579	74	2	9	11	30	6	1954-55	1972-73
• Hillman, Wayne	Chi., NYR, Min., Phi.	13	691	18	86	104	534	28	0	3	3	19	1	1960-61	1972-73
Hilworth, John	Det.	3	57	1	1	2	89	....	....	....	....	....	....	1977-78	1979-80
• Himes, Normie	NYA	9	402	106	113	219	127	2	0	0	0	0	....	1926-27	1934-35
Hindmarch, Dave	Cgy.	4	99	21	17	38	25	10	0	0	0	6	....	1980-81	1983-84
Hinse, Andre	Tor.	1	4	0	0	0	0	....	....	....	....	....	....	1967-68	1967-68
Hinton, Dan	Chi.	1	14	0	0	0	16	....	....	....	....	....	....	1976-77	1976-77
Hirsch, Tom	Min.	3	31	1	7	8	30	12	0	0	0	6	....	1983-84	1987-88
• Hirschfeld, Bert	Mtl.	2	33	1	4	5	2	5	1	0	1	0	....	1949-50	1950-51
Hislop, Jamie	Que., Cgy.	5	345	75	103	178	86	28	3	2	5	11	....	1979-80	1983-84
• Hitchman, Lionel	Ott., Bos.	12	417	28	34	62	523	35	3	1	4	73	2	1922-23	1933-34
Hlinka, Ivan	Van.	2	137	42	81	123	28	16	3	10	13	8	....	1981-82	1982-83
‡ Hlushko, Todd	Phi., Cgy., Pit.	6	79	8	13	21	84	3	0	0	0	2	....	1993-94	1998-99
Hocking, Justin	L.A.	1	1	0	0	0	0	....	....	....	....	....	....	1993-94	1993-94
Hodge, Ken	Chi., Bos., NYR	14	881	328	472	800	779	97	34	47	81	120	2	1964-65	1977-78
Hodge Jr., Ken	Min., Bos., T.B.	4	142	39	48	87	32	15	4	6	10	6	....	1988-89	1992-93
‡ Hodgson, Dan	Tor., Van.	4	114	29	45	74	64	....	....	....	....	....	....	1985-86	1988-89
Hodgson, Rick	Hfd.	1	6	0	0	0	6	1	0	0	0	0	....	1979-80	1979-80
Hodgson, Ted	Bos.	1	4	0	0	0	0	....	....	....	....	....	....	1966-67	1966-67
Hoekstra, Cec	Mtl.	1	4	0	0	0	0	....	....	....	....	....	....	1959-60	1959-60
Hoekstra, Ed	Phi.	1	70	15	21	36	6	7	0	1	1	0	....	1967-68	1967-68
Hoene, Phil	L.A.	3	37	2	4	6	22	....	....	....	....	....	....	1972-73	1974-75
Hoffinger, Val	Chi.	2	28	0	1	1	30	....	....	....	....	....	....	1927-28	1928-29
Hoffman, Mike	Hfd.	3	9	1	3	4	2	....	....	....	....	....	....	1982-83	1985-86
Hoffmeyer, Bob	Chi., Phi., N.J.	6	198	14	52	66	325	3	0	1	1	25	....	1977-78	1984-85
Hofford, Jim	Buf., L.A.	3	18	0	0	0	47	....	....	....	....	....	....	1985-86	1988-89
Hogaboam, Bill	Atl., Det., Min.	8	332	80	109	189	100	2	0	0	0	0	....	1972-73	1979-80
Hoganson, Dale	L.A., Mtl., Que.	7	343	13	77	90	186	11	0	3	3	12	....	1969-70	1981-82
‡ Hoglund, Jonas	Cgy., Mtl., Tor.	7	545	117	145	262	112	59	8	11	19	8	....	1996-97	2002-03
Hogue, Benoit	Buf., NYI, Tor., Dal., T.B., Phx., Bos., Wsh.	15	863	222	321	543	877	92	17	16	33	124	1	1987-88	2001-02
Holan, Milos	Phi., Ana.	3	49	5	11	16	42	....	....	....	....	....	....	1993-94	1995-96
Holbrook, Terry	Min.	2	43	3	6	9	4	6	0	0	0	0	....	1972-73	1973-74
Holland, Jerry	NYR	2	37	8	4	12	6	....	....	....	....	....	....	1974-75	1975-76
• Hollett, Flash	Tor., Ott., Bos., Det.	13	562	132	181	313	358	79	8	26	34	38	2	1933-34	1945-46
‡ Hollinger, Terry	St.L.	2	7	0	0	0	2	....	....	....	....	....	....	1993-94	1994-95
• Hollingworth, Gord	Chi., Det.	4	163	4	14	18	201	3	0	0	0	2	....	1954-55	1957-58
Holloway, Bruce	Van.	1	2	0	0	0	0	....	....	....	....	....	....	1984-85	1984-85
• Holmes, Bill	Mtl., NYA	3	52	6	4	10	35	....	....	....	....	....	....	1925-26	1929-30
Holmes, Chuck	Det.	2	23	1	3	4	10	....	....	....	....	....	....	1958-59	1961-62
Holmes, Lou	Chi.	2	59	1	4	5	6	2	0	0	0	2	....	1931-32	1932-33
Holmes, Warren	L.A.	3	45	8	18	26	7	....	....	....	....	....	....	1981-82	1983-84
Holmgren, Paul	Phi., Min.	10	527	144	179	323	1684	82	19	32	51	195	....	1975-76	1984-85
• Holota, John	Det.	2	15	2	0	2	0	....	....	....	....	....	....	1942-43	1945-46
Holst, Greg	NYR	3	11	0	0	0	0	....	....	....	....	....	....	1975-76	1977-78
Holt, Gary	Cal., Cle., St.L.	5	101	13	11	24	133	....	....	....	....	....	....	1973-74	1977-78
Holt, Randy	Chi., Cle., Van., L.A., Cgy., Wsh., Phi.	10	395	4	37	41	1438	21	2	3	5	83	....	1974-75	1983-84
• Holway, Albert	Tor., Mtl.M., Pit.	5	112	7	2	9	48	6	0	0	0	0	1	1923-24	1928-29
Homenuke, Ron	Van.	1	1	0	0	0	0	....	....	....	....	....	....	1972-73	1972-73
Hoover, Ron	Bos., St.L.	3	18	4	0	4	31	8	0	0	0	18	....	1989-90	1991-92
Hopkins, Dean	L.A., Edm., Que.	6	223	23	51	74	306	18	1	5	6	29	....	1979-80	1988-89
Hopkins, Larry	Tor., Wpg.	4	60	13	16	29	26	6	0	0	0	2	....	1977-78	1982-83
Horacek, Tony	Phi., Chi.	5	154	10	19	29	316	2	1	0	1	2	....	1989-90	1994-95
Horava, Miloslav	NYR	3	80	5	17	22	38	2	0	1	1	0	....	1988-89	1990-91
Horbul, Doug	K.C.	1	4	1	0	1	2	....	....	....	....	....	....	1974-75	1974-75
Hordy, Mike	NYI	2	11	0	0	0	7	....	....	....	....	....	....	1978-79	1979-80
Horeck, Pete	Chi., Det., Bos.	8	426	106	118	224	340	34	6	8	14	43	....	1944-45	1951-52
• Horne, George	Mtl.M., Tor.	3	54	9	3	12	34	4	0	0	0	4	1	1925-26	1928-29
Horner, Red	Tor.	12	490	42	110	152	1254	71	7	10	17	170	1	1928-29	1939-40
• Hornung, Larry	St.L.	2	48	2	9	11	10	11	0	2	2	2	....	1970-71	1971-72
• Horton, Tim	Tor., NYR, Pit., Buf.	24	1446	115	403	518	1611	126	11	39	50	183	4	1949-50	1973-74
Horvath, Bronco	NYR, Mtl., Bos., Chi., Tor., Min.	9	434	141	185	326	319	36	12	9	21	18	....	1955-56	1967-68
Hospodar, Ed	NYR, Hfd., Phi., Min., Buf.	9	450	17	51	68	1314	44	4	1	5	208	....	1979-80	1987-88
Hostak, Martin	Phi.	2	55	3	11	14	24	....	....	....	....	....	....	1990-91	1991-92
Hotham, Greg	Tor., Pit.	6	230	15	74	89	139	5	0	3	3	6	....	1979-80	1984-85
Houck, Paul	Min.	3	16	1	2	3	2	....	....	....	....	....	....	1985-86	1987-88
Houda, Doug	Det., Hfd., L.A., Buf., NYI, Ana.	15	561	19	63	82	1104	18	0	3	3	21	....	1985-86	2002-03
Houde, Claude	K.C.	2	59	3	6	9	40	....	....	....	....	....	....	1974-75	1975-76
‡ Houde, Eric	Mtl.	3	30	2	3	5	4	....	....	....	....	....	....	1996-97	1998-99
Hough, Mike	Que., Fla., NYI	13	707	100	156	256	675	42	5	5	10	38	....	1986-87	1998-99
Houlder, Bill	Wsh., Buf., Ana., St.L., T.B., S.J., Nsh.	16	846	59	191	250	412	30	5	6	11	14	....	1987-88	2002-03
Houle, Rejean	Mtl.	11	635	161	247	408	395	90	14	34	48	66	5	1969-70	1982-83
Housley, Phil	Buf., Wpg., St.L., Cgy., N.J., Wsh., Chi., Tor.	21	1495	338	894	1232	822	85	13	43	56	36	....	1982-83	2002-03
Houston, Ken	Atl., Cgy., Wsh., L.A.	9	570	161	167	328	624	35	10	9	19	66	....	1975-76	1983-84
Howard, Jack	Tor.	1	2	0	0	0	0	....	....	....	....	....	....	1936-37	1936-37
Howatt, Garry	NYI, Hfd., N.J.	12	720	112	156	268	1836	87	12	14	26	289	2	1972-73	1983-84
Howe, Gordie	Det., Hfd.	26	1767	801	1049	1850	1685	157	68	92	160	220	4	1946-47	1979-80
Howe, Mark	Hfd., Phi., Det.	16	929	197	545	742	455	101	10	51	61	34	....	1979-80	1994-95
Howe, Marty	Hfd., Bos.	6	197	2	29	31	99	15	1	2	3	9	....	1979-80	1984-85
• Howe, Syd	Ott., Phi., Tor., St.L., Det.	17	698	237	291	528	212	70	17	27	44	10	3	1929-30	1945-46
Howe, Vic	NYR	3	33	3	4	7	10	....	....	....	....	....	....	1950-51	1954-55
Howell, Harry	NYR, Oak., Cal., L.A.	21	1411	94	324	418	1298	38	3	3	6	32	....	1952-53	1972-73
• Howell, Ron	NYR	2	4	0	0	0	0	....	....	....	....	....	....	1954-55	1955-56
Howse, Don	L.A.	1	33	2	5	7	6	2	0	0	0	0	....	1979-80	1979-80
Howson, Scott	NYI	2	18	5	3	8	4	....	....	....	....	....	....	1984-85	1985-86
Hoyda, Dave	Phi., Wpg.	4	132	6	17	23	299	12	0	0	0	17	....	1977-78	1980-81
Hrdina, Jiri	Cgy., Pit.	5	250	45	85	130	92	46	2	5	7	24	3	1987-88	1991-92
Hrechkosy, Dave	Cal., St.L.	4	140	42	24	66	41	3	1	0	1	2	....	1973-74	1976-77
Hrycuik, Jim	Wsh.	1	21	5	5	10	12	....	....	....	....	....	....	1974-75	1974-75
Hrymnak, Steve	Chi., Det.	2	18	2	1	3	4	2	0	0	0	0	....	1951-52	1952-53
Hrynewich, Tim	Pit.	2	55	6	8	14	82	....	....	....	....	....	....	1982-83	1983-84
Huard, Bill	Bos., Ott., Que., Dal., Edm., L.A.	8	223	16	18	34	594	5	0	0	0	2	....	1992-93	1999-00
Huard, Rolly	Tor.	1	1	1	0	1	0	....	....	....	....	....	....	1930-31	1930-31
Huber, Willie	Det., NYR, Van., Phi.	10	655	104	217	321	950	33	5	5	10	35	....	1978-79	1987-88
Hubick, Greg	Tor., Van.	2	77	6	9	15	10	....	....	....	....	....	....	1975-76	1979-80
Huck, Fran	Mtl., St.L.	3	94	24	30	54	38	11	3	4	7	2	....	1969-70	1972-73
Hucul, Fred	Chi., St.L.	5	164	11	30	41	113	6	1	0	1	10	....	1950-51	1967-68
Huddy, Charlie	Edm., L.A., Buf., St.L.	17	1017	99	354	453	785	183	19	66	85	135	5	1980-81	1996-97
Hudson, Dave	NYI, K.C., Col.	6	409	59	124	183	89	2	1	1	2	0	....	1972-73	1977-78
Hudson, Lex	Pit.	1	2	0	0	0	0	2	0	0	0	0	....	1978-79	1978-79
Hudson, Mike	Chi., Edm., NYR, Pit., Tor., St.L., Phx.	9	416	49	87	136	414	49	4	10	14	64	1	1988-89	1996-97
Hudson, Ron	Det.	2	33	5	2	7	2	....	....	....	....	....	....	1937-38	1939-40
Huffman, Kerry	Phi., Que., Ott.	10	401	37	108	145	361	11	0	0	0	2	....	1986-87	1995-96
Huggins, Al	Mtl.M.	1	20	1	1	2	2	....	....	....	....	....	....	1930-31	1930-31
Hughes, Albert	NYA	2	60	6	8	14	22	....	....	....	....	....	....	1930-31	1931-32
Hughes, Brent	L.A., Phi., St.L., Det., K.C.	8	435	15	117	132	440	22	1	3	4	53	....	1967-68	1974-75
Hughes, Brent	Wpg., Bos., Buf., NYI	8	357	41	39	80	831	29	4	1	5	53	....	1988-89	1996-97
Hughes, Frank	Cal.	1	5	0	0	0	0	....	....	....	....	....	....	1971-72	1971-72
Hughes, Howie	L.A.	3	168	25	32	57	30	14	2	0	2	2	....	1967-68	1969-70
Hughes, Jack	Col.	2	46	2	5	7	104	....	....	....	....	....	....	1980-81	1981-82
Hughes, James	Det.	1	40	0	1	1	48	....	....	....	....	....	....	1929-30	1929-30
Hughes, John	Van., Edm., NYR	2	70	2	14	16	211	7	0	1	1	16	....	1979-80	1980-81
Hughes, Pat	Mtl., Pit., Edm., Buf., St.L., Hfd.	10	573	130	128	258	646	71	8	25	33	77	3	1977-78	1986-87
Hughes, Ryan	Bos.	1	3	0	0	0	0	....	....	....	....	....	....	1995-96	1995-96
Hull, Bobby	Chi., Wpg., Hfd.	16	1063	610	560	1170	640	119	62	67	129	102	1	1957-58	1979-80
Hull, Dennis	Chi., Det.	14	959	303	351	654	261	104	33	34	67	30	....	1964-65	1977-78

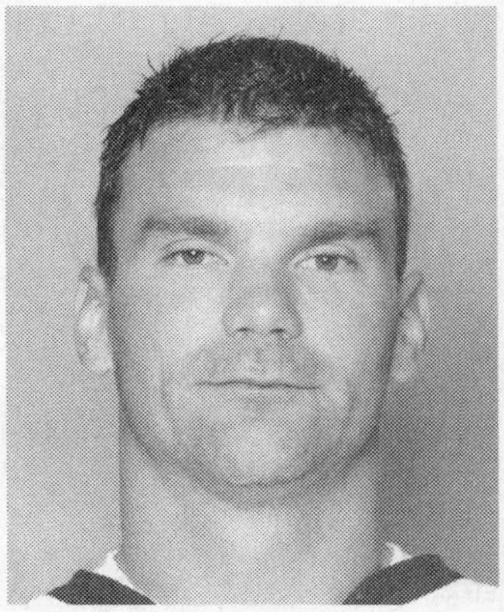
Jonas Hoglund

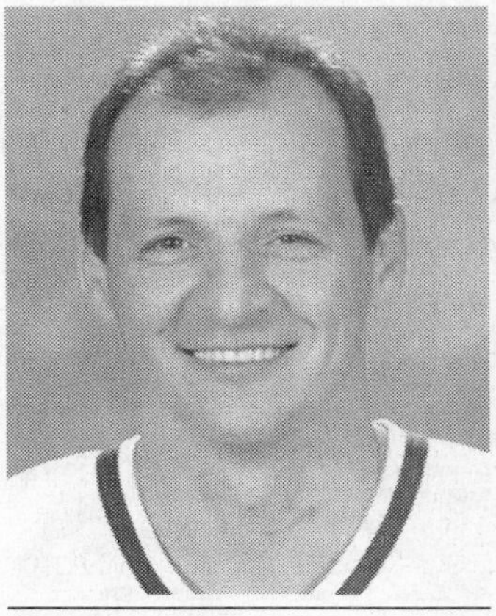
Benoit Hogue

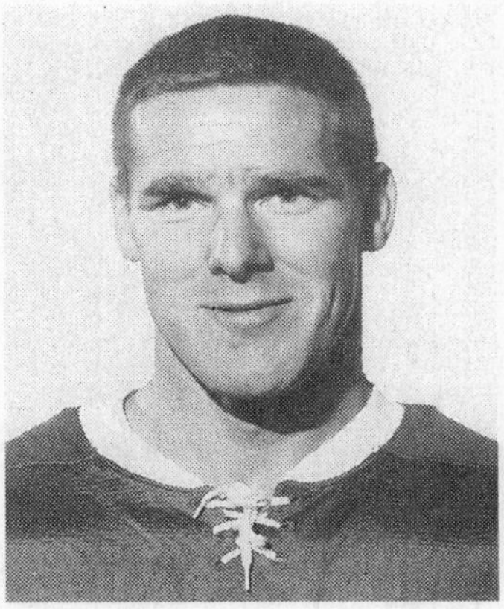
Tim Horton

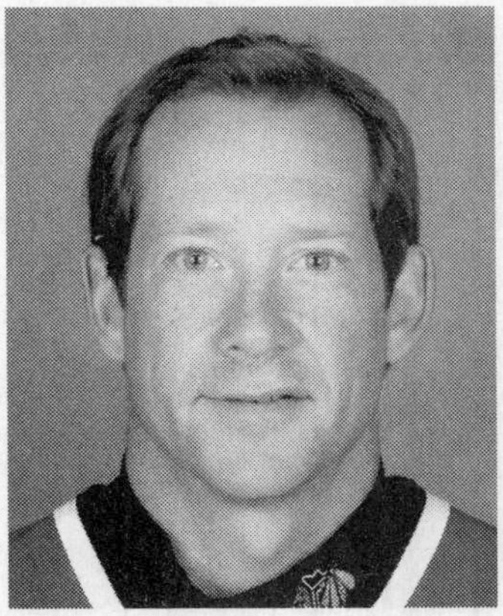
Phil Housley

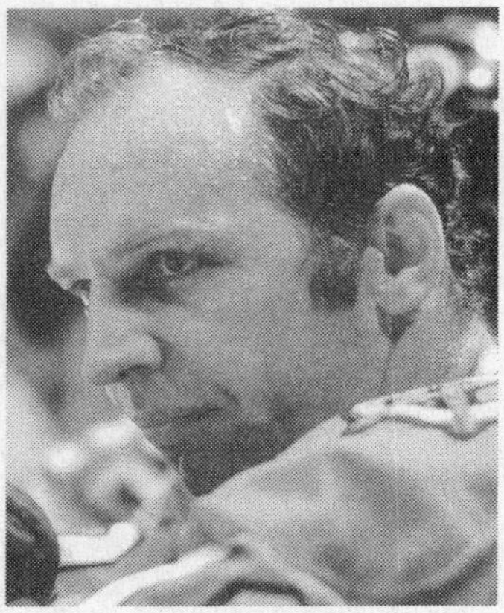

Dennis Hull

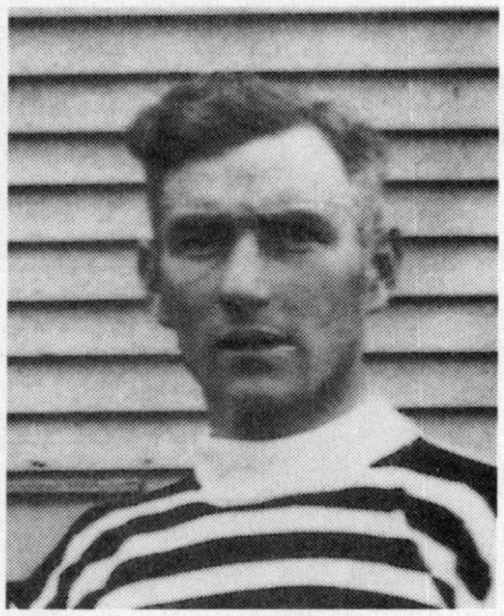

Dick Irvin

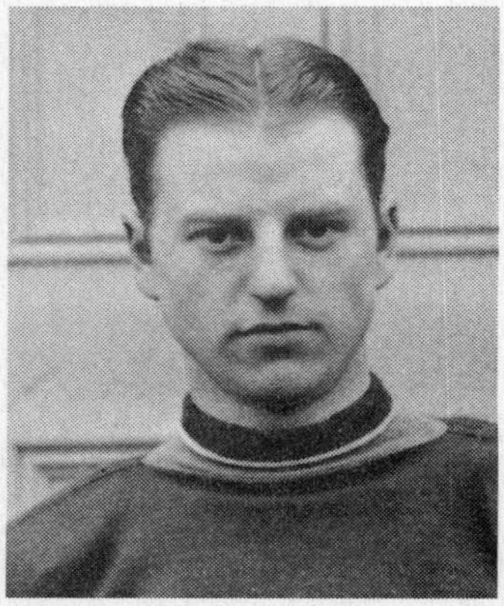

Aurel Joliat

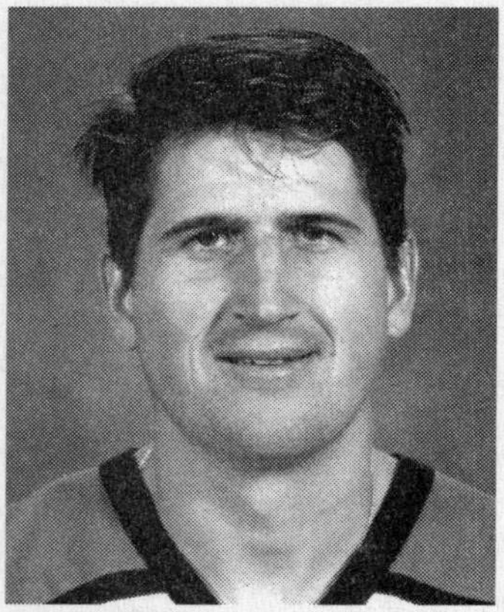

Keith Jones

			Regular Schedule					Playoffs					NHL	First	Last
Name	NHL Teams	NHL Seasons	GP	G	A	TP	PIM	GP	G	A	TP	PIM	Cup Wins	NHL Season	NHL Season
• Hunt, Fred	NYA, NYR	2	59	15	14	29	6	....	....	....	....	....	....	1940-41	1944-45
Hunter, Dale	Que., Wsh., Col.	19	1407	323	697	1020	3565	186	42	76	118	729	....	1980-81	1998-99
Hunter, Dave	Edm., Pit., Wpg.	10	746	133	190	323	918	105	16	24	40	211	3	1979-80	1988-89
Hunter, Mark	Mtl., St.L., Cgy., Hfd., Wsh.	12	628	213	171	384	1426	79	18	20	38	230	1	1981-82	1992-93
Hunter, Tim	Cgy., Que., Van., S.J.	16	815	62	76	138	3146	132	5	7	12	426	1	1981-82	1996-97
Huras, Larry	NYR	1	2	0	0	0	0	....	....	....	....	....	....	1976-77	1976-77
Hurlburt, Bob	Van.	1	1	0	0	0	2	....	....	....	....	....	....	1974-75	1974-75
Hurlbut, Mike	NYR, Que., Buf.	5	29	1	8	9	20	....	....	....	....	....	....	1992-93	1999-00
Hurley, Paul	Bos.	1	1	0	1	1	0	....	....	....	....	....	....	1968-69	1968-69
Hurst, Ron	Tor.	2	64	9	7	16	70	3	0	2	2	4	....	1955-56	1956-57
Huscroft, Jamie	N.J., Bos., Cgy., T.B., Van., Phx., Wsh.	10	352	5	33	38	1065	21	0	1	1	46	....	1988-89	1999-00
Huska, Ryan	Chi.	1	1	0	0	0	0	....	....	....	....	....	....	1997-98	1997-98
Huston, Ron	Cal.	2	79	15	31	46	8	....	....	....	....	....	....	1973-74	1974-75
Hutchinson, Ron	NYR	1	9	0	0	0	0	....	....	....	....	....	....	1960-61	1960-61
Hutchison, Dave	L.A., Tor., Chi., N.J.	10	584	19	97	116	1550	48	2	12	14	149	....	1974-75	1983-84
• Hutton, Bill	Bos., Ott., Phi.	2	64	3	2	5	8	2	0	0	0	0	....	1929-30	1930-31
• Hyland, Harry	Mtl.W., Ott.	1	17	14	2	16	65	....	....	....	....	....	....	1917-18	1917-18
Hynes, Dave	Bos.	2	22	4	0	4	2	....	....	....	....	....	....	1973-74	1974-75
Hynes, Gord	Bos., Phi.	2	52	3	9	12	22	12	1	2	3	6	....	1991-92	1992-93

I

Name	NHL Teams	NHL Seasons	GP	G	A	TP	PIM	GP	G	A	TP	PIM	Cup Wins	First NHL Season	Last NHL Season
Iafrate, Al	Tor., Wsh., Bos., S.J.	12	799	152	311	463	1301	71	19	16	35	77	....	1984-85	1997-98
‡ Ignatjev, Victor	Pit.	1	11	0	1	1	6	1	0	0	0	2	....	1998-99	1998-99
‡ Ihnacak, Miroslav	Tor., Det.	3	56	8	9	17	39	1	0	0	0	0	....	1985-86	1988-89
Ihnacak, Peter	Tor.	8	417	102	165	267	175	28	4	10	14	25	....	1982-83	1989-90
Imlach, Brent	Tor.	2	3	0	0	0	0	....	....	....	....	....	....	1965-66	1966-67
Ingarfield, Earl	NYR, Pit., Oak., Cal.	13	746	179	226	405	239	21	9	8	17	10	....	1958-59	1970-71
Ingarfield, Earl	Atl., Cgy., Det.	2	39	4	4	8	22	2	0	1	1	0	....	1979-80	1980-81
Inglis, Billy	L.A., Buf.	3	36	1	3	4	4	11	1	2	3	4	....	1967-68	1970-71
• Ingoldsby, Johnny	Tor.	2	29	5	1	6	15	....	....	....	....	....	....	1942-43	1943-44
Ingram, Frank	Chi.	3	101	24	16	40	69	11	0	1	1	2	....	1929-30	1931-32
• Ingram, John	Bos.	1	1	0	0	0	0	....	....	....	....	....	....	1924-25	1924-25
Ingram, Ron	Chi., Det., NYR	4	114	5	15	20	81	2	0	0	0	0	....	1956-57	1964-65
‡ Intranuovo, Ralph	Edm., Tor.	3	22	2	4	6	4	....	....	....	....	....	....	1994-95	1996-97
• Irvin, Dick	Chi.	3	94	29	23	52	78	2	2	0	2	4	....	1926-27	1928-29
Irvine, Ted	Bos., L.A., NYR, St.L.	11	724	154	177	331	657	83	16	24	40	115	....	1963-64	1976-77
Irwin, Ivan	Mtl., NYR	5	155	2	27	29	214	5	0	0	0	8	....	1952-53	1957-58
Isaksson, Ulf	L.A.	1	50	7	15	22	10	....	....	....	....	....	....	1982-83	1982-83
Issel, Kim	Edm.	1	4	0	0	0	0	....	....	....	....	....	....	1988-89	1988-89

J

Name	NHL Teams	NHL Seasons	GP	G	A	TP	PIM	GP	G	A	TP	PIM	Cup Wins	First NHL Season	Last NHL Season
• Jackson, Art	Tor., Bos., NYA	11	468	123	178	301	144	52	8	12	20	29	2	1934-35	1944-45
• Jackson, Busher	Tor., NYA, Bos.	15	633	241	234	475	437	71	18	12	30	53	1	1929-30	1943-44
Jackson, Dane	Van., Buf., NYI	4	45	12	6	18	58	6	0	0	0	10	....	1993-94	1997-98
Jackson, Don	Min., Edm., NYR	10	311	16	52	68	640	53	4	5	9	147	2	1977-78	1986-87
• Jackson, Harold	Chi., Det.	8	219	17	34	51	208	31	1	2	3	33	2	1936-37	1946-47
Jackson, Jack	Chi.	1	48	2	5	7	38	....	....	....	....	....	....	1946-47	1946-47
Jackson, Jeff	Tor., NYR, Que., Chi.	8	263	38	48	86	313	6	1	1	2	16	....	1984-85	1991-92
Jackson, Jim	Cgy., Buf.	4	112	17	30	47	20	14	3	2	5	6	....	1982-83	1987-88
• Jackson, Lloyd	NYA	1	14	1	1	2	0	....	....	....	....	....	....	1936-37	1936-37
• Jackson, Stan	Tor., Bos., Ott.	5	86	9	6	15	75	....	....	....	....	....	1	1921-22	1926-27
Jackson, Walter	NYA, Bos.	4	84	16	11	27	18	....	....	....	....	....	....	1932-33	1935-36
• Jacobs, Paul	Tor.	1	1	0	0	0	0	....	....	....	....	....	....	1918-19	1918-19
Jacobs, Tim	Cal.	1	46	0	10	10	35	....	....	....	....	....	....	1975-76	1975-76
Jalo, Risto	Edm.	1	3	0	3	3	0	....	....	....	....	....	....	1985-86	1985-86
Jalonen, Kari	Cgy., Edm.	2	37	9	6	15	4	5	1	0	1	0	....	1982-83	1983-84
James, Gerry	Tor.	5	149	14	26	40	257	15	1	0	1	8	....	1954-55	1959-60
James, Val	Buf., Tor.	2	11	0	0	0	30	....	....	....	....	....	....	1981-82	1986-87
Jamieson, Jim	NYR	1	1	0	1	1	0	....	....	....	....	....	....	1943-44	1943-44
Jankowski, Lou	Det., Chi.	4	127	19	18	37	15	1	0	0	0	0	....	1950-51	1954-55
Janney, Craig	Bos., St.L., S.J., Wpg., Phx., T.B., NYI	12	760	188	563	751	170	120	24	86	110	53	....	1987-88	1998-99
Janssens, Mark	NYR, Min., Hfd., Ana., NYI, Phx., Chi.	14	711	40	73	113	1422	27	5	1	6	33	....	1987-88	2000-01
‡ Jantunen, Marko	Cgy.	1	3	0	0	0	0	....	....	....	....	....	....	1996-97	1996-97
Jarrett, Doug	Chi., NYR	13	775	38	182	220	631	99	7	16	23	82	....	1964-65	1976-77
Jarrett, Gary	Tor., Det., Oak., Cal.	7	341	72	92	164	131	11	3	1	4	9	....	1960-61	1971-72
Jarry, Pierre	NYR, Tor., Det., Min.	7	344	88	117	205	142	5	0	1	1	0	....	1971-72	1977-78
Jarvenpaa, Hannu	Wpg.	3	114	11	26	37	83	....	....	....	....	....	....	1986-87	1988-89
‡ Jarventie, Martti	Mtl.	1	1	0	0	0	0	....	....	....	....	....	....	2001-02	2001-02
Jarvi, Iiro	Que.	2	116	18	43	61	58	....	....	....	....	....	....	1988-89	1989-90
Jarvis, Doug	Mtl., Wsh., Hfd.	13	964	139	264	403	263	105	14	27	41	42	4	1975-76	1987-88
• Jarvis, James	Pit., Phi., Tor.	3	112	17	15	32	62	....	....	....	....	....	....	1929-30	1936-37
Jarvis, Wes	Wsh., Min., L.A., Tor.	9	237	31	55	86	98	2	0	0	0	2	....	1979-80	1987-88
Javanainen, Arto	Pit.	1	14	4	1	5	2	....	....	....	....	....	....	1984-85	1984-85
Jay, Bob	L.A.	1	3	0	1	1	0	....	....	....	....	....	....	1993-94	1993-94
Jeffrey, Larry	Det., Tor., NYR	8	368	39	62	101	293	38	4	10	14	42	1	1961-62	1968-69
Jelinek, Tomas	Ott.	1	49	7	6	13	52	....	....	....	....	....	....	1992-93	1992-93
Jenkins, Dean	L.A.	1	5	0	0	0	2	....	....	....	....	....	....	1983-84	1983-84
Jenkins, Roger	Chi., Tor., Mtl., Bos., Mtl.M., NYA	8	325	15	39	54	253	25	1	7	8	12	2	1930-31	1938-39
Jennings, Bill	Det., Bos.	5	108	32	33	65	45	20	4	4	8	6	....	1940-41	1944-45
Jennings, Grant	Wsh., Hfd., Pit., Tor., Buf.	9	389	14	43	57	804	54	2	1	3	68	2	1987-88	1995-96
Jensen, Chris	NYR, Phi.	6	74	9	12	21	27	....	....	....	....	....	....	1985-86	1991-92
Jensen, David	Min.	3	18	0	2	2	11	....	....	....	....	....	....	1983-84	1985-86
Jensen, David	Hfd., Wsh.	4	69	9	13	22	22	11	0	0	0	2	....	1984-85	1987-88
Jensen, Steve	Min., L.A.	7	438	113	107	220	318	12	0	3	3	9	....	1975-76	1981-82
• Jeremiah, Ed	NYA, Bos.	1	15	0	1	1	0	....	....	....	....	....	....	1931-32	1931-32
Jerrard, Paul	Min.	1	5	0	0	0	4	....	....	....	....	....	....	1988-89	1988-89
• Jerwa, Frank	Bos., St.L.	4	81	11	16	27	53	....	....	....	....	....	....	1931-32	1934-35
• Jerwa, Joe	NYR, Bos., NYA	7	234	29	58	87	309	17	2	3	5	16	....	1930-31	1938-39
Jirik, Jaroslav	St.L.	1	3	0	0	0	0	....	....	....	....	....	....	1969-70	1969-70
• Joanette, Rosario	Mtl.	1	2	0	1	1	4	....	....	....	....	....	....	1944-45	1944-45
Jodzio, Rick	Col., Cle.	1	70	2	8	10	71	....	....	....	....	....	....	1977-78	1977-78
Johannesen, Glenn	NYI	1	2	0	0	0	0	....	....	....	....	....	....	1985-86	1985-86
Johannson, John	N.J.	1	5	0	0	0	0	....	....	....	....	....	....	1983-84	1983-84
• Johansen, Bill	Tor.	1	1	0	0	0	0	....	....	....	....	....	....	1949-50	1949-50
Johansen, Trevor	Tor., Col., L.A.	5	286	11	46	57	282	13	0	3	3	21	....	1977-78	1981-82
Johansson, Bjorn	Cle.	2	15	1	1	2	10	....	....	....	....	....	....	1976-77	1977-78
‡ Johansson, Mathias	Cgy., Pit.	1	58	5	10	15	16	....	....	....	....	....	....	2002-03	2002-03
Johansson, Roger	Cgy., Chi.	4	161	9	34	43	163	5	0	1	1	2	....	1989-90	1994-95
Johns, Don	NYR, Mtl., Min.	6	153	2	21	23	76	....	....	....	....	....	....	1960-61	1967-68
Johnson, Allan	Mtl., Det.	4	105	21	28	49	30	11	2	2	4	6	....	1956-57	1962-63
Johnson, Brian	Det.	1	3	0	0	0	5	....	....	....	....	....	....	1983-84	1983-84
• Johnson, Ching	NYR, NYA	12	436	38	48	86	808	61	5	2	7	161	2	1926-27	1937-38
• Johnson, Danny	Tor., Van., Det.	3	121	18	19	37	24	....	....	....	....	....	....	1969-70	1971-72
Johnson, Earl	Det.	1	1	0	0	0	0	....	....	....	....	....	....	1953-54	1953-54
Johnson, Jim	NYR, Phi., L.A.	8	302	75	111	186	73	7	0	2	2	2	....	1964-65	1971-72
Johnson, Jim	Pit., Min., Dal., Wsh., Phx.	13	829	29	166	195	1197	51	1	11	12	132	....	1985-86	1997-98
Johnson, Mark	Pit., Min., Hfd., St.L., N.J.	11	669	203	305	508	260	37	16	12	28	10	....	1979-80	1989-90
Johnson, Norm	Bos., Chi.	3	61	5	20	25	41	14	4	0	4	6	....	1957-58	1959-60
Johnson, Terry	Que., St.L., Cgy., Tor.	9	285	3	24	27	580	38	0	4	4	118	....	1979-80	1987-88
Johnson, Tom	Mtl., Bos.	17	978	51	213	264	960	111	8	15	23	109	6	1947-48	1964-65
• Johnson, Virgil	Chi.	3	75	1	11	12	27	19	0	3	3	4	1	1937-38	1944-45
Johnston, Bernie	Hfd.	2	57	12	24	36	16	3	0	1	1	0	....	1979-80	1980-81
Johnston, George	Chi.	4	58	20	12	32	2	....	....	....	....	....	....	1941-42	1946-47
Johnston, Greg	Bos., Tor.	9	187	26	29	55	124	22	2	1	3	12	....	1983-84	1991-92
Johnston, Jay	Wsh.	2	8	0	0	0	13	....	....	....	....	....	....	1980-81	1981-82
Johnston, Joey	Min., Cal., Chi.	6	331	85	106	191	320	....	....	....	....	....	....	1968-69	1975-76
Johnston, Larry	L.A., Det., K.C., Col.	7	320	9	64	73	580	....	....	....	....	....	....	1967-68	1976-77
Johnston, Marshall	Min., Cal.	7	251	14	52	66	58	6	0	0	0	2	....	1967-68	1973-74
Johnston, Randy	NYI	1	4	0	0	0	4	....	....	....	....	....	....	1979-80	1979-80
Johnstone, Eddie	NYR, Det.	10	426	122	136	258	375	55	13	10	23	83	....	1975-76	1986-87
Johnstone, Ross	Tor.	2	42	5	4	9	14	3	0	0	0	0	1	1943-44	1944-45
• Joliat, Aurel	Mtl.	16	655	270	190	460	771	46	9	13	22	66	3	1922-23	1937-38
• Joliat, Rene	Mtl.	1	1	0	0	0	0	....	....	....	....	....	....	1924-25	1924-25
Joly, Greg	Wsh., Det.	9	365	21	76	97	250	5	0	0	0	8	....	1974-75	1982-83

Name	NHL Teams	NHL Seasons	Regular Schedule GP	G	A	TP	PIM	Playoffs GP	G	A	TP	PIM	NHL Cup Wins	First NHL Season	Last NHL Season
Joly, Yvan	Mtl.	3	2	0	0	0	0	1	0	0	0	0	....	1979-80	1982-83
‡ Jomphe, Jean-Francois	Ana., Phx., Mtl.	4	111	10	29	39	102	....	....	....	....	....	....	1995-96	1998-99
Jonathan, Stan	Bos., Pit.	8	411	91	110	201	751	63	8	4	12	137	....	1975-76	1982-83
Jones, Bob	NYR	1	2	0	0	0	0	....	....	....	....	....	....	1968-69	1968-69
Jones, Brad	Wpg., L.A., Phi.	6	148	25	31	56	122	9	1	1	2	2	....	1986-87	1991-92
Jones, Buck	Det., Tor.	4	50	2	2	4	36	12	0	1	1	18	....	1938-39	1942-43
Jones, Jim	Cal.	1	2	0	0	0	0	....	....	....	....	....	....	1971-72	1971-72
Jones, Jimmy	Tor.	3	148	13	18	31	68	19	1	5	6	11	....	1977-78	1979-80
Jones, Keith	Wsh., Col., Phi.	9	491	117	141	258	765	63	12	12	24	120	....	1992-93	2000-01
Jones, Ron	Bos., Pit., Wsh.	5	54	1	4	5	31	....	....	....	....	....	....	1971-72	1975-76
‡ Jonsson, Jorgen	NYI, Ana.	1	81	12	19	31	16	....	....	....	....	....	....	1999-00	1999-00
Jonsson, Tomas	NYI, Edm.	8	552	85	259	344	482	80	11	26	37	97	2	1981-82	1988-89
Joseph, Chris	Pit., Edm., T.B., Van., Phi., Phx., Atl.	14	510	39	112	151	567	31	3	4	7	24	....	1987-88	2000-01
Joseph, Tony	Wpg.	1	2	1	0	1	0	....	....	....	....	....	....	1988-89	1988-89
Joyal, Eddie	Det., Tor., L.A., Phi.	9	466	128	134	262	103	50	11	8	19	18	....	1962-63	1971-72
Joyce, Bob	Bos., Wsh., Wpg.	6	158	34	49	83	90	46	15	9	24	29	....	1987-88	1992-93
Joyce, Duane	Dal.	1	3	0	0	0	0	....	....	....	....	....	....	1993-94	1993-94
● Juckes, Bing	NYR	2	16	2	1	3	6	....	....	....	....	....	....	1947-48	1949-50
‡ Juhlin, Patrik	Phi.	2	56	7	6	13	23	13	1	0	1	2	....	1994-95	1995-96
Julien, Claude	Que.	2	14	0	1	1	25	....	....	....	....	....	....	1984-85	1985-86
‡ Junker, Steve	NYI	2	5	0	0	0	0	3	0	1	1	0	....	1992-93	1993-94
Jutila, Timo	Buf.	1	10	1	5	6	13	....	....	....	....	....	....	1984-85	1984-85
Juzda, Bill	NYR, Tor.	9	398	14	54	68	398	42	0	3	3	46	2	1940-41	1951-52
K															
Kabel, Bob	NYR	2	48	5	13	18	34	....	....	....	....	....	....	1959-60	1960-61
Kachowski, Mark	Pit.	3	64	6	5	11	209	....	....	....	....	....	....	1987-88	1989-90
Kachur, Ed	Chi.	2	96	10	14	24	35	....	....	....	....	....	....	1956-57	1957-58
Kaese, Trent	Buf.	1	1	0	0	0	0	....	....	....	....	....	....	1988-89	1988-89
Kaiser, Vern	Mtl.	1	50	7	5	12	33	2	0	0	0	0	....	1950-51	1950-51
● Kalbfleish, Walter	Ott., St.L., NYA, Bos.	4	36	0	4	4	32	5	0	0	0	2	....	1933-34	1936-37
● Kaleta, Alex	Chi., NYR	7	387	92	121	213	190	17	1	6	7	2	....	1941-42	1950-51
‡ Kallio, Tomi	Atl., CBJ, Phi.	3	140	24	31	55	48	....	....	....	....	....	....	2000-01	2002-03
Kallur, Anders	NYI	6	383	101	110	211	149	78	12	23	35	32	4	1979-80	1984-85
‡ Kamensky, Valeri	Que., Col., NYR, Dal., N.J.	11	637	200	301	501	383	66	25	35	60	72	1	1991-92	2001-02
Kaminski, Kevin	Min., Que., Wsh.	7	139	3	10	13	528	8	0	0	0	52	....	1988-89	1996-97
● Kaminsky, Max	Ott., Bos., St.L., Mtl.M.	4	130	22	34	56	38	4	0	0	0	0	....	1933-34	1936-37
Kaminsky, Yan	Wpg., NYI	2	26	3	2	5	4	2	0	0	0	4	....	1993-94	1994-95
● Kampman, Bingo	Tor.	5	189	14	30	44	287	47	1	4	5	38	1	1937-38	1941-42
Kane, Francis	Det.	1	2	0	0	0	0	....	....	....	....	....	....	1943-44	1943-44
Kannegiesser, Gord	St.L.	2	23	0	1	1	15	....	....	....	....	....	....	1967-68	1971-72
Kannegiesser, Sheldon	Pit., NYR, L.A., Van.	8	366	14	67	81	292	18	0	2	2	10	....	1970-71	1977-78
Karabin, Ladislav	Pit.	1	9	0	0	0	2	....	....	....	....	....	....	1993-94	1993-94
Karalahti, Jere	L.A., Nsh.	3	149	8	19	27	97	17	0	1	1	20	....	1999-00	2001-02
Karamnov, Vitali	St.L.	3	92	12	20	32	65	2	0	0	0	2	....	1992-93	1994-95
Karjalainen, Kyosti	L.A.	1	28	1	8	9	12	3	0	1	1	2	....	1991-92	1991-92
Karlander, Al	Det.	4	212	36	56	92	70	4	0	1	1	0	....	1969-70	1972-73
‡ Karlsson, Andreas	Atl.	3	153	11	27	38	50	....	....	....	....	....	....	1999-00	2001-02
‡ Karpa, Dave	Que., Ana., Car., NYR	12	557	18	80	98	1374	19	1	1	2	39	....	1991-92	2002-03
‡ Karpov, Valeri	Ana.	3	76	14	15	29	32	....	....	....	....	....	....	1994-95	1996-97
Kasatonov, Alexei	N.J., Ana., St.L., Bos.	7	383	38	122	160	326	33	4	7	11	40	....	1989-90	1995-96
Kasper, Steve	Bos., L.A., Phi., T.B.	13	821	177	291	468	554	94	20	28	48	82	....	1980-81	1992-93
Kastelic, Ed	Wsh., Hfd.	7	220	11	10	21	719	8	1	0	1	32	....	1985-86	1991-92
Kaszycki, Mike	NYI, Wsh., Tor.	5	226	42	80	122	108	19	2	6	8	10	....	1977-78	1982-83
● Kea, Ed	Atl., St.L.	10	583	30	145	175	508	32	2	4	6	39	....	1973-74	1982-83
Kearns, Dennis	Van.	10	677	31	290	321	386	11	1	2	3	8	....	1971-72	1980-81
● Keating, Jack	Det.	2	11	3	0	3	4	....	....	....	....	....	....	1938-39	1939-40
● Keating, John	NYA	2	35	5	5	10	17	....	....	....	....	....	....	1931-32	1932-33
Keating, Mike	NYR	1	1	0	0	0	0	....	....	....	....	....	....	1977-78	1977-78
● Keats, Duke	Bos., Det., Chi.	3	82	30	19	49	113	....	....	....	....	....	....	1926-27	1928-29
Keczmer, Dan	Min., Hfd., Cgy., Dal., Nsh.	10	235	8	38	46	212	12	0	1	1	8	....	1990-91	1999-00
● Keeling, Butch	Tor., NYR	12	525	157	63	220	331	47	11	11	22	34	1	1926-27	1937-38
Keenan, Larry	Tor., St.L., Buf., Phi.	6	233	38	64	102	28	46	15	16	31	12	....	1961-62	1971-72
Kehoe, Rick	Tor., Pit.	14	906	371	396	767	120	39	4	17	21	4	....	1971-72	1984-85
Kekalainen, Jarmo	Bos., Ott.	5	55	5	8	13	28	....	....	....	....	....	....	1989-90	1993-94
Kelleher, Chris	Bos.	1	1	0	0	0	0	....	....	....	....	....	....	2001-02	2001-02
Keller, Ralph	NYR	1	3	1	0	1	6	....	....	....	....	....	....	1962-63	1962-63
Kellgren, Christer	Col.	1	5	0	0	0	0	....	....	....	....	....	....	1981-82	1981-82
Kelly, Bob	Phi., Wsh.	12	837	154	208	362	1454	101	9	14	23	172	2	1970-71	1981-82
Kelly, Bob	St.L., Pit., Chi.	6	425	87	109	196	687	23	6	3	9	40	....	1973-74	1978-79
Kelly, Dave	Det.	1	16	2	0	2	4	....	....	....	....	....	....	1976-77	1976-77
Kelly, John Paul	L.A.	7	400	54	70	124	366	18	1	1	2	41	....	1979-80	1985-86
● Kelly, Pep	Tor., Chi., Bro.	8	288	74	53	127	105	38	7	6	13	10	....	1934-35	1941-42
Kelly, Pete	St.L., Det., NYA, Bro.	7	177	21	38	59	68	19	3	1	4	2	2	1934-35	1941-42
Kelly, Red	Det., Tor.	20	1316	281	542	823	327	164	33	59	92	51	8	1947-48	1966-67
● Kemp, Kevin	Hfd.	1	3	0	0	0	4	....	....	....	....	....	....	1980-81	1980-81
Kemp, Stan	Tor.	1	1	0	0	0	2	....	....	....	....	....	....	1948-49	1948-49
‡ Kenady, Chris	St.L., NYR	2	7	0	2	2	0	....	....	....	....	....	....	1997-98	1999-00
● Kendall, Bill	Chi., Tor.	5	131	16	10	26	28	6	0	0	0	0	1	1933-34	1937-38
Kennedy, Dean	L.A., NYR, Buf., Wpg., Edm.	12	717	26	108	134	1118	36	1	7	8	59	....	1982-83	1994-95
Kennedy, Forbes	Chi., Det., Bos., Phi., Tor.	11	603	70	108	178	988	12	2	4	6	64	....	1956-57	1968-69
‡ Kennedy, Mike	Dal., Tor., NYI	5	145	16	36	52	112	5	0	0	0	9	....	1994-95	1998-99
Kennedy, Sheldon	Det., Cgy., Bos.	8	310	49	58	107	233	24	6	4	10	20	....	1989-90	1996-97
Kennedy, Ted	Tor.	14	696	231	329	560	432	78	29	31	60	32	5	1942-43	1956-57
● Kenny, Ernest	NYR, Chi.	2	10	0	0	0	18	....	....	....	....	....	....	1930-31	1934-35
Keon, Dave	Tor., Hfd.	18	1296	396	590	986	117	92	32	36	68	6	4	1960-61	1981-82
‡ Kerch, Alexander	Edm.	1	5	0	0	0	2	....	....	....	....	....	....	1993-94	1993-94
Kerr, Alan	NYI, Det., Wpg.	9	391	72	94	166	826	38	5	4	9	70	....	1984-85	1992-93
Kerr, Reg	Cle., Chi., Edm.	6	263	66	94	160	169	7	1	0	1	7	....	1977-78	1983-84
Kerr, Tim	Phi., NYR, Hfd.	13	655	370	304	674	596	81	40	31	71	58	....	1980-81	1992-93
Kesa, Dan	Van., Dal., Pit., T.B.	4	139	8	22	30	66	13	1	0	1	0	....	1993-94	1999-00
Kessell, Rick	Pit., Cal.	5	135	4	24	28	6	....	....	....	....	....	....	1969-70	1973-74
Ketola, Veli-Pekka	Col.	1	44	9	5	14	4	....	....	....	....	....	....	1981-82	1981-82
Ketter, Kerry	Atl.	1	41	0	2	2	58	....	....	....	....	....	....	1972-73	1972-73
Kharin, Sergei	Wpg.	1	7	2	3	5	2	....	....	....	....	....	....	1990-91	1990-91
‡ Kharitonov, Alexander	T.B., NYI	2	71	7	15	22	12	....	....	....	....	....	....	2000-01	2001-02
Khmylev, Yuri	Buf., St.L.	5	263	64	88	152	133	26	8	6	14	24	....	1992-93	1996-97
‡ Khristich, Dmitri	Wsh., L.A., Bos., Tor.	12	811	259	337	596	422	75	15	25	40	41	....	1990-91	2001-02
Kidd, Ian	Van.	2	20	4	7	11	25	....	....	....	....	....	....	1987-88	1988-89
Kiessling, Udo	Min.	1	1	0	0	0	2	....	....	....	....	....	....	1981-82	1981-82
Kilrea, Brian	Det., L.A.	2	26	3	5	8	12	....	....	....	....	....	....	1957-58	1967-68
● Kilrea, Hec	Ott., Det., Tor.	15	633	167	129	296	438	48	8	7	15	18	3	1925-26	1939-40
● Kilrea, Ken	Det.	5	91	16	23	39	8	15	2	2	4	4	....	1938-39	1943-44
● Kilrea, Wally	Ott., Phi., NYA, Mtl.M., Det.	9	329	35	58	93	87	25	2	4	6	6	2	1929-30	1937-38
Kimble, Darin	Que., St.L., Bos., Chi.	7	311	23	20	43	1082	23	0	0	0	52	....	1988-89	1994-95
Kindrachuk, Orest	Phi., Pit., Wsh.	10	508	118	261	379	648	76	20	20	40	53	2	1972-73	1981-82
King, Derek	NYI, Hfd., Tor., St.L.	14	830	261	351	612	417	47	4	17	21	24	....	1986-87	1999-00
King, Frank	Mtl.	1	10	1	0	1	2	....	....	....	....	....	....	1950-51	1950-51
King, Kris	Det., NYR, Wpg., Phx., Tor., Chi.	14	849	66	85	151	2030	67	8	5	13	142	....	1987-88	2000-01
King, Steven	NYR, Ana.	3	67	17	8	25	75	....	....	....	....	....	....	1992-93	1995-96
King, Wayne	Cal.	3	73	5	18	23	34	....	....	....	....	....	....	1973-74	1975-76
Kinnear, Geordie	Atl.	1	4	0	0	0	13	....	....	....	....	....	....	1999-00	1999-00
Kinsella, Brian	Wsh.	2	10	0	1	1	0	....	....	....	....	....	....	1975-76	1976-77
● Kinsella, Ray	Ott.	1	14	0	0	0	0	....	....	....	....	....	....	1930-31	1930-31
‡ Kiprusoff, Marko	Mtl., NYI	2	51	0	10	10	12	....	....	....	....	....	....	1995-96	2001-02
● Kirk, Bobby	NYR	1	39	4	8	12	14	....	....	....	....	....	....	1937-38	1937-38
Kirkpatrick, Bob	NYR	1	49	12	12	24	6	....	....	....	....	....	....	1942-43	1942-43
Kirton, Mark	Tor., Det., Van.	6	266	57	56	113	121	4	1	2	3	7	....	1979-80	1984-85
Kisio, Kelly	Det., NYR, S.J., Cgy.	13	761	229	429	658	768	39	6	15	21	52	....	1982-83	1994-95
Kitchen, Bill	Mtl., Tor.	4	41	1	4	5	40	3	0	1	1	0	....	1981-82	1984-85
● Kitchen, Hobie	Mtl.M., Det.	2	47	5	4	9	58	....	....	....	....	....	1	1925-26	1926-27
Kitchen, Mike	Col., N.J.	8	474	12	62	74	370	2	0	0	0	2	....	1976-77	1983-84
Kjellberg, Patric	Mtl., Nsh., Ana.	6	394	64	96	160	84	10	0	0	0	0	....	1992-93	2002-03
Klassen, Ralph	Cal., Cle., Col., St.L.	9	497	52	93	145	120	26	4	2	6	12	....	1975-76	1983-84
● Klein, Lloyd	Bos., NYA	8	164	30	24	54	68	5	0	0	0	2	1	1928-29	1937-38

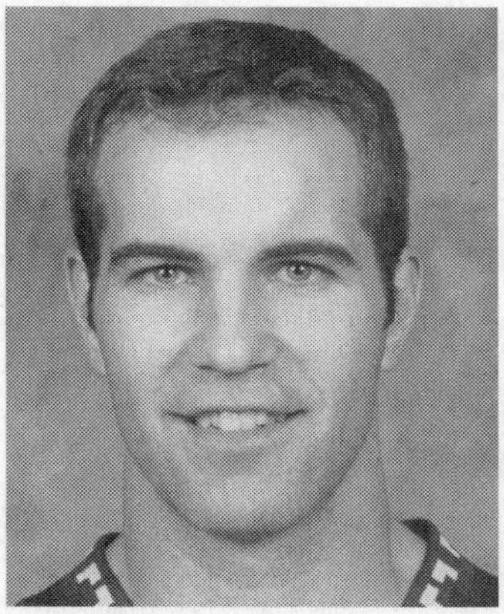

Chris Joseph

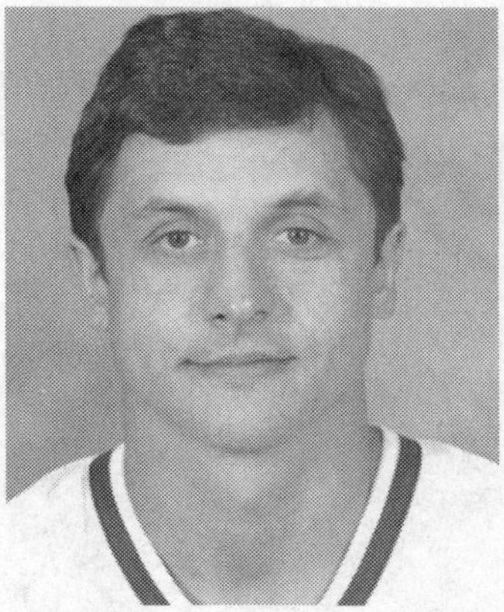

Valeri Kamensky

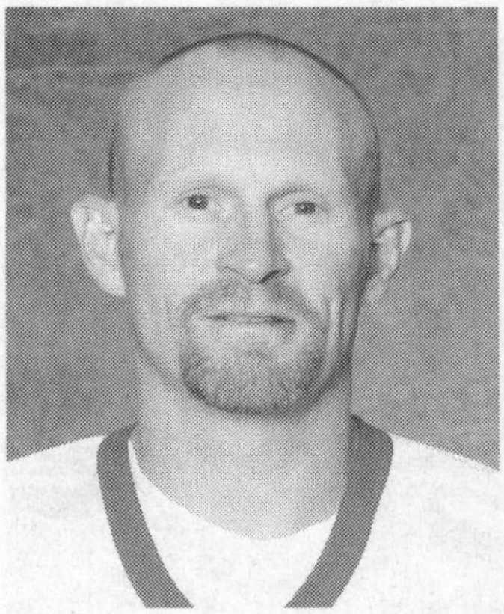

Derek King

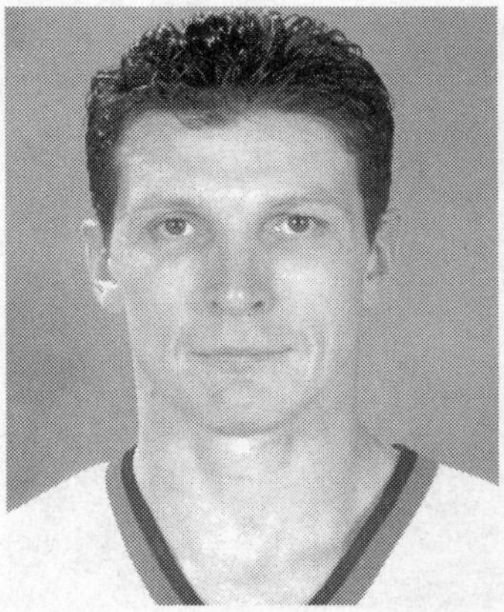

Igor Kravchuk

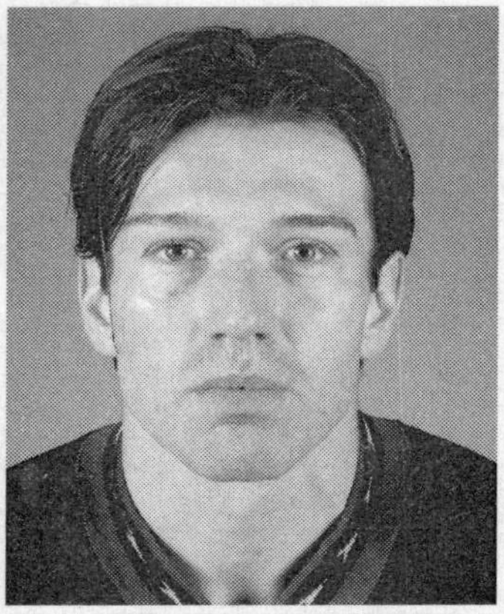

Uwe Krupp

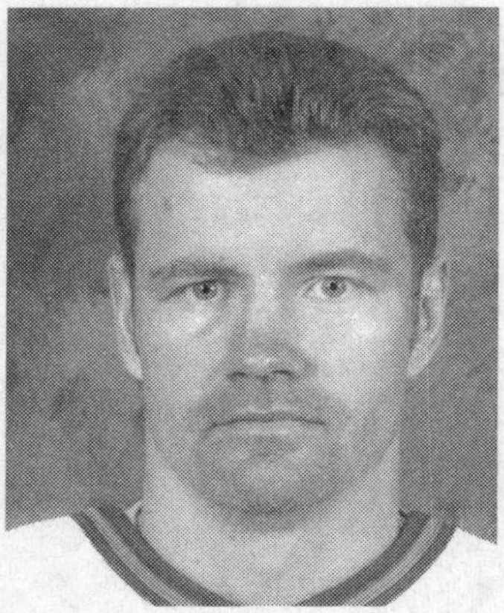

Frantisek Kucera

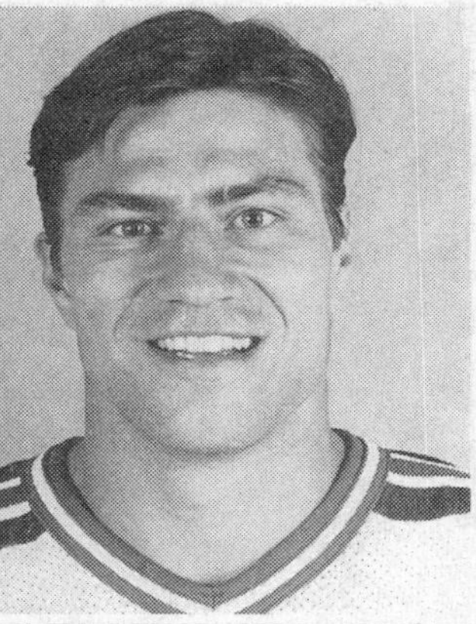

Nick Kypreos

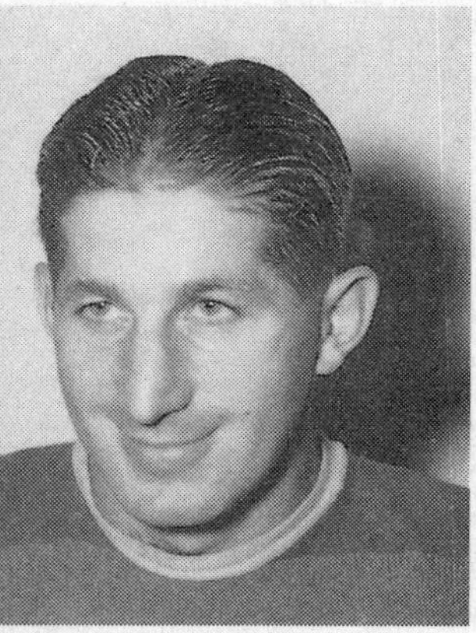

Elmer Lach

Name	NHL Teams	NHL Seasons	Regular Schedule					Playoffs					NHL Cup Wins	First NHL Season	Last NHL Season
			GP	G	A	TP	PIM	GP	G	A	TP	PIM			
Kleinendorst, Scot	NYR, Hfd., Wsh.	8	281	12	46	58	452	26	2	7	9	40	....	1982-83	1989-90
Klima, Petr	Det., Edm., T.B., L.A., Pit.	13	786	313	260	573	671	95	28	24	52	83	1	1985-86	1998-99
‡ Klimovich, Sergei	Chi.	1	1	0	0	0	2	....	....	....	....	....	....	1996-97	1996-97
• Klingbeil, Ike	Chi.	1	5	1	2	3	2	....	....	....	....	....	....	1936-37	1936-37
Klukay, Joe	Tor., Bos.	11	566	109	127	236	189	71	13	10	23	23	4	1942-43	1955-56
Kluzak, Gord	Bos.	7	299	25	98	123	543	46	6	13	19	129	....	1982-83	1990-91
Knibbs, Bill	Bos.	1	53	7	10	17	4	....	....	....	....	....	....	1964-65	1964-65
Knipscheer, Fred	Bos., St.L.	3	28	6	3	9	18	16	2	1	3	6	....	1993-94	1995-96
• Knott, Nick	Bro.	1	14	3	1	4	9	....	....	....	....	....	....	1941-42	1941-42
Knox, Paul	Tor.	1	1	0	0	0	0	....	....	....	....	....	....	1954-55	1954-55
Kocur, Joe	Det., NYR, Van.	15	820	80	82	162	2519	118	10	12	22	231	3	1984-85	1998-99
‡ Koehler, Greg	Car.	1	1	0	0	0	0	....	....	....	....	....	....	2000-01	2000-01
‡ Kohn, Ladislav	Cgy., Tor., Ana., Atl., Det.	7	186	14	28	42	125	2	0	0	0	5	....	1995-96	2002-03
‡ Kolarik, Pavel	Bos.	2	23	0	0	0	10	....	....	....	....	....	....	2000-01	2001-02
‡ Kolesar, Mark	Tor.	2	28	2	2	4	14	3	1	0	1	2	....	1995-96	1996-97
Kolstad, Dean	Min., S.J.	3	40	1	7	8	69	....	....	....	....	....	....	1988-89	1992-93
Komadoski, Neil	L.A., St.L.	8	502	16	76	92	632	23	0	2	2	47	....	1972-73	1979-80
Konik, George	Pit.	1	52	7	8	15	26	....	....	....	....	....	....	1967-68	1967-68
Konroyd, Steve	Cgy., NYI, Chi., Hfd., Det., Ott.	15	895	41	195	236	863	97	10	15	25	99	....	1980-81	1994-95
Konstantinov, Vladimir	Det.	6	446	47	128	175	838	82	5	14	19	107	1	1991-92	1996-97
Kontos, Chris	NYR, Pit., L.A., T.B.	8	230	54	69	123	103	20	11	0	11	12	....	1982-83	1992-93
• Kopak, Russ	Bos.	1	24	7	9	16	0	....	....	....	....	....	....	1943-44	1943-44
Korab, Jerry	Chi., Van., Buf., L.A.	15	975	114	341	455	1629	93	8	18	26	201	....	1970-71	1984-85
Kordic, Dan	Phi.	6	197	4	8	12	584	12	1	0	1	22	....	1991-92	1998-99
• Kordic, John	Mtl., Tor., Wsh., Que.	7	244	17	18	35	997	41	4	3	7	131	1	1985-86	1991-92
Korn, Jim	Det., Tor., Buf., N.J., Cgy.	10	597	66	122	188	1801	16	1	2	3	109	....	1979-80	1989-90
Korney, Mike	Det., NYR	4	77	9	10	19	59	....	....	....	....	....	....	1973-74	1978-79
Koroll, Cliff	Chi.	11	814	208	254	462	376	85	19	29	48	67	....	1969-70	1979-80
Kortko, Roger	NYI	2	79	7	17	24	28	10	0	3	3	17	....	1984-85	1985-86
Kostynski, Doug	Bos.	2	15	3	1	4	4	....	....	....	....	....	....	1983-84	1984-85
Kotanen, Dick	NYR	1	1	0	0	0	0	....	....	....	....	....	....	1950-51	1950-51
Kotsopoulos, Chris	NYR, Hfd., Tor., Det.	10	479	44	109	153	827	31	1	3	4	91	....	1980-81	1989-90
‡ Kovalenko, Andrei	Que., Col., Mtl., Edm., Phi., Car., Bos.	9	620	173	206	379	389	33	5	6	11	20	....	1992-93	2000-01
Kowal, Joe	Buf.	2	22	0	5	5	13	2	0	0	0	0	....	1976-77	1977-78
Kozak, Don	L.A., Van.	7	437	96	86	182	480	29	7	2	9	69	....	1972-73	1978-79
Kozak, Les	Tor.	1	12	1	0	1	2	....	....	....	....	....	....	1961-62	1961-62
• Kraftcheck, Stephen	Bos., NYR, Tor.	4	157	11	18	29	83	6	0	0	0	7	....	1950-51	1958-59
Krake, Skip	Bos., L.A., Buf.	7	249	23	40	63	182	10	1	0	1	17	....	1963-64	1970-71
Kravchuk, Igor	Chi., Edm., St.L., Ott., Cgy., Fla.	12	699	64	210	274	251	51	6	15	21	18	....	1991-92	2002-03
Kravets, Mikhail	S.J.	2	2	0	0	0	0	....	....	....	....	....	....	1991-92	1992-93
Krentz, Dale	Det.	3	30	5	3	8	9	2	0	0	0	0	....	1986-87	1988-89
‡ Krivokrasov, Sergei	Chi., Nsh., Cgy., Min., Ana.	10	450	86	109	195	288	21	2	0	2	14	....	1992-93	2001-02
• Krol, Joe	NYR, Bro.	3	26	10	4	14	8	....	....	....	....	....	....	1936-37	1941-42
Kromm, Richard	Cgy., NYI	9	372	70	103	173	138	36	2	6	8	22	....	1983-84	1992-93
Kron, Robert	Van., Hfd., Car., CBJ	12	771	144	194	338	119	16	3	2	5	2	....	1990-91	2001-02
Krook, Kevin	Col.	1	3	0	0	0	2	....	....	....	....	....	....	1978-79	1978-79
‡ Kroupa, Vlastimil	S.J., N.J.	5	105	4	19	23	66	20	1	2	3	25	....	1993-94	1997-98
Krulicki, Jim	NYR, Det.	1	41	0	3	3	6	....	....	....	....	....	....	1970-71	1970-71
Krupp, Uwe	Buf., NYI, Que., Col., Det., Atl.	15	729	69	212	281	660	81	6	23	29	86	1	1986-87	2002-03
Kruppke, Gord	Det.	3	23	0	0	0	32	....	....	....	....	....	....	1990-91	1993-94
Kruse, Paul	Cgy., NYI, Buf., S.J.	11	423	38	33	71	1074	28	5	2	7	36	....	1990-91	2000-01
Krushelnyski, Mike	Bos., Edm., L.A., Tor., Det.	14	897	241	328	569	699	139	29	43	72	106	3	1981-82	1994-95
Krutov, Vladimir	Van.	1	61	11	23	34	20	....	....	....	....	....	....	1989-90	1989-90
Krygier, Todd	Hfd., Wsh., Ana.	9	543	100	143	243	533	48	10	7	17	40	....	1989-90	1997-98
Kryskow, Dave	Chi., Wsh., Det., Atl.	4	231	33	56	89	174	12	2	0	2	4	....	1972-73	1975-76
Kryzanowski, Ed	Bos., Chi.	5	237	15	22	37	65	18	0	1	1	4	....	1948-49	1952-53
‡ Kucera, Frantisek	Chi., Hfd., Van., Phi., CBJ, Pit., Wsh.	9	465	24	95	119	251	12	0	1	1	0	....	1990-91	2001-02
‡ Kudashov, Alexei	Tor.	1	25	1	0	1	4	....	....	....	....	....	....	1993-94	1993-94
Kudelski, Bob	L.A., Ott., Fla.	9	442	139	102	241	218	22	4	4	8	4	....	1987-88	1995-96
• Kuhn, Gord	NYA	1	12	1	1	2	4	....	....	....	....	....	....	1932-33	1932-33
Kukulowicz, Aggie	NYR	2	4	1	0	1	0	....	....	....	....	....	....	1952-53	1953-54
Kulak, Stu	Van., Edm., NYR, Que., Wpg.	4	90	8	4	12	130	3	0	0	0	2	....	1982-83	1988-89
• Kullman, Arnie	Bos.	2	13	0	1	1	11	....	....	....	....	....	....	1947-48	1949-50
• Kullman, Eddie	NYR	6	343	56	70	126	298	6	1	0	1	2	....	1947-48	1953-54
Kumpel, Mark	Que., Det., Wpg.	6	288	38	46	84	113	39	6	4	10	14	....	1984-85	1990-91
• Kuntz, Alan	NYR	2	45	10	12	22	12	6	1	0	1	2	....	1941-42	1945-46
Kuntz, Murray	St.L.	1	7	1	2	3	0	....	....	....	....	....	....	1974-75	1974-75
Kurri, Jari	Edm., L.A., NYR, Ana., Col.	17	1251	601	797	1398	545	200	106	127	233	123	5	1980-81	1997-98
Kurtenbach, Orland	NYR, Bos., Tor., Van.	13	639	119	213	332	628	19	2	4	6	70	....	1960-61	1973-74
‡ Kurtz, Justin	Van.	1	27	3	5	8	14	....	....	....	....	....	....	2001-02	2001-02
Kurvers, Tom	Mtl., Buf., N.J., Tor., Van., NYI, Ana.	11	659	93	328	421	350	57	8	22	30	68	1	1984-85	1994-95
Kuryluk, Merv	Chi.	1	....	....	....	....	....	2	0	0	0	0	....	1961-62	1961-62
Kushner, Dale	NYI, Phi.	3	84	10	13	23	215	....	....	....	....	....	....	1989-90	1991-92
‡ Kuznik, Greg	Car.	1	1	0	0	0	0	....	....	....	....	....	....	2000-01	2000-01
Kuzyk, Ken	Cle.	2	41	5	9	14	8	....	....	....	....	....	....	1976-77	1977-78
‡ Kvartalnov, Dmitri	Bos.	2	112	42	49	91	26	4	0	0	0	0	....	1992-93	1993-94
Kwong, Larry	NYR	1	1	0	0	0	0	....	....	....	....	....	....	1947-48	1947-48
• Kyle, Bill	NYR	2	3	0	3	3	0	....	....	....	....	....	....	1949-50	1950-51
• Kyle, Gus	NYR, Bos.	3	203	6	20	26	362	14	1	2	3	34	....	1949-50	1951-52
Kyllonen, Markku	Wpg.	1	9	0	2	2	2	....	....	....	....	....	....	1988-89	1988-89
Kypreos, Nick	Wsh., Hfd., NYR, Tor.	8	442	46	44	90	1210	34	1	3	4	65	1	1989-90	1996-97
Kyte, Jim	Wpg., Pit., Cgy., Ott., S.J.	13	598	17	49	66	1342	42	0	6	6	94	....	1982-83	1995-96

L

Name	NHL Teams	NHL Seasons	Regular Schedule					Playoffs					NHL Cup Wins	First NHL Season	Last NHL Season
			GP	G	A	TP	PIM	GP	G	A	TP	PIM			
Labadie, Mike	NYR	1	3	0	0	0	0	....	....	....	....	....	....	1952-53	1952-53
Labatte, Neil	St.L.	2	26	0	2	2	19	....	....	....	....	....	....	1978-79	1981-82
L'Abbe, Moe	Chi.	1	5	0	1	1	0	....	....	....	....	....	....	1972-73	1972-73
Labelle, Marc	Dal.	1	9	0	0	0	46	....	....	....	....	....	....	1996-97	1996-97
Labine, Leo	Bos., Det.	11	643	128	193	321	730	60	12	11	23	82	....	1951-52	1961-62
Labossiere, Gord	NYR, L.A., Min.	6	215	44	62	106	75	10	2	3	5	28	....	1963-64	1971-72
Labovitch, Max	NYR	1	5	0	0	0	4	....	....	....	....	....	....	1943-44	1943-44
Labraaten, Dan	Det., Cgy.	4	268	71	73	144	47	8	1	0	1	4	....	1978-79	1981-82
Labre, Yvon	Pit., Wsh.	9	371	14	87	101	788	....	....	....	....	....	....	1970-71	1980-81
Labrie, Guy	Bos., NYR	2	42	4	9	13	16	....	....	....	....	....	....	1943-44	1944-45
Lach, Elmer	Mtl.	14	664	215	408	623	478	76	19	45	64	36	3	1940-41	1953-54
Lachance, Michel	Col.	1	21	0	4	4	22	....	....	....	....	....	....	1978-79	1978-79
Lacombe, Francois	Oak., Buf., Que.	4	78	2	17	19	54	3	1	0	1	0	....	1968-69	1979-80
Lacombe, Normand	Buf., Edm., Phi.	7	319	53	62	115	196	26	5	1	6	49	1	1984-85	1990-91
Lacroix, Andre	Phi., Chi., Hfd.	6	325	79	119	198	44	16	2	5	7	0	....	1967-68	1979-80
Lacroix, Daniel	NYR, Bos., Phi., Edm., NYI	7	188	11	7	18	379	16	0	1	1	26	....	1993-94	1999-00
Lacroix, Eric	Tor., L.A., Col., NYR, Ott.	8	472	67	70	137	361	30	1	5	6	25	....	1993-94	2000-01
Lacroix, Pierre	Que., Hfd.	4	274	24	108	132	197	8	0	2	2	10	....	1979-80	1982-83
Ladouceur, Randy	Det., Hfd., Ana.	14	930	30	126	156	1322	40	5	8	13	59	....	1982-83	1995-96
LaFayette, Nathan	St.L., Van., NYR, L.A.	6	187	17	20	37	103	32	2	7	9	8	....	1993-94	1998-99
Lafleur, Guy	Mtl., NYR, Que.	17	1126	560	793	1353	399	128	58	76	134	67	5	1971-72	1990-91
• Lafleur, Roland	Mtl.	1	1	0	0	0	0	....	....	....	....	....	....	1924-25	1924-25
LaFontaine, Pat	NYI, Buf., NYR	15	865	468	545	1013	552	69	26	36	62	36	....	1983-84	1997-98
Laforce, Ernie	Mtl.	1	1	0	0	0	0	....	....	....	....	....	....	1942-43	1942-43
LaForest, Bob	L.A.	1	5	1	0	1	2	....	....	....	....	....	....	1983-84	1983-84
Laforge, Claude	Mtl., Det., Phi.	8	193	24	33	57	82	5	1	2	3	15	....	1957-58	1968-69
Laforge, Marc	Hfd., Edm.	2	14	0	0	0	64	....	....	....	....	....	....	1989-90	1993-94
Laframboise, Pete	Cal., Wsh., Pit.	4	227	33	55	88	70	9	1	0	1	0	....	1971-72	1974-75
Lafrance, Adie	Mtl.	1	3	0	0	0	2	2	0	0	0	0	....	1933-34	1933-34
• Lafrance, Leo	Mtl., Chi.	2	33	2	0	2	6	....	....	....	....	....	....	1926-27	1927-28
Lafreniere, Jason	Que., NYR, T.B.	5	146	34	53	87	22	15	1	5	6	19	....	1986-87	1993-94
Lafreniere, Roger	Det., St.L.	2	13	0	0	0	4	....	....	....	....	....	....	1962-63	1972-73
Lagace, Jean-Guy	Pit., Buf., K.C.	6	197	9	39	48	251	....	....	....	....	....	....	1968-69	1975-76
Laidlaw, Tom	NYR, L.A.	10	705	25	139	164	717	69	4	17	21	78	....	1980-81	1989-90
Laird, Robbie	Min.	1	1	0	0	0	0	....	....	....	....	....	....	1979-80	1979-80
Lajeunesse, Serge	Det., Phi.	5	103	1	4	5	103	....	....	....	....	....	....	1970-71	1974-75
‡ Lakovic, Sasha	Cgy., N.J.	3	37	0	4	4	118	....	....	....	....	....	....	1996-97	1998-99
Lalande, Hec	Chi., Det.	4	151	21	39	60	120	....	....	....	....	....	....	1953-54	1957-58
Lalonde, Bobby	Van., Atl., Bos., Cgy.	11	641	124	210	334	298	16	4	2	6	6	....	1971-72	1981-82
• Lalonde, Newsy	Mtl., NYA	6	99	124	41	165	183	7	15	4	19	32	....	1917-18	1926-27
Lalonde, Ron	Pit., Wsh.	7	397	45	78	123	106	....	....	....	....	....	....	1972-73	1978-79

			Regular Schedule					Playoffs							
Name	**NHL Teams**	**NHL Seasons**	**GP**	**G**	**A**	**TP**	**PIM**	**GP**	**G**	**A**	**TP**	**PIM**	**NHL Cup Wins**	**First NHL Season**	**Last NHL Season**
Lalor, Mike	Mtl., St.L., Wsh., Wpg., S.J., Dal.	12	687	17	88	105	677	92	5	10	15	167	1	1985-86	1996-97
● Lamb, Joe	Mtl.M., Ott., NYA, Bos., Mtl., St.L., Det.	11	443	108	101	209	601	18	1	1	2	51	....	1927-28	1937-38
Lamb, Mark	Cgy., Det., Edm., Ott., Phi., Mtl.	11	403	46	100	146	291	70	7	19	26	51	1	1985-86	1995-96
‡ Lambert, Dan	Que.	2	29	6	9	15	22	....	....	....	....	....	....	1990-91	1991-92
Lambert, Denny	Ana., Ott., Nsh., Atl.	8	487	27	66	93	1391	17	0	1	1	28	....	1994-95	2001-02
Lambert, Lane	Det., NYR, Que.	6	283	58	66	124	521	17	2	4	6	40	....	1983-84	1988-89
Lambert, Yvon	Mtl., Buf.	10	683	206	273	479	340	90	27	22	49	67	4	1972-73	1981-82
Lamby, Dick	St.L.	3	22	0	5	5	22	....	....	....	....	....	....	1978-79	1980-81
● Lamirande, Jean-Paul	NYR, Mtl.	4	49	5	5	10	26	8	0	0	0	4	....	1946-47	1954-55
Lammens, Hank	Ott.	1	27	1	2	3	22	....	....	....	....	....	....	1993-94	1993-94
● Lamoureux, Leo	Mtl.	6	235	19	79	98	175	28	1	6	7	16	2	1941-42	1946-47
Lamoureux, Mitch	Pit., Phi.	3	73	11	9	20	59	....	....	....	....	....	....	1983-84	1987-88
Lampman, Mike	St.L., Van., Wsh.	4	96	17	20	37	34	....	....	....	....	....	....	1972-73	1976-77
Lancien, Jack	NYR	4	63	1	5	6	35	6	0	1	1	2	....	1946-47	1950-51
Landon, Larry	Mtl., Tor.	2	9	0	0	0	2	....	....	....	....	....	....	1983-84	1984-85
‡ Landry, Eric	Cgy., Mtl.	4	68	5	9	14	47	....	....	....	....	....	....	1997-98	2001-02
Lane, Gord	Wsh., NYI	10	539	19	94	113	1228	75	3	14	17	214	4	1975-76	1984-85
● Lane, Myles	NYR, Bos.	3	71	4	1	5	41	11	0	0	0	0	1	1928-29	1933-34
Langdon, Steve	Bos.	3	7	0	1	1	2	4	0	0	0	0	....	1974-75	1977-78
Langelle, Pete	Tor.	4	136	22	51	73	11	41	5	9	14	4	1	1938-39	1941-42
Langevin, Chris	Buf.	2	22	3	1	4	22	....	....	....	....	....	....	1983-84	1985-86
Langevin, Dave	NYI, Min., L.A.	8	513	12	107	119	530	87	2	17	19	106	4	1979-80	1986-87
Langlais, Alain	Min.	2	25	4	4	8	10	....	....	....	....	....	....	1973-74	1974-75
Langlois, Albert	Mtl., NYR, Det., Bos.	9	497	21	91	112	488	53	1	5	6	50	3	1957-58	1965-66
● Langlois, Charlie	Ham., NYA, Pit., Mtl.	4	151	22	5	27	189	2	0	0	0	0	....	1924-25	1927-28
Langway, Rod	Mtl., Wsh.	15	994	51	278	329	849	104	5	22	27	97	1	1978-79	1992-93
Lank, Jeff	Phi.	1	2	0	0	0	2	....	....	....	....	....	....	1999-00	1999-00
Lanthier, Jean-Marc	Van.	4	105	16	16	32	29	....	....	....	....	....	....	1983-84	1987-88
Lanyon, Ted	Pit.	1	5	0	0	0	4	....	....	....	....	....	....	1967-68	1967-68
Lanz, Rick	Van., Tor., Chi.	10	569	65	221	286	448	28	3	8	11	35	....	1980-81	1991-92
Laperriere, Daniel	St.L., Ott.	4	48	2	5	7	27	....	....	....	....	....	....	1992-93	1995-96
Laperriere, Jacques	Mtl.	12	691	40	242	282	674	88	9	22	31	101	6	1962-63	1973-74
‡ Laplante, Darryl	Det.	3	35	0	6	6	10	....	....	....	....	....	....	1997-98	1999-00
Lapointe, Guy	Mtl., St.L., Bos.	16	884	171	451	622	893	123	26	44	70	138	6	1968-69	1983-84
● Lapointe, Rick	Det., Phi., St.L., Que., L.A.	11	664	44	176	220	831	46	2	7	9	64	....	1975-76	1985-86
Lappin, Peter	Min., S.J.	2	7	0	0	0	2	....	....	....	....	....	....	1989-90	1991-92
Laprade, Edgar	NYR	10	500	108	172	280	42	18	4	9	13	4	....	1945-46	1954-55
LaPrairie, Benjamin	Chi.	1	7	0	0	0	0	....	....	....	....	....	....	1936-37	1936-37
Lariviere, Garry	Que., Edm.	4	219	6	57	63	167	14	0	5	5	8	....	1979-80	1982-83
Larmer, Jeff	Col., N.J., Chi.	5	158	37	51	88	57	5	1	0	1	2	....	1981-82	1985-86
Larmer, Steve	Chi., NYR	15	1006	441	571	1012	532	140	56	75	131	89	1	1980-81	1994-95
● Larochelle, Wildor	Mtl., Chi.	12	474	92	74	166	211	34	6	4	10	24	2	1925-26	1936-37
Larocque, Denis	L.A.	1	8	0	1	1	18	....	....	....	....	....	....	1987-88	1987-88
‡ Larocque, Mario	T.B.	1	5	0	0	0	16	....	....	....	....	....	....	1998-99	1998-99
● Larose, Bonner	Bos.	1	6	0	0	0	0	....	....	....	....	....	....	1925-26	1925-26
Larose, Claude	Mtl., Min., St.L.	16	943	226	257	483	887	97	14	18	32	143	5	1962-63	1977-78
Larose, Claude	NYR	2	25	4	7	11	2	2	0	0	0	0	....	1979-80	1981-82
‡ Larose, Guy	Wpg., Tor., Cgy., Bos.	6	70	10	9	19	63	4	0	0	0	0	....	1988-89	1994-95
Larouche, Pierre	Pit., Mtl., Hfd., NYR	14	812	395	427	822	237	64	20	34	54	16	2	1974-75	1987-88
‡ Larouche, Steve	Ott., NYR, L.A.	2	26	9	9	18	10	....	....	....	....	....	....	1994-95	1995-96
● Larson, Norm	NYA, Bro., NYR	3	89	25	18	43	12	....	....	....	....	....	....	1940-41	1946-47
Larson, Reed	Det., Bos., Edm., NYI, Min., Buf.	14	904	222	463	685	1391	32	4	7	11	63	....	1976-77	1989-90
Larter, Tyler	Wsh.	1	1	0	0	0	0	....	....	....	....	....	....	1989-90	1989-90
Latal, Jiri	Phi.	3	92	12	36	48	24	....	....	....	....	....	....	1989-90	1991-92
Latos, James	NYR	1	1	0	0	0	0	....	....	....	....	....	....	1988-89	1988-89
Latreille, Phil	NYR	1	4	0	0	0	2	....	....	....	....	....	....	1960-61	1960-61
Latta, David	Que.	4	36	4	8	12	4	....	....	....	....	....	....	1985-86	1990-91
Lauder, Martin	Bos.	1	3	0	0	0	2	....	....	....	....	....	....	1927-28	1927-28
Lauen, Mike	Wpg.	1	4	0	1	1	0	....	....	....	....	....	....	1983-84	1983-84
Lauer, Brad	NYI, Chi., Ott., Pit.	9	323	44	67	111	218	34	7	5	12	24	....	1986-87	1995-96
Laughlin, Craig	Mtl., Wsh., L.A., Tor.	8	549	136	205	341	364	33	6	6	12	20	....	1981-82	1988-89
Laughton, Mike	Oak., Cal.	4	189	39	48	87	101	11	2	4	6	0	....	1967-68	1970-71
‡ Laukkanen, Janne	Que., Col., Ott., Pit., T.B.	9	407	22	99	121	335	59	7	9	16	46	....	1994-95	2002-03
Laurence, Don	Atl., St.L.	2	79	15	22	37	14	....	....	....	....	....	....	1978-79	1979-80
Laus, Paul	Fla.	9	530	14	58	72	1702	30	2	7	9	74	....	1993-94	2001-02
LaVallee, Kevin	Cgy., L.A., St.L., Pit.	7	366	110	125	235	85	32	5	8	13	21	....	1980-81	1986-87
LaVarre, Mark	Chi.	3	78	9	16	25	58	1	0	0	0	2	....	1985-86	1987-88
Lavender, Brian	St.L., NYI, Det., Cal.	4	184	16	26	42	174	3	0	0	0	2	....	1971-72	1974-75
Lavigne, Eric	L.A.	1	1	0	0	0	0	....	....	....	....	....	....	1994-95	1994-95
● Laviolette, Jack	Mtl.	1	18	2	1	3	6	2	0	0	0	0	....	1917-18	1917-18
Laviolette, Peter	NYR	1	12	0	0	0	6	....	....	....	....	....	....	1988-89	1988-89
Lavoie, Dominic	St.L., Ott., Bos., L.A.	6	38	5	8	13	32	....	....	....	....	....	....	1988-89	1993-94
Lawless, Paul	Hfd., Phi., Van., Tor.	7	239	49	77	126	54	3	0	2	2	2	....	1982-83	1989-90
‡ Lawrence, Mark	Dal., NYI	6	142	18	26	44	115	....	....	....	....	....	....	1994-95	2000-01
Lawson, Danny	Det., Min., Buf.	5	219	28	29	57	61	16	0	1	1	2	....	1967-68	1971-72
Lawton, Brian	Min., NYR, Hfd., Que., Bos., S.J.	9	483	112	154	266	401	11	1	1	2	12	....	1983-84	1992-93
Laxdal, Derek	Tor., NYI	6	67	12	7	19	88	1	0	2	2	2	....	1984-85	1990-91
● Laycoe, Hal	NYR, Mtl., Bos.	11	531	25	77	102	292	40	2	5	7	39	....	1945-46	1955-56
Lazaro, Jeff	Bos., Ott.	3	102	14	23	37	114	28	3	3	6	32	....	1990-91	1992-93
Leach, Jamie	Pit., Hfd., Fla.	5	81	11	9	20	12	....	....	....	....	....	1	1989-90	1993-94
Leach, Larry	Bos.	3	126	13	29	42	91	7	1	1	2	8	....	1958-59	1961-62
Leach, Reggie	Bos., Cal., Phi., Det.	13	934	381	285	666	387	94	47	22	69	22	1	1970-71	1982-83
Leach, Stephen	Wsh., Bos., St.L., Car., Ott., Phx., Pit.	15	702	130	153	283	978	92	15	11	26	87	....	1985-86	1999-00
Leavins, Jim	Det., NYR	2	41	2	12	14	30	....	....	....	....	....	....	1985-86	1986-87
‡ Lebeau, Patrick	Mtl., Cgy., Fla., Pit.	4	15	3	2	5	6	....	....	....	....	....	....	1990-91	1998-99
Lebeau, Stephan	Mtl., Ana.	7	373	118	159	277	105	30	9	7	16	12	1	1988-89	1994-95
LeBlanc, Fern	Det.	3	34	5	6	11	0	....	....	....	....	....	....	1976-77	1978-79
LeBlanc, J.P.	Chi., Det.	5	153	14	30	44	87	2	0	0	0	0	....	1968-69	1978-79
LeBlanc, John	Van., Edm., Wpg.	7	83	26	13	39	28	1	0	0	0	0	....	1986-87	1994-95
LeBoutillier, Peter	Ana.	2	35	2	1	3	176	....	....	....	....	....	....	1996-97	1997-98
LeBrun, Al	NYR	2	6	0	2	2	4	....	....	....	....	....	....	1960-61	1965-66
Lecaine, Bill	Pit.	1	4	0	0	0	0	....	....	....	....	....	....	1968-69	1968-69
LeClair, Jack	Mtl.	3	160	20	40	60	56	20	6	1	7	6	2	1954-55	1956-57
Leclerc, Rene	Det.	2	87	10	11	21	105	....	....	....	....	....	....	1968-69	1970-71
Lecuyer, Doug	Chi., Wpg., Pit.	4	126	11	31	42	178	7	4	0	4	15	....	1978-79	1982-83
Ledingham, Walt	Chi., NYI	3	15	0	2	2	4	....	....	....	....	....	....	1972-73	1976-77
● Leduc, Albert	Mtl., Ott., NYR	10	383	57	35	92	614	28	5	6	11	32	2	1925-26	1934-35
LeDuc, Rich	Bos., Que.	4	130	28	38	66	69	5	0	0	0	9	....	1972-73	1980-81
Ledyard, Grant	NYR, L.A., Wsh., Buf., Dal., Van., Bos., Ott., T.B.	18	1028	90	276	366	766	83	6	12	18	96	....	1984-85	2001-02
● Lee, Bobby	Mtl.	1	1	0	0	0	0	....	....	....	....	....	....	1942-43	1942-43
Lee, Edward	Que.	1	2	0	0	0	5	....	....	....	....	....	....	1984-85	1984-85
Lee, Peter	Pit.	6	431	114	131	245	257	19	0	8	8	4	....	1977-78	1982-83
‡ Leeb, Greg	Dal.	1	2	0	0	0	0	....	....	....	....	....	....	2000-01	2000-01
Leeman, Gary	Tor., Cgy., Mtl., Van., St.L.	14	667	199	267	466	531	36	8	16	24	36	1	1982-83	1996-97
‡ Lefebvre, Patrice	Wsh.	1	3	0	0	0	2	....	....	....	....	....	....	1998-99	1998-99
‡ Lefebvre, Sylvain	Mtl., Tor., Que., Col., NYR	14	945	30	154	184	674	129	4	14	18	101	1	1989-90	2002-03
● Lefley, Bryan	NYI, K.C., Col.	5	228	7	29	36	101	2	0	0	0	0	....	1972-73	1977-78
Lefley, Chuck	Mtl., St.L.	9	407	128	164	292	137	29	5	8	13	10	2	1970-71	1980-81
● Leger, Roger	NYR, Mtl.	5	187	18	53	71	71	20	0	7	7	14	....	1943-44	1949-50
Legge, Barry	Que., Wpg.	3	107	1	11	12	144	....	....	....	....	....	....	1979-80	1981-82
Legge, Randy	NYR	1	12	0	2	2	2	....	....	....	....	....	....	1972-73	1972-73
Lehman, Tommy	Bos., Edm.	3	36	5	5	10	16	....	....	....	....	....	....	1987-88	1989-90
Lehto, Petteri	Pit.	1	6	0	0	0	4	....	....	....	....	....	....	1984-85	1984-85
Lehtonen, Antero	Wsh.	1	65	9	12	21	14	....	....	....	....	....	....	1979-80	1979-80
Lehvonen, Henri	K.C.	1	4	0	0	0	0	....	....	....	....	....	....	1974-75	1974-75
Leier, Edward	Chi.	2	16	2	1	3	2	....	....	....	....	....	....	1949-50	1950-51
Leinonen, Mikko	NYR, Wsh.	4	162	31	78	109	71	20	2	11	13	28	....	1981-82	1984-85
Leiter, Bobby	Bos., Pit., Atl.	10	447	98	126	224	144	8	3	0	3	2	....	1962-63	1975-76
Leiter, Ken	NYI, Min.	5	143	14	36	50	62	15	0	6	6	8	....	1984-85	1989-90
Lemaire, Jacques	Mtl.	12	853	366	469	835	217	145	61	78	139	63	8	1967-68	1978-79
Lemay, Moe	Van., Edm., Bos., Wpg.	8	317	72	94	166	442	28	6	3	9	55	1	1981-82	1988-89
Lemelin, Roger	K.C., Col.	4	36	1	2	3	27	....	....	....	....	....	....	1974-75	1977-78
Lemieux, Alain	St.L., Que., Pit.	6	119	28	44	72	38	19	4	6	10	0	....	1981-82	1986-87
Lemieux, Bob	Oak.	1	19	0	1	1	12	....	....	....	....	....	....	1967-68	1967-68
Lemieux, Claude	Mtl., N.J., Col., Phx., Dal.	20	1197	379	406	785	1756	233	80	78	158	529	4	1983-84	2002-03

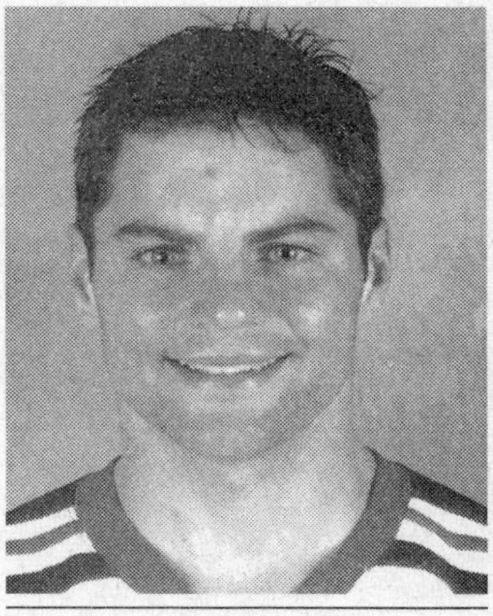
Eric Lacroix

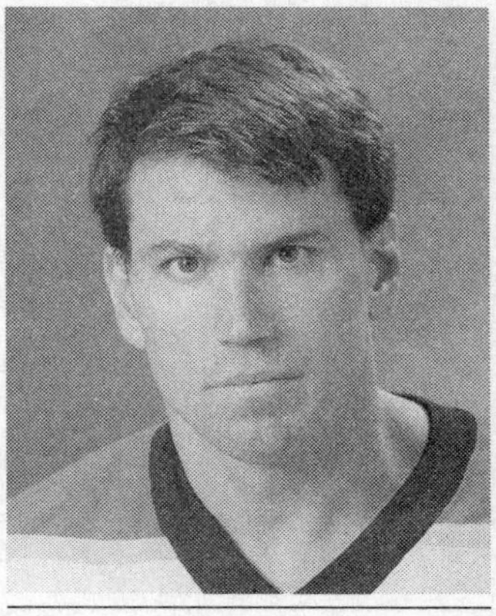
Paul Laus

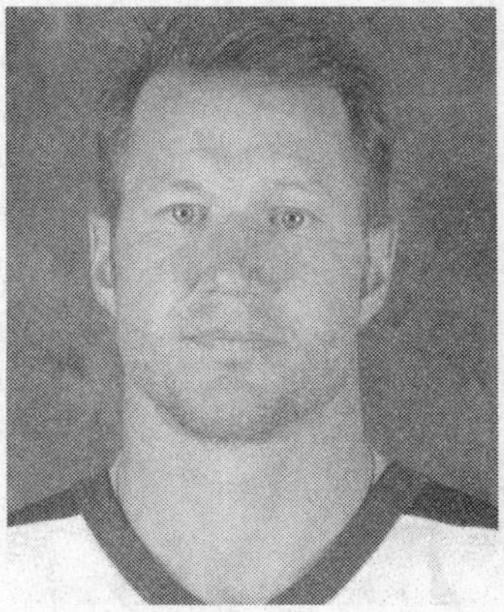
Grant Ledyard

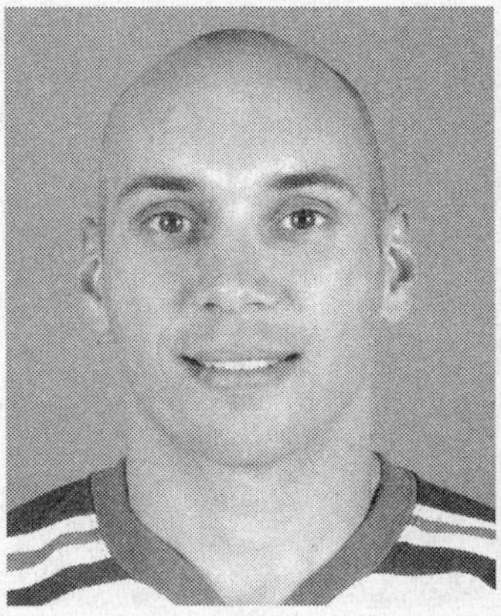
Sylvain Lefebvre

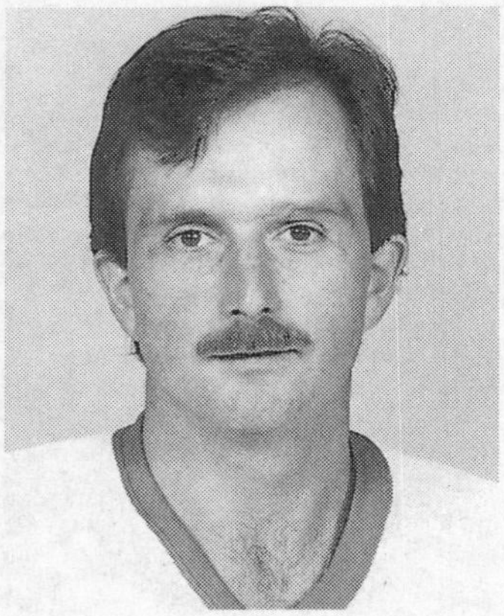

Dave Lewis

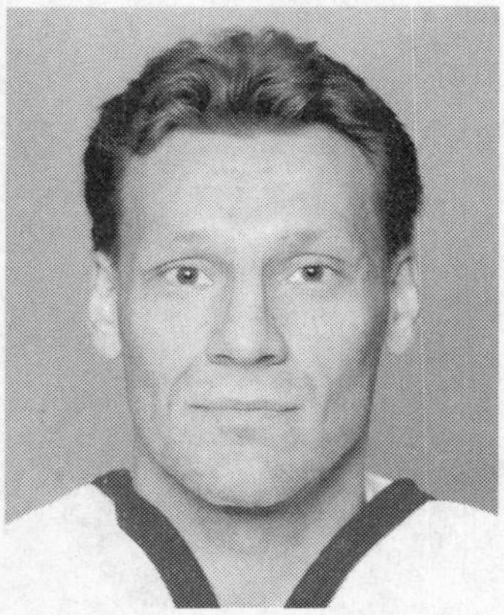

Jyrki Lumme

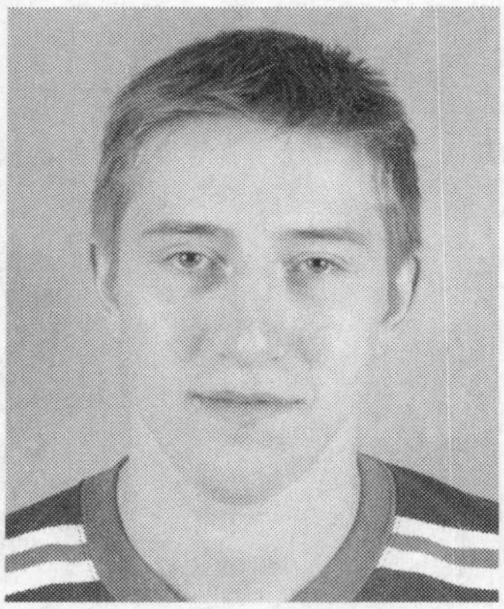

Roman Lyashenko

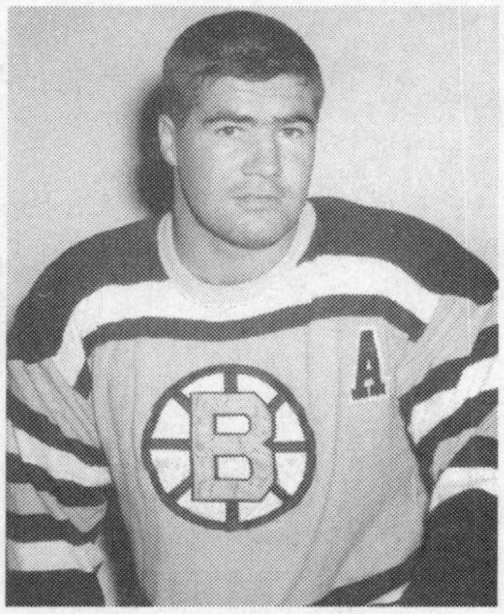

Fleming Mackell

			Regular Schedule					Playoffs							
Name	NHL Teams	NHL Seasons	GP	G	A	TP	PIM	GP	G	A	TP	PIM	NHL Cup Wins	First NHL Season	Last NHL Season
Lemieux, Jacques	L.A.	3	19	0	4	4	8	1	0	0	0	0	....	1967-68	1969-70
Lemieux, Jean	Atl., Wsh.	5	204	23	63	86	39	3	1	1	2	0	....	1973-74	1977-78
Lemieux, Jocelyn	St.L., Mtl., Chi., Hfd., N.J., Cgy., Phx.	12	598	80	84	164	740	60	5	10	15	88	....	1986-87	1997-98
● Lemieux, Real	Det., L.A., NYR, Buf.	8	456	51	104	155	262	18	2	4	6	10	....	1966-67	1973-74
Lemieux, Rich	Van., K.C., Atl.	5	274	39	82	121	132	2	0	0	0	0	....	1971-72	1975-76
Lenardon, Tim	N.J., Van.	2	15	2	1	3	4	....	....	....	....	....	....	1986-87	1989-90
● Lepine, Hec	Mtl.	1	33	5	2	7	2	....	....	....	....	....	....	1925-26	1925-26
● Lepine, Pit	Mtl.	13	526	143	98	241	392	41	7	5	12	26	2	1925-26	1937-38
‡ Leroux, Francois	Edm., Ott., Pit., Col.	10	249	3	20	23	577	33	1	3	4	34	....	1988-89	1997-98
Leroux, Gaston	Mtl.	1	2	0	0	0	0	....	....	....	....	....	....	1935-36	1935-36
‡ Leroux, Jean-Yves	Chi.	5	220	16	22	38	146	....	....	....	....	....	....	1996-97	2000-01
Lesieur, Art	Mtl., Chi.	4	100	4	2	6	50	14	0	0	0	4	1	1928-29	1935-36
Lessard, Rick	Cgy., S.J.	3	15	0	4	4	18	....	....	....	....	....	....	1988-89	1991-92
Lesuk, Bill	Bos., Phi., L.A., Wsh., Wpg.	8	388	44	63	107	368	9	1	0	1	12	1	1968-69	1979-80
● Leswick, Jack	Chi.	1	37	1	7	8	16	....	....	....	....	....	1	1933-34	1933-34
Leswick, Pete	NYA, Bos.	2	3	1	0	1	0	....	....	....	....	....	....	1936-37	1944-45
● Leswick, Tony	NYR, Det., Chi.	12	740	165	159	324	900	59	13	10	23	91	3	1945-46	1957-58
Levandoski, Joe	NYR	1	8	1	1	2	0	....	....	....	....	....	....	1946-47	1946-47
Leveille, Normand	Bos.	2	75	17	25	42	49	....	....	....	....	....	....	1981-82	1982-83
Leveque, Guy	L.A.	2	17	2	2	4	21	....	....	....	....	....	....	1992-93	1993-94
Lever, Don	Van., Atl., Cgy., Col., N.J., Buf.	15	1020	313	367	680	593	30	7	10	17	26	....	1972-73	1986-87
Levie, Craig	Wpg., Min., St.L., Van.	6	183	22	53	75	177	16	2	3	5	32	....	1981-82	1986-87
‡ Levins, Scott	Wpg., Fla., Ott., Phx.	5	124	13	20	33	316	....	....	....	....	....	....	1992-93	1997-98
● Levinsky, Alex	Tor., NYR, Chi.	9	367	19	49	68	307	37	2	1	3	26	2	1930-31	1938-39
Levo, Tapio	Col., N.J.	2	107	16	53	69	36	....	....	....	....	....	....	1981-82	1982-83
Lewicki, Danny	Tor., NYR, Chi.	9	461	105	135	240	177	28	0	4	4	8	1	1950-51	1958-59
Lewis, Dale	NYR	1	8	0	0	0	0	....	....	....	....	....	....	1975-76	1975-76
Lewis, Dave	NYI, L.A., N.J., Det.	15	1008	36	187	223	953	91	1	20	21	143	....	1973-74	1987-88
● Lewis, Doug	Mtl.	1	3	0	0	0	0	....	....	....	....	....	....	1946-47	1946-47
● Lewis, Herbie	Det.	11	483	148	161	309	248	38	13	10	23	6	2	1928-29	1938-39
Ley, Rick	Tor., Hfd.	6	310	12	72	84	528	14	0	2	2	20	....	1968-69	1980-81
Liba, Igor	NYR, L.A.	1	37	7	18	25	36	2	0	0	0	2	....	1988-89	1988-89
Libby, Jeff	NYI	1	1	0	0	0	0	....	....	....	....	....	....	1997-98	1997-98
Libett, Nick	Det., Pit.	14	982	237	268	505	472	16	6	2	8	2	....	1967-68	1980-81
Licari, Tony	Det.	1	9	0	1	1	0	....	....	....	....	....	....	1946-47	1946-47
Liddington, Bob	Tor.	1	11	0	1	1	2	....	....	....	....	....	....	1970-71	1970-71
Lidster, Doug	Van., NYR, St.L., Dal.	16	897	75	268	343	679	80	6	15	21	64	1	1983-84	1998-99
Lilley, John	Ana.	3	23	3	8	11	13	....	....	....	....	....	....	1993-94	1995-96
‡ Lind, Juha	Dal., Mtl.	3	133	9	13	22	20	15	2	2	4	8	....	1997-98	2000-01
Lindberg, Chris	Cgy., Que.	3	116	17	25	42	47	2	0	1	1	2	....	1991-92	1993-94
Lindbom, Johan	NYR	1	38	1	3	4	28	....	....	....	....	....	....	1997-98	1997-98
Linden, Jamie	Fla.	1	4	0	0	0	17	....	....	....	....	....	....	1994-95	1994-95
Lindgren, Lars	Van., Min.	6	394	25	113	138	325	40	5	6	11	20	....	1978-79	1983-84
Lindholm, Mikael	L.A.	1	18	2	2	4	2	....	....	....	....	....	....	1989-90	1989-90
‡ Lindquist, Fredrik	Edm.	1	8	0	0	0	2	....	....	....	....	....	....	1998-99	1998-99
Lindros, Brett	NYI	2	51	2	5	7	147	....	....	....	....	....	....	1994-95	1995-96
Lindsay, Ted	Det., Chi.	17	1068	379	472	851	1808	133	47	49	96	194	4	1944-45	1964-65
Lindstrom, Willy	Wpg., Edm., Pit.	8	582	161	162	323	200	57	14	18	32	24	2	1979-80	1986-87
Linseman, Ken	Phi., Edm., Bos., Tor.	14	860	256	551	807	1727	113	43	77	120	325	1	1978-79	1991-92
‡ Lintner, Richard	Nsh., NYR, Pit.	3	112	8	12	20	54	....	....	....	....	....	....	1999-00	2002-03
Lipuma, Chris	T.B., S.J.	5	72	0	9	9	146	....	....	....	....	....	....	1992-93	1996-97
Liscombe, Carl	Det.	9	373	137	140	277	117	59	22	19	41	20	1	1937-38	1945-46
Litzenberger, Ed	Mtl., Chi., Det., Tor.	12	618	178	238	416	283	40	5	13	18	34	4	1952-53	1963-64
Loach, Lonnie	Ott., L.A., Ana.	2	56	10	13	23	29	1	0	0	0	0	....	1992-93	1993-94
● Locas, Jacques	Mtl.	2	59	7	8	15	66	....	....	....	....	....	....	1947-48	1948-49
Lochead, Bill	Det., Col., NYR	6	330	69	62	131	180	7	3	0	3	6	....	1974-75	1979-80
● Locking, Norm	Chi.	2	48	2	6	8	26	....	....	....	....	....	....	1934-35	1935-36
Loewen, Darcy	Buf., Ott.	5	135	4	8	12	211	....	....	....	....	....	....	1989-90	1993-94
Lofthouse, Mark	Wsh., Det.	6	181	42	38	80	73	....	....	....	....	....	....	1977-78	1982-83
Logan, Dave	Chi., Van.	6	218	5	29	34	470	12	0	0	0	10	....	1975-76	1980-81
Logan, Robert	Buf., L.A.	3	42	10	5	15	0	....	....	....	....	....	....	1986-87	1988-89
Loiselle, Claude	Det., N.J., Que., Tor., NYI	13	616	92	117	209	1149	41	4	11	15	58	....	1981-82	1993-94
Lomakin, Andrei	Phi., Fla.	4	215	42	62	104	92	....	....	....	....	....	....	1991-92	1994-95
Loney, Brian	Van.	1	12	2	3	5	6	....	....	....	....	....	....	1995-96	1995-96
Loney, Troy	Pit., Ana., NYI, NYR	12	624	87	110	197	1091	67	8	14	22	97	2	1983-84	1994-95
Long, Barry	L.A., Det., Wpg.	5	280	11	68	79	250	5	0	1	1	18	....	1972-73	1981-82
● Long, Stan	Mtl.	1	....	....	....	....	....	3	0	0	0	0	....	1951-52	1951-52
Lonsberry, Ross	Bos., L.A., Phi., Pit.	15	968	256	310	566	806	100	21	25	46	87	2	1966-67	1980-81
Loob, Hakan	Cgy.	6	450	193	236	429	189	73	26	28	54	16	1	1983-84	1988-89
Loob, Peter	Que.	1	8	1	2	3	0	....	....	....	....	....	....	1984-85	1984-85
Lorentz, Jim	Bos., St.L., NYR, Buf.	10	659	161	238	399	208	54	12	10	22	30	1	1968-69	1977-78
Lorimer, Bob	NYI, Col., N.J.	10	529	22	90	112	431	49	3	10	13	83	2	1976-77	1985-86
● Lorrain, Rod	Mtl.	6	179	28	39	67	30	11	0	3	3	0	....	1935-36	1941-42
● Loughlin, Clem	Det., Chi.	3	101	8	6	14	77	....	....	....	....	....	....	1926-27	1928-29
● Loughlin, Wilf	Tor.	1	14	0	0	0	2	....	....	....	....	....	....	1923-24	1923-24
Lovsin, Ken	Wsh.	1	1	0	0	0	0	....	....	....	....	....	....	1990-91	1990-91
Lowdermilk, Dwayne	Wsh.	1	2	0	1	1	2	....	....	....	....	....	....	1980-81	1980-81
Lowe, Darren	Pit.	1	8	1	2	3	0	....	....	....	....	....	....	1983-84	1983-84
Lowe, Kevin	Edm., NYR	19	1254	84	347	431	1498	214	10	48	58	192	6	1979-80	1997-98
Lowe, Odie	NYR	1	4	1	1	2	0	....	....	....	....	....	....	1949-50	1949-50
● Lowe, Ross	Bos., Mtl.	3	77	6	8	14	82	2	0	0	0	0	....	1949-50	1951-52
● Lowrey, Ed	Ott., Ham.	3	27	2	2	4	6	....	....	....	....	....	....	1917-18	1920-21
● Lowrey, Fred	Mtl.M., Pit.	2	53	1	1	2	10	2	0	0	0	6	....	1924-25	1925-26
● Lowrey, Gerry	Tor., Pit., Phi., Chi., Ott.	6	211	48	48	96	148	2	1	0	1	2	....	1927-28	1932-33
Lucas, Danny	Phi.	1	6	1	0	1	0	....	....	....	....	....	....	1978-79	1978-79
Lucas, Dave	Det.	1	1	0	0	0	0	....	....	....	....	....	....	1962-63	1962-63
Luce, Don	NYR, Det., Buf., L.A., Tor.	13	894	225	329	554	364	71	17	22	39	52	....	1969-70	1981-82
Ludvig, Jan	N.J., Buf.	7	314	54	87	141	418	....	....	....	....	....	....	1982-83	1988-89
Ludwig, Craig	Mtl., NYI, Min., Dal.	17	1256	38	184	222	1437	177	4	25	29	244	2	1982-83	1998-99
Ludzik, Steve	Chi., Buf.	9	424	46	93	139	333	44	4	8	12	70	....	1981-82	1989-90
Luhning, Warren	NYI, Dal.	3	29	0	1	1	21	....	....	....	....	....	....	1997-98	1999-00
Lukowich, Bernie	Pit., St.L.	2	79	13	15	28	34	2	0	0	0	0	....	1973-74	1974-75
Lukowich, Morris	Wpg., Bos., L.A.	8	582	199	219	418	584	11	0	2	2	24	....	1979-80	1986-87
Luksa, Charlie	Hfd.	1	8	0	1	1	4	....	....	....	....	....	....	1979-80	1979-80
Lumley, Dave	Mtl., Edm., Hfd.	9	437	98	160	258	680	61	6	8	14	131	2	1978-79	1986-87
Lumme, Jyrki	Mtl., Van., Phx., Dal., Tor.	15	985	114	354	468	620	105	9	35	44	52	....	1988-89	2002-03
Lund, Pentti	Bos., NYR	7	259	44	55	99	40	19	7	5	12	0	....	1946-47	1952-53
Lundberg, Brian	Pit.	1	1	0	0	0	2	....	....	....	....	....	....	1982-83	1982-83
Lunde, Len	Det., Chi., Min., Van.	8	321	39	83	122	75	20	3	2	5	2	....	1958-59	1970-71
Lundholm, Bengt	Wpg.	5	275	48	95	143	72	14	3	4	7	14	....	1981-82	1985-86
Lundrigan, Joe	Tor., Wsh.	2	52	2	8	10	22	....	....	....	....	....	....	1972-73	1974-75
Lundstrom, Tord	Det.	1	11	1	1	2	0	....	....	....	....	....	....	1973-74	1973-74
● Lundy, Pat	Det., Chi.	5	150	37	32	69	31	16	2	2	4	2	....	1945-46	1950-51
Luongo, Chris	Det., Ott., NYI	5	218	8	23	31	176	....	....	....	....	....	....	1990-91	1995-96
Lupien, Gilles	Mtl., Pit., Hfd.	5	226	5	25	30	416	25	0	0	0	21	2	1977-78	1981-82
Lupul, Gary	Van.	7	293	70	75	145	243	25	4	7	11	11	....	1979-80	1985-86
● Lyashenko, Roman	Dal., NYR	4	139	14	9	23	55	17	2	1	3	0	....	1999-00	2002-03
Lyle, George	Det., Hfd.	4	99	24	38	62	51	....	....	....	....	....	....	1979-80	1982-83
Lynch, Jack	Pit., Det., Wsh.	7	382	24	106	130	336	....	....	....	....	....	....	1972-73	1978-79
Lynn, Vic	NYR, Det., Mtl., Tor., Bos., Chi.	11	327	49	76	125	274	47	7	10	17	46	3	1942-43	1953-54
Lyon, Steve	Pit.	1	3	0	0	0	2	....	....	....	....	....	....	1976-77	1976-77
Lyons, Ron	Bos., Phi.	1	36	2	4	6	27	5	0	0	0	0	....	1930-31	1930-31
Lysiak, Tom	Atl., Chi.	13	919	292	551	843	567	76	25	38	63	49	....	1973-74	1985-86

M

Name	NHL Teams	NHL Seasons	GP	G	A	TP	PIM	GP	G	A	TP	PIM	NHL Cup Wins	First NHL Season	Last NHL Season
MacAdam, Al	Phi., Cal., Cle., Min., Van.	12	864	240	351	591	509	64	20	24	44	21	1	1973-74	1984-85
MacDermid, Paul	Hfd., Wpg., Wsh., Que.	14	690	116	142	258	1303	43	5	11	16	116	....	1981-82	1994-95
MacDonald, Blair	Edm., Van.	4	219	91	100	191	65	11	0	6	6	2	....	1979-80	1982-83
MacDonald, Brett	Van.	1	1	0	0	0	0	....	....	....	....	....	....	1987-88	1987-88
MacDonald, Doug	Buf.	3	11	1	0	1	2	....	....	....	....	....	....	1992-93	1994-95
MacDonald, Kevin	Ott.	1	1	0	0	0	2	....	....	....	....	....	....	1993-94	1993-94
● MacDonald, Kilby	NYR	4	151	36	34	70	47	15	1	2	3	4	1	1939-40	1944-45
MacDonald, Lowell	Det., L.A., Pit.	13	506	180	210	390	92	30	11	11	22	12	....	1961-62	1977-78
MacDonald, Parker	Tor., NYR, Det., Bos., Min.	14	676	144	179	323	253	75	14	14	28	20	....	1952-53	1968-69
MacDougall, Kim	Min.	1	1	0	0	0	0	....	....	....	....	....	....	1974-75	1974-75

			Regular Schedule					Playoffs					NHL	First	Last
Name	NHL Teams	NHL Seasons	GP	G	A	TP	PIM	GP	G	A	TP	PIM	Cup Wins	NHL Season	NHL Season
MacEachern, Shane	St.L.	1	1	0	0	0	0	....	....	....	....	....	....	1987-88	1987-88
Macey, Hub	NYR, Mtl.	3	30	6	9	15	0	8	0	0	0	0	....	1941-42	1946-47
MacGregor, Bruce	Det., NYR	14	893	213	257	470	217	107	19	28	47	44	....	1960-61	1973-74
MacGregor, Randy	Hfd.	1	2	1	1	2	2	....	....	....	....	....	....	1981-82	1981-82
MacGuigan, Garth	NYI	2	5	0	1	1	2	....	....	....	....	....	....	1979-80	1983-84
MacIntosh, Ian	NYR	1	4	0	0	0	4	....	....	....	....	....	....	1952-53	1952-53
MacIver, Don	Wpg.	1	6	0	0	0	2	....	....	....	....	....	....	1979-80	1979-80
Maciver, Norm	NYR, Hfd., Edm., Ott., Pit., Wpg., Phx.	12	500	55	230	285	350	56	3	11	14	32	....	1986-87	1997-98
MacKasey, Blair	Tor.	1	1	0	0	0	2	....	....	....	....	....	....	1976-77	1976-77
• MacKay, Calum	Det., Mtl.	8	237	50	55	105	214	38	5	13	18	20	1	1946-47	1954-55
MacKay, Dave	Chi.	1	29	3	0	3	26	5	0	1	1	2	....	1940-41	1940-41
• MacKay, Mickey	Chi., Pit., Bos.	4	147	44	19	63	79	11	0	0	0	6	1	1926-27	1929-30
• MacKay, Murdo	Mtl.	4	19	0	3	3	0	15	1	2	3	0	....	1945-46	1948-49
MacKell, Fleming	Tor., Bos.	13	665	149	220	369	562	80	22	41	63	75	2	1947-48	1959-60
• MacKell, Jack	Ott.	2	45	4	2	6	59	2	0	0	0	0	2	1919-20	1920-21
MacKenzie, Barry	Min.	1	6	0	1	1	6	....	....	....	....	....	....	1968-69	1968-69
• MacKenzie, Bill	Chi., Mtl.M., NYR, Mtl.	7	264	15	14	29	145	21	1	1	2	11	1	1932-33	1939-40
Mackey, David	Chi., Min., St.L.	6	126	8	12	20	305	3	0	0	0	2	....	1987-88	1993-94
• Mackey, Reg	NYR	1	34	0	0	0	16	1	0	0	0	0	....	1926-27	1926-27
• Mackie, Howie	Det.	2	20	1	0	1	4	8	0	0	0	0	1	1936-37	1937-38
MacKinnon, Paul	Wsh.	5	147	5	23	28	91	....	....	....	....	....	....	1979-80	1983-84
MacLean, John	N.J., S.J., NYR, Dal.	18	1194	413	429	842	1328	104	35	48	83	152	1	1983-84	2001-02
MacLean, Paul	St.L., Wpg., Det.	11	719	324	349	673	968	53	21	14	35	110	....	1980-81	1990-91
MacLeish, Rick	Phi., Hfd., Pit., Det.	14	846	349	410	759	434	114	54	53	107	38	2	1970-71	1983-84
MacLellan, Brian	L.A., NYR, Min., Cgy., Det.	10	606	172	241	413	551	47	5	9	14	42	1	1982-83	1991-92
MacLeod, Pat	Min., S.J., Dal.	4	53	5	13	18	14	....	....	....	....	....	....	1990-91	1995-96
MacMillan, Billy	Tor., Atl., NYI	7	446	74	77	151	184	53	6	6	12	40	....	1970-71	1976-77
MacMillan, Bob	NYR, St.L., Atl., Cgy., Col., N.J., Chi.	11	753	228	349	577	260	31	8	11	19	16	....	1974-75	1984-85
MacMillan, John	Tor., Det.	5	104	5	10	15	32	12	0	1	1	2	2	1960-61	1964-65
MacNeil, Al	Tor., Mtl., Chi., NYR, Pit.	11	524	17	75	92	617	37	0	4	4	67	....	1955-56	1967-68
MacNeil, Bernie	St.L.	1	4	0	0	0	0	....	....	....	....	....	....	1973-74	1973-74
Macoun, Jamie	Cgy., Tor., Det.	16	1128	76	282	358	1208	159	10	32	42	169	2	1982-83	1998-99
• MacPherson, Bud	Mtl.	7	259	5	33	38	233	29	0	3	3	21	1	1948-49	1956-57
• MacSweyn, Ralph	Phi.	5	47	0	5	5	10	8	0	0	0	6	....	1967-68	1971-72
MacTavish, Craig	Bos., Edm., NYR, Phi., St.L.	17	1093	213	267	480	891	193	20	38	58	218	4	1979-80	1996-97
MacWilliam, Mike	NYI	1	6	0	0	0	14	....	....	....	....	....	....	1995-96	1995-96
Madigan, Connie	St.L.	1	20	0	3	3	25	5	0	0	0	4	....	1972-73	1972-73
Madill, Jeff	N.J.	1	14	4	0	4	46	7	0	2	2	8	....	1990-91	1990-91
Magee, Dean	Min.	1	7	0	0	0	4	....	....	....	....	....	....	1977-78	1977-78
Maggs, Daryl	Chi., Cal., Tor.	3	135	14	19	33	54	4	0	0	0	0	....	1971-72	1979-80
Magnan, Marc	Tor.	1	4	0	1	1	5	....	....	....	....	....	....	1982-83	1982-83
• Magnuson, Keith	Chi.	11	589	14	125	139	1442	68	3	9	12	164	....	1969-70	1979-80
Maguire, Kevin	Tor., Buf., Phi.	6	260	29	30	59	782	11	0	0	0	86	....	1986-87	1991-92
Mahaffy, John	Mtl., NYR	3	37	11	25	36	4	1	0	1	1	0	....	1942-43	1944-45
Mahovlich, Frank	Tor., Det., Mtl.	18	1181	533	570	1103	1056	137	51	67	118	163	6	1956-57	1973-74
Mahovlich, Pete	Det., Mtl., Pit.	16	884	288	485	773	916	88	30	42	72	134	4	1965-66	1980-81
Mailhot, Jacques	Que.	1	5	0	0	0	33	....	....	....	....	....	....	1988-89	1988-89
Mailley, Frank	Mtl.	1	1	0	0	0	0	....	....	....	....	....	....	1942-43	1942-43
Mair, Jim	Phi., NYI, Van.	5	76	4	15	19	49	3	1	2	3	4	....	1970-71	1974-75
• Majeau, Fern	Mtl.	2	56	22	24	46	43	1	0	0	0	0	1	1943-44	1944-45
Major, Bruce	Que.	1	4	0	0	0	0	....	....	....	....	....	....	1990-91	1990-91
‡ Major, Mark	Det.	1	2	0	0	0	5	....	....	....	....	....	....	1996-97	1996-97
Makarov, Sergei	Cgy., S.J., Dal.	7	424	134	250	384	317	34	12	11	23	8	....	1989-90	1996-97
Makela, Mikko	NYI, L.A., Buf., Bos.	7	423	118	147	265	139	18	3	8	11	14	....	1985-86	1994-95
Maki, Chico	Chi.	15	841	143	292	435	345	113	17	36	53	43	1	1960-61	1975-76
• Maki, Wayne	Chi., St.L., Van.	6	246	57	79	136	184	2	1	0	1	2	....	1967-68	1972-73
Makkonen, Kari	Edm.	1	9	2	2	4	0	....	....	....	....	....	....	1979-80	1979-80
Maley, David	Mtl., N.J., Edm., S.J., NYI	9	466	43	81	124	1043	46	5	5	10	111	1	1985-86	1993-94
Malgunas, Stewart	Phi., Wpg., Wsh., Cgy.	7	129	1	5	6	144	....	....	....	....	....	....	1993-94	1999-00
Malinowski, Merlin	Col., N.J., Hfd.	5	282	54	111	165	121	....	....	....	....	....	....	1978-79	1982-83
Malkoc, Dean	Van., Bos., NYI	4	116	1	3	4	299	....	....	....	....	....	....	1995-96	1998-99
Mallette, Troy	NYR, Edm., N.J., Ott., Bos., T.B.	9	456	51	68	119	1226	15	2	2	4	99	....	1989-90	1997-98
Malone, Cliff	Mtl.	1	3	0	0	0	0	....	....	....	....	....	....	1951-52	1951-52
Malone, Greg	Pit., Hfd., Que.	11	704	191	310	501	661	20	3	5	8	32	....	1976-77	1986-87
• Malone, Joe	Mtl., Que., Ham.	7	126	143	32	175	57	9	6	2	8	6	1	1917-18	1923-24
Maloney, Dan	Chi., L.A., Det., Tor.	11	737	192	259	451	1489	40	4	7	11	35	....	1970-71	1981-82
Maloney, Dave	NYR, Buf.	11	657	71	246	317	1154	49	7	17	24	91	....	1974-75	1984-85
Maloney, Don	NYR, Hfd., NYI	13	765	214	350	564	815	94	22	35	57	101	....	1978-79	1990-91
Maloney, Phil	Bos., Tor., Chi.	5	158	28	43	71	16	6	0	0	0	0	....	1949-50	1959-60
‡ Maltais, Steve	Wsh., Min., T.B., Det., CBJ	6	120	9	18	27	53	1	0	0	0	0	....	1989-90	2000-01
Maluta, Ray	Bos.	2	25	2	3	5	6	2	0	0	0	0	....	1975-76	1976-77
Manastersky, Tom	Mtl.	1	6	0	0	0	11	....	....	....	....	....	....	1950-51	1950-51
Mancuso, Gus	Mtl., NYR	4	42	7	9	16	17	....	....	....	....	....	....	1937-38	1942-43
‡ Manderville, Kent	Tor., Edm., Hfd., Car., Phi., Pit.	12	646	37	67	104	348	67	3	3	6	44	....	1991-92	2002-03
Mandich, Dan	Min.	4	111	5	11	16	303	7	0	0	0	2	....	1982-83	1985-86
‡ Maneluk, Mike	Phi., Chi., NYR, CBJ	3	85	11	10	21	57	....	....	....	....	....	....	1998-99	2000-01
Manery, Kris	Cle., Min., Van., Wpg.	4	250	63	64	127	91	....	....	....	....	....	....	1977-78	1980-81
Manery, Randy	Det., Atl., L.A.	10	582	50	206	256	415	13	0	2	2	12	....	1970-71	1979-80
‡ Mann, Cameron	Bos., Nsh.	5	93	14	10	24	40	1	0	0	0	0	....	1997-98	2002-03
Mann, Jack	NYR	2	9	3	4	7	0	....	....	....	....	....	....	1943-44	1944-45
Mann, Jimmy	Wpg., Que., Pit.	8	293	10	20	30	895	22	0	0	0	89	....	1979-80	1987-88
Mann, Ken	Det.	1	1	0	0	0	0	....	....	....	....	....	....	1975-76	1975-76
• Mann, Norm	Tor.	3	31	0	3	3	4	2	0	0	0	0	....	1935-36	1940-41
• Manners, Rennison	Pit., Phi.	2	37	3	2	5	14	....	....	....	....	....	....	1929-30	1930-31
Manno, Bob	Van., Tor., Det.	8	371	41	131	172	274	17	2	4	6	12	....	1976-77	1984-85
Manson, Dave	Chi., Edm., Wpg., Phx., Mtl., Dal., Tor.	16	1103	102	288	390	2792	112	7	24	31	343	....	1986-87	2001-02
Manson, Ray	Bos., NYR	2	2	0	1	1	0	....	....	....	....	....	....	1947-48	1948-49
• Mantha, Georges	Mtl.	13	488	89	102	191	148	36	6	2	8	24	2	1928-29	1940-41
Mantha, Moe	Wpg., Pit., Edm., Min., Phi.	12	656	81	289	370	501	17	5	10	15	18	....	1980-81	1991-92
• Mantha, Sylvio	Mtl., Bos.	14	542	63	78	141	671	39	5	5	10	64	3	1923-24	1936-37
• Maracle, Bud	NYR	1	11	1	3	4	4	4	0	0	0	0	....	1930-31	1930-31
Marcetta, Milan	Tor., Min.	3	54	7	15	22	10	17	7	7	14	4	1	1966-67	1968-69
• March, Mush	Chi.	17	759	153	230	383	540	45	12	15	27	41	2	1928-29	1944-45
Marchinko, Brian	Tor., NYI	4	47	2	6	8	0	....	....	....	....	....	....	1970-71	1973-74
Marcinyshyn, Dave	N.J., Que., NYR	3	16	0	1	1	49	....	....	....	....	....	....	1990-91	1992-93
Marcon, Lou	Det.	3	60	0	4	4	42	....	....	....	....	....	....	1958-59	1962-63
Marcotte, Don	Bos.	15	868	230	254	484	317	132	34	27	61	81	2	1965-66	1981-82
‡ Marha, Josef	Col., Ana., Chi.	6	159	21	32	53	32	....	....	....	....	....	....	1995-96	2000-01
Marini, Hector	NYI, N.J.	5	154	27	46	73	246	10	3	6	9	14	2	1978-79	1983-84
‡ Marinucci, Chris	NYI, L.A.	2	13	1	4	5	2	....	....	....	....	....	....	1994-95	1996-97
• Mario, Frank	Bos.	2	53	9	19	28	24	....	....	....	....	....	....	1941-42	1944-45
• Mariucci, John	Chi.	5	223	11	34	45	308	12	0	3	3	26	....	1940-41	1947-48
Mark, Gordon	N.J., Edm.	4	85	3	10	13	187	....	....	....	....	....	....	1986-87	1994-95
Markell, John	Wpg., St.L., Min.	4	55	11	10	21	36	....	....	....	....	....	....	1979-80	1984-85
• Marker, Gus	Det., Mtl.M., Tor., Bro.	10	322	64	69	133	133	46	5	7	12	36	1	1932-33	1941-42
Markham, Ray	NYR	1	14	1	1	2	21	7	1	0	1	24	....	1979-80	1979-80
• Markle, Jack	Tor.	1	8	0	1	1	0	....	....	....	....	....	....	1935-36	1935-36
• Marks, Jack	Mtl.W., Tor., Que.	2	7	0	0	0	4	....	....	....	....	....	1	1917-18	1919-20
Marks, John	Chi.	10	657	112	163	275	330	57	5	9	14	60	....	1972-73	1981-82
Markwart, Nevin	Bos., Cgy.	8	309	41	68	109	794	19	1	0	1	33	....	1983-84	1991-92
Marois, Daniel	Tor., NYI, Bos., Dal.	8	350	117	93	210	419	19	3	3	6	28	....	1987-88	1995-96
Marois, Mario	NYR, Van., Que., Wpg., St.L.	15	955	76	357	433	1746	100	4	34	38	182	....	1977-78	1991-92
Marotte, Gilles	Bos., Chi., L.A., NYR, St.L.	12	808	56	265	321	919	29	3	3	6	26	....	1965-66	1976-77
Marquess, Mark	Bos.	1	27	5	4	9	6	4	0	0	0	0	....	1946-47	1946-47
Marsh, Brad	Atl., Cgy., Phi., Tor., Det., Ott.	15	1086	23	175	198	1241	97	6	18	24	124	....	1978-79	1992-93
Marsh, Gary	Det., Tor.	2	7	1	3	4	4	....	....	....	....	....	....	1967-68	1968-69
Marsh, Peter	Wpg., Chi.	5	278	48	71	119	224	26	1	5	6	33	....	1979-80	1983-84
Marshall, Bert	Det., Oak., Cal., NYR, NYI	14	868	17	181	198	926	72	4	22	26	99	....	1965-66	1978-79
Marshall, Don	Mtl., NYR, Buf., Tor.	19	1176	265	324	589	127	94	8	15	23	14	5	1951-52	1971-72
Marshall, Paul	Pit., Tor., Hfd.	4	95	15	18	33	17	1	0	0	0	0	....	1979-80	1982-83
Marshall, Willie	Tor.	4	33	1	5	6	2	....	....	....	....	....	....	1952-53	1958-59
Marson, Mike	Wsh., L.A.	6	196	24	24	48	233	....	....	....	....	....	....	1974-75	1979-80
• Martin, Clare	Bos., Det., Chi., NYR	6	237	12	28	40	78	27	0	2	2	6	1	1941-42	1951-52
Martin, Craig	Wpg., Fla.	2	21	0	1	1	24	....	....	....	....	....	....	1994-95	1996-97
Martin, Frank	Bos., Chi.	6	282	11	46	57	122	10	0	2	2	2	....	1952-53	1957-58
Martin, Grant	Van., Wsh.	4	44	0	4	4	55	1	1	0	1	2	....	1983-84	1986-87

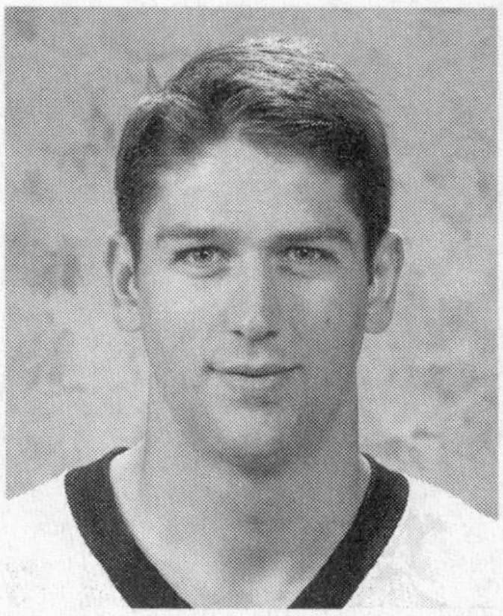

Kent Manderville

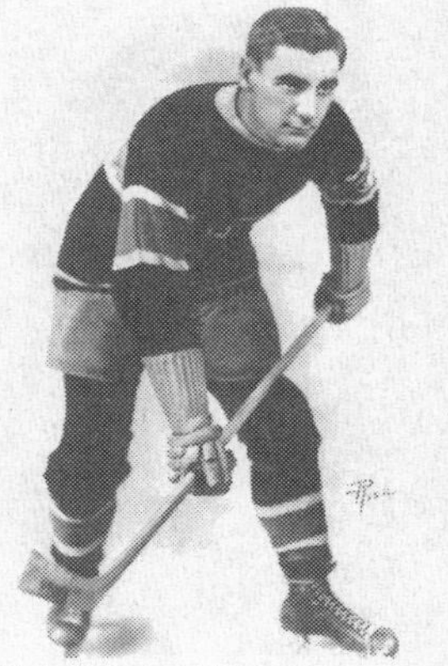

Sylvio Mantha

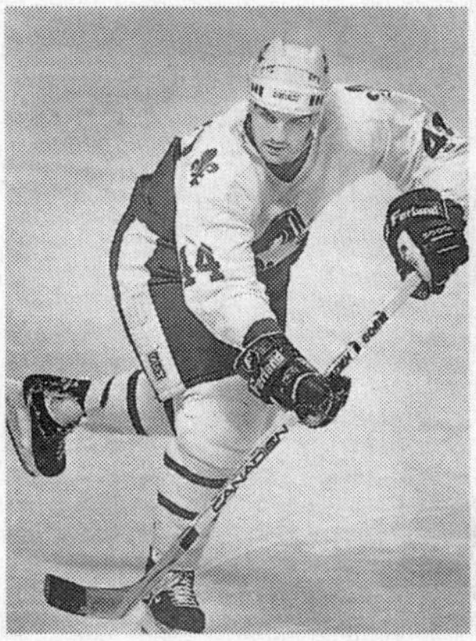

Mario Marois

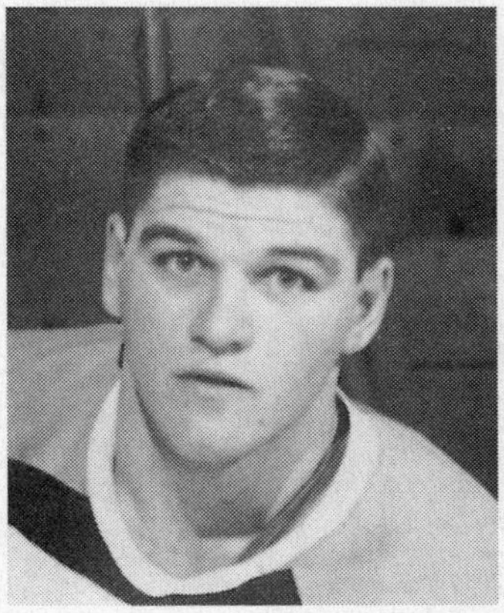

Gilles Marotte

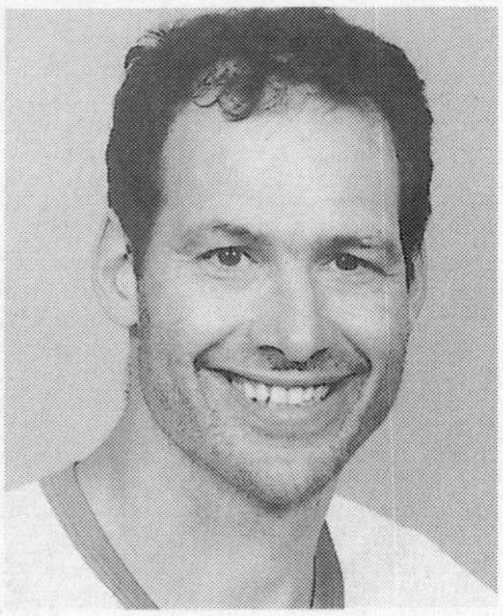

Brad Marsh

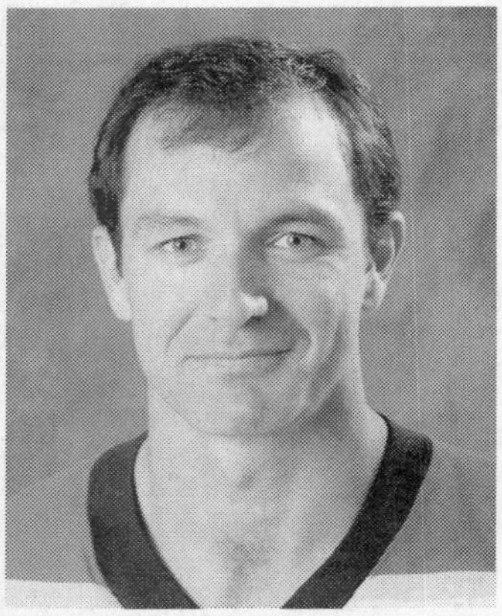

Stephane Matteau

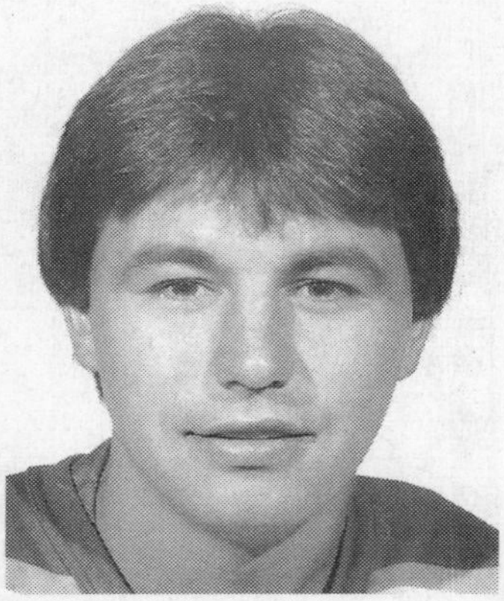

Dale McCourt

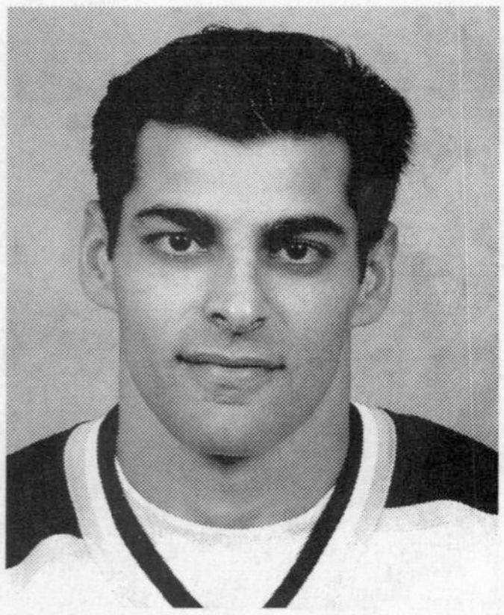

Marty McInnis

			Regular Schedule					Playoffs							
Name	NHL Teams	NHL Seasons	GP	G	A	TP	PIM	GP	G	A	TP	PIM	NHL Cup Wins	First NHL Season	Last NHL Season
Martin, Jack	Tor.	1	1	0	0	0	0	....	....	....	....	....	....	1960-61	1960-61
Martin, Matt	Tor.	4	76	0	5	5	71	....	....	....	....	....	....	1993-94	1996-97
Martin, Pit	Det., Bos., Chi., Van.	17	1101	324	485	809	609	100	27	31	58	56	....	1961-62	1978-79
Martin, Rick	Buf., L.A.	11	685	384	317	701	477	63	24	29	53	74	....	1971-72	1981-82
• Martin, Ron	NYA	2	94	13	16	29	36	....	....	....	....	....	....	1932-33	1933-34
Martin, Terry	Buf., Que., Tor., Edm., Min.	10	479	104	101	205	202	21	4	2	6	26	....	1975-76	1984-85
Martin, Tom	Tor.	1	3	1	0	1	0	....	....	....	....	....	....	1967-68	1967-68
Martin, Tom	Wpg., Hfd., Min.	6	92	12	11	23	249	4	0	0	0	6	....	1984-85	1989-90
Martineau, Don	Atl., Min., Det.	4	90	6	10	16	63	....	....	....	....	....	....	1973-74	1976-77
Martini, Darcy	Edm.	1	2	0	0	0	0	....	....	....	....	....	....	1993-94	1993-94
Martinson, Steve	Det., Mtl., Min.	4	49	2	1	3	244	1	0	0	0	10	....	1987-88	1991-92
Maruk, Dennis	Cal., Cle., Min., Wsh.	14	888	356	522	878	761	34	14	22	36	26	....	1975-76	1988-89
Masnick, Paul	Mtl., Chi., Tor.	6	232	18	41	59	139	33	4	5	9	27	1	1950-51	1957-58
• Mason, Charley	NYR, NYA, Det., Chi.	4	95	7	18	25	44	4	0	1	1	0	....	1934-35	1938-39
• Massecar, George	NYA	3	100	12	11	23	46	....	....	....	....	....	....	1929-30	1931-32
Masters, Jamie	St.L.	3	33	1	13	14	2	2	0	0	0	0	....	1975-76	1978-79
• Masterton, Bill	Min.	1	38	4	8	12	4	....	....	....	....	....	....	1967-68	1967-68
Mathers, Frank	Tor.	3	23	1	3	4	4	....	....	....	....	....	....	1948-49	1951-52
Mathiasen, Dwight	Pit.	3	33	1	7	8	18	....	....	....	....	....	....	1985-86	1987-88
Mathieson, Jim	Wsh.	1	2	0	0	0	4	....	....	....	....	....	....	1989-90	1989-90
‡ Mathieu, Marquis	Bos.	3	16	0	2	2	14	....	....	....	....	....	....	1998-99	2000-01
‡ Matte, Christian	Col., Min.	5	25	2	3	5	12	....	....	....	....	....	....	1996-97	2000-01
• Matte, Joe	Tor., Ham., Bos., Mtl.	4	68	17	15	32	54	....	....	....	....	....	....	1919-20	1925-26
• Matte, Joe	Det., Chi.	2	24	0	3	3	8	....	....	....	....	....	....	1929-30	1942-43
Matteau, Stephane	Cgy., Chi., NYR, St.L., S.J., Fla.	13	848	144	172	316	742	109	12	22	34	80	1	1990-91	2002-03
Mattiussi, Dick	Pit., Oak., Cal.	4	200	8	31	39	124	8	0	1	1	6	....	1967-68	1970-71
• Matz, Johnny	Mtl.	1	30	2	3	5	0	1	0	0	0	0	....	1924-25	1924-25
Maxner, Wayne	Bos.	2	62	8	9	17	48	....	....	....	....	....	....	1964-65	1965-66
Maxwell, Brad	Min., Que., Tor., Van., NYR	10	612	98	270	368	1292	79	12	49	61	178	....	1977-78	1986-87
Maxwell, Bryan	Min., St.L., Wpg., Pit.	8	331	18	77	95	745	15	1	1	2	86	....	1977-78	1984-85
Maxwell, Kevin	Min., Col., N.J.	3	66	6	15	21	61	16	3	4	7	24	....	1980-81	1983-84
Maxwell, Wally	Tor.	1	2	0	0	0	0	....	....	....	....	....	....	1952-53	1952-53
May, Alan	Bos., Edm., Wsh., Dal., Cgy.	8	393	31	45	76	1348	40	1	2	3	80	....	1987-88	1994-95
Mayer, Derek	Ott.	1	17	2	2	4	8	....	....	....	....	....	....	1993-94	1993-94
Mayer, Jim	NYR	1	4	0	0	0	0	....	....	....	....	....	....	1979-80	1979-80
Mayer, Pat	Pit.	1	1	0	0	0	4	....	....	....	....	....	....	1987-88	1987-88
Mayer, Shep	Tor.	1	12	1	2	3	4	....	....	....	....	....	....	1942-43	1942-43
• Mazur, Eddie	Mtl., Chi.	6	107	8	20	28	120	25	4	5	9	22	1	1950-51	1956-57
Mazur, Jay	Van.	4	47	11	7	18	20	6	0	1	1	8	....	1988-89	1991-92
McAdam, Gary	Buf., Pit., Det., Cgy., Wsh., N.J., Tor.	11	534	96	132	228	243	30	6	5	11	16	....	1975-76	1985-86
• McAdam, Sam	NYR	1	5	0	0	0	0	....	....	....	....	....	....	1930-31	1930-31
McAlpine, Chris	N.J., St.L., T.B., Atl., Chi., L.A.	8	289	6	24	30	245	28	0	1	1	18	1	1994-95	2002-03
• McAndrew, Hazen	Bro.	1	7	0	1	1	6	....	....	....	....	....	....	1941-42	1941-42
McAneeley, Ted	Cal.	3	158	8	35	43	141	....	....	....	....	....	....	1972-73	1974-75
McAtee, Jud	Det.	3	46	15	13	28	6	14	2	1	3	0	....	1942-43	1944-45
McAtee, Norm	Bos.	1	13	0	1	1	0	....	....	....	....	....	....	1946-47	1946-47
• McAvoy, George	Mtl.	1	....	....	....	....	....	4	0	0	0	0	....	1954-55	1954-55
McBain, Andrew	Wpg., Pit., Van., Ott.	11	608	129	172	301	633	24	5	7	12	39	....	1983-84	1993-94
‡ McBain, Jason	Hfd.	2	9	0	0	0	0	....	....	....	....	....	....	1995-96	1996-97
‡ McBain, Mike	T.B.	2	64	0	7	7	22	....	....	....	....	....	....	1997-98	1998-99
McBean, Wayne	L.A., NYI, Wpg.	6	211	10	39	49	168	2	1	1	2	0	....	1987-88	1993-94
McBride, Cliff	Mtl.M., Tor.	2	2	0	0	0	0	....	....	....	....	....	....	1928-29	1929-30
McBurney, Jim	Chi.	1	1	0	1	1	0	....	....	....	....	....	....	1952-53	1952-53
• McCabe, Stan	Det., Mtl.M.	4	78	9	4	13	49	....	....	....	....	....	....	1929-30	1933-34
• McCaffrey, Bert	Tor., Pit., Mtl.	7	260	43	30	73	202	8	2	1	3	10	1	1924-25	1930-31
McCahill, John	Col.	1	1	0	0	0	0	....	....	....	....	....	....	1977-78	1977-78
• McCaig, Doug	Det., Chi.	7	263	8	21	29	255	7	0	1	1	10	....	1941-42	1950-51
• McCallum, Dunc	NYR, Pit.	5	187	14	35	49	230	10	1	2	3	12	....	1965-66	1970-71
• McCalmon, Eddie	Chi., Phi.	2	39	5	0	5	14	....	....	....	....	....	....	1927-28	1930-31
McCann, Rick	Det.	6	43	1	4	5	6	....	....	....	....	....	....	1967-68	1974-75
McCarthy, Dan	NYR	1	5	4	0	4	4	....	....	....	....	....	....	1980-81	1980-81
McCarthy, Kevin	Phi., Van., Pit.	10	537	67	191	258	527	21	2	3	5	20	....	1977-78	1986-87
• McCarthy, Thomas	Que., Ham.	2	35	22	7	29	10	....	....	....	....	....	....	1919-20	1920-21
McCarthy, Tom	Det., Bos.	4	60	8	9	17	8	....	....	....	....	....	....	1956-57	1960-61
McCarthy, Tom	Min., Bos.	9	460	178	221	399	330	68	12	26	38	67	....	1979-80	1987-88
• McCartney, Walt	Mtl.	1	2	0	0	0	0	....	....	....	....	....	....	1932-33	1932-33
McCaskill, Ted	Min.	1	4	0	2	2	0	....	....	....	....	....	....	1967-68	1967-68
McClanahan, Rob	Buf., Hfd., NYR	5	224	38	63	101	126	34	4	12	16	31	....	1979-80	1983-84
McCleary, Trent	Ott., Bos., Mtl.	4	192	8	15	23	134	....	....	....	....	....	....	1995-96	1999-00
McClelland, Kevin	Pit., Edm., Det., Tor., Wpg.	12	588	68	112	180	1672	98	11	18	29	281	4	1981-82	1993-94
McCord, Bob	Bos., Det., Min., St.L.	7	316	10	58	68	262	14	2	5	7	10	....	1963-64	1972-73
McCord, Dennis	Van.	1	3	0	0	0	6	....	....	....	....	....	....	1973-74	1973-74
McCormack, John	Tor., Mtl., Chi.	8	311	25	49	74	35	22	1	1	2	0	2	1947-48	1954-55
McCosh, Shawn	L.A., NYR	2	9	1	0	1	6	....	....	....	....	....	....	1991-92	1994-95
McCourt, Dale	Det., Buf., Tor.	7	532	194	284	478	124	21	9	7	16	6	....	1977-78	1983-84
McCreary, Bill	NYR, Det., Mtl., St.L.	8	309	53	62	115	108	48	6	16	22	14	....	1953-54	1970-71
McCreary, Bill	Tor.	1	12	1	0	1	4	....	....	....	....	....	....	1980-81	1980-81
• McCreary, Keith	Mtl., Pit., Atl.	10	532	131	112	243	294	16	0	4	4	6	....	1961-62	1974-75
• McCreedy, John	Tor.	2	64	17	12	29	25	21	4	3	7	16	2	1941-42	1944-45
McCrimmon, Brad	Bos., Phi., Cgy., Det., Hfd., Phx.	18	1222	81	322	403	1416	116	11	18	29	176	1	1979-80	1996-97
McCrimmon, Jim	St.L.	1	2	0	0	0	0	....	....	....	....	....	....	1974-75	1974-75
McCulley, Bob	Mtl.	1	1	0	0	0	0	....	....	....	....	....	....	1934-35	1934-35
• McCurry, Duke	Pit.	4	148	21	11	32	119	4	0	2	2	2	....	1925-26	1928-29
McCutcheon, Brian	Det.	3	37	3	1	4	7	....	....	....	....	....	....	1974-75	1976-77
McCutcheon, Darwin	Tor.	1	1	0	0	0	2	....	....	....	....	....	....	1981-82	1981-82
McDill, Jeff	Chi.	1	1	0	0	0	0	....	....	....	....	....	....	1976-77	1976-77
McDonagh, Bill	NYR	1	4	0	0	0	2	....	....	....	....	....	....	1949-50	1949-50
McDonald, Ab	Mtl., Chi., Bos., Det., Pit., St.L.	15	762	182	248	430	200	84	21	29	50	42	4	1957-58	1971-72
McDonald, Brian	Chi., Buf.	2	12	0	0	0	29	8	0	0	0	2	....	1967-68	1970-71
• McDonald, Bucko	Det., Tor., NYR	11	446	35	88	123	206	50	6	1	7	24	3	1934-35	1944-45
McDonald, Butch	Det., Chi.	2	66	8	20	28	2	5	0	2	2	10	....	1939-40	1944-45
McDonald, Gerry	Hfd.	2	8	0	0	0	4	....	....	....	....	....	....	1981-82	1983-84
• McDonald, Jack	Mtl.W., Mtl., Que., Tor.	5	69	26	14	40	30	7	1	3	4	3	....	1917-18	1921-22
McDonald, Jack	NYR	1	43	10	9	19	6	....	....	....	....	....	....	1943-44	1943-44
McDonald, Lanny	Tor., Col., Cgy.	16	1111	500	506	1006	899	117	44	40	84	120	1	1973-74	1988-89
McDonald, Robert	NYR	1	1	0	0	0	0	....	....	....	....	....	....	1943-44	1943-44
McDonald, Terry	K.C.	1	8	0	1	1	6	....	....	....	....	....	....	1975-76	1975-76
McDonnell, Joe	Van., Pit.	3	50	2	10	12	34	....	....	....	....	....	....	1981-82	1985-86
• McDonnell, Moylan	Ham.	1	22	1	2	3	2	....	....	....	....	....	....	1920-21	1920-21
McDonough, Al	L.A., Pit., Atl., Det.	5	237	73	88	161	73	8	0	1	1	2	....	1970-71	1977-78
McDonough, Hubie	L.A., NYI, S.J.	5	195	40	26	66	67	5	1	0	1	4	....	1988-89	1992-93
McDougal, Mike	NYR, Hfd.	4	61	8	10	18	43	....	....	....	....	....	....	1978-79	1982-83
McDougall, Bill	Det., Edm., T.B.	3	28	5	5	10	12	1	0	0	0	0	....	1990-91	1993-94
McElmury, Jim	Min., K.C., Col.	5	180	14	47	61	49	....	....	....	....	....	....	1972-73	1977-78
McEwen, Mike	NYR, Col., NYI, L.A., Wsh., Det., Hfd.	12	716	108	296	404	460	78	12	36	48	48	3	1976-77	1987-88
McFadden, Jim	Det., Chi.	8	412	100	126	226	89	49	10	9	19	30	1	1946-47	1953-54
McFadyen, Don	Chi.	4	179	12	33	45	77	11	2	2	4	5	1	1932-33	1935-36
McFall, Dan	Wpg.	2	9	0	1	1	0	....	....	....	....	....	....	1984-85	1985-86
• McFarlane, Gord	Chi.	1	2	0	0	0	0	....	....	....	....	....	....	1926-27	1926-27
McGeough, Jim	Wsh., Pit.	4	57	7	10	17	32	....	....	....	....	....	....	1981-82	1986-87
• McGibbon, Irv	Mtl.	1	1	0	0	0	2	....	....	....	....	....	....	1942-43	1942-43
McGill, Bob	Tor., Chi., S.J., Det., NYI, Hfd.	13	705	17	55	72	1766	49	0	0	0	88	....	1981-82	1993-94
• McGill, Jack	Mtl.	3	134	27	10	37	71	3	2	0	2	0	....	1934-35	1936-37
• McGill, Jack	Bos.	4	97	23	36	59	42	27	7	4	11	17	....	1941-42	1946-47
McGill, Ryan	Chi., Phi., Edm.	4	151	4	15	19	391	....	....	....	....	....	....	1991-92	1994-95
McGregor, Sandy	NYR	1	2	0	0	0	2	....	....	....	....	....	....	1963-64	1963-64
• McGuire, Mickey	Pit.	2	36	3	0	3	6	....	....	....	....	....	....	1926-27	1927-28
McHugh, Mike	Min., S.J.	4	20	1	0	1	16	....	....	....	....	....	....	1988-89	1991-92
McIlhargey, Jack	Phi., Van., Hfd.	8	393	11	36	47	1102	27	0	3	3	68	....	1974-75	1981-82
• McInenly, Bert	Det., NYA, Ott., Bos.	6	166	19	15	34	144	4	0	0	0	2	....	1930-31	1935-36
McInnis, Marty	NYI, Cgy., Ana., Bos.	12	796	170	250	420	330	22	3	2	5	4	....	1991-92	2002-03
McIntosh, Bruce	Min.	1	2	0	0	0	0	....	....	....	....	....	....	1972-73	1972-73
McIntosh, Paul	Buf.	2	48	0	2	2	66	2	0	0	0	7	....	1974-75	1975-76
• McIntyre, Jack	Bos., Chi., Det.	11	499	109	102	211	173	29	7	6	13	4	....	1949-50	1959-60
McIntyre, John	Tor., L.A., NYR, Van.	6	351	24	54	78	516	44	0	6	6	54	....	1989-90	1994-95
McIntyre, Larry	Tor.	2	41	0	3	3	26	....	....	....	....	....	....	1969-70	1972-73

			Regular Schedule					Playoffs							
Name	NHL Teams	NHL Seasons	GP	G	A	TP	PIM	GP	G	A	TP	PIM	NHL Cup Wins	First NHL Season	Last NHL Season
McKay, Doug	Det.	1	....	....	....	....	....	1	0	0	0	0	1	1949-50	1949-50
McKay, Randy	Det., N.J., Dal., Mtl.	15	932	162	201	363	1731	123	20	23	43	123	2	1988-89	2002-03
McKay, Ray	Chi., Buf., Cal.	6	140	2	16	18	102	....	....	....	....	....	....	1968-69	1973-74
McKay, Scott	Ana.	1	1	0	0	0	0	....	....	....	....	....	....	1993-94	1993-94
McKechnie, Walt	Min., Cal., Bos., Det., Wsh., Cle., Tor., Col.	16	955	214	392	606	469	15	7	5	12	7	....	1967-68	1982-83
McKee, Mike	Que.	1	48	3	12	15	41	....	....	....	....	....	....	1993-94	1993-94
McKegney, Ian	Chi.	1	3	0	0	0	2	....	....	....	....	....	....	1976-77	1976-77
McKegney, Tony	Buf., Que., Min., NYR, St.L., Det., Chi.	13	912	320	319	639	517	79	24	23	47	56	....	1978-79	1990-91
McKendry, Alex	NYI, Cgy.	4	46	3	6	9	21	6	2	2	4	0	1	1977-78	1980-81
McKenna, Sean	Buf., L.A., Tor.	9	414	82	80	162	181	15	1	2	3	2	....	1981-82	1989-90
McKenney, Don	Bos., NYR, Tor., Det., St.L.	13	798	237	345	582	211	58	18	29	47	10	1	1954-55	1967-68
McKenny, Jim	Tor., Min.	14	604	82	247	329	294	37	7	9	16	10	....	1965-66	1978-79
McKenzie, Brian	Pit.	1	6	1	1	2	4	....	....	....	....	....	....	1971-72	1971-72
McKenzie, John	Chi., Det., NYR, Bos.	12	691	206	268	474	917	69	15	32	47	133	2	1958-59	1971-72
McKim, Andrew	Bos., Det.	3	38	1	4	5	6	....	....	....	....	....	....	1992-93	1994-95
• McKinnon, Alex	Ham., NYA, Chi.	5	193	19	11	30	237	....	....	....	....	....	....	1924-25	1928-29
• McKinnon, John	Mtl., Pit., Phi.	6	208	28	11	39	224	2	0	0	0	4	....	1925-26	1930-31
McLean, Don	Wsh.	1	9	0	0	0	6	....	....	....	....	....	....	1975-76	1975-76
• McLean, Fred	Que., Ham.	2	8	0	0	0	2	....	....	....	....	....	....	1919-20	1920-21
McLean, Jack	Tor.	3	67	14	24	38	76	13	2	2	4	8	1	1942-43	1944-45
McLean, Jeff	S.J.	1	6	1	0	1	0	....	....	....	....	....	....	1993-94	1993-94
• McLellan, John	Tor.	1	2	0	0	0	0	....	....	....	....	....	....	1951-52	1951-52
McLellan, Scott	Bos.	1	2	0	0	0	0	....	....	....	....	....	....	1982-83	1982-83
McLellan, Todd	NYI	1	5	1	1	2	0	....	....	....	....	....	....	1987-88	1987-88
• McLenahan, Rollie	Det.	1	9	2	1	3	10	2	0	0	0	0	....	1945-46	1945-46
McLeod, Al	Det.	1	26	2	2	4	24	....	....	....	....	....	....	1973-74	1973-74
McLeod, Jackie	NYR	5	106	14	23	37	12	7	0	0	0	0	....	1949-50	1954-55
McLlwain, Dave	Pit., Wpg., Buf., NYI, Tor., Ott.	10	501	100	107	207	292	20	0	2	2	2	....	1987-88	1996-97
• McMahon, Mike	Mtl., Bos.	3	57	7	18	25	102	13	1	2	3	30	1	1942-43	1945-46
McMahon, Mike	NYR, Min., Chi., Det., Pit., Buf.	8	224	15	68	83	171	14	3	7	10	4	....	1963-64	1971-72
McManama, Bob	Pit.	3	99	11	25	36	28	8	0	1	1	6	....	1973-74	1975-76
• McManus, Sammy	Mtl.M., Bos.	2	26	0	1	1	8	1	0	0	0	0	1	1934-35	1936-37
McMurchy, Tom	Chi., Edm.	4	55	8	4	12	65	....	....	....	....	....	....	1983-84	1987-88
McNab, Max	Det.	4	128	16	19	35	24	25	1	0	1	4	1	1947-48	1950-51
McNab, Peter	Buf., Bos., Van., N.J.	14	954	363	450	813	179	107	40	42	82	20	....	1973-74	1986-87
• McNabney, Sid	Mtl.	1	....	....	....	....	....	5	0	1	1	2	....	1950-51	1950-51
• McNamara, Howard	Mtl.	1	10	1	0	1	4	....	....	....	....	....	....	1919-20	1919-20
• McNaughton, George	Que.	1	1	0	0	0	0	....	....	....	....	....	....	1919-20	1919-20
McNeill, Billy	Det.	6	257	21	46	67	142	4	1	1	2	4	....	1956-57	1963-64
McNeill, Mike	Chi., Que.	2	63	5	11	16	18	....	....	....	....	....	....	1990-91	1991-92
McNeill, Stu	Det.	3	10	1	1	2	2	....	....	....	....	....	....	1957-58	1959-60
McPhee, George	NYR, N.J.	7	115	24	25	49	257	29	5	3	8	69	....	1982-83	1988-89
McPhee, Mike	Mtl., Min., Dal.	11	744	200	199	399	661	134	28	27	55	193	1	1983-84	1993-94
McRae, Basil	Que., Tor., Det., Min., T.B., St.L., Chi.	16	576	53	83	136	2457	78	8	4	12	349	....	1981-82	1996-97
McRae, Chris	Tor., Det.	3	21	1	0	1	122	....	....	....	....	....	....	1987-88	1989-90
McRae, Ken	Que., Tor.	7	137	14	21	35	364	6	0	0	0	4	....	1987-88	1993-94
• McReavy, Pat	Bos., Det.	4	55	5	10	15	4	22	3	3	6	9	1	1938-39	1941-42
McReynolds, Brian	Wpg., NYR, L.A.	3	30	1	5	6	8	....	....	....	....	....	....	1989-90	1993-94
McSheffrey, Bryan	Van., Buf.	3	90	13	7	20	44	....	....	....	....	....	....	1972-73	1974-75
McSorley, Marty	Pit., Edm., L.A., NYR, S.J., Bos.	17	961	108	251	359	3381	115	10	19	29	374	2	1983-84	1999-00
McSween, Don	Buf., Ana.	5	47	3	10	13	55	....	....	....	....	....	....	1987-88	1995-96
McTaggart, Jim	Wsh.	2	71	3	10	13	205	....	....	....	....	....	....	1980-81	1981-82
‡ McTavish, Dale	Cgy.	1	9	1	2	3	2	....	....	....	....	....	....	1996-97	1996-97
McTavish, Gord	St.L., Wpg.	2	11	1	3	4	2	....	....	....	....	....	....	1978-79	1979-80
• McVeigh, Charley	Chi., NYA	9	397	84	88	172	138	4	0	0	0	2	....	1926-27	1934-35
• McVicar, Jack	Mtl.M.	2	88	2	4	6	63	6	0	0	0	2	....	1930-31	1931-32
Meagher, Rick	Mtl., Hfd., N.J., St.L.	12	691	144	165	309	383	62	8	7	15	41	....	1979-80	1990-91
Meehan, Gerry	Tor., Phi., Buf., Van., Atl., Wsh.	10	670	180	243	423	111	10	0	1	1	0	....	1968-69	1978-79
Meeke, Brent	Cal., Cle.	5	75	9	22	31	8	....	....	....	....	....	....	1972-73	1976-77
Meeker, Howie	Tor.	8	346	83	102	185	329	42	6	9	15	50	4	1946-47	1953-54
Meeker, Mike	Pit.	1	4	0	0	0	5	....	....	....	....	....	....	1978-79	1978-79
• Meeking, Harry	Tor., Det., Bos.	3	64	18	12	30	66	9	3	0	3	6	....	1917-18	1926-27
Meger, Paul	Mtl.	6	212	39	52	91	118	35	3	8	11	16	1	1949-50	1954-55
Meighan, Ron	Min., Pit.	2	48	3	7	10	18	....	....	....	....	....	....	1981-82	1982-83
Meissner, Barrie	Min.	2	6	0	1	1	4	....	....	....	....	....	....	1967-68	1968-69
Meissner, Dick	Bos., NYR	5	171	11	15	26	37	....	....	....	....	....	....	1959-60	1964-65
Melametsa, Anssi	Wpg.	1	27	0	3	3	2	....	....	....	....	....	....	1985-86	1985-86
‡ Melanson, Dean	Buf., Wsh.	2	9	0	0	0	8	....	....	....	....	....	....	1994-95	2001-02
Melin, Roger	Min.	2	3	0	0	0	0	....	....	....	....	....	....	1980-81	1981-82
Mellor, Tom	Det.	2	26	2	4	6	25	....	....	....	....	....	....	1973-74	1974-75
• Melnyk, Gerry	Det., Chi., St.L.	6	269	39	77	116	34	53	6	6	12	6	....	1955-56	1967-68
Melnyk, Larry	Bos., Edm., NYR, Van.	10	432	11	63	74	686	66	2	9	11	127	2	1980-81	1989-90
Melrose, Barry	Wpg., Tor., Det.	6	300	10	23	33	728	7	0	2	2	38	....	1979-80	1985-86
Menard, Hillary	Chi.	1	1	0	0	0	0	....	....	....	....	....	....	1953-54	1953-54
Menard, Howie	Det., L.A., Chi., Oak.	4	151	23	42	65	87	19	3	7	10	36	....	1963-64	1969-70
Mercredi, Vic	Atl.	1	2	0	0	0	0	....	....	....	....	....	....	1974-75	1974-75
Meredith, Greg	Cgy.	2	38	6	4	10	8	5	3	1	4	4	....	1980-81	1982-83
Merkosky, Glenn	Hfd., N.J., Det.	5	66	5	12	17	22	....	....	....	....	....	....	1981-82	1989-90
• Meronek, Bill	Mtl.	2	19	5	8	13	0	1	0	0	0	0	....	1939-40	1942-43
Merrick, Wayne	St.L., Cal., Cle., NYI	12	774	191	265	456	303	102	19	30	49	30	4	1972-73	1983-84
• Merrill, Horace	Ott.	2	8	0	0	0	3	....	....	....	....	....	1	1917-18	1919-20
‡ Mertzig, Jan	NYR	1	23	0	2	2	8	....	....	....	....	....	....	1998-99	1998-99
Messier, Joby	NYR	3	25	0	4	4	24	....	....	....	....	....	....	1992-93	1994-95
Messier, Mitch	Min.	4	20	0	2	2	11	....	....	....	....	....	....	1987-88	1990-91
Messier, Paul	Col.	1	9	0	0	0	4	....	....	....	....	....	....	1978-79	1978-79
Metcalfe, Scott	Edm., Buf.	3	19	1	2	3	18	....	....	....	....	....	....	1987-88	1989-90
‡ Metropolit, Glen	Wsh., T.B.	4	103	10	37	47	26	3	0	0	0	2	....	1999-00	2002-03
Metz, Don	Tor.	9	172	20	35	55	42	42	7	8	15	12	5	1938-39	1948-49
• Metz, Nick	Tor.	12	518	131	119	250	149	76	19	20	39	31	4	1934-35	1947-48
Michaluk, Art	Chi.	1	5	0	0	0	0	....	....	....	....	....	....	1947-48	1947-48
Michaluk, John	Chi.	1	1	0	0	0	0	....	....	....	....	....	....	1950-51	1950-51
Michayluk, Dave	Phi., Pit.	3	14	2	6	8	8	7	1	1	2	0	1	1981-82	1991-92
Micheletti, Joe	St.L., Col.	3	158	11	60	71	114	11	1	11	12	10	....	1979-80	1981-82
Micheletti, Pat	Min.	1	12	2	0	2	8	....	....	....	....	....	....	1987-88	1987-88
• Mickey, Larry	Chi., NYR, Tor., Mtl., L.A., Phi., Buf.	11	292	39	53	92	160	9	1	0	1	10	....	1964-65	1974-75
• Mickoski, Nick	NYR, Chi., Det., Bos.	13	703	158	185	343	319	18	1	6	7	6	....	1947-48	1959-60
Middendorf, Max	Que., Edm.	4	13	2	4	6	6	....	....	....	....	....	....	1986-87	1990-91
Middleton, Rick	NYR, Bos.	14	1005	448	540	988	157	114	45	55	100	19	....	1974-75	1987-88
Miehm, Kevin	St.L.	2	22	1	4	5	8	2	0	1	1	0	....	1992-93	1993-94
Migay, Rudy	Tor.	10	418	59	92	151	293	15	1	0	1	20	....	1949-50	1959-60
‡ Mika, Petr	NYI	1	3	0	0	0	0	....	....	....	....	....	....	1999-00	1999-00
Mikita, Stan	Chi.	22	1394	541	926	1467	1270	155	59	91	150	169	1	1958-59	1979-80
Mikkelson, Bill	L.A., NYI, Wsh.	4	147	4	18	22	105	....	....	....	....	....	....	1971-72	1976-77
Mikol, Jim	Tor., NYR	2	34	1	4	5	8	....	....	....	....	....	....	1962-63	1964-65
Mikulchik, Oleg	Wpg., Ana.	3	37	0	3	3	33	....	....	....	....	....	....	1993-94	1995-96
Milbury, Mike	Bos.	12	754	49	189	238	1552	86	4	24	28	219	....	1975-76	1986-87
• Milks, Hib	Pit., Phi., NYR, Ott.	8	317	87	41	128	179	11	0	0	0	2	....	1925-26	1932-33
Millar, Craig	Edm., Nsh., T.B.	5	114	8	14	22	73	....	....	....	....	....	....	1996-97	2000-01
• Millar, Hugh	Det.	1	4	0	0	0	0	1	0	0	0	0	....	1946-47	1946-47
Millar, Mike	Hfd., Wsh., Bos., Tor.	5	78	18	18	36	12	....	....	....	....	....	....	1986-87	1990-91
Millen, Corey	NYR, L.A., N.J., Dal., Cgy.	8	335	90	119	209	236	47	5	7	12	22	....	1989-90	1996-97
• Miller, Bill	Mtl.M., Mtl.	3	95	7	3	10	16	12	0	0	0	0	1	1934-35	1936-37
Miller, Bob	Bos., Col., L.A.	6	404	75	119	194	220	36	4	7	11	27	....	1977-78	1984-85
Miller, Brad	Buf., Ott., Cgy.	6	82	1	5	6	321	....	....	....	....	....	....	1988-89	1993-94
• Miller, Earl	Chi., Tor.	5	109	19	14	33	124	10	1	0	1	6	1	1927-28	1931-32
Miller, Jack	Chi.	2	17	0	0	0	4	....	....	....	....	....	....	1949-50	1950-51
Miller, Jason	N.J.	3	6	0	0	0	0	....	....	....	....	....	....	1990-91	1992-93
Miller, Jay	Bos., L.A.	7	446	40	44	84	1723	48	2	3	5	243	....	1985-86	1991-92
Miller, Kelly	NYR, Wsh.	15	1057	181	282	463	512	119	20	34	54	65	....	1984-85	1998-99
Miller, Paul	Col.	1	3	0	3	3	0	....	....	....	....	....	....	1981-82	1981-82
Miller, Perry	Det.	4	217	10	51	61	387	....	....	....	....	....	....	1977-78	1980-81
Miller, Tom	Det., NYI	4	118	16	25	41	34	....	....	....	....	....	....	1970-71	1974-75
Miller, Warren	NYR, Hfd.	4	262	40	50	90	137	6	1	0	1	0	....	1979-80	1982-83
Mills, Craig	Wpg., Chi.	3	31	0	5	5	36	1	0	0	0	0	....	1995-96	1998-99
Miner, John	Edm.	1	14	2	3	5	16	....	....	....	....	....	....	1987-88	1987-88

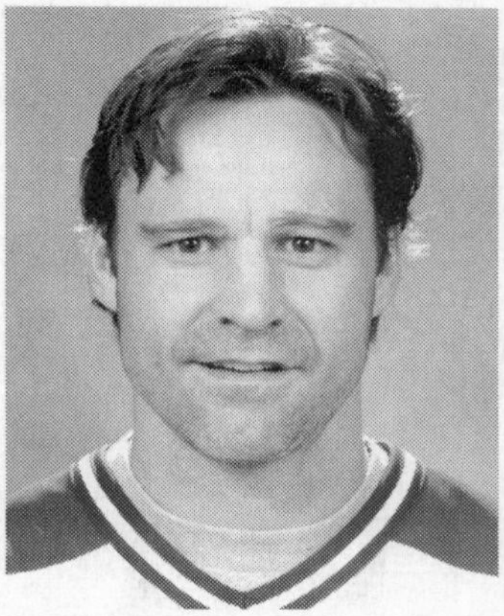
Randy McKay

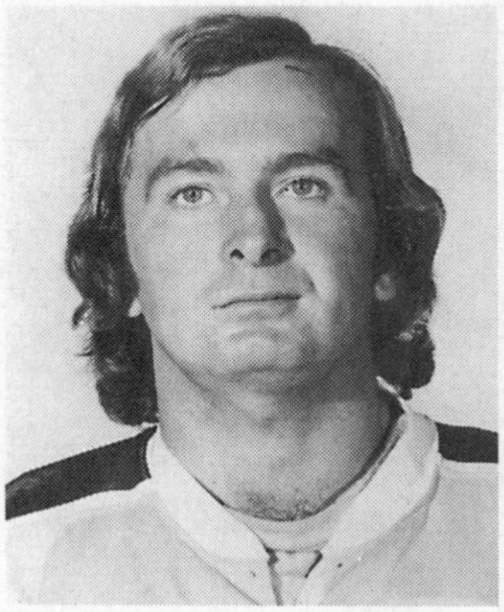
Walt McKechnie

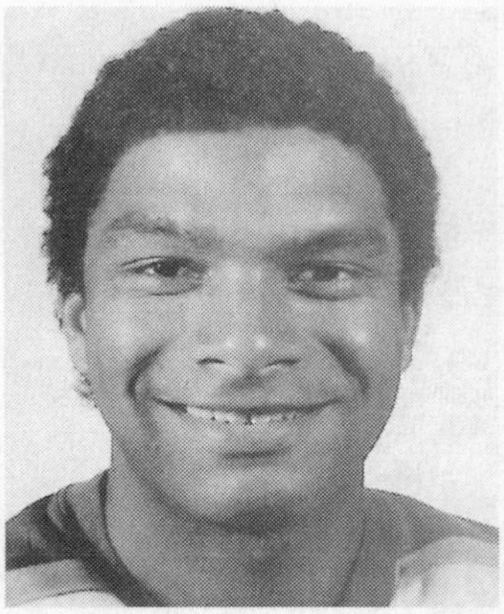
Tony McKegney

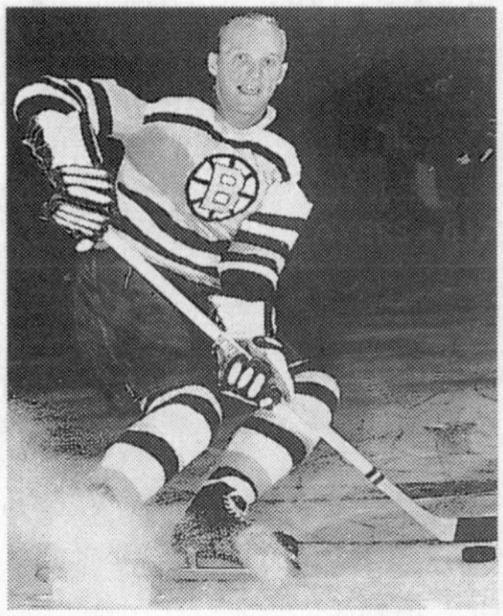
Doug Mohns

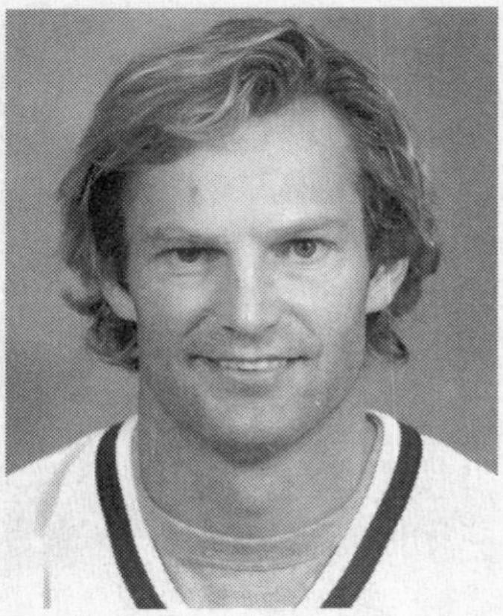

Kirk Muller

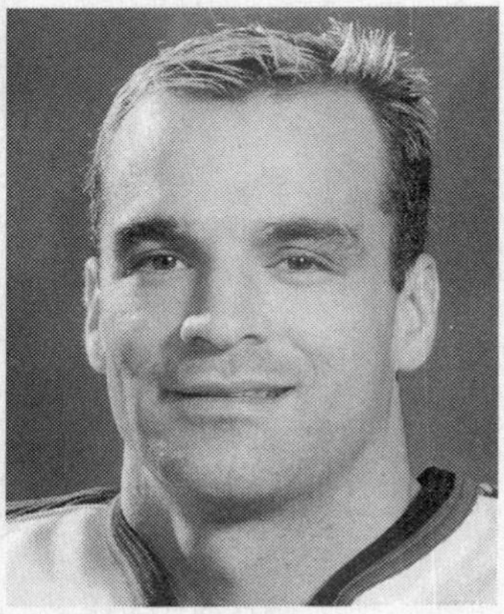

Joe Murphy

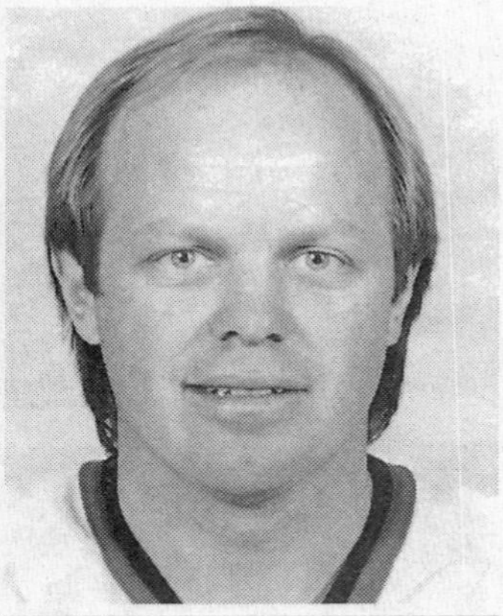

Bob Murray

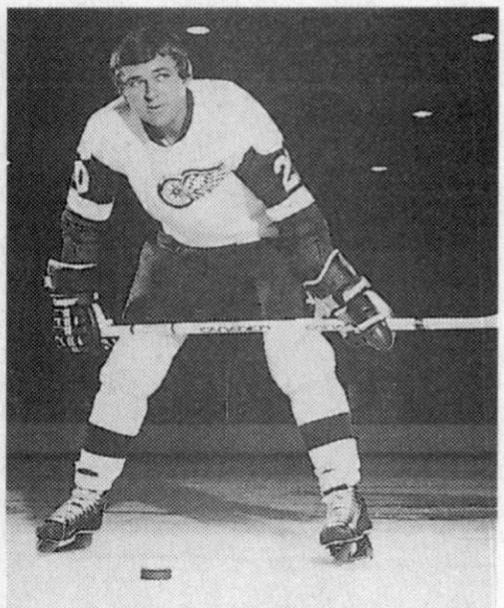

Vaclav Nedomansky

			Regular Schedule					Playoffs					NHL	First	Last
Name	NHL Teams	NHL Seasons	GP	G	A	TP	PIM	GP	G	A	TP	PIM	Cup Wins	NHL Season	NHL Season
Minor, Gerry	Van.	5	140	11	21	32	173	12	1	3	4	25	....	1979-80	1983-84
Mironov, Dmitri	Tor., Pit., Ana., Det., Wsh.	11	556	54	206	260	568	75	10	26	36	48	1	1991-92	2001-02
Miszuk, John	Det., Chi., Phi., Min.	6	237	7	39	46	232	19	0	3	3	19	....	1963-64	1969-70
Mitchell, Bill	Det.	1	1	0	0	0	0	....	....	....	....	....	....	1963-64	1963-64
• Mitchell, Herb	Bos.	2	44	6	0	6	36	....	....	....	....	....	....	1924-25	1925-26
‡ Mitchell, Jeff	Dal.	1	7	0	0	0	7	....	....	....	....	....	....	1997-98	1997-98
Mitchell, Red	Chi.	3	83	4	5	9	67	....	....	....	....	....	....	1941-42	1944-45
Mitchell, Roy	Min.	1	3	0	0	0	0	....	....	....	....	....	....	1992-93	1992-93
• Moe, Bill	NYR	5	261	11	42	53	163	1	0	0	0	0	....	1944-45	1948-49
Moffat, Lyle	Tor., Wpg.	3	97	12	16	28	51	....	....	....	....	....	....	1972-73	1979-80
• Moffat, Ron	Det.	3	37	1	1	2	8	7	0	0	0	0	....	1932-33	1934-35
Moger, Sandy	Bos., L.A.	5	236	41	38	79	212	5	2	2	4	12	....	1994-95	1998-99
Moher, Mike	N.J.	1	9	0	1	1	28	....	....	....	....	....	....	1982-83	1982-83
Mohns, Doug	Bos., Chi., Min., Atl., Wsh.	22	1390	248	462	710	1250	94	14	36	50	122	....	1953-54	1974-75
Mohns, Lloyd	NYR	1	1	0	0	0	0	....	....	....	....	....	....	1943-44	1943-44
Mokosak, Carl	Cgy., L.A., Phi., Pit., Bos.	6	83	11	15	26	170	1	0	0	0	0	....	1981-82	1988-89
Mokosak, John	Det.	2	41	0	2	2	96	....	....	....	....	....	....	1988-89	1989-90
Molin, Lars	Van.	3	172	33	65	98	37	19	2	9	11	7	....	1981-82	1983-84
Moller, Mike	Buf., Edm.	7	134	15	28	43	41	3	0	1	1	0	....	1980-81	1986-87
Moller, Randy	Que., NYR, Buf., Fla.	14	815	45	180	225	1692	78	6	16	22	197	....	1981-82	1994-95
Molloy, Mitch	Buf.	1	2	0	0	0	10	....	....	....	....	....	....	1989-90	1989-90
• Molyneaux, Larry	NYR	2	45	0	1	1	20	10	0	0	0	8	....	1937-38	1938-39
Momesso, Sergio	Mtl., St.L., Van., Tor., NYR	13	710	152	193	345	1557	119	18	26	44	311	....	1983-84	1996-97
Monahan, Garry	Mtl., Det., L.A., Tor., Van.	12	748	116	169	285	484	22	3	1	4	13	....	1967-68	1978-79
Monahan, Hartland	Cal., NYR, Wsh., Pit., L.A., St.L.	7	334	61	80	141	163	6	0	0	0	4	....	1973-74	1980-81
• Mondou, Armand	Mtl.	12	386	47	71	118	99	32	3	5	8	12	2	1928-29	1939-40
Mondou, Pierre	Mtl.	9	548	194	262	456	179	69	17	28	45	26	3	1976-77	1984-85
Mongeau, Michel	St.L., T.B.	4	54	6	19	25	10	2	0	1	1	0	....	1989-90	1992-93
Mongrain, Bob	Buf., L.A.	6	81	13	14	27	14	11	1	2	3	2	....	1979-80	1985-86
Monteith, Hank	Det.	3	77	5	12	17	6	4	0	0	0	0	....	1968-69	1970-71
‡ Montgomery, Jim	St.L., Mtl., Phi., S.J., Dal.	6	122	9	25	34	80	8	1	0	1	2	....	1993-94	2002-03
‡ Moore, Barrie	Buf., Edm., Wsh.	3	39	2	6	8	18	....	....	....	....	....	....	1995-96	1999-00
Moore, Dickie	Mtl., Tor., St.L.	14	719	261	347	608	652	135	46	64	110	122	6	1951-52	1967-68
• Moran, Amby	Mtl., Chi.	2	35	1	1	2	24	....	....	....	....	....	....	1926-27	1927-28
‡ Moravec, David	Buf.	1	1	0	0	0	0	....	....	....	....	....	....	1999-00	1999-00
More, Jay	NYR, Min., S.J., Phx., Chi., Nsh.	10	406	18	54	72	702	31	0	6	6	45	....	1988-89	1998-99
• Morenz, Howie	Mtl., Chi., NYR	14	550	271	201	472	546	39	13	9	22	58	3	1923-24	1936-37
Moretto, Angelo	Cle.	1	5	1	2	3	2	....	....	....	....	....	....	1976-77	1976-77
• Morin, Pete	Mtl.	1	31	10	12	22	7	1	0	0	0	0	....	1941-42	1941-42
• Morin, Stephane	Que., Van.	5	90	16	39	55	52	....	....	....	....	....	....	1989-90	1993-94
‡ Morisset, Dave	Fla.	1	4	0	0	0	5	....	....	....	....	....	....	2001-02	2001-02
Morissette, Dave	Mtl.	2	11	0	0	0	57	....	....	....	....	....	....	1998-99	1999-00
• Morris, Bernie	Bos.	1	6	1	0	1	0	....	....	....	....	....	....	1924-25	1924-25
Morris, Jon	N.J., S.J., Bos.	6	103	16	33	49	47	11	1	7	8	25	....	1988-89	1993-94
• Morris, Moe	Tor., NYR	4	135	13	29	42	58	18	4	2	6	16	1	1943-44	1948-49
Morrison, Dave	L.A., Van.	4	39	3	3	6	4	....	....	....	....	....	....	1980-81	1984-85
Morrison, Don	Det., Chi.	3	112	18	28	46	12	3	0	1	1	0	....	1947-48	1950-51
Morrison, Doug	Bos.	4	23	7	3	10	15	....	....	....	....	....	....	1979-80	1984-85
Morrison, Gary	Phi.	3	43	1	15	16	70	5	0	1	1	2	....	1979-80	1981-82
Morrison, George	St.L.	2	115	17	21	38	13	3	0	0	0	0	....	1970-71	1971-72
Morrison, Jim	Bos., Tor., Det., NYR, Pit.	12	704	40	160	200	542	36	0	12	12	38	....	1951-52	1970-71
• Morrison, John	NYA	1	18	0	0	0	0	....	....	....	....	....	....	1925-26	1925-26
Morrison, Kevin	Col.	1	41	4	11	15	23	....	....	....	....	....	....	1979-80	1979-80
Morrison, Lew	Phi., Atl., Wsh., Pit.	9	564	39	52	91	107	17	0	0	0	2	....	1969-70	1977-78
Morrison, Mark	NYR	2	10	1	1	2	0	....	....	....	....	....	....	1981-82	1983-84
• Morrison, Rod	Det.	1	34	8	7	15	4	3	0	0	0	0	....	1947-48	1947-48
Morrow, Ken	NYI	10	550	17	88	105	309	127	11	22	33	97	4	1979-80	1988-89
Morrow, Scott	Cgy.	1	4	0	0	0	0	....	....	....	....	....	....	1994-95	1994-95
Morton, Dean	Det.	1	1	1	0	1	2	....	....	....	....	....	....	1989-90	1989-90
Mortson, Gus	Tor., Chi., Det.	13	797	46	152	198	1380	54	5	8	13	68	4	1946-47	1958-59
Mosdell, Ken	Bro., Mtl., Chi.	16	693	141	168	309	475	80	16	13	29	48	4	1941-42	1958-59
• Mosienko, Bill	Chi.	14	711	258	282	540	121	22	10	4	14	15	....	1941-42	1954-55
Mott, Morris	Cal.	3	199	18	32	50	49	....	....	....	....	....	....	1972-73	1974-75
• Motter, Alex	Bos., Det.	8	255	39	64	103	135	41	3	9	12	41	1	1934-35	1942-43
Moxey, Jim	Cal., Cle., L.A.	3	127	22	27	49	59	....	....	....	....	....	....	1974-75	1976-77
Mulhern, Richard	Atl., L.A., Tor., Wpg.	6	303	27	93	120	217	7	0	3	3	5	....	1975-76	1980-81
Mulhern, Ryan	Wsh.	1	3	0	0	0	0	....	....	....	....	....	....	1997-98	1997-98
Mullen, Brian	Wpg., NYR, S.J., NYI	11	832	260	362	622	414	62	12	18	30	30	....	1982-83	1992-93
Mullen, Joe	St.L., Cgy., Pit., Bos.	17	1062	502	561	1063	241	143	60	46	106	42	3	1979-80	1996-97
Muller, Kirk	N.J., Mtl., NYI, Tor., Fla., Dal.	19	1349	357	602	959	1223	127	33	36	69	153	1	1984-85	2002-03
Muloin, Wayne	Det., Oak., Cal., Min.	3	147	3	21	24	93	11	0	0	0	2	....	1963-64	1970-71
Mulvenna, Glenn	Pit., Phi.	2	2	0	0	0	4	....	....	....	....	....	....	1991-92	1992-93
Mulvey, Grant	Chi., N.J.	10	586	149	135	284	816	42	10	5	15	70	....	1974-75	1983-84
Mulvey, Paul	Wsh., Pit., L.A.	4	225	30	51	81	613	....	....	....	....	....	....	1978-79	1981-82
• Mummery, Harry	Tor., Que., Mtl., Ham.	6	106	33	19	52	226	2	1	1	2	17	....	1917-18	1922-23
Muni, Craig	Tor., Edm., Chi., Buf., Wpg., Pit., Dal.	16	819	28	119	147	775	113	0	17	17	108	3	1981-82	1997-98
• Munro, Dunc	Mtl.M., Mtl.	8	239	28	18	46	172	21	2	2	4	18	1	1924-25	1931-32
• Munro, Gerry	Mtl.M., Tor.	2	34	1	0	1	37	....	....	....	....	....	....	1924-25	1925-26
Murdoch, Bob	Mtl., L.A., Atl., Cgy.	12	757	60	218	278	764	69	4	18	22	92	2	1970-71	1981-82
Murdoch, Bob	Cal., Cle., St.L.	4	260	72	85	157	127	....	....	....	....	....	....	1975-76	1978-79
Murdoch, Don	NYR, Edm., Det.	6	320	121	117	238	155	24	10	8	18	16	....	1976-77	1981-82
• Murdoch, Murray	NYR	11	508	84	108	192	197	55	9	12	21	28	2	1926-27	1936-37
Murphy, Brian	Det.	1	1	0	0	0	0	....	....	....	....	....	....	1974-75	1974-75
Murphy, Gord	Phi., Bos., Fla., Atl.	14	862	85	238	323	668	53	3	16	19	35	....	1988-89	2001-02
Murphy, Joe	Det., Edm., Chi., St.L., S.J., Bos., Wsh.	15	779	233	295	528	810	120	34	43	77	185	1	1986-87	2000-01
Murphy, Larry	L.A., Wsh., Min., Pit., Tor., Det.	21	1615	287	929	1216	1084	215	37	115	152	201	4	1980-81	2000-01
Murphy, Mike	St.L., NYR, L.A.	12	831	238	318	556	514	66	13	23	36	54	....	1971-72	1982-83
Murphy, Rob	Van., Ott., L.A.	7	125	9	12	21	152	4	0	0	0	2	....	1987-88	1993-94
Murphy, Ron	NYR, Chi., Det., Bos.	18	889	205	274	479	460	53	7	8	15	26	1	1952-53	1969-70
Murray, Allan	NYA	7	271	5	9	14	163	14	0	0	0	10	....	1933-34	1939-40
Murray, Bob	Atl., Van.	4	194	6	16	22	98	10	1	1	2	15	....	1973-74	1976-77
Murray, Bob	Chi.	15	1008	132	382	514	873	112	19	37	56	106	....	1975-76	1989-90
Murray, Chris	Mtl., Hfd., Car., Ott., Chi., Dal.	6	242	16	18	34	550	15	1	0	1	12	....	1994-95	1999-00
Murray, Jim	L.A.	1	30	0	2	2	14	....	....	....	....	....	....	1967-68	1967-68
Murray, Ken	Tor., NYI, Det., K.C.	5	106	1	10	11	135	....	....	....	....	....	....	1969-70	1975-76
• Murray, Leo	Mtl.	1	6	0	0	0	2	....	....	....	....	....	....	1932-33	1932-33
‡ Murray, Mike	Phi.	1	1	0	0	0	0	....	....	....	....	....	....	1987-88	1987-88
Murray, Pat	Phi.	2	25	3	1	4	15	....	....	....	....	....	....	1990-91	1991-92
Murray, Randy	Tor.	1	3	0	0	0	2	....	....	....	....	....	....	1969-70	1969-70
Murray, Rob	Wsh., Wpg., Phx.	8	107	4	15	19	111	9	0	0	0	18	....	1989-90	1998-99
Murray, Terry	Cal., Phi., Det., Wsh.	8	302	4	76	80	199	18	2	2	4	10	....	1972-73	1981-82
Murray, Troy	Chi., Wpg., Ott., Pit., Col.	15	915	230	354	584	875	113	17	26	43	145	1	1981-82	1995-96
Murzyn, Dana	Hfd., Cgy., Van.	14	838	52	152	204	1571	82	9	10	19	166	1	1985-86	1998-99
Musil, Frantisek	Min., Cgy., Ott., Edm.	15	797	34	106	140	1241	42	2	4	6	47	....	1986-87	2000-01
Myers, Hap	Buf.	1	13	0	0	0	6	....	....	....	....	....	....	1970-71	1970-71
Myhres, Brantt	T.B., Phi., S.J., Nsh., Wsh., Bos.	7	154	6	2	8	687	....	....	....	....	....	....	1994-95	2002-03
Myles, Vic	NYR	1	45	6	9	15	57	....	....	....	....	....	....	1942-43	1942-43

N

‡ Nabokov, Dmitri	Chi., NYI	3	55	11	13	24	28	....	....	....	....	....	....	1997-98	1999-00
Nachbaur, Don	Hfd., Edm., Phi.	8	223	23	46	69	465	11	1	1	2	24	....	1980-81	1989-90
Nahrgang, Jim	Det.	3	57	5	12	17	34	....	....	....	....	....	....	1974-75	1976-77
Namestnikov, John	Van., NYI, Nsh.	6	43	0	9	9	24	2	0	0	0	2	....	1993-94	1999-00
Nanne, Lou	Min.	11	635	68	157	225	356	32	4	10	14	8	....	1967-68	1977-78
Nantais, Rich	Min.	3	63	5	4	9	79	....	....	....	....	....	....	1974-75	1976-77
Napier, Mark	Mtl., Min., Edm., Buf.	11	767	235	306	541	157	82	18	24	42	11	2	1978-79	1988-89
Naslund, Mats	Mtl., Bos.	9	651	251	383	634	111	102	35	57	92	33	1	1982-83	1994-95
Nattrass, Ralph	Chi.	4	223	18	38	56	308	....	....	....	....	....	....	1946-47	1949-50
Nattress, Ric	Mtl., St.L., Cgy., Tor., Phi.	11	536	29	135	164	377	67	5	10	15	60	1	1982-83	1992-93
Natyshak, Mike	Que.	1	4	0	0	0	0	....	....	....	....	....	....	1987-88	1987-88
‡ Ndur, Rumun	Buf., NYR, Atl.	4	69	2	3	5	137	....	....	....	....	....	....	1996-97	1999-00
Neaton, Pat	Pit.	1	9	1	1	2	12	....	....	....	....	....	....	1993-94	1993-94
Nechayev, Viktor	L.A.	1	3	1	0	1	0	....	....	....	....	....	....	1982-83	1982-83
Nedomansky, Vaclav	Det., NYR, St.L.	6	421	122	156	278	88	7	3	5	8	0	....	1977-78	1982-83
‡ Nedved, Zdenek	Tor.	3	31	4	6	10	14	....	....	....	....	....	....	1994-95	1996-97

Name	NHL Teams	NHL Seasons	Regular Schedule GP	G	A	TP	PIM	Playoffs GP	G	A	TP	PIM	NHL Cup Wins	First NHL Season	Last NHL Season
Needham, Mike	Pit., Dal.	3	86	9	5	14	16	14	2	0	2	4	1	1991-92	1993-94
Neely, Bob	Tor., Col.	5	283	39	59	98	266	26	5	7	12	15	....	1973-74	1977-78
Neely, Cam	Van., Bos.	13	726	395	299	694	1241	93	57	32	89	168	....	1983-84	1995-96
Neilson, Jim	NYR, Cal., Cle.	16	1023	69	299	368	904	65	1	17	18	61	....	1962-63	1977-78
Nelson, Gordie	Tor.	1	3	0	0	0	11	....	....	....	....	....	....	1969-70	1969-70
Nelson, Todd	Pit., Wsh.	2	3	1	0	1	2	4	0	0	0	0	....	1991-92	1993-94
‡ Nemchinov, Sergei	NYR, Van., NYI, N.J.	11	761	152	193	345	251	105	11	20	31	24	2	1991-92	2001-02
Nemeth, Steve	NYR	1	12	2	0	2	2	....	....	....	....	....	....	1987-88	1987-88
‡ Nemirovsky, David	Fla.	4	91	16	22	38	42	3	1	0	1	0	....	1995-96	1998-99
Nesterenko, Eric	Tor., Chi.	21	1219	250	324	574	1273	124	13	24	37	127	1	1951-52	1971-72
Nethery, Lance	NYR, Edm.	2	41	11	14	25	14	14	5	3	8	9	....	1980-81	1981-82
Neufeld, Ray	Hfd., Wpg., Bos.	11	595	157	200	357	816	28	8	6	14	55	....	1979-80	1989-90
• Neville, Mike	Tor., NYA	3	65	5	5	10	14	2	0	0	0	0	....	1924-25	1930-31
Nevin, Bob	Tor., NYR, Min., L.A.	18	1128	307	419	726	211	84	16	18	34	24	2	1957-58	1975-76
Newberry, John	Mtl., Hfd.	4	22	0	4	4	6	2	0	0	0	0	....	1982-83	1985-86
Newell, Rick	Det.	2	6	0	0	0	0	....	....	....	....	....	....	1972-73	1973-74
Newman, Dan	NYR, Mtl., Edm.	4	126	17	24	41	63	3	0	0	0	4	....	1976-77	1979-80
• Newman, John	Det.	1	8	1	1	2	0	....	....	....	....	....	....	1930-31	1930-31
Nicholls, Bernie	L.A., NYR, Edm., N.J., Chi., S.J.	18	1127	475	734	1209	1292	118	42	72	114	164	....	1981-82	1998-99
Nicholson, Al	Bos.	2	19	0	1	1	4	....	....	....	....	....	....	1955-56	1956-57
• Nicholson, Ed	Det.	1	1	0	0	0	0	....	....	....	....	....	....	1947-48	1947-48
• Nicholson, Hickey	Chi.	1	2	1	0	1	0	....	....	....	....	....	....	1937-38	1937-38
Nicholson, Neil	Oak., NYI	4	39	3	1	4	23	2	0	0	0	0	....	1969-70	1977-78
Nicholson, Paul	Wsh.	3	62	4	8	12	18	....	....	....	....	....	....	1974-75	1976-77
Nicolson, Graeme	Bos., Col., NYR	3	52	2	7	9	60	....	....	....	....	....	....	1978-79	1982-83
Nieckar, Barry	Hfd., Cgy., Ana.	4	8	0	0	0	21	....	....	....	....	....	....	1992-93	1997-98
Niekamp, Jim	Det.	2	29	0	2	2	37	....	....	....	....	....	....	1970-71	1971-72
Nielsen, Jeff	NYR, Ana., Min.	5	252	20	27	47	70	4	0	0	0	2	....	1996-97	2000-01
Nielsen, Kirk	Bos.	1	6	0	0	0	0	....	....	....	....	....	....	1997-98	1997-98
‡ Niemi, Antti-Jussi	Ana.	2	29	1	1	2	22	....	....	....	....	....	....	2000-01	2001-02
Nienhuis, Kraig	Bos.	3	87	20	16	36	39	2	0	0	0	14	....	1985-86	1987-88
• Nighbor, Frank	Ott., Tor.	13	349	139	98	237	249	20	4	9	13	13	4	1917-18	1929-30
Nigro, Frank	Tor.	2	68	8	18	26	39	3	0	0	0	2	....	1982-83	1983-84
‡ Nikulin, Igor	Ana.	1	....	....	....	....	....	1	0	0	0	0	....	1996-97	1996-97
Nilan, Chris	Mtl., NYR, Bos.	13	688	110	115	225	3043	111	8	9	17	541	1	1979-80	1991-92
Nill, Jim	St.L., Van., Bos., Wpg., Det.	9	524	58	87	145	854	59	10	5	15	203	....	1981-82	1989-90
Nilsson, Kent	Atl., Cgy., Min., Edm.	9	553	264	422	686	116	59	11	41	52	14	1	1979-80	1994-95
Nilsson, Ulf	NYR	4	170	57	112	169	85	25	8	14	22	27	....	1978-79	1982-83
Nistico, Lou	Col.	1	3	0	0	0	0	....	....	....	....	....	....	1977-78	1977-78
• Noble, Reg	Tor., Mtl.M., Det.	16	510	168	106	274	916	18	2	2	4	33	3	1917-18	1932-33
Noel, Claude	Wsh.	1	7	0	0	0	0	....	....	....	....	....	....	1979-80	1979-80
• Nolan, Paddy	Tor.	1	2	0	0	0	0	....	....	....	....	....	....	1921-22	1921-22
Nolan, Ted	Det., Pit.	3	78	6	16	22	105	....	....	....	....	....	....	1981-82	1985-86
Nolet, Simon	Phi., K.C., Pit., Col.	10	562	150	182	332	187	34	6	3	9	8	1	1967-68	1976-77
Noonan, Brian	Chi., NYR, St.L., Van., Phx.	12	629	116	159	275	518	71	17	19	36	77	1	1987-88	1998-99
Nordmark, Robert	St.L., Van.	4	236	13	70	83	254	7	3	2	5	8	....	1987-88	1990-91
‡ Nordstrom, Peter	Bos.	1	2	0	0	0	0	....	....	....	....	....	....	1998-99	1998-99
Noris, Joe	Pit., St.L., Buf.	3	55	2	5	7	22	....	....	....	....	....	....	1971-72	1973-74
‡ Norris, Dwayne	Que., Ana.	3	20	2	4	6	8	....	....	....	....	....	....	1993-94	1995-96
Norrish, Rod	Min.	2	21	3	3	6	2	....	....	....	....	....	....	1973-74	1974-75
• Northcott, Baldy	Mtl.M., Chi.	11	446	133	112	245	273	31	8	5	13	14	1	1928-29	1938-39
Norton, Jeff	NYI, S.J., St.L., Edm., T.B., Fla., Pit., Bos.	15	799	52	332	384	615	65	4	21	25	89	....	1987-88	2001-02
Norwich, Craig	Wpg., St.L., Col.	2	104	17	58	75	60	....	....	....	....	....	....	1979-80	1980-81
Norwood, Lee	Que., Wsh., St.L., Det., N.J., Hfd., Cgy.	12	503	58	153	211	1099	65	6	22	28	171	....	1980-81	1993-94
Novy, Milan	Wsh.	1	73	18	30	48	16	2	0	0	0	0	....	1982-83	1982-83
Nowak, Hank	Pit., Det., Bos.	4	180	26	29	55	161	13	1	0	1	8	....	1973-74	1976-77
‡ Nummelin, Petteri	CBJ	1	61	4	12	16	10	....	....	....	....	....	....	2000-01	2000-01
‡ Nurminen, Kai	L.A., Min.	2	69	17	11	28	24	....	....	....	....	....	....	1996-97	2000-01
Nykoluk, Mike	Tor.	1	32	3	1	4	20	....	....	....	....	....	....	1956-57	1956-57
Nylund, Gary	Tor., Chi., NYI	11	608	32	139	171	1235	24	0	6	6	63	....	1982-83	1992-93
• Nyrop, Bill	Mtl., Min.	4	207	12	51	63	101	35	1	7	8	22	3	1975-76	1981-82
Nystrom, Bob	NYI	14	900	235	278	513	1248	157	39	44	83	236	4	1972-73	1985-86

O

Name	NHL Teams	NHL Seasons	Regular Schedule GP	G	A	TP	PIM	Playoffs GP	G	A	TP	PIM	NHL Cup Wins	First NHL Season	Last NHL Season
• Oatman, Russell	Det., Mtl.M., NYR	3	120	20	9	29	100	15	1	0	1	18	....	1926-27	1928-29
O'Brien, Dennis	Min., Col., Cle., Bos.	10	592	31	91	122	1017	34	1	2	3	101	....	1970-71	1979-80
O'Brien, Ellard	Bos.	1	2	0	0	0	0	....	....	....	....	....	....	1955-56	1955-56
O'Callahan, Jack	Chi., N.J.	7	389	27	104	131	541	32	4	11	15	41	....	1982-83	1988-89
O'Connell, Mike	Chi., Bos., Det.	13	860	105	334	439	605	82	8	24	32	64	....	1977-78	1989-90
• O'Connor, Buddy	Mtl., NYR	10	509	140	257	397	34	53	15	21	36	6	2	1941-42	1950-51
O'Connor, Myles	N.J., Ana.	4	43	3	4	7	69	....	....	....	....	....	....	1990-91	1993-94
Oddleifson, Chris	Bos., Van.	9	524	95	191	286	464	14	1	6	7	8	....	1972-73	1980-81
Odelein, Selmar	Edm.	3	18	0	2	2	35	....	....	....	....	....	....	1985-86	1988-89
Odgers, Jeff	S.J., Bos., Col., Atl.	12	821	75	70	145	2364	47	2	1	3	73	....	1991-92	2002-03
Odjick, Gino	Van., NYI, Phi., Mtl.	12	605	64	73	137	2567	44	4	1	5	142	....	1990-91	2001-02
O'Donnell, Fred	Bos.	2	115	15	11	26	98	5	0	1	1	5	....	1972-73	1973-74
O'Donoghue, Don	Oak., Cal.	3	125	18	17	35	35	3	0	0	0	0	....	1969-70	1971-72
Odrowski, Gerry	Det., Oak., St.L.	6	309	12	19	31	111	30	0	1	1	16	....	1960-61	1971-72
O'Dwyer, Bill	L.A., Bos.	5	120	9	13	22	108	10	0	0	0	2	....	1983-84	1989-90
O'Flaherty, Gerry	Tor., Van., Atl.	8	438	99	95	194	168	7	2	2	4	6	....	1971-72	1978-79
O'Flaherty, Peanuts	NYA, Bro.	2	21	5	1	6	0	....	....	....	....	....	....	1940-41	1941-42
Ogilvie, Brian	Chi., St.L.	6	90	15	21	36	29	....	....	....	....	....	....	1972-73	1978-79
• O'Grady, George	Mtl.W.	1	4	0	0	0	0	....	....	....	....	....	....	1917-18	1917-18
Ogrodnick, John	Det., Que., NYR	14	928	402	425	827	260	41	18	8	26	6	....	1979-80	1992-93
‡ Ojanen, Janne	N.J.	4	98	21	23	44	28	3	0	2	2	0	....	1988-89	1992-93
Okerlund, Todd	NYI	1	4	0	0	0	2	....	....	....	....	....	....	1987-88	1987-88
Oksiuta, Roman	Edm., Van., Ana., Pit.	4	153	46	41	87	100	10	2	3	5	0	....	1993-94	1996-97
‡ Olausson, Fredrik	Wpg., Edm., Ana., Pit., Det.	16	1022	147	434	581	450	71	6	23	29	28	1	1986-87	2002-03
Olczyk, Ed	Chi., Tor., Wpg., NYR, L.A., Pit.	16	1031	342	452	794	874	57	19	15	34	57	1	1984-85	1999-00
• Oliver, Harry	Bos., NYA	11	463	127	85	212	147	35	10	6	16	24	1	1926-27	1936-37
Oliver, Murray	Det., Bos., Tor., Min.	17	1127	274	454	728	320	35	9	16	25	10	....	1957-58	1974-75
Olmstead, Bert	Chi., Mtl., Tor.	14	848	181	421	602	884	115	16	43	59	101	5	1948-49	1961-62
Olsen, Darryl	Cgy.	1	1	0	0	0	0	....	....	....	....	....	....	1991-92	1991-92
Olson, Dennis	Det.	1	4	0	0	0	0	....	....	....	....	....	....	1957-58	1957-58
‡ Olsson, Christer	St.L., Ott.	2	56	4	12	16	24	3	0	0	0	0	....	1995-96	1996-97
• O'Neil, Jim	Bos., Mtl.	6	156	6	30	36	109	9	1	1	2	13	....	1933-34	1941-42
O'Neil, Paul	Van., Bos.	2	6	0	0	0	0	....	....	....	....	....	....	1973-74	1975-76
• O'Neill, Tom	Tor.	2	66	10	12	22	53	4	0	0	0	6	1	1943-44	1944-45
Orban, Bill	Chi., Min.	3	114	8	15	23	67	3	0	0	0	0	....	1967-68	1969-70
O'Ree, Willie	Bos.	2	45	4	10	14	26	....	....	....	....	....	....	1957-58	1960-61
O'Regan, Tom	Pit.	3	61	5	12	17	10	....	....	....	....	....	....	1983-84	1985-86
O'Reilly, Terry	Bos.	14	891	204	402	606	2095	108	25	42	67	335	....	1971-72	1984-85
Orlando, Gates	Buf.	3	98	18	26	44	51	5	0	4	4	14	....	1984-85	1986-87
• Orlando, Jimmy	Det.	6	199	6	25	31	375	36	0	9	9	105	1	1936-37	1942-43
Orleski, Dave	Mtl.	2	2	0	0	0	0	....	....	....	....	....	....	1980-81	1981-82
Orr, Bobby	Bos., Chi.	12	657	270	645	915	953	74	26	66	92	107	2	1966-67	1978-79
Osborne, Keith	St.L., T.B.	2	16	1	3	4	16	....	....	....	....	....	....	1989-90	1992-93
Osborne, Mark	Det., NYR, Tor., Wpg.	14	919	212	319	531	1152	87	12	16	28	141	....	1981-82	1994-95
Osburn, Randy	Tor., Phi.	2	27	0	2	2	0	....	....	....	....	....	....	1972-73	1974-75
O'Shea, Danny	Min., Chi., St.L.	5	369	64	115	179	265	39	3	7	10	61	....	1968-69	1972-73
O'Shea, Kevin	Buf., St.L.	3	134	13	18	31	85	12	2	1	3	10	....	1970-71	1972-73
Osiecki, Mark	Cgy., Ott., Wpg., Min.	2	93	3	11	14	43	....	....	....	....	....	....	1991-92	1992-93
O'Sullivan, Chris	Cgy., Van., Ana.	5	62	2	17	19	16	....	....	....	....	....	....	1996-97	2002-03
Otevrel, Jaroslav	S.J.	2	16	3	4	7	2	....	....	....	....	....	....	1992-93	1993-94
Otto, Joel	Cgy., Phi.	14	943	195	313	508	1934	122	27	47	74	207	1	1984-85	1997-98
Ouellette, Eddie	Chi.	1	43	3	2	5	11	1	0	0	0	0	....	1935-36	1935-36
Ouellette, Gerry	Bos.	1	34	5	4	9	0	....	....	....	....	....	....	1960-61	1960-61
Owchar, Dennis	Pit., Col.	6	288	30	85	115	200	10	1	1	2	8	....	1974-75	1979-80
• Owen, George	Bos.	5	183	44	33	77	151	21	2	5	7	25	1	1928-29	1932-33

P

Name	NHL Teams	NHL Seasons	Regular Schedule GP	G	A	TP	PIM	Playoffs GP	G	A	TP	PIM	NHL Cup Wins	First NHL Season	Last NHL Season
Pachal, Clayton	Bos., Col.	3	35	2	3	5	95	....	....	....	....	....	....	1976-77	1978-79
Paddock, John	Wsh., Phi., Que.	5	87	8	14	22	86	5	2	0	2	0	....	1975-76	1982-83

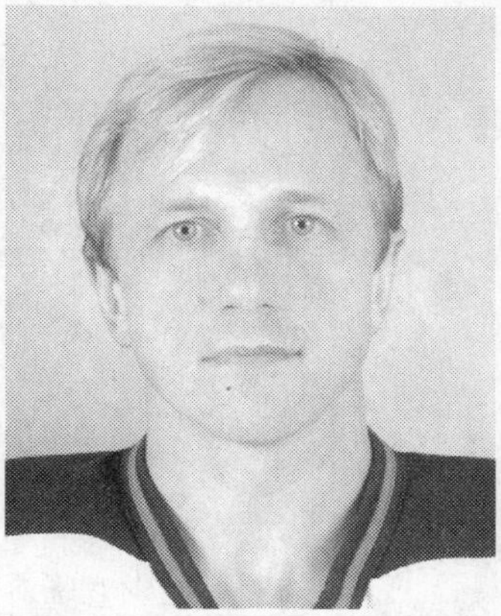

Sergei Nemchinov

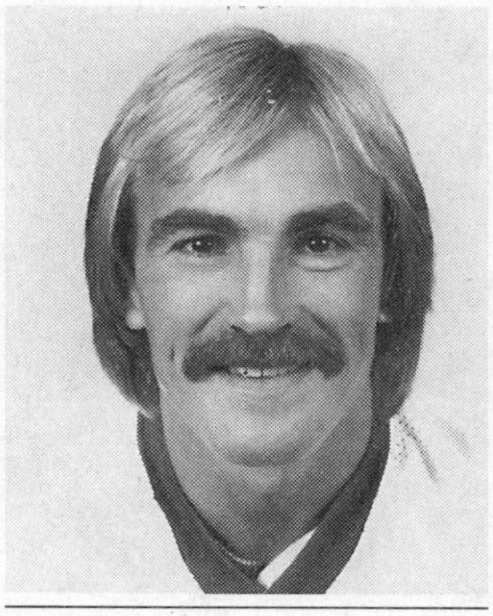

Bob Nystrom

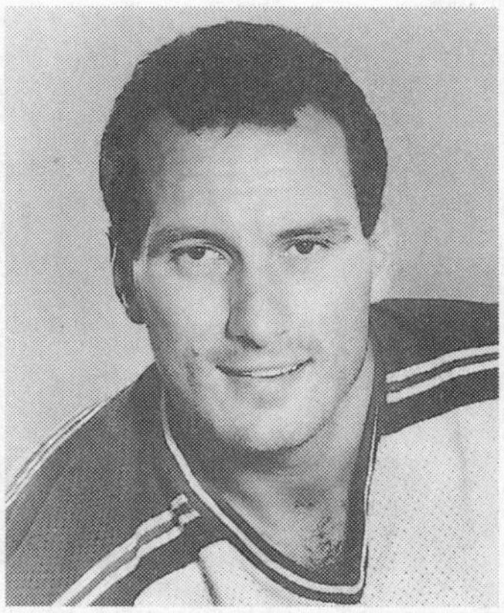

John Ogrodnick

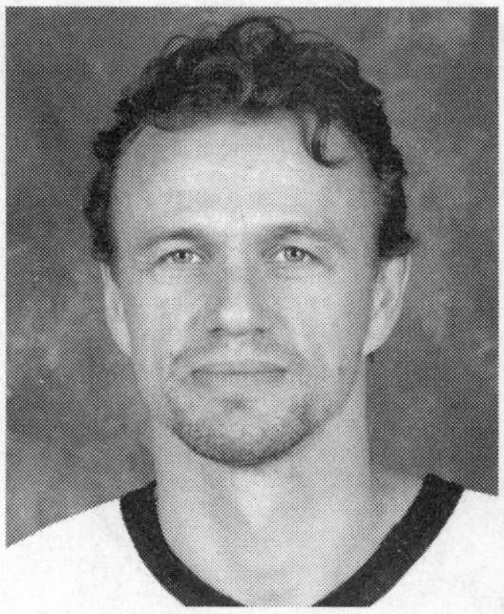

Fredrik Olausson

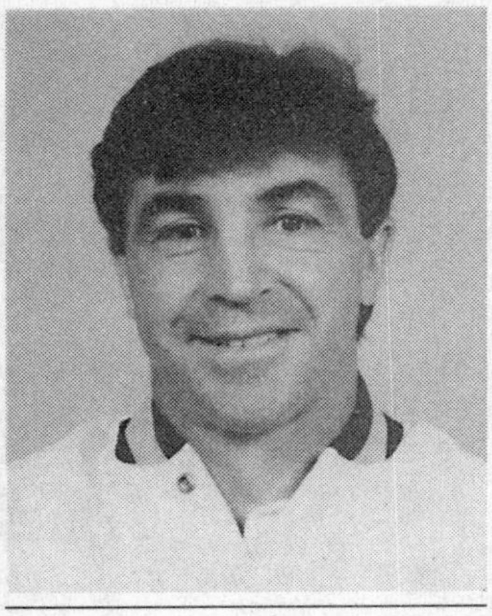

J.P. Parise

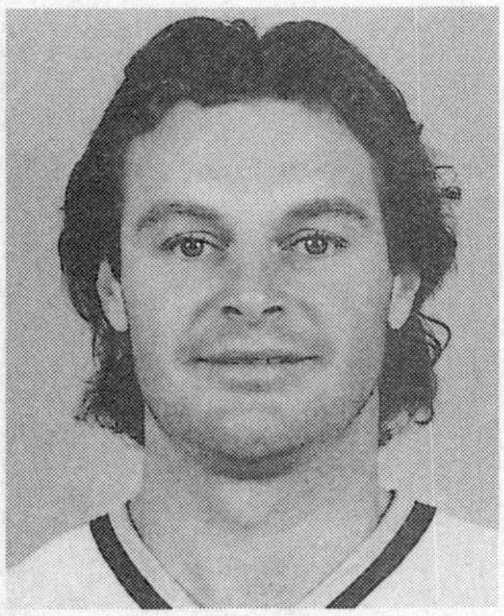

Michel Petit

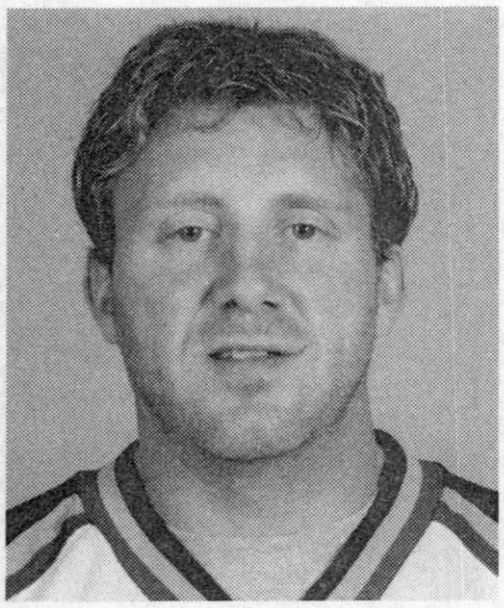

Lance Pitlick

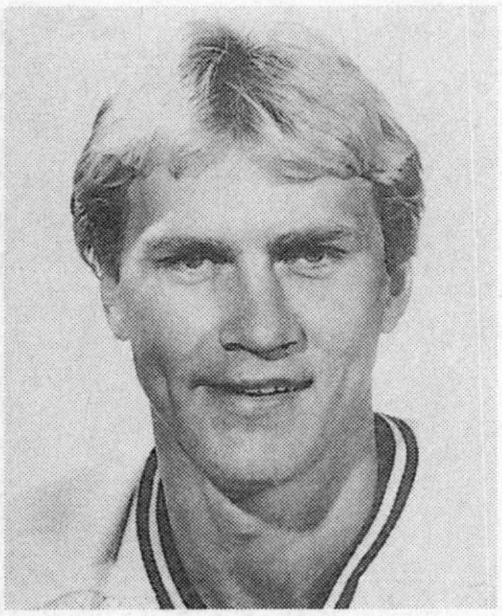

Willi Plett

			Regular Schedule					Playoffs							
Name	NHL Teams	NHL Seasons	GP	G	A	TP	PIM	GP	G	A	TP	PIM	NHL Cup Wins	First NHL Season	Last NHL Season
Paek, Jim	Pit., L.A., Ott.	5	217	5	29	34	155	27	1	4	5	8	2	1990-91	1994-95
Paiement, Rosaire	Phi., Van.	5	190	48	52	100	343	3	3	0	3	0	....	1967-68	1971-72
Paiement, Wilf	K.C., Col., Tor., Que., NYR, Buf., Pit.	14	946	356	458	814	1757	69	18	17	35	185	....	1974-75	1987-88
Palangio, Pete	Mtl., Det., Chi.	5	71	13	10	23	28	7	0	0	0	0	1	1926-27	1937-38
Palazzari, Aldo	Bos., NYR	1	35	8	3	11	4	....	....	....	....	....	....	1943-44	1943-44
Palazzari, Doug	St.L.	4	108	18	20	38	23	2	0	0	0	0	....	1974-75	1978-79
Palmer, Brad	Min., Bos.	3	168	32	38	70	58	29	9	5	14	16	....	1980-81	1982-83
Palmer, Rob	Chi.	3	16	0	3	3	2	....	....	....	....	....	....	1973-74	1975-76
Palmer, Robert	L.A., N.J.	7	320	9	101	110	115	8	1	2	3	6	....	1977-78	1983-84
• Panagabko, Ed	Bos.	2	29	0	3	3	38	....	....	....	....	....	....	1955-56	1956-57
‡ Pankewicz, Greg	Ott., Cgy.	2	21	0	3	3	22	....	....	....	....	....	....	1993-94	1998-99
‡ Panteleev, Grigori	Bos., NYI	4	54	8	6	14	12	....	....	....	....	....	....	1992-93	1995-96
• Papike, Joe	Chi.	3	20	3	3	6	4	5	0	2	2	0	....	1940-41	1944-45
Pappin, Jim	Tor., Chi., Cal., Cle.	14	767	278	295	573	667	92	33	34	67	101	2	1963-64	1976-77
Paradise, Bob	Min., Atl., Pit., Wsh.	8	368	8	54	62	393	12	0	1	1	19	....	1971-72	1978-79
Pargeter, George	Mtl.	1	4	0	0	0	0	....	....	....	....	....	....	1946-47	1946-47
Parise, J.P.	Bos., Tor., Min., NYI, Cle.	14	890	238	356	594	706	86	27	31	58	87	....	1965-66	1978-79
Parizeau, Michel	St.L., Phi.	1	58	3	14	17	18	....	....	....	....	....	....	1971-72	1971-72
Park, Brad	NYR, Bos., Det.	17	1113	213	683	896	1429	161	35	90	125	217	....	1968-69	1984-85
Parker, Jeff	Buf., Hfd.	5	141	16	19	35	163	5	0	0	0	26	....	1986-87	1990-91
• Parkes, Ernie	Mtl.M.	1	17	0	0	0	2	....	....	....	....	....	....	1924-25	1924-25
Parks, Greg	NYI	3	23	1	2	3	6	2	0	0	0	0	....	1990-91	1992-93
• Parsons, George	Tor.	3	78	12	13	25	20	7	3	2	5	11	....	1936-37	1938-39
‡ Parssinen, Timo	Ana.	1	17	0	3	3	2	....	....	....	....	....	....	2001-02	2001-02
• Pasek, Dusan	Min.	1	48	4	10	14	30	2	1	0	1	0	....	1988-89	1988-89
Pasin, Dave	Bos., L.A.	2	76	18	19	37	50	3	0	1	1	0	....	1985-86	1988-89
Paslawski, Greg	Mtl., St.L., Wpg., Buf., Que., Phi., Cgy.	11	650	187	185	372	169	60	19	13	32	25	....	1983-84	1993-94
‡ Patera, Pavel	Dal., Min.	2	32	2	7	9	8	....	....	....	....	....	....	1999-00	2000-01
Paterson, Joe	Det., Phi., L.A., NYR	9	291	19	37	56	829	22	3	4	7	77	....	1980-81	1988-89
Paterson, Mark	Hfd.	4	29	3	3	6	33	....	....	....	....	....	....	1982-83	1985-86
Paterson, Rick	Chi.	9	430	50	43	93	136	61	7	10	17	51	....	1978-79	1986-87
Patey, Doug	Wsh.	3	45	4	2	6	8	....	....	....	....	....	....	1976-77	1978-79
Patey, Larry	Cal., St.L., NYR	12	717	153	163	316	631	40	8	10	18	57	....	1973-74	1984-85
Patrick, Craig	Cal., St.L., K.C., Wsh.	8	401	72	91	163	61	2	0	1	1	0	....	1971-72	1978-79
Patrick, Glenn	St.L., Cal., Cle.	4	38	2	3	5	72	....	....	....	....	....	....	1973-74	1976-77
• Patrick, Lester	NYR	1	1	0	0	0	2	....	....	....	....	....	....	1926-27	1926-27
• Patrick, Lynn	NYR	10	455	145	190	335	240	44	10	6	16	22	1	1934-35	1945-46
• Patrick, Muzz	NYR	5	166	5	26	31	133	25	4	0	4	34	1	1937-38	1945-46
Patrick, Steve	Buf., NYR, Que.	6	250	40	68	108	242	12	0	1	1	12	....	1980-81	1985-86
Patterson, Colin	Cgy., Buf.	10	504	96	109	205	239	85	12	17	29	57	1	1983-84	1992-93
Patterson, Dennis	K.C., Phi.	3	138	6	22	28	67	....	....	....	....	....	....	1974-75	1979-80
Patterson, Ed	Pit.	3	68	3	3	6	56	....	....	....	....	....	....	1993-94	1996-97
• Patterson, George	Tor., Mtl., NYA, Bos., Det., St.L.	9	284	51	27	78	218	3	0	0	0	2	....	1926-27	1934-35
• Paul, Butch	Det.	1	3	0	0	0	0	....	....	....	....	....	....	1964-65	1964-65
• Paulhus, Rollie	Mtl.	1	33	0	0	0	0	....	....	....	....	....	....	1925-26	1925-26
Pavelich, Mark	NYR, Min., S.J.	7	355	137	192	329	340	23	7	17	24	14	....	1981-82	1991-92
Pavelich, Marty	Det.	10	634	93	159	252	454	91	13	15	28	74	4	1947-48	1956-57
Pavese, Jim	St.L., NYR, Det., Hfd.	8	328	13	44	57	689	34	0	6	6	81	....	1981-82	1988-89
• Payer, Evariste	Mtl.	1	1	0	0	0	0	....	....	....	....	....	....	1917-18	1917-18
Payne, Davis	Bos.	2	22	0	1	1	14	....	....	....	....	....	....	1995-96	1996-97
Payne, Steve	Min.	10	613	228	238	466	435	71	35	35	70	60	....	1978-79	1987-88
Paynter, Kent	Chi., Wsh., Wpg., Ott.	7	37	1	3	4	69	4	0	0	0	10	....	1987-88	1993-94
Peake, Pat	Wsh.	5	134	28	41	69	105	13	2	2	4	20	....	1993-94	1997-98
• Pearson, Mel	NYR, Pit.	5	38	2	6	8	25	....	....	....	....	....	....	1959-60	1967-68
Pearson, Rob	Tor., Wsh., St.L.	6	269	56	54	110	645	33	4	2	6	94	....	1991-92	1996-97
Pearson, Scott	Tor., Que., Edm., Buf., NYI	10	292	56	42	98	615	10	2	0	2	14	....	1988-89	1999-00
Pedersen, Allen	Bos., Min., Hfd.	8	428	5	36	41	487	64	0	0	0	91	....	1986-87	1993-94
Pederson, Barry	Bos., Van., Pit., Hfd.	12	701	238	416	654	472	34	22	30	52	25	1	1980-81	1991-92
‡ Pederson, Mark	Mtl., Phi., S.J., Det.	5	169	35	50	85	77	2	0	0	0	0	....	1989-90	1993-94
Pederson, Tom	S.J., Tor.	5	240	20	49	69	142	24	1	11	12	10	....	1992-93	1996-97
• Peer, Bert	Det.	1	1	0	0	0	0	....	....	....	....	....	....	1939-40	1939-40
Peirson, Johnny	Bos.	11	545	153	173	326	315	49	10	16	26	26	....	1946-47	1957-58
Pelensky, Perry	Chi.	1	4	0	0	0	5	....	....	....	....	....	....	1983-84	1983-84
Pelletier, Roger	Phi.	1	1	0	0	0	0	....	....	....	....	....	....	1967-68	1967-68
Peloffy, Andre	Wsh.	1	9	0	0	0	0	....	....	....	....	....	....	1974-75	1974-75
‡ Peltonen, Ville	S.J., Nsh.	5	175	18	42	60	40	....	....	....	....	....	....	1995-96	2000-01
Peluso, Mike	Chi., Ott., N.J., St.L., Cgy.	9	458	38	52	90	1951	62	3	4	7	107	1	1989-90	1997-98
Pelyk, Mike	Tor.	9	441	26	88	114	566	40	0	3	3	41	....	1967-68	1977-78
Penney, Chad	Ott.	1	3	0	0	0	2	....	....	....	....	....	....	1993-94	1993-94
Pennington, Cliff	Mtl., Bos.	3	101	17	42	59	6	....	....	....	....	....	....	1960-61	1962-63
Peplinski, Jim	Cgy.	11	711	161	263	424	1467	99	15	31	46	382	1	1980-81	1994-95
Perlini, Fred	Tor.	2	8	2	3	5	0	....	....	....	....	....	....	1981-82	1983-84
Perreault, Fern	NYR	2	3	0	0	0	0	....	....	....	....	....	....	1947-48	1949-50
Perreault, Gilbert	Buf.	17	1191	512	814	1326	500	90	33	70	103	44	....	1970-71	1986-87
Perry, Brian	Oak., Buf.	3	96	16	29	45	24	8	1	1	2	4	....	1968-69	1970-71
‡ Persson, Ricard	N.J., St.L., Ott.	7	229	10	44	54	262	26	1	3	4	59	....	1995-96	2001-02
Persson, Stefan	NYI	9	622	52	317	369	574	102	7	50	57	69	4	1977-78	1985-86
Pesut, George	Cal.	2	92	3	22	25	130	....	....	....	....	....	....	1974-75	1975-76
• Peters, Frank	NYR	1	43	0	0	0	59	4	0	0	0	2	....	1930-31	1930-31
Peters, Garry	Mtl., NYR, Phi., Bos.	8	311	34	34	68	261	9	2	2	4	31	1	1964-65	1971-72
Peters, Jimmy	Mtl., Bos., Det., Chi.	9	574	125	150	275	186	60	5	9	14	22	3	1945-46	1953-54
Peters, Jimmy	Det., L.A.	9	309	37	36	73	48	11	0	2	2	2	....	1964-65	1974-75
Peters, Steve	Col.	1	2	0	1	1	0	....	....	....	....	....	....	1979-80	1979-80
Peterson, Brent	Det., Buf., Van., Hfd.	11	620	72	141	213	484	31	4	4	8	65	....	1978-79	1988-89
‡ Peterson, Brent	T.B.	3	56	9	1	10	6	....	....	....	....	....	....	1996-97	1998-99
Petit, Michel	Van., NYR, Que., Tor., Cgy., L.A., T.B., Edm., Phi., Phx.	16	827	90	238	328	1839	19	0	2	2	61	....	1982-83	1997-98
‡ Petrenko, Sergei	Buf.	1	14	0	4	4	0	....	....	....	....	....	....	1993-94	1993-94
‡ Petrov, Oleg	Mtl., Nsh.	8	382	72	115	187	101	20	1	6	7	2	....	1992-93	2002-03
‡ Petrovicky, Robert	Hfd., Dal., St.L., T.B., NYI	8	208	27	38	65	118	2	0	0	0	0	....	1992-93	2000-01
Pettersson, Jorgen	St.L., Hfd., Wsh.	6	435	174	192	366	117	44	15	12	27	4	....	1980-81	1985-86
• Pettinger, Eric	Bos., Tor., Ott.	3	98	7	12	19	83	4	1	0	1	8	....	1928-29	1930-31
• Pettinger, Gord	NYR, Det., Bos.	8	292	42	74	116	77	47	4	5	9	11	4	1932-33	1939-40
Phair, Lyle	L.A.	3	48	6	7	13	12	1	0	0	0	0	....	1985-86	1987-88
Phillipoff, Harold	Atl., Chi.	3	141	26	57	83	267	6	0	2	2	9	....	1977-78	1979-80
• Phillips, Bill	Mtl.M.	1	27	1	1	2	6	4	0	0	0	2	....	1929-30	1929-30
Phillips, Charlie	Mtl.	1	17	0	0	0	6	....	....	....	....	....	....	1942-43	1942-43
• Phillips, Merlyn	Mtl.M., NYA	8	302	52	31	83	232	24	5	1	6	19	1	1925-26	1932-33
Picard, Noel	Mtl., St.L., Atl.	7	335	12	63	75	616	50	2	11	13	167	1	1964-65	1972-73
Picard, Robert	Wsh., Tor., Mtl., Wpg., Que., Det.	13	899	104	319	423	1025	36	5	15	20	39	....	1977-78	1989-90
Picard, Roger	St.L.	1	15	2	2	4	21	....	....	....	....	....	....	1967-68	1967-68
Pichette, Dave	Que., St.L., N.J., NYR	7	322	41	140	181	348	28	3	7	10	54	....	1980-81	1987-88
Picketts, Hal	NYA	1	48	3	1	4	32	....	....	....	....	....	....	1933-34	1933-34
Pidhirny, Harry	Bos.	1	2	0	0	0	0	....	....	....	....	....	....	1957-58	1957-58
Pierce, Randy	Col., N.J., Hfd.	8	277	62	76	138	223	2	0	0	0	0	....	1977-78	1984-85
Pike, Alf	NYR	6	234	42	77	119	145	21	4	2	6	12	1	1939-40	1946-47
Pilon, Rich	NYI, NYR, St.L.	14	631	8	69	77	1745	15	0	0	0	50	....	1988-89	2001-02
Pilote, Pierre	Chi., Tor.	14	890	80	418	498	1251	86	8	53	61	102	1	1955-56	1968-69
Pinder, Gerry	Chi., Cal.	3	223	55	69	124	135	17	0	4	4	6	....	1969-70	1971-72
Pirus, Alex	Min., Det.	4	159	30	28	58	94	2	0	1	1	2	....	1976-77	1979-80
Pitlick, Lance	Ott., Fla.	8	393	16	33	49	298	24	0	2	2	21	....	1994-95	2001-02
• Pitre, Didier	Mtl.	6	127	64	34	98	84	9	2	4	6	16	....	1917-18	1922-23
Pivonka, Michal	Wsh.	13	825	181	418	599	478	95	19	36	55	86	....	1986-87	1998-99
• Plager, Barclay	St.L.	10	614	44	187	231	1115	68	3	20	23	182	....	1967-68	1976-77
Plager, Bill	Min., St.L., Atl.	9	263	4	34	38	294	31	0	2	2	26	....	1967-68	1975-76
Plager, Bob	NYR, St.L.	14	644	20	126	146	802	74	2	17	19	195	....	1964-65	1977-78
Plamondon, Gerry	Mtl.	5	74	7	13	20	10	11	5	2	7	2	1	1945-46	1950-51
Plante, Cam	Tor.	1	2	0	0	0	0	....	....	....	....	....	....	1984-85	1984-85
Plante, Dan	NYI	4	159	9	14	23	135	1	1	0	1	2	....	1993-94	1997-98
‡ Plante, Derek	Buf., Dal., Chi., Phi.	8	450	96	152	248	138	41	6	10	16	18	1	1993-94	2000-01
Plante, Pierre	Phi., St.L., Chi., NYR, Que.	9	599	125	172	297	599	33	2	6	8	51	....	1971-72	1979-80
Plantery, Mark	Wpg.	1	25	1	5	6	14	....	....	....	....	....	....	1980-81	1980-81
‡ Plavsic, Adrien	St.L., Van., T.B., Ana.	8	214	16	56	72	161	13	1	7	8	4	....	1989-90	1996-97
• Plaxton, Hugh	Mtl.M.	1	15	1	2	3	4	....	....	....	....	....	....	1932-33	1932-33
Playfair, Jim	Edm., Chi.	3	21	2	4	6	51	....	....	....	....	....	....	1983-84	1988-89
Playfair, Larry	Buf., L.A.	12	688	26	94	120	1812	43	0	6	6	111	....	1978-79	1989-90

Name	NHL Teams	NHL Seasons	Regular Schedule GP	G	A	TP	PIM	Playoffs GP	G	A	TP	PIM	NHL Cup Wins	First NHL Season	Last NHL Season
Pleau, Larry	Mtl.	3	94	9	15	24	27	4	0	0	0	0	....	1969-70	1971-72
• Pletsch, Charles	Ham.	1	1	0	0	0	0	....	....	....	....	....	....	1920-21	1920-21
Plett, Willi	Atl., Cgy., Min., Bos.	13	834	222	215	437	2572	83	24	22	46	466	....	1975-76	1987-88
Plumb, Rob	Det.	2	14	3	2	5	2	....	....	....	....	....	....	1977-78	1978-79
Plumb, Ron	Hfd.	1	26	3	4	7	14	....	....	....	....	....	....	1979-80	1979-80
Pocza, Harvie	Wsh.	2	3	0	0	0	2	....	....	....	....	....	....	1979-80	1981-82
Poddubny, Walt	Edm., Tor., NYR, Que., N.J.	11	468	184	238	422	454	19	7	2	9	12	....	1981-82	1991-92
‡ Podein, Shjon	Edm., Phi., Col., St.L.	11	699	100	106	206	439	127	14	13	27	132	1	1992-93	2002-03
Podloski, Ray	Bos.	1	8	0	1	1	17	....	....	....	....	....	....	1988-89	1988-89
‡ Podollan, Jason	Fla., Tor., L.A., NYI	4	41	1	5	6	19	....	....	....	....	....	....	1996-97	2001-02
Podolsky, Nels	Det.	1	1	0	0	0	0	7	0	0	0	4	....	1948-49	1948-49
Poeschek, Rudy	NYR, Wpg., T.B., St.L.	12	364	6	25	31	817	5	0	0	0	18	....	1987-88	1999-00
• Poeta, Tony	Chi.	1	1	0	0	0	0	....	....	....	....	....	....	1951-52	1951-52
Poile, Bud	Tor., Chi., Det., NYR, Bos.	7	311	107	122	229	91	23	4	5	9	8	1	1942-43	1949-50
Poile, Don	Det.	2	66	7	9	16	12	4	0	0	0	0	....	1954-55	1957-58
Poirier, Gordie	Mtl.	1	10	0	0	0	0	....	....	....	....	....	....	1939-40	1939-40
Polanic, Tom	Min.	2	19	0	2	2	53	5	1	1	2	4	....	1969-70	1970-71
• Polich, John	NYR	2	3	0	1	1	0	....	....	....	....	....	....	1939-40	1940-41
Polich, Mike	Mtl., Min.	5	226	24	29	53	57	23	2	1	3	2	1	1976-77	1980-81
Polis, Greg	Pit., St.L., NYR, Wsh.	10	615	174	169	343	391	7	0	2	2	6	....	1970-71	1979-80
Poliziani, Dan	Bos.	1	1	0	0	0	0	3	0	0	0	0	....	1958-59	1958-59
Polonich, Dennis	Det.	8	390	59	82	141	1242	7	1	0	1	19	....	1974-75	1982-83
Pooley, Paul	Wpg.	2	15	0	3	3	0	....	....	....	....	....	....	1984-85	1985-86
Popein, Larry	NYR, Oak.	8	449	80	141	221	162	16	1	4	5	6	....	1954-55	1967-68
Popiel, Poul	Bos., L.A., Det., Van., Edm.	7	224	13	41	54	210	4	1	0	1	4	....	1965-66	1979-80
‡ Popovic, Peter	Mtl., NYR, Pit., Bos.	8	485	10	63	73	291	35	1	4	5	18	....	1993-94	2000-01
• Portland, Jack	Mtl., Bos., Chi.	10	381	15	56	71	323	33	1	3	4	25	1	1933-34	1942-43
Porvari, Jukka	Col., N.J.	2	39	3	9	12	4	....	....	....	....	....	....	1981-82	1982-83
Posa, Victor	Chi.	1	2	0	0	0	2	....	....	....	....	....	....	1985-86	1985-86
Posavad, Mike	St.L.	2	8	0	0	0	0	....	....	....	....	....	....	1985-86	1986-87
‡ Posmyk, Marek	T.B.	2	19	1	2	3	20	....	....	....	....	....	....	1999-00	2000-01
Potomski, Barry	L.A., S.J.	3	68	6	5	11	227	....	....	....	....	....	....	1995-96	1997-98
Potvin, Denis	NYI	15	1060	310	742	1052	1356	185	56	108	164	253	4	1973-74	1987-88
Potvin, Jean	L.A., Phi., NYI, Cle., Min.	11	613	63	224	287	478	39	2	9	11	17	1	1970-71	1980-81
Potvin, Marc	Det., L.A., Hfd., Bos.	6	121	3	5	8	456	13	0	1	1	50	....	1990-91	1995-96
Poudrier, Daniel	Que.	3	25	1	5	6	10	....	....	....	....	....	....	1985-86	1987-88
Poulin, Daniel	Min.	1	3	1	1	2	2	....	....	....	....	....	....	1981-82	1981-82
Poulin, Dave	Phi., Bos., Wsh.	13	724	205	325	530	482	129	31	42	73	132	....	1982-83	1994-95
Poulin, Patrick	Hfd., Chi., T.B., Mtl.	11	634	101	134	235	299	32	6	2	8	8	....	1991-92	2001-02
Pouzar, Jaroslav	Edm.	4	186	34	48	82	135	29	6	4	10	16	3	1982-83	1986-87
• Powell, Ray	Chi.	1	31	7	15	22	2	....	....	....	....	....	....	1950-51	1950-51
Powis, Geoff	Chi.	1	2	0	0	0	0	....	....	....	....	....	....	1967-68	1967-68
Powis, Lynn	Chi., K.C.	2	130	19	33	52	25	1	0	0	0	0	....	1973-74	1974-75
Prajsler, Petr	L.A., Bos.	4	46	3	10	13	51	4	0	0	0	0	....	1987-88	1991-92
• Pratt, Babe	NYR, Tor., Bos.	12	517	83	209	292	463	63	12	17	29	90	2	1935-36	1946-47
Pratt, Jack	Bos.	2	37	2	0	2	42	4	0	0	0	0	....	1930-31	1931-32
Pratt, Kelly	Pit.	1	22	0	6	6	15	....	....	....	....	....	....	1974-75	1974-75
Pratt, Tracy	Oak., Pit., Buf., Van., Col., Tor.	10	580	17	97	114	1026	25	0	1	1	62	....	1967-68	1976-77
Prentice, Dean	NYR, Bos., Det., Pit., Min.	22	1378	391	469	860	484	54	13	17	30	38	....	1952-53	1973-74
Prentice, Eric	Tor.	1	5	0	0	0	4	....	....	....	....	....	....	1943-44	1943-44
Presley, Wayne	Chi., S.J., Buf., NYR, Tor.	12	684	155	147	302	953	83	26	17	43	142	....	1984-85	1995-96
Preston, Rich	Chi., N.J.	8	580	127	164	291	348	47	4	18	22	56	....	1979-80	1986-87
Preston, Yves	Phi.	2	28	7	3	10	4	....	....	....	....	....	....	1978-79	1980-81
Priakin, Sergei	Cgy.	3	46	3	8	11	2	1	0	0	0	0	....	1988-89	1990-91
Price, Jack	Chi.	3	57	4	6	10	24	4	0	0	0	0	....	1951-52	1953-54
Price, Noel	Tor., NYR, Det., Mtl., Pit., L.A., Atl.	14	499	14	114	128	333	12	0	1	1	8	1	1957-58	1975-76
Price, Pat	NYI, Edm., Pit., Que., NYR, Min.	13	726	43	218	261	1456	74	2	10	12	195	....	1975-76	1987-88
Price, Tom	Cal., Cle., Pit.	5	29	0	2	2	12	....	....	....	....	....	....	1974-75	1978-79
Priestlay, Ken	Buf., Pit.	6	168	27	34	61	63	14	0	0	0	21	1	1986-87	1991-92
• Primeau, Joe	Tor.	9	310	66	177	243	105	38	5	18	23	12	1	1927-28	1935-36
Primeau, Kevin	Van.	1	2	0	0	0	4	....	....	....	....	....	....	1980-81	1980-81
• Pringle, Ellie	NYA	1	6	0	0	0	0	....	....	....	....	....	....	1930-31	1930-31
Probert, Bob	Det., Chi.	16	935	163	221	384	3300	81	16	32	48	274	....	1985-86	2001-02
‡ Prochazka, Martin	Tor., Atl.	2	32	2	5	7	8	....	....	....	....	....	....	1997-98	1999-00
• Prodgers, Goldie	Tor., Ham.	6	111	63	29	92	39	....	....	....	....	....	....	1919-20	1924-25
Prokhorov, Vitali	St.L.	3	83	19	11	30	35	4	0	0	0	0	....	1992-93	1994-95
Prokopec, Mike	Chi.	2	15	0	0	0	11	....	....	....	....	....	....	1995-96	1996-97
Pronovost, Andre	Mtl., Bos., Det., Min.	10	556	94	104	198	408	70	11	11	22	58	4	1956-57	1967-68
Pronovost, Jean	Pit., Atl., Wsh.	14	998	391	383	774	413	35	11	9	20	14	....	1968-69	1981-82
Pronovost, Marcel	Det., Tor.	21	1206	88	257	345	851	134	8	23	31	104	5	1949-50	1969-70
Propp, Brian	Phi., Bos., Min., Hfd.	15	1016	425	579	1004	830	160	64	84	148	151	....	1979-80	1993-94
Proulx, Christian	Mtl.	1	7	1	2	3	20	....	....	....	....	....	....	1993-94	1993-94
• Provost, Claude	Mtl.	15	1005	254	335	589	469	126	25	38	63	86	9	1955-56	1969-70
Prpic, Joel	Bos., Col.	3	18	0	3	3	4	....	....	....	....	....	....	1997-98	2000-01
Pryor, Chris	Min., NYI	6	82	1	4	5	122	....	....	....	....	....	....	1984-85	1989-90
Prystai, Metro	Chi., Det.	11	674	151	179	330	231	43	12	14	26	8	2	1947-48	1957-58
• Pudas, Al	Tor.	1	4	0	0	0	0	....	....	....	....	....	....	1926-27	1926-27
Pulford, Bob	Tor., L.A.	16	1079	281	362	643	792	89	25	26	51	126	4	1956-57	1971-72
Pulkkinen, Dave	NYI	1	2	0	0	0	0	....	....	....	....	....	....	1972-73	1972-73
• Purpur, Fido	St.L., Chi., Det.	5	144	25	35	60	46	16	1	2	3	4	....	1934-35	1944-45
Purves, John	Wsh.	1	7	1	0	1	0	....	....	....	....	....	....	1990-91	1990-91
• Pusie, Jean	Mtl., NYR, Bos.	5	61	1	4	5	28	7	0	0	0	0	1	1930-31	1935-36
Pyatt, Nelson	Det., Wsh., Col.	7	296	71	63	134	69	....	....	....	....	....	....	1973-74	1979-80

Q

Name	NHL Teams	NHL Seasons	Regular Schedule GP	G	A	TP	PIM	Playoffs GP	G	A	TP	PIM	NHL Cup Wins	First NHL Season	Last NHL Season
• Quackenbush, Bill	Det., Bos.	14	774	62	222	284	95	80	2	19	21	8	....	1942-43	1955-56
Quackenbush, Max	Bos., Chi.	2	61	4	7	11	30	6	0	0	0	4	....	1950-51	1951-52
Quenneville, Joel	Tor., Col., N.J., Hfd., Wsh.	13	803	54	136	190	705	32	0	8	8	22	....	1978-79	1990-91
• Quenneville, Leo	NYR	1	25	0	3	3	10	3	0	0	0	0	....	1929-30	1929-30
• Quilty, John	Mtl., Bos.	4	125	36	34	70	81	13	3	5	8	9	....	1940-41	1947-48
Quinn, Dan	Cgy., Pit., Van., St.L., Phi., Min., Ott., L.A.	14	805	266	419	685	533	65	22	26	48	62	....	1983-84	1996-97
Quinn, Pat	Tor., Van., Atl.	9	606	18	113	131	950	11	0	1	1	21	....	1968-69	1976-77
Quinney, Ken	Que.	3	59	7	13	20	23	....	....	....	....	....	....	1986-87	1990-91
Quintin, Jean-Francois	S.J.	2	22	5	5	10	4	....	....	....	....	....	....	1991-92	1992-93

R

Name	NHL Teams	NHL Seasons	Regular Schedule GP	G	A	TP	PIM	Playoffs GP	G	A	TP	PIM	NHL Cup Wins	First NHL Season	Last NHL Season
‡ Racine, Yves	Det., Phi., Mtl., S.J., Cgy., T.B.	9	508	37	194	231	439	25	5	4	9	37	....	1989-90	1997-98
• Radley, Yip	NYA, Mtl.M.	2	18	0	1	1	13	....	....	....	....	....	....	1930-31	1936-37
Raglan, Herb	St.L., Que., T.B., Ott.	9	343	33	56	89	775	32	3	6	9	50	....	1985-86	1993-94
Raglan, Rags	Det., Chi.	3	100	4	9	13	52	3	0	0	0	0	....	1950-51	1952-53
Raleigh, Don	NYR	10	535	101	219	320	96	18	6	5	11	6	....	1943-44	1955-56
‡ Ralph, Brad	Phx.	1	1	0	0	0	0	....	....	....	....	....	....	2000-01	2000-01
Ramage, Rob	Col., St.L., Cgy., Tor., Min., T.B., Mtl., Phi.	15	1044	139	425	564	2226	84	8	42	50	218	2	1979-80	1993-94
• Ramsay, Beattie	Tor.	1	43	0	2	2	10	....	....	....	....	....	....	1927-28	1927-28
Ramsay, Craig	Buf.	14	1070	252	420	672	201	89	17	31	48	27	....	1971-72	1984-85
Ramsay, Les	Chi.	1	11	2	2	4	2	....	....	....	....	....	....	1944-45	1944-45
Ramsey, Mike	Buf., Pit., Det.	18	1070	79	266	345	1012	115	8	29	37	176	....	1979-80	1996-97
Ramsey, Wayne	Buf.	1	2	0	0	0	0	....	....	....	....	....	....	1977-78	1977-78
• Randall, Ken	Tor., Ham., NYA	10	218	68	50	118	533	6	2	1	3	27	2	1917-18	1926-27
Ranheim, Paul	Cgy., Hfd., Car., Phi., Phx.	15	1013	161	199	360	288	36	3	8	11	6	....	1988-89	2002-03
Ranieri, George	Bos.	1	2	0	0	0	0	....	....	....	....	....	....	1956-57	1956-57
‡ Ratchuk, Peter	Fla.	2	32	1	1	2	10	....	....	....	....	....	....	1998-99	2000-01
Ratelle, Jean	NYR, Bos.	21	1281	491	776	1267	276	123	32	66	98	24	....	1960-61	1980-81
Rathwell, Jake	Bos.	1	1	0	0	0	0	....	....	....	....	....	....	1974-75	1974-75
Ratushny, Dan	Van.	1	1	0	1	1	2	....	....	....	....	....	....	1992-93	1992-93
Rausse, Errol	Wsh.	3	31	7	3	10	0	....	....	....	....	....	....	1979-80	1981-82
Rautakallio, Pekka	Atl., Cgy.	3	235	33	121	154	122	23	2	5	7	8	....	1979-80	1981-82
Ravlich, Matt	Bos., Chi., Det., L.A.	10	410	12	78	90	364	24	1	5	6	16	....	1962-63	1972-73
• Raymond, Armand	Mtl.	2	22	0	2	2	10	....	....	....	....	....	....	1937-38	1939-40
• Raymond, Paul	Mtl.	4	76	2	3	5	6	5	0	0	0	2	....	1932-33	1938-39
Read, Mel	NYR	1	1	0	0	0	0	....	....	....	....	....	....	1946-47	1946-47
Reardon, Ken	Mtl.	7	341	26	96	122	604	31	2	5	7	62	1	1940-41	1949-50

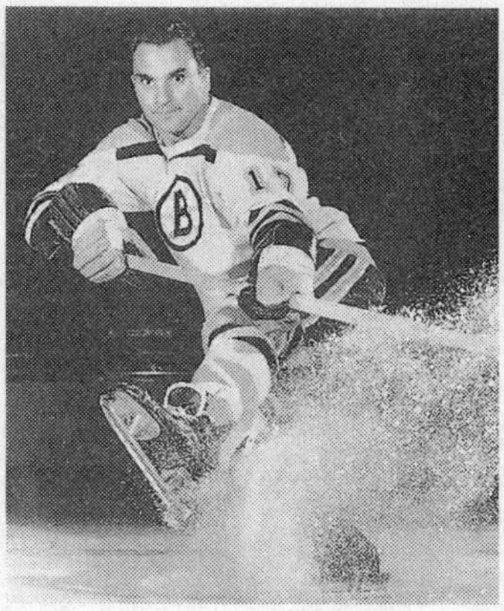
Dean Prentice

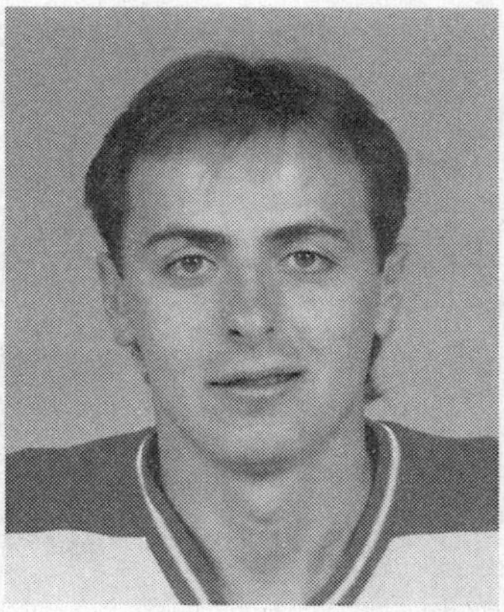
Sergei Priakin

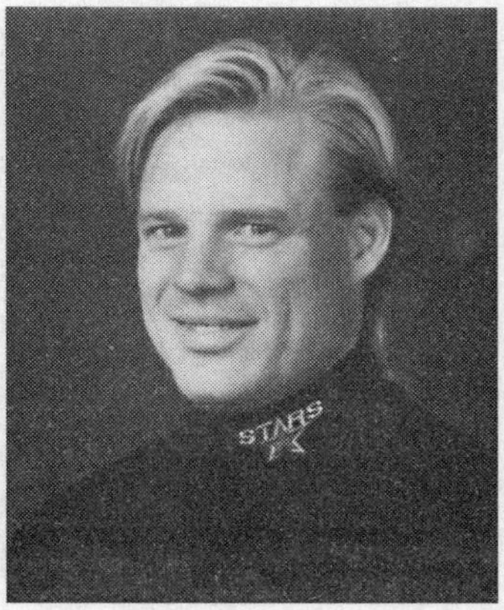

Brian Propp

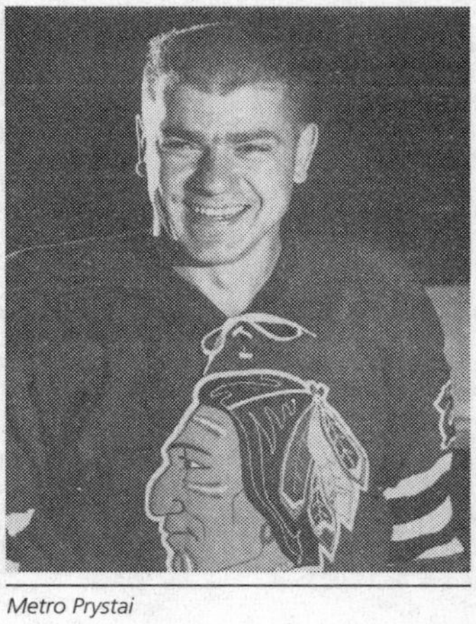
Metro Prystai

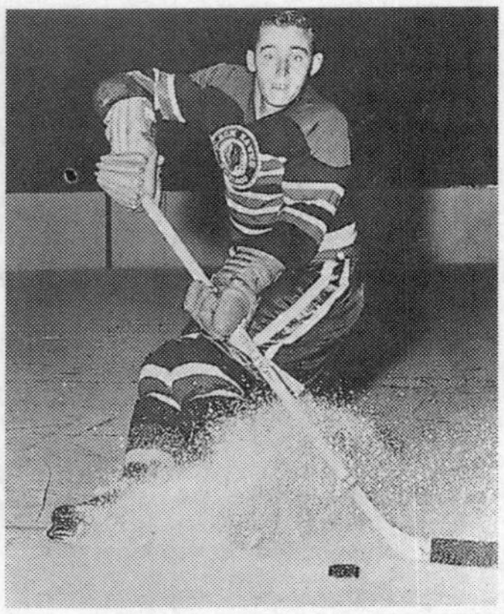

Clare Raglan

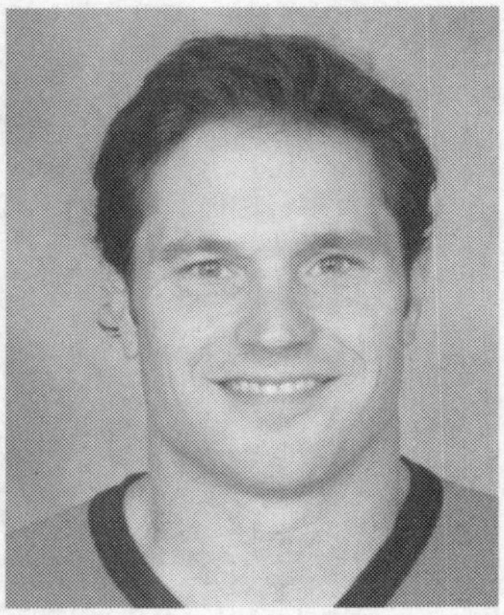

Paul Ranheim

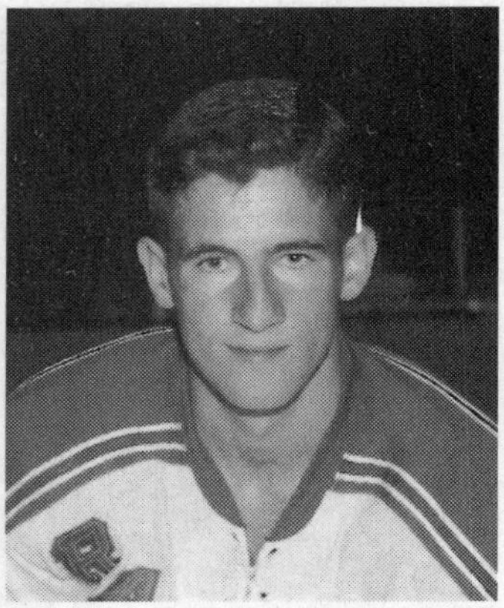

Jean Ratelle

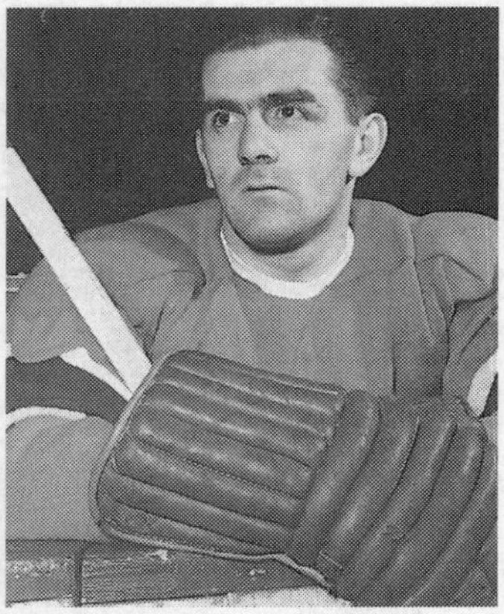

Maurice Richard

			Regular Schedule					Playoffs							
Name	NHL Teams	NHL Seasons	GP	G	A	TP	PIM	GP	G	A	TP	PIM	NHL Cup Wins	First NHL Season	Last NHL Season
● Reardon, Terry	Bos., Mtl.	7	193	47	53	100	73	30	8	10	18	12	1	1938-39	1946-47
Reaume, Marc	Tor., Det., Mtl., Van.	9	344	8	43	51	273	21	0	2	2	8	....	1954-55	1970-71
Reay, Billy	Det., Mtl.	10	479	105	162	267	202	63	13	16	29	43	2	1943-44	1952-53
Redahl, Gord	Bos.	1	18	0	1	1	2	....	....	....	....	....	....	1958-59	1958-59
● Redding, George	Bos.	2	55	3	2	5	23	....	....	....	....	....	....	1924-25	1925-26
Redmond, Craig	L.A., Edm.	5	191	16	68	84	134	3	1	0	1	2	....	1984-85	1988-89
Redmond, Dick	Min., Cal., Chi., St.L., Atl., Bos.	13	771	133	312	445	504	66	9	22	31	27	....	1969-70	1981-82
Redmond, Keith	L.A.	1	12	1	0	1	20	....	....	....	....	....	....	1993-94	1993-94
Redmond, Mickey	Mtl., Det.	9	538	233	195	428	219	16	2	3	5	2	2	1967-68	1975-76
Reeds, Mark	St.L., Hfd.	8	365	45	114	159	135	53	8	9	17	23	....	1981-82	1988-89
Reekie, Joe	Buf., NYI, T.B., Wsh., Chi.	17	902	25	139	164	1326	51	3	4	7	63	....	1985-86	2001-02
● Regan, Bill	NYR, NYA	3	67	3	2	5	67	8	0	0	0	2	....	1929-30	1932-33
Regan, Larry	Bos., Tor.	5	280	41	95	136	71	42	7	14	21	18	....	1956-57	1960-61
Regier, Darcy	Cle., NYI	3	26	0	2	2	35	....	....	....	....	....	....	1977-78	1983-84
Reibel, Dutch	Det., Chi., Bos.	6	409	84	161	245	75	39	6	14	20	4	2	1953-54	1958-59
Reichert, Craig	Ana.	1	3	0	0	0	0	....	....	....	....	....	....	1996-97	1996-97
● Reid, Dave	Tor.	3	7	0	0	0	0	....	....	....	....	....	....	1952-53	1955-56
Reid, Dave	Bos., Tor., Dal., Col.	18	961	165	204	369	253	118	9	26	35	34	2	1983-84	2000-01
Reid, Gerry	Det.	1	....	....	....	....	....	2	0	0	0	2	....	1948-49	1948-49
Reid, Gord	NYA	1	1	0	0	0	2	....	....	....	....	....	....	1936-37	1936-37
● Reid, Reg	Tor.	2	39	1	0	1	4	2	0	0	0	0	....	1924-25	1925-26
Reid, Tom	Chi., Min.	11	701	17	113	130	654	42	1	13	14	49	....	1967-68	1977-78
Reierson, Dave	Cgy.	1	2	0	0	0	2	....	....	....	....	....	....	1988-89	1988-89
Reigle, Ed	Bos.	1	17	0	2	2	25	....	....	....	....	....	....	1950-51	1950-51
Reinhart, Paul	Atl., Cgy., Van.	11	648	133	426	559	277	83	23	54	77	42	....	1979-80	1989-90
● Reinikka, Ollie	NYR	1	16	0	0	0	0	....	....	....	....	....	....	1926-27	1926-27
● Reise, Leo	Ham., NYA, NYR	8	241	43	43	86	187	6	0	0	0	16	....	1920-21	1929-30
Reise, Leo	Chi., Det., NYR	9	494	28	81	109	399	52	8	5	13	68	2	1945-46	1953-54
Renaud, Mark	Hfd., Buf.	5	152	6	50	56	86	....	....	....	....	....	....	1979-80	1983-84
‡ Reynolds, Bobby	Tor.	1	7	1	1	2	0	....	....	....	....	....	....	1989-90	1989-90
Ribble, Pat	Atl., Chi., Tor., Wsh., Cgy.	8	349	19	60	79	365	8	0	1	1	12	....	1975-76	1982-83
Rice, Steven	NYR, Edm., Hfd., Car.	8	329	64	61	125	275	2	2	1	3	6	....	1990-91	1997-98
Richard, Henri	Mtl.	20	1256	358	688	1046	928	180	49	80	129	181	11	1955-56	1974-75
● Richard, Jacques	Atl., Buf., Que.	10	556	160	187	347	307	35	5	5	10	34	....	1972-73	1982-83
Richard, Jean-Marc	Que.	2	5	2	1	3	2	....	....	....	....	....	....	1987-88	1989-90
● Richard, Maurice	Mtl.	18	978	544	421	965	1285	133	82	44	126	188	8	1942-43	1959-60
‡ Richard, Mike	Wsh.	2	7	0	2	2	0	....	....	....	....	....	....	1987-88	1989-90
Richards, Todd	Hfd.	2	8	0	4	4	4	11	0	3	3	6	....	1990-91	1991-92
‡ Richards, Travis	Dal.	2	3	0	0	0	2	....	....	....	....	....	....	1994-95	1995-96
Richardson, Dave	NYR, Chi., Det.	4	45	3	2	5	27	....	....	....	....	....	....	1963-64	1967-68
Richardson, Glen	Van.	1	24	3	6	9	19	....	....	....	....	....	....	1975-76	1975-76
Richardson, Ken	St.L.	3	49	8	13	21	16	....	....	....	....	....	....	1974-75	1978-79
Richer, Bob	Buf.	1	3	0	0	0	0	....	....	....	....	....	....	1972-73	1972-73
Richer, Stephane	Mtl., N.J., T.B., St.L., Pit.	17	1054	421	398	819	614	134	53	45	98	61	2	1984-85	2001-02
Richer, Stephane	T.B., Bos., Fla.	3	27	1	5	6	20	3	0	0	0	0	....	1992-93	1994-95
Richmond, Steve	NYR, Det., N.J., L.A.	5	159	4	23	27	514	4	0	0	0	12	....	1983-84	1988-89
‡ Richter, Barry	NYR, Bos., NYI, Mtl.	5	151	11	34	45	76	....	....	....	....	....	....	1995-96	2000-01
Richter, Dave	Min., Phi., Van., St.L.	9	365	9	40	49	1030	22	1	0	1	80	....	1981-82	1989-90
Ridley, Mike	NYR, Wsh., Tor., Van.	12	866	292	466	758	424	104	28	50	78	70	....	1985-86	1996-97
‡ Riesen, Michel	Edm.	1	12	0	1	1	4	....	....	....	....	....	....	2000-01	2000-01
Riley, Bill	Wsh., Wpg.	5	139	31	30	61	320	....	....	....	....	....	....	1974-75	1979-80
Riley, Jack	Det., Mtl., Bos.	4	104	10	22	32	8	4	0	3	3	0	....	1932-33	1935-36
● Riley, Jim	Chi., Det.	1	9	0	2	2	14	....	....	....	....	....	....	1926-27	1926-27
Riopelle, Rip	Mtl.	3	169	27	16	43	73	8	1	1	2	2	....	1947-48	1949-50
Rioux, Gerry	Wpg.	1	8	0	0	0	6	....	....	....	....	....	....	1979-80	1979-80
Rioux, Pierre	Cgy.	1	14	1	2	3	4	....	....	....	....	....	....	1982-83	1982-83
● Ripley, Vic	Chi., Bos., NYR, St.L.	7	278	51	49	100	173	20	4	1	5	10	....	1928-29	1934-35
Risebrough, Doug	Mtl., Cgy.	13	740	185	286	471	1542	124	21	37	58	238	4	1974-75	1986-87
Rissling, Gary	Wsh., Pit.	7	221	23	30	53	1008	5	0	1	1	4	....	1978-79	1984-85
Ritchie, Bob	Phi., Det.	2	29	8	4	12	10	....	....	....	....	....	....	1976-77	1977-78
● Ritchie, Dave	Mtl.W., Ott., Tor., Que., Mtl.	6	58	15	6	21	50	1	0	0	0	0	....	1917-18	1925-26
Ritson, Alex	NYR	1	1	0	0	0	0	....	....	....	....	....	....	1944-45	1944-45
Rittinger, Alan	Bos.	1	19	3	7	10	0	....	....	....	....	....	....	1943-44	1943-44
Rivard, Bob	Pit.	1	27	5	12	17	4	....	....	....	....	....	....	1967-68	1967-68
● Rivers, Gus	Mtl.	3	88	4	5	9	12	16	2	0	2	2	2	1929-30	1931-32
Rivers, Shawn	T.B.	1	4	0	2	2	2	....	....	....	....	....	....	1992-93	1992-93
Rivers, Wayne	Det., Bos., St.L., NYR	7	108	15	30	45	94	....	....	....	....	....	....	1961-62	1968-69
Rizzuto, Garth	Van.	1	37	3	4	7	16	....	....	....	....	....	....	1970-71	1970-71
● Roach, Mickey	Tor., Ham., NYA	8	211	77	34	111	54	....	....	....	....	....	....	1919-20	1926-27
Roberge, Mario	Mtl.	5	112	7	7	14	314	15	0	0	0	24	1	1990-91	1994-95
Roberge, Serge	Que.	1	9	0	0	0	24	....	....	....	....	....	....	1990-91	1990-91
Robert, Claude	Mtl.	1	23	1	0	1	9	....	....	....	....	....	....	1950-51	1950-51
Robert, Rene	Tor., Pit., Buf., Col.	12	744	284	418	702	597	50	22	19	41	73	....	1970-71	1981-82
Roberto, Phil	Mtl., St.L., Det., K.C., Col., Cle.	8	385	75	106	181	464	31	9	8	17	69	1	1969-70	1976-77
‡ Roberts, David	St.L., Edm., Van.	5	125	20	33	53	85	9	0	0	0	16	....	1993-94	1997-98
Roberts, Doug	Det., Oak., Cal., Bos.	10	419	43	104	147	342	16	2	3	5	46	....	1965-66	1974-75
Roberts, Gordie	Hfd., Min., Phi., St.L., Pit., Bos.	15	1097	61	359	420	1582	153	10	47	57	273	2	1979-80	1993-94
Roberts, Jim	Min.	3	106	17	23	40	33	2	0	0	0	0	....	1976-77	1978-79
Roberts, Jimmy	Mtl., St.L.	15	1006	126	194	320	621	153	20	16	36	160	5	1963-64	1977-78
● Robertson, Fred	Tor., Det.	2	34	1	0	1	35	7	0	0	0	0	1	1931-32	1933-34
Robertson, Geordie	Buf.	1	5	1	2	3	7	....	....	....	....	....	....	1982-83	1982-83
Robertson, George	Mtl.	2	31	2	5	7	6	....	....	....	....	....	....	1947-48	1948-49
Robertson, Torrie	Wsh., Hfd., Det.	10	442	49	99	148	1751	22	2	1	3	90	....	1980-81	1989-90
‡ Robertsson, Bert	Van., Edm., NYR	4	123	4	10	14	75	5	0	0	0	0	....	1997-98	2000-01
Robidoux, Florent	Chi.	3	52	7	4	11	75	....	....	....	....	....	....	1980-81	1983-84
Robinson, Doug	Chi., NYR, L.A.	7	239	44	67	111	34	11	4	3	7	0	....	1963-64	1970-71
● Robinson, Earl	Mtl.M., Chi., Mtl.	11	417	83	98	181	133	25	5	4	9	0	1	1928-29	1939-40
Robinson, Larry	Mtl., L.A.	20	1384	208	750	958	793	227	28	116	144	211	6	1972-73	1991-92
Robinson, Moe	Mtl.	1	1	0	0	0	0	....	....	....	....	....	....	1979-80	1979-80
Robinson, Rob	St.L.	1	22	0	1	1	8	....	....	....	....	....	....	1991-92	1991-92
Robinson, Scott	Min.	1	1	0	0	0	2	....	....	....	....	....	....	1989-90	1989-90
Robitaille, Mike	NYR, Det., Buf., Van.	8	382	23	105	128	280	13	0	1	1	4	....	1969-70	1976-77
● Roche, Des	Mtl.M., Ott., St.L., Mtl., Det.	4	113	20	18	38	44	....	....	....	....	....	....	1930-31	1934-35
● Roche, Earl	Mtl.M., Bos., Ott., St.L., Det.	4	147	25	27	52	48	2	0	0	0	0	....	1930-31	1934-35
Roche, Ernie	Mtl.	1	4	0	0	0	2	....	....	....	....	....	....	1950-51	1950-51
Rochefort, Dave	Det.	1	1	0	0	0	0	....	....	....	....	....	....	1966-67	1966-67
Rochefort, Leon	NYR, Mtl., Phi., L.A., Det., Atl., Van.	15	617	121	147	268	93	39	4	4	8	16	2	1960-61	1975-76
Rochefort, Normand	Que., NYR, T.B.	13	598	39	119	158	570	69	7	5	12	82	....	1980-81	1993-94
● Rockburn, Harvey	Det., Ott.	3	94	4	2	6	254	....	....	....	....	....	....	1929-30	1932-33
● Rodden, Eddie	Chi., Tor., Bos., NYR	4	97	6	14	20	60	2	0	1	1	0	....	1926-27	1930-31
Rodgers, Marc	Det.	1	21	1	1	2	10	....	....	....	....	....	....	1999-00	1999-00
‡ Roest, Stacy	Det., Min.	5	244	28	48	76	54	3	0	0	0	0	....	1998-99	2002-03
Rogers, John	Min.	2	14	2	4	6	0	....	....	....	....	....	....	1973-74	1974-75
Rogers, Mike	Hfd., NYR, Edm.	7	484	202	317	519	184	17	1	13	14	6	....	1979-80	1985-86
Rohlicek, Jeff	Van.	2	9	0	0	0	8	....	....	....	....	....	....	1987-88	1988-89
Rohlin, Leif	Van.	2	96	8	24	32	40	5	0	0	0	0	....	1995-96	1996-97
Rohloff, Jon	Bos.	3	150	7	25	32	129	10	1	2	3	8	....	1994-95	1996-97
Rolfe, Dale	Bos., L.A., Det., NYR	9	509	25	125	150	556	71	5	24	29	89	....	1959-60	1974-75
Romanchych, Larry	Chi., Atl.	6	298	68	97	165	102	7	2	2	4	4	....	1970-71	1976-77
Romaniuk, Russell	Wpg., Phi.	5	102	13	14	27	63	2	0	0	0	0	....	1991-92	1995-96
Rombough, Doug	Buf., NYI, Min.	4	150	24	27	51	80	....	....	....	....	....	....	1972-73	1975-76
Rominski, Dale	T.B.	1	3	0	1	1	2	....	....	....	....	....	....	1999-00	1999-00
● Romnes, Doc	Chi., Tor., NYA	10	360	68	136	204	42	45	7	18	25	4	2	1930-31	1939-40
Ronan, Ed	Mtl., Wpg., Buf.	6	182	13	23	36	101	27	4	3	7	16	1	1991-92	1996-97
● Ronan, Skene	Ott.	1	11	0	0	0	6	....	....	....	....	....	....	1918-19	1918-19
‡ Ronnqvist, Jonas	Ana.	1	38	0	4	4	14	....	....	....	....	....	....	2000-01	2000-01
Ronson, Len	NYR, Oak.	2	18	2	1	3	10	....	....	....	....	....	....	1960-61	1968-69
Ronty, Paul	Bos., NYR, Mtl.	8	488	101	211	312	103	21	1	7	8	6	....	1947-48	1954-55
Rooney, Steve	Mtl., Wpg., N.J.	5	154	15	13	28	496	25	3	2	5	86	1	1984-85	1988-89
Root, Bill	Mtl., Tor., St.L., Phi.	6	247	11	23	34	180	22	1	2	3	25	....	1982-83	1987-88
● Ross, Art	Mtl.W.	1	3	1	0	1	12	....	....	....	....	....	....	1917-18	1917-18
Ross, Jim	NYR	2	62	2	11	13	29	....	....	....	....	....	....	1951-52	1952-53
Rossignol, Roly	Det., Mtl.	3	14	3	5	8	6	1	0	0	0	2	....	1943-44	1945-46
Rota, Darcy	Chi., Atl., Van.	11	794	256	239	495	973	60	14	7	21	147	....	1973-74	1983-84
Rota, Randy	Mtl., L.A., K.C., Col.	5	212	38	39	77	60	5	0	1	1	0	....	1972-73	1976-77
● Rothschild, Sam	Mtl.M., Pit., NYA	4	100	8	6	14	25	6	0	0	0	0	1	1924-25	1927-28

Name	NHL Teams	NHL Seasons	Regular Schedule GP	G	A	TP	PIM	Playoffs GP	G	A	TP	PIM	NHL Cup Wins	First NHL Season	Last NHL Season
● Roulston, Rolly	Det.	3	24	0	6	6	10	....	....	....	....	....	1	1935-36	1937-38
Roulston, Tom	Edm., Pit.	5	195	47	49	96	74	21	2	2	4	2	....	1980-81	1985-86
Roupe, Magnus	Phi.	2	40	3	5	8	42	....	....	....	....	....	....	1987-88	1988-89
Rouse, Bob	Min., Wsh., Tor., Det., S.J.	17	1061	37	181	218	1559	136	7	21	28	198	2	1983-84	1999-00
Rousseau, Bobby	Mtl., Min., NYR	15	942	245	458	703	359	128	27	57	84	69	4	1960-61	1974-75
Rousseau, Guy	Mtl.	2	4	0	1	1	0	....	....	....	....	....	....	1954-55	1956-57
Rousseau, Roland	Mtl.	1	2	0	0	0	0	....	....	....	....	....	....	1952-53	1952-53
Routhier, Jean-Marc	Que.	1	8	0	0	0	9	....	....	....	....	....	....	1989-90	1989-90
● Rowe, Bobby	Bos.	1	4	1	0	1	0	....	....	....	....	....	....	1924-25	1924-25
Rowe, Mike	Pit.	3	11	0	0	0	11	....	....	....	....	....	....	1984-85	1986-87
Rowe, Ron	NYR	1	5	1	0	1	0	....	....	....	....	....	....	1947-48	1947-48
Rowe, Tom	Wsh., Hfd., Det.	7	357	85	100	185	615	3	2	0	2	0	....	1976-77	1982-83
‡ Roy, Jean-Yves	NYR, Ott., Bos.	4	61	12	16	28	26	....	....	....	....	....	....	1994-95	1997-98
Roy, Stephane	Min.	1	12	1	0	1	0	....	....	....	....	....	....	1987-88	1987-88
‡ Royer, Gaetan	T.B.	1	3	0	0	0	2	....	....	....	....	....	....	2001-02	2001-02
‡ Royer, Remi	Chi.	1	18	0	0	0	67	....	....	....	....	....	....	1998-99	1998-99
Rozzini, Gino	Bos.	1	31	5	10	15	20	6	1	2	3	6	....	1944-45	1944-45
Rucinski, Mike	Chi.	2	1	0	0	0	0	2	0	0	0	0	....	1987-88	1988-89
Rucinski, Mike	Car.	3	26	0	2	2	10	....	....	....	....	....	....	1997-98	2000-01
Ruelle, Bernie	Det.	1	2	1	0	1	0	....	....	....	....	....	....	1943-44	1943-44
Ruff, Jason	St.L., T.B.	2	14	3	3	6	10	....	....	....	....	....	....	1992-93	1993-94
Ruff, Lindy	Buf., NYR	12	691	105	195	300	1264	52	11	13	24	193	....	1979-80	1990-91
Ruhnke, Kent	Bos.	1	2	0	1	1	0	....	....	....	....	....	....	1975-76	1975-76
Rundqvist, Thomas	Mtl.	1	2	0	1	1	0	....	....	....	....	....	....	1984-85	1984-85
● Runge, Paul	Bos., Mtl.M., Mtl.	7	140	18	22	40	57	7	0	0	0	6	....	1930-31	1937-38
Ruotsalainen, Reijo	NYR, Edm., N.J.	7	446	107	237	344	180	86	15	32	47	44	2	1981-82	1989-90
Rupp, Duane	NYR, Tor., Min., Pit.	10	374	24	93	117	220	10	2	2	4	8	....	1962-63	1972-73
Ruskowski, Terry	Chi., L.A., Pit., Min.	10	630	113	313	426	1354	21	1	6	7	86	....	1979-80	1988-89
Russell, Cam	Chi., Col.	10	396	9	21	30	872	44	0	5	5	16	....	1989-90	1998-99
● Russell, Church	NYR	3	90	20	16	36	12	....	....	....	....	....	....	1945-46	1947-48
Russell, Phil	Chi., Atl., Cgy., N.J., Buf.	15	1016	99	325	424	2038	73	4	22	26	202	....	1972-73	1986-87
Ruuttu, Christian	Buf., Chi., Van.	9	621	134	298	432	714	42	4	9	13	49	....	1986-87	1994-95
Ruzicka, Vladimir	Edm., Bos., Ott.	5	233	82	85	167	129	30	4	14	18	2	....	1989-90	1993-94
Ryan, Terry	Mtl.	3	8	0	0	0	36	....	....	....	....	....	....	1996-97	1998-99
Rychel, Warren	Chi., L.A., Tor., Col., Ana.	9	406	38	39	77	1422	70	8	13	21	121	1	1988-89	1998-99
Rymsha, Andy	Que.	1	6	0	0	0	23	....	....	....	....	....	....	1991-92	1991-92

S

Name	NHL Teams	NHL Seasons	Regular Schedule GP	G	A	TP	PIM	Playoffs GP	G	A	TP	PIM	NHL Cup Wins	First NHL Season	Last NHL Season
Saarinen, Simo	NYR	1	8	0	0	0	0	....	....	....	....	....	....	1984-85	1984-85
Sabol, Shaun	Phi.	1	2	0	0	0	0	....	....	....	....	....	....	1989-90	1989-90
Sabourin, Bob	Tor.	1	1	0	0	0	2	....	....	....	....	....	....	1951-52	1951-52
Sabourin, Gary	St.L., Tor., Cal., Cle.	10	627	169	188	357	397	62	19	11	30	58	....	1967-68	1976-77
Sabourin, Ken	Cgy., Wsh.	4	74	2	8	10	201	12	0	0	0	34	....	1988-89	1991-92
Sacco, David	Tor., Ana.	3	35	5	13	18	22	....	....	....	....	....	....	1993-94	1995-96
Sacco, Joe	Tor., Ana., NYI, Wsh., Phi.	13	738	94	119	213	421	26	2	0	2	8	....	1990-91	2002-03
Sacharuk, Larry	NYR, St.L.	5	151	29	33	62	42	2	1	1	2	2	....	1972-73	1976-77
Saganiuk, Rocky	Tor., Pit.	6	259	57	65	122	201	6	1	0	1	15	....	1978-79	1983-84
Saleski, Don	Phi., Col.	9	543	128	125	253	629	82	13	17	30	131	2	1971-72	1979-80
Salming, Borje	Tor., Det.	17	1148	150	637	787	1344	81	12	37	49	91	....	1973-74	1989-90
Salovaara, Barry	Det.	2	90	2	13	15	70	....	....	....	....	....	....	1974-75	1975-76
Salvian, Dave	NYI	1	....	....	....	....	....	1	0	1	1	2	....	1976-77	1976-77
Samis, Phil	Tor.	2	2	0	0	0	0	5	0	1	1	2	1	1947-48	1949-50
Sampson, Gary	Wsh.	4	105	13	22	35	25	12	1	0	1	0	....	1983-84	1986-87
Samuelsson, Kjell	NYR, Phi., Pit., T.B.	14	813	48	138	186	1225	123	4	20	24	178	1	1985-86	1998-99
Samuelsson, Ulf	Hfd., Pit., NYR, Det., Phi.	16	1080	57	275	332	2453	132	7	27	34	272	2	1984-85	1999-00
Sandelin, Scott	Mtl., Phi., Min.	4	25	0	4	4	2	....	....	....	....	....	....	1986-87	1991-92
Sanderson, Derek	Bos., NYR, St.L., Van., Pit.	13	598	202	250	452	911	56	18	12	30	187	2	1965-66	1977-78
Sandford, Ed	Bos., Det., Chi.	9	502	106	145	251	355	42	13	11	24	27	....	1947-48	1955-56
Sandlak, Jim	Van., Hfd.	11	549	110	119	229	821	33	7	10	17	30	....	1985-86	1995-96
● Sands, Charlie	Tor., Bos., Mtl., NYR	12	427	99	109	208	58	34	6	6	12	4	1	1932-33	1943-44
Sandstrom, Tomas	NYR, L.A., Pit., Det., Ana.	15	983	394	462	856	1193	139	32	49	81	183	1	1984-85	1998-99
Sandwith, Terran	Edm.	1	8	0	0	0	6	....	....	....	....	....	....	1997-98	1997-98
Sanipass, Everett	Chi., Que.	5	164	25	34	59	358	5	2	0	2	4	....	1986-87	1990-91
‡ Sarault, Yves	Mtl., Cgy., Col., Ott., Atl., Nsh.	8	106	10	10	20	51	5	0	0	0	2	....	1994-95	2001-02
Sargent, Gary	L.A., Min.	8	402	61	161	222	273	20	5	7	12	8	....	1975-76	1982-83
Sarner, Craig	Bos.	1	7	0	0	0	0	....	....	....	....	....	....	1974-75	1974-75
Sarrazin, Dick	Phi.	3	100	20	35	55	22	4	0	0	0	0	....	1968-69	1971-72
Sasakamoose, Fred	Chi.	1	11	0	0	0	6	....	....	....	....	....	....	1953-54	1953-54
Sasser, Grant	Pit.	1	3	0	0	0	0	....	....	....	....	....	....	1983-84	1983-84
Sather, Glen	Bos., Pit., NYR, St.L., Mtl., Min.	10	658	80	113	193	724	72	1	5	6	86	....	1966-67	1975-76
Saunders, Bernie	Que.	2	10	0	1	1	8	....	....	....	....	....	....	1979-80	1980-81
Saunders, David	Van.	1	56	7	13	20	10	....	....	....	....	....	....	1987-88	1987-88
● Saunders, Ted	Ott.	1	18	1	3	4	4	....	....	....	....	....	....	1933-34	1933-34
Sauve, Jean-Francois	Buf., Que.	7	290	65	138	203	114	36	9	12	21	10	....	1980-81	1986-87
‡ Savage, Joel	Buf.	1	3	0	1	1	0	....	....	....	....	....	....	1990-91	1990-91
‡ Savage, Reggie	Wsh., Que.	3	34	5	7	12	28	....	....	....	....	....	....	1990-91	1993-94
● Savage, Tony	Bos., Mtl.	1	49	1	5	6	6	2	0	0	0	0	....	1934-35	1934-35
Savard, Andre	Bos., Buf., Que.	12	790	211	271	482	411	85	13	18	31	77	....	1973-74	1984-85
Savard, Denis	Chi., Mtl., T.B.	17	1196	473	865	1338	1336	169	66	109	175	256	1	1980-81	1996-97
Savard, Jean	Chi., Hfd.	3	43	7	12	19	29	....	....	....	....	....	....	1977-78	1979-80
Savard, Serge	Mtl., Wpg.	17	1040	106	333	439	592	130	19	49	68	88	8	1966-67	1982-83
‡ Savoia, Ryan	Pit.	1	3	0	0	0	0	....	....	....	....	....	....	1998-99	1998-99
Sawyer, Kevin	St.L., Bos., Phx., Ana.	6	110	3	3	6	403	....	....	....	....	....	....	1995-96	2002-03
Scamurra, Peter	Wsh.	4	132	8	25	33	59	....	....	....	....	....	....	1975-76	1979-80
Sceviour, Darin	Chi.	1	1	0	0	0	0	....	....	....	....	....	....	1986-87	1986-87
Schaeffer, Butch	Chi.	1	5	0	0	0	6	....	....	....	....	....	....	1936-37	1936-37
Schamehorn, Kevin	Det., L.A.	3	10	0	0	0	17	....	....	....	....	....	....	1976-77	1980-81
Schella, John	Van.	2	115	2	18	20	224	....	....	....	....	....	....	1970-71	1971-72
Scherza, Chuck	Bos., NYR	2	36	6	6	12	35	....	....	....	....	....	....	1943-44	1944-45
Schinkel, Ken	NYR, Pit.	12	636	127	198	325	163	19	7	2	9	4	....	1959-60	1972-73
‡ Schlegel, Brad	Wsh., Cgy.	3	48	1	8	9	10	7	0	1	1	2	....	1991-92	1993-94
Schliebener, Andy	Van.	3	84	2	11	13	74	6	0	0	0	0	....	1981-82	1984-85
Schmautz, Bobby	Chi., Van., Bos., Edm., Col.	13	764	271	286	557	988	84	28	33	61	92	....	1967-68	1980-81
● Schmautz, Cliff	Buf., Phi.	1	56	13	19	32	33	....	....	....	....	....	....	1970-71	1970-71
● Schmidt, Clarence	Bos.	1	7	1	0	1	2	....	....	....	....	....	....	1943-44	1943-44
Schmidt, Jackie	Bos.	1	45	6	7	13	6	5	0	0	0	0	....	1942-43	1942-43
Schmidt, Milt	Bos.	16	776	229	346	575	466	86	24	25	49	60	2	1936-37	1954-55
Schmidt, Norm	Pit.	4	125	23	33	56	73	....	....	....	....	....	....	1983-84	1987-88
Schmidt, Otto	Bos.	1	2	0	0	0	0	....	....	....	....	....	....	1943-44	1943-44
● Schnarr, Werner	Bos.	2	26	0	0	0	0	....	....	....	....	....	....	1924-25	1925-26
‡ Schneider, Andy	Ott.	1	10	0	0	0	15	....	....	....	....	....	....	1993-94	1993-94
Schock, Danny	Bos., Phi.	2	20	1	2	3	0	1	0	0	0	0	1	1969-70	1970-71
Schock, Ron	Bos., St.L., Pit., Buf.	15	909	166	351	517	260	55	4	16	20	29	....	1963-64	1977-78
Schoenfeld, Jim	Buf., Det., Bos.	13	719	51	204	255	1132	75	3	13	16	151	....	1972-73	1984-85
Schofield, Dwight	Det., Mtl., St.L., Wsh., Pit., Wpg.	7	211	8	22	30	631	9	0	0	0	55	....	1976-77	1987-88
Schreiber, Wally	Min.	2	41	8	10	18	12	....	....	....	....	....	....	1987-88	1988-89
● Schriner, Sweeney	NYA, Tor.	11	484	201	204	405	148	59	18	11	29	54	2	1934-35	1945-46
Schulte, Paxton	Que., Cgy.	2	2	0	0	0	4	....	....	....	....	....	....	1993-94	1996-97
Schultz, Dave	Phi., L.A., Pit., Buf.	9	535	79	121	200	2294	73	8	12	20	412	2	1971-72	1979-80
Schurman, Maynard	Hfd.	1	7	0	0	0	0	....	....	....	....	....	....	1979-80	1979-80
Schutt, Rod	Mtl., Pit., Tor.	8	286	77	92	169	177	22	8	6	14	26	....	1977-78	1985-86
Scissons, Scott	NYI	3	2	0	0	0	0	1	0	0	0	0	....	1990-91	1993-94
Sclisizzi, Enio	Det., Chi.	6	81	12	11	23	26	13	0	0	0	6	....	1946-47	1952-53
● Scott, Ganton	Tor., Ham., Mtl.M.	3	57	1	1	2	0	....	....	....	....	....	....	1922-23	1924-25
● Scott, Laurie	NYA, NYR	2	62	6	3	9	28	....	....	....	....	....	....	1926-27	1927-28
Scremin, Claudio	S.J.	2	17	0	1	1	29	....	....	....	....	....	....	1991-92	1992-93
Scruton, Howard	L.A.	1	4	0	4	4	9	....	....	....	....	....	....	1982-83	1982-83
Seabrooke, Glen	Phi.	3	19	1	6	7	4	....	....	....	....	....	....	1986-87	1988-89
Secord, Al	Bos., Chi., Tor., Phi.	12	766	273	222	495	2093	102	21	34	55	382	....	1978-79	1989-90
Sedlbauer, Ron	Van., Chi., Tor.	7	430	143	86	229	210	19	1	3	4	27	....	1974-75	1980-81
Seftel, Steve	Wsh.	1	4	0	0	0	2	....	....	....	....	....	....	1990-91	1990-91
Seguin, Dan	Min., Van.	2	37	2	6	8	50	....	....	....	....	....	....	1970-71	1973-74
Seguin, Steve	L.A.	1	5	0	0	0	9	....	....	....	....	....	....	1984-85	1984-85
● Seibert, Earl	NYR, Chi., Det.	15	645	89	187	276	746	66	11	8	19	76	2	1931-32	1945-46
Seiling, Ric	Buf., Det.	10	738	179	208	387	573	62	14	14	28	36	....	1977-78	1986-87

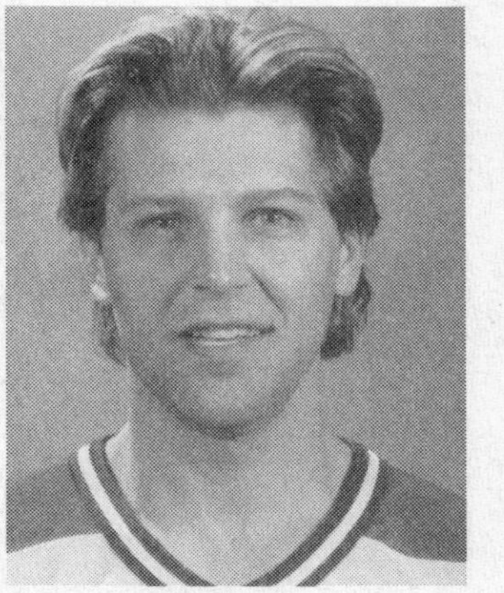
Barry Richter

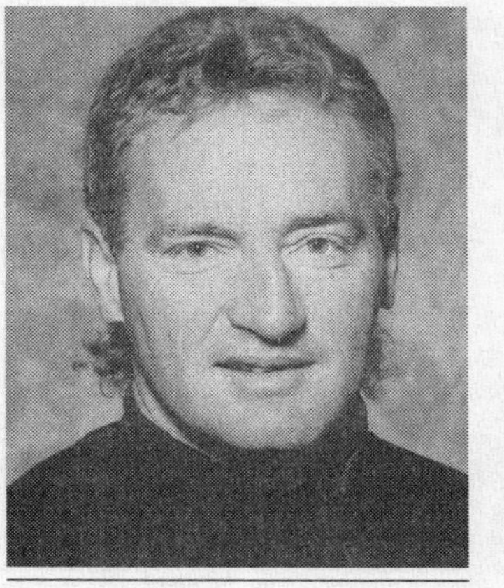
Larry Robinson

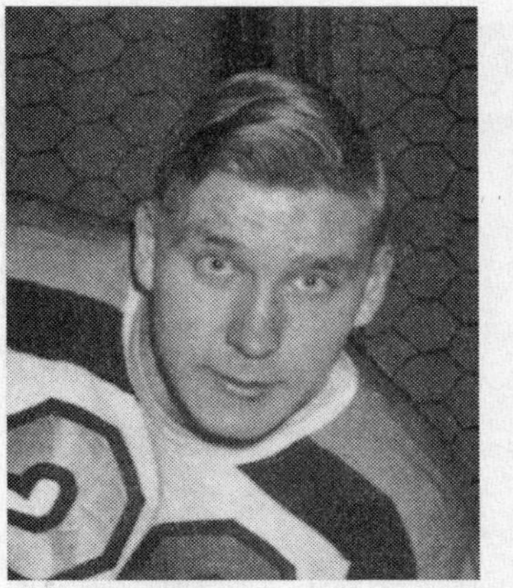
Paul Ronty

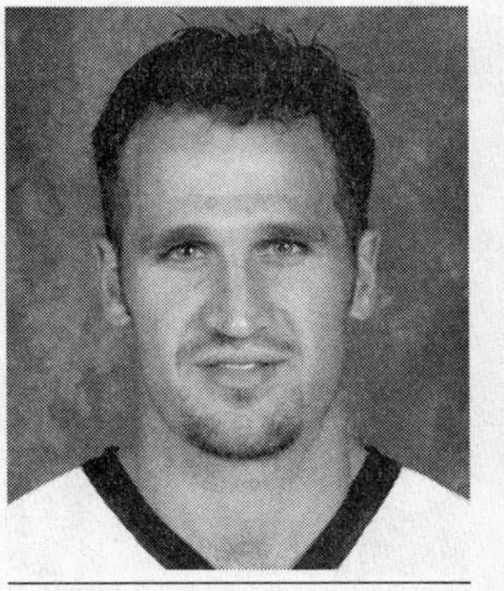
Kevin Sawyer

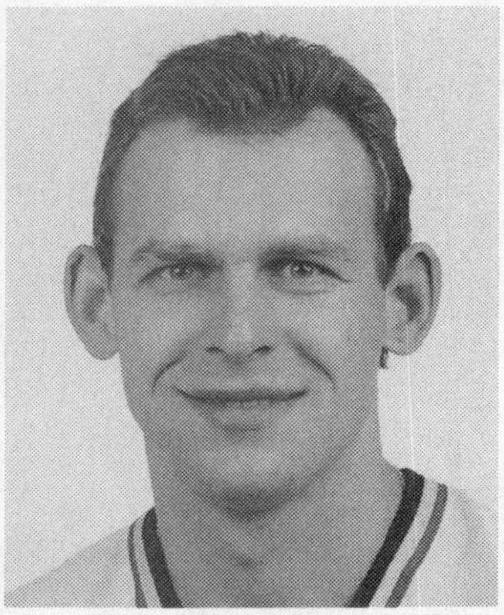

Anatoli Semenov

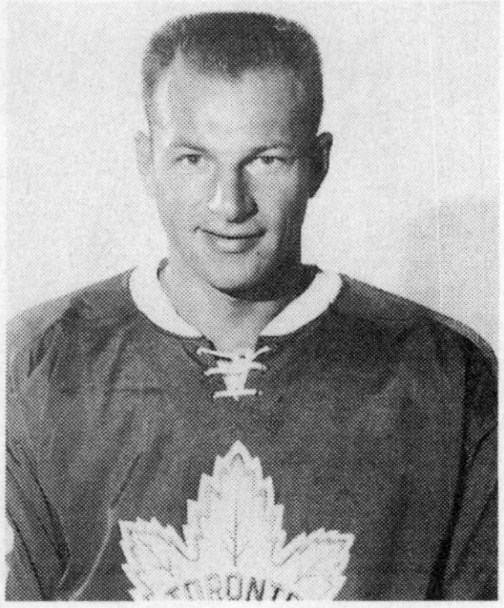

Eddie Shack

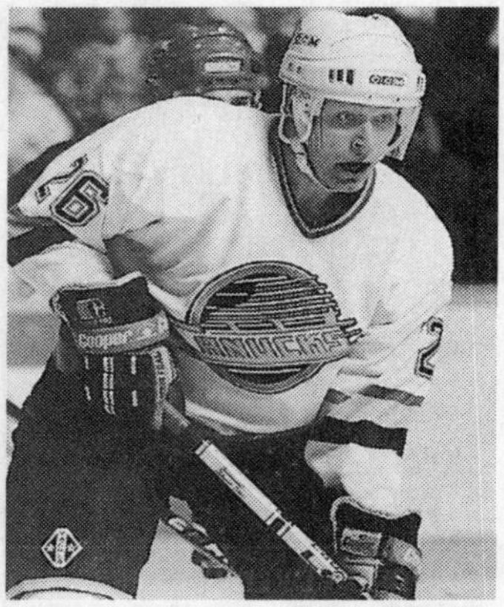

Petri Skriko

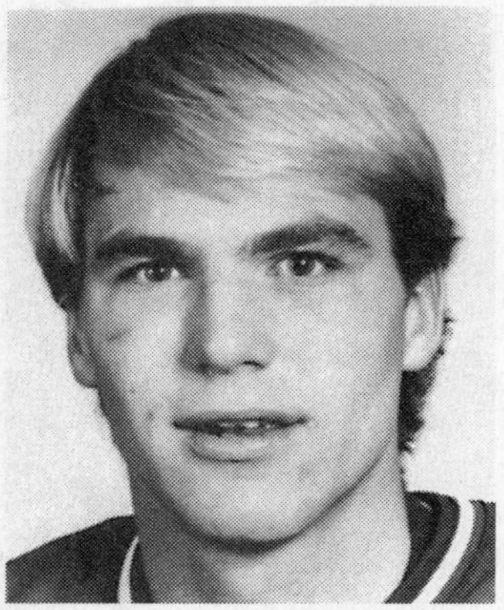

Brian Skrudland

			Regular Schedule					Playoffs					NHL	First	Last
Name	NHL Teams	NHL Seasons	GP	G	A	TP	PIM	GP	G	A	TP	PIM	Cup Wins	NHL Season	NHL Season
Seiling, Rod	Tor., NYR, Wsh., St.L., Atl.	17	979	62	269	331	601	77	4	8	12	55	....	1962-63	1978-79
Sejba, Jiri	Buf.	1	11	0	2	2	8	....	....	....	....	....	....	1990-91	1990-91
Selby, Brit	Tor., Phi., St.L.	8	350	55	62	117	163	16	1	1	2	8	....	1964-65	1971-72
Self, Steve	Wsh.	1	3	0	0	0	0	....	....	....	....	....	....	1976-77	1976-77
Selivanov, Alex	T.B., Edm., CBJ	7	459	121	114	235	379	13	2	3	5	16	....	1994-95	2000-01
Selmser, Sean	CBJ	1	1	0	0	0	5	....	....	....	....	....	....	2000-01	2000-01
Selwood, Brad	Tor., L.A.	3	163	7	40	47	153	6	0	0	0	4	....	1970-71	1979-80
‡ Semak, Alexander	N.J., T.B., NYI, Van.	6	289	83	91	174	187	8	1	1	2	0	....	1991-92	1996-97
Semchuk, Brandy	L.A.	1	1	0	0	0	2	....	....	....	....	....	....	1992-93	1992-93
Semenko, Dave	Edm., Hfd., Tor.	9	575	65	88	153	1175	73	6	6	12	208	2	1979-80	1987-88
Semenov, Anatoli	Edm., T.B., Van., Ana., Phi., Buf.	8	362	68	126	194	122	49	9	13	22	12	....	1989-90	1996-97
Senick, George	NYR	1	13	2	3	5	8	....	....	....	....	....	....	1952-53	1952-53
Seppa, Jyrki	Wpg.	1	13	0	2	2	6	....	....	....	....	....	....	1983-84	1983-84
Serafini, Ron	Cal.	1	2	0	0	0	2	....	....	....	....	....	....	1973-74	1973-74
Serowik, Jeff	Tor., Bos., Pit.	4	28	0	6	6	16	....	....	....	....	....	....	1990-91	1999-00
Servinis, George	Min.	1	5	0	0	0	0	....	....	....	....	....	....	1987-88	1987-88
Sevcik, Jaroslav	Que.	1	13	0	2	2	2	....	....	....	....	....	....	1989-90	1989-90
Severyn, Brent	Que., Fla., NYI, Col., Ana., Dal.	7	328	10	30	40	825	8	0	0	0	12	....	1989-90	1998-99
Sevigny, Pierre	Mtl., NYR	4	78	4	5	9	64	3	0	1	1	0	....	1993-94	1997-98
Shack, Eddie	NYR, Tor., Bos., L.A., Buf., Pit.	17	1047	239	226	465	1437	74	6	7	13	151	4	1958-59	1974-75
● Shack, Joe	NYR	2	70	9	27	36	20	....	....	....	....	....	....	1942-43	1944-45
Shafranov, Konstantin	St.L.	1	5	2	1	3	0	....	....	....	....	....	....	1996-97	1996-97
Shakes, Paul	Cal.	1	21	0	4	4	12	....	....	....	....	....	....	1973-74	1973-74
Shaldybin, Yevgeny	Bos.	1	3	1	0	1	0	....	....	....	....	....	....	1996-97	1996-97
Shanahan, Sean	Mtl., Col., Bos.	3	40	1	3	4	47	....	....	....	....	....	....	1975-76	1977-78
Shand, Dave	Atl., Tor., Wsh.	8	421	19	84	103	544	26	1	2	3	83	....	1976-77	1984-85
Shank, Daniel	Det., Hfd.	3	77	13	14	27	175	5	0	0	0	22	....	1989-90	1991-92
Shannon, Chuck	NYA	1	4	0	0	0	2	....	....	....	....	....	....	1939-40	1939-40
Shannon, Darrin	Buf., Wpg., Phx.	10	506	87	163	250	344	45	7	10	17	38	....	1988-89	1997-98
‡ Shannon, Darryl	Tor., Wpg., Buf., Atl., Cgy., Mtl.	13	544	28	111	139	523	29	4	7	11	16	....	1988-89	2000-01
● Shannon, Gerry	Ott., St.L., Bos., Mtl.M.	5	180	23	29	52	80	9	0	1	1	2	....	1933-34	1937-38
Sharifijanov, Vadim	N.J., Van.	3	92	16	21	37	50	4	0	0	0	0	....	1996-97	1999-00
Sharples, Jeff	Det.	3	105	14	35	49	70	7	0	3	3	6	....	1986-87	1988-89
Sharpley, Glen	Min., Chi.	6	389	117	161	278	199	27	7	11	18	24	....	1976-77	1981-82
Shaunessy, Scott	Que.	2	7	0	0	0	23	....	....	....	....	....	....	1986-87	1988-89
Shaw, Brad	Hfd., Ott., Wsh., St.L.	11	377	22	137	159	208	23	4	8	12	6	....	1985-86	1998-99
Shaw, David	Que., NYR, Edm., Min., Bos., T.B.	16	769	41	153	194	906	45	3	9	12	81	....	1982-83	1997-98
● Shay, Norm	Bos., Tor.	2	53	5	3	8	34	....	....	....	....	....	....	1924-25	1925-26
● Shea, Pat	Chi.	1	10	1	0	1	0	....	....	....	....	....	....	1931-32	1931-32
‡ Shearer, Rob	Col.	1	2	0	0	0	0	....	....	....	....	....	....	2000-01	2000-01
Shedden, Doug	Pit., Det., Que., Tor.	8	416	139	186	325	176	....	....	....	....	....	....	1981-82	1990-91
Sheehan, Bobby	Mtl., Cal., Chi., Det., NYR, Col., L.A.	9	310	48	63	111	40	25	4	3	7	8	1	1969-70	1981-82
Sheehy, Neil	Cgy., Hfd., Wsh.	9	379	18	47	65	1311	54	0	3	3	241	....	1983-84	1991-92
Sheehy, Tim	Det., Hfd.	2	27	2	1	3	0	....	....	....	....	....	....	1977-78	1979-80
Shelton, Doug	Chi.	1	5	0	1	1	2	....	....	....	....	....	....	1967-68	1967-68
● Sheppard, Frank	Det.	1	8	1	1	2	0	....	....	....	....	....	....	1927-28	1927-28
Sheppard, Gregg	Bos., Pit.	10	657	205	293	498	243	82	32	40	72	31	....	1972-73	1981-82
● Sheppard, Johnny	Det., NYA, Bos., Chi.	8	308	68	58	126	224	10	0	0	0	0	1	1926-27	1933-34
Sheppard, Ray	Buf., NYR, Det., S.J., Fla., Car.	13	817	357	300	657	212	81	30	20	50	21	....	1987-88	1999-00
● Sherf, John	Det.	5	19	0	0	0	8	8	0	1	1	2	1	1935-36	1943-44
● Shero, Fred	NYR	3	145	6	14	20	137	13	0	2	2	8	....	1947-48	1949-50
Sherritt, Gordon	Det.	1	8	0	0	0	12	....	....	....	....	....	....	1943-44	1943-44
Sherven, Gord	Edm., Min., Hfd.	5	97	13	22	35	33	3	0	0	0	0	....	1983-84	1987-88
Shevalier, Jeff	L.A., T.B.	3	32	5	9	14	8	....	....	....	....	....	....	1994-95	1999-00
● Shewchuk, Jack	Bos.	6	187	9	19	28	160	20	0	1	1	19	1	1938-39	1944-45
Shibicky, Alex	NYR	8	324	110	91	201	161	39	12	12	24	12	1	1935-36	1945-46
● Shields, Al	Ott., Phi., NYA, Mtl.M., Bos.	11	459	42	46	88	637	17	0	1	1	14	1	1927-28	1937-38
Shill, Bill	Bos.	3	79	21	13	34	18	7	1	2	3	2	....	1942-43	1946-47
● Shill, Jack	Tor., Bos., NYA, Chi.	6	160	15	20	35	70	25	1	6	7	23	1	1933-34	1938-39
Shinske, Rick	Cle., St.L.	3	63	5	16	21	10	....	....	....	....	....	....	1976-77	1978-79
Shires, Jim	Det., St.L., Pit.	3	56	3	6	9	32	....	....	....	....	....	....	1970-71	1972-73
Shmyr, Paul	Chi., Cal., Min., Hfd.	7	343	13	72	85	528	34	3	3	6	44	....	1968-69	1981-82
Shoebottom, Bruce	Bos.	4	35	1	4	5	53	14	1	2	3	77	....	1987-88	1990-91
● Shore, Eddie	Bos., NYA	14	550	105	179	284	1047	55	6	13	19	181	2	1926-27	1939-40
● Shore, Hamby	Ott.	1	18	3	8	11	51	....	....	....	....	....	....	1917-18	1917-18
Short, Steve	L.A., Det.	2	6	0	0	0	2	....	....	....	....	....	....	1977-78	1978-79
‡ Shuchuk, Gary	Det., L.A.	5	142	13	26	39	70	20	2	2	4	12	....	1990-91	1995-96
Shudra, Ron	Edm.	1	10	0	5	5	6	....	....	....	....	....	....	1987-88	1987-88
Shutt, Steve	Mtl., L.A.	13	930	424	393	817	410	99	50	48	98	65	5	1972-73	1984-85
● Siebert, Babe	Mtl.M., NYR, Bos., Mtl.	14	592	140	156	296	982	49	7	5	12	62	2	1925-26	1938-39
Silk, Dave	NYR, Bos., Det., Wpg.	7	249	54	59	113	271	13	2	4	6	13	....	1979-80	1985-86
Siltala, Mike	Wsh., NYR	3	7	1	0	1	2	....	....	....	....	....	....	1981-82	1987-88
Siltanen, Risto	Edm., Hfd., Que.	8	562	90	265	355	266	32	6	12	18	30	....	1979-80	1986-87
Sim, Trevor	Edm.	1	3	0	1	1	2	....	....	....	....	....	....	1989-90	1989-90
Simard, Martin	Cgy., T.B.	3	44	1	5	6	183	....	....	....	....	....	....	1990-91	1992-93
‡ Simicek, Roman	Pit., Min.	2	63	7	10	17	59	....	....	....	....	....	....	2000-01	2001-02
Simmer, Charlie	Cal., Cle., L.A., Bos., Pit.	14	712	342	369	711	544	24	9	9	18	32	....	1974-75	1987-88
Simmons, Al	Cal., Bos.	3	11	0	1	1	21	1	0	0	0	0	....	1971-72	1975-76
● Simon, Cully	Det., Chi.	3	130	4	11	15	121	14	1	0	1	6	1	1942-43	1944-45
Simon, Jason	NYI, Phx.	2	5	0	0	0	34	....	....	....	....	....	....	1993-94	1996-97
Simon, Thain	Det.	1	3	0	0	0	0	....	....	....	....	....	....	1946-47	1946-47
Simon, Todd	Buf.	1	15	0	1	1	0	5	1	0	1	0	....	1993-94	1993-94
Simonetti, Frank	Bos.	4	115	5	8	13	76	12	0	1	1	8	....	1984-85	1987-88
Simpson, Bobby	Atl., St.L., Pit.	5	175	35	29	64	98	6	0	1	1	2	....	1976-77	1982-83
● Simpson, Cliff	Det.	2	6	0	1	1	0	2	0	0	0	2	....	1946-47	1947-48
Simpson, Craig	Pit., Edm., Buf.	10	634	247	250	497	659	67	36	32	68	56	2	1985-86	1994-95
● Simpson, Joe	NYA	6	228	21	19	40	156	2	0	0	0	0	....	1925-26	1930-31
Sims, Al	Bos., Hfd., L.A.	10	475	49	116	165	286	41	0	2	2	14	....	1973-74	1982-83
Sinclair, Reg	NYR, Det.	3	208	49	43	92	139	3	1	0	1	0	....	1950-51	1952-53
● Singbush, Alex	Mtl.	1	32	0	5	5	15	3	0	0	0	4	....	1940-41	1940-41
Sinisalo, Ilkka	Phi., Min., L.A.	11	582	204	222	426	208	68	21	11	32	6	....	1981-82	1991-92
Siren, Ville	Pit., Min.	5	290	14	68	82	276	7	0	0	0	6	....	1985-86	1989-90
Sirois, Bob	Phi., Wsh.	6	286	92	120	212	42	....	....	....	....	....	....	1974-75	1979-80
Sittler, Darryl	Tor., Phi., Det.	15	1096	484	637	1121	948	76	29	45	74	137	....	1970-71	1984-85
● Sjoberg, Lars-Erik	Wpg.	1	79	7	27	34	48	....	....	....	....	....	....	1979-80	1979-80
‡ Sjodin, Tommy	Min., Dal., Que.	2	106	8	40	48	52	....	....	....	....	....	....	1992-93	1993-94
● Skaare, Bjorn	Det.	1	1	0	0	0	0	....	....	....	....	....	....	1978-79	1978-79
Skarda, Randy	St.L.	2	26	0	5	5	11	....	....	....	....	....	....	1989-90	1991-92
● Skilton, Raymie	Mtl.W.	1	1	0	0	0	0	....	....	....	....	....	....	1917-18	1917-18
● Skinner, Alf	Tor., Bos., Mtl.M., Pit.	4	71	26	10	36	87	2	0	1	1	9	1	1917-18	1925-26
Skinner, Larry	Col.	4	47	10	12	22	8	2	0	0	0	0	....	1976-77	1979-80
‡ Skopintsev, Andrei	T.B., Atl.	3	40	2	4	6	32	....	....	....	....	....	....	1998-99	2000-01
Skov, Glen	Det., Chi., Mtl.	12	650	106	136	242	413	53	7	7	14	48	3	1949-50	1960-61
Skriko, Petri	Van., Bos., Wpg., S.J.	9	541	183	222	405	246	28	5	9	14	4	....	1984-85	1992-93
Skrudland, Brian	Mtl., Cgy., Fla., NYR, Dal.	15	881	124	219	343	1107	164	15	46	61	323	2	1985-86	1999-00
Sleaver, John	Chi.	2	13	1	0	1	6	....	....	....	....	....	....	1953-54	1956-57
Sleigher, Louis	Que., Bos.	6	194	46	53	99	146	17	1	1	2	64	....	1979-80	1985-86
Sloan, Tod	Tor., Chi.	13	745	220	262	482	831	47	9	12	21	47	2	1947-48	1960-61
● Slobodian, Peter	NYA	1	41	3	2	5	54	....	....	....	....	....	....	1940-41	1940-41
● Slowinski, Ed	NYR	6	291	58	74	132	63	16	2	6	8	6	....	1947-48	1952-53
Sly, Darryl	Tor., Min., Van.	4	79	1	2	3	20	....	....	....	....	....	....	1965-66	1970-71
Smail, Doug	Wpg., Min., Que., Ott.	13	845	210	249	459	602	42	9	2	11	49	....	1980-81	1992-93
Smart, Alex	Mtl.	1	8	5	2	7	0	....	....	....	....	....	....	1942-43	1942-43
Smedsmo, Dale	Tor.	1	4	0	0	0	0	....	....	....	....	....	....	1972-73	1972-73
Smehlik, Richard	Buf., Atl., N.J.	10	644	49	146	195	415	88	1	14	15	40	1	1992-93	2002-03
Smillie, Don	Bos.	1	12	2	2	4	4	....	....	....	....	....	....	1933-34	1933-34
● Smith, Alex	Ott., Det., Bos., NYA	11	443	41	50	91	645	19	0	2	2	26	1	1924-25	1934-35
● Smith, Art	Tor., Ott.	4	144	15	10	25	249	4	1	1	2	8	....	1927-28	1930-31
Smith, Barry	Bos., Col.	3	114	7	7	14	10	....	....	....	....	....	....	1975-76	1980-81
Smith, Bobby	Min., Mtl.	15	1077	357	679	1036	917	184	64	96	160	245	1	1978-79	1992-93
Smith, Brad	Van., Atl., Cgy., Det., Tor.	9	222	28	34	62	591	20	3	3	6	49	....	1978-79	1986-87
Smith, Brian	Det.	3	61	2	8	10	12	5	0	0	0	0	....	1957-58	1960-61
● Smith, Brian	L.A., Min.	2	67	10	10	20	33	7	0	0	0	0	....	1967-68	1968-69
● Smith, Carl	Det.	1	7	1	1	2	2	....	....	....	....	....	....	1943-44	1943-44
Smith, Clint	NYR, Chi.	11	483	161	236	397	24	42	10	14	24	2	1	1936-37	1946-47
Smith, Dallas	Bos., NYR	16	890	55	252	307	959	86	3	29	32	128	2	1959-60	1977-78

Name	NHL Teams	NHL Seasons	Regular Schedule					Playoffs					NHL Cup Wins	First NHL Season	Last NHL Season
			GP	G	A	TP	PIM	GP	G	A	TP	PIM			
Smith, Dennis	Wsh., L.A.	2	8	0	0	0	4	....	....	....	....	....	....	1989-90	1990-91
Smith, Derek	Buf., Det.	8	335	78	116	194	60	30	9	14	23	13	....	1975-76	1982-83
Smith, Derrick	Phi., Min., Dal.	10	537	82	92	174	373	82	14	11	25	79	....	1984-85	1993-94
• Smith, Des	Mtl.M., Mtl., Chi., Bos.	5	196	22	25	47	236	25	1	4	5	18	1	1937-38	1941-42
• Smith, Don	Mtl.	1	12	1	0	1	6	....	....	....	....	....	....	1919-20	1919-20
Smith, Don	NYR	1	11	1	1	2	0	1	0	0	0	0	....	1949-50	1949-50
Smith, Doug	L.A., Buf., Edm., Van., Pit.	9	535	115	138	253	624	18	4	2	6	21	....	1981-82	1989-90
Smith, Floyd	Bos., NYR, Det., Tor., Buf.	13	616	129	178	307	207	48	12	11	23	16	....	1954-55	1971-72
Smith, Geoff	Edm., Fla., NYR	10	462	18	73	91	282	13	0	1	1	8	1	1989-90	1998-99
Smith, Glen	Chi.	1	2	0	0	0	0	....	....	....	....	....	....	1950-51	1950-51
• Smith, Glenn	Tor.	1	9	0	0	0	0	....	....	....	....	....	....	1921-22	1921-22
Smith, Gord	Wsh., Wpg.	6	299	9	30	39	284	....	....	....	....	....	....	1974-75	1979-80
Smith, Greg	Cal., Cle., Min., Det., Wsh.	13	829	56	232	288	1110	63	4	7	11	106	....	1975-76	1987-88
• Smith, Hooley	Ott., Mtl.M., Bos., NYA	17	715	200	225	425	1013	54	11	8	19	109	2	1924-25	1940-41
• Smith, Ken	Bos.	7	331	78	93	171	49	30	8	13	21	6	....	1944-45	1950-51
Smith, Nakina	Det.	1	10	1	2	3	0	....	....	....	....	....	....	1943-44	1943-44
Smith, Randy	Min.	2	3	0	0	0	0	....	....	....	....	....	....	1985-86	1986-87
Smith, Rick	Bos., Cal., St.L., Det., Wsh.	11	687	52	167	219	560	78	3	23	26	73	1	1968-69	1980-81
• Smith, Rodger	Pit., Phi.	6	210	20	4	24	172	4	3	0	3	0	....	1925-26	1930-31
Smith, Ron	NYI	1	11	1	1	2	14	....	....	....	....	....	....	1972-73	1972-73
• Smith, Sid	Tor.	12	601	186	183	369	94	44	17	10	27	2	3	1946-47	1957-58
Smith, Stan	NYR	2	9	2	1	3	0	1	0	0	0	0	1	1939-40	1940-41
Smith, Steve	Phi., Buf.	6	18	0	1	1	15	....	....	....	....	....	....	1981-82	1988-89
Smith, Steve	Edm., Chi., Cgy.	16	804	72	303	375	2139	134	11	41	52	288	3	1984-85	2000-01
Smith, Stu	Mtl.	2	4	2	2	4	2	1	0	0	0	0	....	1940-41	1941-42
Smith, Stu	Hfd.	4	77	2	10	12	95	....	....	....	....	....	....	1979-80	1982-83
• Smith, Tommy	Que.	1	10	0	1	1	11	....	....	....	....	....	....	1919-20	1919-20
Smith, Vern	NYI	1	1	0	0	0	0	....	....	....	....	....	....	1984-85	1984-85
Smith, Wayne	Chi.	1	2	1	1	2	2	1	0	0	0	0	....	1966-67	1966-67
Smrke, John	St.L., Que.	3	103	11	17	28	33	....	....	....	....	....	....	1977-78	1979-80
• Smrke, Stan	Mtl.	2	9	0	3	3	0	....	....	....	....	....	....	1956-57	1957-58
Smyl, Stan	Van.	13	896	262	411	673	1556	41	16	17	33	64	....	1978-79	1990-91
• Smylie, Rod	Tor., Ott.	6	74	4	2	6	12	4	0	0	0	2	1	1920-21	1925-26
Smyth, Greg	Phi., Que., Cgy., Fla., Tor., Chi.	10	229	4	16	20	783	12	0	0	0	40	....	1986-87	1996-97
Smyth, Kevin	Hfd.	3	58	6	8	14	31	....	....	....	....	....	....	1993-94	1995-96
Snell, Chris	Tor., L.A.	2	34	2	7	9	24	....	....	....	....	....	....	1993-94	1994-95
Snell, Ron	Pit.	2	7	3	2	5	6	....	....	....	....	....	....	1968-69	1969-70
Snell, Ted	Pit., K.C., Det.	2	104	7	18	25	22	....	....	....	....	....	....	1973-74	1974-75
Snepsts, Harold	Van., Min., Det., St.L.	17	1033	38	195	233	2009	93	1	14	15	231	....	1974-75	1990-91
Snow, Sandy	Det.	1	3	0	0	0	2	....	....	....	....	....	....	1968-69	1968-69
Snuggerud, Dave	Buf., S.J., Phi.	4	265	30	54	84	127	12	1	3	4	6	....	1989-90	1992-93
• Snyder, Dan	Atl.	3	49	11	5	16	64	....	....	....	....	....	....	2000-01	2002-03
Sobchuk, Dennis	Det., Que.	2	35	5	6	11	2	....	....	....	....	....	....	1979-80	1982-83
• Sobchuk, Gene	Van.	1	1	0	0	0	0	....	....	....	....	....	....	1973-74	1973-74
Solheim, Ken	Chi., Min., Det., Edm.	5	135	19	20	39	34	3	1	1	2	2	....	1980-81	1985-86
Solinger, Bob	Tor., Det.	5	99	10	11	21	19	....	....	....	....	....	....	1951-52	1959-60
• Somers, Art	Chi., NYR	6	222	33	56	89	189	30	1	5	6	20	1	1929-30	1934-35
Sommer, Roy	Edm.	1	3	1	0	1	7	....	....	....	....	....	....	1980-81	1980-81
Songin, Tom	Bos.	3	43	5	5	10	22	....	....	....	....	....	....	1978-79	1980-81
Sonmor, Glen	NYR	2	28	2	0	2	21	....	....	....	....	....	....	1953-54	1954-55
‡ Sorochan, Lee	Cgy.	2	3	0	0	0	0	....	....	....	....	....	....	1998-99	1999-00
• Sorrell, John	Det., NYA	11	490	127	119	246	100	42	12	15	27	10	2	1930-31	1940-41
• Sparrow, Emory	Bos.	1	8	0	0	0	4	....	....	....	....	....	....	1924-25	1924-25
Speck, Fred	Det., Van.	3	28	1	2	3	2	....	....	....	....	....	....	1968-69	1971-72
• Speer, Bill	Pit., Bos.	4	130	5	20	25	79	8	1	0	1	4	1	1967-68	1970-71
Speers, Ted	Det.	1	4	1	1	2	0	....	....	....	....	....	....	1985-86	1985-86
• Spence, Gordon	Tor.	1	3	0	0	0	0	....	....	....	....	....	....	1925-26	1925-26
• Spencer, Brian	Tor., NYI, Buf., Pit.	10	553	80	143	223	634	37	1	5	6	29	....	1969-70	1978-79
Spencer, Irv	NYR, Bos., Det.	8	230	12	38	50	127	16	0	0	0	8	....	1959-60	1967-68
• Speyer, Chris	Tor., NYA	3	14	0	0	0	0	....	....	....	....	....	....	1923-24	1933-34
Spring, Corey	T.B.	2	16	1	1	2	12	....	....	....	....	....	....	1997-98	1998-99
Spring, Don	Wpg.	4	259	1	54	55	80	6	0	0	0	10	....	1980-81	1983-84
Spring, Frank	Bos., St.L., Cal., Cle.	5	61	14	20	34	12	....	....	....	....	....	....	1969-70	1976-77
• Spring, Jesse	Ham., Pit., Tor., NYA	6	133	11	4	15	74	2	0	2	2	2	....	1923-24	1929-30
Spruce, Andy	Van., Col.	3	172	31	42	73	111	2	0	2	2	0	....	1976-77	1978-79
‡ Srsen, Tomas	Edm.	1	2	0	0	0	0	....	....	....	....	....	....	1990-91	1990-91
St. Amour, Martin	Ott.	1	1	0	0	0	2	....	....	....	....	....	....	1992-93	1992-93
St. Laurent, Andre	NYI, Det., L.A., Pit.	11	644	129	187	316	749	59	8	12	20	48	....	1973-74	1983-84
St. Laurent, Dollard	Mtl., Chi.	12	652	29	133	162	496	92	2	22	24	87	5	1950-51	1961-62
St. Marseille, Frank	St.L., L.A.	10	707	140	285	425	242	88	20	25	45	18	....	1967-68	1976-77
St. Sauveur, Claude	Atl.	1	79	24	24	48	23	2	0	0	0	0	....	1975-76	1975-76
Stackhouse, Ron	Cal., Det., Pit.	12	889	87	372	459	824	32	5	8	13	38	....	1970-71	1981-82
• Stackhouse, Ted	Tor.	1	13	0	0	0	2	1	0	0	0	0	1	1921-22	1921-22
• Stahan, Butch	Mtl.	1	....	....	....	....	....	3	0	1	1	2	....	1944-45	1944-45
Stajduhar, Nick	Edm.	1	2	0	0	0	4	....	....	....	....	....	....	1995-96	1995-96
Staley, Al	NYR	1	1	0	1	1	0	....	....	....	....	....	....	1948-49	1948-49
Stamler, Lorne	L.A., Tor., Wpg.	4	116	14	11	25	16	....	....	....	....	....	....	1976-77	1979-80
Standing, George	Min.	1	2	0	0	0	0	....	....	....	....	....	....	1967-68	1967-68
Stanfield, Fred	Chi., Bos., Min., Buf.	14	914	211	405	616	134	106	21	35	56	10	2	1964-65	1977-78
Stanfield, Jack	Chi.	1	....	....	....	....	....	1	0	0	0	0	....	1965-66	1965-66
Stanfield, Jim	L.A.	3	7	0	1	1	0	....	....	....	....	....	....	1969-70	1971-72
Stankiewicz, Ed	Det.	2	6	0	0	0	2	....	....	....	....	....	....	1953-54	1955-56
Stankiewicz, Myron	St.L., Phi.	1	35	0	7	7	36	1	0	0	0	0	....	1968-69	1968-69
Stanley, Allan	NYR, Chi., Bos., Tor., Phi.	21	1244	100	333	433	792	109	7	36	43	80	4	1948-49	1968-69
• Stanley, Barney	Chi.	1	1	0	0	0	0	....	....	....	....	....	....	1927-28	1927-28
Stanley, Daryl	Phi., Van.	6	189	8	17	25	408	17	0	0	0	30	....	1983-84	1989-90
Stanowski, Wally	Tor., NYR	10	428	23	88	111	160	60	3	14	17	13	4	1939-40	1950-51
‡ Stanton, Paul	Pit., Bos., NYI	5	295	14	49	63	262	44	2	10	12	66	2	1990-91	1994-95
Stapleton, Brian	Wsh.	1	1	0	0	0	0	....	....	....	....	....	....	1975-76	1975-76
Stapleton, Mike	Chi., Pit., Edm., Wpg., Phx., Atl., NYI, Van.	14	697	71	111	182	342	34	1	0	1	39	....	1986-87	2000-01
Stapleton, Pat	Bos., Chi.	10	635	43	294	337	353	65	10	39	49	38	....	1961-62	1972-73
Starikov, Sergei	N.J.	1	16	0	1	1	8	....	....	....	....	....	....	1989-90	1989-90
• Starr, Harold	Ott., Mtl.M., Mtl., NYR	7	205	6	5	11	186	15	1	0	1	4	....	1929-30	1935-36
Starr, Wilf	NYA, Det.	4	87	8	6	14	25	7	0	2	2	2	....	1932-33	1935-36
Stasiuk, Vic	Chi., Det., Bos.	14	745	183	254	437	669	69	16	18	34	40	3	1949-50	1962-63
Stastny, Anton	Que.	9	650	252	384	636	150	66	20	32	52	31	....	1980-81	1988-89
Stastny, Marian	Que., Tor.	5	322	121	173	294	110	32	5	17	22	7	....	1981-82	1985-86
Stastny, Peter	Que., N.J., St.L.	15	977	450	789	1239	824	93	33	72	105	123	....	1980-81	1994-95
Staszak, Ray	Det.	1	4	0	1	1	7	....	....	....	....	....	....	1985-86	1985-86
• Steele, Frank	Det.	1	1	0	0	0	0	....	....	....	....	....	....	1930-31	1930-31
Steen, Anders	Wpg.	1	42	5	11	16	22	....	....	....	....	....	....	1980-81	1980-81
Steen, Thomas	Wpg.	14	950	264	553	817	753	56	12	32	44	62	....	1981-82	1994-95
Stefaniw, Morris	Atl.	1	13	1	1	2	2	....	....	....	....	....	....	1972-73	1972-73
Stefanski, Bud	NYR	1	1	0	0	0	0	....	....	....	....	....	....	1977-78	1977-78
Stemkowski, Pete	Tor., Det., NYR, L.A.	15	967	206	349	555	866	83	25	29	54	136	1	1963-64	1977-78
Stenlund, Vern	Cle.	1	4	0	0	0	0	....	....	....	....	....	....	1976-77	1976-77
Stephenson, Bob	Hfd., Tor.	1	18	2	3	5	4	....	....	....	....	....	....	1979-80	1979-80
Stern, Ron	Van., Cgy., S.J.	12	638	75	86	161	2077	43	7	7	14	119	....	1987-88	1999-00
Sterner, Ulf	NYR	1	4	0	0	0	0	....	....	....	....	....	....	1964-65	1964-65
Stevens, John	Phi., Hfd.	5	53	0	10	10	48	....	....	....	....	....	....	1986-87	1993-94
Stevens, Kevin	Pit., Bos., L.A., NYR, Phi.	15	874	329	397	726	1470	103	46	60	106	170	2	1987-88	2001-02
‡ Stevens, Mike	Van., Bos., NYI, Tor.	4	23	1	4	5	29	....	....	....	....	....	....	1984-85	1989-90
• Stevens, Phil	Mtl.W., Mtl., Bos.	3	25	1	0	1	3	....	....	....	....	....	....	1917-18	1925-26
Stevenson, Shayne	Bos., T.B.	3	27	0	2	2	35	....	....	....	....	....	....	1990-91	1992-93
Stewart, Allan	N.J., Bos.	6	64	6	4	10	243	....	....	....	....	....	....	1985-86	1991-92
Stewart, Bill	Buf., St.L., Tor., Min.	8	261	7	64	71	424	13	1	3	4	11	....	1977-78	1985-86
Stewart, Blair	Det., Wsh., Que.	7	229	34	44	78	326	....	....	....	....	....	....	1973-74	1979-80
Stewart, Bob	Bos., Cal., Cle., St.L., Pit.	9	575	27	101	128	809	5	1	1	2	2	....	1971-72	1979-80
Stewart, Cam	Bos., Fla., Min.	6	202	16	23	39	120	13	1	3	4	9	....	1993-94	2000-01
Stewart, Gaye	Tor., Chi., Det., NYR, Mtl.	11	502	185	159	344	274	25	2	9	11	16	2	1941-42	1953-54
• Stewart, Jack	Det., Chi.	12	565	31	84	115	765	80	5	14	19	143	2	1938-39	1951-52
Stewart, John	Pit., Atl., Cal.	5	258	58	60	118	158	4	0	0	0	10	....	1970-71	1974-75
Stewart, John	Que.	1	2	0	0	0	0	....	....	....	....	....	....	1979-80	1979-80
Stewart, Ken	Chi.	1	6	1	1	2	2	....	....	....	....	....	....	1941-42	1941-42
• Stewart, Nels	Mtl.M., Bos., NYA	15	650	324	191	515	953	50	9	12	21	47	1	1925-26	1939-40

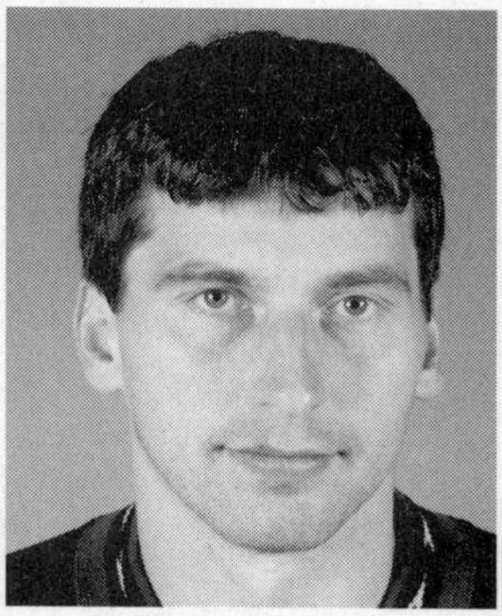

Richard Smehlik

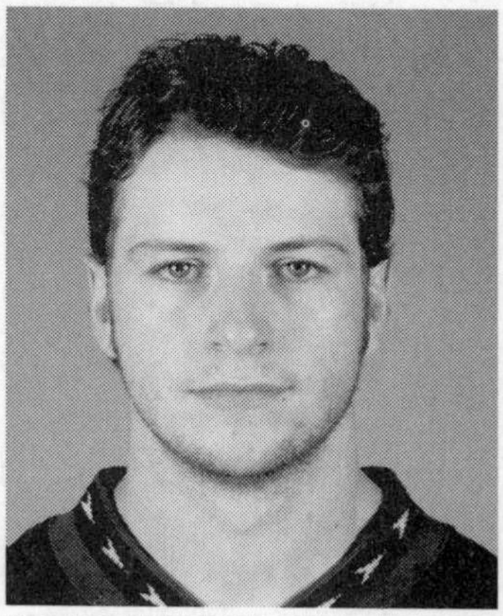

Dan Snyder

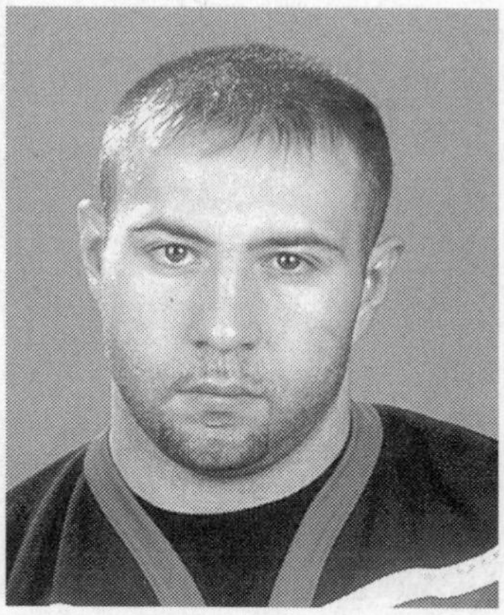

Maxim Sushinsky

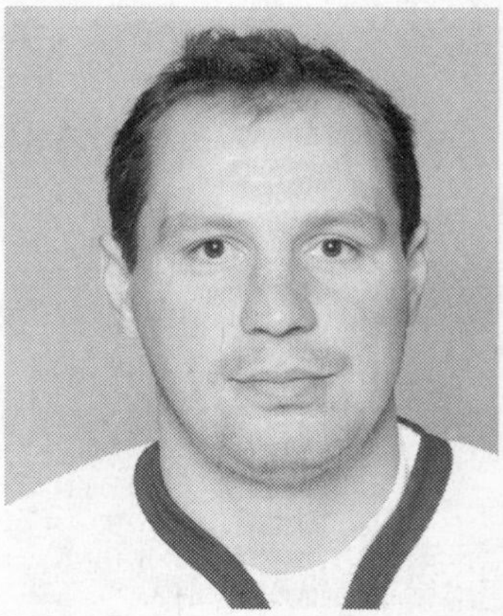

Robert Svehla

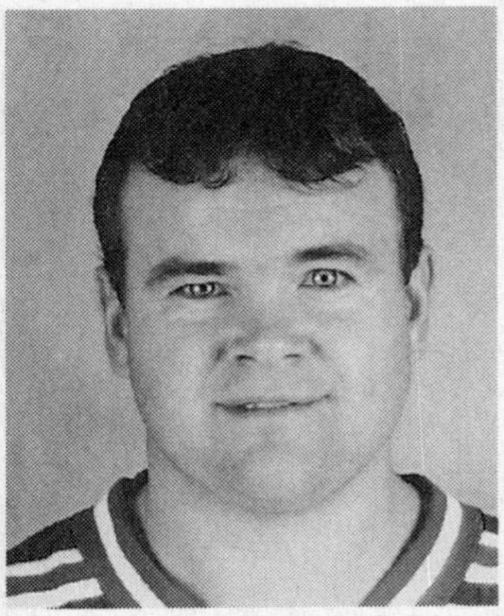

Tim Sweeney

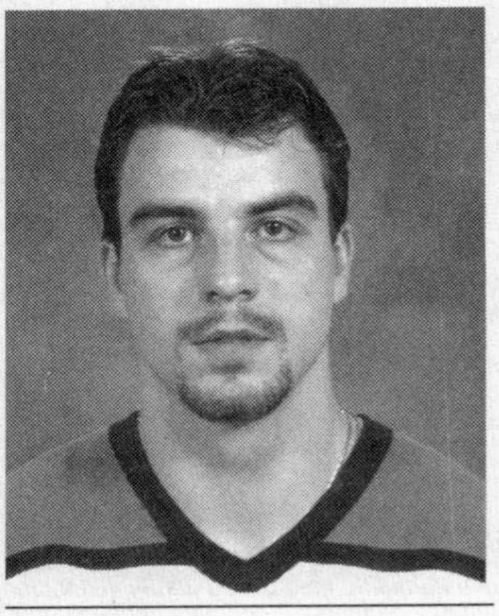

Michal Sykora

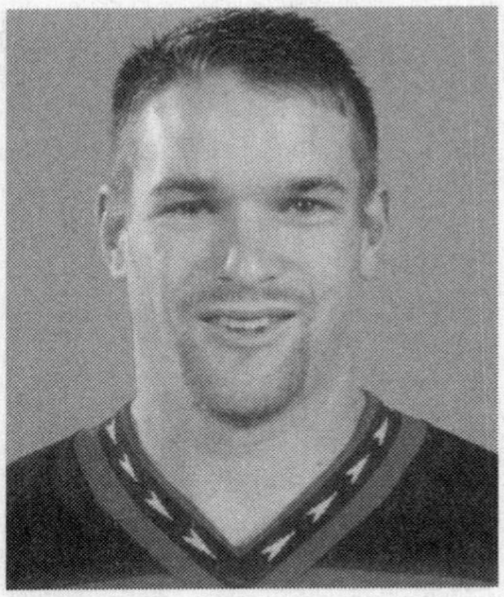

Dean Sylvester

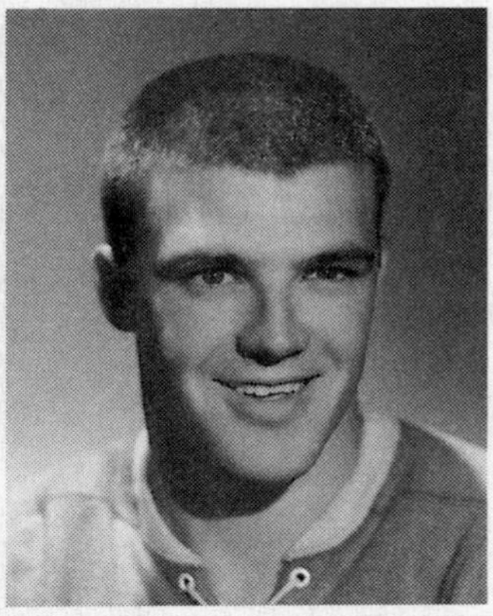

Jean-Guy Talbot

			Regular Schedule					Playoffs							
Name	NHL Teams	NHL Seasons	GP	G	A	TP	PIM	GP	G	A	TP	PIM	NHL Cup Wins	First NHL Season	Last NHL Season
Stewart, Paul	Que.	1	21	2	0	2	74	....	....	....	....	....	....	1979-80	1979-80
Stewart, Ralph	Van., NYI	7	252	57	73	130	28	19	4	4	8	2	....	1970-71	1977-78
Stewart, Ron	Tor., Bos., St.L., NYR, Van., NYI	21	1353	276	253	529	560	119	14	21	35	60	3	1952-53	1972-73
Stewart, Ryan	Wpg.	1	3	1	0	1	0	....	....	....	....	....	....	1985-86	1985-86
Stienburg, Trevor	Que.	4	71	8	4	12	161	1	0	0	0	0	....	1985-86	1988-89
Stiles, Tony	Cgy.	1	30	2	7	9	20	....	....	....	....	....	....	1983-84	1983-84
Stoddard, Jack	NYR	2	80	16	15	31	31	....	....	....	....	....	....	1951-52	1952-53
Stojanov, Alek	Van., Pit.	3	107	2	5	7	222	14	0	0	0	21	....	1994-95	1996-97
Stoltz, Roland	Wsh.	1	14	2	2	4	14	....	....	....	....	....	....	1981-82	1981-82
Stone, Steve	Van.	1	2	0	0	0	0	....	....	....	....	....	....	1973-74	1973-74
Storm, Jim	Hfd., Dal.	3	84	7	15	22	44	....	....	....	....	....	....	1993-94	1995-96
Stothers, Mike	Phi., Tor.	4	30	0	2	2	65	5	0	0	0	11	....	1984-85	1987-88
Stoughton, Blaine	Pit., Tor., Hfd., NYR	8	526	258	191	449	204	8	4	2	6	2	....	1973-74	1983-84
Stoyanovich, Steve	Hfd.	1	23	3	5	8	11	....	....	....	....	....	....	1983-84	1983-84
• Strain, Neil	NYR	1	52	11	13	24	12	....	....	....	....	....	....	1952-53	1952-53
Strate, Gord	Det.	3	61	0	0	0	34	....	....	....	....	....	....	1956-57	1958-59
Stratton, Art	NYR, Det., Chi., Pit., Phi.	4	95	18	33	51	24	5	0	0	0	0	....	1959-60	1967-68
Strobel, Art	NYR	1	7	0	0	0	0	....	....	....	....	....	....	1943-44	1943-44
Strong, Ken	Tor.	3	15	2	2	4	6	....	....	....	....	....	....	1982-83	1984-85
Struch, David	Cgy.	1	4	0	0	0	4	....	....	....	....	....	....	1993-94	1993-94
Strueby, Todd	Edm.	3	5	0	1	1	2	....	....	....	....	....	....	1981-82	1983-84
• Stuart, Billy	Tor., Bos.	7	195	30	20	50	151	12	1	1	2	6	1	1920-21	1926-27
Stumpf, Bob	St.L., Pit.	1	10	1	1	2	20	....	....	....	....	....	....	1974-75	1974-75
Sturgeon, Peter	Col.	2	6	0	1	1	2	....	....	....	....	....	....	1979-80	1980-81
Suikkanen, Kai	Buf.	2	2	0	0	0	0	....	....	....	....	....	....	1981-82	1982-83
Sulliman, Doug	NYR, Hfd., N.J., Phi.	11	631	160	168	328	175	16	1	3	4	2	....	1979-80	1989-90
Sullivan, Barry	Det.	1	1	0	0	0	0	....	....	....	....	....	....	1947-48	1947-48
Sullivan, Bob	Hfd.	1	62	18	19	37	18	....	....	....	....	....	....	1982-83	1982-83
Sullivan, Brian	N.J.	1	2	0	1	1	0	....	....	....	....	....	....	1992-93	1992-93
Sullivan, Frank	Tor., Chi.	4	8	0	0	0	2	....	....	....	....	....	....	1949-50	1955-56
Sullivan, Mike	S.J., Cgy., Bos., Phx.	11	709	54	82	136	203	34	4	8	12	14	....	1991-92	2001-02
Sullivan, Peter	Wpg.	2	126	28	54	82	40	....	....	....	....	....	....	1979-80	1980-81
Sullivan, Red	Bos., Chi., NYR	11	557	107	239	346	441	18	1	2	3	6	....	1949-50	1960-61
Summanen, Raimo	Edm., Van.	5	151	36	40	76	35	10	2	5	7	0	....	1983-84	1987-88
• Summerhill, Bill	Mtl., Bro.	4	72	14	17	31	70	3	0	0	0	2	....	1937-38	1941-42
‡ Sundblad, Niklas	Cgy.	1	2	0	0	0	0	....	....	....	....	....	....	1995-96	1995-96
‡ Sundin, Ronnie	NYR	1	1	0	0	0	0	....	....	....	....	....	....	1997-98	1997-98
Sundstrom, Patrik	Van., N.J.	10	679	219	369	588	349	37	9	17	26	25	....	1982-83	1991-92
Sundstrom, Peter	NYR, Wsh., N.J.	6	338	61	83	144	120	23	3	3	6	8	....	1983-84	1989-90
• Suomi, Al	Chi.	1	5	0	0	0	0	....	....	....	....	....	....	1936-37	1936-37
‡ Sushinsky, Maxim	Min.	1	30	7	4	11	29	....	....	....	....	....	....	2000-01	2000-01
Suter, Gary	Cgy., Chi., S.J.	17	1145	203	641	844	1349	108	17	56	73	120	1	1985-86	2001-02
Sutherland, Bill	Mtl., Phi., Tor., St.L., Det.	6	250	70	58	128	99	14	2	4	6	0	....	1962-63	1971-72
• Sutherland, Max	Bos.	1	2	0	0	0	0	....	....	....	....	....	....	1931-32	1931-32
Sutter, Brent	NYI, Chi.	18	1111	363	466	829	1054	144	30	44	74	164	2	1980-81	1997-98
Sutter, Brian	St.L.	12	779	303	333	636	1786	65	21	21	42	249	....	1976-77	1987-88
Sutter, Darryl	Chi.	8	406	161	118	279	288	51	24	19	43	26	....	1979-80	1986-87
Sutter, Duane	NYI, Chi.	11	731	139	203	342	1333	161	26	32	58	405	4	1979-80	1989-90
Sutter, Rich	Pit., Phi., Van., St.L., Chi., T.B., Tor.	13	874	149	166	315	1411	78	13	5	18	133	....	1982-83	1994-95
Sutter, Ron	Phi., St.L., Que., NYI, Bos., S.J., Cgy.	19	1093	205	329	534	1352	104	8	32	40	193	....	1982-83	2000-01
‡ Sutton, Ken	Buf., Edm., St.L., N.J., S.J., NYI	11	388	23	80	103	338	32	3	4	7	29	1	1990-91	2001-02
Suzor, Mark	Phi., Col.	2	64	4	16	20	60	....	....	....	....	....	....	1976-77	1977-78
‡ Svartvadet, Per	Atl.	4	247	17	34	51	58	....	....	....	....	....	....	1999-00	2002-03
Svehla, Robert	Fla., Tor.	9	655	68	267	335	649	38	1	14	15	42	....	1994-95	2002-03
Svejkovsky, Jaroslav	Wsh., T.B.	4	113	23	19	42	56	1	0	0	0	2	....	1996-97	1999-00
Svensson, Leif	Wsh.	2	121	6	40	46	49	....	....	....	....	....	....	1978-79	1979-80
Svensson, Magnus	Fla.	2	46	4	14	18	31	....	....	....	....	....	....	1994-95	1995-96
Svoboda, Petr	Mtl., Buf., Phi., T.B.	17	1028	58	341	399	1605	127	4	45	49	140	1	1984-85	2000-01
Svoboda, Petr	Tor.	1	18	1	2	3	10	....	....	....	....	....	....	2000-01	2000-01
Swain, Garry	Pit.	1	9	1	1	2	0	....	....	....	....	....	....	1968-69	1968-69
Swarbrick, George	Oak., Pit., Phi.	4	132	17	25	42	173	....	....	....	....	....	....	1967-68	1970-71
• Sweeney, Bill	NYR	1	4	1	0	1	0	....	....	....	....	....	....	1959-60	1959-60
Sweeney, Bob	Bos., Buf., NYI, Cgy.	10	639	125	163	288	799	103	15	18	33	197	....	1986-87	1995-96
Sweeney, Tim	Cgy., Bos., Ana., NYR	8	291	55	83	138	123	4	0	0	0	2	....	1990-91	1997-98
Sykes, Bob	Tor.	1	2	0	0	0	0	....	....	....	....	....	....	1974-75	1974-75
Sykes, Phil	L.A., Wpg.	10	456	79	85	164	519	26	0	3	3	29	....	1982-83	1991-92
‡ Sykora, Michal	S.J., Chi., T.B., Phi.	7	267	15	54	69	185	7	0	1	1	0	....	1993-94	2000-01
Sylvester, Dean	Buf., Atl.	3	96	21	16	37	32	4	0	0	0	0	....	1998-99	2000-01
Szura, Joe	Oak.	2	90	10	15	25	30	7	2	3	5	2	....	1967-68	1968-69

T

Taft, John	Det.	1	15	0	2	2	4	....	....	....	....	....	....	1978-79	1978-79
Taglianetti, Peter	Wpg., Min., Pit., T.B.	11	451	18	74	92	1106	53	2	8	10	103	2	1984-85	1994-95
Talafous, Dean	Atl., Min., NYR	8	497	104	154	258	163	21	4	7	11	11	....	1974-75	1981-82
Talakoski, Ron	NYR	2	9	0	1	1	33	....	....	....	....	....	....	1986-87	1987-88
Talbot, Jean-Guy	Mtl., Min., Det., St.L., Buf.	17	1056	43	242	285	1006	150	4	26	30	142	7	1954-55	1970-71
Tallon, Dale	Van., Chi., Pit.	10	642	98	238	336	568	33	2	10	12	45	....	1970-71	1979-80
Tambellini, Steve	NYI, Col., N.J., Cgy., Van.	10	553	160	150	310	105	2	0	1	1	0	1	1978-79	1987-88
‡ Tancill, Chris	Hfd., Det., Dal., S.J.	8	134	17	32	49	54	11	1	1	2	8	....	1990-91	1997-98
Tanguay, Christian	Que.	1	2	0	0	0	0	....	....	....	....	....	....	1981-82	1981-82
Tannahill, Don	Van.	2	111	30	33	63	25	....	....	....	....	....	....	1972-73	1973-74
Tanti, Tony	Chi., Van., Pit., Buf.	11	697	287	273	560	661	30	3	12	15	27	....	1981-82	1991-92
Tardif, Marc	Mtl., Que.	8	517	194	207	401	443	62	13	15	28	75	2	1969-70	1982-83
Tardif, Patrice	St.L., L.A.	2	65	7	11	18	78	....	....	....	....	....	....	1994-95	1995-96
Tatarinov, Mikhail	Wsh., Que., Bos.	4	161	21	48	69	184	....	....	....	....	....	....	1990-91	1993-94
Tatchell, Spence	NYR	1	1	0	0	0	0	....	....	....	....	....	....	1942-43	1942-43
• Taylor, Billy	Tor., Det., Bos., NYR	7	323	87	180	267	120	33	6	18	24	13	1	1939-40	1947-48
• Taylor, Bob	Bos.	1	8	0	0	0	6	....	....	....	....	....	....	1929-30	1929-30
Taylor, Dave	L.A.	17	1111	431	638	1069	1589	92	26	33	59	145	....	1977-78	1993-94
Taylor, Harry	Tor., Chi.	3	66	5	10	15	30	1	0	0	0	0	1	1946-47	1951-52
Taylor, Mark	Phi., Pit., Wsh.	5	209	42	68	110	73	6	0	0	0	0	....	1981-82	1985-86
• Taylor, Ralph	Chi., NYR	3	99	4	1	5	169	4	0	0	0	10	....	1927-28	1929-30
Taylor, Ted	NYR, Det., Min., Van.	6	166	23	35	58	181	....	....	....	....	....	....	1964-65	1971-72
Taylor Jr., Billy	NYR	1	2	0	0	0	0	....	....	....	....	....	....	1964-65	1964-65
Teal, Jeff	Mtl.	1	6	0	1	1	0	....	....	....	....	....	....	1984-85	1984-85
Teal, Skip	Bos.	1	1	0	0	0	0	....	....	....	....	....	....	1954-55	1954-55
Teal, Vic	NYI	1	1	0	0	0	0	....	....	....	....	....	....	1973-74	1973-74
Tebbutt, Greg	Que., Pit.	2	26	0	3	3	35	....	....	....	....	....	....	1979-80	1983-84
Tepper, Stephen	Chi.	1	1	0	0	0	0	....	....	....	....	....	....	1992-93	1992-93
Terbenche, Paul	Chi., Buf.	5	189	5	26	31	28	12	0	0	0	0	....	1967-68	1973-74
Terrion, Greg	L.A., Tor.	8	561	93	150	243	339	35	2	9	11	41	....	1980-81	1987-88
Terry, Bill	Min.	1	5	0	0	0	0	....	....	....	....	....	....	1987-88	1987-88
• Tertyshny, Dmitri	Phi.	1	62	2	8	10	30	1	0	0	0	0	....	1998-99	1998-99
Tessier, Orval	Mtl., Bos.	3	59	5	7	12	6	....	....	....	....	....	....	1954-55	1960-61
‡ Tezikov, Alexei	Wsh., Van.	3	30	1	1	2	2	....	....	....	....	....	....	1998-99	2001-02
Theberge, Greg	Wsh.	5	153	15	63	78	73	4	0	1	1	0	....	1979-80	1983-84
Thelin, Mats	Bos.	3	163	8	19	27	107	5	0	0	0	6	....	1984-85	1986-87
Thelven, Michael	Bos.	5	207	20	80	100	217	34	4	10	14	34	....	1985-86	1989-90
Therrien, Gaston	Que.	3	22	0	8	8	12	9	0	1	1	4	....	1980-81	1982-83
Thibaudeau, Gilles	Mtl., NYI, Tor.	5	119	25	37	62	40	8	3	3	6	2	....	1986-87	1990-91
Thibeault, Lorrain	Det., Mtl.	2	5	0	2	2	2	....	....	....	....	....	....	1944-45	1945-46
Thiffault, Leo	Min.	1	....	....	....	....	....	5	0	0	0	0	....	1967-68	1967-68
Thomas, Cy	Chi., Tor.	1	14	2	2	4	12	....	....	....	....	....	....	1947-48	1947-48
Thomas, Reg	Que.	1	39	9	7	16	6	....	....	....	....	....	....	1979-80	1979-80
Thomas, Scott	Buf., L.A.	3	63	6	4	10	32	12	1	0	1	4	....	1992-93	2000-01
Thomlinson, Dave	St.L., Bos., L.A.	5	42	1	3	4	50	9	3	1	4	4	....	1989-90	1994-95
‡ Thompson, Brent	L.A., Wpg., Phx.	6	121	1	10	11	352	4	0	0	0	4	....	1991-92	1996-97
• Thompson, Cliff	Bos.	2	13	0	1	1	2	....	....	....	....	....	....	1941-42	1948-49
Thompson, Errol	Tor., Det., Pit.	10	599	208	185	393	184	34	7	5	12	11	....	1970-71	1980-81
• Thompson, Ken	Mtl.W.	1	1	0	0	0	0	....	....	....	....	....	....	1917-18	1917-18
• Thompson, Paul	NYR, Chi.	13	582	153	179	332	336	48	11	11	22	54	3	1926-27	1938-39
• Thoms, Bill	Tor., Chi., Bos.	13	548	135	206	341	154	44	6	10	16	6	....	1932-33	1944-45
• Thomson, Bill	Det.	2	9	2	2	4	0	2	0	0	0	0	....	1938-39	1943-44
Thomson, Floyd	St.L.	8	411	56	97	153	341	10	0	2	2	6	....	1971-72	1979-80
Thomson, Jim	Wsh., Hfd., N.J., L.A., Ott., Ana.	7	115	4	3	7	416	1	0	0	0	0	....	1986-87	1993-94

			Regular Schedule					Playoffs							
Name	NHL Teams	NHL Seasons	GP	G	A	TP	PIM	GP	G	A	TP	PIM	NHL Cup Wins	First NHL Season	Last NHL Season
• Thomson, Jimmy	Tor., Chi.	13	787	19	215	234	920	63	2	13	15	135	4	1945-46	1957-58
• Thomson, Rhys	Mtl., Tor.	2	25	0	2	2	38	....	....	....	....	....	....	1939-40	1942-43
Thornbury, Tom	Pit.	1	14	1	8	9	16	....	....	....	....	....	....	1983-84	1983-84
• Thorsteinson, Joe	NYA	1	4	0	0	0	0	....	....	....	....	....	....	1932-33	1932-33
• Thurier, Fred	NYA, Bro., NYR	3	80	25	27	52	18	....	....	....	....	....	....	1940-41	1944-45
Thurlby, Tom	Oak.	1	20	1	1	2	4	....	....	....	....	....	....	1967-68	1967-68
Thyer, Mario	Min.	1	5	0	0	0	0	1	0	0	0	2	....	1989-90	1989-90
Tichy, Milan	Chi., NYI	3	23	0	5	5	40	....	....	....	....	....	....	1992-93	1995-96
Tidey, Alex	Buf., Edm.	3	9	0	0	0	8	2	0	0	0	0	....	1976-77	1979-80
Tikkanen, Esa	Edm., NYR, St.L., N.J., Van., Fla., Wsh.	15	877	244	386	630	1077	186	72	60	132	275	5	1984-85	1998-99
Tilley, Tom	St.L.	4	174	4	38	42	89	14	1	3	4	19	....	1988-89	1993-94
• Timgren, Ray	Tor., Chi.	6	251	14	44	58	70	30	3	9	12	6	2	1948-49	1954-55
Tinordi, Mark	NYR, Min., Dal., Wsh.	12	663	52	148	200	1514	70	7	11	18	165	....	1987-88	1998-99
Tippett, Dave	Hfd., Wsh., Pit., Phi.	12	721	93	169	262	317	62	6	16	22	34	....	1983-84	1993-94
Titanic, Morris	Buf.	2	19	0	0	0	0	....	....	....	....	....	....	1974-75	1975-76
Titov, German	Cgy., Pit., Edm., Ana.	9	624	157	220	377	311	34	11	12	23	18	....	1993-94	2001-02
‡ Tkaczuk, Daniel	Cgy.	1	19	4	7	11	14	....	....	....	....	....	....	2000-01	2000-01
Tkaczuk, Walt	NYR	14	945	227	451	678	556	93	19	32	51	119	....	1967-68	1980-81
Toal, Mike	Edm.	1	3	0	0	0	0	....	....	....	....	....	....	1979-80	1979-80
Tocchet, Rick	Phi., Pit., L.A., Bos., Wsh., Phx.	18	1144	440	512	952	2972	145	52	60	112	471	1	1984-85	2001-02
Todd, Kevin	N.J., Edm., Chi., L.A., Ana.	9	383	70	133	203	225	12	3	2	5	16	....	1988-89	1997-98
Tomalty, Glenn	Wpg.	1	1	0	0	0	0	....	....	....	....	....	....	1979-80	1979-80
Tomlak, Mike	Hfd.	4	141	15	22	37	103	10	0	1	1	4	....	1989-90	1993-94
‡ Tomlinson, Dave	Tor., Wpg., Fla.	4	42	1	3	4	28	....	....	....	....	....	....	1991-92	1994-95
Tomlinson, Kirk	Min.	1	1	0	0	0	0	....	....	....	....	....	....	1987-88	1987-88
• Tomson, Jack	NYA	3	15	1	1	2	0	2	0	0	0	0	....	1938-39	1940-41
Tonelli, John	NYI, Cgy., L.A., Chi., Que.	14	1028	325	511	836	911	172	40	75	115	200	4	1978-79	1991-92
Tookey, Tim	Wsh., Que., Pit., Phi., L.A.	7	106	22	36	58	71	10	1	3	4	2	....	1980-81	1988-89
Toomey, Sean	Min.	1	1	0	0	0	0	....	....	....	....	....	....	1986-87	1986-87
‡ Toporowski, Shayne	Tor.	1	3	0	0	0	7	....	....	....	....	....	....	1996-97	1996-97
Toppazzini, Jerry	Bos., Chi., Det.	12	783	163	244	407	436	40	13	9	22	13	....	1952-53	1963-64
• Toppazzini, Zellio	Bos., NYR, Chi.	5	123	21	22	43	49	2	0	0	0	0	....	1948-49	1956-57
Torgaev, Pavel	Cgy., T.B.	2	55	6	14	20	20	1	0	0	0	0	....	1995-96	1999-00
Torkki, Jari	Chi.	1	4	1	0	1	0	....	....	....	....	....	....	1988-89	1988-89
‡ Tormanen, Antti	Ott.	1	50	7	8	15	28	....	....	....	....	....	....	1995-96	1995-96
• Touhey, Bill	Mtl.M., Ott., Bos.	7	280	65	40	105	107	2	1	0	1	0	....	1927-28	1933-34
• Toupin, Jacques	Chi.	1	8	1	2	3	0	4	0	0	0	0	....	1943-44	1943-44
• Townsend, Art	Chi.	1	5	0	0	0	0	....	....	....	....	....	....	1926-27	1926-27
Townshend, Graeme	Bos., NYI, Ott.	5	45	3	7	10	28	....	....	....	....	....	....	1989-90	1993-94
Trader, Larry	Det., St.L., Mtl.	4	91	5	13	18	74	3	0	0	0	0	....	1982-83	1987-88
• Trainor, Wes	NYR	1	17	1	2	3	6	....	....	....	....	....	....	1948-49	1948-49
• Trapp, Bob	Chi.	2	82	4	4	8	129	2	0	0	0	4	....	1926-27	1927-28
Trapp, Doug	Buf.	1	2	0	0	0	0	....	....	....	....	....	....	1986-87	1986-87
• Traub, Percy	Chi., Det.	3	130	3	3	6	217	4	0	0	0	6	....	1926-27	1928-29
Trebil, Dan	Ana., Pit., St.L.	5	85	4	4	8	32	10	0	1	1	8	....	1996-97	2000-01
Tredway, Brock	L.A.	1	....	....	....	....	....	1	0	0	0	0	....	1981-82	1981-82
Tremblay, Brent	Wsh.	2	10	1	0	1	6	....	....	....	....	....	....	1978-79	1979-80
Tremblay, Gilles	Mtl.	9	509	168	162	330	161	48	9	14	23	4	3	1960-61	1968-69
• Tremblay, J.C.	Mtl.	13	794	57	306	363	204	108	14	51	65	58	5	1959-60	1971-72
Tremblay, Marcel	Mtl.	1	10	0	2	2	0	....	....	....	....	....	....	1938-39	1938-39
Tremblay, Mario	Mtl.	12	852	258	326	584	1043	101	20	29	49	187	5	1974-75	1985-86
• Tremblay, Nils	Mtl.	2	3	0	1	1	0	2	0	0	0	0	....	1944-45	1945-46
Trimper, Tim	Chi., Wpg., Min.	6	190	30	36	66	153	2	0	0	0	2	....	1979-80	1984-85
Trottier, Bryan	NYI, Pit.	18	1279	524	901	1425	912	221	71	113	184	277	6	1975-76	1993-94
• Trottier, Dave	Mtl.M., Det.	11	446	121	113	234	517	31	4	3	7	39	1	1928-29	1938-39
Trottier, Guy	NYR, Tor.	3	115	28	17	45	37	9	1	0	1	16	....	1968-69	1971-72
Trottier, Rocky	N.J.	2	38	6	4	10	2	....	....	....	....	....	....	1983-84	1984-85
‡ Trudel, Jean-Guy	Phx., Min.	3	5	0	0	0	4	....	....	....	....	....	....	1999-00	2002-03
• Trudel, Lou	Chi., Mtl.	8	306	49	69	118	122	24	1	3	4	4	2	1933-34	1940-41
Trudell, Rene	NYR	3	129	24	28	52	72	5	0	0	0	2	....	1945-46	1947-48
‡ Tsulygin, Nikolai	Ana.	1	22	0	1	1	8	....	....	....	....	....	....	1996-97	1996-97
Tsygurov, Denis	Buf., L.A.	3	51	1	5	6	45	....	....	....	....	....	....	1993-94	1995-96
‡ Tsyplakov, Vladimir	L.A., Buf.	6	331	69	101	170	90	18	1	2	3	16	....	1995-96	2000-01
Tucker, John	Buf., Wsh., NYI, T.B.	12	656	177	259	436	285	31	10	18	28	24	....	1983-84	1995-96
• Tudin, Connie	Mtl.	1	4	0	1	1	4	....	....	....	....	....	....	1941-42	1941-42
Tudor, Rob	Van., St.L.	3	28	4	4	8	19	3	0	0	0	0	....	1978-79	1982-83
Tuer, Allan	L.A., Min., Hfd.	4	57	1	1	2	208	....	....	....	....	....	....	1985-86	1989-90
‡ Tuomainen, Marko	Edm., L.A., NYI	4	79	9	9	18	84	1	0	0	0	0	....	1994-95	2001-02
Turcotte, Alfie	Mtl., Wpg., Wsh.	7	112	17	29	46	49	5	0	0	0	0	....	1983-84	1990-91
Turcotte, Darren	NYR, Hfd., Wpg., S.J., St.L., Nsh.	12	635	195	216	411	301	35	6	8	14	12	....	1988-89	1999-00
Turgeon, Sylvain	Hfd., N.J., Mtl., Ott.	12	669	269	226	495	691	36	4	7	11	22	....	1983-84	1994-95
Turlick, Gord	Bos.	1	2	0	0	0	2	....	....	....	....	....	....	1959-60	1959-60
Turnbull, Ian	Tor., L.A., Pit.	10	628	123	317	440	736	55	13	32	45	94	....	1973-74	1982-83
Turnbull, Perry	St.L., Mtl., Wpg.	9	608	188	163	351	1245	34	6	7	13	86	....	1979-80	1987-88
Turnbull, Randy	Cgy.	1	1	0	0	0	2	....	....	....	....	....	....	1981-82	1981-82
Turner, Bob	Mtl., Chi.	8	478	19	51	70	307	68	1	4	5	44	5	1955-56	1962-63
Turner, Brad	NYI	1	3	0	0	0	0	....	....	....	....	....	....	1991-92	1991-92
Turner, Dean	NYR, Col., L.A.	4	35	1	0	1	59	....	....	....	....	....	....	1978-79	1982-83
• Tustin, Norm	NYR	1	18	2	4	6	0	....	....	....	....	....	....	1941-42	1941-42
Tuten, Aud	Chi.	2	39	4	8	12	48	....	....	....	....	....	....	1941-42	1942-43
Tutt, Brian	Wsh.	1	7	1	0	1	2	....	....	....	....	....	....	1989-90	1989-90
Tuttle, Steve	St.L.	3	144	28	28	56	12	17	1	6	7	2	....	1988-89	1990-91
‡ Tuzzolino, Tony	Ana., NYR, Bos.	3	9	0	0	0	7	....	....	....	....	....	....	1997-98	2001-02
Twist, Tony	St.L., Que.	10	445	10	18	28	1121	18	1	1	2	22	....	1989-90	1998-99

U V

Ubriaco, Gene	Pit., Oak., Chi.	3	177	39	35	74	50	11	2	0	2	4	....	1967-68	1969-70
Ullman, Norm	Det., Tor.	20	1410	490	739	1229	712	106	30	53	83	67	....	1955-56	1974-75
Unger, Garry	Tor., Det., St.L., Atl., L.A., Edm.	16	1105	413	391	804	1075	52	12	18	30	105	....	1967-68	1982-83
‡ Ustorf, Stefan	Wsh.	2	54	7	10	17	16	5	0	0	0	0	....	1995-96	1996-97
Vachon, Nick	NYI	1	1	0	0	0	0	....	....	....	....	....	....	1996-97	1996-97
Vadnais, Carol	Mtl., Oak., Cal., Bos., NYR, N.J.	17	1087	169	418	587	1813	106	10	40	50	185	2	1966-67	1982-83
‡ Vaic, Lubomir	Van.	2	9	1	1	2	2	....	....	....	....	....	....	1997-98	1999-00
Vail, Eric	Atl., Cgy., Det.	9	591	216	260	476	281	20	5	6	11	6	....	1973-74	1981-82
• Vail, Sparky	NYR	2	50	4	1	5	18	10	0	0	0	2	....	1928-29	1929-30
Vaive, Rick	Van., Tor., Chi., Buf.	13	876	441	347	788	1445	54	27	16	43	111	....	1979-80	1991-92
Valentine, Chris	Wsh.	3	105	43	52	95	127	2	0	0	0	4	....	1981-82	1983-84
Valiquette, Jack	Tor., Col.	7	350	84	134	218	79	23	3	6	9	4	....	1974-75	1980-81
Valk, Garry	Van., Ana., Pit., Tor., Chi.	13	777	100	156	256	747	61	6	7	13	79	....	1990-91	2002-03
Vallis, Lindsay	Mtl.	1	1	0	0	0	0	....	....	....	....	....	....	1993-94	1993-94
Van Boxmeer, John	Mtl., Col., Buf., Que.	11	588	84	274	358	465	38	5	15	20	37	1	1973-74	1983-84
Van Dorp, Wayne	Edm., Pit., Chi., Que.	6	125	12	12	24	565	27	0	1	1	42	....	1986-87	1991-92
Van Drunen, David	Ott.	1	1	0	0	0	0	....	....	....	....	....	....	1999-00	1999-00
‡ Van Impe, Darren	Ana., Bos., NYR, Fla., NYI, CBJ	9	411	25	90	115	397	33	3	9	12	28	....	1994-95	2002-03
Van Impe, Ed	Chi., Phi., Pit.	11	700	27	126	153	1025	66	1	12	13	131	2	1966-67	1976-77
‡ Varis, Petri	Chi.	1	1	0	0	0	0	....	....	....	....	....	....	1997-98	1997-98
Varvio, Jarkko	Dal.	2	13	3	4	7	4	....	....	....	....	....	....	1993-94	1994-95
Vasilevski, Alexander	St.L.	2	4	0	0	0	2	....	....	....	....	....	....	1995-96	1996-97
Vasiliev, Alexei	NYR	1	1	0	0	0	2	....	....	....	....	....	....	1999-00	1999-00
‡ Vasiljevs, Herbert	Fla., Atl., Van.	4	51	8	7	15	22	....	....	....	....	....	....	1998-99	2001-02
‡ Vasilyev, Andrei	NYI, Phx.	4	16	2	5	7	6	....	....	....	....	....	....	1994-95	1998-99
Vaske, Dennis	NYI, Bos.	9	235	5	41	46	253	22	0	7	7	16	....	1990-91	1998-99
• Vasko, Moose	Chi., Min.	13	786	34	166	200	719	78	2	7	9	73	1	1956-57	1969-70
Vasko, Rick	Det.	3	31	3	7	10	29	....	....	....	....	....	....	1977-78	1980-81
Vautour, Yvon	NYI, Col., N.J., Que.	6	204	26	33	59	401	....	....	....	....	....	....	1979-80	1984-85
Vaydik, Greg	Chi.	1	5	0	0	0	0	....	....	....	....	....	....	1976-77	1976-77
Veitch, Darren	Wsh., Det., Tor.	10	511	48	209	257	296	33	4	11	15	33	....	1980-81	1990-91
Velischek, Randy	Min., N.J., Que.	10	509	21	76	97	401	44	2	5	7	32	....	1982-83	1991-92
Vellucci, Mike	Hfd.	1	2	0	0	0	11	....	....	....	....	....	....	1987-88	1987-88
Venasky, Vic	L.A.	7	430	61	101	162	66	21	1	5	6	12	....	1972-73	1978-79
Veneruzzo, Gary	St.L.	2	7	1	1	2	0	9	0	2	2	2	....	1967-68	1971-72
Verbeek, Pat	N.J., Hfd., NYR, Dal., Det.	20	1424	522	541	1063	2905	117	26	36	62	225	1	1982-83	2001-02
Vermette, Mark	Que.	4	67	5	13	18	33	....	....	....	....	....	....	1988-89	1991-92
Verret, Claude	Buf.	2	14	2	5	7	2	....	....	....	....	....	....	1983-84	1984-85
Verstraete, Leigh	Tor.	3	8	0	1	1	14	....	....	....	....	....	....	1982-83	1987-88

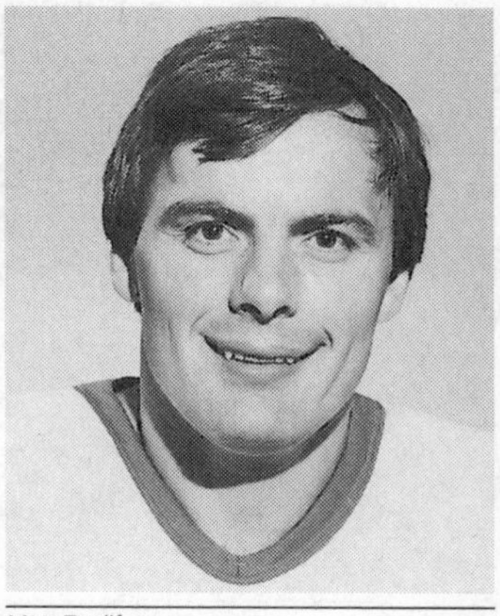

Marc Tardif

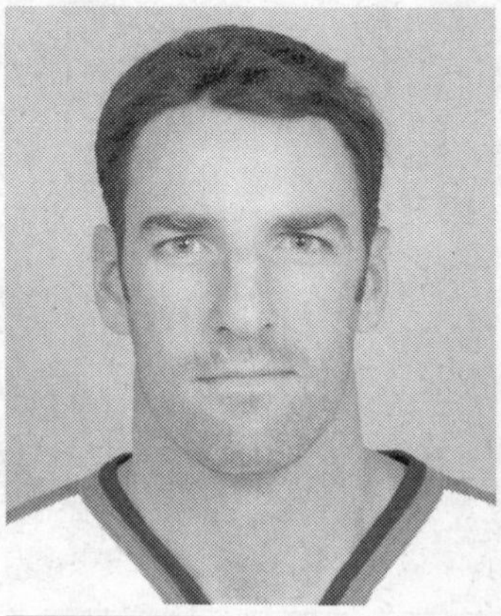

Scott Thomas

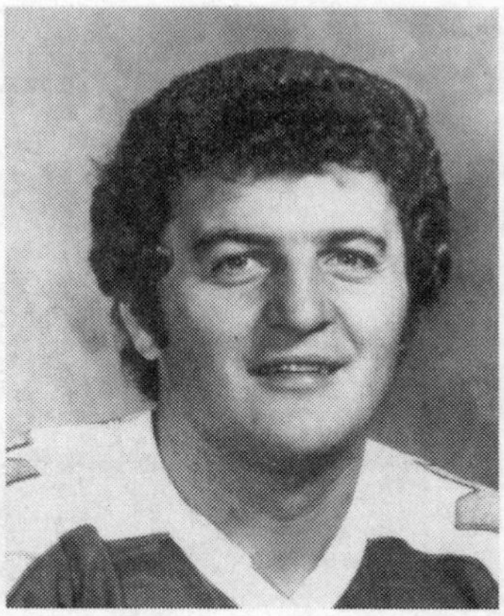

Errol Thompson

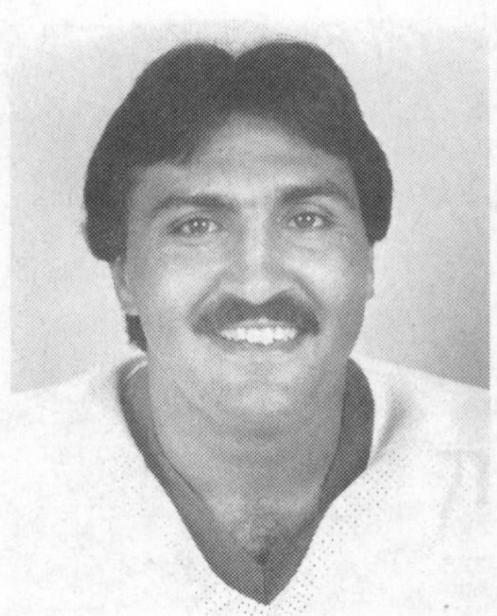

John Tonelli

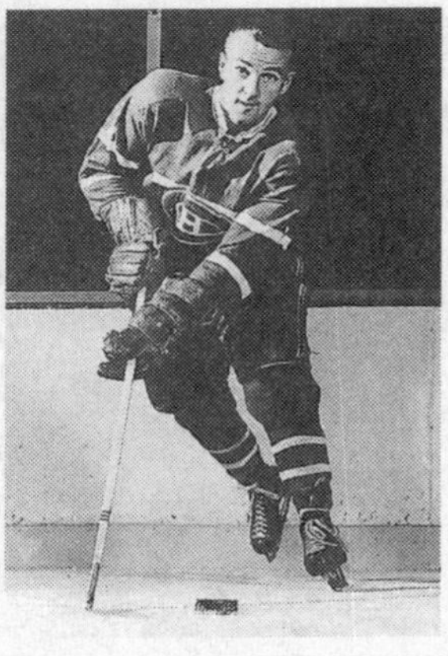

J.C. Tremblay

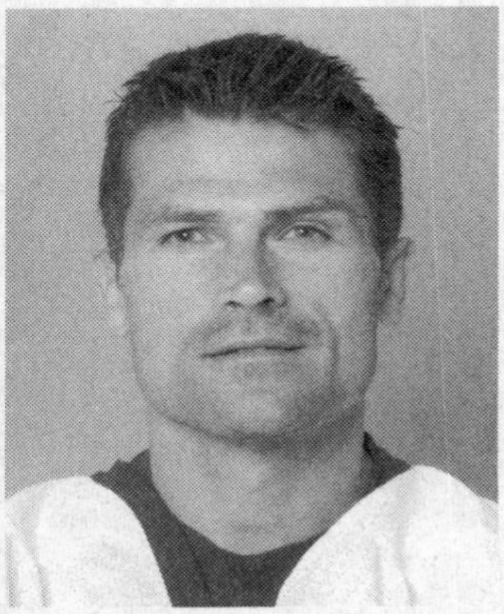

Garry Valk

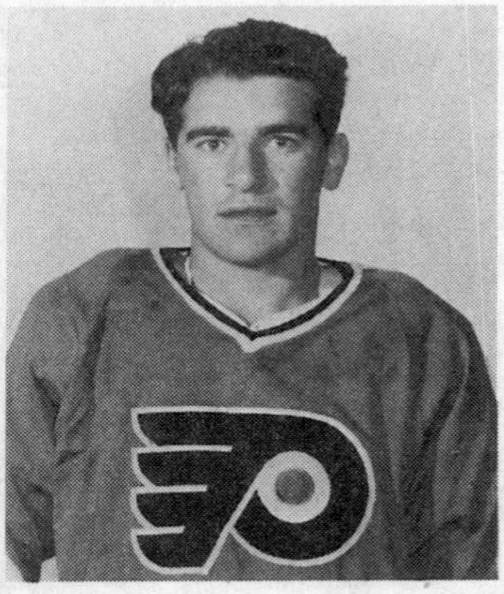

Joe Watson

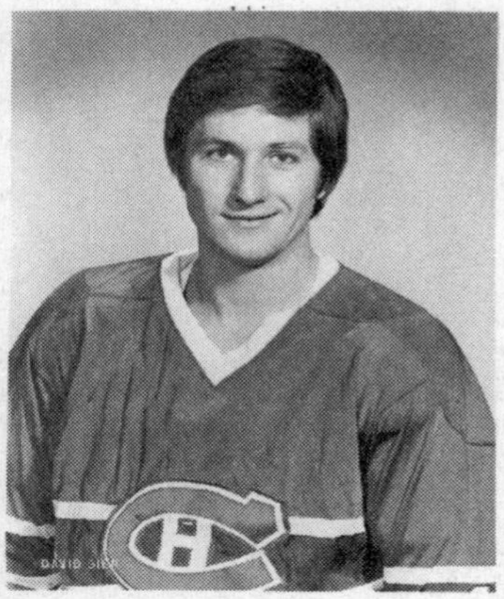

Murray Wilson

			Regular Schedule					Playoffs							
Name	NHL Teams	NHL Seasons	GP	G	A	TP	PIM	GP	G	A	TP	PIM	NHL Cup Wins	First NHL Season	Last NHL Season
Ververgaert, Dennis	Van., Phi., Wsh.	8	583	176	216	392	247	8	1	2	3	6	....	1973-74	1980-81
Vesey, Jim	St.L., Bos.	3	15	1	2	3	7	....	....	....	....	....	....	1988-89	1991-92
Veysey, Sid	Van.	1	1	0	0	0	0	....	....	....	....	....	....	1977-78	1977-78
‡ Vial, Dennis	NYR, Det., Ott.	8	242	4	15	19	794	....	....	....	....	....	....	1990-91	1997-98
Vickers, Steve	NYR	10	698	246	340	586	330	68	24	25	49	58	....	1972-73	1981-82
Vigneault, Alain	St.L.	2	42	2	5	7	82	4	0	1	1	26	....	1981-82	1982-83
‡ Viitakoski, Vesa	Cgy.	3	23	2	4	6	8	....	....	....	....	....	....	1993-94	1995-96
Vilgrain, Claude	Van., N.J., Phi.	5	89	21	32	53	78	11	1	1	2	17	....	1987-88	1993-94
Vincelette, Dan	Chi., Que.	6	193	20	22	42	351	12	0	0	0	4	....	1986-87	1991-92
Vipond, Pete	Cal.	1	3	0	0	0	0	....	....	....	....	....	....	1972-73	1972-73
Virta, Hannu	Buf.	5	245	25	101	126	66	17	1	3	4	6	....	1981-82	1985-86
‡ Virta, Tony	Min.	1	8	2	3	5	0	....	....	....	....	....	....	2001-02	2001-02
Visheau, Mark	Wpg., L.A.	2	29	1	3	4	107	....	....	....	....	....	....	1993-94	1998-99
Vitolinsh, Harijs	Wpg.	1	8	0	0	0	4	....	....	....	....	....	....	1993-94	1993-94
Viveiros, Emanuel	Min.	3	29	1	11	12	6	....	....	....	....	....	....	1985-86	1987-88
‡ Vlasak, Tomas	L.A.	1	10	1	3	4	2	....	....	....	....	....	....	2000-01	2000-01
• Vokes, Ed	Chi.	1	5	0	0	0	0	....	....	....	....	....	....	1930-31	1930-31
Volcan, Mickey	Hfd., Cgy.	4	162	8	33	41	146	....	....	....	....	....	....	1980-81	1983-84
Volchkov, Alexandre	Wsh.	1	3	0	0	0	0	....	....	....	....	....	....	1999-00	1999-00
Volek, David	NYI	6	396	95	154	249	201	15	5	5	10	2	....	1988-89	1993-94
Volmar, Doug	Det., L.A.	4	62	13	8	21	26	2	1	0	1	0	....	1969-70	1972-73
‡ Von Arx, Reto	Chi.	1	19	3	1	4	4	....	....	....	....	....	....	2000-01	2000-01
‡ Von Stefenelli, Phil	Bos., Ott.	2	33	0	5	5	23	....	....	....	....	....	....	1995-96	1996-97
Vopat, Jan	L.A., Nsh.	5	126	11	20	31	70	2	0	1	1	2	....	1995-96	1999-00
‡ Vopat, Roman	St.L., L.A., Chi., Phi.	4	133	6	14	20	253	....	....	....	....	....	....	1995-96	1998-99
Vorobiev, Vladimir	NYR, Edm.	3	33	9	7	16	14	1	0	0	0	0	....	1996-97	1998-99
• Voss, Carl	Tor., NYR, Det., Ott., St.L., NYA, Mtl.M., Chi.	8	261	34	70	104	50	24	5	3	8	0	1	1926-27	1937-38
‡ Vujtek, Vladimir	Mtl., Edm., T.B., Atl., Pit.	6	110	7	30	37	38	....	....	....	....	....	....	1991-92	2002-03
Vukota, Mick	NYI, T.B., Mtl.	11	574	17	29	46	2071	23	0	0	0	73	....	1987-88	1997-98
Vyazmikin, Igor	Edm.	1	4	1	0	1	0	....	....	....	....	....	....	1990-91	1990-91
‡ Vyshedkevich, Sergei	Atl.	2	30	2	5	7	16	....	....	....	....	....	....	1999-00	2000-01

W

Name	NHL Teams	NHL Seasons	GP	G	A	TP	PIM	GP	G	A	TP	PIM	NHL Cup Wins	First NHL Season	Last NHL Season
Waddell, Don	L.A.	1	1	0	0	0	0	....	....	....	....	....	....	1980-81	1980-81
• Waite, Frank	NYR	1	17	1	3	4	4	....	....	....	....	....	....	1930-31	1930-31
Walker, Gord	NYR, L.A.	4	31	3	4	7	23	....	....	....	....	....	....	1986-87	1989-90
Walker, Howard	Wsh., Cgy.	3	83	2	13	15	133	....	....	....	....	....	....	1980-81	1982-83
• Walker, Jack	Det.	2	80	5	8	13	18	....	....	....	....	....	....	1926-27	1927-28
Walker, Kurt	Tor.	3	71	4	5	9	142	16	0	0	0	34	....	1975-76	1977-78
Walker, Russ	L.A.	2	17	1	0	1	41	....	....	....	....	....	....	1976-77	1977-78
Wall, Bob	Det., L.A., St.L.	8	322	30	55	85	155	22	0	3	3	2	....	1964-65	1971-72
Wallin, Peter	NYR	2	52	3	14	17	14	14	2	6	8	6	....	1980-81	1981-82
Walsh, Jim	Buf.	1	4	0	1	1	4	....	....	....	....	....	....	1981-82	1981-82
Walsh, Mike	NYI	2	14	2	0	2	4	....	....	....	....	....	....	1987-88	1988-89
Walter, Ryan	Wsh., Mtl., Van.	15	1003	264	382	646	946	113	16	35	51	62	1	1978-79	1992-93
• Walton, Bobby	Mtl.	1	4	0	0	0	0	....	....	....	....	....	....	1943-44	1943-44
Walton, Mike	Tor., Bos., Van., St.L., Chi.	12	588	201	247	448	357	47	14	10	24	45	2	1965-66	1978-79
Wappel, Gord	Atl., Cgy.	3	20	1	1	2	10	2	0	0	0	4	....	1979-80	1981-82
‡ Ward, Dixon	Van., L.A., Tor., Buf., Bos., NYR	10	537	95	129	224	431	62	14	20	34	46	....	1992-93	2002-03
Ward, Don	Chi., Bos.	2	34	0	1	1	16	....	....	....	....	....	....	1957-58	1959-60
Ward, Ed	Que., Cgy., Atl., Ana., N.J.	8	278	23	26	49	354	....	....	....	....	....	....	1993-94	2000-01
• Ward, Jimmy	Mtl.M., Mtl.	12	527	147	127	274	455	36	4	4	8	26	1	1927-28	1938-39
Ward, Joe	Col.	1	4	0	0	0	2	....	....	....	....	....	....	1980-81	1980-81
Ward, Ron	Tor., Van.	2	89	2	5	7	6	....	....	....	....	....	....	1969-70	1971-72
Ware, Jeff	Tor., Fla.	3	21	0	1	1	12	....	....	....	....	....	....	1996-97	1998-99
Ware, Michael	Edm.	2	5	0	1	1	15	....	....	....	....	....	....	1988-89	1989-90
• Wares, Eddie	NYR, Det., Chi.	9	321	60	102	162	161	45	5	7	12	34	1	1936-37	1946-47
Warner, Bob	Tor.	2	10	1	1	2	4	4	0	0	0	0	....	1975-76	1976-77
Warner, Jim	Hfd.	1	32	0	3	3	10	....	....	....	....	....	....	1979-80	1979-80
Warwick, Bill	NYR	2	14	3	3	6	16	....	....	....	....	....	....	1942-43	1943-44
• Warwick, Grant	NYR, Bos., Mtl.	9	395	147	142	289	220	16	2	4	6	6	....	1941-42	1949-50
‡ Washburn, Steve	Fla., Van., Phi.	6	93	14	15	29	42	1	0	1	1	0	....	1995-96	2000-01
• Wasnie, Nick	Chi., Mtl., NYA, Ott., St.L.	7	248	57	34	91	176	20	6	3	9	20	2	1927-28	1934-35
Watson, Bill	Chi.	4	115	23	36	59	12	6	0	2	2	0	....	1985-86	1988-89
Watson, Bryan	Mtl., Det., Oak., Pit., St.L., Wsh.	16	878	17	135	152	2212	32	2	0	2	70	....	1963-64	1978-79
Watson, Dave	Col.	2	18	0	1	1	10	....	....	....	....	....	....	1979-80	1980-81
• Watson, Harry	Bro., Det., Tor., Chi.	14	809	236	207	443	150	62	16	9	25	27	5	1941-42	1956-57
Watson, Jim	Det., Buf.	8	221	4	19	23	345	....	....	....	....	....	....	1963-64	1971-72
Watson, Jimmy	Phi.	10	613	38	148	186	492	101	5	34	39	89	2	1972-73	1981-82
Watson, Joe	Bos., Phi., Col.	14	835	38	178	216	447	84	3	12	15	82	2	1964-65	1978-79
• Watson, Phil	NYR, Mtl.	13	590	144	265	409	532	54	10	25	35	67	2	1935-36	1947-48
Watters, Tim	Wpg., L.A.	14	741	26	151	177	1289	82	1	5	6	115	....	1981-82	1994-95
Watts, Brian	Det.	1	4	0	0	0	0	....	....	....	....	....	....	1975-76	1975-76
• Webster, Aubrey	Phi., Mtl.M.	2	5	0	0	0	0	....	....	....	....	....	....	1930-31	1934-35
• Webster, Don	Tor.	1	27	7	6	13	28	5	0	0	0	12	....	1943-44	1943-44
Webster, John	NYR	1	14	0	0	0	4	....	....	....	....	....	....	1949-50	1949-50
Webster, Tom	Bos., Det., Cal.	5	102	33	42	75	61	1	0	0	0	0	....	1968-69	1979-80
• Weiland, Cooney	Bos., Ott., Det.	11	509	173	160	333	147	45	12	10	22	12	2	1928-29	1938-39
Weir, Stan	Cal., Tor., Edm., Col., Det.	10	642	139	207	346	183	37	6	5	11	4	....	1972-73	1982-83
Weir, Wally	Que., Hfd., Pit.	6	320	21	45	66	625	23	0	1	1	96	....	1979-80	1984-85
• Wellington, Alex	Quebec Bulldogs	1	1	0	0	0	0	....	....	....	....	....	....	1919-20	1919-20
Wells, Chris	Pit., Fla.	5	195	9	20	29	193	3	0	0	0	0	....	1995-96	1999-00
Wells, Jay	L.A., Phi., Buf., NYR, St.L., T.B.	18	1098	47	216	263	2359	114	3	14	17	213	1	1979-80	1996-97
Wensink, John	St.L., Bos., Que., Col., N.J.	8	403	70	68	138	840	43	2	6	8	86	....	1973-74	1982-83
• Wentworth, Cy	Chi., Mtl.M., Mtl.	13	575	39	68	107	355	35	5	6	11	20	1	1927-28	1939-40
Werenka, Brad	Edm., Que., Chi., Pit., Cgy.	7	320	19	61	80	299	19	2	1	3	14	....	1992-93	2000-01
Wesenberg, Brian	Phi.	1	1	0	0	0	5	....	....	....	....	....	....	1998-99	1998-99
Wesley, Blake	Phi., Hfd., Que., Tor.	7	298	18	46	64	486	19	2	2	4	30	....	1979-80	1985-86
Westfall, Ed	Bos., NYI	18	1220	231	394	625	544	95	22	37	59	41	2	1961-62	1978-79
‡ Westlund, Tommy	Car.	4	203	9	13	22	48	25	1	0	1	17	....	1999-00	2002-03
Wharram, Kenny	Chi.	14	766	252	281	533	222	80	16	27	43	38	1	1951-52	1968-69
Wharton, Len	NYR	1	1	0	0	0	0	....	....	....	....	....	....	1944-45	1944-45
Wheeldon, Simon	NYR, Wpg.	3	15	0	2	2	10	....	....	....	....	....	....	1987-88	1990-91
• Wheldon, Don	St.L.	1	2	0	0	0	0	....	....	....	....	....	....	1974-75	1974-75
Whelton, Bill	Wpg.	1	2	0	0	0	0	....	....	....	....	....	....	1980-81	1980-81
Whistle, Rob	NYR, St.L.	2	51	7	5	12	16	4	0	0	0	2	....	1985-86	1987-88
White, Bill	L.A., Chi.	9	604	50	215	265	495	91	7	32	39	76	....	1967-68	1975-76
White, Moe	Mtl.	1	4	0	1	1	2	....	....	....	....	....	....	1945-46	1945-46
• White, Sherman	NYR	2	4	0	2	2	0	....	....	....	....	....	....	1946-47	1949-50
• White, Tex	Pit., NYA, Phi.	6	203	33	12	45	141	4	0	0	0	4	....	1925-26	1930-31
White, Tony	Wsh., Min.	5	164	37	28	65	104	....	....	....	....	....	....	1974-75	1979-80
Whitelaw, Bob	Det.	2	32	0	2	2	2	8	0	0	0	0	....	1940-41	1941-42
Whitlock, Bob	Min.	1	1	0	0	0	0	....	....	....	....	....	....	1969-70	1969-70
Whyte, Sean	L.A.	2	21	0	2	2	12	....	....	....	....	....	....	1991-92	1992-93
• Wickenheiser, Doug	Mtl., St.L., Van., NYR, Wsh.	10	556	111	165	276	286	41	4	7	11	18	....	1980-81	1989-90
• Widing, Juha	NYR, L.A., Cle.	8	575	144	226	370	208	8	1	2	3	2	....	1969-70	1976-77
Widmer, Jason	NYI, S.J.	3	7	0	1	1	7	....	....	....	....	....	....	1994-95	1996-97
• Wiebe, Art	Chi.	11	414	14	27	41	201	31	1	3	4	10	1	1932-33	1943-44
Wiemer, Jim	Buf., NYR, Edm., L.A., Bos.	11	325	29	72	101	378	62	5	8	13	63	....	1982-83	1993-94
• Wilcox, Archie	Mtl.M., Bos., St.L.	6	208	8	14	22	158	12	1	0	1	8	....	1929-30	1934-35
Wilcox, Barry	Van.	2	33	3	2	5	15	....	....	....	....	....	....	1972-73	1974-75
Wilder, Arch	Det.	1	18	0	2	2	2	....	....	....	....	....	....	1940-41	1940-41
Wiley, Jim	Pit., Van.	5	63	4	10	14	8	....	....	....	....	....	....	1972-73	1976-77
Wilkie, Bob	Det., Phi.	2	18	2	5	7	10	....	....	....	....	....	....	1990-91	1993-94
Wilkie, David	Mtl., T.B., NYR	6	167	10	26	36	165	8	1	2	3	14	....	1994-95	2000-01
Wilkins, Barry	Bos., Van., Pit.	9	418	27	125	152	663	6	0	1	1	4	....	1966-67	1975-76
• Wilkinson, John	Bos.	1	9	0	0	0	6	....	....	....	....	....	....	1943-44	1943-44
Wilkinson, Neil	Min., S.J., Chi., Wpg., Pit.	10	460	16	67	83	813	53	3	6	9	41	....	1989-90	1998-99
Wilks, Brian	L.A.	4	48	4	8	12	27	....	....	....	....	....	....	1984-85	1988-89
Willard, Rod	Tor.	1	1	0	0	0	0	....	....	....	....	....	....	1982-83	1982-83
• Williams, Burr	Det., St.L., Bos.	3	19	0	1	1	28	7	0	0	0	8	....	1933-34	1936-37
Williams, Butch	St.L., Cal.	3	108	14	35	49	131	....	....	....	....	....	....	1973-74	1975-76
Williams, Darryl	L.A.	1	2	0	0	0	10	....	....	....	....	....	....	1992-93	1992-93
Williams, David	S.J., Ana.	4	173	11	53	64	157	....	....	....	....	....	....	1991-92	1994-95

Name	NHL Teams	NHL Seasons	Regular Schedule GP	G	A	TP	PIM	Playoffs GP	G	A	TP	PIM	NHL Cup Wins	First NHL Season	Last NHL Season
Williams, Fred	Det.	1	44	2	5	7	10	....	....	....	....	....	....	1976-77	1976-77
Williams, Gord	Phi.	2	2	0	0	0	2	....	....	....	....	....	....	1981-82	1982-83
Williams, Sean	Chi.	1	2	0	0	0	4	....	....	....	....	....	....	1991-92	1991-92
Williams, Tiger	Tor., Van., Det., L.A., Hfd.	14	962	241	272	513	3966	83	12	23	35	455	....	1974-75	1987-88
Williams, Tom	NYR, L.A.	8	397	115	138	253	73	29	8	7	15	4	....	1971-72	1978-79
• Williams, Tommy	Bos., Min., Cal., Wsh.	13	663	161	269	430	177	10	2	5	7	2	....	1961-62	1975-76
Willson, Don	Mtl.	2	22	2	7	9	0	3	0	0	0	0	....	1937-38	1938-39
Wilson, Behn	Phi., Chi.	9	601	98	260	358	1480	67	12	29	41	190	....	1978-79	1987-88
• Wilson, Bert	NYR, St.L., L.A., Cgy.	8	478	37	44	81	646	21	0	2	2	42	....	1973-74	1980-81
Wilson, Bob	Chi.	1	1	0	0	0	0	....	....	....	....	....	....	1953-54	1953-54
Wilson, Carey	Cgy., Hfd., NYR	10	552	169	258	427	314	52	11	13	24	14	....	1983-84	1992-93
• Wilson, Cully	Tor., Mtl., Ham., Chi.	5	127	59	28	87	243	2	1	0	1	6	....	1919-20	1926-27
Wilson, Doug	Chi., S.J.	16	1024	237	590	827	830	95	19	61	80	88	....	1977-78	1992-93
Wilson, Gord	Bos.	1	....	....	....	....	....	2	0	0	0	0	....	1954-55	1954-55
Wilson, Hub	NYA	1	2	0	0	0	0	....	....	....	....	....	....	1931-32	1931-32
Wilson, Jerry	Mtl.	1	3	0	0	0	2	....	....	....	....	....	....	1956-57	1956-57
Wilson, Johnny	Det., Chi., Tor., NYR	13	688	161	171	332	190	66	14	13	27	11	4	1949-50	1961-62
• Wilson, Larry	Det., Chi.	6	152	21	48	69	75	4	0	0	0	0	1	1949-50	1955-56
Wilson, Mitch	N.J., Pit.	2	26	2	3	5	104	....	....	....	....	....	....	1984-85	1986-87
Wilson, Murray	Mtl., L.A.	7	386	94	95	189	162	53	5	14	19	32	4	1972-73	1978-79
Wilson, Rick	Mtl., St.L., Det.	4	239	6	26	32	165	3	0	0	0	0	....	1973-74	1976-77
Wilson, Rik	St.L., Cgy., Chi.	6	251	25	65	90	220	22	0	4	4	23	....	1981-82	1987-88
Wilson, Roger	Chi.	1	7	0	2	2	6	....	....	....	....	....	....	1974-75	1974-75
Wilson, Ron	Tor., Min.	7	177	26	67	93	68	20	4	13	17	8	....	1977-78	1987-88
Wilson, Ron	Wpg., St.L., Mtl.	14	832	110	216	326	415	63	10	12	22	64	....	1979-80	1993-94
Wilson, Wally	Bos.	1	53	11	8	19	18	1	0	0	0	0	....	1947-48	1947-48
Wing, Murray	Det.	1	1	0	1	1	0	....	....	....	....	....	....	1973-74	1973-74
Winnes, Chris	Bos., Phi.	4	33	1	6	7	6	1	0	0	0	0	....	1990-91	1993-94
Wiseman, Brian	Tor.	1	3	0	0	0	0	....	....	....	....	....	....	1996-97	1996-97
• Wiseman, Eddie	Det., NYA, Bos.	10	456	115	165	280	136	43	10	10	20	16	1	1932-33	1941-42
Wiste, Jim	Chi., Van.	3	52	1	10	11	8	....	....	....	....	....	....	1968-69	1970-71
‡ Witehall, Johan	NYR, Mtl.	3	54	2	5	7	16	....	....	....	....	....	....	1998-99	2000-01
Witherspoon, Jim	L.A.	1	2	0	0	0	2	....	....	....	....	....	....	1975-76	1975-76
Witiuk, Steve	Chi.	1	33	3	8	11	14	....	....	....	....	....	....	1951-52	1951-52
Woit, Benny	Det., Chi.	7	334	7	26	33	170	41	2	6	8	18	3	1950-51	1956-57
Wojciechowski, Steve	Det.	2	54	19	20	39	17	6	0	1	1	0	....	1944-45	1946-47
Wolanin, Craig	N.J., Que., Col., T.B., Tor.	13	695	40	133	173	894	35	4	6	10	67	1	1985-86	1997-98
Wolf, Bennett	Pit.	3	30	0	1	1	133	....	....	....	....	....	....	1980-81	1982-83
Wong, Mike	Det.	1	22	1	1	2	12	....	....	....	....	....	....	1975-76	1975-76
‡ Wood, Dody	S.J.	5	106	8	10	18	471	....	....	....	....	....	....	1992-93	1997-98
Wood, Randy	NYI, Buf., Tor., Dal.	11	741	175	159	334	603	51	8	9	17	40	....	1986-87	1996-97
Wood, Robert	NYR	1	1	0	0	0	0	....	....	....	....	....	....	1950-51	1950-51
Woodley, Dan	Van.	1	5	2	0	2	17	....	....	....	....	....	....	1987-88	1987-88
Woods, Paul	Det.	7	501	72	124	196	276	7	0	5	5	4	....	1977-78	1983-84
Wortman, Kevin	Cgy.	1	5	0	0	0	2	....	....	....	....	....	....	1993-94	1993-94
• Woytowich, Bob	Bos., Min., Pit., L.A.	8	503	32	126	158	352	24	1	3	4	20	....	1964-65	1971-72
‡ Wren, Bob	Ana., Tor.	3	5	0	0	0	0	1	0	0	0	0	....	1997-98	2001-02
Wright, John	Van., St.L., K.C.	3	127	16	36	52	67	....	....	....	....	....	....	1972-73	1974-75
Wright, Keith	Phi.	1	1	0	0	0	0	....	....	....	....	....	....	1967-68	1967-68
Wright, Larry	Phi., Cal., Det.	5	106	4	8	12	19	....	....	....	....	....	....	1971-72	1977-78
Wycherley, Ralph	NYA, Bro.	2	28	4	7	11	6	....	....	....	....	....	....	1940-41	1941-42
• Wylie, Bill	NYR	1	1	0	0	0	0	....	....	....	....	....	....	1950-51	1950-51
Wylie, Duane	Chi.	2	14	3	3	6	2	....	....	....	....	....	....	1974-75	1976-77
Wyrozub, Randy	Buf.	4	100	8	10	18	10	....	....	....	....	....	....	1970-71	1973-74

Y Z

Name	NHL Teams	NHL Seasons	Regular Schedule GP	G	A	TP	PIM	Playoffs GP	G	A	TP	PIM	NHL Cup Wins	First NHL Season	Last NHL Season
‡ Yachmenev, Vitali	L.A., Nsh.	8	487	83	133	216	88	....	....	....	....	....	....	1995-96	2002-03
• Yackel, Ken	Bos.	1	6	0	0	0	2	2	0	0	0	2	....	1958-59	1958-59
‡ Yake, Terry	Hfd., Ana., Tor., St.L., Wsh.	11	403	77	120	197	220	32	4	4	8	36	....	1988-89	2000-01
‡ Yakushin, Dmitri	Tor.	1	2	0	0	0	2	....	....	....	....	....	....	1999-00	1999-00
Yaremchuk, Gary	Tor.	4	34	1	4	5	28	....	....	....	....	....	....	1981-82	1984-85
Yaremchuk, Ken	Chi., Tor.	6	235	36	56	92	106	31	6	8	14	49	....	1983-84	1988-89
Yates, Ross	Hfd.	1	7	1	1	2	4	....	....	....	....	....	....	1983-84	1983-84
Yawney, Trent	Chi., Cgy., St.L.	12	593	27	102	129	783	60	9	17	26	81	....	1987-88	1998-99
• Yegorov, Alexei	S.J.	2	11	3	3	6	2	....	....	....	....	....	....	1995-96	1996-97
‡ Ylonen, Juha	Phx., T.B., Ott.	6	341	26	76	102	90	15	0	7	7	4	....	1996-97	2001-02
York, Harry	St.L., NYR, Pit., Van.	4	244	29	46	75	99	5	0	0	0	2	....	1996-97	1999-00
Young, B.J.	Det.	1	1	0	0	0	0	....	....	....	....	....	....	1999-00	1999-00
Young, Brian	Chi.	1	8	0	2	2	6	....	....	....	....	....	....	1980-81	1980-81
Young, C.J.	Cgy., Bos.	1	43	7	7	14	32	....	....	....	....	....	....	1992-93	1992-93
• Young, Doug	Det., Mtl.	10	388	35	45	80	303	28	1	5	6	16	2	1931-32	1940-41
• Young, Howie	Det., Chi., Van.	8	336	12	62	74	851	19	2	4	6	46	....	1960-61	1970-71
Young, Tim	Min., Wpg., Phi.	10	628	195	341	536	438	36	7	24	31	27	....	1975-76	1984-85
Young, Warren	Min., Pit., Det.	7	236	72	77	149	472	....	....	....	....	....	....	1981-82	1987-88
Younghans, Tom	Min., NYR	6	429	44	41	85	373	24	2	1	3	21	....	1976-77	1981-82
Ysebaert, Paul	N.J., Det., Wpg., Chi., T.B.	11	532	149	187	336	217	30	4	3	7	20	....	1988-89	1998-99
‡ Zabransky, Libor	St.L.	2	40	1	6	7	50	....	....	....	....	....	....	1996-97	1997-98
Zaharko, Miles	Atl., Chi.	4	129	5	32	37	84	3	0	0	0	0	....	1977-78	1981-82
Zaine, Rod	Pit., Buf.	2	61	10	6	16	25	....	....	....	....	....	....	1970-71	1971-72
Zalapski, Zarley	Pit., Hfd., Cgy., Mtl., Phi.	12	637	99	285	384	684	48	4	23	27	47	....	1987-88	1999-00
Zanussi, Joe	NYR, Bos., St.L.	3	87	1	13	14	46	4	0	1	1	2	....	1974-75	1976-77
Zanussi, Ron	Min., Tor.	5	299	52	83	135	373	17	0	4	4	17	....	1977-78	1981-82
Zavisha, Brad	Edm.	1	2	0	0	0	0	....	....	....	....	....	....	1993-94	1993-94
‡ Zehr, Jeff	Bos.	1	4	0	0	0	2	....	....	....	....	....	....	1999-00	1999-00
Zeidel, Larry	Det., Chi., Phi.	5	158	3	16	19	198	12	0	1	1	12	1	1951-52	1968-69
‡ Zelepukin, Valeri	N.J., Edm., Phi., Chi.	10	595	117	177	294	527	85	13	13	26	48	1	1991-92	2000-01
Zemlak, Richard	Que., Min., Pit., Cgy.	5	132	2	12	14	587	1	0	0	0	10	....	1986-87	1991-92
Zeniuk, Ed	Det.	1	2	0	0	0	0	....	....	....	....	....	....	1954-55	1954-55
Zent, Jason	Ott., Phi.	3	27	3	3	6	13	....	....	....	....	....	....	1996-97	1998-99
Zetterstrom, Lars	Van.	1	14	0	1	1	2	....	....	....	....	....	....	1978-79	1978-79
Zettler, Rob	Min., S.J., Phi., Tor., Nsh., Wsh.	14	569	5	65	70	920	14	0	0	0	4	....	1988-89	2001-02
Zezel, Peter	Phi., St.L., Wsh., Tor., Dal., N.J., Van.	15	873	219	389	608	435	131	25	39	64	83	....	1984-85	1998-99
‡ Ziegler, Thomas	T.B.	1	5	0	0	0	0	....	....	....	....	....	....	2000-01	2000-01
Zmolek, Doug	S.J., Dal., L.A., Chi.	8	467	11	53	64	905	14	0	1	1	16	....	1992-93	1999-00
Zoborosky, Marty	Chi.	1	1	0	0	0	2	....	....	....	....	....	....	1944-45	1944-45
Zombo, Rick	Det., St.L., Bos.	12	652	24	130	154	728	60	1	11	12	127	....	1984-85	1995-96
Zuke, Mike	St.L., Hfd.	8	455	86	196	282	220	26	6	6	12	12	....	1978-79	1985-86
Zunich, Rudy	Det.	1	2	0	0	0	2	....	....	....	....	....	....	1943-44	1943-44

Retired Players, Goaltenders and Coaches Research Project

Throughout the Retired Players and Retired Goaltenders sections of this book, you will notice many players with a bullet (•) by their names. These players, according to our records, are deceased. The editors recognize that our information on the death dates of NHLers is incomplete. If you have documented information on the passing of any player not marked with a bullet (•) in this edition, we would like to hear from you. We also welcome information on deceased NHL head coaches. Please send this information to:

Retired Player
Research Project
c/o NHL Publishing
194 Dovercourt Road
Toronto, Ontario
M6J 3C8 Canada
Fax: 416/531-3939

Many thanks to the following contributors in 2003-04:

Tim Bateman, Corey Bryant, Paul R. Carroll, Jr., Bob Duff, Peter Fillman, Ernie Fitzsimmons, Gary J. Pearce, Drew "Whitey" White.

Retired NHL Goaltender Index

Abbreviations: Teams/Cities: – **Ana.** – Anaheim; **Atl.** – Atlanta; **Bos.** – Boston; **Bro.** – Brooklyn; **Buf.** – Buffalo; **Cal.** – California; **Cgy.** – Calgary; **Cle.** – Cleveland; **Col.** – Colorado; **CBJ** – Columbus; **Dal.** – Dallas; **Det.** – Detroit; **Edm.** – Edmonton; **Fla.** – Florida; **Ham.** – Hamilton; **Hfd.** – Hartford; **K.C.** – Kansas City; **L.A.** – Los Angeles; **Min.** – Minnesota; **Mtl.** – Montreal; **Mtl.M.** – Montreal Maroons; **Mtl.W.** – Montreal Wanderers; **N.J.** – New Jersey; **NYA** – NY Americans; **NYI** – NY Islanders; **NYR** – New York Rangers; – **Oak.** – Oakland; **Ott.** – Ottawa; – **Phi.** – Philadelphia; **Phx.** – Phoenix; **Pit.** – Pittsburgh; **Que.** – Quebec; **St.L.** – St. Louis; **S.J.** – San Jose; **T.B.** – Tampa Bay; **Tor.** – Toronto; **Van.** – Vancouver; **Wpg.** – Winnipeg; **Wsh.** – Washington

Avg. – goals against per 60 minutes played; **GA** – goals agains; **GP** – games played; **Mins** – minutes played; **SO** – shutouts.
● – deceased. § – Forward, defenseman or coach who appeared in goal. For complete career, see Retired Player Index. ‡ – Remains active in other leagues.

			Regular Schedule								Playoffs										
Name	NHL Teams	NHL Seasons	GP	W	L	T	Mins	GA	SO	Avg	GP	W	L	T	Mins	GA	SO	Avg	NHL Cup Wins	First NHL Season	Last NHL Season
Abbott, George	Bos.	1	1	0	1	0	60	7	0	7.00	....	....	....	....	....	....	....	....		1943-44	1943-44
Adams, John	Bos., Wsh.	2	22	9	10	1	1180	85	1	4.32	....	....	....	....	....	....	....	....		1972-73	1974-75
Aiken, Don	Mtl.	1	1	0	1	0	34	6	0	10.59	....	....	....	....	....	....	....	....		1957-58	1957-58
● Aitkenhead, Andy	NYR	3	106	47	43	16	6570	257	11	2.35	10	6	2	2	608	15	3	1.48	1	1932-33	1934-35
● Almas, Red	Det., Chi.	3	3	0	2	1	180	13	0	4.33	5	1	3	....	263	13	0	2.97		1946-47	1952-53
● Anderson, Lorne	NYR	1	3	1	2	0	180	18	0	6.00	....	....	....	....	....	....	....	....		1951-52	1951-52
Astrom, Hardy	NYR, Col.	3	83	17	44	12	4456	278	0	3.74	....	....	....	....	....	....	....	....		1977-78	1980-81
‡ Bach, Ryan	L.A.	1	3	0	3	0	108	8	0	4.44	....	....	....	....	....	....	....	....		1998-99	1998-99
Bailey, Scott	Bos.	2	19	6	6	2	965	55	0	3.42	....	....	....	....	....	....	....	....		1995-96	1996-97
Baker, Steve	NYR	4	57	20	20	11	3081	190	3	3.70	14	7	7	....	826	55	0	4.00		1979-80	1982-83
‡ Bales, Mike	Bos., Ott.	4	23	2	15	1	1120	77	0	4.13	....	....	....	....	....	....	....	....		1992-93	1996-97
Bannerman, Murray	Van., Chi.	8	289	116	125	33	16470	1051	8	3.83	40	20	18	....	2322	165	0	4.26		1977-78	1986-87
Baron, Marco	Bos., L.A., Edm.	6	86	34	38	9	4822	292	1	3.63	1	0	1	....	20	3	0	9.00		1979-80	1984-85
Barrasso, Tom	Buf., Pit., Ott., Car., Tor., St.L.	19	777	369	277	86	44180	2385	38	3.24	119	61	54	....	6953	349	6	3.01	2	1983-84	2002-03
Bassen, Hank	Chi., Det., Pit.	9	156	46	66	31	8759	434	5	2.97	5	1	3	....	274	11	0	2.41		1954-55	1967-68
● Bastien, Baz	Tor.	1	5	0	4	1	300	20	0	4.00	....	....	....	....	....	....	....	....		1945-46	1945-46
Bauman, Gary	Mtl., Min.	3	35	6	18	6	1718	102	0	3.56	....	....	....	....	....	....	....	....		1966-67	1968-69
Beaupre, Don	Min., Wsh., Ott., Tor.	17	667	268	277	75	37396	2151	17	3.45	72	33	31	....	3943	220	3	3.35		1980-81	1996-97
Beauregard, Stephane	Wpg., Phi.	5	90	19	39	11	4402	268	2	3.65	4	1	3	....	238	12	0	3.03		1989-90	1993-94
Bedard, Jim	Wsh.	2	73	17	40	13	4232	278	1	3.94	....	....	....	....	....	....	....	....		1977-78	1978-79
Behrend, Marc	Wpg.	3	39	12	19	3	1991	160	1	4.82	7	1	3	0	312	19	0	3.65		1983-84	1985-86
Belanger, Yves	St.L., Atl., Bos.	6	78	29	33	6	4134	259	2	3.76	....	....	....	....	....	....	....	....		1974-75	1979-80
Belhumeur, Michel	Phi., Wsh.	3	65	9	36	7	3306	254	0	4.61	1	0	0	....	10	1	0	6.00		1972-73	1975-76
● Bell, Gordie	Tor., NYR	2	8	3	5	0	480	31	0	3.88	2	1	1	....	120	9	0	4.50		1945-46	1955-56
● Benedict, Clint	Ott., Mtl.M.	13	362	190	143	28	22367	863	58	2.32	28	11	12	5	1707	53	9	1.86	4	1917-18	1929-30
Bennett, Harvey	Bos.	1	25	10	12	2	1470	103	0	4.20	....	....	....	....	....	....	....	....		1944-45	1944-45
Bergeron, Jean-Claude	Mtl., T.B., L.A.	6	72	21	33	7	3772	232	1	3.69	....	....	....	....	....	....	....	....		1990-91	1996-97
Bernhardt, Tim	Cgy., Tor.	4	67	17	36	7	3748	267	0	4.27	....	....	....	....	....	....	....	....		1982-83	1986-87
‡ Berthiaume, Daniel	Wpg., Min., L.A., Bos., Ott.	9	215	81	90	21	11662	714	5	3.67	14	5	9	....	807	50	0	3.72		1985-86	1993-94
Bester, Allan	Tor., Det., Dal.	10	219	73	99	17	11773	786	7	4.01	11	2	6	....	508	37	0	4.37		1983-84	1995-96
● Beveridge, Bill	Det., Ott., St.L., Mtl.M., NYR	9	297	87	166	42	18375	879	18	2.87	5	2	3	....	300	11	0	2.20		1929-30	1942-43
● Bibeault, Paul	Mtl., Tor., Bos., Chi.	7	214	81	107	25	12890	785	10	3.65	20	6	14	....	1237	71	2	3.44		1940-41	1946-47
Billington, Craig	N.J., Ott., Bos., Col., Wsh.	15	332	110	149	31	17097	1034	9	3.63	8	0	2	....	213	15	0	4.23		1985-86	2002-03
Binette, Andre	Mtl.	1	1	1	0	0	60	4	0	4.00	....	....	....	....	....	....	....	....		1954-55	1954-55
Binkley, Les	Pit.	5	196	58	94	34	11046	575	11	3.12	7	5	2	....	428	15	0	2.10		1967-68	1971-72
Bittner, Richard	Bos.	1	1	0	0	1	60	3	0	3.00	....	....	....	....	....	....	....	....		1949-50	1949-50
Blake, Mike	L.A.	3	40	13	15	5	2117	150	0	4.25	....	....	....	....	....	....	....	....		1981-82	1983-84
Blue, John	Bos., Buf.	3	46	16	18	7	2521	126	1	3.00	2	0	1	....	96	5	0	3.13		1992-93	1995-96
Boisvert, Gilles	Det.	1	3	0	3	0	180	9	0	3.00	....	....	....	....	....	....	....	....		1959-60	1959-60
Bouchard, Dan	Atl., Cgy., Que., Wpg.	14	655	286	232	113	37919	2061	27	3.26	43	13	30	....	2549	147	1	3.46		1972-73	1985-86
● Bourque, Claude	Mtl., Det.	2	62	16	38	8	3830	193	4	3.02	3	1	2	....	188	8	1	2.55		1938-39	1939-40
Boutin, Rollie	Wsh.	3	22	7	10	1	1137	75	0	3.96	....	....	....	....	....	....	....	....		1978-79	1980-81
● Bouvrette, Lionel	NYR	1	1	0	1	0	60	6	0	6.00	....	....	....	....	....	....	....	....		1942-43	1942-43
Bower, Johnny	NYR, Tor.	15	552	250	195	90	32016	1340	37	2.51	74	35	34	....	4378	180	5	2.47	4	1953-54	1969-70
§ ● Branigan, Andy	NYA	1	1	0	0	0	7	0	0	0.00	....	....	....	....	....	....	....	....		1940-41	1940-41
● Brimsek, Frank	Bos., Chi.	10	514	252	182	80	31210	1404	40	2.70	68	32	36	....	4395	186	2	2.54	2	1938-39	1949-50
● Broda, Turk	Tor.	14	629	302	224	101	38167	1609	62	2.53	101	60	39	....	6389	211	13	1.98	5	1936-37	1951-52
Broderick, Ken	Min., Bos.	3	27	11	12	1	1464	74	1	3.03	....	....	....	....	....	....	....	....		1969-70	1974-75
Broderick, Len	Mtl.	1	1	1	0	0	60	2	0	2.00	....	....	....	....	....	....	....	....		1957-58	1957-58
Brodeur, Richard	NYI, Van., Hfd.	9	385	131	175	62	21968	1410	6	3.85	33	13	20	....	2009	111	1	3.32		1979-80	1987-88
Bromley, Gary	Buf., Van.	6	136	54	44	28	7427	425	7	3.43	7	2	5	....	360	25	0	4.17		1973-74	1980-81
● Brooks, Art	Tor.	1	4	2	2	0	220	23	0	6.27	....	....	....	....	....	....	....	....		1917-18	1917-18
Brooks, Ross	Bos.	3	54	37	7	6	3047	134	4	2.64	1	0	0	....	20	3	0	9.00		1972-73	1974-75
● Brophy, Frank	Que.	1	21	3	18	0	1249	148	0	7.11	....	....	....	....	....	....	....	....		1919-20	1919-20
Brown, Andy	Det., Pit.	3	62	22	26	9	3373	213	1	3.79	....	....	....	....	....	....	....	....		1971-72	1973-74
Brown, Ken	Chi.	1	1	0	0	0	18	1	0	3.33	....	....	....	....	....	....	....	....		1970-71	1970-71
Brunetta, Mario	Que.	3	40	12	17	1	1967	128	0	3.90	....	....	....	....	....	....	....	....		1987-88	1989-90
Bullock, Bruce	Van.	3	16	3	9	3	927	74	0	4.79	....	....	....	....	....	....	....	....		1972-73	1976-77
● Buzinski, Steve	NYR	1	9	2	6	1	560	55	0	5.89	....	....	....	....	....	....	....	....		1942-43	1942-43
Caley, Don	St.L.	1	1	0	0	0	30	3	0	6.00	....	....	....	....	....	....	....	....		1967-68	1967-68
Caprice, Frank	Van.	6	102	31	46	11	5589	391	1	4.20	....	....	....	....	....	....	....	....		1982-83	1987-88
Carey, Jim	Wsh., Bos., St.L.	5	172	79	65	16	9668	416	16	2.58	10	2	5	....	455	35	0	4.62		1994-95	1998-99
Caron, Jacques	L.A., St.L., Van.	5	72	24	29	11	3846	211	2	3.29	12	4	7	....	639	34	0	3.19		1967-68	1973-74
Carter, Lyle	Cal.	1	15	4	7	0	721	50	0	4.16	....	....	....	....	....	....	....	....		1971-72	1971-72
Casey, Jon	Min., Bos., St.L.	12	425	170	157	55	23255	1246	16	3.21	66	32	31	....	3743	192	3	3.08		1983-84	1996-97
‡ Chabot, Frederic	Mtl., Phi., L.A.	5	32	4	8	4	1262	62	0	2.95	....	....	....	....	....	....	....	....		1990-91	1998-99
● Chabot, Lorne	NYR, Tor., Mtl., Chi., Mtl.M., NYA	11	411	201	148	62	25307	860	73	2.04	37	13	17	6	2498	64	5	1.54	2	1926-27	1936-37
Chadwick, Ed	Tor., Bos.	6	184	57	92	35	11040	541	14	2.94	....	....	....	....	....	....	....	....		1955-56	1961-62
Champoux, Bob	Det., Cal.	2	17	2	11	3	923	80	0	5.20	1	1	0	....	55	4	0	4.36		1963-64	1973-74
Cheevers, Gerry	Tor., Bos.	13	418	230	102	74	24394	1174	26	2.89	88	53	34	....	5396	242	8	2.69	2	1961-62	1979-80
Cheveldae, Tim	Det., Wpg., Bos.	9	340	149	136	37	19172	1116	10	3.49	25	9	15	....	1418	71	2	3.00		1988-89	1996-97
Chevrier, Alain	N.J., Wpg., Chi., Pit., Det.	6	234	91	100	14	12202	845	2	4.16	16	9	7	....	1013	44	0	2.61		1985-86	1990-91
§ ● Clancy, King	Ott., Tor.	2	2	0	0	0	3	1	0	20.00	....	....	....	....	....	....	....	....		1924-25	1931-32
§ ● Cleghorn, Odie	Pit.	1	1	1	0	0	60	2	0	2.00	....	....	....	....	....	....	....	....		1925-26	1925-26
§ ● Cleghorn, Sprague	Ott., Mtl.	2	2	0	0	0	5	0	0	0.00	....	....	....	....	....	....	....	....		1918-19	1921-22
Clifford, Chris	Chi.	2	2	0	0	0	24	0	0	0.00	....	....	....	....	....	....	....	....		1984-85	1988-89
Cloutier, Jacques	Buf., Chi., Que.	12	255	82	102	24	12826	778	3	3.64	8	1	5	....	413	18	1	2.62		1981-82	1993-94
Colvin, Les	Bos.	1	1	0	1	0	60	4	0	4.00	....	....	....	....	....	....	....	....		1948-49	1948-49
§ ● Conacher, Charlie	Tor., Det.	3	4	0	0	0	10	0	0	0.00	....	....	....	....	....	....	....	....		1932-33	1938-39
● Connell, Alec	Ott., Det., NYA, Mtl.M.	12	417	193	156	67	26050	830	81	1.91	21	8	5	8	1309	26	4	1.19	2	1924-25	1936-37
Corsi, Jim	Edm.	1	26	8	14	3	1366	83	0	3.65	....	....	....	....	....	....	....	....		1979-80	1979-80
Courteau, Maurice	Bos.	1	6	2	4	0	360	33	0	5.50	....	....	....	....	....	....	....	....		1943-44	1943-44
‡ Cousineau, Marcel	Tor., NYI, L.A.	4	26	4	10	1	1047	51	1	2.92	....	....	....	....	....	....	....	....		1996-97	1999-00
Cowley, Wayne	Edm.	1	1	0	1	0	57	3	0	3.16	....	....	....	....	....	....	....	....		1993-94	1993-94
Cox, Abbie	Mtl.M., NYA, Det., Mtl.	3	5	1	1	2	263	11	0	2.51	....	....	....	....	....	....	....	....		1929-30	1935-36
Craig, Jim	Atl., Bos., Min.	3	30	11	10	7	1588	100	0	3.78	....	....	....	....	....	....	....	....		1979-80	1983-84
Crha, Jiri	Tor.	2	69	28	27	11	3942	261	0	3.97	5	0	4	....	186	21	0	6.77		1979-80	1980-81
● Crozier, Roger	Det., Buf., Wsh.	14	518	206	197	70	28567	1446	30	3.04	32	14	16	....	1789	82	1	2.75		1963-64	1976-77
● Cude, Wilf	Phi., Bos., Chi., Mtl., Det.	10	282	100	132	49	17586	798	24	2.72	19	7	11	1	1257	51	1	2.43		1930-31	1940-41
Cutts, Don	Edm.	1	6	1	2	1	269	16	0	3.57	....	....	....	....	....	....	....	....		1979-80	1979-80
● Cyr, Claude	Mtl.	1	1	0	0	0	20	1	0	3.00	....	....	....	....	....	....	....	....		1958-59	1958-59
Dadswell, Doug	Cgy.	2	27	8	8	3	1346	99	0	4.41	....	....	....	....	....	....	....	....		1986-87	1987-88
D'Alessio, Corrie	Hfd.	1	1	0	0	0	11	0	0	0.00	....	....	....	....	....	....	....	....		1992-93	1992-93
Daley, Joe	Pit., Buf., Det.	4	105	34	44	19	5836	326	3	3.35	....	....	....	....	....	....	....	....		1968-69	1971-72
Damore, Nick	Bos.	1	1	1	0	0	60	3	0	3.00	....	....	....	....	....	....	....	....		1941-42	1941-42
D'Amour, Marc	Cgy., Phi.	2	16	2	4	2	579	32	0	3.32	....	....	....	....	....	....	....	....		1985-86	1988-89
§ ● Darragh, Jack	Ott.	1	1	0	0	0	2	0	0	0.00	....	....	....	....	....	....	....	....		1919-20	1919-20

			Regular Schedule								Playoffs										
Name	NHL Teams	NHL Seasons	GP	W	L	T	Mins	GA	SO	Avg	GP	W	L	T	Mins	GA	SO	Avg	NHL Cup Wins	First NHL Season	Last NHL Season
Daskalakis, Cleon	Bos.	3	12	3	4	1	506	41	0	4.86	....	....	....	....	....	....	....	....		1984-85	1986-87
Davidson, John	St.L., NYR	10	301	123	124	39	17109	1004	7	3.52	31	16	14	....	1862	77	1	2.48		1973-74	1982-83
Decourcy, Bob	NYR	1	1	0	1	0	29	6	0	12.41	....	....	....	....	....	....	....	....		1947-48	1947-48
Defelice, Norm	Bos.	1	10	3	5	2	600	30	0	3.00	....	....	....	....	....	....	....	....		1956-57	1956-57
DeJordy, Denis	Chi., L.A., Mtl., Det.	12	316	124	128	51	17798	929	15	3.13	18	6	9	....	946	55	0	3.49	1	1960-61	1973-74
DelGuidice, Matt	Bos.	2	11	2	5	1	434	28	0	3.87	....	....	....	....	....	....	....	....		1990-91	1991-92
DeRouville, Philippe	Pit.	2	3	1	2	0	171	9	0	3.16	....	....	....	....	....	....	....	....		1994-95	1996-97
Desjardins, Gerry	L.A., Chi., NYI, Buf.	10	331	122	153	44	19014	1042	12	3.29	35	15	15	....	1874	108	0	3.46		1968-69	1977-78
• Dickie, Bill	Chi.	1	1	1	0	0	60	3	0	3.00	....	....	....	....	....	....	....	....		1941-42	1941-42
Dion, Connie	Det.	2	38	23	11	4	2280	119	1	3.13	5	1	4	....	300	17	0	3.40		1943-44	1944-45
Dion, Michel	Que., Wpg., Pit.	6	227	60	118	32	12695	898	2	4.24	5	2	3	....	304	22	0	4.34		1979-80	1984-85
Dolson, Dolly	Det.	3	93	35	41	17	5820	192	16	1.98	2	0	2	0	120	7	0	3.50		1928-29	1930-31
Dopson, Rob	Pit.	1	2	0	0	0	45	3	0	4.00	....	....	....	....	....	....	....	....		1993-94	1993-94
Dowie, Bruce	Tor.	1	2	0	1	0	72	4	0	3.33	....	....	....	....	....	....	....	....		1983-84	1983-84
‡ Draper, Tom	Wpg., Buf., NYI	6	53	19	23	5	2807	173	1	3.70	7	3	4	....	433	19	1	2.63		1988-89	1995-96
Dryden, Dave	NYR, Chi., Buf., Edm.	9	203	66	76	31	10424	555	9	3.19	3	0	2	....	133	9	0	4.06		1961-62	1979-80
Dryden, Ken	Mtl.	8	397	258	57	74	23352	870	46	2.24	112	80	32	....	6846	274	10	2.40	6	1970-71	1978-79
Duffus, Parris	Phx.	1	1	0	0	0	29	1	0	2.07	....	....	....	....	....	....	....	....		1996-97	1996-97
Dumas, Michel	Chi.	3	8	2	1	2	362	24	0	3.98	1	0	0	....	19	1	0	3.16		1974-75	1976-77
Dupuis, Bob	Edm.	1	1	0	1	0	60	4	0	4.00	....	....	....	....	....	....	....	....		1979-80	1979-80
• Durnan, Bill	Mtl.	7	383	208	112	62	22945	901	34	2.36	45	27	18	....	2871	99	2	2.07	2	1943-44	1949-50
Dyck, Ed	Van.	3	49	8	28	5	2453	178	1	4.35	....	....	....	....	....	....	....	....		1971-72	1973-74
Edwards, Don	Buf., Cgy., Tor.	10	459	208	155	74	26181	1449	16	3.32	42	16	21	....	2302	132	1	3.44		1976-77	1985-86
Edwards, Gary	St.L., L.A., Cle., Min., Edm., Pit.	13	286	88	125	51	16002	973	10	3.65	11	5	4	....	537	34	0	3.80		1968-69	1981-82
Edwards, Marv	Pit., Tor., Cal.	4	61	15	34	7	3467	218	2	3.77	....	....	....	....	....	....	....	....		1968-69	1973-74
• Edwards, Roy	Det., Pit.	7	236	97	88	38	13109	637	12	2.92	4	0	3	....	206	11	0	3.20		1967-68	1973-74
Eliot, Darren	L.A., Det., Buf.	5	89	25	41	12	4931	377	1	4.59	1	0	0	....	40	7	0	10.50		1984-85	1988-89
Ellacott, Ken	Van.	1	12	2	3	4	555	41	0	4.43	....	....	....	....	....	....	....	....		1982-83	1982-83
Erickson, Chad	N.J.	1	2	1	1	0	120	9	0	4.50	....	....	....	....	....	....	....	....		1991-92	1991-92
Esposito, Tony	Mtl., Chi.	16	886	423	306	151	52585	2563	76	2.92	99	45	53	....	6017	308	6	3.07	1	1968-69	1983-84
Essensa, Bob	Wpg., Det., Edm., Phx., Van., Buf.	12	446	173	176	47	24215	1270	18	3.15	16	4	9	0	864	51	0	3.54		1988-89	2001-02
• Evans, Claude	Mtl., Bos.	2	5	1	2	1	260	16	0	3.69	....	....	....	....	....	....	....	....		1954-55	1957-58
Exelby, Randy	Mtl., Edm.	2	2	0	1	0	63	5	0	4.76	....	....	....	....	....	....	....	....		1988-89	1989-90
‡ Fankhouser, Scott	Atl.	2	23	4	12	2	1180	65	0	3.31	....	....	....	....	....	....	....	....		1999-00	2000-01
Farr, Rocky	Buf.	3	19	2	6	3	722	42	0	3.49	....	....	....	....	....	....	....	....		1972-73	1974-75
Favell, Doug	Phi., Tor., Col.	12	373	123	153	69	20771	1096	18	3.17	21	6	15	....	1270	66	1	3.12		1967-68	1978-79
Fiset, Stephane	Que., Col., L.A., Mtl.	13	390	164	153	44	21785	1114	16	3.07	14	1	7	0	563	37	0	3.94	1	1989-90	2001-02
Fitzpatrick, Mark	L.A., NYI, Fla., T.B., Chi., Car.	12	329	113	136	49	18329	953	8	3.12	9	0	3	....	289	23	0	4.78		1988-89	1999-00
• Forbes, Jake	Tor., Ham., NYA, Phi.	13	210	85	114	11	12922	594	19	2.76	2	0	2	0	120	7	0	3.50		1919-20	1932-33
Ford, Brian	Que., Pit.	2	11	3	7	0	580	61	0	6.31	....	....	....	....	....	....	....	....		1983-84	1984-85
Foster, Norm	Bos., Edm.	2	13	7	4	0	623	34	0	3.27	....	....	....	....	....	....	....	....		1990-91	1991-92
‡ Fountain, Mike	Van., Car., Ott.	4	11	2	6	0	483	28	1	3.48	....	....	....	....	....	....	....	....		1996-97	2000-01
• Fowler, Hec	Bos.	1	7	1	6	0	409	42	0	6.16	....	....	....	....	....	....	....	....		1924-25	1924-25
Francis, Emile	Chi., NYR	6	95	31	52	11	5660	355	1	3.76	....	....	....	....	....	....	....	....		1946-47	1951-52
• Franks, Jimmy	Det., NYR, Bos.	4	42	12	23	7	2520	181	1	4.31	1	0	1	....	30	2	0	4.00	1	1936-37	1943-44
Frederick, Ray	Chi.	1	5	0	4	1	300	22	0	4.40	....	....	....	....	....	....	....	....		1954-55	1954-55
Friesen, Karl	N.J.	1	4	0	2	1	130	16	0	7.38	....	....	....	....	....	....	....	....		1986-87	1986-87
Froese, Bob	Phi., NYR	8	242	128	72	20	13451	694	13	3.10	18	3	9	....	830	55	0	3.98		1982-83	1989-90
Fuhr, Grant	Edm., Tor., Buf., L.A., St.L., Cgy.	19	868	403	295	114	48945	2756	25	3.38	150	92	50	....	8834	430	6	2.92	5	1981-82	1999-00
‡ Gage, Joaquin	Edm.	3	23	4	12	1	1076	67	0	3.74	....	....	....	....	....	....	....	....		1994-95	2000-01
Gagnon, David	Det.	1	2	0	1	0	35	6	0	10.29	....	....	....	....	....	....	....	....		1990-91	1990-91
• Gamble, Bruce	NYR, Bos., Tor., Phi.	10	327	110	150	46	18442	988	22	3.21	5	0	4	....	206	25	0	7.28	1	1958-59	1971-72
Gamble, Troy	Van.	4	72	22	29	9	3804	229	1	3.61	4	1	3	....	249	16	0	3.86		1986-87	1991-92
• Gardiner, Bert	NYR, Mtl., Chi., Bos.	6	144	49	68	27	8760	554	4	3.79	9	4	5	....	647	20	0	1.85		1935-36	1943-44
• Gardiner, Charlie	Chi.	7	316	112	152	52	19687	664	42	2.02	21	12	6	3	1472	35	5	1.43	1	1927-28	1933-34
Gardner, George	Det., Van.	5	66	16	30	6	3313	207	0	3.75	....	....	....	....	....	....	....	....		1965-66	1971-72
‡ Garner, Tyrone	Cgy.	1	3	0	2	0	139	12	0	5.18	....	....	....	....	....	....	....	....		1998-99	1998-99
Garrett, John	Hfd., Que., Van.	6	207	68	91	37	11763	837	1	4.27	9	4	3	....	461	33	0	4.30		1979-80	1984-85
Gatherum, Dave	Det.	1	3	2	0	1	180	3	1	1.00	....	....	....	....	....	....	....	....	1	1953-54	1953-54
Gauthier, Paul	Mtl.	1	1	0	0	1	70	2	0	1.71	....	....	....	....	....	....	....	....		1937-38	1937-38
‡ Gauthier, Sean	S.J.	1	1	0	0	0	3	0	0	0.00	....	....	....	....	....	....	....	....		1998-99	1998-99
• Gelineau, Jack	Bos., Chi.	4	143	46	64	33	8580	447	7	3.13	4	1	2	....	260	7	1	1.62		1948-49	1953-54
Giacomin, Ed	NYR, Det.	13	609	289	209	96	35633	1672	54	2.82	65	29	35	....	3838	180	1	2.81		1965-66	1977-78
Gilbert, Gilles	Min., Bos., Det.	14	416	192	143	60	23677	1290	18	3.27	32	17	15	....	1919	97	3	3.03		1969-70	1982-83
Gill, Andre	Bos.	1	5	3	2	0	270	13	1	2.89	....	....	....	....	....	....	....	....		1967-68	1967-68
• Goodman, Paul	Chi.	3	52	23	20	9	3240	117	6	2.17	3	0	3	....	187	10	0	3.21	1	1937-38	1940-41
Gordon, Scott	Que.	2	23	2	16	0	1082	101	0	5.60	....	....	....	....	....	....	....	....		1989-90	1990-91
Gosselin, Mario	Que., L.A., Hfd.	9	241	91	107	14	12857	801	6	3.74	32	16	15	....	1816	99	0	3.27		1983-84	1993-94
‡ Goverde, David	L.A.	3	5	1	4	0	278	29	0	6.26	....	....	....	....	....	....	....	....		1991-92	1993-94
Grahame, Ron	Bos., L.A., Que.	4	114	50	43	15	6472	409	5	3.79	4	2	1	....	202	7	0	2.08		1977-78	1980-81
• Grant, Benny	Tor., NYA, Bos.	6	50	17	26	4	2990	187	4	3.75	....	....	....	....	....	....	....	....		1928-29	1943-44
Grant, Doug	Det., St.L.	7	77	27	34	8	4199	280	2	4.00	....	....	....	....	....	....	....	....		1973-74	1979-80
Gratton, Gilles	St.L., NYR	2	47	13	18	9	2299	154	0	4.02	....	....	....	....	....	....	....	....		1975-76	1976-77
Gray, Gerry	Det., NYI	2	8	1	5	1	440	35	0	4.77	....	....	....	....	....	....	....	....		1970-71	1972-73
Gray, Harrison	Det.	1	1	0	1	0	40	5	0	7.50	....	....	....	....	....	....	....	....		1963-64	1963-64
Greenlay, Mike	Edm.	1	2	0	0	0	20	4	0	12.00	....	....	....	....	....	....	....	....		1989-90	1989-90
Guenette, Steve	Pit., Cgy.	5	35	19	16	0	1958	122	1	3.74	....	....	....	....	....	....	....	....		1986-87	1990-91
• Hainsworth, George	Mtl., Tor.	11	465	246	145	74	29087	937	94	1.93	52	22	25	5	3486	112	8	1.93	2	1926-27	1936-37
Hall, Glenn	Det., Chi., St.L.	19	906	407	326	163	53484	2222	84	2.49	115	49	65	....	6899	320	6	2.78	2	1951-52	1970-71
Hamel, Pierre	Tor., Wpg.	4	69	13	41	7	3766	276	0	4.40	....	....	....	....	....	....	....	....		1974-75	1980-81
Hanlon, Glen	Van., St.L., NYR, Det.	15	477	167	202	61	26037	1561	13	3.60	35	11	15	....	1756	92	4	3.14		1977-78	1990-91
Harrison, Paul	Min., Tor., Pit., Buf.	7	109	28	59	9	5806	408	2	4.22	4	0	1	....	157	9	0	3.44		1975-76	1981-82
Hayward, Brian	Wpg., Mtl., Min., S.J.	11	357	143	156	37	20025	1242	8	3.72	37	11	18	....	1803	104	0	3.46		1982-83	1992-93
Head, Don	Bos.	1	38	9	26	3	2280	158	2	4.16	....	....	....	....	....	....	....	....		1961-62	1961-62
Healy, Glenn	L.A., NYI, NYR, Tor.	15	437	166	190	47	24256	1361	13	3.37	37	13	15	....	1930	108	0	3.36	1	1985-86	2000-01
Hebert, Guy	St.L., Ana., NYR	10	491	191	222	56	27889	1307	28	2.81	14	4	7	....	744	33	1	2.66		1991-92	2000-01
• Hebert, Sammy	Tor., Ott.	2	4	2	1	0	200	19	0	5.70	....	....	....	....	....	....	....	....	1	1917-18	1923-24
Heinz, Rick	St.L., Van.	5	49	14	19	5	2356	159	2	4.05	1	0	0	....	8	1	0	7.50		1980-81	1984-85
Henderson, John	Bos.	2	46	15	15	15	2688	113	5	2.52	2	0	2	....	120	8	0	4.00		1954-55	1955-56
• Henry, Gord	Bos.	4	3	1	2	0	180	5	1	1.67	5	0	4	....	283	21	0	4.45		1948-49	1952-53
• Henry, Jim	NYR, Chi., Bos.	9	406	161	173	70	24355	1166	27	2.87	29	11	18	....	1741	81	2	2.79		1941-42	1954-55
Herron, Denis	Pit., K.C., Mtl.	14	462	146	203	76	25608	1579	10	3.70	15	5	10	....	901	50	0	3.33		1972-73	1985-86
Hextall, Ron	Phi., Que., NYI	13	608	296	214	69	34750	1723	23	2.97	93	47	43	....	5456	276	2	3.04		1986-87	1998-99
Highton, Hec	Chi.	1	24	10	14	0	1440	108	0	4.50	....	....	....	....	....	....	....	....		1943-44	1943-44
§ • Himes, Normie	NYA	2	2	0	1	0	79	3	0	2.28	....	....	....	....	....	....	....	....		1927-28	1928-29
‡ Hirsch, Corey	NYR, Van., Wsh., Dal.	7	108	34	45	14	5775	301	4	3.13	6	2	3	....	338	21	0	3.73		1992-93	2002-03
Hodge, Charlie	Mtl., Oak., Van.	14	358	150	125	61	20573	925	24	2.70	16	7	8	....	804	32	2	2.39	5	1954-55	1970-71
Hodson, Kevin	Det., T.B.	6	71	17	18	10	2910	134	4	2.76	1	0	0	....	1	0	0	0.00	2	1995-96	2002-03
Hoffort, Bruce	Phi.	2	9	4	0	3	368	22	0	3.59	....	....	....	....	....	....	....	....		1989-90	1990-91
Hoganson, Paul	Pit.	1	2	0	1	0	57	7	0	7.37	....	....	....	....	....	....	....	....		1970-71	1970-71
Hogosta, Goran	NYI, Que.	2	22	5	12	3	1208	83	1	4.12	....	....	....	....	....	....	....	....		1977-78	1979-80
Holden, Mark	Mtl., Wpg.	4	8	2	2	1	372	25	0	4.03	....	....	....	....	....	....	....	....		1981-82	1984-85
Holland, Ken	Hfd., Det.	2	4	0	2	1	206	17	0	4.95	....	....	....	....	....	....	....	....		1980-81	1983-84
Holland, Robbie	Pit.	2	44	11	22	9	2513	171	1	4.08	....	....	....	....	....	....	....	....		1979-80	1980-81
• Holmes, Hap	Tor., Det.	4	103	39	54	10	6510	264	17	2.43	2	1	1	0	120	7	0	3.50	1	1917-18	1927-28
§ Horner, Red	Tor.	1	1	0	0	0	1	1	0	60.00	....	....	....	....	....	....	....	....		1931-32	1931-32
Hrivnak, Jim	Wsh., Wpg., St.L.	5	85	34	30	3	4217	262	0	3.73	....	....	....	....	....	....	....	....		1989-90	1993-94
Hrudey, Kelly	NYI, L.A., S.J.	15	677	271	265	88	38084	2174	17	3.43	85	36	46	....	5163	283	0	3.29		1983-84	1997-98
Ing, Peter	Tor., Edm., Det.	4	74	20	37	9	3941	266	1	4.05	....	....	....	....	....	....	....	....		1989-90	1993-94
Inness, Gary	Pit., Phi., Wsh.	7	162	58	61	27	8710	494	2	3.40	9	5	4	....	540	24	0	2.67		1973-74	1980-81

Name	NHL Teams	NHL Seasons	Regular Schedule GP	W	L	T	Mins	GA	SO	Avg	Playoffs GP	W	L	T	Mins	GA	SO	Avg	NHL Cup Wins	First NHL Season	Last NHL Season
Ireland, Randy	Buf.	1	2	0	0	0	30	3	0	6.00	....	....	....	....	....	....	....	....		1978-79	1978-79
Irons, Robbie	St.L.	1	1	0	0	0	3	0	0	0.00	....	....	....	....	....	....	....	....		1968-69	1968-69
• Ironstone, Joe	Ott., NYA, Tor.	3	2	0	0	1	110	3	1	1.64	....	....	....	....	....	....	....	....		1924-25	1927-28
Jablonski, Pat	St.L., T.B., Mtl., Phx., Car.	8	128	28	62	18	6634	413	1	3.74	4	0	0	....	139	6	0	2.59		1989-90	1997-98
Jackson, Doug	Chi.	1	6	2	3	1	360	42	0	7.00	....	....	....	....	....	....	....	....		1947-48	1947-48
Jackson, Percy	Bos., NYA, NYR	4	7	1	3	1	392	26	0	3.98	....	....	....	....	....	....	....	....		1931-32	1935-36
‡ Jaks, Pauli	L.A.	1	1	0	0	0	40	2	0	3.00	....	....	....	....	....	....	....	....		1994-95	1994-95
Janaszak, Steve	Min., Col.	2	3	0	1	1	160	15	0	5.63	....	....	....	....	....	....	....	....		1979-80	1981-82
Janecyk, Bob	Chi., L.A.	6	110	43	47	13	6250	432	2	4.15	3	0	3	....	184	10	0	3.26		1983-84	1988-89
§ Jenkins, Roger	NYA	1	1	0	1	0	30	7	0	14.00	....	....	....	....	....	....	....	....		1938-39	1938-39
Jensen, Al	Det., Wsh., L.A.	7	179	95	53	18	9974	557	8	3.35	12	5	5	....	598	32	0	3.21		1980-81	1986-87
Jensen, Darren	Phi.	2	30	15	10	1	1496	95	2	3.81	....	....	....	....	....	....	....	....		1984-85	1985-86
Johnson, Bob	St.L., Pit.	2	24	9	9	1	1059	66	0	3.74	....	....	....	....	....	....	....	....		1972-73	1974-75
Johnston, Eddie	Bos., Tor., St.L., Chi.	16	592	234	257	80	34216	1852	32	3.25	18	7	10	....	1023	57	1	3.34	2	1962-63	1977-78
Junkin, Joe	Bos.	1	1	0	0	0	8	0	0	0.00	....	....	....	....	....	....	....	....		1968-69	1968-69
Kaarela, Jari	Col.	1	5	2	2	0	220	22	0	6.00	....	....	....	....	....	....	....	....		1980-81	1980-81
Kamppuri, Hannu	N.J.	1	13	1	10	1	645	54	0	5.02	....	....	....	....	....	....	....	....		1984-85	1984-85
• Karakas, Mike	Chi., Mtl.	8	336	114	169	53	20616	1002	28	2.92	23	11	12	0	1434	72	3	3.01	1	1935-36	1945-46
Keans, Doug	L.A., Bos.	9	210	96	64	26	11388	666	4	3.51	9	2	6	....	432	34	0	4.72		1979-80	1987-88
Keenan, Don	Bos.	1	1	0	1	0	60	4	0	4.00	....	....	....	....	....	....	....	....		1958-59	1958-59
• Kerr, Dave	Mtl.M., NYA, NYR	11	427	203	148	75	26639	954	51	2.15	40	18	19	3	2616	76	8	1.74	1	1930-31	1940-41
King, Scott	Det.	2	2	0	0	0	61	3	0	2.95	....	....	....	....	....	....	....	....		1990-91	1991-92
Kleisinger, Terry	NYR	1	4	0	2	0	191	14	0	4.40	....	....	....	....	....	....	....	....		1985-86	1985-86
Klymkiw, Julian	NYR	1	1	0	0	0	19	2	0	6.32	....	....	....	....	....	....	....	....		1958-59	1958-59
Knickle, Rick	L.A.	2	14	7	6	0	706	44	0	3.74	....	....	....	....	....	....	....	....		1992-93	1993-94
Kuntar, Les	Mtl.	1	6	2	2	0	302	16	0	3.18	....	....	....	....	....	....	....	....		1993-94	1993-94
Kurt, Gary	Cal.	1	16	1	7	5	838	60	0	4.30	....	....	....	....	....	....	....	....		1971-72	1971-72
Labrecque, Patrick	Mtl.	1	2	0	1	0	98	7	0	4.29	....	....	....	....	....	....	....	....		1995-96	1995-96
Lacher, Blaine	Bos.	2	47	22	16	4	2636	123	4	2.80	5	1	4	....	283	12	0	2.54		1994-95	1995-96
• Lacroix, Frenchy	Mtl.	2	5	1	4	0	280	16	0	3.43	....	....	....	....	....	....	....	....		1925-26	1926-27
LaFerriere, Rick	Col.	1	1	0	0	0	20	1	0	3.00	....	....	....	....	....	....	....	....		1981-82	1981-82
LaForest, Mark	Det., Phi., Tor., Ott.	6	103	25	54	4	5032	354	2	4.22	2	1	0	....	48	1	0	1.25		1985-86	1993-94
‡ Langkow, Scott	Wpg., Phx., Atl.	4	20	3	12	1	943	68	0	4.33	....	....	....	....	....	....	....	....		1995-96	1999-00
• Larocque, Michel	Mtl., Tor., Phi., St.L.	11	312	160	89	45	17615	978	17	3.33	14	6	6	....	759	37	1	2.92	4	1973-74	1983-84
Larocque, Michel	Chi.	1	3	0	2	0	152	9	0	3.55	....	....	....	....	....	....	....	....		2000-01	2000-01
‡ Lasak, Jan	Nsh.	2	6	0	4	0	267	18	0	4.04	....	....	....	....	....	....	....	....		2001-02	2002-03
Laskowski, Gary	L.A.	2	59	19	27	5	2942	228	0	4.65	....	....	....	....	....	....	....	....		1982-83	1983-84
Laxton, Gord	Pit.	4	17	4	9	0	800	74	0	5.55	....	....	....	....	....	....	....	....		1975-76	1978-79
LeBlanc, Ray	Chi.	1	1	1	0	0	60	1	0	1.00	....	....	....	....	....	....	....	....		1991-92	1991-92
§ • Leduc, Albert	Mtl.	1	1	0	0	0	2	1	0	30.00	....	....	....	....	....	....	....	....		1931-32	1931-32
Legris, Claude	Det.	2	4	0	1	1	91	4	0	2.64	....	....	....	....	....	....	....	....		1980-81	1981-82
• Lehman, Hugh	Chi.	2	48	20	24	4	3047	136	6	2.68	2	0	1	1	120	10	0	5.00		1926-27	1927-28
Lemelin, Reggie	Atl., Cgy., Bos.	15	507	236	162	63	28006	1613	12	3.46	59	23	25	....	3119	186	2	3.58		1978-79	1992-93
Lenarduzzi, Mike	Hfd.	2	4	1	1	1	189	10	0	3.17	....	....	....	....	....	....	....	....		1992-93	1993-94
Lessard, Mario	L.A.	6	240	92	97	39	13529	843	9	3.74	20	6	12	....	1136	83	0	4.38		1978-79	1983-84
Levasseur, Jean-Louis	Min.	1	1	0	1	0	60	7	0	7.00	....	....	....	....	....	....	....	....		1979-80	1979-80
§ • Levinsky, Alex	Tor.	1	1	0	0	0	1	1	0	60.00	....	....	....	....	....	....	....	....		1931-32	1931-32
• Lindbergh, Pelle	Phi.	5	157	87	49	15	9150	503	7	3.30	23	12	10	....	1214	63	3	3.11		1981-82	1985-86
• Lindsay, Bert	Mtl.W., Tor.	2	20	6	14	0	1238	118	0	5.72	....	....	....	....	....	....	....	....		1917-18	1918-19
Littman, David	Buf., T.B.	3	3	0	2	0	141	14	0	5.96	....	....	....	....	....	....	....	....		1990-91	1992-93
Liut, Mike	St.L., Hfd., Wsh.	13	664	294	271	74	38215	2221	25	3.49	67	29	32	....	3814	215	2	3.38		1979-80	1991-92
Lockett, Ken	Van.	2	55	13	15	8	2348	131	2	3.35	1	0	1	....	60	6	0	6.00		1974-75	1975-76
• Lockhart, Howard	Tor., Que., Ham., Bos.	5	59	16	41	0	3413	287	1	5.05	....	....	....	....	....	....	....	....		1919-20	1924-25
LoPresti, Pete	Min., Edm.	6	175	43	102	20	9858	668	5	4.07	2	0	2	....	77	6	0	4.68		1974-75	1980-81
• LoPresti, Sam	Chi.	2	74	30	38	6	4530	236	4	3.13	8	3	5	....	530	17	1	1.92		1940-41	1941-42
‡ Lorenz, Danny	NYI	3	8	1	5	0	357	25	0	4.20	....	....	....	....	....	....	....	....		1990-91	1992-93
Loustel, Ron	Wpg.	1	1	0	1	0	60	10	0	10.00	....	....	....	....	....	....	....	....		1980-81	1980-81
Low, Ron	Tor., Wsh., Det., Que., Edm., N.J.	11	382	102	203	38	20502	1463	4	4.28	7	1	6	....	452	29	0	3.85		1972-73	1984-85
Lozinski, Larry	Det.	1	30	6	11	7	1459	105	0	4.32	....	....	....	....	....	....	....	....		1980-81	1980-81
• Lumley, Harry	Det., NYR, Chi., Tor., Bos.	16	803	330	329	142	48044	2206	71	2.75	76	29	47	....	4778	198	7	2.49	1	1943-44	1959-60
MacKenzie, Shawn	N.J.	1	4	0	1	0	130	15	0	6.92	....	....	....	....	....	....	....	....		1982-83	1982-83
Madeley, Darrin	Ott.	3	39	4	23	5	1928	140	0	4.36	....	....	....	....	....	....	....	....		1992-93	1994-95
Malarchuk, Clint	Que., Wsh., Buf.	11	338	141	130	45	19030	1100	12	3.47	15	2	9	0	781	56	0	4.30		1981-82	1991-92
Maneluk, George	NYI	1	4	1	1	0	140	15	0	6.43	....	....	....	....	....	....	....	....		1990-91	1990-91
Maniago, Cesare	Tor., Mtl., NYR, Min., Van.	15	568	189	257	97	32570	1773	30	3.27	36	15	21	....	2245	100	3	2.67		1960-61	1977-78
Marois, Jean	Tor., Chi.	2	3	1	2	0	180	15	0	5.00	....	....	....	....	....	....	....	....		1943-44	1953-54
Martin, Seth	St.L.	1	30	8	10	7	1552	67	1	2.59	2	0	0	....	73	5	0	4.11		1967-68	1967-68
Mason, Bob	Wsh., Chi., Que., Van.	8	145	55	65	16	7988	500	1	3.76	5	2	3	....	369	12	1	1.95		1983-84	1990-91
Mattsson, Markus	Wpg., Min., L.A.	4	92	21	46	14	5007	343	6	4.11	....	....	....	....	....	....	....	....		1979-80	1983-84
May, Darrell	St.L.	2	6	1	5	0	364	31	0	5.11	....	....	....	....	....	....	....	....		1985-86	1987-88
Mayer, Gilles	Tor.	4	9	2	6	1	540	24	0	2.67	....	....	....	....	....	....	....	....		1949-50	1955-56
• McAuley, Ken	NYR	2	96	17	64	15	5740	537	1	5.61	....	....	....	....	....	....	....	....		1943-44	1944-45
McCartan, Jack	NYR	2	12	2	7	3	680	42	1	3.71	....	....	....	....	....	....	....	....		1959-60	1960-61
• McCool, Frank	Tor.	2	72	34	31	7	4320	242	4	3.36	13	8	5	....	807	30	4	2.23	1	1944-45	1945-46
McDuffe, Peter	St.L., NYR, K.C., Det.	5	57	11	36	6	3207	218	0	4.08	1	0	1	....	60	7	0	7.00		1971-72	1975-76
McGrattan, Tom	Det.	1	1	0	0	0	8	1	0	7.50	....	....	....	....	....	....	....	....		1947-48	1947-48
McKay, Ross	Hfd.	1	1	0	0	0	35	3	0	5.14	....	....	....	....	....	....	....	....		1990-91	1990-91
McKenzie, Bill	Det., K.C., Col.	6	91	18	49	13	4776	326	2	4.10	....	....	....	....	....	....	....	....		1973-74	1979-80
McKichan, Steve	Van.	1	1	0	0	0	20	2	0	6.00	....	....	....	....	....	....	....	....		1990-91	1990-91
McLachlan, Murray	Tor.	1	2	0	1	0	25	4	0	9.60	....	....	....	....	....	....	....	....		1970-71	1970-71
McLean, Kirk	N.J., Van., Car., Fla., NYR	16	612	245	262	72	35090	1904	22	3.26	68	34	34	....	4189	198	6	2.84		1985-86	2000-01
McLelland, Dave	Van.	1	2	1	1	0	120	10	0	5.00	....	....	....	....	....	....	....	....		1972-73	1972-73
McLeod, Don	Det., Phi.	2	18	3	10	1	879	74	0	5.05	....	....	....	....	....	....	....	....		1970-71	1971-72
McLeod, Jim	St.L.	1	16	6	6	4	880	44	0	3.00	....	....	....	....	....	....	....	....		1971-72	1971-72
McNamara, Gerry	Tor.	2	7	2	2	1	323	14	0	2.60	....	....	....	....	....	....	....	....		1960-61	1969-70
• McNeil, Gerry	Mtl.	8	276	119	105	52	16535	649	28	2.36	35	17	18	....	2284	72	5	1.89	3	1947-48	1957-58
McRae, Gord	Tor.	5	71	30	22	10	3799	221	1	3.49	8	2	5	....	454	22	0	2.91		1972-73	1977-78
Melanson, Roland	NYI, Min., L.A., N.J., Mtl.	11	291	129	106	33	16452	995	6	3.63	23	4	9	....	801	59	0	4.42	3	1980-81	1991-92
Meloche, Gilles	Chi., Cal., Cle., Min., Pit.	18	788	270	351	131	45401	2756	20	3.64	45	21	19	....	2464	143	2	3.48		1970-71	1987-88
Micalef, Corrado	Det.	5	113	26	59	15	5794	409	2	4.24	3	0	0	....	49	8	0	9.80		1981-82	1985-86
‡ Michaud, Alfie	Van.	1	2	0	1	0	69	5	0	4.35	....	....	....	....	....	....	....	....		1999-00	1999-00
Middlebrook, Lindsay	Wpg., Min., N.J., Edm.	4	37	3	23	6	1845	152	0	4.94	....	....	....	....	....	....	....	....		1979-80	1982-83
• Millar, Al	Bos.	1	6	1	4	1	360	25	0	4.17	....	....	....	....	....	....	....	....		1957-58	1957-58
Millen, Greg	Pit., Hfd., St.L., Que., Chi., Det.	14	604	215	284	89	35377	2281	17	3.87	59	27	29	....	3383	193	0	3.42		1978-79	1991-92
• Miller, Joe	NYA, NYR, Pit., Phi.	4	127	24	87	16	7871	383	16	2.92	3	2	1	0	180	3	1	1.00	1	1927-28	1930-31
‡ Minard, Mike	Edm.	1	1	1	0	0	60	3	0	3.00	....	....	....	....	....	....	....	....		1999-00	1999-00
Mio, Eddie	Edm., NYR, Det.	7	192	64	73	30	10428	705	4	4.06	17	9	7	....	986	63	0	3.83		1979-80	1985-86
• Mitchell, Ivan	Tor.	3	22	10	9	0	1190	88	0	4.44	....	....	....	....	....	....	....	....	1	1919-20	1921-22
Moffat, Mike	Bos.	3	19	7	7	2	979	70	0	4.29	11	6	5	....	663	38	0	3.44		1981-82	1983-84
Moog, Andy	Edm., Bos., Dal., Mtl.	18	713	372	209	88	40151	2097	28	3.13	132	68	57	....	7452	377	4	3.04	3	1980-81	1997-98
Moore, Alfie	NYA, Chi., Det.	4	21	7	14	0	1290	81	1	3.77	3	1	2	....	180	7	0	2.33	1	1936-37	1939-40
Moore, Robbie	Phi., Wsh.	2	6	3	1	1	257	8	2	1.87	5	3	2	....	268	18	0	4.03		1978-79	1982-83
Morissette, Jean-Guy	Mtl.	1	1	0	1	0	36	4	0	6.67	....	....	....	....	....	....	....	....		1963-64	1963-64
• Mowers, Johnny	Det.	4	152	65	61	26	9350	399	15	2.56	32	19	13	....	2000	85	2	2.55	1	1940-41	1946-47
Mrazek, Jerome	Phi.	1	1	0	0	0	6	1	0	10.00	....	....	....	....	....	....	....	....		1975-76	1975-76
§ • Mummery, Harry	Que., Ham.	2	4	2	1	0	192	20	0	6.25	....	....	....	....	....	....	....	....		1919-20	1921-22
§ • Munro, Dunc	Mtl.M.	1	1	0	0	0	2	0	0	0.00	....	....	....	....	....	....	....	....		1924-25	1924-25
• Murphy, Hal	Mtl.	1	1	1	0	0	60	4	0	4.00	....	....	....	....	....	....	....	....		1952-53	1952-53
• Murray, Mickey	Mtl.	1	1	0	1	0	60	4	0	4.00	....	....	....	....	....	....	....	....		1929-30	1929-30
Muzzatti, Jason	Cgy., Hfd., NYR, S.J.	5	62	13	25	10	3014	167	1	3.32	....	....	....	....	....	....	....	....		1993-94	1997-98

Name	NHL Teams	NHL Seasons	Regular Schedule GP	W	L	T	Mins	GA	SO	Avg	Playoffs GP	W	L	T	Mins	GA	SO	Avg	NHL Cup Wins	First NHL Season	Last NHL Season
‡ Myllys, Jarmo	Min., S.J.	4	39	4	27	1	1846	161	0	5.23	....	....	....	....	....	....	....	....		1988-89	1991-92
Mylnikov, Sergei	Que.	1	10	1	7	2	568	47	0	4.96	....	....	....	....	....	....	....	....		1989-90	1989-90
Myre, Phil	Mtl., Atl., St.L., Phi., Col., Buf.	14	439	149	198	76	25220	1482	14	3.53	12	6	5	....	747	41	1	3.29	1	1969-70	1982-83
‡ Naumenko, Gregg	Ana.	1	2	0	1	0	70	7	0	6.00	....	....	....	....	....	....	....	....		2000-01	2000-01
Newton, Cam	Pit.	2	16	4	7	1	814	51	0	3.76	....	....	....	....	....	....	....	....		1970-71	1972-73
Norris, Jack	Bos., Chi., L.A.	4	58	20	25	4	3119	202	2	3.89	....	....	....	....	....	....	....	....		1964-65	1970-71
Oleschuk, Bill	K.C., Col.	4	55	7	28	10	2835	188	1	3.98	....	....	....	....	....	....	....	....		1975-76	1979-80
• Olesevich, Dan	NYR	1	1	0	0	1	29	2	0	4.14	....	....	....	....	....	....	....	....		1961-62	1961-62
O'Neill, Mike	Wpg., Ana.	4	21	0	9	2	855	61	0	4.28	....	....	....	....	....	....	....	....		1991-92	1996-97
Ouimet, Ted	St.L.	1	1	0	1	0	60	2	0	2.00	....	....	....	....	....	....	....	....		1968-69	1968-69
Pageau, Paul	L.A.	1	1	0	1	0	60	8	0	8.00	....	....	....	....	....	....	....	....		1980-81	1980-81
• Paille, Marcel	NYR	7	107	32	52	22	6342	362	2	3.42	....	....	....	....	....	....	....	....		1957-58	1964-65
Palmateer, Mike	Tor., Wsh.	8	356	149	138	52	20131	1183	17	3.53	29	12	17	....	1765	89	2	3.03		1976-77	1983-84
Pang, Darren	Chi.	3	81	27	35	7	4252	287	0	4.05	6	1	3	....	250	18	0	4.32		1984-85	1988-89
Parent, Bernie	Bos., Phi., Tor.	13	608	271	198	121	35136	1493	54	2.55	71	38	33	....	4302	174	6	2.43	2	1965-66	1978-79
Parent, Bob	Tor.	2	3	0	2	0	160	15	0	5.63	....	....	....	....	....	....	....	....		1981-82	1982-83
‡ Parent, Rich	St.L., T.B., Pit.	4	32	7	11	5	1561	82	1	3.15	....	....	....	....	....	....	....	....		1997-98	2000-01
Parro, Dave	Wsh.	4	77	21	36	10	4015	274	2	4.09	....	....	....	....	....	....	....	....		1980-81	1983-84
§ • Patrick, Lester	NYR	1	....	....	....	....	....	....	....	....	1	1	0	0	46	1	0	1.30	1	1927-28	1927-28
Peeters, Pete	Phi., Bos., Wsh.	13	489	246	155	51	27699	1424	21	3.08	71	35	35	....	4200	232	2	3.31		1978-79	1990-91
Pelletier, Marcel	Chi., NYR	2	8	1	6	0	395	32	0	4.86	....	....	....	....	....	....	....	....		1950-51	1962-63
Penney, Steve	Mtl., Wpg.	5	91	35	38	12	5194	313	1	3.62	27	15	12	....	1604	72	4	2.69		1983-84	1987-88
• Perreault, Bob	Mtl., Det., Bos.	3	31	8	16	7	1827	103	3	3.38	....	....	....	....	....	....	....	....		1955-56	1962-63
Pettie, Jim	Bos.	3	21	9	7	2	1157	71	1	3.68	....	....	....	....	....	....	....	....		1976-77	1978-79
Pietrangelo, Frank	Pit., Hfd.	7	141	46	59	6	7141	490	1	4.12	12	7	5	....	713	34	1	2.86	1	1987-88	1993-94
• Plante, Jacques	Mtl., NYR, St.L., Tor., Bos.	18	837	437	246	145	49533	1964	82	2.38	112	71	36	....	6651	237	14	2.14	6	1952-53	1972-73
Plasse, Michel	St.L., Mtl., K.C., Pit., Col., Que.	11	299	92	136	54	16760	1058	2	3.79	4	1	2	....	195	9	1	2.77	1	1970-71	1981-82
§ • Plaxton, Hugh	Mtl.M.	1	1	0	1	0	57	5	0	5.26	....	....	....	....	....	....	....	....		1932-33	1932-33
Pronovost, Claude	Bos., Mtl.	2	3	1	1	0	120	7	1	3.50	....	....	....	....	....	....	....	....		1955-56	1958-59
Puppa, Daren	Buf., Tor., T.B.	15	429	179	161	54	23819	1204	19	3.03	16	4	9	....	786	51	0	3.89		1985-86	1999-00
Pusey, Chris	Det.	1	1	0	0	0	40	3	0	4.50	....	....	....	....	....	....	....	....		1985-86	1985-86
Racicot, Andre	Mtl.	5	68	26	23	8	3357	196	2	3.50	4	0	1	....	31	4	0	7.74	1	1989-90	1993-94
Racine, Bruce	St.L.	1	11	0	3	0	230	12	0	3.13	1	0	0	....	1	0	0	0.00		1995-96	1995-96
‡ Ram, Jamie	NYR	1	1	0	0	0	27	0	0	0.00	....	....	....	....	....	....	....	....		1995-96	1995-96
Ranford, Bill	Bos., Edm., Wsh., T.B., Det.	15	647	240	279	76	35936	2042	15	3.41	53	28	25	....	3110	159	4	3.07	2	1985-86	1999-00
Raymond, Alain	Wsh.	1	1	0	1	0	40	2	0	3.00	....	....	....	....	....	....	....	....		1987-88	1987-88
• Rayner, Chuck	NYA, Bro., NYR	10	424	138	208	77	25491	1294	25	3.05	18	9	9	....	1135	46	1	2.43		1940-41	1952-53
Reaugh, Daryl	Edm., Hfd.	3	27	8	9	1	1246	72	1	3.47	....	....	....	....	....	....	....	....		1984-85	1990-91
Reddick, Pokey	Wpg., Edm., Fla.	6	132	46	58	16	7162	443	0	3.71	4	0	2	....	168	10	0	3.57	1	1986-87	1993-94
§ • Redding, George	Bos.	1	1	0	0	0	11	1	0	5.45	....	....	....	....	....	....	....	....		1924-25	1924-25
Redquest, Greg	Pit.	1	1	0	0	0	13	3	0	13.85	....	....	....	....	....	....	....	....		1977-78	1977-78
Reece, Dave	Bos.	1	14	7	5	2	777	43	2	3.32	....	....	....	....	....	....	....	....		1975-76	1975-76
Reese, Jeff	Tor., Cgy., Hfd., T.B., N.J.	11	174	53	65	17	8667	529	5	3.66	11	3	5	....	515	35	0	4.08		1987-88	1998-99
Resch, Glenn	NYI, Col., N.J., Phi.	14	571	231	224	82	32279	1761	26	3.27	41	17	17	....	2044	85	2	2.50	1	1973-74	1986-87
• Rheaume, Herb	Mtl.	1	31	10	20	1	1889	92	0	2.92	....	....	....	....	....	....	....	....		1925-26	1925-26
Ricci, Nick	Pit.	4	19	7	12	0	1087	79	0	4.36	....	....	....	....	....	....	....	....		1979-80	1982-83
Richardson, Terry	Det., St.L.	5	20	3	11	0	906	85	0	5.63	....	....	....	....	....	....	....	....		1973-74	1978-79
Richter, Mike	NYR	15	666	301	258	73	38183	1840	24	2.89	76	41	33	....	4514	202	9	2.68	1	1988-89	2002-03
Ridley, Curt	NYR, Van., Tor.	6	104	27	47	16	5498	355	1	3.87	2	0	2	....	120	8	0	4.00		1974-75	1980-81
Riendeau, Vincent	Mtl., St.L., Det., Bos.	8	184	85	65	20	10423	573	5	3.30	25	11	12	....	1277	71	1	3.34		1987-88	1994-95
Riggin, Dennis	Det.	2	18	6	10	2	999	52	1	3.12	....	....	....	....	....	....	....	....		1959-60	1962-63
Riggin, Pat	Atl., Cgy., Wsh., Bos., Pit.	9	350	153	120	52	19872	1135	11	3.43	25	8	13	....	1336	72	0	3.23		1979-80	1987-88
Ring, Bob	Bos.	1	1	0	0	0	33	4	0	7.27	....	....	....	....	....	....	....	....		1965-66	1965-66
Rivard, Fern	Min.	4	55	9	26	11	2865	190	2	3.98	....	....	....	....	....	....	....	....		1968-69	1974-75
• Roach, John Ross	Tor., NYR, Det.	14	492	219	204	68	30444	1246	58	2.46	29	12	14	3	1901	60	7	1.89	1	1921-22	1934-35
• Roberts, Moe	Bos., NYA, Chi.	4	10	3	5	0	501	31	0	3.71	....	....	....	....	....	....	....	....		1925-26	1951-52
• Robertson, Earl	Det., NYA, Bro.	6	190	60	95	34	11820	575	16	2.92	15	7	7	....	995	29	2	1.75	1	1936-37	1941-42
• Rollins, Al	Tor., Chi., NYR	9	430	141	205	83	25723	1192	28	2.78	13	6	7	....	755	30	0	2.38	1	1949-50	1959-60
Romano, Roberto	Pit., Bos.	6	126	46	63	8	7111	471	4	3.97	....	....	....	....	....	....	....	....		1982-83	1993-94
Rosati, Mike	Wsh.	1	1	1	0	0	28	0	0	0.00	....	....	....	....	....	....	....	....		1998-99	1998-99
Roussel, Dominic	Phi., Wpg., Ana., Edm.	8	205	77	70	23	10665	555	7	3.12	1	0	0	....	23	0	0	0.00		1991-92	2000-01
Roy, Patrick	Mtl., Col.	19	1029	551	315	131	60235	2546	66	2.54	247	151	94	0	15209	584	23	2.30	4	1984-85	2002-03
Rupp, Pat	Det.	1	1	0	1	0	60	4	0	4.00	....	....	....	....	....	....	....	....		1963-64	1963-64
Rutherford, Jim	Det., Pit., Tor., L.A.	13	457	151	227	59	25895	1576	14	3.65	8	2	5	....	440	28	0	3.82		1970-71	1982-83
Rutledge, Wayne	L.A.	3	82	28	37	9	4325	241	2	3.34	8	2	4	....	378	20	0	3.17		1967-68	1969-70
St. Croix, Rick	Phi., Tor.	8	130	49	54	18	7295	451	2	3.71	11	4	6	....	562	29	1	3.10		1977-78	1984-85
St. Laurent, Sam	N.J., Det.	5	34	7	12	4	1572	92	1	3.51	1	0	0	....	10	1	0	6.00		1985-86	1989-90
§ • Sands, Charlie	Mtl.	1	1	0	0	0	25	5	0	12.00	....	....	....	....	....	....	....	....		1939-40	1939-40
Sands, Mike	Min.	2	6	0	5	0	302	26	0	5.17	....	....	....	....	....	....	....	....		1984-85	1986-87
Sarjeant, Geoff	St.L., S.J.	2	8	1	2	1	291	20	0	4.12	....	....	....	....	....	....	....	....		1994-95	1995-96
Sauve, Bob	Buf., Det., Chi., N.J.	13	420	182	154	54	23711	1377	8	3.48	34	15	16	....	1850	95	4	3.08		1976-77	1988-89
• Sawchuk, Terry	Det., Bos., Tor., L.A., NYR	21	971	447	330	172	57194	2389	103	2.51	106	54	48	....	6290	266	12	2.54	4	1949-50	1969-70
• Schaefer, Joe	NYR	2	2	0	2	0	86	8	0	5.58	....	....	....	....	....	....	....	....		1959-60	1960-61
Schafer, Paxton	Bos.	1	3	0	0	0	77	6	0	4.68	....	....	....	....	....	....	....	....		1996-97	1996-97
Scott, Ron	NYR, L.A.	5	28	8	13	4	1450	91	0	3.77	1	0	0	....	32	4	0	7.50		1983-84	1989-90
Sevigny, Richard	Mtl., Que.	9	176	80	54	20	9485	507	5	3.21	4	0	3	....	208	13	0	3.75	1	1978-79	1986-87
Sharples, Scott	Cgy.	1	1	0	0	1	65	4	0	3.69	....	....	....	....	....	....	....	....		1991-92	1991-92
§ • Shields, Al	NYA	1	2	0	0	0	41	9	0	13.17	....	....	....	....	....	....	....	....		1931-32	1931-32
Shtalenkov, Mikhail	Ana., Edm., Phx., Fla.	7	190	62	82	19	9966	480	8	2.89	4	0	3	....	211	10	0	2.84		1993-94	1999-00
‡ Shulmistra, Richard	N.J., Fla.	2	2	1	1	0	122	3	0	1.48	....	....	....	....	....	....	....	....		1997-98	1999-00
Sidorkiewicz, Peter	Hfd., Ott., N.J.	8	246	79	128	27	13884	832	8	3.60	15	5	10	....	912	55	0	3.62		1987-88	1997-98
Simmons, Don	Bos., Tor., NYR	11	249	101	101	41	14555	701	20	2.89	24	13	11	....	1436	62	3	2.59	3	1956-57	1968-69
Simmons, Gary	Cal., Cle., L.A.	4	107	30	57	15	6162	366	5	3.56	1	0	0	....	20	1	0	3.00		1974-75	1977-78
Skidmore, Paul	St.L.	1	2	1	1	0	120	6	0	3.00	....	....	....	....	....	....	....	....		1981-82	1981-82
Skorodenski, Warren	Chi., Edm.	5	35	12	11	4	1732	100	2	3.46	2	0	0	....	33	6	0	10.91		1981-82	1987-88
• Smith, Al	Tor., Pit., Det., Buf., Hfd., Col.	10	233	74	99	36	12752	735	10	3.46	6	1	4	....	317	21	0	3.97		1965-66	1980-81
Smith, Billy	L.A., NYI	18	680	305	233	105	38431	2031	22	3.17	132	88	36	....	7645	348	5	2.73	4	1971-72	1988-89
Smith, Gary	Tor., Oak., Cal., Chi., Van., Min., Wsh., Wpg.	14	532	173	261	74	29619	1675	26	3.39	20	5	13	....	1153	62	1	3.23		1965-66	1979-80
• Smith, Normie	Mtl.M., Det.	8	199	81	83	35	12357	479	17	2.33	12	9	2	0	820	18	3	1.32	2	1931-32	1944-45
Sneddon, Bob	Cal.	1	5	0	2	0	225	21	0	5.60	....	....	....	....	....	....	....	....		1970-71	1970-71
Soderstrom, Tommy	Phi., NYI	5	156	45	69	19	8189	496	10	3.63	....	....	....	....	....	....	....	....		1992-93	1996-97
Soetaert, Doug	NYR, Wpg., Mtl.	12	284	110	104	42	15583	1030	6	3.97	5	1	2	....	180	14	0	4.67	1	1975-76	1986-87
Soucy, Christian	Chi.	1	1	0	0	0	3	0	0	0.00	....	....	....	....	....	....	....	....		1993-94	1993-94
• Spooner, Red	Pit.	1	1	0	1	0	60	6	0	6.00	....	....	....	....	....	....	....	....		1929-30	1929-30
§ • Spring, Jesse	Ham.	1	1	0	0	0	2	0	0	0.00	....	....	....	....	....	....	....	....		1924-25	1924-25
Staniowski, Ed	St.L., Wpg., Hfd.	10	219	67	104	21	12075	818	2	4.06	8	1	6	....	428	28	0	3.93		1975-76	1984-85
§ • Starr, Harold	Mtl.M.	1	1	0	0	0	3	0	0	0.00	....	....	....	....	....	....	....	....		1931-32	1931-32
Stauber, Robb	L.A., Buf.	4	62	21	23	9	3295	209	1	3.81	4	3	1	....	240	16	0	4.00		1989-90	1994-95
Stefan, Greg	Det.	9	299	115	127	30	16333	1068	5	3.92	30	12	17	....	1681	99	1	3.53		1981-82	1989-90
Stein, Phil	Tor.	1	1	0	0	1	70	2	0	1.71	....	....	....	....	....	....	....	....		1939-40	1939-40
Stephenson, Wayne	St.L., Phi., Wsh.	10	328	146	103	49	18343	937	14	3.06	26	11	12	....	1522	79	2	3.11	1	1971-72	1980-81
Stevenson, Doug	NYR, Chi.	3	8	2	6	0	480	39	0	4.88	....	....	....	....	....	....	....	....		1944-45	1945-46
Stewart, Charles	Bos.	3	77	30	41	5	4742	194	10	2.45	....	....	....	....	....	....	....	....		1924-25	1926-27
Stewart, Jim	Bos.	1	1	0	1	0	20	5	0	15.00	....	....	....	....	....	....	....	....		1979-80	1979-80
• Stuart, Herb	Det.	1	3	1	2	0	180	5	0	1.67	....	....	....	....	....	....	....	....		1926-27	1926-27
Sylvestri, Don	Bos.	1	3	0	0	2	102	6	0	3.53	....	....	....	....	....	....	....	....		1984-85	1984-85
Tabaracci, Rick	Pit., Wpg., Wsh., Cgy., T.B., Atl., Col.	11	286	93	125	30	15255	760	15	2.99	17	4	12	....	1025	53	0	3.10		1988-89	1999-00

Name	NHL Teams	NHL Seasons	GP	W	L	T	Mins	GA	SO	Avg	GP	W	L	T	Mins	GA	SO	Avg	NHL Cup Wins	First NHL Season	Last NHL Season
							Regular Schedule								Playoffs						
Takko, Kari	Min., Edm.	6	142	37	71	14	7317	475	1	3.90	4	0	1	....	109	7	0	3.85		1985-86	1990-91
‡ Tallas, Robbie	Bos., Chi.	6	99	28	42	10	5069	246	3	2.91	....	....	....	....	....	....	....	....		1995-96	2000-01
Tanner, John	Que.	3	21	2	11	5	1084	65	1	3.60	....	....	....	....	....	....	....	....		1989-90	1991-92
Tataryn, Dave	NYR	1	2	1	1	0	80	10	0	7.50	....	....	....	....	....	....	....	....		1976-77	1976-77
Taylor, Bobby	Phi., Pit.	5	46	15	17	6	2268	155	0	4.10	....	....	....	....	....	....	....	....	1	1971-72	1975-76
● Teno, Harvey	Det.	1	5	2	3	0	300	15	0	3.00	....	....	....	....	....	....	....	....		1938-39	1938-39
Terreri, Chris	N.J., S.J., Chi., NYI	14	406	151	172	43	22369	1143	9	3.07	29	12	12	....	1523	86	0	3.39	2	1986-87	2000-01
Thomas, Wayne	Mtl., Tor., NYR	9	243	103	93	34	13768	766	10	3.34	15	6	8	....	849	50	1	3.53		1972-73	1980-81
● Thompson, Tiny	Bos., Det.	12	553	284	194	75	34175	1183	81	2.08	44	20	24	0	2974	93	7	1.88	1	1928-29	1939-40
§ Toppazzini, Jerry	Bos.	1	1	0	0	0	1	0	0	0.00	....	....	....	....	....	....	....	....		1960-61	1960-61
Torchia, Mike	Dal.	1	6	3	2	1	327	18	0	3.30	....	....	....	....	....	....	....	....		1994-95	1994-95
‡ Trefilov, Andrei	Cgy., Buf., Chi.	7	54	12	25	4	2663	153	2	3.45	1	0	0	....	5	0	0	0.00		1992-93	1998-99
Tremblay, Vincent	Tor., Pit.	5	58	12	26	8	2785	223	1	4.80	....	....	....	....	....	....	....	....		1979-80	1983-84
Tucker, Ted	Cal.	1	5	1	1	1	177	10	0	3.39	....	....	....	....	....	....	....	....		1973-74	1973-74
● Turner, Joe	Det.	1	1	0	0	1	70	3	0	2.57	....	....	....	....	....	....	....	....		1941-42	1941-42
Vachon, Rogie	Mtl., L.A., Det., Bos.	16	795	355	291	127	46298	2310	51	2.99	48	23	23	....	2876	133	2	2.77	3	1966-67	1981-82
Vanbiesbrouck, John	NYR, Fla., Phi., NYI, N.J.	20	882	374	346	119	50475	2503	40	2.98	71	28	38	....	3969	177	5	2.68		1981-82	2001-02
Veisor, Mike	Chi., Hfd., Wpg.	10	139	41	62	26	7806	532	5	4.09	4	0	2	....	180	15	0	5.00		1973-74	1983-84
Vernon, Mike	Cgy., Det., S.J., Fla.	19	781	385	273	92	44449	2206	27	2.98	138	77	56	....	8214	367	6	2.68	2	1982-83	2001-02
● Vezina, Georges	Mtl.	9	190	103	81	5	11592	633	13	3.28	13	10	3	0	780	35	2	2.69	1	1917-18	1925-26
Villemure, Gilles	NYR, Chi.	10	205	100	64	29	11581	542	13	2.81	14	5	5	....	656	32	0	2.93		1963-64	1976-77
‡ Waite, Jimmy	Chi., S.J., Phx.	11	106	28	41	12	5253	293	4	3.35	6	0	3	....	211	14	0	3.98		1988-89	1998-99
Wakaluk, Darcy	Buf., Min., Dal., Phx.	8	191	67	75	21	9756	524	9	3.22	8	4	2	....	364	18	0	2.97		1988-89	1996-97
Wakely, Ernie	Mtl., St.L.	5	113	41	42	17	6244	290	8	2.79	10	2	6	....	509	37	1	4.36		1962-63	1971-72
● Walsh, Flat	Mtl.M., NYA	7	108	48	43	16	6641	256	12	2.31	8	2	4	2	570	16	2	1.68		1926-27	1932-33
Wamsley, Rick	Mtl., St.L., Cgy., Tor.	13	407	204	131	46	23123	1287	12	3.34	27	7	18	....	1397	81	0	3.48	1	1980-81	1992-93
Watt, Jim	St.L.	1	1	0	0	0	20	2	0	6.00	....	....	....	....	....	....	....	....		1973-74	1973-74
Weeks, Steve	NYR, Hfd., Van., NYI, L.A., Ott.	18	290	111	119	33	15879	989	5	3.74	12	3	5	....	486	27	0	3.33		1980-81	1992-93
Wetzel, Carl	Det., Min.	2	7	1	3	1	301	22	0	4.39	....	....	....	....	....	....	....	....		1964-65	1967-68
Whitmore, Kay	Hfd., Van., Bos., Cgy.	9	155	60	64	16	8596	508	4	3.55	4	0	2	....	174	13	0	4.48		1988-89	2001-02
Wilkinson, Derek	T.B.	4	22	3	12	3	933	57	0	3.67	....	....	....	....	....	....	....	....		1995-96	1998-99
Willis, Jordan	Dal.	1	1	0	1	0	19	1	0	3.16	....	....	....	....	....	....	....	....		1995-96	1995-96
Wilson, Dunc	Phi., Van., Tor., NYR, Pit.	10	287	80	150	33	15851	988	8	3.74	....	....	....	....	....	....	....	....		1969-70	1978-79
● Wilson, Lefty	Det., Tor., Bos.	3	3	0	0	1	81	1	0	0.74	....	....	....	....	....	....	....	....		1953-54	1957-58
● Winkler, Hal	NYR, Bos.	2	75	35	26	14	6601	175	21	1.60	10	2	3	5	640	18	2	1.69		1926-27	1927-28
Wolfe, Bernie	Wsh.	4	120	20	61	21	6104	424	1	4.17	....	....	....	....	....	....	....	....		1975-76	1978-79
Wood, Alex	NYA	1	1	0	1	0	70	3	0	2.57	....	....	....	....	....	....	....	....		1936-37	1936-37
Worsley, Gump	NYR, Mtl., Min.	21	861	335	352	150	50183	2407	43	2.88	70	40	26	....	4084	189	5	2.78	4	1952-53	1973-74
● Worters, Roy	Pit., NYA, Mtl.	12	484	171	229	83	30175	1143	67	2.27	11	3	6	2	690	24	3	2.09		1925-26	1936-37
Worthy, Chris	Oak., Cal.	3	26	5	10	4	1326	98	0	4.43	....	....	....	....	....	....	....	....		1968-69	1970-71
Wregget, Ken	Tor., Phi., Pit., Cgy., Det.	17	575	225	248	53	31663	1917	9	3.63	56	28	25	....	3341	160	3	2.87	1	1983-84	1999-00
‡ Yeremeyev, Vitali	NYR	1	4	0	4	0	212	16	0	4.53	....	....	....	....	....	....	....	....		2000-01	2000-01
§ Young, Doug	Det.	1	1	0	0	0	21	1	0	2.86	....	....	....	....	....	....	....	....		1933-34	1933-34
Young, Wendell	Van., Phi., Pit., T.B.	10	187	59	86	12	9410	618	2	3.94	2	0	1	....	99	6	0	3.64	2	1985-86	1994-95
Zanier, Mike	Edm.	1	3	1	1	1	185	12	0	3.89	....	....	....	....	....	....	....	....		1984-85	1984-85

Tom Barrasso

Roger Crozier

Michel Larocque

Patrick Roy

Craig Billington

Kevin Hodson

Mike Richter

Tiny Thompson

List of NHL Free Agents

The following players became free agents on July 1, 2004:

GROUP II FREE AGENTS

SUBJECT TO COMPENSATION AND RIGHT TO MATCH

The players listed below have been tendered a qualifying offer by their respective clubs and are subject to draft-choice compensation and right to match.

Anaheim
Ilja Bryzgalov, Kurtis Foster, Michael Holmqvist, Tony Martensson, Rob Niedermayer, Ruslan Salei, Vitaly Vishnevski

Atlanta
Kip Brennan, Garnet Exelby, Dany Heatley, Tomas Kloucek, Ilya Kovalchuk, Francis Lessard, Derek MacKenzie, Brian Maloney, Ronald Petrovicky, Kyle Rossiter, Tommi Santala, Marc Savard, Luke Sellars, Patrik Stefan

Boston
Hal Gill, Jonathan Girard, Sergei Gonchar, Andy Hilbert, Ivan Huml, Zdenek Kutlak, Andrew Raycroft, Sergei Samsonov, Joe Thornton

Buffalo
Maxim Afinogenov, Milan Bartovic, Martin Biron, Daniel Briere, Brad Brown, Brian Campbell, Tim Connolly, Jean-Pierre Dumont, Rory Fitzpatrick, Mike Grier, Jochen Hecht, Doug Janik, Jeff Jillson, Dmitri Kalinin, Ryan Miller, Norm Milley, Mika Noronen, Andrew Peters, Taylor Pyatt, Henrik Tallinder

Calgary
Mike Commodore, Denis Gauthier, Jarome Iginla, Miikka Kiprusoff, Jordan Leopold, Lynn Loyns, Marcus Nilson

Carolina
Kevyn Adams, Jesse Boulerice, Pavel Brendl, Erik Cole, Martin Gerber, Jeff O'Neill, Allan Rourke, Bruno St. Jacques, Josef Vasicek, Radim Vrbata, Niclas Wallin, Justin Williams, Rob Zepp, Mike Zigomanis

Chicago
Craig Anderson, Mark Bell, Bryan Berard, Kyle Calder, Eric Daze, Michael Leighton, Steve McCarthy, Stephane Robidas, Jocelyn Thibault, Jim Vandermeer

Colorado
David Aebischer, Peter Forsberg, Riku Hahl, Milan Hejduk, Dan Hinote, Tom Lawson, Karlis Skrastins, Alex Tanguay, Peter Worrell

Columbus
Marc Denis, Alexander Guskov, Andrej Nedorost, Mike Pandolfo, Martin Paroulek, Jaroslav Spacek, David Vyborny, Derrick Walser

Dallas
John Erskine, Dan Jancevski, Mike Siklenka, Jaroslav Svoboda, Mathias Tjarnqvist

Detroit
Mathieu Dandenault, Pavel Datsyuk, Jiri Fischer, Jason Williams

Edmonton
Kristian Antila, Marc-Andre Bergeron, Mike Bishai, Eric Brewer, Ty Conklin, Nate DiCasmirro, Radek Dvorak, J.J. Hunter, Brad Isbister, Mikko Luoma, Sean McAslan, Mike Morrison, Tyler Moss, Jani Rita, Alexei Semenov, Jason Smith

Florida
Eric Beaudoin, Christian Berglund, Niklas Hagman, Darcy Hordichuk, Ryan Jardine, Olli Jokinen, Juraj Kolnik, Vaclav Nedorost, Denis Shvidki, Mike Van Ryn

Los Angeles
Sean Avery, Eric Belanger, Noah Clarke, Joe Corvo, Jeff Cowan, Ryan Flinn, Steve Kelly, Bryan Muir, Joe Rullier, Lubomir Visnovsky, Tomas Zizka

Minnesota
Christoph Brandner, Andrew Brunette, Dan Cavanaugh, Mark Cullen, Manny Fernandez, Mika Hannula, Alex Henry, Jeff Hoggan, Willie Mitchell, Richard Park, Nick Schultz, Stephane Veilleux, Rickard Wallin, Kyle Wanvig

Montreal
Steve Begin, Radek Bonk, Ron Hainsey, Marcel Hossa, Cristobal Huet, Mike Ribeiro, Michael Ryder, Sheldon Souray, Marc-Andre Thinel, Rene Vydareny, Richard Zednik

Nashville
Mark Eaton, Martin Erat, Vernon Fiddler, Simon Gamache, Adam Hall, Scott Hartnell, Darren Haydar, Shane Hnidy, Andrew Hutchinson, Vladimir Orszagh, Konstantin Panov, Kirill Safronov, Wyatt Smith, Steve Sullivan, Tomas Vokoun, Marek Zidlicky

New Jersey
Ari Ahonen, Jeff Friesen, Scott Gomez, Viktor Kozlov, Scott Niedermayer, Jay Pandolfo, Brian Rafalski

NY Islanders
Adrian Aucoin, Jason Blake, Martin Chabada, Rick DiPietro, Jeff Hamilton, Roman Hamrlik, Trent Hunter, Oleg Kvasha, Justin Mapletoft, Janne Niinimaa, Justin Papineau, Mark Parrish, Tomi Pettinen, Dave Scatchard, Mattias Weinhandl

NY Rangers
Mike Green, Martin Grenier, Matthew Kinch, Lucas Lawson, Jamie Lundmark, Dale Purinton, Karel Rachunek, Layne Ulmer, Chad Wiseman

Ottawa
Zdeno Chara, Martin Havlat, Chris Kelly, Chris Phillips, Brian Pothier, Martin Prusek, Peter Schaefer, Vaclav Varada, Julien Vauclair

Philadelphia
Nick Deschenes, Simon Gagne, Michal Handzus, Kim Johnsson, Antero Niittymaki, Branko Radivojevic, Mattias Timander

Phoenix
Brian Boucher, Jason Chimera, Mike Comrie, Jason Jaspers, Mike Johnson, Daymond Langkow, Derek Morris, Ladislav Nagy, Mike Stutzel, Erik Westrum

Pittsburgh
Ramzi Abid, Kris Beech, Matt Bradley, Shane Endicott, Rico Fata, Matt Hussey, Ric Jackman, David Koci, Milan Kraft, Guillaume Lefebvre, Ross Lupaschuk, Aleksey Morozov, Matt Murley, Brooks Orpik, Lasse Pirjeta, Darcy Robinson, Michal Sivek, Tomas Surovy

St. Louis
Christian Backman, Petr Cajanek, Barret Jackman, Patrick Lalime, Jamal Mayers, Chris Pronger, Curtis Sanford, Igor Valeev

San Jose
Matt Carkner, Rob Davison, Nicholas Dimitrakos, Nisse Ekman, Jim Fahey, Scott Hannan, Evgeni Nabokov, Scott Parker, Wayne Primeau, Pat Rissmiller, Mark Smith, Vesa Toskala, Miroslav Zalesak

Tampa Bay
Dimitri Afanasenkov, Nikita Alexeev, Martin Cibak, Chris Dingman, Brian Eklund, Ruslan Fedotenko, Timo Helbling, Pavel Kubina, Fredrik Modin, Jimmie Olvestad, Nolan Pratt, Cory Sarich, Eero Somervuori, Martin St. Louis, Cory Stillman, Shane Willis

Toronto
Nik Antropov, Luca Cereda, Harold Druken, Tomas Kaberle, Brad Leeb, Bryan McCabe, Alexei Ponikarovsky, Mikael Tellqvist, Clarke Wilm

Vancouver
Bryan Allen, Alex Auld, Artem Chubarov, Dan Cloutier, Fedor Fedorov, Mikko Jokela, Brendan Morrison, Justin Morrison, Brandon Reid, Daniel Sedin, Henrik Sedin

Washington
Jeff Halpern, Graham Mink, Maxime Ouellet, Stephen Peat, Matt Pettinger, Rastislav Stana, Brendan Witt, Dainius Zubrus

GROUP III FREE AGENTS

UNRESTRICTED

The following players qualified for Group III Free Agency (age 31 or older with at least four years of NHL experience) and are unrestricted Free Agents.

Anaheim
Dan Bylsma

Atlanta
Byron Dafoe, Bill Lindsay, Chris Tamer

Boston
Ted Donato, Travis Green, Mike Knuble, Dan McGillis, Ian Moran, Glen Murray, Michael Nylander, Sean O'Donnell, Felix Potvin, Brian Rolston, Jiri Slegr, Rob Zamuner

Buffalo
James Patrick, Alexei Zhitnik

Calgary
Craig Conroy, Dave Lowry, Dean McAmmond, Krzysztof Oliwa, Chris Simon, Brad Werenka

Carolina
Sean Hill, Glen Wesley

Chicago
Theoren Fleury, Igor Korolev, Steve Passmore, Steve Poapst, Ryan Vandenbussche

Colorado
Matthew Barnaby, Jim Cummins, Andrei Nikolishin, Tommy Salo, Teemu Selanne

Columbus
Fred Brathwaite, Brian Holzinger

Dallas
Shayne Corson, Richard Matvichuk, Teppo Numminen, David Oliver, Chris Therien, Ron Tugnutt, Scott Young

Detroit
Chris Chelios, Kris Draper, Dominik Hasek, Brett Hull, Derek King, Kevin Miller, Michel Picard, Mathieu Schneider, Brendan Shanahan, Steve Thomas, Steve Yzerman

Edmonton
Petr Nedved, Adam Oates

Florida
Donald Audette, Paul Laus, Lyle Odelein, Steve Shields

Los Angeles
Milan Hnilicka, Jaroslav Modry, Zigmund Palffy, Stephane Quintal, Luc Robitaille, Jozef Stumpel

Minnesota
None

Montreal
Andreas Dackell, Jim Dowd, Joe Juneau, Alex Kovalev, Darren Langdon, Yanic Perreault

Nashville
Brad Bombardir, Wade Flaherty, Tony Hrkac, Andreas Johansson, Rem Murray, Jason York, Sergei Zholtok

New Jersey
Tommy Albelin, Igor Larionov, John Madden, Grant Marshall, Corey Schwab, Turner Stevenson

NY Islanders
Mariusz Czerkawski, Alexander Karpovtsev, Cliff Ronning, Garth Snow

NY Rangers
Pavel Bure, Eric Lindros, Sandy McCarthy, Jamie McLennan, Mark Messier, Boris Mironov, Jamie Pushor

Ottawa
Peter Bondra, Jody Hull, Curtis Leschyshyn, Rob Ray, Todd Simpson, Shaun Van Allen

Philadelphia
Vladimir Malakhov, Mark Recchi, Alexei Zhamnov

Phoenix
None

Pittsburgh
Kelly Buchberger, Mario Lemieux, Reid Simpson

St. Louis
Murray Baron, Jeff Finley, Alexander Khavanov, Al MacInnis, Steve Martins, Scott Mellanby, Chris Osgood, Scott Pellerin, Pascal Rheaume, Mike Sillinger, Eric Weinrich

San Jose
Vincent Damphousse, Jason Marshall, Mike Ricci

Tampa Bay
Dave Andreychuk, Jassen Cullimore, Darren Rumble

Toronto
Drake Berehowsky, Tom Fitzgerald, Ron Francis, Calle Johansson, Trevor Kidd, Bryan Marchment, Robert Reichel, Mikael Renberg

Vancouver
Magnus Arvedson, Marc Bergevin, Mike Keane, Sean Pronger, Martin Rucinsky

Washington
Craig Johnson, Kip Miller

POTENTIAL GROUP V FREE AGENTS

The following players: (i) have completed 10 pro seasons or more (NHL or Minors, excluding Junior hockey), and (ii) in the 2003-2004 season earned less than the League average salary and (iii) received a timely qualifying offer

These players have the right to elect once in their careers to become unrestricted Free Agents. Should a player not elect to become an unrestricted Free Agent, since his prior club has tendered him a qualifying offer he would remain subject to draft choice compensation and right to match as applies to Group II Free Agents. The players listed below elected Group V status.

Colorado
Paul Kariya

Los Angeles
Ian Laperriere

New Jersey
Sergei Brylin

GROUP VI FREE AGENTS
UNRESTRICTED FREE AGENTS

The following players qualify for unrestricted free agency, having met the requirements for Group VI free agency. These players, whose contracts have expired, are age 25 or older, have completed three or more professional seasons, and (i) in the case of a player other than a goaltender have played fewer than 80 NHL games (regular-season and playoff), or (ii) in the case of a goaltender have played fewer than 28 NHL games (regular-season and playoff).

Anaheim
Chris Armstrong, Garrett Burnett, Casey Hankinson, Mike Mottau, Nick Smith

Atlanta
Frederic Cassivi, Joe DiPenta, Eric Healey, Brian Swanson, Mike Weaver

Boston
Rich Brennan, Ed Campbell, Carl Corazzini, Doug Doull, Matt Herr, Tim Thomas, Darren Van Oene

Buffalo
Brian Chapman, David Cullen, Rick Mrozik

Calgary
Matt Davidson, Robert Dome, Martin Sonnenberg, Jesse Wallin

Carolina
Brad Defauw, Randy Petruk, Joey Tetarenko

Chicago
Johnathan Aitken, Burke Henry, Brett McLean, Jason Morgan

Colorado
Travis Brigley, Steve Moore, D.J. Smith

Columbus
Mark Hartigan, Don MacLean

Dallas
Bubba Berenzweig, Marc Kristoffersson, Jeff MacMillan, Gavin Morgan, Mark Wotton

Detroit
Marc Lamothe, Anders Myrvold

Edmonton
Bobby Allen, Chad Hinz, Jan Horacek

Florida
Lee Goren, Kent Huskins

Los Angeles
Pavel Rosa, Richard Seeley, Jerred Smithson, John Tripp

Minnesota
Travis Roche

Montreal
Benoit Gratton

Nashville
Mathieu Darche, Mike Farrell, Jan Lasak, Curtis Murphy, Robert Schnabel, Ray Schultz

New Jersey
Maxim Balmochnykh, Scott Clemmensen, Greg Crozier, Raymond Giroux, Joe Hulbig, Steve Kariya, Mike Matteucci, Ryan Murphy

NY Islanders
Derek Bekar, Alan Letang, Eric Manlow, Brandon Smith

NY Rangers
Bobby Andrews, Cory Larose, Jeff Paul

Ottawa
Serge Payer, Peter Smrek, Brad Tapper

Philadelphia
Steve Gainey, Kirby Law, Ian MacNeil, Mark Murphy, Mike Peluso, Andre Savage, Pete Vandermeer

Phoenix
Chris Ferraro

Pittsburgh
Patrick Boileau, Martin Brochu, Tom Kostopoulos, Eric Meloche, Alain Nasreddine

St. Louis
Marc Brown, Steve McLaren, Ryan Ready, Cody Rudkowsky

San Jose
Jesse Fibiger, Tavis Hansen

Tampa Bay
Dwayne Hay

Toronto
Josh Holden, Mike Minard

Vancouver
Nolan Baumgartner, Pat Kavanagh, Jaroslav Obsut, Sergei Varlamov

Washington
Mel Angelstad, Josef Boumedienne, Sebastien Charpentier, Jean-Francois Fortin, Chris Hajt, Francois Methot, Andrei Podkonicky, Todd Rohloff, Darcy Verot

UNRESTRICTED FREE AGENTS

The following players were not tendered a qualifying offer and are therefore unrestricted Free Agents not subject to a right to match or draft choice compensation

Anaheim
Keith Aucoin, Brian Gornick, Jason Krog, Petr Schastlivy, Cam Severson

Atlanta
Zdenek Blatny, Daniel Corso, Shawn Heins, Frantisek Kaberle, David Kaczowka, Randy Robitaille, Yannick Tremblay

Boston
Andy Delmore, Mike Gellard, Michal Grosek, Patrick Leahy, Craig MacDonald, Peter Metcalf, Chris Paradise

Buffalo
Jason Botterill, Karel Mosovsky, Domenic Pittis, Scott Ricci

Calgary
Garett Bembridge, Petr Buzek, Dany Sabourin

Carolina
Craig Adams, Patrick Desrochers, Tomas Kurka, Brett Lysak, Peter Reynolds, Jamie Storr, Damian Surma, Kevin Weekes

Chicago
Deron Quint, Jason Strudwick, Yorick Treille, Matt Underhill

Colorado
Chris Gratton, Mikhail Kuleshov

Columbus
Brendan Buckley, Anders Eriksson, David Ling, Tyler Sloan

Dallas
Jeff Bateman, Valeri Bure, Justin Cox, Aaron Downey, Brett Draney, Barrett Heisten, Lubomir Sekeras, Michael Sgroi, Jarrod Skalde, Blake Sloan, Rob Valicevic

Detroit
Ryan Barnes, Boyd Devereaux, Jamie Rivers

Edmonton
Scott Ferguson, Michael Henrich

Florida
Matt Cullen, Paul Elliott, Paul Healey, Kristian Kudroc, Simon Lajeunesse, Andreas Lilja, Eric Messier, David Morisset, Sean O'Connor, Byron Ritchie, Mikael Samuelsson, Pavel Trnka

Los Angeles
Jason Allison, Anson Carter, Brad Chartrand, Mathieu Chouinard, Adam Deadmarsh, Maxim Kuznetsov

Minnesota
Frederic Cloutier, Antti Laaksonen, Bill Muckalt, Michael Schutte, Jason Wiemer

Montreal
Jean-Francois Damphousse, Gordie Dwyer, Eric Fichaud, Jerome Marois, Niklas Sundstrom, Patrick Traverse

Nashville
Jamie Allison, Greg Classen, Jeremy Stevenson

New Jersey
Craig Darby, Chris Hartsburg

NY Islanders
Eric Cairns, Cail MacLean, Steve Webb

NY Rangers
Joel Bouchard, Benoit Dusablon, Josh Green, Jeff Heerema, Jan Hlavac, John Jakopin, Dan Lacouture, Chris McAllister

Ottawa
Andrew Allen

Philadelphia
None

Phoenix
Goran Bezina, Zac Bierk, Chris Dyment, Peter Ferraro, Bryan Helmer, Tom Koivisto, Ivan Novoseltsev, Todd Reirden, Gary Shuchuk, Mike Wilson

Pittsburgh
Jean-Sebastien Aubin, Dan Focht, Pauli Levokari, Steve McKenna, Toby Petersen, Jonathan Sim, Landon Wilson

St. Louis
Mike Danton, Pavol Demitra, Christian Laflamme

San Jose
Curtis Brown, Todd Harvey, Seamus Kotyk, Willie Levesque, Yuri Moscevsky, Robert Mulick

Tampa Bay
Ben Clymer, Sheldon Keefe, Evgeny Konstantinov, Stan Neckar, Pascal Trepanier, Jeremy Van Hoof

Toronto
Sebastien Centomo, Christian Chartier, Aaron Gavey, Jamie Hodson

Vancouver
Sylvain Blouin, Dallas Eakins, Johan Hedberg, Mats Lindgren, Chris Nielsen

Washington
Bates Battaglia, Rick Berry, Ivan Ciernik, Colin Forbes, Jean-Luc Grand-Pierre, John Gruden, Joel Kwiatkowski, Brad Norton, Roman Tvrdon, Trent Whitfield, Matthew Yeats

2003-04 NHL Trade Register

(listed in chronological order)

September 2003

10 – Florida traded C **Serge Payer** to Ottawa for Ottawa's 9th-round choice (D **Luke Beaverson**) in the 2004 Entry Draft.

15 – Atlanta traded G **Milan Hnilicka** to Los Angeles for future considerations.

October 2003

3 – Carolina traded G **Jani Hurme** to Atlanta for Atlanta's 4th-round choice (D **Brett Carson**) in the 2004 Entry Draft.

3 – Columbus traded C **Travis Green** to Boston for Boston's 6th-round choice (C **Lennart Petrell**) in the 2004 Entry Draft.

5 – Boston traded G **Steve Shields** to Florida for future considerations.

5 – Washington traded LW **Denis Hamel** to Ottawa for future considerations.

23 – Washington traded LW **Steve Konowalchuk** and its 3rd-round choice (later traded to Carolina – Carolina selected D **Casey Borer**) in the 2004 Entry Draft to Colorado for LW **Bates Battaglia** and RW **Jonas Johansson**.

27 – Tampa Bay traded LW **Erkki Rajamaki** to St. Louis for St. Louis' 8th-round choice (LW **Justin Keller**) in the 2004 Entry Draft.

30 – Columbus traded C **Sean Pronger** to Vancouver for LW **Zenith Komarniski**.

November 2003

16 – San Jose traded G **Miikka Kiprusoff** to Calgary for a conditional choice in the 2005 Entry Draft.

17 – Dallas traded D **Stephane Robidas** and its 2nd-round choice (C **Jakub Sindel**) in the 2004 Entry Draft to Chicago for D **Jon Klemm** and NY Rangers' 4th-round choice (previously acquired – Dallas selected LW **Fredrik Naslund**) in the 2004 Entry Draft.

30 – Pittsburgh traded C **Martin Straka** to Los Angeles for D **Martin Strbak** and LW **Sergei Anshakov**.

December 2003

2 – Atlanta traded C **Simon Gamache** and D **Kirill Safranov** to Nashville for LW **Ben Simon** and D **Tomas Kloucek**.

9 – Minnesota traded D **Chris Dyment** to Phoenix for D **Michael Schutte**.

16 – Edmonton traded C **Mike Comrie** to Philadelphia for D **Jeff Woywitka**, Philadelphia's 1st-round choice (C **Rob Schremp**) in the 2004 Entry Draft and 3rd-round choice in the 2005 Entry Draft.

17 – Nashville traded D **Wade Brookbank** to Vancouver for future considerations.

17 – Philadelphia traded RW **Eric Chouinard** to Minnesota for Minnesota's 5th-round choice (D **Chris Zarb**) in the 2004 Entry Draft.

29 – Ottawa traded D **Wade Brookbank** to Florida for future considerations.

30 – Florida traded RW **Ivan Novoseltsev** to Phoenix for future considerations.

31 – Columbus traded D **Jean-Luc Grand-Pierre** to Atlanta for future considerations.

January 2004

6 – Atlanta traded RW **Brad Tapper** to Ottawa for C **Daniel Corso**.

9 – San Jose traded LW **Lynn Loyns** to Calgary for a conditional 5th-round choice (later traded to Florida – Florida selected D **Bret Nasby**) in the 2004 Entry Draft.

17 – Anaheim traded D **Todd Reirden** to Phoenix for future considerations.

17 – Vancouver traded D **Jiri Slegr** to Boston for future considerations.

20 – Philadelphia traded RW **Justin Williams** to Carolina for D **Danny Markov**.

22 – NY Islanders traded D **Mattias Timander** to Philadelphia for Tampa Bay's 7th-round choice (previously acquired – NY Islanders selected D **Chris Campoli**) in the 2004 Entry Draft.

23 – Columbus traded D **Jamie Pushor** to NY Rangers for NY Rangers' 8th-round choice (RW **Matt Greer**) in the 2004 Entry Draft.

23 – Ottawa traded RW **Dennis Bonvie** to Colorado for C/RW **Charlie Stephens**.

23 – Washington traded RW **Jaromir Jagr** to NY Rangers for RW **Anson Carter**.

27 – Columbus traded D **Darryl Sydor** and its 4th-round choice (D **Mike Lundin**) in the 2004 Entry Draft to Tampa Bay for C **Alexander Svitov** and Tampa Bay's 3rd-round choice (later traded to Calgary – Calgary selected C **Dustin Boyd**) in the 2004 Entry Draft.

February 2004

4 – Ottawa traded LW **Petr Schastlivy** to Anaheim for D **Todd Simpson**.

9 – Philadelphia traded D **Eric Weinrich** to St. Louis for St. Louis' 5th-round choice (RW **Gino Pisellini**) in the 2004 Entry Draft.

9 – Philadelphia traded C **Mike Comrie** to Phoenix for G **Sean Burke**, RW **Branko Radivojevic** and LW **Ben Eager**.

10 – Columbus traded D **Pauli Levokari** to Pittsburgh for D **Brendan Buckley**.

11 – Toronto traded D **Ric Jackman** to Pittsburgh for D **Drake Berehowsky**.

16 – Dallas traded LW **Steve Gainey** to Philadelphia for RW **Mike Siklenka**.

16 – Chicago traded LW **Steve Sullivan** to Nashville for Nashville's 2nd-round choices in the 2004 (C **Ryan Garlock**) and 2005 Entry Drafts.

16 – Edmonton traded C **Peter Sarno** to Vancouver for G **Tyler Moss**.

18 – Washington traded RW **Peter Bondra** to Ottawa for C **Brooks Laich**, Ottawa's 2nd-round choice in the 2005 Entry Draft and future considerations.

19 – Chicago traded C **Alex Zhamnov** and Washington's 4th-round choice in the 2004 Entry Draft (previously acquired – Philadelphia selected **R.J. Anderson**) to Philadelphia for D **Jim Vandermeer**, C **Colin Fraser** and Los Angeles' 2nd-round choice (previously acquired – Chicago selected **Bryan Bickell**) in the 2004 Entry Draft.

20 – Carolina traded D **Bob Boughner** to Colorado for D **Chris Bahen** and Washington's 3rd-round choice (previously acquired – Carolina selected D **Casey Borer**) in the 2004 Entry Draft.

21 – Anaheim traded D **Kurt Sauer** and its 4th-round choice in the 2005 Entry Draft to Colorado for D **Martin Skoula**.

22 – Phoenix traded RW **Landon Wilson** to Pittsburgh for future considerations.

24 – Chicago traded LW **Ville Nieminen** to Calgary for **C Jason Morgan** and a conditional choice in the 2005 Entry Draft.

25 – Nashville traded D **Timo Helbling** to Tampa Bay for Tampa Bay's 8th-round choice (G **Pekka Rinne**) in the 2004 Entry Draft.

25 – Minnesota traded C **Darby Hendrickson** and its 8th-round choice (RW **Brandon Yip**)in the 2004 Entry Draft to Colorado for Colorado's 4th-round choice in the 2005 Entry Draft.

27 – Washington traded C **Robert Lang** to Detroit for LW **Tomas Fleischmann**, Detroit's 1st-round choice (D **Mike Green**) in the 2004 Entry Draft and a 4th-round choice in the 2006 Entry Draft.

March 2004

1 – Florida traded C **Viktor Kozlov** to New Jersey for LW **Christian Berglund** and D **Victor Uchevatov**.

2 – Chicago traded RW **Ty Jones** to Florida for a conditional choice in the 2006 Entry Draft.

2 – Chicago traded D **Nathan Dempsey** to Los Angeles for Los Angeles' 5th-round choice in the 2005 Entry Draft and future considerations.

2 – NY Rangers traded RW **Alex Kovalev** to Montreal for RW **Jozef Balej** and Montreal's 2nd-round choice (C **Bruce Graham**) in the 2004 Entry Draft.

3 – Washington traded D **Sergei Gonchar** to Boston for D **Shaone Morrisonn** and Boston's 1st- and 2nd-round choices (D **Jeff Schultz** and C **Michail Yunkov**) in the 2004 Entry Draft.

3 – NY Rangers traded C **Petr Nedved** and G **Jussi Markkanen** to Edmonton for G **Stephen Valiquette**, C **Dwight Helminen**, Edmonton's 2nd-round compensatory choice (LW **Dane Byers**) in the 2004 Entry Draft and a conditional 3rd-round choice in the 2005 Entry Draft.

3 – Minnesota traded D **Jason Marshall** to San Jose for San Jose's 5th-round choice (D **Jean-Claude Sawyer**) in the 2004 Entry Draft.

3 – Toronto traded D **Maxim Kondratiev**, C **Jarkko Immonen**, Toronto's 1st-round choice (later traded to Calgary – Calgary selected LW **Kris Chucko**) in the 2004 Entry Draft and 2nd-round choice in 2005 to NY Rangers for D **Brian Leetch** and Edmonton's 4th-round choice (previously acquired – Toronto selected **Roman Kukumberg**).

4 – Washington traded C **Michael Nylander** to Boston for Boston's 2nd-round choice in the 2006 Entry Draft and future considerations.

4 – Phoenix traded C **Mike Sillinger** to St. Louis for G **Brent Johnson**.

4 – Minnesota traded C **Jim Dowd** to Montreal for Montreal's 4th-round choice (RW **Julien Sprunger**) in the 2004 Entry Draft.

5 – Phoenix traded C **Jan Hrdina** to New Jersey for RW **Mike Rupp** and New Jersey's 2nd-round choice (later traded to Edmonton – Edmonton selected LW **Geoff Paukovich**) in the 2004 Entry Draft.

5 – Minnesota traded D **Brad Bombardir** and C **Sergei Zholtok** to Nashville for Buffalo's 3rd-round choice in the 2004 Entry Draft (previously acquired – Minnesota selected D **Clayton Stoner**) and Nashville's 4th-round choice (LW **Patrick Bordeleau**) in the 2004 Entry Draft.

6 – NY Rangers traded LW **Chris Simon** and its 7th-round choice (C **Matt Schneider**) in the 2004 Entry Draft to Calgary for G **Jamie McLennan**, C **Blair Betts** and RW **Greg Moore**.

8 – NY Rangers traded D **Vladimir Malakhov** to Philadelphia for RW **Rick Kozak** and Philadelphia's 2nd-round choice in the 2005 Entry Draft.

8 – Philadelphia traded D **Chris Therien** to Dallas for Phoenix's 8th-round choice (previously acquired – Philadelphia selected G **Martin Houle**) in the 2004 Entry Draft and Dallas' 3rd-round choice in the 2005 Entry Draft.

8 – Atlanta traded LW **Kamil Piros** to Florida for D **Kyle Rossiter**.

8 – Pittsburgh traded RW **Steve Webb** to NY Islanders for D **Alain Nasreddine**.

8 – Washington traded RW **Anson Carter** to Los Angeles for C/RW **Jared Aulin**.

8 – Minnesota traded D **Brad Brown** and its 6th-round choice in the 2005 Entry Draft to Buffalo for a 4th-round choice in the 2005 Entry Draft.

8 – Florida traded LW **Marcus Nilson** to Calgary for Calgary's 2nd-round choice (LW **David Booth**) in the 2004 Entry Draft.

8 – Colorado traded D **Chris McAllister**, D **David Liffiton** and Florida's 2nd-round choice (previously acquired and later traded back to Florida – Florida selected G **David Shantz**) in the 2004 Entry Draft to NY Rangers for RW **Matthew Barnaby** and the NY Rangers' 3rd-round choice (RW **Denis Parshin**) in the 2004 Entry Draft.

8 – Florida traded RW **Valeri Bure** to Dallas for D **Drew Bagnell** and a 2nd-round compensatory choice (later traded to Phoenix – Phoenix selected RW **Enver Lisin**) in the 2004 Entry Draft awarded to Dallas for the free-agent signing of **Derian Hatcher**.

8 – Colorado traded D **Derek Morris** and D **Keith Ballard** to Phoenix for D **Ossi Vaananen**, C **Chris Gratton** and Phoenix's 2nd-round choice in the 2005 Entry Draft.

8 – Edmonton traded G **Tommy Salo** and its 6th-round choice in the 2005 Entry Draft to Colorado for D **Tom Gilbert**.

9 – Atlanta traded LW **Jeff Cowan** to Los Angeles for LW **Kip Brennan**.

9 – Boston traded D **Jeff Jillson** to San Jose for C **Brad Boyes**; San Jose traded **Jillson** and its 9th-round choice in the 2005 Entry Draft to Buffalo for C **Curtis Brown** and D **Andy Delmore**; San Jose traded **Delmore** to Boston for future considerations.

9 – Carolina traded C **Ron Francis** to Toronto for Toronto's 4th-round choice in the 2005 Entry Draft.

9 – Chicago traded D **Alexander Karpovtsev** to NY Islanders for NY Islanders' 4th-round choice in the 2005 Entry Draft.

9 – Colorado traded LW **Jordan Krestanovich** to Minnesota for LW **Chris Bala**.

9 – Columbus traded LW **Lasse Pirjeta** to Pittsburgh for C **Brian Holzinger**.

9 – Columbus traded LW **Geoff Sanderson** to Vancouver for Vancouver's 3rd-round choice (G **Daniel Lacosta**) in the 2004 Entry Draft.

9 – Florida traded D **Jeff Paul** to NY Rangers for LW **Paul Healey**.

9 – Montreal traded LW **Sylvain Blouin** to Vancouver for D **Rene Vydareny**.

9 – Nashville traded D **Stan Neckar** to Tampa Bay for Tampa Bay's 6th-round choice (D **Kevin Schaeffer**) in the 2004 Entry Draft.

9 – NY Rangers traded D **Greg de Vries** to Ottawa for D **Karel Rachunek** and C/LW **Alexandre Giroux**.

9 – NY Rangers traded LW **Martin Rucinsky** to Vancouver for C **R.J. Umberger** and D **Martin Grenier**.

9 – Ottawa traded D **Shane Hnidy** to Nashville for Colorado's 3rd-round choice (previously acquired – Ottawa selected C **Peter Regin Jensen**) in the 2004 Entry Draft.

9 – Phoenix traded LW **Brian Savage** to St. Louis for future considerations.

9 – Pittsburgh traded D **Marc Bergevin** to Vancouver for Vancouver's 7th-round choice (C **Jordan Morrison**) in the 2004 Entry Draft.

9 – St. Louis traded D **Tom Koivisto** to Phoenix for future considerations.

9 – St. Louis traded LW **Sergei Varlamov** to Vancouver for **LW Ryan Ready**.

9 – Washington traded RW **Mike Grier** to Buffalo for C **Jakub Klepis**.

June 2004

16 – Carolina traded G **Arturs Irbe** to Columbus for future considerations.

18 – Anaheim traded G **Martin Gerber** to Carolina for D **Tomas Malec** and Carolina's 3rd-round choice (D **Kyle Kluberantz**) in the 2004 Entry Draft.

25 – Dallas traded G **Jason Bacashihua** to St. Louis for the rights to D **Shawn Belle**.

26 – Anaheim traded D **Niclas Havelid** to Atlanta for D **Kurtis Foster**.

26 – Carolina traded its 1st-round choice (LW **Alexandre Picard**) and Toronto's 2nd-round choice (previously acquired – Columbus selected D **Kyle Wharton**) in the 2004 Entry Draft to Columbus for Columbus' 1st-round choice (LW **Andrew Ladd**) in the 2004 Entry Draft.

26 – Calgary traded its 1st and 8th-round choices (LW **Lauri Korpikoski** and D **Jonathan Paiement**) in the 2004 Entry Draft to NY Rangers for Toronto's 1st-round choice (previously acquired – Calgary selected LW **Chris Chucko**) and the Rangers' 2nd-round compensatory choice (RW **Adam Pineault**) in the 2004 Entry Draft.

26 – Dallas traded its 1st-round choice (C **Travis Zajac**) in the 2004 Entry Draft to New Jersey for New Jersey's 1st- round choice (later traded to San Jose – San Jose selected RW **Lukas Kaspar**) and 3rd-round choice (later traded to Washington – Washington selected D **Clayton Barthel**) in the 2004 Entry Draft.

2003-04 NHL Player Transactions *continued*

26 – Dallas traded New Jersey's 1st-round choice (previously acquired – San Jose selected RW **Lukas Kaspar**) in the 2004 Entry Draft and Dallas' 5th-round choice (C **Steven Zalewski**) in 2004 to San Jose for San Jose's 1st-round choice (D **Mark Fistric**), 2nd-round compensatory choice (RW **Raymond Sawada**) and 3rd-round compensatory choice (later traded to Vancouver – Vancouver selected D **Alexander Elder**) in the 2004 Entry Draft .

26 – Calgary traded the NY Rangers' 2nd-round compensatory choice (previously acquired – Columbus selected RW **Adam Pineault**) in the 2004 Entry Draft to Columbus for Columbus' 3rd-round choice (C/LW **Brandon Prust**) and Tampa Bay's 3rd-round choice (previously acquired – Calgary selected C **Dustin Boyd**) in the 2004 Entry Draft.

26 – Florida traded Dallas' 2nd-round compensatory choice (previously acquired and later traded to Phoenix – Phoenix selected RW **Enver Lisin**) and Florida's 3rd-round choice (RW **Zdenek Bahensky**) in the 2004 Entry Draft to NY Rangers for Florida's 2nd-round choice (previously acquired – Florida selected G **David Shantz**) in the 2004 Entry Draft.

26 – Los Angeles traded its 3rd-round choice (LW **Shawn Weller**) in the 2004 Entry Draft to Ottawa for C **Radek Bonk**.

26 – Edmonton traded LW **Jason Chimera** and its 3rd-round choice (later traded to NY Rangers – NY Rangers selected C **Billy Ryan**) in the 2004 Entry Draft to Phoenix for New Jersey's 2nd-round choice (previously acquired – Edmonton selected LW **Geoff Paukovich**) and Buffalo's 4th-round choice (previously acquired – Edmonton selected LW **Liam Reddox**) in the 2004 Entry Draft. (Note – under the terms of a June 21, 2003 trade between Carolina and Phoenix, Phoenix transferred the 80th overall choice to Carolina).

26 – Carolina traded Edmonton's 3rd-round choice (previously acquired and later traded to NY Rangers – NY Rangers selected C **Billy Ryan**) in the 2004 Entry Draft to Phoenix for Phoenix's 3rd-round choice in the 2005 Entry Draft.

26 – NY Rangers traded Dallas' 2nd-round compensatory choice (previously acquired – Phoenix selected RW **Enver Lisin**) in the 2004 Entry Draft to Phoenix for Philadelphia's 2nd-round choice (previously acquired – NY Rangers selected C **Brandon Dubinsky**) and Edmonton's 3rd-round choice (previously acquired – NY Rangers selected C **Billy Ryan**) in the 2004 Entry Draft.

26 – Dallas traded New Jersey's 3rd-round choice (previously acquired – Washington selected D **Clayton Barthel**) in the 2004 Entry Draft to Washington for Washington's 3rd-round choice in the 2005 Entry Draft.

26 – Dallas traded San Jose's 3rd-round compensatory choice (previously acquired – Vancouver selected D **Alexander Elder**) in the 2004 Entry Draft to Vancouver for Vancouver's 3rd-round choice in the 2005 Entry Draft.

26 – Boston traded its 3rd-round choice (later traded to San Jose – San Jose selected G **Thomas Greiss**), Tampa Bay's 4th-round choice (previously acquired – San Jose selected G **Jason Churchill**) and its 9th-round choice (G **Brian Mahoney-Wilson**) in the 2004 Entry Draft to San Jose for San Jose's 2nd-round choice (C **David Krejci**) in the 2004 Entry Draft.

26 – Los Angeles traded G **Cristobal Huet** and C **Radek Bonk** to Montreal for G **Mathieu Garon** and San Jose's 3rd-round choice (previously acquired – Los Angeles selected D **Paul Baier**) in the 2004 Entry Draft.

27 – Atlanta traded its 3rd-round choice in the 2005 Entry Draft to Carolina for Carolina's 4th-round choice (LW **Chad Painchaud**) in the 2004 Entry Draft.

27 – San Jose traded Calgary's 5th-round choice (previously acquired and later traded to Florida – Florida selected D **Bret Nasby**) in the 2004 Entry Draft to Florida for Florida's 7th- and 8th-round choices (D **Michael Vernace** and G **Derek MacIntyre**) in the 2004 Entry Draft.

27 – Philadelphia traded its 5th-round choice (D **Brandon Elliott**), 6th-round choice (D **Jan Zapletal**) and San Jose's 6th-round choice (previously acquired – Tampa Bay selected G **Kari Ramo**) in the 2004 Entry Draft to Tampa Bay for Tampa Bay's 3rd-round choice in the 2005 Entry Draft.

27 – Ottawa traded G **Patrick Lalime** to St. Louis for a conditional 4th-round choice in the 2005 Entry Draft.

27 – Los Angeles traded its 9th-round choice (D **Grant Clitsome**) in the 2004 Entry Draft to Columbus for Columbus' 8th-round choice in the 2005 Entry Draft.

27 – Montreal traded D **Stephane Quintal** to Los Angeles for future considerations.

27 – Atlanta traded a conditional 7th-round choice in the 2005 Entry Draft to Chicago for G **Adam Berkhoel**.

29 – Carolina traded LW **Jaroslav Svoboda** to Dallas for Dallas' 4th-round choice in the 2005 Entry Draft.

July 2004

6 – Phoenix traded D **Radoslav Suchy** and Phoenix's 6th-round choice in the 2005 Entry Draft to Columbus for Columbus' 4th-round choice in the 2005 Entry Draft.

Trades and free agent signings after August 12, 2004 are listed on page 338.

Hockey Fights Cancer is a joint initiative created by the National Hockey League and the National Hockey League Players' Association that honors those in the hockey community who have struggled, or continue to struggle, with the disease.

The goal of Hockey Fights Cancer is to raise money and visibility for local cancer care or research, as well as to support the American Cancer Society and Canadian Cancer Society national organizations. Founded by the NHL and the NHLPA, Hockey Fights Cancer is supported by NHL member clubs, NHL Alumni, the NHL Officials Association, Professional Hockey Trainers and Equipment Managers, corporate marketing partners, broadcast partners and fans throughout North America.

Join the Fight! If you would like to make a contribution to Hockey Fights Cancer, please forward a check made payable to Hockey Fights Cancer to one of the following addresses:

For Canadian Residents:
Hockey Fights Cancer
P.O. Box 1282, Station B
Montreal, Quebec H3B 3K9

For U.S. Residents:
Hockey Fights Cancer
P.O. Box 5037
New York, NY 10185-5037

Please include your name and current address so that your donation can be acknowledged. All donations are tax-deductible.

For more information, log-on to www.hockeyfightscancer.com or call 1-800-540-6500.

NHL League and Team Websites

National Hockey League ....www.nhl.com

NHL Site for Kids ....www.nhl.com/kids

NHL Merchandise Shop ....shop.nhl.com

NHL Job Postings.......................hockeyjobs.nhl.com

Hockey Fights Cancer ....www.nhl.com/nhlhq/hockeyfightscancer/index.html

Official NHL Team Websites:

Anaheim..www.mightyducks.com

Atlanta ....www.atlantathrashers.com

Boston...www.bostonbruins.com

Buffalo ....www.sabres.com

Calgary..www.calgaryflames.com

Carolina...www.carolinahurricanes.com

Chicago..www.chicagoblackhawks.com

Colorado ....www.coloradoavalanche.com

Columbus ....www.bluejackets.com

Dallas ....www.dallasstars.com

Detroit...www.detroitredwings.com

Edmonton..www.edmontonoilers.com

Florida ....www.floridapanthers.com

Los Angeles ....www.lakings.com

Minnesota ....www.wild.com

Montreal ....www.canadiens.com

Nashville..www.nashvillepredators.com

New Jersey ....www.newjerseydevils.com

NY Islanders ....www.newyorkislanders.com

NY Rangers ....www.newyorkrangers.com

Ottawa...www.ottawasenators.com

Philadelphia.......................................www.philadelphiaflyers.com

Phoenix..www.phoenixcoyotes.com

Pittsburgh..www.pittsburghpenguins.com

St. Louis ....www.stlouisblues.com

San Jose ....www.sjsharks.com

Tampa Bay...www.tampabaylightning.com

Toronto..www.mapleleafs.com

Vancouver ....www.canucks.com

Washington..www.washingtoncaps.com

To order the *NHL Official Guide & Record Book* and other books about hockey:

www.nhlofficialguide.com

Contributors

The NHL Official Guide & Record Book is produced with the help of many.

Special thanks to: the Communications staff of each NHL club, Kerry Banks, Aaron Bell (OHL), Case and Nellie Bontje; Bob Borgen, Craig Campbell, Trish Campbell, Jack Carnefix (ECHL), Paul R. Carroll Jr., Jason Chaimovitch (AHL), Steve Cherwonak (CHL), Denis Demers (QMJHL), Leith Dunick, Bob Duff, Peter Fillman, Ernie Fitzsimmons, Mel Foster, Tom Gronek, Hockey Hall of Fame, Patrick Houda, Peter Jagla, Eric Kay, Danny S. Kobayashi, Len Kotylo, Dennis Lennox II (HockeyRefs.com), Derek Lunney, Roy Mackie, Al Mason, Leroy McKinnon (WHL), Dave McMahon, Herb Morell (OHL), Anna Mormina, NCAA Conference and School Sports Information Departments, NHL Broadcasters' Association, NHL Central Registry, NHL Officiating, NHL Players' Association, Joseph Nieforth, John Paton, Gary J. Pearce, Lisa Peppin (UHL), Phil Pritchard, Valentina Riazanova, Frank and Rita Rocys, Mrs. Claude Rompré (QMJHL), Minako Saki, Ralph Slate, Paul Tackaberry, Toronto Public Library/Globe and Mail – Canada's Heritage from 1844, U.S. Hockey Hall of Fame, Tyler Wolosewich.

Researchers and Historians: contact the Society for International Hockey Research www.sihrhockey.org

Photo Credits

NHL Images: Anita Cechowski.

Photographers: Graig Abel, Toronto; Scott Audette, Tampa; Steve and Brian Babineau, Boston; Bruce Bennett Studios, New York/New Jersey; Andrew D. Bernstein Associates, Los Angeles; Mark Buckner, St. Louis; Scott Cunningham, Atlanta; Tim Defrisco, Colorado; Getty Images (Victor Decolongon, Elsa, Harry How, Charles Laberge, Robert Laberge, Doug Pensinger, Tom Pidgeon, Dave Sandford, Eliot J. Schechter, Rick Stewart, Ian Tomlinson, Jeff Vinnick) Barry Gossage, Phoenix; Glenn James, Dallas; Bruce Kluckhohn, Minnesota; Mitchell Layton, Washington; Richard Lewis, Florida; Dale McMillan, Edmonton; Matt Polk, Pittsburgh; Deborah Robinson, Anaheim; John Russell, Nashville; Jamie Sabau, Columbus; Bill Smith, Chicago; Don Smith, San Jose; Gerry Thomas, Edmonton; Rocky Widner, San Jose; Bill Wippert, Buffalo.

THREE STAR SELECTION...

NHL OFFICIAL GUIDE
IS PLEASED TO OFFER...

NHL PUBLICATIONS
ORDER FORM

Please send

☐ copies of **next** year's
NHL Guide & Record Book/2006 (available Sept. 2005)

☐ copies of **this** year's
NHL Guide & Record Book/2005 (available now)

☐ copies of **the limited edition**
World Cup of Hockey 2004 Media Guide (available now)

☐ copies of **next** year's
NHL Yearbook 2006 magazine (available Sept. 2005)

☐ copies of **next** year's
NHL Rule Book/2005-06 (available Sept. 2005)

PRICES:	CANADA	USA	OVERSEAS
GUIDE & RECORD BOOK	$27.95	$24.95	$24.95 U.S.$
Handling (per copy)	$ 5.65	$10.00	$15.00 U.S.$
7% GST	$ 2.35		
Total (per copy)	**$35.95**	**$34.95**	**$39.95** U.S.$
Add Extra for airmail	$ 9.00	$ 9.00	$17.00 U.S.$
WORLD CUP MEDIA GUIDE	$19.95	$14.95	$14.95 U.S.$
Handling (per copy)	$ 4.55	$ 7.00	$12.00 U.S.$
7% GST	$ 1.72	—	—
Total (per copy)	**$26.22**	**$21.95**	**$26.95** U.S.$
YEARBOOK	$ 9.95	$ 7.99	$ 9.95 U.S.$
Handling (per copy)	$ 4.55	$ 6.01	$ 7.00 U.S.$
7% GST	$ 1.02	—	—
Total (per copy)	**$15.52**	**$14.00**	**$16.95** U.S.$
RULE BOOK	$11.95	$ 8.95	$ 7.95 U.S.$
Handling (per copy)	$ 2.54	$ 3.00	$ 3.55 U.S.$
7% GST	$ 1.01	—	—
Total (per copy)	**$15.50**	**$11.95**	**$11.50** U.S.$

Charge my ☐ Visa ☐ MasterCard/EuroCard ☐ Am Ex

Credit Card Account Number   Expiry Date (important)

Signature

☐ Enclosed is my cheque/check or money order.

Name

Address

Province/State   Postal/Zip Code

IN CANADA
Mail completed form to:
NHL Official Guide
194 Dovercourt Rd.
Toronto, Ontario
M6J 3C8

IN USA
Mail completed form to:
NHL Official Guide
194 Dovercourt Rd.
Toronto, Ontario
CANADA M6J 3C8
Remit in U.S. funds

OVERSEAS
Mail completed form to:
NHL Official Guide
194 Dovercourt Rd.
Toronto, Ontario
CANADA M6J 3C8
Money order or
credit card only.
No cheques please.

DELIVERY: Canada & USA – up to three weeks. Overseas – up to five weeks.

1. **THE NHL OFFICIAL GUIDE & RECORD BOOK**
The NHL's authoritative information source. 73rd year in print. 640 pages. The "Bible of Hockey". Read worldwide.

2. **WORLD CUP OF HOCKEY 2004 MEDIA GUIDE**
A limited edition 192-page, large-format softcover book with complete info on hockey's elite best-on-best competition.

3. **THE NHL YEARBOOK**
216-page, full-color magazine with features on each club. Award winners, All-Stars and special statistics.

4. **THE NHL RULE BOOK**
Complete playing rules, rink dimensions and officials' signals.

Free Book List with each order.

SECURE ONLINE ORDERING and many more hockey books available at www.nhlofficialguide.com

3 Ways to Order with your Credit Card :
ONLINE, by FAX or by E-MAIL
ONLINE www.nhlofficialguide.com
FAX **416/531-3939 or**
(OVERSEAS CUSTOMERS: USE INTERNATIONAL DIALING CODE FOR CANADA)
E-MAIL **dda.nhl@sympatico.ca**
24 HOURS
PLEASE INCLUDE YOUR CARD'S EXPIRY DATE